Longn
Crossw
Key

D0130246

Longman

Longman Group UK Limited
Longman House, Burnt Mill, Harlow,
Essex CM20 2JE, England
and Associated Companies throughout the world.

© Evelyn Marshall
All rights reserved. No part of this publication may be reproduced, stored
in a retrieval system or transmitted in any form or by any means
electronic, mechanical, photocopying, recording or otherwise, without
the prior permission of the Copyright owner.

Cased Edition first published 1982
Fourth impression 1988
Paperback Edition first published 1988
Second impression 1989

ISBN 0 582 55620 1 (Standard edition)
ISBN 0 582 55562 0 (De luxe edition)
ISBN 0 582 03782 4 (Paperback edition)

Printed in Great Britain by
Richard Clay Ltd, Bungay, Suffolk

Author's preface

In these days of increased leisure, more and more people find the fascination of word games hard to resist.

The *Longman Crossword Key* has been compiled to alleviate the frustrating and time-wasting search for that elusive word which gets no further than 'the tip of one's tongue'. With the aid of this book not only can those sought-after words be found at a glance, but also arguments can be settled finally and tension eliminated.

Crosswords are available at all levels, ranging from those whose challenge is the speed at which they can be solved, to those whose intractable clues tease the brain for days. The *Longman Crossword Key* lists all words both by length and by letter position. It contains over 750,000 words from three to fifteen letters long. Previous crossword dictionaries listed words in alphabetical order only by length.

In this book, if, for instance, you wanted a six-letter word whose third letter was 'e' (xxexxx) you would turn to the section for six-letter words. Then you would find 'position = 3' and look through the letters printed in heavy type until you came to 'e'. In an ordinary dictionary it would take hours to find all the possible words with 'e' as the third letter, but this method provides a quick reference thus allowing you far more time to match the words available with the clue you have been given.

The solution to crossword problems you had previously thought insoluble will now be well

within your reach. The *Crossword Key* will also prove to be an invaluable aid to compilers in their work. Then there are also the thousands of other word games, puzzles and competitions which can be solved with the aid of this book. Why not keep the children occupied on long journeys by using the *Longman Crossword Key* to invent guessing games for them?

Happy hours... Evelyn Marshall

A note on the author

Evelyn Marshall is a retired businesswoman who lives in Stourport-on-Severn. In addition to being a keen solver of crosswords she has also been a compiler of them for many years, in particular for the *Birmingham Mail*.

Six years ago she started working on her idea for a crossword dictionary based on first and last letters. This project became known and she was interviewed by the *Birmingham Mail* and ATV's 'Today's People', which resulted in her being 'inundated with requests for copies of the book'. It was brought to the attention of the Longman Dictionary and Reference Book Department who used their unique and extensive computer-based text-processing facilities to extend her idea.

The result is the *Longman Crossword Key* which has a separate section for letters in all positions, thus making it the first truly comprehensive crossword dictionary.

How to use the Crossword Key

The words are arranged in sections, the first covering words of three letters and the last covering words of fifteen letters.

Each section contains words listed alphabetically with

☐ first letter in bold type in the first section
☐ second letter in bold type in the second section
☐ and so on, until the last letter is reached.

Thus, every word in the *Key* will appear as many times as it has letters – a three-letter word will appear three times, a ten-letter word ten times, etc.

So, if you need a six-letter word with 'p' as the fourth letter

☐ turn to the section for six-letter words
☐ look for 'position = 4' at the top of the page
☐ find 'p' in the bold letters.

Now comes the real display of skill. Which word is the one that will fit your requirements?

3 letter words

```
aba bit dim fie hen key mog pap rom ted wig fag pat odd ree bib sic cod
ABC biz din fig hep kid mol par rot tee win fah paw ode ref bid sin cog
abo boa dip fin her kif mom pas row teg wis fan pax bed rem big sip col
aby bob dit fir het kin moo pat rub ten wit far pay bee rep bin sir con
ace bod div fit hew kip mop paw rue tew wiz fat rad beg rto bis sit coo
act bog doe fix hex kit mor pax rug the woe fay rag bel rev bio sis cop
add bok dog flu hey koa mot pay rum tho wog gab rah ben Rex bit six cor
ado boo doh fly hic kob mow pea run two won gad raj bet sea biz tic cos
adz bop Dom fob hid kop Mrs ped rut tic woo gag ram bey sec dib tie cot
aft bot don foe hie lab mud peg rye tie wop gal ran deb see did tig cow
aga bow dop fog him lac mug pen sac tig wot gam rap dee sei die til cox
age box dor foo his lad mum pep sad til wow gan rat den sen dig tin coy
ago boy dot for hip lag nab per sag tin wry gap raw dew set dim tip coz
aha bra dow fou his lah nae pet sai tip wud gar rax dey sew din tit doe
aid bub dry fox hit lam nag pew sal tit wye gas ray eel sex dip via dog
ail bud dso foy hob lap nap phi sap tod yah gat sac een sez dit vie doh
aim bug dub Fra hod lar nay pie sat toe yak gay sad fed tea div vim Dom
ain bum dud fro hoe lat neb pig saw tog yam had sag fee tec fib vis don
air bun due fry hog law nee pin sax tom yap hae sai fen ted fid wig dop
ait bur dug fud hon lax net pip say ton yaw hag sal feu tee fie win dor
ala bus dun fug hop lay new pit sea too yea hah sap few teg fig wis dot
alb but duo fun hot lea nib pix sec top yen ham sat fey ten fin wit dow
ale buy dux fur how led nil ply sec tor yep han saw fez tew fir wiz eon
all bye dye gab hoy lee nim pod sei tot yes hap sax ged vee fit yin fob
alp cab dye gad hub leg nip poe sen tow yet has say gee veg fix yip foe
alt cad dzo gag hue lei nit poi set toy yew hat tab gel vet gib zip fog
ama cam ear gal hug Leo nix pom sew try yin haw tag gem vex gid eke fop
amp can eat gam huh let nob pon sex tub yip hay tai gen web gie oke for
ana cap eau gan hum leu nod pop sez tug yob jab taj get wed gig ski fou
and car ebb gap hun lev nog pot she tui yod jag tam gey wee gin sky fox
ane cat ecu gar hup lex Noh pow shy tum yon jam tan heh wen git ala Goa
ani caw edh gas hut ley non pox sib tun you Jap tap hem wet hic alb Goa
ant cay eel gat hyp lib Ibo pro sic tup zap jar tar hen wey hid ale gob
any chi een gay ice lid not pry sin tut zax Jat tat hep yea hie all god
ape cob eff ged ice lie now psi sin tux zed jaw tau her yen him alp goo
apt cod eft gee icy lip nth pub sit two zee jay taw het yep hin alt got
arc cog egg gel Ido lis nub pud sis Twi zel kai tax hew yet hip eld gov
are col ego gem ilk lit nun pug sit ufo zho lab van hey yew his elf goy
ark con eke gen ill lob nut pun six ugh zip lac vas jet zed hit elk hob
arm coo eld get imp log oaf pup ski ule zip lac vas jet zed jib ell hod
art cop elf gey ilk loo oak pur sky ule zoa lad vat jeu zee jig elm hoe
ash cor elk ghi ink lop oar pus sly ure zoo lag wad Jew zel kid flu hog
ask cos ell gib inn lor oat put sob urn —— lah wae kea Zen kif fly hon
asp cot elm gid ion lot obi puy soc use baa lam wag ked aft kin ilk hop
ass cow emu gie ire low oca pye sod vac bad lap wan kef eff kip ill hot
ate cox end gig irk lox och pyx soh van bag lar wap keg eft kit old how
auk coy eon gin ism loy odd qua sol vas bah lat war ken off lib ply hoy
ave coz era git ita lud oer rad son vat bam law was key off lid sly ion
awe cru ere gnu its lug off rag sop vee ban lax waw lea ufo lie ule job
awl cry erf Goa ivy lum off rah sot veg bap lay wax led aga lip ama jog
awn cub erg gob jab lur oft raj sou vet bar mac way lee age lis amp jot
axe cud erk god jag lux ohm ram sow vex bat mad yah leg ago lit emu jow
aye cue ern goo jam luz oho ran sox via bay mag yak lei egg mid imp joy
azo cur err got Jap lye oil rap soy vie cab man yam Leo mil ana koa
baa cup ess gov jar mac oke rat spa vim cad man yap let ugh mim and kob
bad cut eta goy Jat mad old raw spy vis cam map yaw leu aha mir ane kop
bag cur eth gum jaw mag one rax sri voe can mar zap lev chi mix ani lob
bah cwm eve gun jay mam oof ray sty vow cap mat zax lex ghi nib ant log
bam dab ewe gup jet man ooh red sub vug car maw aba ley mho nil any loo
ban dad eye gut jeu map ope ree sue wae caw may ABC men ohm end lop
bap dag fab guv Jew mar opt ref sum wae caw nab abo met oho nip gnu lor
bar dak fad guy jib mat orb rem sun wag cay nae aby meu phi nit Ind lot
bat dal fag gym jig maw orc rep sup wan dab nap Ibo neb she nix ink low
bay dam fah had jog men ort rev tag war dag nay obi nee shy oil inn lox
bed dan fan had jot met our Rex tai was dak oaf ace net the pig boa moa
bee dap far hae jow meu out rho taj waw dal oak act new tho pin bob mob
beg daw fat hag joy mew ova ria tam wad dam ope oer thy pip bod mog
bel day fay hah jug mho owe rib tan way dan oat ecu pea who pit bog mol
ben deb fed ham jut mid owl rid tap web dap pad ice ped why pix bok mol
bet dee fee han kai mil own rig tar daw pal icy pen pea who pix bok mom
bey den fen hap kat mim oxy rim tat wee day pam oca peg zho ria boo mom
bib dew feu has kea mir pad rip tau eat day pal add pep mix rid bot mop
bid dey few hat ked mix pah rob taw eau pap ado per aim rig bow mot
big dib fey haw kef moa pal roc tax wey eau pap adz pet ain rim box mot
bin did fez hay keg mob pam rod tea who fab par edh pew air rip boy mow
bio die fib heh ken mod pan roe tec why fad pas Ido red ait sib cob nob
bis dig fid hem
```

```
nod yon auk pub wye lib hid foe cog och arm fin Ibo sip pus out mew fay
nog you bub azo lob hod gee dag dob bam fun gan Leo sop sis pat mow fey
Noh zoa bud pug dzo mob Ind gie gig pah bum gan Leo sup vas pet new fly
non zoo bug pun ——  nab ked hae dog rah cam gen loo tap vis pit now foy
nor ape bum pup aba neb kid hie dug soh cum gin mho tip was pot paw fry
not apt bun pur aga nib lad hoe egg ugh cwm gun moo top wis put pew gay
now ope bur pus aha nob led hue erg yah dam han oho tup yes rat pow gey
oof opt bus put ala nub lid ice fag ani dim hen pro wap act raw raw goy
ooh spa but puy ama orb lud ire fig chi Dom hin rho wop aft rot row guy
pod spy buy qua ana pub mad lee fog ghi elm hon tho yap ait rut saw hay
poe arc cub rub baa rib mie lie fug kai gam Hun two yep alt sat sew hey
poi are cud rue boa rob mod lye lei gem inn two yip ant set sow hoy
pom ark cue rug bra rub nae gig obi gum ion ufo zap apt sit taw icy
pon arm cum run era sib nod nee hag phi gym ken who zip art sot tew ivy
pop art cup run eta sob odd ode hog poi ham kin woo air bat tat tow jay
pot bra cur rut Fra sub old oke hug psi hem man zho bar bet tit vow joy
pow cru cut sub Goa tab pad one jag sai him man zoo bur bit tot waw key
pox cry dub sue ita tub ped ope jig sei hum non alp car bot tut wow lay
rob dry dud sun kea web bod ore jog ski ism nun amp cor but vat yaw ley
roc era due sun koa yob pud owe jug Sri jam own asp cur cat vet yew loy
rod ere dug sup lea ABC rad pie tai lam bap nap dor cot wet box may
roe erf dun tub moa arc red poe lag tui lum pen bop ear cut wit cox nay
rom erg duo tug oca hic rid pye leg Twi mam pin cap err dit wot dux oxy
rot erk dup tui ova lac rod ree log raj mim pon cop far dot yet fix pay
row ern dux tum pea mac sad roe lug taj mom pun cup fir eat cru fox ply
sob err fud tun qua orc sod rue mag ark mum ran dap for eft eau hex pry
soc Fra fug tup ria roc ted rye mog ask nim run dip fur fat ecu lax puy
sod fro fun tut sea sac tod see mug auk ohm sen dog gar fit emu lex ray
soh fry fur tux spa sec wad she nag bok pam sin dup her gat feu lox say
sol ire gum vug tea sic wed sue nog dak pom son fop jar get flu lux shy
son irk gun wud twa soc wud tee peg elk ram sun gap lar git fou mix sky
sop Mrs gup ave via tec yod the pig erk rem tan gup lor got gnu nix sly
sot orb gut eve yea tic zed tie pug ilk rim ten gyp lur gut jeu pax soy
sou orc guv ivy zoa vac ace toe rag ink rum tin hap mar hat leu pix spy
sow ore guy ova alb add age ule rig irk rum tun hep mir het meu pox sty
sox ort hub awe bib aid ale use rug oak sum tun hip mor hit sou pyx thy
soy pro hue awl bob and ane sag yak tam urn hop nor hot tau rax toy
tod pry hug awn bub bad ape vee tag ail tom van hup oar hut you Rex try
toe Sri huh cwm cab bed are vie teg all tum wan hyp oer Jat div sax way
tog try hum ewe cob bid ate voe teg awl vim wen imp our jet gov sex wey
tom ure Hun owe cub bod ave wae tog bel yam win Jap par jot guv six why
ton urn hup owl dab bud awe wee tug ain won kip per jut lev sox wry
too wry hut own deb cad axe woe veg dal awn yen kop pur kat rev tax adz
top ash jug twa dib cod aye wye vug eel ban yin lap sir kit bow tux biz
tor ask jut Twi dub cud bee zee wag ell ben yon lip tar law caw vex coz
tot asp lud two ebb dad bye eff wig gal bin Zen lop tor let cow wax fez
tow ass lug axe fab did cue elf wog gel bun abo map war lit daw zax luz
toy dso lum oxy fib dud dee erf ash ill can ado mop ass lot dew aby sez
voe ess lur aye fob eld die kef bah mil con ago nap bis mat dow any wiz
vow ism lux bye gab end doe kif doh mol dan azo nip bus met few bay
woe psi luz dye gib fad due oaf eth nil den bio pap cos mot haw bey
wog use mud eye gob fed dye off eth oil din boo pep ess net hew boy
won ate mug gym hob fid eke oof fah owl don coo pip gas nit how buy
woo eta mum gyp hub fud ere ref hah pal dun dso pop has not jaw cay
wop eth nub hyp jab gad eve bag heh sal een duo pup his nut Jew coy
wot ita nun lye jib ged ewe beg huh sol eon dzo rap its oat jow cry
wow its nut pye job gid eye big lah til ern ego rep lis oft law day
yob nth our pyx kob god fee bog Noh zel fan fro rip Mrs opt low dey
yod sty out rye lab had fie bug nth aim fen goo sap pas ort maw dry
```

4 letter words

```
abba Acts agio alas amir apse asci awry back bank bats Beeb best bint
abbe acyl agog alee ammo aqua ashy axel bade bant batt beef beta bird
abed Adam agon alfa amok Arab Asti axes bael barb baud been bevy birk
abet Adar ague alga amyl arak atom axil bail bard bawd beep bias birl
able adit ahem ally anew arch atop axis bait bare bawl beer bice bise
ably adze ahoy alms anil area auld axle bake bark bawn beet bide bisk
abut aeon aide aloe ankh Ares aunt axon bald barm bays bell bier bite
abye aero aine alow anna aria aura ayah bale barn bead belt biff bitt
ache aery Ainu also anoa arid auto baas balk base beak bema bigg blab
achy afar airy alto anon aril aver baba ball bash beam bend bike blae
acid Afro ajar alum anta arms avid babe balm bask bean bent bile blah
acme agar akee amah ante army avow Babi banc bass bear bere bilk blat
acne aged akin ambo anti arty away baby band bast beat berg bill bleb
acol agha alae amen apex arum awed babu bane bate beau berk bind bled
acre agin alar amid apod aryl awny bach bang bath beck berm bine blew
```

```
blin bund chop coup deed dost eery feet fore germ grow helm hwyl joss
blip bung chou cove deem dote egad feis fork gest grub help hyle jota
blob bunk chow cowl deep doth egal fell form geum grum heme hymn jowl
bloc bunt chub coxa deer doup eger felt fort ghat guan hemp hype juba
blot buoy chug coxy deft dour eggy feme foss ghee guar hent hypo judo
blow burd chum coze defy dove egis fend foul gibe guff herb iamb judy
blub burg chut crab deil down ekka fere four gift gula herd ibex juju
blue burk ciao crag dele doxy elan fern fowl gila gulf here ibid July
blur burl cine cram delf doze elmy fess foxy gild gull herl ibis jump
boar burn cire cran dell dozy else frae gill gulp herm icky June
boat burp cist crap deme drab emeu fete frap gilt gump hern icon junk
bock burr cite craw demo drag emir feud frat gimp gunk hero idea Juno
bode bury city cree demy dram emit fiat Frau gink guru Herr idem jury
body bush clad crew dene drat Emmy fico fray gird gush hers ides just
Boer busk clam crib dent draw enow fief frit girn gust hest idle jute
bogy buss clan crit dray envy fief frit girt guts hewn idly kadi
boil bust clap crop derm drip epha fife froe giro gybe hick idol kago
boko busy claw crow derv drop epee file froe giro gymp hide iffy kail
bold butt clay crud desk drew epic fill frog girt gyms hick ilex kaka
bole buzz clef crux dewy drey epos film froe give gyre high ilea kale
boll byre cleg cube dhal drib ergo fils frow glad gyri high ikon kali
bolt byte clem cuff dhow drip Erin find fuci glam gyve hila ilea kame
boma cade clew cuit dial drop erne fine fuel glee haaf hill ilka kana
bomb cadi clip cull dice drub Eros fink full gleg haar hilt illy kaon
bond cafe clod culm dick drug Erse Finn fume glen hack hind imam kart
bone caff clog cult dido drum erst fino fumy glen hade hint impi kava
bong cage clop cups diet Druz esne fire fund glia hadj hipt inby kayo
bony cagy clot curb dike drey esne fire fund glia haem hire Inca keck
boob cake clou curd dill duad espy firm funk glib haet hiss inch keek
book calf cloy curl dime duce etch firn furl glim haik hist info keel
boom calk club curn dine duck etna fisc fury glob hail hive inky keen
boon call clue curr dint duct etui fish fuse glop haik hoar inly keep
boor calm coal curt dire dues euro fisk fuze glow haik hoax into kelp
boot calx coat cush dirk duel even fist fuzz glue hail hobo iota Kelt
bora came coca cusp dirl dues ever five fyrd glum hajj hock iris kemp
bore camp coco cuss dirt evil fizz gaby gade gnar haka hoer iron kent
born camp cock cusp dirl duet ewer flab gade gnar hale hogg isle kepi
bort cane code cyan dint duff exam flag gadi gnat hale hoho isnt kept
bosh cang coda cyma dish duke exes flak Gael gnaw half hold itch kerb
bosk cant code cyme duma dull exit flam gaff goad hall hole item kerf
boss cape coed cyma disk duly exon flan gaga goal halm holm iwis kern
both capo coho cyme dite duma expo flap gage goat halo holp jack khan
bott card coif cyst doit dumb eyas flat gain goby halt hols jade khat
bout care coil czar ditt dump eyed flaw gait goer hame holt jail kibe
bowl cark coin dace diva dune eyes flax gala goes hand holy Jain kick
boxy carl coir Dada dive dung eyot flay gale gogo hang home jake kier
boyg carp cola dado divi dunk eyra flea gall gold hank homo jamb kill
boyo cart coke daff dixy dupe eyre fled gamb golf hank homy jane kiln
bozo case cold dahl doat dura eyry flee game gone hare hone jape kilo
brad cash cole dago dock durn face flew gamp gong hark hong jarl kilt
brae cask colt dahl dodo duro fact flex gang good harm hood Java kind
brag cast coma Dail doer dusk fade fley gaol goof harn hoof jato kine
bran cate comb dais does dust fado flic gaol goof harp hook jean king
brat caul come dale doff duty faff flip garb goon harp hoop jeep kino
braw cave comp dame doge dyad fail flit floc garn hart hoot jeer kiri
bray cavy cone damn dogy Dyak fain floc garn hash hate hope jehu kirk
bred cede conk damp doit dyer fair floe gash gory hasp hope jell kiss
bree cedi conn Dane dojo dyke fake flog gasp Goth hast horn jerk kist
bren ceil dang dole dyne fall flop gast gout hath horn jess kite
brer cell cook dank doll each falx flow gate gowk haul horn jest kith
brew celt cool dare dolt earl fame flub gaud gown haul hose hour jete kiwi
Brie cent coon darg dome easy fane flue Gaul gram grab have hove jibe knag
brig cere coop dark domy ease fang flux gaum graf hawk howl jiff knap
brim cert coot darn dona east fard flys gaup gram haze hued jill knar
brio cess cope dart done easy fare foal gaur gran hazy huff jilt knee
brit chad Copt dash dong eath farl foam gave grat head huge jimp knew
brog cham copy data dont eats farm foci gawk gray heal huge jink knit
brow chap chat cord date daub doom echo fash flog garn gaze grew hear hulk jinn knob
brut chat char core daub door echt fast foil gean grey heat hull jinx knop
bubo chaw chat corf dawk doom echo fate foin gear grid heck hump jive knot
buck chef core cork dawn dope ecru faun fold geat grig heed hung jock know
buff chew corm daze dorm Edam fawn folk geld grim heel hunk joey knur
buhl chic corn dead dorr Edda faze fond Geez grin heft hunt john knut
bulb chid cose deaf dorp eddy fear font geld grip heil hurl join koan
bulk chin cosh deal dorr Eden fear food gelt gris heir hurt joke koel
bull chin cost dean dort edge feat food fool gene grit held hush joky kohl
bumf chip cosy dear dory edgy feck fool gene grit heir hush josh kola
bump chit cote debt dose edit feed foot gens grog hele husk jolt kola
buna choc cott deck doss eely feel ford gent grot hell huss josh kolo
```

```
kook lift lurk mica myna ogee past plum quad rima sard sick soap suit
koto like lush mice myth ogle pate plus quag rime sari side soar sulk
kris lilo lust mick Naga ogre path pock quay rimy sark sift sock sumo
kudu lilt lute midi naif oily paua poco quid rind sash sigh soda sump
Kurd lily luxe mien nail oink paul poem quin ring sass sign sofa sung
kyat lima lyam miff name okay pave poet quip rink sate sika soft sunk
kyle limb lych mike nana okra pawl pogo quit riot sati sike soho sunn
lace lime lyme mild nape oleo pawn poke quiz ripe save Sikh soil sura
lack limn lynx mile nard olid peak poky quod rise sawn sild soke surd
lacy limo Lyon milk nark olio peal pole rabi risk saxe silk sola sure
lade limp lyre mill nary olla pean poll race rite scab sill sold surf
lady limy lyse milt nave omen pear polo rack rive scad silo sole swab
laic line maam mime navy omer peat poly racy road scan silt soli swag
laid ling mace mina naze omit peck pome raff roam scar sima solo swam
lain link Mach mind Nazi once peek pomp raft roan scat sine soma swan
lair linn mack mine neap oner peel pond raga roar scot sing some swat
lake lino made Ming near only peen pone rage robe scow sinh sone sway
lakh lint mage mini neat onto peep pong ragi rock scry sink song swig
laky liny magi mink neck onus peer pons raid rode scud Sion soon swim
lama lion maid mint need onyx peke pony rail roil scug sire soot swiz
lamb lira mail minx neem oont pelf pood rain role scum site soph swob
lame lire maim mire neer oops pelt poof raja roll scup sith sora swop
lamp lisp main mirk nene ooze pent pooh rake romp scut Siva sorb swot
land list make miry neon opah peon pool raki rood seal size sore swum
lane live mako mise ness opal peri poon rale roof seam sizy sori syce
lang load male miss nest open perk poor ramp room sear skat sorn sync
lank loaf mali mist nett opus pern pore rand root seat skaw sort syne
Lapp loam mall mite neum oral pern pork rang rope sect skep souk taal
lard loan malm moan news orca pert porn rani rose seed skew soul tabu
lark loch malt moat newt orfe peso port rank rosy seek skid soup tace
larn loci mama mock next orgy pest post rant rote seel skim sour tach
lase lock mana mode nice orle phew posh rape rota self slab spae taco
lash loco mane mods nick orra phiz post rapt rote sell slag spar tact
lass loco Manx moho nide orts phon post rare rotl self slam spat tael
last lode many moho nidi oryx phot posy rase rotl seer slap spay tahr
late loft marc moil niff otic pica pouf rash roue sego slat spec tail
lath loge mare moke nigh otto pice pour rasp roup seme slaw sped take
laud logo mark moko nigh ouch pick pout rata roux semi slay spin talc
lava loin marl moll nill ouch pick pout rata roux self slag spar tail
lave loir marm moll nine ouph Pict poxy rate rove semi slat spec tala
lawk loll Mars moly nipa ours pied pram rath roux seme slap spay take
lawn lone mart mome nisi oust pier prat rave ruby slaw spew tale
laze long mash mona nixy ouzo pika pray razz rude sept slay spit tame
lazy look mask monk nock oval pike pray razz rude sera slew spiv tall
lead loom mass mono node oven oxen pile pree real ruin Serb sley spot tame
leaf loon mast mood nodi ovum pili prep ream rule sere slid spry tamp
leak loop mate moon noel oven pill prex ream ruff sera slew spud tana
leal loot math moor noil oxen pimp prey reap rune serf slim spue tang
lean lope matt moot nome oxer pine prig rear rung seta slip spud tank
leap lord maud mope none oyes ping prim reck runt sewn slob spur tapa
leat lore maul mora nonU oyez pint prod rede ruse slay sloe stab tape
leek lorn maun more nook paca piny prof redo rush sexy slog stag taps
lees lory maxi Moro nope pace pion prog reed rusk shad slop stap tara
leet lose maya mort norm pack pipa prom reef Russ shag slot star tare
left loss mazy moss nose pact pipe prop reek rust shah slow stay tarn
lehr lost mead most nosh page pipy prow reel ruth sham slub stay taro
lend loth mead mote paid pirn puce refs ryal Shan slue sten tarp
leno loud meal moth note pail pise puck reft ryot shaw slug step tart
lens loup mean moue noun pain piss puja reis rype shea slum slur stew tash
less lout Mede mown nova pale pith pull rent saga shed slut stir tass
lest love meed much nude pall pity pull rent saga shew smew stoa tata
Lett lowe meek much nude pall pity pull rent saga shew smew stoa taut
leva lown meld muff numb palm pixy puma rest said ship smug stot taws
levy luau meld muff numb palm pixy puma rest said ship smug stot taxa
lewd luce mell mule nuts paly plan pump puna rhea sail shiv smut stow taxi
liar luck melt mull oary pane plat puna rhea sain shod snag stub teak
Lias ludo memo oast pang play punk rhus sake shoe snap stud teal
lice lues mend muon oath pant plea punt rial saki shog sned stum team
lich luff menu mure oats papa pleb puny rich sale shoo snib stun tear
lick luge meow murk obey para pled pupa rick salt shop snip stye teat
lido lull mere muse obit pard plie pure ride same shot snob such teem
lied lulu mesa mush oboe pare plod purl rife samp Shri snot suck teen
lief lump mesh musk obol park plop purr riff sane shun snow sudd teff
lien lune mess muss odds parr plot push rift sang shut snub suds tegg
lier lung mete must odea part plow puss rift sank sial snug suer tele
lieu lunt mewl mute odic pash ploy putt rile sans sice soak suet tell
life lure mews mutt ogam pass plug pyre rill sans sice soak Sufi temp
```

```
tend tore uric warm wits Zion cart gala Java Mars rail tara abba beer
tent tori urim wive zoea case gale jazz mart rain tare abbe beet
term torn urus warp woad zoic cash gall kadi mash raja tarn abed bell
tern torr used wart woes zone cask gamb kago mask rake taro abet belt
test tort user wary woom zoom cast game kail mass raki tarp able bema
text Tory uvea wash wold zoon cate gamp kaka mast rale tart ably bend
Thai tosh vagi wasp wolf zoot caul gamy kale mate rami tash abut bent
than toss vail watt womb zori cave gang kali math ramp task abye bere
thar tote vain watt wont Zulu cavy gaol kame matt rand tass ebon berg
that tour vair waul wood ——  dace gape kana maty rang tata ibex berk
thaw tout vale wave woof baas Dada garb kaon maud rani taut ibid berm
thee town vali wavy wool baba dado garn kart maul rank taws ibis best
them towy vamp wawl word babe daff gash kava maun rant taxa obey beta
then trad vane waxy wore Babi daft gasp kayo maxi rape taxi obit bevy
thew tram vang ways work babu dago gast lace maya rapt vagi oboe cede
they trap vara weak worm baby dahl gate lack maze rare vail obol cedi
thig tray vary weal worn bach Dail gaud lacy mazy rase vain ache ceil
thin tree vasa wean wort back dais Gaul lade Naga rash vair achy cell
thir trek vase wear wost bade dale gaum lady naif rasp vale acid celt
this tret vast weed wove bael dame gaup laic nail rata vali acme cent
thou trey veal week wrap bail damn gaur laid name rate vamp acne cere
thro trig Veda ween wren bait damp gave lain nana rath vane acol cert
thud trim veer weep writ bake Dane gawk lair nape rave vang acre cess
thug trio vehm weet wynd bald dang gawp lake nard raze vara Acts dead
thus trip veil weft Xmas bale dank gaze lakh nark razz vary acyl deaf
tice trod vein weir Xray balk dare haaf laky nary sack vasa echo deal
tick tron vela weka yack ball darg haar lama nave safe vase echt dean
tide trot veld weld yang balm dark hack lamb navy saga vast ecru dear
tidy trow vena well yank banc darn hade lame naze sage Waac icky debt
tied troy vend wels yapp band dart hadj lamp Nazi sago Waaf icon deck
tier true vent welt yard bane dash haem land oary said wade scab deed
tiff trug verb wend yare bang data haet lane oast sail wadi scad deem
tige tsar vert went yarn bank date haft lang oath sain wady scan deep
tike Tshi vest wept yaup bant daub haha lank oats sake waff scar deer
tiki tuan veto were yawl barb dawk haik Lapp paca saki waft scat deft
tile tuba vice west yaws bard dawn hair lard pace sale wage scot defy
till tube vide wert yeah bare daze hair lard lard pace sale waif scow deil
tilt tuck vide wham yeah bark each hajj larn pact same wail scry dele
time tufa view whap yegg barm earl haka lase page samp wain scud delf
tine tuff vile what year barn earn hake lash paid sand wait scug dell
ting tuft vill whee yegg base ease hale lass pail sane wake scum deme
tint tule vina when yeld bash east half last pain sang wale scup demo
tiny tump vine whet yell bask easy hall late pair sank walk scut demy
tire tuna vino whew yelp bass eath halm lath pale sans wall Adam dene
tirl tune vint whey yerk bast eats halo laud Pali sard wame Adar dent
tiro tung viny whid yeti bate face halt lava pall sari wand adit deny
titi Tupi viol Whig yeuk bath fact hame lave palm sark wane adze derm
tizz turf virl whim yill bats fade hand lawk palp sash want Edam derv
toad Turk visa whin ylem batt fado hang lawn paly sass ward Edda desk
toby turn vise whip yoga baud faff hank laze pane sate ware eddy dewy
toco tush viva whir yogh bawd fail hard lazy pang sati warm Eden eely
todo tusk vive whit yogi bawl fain hare maam pant save warn edge eery
tody tutu vlei whiz yoke bawn fair hark mace papa sawn warp edgy fear
toed twae void whoa yolk bays fake harl Mach para saxe wart edit feat
toff twee vole whom yond cade fall harm mack pard taal wary idea feck
toft twig volt whop yoni cadi falx harn made pare tabu wash idem feed
tofu twin vote wick yore cafe fame harp mage park tace wasp ides feel
toga twit Waac wide york caff fane hart magi parr tach wast idle feet
togs tyke Waaf wife yowl cage fang hash maid part tack watt idly feis
toil type wade wild yowl cagy fard hasp mail pash taco waul idol fell
toko typo wadi wile yoyo cake fare hast maim pass tact wave odds felt
tola tyre wady will yuan calf farl hate main past tael wavy odea feme
told tyro waff wilt yuca calk farm hath make pate tahr wawl odic fend
tole tzar waft wily yuga call faro haul mako path tail waxy udal fere
toll udal wage wind yule calm fash have male paua tala yack aeon fern
tolu ugli waif wine yurt calp fast hawk mali paul tala yack aero fess
tomb ugly wail wing ywis calx fate haze mall pave talc yang aery fest
tome ulna wain wink zack came faun hazy malm pawl tale yank bead fete
tone umbo wait wino zany camp fawn iamb malt pawn tali yapp beak feud
tong unci wake winy zati cane faze jack mama rabi talk yard beam gean
tony unco wale wipe zeal cang gaby jade mane rack tall yare bean gear
took undo walk wire zebu cant gade jail mane racy tame yarn bear geat
tool unit wall wiry zein cape gadi Jain Manx racy tamp yaup beat geck
toom unto wame wise Zend capo Gael jake many raff tana yawl beau Geez
toon upas wand wish zero card gaff jamb marc raft tang yawn beck geld
tope upon wane wisp zest care gaga jane mare raga tank yaws Beeb gelt
topi Urdu want wist zeta cark gage jape mark rage tapa zany been gene
tops urea ward wite zinc carl gain jarl marl ragi tape zany beep gens
torc urge ware with zing carp gait jato marm raid taps zati beep gent
```

```
germ mead reis weft khan bigg gird lint pixy vina blob olio ante boss
gest meal rely weir khat bike girl liny rial vine bloc olla anti both
geum mean rend weka phew bile girn lion rice vino blot plan enow bott
head meat rent weld phiz bilk giro lira rich vint blow plat envy bout
heal Mede repp well phon bill girt lire rick viny blub play gnar bowl
heap meed rest wels phot bind gist lisp ride viol blue plea gnat boxy
hear meek rete welt rhea bine give list rife virl blur pleb gnaw boyg
heat meet seal wend rhus bint hick live riff visa clad pled inby boyo
heck meld seam went shad bird hide mica rift vise clam plie Inca bozo
heed mell sear wept shag birk hifi mice rile viva clan plod inch coal
heel melt seat were shah birl high mick rill vive clap plop info coat
heft memo sect wert sham bise hike midi rima wick claw plot inky coax
heil mend seed west Shan bisk hila mien rime wide clay plow inly coca
heir menu seek yeah shaw bite hill miff rimy wife clef ploy into cock
held meow seel yean shay bitt hilt mike rind wild cleg plug knag coco
hele mere seem year shea ciao hind mild ring wile clem plum knap coda
hell mesa seen yegg shed cine hint mile rink will clew plus knar code
helm mesh seep yeld shew cire hipt milk riot wilt clip slab knee coed
help mess seer yell shim cist hire mill ripe wily clod slag knew coho
heme mete sego yelp shin cite hiss milt rise wind clog slam knit coif
hemp mewl self yerk ship city hist mime risk wine clop slap knob coil
hent mews sell yeti shiv dial hive mina rite wing clot slat knop coin
herb neap seme yeuk shod dice jibe mind rive wink clou Slav knot coir
herd near semi zeal shoe dick jiff mine sial wino cloy slaw know coke
here neat send zebu shog dido jill Ming sice winy club slay knur cola
herl neck sent zein shoo diet jilt mini sick wipe clue sled knut cold
herm need seps Zend shop dike jimp mink side wire elan slew once cole
hern neem sept zero shot dill jink mint sift wiry elmy sley oner colt
hero neer sera zest show dime jinn minx sigh wise else slid only coma
Herr nene Serb zeta Shri dine jinx mire sign wish flab slim onto comb
hers neon sere afar shun ding jive mirk sika wisp flag slip onus come
hest ness serf Afro shut dink kibe miry sike wist flak slit onyx comp
hewn nest seta iffy Thai dint kick mise Sikh wite flam slob snag cone
jean nett sett agar than dire kier miss sild with flan sloe snap conk
jeep neum sewn aged thar dirk kill mist silk wits flap slog sned conn
jeer neve sext agha that dirl kiln mite sill wive flat slop snib cony
jehu news sexy agin thaw dirt kilo mitt silo yill flaw slot snip cook
jell newt teak agio thee disc kilt nice silt zinc flax slow snob cool
jerk next teal agog them dish kind nick sima zing flay slub snog coon
jess peak team agon then disk king nide sine Zion flea slue snot coop
jest peal tear ague thew diss kino nidi sing ajar fled slug snow coot
jete pean teat egad they dite kink niff sinh akee flee slum snub cope
keck pear teem egal thig ditt kino nigh sink akin flew slur snug Copt
keek peat teen eger thin diva kiri nill Sion ekka flex slut unci copy
keel peck teff eggy thir dive kirk nine sire ikon fley ulna unco cord
keen peek tegg egis this divi kiss nipa site okay flic vlei undo core
keep peel tele ogam thou dixy kist nisi sith okra flip ylem unit corf
kelp peen tell ogee thro fiat kite nixy Siva skat flit amah unto cork
Kelt peep temp ogle thud fico kith oily size skaw floc ambo boar corm
kemp peer tend ogre thug fido kiwi oink sizy skep floe amen boat corn
kent peke tent ugli thus fief kino pica tice skew flog amid bock cose
kepi pelf term ugly wham fife kiri pice tick skid flop amir bode cosh
kept pelt tern ahoy whap file lice pick tide skim flow ammo body cost
kerb pent test chad what fill lich Pict tidy skin flub amok Boer cosy
kerf peon text cham whee film lick pied tied skip flue amyl bogy cote
kern pepo veal Veda when fils lido pier tier skit flux emeu boil cott
lead peri Veda chap whet find lied pika tiff skua flys emir boko coup
leaf perk veer char whew fine lief pike tige alae glad emit bold cove
leak perm vehm chat whey fink lien pile tike alar glam Emmy bole cowl
leal pern veil chaw whid Finn lier pili tiki alas glee Gman boll coxa
lean pert vein chef Whig fino lieu pill tile alee gleg imam bolt coxy
leap peso vela chew whim fire life pimp tilt alfa glen impi boma coze
leat pest veld chic whin firm lift pine tine alga gley omen bomb doat
leek read vena chid whip firn like ping time ally glia omer book doge
leer real vend chin whir fisc lilo pink tine alms glib omit bone dock
lees ream vent chip whit fish lilt pint ting aloe glim smew bong doer
leet reap verb chit whiz fisk lily piny tint alow glob smit bony does
left rear vert choc whoa fist lima pion tiny also glop smog boob doff
lehr reck vest chop whom fitz limb pipa tire alto glow smug book doge
lend redd veto chou whop five lime pipe tirl alum glue smut boom dogy
leno rede weak chow aide fizz limn pipy tiro blab glum umbo boon doit
lens redo weal chub aine gibe limo pirn titi blae glut Xmas boor dojo
Lent reed wean chug Ainu gift limp pise tizz blah ilea anew boot dole
less reef wear chum airy gila limy pish vial blat ilex anil bora doll
lest reek weed chut bias gild line piss vice bleb ilia ankh bore dolt
Lett reel week dhal bice gill ling pita vide bled ilka anna born dome
leva refs ween dhow bide gilt link pith view blew illy anoa bort domy
levy reft weep ghat bier gimp linn pity vile blin oleo anon bosh dona
lewd rein weet ghee biff gink lino pium vill blip olid anta bosk done
```

```
dong holm lout pony soul york crap prau stot dunk lush suds axes alas
dont holp love pood soup your pray stow dupe lust lute suet axil amah
dook hols lowe poof sour yowl cree pree stub dura lute suet axis Arab
doom holt lown pooh sown yoyo crew prep stud durn luxe Sufi axle arak
door holy moan pool soya zoea crib prex stum duro suit      axon away
dope home moat poon toad zoic crit prey stun dusk muck suit exam ayah
dopy homo mock poop toby zone crop prig stye dust muff sumo exes baas
dorm homy mode poor toco zoom crow prim duro mute mule sump exit bead
dorp hone moho pope todo zoon crud proa aunt fuci mull sung exon beak
dorr hong moil pore tody zoot crux prod aura fuel mump sunk expo beam
dort honk pork toed zori drab prof auto fuci mump muon sunn oxen bean
dory hood moke port toff apex drag prog bubo full mure sura oxer bear
dose hoof mole pose tofu apod dram prom buck fume murk surd ayah beat
doss hook mole tofu apse drat prop buff fumy muse sure byre beau
dost hoop moll posh toga epee draw prow buhl fund mush surf byte bias
dote hoot moly post togs epha dray trad bulb funk musk tuan cyan blab
doth hope mome posy toil epic dree tram bulk furl muss tuba cyma blae
doup horn mona pouf toko epos dreg trap bull fury must tube cyme blah
dour hose monk pour tola opah drew tray bumf fuse mute tuck cyst blat
dove hoss mono pout told opal drey tree bump fuss mutt tufa dyad boar
down host mood poxy tole open drib trek buna fuze nude tuff Dyak boat
doxy hour moon road toll opus drip tret bund fuzz null tuft dyer brad
doze hove moor roam tolu drop trey bung guan numb tule dyke brae
dozy howl moot roan tomb span drub trig bunk guar nuts tump dyne brag
foal iota mope roar tone spar drug trim bunt guff ouch tuna eyas bran
foam jock mora robe tone spat drum trio buoy gula ouph tune eyed brat
foci joey more rock tong spay Druz trip burd gulf ours tung eyne braw
fogy john rode tony cego trod tron burk gulp oust Tupi eyot bray
fohn join Moro roil took sped Erin tron burk gulp ouzo turf eyra chad
foil joke mort role tool spew erne trot burl gump puce Turk eyre cham
foin joky moss roll toom spin Eros trow burn gunk puck turn eyry chap
fold jolt most romp toon spit Erse troy burp guru puff tush fyrd char
folk josh mote rood tope spiv erst true burr gush puja tusk gybe chat
fond joss moth roof topi spot frae trug bury gust puke tutu gymp chaw
font jota moue rook tops spry frap Urdu bush guts pule yuan gyre ciao
food jowl move room torc spud frat urea busk hued pull yuca gyri clad
fool koan mown root tore spue Frau urge buss huff pulp yuga gyro clam
foot koel moxa rope tori spun fray uric bust huge puma yule gyve clan
ford kohl nock ropy torn spur free urim busy hula pump yurt hyle clap
fore kola node rose tort upas fret urus butt hulk puna Zulu hyle claw
fork kolo nodi rosy tort upon frit wrap buzz hull punk puna hymn clay
form kook noel rota Tory aqua froe wren cube hump punt aver hype coal
fort koto noil rote tosh Arab frog writ cuff hung puny avid hypo coat
foss load nome rotl toss arak from Xray cuit hunk pupa even ever coax
foul loaf none roue arch frow asci cull hunt pure ever lyam crab
four loam nonU roup tour area grab ashy culm hurl purl evil lyme cram
fowl loan noon roux town Ares graf Asti cult hurt purr oval lynx cran
foxy lobe noon roux town aria gram esne cups hush push oven Lyon crap
goad loch nope rove towy arid gran espy curb husk puss over lyre craw
goal loci norm soak void aril grat esse curd huss putt ovum lyse cyan
goat lock nose soap vole arms gray isle cure juba quad uvea myna czar
goby loco nosh soar volt army gree isnt curl judo quag away myth oyer dead
goer lode nosy sock vote arty grew tsar curn judy quay awed myth oyer deaf
goes loft note soda woad arum grey Tshi curr juju quid awny oyer deal
gogo loge noun sofa woes aryl grid used curt July quin awry oyes dean
gold logo nous soft woke brad grig user cush junk quip ewer oyez dear
golf loin nova soho wold brae grim atom cusk June quit hwyl pyre dhal
gone loir nowt soil wolf brag grin atop cusp junk quiz iwis ryal dial
gong loll oont soke womb bran grip etch cuss Juno quod swab ryot doat
gonk lone oops sola wont brat gris etna cute jury ruby swag rype drab
good long ooze sold wood braw grit etui duad just ruck swam syce drag
goof look oozy sole worf bray grog itch dual jute rudd swan sync dram
gook loom pock soli wool bred grot item duce kudu rude swap syne drat
goon loon poco solo word bree grow otic duck Kurd ruff swat tyke draw
goop loop poem soma wore bren grub otto duct luau ruin swam type dray
gory loot poet some work brer grum stab dude luce rule swig typo duad
Goth lope pogo sone worm brew iris stag duds luck rump swim tyre dual
gout lord poke song worn Brie iron stap duel ludo rune swiz tyro duad
gowk lore poky soon wort brig kris star dues lues rung swob wynd dyad
gown lorn pole soot wost brim oral stay duet luff runt swop czar Dyak
hoar lory poll soph wove brio orca stem duff luge ruse swot tzar Edam
hoax lose polo sora yoga brit orfe sten duke luli rush swum ──── egad
hobo loss poly sorb yogh brog orgy step dull lulu rusk twae Adam egal
hock lost pome sore yogi brow orle stet duly lump Russ twee Adar elan
hoer lota pomp sori yoke brut orra stew duma lune rust twig afar exam
hogg loth pond sork crab orts stir dumb lung ruth twin agar eyas
hoho loud pone sort yond crag oryx stoa dump lunt such twit ajar fear
hold loup pong soso yoni cram pram stob dune lure suck ywis alae feat
hole lour pons souk yore cran prat stop dung lurk sudd axel alar fiat
```

```
flab near swan back rack odds dyer ogee used alga amir Jain trig sike
flag neat swap beck racy redd Eden oleo user bigg anil join trim Sikh
flak ogam swat bice reck rede eger omen uvea bogy aria kail trio soke
flam okay sway bock rice redo emeu omer veer cage arid knit trip take
flan opah taal buck rich ride epee oner view vlei dago avid laic twin tiki
flap opal teak coca rick rode even open weed doge axil laid twit toko
flat oral teal cock rock rudd ever oven week dogy axis lain unit tyke
flaw oval team coco ruck rude ewer over week edge bail lair uric wake
flax peak tear dace sice side exes oxen ween edgy bait loin urim weka
flay peal teat deck sect soda eyed oxer weep eggy blin loir vail woke
foal pean Thai dice sick sudd feed oyer weet ergo boil maid vain yoke
foam pear than dick sick suds feel oyes whee blip maid vain yoke
frae peat thar dock tide feet feet oyez when fogy boil mail vair able
frap plan that duce such tidy fief peek whet gaga Brie maim veil ably
frat plat thaw duck suck todo flea peel whew gage brig main vein ally
Frau play toad duct syce tody fled peen whey gogo brim moil void auld
fray pram trad each tace undo flee peep woes high brio naif waif axle
gean prat tram etch tach Urdu flew peer wren hogg brit nail wail bald
gear prau trap face tack Veda flex phew huge ceil noil wain bale
geat pray tray fact taco vide fley pied zoea kago obit wait balk
ghat quad tsar feck tact wade free pier alfa loge chid odic weir ball
glad quag tuan fico tice wadi fret plea biff logo chin olid whid balm
glam quay twae foci tick wady fuel pleb buff luge chip chin whid balm
Gman read tzar fuci toco wide Gael pled cafe mage chit omit Whig belt
gnar real udal geck tuck abed Geez poem caff magi otic whin bile
gnat ream upas hack unci abet ghee poet cuff Naga coif paid whip bilk
gnaw reap veal heck unco aged glee pree daff nigh coil pail whir bill
goad rear vial hick vice ahem gleg prep daft orgy coin pain whit bold
goal rial Waac hock wick akee glen prex deft page coir pair whiz bole
goat road Waaf Inca yack alee gley prey defy pogo crib phiz writ boll
grab roam weak inch yuca amen goer reed doff raga crit plie ywis bolt
graf roan weal itch zack anew goes reef duff rage cuit prig zein bulb
gram roar wean jack aide apex gree reek faff ragi Dail prim zoic bulk
gran ryal wear jock bade area grew reel fife saga dais quid dojo bull
grat scab wham keck bide Ares grey rhea gaff sage deil quin hajj calf
gray scad whap kick bode aver haem seed gift sago doit quip juju calk
guan scan what lace cade awed haet seek guff sego drib quit puja call
guar scar woad lack cadi axel haft sigh drip quiz raja calm
haaf scat wrap lacy cadi axes heed sign sign edit raid ankh calp
haar seal Xmas lice cede bael heel seem heft egis rail bake calx
head seam Xray lich cedi Beeb hued seen hifi tegg emir rain bike cell
heal sear yeah lick coda beef ibex seep tige emir boko celt
heap seat yean loch code been idea shea info togs epic reis cake cola
hear shad year loci Dada beep idem shed jiff urge Erin roil coke cold
heat shag yuan lock dado beer ides shew left vagi evil ruin dike cole
hoar shah zeal loco dido beet ilea skep life yegg exit said duke colt
hoax sham abba luce dodo bier ilex skew lift yoga fail sail dyke cull
imam Shan abbe luck dude bleb item sled loft yogh fain sain ekka culm
jean shaw ambo lych duds bled jeep slew luff yogi fair shim fake cult
khan shay baba mace Edda blew jeer sley miff yuga feis shin haka dale
khat sial babe Mach eddy Boer joey smew muff flic ship hake dele
knag skat Babi mack fade bred keek sned niff ache flip shiv hike delf
knap skaw babu mica fado bree keel spec orfe achy flit skid icky dell
knar slab baby mice fido bren keen sped puff agha foil skim ilka dill
koan slag bubo mick gade brer keep spew raff ashy foin skin inky dole
kyat slam cube mock gadi brew kier stem raft buhl frit skip jake doll
lead slap debt much hade chef knee sten refs coho gain skit joke doll
leaf slat gaby muck hadj chew knew step reft dahl gait slid joky dull
leak Slav gibe neck hide clef koel stet rife echo glia slim kaka duly
leal slaw goby nice jade cleg leek stew riff echt glib slip lake eely
lean slay gybe nick judo clem leer suer rift epha glim slit lakh fall
leap snag hobo nock judy clew lees suet ruff fohn grid smit laky falx
leat snap inby once kadi coed leet tael safe haha grig snib like fell
liar soak jibe orca kudu cree lied teem sift hoho grim snip make felt
Lias soap juba ouch lade crew lief teen sofa jehu grin soil mako file
load soar kibe paca lady deed lien thee soft john grip spin mike fill
loaf spae lobe pace lido deem lier them Sufi kohl gris spit moke film
loam span rabi pack lode deep lieu then teff lehr grit spiv moko fils
loan spar robe pact ludo deer lues thew tiff moho haik stir peke fold
luau spat ruby peck made diet meed they toff soho hail suit pika folk
lyam spay tabu pica Mede doer meek tied toft tahr hair swig poke full
maam stab toby pice midi does meet tier tofu Tshi heil swim poky gala
mead stag tuba pick mode dree mien toed tufa vehm heir swiz poky gale
meal stap tube Pict mods dreg need tree tuff acid ibid tail huge gall
mean star umbo pock nide drew neem trek tuft adit ibis thig rake geld
meat stay zebu poco nidi drey neer tret waff agin ilia thin raki gelt
moan swab arch puce node duel noel trey waft agio iris thir sake gila
moat swag asci puck nodi dues obey twee weft akin iwis this saki gild
neap swam bach race nude duet odea urea wife amid jail toil sika gill
```

```
gilt ogle wild limo Dane ling sone boot mood tron awry farm mire Tory
gold oily wile limp dang link song brog moon trot barb faro mirk turf
golf olla will limy dank linn sung brow moor trow bard fere miry Turk
gula only wilt lump dene lino sunk buoy moot troy bare fern mora turn
gulf orle wily lyme dent lint sunn choc muon upon bark fire more tyre
gull pale wold mama deny liny sync chop neon viol barm firm morn tyro
gulp Pali wolf memo dine lone syne chou nook whoa barn firn Moro vara
hale pall yeld mime ding long tana chou noon whom bere ford mort vary
half palm yell mome dink lune tang clod oboe whop berg fore mure verb
hall palp yelp mump dint lung tank clog obol wood berk fork murk vert
halm paly yill name dona lunt tend clop peon woof berm form nard virl
halo pelf yolk nome done lynx tent clot phon wool bird fort nark ward
halt pelt yule numb dong mana tine clou      Zion birk furl nary ware
held pile Zulu pimp dont mane tiny cloy pion zoom birl fury norm warm
hele pili acme pome dune Manx tint cook plod zoon bora fyrd oary warn
hell pill alms pomp dung many tiny cool plop zoot bore garb ogre warp
helm pole ammo puma dunk mend tone coon plot cape born garn okra wart
help poll arms pump dyne menu tong coot ploy capo bort germ orra wary
hila polo army rami erne mina tony crop pood      burd gird ours were
hill pule bema ramp esne mind tuna crow pooh copy burg girl para wert
hilt pull boma rima etna mine tune dhow pool burk girn pard wire
hold pulp bomb rime eyne Ming tung dook poon burl giro pare wiry
hole rale bumf rimy fane mini ulna doom pool dope burn girt park word
holm rile bump romp fang mink vane door poon dopy burp gory parr wore
holp rely came rump fend mint door poop dupe burr guru part work
hols rill camp same find minx vena drop poor espy bury gyre peri worm
holt role coma samp fine mona vend ebon proa expo byre gyri perk worn
holy rule comb seme font mono vent enow prod gape card gyro perm wort
hula sale come semi fino myna vina vine prof hipt care hard pern yard
hulk salt comp sima Finn mona vine Eros prog hype cark hare pert yare
hull self cyma soma fond myna vint exon prom hypo carl hark pirn yarn
hyle damn cyme some font nene nana exon prop impi cart harm pork yore
idle sild dame sumo fund nine none wand floe jape cere harn pore yore
idly silk damn sump funk nonU wane flog riot kepi cert harp porn york
illy silo deme tame gang oink want flop rood kept cire hart port yurt
inly silt demo tamp gene oont wend flow roof Lapp cord herb purl zero
isle silt demy temp gens pane went food rook lope core herd purr zori
jell silo dime time gent pang wind fool room mope corf here pyre also
jill silt tomb tome gone pant wine foot root nape cork herl rare apse
jilt sola dome tome gone pent wing froe ryot nipa corm herm sard base
jolt sold domy tump gong pent wink frog scot nope corn hern sari bash
July sole duma vamp pine ping wino from shod oops curb hero sark bask
kale soli dumb wame gunk hand pink winy frow shod ouph curd Herr scry bass
kali solo dump womb hand pink winy wynd glob shog papa cure curl hers sera bast
kelp sulk elmy acne hang pint wont gaol shoe pupa cure curl hire Serb bise
Kelt tala Emmy aine hank piny wynd glob shoo pipa curn horn sere bisk
kill talc fame Ainu hent pond yang glop shop pipe curr hurl serf bosh
kiln tale feme anna hind pone yank glow shot pipy curt hurt Shri bosk
kilo tali fume aunt hint pong yond good show pope dare jarl sire boss
kilt talk fumy awny hone pons yoni goof shot pipy dark jerk sora bush
kola tall gamb banc hong pony zany gook Sion pupa darg jury sorb busk
kolo tele game band honk puna Zend goon slob sloe rape dark kart sora buss
kyle tell gamp bane hung punk zinc goop sloe rapt darn kart kerb sori bust
lilo tile gamy bang hunk punt zing grog slog repp derm kerf sorn busy
lilt tilt gimp bank hunt puny zone grot slop ripe derv kern sort case
lily till gump bant isnt rand acol grow slot rope dire kiri spry cash
loll tola gymp bend jane rang aeon hood slow ropy dirk kirk sura cask
lull told hame bent jink rani agog hoof smog rype dirt dirk Kurd surd cast
lulu tole heme bind jinn rank agon hook snob seps dirl Kurd surd cess
male tolu hemp bine jinx rant ahoy hoop snog sept dirt lard sure cist
mali tolu home bint June rend aloe hoot snot soph dorm lark surf cose
mall tule homo bond junk rent alow icon snow tapa dorp larn tara cosh
malm ugli homy bone kana rind amok idol soon tape dorr lira tare cost
malt ugly hump bong kent ring anoa ikon spot taps dort lire tarn cosy
meld vale hymn bony kind rink iron soot stoa topi dura lord taro cush
mell vali iamb buna kine rune apod atom knob stob tops durn lorn tart cusk
melt vela jamb bund king runt atop knop stop Tupi duro lory term cusp
mild veld jimp bung kink sand avow knot stot type earl lure tern cuss
mile vile jump bunk kino sane axon know stow typo earn lurk thro cyst
milk vill kame bunt kino sane axon know stow typo earn lurk thro cyst
mill vole kemp cane land sang blob lion swob wept ecru lyre tire dash
milt volt kemp cang lane sank bloc lion swop wipe eery marc tirl desk
mole wale lamb cant lang sans blot look loom swot yapp euro mare tiro disc
moll wall lamp cine lend sent boob loon took aero eyra mark torc dish
moly wall lamp cine lend sent boob loon took aero eyra marl tore disk
mule weld lima cone sine sing boom boon Lyon toon airy fard Mars torn dose
mull wels limb conn lent sinh book boor meow trod aura farl mere tort dost
null welt limn cony line sink boor meow trod aura farl mere tort dost
```

```
dusk nisi cate tata opus lava poxy data sera limb dyad rood bice dude
dust nose cite titi ovum lave saxe diva seta numb egad rudd bide duke
ease nosh city tote paua leva sext dona shea pleb eyed said bike dune
east nosy cote tutu paul levy sexy duma sika scab fard sand bile dupe
easy oast cott unto pium live taxa dura sima Serb feed sard bine dyke
else oust cute veto plug love taxi Edda Siva slab scad bise dyne
Erse pash data vote plum move text ekka skua slob feud scud bite ease
erst pass date watt plus nave waxy epha soda slub find seed blae edge
esse past dite wite pouf navy abye etna sofa snib fled send blue else
fash peso ditt with pour neve acyl eyra sola snob fold shad bode epee
fast pest dote wits pout nova amyl flea soma snub fond shed bole erne
fess pise doth yeti rhus pave aryl gaga sora sorb food shod bone Erse
fest pish duty zati roue rave bays gala soya stab ford sild bore esne
fisc piss eath zeta roup rive boyg gila stoa stob fund skid brae esse
fish pose eats abut rout rove boyo glia sura stub fyrd sled bree eyne
fisk posh fate ague roux save flys gula tala swab gaud slid Brie eyre
fist post fete alum scud Siva hwyl haha tana swob geld sned byre face
foss posy fitz aqua scug viva kayo haka tapa tomb gild sold byte fade
fuse push gate arum scum vive maya hila tara verb gird sped cade fake
fuss puss Goth baud scup wave onyx hula tata womb glad spud cafe fame
gash rase guts blub scut wavy oryx idea taxa banc goad stud cage fane
gasp rash hate blue shun wive soya ilea toga bloc gold sudd cake fare
gast rasp hath blur shut wove stye ilia tola chic good surd came fate
gest rest into bout skua bawd ways ilka tuba choc grid tend cane faze
gist rise iota brut slub bawl yoyo Inca tufa disc hand thud cape feme
gush risk jato caul slue bawn adze iota tuna epic hard tied care fere
gust rose jete chub slug bowl bozo Java ulna fisc head toad case fete
hash rosy jota chug slum cowl buzz jota urea flic heed toed cate fife
hasp ruse jute chum slur dawk coze juba uvea floc held told cave file
hast rush kite chut slut dawn daze kaka vara laic herd trad cede fine
hest rusk kith club smug dewy doze kana vasa marc hind trod cere fire
hiss Russ koto clue smut down dozy kava Veda odic hold used cine five
hist rust late coup snub fawn faze kola vela otic hood veld cire flee
hose sash lath crud snug fowl fizz lama vena spec hued vine cite floe
hoss sass Lett crux souk gawk fuze lava vina sync ibid void clue flue
host soso lota daub soul gawp fuzz leva visa talc kind wand code fore
hush tash loth doup soup gowk gaze lima viva torc Kurd ward coke frae
husk task lute dour sour gown haze lira weka uric laid weed cole free
huss tass mate drub spud hawk hazy lota whoa Waac land weld come froe
jess test math drug spue hewn jazz mama yoga zinc lard wend cone fume
jest tosh matt drum spun howl laze mana yuca zoic laud whid cope fuse
josh toss maty Druz spur jowl lazy maya yuga abed lead wild core fuze
joss tush mete etui stub kiwi maze mesa zeta acid lend wind cose gade
just tusk mite faun stud lawk mazy mica zoea aged lewd woad cote gage
kiss vasa mitt feud stum lawn naze mina Arab amid lied wold cove gale
kist vase mote flub stun lewd Nazi mona barb apod load wood coze game
lase vast moth flue swum lowe ooze mora Beeb arid lord word cree gape
lash vest mute flux taut lown oozy moxa blab auld loud wynd cube gate
lass visa mutt foul thud mewl ouzo myna bleb avid maid yard cure gave
last vise myth four thug mews raze Naga blob awed maud yeld cute gaze
less wash nett gaud thus mown razz nana blub bald mead yond cyme gene
lest wasp note Gaul tour news size nipa bomb band meed Zend dace ghee
lisp wast nuts gaum tout newt sizy nova boob bard meld abbe dale gibe
list west oath gaup true nowt tizz odea bulb baud mend able Dame give
lose wise oats gaur trug pawl ———— okra chub bawd mild abye Dane glee
loss wish onto geum urus pawn abba olla club bead mind ache dare glue
lost wisp orts glue waul sawn agha orca comb bend mood acme date gone
lush wist otto glum yaup sewn alfa orra crab bind nard acne daze gree
lust wost pate glut yeuk sown alga paca crib bird need acre dele gybe
lyse zest path gout your taws anna papa curb bled olid adze deme gyre
mash Acts pita grub bevy town anoa para daub bold paid ague dene gyve
mask alto pith grum cave towy anta paua drab bond pard aide dice hade
mass anta pity haul cavy wawl aqua pica drib brad pied aine dike hake
mast ante putt hour cove yawl area pika drub bred pled akee dime hale
mesa anti rata knur diva yawn aria pipa dumb bund plod alae dire hame
mesh arty rate knut dive yaws aura pita flab burd pond alee dire hare
mess Asti rath laud divi yowl baba plea flub card pood aloe dite hate
mise auto rete loud dove boxy bema proa gamb chad prod ante dive have
miss bate rite loup envy coxa beta puja garb chid quad apse doge haze
mist bath rota lour five coxy boma puma glib clad quid axle dole hele
moss bats rote lout gave dixy bora puna glob clod quod babe dome heme
most batt rotl maud give doxy buna pupa grab coed raid bade done here
muse beta ruth maul gyve foxy coca raga grub cold rand bake dope hide
mush bite sate maun have luxe coda raja herb cord read bale dose hike
musk bitt sati moue hive maxi cola rata iamb crud redd bane dote hire
muss both seta neum hove moxa coma rhea jamb curd reed bare dove hive
must bott sett noun Java next coxa rima kerb dead reed base doze hole
ness butt site nous jive nixy cyma rota knob deed rind bate dree home
nest byte sith onus kava pixy Dada saga lamb duad road bere duce hone
```

```
hope mode rife twae muff rung mesh sati gawk rink dell opal corm trim
hose moke rile twee naif sang moth semi geck risk dhal oral cram urim
hove mole rime tyke niff scug much Shri gink rock dial oval culm vehm
huge mome ripe type pelf shag mush soli gonk rook dill pail deem warm
hyle mope rise tyre poof shog myth sori gook ruck dirl pall derm wham
hype more rite urge pouf sing nigh Sufi gowk rusk doll paul doom whim
idle mote rive vale prof slag nosh tali gunk sack dual pawl dorm whom
isle moue robe vane puff slog oath taxi hack sank duel peal dram worm
jade move rode vase raff slug opah Thai haik sark dull peel drum ylem
jake mule role vice reef smog ouch tiki hank seek earl pill Edam zoom
jane mure rope vide riff smug ouph titi hark sick egal poll exam aeon
jape muse rose vile roof snag pash topi hawk silk evil pool farm agin
jete mute rote vine ruff snog path tori heck sink fail pull film agon
jibe name roue vise self snug pish Tshi hick soak fall purl firm akin
jive nape rove vive serf song pith Tupi hock sock farl rail flam amen
joke nave rude vole surf stag pooh ugli honk souk feel real foam anon
June naze rule vote teff sung posh unci hook suck fell reel form axon
jute nene rune wade tiff swag push vagi hulk sulk fill rial from barn
kale neve ruse wage toff swig rash vali hunk sunk foal rill gaum bawn
kame nice rype wake tuff tang rath vlei husk tack foil roil germ bean
kibe nide safe wale turf tegg rich wadi jack talk fool roll geum been
kine nine sage wame Waaf thig rush yeti jerk tank foul rotl glam blin
kite node sake wane waff thug ruth yogi jink task fowl ryal glim boon
knee nome sale ware waif ting sash yoni jock teak fuel sail glum born
kyle none same wave wolf tong shah zati junk tick full seal gram bran
lace nope sane were woof trig sigh zori keck took furl seel grim bren
lade nose sate whee agog trug Sikh hadj keek trek Gael sell grum burn
lake note save wide bang sinh hajj kick tuck gall sial haem chin
lame nude saxe wife berg twig sith amok kink Turk gaol sill halm clan
lane oboe seme wile bigg vang soph arak kirk tusk Gaul soil harm coin
lase ogee sere wine bong Whig such back kook walk gill soul helm conn
late ogle shoe wipe boyg wing tach balk lack weak girl taal herm coon
lave ogre sice wire brag yang tash bank lank week goal tael holm corn
laze once side wise brig yegg tosh bark lark wick gull tail idem cran
lice ooze sike wite brog zing tush bask lawk wink hail tall imam curn
life orfe sine wive bung amah wash beak leak work hall teal item cyan
like orle sire woke burg ankh wish beck leek yack harl tell loam damn
lime pace site wore cang arch with berk lick yank haul till loom darn
line page size wove chug ayah yeah bilk link yerk heal tirl lyam dawn
lire pale sloe yare cleg bach yogh birk lock yeuk heel toil maam dean
live pane slue yoke clog bash anti bisk look yolk heil toll maim down
lobe pare soke yore crag bath asci bock luck york hell tool malm durn
lode pate sole yule dang blah Asti book lurk zack herl udal marm earn
loge pave some zone darg bosh Babi bosk mack acol hill vail neem ebon
lone peke sone beef ding both cadi buck mark acyl howl veal neum Eden
lope pice sore biff dong bush cedi bulk mask amyl hull veil norm elan
lore pike spae buff drag cash divi bunk meek anil hurl vial ogam Erin
lose pile spue bumf dreg cosh etui burk mick aril hwyl vill ovum even
love pine stye caff drug cush foci busk milk aryl idol viol palm exon
lowe pipe sure calf dung dash fuci calk mink axel jail virl perm fain
luce pise syce chef dish gadi gash dick cark cask jell wall plum fawn
luge plie syne clef flag gyri hajj dink cask bael jell waul poem fern
lune poke tace coif flog each hifi cock conk bail jill jowl pram Finn
lure pole take corf frog eath impi conk muck bail jill weal prim firn
lute pome tale cuff gang etch kadi cook murk bawl kail weal prom flan
luxe pone tame daff gleg fash kali cork musk bell keel well ream flan
lyme pope tape deaf gong fish kepi cusk nark bill kill will ream fohn
lyre pore tare delf grig gash kiri dank neck birl koel wool roam foin
lyse pose tele doff grog Goth kiwi dark nick boil kohl yawl room gain
mace pree thee duff hang gush loci dawk nock boll leal yell scum garn
made puce tice faff hogg hash magi deck nook bowl loll yill seam gean
mage puke tide fief hong hath mali desk oink buhl lull yowl seem girn
make pule tige gaff hung high maxi dick park bull mail zeal sham glen
male pure tike golf king hush midi dink park burl mall Adam shim Gman
mane pyre tile goof knag inch mini park peak call marl maul ahem skim goon
mare race time graf lang itch Nazi disk peck carl maul alum slam gown
mate rage tine guff ling josh nidi dock peek caul meal arum slim gran
maze rake tire gulf long kith nisi dook perk ceil mell atom slum grin
Mede rale tole haaf lung lakh nodi duck pick cell mewl balm stem guan
mere rape tome half Ming lash Pali dink pink coal mill barm stum harn
mete rare tone hoof pang lath peri dusk pock coil mill beam swam hern
mice rase tope huff ping lich pili Dyak pork cool moll berm swim hewn
mike rate tore jiff plug loch rabi feck puck cowl mull boom swum horn
mile rave tote kerf pong loth ragi fink punk cull nail brim team hymn
mime raze tree leaf prig lush raki fisk rack curl nill calm teem icon
mine rede true lief prog lych rami flak rank dahl noel cham term ikon
mire rete tube loaf quag Mach rani folk reck Dail noil chum them iron
mise rice tule luff rang mash saki fork reek deal null clam toom Jain
mite ride tune miff ring math sari funk rick deil obol clem tram jean
```

```
jinn tern kino drip sump moor foss aunt fest lunt skat jehu flax gamy
john than kolo drop swap near fuss bait fiat lust skit juju flex gley
join then koto dump swop neer gens bant fist malt slat kudu flux goby
kaon thin leno flap tamp omer goes bast flat mart slit lieu hoax gory
keen toon lido flip tarp oner gris batt flit mast slot luau ibex gray
kern torn lilo flop temp over guts beat font matt slut lulu ilex grey
khan town limo frap trap oxer hers beet foot meat smit menu jinx hazy
kiln tron lino gamp trip oyer hiss belt fort meet smut nonU lynx holy
koan tuan loco gasp tump pair hols bent frat melt snot prau Manx homy
lain turn logo gaup vamp parr hoss best fret milt soft tabu minx icky
larn twin ludo gawp warp pear huss bint frit mint soot thou onyx idly
lawn upon mako gimp wasp peer ibis bitt gait mist sort tofu oryx iffy
lean vain memo glop weep pier ides blat gast mitt spat tolu prex illy
lien vein moho goop poor iris blot geat gelt moat spit tutu roux inby
limn wain moko grip whap poor iwis boat gent mort spot Urdu ably inky
linn warn mono gulp whop purr jess bolt gest most stet zebu achy inly
lion wean Moro gump wisp rear joss boot ghat must stot Zulu aery joey
loan ween oleo gymp wrap roar kiss bort gift mutt suet derv ahoy joky
loin when olio harp yapp scar kris bott gilt neat suit shiv airy judy
loon whin onto hasp yaup sear lass bout gilt neat swat Slav ally July
lorn worn otto heap yelp seer lees brat girt nest swot spiv army jury
lown ouzo help Adar slur lens brit gist nett tact alow arty lacy
Lyon yarn pepo hemp afar soar less brut glut gnat newt tart anew ashy lady
main yawn peso holp agar sour Lias bunt gnat next taut avow away laky
maun yean poco ajar spar loss bust goat nowt teat blew awny lazy
mean yuan pogo hump alar spur lues butt gout oast tent blow awry levy
mien zein polo jeep amir star Mars cant grat obit test braw baby lily
moan Zion redo jimp aver stir mass cart grit omit text brew bevy limy
moon zoon sago jump bear suer mess cast grot oont that brow body liny
morn aero sego keep beer tahr mews celt gust oust tilt chaw bogy lory
mown Afro shoo kelp bier tear miss cent haet pact tint chew bony many
muon agio silo kemp blur thar mods cert haft pant toft chow boxy maty
neon also soho knap boar thir moss chat halt part toft claw bray mazy
noon alto solo knop Boer tier muss chit hart past tort claw buoy miry
noun ambo soso lamp boor torr ness chut hast peat tret craw bury moly
omen ammo sumo Lapp boor tour news cist heat pelt trot crew busy nary
open auto taco leap burr char tzar nuts coat hent pert twit dhow cavy navy
oven boko taro limp coir user oats colt hest pest unit draw city nixy
oxen boyo thro lisp curr vair odds coot hilt phot vast drew clay nosy
pain bozo tiro loop vair veer onus Copt hint Pict vent enow cloy oary
pawn brio toco loup czar veer cost onus hipt pint vert flaw cony obey
pean bubo todo lump dear wear opus cott hist plat vest flew copy oily
peen capo toko mump deer weir oust cuit orts crit holt plot flaw okay
peon ciao trio neap doer whir orts crit holt plot vint flow cosy only
pern typo coco palp door ours cuit oyes poet volt frow coxy oozy
phon coho tyro peep dyer your cult hoot port volt waft glow defy orgy
pion dado umbo pimp dour Acts pass curt hunt post wait gnaw demy paly
pirn dago unco plop dyer alas piss cyst hurt pout want grew deny piny
plan demo undo pomp eger alms plus daft isnt prat wart grow dewy pipy
poon dido unto poop emir Ares pons dart jest punt wait gnaw demy pity
porn dodo veto prep ever arms puss debt jilt putt watt know dixy pixy
quin dojo vino prop ewer axes refs deft jolt quit meow domy play
rain duro wino pulp fair axis reis dent just raft weft phew dopy ploy
rein echo yoyo pump fear baas rhus diet kart welt plow dory poky
roan ergo zero quip four bass Russ dint Kelt rapt prow doxy poly
ruin euro atop ramp gaur bats sans dirt kent reft scow dozy pony
sain expo beep rasp gear bays sass ditt kept rent shaw dray posy
sawn fado blip reap gnar bias seps doat khat rest west shew drey poxy
scan faro bump repp goer buds suds doit kilt riot whet skaw duly pray
seen fico burp romp guar buss taps dolt kist root wilt slaw duty prey
sewn fido calp roup haar cess tass dont knit rout wist slew easy puny
Shan fino camp hair samp hear cups taws dort knot rust wont slow eddy quay
shin giro carp samp hear dais togs duct last ryot wort smew edgy racy
shun gogo chap scup heir dais thus drat kyat rust ryot wort smew eely rely
sign gyro chip seep Herr diss togs duct last ryot wort smew eery rimy
Sion halo chop ship hoar does duet leat salt wost snow eggy ropy
skin hero clap shop hoer doss toss dust leet scat writ spew elmy rosy
soon hobo clip skep hour duds upas east left scot stew Emmy ruby
sorn hoho clop skip jeer dues urus echt lent lest seat zest stow envy scry
sown homo comp slap kier eats ways edit lest seat zoot thaw espy sexy
span hypo coop slip knar egis wels emit lift sent babu trow flay shay
spin info coup slop knur epos wits erst lift sept beau view fley sizy
spun into crap snap lair Eros woes exit lilt sept beau view fley slay
sten jato crop snip leer exes eyot fact list loft shot clou apex foxy spay
stun judo cusp soap lehr eyas yaws fact loft shot ecru calx fray spry
sunn Juno damp soup liar feis ywis fast loft shot ecru calx fury spry
swan kago deep stap lier fess abet feat loot lost sift Frau crux fury sway
tarn kayo dorp step loir fils abut feet lost sift guru falx fury sway
teen kilo doup stop lour flys adit felt lout silt guru falx gaby they
```

tidy tody towy troy viny wavy wily Xray Druz fuzz oyez razz whiz
tiny tony tray ugly wady waxy winy zany fitz Geez phiz swiz
toby Tory trey vary wary whey wiry buzz fizz jazz quiz tizz

5 letter words

abaca again alway apply aunty bason bield boast brava bunko carat chimp
abaci agami amain appro aurae bassi bifid bobby brave bunny carer china
aback agape amass appui aural basso bight boche bravi bunty caret chine
abaft agate Amati appuy auras baste bigot bodge bravo bunya cargo chink
abase agave amaze April auric batch bijou bogey brawl buran Carib chirk
abash agaze amban apron auxin bated biker boggy brawn burgh carny chirp
abate agent ambit aptly avast baths bilbo bogie braxy burin carob chirr
abaya aggro amble Araby avens batik bilge bogle braze burka carol chive
abbey agile ambos arbor avert baton bilgy bogus bread burke carom chivy
abbot aging ambry areal avian batty bimbo bolas bream burly carpi chizz
abeam agist ameer areca avoid baulk binge bolus brede burnt carry chock
abele aglet amend arena await bawdy bingo bombe breed burro carve choir
abhor agley ament argil awake bayou biome bonce breer burry caste choke
abide aglow amice argol award beach biota boned brent bursa catch choky
ablow agogo amide argon aware beady biped boner breve burse cater choli
abode agone amine argot awash beamy bipod boney briar burst cates chomp
aboil agony amigo argue awful beano birch bongo bribe busby catty chops
Abomb agora amine Argus awned beard birth bonne brick bused cauli chord
abort agree amino Arian awoke beast bison bonny bride bushy caulk chore
about agued Amish ariel axial beaus bitch bonus brief busty cause chose
above ahead amiss arise axile beaut biter bonze brier butch caver choux
abrim ahold amity armed axiom beaux bitsy booby brill butte cavil chuck
abuse ahull amnia aroid ayrie bebop bitts booed brine butty cease chuff
abuzz aider among aroma azoic bedad bitty boost bring butyl cedar chump
abysm ainee amort arose azote bedel bivvy booth brink buxom cello chunk
abyss aioli amour arrah azoth bedew black boots briny buyer cense churl
acari airer ample arras Aztec bedim blade booty brisk bwana cento churn
acerb aisle amply array azure beech blain booze brize byend ceorl churr
acini aitch amuck arris babel beefs bland boozy broad byway cesti chuse
ackee akene amuse arrow baboo beefy blank borax broch cabal chafe chute
acock alack ancon arsis babul beery blare borer brock cabby chaff chyle
acold alarm anele arson bacca befit blase boric broil caber chain chyme
acorn alary anent artel baccy befog blast borne bronc cabin chair cider
acred alate angel arval bacon begad blate boron brood caboc chalk cigar
acrid album anger Aryan baddy began blaze bosky brook cabob champ cilia
actin alder angle ascot badge begat bleak bosom broom cable chant cimex
acton aleph Anglo ascus badly beget blear boson brose cacti chaos cinch
actor alert angst ashen baffs begin bleat bossy broth caddy chape circa
acute algae anigh ashet bagel begot bleed bosun brown cadet chaps cirri
adage algal anile aside baggy begum bleep botch bruin cadge chard cisco
adapt algid anima asker bairn begun blend botel brule cadre chare cissy
addax algin anion askew baize beige blent bothy brume caeca chary civet
adder Algol anise aspen baker being bless bough brunt cafes chase civic
addle alias anker asper balas belay blest boule brush cagey chasm civil
adept alibi ankle aspic baler belch blimp boult brute caird cheap civvy
adieu alien annal assai balky belga blimy bound bubal cairn cheat clack
adios align annex assay bally belie blind bourg bubby caked cheek claim
adlib alike annoy asset balmy belle blini bourn bucko calid cheep clamp
adman alive annul assot balsa belly blips bouse buddy calif cheer clang
admit alkyd anode aster banal below bliss bousy budge calix chefs clank
admix alkyl anomy astir banco bench blitz bowed buffi calla cheka clary
adobe Allah antae aswim bandy bends bloat bowel buffo calpa chela clash
adopt allay antic ataxy banjo bendy block bower buggy calks chelp clasp
adore alley antra atilt banks benni bloke bowls bugle calyx chemo class
adorn allin antre atlas banns benny blond boyar build camas chert clave
adown allod anvil atman barbe beret blood brace built camel chess clean
adoze allot Anzac atoll bardy berry bloom brach bulge cameo chest clear
adult allow aorta atomy barge berth blown bract bulgy campy chevy cleat
adunc alloy apace atone baric beryl blowy braid bulky camus chewy cleek
adust allyl apart atony barky beset blude brail bulla canal chiao cleft
adyta aloft apeak atria barmy besom blues brain bully candy chick clepe
aegis aloha apery atrip baron besot bluet brake bumbo canna chide clerk
aerie alone aphid attar barre betel bluey brame bumph canny chief click
affix along aphis attic basal beton bluff braky bumpy canoe chiel cliff
afire aloof apian audio basan bevel blunt brand bunch canon child climb
afoot aloud apish audit bases bezel blurb brank bunce canst chile clime
afore alpha apode auger basic bhang blurt brans bunco canto chili cline
Afric altar aport aught basil bible blush brant bunds canty chill cling
afrit alter appal augur basin biddy board brash bungs caper chimb clink
after alula apple aulic basis bidet boart brass bunia capon chime clock

```
cloke  corse  crush  debug  dizzy  drops  elfin  event  fetid  fluke  fundi  ghyll
clone  coset  crust  debut  djinn  dross  elide  evert  fetor  fluky  funds  giant
clonk  costa  crwth  decal  dobby  drove  elite  every  fetus  flume  fungi  giber
cloot  cotta  cryer  decay  docht  drown  elite  evict  fever  flump  funky  giddy
close  couch  crypt  decor  dodge  druid  eloin  evite  fibre  flung  funny  gigot
cloth  cough  Cuban  decoy  dodgy  drupe  elope  evoke  fiche  fluor  furan  gilpy
cloud  could  cubby  decry  dodos  drunk  elude  exact  fichu  flush  furor  gigue
clout  count  cubeb  deedy  doest  druse  elvan  exalt  field  flute  fural  gimme
clove  coupe  cubic  defer  doggo  dryad  elver  excel  fiend  fluty  furry  ginny
clown  court  cubit  degas  doggy  dryer  elves  exeat  fiery  flyer  furze  gipsy
clubs  couth  cuddy  degum  dogie  dryly  exert  fifer  flyby  furzy  girly
cluck  coven  cuish  deice  doily  ducal  embay  exile  fifth  foamy  fusee  giron
clump  cover  Cufic  deify  doing  ducat  embed  exine  fifty  focal  fusil  girth
clung  covet  culch  deism  dolce  duchy  embow  exist  fight  focus  fussy  gismo
clunk  covey  culet  deist  dolly  ducks  embus  exode  filch  foehn  fusty  given
cnida  covin  cully  deity  domed  ducky  emcee  expel  filet  fogey  fytte  giver
coach  cowed  cumin  dekko  donah  duddy  emeer  extol  filly  foggy  gabby  glace
coact  cower  cupel  delay  donee  dulia  emend  extra  filmy  foist  gable  glade
coapt  cowry  Cupid  delft  donga  dully  emery  exude  filth  folia  gaffe  glady
coast  coxae  cuppa  delta  donna  dulse  emmer  exult  final  folio  gaily  glair
coati  coxal  curch  delve  donor  dumka  emmet  exurb  folia  gaily  galah  gland
cobby  coxal  curds  demit  donut  dumky  emote  eying  finch  folly  galah  glare
cobia  coyly  curdy  demob  doper  dumky  empty  eyrie  fines  foots  galea  glary
coble  coypu  curer  demon  dopey  dumpy  enact  fable  finis  footy  Galla  glass
Cobol  cozen  curie  demos  Doric  dunce  enate  faced  finny  foray  gally  glaur
cobra  crack  curio  demur  dormy  dungy  endow  facer  fiord  forby  galop  glaze
cocci  craft  curie  denim  dungy  dunno  endow  facet  firer  force  gamba  glazy
cocky  crake  curio  dense  dorts  dunno  endue  facia  firry  fordo  games  gleam
cocoa  cramp  curly  dense  dorty  dunno  enema  facta  first  forge  gamic  glean
coder  crane  curry  depot  dotal  enemy  enemy  faddy  firth  forgo  gamin  glebe
codex  crank  curse  depth  doter  dotty  enjoy  faery  fishy  forme  gamma  glede
codon  crape  curst  derby  dotty  duomo  ennui  fagin  fitch  forte  gammy  gleed
cogue  craps  curve  derma  Douay  duper  enol   fagot  fitly  forth  gamut  gleek
cohoe  crash  curvy  desex  doubt  duple  ensew  faint  fiver  forty  ganja  gleet
coign  crass  cusec  deter  dough  duppy  ensky  fairy  fives  forum  gaper  glial
coley  crate  cushy  deuce  douma  durra  ensue  faith  fixed  fossa  gappy  glide
colic  crave  cutch  devil  douse  durst  enter  faker  fixer  fosse  garth  glint
colin  crawl  cutey  dewan  dowed  durum  entia  fakir  fizzy  found  gassy  gloat
colly  craze  cutie  dhobi  dowel  dusky  entry  falls  fjeld  fount  gaudy  globe
colon  crazy  cutin  dhole  dower  dusty  enure  false  fjord  fovea  gauge  gloom
colza  creak  cutis  dhoti  dowdy  dutch  envoi  famed  flack  foyer  gault  glory
comae  cream  cutty  Diana  dowel  duvet  envoy  fancy  flail  frail  gaumy  gloss
comal  credo  cycad  diary  dwale  dwarf  Eolic  fanny  flair  frame  gaunt  glout
combe  creed  cycle  diazo  downa  dwell  eosin  Fanti  flake  franc  gauss  glove
combo  creek  cyclo  dicer  downy  dwelt  epact  farad  flaky  frank  gauze  gloze
comer  creel  cyder  dicey  dowry  dying  ephah  farce  flame  fraud  gauzy  gluey
comet  creep  cymar  dicky  dowse  eager  ephod  farci  flamy  freak  gavel  glume
comfy  creme  Cymry  dicot  doyen  eagle  ephor  farcy  flank  freer  gawky  glyph
comic  crepe  cynic  dicta  dozen  eagre  epoch  farle  flare  frena  gawsy  gnarl
comma  crept  Czech  didst  dozer  eared  epode  fatal  flash  fresh  gazer  gnarr
compo  cress  dacha  diene  Draco  early  epoxy  fated  flask  friar  gecko  gnash
compt  crest  daddy  dight  draff  earth  equal  fatly  flaxy  frier  geese  gnawn
conch  crick  daffy  digit  draft  easel  equip  fatso  fleam  frill  geist  gnome
coney  crier  dagga  diker  drail  eaten  erase  fatty  fleck  frisk  gelid  goaty
conga  cries  dagos  dilly  drain  eater  erect  faugh  fleer  frith  gelly  godet
conge  crime  daily  dimer  drake  eaves  erect  fault  fleet  fritz  gemma  godly
conic  crimp  dairy  dimly  drama  ebony  ergot  fauna  flesh  frizz  gemmy  goest
conky  crisp  daisy  dinar  drank  eclat  erica  favus  flews  frock  gemot  goeth
conte  croak  dalek  diner  drape  Eddic  Ernie  fawny  flick  frond  genet  goety
cooee  crock  dally  dingo  drawl  edged  erode  fayre  flied  frons  genic  going
cooey  croft  daman  dingy  drawn  edict  erose  feast  flier  front  genie  golem
cooky  crone  damar  dinky  dread  edify  error  feaze  flimp  frore  genii  golly
cooly  crony  dance  diode  dream  educe  eruct  feign  fling  frost  genoa  gonad
coomb  cronk  dandy  dippy  drear  educt  erupt  feint  flint  froth  genre  goner
coopt  crook  dandy  dirge  dregs  eerie  escot  fella  flirt  frown  genro  gonna
copal  croon  daric  dirty  dress  eggar  esker  felly  float  froze  gents  goody
coper  crore  darky  disco  dried  egger  essay  felon  flock  fruit  genus  gooey
copra  cross  darts  dishy  drier  egger  ester  femur  flong  frump  geode  goofy
copse  croup  dated  disme  drift  egret  estoc  fence  flood  fryer  geoid  goopy
copsy  crowd  datum  ditch  drill  eider  estop  fenny  floor  fryup  gerah  goose
coral  crown  dauby  ditto  drily  eight  ether  feoff  flora  fubsy  germy  goral
cords  cruck  daunt  ditty  drink  eland  ethic  feral  flory  fucus  gesso  gorge
corer  crude  davit  divan  drive  elate  ethos  ferly  floss  fudge  geste  gorse
corgi  cruel  dealt  diver  droit  elbow  ethyl  fermi  flota  fugal  getup  gorsy
corky  cruet  deary  Dives  droll  elder  etude  ferny  flour  fuggy  ghast  gotta
corno  cruel  death  divot  drome  etwee  etwee  ferry  flout  fugle  ghaut  Gouda
cornu  crumb  debag  divvy  drone  elect  etyma  fesse  flown  fugue  ghost  gouge
corny  crump  debar  dixie  drool  elegy  evade  fetal  fluff  fully  ghoul  gourd
corps  cruse  debit  dizen  droop  elemi  evens  fetch  fluid  fumet  ghoul  gourd
```

```
gouty  gunge  herby  hurry  inure  kalif  lacey  lever  loris  mange  metic  morra
gowan  gunny  herma  hurst  inurn  kalpa  laded  levin  lorry  mango  metif  morse
goyim  guppy  heron  husky  iodic  kapok  laden  lewis  losel  mangy  metis  mosey
graal  gurry  hertz  hussy  ionic  kappa  ladle  lexis  loser  mania  metre  mossy
grace  gushy  hewer  hutch  irade  kaput  ladle  liana  lotah  manic  metro  motel
grade  gusto  hexad  hutia  Iraqi  karma  lagan  liane  lotto  manly  mezzo  motet
graft  gusty  hight  huzza  irate  karoo  lager  liang  lotus  manna  miaow  mothy
grail  gutsy  hiker  huzzy  Irish  karst  lahar  liang  lough  manor  miaul  motif
grain  gutta  hilar  hydra  irony  kauri  laigh  liard  louis  manse  micky  motor
graip  gutty  hillo  hydro  Islam  kayak  laird  liber  lound  manta  micro  motte
grama  gutty  hilly  hyena  islet  kazoo  laird  libel  lowne  manto  middy  motto
grand  guyot  hilum  hying  issei  kebab  lairy  libra  loupe  manul  midge  mould
grant  gypsy  hinge  hyoid  issue  kebob  laity  licht  loury  manus  midon  moult
grape  gyral  hinny  hylic  istle  kedge  lance  licit  louse  manus  midst  mound
graph  gyron  hippo  hyrax  itchy  kefir  lanky  liege  lousy  Maori  might  mount
grapy  gyrus  hippy  hyson  ivory  kelpy  lapel  liein  lover  maple  milch  mourn
grasp  habit  hirer  iambi  ivied  kempt  lapse  lifer  lovey  marah  miler  mouse
grass  hadal  hitch  izard  ixtle  kenaf  larch  ligan  lower  march  milky  mouth
grate  hadji  hives  iambi  izard  kendo  lardy  liger  lowly  mardy  mille  mover
grave  hadst  icily  ichor  izzat  kerne  lares  light  loyal  mares  mimer  movie
gravy  haick  hives  icily  jabot  kerry  large  liken  Lucan  marge  mimic  mower
graze  haiku  hoard  icing  jacks  ketch  largo  limbo  lucid  maria  minar  mucic
great  haily  hobby  icker  jaded  keyed  larum  limen  lucky  marid  mince  mucin
grebe  hairy  hocus  ictus  jaggy  khadi  larva  limey  lucre  marly  miner  mucky
greed  hajji  hodge  idead  Jaina  khaki  laser  limit  luffa  marry  mingy  mucro
Greek  hakim  hogan  ideal  jakes  Khmer  lasso  linen  lumen  marsh  minim  mucus
green  halal  hohum  idiom  jalap  kiang  latch  liner  lumme  maser  minor  muddy
greet  halla  hoick  idiot  jammy  kiddy  lated  lines  lumpy  mashy  minty  mudir
grege  hallo  hoise  idler  japan  kinin  laten  lingo  lunar  mason  minus  mufti
gride  halma  hoist  idola  jaspe  kinky  latex  linin  lunch  massa  mirky  muggy
grief  halos  hokey  idyll  jaunt  kiosk  lathe  links  lunge  masse  mirth  mujik
griff  halva  hokku  igloo  jazzy  kitty  lathi  linny  lungi  massy  misdo  mulch
grift  halve  hokum  ihram  jeans  kloof  lipid  lupin  lurch  match  miser  mulct
grike  hamal  holey  ileac  jehad  knack  Latin  lippy  lurid  matey  missy  mulga
grill  hammy  holla  ileal  jelly  knave  lauds  lisle  lushy  maths  misty  mulla
grime  handy  holly  ileum  jemmy  knead  laugh  lists  lusty  matin  mitre  multi
grimy  hanky  hollo  ileus  jenny  kneed  laura  lithe  lyart  matlo  mixed  muley
grind  Hanse  hoick  iliac  jerky  kneel  laver  litho  lycee  matte  mixen  mummy
gripe  haply  homer  Iliad  Jerry  knell  lawks  litre  lymph  matzo  mixer  mumps
grise  happy  homey  ilial  Jesse  knelt  lawny  liven  lying  maund  mixup  munch
grist  haram  honey  ilium  jetty  knife  laxly  liver  mauve  mizen  mungo
grith  hardy  honky  image  jewel  knish  layby  lives  lynch  mavis  mneme  mural
grits  harem  hooch  imago  Jewry  knock  layer  livid  lyric  maxim  mobby  murex
groan  harpy  hooky  imaum  jibba  knoll  layup  livre  Mayan  mocha  murky
groat  harry  hoots  imbed  jiber  knout  lazar  llama  lyses  maybe  modal  murra
groin  harsh  horal  imbue  jiffy  known  leach  llano  lysin  mayor  model  murre
groom  haste  horde  imide  jihad  knurl  leads  loach  lysis  mazer  mogul  muser
grope  hasty  horme  immit  jingo  knurr  leady  loamy  lysol  mealy  mohur  mushy
gross  hatch  horny  immix  jinks  koala  leafy  loath  lythe  McCoy  moire  music
group  hater  horse  impel  jinni  koine  leaky  lobar  lytta  McCoy  moist  musky
grout  haugh  horst  imply  jocko  kooky  leant  lobby  macaw  means  moksa  mussy
grove  haulm  hosen  inane  joint  kopek  leapt  lobed  macer  meant  molal  musth
growl  Hausa  hosta  inapt  joist  kopje  learn  lobus  macho  meany  molar  musty
grown  haven  hotel  inarm  joker  Koran  lease  local  macle  meaty  molto  muted
gruel  haver  hotly  incur  jokey  kotow  leash  locum  macro  mecca  molly  mutch
gruff  havoc  hotch  incus  jokul  kraal  least  locus  madam  medal  molto  muted
grume  hawse  hotel  index  jolly  krait  leave  loden  media  madge  momma  muzzy
grump  hazel  hotly  Indic  jolty  krans  ledge  lodge  madge  medic  monad  myall
grunt  hazer  hough  indri  Jonah  kraut  ledgy  loess  madly  Medoc  monas  mynah
guana  heady  house  indue  jorum  krill  leech  lofty  Mafia  meiny  monde  myoid
guano  heard  hovel  inept  joule  krona  leery  logan  magic  melee  money  myoma
guard  heart  hover  inert  joust  krone  lefty  logia  magma  melic  monte  myope
guava  heath  howdy  infer  jowar  kudos  legal  logic  magus  melon  month  myrrh
Guelf  heave  howff  infix  judas  kudzu  leger  Logos  Mahdi  mense  mooch  nabob
guess  heavy  howff  infra  judge  Kufic  leges  lolly  mains  mercy  moody  nacre
guest  hedge  hubby  ingle  juice  kukri  leggy  loner  maize  merge  moola  nadir
guide  hefty  hubby  ingot  juicy  kulak  longa  major  maker  merit  moose  naevi
guild  heigh  huffy  injun  julep  kulan  leman  longe  makar  merle  moped  naiad
guile  heist  hullo  inker  jumbo  kumis  lemma  looby  maker  merry  moper  naive
guilt  helix  human  inlaw  jumpy  kvass  lemur  loofa  malar  mesel  mopup  naked
guimp  hello  humic  inlay  junky  kwela  lento  looks  Malay  mesic  mopus  naker
guise  helot  humid  inlet  junta  kyang  Lents  loony  malic  mesne  moral  namer
gular  helve  humpy  inner  junto  kylin  leper  loopy  malty  meson  morat  nancy
gulch  heman  humus  inoff  jural  kyloe  lepta  loose  mamba  mesto  morel  nanna
gules  hence  hunch  input  jurat  kyrie  lethe  loral  mambo  metal  mores  nanny
gully  henge  hunks  inset  Kaaba  labia  letup  loran  mamma  meter  morel  nappe
gulph  henge  hunks  inset  Kaaba  labia  letup  loral  mammy  metal  mores  nappy
gumbo  henna  hunky  inter  kabob  labra  levee  lordy  maned  meter  moron  nares
gummy  henry  hurly  intro  Kafir  lacet  level  lorel  manes  meths  morph  naris
```

```
narky novel orpin parry piety pommy pudgy raggy remit rouge satyr secco
nasal noway orris parse piezo ponce puffy rainy renal rough sauce sedan
nasty Nowel ortho Parsi piggy poncy puggy raise renew round sauch Seder
natal noyau Osage parti pigmy pongo pukka rajah rente roupy saucy sedge
nates nucha Oscan party piker pooch puler raker repay rouse Saudi sedgy
natty nudge Oscar Pasch pilaf pooja pulpy rally repel roust saugh sedum
naval nulla osier pasha pilau pools pulse ramal reply route sault seedy
navel numen ossia pashm pilaw poort punch ramie repot routh sauna seely
navvy nurse ostia passe pilch poppy Punic ramus repro rover saury seepy
nawab nutty otary pasta pilei popsy punty ranch reran rowan saute segno
neath nyala other paste pilot porch pupae randy rerun rowdy saver segue
necks nylon otter pasty pilus porgy pupal ranee resat rowel savin seine
neddy nymph ought patch pilus porky pupil range reset rowen savoy seise
needs oaken ounce paten pinch porno puppy rangy resin rower savvy seism
needy oakum ouphe pater piney Porte puree raper resit royal Saxon seize
Negro oared ousel patio pinko poser purge raphe retch rubin sayer sekos
negus oases outby patsy pinky posit Purim rapid retry ruble sayso selah
neigh oasis outdo patty pinna posse purin raspy reuse rubus sayst sells
neive oaten outer pause pinny potto purse rasse revel ruche scald selva
nelly oaves outgo pavan pinon potty pursy ratan revet ruddy scale semee
nerka obang outre paver pinta pouch pushy ratch revue rugby scall semen
nerve obeah ouzel pavid pinto poult pussy ratel rheum ruler scalp senna
nervy obeli ovary pavis pinup pound puton rater rhine rumba scaly senor
netty obese ovate pawky pious pouty putti rathe rhino rumen scamp sensa
neume occur overs payee pipal powan putto ratio rhomb rumly scant sense
never ocean overt payer piper power putty ratty rhumb rummy scape sepal
newel ochre ovine peace pipit praam pygmy ravel rhyme rumpy scare sepia
newly ochry ovoid peach pipul prahu pylon raven riant runic scarf sepoy
newsy octal ovoli peaky pique prang pyxie raver riata runny scarp septa
nexus octet ovolo pearl piste prank pyxis ravin ribes runty scart serac
niche oddly ovule peart pitch prase Qboat rawly ricer runup scary serai
nidus odeon owing pease pithy prate quack rayed rider rupee scatt seral
niece odeum owlet peaty piton prawn quaff razee ridge rural scaup serge
nieve odium owner pecan pitta preen quail razor ridgy rushy scaur Seric
niffy odour oxbow pedal pivot press quake reach rifle rusty sceat serif
nifty offal oxeye peeve pixie prest quaky react right rutty scena serin
night offer oxide peggy pizza prexy qualm ready rigid sable scend serow
nimbi often oxlip pekan place price quant realm rigor sabot scene serra
ninny ogham oxter pekoe plage prick quark reams rille sabra scent serry
ninon ogive ozone pelta plaid pricy quart rearm rinse sabre schmo serum
ninth ogler pacer penal plain pride quash reata ripen sacra schwa serve
nippy ohmic pacha pence plait prier quasi reave riser sadhu scifi servo
nisei ohone paddy penna plane prima quean rebec rishi sadly scion setae
nisus oidia padre penny plank prime queen rebel risky saggy scoff seton
nitid oiled paean peony plant primo queer rebid ritzy sahib scold setto
niton oiler paeon peppy plash primp quell rebus rival saiga scone setup
nitre okapi pagan perai plasm prink quern rebut rived saint scoop seven
nitro olden paint perch plate print query recap rivel saith scoot sever
nival oldie paisa perdu playa prior quest recce riven saker scopa sewer
nixie oleic palay peril plaza prise queue recto rivet Sakta scope sewin
nizam olein palea perky plead prism quick redan river salad scorn sexed
nobby oleum pally perry pleat privy quiet redia roach salep Scots sexto
noble olive palmy perse plebs prize quiff reddy roast sales scour shack
nobly ology palpi pesky plica probe quill redia robin salic scout shade
nodal omasa palsy petal plonk proem quilt redid roble sally scowl shady
noddy ombre pampa peter pluck prole quins redly robot salmi scrag shaft
nodus omega panda petit plumb prone quint redox rocks salon scram shake
nohow oncer pandy petri plume prong quipu reedy rocky salse scrap shako
noise oneup panel petty plump proof quire reeky rodeo salts scray shaky
noisy onion panga pewit plumy prose quirk reest roger salty scree shale
nomad onset panic phage plunk prowl quirt refel rogue salve screw shall
nomen oomph panne phase plush proud quite refer roily salvo scrim shalt
nonce opera pansy phene Pluto Provo quits refit roker samba scrip shaly
nones opine panto pheon poach prowl quoin regal rolls sambo scrod shame
nonet opium pants phial pocky proxy quoit regie roman samel scrub shank
nonny optic panty phlox poddy prude quota regal Romeo sandy scrum shant
nooky orach papal phone podge prune quote reign rondo sapan scuba shape
noone oracy papaw phono podgy prunt quoth reify rooky sapid scudi shard
noose orate paper photo poesy pryer Quran reign roomy sapor scudo share
nopal orbed pappy phyla poilu psalm rabbi reins roost sappy scuff shark
noria orbit parch phyle point pseud rabic reive rooty saree scull sharp
Norse order pardi piano poise pshaw rabid rejig roper sarge sculp shave
north oread pardy picky poise psoas racer relax ropey sarky scurf shawl
noser organ parer picot poker psora radar relay rorty saros scuta shawm
nosey oribi parge picul pubic psych radii relet roset sasin scute sheaf
notch oriel parka pidog polar pubic radio relic rosin Satan scuff shear
noted Oriya parky piece polio pubis radix relit rotch sated sebum sheen
notum orlop parle pieta polka pucka radon reman rotor satin secco sheep
novae ormer parol pieta polyp pudge radon remex rotor satin sebum sheer
```

5 letter words   position = 1

sheet	sizar	smirk	sower	squid	stoup	sweal	tatou	those	torse	tufty	unlit
sheik	sizer	smite	space	squit	stour	swear	tatty	thraw	torsk	tuism	unman
shelf	skald	smith	spade	stack	stout	sweat	taunt	three	torso	tulip	unpeg
shell	skate	smock	spado	staff	stove	swede	taupe	threw	torte	tulle	unpin
shend	skean	smoke	spahi	stage	strad	sweep	tawer	thrid	torus	tumid	unrig
shent	skeet	smoko	spake	stagy	strap	sweet	tawie	throb	total	tummy	unrip
Sheol	skein	smoky	spall	staid	straw	swell	tawny	throe	totem	tuner	unsay
sherd	skelm	smolt	spang	stain	stray	swept	tawse	throw	touch	tunic	unset
sheva	skelp	smote	spank	stair	strep	swift	taxer	thrum	tough	tunny	unsex
shewn	skene	snack	spare	stake	strew	swill	taxis	thuja	touse	tuque	untie
Shiah	skier	snafu	spark	stale	stria	swine	taxon	thumb	tousy	turbo	until
shiel	skiey	snail	spasm	stalk	strip	swing	taxus	thump	towel	turfy	unzip
shier	skiff	snake	spate	stall	strop	swink	tazza	thuya	tower	Turki	upend
shift	skill	snaky	spawn	stamp	strow	swipe	teach	thyme	towny	turps	upped
shill	skimp	snare	speak	stand	stroy	swirl	teary	thymy	toxic	tusky	upper
shily	skink	snark	spean	stane	strum	swish	tease	tiara	toxin	tutee	upset
shine	skint	snarl	spear	stang	strut	Swiss	techy	tibia	trace	tutor	uraei
shiny	skirl	snash	speck	stank	stuck	swith	teens	tical	track	tutti	urate
shire	skirr	snath	specs	staph	study	swizz	teeny	tidal	tract	tutty	urban
shirk	skirt	sneak	speed	stare	stuff	swoon	tehee	tiein	trade	twain	ureal
shirr	skite	sneap	speel	stark	stull	swoop	teind	tiger	trail	twang	uredo
shirt	skive	sneck	speer	start	stump	sword	telex	tight	train	tweak	urger
Shiva	skoal	sneer	speir	stash	stung	swore	telic	tigon	trait	tweed	urial
shoal	skulk	snell	spell	state	stunk	sworn	telly	tilde	tramp	tweet	urine
shoat	skull	snick	spelt	stave	stunt	swung	tempi	tiler	traps	twere	urubu
shock	skunk	snide	spend	stays	stupa	sybil	tempo	tilth	trash	twerp	usage
shoer	skyer	sniff	spent	stead	stupe	sycee	tench	timer	trass	twice	usher
shoji	skyey	snipe	sperm	steak	sturt	sylph	tenet	timid	trawl	twill	usual
shone	slack	snips	spica	steal	styes	sylva	tenne	tinct	tread	twine	usurp
shook	slain	snoek	spice	steam	style	synch	tenon	tinea	treat	twink	usury
shoon	slake	snood	spick	steed	styli	synod	tenor	tined	treen	twiny	uteri
shoot	slang	snook	spicy	steek	stylo	syren	tense	tinge	trend	twirl	utile
shore	slant	snoop	spiel	steel	suave	syrup	tepee	tinny	tress	twirp	utter
shorn	slash	snoot	spier	steep	suber	tabby	terai	tinty	trews	twist	uveal
short	slate	snore	spike	steer	sucre	tabes	terce	tippy	treys	twite	uvula
shout	slaty	snort	spiky	stein	sudor	tabla	terga	tipsy	triac	twixt	Uzbeg
shove	slave	snout	spile	stela	Sudra	table	terms	tired	triad	twyer	Uzbek
shown	sleek	snowy	spill	stele	sudsy	taboo	terne	tirls	trial	tying	vacua
showy	sleep	snuff	spilt	steno	suede	tabor	terra	tiros	tribe	tyler	vagal
shred	sleet	soapy	spine	steps	suety	tache	terry	titan	trice	typal	vague
shrew	slept	sober	spiny	stere	Sufic	tacit	terse	titer	trick	typic	vagus
shrub	slice	socle	spire	stern	sugar	tacky	tesla	tithe	tried	Uboat	vails
shrug	slick	sodic	spirt	stich	suint	tafia	testa	titis	trier	udder	valet
shuck	slide	Sodom	spiry	stick	suite	taffy	testy	title	trill	Ugric	valid
shunt	slily	softa	spite	sties	sulci	taiga	tetra	titre	trine	uhlan	valse
shush	slime	softy	spitz	stiff	sulfa	tails	tewit	tizzy	trior	ukase	value
shyer	slimy	soggy	splat	stile	sulky	taint	texas	toady	tripe	ulcer	valve
shyly	sling	solan	splay	still	sully	taken	thack	toast	trist	ulema	vaned
sibyl	slink	solar	split	stilt	sumac	taker	thana	today	troat	ulmin	vapid
sided	slips	soldi	Spode	stime	summa	takin	thane	toddy	trode	ulnae	varan
sidle	sloid	soldo	spoil	sting	Sunna	taler	thank	toile	troke	ulnar	varec
siege	sloop	solen	spoke	stink	Sunni	tales	thawy	toils	troll	ultra	varix
sieve	sloot	solfa	spoof	stint	sunny	tally	theca	toits	tromp	umbel	varus
sight	slope	solid	spook	stipe	sunup	talon	theft	tokay	trona	umber	varve
sigil	slops	solon	spool	stirk	super	taluk	thegn	token	trone	umble	vasal
sigla	slosh	solum	spoom	stirp	supra	talus	thein	toman	troop	umbra	vasty
sigma	sloth	solus	spoon	stoae	surah	tamer	their	tonal	trope	umiak	vatic
silex	sloyd	solve	spoor	stoat	sural	Tamil	thema	tondi	troth	umpty	vault
silks	slubb	sonar	spore	stoep	surat	tamis	theme	tondo	trots	unapt	vaunt
silky	sluit	sonde	sport	stogy	surfy	tango	there	toner	trout	unarm	vealy
silly	slump	sonic	spout	stoic	surge	tangy	these	tonga	trove	unbar	Vedda
silty	slung	sonny	sprag	stoke	surly	tanka	theta	tongs	truce	unbed	Vedic
silva	slunk	sonsy	sprat	stola	surra	tansy	thews	tonic	truck	uncap	veena
simar	slurp	sooth	spray	stole	sutor	taper	thewy	tonne	truer	uncle	veery
since	slush	sooty	spree	stoln	sutra	tapir	thick	tonus	trull	uncus	vegan
sinew	slyer	sophy	sprig	stoma	swage	tapis	thief	toons	trump	uncut	veiny
singe	slyly	sopor	sprit	stomp	swain	tardy	thigh	tooth	trunk	under	velar
Singh	slype	soppy	sprue	stone	swale	targe	thill	topaz	truss	undid	veldt
sinus	smack	soral	spume	stonk	swami	tarok	thine	topee	trust	undue	velum
Sioux	small	sorel	spumy	stony	swamp	tarot	thing	toper	truth	unfit	venae
siren	smalt	sorgo	spunk	stood	swank	tarre	think	tophi	tryon	unfix	venal
sisal	smarm	sorra	spurn	stook	sward	tarry	thins	topic	tryst	ungot	venge
sissy	smart	sorry	spurt	stool	sware	tarsi	third	topoi	tsade	ungum	venin
sitar	smash	sorus	sputa	stoop	swarf	tarty	thirl	topos	tubae	unhip	venom
sitin	smaze	sough	squab	stope	swarm	tasse	thole	toque	tubal	Uniat	venue
sixer	smear	sound	squad	store	swart	taste	tholi	Torah	tubby	union	Venus
sixte	smell	souse	squat	stork	swash	tasty	thong	torch	tuber	unite	verge
sixth	smelt	south	squaw	storm	swath	Tatar	thorn	toric	tucum	unity	verse
sixty	smile	sowar	squib	story	swayl	tater	thorp	torii	Tudor	unlay	verso

```
verst  waney  wingy  yours  batty  dance  gaudy  karst  mammy  oared  radon  sauce
vertu  wanly  winze  youth  baulk  dandy  gauge  kauri  maned  oases  raggy  sauch
verve  wares  wiper  yucca  bawdy  daric  gault  kayak  manes  oasis  rainy  saucy
vesta  warty  wispy  yucky  bayou  darky  gaumy  kazoo  mange  oaten  raise  Saudi
vetch  washy  witan  yukky  Caaba  darts  gaunt  label  mango  oaves  rajah  saugh
viand  waste  witch  yulan  cabal  dated  gauss  labia  mangy  pacer  raker  sault
vibes  watch  withe  yummy  cabby  dater  gauze  labra  mania  pacha  rally  sauna
vicar  water  withy  zambo  caber  datum  gauzy  lacet  manic  paddy  ramal  saury
Vichy  waved  witty  zanze  cabin  dauby  gavel  lacey  manly  padre  ramie  saute
video  waver  wives  zebec  cabob  davit  gawky  laded  manna  paean  ramus  saver
viewy  wavey  wizen  zebra  caboc  eager  gazer  laden  manor  paeon  ranch  savin
vigil  waxen  wodge  zesty  cacao  eagle  habit  ladle  manse  pagan  randy  savoy
villa  waxer  woful  zibet  cache  eagre  hadal  lagan  manta  paint  ranee  savvy
villi  weald  woken  zinco  cacti  eared  Hades  lager  manto  paisa  range  Saxon
vinal  weary  woman  zincy  caddy  early  hadji  lahar  manul  palay  rangy  sayer
vinca  weave  women  zingy  cadet  earth  haick  laigh  manus  palea  raper  sayso
vinyl  webby  wonga  zinky  cadge  easel  haiku  laird  maple  palmy  raphe  sayst
viola  weber  wonky  zippy  cadre  eaten  haily  lairy  marah  palpi  rapid  tabby
viper  wedge  woods  zloty  caeca  eater  hairy  laity  march  palsy  raspy  tabes
viral  weeds  woody  zombi  cagey  eaves  hajji  lance  mardy  pampa  rasse  tabla
vireo  weedy  wooer  zonal  caird  fable  hakim  lanky  mares  panda  ratan  table
vires  weeny  woozy  zonda  cairn  faced  halal  lapel  marge  pandy  ratch  taboo
virga  weepy  words  zooid  calid  facer  hallo  lapse  maria  panel  ratel  tabor
Virgo  weigh  wordy  zooks  calif  facet  halma  larch  marid  panga  rater  tache
virid  weird  works  zoril  calix  facia  halos  lardy  marly  panic  rathe  tacit
virtu  welch  world  zygal  calla  facta  halva  lares  marry  panne  ratio  tacky
virus  wells  worms  ─────  calpa  faddy  halve  large  mashy  pansy  ratty  taffy
visit  welsh  wormy  babel  calpa  faery  halve  largo  mashy  panto  ravel  tafia
visor  wench  worry  baboo  calva  fagin  hamal  larky  mashy  pants  raven  taiga
vista  wetly  worse  babul  calve  fagot  hammy  larum  massa  panty  raver  tails
vital  whack  worst  bacca  calyx  faint  handy  larva  massa  papal  ravin  taint
vitta  whale  worth  baccy  camas  fairy  hanky  laser  masse  papaw  rawly  taken
vivat  whang  would  bacon  camel  faith  Hanse  lasso  massy  paper  rayed  taker
vives  whaup  woven  baddy  cameo  faker  haply  latch  mater  razee  razee  takin
vivid  wheal  wrack  badge  campy  fakir  happy  lated  match  parch  razor  tales
vixen  wheat  wrapt  badly  canal  falls  haram  laten  matey  pardi  sable  tally
vizor  wheel  wrath  bagel  canna  false  hardy  latex  maths  pardy  sabot  talon
Vlach  wheen  wreak  baggy  canny  famed  harem  lathe  matin  parer  sabra  taluk
vocal  whelk  wreck  Bahai  canoe  fancy  harpy  lathi  matlo  parge  sabre  talus
vodka  whelm  wrick  bairn  canon  fanny  harry  Latin  matte  parka  sacra  tamer
vogie  whelp  wring  baize  canst  Fanti  harsh  matzo  maund  parky  sadhu  Tamil
vogue  where  wrist  baker  canto  farad  haste  laugh  mauve  parle  sadly  tamis
voice  which  write  balas  canty  farce  hasty  lauds  mavis  parol  saggy  tammy
voile  whiff  wrong  baler  caper  farci  hatch  laura  Mayan  parry  sahib  tango
volar  while  wrote  balky  capon  farcy  hater  laver  maybe  parse  saiga  tangy
volet  whine  wroth  bally  carat  farle  haugh  lawks  mayor  Parsi  saint  tanka
volta  whiny  wrung  balmy  carer  fatal  haulm  lawny  mayst  parti  saith  tansy
volte  whirl  wryly  balsa  caret  fated  haunt  laxly  mazer  party  Sakta  tapir
volti  whirr  xebec  banal  cargo  fatly  Hausa  layby  macaw  pasha  salad  tapis
volva  whish  xenia  banco  Carib  fatso  haven  layer  macer  pashm  salep  targe
vomer  whisk  xenon  bandy  carny  fatty  haver  layup  macho  passe  sales  tarok
vomit  whist  xeric  banjo  carob  faugh  havoc  lazar  macle  pasta  salic  tarot
voter  white  Xhosa  banns  carol  fault  hawse  macaw  macro  paste  sally  tarre
vouch  whity  Xrays  Bantu  carom  fauna  hazel  macer  madam  pasty  salmi  tarry
vouge  whizz  xylem  barbe  carpi  favus  hazer  macho  madge  patch  salon  tarsi
vowel  whole  xylol  bardy  carry  fawny  iambi  macle  madly  paten  salse  tarty
vraic  whoop  xysti  barge  carve  fayre  jabot  macro  Mafia  pater  salts  tasse
vrouw  whore  yacht  baric  caste  fatly  jacks  madam  magic  patio  salty  taste
vuggy  whose  yager  barky  catch  fatso  jaded  madge  magma  patsy  salve  tasty
vying  whoso  yahoo  barmy  cater  gabby  jaggy  madly  magus  pause  salvo  Tatar
wacke  widdy  yamen  baron  cates  gable  jakes  Mafia  Mahdi  pavan  samba  tater
wacky  widen  yapok  barre  catty  gaffe  jalap  magic  mains  paver  sambo  tatou
waddy  widow  yauld  basal  cauli  gaily  jammy  magma  maize  pavid  samel  tatty
wader  width  yawny  basan  caulk  galah  japan  magus  major  pavis  sandy  taunt
wafer  wield  years  bases  cause  galea  jaspe  Mahdi  makar  pawky  sapan  taupe
wager  wigan  yearn  basic  caver  Galla  jaunt  mains  maker  payee  sapid  tawer
wages  wight  yeast  basin  cavil  gally  jazzy  maize  malar  payer  sapor  tawie
wagon  wilco  yerba  basis  dacha  galop  kabob  major  malty  saree  sappy  tawny
wahoo  wilds  yield  bason  daddy  gamba  Kafir  makar  mamba  sarge  saree  tawse
waist  willy  yippy  basso  dagga  games  kalif  maker  mambo  salad  sarky  taxer
waits  wince  yobbo  baste  dagos  gamic  kalpa  malar  mamma  naval  saros  taxis
waive  winch  yodel  batch  daily  gamin  kaput  Malay  namer  navel  Satan  taxon
waken  windy  yokel  bated  dairy  gamma  kapok  malic  nancy  navvy  sasin  taxus
waker  winey  yolky  bathe  daisy  gammy  kappa  malty  nanna  nawab  sassy  tazza
wakes  winge  yonks  batik  dalek  gamut  kapur  mamba  nanny  oaken  sated  vacua
waler  wings  young  baton  dally  ganja  kapok  mambo  nappe  radii  satin  vagal
walla                       daman  garth  karma  mambo  nappy  radio  satyr  vague
wally                       damar  gassy  karoo  mamma  nares
waltz
```

```
vagus abort scowl beech denim herma melon ready seism veena agree chuff
vails about scrag beefs dense heron mense realm seize veery agued chump
valet above scram beefy depot hertz mercy reams sekos vegan egest chunk
valid abrim scran beery depth hewer merge rearm selah veiny eggar churl
valse abuse scrap befit derby hexad meril reata sells velar egger churn
value abuzz scray befog derma jeans merit reave selva veldt egret churr
valve abysm scree begad desex jehad merle rebec semee velum igloo chuse
vaned abyss screw began deter jelly merry rebel semen venae ogham chute
vapid ebony scrim begat deuce jemmy mesel rebid senna venal ogive chyle
varan Hbomb scrip beget devil jenny mesic rebus senor venge ogler chyme
varec obang scrod begin dewan jerky mesne rebut sensa venin Ugric dhobi
varix obeah scrub begot eerie Jerry meson recap sense venom ahead dhole
varus obeli scrum begum feast Jesse messy recce sepal venue ahold dhoti
varve obese scuba begun feeze jetty mesto recto sepia Venus ahull ghast
vasal Qboat scudi beige feign jewel metal recur sepoy verge bhang ghaut
vasty Uboat scudo being feint Jewry meter redan septa verse chafe Ghazi
vatic acari scuff belay fella kebab meths reddy serac verso chaff ghost
vault acerb scull belch felly kebob metic redia serai verst chain ghoul
vaunt acini sculp belga felon kedge metif redid seral vertu chair ghyll
wacke ackee scuta belie femur kefir metis redly serge verve chalk ihram
wacky acock scute belle fence kelpy metre redox Seric vesta champ khadi
waddy acold scurf belly fenny kempt metro reedy serif vetch chant khaki
wader acorn adage below feoff kenaf mezzo reeky serin weald chaos Khmer
wafer acred adapt bench feral kendo neath reest serow weary chape ohmic
wager acrid addax bends ferly kerne necks reeve serra weave chaps ohone
wages actin adder bendy fermi kerry neddy refel serry webby chard phage
wagon acton addle benni ferny ketch needs refer serum weber chare phase
wahoo actor adept benny ferry keyed needy refit serve wedge charm phene
waist acute adieu beret fesse leach Negro regal servo weeds charr pheon
waits eclat adios berry fetal leads negus regie setae weedy chart phial
waive ichor adlib berth fetch leady neigh Reich seton weeny chary phlox
waken icily adman beryl fetid leafy neive reify setto weepy chase phone
waker icing admit beset fetor leaky nelly reign setup weigh chasm phono
wakes icker admix besom fetus leant nerka reins seven weird cheap phony
waler ictus adobe besot fever leapt nerve reive sever welch cheat photo
walla McCoy adopt betel gecko learn nervy rejig sewer wells check phyla
wally occur adore beton geese lease netty relax sewin welsh cheek phyle
waltz ocean adorn bevel geist leash neume relay sexed wench cheep rheum
waney ochre adown bezel gelid least never relet sexto wetly cheer rhine
wanly ochry adoze cease gelly leave newel relic teach xebec cheka rhino
wares octal adult cedar gemma ledge newly relit teary xenia chela rhomb
warty octet adunc cello gemmy ledgy newsy reman tease xenon chert rhumb
washy scald adust cense gemot leech nexus remex techy xeric chess rhyme
waste scale adyta cento genet leery peace remit teens yarns chest shack
watch scall Eddic ceorl genic lefty peach renal teeny years chevy shade
water scalp edged cesti genie legal peaky renew teeth yeast chewy shady
waved scaly edict dealt genii leger pearl rente tehee yerba chiao shaft
waver scamp edify deary genoa leges peart repay teind zebec chick shake
wavey scant educe death genre leggy pease repel telex zebra chide shako
waxen scape educt debag genro legit peaty reply telic zesty chief shaky
waxer scare idead debar gents leman pecan repot tempi affix chiel shale
yacht scarf ideal debit genus lemma pedal repro tempo afire child shall
yager scarp idiom debug geode lemon peeve rerun tempt afoot chile shalt
yahoo scart idiot debut geoid lemur peggy resat tench afore chili shaly
yamen scary idler decal gerah lento pekan reset tenet Afric chill shame
yapok scatt idola decay germy Lents pekoe reset tenne afrit chimb shank
yauld scaup idyll decor gesso leper pelta resin tenon after chime shant
yawny scaur oddly decoy geste lepta penal resit tenor offal chimp shape
zambo sceat odeon decry getup lethe pence retch tense offer china shard
zanze scena odeum deedy heady letup penna retry tense often chine share
abaca scend odium defer heard levee penny reuse tenth again chink shark
abaci scene odour degas heart level peony revel tenty agami chirk sharp
aback scent udder degum heath lever peppy revet tepee agape chirp shave
abaft schmo aegis deice heave levin perai revue tepid agate chirr shawl
abase schwa aerie deify heavy lewis perch seamy terai agave chive shawm
abash scifi beach deign hedge mealy perdu sebum terms agaze chivy sheaf
abask scion beady deism hefty means peril secco terne agene chizz shear
abate scoff beamy deist heigh meant perky sedan terra agent chock sheen
abaya scold beano deity heist meany perry Seder terry aggro choir sheep
abbey scone beard dekko helix meaty perse sedge terse agile choke sheer
abbot scoop beast delay hello mecca pesky sedgy tesla aging choky sheet
abeam scoot beaus delft helot medal petal sedum testa agist choli sheik
abele scopa beaut delta helve media peter seedy testy aglet chomp shelf
abhor scope beaux delve heman medic petit seely tetra agley chops shell
abide score bebop demit hence medii petri seepy Tevet aglow chord shend
ablow scorn bedad demob henge Medoc petty segno texas agogo chore shent
abode Scots bedel demon henna meiny pewit segue vealy agone chose Sheol
aboil scour bedew demos henry melee reach seine Vedda agony choux sherd
Abomb scout bedim demur herby melic react seise Vedic agora chuck sheva
```

```
shewn thump cirri fixed litho pilau sisal wilds aline cleek flota playa
Shiah thuya cisco fixer litre pilaw sissy wiles alive cleft flour plaza
shiel thyme cissy fizzy liven pilch sitar willy alkyd clepe flout plead
shier thymy civet giant liver pilea sitin wince alkyl clerk flown pleat
shift uhlan civic giber lives pilei sixer winch Allah click fluff plebs
shill whack civil giddy livid pilot sixte windy allay cliff fluid plica
shily whale civvy gigot livre pilus sixth winey alley climb fluke plonk
shine whang Diana gigue miaow pinch sixty winge allin clime fluky pluck
shiny wharf diary gilpy miaul piney sizar wings allot cline flume plumb
shire whaup diazo gimme micky pinko sizer wingy allow cling flump plume
shirk wheal dicer ginny micro pinky tiara winze alloy clink flung plump
shirr wheat dicey gipsy middy pinna tibia wiper allyl cloak flunk plumy
shirt wheel dicky girly midge pinny tical wispy aloft clock fluor plunk
Shiva wheen dicot giron midon pinon tidal witan aloha cloke flush plush
shoal whelk dicta girth midst pinta tiein witch alone clone flute Pluto
shoat whelm didst gismo might pinto tieup withe along clonk fluty slack
shock whelp diene given milch pinup tiger withy aloof cloot flyby slain
shoer where dight giver miler pious tight witty aloud close flyer slake
shoji which digit hight milky pipal tigon wives alpha cloth glace slang
shone whiff diker hiker mille piper tilde wizen altar cloud glade slant
shook while dilly hilar mimer pipit tiler yield alter clout glady slash
shoon whine dimer hillo mimic pipul tilth yippy alula clove glair slate
shoot whiny dimly hilly minar pique timer zibet alway clown gland slaty
shore whirl dinar hilum mince piste times zinco black clubs glare slave
shorn whirr diner Hindi miner pitch timid zincy blade cluck glary sleek
short whish dingo Hindu mingy pithy tinct zingy blain clump glass sleep
shout whisk dingy hinge minim piton tinea zinky blame clung glaur sleet
shove whist dinky hippo minor pitta tined zippy bland clunk glaze slept
shown white diode hippy minty pivot tinge djinn blank eland glazy slice
showy whity dippy hirer minus pixie tinny eject blare elate gleam slick
shred whizz dirge hitch mirky pizza tinty fjeld blase elbow glean slide
shrew whole dirty hives mirth riant tippy fjord blast elder glebe slily
shrub whoop disco hitch misdo riata tipsy akene blate elect glede slime
shrug whore dishy jibba miser ribes tipup okapi blaze elegy gleed slimy
shuck whorl disme jiber missy ricer titan skald bleak elemi gleek sling
shunt whose ditch jiffy misty rider tithe skate blear elfin gleet slink
shush whoso ditto jihad mitre ridge title skean bleat elide glial slips
shyer Xhosa ditty jingo mixed ridgy titre skeet bleed elite glide sloid
shyly aider divan jinks mixen rifle tizzy skein bleep eloge glint sloop
thane ainee diver jinni mixer right viand skelm blend eloin gloat sloot
thank aioli Dives kiang mixup rigid vibes skelp blent elope globe slope
thawy airer divot kiddy mizen rigor vicar skene bless elude gloom slops
theca aisle divvy kinin niche rille Vichy skier blest elute glory slosh
theft aitch dixie kinky nidus rinse video skiey blimp elvan gloss sloth
thegn bible dizen kiosk niece ripen viewy skiff blimy elver glout sloyd
their biddy dizzy kitty nieve risen vigil skill blind elves glove slubb
thema bidet eider liana niffy riser villa skimp blink flack gloze sluit
theme bield eight liane nifty rishi villi skink bliss flail gluey slump
there bifid fibre liang night risky vinal skint blitz flair glume slung
therm bight fiche liard nimbi ritzy vinca skirl bloat flake glyph slunk
these bigot fichu libel ninny rival vinyl skirr block flaky ileac slurp
theta bijou field liber ninon rived viola skirt bloke flame ileal slush
thews biker fiend libra ninth rivel viper skite blond flamy ileum slyer
thewy bilbo fiery licht nippy riven viral skive blood flank ileus slyly
thick bilge fifer licit nisei river vireo skoal bloom flare iliac slype
thief bilgy fifth liege nisus rivet vires skulk blown flash Iliad ulcer
thigh billy fifty liein nitid sibyl Virgo skull blowy flask ilial ulema
thill bimbo fight lifer niton sided virid skunk blude flaxy ilium ulmin
thine binge filch ligan nitre sidle virtu skyer blues fleam kloof ulnae
thing bingo filet liger nitro siege virus skyey bluet fleck llama ulnar
think biome fille light nival sieve virus ukase bluey fleer llano ultra
third biota filly liken nixie sight visit alack bluff fleet olden Vlach
thirl biped filmy lilac nizam sigil visor alarm blunt flesh oldie zloty
thole bipod filth limbo oidia sigla vista alary blurb flews oleic amain
tholi birch final limen oiled sigma vital alate blurt flick olein amass
thong birth finch limey oiler silex vitta album blush flied oleum Amati
thorn bison fines limit piano silks vivat alder clack flier olive amaze
thorp biter finis linen picky silky vives aleph claim flimp ology amban
those bitsy finny liner picot silly vivid alert clamp fling place amber
thraw bitts fiord lines picul silty vixen algae clang flint plage ambit
three bitty firer lingo pidog silva vizor algal clank flirt plaid amble
threw bivvy firry linin piece simar widdy algid clary float plain ambos
thrid cider first links pieta since widen algin clash flock plait ambry
throb cigar firth linny piety sinew widow Algol clasp flood plane ameer
throe cigar fishy lipid piezo singe width alias class flora plank amend
throw cilia fitch lippy pigmy Singh wield alibi clave floor plant ament
thrum cimex fitly lisle pigmy sinus wight align clear flory plash amice
thuja cinch fiver lists piker Sioux wight alike cleat floss plasm amide
thumb circa fives lithe pilaf siren wilco aline cleat floss plate amido
```

```
amigo ankle knout bogey comae donah goose kotow moose polar soggy tousy
amine annal known boggy comal donee gopak loach moped polio solan towel
amino annex knurl bogie combe donga goral loamy moper polka solar tower
Amish annoy knurr bogle combo donna gorge loath mopup polyp soldi towny
amiss annul mneme bogus comer donor gorse lobar mopus pommy soldo toxic
amity anode oncer bohea comet donut gorsy lobed morat poncy solen toxin
amnia anomy oneup bolas comfy doper gotta lobby moral ponce solfa vocal
among antae onion bolus comic dopey Gouda lobus moray pongo solid vodka
amort antic onset bombe comma Doric gouge local morel pooch solon vogie
amour antra snack bonce compo dormy gourd locum mores pooja solum vogue
ample antre snafu boned compt dorts gouty locus moron pools solus voice
amply anvil snail boner conch dorty gowan loden morph poort solve voile
amuck Anzac snake boney coney dotal goyim lodge morra poppy sonar volar
amuse cnida snaky bongo conga doter hoard loess morse popsy sonde volet
embay enact snare bonne conge dotty hoary lofty mosey porch sonic volta
embed enate snark bonny conic Douay hobby logan mossy porgy sonny volte
ember ended snarl bonus conky doubt hocus logia motel porky sonsy volti
embow endow snash bonze conte douce hodge logic motet porno sooth volva
embus endue snath booby cooee dough hogan Logos mothy Porte sooty vomer
emcee enema sneak booed cooey douma hohum lolly motif poser sophy vomit
emeer enemy sneap boost cooky douse hoick loner motor posit sopor voter
emend enjoy sneck booth cooly dowdy hoise longa motte posse soppy vouch
emery ennui sneer boots coomb dowed hoist longe motto potto sorel vouge
emmer enrol snell booty coopt dowel hokey looby mould potty sorgo vowel
emmet ensew snick booze copal dower hokku loofa moult pouch sorra wodge
emote ensky snide boozy coper downa hokum looks mound poult sorry woful
empty ensue sniff borax copra downy holey loony mount pound sorus woken
image enter snipe borer copse dowry holla loopy mourn pouty sough woman
imago entia snips boric copsy dowse hollo loose mouse powan sound women
imaum entry snoek borne coral doyen holly loppy mousy power soupy wonga
imbed envoi snook boron cords dozen homer loral mouth roach souse wonky
imbue envoy snoop bosom corer dozer homey loran mover roast south woods
imide envoy snoot boson corgi Eolic honey lordy movie robin sowar woody
immit gnarl snore bosky corky eosin honky lorel mower roble sower wooer
immix gnarr snort bossy corno foamy hooch loris nobby robot toady woozy
impel gnash snout bosun cornu focal hooey lorry noble rocks toast words
imply gnawn snowy botch corny focus hooky losel nobly rocky today wordy
omasa gnome snuff botel corps foehn hoots loser nodal rodeo toddy works
ombre inane unapt bothy corse fogey horal lotah noddy roger togue world
omega inapt unarm bough coset foggy horde lotto nomad rogue toils worms
smack inarm unbar boule costa foist horme lotus nomen roily Tokay wormy
smalt incur unbed boult cotta folia horny loupe nonce roker token worry
smart incus uncap bound couch folio horse loury nones roble toman worse
smash index uncle bourg coude folly horst louse nonet roman tommy worst
smaze Indic uncus bourn cough foots horsy louis nomad Romeo tonal worth
smalt indri uncut bouse could footy hosen loury nomen rondo tondi would
smarm indue undid bousy count foray hosta louse nonce rooky tondo wound
smear inept under bowed coupe forby hotch lousy nones roost tonga woven
smell inert undue bowel court force hotel lover nonny roomy tongs yobbo
smelt infer unfit bower couth fordo hotly lowly nooky roper tonic yodel
smile infra unfix bowls coven forge hough loose noose ropey tonka yogic
smirk ingle ungot bowse cover forgo hound loyal noone rorty tonne yokel
smite ingot ungum boxer covet forme houri Norse nopal roset tonus yolky
smith injun Uniat boyar covey forth house north noria rosin tooth yonks
smock inker unify coach covin forty hovel noser north rotch topaz young
smoke inkle union coact cowed forum hover rouge nosey rotor topee yours
smoko inlaw unite coapt cower fossa howdy route notch round toper youth
smoky inlay unity coast cowry fosse howff rouse noted rough tophi apace
smolt inlet unlaw coati coxae found iodic roupy novel roust topic apart
smote inner unlay cobia coxal fount ionic rouse novae rouse topoi apeak
umbel inoff unlit cobra coyly fovea jocko roust noway route topos apery
umber input unman Cobol coypu foyer joint routh Nowel routh toque aphid
umbra inset unpeg coble cozen goaty joist novae noyau rover Torah aphis
umiak inter unpin cocci codex godet joker rover roman rowan torch apian
umpty intro unrig cocky codon godly joker roset Romeo rowdy toric apish
ancon inure unrip cocoa coder going jokey rosin rondo rowel torii apode
anele inurn unsay codas cogue golem jokul rotch rooky rowen torse aport
anent knack unset coign cohoe golly jolly rotor roost rower torsk appal
angel knave unsex colic coign gonad jolty rouge roomy royal torso apple
anger knave untie colin colic gonna Jonah round roper rowan torte apply
angle knead until colly colin goner jorum roupy ropey rowdy torus appro
Anglo kneed unzip colon colly goody joule rouse rorty rowel total appui
angst kneel aorta colza colon goofy joust roust roset rowen totem appuy
anigh knell board     colza goopy jowar routh rosin rower touch
anile knelt boart           goosy koala    rotch royal touse
anima knife boast                kooky
anion knish bobby                kopek
anise knock boche                kopje
anker knoll bodge                Koran
```

```
April sprig briar cruck frock krona trews aster stead stupe culet fussy
apron sprit bribe crude frond krone triad astir steak sturt culex fusty
apsis sprue brick cruel frons orach trial aswim steal styes cully fuzzy
aptly spume bride cruet front oracy Trias escot steam style cumin guana
epact spumy brief crumb frore orate tribe esker stean styli cupel guano
ephah spunk brier crump frost orbed trice essay steed stylo cupid guard
ephod spurn brill cruse froth orbit trick ester steek uteri cuppa guava
ephor spurt brine crush frown order tried estoc steel utile curch Guelf
epoch sputa bring crust froze oread trier estop steep utter curds guess
epode upend brink crwth fruit organ trike Islam steer audio curdy guest
epoxy upped briny cryer frump oribi trill islet stein audit curer guide
opera upper brisk crypt fryer oriel trine issei stela auger curia guild
opine upset brize Draco fryup Oriya trior issue stele aught curie guile
opium equal broad draff graal orlop tripe istle steno augur curio guilt
optic equip broch draft grace ormer trist Osage steps aulic curly guimp
space squab brock drail grade orpin trite Oscan stere aunty curry guise
spade squad broil drain graff orris troat Oscar stern aurae curse gular
spado squat broke drake graft ortho trode osier stich aural curst gulch
spahi squaw bronc drama grail praam troll ossia stick auras curve gules
spake squib brood drank grain prahu tromp ostia sties auric curvy gully
spall squid brook drape graip prang trona psalm stiff auxin cusec gulph
spang squit broom drawl grama prank trone pseud stile bubal cushy gumbo
spank Araby brose drawn grand prase troop pshaw still bubby cutch gummy
spare arbor broth dread grant prate trope psoas stilt bucko cutey gunge
spark areal brown dream grape prawn troth psora stime buddy cutie gunny
spasm areca bruin drear graph preen trout psych sting budge cutin guppy
spate arena bruit dregs grapy press trove tsade stink buffi cutis gurry
spawn argil brule dress grasp prest truce usage stint buffo cutty gushy
speak argol brume dried grass prexy truck usher stipe buggy ducal gusto
spean argon brunt drier grate price trull usual stirk bugle ducat gusty
spear argot brush drift grave prick truly usurp stirp build duchy gutsy
speck argue brute drill gravy pricy trump usury stoae built ducks gutta
specs Argus crack drily graze pride trunk ataxy stoat buist ducky gutty
speed Arian craft drink great prier truss atilt stock bulge duddy guyot
speel ariel crake drive grebe prima trust atlas stoep bulgy dulia hubby
speer arise cramp droit greed prime truth atman stogy bulky dully huffy
speir armed crane droll Greek primo tryon atoll stoic bulla dulse hullo
spell aroid crank drome green primp tryst atomy stoke bully dumka human
spelt aroma crape drone greet prink uraei atone stola bumbo dumky humic
spend arose craps drool grege print urate atony stole bumph dummy humid
spent arrah crash droop gride prior urban atria stoln bumpy dumps humph
sperm arras crass drops grief prise ureal atrip stoma bunce dumpy humpy
spica arris crate dross griff prism uredo attar stomp bunch dunce humus
spice arris crave drove grift privy urger attic stonk bunco dungy hunch
spick arrow crawl drown grike prize urial ether stony bundh dunno hunks
spicy arsis craze druid grill probe urine ethic stood bundy dunny hunky
spiel arson crazy drunk grime proem urubu ethos stook bunia duomo hurly
spier artel creak drupe grimy prole vraic ethyl stool bunje duple hurry
spike arval cream druse griot prone vrouw etude stoop bunko duppy hurst
spiky Aryan credo Druze gripe prong wrack etwee stoor bunny duper husky
spile brace creed dryad grise proof wrapt etyma stope bunty durra hussy
spill brach creek dryer grist prose wrath itchy store buran durst hutch
spilt bract creel dryly grith prosy wreak otary stork burgh durum hutia
spine braid creep erase grits proud wreck other storm burin dusky huzza
spiny brail creme erbia groan Provo wrest otter story burka dusty huzzy
spire brain crepe erect groat prowl wrick stack stoup burke dutch judas
spirt brake crept ergot groin proxy wring staff stour burly duvet judge
spiry braky cress erica groom prude wrist stage stout burnt fubsy juice
spite brand crest Ernie grope prune write stagy stove burro fucus juicy
spitz brank crick erode gross pryer wrong staid strad burry fudge julep
splat brant crier error grout trace wrote stain strap bursa fugal jumbo
splay brash cries eruct grove track wroth stair straw burse fuggy jumpy
split brass crime erupt growl tract wrung stake stray burst fugle junky
Spode brava crimp frail grown tragi wryly stale strep busby fugue junta
spoil brave crisp frame gruel trail Xrays stalk strew bused fully junto
spoke bravi croak franc gruff train ascot stall stria bushy fumet jural
spoof bravo Croat frank grume trait ascus stamp strip busty fundi jurat
spook brawl crock fraud grump tramp asdic stand strop butch funds juror
spool brawn croft freak grunt traps ashen stane strow butte fungi kudos
spoom braxy crone freer irade trash ashet stang strum butty funky kudzu
spoon braze cronk frena Iraqi trass Asian stank strut buxom funny Kufic
spoor bread crony fresh irate trawl aside staph stuck buyer fural kukri
spore break crook friar Irish tread asker stare study cubby furan kulak
sport bream croon frier irony treat askew stark stuff cubeb furor kulan
spout brede croup frill kraal treck aspen start stull cubic furry kumis
sprag breed cross frisk krait treed aspic stash stump cubit furze Lucan
sprat breer crore frith krans treen assai state stunk cuddy furzy lucid
spray brent crowd fritz kraut trend assay stave stunt cuish fusee lucky
spree breve crown frizz krill tress asset stays stupa culch fusil lucre
```

```
luffa pupae Sudra overs twirp myrrh beast cramp graal meant scant staid
lumen pupal sudsy overt twist nyala beaus crane grace meany scape stain
lumme pupil suede ovine twite nylon beaut crank grade meaty scare stair
lumpy puppy suety ovoid twixt nymph beaux crape graft miaow scarf stake
lunar puree Sufic ovoli twyer pygmy bhang craps grail miaul scarp stale
lunch purge sugar ovolo axial pylon black crash grain myall scart stalk
lunge Purim suint ovule axile pyxie blade crass graip neath scary stall
lungi purin suite uveal axiom pyxis blain crate grama nyala scatt stamp
lupin purse sulci uvula exact sybil blame crave grand obang scaup stand
lupus pursy sulfa await exalt sycee bland crawl grant okapi scaur stane
lurch pushy sulky awake excel sylph blank craze grape omasa seamy stang
lurid pussy sully award exeat sylva blare crazy graph orach shack stank
lushy puton sumac aware exert synch blase dealt grapy oracy shade staph
lusty putti summa awash exile synod blast deary grasp orate shady stare
mucic putto Sunna awful exine syren blate death grass Osage shaft stark
mucin putty Sunni awned exist syrup blaze Diana grate otary shake start
mucky quack sunny awoke exode tying board diary grave ovary shako stash
mucro quaff sunup bwana expel tyler boart diazo gravy ovate shaky state
mucus quail super dwale extol typal boast Draco graze peace shale stave
muddy quake supra dwarf extra typic brace draff guana peach shall stays
mudir quaky surah dwell exude vying brach draft guano peaky shalt suave
mufti qualm sural dwelt exult xylem bract drail guard pearl shaly swage
muggy quant surat kwela exurb xylol braid drain guava peart shame swain
mujik quark surfy owing ixtle xysti brail drake heady pease shank swale
mulch quart surge owlet oxbow zygal brain drama heard peaty shant swami
mulct quash surly owner oxeye azoic brake drank heart phage shape swamp
muley quasi surra swage oxide azote braky drape heath phase shard swank
mulga quean sutor swain oxlip azoth brand drawl heave piano share sward
mulla queen sutra swale oxter Aztec brank drawn heavy place shark sware
multi queer tubae swami ayrie azure brant dwale hoard plage sharp swarf
mummy quell tubal swamp byend Czech brash dwarf hoary plaid shave swarm
mumps quern tubby swank bylaw izard brass eland image plain shawl swart
munch query tuber sward byway izzat brava elate imago plait shawm swash
mungo quest tucum sware cycad ozone brave enact imaum plane skald swath
mural queue Tudor swarf cycle Uzbeg bravi enate inane plank skate swayl
murex quick tufty swarm cyclo Uzbek bravo epact inapt plant slack teach
murky quiet tuism swart cyder ----- brawl erase inarm plash slain teary
murra quiff tulip swash cymar abaca brawn evade irade plasm slake tease
murre quill tulle swath Cymry abaci braxy exact Iraqi plate slang thane
muser quilt tumid swayl cynic aback braze exalt irate playa slant thank
mushy quins tummy sweal dying abaft bwana feast izard plaza slash thawy
music quint tuner swear eying abase Caaba flack jeans poach slate tiara
musky quipu tunic sweat eyrie abash cease flail Kaaba praam slaty toady
mussy quire tunny swede fytte abask chafe flair khadi prahu slave toast
musth quirk tuque sweep gypsy abate chaff flake khaki prang smack trace
musty quirt turbo sweet gyral abaya chain flaky kiang prank small track
mutch quite turfy swell gyron acari chair flame knack prase smalt tract
muted quits Turki swept gyrus adage chalk flamy knave prate smarm trade
muzzy quoin turps swift hydra again champ flank koala prawn smart tragi
nucha quoit tusky swill hydro agami chant flare kraal psalm smash trail
nudge quota tutee swine hyena agape chape flask krait quack smaze train
nulla quote tutor swing hying agate chaps flaxy krans quaff snack trait
numen quoth tutti swink Hykos agaze chard foamy kvass quail snafu tramp
nurse Quran tutty swipe hylic agave chare frail kyang quake snail traps
nutty rubin vuggy swirl hyoid agaze charm frame leach quaky snake trash
ought ruble yucca swish hypha alack charr franc leads quark snare trawl
ounce rubus yucky Swiss hyrax alarm chart frank leady quart snark tsade
ouphe ruche yukky swith hyson alary chary fraud leafy quash snarl twain
ousel ruddy yulan swizz kylin alate chase ghast leaky quasi snash twang
outby rugby yummy swoon kyloe amain chasm ghaut leant quash snath ukase
outdo ruler avail swoop kyrie amass clack Ghazi leapt reach soapy unapt
outer rumba avast sword lyart Amati claim Ghazi learn react space unarm
outgo rumen avens swore lyart amaze claim giant learn react space unarm
outre rumly avert sworn lycee apace clamp glace lease ready spade uraei
ouzel rummy avian swung lying apart clang glade leash realm spado urate
pubic rumpy avoid twain lymph Araby clank glady least reams spahi usage
pubis runic evade twang lynch ataxy clary glair leave rearm spake vealy
pucka runny evens tweak lyric avail clash gland liana reata spall viand
pudge runty event tweed lyses avast clasp glare liane reave spang Vlach
pudgy runup evert tween lysin await class glary liang riant spank vraic
puffy rupee every tweet lysis awake clave glass liard riata spare weald
puggy rural evict twere lysol award coach glaur llama roach spark weary
pukka rushy evite twerp lythe aware coact glaze llano roast spasm weave
puler rusty evoke twice lytta awash coapt glazy loach scald spate whack
pulpy rutty ivied twill myall beach coast gnarl loamy scale spawn whale
pulse suave ivory twine mynah beady coati gnarr loath scall stack whang
punch suber kvass twink myoid beamy crack gnash lyart scalp staff wharf
Punic sucre ovary twiny myoma beano craft gnawn mealy scaly stage whaup
punty sudor ovate twirl myope beard crake goaty means scamp stagy wrack
```

```
wrapt lobus cyclo picul endow reddy bless fleam piece spelt where begad
wrath mobby dacha pocky endue redia blest fleck pieta spend wield began
Xrays nabob decal pucka faddy redid bread fleer piety spent wreak begat
yearn nobby decay racer fudge redly break fleet piezo sperm wreck beget
years noble decor races giddy redox bream flesh plead stead wrest begin
yeast nobly decoy recap godet rider brede flews pleat steak yield begot
abbey ombre decry recce godly ridge breed foehn plebs steal affix begum
abbot orbed dicer recto hadal ridgy breer freak poesy steam awful begun
album orbit dicey recur Hades rodeo brent freer preen steed befit bight
amban oxbow dicky ricer hadji ruddy breve frena press steek befog bigot
amber pubic dicot rocks hadst sadhu byend fresh prest steel bifid bogey
ambit pubis dicta rocky hedge sadly caeca geese prexy steep buffi boggy
amble rabbi docht ruche hodge sedan cheap gleam pseud steer buffo bogie
ambos rabic ducal sacra hydra Seder cheat glean quean stein Cufic bogle
ambry rabid ducat secco hydro sedge check glebe queen stela daffy bogus
arbor rebec duchy socle index sedgy cheek glede queer stele defer buggy
babel rebel ducks sucre Indic sedum cheep gleed quell steno elfin bugle
baboo rebid ducky sycee indri sided cheer gleek quern steps fifer cagey
babul rebus emcee tache indue sidle cheka gleet query stere fifth cigar
bebop rebut escot tacit iodic Sodom chert goeth quest stern fifty cogue
bible ribes excel tacky jaded sudor chess goety queue suede gaffe dagga
bobby robin faced techy judas Sudra chest grebe reedy swede hefty dagos
bubal roble facer tical judge sudsy chevy greed reeky swear huffy degas
bubby robot facet tucum kedge tidal chewy green reest sweal infer degum
cabal rubin facia ulcer kiddy today clean greet reeve sweat infix dight
cabby ruble facta uncap kudos toddy clear grege rheum sweep jiffy digit
caber rubus fiche uncle kudzu Tudor cleat Greek scena sweet Kafir doggo
cabin sable fichu uncus laded udder cleek scend scend swell kefir doggy
cable sabot focal uncut laden under cleft Guelf scend swept Kufic dogie
cabob sabra focus vacua Ladin undid clepe guess scena scene lefty dogma
caboc sabre fucus vicar ladle undue clerk guest scene scent lifer eager
cobby sebum gecko Vichy ledge Vedda creak hyena scent teens lofty eagle
cobia sibyl hocus wacke ledgy Vedic cream idead seedy teeny luffa eagre
coble sober incur wacky loden video credo ideal seely teeth Mafia edged
Cobol suber incus yacht lodge vodka creed sheaf seepy theca mufti eggar
cobra sybil itchy yucca madam waddy creek shear sheaf theft niffy ergot
Cuban tabby jacks yucky madge wader creel sheen shear thegn nifty fagin
cubby tabes jocko addax madly wedge creep sheep sheer their offal fagot
cubeb tabla lacet adder medal widdy crepe sheer sheet thema offer fogey
cubic table lacey addle media widen crept sheik sheik theme puffy foggy
cubit taboo licht aider medic widow cress shelf shelf there refel fight
debag tabor licit alder Medoc wodge crest shell theta therm refer fogey
debar tibia local asdic middy yodel Czech shend thews these refit fuggy
debit tubae locum audio midge abeam deedy shent thewy theta rifle fugal
debug tubal locus audit midon abele diene Sheol tiein thews softa fugle
debut tubby Lucan baddy midst acerb doest sheva tieup these softy fugue
dobby tuber lucid badge modal adept doeth shewn tread thewy taffy gigot
elbow umbel lucky badly model agene dread skean treat tiein tafia gigue
embay umber lucre bedad modus agent dream skein treen tieup toffy hight
embed umbra lycee bedel muddy ahead drear skeet tress tread tufty hogan
ember unbar macaw bedew mudir akene dregs skelm trews treat unfit ingle
embow unbed macho bedim nadir aleph dress skelp tween treen unfix ingot
embus urban macle biddy neddy alert dwell skene tweed trend wafer jaggy
fable Uzbeg Macon bidet nidus ameer dwelt sleek tweet tress woful lagan
fibre Uzbek macro bodge nodal amend egest sleep twere trews aegis lager
fubsy vibes McCoy buddy noddy anele eject sleet twerp tween aggro leger
gabby webby mecca budge nodus anent elect slept ulema tweet algae leges
gable weber micky caddy nudge apeak elegy smear upend twere algal legit
giber xebec micro cadet oddly apery elemi smell ureal twerp algid ligan
habit zebec mocha cadge oidia areal emend smelt uredo ulema algin liger
hobby zebra mucic cadre olden areca emery sneak uteri upend angel light
hubby zibet mucin cedar order arena enema sneap uveal ureal anger logan
imbed ancon mucho cider paddy avens enemy sneck veena uredo angle logia
imbue ascot mucky coder padre avert erect oleum snell steno Anglo logic
jabot ascus mucro codec pedal beech erect oleic snell steno angst Logos
jibba bacca mucus codex pidog beefs evens olein sneap speak argil magic
jiber baccy nacre codon poddy beefy event oleum sneck spear argol magma
kabob bacon necks cuddy podge beery evert omega snell speck argon magus
kebab bacon niche cyder podgy bield every oneup speak speed argot might
kebob boche nucha daddy podia bleak exeat opera speal speel argue mogul
label bucko occur didst pudge blear exert obeah speak spell Argus muggy
labia cacao oncer dodge pudgy bleat feeze obeli peaen speed auger Negro
labra cache Oscan dodgy radar bleed field obese paeon speel wheel auger negus
libel cacti Oscar eider radii bleed field feeze paeon speer wheen aught
liber cocci pacer elder radio bleep fiend peeve speer whelk augur night
libra cocky pacha Eddic radix bleep fiery phene spell whelm bagel organ
lobar cocoa pecan eider radon blend fjeld phone speir whelm baggy ought
lobby cycad picky radio ended fiend peeve speer whelp augur night
lobed cycle picot ended redan blent fjeld pheon spell whelp baggy ought
```

```
pagan usher chili fritz opium skiff thigh rejig belay gules palsy tilth
peggy wahoo chill frizz oribi skill thill ackee belch gully pelta tulip
piggy yahoo chimb gaily oriel skimp thine alkyd belga gulph phlox tulle
pigmy abide chime geist Oriya skink thing alkyl belie halal pilaf tyler
puggy acini chimp glial osier skint think anker belle hallo pilau uhlan
pygmy adieu china glide ovine skirl third ankle belly halma pilaw unlay
raggy adios chine glint owing skirr thirl asker below halos pilch unlit
regal afire chink going oxide skirt toile askew bilbo halva pilea valet
regie agile chirk gride paint skite toils baker bilge halve pilei valid
right aging chirp grief paisa skive triad biker bilgy helix pilot valse
rigid agist chirr griff phial slice trial dekko billy hello pilus value
rigor alias chive grift plica slick Trias diker bolas helot polar valve
roger alibi chivy grike poilu slide tribe esker bolus helve polio velar
rogue alien chizz grill poind slily trice faker bulge hilar polka veldt
rugby align click grime point slime trick fakir bulgy hillo polyp velum
saggy alike cliff grimy poise slimy tried hakim bulky hilly puler villa
segno aline climb grind price sling trier hiker bulla hilum pulpy villi
segue alive clime gripe prick slink trike hokey bully holey pulse volar
sight amice cline grise pricy slips trill hokku bylaw holla pylon volet
sigil amide cling grist pride smile trine hokum calid hollo rally volta
sigla amido clink grith prier smirk trior Hykos calif holly relax volte
sigma amigo cnida grits prima smite tripe icker calix hullo relay volti
soggy amine coign guide prime smith trist inker calla hylic relet volva
sugar amino crick guild primo snick trite inkle calpa idler relic waler
tiger Amish crier guile primp snide tuism jakes calve igloo relit walla
tight amiss cries guilt prink sniff twice joker calyx inlaw rille wally
tigon amity crime guimp print snipe twill jokey cello inlay rolls waltz
togue anigh crimp guise prior snips twine jokul cilia inlet ruler welch
ungot anile crisp haick prise spica twink kukri coley Islam salad wells
ungum anima cuish haiku prism spice twiny liken colic islet salep welsh
urger anion daily haily privy spick twirl makar colin jalap sales wilco
vagal anise dairy hairy prize spicy twirp maker colly jelly salic wilds
vague apian daisy heigh quick spiel twist moksa colon jolly sally wiles
vagus apish deice heist quiet spier twite naked colza jolty salmi willy
vegan Arian deify hoick quiff spike twixt naker culch julep salon xylem
vigil ariel deign hoise quill spiky tying oaken culet kalif salse xylol
vogie arise deism hoist quilt spile umiak oakum culex kalpa salts yolky
vogue Asian deist hying quins spill Uniat pekan cully kelpy salty yulan
vuggy aside deity icily quint spilt unify pekoe dalek kulak salve adman
wager atilt djinn icing quipu spine union piker dally kulan salvo admit
wages avian doily idiom quire spiny unite poker delay kylin selah admix
wagon axial doing idiot quirk spirt unity pukka delft kyloe sells armed
wigan axile dried iliac quirt spiry urial raker delta lilac selva atman
wight axiom drier Iliad quite spite urine roker delve lolly silex bimbo
yager bairn drift ilial quits stich utile saker dilly malar silks bombe
yogic baize drill ilium rainy stick veiny sekos dolce Malay silky bumbo
zygal beige drily imide raise stied voice Sikhs dolly malic silly bumph
abhor being drink Irish reins stiff voile Sakta dulia malty silty bumpy
aphid blimp drive ivied reist stile vying takin dully melee silva camas
aphis blimy dying Jaina reive still waist taken dulse melic solan camel
ashen blind edict joint reify stilb waits taker eclat melon solar cameo
ashet blini edify joist reign stilt waive takes Eolic milch soldi campy
Bahai blink elide juice Reich stime waken Tokay falls milky soldo cimex
bohea bliss elite juicy rhine stink weigh token false mille solen comae
cohoe blitz erica knife rhino stipe weird waken fella molal solfa comal
ephah briar evict knish roily stint which waker felly molar solid combe
ephod bribe evite koine saiga stirk whiff wakes felon molla solon combo
ephor brick exile krill saint stirp while woken filch molly solum comer
ether bride exine laigh saith stirs whine yokel filet mulch solus comet
ethic brief exist laird scifi stive whirl yukky fille mulct solve comfy
ethos brier eying lairy scion suint whirr adlib filly mulga splat comic
ethyl brill faint laity seine suite whish aglet filmy mulla splay comma
hohum brine fairy lying seism suits whisk agley filth multi split compo
ichor bring faith mains seize Swiss whist aglow folia nelly sulci compt
jehad brink feign maize seity swift white Allah folic nulla sulfa cumin
jihad briny feint meiny shiel swill whits allay folio nylon sulky cymar
lahar brisk flick moire shier swims whity alley folly ogler sully Cymry
Mahdi brize flied moist shift swine whizz allin fully oiled sylph daman
mohur build flier naiad shill swing wrick allot galah orlop sylva damar
nohow built flimp naive shily swink wring allow galea owlet tales demob
ochre buist fling neigh shine swipe wrist alloy Galla oxlip talon demit
ochry caird flint neive shiny swirl write allyl galop palay taluk demon
ogham cairn flirt noise shire swish bijou atlas gelid palea talus demos
other chiao foist noisy shirk swith enjoy aulic gelly paled telex demur
pshaw chide friar odium shirr swizz injun balas gilpy palki telic dimer
sahib chief frier ogive shirt teind major baler golem palla tells dimly
schmo chiel frill olive Shiva thick mujik balky golly pally telly domed
schwa child frisk onion skier thief rajah balmy gular palmy tiler dumka
tehee chile frith opine skiey thief rajah balsa gulch palpi tiler dumky
```

```
dummy remit canna hinge nonce tenor agora clout ghoul pools snout wrong
dumps roman canny hinny nones tense ahold clove gloat poort snowy wrote
dumpy Romeo canoe honey nonet tenth aioli clown globe probe sooth wroth
emmer rumba canon honky nonny tenty aloft cooee gloom proem sooty Xhosa
emmet rumen canst hunch ounce tinct aloha cooey glory prole Spode zloty
famed rumly canto hunks owner tinea alone cooky gloss prone spoil zooid
femur rummy canty hunky panda tined along cooly glout prong spoke zooks
fumet rumpy cense inner pandy tinge aloof coomb glove proof spoof alpha
gamba samba cento ionic panel tinny aloud coopt gloze prose spook ample
games sambo cinch jenny panga tinty among croak gnome prosy spool amply
gamic samel conch jingo panic tonal amort Croat goody proud spoom appal
gamin semee conga jinks panne tondi amour crock gooey Provo spoon apple
gamma semen conge jinni pansy tondo anomy croft goofy prowl spoor apply
gammy simar conic Jonah panto toner anode crone goopy proxy spore appro
gamut sumac conky junky pants tonga apode cronk goose psoas sport appui
gemma summa conte junta panty tongs aport crony groan psora spout appuy
gemmy tamer conto junto penal tonic aroid crook groat Qboat stoae aspen
gemot Tamil cynic lance pence tunic aroma croon groin quoin stoat aspic
gimme tamis dance lanky penna tunny arose crore groom quoit stock biped
gumbo tammy dandy lento penny ulnae atoll cross grope quota stoep bipod
gummy tempi denim linen pinch ulnar atomy croup gross quote stogy caper
hamal tempo dense lines piney vaned atone crowd group quoth stoic capon
hammy tempt dinar lingo pinko venae atony crown grout rhomb stoke copal
heman timer diner linin pinky venal avoid dhobi grove rooky stola coper
homer times dingo links pinna venge awoke dhole growl roomy stole copra
homey timid dingy linny pinny venin azoic dhoti grown roost stoma copse
human toman dinky liner pinon venom azote diode hooch rooty stomp copsy
humic tommy donah loner pinta venue azoth droit hooey scoff stone cupel
humid tumid donee longa pinto Venus biome droll hooky scold stonk Cupid
humph tummy donga longe pinup vinal biota drome hoots scone stony cuppa
humpy ulmin donna lunar ponce vinca bloat drone hyoid scoop stood depot
humus unman donor lunch pongo vinyl block drool idola scoot stook depth
iambi vomer donut lunge Punic waney bloke droop inoff scopa stool dippy
immit vomit dunce lungi punch wanly blond drops irony scope stoop doper
immix woman dungy lynch ranch wench blood dross ivory score stope duper
jammy women dunno maned randy wince bloom drove kiosk scorn store duple
jemmy yamen dunny manes ranee winch blowy drown knock Scots stork duppy
jumbo yummy Ernie mange range windy booby ebony knoll scout storm empty
jumpy zambo fancy mango rangy winey booed eloge knout scowl story expel
kempt zombi fanny mangy renal wingy boost elope known shoal stoup gaper
Khmer ainee Fanti mania renew wings booth eloin krona shoat stour gappy
kumis amnia fence manic rente wingy booty emote krone shock stout gipsy
leman annal fenny manly rinse winze booze epoch looby shoer stove gopak
lemma annex final manna rondo wonga boozy epode looks shoji swoon guppy
lemon annul finch manor runic wonky broad epoxy loofa shone swoop gypsy
lemur aunty fines manse runny xenia broch erode loony shook sword haply
limbo awned finis manta runty xenon brock erose looks shoon sworn happy
limen banal finny manto runup yonks broil evoke loose shoot thole hippo
limey banco fundi manul senna zanze bronc exode loopy shore thong hippy
limit banco funds manus senor zincy brood feoff loory shorn thorn hypha
lumen bands fungi mense sensa zingy brook fiord Maori short thorp impel
lumme banjo funky minar sense zonal broom fjord mooch shout those imply
lumpy banns funny mince since zonda brose float moody shove tooth input
lymph Bantu ganja miner singe abode brown flock moola shown troat japan
mamba bench genet mingy Singh aboil chock flong moony showy trode kapok
mambo bends genic minim sinew about choir flood moose Sioux troll kappa
mamma benni genie minor sinus above choke floor myoid skoal tromp kaput
mammy benny genii minty sonar acock choky flora myoma sloid trona kopek
mimer binge genoa minus sonde acold choli flory myope sloop trone kopje
mimic bingo genre monad sonic acorn chomp floss nooky sloot troop lapel
momma bonce genro monas sonny adobe chops flota noone slope trope lapse
mummy boned gents monde sunny adopt chord flout odour slops troth leper
mumps boner genus money sunup adore chore flown ology slosh trout lepta
namer boney ginny monte synch adorn chose frond ovoid sloth trove lipid
nimbi bongo gonad month synod adown choux frons ovoli sloyd Uboat lippy
nomad bonne goner munch tango adoze cloak frock ovolo smock viola loppy
nomen bonny gonna mungo tanka afoot cloke frore ozone smoke vrouw lupin
numen bonus gunge mynah tangy afore clock frost peony smoko whole lupus
nymph bonze gunny nancy tansy agogo cloke froth phone smoky whore maple
ohmic bunch handy nanna tench agone cloak frown phono snoek whorl moped
oomph bunco hanky nanny tenet agony cloot froze photo snood whose moper
ormer bunia Hanse mungo tango adorn choux frock phono smoke whore mopup
pampa bunko hence mynah tanka adown cloak frore photo smoko whorl mopus
pommy bunny henge nancy tangy adoze cloke frost pious smoky whose nappe
ramal bunty henna nanna tansy afoot clonk froth plonk smolt whoso nappy
ramie bunya henny nanny tench afore cloot frown pooch smote woods nippy
ramus canal henry ninny tenet agogo cloth froze pious snoek wooer nopal
reman candy Hindi ninon tenne agone close geode plonk snoot woody nippy
remex candy Hindu ninth tenon agony cloud ghost pooja snort woozy orpin
```

```
ouphe airer curry herma nares shrew varix ensky Pasch betel kitty peter
papal aorta curse heron naris shrub varus ensue pasha beton kotow petit
papaw April curst hertz narky shrug varve eosin pashm bitch latch petri
paper apron curve hirer nerka siren verge essay passe biter lated petty
pappy arrah curvy horal nerve sorel verse fesse pasta bitsy laten pitch
peppy arras daric horde nervy sorgo verso fishy pasta bitts latex pithy
pipal array darky horme noria sorra verst fossa pasty bitty lathe piton
piper arris darts horny Norse sorry vertu fosse pesky botch lathi pitta
pipit arrow derby horse north sorus verve fusee piste botel lathy potto
pipul atria derma horst nurse sprag viral fusil poser bothy Latin potty
poppy atrip dirge horsy oared sprat vireo fussy posit butch lethe puton
popsy aurae dirty hurly orris spray vires fusty posse butte letup putti
pupae aural Doric hurry parch spree virga gassy pushy butty lithe putto
pupal auras dormy hurst pardi sprig Virgo gesso pussy butyl litho putty
pupil auric dorts hyrax pardy sprit virid geste raspy catch litre ratan
puppy ayrie dorty ihram parer sprue virtu gismo rasse cater lotah ratch
raper barbe durra jerky parge strad wares gushy resat cates lotto ratel
raphe bardy durst jural parle strap warty gusto reset catty lotus rater
rapid barge durum jurat parka straw words gusty resit cutch lytta ratio
repay baric eared juror parky stray wordy haste risen cutey match ratty
repel barky early karma parol strep works hasty riser cutie mater retch
reply barmy earth karoo parry strew world hosen rishi cutin matey retry
repot baron eerie karst parse stria wormy hosta risky cutis maths ritzy
repro barre egret kerne Parsi strip worms husky roset cutty matin rotch
ripen beret enrol kerry parti strop worry hussy rosin dated matlo rotor
roper berry error Koran party strow worse hyson rushy dater matte rutty
ropey berth eyrie kyrie perai stroy worst inset rusty datum matzo Satan
rupee beryl farad larch perch strum worth issei sasin deter metal sated
sapan birch farce lardy perdu strut xeric issue sassy ditch meter satin
sapid birth farci lares peril surah yerba jaspe sisal ditto meths satyr
sapor borax farcy large perky sural aisle Jesse sissy ditty metic setae
sappy borer feral largo perry surat apsis lasso tasse dotal metif seton
sepal boric ferly larky perse surfy arsis lisle taste doter metis setto
sepia borne fermi larum porch surge arson lists tasty dotty metre setup
sepoy boron ferny larva porgy surly assai losel testa dutch metro sitar
septa buran ferry loral porky surra assay loser testa eaten mitre sitin
sophy burgh firer loran porno syren asset lushy testy eater motel sutor
sopor burin firry lordy Porte syrup basal lusty tusky enter motet sutra
soppy burka first lorel puree targe basan lyses unsay entia mothy Tatar
super burke firth loris purge tarok bases lysin unset entry motif tater
supra burly foray lorry Purim tarot basic lysis unsex ester motor tatou
taper burnt forby lurch purin tarre basil lysol upset estoc motte tatty
tapir burro force lurid purse tarsi basin maser vasal estop motto tetra
tapis burry fordo lyric pursy tarty basis mashy vasty extol mutch titan
tepee bursa forge marah Quran terai bason mason visit extra muted tithe
tepid burse forgo march reran terce bassi massa visor fatal natal title
tippy burst forme mardy rerun terms basso masse vista fated nates titre
tipsy carat forte mares rural terne baste massy waste fatly natty total
tipup caret forth marge saree terra beset mesel washy fatso netty totem
topaz cargo forty maria sarge terry besom mesic waste fatty nitid tutee
topee Carib forum marid saros terse besot mesne wispy fetal niton tutor
toper carny fural marly scrag thraw bison meson xysti fetch nitre tutti
tophi carob furan marry scram three bosky messy zesty fetid nitro tutty
topic carol furor marsh scran threw bosom mesto actin fetor notum ultra
topoi carom furry mercy scrap thrid boson miser acton fetus noted untie
topos carry furze merge scray throb bossy misdo antae fitch notch until
typal carve furzy meril scrip throe bosun misty antic fitly natum utter
typic circa garth merit scree throw busby mosey antra fytte oaten vatic
umpty cirri gerah merle screw thrum busby mossy aitch getup octal vetch
unpeg coral germy merry scrim Torah bushy muser altar gotta octet vital
unpin cords girly mirky scrip torch busty mushy alter gutsy often vitta
upped corer giron mirth scrod toric bushy music antic gutta optic voter
upper corgi girth moral scrub torii caste musky antra gutty ortho watch
vapid corky goral morat scrum torse cesti mussy antre hatch ostia water
viper corno gorge moray serac torsk cisco musth aptly hater otter wetly
wiper cornu gorse morel serai torso cissy musty artel hitch outby witan
yapok corny gorsy mores Seric torte coset nasal astir hotch outdo witch
yippy corps gurry moron serif torus cusec nasty attar hotel outgo withe
zippy corse gyral morph serin turbo cushy nisei attic hotly outre withy
pique curch gyron morra serow turfy desex nisus Aztec hutch oxter witty
toque curds gyrus morse serra Turki disco noser batch hutia patch abuse
tuque curer haram mural serry turps dishy nosey bated ictus paten abuzz
abrim curet hardy murex serum Ugric disme oases bathe inter pater acute
acred curia harem murky serve Ugric dusky oasis baths intro patio adult
acrid curio harpy murra servo unrig dusty onset baton istle patsy adunc
aerie curio harry murre shred unrip easel ossia batik ixtle patty adust
Afric curly harsh myrrh shred varec ensew ousel batty jetty petal agued
afrit       herby       varan       ketch             aerie ahull
```

```
alula elude mound squat envoi bowse nexus slyly aural elvan legal pupae
amuck elute mount squaw envoy byway nixie slype auras embay leman pupal
amuse enure mourn squib favus cowed pixie styes avian ephah ligan Qboat
azure equal mouse squid fever cower pyxie style axial equal lilac quean
baulk equip mousy squit fiver cowry pyxis styli Bahai essay lobar Quran
blude eruct mouth stuck fives crwth Saxon stylo balas exeat local radar
blues erupt neume study fovea dewan sexed thyme banal farad logan rajah
bluet etude ovule stuff gavel dowdy sexto thymy basal fatal loral ramal
bluey exude pause stull given dowed sixer tryon basan feral loran ratan
bluff exult pluck stump giver dowel sixte tryst bedad fetal lotah recap
blunt exurb plumb stung haven dower sixth twyer begad final loyal redan
blurb faugh plume stunk haver downa sixty wryly began fleam Lucan regal
blurt fault plump stunt havoc downy taxer Anzac begat float lunar relax
blush fauna plumy stupa hives dowry taxis bezel belay focal macaw relay
bough fluff plunk stupe hovel dowse taxon cozen bleak foray madam reman
boule fluid plush sturt hover etwee taxus dizen blear freak makar renal
boult fluke Pluto swung laver fawny texas dizzy bleat friar malar repay
bound fluky pouch taunt levee gawky toxic dozen bloat fugal Malay reran
bourg flume poult taupe level gawsy toxin dozer bolas fural marah resat
bourn flump pound thuja lever gowan vixen fizzy borax furan Mayan rival
bouse flung pouty thumb levin hawse waxen fuzzy boyar galah medal roman
bousy flunk prude thump liven hewer waxer gazer bread gerah metal rowan
bruin fluor prune thuya liver howdy abysm hazel break gleam minar royal
bruit flush prunt touch lives howff abyss hazer bream glean modal rural
brule flute reuse tough livid jewel adyta huzza briar glial molal salad
brume fluty rhumb touse livre Jewry Aryan huzzy broad gloat molar sapan
brunt found rouge tousy lover jowar bayou izzat bubal gonad monad Satan
brush fount rough truce lovey lawks boyar jazzy buran gopak monas sceat
brute fruit round truck mavis lawny buyer kazoo bylaw goral moral scrag
cauli frump roupy trull mover lewis chyle lazar byway gowan morat scram
caulk gaudy rouse truly movie lower chyme mazer cabal graal moray scran
cause gauge roust trump naval lowly coyly mezzo cacao great mural scrap
chuck gault route trunk navel lowne coypu mizen camas groan mynah scray
chuff gaumy routh truss navvy mower cryer muzzy canal groat naiad sedan
chump gaunt sauce trust never nawab crypt nizam carat gular nasal selah
chunk gauss sauch truth nival newel doyen ouzel cedar gyral natal sepal
churl gauze saucy urubu novae newly dryad pizza cheap hadal naval serac
churn gauzy Saudi usual novel newsy dryer razee cheat halal nawab serai
churr gluey saugh usurp oaves noway dryly razor chiao hamal nival seral
chuse glume sault usury pavan Nowel etyma sizar cigar haram nizam setae
chute Gouda sauna uvula paver pawky fayre sizer clean heman nodal sheaf
clubs gouge saury vault pavid pewit flyby tazza clear hexad nomad shear
cluck gourd saute vaunt pavis powan flyer tizzy cleat hilar nopal Shiah
clump gouty scuba vouch pivot power foyer unzip cloak hogan novae shoal
clung gruel scudi vouge ravel rawly fryer vizor comae horal noway shoat
clunk gruff scudo would raven rowan fryup wizen comal human noyau simar
couch grume scuff wound raver rowdy ghyll ——— copal hyrax obeah sisal
coude grump scull wrung ravin rowel glyph abeam coral idead ocean sitar
cough grunt sculp yauld revel rowen goyim addax coxae ideal octal sizar
could haugh scurf young revet rower guyot adman coxal ihram offal skean
count haulm scuta yours revue sewer idyll ahead creak ileac ogham skoal
coupe haunt scute youth rival sewin kayak algae cream ileal oread smear
court Hausa shuck anvil rived sowar keyed algal croak iliac organ sneak
couth hough shunt arval rivel sower layby alias Croat Iliad Oscan sneap
cruck hound shush bevel riven tawer layer Allah Cuban ilial Oscar solan
crude houri skulk bivvy river tawie layup allay cycad inlaw paean solar
cruel house skull caver rivet tawny loyal altar cymar inlay pagan sonar
cruet inure skunk cavil rover tawse Mayan alway daman Islam palay sowar
crumb inurn slubb civet saver towel maybe amban damar izzat papal speak
crump jaunt sluit civic savin tower mayor annal debag jalap papaw spean
cruse joule slump civil savoy towny mayst antae debar japan pavan spear
crush joust slung civvy savvy vowel noyau Anzac decal jehad pecan splat
crust kauri slunk coven seven yawny payee apeak decay jihad pedal splay
dauby knurl slurp cover sever auxin payer apian degas Jonah pekan sprag
daunt knurr slush covet vivat boxer phyla appal delay jowar penal sprat
deuce lauds snuff covey vives buxom phyle areal dewan judas perai spray
Douay laugh sough covin vivid coxae pryer Arian dinar jural petal squab
doubt laura sound davit waved coxal psych arrah divan jurat phial squad
douce lough soupy devil waver dixie rayed arras donah kayak pilaf squat
dough louis souse divan wavey fixed rhyme array dotal kebab pilau squaw
douma lound south diver wives fixer royal arval Douay kenaf pilaw stead
douse loupe spume Dives woven hexad sayer Aryan dread knead pipal steak
druid loury spumy divot alway laxly sayso Asian dream Koran plead steal
drunk louse spunk divvy aswim lexis sayst assai drear kraal pleat steam
drupe lousy spurn duvet bawdy maxim shyer assay dryad kulak polar stoae
druse maund spurt eaves bowed mixed shyly atlas ducal kulan powan stoat
Druze mauve sputa elvan bowel mixen skyer atman ducat lagan praam strad
educe mould squab elver bower mixer skyey attar eclat lahar pshaw strap
educt moult squad elves bowls mixup slyer aurae eggar lazar psoas straw
```

```
stray bombe beech flock Reich bardy noddy angel codex emcee homey maker
sugar booby belch force retch bawdy outdo anger coley emeer honey maned
sumac bribe bench frock roach beady oxide anker comer emmer hooey manes
surah bubby birch glace rotch bends paddy annex comet emmet hosen mares
sural bumbo bitch grace sauce bendy panda ariel coney ended hotel maser
surat busby black gulch sauch biddy pandy armed cooee ensew hovel mater
sweal Caaba block haick saucy blade pardi artel cooey enter hover matey
swear cabby bonce hatch secco blude pardy ashen coper esker icker mazer
sweat clubs botch hence shack brede perdu ashet corer ester idler melee
Tatar cobby brace hitch shock bride poddy asker coset ether imbed mesel
terai combe brach hoick shuck buddy pride askew coven etwee impel meter
texas combo bract hooch since caddy prude aspen cover excel index miler
thraw cubby brick hotch slack candy randy asset covet expel infer mimer
tical dauby broch hunch slice chide ready aster covey faced inker miner
tidal derby brock hutch slick cnida reddy auger cowed facer inlet miser
titan dhobi bunch juice smack cords reedy awned cower facet inner mixed
today dobby bunco juicy smock coude rondo Aztec cozen faker inset mixen
Tokay doubt butch ketch snack credo rowdy babel creed famed inter mixer
toman flyby caeca knack sneck crude ruddy bagel creek fated islet mizen
tonal forby catch knock snick cuddy sandy baker creel fever issei model
topaz gabby check lance space curds Saudi baler creep fifer ivied money
Torah gamba chick larch speck curdy scudi bases crier filet jaded moped
total glebe chock latch specs daddy scudo bated cries fines jakes moper
tread globe chuck leach spica dandy seedy bedel cruel firer jewel morel
treat grebe cinch leech spice deedy shade bedew cruet fiver jiber mores
triad gumbo circa loach spick diode shady beget cryer fives joker mosey
trial herby cisco lunch spicy dowdy slide beret cubeb fixed jokey motel
Trias hobby clack lurch stich elide soldi beset culet fixer julep motet
troat hubby click lynch stick elude soldo betel culex fleer keyed mover
tubae iambi clock march stick epode sonde bevel cupel fleet Khmer mower
tubal jibba cluck match stock erode spade bezel curer flied kneed muley
tweak jumbo coach mecca stuck etude spado bidet cusec flier kneel murex
typal Kaaba coact mercy sulci etude Spode biker cutey flyer kopek muser
Uboat layby cocci milch synch evade Spode biped cyder fogey label muted
uhlan limbo conch mince teach exode study biter dalek fovea lacet naked
ulnae lobby couch mooch tench exude suede bleed dated foyer lacey naker
ulnar looby crack mulch terce faddy swede bleep dater freer laded namer
umiak mamba crick mulct theca fordo tardy blues defer frier laden nares
unbar mambo crock munch thick fundi tilde bluet desex fryer lager nates
uncap maybe cruck mutch tinct funds toady bluey deter fumet lapel navel
Uniat mobby culch nancy torch gaudy toddy bogey dicer fusee lares never
unlay nimbi curch niece touch geode tondi bohea dicey galea laser newel
unman nobby cutch nonce trace giddy tondo boned diker games lated nisei
unsay oribi Czech notch track glade trade boner dimer gaper laten nomen
urban outby dance orach tract glady trode boney diner gavel latex nones
ureal plebs deice oracy trice glede tsade booed diver gazer laver nonet
urial probe deuce ounce trick glide uredo borer Dives genet layer noser
usual rabbi disco parch truce goody Vedda botel dizen giber leger nosey
uveal rugby ditch Pasch truck Gouda veldt bowed domed given leges noted
vagal rumba dolce patch twice grade waddy bowel donee giver leper novel
varan samba douce peace vetch gride weeds bower doper gleed levee Nowel
vasal sambo Draco peach vinca guide weedy boxer dopey gleek level numen
vegan scuba dunce pence Vlach handy widdy breed doter gleet lever oaken
velar slubb dutch perch voice hardy wilds breer dowed gluey libel oared
venae tabby edict piece vouch heady windy brief dowel godet liber oases
venal tribe educe pilch watch Hindi woods brier dower golem lifer oaten
vicar tubby educt pinch welch Hindu woody bused doyen goner liger oaves
vinal turbo eject pitch wench horde words buyer dozen gooey liken octet
viral urubu elect place whack howdy wordy caber dozer greed limen offer
vital webby enact plica which imide zonda cadet dried Greek limey often
vivat yerba epact pluck wilco irade abbey cagey drier green linen ogler
vocal yobbo epoch poach wince kendo ackee camel dryer greet liner oiled
volar zambo erect ponce winch khadi acred cameo duper grief lines oiler
wheal zombi erica poncy witch kiddy adder caper duvet gruel liven olden
wheat abaca eruct pooch wrack lardy adieu carer eager gules liver oncer
wigan abaci evict porch wreck leads after caret eared Hades lives onset
witan aback exact pouch wrick leady aglet cater easel harem lobed orbed
woman acock fancy price yucca leady agley cates eaten hater loden order
wreak aitch farce prick zinco lordy agree caver eater haven loner oriel
yulan alack farci pricy zincy Mahdi agued cheek eaves haver lorel ormer
zonal amice farcy psych abide mardy aider cheep edged hazel losel osier
zygal amuck fence punch abode middy ainee cheer egger hazer loser other
adobe apace fetch quack amide misdo airer chief egret hewer lover otter
alibi areca filch quick amido monde alder chiel eider hiker lovey ousel
Araby bacca finch ranch anode moody alien cider elder hirer lower outer
barbe baccy fitch ratch apode muddy alley cimex elver hives lumen ouzel
bilbo banco flack reach aside neddy alter civet elves hokey lycee owlet
bimbo batch fleck react baddy needs amber cleek embed holey lyses owner
bobby beach flick recce bandy needy ameer coder ember homer macer oxter
```

```
pacer samel tepee widen toffy ledge usage sophy bunia glair music scrip
palea saree thief wiles turfy ledgy venge spahi burin goyim myoid sepia
panel sated three winey unify leggy verge tache cabin grail nadir Seric
paper saver threw wiper whiff liege virga techy calid grain naris serif
parer sayer tiger wives adage lingo Virgo tight calif graip nitid serin
paten scree tiler wizen agogo lodge vouge tithe calix groin nixie sewin
pater screw timer woken align longa vuggy tophi Carib habit noria sheik
paver Seder times women amigo longe wedge Vichy cavil hakim oasis sigil
payee semee tinea wooer anigh lough weigh washy chain helix ohmic sitin
payer semen tined woven badge lunge winge wight chair humic oidia skein
peter seven token xebec baggy lungi wings withe choir humid oldie slain
piker sever toner xylem barge madge wingy withy cilia hutia oleic sloid
pilea sewer topee yager beige mange wodge yacht civic hylic olein sluit
pilei sexed toper yamen belga mango wonga aboil civil hyoid optic snail
piney sheen totem yodel bilge mangy zingy abrim claim immit orbit sodic
piper sheep towel yokel bilgy marge aloha acrid cobia immix orpin solid
poker sheer tower zebec binge merge alpha actin colic Indic orris sonic
poser sheet treen zibet bingo midge aught adlib conic iodic ossia speir
power shiel tried abaft bodge mingy bathe admit comic iodic ostia split
preen shier trier aloft boggy muggy baths admix conic ionic ovoid spoil
prier shoer tuber beefs bough mulga bight aegis covin Kafir oxlip sprig
proem shred tuner beefy bough mungo boche aerie cubic kalif panic sprit
pryer shrew tutee bluff budge neigh bothy affix cubit kefir patio squib
puler shyer tweed buffi buggy nudge bushy Afric Cufic kinin pavid squid
puree sided tween buffo bulge ology cache afrit cumin krait pavis squit
queen silex tweet chafe bulgy omega cushy again Cupid Kufic peril staid
queer sinew twyer chaff burgh Osage dacha algid curia kumis petit stain
quiet siren tyler chuff cadge outgo dight algin curie kylin pewit stair
racer sixer udder cleft cargo panga dishy allin curio kyrie pipit stein
races sizer ulcer cliff coign parge docht amain cutie labia pixie stoic
raker skeet umbel comfy conga peggy duchy ambit cutin Ladin plaid stria
ranee skier umber craft conge phage eight amnia cutis Latin plain strip
raper skiey unbed croft corgi piggy fiche antic cynic legit plait Sufic
ratel skyer under daffy cough plage fichu anvil daric levin podia swain
rater skyey unpeg dagga deify podge fight aphid davit lewis polio sybil
ravel sleek unset delft deign podgy fishy aphis debit lexis posit tacit
raven sleep unsex draff dingo pongo foehn April demit licit pubic tafia
raver sleet upped draft dingy porgy gushy apsis denim liein pubis takin
rayed slyer upper drift dirge pudge hight argil devil limit Punic Tamil
razee sneer upset edify dodge pudgy hypha aroid digit linin pupil tamis
rebec snoek uraei feoff dodgy       itchy arris dixie lipid Purim tapir
rebel sober urger fluff doggo purge lathe arsis dogie livid purin tapis
refel solen usher gaffe doggy raggy lathi asdic Doric logia pyxie tawie
refer sorel utter goofy donga range lathy aspic drail logic pyxis taxis
relet sower Uzbeg graft dough rangy lethe astir drain loris quail telic
remex speed Uzbek griff dregs reign licht aswim droit louis quoin tepid
renew speel valet grift dungy ridge light atria druid lucid quoit their
repel speer vaned gruff elegy ridgy lithe atrip dulia lupin rabic thrid
reset spiel varec howff eloge rouge litho attic Eddic lurid rabid tibia
revel spier vibes huffy faugh rough lushy audio eerie lyric radii tiein
revet spree video inoff feign saggy lythe audit elfin lysin radio timid
ribes steed viper jiffy foggy saiga macho aulic eloin lysis radix tonic
ricer steek vireo knife forge sarge mashy auric entia Mafia ramie topic
rider steel vires leafy forgo saugh maths auxin Eolic magic rapid toric
ripen steep vives loofa fudge sedge meths avail eosin malic ratio torii
risen steer vixen luffa fuggy sedgy might avoid equip mania ravin toxic
riser sties volet niffy fungi serge mocha await Ernie manic rebid toxin
rived stoep vomer puffy gauge siege mothy ayrie ethic maria redia trail
rivel strep voter quaff gorge singe mushy azoic eyrie marid redid train
riven strew vowel quiff gouge Singh niche baric facia matin refit trait
river styes wader reify grege soggy night basic fagin mavis regie tulip
rivet suber wafer scifi gunge sorgo nucha basil fakir maxim rejig tumid
rodeo super wager scoff haugh sough ortho basin fetid media relic tunic
roger sweep wages scuff hedge stage ought basis finis medic relit twain
roker sweet waken shaft heigh stagy ouphe batik flail melic remit typic
Romeo sycee waker shift henge stogy pacha bedim flair meril resin Ugric
roper syren wakes skiff hinge surge pasha befit fluid merit resit ulmin
ropey tabes waler snafu hodge swage pashm begin folia mesic rigid undid
roset taken waney sniff hough taiga pithy belie folio metic robin unfit
rover taker wares snuff image tango prahu bifid frail metif rosin unfix
rowel tales water solfa imago tangy pushy blain fruit metis rubin unlit
rowen tamer waved staff jaggy targe raphe bogie fusil mimic runic unpin
rower taper waver stiff jingo thegn rathe boric gamic minim sahib unrig
ruler tater wavey stuff judge thigh right braid gamin motif salic unrip
rumen tawer waxen sulfa kedge tinge rishi brail gelid movie sapid untie
rupee taxer waxer surfy laigh tonga ruche brain genic mucic sasin until
saker tehee weber swift large tongs rushy broil genie mucin satin unzip
salep telex wheel taffy largo tough sadhu bruin genii mudir savin valid
sales tenet wheen theft laugh tragi sight bruit geoid mujik scrim vapid
```

```
varix jocko abele duple manly skulk world halma aging doing lawny scone
vatic junky acold dwale maple skull would hammy agone donna leant segno
Vedic khaki addle dwell marly slily wryly Hbomb agony downa liana seine
venin kinky adult dwelt matlo slyly yauld herma akene downy liane senna
vigil kooky agile eagle mealy small yield horme aline drank liang shank
virid lanky ahold early merle smalt Abomb jammy alone drink linny shant
visit larky ahull exalt mille smell agami jemmy along drone llano shend
vivid lawks aioli exile molly smelt anima karma amend drunk loony shent
vogie leaky aisle exult moola smile anomy lemma ament dunno lound shine
vomit links alula fable mould smolt aroma llama amine dunny lowne shiny
vraic looks amble falls moult snell atomy loamy amino dying lying shone
xenia lucky ample farle mulla socle balmy lumme among ebony mains shunt
xeric micky amply fatly myall spall barmy magma anent eland manna skene
yogic milky anele fault nelly spell beamy mamma arena emend maund skink
zooid mirky angle fella newly spelt biome mammy atone evens means skint
zoril mucky Anglo felly noble spile blame mneme atony event meant skunk
banjo murky anile ferly nobly spill blimp momma avens exine meany slang
ganja musky ankle field nulla spilt blimy mummy banns eying meiny slant
hadji narky apple fille nyala stale brume myoma beano faint mesne sling
hajji necks apply filly obeli stalk champ neume being fanny moony slink
kopje nerka aptly fitly oddly stall chimb palmy benni fauna mound slung
pooja nooky atilt fjeld ovoli stela chime pigmy benny fawny mount slunk
shoji parka atoll folly ovolo stele chimp plumb bhang feint nanna sonny
thuja parky axile frill ovule stile chomp plume bland fenny nanny sound
alike pawky badly fugle pally still chump plump blank ferny ninny spang
awake peaky bally fully parle stilt chyme plumy blend fiend nonny spank
awoke perky baulk gable phyla stola clamp pommy blent finny noone spend
balky pesky belle gaily phyle stole climb prima blind flank obang spent
barky picky belly Galla poilu stull clime prime blink fling ohone spine
bloke pinko bible gally pools style clump primo blond flint opine spiny
bosky pinky bield gault poult styli comma primp blunt flong ovine spunk
brake pocky billy gelly prole stylo coomb pygmy bonne flung owing stand
braky polka bogle ghyll psalm sully cramp reams bonny flunk ozone stane
broke porky boule girly qualm surly creme rhomb borne found paint stang
bucko pucka boult godly quell swale crime rhumb bound fount panne stank
bulky pukka bowls golly quill swell crimp rhyme brand franc penna steno
bunko quake brill grill quilt swill crump roomy brank frank penny sting
burka quaky brule Guelf rally tabla crump rummy brant frena peony stink
burke reeky bugle guild rawly table derma salmi brent frond phene stint
cheka risky build guile realm tails disme scamp brine frons phone stone
choke rocks built guilt redly tally dogma schmo bring front phono stonk
choky rocky bulla gully reply telly dormy seamy brink funny phony stony
cloke rooky bully haily rifle tesla douma shame briny gaunt piano stung
cocky sarky burly hallo rille thill drama sigma bronc giant pinna stunk
conky shake cable haply roble thole drome skimp brunt ginny pinny stunt
cooky shako calla haulm roily tholi dummy slime bunny gland plane suint
corky shaky cauli hello rolls title duomo slimy burnt glint plank Sunna
crake silks caulk hillo ruble toile elemi slump bwana going plant Sunni
darky silky cello hilly rumly toils enema spume byend gonna plonk sunny
dekko slake chalk holla sable trill enemy spumy canna grand plunk swank
dicky smoke chela hollo sadly troll etyma stamp canny grant poind swine
dinky smoko child holly sally trull fermi stime carny grind point swing
drake smoky chile hotly sault truly filmy stoma chant grunt porno swink
ducks snake chili hullo scald tulle flame stomp china guano pound swung
ducky snaky chill hurly scale twill flamy stump chine guano prang taint
dumka spake choli icily scall uncle flimp summa chink gunny prank taunt
dumky spike chyle idola scalp utile flume swami chunk haunt prink tawny
dusky spiky coble idyll scaly uvula flump swamp clang henna print teens
ensky spoke colly imply scold vails foamy tammy clank hinny prone teeny
evoke stake cooly ingle scull vault forme terms cline horny prong teind
flake stoke could inkle sculp vealy frame thema cling hound prune tenne
flaky sulky coyly istle seely villa frump theme clink hyena prunt terne
fluke tacky cully ixtle sells villi gamma thumb clone hying quant thane
fluky tanka curly jelly shale viola gammy thump clonk icing quins thank
funky tonka cycle jolly shall voile gaumy thyme clung inane quint thine
gawky trike cyclo joule shalt walla gemma thymy clunk irony rainy thing
gecko Turki daily knell shaly wally gemmy tommy corno Jaina reins think
grike tusky dally knelt shelf wanly germy tramp cornu jaunt rhine thong
haiku vodka dealt knoll shell weald gimme tromp corny jeans rhino tinny
hanky wacke dhole koala shill wells gismo trump count jenny riant tonne
hokku wacky dilly krill shily wetly glume tummy crane jinni round towny
honky wonky dimly kwela shyly whale gnome ulema crank joint runny trend
hooky works doily ladle sidle whelk grama worms crone kerne saint trine
hunks yolky dolly laxly sigla whelm grime wormy cronk kiang sauna trona
hunky yonks drill lisle silly whelp grimy yummy crony koine scant trone
husky yucky drily lolly skald while grume acini daunt krans scena trunk
jacks yukky droll lowly skelm whole grump adunc Diana krona scend tunny
jerky zinky dryly macle skelp wield guimp agene diene krone scene twang
jinks zooks dully madly skill willy gummy agent djinn kyang scent twine
```

```
twink carom lysol spoor duppy sylph cobra learn shore weird crest horst
twiny chaos Macon stood elope taupe copra leery shorn wharf crisp horsy
tying cloot major stook erupt tempi court liard short where cross house
upend Cobol manor stool gappy tempo cowry libra skirl whirl cruse hurst
urine cocoa mason stoop gilpy tempt crore litre skirr whirr crush hussy
vaunt codon mayor strop glyph tippy curry livre skirt whore crust Irish
veena cohoe McCoy strow goopy traps Cymry lorry slurp whorl cuish Jesse
veiny colon Medoc stroy grape tripe dairy loury smarm worry curse joist
viand crook melon sudor graph trope deary lucre smart yearn curst joust
vying croon meson sutor grapy turps decry lyart smirk years daisy karst
weeny dagos miaow swoon gripe unapt diary macro snare yours deism kiosk
whang decor midon swoop grope weepy dowry Maori snark zebra deist knish
whine decoy minor synod gulph wispy durra marry snarl abase dense kvass
whiny demob moron taboo guppy wrapt dwarf merry snore abash didst lapse
wound demon motor tabor happy yippy eagre metre snort abask doest lasso
wring demos nabob talon harpy zippy emery metro sorra abuse douse lease
wrong depot ninon tarok hippo Iraqi entry micro sorry abysm dowse leash
wrung dicot niton tarot hippy abort enure mitre spare abyss dress least
yawny divot nohow tatou humph acari evert moire spark adust dross loess
young dodos nylon taxon humpy acerb every morra sperm agist druse loose
abbot donor odeon tenon inapt acorn exert mourn spire amass dulse louse
abhor drool onion tenor inept adore extra mucro spirt Amish durst lousy
ablow droop orlop throb jaspe adorn exurb murra spiry amiss egest manse
acton elbow oxbow throe jumpy afire faery murre spore amuse erase marsh
actor embow paeon throw kalpa afore fairy myrrh sport angst erose massa
adios endow parol tigon kappa aggro fayre nacre spurn anise exist masse
afoot enjoy pekoe topoi kelpy agora ferry Negro spurt apish false massy
aglow enrol pheon topos kempt alarm fibre nitre stare arise fatso mayst
Algol envoi phlox trior leapt alary fiery nitro stark arose feast mense
allot envoy picot troop lippy alert fiord ochre start avast fesse messy
allow ephod pidog tryon loopy ambry firry ochry stere awash first midst
alloy ephor pilot Tudor loppy amort fjord ombre stern balsa flash missy
aloof ergot pinon tutor loupe antra flare opera stirk bassi flask moist
ambos error piton ungot lumpy antre flirt otary stirp basso flesh moksa
ancon escot pivot union lymph apart flora outre store beast floss moose
anion estoc prior venom morph apery flory ovary stork bitsy flush morse
annoy estop proof visor mumps aport frore overs storm blase foist mossy
apron ethos puton vizor myope appro furry overt story blast fossa mouse
arbor extol pylon wagon nappe avert genre padre sturt bless fosse mousy
argol fagot radon wahoo nappy award genro parry sucre blest fresh mussy
argon felon razor whoop nippy aware glare pearl Sudra bliss frisk newsy
argot fetor redox widow nymph azure glary peart supra blush frost noise
arrow flood repot xenon okapi bairn glory perry surra boast fubsy noisy
arson floor rigor xylol oomph barre gnarl petri sutra boost fussy noose
ascot fluor robot yahoo palpi beard gnarr poort sward bossy gassy Norse
axiom furor rotor yapok pampa beery gourd psora sware bouse gauss nurse
baboo galop sabot adapt pappy berry guard quark swarf bousy gawsy obese
bacon gemot salon adept peppy blare gurry quart swarm bowse geese omasa
baron genoa sapor adopt poppy blurb hairy quern swart brash geist paisa
bason gigot saros agape pulpy blurt harry query swirl brass gesso palsy
baton giron savoy aleph puppy board heard quire sword brisk ghast pansy
bayou gloom Saxon bumph quipu boart heart quirk swore brose ghost parse
bebop groom scion bumpy raspy bourg henry quirt sworn brush gipsy Parsi
befog guyot scoop calpa roupy bourn hoard rearm tarre buist glass passe
begot gyron scoot campy rumpy burro hoary repro tarry bursa gloss patsy
below halos scrod carpi sappy burry houri retry teary burse gnash pause
besom havoc sekos chape scape cadre hurry sabra terra burst goest pease
besot helot senor chaps scopa caird hydra sabre terry canst goose perse
beton heron sepoy chops scope cairn hydro sacra tetra cause gorse phase
bigot hyson serow clepe seepy carry inarm saury there cease gorsy plash
bijou Hykos seton coapt shape ceorl indri scare therm cense grasp plasm
bipod ichor Sheol compo slept chard inert scarf third chase grasp plush
bison idiom shook compt slips chare infra scarp thirl chasm grise poesy
blood idiot shoon coopt slope charm intro scart thorn chess grist poise
bloom igloo shoot corps slops charr inure scary thorp chest gross popsy
boron ingot sloop coupe slype chart inurn score tiara chose guess posse
bosom jabot sloot coypu snipe chary ivory scorn titre chuse guest prase
boson juror snood crape snips chert izard scurf twere cissy guise press
brood kabob snook craps soapy chirk Jerry serra twerp clash gutsy prest
brook kapok snoop crepe soppy chirp Jewry serry twirl clasp gypsy prise
broom karoo snoot crept soupy chirr kauri shard twirp class hadst prism
buxom kazoo Sodom crypt staph chord knurl share ultra close Hanse prose
cabob kebob solon cuppa steps chore knurr sharp unarm copse Hausa prosy
caboc kloof sopor dippy stipe churl knurr sherd usurp corse hawse pulse
canoe kotow spoof drape stope churn kukri shire usury corse heist pursy
canon kudos spook drops stupa churr labra shirr veery crash hoise purse
capon kyloe spool drupe stupe cirri laird shirk uteri crash hoist pussy
carob lemon spoom dumps swept clary lairy shirr veery cress horse quash
carol Logos spoon dumpy swipe clerk laura shirt weary cress horse quasi
```

```
quest agate footy pants sputa choux mopus undue silva vinyl bunia huzza
raise alate forte panty state cloud mucus ungum skive Xrays bunya hydra
rasse Amati forth parti suety clout negus vacua slave abuzz burka hyena
reest amity forty party suite cogue nexus vague solve adoze bursa hypha
reuse aorta frith pasta swath croup nidus vagus stave agaze bwana idola
rinse aunty fritz paste swith datum nisus value stove amaze Caaba infra
roast azote froth pasty tarty debug nodus varus suave baize caeca Jaina
roost azoth fusty patty taste debut notum velum sylva blaze calla jibba
rouse Bantu fytte peaty tasty degum oakum venue trove bonze calpa junta
roust baste garth pelta tatty demur occur Venus valve booze canna Kaaba
salse batty gents petty teeth donut odeum virus varve boozy cheka kalpa
sassy berth geste photo tenth durum odium vogue verve braze chela kappa
sayso biota girth pieta tenty embus odour vrouw volva brize china karma
sayst birth goaty piety testa endue oleum waive       chizz cilia koala
seise bitts goeth pinta testy ennui oneup woful weave colza circa krona
seism bitty goety pinto theta ensue opium above adown craze cnida kwela
sensa blate gotta piste tilth favus picul agave blown crazy cobia labia
sense blitz gouty pitta tinty femur pilus alive blowy diazo cobra labra
shush booth grate plate tooth fetus pinup bivvy brawl dizzy cocoa larva
sissy boots grith Pluto torte flour pious brava brawn Druze colza laura
slash booty grits Porte trite flout pipul brave brown feeze comma lemma
slosh broth gusto potto troth focus pique bravi chewy fizzy conga lepta
slush brute gusty potty truth forum proud bravo clown frizz copra liana
smash bunty gutta pouty tufty fraud pseud breve crawl froze costa libra
snash busty gutty prate tutti fryup queue calve crowd furze cotta llama
sonsy butte haste punty tutty fucus ramus carve crown furzy cuppa logia
souse butty hasty putti twite fugue rebus chevy drawl fuzzy curia longa
spasm cacti heath putto umpty gamut rebut chive drawn gauze dacha loofa
stash canto hefty putty unite genus recur chivy drown gauzy dagga luffa
sudsy canty hertz quite unity getup rerun civvy flews Ghazi delta lytta
swash caste hoots quits urate ghaut revue clave flown glaze derma Mafia
swish catty hosta quota vasty ghoul rheum clove frown glazy Diana magma
Swiss cento irate quote vertu gigue rogue crave gnawn gloze dicta mamba
tansy cesti jetty quoth vesta glaur rubus curve growl graze dogma mamma
tarsi chute jolty ratty virtu glout runup curvy grown huzza donga mania
tasse cloth junta reata vista group scaup delve known huzzy donna manna
tawse coati junto recto vitta grout scaur divvy prawn jazzy douma manta
tease conte kitty rente volta gyrus scour drive prowl kudzu downa maria
tense costa laity riata volte hilum scout drove schwa maize drama massa
terse cotta lefty rooty volti hocus scrub glove scowl matzo dulia mecca
these couth lento rorty waits hohum scrum grave shawl mezzo dumka media
those crate Lents route waltz hokum sebum gravy shawm muzzy durra mocha
tipsy crwth lepta routh warty humus sedum grove shewn piezo enema moksa
toast cutty lists runty waste ictus segue guava shown pizza entia momma
torse darts loath rusty white ileum serum halva showy plaza erica moola
torsk death lofty rutty whity ileus setup halve snowy prize etyma morra
torso deity lotto saith width ilium shout heave spawn ritzy extra mulga
touse delta lusty Sakta witty imaum shrub heavy       seize facia mulla
tousy depth lytta salts worth imbue shrug helve thews smaze facta murra
trash dhoti malty salty wrath incur sinus knave thewy swizz fauna myoma
trass dicta manta saute write incus Sioux larva trawl tazza fella nanna
tress dirty manto scatt wrote indue snout leave trews tizzy flora nerka
trist ditto matte Scots wroth injun solum mauve viewy whizz flota noria
truss ditty meaty scuta xysti input solus naevi ataxy winze folia nucha
trust doeth mesto scute youth issue sorus naive braxy woozy fossa nulla
tryst dorts minty septa zesty jokul spout navvy epoxy zanze fovea nyala
tuism dorty mirth setto zloty jorum sprue neive flaxy ——— frena oidia
twist dotty misty sexto about kaput stoup nerve prexy abaca galea omasa
ukase dusty molto silty album knout stour nervy proxy abaya Galla omega
valse earth monte sixte aloud kraut strum ogive abaya agora gamba opera
verse elate month sixth amour larum strut olive alkyd aloha gamma Oriya
verso elite motte sixty annul layup sunup peeve alkyl alpha ganja ossia
verst elute motto skate appui lemur setup privy allyl alula genoa ostia
waist emote mouth skite appuy letup syrup privy allyl alula genoa pacha
welsh empty mufti slate argue lobus taluk Provo beryl amnia gonna paisa
whish enate multi slaty Argus locum talus reave bunya anima gotta palea
whisk evite musth sloth ascus locus taxus reeve butyl antra Gouda pampa
whist facta musty smite augur lotus thrum reive calyx aorta grama panda
whose faith nasty smith awful lupus tieup salve ethyl areca guana panga
whoso Fanti natty smote babul magus tipup salvo Oriya arena guava parka
worse fatty neath snath beaus manul togue savvy oxeye aroma gutta pasha
worst fifth netty softa beaut manus tonus selva playa atria halma pasta
wrest fifty nifty softy beaux miaul toque serve polyp bacca halva pelta
wrist filth ninth sooth begum minus torus servo satyr balsa Hausa penna
Xhosa firth north sooty begun mixup trout shave sibyl belga henna phyla
yeast flota nutty south bogus modus tucum sheva sloyd biota herma pieta
abate flute orate spate bolus mogul tuque Shiva stays bohea holla pilea
acute fluty ovate spite bonus mohur uncus shove swayl brava hosta pinna
adyta foots panto spitz bosun mopup uncut sieve thuya bulla hutia pinta
```

```
pitta umbra Doric award grand sided akene bribe cutie fluke house monte
pizza uvula Eddic awned greed skald alate bride cycle flume image moose
playa vacua Eolic bated grind sloid algae brine dance flute imbue morse
plaza Vedda estoc beard guard sloyd alike brize deice force imide motte
plica veena ethic bedad guild snood aline broke delve forge inane mouse
podia vesta franc begad heard solid alive brose dense forme indue movie
polka villa gamic bield hexad sound alone brule deuce forte ingle murre
pooja vinca genic bifid hoard speed amaze brume dhole fosse inkle myope
prima viola havoc biped hound spend amble brute diene frame inure nacre
psora virga humic bipod humid squad amice budge diode frore irade naive
pucka vista hylic bland hyoid squid amide bugle dirge froze irate nappe
pukka vitta ileac bleed idead staid amine bulge disme fudge issue neive
quota vodka iliac blend Iliad stand ample burke dixie fugle istle nerve
reata volta Indic blind imbed stead amuse burse dodge fugue ixtle neume
redia volva iodic blond ivied steed anele butte dogie furze jaspe niche
riata walla ionic blood izard stood angle cable dolce fusee Jesse niece
rumba wonga Kufic board jaded strad anile cache donee fytte joule nieve
sabra xenia lilac boned jehad sward anise cadge douce gable judge nitre
sacra Xhosa logic booed jihad sword ankle cadre douse gaffe juice nixie
saiga yerba lyric bound keyed synod anode calve dowse gauge kedge noble
Sakta yucca magic bowed knead teind antae canoe drake gauze kerne noise
samba zebra malic braid kneed tepid antre carve drape geese knave nonce
sauna zonda manic brand laded third apace caste drive genie knife noone
scena Abomb medic bread laird thrid apode cause drome genre koine noose
schwa acerb Medoc breed lated timid apple cease drone geode kopje Norse
scopa adlib melic broad liard tined argue cense drove geste krone novae
scuba blurb mesic brood lipid tread arise chafe drupe gigue kyloe nudge
scuta cabob metic build livid trend arose chape druse gimme kyrie nurse
selva Carib mimic bused lobed triad aside chare Druze glace ladle obese
senna carob mucic byend lound tried atone chase dulse glade lance ochre
sensa chimb music caird lucid tumid aurae chide dunce glare lapse ogive
sepia climb ohmic calid lurid tweed awake chile duple glaze large ohone
septa coomb oleic chard maned unbed aware chime dwale glebe lathe oldie
serra crumb optic child marid undid awoke chine eagle glede lease olive
sheva cubeb panic chord maund upend axile chive eagre glide leave ombre
Shiva demob pubic cloud mixed upped ayrie choke educe globe ledge opine
sigla exurb Punic could monad valid azote chore eerie glove lethe orate
sigma Hbomb rabic cowed moped vaned azure chose elate gloze levee Osage
silva kabob rebec creed mould vapid badge chuse elide glume liane ounce
softa kebab relic crowd mound viand baize chute elite gnome liege ouphe
solfa kebob runic Cupid muted virid barbe chyle eloge goose lisle outre
sorra nabob salic cycad myoid vivid barge chyme elope gorge lithe ovate
spica nawab serac dated naiad waved barre clave elude gorse litre ovine
sputa plumb Seric domed naked weald baste clepe elute gouge livre ovule
stela rhomb sodic dowed nitid weird bathe clime emcee grace lodge oxeye
stola rhumb sonic dread nomad wield beige cline emote grade longe oxide
stoma sahib stoic dried noted world belie cloke enate grape loose ozone
stria scrub Sufic druid oared would belle clone endue grate loupe padre
stupa shrub sumac dryad oiled wound bible close ensue grave louse panne
Sudra slubb telic eared orbed yauld bilge clove enure graze lowne parge
sulfa squab tonic edged oread yield binge coble epode grebe lucre parle
summa squib topic eland ovoid zooid biome cogue erase grege lumme parse
Sunna throb toric embed pavid abase blade cohoe Ernie gride lunge passe
supra thumb toxic emend plaid abate blame comae erode grike lycee paste
surra adunc tunic ended plead abele blare combe erose grime lythe pause
sutra Afric typic ephod poind abide blase conge etude gripe macle payee
sylva antic Ugric faced pound abode blate conte etwee grise madge peace
tabla Anzac varec famed proud above blaze cooee evade grope maize pease
tafia asdic vatic farad pseud abuse bloke copse evite grove mange peeve
taiga aspic Vedic fated rabid ackee blude corse evoke grume manse pekoe
tanka attic vraic fetid rapid acute boche coude exile guide maple pence
tazza aulic xebec field rayed adage bodge coupe exine guile marge perse
terra auric xeric fiend rebid addle bogie coxae exode guise masse phage
tesla azoic yogic fiord redid adobe bogle crake exude gunge matte phase
testa Aztec zebec fixed rigid adore bombe crane eyrie halve mauve phene
tetra baric acold fjeld rived adoze bonce crape fable Hanse maybe phone
theca basic acred fjord round aerie bonne crate false haste melee phyle
thema boric acrid flied salad afire bonze crave farce hawse mense piece
theta bronc agued flood sapid afore booze craze farle heave merge pique
thuja caboc ahead fluid sated agape borne creme fayre hedge merle piste
thuya civic ahold found scald agate boule crepe feeze helve mesne pixie
tiara colic algid fraud scend agave bouse crime fence hence metre place
tibia comic alkyd frond scold agaze bowse crone fesse henge midge plage
tinea conic aloud gelid scrod agene brace crore fibre hinge mille plane
tonga cubic amend geoid sexed agile brake crude fiche hodge mince plate
tonka Cufic aphid gland shard agone brave cruse fille hoise mitre plume
trona cusec armed gleed shend agree braze curie flake horde mneme podge
ulema cynic aroid gonad sherd ainee brede curse flame horme moire poise
ultra daric avoid gourd shred aisle breve curve flare horse monde ponce
```

```
Porte semee stoke twere quiff aleph goeth rajah Bahai terai frisk thick
posse sense stole twice scarf Allah graph ranch bassi tholi frock think
prase serge stone twine scoff Amish grith ratch benni tondi gleek torsk
prate serve stope twite scuff anigh gulch reach bravi tophi gopak track
price setae store ukase scurf apish gulph Reich buffi topoi Greek trick
pride shade stove ulnae serif arrah harsh retch cacti torii haick truck
prime shake stupe uncle sheaf awash hatch roach carpi tragi hoick trunk
prise shale style undue shelf azoth haugh rotch cauli Turki kapok tweak
prize shame suave unite skiff batch heath rough cesti tutti kayak twink
probe shape sucre untie sniff beach heigh routh chili uraei kiosk umiak
prole share suede urate snuff beech hitch saith choli uteri knack Uzbek
prone shave suite urine spoof belch hooch sauch cirri villi knock whack
prose shine surge usage staff bench hotch saugh coati volti kopek whelk
prude shire swage utile stiff berth hough selah cocci xysti kulak whisk
prune shone swale vague stuff birch humph Shiah corgi zombi mujik wrack
pudge shore sware valse swarf birth hunch shush dhobi aback plank wreak
pulse shove value thief witch hutch Singh dhoti abask plonk wreck
pupae sidle swine valve wharf blush Irish sixth elemi acock pluck wrick
puree siege swipe varve whiff booth Jonah slash ennui alack plunk yapok
purge sieve swore venae aging botch ketch slosh envoi amuck prank aboil
purse since sycee venge along bough knish sloth Fanti apeak prick ahull
pyxie singe table venue among brach laigh slush farci batik prink algal
quake sixte tache verge befog brash larch smash fermi baulk quack Algol
queue skate targe verse being broch latch smith fundi black quark alkyl
quire skene tarre verve bhang broth laugh snash fungi blank quick allyl
quite skite tasse vogie bourg brush leach snath genii bleak quirk angel
quote skive taste vogue bring bumph leash sooth Ghazi blink shack annal
raise slake taupe voice clang bunch leech sough hadji block shank annul
ramie slate tawie voile cling burgh loach south hajji brank shark anvil
ranee slave tawse volte clung butch loath staph Hindi break sheik appal
range slice tease vouge catch lotah stash houri brick shirk April
raphe slide tehee wacke cinch lough stich iambi brink shock areal
rasse slime tenne waive doing clash lunch surah indri brisk shook argil
rathe slope tense waste dying cloth lurch swash Iraqi brock shook argol
razee slype tepee weave eying coach lymph swath issei brook skink ariel
reave smaze terce wedge fling conch lynch swish jinni caulk skulk artel
recce smile terne whale flong couch marah swith kauri chalk skunk arval
reeve smite terse where flung cough march sylph khadi check slack atoll
regie smoke thane while going couth marsh synch khaki cheek sleek aural
reive smote theme whine hying crash teach khaki chick slick avail
rente snake there white icing crush milch tench lathi chink slink awful
reuse snare these whole kiang crwth mirth teeth lungi chirk slunk axial
revue snide thine whore kyang cuish month tenth Mahdi chock smack babel
rhine snipe thole whose liang culch mooch thigh Maori chuck smirk babul
rhyme snore those wince lying curch morph tilth mufti chunk smock bagel
ridge socle three winge obang cutch mouth tooth multi clack snack banal
rifle solve throe winze owing Czech mulch Torah naevi clank snark basal
rille sonde thyme withe pidog death munch torch nimbi cleek sneak basil
rinse souse tilde wodge prang depth musth touch nisei clerk sneck bedel
roble space tinge worse prong ditch mutch tough obeli click snick beryl
rogue spade tithe write rejig doeth mynah trash okapi clink snoek betel
rouge spake title wrote scrag donah myrrh troth oribi cloak snook bevel
rouse spare titre zanze shrug dough neath truth ovoli clock spank bezel
route spate togue aloof slang dutch neigh vetch palpi clonk spark botel
ruble spice toile bluff sling earth ninth Vlach pardi cloud speak bowel
ruche spike tonne brief slung ephah north vouch Parsi cluck speck brail
rupee spile topee calif spang epoch notch watch parti crack spick brawl
sable spine toque chaff sprag faith nymph weigh perai crank spook brill
sabre spire torse chief sprig faugh obeah welch petri creak spunk broil
salse spite torte chuff stang fetch oomph welsh pilei creek stack bubal
salve Spode touse cliff sting fifth orach wench putti crick stalk butyl
saree spoke trace draff stung filch parch which quasi croak stank cabal
sarge spore trade dwarf swung filth Pasch whish rabbi crock stark camel
sauce spree tribe feoff swung finch patch width radii cronk steak canal
saute sprue trice fluff thing firth peach winch rishi crook steek carol
scale spume trike grief thong fitch perch witch salmi cruck stick cavil
scape stage trine griff twang flash pilch worth Saudi dalek stink ceorl
scare stake tripe gruff tying flesh pinch wrath scifi drank stirk chiel
scene stale trite Guelf unpeg flush pitch wroth scudi drink stock chill
scone stane trode howff unrig forth plash youth serai drunk stonk churl
scope stare trone inoff Uzbeg fresh plush abaci shoji flack stook civil
score state trope kalif vying frith poach acari soldi flank stork Cobol
scree stave trove kenaf whang froth pooch acini spahi flask stuck comal
scute stele truce kloof wring galah porch agami styli fleck stunk copal
sedge stere tsade metif wrong garth pouch aioli sulci flick swank coral
segue stile tubae motif wrung gerah psych alibi Sunni flock swink coxal
seine stime tulle pilaf young girth punch Amati swami fluke taluk crawl
seise stipe tuque proof abash glyph quash appui tarsi frank tarok creel
seize stoae tutee quaff aitch gnash quoth assai tempi freak thank cruel
```

```
cupel miaul snail bloom strum croon Macon scran amino macho zambo strep
decal modal snarl bosom swarm crown mason sedan Anglo macro zinco strip
devil model snell bream therm Cuban matin semen appro mambo atrip strop
dotal mogul snell broom thrum cumin Mayan serin audio mango bebop stump
dowel molal spall buxom totem cutin melon seton baboo manto bleep sunup
drail moral speel carom tucum daman meson seven banco matlo blimp swamp
drawl morel spell charm tuism deign midon sewin banjo matzo champ sweep
drill motel spiel chasm unarm demon mixen sheen basso mesto cheap swoop
droll mural spill claim ungum dewan mizen shewn beano metro cheep syrup
drool myall spoil cream velum divan moron shoon bilbo mezzo chimp thorp
ducal nasal spool datum venom dizen mourn shorn bimbo micro chirp thump
dwell natal stall degum whelm djinn mucin shown bingo misdo chomp tieup
easel naval steal deism xylem doyen ninon siren bongo molto chump tipup
enrol navel steel denim acorn dozen nomen sitin bravo motto clamp tramp
equal newel still dream actin drain numen skean bucko mucro clasp tromp
ethyl nival stool durum acton drawn numen skein buffo mungo clump troop
excel nodal stull fleam adman drown nylon slain bumbo Negro cramp trump
expel nopal sural forum adorn eaten oaken solan bunco nitro creep tulip
extol novel swayl gleam adown elfin oaten solen bunko ortho crimp twerp
fatal Nowel sweal gloom again eloin ocean solon burro outdo crisp twirp
feral octal swell golem algin elvan odeon spawn cacao outgo croup uncap
fetal offal swill goyim alien eosin often spean cameo ovolo crump unrip
final oriel swirl groom align fagin olden spoon canto panto droop unzip
flail ousel sybil hakim allin feign olein spurn cargo patio equip usurp
focal ouzel Tamil haram amain felon onion stain cello phono estop whaup
frail panel thill harem amban flown organ stein cento photo flimp whelp
frill papal thirl haulm ancon foehn orpin stern chiao piano flump whoop
fugal parol tical hilum anion frown Oscan swain cisco piezo frump abhor
fural pearl tidal hohum apian furan paean swoon combo pinko fryup actor
fusil pedal tonal hokum apron gamin paeon sworn compo pinto galop adder
gavel penal total idiom argon giron pagan syren corno Pluto getup after
ghoul peril towel ihram Arian given paten taken credo polio graip aider
ghyll petal trail ileum arson glean pavan takin curio pongo grasp airer
glial phial trawl ilium Aryan gnawn pecan talon cyclo porno group alder
gnarl picul trial imaum ashen gowan pekan taxon dekko potto grump altar
goral pipal trill inarm Asian grain pheon tenon diazo primo guimp alter
graal pipul troll Islam aspen green pinon thegn dingo Provo jalap amber
grail prowl trull jorum atman groan piton thorn disco putto julep ameer
grill pupal tubal larum auxin groin plain tiein ditto radio layup amour
growl pupil twill locum avian grown powan tigon doggo ratio letup anger
gruel quail twirl madam bacon gyron prawn titan Draco recto mixup anker
gyral quell typal maxim bairn haven preen token dunno repro mopup arbor
hadal quill umbel minim baron heman purin toman duomo rhino oneup asker
halal ramal until nizam basan heron puton toxin fatso rodeo orlop aster
hamal ratel ureal notum basin hogan pylon train folio Romeo oxlip astir
hazel ravel urial oakum bason hosen quean treen fordo rondo pinup attar
horal rebel usual odeum baton human queen tryon forgo salvo plump auger
hotel refel uveal odium began hyson quern twain gecko sambo polyp augur
hovel regal vagal ogham begin injun quoin tween genro sayso primp baker
ideal renal vasal oleum begun inurn Quran uhlan gesso schmo recap baler
idyll repel venal opium beton japan radon ulmin gismo scudo runup biker
ileal revel vigil pashm bison kinin ratan union guano secco salep biter
ilial rival vinal plasm blain known raven unman gumbo segno scalp blear
impel rivel vinyl praam blown Koran ravin unpin gusto servo scamp boner
jewel rowel viral prism boron kulan redan urban hallo setto scarp borer
jokul royal vital proem boson kylin reign varan hello sexto scaup bower
jural rural vocal psalm       laden reman vegan hillo shako scoop boxer
kneel samel vowel Purim bourn Ladin reran venin hippo smoko scrap boyar
knell scall wheal qualm brain lagan rerun vixen hollo soldo scrip breer
knoll scowl wheel realm brawn laten resin wagon hullo sorgo sculp briar
knurl scull whirl rearm brown Latin ripen waken hydro spado setup brier
kraal sepal whorl rheum bruin learn risen waxen igloo steno sharp buyer
krill seral woful scram burin leman riven wheen imago stylo sheep caber
label shall xylol scrim burin lemon robin widen intro taboo skelp caper
lapel shawl yodel scrum cabin levin roman wigan jingo tango skimp carer
legal shell yokel sebum cairn liein rosin witan jocko tempo sleep cater
level Sheol zonal sedum canon ligan rowan wizen jumbo tondo sloop caver
libel shiel zoril seism capon liken rowen woken karoo torso slump cedar
local shill zygal serum chain limen rubin woman kazoo turbo slurp chair
loral shoal abeam shawm churn linen rumen women kendo uredo sneap charr
lorel sibyl abrim skelm clean linin salon woven kenko verso snoop cheer
losel sigil abysm smarm clown liven sapan xenon largo video stamp chirr
loyal sisal alarm Sodom codon loden sasin yamen lasso vireo steep choir
lysol skill album solum       logan Satan yearn lento Virgo stirp churr
manul skirl aswim spasm colin loran satin yulan limbo wahoo stoep cigar
medal skoal axiom sperm colon Lucan savin aggro lingo whoso stomp clear
meril skull bedim spoom coven lumen Saxon agogo litho wilco stoop coder
mesel small begum steam covin lupin scion amido llano yahoo stoup coder
metal smell besom storm cozen lysin scorn amigo lotto yobbo strap comer
```

```
coper hater offer sneer aegis frons needs vails blunt egret hurst quirt
corer haver ogler sober alias fucus negus varus blurt eight idiot quoit
cover hazer oiler solar amass funds nexus Venus boart eject immit react
cower hewer oncer sonar ambos games nidus vibes boast elect inapt rebut
crier hiker order sopor amiss gauss nisus vires boost emmet inept reest
cryer hilar ormer sowar aphis gents nodus virus boult enact inert refit
curer hirer Oscar sower apsis genus nones vives bract epact ingot relet
cyder homer osier spear Argus glass oases wages brant erect inlet relit
cymar hover other speer arras gloss oasis waits brent ergot input remit
damar ichor otter speir arris grass oaves wakes bruit eruct inset repot
dater icker outer spier arsis grits orris wares brunt erupt islet resat
debar idler owner spoor ascus gross overs weeds built escot izzat reset
decor incur oxter stair atlas guess pants wells buist event jabot resit
defer infer pacer steer auras gules pavis wilds burnt evert jaunt revet
demur inker paper stour avens gyrus pilus wiles burst evict joint riant
deter inner parer suber balas Hades pious wings cadet exact joist right
dicer inter pater sudor banns halos plebs wives canst exalt joust rivet
diker jiber paver sugar bases hives pools woods carat exeat jurat roast
dimer joker payer super basis hocus press words caret exert kaput robot
dinar jowar peter sutor baths hoots psoas works chant exist karst roost
diner juror piker swear beaus humus pubis worms chart exult kempt roset
diver Kafir piper tabor beefs hunks pyxis Xrays cheat facet knelt roust
donor kefir poker taker bends Hykos quins years chert fagot knout sabot
doper Khmer polar tamer bitts ictus quits yonks chest faint krait saint
doter knurr poser taper bless ileus races yours civet fault kraut sault
dower lager power tapir bliss incus ramus zooks cleat feast lacet sayst
dozer lahar prier Tatar blues jacks reams abaft cleft feint leant scant
drear laser prior tater bogus jakes rebus abbot cloot fight leapt scart
drier laver pryer tawer bolas jeans reins abort clout filet least scatt
dryer layer puler taxer bolus jinks ribes about coact first legit sceat
duper lazar queer tenor bonus judas rocks adapt coapt fleet licht scent
eager leger racer their boots krans rolls adept coast flint licit scoot
eater lemur radar tiger bowls kudos rubus admit comet flirt light scout
eggar leper raker tiler brass kumis sales adopt compt float limit shaft
egger lever raper timer camas kvass salts adult coopt flout lyart shalt
eider liber rater toner cates lares saros adust coset foist mayst shant
elder lifer raver toper chaos lauds Scots afoot count fount meant sheet
elver liger razor tower chaps lawks sekos afrit court front merit shent
ember liner recur trier chess leads sells agent covet frost midst shift
emeer liver refer trior chops leges silks agist craft fruit might shirt
emmer lobar ricer tuber class Lents sinus aglet crept fumet moist shoat
enter loner rider Tudor       lewis slips alert crest gamut morat shoot
ephor loser rigor tuner cords lexis slops allot Croat gault motet short
error lover riser tutor corps lines snips aloft croft gaunt moult shout
esker lower river twyer craps links solus ambit cruet geist mount shunt
ester lunar roger tyler crass lists sorus ament crust gemot mulct sight
ether macer roker udder cress lives specs amort crypt genet night skeet
facer major roper ulcer cries lobus stays anent cubit ghast nonet skint
faker makar roper ulnar cross locus steps angst culet ghaut octet skirt
fakir maker rotor umber curds loess sties apart daunt ghost orbit slant
femur malar rover unbar cutis Logos styes aport davit giant ought sleet
fetor manor ruler under dagos looks tabes argot dealt gigot overt slept
fever maser saker upper darts loris tails ascot debit glint owlet sloot
fifer mater sapor urger degas lotus tales ashet debut gloat paint smalt
firer mayor satyr usher demos louis talus asset deist glout peart smart
fiver mazer saver utter Dives lupus tamis atilt delft godet petit smelt
fixer meter sayer velar dodos lyses tapis avast demit goest pewit smolt
flair miler scaur vicar dorts lysis taxis avert deist goest peart smolt
fleer mimer scour visor dregs magus taxis avast delft grant pewit snoot
flier minar Seder vizor dress mains taxus avert demit graft picot snort
floor miner senor volar drops manes teens await depot great pilot snout
flour minor sever vomer dross manus terms beast dicot greet pipit spelt
fluor miser sewer voter ducks mares texas beaut didst grift pivot spent
flyer mixer shear wader dumps maths thews befit dight grist plait spilt
foyer mohur sheer wafer eaves mavis times begat digit groat plant spirt
freer molar shier wager elves means toils beget divot grout pleat splat
friar moper shirr waker embus meths tongs begot docht grunt point split
frier motor shyer waler ethos metis tonus beret donut guest poort sport
fryer mover simar water evens minus topos beset doubt guilt posit spout
furor mower sitar waver falls modus torus besot draft guyot poult sprat
gaper mudir sixer waxer favus monas traps bidet drift habit prest sprit
gazer muser sizar weber fetus mopus trass bight droit hadst prunt spurt
giber nadir sizar whirr fines mores tress bigot ducat haunt Qboat squat
giver naker skier wiper finis mucus trews blast durst heart quant squit
glair namer skirr wooer fives mumps Trias bleat dwelt heist quart start
glaur never slyer yager flews nares truss blent eclat helot quest stilt
gnarr noser slyer abyss floss naris turps blest edict hight quiet stint
goner occur smear adios focus nates uncus bloat educt hoist quilt stoat
gular odour       smear foots necks vagus bluet egest horst quint stout
```

```
strut tatou amity cagey doily fully homey lovey nosey rally snaky unify
stunt urubu amply campy dolly funky honey lowly noway randy snowy unity
sturt vertu annoy candy dopey funny honky lucky nutty rangy soapy unlay
suint virtu anomy canny dormy furry hooey lumpy ochry raspy softy unsay
surat ablow apery canty dorty furzy hooky lushy oddly ratty soggy usury
swart aglow apply carny dotty fussy horny lusty ology rawly sonny vasty
sweat allow appuy carry Douay fusty horsy madly oracy ready sonsy vealy
sweet arrow aptly catty dowdy fuzzy hotly Malay otary reddy sooty veery
swept askew Araby chary downy gabby howdy malty outby redly sophy veiny
swift bedew array chevy dowry gaily hubby mammy ovary reedy soppy Vichy
tacit below assay chewy drily gally huffy mangy paddy reeky sorry viewy
taint bylaw ataxy chivy dryly gammy humpy manly palay reify soupy vuggy
tarot elbow atomy choky duchy gappy hunky mardy pally relay spicy wacky
taunt embow atony cissy ducky gassy hurly marly palmy repay spiky waddy
tempt endow aunty civvy duddy gaudy husky marry palsy retry spiny wally
tenet ensew baccy clary dumky gaumy hussy mashy pandy ridgy spiry waney
theft inlaw baddy cobby dummy gauzy icily massy pansy risky splay wanly
tight kotow badly cocky dumpy gawky imply matey panty ritzy spray warty
tinct macaw baggy coley dungy gawsy inlay mealy pappy rocky spumy washy
toast miaow balky colly dunny gelly irony meany pardy roily stagy wavey
tract nohow bally comfy duppy gemmy itchy meaty parky rooky stogy weary
trait oxbow bandy coney durry germy ivory meiny parry roomy stony webby
treat papaw bardy conky dusky giddy jaggy mercy party rooty story weedy
trist pilaw barky cooey dusty gilpy jammy merry pasty ropey stray weeny
troat pshaw barmy cooky early ginny jazzy messy patsy rorty stroy weepy
trout renew barny cooly ebony gipsy jelly micky patty roupy study wetly
trust screw batty copsy edify girny jemmy middy pawky rowdy sudsy whiny
tryst serow bawdy corky elegy girly jenny milky peaky ruddy suety whity
tweet shrew beady corny embay glady jerky mingy peaty rugby sulky widdy
twist sinew beaky covey emery glary Jerry minty peggy rumly sully willy
twixt squaw beamy cowry empty glazy jetty mirky penny rummy sunny windy
Uboat straw beany coyly enemy gluey Jewry missy peony rumpy surfy winey
unapt strew beefy crazy enjoy goaty jiffy misty peppy runny surly wingy
uncut strow beery crony ensky godly jimpy mobby perky runty tabby wispy
unfit thraw belay cubby entry golly jokey molly perry rushy tacky withy
ungot threw belly cuddy envoy goody jolly money pesky rusty taffy witty
Uniat throw bendy cully epoxy gooey jolty moody petty rutty tally wonky
unlit vrouw benny curdy essay goofy juicy moony phony sadly tammy woody
unset widow berry curly every goopy jumpy moray picky saggy tangy woozy
upset addax biddy curry faddy gorsy junky mosey piety sally tansy wordy
valet admix biffy curvy faery gouty kelpy mossy piggy salty tardy wormy
vault affix bilgy cushy fairy grapy kerry mothy pigmy sandy tarry worry
vaunt annex billy cutey fancy gravy kicky mousy piney sappy tarty wryly
veldt beaux bitsy cutty fanny grimy kiddy mucky pinky sarky tasty yawny
verst blowy bitty Cymry fatly gripy kinky muddy pinny sassy tatty yippy
visit borax bivvy daddy fatty gully kitty muggy pithy saucy tawny yolky
vivat calix blimy daffy fawny gummy kooky muley plumy saury teary yucky
volet calyx bluey daily feely gunny lacey mummy pocky savoy techy yukky
vomit choux bobby dairy felly guppy laity murky poddy savvy teeny yummy
waist codex boggy daisy fenny gurry lairy mushy podgy sawny telly zesty
wheat culex boney dally ferly gushy lammy musky poesy scaly tenty zincy
whist desex booby dandy ferny gusty lanky mussy pokey scary terry zingy
wight helix booty darky ferry gutsy lardy musty pommy scray testy zinky
worst hyrax boozy dauby fiery gutty larky muzzy poncy seamy thawy zippy
wrapt immix bosky deary fifty gypsy lathy nancy poppy sedgy thewy zloty
wrest index bossy decay filly haily laxly nanny popsy seedy thymy abuzz
wrist infix bothy decoy filmy hairy layby nappy porgy seely tinny blitz
yacht latex bousy decry finny hammy leady narky porky seepy tinty chizz
yeast murex braky deedy firry handy leafy nasty potty sepoy tippy fritz
zibet phlox braxy deify fishy hanky leaky natty pouty serry tipsy frizz
adieu radix briny deity fitly haply ledgy navvy prexy shady tizzy hertz
Bantu redox bubby delay fizzy happy leery neddy pricy shaky toady spitz
bayou relax buddy derby flaky hardy lefty needy privy shaly today swizz
bijou remex buggy diary flamy harpy leggy nelly prosy shily toddy topaz
cornu silex bulgy dicey flaxy harry limey nerdy proxy shiny toffy waltz
coypu Sioux bulky dicky flory hasty limpy netty pudgy showy Tokay whizz
fichu telex bully dilly fluky heady linny nervy puffy shyly tommy
haiku unfix bumpy dimly fluty heavy lippy newly puggy silky tousy
Hindu unsex bunny dingy flyby hefty lobby newsy pulpy silly towny
hokku varix bunty dinky foamy henry lofty niffy puppy silty truly
kudzu abbey burly dippy fogey herby lolly nifty pursy sissy tubby
noyau agley burry dirty foggy hilly looby ninny pushy sixty tufty
perdu agony busby dishy folly hinny loony nippy pussy skiey tummy
pilau alary bushy ditty footy hippy loopy nobby putty skyey tunny
poilu allay busty divvy foray hoary loppy nobly pygmy slaty turfy
prahu alley butty dizzy forby hobby lordy noddy quaky slily tusky
quipu alloy byway dobby forty hokey lorry noisy query slimy tutty
sadhu alway cabby dodgy fubsy holey loury nonny raggy slyly twiny
snafu ambry caddy doggy fuggy holly lousy nooky rainy smoky umpty
```

6 letter words

abacus adorer aldrin anoxic arrant autism banned Beaune betide bloody
abater adrift alegar answer arrest autumn banner beauty betony bloomy
abatis adroit alevin anthem arrive avatar bantam beaver betook blotch
abbacy adsorb alexia anther arroba avaunt banter becall betray blotto
abbess advent alexin antiar arrowy avenge banyan becalm betted blouse
abduce adverb algoid anting arroyo avenue banzai became better blowed
abduct advert alight antler arsine averse baobab becket bettor blower
abject advice aliped antral artery Avesta barbed beckon bewail blowsy
abjure advise alkali antrum artful aviary barbel become beware blowup
ablate adytum alkane anyhow artist aviate barber bedaub bewray blowzy
ablaut aedile alkene anyone ascend avidly barbet bedaze beyond bluing
ablaze Aegean alkyne anyway ascent avocet bardic bedbug bezant bluish
abloom Aeolic allege aorist aseity avouch barege bedded bezoar blunge
ablush aerate allele aortal ashbin avowal barely bedder bharal blurry
aboard aerial allied aortic ashcan avowed barfly bedeck bhisti boatel
aboral aerily allium ashlar aoudad avulse bargee bedell bibbed boater
abound aerobe allout apache ashore awaked barite bedlam bibber bobbed
abrade aether allred apathy ashpan awaken barium bedpan biceps bobbin
abroad afeard allude apexes ashram aweary barker bedsit bicker bobble
abrupt affair allure aphony askant aweigh barley beduin bidden bobcat
abseil affect almond apiary askari awheel barman beeper bidder boblet
absent affeer almost apical aslant awhile barney beetle bieldy bobwig
absorb affine alpaca apices asleep awmous barony beeves biffin bocage
absurd affirm alpine apiece aslope awning barque befall biform bodega
abulia afflux alsike aplomb aspect awoken barred befell bigamy bodger
abuser afford alulae apnoea aspire axilla barrel befool bigger bodice
acacia affray alumna apodal assail ayeaye barren before biggin bodily
acajou Afghan alumni apogee assent azalea barret befoul bigwig boding
acarid afield always apozem assert azonal barrio beggar Bihari bodkin
acarus aflame amadou appeal assess azotic barrow begged bijoux boffin
accede afloat amatol appear assign Baalim barter begird bikini bogged
accent afraid amazon append assist babble barton begirt bilbos boggle
accept afreet ambler appose assize babbly baryon begone bilker bohunk
access afresh ambush Arabic assoil Babism baryta behalf billet boiler
accord afrite amends arable assort Babist basalt behave billon boldly
accost afters amenta arbour assume baboon basely behead billow bolero
accrue agamic amerce arcade assure backer bashaw beheld billyo bolide
accuse agamid amidst Arcady astern backup basher behest binary bollix
acedia agaric amnion arcana asthma baddie basics behind binate bolshy
acetal ageing amoeba arcane astral badger basket behold binder bolter
acetic agency amoral arched astray baffle basnet behoof binful bomber
acetyl agenda amount archer astute bagful Basque behove bionic bonbon
achene ageold ampere archil aswoon bagged basset beigel biopsy bonded
acidic aghast amulet archly asylum bagman bassos belaud biotic bonder
acidly agnail amuser archon ataman bagnio baster beldam biotin bongos
acinar agnate amylum arctic ataxia bagwig bather belfry birdie bonism
acinus agnise anabas ardent ataxic bailee bathos belike bireme bonist
ackack agonal anadem ardour athome bailey bating belong birkie bonito
acquit agonic ananas areola atomic bailie batman beloved birler bonnet
across agouti anarch areole atonal bailor batata bemire bisect bonnie
acting agrafe anatta argala atomic baiter bateau bemoan bishop bonsai
action aguish anatto argali atrial baker batter bemock bisque bonxie
active ahimsa anchor argand atrium bakery bathos bemuse bister bonzer
actual aikido angary argent attach balata batted bender bistre booboo
acuity airbed angina Argive attack balboa batten bemire bistro boodle
acumen airbus angled argosy attain baldly batter bemoan bitchy boohoo
adagio airgun angler arguer attend baleen battle bemock biting booing
Adamic airily angora argufy attest balker battue bemuse bitted booker
addend airing anicut argute attire ballad bauble bender bitten bookie
addict airman animal argyle attorn ballet bawbee benign bitter booksy
addled airsac animus aright attune ballon bawble bennet bizone boomer
adduce airway anklet ariled aubade ballot bawdry benumb bladed booted
adenyl akimbo anlace ariosi auburn balsam bawler benzol blanch bootee
adhere alalia anlage arioso audile Baltic bawley benzyl blanky boozer
adieus alarum anneal arisen Augean bamboo bayard berate blazer bopeep
adieux alated annexe armada augite banana bazaar Berber bereft blazes bopped
adipic albata annual armful august bandit beachy bereft blazon bopper
adjoin albedo annuli armlet auklet bandog beacon berlin bleach borage
adjure albeit anodal armour aumbry banger beadle bertha bleary borane
adjust albert anodic armpit auntie bangle beagle berthe blench borate
admass albino anoint arnica aurist banian beaked beseem blende bordel
admire albite anomic aroint aurora banish beaker beside blenny border
adnate alcaic anomie around aurous banjax beamer bested blight boreal
adnexa alcove anonym arouse Aussie banjos bearer bestir blimey Boreas
Adonic Aldine anorak arpent Austin banker beaten bestow blintz boride
Adonis aldose anoxia arrack author banket beater bethel blonde borrow

borsch	bridle	burbot	cahoot	carnal	cerium	chroma	coated	conger	coulee
borzoi	briefs	burden	caiman	carnet	cermet	chrome	coatee	congou	county
bosche	briery	bureau	caique	carney	certes	chromo	cobalt	conics	couple
bosket	bright	burgee	cajole	carpal	ceruse	chubby	cobber	conker	coupon
bosomy	briner	burger	caking	carpel	cervix	chuffy	cobble	conman	course
boston	briony	burgle	calami	carper	cesser	chukar	cobnut	conned	cousin
botany	Briton	burgoo	calash	carpet	cestus	chukka	cobweb	conner	covert
botchy	broach	burhel	calcar	carpus	cesura	chummy	coccal	conoid	coving
botfly	broche	burial	calces	carrel	cetane	chunky	coccid	consul	cowage
bother	brogue	burkha	calcic	carrot	chacha	chypre	coccus	convex	coward
bothie	broken	burlap	calico	cartel	chacma	cicada	coccyx	convey	cowboy
botone	broker	burler	caliph	carter	chaeta	cicala	cochin	convoy	cowish
bottle	brolly	Burman	calker	carton	chafer	cicely	cocked	cooker	cowled
bottom	bromic	burner	calkin	carvel	chaffy	cigala	cocker	cookie	cowman
boucle	bronco	burnet	caller	carven	chaise	cilice	cockle	cooler	cowpat
bought	bronze	burnup	callet	carver	chalet	cilium	cocoon	coolie	cowpea
bougie	bronzy	burrel	callow	casbah	chalky	cinder	coddle	coolly	cowpox
boulle	brooch	burrow	callup	casein	chance	cineol	codger	coolth	cowrie
bounce	broody	bursae	callus	casern	chancy	cinema	codify	coonty	coyote
bouncy	browny	bursal	calmly	cashew	change	cinque	codlin	cooper	crabby
bounds	browse	bursar	calory	cashoo	chanty	cipher	coelom	coopts	cradle
bounty	bruise	bursas	calpac	casing	chapel	circle	coerce	cootie	crafty
bourne	brumal	burton	calque	casino	chappy	circus	coeval	copeck	craggy
bourse	brumby	busbar	calves	casket	charas	cirque	coffee	copier	crambo
bovine	brunch	busboy	calxes	Caslon	charge	cirrus	coffer	coping	cranch
bovver	brunet	bushed	camass	casque	charka	cistus	coffin	copita	crania
bowels	brushy	bushel	camber	cassia	Charon	cither	coffle	copout	cranky
bowery	brutal	busily	camera	cassis	chaser	citole	cogent	copped	cranny
bowfin	brutus	busing	camion	caster	chaste	citric	cogged	copper	crappy
bowing	bryony	busker	camise	castle	chaunt	citron	cogito	Coptic	crases
bowleg	bubble	buskin	camlet	castor	cheeky	citrus	cognac	copula	crasis
bowler	bubbly	busman	camper	casual	cheers	civics	coheir	corban	cratch
bowman	buccal	bussed	campus	catalo	cheery	claggy	cohere	corbel	crater
bowsaw	bucker	busted	canape	catchy	cheese	clammy	cohort	corbie	cravat
bowtie	bucket	buster	canard	catena	cheesy	claque	coigne	corded	craven
bowwow	buckle	bustee	canary	catgut	chelae	claret	coiner	cordon	craver
bowyer	buckra	bustle	cancan	Cathar	chemic	clause	coinop	corder	crawly
boxbed	budded	bustup	cancel	cation	cherry	claver	coital	corium	crayon
boxcar	Buddha	butane	cancer	catkin	cherty	clavis	coitus	corked	crazed
boxful	buddle	butene	candid	catnap	cherub	clayey	coldly	cornea	creaky
boxing	budget	butler	candle	catnep	chesil	cleave	coleus	corned	creamy
boyish	budgie	butter	canful	catnip	chesty	clench	collar	corner	crease
bracer	buffer	button	cangue	catsup	chevet	clergy	collet	cornet	create
braces	buffet	buzzer	canine	cattle	chiasm	cleric	collie	cornua	creche
Brahma	bugged	byblow	canker	caucus	chiaus	clerid	collop	corody	credal
Brahmi	bugler	byebye	canned	caudal	chichi	clevis	colony	corona	credit
brains	buglet	byelaw	cannel	caudex	chicle	client	colour	corpse	creeps
brainy	bulbar	byform	canner	caudle	chield	cliffy	colter	corpus	creepy
braird	bulbed	bygone	cannie	caught	chigoe	climax	column	corral	creese
braise	bulbil	bylane	cannon	caulis	chilli	clinch	colure	corrie	crenel
branch	bulbul	byline	cannot	causal	chilly	clinic	colugo	corsac	creole
brandy	Bulgar	byname	canopy	causer	chimer	clipon	comate	corsak	Cretan
branle	bulger	bypass	canter	causey	chintz	clique	combat	corset	cretic
brassy	bulimy	bypast	canthi	caveat	chippy	cliquy	combed	cortex	cretin
brawly	bulker	bypath	cantle	cavern	chirpy	cloaca	comber	corvee	crewel
brawny	bullae	byplay	canton	caviar	chisel	cloche	comedo	corves	crikey
brayer	buller	byroad	cantor	cavies	chital	cloddy	comedy	Corvus	crimpy
brazen	bullet	byssus	cantus	caving	chitin	cloggy	comely	corymb	cringe
brazil	bumalo	byword	Canuck	cavity	chiton	clonal	comeon	coryza	crinum
breach	bumble	bywork	canvas	cayman	chitty	clonic	comfit	cosher	cripes
breast	bumkin	cabala	canyon	cayuse	chives	clonks	coming	cosier	crises
breath	bummed	cabana	capful	cedarn	chivvy	clonus	comity	cosily	crispy
breech	bummer	cabman	capias	celiac	choice	cloots	commie	cosine	crista
breeks	bummle	cachet	caplin	cellar	chokey	closed	commis	cosmic	critic
breese	bumper	cachou	capote	celled	choker	closet	commit	cosmos	croaky
breeze	bunchy	cackle	capric	Celtic	choler	clothe	commix	cosset	crocus
breezy	bunder	cacoon	capsid	cement	choose	cloudy	common	cossie	crofts
bregma	bundle	cactus	captor	censer	choosy	clough	comose	costae	croppy
brehon	bungle	caddie	carafe	censor	chopin	cloven	comous	costal	crosse
Breton	bunion	caddis	carbon	census	choppy	clover	compel	costar	crotal
brevet	bunker	cadent	carboy	cental	choral	cloyed	comply	coster	crotch
brewer	bunkum	cadger	carder	centre	chorea	clumps	comsat	costly	croton
brewis	bunnia	caecal	career	centum	choric	clumpy	concha	cottar	crouch
briard	bunsen	caecum	caress	cerate	chorus	clumsy	conchy	cottas	croupy
briary	bunted	cafard	carfax	cercus	chosen	clunch	concur	cotted	crouse
briber	bunter	Caffre	carful	cereal	chough	clutch	condor	cotter	cruces
bricky	bunyip	caftan	caries	cereus	chouse	clypei	confab	cotton	cruddy
bridal	burble	cagily	carina	ceriph	chrism	coaita	confer	coucal	cruise
bridge	burbly	cahier	carman	cerise	Christ	coarse	congee	cougar	cruive

```
crumby cygnet debris deride diploe dorado duffel elated enroll eunuch
crummy cymbal debtor derive diplon Dorian duffer elater enroot eureka
crunch cymose debunk dermal dipnet dormer duffle eldest ensate eutaxy
crural Cymric decade dermic dipody dormie dugong eleven ensign evader
cruset cypher decamp dermis dipole dorsal dugout elevon ensile evener
crusty cyprid decani derris dipped dorsum duiker elfish ensoul evenly
crutch cystic decant desalt dipper dorter dukery elicit ensure evilly
cruxes cystid deceit descry dipsas dosage dulcet elixir entail evince
crying dabbed decent desert dirdum dossal dumbly elodea entera evolue
crypto dabber decide design direct dossel dumdum eloign entice evolve
cubage dabble decker desire direly dosser dumose eloper entire evzone
cubism dacoit deckle desist dirham dotage dumper eluant entity examen
cubist dactyl decoct desman dirhem dotard dunite eluate entoil exarch
cuboid daedal decode desmid dirndl dotted Dunker eluent entomb exceed
cuckoo daemon decoke desorb disarm dottle dunlin elvish entrap except
cuddie daftly decree despot disbar douane dunned elytra entree excess
cuddle dagger deduce detach disbud double dupery embalm envier excide
cuddly daggle deduct detail discal doubly duplet embank enwind excise
cudgel dagoes deejay detain discus douche duplex embark enwomb excite
cueing dahlia deepen detect diseur dought durbar embars enwrap excuse
cueist daimen deeply detent dismal doughy duress emblem enzyme exedra
cuesta daimio deface detest dismay dourly durgan emblic Eocene exempt
cuffed daimyo defame detour disown douser Durham emboli eolian exequy
cuisse daimon defeat deuced dispel dowlas durian emboly eolith exeunt
culler dainty defend devest distal downer during emboss eonian exhale
cullet daises defier device distil dowser durned embrue eonism exhort
cullis damage defile devise disuse doyley durrie embryo Eozoic exhume
cultch damask deform devoid dither dozily duster emerge Eozoon exilic
cultic dammar defray devoir dittos drably dustup emeses eparch exodus
cultus dammed defuse devote divers drachm duyker emesis ephebe exogen
culver damned degras devour divert drafty dyadic emetic ephebi exomis
cumber dampen degree devout divest dragee dybbuk emetin epical exotic
cummer damper degust dewily divide draggy dyeing emeute epimer expand
cummin damply dehorn dewlap divine dragon dynamo emodin epizoa expect
cumuli damsel deicer dexter diving draper dynast empale epodic expend
cunner damson deific dharma djibba drawee eaglet empery eponym expert
cupful dancer deject dhooti djinni drawer earful empire epopee expire
cupola dander delate dhurra doable dreamt earing employ equals expiry
cupped dandle delete diacid dobbin dreamy earner empusa equate export
cupric dangle delict diadem docent dreary earthy emulge equine expose
cuptie danger delude diaper docile dredge earwax enable equips exsect
cupule Daniel deluge diatom docker dreggy earwig enamel equity exsert
curacy Danish deluxe dibbed docket dreich easily enatic eraser extant
curare daphne delver dibber doctor drench easter encage erbium extasy
curari dapper demand dibble dodder dressy eatery encamp erenow extend
curate darbar demark dicast doddle drifty eating encase ergate extent
curdle daring demean dicker dodgem drippy ecarte encash eringo extern
curfew darken dement dickey dodger drivel echoer encode ermine extort
curiae darkey demise dictum dodoes driven echoic encore erotic eyalet
curial darkie demist diddle dogate driver eclair encyst errand eyecup
curium darkle demode didoes dogear droger eczema endart errant eyeful
curler darkly demote diesel dogend drogue Eddaic endear errata eyeing
curlew darned demure dieses dogfox droich Edenic endive ersatz eyelet
currie darnel denary diesis dogged drolly edgily endrin eryngo eyelid
cursed darner dengue dieter doggie drongo edible endure escape Eyetie
cursor darter denial differ dogleg droopy edited enface escarp Fabian
cursus dartle denier digamy dogood dropsy editor enfold eschar fabled
curtal dasher denims digest doited drosky eerily engage eschew fabler
curtly dassie denote digger dolium drossy efface engild escort fabric
curtsy datary dental diglot dollar drouth effect engine escrow facade
curule dative dentel dikdik dollop drover effete engird escudo facete
curvet datura dentex diktat dolman drowse effigy engirt espial facial
cuscus dauber dentil dilate dolmen drowsy efflux englut esprit facies
cushat dawdle dentin dilute dolour drudge effort engram essive facile
cusped daybed denude dimity domain drupel effuse engulf essoin facing
cuspid dayfly deodan dimmed domett drybob Egeria enhalo estate factor
cussed dazzle deodar dimmer domino dryfly egesta enisle esteem factum
custom deacon depart dimple donate dryish eggcup enjoin estray facula
cutely deaden depend dimply donjon dryrot eggler enlace etcher fadein
cutler deadly deperm dimwit donkey dryrun eggnog enlist eterne faerie
cutlet deafen depict dingey donned dually egoism enmesh ethane fagend
cutoff dealer deploy dinghy donsie dubbed egoist enmity ethene fagged
cutout dearie depone dingle doocot dubbin egress ennead ethics faggot
cutter dearly deport dingus doodad ducker eidola ennuye ethnic failed
cuttle dearth depose dining doodah dudeen eighth enough ethyne faille
cyanic deasil depute dinkum doodle dudish eighty enrage etrier fainly
cyanin debark deputy dinned doolie duello either enrapt etymon fairly
cycler debase derail dinner dopant duende ejecta enrich euchre fakery
cyclic debate derate diplex Dopper duenna elapse enrobe eulogy falcon
```

```
fallal ferule flange forbid fugato gangly giaour golden groper halloa
fallen fervid flappy forbye fugged gangue gibber golfer grotto halloo
fallow fescue flashy forced fuhrer gannet gibbet gollop grotty hallow
falsie festal flatly forcer fulcra ganoid gibbon golosh grouch hallux
falter fester flatus fordid fulfil gantry giddap goober ground haloes
family fetial flaunt forego fulgid gaoler gifted goodie grouse halter
famine fetich flavin forest fulham gapped gigged goodly grovel halvah
famish fetish flaxen forger fullam garage giggle googly grower halves
famous fetter fleche forget fuller garbed giggly googol growly hamate
famuli fettle fledge forgot fulmar garble giglet gooier growth Hamite
fandom feudal fleece forint fumble garcon giglot gooney groyne hamlet
fanged fezzed fleech forked fundus garden gigman gooses grubby hammal
fanion fezzes fleecy formal fungal garget gigolo gopher grudge hammam
fanjet fiacre flench format fungus gargle gilder goramy grugru hammed
fanned fiance flense formed funkia garial gilled gorget grumly hammer
fanner fiasco fleshy former funned garish gillie gorgio grumps hamper
fantan fibbed fletch formic funnel garlic gimbal gorgon grumpy handed
Fantee fibber fleury fornix furfur garner gimlet gorily grutch handle
fantod fibred flexor forrad furore garnet gimmal goslow guaiac hangar
fantom fibril flight forrit furred garran gimmer gospel guanin hanged
faquir fibrin flimsy forsay furrow garret gingal gossan guddle hanger
fardel fibula flinch fossae fusain garron ginger gossip Guelph hangup
farfel fickle flinty fossil fusile garrot gingko Gothic guenon hanker
farina fiddle flirty fossor fusion garter ginkgo gotten guffaw hankie
farmer fiddly flitch foster fusser garuda ginned gourde guggle hansel
faroff fidget floaty fother fustic garvie ginner govern guider hansom
farout fierce flocci fought futile garvey ginger gowany guidon happed
farrow fiesta floozy foully future Gascon girdle goyish guilty happen
fasces figged floppy foulup fylfot gasbag girder gozzan guinea haptic
fascia figure florae fourth gabbed gasify girlie grabby guiser harass
fasten filfot floral foveae gabber gasket glacis graben guitar harden
faster filial floras foveal gabble gasman glairy grader gulden hardly
fathen filing floret fowler gabbro gasper glaive gradin Gullah hardup
father filler florid fracas gabion gassed glance gradus gullet harken
fathom fillet florin fraena gabled gasser glassy grainy gulley harlot
fatted fillip flossy fraise gablet gateau glazer gramme gummed harper
fatten filmic floury framer gadded gather gleamy Grammy gundog harrow
fatter filose flower frappe gadder gauche gleety gramps gunman hartal
faucal filter fluent fratch gadfly gaucho glibly grange gunned haslet
fauces filthy fluffy fridge gadget gauger glider granny gunnel hassle
faucet fimble flukey Frauen Gadhel gavage glitch Granth gunner hasten
faulty finale flunky frazil gadoid gavial global grappa gunsel hatbox
faunae finals flurry freaky Gaelic gazebo gloomy grassy gunshy hatful
faunal finder fluted freely gaffer gazump gloria grater gunter hatpeg
faunas finely fluter freest gagged geckos glossy gratin gunyah hatpin
favour finery flying freeze gagger geegee glover gratis gurgle hatred
fawner finger flyman french gaggle geezer glower graved gurjun hatted
fealty finial flysch frenum gagman geisha glumly gravel Gurkha hatter
featly fining flyway frenzy gaiety gelled glumpy graven gurnet hauler
feckly finish fobbed fresco gainer Gemara glutei graver gurrah haunch
fecula finite focsle friary gainly Gemini gluten Graves gusher Havana
fecund finnan fodder Friday gainst gemmae glycin gravid gusset havers
fedora finned foeman fridge gaited gemmed glycol grazer guttae hawhaw
feeble finner foetal friend gaiter gender gnarly grease gutted hawked
feebly Finnic foetid frieze galago genera gnawer greasy gutter hawker
feeder fiorin foetus fright galaxy geneva gneiss greave guvnor hawser
feeing fipple fogbow frigid galena genial gnomic greedy guzzle haybox
feeler firing fogdog frijol galiot genius gnomon greens gypped haymow
feirie firkin fogged frilly galley genned gnosis greeny gypsum hazard
feisty firlot foible fringe Gallic genome goalie greige gyrate hazily
feline firman foiled fringy Gallio gentes goanna greyly habile headed
fellah firmly foison frisky gallon gentle goatee grieve hackle header
feller fiscal folder frivol gallop gently gobang grigri hackly headon
felloe fisher foliar frizzy galoot gentoo gobbet grille haddie healer
fellow fistic folium froggy galore gentry gobble grilse hadron health
felony fitful folksy frolic galosh geodic goblet grimly haemal hearer
female fitted follow frosty gambir George goblin gringo haemin hearse
femora fitter foment frothy gambit gerbil gocart griper haffet hearth
fencer fixate fondle frowst gamble gerent goddam grippe haffit hearty
fender fixity fondly frowsy gambol german godown grippy hagbut heated
Fenian fizgig fondue frowzy gamely germen godson grisly haggis heater
fenman fizzle fontal frozen gamete gerund godwit grison haggle heathy
fennec flabby fooler frugal gamily getout goffer gritty hailer heaven
fennel flacon footed fruity gamine getter goglet grivet hairdo heaver
ferial flaggy footer frumpy gaming gewgaw goggly groats haired Hebrew
ferine flagon footle frusta gammer geyser goglet grocer haleru heckle
ferret flambe foozle frutex gammon gharry Goidel groggy halide hectic
ferric flamen forage fucoid gander ghetto goitre groove halite hector
ferula flanch forbad fuddle ganger ghosty gokart groovy hallal heddle
```

```
hedera holden hungry inclip invent jibber keeper labial lavabo lifter
hedger holder hunker income invert jigged kelpie labile lavage liftup
heehaw holdup hunter incubi invest jigger kelson labium laveer ligate
heeled holily hurdle incult invite jiggle kelter labour lavish ligger
heeler holism hurler incuse invoke jiggly Keltic labret lavolt lights
hegira holler hurley indaba inward jigsaw kelvin labrum lawful lignin
heifer holloa hurrah indeed inwick jilter kenned laceup lawman ligula
height hollow hurray indene inwove jingle kennel laches lawyer ligule
hejira holpen hurter indent inwrap jingly kermes lacing laxity ligure
helium homage hurtle Indian inyala jinnee kermis lackey layday likely
heller hombre husker indict iodate jitney kerned lactic layman liking
helmet homely hussar indign iodide jitter kernel lacuna layoff lilied
helper homily hustle indigo iodine jobber ketone laddie layout limbec
hemmed homing hutted indite iodise joblot kettle ladder lazily limbed
hempen hominy huzoor indium iodism jockey kewpie ladify lazuli limber
henrun honest hyaena indole iolite jocose keyway lading leaden limbic
henrys honied hybrid indoor Ionian jocund kiaugh ladino leader limbus
hepcat honour hybris induce ionise jogged kibble ladyfy leadin liming
heptad hooded hydric induct ionium jogger kibitz lagged leadup limner
herald hoodie hymnal indult ireful joggle kiblah lagger leafed limper
herbal hoodoo hymnic induna irenic johnny kibosh lagoon league limpet
herder hoofed hyphae infamy irides joiner kicker laguna lealty limpid
herdic hoofer hyphal infant iritis jolter kidded laical leanly limply
hereat hookah hyphen infare ironer jolter kidder lallan leanto limuli
hereby hooked hyssop infect ironic josher kiddie lambda leaper linage
herein hooker iambic infelt irrupt josser kidnap lamber learnt linden
hereof hookey iambus infest isabel jostle kidney lamely leaved lineal
hereon hookup ibexes infirm isatin jotted kidney lament leaven linear
heresy hooper ibices inflow ischia jotter kiekie lamina leaver lineup
hereto hoopla ibidem influx island jounce killer lamish leaves linger
heriot hoopoe iceaxe infold isobar jouncy kilted Lammas lecher lingua
hermit hooray icebag inform isohel jovial kilter lammed lector linhay
hernia hootch icebox infula isomer Jovian kimono lanate ledged lining
heroic hooter icecap ingest isopod joyful kincob lancer ledger linkup
heroin hooves iceman ingulf italic joyous kindle lancet leeway linnet
herpes hopped icicle inhale itself Judaic kindly landau legacy linney
Herren hopper iconic inhere izzard judder kinema landed legate linsey
hetero horary ideaed inhume jabbed Judean kingly lander legato lintel
hetman horned ideate inject jabber judger kipper langue legbye lintie
hexact horner idiocy injure jabiru judoka kirsch langur legend lionel
hexane hornet idolum injury jacana jugate kirtle lankly legged lipase
hexose horrid ignite inkpot jackal jugful kismet lanner legion lipide
heyday horror ignore inlaid jacket jugged kitbag lanugo legist lipoid
hiatus horsey iguana inland jaeger juggle kitcat lapdog legman lipoma
hiccup hosier illume inlaws jagged jujube kitsch lapful legume lipped
hickey hostel illuse inlier jagger Julian kitten lapped lemony lippen
hidden hotbed imbibe inmate jaguar jumbal kittle lappet lender lippie
hiding hotdog imbrex inmost jailer jumble kittul lappie length liquid
hieing hotpot imbrue innate jailor jumbly knaggy lapsed lenity liquor
higgle hotter immane inroad jalopy jumper knight lapsus lensed lisper
higher houdan immesh inrush jammed jungle knives larder Lenten lissom
highly hourly immune inseam jammer jungly knobby lardon lentil listed
hijack housel immure insect jangle junior knotty lariat Leonid listel
hinder housey impact insert jarful junker knower larker lepton listen
Hindoo howdah impair inside jargon junket kobold larrup lesion lister
hinged howler impala insist jarrah junkie koedoe larvae lessee litany
hipped hoyden impale insole jarred jurist kookie larval lessen litchi
hippie hubbub impark inspan jarvey justly koolah larynx lesson lithia
hirple hubcap impart instal jasper Jutish kopeck lascar lessor lithic
hispid hubris impawn instar jaunce jutted koppie lasher lethal litmus
hisser huckle impede instep jaunty kabala Korean lashup letoff litter
hither huddle impend insult jeerer kabuki kosher lasque letter little
hitman hugely impone insure jejune Kabyle kowhai lassie Lettic livein
hoarse hugged import intact jennet Kaffir kowtow lassos levant lively
hoaxer humane impose intake jerbil kaftan kraken laster Levite livery
hobbit humble impost intend jerboa kainit krantz lastly levity living
hobble humbly impugn intent jerkin kaiser kronen lateen lewdly lizard
hobnob humbug impure intern jerker kakapo kroner lately liable loaded
hocker humect impute intine jersey kalong kronur latent liaise loader
hockey humeri inarch intoed jester kanaka kultur latest libber loafer
hodden humify inborn intern Jesuit kaolin kronen lather libido loaner
hodman hummed inbred intine jetlag kaputt kroner latish libido loathe
hoeing hummel incase intoed jetsam karate kronur Libyan lichee loaves
hogged hummer incept intone jetted karmic kultur latria lichen lobate
hogget hummum incest intray Jewess kaross kumiss latron lictor lobbed
hoggin humour inches intuit Jewish karroo kummel latten lidded lobose
hogtie humped incise inulin jezail kasbah kurgan latter lieder lobule
hoicks hunger incite invade jibbah kation laager launce lierne locale
hoised hunger incite invade jibbed keenly laager launch lierne locate
```

```
lochan luting mantel mazily midgut moggie muddle natant noggin ocelli
locker luxate mantes meadow midoff mohair muesli nation nomism ocelot
locket luxury mantic meagre midrib Mohawk muffin native nonage ochone
lockup lyceum mantid mealie midway Mohock muffle natron nonary oclock
loculi lychee mantis meanie miffed mohole muflon natter noncom octane
locust Lydian mantle meanly mighty moider mugged nature nonego octant
lodger lyrate mantua measly mignon moiety mugger naught nonfat octave
lofter lyrics mantus meatus mihrab moiler mukluk nausea nonius octavo
loggat lyrism manual meddle mikado molest mulish nautch nonuse octroi
logged lyrist manuka mediae milady moline mullah Nazify noodle ocular
logger lysine manure medial milage mollie muller Nazism Nordic oddity
loggia macaco Maoism median mildew Moloch mullet neaped normal oddjob
logion machan Maoist medick mildly molten mulley nearby Norman oddson
logjam mackle mapped medico milieu moment multum nearer noshup odious
loiter macron mapper medium milker Monday mumble nearly nosily oecist
loller macula maquis medius milled moneys mummer neaten nosing oedema
lollop macule maraca medlar miller monger mumper neatly nostoc oeuvre
loment Madame maraud medley millet Mongol mundic nebula notary offend
lonely madcap marble medusa milord monial Munich nebuly notate offent
longan madden marbly meekly milter monied muntin nectar notice office
loofah madder marcel meetly mimosa monies murder needle notify offing
looker madman margay megilp mincer monism murine neednt notion offish
lookin madras margin megohm minded monist murmur negate nougat offkey
looper maduro marina megrim minder monkey murphy nekton nought offset
loosen maenad marine meinie mingle monody murrey nelson nounal ogamic
looter maggot marish mellow minify moocow muscat Nepali novena ogival
lopped Magian Marist melody minima mooing muscle nephew novice ogress
lopper magilp marked melton mining moolah museum nereid Nowell ogrish
loquat magnet marker member minion mopish musing nerine nowise ohmage
lorcha magnum market memoir minish mopoke muskeg nerite noyade oidium
lordly magpie markup memory minium mopped musket neroli nozzle oilcan
lorica maguey marlin menace minnow mopper muskox nestle nuance oilman
loriot Magyar marmot menage Minoan moppet Muslim Nestor nubble oilnut
lotion mahout maroon mender minter morale muslin netful nubbly oldish
lotted maidan marque menhir minuet morals mussel nether nubile oleate
louche maiden marram menial minute morass muster netted nuchal olefin
louden maigre marred meninx miosis morbid mutant nettle nuclei oliver
loudly mailed marron mensal miotic morbus mutate neural nudely omasum
lounge mainly marrow menses mirage moreen mutely neuron nudism omelet
loupen Majlis marten mental mirror morgen mutine neuter nudist omenta
loupit makedo marshy mentor miscue morgue mutiny newish nudity onager
louver makeup marten mentum misdid morion mutism newton nugget oncost
louvre making martin mercer misere morish mutter niacin nullah oneoff
lovage malady martyr merely misery Mormon mutton nibbed number oneway
lovein Malaga marvel merest misfit mornay mutual nibble numbly onfall
lovely malate mascle merger mishap morose mutule nicely numina online
loving maleic mascon merils mishit morpho mutuum nicety nuncio onrush
lowboy malice mascot merino mishmi morris muumuu nicish nuncle onside
lowery malign masher merism Mishna morrow muzhik nickel nurser onward
lowing malism mashie merlin mislay morsel muzzle nicker nutant oocyte
lowish malkin masker merlon misled mortal myelin nidget nutate oodles
lowkey mallee maslin merman missal mortar mygale nidify nutmeg oogamy
lubber mallei Masora merrie missel morula myopia nielli nutria oogeny
lubric mallet masque mescal missis mosaic myopic niello nutter oolite
lucent mallow massif mesial missus moshav myosin nigger nuzzle oology
lucern maltha masted messan mister Moslem myosis niggle nympho oolong
luetic mammae master Messrs mistle mosque myotic nighty oafish oomiak
lugged mammal mastic mestee misuse mostly myriad nignog oarage opaque
lugger mammee matico metage mitral motett myrica nilgai obeche opener
luggie mammer matins metals mitten mother myrtle nimble obelus openly
lumbar mammon matlow meteor mizzen motile myself nimbly obeyer ophite
lumber manage matrix method mizzle motion mystic nimbus obital opiate
lumina manana matron methyl mizzly motive mythic nimrod object oppose
lummox manche matted metier moaner motley mythos ninety objure oppugn
lumpen Manchu matter metope moated motmot myxoma nipped oblast optant
lumper manday mature metred mobbed motory nabbed nipper oblate optics
lunacy manege matzoh metric mobcap mottle naevus nipple oblige optima
lunate manful maugre mettle mobile moujik nagana nitric oblong option
lunger mangel maundy mezuza mocker mouldy nagged nitwit oboist orache
lunula manger maxima miasma mockup moulin nagger nobble obsess oracle
lunule mangle maxixe mickey modena mouser nailer nobbut obtain orally
lupine mangos maybug mickle modern mousse namely nobody obtect orange
lurdan maniac mayday micron modest mouthy nanism nocent obtest orator
lurker manila mayest midage modify moving napalm nodded obtund orcein
lushly manioc mayfly midair modish mucker napkin noddle obtuse orchid
lustra manito mayhap midday modius muckle napped nodose obvert orchil
lustre manned mayhem midden module mucoid nardoo nodule occamy orchis
luteal manner maying middle moduli mucosa narrow noesis occult ordain
lutein manque mazard midget modulo mucous nastic noetic occupy ordeal
```

```
ordure padded pascal people pilose plucky potato puddly Quaker rancid
orexis paddle Pashto peplum pilous plumed potboy pueblo qualmy randan
orfray paella passer pepped pilule plummy poteen puffed quanta randem
orgasm paeony passim pepper pimple plumpy potent puffer quarry random
orgeat pagoda pastel pepsin pimply plunge potful puffin quarte ranger
orient paidup pastil peptic pincer plural pother pugdog quarto ranker
origan pajama pastor perdue pineal plushy potion puisne quartz rankle
origin pakeha pastry period pinery pluton potman puller quasar rankly
oriole palace patchy perish pineta pneuma potpie pullet quaver ransom
orison palais patent permit pinger pocked potted pulley queasy ranter
ormolu palate Pathan perron pinion pocket potter pullin queazy ranula
ornate paleae pathic person pinkie podded pottle pullon quench raphia
ornery palely pathos pertly pinnae podite pouchy pullup queuer raphis
orphan paling patina peruke pinned podium pouffe pulper quiche rapids
orphic palish patois peruse pinner podsol pounce pulpit quince rapier
orpine pallet patrol pesade pinole podzol pourer pulque quinoa rapine
orrery pallia patron peseta pintle poetic pouter pulsar quinol rapist
oscine pallid patted pesewa piolet poetry powder pulser quinsy rapped
oscula pallor patten pester pionic pogrom powwow pulvil quinta rappee
osmium palmar patter pestle piping pointe praise pumice quirky rappel
osmose palmer paunch petara pipkin points prance pummel quitch rapper
osprey palolo pauper petard pipped poison prater pumper quiver raptly
ossein palpal pavage petite pippin Polack pratie punchy quoits raptor
ossify palpus pavane petrel piquet polder praxis puncta quorum rarefy
osteal palter paving petrol piracy police prayer pundit quotes rarely
ostial paltry pavior petted pirate policy preach punily quotha raring
ostium pampas pavise petter piraya polish precis punish rabato rarity
ostler pamper pawnee pewter Pisces polite prefab punkah rabbet rascal
otiose panada pawner peyote pissed polity prefer punned rabbin rasher
otitis panama pawpaw peyotl pistil pollan prefix punner rabbit rashly
ottava panary payday phalli pistol polled prelim punnet rabble rasper
ouster pander paynim pharos piston pollen premed puntee rabies raster
outact pandit payoff phasic pitchy poller premix punter raceme rasure
outage panful payola phasis pithos pollex prepay pupate rachis ratbag
outbid panned peachy phatic pitier polony preses pupped racial ratels
outbye pantry peahen phenol pitman polypi preset puppet racily rather
outcry panzer peaked phenyl pitpan pomace presto purdah racism ratify
outdid papacy peanut phlegm pitsaw pomade pretax purely racist ratine
outfit papain pearly phloem pitted pomelo pretty purfle racker rating
outfox papaya peavey phobia pitter pommel prewar purger racket ratite
outgun papery pebble phobic pizzle pommie pricey purify racoon ratlin
outing papism pebbly phoebe placed pompom priest purine raddle ratoon
outlaw papist pecker phoney placer poncho primal purism radial rattan
outlay pappus pecten phonic placet ponder primer purist radian rattat
outlet papula pectic phonon placid pongee primly purity radish ratted
output papule pectin phooey plagal pontie primus purler radium ratter
outran papyri pedalo photic plague pontil prince purlin radome rattle
outrun parade pedant photon plaguy ponton priory purple radula ravage
outsat paramo pedate phrase plaice poodle prison purply raffia ravine
outset parang peddle phylum plains pooped prissy purser raffle raving
outsit paraph pedlar physic plaint poorly privet pursue rafter ravish
outtop parcel peeler piaffe planar popery prizer purvey ragbag razzia
outvie pardah peeper piazza planer popgun prober pusher ragged razzle
outwit pardie peepul picker planet popish probit pushup raggee reader
ovally pardon peewit picket plashy poplar proleg putlog raggle really
overdo parent pegged pickle plasma poplin prolix putoff raglan realty
overly parget pegleg pickup platan popped prompt putrid ragman reamer
ovisac pariah pegtop picnic platen popper pronto putsch ragout reaper
ovular parian pelage picric plater poppet propel puttee ragtag rearer
owlish paring pelham piddle player popple proper putter ragtop reason
oxalic parish pellet piecer pleach popply propyl puttie raguly reaver
oxalis parity pelmet piedog pleads popsie proser puzzle raider rebate
oxbird parkas pelota pieman please porgie prosit pycnic railer rebato
oxford parkin peltae pierce plebby porism protea pyemia raiser rebeck
oxgall parlay pelter piffle pledge porker proton pyknic raisin rebore
oxgang parley peltry pigeon plenty porose proven pylori raited reborn
oxgate parlor pelves pigged plenum porous prover pyrene Rajput rebuff
oxherd parody pelvic piggin pleura portal pruina pyrite rakish rebuke
oxhide parole pelvis pigsty plexor portly pruner pyrola ramate recall
oxland parral pencil piglet plexus posada prying pyrope ramble recant
oxtail parrel penman pignut pliant poseur pseudo python ramify recast
oxygen parrot pennae pigpen plicae posset psyche pyuria ramjet recede
oxymel parsec penned pilaff pliers possum psycho quaere rammed recent
oyster Parsee pennon pileum plight postal pterin quagga rammer recess
ozonic parson pentad pileup plisse poster ptisan quaggy ramose recipe
pacify partan pentup pileus ploidy postil ptosis quahog ramous recite
packer partly pentyl pilfer plotty potage public quaich ramrod reckon
packet parure penult pillar plough potale pucker quaigh ramson recoil
padauk parvis penury pillow plover potash puddle quaint rancho recoin
```

record	remote	revoke	rococo	runner	sangar	scorch	select	Shakta	sialic
recoup	remove	revolt	rodent	runoff	sanies	scorer	Seljuk	Shakti	sicken
rector	remuda	revved	rodman	runrig	sanify	scoria	seller	shalom	sicker
rectum	rename	reward	roller	runway	sanity	scotch	selves	shaman	sickle
rectus	render	rewind	rollon	rupiah	sanjak	scoter	semble	shammy	sickly
redact	renege	rewire	Romaic	rusher	sannup	scotia	Semite	shamus	siding
redbud	rennet	rewoke	Romany	rushes	santal	Scotic	semmit	shandy	sienna
redcap	renown	reword	Romish	russet	santir	scouse	semple	shanny	sierra
redden	rental	rework	romper	russia	sapele	scouth	sempre	shanty	siesta
redder	renter	rhaphe	rondel	rustic	sapful	scrape	senary	shaped	sifter
reddle	reopen	rhebok	ronyon	rustle	sapota	scrawl	senate	shapen	sigher
redeem	repaid	rhesus	roofer	rutile	sappan	screak	sendal	shaper	siglum
redeye	repair	rhetor	rookie	rutted	sapped	scream	sender	sharer	signal
redhot	repand	rheumy	roomer	sabbat	sapper	screed	sendup	sharif	signer
rediae	repass	rhinal	rooted	Sabian	sarape	screen	senega	sharps	signet
redone	repast	rhombi	rooter	Sabine	sardel	screwy	senhor	shaven	signor
redraw	repeal	rhumba	ropery	sables	sarong	scribe	senile	shaver	silage
redtop	repeat	rhymer	roping	sachem	sarsen	scrimp	senior	shavie	sileni
reduce	repent	rhythm	roquet	sachet	sashay	script	sennet	shears	silent
reebok	repine	ribald	rorted	sacque	sasine	scroll	sennit	sheass	silica
reecho	replay	riband	rosace	sacral	sateen	scroop	senora	sheath	silken
reedit	replum	ribbed	rosary	sacred	satiny	scruff	senses	sheave	siller
reefer	report	ribbon	rosery	sacrum	satire	scrump	sensor	sheeny	silvan
reeler	repose	ribose	rosily	sadden	satori	scryer	sensum	sheets	silver
reface	repugn	richen	rosiny	sadder	satrap	sculpt	sentry	sheikh	simian
refect	repute	riches	roster	saddhu	Saturn	scummy	sephen	sheila	simile
refill	reread	richly	rostra	saddle	satyra	scurfy	sepsis	shekel	simmer
refine	resale	ricker	rosula	sadism	saucer	scurry	septal	shelly	simnel
reflex	rescue	rickey	rotary	sadist	sauger	scurvy	septet	Shelta	simony
reflow	reseat	ricrac	rotate	saeter	saurel	scutal	septic	shelty	simoom
reflux	reseau	rictal	rotche	safari	savage	scutch	septum	shelve	simoon
reform	resect	rictus	rotgut	safely	savant	scutum	sequel	sheoak	simper
refuel	reseda	ridded	rotted	safety	savate	scyphi	sequin	sherif	simple
refuge	resell	ridden	rotten	sagely	savine	scythe	serang	Sherpa	simply
refund	resent	riddle	rotter	saggar	saving	seaair	serape	sherry	simurg
refuse	reship	rident	rotund	sagged	savory	seabed	seraph	sheugh	sinewy
refute	reside	ridged	rouble	sagger	savour	seabee	serein	shield	sinful
regain	resign	riding	roucou	saidst	sawder	seacow	serene	shiest	singer
regale	resile	rifely	rouncy	sailed	sawfly	seadog	serial	shifty	single
regard	resist	riffle	rouser	sailer	sawney	seaear	series	Shiite	singly
regent	resold	rifler	router	sailor	sawpit	seafan	seriph	shikar	sinker
reggae	resole	rigged	roving	saithe	sawset	seafog	sermon	shiksa	sinned
regime	resorb	rigger	rowing	salaam	sawyer	seafox	serosa	shimmy	sinner
regina	resort	righto	royals	salade	saxony	sealer	serous	shindy	sinnet
region	rester	rigour	rozzer	salami	sayest	seaman	serrae	shiner	sinter
regius	result	rigout	rubato	salary	saying	seamat	serran	shinny	Siouan
reglet	resume	rillet	rubbed	Salian	sayyid	seamer	serval	Shinto	siphon
regnal	retail	rimmed	rubber	salify	scabby	seamew	server	shinty	sipped
regret	retain	rimose	rubble	salina	scalar	seance	sesame	shirty	sipper
regulo	retake	rimous	rubbly	saline	scaled	seapen	seseli	shiver	sippet
rehash	retard	ringed	rubefy	saliva	scaler	seapig	sestet	shoaly	sircar
rehear	retell	ringer	rubify	sallee	scales	search	setoff	shoddy	sirdar
reheat	retene	rinser	rubric	sallet	scampi	season	setose	shofar	sirkar
reheel	retest	rioter	ruched	sallow	scanty	seater	setout	shogun	sirrah
reiver	retial	ripely	ruckle	salmon	scarab	seaway	settee	shoppy	sirree
reject	retina	ripoff	ruckus	saloon	scarce	secant	setter	shoran	siskin
rejoin	retire	ripped	rudder	saloop	scarer	secede	settle	shorts	sissoo
relaid	retold	ripper	ruddle	salter	scarry	secern	sevens	shorty	sister
relate	retook	ripple	rudely	saltus	scarus	second	severe	should	sistra
relent	retool	ripply	rudish	saluki	scathe	secret	severy	shovel	sittar
relict	retort	riprap	rueful	salute	scatty	sector	Sevres	shover	sitter
relief	retral	ripsaw	ruelle	salver	scazon	secund	sewage	shower	sixain
reline	retrod	rising	ruffed	salvia	scenic	secure	sewing	shrank	sixgun
relish	returf	risker	ruffle	salvor	schema	sedate	sexily	shrewd	sizing
relive	return	risque	rufous	salvos	scheme	sedile	sexism	shriek	sizzle
reload	retuse	ritual	rugged	samara	schism	seduce	sexist	shrift	skater
reluct	revamp	rivage	rugger	sambar	schist	seeder	sexpot	shrike	skeely
relume	reveal	rizzar	rugose	sambur	schizo	seeing	sextan	shrill	skeigh
remade	reverb	rizzer	ruiner	Samian	schlep	seemly	sextet	shrimp	skerry
remain	revere	roadie	ruling	samite	schorl	seesaw	sexton	shrine	sketch
remake	revers	roamer	rumble	samlet	school	seethe	sexual	shrink	skewer
remand	revert	roarer	rumbly	Samoan	schuss	seiche	shabby	shrive	skibob
remark	revery	robalo	rummer	sampan	scilla	seiner	shader	shroff	skiddy
remedy	revest	robbed	rumour	sample	sclaff	seisin	shades	shroud	skiing
remind	revets	robber	rumple	Samson	sclera	seizer	shadow	shrove	skilly
remint	review	robust	rumpus	sandal	scolex	seizes	shaduf	shrunk	skimpy
remise	revile	rochet	rundle	sander	sconce	seizin	shaggy	shucks	skinny
remiss	revise	rocker	runlet	sandhi	scopae	sejant	shaken	shutin	skirun
remora	revive	rocket	runnel	sanely	scopas	seldom	shaker	shyest	skiver

```
skivvy sneesh spacer squire storax sudden syrinx tatter tetter tiewig
skylab sneeze spadix squirm stores suffer syrupy tattle Teuton tiffin
skyman sneezy sparer squirt storey suffix system tattoo thaler tights
skyway sniffy sparge squish stormy Sufism syzygy taught thalli tiling
slacks sniper sparks stable stound sugary tabard Taurus thanks tiller
slaggy snippy sparry stably stover suitor tabbed tauten thatch tilter
slalom snitch sparse stacte strafe sulcus tablet tautly Theban timbal
slangy snivel spathe stadia strain sullen tabour tautog thecae timber
slapup snobby spavin stager strait sultan tacker tavern thecal timbre
slater snoopy specie stagey strake sultry tacket tawdry theine timely
slaver snooty speech stairs strand sumach tackle tawery theirs timing
slavey snooze speedo staith strass summae tactic tawpie theism timous
Slavic snorer speedy stakes strata summed taenia taxies theist tincal
slayer snotty speiss stalag strath summer tagend taxman thenar tindal
sleave snouty spence stalky strati summit tagged teabag thence tinder
sleazy snubby spewer stamen strawy summon tagrag teacup theory tinful
sledge snuffy sphene stance strays sunbow tahini teapot theses tingle
sleepy snugly sphere stanch streak sundae tahsil teapoy thesis tingly
sleety soaker sphery stanza stream Sunday tailor teasel thetic tinily
sleeve sobbed sphinx stapes streek sunder taipan teaser thieve tinker
sleigh sobeit spider staple street sundew takahe teaset things tinkle
sleuth socage spiffy starch stress sundog takein teazel thingy tinkly
slicer soccer spigot starer strewn sundry taking teazle thinly tinman
slider social spilth starry striae sungod talbot tedded thirst tinned
slight socket spinal starve strict sunhat talcky tedder thirty tinner
slimly sodden spined stases stride sunken talcum tedium tholoi tinpot
slinky sodium spinel stasis strife sunlit talent teemer tholos tinsel
slipon sodomy spinet statal strike sunned talion teensy tholus tinter
slippy soever spiral stated Strine sunray talker teepee thorax tipcat
slipup soffit spirit stater string sunset talkie teeter thoria tipoff
sliver soften spital states stripe suntan tallow teethe thorny tipped
slogan softie splash static stripy superb Talmud tegmen thoron tipper
sloppy softly spleen stator strive supine tamale tegula thorpe tippet
sloshy soigne splent statue strobe supped tamara teledu though tipple
slouch soiree splice status strode supper tamely telega thrall tiptoe
slough soline spline stayer stroke supple taming teller thrash tiptop
Slovak solano splint steady stroll supply tampan telson thrawn tirade
sloven soldan splits steamy stroma surely tamper Telugu thread tisane
slowly solder splore steely stromb surety tampon temper threap tissue
sludge solely splosh steeve strong surfer tamtam temple threat titbit
sludgy solemn spoffy stelae stroud surrey tandem tenace thresh titfer
sluice solidi spoilt stelar strout surtax tangle tenant thrice tither
sluicy solids spoken stemma strove survey tangly tender thrift titian
slummy solute sponge stench strown suslik tanist tendon thrill titled
slurry solver spongy stepin struck sutile tanked tenner thrips titter
slushy sombre spooky steppe struma sutler tanker tennis thrive tittle
slyest somite spoony stepup strung suttee tanned tenour throat tittup
smalls sonant sports stereo strunt suture tanner tenpin throes tmeses
smalto sonata sporty steric Stuart svelte tannic tenrec throne tmesis
smarmy sonnet spotty sterna stubby swaddy tannin tenson throng tocher
smarty sonsie spouse sterol stucco swampy tanrec tensor throve tocsin
smatch sooner sprain stewed studio swanky tantra tenter thrown toddle
smeary soothe sprang sticky stuffy swaraj Taoism tentie thrush toecap
smeech sophic sprawl stifle stumer swarth Taoist tenues thrust toeing
smelly sopite spread stigma stumpy swatch tapeta tenuis thulia toffee
smilax sopped sprent stilly stupid swathe tapped tenure thwack togaed
smiler sorage spring stingo stupor swayer tapper tenuto thwart togged
smirch sorbet sprint stingy sturdy sweaty tappet tenzon thymol toggle
smirky sordid sprite stinko stylar sweeny tappit tepefy thymus toiler
smiter sorely sprout stipel stylet sweets target tercel thyrse toilet
smithy sorgho spruce stipes stylus swerve Targum tercet tibiae Toledo
smoggy sorner spruit stirps stymie sweven tariff teredo tibial toluic
smoker sorrel sprung stitch suable swinge tarmac terete ticked toluol
smooch sorrow spryer stithy subbed swiper tarpan tergal ticker tomato
smooth sorter spryly stiver subdue swipes tarpon tergum ticket tombac
smouch sortes spunky stocks sublet swirly tarras termer tickey tomboy
smudge sortie spurge stocky subman swishy tarred termly tickle tomcat
smudgy Sothic spurry stodge submit switch tarsal termor tickly tomcod
smugly sotted sputum stodgy suborn swivel tarsia terret tictac tomtit
smutch sought squail stogie subsea swoosh tarsus territ tictoc tomtom
smutty souari squall stoked subset swound tartan terror tidbit toneme
snaggy souled squama stoker subtil sylphs tartar terser tiddly tonger
snappy source square stolen subtle sylvan Tarzan tester tidily tongue
snarer sourly squash stolid subtly symbol tassel testes tiebar tonish
snarly souter squawk stolon suburb syndic tasset teston tiedye tonsil
snatch soviet squeak stoned subway syntax tassie tetany tiepin tooter
snathe sovran squeal stoner sucker syphon taster tetchy tierce toothy
snazzy sowans squill stooge suckle Syriac tatami tether tiered tootle
sneaky sowens squint stopgo sudary Syrian tatted tetrad tierod tootsy
```

```
Tophet  triune  tuxedo  ungues  unwrap  vassal  virago  wangle  whinge  wonted
tophus  trivet  tuyere  unguis  unyoke  vastly  virgin  wanion  whinny  wonton
topman  trivia  twangy  ungula  upbear  vatful  virile  wanted  whippy  wooded
topped  trocar  tweeds  unhair  upbeat  vatted  virose  wanton  whirly  wooden
topper  troche  tweedy  unhand  upcast  vaudoo  virtue  wapiti  whisht  woodsy
topple  trogon  tweeny  unholy  update  vaulty  visage  warble  whisky  woofer
torero  troika  twelve  unhook  upheld  vaward  viscid  warcry  whited  wooled
Tories  Trojan  twenty  Uniate  uphill  vector  viscus  warden  whiten  woolly
toroid  trolly  twicer  unific  uphold  Vedist  Vishnu  warder  whites  worker
torose  trompe  twiggy  uniped  uphroe  vegete  visile  wardog  whitey  wormer
torpid  trophy  twilit  unipod  upkeep  veiled  vision  warily  wholly  worrit
torpor  tropic  twiner  unique  upland  veined  visive  warmer  whomso  worsen
torque  troppo  twinge  unisex  uplift  veleta  visual  warmly  whoops  worthy
torrid  trough  twirly  unison  upmost  vellum  vitals  warmth  whoosh  wortle
torsel  troupe  twisty  united  upping  velour  vitric  warped  whydah  woundy
torten  trouty  twitch  uniter  uppish  velure  vittae  warper  wicked  wowser
torula  trover  twoply  unjoin  uppity  velvet  vivace  warred  wicker  wraith
tosher  trowel  twould  unjust  uprise  vendee  vivers  warren  wicket  wrasse
tosser  truant  twoway  unkind  uproar  vender  vivify  warsle  widely  wrathy
tossup  trudge  tycoon  unking  uproot  vendor  vizard  warted  widget  wreath
tother  truism  tymbal  unkink  uprush  vendue  vizier  washer  widish  wrench
totted  trumps  tympan  unknit  upshot  veneer  vizsla  wasted  wieldy  wretch
totter  trusty  typhus  unknot  upside  venery  voiced  waster  wiener  wright
toucan  trying  typify  unlace  uptake  venial  voider  waters  wifely  writer
touche  tryout  typing  unlade  uptown  venire  voided  wattle  wigeon  writhe
touchy  tsamba  typist  unlaid  upturn  venose  volant  waught  wigged  wyvern
toupee  tsetse  tyrant  unlash  upward  venous  volley  wavery  wiggle  xenial
toupet  Tshirt  Tyrian  unless  upwind  venter  volost  wavily  wiggly  xenium
tourer  tsotsi  ubiety  unlike  uracil  ventil  volume  waxily  wigwag  xylene
tousle  Tswana  uglify  unlink  uraeus  ventre  volute  waylay  wigwam  xyloid
touter  Tuareg  uglily  unload  Uralic  venule  volvox  wayout  wilder  xylose
towage  tubber  ugsome  unlock  Urania  verbal  voodoo  waxily  wildly  xystus
toward  tubful  Ugrian  unmade  uranic  verger  vorant  weaken  wilful  yabber
towery  tubing  ugsome  unmake  Uranus  verify  vortex  weaker  willed  yaffle
towhee  tubule  ullage  unmask  uranyl  verily  votary  wealth  willet  Yahveh
townee  tuchun  ulster  unmeet  urbane  verism  voting  weaken  willow  Yahweh
toxoid  tucker  ultima  unmoor  urchin  verist  votive  weapon  Wilton  Yankee
tracer  tucket  ultimo  unnail  ureter  verity  voulge  weaner  wimble  yaourt
traces  tuckin  umbles  unpack  urgent  vermin  voyage  wearer  wimple  yapock
tracks  tuffet  umbrae  unpaid  urinal  vernal  voyeur  weasel  wincey  yapped
trader  tufted  umbral  unpick  urnful  vernal  vulcan  weazen  winded  yapper
tragic  tufter  umbras  unplug  ursine  versed  vulgar  wabble  winder  yarely
tragus  tugged  umlaut  unread  usable  verser  vulgus  wabain  window  yarrow
trance  tuille  umpire  unreal  usance  verset  wabain  webbed  windup  yatter
trapan  tulwar  unable  unreel  useful  versus  wabble  wedded  winery  yaupon
trapes  tumble  unbend  unrest  ustion  vertex  wadded  weeder  winged  yclept
trappy  tumefy  unbent  unripe  usurer  vervet  waddie  weekly  winger  yearly
trashy  tumour  unbind  unrobe  uterus  vesica  waddle  weeper  winker  yeasty
trauma  tumtum  unbitt  unroll  utmost  vesper  waders  weepie  winkle  yellow
travel  tumuli  unbolt  unroof  utopia  vessel  wadmal  weevil  winnow  yelper
treaty  tumult  unborn  unroot  uvulae  vestal  wadmol  weight  winner  yenned
treble  tundra  unbred  unrope  uvular  vested  wafery  weirdo  winsey  yeoman
trebly  tuning  uncage  unruly  vacant  vestee  waffle  weirdy  wintle  yesman
tremie  tunnel  uncate  unsafe  vacate  vestry  wafter  welder  wintry  yester
tremor  tupelo  uncial  unsaid  vacuum  vetted  wagged  weldor  wiring  yipped
trench  turban  uncini  unseal  vagary  viable  waggle  welkin  wisdom  yippee
trendy  turbid  unclad  unseam  vagile  viands  waggly  welter  wisely  yippie
trepan  turbit  uncoil  unseat  vagrom  viator  waggon  welter  wisent  yogism
trepid  turbot  uncool  unseen  vainly  vibist  Wahabi  welter  wisher  yogurt
tressy  tureen  uncork  unself  Vaisya  vibrio  wahine  Wendic  wisely  yoicks
triage  turgid  uncurl  unship  valeta  victim  wailer  wester  wisent  yolked
tribal  turgor  undate  unshod  valgus  victor  waiter  wether  wither  yonder
tricar  turion  undies  unshoe  valine  vicuna  waiver  wetted  withal  yoohoo
tricky  turkey  undine  unstop  valise  vidual  walker  wetter  within  yorker
tricot  Turkic  undock  unsung  valley  vielle  walkin  whaler  withit  Yoruba
trifid  turner  undoer  untidy  vallum  vidual  walkon  whatso  witted  yttria
trifle  turnip  undone  untied  valour  vieller valuer  whaler  wittol  yumyum
trigon  turnup  unduly  untold  valuer  viewer  walled  wheeze  wittol  zaffer
trilby  turret  unease  untrue  valuta  vigour  waller  wheezy  wivern  zaffre
trimer  turtle  uneasy  untuck  valved  vihara  wallet  whenas  wizard  zander
trimly  turves  uneath  untune  vamper  Viking  wallop  whence  wizier  zanily
trinal  Tuscan  uneven  unused  vandal  vilely  wallow  wherry  wobble  zapped
triode  tusked  unfair  unveil  vanish  vilify  walnut  wheyey  wobbly  zarape
triple  tusker  unfold  unwary  vanity  villus  wamble  whidah  woeful  zareba
triply  tussah  unfurl  unwell  vanner  vinery  wambly  whiles  woggle  zariba
tripod  tusser  ungird  unwept  vapour  vinous  wampee  whilom  wolves  zealot
tripos  tussle  ungirt  unwind  varied  vintry  wampum  whilst  wombat  zebeck
triste  tutsan  unglue  unwise  varlet  violet  whimsy  whilst  womera  zeloso
triton  tutted  ungual  unworn  varved  violin  wander  whiner  wonder  zeloso
```

```
zenana banner cafard carfax damage fallen gallop hallal jarful lariat
zenith bantam Caffre carful damask fallow galoot halloa jargon larker
zephyr banter caftan caries dammar falsie galore halloo jarrah larrup
zeugma banyan cagily carina dammed falter galosh hallow jarred larvae
zigzag banzai cahier carman damned family gambir hallux jarvey larval
zillah baobab cahoot carnal dampen famine gambit haloes jasper larynx
zinced barbed caiman carnet damper famish gamble halter jaunce lascar
zincic barbel caique carney damply famous gambol halvah jaunty lasher
zincky barber cajole carpal damsel famuli gamely halves kabala lashup
zingel barbet calami carpel damson fandom gamete hamate kabuki lasque
zinked bardic calash carper dancer fanged gamily Hamite Kabyle lassie
zinnia barege calcar carpet dander fanion gamine hamlet Kaffir lassos
zipped barely calces carpus dandle fanjet gaming hammal kaftan laster
zipper barfly calcic carrel danger fanned gammer hammam kainit lastly
zircon bargee calico carrot dangle fanner gammon hammed kaiser lateen
zither barite caliph cartel Daniel fantan gander hammer kakapo lately
zlotys barium calker carter Danish Fantee ganger hamper kalong latent
zodiac barker calkin carton dankly fantod gangly handed kanaka latest
zombie barley caller carvel daphne fantom gangue handle kaolin lather
zonary barman callet carven dapper faquir gannet hangar kaput  latish
zonate barney callow carver dapple fardel ganoid hanged karate latria
zoning barony callup casbah daring farfel gantry hanger karmic latron
zonked barque callus casein darken farina gaoler hangup kaross latten
Zouave barred calmly casern darkey farmer gapped hanker karroo latter
zounds barrel calory cashew darkie faroff garage hankie kasbah launce
zufolo barren calpac casing darkle farout garbed hansel kation launch
zygoma barret calque casino darkly farrow garble hansom laager laurel
zygote barrio calves casket darned fasces garcon happed labial lavabo
zymase barrow calxes Caslon darnel fascia garden happen labile lavage
zythum barter camass casque darner fasten garget haptic labium laveer
────── barton camber cassia darter faster gargle harass labour lavish
Baalim baryon camera cassis dartle fathen garial harden labret lavolt
babble baryta camion caster dartre father garish hardly labrum lawful
babbly basalt camise castle dasher fathom garlic hardup laceup lawman
Babism basely camlet castor dassie fatted garner harken laches lawyer
Babist bashaw camper casual datary fatten garnet harlot lacing laxity
baboon basher campus catalo dative fatter garran harper lackey layday
backer basics canape catchy datura faucal garret harrow lactic layman
backup basket canard catena dauber fauces garron hartal lacuna layoff
baddie basnet canary catgut dawdle faucet garrot haslet ladder layout
badger Basque cancan Cathar daybed faulty garter hassle laddie lazily
baffle basset cancel cation dayfly faunae garuda hasten ladify lazuli
bagful bassos cancer catkin dazzle faunal garvie hatbox lading macaco
bagged baster candid catnap eaglet favour Gascon hatful ladino machan
bagman Basuto candle catnip earful fawner gasbag hatpeg ladyfy mackle
bagnio Basutu canful catsup earing gabbed gasify hatpin lagged macron
bagwig batata cangue cattle earner gabber gasket hatred lagger macula
bailee bateau canine caucus earthy gabble gaskin hatted lagoon macule
bailer bather canker caudal earwax gabbro gasman hatter laguna Madame
bailey bathos canned caudex earwig gabion gassed hauler laical madcap
bailie bating cannel caudle easily gabled gasser haunch lallan madden
bailor batman canner caught easter gablet gateau havers lambda madder
baiter batted cannon caulis eatery gadded gather hawhaw lamber madman
bakery batten cannot causal eating gadder gauche hawked lamely madras
balata batter canopy causer Fabian gadfly gaucho hawker lament maduro
balboa battle canter causey fabled gadget gauger hawser lamina maenad
baldly battue canthi caveat fabler gadoid gavial haybox Lammas Magian
baleen bauble cantle cavern fabric Gadhel gavage haymow lammed magilp
balker bawbee cantor caviar facade Gaelic gazebo hazard lanate magnet
ballad bawble cantus caving facete gaffer gazump hazily lancer magnum
ballet bawdry Canuck cavity facial gagged habile iambic lancet magpie
ballon bawler canvas cavort facile gagger hackle iambus landau maguey
ballot bawley canyon cayman facing gaggle hackly jabbed landed Magyar
balsam bayard capful cayuse factor gagman haddie jabber lander mahout
Baltic bazaar capias dabbed factum gainer haemal jabiru langue maidan
bamboo cabala caplin dabber facula gainly haemin jacana langur maiden
banana cabana capote dabble fadein gainst haffet jackal lanner maigre
bandit cabman capric dacoit faerie gaited haffit jacket lanugo mailed
bandog cachet capsid dactyl fagend gaiter hagbut jaeger lapdog mainly
banger cachou captor daedal fagged galago haggis jagged lapful makedo
bangle cackle carafe daemon faggot galaxy haggle jaguar lapped makeup
bangup cacoon carbon daftly failed galena hailer jailer lappet making
banian cactus carboy dagger faille galiot hairdo jailor lappie malady
banish caddie carder dagoes fainly galley haired jalopy lapsed Malaga
banjax caddis careen dahlia fairly Gallic haleru jammed lapsus malate
banjos cadent career daimen fakery Gallio halide jammer larder maleic
banker cadger caress daimio falcon gallon halite jangle lardon malice
banket caecal ...    daimon fallal ...    ...    ...    ...    ...
banned caecum caress dainty fallal gallon halite jangle lardon malice
```

```
malign masher pallia patron ransom salify tabard Taurus wander absent
malism mashie pallid patted ranter salina tabbed tauten wangle absorb
malkin masker pallor patten ranula saline tablet tautly wanion absurd
mallee maslin palmar patter raphia saliva tabour tautog wanted abulia
mallei Masora palmer paunch raphis sallee tacker tavern wanton abuser
mallet masque palolo pauper rapids sallet tacket tawdry wapiti ibexes
mallow massif palpal pavage rapier sallow tackle tawery wapper ibices
maltha masted palpus pavane rapine salmon tactic tawpie warble ibidem
mammae master palter paving rapist saloon taenia taxies warcry obeche
mammal mastic paltry pavior rapped saloop tagend taxman warden obelus
mammee matico pampas pavise rappee salter tagged taxman warder obeyer
mammer matins pamper pawner rappel saltus tagrag vacant wardog obital
mammon matlow panada pawnee rapper saluki tahini vacate wargod object
manage matrix panama pawpaw raptly salute tahsil vacuum warily objure
manana matron panary payday raptor salver taipan vagary warmer oblast
manche matted pandit payoff rarefy salvia takahe vagile warmly oblate
Manchu matter pander paynim rarely salvor takein vagrom warmth oblige
manday mature pandit payola rarity salvos taking vainly warmup oblong
manege matzoh panful rabato rascal samara talbot Vaisya warped oboist
manful maugre panzer rabbet rasher sambar talcky valeta warper obsess
mangel maundy papacy rabbin rashly sambur talcum valgus warred obtain
manger maxima papain rabbit rasper Samian talent valine warren obtect
mangle maxixe papaya rabble raster samite talion valise warsle obtest
mangos maybug papers rabies rasure samlet talker valley warted obtund
maniac mayday papery raceme ratbag Samoan talkie valuer washer obtuse
manila mayest papism rachis rather sampan tallow vallum waster obvert
manioc mayfly papist racial ratify sample Talmud valour waters ubiety
manito mayhap pappus racily ratine Samson tamale valuta watery acacia
manned mayhem papula racism rating sandal tamara valued wattle acajou
manner maying papule racist ration sander tamely valuer waught acarid
manque mazard papyri racker ratite sandhi taming valved wavery acarus
mantel mazily parade racket ratlin sangar tampan vamper wavily accede
mantes nabbed paramo racoon ratoon sanies tamper vandal waxily accent
mantic naevus parang raddle rattan sanify tampon vanish waylay accept
mantid nagana paraph radial rattat sanity tamtam vanity waylay access
mantis nagged parcel radian ratted sanjak tandem vanner wayout accord
mantle nagger pardie radish ratter santal tangle varied yabber accost
mantra nailer pardon radium rattle Taoism tangly varlet yaffle accrue
mantua namely parent radius ravage Taoist tanist varved yammer accuse
manual nanism parget radome ravine santir tanked vassal Yankee acedia
manuka napalm pariah radula raving sapele tanker vatful yapock acetal
manure napkin parian raffia ravish sapful tanned vatted yapped acetic
Maoism napped paring raffle razzia sapota tanner vaudoo yapper acetyl
Maoist nardoo parish rafter razzle sappan tannic vaulty yarely achene
mapped narrow parity ragbag sabbat sapped tannin vaward yarrow acidic
mapper nastic parkin ragged Sabian sapper tanrec wabain yatter acidly
maquis natant parlay raggee Sabine sarape tantra wabble yaupon acinar
maraca nation parley raggle sachem sardel Taoism wadded yawned acinus
maraud native raglan raglan sachet sarong Taoist waddie zaffer ackack
marble natron raglan raglan sacral sarsen tapeta waddle zaffre acquit
marbly natter parody ragman sacred sachem tapper waders zander across
marcel nature parole ragout sachet sashay tappet wadmal zanily acting
margay naught parpen ragtag sacque sacque tappit wadmol zarape action
margin nausea parral raguly sacral sateen target wafery zareba active
marina nautch parrel raider sacred satiny Targum waffle zariba actual
marine Nazify parrot railer sacrum satire tariff wafter abacus acuity
marish Nazism raisin raiser sadden satori tarmac wagged abater acumen
Marist oafish Parsee raisin sadder satrap tarpan waggle abatis ecarte
marked oarage parson Rajput saddhu Saturn tarpon waggly abbacy echoer
marker pacify partan rakish saddle saucer tarras waggon abbess echoic
market packer partly ramate sadism sauger tarred wahine abduce eclair
markup packet parure ramble sadist saurel tarsal wailer abduct eczema
marlin padauk parvis ramify safari savage tarpon waiter abject iceaxe
marmot padded pascal ramjet safely savant tarsal waiver abjure icebag
maroon paddle Pashto rammed safety savate tarsia walker abduct icebox
marque paella passer ramose sagely savine tarsus walkin abject icecap
marram pagoda passim ramous saggar saving tartan walkon abjure iceman
marred paidup pastel ramper sagged savory tartar wallah ablate icicle
marron pajama pastil ramrod sagger savour tartly walled ablaut iconic
marrow pakeha pastor ramson saidst sawder Tarzan waller ablaze occamy
marrum palace pastry rancho sailed sawfly tassel wallet abloom occult
marshy palais patchy rancid sailer sawney tassie wallop ablush occupy
marten palais patent randan sailor sawpit taster wallow aboard ocelli
martin palate Pathan random saithe sawset tatami walnut aboral ocelot
martyr paleae pathic ranger salaam sawyer tatted walrus abound ochone
marvel palely pathos ranker salade saxony tatter wamble abrade oclock
mascle paling patina rankle salami sayest tattle wambly abroad octane
mascon palish patois rankle salary saying tattoo wampee abrupt octant
mascot pallet patrol rankly Salian sayyid taught wampum abseil octave
```

```
octavo adieus befell centum demean fellah hectic keyway melody peaked
octroi adieux befool cerate dement feller hector leaden melton peanut
ocular adipic before cercus demise felloe heddle leader member pearly
scabby adjoin befoul cereal demist fellow hedera leadin memoir peavey
scalar adjure beggar cereus demode felony hedger leadup memory pebble
scaled adjust begged ceriph demote female heehaw leafed menace pebbly
scaler admass begird cerise demure femora heeled league menage pecker
scales admire begirt cerium denary fencer heeler lealty mender pecten
scampi adnate begone cermet dengue fender hegira leanly menhir pectic
scanty adnexa behalf certes denial Fenian heifer leanto menial pectin
scarab Adonic behave ceruse denier fenman height leaper meninx pedalo
scarce Adonis behead cervix denims fennec hejira learnt mensal pedant
scarer adorer beheld cesser denote fennel helium leaved menses pedate
scarry adrift behest cestus dental ferial heller leaven mental peddle
scarus adroit behind cesura dentel ferine helmet leaver mentor pedlar
scathe adsorb behold cetane dentil ferret helper leaves mentum peeler
scatty advent behoof deacon denude ferric hemmed lecher mercer peeper
scazon adverb behove deaden deodar ferula hempen lector merely peepul
scenic advert beigel deadly depart ferule henrun ledged merest peewit
schema advice belaud deafen depend fervid henrys ledger merger pegged
scheme advise beldam deafly depict fescue hepcat leeway merils pegleg
schism adytum belfry dealer deploy festal heptad legacy merino pegtop
schist Eddaic Belgic dearie depone fester herald legate merism pelage
schizo Edenic belief dearly deport fetial herbal legato merlin pelham
schlep edgily belike dearth depose fetich herder legbye merlon pellet
school edging belive deasil depute fetish herdic legend merman pelmet
schorl edible bellow debark deputy fetter hereat legged merrie pelota
schuss editor belong debase derail feudal hereby legion mescal peltae
scilla ideaed belted debate derate fezzed herein legist mesial pelter
sclaff ideate beluga debris deride fezzes hereof legman messan peltry
sclera idiocy bemire debtor derive fezzes hereon legume Messrs pelves
scolex idolum bemoan debunk dermal geckos heresy lemony mestee pelvic
sconce oddity bemock decade dermic geegee hereto lender metage pelvis
scopae oddjob bemuse decamp dermis geezer heriot length metals pencil
scopas oddson bender decani derris geisha hermit lenity meteor penman
scorch odious benign decant desalt gelled hernia lensed method pennae
scorer aedile bennet deceit descry Gemara heroic Lenten methyl penned
scoria Aegean benumb decent desert Gemini heroin lentil metier pennon
scotch Aeolic benzol decide design gemmae herpes Leonid metope pentad
scoter aerate benzyl decker desire gemmed Herren lepton metred pentup
scotia aerial berate deckle desist gender hetero lesion metric pentyl
Scotic aerily Berber decoct desman genera hetman lessee mettle penult
scouse aerobe bereft decode desmid geneva hexact lessen mezuza penury
scouth aether berlin decoke desorb genial hexane lesser neaped people
scrape beachy bertha decree despot genius hexose lesson nearby peplum
scrawl beacon berthe dedans detach genned heyday lessor nearer pepped
screak beadle beseem deduce detail gentes jeerer lethal nearly pepper
scream beagle beside deduct detain gentle jejune letoff neaten pepsin
screed beaked bested deejay detect gentoo jennet letter neatly peptic
screen beaker bestir deepen detent gently jerbil Lettic nebula perdue
screwy beamer bestow deeply detest gerboa jerboa levant nebuly period
scribe beanie betake deface detour gentry jerker Levite nectar perish
scrimp bearer bethel defame deuced geodic jerkin levity needle permit
script beaten betide defeat devest George jersey lewdly neednt perron
scroll beater betony defect device gerbil jester meadow negate person
scroop Beaune betook defend devise gerent Jesuit meagre nekton pertly
scruff beauty betray defier devoid german jetlag mealie Nepali peruke
scrump beaver betted defile devoir germen jetsam meanie nephew peruse
scryer becall better define devote gerund jetted meanly nereid pesade
sculpt becalm bettor deform devour getout Jewess measly nerine peseta
scummy became bewail defray devout getter Jewish meatus nerite pesewa
scurfy becket beware deftly dewily gewgaw jezail meddle nerite pester
scurry beckon bewray defuse dewlap geyser keenly mediae neroli pestle
scurvy become beyond degras dexter headed kelpie medial nestle petara
scutal bedaub bezant degree eerily header kelson medick netful petard
scutch bedaze bezoar degust fealty headon kelter medico nether petite
scutum bedbug cecity dehorn featly healer kelvin medium nettle petrel
scyphi bedded cedarn deicer feckly health Keltic medius netted petrol
scythe bedder celery deific fecula hearer kelvin medlar nettle petted
yclept bedeck celiac deject fecund hearse kenned medley neural petter
adagio bedell cellar delate fedora hearth kennel medusa neuron pewter
Adamic bedlam celled delete feeble hearty kermes meekly neuter peyote
addend bedpan Celtic delict feebly heated kermis meetly newish peyotl
addict bedsit cement delude feeder heater kerned megilp newton reader
addled beduin censer deluge feeing heathy kernel megohm oecist really
adduce beeper censor deluxe feeler heaven kersey megrim oedema realty
adduct beetle census delver feirie heaver ketone meinie oeuvre reamer
adenyl beeves cental demand feisty Hebrew ketone meinie peachy reaper
adhere befall centre demark feline heckle kettle mellow peahen rearer
```

```
reason relent retool Semite teensy venule affray chaste phloem shirty
reaver relict retort semmit teepee verbal Afghan chatty phobia shiver
rebate relief retral semple teeter verger afield chaunt phobic shoaly
rebato reline retrod sempre teethe verify aflame cheeky phoebe shoddy
rebeck relish retted senary tegmen verily afloat cheers phoney shofar
rebore relive returf senate tegula verism afraid cheery phonic shogun
reborn reload return sendal teledu verist afreet cheese phonon shoppy
rebuff reluct retuse senega telega verity afresh cheesy phooey shoran
rebuke relume revamp sender teller vermin afrite chelae photic shorts
recall remade reveal sendup telson vernal afters chemic photon shorty
recant remain reverb senhor Telugu versal efface cheque phrase should
recast remake revere senile temper versed effect cherry phylum shovel
recede remand revers senior temple verser effete cherty physic shover
recent remark revert sennet tenace verset effigy cherub rhaphe shower
recess remedy revery sennit tenant versus efflux chesil rhebok shrank
recipe remind revest senora tender vertex effort chesty rhesus shrewd
recite remint review senses tendon vervet effuse chevet rhetor shriek
reckon remise revile sensor tenner vesica offend chiasm rheumy shrift
recoil remiss revise sensum tennis vesper offent chiaus rhinal shrike
recoin remora revive sentry tenour vessel office chichi rhombi shrill
record remote revoke sephen tenpin vestal offing chicle rhumba shrimp
recoup remuda revolt sepsis tenrec vested offish chield rhymer shrine
rector remove revved septal tenson vestee offkey chigoe rhythm shrink
rectum rename reward septet tensor vestry offset chilli shabby shrive
rectus render rewind septic tenter vetted agamic chilly shader shroff
redact renege rewire septum tentie weaken agamid chimer shades shroud
redbud rennet rewoke sequel tenues weakly agaric chintz shadow shrove
redcap renown reword sequin tenuis wealth ageing chippy shaduf shrunk
redden rental rework serang tenure weaner agency chirpy shaggy shucks
redder renter seaair serape tenuto weapon agenda chisel shaken shutin
reddle reopen seabed seraph tenzon wearer ageold chital shaker shyest
redeem repaid seabee serein tepefy weasel aghast chitin Shakta thaler
redeye repair seacow serene teraph weaver agnail chiton Shakti thalli
redhot repand seadog serial tercel weazen agnate chitty shalom thanks
rediae repass seaear series tercet webbed agnise chives shaman thatch
redone repast seafan seriph teredo wedded agonal chivvy shammy Theban
redraw repeal seafog sermon terete weeder agonic choice shamus thecae
redtop repeat seafox serosa tergal weekly agouti choker shandy thecal
reduce repent sealer serous tergum weeper agrafe chokey shanny theine
reebok repine seaman serrae termer weepie aguish choler shanty theirs
reecho replay seamat serran termly weever Egeria choose shaped theism
reedit replum seamer serval termor weevil egesta choosy shapen theist
reefer report seamew server terret weight eggcup chopin sharer thenar
reeler repose seance serret territ weirdo eggler choppy sharif thence
reface repugn seapen seseli terror weirdy eggnog choral sharps theory
refect repute seapig sestet testae welder egoism chorea shaven theses
refill reread search setoff tester weldor egoist choric shaver thesis
refine resale season setose teston welkin egress chorus shavie thetic
reflex rescue seater setout tetany welter ignite chosen shears thieve
reflow reseat seaway settee tetchy Wendic ignore chough sheass things
reflux reseau secant setter tether wester iguana chouse sheath thingy
reform resect secede settle tetrad wether ogamic chrism sheave thinly
refuel reseda secern sevens tetter wetted ogival Christ sheeny thirst
refuge resell second severe Teuton wetter ogress chroma sheets thirty
refund resent secret severy vector xenial ogrish chromo sheikh tholoi
refuse reship sector Sevres Vedist xenium uglify chubby sheila tholos
refute reside secund sewage vegete yearly uglily chuffy shekel tholus
regain resign secure sewing veiled yeasty Ugrian chukar shelly thorax
regale resile sedate sexily veined yellow ugsome chukka Shelta thoria
regard resist sedile sexism veleta yelper ahimsa chukor shelty thorny
regent resold seduce sexist vellum yenned bharal chummy shelve thoron
reggae resole seeder sexpot veloce yeoman bhisti chunky shends thorpe
regime resorb seeing sextan velour yesman chacha church sheoak though
regina resort seeker sextet velure yester chacma chypre sherif thrall
region rester seemly sexton velvet zealot chafer dharma Sherpa thrash
regius result seesaw sexual vendee zebeck chaffy dhooti sherry thrawn
reglet resume seethe teabag vender zeloso chalet dhurra sheugh thread
regnal retail seiche teacup vendor zenana chalks gharry shield threap
regret retain seiner teapot vendue zenith chalky ghetto shiest threat
regulo retake seisin teapoy veneer zephyr chance ghosty shifty thresh
rehash retard seizer teasel venery zeugma chancy ohmage Shiite thrice
rehear retell seizin teaser venial afeard change phalli shikar thrift
reheat retene sejant teaset venire affair chanty pharos shiksa thrill
reheel retest seldom teazel Venite affect chapel phasic shimmy thrips
reiver retial select teazle venose affeer chappy phatic shindy thrive
reject retina Seljuk tedded venous affine charas phenol shiner throat
rejoin retire seller tedder venter affirm charge phenom shinny throes
relaid retold selves tedium ventil afflux Charon phenyl Shinto throne
relate retook semble teemer ventre afford chaser phlegm shinty throng
```

```
throve biotic dinner finnan jingle lingua Minoan piggin rillet sissoo
thrown biotin diplex finned jingly linhay minter piglet rimmed sister
thrush birdie diploe finner jinnee lining minuet pignut rimose sistra
thrust bireme diplon Finnic jitney linkup minute pigsty rimous sittar
thulia birkie dipnet fiorin jitter linnet miosis pilaff ringed sitter
thwack birler dipody fipple kiaugh linney miotic pileum ringer sixain
thwart bisect dipole firing kibble linsey mirage pileup rinser sixgun
thymol bishop dipped firkin kibitz lintel mirror pileus rioter sizing
thymus bisque dipper firlot kiblah lintie miscue pilfer ripely sizzle
thyrse bister dipsas firman kibosh lionel misdid pillar ripoff tibiae
thyrsi bistre dirdum firmly kicker lipase misere pillow ripped tibial
whacky bistro direct fiscal kidded lipide misery pilose ripper ticked
whaler bitchy direly fisher kidder lipoid misfit pilous ripple ticker
whatso biting dirham fistic kiddie lipoma mishap pilule ripply ticket
wheeze bitted dirhem fitful kidnap lipped mishit pimple riprap tickey
wheezy bitten dirndl fitted kidney lippen mishmi pimply ripsaw tickle
whenas bitter disarm fitter kiekie lippie Mishna pincer rising tickly
whence bizone disbar fixate killer liquid mislay pineal risker tictac
wherry cicada disbud fixity kilted liquor misled pinery risque tidbit
wheyey cicala discal fizgig kilter lisper missal pineta ritual tiddly
whidah cicely discus fizzle kimono lissom missel pinger rivage tidily
whiles cigala diseur giaour kincob listed missis pinion rizzar tiebar
whilom cilice dismal gibber kindle listel missus pinkie rizzer tiedye
whilst cilium dismay gibbet kindly listen mister pinnae sialic tiepin
whimsy cinder disown gibbon kinema lister mistle pinned sicken tierce
whiner cinema dispel giddap kingly litany misuse pinner sicker tiered
whinge cineol distal gifted kipper litchi mitral pinole sickle tierod
whinny cinque distil gigged kirsch lithia mitten pintle sickly tiewig
whippy cipher disuse giggle kirtle lithic mizzen piolet siding tiffin
whirly circle dither giggly kismet litmus mizzle pionic sienna tights
whisht circus dittos giglet kisser litter mizzly piping sierra tiling
whisky cirque divers giglot kitbag little niacin pipkin siesta tiller
whited cirrus divert gigman kitcat livein nibbed pipped sifter tilter
whiten cistus divest gigolo kitool lively nibble pippin sigher timbal
whites cither divide gilder kitsch livery nicely piquet siglum timber
whitey citole divine gilled kitten living nicety piracy signal timbre
wholly citric diving gillie kittle lizard nicish pirate signer timely
whomso citron eidola gimbal kittul miasma nickel piraya signet timing
whoops citrus eighth gimlet liable mickey nicker Pisces signor timous
whoosh civics eighty gimmal liaise mickle nidget pissed silage tincal
whydah diacid either gimmer libber micron nidify pistil sileni tindal
aikido diadem fiacre gingal libido midage nielli pistol silent tinder
airbed diaper fiance ginger Libyan midair niello piston silica tinful
airbus diatom fiasco gingko lichee midday nigger pitchy silken tingle
airgun dibbed fibbed ginkgo lichen midden niggle pithos siller tingly
airily dibber fibber ginned lictor middle nighty pitier silvan tinily
airing dibble fibred ginner lidded midget nignog pitman silver tinker
airman dicast fibril girder lieder midgut nilgai pitpan simian tinkle
airsac dicker fibrin girdle lierne midoff nimble pitsaw simile tinkly
airway dickey fibula girlie lifter midrib nimbly pitted simmer tinman
aisled dictum fickle hiatus liftup midway nimbus pitter simnel tinned
bibbed diddle fiddle hiccup ligate miffed Nimrod pizzle simony tinner
bibber didoes fiddly hickey ligger mighty ninety ribald simoom tinpot
biceps diesel fidget hidden lights mignon nipped riband simoon tinsel
bicker dieses fierce hiding lignin mihrab nipper ribbed simper tinter
bidden diesis fiesta hieing ligula mikado nipple ribbon simple tipcat
bidder dieter figged higgle ligule milady nitric ribose simply tipoff
bieldy differ figure higher ligure milage nitwit richen simurg tipped
biffin digamy filfot highly likely mildew oidium riches sinewy tipper
biform digest filial hijack liking mildly oilcan richly sinful tippet
bigamy digger filing hinder lilied milieu oilman ricker singer tipple
bigger diglot filler Hindoo limbec milker oilnut rickey single tiptoe
biggin dikdik fillet hinged limbed milled piaffe ricrac sinker tiptop
bigwig diktat fillip hipped limber milord piazza rictal sinned tirade
Bihari dilate filmic hippie limbic milter picker rictus sinner tisane
bijoux dilute filose hirple limbus mimosa picket ridded sinnet tissue
bikini dimity filter hispid liming mincer pickle ridden sinter titbit
bilbos dimmed filthy hisser limner minded picnic riddle sinuet titfer
bilker dimmer fimble hither limper minder picric riding siphon tither
billet dimple finale hitman limpet mingle piddle ridged sipped titian
billon dimply finals jibbah limpid mingly pidgin ridges sipper titter
billow dimwit finder jibbed limply minify piecer rifely sippet tittle
billyo dingey finely jibber limuli minima piedog riffle sircar tittup
binary dinghy finery jigged linage minims pieing rifler sirdar viable
binate dingle finger jigger linden mining pieman rigged sirkar viands
binder dingus finial jiggle lineal minion pierce rigger siroco viatic
binful dining fining jiggly linear minish piffle righto sirrah viator
bionic dinkum finish jigsaw lineup minium pigeon rigour sirree vibist
biopsy dinned finite jilter linger minnow pigged rigout siskin vibrio
```

```
victim wintry allele closet fluter plural embryo angina ensile inmate
victor wirily allied clothe flying plushy emerge angled ensoul inmost
vicuna wiring allium cloudy flyman pluton emerse angler ensure innate
vidual wisdom allout clough flysch slacks emesis angora entail inning
vielle wisely allred cloven flyway slaggy emetic anicut entera inroad
viewer wisent allude clover glacis slalom emetin animal entice inrush
vigour wisher allure clumpy gladly slangy emeute animus entire insane
vihara withal almond clumsy glairy slapup empery anklet entity inseam
Viking wither almost clunch glaive slater empire anlace entoil insect
vilely within alpaca clutch glance slaver employ anlage entomb insert
vilify withit alpine clypei glassy slavey empusa annals entrap inside
villus witted alsike elapse glazer Slavic emulge anneal entree insist
vinery wittol alulae elated gleamy slayer imbibe annexe envier insole
vinous wivern alumna elater gleety sleave imbrex annual enwind inspan
vintry wizard alumni eldest glibly sleazy imbrue annuli enwomb instal
violet wizier always eleven glider sledge immane anodal enwrap instar
violin yipped bladed elevon glitch sleepy immesh anodic enzyme instep
virago yippee blanch elfish global sleety immune anoint gnarly instil
virgin yippie blanky elicit gloomy sleeve immure anomic gnawer insult
virile zigzag blazer elixir gloria sleigh impact anomie gneiss insure
virose zillah blazes elodea glossy sleuth impair anonym gnomic intact
virtue zinced blazon eloign glover slicer impala anorak gnomon intake
visage zincic bleach eloper glower slider impale anoxia gnosis intend
viscid zincky bleary eluant glumly slight impark anoxic inarch intent
viscus zingel blench eluate glumpy slimly impart answer inborn intern
Vishnu zinked blende eluent glutei slinky impawn anthem inbred intine
visile zinnia blenny elvish gluten slipon impede anther incase intoed
vision zipped blight elytra glycin slippy impend antiar incept intone
visive zipper blimey flabby glycol slipup impish anting incest intray
visual zircon blintz flacon illume sliver impone antler inches intuit
vitals zither blithe flaggy illuse slogan import antral incise inulin
vitric djibba blonde flagon klepht sloppy impose antrum incite invade
vittae djinni bloody flambe oldish sloshy impost anyhow inclip invent
vivace ejecta bloomy flamen oleate slouch impugn anyone income invert
vivers akimbo blotch flanch olefin slough impure anyway incubi invest
vivify skater blotto flange oliver Slovak impute enable incult invite
vizard skeely blouse flappy placed sloven omasum enamel incuse invoke
vizier skeigh blowed flashy placer slowly omelet encage indaba inward
vizsla skerry blower flatly placet sludge omenta encamp indeed inwick
wicked sketch blowsy flatus placid sludgy smalls encash indene inwowe
wicker skewer blowup flaunt plagal sluice smalto encode indent inwrap
wicket skibob blowzy flavin plague sluicy smarmy encore Indian inyala
widely skiddy bluing flaxen plaguy slummy smarty encyst indict knaggy
widget skiing bluish fleche plaice slurry smatch endear indign knight
widish skilly blunge fledge plaint slushy smeary ending indigo knives
wieldy skimpy blurry fleece planar slyest smeech endive indite knobby
wiener skinny claggy fleech planer ullage smelly endure indium knotty
wifely skirun clammy fleecy planet ulster smilax energy indole knower
wigeon skiver claque flench plaque ultima smiler enface indoor onager
wigged skivvy claret flense plashy ultimo smirch enfold induce oncost
wiggle skylab classy fleshy plasma zlotys smirky engage induct oneoff
wiggly skyman clause fletch platan amadou smiter engild indult oneway
wigwag skyway claver fleury platen amatol smithy engine induna onfall
wigwam alalia clavis flexor plater amazon smoggy engird infamy online
wilder alarum clayey flicks player ambler smoker engirt infant onrush
wildly alated cleave flight pleach ambush smooch englut infare onside
wilful albata clench flimsy please amends smooth engram infect onward
wilily albedo clergy flinch plebby amerce smouch engulf infelt pneuma
willed albeit cleric flinty pledge amidst smudge enhalo infest snaggy
willet albert clever flitch plenty amnion smudgy enigma infirm snappy
willow albino clevis floaty plenum amoeba smugly enisle inflow snarer
Wilton albite cliche flocci pleura amoral smutch enjoin influx snarly
wimble alcaic client floozy plexor amount umbels enlace infold snatch
wimple alcove cliffy floppy plexus ampere umbrae enlist inform snathe
wincey Aldine climax floral pliant amulet umbral enmesh infula snazzy
winded aldose clinch floras plicae amuser umbras enmity infuse sneaky
winder aldrin clingy floret pliers amylum umlaut ennead ingest sneesh
window alegar clinic florid plight embalm umpire ennuye ingulf sneeze
windup alevin clipon florin plinth embank anabas enosis inhale sneezy
winery alexia clique flossy plisse embark anadem enough inhere sniffy
winged alexin cliquy floury ploidy embays ananas enrage inhume sniper
winger algoid cloaca flower plotty embers anarch enrapt inject snippy
winker alight cloche fluent plough emblem anatta enrich injure snitch
winkle aliped cloddy fluffy plover emblic anatto enrobe injury snivel
winner alkali cloggy flukey plucky embody anchor enroll inkpot snobby
winnow alkane clonal flumes plumed emboli ancone enroot inlaid snoopy
winsey alkene clonic flunky plummy emboly aneled ensate inland snooty
winter alkyne clonus flurry plumpy emboss anenst enseam inlaws snooze
wintle allege closed fluted plunge embrue angary ensign inlier snorer
```

```
snotty unpaid bonito cobnut conned cousin dowlas gobbet hooded Korean
snouty unpick bonnet cobweb conner covert downer gobble hoodie kosher
snubby unplug bonnie coccal conoid coving dowser goblet hoodoo kowhai
snuffy unread bonsai coccid consul cowage doyley goblin hoofed kowtow
snugly unreal bonxie coccus convex coward dozily gocart hoofer loaded
unable unreel bonzer coccyx convey cowboy Eocene goddam hookah loader
unbend unrest booboo cochin convoy cowish eolian godown hooked loafer
unbent unripe boodle cocked cooker cowled eolith godson hooker loaner
unbind unrobe boohoo cocker cookie cowman eonian godwit hookey loathe
unbitt unroll booing cockle cooler cowpat eonism goffer hookup loaves
unbolt unroof booker cocoon coolie cowpea Eozoic goggle hooper lobate
unborn unroot bookie coddle coolly cowpox Eozoon goggly hoopla lobbed
unbred unrope booksy codger coolth cowrie fobbed goglet hoopoe lobose
uncage unruly boomer codify coonty coyote focsle Goidel hooray lobule
uncate unsafe booted codlin cooper doable fodder goitre hootch locale
uncial unsaid bootee coelom cootie dobbin foeman gokart hooter locate
uncini unseal bootie coerce copeck docent foetal golden hooves lochan
unclad unseam bopeep coeval copier docile foetid golfer hopped locker
uncoil unseat bopped coffee coping docker foetus gollop hopper locket
uncool unseen bopper coffer copita docket fogbow golosh hopple lockup
uncork unself borage coffin copout doctor fogdog goober horary loculi
uncurl unship borane coffle copped dodder fogged goodie horned locust
undate unshod borate cogent copper doddle foible goodly horner lodger
undies unshoe bordel cogged Coptic dodgem foiled googly hornet lofter
undine unstop border cogito copula dodger foison googol horrid loggat
undock unsung boreal cognac coquet dodoes foliar googly horror logged
undoer untidy Boreas coheir corban dogate folium gooier horsey logger
undone untied boride cohere corbel dogear foliar gooney hosier loggia
unduly untold boring cohort corbie dogend folksy gooses hostel logion
unease untrue borrow coigne corded dogfox follow gopher hotbed logjam
uneasy untuck borsch coiner corder dogged foment goramy hotdog loiter
uneath untune borzoi coinop cordon dogger gorget gorget hotpot loller
uneven unused bosche coital corium doggie gorgio gorgio hotter lollop
unfair unveil bosket coitus corked dogleg gorgon gorgon houdan loment
unfold unwary bosomy coldly corker dogood gorily goslow hourly lonely
unfurl unwell boston coleus cornea doited fooler gospel housel longan
ungird unwept botany collar corned dolium footed gossan housey loofah
ungirt unwind botchy collet cornel dollar footer gossip howdah looker
unglue unwise botfly collie corner dollop footle Gothic howler lookin
ungual unworn bother collop cornua dolman foozle gotten hoyden looper
ungues unwrap bothie colony corody dolmen forage gourde iodate loosen
unguis unyoke botone colour corozo dolour forbad govern iodide looter
ungula aorist bottle colter corona domain forbid gowany iodine lopped
unhair aortal bottom column corpse domett forbye goyish iodise lopper
unhand aortic boucle colure corpus domino forced gozzan iodism loquat
unholy aoudad bought colugo corral donate forcer hoarse iolite lorcha
unhook boatel bougie comate corrie donjon forego hobbit Ionian lordly
Uniate boater boulle combat corsac donkey forest hobble ionium lorica
unific bobbed bounce combed corset donned forger hobnob joanna loriot
uniped bobbin bounds comber cortex donsie forget hocker jobber lotion
unipod bobble bounty comedo corvee doodad forgot hockey joblot lotted
unique bobcat bourne comedy corves doodah forint hockey jockey louche
unisex boblet bovine comely Corvus doodle formal hodden jocose louden
unison bobwig bovver comeon coryza doolie format hodman jocund loudly
united bocage bowels comfit corymb dopant former hoeing jogged lounge
uniter bodega bowery coming cosher Dopper formic hogged jogger loupen
unjoin bodger bowfin comity cosily dorado fornix hoggin joggle loupit
unjust bodice bowleg commie cosine Dorian forbad hogtie johnny louver
unkind bodily bowler commis cosmic dormer forrad hoicks joiner louvre
unking boding bowman commit cosmos dormie forrit hoised jolter lovage
unkink bodkin bowsaw commix cosset dorsal forsay holden josher lovein
unknit boffin bowtie common costae dorsum fossae holder josser lovely
unknot bogged bowwow comose costal dorter fossil holdup jostle loving
unlace boggle bowyer comous costar dosage fossor holily jotted lowboy
unlade bohunk boxbed compel coster dossal foster holism jotter lowery
unlaid boiler boxcar comply costly dossel fother holler jounce lowing
unlash bolero boxful comsat cottar dosser holloa holloa jouncy lowish
unless bolero boxing concha cotted dotage fought hollow lowkey lowkey
unlike bolide bollix concur conchy dotard foully holpen jovial moaner
unlink bolide boxing confab cotton dottle foulup homage Jovian moated
unload bolshy boyish confer cottar douane fourth hombre joyful mobbed
unlock bolter cooter? concur cotton dourly hombre hombre joyous mobcap
unmade bomber coaita confer coucal double foveae homely kobold mobile
unmake bonbon coarse congee cougar doubly foveal homily koedoe mocker
unmask bonded coated conger coulee douche fowler homing koodoo mockup
unmeet bonder coatee congou county dought goalie hominy kookie modena
unmoor bongos cobalt conics couple doughy goanna honest koolah modern
unnail bonism cobber conker coupon dourly goatee honied kopeck modest
unpack bonist cobble conman course douser gobang honour koppie modify
```

```
modish  nobble  pommel  ronyon  sorrow  towery  ephebe  spruce  aright  bronze
modius  nobbut  pommie  roofer  sorter  towhee  ephebi  spruit  ariled  bronzy
module  nobody  pompom  rookie  sortes  townee  epical  sprung  ariosi  brooch
moduli  nocent  poncho  roomer  sortie  toxoid  epimer  spryer  arioso  broody
modulo  nodded  ponder  rooted  Sothic  voiced  epizoa  spryly  arisen  browny
moggie  noddle  pongee  rooter  sotted  voided  epodic  spunky  arista  browse
mohair  nodose  pontie  ropery  souari  voider  eponym  spurge  armada  bruise
Mohawk  nodule  pontil  roping  sought  volant  epopee  spurry  armful  brumal
Mohock  noesis  ponton  roquet  souled  volley  opaque  sputum  armlet  brumby
mohole  noetic  poodle  rosace  source  volost  opener  upbear  armour  brunch
moider  noggin  pooped  rosary  sourly  volume  openly  upbeat  armpit  brunet
moiety  nomism  poorly  rosery  souter  volute  ophite  upcast  arnica  brushy
moiler  nonage  popery  rosily  soviet  volvox  opiate  update  aroint  brutal
molest  nonary  popgun  rosiny  sovran  voodoo  oppose  upheld  around  brutus
moline  noncom  popish  roster  sowans  vorant  oppugn  uphill  arouse  bryony
mollie  nonego  poplar  rostra  sowens  vortex  optant  uphold  arpent  crabby
Moloch  nonfat  poplin  rosula  tocher  votary  optics  uphroe  arrack  cradle
molten  nonius  popped  rotary  tocsin  voting  optima  upkeep  arrant  crafty
moment  nonuse  popper  rotate  toddle  votive  option  upland  arrest  craggy
Monday  noodle  poppet  rotche  toecap  voulge  spacer  uplift  arrive  crambo
moneys  Nordic  popple  rotgut  toeing  voyage  spadix  upmost  arroba  cranch
monger  normal  popply  rotted  toffee  voyeur  sparer  upping  arrowy  crania
Mongol  Norman  porgie  rotten  togaed  wobble  sparge  uppish  arroyo  cranky
monial  noshup  porism  rotter  togged  wobbly  sparks  uppity  arsine  cranny
monied  nosily  porker  rotund  toggle  woeful  sparry  uprise  artery  crappy
monies  nosing  porose  rouble  toiler  woggle  sparse  uproar  artful  crases
monism  nostoc  porous  roucou  toilet  wolves  spathe  uproot  artist  crasis
monist  notary  portal  rouncy  Toledo  wombat  spavin  uprush  bracer  cratch
monkey  notate  porter  rouser  toluic  womera  specie  upshot  braces  crater
monody  notice  portly  router  toluol  wonder  speech  upside  Brahma  cravat
moocow  notify  posada  roving  tomato  wonted  speedo  uptake  Brahmi  craven
mooing  notion  poseur  rowing  tombac  wonton  speedy  uptown  brains  craver
moolah  nougat  posset  royals  tombak  wooded  speiss  upturn  brainy  crawly
mopish  nought  possum  rozzer  tomboy  wooden  spence  upward  braird  crayon
mopoke  nounal  postal  soaker  tomcat  woodsy  spewer  upwind  braise  crazed
mopped  novena  poster  sobbed  tomcod  woofer  sphene  equate  branch  creaky
mopper  novice  postil  sobeit  tomtit  wooled  sphere  equine  brandy  creamy
moppet  Nowell  potage  socage  tomtom  woolly  sphery  equity  branle  crease
morale  nowise  potale  soccer  toneme  worker  sphinx  squail  brassy  create
morals  noyade  potash  social  tongue  wormer  spider  squall  brawly  creche
morass  nozzle  potato  socket  tonish  worrit  spiffy  squama  brawny  credal
morbid  oocyte  potboy  sodden  tonsil  worsen  spigot  square  brayer  credit
morbus  oodles  poteen  sodium  tooter  worthy  spilth  squash  brazen  creeps
moreen  oogamy  potent  sodomy  toothy  wortle  spinal  squawk  brazil  creepy
morgen  oogeny  potful  soever  tootle  woundy  spined  squeak  breach  creese
morgue  oolite  pother  soffit  tootsy  wowser  spinel  squeal  breast  crenel
morion  oology  potion  soften  Tophet  yogism  spinet  squill  breath  creole
morish  oolong  potman  softie  tophus  yogurt  spiral  squint  breech  cresol
Mormon  oomiak  potpie  softly  topman  yoicks  spirit  squire  breeks  Cretan
mornay  pocked  potted  soigne  topped  yolked  spital  squirm  breese  cretic
morose  pocket  potter  soiree  topper  yonder  splash  squirt  breeze  cretin
morpho  podded  pottle  solace  topple  yoohoo  spleen  squish  breezy  crewel
morris  podite  pouchy  solano  torero  yorker  splent  Arabic  bregma  crikey
morrow  podium  pouffe  soldan  Tories  Yoruba  splice  arable  brehon  crimpy
morsel  podsol  pounce  solder  toroid  zodiac  spline  arbour  Breton  cringe
mortal  podzol  pourer  solely  torose  zombie  splint  arcade  brevet  cripes
mortar  poetic  pouter  solemn  torpid  zonary  splits  Arcady  brewer  crises
morula  poetry  powder  solidi  torpor  zonate  splore  arcana  brewis  crisis
mosaic  pogrom  powwow  solids  torque  zoning  splosh  arcane  briard  crispy
moshav  pointe  roadie  solute  torrid  zonked  spoffy  arched  briary  crista
Moslem  points  roamer  solver  torsel  Zouave  spoilt  archer  briber  critic
mosque  poison  roarer  sombre  torten  zounds  spoken  archil  bricky  croaky
mostly  Polack  robalo  somite  torula  apache  sponge  archly  bridal  crocus
motett  polder  robbed  sonant  tosher  apathy  spongy  archon  bridge  croppy
mother  police  robber  sonata  tosser  apexes  spooky  arctic  bridle  crosse
motile  policy  robust  sonnet  tossup  aphony  spoony  ardent  briefs  crotal
motion  polish  rochet  sonsie  tother  apiary  sports  ardour  briery  crotch
motive  polite  rocker  sooner  totted  apical  sporty  areola  bright  croton
motley  polity  rocket  soothe  totter  apices  spotty  areole  briner  crouch
motmot  pollan  rococo  sophic  toucan  apiece  spouse  argala  briony  croupy
motory  polled  rodent  sopite  touche  aplomb  sprain  argali  Briton  crouse
mottle  pollen  rodman  sopped  touchy  apnoea  sprang  argand  broach  cruces
moujik  poller  roller  sorage  toupee  apodal  sprawl  argent  broche  cruddy
mouldy  pollex  rollon  sorbet  toupet  apogee  spread  Argive  brogue  cruise
moulin  polony  Romaic  sordid  tourer  apozem  sprent  argosy  broken  cruive
mouser  polypi  Romany  sorely  tousle  appeal  spring  arguer  broker  crumby
mousse  pomace  Romish  sorgho  touter  appear  sprint  argufy  brolly  crummy
mouthy  pomade  romper  sorner  towage  append  sprite  argute  bromic  crunch
moving  pomelo  rondel  sorrel  toward  appose  sprout  argyle  bronco  crural
```

```
cruset fridge ground primer trophy Eskimo stadia strain bubbly busman
crusty friend grouse primly tropic espial stager strait buccal bussed
crutch frieze grovel primus troppo esprit stagey strake bucker busted
cruxes fright grower prince trough Essene stairs strand bucket bustee
crying frigid growly priory troupe essive staith strass buckle buster
crypto frijol growth prison trouty essoin stakes strata buckra bustle
drably frilly groyne prissy trover estate stalag strath budded bustup
drachm fringe grubby privet trowel esteem stalky strawy Buddha butane
drafty fringy grudge prizer truant estray stamen strays buddle butene
dragee frisky grugru prober trudge isabel stance streak budget butler
draggy frivol grumly probit truism isatin stanch streek budgie butter
dragon frizzy grumps profit trumps ischia stanza stream buffer button
draper froggy grumpy proleg trusty island stapes street buffet buzzer
drawee frolic grutch prolix trying isobar staple stress bugged cubage
drawer frosty ireful prompt tryout isohel starch strewn bugler cubism
dreamt frothy irenic pronto uracil isomer starer strict buglet cubist
dreamy frowst irides propel uraeus isopod starry stride bulbar cuboid
dreary frowsy iritis proper Uralic oscine starve strife bulbed cuckoo
dredge frowzy ironer propyl Urania oscula stases strike bulbil cuddie
dreggy frozen ironic proser uranic osmium stasis Strine bulbul cuddle
dreich frugal irrupt prosit Uranus osmose statal string Bulgar cuddly
drench fruity kraken protea uranyl osprey stated stripe bulger cudgel
dressy frumpy krantz proton urbane ossein stater stripy bulimy cueing
drifty frusta kronen proven urchin ossify states strive bulker cueist
drippy frutex kroner pruina ureter osteal static strobe bullae cuesta
drivel grabby kronor pruner urgent ostial stator strode buller cuffed
driven graben kronur prying urinal ostium statue stroke bullet cuisse
driver grader orache tracer urnful ostler status stroll bumalo culler
droger gradin oracle traces ursine pseudo stayer stroma bumble cullet
drogue gradus orally tracks wraith psyche steady stromb bumkin cullis
droich grainy orange trader wrasse psycho steamy strong bummed cultch
drolly gramme orator tragic wrathy tsamba steely stroud bummer cultic
drongo Grammy orcein tragus wreath tsetse steeve strout bummle cultus
droopy gramps orchid trance wrench Tshirt stelae strove bumper culver
dropsy grange orchil trapan wretch tsotsi stelar strown bunchy cumber
drosky granny orchis trapes wright Tswana stemma struck bunder cummer
drossy Granth ordain trappy writer usable stench struma bundle cummin
drouth grappa ordeal trashy writhe usance stepin strung bungle cumuli
drover grassy ordure trauma ascend useful steppe strunt bunion cunner
drowse grater orexis travel ascent ustion stepup Stuart bunker cupful
drowsy gratin orfray treaty aseity usurer stereo stubby bunkum cupola
drudge gratis orgasm treble ashbin ataman steric stucco bunnia cupped
drupel graved orgeat trebly ashcan ataxia sterna studio bunsen cupric
drybob gravel orient tremie ashlar ataxic sterol stuffy bunted cuptie
dryfly graven origan tremor ashore athome stewed stumer bunter cupule
dryish graver origin trench ashpan atomic sticky stumpy burble curacy
dryrot Graves oriole trendy ashram atonal stifle stupid burbot curare
dryrun gravid orison trepan askant atonic stigma stupor burbly curari
eraser grazer ormolu trepid askari atrial stilly sturdy burden curate
erbium grease ornate tressy aslant atrium stingo stylar bureau curdle
eremic greasy ornery triage asleep attach stingy stylet burgee curfew
erenow greave orphan tribal aslope attack stinko stylus burger curiae
ergate greedy orphic tricar aspect attain stipel stymie burghs curial
ermine greens orpine tricot aspire attend stipes styrax burgle curium
erotic greeny orrery trifid assail attest stirps uterus burgoo curler
errand greige praise trifle assent attire stitch utmost burhel curlew
errant greyly prance trigon assert attorn stithy utopia burial currie
errata grieve prater trilby assess attune stiver yttria burkha cursed
ersatz grigri pratie trimer assign etcher stoats aubade burlap cursor
eryngo grille praxis trimly assist eterne stocks auburn burler cursus
fracas grilse prayer trinal assize ethane stocky audile Burman curtal
fraena grimly preach triode assoil ethene stodge audios burner curtly
fraise gringo precis triple assort ethics stodgy Augean burnet curtsy
framer griper prefab triply assume Ethiop stogie augend burnup curule
frappe grippe prefer tripod assure ethnic stoker augite burrel curvet
fratch grippy prefix tripos astern ethyne stokes augury burrow cuscus
frater grisly prelim trippy asthma etrier stolen august bursae cushat
Frauen grison premed triste astral etymon stolid auklet bursal cusped
frazil gritty premix triton astray italic stolon aumbry bursar cuspid
freaky grivet prepay triune astute itself stoned auntie bursas cussed
freely groats preses trivet aswoon otiose stoner aurate burton custom
freest grocer preset trivia asylum otitis stooge aurist busbar cutely
freeze groggy presto trocar escape ottava stopgo aurora busboy cutler
french groove pretax troche escarp otters storax aurous bushed cutlet
frenum groovy pretty trogon eschar pterin stores Aussie bushel cutoff
frenzy groper prewar troika eschew ptisan storey Austin busily cutout
fresco grotto pricey Trojan escort ptosis stormy author busing cutter
friary grotty priest trolly escrow stable stover autism busker cuttle
Friday grouch primal trompe escudo stacte strafe autumn buskin dually
```

```
dubbed guggle Julian muscat puffin quiche suffix turkey swipes byelaw
dubbin guider jumbal muscle pugdog quince Sufism Turkic swirly byform
ducker guidon jumble museum puisne quinoa sugary turner swishy bygone
dudeen guilty jumbly musing puller quinol suitor turnip switch bylane
dudish guinea jumper muskeg pullet quinsy sulcus turnup swivel byline
duello guiser jungle musket pulley quinta sullen turret swoosh byname
duende guitar jungly muskox pullin quirky sultan turtle swound bypass
duenna gulden junior Muslim pullon quitch sultry turves twangy bypast
duffel Gullah junker muslin pullup quiver sumach Tuscan tweeds bypath
duffer gullet junket mussel pulper quoits summae tusked tweedy byplay
duffle gulley junkie muster pulpit quorum summed tusker tweeny byroad
dugong gummed jurist mutant pulque quotes summer tussah twelve byssus
dugout gundog justly mutate pulsar quotha summit tusser twenty byword
duiker gunman Jutish mutine pulser rubato summon tussle twicer bywork
dukery gunned jutted mutiny pulvil rubbed sunbow tutsan twiggy cyanic
dulcet gunnel kultur mutism pumice rubber sundae tutted twilit cyanin
dumbly gunner kumiss mutter pummel rubble Sunday tuxedo twiner cycler
dumdum gunsel kummel mutton pumper rubefy sunder tuyere twinge cyclic
dumose gunshy kurgan mutual punchy rubify sundew vulcan twirly cygnet
dumper gunter lubber mutule puncta rubric sundog vulgar twisty cymbal
dunite gunyah lubric mutuum pundit ruched sundry vulgus twitch cymose
Dunker gurgle lucent muumuu punily ruckle sungod yumyum twoply Cymric
dunlin gurjun lucern muzhik punish ruckus sunhat zufolo twould cypher
dunned Gurkha luetic muzzle punkah rudder sunken avatar twoway cyprid
dupery gurnet lugged nubble punned ruddle sunlit avaunt twyere cystic
duplet gurrah lugger nubile punner rudely sunned avenge axilla cystid
duplex gusher luggie nuchal punnet rudish sunray avenue examen dyadic
durbar gusset lumbar nuclei puntee rueful sunset averse exarch dybbuk
duress guttae lumber nudely punter ruelle suntan Avesta exceed dyeing
durgan gutted lumina nudism pupate ruffed superb aviary except dynamo
Durham gutter lummox nudist pupped ruffle supine aviate excess dynast
durian guvnor lumpen nudity puppet rufous supped avidly excide eyalet
during guzzle lumper nugget purdah rugged supper avocet excise eyecup
durned hubbub lunacy number purfle rugger supple avouch excite eyeful
durrie hubcap lunate numbly purger rugose supply avowal excuse eyeing
duster hubris lunger numina purify ruiner surely avowed exedra eyelet
dustup huckle lunula nuncio purine ruling surety avower exempt eyelid
duyker huddle lunule nuncle purism rumble surfer avulse exequy Eyetie
euchre hugely lupine nurser purist rumbly surrey evader exeunt fylfot
eulogy hugged lurdan nutant purity rumina surtax evener exhale gypped
eunuch humane lurker nutate purler rummer survey evenly exhort gypsum
eureka humble lushly nutmeg purlin rumour suslik evilly exhume gyrate
eutaxy humbly lustra nutria purple rumple sutile evince exilic hyaena
fucoid humbug lustre nutter purply rumpus sutler evolue exodus hybrid
fuddle humect luteal nuzzle purser rundle suttee evolve exogen hybris
fugato humeri lutein ouster pursue runlet suture evzone exomis hydric
fugged humify luting outact purvey runnel Tuareg overdo exotic hymnal
fuhrer hummed luxate outage pusher runner tubber overly expand hymnic
fulcra hummel luxury outbid Pushtu runoff tubful ovisac expect hyphae
fulfil hummum mucker outbye pushup runrig tubing ovular expend hyphal
fulgid humour muckle outcry putlog runway tubule svelte expert hyphen
fulham humped mucoid outdid putoff rupiah tuchun uvulae expire hyssop
fullam hunger mucosa outfit putrid rusher tucker uvular expiry lyceum
fuller hunker mucous outfox putsch rushes tucket awaked export lychee
fulmar hunter muddle outgun puttee russet tuckin awaken expose Lydian
fumble hurdle muesli outing putter russia tuffet aweary exsect lyrate
fundus hurler muffin outlaw puttie rustic tufted aweigh exsert lyrics
fungal hurrah muffle outlay puzzle rustle tufter awheel extant lyrism
fungus hurray muflon outlet quaere rutile tugged awhile extend lyrist
funkia hurter mugged output quagga rutted tulwar awmous extent lysine
funned hurtle mugger outran quaggy suable tumble awning extern myelin
funnel husker mukluk outrun quahog subbed tumefy awoken extort mygale
furfur hussar mulish outsat quaich subdue tumour owlish extasy myopia
furore hustle mullah outset quaigh sublet tumtum swaddy oxalic myopic
furred hutted muller outsit quaint subman tumuli swampy oxalis myosin
furrow huzoor mullet outtop Quaker submit tumult swanky oxbird myosis
fusain Judaic mulley outvie qualmy suborn tundra swaraj oxford myotic
fusile judder multum outwit quanta subset tuning swarth oxgall myriad
fusion Judean mumble public quarry subtil tunnel swatch oxgang myrica
fusser judger mummer pucker quarte subtle tupelo swathe oxgate myrtle
fustic judoka mumper puddle quarto subtly turban swayer oxherd myself
futile jugate mundic puddly quartz suburb turbid sweaty oxhide mystic
future jugful Munich pueblo quasar sucker turbit sweeny oxland mythic
guaiac jugged muntin puffed quaver suckle turbot sweets oxtail mythos
guanin juggle murder puffer queasy sudary turgid swerve oxygen myxoma
guddle jujube murine        queazy sudden turgor sweven oxymel nympho
Guelph        murmur        quench        turion swimmy ayeaye oyster
guenon        murphy        queuer               swinge byblow pycnic
guffaw        murrey                              swiper byebye pyedog
```

```
pyknic beachy crania fratch leanly prance shalom statue albite gabled
pylori beacon cranky frater leanto prater shaman status ambler gablet
pyrene beadle cranny Frauen leaper pratie shammy stayer ambush gibber
pyrite beagle crappy frazil learnt praxis shamus suable arbour gibbet
pyrola beaked crases gharry leaved prayer shandy swaddy aubade gibbon
pyrope beaker crasis giaour leaven quaere shanny swampy auburn gobang
python beamer cratch glacis leaver quagga shanty swanky babble gobbet
sylvan beanie crater gladly leaves quaggy shaped swaraj babbly gobble
symbol bearer cravat glairy liable quahog shapen swarth Babism goblet
syndic beaten craven glaive liaise quaich shaper swatch Babist goblin
syntax beater craver glance loaded quaigh sharer swathe baboon habile
syphon Beaune crawly glassy loader quaint sharif swayer bibbed Hebrew
Syriac beauty crayon glazer loafer Quaker sharps teabag bibber hobbit
Syrian beaver crazed gnarly loaner qualmy shaven teacup bobbed hobble
syrinx bharal cyanic gnawer loathe quanta shaver teapot bobbin hobnob
syrupy bladed cyanin goalie loaves quarry shavie teapoy bobble hubbub
system blanch deacon goanna meadow quarte sialic teasel bobcat hubcap
syzygy blanky deaden goatee meagre quarto skater teaser boblet hubris
tycoon blazer deadly grabby mealie quartz slacks teaset bobwig hybrid
tymbal blazes deafen graben meanie quasar slaggy teazel bubble hybris
tympan blazon deafly grader meanly quaver slalom teazle bubbly imbibe
typhus boatel dealer gradin measly reader slangy thaler byblow imbrex
typify boater dearie gradus meatus really slapup thalli cabala imbrue
typing bracer dearly grainy miasma realty slater thanks cabana inborn
typist braces dearth gramme moaner reamer slaver thatch cabman inbred
tyrant Brahma deasil Grammy moated reaper slavey tracer cobalt jabbed
Tyrian Brahmi dharma gramps neaped rearer Slavic traces cobber jabber
wyvern brains diacid grange nearby reason slayer tracks cobble jabiru
xylene brainy diadem granny nearer reaver smalls trader cobnut jibbah
xyloid braird diaper Granth nearly rhaphe smalto tragic cobweb jibbed
xylose braise diatom grappa neaten roadie smarmy tragus cubage jibber
xystus branch doable grassy neatly roamer smarty trance cubism jobber
zygoma brandy drably grater niacin roarer smatch trapan cubist joblot
zygote branle drachm gratin nuance scabby snaggy trapes cuboid kabala
zymase brassy drafty gratis ogamic scalar snappy trappy dabbed kabuki
zythum brawly dragee graved omasum scaled snarer trashy dabber Kabyle
azalea brawny draggy gravel onager scaler snarly trauma dabble kibble
azonal brayer dragon graven opaque scales snatch travel debark kibitz
azotic brazen draper graver orache scampi snathe tsamba debase kibosh
izzard brazil drawee Graves oracle scanty snazzy Tuareg debate kobold
ozonic chacha drawer gravid orally scarab soaker twangy debris labial
────── chacma dually grazer orange scarce spacer unable debtor labile
abacus chafer dyadic guaiac orator scarer spadix uracil debunk labium
abater chaffy ecarte guanin ovally scarry sparer uraeus dibbed labour
abatis chaise elapse headed oxalic scarus sparge Uralic dibber labret
acacia chalet elated header oxalis scathe sparks Urania dibble labrum
acajou chalky elater headon peachy scatty sparry uranic dobbin libber
acarid chance enable healer peahen scazon sparse Uranus dubbed libido
acarus chancy enamel health peaked seaair spathe uranyl dubbin Libyan
adagio change eraser hearer peanut seabed spavin usable dybbuk lobate
Adamic chanty evader hearse pearly seabee stable usance embalm lobbed
agamic chapel examen hearth peavey seacow stably viable embank lobber
agamid chappy exarch hearty phalli seadog stacte viands embark lobose
agaric charas eyalet heated pharos seaear stadia viator embers lobule
alalia charge fealty heater phasic seafan stager weaken emblem lubber
alarum Charon featly heathy phasis seafog stagey weakly emblic lubric
alated chaser fiacre heaven phatic seafox stairs wealth embody mobbed
amadou chaste fiance heaver piaffe sealer staith weaner emboli mobcap
amatol chatty fiasco hiatus piazza seaman stakes weapon embosk mobile
amazon chaunt flabby hoarse placed seamat stalag wearer emboss nabbed
anabas claggy flacon hoaxer placer seamer stalky weasel embrue nebula
anadem clammy flaggy hyaena placet seamew stamen weaver embryo nebuly
ananas claque flagon inarch placid seance stance weazen erbium nibbed
anarch claret flambe isabel plagal seapen stanch whacky Fabian nibble
anatta classy flamen isatin plague seapig stanza whaler fabled nobble
anatto clause flanch italic plaguy search stapes whatso fabler nobbut
apache claver flange joanna plaice season staple wraith fabric nobody
apathy clavis flappy kiaugh plaint seater starch wrasse fibbed nubble
Arabic clayey flashy knaggy planar seaway starer wrathy fibber nubbly
arable coaita flatly kraken planer shabby starry yearly fibred nubile
ataman coarse flatus krantz planet shader starve yeasty fibril oxbird
ataxia coated flaunt laager plaque shades stases zealot fibrin pebble
ataxic coatee flavin leaden plashy shadow stasis abbacy fibula pebbly
avatar crabby flaxen leader plasma shaduf statal abbess fobbed public
avaunt cradle fracas leadin platan shaggy stated albata gabbed rabato
awaked crafty fraena leadup platen shaken stater albedo gabber rabbet
awaken craggy fraise leafed plater shaker states albeit gabble rabbin
azalea crambo framer league player Shakta static albert gabbro rabbit
Baalim cranch frappe lealty praise Shakti stator albino gabion rabble
```

rabies access docket lecher racoon uncoil dudeen lodger radian adenyl
rebate accord doctor lector recall uncool dudish Lydian radish afeard
rebato accost ducker lichee recant uncork Eddaic Madame radium ageing
rebeck accrue encage lichen recast uncurl eidola madcap radius agency
rebore accuse encamp lictor recede upcast eldest madden radome agenda
reborn alcaic encase locale recent urchin endear madder radula ageold
rebuff alcove encash locate recess vacant ending madman redact alegar
rebuke anchor encode lochan recipe vacate endive madras redbud alevin
ribald arcade encore locker recite vacuum endure maduro redcap alexia
riband Arcady encyst locket reckon vector fadein meddle redden alexin
ribbed arcana Eocene lockup recoil victim fedora mediae redder amends
ribbon arcane escape loculi recoin victor fiddle medial reddle amenta
ribose arched escarp locust record vicuna fiddly median redeem amerce
robalo archer eschar lucent recoup wicked fidget medick redeye apexes
robbed archil eschew lucern rector wicker fodder medico redhot areola
robber archly escort lyceum rectum wicket fuddle medium rediae areole
robust archon escrow lychee rectus abduce gadded medius redone aseity
rubato arctic escudo macaco richen abduct gadder medlar redraw avenge
rubbed ascend etcher machan riches addend gadfly medley redtop avenue
rubber ascent euchre mackle richly addict gadget medusa reduce averse
rubble backer exceed macron ricker addled Gadhel midage ridded Avesta
rubbly backup except macula rickey adduce gadoid midair ridden aweary
rubefy becall excess macule ricrac adduct giddap midday riddle aweigh
rubify becalm excide mickey rictal aedile gidday midden rident ayeaye
rubric became excise mickle rictus Aldine goddam middle ridged beeper
sabbat becket excite micron rochet aldose godown midget riding beetle
Sabian beckon excuse mocker rocker aldrin godson midgut rodent beeves
Sabine become facade mockup rocket ardent godwit midoff rodman bieldy
sables biceps facete mucker rococo ardour guddle midrib rudder bleach
sobbed bicker facial muckle ruched audile haddie midway ruddle bleary
sobeit bocage facies mucoid ruckle baddie hadron modena rudely blench
subbed buccal facile mucosa ruckus badger heddle modern rudish blende
subdue bucker facing mucous sachem bedaub hedera modest sadden blenny
sublet bucket factor nectar sachet bedaze hedger modify sadder breach
subman buckle factum nicely sacque bedbug hidden modish saddhu breast
submit buckra facula nicety sacral bedded hiding modius saddle breath
suborn cachet fecula nicish sacred bedder hodden module sadism breech
subset cachou feckly nickel sacrum bedeck hodman moduli sadist breeks
subtil cackle fecund nicker secant bedell huddle modulo sedate breese
subtle cacoon fickle nocent secede bedlam hydric muddle sedile breeze
subtly cactus focsle nuchal secern bedpan indaba nidget seduce breezy
suburb cecity fucoid nuclei second bedsit indeed nidify siding bregma
subway cicada geckos occamy secret beduin indene nodded sodden brehon
tabard cicala gocart occult sector bidden indent nodder sodium Breton
tabbed cicely hackle occupy secund bidder indict noddle sodomy brevet
tablet coccal hackly oecist secure bodega indign nodose sudary brewer
tabour coccid heckle oncost sicken bodger indigo nodule sudden brewis
tibiae coccus hectic oocyte sicker bodice indite nudely tedded byebye
tibial coccyx hector orcein sickle bodily indium nudism tedder byelaw
tubber cochin hiccup orchid sickly boding indole nudist tedium caecal
tubful cocked hickey orchil socage bodkin indoor nudity tidbit caecum
tubing cocker hocker orchis soccer budded induce oddity tiddly cheder
tubule cockle hockey oscine social budget induct oddjob tidily cheeky
umbles cocoon huckle oscula socket budgie indult oddson toddle cheers
umbrae cuckoo incase pacify sucker buddle induna oedema todies cheery
umbral cycler incept packer suckle Buddha iodate oldish undate cheese
umbras cyclic incest packet tacker caddie iodide oodles undies cheesy
unbend dacoit inches pecker tackle caddis iodine ordain undine chelae
unbent dactyl incise pecten tacket cadent iodise ordeal undock chemic
unbind decade incite pectic tactic cadger iodism ordure undoer cheque
unbitt decani inclip pectin ticked coddle Judaic padauk undone cherry
unbolt decamp income picker ticker codger Judean padded unduly cherty
unborn decant incubi picket ticket codify judger paddle update cherub
unbred deceit incult pickle tickey codlin judoka pedalo Vedist chesil
upbear decent incuse pickup tickle cuddie kidded pedant vidual chesty
upbeat decide ischia picnic tickly cuddle kidder pedate wadded chevet
urbane decker jacana picric tictac cuddly kiddie peddle waddie cleave
vibist deckle jackal pocked tocher cudgel kidnap pedlar waders clench
vibrio decoct jacket pocket tocsin dedans kidney piddle wadmal clergy
wabain decode jockey pucker tuchun deduce kidvid pidgin wadmol cleric
wabble decoke jocose pycnic tucker deduct ladder podded widdie clever
webbed decree jocund raceme tucket diddle laddie podite widely clevis
wobble dicast kicker rachis tuckin diddly ladify podium widget coelom
wobbly dicker laceup racial tycoon didoes lading podsol widish coeval
yabber dickey lacing racily uncage doddle ladino podzol zodiac creaky
zebeck dictum lacked racism uncate dodder ladyfy puddle acedia creamy
accede docent lackey racist uncial dodgem ledged puddly acetal crease
accent docile lactic racker uncini dodger ledger raddle acetic create
accept docker lacuna racket unclad dodoes lidded radial acetyl creche

```
credal fleshy olefin sheave theism buffer puffer begged goggle mugger
credit fletch omelet sheeny theist buffet puffin begird goggly mygale
creeps fleury omenta sheets thenar byform raffia begirt goglet nagana
creepy flexor oneoff sheikh thence cafard raffle begone guggle nagged
creese foeman oneway sheila theory Caffre rafter bigamy hagbut nagger
crenel foetal opener shekel theses caftan reface bigger haggis negate
creole foetid openly shelly thesis coffee refect biggin haggle nigger
cresol foetus orexis Shelta thetic coffer refill bigwig hegira niggle
Cretan freaky overdo shelty tiebar coffin refine bogged higgle nighty
cretic freely overly shelve tiedye coffle reflex boggle higher nignog
cretin freest paella sheoak tiepin cuffed reflow bugler highly noggin
crewel freeze paeony sherif tierce daftly reflux buglet hogged nugget
cueing french peeler Sherpa tiered deface reform bygone hogget oogamy
cueist frenum peeper sherry tierod defame refuel cagily hoggin oogeny
cuesta frenzy peepul sheugh tiewig defeat refuge cigala hogtie orgasm
daedal fresco peewit sienna tmeses defect refund cigala hugely orgeat
daemon Gaelic phenol sierra tmesis defend refuse cogent hugged oxgall
deejay geegee phenyl siesta toecap defier refute cogito ingest oxgang
deepen geezer piecer skeely toeing defile rifely cogito ingulf oxgate
deeply ghetto piedog skeigh treaty define riffle cognac jagged pagoda
diesel gleamy pieman skerry treble deform rifler cygnet jagger pegged
dieses gleety pierce sketch trebly defray ruffed dagger jaguar pegleg
diesis gneiss pleach sleave tremie deftly ruffle dagoes jigged pegtop
dieter grease pledge sledge tremor defuse rufous degras jigger pigeon
dreamt greasy plenty sleepy trench differ safari degree jiggle pigged
dreamy greave plenum sleety trendy duffel safely degust jiggly piggin
dreary greedy pleura sleeve trepan duffer safety digamy jigsaw piglet
dredge greens plexor sleigh trepid duffle sifter digest jogged pignut
dreggy greeny plexus sleuth tressy efface soffit digger joggle pigsty
dreich greige pneuma smeary tsetse effect soften diglot jogger pogrom
drench greyly poetic smeech tweeds effigy softie dogate jugate pugdog
dressy Guelph poetry smelly tweedy efflux softly dogear jugful ragbag
duello guenon precis sneeze tweeny effort suffer dogend jugged ragged
duende haemal prefab sneezy twelve effuse suffix dogfox juggle raggee
duenna haemin prefer soever twenty elfish Sufism dogged lagged raggle
dyeing heehaw prefix specie unease enface tiffin dogger lagger raglan
Edenic heeled prelim speedo uneasy enfold toffee doggie lagoon ragman
Egeria heeler premed speedy uneath gaffer tuffet dogleg laguna ragout
ejecta hieing premix spence uneven gifted tufted dogood legacy ragtag
eleven hoeing prepay spewer ureter goffer tufter dugong legate raguly
elevon ibexes preses speiss uterus guffaw unfair dugout legato regain
emerge iceaxe preset steady vielle haffet unfold edgily legbye regale
emeses icebag presto steamy viewer haffit unfurl edging legend regard
emesis icebox pretax steely weeded wafery waffle eggcup legged regent
emetic icecap pretty steeve weeper infamy wafter eggler legion reggae
emetin iceman prewar stelae weepie infant wifely eggnog legist regime
emeute ideaed pseudo stelar weever infare yaffle eighth legman regina
energy ideate pterin stemma weevil infect zaffer eighty legume region
eremic ireful pueblo stench wheeze infelt zaffre engage ligate regius
erenow irenic pyedog stepin wheezy infest zufolo engild ligger reglet
eterne jaeger queasy steppe whenas infirm Aegean engine lights regnal
evener jeerer queazy stereo whence inflow Afghan engird lignin regret
evenly keenly quench steric wherry influx algoid engirt ligula regulo
exedra keeper queuer sterna wheyey infold angary englut ligule rigged
exempt kiekie reebok sterol wieldy inform angina engram ligure rigger
exequy klepht reecho stewed wiener infula angled engulf loggat righto
exeunt koedoe reedit svelte woeful infuse angler ergate logged rigour
eyecup leeway reefer sweaty wreath Kaffir angora fagend logger rigout
eyeful lieder reeler sweeny wrench kaftan argala faggot loggia rugged
eyeing lierne rhebok sweets wrest  lifter argali figged logion rugger
eyelet luetic rhesus swerve affair liftup argand fogbow logjam rugose
eyelid meekly rhetor sweven affect lofter argent fogdog lugged saggar
Eyetie meetly rueful taenia affeer miffed Argive fogged lugger sagely
faerie muesli ruelle teemer affine muffin argosy fugato luggie sagged
feeble myelin saeter teensy affirm muffle arguer fugged maggot sagger
feebly naevus scenic teepee afflux muflon argufy gagged Magian sigher
feeder needle seeder teeter afford oafish argute gagger magilp siglum
feeing neednt seeing teethe affray offend Augean gaggle magnet signal
feeler nielli seeker thecae baffle offent augite gagman magnum signer
fierce niello seemly thecal befall office augury gigged magpie signet
fiesta noesis seesaw theine befell offing august giggle maguey signor
fleche noetic seethe theirs befool offish Argive giggly Magyar sugary
fledge obeche shears wreath befoul offkey argute giglet megilp tagend
fleece obelus sheass wrench biffin offset augite gigman megohm tagged
fleech obeyer sheath thecae biform onfall augury mignon megrim tagrag
fleecy ocelli theine thecal boffin orfray august moggie mignon tegmen
flench ocelot sheass theine biform oxford orfray gigman moggie tegula
flense oleate sheath theirs boffin puffed beggar gigolo mugged togaed
```

```
togged inhere bailie drippy haired raisin stipes whidah taking calces
toggle inhume bailor drivel heifer reiver stirps whiles unkind calcic
tugged johnny baiter driven height rhinal stitch whilom unking calico
ungird mahout beigel driver hoicks ruiner stithy whilst unkink caliph
ungirt mihrab bhisti duiker hoised saidst stiver whimsy unknit calker
unglue mohair blight edible ibices sailed suitor whiner unknot calkin
ungual Mohawk blimey editor ibidem sailer swimmy whinge upkeep caller
ungues Mohock blintz elicit icicle sailor swinge whinny Viking callet
unguis mohole blithe elixir idiocy saithe swiper whippy ablate callow
ungula ochone boiler enigma irides scilla swipes whirly ablaut callup
urgent ophite briard enisle iritis seiche swirly whisht ablaze callus
vagary oxherd briary epical jailer seiner swishy whisky abloom calmly
vagile oxhide briber epimer jailor seisin switch whited ablush calory
vagrom rehash bricky epizoa joiner seizer swivel whiten aflame calpac
vegete rehear bridal evilly kainit seizin tailor whites afloat calque
vigour reheat bridge evince kaiser shield taipan whitey allege calves
wagged reheel bridle exilic knight shiest thieve wright allele calxes
waggle schema briefs failed knives shifty things writer allied celery
waggly scheme briery faille laical Shiite thingy writhe allium celiac
waggon schism bright fainly loiter shikar thinly yoicks allout cellar
wigeon schist briner fairly maidan shiksa thirst abject allred celled
wigged schizo briony feirie maiden shimmy thirty abjure allude Celtic
wiggle schlep Briton feisty maigre shindy toiler adjoin allure cilice
wiggly school caiman flight mailed shiner toilet adjure anlace cilium
wigwag schorl caique flimsy mainly shinny triage adjust anlage coldly
wigwam schuss chiasm flinch meinie Shinto tribal bijoux aplomb coleus
woggle sphene chiaus flinty moider shinty tricar cajole aslant collar
yogism sphere chichi flirty moiety shirty tricky deject asleep collet
yogurt sphery chicle flitch moiler shiver tricot enjoin aslope collie
zigzag sphinx chield foible nailer skibob trifid hejira balata collop
zygoma tahini chigoe foiled obital skiddy trifle hijack balboa colony
zygote tahsil chilli foison odious skiing trigon inject baldly colour
achene Tshirt chilly friary ogival skilly trilby injure baleen colter
adhere unhair chimer Friday oliver skimpy trimer injury balker colugo
aghast unhand chintz fridge opiate skinny trimly jejune ballad column
aphony unholy chippy friend orient skirun trinal jujube ballet colure
ashbin unhook chirpy frieze origan skiver triode Majlis ballon culler
ashcan upheld chisel fright origin skivvy triple object ballot cullet
ashlar uphill chital frigid oriole slicer triply objure balsam cullis
ashore uphold chitin frijol orison slider tripod pajama Baltic cultch
ashpan uphroe chiton frilly otiose slight tripos Rajput belaud cultic
ashram vihara chitty fringe otitis slimly triste reject beldam cultus
athome Wahabi chives fringy ovisac slinky triton rejoin belfry culver
awheel wahine chivvy frisky paidup slipon triune sejant Belgic delate
awhile Yahveh cliche frivol pliant slippy trivet unjoin belief delete
behalf Yahweh client frizzy plicae slipup trivia unjust belike delict
behave acidic cliffy gaiety pliers sliver tuille ackack belive delude
behead acidly climax gainer plight smilax twicer aikido bellow deluge
beheld acinar clinch gainly plinth smiler twiggy alkali belong deluxe
behest acinus clingy gainst plisse smirch twilit alkane belted delver
behind adieus clinic gaited pointe smirky twiner alkene beluga dilate
behold adieux clipon gaiter points smiter twinge alkyne bilbos dilute
behoof adipic clique geisha poison smithy twirly anklet bilker dolium
behove afield cliquy glibly pricey sniffy twisty askant billet dollar
Bihari ahimsa coigne glider priest sniper twitch askari billon dollop
bohunk akimbo coiner glitch primal snitch ubiety auklet billow dolman
cahier alight coinop Goidel primer snivel Uniate bakery billyo dolmen
cahoot aliped coital goitre primly soigne unific bikini boldly dolour
coheir amidst coitus grieve primus soiree uniped dikdik bolero dulcet
cohere anicut crikey grigri prince soiree unipod diktat bolide eclair
cohort animal crimpy grille priory spider unique dukery bollix enlace
dahlia animus cringe grilse prison spiffy unisex Eskimo bolshy enlist
dehorn apiary cripes grimly prissy spigot unison fakery bolter eolian
echoer apical crises gringo privet spilth united gokart bulbar eolith
echoic apices crisis griper prizer spinal uniter inkpot bulbed eulogy
enhalo apiece crispy grippe ptisan spined urinal kakapo bulbil falcon
ephebe aright crista grippy puisne spinel vainly likely bulbul fallal
ephebi ariled critic grisly quiche spinet Vaisya liking Bulgar fallen
ethane ariosi cuisse grison quince spiral veiled makedo bulger fallow
ethene arioso daimen gritty quinoa spirit veined makeup bulimy falsie
ethics arisen daimio grivet quinol spital voiced making bulker falter
Ethiop arista daimon guider quinsy sticky voided mikado bullae feline
ethnic aviary dainty guidon quinta stifle voider mukluk buller fellah
ethyne aviate deicer guilty quirky stigma wailer nekton bullet feller
exhale avidly deific guinea quitch stilly waiter pakeha bylane felloe
exhort axilla djibba guiser quiver stingo waiver pyknic byline fellow
exhume bailee djinni guitar raider stingy weight rakish calami felony
fuhrer bailer doited hailer railer stinko weirdo takahe calash filfot
inhale bailey drifty hairdo raiser stipel weirdy takein calcar filial
```

```
filing jilter pallet salary tulwar almond dimmed immesh pompom tamara
filler jolter pallia Salian uglify almost dimmer immune pumice tamely
fillet Julian pallid salify uglily armada dimple immure pummel taming
fillip kalong pallor salina ullage armful dimply inmate pumper tampan
filmic kelpie palmar saline umlaut armlet dimwit inmost ramate tamper
filose kelson palmer saliva unlace armour domain jammed ramble tampon
filter kelter palolo sallee unlade armpit domett jammer ramify tamtam
filthy Keltic palpal sallet unlaid aumbry domino jumbal ramjet temper
folder kelvin palpus sallow unlash awmous dumbly jumble rammed temple
foliar killer palter salmon unless bamboo dumdum jumbly rammer timbal
folium kilted paltry saloon unlike bemire dumose jumper ramose timber
folksy kilter pelage saloop unlink bemoan dumper ramous timbre
follow kultur pelham salter unload bemock enmesh kumiss ramper timely
fulcra lallan pellet saltus unlock bemuse enmity kummel ramrod timing
fulfil lilied pelmet saluki upland bomber ermine lambda ramson timous
fulgid loller pelota salute uplift bumalo family lamber remade tomato
fulham lollop peltae salver valeta bumble famine lamely remain tombac
fullam malady pelter salvia valgus bumkin famish lament remake tombak
fuller Malaga peltry salvor valine bummed famous lamina remand tomboy
fulmar malate pelves salvos valise bummer famuli lamish remark tomcat
fylfot maleic pelvic sclaff valley bummle female Lammas remedy tomcod
galago malice pelvis sclera vallum bumper femora lammed remind tomtit
galaxy malign phlegm seldom valour camass fimble lemony remint tomtom
galena malism phloem select valuer camber foment limbec remise tumble
galiot malist pilaff Seljuk valuta camera fumble limbed remiss tumefy
galley mallee pileum seller valved camion gambir limber remora tumour
Gallic mallei pileup selves veleta camise gambit limbic remote tumtum
Gallio mallet pileus silage vellum camlet gamble limbus remove tumuli
gallon mallow pilfer sileni veloce camper gambol liming remuda tumult
gallop maltha pillar silent velour campus gamely limner rimmed tymbal
galoot melton pillow silica velure cement gamete limper rimose tympan
galore melody pilose silken velvet comate gamily limpet rimous unmade
galosh melton pilous siller vilely combat gamine limpid Romaic unmake
gelled milady pilule silvan vilify combed gaming limply Romany unmask
gilder milage Polack silver villus comber gammer limuli Romish unmeet
gilled mildew polder solace volant comedo gammon loment romper unmoor
gillie mildly police solano volley comedy Gemara lumbar rumble upmost
golden milieu policy solder volost comely Gemini lumber rumbly utmost
golfer milker polish soldan volume comeon gemmae lumina rumina vamper
gollop milled polite solely volute comfit gemmed lummox rummer wamble
golosh miller polity solemn volvox coming gimbal lumpen rumour wambly
gulden milord pollan solidi vulcan comity gimlet lumper rumple wampee
Gullah milord polled solids vulgar commie gimmal mammae rumpus wampum
gullet milter pollen solute vulgus commis gimmer mammal samara wimble
gulley molest poller solver walker commit gummed mammee sambar wimple
haleru moline pollex splash walkin commix hamate mammer sambur wombat
halide mollie polony spleen walkon common Hamite mammon Samian womera
halite Moloch polypi splent wallah comose hamlet member samite yammer
hallal molten puller splice walled comous hammal memoir samlet yumyum
halloa mulish pullet spline waller compel hammam memory Samoan zombie
halloo mullah pulley splint wallet comply hammed mimosa sampan zymase
hallow muller pullin splits wallop comsat hammer moment sample adnate
hallux mullet pullon splore wallow cumber hamper mumble Samson adnexa
haloes mulley pullup splosh walnut cummer hemmed mummer semble agnail
halter multum pulper sulcus walrus cummin hempen mumper Semite agnate
halvah nelson pulpit sullen welder cumuli homage namely semmit agnise
halves nilgai pulque sultan weldor cymbal hombre nimble semple amnion
helium nullah pulsar sultry welkin cymose homely nimbly sempre annals
heller oblast pulser sylvan welter Cymric homily nimbus simian anneal
helmet oblate pulvil talbot wilder damage homing Nimrod simile annexe
helper oblige pylori talcky wildly damask hominy nomism simmer annual
holden oblong relaid talcum wilful dammar humane number simnel annuli
holder oclock relate talent willed dammed humble numbly simony apnoea
holdup oilcan relent talion willed dampen humbly numina simoom arnica
holily oilman relict talker willet dampen humbug nympho simoon auntie
holism oilnut relief talkie willow damper humect ohmage simper awning
holler online reline tallow Wilton damply humeri oomiak simple banana
holloa oolite relish Talmud wolves damsel humify ormolu simply bandit
hollow oology relive teledu xylene damson hummed osmium simurg bandog
holpen oolong reload telega xyloid demand hummel osmose sombre banger
illume owlish reluct teller xylose demark hummer pampas somite bangle
illuse oxland relume telson yclept demean hummum pamper sumach bangup
inlaid palace rillet Telugu yellow dement humour pimple summae banian
inland palais roller tiling yelper demise humped pimply summed banish
inlaws palate rollon tiller yolked demist hymnal pomace summer banjax
inlier paleae ruling tilter zeloso demode hymnic pomade summit banjos
iolite palely salaam Toledo zillah demote iambic pomelo summon banker
island paling salade toluic admass demure iambus pommel symbol banket
jalopy palish salami toluol admire dimity immane pommie tamale banned
```

```
banner concur finely innate manner pennon senate tinful zincic brolly
bantam condor finery inning manque pentad sendal tingle zincky bromic
banter confab finger Ionian mantel pentup sender tingly zingel bronco
banyan confer finial ionise mantes pentyl sendup tinily zinked bronze
banzai congee fining ionium mantic penult senega tinker zinnia bronzy
bender conger finish jangle mantid penury senhor tinkle zonary brooch
benign congou finite jennet mantis pincer senile tinkly zonate broody
bennet conics finnan jingle mantle pineal senior tinman zoning browny
benumb conker finned jingly mantra pinery sennet tinned zonked browse
benzol conman finner jinnee mantua pineta sennit tinner aboard choice
benzyl conned Finnic jungle manual pinger senora tinpot aboral choker
binary conner fondle jungly manuka pinion senses tinsel abound chokey
binate conoid fondly junior manure pinkie sensor tinter Adonic choler
binder consul fondue junker menace pinnae sensum toneme Adonis choose
binful convex fontal junket menage pinned sentry tongue adorer choosy
bonbon convey fundus junkie mender pinner sinewy tonish Aeolic chopin
bonded convoy fungal kanaka menhir pinole sinful tonsil agonal choppy
bonder cunner fungus kenned menial pintle singer tundra agonic choral
bongos dancer funkia kennel meninx poncho single tuning agouti chorea
bonism dander funned kincob mensal ponder singly tunnel amoeba choric
bonist dandle funnel kindle menses pongee sinker unnail amoral chorus
bonito danger gander kindly mental pontie sinned urnful amount chosen
bonnet dangle ganger kinema mentor pontil sinner vandal anodal chough
bonnie Daniel gangly kingly mentum ponton sinnet vanish anodic chouse
bonsai Danish gangue lanate mincer punchy sinter vanity anoint cloaca
bonxie dankly gannet lancer minded puncta sonant vanner anomic cloche
bonzer denary ganoid lancet minder pundit sonata vendee anomie cloddy
bunchy dengue gantry landau mingle punily sonnet vender anonym cloggy
bunder denial gender landed minify punish sonsie vendor anorak clonal
bundle denier genera lander minima punkah sunbow vendue anoxia clonic
bungle denims geneva langue mining punned sundae veneer anoxic clonus
bunion denote genial langur minion punner Sunday venery apodal closed
bunker dental genius lankly minish punnet sunder venial apogee closet
bunkum dentel genned lanner minium puntee sundew venire apozem clothe
bunnia dentil genome lanugo minnow punter sundog Venite aroint cloudy
bunsen denude gentes lender Minoan rancho sundry venose around clough
bunted dingey gentle length minter rancid sungod venous arouse cloven
bunter dinghy gently lenity minuet randan sunhat venter atomic clover
bunyip dingle gentoo lensed minute randem sunken ventil atonal cooker
byname dingus gentry Lenten Monday random sunlit ventre atonic cookie
canape dining gingal lentil moneys ranger sunned venule avocet cooler
canard dinkum ginger linage monger ranker sunray vinery avouch coolie
canary dinned gingko linden Mongol rankle sunset vinous avowal coolly
cancan dinner ginkgo lineal monial rankly suntan vintry avowed coolth
cancel donate ginned linear monied ransom syndic wander awoken coonty
cancer donjon ginner lineup monies ranter syntax wangle azonal cooper
candid donkey gundog linger monism ranula tandem wanion azotic cootie
candle donned gunman lingua monist rename tangle wanted baobab croaky
canful donsie gunned linhay monkey renege tangly wanton bionic crocus
cangue dunite gunnel lining monody rennet tanist Wendic biopsy croppy
canine Dunker gunner linkup mundic renown tanker winced biotic crosse
canker dunlin gunsel linnet Munich rental tanned wincey biotin crotal
canned dunned gunshy linney muntin rented tanner winder blonde crotch
cannel dynamo gunter linsey nanism renter tannic window bloody croton
canner dynast gunyah lintel ninety ringed tannin winery bloomy crouch
cannon ennead handed lintie nonage ringer tanrec winged blotch croupy
cannot ennuye handle lonely nonary rinser tantra winger blotto crouse
canopy eonian hangar longan noncom rondel tenace winker blouse deodar
canter eonism hanged lunacy nonego ronyon tenant winkle blowed dhooti
canthi eunuch hanger lunate nonfat rundle tender winner blower doodad
cantle fandom hangup lunger nonius runlet tendon winnow blowsy doodah
canton fanged hanker lunula nonuse runnel tenner winsey blowup doodle
cantor fanion hankie lunule nuncio runner tennis winter blowzy doolie
cantus fanjet hansel manage nuncle runoff tenour wintle booboo droger
Canuck fanner hansom manana ornate runrig tenpin wintry boohoo drogue
canvas fantan henrun manche ornery runway tenrec wonder booing droich
canyon Fantee henrys Manchu panada sandal tenson wonted booker drolly
censer fantod hinder manday panama sander tensor wonton bookie drongo
censor fantom Hindoo manege panary sandhi tenter xenial boomer droopy
census fencer hinged mangel pander sanely tentie xenium booted dropsy
cental fender honest manger panful sanies tenues Yankee bootee drosky
centre Fenian honied mangle panned sanify tenuis yenned boozer drossy
centum fenman honour mangos pantry sanity tenure yonder broach drouth
cinder fennec hunger maniac panzer sanjak tenuto zander broche drover
cinema fennel hungry manila pencil sannup tenzon zenana brogue drowse
cineol finale hunker manioc penman santal tincal zenith broken drowsy
cinque finals hunter manito pennae santir tindal zinced broker egoism
concha finder ignite manned penned senary tinder               egoist
conchy        ignore                                           elodea
```

```
eloign hoodie profit spooky zlotys expert orphan sapped abrade border
eloper hoodoo proleg spoony alpaca expire orphic sapper abroad boreal
enosis hoofed prolix sports alpine expiry orpine sephen abrupt Boreas
enough hoofer prompt sporty ampere export osprey sepsis across boride
epodic hookah pronto spotty appeal expose papacy septal adrift boring
eponym hooked propel spouse appear fipple papain septet adroit borrow
epopee hooker proper stocks append gapped papaya septic aerate borsch
erotic hookey propyl stocky appose gopher papers septum aerial borzoi
evolue hookup proser stodge arpent gypped papery siphon aerily burble
evolve hooper prosit stodgy aspect gypsum papism sipped aerobe burbly
exodus hoopla protea stogie aspire happed papist sipper afraid burbot
exogen hoopoe proton stoker bopeep happen pappus sippet afreet burden
exomis hooray proven stokes bopped haptic papula sophic afresh bureau
exotic hootch ptosis stolen bopper hepcat papule sopite afrite burgee
fiorin hooter quoits stolid bypass heptad papyri sopped agrafe burger
floaty hooves quorum stolon bypast hipped peplum superb airbed burgle
flocci iconic quotes stoned bypath hippie pepped supine airbus burgoo
floozy idolum quotha stoner byplay hopped pepper supped airgun burhel
floppy ironer reopen stooge capful hopper pepsin supper airily burial
florae ironic rhombi stopgo capias hopple peptic supple airing burkha
floral isobar rioter storax caplin hyphae piping supply airman burlap
floras isohel roofer stores capote hyphal pipkin syphon airsac burler
floret isomer rookie storey capped hyphen pipped tapeta airway Burman
florid isopod roomer stormy capric impact pippin tapped aorist burner
florin kaolin rooted stound capsid impair popery tapper aortal burnet
flossy knobby rooter stover captor impala popgun tappet aortic burnup
floury knotty scolex swoosh cipher impale popish tappit arrack burrel
flower knower sconce swound copeck impark poplar tepefy arrant burrow
fooler koodoo scopae Taoism copier impart poplin tipcat arrest bursae
footed kookie scopas Taoist coping impawn popped tipoff arrive bursal
footer koolah scorch tholoi copita impede popper tipped arroba bursar
footle kronen scorer tholos copout impend poppet tipper arrowy bursas
foozle kroner scoria tholus copped impish popple tippet arroyo burton
froggy kronor scotch thorax copper impone popply tipple atrial byroad
frolic kronur scoter thoria Coptic import pupate tiptoe atrium carafe
frosty Leonid scotia thorny copula impose pupped tiptop aurist carbon
frothy lionel Scotic thoron cupful impost puppet Tophet aurora carboy
frowst loofah scouse thorpe cupola impugn raphia tophus aurous carder
frowsy looker scouth though cupped impure raphis topman barbed careen
frowzy lookin shoaly tooter cupric impute rapids topped barbel career
frozen looper shoddy toothy cuptie kaputt rapier topper barber caress
gaoler loosen shofar tootle cupule kipper rapine topple barbet carfax
geodic looser shogun tootsy cypher kopeck rapist tupelo bardic carful
George Maoism shoppy trocar cyprid koppie rapped typhus barege caries
ghosty Maoist shoran troche daphne lapdog rappee typify barely carina
global miosis shorts trogon dapper lapful rappel typing barfly carman
gloomy miotic shorty troika dapple lapped rapper typist bargee carnal
gloria moocow should Trojan depart lappet raptly umpire barite carnet
glossy mooing shovel trolly depend lappie raptor unpack barium carney
glover moolah shover trompe depict lapsed repaid unpaid barker carpal
glower myopia shower trophy deploy lapsus repair unpick barley carpel
gnomic myopic Siouan tropic depone lepton repand unplug barman carper
gnomon myosin slogan troppo deport lipase repass upping barney carpet
gnosis myosis sloppy trough depose lipide repast uppish barony carpus
goober myotic sloshy troupe depute lipoid repeal uppity barque carrel
goodie noodle slouch trouty diplex lipoma repeat vapour barred carrot
goodly oboist slough trover diploe lipped repent wapiti barrel cartel
googly ozonic Slovak trowel diplon lippen repine yapock barren carter
googol people sloven tsotsi diplon lippie replay yapped barret carton
gooier phobia slowly twoply dipnet lopped replum yapper barrio carvel
gooney phobic smoggy twould dipody lopper report yipped barrow carven
gooses phoebe smoker twoway dipole lupine repose yippee barter carver
groats phoney smooch utopia dipped mapped repugn yippie barton cerate
grocer phonic smooth violet dipper mapper repute yippie baryon cercus
groggy phonon smouch violin dipsas mopish ripely zapped baryta cereal
groove phooey snobby voodoo dopant mopoke ripoff zephyr berate cereus
groovy photic snoopy wholly Dopper mopped ripost zipped Berber ceriph
groper photon snooty whomso dupery mopper ripper zipper bereft cerise
grotto piolet snooze whoops duplet moppet ripple acquit berlin cerium
grotty pionic snorer whoosh duplex napalm ripply coquet bertha cermet
grouch ploidy snotty wooded empery napkin riprap faquir berthe certes
ground plotty snouty wooden empire napped ripsaw liquid birdie ceruse
grouse plough sooner woodsy employ Nepali ropery liquor bireme cervix
grovel plover soothe woofer empusa nephew roping loquat birkie chrism
grower poodle spoffy wooled espial nipped rupiah maquis birler Christ
growly pooped spoilt woolly esprit nipper sapele piquet borage chroma
growth poorly spoken yaourt expand nipple sapful roquet borane chrome
groyne prober sponge yeoman expect oppose sapota sequel borate chromo
hooded probit spongy yoohoo expend oppugn sappan sequin bordel circle
```

circus	dirndl	furred	hurray	merest	Parsee	sermon	strode	torque	warren
cirque	dorado	furrow	hurter	merger	parson	serosa	stroke	torrid	warsle
cirrus	Dorian	garage	hurtle	merils	partan	serous	stroll	torsel	warted
corban	dormer	garbed	inroad	merino	partly	serrae	stroma	torten	wirily
corbel	dormie	garble	inrush	merism	parure	serran	stromb	torula	wiring
corbie	dorsal	garcon	irrupt	merlin	parvis	serval	strong	turban	worker
corded	dorsum	garden	jarful	merlon	perdue	server	stroud	turbid	wormer
corder	dorter	garget	jargon	merman	period	shrank	strout	turbit	worrit
cordon	durbar	gargle	jarrah	merrie	perish	shrewd	strove	turbot	worsen
corium	duress	garial	jarred	mirage	permit	shriek	struma	tureen	worthy
corked	durgan	garish	jarvey	mirror	perron	shrift	struck	turgid	wortle
corker	Durham	garlic	jerbil	morale	person	shrike	strung	turgor	yarely
cornea	durian	garner	jerboa	morals	pertly	shrill	strunt	turion	yarrow
corned	during	garnet	jerker	morass	peruke	shrimp	struts	turkey	yorker
cornel	durned	garran	jerkin	morbid	peruse	shrine	surely	Turkic	Yoruba
corner	durrie	garret	jersey	morbus	phrase	shrink	surety	turner	zarape
cornet	earful	garron	jurist	moreen	piracy	shrive	surfer	turnip	zareba
cornua	earing	garrot	karate	morgen	pirate	shroff	surrey	turnup	zariba
corody	earner	garter	karmic	morgue	piraya	shroud	surtax	turret	zircon
corona	earthy	garuda	kaross	morion	porgie	shrove	survey	turtle	abseil
corozo	earwax	garvie	karroo	morish	porism	shrunk	Syriac	turves	absent
corpse	earwig	gerbil	kermes	Mormon	porker	sircar	Syrian	tyrant	absorb
corpus	eerily	gerent	kermis	mornay	porose	sirdar	syrinx	Tyrian	absurd
corral	egress	german	kerned	morose	porous	sirkar	syrupy	Ugrian	adsorb
corrie	enrage	germen	kernel	morpho	portal	sirrah	target	unread	aisled
corsac	enrapt	gerund	kersey	morris	porter	sirree	Targum	unreal	alsike
corsak	enrich	girder	kirsch	morrow	portly	sorage	tariff	unreel	answer
corset	enrobe	girdle	kirtle	morsel	purdah	sorbet	tarmac	unrest	arsine
cortex	enroll	girlie	Korean	mortal	purely	sordid	tarpan	unripe	assail
corvee	enroot	goramy	kurgan	mortar	purfle	sorely	tarpon	unrobe	assent
corves	errand	gorget	larder	morula	purger	sorgho	tarras	unroll	assert
Corvus	errant	gorgio	lardon	murder	purify	sorner	tarred	unroof	assess
corymb	errata	gorgon	lariat	murine	purine	sorrel	tarsal	unroot	assign
coryza	etrier	gorily	larker	murmur	purism	sorrow	tarsia	unrope	assist
curacy	eureka	gurgle	larrup	murphy	purist	sorter	tarsus	unruly	assize
curare	fardel	gurjun	larvae	murrey	purity	sortes	tartan	uprise	assoil
curari	farfel	Gurkha	larval	myriad	purler	sortie	tartar	uproar	assort
curate	farina	gurnet	larynx	myrica	purlin	sprain	tartly	uproot	assume
curdle	farmer	gurrah	lorcha	myrtle	purple	sprang	Tarzan	uprush	assure
curfew	faroff	gyrate	lordly	nardoo	purply	sprawl	teraph	varied	Aussie
curiae	farout	harass	lorica	narrow	purser	spread	tercel	varlet	Austin
curial	farrow	harden	loriot	nereid	pursue	sprent	tercet	varved	basalt
curium	ferial	hardly	lurdan	nerine	purvey	spring	teredo	verbal	basely
curler	ferine	hardup	lurker	nerite	pyrene	sprint	terete	verger	bashaw
curlew	ferret	harken	lyrate	neroli	pyrite	sprite	tergal	verify	basher
currie	ferric	harlot	lyrics	Nordic	pyrola	sprout	tergum	verily	basics
cursed	ferula	harper	lyrism	normal	pyrope	spruce	termer	verism	basket
cursor	ferule	harrow	lyrist	Norman	rarefy	spruit	termly	verist	basnet
cursus	fervid	hartal	maraca	nurser	rarely	sprung	termor	verity	Basque
curtal	firing	herald	maraud	oarage	raring	spryer	terret	vermin	basset
curtly	firkin	herbal	marble	ogress	rarity	spryly	territ	vernal	bassos
curtsy	firlot	herder	marbly	ogrish	reread	strafe	terror	versal	baster
curule	firman	herdic	marcel	onrush	sarape	strain	thrall	versed	Basuto
curvet	firmly	hereat	margay	orrery	sardel	strait	thrash	verser	Basutu
daring	forage	hereby	margin	parade	sarong	strake	thrawn	verset	beseem
darken	forbad	herein	marina	paramo	sarsen	strand	thread	versus	beside
darkey	forbid	hereof	marine	parang	scrape	strass	threap	vertex	bested
darkie	forbye	hereon	marish	paraph	scrawl	strata	threat	vervet	bestir
darkle	forced	heresy	Marist	parcel	screak	strath	thresh	virago	bestow
darkly	forcer	hereto	marked	pardie	scream	strawy	thrice	virgin	bisect
darned	fordid	heriot	marker	pardon	screed	strays	thrift	virile	bishop
darnel	forego	hermit	markup	parent	screen	streak	thrill	virose	bisque
darner	forest	hernia	marlin	pareve	screwy	stream	thrips	virtue	bister
darter	forgat	heroic	marmot	parget	scribe	streek	thrive	vorant	bistre
dartle	forger	heroin	maroon	pariah	scrimp	street	throat	vortex	bistro
dartre	forgot	herpes	marque	parian	script	stress	throbs	warble	bosche
derail	forint	Herren	marram	paring	scroll	strewn	throes	warcry	bosket
derate	formal	hirple	marred	parish	scroop	striae	throne	warden	bosomy
deride	format	horary	marron	parkin	scruff	strict	throng	warder	boston
derive	formed	horned	marrow	parlay	scrump	stride	throve	wardog	busbar
dermal	former	horner	marrum	parley	scryer	strife	thrown	wargod	busboy
dermic	formic	hornet	marshy	parody	serang	strike	thrums	warily	bushed
dermis	fornix	horrid	martel	parole	serape	Strine	thrush	warmer	bushel
derris	forpet	horror	marten	parous	seraph	string	thrust	warmly	busily
dirdum	forrad	horsey	martin	parpen	serein	stripe	tirade	warmth	busing
direct	forrit	hurdle	martyr	parral	serene	strips	toroid	warmup	busker
direly	forsay	hurler	marvel	parrel	serial	stripy	torose	warped	buskin
dirham	furfur	hurley	mercer	parrot	series	strive	torpid	warper	busman
dirhem	furore	hurrah	merely	parsec	seriph	strobe	torpor	warred	bussed

6 letter words   position = 3

busted	ensile	kosher	nastic	rushes	action	cattle	guttae	matted	outact
bustee	ensoul	lascar	nestle	russet	active	cetane	gutted	matter	outage
buster	ensure	lasher	Nestor	russia	actual	cither	gutter	mature	outbid
bustle	ersatz	lashup	noshup	rustic	aether	citole	hatbox	matzoh	outbye
bustup	Essene	lasque	nosily	rustle	afters	citric	hatful	metage	outcry
byssus	essive	lassie	nosing	sashay	anthem	citron	hatpeg	metals	outdid
casbah	essoin	lassos	nostoc	sasine	anther	citrus	hatpin	meteor	outfit
casein	exsect	laster	obsess	sesame	antiar	cottar	hatred	method	outfox
casern	exsert	lastly	onside	seseli	anting	cotted	hatted	methyl	outgun
cashew	fasces	lesion	ossein	sestet	antler	cotter	hatter	metier	outing
casing	fascia	lessee	ossify	siskin	antral	cotton	hetero	metope	outlaw
casino	fasten	lessen	ouster	sissoo	antrum	cutely	hetman	metred	outlay
casket	faster	lesser	oyster	sister	artery	cutler	hither	metric	outlet
Caslon	fescue	lesson	pascal	sistra	artful	cutlet	hitman	mettle	output
casque	festal	lessor	Pashto	suslik	artist	cutoff	hotbed	mitral	outran
cassia	fester	lisper	passer	system	astern	cutout	hotdog	mitten	outrun
cassis	fiscal	lissom	passim	tassel	asthma	cutter	hotpot	motett	outsat
caster	fisher	listed	pastel	tassie	astral	cuttle	hotter	mother	outset
castle	fistic	listel	pastil	taster	astray	datary	hutted	motile	outsit
castor	fossae	listen	pastor	testae	astute	dative	intact	motion	outtop
casual	fossil	lister	pastry	tester	attach	datura	intake	motive	outvie
cesser	fossor	lushly	pesade	teston	attack	detach	intend	motley	outwit
cestus	foster	lustra	peseta	tisane	attain	detail	intent	motmot	oxtail
cesura	fusain	lustre	pesewa	tissue	attend	detain	intern	motory	patchy
cistus	fusile	lysine	pester	tosher	attest	detect	intine	mottle	patent
cosher	fusion	mascle	pestle	tosser	attire	detent	intoed	mutant	Pathan
cosily	fusser	mascon	Pisces	tossup	attorn	detest	intone	mutate	pathic
cosine	fustic	mascot	pissed	Tuscan	attune	detour	intray	mutely	pathos
cosmic	gasbag	masher	pistil	tusked	author	dither	intuit	mutine	patina
cosmos	Gascon	mashie	pistol	tusker	autism	dittos	jetlag	mutiny	patois
cosset	gasify	masker	piston	tussah	autumn	dotage	jetsam	mutism	patrol
costae	gasket	maslin	posada	tusser	batata	dotard	jetted	mutter	patron
costal	gaskin	Masora	poseur	tussle	bateau	dotted	jitney	mutton	patted
costar	gasman	masque	posset	ugsome	bather	dottle	jitter	mutual	patten
coster	gasper	massif	possum	ulster	bathos	eatery	jotted	mutule	patter
costly	gassed	masted	postal	unsafe	bating	eating	jotter	mutuum	petara
cuscus	gasser	master	poster	unsaid	batman	either	Jutish	mythic	petard
cushat	goslow	mastic	postil	unseal	batted	entail	jutted	mythos	petite
cusped	gospel	mescal	pusher	unseam	batten	entera	kation	natant	petrel
cuspid	gossan	mesial	Pushtu	unseat	batter	entice	ketone	nation	petrol
cussed	gossip	messan	pushup	unseen	battle	entire	kettle	native	petted
custom	gusher	Messrs	rascal	unself	battue	entity	kitbag	natron	petter
cystic	gusset	mestee	rasher	unship	betake	entoil	kitcat	natter	pitchy
cystid	haslet	miscue	rashly	unshod	bethel	entomb	kitool	nature	pithos
dasher	hassle	misdid	rasper	unshoe	betide	entrap	kitsch	netful	pitier
dassie	hasten	misere	raster	unstop	betony	entree	kitten	nether	pitman
desalt	hispid	misery	rasure	unsung	betook	estate	kittle	netted	pitpan
descry	hisser	misfit	resale	upshot	betray	esteem	kittul	nettle	pitsaw
desert	hostel	mishap	rescue	upside	betted	estray	lateen	nitric	pitted
design	hushed	mishit	reseal	ursine	better	eutaxy	lately	nitwit	pitter
desire	husker	mishmi	reseat	vassal	bettor	extant	latent	notary	potage
desist	hussar	Mishna	reseau	vastly	bitchy	extasy	latest	notate	potale
desman	hustle	mislay	resect	vesica	biting	extend	lather	notice	potash
desmid	hyssop	misled	reseda	vesper	bitted	extent	latish	notify	potato
desorb	insane	missal	resell	vessel	bitten	extern	latria	notion	potboy
despot	inseam	missel	resent	vestal	bitter	extort	latron	nutant	poteen
disarm	insect	missis	reship	vested	botany	fathen	latten	nutate	potent
disbar	insert	missus	reside	vestee	botchy	father	latter	nutmeg	potful
disbud	inside	mister	resign	vestry	botfly	fathom	lethal	nutria	pother
discal	insist	mistle	resile	visage	bother	fatted	letoff	nutter	potion
discus	insole	misuse	resist	viscid	bothie	fatten	letter	obtain	potman
diseur	inspan	mosaic	resold	viscus	botone	fatter	Lettic	obtect	potpie
dismal	instal	moshav	resorb	Vishnu	bottle	fetial	litany	obtest	potted
dismay	instar	Moslem	resort	visile	bottom	fetich	litchi	obtund	potter
disown	instep	mosque	rester	vision	butane	fetish	lithia	obtuse	pottle
dispel	instil	mostly	result	visive	butene	fetter	lithic	octane	putlog
distal	insult	muscat	resume	visual	butler	fettle	litmus	octant	putoff
distil	insure	muscle	rising	washer	butter	fitful	litter	octave	putrid
disuse	itself	museum	risker	wasted	button	fitted	little	octavo	putsch
dosage	jasper	musing	risque	waster	catalo	fitter	lotion	octroi	puttee
dossal	jester	muskeg	rosace	wester	catchy	fother	lotted	optant	putter
dossel	Jesuit	musket	rosary	wisdom	catena	futile	luteal	optics	puttie
dosser	josher	muskox	rosery	wisely	catgut	future	lutein	optima	python
duster	josser	Muslim	rosily	wisent	Cathar	gateau	luting	option	ratbag
dustup	jostle	muslin	rosiny	wisher	cation	gather	matico	osteal	rather
easily	justly	mussel	roster	xystus	catkin	getout	matins	ostial	ratify
easter	kasbah	muster	rostra	yesman	catnap	getter	matlow	ostium	ratine
ensate	kismet	myself	rosula	yester	catnip	Gothic	matrix	ostler	rating
ensign	kisser	mystic	rusher	acting	catsup	gotten	matron	ottava	ration

ratite	totted	caudle	frusta	rouble	tourer	lively	bowyer	tawery	elytra
ratlin	totter	caught	frutex	roucou	tousle	livery	byword	tawpie	eryngo
ratoon	tutsan	caulis	gauche	rouncy	touter	living	bywork	thwack	etymon
rattan	tutted	causal	gaucho	rouser	truant	lovage	cowage	thwart	flying
rattat	ultima	causer	gauger	router	trudge	lovein	coward	towage	flyman
ratted	ultimo	causey	glumly	saucer	truism	lovely	cowboy	toward	flysch
ratter	untidy	chubby	glumpy	sauger	trumps	loving	cowish	towery	flyway
rattle	untied	chuffy	glutei	saurel	trusty	moving	cowled	towhee	geyser
retail	untold	chukar	gluten	sculpt	unused	novena	cowman	townee	glycin
retain	untrue	chukka	gourde	scummy	usurer	novice	cowpat	Tswana	glycol
retake	untuck	chummy	grubby	scurfy	uvulae	obvert	cowpea	unwary	goyish
retard	untune	chunky	grudge	scurry	uvular	pavage	cowpox	unwell	haybox
retell	uptake	church	grugru	scurvy	vaudoo	pavane	cowrie	unwept	haymow
retene	uptown	clumpy	grumly	scutal	vaulty	paving	dawdle	unwind	heyday
retest	upturn	clumsy	grumps	scutch	voulge	pavior	dewily	unwise	hoyden
retial	ustion	clunch	grumpy	scutum	waught	pavise	dewlap	unworn	inyala
retina	vatful	clutch	grutch	shucks	woundy	ravage	dowlas	unwrap	joyful
retire	vatted	coucal	hauler	shutin	yaupon	ravine	downer	upward	joyous
retold	vetted	cougar	haunch	sludge	zeugma	raving	dowser	upwind	keyway
retook	vitals	coulee	houdan	sludgy	Zouave	ravish	enwind	vaward	layday
retool	vitric	county	hourly	sluice	zounds	revamp	enwomb	wowser	layman
retort	vittae	couple	housel	sluicy	advent	reveal	enwrap	boxbed	layoff
retral	votary	coupon	housey	slummy	adverb	reverb	fawner	boxcar	layout
retrod	voting	course	iguana	slurry	advert	revere	fowler	boxful	maybug
retted	votive	cousin	inulin	slushy	advice	revers	gewgaw	boxing	mayday
returf	waters	cruces	jaunce	smudge	advise	revert	gowany	dexter	mayest
return	watery	cruddy	jaunty	smudgy	bovine	revery	hawhaw	fixate	mayfly
retuse	wattle	cruise	jounce	smugly	bovver	revest	hawked	fixity	mayhap
ritual	wether	cruive	jouncy	smutch	caveat	review	hawker	hexact	mayhem
rotary	wetted	crumby	launce	smutty	cavern	revile	hawser	hexane	maying
rotate	wetter	crummy	launch	snubby	caviar	revise	howdah	hexose	noyade
rotche	withal	crunch	laurel	snuffy	caving	revive	howler	laxity	oxygen
rotgut	wither	crural	louche	snugly	cavity	revoke	inward	luxate	oxymel
rotted	within	cruset	louden	souari	cavort	revolt	inwick	luxury	payday
rotten·withit	crusty	loudly	sought	civics	revved	inwove	maxima	paynim	
rotter	witted	crutch	lounge	souled	covert	rivage	inwrap	maxixe	payoff
rotund	wittol	cruxes	loupen	source	coving	roving	Jewess	myxoma	payola
rutile	yatter	dauber	loupit	sourly	devest	savage	Jewish	saxony	peyote
rutted	yttria	deuced	louver	souter	device	savant	kewpie	sexily	peyotl
sateen	zither	dhurra	louvre	spunky	devise	savate	kowhai	sexism	phylum
satiny	zythum	douane	maugre	spurge	devoid	savine	kowtow	sexist	physic
satire	abulia	double	maundy	spurry	devoir	saving	lawful	sexpot	prying
satori	abuser	doubly	moujik	sputum	devote	savory	lawman	sextan	psyche
satrap	acuity	douche	mouldy	squail	devour	savour	lawyer	sextet	psycho
Saturn	acumen	dought	moulin	squall	devout	sevens	lewdly	sexton	rhymer
satyra	aguish	doughy	mouser	squama	divers	severe	lowboy	sexual	rhythm
setoff	alulae	dourly	mousse	square	divert	severy	lowery	sixain	royals
setose	alumna	douser	mouthy	squash	divest	Sevres	lowing	sixgun	sayest
setout	alumni	drudge	muumuu	squawk	divide	soviet	lowish	taxies	saying
settee	amulet	drupel	naught	squeak	divine	sovran	lowkey	taxman	sayyid
setter	amuser	eluant	nausea	squeal	diving	tavern	newish	toxoid	scyphi
settle	aoudad	eluate	nautch	squill	elvish	unveil	newton	tuxedo	scythe
sittar	avulse	eluent	neural	squint	envier	vivace	Nowell	waxily	shyest
sitter	bauble	emulge	neuron	squire	favour	vivers	nowise	adytum	skylab
Sothic	bluing	equate	neuter	squirm	foveae	vivify	onward	amylum	skyman
sotted	bluish	equine	nougat	squirt	foveal	wavery	pawnee	anyhow	skyway
sutile	blunge	equity	nought	squish	gavage	wavily	pawner	anyone	slyest
sutler	blurry	faucal	nounal	Stuart	gavial	wivern	pawpaw	anyway	stylar
suttee	boucle	fauces	ocular	stubby	govern	wyvern	pewter	asylum	stylet
suture	bought	faucet	oeuvre	stucco	guvnor	always	powder	bayard	stylus
tatami	bougie	faulty	ovular	studio	Havana	aswoon	powwow	beyond	stymie
tatted	boulle	faunae	paunch	stuffy	havers	bawbee	reward	boyish	styrax
tatter	bounce	faunal	pauper	stumer	invade	bawble	rewind	bryony	thymol
tattle	bouncy	faunas	plucky	stumpy	invent	bawdry	rewire	cayman	thymus
tattoo	bounds	feudal	plumed	stupid	invert	bawler	rewoke	cayuse	thyrse
tetany	bounty	fluent	plummy	stupor	invest	bawley	reword	chypre	thyrsi
tetchy	bourne	fluffy	plumpy	sturdy	invite	bewail	rework	clypei	trying
tether	bourse	flukey	plunge	taught	invoke	beware	rowing	coyote	tryout
tetrad	bruise	flunky	plural	Taurus	jovial	bewray	sawder	crying	tuyere
tetter	brumal	flurry	plushy	tauten	Jovian	bowels	sawfly	crypto	twyere
titbit	brumby	fluted	pluton	tautly	lavabo	bowery	sawney	daybed	unyoke
titfer	brunch	fluter	pouchy	tautog	lavage	bowfin	sawpit	dayfly	voyage
tither	brunet	fought	pouffe	Teuton	laveer	bowing	sawset	doyley	voyeur
titian	brushy	foully	pounce	thulia	lavish	bowleg	sawyer	drybob	waylay
titled	brutal	foulup	pourer	toucan	lavolt	bowler	sewage	dryfly	wayout
titter	brutus	fourth	pouter	touche	levant	bowman	sewing	dryish	whydah
tittle	caucus	frugal	pruina	touchy	Levite	bowsaw	sowans	dryrot	bazaar
tittup	caudal	fruity	pruner	toupee	levity	bowtie	sowens	dryrun	bezant
tother	caudex	frumpy	rhumba	toupet	livein	bowwow	tawdry	duyker	bezoar

```
bizone anlage catalo enface inlaid notate rebato solace unnail busboy
buzzer annals cedarn engage inland noyade recall solano unpack byebye
dazzle apiary cerate enhalo inlaws nutant recant sonant unpaid camber
dozily arcade cetane enlace inmate nutate recast sonata unsafe carbon
eczema Arcady chiasm enrage innate oarage redact sorage unsaid carboy
enzyme arcana chiaus enrapt insane oblast reface souari unwary casbah
Eozoic arcane cicada ensate intact oblate regain sowans upcast chubby
Eozoon argala cicala entail intake obtain regale splash update cobber
evzone argali cigala equate invade occamy regard sprain upland cobble
fezzed argand cleave ergate inward octane rehash sprang uptake combat
fezzes armada cloaca errand inyala octant relaid sprawl upward combed
fizgig arrack cobalt errant iodate octave relate squail urbane comber
fizzle arrant comate errata island octavo remade squall vacant corban
gazebo askant cowage ersatz izzard ohmage remain squama vacate corbel
gazump askari coward escape jacana oleate remake square vagary corbie
gozzan aslant creaky escarp jezail onfall remand squash vaward cowboy
guzzle assail creamy estate Judaic onward remark squawk vihara crabby
hazard attach crease ethane jugate oogamy rename steady virago cumber
hazily attack create eutaxy kabala opiate repaid steamy visage cymbal
huzoor attain croaky exhale kakapo optant repair strafe vitals dabbed
izzard aubade cubage expand kanaka ordain repand strain vivace dabber
jezail aviary curacy extant karate orgasm repass strait vizard dabble
lazily aviate curare extasy lanate ornate repast strake volant dauber
lazuli aweary curari facade lavabo ottava resale strand vorant daybed
lizard ayeaye curate female lavage outact retail strass votary dibbed
mazard balata damage finale legacy outage retain strata voyage dibber
mazily banana damask finals legate oxgall retake strath wabain dibble
mezuza basalt datary fixate legato oxgang retard strati Wahabi disbar
mizzen batata debark floaty levant oxgate revamp strawy wizard disbud
mizzle bayard debase forage ligate oxland reward strays wreath djibba
mizzly bazaar debate freaky linage oxtail ribald Stuart zarape doable
muzhik becall decade friary lipase padauk riband sudary zenana dobbin
muzzle becalm decamp fugato litany pajama rivage sugary zonary double
Nazify became decani fusain lizard palace robalo sumach zonate doubly
Nazism bedaub decant galago lobate palais Romaic sweaty Zouave drably
nozzle bedaze dedans galaxy locale palate Romany tabard zymase drybob
nuzzle befall deface garage locate panada rosace takahe airbed dubbed
pizzle behalf defame gavage lovage panama rosary tamale airbus dubbin
puzzle behave delate Gemara lunacy panary rotary tamara anabas dumbly
razzia belaud demand gleamy lunate papacy rotate tatami Arabic durbar
razzle berate demark gobang luxate papain royals tenace arable dybbuk
rizzar betake denary gocart lyrate papaya rubato tenant ashbin edible
rizzer bewail depart gokart macaco parade safari teraph aumbry enable
rozzer beware derail goramy Madame paramo salaam tetany babble feeble
sizing bezant derate gowany malady parang salade thrall babbly feebly
sizzle bigamy desalt grease Malaga paraph salami thrash balboa fibbed
syzygy Bihari detach greasy malate pavage salary thrawn bamboo fibber
vizard binary detail greave manage pavane samara thwack baobab fimble
vizier binate detain groats manana pedalo sarape thwart barbed flabby
vizsla bleach dicast gyrate maraca pedant savage tirade barbel fobbed
wizard bleary digamy hamate maraud pedate savant tisane barber fogbow
wizier bocage dilate harass mazard pelage savate togaed barbet foible
─────  borage disarm Havana menace pesade sclaff tomato bauble forbad
abbacy borane dogate hazard menage petara scrape towage bawbee forbid
ablate borate domain herald metage petard scrawl toward bawble forbye
ablaut botany donate hexact metals phrase seaair treaty bedbug fumble
ablaze breach dopant hexane midage pilaff secant triage Berber gabbed
aboard breast dorado hijack midair piracy sedate truant bibbed gabber
abrade breath dosage homage mikado pirate sejant Tswana bibber gabble
ackack briard dotage horary milady piraya senary tyrant bilbos gabbro
admass briary dotard humane milage pleach senate ullage bobbed gambir
adnate broach douane ideaed mirage pliant serang umlaut bobbin gambit
aerate bumalo dreamt ideate mohair please serape uncage bobble gamble
afeard butane dreamy ideate Mohawk Polack seraph uncate bomber gambol
affair bylane dreary iguana morale pomace sesame undate bonbon garbed
aflame byname dynamo immane morals pomade sewage unease booboo garble
afraid bypass dynast impact morass posada shears uneasy boxbed gasbag
aghast bypast eclair impair mosaic potage sheass uneath briber gerbil
agnail bypath Eddaic impala mutant potale sheath unfair bubble gibber
agnate cabala efface impale mutate potash sheave unhair bubbly gibbet
agrafe cabana eluant impark mygale potato shoaly unhand bulbar gibbon
albata cafard eluate impart nagana preach shrank Uniate bulbed gimbal
alcaic calami embalm impawn napalm pupate silage unlace bulbil glibly
alkali calash embank incase natant queasy sixain unlade bulbul global
alkane camass embark indaba negate queazy sleave unlaid bumble gobbet
alpaca canape encage infamy Nepali rabato sleazy unlash burble gobble
always canard encamp infant nonage ramate smeary unmade burbly goober
angary canary encase infare nonary ravage sneaky unmake burbot grabby
anlace carafe encash inhale notary rebate socage unmask busbar graben
```

grubby	pueblo	yabber	fiacre	puncta	bandog	feeder	kindle	pundit	tindal
hagbut	rabbet	zombie	fiscal	quiche	bardic	fender	kindly	purdah	tinder
hatbox	rabbin	abacus	flacon	rancho	bawdry	feudal	koedoe	pyedog	toddle
haybox	rabbit	acacia	fleche	rancid	beadle	fiddle	koodoo	raddle	trader
herbal	rabble	anicut	flocci	rascal	bedded	fiddly	ladder	raider	trudge
hobbit	ragbag	apache	forced	redcap	bedder	finder	laddie	randan	tundra
hobble	ramble	apical	forcer	reecho	beldam	fledge	landau	random	vandal
hombre	ratbag	apices	fracas	rescue	bender	fodder	landed	randon	vaudoo
hotbed	redbud	ashcan	fulcra	rotche	bidden	fogdog	lander	reader	vendee
hubbub	reebok	avocet	garcon	roucou	bidder	folder	lapdog	redden	vender
humble	rhebok	beachy	Gascon	saucer	binder	fondle	larder	redder	vendor
humbly	ribbed	beacon	gauche	seacow	birdie	fondly	lardon	reddle	vendue
humbug	ribbon	bitchy	gaucho	seiche	bladed	fondue	layday	reedit	voided
iambic	robbed	bobcat	glacis	shucks	boldly	fordid	leaden	render	voider
iambus	robber	bosche	glycin	sircar	bonded	Friday	leader	ridded	voodoo
icebag	rouble	botchy	glycol	slacks	bonder	fridge	leadin	ridden	wadded
icebox	rubbed	boucle	grocer	slicer	boodle	fuddle	leadup	riddle	waddie
isabel	rubber	boxcar	hepcat	soccer	bordel	fundus	lender	roadie	waddle
isobar	rubble	bracer	hiccup	spacer	border	gadded	lewdly	rondel	waddle
jabbed	rubbly	braces	hoicks	specie	bridal	gadder	lidded	rudder	wander
jabber	rumble	bricky	hubcap	stacte	bridge	gander	lieder	ruddle	warden
jerbil	rumbly	broche	ibices	sticky	bridle	garden	linden	rundle	warder
jerboa	sabbat	buccal	icecap	stocks	budded	gender	loaded	sadden	wardog
jibbah	sambar	bunchy	icicle	stocky	Buddha	geodic	loader	sadder	wedded
jibbed	sambur	caecal	kincob	stucco	buddle	giddap	lordly	saddhu	welder
jibber	scabby	caecum	kitcat	sulcus	bunder	gilder	louden	saddle	weldor
jobber	seabed	calcar	laical	talcky	bundle	girder	loudly	saidst	Wendic
jumbal	seabee	calces	lancer	talcum	burden	girdle	lurdan	sandal	whidah
jumble	semble	calcic	lancet	teacup	caddie	gladly	madden	sander	whydah
jumbly	shabby	cancan	lascar	tercel	caddis	glider	madder	sandhi	wilder
kasbah	skibob	cancel	litchi	tercet	candid	goddam	maidan	sardel	wildly
kibble	snobby	cancer	lorcha	tetchy	candle	Goidel	maiden	sawder	winded
kitbag	snubby	catchy	louche	thecae	carder	golden	manday	seadog	winder
knobby	sobbed	caucus	madcap	thecal	caudal	goodie	mayday	seeder	window
lambda	sombre	cercus	manche	tincal	caudex	goodly	meadow	seldom	windup
lamber	sorbet	chacha	Manchu	tipcat	caudle	grader	meddle	sendal	wisdom
legbye	stable	chacma	marcel	toecap	cinder	gradin	mender	sender	wonder
liable	stably	chichi	mascle	tomcat	cloddy	gradus	midday	sendup	wooded
libber	stubby	chicle	mascon	tomcod	coddle	grudge	midden	shader	wooden
limbec	suable	circle	mascot	toucan	coldly	guddle	middle	shades	woodsy
limbed	subbed	circus	mercer	touche	condor	guider	mildew	shadow	yonder
limber	sunbow	cliche	mescal	touchy	corded	guidon	mildly	shaduf	zander
limbic	symbol	cloche	mincer	tracer	corder	gulden	minded	shoddy	abbess
limbus	tabbed	coccal	miscue	traces	cordon	gundog	minder	sirdar	abject
lobbed	talbot	coccid	mobcap	tracks	cradle	haddie	misdid	skiddy	abseil
lowboy	teabag	coccus	moocow	tricar	credal	handed	moider	sledge	absent
lubber	Theban	coccyx	muscat	tricky	credit	handle	Monday	slider	accede
lumbar	tidbit	concha	muscle	tricot	cruddy	harden	muddle	sludge	accent
lumber	tiebar	conchy	niacin	trocar	cuddie	hardly	mundic	sludgy	accept
marble	timbal	concur	noncom	troche	cuddle	hardup	murder	smudge	access
marbly	timber	coucal	nuncio	Tuscan	cuddly	headed	nardoo	smudgy	achene
maybug	timbre	creche	nuncle	twicer	curdle	header	needle	sodden	addend
member	titbit	crocus	obeche	uracil	daedal	headon	neednt	soldan	adhere
mobbed	tombac	cruces	oilcan	viscid	dander	heddle	nodded	solder	adieus
morbid	tombak	cuscus	orache	viscus	dandle	herder	noddle	sordid	adieux
morbus	tomboy	dancer	oracle	voiced	dawdle	herdic	noodle	spadix	adnexa
mumble	treble	deacon	outcry	vulcan	deaden	heyday	Nordic	spider	advent
nabbed	trebly	deicer	parcel	warcry	deadly	hidden	outdid	stadia	adverb
nibbed	tribal	descry	pascal	whacky	deodar	hinder	padded	stodge	advert
nibble	tubber	deuced	patchy	wincey	diadem	Hindoo	paddle	stodgy	Aegean
nimble	tumble	diacid	peachy	yoicks	diddle	hodden	paidup	studio	affect
nimbly	turban	discal	pencil	zinced	dikdik	holden	pander	subdue	affeer
nimbus	turbid	discus	piecer	zincic	dirdum	holder	pandit	sudden	afield
nobble	turbit	douche	pincer	zincky	dodder	holdup	pardie	sundae	afreet
nobbut	turbot	drachm	Pisces	zircon	doddle	hooded	pardon	Sunday	afresh
nubble	tymbal	dulcet	pitchy	acedia	doodad	hoodie	payday	sunder	afters
nubbly	unable	eggcup	placed	acidic	doodah	hoodoo	peddle	sundew	albedo
number	usable	ejecta	placer	acidly	doodle	hotdog	perdue	sundog	albeit
numbly	verbal	elicit	placet	amadou	dredge	houdan	piddle	sundry	albert
outbid	viable	epical	placid	amidst	drudge	howdah	piedog	swaddy	alkene
outbye	wabble	eyecup	plicae	anadem	dumdum	hoyden	pledge	syndic	allege
pebble	wamble	falcon	plucky	anodal	dyadic	huddle	podded	tandem	allele
pebbly	wambly	fasces	poncho	anodic	elodea	hurdle	polder	tawdry	amoeba
phobia	warble	fascia	pouchy	aoudad	epodic	ibidem	ponder	tedded	ampere
phobic	webbed	faucal	precis	apodal	evader	irides	poodle	tedder	anneal
plebby	wimble	fauces	pricey	avidly	exedra	judder	powder	tender	annexe
potboy	wobble	faucet	psyche	baddie	exodus	kidded	puddle	tendon	apiece
prober	wobbly	fencer	psycho	baldly	fandom	kidder	puddly	tiddly	appeal
probit	wombat	fescue	punchy	bandit	fardel	kiddie	pugdog	tiedye	appear

append	comedo	fleecy	latent	peseta	screed	timely	buffer	potful	bought
ardent	comedy	fluent	latest	pesewa	screen	Toledo	buffet	pouffe	bougie
argent	comely	foment	laveer	phlegm	screwy	toneme	Caffre	prefab	bregma
arpent	comeon	forego	legend	phoebe	seaear	torero	canful	prefer	bright
arrest	copeck	forest	likely	pigeon	secede	towery	capful	prefix	brogue
artery	covert	foveae	lineal	pileum	secern	tumefy	carfax	profit	budget
ascend	creeps	foveal	linear	pileup	select	tupelo	carful	puffed	budgie
ascent	creepy	fraena	lineup	pileus	senega	tureen	chafer	puffer	bugged
asleep	creese	freely	livein	pineal	serein	tuxedo	chaffy	puffin	Bulgar
aspect	cutely	freest	lively	pinery	serene	tuyere	chuffy	purfle	bulger
assent	deceit	freeze	livery	pineta	seseli	tweeds	cliffy	raffia	bungle
assert	decent	friend	loment	pliers	sevens	tweedy	coffee	raffle	burgee
assess	defeat	frieze	lonely	pomelo	severe	tweeny	coffer	reefer	burger
astern	defect	gaiety	lovein	popery	severy	twyere	coffin	riffle	burgle
attend	defend	galena	lovely	poseur	sheeny	ubiety	coffle	roofer	burgoo
attest	deject	gamely	lowery	poteen	sheets	unbend	comfit	rueful	cadger
Augean	delete	gamete	lucent	potent	shield	unbent	confab	ruffed	cangue
awheel	demean	gateau	lucern	priest	shiest	unless	confer	ruffle	catgut
bakery	dement	gazebo	luteal	purely	shrewd	unmeet	crafty	sapful	caught
baleen	depend	genera	lutein	pyrene	shyest	unread	cuffed	sawfly	chigoe
barege	desert	geneva	lyceum	quaere	sileni	unreal	cupful	seafan	claggy
barely	detect	gerent	makedo	raceme	silent	unreel	curfew	seafog	cloggy
basely	detent	gleety	makeup	rarefy	sinewy	unrest	dayfly	seafox	codger
bateau	detest	govern	maleic	rarely	skeely	unseal	deafen	shifty	cogged
bedeck	devest	greedy	manege	rebeck	sleepy	unseam	deafly	shofar	coigne
bedell	digest	greens	mayest	recede	sleety	unseat	deific	sinful	congee
befell	direct	greeny	merely	recent	sleeve	unseen	differ	sniffy	conger
behead	direly	grieve	merest	recess	slyest	unself	dogfox	snuffy	congou
beheld	diseur	haleru	meteor	redeem	smeech	unveil	drafty	soffit	cougar
behest	divers	havers	misere	redeye	sneesh	unwell	drifty	spiffy	craggy
bereft	divert	hedera	misery	refect	sneeze	unwept	dryfly	spoffy	cudgel
beseem	divest	hereat	modena	regent	sneezy	upbear	duffel	stifle	dagger
biceps	docent	hereby	modern	rehear	sobeit	upbeat	duffer	stuffy	danger
bireme	dogear	herein	modest	reheat	solely	upheld	duffle	suffer	dangle
bisect	dogend	hereof	moiety	reheel	solemn	upkeep	earful	suffix	dengue
bodega	domett	hereon	molest	reject	sorely	uraeus	eyeful	surfer	digger
bolero	dudeen	heresy	moment	relent	sowens	urgent	farfel	tiffin	dingey
bopeep	dukery	hereto	moneys	remedy	speech	valeta	filfot	tinful	dinghy
boreal	dupery	hetero	moreen	renege	speedo	vegete	fitful	titfer	dingle
Boreas	duress	homely	motett	repeal	speedy	veleta	fluffy	toffee	dingus
bowels	eatery	honest	museum	repeat	sphene	veneer	fulfil	trifid	dodgem
bowery	eczema	hugely	mutely	repent	sphere	venery	furfur	trifle	dodger
breech	effect	humect	myself	reread	sphery	vilely	fylfot	tubful	dogged
breeks	effete	humeri	namely	reseat	spleen	vinery	gadfly	tuffet	dogger
breese	egress	hyaena	nereid	reseau	splent	vivers	gaffer	unific	doggie
breeze	eldest	immesh	nicely	resect	spread	voyeur	goffer	urnful	dought
breezy	eluent	impede	nicety	reseda	sprent	waders	golfer	useful	doughy
briefs	embers	impend	ninety	resell	squeak	wafery	guffaw	vatful	dragee
briery	empery	incept	nocent	resent	squeal	waters	haffet	waffle	draggy
bureau	endear	incest	nonego	retell	steely	watery	haffit	wilful	dragon
butene	enmesh	indeed	novena	retene	steeve	wavery	hatful	woeful	dreggy
cadent	ennead	indene	Nowell	retest	streak	wheeze	heifer	woofer	droger
camera	entera	indent	nudely	reveal	stream	wheezy	hoofed	yaffle	drogue
careen	Eocene	infect	object	reverb	streek	widely	hoofer	zaffer	durgan
career	ephebe	infelt	obsess	revere	street	wifely	ireful	zaffre	enigma
caress	ephebi	infest	obtect	revers	stress	wigeon	jarful	adagio	exogen
casein	Essene	ingest	obtest	revert	strewn	winery	joyful	airgun	fagged
casern	esteem	inhere	obvert	revery	superb	wisely	jugful	alegar	faggot
catena	ethene	inject	oedema	revest	surely	wisent	Kaffir	alight	fanged
caveat	eureka	inseam	offend	rident	surety	wivern	lapful	apogee	fidget
cavern	exceed	insect	offent	rifely	sweeny	womera	lawful	aright	figged
celery	except	insert	ogress	ripely	sweets	wyvern	leafed	badger	finger
cement	excess	intend	oogeny	rodent	tagend	xylene	loafer	bagged	fizgig
cereal	expect	intent	orcein	ropery	takein	yarely	loofah	banger	flaggy
cereus	expend	intern	ordeal	rosery	talent	yclept	manful	bangle	flagon
cheeky	expert	invent	orgeat	rubefy	tamely	zareba	mayfly	bangup	flight
cheers	exsect	invert	orient	rudely	tapeta	zebeck	miffed	bargee	fogged
cheery	exsert	invest	ornery	safely	tavern	armful	misfit	beagle	forger
cheese	extend	itself	orrery	safety	tawery	artful	muffin	beggar	forget
cheesy	extent	Jewess	ossein	sagely	teledu	baffle	muffle	begged	forgot
chield	extern	Judean	osteal	sanely	telega	bagful	netful	beigel	fought
cicely	facete	kinema	oxherd	sapele	tepefy	barfly	nonfat	Belgic	fright
cinema	fadein	kopeck	pakeha	sateen	teredo	belfry	outfit	bigger	frigid
cineol	fagend	Korean	paleae	sayest	terete	biffin	outfox	biggin	froggy
client	fakery	laceup	palely	schema	thieve	binful	panful	blight	frugal
cogent	finely	lamely	papers	scheme	thread	boffin	perfin	bodger	fugged
coheir	finery	lament	papery	sclera	threap	botfly	piaffe	bogged	fulgid
cohere	fleece	lateen	parent	screak	threat	bowfin	piffle	boggle	fungal
coleus	fleech	lately	patent	scream	thresh	boxful	pilfer	bongos	fungus

gadget	ligger	saggar	archil	lithic	tother	banish	coping	enrich	gorily
gagged	linger	sagged	archly	lochan	towhee	barite	copita	ensign	goyish
gagger	lingua	sagger	archon	lushly	tuchun	barium	corium	ensile	grainy
gaggle	lodger	sangar	asthma	lychee	typhus	basics	cosily	entice	greige
ganger	loggat	sauger	author	machan	unship	bating	cosine	entire	guaiac
gangly	logged	shaggy	bashaw	masher	unshod	begird	coving	entity	habile
gangue	logger	shogun	basher	mashie	unshoe	begirt	cowish	envier	halide
garget	loggia	singer	bather	mayhap	upshot	behind	cruise	enwind	halite
gargle	longan	single	bathos	mayhem	urchin	belief	cruive	eolian	Hamite
gauger	lugged	singly	bethel	menhir	Vishnu	belike	crying	eolith	hazily
geegee	lugger	sixgun	bishop	method	washer	belive	cubism	eonian	hegira
gewgaw	luggie	slaggy	boohoo	methyl	wether	bemire	cubist	eonism	hejira
gigged	lunger	slight	bother	mighty	wisher	benign	cueing	equine	helium
giggle	maggot	slogan	bothie	mishap	withal	beside	cueist	equity	heriot
giggly	maigre	smoggy	Brahma	mishit	wither	betide	curiae	erbium	hiding
gingal	mangel	smugly	Brahmi	mishmi	within	bikini	curial	ermine	hieing
ginger	manger	snaggy	brehon	Mishna	withit	biting	curium	Eskimo	hoeing
gingko	mangle	snugly	burhel	moshav	yoohoo	bluing	Daniel	espial	holily
goggle	mangos	soigne	bushed	mother	zephyr	bluish	Danish	essive	holism
goggly	margay	sorgho	bushel	muzhik	zither	bodice	daring	ethics	homily
googly	margin	sought	cachet	mythic	zythum	bodily	dative	Ethiop	homing
googol	maugre	spigot	cachou	mythos	acting	boding	decide	etrier	hominy
gorget	meagre	stager	cashew	nephew	action	bolide	defier	excide	honied
gorgio	merger	stagey	Cathar	nether	active	bonism	defile	excise	hosier
gorgon	midget	stigma	cipher	nighty	acuity	bonist	define	excite	humify
grigri	midgut	stogie	cither	noshup	addict	bonito	delict	expire	ignite
groggy	mingle	sungod	cochin	nuchal	admire	booing	demise	expiry	imbibe
grugru	moggie	tagged	cosher	orchid	adrift	boride	demist	eyeing	impish
guggle	monger	tangle	cushat	orchil	advice	boring	denial	Fabian	incise
gurgle	Mongol	tangly	cypher	orchis	advise	bovine	denier	facial	incite
haggis	morgen	target	daphne	orphan	aedile	bowing	denims	facies	Indian
haggle	morgue	Targum	dasher	orphic	aerial	boxing	depict	facile	indict
hangar	mugged	taught	dirham	Pashto	aerily	boyish	deride	facing	indign
hanged	mugger	tergal	dirham	Pathan	affine	brains	derive	family	indigo
hanger	nagged	tergum	dither	pathic	affirm	brainy	design	famine	indite
hangup	nagger	tingle	Durham	pathos	afrite	braird	desire	famish	indium
hedger	naught	tingly	eighth	peahen	ageing	braise	desist	fanion	infirm
height	nidget	togged	eighty	pelham	agnise	bruise	device	farina	inlier
higgle	nigger	toggle	either	pithos	aguish	bulimy	devise	feeing	inning
hinged	niggle	tongue	eschar	pother	aikido	bunion	dewily	feline	inside
hogged	nilgai	tragic	eschew	pusher	airily	burial	dimity	Fenian	insist
hogget	noggin	tragus	etcher	Pushtu	airing	busily	dining	ferial	intine
hoggin	nougat	trigon	euchre	pushup	albino	busing	divide	ferine	invite
hugged	nought	trogon	fathen	python	albite	byline	divine	fetial	inwick
hunger	nugget	tugged	father	quahog	Aldine	cagily	diving	fetich	iodide
hungry	onager	turgid	fathom	rachis	allied	cahier	docile	fetish	iodine
jaeger	origan	turgor	fisher	raphia	allium	calico	dolium	filial	iodise
jagged	origin	twiggy	fother	raphis	alpine	caliph	domino	filing	iodism
jagger	outgun	valgus	fulham	rasher	alsike	camion	Dorian	finial	iolite
jangle	oxygen	verger	Gadhel	rashly	amnion	camise	dozily	fining	Ionian
jargon	parget	virgin	gather	rather	angina	canine	dreich	finish	ionise
jigged	pegged	vulgar	gopher	redhot	anoint	capias	droich	finite	ionium
jigger	pidgin	vulgus	Gothic	reship	antiar	carina	dryish	firing	jabiru
jiggle	pigged	wagged	gusher	richen	anting	caries	dudish	fixity	Jewish
jiggly	piggin	waggle	hawhaw	riches	aorist	casing	dunite	flying	jovial
jingle	pinger	waggly	heehaw	richly	Argive	casino	durian	foliar	Jovian
jingly	plagal	waggon	higher	righto	arnica	cation	during	folium	Julian
jogged	plague	wangle	highly	rochet	aroint	caviar	dyeing	forint	junior
jogger	plaguy	wargod	hither	ruched	arrive	caving	earing	fraise	jurist
joggle	plight	waught	hyphae	rusher	arsine	cavity	easily	fruity	Jutish
judger	pongee	weight	hyphal	rushes	artist	cecity	eating	fusile	kation
jugged	popgun	widget	hyphen	sachem	aseity	celiac	edgily	fusion	kibitz
juggle	porgie	wigged	inches	sachet	aspire	ceriph	edging	futile	kumiss
jungle	purger	wiggle	ischia	sashay	assign	cerise	eerily	gabion	labial
jungly	quaggy	wiggly	isohel	senhor	assist	cerium	effigy	galiot	labile
kingly	quagga	winged	josher	sephen	assize	chaise	egoism	gamily	labium
knaggy	ragged	winger	kosher	sigher	atrial	choice	egoist	gamine	lacing
knight	raggee	woggle	kowhai	siphon	atrium	chrism	elfish	gaming	ladify
kurgan	raggle	wright	laches	sophic	attire	Christ	eloign	garial	lading
laager	ranger	zeugma	lasher	Sothic	audile	cilice	elvish	garish	ladino
lagged	reggae	zingel	lashup	sunhat	augite	cilium	empire	gasify	lamina
lagger	ridged	aether	lather	syphon	aurist	civics	ending	gavial	lamish
langue	rigged	Afghan	lecher	tether	autism	coaita	endive	Gemini	lariat
langur	rigger	anchor	lethal	tights	aweigh	codify	engild	genial	latish
league	ringed	anthem	lichee	tither	awhile	cogito	engine	genius	lavish
ledged	ringer	anther	lichen	tocher	awning	coming	engird	glairy	laxity
ledger	rotgut	anyhow	lights	Tophet	Babism	comity	engirt	glaive	lazily
legged	rugged	arched	linhay	tophus	Babist	conics	enlist	gneiss	legion
length	rugger	archer	lithia	tosher	banian	copier	enmity	gooier	legist

lenity	monism	paring	reline	shrill	timing	wahine	chukka	looker	stoker
lesion	monist	parish	relish	shrimp	tinily	wanion	cocked	lookin	stokes
Levite	mooing	parity	relive	shrine	titian	wapiti	cocker	lowkey	sucker
levity	mopish	patina	remind	shrink	toeing	warily	cockle	lurker	suckle
liaise	morion	paving	remint	shrive	tonish	wavily	conker	mackle	sunken
libido	morish	pavior	remise	siding	Tories	waxily	cooker	malkin	tacker
liking	motile	pavise	remiss	silica	troika	widish	cookie	marked	tacket
lilied	motion	period	repine	simian	truism	wilily	corked	marker	tackle
liming	motive	perish	reside	simile	trying	wirily	corker	market	talker
lining	moving	petite	resign	sizing	Tshirt	wiring	crikey	markup	talkie
lipide	mulish	pinion	resile	skeigh	tubing	wizier	cuckoo	masker	tanked
living	Munich	piping	resist	skiing	tuning	wraith	dankly	meekly	tanker
logion	murine	pitier	retial	sleigh	turion	xenial	darken	mickey	ticked
lorica	musing	plaice	retina	sluice	typify	xenium	darkey	mickle	ticker
loriot	mutine	plaint	retire	sluicy	typing	yogism	darkie	milker	ticket
lotion	mutiny	ploidy	review	social	typist	zanily	darkle	mocker	tickey
loving	mutism	podite	revile	sodium	Tyrian	zariba	darkly	mockup	tickle
lowing	myriad	podium	revise	solidi	uglify	zenith	decker	monkey	tickly
lowish	myrica	police	revive	solids	uglily	zodiac	deckle	mucker	tinker
lumina	nanism	policy	rewind	somite	Ugrian	zoning	dicker	muckle	tinkle
lupine	nation	polish	rewire	sopite	ultima	acajou	dickey	muskeg	tinkly
luting	native	polite	riding	soviet	ultimo	banjax	dinkum	musket	tucker
Lydian	Nazify	polity	rising	speiss	umpire	banjos	docker	muskox	tucket
lyrics	Nazism	popish	Romish	sphinx	unbind	deejay	docket	napkin	tuckin
lyrism	nerine	porism	roping	splice	unbitt	donjon	donkey	nickel	turkey
lyrist	nerite	potion	rosily	spline	uncial	fanjet	ducker	nicker	Turkic
lysine	newish	praise	rosiny	splint	uncini	frijol	duiker	offkey	tusked
Magian	nicish	pruina	roving	splits	undies	gurjun	Dunker	packer	tusker
magilp	nidify	prying	rowing	spoilt	undine	logjam	duyker	packet	walker
making	nomism	pumice	rubify	spring	ungird	moujik	feckly	parkin	walkin
malice	nonius	punily	rudish	sprint	ungirt	oddjob	fickle	peaked	walkon
malign	nosily	punish	ruling	sprite	unkind	ramjet	firkin	pecker	weaken
malism	nosing	purify	rumina	squill	unking	sanjak	flukey	picker	weakly
maniac	notice	purine	rupiah	squint	unkink	Seljuk	folksy	picket	weekly
manila	notify	purism	rutile	squire	unlike	Trojan	forked	pickle	welkin
manioc	notion	purist	Sabian	squirm	unlink	awaked	funkia	pickup	wicked
manito	novice	purity	Sabine	squirt	unpick	awaken	gasket	pinkie	wicker
Maoism	nowise	pyrite	sadism	squish	unripe	awoken	gaskin	pipkin	wicket
Maoist	nubile	quaich	sadist	stairs	untidy	backer	geckos	pocked	winker
marina	nudism	quaigh	Salian	staith	untied	backup	ginkgo	pocket	winkle
marine	nudist	quaint	salify	striae	unwind	balker	Gurkha	porker	worker
marish	nudity	quoits	salina	strict	unwise	banker	hackle	pucker	Yankee
Marist	numina	rabies	saline	stride	uphill	banket	hackly	punkah	yolked
matico	oafish	racial	saliva	strife	uplift	barker	hanker	Quaker	yorker
matins	oblige	racily	Samian	strike	upping	basket	hankie	racker	zinked
maxima	oboist	racism	samite	Strine	uppish	beaked	harken	racket	zonked
maxixe	oddity	racist	sanies	string	uppity	beaker	hawked	ranker	abulia
maying	oecist	radial	sanify	stripe	uprise	becket	hawker	rankle	addled
mazily	office	radian	sanity	stripy	upside	beckon	heckle	rankly	Aeolic
mediae	offing	radish	sasine	strive	upwind	bicker	hickey	reckon	afflux
medial	offish	radium	satiny	Sufism	ursine	bilker	hocker	ricker	aisled
median	ogrish	radius	satire	supine	ustion	birkie	hockey	rickey	alalia
medick	oidium	rakish	savine	sutile	vagile	bodkin	hookah	risker	alulae
medico	oldish	ramify	saving	Syriac	valine	booker	hooked	rocker	ambler
medium	online	rapids	saying	Syrian	valise	bookie	hooker	rocket	amulet
medius	onside	rapier	schism	syrinx	vanish	booksy	hookey	rookie	amylum
megilp	oolite	rapine	schist	tahini	vanity	bosket	hookup	ruckle	angled
menial	oomiak	rapist	schizo	taking	varied	broken	huckle	ruckus	angler
meninx	ophite	raring	scribe	talion	Vedist	broker	hunker	seeker	anklet
merils	optics	rarity	scrimp	taming	venial	bucker	husker	shaken	antler
merino	optima	ratify	script	tanist	venire	bucket	jackal	shaker	ariled
merism	option	ratine	sedile	tariff	verify	buckle	jacket	Shakta	armlet
mesial	orpine	rating	seeing	Taoism	verily	buckra	jerker	Shakti	ashlar
metier	oscine	ration	Semite	Taoist	verism	bulker	jerkin	shekel	asylum
milieu	osmium	ratite	senile	taxies	verist	bumkin	jockey	shikar	auklet
minify	ossify	ravine	senior	tedium	verity	bunker	junker	shiksa	avulse
minima	ostial	raving	serial	theine	vesica	bunkum	junkie	sicken	axilla
mining	ostium	ravish	series	theirs	vibist	burkha	junkie	sicker	azalea
minion	outing	recipe	seriph	theism	Viking	busker	kicker	sickle	Baalim
minish	owlish	recite	sewing	theist	vilify	buskin	kiekie	sickly	bailee
minium	oxbird	rediae	sexily	thrice	virile	cackle	kookie	silken	bailer
mobile	oxhide	refill	sexism	thrift	visile	calker	kraken	sinker	bailey
modify	pacify	refine	sexist	thrill	vision	calkin	lackey	sirkar	bailie
modish	paling	regime	sheikh	thrips	visive	canker	lankly	siskin	bailor
modius	palish	regina	sheila	thrive	voting	casket	larker	smoker	ballad
moline	papism	region	Shiite	tibiae	vivify	catkin	larker	soaker	ballet
monial	papist	regius	shriek	tibial	vizier	choker	linkup	socket	ballon
monied	pariah	relict	shrift	tidily	voting	chokey	locker	spoken	ballot
monies	parian	relief	shrike	tiling	votive	chukar	lockup	stakes	barley

```
bawler dowlas gullet niello sallee veiled conman haemin rimmed amends
bawley doyley gulley nuclei sallet vellum cosmic hammal roamer amenta
bedlam drolly hailer nullah sallow vielle cosmos hammam rodman ananas
bellow dually hallal obelus samlet villus cowman hammed roomer anonym
berlin duello halloa ocelli scalar violet crambo hammer rummer atonal
bieldy dunlin halloo ocelot scaled violin crimpy haymow salmon atonic
billet duplet hallow ocular scaler volley crumby helmet scampi avenge
billon duplex hallux omelet scales voulge crummy hemmed scummy avenue
billow eaglet hamlet oodles schlep wailer cummer seaman azonal
billyo efflux harlot orally scilla wallah cummin seamat bagnio
birler eggler haslet ostler scolex walled daemon hetman seamew banned
boblet emblem hauler outlaw sculpt waller daimen hitman seamer banner
boiler emblic healer outlay sealer wallet daimio hodman seamew barney
bollix employ health outlet seller wallop daimon hummed seemly basnet
boulle emulge heeled ovally shalom wallow dammar hummel semmit beanie
bowleg englut heeler ovular shelly waylay dammed hummer sermon bennet
bowler evilly heller oxalic Shelta wealth dermal hummum shaman bionic
brolly evolue holler oxalis shelty whaler dermic isomer shammy blanch
bugler evolve holloa paella shelve whiles dermis jammed shamus blanky
buglet exilic hollow pallet sialic whilom desman jammer shimmy blench
bullae eyalet howler pallia siglum whilst desmid karmic simmer blende
buller eyelet hurler pallid siller wholly dimmed kermes skimpy blenny
bullet eyelid hurley pallor skilly wieldy dimmer kermis skyman blintz
burlap fabled idolum parlay skylab willed dismal kismet slimly blonde
burler fabler inclip parley slalom willet dismay kummel slummy blonde
butler failed inflow pedlar smalls willow dolman Lammas stamen blunge
byblow faille influx peeler smalto wooled dolmen lammed stemma bonnet
byelaw fallal inulin pegleg smelly woolly dormer lawman stumer bonnie
byplay fallen italic pellet smilax yellow dormie layman stumpy bounce
caller fallow jailer peplum smiler zealot enamel legman stymie bouncy
callet faulty jailor phalli souled zillah epimer subman bounds
callow fealty jetlag phylum spilth acumen eremic lummox submit bounty
callup feeler joblot piglet stalag Adamic etymon madman summae branch
callus fellah kaolin pillar stalky agamic examen mammae summed brandy
camlet feller kiblah pillow stelae agamid exempt mammal summer branle
caplin felloe killer piolet stelar ahimsa exomis mammee summit briner
Caslon fellow koolah pollan stilly airman farmer mammer summon bronco
caulis filler lallan polled stolen akimbo fenman mammon swampy bronze
cellar fillet lealty pollen stolid alumna filmic marmot swimmy bronzy
celled fillip loller poller stolon alumni firman merman Talmud brunch
chalet firlot lollop pollex stylar animal firmly Mormon tarmac brunet
chalky foiled mailed poplar stylet animus flambe motmot taxman bunnia
chelae follow Majlis poplin stylus anomic flamen mummer teemer burner
chilli fooler mallee prelim sublet anomie flimsy murmur tegmen burnet
chilly foully mallei proleg sullen ataman flyman muumuu termer burnup
choler foulup mallet prolix sunlit atomic foeman normal termly canned
codlin fowler mallow public suslik bagman formal Norman termor cannel
coelom frilly marlin puller sutler barman format nutmeg thymol canner
collar frolic maslin pullet svelte batman formed ogamic thymus cannon
collet fullam matlow pulley tablet beamer former oilman tinman cannot
collie fuller mealie pullin tailor blimey formic oxymel topman carnal
collop gabled medlar pullon tallow boomer framer palmar tremie carnet
cooler gablet medley pullup teller bowman frumpy palmer tremor carney
coolie Gaelic mellow purler thaler bromic fulmar pelmet trimer catnap
coolly galley merlin purlin thalli brumal gagman penman trimly catnip
coolth Gallic merlon putlog tholoi brumby gammer permit trompe chance
coulee Gallio milled qualmy tholos bummed gammon pieman trumps chancy
cowled gallon miller raglan tholus bummer gasman pitman tsamba change
culler gallop millet railer thulia bummle gemmae plumed vermin chanty
cullet gaoler mislay ratlin tiller Burman gemmed wadmal chintz
cullis garlic misled really titled busman german plummy wadmol chunky
curler gelled moiler realty toiler cabman germen plumpy warmer clench
curlew giglet mollie reeler toilet caiman gigman pommel warmly clinch
cutler giglot moolah reflex trilby calmly gimmal pommie warmth clingy
cutlet gilled Moslem reflow trolly carman gimmer potman warmup clinic
cycler gillie motley reflux tuille cayman glumly premed whimsy clonal
cyclic gimlet mouldy reglet twelve cermet glumpy premix whomso clonic
dahlia girlie moulin replay twilit chemic gnomic primal wormer clonus
dealer goalie muflon replum umbles chimer gnomon primer yammer clunch
deploy goblet mukluk rifler unclad chummy gramme primly yeoman cobnut
dewlap goblin mullah rillet unglue clammy Grammy prompt yesman cognac
diglot goglet muller rollon unplug climax gramps pummel acinar coiner
diplex gollop mullet rollon Uralic clumpy grimly ragman adenyl coinop
diploe goslow mulley ruelle uvulae clumsy grumly rammed Adonic conned
diplon grille Muslim runlet uvular commie grumps rammer Adonis coonty
dogleg grilse muslin sables valley commis grumpy reamer agency cornea
dollar Guelph myelin sailed vallum commit gummed rhombi agenda corned
dollop guilty nailer sailer varlet commix gunman rhumba agonal cornel
doolie Gullah nielli sailor vaulty common haemal rhymer agonic corner
```

cornet	ginner	nounal	signal	whence	bloomy	embody	judoka	putoff	snoopy
cornua	glance	nuance	signer	whiner	bosomy	emboli	kalong	pylori	snooty
county	goanna	oilnut	signet	whinge	botone	emboly	kaross	pyrola	snooze
cranch	gooney	omenta	signor	whinny	briony	emboss	ketone	pyrope	sodomy
crania	grange	opener	simnel	wiener	brooch	encode	kibosh	racoon	splore
cranky	granny	openly	sinned	winner	broody	encore	kimono	radome	splosh
cranny	Granth	orange	sinner	winnow	bryony	enfold	kitool	ragout	spooky
crenel	gringo	ozonic	sinnet	woundy	byform	enjoin	kobold	ramose	spoony
cringe	guanin	panned	skinny	wrench	bygone	enrobe	labour	ramous	sprout
crunch	guenon	paunch	slangy	yenned	byroad	enroll	lagoon	ratoon	stooge
cunner	guinea	pawnee	slinky	zinnia	byword	enroot	lavolt	rebore	strobe
cyanic	gunned	pawner	sonnet	zounds	bywork	ensoul	layoff	reborn	strode
cyanin	gunnel	paynim	sooner	abloom	cacoon	entoil	layout	recoil	stroke
cygnet	gunner	peanut	sorner	abroad	cahoot	entomb	lemony	recoin	stroll
dainty	gurnet	pennae	spence	absorb	cajole	enwomb	letoff	record	stroma
damned	guvnor	penned	spinal	accord	calory	Eozoic	lipoid	recoup	stromb
darned	haunch	pennon	spined	accost	canopy	Eozoon	lipoma	redone	strong
darnel	hernia	phenol	spinel	across	capote	escort	lobose	reform	stroud
darner	hobnob	phenyl	spinet	adjoin	cavort	essoin	mahout	rejoin	strout
dinned	horned	phoney	sponge	adroit	choose	eulogy	maroon	reload	strove
dinner	horner	phonic	spongy	adsorb	choosy	evzone	Masora	remora	strown
dipnet	hornet	phonon	spunky	aerobe	chroma	exhort	megohm	remote	suborn
dirndl	hymnal	picnic	stance	afford	chrome	export	melody	remove	swoosh
djinni	hymnic	pignut	stanch	afloat	chromo	expose	memoir	renown	tabour
donned	iconic	pinnae	stanza	ageold	citole	extort	memory	report	tenour
downer	irenic	pinned	stench	alcove	cocoon	famous	metope	repose	theory
drench	ironer	pinner	stingo	aldose	cohort	faroff	midoff	resold	throat
drongo	ironic	pionic	stingy	algoid	colony	farout	milord	resole	throes
duende	jaunce	planar	stinko	allout	colour	favour	mimosa	resorb	throne
duenna	jaunty	planer	stoned	almond	comose	fedora	Minoan	resort	throng
dunned	jennet	planet	stoner	almost	comous	felony	Mohock	retold	throve
durned	jinnee	plenty	sunned	angora	conoid	femora	mohole	retook	thrown
earner	jitney	plenum	swanky	anyone	copout	filose	Moloch	retool	timous
Edenic	joanna	plinth	swinge	aphony	corody	floozy	monody	retort	tipoff
eggnog	johnny	plunge	taenia	aplomb	corona	fucoid	mopoke	revoke	toroid
eponym	joiner	pointe	tanned	apnoea	corozo	furore	morose	revolt	torose
erenow	jounce	points	tanner	appose	coyote	gadoid	motory	rewoke	toxoid
eryngo	jouncy	pounce	tannic	arbour	creole	galoot	mucoid	reword	triode
ethnic	kainit	prance	tannin	ardour	cuboid	galore	mucosa	rework	tryout
evener	keenly	prince	teensy	areola	cupola	galosh	mucous	ribose	tumour
evenly	kenned	pronto	tenner	areole	cutoff	ganoid	myxoma	rigour	tycoon
evince	kennel	pruner	tennis	argosy	cutout	genome	neroli	rigout	ugsome
fainly	kerned	punned	thanks	ariosi	cymose	getout	nobody	rimose	unbolt
fanned	kernel	punner	thenar	arioso	dacoit	giaour	nodose	rimous	unborn
fanner	kidnap	punnet	thence	armour	dagoes	gigolo	oblong	ripoff	uncoil
faunae	kidney	pycnic	things	arroba	decoct	gloomy	ochone	rococo	uncool
faunal	krantz	pyknic	thingy	arrowy	decode	godown	oclock	rufous	uncork
faunas	kronen	quanta	thinly	arroyo	decoke	golosh	odious	rugose	undock
fawner	kroner	quench	tinned	ashore	deform	groove	oncost	rumour	undoer
fennec	kronor	quince	tinner	aslope	dehorn	groovy	oneoff	runoff	undone
fennel	kronur	quinoa	townee	assoil	demode	haloes	oology	saloon	unfold
fiance	lanner	quinol	trance	assort	demote	heroic	oolong	saloop	unholy
finnan	launce	quinsy	trench	aswoon	denote	heroin	oppose	Samoan	unhook
finned	launch	quinta	trendy	athome	depone	hexose	oriole	sapota	unjoin
finner	leanly	regnal	trinal	attorn	deport	honour	ormolu	sarong	unload
Finnic	leanto	rennet	tunnel	aurora	depose	humour	osmose	satori	unlock
flanch	Leonid	rhinal	turner	aurous	desorb	huzoor	otiose	savory	unmoor
flange	lignin	rouncy	turnip	awmous	detour	idiocy	oxford	savour	unrobe
flench	limner	ruiner	turnup	baboon	devoid	ignore	paeony	saxony	unroof
flense	linnet	runnel	twangy	barony	devoir	impone	pagoda	school	unroot
flinch	linney	runner	twenty	become	devote	import	palolo	schorl	unrope
flinty	lionel	sannup	twiner	befool	devout	impose	parody	scroll	unruly
flunky	loaner	sawney	twinge	before	dhooly	impost	parole	scroop	untold
fornix	lounge	scanty	unknit	befoul	dhooti	inborn	parous	second	unworn
french	maenad	scenic	unknot	begone	didoes	income	patois	senora	unyoke
frenum	magnet	sconce	Urania	behold	dipody	indole	payoff	serosa	uphold
frenzy	magnum	seance	uranic	behoof	dipole	indoor	payola	serous	upmost
fringe	mainly	seiner	Uranus	behove	disown	infold	pelota	setoff	uproar
fringy	manned	sennet	uranyl	belong	dodoes	inform	peyotl	setout	uptown
funned	manner	sennit	urinal	bemoan	dogood	inmost	peyote	setose	uproot
funnel	maundy	shandy	usance	bemock	dolour	inroad	phloem	sheoak	utmost
gainer	meanie	shanny	vainly	betony	droopy	insole	phooey	shroff	valour
gainly	meanly	shanty	vanner	betook	dugong	intoed	pilose	shroud	vapour
gainst	meinie	shindy	veined	beyond	dugout	intone	pilous	shrove	veloce
gannet	mignon	shiner	vernal	bezoar	dumose	invoke	pinole	simony	velour
garner	minnow	shinny	viands	biform	echoer	inwove	polony	simoom	venose
garnet	moaner	Shinto	walnut	bijoux	echoic	jalopy	porose	simoon	venous
genned	mornay	shinty	weaner	bizone	effort	jocose	porous	smooch	vigour
ginned	nignog	sienna	whenas	bloody	eidola	joyous	priory	smooth	vinous

```
virose eloper neaped simple wampee burrel floral midrib Sevres thyrse
volost epopee nipped simply wampum burrow floras mihrab sharer thyrsi
wayout fipple nipper sipped wapper capric floret mirror sharif tierce
whoops flappy nipple sipper warped carrel florid mitral sharps tiered
whoosh floppy nympho sippet warper carrot florin morris sherif tierod
xyloid frappe output slapup weapon charas flurry morrow Sherpa torrid
xylose gapped palpal slipon weeper charge forrad murrey sherry tourer
yapock gasper palpus slippy weepie Charon forrit narrow shirty Tuareg
zeloso gospel pampas slipup whippy cherry fourth natron shoran turret
zufolo grappa pamper sloppy wimple cherty fuhrer nearby shorts twirly
zygoma griper pappus snappy yapped cherub furred nearer shorty umbrae
zygote grippe parpen sniper yapper chirpy furrow nearly sierra umbral
adipic grippy pauper snippy yaupon choral garran neural sirrah umbras
aliped groper pawpaw sopped yelper chorea garret neuron sirree unbred
armpit gypped peeper stapes yipped choric garron Nimrod skerry untrue
ashpan hamper peepul staple yippee chorus garrot nitric skirun unwrap
bedpan happed people stepin yippie church George nutria slurry uphroe
beeper happen pepped steppe zapped cirrus gharry octroi smarmy usurer
biopsy harper pepper stepup zipped citric gloria orfray smarty uterus
bopped hatpeg pimple stipel zipper citron gnarly osprey smirch vagrom
bopper hatpin pimply stipes barque citrus gourde outran smirky vibrio
bumper helper pipped stopgo Basque claret gurrah outrun snarer vitric
calpac hempen pippin stupid bisque clergy hadron overdo snarly walrus
camper herpes pitpan stupor caique cleric hairdo overly snorer warred
campus hipped pompom supped calque coarse haired parral soiree warren
capped hippie pooped supper casque coerce harrow parrel sorrel wearer
carpal hirple popped supple cheque corral hatred parrot sorrow weirdo
carpel hispid popper supply cinque corrie hearer patrol source weirdy
carper holpen poppet swiper cirque course hearse patron sourly wherry
carpet hooper popple swipes claque cowrie hearth pearly sovran whirly
carpus hoopla popply taipan clique crural hearty perron sparer worrit
chapel hoopoe potpie tampan cliquy cupric Hebrew petrel sparge yarrow
chappy hopped prepay tamper exequy currie henrun petrol sparks yearly
chippy hopper propel tampon lasque Cymric henrys pharos sparry yttria
chopin hopple proper tapped manque cyprid Herren picric sparse abuser
choppy hotpot propyl tapper marque dearie hoarse pierce spiral airsac
chypre humped pulper tappet masque dearly hooray plural spirit amuser
clipon inkpot pulpit tappit mosque dearth horrid pogrom sports arisen
clypei inspan pumper tarpan opaque debris horror poorly sporty arista
compel isopod pupped tarpon plaque decree hourly pourer spurge Aussie
comply jasper puppet tawpie pulque degras hubris pterin spurry Avesta
cooper jumper purple teapot risque degree hurrah putrid starch balsam
copped keeper purply teapoy sacque derris hurray quarry starer basset
copper kelpie Rajput teepee torque dharma hybrid quarte starry bassos
corpse kewpie ramper temper unique dhurra hybris quarto starve bedsit
corpus kipper rapped temple aboral dourly hydric quartz stereo bhisti
couple klepht rappee tenpin acarid dryrot imbrex quirky steric bolshy
coupon koppie rappel tiepin acarus dryrun imbrue quorum sterna bonsai
cowpat lapped rapper tinpot accrue durrie inarch ramrod sterol borsch
cowpea lappet reaper tipped adorer ecarte inbred rearer stirps bowsaw
cowpox lappie reopen tipper affray Egeria intray redraw storax brassy
crappy leaper rhaphe tippet agaric embrue inwrap regret stores brushy
cripes limper ripped tipple alarum embryo jarrah retral storey bunsen
croppy limpet ripper topped aldrin amerce jarred retrod stormy bursae
crypto limpid ripple topper allred emerge jeerer ricrac sturdy bursal
cupped limply ripply topple amerce energy karroo riprap styrax bursar
cusped lipped romper torpid amoral engram labret roarer sunray bursas
cuspid lippen rumble torpor anarch entrap labrum rubric surrey bussed
dampen lippie rumpus toupee anorak entree larrup runrig swaraj byssus
damper lisper sampan toupet antral enwrap latria sacral swarth capsid
damply looper sample trapan antrum escrow latron sacred swerve cassia
dapper lopped scopae trapes astral esprit laurel sacrum swirly cassis
dapple lopper scopas trappy astray estray learnt satrap tagrag catsup
deepen loupen scyphi trepan averse eterne lierne saurel tanrec causal
deeply loupit seapen trepid barred exarch lubric scarab tarras causer
despot lumpen seapig triple barrel fabric macron scarce tarred causey
diaper lumper semple triply barren faerie madras scarer Taurus censer
dimple magpie sempre tripod barret fairly marram scarry tenrec censor
dimply mapped sexpot tripos barrio farrow marred scarus terret census
dipped mapper shaped trophy barrow feirie marron scorch terror cesser
dipper mopped shapen tropic bearer ferret marrow scorer terror chaser
dispel mopper shaper troppo betray ferric marrum scoria tetrad chaste
Dopper moppet shoppy twoply bewray fibred matrix scurfy thirst chesil
draper morpho simper tympan bharal fibril matron scurry thirty chesty
drippy mumper shaped uniped blurry fierce merrie scurvy thorax chisel
dropsy murphy shapen unipod borrow fiorin metred secret thoria chosen
drupel myopia shaper utopia borrow flirty metric serrae thorny classy
dumper myopic shoppy vamper bourne flirty metric serran thorpe closed
elapse napped simper vesper bourse florae micron serran thorpe closet
```

comsat	grassy	pepsin	tmeses	bettor	cotted	filthy	instil	mestee	pistol
consul	grisly	person	tmesis	biotic	cotter	fistic	iritis	mettle	piston
corsac	grison	phasic	tocsin	biotin	cotton	fitted	isatin	milter	pitted
corsak	guiser	phasis	tonsil	bister	cratch	fitter	jester	minter	pitter
corset	gunsel	physic	torsel	bistre	crater	flatly	jetted	miotic	platan
cosset	gunshy	pigsty	tosser	bistro	Cretan	flatus	jilter	mister	platen
cousin	gusset	pissed	tossup	bitted	cretic	fletch	jitter	mistle	plater
crases	gypsum	pitsaw	tousle	bitten	cretin	flitch	jolter	mitten	plotty
crasis	hansel	plashy	trashy	bitter	critic	fluted	jostle	moated	pluton
cresol	hansom	plasma	tressy	blithe	crotal	fluter	jotted	molten	poetic
crises	hassle	plisse	triste	blotch	crotch	foetal	jotter	mortal	poetry
crisis	hawser	plushy	trusty	blotto	croton	foetid	justly	mortar	pontie
crispy	hisser	podsol	tussah	boatel	crutch	foetus	kaftan	mostly	pontil
crista	hoised	poison	tusser	boater	cultch	fontal	kelter	mottle	ponton
crosse	horsey	posset	tussle	bolter	cultic	footed	Keltic	mouthy	portal
cruset	housel	possum	tutsan	booted	cultus	footer	kettle	multum	porter
crusty	housey	preses	twisty	bootee	cuptie	footle	kilted	muntin	portly
cuesta	hussar	preset	unisex	boston	curtal	foster	kilter	muster	postal
cuisse	hyssop	presto	unison	bottle	curtly	fratch	kirtle	mutter	poster
cursed	jersey	prison	unused	bottom	curtsy	frater	kittle	mutton	postil
cursor	jetsam	prissy	Vaisya	bowtie	custom	frothy	kitten	myotic	potted
cursus	jigsaw	proser	vassal	Breton	cutter	frutex	kittle	myrtle	potter
cussed	josser	prosit	versal	Briton	cuttle	fustic	kittul	mystic	pottle
damsel	kaiser	ptisan	versed	brutal	cystic	gaited	knotty	nastic	pouter
damson	kelson	ptosis	verset	brutus	cystid	gaiter	kowtow	natter	prater
dassie	kersey	puisne	verset	bunted	dactyl	gantry	kultur	nautch	pratie
deasil	kirsch	pulsar	versus	bunter	daftly	garter	lactic	neaten	pretax
diesel	kisser	pulser	vessel	burton	darter	gentes	laster	neatly	pretty
dieses	kitsch	purser	vizsla	busted	dartle	gentle	lastly	nectar	protea
diesis	lapsed	pursue	warsle	bustee	dartre	gently	latten	nekton	proton
dipsas	lapsus	putsch	weasel	buster	debtor	gentoo	latter	nestle	puntee
donsie	lassie	quasar	whisht	bustle	deftly	gentry	lector	Nestor	punter
dorsal	lassos	raiser	whisky	bustup	dental	getter	Lenten	netted	puttee
dorsum	lensed	raisin	winsey	butter	dentel	ghetto	lentil	nettle	putter
dossal	lessee	ramson	worsen	button	dentil	gifted	lepton	neuter	puttie
dossel	lessen	ransom	wowser	cactus	dexter	glitch	letter	newton	quitch
dosser	lesser	reason	wrasse	caftan	diatom	glutei	Lettic	noetic	quotes
douser	lesson	rhesus	yeasty	canter	dictum	gluten	lictor	nostoc	quotha
dowser	lessor	rinser	abater	canthi	dieter	goatee	lifter	nutter	rafter
dressy	linsey	ripsaw	abatis	cantle	diktat	gotten	lintel	obital	ragtag
drosky	lissom	rouser	acetal	canton	distal	grater	lintie	orator	ranter
drossy	loosen	russet	acetic	cantor	distil	gratin	listed	otitis	raptly
egesta	marshy	russia	acetyl	cantus	dittos	gratis	listel	ouster	raptor
emeses	massif	Samson	adytum	captor	doctor	gritty	listen	outtop	raster
emesis	measly	sarsen	alated	cartel	doited	gritty	listen	oyster	rattan
enisle	mensal	sawset	amatol	carter	dorter	grotto	lister	palter	rattat
enosis	menses	season	anatta	carton	dotted	grotty	litter	paltry	ratted
eraser	messan	seesaw	anatto	caster	dottle	grutch	little	pantry	ratter
falsie	Messrs	seisin	aortal	castle	duster	guitar	loathe	partan	rattle
feisty	miasma	senses	aortic	castor	dustup	gunter	lofter	partly	rector
fiasco	miosis	sensor	apathy	cattle	earthy	guttae	loiter	pastel	rectum
fiesta	missal	sensum	arctic	Celtic	easter	guttas	looter	pastil	rectus
flashy	missel	sepsis	auntie	cental	editor	gutted	lister	pastor	redtop
fleshy	missis	siesta	Austin	centre	elated	gutter	luetic	pastry	rental
flossy	missus	sissoo	avatar	centum	elater	haptic	lustra	patted	renter
flysch	morsel	sloshy	azotic	certes	elytra	hartal	lustre	patten	rester
focsle	mouser	slushy	baiter	cestus	emetic	hasten	maltha	patter	retted
foison	mousse	sonsie	Baltic	chatty	emetin	hatted	mantel	pecten	rhetor
forsay	muesli	stases	bantam	chital	erotic	hatter	mantes	pectic	rhythm
fossae	mussel	stasis	banter	chitin	exotic	heated	mantic	pectin	rictal
fossil	myosin	subset	barter	chiton	Eyetie	heater	mantid	pegtop	rictus
fossor	myosis	sunset	barton	chitty	factor	heathy	mantis	peltae	rioter
fresco	nausea	swishy	baster	cistus	factum	hectic	mantle	pelter	rooted
frisky	nelson	tahsil	batted	clothe	falter	hector	mantra	peltry	rooter
frosty	noesis	tarsal	batten	clutch	fantan	heptad	mantua	pentad	roster
frusta	nurser	tarsia	batter	coated	Fantee	hiatus	marten	pentup	rostra
fusser	oddson	tarsus	battle	coatee	fantod	hogtie	martin	pentyl	rotted
gassed	offset	tassel	battue	coital	fantom	hootch	martyr	peptic	rotten
gasser	omasum	tassie	beaten	coitus	fasten	hooter	masted	pertly	rotter
geisha	orison	teasel	beater	colter	faster	hostel	master	pester	router
geyser	outsat	teaser	beetle	cootie	fatted	hotter	mastic	pestle	rustic
ghosty	outset	teaset	belted	Coptic	fatten	hunter	matted	petted	rustle
glassy	outsit	telson	bertha	cortex	fatter	hurter	matter	petter	rutted
glossy	ovisac	tenson	berthe	costae	featly	hurtle	meatus	pewter	saeter
gnosis	parsec	tensor	bested	costal	festal	hustle	meetly	phatic	saithe
godson	Parsee	theses	bestir	costar	fester	hutted	melton	photic	salter
gooses	parson	thesis	bestow	coster	fetter	instal	mental	photon	saltus
gossan	passer	tinsel	betted	costly	fettle	instar	mentor	pintle	santal
gossip	passim	tissue	better	cottar	filter	instep	mentum	pistil	santir

```
scathe syntax waiter bohunk incubi papula swound craver slavey outwit
scatty system wanted Canuck incult papule syrupy culver Slavic peewit
scotch tactic wanton casual incuse parure tegula curvet sliver powwow
scoter tamtam warted cayuse ceruse penult Telugu delver Slovak prewar
scotia tantra wasted ceruse induct penury tenues drivel sloven runway
Scotic tartan waster cesura indult peruke tenuis driven snivel seaway
scutal tartar wattle chaunt induna peruse tenure driver soever shower
scutch tartly welter chough infula pilule tenuto drover solver skewer
scutum taster wester chouse infuse piquet though eleven spavin skyway
scythe tatted wetted clause ingulf pleura thrush elevon stiver slowly
seater tatter wetter cloudy inhume plough thrust fervid stover spewer
sector tattle whatso clough injure pneuma toluic flavin survey stewed
seethe tattoo whited colugo injury pseudo toluol frivol sweven subway
sentry tauten whiten column inrush queuer torula garvie swivel tiewig
septal tautly whites colure insult radula trauma glover sylvan trowel
septet tautog whitey copula insure raguly triune graved travel tulwar
septic teeter Wilton coquet intuit ranula trough gravel trivet twoway
septum teethe winter crouch irrupt rasure troupe graven trivia viewer
sestet tenter wintle croupy jaguar rebuff trouty graver trover wigwag
settee tentie wintry crouse jejune rebuke tubule Graves turves wigwam
setter testae witted cumuli Jesuit reduce tumuli gravid uneven Yahweh
settle tester wittol cupule jocund refuel tumult grivet valved alexia
sextan teston wonted curule jujube refuge twould grovel varved alexin
sextet tetter wonton datura kabuki refund uncurl halvah velvet anoxia
sexton Teuton worthy debunk kaputt refuse unduly halves vervet anoxic
shutin thatch wortle deduce kiaugh refute unfurl heaven volvox apexes
sifter thetic wrathy deduct lacuna regulo ungual heaver waiver ataxia
sinter tictac wretch defuse laguna reluct ungues hooves weaver ataxic
sister tilter writer degust lanugo relume unguis jarvey weever bonxie
sistra tinter writhe delude lazuli remuda ungula kelvin weevil calxes
sittar tiptoe xystus deluge legume repugn unjust knives wolves cruxes
sitter tiptop yatter deluxe ligula repute unruly larvae Yahveh elixir
skater titter yester demure ligule result unsung larval airway flaxen
sketch tittle zlotys denude ligure resume untuck leaved answer flexor
slater tittup abduce depute limuli returf untune leaven anyway hoaxer
smatch tomtit abduct deputy liquid return uprush leaver avowal ibexes
smiter tomtom abjure dilute liquor retuse upturn leaves avowed orexis
smithy tooter ablush disuse lobule rheumy vacuum loaves bagwig plexor
smutch toothy abound drouth loculi ritual valuer louver bigwig plexus
smutty tootle abrupt effuse locust robust valuta louvre blowed praxis
snatch tootsy absurd emeute loquat roquet velure marvel blower alkyne
snathe torten accuse empusa lunula rosula venule naevus blowsy argyle
snitch totted acquit endure lunule rotund vicuna oeuvre blowup banyan
snotty totter actual engulf luxury saluki vidual ogival blowzy baryon
soften touter adduce ennuye macula salute visual oliver bobwig baryta
softie triton adduct enough macule Saturn volume outvie bowwow bowyer
softly tsetse adjure ensure maduro schuss volute parvis brawly brayer
soothe tsotsi adjust escudo maguey scouse yaourt peavey brawny bunyip
sorter tufted agouti eunuch manual scouth yogurt pelves brewer canyon
sortes tufter allude excuse manuka scruff Yoruba pelvic brewis clayey
sortie tumtum allure exeunt manure scrump alevin pelvis browny corymb
sotted turtle ambush exhume maquis secund beaver plover browse coryza
souter tutted amount facula mature secure beeves privet cobweb crayon
spathe twitch annual famuli medusa seduce bovver proven crawly encyst
spital ulster annuli faquir mezuza sequel brevet pulvil crewel enzyme
spotty united arguer fecula minuet sequin calves purvey dimwit ethyne
sputum uniter argufy fecund minute sexual canvas quaver drawee greyly
statal unstop argute ferula misuse sheugh carvel quiver drawer groyne
stated ureter around ferule module should carven reaver drowse gunyah
stater vastly arouse fibula moduli shrunk carver reiver drowsy Kabyle
states vatted assume figure modulo simurg cervix revved earwax ladyfy
static vector assure flaunt morula Siouan chevet salver earwig larynx
stator venter astute fleury mutual sleuth chives salvia flower lawyer
statue ventil attune floury mutule slouch chivvy salvor flyway Libyan
status ventre auburn Frauen mutuum slough claver salvos frowst Magyar
stitch vertex augury future nature smouch clavis selves frowsy obeyer
stithy vestal august garuda nebula snouty clever serval frowzy oocyte
subtil vested autumn gazump nebuly solute clevis server glower papyri
subtle vestee avaunt gerund nodule spouse cloven shaven gnawer player
subtly vestry avouch grouch nonuse spruce clover shaver godwit polypi
suitor vetted Basuto ground objure spruit coeval shavie grower prayer
sultan viator Basutu grouse obtund sprung convex shiver growly ronyon
sultry victim Beaune illume obtuse stound convey shovel growth satyra
suntan victor beauty illuse occult struck convoy shover keyway sawyer
surtax vintry beduin immune occupy struma corvee silvan knower sayyid
suttee virtue beluga immure onrush strung corves silver leeway scryer
swatch vittae bemuse impugn oppugn strunt Corvus skiver midway slayer
swathe vortex benumb impure ordure suburb cravat skivvy nitwit spryer
switch wafter blouse impute oscula suture craven slaver oneway spryly
```

```
stayer alulae byelaw dewlap garial jumbal monial prewar serial thenar
swayer amoral byplay diktat garran kaftan moolah primal serrae thorax
syzygy anabas byroad dipsas gasbag kasbah mornay ptisan serran thread
wheyey ananas cabman dirham gasman keyway mortal pulsar serval threap
yumyum animal caecal disbar gateau kiblah mortar punkah sextan threat
amazon anneal caftan discal gavial kidnap moshav purdah sexual throat
apozem annual caiman dismal gemmae kitbag mullah quasar shaman tibiae
banzai anodal calcar dismay genial kitcat muscat racial sheoak tibial
benzol anorak calpac distal german koolah mutual radial shikar tictac
benzyl antiar cancan dogear gewgaw Korean myriad radian shofar tiebar
blazer antral canvas dollar giddap kowhai nectar ragbag shoran timbal
blazes anyway capias dolman gigman kurgan neural raglan signal tincal
blazon aortal carfax doodad gimbal labial nilgai ragman silvan tindal
bonzer aoudal carman doodah gimmal laical nonfat ragtag simian tinman
boozer apical carnal Dorian gingal lallan normal randan Siouan tipcat
borzoi apodal carpal dorsal global Lammas Norman rascal sircar titian
brazen appeal casbah dossal goddam landau nougat ratbag sirdar toecap
brazil appear casual dowlas gossan lariat nounal rattan sirkar tombac
buzzer ashcan Cathar durbar gozzan larvae nuchal rattat sirrah tombak
crazed ashlar catnap durgan guaiac larval nullah redcap sittar tomcat
dazzle ashpan caudal Durham guffaw lascar obital rediae skylab topman
epizoa ashram causal durian guitar lawman ocular redraw skyman toucan
fezzed astral caveat earwax Gullah layday ogival reggae skyway trapan
fezzes astray caviar endear gunman layman oilcan regnal slogan trepan
fizzle ataman cayman engram gunyah leeway oilman rehear Slovak tribal
foozle atonal celiac ennead gurrah legman oneway reheat smilax tricar
frazil atrial cellar entrap guttae lethal oomiak reload social trinal
frizzy Augean cental enwrap haemal Libyan ordeal rental soldan trocar
frozen avatar cereal eolian hallal lineal orfray repeal sovran Trojan
geezer avowal charas eonian halvah linear orgeat repeat spinal tulwar
glazer azonal chelae epical hammal linhay origan replay spiral turban
gozzan bagman chital eschar hammam lochan orphan reread spital Tuscan
grazer ballad choral espial hangar loggat osteal reseat spread tussah
guzzle balsam chukar estray hartal logjam ostial reseau squeak tutsan
matzoh banian climax Fabian hawhaw longan outlaw retial squeal twoway
mizzen banjax clonal facial heehaw loofah outlay retral stalag tymbal
mizzle bantam coccal fallal hepcat loquat outran reveal statal tympan
mizzly banyan coeval fantan heptad lumbar outsat rhinal stelae Tyrian
muzzle banzai cognac faucal herbal lurdan ovisac ricrac stelar Ugrian
nozzle baobab coital faunae hereat luteal ovular rictal storax umbrae
nuzzle barman collar faunal hetman Lydian paleae riprap streak umbral
panzer bashaw combat faunas heyday machan palmar ripsaw stream umbras
piazza bateau comsat fellah hitman madcap palpal ritual striae uncial
pizzle batman confab Fenian hodman madman pampas rizzar stylar unclad
podzol bazaar conman fenman hookah madras pariah rodman styrax ungual
prizer bedlam corban ferial hooray maenad parian runway subman unload
puzzle bedpan corral festal houdan Magian parlay rupiah subway unread
razzia beggar corsac fetial howdah Magyar parral sabbat sultan unreal
razzle behead corsak feudal hubcap maidan partan Sabian summae unseal
rizzar beldam costae filial hurrah mammae pascal sacral sundae unseam
rizzer bemoan costal finial hurray mammal Pathan saggar Sunday unseat
rozzer betray costar finnan hussar manday pawpaw salaam sunhat unwrap
scazon bewray cottar firman hymnal maniac payday Salian sunray upbear
seizer bezoar coucal fiscal hyphae manual pedlar sambar suntan upbeat
seizin bharal cougar florae hyphal margay pelham Samian surtax uproar
sizzle bobcat cowman floral icebag marram peltae Samoan swaraj urinal
snazzy bonsai cowpat floras icecap mayday penman sampan sylvan uvulae
Tarzan boreal cravat flyman iceman mayhap pennae sandal syntax uvular
teazel Boreas credal flyway Indian mediae pentad sangar Syriac vandal
teazle bowman Cretan foeman inroad medial pieman sanjak Syrian vassal
tenzon bowsaw crotal foetal inseam median pillar santal tagrag venial
weazen boxcar crural foliar inspan medlar pineal sappan taipan verbal
zigzag bridal curiae fontal instal menial pinnae sashay tampan vernal
       brumal curial forbad instar mensal pitman satrap tamtam versal
aboral brutal curtal formal intray mental pitpan scalar tarmac vestal
abroad buccal cushat format inwrap merman pitsaw scarab tarpan vidual
acetal bulbar cymbal forrad Ionian mescal plagal scopae tarras visual
acinar Bulgar daedal forsay isobar mesial planar scopas tarsal vittae
actual bullae dammar fossae jackal messan platan screak tartan vulcan
Aegean bureau deejay foveae jaguar midday plicae scream tartar vulgar
aerial burial defeat foveal jarrah midway plural scutal Tarzan wadmal
affray burlap defray fracas jetlag mihrab pollan seaear taxman wallah
Afghan Burman degras Friday jetsam Minoan poplar seafan teabag waylay
afloat bursae demean frugal jibbah mishap portal seaman tergal whenas
agonal bursal denial fulham jigsaw mislay postal seamat testae whidah
airman bursar dental fullam jovial missal potman seaway tetrad whydah
airsac bursar deodar fulmar Jovian mitral prefab seesaw Theban wigwag
airway busbar dermal fungal Judean mobcap prepay sendal thecae wigwam
alegar busman desman gagman Julian Monday pretax septal thecal withal
```

```
wombat blench french reface arcade reside azalea bitter bushel clypei
xenial blotch fresco refect Arcady salade backer bladed busker coated
yeoman bodice glance reject armada secede badger blazer bussed coatee
yesman borsch glitch relict aubade shandy bagged blazes busted cobber
zigzag bounce grouch reluct beside shindy bailee blimey bustee cobweb
zillah bouncy grutch resect betide shoddy bailer blowed buster cocked
zodiac branch haunch rococo bieldy skiddy bailey blower butler cocker
aerobe breach hexact rosace blende solidi baiter boatel butter codger
akimbo breech hijack rouncy blonde solids baleen boater buzzer coffee
amoeba broach hootch scarce bloody speedo balker bobbed cachet coffer
arroba bronco humect sconce bolide speedy ballet boblet cadger cogged
brumby brooch idiocy scorch boride steady banger bodger cahier coiner
chubby brunch impact scotch bounds stride banker bogged calces collet
crabby calico inarch scutch brandy strode banket boiler calker colter
crambo Canuck indict seance broody sturdy banned bolter caller combed
crumby chance induce search cicada swaddy bomber bonnet callet comber
djibba chancy induct seduce cloddy teledu banter bonder calves compel
enrobe choice infect select cloudy teredo barbed bonxie calxes confer
ephebe church inject silica comedo tirade barbel bonzer camber congee
ephebi cilice insect sketch comedy Toledo barber booker camlet conger
flabby civics intact slouch corody trendy barbet boomer camper conker
flambe clench inwick sluice cruddy triode bargee booted cancel conned
gazebo clinch jaunce sluicy decade tuxedo barker bootee cancer conner
grabby cloaca jounce smatch decide tweeds barley boozer canker convex
grubby clunch jouncy smeech decode tweedy barney bopeep canned convey
hereby clutch kirsch smirch delude unlade barred bopped canner cooker
imbibe coerce kopeck smooch denude unmade barrel bopper canter cooler
incubi kitsch launce smouch deride untidy barren bordel capped copier
indaba copeck launch smutch dipody upside barret border carder copped
jujube cranch legacy snatch dirndl viands barter bordar career copper
knobby cratch lorica snitch divide weirdo basher bosket careen coquet
lavabo crotch lunacy solace dorado weirdy basket bother caries corbel
nearby crouch lyrics source duende wieldy basnet bovver carnet corded
phoebe crunch macaco speech embody woundy basset bowleg carney corder
plebby crutch malice spence encode zounds baster bowler carpal cornea
rhombi cultch maraca splice escudo abater bather bowyer carpel corned
rhumba curacy matico spruce excide abuser batted boxbed carper cornel
scabby decoct medick stance facade acumen batten bracer carpet corner
scribe deduce medico stanch garuda addled batter braces carrel cornet
shabby deduct menace starch gourde adorer bawbee brayer cartel corset
snobby deface Mohock stench greedy aether bawler brazen carter cortex
snubby defect Moloch stitch hairdo affeer bawley brewer carven corves
strobe deject Munich strict halide afreet beaked briber carver cosher
stubby delict myrica struck impede airbed beaker briner casein cosset
trilby depict nautch stucco inside aisled beamer broken casket coster
tsamba detach notice sumach invade alated bearer broker caster cotted
unrobe detect novice swatch iodide aliped beaten brunet causer cotter
Wahabi device nuance switch lambda allied beater bucker causey coulee
Yoruba direct object tenace libido allred beaver bucket celled cowled
zareba dreich obtect thatch lipide ambler becket budded censer cowpea
zariba drench oclock thence makedo amulet bedded budget cermet crases
abbacy droich office thrice malady anadem bedder buffer certes crater
abduce efface optics thwack maundy angled beeper buffet cesser craven
abduct effect outact tierce melody angler beeves bugged chafer craver
abject enface palace trance mikado anklet begged bugler chalet crazed
ackack enlace papacy trench milady answer beigel buglet chapel crenel
addict enrich paunch twitch monody anthem belief bulbed chaser crewel
adduce entice pierce undock mouldy anther belted bulger chevet crikey
adduct ethics piracy unlace nobody antler bender bulker chimer cripes
advice eunuch plaice unlock noyade apexes bennet buller chisel crises
affect evince pleach unpack onside apices Berber bullet chives cruces
agency exarch Polack unpick overdo apnoea beseem bummed choker cruset
alpaca expect police untuck oxhide apogee bested bummer chokey cruxes
amerce exsect policy usance pagoda apozem betted bumper choler cudgel
anarch fetich pomace veloce panada arched better bunder chorea cuffed
anlace fiance pounce vesica parade archer bibbed bunsen cinder culler
apiece fiasco prance vivace parody arguer bibber bunted cipher cullet
arnica fierce preach whence pesade ariled bicker bunter cither culver
arrack flanch prince wrench ploidy arisen bidden burden claret cumber
aspect fleece pumice wretch pomade armlet bidder burgee claver cummer
attach fleech putsch yapock posada asleep bigger burger clayey cunner
attack fleecy quaich zebeck pseudo avocet bilker burhel clever cupped
avouch flench quench abrade rapids avowed billet burler closed curfew
basics fletch quince accede recede awaked binder burner closet curler
bedeck flinch quitch agenda remade awaken birler burnet cloven curlew
bemock flitch rebeck aikido remedy awheel bister burrel clover
bisect flocci redact albedo remuda awoken bitted bushed
blanch flysch reduce allude reseda       bitten
bleach fratch        amends
```

```
cursed dogger fanjet funnel gopher heifer isabel lagger lofter minded
curvet dogleg fanned furred gorget heller isohel lamber logged minder
cusped doited fanner fusser gospel helmet isomer lammed logger minter
cussed dolmen Fantee gabbed gotten helper jabbed lancer loiter minuet
cutler donkey fardel gabber graben hemmed jabber lancet loller misled
cutlet donned farfel gabled grader hempen jacket landed looker missel
cutter Dopper farmer gablet grater herder jaeger lander looper mister
cycler dormer fasces gadded graved herpes jagged lanner loosen mitten
cygnet dorter fasten gadder gravel Herren jagger lapped looter mizzen
cypher dossel faster gadget graven hickey jailer lappet lopped moaner
dabbed dosser fathen Gadhel graver hidden jammed lapsed lopper moated
dabber dotted father gaffer Graves higher jammer larder lotted mobbed
dagger douser fatted gagged grazer hinder jarred larker louden mocker
dagoes downer fatten gagger griper hinged jarvey lasher loupen moider
daimen dowser fatter gainer grivet hipped jasper laster louver moiler
dammed doyley fauces gaited grocer hisser jeerer lateen lowkey molten
damned dragee faucet gaiter groper hither jennet lather lubber monger
dampen draper fawner galley grovel hoaxer jerker latten lugged monied
damper drawee feeder gammer grower hocker jersey latter lugger monies
damsel drawer feeler gander guider hockey jester laurel lumber monkey
dancer drivel feller ganger guinea hodden jetted laveer lumpen mopped
dander driven fencer gannet guiser hogged jibbed lawyer lumper mopper
danger driver fender gaoler gulden hogget jibber leaden lunger moppet
Daniel droger fennec gapped gullet hoised jigged leader lurker moreen
dapper drover fennel garbed gulley holden jigger leafed lychee morgen
darken drupel ferret garden gummed holder jilter leaper madden morsel
darkey dubbed fester garget gunned holler jinnee leaved madder Moslem
darned ducker fetter garner gunnel holpen jitney leaven magnet mother
darnel dudeen fezzed garnet gunner honied jitter leaver maguey motley
darner duffel fezzes garret gunsel hooded jobber leaves maiden mouser
darter duffer fibbed garter gunter hoofed jockey lecher mailed mucker
dasher duiker fibber gasket gurnet hoofer jogged ledged mallee mugged
dauber dulcet fibred gasper gusher hooked jogger ledger mallei mugger
daybed dumper fidget gasser gusset hooker joiner legged mallet muller
deaden Dunker figged gather gutted hookey jolter lender mammee mullet
deafen dunned filler gauger gutter hooper josher lensed mammer mulley
dealer duplet fillet geegee gypped hooter josser Lenten mangel mummer
decker duplex filter geezer haffet hooves jotted lessee manger mumper
decree durned finder gelled hailer hopped jotter lessen manned murder
deepen duster finger gemmed haired hopper judder lesser manner murrey
defier duyker finned gender haloes horned judger letter mantel muskeg
degree eaglet finner genned halter horner jugged libber mantes musket
deicer earner fisher gentes halves horsey junker lichee mapped mussel
delver easter fitted germen hamlet hosier junket lichen mapper muster
denier echoer fitter getter hammed hostel jutted lidded marcel mutter
dental eggler flamen geyser hammer hotbed kaiser lieder marked nabbed
deuced either flaxen gibber hamper hotrod keeper lifter market nagged
dexter elated floret gibbet handed hotter keloid ligger marred nagger
diadem elater flower gifted hanged housel kelter lilied marten nailer
diaper eleven flukey gigged hanger housey kenned limbec marvel napped
dibbed elodea fluted giglet hanker howler kennel limbed masher natter
dibber eloper fluter gilded hansel hoyden kermes limber masked nausea
dicker emblem fobbed gilder happed hugged kerned limner masker neaped
dickey emeses fodder gilled happen hummed kernel limper masted nearer
didoes enamel fogged gimlet harden hummel kersey limpet master neaten
diesel entree foiled gimmer harken hummer kicker linden matted nephew
dieses envier folder ginger harper humped kidded linger matter nether
dieter epimer fooler ginned haslet hunger kidder linnet mayhem netted
differ epopee footed ginner hasten hunker kidney linney medley neuter
digger eraser footer girder hatpeg hunter killer linsey member nibbed
dimmed eschew forced glazer hatred hurler kilted lintel mender nickel
dimmer esteem forcer glider hatted hurley kilter lionel menses nicker
dingey etcher forger glover hatter hurter kipper lipped mercer nidget
dinned etrier forget glower hauler husker kismet lippen merger nigger
dinner evader forgot gluten hawked hutted kisser lisper mestee nipped
diplex evener forked glutei hawker hyphen kitten listed metier nipper
dipnet examen formed gnawer hawser ibexes knifed listel metred nodded
dipped exceed former goatee headed ibices knives listen mickey nuclei
dipper exogen foster gobbet header ibidem knower lister midden nugget
dirhem eyalet fother goblet healer ideaed kosher litter midget number
dispel eyelet fowler goffer hearer imbrex kraken loaded miffed nurser
dither fabled framer goglet heated inbred kronen loader mildew nutmeg
docker fabler frater golden heater inches kroner loafer milieu nutter
docket facies frozen golfer heaved indeed kummel loaner milker obeyer
dodder fagged frutex goober heaven inlier laager loaves milled offkey
dodgem failed fugged Goidel heaver instep labret lobbed miller offset
dodger fallen fuhrer gooier hedger intoed lackey locker millet oliver
dodoes falter fuller gooney heeled irides ladder locket milter omelet
dogged fanged funned gooses heeler ironer lagged lodger mincer onager
```

```
oodles placet quiver roarer seabee smiter sunset tipped usurer wheyey
opener planer quotes robbed sealer smoker supped tipper valley whiles
osprey planet rabbet robber seamer snarer supper tippet valuer whiner
ostler platen rabies rochet seamew sniper surfer titfer valved whited
ouster plater racker rocker seapen snivel surrey tither vamper whiten
outlet player racket rocket seater snorer survey titled vanner whites
outset plover rafter roller secret soaker sutler titter varied whitey
oxygen plumed ragged romper seeder sobbed suttee tmeses varlet wicked
oxymel pocked raggee rondel seeker soccer swayer tocher varved wicker
oyster pocket raider roofer seiner socket sweven toffee vatted wicket
packer podded railer roomer seizer sodden swiper togaed veiled widget
packet polder raiser rooted seller soever swipes togged veined wiener
padded polled ramjet rooter selves soften swivel toiler velvet wigged
pallet pollen rammed roquet sender soiree system toilet vendee wilder
palmer poller rammer roster sennet solder tabbed tooter vender willed
palter pollex ramper rotted senses solver tablet Tophet veneer willet
pamper pommel random rotten sephen sonnet tacker topped venter wincey
pander ponder ranger rotter septet sooner tacket topper verger winded
panned pongee ranker rouser sequel sopped tagged Tories versed winder
panzer pooped ranter router series sorbet talker torsel verser winged
parcel popped rapier rozzer server sorner tamper torten verset winger
parget popper rapped rubbed sestet sorrel tandem tosher vertex winker
parley poppet rappee rubber settee sorter tanked tosser vervet winner
parpen porker rappel ruched setter sortes tanker tother vesper winsey
parrel porter rapper rudder Sevres sotted tanned totted vessel winter
parsec posset rasher ruffed sextet souled tanner totter vested wisher
Parsee poster rasper rugged shader souter tanrec toupee vestee wither
passer poteen raster rugger shades soviet tapped toupet vetted witted
pastel pother rather ruiner shaken spacer tapper tourer viewer wizier
patted potted ratted rummer shaker sparer tappet touter violet wolves
patten potter ratter runlet shaped spewer target towhee vizier wonder
patter pourer reader runnel shapen spider tarred townee voiced wonted
pauper pouter reamer runner shaper spined tassel tracer voided wooded
pawnee powder reaper rusher sharer spinel taster traces voider wooden
pawner prater rearer rushes shaven spinet tatted trader volley woofer
peahen prayer reaver russet shaver spleen tatter trapes vortex wooled
peaked prefer redden rutted shekel spoken tauten travel wadded worker
peavey premed redder sables shiner spryer taxies trimer wafter wormer
pecker preses redeem sachem shiver stager teasel trivet wagged worsen
pecten preset reefer sachet shovel stagey teaser trover wailer wowser
peeler pricey reeler sacred shover stakes teaset trowel waiter writer
peeper primer reflex sadden shower stamen teazel Tuareg waiver yabber
pegged privet refuel sadder shriek stapes tedded tubber walker Yahveh
pegleg prizer reglet saeter sicken starer tedder tucker walled Yahweh
pellet prober regret sagged sicker stases teemer tucket waller Yankee
pelmet proleg reheel sagger sifter stated teepee tuffet wallet yammer
pelter propel reiver sailed sigher stater teeter tufted wander yapped
pelves proper relief sailer signer states tegmen tufter wanted yapper
penned proser render sallee signet stayer teller tugged wapped yatter
pepped protea rennet sallet silken stereo temper tunnel wapper yelper
pepper proven renter salter siller stewed tender tureen warden yenned
pester pruner reopen salver silver stipel tenner turkey warder yester
petrel pucker rester samlet simmer stipes tenrec turner warmer yipped
petted puffed retted sander simnel stiver tenter turret warped yippee
petter puffer review sanies simper stoker tenues turves warper yolked
pewter puller revved sapped singer stokes tercel tusked warred yonder
phloem pullet rhymer sapper sinker stolen tercet tusker warren yorker
phoney pulley ribbed sardel sinned stoned termer tusser warted zaffer
phooey pulper richen sarsen sinner stoner terret tutted washer zander
picker pulser riches sateen sinnet stores tester twicer wasted zapped
picket pummel ricker saucer sinter storey tether twiner waster zinced
piecer pumper rickey sauger sipped stover tetter ulster weaken zingel
pigged punned ridded saurel sipper streek thaler umbles weaner zinked
piglet punner ridden sawder sippet street theses unbred wearer zipped
pilfer punnet ridged sawney sirree stumer throes undies weasel zipper
pincer puntee rifler sawset sister stylet ticked undoer weaver zither
pinger punter rigged sawyer sitter subbed ticker uneven weazen zonked
pinned pupped rigger scaled skater sublet ticket ungues webbed adrift
pinner puppet rillet scaler skewer subset tickey uniped wedded agrafe
piolet purger rimmed scales skiver sucker tiered unisex weeder argufy
pipped purler ringed scarer slater sudden tiller united weeper bereft
piquet purser ringer schlep slaver suffer tilter uniter weever briefs
Pisces purvey rinser scolex slavey sullen timber unmeet welder carafe
pissed pusher rioter scorer slayer summed tinder unreel welter chaffy
pitier puttee ripped scoter slicer summer tinker unseen wester chuffy
pitted putter ripper screed slider sunder tinned untied wether cliffy
pitter Quaker risker screen sliver sundew tinner unused wetted codify
placed quaver rizzer scryer sloven sunken tinsel upkeep wetter cutoff
placer queuer roamer seabed smiler sunned tinter ureter whaler faroff
```

fluffy	cowage	plunge	Buddha	seethe	atonic	cochin	echoic	gloria	latria
gasify	craggy	potage	bunchy	seiche	attain	codlin	eclair	glycin	leadin
humify	cringe	quagga	burkha	slight	auntie	coffin	Eddaic	gnomic	lentil
ladify	cubage	quaggy	canthi	sloshy	Aussie	coheir	Edenic	gnosis	Leonid
ladyfy	damage	quaigh	catchy	slushy	Austin	collie	Egeria	goalie	Lettic
layoff	deluge	ravage	caught	smithy	azotic	comfit	elicit	goblin	lignin
letoff	design	refuge	chacha	snathe	Baalim	commie	elixir	godwit	limbic
midoff	dosage	renege	chichi	soothe	baddie	commis	emblic	goodie	limpid
minify	dotage	repugn	cliche	sorgho	bagnio	commit	emesis	gorgio	lintie
modify	draggy	resign	cloche	sought	bagwig	conoid	emetic	gossip	lipoid
Nazify	dredge	rivage	clothe	spathe	bailie	cookie	emetin	Gothic	lippie
nidify	dreggy	savage	concha	stithy	Baltic	coolie	enjoin	gradin	liquid
notify	drongo	senega	conchy	swathe	bandit	cootie	enosis	gratin	lithia
oneoff	drudge	sewage	creche	swishy	bardic	Coptic	entail	gratis	lithic
ossify	effigy	shaggy	dinghy	takahe	barrio	corbie	entoil	gravid	livein
pacify	eloign	sheugh	douche	taught	beanie	corrie	Eozoic	guanin	loggia
payoff	emerge	silage	dought	teethe	bedsit	cosmic	epodic	haddie	lookin
piaffe	emulge	skeigh	doughy	tetchy	beduin	cousin	eremic	haemin	loupit
pilaff	encage	slaggy	drachm	toothy	Belgic	cowrie	erotic	haffit	lovein
pouffe	energy	slangy	earthy	touche	berlin	crania	esprit	haggis	lubric
purify	engage	sledge	filthy	touchy	bestir	credit	essoin	hankie	luetic
putoff	enough	sleigh	flashy	trashy	bewail	cretic	ethnic	haptic	luggie
ramify	enrage	slough	fleche	troche	biffin	cretin	exilic	hatpin	lutein
rarefy	ensign	sludge	fleshy	trophy	biggin	crisis	exomis	hectic	magpie
ratify	eryngo	sludgy	flight	waught	bigwig	critic	eyelid	herdic	Majlis
rebuff	eulogy	smoggy	fought	weight	bionic	cuboid	Eyetie	herein	maleic
rubefy	flaggy	smudge	fright	whisht	biotic	cuddie	fabric	hermit	malkin
rubify	flange	smudgy	frothy	worthy	biotin	cullis	fadein	hernia	mantic
runoff	fledge	snaggy	gauche	abatis	birdie	cummin	faerie	heroic	mantid
salify	forage	socage	gaucho	abseil	birkie	cupric	falsie	heroin	mantis
sanify	forego	sorage	geisha	abulia	bobbin	cuptie	faquir	hippie	maquis
sclaff	fridge	sparge	gunshy	acacia	bobwig	currie	fascia	hispid	margin
scruff	fringe	sponge	Gurkha	acarid	bodkin	cuspid	feirie	hoggin	marlin
scurfy	fringy	spongy	heathy	acedia	boffin	cyanic	ferric	hogtie	martin
setoff	froggy	spurge	height	acetic	bollix	cyanin	fervid	hoodie	mashie
shrift	galago	stingo	klepht	acidic	bonnie	cyclic	fibril	horrid	maslin
shroff	garage	stingy	knight	acquit	bonxie	Cymric	fibrin	hubris	massif
sniffy	gavage	stodge	litchi	adagio	bookie	cyprid	fillip	hybrid	mastic
snuffy	George	stodgy	loathe	Adamic	bothie	cystic	filmic	hybris	matrix
spiffy	ginkgo	stooge	lorcha	adipic	bougie	cystid	Finnic	hydric	mealie
spoffy	grange	stopgo	louche	adjoin	bowfin	dacoit	fiorin	hymnic	meanie
strafe	greige	swinge	maltha	Adonic	bowtie	dahlia	firkin	iambic	megrim
strife	gringo	syzygy	manche	Adonis	brazil	daimio	fizgig	iconic	meinie
stuffy	groggy	telega	Manchu	adroit	brewis	darkie	flavin	impair	memoir
tariff	grudge	Telugu	marshy	Aeolic	bromic	dassie	florid	inclip	menhir
tepefy	homage	things	megohm	affair	budgie	dearie	florin	inlaid	merlin
thrift	impugn	thingy	morpho	afraid	bulbil	deasil	foetid	instil	metric
tipoff	indign	though	mouthy	agamic	bumkin	debris	forbid	intuit	midair
tumefy	indigo	towage	murphy	agamid	bunnia	deceit	fordid	inulin	midrib
typify	kiaugh	triage	naught	agaric	bunyip	deific	formic	irenic	miosis
uglify	knaggy	trough	nought	agnail	buskin	dentil	fornix	iritis	miotic
unsafe	lanugo	trudge	nympho	agonic	caddie	derail	forrit	ironic	misdid
uplift	lavage	twangy	obeche	albeit	caddis	dermic	fossil	isatin	misfit
verify	linage	twiggy	orache	alcaic	calcic	dermis	frazil	ischia	mishit
vilify	lounge	twinge	pakeha	aldrin	calkin	derris	frigid	italic	missis
vivify	lovage	ullage	patchy	alevin	caplin	desmid	frolic	jerbil	moggie
allege	Malaga	uncage	peachy	alexia	capric	detail	fucoid	jerkin	mohair
anlage	malign	virago	pitchy	alexin	capsid	detain	fulfil	Jesuit	mollie
assign	manage	visage	plashy	algoid	casein	devoid	fulgid	jezail	morbid
avenge	manege	voulge	plushy	anodic	cassia	devoir	funkia	Judaic	morris
aweigh	menage	voyage	poncho	anomic	cassis	diacid	fusain	junkie	mosaic
barege	metage	whinge	pouchy	anomie	catkin	diesis	gadoid	Kaffir	moujik
beluga	midage	alight	psyche	anoxia	catnip	dikdik	Gaelic	kainit	moulin
benign	milage	apache	psycho	anoxic	caulis	dimwit	Gallic	kaolin	mucoid
blunge	mirage	apathy	punchy	aortic	Celtic	distil	Gallio	karmic	muffin
bocage	nonage	aright	quiche	Arabic	cervix	dobbin	gambir	kelvin	mundic
bodega	oarage	beachy	quotha	archil	chemic	doggie	gambit	kelpie	muntin
borage	oblige	bertha	rancho	arctic	chesil	domain	ganoid	Keltic	Muslim
bridge	ohmage	berthe	reecho	armpit	chitin	donsie	garlic	kermis	muslin
change	oology	blight	rhaphe	ashbin	chopin	doolie	garvie	kiddie	muzhik
charge	oppugn	blithe	rhythm	assail	choric	dormie	gaskin	kiekie	myelin
chough	orange	bolshy	rotche	assoil	citric	dubbin	geodic	kookie	myopia
claggy	outage	bosche	saddhu	ataxia	clavis	dunlin	gerbil	koppie	myopic
clergy	pavage	botchy	saithe	ataxic	cleric	durrie	gillie	lactic	myosin
clingy	pelage	bought	sandhi	atomic	clevis	dyadic	girlie	laddie	myosis
cloggy	phlegm	bright	scathe		clinic	earwig	glacis	lappie	myotic
clough	pledge	broche	scyphi		clonic			lassie	mystic
colugo	plough	brushy	scythe		coccid				mythic

```
napkin poplin siskin turbit rebuke behalf damply fickle hopple macule
nastic porgie sixain turgid remake beheld dandle fiddle hourly magilp
nereid postil Slavic Turkic retake behold dangle fiddly huckle mainly
niacin potpie sobeit turnip revoke bobble dankly fimble huddle mangle
nitric pratie soffit twilit rewoke bodily dapple finale hugely manila
nitwit praxis softie uncoil saluki boggle darkle finals humble manila
noesis precis sonsie unfair sheikh boldly darkly finely humbly mantle
noetic prefix sophic unguis shrike boodle dartle fipple hurdle marble
noggin prelim sordid unhair shucks botfly dawdle firmly hurtle marbly
Nordic premix sortie unific slacks bottle dayfly fizzle hustle mascle
nuncio probit Sothic unjoin slinky boucle dazzle flatly icicle mayfly
nutria profit spadix unknit smirky boulle deadly focsle impala mazily
obtain prolix spavin unlaid sneaky bowels deafly foible impale meanly
ogamic prosit specie unnail sparks branle dearly fondle incult measly
olefin pterin spirit unpaid spooky brawly deckle fondly indole meddle
orcein ptosis sprain unsaid spunky bridle deeply footle indult meekly
orchid public spruit unship stalky brolly defile foozle infelt meetly
orchil puffin squail unveil sticky bubble deftly foully infold megilp
orchis pullin stadia uracil stinko bubbly desalt freely infula merely
ordain pulpit stasis Uralic stocks buckle dewily frilly ingulf merils
orexis pulvil static Urania stocky buddle dibble fuddle inhale metals
origin pundit stepin uranic strake bumalo diddle fumble insole mettle
orphic purlin steric urchin strike bumble dimple fusile insult mickle
ossein putrid stogie utopia stroke bummle dimply futile inyala middle
otitis puttie stolid ventil swanky bundle dingle gabble itself mildly
outbid pycnic strain vermin talcky bungle dipole gadfly jangle mingle
outdid pyknic strait vibrio thanks burble direly gaggle jiggle mistle
outfit rabbin studio victim tracks burbly doable gainly jiggly mizzle
outsit rabbit stupid violin tricky burgle docile gamble jingle mizzly
outvie rachis stymie virgin troika busily doddle gamely jingly mobile
outwit raffia submit viscid unlike bustle doodle gamily joggle module
oxalic raisin subtil wabain unmake cabala dottle gangly moduli
oxalis rancid suffix walkin unyoke cackle double garble jostle modulo
oxtail raphia summit waddie uptake cagily doubly gargle jumble mohole
ozonic raphis sunlit walkin whacky cajole dourly gentle jumbly morale
palais ratlin suslik weepie whisky calmly dozily gently jungle morals
pallia razzia syndic weevil yoicks candle drably giggle jungly morula
pallid recoil tactic welkin zincky cantle drolly giggly justly motile
pandit recoin taenia Wendic acidly castle dryfly gigolo kabala mottle
papain reedit tahsil within aedile catalo dually girdle Kabyle muckle
pardie regain takein withit aerily cattle duello gladly keenly muddle
parkin rejoin talkie worrit afield caudle duffle glibly kettle muesli
parvis relaid tannic xyloid ageold chicle dumbly glumly kibble muffle
passim remain tannin yippie airily chield easily gnarly kindle mumble
pastil repaid tappit yttria alkali chilli edgily gobble kindly muscle
pathic repair tarsia zincic allele chilly edible goggle kingly mutely
patois reship tassie zinnia annals cicala eerily goggly kirtle mutule
paynim retail tawpie zombie annuli cicely eidola goodly kittle muzzle
pectic retain tennis alsike arable cigala embalm googly kobold mygale
pectin roadie tenpin belike archly circle emboli gorily labile myrtle
peewit Romaic tentie betake areola citole emboly greyly lamely myself
pelvic rookie tenuis blanky areole cobalt enable grille lankly namely
pelvis rubric territ breeks argala cobble enfold grimly lastly napalm
pencil runrig thesis bricky argali cockle engild grisly lately nearly
pepsin russia thetic chalky argyle coddle engulf growly lavolt neatly
peptic rustic thoria cheeky audile coffle enhalo grumly lazily nebula
permit salvia thulia chukka avidly coldly enisle guddle lazuli nebuly
phasic santir tidbit chunky awhile comely enroll guggle leanly needle
phasis sawpit tiepin cranky axilla comply ensile gurgle lewdly Nepali
phatic sayyid tiewig creaky babble coolly evenly guzzle liable neroli
phobia scenic tiffin croaky babbly copula evilly habile ligula nestle
phobic scoria titbit decoke baffle cosily exhale hackle ligule nettle
phonic scotia tmesis drosky baldly costly facile hackly likely nibble
photic Scotic tocsin eureka bangle couple facula haggle limply nicely
physic seaair toluic flunky barely cradle faille handle limuli nielli
picnic seapig tomtit freaky barfly crawly fainly hardly little niello
picric seisin tonsil frisky basalt creole fairly hassle lively niggle
pidgin seizin toroid gingko basely cuddle family hazily lobule nimble
piggin semmit torpid hoicks battle cuddly famuli heckle locale nimbly
pinkie sennit torrid intake bauble cumuli featly heddle loculi nipple
pionic sepsis toxoid invoke bawble cupola feckly herald lonely nobble
pipkin septic tragic judoka beadle cupule fecula higgle lordly noddle
pippin sequin tremie kabuki beagle curdle feeble highly loudly nodule
pistil serein trepid kanaka becall curtly feebly hirple lovely noodle
placid sharif trifid manuka becalm curule female hobble lunula nosily
poetic shavie trivia mopoke bedell cutely ferula holily lunule Nowell
pommie sherif tropic peruke beetle cuttle ferule homely lushly nozzle
pontie shutin tuckin plucky befall dabble fettle homily mackle nubble
pontil sialic turbid quirky befell daftly fibula hoopla macula nubbly
```

nubile	razzle	smelly	twould	bigamy	scrimp	behind	duenna	indene	obtund
nudely	really	smugly	uglily	bireme	scrump	belong	dugong	indent	ochone
numbly	recall	snarly	unable	bloomy	scummy	betony	during	induna	octane
nuncle	reddle	snugly	unbolt	bosomy	sesame	beyond	dyeing	infant	octant
nuzzle	refill	softly	unduly	Brahma	shammy	bezant	earing	inland	offend
occult	regale	solely	unfold	Brahmi	shimmy	bikini	eating	inning	offent
ocelli	regulo	sorely	ungula	bregma	shrimp	biting	edging	insane	offing
onfall	resale	sourly	unholy	bulimy	slummy	bizone	eluant	intend	online
openly	resell	spoilt	unroll	byname	smarmy	blenny	eluent	intent	oogeny
oracle	resile	spryly	unruly	calami	sodomy	bluing	embank	intine	oolong
orally	resold	squall	unself	chacma	solemn	boding	ending	intone	optant
oriole	resole	squill	untold	chroma	squama	bohunk	engine	invent	orient
ormolu	result	stable	unwell	chrome	steamy	booing	enwind	iodine	orpine
oscula	retell	stably	upheld	chromo	stemma	borane	Eocene	island	oscine
ovally	retold	staple	uphill	chummy	stigma	boring	equine	jacana	outing
overly	revile	steely	uphold	cinema	stormy	botany	ermine	jejune	oxgang
oxgall	revolt	stifle	usable	clammy	stroma	botone	errand	joanna	oxland
paddle	ribald	stilly	vagile	column	stromb	bourne	errant	jocund	paeony
paella	richly	stroll	vainly	corymb	struma	bovine	Essene	johnny	paling
palely	riddle	suable	vastly	creamy	swimmy	bowing	eterne	kalong	parang
palolo	rifely	subtle	venule	crummy	tatami	boxing	ethane	ketone	parent
papula	riffle	subtly	verily	decamp	toneme	brains	ethene	kimono	paring
papule	ripely	suckle	viable	defame	trauma	brainy	ethyne	lacing	patent
parole	ripple	supple	vielle	denims	ugsome	brawny	evzone	lacuna	patina
partly	ripply	supply	vilely	dharma	ultima	briony	exeunt	lading	pavane
payola	robalo	surely	virile	digamy	ultimo	browny	expand	ladino	paving
pearly	rosily	sutile	visile	dreamt	volume	bryony	expend	laguna	pedant
pebble	rosula	swirly	vitals	dreamy	zeugma	busing	extant	lament	piping
pebbly	rouble	swirly	vizsla	dynamo	zygoma	butane	extend	lamina	plaint
pedalo	royals	tamale	wabble	eczema	abound	butene	extent	larynx	pliant
peddle	rubble	tamely	waddle	encamp	absent	bygone	eyeing	latent	polony
penult	rubbly	tangle	waffle	enigma	accent	bylane	facing	learnt	potent
people	ruckle	tangly	waggle	entomb	achene	byline	fagend	legend	pruina
pertly	ruddle	tartly	waggly	enwomb	acting	cabana	famine	lemony	prying
pestle	rudely	tattle	wamble	enzyme	addend	cadent	farina	levant	puisne
phalli	ruelle	tautly	wambly	Eskimo	advent	canine	fecund	lierne	purine
pickle	ruffle	teazle	wangle	exhume	affine	carina	feeing	liking	pyrene
piddle	rumble	tegula	warble	gazump	ageing	casing	feline	liming	quaint
piffle	rumbly	temple	warily	genome	airing	casino	felony	lining	rapine
pilule	rumple	termly	warmly	gleamy	albino	catena	ferine	litany	raring
pimple	rundle	thalli	warsle	gloomy	Aldine	caving	filing	living	ratine
pimply	rustle	thinly	wattle	goramy	alkane	cement	fining	loment	rating
pinole	rutile	thrall	wavily	gramme	alkene	cetane	firing	loving	ravine
pintle	saddle	thrill	waxily	Grammy	alkyne	chaunt	flaunt	lowing	raving
pizzle	safely	tickle	weakly	illume	almond	client	fluent	lucent	recant
pomelo	sagely	tickly	weekly	income	alpine	cogent	flying	lumina	recent
poodle	sample	tiddly	whirly	infamy	alumna	coigne	foment	lupine	redone
poorly	sanely	tidily	wholly	inhume	alumni	colony	forint	luting	refine
popple	sapele	timely	widely	kinema	amount	coming	fraena	lysine	refund
popply	sawfly	tingle	wifely	legume	angina	coping	friend	making	regent
portly	scilla	tingly	wiggle	lipoma	anoint	corona	galena	manana	regina
potale	scroll	tinily	wiggly	Madame	anting	cosine	gamine	marina	relent
pottle	sedile	tinkle	wildly	maxima	anyone	coving	gaming	marine	reline
primly	seemly	tinkly	wilily	miasma	aphony	cranny	Gemini	matins	remand
puddle	semble	tipple	wimble	minima	append	crying	gerent	maying	remind
puddly	semple	tittle	wimple	mishmi	arcana	cueing	gerund	meninx	remint
pueblo	senile	toddle	winkle	myxoma	arcane	daphne	goanna	merino	repand
punily	seseli	toggle	wintle	occamy	ardent	daring	gobang	mining	repent
purely	settle	tootle	wirily	oedema	argand	debunk	gowany	Mishna	resent
purfle	sexily	topple	wisely	oogamy	argent	decani	grainy	modena	retene
purple	sheila	torula	wobble	optima	aroint	decant	granny	moline	retina
purply	shelly	tousle	wobbly	pajama	around	decent	greens	moment	rewind
puzzle	shield	treble	woggle	panama	arpent	dedans	greeny	mooing	riband
pyrola	shoaly	trebly	woolly	paramo	arrant	defend	ground	moving	rident
rabble	should	trifle	wortle	plasma	arsine	define	groyne	murine	riding
racily	shrill	triple	yaffle	plummy	ascend	demand	Havana	musing	rising
raddle	sickle	triple	yarely	pneuma	ascent	dement	hexane	mutant	rodent
radula	sickly	triply	yearly	qualmy	askant	depend	hiding	mutine	Romany
raffle	simile	trolly	zanily	raceme	aslant	depone	hieing	mutiny	ropily
raggle	simple	tubule	zufolo	radome	assent	detent	hoeing	nagana	roping
raguly	simply	tuille	aflame	regime	attend	dining	homing	natant	rosiny
ramble	single	tumble	aplomb	relume	attune	divine	hominy	neednt	rotund
rankle	singly	tumuli	assume	rename	avaunt	diving	humane	nerine	roving
rankly	sizzle	tumult	asthma	resume	awning	djinni	hyaena	nocent	rowing
ranula	skeely	tupelo	athome	revamp	banana	docent	iguana	nosing	ruling
raptly	skilly	turtle	autumn	rheumy	barony	dogend	immane	novena	rumina
rarely	slimly	tussle	became	salami	bating	domino	immune	numina	Sabine
rashly	slowly	twirly	become	schema	Beaune	dopant	impend	nutant	salina
rattle	smalls	twoply	benumb	scheme	begone	douane	impone	oblong	saline

```
sarong Tswana blazon doctor harlot merlon prison sungod weapon sleepy
sasine tubing bonbon dogfox harrow meteor proton symbol weldor slippy
satiny tuning bongos dogood hatbox method pugdog syphon whilom sloppy
savant tweeny booboo dollop haybox micron pullon tailor wigeon snappy
savine typing boohoo donjon haymow mignon putlog talbot willow snippy
saving tyrant borrow dragon headon minion pyedog talion Wilton snoopy
saxony unbend borzoi drybob hector minnow python tallow window steppe
saying unbent boston dryrot hereof mirror quahog tampon winnow stirps
secant unbind bottom editor hereon Mongol quinoa tarpon wisdom stripe
second uncini bowwow eggnog heriot moocow quinol tattoo wittol stripy
secund undine brehon elevon Hindoo morion racoon tautog wonton stumpy
seeing undone Breton employ hobnob Mormon ramrod teapot yarrow swampy
sejant unhand Briton enroot holloa morrow ramson teapoy yaupon syrupy
serang unkind bunion Eozoon hollow motion random telson yellow teraph
serene unking burbot epizoa hoodoo motmot ransom tendon yoohoo thorpe
sevens unkink burgoo erenow hoopoe muflon raptor tenson zealot thrips
sewing unlink burrow escrow horror muskox ration tensor zircon trappy
shanny unsung burton Ethiop hotdog mutton ratoon tenzon abrupt trompe
sheeny untune busboy etymon hotpot mythos reason termor accept troppo
shinny unwind button factor huzoor nardoo reckon terror aslope troupe
shrank upland byblow faggot hyssop narrow rector teston biceps trumps
shrine upping cachou falcon icebox nation redhot Teuton caliph unripe
shrink upwind cacoon fallow indoor natron redtop tholoi canape unrope
shrunk urbane cahoot fandom inflow nekton reebok tholos canopy unwept
siding urgent callow fanion inkpot nelson reflow thoron ceriph whippy
sienna ursine camion fantod isopod Nestor region thymol chappy whoops
sileni vacant cannon fantom jailor neuron retook tierod chippy yclept
silent valine cannot farrow jargon newton retool tinpot chirpy zarape
simony vicuna canton fathom jerboa nignog retrod tiptoe choppy abjure
sizing Viking cantor felloe joblot Nimrod rhebok tiptop clumpy aboard
skiing Vishnu canyon fellow junior noncom rhetor toluol crappy absorb
skinny volant captor filfot karroo nostoc ribbon tomboy creeps absurd
soigne vorant carbon firlot kation notion rollon tomcod creepy accord
solano voting carboy flacon kelson ocelot ronyon tomtom crimpy adhere
sonant wahine carrot flagon kincob octroi roucou torpor crispy adjure
sowans whinny carton flexor kitool oddjob sailor tremor croppy admire
sowens wiring Caslon fogbow koedoe oddson sallow tricot croupy adsorb
sphene wisent castor fogdog koodoo option salmon trigon drippy adverb
sphinx xylene cation foison kowtow orator saloon tripod droopy advert
splent zenana censor follow kronor orison saloop tripos enrapt afeard
spline zoning Charon forgot lagoon outfox salvor triton escape affirm
splint abloom chigoe fossor lapdog outtop salvos trogon except afford
spoony acajou chiton frijol lardon pallor Samson turbot exempt afters
sprang action cineol frivol lassos pardon scazon turgor flappy albert
sprent amadou citron furrow latron parrot school turion floppy allure
spring amatol clipon fusion lector parson scroop tycoon frappe ampere
sprint amazon cocoon fylfot legion pastor seacow uncool frumpy angary
sprung amnion coelom gabion lepton pathos seadog unhook glumpy angora
squint anchor coinop galiot lesion patrol seafog unipod gramps apiary
sterna anyhow collop gallon lesson patron seafox unison grappa artery
stound archon comeon gallop lessor pavior season sector grippe ashore
strand aswoon common galoot lictor pegtop sector unknot grippy askari
Strine author condor gambol liquor pennon seldom unroof grumps aspire
string baboon congou gammon lissom period senhor unroot grumpy assert
strong bailor convoy garcon logion perron senior unshod Guelph assort
strung balboa cordon garron lollop person sensor unshoe incept assure
strunt ballon cosmos garrot loriot petrol sermon unstop irrupt astern
supine ballot cotton Gascon lotion pharos sexpot uphroe jalopy attire
sweeny bamboo coupon geckos lowboy phenol sexton uproot kakapo attorn
swound bandog cowboy gentoo lummox phonon shadow upshot metope auburn
syrinx banjos cowpox gibbon macron photon shalom ustion occupy augury
tagend barrow crayon giglot maggot piedog signor vagrom paraph aumbry
tahini barton cresol glycol mallow pigeon simoom vaudoo plumpy aurora
taking baryon croton gnomon mammon pinion simoon vector polypi aviary
talent bassos cuckoo godson mangos pistol siphon vendor prompt aweary
taming bathos cursor gollop manioc piston sissoo viator pyrope bakery
tenant beacon custom googol marmot pithos skibob victor recipe bawdry
tetany beckon daemon gorgon maroon plexor slalom vision sarape bayard
theine befool daimon goslow marron pluton slipon volvox scampi before
thorny behoof damson grison marrow podsol sorrow voodoo scrape begird
throne bellow deacon guenon mascon podzol spigot wadmol script begirt
throng benzol debtor guidon mascot pogrom stator waggon sculpt belfry
tiling bestow deploy gundog matlow poison sterol walkon serape bemire
timing betook despot guvnor matron pompom stolen wallop seraph beware
tisane bettor diatom hadron matzoh pompon stolon wallow seriph biform
toeing bilbos diglot halloa meadow ponton stupor wanion sharps Bihari
triune billon diplee halloo mellow potboy suitor wanton Sherpa binary
truant billow diplon hallow melton potion summon wardog shoppy bistre
trying bishop dittos hansom mentor powwow sundog wargod skimpy bistro
```

```
bleary expire maugre satori venire bruise eonism Maoism rakish unless
blurry expiry mazard Saturn ventre bypass excess Maoist ramose unmask
bolero export meagre satyra vestry bypast excise marish rapist unrest
bowery exsert memory savory vihara calash excuse Marist ravish unwise
braird extern Messrs scarry vinery camass expose mayest recast upcast
briard extort milord schorl vintry camise extasy medusa recess upmost
briary fakery misere sclera vivers caress famish merest refuse uppish
briery fedora misery scurry vizard cayuse fetish merism rehash uprise
buckra femora modern secern votary cerise filose mimosa relish uprush
byform fiacre motory secure waders ceruse finish minish remise utmost
byword figure nature sempre wafery chaise flense misuse remiss valise
bywork finery nonary senary warcry cheese flimsy modest repass vanish
cafard fleury notary senora waters cheesy flossy modish repast Vedist
Caffre floury objure sentry watery chiasm folksy molest repose venose
calory flurry obvert severe wavery choose forest monism resist verism
camera friary oeuvre severy wherry choosy fraise monist retest verist
canard fulcra onward shears winery chouse freest mopish retuse vibist
canary furore ordure sherry wintry chrism frowst morass revest virose
casern future ornery sierra wivern Christ frowsy morish revise volost
cavern gabbro orrery simurg wizard classy gainst morose ribose whatso
cavort galore outcry sistra womera clause galosh mousse rimose whilst
cedarn gantry oxbird skerry wyvern clumsy garish mucosa robust whimsy
celery Gemara oxford slurry yaourt coarse glassy mulish Romish whomso
centre genera oxherd smeary yogurt comose glossy mutism rudish whoosh
cesura gentry paltry sombre zaffre corpse gneiss nanism rugose widish
cheers gharry panary souari zonary course golosh Nazism sadism woodsy
cheery glairy pantry sparry abbess cowish goyish newish sadist wrasse
cherry gocart papers sphere ablush crease grassy nicish saidst xylose
chypre goitre papery sphery access creese grease nodose sayest yogism
cohere gokart papyri splore accost crosse greasy nomish schism zeloso
cohort govern pastry spurry accuse crouse grilse nomism schist zymase
colure grigri pastry square across cruise grouse nowise schuss ablate
covert grugru peltry squire adjust cubism harass nowise scouse acuity
coward haleru penury squirm admass cubist hearse nudism serosa adnate
curare havers petara squirt advise cueist heresy nudist setose aerate
curari hazard petard stairs afresh cuisse hexose oafish sexism afrite
dartre hedera pinery starry aghast curtsy hoarse oblast sexist agnate
datary hegira pleura Stuart agnise cymose holism oboist sheass agouti
datura hejira pliers suborn aguish damask honest obsess shiest albata
debark hetero poetry suburb ahimsa Danish illuse obtuse shiksa albite
deform hombre popery sudary aldose debase immesh oecist shyest amenta
dehorn horary priory sugary almost defuse impish offish slyest anatta
demark humeri pylori sultry ambush degust impose ogress sneesh anatto
demure hungry quaere sundry amidst demise impost ogrish sparse argute
denary ignore quarry superb aorist demist incase oldish speiss arista
depart immure rasure suture appose depose incest oncost splash aseity
deport impark rebore tabard argosy desist incise onrush splosh astute
descry impart reborn tamara ariosi detest incuse oppose spouse augite
desert import record tantra arioso devest infest orgasm squash Avesta
desire impure reform tavern arouse devise infuse osmose squish aviate
desorb inborn regard tawdry arrest dicast ingest otiose strass balata
dhurra infare remark tawery artist digest inmost owlish stress barite
disarm infirm remora tenure assess disuse inrush palish Sufism baryta
divers inform report theirs assist divest insist papism swoosh Basuto
divert inhere resorb theory attest dressy invest papist tanist Basutu
dotard injure resort thwart august dropsy iodise parish Taoism batata
dreary injury retard timbre aurist drossy iodism pavise Taoist beauty
dukery insert retire torero autism drowse ionise perish teensy berate
dupery insure retort toward averse drowsy Jewess peruse theism bhisti
eatery intern returf towery avulse dryish Jewish phrase theist binate
effort invert return Tshirt Babism dudish jocose pilose thirst blintz
elytra inward reverb tundra Babist dumose jurist please thrash blotto
embark izzard revere tuyere banish duress Jutish plisse thresh bonito
embers jabiru revers twyere behest dynast kaross polish thrush borate
empery ligure revert umpire bemuse effuse kibosh popish thrust bounty
empire livery revery unborn biopsy egoism kumiss porism thyrse breath
encore lizard reward uncork blouse egoist lamish porose thyrsi bypath
endure louvre rewire uncurl blowsy egress latest potash tonish capote
engird lowery reword unfurl bluish elapse latish praise tootsy cavity
engirt lucern rework ungird bonism eldest lavish priest torose cecity
ensure lustra ropery ungirt bonist elfish legist prissy tressy cerate
entera lustre rosary unwary booksy elvish liaise punish truism chanty
entire luxury rosery unworn bourse emboss lipase purism tsetse chaste
escarp maduro rostra upturn boyish empusa lobose purist tsotsi chatty
escort maigre rotary upward braise encase locust queasy typist cherty
euchre mantra safari vagary brassy encash lowish quinsy unease chesty
exedra manure salary vaward breast encyst lyrism racism uneasy chintz
exhort Masora samara velure breese enlist lyrist racist unjust chitty
expert mature satire venery browse enmesh malism radish unlash coaita
```

```
cogito groats peyote solute armful cornua humour oilnut sensum voyeur
comate grotto peyotl somite armour corpus iambus omasum septum vulgus
comity grotty pigsty sonata artful Corvus idolum opaque serous walnut
coolth growth pineta sopite asylum crocus imbrue osmium setout walrus
coonty guilty pirate spilth atrium cultus indium ostium shaduf wampum
copita gyrate plenty splits aurous cupful influx outgun shamus warmup
county halite plinth sports avenue curium ionium output shogun wayout
coyote hamate plotty sporty awmous cursus ireful outrun shroud wilful
crafty Hamite podite spotty backup cuscus jarful padauk siglum windup
create health pointe sprite bagful cutout joyful paidup sinful woeful
crista hearth points stacte bangup dengue joyous palpus sixgun xenium
crusty hearty polite staith barium detour jugful panful skirun xystus
crypto hereto polity strata barque devour kittul parous slapup yumyum
cuesta ideate potato strath Basque devout kronur pappus slipup zythum
curate ignite presto strati battue dictum kultur peanut sodium active
dainty impute pretty surety bedaub dingus labium peepul sprout alcove
dearth incite pronto svelte bedbug dinkum labour pentup sputum Argive
debate indite puncta swarth befoul dirdum labrum peplum statue arrive
delate inmate pupate sweaty belaud disbud laceup perdue status behave
delete innate purity sweets bijoux discus langue phylum stepup behove
demote invite Pushtu tapeta binful diseur langur pickup stroud belive
denote iodate pyruto tenuto bisque dolium lapful pignut strout chivvy
depute iolite quanta terete blowup dolour lapsus pileum stylus cleave
deputy jaunty quarte thirty boxful dorsum larrup pileup subdue cruive
derate jugate quarto tights brogue drogue lashup pileus sulcus dative
devote kaputt quartz tomato brutus dryrun lasque pilous tabour derive
dhooti karate quinta treaty bulbul dugout lawful plague talcum endive
dilate kibitz quoits triste bunkum dumdum layout plaguy Talmud essive
dilute knotty rabato trouty burnup dustup leadup plaque Targum evolve
dimity krantz ramate trusty bustup dybbuk league plenum tarsus geneva
dogate lanate rarity twenty byssus earful liftup plexus Taurus glaive
domett laxity ratite twisty cactus efflux limbus podium teacup greave
donate lealty realty ubiety caecum eggcup lineup popgun tedium grieve
drafty leanto rebate unbitt caique embrue lingua porous tenour groove
drifty legate rebato uncate callup englut linkup poseur tergum groovy
drouth legato recite undate callus ensoul litmus possum tholus inwove
dunite length refute uneath campus erbium lockup potful thymus motive
ecarte lenity relate Uniate canful evolue lyceum primus timous native
effete Levite remote update cangue exequy magnum pullup tinful octave
egesta levity repute uppity cantus exodus mahout pulque tissue octavo
eighth ligate righto vacate capful eyecup makeup pursue tittup ottava
eighty lights rotate valeta carful eyeful manful pushup tongue relive
ejecta lobate rubato valuta carpus factum manque quorum torque remove
eluate locate safety vanity casque farout mantua radium tossup revive
emeute lunate salute vaulty catgut favour maraud radius tragus saliva
enmity luxate samite vegete catsup fescue markup ragout tryout scurvy
ensate lyrate sanity veleta caucus fitful marque Rajput tuchun sheave
entity malate sapota Venite census flatus marrum ramous tubful shelve
eolith manito savate verity centum foetus masque recoup tumour shrive
equate mighty scanty volute cercus folium maybug rectum tumtum shrove
equity minute scatty wapiti cereus fondue meatus rectus turnup skivvy
ergate moiety scouth warmth cerium foulup medium redbud typhus sleave
errata motett sedate wealth cestus frenum medius reflux umlaut sleeve
ersatz mutate Semite wraith cheque fundus mentum regius unglue strive
estate negate senate wreath cherub fungus minium replum unique steeve
excite nerite Shakta yeasty chiaus furfur miscue rescue unplug strove
facete nicety Shakti zenith chorus gangue mockup rhesus untrue thieve
faulty nighty shanty zonate cilium genius mockup rigour uraeus thieve
fealty ninety sheath zygote cinque getout modius rigout Uranus thrive
feisty notate sheets abacus circus giaour morbus rimous urnful throve
fiesta nudity Shelta ablaut cirque gradus morgue risque useful twelve
finite nutate shelty acarus cirrus gurjun mosque rotgut uterus visive
fixate oblate shifty accrue cistus gypsum mucous ruckus vacuum votive
fixity oddity Shiite acinus citrus hagbut mukluk rufous valgus Zouave
flinty oleate Shinto adieus claque hallux multum rumour vallum arrowy
flirty omenta shinty adieux clique hangup murmur rumpus valour disown
floaty oocyte shirty adytum cliquy hatful museum mutuum vapour godown
fourth oolite shorts afflux clonus helium multum sacque vatful impawn
frosty ophite shorty airbus cobnut henrun muumuu sacrum vellum inlaws
fruity opiate siesta airgun coccus hiatus mutuum saltus velour Mohawk
frusta ornate sleety alarum coitus hiccup naevus sambur vendue pesewa
fugato oxgate sleuth allium coleus holdup netful sannup venous renown
gaiety palate smalto allout colour hiccup nimbus sapful venous renown
gamete parity smarty amylum colour holdup nobbut sapful versus scrawl
ghetto Pashto smooth anicut comous honour nonius savour vigour screwy
ghosty pedate smutty animus concur hookup noshup scarus villus shrewd
gleety pelota snooty antrum consul hubbub obelus scutum vinous sinewy
Granth peseta snotty arbour copout humbug odious Seljuk virtue sprawl
gritty petite snouty ardour corium hummum oidium sendup viscus squawk
```

```
strawy agenda egesta mantra salvia corymb epodic pionic beaked diacid
strewn ahimsa eidola mantua samara desorb eremic poetic bedded dibbed
strown alalia ejecta manuka sapota drybob erotic public begged dimmed
thrawn albata elodea maraca satyra entomb ethnic pycnic begird dinned
thrown alexia elytra marina schema enwomb exilic pyknic behead dipped
uptown alpaca empusa Masora scilla hobnob exotic ricrac beheld disbud
adnexa alumna enigma maxima sclera hubbub fabric Romaic behind dogend
annexe amenta entera medusa scoria kincob fennec rubric behold dogged
deluxe amoeba epizoa mezuza scotia midrib ferric rustic belaud dogood
eutaxy anatta errata miasma senega mihrab filmic scenic belted doited
galaxy angina eureka mimosa senora oddjob Finnic Scotic bested donned
iceaxe angora exedra minima serosa prefab fistic septic betted doodad
maxixe anoxia facula Mishna Shakta resorb formic sialic beyond dotard
acetyl apnoea farina modena sheila reverb frolic Slavic bibbed dotted
adenyl arcana fascia morula Shelta scarab fustic sophic bitted dubbed
always areola fecula mucosa Sherpa skibob Gaelic Sothic bladed dunned
anonym argala fedora myopia shiksa skylab Gallic static blowed durned
arroyo arista femora myrica sienna stromb garlic steric bobbed elated
ayeaye armada ferula myxoma sierra suburb geodic syndic bogged enfold
benzyl arnica fibula nagana siesta superb gnomic Syriac bonded engild
billyo arroba fiesta nausea silica acetic Gothic tactic booted engird
byebye asthma fraena nebula sistra acidic guaiac tannic bopped ennead
coccyx ataxia frusta novena sonata Adamic haptic tanrec boxbed enwind
dactyl aurora fulcra numina squama adipic hectic tarmac braird errand
embryo Avesta funkia nutria stadia Adonic herdic tenrec briard exceed
ennuye axilla galena oedema stanza Aeolic heroic thetic budded expand
eponym azalea garuda omenta stemma agamic hydric tictac bugged expend
forbye balata geisha optima sterna agaric hymnic toluic bulbed extend
henrys balboa Gemara oscula stigma agonic iambic tombac bummed eyelid
legbye banana genera ottava strata airsac iconic tragic bunted fabled
martyr baryta geneva paella stroma alcaic irenic tropic bushed fagend
methyl batata gloria pagoda struma anodic ironic Turkic bussed fagged
moneys beluga goanna pajama taenia anomic italic unific busted failed
outbye bertha grappa pakeha tamara anoxic Judaic Uralic byroad fanged
papaya bodega guinea pallia tantra aortic karmic uranic byword fanned
pentyl Brahma Gurkha panada tapeta Arabic Keltic vitric cafard fantod
phenyl bregma halloa panama tarsia arctic lactic Wendic canard fatted
piraya buckra Havana papaya tegula ataxic Lettic zincic candid fecund
propyl Buddha hedera papula telega atomic limbec zodiac canned fervid
redeye bunnia hegira patina thoria atonic limbic aboard capped fezzed
strays burkha hejira payola thulia azotic lithic abound capsid fibbed
tiedye cabala hernia pelota torula Baltic lubric abroad celled fibred
uranyl cabana holloa peseta trauma bardic luetic absurd chield figged
Vaisya camera hoopla pesewa trivia Belgic maleic acarid closed finned
zephyr carina hyaena petara troika bionic maniac accord coated fitted
zlotys cassia iguana phobia tsamba biotic manioc addend coccid florid
ablaze catena impala piazza Tswana bromic mantic addled cocked fluted
assize cesura indaba pineta tundra calcic mastic afeard cogged fobbed
bedaze chacha induna piraya ultima calpac metric afford combed foetid
blowzy chacma infula plasma ungula capric miotic afield conned fogged
breeze chorea inyala pleura Urania celiac mosaic afraid conoid foiled
breezy chroma ischia pneuma utopia Celtic mundic agamid copped footed
bronze chukka jacana posada Vaisya chemic myopic ageold corded forbad
bronzy cicada jerboa protea valeta choric myotic airbed corked forbid
corozo cicala joanna pruina valuta citric mystic aisled corned forced
coryza cigala judoka puncta veleta cleric mythic alated cotted fordid
floozy cinema kabala pyrola vesica clinic nastic algoid coward forked
freeze cloaca kanaka quagga vicuna clonic nitric aliped cowled formed
frenzy coaita kinema quanta vihara cognac noetic allied crazed forrad
frieze concha lacuna quinoa vizsla Coptic Nordic allred cuboid friend
frizzy copita laguna quinta womera corsac nostoc almond cuffed frigid
frowzy copula lambda quotha Yoruba cosmic ogamic angled cupped fucoid
mezuza cornea lamina radula yttria cretic orphic aoudad cursed fugged
piazza cornua latria raffia zareba critic ovisac append cusped fulgid
queazy corona ligula ranula zariba cultic oxalic arched cuspid funned
schizo coryza lingua raphia zenana cupric ozonic argand cussed furred
sleazy cowpea lipoma razzia zeugma cyanic parsec ariled cyprid gabbed
snazzy crania lithia regina zinnia cyclic pathic around cystid gabled
sneeze crista loggia remora zygoma Cymric pectic ascend dabbed gadded
sneezy cuesta lorcha remuda absorb cystic pelvic attend dammed gadoid
snooze cupola lorica reseda adsorb deific peptic avowed damned gagged
stanza dahlia lumina retina adverb dermic phasic awaked darned gaited
wheeze datura lunula rhumba aplomb dyadic phatic bagged daybed ganoid
wheezy dharma lustra rostra baobab echoic phobic ballad defend gapped
—————— dhurra macula rosula bedaub Eddaic phonic banned demand garbed
abulia djibba Malaga rumina benumb Edenic photic barbed depend gassed
acacia duenna maltha russia cherub emblic physic barred desmid gelled
acedia eczema manana salina cobweb emetic picnic batted deuced gemmed
adnexa Egeria manila saliva confab Eozoic picric bayard devoid genned
```

```
gerund lapped pepped should unread affine beadle bungle comose demote
gifted lapsed period shrewd unsaid aflame beagle burble congee demure
gigged leafed petard shroud unshod afrite beanie burgee cookie dengue
gilled leaved petted sinned untied agnate Beaune burgle coolie denote
ginned ledged pigged sipped untold agnise became bursae cootie denude
graved legend pinned sobbed unused agrafe become bustee corbie depone
gravid legged pipped sopped unwind albite bedaze bustle corpse depose
ground lensed pissed sordid upheld alcove beetle butane corrie depute
gummed Leonid pitted sotted uphold Aldine before butene corvee derate
gunned lidded placed souled upland alkane begone byebye cosine deride
gutted lilied placid spined upward alkene behave bygone costae derive
gypped limbed plumed spread upwind alkyne behove bylane coulee desire
haired limpid pocked stated valved aldose belike byline couple device
hammed lipoid podded stewed varied allege belive byname course devise
handed lipped polled stolid varved allele bemire cackle cowage devote
hanged liquid pooped stoned vatted allude bemuse caddie cowrie dibble
happed listed popped stound vaward allure berate caique cradle diddle
hatred lizard potted strand veiled alpine berthe cajole crease dilate
hatted loaded premed stroud veined alsike beside calque create dimple
hawked lobbed puffed stupid versed alulae betake camise creche dingle
hazard logged punned subbed vested amerce betide candle creese diploe
headed lopped pupped summed vetted ampere beware cangue cringe dipole
heated lotted putrid sungod viscid anlace binate canine crosse disuse
heeled lugged ragged sunned vizard anlage birdie cantle crouse divide
hemmed maenad ramrod swound voiced annexe bireme capote cruise divine
heptad mailed rancid tabard voided anomie birkie carafe cruive doable
herald manned rapped tabbed wadded anyone bisque casque cubage docile
hinged mantid rasped tagend wagged apache bistre castle cuddie doddle
hipped mapped ratted tagged walled apiece bizone cattle cuddle dogate
hispid maraud record Talmud wanted apogee blende caudle cuisse doggie
hogged marked redbud tanked warded appose blithe cayuse cuptie donate
hoised marred refund tanned warped arable blonde centre cupule donsie
honied masted regard tapped warred arcade blouse cerate curare doodle
hooded matted relaid tarred warted arcane blunge cerise curate doolie
hoofed mazard reload tatted wasted areole bobble ceruse curdle dormie
hooked method remand tented webbed Argive bocage cetane curiae dosage
hopped metred remind tetrad wedded argute bodice chaise currie dotage
horned miffed repaid thread wetted argyle boggle chance curule dottle
horrid milled reread ticked wicked arouse bolide change cushie douane
hotbed milord resold tiered wigged arrive bonnie charge cuttle double
hugged minded rested tierod willed arsine bonxie chasse cymose douche
hummed misdid retard tinned winded ashore boodle chaste damage dragee
humped misled retold tinted winged aslope bookie cheese dandle drawee
hutted moated retrod tipped winked aspire bootee chelae dangle dredge
hybrid mobbed retted titled witted assize borage cheque daphne drogue
ideaed monied revved togaed wizard assume borane chicle dapple drowse
impend mopped reward togged wonted assure borate chigoe darkie drudge
inbred morbid rewind tomcod wooded astute boride choice darkle duende
indeed mucoid reword topped wooled athome bosche choose dartle duffle
infold mugged ribald toroid xyloid attire bothie chouse dartre dumose
inlaid myriad riband torpid yapped attune botone chrome dassie dunite
inland nabbed ribbed torrid yenned aubade bottle chypre dative durrie
inroad nagged ridded tossed yipped audile boucle cilice dautie ecarte
intend napped ridged totted yolked augite bougie cinque dawdle edible
intoed neaped rigged toward zapped auntie boulle cirque dazzle efface
inward nereid rimmed toxoid zinced Aussie bounce citole dearie effete
island netted ringed trepid zinked avenge bourne claque debase effuse
isopod nibbed rinsed trifid zipped avenue bourse clause debate elapse
izzard Nimrod ripped tripod zonked averse bovine cleave decade eluate
jabbed nipped roofed tufted abduce aviate bowtie cleome decare embrue
jagged nodded rooted tugged abjure avulse braise cliche decide emerge
jammed obtund rotted turbid ablate awhile braize clique decode emeute
jarred offend rotund turgid ablaze ayeaye branle cloche decoke emigre
jetted onward rubbed tusked abrade babble breese clothe decree empire
jibbed orchid ruched tutted accede baddie breeze coarse deduce emulge
jigged outbid ruffed twould accrue baffle bridge coatee deface enable
jocund outdid rugged unbend accuse baggie bridle cobble defame encage
jogged oxbird rutted unbind achene bailee broche cockle defile encase
jotted oxford sacred unclad active bailie brogue coddle define encode
jugged oxherd sailed unfold adduce bangle bronze coerce defuse encore
jutted oxland sapped ungird adhere barege browse coffee degage endive
kenned padded sayyid unhand adjure bargee bruise coffle degree endure
kerned pallid scaled uniped admire barite buckle cohere delate enface
kidded panned screed unipod adnate Basque buddle cohune delete engage
kilted patted seabed united advice battle budgie coigne delude engine
kobold peaked second unkind advise battue bullae collie deluge enisle
lagged pegged secund unlaid aedile bauble bumble colure deluxe enlace
lammed penned shaped unload aerate bawbee bummle comate demise ennuye
landed pentad shield unpaid aerobe bawble bundle commie demode enrage
```

enrobe	footle	hearse	jiggle	magpie	nerine	peddle	quince	roadie	single
ensate	foozle	heckle	jingle	maigre	nerite	pelage	rabble	rookie	sirree
ensile	forage	heddle	jinnee	malate	nestle	peltae	raceme	rosace	sizzle
ensure	forbye	hexane	jocose	malice	nettle	pennae	raddle	rotate	sleave
entice	fossae	hexose	joggle	mallee	nibble	people	radome	rotche	sledge
entire	foveae	higgle	jostle	mammae	niggle	perdue	raffle	rouble	sleeve
entree	fraise	hippie	jounce	mammee	nimble	peruke	raggee	rubble	sludge
enzyme	frappe	hirple	jugate	manage	nipple	peruse	raggle	ruckle	sluice
Eocene	freeze	hoarse	juggle	manche	nobble	pesade	ramate	ruddle	smudge
ephebe	fridge	hobble	jujube	manege	noddle	pestle	ramble	ruelle	snathe
epopee	frieze	hogtie	jumble	mangle	nodose	petite	ramose	ruffle	sneeze
equate	fringe	homage	jungle	manque	nodule	peyote	rankle	rugose	snooze
equine	fuddle	hombre	junkie	mantle	nonage	phoebe	rapine	rumble	socage
ergate	fumble	hoodie	Kabyle	manure	nonuse	phrase	rappee	rumple	softie
ermine	furore	hoopoe	karate	marble	noodle	piaffe	rasure	rundle	soigne
escape	fusile	hopple	kelpie	marine	notate	pickle	ratine	rustle	soiree
Essene	futile	huckle	ketone	marque	notice	piddle	ratite	rutile	solace
essive	future	huddle	kettle	mascle	novice	pierce	rattle	Sabine	solute
estate	gabble	humane	kewpie	mashie	nowise	piffle	ravage	sacque	sombre
eterne	gaggle	humble	kibble	masque	noyade	pilose	ravine	saddle	somite
ethane	galore	hurdle	kiddie	mature	nozzle	pilule	razzle	saithe	sonsie
ethene	gamble	hurtle	kiekie	maugre	nuance	pimple	rebate	salade	soothe
ethyne	gamete	hustle	kindle	maxixe	nubble	pinkie	rebore	saline	sopite
euchre	gamine	hyphae	kirtle	meagre	nubile	pinnae	rebuke	sallee	sorage
evince	gangue	iceaxe	kittle	mealie	nuncle	pinole	recede	salute	sortie
evolue	garage	icicle	koedoe	meanie	nutate	pintle	recipe	samite	source
evolve	garble	ideate	kookie	meddle	nuzzle	pirate	recite	sample	sparge
evzone	gargle	ignite	koppie	mediae	oarage	pizzle	reddle	sapele	sparse
excide	garvie	ignore	labile	meinie	obeche	plague	redeye	sarape	spathe
excise	gauche	illume	laddie	menace	objure	plaice	rediae	sasine	specie
excite	gavage	illuse	lanate	menage	oblate	plaque	redone	satire	spence
excuse	geegee	imbibe	langue	merrie	oblige	please	reduce	savage	sphene
exhale	gemmae	imbrue	lappie	mestee	obtuse	pledge	reface	savate	sphere
exhume	genome	immane	larvae	metage	ochone	plicae	refine	savine	splice
expire	gentle	immune	lasque	metope	octane	plisse	refuge	scarce	spline
expose	George	immure	lassie	mettle	octave	plunge	refuse	scathe	splore
Eyetie	giggle	impale	launce	mickle	oeuvre	podite	refute	scheme	sponge
facade	gillie	impede	lavage	midage	office	pointe	regale	sconce	spouse
facete	girdle	impone	league	middle	ohmage	police	reggae	scopae	sprite
facile	girlie	impose	legate	milage	oleate	polite	regime	scouse	spruce
faerie	glaive	impure	legbye	mingle	online	pomace	relate	scrape	spurge
faille	glance	impute	legume	minute	onside	pomade	reline	scribe	square
falsie	goalie	incase	lessee	mirage	oocyte	pommie	relive	scythe	squire
famine	goatee	incise	Levite	miscue	oolite	pongee	relume	seabee	stable
Fantee	gobble	incite	liable	misere	opaque	pontie	remade	seance	stacte
faunae	goggle	income	liaise	mistle	ophite	poodle	remake	secede	stance
feeble	goitre	incuse	lichee	misuse	opiate	popple	remise	secure	staple
feirie	goodie	indene	lierne	mizzle	oppose	porgie	remote	sedate	starve
feline	gourde	indite	ligate	mobile	orache	porose	remove	sedile	statue
felloe	gramme	indole	ligule	module	oracle	potage	rename	seduce	steeve
female	grange	induce	ligure	moggie	orange	potale	renege	seethe	stelae
ferine	grease	infare	linage	mohole	ordure	potpie	repine	seiche	steppe
ferule	greave	infuse	lintie	moline	oriole	pottle	repose	semble	stifle
fescue	greige	inhale	lipase	mollie	ornate	pouffe	repute	Semite	stodge
fettle	grieve	inhere	lipide	mopoke	orpine	pounce	resale	semple	stogie
fiacre	grille	inhume	lippie	morale	oscine	praise	rescue	sempre	stooge
fiance	grilse	injure	little	morgue	osmose	prance	reside	senate	strafe
fickle	grippe	inmate	loathe	morose	otiose	pratie	resile	senile	strake
fiddle	groove	innate	lobate	mosque	outage	prince	resole	serape	striae
fierce	grouse	insane	lobose	motile	outbye	psyche	resume	serene	stride
figure	groyne	inside	lobule	motive	outvie	puddle	retake	serrae	strife
filose	grudge	insole	locale	mottle	oxgate	puisne	retene	sesame	strike
fimble	guddle	insure	locate	mousse	oxhide	pulque	retire	setose	Strine
finale	guggle	intake	louche	muckle	paddle	pumice	retuse	settee	stripe
finite	gurgle	intine	lounge	muddle	palace	puntee	revere	settle	strive
fipple	guttae	intone	louvre	muffle	palate	pupate	revile	severe	strobe
fixate	guzzle	invade	lovage	mumble	paleae	purfle	revise	sewage	strode
fizzle	gyrate	invite	luggie	murine	papule	purine	revive	shavie	stroke
flambe	habile	invoke	lunate	muscle	parade	purple	revoke	sheave	strove
flange	hackle	inwove	lunule	mutate	pardie	pursue	rewire	shelve	stymie
fleche	haddie	iodate	lupine	mutine	parole	puttee	rewoke	Shiite	suable
fledge	haggle	iodide	lustre	mutule	Parsee	puttie	rhaphe	shrike	subdue
fleece	halide	iodine	luxate	muzzle	parure	puzzle	ribose	shrine	subtle
flense	halite	iodise	lychee	mygale	pavage	pyrene	riddle	shrive	suckle
florae	hamate	iolite	lyrate	myrtle	pavane	pyrite	riffle	shrove	summae
focsle	Hamite	ionise	lysine	native	pavise	pyrope	rimose	sickle	sundae
foible	handle	jangle	mackle	nature	pawnee	quaere	ripple	silage	supine
fondle	hankie	jaunce	macule	needle	pebble	quarte	risque	simile	supple
fondue	hassle	jejune	Madame	negate	pedate	quiche	rivage	simple	sutile

```
suttee tussle wamble bluing oxgang attach Granth quitch wretch tumuli
suture tuyere wampee bobwig paling avouch grouch radish Yahveh uncini
svelte twelve wangle boding parang aweigh growth rakish Yahweh Wahabi
swathe twinge warble booing paring banish grutch ravish zenith wapiti
swerve twyere warsle boring paving blanch Guelph rehash zillah swaraj
swinge ugsome wattle bowing pegleg bleach Gullah relish zinnah ackack
tackle ullage weepie bowleg piedog blench gunyah Romish alkali anorak
takahe umbrae wheeze boxing piping blotch gurrah rudish alumni arrack
talkie umpire whence busing proleg bluish halvah rupiah annuli attack
tamale unable whinge casing prying borsch haunch scorch argali bedeck
tangle uncage wiggle caving pugdog boyish health scotch ariosi bemock
tassie uncate wimble coming putlog branch hearth scouth askari betook
tattle undate wimple coping pyedog breach hookah scutch banzai bohunk
tawpie undine winkle coving quahog breath hootch search bhisti bywork
teazle undone wintle crying ragbag breech howdah seraph Bihari Canuck
teepee unease wobble cueing ragtag broach hurrah seriph bikini copeck
teethe unglue woggle daring raring brooch immesh sheath bonsai corsak
temple Uniate wortle dining ratbag brunch impish sheikh borzoi damask
tenace unique wrasse diving rating bypath inarch sheugh Brahmi debark
tentie unlace writhe dogleg raving calash inrush sirrah calami debunk
tenure unlade xylene dugong riding caliph jarrah skeigh canthi demark
terete unlike xylose during rising casbah Jewish sketch chichi dikdik
testae unmade yaffle dyeing roping ceriph jibbah sleigh chilli dybbuk
thecae unmake Yankee earing roving chough Jutish sleuth clypei embank
theine unripe yippee earwig rowing church kasbah slouch cumuli embark
thence unrobe yippie eating ruling clench kiaugh slough curari hijack
thieve unrope zaffre edging runrig clinch kiblah smatch decani impark
thorpe unsafe zarape eggnog sarong clough kibosh smeech dhooti inwick
thrice unshoe zombie ending saving clunch kirsch smirch djinni kopeck
thrive untrue zonate eyeing saying clutch kitsch smooch emboli medick
throne untune Zouave facing seadog coolth koolah smooth ephebi Mohawk
throve unwise zygote feeing seafog cowish lamish smouch famuli Mohock
thyrse unyoke zymase filing seapig cranch latish smutch flocci moujik
tibiae .update behalf fining seeing cratch launch snatch Gemini mukluk
tickle uphroe behoof firing serang crotch lavish sneesh glutei muzhik
tiedye uprise belief fizgig sewing crouch length snitch grigri oclock
tierce upside cutoff flying siding crunch loofah speech humeri oomiak
timbre uptake engulf fogdog simurg crutch lowish spilth incubi padauk
tingle urbane faroff gaming sizing cultch marish splash kabuki Polack
tinkle ursine hereof gasbag skiing Danish matzoh splosh kowhai rebeck
tipple usable ingulf gobang sprang dearth minish squash lazuli reebok
tiptoe usance itself gundog spring detach modish squish limuli remark
tirade uvulae layoff hatpeg sprung doodah Moloch staith litchi retook
tisane vacate letoff hiding stalag dreich moolah stanch loculi rework
tissue vagile massif hieing string drench mopish starch mallei rhebok
tittle valine midoff hoeing strong droich morish stench mishmi sanjak
toddle valise myself homing strung drouth mulish stitch moduli screak
toffee vegete oneoff hotdog sundog dryish mullah strath muesli Seljuk
toggle veloce payoff humbug tagrag dudish Munich sumach Nepali sheoak
toneme velure pilaff icebag taking eighth nautch swarth neroli shrank
tongue vendee putoff inning taming elfish newish swatch nielli shriek
tootle vendue rebuff jetlag tautog elvish nicish switch nilgai shrink
topple venire relief kalong teabag encash nullah swoosh nuclei shrunk
torose Venite returf kitbag throng enmesh oafish teraph ocelli Slovak
torque venose ripoff lacing tiewig enough offish thatch octroi squawk
touche ventre runoff lading tiling enrich ogrish though papyri squeak
toupee venule sclaff lapdog timing eolith oldish thrash phalli streak
tousle vestee scruff liking toeing eunuch onrush thresh polypi streek
towage viable setoff liming trying exarch owlish thrush pylori struck
towhee vielle shaduf lining Tuareg famish palish tonish rhombi suslik
townee virile sharif living tubing fellah paraph trench safari thwack
trance virose sherif loving tuning fetich pariah trough salami tombak
treble virtue shroff lowing typing fetish parish tussah saluki uncork
tremie visage tariff luting unking finish parish twitch sandhi undock
triage visile tipoff making unplug flanch perish uneath satori unhook
trifle visive unroof maybug unsung fleech pleach unlash scampi unkink
triode vittae unself maying upping flench plinth uppish scyphi unlink
triple vivace acting mining Viking fletch plough uprush seseli unlock
triste volume ageing mooing voting flinch polish vanish Shakti unmask
triune volute airing moving wardog flitch popish wallah sileni unpack
troche votive anting musing wigwag flysch potash warmth solidi unpick
trompe voulge awning muskeg wiring fourth preach wealth souari untuck
troupe voyage bagwig nignog zigzag fratch punish whidah strati yapock
trudge wabble bandog nosing zoning french punkah whoosh tahini zebeck
tsetse waddie bating nutmeg ablush galosh purdah whydah tatami aboral
tubule waddle bedbug oblong afresh garish putsch widish thalli abseil
tuille waffle belong offing aguish glitch quaich wraith tholoi acetal
tumble waggle bigwig oolong ambush golosh quaigh wreath thyrsi acetyl
turtle wahine biting outing anarch goyish quench wrench tsotsi actual
```

```
adenyl choral fossil mensal resell tubful cilium napalm wigwam burton
aerial cineol foveal mental retail tunnel coelom Nazism wisdom buskin
agnail clonal frazil mescal retell tymbal corium nomism xenium busman
agonal coccal frijol mesial retial umbral cubism noncom yogism button
amatol coeval frivol methyl retool uncial curium nudism yumyum cabman
amoral coital frugal missal retral uncoil custom oidium zythum cacoon
animal compel fulfil missel reveal uncool deform omasum action caftan
anneal consul fungal mitral rhinal uncurl diadem orgasm acumen caiman
annual corbel funnel Mongol rictal unfurl diatom osmium adjoin calkin
anodal cornel Gadhel monial ritual ungual dictum ostium Aegean camion
antral corral gambol morsel rondel unnail dinkum papism Afghan cancan
aortal costal garial mortal rueful unreal dirdum passim airgun cannon
apical coucal gavial mussel runnel unreel dirham paynim airman canton
apodal credal genial mutual sacral unroll dirhem pelham aldrin canyon
appeal crenel gerbil netful sandal unseal disarm peplum alevin caplin
archil cresol gimbal neural santal unveil dodgem phlegm alexin carbon
armful crewel gimmal nickel sapful unwell dolium phloem amazon careen
artful crotal gingal normal sardel uphill dorsum phylum amnion carman
assail crural global nounal saurel uracil drachm pileum archon carton
assoil cudgel glycol Nowell school uranyl dumdum plenum arisen carven
astral cupful Goidel nuchal schorl urinal Durham podium ashbin casein
atonal curial googol obital scrawl urnful egoism pogrom ashcan casern
atrial curtal gospel ogival scroll useful embalm pompom ashpan Caslon
avowal cymbal gravel onfall scutal vandal emblem porism assign cation
awheel dactyl grovel orchil sendal vassal engram possum astern catkin
azonal daedal gunnel ordeal septal vatful eonism prelim aswoon cavern
bagful damsel gunsel osteal sequel venial eponym purism ataman cayman
barbel Daniel haemal ostial serial ventil erbium quorum attain cedarn
barrel darnel hallal oxgall serval verbal esteem racism attorn Charon
becall deasil hammal oxtail sexual vernal factum radium auburn chitin
bedell denial hansel oxymel shekel versal fandom random Augean chiton
befall dental hartal palpal shovel vessel fantom random Austin chopin
befell dentel hatful panful shrill vestal fathom ransom autumn chosen
befool dentil herbal parcel signal vidual folium rectum awaken citron
befoul derail hostel parral simnel visual frenum redeem awoken clipon
beigel dermal housel parrel sinful wadmal fulham reform baboon cloven
benzol detail hummel pascal snivel wadmol fullam replum bagman cochin
benzyl diesel hymnal pastel social weasel goddam rhythm baleen cocoon
bethel dirndl hyphal pastil sorrel weevil gypsum sachem ballon codlin
bewail discal instal patrol spinal wilful hammam sacrum banian coffin
bharal dismal instil peepul spinel withal hansom sadism banyan column
binful dispel ireful pencil spiral wittol helium salaam barman comeon
boatel distal isabel pentyl spital woeful holism schism barren common
bordel distil isohel petrel sprawl xenial hummum scream barton conman
boreal dorsal jackal petrol squail zingel ibidem scutum baryon corban
boxful dossal jarful peyotl squall abloom idolum seldom batman cordon
brazil dossel jerbil phenol squeal adytum indium sensum batten cotton
bridal drivel jezail phenyl squill affirm infirm septum beacon coupon
brumal drupel jovial pineal statal alarum inform sexism beaten cousin
brutal duffel joyful pistil sterol allium inseam shalom beckon cowman
buccal earful jugful pistol stipel amylum iodism siglum bedpan craven
bulbil enamel jumbal plagal stroll anadem ionium simoom beduin crayon
bulbul enroll kennel plural subtil anonym jetsam slalom bemoan Cretan
burhel ensoul kernel podsol swivel anthem labium sodium benign cretin
burial entail kitool podzol symbol antrum labrum sputum berlin croton
burrel entoil kittul pommel tahsil apozem lissom squirm bidden cummin
bursal epical kummel pontil tarsal ashram logjam stream biffin cyanin
bushel espial labial portal tassel asylum lyceum Sufism biggin daemon
caecal eyeful laical postal teasel atrium lyrism system billon daimen
cancel facial lapful postil teazel autism magnum talcum biotin daimon
canful fallal larval potful tercel Baalim malism tamtam bitten dampen
cannel fardel laurel primal tergal Babism Maoism tandem blazon damson
capful farfel lawful propel thecal balsam marram Taoism bobbin darken
carful faucal lentil propyl thrall bantam marrum Targum bodkin deacon
carnal faunal lethal pulvil thrill barium mayhem tedium boffin deaden
carpal fennel lineal pummel thymol becalm medium tergum bonbon deafen
carpel ferial lintel quinol tibial bedlam megohm theism boston deepen
carrel festal lionel racial timbal beldam megrim tomtom bowfin dehorn
cartel fetial listel radial tincal beseem mentum truism bowman demean
carvel feudal luteal rappel tindal biform merism tumtum brazen design
casual fibril mammal rascal tinful bonism minium unseam brehon desman
caudal filial manful recall tinsel bottom monism vacuum Breton detain
causal finial mangel recoil toluol bunkum Moslem vagrom Briton diplon
cental fiscal mantel refill tonsil byform multum vallum broken disown
cereal fitful manual refuel torsel caecum museum vellum bumkin dobbin
chapel floral marcel regnal travel centum Muslim verism bunion dolman
chesil foetal marvel reheel tribal cerium mutism victim bunsen dolmen
chisel fontal medial rental trinal chiasm mutuum wampum burden domain
chital formal menial repeal trowel chrism nanism whilom Burman donjon
```

Dorian	graben	lessen	noggin	ramson	sodden	uneven	enhalo	sissoo	lashup
dragon	gradin	lesson	Norman	randan	soften	unison	eryngo	smalto	leadup
driven	gratin	Libyan	notion	ration	soldan	unjoin	escudo	solano	liftup
dryrun	graven	lichen	obtain	ratlin	solemn	unseen	Eskimo	sorgho	lineup
dubbin	grison	lignin	oddson	ratoon	sovran	unworn	fiasco	speedo	linkup
dudeen	guanin	linden	oilcan	rattan	spavin	uptown	forego	stereo	lockup
dunlin	guenon	lippen	oilman	reason	spleen	upturn	fresco	stingo	lollop
durgan	guidon	listen	olefin	reborn	spoken	urchin	fugato	stinko	madcap
durian	gulden	livein	oppugn	reckon	sprain	ustion	gabbro	stopgo	magilp
eleven	gunman	lochan	option	recoin	stamen	vermin	galago	stucco	makeup
elevon	gurjun	logion	orcein	redden	stepin	violin	Gallio	studio	markup
eloign	hadron	longan	ordain	regain	stolen	virgin	gaucho	tattoo	mayhap
emetin	haemin	lookin	origan	region	stolon	vision	gazebo	tenuto	megilp
enjoin	happen	loosen	origin	rejoin	strain	vulcan	gentoo	teredo	mishap
ensign	harden	lotion	orison	remain	strewn	wabain	ghetto	Toledo	mobcap
eolian	harken	louden	orphan	renown	strown	waggon	gigolo	tomato	mockup
eonian	hasten	loupen	ossein	reopen	subman	walkin	gingko	torero	noshup
Eozoon	hatpin	lovein	outgun	repugn	suborn	walkon	gingko	troppo	outtop
essoin	headon	lucern	outran	resign	sudden	wanion	gorgio	tupelo	paidup
etymon	heaven	lumpen	outrun	retain	sullen	wanton	gringo	tuxedo	pegtop
examen	hempen	lurdan	oxygen	return	sultan	warden	grotto	ultimo	pentup
exogen	henrun	lutein	papain	ribbon	summon	warren	hairdo	vaudoo	pickup
extern	herein	Lydian	pardon	richen	sunken	weaken	halloo	vibrio	pileup
Fabian	hereon	machan	parian	ridden	suntan	weapon	hereto	virago	pullup
fadein	heroin	macron	parkin	rodman	sweven	weazen	hetero	voodoo	pushup
falcon	Herren	madden	parpen	rollon	sylvan	welkin	Hindoo	weirdo	recoup
fallen	hetman	madman	parson	ronyon	syphon	whiten	hoodoo	whatso	redcap
fanion	hidden	Magian	partan	rotten	Syrian	wigeon	indigo	whomso	redtop
fantan	hitman	maidan	Pathan	Sabian	taipan	Wilton	kakapo	yoohoo	reship
fasten	hodden	maiden	patron	sadden	takein	within	karroo	zeloso	revamp
fathen	hodman	malign	patten	Salian	talion	wivern	kimono	zufolo	riprap
fatten	hoggin	malkin	peahen	salmon	tampan	wonton	koodoo	asleep	saloop
Fenian	holden	mammon	pecten	saloon	tampon	wooden	ladino	backup	sannup
fenman	holpen	margin	pectin	Samian	tannin	worsen	lanugo	bangup	satrap
fibrin	houdan	marlin	penman	Samoan	tarpan	wyvern	lavabo	bishop	schlep
finnan	hoyden	maroon	pennon	sampan	tarpon	yaupon	leanto	blowup	scrimp
fiorin	hyphen	marron	pepsin	Samson	tartan	yeoman	legato	bopeep	scroop
firkin	iceman	marten	perron	person	Tarzan	yesman	libido	bunyip	scrump
firman	impawn	martin	person	sarsen	tauten	zircon	macaco	burlap	sendup
flacon	impugn	mascon	phonon	sateen	tavern	adagio	maduro	burnup	shrimp
flagon	inborn	maslin	photon	Saturn	taxman	aikido	makedo	bustup	slapup
flamen	Indian	matron	pidgin	scazon	tegmen	akimbo	manito	callup	slipup
flavin	indign	median	pieman	screen	telson	albedo	matico	catnap	stepup
flaxen	inspan	melton	pigeon	seafan	tendon	albino	medico	catnip	teacup
florin	intern	merlin	piggin	seaman	tenpin	anatto	merino	catsup	threap
flyman	inulin	merlon	pinion	seapen	tenson	arioso	mikado	coinop	tiptop
foeman	Ionian	merman	pipkin	season	tenzon	arroyo	modulo	collop	tittup
foison	isatin	messan	pippin	secern	teston	bagnio	morpho	decamp	toecap
Frauen	jargon	micron	piston	seisin	Teuton	bamboo	nardoo	dewlap	tossup
frozen	jerkin	midden	pitman	seizin	Theban	barrio	niello	dollop	turnip
fusain	Jovian	mignon	pitpan	sephen	thoron	Basuto	nonego	dustup	turnup
fusion	Judean	minion	platan	sequin	thrawn	billyo	nuncio	eggcup	unship
gabion	Julian	Minoan	platen	serein	thrown	bistro	nympho	encamp	unstop
gagman	kaftan	mitten	pluton	sermon	tiepin	blotto	octavo	entrap	unwrap
gallon	kaolin	mizzen	poison	serran	tiffin	bolero	overdo	enwrap	upkeep
gammon	kation	modern	pollan	sextan	tinman	bonito	palolo	escarp	wallop
garcon	kelson	molten	pollen	sexton	titian	booboo	paramo	Ethiop	warmup
garden	kelvin	moreen	ponton	shaken	tocsin	boohoo	Pashto	eyecup	windup
garran	kitten	morgen	popgun	shaman	topman	bronco	pedalo	fillip	abater
garron	Korean	morion	poplin	shapen	torten	bumalo	pomelo	foulup	abuser
Gascon	kraken	Mormon	poteen	shaven	toucan	burgoo	poncho	gallop	acinar
gaskin	kronen	motion	potion	shogun	trapan	calico	potato	gazump	adorer
gasman	kurgan	moulin	potman	shoran	trepan	casino	presto	giddap	aether
german	lagoon	muffin	prison	shutin	trigon	catalo	pronto	gollop	affair
germen	lallan	muflon	proton	sicken	triton	chromo	pseudo	gossip	affeer
gibbon	lardon	muntin	proven	silken	trogon	cogito	psycho	hangup	alegar
gigman	lateen	muslin	pterin	silvan	Trojan	colugo	pueblo	hardup	ambler
gluten	latron	mutton	ptisan	simian	tuchun	comedo	quarto	hiccup	amuser
glycin	latten	myelin	puffin	simoon	tuckin	corozo	rabato	holdup	anchor
gnomon	lawman	myosin	pullin	Siouan	turban	crambo	rancho	hookup	angler
goblin	layman	napkin	pullon	siphon	tureen	crypto	rebato	hubcap	answer
godown	leaden	nation	purlin	siskin	turion	cuckoo	reecho	hyssop	anther
godson	leadin	natron	python	sixain	Tuscan	daimio	regulo	icecap	antiar
golden	leaven	neaten	rabbin	sixgun	tutsan	domino	righto	inclip	antler
gorgon	legion	nekton	racoon	skirun	tycoon	dorado	robalo	instep	appear
gossan	legman	nelson	radian	skyman	tympan	drongo	rococo	inwrap	arbour
gotten	Lenten	neuron	raglan	slipon	Tyrian	duello	rubato	kidnap	archer
govern	lepton	newton	ragman	slogan	Ugrian	dynamo	schizo	laceup	ardour
gozzan	lesion	niacin	raisin	sloven	unborn	embryo	Shinto	larrup	arguer

```
armour bummer costar durbar ganger hooker larker mincer pitter reiver
ashlar bumper coster duster gaoler hooper lascar minder placer render
author bunder cottar duyker garner hooter lasher minter planar renter
avatar bunker cotter earner garter hopper laster mirror planer repair
backer bunter cougar easter gasper horner lather mister plater rester
badger burger crater echoer gasser horror latter moaner player rhetor
bailer burler craver eclair gather hosier laveer mocker plexor rhymer
bailor burner culler editor gauger hotter lawyer mohair plover ricker
baiter bursar culver eggler geezer howler leader moider polder rifler
balker busbar cumber either gender hummer leaper moiler poller rigger
banger busker cummer elater getter humour leaver monger ponder rigour
banker buster cunner elixir geyser hunger lecher mopper poplar ringer
banner butler curler eloper giaour hunker lector mortar popper rinser
banter butter cursor endear gibber hunter ledger mother porker rioter
barber buzzer cutler envier gilder hurler lender mouser porter ripper
barker cadger cutter epimer gimmer hurter lesser mucker poseur risker
barter cahier cycler eraser ginger husker lessor mugger poster rizzar
basher calcar cypher eschar ginner hussar letter muller pother rizzer
baster calker dabber etcher girder huzoor libber mummer potter roamer
bather caller dagger etrier glazer impair lictor mumper pourer roarer
batter camber dammar evader glider indoor lieder murder pouter robber
bawler camper damper evener glover inlier lifter murmur powder rocker
bazaar cancer dancer fabler glower instar ligger muster prater roller
beaker canker dander factor gnawer ironer limber mutter prayer romper
beamer canner danger falter goffer isobar limner nagger prefer roofer
bearer canter dapper fanner golfer isomer limper nailer prewar roomer
beater cantor darner faquir goober jabber linear natter primer rooter
beaver captor darter farmer gooier jaeger linger nearer prizer roster
bedder carder dasher faster gopher jagger liquor nectar prober rotter
beeper career dauber father grader jaguar lisper Nestor proper rouser
beggar carper dealer fatter grater jailer lister nether proser router
bender carter debtor favour graver jailor litter neuter pruner rozzer
Berber carver decker fawner grazer jammer loader nicker pucker rubber
bestir caster defier feeder griper jasper loafer nigger puffer rudder
better castor deicer feeler grocer jeerer loaner nipper puller rugger
bettor Cathar delver feller groper jerker locker number pulper ruiner
bezoar causer denier fencer grower jester lodger nurser pulsar rummer
bibber caviar deodar fender guider jibber lofter nutter pulser rumour
bicker cellar detour fester guiser jigger logger obeyer pumper runner
bidder censer devoir fetter guitar jilter loiter ocular punner rusher
bigger censor devour fibber gunner jitter loller oliver punter sadder
bilker cesser dexter filler gunter jobber looker onager purger saeter
binder chafer diaper filter gusher jogger looper opener purler saggar
birler chaser dibber finder gutter joiner looter orator purser sagger
bister chimer dicker finger guvnor jolter lopper ostler pusher sailer
bitter choker dieter finner hailer josher louver ouster putter sailor
blazer choler differ fisher halter josser lubber ovular Quaker salter
blower chukar digger fitter hammer jotter lugger oyster quasar salver
boater cinder dimmer flexor hamper judder lumbar packer quaver salvor
bodger cipher dinner flower hangar judger lumber pallor queuer sambar
boiler cither dipper fluter hanger jumper lumper palmar quiver sambur
bolter claver disbar fodder hanker junior lunger palmer racker sander
bomber clever diseur folder harper junker lurker palter rafter sangar
bonder clover dither foliar hatter Kaffir madder pamper raider santir
bonzer cobber docker fooler hauler kaiser Magyar pander railer sapper
booker cocker doctor footer hawker keeper mammer panzer raiser saucer
boomer codger dodder forcer hawser kelter manger passer rammer sauger
boozer coffer dodger forger header kicker manner pastor ramper savour
bopper coheir dogear former healer kidder mapper patter ranger sawder
border coiner dogger fossor hearer killer marker pauper ranker sawyer
bother collar dollar foster heater kilter martyr pavior ranter scalar
bovver colour dolour fother heaver kipper masher pawner rapier scaler
bowler colter Dopper fowler hector kisser masker pecker rapper scarer
bowyer comber dormer framer hedger knower master pedlar raptor scorer
boxcar concur dorter frater heeler kosher matter peeler rasher scoter
bracer condor dosser fuhrer heifer kroner medlar peeper rasper scryer
brayer confer douser fuller heller kronor member pelter raster seaair
brewer conger downer fulmar helper kronur memoir pepper rather seaear
briber conker dowser furfur herder kultur mender pester ratter sealer
briner conner draper fusser higher laager menhir petter reader seamer
broker cooker drawer gabber hinder labour mentor pewter reamer seater
bucker cooler driver gadder hisser ladder mercer picker reaper sector
buffer cooper droger gaffer hither lagger merger piecer rearer seeder
bugler copier drover gagger hoaxer lamber meteor pilfer reaver seeker
bulbar copper ducker gainer hocker lancer metier pillar rector seiner
Bulgar corder duffer gaiter holder lander midair pincer redder seizer
bulger corker duiker gambir holler langur milker pinger reefer seller
bulker corner dumper gammer honour lanner miller pinner reeler sender
buller cosher Dunker gander hoofer larder milter pitier rehear senhor
```

```
senior  suitor  twiner  yammer  cheers  glacis  odious  shucks  vivers  basnet
sensor  summer  ulster  yapper  chiaus  gneiss  ogress  slacks  vulgus  basset
server  sunder  undoer  yatter  chives  gnosis  oodles  smalls  waders  becket
setter  supper  unfair  yelper  chorus  gooses  optics  solids  walrus  bedsit
shader  surfer  unhair  yester  circus  gradus  orchis  sortes  waters  begirt
shaker  sutler  uniter  yonder  cirrus  gramps  orexis  sowans  whenas  behest
shaper  swayer  unmoor  yorker  cistus  gratis  otitis  sowens  whiles  bennet
sharer  swiper  upbear  zaffer  citrus  Graves  oxalis  sparks  whites  bereft
shaver  tabour  uproar  zander  civics  greens  palais  speiss  whoops  bezant
shikar  tacker  ureter  zephyr  clavis  groats  palpus  splits  wolves  billet
shiner  tailor  usurer  zipper  clevis  grumps  pampas  sports  xystus  bisect
shiver  talker  uvular  zither  clonus  haggis  papers  stairs  yoicks  blight
shofar  tamper  valour  abacus  coccus  haloes  pappus  stakes  zlotys  bobcat
shover  tanker  valuer  abatis  coitus  halves  parous  stapes  zounds  boblet
shower  tanner  vamper  abbess  coleus  harass  parvis  stases  abduct  bonist
sicker  tapper  vanner  acarus  commis  havers  pathos  stasis  abject  bonnet
sifter  tartar  vector  access  comous  henrys  patois  states  ablaut  bosket
sigher  taster  velour  acinus  conics  herpes  pelves  status  abrupt  bought
signer  tatter  vendor  across  corpus  hiatus  pelvis  stipes  absent  breast
signor  teaser  veneer  adieus  corves  hoicks  pharos  stocks  accent  brevet
siller  tedder  venter  admass  Corvus  hooves  phasis  stokes  accost  bright
silver  teemer  verger  Adonis  cosmos  hubris  pileus  stores  acquit  brunet
simmer  teener  verser  afters  crases  hybris  pilous  strass  addict  bucket
simper  teller  vesper  airbus  crasis  iambus  Pisces  strays  adduct  budget
singer  temper  viator  always  creeps  ibexes  pithos  stress  adjust  buffet
sinker  tenner  victor  amends  cripes  ibices  plexus  stylus  adrift  buglet
sinner  tenour  viewer  anabas  crises  inches  pliers  sulcus  adroit  bullet
sinter  tenser  vigour  ananas  crisis  inlaws  points  sweets  advent  burbot
sipper  tensor  vizier  animus  crocus  irides  porous  swipes  advert  burnet
sircar  tenter  voider  annals  cruces  iritis  praxis  tarras  affect  bypast
sirdar  termer  voyeur  apexes  cruxes  Jewess  precis  tarsus  afloat  cachet
sirkar  termor  vulgar  apices  cullis  joyous  preses  Taurus  afreet  cadent
sister  tester  wafter  arenas  cultus  kaross  primus  taxies  aghast  cahoot
sittar  tether  wailer  assess  cursus  kermes  ptosis  tennis  albeit  callet
sitter  tetter  waiter  aurous  cuscus  kermis  quoits  tenues  albert  camlet
skater  thaler  waiver  awmous  dagoes  knives  quotes  tenuis  alight  cannot
skewer  thenar  walker  banjos  debris  kumiss  rabies  thanks  allout  carnet
skiver  ticker  waller  basics  dedans  laches  rachis  theirs  almost  carpet
slater  tidier  wander  bassos  degras  Lammas  radius  theses  amidst  carrot
slaver  tiebar  wanner  bathos  denims  lapsus  ramous  thesis  amount  casket
slayer  tiller  wapper  beeves  dermis  lassos  raphis  things  amulet  catgut
slicer  tilter  warder  biceps  derris  leaves  rapids  tholos  anicut  caught
slider  timber  warmer  bilbos  didoes  lights  recess  tholus  anklet  caveat
sliver  tinder  warner  blazes  dieses  limbus  rectus  thrips  anoint  cavort
smiler  tinker  warper  bongos  diesis  litmus  regius  throes  aorist  cement
smiter  tinner  washer  Boreas  dingus  loaves  remiss  thymus  ardent  cermet
smoker  tinter  waster  bounds  dipsas  lyrics  repass  tights  argent  chalet
snarer  tipper  weaner  bowels  discus  madras  revers  timous  aright  chaunt
sniper  titfer  wearer  braces  dittos  Majlis  rhesus  tmeses  armlet  chevet
snorer  tither  weaver  brains  divers  mangos  riches  tmesis  armpit  Christ
soaker  titter  weeder  breeks  dodoes  mantes  rictus  tophus  aroint  claret
soccer  tocher  weeper  brewis  dowlas  mantis  rimous  Tories  arpent  client
soever  toiler  weever  briefs  duress  maquis  royals  traces  arrant  closet
solder  tooter  welder  brutus  egress  matins  ruckus  tracks  arrest  cobalt
solver  topper  weldor  bursas  embers  meatus  rufous  tragus  artist  cobnut
sooner  torpor  welter  byssus  emboss  medius  rumpus  trapes  ascent  cogent
sorner  tosher  wester  cactus  emeses  menses  rushes  tripos  askant  cohort
sorter  tosser  wether  caddis  emesis  merils  sables  trumps  aslant  collet
souter  tother  wetter  calces  enosis  Messrs  saltus  turves  aspect  combat
spacer  totter  whaler  callus  ethics  metals  salvos  tweeds  assent  comfit
sparer  tourer  whiner  calves  excess  miosis  sanies  typhus  assert  commit
spewer  touter  wicker  calxes  exodus  missis  scales  umbles  assist  comsat
spider  tracer  wiener  camass  exomis  missus  scarus  umbras  assort  copout
spryer  trader  wilder  campus  facies  modius  schuss  undies  attest  coquet
stager  tremor  winder  cantus  famous  moneys  scopas  ungues  august  cornet
starer  tricar  winger  canvas  fasces  monies  selves  unguis  auklet  corset
stater  trimer  winker  capias  fauces  morals  senses  unless  aurist  cosset
stator  trocar  winner  caress  faunas  morass  sepsis  uraeus  avaunt  covert
stayer  trover  winter  caries  fezzes  morbus  series  Uranus  avocet  cowpat
stelar  tubber  wisher  carpus  finals  morris  serous  uterus  babbit  cravat
stiver  tucker  wither  cassis  flatus  mucous  sevens  valgus  Babist  credit
stoker  tufter  wizier  caucus  floras  myosis  Sevres  venous  ballet  cruset
stoner  tulwar  wonder  caulis  foetus  mythos  shades  versus  ballot  cubist
stover  tumour  woofer  census  fracas  naevus  shamus  viands  banket  cueist
stumer  turgor  worker  cercus  fundus  nimbus  sharps  villus  bannet  cullet
stupor  turner  wormer  cereus  fungus  noesis  shears  vinous  barbet  curvet
stylar  tusker  wowser  certes  geckos  nonius  sheass  virtus  barret  cushat
sucker  tusser  writer  cestus  genius  obelus  sheets  viscus  basalt  cutlet
suffer  twicer  yabber  charas  gentes  obsess  shorts  vitals  basket  cutout
```

```
cygnet farout indict motett prompt semmit tippet congou seesaw aphony
dacoit faucet induct motmot prosit sennet titbit gateau shadow apiary
decant ferret indult mullet pullet sennit toilet grugru sorrow Arcady
deceit fidget infant muscat pulpit septet tomcat haleru sunbow archly
decent filfot infect musket pundit sestet tomtit jabiru sundew argosy
decoct fillet infelt mutant punnet setout Tophet landau tallow argufy
deduct firlot infest natant puppet sexist toupet Manchu wallow arrowy
defeat flaunt ingest naught purist sexpot tricot milieu willow artery
defect flight inject neednt quaint sextet trivet muumuu window aseity
degust floret inkpot nidget rabbet shiest truant ormolu winnow astray
deject fluent inmost nitwit rabbit shrift tryout Pushtu yarrow augury
delict foment insect nobbut racist shyest Tshirt reseau yellow aumbry
dement forest insert nocent racket signet tucket roucou adieux aviary
demist forget insist nonfat ragout silent tuffet saddhu afflux avidly
depart forgot insult nougat Rajput sinnet tumult teledu banjax aweary
depict forint intact nought ramjet sippet turbit Telugu bijoux babbly
deport format intent nudist rapist slight turbot Vishnu bollix bailey
desalt forrit intuit nugget rattat slyest turret moshav carfax bakery
desert fought invent nutant recant sobeit twilit anyhow caudex baldly
desist freest invert object recast socket typist barrow cervix barely
despot fright invest oblast recent soffit tyrant bashaw climax barfly
detect frowst irrupt oboist redact sonant umlaut bellow coccyx barley
detent fylfot jacket obtect redhot sonnet unbent bestow commix barney
detest gablet jennet obtest reedit sorbet unbitt billow convex barony
devest gadget Jesuit obvert refect sought unbolt borrow cortex basely
devout gainst joblot occult regent soviet ungirt bowsaw cowpox bawdry
dicast galiot junket ocelot reglet spigot unjust bowwow diplex bawley
digest galoot jurist octant regret spinet unknit burrow dogfox beachy
diglot gambit kainit oecist reheat spirit unknot byblow duplex beauty
diktat gannet kaputt offent reject splent unmeet byelaw earwax belfry
dimwit garget kismet offset relent splint unrest callow efflux betony
dipnet garnet kitcat oilnut relict spoilt unroot cashew fornix betray
direct garret klepht omelet reluct sprent unseat curfew frutex bewray
divert garrot knight oncost remint sprint unwept curlew hallux bieldy
divest gasket labret optant rennet sprout upbeat erenow hatbox bigamy
docent gerent lament orgeat repast spruit upcast eschew haybox binary
docket getout lancet orient repeat squint uplift escrow icebox biopsy
domett gibbet lappet outact repent squirt upmost fallow imbrex bitchy
dopant giglet lariat outfit report strait uproot farrow influx blanky
dought giglot latent outlet reseat street upshot fellow larynx bleary
dreamt gimlet latest output resect strict urgent fogbow lummox blenny
dryrot gobbet lavolt outsat resent strout utmost follow matrix blimey
dugout goblet layout outset resist strunt vacant furrow meninx bloody
dulcet gocart learnt outsit resort Stuart varlet gewgaw muskox bloomy
duplet godwit legist outwit result stylet Vedist goslow outfox blowsy
dynast goglet levant packet retest sublet velvet guffaw pollex blowzy
eaglet gokart limpet pallet retort submit verist hallow prefix blurry
effect gorget linnet pandit revert subset verset harrow premix bodily
effort grivet locket papist revest summit vervet hawhaw pretax boldly
egoist gullet locust parent revolt sunhat vibist haymow prolix bolshy
eldest gurnet loggat parget rident sunlit violet Hebrew reflex booksy
elicit gusset loment parrot rigout sunset volant heehaw reflux bosomy
eluant haffet loquat patent rillet tablet volost hollow scolex botany
eluent haffit loriot peanut robust tacket vorant inflow seafox botchy
encyst hagbut loupit pedant rochet talbot wallet jigsaw smilax botfly
engirt hamlet lucent peewit rocket talent walnut kowtow spadix bouncy
englut harlot lyrist pellet rodent tanist waught mallow sphinx bounty
enlist haslet maggot pelmet roquet Taoist wayout marrow storax bowery
enrapt height magnet penult rotgut tappet weight matlow styrax brainy
enroot helmet mahout permit runlet tappit whilst meadow suffix brandy
errant hepcat mallet picket russet target whisht mellow surtax brassy
escort hereat Maoist piglet sabbat taught wicket mildew syntax brawly
esprit heriot Marist pignut sachet teapot widget minnow syrinx brawny
except hermit market piolet sadist teaset willet moocow thorax breezy
exempt hexact marmot piquet saidst tenant wisent morrow unisex briary
exeunt hobbit mascot placet sallet tercet withit narrow vertex bricky
exhort hogget mayest plaint samlet terret wombat nephew volvox briery
expect honest merest planet savant territ worrit outlaw vortex briony
expert hornet midget pliant sawpit theist wright pawpaw abbacy brolly
export hotpot midgut plight sawset thirst yaourt pillow acidly bronzy
exsect humect millet pocket sayest threat yclept pitsaw acuity broody
exsert impact minuet poppet schist thrift yogurt powwow aerily browny
extant impart misfit posset script throat zealot redraw affray brumby
extent import mishit potent preset thrust acajou reflow agency brushy
extort impost modest preset seamat thwart amadou review airily bryony
eyalet incept molest priest secant ticket Basutu ripsaw airway bubbly
eyelet incest moment privet secret tidbit bateau sallow angary bulimy
faggot incult monist probit sejant tinpot bureau seacow anyway bunchy
fanjet indent moppet profit select tipcat cachou seamew apathy burbly
```

busboy	creepy	emboly	gamily	injury	mickey	pastry	ripply	slavey	sturdy
busily	crikey	empery	gangly	intray	midday	patchy	Romany	sleazy	subtly
byplay	crimpy	employ	gantry	jalopy	midway	payday	ropery	sleepy	subway
cagily	crispy	energy	gasify	jarvey	mighty	peachy	rosary	sleety	sudary
calmly	croaky	enmity	gently	jaunty	milady	pearly	rosery	slimly	sugary
calory	croppy	entity	gentry	jersey	mildly	peavey	rosily	slinky	sultry
canary	croupy	equity	gharry	jiggly	minify	pebbly	rosiny	slippy	Sunday
canopy	cruddy	estray	ghosty	jingly	misery	peltry	rotary	sloppy	sundry
carboy	crumby	eulogy	giggly	jitney	mislay	penury	rouncy	sloshy	sunray
carney	crummy	eutaxy	gladly	jockey	mizzly	pertly	rubbly	slowly	supply
catchy	crusty	evenly	glairy	johnny	modify	phoney	rubefy	sludgy	surely
causey	cuddly	evilly	glassy	jouncy	moiety	phooey	rubify	sluicy	surety
cavity	curacy	exequy	gleamy	jumbly	Monday	pigsty	rudely	slummy	surrey
cecity	curtly	expiry	gleety	jungly	monkey	pimply	rumbly	slurry	survey
celery	curtsy	extasy	glibly	justly	monody	pinery	runway	slushy	swaddy
chaffy	cutely	fainly	gloomy	keenly	mornay	piracy	safely	smarmy	swampy
chalky	daftly	fairly	glossy	kersey	mostly	pitchy	safety	smarty	swanky
chancy	dainty	fakery	glumly	keyway	motley	plaguy	sagely	smeary	sweaty
chanty	damply	family	glumpy	kidney	motory	plashy	salary	smelly	sweeny
chappy	dankly	faulty	gnarly	kindly	mouldy	plebby	salify	smirky	swimmy
chatty	darkey	fealty	goggly	kingly	mouthy	plenty	sanely	smithy	swirly
cheeky	darkly	featly	goodly	knaggy	mulley	ploidy	sanify	smoggy	swishy
cheery	datary	feckly	googly	knobby	murphy	plotty	sanity	smudgy	syrupy
cheesy	dayfly	feebly	googly	knotty	murrey	plucky	sashay	smugly	syzygy
cherry	deadly	felony	goramy	lackey	mutely	plummy	satiny	smutty	talcky
cherty	deafly	feisty	gorily	ladify	mutiny	plumpy	savory	snaggy	tamely
chesty	dearly	fiddly	gowany	ladyfy	namely	plushy	sawfly	snappy	tangly
chilly	deejay	filthy	grabby	lamely	Nazify	poetry	sawney	snarly	tartly
chippy	deeply	finely	grainy	lankly	nearby	policy	saxony	snazzy	tautly
chirpy	defray	finery	Grammy	lastly	nearly	polity	scabby	sneaky	tawdry
chitty	deftly	firmly	granny	lately	neatly	polony	scanty	sneezy	tawery
chivvy	denary	fixity	grassy	laxity	nebuly	poorly	scarry	sniffy	teapoy
chokey	deploy	flabby	greasy	layday	nicely	popery	scatty	snippy	teensy
choosy	deputy	flaggy	greedy	lazily	nicety	popply	screwy	snobby	tepefy
choppy	descry	flappy	greeny	lealty	nidify	portly	scummy	snoopy	termly
chubby	dewily	flashy	greyly	leeway	nighty	potboy	scurfy	snooty	tetany
chuffy	dickey	flatly	grimly	leanly	nimbly	pouchy	scurry	snotty	tetchy
chummy	digamy	fleecy	grippy	legacy	ninety	prepay	scurvy	snubby	theory
chunky	dimity	fleshy	grisly	lemony	nobody	pretty	seaway	snuffy	thingy
cicely	dimply	fleury	gritty	lenity	nonary	pricey	seemly	snugly	thinly
claggy	dingey	flimsy	groggy	levity	nosily	primly	senary	snugly	thirty
clammy	dinghy	flinty	groovy	lewdly	notary	priory	sentry	sodomy	thorny
classy	dipody	flirty	grotty	likely	notify	prissy	severy	softly	tickey
clayey	direly	floaty	growly	limply	nubbly	puddly	sexily	solely	tickly
clergy	dismay	floozy	grubby	linney	nudely	pulley	shabby	sorely	tiddly
cliffy	donkey	floppy	grumly	linhay	nudity	punchy	shaggy	sourly	tidily
clingy	doubly	flossy	grumpy	linsey	nudily	punily	shammy	sparry	timely
cliquy	doughy	floury	guilty	litany	occamy	purely	shandy	speedy	tingly
cloddy	dourly	fluffy	gulley	lively	occupy	purify	shanny	sphery	tinily
cloggy	doyley	flukey	gunshy	livery	oddity	purity	shanty	spiffy	tinkly
cloudy	dozily	flunky	hackly	lonely	offkey	purply	sheeny	spoffy	tomboy
clumpy	drably	flurry	hardly	lordly	oneway	purvey	shelly	spongy	toothy
clumsy	drafty	flyway	hazily	loudly	oogamy	quaggy	shelty	spooky	tootsy
codify	draggy	folksy	hearty	lovely	oogeny	qualmy	sherry	spoony	touchy
coldly	dreamy	fondly	heathy	lowboy	oology	quarry	shifty	sporty	towery
colony	dreary	forsay	hereby	lowery	openly	queasy	shimmy	spotty	trappy
comedy	dreggy	foully	heresy	lowkey	orally	queazy	shindy	spryly	trashy
comely	dressy	freaky	heyday	lunacy	orfray	quinsy	shinny	spunky	treaty
comity	drifty	freely	hickey	lushly	ornery	quirky	shinty	spurry	trebly
comply	drippy	frenzy	highly	luxury	orrery	racily	shirty	stably	trendy
conchy	drolly	friary	hockey	maguey	osprey	raguly	shoaly	stagey	tressy
convey	droopy	Friday	holily	mainly	ossify	ramify	shoddy	stalky	tricky
convoy	dropsy	frilly	homely	malady	outcry	rankly	shoppy	starry	trilby
coolly	drosky	fringy	homily	manday	outlay	raptly	shorty	steady	trimly
coonty	drossy	frisky	hominy	marbly	ovally	rarefy	sickly	steamy	triply
corody	drowsy	frizzy	hookey	margay	overly	rarely	simony	steely	trolly
cosily	dryfly	froggy	hooray	marshy	pacify	rarity	simply	sticky	trophy
costly	dually	frosty	horary	maundy	palely	rashly	sinewy	stilly	trouty
county	dukery	frothy	horsey	mayday	paltry	ratify	singly	stingy	trusty
cowboy	dumbly	frowsy	hourly	mayfly	paltry	really	skeely	stithy	tumefy
crabby	dupery	frowzy	housey	mazily	panary	realty	skerry	stocky	turkey
crafty	earthy	fruity	hugely	meanly	pantry	remedy	skiddy	stodgy	twangy
craggy	easily	frumpy	humbly	measly	papacy	replay	skilly	storey	tweedy
cranky	eatery	gadfly	humify	medley	papery	revery	skimpy	stormy	tweeny
cranny	edgily	gaiety	hungry	meekly	parity	rheumy	skinny	strawy	twenty
crappy	eerily	gainly	hurley	meetly	parlay	richly	skivvy	stripy	twiggy
crawly	effigy	galaxy	hurray	melody	parley	rickey	skyway	stubby	twirly
creaky	eighty	galley	idiocy	memory	parody	rifely	slaggy	stuffy	twisty
creamy	embody	gamely	infamy	merely	partly	ripely	slangy	stumpy	twoply

```
two¯way untidy venery vivify watery wheezy wholly winsey wrathy ersatz
typify  unwary verify volley wavery wherry widely wintry yarely kibitz
ubiety  uppity verily votary wavily wheyey wieldy wirily yearly krantz
uglify  vagary verity wafery waxily whimsy wifely wisely yeasty quartz
uglily  vainly vestry waggly waylay whinny wiggly wobbly zanily
unduly  valley vilely wambly weakly whippy wildly woodsy zincky
uneasy  vanity vilify warcry weekly whirly wilily woolly zonary
unholy  vastly vinery warily weirdy whisky wincey worthy blintz
unruly  vaulty vintry warmly whacky whitey winery woundy chintz
```

7 letter words

```
abaddon Achaian aerobic alfalfa amiable animist apostle arraign attaboy
abalone Achates aerosol alforja amiably anionic apothem arrange attache
abandon achieve afeared algebra amildar aniseed apparat arrayer attaint
abashed acicula affable alginic ammeter annates apparel arrears attempt
abattis acidify affably alidade ammonal annatta appease arrival attract
abaxial acidity affaire alienly ammonia annatto applaud arriver attrite
Abbasid acinous affined aliform amnesia annelid applied arsenal auction
abdomen ackemma afflict aliment amnesic annicut applier arsenic audible
Abelian acolyte affront alimony amnesty annuity appoint article audient
abetted aconite African aliquot amoebae annular apprise artisan auditor
abetter acouchy against alkalis amoebas annulet approve artiste augment
abettor acquest agamous alkanet amoebic annulus apraxia artless augural
abeyant acquire ageless Alkoran amongst anodise apricot artwork aurally
abiding acrasin agelong alleged amorist anodyne apropos ascarid aureate
abigail acreage aggress allegro amorous anoesis apsidal ascaris aurelia
ability acridly agilely allelic amphora anoetic apsides ascesis aureola
abiotic acrobat agility allergy amplify anomaly apteryx ascetic aureole
abjurer acrogen agitate allheal ampoule anosmia aptness ascidia auricle
ablator acronym agitato allonge ampulla anosmic aquaria ascites aurochs
abolish acroter agnatic allover amputee another aquatic ascitic aurorae
abomasa acrylic agnomen allseed amusive antacid aquavit ascribe auroral
aborter actinia agonise allstar amylase antbear aqueous asepsis auroras
abought actinic agonist alltime amyloid antefix aquifer aseptic auspice
aboulia actinon agraffe alluvia amyloin antenna aquiver asexual austere
abrader actress agrapha almanac amylose anthill Arabian ashamed austral
abreact actuary aground almirah anaemia anthrax arabise ashtray autarky
abreast actuate aiblins almoner anaemic antigen Arabist Asiatic autobus
abridge acutely aileron almonry anagoge antilog Aramaic asinine autocar
abroach acyclic ailment almsman anagogy antique araneid askance autocue
abscess adamant aimless alodial anagram antlion Arapaho askesis autopsy
abscise Adamite aircrew alodium analogy antonym arbiter asocial auxesis
abscond adapter airdrop aloetic analyse anurous arbutus asperse auxetic
absence adaptor airfare aloofly analyst anxiety arcaded asphalt avarice
absinth adaxial airflow alphorn Ananias anxious arcadia aspirer avenger
absolve addable airglow already anarchy anybody arcanum aspirin average
abstain addenda airhole alright anatase anymore archaic asquint averred
abubble addible airless alsoran anatomy anyroad archery assagai Avestan
abusive address airlift althaea anchovy anytime archive assault Avestic
abutted adducer airline althorn anchusa anyways archway assayer aviator
abutter adenine airlock alumina ancient anywise arctoid assegai avidity
abysmal adenoid airmail alumnae ancones apagoge arcuate assizes avionic
abyssal adenoma airmiss alumnus ancress apanage arcweld assuage avocado
academe adeptly airport alunite andante apatite ardency assured awarder
academy adherer airpost alveoli andiron apetaly arduous assurer aweless
Acadian adhibit airship alyssum android aphasia areally astable awesome
acantha adipose airsick amalgam anemone aphasic areaway astatic awfully
acarian adjoint airwave amanita aneroid aphelia areolae asteria awkward
accidie adjourn ajutage amarant aneurin apheses areolar astound awnless
acclaim adjudge akvavit amateur angelic aphesis areolas astride axially
account adjunct alameda amative angelus aphetic aridity asunder axillae
accrete admiral alanine amatory Angevin aphides arietta ataraxy axillar
accrual admirer alation amazing anginal aphonia aristae atavism axolotl
accurst adnexal albumen ambages angioma aphonic aristas atavist Azilean
accusal adopter albumin ambatch Anglian aphotic armband atelier azimuth
accused adrenal alcaide ambient anglice aphylly armfuls atheism azurine
accuser adulate alcalde amboina angling apishly armhole atheist azurite
acequia adultly alcayde ambones Anglist aplasia armiger athirst azygous
acerbic advance alcazar amboyna angrily aplenty armlike athlete Baalism
acerola adverse alchemy ambsace anguine apocope armoire athwart babassu
acerose advised alcohol amender anguish apodous armoury atingle babbitt
acetate adviser Alcoran amenity angular apogamy Armoric atomise babbler
acetify advisor alembic amentia aniline apogean armpits atomism babyish
acetone aeolian alertly amercer anility apology armrest atomist babysit
acetous aeonian aleuron Amerind animate apolune armsful atresia baccara
Achaean aerator alewife Amharic animism apostil arousal atrophy baccate
```

```
bacchic  bassist  Benelux  bionics  boarder  bounden  brisken  bumpily  calamus
bacilli  bassoon  Bengali  biotite  boarish  bounder  brisket  bumpkin  calando
backing  bastard  benison  bipedal  boaster  bouquet  briskly  bungler  calcify
backlog  basting  benthic  biplane  boating  bourbon  bristle  bunraku  calcine
backsaw  bastion  benthos  bipolar  boatman  bourdon  bristly  bunting  calcite
backset  bateaux  benzene  birchen  bobbery  bourree  British  buoyage  calcium
baddish  bathing  benzine  birddog  bobbing  bowhead  brittle  buoyant  calculi
badmash  bathtub  benzoic  birdman  bobbish  bowlder  brittly  burbler  caldera
badness  batiste  benzoin  biretta  bobeche  bowlful  britzka  burdock  caldron
baffler  batsman  benzole  biriani  bobsled  bowline  broaden  bureaus  calends
bagasse  battels  benzoyl  biscuit  bobstay  bowling  broadly  bureaux  calibre
baggage  battery  bepaint  bismuth  bobtail  bowshot  brocade  burette  calices
baggily  batting  bequest  bistort  bodeful  boxcalf  brocket  burgage  caliche
bagging  Bauhaus  bereave  bistred  bogbean  boxhaul  broider  burgeon  calicle
bagpipe  bauxite  bergylt  bittern  boggler  boxkite  broiler  burgess  calipee
Bahadur  bawcock  berhyme  bitters  bogyman  boxlike  brokage  burghal  caliper
Bahaism  bawdily  berline  bitting  bohemia  boxroom  broking  burgher  callant
Bahaist  bayonet  berried  bittock  boiling  boxseat  bromate  burglar  callbox
Bahaite  bazooka  berserk  bitumen  boletus  boxwood  bromide  Burmese  callboy
bailiff  beading  beseech  bivalve  bolivar  boycott  bromine  burning  calling
baklava  beamish  beshrew  bivouac  bollard  boyhood  bromism  burnish  callous
balance  beanbag  besides  bizarre  bologna  brabble  bronchi  burnous  calomel
balcony  bearded  besiege  blabbed  boloney  bracing  broncho  bursary  caloric
balding  bearing  besmear  blabber  bolshie  bracken  brooder  burster  calorie
baldish  bearish  bespeak  blacken  bolster  bracket  brothel  burthen  calotte
baldric  beastly  bespoke  blackly  bombard  bradawl  brother  burweed  caloyer
baleful  beatify  bestead  bladder  bombast  bragged  brought  bushido  calpack
ballade  beating  bestial  blandly  bonanza  bragger  brownie  bushman  caltrap
ballast  beatnik  bestrew  blanket  bondage  Brahman  browser  bushtit  caltrop
ballboy  because  betaken  blankly  bondman  Brahmin  brucine  busking  calumet
balloon  becloud  bethink  blarney  bonedry  braille  brucite  bussing  calumny
balmily  bedding  betimes  blasted  boneset  bramble  bruhaha  bustard  calvary
baloney  bedevil  betoken  blaster  bonfire  brambly  bruiser  bustler  calyces
bambini  bedfast  betroth  blatant  bongoes  branchy  brumous  butcher  calycle
bambino  bedight  betting  blather  bonkers  brander  brusher  buttend  calypso
banally  bedizen  between  blatter  bonnily  brannew  brusque  buttery  calyxes
bananas  bedouin  betwixt  bleakly  boobook  bransle  brutish  buttock  camaron
bandage  bedpost  bewitch  bleater  bookend  brantle  bruxism  buttons  cambial
bandana  bedrock  bezique  bleeder  bookful  brantub  Brython  buttony  cambist
bandbox  bedroll  bheesty  bleeper  booking  brashly  bubonic  butyric  cambium
bandeau  bedroom  bheetie  blemish  bookish  brassie  buccina  buyable  cambrel
bandore  bedside  Biafran  blender  booklet  brattle  buckeye  buzzard  cambric
bandsaw  bedsock  biassed  blesbok  bookman  braunch  buckler  buzzsaw  camelot
baneful  bedsore  biaxial  blessed  booksie  bravado  buckram  byebyes  camelry
banjoes  bedtime  bibbery  blether  Boolean  bravely  bucksaw  bygones  cameral
banking  beechen  bibbing  blewits  boomlet  bravery  bucolic  Byronic  camorra
banksia  beehive  bibcock  blighty  boorish  bravura  budding  bywoner  campbed
banning  beeline  bibelot  blinder  booster  brawler  buffalo  cabaret  camphor
bannock  beeswax  biblist  blindly  bootleg  brazier  buffoon  cabbage  camping
banquet  beggary  bicycle  blinker  boozeup  breaded  bugaboo  cabbagy  campion
banshee  begging  bidding  blintze  boozily  breadth  bugbane  cabbala  camwood
banteng  begonia  biennia  blister  bopping  breaker  bugbear  cabinet  canakin
banting  begorra  bifilar  blither  boracic  breakin  bugeyed  cabling  canasta
baptise  begrime  bifocal  bloated  borazon  breakup  bugging  caboose  candela
baptism  beguile  bigener  bloater  bordure  breathe  bugloss  cabrank  candent
baptist  beguine  biggest  blocker  boredom  breathy  builded  cacanny  candied
barbate  behaver  biggish  blooded  borings  breccia  builder  cachexy  candour
barbell  behoove  bighead  bloomer  bornite  breeder  buildup  cacique  canikin
barbule  beignet  bighorn  blossom  borough  brevier  builtin  cackler  cannery
bargain  bejewel  bigname  blotchy  borscht  brevity  buirdly  cacodyl  cannily
barilla  beknown  bigness  blotted  borstal  brewage  bulbous  cacoepy  canning
barline  belated  bigoted  blotter  bortsch  brewery  bulimia  cacumen  cannula
barmaid  belcher  bigotry  blouson  boscage  bribery  bulkily  cadaver  canonic
baronet  beldame  bigtime  blowdry  boskage  brickie  bullace  caddice  canonry
baroque  Belgian  bilboes  blowfly  bossism  brickle  bullary  caddied  Canopic
barrack  believe  biliary  blowgun  Boswell  bricole  bullate  caddies  cantata
barrage  bellboy  bilimbi  blowout  botanic  bridoon  bullbat  caddish  cantate
barrier  bellhop  bilious  blowzed  botargo  briefly  bulldog  cadence  canteen
barring  belljar  billing  blubber  botcher  brigade  bullion  cadency  canthus
barroom  bellman  billion  blucher  bottega  brigand  bullish  cadenza  cantina
barytes  bellows  billowy  blueing  bottled  brimful  bullock  Cadmean  canting
barytic  beloved  bilobar  bluffer  bottony  brimmed  bullous  cadmium  cantrip
bascule  Beltane  bilobed  bluffly  botulin  brimmer  bullpen  caesium  canvass
baseman  belting  biltong  blunder  bouchee  brinded  bulrush  caesura  canzone
basenji  belying  bimanal  blunger  boudoir  brindle  bulwark  cahoots  canzoni
bashful  bencher  bindery  bluntly  bouilli  bringer  bumbler  caimans  capable
basidia  beneath  binding  blurred  boulder  brinjal  bumboat  caisson  capably
basilar  benefic  biology  blusher  boulter  brioche  bummalo  caitiff  capelin
basinet  benefit  biomass  bluster  bouncer  briquet  bumming  cajoler  caperer
```

capital	catbird	chalone	chimney	clamant	coconut	compote	cooking	council
capitol	catboat	chamber	chindit	clamber	cocotte	compute	cookout	counsel
caporal	catcall	chamfer	Chinese	clammed	codable	comrade	coolant	counter
capping	catcher	chamois	Chinook	clamour	coddler	Comtian	coolish	country
caprice	catchup	champac	chintzy	clanger	codeine	Comtism	cooncan	coupler
caprine	catechu	champak	chinwag	clapped	codfish	Comtist	coontie	couplet
caproic	catenae	chancel	chipped	clapper	codices	conacre	copaiba	courage
Capsian	catenas	chancre	chipper	clarify	codicil	conatus	copaiva	courier
capsize	cateran	changer	chirrup	clarion	codling	concave	copepod	courlan
capstan	caterer	channel	chitter	clarity	coeliac	conceal	copilot	courser
capsule	catfish	chanson	chlamys	clarkia	coequal	concede	copious	courtly
captain	Cathari	chanter	chloral	classes	coexist	conceit	coppery	couthie
caption	Cathars	chantry	chloric	classic	coffers	concent	coppice	couture
captive	cathead	chaotic	cholera	classis	cogency	concept	copular	couvade
capture	cathode	chapati	choline	clastic	cogging	concern	copycat	couvert
capuche	cathood	chaplet	chooser	clatter	cognate	concert	copyist	coverup
caracal	catlike	chapman	choosey	clausal	cognise	conchae	coquito	cowbane
caracul	catling	chapped	chopine	clavate	cohabit	conchie	coracle	cowbell
caramel	catmint	chappie	chopped	clavier	coherer	concise	coranto	cowbird
caravan	catseye	chapter	chopper	claypan	coinage	concoct	corbeil	cowfish
caravel	catspaw	charade	chorale	cleaner	coinbox	concord	cordage	cowhage
caraway	catsuit	chariot	chordal	cleanly	coition	concuss	cordate	cowhand
carbide	cattalo	charily	chorine	cleanse	coldish	condemn	cordial	cowheel
carbine	cattily	charism	chorion	cleanup	colicky	condign	cordite	cowherd
carcase	catwalk	charity	choroid	clearly	colitis	condole	cordoba	cowhide
carcass	caudate	charley	chortle	cleaver	collage	condone	corella	cowlick
cardiac	caulker	charlie	chrisom	clement	collard	conduce	corkage	cowling
cardoon	caustic	charmer	christy	clerisy	collect	conduct	corking	cowpoke
careful	cautery	charnel	chromic	clerkly	colleen	conduit	cornage	cowshed
caribou	caution	charpoy	chronic	clicker	college	condyle	corneal	cowslip
carinae	cavally	charqui	chuckle	climate	collide	confect	cornett	coxcomb
carinal	cavalry	charred	chuddah	climber	collier	confess	cornfed	coyness
carinas	caveman	charter	chuddar	clinker	collins	confide	cornice	cozener
carioca	cavetti	chassis	chuffed	clipped	colloid	confine	cornily	crabbed
cariole	cavetto	chasten	chugged	clipper	collude	confirm	Cornish	cracked
carious	caviare	chateau	chukker	clippie	colobus	conflux	cornist	cracker
carking	cayenne	chatted	chummed	cliquey	cologne	conform	cornual	crackle
carline	caymans	chattel	chunnel	clivers	colonel	confuse	cornuto	crackly
Carlism	cedilla	chatter	chunter	cloacae	colonic	confute	corolla	crackup
Carlist	ceilidh	cheapen	chupati	cloacal	colossi	congeal	coronae	cragged
carload	ceiling	cheaply	churchy	clobber	colours	congest	coronal	crammed
carmine	celadon	cheater	chutney	clocker	coloury	conidia	coronas	crammer
carnage	celesta	checker	chymous	clogged	coltish	conifer	coroner	crampet
caroche	celeste	checkup	ciboria	clogger	combine	coniine	coronet	crampit
carotid	cellist	cheddar	cichlid	closely	combout	conjoin	corpora	crampon
carotin	cellule	cheerer	cidaris	closeup	combust	conjure	correct	cranage
carouse	Celsius	cheerio	ciliary	closure	comedic	conkers	corrida	cranial
carping	cembalo	cheetah	ciliate	clothes	cometic	connate	corrode	cranium
carport	cenacle	chelate	cimices	clotted	comfort	connect	corrody	crankle
carrack	censure	chemise	cindery	cloture	comfrey	conning	corsage	crannog
carrier	centaur	chemism	cineast	clubbed	comical	connive	corsair	crappie
carrion	centavo	chemist	cineole	clubman	comitia	connote	corslet	crassly
carroty	centime	chequer	cingula	clumber	command	conquer	cortege	craunch
carryon	centner	cherish	cipolin	cluster	commend	consent	cortile	craving
carsick	central	cheroot	Circean	clutter	comment	consign	corvina	crawler
cartage	centred	chervil	circler	clypeal	commode	consist	corvine	crazily
cartful	centric	chessel	circlet	clypeus	commons	console	corydon	creamer
cartoon	centrum	chested	circuit	clyster	commove	consort	cosmism	creator
carving	century	cheviot	circusy	coacher	commune	consult	cosmist	credent
cascade	cepheid	chevron	cirrose	coaling	commute	consume	cossack	creedal
cascara	ceramic	Chianti	cirrous	coaltit	compact	contact	costard	creeper
caseous	cerebra	chiasma	cistern	coaming	company	contain	costate	cremate
caserne	ceresin	chibouk	citable	coarsen	compare	contemn	costean	cremona
cashier	certain	chicane	citadel	coastal	compart	contend	costing	crenate
cassata	certify	Chicano	cithara	coaster	compass	content	costrel	cresset
cassava	cerumen	chicken	cithern	coating	compeer	contest	costume	crested
cassino	cervine	chicory	citizen	coaxial	compend	context	coterie	crevice
cassock	cession	chidden	citrate	cobbler	compere	contort	cotidal	cribbed
castile	cestode	chiffon	citrine	cocaine	compete	contour	cottage	cribble
casting	cestoid	chigger	civilly	coccoid	compile	control	cottier	cricket
castled	Chablis	chignon	civvies	cochlea	complex	contuse	cottony	cricoid
castoff	chaffer	childer	clabber	cockade	complin	convect	Coueism	crimine
casuals	chagrin	childly	clacker	cockeye	complot	convene	couldst	crimper
casuist	chalaza	chiliad	cladode	cockily	compony	convent	couloir	crimple
Catalan	Chaldee	chillum	claimer	cockney	comport	convert	coulomb	crimson
catalos	chalice	chimera		cockpit	compose	convict	coulter	cringer
catalpa	challis	chimere		cockshy	compost	convoke		cringle
catarrh								crinite
catawba								crinkle

crinkly	cunette	dampish	deforce	devious	discant	dogwood	dropper	earlobe
crinoid	cunning	dandify	defraud	devisal	discard	doleful	drosera	earlock
criollo	cupcake	Danelaw	defrock	devisee	discern	dollish	droshky	earmark
cripple	cupmoss	dangler	defrost	deviser	discerp	dolphin	drought	earmuff
crisper	cupping	danseur	defunct	devisor	discoid	doltish	drouthy	earnest
crisply	cuprite	Dantean	degauss	devolve	discord	domical	droving	earplug
cristae	cuprous	dapsone	degrade	devoted	discuss	dominie	drubbed	earring
critter	cupsful	darbies	dehisce	devotee	disdain	donator	drudger	earshot
croaker	cupular	dariole	deicide	dewclaw	disease	donning	drugged	earthen
crochet	curable	darkish	deiform	dewdrop	diseuse	donnish	drugget	earthly
crocket	curacao	darling	deictic	dewfall	disfame	doodler	druidic	easeful
Croesus	curacoa	darning	deistic	dewpond	disgust	doomful	drumlin	eastern
crofter	curator	darshan	delaine	dextral	dishorn	doorman	drummed	easting
crooked	curcuma	dashiki	delator	dextran	disjoin	doormat	drummer	eatable
crooner	cureall	dashing	delayer	dextrin	dislike	doorway	drunken	ebbtide
cropped	curette	dashpot	delight	diabase	dislimn	dorhawk	drycell	ebonise
cropper	curiosa	dastard	Delilah	diabolo	dismast	Dorking	drydock	ebonite
croquet	curious	dasyure	delimit	diadrom	dismiss	dormant	dryeyed	ebriate
croquis	curling	datable	deliver	diagram	disobey	dormice	dryness	ebriety
crosier	currach	datival	delouse	dialect	dispark	dornick	drysalt	eccrine
crossly	curragh	dauphin	Delphic	dialled	dispart	dortour	dryshod	ecdyses
crouton	currant	dawdler	deltaic	dialyse	display	dossier	dualise	ecdysis
crowbar	current	dawning	deltoid	diamond	disport	dotting	dualism	echelon
crowdie	currier	daybook	deluder	diarchy	dispose	doubler	dualist	echidna
crowned	currish	daylong	demerit	diarise	dispute	doubles	duality	echinus
crowner	cursive	dayroom	demesne	diarist	disrank	doublet	dubbing	echoism
crownet	cursory	daystar	demigod	dibasic	disrate	doubter	dubiety	eclipse
crowtoe	curtail	daytime	demirep	dibbing	disrobe	doucely	dubious	eclogue
crozier	curtain	daywork	demoded	dickens	disroot	douceur	ducally	ecology
crucial	curtana	dazedly	demonic	dictate	disrupt	doughty	duchess	economy
crucian	curtsey	dazzler	demount	diction	dissave	dovecot	ducking	ecstasy
crucify	curvate	deadend	demotic	diddler	disseat	dovekie	duckpin	ectopic
crudely	cushion	deadeye	denarii	diehard	dissect	dowager	ductile	edacity
crudity	cuspate	deadpan	denizen	dietary	dissent	dowdily	ducting	edaphic
cruelly	custard	deafaid	densely	diffuse	distaff	downbow	dudgeon	edictal
cruelty	custody	dealing	density	digamma	distain	doyenne	duelled	edifice
cruiser	customs	deanery	dentate	digging	distant	dozenth	dueller	edition
cruller	cutaway	deathly	dentine	digital	distend	drabber	dukedom	educate
crumble	cutback	debacle	dentist	dignify	distent	drabbet	dulcify	eductor
crumbly	cuticle	debater	denture	dignity	distich	drabble	dullard	eelpout
crumpet	cutlass	debauch	deodand	digraph	distill	drabler	dullish	eelworm
crumple	cutlery	debouch	deodara	digress	distort	drachma	dulness	effects
crunchy	cutline	Debrett	deplane	dilated	disturb	draftee	dumpish	effendi
crupper	cutrate	debrief	deplete	dilator	ditcher	drafter	dunbird	effulge
crusade	cutting	decadal	deplore	dilemma	dithery	dragged	dungeon	egality
crusado	cutworm	decagon	deplume	diluent	dittany	draggle	Dunkirk	eggcosy
crusher	cuvette	decanal	deposal	dilutee	diurnal	dragnet	dunnage	eggflip
crustal	cyanide	decapod	deposit	diluter	diverge	dragoon	dunning	egghead
crusted	cyanine	decease	deprave	dilutor	diverse	drainer	dunnock	egotise
crybaby	cyanite	deceive	depress	dimeric	divider	drapery	duodena	egotism
cryogen	cyathus	decency	deprive	dimeter	diviner	drastic	duopoly	egotist
cryptal	cyclist	deciare	derange	dimmest	divisor	dratted	dupable	egotrip
cryptic	cycloid	decibel	derider	dimming	divorce	draught	durable	eidetic
crystal	cyclone	decided	derrick	dimmish	divulge	drawbar	durably	eidolon
csardas	cyclops	decider	dervish	dimness	dizzard	drawing	duramen	einkorn
ctenoid	cymbalo	decidua	descant	dinette	dizzily	drawler	durance	eirenic
cubbing	cynical	decimal	descend	dingily	djibbah	drayage	durmast	ejector
cubhood	cypress	decking	descent	dingoes	docetic	drayman	duskily	ekistic
cubical	Cyprian	declaim	deserve	dinning	dockage	dreamed	dustbin	elastic
cubicle	Cypriot	declare	despair	diocese	dockise	dreamer	dustily	elastin
cubital	cypsela	declass	despise	diopter	doddard	dredger	dustman	elation
cuckold	cystine	decline	despite	dioptre	doddery	dresser	dustpan	elderly
cudbear	cystoid	decoder	despoil	diorama	dodgems	dribble	duteous	Eleatic
cudweed	czardas	decorum	despond	diorism	dodgery	driblet	dutiful	elector
cuirass	czardom	decrier	dessert	diorite	doeskin	driedup	duumvir	electro
cuisine	czarina	decrypt	destine	dioxide	dogbane	drifter	dwarves	elegant
cuittle	czarist	decuman	destiny	diploid	dogcart	driller	dweller	elegiac
culices	dabbers	decuple	destroy	diploma	dogdays	drinker	dwindle	elegise
cullion	dabbing	deepfry	deterge	dipnoan	dogeate	dripdry	dyarchy	elegist
culotte	dabbler	deepsea	detinue	dipolar	dogfish	dripped	dyewood	element
culprit	dacoity	default	detract	dipping	doggery	drivein	dynamic	elenchi
cultism	Dadaism	defence	detrain	diptera	dogging	driving	dynasty	elevate
cultist	Dadaist	defiant	detrude	diptych	doggish	drizzle	eagerly	elevens
culture	dallier	deficit	deutzia	direful	doggone	drizzly	earache	elfbolt
culvert	damming	defiler	devalue	dirtily	dogrose	drogher	eardrop	elfland
cumquat	damnify	definer	develop	disable	dogskin	dromond	eardrum	elflock
cumshaw	damning	deflate	deviant	disavow	dogstar	droplet	earflap	elision
cumulus	damosel	deflect	deviate	disband	dogtrot	dropout	earhole	elitism
cuneate	damozel	defocus	devilry	disbark	dogvane	dropped	earldom	elitist

ellipse	enemata	epochal	exactly	faculae	feather	filaria	flecker	foliage
Elohism	energid	eponymy	exactor	faculty	feature	filasse	fleeced	foliate
Elohist	enfeoff	epoxide	examine	faddish	febrile	filbert	fleecer	foliole
elusion	enfiled	epsilon	example	faddism	fedayee	filemot	fleeing	foliose
elusive	enforce	equable	exarate	faddist	federal	filiate	fleetly	folkway
elusory	enframe	equably	excerpt	fadedly	feeding	filibeg	Fleming	follies
elution	engaged	equally	excited	fadeout	feedlot	filings	Flemish	fondant
eluvial	English	equator	exciter	fagging	feeling	filling	fleshed	fondler
eluvium	engorge	equerry	exciton	fagotto	feigner	filmdom	flesher	foolery
elysian	engraft	equinal	excitor	faience	felonry	filmset	fleshly	foolish
Elysium	engrail	equinox	exclaim	failing	felsite	fimbria	fletton	footage
elytron	engrain	erasure	exclave	failure	felspar	finagle	fleuret	footboy
elytrum	engrave	erectly	exclude	faintly	felting	finally	fleuron	footing
Elzevir	engross	erector	excrete	fairing	felucca	finance	flexile	footman
emanate	enhance	erelong	excurse	fairish	felwort	finback	flexion	footpad
embargo	enlarge	eremite	excusal	fairway	feminal	finding	flexure	footrot
embassy	enliven	erepsin	execute	Falange	femoral	finesse	flicker	footsie
emblaze	ennoble	ergates	exedrae	falbala	fencing	finical	flighty	footway
embolic	enounce	ergodic	exegete	falcate	fenfire	finicky	flipped	fopling
embolus	enplane	ericoid	exempla	falcula	fenland	finikin	flipper	foppery
embosom	enprint	eristic	exergue	fallacy	feoffee	finings	flitted	foppish
embowed	enquire	erlking	exhaust	fallguy	feoffer	finning	flitter	forager
embowel	enquiry	ermined	exhibit	falling	feoffor	Finnish	flivver	foramen
embower	enslave	erodent	exhumer	falloff	fermata	firearm	floater	forayer
embrace	ensnare	erosion	exigent	fallout	ferment	firebox	floccus	forbade
embroil	ensnarl	erosive	exocarp	falsely	fermion	firebug	flogged	forbear
embrown	entasis	erotica	exogamy	falsies	fermium	firedog	floorer	forbode
embryon	entente	erotism	exordia	falsify	fernery	firefly	floosie	forbore
emerald	enteral	errancy	exotica	falsity	fernowl	fireman	floozie	forceps
emeriti	enteric	erratic	expanse	famulus	ferrate	firenew	flopped	fordone
emersed	enteron	erratum	expense	fanatic	ferrety	firstly	floreat	forearm
emetine	enthral	erudite	expiate	fancier	ferrite	firtree	florist	foreign
emicate	enthuse	escapee	explain	fancily	ferrous	fishery	floruit	foreleg
eminent	entitle	escaper	explant	fanclub	ferrugo	fisheye	flotage	foreman
emirate	entomic	escheat	explode	fanfare	ferrule	fishily	flotsam	forepaw
emitted	entotic	escolar	exploit	fanfold	fertile	fishing	flounce	foreran
emitter	entozoa	escribe	explore	fanmail	fervent	fishnet	flowage	forerun
emotion	entrain	esotery	exposal	fanning	fervour	fishway	flowery	foresaw
emotive	entrant	esparto	exposed	fantail	festive	fissile	flubbed	foresay
empanel	entreat	espouse	exposer	fantasm	festoon	fission	fluence	foresee
empathy	entropy	esquire	exposit	fantast	fetidly	fissure	fluency	foretop
emperor	entrust	essayer	expound	fantasy	fetlock	fistful	fluidal	forever
empiric	entwine	essence	express	fantods	fetters	fistula	fluidic	forfeit
emplace	entwist	essoyne	expulse	faraday	feudist	fitchet	fluidly	forfend
emplane	envelop	estrade	expunge	faradic	fewness	fitchew	flummox	forgave
emporia	envenom	estreat	exscind	faraway	feyness	fitment	flunkey	forgery
empower	envious	estuary	externe	farceur	fiancee	fitness	fluster	forging
empress	environ	etaerio	extinct	farcing	fibbing	fittest	fluting	forgive
emprise	enwheel	etamine	extract	fargone	fibroid	fitting	flutist	forgoer
emptier	enwound	etching	extreme	farming	fibroin	fixable	flutter	forgone
emptily	enzymic	eternal	extrude	farmost	fibroma	fixedly	fluvial	forkful
emption	eparchy	etesian	exudate	Faroese	fibrous	fixings	fluxion	forlorn
empyema	epatant	ethanol	exurban	farrago	fibster	fixture	flyable	formant
emulate	epaulet	etheric	exurbia	farrier	fibulae	flaccid	flyaway	formate
emulous	epergne	ethical	exuviae	farruca	fibular	flagday	flyback	formula
enactor	ephebus	ethiops	exuvial	farther	fibulas	flagged	flybane	forsake
enamour	ephedra	ethmoid	eyeball	fascial	fictile	flagman	flybelt	forsook
enation	epicarp	Etonian	eyebath	fascine	fiction	flamfew	flyblow	forties
enchain	epicede	euclase	eyebolt	Fascism	fictive	flaming	flyboat	fortify
enchant	epicene	eucrite	eyebrow	Fascist	fiddler	flaneur	flybook	Fortran
enchase	epicure	eugenic	eyedrop	fashion	fideism	flanker	flyhalf	fortune
enclasp	epidote	euglena	eyehole	fastday	fideist	flannel	flyleaf	forward
enclave	epigeal	eulogia	eyelash	fatally	fidgets	flapped	flyover	forwent
enclose	epigean	eupepsy	eyeless	fateful	fidgety	flapper	flypast	forworn
encoder	epigene	euphony	eyelike	fathead	fiefdom	flareup	flyting	fossick
encomia	epigone	Euratom	eyeshot	fatigue	fielder	flasher	flytrap	fossula
Encraty	epigoni	eustasy	eyesore	fatling	fierily	flatcap	fobbing	fouette
encrust	epigram	eutexia	eyespot	fatness	fifteen	flatcar	focused	foulard
endarch	epigyny	evacuee	eyewash	fattest	fifthly	flatlet	fogbank	foumart
endemic	epilate	evangel	eyewink	fatting	fifties	flatout	foggage	founder
enderon	episode	evanish	Faberge	fattish	figging	flatten	foggily	foundry
endless	epistle	evasion	fabliau	fatuity	fighter	flatter	fogging	fourale
endlong	epitaph	evasive	fabular	fatuous	figleaf	flattop	foghorn	fourgon
endmost	epitaxy	evening	faceoff	faucial	figment	flaught	foglamp	foveate
endogen	epithem	evictor	faceted	faunist	figtree	flaunty	fogydom	foveola
endorse	epithet	evident	faction	fauvism	figural	flavine	fogyish	fowling
endozoa	epitome	evolute	factory	fauvist	figured	flavour	fogyism	foxhole
endways	epizoic	ewelamb	factual	fearful	figwort	fleabag	folding	foxhunt
endwise	epizoon	eweneck	facture	feaster	filacer	fleapit	foldout	foxtail

foxtrot	fumbler	gangrel	gharial	Gobelin	grapple	guarded	Hamitic	headman
fracted	funeral	gangway	ghastly	goddamn	grasper	guardee	hamming	headpin
fraenum	funfair	gantlet	gherkin	goddess	gratify	guayule	hammock	headset
fragile	fungoid	garbage	ghettos	godetia	grating	gubbins	hamster	headway
frailly	fungous	garbler	ghillie	godevil	graunch	gudgeon	hamulus	healthy
frailty	funicle	garboil	ghostly	godhead	gravely	Guelfic	handbag	hearing
Fraktur	funnies	gardant	giantry	godhood	gravity	guerdon	handcar	hearken
frameup	funnily	garfish	gibbous	godless	gravure	guereza	handful	hearsay
frankly	funning	garland	giblets	godlike	grazier	guesser	handgun	hearted
frantic	furbish	garment	giddily	godling	grazing	guichet	handily	hearten
frapped	furcate	garnish	gigging	godroon	greaser	Guignol	handler	heathen
fratery	furcula	garotte	giggler	godsend	greaten	guilder	handoff	heather
fraught	furioso	garpike	gilbert	godship	greatly	guipure	handout	heating
frazzle	furious	gascoal	gilding	godward	greaves	guisard	handsaw	heavily
freaked	furlong	gaseous	giltcup	goggler	Grecian	gullery	handsel	hebenon
freckle	furmety	gasfire	gimbals	goggles	grecise	gumboil	handset	Hebraic
freckly	furmity	gasmask	gimmick	goitred	Grecism	gumboot	hangdog	heckler
freebie	furnace	gasring	gingery	goldbug	greenly	gumdrop	hanging	hectare
freedom	furrier	gassing	gingham	goldeye	greenth	gumming	hangman	hedonic
freeman	furring	gastric	gingili	golfbag	greisen	gummite	hangout	heedful
freesia	furrowy	gateaux	ginning	golfing	gremial	gumshoe	Hansard	heeltap
freeway	further	gateleg	ginseng	gombeen	gremlin	gunboat	hanuman	heftily
freezer	furtive	gateway	giraffe	gomeral	grenade	gunfire	hapence	heighho
freight	fuscous	gathers	girasol	gomeril	greyhen	gunlock	hapenny	heinous
Frenchy	fusible	gatling	girdler	gonadal	greyish	gunnera	hapless	heiress
frenula	fussily	gaudery	girlish	gondola	greylag	gunnery	haploid	helical
frescos	fusspot	gaudily	gittern	gonidia	gribble	gunning	happily	helices
freshen	fustian	Gaulish	gizzard	goodbye	griddle	gunplay	happing	helicon
fresher	fustily	gauntly	glacial	goodday	griffin	gunroom	harbour	hellbox
freshet	futhark	gauntry	glacier	goodish	griffon	gunship	hardhit	hellcat
freshly	futhorc	gavotte	gladded	goodman	grifter	gunshot	hardpan	Hellene
fretful	futhork	gawkily	gladden	gooiest	grilled	gunwale	hardset	hellion
fretsaw	futtock	gayness	gladder	gorcock	griller	gurnard	hardtop	hellish
fretted	fuzzily	gazelle	glaikit	gorcrow	grimace	gushing	harelip	helluva
friable	gabbing	gazette	glamour	Gordian	grimmer	gustily	harijan	helotry
friarly	gabbler	gearbox	glaring	gorget	grinder	gutless	harmala	helpful
fribble	gabbros	gearing	glassen	gorilla	grinned	gutsily	harmful	helping
frigate	gabelle	geckoes	glasses	gorsedd	gripped	guttate	harmine	hemiola
frijole	gabfest	geebung	glazier	goshawk	gripper	gutting	harmony	hemione
fripper	gabnash	Gehenna	glazing	gosling	griskin	guzzler	harness	hemline
friseur	gadding	gelatin	gleaner	gossipy	gristle	gwyniad	harpist	hemlock
Frisian	gadgety	gelding	gleeful	gossoon	gristly	gymnast	harpoon	hemming
frisker	gadroon	gelidly	gleeman	gouache	gritted	gymslip	harrier	henbane
frisket	gadwall	gelling	glenoid	goulash	grizzle	gypping	harshen	hencoop
frisson	gagging	gemmate	gliadin	gourami	grizzly	habitat	harshly	hennery
fritted	gagster	gemmery	glimmer	gourmet	Grobian	habited	harslet	henpeck
fritter	gahnite	gemming	glimpse	grabbed	groaner	habitue	harvest	henwife
frizzle	gainful	gemmule	glisten	grabber	grocery	hachure	hasbeen	heparin
frizzly	gainsay	gemsbok	glister	grabble	Grolier	hackbut	hashish	hepatic
frogeye	Galahad	general	glitter	gracile	grommet	hackery	hassock	heptane
frogged	galanga	generic	globoid	grackle	groover	hacking	hastate	herbage
frogman	galatea	geneses	globose	gradate	grossly	hackler	hastily	heretic
fronded	galeate	genesis	globule	gradely	grottos	hackney	hatable	heritor
frontal	galenic	genetic	glorify	gradine	grouchy	hacksaw	hatband	herniae
fronton	galilee	genette	glossal	gradual	grouper	haddock	hatcher	hernial
frosted	galipot	Genevan	glottal	grafter	groupie	hafnium	hatchet	hernias
froward	gallant	genista	glottic	grained	grouser	hagborn	hateful	heroics
frowsty	gallate	genitor	glottis	grainer	growler	hagfish	hatless	heroine
fructed	galleon	genizah	glozing	gramary	grownup	Haggada	hatting	heroise
fruited	gallery	genning	glucose	grammar	grubbed	haggard	hauberk	heroism
fruiter	gallfly	Genoese	glueing	grampus	grubber	haggish	haughty	heronry
frustum	gallice	genteel	glummer	granary	gruffly	haggler	haulage	herring
fuchsia	galling	gentian	gluteal	grandad	grumble	hagweed	hauler	herself
fuddler	galliot	gentile	gluteus	grandam	grumbly	haircut	haulier	hessian
Fuehrer	gallium	genuine	glutted	grandee	grummet	hairnet	haunted	hetaera
fuelled	gallnut	geodesy	glutton	grandly	grumose	hairpin	haunter	hetaira
fueller	galloon	geoduck	glyphic	grandma	grumous	Halakah	hautboy	hexadic
fugally	gallows	geogony	glycine	grandpa	grunion	halberd	hauteur	hexagon
fugging	galumph	geoidal	glyptal	granger	grunter	halbert	havenot	hexapla
fuguist	gambade	geology	glyptic	granita	gruntle	halcyon	hawkish	hexapod
fulcrum	gambado	Geordie	gnarled	granite	grutten	halibut	haycock	heyduck
fulgent	gambier	georgic	gnathic	grannie	gruyere	halidom	hayfork	hiccupy
fulgour	gambler	germane	gnocchi	grantee	gryphon	hallali	hayloft	hickory
fullage	gamboge	gestalt	gnomish	granter	grysbok	hallway	hayrick	hidalga
fullout	gambrel	gestapo	gnostic	grantor	Gstring	halogen	hayseed	hidalgo
fulmine	gamebag	gestate	goahead	granule	guanaco	halting	hayward	hideous
fulness	gamelan	gesture	goatgod	grapery	guanine	halvers	haywire	hideout
fulsome	gametic	getaway	goatish	graphic	guarana	halyard	headily	higgler
fulvous	ganglia	getting	gobbler	grapnel	guarani	Hamburg	heading	highboy

7 letter words   position = 1

```
highhat hostler ideally indices intense January Kalmuck knowhow latakia
highman hotfoot identic indicia interim japonic kalpack knowing latchet
highway hothead idiotic inditer interne jargoon kampong knuckle latency
hilding hotness idlesse indoors intoner jarring Kannada knurled lateral
hillman hotshot idolise indorse intrant jasmine Kantian kolkhoz latexes
hillock hottest idyllic indraft intreat javelin Karaite Koranic lathery
hilltop hottish igneous indrawn introit jawbone karakul koumiss lathing
himself housing igniter inducer intrude jaybird karting kremlin latices
hindgut howbeit ignoble indulge intrust jaywalk kathode krimmer latrine
hipbath however ignobly indusia intwine jazzily katydid Krishna lattice
hipbone howling ignorer indwell inutile jazzman keelson krypton Latvian
hipness huanaco ikebana indwelt invader jealous keeping kumquat laugher
hipping hueless ileitis ineptly invalid jejunum kenning Kurdish launder
hiproof huffish ilkaday inertia inveigh jellaba kenosis kursaal laundry
hipster hugeous illbred inertly inverse jellied kenotic kyanise laurels
hirable hugging illegal inexact invitee jemadar kentish kyanite lavolta
hircine hulking illicit infancy inviter jerkily keramic labarum lavrock
hirsute humanly illness infanta invoice jetting keratin labella lawhand
hirudin humbles imagery infante involve jewelry kermess labiate lawless
histone humbuzz imagine infarct inwards jewfish kerogen lacking lawlist
history humdrum imagism infauna inweave Jezebel kerygma laconic lawlord
hitcher humeral imagist inferno inwoven jibbing kestrel lacquer lawsuit
hitting humerus imamate infidel ipomoea jibboom ketchup lactate laxness
Hittite humidly imbiber infield Iranian jibdoor keyhole lacteal layered
hoarsen humidor imbower inflame irately jigging keyless lactose layette
hoatzin humming imbrute inflate irideal jimjams keynote lacunae lazaret
Hobbian hummock imitate inflect iridise jingler keyring lacunal leading
Hobbism humoral immense inflict iridium jitters keyword lacunar leadoff
Hobbist hundred immerge infract Irishry jittery khaddar lacunas leafage
hobbler hunkers immerse infulae irksome jobbery khamsin ladanum leafbud
hobnail Hunnish immoral ingenue ironing jobbing khanate ladybug leaflet
hockday hunting impaint ingesta ironist jocular khedive ladykin leaguer
hocused hurdler impanel ingoing ischial jogging kibbutz laggard leakage
hoecake hurdles impasse ingraft ischium jogtrot kickoff lagging leaning
hoedown hurling impaste ingrain Ishmael joinder kidding laicise learned
hogback hurried impasto ingrate Islamic joinery kiddish laicism learner
hogfish hurtful impeach ingress Ismaili joining kidskin lairage leather
hoggery husband impearl ingroup isobath jointer killick lakelet lechery
hogging hushaby imperil ingrown isochor jointly killing Lallans lectern
hoggish huskily impetus inhabit isogamy jollify killjoy Lamaism lection
hogwash husking impiety inhaler isogeny jollity kilobar Lamaist lecture
hogweed Hussite impinge inherit isogram jonquil kiloton lambast leeward
holdall hustler impious inhibit isohyet jotting kinchin lambent leftism
holding hutment implant inhouse isokont journal kindler lambert leftist
holibut hutting implead inhuman isolate journey kindred lambkin legally
holiday hyaline implete injurer isonomy jouster kinesis lamella legatee
holland hyalite implode inkhorn isotope joyance kinetic laminae legator
holmium hyaloid implore inkling isotopy joyless kinfolk laminar legbail
holmoak hydatid imposer inkwell isotron joyride kingcup lamming legging
holster hydrant impound inlayer Israeli jubilee kingdom lampion leghorn
homager hydrate impresa innards issuant Judaean kinglet lampoon legible
homburg hydride impress innerve isthmus Judaise kingpin lamprey legibly
Homeric hydroid imprest innings itacism Judaism kinship lancers legiron
Homerid hydrous imprint inocula Italian Judaist kinsman landing legless
hominid hygeian improve inphase Italiot judoist Kirghiz languet legpull
homonym hygiene impulse inquest itemise jugging kissing languid legrest
honesty hymenia inanely inquire iterant juggins kitchen languor legroom
honeyed hymnary inanity inquiry iterate juggler kitschy laniary legshow
honours hymnist inaptly insculp ivories jugular klipdas lankily legwork
hoodlum hymnody inboard insecty jabbing juicily knacker lanolin leister
hooklet hyperon inbreed inshore jacamar jujitsu knapped lantana lemmata
hopbind hypnoid inbuilt insider jacinth jukebox knapper lantern lemming
hopeful hypogea incense insight jackass jumbuck knavery lanyard lending
hophead hypoxia incipit insigne jackdaw jumpjet knavish Laotian lengthy
hoplite hypoxic incised insipid jackpot jumpoff kneader lapilli lenient
hopping Iberian incisor insofar jacktar juncoes kneecap lapping lentigo
hopsack iceberg inciter inspect Jacobin Jungian kneeler Laputan lentisk
horizon iceboat incline inspire jacobus juniper kneepan lapwing lentoid
hormone icecold inclose install jaconet Jupiter kneesup larceny leonine
hornmad icefall include instant jadedly jurally knitted lardoon leopard
horrent icefloe incomer instate jadeite juryman knitter largely leotard
horrify icefoot incrust instead jaggery jussive knobbed largess leprosy
horsily icepack incubus insular Jainism justice knobble largish leprous
hosanna icerink incudes insulin jaloppy justify knobbly lasagna lesbian
hosiery iceshow incurve insured jamming jutting knocker lasagne letdown
hospice ichabod incused insurer Janeite kabbala knockon lashing lethean
hostage iciness indepth inswept jangler Kaddish knotted lashkar letters
hostess icteric indexer inswing janitor kainite knotter lassoes letting
hostile icterus indican integer jannock kalends knowall lasting lettuce
```

Lettish	liveoak	lugsail	maintop	margent	meddler	milkleg	mixture	mounter
lettuce	llanero	lugworm	majesty	marimba	mediacy	milkman	Moabite	Mountie
leucine	loading	lullaby	makings	mariner	mediant	milksop	mobbing	mourner
leucite	loaning	lumbago	malacia	marital	mediate	milldam	mobbish	mousaka
leucoma	loather	lumbang	malaise	markhor	medical	million	mobster	mousing
levator	loathly	lumenal	malaria	marking	medulla	milreis	mockery	mousmee
levelly	lobbing	luminal	Malayan	marline	medusae	mimesis	modally	mouther
leveret	lobelia	lumpily	malefic	marlite	medusan	mimetic	modesty	movable
lexical	lobster	lumpish	malines	marmite	medusas	mimical	modicum	mowburn
lexicon	lobular	lunatic	malison	marplot	meerkat	mimicry	modiste	mozetta
liaison	lobworm	luncher	mallard	marquee	meeting	mimulus	modular	mudbath
Liassic	locally	lunette	malleus	marquis	megaron	minaret	modulus	muddily
liberal	locater	lunular	malmsey	Marrano	megaton	mincing	mofette	muddler
liberty	lockage	lupulin	maltase	married	meiosis	mindful	moidore	mudfish
library	lockjaw	lurcher	Maltese	marring	meiotic	mineral	moisten	mudflat
librate	locknut	lurdane	malting	marrowy	Meissen	minever	moistly	mudlark
licence	lockout	luridly	maltose	Marsala	melange	miniate	moither	mudpack
license	locular	lustful	mamelon	marshal	melanic	minibus	molimen	muezzin
lichowl	loculus	lustily	mamilla	martial	melanin	minicab	mollify	muffler
licitly	lodging	lustral	mammary	Martian	melilot	minicar	mollusc	mugging
licking	loftily	lustrum	mammate	martini	melisma	minikin	molossi	muggins
lidless	logbook	luteous	mammock	martlet	melodic	minimal	momenta	mugwort
lieabed	logging	lychnis	mammoth	martyry	melting	minimum	monacal	mugwump
lifeful	logical	lychowl	manacle	Marxian	memento	minimus	monadic	mulatto
liftoff	logline	lycopod	manager	Marxism	memoirs	miniver	monarch	mullein
lighted	logwood	lyddite	manakin	Marxist	mending	minorca	mondial	mullion
lighten	Lollard	lyingin	manatee	marybud	menfolk	minster	moneyed	mullock
lighter	Lombard	lyingly	manchet	mascara	menisci	mintage	moneyer	multure
lightly	lomenta	lymphad	mandala	mashtub	menorah	minuend	mongrel	mumbler
lignify	lyncean	lyrated	mandate	Masonic	menthol	minutes	moniker	mummery
lignite	longbow	lynchet	mandola	masonry	mention	minutia	monitor	mummify
ligroin	longday	lyrical	mandora	Masorah	mercery	Miocene	monkery	mumming
likable	longhop	macabre	mandrel	masquer	merchet	miracle	monkish	mumpish
lilting	longing	macadam	mandril	massage	mercury	mirador	monocle	mundane
limbate	longish	macaque	mangily	masseur	mermaid	mirkily	monocot	mundify
limbeck	looking	mangoes	mangold	massive	merrily	miscall	monodic	munnion
limbous	lookout	machair	mangold	mastaba	meseems	miscast	monomer	munting
liminal	looksee	machete	manhole	masters	mesonic	miscopy	monsoon	muntjac
limited	loosely	machine	manhood	mastery	message	misdate	monster	muntjak
limiter	lopping	macrame	manhour	mastich	messiah	misdeal	montage	muonium
limosis	lording	macrami	manhunt	mastiff	Messias	misdeed	montane	muraena
limpkin	lorette	maculae	manihot	mastoid	messily	misdeem	montero	murexes
limulus	lorgnon	macular	manikin	matador	messtin	misdone	monthly	muriate
linctus	loricae	maddest	manilla	matchet	mestiza	miserly	moocher	murices
lindane	lorimer	madding	manille	matelot	mestizo	misfire	moodily	murkily
lineage	loriner	Madeira	maniple	matinal	metamer	misgave	mooneye	murrain
lineate	losable	madness	manitou	matinee	metayer	misgive	moonlit	murther
lineman	lottery	madonna	manjack	matrass	metazoa	mishear	moonset	muscled
lineout	lotting	madrona	mankind	mattery	methane	misknow	moorage	musette
lingual	loudish	madrono	manless	matting	metonym	mislaid	moorhen	musical
linkage	lounger	madwort	manlike	mattins	metopic	mislead	mooring	muskrat
linkboy	lousily	maestri	manmade	mattock	metopon	mislike	Moorish	mustang
linkman	loutish	maestro	manners	mattoid	metrics	mislive	moorlog	mustard
Linnean	louvred	maffick	manning	matzoth	metrist	mismate	mopping	mutable
linocut	lovable	mafiosi	mannish	maudlin	mettled	misname	moraine	mutably
linsang	lovably	mafioso	mannite	maunder	Mexican	misplay	morally	mutagen
linseed	loverly	magenta	mannose	mauther	mezuzah	misread	morassy	muttony
lioncel	lowborn	maggoty	mansard	mawkish	miasmal	misrule	mordant	muzzily
lioness	lowbred	magical	mansion	mawworm	miasmic	missend	mordent	muzzler
lionise	lowbrow	magmata	mansize	maxilla	micelle	missent	moreish	myalgia
lipdeep	lowdown	magnate	manteau	maximal	microbe	missile	morello	myalgic
lipless	lowland	magneto	mantlet	maximum	midland	missing	morendo	myalism
lipping	lowlily	magnify	mantram	maxwell	midline	mission	Moresco	mycelia
lipread	lowness	mahaleb	mantrap	mayoral	midmost	missish	Morisco	mycoses
liquate	lowrise	mahatma	manumit	maypole	midriff	missive	morning	mycosis
liquefy	loyally	Mahdism	manward	Maytime	midship	misstep	morocco	mycotic
liqueur	loyalty	Mahdist	manweek	mayweed	midweek	mistake	moronic	myeloid
lissome	lozenge	mahjong	Manxcat	mazurka	Midwest	mistful	morphia	myeloma
listeth	lubbard	mahonia	Manxman	mazzard	midwife	mistily	mortice	myiasis
listing	lucarne	mahound	manyear	meadowy	midyear	mistime	mortify	mylodon
literal	lucency	mahseer	mapping	mealies	mightst	misting	mortise	mynheer
lithely	lucerne	maidish	marabou	meander	migrant	mistook	morulae	myogram
lithium	lucidly	maidism	Maratha	meaning	migrate	mistral	morular	myology
lithoid	Lucifer	mailbag	Marathi	measles	mildewy	mitoses	morwong	myomata
litotes	luckily	mailbox	marbled	measure	mileage	mitosis	Moselle	mystery
littery	Luddite	mailing	marbles	meatfly	milfoil	mitotic	mosshag	mystify
liturgy	luggage	maillot	marcher	meatman	miliary	mitzvah	mottled	mythise
livable	lugging	mailman	marconi	Mechlin	militia	mixedly	mouflon	mythist
livebox	lughole	mailvan	maremma	meconic	milking	mixedup	moulder	myxomas

nabbing
nacarat
nacelle
nacrous
nagging
Nahuatl
naiades
nailery
naively
naivete
naivety
nakedly
namable
nameday
nankeen
naphtha
napless
napping
narrate
narrows
narthex
narwhal
nasally
nascent
nastily
nattily
natural
naughty
nauplii
nautics
nautili
navarin
Naziism
nearest
nebbish
nebulae
nebular
nebulas
necklet
necktie
necrose
nectary
needful
needler
neglect
neglige
Negress
Negrito
negroid
neither
nelumbo
nemesia
nemesis
Neogaea
neolith
neology
neonate
neoteny
neozoic
nephric
Neptune
neritic
nervate
nervine
nervous
nervure
nesting
netball
netfish
netlike
netsuke
netting
network
neurine
neuroma
neurone
neuston
neutral
neutron
newborn
newcome
newlaid
newmown
newness
newsboy
newsman
nibbler
niblick
niceish
nictate
niggard
niggler
nightie
nightly
nigrify
Nilotic
nimiety
ninepin
niobium
nippers
nippily
nipping
nirvana
nitrate
nitride
nitrify
nitrile
nitrite
nitrous
niveous
Noachic
nobbler
noctuid
noctule
nocturn
nocuous
nodally
nodated
nodding
nodical
nodular
nogging
noisily
noisome
nomadic
nomarch
nombril
nominal
nominee
nonagon
noniron
nonplus
nonskid
nonslip
nonstop
nonsuch
nonsuit
nonuser
noology
noonday
nooning
norland
norther
norward
nosebag
nosegay
noserag
nostril
nostrum
notable
notably
notched
notedly
notelet
notepad
nothing
notitia
noumena
nourish
novella
novelle
novelty
nowhere
noxious
nuclear
nucleic
nuclein
nucleon
nucleus
nuclide
nullify
nullity
numbles
numeral
numeric
nummary
nunatak
nunhood
nunnery
nunnish
nunship
nuptial
nursery
nursing
nurture
nutcase
nutgall
nutlike
nutpine
nutting
nylghau
nymphal
nymphet
oakfern
oakgall
oakling
oaktree
oakwood
oarfish
oarless
oarlock
oarsman
oarweed
oatcake
oatmeal
obconic
obelise
obelisk
obesity
obitual
obligee
obligor
oblique
obloquy
obolary
obovate
obovoid
obscene
obscure
observe
obtrude
obverse
obviate
obvious
ocarina
occiput
occlude
oceanic
ocellar
ocellus
ochrous
octagon
octaval
octette
October
octopod
octopus
octuple
oculate
oculist
odalisk
oddball
oddment
oddness
odontic
odorant
odorous
odoured
odyssey
oedipal
oenomel
oersted
oestral
oestrum
oestrus
offbeat
offence
offhand
officer
offload
offpeak
offside
oghamic
ogreish
oilbath
oilbird
oilcake
oildrum
oilseed
oilskin
oilwell
oldster
oldtime
olefine
olivary
olivine
oloroso
Olympic
omental
omentum
omicron
ominous
omitted
omneity
omnibus
omnific
onanism
oneeyed
oneiric
oneness
onerous
oneself
oneshot
onestep
onetime
ongoing
onshore
onstage
onwards
onymous
oolitic
oomiack
oophyte
oosperm
oospore
opacity
opaline
openair
openend
opening
operand
operant
operate
operose
ophitic
opinion
opossum
oppidan
opposer
oppress
opsonic
opsonin
optical
optimal
optimum
opulent
opuntia
opuscle
oration
oratory
oratrix
orbital
orchard
orderer
orderly
ordinal
orectic
oregano
organic
organon
organum
organza
orifice
origami
orogeny
orology
orotund
Orphean
Orphism
orphrey
ortolan
osculum
osmosis
osmotic
osmunda
osselet
osseous
osseter
ossicle
ossific
ossuary
osteoid
ostiary
ostiole
ostraca
ostraka
ostrich
otolith
otology
ottoman
ouabain
ourself
outback
outcast
outcome
outcrop
outdone
outdoor
outface
outfall
outflow
outfoot
outgone
outgrew
outgrow
outhaul
outland
outlast
outlier
outline
outlive
outlook
outmost
outpace
outplay
outport
outpost
outrage
outrank
outride
outrode
outrush
outsell
outshot
outside
outsize
outsold
outsole
outstay
outtake
outtalk
outturn
outvote
outward
outwear
outwent
outwore
outwork
outworn
ovarian
ovation
overact
overage
overall
overarm
overate
overawe
overbid
overbuy
overdid
overdue
overeat
overfed
overfly
overlap
overlay
overlie
overman
overpay
overran
overrun
oversaw
oversea
oversee
overset
oversew
overtax
overtly
overtop
overuse
ovicide
oviduct
oviform
ovoidal
ovulate
oxalate
oxfence
oxidant
oxidase
oxidate
oxidise
Oxonian
oxyacid
oxytone
ozonise
pabulum
pachisi
pacific
package
packice
packing
packman
padding
paddler
paddock
padlock
padrone
padroni
paeonic
pageant
pageboy
paginal
pahlavi
pailful
painful
painter
pairoar
paisley
pajamas
paladin
palatal
palaver
paletot
palette
palfrey
palings
pallium
palmary
palmate
palmist
palmoil
palmyra
palpate
palsied
paludal
pampean
pampero
panacea
panache
pancake
Pandean
pandect
pandora
pandore
panicky
panicle
Panjabi
pannage
pannier
panning
panocha
panoply
panther
panties
pantile
papadam
papally
paperer
Paphian
papilla
papoose
pappose
paprika
papulae
papular
papyrus
parable
parader
parados
paradox
paragon
parapet
parasol
parboil
pardner
parerga
paresis
paretic
parfait
pargana
parkway
parlour
parlous
parodic
parolee
paronym
parotid
parpend
parquet
parsley
parsnip
partake
partial
parting
partita
partite
partlet
partner
partook
parvenu
parvise
paschal
passade
passado
passage
passant
passing
passion
passive
passkey
pastern
pasteup
pastime
pasture
patagia
patella
patency
pathway
patient
patrial
patriot
patroon
pattern
patting
paucity
Pauline
paunchy
paviour
payable
paydesk
payload
payment
payroll
paysage
peacock
peafowl
pearled
pearler
peartly
peasant
peascod
peasoup
pebrine
peccant
peccary
peckish
peddler
pedicab
pedicel
pedicle
pedlary
peerage
peeress
peevish
Pegasus
pegging
pelagic
pelican
pelisse
peloria
peloric
pelorus
peltate
pelting
pemican
penally
penalty
penance
pendant
pendent
pending
penguin
penname
pennant
pennate
pennies
pennill
pennine
penning
pensile
pension
pensive
pentane
pentode
pentose
peonage
peppery
peppill
pepping
peptalk
peptide
peptise
peptone
percale
percent
percept
percher
percine
percoid
percuss
perdure
perfect
perfidy
perform
perfume
perfuse
pergola
perhaps
periapt
peridot
perigee
perique
periwig
perjure
perjury
perkily
perlite
Permian
permute
perpend
perpent
perplex
Persian
persist
persona
pertain
perturb
pertuse
perusal
peruser
pervade
pervert
pessary
petasus
petiole
petrify
Petrine
petrous
pettily
petting
pettish

```
petunia pinetum playboy polypod precast profile pulvini quetzal rapport
pfennig pinfire playful polypus precede profuse pumpkin queuing rapture
phaeton pinfish playing pomatum precept progeny puncher quibble rarebit
phalanx pinfold playlet pomfret precise program punchup quicken raschel
phallic pinguid playoff pompano precook project punctum quickie rasping
phallus pinhead playpen pompion predate prolate pungent quickly ratable
phantom pinhole pleader pompous predial prolong Punjabi quieten ratafia
pharaoh pinkeye pleased pondage predict promise punning quietly ratatat
pharynx pinking plectra poniard predoom promote punster quietus ratchet
phasmid pinkish pledgee pontage preempt pronaoi puparia quillet rations
phellem pinnace pledger pontiff preface pronaos pupilar quiller ratline
philter pinnate pledget pontify prefect pronate pupping quilter ratlike
philtre pinning pledgor pontoon preform pronely puritan quinary ratling
phlegmy pinnule plenary poofter preheat pronged purlieu quinate rattail
phoenix pintado plenish poohbah prelacy pronoun purloin quinine ratteen
phonate pintail pleurae poorish prelate propane purport quinone ratting
phoneme pintuck pleural popadum prelect propend purpose quintal rattler
phonics pinworm pleuron popcorn prelims prophet purpura quintan rattrap
phonily pioneer pliable popeyed prelude propine purpure quintet raucous
photism piously pliably popover premier propjet pursuer quintic raunchy
phrasal pipeful plicate poppied premise propone pursuit quipped ravager
phratry piperic pliskie popping premiss propose purview quitted ravelin
phrenic pipette plodded popular premium propped pushful quitter ravined
phrensy pipping plodder porcine preoral prorate pushing quittor ravings
physics piquant plopped porifer prepack prosaic pushrod quivery ravioli
piaffer piragua plosion porrect prepaid prosify pustule quixote rawhide
pianism piranha plosive portage prepare prosily putamen quizzed rawness
pianist piratic plotted portend preplan prosody putdown quizzer rayless
piastre pirogue plotter portent presage prosper putlock quizzes reacher
pibroch piscary plucker portico presell protean putrefy quondam reactor
picador piscina plugged portion present protect puttier rabbity readily
piccolo piscine plugger portray preside protege putting rabbler reading
piceous pismire plumage posaune presoak proteid puzzler raccoon readout
pickaxe pissoir plumate poseuse presser protein pyaemia racemic reagent
pickeer pistole plumber possess pressup protend pyaemic rackety realgar
pickled pitapat plumbic postage presume protest pycnite racquet realign
picotee pitched plumbob postbag pretend proteus pygmean radiant realise
picquet pitcher plumery postbox pretest protist pygmoid radiate realism
picrate piteous plummet postboy pretext protium pyjamas radical realist
Pictish pitfall plumose posteen pretzel proudly pyloric radices reality
picture pithead plumper postern prevail proverb pylorus radicle reallot
piddock pithhat plumply postfix prevent provide pyralid radulae realtor
pidgeon pithily plumule posting preview proviso pyralis radular rebirth
piebald pitiful plunder postman previse provoke pyramid raffish reboant
pieeyed pitpony plunger posture priapic provost pyretic ragbolt rebound
pierrot pitprop plunker postwar pricker prowess pyrexia ragdoll rebuild
pietism pitting plusage potable pricket prowler pyrexic raggedy rebuilt
pietist pivotal plushly potamic prickle proximo pyrites ragging rebuker
piffler pivoter pluvial pothead prickly prudent pyritic ragtime receipt
piggery placard plywood potheen primacy prudery pyrosis ragweed receive
pigging placate poacher potherb primage prudish pyrrhic ragworm recency
piggish placebo pochard pothole primary pruning Pythian ragwort recital
pigiron placket podagra pothook primate prurigo pyxides railcar reciter
piglead placoid podding potluck primely prussic pyxidia railing reclaim
pigling plafond podesta potshot primero psalter quadrat railman reclame
pigmean plaided poetess pottage priming psychic quadric railway recline
pigment plainly poetics potteen primmed pteroic quaffer raiment recluse
pigskin planish poetise pottery primula pteryla quahaug Rajpoot recount
pigtail planned pofaced potting printer ptyalin qualify rakeoff recover
pigwash planner poinder pouched prithee puberal quality rallier recruit
pigweed plantar pointed pouffes privacy puberty quamash ralline rectify
pikelet planter pointer poulard private puccoon quantic Ramadan rectory
pikeman planula poitrel poulter privily puckery quantum rambler rectrix
pileate planxty polacca poultry privity puckish quarrel ramekin recurve
pilgrim plasmic polacre poundal prizing pudding quartan ramenta recycle
pillage plasmid poleaxe pounder proband puddler quarter ramming redcoat
pillbox plasmin polecat poussin probang pudency quartet rampage reddest
pillion plaster polemic pouting probate pudenda quartic rampant reddish
pillock plastic polenta poverty probity puerile quassia rampart redhead
pillory plastid politic powdery problem puffery quavery rampion redlegs
pillowy platane pollack praetor proceed pugging quayage ramsons redneck
pillule plateau pollard prairie process puggish Quechua rancher redness
pilsner platina pollock praiser procure puggree queenly rancour redoubt
pilular plating pollute praline prodded pugmill queerly ranking redound
pimento platoon poloist prancer prodder pugnose queller ransack redpoll
pimping platted polygon prattle prodigy Pullman querist rapeoil redraft
pinball platter polymer pravity produce pullout quester raphide redress
pincers plaudit polynia preachy product pulpous questor rapidly redskin
pincher playact polynya prebend proffer pulsate quetsch rapping reducer
```

redwing	replica	reviver	rockoil	ruddock	Sanctus	scalder	scrieve	selenic
redwood	replier	revivor	rocktar	ruderal	sandbag	scaldic	scrimpy	selffed
reeding	reposal	revolve	rodding	rudesby	sandbar	scalene	scrooge	selfish
reelect	reposit	revving	rodlike	ruffian	sandbed	scallop	scrouge	sellout
reenact	repress	rewound	rodsman	ruffler	sandbox	scalpel	scrubby	seltzer
reenter	reprint	rewrite	roebuck	ruinate	sandboy	scalper	scruffy	selvage
reentry	reprise	rewrote	roedeer	ruinous	sanders	scamper	scrumpy	sematic
referee	reproof	reynard	roguery	rumbler	sandfly	scandal	scrunch	semilog
refined	reprove	rhabdom	roguish	rummage	sandlot	scanned	scruple	seminal
refiner	reptile	Rhaetic	roister	rumness	sandman	scanner	scudded	seminar
reflate	repulse	rhamnus	rollick	rumshop	sandpit	scantly	scuffle	semiped
reflect	reputed	rhatany	rolling	runaway	sangria	scapple	sculler	Semitic
refloat	request	rhenium	rollmop	rundale	sanicle	scapula	sculpin	senarii
refocus	requiem	rhiancy	rolltop	rundlet	santour	scarfed	scumble	senator
refract	require	rhizoid	romance	rundown	sapajou	scarify	scummed	senatus
refrain	requite	rhizome	Romanic	runless	saphead	scarlet	scunner	sendoff
refresh	reredos	rhodium	Romansh	running	sapient	scarper	scupper	senecio
refugee	rescale	rhodora	romaunt	rupture	sapless	scarred	scurril	senhora
refusal	rescind	rhombic	Rommany	rurally	sapling	scarves	scutage	senores
refuser	rescuer	rhombus	rondeau	russety	saponin	scatted	scutate	sensory
refutal	reseaux	rhubarb	rondure	Russian	sapphic	scatter	scutter	sensual
refuter	reserve	rhymist	rontgen	Russify	sapping	scauper	scuttle	Senussi
regalia	reshape	ribband	roofing	rustily	saprobe	scenery	seabass	seppuku
regally	residua	ribbing	rooftop	rustler	sapsago	scented	seabear	septate
regards	residue	ribston	rooinek	ruthful	sapwood	scepsis	seabird	septime
regatta	resolve	ribwork	rookery	rutting	Saracen	sceptic	seablue	sequela
regency	resound	ribwort	roomful	ruttish	sarangi	sceptre	seaboot	sequent
regimen	respect	rickets	rooster	Sabaism	sarcasm	schappe	seafish	sequoia
reginal	respell	rickety	rootage	Sabaoth	sarcode	schemer	seafood	Serbian
regnant	respelt	ricksha	rootlet	Sabbath	sarcoid	scherzi	seafowl	serfage
regorge	respire	ricotta	ropable	saccade	sarcoma	scherzo	seagirt	serfdom
regrant	respite	ridable	ropeway	saccate	sarcous	schlepp	seagull	seriate
regrate	respond	ridding	rorqual	saccule	sardine	schlock	seakale	sericin
regress	respray	riddler	roseate	sacculi	sardius	schmuck	sealane	seriema
regrets	restart	ridging	rosebay	sackbut	sarking	schnook	sealant	seringa
regroup	restate	ridotto	rosebud	sackful	sashimi	scholar	sealegs	serious
regular	restful	riffler	rosecut	sacking	sassaby	scholia	sealery	serpent
regulus	restiff	rifling	rosehip	sacring	satanic	sciarid	seamaid	serpigo
reheard	restive	rigging	rosella	sacrist	satchel	sciatic	seamark	serpula
rehouse	restock	righten	roseola	saddest	satiate	science	seapink	serrate
reissue	restore	righter	rosered	saddish	satiety	scirrhi	seaport	serried
rejoice	restyle	rightly	rosette	saddler	satinet	scissel	searoom	servant
relapse	resurge	rigidly	rostral	sadness	satiric	scissor	seasick	servery
related	retable	rilievo	rostrum	saffron	satisfy	scleral	seaside	Servian
relater	retaken	rimming	rotator	sagging	satrapy	scoffer	seaslug	service
relator	rethink	ringent	rotifer	sagitta	satsuma	scolder	seatang	servile
relayed	retiary	ringing	rotting	saguaro	satyral	scollop	seating	serving
release	reticle	ringlet	rotunda	saidest	satyric	scomber	seawall	Servite
reliant	retinae	ringtaw	roughen	sailing	satyrid	scooper	seaward	sessile
relieve	retinal	riotous	roughly	sainted	saucily	scooter	seaware	session
relievo	retinas	ripcord	roulade	saintly	saunter	scopula	seaweed	sestina
relight	retinol	ripieni	rouleau	sakeret	saurian	scoriae	seawhip	setback
relique	retinue	ripieno	rounded	Saktism	sauroid	scorify	seawife	setdown
remains	retired	riposte	roundel	salable	sausage	scoring	seawolf	setting
remarry	retouch	ripping	rounder	salicet	savable	scorner	seceder	settler
remblai	retrace	ripplet	roundly	salicin	savanna	scorper	seclude	settlor
remiges	retract	riptide	roundup	salient	saveall	Scorpio	seconde	setwall
remnant	retrain	risible	rousing	Salique	saveloy	scotice	secondi	seventh
remodel	retread	risotto	rouster	sallowy	savings	Scotism	secondo	seventy
remorse	retreat	rissole	routine	salpinx	saviour	Scotist	secrecy	several
remould	retrial	rivalry	rowboat	salsify	savoury	scotoma	secrete	sexfoil
remount	retsina	rivered	rowdily	saltant	sawbill	Scottie	sectary	sexless
removal	rettery	riveter	rowlock	saltbox	sawbuck	scourer	sectile	Sextans
removed	retting	riviera	royally	saltcat	sawdust	scourge	section	sextant
remover	returns	riviere	royalty	saltern	sawfish	scouter	secular	sextile
reneger	reunion	rivulet	royster	salting	sawgate	scraggy	securer	sferics
renegue	reunite	roadbed	rubadub	saltire	sawmill	scranny	sedilia	sfumato
renewal	revalue	roadhog	rubbers	saltish	sawnoff	scraper	seducer	shackle
renewer	revelry	roadman	rubbery	saltpan	sawwort	scrapie	seeable	shadily
rentier	revenge	roadway	rubbing	saluter	saxhorn	scrappy	seedbed	shading
reorder	revenue	roaring	rubbish	salvage	saxtuba	scratch	seedily	shadoof
repaint	reverie	roaster	rubdown	salvoes	sayable	scrawly	seedlip	shadowy
repaper	reverse	robbery	rubella	sambuca	scabbed	scrawny	seeming	shaitan
repiner	reversi	robbing	rubeola	samisen	scabble	screech	seepage	shakeup
repique	reviler	rockery	rubicon	samovar	scabies	screeve	segment	shakily
replace	revisal	rockier	rubious	Samoyed	scabrid	screwed	seismal	shallop
replant	reviser	rockily	ruching	sampler	scaglia	screwer	seismic	shallot
replete	revisit	rocking	ruction	samurai	scalade	scribal	seizing	shallow
replevy	revival	rocklet	ruddily	sanctum	scalado	scriber	seizure	shamble

shammed	shrinal	sitting	sleeved	snorkel	sounder	spitted	stalked	stinker
shammer	shrivel	situate	sleight	snorter	soundly	spitter	stalker	stipend
shampoo	shriven	Sivaism	slender	snouted	soupcon	spittle	stamina	stipple
shanked	shrubby	Sivaite	slicker	snowcap	sourish	splashy	stammel	stipule
shapely	shucker	sixaine	slickly	snowily	soursop	spleeny	stammer	stirpes
sharpen	shudder	sixfold	slidden	snowman	soutane	splenic	stamper	stirred
sharper	shuffle	sixteen	slimily	snubbed	souther	splicer	standby	stirrer
sharply	shunned	sixthly	slimmer	snubber	sowback	splodge	stander	stirrup
shaslik	shunner	sixties	slinger	snuffer	soybean	splotch	standin	stocker
shaster	shunter	Sixtine	slinker	snuffle	sozzled	splurge	standup	stoical
shastra	shuteye	sizable	slipped	snuggle	spacial	spodium	staniel	stomach
shatter	shutout	sizably	slipper	soakage	spacing	spoiler	stannic	stomata
Shavian	shutter	sizzler	slipway	soaking	spadger	spondee	stapler	stonily
shaving	shuttle	sjambok	slither	soapbox	spancel	spondyl	starchy	stonker
shearer	shylock	skaldic	slobber	soapily	spangle	sponger	stardom	stopgap
sheathe	shyness	skating	sloegin	soaring	spangly	spongin	starkly	stopoff
sheaves	shyster	skeeter	slogged	sobbing	spaniel	sponson	starlet	stopped
shebang	sialoid	skegger	slogger	soberly	Spanish	sponsor	starlit	stopper
shebear	siamang	skellum	slopped	socager	spanker	spoofer	starred	stopple
shebeen	Siamese	skelter	sloshed	soccage	spanned	spooney	starter	storage
shedder	sibling	skepsis	slotcar	society	spanner	spoorer	startle	storied
sheerly	sibship	sketchy	slotted	sockeye	sparely	sporran	statant	stouten
shellac	sickbay	skiable	slouchy	sofabed	sparger	sporter	stately	stoutly
shelled	sickbed	skidded	sloughy	softish	sparing	sporule	statice	stovies
sheller	sickish	skidlid	Slovene	soggily	sparkle	spotted	statics	stowage
shelter	sickpay	skidpan	slowish	soignee	sparoid	spotter	station	straits
sheltie	sidecar	skiffle	slubbed	soilure	sparred	spousal	statism	strange
shelved	sideway	skijump	slubber	sojourn	sparrow	spouter	statist	stratum
shelves	siemens	skilful	slugged	sokeman	Spartan	sprawly	stative	stratus
Shemite	sierran	skilift	slugger	solanum	spastic	sprayer	statued	strayer
sherbet	sighted	skilled	slumber	solaria	spathic	sprayey	stature	streaky
shereef	sightly	skillet	slummed	solatia	spatial	spriggy	statute	stretch
sheriff	sigmate	skimmed	slummer	soldier	spatted	springe	staunch	stretta
sherris	sigmoid	skimmer	slurred	solicit	spattee	springy	stealer	stretto
shicker	signary	skimmia	slyness	solidly	spatter	spryest	stealth	strewth
shifter	signify	skinful	smacker	solidus	spatula	spumous	steamer	striate
shikari	signior	skinker	smaragd	soliped	spawner	spunkie	stearic	strider
shilpit	signora	skinned	smarten	soloist	speaker	spurner	stearin	stridor
shimmer	signore	skinner	smartly	Solomon	special	spurred	steekit	strigil
shindig	signori	skipped	smasher	soluble	species	spurrey	steepen	striker
shingle	signory	skipper	smashup	solvate	specify	spurtle	steeple	stringy
shingly	Sikhism	skippet	smatter	solvent	speckle	sputnik	steeply	striped
shinned	silence	skinret	smeddum	somatic	spectra	sputter	steerer	striven
shinpad	silenus	skirted	smeller	someday	spectre	spyhole	stellar	striver
shiplap	silesia	skirter	smelter	somehow	specula	squabby	stemmed	strophe
shipman	silicic	skitter	smidgen	someone	speeder	squacco	stemple	stroppy
shipped	silicle	skittle	smidgin	someway	speedup	squaddy	stemson	strudel
shippen	silicon	skolion	smitten	somitic	speller	squails	stenchy	strumae
shipper	siliqua	skulker	smokeho	sonance	spelter	squalid	stencil	stubbed
shippon	silique	skyblue	smokily	sonancy	spencer	squally	stentor	stubble
shipway	silkily	skyborn	smoking	songful	spender	squalor	stepney	stubbly
shirker	sillily	skyhigh	smoochy	sonless	sphenic	squamae	stepped	stuccos
shittim	silvern	skyjack	smother	sonship	spheral	squarer	stepper	stuckup
shivers	silvery	skylark	smuggle	soonish	spheric	squashy	stepson	studded
shivery	similar	skyline	smutted	soother	spicate	squatty	sterile	student
shocker	similor	skysail	snaffle	soothly	spicery	squeaky	sterlet	studied
shoeing	simitar	skyward	snagged	sootily	spicily	squeeze	sternal	stuffer
shogged	simpler	slabbed	snakily	sophism	spicula	squelch	sterned	stumble
shoofly	simplex	slabber	snapped	sophist	spicule	squiffy	sternly	stummed
shooter	simular	slacken	snapper	soppily	spidery	squinch	sternum	stumper
shopboy	sincere	slacker	snarler	sopping	spieler	squinny	steroid	stunned
shopman	singlet	slackly	snarlup	soprani	spignel	squirmy	stetson	stunner
shopped	sinkage	slagged	snatchy	soprano	spikily	squishy	stetted	stunted
shopper	sinless	slammed	sneaker	sorbent	spiller	squitch	steward	stupefy
shoring	sinning	slander	sneerer	Sorbian	spinach	stabbed	stewpan	stutter
shorten	sinopia	slantly	sneezer	sorcery	spindle	stabber	stewpot	stygian
shortie	sinsyne	slapped	snicker	sordini	spindly	stabile	sthenic	stylise
shortly	sintery	slasher	sniffer	sordino	spindry	stabler	stibine	stylish
shotgun	sinuate	slather	sniffle	sorghum	spinner	stables	sticker	stylist
shotten	sinuous	slating	snifter	sorites	spinney	stacker	stickit	stylite
shouter	sipping	slatted	snigger	soroban	spinode	staddle	stickle	styloid
showbiz	sirgang	slavery	sniggle	sororal	spinoff	stadium	stickup	styptic
showery	sirloin	slavish	snipped	sorosis	spinose	stagger	stiffen	styrene
showily	sirocco	Slavism	snipper	sorrily	spinous	stagily	stiffly	suasion
showing	Sistine	sledded	snippet	sotting	spinule	staging	stifler	suasive
showman	sistrum	sleeken	snooker	sottish	spiraea	staidly	stilted	suavely
showoff	sitdown	sleekit	snooper	soubise	spirant	stainer	Stilton	suavity
shrieve	sitfast	sleekly	snoozer	souffle	spireme	staithe	stimuli	subacid
shrilly	sithens	sleeper	snoozle	soulful	spirits	stalely	stinger	subadar

subaqua	supping	synapse	tannery	tenancy	thieves	tipsily	touchup	triceps
subbing	support	syncarp	tanning	tendril	thigger	tipster	toughen	tricker
subdean	suppose	syncope	tannish	tenfold	thiller	titanic	toughly	trickle
subdual	supreme	synergy	tanooze	tenoner	thimble	tithing	touraco	tricksy
subduct	supremo	synesis	tantara	tenpins	thinker	titlark	touring	tricorn
subdued	surbase	syngamy	tantivy	tensely	thinned	titling	tourism	trident
subedit	surcoat	synodal	tantric	tensile	thinner	titmice	tourist	triduan
suberic	surface	synodic	tantrum	tension	thirdly	Titoism	tourney	triduum
suberin	surfeit	synonym	tanyard	tensity	thirsty	Titoist	towards	trifler
subfusc	surfing	synovia	taperer	tensive	thistle	titrate	towboat	triform
subhead	surfman	syringa	tapetal	tentbed	thistly	tittupy	towered	trigamy
subject	surgeon	syringe	tapetum	tentfly	thither	titular	towhead	trigger
subjoin	surgery	syrphid	tapioca	tenthly	Thomism	toaster	towline	trilith
sublate	surlily	systole	tapping	tentpeg	Thomist	tobacco	towmond	trilogy
sublime	surmise	tabanid	taproom	tenuity	thorite	toccata	towmont	trimmed
subplot	surname	tabaret	taproot	tenuous	thorium	toddler	townish	trimmer
subside	surpass	tabasco	tapsman	tepidly	thorned	toeclip	townlet	trinary
subsidy	surplus	tabbing	tapster	tequila	thought	toehold	towpath	trindle
subsist	surreal	tabetic	tarbush	terbium	thready	toeless	towrope	tringle
subsoil	surtout	tabinet	tardily	terebra	thrifty	toenail	toyshop	trinity
subsume	survive	tableau	tarnish	tergite	thriven	toggery	tracery	trinket
subtend	suspect	tabloid	tarrier	termini	throaty	toilful	trachea	trinkum
subtile	suspend	taborer	tarring	termite	thrombi	tollbar	tracker	triolet
suburbs	suspire	tabular	tartare	ternary	throned	tollman	tractor	tripery
subvert	sustain	tachism	tartish	ternate	through	toluene	tradein	triplet
subzero	sutural	tachist	tartlet	terpene	thrower	tombola	trading	triplex
succade	sutured	tacitly	Tartufe	terrace	throwin	tombolo	traduce	tripody
succeed	swabbed	tacking	tastily	terrain	thrummy	tomenta	traffic	tripoli
success	swabber	tackler	tatters	terrene	thudded	tomfool	tragedy	tripped
succory	swaddle	tactful	tattery	terrier	thuggee	tompion	trailer	tripper
succour	swagged	tactics	tattily	terrify	thulium	tonally	trainee	trippet
succuba	swagger	tactile	tatting	terrine	thummim	tonemic	trainer	tripple
succubi	swagman	taction	tattler	tersely	thumper	tonerow	traipse	trireme
succumb	Swahili	tactual	taunter	tertial	thunder	tonight	traitor	trisect
sucking	swallow	tadpole	taurine	tertian	thymine	tonnage	traject	trishaw
suckler	swanker	taeniae	taxable	tessera	thyroid	tonneau	tramcar	trismus
sucrose	swanned	taffeta	taxfree	testacy	thyrsus	tonsure	trammel	tritely
suction	swapped	Tagalog	taxicab	testate	thyself	tontine	trample	tritium
sudaria	swapper	tagetes	taxiing	testban	Tibetan	toolbox	tramway	tritone
suffice	swarded	tagging	taximan	testbed	ticking	tooling	tranche	triumph
Suffolk	swarmer	tailend	taxless	testfly	tickler	toothed	trangam	trivial
suffuse	swarthy	tailing	taxying	testify	tidally	tootsie	transit	trivium
suggest	swasher	takeoff	teacake	testily	tiddler	topcoat	transom	trochal
suicide	swatted	takings	teacher	testoon	tiddley	topfull	tranter	trochee
suiting	swatter	talaria	teachin	testudo	tiderip	tophole	trapeze	trochus
sulcate	swearer	talayot	teacosy	tetanic	tideway	topiary	trapped	trodden
sulkily	sweater	talcose	teagown	tetanus	tidings	topical	trapper	troller
sullage	Swedish	talcous	tealeaf	tetrode	tieback	topknot	travail	trolley
sulphur	sweeper	talipes	tearful	textile	tiebeam	topless	travois	trollop
sultana	sweeten	talipot	teargas	textual	tiercel	topmast	trawler	trommel
summand	sweetie	talking	tearing	texture	tiercet	topmost	trayful	trooper
summary	sweetly	tallage	tearoom	thalami	tiffany	toponym	treacle	trophic
summery	swelter	tallboy	tearose	thallic	tighten	topping	treacly	tropics
summing	swiftly	tallish	teashop	thallus	tightly	topsail	treader	tropism
summons	swigged	tallith	teatime	thalweg	tigress	topside	treadle	trotted
sumpter	swiller	tallowy	teatray	thanage	tigrish	topsoil	treason	trotter
sunbath	swimmer	tallyho	technic	thankee	tilbury	torchon	treater	trouble
sunbeam	swindle	taloned	tectrix	thanker	tillage	torgoch	treetop	trounce
sunbear	swinery	tamable	tedding	theatre	timbale	torment	trefoil	trouper
sunbird	swinger	tamarin	tedious	thecate	timbrel	tormina	trehala	trouser
sunburn	swingle	tamasha	teeming	themata	timelag	tornado	trekked	truancy
sundeck	swinish	tambour	teenage	theorbo	timeous	torpedo	trekker	trucial
sundial	swipple	Tammany	tegmina	theorem	timidly	torpids	trellis	trucker
sundisc	swither	tamping	tegular	therapy	timothy	torrefy	tremble	truckle
sundown	Switzer	tampion	tektite	thereat	timpani	torrent	trembly	trudgen
sunfish	swizzle	tanager	telamon	thereby	timpano	torsade	tremolo	truffle
sunlamp	swobbed	tanagra	teleost	therein	tinamou	torsion	trenail	trumeau
sunless	swollen	tanbark	telergy	thereof	tindery	tortile	trental	trumpet
sunnily	swopped	tandoor	telling	thereon	tinfoil	tortrix	trepang	truncal
sunning	swopper	tangelo	telpher	thereto	tingler	torture	tressed	trundle
Sunnite	swotted	tangent	Telstar	theriac	tinhorn	torulae	tressel	trusser
sunrise	syconia	tanghin	tempera	thermae	tinnily	Toryism	trestle	trustee
sunroof	sycosis	tangram	tempest	thermal	tinning	tosspot	triable	truster
sunspot	syenite	tankage	Templar	thermic	tintack	totally	triacid	trypsin
sunstar	syllabi	tankard	templet	theurgy	tinware	totemic	triadic	tryptic
sunsuit	sylphid	tankcar	tempter	thiamin	tipcart	tottery	tribade	trysail
suntrap	sylvine	tankful	tempura	thicken	tipping	totting	triblet	tsardom
sunward	sylvite	tannage	tenable	thicket	tippler	touched	tribune	tsarina
sunwise	symptom	tannate	tenably	thickly	tipsify	toucher	tribute	tsarism

tsarist	tympano	unideal	uranism	Veddoid	vintage	Walloon	welloff	willowy
Tsquare	tympany	unifier	uranium	vedette	vintner	wallrue	wellset	windage
tsunami	Tynwald	uniform	uranous	vegetal	violate	waltzer	welsher	windbag
tuatara	typebar	unitary	urethan	vehicle	violent	wanigan	wencher	windegg
tubbing	typeset	unitive	urethra	veiling	violist	wanness	Wendish	windily
tubbish	typhoid	unjoint	urgency	veining	violone	wannish	wergild	winding
tubular	typhoon	unkempt	urinary	veinlet	virelay	wanting	werwolf	windrow
tuckbox	typhous	unknown	urodele	velamen	virgate	waratah	western	Windsor
Tuesday	typical	unladen	urology	velaria	virgule	warbler	westing	winesap
tugboat	typonym	unlatch	useless	veliger	virtual	warfare	wetback	winglet
tugging	tyranny	unlearn	usually	velours	visaged	wargame	wetness	wingnut
tuition	tzigane	unleash	usurper	veloute	viscera	warhead	wettest	winkers
tulchan	tzigany	unlined	utensil	velvety	viscose	warison	wetting	winning
tumbler	uberous	unloose	uterine	venally	viscous	warlike	wettish	winnock
tumbrel	udaller	unlucky	utilise	venatic	visible	warlock	whacker	winsome
tumbril	ukelele	unmanly	utility	vendace	visibly	warlord	whaling	wintery
tumidly	ukulele	unmeant	utopian	venefic	visitor	warmish	whangee	wireman
tumular	ulcered	unmixed	utopism	venerer	visored	warning	wharves	wiretap
tumulus	ululant	unmoral	utopist	venison	vistaed	warpath	whatnot	wishful
tunable	ululate	unmoved	utricle	ventage	vitally	warrant	wheaten	wishing
tunably	umbonal	unnerve	utterer	ventail	vitamin	warring	wheedle	wistful
tundish	umbones	unpaged	utterly	ventral	vitelli	warrior	wheeled	withers
tuneful	umbrage	unquiet	uveitis	venture	vitiate	warship	wheeler	without
tunicle	Umbrian	unquote	uxorial	venturi	vitrify	warthog	whereas	witless
tunning	umpteen	unravel	vacancy	veranda	vitrine	wartime	whereat	witling
turbary	unaptly	unready	vaccine	verbena	vitriol	washing	whereby	witloof
turbine	unarmed	unright	vacuity	verbose	vittate	washout	wherein	witness
turdine	unasked	unroost	vacuole	verdant	vittles	washpot	whereof	wittily
turdoid	unaware	unsaved	vacuous	verdict	vitular	washtub	whereon	witting
turfite	unbated	unscrew	vagally	verdure	vivaria	waspish	whereto	wizened
turfman	unblest	unsexed	vagrant	verglas	vividly	wassail	whether	wobbler
turgent	unblock	unshell	vaguely	veriest	vivific	wastage	whetted	wolfcub
Turkish	unbosom	unsight	vaguish	verismo	vixenly	wastrel	whetter	wolfdog
turmoil	unbound	unsnarl	Vaishya	vermeil	vocable	watcher	wheyish	wolfish
turnery	unbowed	unsound	valance	vermian	vocalic	watered	whicker	wolfram
turning	unboxed	unstick	valence	vernier	vocally	waterer	whidder	wolvish
turnipy	unbrace	unstuck	valency	verruca	voguish	wattage	whiffle	womanly
turnkey	unbuild	unswear	valeric	versant	voivode	Watteau	whimper	woodcut
turnout	unbuilt	unswore	valiant	versify	volante	wattled	whimsey	woodman
turpeth	uncanny	unsworn	validly	versine	volcano	wattles	whinger	woodpie
tushery	unchain	unteach	vallate	version	voltage	wavelet	whipped	woolfat
tussive	uncinus	unthink	valonia	vertigo	voltaic	waverer	whipper	woolled
tussock	uncivil	untried	valuate	vervain	voluble	waxbill	whippet	woollen
tussore	unclasp	untruly	valvate	vesicae	volubly	waxtree	whipsaw	wooloil
tutelar	unclean	untruss	valvula	vesical	volumed	waxwing	whirler	woolsey
tutenag	uncloak	untruth	valvule	vesicle	voluted	waxwork	whirred	woomera
tutting	unclose	untuned	vamoose	vespers	volutin	waybill	whisker	woozily
tutwork	uncouth	untwine	vampire	vespine	votable	waylaid	whiskey	wordage
twaddle	uncover	untwist	vampish	vestige	vouchee	wayless	whisper	wordily
twaddly	uncross	untying	vanadic	vestral	voucher	waymark	whistle	wording
twangle	uncrown	unusual	Vandyke	vesture	vowelly	wayside	whitely	workbag
twankay	unction	unweave	vanessa	veteran	voyager	wayward	whither	workbox
tweeter	underdo	unwound	vanilla	vetiver	vulgate	wayworn	whiting	workday
tweezer	undergo	unwoven	vantage	vetting	vulpine	weakish	whitish	working
twelfth	undoing	upbraid	vanward	vexedly	vulture	wealden	whitlow	workman
twelves	undress	upfield	vapidly	vexilla	wadable	wealthy	Whitsun	workout
twibill	undying	upgrade	vapours	viaduct	wadding	wearily	whittle	worldly
twiddle	unearth	upheave	vapoury	viatica	waddler	wearing	whizkid	wornout
twiddly	unequal	upraise	vaquero	vibrant	waftage	weasand	whizzed	worrier
twigged	unfaith	upright	variant	vibrate	wafture	weather	whoever	worship
twilled	unfitly	upriser	variate	vibrato	wagerer	webbing	whoopee	worsted
twinkle	unfrock	upsides	varices	viceroy	waggery	webfoot	whooper	wottest
twinkly	unfroze	upsilon	variety	vicinal	wagging	webster	whopper	wouldbe
twinned	unfunny	upstage	variola	vicious	waggish	webworm	whorish	wouldst
twister	unfussy	upstair	variole	victory	wagoner	wedding	whorled	wrangle
twitchy	ungodly	upstart	various	victual	wagtail	wedging	whoseso	wrapped
twitted	unguard	upsurge	varment	vidette	Wahabee	wedlock	wickiup	wrapper
twitter	unguent	upsweep	varmint	vidimus	wailful	weekday	widgeon	wreathe
twofold	ungulae	upswept	varnish	viduity	waisted	weekend	widowed	wreathy
twoline	unhandy	upswing	varsity	viewing	waister	weevily	widower	wrecker
twoness	unhappy	upthrew	vascula	vilayet	waiting	weigher	wielder	wrestle
twosome	unheard	upthrow	vastity	village	wakeful	weighin	wigging	wriggle
twostep	unhinge	uptight	Vatican	villain	wakener	weighty	wiggler	wriggly
twotime	unhitch	uptrend	vatting	villein	walking	weirdie	wigless	wringer
twotone	unhoped	upwards	Vaudois	villose	walkout	weirdly	wildcat	wrinkle
tychism	unhorse	uraemia	vaulted	villous	walkway	welcher	wilding	wrinkly
tylopod	unhouse	Uralian	vaulter	vinasse	wallaby	welcome	wildish	writeup
tympana	unicity	uralite	vaunter	vincula	walleye	welfare	willies	writhen
tympani	unicorn	uranide	Vedanta	vinegar	walling	wellies	willing	writing

```
written Baalism barytic callous caravel catspaw eastern fatness gaudery
wrongly babassu bascule calomel caraway catsuit easting fattest gaudily
wrought babbitt baseman caloric carbide cattalo eatable fatting Gaulish
wrybill babbler basenji calorie carbine cattery Faberge fattish gauntly
wryneck babyish bashful calotte carcase cattily fabliau fatuity gauntry
wryness babysit basidia caloyer carcass catwalk fabular fatuous gavotte
wychelm baccara basilar calpack cardiac caudate faceoff faucial gawkily
xanthic baccate basinet caltrap cardoon caulker faceted faunist gayness
xanthin bacchic bassist caltrop careful caustic faction fauvism gazelle
xiphoid bacilli bassoon calumet caribou cautery factory fauvist gazette
Yahvist backing bastard calumny carinae caution factual gabbing habitat
Yahwist backlog basting calvary carinal cavally facture gabbler habitue
yapping backsaw bastion calyces carinas cavalry faculae gabelle hachure
yardage backset bateaux calycle carioca caveman faculty gabfest hackbut
yardang baddish bathing calypso cariole cavetti faddish gabnash hackery
yardarm badmash bathtub calyxes carious cavetto faddism gadding hacking
yardman badness batiste camaron carking caviare faddist gadgety hackler
yashmak baffler batsman cambial carline cayenne fadedly gadroon hackney
yatagan bagasse battels cambist Carlism caymans fadeout gadwall hacksaw
ycleped baggage battery cambium Carlist dabbing fagging gagging haddock
yeggman baggily batting cambrel carload dabbler fagotto gagster hafnium
yellowy bagging Bauhaus cambric carmine dacoity faience gahnite hagfish
yenning bagpipe bauxite camelot carnage Dadaism failing gainful Haggada
yestern Bahadur bawcock camelry caroche Dadaist failure gainsay haggard
yewtree Bahaism bawdily cameral carotid dallier faintly Galahad haggish
Yiddish Bahaist bayonet camorra carotin damming fairing galanga haggler
yielder Bahaite bazooka campbed carouse damnify fairish galatea hagweed
yipping bailiff cabaret camphor carping damning fairway galeate haircut
yoghurt baklava cabbage camping carport damosel Falange galenic hairnet
yolksac balance cabbagy campion carrack damozel falbala galilee hairpin
Yorkist balcony cabbala camwood carrier dampish falcate galipot Halakah
younger balding cabinet canakin carrion dandify falcula gallant halberd
younker baldish cabling canasta carroty Danelaw fallacy gallate halbert
yttrium baldric caboose candela carryon dangler fallguy galleon halcyon
yulelog baleful cabrank candent carsick danseur falling gallery halfway
zapping ballade cacanny candied cartage Dantean falloff gallfly halfwit
zaptieh ballast cachexy candour cartful dapsone fallout gallice halibut
zealous ballboy cacique canikin cartoon darbies falsely galling halidom
zebrine balloon cackler cannery carving dariole falsies galliot hallali
zebroid balmily cacodyl cannily cascade darkish falsify gallium hallway
zedoary baloney cacoepy canning cascara darling falsity gallnut halogen
zemstvo bambini cacumen cannula caseous darning famulus galloon halting
zeolite bambino cadaver canonic caserne darshan fanatic gallows halvers
zestful banally caddice canonry cashier dashiki fancier galumph halyard
zetetic bananas caddish Canopic cassata dashing fancily gambade Hamburg
ziganka bandage cadence cantata cassava dashpot fanclub gambado Hamitic
zillion bandana cadency cantate cassino dastard fanfare gambier hamming
zincify bandbox cadenza canteen cassock dasyure fanfold gambler hammock
zincing bandeau Cadmean canthus castile datable fanmail gamboge hamster
zincite bandore cadmium cantina casting datival fanning gambrel hamulus
zincked bandsaw caducei canting castled dauphin fantail gamebag handbag
Zingari baneful caesium cantrip castoff dawdler fantasm gamelan handcar
Zingaro banjoes caesura canvass casuals dawning fantast gametic handful
zinkify banking cagoule canzone casuist daybook fantasy ganglia handgun
zinking banksia cahoots canzoni Catalan daylong fantods gangrel handily
Zionism banning caimans capable catalos dayroom faraday gangway handler
Zionist bannock caisson capably catalpa daystar faradic gantlet handoff
zipcode banquet caitiff capelin catarrh daytime faraway garbage handout
zipping banshee cajoler caperer catawba daywork farceur garbler handsaw
zithern banteng calamus capital catbird dazedly farcing garboil handsel
zoarium banting calando capitol catboat dazzler fargone gardant handset
Zoilism baptise calcify caporal catcall eagerly farming garfish hangdog
Zoilist baptism calcine caprice catcher earache farmost garland hanging
zonated baptist calcite caprine catchup eardrum Faroese garment hangman
zoogamy barbate calcium caproic catechu eardrop farrago garnish hangout
zoogeny barbell calculi caprock catenae earflap farrier garotte Hansard
zoogony barbule caldera Capsian catenas earhole farruca garpike hanuman
zooidal bargain caldron capsize cateran earldom farther gascoal hapence
zoology barilla calends capstan caterer earlobe fascial gaseous hapenny
zoonomy barline calibre capsule catfish earlock fascine gasfire hapless
zootaxy barmaid calices captain Cathari earmark Fascism gasmask haploid
zootomy baronet caliche caption Cathars earmuff Fascist gasring haporth
zygosis baroque calicle captive cathead earnest fashion gassing happily
zygotic barrack calipee capture cathode earplug fastday gastric happing
zymogen barrage caliper capuche cathood earring fatally gateaux harbour
zymosis barrier callant caracal catlike earshot fateful gateleg hardhit
zymotic barring callbox caracul catling earthen fathead gateway hardpan
zymurgy barroom callboy caramel catmint earthly fatigue gathers hardset
─────── barytes calling caravan catseye easeful fatling gatling hardtop
```

harelip	kalpack	latices	Maltese	marring	nastily	panties	payroll	rawness
haricot	kampong	latrine	malting	marrowy	nattily	pantile	paysage	rayless
harijan	Kannada	lattice	maltose	Marsala	natural	papadam	rabbity	Sabaism
harmala	Kantian	Latvian	mamelon	marshal	naughty	papally	rabbler	Sabaoth
harmful	Karaite	laugher	mamilla	martial	nauplii	paperer	rabidly	Sabbath
harmony	karakul	launder	mammary	Martian	nautics	Paphian	raccoon	saccade
harness	karting	laundry	mammate	martini	nautili	papilla	racemic	saccate
harpist	kathode	laurels	mammock	martlet	navarin	papoose	rackety	saccule
harpoon	katydid	lavolta	mammoth	martyry	Naziism	pappose	racquet	sacculi
harrier	labarum	lavrock	manacle	Marxian	oakfern	paprika	radiant	sackbut
harshen	labella	lawhand	manager	Marxism	oakgall	papulae	radiate	sackful
harshly	labiate	lawless	manakin	Marxist	oakling	papular	radical	sacking
harslet	lacking	lawlist	manatee	marybud	oaktree	papyrus	radices	sacring
harvest	laconic	lawlord	manchet	mascara	oakwood	parable	radicle	sacrist
hasbeen	lacquer	lawsuit	mandala	mashtub	oarfish	parader	radulae	saddest
hashish	lactate	laxness	mandate	Masonic	oarless	parados	radular	saddish
hassock	lacteal	layered	mandola	masonry	oarlock	paradox	raffish	saddler
hastate	lactose	layette	mandora	Masorah	oarsman	paragon	ragbolt	sadness
hastily	lacunae	lazaret	mandrel	masquer	oarweed	parapet	ragdoll	saffron
hatable	lacunal	macabre	mandril	massage	oatcake	parasol	ragged y	sagging
hatband	lacunar	macadam	mangily	masseur	oatmeal	parboil	ragging	sagitta
hatcher	lacunas	macaque	mangoes	massive	pabulum	pardner	ragtime	saguaro
hatchet	ladanum	machair	mangold	mastaba	pachisi	parerga	ragweed	saidest
hateful	ladybug	machete	manhole	mastery	pacific	paresis	ragworm	sailing
hatless	ladykin	machine	manhood	mastich	package	paretic	ragwort	sainted
hatting	laggard	macrame	manhour	mastich	packice	parfait	railcar	saintly
hauberk	lagging	macrami	manhunt	mastiff	packing	pargana	railing	sakeret
haughty	laicise	maculae	manihot	mastoid	packman	parkway	railman	Saktism
haulage	laicism	macular	manikin	matador	padding	parlour	railway	salable
haulier	lairage	maddest	manilla	matchet	paddler	parlous	raiment	salicet
haunted	lakelet	madding	manille	matelot	paddock	parodic	rainbow	salicin
haunter	Lallans	Madeira	maniple	matinal	padlock	parolee	Rajpoot	salient
hautboy	Lamaism	madness	manitou	matinee	padrone	paronym	rakeoff	Salique
hauteur	Lamaist	madonna	manjack	matrass	padroni	parotid	rallier	sallowy
havenot	lambast	madrona	mankind	mattery	paeonia	parpend	ralline	salpinx
hawkish	lambent	madrono	manless	matting	pageant	parquet	Ramadan	salsify
haycock	lambert	madwort	manlike	mattins	pageboy	parsley	rambler	saltant
hayfork	lambkin	maestri	manmade	mattock	paginal	parsnip	ramekin	saltbox
hayloft	lamella	maestro	manners	mattoid	pahlavi	partake	ramenta	saltcat
hayrick	laminae	maffick	manning	matzoth	pailful	partial	ramming	saltern
hayseed	laminar	mafiosi	mannish	maudlin	painful	parting	rampage	salting
hayward	lamming	mafioso	mannite	maunder	painter	partita	rampant	saltire
haywire	lampion	magenta	mannose	mauther	pairoar	partite	rampart	saltish
jabbing	lampoon	maggoty	mansard	mawkish	paisley	partlet	rampion	saltpan
jacamar	lamprey	magical	mansion	mawworm	pajamas	partner	ramsons	saluter
jacinth	lancers	magmata	mansize	maxilla	paladin	partook	rancher	salvage
jackass	landing	magnate	manteau	maximal	palatal	parvenu	rancour	salvoes
jackdaw	languet	magneto	mantlet	maximum	palaver	parvise	ranking	sambuca
jackpot	languid	magnify	mantram	maxwell	palette	paschal	ransack	samisen
jacktar	languor	mahaleb	mantrap	mayoral	palette	passade	rapeoil	samovar
Jacobin	laniary	mahatma	manumit	maypole	palfrey	passado	raphide	Samoyed
jacobus	lankily	Mahdism	manward	Maytime	palings	passage	rapidly	sampler
jaconet	lanolin	Mahdist	manweek	mayweed	pallium	passant	rapping	samurai
jadedly	lantana	mahjong	Manxcat	mazurka	palmary	passing	rapport	sanctum
jadeite	lantern	mahonia	Manxman	mazzard	palmate	passion	rapture	Sanctus
jaggery	lanyard	mahound	manyear	nabbing	palmist	passive	rarebit	sandbag
Jainism	Laotian	mahseer	mapping	nacarat	palmoil	passkey	raschel	sandbar
jaloppy	lapilli	maidish	marabou	nacelle	palmyra	pastern	rasping	sandbed
jamming	lapping	maidism	Maratha	nacrous	palpate	pasteup	ratable	sandbox
Janeite	Laputan	mailbag	Marathi	nagging	palsied	pastime	ratafia	sandboy
jangler	lapwing	mailbox	marbled	Nahuatl	paludal	pasture	ratatat	sanders
janitor	larceny	mailing	marbles	naiades	pampean	patagia	ratchet	sandfly
jannock	lardoon	maillot	marcher	nailery	pampero	patella	rations	sandlot
January	largely	mailman	marconi	naively	panacea	patency	ratlike	sandman
japonic	largess	mailvan	maremma	naivete	panache	pathway	ratling	sandpit
jargoon	largish	maintop	margent	naivety	pancake	patient	rattail	sangria
jarring	lasagna	majesty	marimba	nakedly	Pandean	patrial	ratteen	sanicle
jasmine	lasagne	makings	mariner	namable	pandect	patriot	rattery	santour
javelin	lashing	malacca	marital	nameday	pandora	patroon	ratting	sapajou
jawbone	lashkar	malaise	markhor	nankeen	pandore	pattern	rattler	saphead
jaybird	lassoes	malaria	marking	naphtha	panicky	patting	rattrap	sapient
jaywalk	lasting	Malayan	marline	napless	panicle	paucity	raucous	sapless
jazzily	latakia	malefic	marlite	napping	Panjabi	Pauline	raunchy	sapling
jazzman	latchet	malines	marmite	narrate	pannage	paunchy	ravager	saponin
kabbala	latency	malison	marplot	narrows	pannier	paviour	ravelin	sapphic
Kaddish	lateral	mallard	marquee	narthex	panning	payable	ravined	sapping
kainite	latexes	malleus	marquis	narwhal	panocha	paydesk	ravings	saprobe
kalends	lathery	malmsey	Marrano	nasally	panoply	payload	ravioli	sapsago
Kalmuck	lathing	maltase	married	nascent	panther	payment	rawhide	sapwood

Saracen	talcose	vacuous	wannish	ablator	acinous	scandal	scrunch	beanbag
sarangi	talcous	vagally	wanting	abolish	ackemma	scanned	scruple	bearded
sarcasm	talipes	vagrant	waratah	abomasa	acolyte	scanner	scudded	bearing
sarcode	talipot	vaguely	warbler	aborter	aconite	scantly	scuffle	bearish
sarcoid	talking	vaguish	warfare	abought	acouchy	scapple	sculler	beastly
sarcoma	tallage	Vaishya	wargame	aboulia	acquest	scapula	sculpin	beatify
sarcous	tallboy	valance	warhead	abrader	acquire	scarfed	scumble	beating
sardine	tallish	valence	warison	abreact	acrasin	scarify	scummed	beatnik
sardius	tallith	valency	warlike	abreast	acreage	scarlet	scunner	because
sarking	tallowy	valeric	warlock	abridge	acridly	scarper	scupper	becloud
sashimi	tallyho	valiant	warlord	abroach	acrobat	scarred	scurril	bedding
sassaby	taloned	validly	warmish	abscess	acrogen	scarves	scutage	bedevil
satanic	tamable	vallate	warning	abscise	acronym	scatted	scutate	bedfast
satchel	tamarin	valonia	warpath	abscond	acroter	scatter	scutter	bedight
satiate	tamasha	valuate	warrant	absence	acrylic	scauper	scuttle	bedizen
satiety	tambour	valvate	warring	absinth	actinia	scenery	ycleped	bedouin
satinet	Tammany	valvula	warrior	absolve	actinic	scented	adamant	bedpost
satiric	tamping	valvule	warship	abstain	actinon	scepsis	Adamite	bedrock
satisfy	tampion	vamoose	warthog	abubble	actress	sceptic	adapter	bedroll
satrapy	tanager	vampire	wartime	abusive	actuary	sceptre	adaptor	bedroom
satsuma	tanagra	vampish	washing	abutted	actuate	schappe	adaxial	bedside
satyral	tanbark	vanadic	washout	abutter	acutely	schemer	addable	bedsock
satyric	tandoor	Vandyke	washpot	abysmal	acyclic	scherzi	addenda	bedsore
satyrid	tangelo	vanessa	washtub	abyssal	eccrine	scherzo	addible	bedtime
saucily	tangent	vanilla	waspish	ebbtide	ecdyses	schlepp	address	beechen
saunter	tanghin	vantage	wassail	ebonise	ecdysis	schlock	adducer	beehive
saurian	tangram	vanward	wastage	ebonite	echelon	schmuck	adenine	beeline
sauroid	tankage	vapidly	wastrel	ebriate	echidna	schnook	adenoid	beeswax
sausage	tankard	vapours	watcher	ebriety	echinus	scholar	adenoma	beggary
savable	tankcar	vapoury	watered	Iberian	echoism	scholia	adeptly	begging
savanna	tankful	vaquero	waterer	obconic	eclipse	sciarid	adherer	begonia
saveall	tannage	variant	wattage	obelise	eclogue	sciatic	adhibit	begorra
saveloy	tannate	variate	Watteau	obelisk	ecology	science	adipose	begrime
savings	tannery	varices	wattled	obesity	economy	scirrhi	adjoint	beguile
saviour	tanning	variety	wattles	obitual	ecstasy	scissel	adjourn	beguine
savoury	tannish	variola	wavelet	obligee	ectopic	scissor	adjudge	behaver
sawbill	tanooze	variole	waverer	obligor	iceberg	scleral	adjunct	behoove
sawbuck	tantara	various	waxbill	oblique	iceboat	scoffer	admiral	beignet
sawdust	tantivy	varment	waxtree	obloquy	icecold	scolder	admirer	bejewel
sawfish	tantric	varmint	waxwing	obolary	icefall	scollop	adnexal	beknown
sawgate	tantrum	varnish	waxwork	obovate	icefloe	scomber	adopter	belated
sawmill	tanyard	varsity	waybill	obovoid	icefoot	scooper	adrenal	belcher
sawnoff	taperer	vascula	waylaid	obscene	icepack	scooter	adulate	beldame
sawwort	tapetal	vastity	wayless	obscure	icerink	scopula	adultly	Belgian
saxhorn	tapetum	Vatican	waymark	observe	iceshow	scoriae	advance	believe
saxtuba	tapioca	vatting	wayside	obtrude	ichabod	scorify	adverse	bellboy
sayable	tapping	Vaudois	wayward	obverse	iciness	scoring	advised	bellhop
tabanid	taproom	vaulted	wayworn	obviate	icteric	scorner	adviser	belljar
tabaret	taproot	vaulter	xanthic	obvious	icterus	scorper	advisor	bellman
tabasco	tapsman	vaunter	xanthin	uberous	ocarina	Scorpio	edacity	bellows
tabbing	tapster	wadable	Yahweh	academe	occiput	scotice	edaphic	beloved
tabetic	tarbush	wadding	Yahwist	academy	occlude	Scotism	edictal	Beltane
tabinet	tardily	waddler	yapping	Acadian	oceanic	Scotist	edifice	belting
tableau	tarnish	waftage	yardage	acantha	ocellar	scotoma	edition	belying
tabloid	tarrier	wafture	yardang	acarian	ocellus	Scottie	educate	bencher
taborer	tarring	wagerer	yardarm	accidie	ochrous	scourer	eductor	beneath
tabular	tartare	waggery	yardman	acclaim	octagon	scourge	ideally	benefic
tachism	tartish	wagging	yashmak	account	octaval	scouter	identic	benefit
tachist	tartlet	waggish	yatagan	accrete	octette	scraggy	idiotic	Benelux
tacitly	Tartufe	wagoner	zapping	accrual	October	scranny	idlesse	Bengali
tacking	tastily	wagtail	zaptieh	accurst	octopod	scraper	idolise	benison
tackler	tatters	Wahabee	abaddon	accusal	octopus	scrapie	idyllic	benthic
tactful	tattery	wailful	abalone	accused	octuple	scrappy	odalisk	benthos
tactics	tattily	waisted	abandon	accuser	oculate	scratch	oddball	benzene
tactile	tatting	waister	abashed	acequia	oculist	scrawly	oddment	benzine
taction	tattler	waiting	abattis	acerbic	scabbed	scrawny	oddness	benzoic
tactual	taunter	wakeful	abaxial	acerola	scabble	screech	odontic	benzoin
tadpole	taurine	wakener	Abbasid	acerose	scabies	screeve	odorant	benzole
taeniae	taxable	walking	abdomen	acetate	scabrid	screwed	odorous	benzoyl
taffeta	taxfree	walkout	Abelian	acetify	scaglia	screwer	odoured	bepaint
Tagalog	taxicab	walkway	abetted	acetone	scalade	scribal	odyssey	bequest
tagetes	taxiing	wallaby	abetter	acetous	scalado	scriber	udaller	bereave
tagging	taximan	walleye	abettor	Achaean	scalder	scrieve	aeolian	bergylt
tailend	taxless	walling	abeyant	Achaian	scaldic	scrimpy	aeonian	berhyme
tailing	taxying	Walloon	abiding	Achates	scalene	scrooge	aerator	berline
takeoff	vacancy	wallrue	abigail	achieve	scallop	scrouge	aerobic	berried
takings	vaccine	waltzer	ability	acicula	scalpel	scrubby	aerosol	berserk
talaria	vacuity	wanigan	abiotic	acidify	scalper	scruffy	beading	beseech
talayot	vacuole	wanness	abjurer	acidity	scamper	scrumpy	beamish	beshrew

```
besides declare despair fetidly helicon leaning meiosis netfish peptalk
besiege declass despise fetlock hellbox learned meiotic netlike peptide
besmear decline despite fetters hellcat learner Meissen netsuke peptise
bespeak decoder despoil feudist Hellene leather melange netting peptone
bespoke decorum despond fewness hellion lechery melanic network percale
bestead decrier dessert feyness hellish lectern melanin neurine percent
bestial decrypt destine gearbox helluva lection melilot neuroma percept
bestrew decuman destiny gearing helotry lecture melisma neurone percher
betaken decuple destroy geckoes helpful leeward melodic neuston percine
bethink deepfry deterge geebung helping leftism melting neutral percoid
betimes deepsea detinue Gehenna hemiola leftist memento neutron percuss
betoken default detract gelatin hemione legally memoirs newborn perdure
betroth defence detrain gelding hemline legatee mending newcome perfect
betting defiant detrude gelidly hemlock legator menfolk newlaid perfidy
between deficit deutzia gelling hemming legbail menisci newmown perform
betwixt defiler devalue gemmate henbane legging menorah newness perfume
bewitch definer develop gemmery hencoop leghorn menthol newsboy perfuse
bezique deflate deviant gemming hennery legible mention newsman pergola
cedilla deflect deviate gemmule henpeck legibly mercery oedipal perhaps
ceilidh defocus devilry gemsbok heparin legiron merchet oenomel periapt
ceiling deforce devious general hepatic legless mercury oersted peridot
celadon defraud devisal generic heptane legpull mermaid oestral perigee
celesta defrock devisee geneses herbage legrest merrily oestrum perique
celeste defrost deviser genesis heretic legroom meseems oestrus periwig
cellist defunct devisor genetic heritor legshow mesonic peacock perjure
cellule degauss devolve genette herniae legwork message peafowl perjury
Celsius degrade devoted Genevan hernial leister messiah pearled perkily
cembalo dehisce devotee genista hernias leisure Messias pearler perlite
cenacle deicide dewclaw genitor heroics lemmata messily peartly Permian
censure deictic dewdrop genizah heroine lemming messtin peasant permute
centaur deiform dewfall genning heroise lending mestiza peascod perpend
centavo deistic dewpond Genoese heroism lengthy mestizo peasoup perpent
centime delaine dextral genteel heroize lenient metamer pebrine perplex
centner delator dextran gentian heronry lentigo metayer peccant Persian
central delayer dextrin gentile herring lentisk metazoa peccary persist
centred delight eelpout genuine herself lentoid methane peckish persona
centric Delilah eelworm geodesy hessian leonine metonym peddler pertain
centrum delimit fearful geogony hetaera leopard metopic pedicab perturb
century deliver feaster geoidal hetaira leotard metopon pedicel pertuse
cepheid delouse feather geology hexadic leprosy metrics pedicle perusal
ceramic Delphic feature Geordie hexagon leprous metrist pedlary peruser
cerebra deltaic febrile georgic hexapla lesbian mettled peerage pervade
ceresin deltoid fedayee gerbera hexapod letdown Mexican peeress pervert
certain deluder federal germane heyduck lethean mezuzah peevish pessary
certify demerit feeding gestalt jealous letters nearest Pegasus petasus
cerumen demesne feedlot gestapo jejunum letting nebbish pegging petiole
cervine demigod feeling gestate jellaba Lettish nebulae pelagic petrify
cession demirep feigner gesture jellied lettuce nebular pelican Petrine
cesspit demoded felonry getaway jemadar leucine nebulas pelisse petrous
cestode demonic felsite getting jerkily leucite necklet peloria pettily
cestoid demotic felspar headily jetting leucoma necktie peloric petting
deadend demount felting heading jewelry levator necrose pelorus pettish
deadeye denarii felucca headman jewfish levelly nectary peltate petunia
deadpan denizen felwort headpin Jezebel leveret needful pelting reacher
deafaid densely feminal headset keelson lexical needler pemican reactor
dealing density fencing headway keeping lexicon neglect penally readily
deanery dentate fenfire healthy kenning meadowy neglige penalty reading
deathly dentine fenland hearing kenosis mealies Negress penance readout
debacle dentist fennecs hearken kenotic meander Negrito pendant reagent
debater denture feoffee hearsay kentish meaning negroid pendent realgar
debauch deodand feoffer hearted keramic measles neither pending realign
debouch deodara feoffor hearten keratin measure nelumbo penguin realise
Debrett deplane fermata heathen kermess meatfly nemesia penname realism
debrief deplete ferment heather kerogen meatman nemesis pennant realist
decadal deplume fermion heating kerygma Mechlin Neogaea pennate reality
decagon deposal fermium heavily kestrel meconic neolith pennies reallot
decanal deposer fernery hebenon ketchup meddler neology pennill realtor
decapod deposit fernowl Hebraic keyhole mediacy neonate pennine rebirth
decease deprave ferrate heckler keyless mediads neoteny penning reboant
deceive depress ferrety hectare keynote mediant neozoic pensile rebound
decency deprive ferrite hedonic keyring mediate nephric pension rebuild
deciare derange ferrous heedful keyword medical Neptune pensive rebuilt
decibel derider ferrugo heeltap leading medulla neritic pentane rebuker
decided derrick ferrule heftily leadoff medusae nervate pentode receipt
decider dervish fertile heighho leafage medusas nervine pentose receive
decidua descant fervent heinous leafbud meerkat nervous peonage recency
decimal descend fervour heiress leaflet meeting nervure peppery recital
decking descent festive helical leaguer megaron nesting peppill reciter
declaim deserve festoon helices leakage megaton netball pepping reclaim
```

reclame	remarry	retouch	seeable	teacosy	tetanic	weevily	egotism	chevron
recline	remblai	retrace	seedbed	teagown	tetanus	weigher	egotist	Chianti
recluse	remiges	retract	seedily	tealeaf	tetrode	weighin	egotrip	chiasma
recount	remnant	retrain	seedlip	tearful	textile	weighty	igneous	chibouk
recover	remodel	retread	seeming	teargas	textual	weirdie	igniter	chicane
recruit	remorse	retreat	seepage	tearing	texture	weirdly	ignoble	Chicano
rectify	remould	retrial	segment	tearoom	Vedanta	welcher	ignobly	chicken
rectory	remount	retsina	seismal	tearose	Veddoid	welcome	ignorer	chicory
rectrix	removal	rettery	seismic	teashop	vedette	welfare	oghamic	chidden
recurve	removed	retting	seizing	teatime	vegetal	wellies	ogreish	chiefly
recycle	remover	returns	seizure	teatray	vehicle	welloff	bheesty	chiffon
redcoat	reneger	reunion	selenic	technic	veiling	wellset	bheetie	chigger
reddest	renegue	reunite	selffed	tectrix	veining	welsher	Chablis	chignon
reddish	renewal	revalue	selfish	tedding	veinlet	wencher	chaffer	childer
redhead	renewer	revelry	sellout	tedious	velamen	Wendish	chagrin	childly
redlegs	rentier	revenge	seltzer	teeming	velaria	wergild	chalaza	chiliad
redneck	reorder	revenue	selvage	teenage	veliger	werwolf	Chaldee	chillum
redness	repaint	reverie	sematic	tegmina	velours	western	chalice	chimera
redoubt	repaper	reverse	semilog	tegular	veloute	westing	challis	chimere
redound	repiner	reversi	seminal	tektite	velvety	wetback	chalone	chimney
redpoll	repique	reviler	seminar	telamon	venally	wetness	chamber	chindit
redraft	replace	revisal	semiped	teleost	venatic	wettest	chamfer	Chinese
redress	replant	reviser	Semitic	telergy	vendace	wetting	chamois	Chinook
redskin	replete	revisit	senarii	telling	venefic	wettish	champac	chintzy
reducer	replevy	revival	senator	telpher	venerer	yeggman	champak	chinwag
redwing	replica	reviver	senatus	Telstar	venison	yellowy	chancel	chipped
redwood	replier	revivor	sendoff	tempera	ventage	yenning	chancre	chipper
reeding	reposal	revolve	senecio	tempest	ventail	yestern	changer	chirrup
reelect	reposit	revving	senhora	Templar	ventral	yewtree	channel	chitter
reenact	repress	rewound	senores	templet	venture	zealous	chanson	chlamys
reenter	reprint	rewrite	sensory	tempter	venturi	zebrine	chanter	chloral
reentry	reprise	rewrote	sensual	tempura	veranda	zebroid	chantry	chloric
referee	reproof	reynard	Senussi	tenable	verbena	zedoary	chaotic	chocice
refined	reprove	seabass	seppuku	tenably	verbose	zemstvo	chapati	Choctaw
refiner	reptile	seabear	septate	tenancy	verdant	zeolite	chaplet	cholera
reflate	repulse	seabird	septime	tendril	verdict	zestful	chapman	choline
reflect	reputed	seablue	sequela	tenfold	verdure	zetetic	chapped	chooser
refloat	request	seaboot	sequent	tenoner	verglas	afeared	chappie	choosey
refocus	requiem	seafish	sequoia	tenpins	veriest	affable	chapter	chopine
refract	require	seafood	Serbian	tensely	verismo	affably	charade	chopped
refrain	requite	seafowl	serfage	tensile	vermeil	affaire	charger	chopper
refresh	reredos	seagirt	serfdom	tension	vermian	affined	charily	chorale
refugee	rescale	seagull	seriate	tensity	vernier	afflict	chariot	chordal
refusal	rescind	seakale	sericin	tensive	verruca	affront	charism	chorine
refuser	rescuer	sealane	seriema	tentbed	versant	African	charity	chorion
refutal	reseaux	sealant	seringa	tentfly	versify	effects	charley	choroid
refuter	reserve	sealegs	serious	tenthly	versine	effendi	charlie	chortle
regalia	reshape	sealery	serpent	tentpeg	version	effulge	charmer	chowder
regally	residua	seamaid	serpigo	tenuity	vertigo	offbeat	charnel	chrisom
regards	residue	seamark	serpula	tenuous	vervain	offence	charpoy	christy
regatta	resolve	seapink	serrate	tepidly	vesicae	offhand	charqui	chromic
regency	resound	seaport	serried	tequila	vesical	officer	charred	chronic
regimen	respect	searoom	servant	terbium	vesicle	offload	charter	chuckle
reginal	respell	seasick	servery	terebra	vespers	offpeak	chassis	chuddah
regnant	respelt	seaside	Servian	tergite	vespine	offside	chasten	chuddar
regorge	respire	seaslug	service	termini	vestige	pfennig	chateau	chuffed
regrant	respite	seatang	servile	termite	vestral	chatted	chattel	chugged
regrate	respond	seating	serving	ternary	vesture	against	chattel	chukker
regress	respray	seawall	Servite	ternate	veteran	agamous	chatter	chummed
regrets	restart	seaward	sessile	terpene	vetiver	ageless	cheapen	chunnel
regroup	restate	seaware	session	terrace	vetting	agelong	cheaply	chunter
regular	restful	seaweed	sestina	terrain	vexedly	aggress	cheater	chupati
regulus	restiff	seawhip	setback	terrene	vexilla	agilely	checker	churchy
reheard	restive	seawife	setdown	terrier	weakish	agility	checkup	chutney
rehouse	restock	seawolf	setting	terrify	wealden	agitate	cheddar	chymous
reissue	restore	seceder	settler	terrine	wealthy	agitato	cheerer	gharial
rejoice	restyle	seclude	settlor	tersely	wearily	agnatic	cheerio	ghastly
relapse	resurge	seconde	setwall	tertial	wearing	agnomen	cheetah	gherkin
related	retable	secondi	seventh	tertian	weasand	agonise	chelate	ghettos
relater	retaken	secondo	seventy	tessera	weather	agonist	chemise	ghillie
relator	rethink	secrecy	several	testacy	webbing	agraffe	chemism	ghostly
relayed	retiary	secrete	sexfoil	testate	webfoot	aground	chemist	khaddar
release	reticle	sectary	sexless	testban	webster	agrapha	chequer	khamsin
reliant	retinae	sectile	Sextans	testbed	webworm	aground	cherish	khanate
relieve	retinal	section	sextant	testfly	wedding	egality	cheroot	khedive
relievo	retinas	secular	sextile	testify	wedging	eggcosy	chervil	phaeton
relight	retinol	securer	teacake	testily	wedlock	eggflip	chessel	phalanx
relique	retinue	sedilia	teacher	testoon	weekday	egghead	chested	phallic
remains	retired	seducer	teachin	testudo	weekend	egotise	cheviot	phallus

```
phantom  shicker  thereon  whirler  biology  digress  distort  firefly  hitting
pharaoh  shifter  thereto  whirred  biomass  dilated  disturb  fireman  Hittite
pharynx  shikari  theriac  whisker  bionics  dilator  ditcher  firenew  jibbing
phasmid  shilpit  thermae  whiskey  biotite  dilemma  dithery  firstly  jibboom
phellem  shimmer  thermal  whisper  bipedal  diluent  dittany  firtree  jibdoor
philter  shindig  thermic  whistle  biplane  dilutee  diurnal  fishery  jigging
philtre  shingle  theurgy  whitely  bipolar  diluter  diverge  fisheye  jimjams
phlegmy  shingly  thiamin  whither  birchen  dilutor  diverse  fishily  jingler
phoenix  shinned  thicken  whiting  birddog  dimeric  divider  fishing  jitters
phonate  shinpad  thicket  whitish  birdman  dimeter  diviner  fishnet  jittery
phoneme  shiplap  thickly  whitlow  biretta  dimmest  divisor  fishway  kibbutz
phonics  shipman  thieves  Whitsun  biriani  dimming  divorce  fissile  kickoff
phonily  shipped  thigger  whittle  biscuit  dimmish  divulge  fission  kidding
photism  shippen  thiller  whizkid  bismuth  dimness  dizzard  fissure  kiddish
phrasal  shipper  thimble  whizzed  bistort  dinette  dizzily  fistful  kidskin
phratry  shippon  thinker  whoever  bistred  dingily  eidetic  fistula  killick
phrenic  shipway  thinned  whoopee  bittern  dingoes  eidolon  fitchet  killing
phrensy  shirker  thinner  whooper  bitters  dinning  einkorn  fitchew  killjoy
physics  shittim  thirdly  whopper  bitting  diocese  eirenic  fitment  kilobar
rhabdom  shivers  thirsty  whorish  bittock  diopter  fiancee  fitness  kiloton
Rhaetic  shivery  thistle  whorled  bitumen  dioptre  fibbing  fittest  kinchin
rhamnus  shocker  thistly  whoseso  bivalve  diorama  fibroid  fitting  kindler
rhatany  shoeing  thither  aiblins  bivouac  diorism  fibroin  fixable  kindred
rhenium  shogged  Thomism  aileron  bizarre  diorite  fibroma  fixedly  kinesis
rhiancy  shoofly  Thomist  aimless  ciboria  dioxide  fibrous  fixings  kinetic
rhizoid  shooter  thorite  aircrew  cidaris  diploid  fibster  fixture  kinfolk
rhizome  shopboy  thorium  airdrop  ciliary  diploma  fibulae  giantry  kingcup
rhodium  shopman  thorned  airfare  ciliate  dipnoan  fibular  gibbous  kingdom
rhodora  shopped  thought  airflow  cimices  dipolar  fibulas  giblets  kinglet
rhombic  shopper  thready  airglow  cindery  diptera  fictile  giddily  kingpin
rhombus  shoring  thrifty  airhole  cineast  diptych  fiction  gigging  kinship
rhubarb  shorten  thriven  airless  cineole  direful  fictive  giggler  kinsman
rhymist  shortie  throaty  airlift  cingula  dirtily  fiddler  gilbert  Kirghiz
shackle  shortly  thrombi  airline  cipolin  disable  fideism  gilding  kissing
shadily  shotgun  throned  airlock  Circean  disavow  fideist  gillnet  kitchen
shading  shotten  through  airmail  circler  disband  fidgets  giltcup  kitschy
shadoof  shouter  thrower  airmiss  circlet  disbark  fidgety  gimbals  liaison
shadowy  showbiz  throwin  airport  circuit  discant  fiefdom  gimmick  Liassic
shaitan  showery  thrummy  airpost  circusy  discard  fielder  gingery  liberal
shakeup  showily  thudded  airship  cirrose  discern  fierily  gingham  liberty
shakily  showing  thuggee  airsick  cirrous  discerp  fifteen  gingili  library
shallop  showman  thulium  airwave  cistern  discoid  fifthly  ginning  librate
shallot  showoff  thummim  Biafran  citable  discord  fifties  ginseng  licence
shallow  shrieve  thumper  biassed  citadel  discuss  figging  giraffe  license
shamble  shrilly  thunder  biaxial  cithara  disdain  fighter  girasol  lichowl
shammed  shrinal  thymine  bibbery  cithern  disease  figleaf  girdler  licitly
shammer  shrivel  thyroid  bibbing  citizen  diseuse  figment  girlish  licking
shampoo  shriven  thyrsus  bibcock  citrate  disfame  figtree  gittern  lidless
shanked  shrubby  thyself  bibelot  citrine  disgust  figural  gizzard  lieabed
shapely  shucker  whacker  biblist  cittern  dishorn  figured  hiccupy  lifeful
sharpen  shudder  whaling  bicycle  civilly  disjoin  filacer  hickory  liftoff
sharper  shuffle  whangee  bidding  civvies  dislike  filaria  hidalga  lighted
sharply  shunned  wharves  biennia  diabase  dislimn  filasse  hidalgo  lighten
shaslik  shunner  whatnot  bifilar  diabolo  dismast  filbert  hideous  lighter
shaster  shunter  wheaten  bifocal  diadrom  dismiss  filemot  hideout  lightly
shastra  shuteye  wheedle  bigener  diagram  disobey  filiate  higgler  lignify
shatter  shutout  wheeled  biggest  dialect  dispark  filibeg  highboy  lignite
Shavian  shutter  wheeler  biggish  dialled  dispart  filings  highhat  ligroin
shaving  shuttle  whereas  bighead  dialyse  display  filling  highway  likable
shearer  shylock  whereat  bighorn  diamond  disport  filmdom  hilding  lilting
sheathe  shyness  whereby  bigname  diarchy  dispose  filmset  hillman  limbate
sheaves  shyster  wherein  bigness  diarise  dispute  fimbria  hillock  limbeck
shebang  thalami  whereof  bigoted  diarist  disrank  finagle  hilltop  limbous
shebear  thallic  whereon  bigotry  dibasic  disrate  finally  himself  liminal
shebeen  thallus  whereto  bigtime  dibbing  disrobe  finance  hindgut  limited
shedder  thalweg  whether  bilboes  dickens  disroot  finback  hipbath  limiter
sheerly  thanage  whetted  biliary  dictate  disrupt  finding  hipbone  limosis
shellac  thankee  whetter  bilimbi  diction  dissave  finesse  hipness  limpkin
shelled  thanker  wheyish  bilious  diddler  disseat  finical  hipping  limulus
sheller  theatre  whicker  billing  diehard  dissect  finicky  hiproof  linctus
shelter  thecate  whidder  billion  dietary  dissent  finikin  hipster  lindane
sheltie  themata  whiffle  bilobar  diffuse  distaff  finings  hirable  lineage
shelved  theorbo  whimper  bilobed  digamma  distain  finning  hircine  lineate
shelves  theorem  whimsey  biltong  digging  distant  Finnish  hirsute  lineman
Shemite  therapy  whinger  bimanal  digital  distend  firearm  hirudin  lineout
sherbet  thereat  whipped  bindery  dignify  distent  firebox  histone  lingual
shereef  thereby  whipper  binding  dignity  distich  firebug  history  linkage
sheriff  therein  whippet  bindery  dignity  distill  firedog  hitcher  linkboy
sherris  thereof  whipsaw  binding  digraph  distill  firedog  hitcher  linkman
```

```
Linnean minutia oilskin pipping sidecar tiffany visitor ajutage alkanet
linocut Miocene oilwell piquant sideway tighten visored djibbah Alkoran
linsang miracle piaffer piragua siemens tightly vistaed ejector alleged
linseed mirador pianism piranha sierran tigress vitally sjambok allegro
lioncel mirkily pianist piratic sighted tigrish vitamin akvavit allelic
lioness miscall piastre pirogue sightly tilbury vitelli ekistic allergy
lionise miscast pibroch piscary sigmate tillage vitiate ikebana allheal
lipdeep miscopy picador piscina sigmoid timbale vitrify skaldic allonge
lipless misdate piccolo piscine signary timbrel vitrine skating allover
lipping misdeal piceous pismire signify timelag vitriol skeeter allseed
lipread misdeed pickaxe pissoir signior timeous vittate skegger allstar
liquate misdeem pickeer pistole signora timidly vittles skellum alltime
liquefy misdone pickled pitapat signore timothy vitular skelter alluvia
liqueur miserly picotee pitched signori timpani vivaria skepsis almanac
lissome misfire picquet pitcher signory timpano vividly sketchy almirah
listeth misgave picrate piteous Sikhism tinamou vivific skiable almoner
listing misgive Pictish pitfall silence tindery vixenly skidded almonry
literal mishear picture pithead silenus tinfoil wickiup skidlid almsman
lithely Mishnah piddock pithhat silesia tingler widgeon skidpan alodial
lithium misknow pidgeon pithily silicic tinhorn widowed skiffle alodium
lithoid mislaid piebald pitiful silicle tinnily widower skijump aloetic
litotes mislead pieeyed pitpony silicon tinning wielder skilful aloofly
littery mislike pierrot pitprop siliqua tintack wigging skilift alphorn
liturgy mismate pietism pitting silique tinware wiggler skilled already
livable misname pietist pivotal silkily tipcart wigless skillet alright
livebox misplay piffler pivoter sillily tipping wildcat skimmed alsoran
liveoak misread piggery ribband silvern tippler wilding skimmer althaea
miasmal misrule pigging ribbing silvery tipsify wildish skimmia althorn
miasmic missend piggish ribston similar tipsily willies skinful alumina
micelle missent pigiron ribwork similor tipster willing skinker alumnae
microbe missile piglead ribwort simitar titanic willowy skinned alumnus
midland missing pigling rickets simpler tithing windage skinner alunite
midline mission pigmean rickety simplex titlark windbag skipped alveoli
midmost missish pigment ricksha simular titling windegg skipper alyssum
midriff missive pigskin ricotta sincere titmice windily skippet blabbed
midship misstep pigtail ridable singlet Titoism winding skirret blabber
midweek mistake pigwash ridding sinkage Titoist windrow skirted blacken
Midwest mistful pigweed riddler sinless titrate Windsor skirter blackly
midwife mistily pikelet ridging sinning tittupy winesap skitter bladder
midyear mistime pikeman ridotto sinopia titular winglet skittle blandly
mightst misting pileate riffler sinsyne viaduct wingnut skolion blanket
migrant mistook pilgrim rifling sintery viatica winkers skulker blankly
migrate mistral pillage rigging sinuate vibrant winning skyblue blarney
mildewy mitoses pillbox righten sinuous vibrate winnock skyborn blasted
mileage mitosis pillion righter sipping vibrato winsome skyhigh blaster
milfoil mitotic pillock rightly sirgang viceroy wintery skyjack blatant
miliary mitzvah pillory rigidly sirloin vicinal wireman skylark blather
militia mixedly pillowy rilievo sirocco vicious wiretap skyline blatter
milking mixedup pillule rimming Sistine victory wishful skysail bleakly
milkleg mixture pilsner ringent sistrum victual wishing skyward bleater
milkman nibbler pilular ringing sitdown vidette wistful ukelele bleeder
milksop niblick pimento ringlet sitfast vidimus withers ukulele bleeper
milldam niceish pimping ringtaw sithens viduity without alameda blemish
million nictate pinball riotous sitting viewing witless alanine blender
milreis niggard pincers ripcord situate vilayet witling alation blesbok
mimesis niggler pincher ripieni Sivaism village witloof albumen blessed
mimetic nightie pinetum ripieno Sivaite villain witness albumin blether
mimical nightly pinfire riposte sixaine villein wittily alcaide blewits
mimicry nigrify pinfish ripping sixfold villose witting alcalde blighty
mimulus Nilotic pinfold ripplet sixteen villous wizened alcayde blinder
minaret nimiety pinguid riptide sixthly vinasse xiphoid alcazar blindly
mincing ninepin pinhead risible sixties vincula Yiddish alchemy blinker
mindful niobium pinhole risotto Sixtine vinegar yielder alcohol blintze
mineral nippers pinkeye rissole sizable vintage yipping Alcoran blister
minever nippily pinking rivalry sizably vintner ziganka alembic blither
miniate nipping pinkish rivered sizzler violate zillion alertly bloated
minibus nirvana pinnace riveter Tibetan violent zincify aleuron bloater
minicab nitrate pinnate riviera ticking violist zincing alewife blocker
minicar nitride pinning riviere tickler violone zincite alfalfa blooded
minikin nitrify pinnule rivulet tidally virelay zincked alforja bloomer
minimal nitrile pintado sialoid tiddler virgate Zingari algebra blossom
minimum nitrite pintail siamang tiddley virgule Zingaro alginic blotchy
minimus nitrous pintuck Siamese tiderip virtual zinkify alidade blotted
miniver niveous pinworm sibling tideway visaged zinnia alienly blotter
minorca oilbath pioneer sibship tidings viscera Zionism aliform blouson
minster oilbird piously sickbay tieback viscose Zionist aliment blowdry
mintage oilcake pipeful sickbed tiebeam viscous zipcode alimony blowfly
minuend oildrum piperic sickish tiercel visible zipping aliquot blowgun
minutes oilseed pipette sickpay tiercet visibly zithern alkalis blowout
```

```
blowzed  elderly  flitter  gluteus  plosive  slurred  emplace  umbones  anymore
blubber  Eleatic  flivver  glutted  plotted  slyness  emplane  umbrage  anyroad
blucher  elector  floater  glutton  plotter  ulcered  emporia  Umbrian  anytime
blueing  electro  floccus  glycine  plucker  ululant  empower  umpteen  anyways
bluffer  elegant  flogged  glyphic  plugged  ululate  empress  anaemia  anywise
bluffly  elegiac  floorer  glyptal  plugger  amalgam  emprise  anaemic  enactor
blunder  elegise  floosie  glyptic  plumage  amanita  emptier  anagoge  enamour
blunger  elegist  floozie  ileitis  plumate  amarant  emptily  anagogy  enation
bluntly  element  flopped  ilkaday  plumber  amateur  emption  anagram  enchain
blurred  elenchi  floreat  illbred  plumbic  amative  empyema  analogy  enchant
blusher  elevate  florist  illegal  plumbob  amatory  emulate  analyse  enchase
bluster  elevens  floruit  illicit  plumery  amazing  emulous  analyst  enclasp
clabber  elfbolt  flotage  illness  plummet  ambages  imagery  Ananias  enclave
clacker  elfland  flotsam  klipdas  plumose  ambatch  imagine  anarchy  enclose
cladode  elflock  flounce  llanero  plumper  ambient  imagism  anatase  encoder
claimer  elision  flowage  oldster  plumply  amboina  imagist  anatomy  encomia
clamant  elitism  flowery  oldtime  plumule  ambones  imamate  anchovy  Encraty
clamber  elitist  flubbed  olefine  plunder  amboyna  imbiber  anchusa  encrust
clammed  ellipse  fluence  olivary  plunger  ambsace  imbower  ancient  endarch
clamour  Elohism  fluency  olivine  plunker  amender  imbrute  ancones  endemic
clanger  Elohist  fluidal  oloroso  plusage  amenity  imitate  ancress  enderon
clapped  elusion  fluidic  Olympic  plushly  amentia  immense  andante  endless
clapper  elusive  fluidly  placard  pluvial  amentum  immerge  andiron  endlong
clarify  elusory  flummox  placate  plywood  Amerind  immerse  android  endmost
clarion  elution  flunkey  placebo  slabbed  Amharic  immoral  anemone  endogen
clarity  eluvial  fluster  placket  slabber  amiable  impaint  aneroid  endorse
clarkia  eluvium  fluting  placoid  slacken  amiably  impanel  aneurin  endozoa
classes  elysian  flutist  plafond  slacker  amildar  impasse  angelic  endways
classic  Elysium  flutter  plaided  slackly  ammeter  impaste  angelus  endwise
classis  elytron  fluvial  plainly  slagged  ammonal  impasto  Angevin  enemata
clastic  elytrum  fluxion  planish  slammed  ammonia  impeach  anginal  energid
clatter  Elzevir  flyable  planned  slander  amnesia  impearl  angioma  enfeoff
clausal  flaccid  flyaway  planner  slantly  amnesic  imperil  Anglian  enfiled
clavate  flagday  flyback  plantar  slapped  amnesty  impetus  anglice  enforce
clavier  flagged  flybane  planter  slasher  amoebae  impiety  angling  enframe
claypan  flagman  flybelt  planula  slather  amoebas  impinge  Anglist  engaged
cleaner  flamfew  flyblow  planxty  slating  amoebic  impious  angrily  English
cleanly  flaming  flyboat  plasmic  slatted  amongst  implant  anguine  engorge
cleanse  flaneur  flybook  plasmid  slavery  amorist  implead  anguish  engraft
cleanup  flanker  flyhalf  plasmin  slavish  amorous  implete  angular  engrail
clearly  flannel  flyleaf  plaster  Slavism  amphora  implode  aniline  engrain
cleaver  flapped  flyover  plastic  sledded  amplify  implore  anility  engrave
clement  flapper  flypast  plastid  sleeken  ampoule  imposer  animate  engross
clerisy  flareup  flyting  platane  sleekit  ampulla  impound  animism  enhance
clerkly  flasher  flytrap  plateau  sleekly  amputee  impresa  animist  enlarge
clicker  flatcap  glacial  platina  sleeper  amtrack  impress  anionic  enliven
climate  flatcar  glacier  plating  sleeved  amusive  imprest  aniseed  ennoble
climber  flatlet  gladded  platoon  sleight  amylase  imprint  annates  enounce
clinker  flatout  gladden  platted  slender  amyloid  improve  annatta  enplane
clipped  flatten  gladder  platter  slicker  amylose  impulse  annatto  enprint
clipper  flatter  glaikit  plaudit  slickly  emanate  omental  annelid  enquire
clippie  flattop  glamour  playact  slidden  embargo  omentum  annicut  enquiry
cliquey  flaught  glaring  playboy  slimily  embassy  omicron  annuity  enslave
clivers  flaunty  glassen  playful  slimmer  emblaze  ominous  annular  ensnare
cloacae  flavine  glasses  playing  slinger  embolic  omitted  annulet  ensnarl
cloacal  flavour  glazier  playlet  slinker  embolus  omneity  annulus  entasis
clobber  fleabag  glazing  playoff  slipped  embosom  omnibus  anodise  entente
clocker  fleapit  gleaner  playpen  slipper  embowed  omnific  anodyne  enteral
clogged  flecker  gleeful  pleader  slipway  embowel  anoesis  anomaly  enteric
clogger  fleeced  gleeman  pleased  slither  embower  anoetic  anosmia  enteron
closely  fleecer  glenoid  plectra  slobber  embrace  smarten  another  enthral
closeup  fleeing  gliadin  pledgee  sloegin  embroil  smartly  anosmia  enthuse
closure  fleetly  glimmer  pledger  slogged  embrown  smasher  anosmic  entitle
clothes  Fleming  glimpse  pledget  slogger  embryon  smashup  another  entomic
clotted  Flemish  glisten  pledgor  slopped  emerald  smatter  antacid  entotic
cloture  fleshed  glister  plenary  sloshed  emeriti  smeddum  antbear  entozoa
clubbed  flesher  glitter  plenish  slotcar  emersed  smeller  antefix  entrain
clubman  fleshly  globoid  pleurae  slotted  emetine  smelter  antenna  entrant
clumber  fletton  globose  pleural  slouchy  emicate  smidgen  anthill  entreat
Cluniac  fleuret  globule  pleuron  sloughy  eminent  smidgin  anthrax  entropy
clupeid  fleuron  glorify  pliable  Slovene  emirate  smitten  antigen  entrust
cluster  flexile  glossal  pliably  slowish  emitted  smokeho  antilog  entwine
clutter  flexion  Glossic  pliancy  slubbed  emitter  smokily  antique  entwist
clypeal  flexure  glottal  plicate  slubber  emotion  smoking  antlion  envelop
clypeus  flicker  glottis  pliskie  slugged  emotive  smoochy  antonym  envenom
clyster  flighty  glozing  plodded  slugger  empanel  smother  anurous  environ
elastic  flipped  glucose  plodder  slummer  empathy  smuggle  anxiety  enviros
elastin  flipper  glummer  plopped  slummed  emperor  smutted  anxious  enwheel
elation  flitted  gluteal  plosion  slummer  empiric  umbonal  anybody  enwound
```

```
enzymic inlayer onerous unfaith bobbery bourree coltish coniine coronet
gnarled innards oneself unfitly bobbing bowhead combine conjoin corpora
gnathic innerve oneshot unfrock bobbish bowlder combout conjure correct
gnocchi innings onestep unfroze bobeche bowlful combust conkers corrida
gnomish inocula onetime unfunny bobsled bowline comedic connate corrode
gnostic inphase ongoing unfussy bobstay bowling cometic connect corrody
inanely inquest onshore ungodly bobtail bowshot comfort conning corrupt
inanity inquire onstage unguard bodeful boxcalf comfrey connive corsage
inaptly inquiry onwards unguent bogbean boxhaul comical connote corsair
inboard insculp onymous ungulae boggler boxkite comitia conquer corslet
inbreed insecty snaffle unhandy bogyman boxlike command consent cortege
inbuilt inshore snagged unhappy bohemia boxroom commend consign cortile
incense insider snakily unheard boiling boxseat comment consist corvina
incipit insight snapped unhinge boletus boxwood commode console corvine
incised insigne snapper unhitch bolivar boycott commons consort corydon
incisor insipid snarler unhoped bollard boyhood commove consult cosmism
inciter insofar snarlup unhorse bologna coacher commune consume cosmist
incline inspect snatchy unhouse boloney coagula commute contact cossack
inclose inspire sneaker unicity bolshie coaltit compact contain costard
include install sneerer unicorn bolster coaming company contemn costate
incomer instant sneezer unideal bombard coarsen compare contend costean
incrust instate snicker unifier bombast coastal compart content costing
incubus instead sniffer uniform bonanza coaster compass contest costive
incudes insular sniffle unitary bondage coating compeer context costrel
incurve insulin snifter unitive bondman coaxial compend contort costume
incused insured snigger unjoint bonedry cobbler compere contour coterie
indepth insurer sniggle unkempt boneset cocaine compete control cotidal
indexer inswing snipped unknown bonfire coccoid compile contuse cottage
indican integer snipper unladen bongoes cochlea complex convect cottier
indices intense snippet unlatch bonkers cockade complin convene cottony
indicia interim snooker unlearn bonnily cockeye complot convent Coueism
inditer interne snooper unleash boobook cockily compony convert couldst
indoors intoner snoozer unlined bookend cockney comport convict couloir
indorse intrant snoozle unloose bookful cockpit compose convoke coulomb
indraft intreat snorkel unlucky booking cockshy compost cookery coulter
indrawn introit snorter unmanly bookish coconut compote cooking council
inducer intrude snouted unmeant booklet cocotte compute cookout counsel
indulge intrust snowcap unmixed bookman codable comrade coolant counter
indusia intwine snowily unmoral booksie coddler Comtian coolish country
indwell inutile snowman unmoved Boolean codeine Comtism cooncan coupler
indwelt invader snubbed unnerve boomlet codfish Comtist coontie couplet
ineptly invalid snubber unpaged boorish codices conacre copaiba courage
inertia inveigh snuffer unquiet booster codicil conatus copaiva courier
inertly inverse snuffle unquote bootleg codling concave copepod courlan
inexact invitee snuggle unravel boozeup coeliac conceal copilot courser
infancy inviter unaptly unready boozily coequal concede copious courtly
infanta invoice unarmed unright bopping coexist conceit coppery couthie
infante involve unasked unroost boracic coffers concent coppice couture
infarct inwards unaware unsaved borazon cogency concept copular couvade
infauna inweave unbated unscrew bordure cogging concern copycat couvert
inferno inwoven unblest unsexed boredom cognate concert copyist coverup
infidel knacker unblock unshell borings cognise conchae coquito cowbane
infield knapped unbosom unsight bornite cohabit conchie coracle cowbell
inflame knapper unbound unsnarl borough coherer concise coranto cowbird
inflate knavery unbowed unsound borscht coinage concoct corbeil cowfish
inflect knavish unboxed unstick borstal coinbox concord cordage cowhage
inflict kneader unbrace unstuck bortsch coition concuss cordate cowhand
infract kneecap unbuild unswear boscage coldish condemn cordial cowheel
infulae kneeler unbuilt unswore boskage coletit condign cordite cowherd
ingenue keenpan uncanny unsworn bossism colicky condole cordoba cowhide
ingesta kneesup unchain unteach Boswell colitis condone corella cowlick
ingoing knitted uncinus unthink botanic collage conduce corkage cowling
ingraft knitter uncivil untried botargo collard conduct cornage cowpoke
ingrain knobbed unclasp untruly botcher collate conduit corncob cowshed
ingrate knobble unclean untruss bottega collect condyle corncob cowslip
ingress knobbly uncloak untruth bottled colleen confect corneal coxcomb
ingroup knocker unclose untuned bottony college confess cornett coyness
ingrown knockon uncouth untwine botulin collide confide cornfed cozener
inhabit knotted uncover untwist bouchee collier confine cornice docetic
inhaler knotter uncross untying boudoir collins confirm cornily dockage
inherit knowall uncrown unusual bouilli colloid conflux Cornish dockise
inhibit knowhow unction unweave boulder collude conform cornist doddard
inhouse knowing underdo unwound boulter colobus confuse cornual doddery
inhuman knuckle undergo unwoven bouncer cologne confute cornuto dodgems
initial knurled undoing boarder bounden colonel congeal corolla dodgery
injurer onanism undress boarish bounder colonic congest coronae doeskin
inkhorn oneeyed undying boaster bouquet colossi conical coronal dogbane
inkling oneiric unearth boating bourbon colours conidia coronas dogcart
inkwell oneness unequal boatman bourdon coloury conifer coroner dogdays
```

```
dogeate fopling goggler horrent loosely mooring notably possess rootlet
dogfish foppery goggles horrify lopping Moorish notched postage ropable
doggery foppish goitred horsily lording moorlog notedly postbag ropeway
dogging forager goldbug hosanna lorette mopping notelet postbox rorqual
doggish foramen golfbag hosiery lorgnon moraine notepad postboy roseate
doggone forayer golfing hospice loricae morally nothing posteen rosebay
dogrose forbade goliard hostage lorimer morassy notitia postern rosebud
dogskin forbear Goliath hostile loriner mordant noumena postfix rosecut
dogstar forbode gombeen hostler losable mordent nourish posting rosehip
dogtrot forbore gomeral hotfoot lottery moreish novella postman rosella
dogvane forceps gomeril hothead lotting morello novelle posture roseola
dogwood fordone gonadal hotness loudish morendo novelty postwar rosered
doleful forearm gondola hotshot lounger Moresco nowhere potable rosette
dollish foreign gonidia hottest lousily Morisco noxious potamic rostral
dolphin foreleg goodbye hottish loutish morning oolitic potbank rostrum
doltish foreman goodday housing louvred morocco oomiack potence rotator
domical forepaw goodish howbeit lovable moronic oophyte potency rotifer
dominie foreran goodman however lovably morphia oosperm pothead rotting
donator forerun gooiest howling loverly mortice oospore potheen rotunda
donning foresaw gorcock jobbery lowborn mortify poacher potherb roughen
donnish foresay gorcrow jobbing lowbred mortise pochard pothole roughly
doodler foresee Gordian jocular lowbrow morulae podagra pothook roulade
doomful foretop gorilla jogging lowdown morular podding potluck rouleau
doorman forever gorsedh jogtrot lowland morwong podesta potshot rounded
doormat forfeit goshawk joinder lowlily Moselle poetess pottage roundel
doorway forfend gosling joinery lowness mosshag poetics pottery rounder
dorhawk forgave gossipy joining lowrise mottled poetise potting roundly
Dorking forgery gossoon jointer loyally mouflon pofaced pouched roundup
dormant forging gouache jointly loyalty moulder poinder poulard rousing
dormice forgive goulash jollify lozenge mounter pointed poulter rouster
dornick forgoer gourami jollity Moabite Mountie pointer poultry routine
dortour forgone gourmet jonquil mobbing mourner polacca poundal rowboat
dossier forkful goutfly jotting mobbish mousaka polacre pounder rowdily
dotting forlorn hoarsen journal mobster mousing poleaxe pouting rowlock
doubler formant hoatzin journey mockery mousmee polecat poverty royally
doubles formate Hobbian jouster modally mouther polemic powdery royalty
doublet formula Hobbism joyance modesty movable polenta roadbed royster
doubter forsake Hobbist joyless modicum mowburn politic roadhog soakage
doucely forsook hobbler joyride modiste Noachic pollack roadman soaking
douceur forties hobnail kolkhoz modular nobbler pollard roadway soapbox
doughty Fortran hockday komatik modulus noctuid pollock roaming soapily
dovecot fortune hocused Koranic mofette noctule pollute roaring soaring
dovekie forward hoecake koumiss moidore nocturn poloist roaster sobbing
dowager forwent hoedown loading moisten nodally polygon robbery soberly
dowdily forworn hogback loaning moistly nodated polymer robbing socager
downbow fossick hogfish loather moither nodding polynia rockery soccage
doyenne fossula hoggery loathly molimen nodical polynya rockier society
dozenth fouette hogging lobbing mollify nodular polypod rockily sockeye
fobbing foulard hoggish lobelia mollusc nogging polypus rocking sofabed
focused foumart hogwash lobster molossi noggins pomatum rocklet softish
fogbank founder hogweed lobular momenta noisily pomfret rockoil soggily
foggage foundry holdall lobworm monacal noisome pompano rocktar soignee
foggily fourale holding locally monadic nomadic pompous rodding soilure
fogging fourale holibut locater monarch nomarch pondage rodlike sojourn
foghorn fourgon holiday lockage monauls nombles poniard rodsman sokeman
foglamp foveate holland lockjaw mondial nombril pontage roebuck solanum
fogydom foveola holmium locknut moneyed nominal pontiff roedeer solaria
fogyish fowling holmoak lockout mongers nominee pontify roguery solatia
fogyism foxhole holster locular mongrel nonagon pontoon roguish soldier
folding foxhunt homager loculus moniker noniron poofter roister solicit
foldout foxtail homburg lodging monkery nonplus poohbah rollick solidly
foliage foxtrot Homeric loftily monkish nonskid poorish rolling solidus
foliate goahead Homerid logbook monocle nonslip popadum rollmop soliped
foliole goatgod hominid logging monocot nonstop popcorn rolltop soloist
foliose goatish homonym logline monodic nonsuch popeyed romance Solomon
folkway gobbler honesty logwood monomer nonsuit popover Romanic soluble
follies Gobelin honeyed Lollard monsoon nonuser poppied Romansh solvate
fondant goddamn honours Lombard monster noology popping romaunt solvent
fondler goddess hoodlum lomenta montage noonday popular Rommany somatic
foolery godetia hoodman longago montane nooning porcine rondeau someday
foolish godevil hooklet longans montero norland porrect rondure somehow
footage godhead hopbind longbow monthly norther portage rontgen someone
footboy godhood hopeful longday moocher norward portend roofing someway
footing godless hoplite longhop moodily nosebag portent rooftop somitic
footman godlike hopping longing mooneye nosegay portico rooinek sonance
footpad godling hopsack longish moonlit noserag portion roomful sonancy
footrot godsend horizon looking moonset nostril portray roosted songful
footsie godship hormone lookout moorage nostrum poseurs rooster sonless
footway godward hornmad looksee moorhen notable poseuse rootage sonship
```

soonish	topsoil	woozily	epatant	spatter	spryest	arctoid	brewery	crazily
soother	torchon	wordage	epaulet	spatula	spumous	arcuate	bribery	creamer
soothly	torgoch	wordily	epergne	spawner	spunkie	arcweld	brickie	creator
sootily	torment	wording	ephebus	speaker	spurner	ardency	brickle	credent
sophism	tormina	workbag	ephedra	special	spurred	arduous	bricole	creedal
sophist	tornado	workbox	epicarp	species	spurrey	areally	bridoon	creeper
soppily	torpedo	workday	epicede	specify	spurtle	areaway	briefly	cremate
sopping	torpids	working	epicene	speckle	sputnik	areolae	brigade	cremona
soprani	torrefy	workman	epicure	spectra	sputter	areolar	brigand	crenate
soprano	torrent	workout	epidote	spectre	spyhole	areolas	brimful	cresset
sorbent	torsade	worldly	epigeal	specula	upbraid	aridity	brimmed	crested
Sorbian	torsion	wornout	epigean	speeder	upfield	arietta	brimmer	crevice
sorcery	tortile	worrier	epigene	speedup	upgrade	aristae	brinded	cribbed
sordini	tortrix	worship	epigone	speller	upheave	aristas	brindle	cribble
sordino	torture	worsted	epigoni	spelter	upraise	armband	bringer	cricket
sorghum	torulae	wottest	epigram	spencer	upright	armfuls	brinjal	cricoid
sorites	Toryism	wouldbe	epigyny	spender	upriser	armhole	brioche	crimine
soroban	tosspot	wouldst	epilate	sphenic	upsides	armiger	briquet	crimper
sororal	totally	yoghurt	episode	spheral	upsilon	armless	brisken	crimple
sorosis	totemic	yolksac	epistle	spheric	upstage	armlike	brisket	crimson
sorrily	tottery	Yorkist	epitaph	spicate	upstair	armoire	briskly	cringer
sotting	totting	younger	epitaxy	spicery	upstart	Armoric	bristle	cringle
sottish	touched	younker	epithem	spicily	upsurge	armoury	bristly	crinite
soubise	toucher	zoarium	epithet	spicula	upsweep	armrest	British	crinkle
souffle	touchup	Zoilism	epitome	spicule	upswept	armsful	brittle	crinkly
soulful	toughen	Zoilist	epizoic	spidery	upswing	arousal	brittly	crinoid
sounder	toughly	zonated	epizoon	spieler	upthrew	arraign	britzka	criollo
soundly	touraco	zoogamy	epochal	spignel	upthrow	arrange	broaden	cripple
soupcon	touring	zoogeny	eponymy	spikily	uptight	arrayer	broadly	crisper
sourish	tourism	zoogony	epoxide	spiller	uptrend	arrears	brocade	crisply
soursop	tourist	zooidal	epsilon	spinach	upwards	arrival	brocket	cristae
soutane	tourney	zoology	ipomoea	spindle	aquaria	arriver	broider	critter
souther	towards	zoonomy	opacity	spindly	aquatic	arsenal	broiler	croaker
sowback	towboat	zootaxy	opaline	spindry	aquavit	arsenic	brokage	crochet
soybean	towered	zootomy	openair	spinner	aqueous	article	broking	crocket
sozzled	towhead	apagoge	openend	spinney	aquifer	artisan	bromate	Croesus
toaster	towline	apanage	opening	spinode	aquiver	artiste	bromide	crofter
tobacco	towmond	apatite	operand	spinoff	equable	artless	bromine	crooked
toccata	towmont	apetaly	operant	spinose	equably	artwork	bromism	crooner
toddler	townish	aphasia	operate	spinous	equally	brabble	bronchi	cropped
toeclip	townlet	aphasic	operose	spinule	equator	bracing	broncho	cropper
toehold	towpath	aphelia	ophitic	spiraea	equerry	bracken	brooder	croquet
toeless	towrope	apheses	opinion	spirant	equinal	bracket	brothel	croquis
toenail	toyshop	aphesis	opossum	spireme	equinox	bradawl	brother	crosier
toggery	vocable	aphetic	oppidan	spirits	squabby	bragged	brought	crossly
toilful	vocalic	aphides	opposer	spitted	squacco	bragger	brownie	crouton
tollbar	vocally	aphonia	oppress	spitter	squaddy	Brahman	browser	crowbar
tollman	voguish	aphonic	opsonic	spittle	squails	Brahmin	brucine	crowdie
toluene	voivode	aphotic	opsonin	splashy	squalid	braille	brucite	crowned
tombola	volante	aphylly	optical	spleeny	squally	bramble	bruhaha	crowner
tombolo	volcano	apishly	optimal	splenic	squalor	brambly	bruiser	crownet
tomenta	voltage	aplasia	optimum	splicer	squamae	branchy	brumous	crowtoe
tomfool	voltaic	aplenty	opulent	splodge	squarer	brander	brusher	crozier
tompion	voluble	apocope	opuntia	splotch	squashy	brannew	brusque	crucial
tonally	volubly	apodous	opuscle	splurge	squatty	bransle	brutish	crucian
tonemic	volumed	apogamy	spacial	spodium	squeaky	brantle	bruxism	crucify
tonerow	voluted	apogean	spacing	spoiler	squeeze	brantub	Brython	crudely
tonight	volutin	apology	spadger	spondee	squelch	brashly	crabbed	crudity
tonnage	votable	apolune	spancel	spondyl	squiffy	brassie	cracked	cruelly
tonneau	vouchee	apostil	spangle	sponger	squinch	brattle	cracker	cruelty
tonsure	voucher	apostle	spangly	spongin	squinny	braunch	crackle	cruiser
tontine	vowelly	apothem	spaniel	sponson	squirmy	bravado	crackly	cruller
toolbox	voyager	apparat	Spanish	sponsor	squishy	bravely	crackup	crumble
tooling	wobbler	apparel	spanker	spoofer	squitch	bravery	cragged	crumbly
toothed	wolfcub	appease	spanned	spooney	Arabian	bravura	crammed	crumpet
tootsie	wolfdog	applaud	spanner	spoorer	arabise	brawler	crammer	crumple
topcoat	wolfish	applied	sparely	sporran	Arabist	brazier	crampet	crunchy
topfull	wolfram	applier	sparger	sporter	Aramaic	breaded	crampit	crupper
tophole	wolvish	appoint	sparing	sporule	araneid	breadth	crampon	crusade
topiary	womanly	apprise	sparkle	spotted	Arapaho	breaker	cranage	crusado
topical	woodcut	approve	sparoid	spotter	arbiter	breakin	cranial	crusher
topknot	woodman	apraxia	sparred	spousal	arbutus	breakup	cranium	crustal
topless	woodpie	apricot	sparrow	spouter	arcaded	breathe	crannog	crybaby
topmast	woolfat	apropos	Spartan	sprawly	arcadia	breathy	crappie	cryogen
topmost	woolled	apsidal	spastic	sprayer	arcanum	breccia	crapply	cryptal
toponym	woollen	apsides	spathic	sprayey	archaic	breeder	crassly	cryptic
topping	wooloil	apteryx	spatial	spriggy	archery	brevier	craunch	cryptic
topsail	woolsey	aptness	spatted	springe	archive	brevity	craving	crystal
topside	woomera	eparchy	spattee	springy	archway	brewage	crawler	drabber

drabbet	errancy	grampus	grubber	premier	propjet	trembly	trudgen	asteria
drabble	erratic	granary	gruffly	premise	propone	tremolo	truffle	astound
drabler	erratum	grandad	grumble	premiss	propose	trenail	trumeau	astride
drachma	erudite	grandam	grumbly	premium	propped	trental	trumpet	asunder
draftee	fracted	grandee	grummet	prepack	prorate	trepang	truncal	csardas
drafter	fraenum	grandly	grumose	prepaid	prosaic	tressed	trundle	escapee
dragged	fragile	grandma	grumous	prepare	prosify	tressel	trusser	escaper
draggle	frailly	grandpa	grunion	preplan	prosily	trestle	trustee	escheat
dragnet	frailty	granger	grunter	presage	prosody	triable	truster	escolar
dragoon	Fraktur	granita	gruntle	present	prosper	triacid	trypsin	escribe
drainer	frameup	granite	grutten	preside	protean	triadic	tryptic	esotery
drapery	frankly	grannie	gruyere	presoak	protect	tribade	trysail	esparto
drastic	frantic	grantee	gryphon	presser	protege	triblet	uraemia	espouse
dratted	frapped	granter	grysbok	pressup	proteid	tribune	Uralian	esquire
draught	fratery	grantor	Iranian	presume	protein	tribute	uralite	essayer
drawbar	fraught	granule	irately	pretend	protend	triceps	uranide	essence
drawing	frazzle	grapery	irideal	pretest	protest	tricker	uranism	essoyne
drawler	freaked	graphic	iridise	pretext	proteus	trickle	uranium	estrade
drayage	freckle	grapnel	iridium	pretzel	protist	tricksy	uranous	estreat
drayman	freckly	grapple	Irishry	prevail	protium	tricorn	urethan	estuary
dreamed	freebie	grasper	irksome	prevent	proudly	trident	urethra	Gstring
dreamer	freedom	gratify	ironing	preview	proverb	triduan	urgency	ischial
dredger	freeman	grating	ironist	previse	provide	triduum	urinary	ischium
dresser	freesia	graunch	kremlin	priapic	proviso	trifler	urodele	Ishmael
dribble	freeway	gravely	krimmer	pricker	provoke	triform	urology	Islamic
driblet	freezer	gravity	Krishna	pricket	provost	trigamy	wrangle	Ismaili
driedup	freight	gravure	krypton	prickle	prowess	trigger	wrapped	isobath
drifter	Frenchy	grazier	oration	prickly	prowler	trilith	wrapper	isochor
driller	frenula	grazing	oratory	primacy	proximo	trilogy	wreathe	isogamy
drinker	frescos	greaser	oratrix	primage	prudent	trimmed	wreathy	isogeny
dripdry	freshen	greaten	orbital	primary	prudery	trimmer	wrecker	isogram
dripped	fresher	greatly	orchard	primate	prudish	trinary	wrestle	isohyet
drivein	freshet	greaves	orderer	primely	pruning	trindle	wriggle	isokont
driving	freshly	Grecian	orderly	primero	prurigo	tringle	wriggly	isolate
drizzle	fretful	grecise	ordinal	priming	prussic	trinity	wringer	isonomy
drizzly	fretsaw	Grecism	orectic	primmed	tracery	trinket	wrinkle	isotope
drogher	fretted	greenly	oregano	primula	trachea	trinkum	wrinkly	isotopy
dromond	friable	greenth	organic	printer	tracker	triolet	writeup	isotron
droplet	friarly	greisen	organon	prithee	tractor	tripery	writhen	Israeli
dropout	fribble	gremial	organum	privacy	tradein	triplet	writing	issuant
dropped	frigate	gremlin	organza	private	trading	triplex	written	isthmus
dropper	frijole	grenade	orifice	privily	traduce	tripody	wrongly	osculum
drosera	fripper	greyhen	origami	privity	traffic	tripoli	wrought	osmosis
droshky	friseur	greyish	orogeny	proband	tragedy	tripped	wrybill	osmotic
drought	Frisian	greylag	orology	probang	trailer	tripper	wryneck	osmunda
drouthy	frisker	gribble	orotund	probate	trainee	trippet	wryness	osselet
droving	frisket	griddle	Orphean	probity	trainer	tripple	ascarid	osseous
drubbed	frisson	griffin	Orphism	problem	traipse	trireme	ascaris	osseter
drudger	fritted	griffon	orphrey	proceed	traitor	trisect	ascesis	ossicle
drugged	fritter	grifter	ortolan	process	traject	trishaw	ascetic	ossific
drugget	frizzle	grilled	praetor	proctor	tramcar	trismus	ascidia	ossuary
druidic	frizzly	griller	prairie	procure	trammel	tritely	ascites	osteoid
drumlin	frogeye	grimace	praiser	prodded	trample	tritium	ascitic	ostiary
drummed	frogged	grimmer	Prakrit	prodder	tramway	tritone	ascribe	ostiole
drummer	frogman	grinder	praline	prodigy	tranche	triumph	asepsis	ostraca
drunken	fronded	grinned	prancer	produce	trangam	trivial	aseptic	ostraka
drycell	frontal	gripped	prattle	product	transit	trivium	asexual	ostrich
drydock	fronton	gripper	pravity	profane	transom	trochal	ashamed	psalter
dryeyed	frosted	griskin	preachy	profess	tranter	trochee	ashtray	psychic
dryness	froward	gristle	prebend	proffer	trapeze	trochus	Asiatic	tsardom
drysalt	frowsty	gristly	precast	profile	trapped	trodden	asinine	tsarina
dryshod	fructed	gritted	precede	profuse	trapper	troller	askance	tsarism
erasure	fruited	grizzle	precept	progeny	travail	trolley	askesis	tsarist
erectly	fruiter	grizzly	precise	program	travois	trollop	asocial	Tsquare
erector	frustum	Grobian	precook	project	trawler	trommel	asperse	tsunami
erelong	grabbed	grocery	predate	prolate	trayful	trooper	asphalt	useless
eremite	grabber	grogram	predial	prolong	treacle	trophic	aspirer	usually
erepsin	grabble	Grolier	predict	promise	treacly	tropics	aspirin	usurper
ergates	gracile	grommet	predoom	promote	treader	tropism	asquint	ataraxy
ergodic	grackle	groover	preempt	pronaoi	treadle	trotted	assagai	atavism
ericoid	gradate	grossly	preface	pronaos	treason	trotter	assault	atavist
eristic	gradely	grottos	prefect	pronate	treater	trouble	assayer	atelier
erlking	gradine	grouchy	preform	pronely	treetop	trounce	assegai	atheism
ermined	gradual	grouper	preheat	pronged	trefoil	trouper	assizes	atheist
erodent	grafter	groupie	prelacy	pronoun	trehala	trouser	assuage	athirst
erosion	grained	grouser	prelate	propane	trekked	truancy	assured	athlete
erosive	grainer	growler	prelect	propend	trekker	trucial	assurer	athwart
erotica	gramary	grownup	prelims	prophet	trellis	trucker	astable	atingle
erotism	grammar	grubbed	prelude	propine	tremble	truckle	astatic	atomise

```
atomism stature streaky auxetic buttony dubbing furioso humidly lustful
atomist statute stretch bubonic butyric dubiety furious humidor lustily
atresia staunch stretta buccina buyable dubious furlong humming lustral
atrophy stealer stretto buckeye buzzard ducally furmety humming lustrum
attaboy stealth strewth buckler buzzsaw duchess furmity hummock luteous
attache steamer striate buckram cubbing ducking furnace humoral mudbath
attaint stearic strider bucksaw cubhood duckpin furnish hundred muddily
attempt stearin stridor bucolic cubical ductile furrier hunkers muddler
attract steekit strigil budding cubicle ducting furring hunting mudfish
attrite steepen striker buffalo cubital dudgeon furrowy hurdler mudflat
ctenoid steeple stringy buffoon cuckold duelled further hurdles mudlark
etaerio steeply striped bugaboo cudbear dueller furtive hurling mudpack
etamine steerer striven bugbane cudweed dukedom fuscous hurried muezzin
etching stellar striver bugbear cuirass dulcify fusible hurtful muffler
eternal stemmed strophe bugeyed cuisine dullard fussily husband mugging
etesian stemple stroppy bugging cuittle dullish fusspot hushaby muggins
ethanol stemson strudel bugloss culices dulness fustian huskily mugwort
etheric stenchy strumae builded cullion dumpish fustily husking mugwump
ethical stencil stubbed builder culotte dunbird futhark Hussite mulatto
ethiops stentor stubble buildup culprit dungeon futhorc hustler mullein
ethmoid stepney stubbly builtin cultism Dunkirk futhork hutment mullion
Etonian stepped stuccos builtup cultist dunnage futtock hutting mullock
itacism stepper stuckup buirdly culture dunning fuzzily jubilee multure
Italian stepson studded bulbous culvert dunnock guanaco Judaean mumbler
Italiot sterile student bulimia cumquat duodena guanine Judaise mummery
itemise sterlet studied bulkily cumshaw duopoly guarana Judaism mummify
iterant sternal stuffer bullace cumulus dupable guarani Judaist mumming
iterate sterned stumble bullary cuneate durable guarded judoist mumpish
otolith sternly stummed bullate cunette durably guardee jugging mundane
otology sternum stumper bullbat cunning duramen guayule juggins mundify
ottoman steroid stunned bulldog cupcake durance gubbins juggler munnion
pteroic stetson stunner bullion cupmoss durmast gudgeon jugular munting
pteryla stetted stunted bullish cupping duskily Guelfic juicily muntjac
ptyalin steward stupefy bullock cuprite dustbin guerdon jujitsu muntjak
stabbed stewpan stutter bullpen cuprous dustily guereza jukebox muonium
stabber stewpot stygian bulrush cupsful dustman guesser jumbuck muraena
stabile sthenic stylise bulwark cupular dustpan guichet jumpjet murexes
stabler stibine stylish bumbler curable duteous Guignol jumpoff muriate
stables sticker stylist bumboat curacao dutiful guilder juncoes murices
stacker stickit stylite bummalo curacoa duumvir guipure Jungian murkily
staddle stickle styloid bumming curator euclase guisard juniper murrain
stadium stickup styptic bumpily curcuma eucrite gullery Jupiter murther
stagger stiffen styrene bumpkin cureall eugenic gumboil jurally muscled
stagily stiffly utensil bungler curette euglena gumboot juryman musette
staging stifler uterine bunraku curiosa eulogia gumdrop jussive musical
staidly stilted utilise bunting curious eupepsy gumming justice muskrat
stainer Stilton utility buoyage curling euphony gummite justify mustang
staithe stimuli utopian buoyant currach Euratom gumshoe jutting mustard
stalely stinger utopism burbler curragh eustasy gunboat kumquat mutable
stalked stinker utopist burdock currant eutexia gunfire Kurdish mutably
stalker stipend utricle bureaus current fuchsia gunlock kursaal mutagen
stamina stipple utterer bureaux currier fuddler gunnera lubbard muttony
stammel stipule utterly burette currish Fuehrer gunnery lucarne muzzily
stammer stirpes yttrium burgage cursive fuelled gunning lucency muzzler
stamper stirred auction burgeon cursory fueller gunplay lucerne nuclear
standby stirrer audible burgess curtail fugally gunroom lucidly nucleic
stander stirrup audient burghal curtain fugging gunship Lucifer nuclein
standin stocker auditor burgher curtana fuguist gunshot luckily nucleon
standup stoical augment burglar curtsey fulcrum gunwale Luddite nucleus
staniel stomach augural Burmese curvate fulgent gurnard luggage nuclide
stannic stomata aurally burning cushion fulgour gushing lugging nullify
stapler stonily aureate burnish cuspate fullage gustily lughole nullity
starchy stonker aurelia burnous custard fullout gutless lugsail numbles
stardom stopgap aureola bursary customs fulmine gutsily lugworm numeral
starkly stopoff aureole burster cutaway fulness guttate lullaby numeric
starlet stopped auricle burthen cutback fulsome gutting lumbago nummary
starlit stopper aurochs burweed cutdown fulvous guzzler lumbang nunatak
starred stopple aurorae bushido cuticle fumbler huanaco lumenal nunhood
starter storage auroral bushman cutlass funeral hueless luminal nunnery
startle storied auroras bushtit cutlery funfair huffish lumpily nunnish
statant stouten auspice busking cutline fungoid hugeous lumpish nunship
stately stoutly austere bussing cutrate fungous hugging lunatic nuptial
statice stovies austral bustard cutting funicle hulking luncher nursery
statics stowage autarky bustler cutworm funnies humanly lunette nursing
station straits autobus butcher cuvette funnily humbles lunular nurture
statism strange autocar buttend dualise funning humbuzz lupulin nutcase
statist stratum autocue buttery dualism furbish humdrum lurcher nutgall
stative stratus autopsy buttock dualist furcate humeral lurdane nutlike
statued strayer auxesis buttons duality furcula humerus luridly nutpine
```

```
nutting  puparia  rubbery  suckler  tuition  overman  tweeter  exurban  lycopod
ouabain  pupilar  rubbing  sucrose  tulchan  overpay  tweezer  exurbia  lyddite
ourself  pupping  rubbish  suction  tumbler  overran  twelfth  exuviae  lyingin
outback  puritan  rubdown  sudaria  tumbrel  overrun  twelves  exuvial  lyingly
outcast  purlieu  rubella  suffice  tumbril  oversaw  twibill  oxalate  lymphad
outcome  purloin  rubeola  Suffolk  tumidly  oversea  twiddle  oxfence  lyncean
outcrop  purport  rubicon  suffuse  tumular  oversee  twiddly  oxidant  lynchet
outdone  purpose  rubious  suggest  tumulus  overset  twigged  oxidase  lyrated
outdoor  purpura  ruching  suicide  tunable  oversew  twilled  oxidate  lyrical
outface  purpure  ruction  suiting  tunably  overtax  twinkle  oxidise  myalgia
outfall  pursuer  ruddily  sulcate  tundish  overtly  twinkly  Oxonian  myalgic
outflow  pursuit  ruddock  sulkily  tuneful  overtop  twinned  oxyacid  myalism
outfoot  purview  ruderal  sullage  tunicle  overuse  twister  oxytone  mycelia
outgone  pushful  rudesby  sulphur  tunning  ovicide  twitchy  uxorial  mycoses
outgrew  pushing  ruffian  sultana  turbary  oviduct  twitted  byebyes  mycosis
outgrow  pushrod  ruffler  summand  turbine  oviform  twitter  bygones  mycotic
outhaul  pustule  ruinate  summary  turdine  ovoidal  twofold  Byronic  myeloid
outland  putamen  ruinous  summery  turdoid  ovulate  twoline  bywoner  myeloma
outlast  putdown  rumbler  summing  turfite  uveitis  twoness  cyanide  myiasis
outlier  putlock  rummage  summons  turfman  awarder  twosome  cyanine  mylodon
outline  putrefy  rumness  sumpter  turgent  aweless  twostep  cyanite  mynheer
outlive  puttier  rumshop  sunbath  Turkish  awesome  twotime  cyathus  myogram
outlook  putting  runaway  sunbeam  turmoil  awfully  twotone  cyclist  myology
outmost  puzzler  rundale  sunbear  turnery  awkward  axially  cycloid  myomata
outpace  quadrat  rundlet  sunbird  turning  awnless  axillae  cyclone  mystery
outplay  quadric  rundown  sunburn  turnipy  dwarves  axillar  cyclops  mystify
outport  quaffer  runless  sundeck  turnkey  dweller  axolotl  cymbalo  mythise
outpost  quahaug  running  sundial  turnout  dwindle  exactly  cynical  mythist
outrage  qualify  rupture  sundisc  turpeth  ewelamb  exactor  cypress  myxomas
outrank  quality  rurally  sundown  tushery  eweneck  examine  Cyprian  nylghau
outride  quamash  russety  sunfish  tussive  gwyniad  example  Cypriot  nymphal
outrode  quantic  Russian  sunlamp  tussock  swabbed  exarate  cypsela  nymphet
outrush  quantum  Russify  sunless  tussore  swabber  excerpt  cystine  pyaemia
outsell  quarrel  rustily  sunnily  tutelar  swaddle  excited  cystoid  pyaemic
outshot  quartan  rustler  sunning  tutenag  swagged  exciter  dyarchy  pycnite
outside  quarter  ruthful  Sunnite  tutting  swagger  exciton  dyewood  pygmean
outsize  quartet  rutting  sunrise  tutwork  swagman  excitor  dynamic  pygmoid
outsold  quartic  ruttish  sunroof  vulgate  Swahili  exclaim  dynasty  pyjamas
outsole  quassia  suasion  sunspot  vulpine  swallow  exclave  eyeball  pyloric
outstay  quavery  suasive  sunstar  vulture  swanker  exclude  eyebath  pylorus
outtake  quayage  suavely  sunsuit  yulelog  swanned  excrete  eyebolt  pyralid
outtalk  Quechua  suavity  suntrap  avarice  swapped  excurse  eyebrow  pyralis
outturn  queenly  subacid  sunward  avenger  swapper  excusal  eyedrop  pyramid
outvote  queerly  subadar  sunwise  average  swarded  execute  eyehole  pyretic
outward  queller  subaqua  supping  averred  swarmer  exedrae  eyelash  pyrexia
outwear  querist  subbing  support  Avestan  swarthy  exegete  eyeless  pyrexic
outwent  quester  subdean  suppose  Avestic  swasher  exempla  eyelike  pyrites
outwore  questor  subdual  supreme  aviator  swatted  exergue  eyeshot  pyritic
outwork  quetsch  subduct  supremo  avidity  swatter  exhaust  eyesore  pyrosis
outworn  quetzal  subdued  surbase  avionic  swearer  exhibit  eyespot  pyrrhic
puberal  queuing  subedit  surcoat  avocado  sweater  exhumer  eyewash  Pythian
puberty  quibble  suberic  surface  evacuee  Swedish  exigent  eyewink  pyxides
publish  quicken  suberin  surfeit  evangel  sweeper  exocarp  gymnast  pyxidia
puccoon  quickie  subfusc  surfing  evanish  sweeten  exogamy  gymslip  syconia
puckery  quickly  subhead  surfman  evasion  sweetie  exordia  gypping  sycosis
puckish  quieten  subject  surgeon  evasive  sweetly  exotica  hyaline  syenite
pudding  quietly  subjoin  surgery  evening  swelter  expanse  hyalite  syllabi
puddler  quietus  sublate  surlily  evictor  swiftly  expense  hyaloid  sylphid
pudency  quillet  sublime  surmise  evident  swigged  expiate  hydatid  sylvine
puerile  quilter  subplot  surname  evolute  swiller  explain  hydrant  sylvite
puffery  quinary  subside  surpass  ivories  swimmer  explant  hydrate  symptom
pugging  quinate  subsidy  surplus  ovarian  swindle  explode  hydride  synapse
puggish  quinine  subsist  surreal  ovation  swinery  exploit  hydroid  syncarp
puggree  quinone  subsoil  surtout  overact  swinger  explore  hydrous  syncope
pugmill  quintal  subsume  survive  overage  swingle  exposal  hygeian  synergy
pugnose  quintan  subtend  suspect  overall  swinish  exposed  hygiene  synesis
Pullman  quintet  subtile  suspend  overarm  swipple  exposer  hymenia  syngamy
pullout  quintic  suburbs  suspire  overate  swither  exposit  hymnary  synodal
pulpous  quipped  subvert  sustain  overawe  Switzer  expound  hymnist  synodic
pulsate  quitted  subzero  sutural  overbid  swizzle  express  hymnody  synonym
pulvini  quitter  succade  sutured  overbuy  swobbed  expulse  hyperon  synovia
pumpkin  quivery  succeed  tuatara  overdid  swollen  expunge  hypnoid  syringa
puncher  quixote  success  tubbing  overdue  swopped  exscind  hypogea  syringe
punchup  quizzed  succory  tubbish  overeat  swopper  externe  hypoxia  syrphid
punctum  quizzer  succour  tubular  overfed  swotted  extinct  hypoxic  systole
pungent  quizzes  succuba  tuckbox  overfly  twaddle  extract  kyanise  tychism
Punjabi  quondam  succubi  Tuesday  overlap  twaddly  extreme  kyanite  tylopod
punning  rubadub  succumb  tugboat  overlay  twangle  extrude  lychnis  tympana
punster  rubbers  sucking  tugging  overlie  twankay  exudate  lychowl  tympani
```

```
tympano araneid champac crampit epatant grabbed inaptly piaffer realist
tympany Arapaho champak crampon epaulet grabber Iranian pianism reality
Tynwald ataraxy chancel cranage erasure grabble irately pianist reallot
typebar atavism chancre cranial etaerio gracile itacism piastre realtor
typeset atavist changer cranium etamine grackle Italian placard rhabdom
typhoid avarice channel crankle evacuee gradate Italiot placate Rhaetic
typhoon awarder chanson crannog evangel gradely jealous placebo rhamnus
typhous Baalism chanter crappie evanish gradine khaddar placket rhatany
typical beading chantry crassly evasion gradual khamsin placoid roadbed
typonym beamish chaotic craunch evasive grafter khanate plafond roadhog
tyranny beanbag chapati craving exactly grained knacker plaided roadman
wychelm bearded chaplet crawler exactor grainer knapped plainly roadway
zygosis bearing chapman crazily examine gramary knapper planish roaring
zygotic bearish chapped csardas example grammar knavery planned roaster
zymogen beastly chappie cyanide exarate grampus knavish planner scabbed
zymosis beatify chapter cyanine fearful granary kyanise plantar scabble
zymotic beating charade cyanite feaster grandad kyanite planter scabies
zymurgy beatnik charger cyathus feather grandam leading planula scabrid
Azilean Biafran charily czardas feature grandee leadoff planxty scaglia
azimuth biassed chariot czardom fiancee grandly leafage plasmic scalade
azurine biaxial charism czarina flaccid grandma leafbud plasmid scalado
azurite blabbed charity czarism flagday grandpa leaflet plasmin scalder
azygous blabber charley czarist flagged granger leaguer plaster scaldic
czardas blacken charlie deadend flagman granita leakage plastic scalene
czardom blackly charmer deadeye flamfew granite leaning plastid scallop
czarina bladder charnel deadpan flaming grannie learned platane scalpel
czarism blandly charpoy deafaid flaneur grantee learner plateau scalper
czarist blanket charqui dealing flanker granter leather platina scamper
ozonise blankly charred deanery flannel grantor liaison plating scandal
tzigane blarney charter deathly flapped granule Liassic platoon scanned
tzigany blasted chassis diabase flapper grapery llanero platted scanner
——————— blaster chasten diabolo flareup graphic loading platter scantly
abaddon blatant chateau diadrom flasher grapnel loaning plaudit scapple
abalone blather chatted diagram flatcap grapple loather playact scapula
abandon blatter chattel dialect flatcar grasper loathly playboy scarfed
abashed boarder chatter dialled flatlet gratify meadowy playful scarify
abattis boarish clabber dialyse flatout grating mealies playing scarlet
abaxial boaster clacker diamond flatten graunch meander playlet scarper
academe boating cladode diarchy flatter gravely meaning playoff scarred
academy boatman claimer diarise flattop gravity measles playpen scarves
Acadian brabble clamant diarist flaught gravure measure poacher scatted
acantha bracing clamber drabber flaunty grazier meatfly praetor scatter
acarian bracken clammed drabbet flavine grazing meatman prairie scauper
adamant bracket clamour drabble flavour guanaco miasmal praiser seabass
Adamite bradawl clanger drabler fracted guanine miasmic Prakrit seabear
adapter bragged clapped drachma fraenum guarana Moabite praline seabird
adaptor bragger clapper draftee fragile guarani myalgia prancer seablue
adaxial Brahman clarify drafter frailly guarded myalgic prattle seaboot
against Brahmin clarion dragged frailty guardee myalism pravity seafish
agamous braille clarity draggle Fraktur guayule nearest psalter seafood
alameda bramble clarkia dragnet frameup headily Noachic pyaemia seafowl
alanine brambly classes dragoon frankly heading ocarina pyaemic seagirt
alation branchy classic drainer frantic headman odalisk quadrat seagull
amalgam brander classis drapery frapped headpin onanism quadric seakale
amanita brannew clastic drastic fratery headset opacity quaffer sealane
amarant bransle clatter dratted fraught headway opaline quahaug sealant
amateur brantle clausal draught frazzle healthy oration qualify sealegs
amative brantub clavate drawbar gearbox hearing oratory quality sealery
amatory brashly clavier drawing gearing hearken oratrix quamash seamaid
amazing brassie claypan drawler gharial hearsay ouabain quantic seamark
anaemia brattle coacher drayage ghastly hearted ovarian quantum seapink
anaemic braunch coagula drayman giantry hearten ovation quarrel seaport
anagoge bravado coaltit dualise glacial heathen oxalate quartan searoom
anagogy bravely coaming dualism glacier heather peacock quarter seasick
anagram bravery coarsen dualist gladded heating peafowl quartet seaside
analogy bravura coastal duality gladden heavily pearled quartic seaslug
analyse brawler coaster dwarves gladder hoarsen pearler quassia seatang
analyst brazier coating dyarchy glaikit hoatzin peartly quavery seating
Ananias Chablis coaxial edacity glamour huanaco peasant quayage seawall
anarchy chaffer crabbed edaphic glaring hyaline peascod reacher seaward
anatase chagrin cracked egality glassen hyalite peasoup reactor seaware
anatomy chalaza cracker elastic glasses hyaloid phaeton readily seaweed
apagoge Chaldee crackle elastin glazier imagery phalanx reading seawhip
apanage chalice crackly elation glazing imagine phallic readout seawife
apatite challis crackup emanate gnarled imagism phallus reagent seawolf
Arabian chalone cragged enactor gnathic imagist phantom realgar shackle
arabise chamber crammed enamour goahead imamate pharaoh realign shadily
Arabist chamfer crammer enation goatgod inanely pharynx realise shading
Aramaic chamois crampet eparchy goatish inanity phasmid realism shadoof
```

```
shadowy sparkle swarthy viatica embassy nebular tableau backlog enclose
shaitan sparoid swasher weakish emblaze nebulas tabloid backsaw encoder
shakeup sparred swatted wealden embolic nibbler taborer backset encomia
shakily sparrow swatter wealthy embolus niblick tabular because Encraty
shallop Spartan teacake wearily embosom nobbler Tibetan becloud encrust
shallot spastic teacher wearing embowed orbital tobacco bicycle escapee
shallow spathic teachin weasand embowel pabulum tubbing buccina escaper
shamble spatial teacosy weather embower pebrine tubbish buckeye escheat
shammed spatted teagown whacker embrace pibroch tubular buckler escolar
shammer spattee tealeaf whaling embroil puberal umbonal buckram escribe
shampoo spatter tearful whangee embrown puberty umbones bucksaw etching
shanked spatula teargas wharves embryon umbrage bucolic euclase
shapely spawner tearing whatnot Faberge rabbity Umbrian cacanny eucrite
sharpen stabbed tearoom wrangle fabliau rabbler unbated cachexy excerpt
sharper stabber tearose wrapped fabular rabidly unblest cacique excited
sharply stabile teashop wrapper febrile rebirth unblock cackler exciter
shaslik stabler teatime zealous fibbing reboant unbosom cacodyl exciton
shaster stables teatray zoarium fibroid rebound unbound cacoepy excitor
shastra stacker thalami Abbasid fibroin rebuild unbowed cacumen exclaim
shatter staddle thallic aiblins fibroma rebuilt unboxed cichlid exclave
Shavian stadium thallus albumen fibrous rebuker unbrace cocaine exclude
shaving stagger thalweg albumin fibster ribband unbuild coccoid excrete
sialoid stagily thanage ambages fibulae ribbing unbuilt cochlea excurse
siamang staging thankee ambatch fibular ribston upbraid cockade excusal
Siamese staidly thanker ambient fibulas ribwork vibrant cockeye faceoff
sjambok stainer toaster amboina fobbing ribwort vibrate cockily faceted
skaldic staithe tracery ambones gabbing robbery vibrato cockney faction
skating stalely trachea amboyna gabbler robbing webbing cockpit factory
slabbed stalked tracker ambsace gabelle rubadub webfoot cockshy factual
slabber stalker tractor arbiter gabfest rubbers webster coconut facture
slacken stamina tradein arbutus gabnash rubbery webworm cocotte faculae
slacker stammel trading babassu gibbous rubbing wobbler cuckold faculty
slackly stammer traduce babbitt giblets rubbish zebrine cyclist fictile
slagged stamper traffic babbler gobbler rubdown zebroid cycloid fiction
slammed standby tragedy babyish Gobelin rubella accidie cyclone fictive
slander stander trailer babysit gubbins rubeola acclaim cyclops focused
slantly standin trainee bibbery habitat rubicon account dacoity fuchsia
slapped standup trainer bibbing habitue rubious accrete decadal geckoes
slasher staniel traipse bibcock hebenon Sabaism accrual decagon hachure
slather stannic traitor bibelot Hebraic Sabaoth accurst decanal hackbut
slating stapler traject biblist Hobbian Sabbath accusal decapod hackery
slatted starchy tramcar bobbery Hobbism sibling accused decease hacking
slavery stardom trammel bobbing Hobbist sibship accuser deceive hackler
slavish starkly trample bobbish hobbler sobbing alcaide decency hackney
Slavism starlet tramway bobeche hobnail soberly alcalde deciare hacksaw
smacker starlit tranche bobsled imbiber subacid alcayde decibel heckler
smaragd starred trangam bobstay imbower subadar alcazar decided hectare
smarten starter transit bobtail imbrute subaqua alchemy decider hiccupy
smartly startle transom bubonic inboard subbing alcohol decidua hickory
smasher statant tranter cabaret inbreed subdean Alcoran decimal hockday
smashup stately trapeze cabbage inbuilt subdual anchovy decking hocused
smatter statice trapped cabbagy jabbing subduct anchusa declaim incense
snaffle statics trapper cabbala jibbing subdued ancient declare incipit
snagged station travail cabinet jibboom subedit ancones declass incised
snakily statism travois cabling jibdoor suberic ancress decline incisor
snapped statist trawler caboose jobbery suberin arcaded decoder inciter
snapper stative trayful cabrank jobbing subfusc arcadia decorum incline
snarler statued tsardom ciboria jubilee subhead arcanum decrier inclose
snarlup stature tsarina cobbler kabbala subject archaic decrypt include
snatchy statute tsarism cubbing kibbutz subjoin archery decuman incomer
soakage staunch tsarist cubhood labarum sublate archive decuple incrust
soaking suasion tuatara cubical labella sublime archway dickens incubus
soapbox suasive twaddle cubicle labiate subplot arctoid dictate incudes
soapily suavely twaddly cubital liberal subside arcuate diction incurve
soaring suavity twangle dabbing liberty subsidy arcweld docetic incused
spacial swabbed twankay dabbler library subsist ascarid dockage ischial
spacing swabber udaller debacle librate subsoil ascaris dockise ischium
spadger swaddle unaptly debater lobbing subsume ascesis ducally jacamar
spancel swagged unarmed debauch lobelia subtend ascetic duchess jacinth
spangle swagger unasked debouch lobster subtile ascidia ducking jackass
spangly swagman unaware Debrett lobular suburbs ascites duckpin jackdaw
spaniel Swahili uraemia debrief lobworm subvert ascitic ductile jackpot
Spanish swallow Uralian dibasic lubbard subzero ascribe ducting jacktar
spanker swanker uralite dibbing mobbing tabanid auction eccrine Jacobin
spanned swanned uranide dubbing mobbish tabaret baccara enchain jacobus
spanner swapped uranism dubiety mobster tabasco baccate enchant jaconet
sparely swapper uranium dubious nabbing tabbing bacchic enchase jocular
sparger swarded uranous ebbtide nebbish tabetic bacilli enclasp kickoff
sparing swarmer viaduct embargo nebulae tabinet backing enclave lacking
```

```
laconic pacific sickbay audible fuddler medusan redwood amenity cleanly
lacquer package sickbed audient gadding medusas ridable amentia cleanse
lactate packice sickish auditor gadgety midland ridding amentum cleanup
lacteal packing sickpay baddish gadroon midline riddler Amerind clearly
lactose packman socager badmash gadwall midmost ridging anemone cleaver
lacunae peccant soccage badness giddily midriff ridotto aneroid clement
lacunal peccary society bedding goddamn midship rodding aneurin clerisy
lacunar peckish sockeye bedevil goddess midweek rodlike apetaly clerkly
lacunas picador succade bedfast godetia Midwest rodsman areally coeliac
lechery piccolo succeed bedight godevil midwife ruddily areaway coequal
lectern piceous success bedizen godhead midyear ruddock areolae coexist
lection pickaxe succory bedouin godhood modally ruderal areolar creamer
lecture pickeer succour bedpost godless modesty rudesby areolas creator
licence pickled succuba bedrock godlike modicum saddest asepsis credent
license picotee succubi bedroll godling modiste saddish aseptic creedal
lichowl picquet succumb bedroom godsend modular saddler asexual creeper
licitly picrate sucking bedside godship modulus sadness atelier cremate
licking Pictish suckler bedsock godward mudbath sedilia avenger cremona
locally picture sucrose bedsore gudgeon muddily seducer average crenate
locater pochard suction bedtime haddock muddler sidecar averred cresset
lockage puccoon syconia bidding hedonic mudfish sideway Avestan crested
lockjaw puckery sycosis bodeful hidalga mudflat sudaria Avestic crevice
locknut puckish tachism budding hidalgo mudlark tadpole aweless ctenoid
lockout pycnite tachist cadaver hideous mudpack tedding awesome deepfry
locular raccoon tacitly caddice hideout nodally tedious beechen deepsea
loculus racemic tacking caddish hydatid nodated tidally beehive diehard
lucarne rackety tackler cadence hydrant nodding tiddler beeline dietary
lucency racquet tactful cadency hydrate nodical tiddley beeswax doeskin
lucerne receipt tactics cadenza hydride nodular tiderip bheesty dreamed
lucidly receive tactile Cadmean hydroid oddball tideway bheetie dreamer
Lucifer recency taction cadmium hydrous oddment tidings biennia dredger
luckily recital tactual caducei indepth oddness toddler bleakly dresser
lychnis reciter technic cedilla indexer oedipal underdo bleater duelled
lychowl reclaim tectrix cidaris indican oldster undergo bleeder dueller
lycopod reclame ticking codable indices oldtime undoing bleeper dweller
macabre recline tickler coddler indicia orderer undress blemish dyewood
macadam recluse toccata codeine inditer orderly undying blender ejector
macaque recount tuckbox codfish indoors ordinal Vedanta blesbok Eleatic
machair recover tychism codices indorse padding Veddoid blessed elector
machete recruit ulcered codicil indraft paddler vedette blether electro
machine rectify uncanny codling indrawn paddock vidette blewits elegant
macrame rectory unchain cudbear inducer padlock vidimus breaded elegiac
macrami rectrix uncinus cudweed indulge padrone viduity breadth elegise
maculae recurve uncivil Dadaism indusia padroni wadable breaker elegist
macular recycle unclasp Dadaist indwell peddler wadding breakin element
Mechlin rickets unclean diddler indwelt pedicab waddler breakup elenchi
meconic rickety uncloak doddard jadedly pedicel wedding breathe elevate
micelle ricksha unclose doddery jadeite pedicle wedging breathy elevens
microbe ricotta uncouth dodgems Judaean pedlary wedlock breccia emerald
mockery rockery uncover dodgery Judaise piddock widgeon breeder emeriti
mycelia rockier uncross dudgeon Judaism pidgeon widowed brevier emersed
mycoses rockily uncrown ecdyses Judaist podagra widower brevity emetine
mycosis rocking unction ecdysis judoist podding Yiddish brewage enemata
mycotic rocklet vacancy eidetic Kaddish podesta zedoary brewery energid
nacarat rockoil vaccine eidolon kidding pudding Abelian byebyes epergne
nacelle rocktar vacuity elderly kiddish puddler abetted caesium erectly
nacrous ruching vacuole endarch kidskin pudency abetter caesura erector
necklet ruction viceroy endemic ladanum radiant abettor cheapen erelong
necktie saccade vicinal endless ladybug radiate abeyant cheaply eremite
necrose saccate vicious endlong ladykin radical acequia cheater erepsin
nectary saccule victory endmost lidless radices acerbic checker eternal
niceish sacculi victual endogen Luddite radicle acerola checkup etesian
nictate sackbut vocable endorse lyddite radulae acerose cheddar evening
noctuid sackful vocalic endozoa maddest redcoat acetate cheerer ewelamb
noctule sacking vocally endways madding reddest acetone cheetah execute
nocturn sacring wickiup endwise Madeira reddish acetous chelate exedrae
nocuous sacrist wychelm faddish madness redhead adenine chemise exegete
nuclear seceder abdomen faddism madonna redlegs adenoid chemism exempla
nucleic seclude addable faddist madrona redneck adenoma chemist exergue
nuclein seconde addenda fadedly madrono redness adeptly chequer eyeball
nucleon secondi addible fadeout madwort redoubt afeared cherish eyebath
nucleus secondo address fedayee meddler redound ageless cheroot eyebolt
nuclide secrecy adducer federal mediacy redpoll agelong chervil eyebrow
obconic secrete andante fiddler mediant redraft alembic chessel eyedrop
occiput sectary andiron fideism mediate redress alertly chested eyehole
occlude sectile android fideist medical redskin aleuron cheviot eyelash
orchard section ardency fidgets medulla reducer alewife chevron eyeless
osculum secular arduous fidgety medusae redwing amender cleaner eyelike
```

```
eyeshot heedful overbuy preside sleeved thereto afflict refined bugbane
eyesore heeltap overdid presoak sleight theriac affront refiner bugbear
eyespot hoecake overdue presser slender thermae alfalfa reflate bugeyed
eyewash hoedown overeat pressup smeddum thermal alforja reflect bugging
eyewink hueless overfed presume smeller thermic awfully refloat bugloss
feeding Iberian overfly pretend smelter theurgy baffler refocus bygones
feedlot iceberg overlap pretest sneaker tieback bifilar refract cagoule
feeling iceboat overlay pretext sneerer tiebeam bifocal refrain cogency
fiefdom icecold overlie pretzel sneezer tiercel buffalo refresh cogging
fielder icefall overman prevail speaker tiercet buffoon refugee cognate
fierily icefloe overpay prevent special toeclip coffers refusal cognise
fleabag icefoot overran preview species toehold default refuser degauss
fleapit icepack overrun previse specify toeless defence refutal degrade
flecker icerink oversaw pteroic speckle toenail defiant refuter digamma
fleeced iceshow oversea pteryla spectra treacle deficit riffler digging
fleecer ideally oversee puerile spectre treacly defiler rifling digital
fleeing identic overset Quechua specula treader definer ruffian dignify
fleetly ikebana oversew queenly speeder treadle deflate ruffler dignity
Fleming ileitis overtax queerly speedup treason deflect saffron digraph
Flemish ineptly overtly queller speller treater defocus sofabed digress
fleshed inertia overtop querist spelter treetop deforce softish dogbane
flesher inertly overuse quester spencer trefoil defraud suffice dogcart
fleshly inexact paeonic questor spender trehala defrock Suffolk dogdays
fletton itemise peerage quetsch stealer trekked defrost suffuse dogeate
fleuret iterant peeress quetzal stealth trekker defunct taffeta dogfish
fleuron iterate peevish queuing steamer trellis diffuse tiffany doggery
flexile keelson pfennig reeding stearic tremble effects unfaith dogging
flexion keeping phellem reelect stearin trembly effendi unfitly doggish
flexure khedive piebald reenact steekit tremolo effulge unfrock doggone
freaked kneader pieeyed reenter steepen trenail elfbolt unfroze dogrose
freckle kneecap pierrot reentry steeple trental elfland unfunny dogskin
freckly kneeler pietism rhenium steeply trepang elflock unfussy dogstar
freebie kneepan pietist roebuck steerer tressed enfeoff upfield dogtrot
freedom kneesup pleader roedeer stellar tressel enfiled waftage dogvane
freeman kremlin pleased scenery stemmed trestle enforce wafture dogwood
freesia leeward plectra scented stemple Tuesday enframe aggress eagerly
freeway lieabed pledgee scepsis stemson tweeter fifteen algebra eggcosy
freezer maestri pledger sceptic stenchy tweezer fifthly alginic eggflip
freight maestro pledget sceptre stencil twelfth fifties angelic egghead
Frenchy meerkat pledgor seeable stentor twelves hafnium angelus engaged
frenula meeting plenary seedbed stepney uberous heftily Angevin English
frescos muezzin plenish seedily stepped ukelele huffish anginal engorge
freshen myeloid pleurae seedlip stepper unearth infancy angioma engraft
fresher myeloma pleural seeming stepson unequal infanta Anglian engrail
freshet needful pleuron seepage sterile urethan infante anglice engrain
freshly needler poetess sferics sterlet urethra infarct angling engrave
fretful obelise poetics shearer sternal useless infauna Anglist engross
fretsaw obelisk poetise sheathe sterned utensil inferno angrily ergates
fretted obesity preachy sheaves sternly uterine infidel anguine ergodic
Fuehrer oceanic prebend shebang sternum uveitis infield anguish eugenic
fuelled ocellar precast shebear steroid viewing inflame angular euglena
fueller ocellus precede shebeen stetson weekday inflate augment fagging
geebung olefine precept shedder stetted weekend inflect augural fagotto
gherkin omental precise sheerly steward weevily inflict bagasse figging
ghettos omentum precook shellac stewpan wheaten infract baggage fighter
gleaner oneeyed predate shelled stewpot wheedle infulae baggily figleaf
gleeful oneiric predial sheller swearer wheeled leftism bagging figment
gleeman oneness predict shelter sweater wheeler leftist bagpipe figtree
glenoid onerous predoom sheltie Swedish whereas lifeful beggary figural
greaser oneself preempt shelved sweeper whereat liftoff begging figured
greaten oneshot preface shelves sweeten whereby loftily begonia figwort
greatly onestep prefect Shemite sweetie wherein maffick begorra fogbank
greaves onetime preform sherbet sweetly whereof mafiosi begrime foggage
Grecian openair preheat shereef swelter whereon mafioso beguile foggily
grecise openend prelacy sheriff syenite whereto mofette beguine fogging
Grecism opening prelate sherris taeniae whether muffler bigener foghorn
greenly operand prelect siemens teeming whetted offbeat biggest foglamp
greenth operant prelims sierran teenage whetter offence biggish fogydom
greisen operate prelude skeeter theatre wheyish officer bighead fogyish
gremial operose premier skegger thecate wielder offload bighorn fogyism
gremlin orectic premise skellum themata wreathe offpeak bigname fugally
grenade oregano premiss skelter theorbo wreathy offside bigness fugging
greyhen overact premium skepsis theorem wrecker oxfence bigoted fuguist
greyish overage prepack sketchy therapy wrestle piffler bigotry gagging
greylag overall prepaid sledded threat  yielder pofaced bigtime gagster
Guelfic overarm prepare sleeken thereby affable         bogbean gigging
guerdon overate preplan sleekit therein affably puffery boggler giggler
guereza overawe presage sleekly thereof affaire raffish bogyman goggler
guesser overbid present sleeper thereon affined referee bugaboo goggles
```

```
hagfish magnify rigidly atheist Wahabee bristly deicide Frisian mailbox
Haggada megaron roguery athirst Yahvist British deictic frisker mailing
haggard megaton roguish athlete Yahwist brittle deiform frisket maillot
haggish mightst sagging athwart abiding brittly deistic frisson mailman
haggler migrant sagitta Bahadur abigail britzka djibbah fritted mailvan
hagweed migrate saguaro Bahaism ability builded dribble fritter maintop
higgler mugging segment Bahaist abiotic builder driblet frizzle meiosis
highboy muggins sighted Bahaite acicula buildup driedup frizzly meiotic
highhat mugwort sightly behaver acidify builtin drifter gainful Meissen
highman mugwump sigmate behoove acidity builtup driller gainsay moidore
highway nagging sigmoid bohemia acinous buirdly drinker ghillie moisten
hogback neglect signary cahoots adipose caimans dripdry gliadin moistly
hogfish neglige signify cohabit agilely caisson dripped glimmer moither
hoggery Negress signior coherer agility caitiff drivein glimpse myiasis
hogging Negrito signora dehisce agitate ceilidh driving glisten naiades
hoggish negroid signore echelon agitato ceiling drizzle glister nailery
hogwash niggard signori echidna alidade Chianti drizzly glitter naively
hogweed niggler signory echinus alienly chiasma dwindle goitred naivete
hugeous nightie soggily echoism aliform chibouk edictal gribble naivety
hugging nightly suggest enhance aliment chicane edifice griddle neither
hygeian nigrify Tagalog ephebus alimony Chicano edition griffin noisily
hygiene nogging tagetes ephedra aliquot chicken ekistic griffon noisome
ingenue ongoing tagging ethanol amiable chicory elision grifter obitual
ingesta organic tegmina etheric amiably chidden elitism grilled olivary
ingoing organon tegular ethical amildar chiefly elitist griller olivine
ingraft organum tighten ethiops aniline chiffon emicate grimace omicron
ingrain organza tightly ethmoid anility chigger eminent grimmer ominous
ingrate pageant tigress exhaust animate chignon emirate grinder omitted
ingress pageboy tigrish exhibit animism childer emitted grinned opinion
ingroup paginal toggery exhumer animist childly emitter gripped orifice
ingrown Pegasus tugboat gahnite anionic chiliad epicarp gripper origami
jaggery pegging tugging Gehenna aniseed chillum epicede griskin ovicide
jigging piggery ungodly ichabod apishly chimera epicene gristle oviduct
jogging pigging unguard inhabit aridity chimere epicure gristly oviform
jogtrot piggish unguent inhaler arietta chimney epidote gritted oxidant
jugging pigiron ungulae inherit aristae chindit epigeal grizzle oxidase
juggins piglead upgrade inhibit aristas Chinese epigene grizzly oxidate
juggler pigling urgency inhouse Asiatic Chinook epigene guichet oxidise
jugular pigmean vagally inhuman asinine chintzy epigone Guignol pailful
laggard pigment vagrant Ishmael atingle chinwag epigoni guilder painful
lagging pigskin vaguely mahaleb aviator chipped epigram guipure painter
legally pigtail vaguish mahatma avidity chipper epigyny guisard pairoar
legatee pigwash vegetal Mahdism avionic chirrup epilate haircut paisley
legator pigweed voguish Mahdist axially chitter episode hairnet philter
legbail pugging wagerer mahjong axillae clicker epistle hairpin philtre
legging puggish waggery mahonia axillar climate epitaph heighho pliable
leghorn puggree wagging mahound Azilean climber epitaxy heinous pliably
legible pugmill waggish mahseer azimuth clinker epithem heiress pliancy
legibly pugnose wagoner Nahuatl bailiff clipped epithet iciness plicate
legiron pygmean wagtail ochrous beignet clipper epitome idiotic pliskie
legless pygmoid wigging oghamic blighty clippie epizoic imitate poinder
legpull ragbolt wiggler ophitic blinder cliquey epizoon initial pointed
legrest ragdoll wigless pahlavi blindly clivers ericoid irideal pointer
legroom raggedy yeggman reheard blinker coinage eristic iridise priapic
legshow ragging yoghurt rehouse blintze coinbox evictor iridium pricker
legwork ragtime ziganka schappe blister coition evident Irishry pricket
lighted ragweed zygosis schemer blither cribbed exigent Jainism prickle
lighten ragworm zygotic scherzi boiling cribble faience joinder prickly
lighter ragwort Achaean scherzo bribery cricket failing joinery primacy
lightly regalia Achaian schlepp brickie cricoid failure joining primage
lignify regally Achates schlock brickle crimine faintly jointer primary
lignite regards achieve schmuck bricole crimper fairing jointly primate
ligroin regatta adherer schnook bridoon crimple fairish juicily primely
logbook regency adhibit scholar briefly crimson fairway kainite primero
logging regimen Amharic scholia brigade cringer feigner klipdas priming
logical reginal aphasia sphenic brigand cringle flicker knitted primmed
logline regnant aphasic spheral brimful crinite flighty knitter primula
logwood regorge aphelia spheric brimmed crinkle flipped krimmer printer
luggage regrant apheses sthenic brimmer crinkly flipper Krishna prithee
lugging regrate aphesis unhandy brinded crinoid flitted laicise privacy
lughole regress aphetic unhappy brindle criollo flitter laicism private
lugsail regrets aphides unheard bringer cripple flivver lairage privily
lugworm regroup aphonia unhinge brinjal crisper friable leister privity
magenta regular aphonic unhitch brioche crisply friarly leisure quibble
maggoty regulus aphotic unhoped briquet cristae fribble lyingin quicken
magical rigging aphylly unhorse brisken critter frigate lyingly quickie
magmata righten ashamed unhouse brisket cuirass frijole maidish quickly
magnate righter ashtray upheave briskly cuisine fripper maidism quieten
magneto rightly atheism vehicle bristle cuittle friseur mailbag quietly
```

```
quietus skimmia stipend tripple wrinkly balance caloric doltish gallows
quillet skinful stipple trireme writeup balcony calorie dulcify galumph
quilter skinker stipule trisect writhen balding calotte dullard gelatin
quinary skinned stirpes trishaw writing baldish caloyer dullish gelding
quinate skinner stirred trismus written baldric calpack dulness gelidly
quinine skipped stirrer tritely Zoilism baleful caltrap eclipse gelling
quinone skipper stirrup tritium Zoilist ballade caltrop eclogue gilbert
quintal skippet suicide tritone abjurer ballast calumet eelpout gilding
quintan skirret suiting triumph adjoint ballboy calumny eelworm gillnet
quintet skirted swiftly trivial adjourn balloon calvary ellipse giltcup
quintic skirter swigged trivium adjudge balmily calyces enlarge goldbug
quipped skitter swiller tuition adjunct baloney calycle enliven golfbag
quitted skittle swindle twibill bejewel belated calypso erlking golfing
quitter slicker swinery twiddle cajoler belcher calyxes eulogia goliard
quivery slickly swinery twiddly injurer beldame celadon Falange Goliath
quixote slidden swinger twigged jejunum Belgian celesta falbala gullery
quizzed slimily swingle twilled jujitsu believe celeste falcate Halakah
quizzer slimmer swinish twinkle majesty bellboy cellist falcula halberd
quizzes slinger swipple twinkly pajamas bellhop cellule fallacy halbert
railcar slinker swither twinned pyjamas belljar Celsius fallguy halcyon
railing slipped Switzer twister Rajpoot bellman chlamys falling halfway
railman slipper swizzle twitchy rejoice bellows chloral falloff halfwit
railway slipway tailend twitted sojourn beloved chloric fallout halibut
raiment slither tailing twitter unjoint Beltane ciliary falsely halidom
rainbow smidgen thiamin tzigane ackemma belting ciliate falsies hallali
reissue smidgin thicken tzigany alkalis belying coldish falsify hallway
rhiancy smitten thicket unicity alkanet bilboes coletit falsity halogen
rhizoid snicker thickly unicorn Alkoran biliary colicky felonry halting
rhizome sniffer thieves unideal askance bilimbi colitis felsite halvers
roister sniffle thigger unifier askesis bilious collage felspar halyard
ruinate snifter thiller uniform awkward billing collard felting helical
ruinous snigger thimble unitary baklava billion collate felucca helices
saidest sniggle thinker unitive beknown billowy collect felwort helicon
sailing snipped thinned urinary bilobar colleen filacer hellbox
sainted snipper thinner utilise ilkaday bilobed college filaria hellcat
saintly snippet thirdly utility inkhorn biltong collide filasse Hellene
sciarid soignee thirsty Vaishya inkling boletus collier filbert hellion
sciatic soilure thistle veiling inkwell bolivar collins filemot hellish
science spicate thistly veinlet irksome bollard colloid filiate helluva
scirrhi spicery thither veinlet jukebox bologna collude filibeg helotry
scissel spicily toilful voivode lakelet boloney colobus filings helpful
scissor spicula triable wailful likable bolshie cologne filling helping
seismal spicule triacid waisted makings bolster colonel filmdom hilding
seismic spidery triadic waister nakedly bulbous colonic filmset hillman
seizing spieler tribade waiting oakfern bulimia colossi folding hillock
seizure spignel triblet weigher oakgall bulkily colours foldout hilltop
shicker spikily tribune weighin oakling bullace coloury foliage holdall
shifter spiller tribute weighty oaktree bullary coltish foliate holding
shikari spinach triceps weirdie oakwood bullate culices foliole holibut
shilpit spindle tricker weirdly pikelet bullbat cullion foliose holiday
shimmer spindly trickle whicker pikeman bulldog culotte folkway holland
shindig spindry tricksy whidder rakeoff bullion culprit follies holmium
shingle spinner tricorn whiffle sakeret bullish cultism fulcrum holmoak
shingly spinney trident whimper Saktism bullock cultist fulgent holster
shinned spinode triduan whimsey Sikhism bullpen culture fulgour hulking
shinpad spinoff triduum whinger sokeman bulrush culvert fullage idlesse
shiplap spinose trifler whipped takeoff bulwark dallier fullout illbred
shipman spinous triform whipper takings calamus delaine fulmine illegal
shipped spinule trigamy whippet tektite calando delator fulness illicit
shippen spiraea trigger whipsaw unkempt calcify delayer fulsome illness
shipper spirant trilith whirler unknown calcine delight fulvous inlayer
shippon spireme trilogy whirred wakeful calcite Delilah Galahad Islamic
shipway spirits trimmed whisker wakener calcium delimit galanga jaloppy
shirker spitted trimmer whiskey ablator calculi deliver galatea jellaba
shittim spitter trinary whisper aileron caldera delouse galeate jellied
shivers spittle trindle whistle ailment caldron Delphic galenic jollify
shivery stibine tringle whitely alleged calends deltaic galilee jollity
skiable sticker trinity whither allegro calibre deltoid galipot kalends
skidded stickit trinket whiting allelic calices deluder gallant Kalmuck
skidlid stickle trinkum whitish allergo caliche dilated gallate kalpack
skidpan stickup triolet whitlow allheal calicle dilator galleon killick
skiffle stiffen tripery Whitsun allonge calipee dilemma gallery killing
skijump stiffly triplet whittle allover caliper diluent gallfly killjoy
skilful stifler triplex whizkid allseed callant dilutee gallice kilobar
skilift stilted tripody whizzed allstar callbox diluter galling kiloton
skilled Stilton tripoli wriggle alltime callboy dilutor galliot kolkhoz
skillet stimuli tripped wriggly alluvia calling doleful gallium Lallans
skimmed stinger tripper wringer aplasia callous dollish lilting
skimmer stinker trippet wrinkle aplenty calomel dolphin galloon Lollard
```

```
lullaby  pelisse  salvoes  unleash  almsman  comrade  Homerid  mummery  similor
malacia  peloria  scleral  unlined  ammeter  Comtian  hominid  mummify  simitar
malaise  peloric  selenic  unloose  ammonal  Comtism  homonym  mumming  simpler
malaria  pelorus  selffed  unlucky  ammonia  Comtist  humanly  mumpish  simplex
Malayan  peltate  selfish  valance  armband  cumquat  humbles  namable  simular
malefic  pelting  sellout  valence  armfuls  cumshaw  humbuzz  nameday  somatic
malines  phlegmy  seltzer  valency  armhole  cumulus  humdrum  nemesia  someday
malison  pileate  selvage  valeric  armiger  cymbalo  humeral  nemesis  somehow
mallard  pilgrim  silence  valiant  armless  damming  humerus  nimiety  someone
malleus  pillage  silenus  validly  armlike  damnify  humidly  nomadic  someway
malmsey  pillbox  silesia  vallate  armoire  damning  humidor  nomarch  somitic
maltase  pillion  silicic  valonia  Armoric  damosel  humming  nombril  summand
Maltese  pillock  silicle  valuate  armoury  damozel  hummock  nominal  summary
malting  pillory  silicon  valvate  armrest  dampish  humoral  nominee  summery
maltose  pillowy  siliqua  valvula  armsful  demerit  hymenia  numbles  summing
melange  pillule  silique  valvule  bambini  demesne  hymnary  numeral  summons
melanic  pilsner  silkily  velamen  bambino  demigod  hymnist  numeric  sumpter
melanin  pilular  sillily  velaria  bimanal  demirep  hymnody  nummary  symptom
melilot  polacca  silvern  veliger  bombard  demoded  immense  nymphal  tamable
melisma  polacre  silvery  velours  bombast  demonic  immerge  nymphet  tamarin
melodic  poleaxe  solanum  veloute  bumbler  demotic  immerse  oomiack  tamasha
melting  polecat  solaria  velvety  bumboat  demount  immoral  osmosis  tambour
mildewy  polemic  solatia  vilayet  bummalo  dimeric  Ismaili  osmotic  Tammany
mileage  polenta  soldier  village  bumming  dimeter  jamming  osmunda  tamping
milfoil  politic  solicit  villain  bumpily  dimmest  jemadar  pampean  tampion
miliary  pollack  solidly  villein  bumpkin  dimming  jimjams  pampero  tempera
militia  pollard  solidus  villose  camaron  dimmish  jumbuck  pemican  tempest
milking  pollock  soliped  villous  cambial  dimness  jumpjet  pimento  Templar
milkleg  pollute  soloist  volante  cambist  domical  jumpoff  pimping  templet
milkman  poloist  Solomon  volcano  cambium  dominie  kampong  pomatum  tempter
milksop  polygon  soluble  voltage  cambrel  dumpish  kumquat  pomfret  tempura
milldam  polymer  solvate  voltaic  cambric  ermined  Lamaism  pompano  timbale
million  polynia  solvent  voluble  camelot  famulus  Lamaist  pompous  timbrel
milreis  polynya  splashy  volubly  camelry  feminal  lambast  pumpkin  timelag
molimen  polypod  spleeny  volumed  cameral  femoral  lambent  Ramadan  timeous
mollify  polypus  splenic  volutin  campbed  fimbria  lambert  rambler  timidly
mollusc  Pullman  splicer  vulgate  camphor  fumbler  lambkin  ramekin  timothy
molossi  pullout  splodge  vulpine  campion  gambade  lamella  ramenta  timpani
mulatto  pulpous  splotch  vulture  camping  gambado  laminae  ramming  timpano
mullein  pulsate  splurge  walking  camwood  gambier  laminar  rampage  tombola
mullion  pulvini  sulcate  walkout  cembalo  gamboge  lamming  rampant  tombolo
mullock  pyloric  sulkily  walkway  cimices  gambrel  lampion  rampart  tomenta
multure  pylorus  sullage  wallaby  combine  gamebag  lampoon  rampion  tomfool
mylodon  rallier  sulphur  walleye  combout  gamelan  lamprey  ramsons  tompion
nelumbo  ralline  sultana  walling  combust  gametic  lemmata  remains  tumbler
Nilotic  relapse  syllabi  wallrue  comedic  gemmate  lemming  remarry  tumbrel
nullify  related  sylphid  waltzer  cometic  gemmery  limbate  remblai  tumbril
nullity  relater  sylvine  welcher  comfort  gemming  limbeck  remiges  tumidly
nylghau  relator  sylvite  welcome  comfrey  gemmule  limbous  remnant  tumular
obligee  relayed  talaria  welfare  comical  gemsbok  liminal  remodel  tumulus
obligor  release  talayot  welloff  comitia  gimbals  limited  remorse  tympana
oblique  reliant  talcose  wellset  command  gimmick  limiter  remould  tympani
obloquy  relieve  talcous  welsher  commend  gombeen  limosis  remount  tympano
oilbath  relievo  talipes  wildcat  commode  gomeral  limpkin  removal  tympany
oilbird  relight  talipot  wilding  commons  gomeril  limulus  removed  unmanly
oilcake  relique  talking  wildish  commove  gumboil  Lombard  remover  unmeant
oildrum  rilievo  tallage  willies  commune  gumboot  lomenta  rimming  unmixed
oilseed  rollick  tallboy  willing  commute  gumdrop  lumbago  romance  unmoral
oilskin  rolling  tallish  willowy  compact  gumming  lumbang  Romanic  unmoved
oilwell  rollmop  tallith  wolfcub  compare  gummite  lumenal  Romansh  vamoose
oolitic  rolltop  tallowy  wolfdog  compart  gumshoe  luminal  romaunt  vampire
paladin  salable  telamon  wolfish  compass  gymnast  lumpily  Rommany  vampish
palatal  salicet  teleost  wolfram  compeer  gymslip  lumpish  rumbler  womanly
palaver  salicin  telergy  wolvish  compend  Hamburg  mamelon  rumness  zemstvo
paletot  salient  telling  ycleped  compere  Hamitic  mamilla  rummage  zymogen
palette  Salique  telpher  yellowy  compete  hamming  mammary  rumshop  zymosis
palfrey  sallowy  Telstar  yolksac  compile  hammock  mammate  samisen  zymotic
palings  salpinx  tilbury  yulelog  complex  hamster  mammock  samovar  zymurgy
pallium  salsify  tillage  zillion  complin  hamulus  mammoth  Samoyed  adnexal
palmary  saltant  tollbar  admiral  complot  hemiola  memento  sampler  agnatic
palmate  saltbox  tollman  admirer  compony  hemione  memoirs  samurai  agnomen
palmist  saltcat  toluene  aimless  comport  hemline  mimesis  sematic  amnesia
palmoil  saltern  tulchan  almanac  compose  hemlock  mimetic  semilog  amnesic
palmyra  salting  tylopod  almirah  compost  hemming  mimical  seminal  amnesty
palpate  saltire  unladen  almoner  compote  himself  mimicry  seminar  annates
palsied  saltish  unlatch  almonry  compute  homager  mimulus  semiped  annatta
paludal  saltpan  unlearn  almsman  comrade  homburg  momenta  Semitic  annatto
pelagic  saluter  ...      ...      ...      Homeric  mimesis  similar  annelid
pelican  salvage  unlearn  almonry  compute  Homeric  mumbler  similar  annicut
```

annuity	centavo	convene	gangway	January	mangoes	montane	pinking	sinuous
annular	centime	convent	gantlet	jingler	mangold	montero	pinkish	sonance
annulet	centner	convert	general	jonquil	manhole	monthly	pinnace	sonancy
annulus	central	convict	generic	juncoes	manhood	mundane	pinnate	songful
awnless	centred	convoke	geneses	Jungian	manhour	mundify	pinning	sonless
banally	centric	cuneate	genesis	juniper	manhunt	munnion	pinnule	sonship
bananas	centrum	cunette	genetic	Kannada	manihot	munting	pintado	sunbath
bandage	century	cunning	genette	Kantian	manikin	muntjac	pintail	sunbeam
bandana	cindery	cynical	Genevan	kenning	manilla	muntjak	pintuck	sunbear
bandbox	cineast	dandify	genista	kenosis	manille	mynheer	pinworm	sunbird
bandeau	cineole	Danelaw	genitor	kenotic	maniple	nankeen	pondage	sunburn
bandore	cingula	dangler	genizah	kentish	manitou	ninepin	poniard	sundeck
bandsaw	conacre	danseur	genning	kinchin	manjack	nonagon	pontage	sundial
baneful	conatus	Dantean	Genoese	kindler	mankind	noniron	pontiff	sundisc
banjoes	concave	denarii	genteel	kindred	manless	nonplus	pontify	sundown
banking	conceal	denizen	gentian	kinesis	manlike	nonskid	pontoon	sunfish
banksia	concede	densely	gentile	kinetic	manmade	nonslip	puncher	sunlamp
banning	conceit	density	genuine	kinfolk	manners	nonstop	punchup	sunless
bannock	concent	dentate	gingery	kingcup	manning	nonsuch	punctum	sunnily
banquet	concept	dentine	gingham	kingdom	mannish	nonsuit	pungent	sunning
banshee	concern	dentist	gingili	kinglet	mannite	nonuser	Punjabi	Sunnite
banteng	concert	denture	ginning	kingpin	mannose	nunatak	punning	sunrise
banting	conchae	dinette	ginseng	kinship	mansard	nunhood	punster	sunroof
bencher	conchie	dingily	gonadal	kinsman	mansion	nunnery	rancher	sunspot
beneath	concise	dingoes	gondola	lancers	mansize	nunnish	rancour	sunstar
benefic	concoct	dinning	gonidia	landing	manteau	nunship	ranking	sunsuit
benefit	concord	donator	gunboat	languet	mantlet	oenomel	ransack	suntrap
Benelux	concuss	donning	gunfire	languid	mantram	omneity	reneger	sunward
Bengali	condemn	donnish	gunlock	languor	mantrap	omnibus	renewal	sunwise
benison	condign	dunbird	gunnera	laniary	manumit	omnific	renewer	synapse
benthic	condole	dungeon	gunnery	lankily	manward	panacea	rentier	syncarp
benthos	condone	Dunkirk	gunning	lanolin	manweek	panache	ringent	syncope
benzene	conduce	dunnage	gunplay	lantana	Manxcat	pancake	ringing	synergy
benzine	conduct	dunning	gunroom	lantern	Manxman	Pandean	ringlet	synesis
benzoic	conduit	dunnock	gunship	lanyard	manyear	pandect	rondeau	syngamy
benzoin	condyle	dynamic	gunshot	lending	mending	pandora	rondure	synodal
benzole	confect	dynasty	gunwale	lengthy	menfolk	pandore	rondure	synodic
benzoyl	confess	einkorn	handbag	lenient	menisci	panicky	rontgen	synonym
bindery	confide	ennoble	handcar	lentigo	menorah	panicle	runaway	synovia
binding	confine	fanatic	handful	lentisk	menthol	Panjabi	rundale	tanager
bonanza	confirm	fancier	handgun	lentoid	mention	pannage	rundlet	tanagra
bondage	conflux	fancily	handily	linctus	minaret	pannier	rundown	tanbark
bondman	conform	fanclub	handler	lindane	mincing	panning	runless	tandoor
bonedry	confuse	fanfare	handoff	lineage	mindful	panocha	running	tangelo
boneset	confute	fanfold	handout	lineate	mineral	panoply	sanctum	tangent
bonfire	congeal	fanmail	handsaw	lineman	minever	panther	sanctus	tanghin
bongoes	congest	fanning	handsel	lineout	miniate	panties	Sanctus	tangram
bonkers	conical	fantail	handset	lingual	minibus	pantile	sandbag	tankage
bonnily	conidia	fantasm	hangdog	linkage	minicab	penally	sandbar	tankard
bungler	conifer	fantast	hanging	linkboy	minicar	penalty	sandbed	tankcar
bunraku	coniine	fantasy	hangman	linkman	minikin	penance	sandbox	tankful
bunting	conjoin	fantods	hangout	Linnean	minimal	pendant	sandboy	tannage
canakin	conjure	fencing	Hansard	linocut	minimum	pendent	sanders	tannate
canasta	conkers	fenfire	hanuman	linsang	minimus	pending	sandfly	tannery
candela	connate	fenland	henbane	linseed	miniver	penguin	sandlot	tanning
candent	connect	finagle	hencoop	longago	minorca	penname	sandman	tannish
candied	conning	finally	hennery	longbow	minster	pennant	sandpit	tanooze
candour	connive	finance	henpeck	longday	mintage	pennate	sangria	tantara
canikin	connote	finback	henwife	longhop	minuend	pennies	sanicle	tantivy
cannery	conquer	finding	hindgut	longing	minutes	pennill	santour	tantric
cannily	consent	finesse	honesty	longish	minutia	pennine	senarii	tantrum
canning	consign	finical	honeyed	lunatic	monacal	penning	senator	tanyard
cannula	consist	finicky	honours	luncher	monadic	pension	senatus	tenable
canonic	console	finikin	hundred	lunette	monarch	pensile	sendoff	tenably
canonry	consort	finings	hunkers	lunular	mondial	pensive	senecio	tenancy
Canopic	consult	finning	Hunnish	lyncean	moneyed	pentane	senhora	tendril
cantata	consume	Finnish	hunting	lynchet	moneyer	pentode	senores	tenfold
cantate	contact	fondant	igneous	manacle	mongrel	pentose	sensory	tenoner
canteen	contain	fondler	igniter	manager	moniker	pinball	sensual	tenpins
canthus	contemn	funeral	ignoble	manakin	monitor	pincers	Senussi	tensely
cantina	contend	funfair	ignobly	manatee	monkery	pincher	sincere	tensile
canting	content	fungoid	ignorer	manchet	monkish	pinetum	singlet	tension
cantrip	contest	fungous	innards	mandala	monocle	pinfire	sinkage	tensity
canvass	context	funicle	innerve	mandate	monocot	pinfish	sinless	tensive
canzone	contort	funnies	innings	mandola	monodic	pinfold	sinning	tentbed
canzoni	contour	funnily	Janeite	mandora	monomer	pinguid	sinopia	tentfly
cenacle	control	funning	jangler	mandrel	monsoon	pinhead	sinsyne	tenthly
censure	contuse	ganglia	janitor	mandril	monster	pinhole	sintery	tentpeg
centaur	convect	gangrel	jannock	mangily	montage	pinkeye	sinuate	tenuity

```
tenuous zinking booster crownet footboy knotted probate scolder spongin
tinamos zonated bootleg crowtoe footing knotter probity scollop sponson
tindery abolish boozeup crozier footman knowall problem scomber sponsor
tinfoil abomasa boozily deodand footpad knowhow proceed scooper spoofer
tingler aborter broaden deodara footrot knowing process scooter spooney
tinhorn abought broadly diocese footsie Laotian proctor scopula spoorer
tinnily aboulia brocade diopter footway leonine procure scoriae sporran
tinning acolyte brocket dioptre frogeye leopard prodded scorify sporter
tintack aconite broider diorama frogged leotard prodder scoring sporule
tinware acouchy broiler diorism frogman lioncel prodigy scorner spotted
tonally adopter brokage diorite fronded lioness produce scorper spotter
tonemic aeolian broking dioxide frontal lionise product Scorpio spousal
tonerow aeonian bromate doodler fronton looking profane scotice spouter
tonight agonise bromide doomful frosted lookout profess Scotism stocker
tonnage agonist bromine doorman froward looksee proffer Scotist stoical
tonneau alodial bromism doormat frowsty loosely profile scotoma stomach
tonsure alodium bronchi doorway geodesy Miocene profuse Scottie stomata
tontine aloetic broncho drogher geogony moocher progeny scourer stonily
tunable aloofly brooder dromond geoidal moodily program scourge stonker
tunably amoebae brothel droplet geology mooneye project scouter stopgap
tundish amoebas brother dropout Geordie moonlit prolate shocker stopoff
tuneful amoebic brought dropped georgic moonset prolong shoeing stopped
tunicle amongst brownie dropper ghostly moorage promise shogged stopper
tunning amorist browser drosera globoid moorhen promote shoofly stopple
Tynwald amorous buoyage droshky globose mooring pronaoi shooter storage
unnerve anodise buoyant drought globule Moorish pronaos shopboy storied
vanadic anodyne chocice drouthy glorify moorlog pronate shopman stouten
Vandyke anoesis Choctaw droving glossal muonium pronely shopped stoutly
vanessa anoetic cholera duodena Glossic myogram pronged shopper stovies
vanilla anomaly choline duopoly glottal myology pronoun shoring stowage
vantage anosmia chooser ebonise glottis myomata propane shorten swobbed
vanward anosmic choosey ebonite glozing Neogaea propend shortie swollen
venally another chopine ecology gnocchi neolith prophet shortly swopped
venatic apocope chopped economy gnomish neology propine shotgun swopper
vendace apodous chopper egotise gnostic neonate propjet shotten swotted
venefic apogamy chorale egotism goodbye neoteny propone shouter Thomism
venerer apogean chordal egotist goodday neozoic propose showbiz Thomist
venison apology chorine egotrip goodish niobium propped showery thorite
ventage apolune chorion Elohism goodman noology prorate showily thorium
ventail apostil choroid Elohist gooiest noonday prosaic showing thorned
ventral apostle chortle emotion Grobian nooning prosify showman thought
venture apothem chowder emotive grocery obolary prosily showoff toolbox
venturi arousal cloacae enounce grogram obovate prosody skolion tooling
vinasse asocial cloacal epochal Grolier obovoid prosper slobber toothed
vincula atomise clobber eponymy grommet odontic protean sloegin tootsie
vinegar atomism clocker epoxide groover odorant protect slogged trochal
vintage atomist clogged erodent grossly odorous protege slogger trochee
vintner avocado clogger erosion grottos odoured proteid slopped trochus
wanigan axolotl closely erosive grouchy oloroso protein sloshed trodden
wanness biology closeup erotica grouper opossum protend slotcar troller
wannish biomass closure erotism groupie orogeny protest slotted trolley
wanting bionics clothes esotery grouser orology proteus slouchy trollop
wencher biotite clotted Etonian growler orotund protist sloughy trommel
Wendish bloated cloture evolute grownup otolith protium Slovene trooper
windage bloater cookery exocarp hoodlum otology proudly slowish trophic
windbag blocker cooking exogamy hooklet ovoidal proverb smokeho tropics
windegg blooded cookout exordia idolise Oxonian provide smokily tropism
windily bloomer coolant exotica inocula ozonise proviso smoking trotted
winding blossom coolish feoffee ipomoea peonage provoke smoochy trotter
windrow blotchy cooncan feoffer ironing phoenix provost smother trouble
Windsor blotted coontie feoffor ironist phonate prowess snooker trounce
winesap blotter croaker floater isobath phoneme prowler snooper trouper
winglet blouson crochet floccus isochor phonics proximo snoozer trouser
wingnut blowdry crocket flogged isogamy phonily quondam snoozle twofold
winkers blowfly Croesus floorer isogeny photism reorder snorkel twoline
winning blowgun crofter floosie isogram pioneer rhodium snorter twoness
winnock blowout crooked floozie isohyet piously rhodora snouted twosome
winsome blowzed crooner flopped isokont plodded rhombic snowcap twostep
wintery boobook cropped floreat isolate plodder rhombus snowily twotime
xanthic bookend cropper florist isonomy plopped riotous snowman twotone
xanthin bookful croquet floruit isotope plosion roofing soonish urodele
yenning booking croquis flotage isotopy plosive rooftop soother urology
zincify bookish crosier flotsam isotron plotted rooinek soothly utopian
zincing booklet crossly flounce ivories plotter rookery sootily utopism
zincite bookman crouton flowage knobbed poofter roomful spodium utopist
zincked booksie crowbar flowery knobble poohbah rooster spoiler uxorial
Zingari boomlet crowdie foolery knobbly poorish rootage spondee violate
Zingaro Boolean crowned foolish knocker proband rootlet spondyl violent
zinkify boorish crowner footage knockon probang scoffer sponger violist
```

violone	cipolin	gypping	oophyte	sapling	inquest	auroras	carline	corvina
whoever	copaiba	hapence	oppidan	saponin	inquire	barbate	Carlism	corvine
whoopee	copaiva	hapenny	opposer	sapphic	inquiry	barbell	Carlist	corydon
whooper	copepod	hapless	oppress	sapping	liquate	barbule	carload	curable
whopper	copilot	haploid	Orphean	saprobe	liquefy	bargain	carmine	curacao
whorish	copious	haporth	Orphism	sapsago	liqueur	barilla	carnage	curacoa
whorled	coppery	happily	orphrey	sapwood	piquant	barline	caroche	curator
whoseso	coppice	happing	papadam	seppuku	request	barmaid	carotid	curcuma
woodcut	copular	heparin	papally	septate	requiem	baronet	carotin	cureall
woodman	copycat	hepatic	paperer	septime	require	baroque	carouse	curette
woodpie	copyist	heptane	Paphian	sipping	requite	barrack	carping	curiosa
woolfat	cupcake	hipbath	papilla	sophism	sequela	barrage	carport	curious
woolled	cupmoss	hipbone	papoose	sophist	sequent	barrier	carrack	curling
woollen	cupping	hipness	pappose	soppily	sequoia	barring	carrier	currach
wooloil	cuprite	hipping	paprika	sopping	tequila	barroom	carrion	curragh
woolsey	cuprous	hiproof	papulae	soprani	Tsquare	barytes	carroty	currant
woomera	cupsful	hipster	papular	soprano	unquiet	barytic	carryon	current
woozily	cupular	hopbind	papyrus	supping	unquote	bereave	carsick	currier
wrongly	cypress	hopeful	peppery	support	vaquero	bergylt	cartage	currish
wrought	Cyprian	hophead	peppill	suppose	abrader	berhyme	cartful	cursive
zeolite	Cypriot	hoplite	pepping	supreme	abreact	berline	cartoon	cursory
Zionism	cypsela	hopping	peptalk	supremo	abreast	berried	carving	curtail
Zionist	dapsone	hopsack	peptide	taperer	abridge	berserk	ceramic	curtain
zoogamy	deplane	hyperon	peptise	tapetal	abroach	birchen	cerebra	curtana
zoogeny	deplete	hypnoid	peptone	tapetum	acrasin	birddog	ceresin	curtsey
zoogony	deplore	hypogea	pipeful	tapioca	acreage	birdman	certain	curvate
zooidal	deplume	hypoxia	piperic	tapping	acridly	biretta	certify	darbies
zoology	deposal	hypoxic	pipette	taproom	acrobat	biriani	cerumen	dariole
zoonomy	deposit	impaint	pipping	taproot	acrogen	boracic	cervine	darkish
zootaxy	deprave	impanel	popadum	tapsman	acronym	borazon	chrisom	darling
zootomy	depress	impasse	popcorn	tapster	acroter	bordure	christy	darning
alphorn	deprive	impaste	popeyed	tepidly	acrylic	boredom	chromic	darshan
amphora	diploid	impasto	popover	tipcart	adrenal	borings	chronic	derange
amplify	diploma	impeach	poppied	tipping	aerator	bornite	Circean	derider
ampoule	dipnoan	impearl	popping	tippler	aerobic	borough	circler	derrick
ampulla	dipolar	imperil	popular	tipsify	aerosol	borscht	circlet	dervish
amputee	dipping	impetus	puparia	tipsily	African	borstal	circuit	direful
apparat	diptera	impiety	pupilar	tipster	agraffe	bortsch	circusy	dirtily
apparel	diptych	impinge	pupping	topcoat	agrapha	burbler	cirrose	dorhawk
appease	dupable	impious	rapeoil	topfull	aground	burdock	cirrous	Dorking
applaud	empanel	implant	raphide	tophole	aircrew	bureaus	coracle	dormant
applied	empathy	implead	rapidly	topiary	airdrop	bureaux	coranto	dormice
applier	emperor	implete	rapping	topical	airfare	burette	corbeil	dornick
appoint	empiric	implode	rapport	topknot	airflow	burgage	cordage	dortour
apprise	emplace	implore	rapture	topless	airglow	burgeon	cordate	durable
approve	emplane	imposer	repaint	topmast	airhole	burgess	cordial	durably
asperse	emporia	impound	repaper	topmost	airless	burghal	cordite	duramen
asphalt	empower	impresa	repiner	toponym	airlift	burgher	cordoba	durance
aspirer	empress	impress	repique	topping	airline	burglar	corella	durmast
aspirin	emprise	imprest	replace	topsail	airlock	Burmese	corkage	earache
baptise	emptier	imprint	replant	topside	airmail	burning	corking	eardrop
baptism	emptily	improve	replete	topsoil	airmiss	burnish	cornage	eardrum
baptist	emption	impulse	replevy	typebar	airport	burnous	corncob	earflap
bepaint	empyema	inphase	replica	typeset	airpost	bursary	corneal	earhole
bipedal	enplane	japonic	replier	typhoid	airship	burster	cornett	earldom
biplane	enprint	Jupiter	reposal	typhoon	airsick	burthen	cornfed	earlobe
bipolar	esparto	lapilli	reposit	typhous	airwave	burweed	cornice	earlock
bopping	espouse	lapping	repress	typical	already	Byronic	cornily	earmark
capable	eupepsy	Laputan	reprint	typonym	alright	caracal	Cornish	earmuff
capably	euphony	lapwing	reprise	umpteen	apraxia	caracul	cornist	earnest
capelin	expanse	leprosy	reproof	unpaged	apricot	caramel	cornual	earplug
caperer	expense	leprous	reprove	vapidly	apropos	caravan	cornuto	earring
capital	expiate	lipdeep	reptile	vapours	arraign	caravel	corolla	earshot
capitol	explain	lipless	repulse	vapoury	arrange	caraway	coronae	earthen
caporal	explant	lipping	reputed	xiphoid	arrayer	carbide	coronal	earthly
capping	explode	lipread	ripcord	yapping	arrears	carbine	coronas	ebriate
caprice	exploit	lopping	ripieni	yipping	arrival	carcase	coroner	ebriety
caprine	explore	lupulin	ripieno	zapping	arriver	carcass	coronet	eirenic
caproic	exposal	mapping	riposte	zaptieh	atresia	cardiac	corpora	errancy
Capsian	exposed	mopping	ripping	zipcode	atrophy	cardoon	correct	erratic
capsize	exposer	naphtha	ripplet	zipping	aurally	careful	corrida	erratum
capstan	exposit	napless	riptide	acquest	aureate	caribou	corrode	Euratom
capsule	expound	napping	ropable	acquire	aurelia	carinae	corrody	faraday
captain	express	nephric	ropeway	asquint	aureola	carinal	corrupt	faradic
caption	expulse	Neptune	rupture	bequest	aureole	carinas	corsage	faraway
captive	expunge	nippers	sapajou	coquito	auricle	carioca	corsair	farceur
capture	fopling	nippily	saphead	enquire	aurochs	cariole	corslet	farcing
capuche	foppery	nipping	sapient	enquiry	aurorae	carious	cortege	fargone
cepheid	foppish	nuptial	sapless	esquire	auroral	carking	cortile	farming

```
farmost furmety jargoon mordant partner pyrrhic sprayer throned waratah
Faroese furmity jarring mordent partook rarebit sprayey through warbler
farrago furnace jerkily moreish parvenu reredos spriggy thrower warfare
farrier furnish jurally morello parvise rorqual springe throwin wargame
farruca furrier juryman morendo percale rurally springy thrummy warhead
farther furring Karaite Moresco percent Saracen spryest torchon warison
fermata furrowy karakul Morisco percept sarangi straits torgoch warlike
ferment further karting morning percher sarcasm strange torment warlock
fermion furtive keramic morocco percine sarcode stratum tormina warlord
fermium garbage keratin moronic percoid sarcoid stratus tornado warmish
fernery garbler kermess morphia percuss sarcoma strayer torpedo warning
fernowl garboil kerogen mortice perdure sarcous streaky torpids warpath
ferrate gardant kerygma mortify perfect sardine stretch torrefy warrant
ferrety garfish Kirghiz mortise perfidy sardius stretta torrent warring
ferrite garland Koranic morulae perform sarking stretto torsade warrior
ferrous garment Kurdish morular perfume scraggy strewth torsion warship
ferrugo garnish kursaal morwong perfuse scranny striate tortile warthog
ferrule garotte larceny muraena pergola scraper strider tortrix wartime
fertile garpike lardoon murexes perhaps scrapie stridor torture wergild
fervent gerbera largely muriate periapt scrappy strigil torulae werwolf
fervour germane largess murices peridot scratch striker Toryism wireman
firearm giraffe largish murkily perigee scrawly stringy turbary wiretap
firebox girasol lording murrain perique scrawny striped turbine wordage
firebug girdler lorette murther periwig screech striven turdine wordily
firedog girlish lorgnon narrate perjure screeve striver turdoid wording
firefly gorcock loricae narrows perjury screwed strophe turfite workbag
fireman gorcrow lorimer narthex perkily screwer stroppy turfman workbox
firenew Gordian loriner narwhal perlite scribal strudel turgent workday
firstly gorilla lurcher neritic Permian scriber strumae Turkish working
firtree gorsedd lurdane nervate permute scrieve surbase turmoil workman
forager gurnard luridly nervine perpend scrimpy surcoat turnery workout
foramen harbour lyrated nervous perpent scrooge surface turning worldly
forayer hardhit lyrical nervure perplex scrouge surfeit turnipy wornout
forbade hardpan marabou nirvana Persian scrubby surfing turnkey worrier
forbear hardset Maratha norland persist scruffy surfman turnout worship
forbode hardtop Marathi norther persona scrumpy surgeon turpeth worsted
forbore harelip marbled norward pertain scrunch surgery tyranny yardage
forceps haricot marbles nursery perturb scruple surlily unravel yardang
fordone harijan marcher nursing pertuse Serbian surmise unready yardarm
forearm harmala marconi nurture perusal serfage surname unright yardman
foreign harmful maremma oarfish peruser serfdom surpass unroost Yorkist
foreleg harmony margent oarless pervade seriate surplus upraise abscess
foreman harness marimba oarlock pervert sericin surreal upright abscise
forepaw harpist mariner oarsman phrasal seriema surtout upriser abscond
foreran harpoon marital oarweed phratry seringa survive utricle absence
forerun harrier markhor oersted phrenic serious syringa variant absinth
foresaw harshen marking ogreish phrensy serpent syringe variate absolve
foresay harshly marline ourself piragua serpigo syrphid varices abstain
foresee harslet marlite parable piranha serpula tarbush variety alsoran
foretop harvest marmite parader piratic serrate tardily variola apsidal
forever herbage marplot parados pirogue serried tarnish variole apsides
forfeit heretic marquee paradox porcine servant tarrier various arsenal
forfend heritor marquis paragon porifer servery tarring varment arsenic
forgave herniae Marrano parapet porrect Servian tartare varmint assagai
forgery hernial married parasol portage service tartish varnish assault
forging hernias marring parboil portend servile tartlet varsity assayer
forgive heroics marrowy pardner portent serving Tartufe veranda assegai
forgoer heroine Marsala parerga portico Servite terbium verbena assizes
forgone heroism marshal paresis portion shrieve terebra verbose assuage
forkful heronry martial paretic portray shrilly tergite verdant assured
forlorn herring Martian parfait puritan shrinal termini verdict assurer
formant herself martini pargana purlieu shrivel termite verdure auspice
formate hirable martlet parkway purloin shriven ternary verglas austere
formula hircine martyry parlour purport shrubby ternate veriest austral
forsake hirsute Marxian parlous purpose sirgang terpene verismo bascule
forsook hirudin Marxism parodic purpura sirloin terrace vermeil baseman
forties horizon Marxist parolee purpure sirocco terrain vermian basenji
fortify hormone marybud paronym pursuer sorbent terrene vernier bashful
Fortran hornito mercery parotid pursuit Sorbian terrier verruca basidia
fortune hornmad merchet parpend purview sorcery terrify versant basilar
forward horrent mercury parquet pyralid sordini terrine versify basinet
forwent horrify mermaid parsley pyralis sordino tersely versine bassist
forworn horsily miracle parsnip pyramid sorghum tertial version bassoon
furbish hurdler mirador partake pyretic sorites tertian vertigo bastard
furcate hurdles mirbane partial pyrexia soroban thready vervain basting
furcula hurling mirkily parting pyrexic sororal thrifty virelay bastion
furioso hurried moraine partita pyrites sorosis thriven virgate beseech
furious hurtful morally partite pyritic sorrily throaty virgule beshrew
furlong Israeli morassy partlet pyrosis sprawly thrombi virtual besides
```

besiege	disband	fission	lashkar	muskrat	resolve	upstage	attrite	cittern
besmear	disbark	fissure	lassoes	mustang	resound	upstair	autarky	coterie
bespeak	discant	fistful	lasting	mustard	respect	upstart	autobus	cotidal
bespoke	discard	fistula	lesbian	mystery	respell	upsurge	autocar	cottage
bestead	discern	fossick	lissome	mystify	respell	upsweep	autocue	cottier
bestial	discerp	fossula	listeth	nasally	respire	upswept	autopsy	cottony
bestrew	discoid	fuscous	listing	nascent	respite	upswing	bateaux	cutaway
biscuit	discord	fusible	losable	nastily	respond	vascula	bathing	cutback
bismuth	discuss	fussily	lustful	nesting	respray	vastity	bathtub	cuticle
bistort	disdain	fusspot	lustily	nosebag	restart	vesicae	batiste	cutlass
bistred	disease	fustian	lustral	nosegay	restate	vesical	batsman	cutlery
boscage	diseuse	fustily	lustrum	noserag	restful	vesicle	battels	cutline
boskage	disfame	gascoal	mascara	nostril	restiff	vespers	battery	cutrate
bossism	disgust	gaseous	mashtub	nostrum	restive	vespine	batting	cutting
Boswell	dishorn	gasfire	Masonic	obscene	restock	vestige	betaken	cutworm
bushido	disjoin	gasmask	masonry	obscure	restore	vestral	bethink	datable
bushman	dislike	gasring	Masorah	observe	restyle	vesture	betimes	datival
bushtit	dislimn	gassing	masquer	oestral	resurge	visaged	betoken	deterge
busking	dismast	gastric	massage	oestrum	risible	viscera	betroth	detinue
bussing	dismiss	gestalt	masseur	oestrus	risotto	viscose	betting	detract
bustard	disobey	gestapo	massive	onshore	rissole	viscous	between	detrain
bustler	dispark	gestate	mastaba	onstage	roseate	visible	betwixt	detrude
cascade	dispart	gesture	masters	oosperm	rosebay	visibly	bittern	ditcher
cascara	display	goshawk	mastery	oospore	rosebud	visitor	bitters	dithery
caseous	disport	gosling	mastich	opsonic	rosecut	visored	bitting	dittany
caserne	dispose	gossipy	mastiff	opsonin	rosehip	vistaed	bittock	dotting
cashier	dispute	gossoon	mastoid	osselet	rosella	washing	bitumen	duteous
cassata	disrank	gushing	meseems	osseous	roseola	washout	botanic	dutiful
cassava	disrate	gustily	mesonic	osseter	rosered	washpot	botargo	eatable
cassino	disrobe	hasbeen	message	ossicle	rosette	washtub	botcher	ectopic
cassock	disroot	hashish	messiah	ossific	rostral	waspish	bottega	entasis
castile	disrupt	hassock	Messias	ossuary	rostrum	wassail	bottled	entente
casting	dissave	hastate	messily	paschal	russety	wastage	bottony	enteral
castled	disseat	hastily	messtin	passade	Russian	wastrel	botulin	enteric
castoff	dissect	hessian	mestiza	passado	Russify	western	butcher	enteron
casuals	dissent	histone	mestizo	passage	rustily	westing	buttend	enthral
casuist	distaff	history	miscall	passant	rustler	wishful	buttery	enthuse
cession	distain	hosanna	miscast	passing	sashimi	wishing	buttock	entitle
cesspit	distant	hosiery	miscopy	passion	sassaby	wistful	buttons	entomic
cestode	distend	hospice	misdate	passive	sessile	yashmak	buttony	entotic
cestoid	distent	hostage	misdeal	passkey	session	yestern	butyric	entozoa
cistern	distich	hostess	misdeed	pastern	sestina	zestful	Catalan	entrain
cosmism	distill	hostile	misdeem	pasteup	Sistine	actinia	catalos	entrant
cosmist	distort	hostler	misdone	pastime	sistrum	actinic	catalpa	entreat
cossack	disturb	husband	miserly	pasture	suspect	actinon	catarrh	entropy
costard	dossier	hushaby	misfire	pessary	suspend	actress	catawba	entrust
costate	duskily	huskily	misgave	piscary	suspire	actuary	catbird	entwine
costean	dustbin	husking	misgive	piscina	sustain	actuate	catboat	entwist
costing	dustily	Hussite	mishear	piscine	systole	althaea	catcall	estrade
costive	dustman	hustler	Mishnah	pismire	tastily	althorn	catcher	estreat
costrel	dustpan	insculp	misknow	pissoir	tessera	amtrack	catchup	estuary
costume	easeful	insecty	mislaid	pistole	testacy	antacid	catechu	eutexia
cushion	eastern	inshore	mislead	poseuse	testate	antbear	catenae	externe
cuspate	easting	insider	mislike	possess	testban	antefix	catenas	extinct
custard	ecstasy	insight	mismate	postage	testbed	antenna	cateran	extract
custody	enslave	insigne	misname	postbag	testfly	anthill	caterer	extreme
customs	ensnare	insipid	misplay	postbox	testify	anthrax	catfish	extrude
cystine	ensnarl	insofar	misread	postboy	testily	antigen	Cathari	fatally
cystoid	epsilon	inspect	misrule	posteen	testoon	antilog	Cathars	fateful
dashiki	essayer	inspire	missend	postern	testudo	antique	cathead	fathead
dashing	essence	install	missent	postfix	tosspot	antlion	cathode	fatigue
dashpot	essoyne	instant	missile	posting	tushery	antonym	cathood	fatling
dastard	eustasy	instate	missing	postman	tussive	apteryx	catlike	fatness
dasyure	exscind	instead	mission	posture	tussock	aptness	catling	fattest
descant	fascial	insular	missish	postwar	tussore	article	catmint	fatting
descend	fascine	insulin	missive	pushful	unsaved	artisan	catseye	fattish
descent	Fascism	insured	misstep	pushing	unscrew	artiste	catspaw	fatuity
deserve	Fascist	insurer	mistake	pushrod	unsexed	artless	catsuit	fatuous
despair	fashion	inswing	mistful	pustule	unshell	artwork	cattalo	fetidly
despise	fastday	issuant	mistily	raschel	unsight	astable	cattery	fetlock
despite	festive	jasmine	mistime	rasping	unsnarl	astatic	cattily	fetters
despoil	festoon	jussive	misting	rescale	unsound	asteria	catwalk	fitchet
despond	fishery	justice	mistook	rescind	unstick	astound	citable	fitchew
dessert	fisheye	justify	mistral	rescuer	unstuck	astride	citadel	fitment
destine	fishily	kestrel	Moselle	reseaux	unswear	attaboy	cithara	fitness
destiny	fishing	kissing	mosshag	reserve	unsworn	attache	cithern	fittest
destroy	fishnet	lasagna	muscled	reshape	upsides	attempt	citizen	fitting
disable	fishway	lasagne	musette	residua	upsilon	attract	citrate	futhark
disavow	fissile	lashing	musical	residue	upstage	attrite	citrine	futhorc

```
futhork lithoid optimum pitfall satrapy watered brutish drugget grumble
futtock litotes ortolan pithead satsuma waterer bruxism druidic grumbly
gateaux littery osteoid pithhat satyral wattage caudate drumlin grummet
gateleg liturgy ostiary pithily satyric Watteau caulker drummed grumose
gateway lottery ostiole pitiful satyrid wattled caustic drummer grumous
gathers lotting ostraca pitpony setback wattles cautery drunken grunion
gatling luteous ostraka pitprop setdown wetback caution duumvir grunter
getaway matador ostrich pitting setting wetness chuckle educate gruntle
getting matchet ottoman potable settler wettest chuddah eductor grutten
gittern matelot outback potamic settlor wetting chuddar elusion gruyere
Gstring matinal outcast potbank setwall wettish chuffed elusive hauberk
gutless matinee outcome potence sitdown withers chugged elusory haughty
gutsily matrass outcrop potency sitfast without chukker elution haulage
guttate mattery outdone pothead sithens witless chummed eluvial haulier
gutting matting outdoor potheen sitting witling chunnel eluvium haunted
hatable mattins outface potherb situate witloof chunter emulate haunter
hatband mattock outfall pothole sotting witness chupati emulous hautboy
hatcher mattoid outflow pothook sottish wittily churchy equable hauteur
hatchet matzoth outfoot potluck sutural witting chutney equably housing
hateful metamer outgone potshot sutured wottest clubbed equally inutile
hatless metayer outgrew pottage tatters yatagan clubman equator journal
hatting metazoa outgrow pottery tattery yttrium clumber equerry journey
hetaera methane outhaul potting tattily zetetic Cluniac equinal jouster
hetaira metonym outland putamen tatting zithern clupeid equinox knuckle
hitcher metopic outlast putdown tattler abubble cluster erudite knurled
hitting metopon outlier putlock tetanic abusive clutter exudate koumiss
Hittite metrics outline putrefy tetanus abutted Coueism exurban laugher
hotfoot metrist outlive puttier tetrode abutter couldst exurbia launder
hothead mettled outlook putting titanic acutely couloir exuviae laundry
hotness mitoses outmost Pythian tithing adulate coulomb exuvial laurels
hotshot mitosis outpace ratable titlark adultly coulter faucial leucine
hottest mitotic outplay ratafia titling ajutage council faunist leucite
hottish mitzvah outport ratatat titmice alumina counsel fauvism leucoma
hutment mottled outpost ratchet Titoism alumnae counter fauvist loudish
hutting mutable outrage rations Titoist alumnus country feudist lounger
icteric mutably outrank ratlike titrate alunite coupler flubbed lousily
icterus mutagen outride ratling tittupy amusive couplet fluence loutish
integer muttony outrode rattail titular anurous courage fluency louvred
intense mythise outrush ratteen totally aquaria courier fluidal maudlin
interim mythist outsell rattery totemic aquatic courlan fluidic maunder
interne nattily outshot ratting tottery aquavit courser fluidly mauther
intoner natural outside rattler totting aqueous courtly flummox mouflon
intrant netball outsize rattrap tutelar aquifer couthie flunkey moulder
intreat netfish outsold retable tutenag aquiver couture fluster mounter
introit netlike outsole retaken tutting asunder couvade fluting Mountie
intrude netsuke outstay rethink tutwork azurine couvert flutist mourner
intrust netting outtake retiary unteach azurite crucial flutter mousaka
intwine network outtalk reticle unthink Bauhaus crucian fluvial mousing
isthmus nitrate outturn retinae untried bauxite crucify fluxion mousmee
jetting nitride outvote retinal untruly blubber crudely fouette mouther
jitters nitrify outward retinas untruss blucher crudity foulard naughty
jittery nitrile outwear retinol untruth blueing cruelly foumart nauplii
jotting nitrite outwent retinue untuned bluffer cruelty founder nautics
jutting nitrous outwore retired untwine bluffly cruiser foundry nautili
kathode notable outwork retouch untwist blunder cruller fourale neurine
katydid notably outworn retrace untying blunger crumble fourgon neuroma
ketchup notched patagia retract upthrew bluntly crumbly fructed neurone
kitchen notedly patella retrain upthrow blurred crumpet fruited neuston
kitschy notelet patency retread uptight blusher crumple fruiter neutral
latakia notepad pathway retreat uptrend bluster crunchy frustum neutron
latchet nothing patient retrial utterer bouchee crupper gaudery noumena
latency notitia patrial retsina utterly boudoir crusade gaudily nourish
lateral nutcase patriot retting vatting boulder crusado Gaulish oculate
latexes nutgall patroon returns veteran boulter crusher gauntly oculist
lathery nutlike pattern retting vetiver bouncer crustal gauntry opulent
lathing nutpine patting rotator vetting bounden dauphin glucose opuntia
latices nutting petasus rotifer vitally bounder deutzia glummer opuscle
latrine oatcake petiole rotting vitamin bouquet diurnal gluteal ovulate
lattice oatmeal petrify rotunda vitelli bourbon doubler gluteus paucity
Latvian obtrude Petrine ruthful vitelli bourdon doubles glutted Pauline
letdown octagon petrous rutting vitiate bourree doublet glutton paunchy
lethean octaval pettily ruttish vitrify bourree doubter gouache plucker
letters octette petting satanic vitrine brucine doucely goulash plugged
letting October pettish satchel vitriol brucite doucely gourami plugger
Lettish octopod petunia satiate vittate bruhaha douceur gourmet plumage
lettuce octopus pitapat satiety vittles bruiser doughty goutfly plumate
literal octuple pitched satinet vitular brumous drubbed grubbed plumber
lithely optical pitcher satiric votable brusher drudger grubber plumbic
lithium optimal piteous satisfy watcher brusque drugged gruffly plumbob
```

```
plumery  slummer  tourism  foveola  waverer  rewrote  sixaine  flybook  stygian
plummet  slurred  tourist  gavotte  bawcock  rowboat  sixfold  flyhalf  stylise
plumose  smuggle  tourney  havenot  bawdily  rowdily  sixteen  flyleaf  stylish
plumper  smutted  truancy  invader  bewitch  rowlock  sixthly  flyover  stylist
plumply  snubbed  trucial  invalid  bowhead  sawbill  sixties  flypast  stylite
plumule  snubber  trucker  inveigh  bowlder  sawbuck  Sixtine  flyting  styloid
plunder  snuffer  truckle  inverse  bowlful  sawdust  taxable  flytrap  styptic
plunger  snuffle  trudgen  invitee  bowline  sawfish  taxfree  gayness  styrene
plunker  snuggle  truffle  inviter  bowling  sawgate  taxicab  glycine  thymine
plusage  soubise  trumeau  invoice  bowshot  sawmill  taxiing  glyphic  thyroid
plushly  souffle  trumpet  involve  bywoner  sawnoff  taximan  glyptal  thyrsus
pluvial  soulful  truncal  javelin  cowbane  sawwort  taxless  glyptic  thyself
pouched  sounder  trundle  lavolta  cowbell  sowback  taxying  gryphon  toyshop
poulard  soundly  trusser  lavrock  cowbird  towards  textile  grysbok  trypsin
poulter  soupcon  trustee  levator  cowfish  towboat  textual  gwyniad  tryptic
poultry  sourish  truster  levelly  cowhage  towered  texture  haycock  trysail
poundal  soursop  tsunami  leveret  cowhand  towhead  vexedly  hayfork  voyager
pounder  soutane  ukulele  livable  cowheel  towline  vexilla  hayloft  waybill
poussin  souther  ululant  livebox  cowherd  towmond  vixenly  hayrick  waylaid
pouting  spumous  ululate  liveoak  cowhide  towmont  waxbill  hayseed  wayless
prudent  spunkie  unusual  lovable  cowlick  townish  waxtree  hayward  waymark
prudery  spurner  usually  lovably  cowling  townlet  waxwing  haywire  wayside
prudish  spurred  usurper  loverly  cowpoke  towpath  waxwork  heyduck  wayward
pruning  spurrey  Vaudois  movable  cowshed  towrope  abysmal  idyllic  wayworn
prurigo  spurtle  vaulted  navarin  cowslip  unweave  abyssal  jaybird  wrybill
prussic  sputnik  vaulter  niveous  dawdler  unwound  acyclic  jaywalk  wryneck
raucous  sputter  vaunter  novella  dawning  unwoven  alyssum  joyance  wryness
raunchy  squabby  vouchee  novelle  dewclaw  upwards  amylase  joyless  bazooka
reunion  squacco  voucher  novelty  dewdrop  vowelly  amyloid  joyride  bezique
reunite  squaddy  wouldbe  obverse  dewfall  yewtree  amylose  keyhole  bizarre
rhubarb  squails  wouldst  obviate  dewpond  anxiety  anybody  keyless  buzzard
roughen  squalid  younger  obvious  dowager  anxious  anymore  keynote  buzzsaw
roughly  squally  younker  paviour  dowdily  auxesis  anyroad  keyring  cozener
roulade  squalor  advance  pivotal  downbow  auxetic  anytime  keyword  dazedly
rouleau  squamae  adverse  pivoter  enwheel  boxcalf  anyways  krypton  dazzler
rounded  squarer  advised  poverty  enwound  boxhaul  anywise  layered  dizzard
roundel  squashy  adviser  ravager  fewness  boxkite  azygous  layette  dizzily
rounder  squatty  advisor  ravelin  fowling  boxlike  bayonet  loyally  dozenth
roundly  squeaky  akvavit  ravined  gawkily  boxroom  boycott  loyalty  Elzevir
roundup  squeeze  alveoli  ravings  hawkish  boxseat  boyhood  mayoral  enzymic
rousing  squelch  bivalve  ravioli  howbeit  boxwood  Brython  maypole  fuzzily
rouster  squiffy  bivouac  revalue  however  coxcomb  buyable  Maytime  gazelle
routine  squinch  cavally  revelry  howling  dextral  cayenne  mayweed  gazette
saucily  squinny  cavalry  revenge  inwards  dextran  caymans  odyssey  gizzard
saunter  squirmy  caveman  revenue  inweave  dextrin  chymous  Olympic  guzzler
saurian  squishy  cavetti  reverie  inwoven  fixable  clypeal  onymous  jazzily
sauroid  squitch  cavetto  reverse  jawbone  fixedly  clypeus  oxyacid  jazzman
sausage  stubbed  caviare  reversi  jewelry  fixings  clyster  oxytone  Jezebel
scudded  stubble  civilly  reviler  jewfish  fixture  coyness  payable  lazaret
scuffle  stubbly  civvies  revisal  lawhand  foxhole  crybaby  paydesk  lozenge
sculler  stuccos  coverup  reviser  lawless  foxhunt  cryogen  payload  mazurka
sculpin  stuckup  cuvette  revisit  lawlist  foxtail  cryptal  payment  mazzard
scumble  studded  devalue  revival  lawlord  foxtrot  cryptic  payroll  mezuzah
scummed  student  develop  reviver  lawsuit  hexadic  crystal  paysage  mozetta
scunner  studied  deviant  revivor  lowborn  hexagon  daybook  physics  muzzily
scupper  stuffer  deviate  revolve  lowbred  hexapla  daylong  plywood  muzzler
scurril  stumble  devilry  revving  lowbrow  hexapod  dayroom  psychic  Naziism
scutage  stummed  devious  rivalry  lowdown  laxness  daystar  ptyalin  puzzler
scutate  stumper  devisal  rivered  lowland  lexical  daytime  rayless  sizable
scutter  stunned  devisee  riveter  lowlily  lexicon  daywork  reynard  sizably
scuttle  stunner  deviser  riviera  lowness  maxilla  doyenne  rhymist  sizzler
sfumato  stunted  devisor  riviere  lowrise  maximal  drycell  royally  sozzled
shucker  stupefy  devolve  rivulet  mawkish  maximum  drydock  royalty  wizened
shudder  stutter  devoted  savable  mawworm  maxwell  dryeyed  royster  ──────
shuffle  taunter  devotee  savanna  mowburn  Mexican  dryness  sayable  Abbasid
shunned  taurine  diverge  saveall  newborn  mixedly  drysalt  shylock  ablator
shunner  thudded  diverse  saveloy  newcome  mixedup  dryshod  shyness  abrader
shunter  thuggee  divider  savings  newlaid  mixture  elysian  shyster  Achaean
shuteye  thulium  diviner  saviour  newmown  myxomas  Elysium  skyblue  Achaian
shutout  thummim  divisor  savoury  newness  noxious  elytron  skyborn  Achates
shutter  thumper  divorce  seventh  newsboy  pyxides  elytrum  skyhigh  acrasin
shuttle  thunder  divulge  seventy  newsman  pyxidia  feyness  skyjack  addable
skulker  touched  dovecot  several  nowhere  saxhorn  flyable  skylark  advance
slubbed  toucher  dovekie  Sivaism  onwards  saxtuba  flyaway  skyline  aerator
slubber  touchup  envelop  Sivaite  powdery  sexfoil  flyback  skysail  afeared
slugged  toughen  envenom  vivaria  rawhide  sexless  flybane  skyward  affable
slugger  toughly  envious  vividly  rawness  Sextans  flybelt  slyness  affably
slumber  touraco  environ  vivific  rewound  sextant  flyblow  soybean  affaire
slummed  touring  foveate  wavelet  rewrite  sextile  flyboat  spyhole  agnatic
```

agraffe	botanic	decadal	forayer	lasagne	onwards	rhiancy	straits	visaged
agrapha	botargo	decagon	freaked	latakia	organic	ridable	strange	vitally
akvavit	breaded	decanal	friable	lazaret	organon	rivalry	stratum	vitamin
alcaide	breadth	decapod	friarly	legally	organum	romance	stratus	vivaria
alcalde	breaker	default	fugally	legatee	organza	Romanic	strayer	vocable
alcayde	breakin	degauss	Galahad	legator	oxyacid	Romansh	subacid	vocalic
alcazar	breakup	delaine	galanga	levator	pajamas	romaunt	subadar	vocally
alfalfa	breathe	delator	galatea	lieabed	paladin	ropable	subaqua	volante
alkalis	breathy	delayer	gelatin	likable	palatal	rotator	sudaria	votable
alkanet	broaden	denarii	getaway	livable	palaver	royally	swearer	voyager
almanac	broadly	derange	giraffe	locally	panacea	royalty	sweater	wadable
ambages	bugaboo	devalue	girasol	locater	panache	rubadub	synapse	Wahabee
ambatch	buyable	dibasic	gleaner	losable	papadam	runaway	tabanid	waratah
Amharic	cabaret	digamma	gliadin	lovable	papally	rurally	tabaret	wheaten
amiable	cacanny	dilated	gonadal	lovably	parable	Sabaism	tabasco	womanly
amiably	cadaver	dilator	gouache	loyally	parader	Sabaoth	Tagalog	wreathe
andante	calamus	disable	greaser	loyalty	parados	salable	talaria	wreathy
annates	calando	disavow	greaten	lucarne	paradox	sapajou	talayot	yatagan
annatta	camaron	donator	greatly	lunatic	paragon	Saracen	tamable	ziganka
annatto	canakin	dowager	greaves	lyrated	parapet	sarangi	tamarin	zonated
antacid	canasta	dreamed	Halakah	macabre	parasol	satanic	tamasha	abubble
aphasia	capable	dreamer	hatable	macadam	patagia	savable	tanager	antbear
aphasic	capably	ducally	heparin	macaque	payable	savanna	tanagra	anybody
aplasia	caracal	dupable	hepatic	mahaleb	Pegasus	sayable	taxable	Arabian
apparat	caracul	durable	hetaera	mahatma	pelagic	schappe	telamon	arabise
apparel	caramel	durably	hetaira	malacia	penally	sciarid	tenable	Arabist
apraxia	caravan	duramen	hexadic	malaise	penalty	sciatic	tenably	armband
aquaria	caravel	durance	hexagon	malaria	penance	scraggy	tenancy	babbitt
aquatic	caraway	dynamic	hexapla	Malayan	petasus	scranny	tetanic	babbler
aquavit	Catalan	dynasty	hexapod	manacle	phrasal	scraper	tetanus	bambini
arcaded	catalos	earache	hidalga	manager	phratry	scrapie	theatre	bambino
arcadia	catalpa	eatable	hidalgo	manakin	picador	scrappy	thiamin	barbate
arcanum	catarrh	Eleatic	hirable	manatee	piragua	scratch	tidally	barbell
areally	catawba	embargo	homager	marabou	piranha	scrawly	tinamou	barbule
areaway	cavally	embassy	hosanna	Maratha	piratic	scrawny	titanic	bibbery
arraign	cavalry	empanel	humanly	Marathi	pitapat	seeable	tobacco	bibbing
arrange	celadon	empathy	hydatid	matador	pleader	sematic	tonally	bilboes
arrayer	cenacle	endarch	ichabod	megaron	pleased	senarii	totally	blabbed
ascarid	ceramic	engaged	ideally	megaton	pliable	senator	towards	blabber
ascaris	cheapen	enhance	ilkaday	melange	pliably	senatus	treacle	blubber
ashamed	cheaply	enlarge	impaint	melanic	pliancy	shearer	treacly	bobbery
Asiatic	cheater	entasis	impanel	melanin	podagra	sheathe	treader	bobbing
askance	Chianti	equable	impasse	metamer	pofaced	sheaves	treadle	bobbish
assagai	chiasma	equably	impaste	metayer	polacca	Sivaism	treason	bogbean
assault	chlamys	equally	impasto	metazoa	polacre	Sivaite	treater	bombard
assayer	cidaris	equator	infancy	minaret	pomatum	sixaine	triable	bombast
astable	citable	ergates	infanta	miracle	popadum	sizable	triacid	boobook
astatic	citadel	errancy	infante	mirador	potable	sizably	triadic	brabble
attaboy	cleaner	erratic	infarct	modally	potamic	skiable	truancy	bribery
attache	cleanly	erratum	infauna	monacal	preachy	sneaker	tunable	bugbane
attaint	cleanse	escapee	inhabit	monadic	priapic	socager	tunably	bugbear
aurally	cleanup	escaper	inhaler	monarch	ptyalin	sofabed	tyranny	bulbous
autarky	clearly	esparto	inlayer	moraine	puparia	solanum	unbated	bumbler
aviator	cleaver	essayer	innards	morally	putamen	solaria	uncanny	bumboat
axially	cloacae	ethanol	invader	morassy	pyjamas	solatia	unearth	burbler
babassu	cloacal	Euratom	invalid	movable	pyralid	somatic	unfaith	byebyes
bagasse	cocaine	exhaust	inwards	mulatto	pyralis	sonance	unhandy	cabbage
Bahadur	codable	expanse	Islamic	muraena	pyramid	sonancy	unhappy	cabbagy
Bahaism	cohabit	Falange	Ismaili	mutable	Ramadan	speaker	unladen	cabbala
Bahaist	conacre	fanatic	Israeli	mutagen	ratable	splashy	unlatch	cambial
Bahaite	conatus	faraday	jacamar	mutably	ratafia	sprawly	unmanly	cambist
balance	copaiba	faradic	jemadar	myiasis	ratatat	sprayer	unpaged	cambium
banally	copaiva	faraway	joyance	nacarat	ravager	sprayey	unravel	cambrel
bananas	coracle	fatally	Judaean	naiades	regalia	squabby	unsaved	cambric
because	coranto	fedayee	Judaise	namable	regally	squacco	upraise	carbide
behaver	creamer	filacer	Judaism	nasally	regards	squaddy	upwards	carbine
belated	creator	filaria	Judaist	navarin	regatta	squails	usually	catbird
bepaint	croaker	filasse	jurally	nodally	relapse	squalid	vacancy	catboat
betaken	curable	finagle	Karaite	nodated	related	squally	vagally	cembalo
bimanal	curacao	finally	karakul	nomadic	relater	squalor	valance	Chablis
bivalve	curacoa	finance	keramic	nomarch	relator	squamae	vanadic	chibouk
bizarre	curator	fixable	keratin	nonagon	relayed	squarer	Vedanta	clabber
bleakly	cutaway	fleabag	kneader	notable	remains	squashy	velamen	clobber
bleater	Dadaism	fleapit	Koranic	notably	remarry	squatty	velaria	clubbed
bloated	Dadaist	floater	labarum	nunatak	repaint	stealer	venally	clubman
bloater	datable	flyable	ladanum	oceanic	repaper	stealth	venatic	cobbler
bonanza	debacle	flyaway	Lamaism	octagon	retable	steamer	veranda	combine
boracic	debater	forager	Lamaist	octaval	retaken	stearic	vilayet	combout
borazon	debauch	foramen	lasagna	oghamic	revalue	stearin	vinasse	combust

```
corbeil globose mudbath stabbed boscage deictic gorcock peacock shicker
cowbane globule mumbler stabber botcher descant gorcrow peccant shocker
cowbell gobbler nabbing stabile bouchee descend gracile peccary shucker
cowbird gombeen nebbish stabler boxcalf descent grackle percale sincere
crabbed grabbed netball stables boycott dewclaw Grecian percent slacken
cribbed grabber newborn stibine bracing diocese grecise percept slacker
cribble grabble nibbler stubbed bracken discant Grecism percher slackly
crybaby gribble niobium stubble bracket discard grocery percine slicker
cubbing Grobian nobbler stubbly breccia discern guichet percoid slickly
cudbear grubbed nombril subbing brickie discerp halcyon percuss smacker
cutback grubber numbles sunbath brickle discoid hatcher piccolo snicker
cymbalo gubbins oddball sunbeam bricole discord hatchet pincers soccage
dabbing gumboil offbeat sunbear brocade discuss haycock pincher sorcery
dabbler gumboot oilbath sunbird brocket ditcher hencoop piscary spacial
darbies gunboat oilbird sunburn brucine dogcart hiccupy piscina spacing
daybook halberd ouabain surbase brucite doucely hircine piscine special
diabase halbert outbath swabbed buccina douceur hitcher pitched species
diabolo Hamburg parboil swabber butcher drachma hoecake pitcher specify
dibbing harbour piebald swobbed calcify drycell icecold placard speckle
disband hasbeen pinball tabbing calcine dulcify inocula placate spectra
disbark hatband potbank tambour calcite edacity insculp placebo spectre
djibbah hauberk prebend tanbark calcium edictal isochor placket specula
dogbane henbane proband tarbush calculi educate itacism placoid spicate
doubler herbage probang terbium carcase eductor juicily plectra spicery
doubles hipbath probate tieback carcass eggcosy juncoes plicate spicily
doublet hipbone probity tiebeam cascade ejector ketchup plucker spicula
doubter Hobbian problem tilbury cascara elector kinchin poacher spicule
drabber Hobbism quibble timbale catcall electro kitchen popcorn stacker
drabbet Hobbist rabbity timbrel catcher emicate knacker porcine sticker
drabble hobbler rabbler tombola catchup enactor knocker pouched stickit
drabler hogback ragbolt tombolo checker epicarp knockon precast stickle
dribble homburg rambler towboat checkup epicede knuckle precede stickup
driblet hopbind remblai tribade chicane epicene laicise precept stocker
drubbed howbeit rhabdom triblet Chicano epicure laicism precise stuccos
dubbing humbles rhubarb tribune chicken epochal lancers precook stuckup
dunbird humbuzz ribband tribute chicory erectly larceny pricker succade
elfbolt husband ribbing tubbing chocice erector latchet pricket succeed
eyeball iceberg robbery tubbish Choctaw ericoid leucine prickle success
eyebath iceboat robbing tugboat chuckle evacuee leucite prickly succory
eyebolt ikebana roebuck tumbler Circean evictor leucoma proceed succour
eyebrow illbred rowboat tumbrel circler exactly linctus process succuba
falbala isobath rubbers tumbril circlet exactor luncher proctor succubi
fibbing jabbing rubbery turbary circuit execute lurcher procure succumb
filbert jawbone rubbing turbine circusy exocarp lyncean psychic suicide
fimbria jaybird rubbish twibill clacker exscind lynchet puccoon sulcate
finback jibbing rumbler verbena clicker falcate manchet puncher surcoat
flubbed jibboom Sabbath verbose clocker falcula marcher punchup syncarp
flyback jobbery sambuca warbler coacher fancier marconi punctum syncope
flybane jobbing sawbill waxbill coccoid fancily mascara Quechua talcose
flybelt jumbuck sawbuck waybill concave fanclub matchet quicken talcous
flyblow kabbala scabbed webbing conceal farceur mercery quickie teacake
flyboat kibbutz scabble wetback concede farcing merchet quickly teacher
flybook knobbed scabies wobbler conceit fascial mercury raccoon teachin
fobbing knobble scabrid wrybill concent fascine mincing rancher teacosy
fogbank knobbly seabass abscess concept Fascism Miocene rancour thecate
forbade lambast seabear abscise concern Fascist miscall raschel thicken
forbear lambent seabird abscond concert faucial miscast ratchet thicket
forbode lambert seablue acicula conchae fencing miscopy raucous thickly
forbore lambkin seaboot acyclic conchie fitchet moocher reacher tipcart
fribble legbail Serbian aircrew concise fitchew muscled reactor toccata
fumbler lesbian setback apocope concoct flaccid nascent redcoat toeclip
furbish limbate shebang asocial concord flecker newcome rescale topcoat
gabbing limbeck shebear avocado concuss flicker Noachic rescind torchon
gabbler limbous shebeen baccara coxcomb floccus notched rescuer touched
gambade lobbing skyblue baccate cracked forceps nutcase ripcord toucher
gambado logbook skyborn bacchic cracker fracted oatcake saccade touchup
gambier Lombard slabbed balcony crackle freckle obscene saccate tracery
gambler lowborn slabber bascule crackly freckly obscure saccule trachea
gamboge lowbred slobber bawcock crackup fructed oilcake sacculi tracker
gambrel lowbrow slubbed beechen cricket fulcrum omicron sanctum tractor
garbage lubbard slubber belcher cricoid furcate opacity Sanctus triceps
garbler lumbago snubbed bencher crochet furcula orectic sarcasm tricker
garboil lumbang snubber bibcock crocket fuscous outcast sarcode trickle
geebung marbled sobbing birchen crucial gascoal outcome sarcoid tricksy
gerbera marbles sorbent biscuit crucian glacial outcrop sarcoma tricorn
gibbous Moabite Sorbian blacken crucify glacier ovicide sarcous trochal
gilbert mobbing soubise blackly cupcake glucose pancake satchel trochee
gimbals mobbish sowback blocker curcuma glycine paschal saucily trochus
globoid mowburn soybean blucher deicide gnocchi paucity shackle trucial
```

```
trucker cardiac gladded maddest pudding studied adrenal blueing dimeric
truckle cardoon gladden madding puddler subdean adverse bobeche dimeter
tulchan caudate gladder Mahdism putdown subdual aileron bodeful dinette
unicity cheddar goddamn Mahdist quadrat subduct algebra bohemia direful
unicorn chidden goddess maidish quadric subdued alienly boletus disease
unscrew chuddah goldbug maidism ragdoll sundeck alleged bonedry diseuse
vaccine chuddar gondola mandala readily sundial allegro boneset diverge
vascula cindery goodbye mandate reading sundisc allelic boredom diverse
vincula cladode goodday mandola readout sundown allergy breeder docetic
viscera coddler goodish mandora reddest swaddle aloetic briefly dogeate
viscose coldish goodman mandrel reddish Swedish already bugeyed doleful
viscous condemn Gordian mandril reeding tandoor alveoli bureaus dovecot
volcano condign gradate maudlin rhodium tardily ammeter bureaux dovekie
vouchee condole gradely meadowy rhodora tedding amnesia burette doyenne
voucher condone gradine meddler ridding tendril amnesic cadence dozenth
watcher conduce gradual mending riddler thudded amnesty cadency driedup
welcher conduct griddle mildewy roadbed tiddler amoebae cadenza dryeyed
welcome conduit gumdrop mindful roadhog tiddley amoebas calends dukedom
wencher condyle haddock misdate roadman tindery amoebic camelot duteous
whacker cordage handbag misdeal roadway toddler anaemia camelry eagerly
whicker cordate handcar misdeed rodding tradein anaemic cameral easeful
wrecker cordial handful misdeem roedeer trading angelic capelin echelon
zincify cordite handgun misdone rondeau traduce angelus caperer effects
zincing cordoba handily moidore rondure trident Angevin careful effendi
zincite credent handler mondial rowdily triduan annelid caseous eidetic
zincked crudely handoff moodily rubdown triduum anoesis caserne eirenic
zipcode crudity handout mordant ruddily trodden anoetic catechu elderly
abaddon dandify handsaw mordent ruddock trudgen antefix catenae Elzevir
abiding dawdler handsel muddily rundale tundish antenna catenas emperor
academe deadend handset muddler rundlet turdine aphelia cateran endemic
academy deadeye hardhit mundane rundown turdoid apheses caterer enderon
Acadian deadpan hardpan mundify saddest twaddle aphesis caveman enfeoff
acidify deodand hardset needful saddish twaddly aphetic cavetti entente
acidity deodara hardtop needler saddler twiddle aplenty cavetto enteral
airdrop dewdrop headily nodding saidest twiddly appease cayenne enteric
alidade diddler heading oildrum sandbag unideal apteryx celeste enteron
alodial disdain headman outdone sandbar urodele aqueous celesta envelop
alodium doddard headpin outdoor sandbed Vandyke ardency cerebra envenom
anodise doddery headset oviduct sandbox Vaudois arietta ceresin ephebus
anodyne dogdays headway oxidant sandboy Veddoid arrears cheerer ephedra
apodous doodler heedful oxidase sanders vendace arsenal cheerio equerry
aridity dowdily heyduck oxidate sandfly verdant arsenic cheetah essence
avidity dredger hilding oxidise sandlot verdict ascesis chiefly etaerio
baddish drudger hindgut padding sandman verdure ascetic cineast etheric
balding drydock hoedown paddler sandpit viaduct askesis cineole eugenic
baldish duodena holdall paddock sardine wadding asperse codeine eupepsy
baldric eardrop holding Pandean sardius waddler assegai cogency eutexia
bandage eardrum hoodlum pandect sawdust wedding asteria coherer excerpt
bandana epidote humdrum pandora scudded Wendish atheism coletit expense
bandbox erodent hundred pandore seedbed whidder atheist comedic externe
bandeau erudite hurdler pardner seedily wildcat atresia cometic Faberge
bandore evident hurdles paydesk seedlip wilding attempt copepod faceoff
bandsaw exedrae irideal peddler sendoff wildish aureate corella faceted
bawdily exudate iridise pendant setdown windage aurelia coterie fadedly
beading eyedrop iridium pendent shadily windbag aureola Coueism fadeout
bedding faddish jibdoor pending shading windegg aureole coverup faience
beldame faddism Kaddish perdure shadoof windily auxesis cozener fateful
bidding faddist khaddar piddock shadowy winding auxetic creedal federal
bindery feeding khedive pledgee shedder windrow baleful creeper fideism
binding feedlot kidding pledger shudder Windsor baneful Croesus fideist
birddog feudist kiddish pledget sitdown woodcut baseman cruelly filemot
birdman fiddler kindler pledgor skidded woodman basenji cruelty finesse
bladder finding kindred plodded skidlid woodpie bateaux cuneate firearm
bondage folding Kurdish plodder skidpan wordage bedevil cunette firebox
bondman foldout landing podding sledded wordily bejewel cureall firebug
bordure fondant lardoon pondage slidden wording beneath curette firedog
boudoir fondler leading powdery smeddum yardage benefic cuvette firefly
bradawl fordone leadoff predate smidgen yardang benefit Danelaw fireman
bridoon fuddler lending predial smidgin yardarm Benelux dazedly firenew
budding gadding letdown predict soldier yardman bereave decease fixedly
burdock gardant lindane predoom sordini Yiddish beseech deceive fleeced
caddice gaudery lipdeep prodded sordino abreact bheesty decency fleecer
caddish gaudier loading prodder spadger abreast bheetie defence fleeing
caldera gaudily lording prodigy spidery absence bibelot demerit fleetly
caldron gelding loudish produce spodium ackemma bigener demesne fluence
candela geodesy lowdown product staddle acreage bipedal deserve fluency
candent giddily Luddite prudent stadium addenda biretta deterge forearm
candied gilding lurdane prudery studded adherer bleeder develop foreign
candour girdler lyddite prudish student adnexal bleeper dilemma foreleg
```

```
foreman  impearl  minever  polecat  seceder  towered  coffers  oviform  traffic
forepaw  imperil  miserly  polemic  selenic  treetop  comfort  palfrey  trefoil
foreran  impetus  mixedly  polenta  senecio  tuneful  comfrey  parfait  trifler
forerun  incense  mixedup  popeyed  seventh  tutelar  confect  peafowl  triform
foresaw  indepth  modesty  poseuse  seventy  tutenag  confess  perfect  truffle
foresay  indexer  mofette  potence  several  tweeter  confide  perfidy  turfite
foresee  inferno  momenta  potency  sheerly  tweezer  confine  perform  turfman
foretop  ingenue  moneyed  poverty  shoeing  typebar  confirm  perfume  twofold
forever  ingesta  moneyer  praetor  sidecar  typeset  conflux  perfuse  unifier
fouette  inherit  moreish  preempt  sideway  ulcered  conform  piaffer  uniform
foveate  innerve  morello  puberal  silence  underdo  confuse  piffler  warfare
foveola  insecty  morendo  puberty  silenus  undergo  confute  pinfire  webfoot
fraenum  integer  Moresco  pudency  silesia  unheard  cowfish  pinfish  welfare
freebie  intense  Moselle  pyaemia  skeeter  unkempt  crofter  pinfold  whiffle
freedom  interim  mozetta  pyaemic  sleeken  unlearn  deafaid  pitfall  wolfcub
freeman  interne  murexes  pyretic  sleekit  unleash  deiform  plafond  wolfdog
freesia  inveigh  musette  pyrexia  sleekly  unmeant  dewfall  pomfret  wolfish
freeway  inverse  mycelia  pyrexic  sleeper  unnerve  diffuse  poofter  wolfram
freezer  inweave  nacelle  queenly  sleeved  unready  disfame  preface  abigail
funeral  jadedly  nakedly  queerly  sloegin  unsexed  dogfish  prefect  airglow
gabelle  jadeite  nameday  quieten  sneerer  unteach  draftee  preform  anagoge
galeate  Janeite  nemesia  quietly  sneezer  unweave  drafter  profane  anagogy
galenic  javelin  nemesis  quietus  soberly  upheave  drifter  profess  anagram
gamebag  jewelry  niceish  racemic  sokeman  uraemia  earflap  proffer  apagoge
gamelan  Jezebel  ninepin  rakeoff  someday  urgency  edifice  profile  apogamy
gametic  jukebox  niveous  ramekin  somehow  utterer  eggflip  profuse  apogean
gaseous  kalends  nosebag  ramenta  someone  utterly  fanfare  puffery  azygous
gateaux  kinesis  nosegay  rapeoil  someway  valence  fanfold  quaffer  baggage
gateleg  kinetic  noserag  rarebit  speeder  valency  fenfire  raffish  baggily
gateway  kneecap  notedly  ravelin  speedup  valeric  feoffee  riffler  bagging
gazelle  kneeler  notelet  receipt  sphenic  vanessa  feoffer  roofing  bargain
gazette  kneepan  notepad  receive  spheral  vedette  feoffor  rooftop  beggary
Gehenna  kneesup  novella  recency  spheric  vegetal  fiefdom  ruffian  begging
general  labella  novelle  referee  spieler  venefic  forfeit  ruffler  beignet
generic  lakelet  novelty  regency  spleeny  venerer  forfend  saffron  Belgian
geneses  lamella  numeral  reheard  splenic  veteran  funfair  sawfish  Bengali
genesis  latency  numeric  release  squeaky  vexedly  gabfest  scoffer  bergylt
genetic  lateral  observe  reneger  squeeze  viceroy  garfish  scuffle  biggest
genette  latexes  obverse  renegue  squelch  vidette  gasfire  seafish  biggish
Genevan  layered  octette  renewal  steekit  vinegar  golfbag  seafood  blighty
gleeful  layette  offence  renewer  steepen  virelay  golfing  seafowl  boggler
gleeman  levelly  ogreish  reredos  steeple  vitelli  grafter  selffed  bongoes
Gobelin  leveret  omneity  reseaux  steeply  vixenly  griffin  selfish  bragged
godetia  liberal  oneeyed  reserve  steerer  vowelly  griffon  serfage  bragger
godevil  liberty  orderer  revelry  sthenic  wagerer  grifter  serfdom  brigade
gomeral  licence  orderly  revenge  streaky  wakeful  gruffly  sexfoil  brigand
gomeril  license  osselet  revenue  stretch  wakener  gunfire  shifter  bugging
greenly  lifeful  osseous  reverie  stretta  watered  hagfish  shuffle  bungler
greenth  lineage  osseter  reverse  stretto  waterer  halfway  sitfast  burgage
hapence  lineate  osteoid  reversi  subedit  wavelet  halfwit  sixfold  burgeon
hapenny  lineman  oxfence  Rhaetic  suberic  waverer  hayfork  skiffle  burgess
harelip  lineout  pageant  rivered  suberin  wheedle  hogfish  snaffle  burghal
hateful  literal  pageboy  riveter  sweeper  wheeled  hotfoot  sniffer  burgher
havenot  livebox  paletot  ropeway  sweeten  wheeler  huffish  sniffle  burglar
hebenon  liveoak  palette  roseate  sweetie  whoever  icefall  snifter  chagrin
heretic  lobelia  paperer  rosebay  sweetly  winesap  icefloe  snuffer  chigger
hideous  lomenta  parerga  rosebud  wireman  wireman  icefoot  snuffle  chignon
hideout  lorette  paresis  rosecut  synergy  wiretap  jewfish  souffle  chugged
Homeric  loverly  paretic  rosehip  synesis  wizened  kinfolk  stiffen  cingula
Homerid  lozenge  patella  rosella  tabetic  ycleped  leafage  stiffly  clogged
honesty  lucency  patency  roseola  tagetes  yulelog  leafbud  stifler  clogger
honeyed  lucerne  phaeton  rosered  takeoff  zetetic  leaflet  stuffer  coagula
hopeful  lumenal  phlegmy  rosette  taperer  airfare  maffick  subfusc  cogging
however  lunette  phoenix  rubella  tapetal  airflow  menfolk  suffice  congeal
hugeous  luteous  phrenic  rubeola  tapetum  aliform  milfoil  Suffolk  congest
humeral  Madeira  phrensy  ruderal  teleost  armfuls  misfire  suffuse  cragged
humerus  magenta  piceous  rudesby  telergy  baffler  mouflon  sunfish  dangler
hygeian  majesty  pieeyed  sakeret  terebra  bedfast  mudfish  surface  diagram
hymenia  malefic  pikelet  saveall  thieves  Biafran  mudflat  surfeit  digging
hyperon  mamelon  pikeman  saveloy  thready  bluffer  muffler  surfing  dingily
icteric  maremma  pileate  schemer  Tibetan  bluffly  netfish  surfman  dingoes
icterus  matelot  pimento  scherzi  tiderip  bonfire  oakfern  swiftly  disgust
idlesse  memento  pinetum  scherzo  tideway  buffalo  oarfish  taffeta  dodgems
igneous  meseems  pipeful  science  timelag  buffoon  olefine  taxfree  dodgery
illegal  micelle  piperic  scleral  timeous  catfish  orifice  tenfold  doggery
immense  mileage  pipette  screech  tomenta  chaffer  outface  tiffany  dogging
immerge  mimesis  piteous  screeve  tonemic  chiffon  outfall  tinfoil  doggish
immerse  mimetic  podesta  screwed  tonerow  chuffed  outflow  tomfool  doggone
impeach  mineral  poleaxe  screwer  totemic  codfish  outfoot  topfull  doughty
```

```
dragged higgler penguin trigamy cithern leghorn senhora apricot codices
draggle hoggery pergola trigger cochlea lethean sighted apsidal codicil
dragnet hogging pidgeon tugging cowhage lichowl sightly apsides colicky
dragoon hoggish piggery turgent cowhand lighted Sikhism aquifer colitis
drogher hugging pigging twigged cowheel lighten sithens aquiver comical
drugged imagery piggish tzigane cowherd lighter skyhigh arbiter comitia
drugget imagine pilgrim tzigany cowhide lightly sophism armiger conical
dudgeon imagism pinguid verglas cubhood lithely sophist arrival conidia
dungeon imagist plugged virgate cushion lithium spyhole arriver conifer
elegant isogamy plugger virgule dashiki lithoid subhead article coniine
elegiac isogeny progeny vulgate dashing lughole Swahili artisan copilot
elegise isogram program waggery dashpot lychnis tachism artiste copious
elegist jaggery pugging wagging diehard lychowl tachist ascidia cotidal
epigeal jangler puggish waggish dishorn machair technic ascites cruiser
epigean jargoon puggree wargame dithery machete tighten ascitic cubical
epigene jigging pungent wedging dorhawk machine tightly aspirer cubicle
epigone jingler raggedy weigher duchess manhole tinhorn aspirin cubital
epigoni jogging ragging weighin earhole manhood tithing assizes culices
epigram jugging reagent weighty egghead manhour toehold athirst curiosa
epigyny juggins ridging wergild Elohism manhunt tophole audible curious
exegete juggler rigging widgeon Elohist mashtub towhead audient cuticle
exigent Jungian ringent wigging enchain Mechlin trehala auditor cynical
exogamy kingcup ringing wiggler enchant methane tushery auricle dariole
fagging kingdom ringlet winglet enchase mightst tychism bacilli datival
fargone kinglet ringtaw wingnut         mishear typhoid barilla deciare
feigner kingpin roughen wriggle enthuse Mishnah typhoon basidia decibel
fidgets Kirghiz roughly wriggly enwheel mynheer typhous basilar decided
fidgety laggard sagging yeggman escheat mythise unchain basinet decider
figging lagging sangria Zingari etching mythist unshell batiste decidua
flagday languet sawgate Zingaro euphony naphtha unthink bedight decimal
flagged languid scaglia zoogamy eyehole nephric upthrew bedizen defiant
flagman languor seagirt zoogeny fashion nightie upthrow believe deficit
flighty largely seagull zoogony fathead nightly warhead benison defiler
flogged largess shogged airhole fighter nothing washing besides definer
foggage largish singlet alchemy fishery nowhere washout besiege dehisce
foggily laugher sirgang allheal fisheye nunhood washpot betimes delight
fogging leaguer skegger alphorn fishily offhand washtub bewitch Delilah
forgave legging slagged althaea fishing onshore wishful bezique delimit
forgery lengthy slogged althorn fishnet oophyte wishing bifilar deliver
forging lingual slogger amphora fishway orchard withers biliary demigod
forgive lodging slugged anchovy flyhalf Orphean without bilimbi demirep
forgoer logging slugger anchusa foghorn Orphism wychelm bilious denizen
forgone longago smuggle anthill foxhole orphrey xiphoid biriani derider
fragile longbow snagged anthrax foxhunt outhaul yashmak bolivar detinue
frigate longday snigger archaic fuchsia pachisi yoghurt borings deviant
frogeye longhop sniggle archery Fuehrer Paphian zithern bouilli deviate
frogged longing snuggle archive futhark pathway abridge braille devilry
frogman longish soggily archway futhorc perhaps absinth broider devious
fugging lorgnon soignee armhole futhork pinhead accidie broiler devisal
fulgent luggage songful asphalt gathers pinhole achieve bruiser devisee
fulgour lugging sorghum bashful goahead pithead acridly bulimia deviser
fungoid maggoty spignel bathing godhead pithhat actinia cabinet devisor
fungous mangily stagger bathtub godhood pithily actinic cacique digital
gadgety mangoes stagily Bauhaus goshawk pochard actinon calibre divider
gagging mangold staging beehive gushing poohbah addible calices diviner
ganglia margent stygian berhyme hachure pothead adhibit caliche divisor
gangrel misgave suggest beshrew hashish potheen admiral calicle domical
gangway misgive surgeon bethink highboy potherb admirer calipee dominie
geogony mongrel surgery bighead highhat pothole advised caliper drainer
gigging mugging swagged bighorn highman pothook adviser canikin druidic
giggler muggins swagger bowhead highway preheat advisor capital dubiety
gingery myogram swagman boxhaul hophead pushful affined capitol dubious
gingham nagging swigged boyhood hothead pushing African caribou dutiful
gingili naughty syngamy Brahman hushaby pushrod against carinae ebriate
goggler Neogaea tagging Brahmin inkhorn Pythian alginic carinal ebriety
goggles niggard tangelo bruhaha inphase quahaug almirah carinas echidna
grogram niggler tangent bushido inshore raphide alright carioca echinus
gudgeon nogging tanghin bushman ischial rawhide ambient cariole eclipse
Guignol nutgall tangram bushtit ischium redhead ancient carious ellipse
Haggada nylghau teagown cachexy isohyet reshape andiron caviare empiric
haggard oakgall tergite cashier isthmus rethink anginal cedilla enfiled
haggish oregano thigger Cathari kathode righten angioma chrisom enliven
haggler origami thuggee Cathars keyhole righter annicut christy entitle
hangdog orogeny tingler cathead lashing rightly antigen ciliary envious
hanging outgone toggery cathode lashkar ruching antilog ciliate environ
hangman outgrew torgoch cathood lathery ruthful antique cimices epsilon
hangout outgrow toughen cepheid lathing saphead anxiety citizen equinal
haughty pargana toughly cichlid lawhand sashimi anxious civilly equinox
heighho pegging tragedy cithara lechery saxhorn aphides claimer ermined
```

```
ethical impious Mexican plaided satisfy tidings subject jacktar sinkage
ethiops incipit miliary plainly savings timidly subjoin jerkily smokeho
excited incised militia politic saviour tonight traject kickoff smokily
exciter incisor mimical poniard scribal topiary backing kolkhoz smoking
exciton inciter mimicry porifer scriber topical backlog lacking snakily
excitor indican miniate prairie scrieve trailer backsaw lankily soakage
exhibit indices minibus praiser scrimpy trainee backset leakage soaking
expiate indicia minicab pupilar sedilia trainer banking licking sockeye
extinct inditer minicar puritan semilog traipse banksia linkage spikily
fatigue infidel minikin pyrites seminal traitor bonkers linkboy sucking
feminal infield minimal pyritic seminar tumidly bookend linkman suckler
fetidly inhibit minimum pyxides semiped tunicle bookful lockage sulkily
filiate innings minimus pyxidia Semitic typical booking lockjaw tacking
filibeg insider miniver rabidly seriate uncinus bookish locknut tackler
filings insight modicum radiant sericin uncivil booklet lockout talking
finical insigne modiste radiate seriema unfitly bookman looking tankage
finicky insipid molimen radical seringa unhinge booksie lookout tankard
finikin invitee moniker radices serious unhitch boskage looksee tankcar
finings inviter monitor radicle shaitan unlined boxkite luckily tankful
fixings jacinth Morisco rapidly shrieve unmixed brokage mankind ticking
fluidal janitor muriate rations shrilly unright broking markhor tickler
fluidic jubilee murices ravined shrinal unsight buckeye marking topknot
fluidly jujitsu musical ravings shrivel upfield buckler mawkish trekked
foliage juniper Naziism ravioli shriven upright buckram milking trekker
foliate Jupiter neritic rebirth silicic upriser bucksaw milkleg tuckbox
foliole labiate nimiety recital silicle upsides bulkily milkman Turkish
foliose laminae nodical reciter silicon upsilon busking milksop walking
frailly laminar nominal refined siliqua uptight cackler mirkily walkout
frailty laniary nominee refiner silique utricle carking misknow walkway
freight lapilli noniron regimen similar uveitis chukker mockery weakish
fruited latices notitia reginal similor valiant cockade monkery weekday
fruiter legible noxious reliant simitar validly cockeye monkish weekend
funicle legibly obligee relieve sleight vanilla cockily murkily wickiup
furioso legiron obliger relievo society vapidly cockney muskrat winkers
furious lenient oblique relight solicit variant cockpit nankeen workbag
fusible lexical obviate relique solidly variate cockshy necklet workbox
galilee lexicon obvious remiges solidus varices conkers necktie workday
galipot liaison occiput repiner soliped variety cookery package working
gelidly licitly oedipal repique somitic variola cooking packice workman
genista liminal officer residua sorites variole cookout packing workout
genitor limited omnibus residue splicer various corkage packman yolksac
genizah limiter omnific retiary spoiler Vatican corking parkway Yorkist
geoidal logical oneiric reticle spriggy vehicle cuckold peckish zinkify
glaikit loricae oolitic retinae springe veliger darkish perkily zinking
goliard lorimer oomiack retinal springy venison decking pickaxe abalone
Goliath loriner ophitic retinas squiffy veriest dickens pickeer Abelian
gonidia lucidly oppidan retinol squinch verismo dockage pickled ability
gooiest Lucifer optical retinue squinny vesicae dockise pinkeye abolish
gorilla luminal optimal retired squirmy vesical Dorking pinking acclaim
grained luridly optimum reviler squishy vesicle ducking pinkish acolyte
grainer lyrical orbital revisal squitch vetiver duckpin Prakrit adulate
greisen mafiosi ordinal reviser staidly vexilla Dunkirk puckery adultly
habitat mafioso ossicle revisit stainer vicinal duskily puckish aeolian
habitue magical ossific revival staithe vicious einkorn rackety afflict
halibut makings ostiary reviver stoical vidimus erlking ranking ageless
halidom malines ostiole revivor striate visible folkway rickets agelong
Hamitic malison ovoidal rigidly strider visibly forkful rickety agilely
haricot mamilla pacific rilievo stridor visitor Fraktur ricksha agility
harijan manihot paginal ripieni strigil vitiate gawkily rockery aiblins
helical manikin palings ripieno striker vividly geckoes rockier aimless
helices manilla panicky risible stringy vivific hackbut rockily airless
helicon manille panicle riviera striped wanigan hackery rocking airlift
hemiola maniple papilla riviere striven warison hacking rocklet airline
hemione manitou patient rooinek striver zooidal hackler rockoil airlock
heritor marimba paviour rotifer syringa banjoes hackney rocktar amalgam
holibut mariner pedicab rubicon syringe conjoin hacksaw rookery amildar
holiday marital pedicel rubious tabinet conjure hawkish sackbut amplify
hominid matinal pedicle sagitta tacitly disjoin heckler sackful amylase
horizon matinee pelican salicet takings frijole hickory sacking amyloid
hosiery maxilla pelisse salicin talipes jimjams hockday sarking amylose
humidly maximal pemican salient talipot mahjong hooklet seakale analogy
humidor maximum periapt Salique tapioca manjack hulking shakeup analyse
hygiene mediacy peridot samisen taxicab Panjabi hunkers shakily analyst
igniter mediant perigee sanicle taxiing perjure huskily shikari Anglian
ileitis mediate perique sapient taximan perjury husking sickbay anglice
illicit medical periwig satiate tedious project isokont sickbed angling
imbiber melilot petiole satiety tepidly Punjabi jackass sickish Anglist
impiety melisma pigiron satinet thrifty skijump jackdaw sickpay aniline
impinge menisci pitiful satiric thriven skyjack jackpot silkily anility
```

antlion	cellist	earlobe	Gaulish	lawless	orology	reallot	skyline	unclean
apology	cellule	earlock	gelling	lawlist	otolith	realtor	smeller	uncloak
apolune	chalaza	ecology	geology	lawlord	otology	reclaim	smelter	unclose
applaud	Chaldee	egality	ghillie	legless	outland	reclame	soilure	Uralian
applied	chalice	elfland	giblets	lidless	outlast	recline	sonless	uralite
applier	challis	elflock	gillnet	lipless	outlier	recluse	soulful	urology
armless	chalone	emblaze	girlish	logline	outline	redlegs	speller	useless
armlike	chelate	emplace	godless	Lollard	outlive	reelect	spelter	utilise
artless	childer	emplace	godlike	lowland	outlook	reflate	spiller	utility
atelier	childly	emulate	godling	lowlily	ovulate	reflect	stalely	vallate
athlete	chiliad	emulous	gosling	lullaby	oxalate	refloat	stalked	vaulted
aweless	chillum	enclasp	goulash	mailbag	padlock	replace	stalker	vaulter
awnless	cholera	enclave	grilled	mailbox	pahlavi	replant	stellar	veiling
axillae	choline	enclose	griller	mailing	pailful	replete	stilted	village
axillar	coaltit	endless	Grolier	maillot	pallium	replevy	Stilton	villain
axolotl	codling	endlong	Guelfic	mailman	parlour	replica	stylise	villein
Azilean	coeliac	English	guilder	mailvan	parlous	replier	stylish	villose
Baalism	collage	enplane	gullery	mallard	Pauline	rifling	stylist	villous
bailiff	collard	enslave	gunlock	malleus	payload	rodlike	stylite	violate
baklava	collate	epilate	gutless	manless	pedlary	rollick	styloid	violent
ballade	collect	erelong	hallali	manlike	perlite	rolling	sublate	violist
ballast	colleen	euclase	hallway	marline	phalanx	rollmop	sublime	violone
ballboy	college	euglena	hapless	marlite	phallic	rolltop	sullage	wailful
balloon	collide	evolute	haploid	mealies	phallus	roulade	sunlamp	wallaby
barline	collier	ewelamb	hatless	midland	phellem	rouleau	sunless	walleye
becloud	collins	exclaim	haulage	midline	philter	rowlock	surlily	walling
beeline	colloid	exclave	haulier	milldam	philtre	runless	swallow	Walloon
bellboy	collude	exclude	hayloft	million	pighead	sailing	swelter	wallrue
bellhop	coolant	explain	healthy	mislaid	pigling	sallowy	swiller	warlike
belljar	coolish	explant	heeltap	mislead	pillage	sapless	swollen	warlock
bellman	couldst	explode	hellbox	mislike	pillbox	sapling	syllabi	warlord
bellows	couloir	exploit	hellcat	mollify	pillion	scalade	tableau	waylaid
berline	coulomb	explore	Hellene	mollusc	pillock	scalado	tabloid	wayless
biblist	coulter	eyelash	hellion	moulder	pillory	scalder	tailend	wealden
billing	cowlick	eyeless	hellish	mudlark	pillowy	scaldic	tailing	wealthy
billion	cowling	eyelike	helluva	mullein	pillule	scalene	tallage	wedlock
billowy	cruller	fabliau	hemline	mullion	pollack	scallop	tallboy	wellies
biology	cullion	failing	hemlock	mullock	pollard	scalpel	tallish	welloff
biplane	curling	failure	hillman	myalgia	pollock	scalper	tallith	wellset
boiling	cutlass	fallacy	hillock	myalgic	pollute	schlepp	tallowy	whaling
bollard	cutlery	fallguy	hilltop	myalism	potluck	schlock	tallyho	wielder
Boolean	cutline	falling	holland	myeloid	poulard	scolder	taxless	wigless
boulder	cyclist	falloff	hoplite	myeloma	poulter	scollop	tealeaf	willies
boulter	cycloid	fallout	howling	myology	poultry	sculler	telling	willing
bowlder	cyclone	fatling	hueless	nailery	praline	sculpin	thalami	willowy
bowlful	cyclops	feeling	hurling	napless	prelacy	sealane	thallic	witless
bowline	dallier	fenland	hyaline	neglect	prelate	sealant	thallus	witling
bowling	darling	fetlock	hyalite	neglige	prelect	sealegs	thalweg	witloof
boxlike	daylong	fielder	hyaloid	neolith	prelims	sealery	thiller	woolfat
bugloss	dealing	figleaf	idolise	neology	prelude	seclude	thulium	woolled
builded	declaim	filling	idyllic	netlike	prolate	sellout	tillage	woollen
builder	declare	flyleaf	implant	newlaid	prolong	sexless	titlark	wooloil
buildup	declass	foglamp	implead	niblick	psalter	shallop	titling	woolsey
builtin	decline	follies	implete	noology	publish	shallot	toeless	worldly
builtup	deflate	foolery	implode	norland	Pullman	shallow	toilful	wouldbe
bullace	deflect	foolish	implore	nuclear	pullout	shellac	tollbar	wouldst
bullary	deplane	fopling	incline	nucleic	purlieu	shelled	tollman	yellowy
bullate	deplete	forlorn	inclose	nuclein	purloin	sheller	toolbox	yielder
bullbat	deplore	foulard	include	nucleon	putlock	shelter	tooling	zealous
bulldog	deplume	fowling	inflame	nucleus	qualify	sheltie	topless	zeolite
bullion	dialect	fuelled	inflate	nuclide	quality	shelved	towline	zillion
bullish	dialled	fueller	inflect	nullify	queller	shelves	trellis	Zoilism
bullock	dialyse	fullage	inflict	nullity	quillet	shilpit	trilith	Zoilist
bullpen	diploid	fullout	inkling	nutlike	quilter	shylock	trilogy	zoology
cabling	diploma	furlong	isolate	oakling	railcar	sialoid	troller	abomasa
callant	dislike	gallant	Italian	oarless	railing	sibling	trolley	adamant
callbox	dislimn	gallate	Italiot	oarlock	railman	sillily	trollop	Adamite
callboy	dollish	galleon	jealous	obelise	railway	sinless	twelfth	agamous
calling	driller	gallery	jellaba	obelisk	rallier	sirloin	twelves	ailment
callous	dualise	gallfly	jellied	obolary	ralline	skaldic	twilled	airmail
carline	dualism	gallice	jollify	occlude	ratlike	skellum	twoline	airmiss
Carlism	dualist	galling	jollity	ocellar	ratling	skelter	udaller	alameda
Carlist	duality	galliot	joyless	ocellus	rayless	skilful	ukelele	alembic
carload	duelled	gallium	keelson	oculate	realgar	skilift	ukulele	aliment
catlike	dueller	gallnut	keyless	oculist	realign	skilled	ululant	alimony
catling	dullard	galloon	killick	odalisk	realise	skillet	ululate	alumina
caulker	dullish	gallows	killing	offload	realism	skolion	unblest	alumnae
ceilidh	dweller	garland	killjoy	opaline	realist	skulker	unblock	alumnus
ceiling	earldom	gatling	Lallans	opulent	reality	skylark	unclasp	anemone

animate	crimper	grimmer	plumply	summery	bigness	counter	frenula	Jainism
animism	crimple	grommet	plumule	summing	bionics	country	fronded	jannock
animist	crimson	grumble	premier	summons	blandly	coyness	frontal	joinder
anomaly	crumble	grumbly	premise	surmise	blanket	cranage	fronton	joinery
anymore	crumbly	grummet	premiss	swimmer	blankly	cranial	fulness	joining
Aramaic	crumpet	grumose	premium	Tammany	blender	cranium	funnies	jointer
atomise	crumple	grumous	primacy	teeming	blinder	crankle	funnily	jointly
atomism	cupmoss	gumming	primage	tegmina	blindly	crannog	funning	kainite
atomist	damming	gummite	primary	termini	blinker	crenate	furnace	Kannada
augment	diamond	hamming	primate	termite	blintze	cringer	furnish	kenning
azimuth	dimmest	hammock	primely	themata	blunder	cringle	gabnash	keynote
badmash	dimming	harmala	primero	thimble	blunger	crinite	gahnite	khanate
balmily	dimmish	harmful	priming	Thomism	bluntly	crinkle	gainful	kyanise
barmaid	dismast	harmony	primmed	Thomist	bonnily	crinkly	gainsay	kyanite
beamish	dismiss	hemming	primula	thummim	bornite	crinoid	garnish	launder
besmear	doomful	holmium	promise	thumper	bouncer	crunchy	gauntly	laundry
biomass	dormant	holmoak	promote	thymine	bounden	ctenoid	gauntry	laxness
bismuth	dormice	hormone	pugmill	titmice	bounder	cunning	gayness	leaning
blemish	dromond	humming	pygmean	topmast	branchy	cyanide	genning	leonine
boomlet	drumlin	hummock	pygmoid	topmost	brander	cyanine	giantry	lignify
bramble	drummed	hutment	quamash	torment	brannew	cyanite	ginning	lignite
brambly	drummer	imamate	raiment	tormina	bransle	damnify	glenoid	Linnean
brimful	durmast	ipomoea	ramming	towmond	brantle	damning	granary	lioncel
brimmed	duumvir	Ishmael	rhamnus	towmont	brantub	darning	grandad	lioness
brimmer	earmark	itemise	rhombic	tramcar	brinded	dawning	grandam	lionise
bromate	earmuff	jamming	rhombus	trammel	brindle	deanery	grandee	llanero
bromide	element	jasmine	rhymist	trample	bringer	dignify	grandly	loaning
bromine	enamour	Kalmuck	rimming	tramway	brinjal	dignity	grandma	lounger
bromism	endmost	kermess	Rommany	tremble	bronchi	dimness	grandpa	lowness
brumous	enemata	khamsin	roomful	trembly	broncho	dinning	granger	lyingin
bummalo	eremite	koumiss	rummage	tremolo	burning	dipnoan	granita	lyingly
bumming	etamine	kremlin	sawmill	trimmed	burnish	donning	granite	madness
Burmese	ethmoid	krimmer	scamper	trimmer	burnous	donnish	grannie	magnate
Cadmean	examine	lamming	schmuck	trommel	cannery	dornick	grantee	magneto
cadmium	example	lemmata	scomber	trumeau	cannily	downbow	granter	magnify
caimans	exempla	lemming	scumble	trumpet	canning	drinker	grantor	maintop
carmine	fanmail	magmata	scummed	turmoil	cannula	drunken	granule	manners
catmint	farming	malmsey	seamaid	varment	carnage	dryness	grenade	manning
caymans	farmost	mammary	seamark	varmint	chancel	dulness	grinder	mannish
chamber	fermata	mammate	seeming	vermeil	chancre	dunnage	grinned	mannite
chamfer	ferment	mammock	segment	vermian	changer	dunning	grunion	mannose
chamois	fermion	mammoth	sfumato	warmish	channel	dunnock	grunter	maunder
champac	fermium	manmade	shamble	waymark	chanson	dwindle	gruntle	meander
champak	figment	marmite	shammed	whimper	chanter	earnest	guanaco	meaning
chemise	filmdom	mermaid	shammer	whimsey	chantry	ebonise	guanine	misname
chemism	filmset	midmost	shampoo	woomera	chindit	ebonite	gunnera	mooneye
chemist	fitment	mismate	Shemite	abandon	Chinese	economy	gunnery	moonlit
chimera	flamfew	mummery	shimmer	acantha	Chinook	elenchi	gunning	moonset
chimere	flaming	mummify	siamang	acinous	chintzy	emanate	gurnard	morning
chimney	Fleming	mumming	Siamese	aconite	chinwag	eminent	gwyniad	mounter
chummed	Flemish	myomata	siemens	adenine	chunnel	ensnare	gymnast	Mountie
chymous	flummox	newmown	sigmate	adenoid	chunter	ensnarl	hafnium	munnion
clamant	formant	noumena	sigmoid	adenoma	clanger	eponymy	harness	muonium
clamber	formate	nummary	sjambok	aeonian	clinker	Etonian	haunted	neonate
clammed	formula	oatmeal	skimmed	agonise	Cluniac	evangel	haunter	newness
clamour	foumart	oddment	skimmer	agonist	cognate	evanish	heinous	noonday
clement	frameup	Olympic	skimmia	alanine	cognise	evening	hennery	nooning
climate	fulmine	onymous	slammed	alunite	coinage	eweneck	herniae	nunnery
climber	furmety	outmost	slimily	amanita	coinbox	faintly	hernial	nunnish
clumber	furmity	palmary	slimmer	amender	connate	fanning	hernias	oddness
coaming	garment	palmate	slumber	amenity	connect	fatness	hipness	odontic
command	gasmask	palmist	slummed	amentia	conning	faunist	hobnail	omental
commend	gemmate	palmoil	slummer	amentum	connive	fernery	hornmad	omentum
comment	gemmery	palmyra	spumous	amongst	connote	fernowl	hotness	ominous
commode	gemming	payment	stamina	Ananias	cooncan	fewness	huanaco	onanism
commons	gemmule	Permian	stammel	apanage	coontie	feyness	Hunnish	oneness
commove	germane	permute	stammer	aptness	cornage	fiancee	hymnary	openair
commune	gimmick	pigmean	stamper	araneid	corncob	finning	hymnist	openend
commute	glamour	pigment	stemmed	asinine	corneal	Finnish	hymnody	opening
cosmism	glimmer	pismire	stemple	asunder	cornett	fitness	hymnoid	opinion
cosmist	glimpse	plumage	stemson	atingle	cornfed	flaneur	hypnoid	opuntia
crammed	glummer	plumate	stimuli	avenger	cornice	flanker	iciness	Oxonian
crammer	gnomish	plumber	stomach	badness	cornily	flannel	identic	ozonise
crampet	gramary	plumbic	stomata	banning	Cornish	flunkey	illness	painful
crampit	grammar	plumbob	stumble	bannock	cornist	founder	inanely	painter
crampon	grampus	plumery	stummed	beanbag	cornual	foundry	inanity	pannage
cremate	gremial	plummet	stumper	beknown	cornuto	frankly	ironing	pannier
cremona	gremlin	plumose	summand	biennia	council	frantic	ironist	panning
crimine	grimace	plumper	summary	bigname	counsel	Frenchy	isonomy	paunchy

```
penname roundup standin twoness armoire colossi Genoese monomer scrooge
pennant ruinate standup unknown Armoric colours groover morocco scrouge
pennate ruinous staniel unsnarl armoury coloury halogen moronic seconde
pennies rumness stannic uranide astound corolla haporth mycoses secondi
pennill running stenchy uranism atrophy coronae hedonic mycosis secondo
pennine sadness stencil uranium aurochs coronal helotry mycotic senores
penning sainted stentor uranous aurorae coronas heroics mylodon shoofly
peonage saintly stinger urinary auroral coroner heroine myxomas shooter
pfennig saunter stinker utensil auroras coronet heroise Nilotic sinopia
phantom sawnoff stonily varnish autobus criollo heroism obconic sirocco
phonate scandal stonker vaunter autocar crooked heronry obloquy smoochy
phoneme scanned stunned veining autocue crooner homonym October snooker
phonics scanner stunner veinlet autopsy cryogen honours octopod snooper
phonily scantly stunted vernier avionic culotte humoral octopus snoozer
pianism scenery sunnily wanness baloney dacoity hypogea oenomel snoozle
pianist scented sunning wannish baronet damosel hypoxia ongoing sojourn
pinnace schnook Sunnite warning baroque damozel hypoxic opposer soloist
pinnate scunner surname wetness bayonet debouch idiotic opsonic Solomon
pinning shanked swanker whangee bazooka decoder ignoble opsonin soroban
pinnule shindig swanned whinger bedouin decorum ignobly ortolan sororal
pioneer shingle swindle winning begonia defocus ignorer osmosis sorosis
planish shingly swinery winnock begorra deforce imbower osmotic splodge
planned shinned swinger witness behoove delouse immoral ottoman splotch
planner shinpad swingle wornout beloved demoded imposer paeonic spoofer
plantar shunned swinish wrangle betoken demonic impound panocha spooney
planter shunner syenite wringer bifocal demotic inboard panoply spoorer
planula shunter taeniae wrinkle bigoted demount incomer papoose strophe
planxty shyness tannage wrinkly bigotry deposal indoors parodic stroppy
plenary signary tannate wrongly bilobar deposit indorse parolee syconia
plenish signify tannery wryneck bilobed devolve ingoing paronym sycosis
plunder signior tanning wryness bipolar devoted inhouse parotid synodal
plunger signora tannish yenning bivouac devotee insofar peloria synodic
plunker signore tarnish younger blooded dipolar intoner peloric synonym
poinder signori taunter younker bloomer disobey invoice pelorus synovia
pointed signory teenage Zionism bologna divorce involve picotee taborer
pointer sinning ternary Zionist boloney echoism inwoven pirogue taloned
poundal skinful ternate zoonomy borough eclogue Jacobin pivotal tanooze
pounder skinker thanage abdomen brioche ectopic jacobus pivoter tenoner
prancer skinned thankee abiotic brooder eidolon jaconet poloist theorbo
printer skinner thanker abroach bubonic embolic jaloppy popover theorem
pronaoi slander thinker absolve bucolic embolus japonic pyloric throaty
pronaos slantly thinned account bygones embosom judoist pylorus thrombi
pronate slender thinner acrobat Byronic embowed kenosis pyrosis throned
pronely slinger thunder acrogen bywoner embowel kenotic reboant through
pronged slinker tinnily acronym caboose embower kerogen rebound thrower
pronoun slyness tinning acroter cacodyl emporia kilobar recount throwin
pruning soonish toenail adjoint cacoepy empower kiloton recover timothy
pugnose sounder tonnage adjourn cagoule encoder laconic redoubt Titoism
punning soundly tonneau aerobic cahoots encomia lanolin redound Titoist
pycnite spancel tornado aerosol cajoler endogen lavolta refocus toponym
quantic spangle townish agnomen calomel endorse limosis regorge triolet
quantum spangly townlet aground caloric endozoa linocut rehouse trooper
quinary spaniel tranche alcohol calorie enforce litotes rejoice tylopod
quinate Spanish trangam Alcoran calotte engorge lycopod remodel typonym
quinine spanker transit alforja caloyer ennoble madonna remorse umbonal
quinone spanned transom Alkoran camorra entomic mahonia remould umbones
quintal spanner tranter allonge canonic entotic mahound remount unbosom
quintan spencer trenail allover canonry entozoa Masonic removal unbound
quintet spender trental almoner Canopic enwound masonry removed unbowed
quintic spinach trinary almonry caporal ergodic Masorah remover unboxed
quondam spindle trindle aloofly caroche escolar mayoral reposal uncouth
rainbow spindly tringle alsoran carotid espouse meconic reposit uncover
raunchy spindry trinity amboina carotin essoyne meiosis resolve undoing
rawness spinner trinket ambones carouse eulogia meiotic resound ungodly
redneck spinney trinkum amboyna chaotic exposal melodic retouch unhoped
redness spinode truncal ammonal chloral exposed memoirs revolve unhorse
reenact spinoff trundle ammonia chloric exposer menorah rewound unhouse
reenter spinose tsunami ampoule chooser exposit mesonic ricotta unjoint
reentry spinous tunning ancones choosey expound metonym ridotto unloose
regnant spinule turnery anionic chromic fagotto metopic riposte unmoral
remnant spondee turning antonym chronic Faroese metopon risotto unmoved
reunion spondyl turnipy aphonia ciboria felonry minorca samovar unroost
reunite sponger turnkey aphonic cipolin femoral mitoses Samoyed unsound
reynard spongin turnout aphotic coconut floorer mitosis saponin unwound
rhenium sponson twangle appoint cocotte floosie mitotic savoury unwoven
rounded sponsor twankay apropos colobus floozie molossi scholar valonia
roundel spunkie twinkle areolae cologne flyover monocle scholia vamoose
rounder standby twinkly areolar colonel garotte monocot scooper vapours
roundly stander twinned areolas colonic gavotte monodic scooter vapoury
```

```
velours  coppery  helping  propane  snipper  trypsin  ascribe  clerisy  empress
veloute  coppice  henpeck  propend  snippet  tryptic  astride  clerkly  emprise
visored  corpora  hipping  prophet  soapbox  turpeth  ataraxy  coarsen  Encraty
wagoner  coupler  hopping  propine  soapily  tympana  attract  comrade  encrust
whoopee  couplet  hospice  propjet  soppily  tympani  attrite  correct  energid
whooper  cowpoke  icepack  propone  sopping  tympano  avarice  corrida  enframe
widowed  crappie  inaptly  propose  soupcon  tympany  average  corrode  engraft
widower  cripple  ineptly  propped  stapler  unaptly  averred  corrody  engrail
zedoary  cropped  inspect  pulpous  stepney  utopian  awarder  corrupt  engrain
zygosis  cropper  inspire  pumpkin  stepped  utopism  azurine  courage  engrave
zygotic  crupper  jumpjet  pupping  stepper  utopist  azurite  courier  engross
zymogen  cryptal  jumpoff  purport  stepson  vampire  barrack  courlan  enprint
zymosis  cryptic  kalpack  purpose  stipend  vampish  barrage  courser  entrain
zymotic  culprit  kampong  purpura  stipple  vespers  barrier  courtly  entrant
adapter  cupping  keeping  purpure  stipule  vespine  barring  csardas  entreat
adaptor  cuspate  klipdas  quipped  stopgap  vulpine  barroom  cuirass  entropy
adeptly  dampish  knapped  Rajpoot  stopoff  warpath  bearded  cuprite  entrust
adipose  dauphin  knapper  rampage  stopped  waspish  bearing  cuprous  eparchy
adopter  deepsea  krypton  rampant  stopper  whipped  bearish  currach  epergne
airport  deepfry  lampion  rampart  stopple  whipper  bedrock  curragh  escribe
airpost  Delphic  lampoon  rampion  stupefy  whippet  bedroll  currant  estrade
Arapaho  despair  lamprey  rapping  styptic  whipsaw  bedroom  current  estreat
asepsis  despise  lapping  rapport  subplot  whopper  begrime  currier  eternal
aseptic  despite  legpull  rasping  sulphur  wrapped  berried  currish  eucrite
auspice  despoil  leopard  redpoll  sumpter  wrapper  betroth  cutrate  exarate
bagpipe  despond  limpkin  respect  supping  yapping  blarney  cypress  excrete
bedpost  dewpond  lipping  respell  support  yipping  blurred  Cyprian  exergue
bespeak  diopter  lopping  respell  suppose  zapping  boarder  Cypriot  exordia
bespoke  dioptre  lumpily  respire  surpass  zipping  boarish  czardas  express
bopping  dipping  lumpish  respite  surplus  acequia  boorish  czardom  extract
bumpily  dispark  lymphad  respond  suspect  aliquot  bourbon  czarina  extreme
bumpkin  dispart  mapping  respray  suspend  banquet  bourdon  czarism  extrude
calpack  display  marplot  ripping  suspire  bouquet  bourree  czarist  exurban
campbed  disport  maypole  ripplet  swapped  briquet  boxroom  dayroom  exurbia
camphor  dispose  misplay  salpinx  swapper  chequer  buirdly  Debrett  fairing
camping  dispute  mopping  sampler  swipple  cliquey  bulrush  debrief  fairish
campion  dolphin  morphia  sapphic  swopped  croquet  bunraku  decrier  fairway
capping  drapery  mudpack  sapping  swopper  conquer  cabrank  decrypt  farrago
carping  dripdry  mumpish  scapple  sylphid  croquis  caprice  defraud  farrier
carport  dripped  napping  scapula  symptom  cumquat  caprine  defrock  farruca
chapati  droplet  nauplii  scepsis  syrphid  jonquil  caproic  defrost  fearful
chaplet  dropout  nippers  sceptic  tadpole  kumquat  carrack  degrade  febrile
chapman  dropped  nippily  sceptre  tamping  lacquer  carrier  deprave  ferrate
chapped  dropper  nipping  scopula  tampion  marquee  carrion  depress  ferrety
chappie  dumpish  nonplus  scupper  tapping  marquis  carroty  deprive  ferrite
chapter  duopoly  nutpine  seapink  telpher  masquer  carryon  derrick  ferrous
chipped  earplug  nymphal  seaport  tempera  parquet  charade  detract  ferrugo
chipper  edaphic  nymphet  seepage  tempest  picquet  charger  detrain  ferrule
chopine  eelpout  offpeak  seppuku  Templar  racquet  charily  detrude  fibroid
chopped  erepsin  oosperm  serpent  templet  rorqual  chariot  diarchy  fibroin
chopper  flapped  oospore  serpigo  tempter  unequal  charism  diarise  fibroma
chupati  flapper  outpace  serpula  tempura  acarian  charity  diarist  fibrous
clapped  flipped  outplay  shapely  tenpins  aborter  charley  digraph  fierily
clapper  flipper  outport  shiplap  terpene  acarine  charlie  diorama  flareup
clipped  flopped  outpost  shipman  timpani  accrete  charmer  diorism  floreat
clipper  flypast  palpate  shipped  timpano  accrual  charnel  diorite  florist
clippie  foppery  pampean  shippen  tipping  acerbic  charpoy  disrank  floruit
clupeid  foppish  pampero  shipper  tippler  acerola  charqui  disrate  fourale
clypeal  frapped  pappose  shippon  tompion  acerose  charred  disrobe  fourgon
clypeus  fripper  parpend  shipway  topping  actress  charter  disroot  furrier
compact  garpike  peppery  shopboy  torpedo  address  cherish  diurnal  furring
company  glyphic  peppill  shopman  torpids  affront  cheroot  dogrose  furrowy
compare  glyptal  pepping  shopped  towpath  aggress  chervil  doorman  gadroon
compart  glyptic  perpend  shopper  trapeze  alertly  chirrup  doormat  gasring
compass  grapery  perpent  simpler  trapped  amarant  chorale  doorway  gearbox
compeer  graphic  perplex  simplex  trapper  Amerind  chordal  dormant  gearing
compend  grapnel  pimping  sipping  trepang  amorist  chorine  dwarves  Geordie
compere  grapple  pipping  skepsis  tripery  amorous  chorion  dyarchy  georgic
compete  gripped  pitpony  skipped  triplet  amtrack  choroid  earring  gharial
compile  gripper  pitprop  skipper  triplex  anarchy  chortle  eccrine  gherkin
complex  gryphon  plopped  skippet  tripody  ancress  churchy  embrace  glaring
complin  guipure  pompano  slapped  tripoli  android  cirrose  embroil  glorify
complot  gunplay  pompous  slipped  tripos   aneroid  cirrous  embrown  gnarled
compony  gypping  poppied  slipper  tripped  angrily  citrate  embryon  gourami
comport  happily  popping  slipway  tripper  anurous  citrine  emerald  gourmet
compose  happing  prepack  slopped  trippet  anyroad  clarify  emerged  Gstring
compost  harpist  prepaid  snapped  trophic  apprise  clarion  emeriti  guarana
compote  harpoon  prepare  snapper  tropics  approve  clarity  emersed  guarani
compute  helpful  preplan  snipped  tropism  armrest  clarkia  emirate  guarded
```

```
guardee madrona overlay sacrist starred uberous batsman consult fibster
guerdon madrono overlie saprobe starter umbrage beastly consume firstly
guereza Marrano overman satrapy startle Umbrian bedside corsage fissile
gunroom married overpay saurian sterile unarmed bedsock corsair fission
haircut marring overran sauroid sterlet unbrace bedsore corslet fissure
hairnet marrowy overrun scarfed sternal uncross beeswax cossack flasher
hairpin matrass oversaw scarify sterned uncrown berserk cowshed fleshed
harrier meerkat oversea scarlet sternly undress biassed cowslip flesher
hayrick merrily oversee scarper sternum unfrock blasted crassly fleshly
hearing metrics overset scarred steroid unfroze blaster cresset fluster
hearken metrist oversew scarves stirpes untried blesbok crested forsake
hearsay microbe overtax scirrhi stirred untruly blessed crisper forsook
hearted midriff overtly scoriae stirrer untruss blister crisply fossick
hearten migrant overtop scorify stirrup untruth blossom cristae fossula
Hebraic migrate overuse scoring storage upbraid blusher crosier frescos
heiress milreis padrone scorner storied upgrade bluster crossly freshen
herring misread padroni scorper styrene uptrend boaster crusade fresher
hiproof misrule pairoar Scorpio sucrose usurper bobsled crusado freshet
hoarsen moorage paprika scurril sunrise uterine bobstay crusher freshly
horrent moorhen patrial searoom sunroof uxorial bolshie crustal friseur
horrify mooring patriot secrecy supreme vagrant bolster crusted Frisian
hurried Moorish patroon secrete supremo verruca booster crystal frisker
hydrant moorlog payroll serrate surreal vibrant borscht cuisine frisket
hydrate mourner pearled serried swarded vibrate borstal cumshaw frisson
hydride murrain pearler sferics swarmer vibrato bossism cupsful frosted
hydroid nacrous peartly sharpen swarthy vitrify bowshot cursive frustum
hydrous narrate pebrine sharper taproom vitrine boxseat cursory fulsome
Iberian narrows peerage sharply taproot vitriol brashly cypsela fussily
icerink nearest peeress sherbet tarrier warrant brassie danseur fusspot
imbrute necrose petrify shereef tarring warring brisken dapsone gagster
impresa Negress Petrine sheriff taurine warrior brisket darshan gassing
impress Negrito petrous sherris tearful wearily briskly daystar gemsbok
imprest negroid pharaoh shirker teargas wearing bristle deistic ghastly
imprint neurine pharynx shoring tearing weirdie bristly densely ghostly
improve neuroma pibroch shorten tearoom weirdly brusher density ginseng
inbreed neurone picrate shortie tearose wharves brusque dessert glassen
incrust nigrify pierrot shortly terrace whereas bursary dissave glasses
indraft nitrate poorish sierran terrain whereat burster disseat glisten
indrawn nitride porrect skirret terrene whereby bussing dissect glister
inertia nitrify prorate skirted terrier wherein caesium dissent glossal
inertly nitrile prurigo skirter terrify whereof caesura doeskin Glossic
infract nitrite pteroic slurred terrine whereon caisson dogskin gnostic
ingraft nitrous pteryla smaragd tetrode whereto Capsian dogstar godsend
ingrain nourish puerile smarten therapy whirler capsize dossier godship
ingrate obtrude putrefy smartly thereat whirred capstan drastic gorsedd
ingress ocarina pyrrhic snarler thereby whorish capsule dresser gossipy
ingroup ochrous quarrel snarlup therein whorled carsick drosera gossoon
ingrown odorant quartan snorkel thereof worrier cassata droshky grasper
intrant odorous quarter snorter thereon yttrium cassava drysalt griskin
intreat oloroso quartet soaring thereto zebrine cassino dryshod gristle
introit onerous quartic soprani theriac zebroid cassock earshot gristly
intrude operand querist soprano thermae zoarium catseye ekistic grossly
intrust operant recruit sorrily thermal abashed catspaw elastic grysbok
iterant operate redraft sourish thermic abusive catsuit elastin guesser
iterate operose redress soursop thirdly abysmal caustic elision guisard
ivories oppress refract sparely thirsty abyssal Celsius elusion gumshoe
jarring ostraca refrain sparger thorite airship cession elusive gunship
journal ostraka refresh sparing thorium airsick censure elusory gunshot
journey ostrich regrant sparkle thorned allseed cesspit elysian gutsily
joyride outrage regrate sparoid thyroid allstar chassis Elysium gymslip
keyring outrank regress sparred thyrsus almsman chasten episode hamster
knurled outride regrets sparrow tiercel alyssum chessel epistle Hansard
lairage outrode regroup Spartan tiercet ambsace chested erasure harshen
latrine outrush reorder spiraea tigress amusive classes eristic harshly
laurels ovarian repress spirant tigrish aniseed classic erosion harslet
lavrock overact reprint spireme titrate anosmia classis erosive hassock
learned overage reprise spirits torrefy anosmic clastic etesian hayseed
learner overall reproof sporran torrent apishly closely evasion herself
legrest overarm reprove sporter touraco apostil closeup evasive hessian
legroom overate retrace sporule touring apostle closure eyeshot himself
leprosy overawe retract spurner tourism aristae cluster eyesore hipster
leprous overbid retrain spurred tourist aristas clyster eyespot hirsute
library overbuy retread spurrey tourney armsful coastal falsely holster
librate overdid retreat spurtle towrope Avestan coaster falsies hopsack
ligroin overdue retrial starchy trireme Avestic consent falsify horsily
lipread overeat rewrite stardom tsardom awesome consign falsity hotshot
lowrise overfed rewrote starkly tsarina banshee consist feaster housing
macrame overfly roaring starlet tsarism bassist console felsite Hussite
macrami overlap sacring starlit tsarist bassoon consort felspar iceshow
```

```
Irishry obesity pursuit toaster arctoid canting culture emptily fratery
irksome odyssey quassia tonsure ashtray cantrip curtail emption fretful
jouster oersted quester topsail auction captain curtain enation fretsaw
jussive offside questor topside austere caption curtana epatant fretted
kidskin oilseed ramsons topsoil austral captive curtsey epitaph fritted
kinship oilskin ransack torsade banteng capture custard epitaxy fritter
kinsman oldster redskin torsion banting cartage custody epithem further
kissing oneself reissue tosspot baptise cartful customs epithet furtive
kitschy oneshot retsina toyshop baptism cartoon cutting epitome fustian
Krishna onestep ribston tressed baptist castile cyathus erotica fustily
kursaal opossum rissole tressel bastard casting cystine erotism futtock
lassoes opuscle roaster trestle basting castled cystoid esotery gantlet
lawsuit ourself rodsman trisect bastion castoff Dantean eustasy gastric
legshow outsell roister trishaw battels cattalo dastard exotica genteel
leister outshot rooster trismus battery cattery daytime faction gentian
leisure outside rousing trusser batting cattily deathly factory gentile
Liassic outsize rouster trustee beatify cautery deltaic factual gestalt
linsang outsold royster truster beating caution deltoid facture gestapo
linseed outsole rumshop trysoil beatnik centaur dentate fantail gestate
lissome outstay russety Tuesday bedtime centavo dentine fantasm gesture
lobster paisley Russian tussive Beltane centime dentist fantast getting
loosely palsied Russify tussock belting centner denture fantasy ghettos
lousily parsley salsify tussore benthic central destine fantods giltcup
lugsail parsnip sapsago twister benthos centred destiny farther gittern
maestri passade sassaby twosome bestead centric destroy fastday glitter
maestro passado satsuma twostep bestial centrum deutzia fattest glottal
mahseer passage sausage unasked bestrew century dextral fatting glottis
mansard passant scissel unusual betting certain dextran fattish gluteal
mansion passing scissor Vaishya bigtime certify dextrin feather gluteus
mansize passion seasick varsity biltong cestode dictate feature glutted
Marsala passive seaside versant biotite cestoid diction felting glutton
marshal passkey seaslug versify bistort chateau dietary fertile gnathic
massage paysage seismal versine bistred chatted diptera festive goatgod
masseur peasant seismic version bittern chattel diptych festoon goatish
massive peascod sensory waisted bitters chatter dirtily fetters goitred
measles peasoup sensual waister bitting chitter distaff fictile goutfly
measure pensile sessile warship bittock chutney distain fiction gratify
Meissen pension session wassail blatant cistern distant fictive grating
message pensive shaslik wayside blather cittern distend fifteen gritted
messiah Persian shaster weasand blatter clatter distent fifthly grottos
Messias persist shastra webster blether clothes distich fifties grutten
messily persona shyster welsher blither clotted distill figtree gustily
messtin pessary sibship whisker blotchy cloture distort firtree guttate
miasmal phasmid sinsyne whiskey blotted clutter disturb fistful gutting
miasmic physics skysail whisper blotter coating dittany fistula halting
midship piastre slasher whistle boating coition dogtrot fittest hastate
minster pigskin sloshed whoseso boatman coltish doltish fitting hastily
missend pilsner smasher winsome bobtail Comtian dortour fixture hatting
missent pissoir smashup worship bootleg Comtism dotting flatcap hautboy
missile plasmic sonship worsted bortsch Comtist dratted flatcar hauteur
missing plasmid spastic wrestle bottega contact ductile flatlet heathen
mission plasmin suasion zemstvo bottled contain ducting flatout heather
missish plaster suasive abattis bottony contemn dustbin flatten heating
missive plastic subside abetted brattle contend dustily flatter hectare
misstep plastid subsidy abetter British content dustman flattop heftily
mobster pliskie subsist abettor brittle contest dustpan fletton heptane
moisten plosion subsoil abstain brittly context earthen flitted histone
moistly plosive subsume abutted britzka contort earthly flitter history
monsoon plusage sunspot abutter brothel contour eastern flotage hitting
monster plushly sunstar acetate brother control easting flotsam Hittite
mosshag possess sunsuit acetify brutish contuse ebbtide fluting hoatzin
mousaka potshot swasher acetone Brython cortege ecstasy flutist hostage
mousing poussin tapsman acetous bunting cortile edition flutter hostess
mousmee presage tapster acutely burthen costard egotise flyting hostile
netsuke present teashop agitate bustard costate egotism flytrap hostler
neuston preside Telstar agitato bustler costean egotist footage hottest
newsboy presoak tensely ajutage buttend costing egotrip footboy hottish
newsman presser tensile alation buttery costive elation footing hunting
noisily pressup tension alltime buttock costrel elitism footman hurtful
noisome presume tensity amateur buttons costume elitist footpad hustler
nonskid prosaic tensive amative buttony cottage elution footrot hutting
nonslip prosify tersely amatory caitiff cottier elytron footsie imitate
nonstop prosily tessera anatase caltrap cottony elytrum footway initial
nonsuch prosody thistle anatomy caltrop couthie emetine forties install
nonsuit prosper thistly another cantata couture emitted fortify instant
nunship prussic thyself anytime cantate critter emitter Fortran instate
nursery pulsate tipsify apatite canteen cuittle emotion fortune instead
nursing punster tipsily apetaly canthus cultism emotive foxtail inutile
oarsman pursuer tipster apothem cantina cultist emptier foxtrot irately
```

isotope	mattoid	outturn	pottage	scotice	statics	tritone	wintery	decuman
isotopy	mauther	ovation	pottery	Scotish	station	trotted	wistful	decuple
isotron	Maytime	oxytone	potting	Scotist	statism	trotter	wittily	defunct
jetting	meatfly	panther	pouting	scotoma	statist	tuatara	witting	deluder
jitters	meatman	panties	prattle	Scottie	stative	tuition	wottest	diluent
jittery	meeting	pantile	pretend	scutage	statued	tutting	writeup	dilutee
jogtrot	melting	partake	pretest	scutate	stature	twitchy	writhen	diluter
jotting	menthol	partial	pretext	scutter	statute	twitted	writing	dilutor
justice	mention	parting	pretzel	scuttle	stetson	twitter	written	divulge
justify	mestiza	partita	prithee	seatang	stetted	twotime	xanthic	draught
jutting	mestizo	partite	protean	seating	stutter	twotone	xanthin	drought
Kantian	mettled	partlet	protect	sectary	subtend	umpteen	yestern	drouthy
karting	mintage	partner	protege	sectile	subtile	unction	yewtree	effulge
kentish	mistake	partook	proteid	section	suction	unitary	zaptieh	enounce
kestrel	mistful	pastern	protein	seltzer	suiting	unitive	zestful	enquire
knitted	mistily	pasteup	protend	septate	sultana	unstick	zootaxy	enquiry
knitter	mistime	pastime	protest	septime	suntrap	unstuck	zootomy	epaulet
knotted	misting	pasture	proteus	sestina	surtout	upstage	abjurer	esquire
knotter	mistook	pattern	protist	setting	sustain	upstair	abought	estuary
lactate	mistral	patting	protium	settler	swatted	upstart	aboulia	excurse
lacteal	mixture	peltate	pustule	settlor	swatter	urethan	accurst	excusal
lactose	moither	pelting	puttier	Sextans	swither	urethra	accusal	exhumer
lantana	montage	pentane	putting	sextant	Switzer	vantage	accused	expulse
lantern	montane	pentode	quetsch	sextile	swotted	vastity	accuser	expunge
Laotian	montero	pentose	quetzal	shatter	systole	vatting	acouchy	fabular
lasting	monthly	peptalk	quitted	shittim	tactful	ventage	acquest	faculae
lattice	mortice	peptide	quitter	shotgun	tactics	ventail	acquire	faculty
leather	mortify	peptise	ragtime	shotten	tactile	ventral	actuary	famulus
lectern	mortise	peptone	rapture	shuteye	taction	venture	actuate	fatuity
lection	mottled	pertain	rattail	shutout	tactual	venturi	adducer	fatuous
lecture	mouther	perturb	ratteen	shutter	tantara	vertigo	adjudge	felucca
leftism	multure	pertuse	rattery	shuttle	tantivy	vestige	adjunct	fibulae
leftist	munting	pettily	ratting	sintery	tantric	vestral	albumen	fibular
lentigo	muntjac	petting	rattler	Sistine	tantrum	vesture	albumin	fibulas
lentisk	muntjak	pettish	rattrap	sistrum	tartare	vetting	aleuron	figural
lentoid	murther	photism	rectify	sitting	tartish	viatica	alluvia	figured
leotard	mustang	Pictish	rectory	sixteen	tartlet	victory	ampulla	flaught
letters	mustard	picture	rectrix	sixthly	Tartufe	victual	amputee	flaunty
letting	muttony	pietism	rentier	sixties	tastily	vintage	aneurin	fleuret
Lettish	mystery	pietist	reptile	Sixtine	tatters	vintner	anguine	fleuron
lettuce	mystify	pigtail	restart	skating	tattery	virtual	anguish	flounce
liftoff	narthex	pintado	restate	sketchy	tattily	vistaed	angular	focused
lilting	nastily	pintail	restful	skitter	tatting	vittate	annuity	fraught
listeth	nattily	pintuck	restiff	skittle	tattler	vittles	annular	fuguist
listing	nautics	pistole	restive	slasher	teatime	voltage	annulet	galumph
littery	nautili	pitting	restock	slating	teatray	voltaic	annulus	genuine
loather	nectary	platane	restore	slatted	tectrix	vulture	arbutus	graunch
loathly	neither	plateau	restyle	slither	tektite	waftage	arcuate	grouchy
loftily	neoteny	platina	rettery	slotcar	tentbed	wafture	arduous	grouper
lottery	Neptune	plating	retting	slotted	tentfly	wagtail	arousal	groupie
lotting	nesting	platoon	rhatany	smatter	tenthly	waiting	asquint	grouser
loutish	netting	platted	riotous	smitten	tentpeg	waltzer	assuage	hamulus
lustful	neutral	platter	riptide	smother	tertial	wanting	assured	hanuman
lustily	neutron	plotted	rontgen	smutted	tertian	warthog	assurer	hirudin
lustral	nictate	plotter	rootage	snatchy	testacy	wartime	augural	hocused
lustrum	noctuid	poetess	rootlet	softish	testate	wastage	awfully	impulse
maltase	noctule	poetics	rostral	soother	testban	wastrel	beguile	inbuilt
Maltese	nocturn	poetise	rostrum	soothly	testbed	wattage	beguine	incubus
malting	norther	pontage	rotting	sootily	testfly	Watteau	bequest	incudes
maltose	nostril	pontiff	routine	sotting	testify	wattled	bitumen	incurve
manteau	nostrum	pontify	ruction	sottish	testily	wattles	blouson	incused
mantlet	nuptial	pontoon	rupture	soutane	testoon	waxtree	botulin	inducer
mantram	nurture	portage	rustily	souther	testudo	weather	braunch	indulge
mantrap	nutting	portend	rustler	spathic	textile	western	brought	indusia
martial	oaktree	portent	rutting	spatial	textual	westing	cacumen	infulae
Martian	obitual	portico	ruttish	spatted	texture	wettest	caducei	inhuman
martini	oestral	portion	Saktism	spattee	thither	wetting	calumet	injurer
martlet	oestrum	portray	saltant	spatter	tintack	wettish	calumny	inquest
martyry	oestrus	postage	saltbox	spatula	tittupy	whatnot	capuche	inquire
mastaba	oldtime	postbag	saltcat	spitted	tontine	whether	casuals	inquiry
masters	omitted	postbox	saltern	spitter	toothed	whetted	casuist	insular
mastery	onetime	postboy	salting	spittle	tootsie	whetter	cerumen	insulin
mastich	onstage	posteen	saltire	spotted	tortile	whitely	clausal	insured
mastiff	oration	postern	saltish	spotter	tortrix	whither	copular	insurer
mastoid	oratory	postfix	saltpan	sputnik	torture	whiting	coquito	issuant
mattery	oratrix	posting	santour	sputter	tottery	whitish	cacumen	January
matting	orotund	postman	saxtuba	statant	totting	whitlow	crouton	jejunum
mattins	outtake	posture	scatted	stately	tritely	Whitsun	cumulus	jocular
mattock	outtalk	postwar	scatter	statice	tritium	whittle	cupular	jugular

```
lacunae request unquote knavish voivode jaywalk Tynwald katydid neozoic
lacunal requiem untuned Latvian weevily keyword unaware kerygma puzzler
lacunar require upsurge louvred wolvish knowall unswear ladybug quizzed
lacunas requite vacuity naively Yahvist knowhow unswore ladykin quizzer
Laputan resurge vacuole naivete airwave knowing unsworn lanyard quizzes
limulus returns vacuous naivety alewife lapwing untwine manyear rhizoid
liquate rivulet vaguely nervate anyways leeward untwist marybud rhizome
liquefy roguery vaguish nervine anywise legwork upsweep midyear seizing
liqueur roguish valuate nervous arcweld lobworm upswept papyrus seizure
liturgy rotunda vaquero nervure artwork logwood upswing playact sizzler
lobular saguaro viduity nirvana athwart lugworm vanward playboy sozzled
locular saluter vitular obovate awkward madwort viewing playful subzero
loculus samurai voguish obovoid between manward waxwing playing swizzle
lunular scauper voluble olivary betwixt manweek waxwork playlet whizkid
lupulin scourer volubly olivine blewits mawworn wayward playoff whizzed
maculae scourge volumed outvote blowdry maxwell wayworn playpen woozily
macular scouter voluted parvenu blowfly mayweed webworm polygon ───────
manumit scrubby volutin parvise blowgun midweek werwolf polymer abeyant
mazurka scruffy wrought peevish blowout Midwest Yahwist polynia abigail
medulla scrumpy zymurgy pervade blowzed midwife abaxial polynya abomasa
medusae scrunch atavism pervert Boswell morwong adaxial polypod abreact
medusan scruple atavist pluvial boxwood mugwort asexual polypus abreast
medusas secular bravado pravity brawler mugwump bauxite quayage abroach
mezuzah securer bravely prevail brewage narwhal biaxial recycle abstain
mimulus seducer bravery prevent brewery network bruxism satyral acclaim
minuend Senussi bravura preview brownie norward coaxial satyric acetate
minutes sequela brevier previse browser oakwood coexist satyrid acreage
minutia sequent brevity privacy bulwark oarweed dioxide spryest actuary
modular sequoia calvary private burweed oilwell epoxide tanyard actuate
modulus shouter canvass privily camwood outward flexile taxying adamant
morulae shrubby carving privity catwalk outwear flexion Toryism adulate
morular simular cervine proverb chowder outwent flexure trayful agitate
Nahuatl sinuate cheviot provide crawler outwore fluxion undying agitato
natural sinuous chevron proviso crowbar outwork inexact untying airfare
nebulae situate civvies provoke crowdie outworn Manxcat wheyish airmail
nebular slouchy clavate provost crowned pigwash Manxman amazing airwave
nebulas sloughy clavier pulvini crowner pigweed Marxian benzene ajutage
nelumbo snouted clivers purview crownet pinworm Marxism benzine alidade
nocuous soluble connect quavery crowtoe plywood Marxist benzoic already
nodular splurge convene quivery cudweed prowess proximo benzoin althaea
nonuser spousal convent revving cutworm prowler quixote benzole amarant
octuple spouter convert salvage daywork ragweed abeyant benzoyl ambsace
odoured staunch convict salvoes dogwood ragworm acrylic boozeup amtrack
osculum stouten convoke selvage drawbar ragwort aphylly boozily amylase
osmunda stoutly corvina servant drawing redwing babyish brazier anatase
ossuary strudel corvine servery drawler redwood babysit buzzard animate
pabulum strumae couvade Servian dyewood ribwork barytes buzzsaw anomaly
paludal suburbs couvert service eelworm ribwort barytic canzone anyways
papulae sutural craving servile endways sapwood belying canzoni apanage
papular sutured crevice serving endwise sawwort bicycle crazily apetaly
perusal tabular culvert Servite entwine seawall bogyman crozier apogamy
peruser tegular curvate Shavian entwist seaward buoyage dazzler appease
petunia tenuity dervish shaving eyewash seaware buoyant dizzard applaud
pilular tenuous dogvane shivers eyewink seaweed butyric dizzily Aramaic
piously tequila drivein shivery felwort seawhip calyces drizzle Arapaho
piquant theurgy driving silvern figwort seawife calycle drizzly archaic
plaudit thought droving silvery flowage seawolf calypso epizoic arcuate
pleurae thrummy elevate slavery flowery setwall calyxes epizoon armband
pleural titular elevens slavish forward showbiz claypan frazzle arrears
pleuron toluene eluvial Slavism forwent showery copycat frizzle asphalt
popular torulae eluvium Slovene forworn showily copyist frizzly assuage
proudly triumph exuviae solvate froward showing corydon fuzzily ataraxy
queuing trouble exuvial solvent frowsty showman dasyure gizzard athwart
radulae trounce fauvism stovies gadwall showoff drayage glazier attract
radular trouper fauvist suavely godward skyward drayman glazing aureate
rebuild Tsquare fervent suavity growler slowish ecdyses glozing average
rebuilt tubular flavine subvert grownup snowcap ecdysis grazier avocado
rebuker tumular flavour survive gunwale snowily empyema grazing awkward
recurve tumulus flivver sylvine hagweed spawner enzymic grizzle baccara
reducer unbuild fluvial sylvite hayward steward fogydom grizzly baccate
refugee unbuilt fulvous travail haywire stewpan fogyish guzzler badmash
refusal unfunny gravely travois henwife stewpot fogyism jazzily baggage
refuser unfussy gravity trivial hogwash stowage greyhen jazzman baklava
refutal unguard gravure trivium hogweed sunward greyish matzoth ballade
refuter unguent halvers valvate indwell sunwise greylag mazzard ballast
regular ungulae harvest valvula indwelt gruyere mitzvah bandage
regulus ungulae heavily velvety inkwell sunwise guayule muezzin bandana
repulse unlucky knavery vervain inswing trawler halyard muzzily barbate
reputed unquiet knavery vervain intwine tutwork juryman muzzler bargain
```

barmaid	catwalk	cymbalo	enchain	foulard	hydrate	lumbago	obolary	perhaps
barrack	caudate	dastard	enchant	foumart	hymnary	lumbang	obovate	periapt
barrage	caviare	deafaid	enchase	fourale	icefall	lurdane	obviate	pertain
bastard	caymans	decease	enclasp	foveate	icepack	machair	oculate	pervade
bateaux	cembalo	deciare	enclave	foxtail	ikebana	macrame	oddball	pessary
Bauhaus	centaur	declaim	Encraty	frigate	imamate	macrami	odorant	phalanx
bedfast	centavo	declare	endways	froward	imitate	magmata	offhand	pharaoh
beggary	certain	declass	enemata	fullage	impeach	magnate	oilbath	phonate
beldame	chalaza	defiant	enframe	funfair	impearl	mallard	oilcake	pickaxe
Beltane	chapati	deflate	engraft	furcate	implant	maltase	olivary	picrate
beneath	charade	defraud	engrail	furnace	inboard	mammary	onstage	piebald
Bengali	chelate	degrade	engrain	futhark	indraft	mammate	oomiack	pigtail
bereave	chicane	deltaic	engrave	gabnash	indrawn	mandala	openair	pigwash
bigname	Chicano	dentate	enplane	gadwall	inexact	mandate	operand	pileate
biliary	chorale	deodand	enslave	galeate	inflame	manjack	operant	pillage
biomass	chupati	deodara	ensnare	gallant	inflate	manmade	operate	pinball
biplane	ciliary	deplane	ensnarl	gallate	infract	mansard	orchard	pinnace
biriani	ciliate	deprave	entrain	gambade	ingraft	manward	oregano	pinnate
blatant	cineast	descant	entrant	gambado	ingrain	Marrano	origami	pintado
bobtail	cithara	despair	epatant	garbage	ingrate	Marsala	ossuary	pintail
bollard	citrate	detract	epicarp	gardant	inphase	mascara	ostiary	piquant
bombard	clamant	detrain	epilate	garland	install	massage	ostraca	piscary
bombast	clavate	deviant	epitaph	gasmask	instant	mastaba	ostraka	pitfall
bondage	climate	deviate	epitaxy	gateaux	instate	matrass	ouabain	placard
boscage	cockade	dewfall	estrade	gemmate	intrant	mazzard	outback	placate
boskage	cognate	diabase	estuary	germane	inweave	mediacy	outcast	platane
boxcalf	coinage	dictate	euclase	gestalt	Ishmael	mediant	outface	playact
boxhaul	collard	diehard	eustasy	gestapo	isobath	mediate	outfall	plenary
bradawl	collate	dietary	ewelamb	gestate	isogamy	mermaid	outhaul	plicate
bravado	digraph	exarate	gimbals	isolate	message	outland	plumage
brewage	command	diorama	exclaim	gizzard	issuant	methane	outlast	plumate
brigade	compact	disband	exclave	goddamn	iterant	midland	outpace	plusage
brigand	company	disbark	exocarp	godward	iterate	migrant	outrage	pochard
brocade	compare	discant	exogamy	goliard	jackass	migrate	outrank	poleaxe
brokage	compart	discard	expiate	Goliath	January	mileage	outtake	pollack
bromate	compass	disdain	explain	goshawk	jaywalk	miliary	outtalk	pollard
bruhaha	comrade	disease	explant	goulash	jellaba	miniate	outward	pompano
buffalo	concave	disfame	extract	gourami	jimjams	mintage	overact	pondage
bugbane	connate	dismast	exudate	gradate	kabbala	miscall	overage	poniard
bullace	contact	dispark	eyeball	gramary	kalpack	miscast	overall	pontage
bullary	contain	dispart	eyebath	granary	Kannada	misdate	overarm	portage
bullate	coolant	disrank	eyelash	grenade	khanate	misgave	overate	postage
bulwark	cordage	disrate	eyewash	grimace	knowall	mislaid	overawe	potbank
bummalo	cordate	dissave	falbala	guanaco	kursaal	mismate	ovulate	pottage
bunraku	corkage	distaff	falcate	guarana	labiate	misname	oxalate	poulard
buoyage	cornage	distain	fallacy	guarani	lactate	mistake	oxidant	precast
buoyant	corsage	distant	fanfare	guisard	laggard	montage	oxidase	predate
bureaus	corsair	dittany	fanmail	gunwale	lairage	montane	oxidate	preface
bureaux	cossack	dizzard	fantail	gurnard	Lallans	moorage	package	prelacy
burgage	costard	dockage	fantasm	guttate	lambast	mordant	pageant	prelate
bursary	costate	doddard	fantast	gymnast	laniary	mousaka	pahlavi	prepack
bustard	cottage	dogbane	fantasy	Haggada	lantana	mudbath	palmary	prepaid
buzzard	courage	dogcart	farrago	haggard	lanyard	mudlark	palmate	prepare
cabbage	couvade	dogdays	fenland	hallali	lawhand	mudpack	palpate	presage
cabbagy	cowbane	dogeate	fermata	halyard	leafage	mundane	pancake	prevail
cabbala	cowhage	dogvane	ferrate	Hansard	leakage	muriate	Panjabi	primacy
cabrank	cowherd	dorhawk	filiate	harmala	leeward	murrain	pannage	primage
caimans	cranage	dormant	finback	hastate	legbail	mustang	parfait	primary
callant	cremate	drayage	firearm	hatband	lemmata	mustard	pargana	primate
calpack	crenate	drysalt	flotage	haulage	leopard	myomata	partake	privacy
calvary	crusade	dullard	flowage	hayward	leotard	Nahuatl	passade	private
cantata	crusado	dunnage	flyback	Hebraic	library	narrate	passado	proband
cantate	crybaby	durmast	flybane	hectare	librate	nectary	passage	probang
canvass	cuirass	earmark	flyhalf	henbane	limbate	Neogaea	passant	probate
captain	cuneate	ebriate	flypast	heptane	lindane	neonate	paysage	profane
carcase	cupcake	ecstasy	fogbank	herbage	lineage	nervate	peasant	prolate
carcass	cureall	educate	foggage	hipbath	lineate	netball	peccant	pronaoi
carnage	currach	elegant	foglamp	hobnail	linkage	newlaid	peccary	pronaos
carrack	curragh	elevate	foliage	hoecake	linsang	nictate	pedlary	pronate
cartage	currant	elfland	foliate	hogback	liquate	niggard	peerage	propane
cascade	curtail	emanate	fondant	hogwash	lockage	nirvana	peltate	prorate
cascara	curtain	emblaze	footage	holdall	Lollard	nitrate	pendant	prosaic
cassata	curtana	embrace	forbade	holland	Lombard	norland	penname	pulsate
cassava	curvate	emerald	forearm	hopsack	longago	norward	pennant	Punjabi
casuals	cuspate	emicate	forgave	hostage	lowland	nummary	pennate	quahaug
catcall	custard	emirate	formant	huanaco	lubbard	nutcase	pentane	quamash
Cathari	cutback	emplace	formate	husband	luggage	nutgall	peonage	quayage
Cathars	cutlass	emplane	forsake	hushaby	lugsail	oakgall	peptalk	quinary
cattalo	cutrate	emulate	forward	hydrant	lullaby	oatcake	percale	quinate

```
radiant servant thecate ventage brambly grumble rhombus visible dyarchy
radiate setback themata ventail bugaboo grumbly ridable visibly earache
rampage setwall therapy verdant bullbat grysbok risible vocable effects
rampant Sextans thready versant buyable hackbut roadbed voluble elenchi
rampart sextant throaty vervain calibre halibut ropable volubly eparchy
ransack sfumato tieback vibrant callbox handbag rosebay votable ethical
rattail shebang tiffany vibrate callboy hatable rosebud wadable felucca
reboant shikari tillage vibrato campbed hautboy sackbut Wahabee fiancee
reclaim siamang timbale village capable hellbox salable windbag filacer
reclame sigmate village villain capably highboy saltbox workbag finical
redraft signary timpani vintage caribou hirable sandbag workbox finicky
reenact sinkage timpano violate cerebra holibut sandbar acouchy flaccid
reflate sinuate tintack virgate chamber ichabod sandbed adducer flatcap
refract sirgang tinware vistaed citable ignoble sandbox African flatcar
refrain sitfast tipcart vitiate clabber ignobly sandboy anarchy fleeced
regnant situate titlark vittate clamber imbiber savable annicut fleecer
regrant skyjack titrate volcano climber incubus sayable antacid floccus
regrate skylark toccata voltage clobber inhabit scabbed apricot Frenchy
reheard skysail toenail voltaic clubbed inhibit scabble article frescos
release smaragd tonnage vulgate clumber Jacobin scomber attache funicle
reliant soakage topiary waftage codable jacobus scribal auricle giltcup
remnant soccage topmast wagtail cohabit jukebox scriber aurochs gnocchi
replace solvate topsail wallaby coinbox kilobar scrubby autocar gouache
replant soprani tornado warfare colobus knobbed scumble autocue grouchy
rescale soprano torsade wargame crabbed knobble seeable bicycle haircut
reseaux soutane touraco warpath cribbed knobbly seedbed bifocal handcar
reshape sowback towpath warrant cribble ladybug shamble blotchy haricot
restart spicate travail wassail crowbar leafbud sherbet bobeche helical
restate spinach trehala wastage crumble legible shopboy boracic helices
retiary spiraea trenail waylaid crumbly legibly showbiz borscht helicon
retrace spirant trepang waymark curable likable shrubby bouncer hellcat
retract squeaky tribade wayward datable linkboy sickbay branchy illicit
retrain statant trigamy weasand decibel livable sickbed breccia indican
reynard steward trinary welfare disable livebox sizable brioche indices
rhatany stomach trysail wetback disobey longbow sizably bronchi indicia
rhubarb stomata Tsquare windage djibbah losable sjambok broncho inducer
ribband storage tsunami wordage downbow lovable skiable caducei insecty
Rommany stowage tuatara yardage drabber lovably slabbed calices kingcup
rootage streaky turbary yardang drabbet macabre slabber caliche kitschy
roseate striate tympana yardarm drabble mailbag slobber calicle kneecap
roulade sublate tympani zedoary drawbar mailbox slubbed calyces latices
ruinate succade tympano Zingari dribble marabou slubber calycle lexical
rummage sulcate tympany Zingaro drubbed marybud slumber capuche lexicon
rundale sullage Tynwald zoogamy dupable minibus snubbed caracal linocut
Sabbath sultana tzigane zootaxy durable movable snubber caracul lioncel
saccade summand tzigany abubble durably mutable soapbox caroche logical
saccate summary ululant acerbic dustbin mutably sofabed catechu loricae
saguaro sunbath ululate acrobat eatable namable soluble cenacle lyrical
saltant sunlamp umbrage addable ennoble newsboy soroban chancel magical
salvage sunward unaware addible ephebus nosebag squabby chancre malacia
sapsago surbase unbrace adhibit equable notable stabbed churchy manacle
sarcasm surface unchain aerobic equably notably stabber cimices Manxcat
sassaby surname unclasp affable exhibit October stubbed cloacae medical
satiate surpass unguard affably exurban omnibus stubble cloacal Mexican
satrapy sustain unheard alembic exurbia overbid stubbly codices mimical
sausage syllabi unitary algebra filibeg overbuy stumble codicil mimicry
saveall syncarp unlearn amiable firebox pageboy swabbed colicky minicab
sawgate syngamy unleash amiably firebug parable swabber comical minicar
scalade tallage unmeant amoebae fixable payable swobbed conacre miracle
scalado Tammany unready amoebas fleabag pillbox tallboy conical modicum
scutage tanbark unsnarl amoebic flubbed playboy tamable cooncan monacal
scutate tankage unteach astable flyable pliable taxable copycat monacle
seabass tankard unweave attaboy footboy pliably tenable coracle monocot
seakale tannage upbraid audible freebie plumber tenably corncob morocco
sealane tannate upgrade autobus friable plumbic tentbed council murices
sealant tantara upheave ballboy fribble plumbob terebra crunchy musical
seamaid tanyard upstage bandbox fusible poohbah testban cubical nodical
seamark tartare upstair beanbag gamebag postbag testbed cubicle officer
seatang teacake upstart bellboy gearbox postbox thimble culices optical
seawall teenage urinary bilobar gemsbok postboy tollbar curacao opuscle
seaward ternary vagrant bilobed goldbug potable toolbox curacoa ossicle
seaware ternate valiant blabbed golfbag quibble tremble cuticle oxyacid
sectary terrace vallate blabber goodbye rainbow trembly cynical panacea
seepage testacy valuate blesbok grabbed rarebit triable debacle panache
selvage testate valvate blubber grabber ratable trouble deficit panicky
septate thalami vantage bourbon grabble retable tuckbox defocus panicle
serfage thanage vanward brabble grubbed rhombic tunable diarchy panocha
seriate         variant bramble grubber         tunably domical paunchy
serrate         variate                         typebar dovecot peascod
                vendace
```

```
pedicab abaddon decadal khaddar serfdom worldly bowhead cookery enwheel
pedicel abandon decided kingdom shedder wouldbe boxseat coppery epicede
pedicle abrader decider klipdas shindig wouldst bravely corbeil epicene
pelican abridge decidua kneader shudder yielder bravery corneal epigeal
pemican accidie decoder launder skaldic zooidal brewery cornett epigean
pofaced acridly deluder laundry skidded abscess bribery correct epigene
polacca adjudge demoded longday slander academe buckeye cortege erodent
polacre amender derider lucidly sledded academy bugbear costean escheat
polecat amildar divider luridly slender accrete burgeon couvert esotery
prancer aphides driedup macadam slidden Achaean burgess cowbell estreat
preachy apsidal dripdry matador smeddum achieve Burmese cowheel euglena
radical apsides druidic maunder solidly acquest burweed cowherd evident
radices arcaded dukedom meander solidus actress buttend coyness eweneck
radicle arcadia dwindle melodic someday acutely buttery credent excrete
railcar ascidia earldom milldam sounder address cachexy crudely exegete
raunchy asunder echidna mirador soundly ageless cacoepy cudbear exigent
recycle awarder encoder mixedly speeder aggress Cadmean cudweed express
reducer Bahadur ephedra mixedup speedup agilely caldera culvert extreme
refocus basidia ergodic monadic spender ailment candela current eyeless
reticle bearded exordia monodic spindle aimless candent cutlery falsely
rosecut besides fadedly moulder spindly airless cannery cypress farceur
rubicon bipedal faraday mylodon spindry alameda canteen cypsela Faroese
salicet birddog faradic naiades splodge alchemy cathead danseur fathead
salicin bladder fastday nakedly spondee aliment catseye Dantean fatness
saltcat blandly fetidly nameday spondyl allheal cattery deadend fattest
sanicle bleeder fiefdom nomadic squaddy allseed cautery deadeye ferment
Saracen blender fielder noonday staddle amateur cepheid deanery fernery
seducer blinder filmdom notedly staidly ambient chateau Debrett ferrety
senecio blindly firedog oppidan standby ancient chimera deflect fervent
sericin blooded fixedly overdid stander ancress chimere densely fetters
sidecar blowdry flagday overdue standin aniseed Chinese deplete fewness
silicic blunder fluidal ovoidal standup antbear cholera depress feyness
silicle boarder fluidic paladin stardom anxiety cindery descend fidgets
silicon bonedry fluidly paludal strider apogean Circean descent fidgety
sirocco boredom fogydom papadam stridor aptness cistern dessert fifteen
sketchy boulder founder parader strudel araneid cithern dialect figleaf
slotcar bounden foundry parades studded archery cittern dickens figment
slouchy bounder freedom paradox subadar arcweld clement digress filbert
smoochy bourdon fronded parodic subedit armless clivers diluent fishery
snatchy bowlder gelidly peridot swaddle armrest closely dimmest fisheye
snowcap brander geoidal picador swarded artless closeup dimness fitment
solicit breaded Geordie plaided swindle athlete clupeid diocese fitness
soupcon breadth gladded plaudit synodal audient clypeal diptera fittest
spancel breeder gladden pleader synodic augment clypeus discern flaneur
spencer brinded gladder plodded tepidly austere cockeye discerp flareup
splicer brindle gliadin plodder thirdly aweless coffers disseat floreat
squacco broaden gonadal plunder thudded awnless collect dissect flowery
starchy broadly gonidia poinder thunder Azilean colleen dissent flybelt
stenchy broider goodday popadum timidly badness college distend flyleaf
stencil brooder grandad poundal treader bandeau commend distent foolery
stoical builded grandam pounder treadle banteng comment dithery foppery
stuccos builder grandee prodded triadic barbell compeer doddery forbear
subacid buildup grandly prodder trindle battels compend dodgems forceps
tankcar buirdly grandma proudly trodden battery compere dodgery forfeit
taxicab bulldog grandpa pyxides trundle believe compete doggery forfend
tiercel cacodyl griddle pyxidia tsardom benzene conceal doucely forgery
tiercet celadon grinder quondam Tuesday bequest concede douceur forwent
tobacco Chaldee guarded rabidly tumidly berserk conceit drapery frameup
topical cheddar guardee Ramadan twaddle beseech concent drivein fratery
tramcar chidden guerdon rapidly twaddly besiege concept drosera friseur
tranche childer guilder remodel twiddle besmear concern drycell frogeye
treacle childly halidom reorder twiddly bespeak concert dryness fulgent
treacly chindit hangdog reredos ungodly bestead condemn dubiety fulness
triacid chordal hexadic residua unladen between confect duchess furmety
truncal chowder hirudin residue upsides bibbery confess dudgeon gabfest
tunicle chuddah hockday rhabdom validly biggest congeal dulness gadgety
twitchy chuddar holiday rigidly vanadic bighead congest dungeon galleon
typical citadel humidly rounded vapidly bigness conkers duodena gallery
unlucky comedic humidor roundel vexedly bindery connect earnest garment
utricle conidia ilkaday rounder vividly bittern consent eastern gathers
varices corydon incudes roundly wealden bitters contemn ebriety gaudery
Vatican cotidal infidel roundup weekday bobbery contend egghead gayness
vehicle couldst insider rubadub weirdie bogbean content element gemmery
vesicae creedal invader scalder weirdly bonkers contest elevens Genoese
vesical crowdie jackdaw scaldic wheedle bookend context eminent genteel
vesicle csardas jadedly scandal whidder Boolean convect empress geodesy
wildcat czardas jemadar scolder wielder boozeup convene empyema gerbera
wolfcub czardom joinder scudded wolfdog Boswell convent endless giblets
woodcut dazedly katydid seceder workday bottega convert entreat gilbert
```

gingery	instead	minuend	peeress	raiment	shapely	tensely	wetness	gruffly
ginseng	intreat	Miocene	pendent	ratteen	shebear	terpene	wettest	Guelfic
gittern	irately	misdeal	peppery	rattery	shebeen	terrene	whereas	handful
gluteal	irideal	misdeed	percent	rawness	shereef	tersely	whereat	harmful
gluteus	isogeny	misdeem	percept	rayless	shivers	tessera	whereby	hateful
goahead	Israeli	mishear	perfect	reagent	shivery	thereat	wherein	heedful
goddess	jaggery	mislead	perpend	reddest	showery	thereby	whereof	helpful
godhead	jitters	misread	perpent	redhead	shrieve	therein	whereon	hopeful
godless	jittery	missend	pervert	redlegs	shuteye	thereof	whereto	hurtful
godsend	jobbery	missent	phoneme	redneck	shyness	thereon	whitely	insofar
gombeen	joinery	mockery	pickeer	redness	Siamese	thereto	whoseso	lifeful
gooiest	joyless	monkery	pidgeon	redress	siemens	thyself	widgeon	Lucifer
gorsedd	Judaean	montero	piggery	reelect	silvern	tiebeam	wigless	lustful
gradely	kermess	mooneye	piglead	reflect	silvery	tigress	windegg	malefic
grapery	keyless	mordent	pigmean	refresh	sincere	tindery	winkers	meatfly
gravely	knavery	mullein	pigment	regress	sinless	toeless	wintery	mindful
grocery	lacteal	mummery	pigweed	regrets	sintery	toggery	withers	mistful
gruyere	lambent	muraena	pincers	relieve	sithens	toluene	witless	needful
gudgeon	lambert	mynheer	pinhead	relievo	sixteen	tonneau	witness	omnific
guereza	lancers	mystery	pinkeye	replete	slavery	topless	woomera	ossific
gullery	lantern	nailery	pioneer	replevy	Slovene	torment	wottest	overfed
gunnera	larceny	naively	pithead	repress	slyness	torpedo	writeup	overfly
gunnery	largely	naivete	placebo	request	smokeho	torrefy	wryneck	pacific
gutless	largess	naivety	plateau	respect	society	torrent	wryness	pailful
hackery	lathery	nankeen	plumery	respell	sockeye	tottery	wychelm	painful
hagweed	laurels	napless	poetess	respelt	solvent	towhead	yestern	piaffer
halberd	lawless	nascent	porrect	retread	sonless	tracery	zithern	pipeful
halbert	laxness	nearest	portend	retreat	sorbent	tradein	zoogeny	pitiful
halvers	lechery	neglect	portent	rettery	sorcery	tragedy	agraffe	playful
hapless	lectern	Negress	possess	rickets	soybean	traject	aloofly	porifer
harness	legless	neoteny	posteen	rickety	sparely	trapeze	antefix	postfix
harvest	legrest	newness	postern	rilievo	spicery	triceps	aquifer	proffer
hasbeen	lenient	nimiety	pothead	ringent	spidery	trident	armsful	pushful
hatless	lethean	nippers	potheen	ripieni	spireme	tripery	baleful	quaffer
hauberk	letters	noumena	potherb	ripieno	spleeny	trireme	baneful	ratafia
hauteur	lidless	nowhere	pottery	riviera	spryest	trisect	bashful	restful
hayseed	limbeck	nuclear	powdery	riviere	squeeze	tritely	benefic	roomful
heiress	Linnean	nucleic	prebend	robbery	stalely	trumeau	benefit	rotifer
Hellene	linseed	nuclein	precede	rockery	stately	turgent	blowfly	ruthful
hennery	lioness	nucleon	precept	roedeer	stipend	turnery	bluffer	sackful
henpeck	lipdeep	nucleus	prefect	roguery	student	turpeth	bluffly	sandfly
herself	lipless	nunnery	preheat	rondeau	stupefy	tushery	bodeful	scarfed
hetaera	lipread	nursery	prelect	rookery	styrene	twoness	bookful	scoffer
himself	liquefy	oakfern	present	rouleau	suavely	ukelele	bowlful	scruffy
hipness	liqueur	oarless	pretend	rubbers	subdean	ukulele	briefly	scuffle
hoggery	listeth	oarweed	pretest	rubbery	subhead	umpteen	brimful	selffed
hogweed	lithely	oatmeal	pretext	rumness	subject	unblest	careful	shoofly
hophead	littery	obscene	prevent	runless	subtend	unclean	cartful	shuffle
horrent	llanero	oddment	primely	russety	subvert	undress	chaffer	skiffle
hosiery	loosely	oddness	primero	saddest	subzero	unguent	chamfer	skilful
hostess	lottery	offbeat	proceed	sadness	succeed	unideal	chiefly	skinful
hothead	lowness	offpeak	process	saidest	success	unshell	chiffon	snaffle
hotness	lyncean	oilseed	profess	salient	suggest	unswear	chuffed	sniffer
hottest	machete	oilwell	progeny	saltern	summery	upfield	conifer	sniffle
howbeit	maddest	oneness	project	sanders	sunbeam	upsweep	cornfed	snuffer
hueless	madness	oneself	pronely	saphead	sunbear	upswept	cupsful	snuffle
hunkers	magneto	oosperm	propend	sapient	sundeck	uptrend	deepfry	songful
hutment	mahseer	openend	protean	sapless	sunless	urodele	direful	souffle
hygiene	malleus	oppress	protect	satiety	supreme	useless	doleful	soulful
iceberg	Maltese	opulent	protege	scalene	supremo	vaguely	doomful	spoofer
iciness	manless	orogeny	proteid	scenery	surfeit	vaquero	dutiful	squiffy
illness	manners	Orphean	protein	schlepp	surgeon	variety	easeful	stiffen
imagery	manteau	ourself	protend	screech	surgery	varment	fateful	stiffly
impiety	manweek	outsell	protest	screeve	surreal	velvety	fearful	stuffer
implead	manyear	outwear	proteus	scrieve	suspect	verbena	feoffee	tactful
implete	margent	outwent	proverb	seabear	suspend	veriest	feoffer	tankful
impresa	masseur	overeat	prowess	sealegs	swinery	vermeil	feoffor	tearful
impress	masters	pampean	prudent	sealery	tableau	vespers	firefly	tentfly
imprest	mastery	pampero	prudery	seaweed	taffeta	villein	fistful	testfly
inanely	mattery	Pandean	puckery	secrecy	tailend	violent	flamfew	thrifty
inbreed	maxwell	pandect	puffery	secrete	tangelo	viscera	forkful	toilful
indwell	mayweed	parpend	pungent	segment	tangent	waggery	fretful	traffic
indwelt	mercery	parvenu	putrefy	sequela	tannery	walleye	gainful	trayful
infield	meseems	pastern	pygmean	sequent	tatters	wanness	gallfly	truffle
inflect	midweek	pasteup	quavery	seriema	tattery	warhead	giraffe	tuneful
ingress	Midwest	patient	quivery	serpent	taxless	Watteau	gleeful	twelfth
inkwell	midyear	pattern	rackety	servery	tealeaf	wayless	goutfly	venefic
inquest	mildewy	paydesk	raggedy	sexless	tempera	weekend	griffin	vivific
inspect	milreis	payment	ragweed	shakeup	tempest	western	griffon	wailful

```
wakeful hypogea strigil coacher laugher smother agility babbitt bonnily
whiffle illegal swagged conchae leather somehow agonise babyish booking
wishful insight swagger conchie legshow sonship agonist backing bookish
wistful insigne swigged couthie loather soother aiblins baddish boorish
woolfat integer swinger cowshed loathly soothly airlift baggily boozily
zestful kerogen swingle crochet longhop sorghum airline bagging bopping
abought kerygma tanager crusher luncher souther airmiss bagpipe bornite
acrogen lasagna tanagra cumshaw lurcher spathic airsick Bahaism bossism
alleged lasagne teargas cyathus lymphad sulphur alanine Bahaist bowline
allegro lounger thigger darshan lynchet swasher alation Bahaite bowling
alright lyingin thought dauphin manchet swither alcaide bailiff boxkite
amalgam lyingly thuggee deathly manihot sylphid alewife balding boxlike
ambages manager tonight Delphic marcher syrphid alltime baldish bracing
amongst mutagen trangam ditcher markhor tanghin alodial balmily brazier
antigen myalgia trigger dolphin marshal teacher alodium bambini brevier
armiger myalgic tringle doughty matchet teachin alumina bambino brevity
assagai nonagon trudgen drachma mauther teashop alunite banking British
assegai nosegay twangle drogher menthol telpher amanita banning broking
atingle obligee twigged droshky merchet tenthly amative banting bromide
avenger obligor unpaged dryshod midship thither amazing baptise bromine
bedight octagon unright earshot moither toothed amboina baptism bromism
blowgun paragon unsight earthen monthly torchon amenity baptist brucine
blunger patagia upright earthly moocher touched Amerind barline brucite
bologna pelagic uptight edaphic moorhen toucher amorist barrier brutish
bragged perigee veliger epithem morphia touchup amplify barring bruxism
bragger phlegmy vinegar epithet mosshag toughen amusive bassist buccina
bringer piragua visaged epochal mouther toughly Ananias basting budding
brought pirogue voyager eyeshot murther toyshop Anglian bastion bugging
changer pledgee wanigan farther narthex trachea anglice bathing bulkily
charger pledger whangee feather narwhal trishaw angling batting bullion
chigger pledget whinger fifthly naughty trochal Anglist bauxite bullish
chugged pledgor wrangle fitchet neither trochee angrily bawdily bumming
clanger plugged wriggle fitchew Noachic trochus anguine beading bumpily
clogged plugger wriggly flasher norther trophic anguish beamish bunting
clogger plunger wringer fleshed notched tulchan aniline bearing burning
cologne podagra wrongly flesher nunship urethan anility bearish burnish
cragged polygon wrought fleshly nylghau urethra animism beatify bushido
cringer pronged yatagan flighty nymphal Vaishya animist beating busking
cringle ravager younger freshen nymphet vouchee annuity bedding bussing
cryogen realgar zymogen fresher oneshot voucher anodise bedside cabling
decagon refugee abashed freshet outshot warship anthill bedtime caddice
delight relight airship freshly panther warthog antlion beehive caddish
demigod remiges alcohol further paschal watcher anytime beeline cadmium
dowager reneger another Galahad percher weather anywise begging caesium
dragged renegue apishly gingham pincher weigher apatite begrime caitiff
draggle rontgen apothem glyphic pitched weighin applied beguile calcify
draught scraggy bacchic gnathic pitcher weighty applier beguine calcine
dredger shingle banshee godship pithhat welcher appoint Belgian calcite
drought shingly beechen graphic plushly welsher apprise belting calcium
drudger shogged belcher greyhen poacher wencher Arabian belying calling
drugged shotgun bellhop gryphon potshot whether arabise benzine cambial
drugget skegger bencher guichet pouched whither Arabist bepaint cambist
eclogue slagged benthic gumshoe prithee worship archive berline cambium
endogen sleight benthos gunship prophet writhen aridity berried camping
energid slinger birchen gunshot psychic xanthic armlike bestial campion
engaged sloegin blather hardhit puncher xanthin armoire bethink candied
epergne slogged blether harshen punchup abaxial arraign betting cannily
eulogia slogger blighty harshly pyrrhic Abelian ascribe betwixt canning
evangel sloughy blither hatcher Quechua abiding asinine biaxial cantina
exergue slugged blucher hatchet rancher ability asocial bibbing canting
fallguy slugger blusher haughty raschel abolish asquint biblist capping
fatigue smidgen bolshie heathen ratchet abscise astride bidding caprice
finagle smidgin botcher heather reacher abusive atavism biggish caprine
flagged smuggle bouchee heighho roadhog Acadian atavist bigtime Capsian
flaught snagged bowshot highhat rosehip acarian atelier billing capsize
flogged snigger brashly hitcher roughen acetify atheism billion caption
forager sniggle brothel hotshot roughly Achaian atheist binding captive
fourgon snuggle brother iceshow rumshop acidify atomise bionics carbide
fraught socager brusher Irishry sapphic acidity atomism biotite carbine
freight spadger Brython isochor satchel aconite atomist bitting cardiac
frogged spangle burghal ketchup seawhip acquire attaint blemish carking
georgic spangly burgher kinchin sibship Adamite attrite blewits carline
goatgod sparger burthen kinship sixthly adaxial auction blueing Carlism
granger sponger butcher Kirghiz slasher adenine auspice boarish Carlist
halogen spongin camphor kitchen slather adjoint avarice boating carmine
handgun spriggy canthus knowhow slither aeolian avidity bobbing carping
hexagon stagger catcher kolkhoz sloshed aeonian azurine bobbish carrier
hindgut stinger catchup Krishna smasher affaire azurite boiling carrion
homager stopgap clothes latchet smashup afflict Baalism bonfire carsick
```

```
carving cooking darkish dustily failing fopling gossipy Hobbist jerkily
cashier coolish darling earring fairing foppish gracile hogfish jetting
cassino copaiba darning easting fairish foreign gradine hogging jewfish
castile copaiva dashiki ebbtide falling forging granita hoggish jibbing
casting coppice dashing ebonise falsies forgive granite holding jigging
casuist copyist dawning ebonite falsify forties gratify holmium jobbing
catbird coquito daytime eccrine falsity fortify grating hopbind jogging
catfish cordial dealing echoism fancier fossick gravity hoplite joining
catlike cordite debrief edacity fancily fowling grazier hopping jollify
catling corking deceive edifice fanning fragile grazing horrify jollity
catmint cornice decking edition farcing Frisian Grecian horsily jotting
cattily cornily decline egality farming fugging grecise hospice joyride
caution Cornish decrier egotise farrier fuguist Grecism hostile Judaise
ceilidh cornist deicide egotism fascal  fulmine gremial hottish Judaism
ceiling corrida delaine egotist fascine funnies greyish housing Judaist
cellist cortile density elation Fascism funnily Grobian howling judoist
Celsius corvina dentine elegiac Fascist funning Grolier huffish jugging
centime corvine dentist elegise fashion furbish grunion hugging juggins
certify cosmism deprive elegist fatling furmity Gstring hulking juicily
cervine cosmist derrick elision fatting furnish guanine humming Jungian
cession costing dervish elitism fattish furrier gubbins Hunnish jussive
chalice costive despise elitist fatuity furring gumming hunting justice
charily cottier despite Elohism faucial furtive gummite hurling justify
chariot Coueism destine Elohist faunist fussily gunfire hurried jutting
charism courier destiny elusion fauvism fustian gunning huskily Kaddish
charity cowbird diarise elusive fauvist fustily gushing husking kainite
chemise cowfish diarist elution febrile fuzzily gustily Hussite Kantian
chemism cowhide dibbing eluvial feeding gabbing gutsily hutting Karaite
chemist cowlick diction eluvium feeling gadding gutting hyaline karting
cherish cowling digging elysian felsite gagging gwyniad hyalite keeping
cheviot cranial dignify Elysium felting gahnite gypping hydride kenning
chiliad cranium dignity emeriti fencing gallice hacking hygeian kentish
chocice craving dimming emetine fenfire galling hafnium hymnist keyring
choline crazily dimmish emotion fermion galliot hagfish Iberian khedive
chopine crevice dingily emotive fermium gallium haggish icerink kidding
chorine crimine dinning emprise ferrite gambier halting idolise kiddish
chorion crinite diorism emptier fertile garfish hamming imagine killick
citrine crosier diorite emptily festive garnish handily imagism killing
civvies crozier dioxide emption feudist garpike hanging imagist kissing
clarify crucial dipping enation fibbing gasfire happily impaint knavish
clarion crucian dirtily endwise fictile gasring happing imprint knowing
clarity crucify dislike English fiction gassing harpist inanity koumiss
clavier crudity dislimn enprint fictive gatling harrier inbuilt Kurdish
clerisy cubbing dismiss enquire fideism gaudily hashish incline kyanise
Cluniac cuisine distich enquiry fideist Gaulish hastily inflict kyanite
coaming cullion distill entwine fierily gawkily hatting ingoing lacking
coating cultism dizzily entwist fifties gearing haulier initial lagging
coaxial cultist dockise epoxide figging gelding hawkish inkling laicise
cocaine cunning dogfish eremite filling gelling hayrick inquire laicism
cockily cupping dogging erlking finding gemming haywire inquiry Lamaism
codeine cuprite doggish erosion finning genning headily inspire Lamaist
codfish curling dollish erosive Finnish gentian heading inswing lamming
codling currier doltish erotica fishily gentile hearing intwine lampion
coeliac currish donning erotism fishing genuine heating inutile landing
coexist cursive donnish erudite fissile getting heavily inveigh lankily
cogging cushion Dorking escribe fission gharial heftily invoice Laotian
cognise cutline dormice esquire fitting giddily hellion Iranian lapping
coition cutting dornick etamine flaming gigging hellish iridise lapwing
coldish cyanide dossier etching flavine gilding helping iridium largish
collide cyanine dotting etesian fleeing gimmick hemline ironing lashing
collier cyanite dowdily Etonian Fleming gingili hemming ironist lasting
collins cyclist drawing eucrite Flemish ginning henwife ischial lathing
coltish Cyprian driving evanish flexile girlish herniae ischium latrine
combine Cypriot droving evasion flexion glacial hernial Ismaili lattice
compile cystine dualise evasive florist glacier hernias itacism Latvian
Comtian czarina dualism evening fluting glaring heroics Italian lawlist
Comtism czarism dualist examine flutist glazier heroine Italiot leading
Comtist czarist duality exotica fluvial glazing heroise itemise leaning
concise dabbing dubbing exscind fluxion glorify heroism ivories lection
condign dacoity ducking exuviae flyting glozing herring jabbing leftism
confide Dadaism ductile exuvial fobbing glycine hessian jadeite leftist
confine Dadaist ducting eyelike foggily gnomish hetaira Jainism legging
confirm dallier dulcify eyewink fogging goatish hilding jamming lemming
coniine damming dullish fabliau fogyish godlike hipping Janeite lending
conning damnify dumpish faction fogyism godling hircine jarring lentigo
connive damning dunbird faddish folding golfing hitting jasmine lentisk
consign dampish Dunkirk faddism follies goodish Hittite jaybird leonine
consist dandify dunning faddist foolish Gordian Hobbian jazzily lesbian
convict darbies duskily fagging footing gosling Hobbism jellied letting
```

```
Lettish melting netfish Paphian poetics rasping running sickish stonily
leucine memoirs netlike paprika poetise ratlike Russian signify storied
leucite mending netting partial poloist ratling Russify signior stovies
licking mention neurine parting pontiff ratting rustily Sikhism straits
lignify merrily niblick partita pontify rawhide rutting silkily studied
lignite messiah niceish partite poorish readily ruttish sillily stygian
lilting Messias nigrify parvise poppied reading Sabaism sinning stylise
lionise messily niobium passing popping realign sacking sipping stylish
lipping mestiza nippily passion porcine realise sacring Sistine stylist
listing mestizo nipping passive portico realism sacrist sitting stylite
lithium metrics nitride pastime portion realist saddish Sivaism suasion
loading metrist nitrify patrial posting reality sagging Sivaite suasive
loaning midline nitrile patriot potting rebuild sailing sixaine suavity
lobbing midriff nitrite patting pouting rebuilt Saktism sixties subbing
lodging midwife nodding paucity praline receipt salpinx Sixtine sublime
loftily milking nogging Pauline pravity receive salsify skating subside
logging million noisily pebrine precise recline salting skilift subsidy
logline mincing nooning peckish predial rectify saltire skolion subsist
longing mirkily nothing peevish predict reddish saltish skyhigh subtile
longish misfire nourish pegging prelims redwing sapling skyline sucking
looking misgive nuclide pelting premier reeding sapping slating suction
lopping mislike nullify pending premise rejoice sardine slavish suffice
lording missile nullity pennies premiss remains sardius Slavism suicide
lotting missing nunnish pennill premium rentier sarking slimily suiting
loudish mission nuptial pennine preside repaint sashimi slowish sulkily
lousily missish nursing penning preview replica saucily smokily summing
loutish missive nutlike pensile previse replier saurian smoking sunbird
lowlily mistily nutpine pension priming reprint sawbill snakily sundial
lowrise mistime nutting pensive privily reprise sawfish snowily sundisc
luckily misting oakling peppill privity reptile sawmill soaking sunfish
Luddite Moabite oarfish pepping probity requiem scabies soapily sunnily
lugging mobbing obelise peptide prodigy require scarify soaring sunning
lumpily mobbish obelisk peptise profile requite scoriae sobbing Sunnite
lumpish mollify obesity percine promise rescind scorify softish sunrise
lustily mondial ocarina perfidy propine respire scoring soggily sunwise
lyddite monkish odalisk perkily prosify respite scotice soldier supping
machine moodily offside perlite prosily restiff Scotism soloist surfing
madding mooring ogreish Permian protist restive Scotist soonish surlily
Madeira Moorish oilbird Persian protium rethink seabird sootily surmise
maffick mopping oldtime persist provide retrial seafish sophism survive
magnify moraine olefine petrify proviso retsina seagirt sophist suspire
Mahdism moreish olivine Petrine proximo retting seapink soppily Swahili
Mahdist morning omneity pettily prudish reunion seasick sopping Swedish
maidish mortice onanism petting pruning reunite seaside Sorbian swinish
maidism mortify oncotee pettish prurigo revving seating sordini syenite
mailing mortise onetime phonics publish rewrite seawife sordino sylvine
malaise mousing ongoing phonily puckish rhenium sectile sorrily sylvite
malting muddily opacity photism pudding rhodium section sotting tabbing
mangily mudfish opaline physics puerile rhymist seedily sottish tachism
mankind mugging opening pianism puggish ribbing seeming soubise tachist
manlike muggins opinion pianist pugging ridding seizing sourish tacking
manning mullion oration Pictish pugmill ridging selfish spacial tactics
mannish mummify orifice pietism pulvini rifling septime spacing tactile
mannite mumming Orphism pietist punning rigging Serbian spaniel taction
mansion mumpish ostrich pigging pupping rimming serpigo Spanish taeniae
mansize mundify otolith piggish purlieu ringing serried sparing tagging
mapping munnion outlier pigling purview ripping Servian spatial tailing
marking munting outline pillion pushing riptide service special talking
marline muonium outlive pimping puttier roaring servile species tallish
marlite murkily outride pinfire putting robbing serving specify tallith
marmite muzzily outside pinfish pycnite rockier Servite spicily tamping
married myalism outsize pinking Pythian rockily sessile spikily tampion
marring mystify ovarian pinkish qualify rocking session spirits tanning
martial mythise ovation pinning quality rodding sestina spodium tannish
Martian mythist ovicide piscina queuing rodlike setting squails tantivy
martini nabbing oxidise piscine quinine rollick sferics stadium tardily
Marxian nagging Oxonian pismire rabbity rolling shadily stagily tarnish
Marxism napping ozonise pithily raffish roofing shading staging tarrier
Marxist nastily pachisi pitting ragging rotting shakily stamina tarring
massive nattily packice planish ragtime rousing Shavian staniel tartish
mastich nautics packing platina railing routine shaving statice tastily
mastiff nautili padding plating rallier rowdily Shemite statics tattily
matting Naziism pallium playing ralline rubbing sheriff station tatting
mattins nebbish palmist plenish ramming rubbish shoeing statism taurine
mawkish neglige palsied plosion rampion ruching shoring statist taxiing
Maytime Negrito pannier plosive ranking ruction showily stative taxying
mealies neolith panning pluvial raphide ruddily showing sterile tearing
meaning nervine panties podding rapping ruffian sibling stibine teatime
```

```
tedding  turfite  wannish  brinjal  kidskin  thicken  bouilli  drawler  harslet
teeming  Turkish  wanting  harijan  knacker  thicket  braille  driblet  heckler
tegmina  turning  warlike  jumpjet  knocker  thickly  brawler  driller  hidalga
tektite  turnipy  warmish  killjoy  knockon  thinker  broiler  droplet  hidalgo
telling  tussive  warning  lockjaw  knuckle  tracker  buckler  drumlin  higgler
tenpins  tutting  warring  muntjac  ladykin  trekked  bucolic  ducally  hobbler
tensile  twibill  warrior  muntjak  lambkin  trekker  bumbler  duelled  hoodlum
tension  twoline  wartime  propjet  lashkar  tricker  bungler  dueller  hooklet
tensity  twotime  washing  sapajou  latakia  trickle  burbler  dweller  hostler
tensive  tychism  waspish  betaken  limpkin  tricksy  burglar  earflap  humbles
tenuity  Umbrian  waxbill  betoken  manakin  trinket  bustler  earplug  hurdler
tequila  unbuild  waxwing  blacken  manikin  trinkum  cackler  echelon  hurdles
terbium  unbuilt  waybill  blackly  meerkat  trucker  cajoler  effulge  hustler
tergite  unction  wayside  blanket  minikin  truckle  camelot  eggflip  icefloe
termini  undoing  weakish  blankly  moniker  turnkey  camelry  eidolon  ideally
termite  undying  wearily  bleakly  nonskid  twankay  capelin  embolic  idyllic
terrier  unfaith  wearing  blinker  oilskin  twinkle  castled  embolus  impulse
terrify  unicity  webbing  blocker  passkey  twinkly  Catalan  enfiled  indulge
terrine  unifier  wedding  bracken  pigskin  unasked  catalos  envelop  infulae
tertial  unitive  wedging  bracket  placket  whacker  catalpa  epaulet  inhaler
tertian  unjoint  weevily  breaker  pliskie  whicker  cavally  epsilon  insular
testify  unquiet  wellies  breakin  plucker  whisker  cavalry  equally  insulin
testily  unstick  Wendish  breakup  plunker  whiskey  cedilla  escolar  invalid
textile  unthink  wergild  brickie  pricker  whizkid  Chablis  expulse  involve
theriac  untried  westing  brickle  pricket  wrecker  challis  fabular  jangler
Thomism  untwine  wetting  brisken  prickle  wrinkle  chaplet  faculae  javelin
Thomist  untwist  wettish  brisket  prickly  wrinkly  charley  faculty  jewelry
thorite  untying  whaling  briskly  pumpkin  younker  charlie  famulus  jingler
thorium  upraise  wheyish  brocket  quicken  zincked  chillum  fanclub  jocular
thulium  upswing  whiting  bumpkin  quickie  aboulia  cichlid  fatally  jubilee
thymine  Uralian  whitish  canakin  quickly  absolve  cipolin  feedlot  juggler
ticking  uralite  whorish  canikin  ramekin  acrylic  circler  fibulae  jugular
tigrish  uranide  wickiup  caulker  rebuker  acyclic  circlet  fibular  jurally
tinnily  uranism  wigging  checker  redskin  airflow  civilly  fibulas  kindler
tinning  uranium  wilding  checkup  retaken  airglow  cobbler  fiddler  kinglet
tipping  uterine  wildish  chicken  shackle  alcalde  cochlea  finally  kneeler
tipsify  utilise  willies  chuckle  shanked  alfalfa  coddler  flatlet  knurled
tipsily  utility  willing  chukker  shicker  alkalis  complex  flyblow  kremlin
tithing  utopian  windily  clacker  shirker  allelic  complin  fondler  labella
titling  utopism  winding  clarkia  shocker  ampulla  complot  foreleg  lakelet
titmice  utopist  winning  clerkly  shucker  angelic  conflux  frailly  lamella
Titoism  uxorial  wishing  clicker  skinker  angelus  copilot  frailty  lanolin
Titoist  vaccine  witling  clinker  skulker  angular  copular  fuddler  lapilli
tompion  vacuity  wittily  clocker  slacken  annelid  corella  fuelled  lavolta
tontine  vaguish  witting  cracked  slacker  annular  corolla  fueller  leaflet
tooling  vampire  wolfish  cracker  slackly  annulet  corslet  fugally  legally
topping  vampish  wolvish  crackle  sleeken  annulus  coupler  fumbler  levelly
topside  varmint  woozily  crackly  sleekit  antilog  couplet  gabbler  limulus
tormina  varnish  wordily  crackup  sleekly  aphelia  courlan  gabelle  lobelia
torpids  varsity  wording  crankle  slicker  aphylly  cowslip  galilee  lobular
torsion  vastity  working  cricket  slickly  areally  crawler  gambler  locally
tortile  vatting  worrier  crinkle  slinker  areolae  criollo  gamelan  locular
Toryism  veiling  writing  crinkly  smacker  areolas  cruelly  ganglia  loculus
totting  veining  wrybill  croaker  sneaker  aurally  cruelty  gantlet  loyally
touring  verdict  Yahvist  crocket  snicker  aurelia  cruller  garbler  loyalty
tourism  vermian  Yahwist  crooked  snooker  availed  cumulus  gateleg  lunular
tourist  vernier  yapping  doeskin  snorkel  awfully  cupular  gazelle  lupulin
towline  versify  yenning  dogskin  spanker  axially  dabbler  ghillie  maculae
townish  versine  Yiddish  dovekie  sparkle  axillae  dangler  giggler  macular
trading  version  yipping  drinker  speaker  axillar  dawdler  girdler  mahaleb
trilith  vertigo  Yorkist  drunken  speckle  babbler  dazzler  gnarled  maillot
trinity  vespine  yttrium  finikin  spunkie  bacilli  defiler  gobbler  mamelon
tritium  vestige  zapping  flanker  stacker  backlog  Gobelin  goggler  mamilla
trivial  vetting  zaptieh  flecker  stalked  baffler  Delilah  goggles  manilla
trivium  viatica  zebrine  flicker  stalker  banally  devalue  gorilla  manille
tropics  viduity  zeolite  flunkey  starkly  barilla  develop  graplin  mantlet
tropism  viewing  zillion  frankly  steekit  basilar  devilry  gremlin  marbled
trucial  violist  zincify  freaked  sticker  Benelux  devolve  greylag  marbles
tsarina  vitrify  zincing  freckle  stickit  bibelot  dewclaw  grilled  marplot
tsarism  vitrine  zincite  freckly  stickle  bifilar  dialled  griller  martlet
tsarist  vitriol  zinkify  frisker  stickup  bipolar  diddler  growler  matelot
tubbing  voguish  zinking  frisket  stinker  bivalve  dipolar  guzzler  maxilla
tubbish  vulpine  Zionism  gherkin  stocker  bobsled  display  gymslip  measles
tugging  wadding  Zionist  glaikit  stonker  boggler  divulge  hackler  Mechlin
tuition  wagging  zipping  grackle  striker  booklet  doodler  haggler  meddler
tundish  waggish  zoarium  griskin  stuckup  boomlet  doubler  hamular  medulla
tunning  waiting  Zoilism  Halakah  swanker  bootleg  doubles  hamulus  melilot
turbine  walking  Zoilist  hearken  thankee  bottled  doublet  handler  metaled
turdine  walling  belljar  karakul  thanker  botulin  drabler  harelip  mettled
```

```
micelle preplan singlet upsilon clammed monomer thrombi bimanal enhance
milkleg problem sizzler usually clubman mousmee thrummy blarney enounce
mimulus prowler skellum vagally crammed myxomas thummim boloney entente
misplay ptyalin skidlid vanilla crammer nelumbo tinamou bonanza envenom
modally puddler skilled veinlet creamer newsman tollman borings equinal
modular pupilar skillet venally decimal oarsman tonemic botanic equinox
modulus puzzler skyblue verglas decuman oenomel totemic brannew ermined
moonlit pyralid smeller vexilla delimit oghamic trammel braunch errancy
moorlog pyralis snarler virelay digamma optimal trimmed brownie essence
morally queller snarlup vitally dilemma optimum trimmer bubonic eternal
morello quillet sozzled vitelli doorman ottoman trismus bygones ethanol
morulae rabbler speller vittles doormat overman triumph Byronic eugenic
morular radulae spieler vitular drayman packman trommel bywoner expanse
Moselle radular spiller vocalic dreamed pajamas turfman cabinet expense
mottled rambler spoiler vocally dreamer phasmid unarmed cacanny expunge
mouflon rattler squalid vowelly drummed pikeman unkempt cadence extinct
muddler ravelin squally waddler drummer plasmic uraemia cadency faience
mudflat reallot squalor warbler duramen plasmid velamen cadenza Falange
muffler regalia squelch wattled dustman plasmin vidimus calando feigner
mumbler regally stabler wattles dynamic plummet vitamin calends felonry
muscled regular stables wavelet encomia polemic volumed canonic feminal
muzzler regulus stapler wheeled endemic polymer wireman canonry filings
mycelia remblai starlet wheeler entomic postman woodman carinae finance
nacelle repulse starlit whirler enzymic potamic workman carinal finings
nasally resolve stealer whitlow exhumer preempt yardman carinas firenew
nauplii revalue stealth whorled filemot primmed yashmak catenae fishnet
nebulae revelry stellar wiggler fireman Pullman yeggman catenas fixings
nebular reviler sterlet winglet flagman putamen absence cayenne flannel
nebulas revolve stifler wobbler flummox pyaemia absinth centner flaunty
necklet riddler subplot woolled footman pyaemic acronym channel flounce
needler riffler suckler woollen foramen pyjamas actinia charnel fluence
nibbler ringlet surplus yulelog foreman pyramid actinic Chianti fluency
niggler ripplet swallow abdomen freeman racemic actinon chignon fraenum
nobbler rivalry swiller abysmal frogman railman addenda chimney galanga
nodally rivulet swollen ackemma galumph regimen adjunct chronic galenic
nodular rocklet tabular agnomen gleeman roadman adrenal chunnel gallnut
nonplus rootlet tackler albumen glimmer rodsman advance chutney Gehenna
nonslip rosella Tagalog albumin glummer rollmop affined cleaner gillnet
notelet royally tartlet almsman goodman sandman against cleanly gleaner
novella royalty tattler anaemia gourmet schemer alginic cleanse grained
novelle rubella tegular anaemic grammar scrimpy alienly cleanup grainer
novelty ruffler Templar anosmia grimmer scrumpy alkanet cockney grannie
numbles rumbler templet anosmic grommet scummed allonge coconut grapnel
ocellar rundlet thallic ashamed grummet seismal almanac cogency graunch
ocellus rurally thallus attempt hangman seismic almoner colonel greenly
ortolan rustler thiller baseman hanuman shammed almonry colonic greenth
osculum saddler tickler batsman headman shammer alumnae coranto grinned
osselet sampler tidally bellman highman shimmer alumnus coronae grownup
outflow sandlot tiddler betimes hillman shipman ambones coronal Guignol
outplay saveloy tiddley bilimbi hornmad shopman ammonal coronas hackney
overlap scaglia timelag birdman incomer showman ammonia coroner hairnet
overlay scallop tingler bitumen inhuman skimmed ancones coronet hapence
overlie scarlet tippler bloomer Islamic skimmer andante cozener hapenny
pabulum scholar titular boatman isthmus skimmia anginal crannog havenot
paddler scholia toddler bogyman jacamar slammed anionic craunch hebenon
paisley scollop toeclip bohemia jazzman slimmer antenna crooner hedonic
papally sculler tonally bondman juryman slummed antonym crowned heronry
papilla seablue torulae bookman keramic slummer aphonia crowner hominid
papulae seaslug totally Brahman kinsman snowman aphonic crownet homonym
papular secular townlet Brahmin krimmer sokeman aplenty decanal hosanna
parolee sedilia trailer brimmed lineman Solomon arcanum decency humanly
parsley seedlip trawler brimmer linkman squamae ardency defence hymenia
partlet semilog trellis bulimia lorimer stammel arrange definer immense
patella settler triblet bushman mailman stammer arsenal defunct impanel
pearled settlor trifler cacumen manumit steamer arsenic demonic impinge
pearler shallop triolet calamus Manxman stemmed askance derange incense
peddler shallot triplet calomel maremma strumae avionic detinue infancy
penally shallow triplex calumet marimba stummed balance diurnal infanta
penalty shaslik troller calumny maximal surfman baloney diviner infante
perplex shellac trolley caramel maximum swagman bananas dominie ingenue
phallic shelled trollop caveman meatman swarmer baronet doyenne innings
phallus sheller tubular ceramic metamer swimmer basenji dozenth intense
phellem shiplap tumbler cerumen miasmal tapsman basinet dragnet intoner
pickled shrilly tumular chapman miasmic taximan bayonet drainer jacinth
piffler similar tumulus charmer milkman telamon beatnik durance jaconet
pikelet similor tutelar chlamys minimal thermae begonia echinus japonic
pilular simpler twilled chromic minimum thermal beignet effendi jejunum
playlet simplex udaller chummed minimus thermic biennia eirenic journal
popular simular ungulae claimer molimen thiamin bigener empanel journey
```

```
joyance piranha springy abalone bespoke compose dromond forbore hormone
kalends plainly spurner abscond betroth compost dropout fordone hotfoot
Koranic planned sputnik acerola bibcock compote drydock forgoer hugeous
laconic planner squinch acerose bighorn concoct dubious forgone hummock
lacunae pliancy squinny acetone bilboes concord dunnock forlorn hyaloid
lacunal polenta stainer acetous bilious condole duopoly forsook hydroid
lacunar polynia stannic acinous billowy condone duteous forworn hydrous
lacunas polynya staunch adenoid biltong conform dyewood foveola hymnody
ladanum potence stepney adenoma biology conjoin earhole foxhole hypnoid
laminae potency sternal adipose bistort connote earlobe frijole iceboat
laminar pudency sterned affront bittock console earlock fulgour icecold
latency queenly sternly agamous blowout consort ecology fullout icefoot
learned ramenta sternum agelong bongoes contort economy fulsome igneous
learner ravined sthenic airhole boobook contour eelpout fulvous impious
licence ravings strange airlock bottony convoke eelworm fungoid implode
license recency stringy airport boudoir cookout eggcosy fungous implore
liminal refined stunned airpost boxroom copious einkorn furioso improve
locknut refiner stunner aliform boxwood cordoba elfbolt furious inclose
lomenta regency swanned alimony boycott corpora elflock furlong indoors
lorgnon reginal syconia alphorn boyhood corrode elusory furrowy ingroup
loriner repiner synonym althorn bricole corrody embroil fuscous ingrown
lozenge retinae syringa alveoli bridoon cottony embrown futhorc inkhorn
lucency retinal syringe amatory brumous couloir emulous futhork inshore
lumenal retinas tabanid amorous buffoon coulomb enamour futtock introit
luminal retinol tabinet amphora bugloss cowpoke enclose gadroon ipomoea
lychnis retinue takings amyloid bulbous coxcomb endlong galloon irksome
madonna revenge taloned amylose bullock cremona endmost gallows isokont
magenta revenue technic anagoge bumboat cricoid enfeoff gamboge isonomy
mahonia rhamnus tenancy anagogy burdock crinoid engross garboil isotope
makings rhiancy tenoner analogy burnous ctenoid entropy gascoal isotopy
malines romance tetanic anatomy buttock cubhood envious gaseous jannock
mariner Romanic tetanus anchovy buttons cuckold epidote geckoes jargoon
Masonic Romansh thinned android buttony cupmoss epigone geogony jawbone
masonry rooinek thinner anemone caboose cuprous epigoni geology jealous
matinal rotunda thorned aneroid cahoots curiosa episode gibbous jibboom
matinee saponin throned angioma callous curious epitome glamour jibdoor
meconic sarangi tidings anurous camwood cursory epizoic glenoid jumpoff
melange satanic titanic anxious candour custody epizoon globoid juncoes
melanic satinet tomenta anybody canzone customs erelong globose kampong
melanin savanna topknot anymore canzoni cutworm ericoid glucose kathode
memento savings toponym anyroad caproic cycloid ethiops godhood keyhole
mesonic scanned tourney apagoge cardoon cyclone ethmoid gondola keynote
metonym scanner trainee apocope carioca cyclops euphony gorcock keyword
Mishnah science trainer apodous cariole cystoid explode gossoon kickoff
misknow scorner trounce apology carious dapsone exploit grumose kinfolk
momenta scranny truancy approve carload dariole explore grumous lactose
morendo scrunch tutenag aqueous carport daybook eyebolt gumboil lampoon
moronic scunner twinned arctoid carroty daylong eyehole gumboot lardoon
mourner seconde typonym arduous cartoon dayroom eyesore gunboat lassoes
nominal secondi tyranny armhole caseous daywork faceoff gunlock lavrock
nominee secondo umbonal artwork cassock defrock factory gunroom lawlord
obconic selenic umbones aureola castoff defrost fadeout haddock leadoff
oceanic seminal uncanny aureole catboat deiform falloff hammock leghorn
offence seminar uncinus awesome cathode deltoid fallout handoff legroom
opsonic seringa unfunny axolotl cathood deplore fanfold handout legwork
opsonin seventh unhandy azygous cestode despoil fantods hangout lentoid
ordinal seventy unhinge balcony cestoid despond fargone haploid leprosy
organic shinned unlined balloon chalone devious farmost harbour leprous
organon shrinal unmanly bandore chamois dewpond fatuous harmony letdown
organum shunned untuned banjoes cheroot diabolo felwort harpoon leucoma
organza shunner urgency bannock chibouk diamond fernowl hassock lichowl
osmunda silence vacancy barroom chicory dingoes ferrous haycock liftoff
oxfence silenus valance bassoon Chinook diploid fervour hayfork ligroin
paeonic skinned valence bawcock choroid diploma festoon hayloft limbous
paginal skinner valency bazooka chymous dipnoan fetlock heinous lineout
palings soignee valonia becloud cineole discoid fibroid hemiola lissome
pardner solanum Vedanta bedpost cirrose discord fibroin hemione lithoid
paronym sonance veranda bedrock cirrous dishorn fibroma hemlock liveoak
parsnip sonancy vicinal bedroll cladode disjoin fibrous hencoop lobworm
partner spanned vintner bedroom clamour disport figwort hickory lockout
patency spanner vixenly bedsock coccoid dispose flatout hideous logbook
penance spawner volante bedsore colloid disrobe flavour hideout logwood
petunia sphenic wagoner behoove combout disroot flyboat hillock lookout
pfennig spignel wakener beknown comfort distort flybook hipbone lowborn
phoenix whatnot bellows commode doggone foghorn hiproof lowdown
phrenic spinney wingnut benzoic commons dogrose foldout histone lughole
phrensy splenic wizened benzoin commove dogwood foliole history lugworm
pilsner spooney womanly benzole compony dortour foliose hoedown luteous
pimento springe ziganka benzoyl comport dragoon forbode holmoak lychowl
```

```
madrona osseous predoom sauroid tearoom viscose dashpot quipped talipot
madrono osteoid preform saviour tearose viscous deadpan relapse tentpeg
madwort ostiole presoak sawnoff tedious voivode decapod repaper thumper
mafiosi otology prolong sawwort teleost walkout decuple saltpan tosspot
mafioso outcome promote saxhorn tenfold Walloon dripped sandpit traipse
maggoty outdone pronoun schlock tenuous warlock dropped scalpel trample
mahjong outdoor propone schnook testoon warlord dropper scalper trapped
maltose outfoot propose scotoma tetrode washout duckpin scamper trapper
mammock outgone prosody scrooge thyroid waxwork dustpan scapple tripped
mammoth outlook provoke seaboot timeous wayworn eclipse scarper tripper
mandola outmost provost seafood tinfoil webfoot ectopic scauper trippet
mandora outport pteroic seafowl tinhorn webworm ellipse schappe tripple
mangoes outpost puccoon seaport toehold wedlock escapee scooper trooper
mangold outrode pugnose searoom tombola welcome escaper scorper trouper
manhole outsold pullout seawolf tombolo welloff eupepsy Scorpio trumpet
manhood outsole pulpous sellout tomfool werwolf example scraper tylopod
manhour outvote purloin sendoff topcoat willowy exempla scrapie unhappy
mannose outwore purport senhora tophole winnock eyespot scrappy unhoped
marconi outwork purpose sensory topmost winsome felspar scruple usurper
marrowy outworn putdown sequoia topsoil without flapped sculpin washpot
mastoid oviform putlock serious torgoch witloof flapper scupper whimper
mattock oxytone pygmoid setdown towboat wooloil fleapit semiped whipped
mattoid paddock quinone sexfoil towmond workout flipped shampoo whipper
matzoth padlock quixote shadoof towmont wornout flipper sharpen whippet
mawworm padrone raccoon shadowy towrope xiphoid flopped sharper whisper
maypole padroni ragbolt showoff travois yellowy footpad sharply whoopee
meadowy pairoar ragdoll shutout trefoil zealous forepaw shilpit whooper
menfolk palmoil ragworm shylock tremolo zebroid frapped shinpad whopper
microbe pandora ragwort sialoid tricorn zipcode fripper shipped woodpie
midmost pandore Rajpoot sigmoid triform zoogony fusspot shippen wrapped
milfoil papoose rakeoff signora trilogy zoology galipot shipper wrapper
miscopy pappose ramsons signore tripody zoonomy glimpse shippon ycleped
misdone parboil rancour signori tripoli zootomy grampus shopped antique
mistook parlour rapeoil signory tritone agrapha grapple shopper baroque
moidore parlous rapport sinuous tugboat apropos grasper sickpay bezique
monsoon partook rations sirloin turdoid atrophy gripped sinopia brusque
morwong patroon raucous sitdown turmoil autopsy gripper skidpan cacique
mugwort paviour ravioli sixfold turnout bleeper grouper skipped charqui
mullock payload readout skyborn tussock bullpen groupie skipper macaque
muttony payroll rectory someone tussore calipee hairpin skippet oblique
myeloid peacock redcoat sparoid tutwork caliper hardpan slapped obloquy
myeloma peafowl redpoll spinode twofold calypso headpin sleeper perique
myology peasoup redwood spinoff twosome Canopic hexapla slipped relique
nacrous pentode refloat spinose twotone catspaw hexapod slipper repique
narrows pentose regroup spinous typhoid cesspit incipit slopped Salique
necrose peptone reproof spumous typhoon champac indepth snapped siliqua
negroid percoid reprove spyhole typhous champak insipid snapper silique
neology perform respond steroid uberous chapped jackpot snipped subaqua
neozoic pergola restock stopoff unblock chappie jaloppy snipper abjurer
nervous persona restore styloid uncloak charpoy juniper snippet accurst
network petiole rewrote subjoin unclose cheapen kingpin snooper adherer
neuroma petrous rhizoid subsoil uncross cheaply knapped soliped admiral
neurone pibroch rhizome succory uncrown chipped knapper stamper admirer
newborn piccolo rhodora succour unfrock chipper kneepan steepen adverse
newcome piceous ribwork sucrose unfroze chopped lycopod steeple afeared
newmown piddock ribwort Suffolk unicorn chopper maniple steeply aileron
nitrous pillock riotous summons uniform clapped metopic stemple aircrew
niveous pillory ripcord sundown unknown clapper metopon stepped airdrop
nocuous pillowy rissole sunroof unloose claypan ninepin stepper Alcoran
noisome pinfold rockoil support unquote clipped notepad stewpan aleuron
noology pinhole roseola suppose unroost clipper occiput stewpot alforja
noxious pinwork rowboat surcoat unsnore clippie octopod stipple Alkoran
nunhood pissoir rowlock surtout unsworn cockpit octopus stirpes allergy
oakwood pistole rubdown syncope uranous copepod octuple stopped almirah
oarlock piteous rubeola systole urology crampet oedipal stopper alsoran
obovoid pitpony rubious tabloid vacuole crampit Olympic stopple Amharic
obvious placoid ruddock tadpole vacuous crampon overpay striped anagram
ochrous plafond ruinous takeoff vamoose crappie panoply strophe andiron
odorous platoon rundown talcose variola creeper parapet stroppy aneurin
offload playoff Sabaoth talcous variole crimper pitapat stumper anthrax
oloroso plumose sallowy tallowy variola crimple playpen sunspot apparat
ominous plywood salvoes tambour Vaudois cripple plopped swapped apparel
onerous pollock santour tandoor Veddoid crisper plumper swapper apteryx
onshore pompous saprobe tanooze verbose crisply plumply sweeper aquaria
onymous pontoon sapwood tapioca vicious cropped polypod swipple Armoric
oospore popcorn sarcode taproom victory cropper polypus swopped ascarid
operose pothole sarcoid taproot villose crumpet priapic swopper ascaris
oratory pothook sarcoma teacosy villous crumple propped synapse ashtray
orology precook sarcous teagown violone crupper prosper talipes asperse
```

aspirer	dimeric	hundred	numeral	sangria	tumbrel	boneset	gainsay	parasol
aspirin	diverge	hyperon	numeric	satiric	tumbril	booksie	geneses	paresis
assured	diverse	icteric	oaktree	satyral	ulcered	bortsch	genesis	Pegasus
assurer	divorce	icterus	observe	satyric	underdo	bransle	genista	pelisse
asteria	dogtrot	ignorer	obverse	satyrid	undergo	brassie	girasol	perusal
athirst	eagerly	illbred	odoured	scabrid	unearth	browser	glassen	peruser
augural	eardrop	immerge	oestral	scarred	unhorse	bruiser	glasses	petasus
aurorae	eardrum	immerse	oestrum	scherzi	unmoral	bucksaw	glossal	phrasal
auroral	egotrip	immoral	oestrus	scherzo	unnerve	buzzsaw	Glossic	piously
auroras	elderly	imperil	oildrum	sciarid	unscrew	caisson	greaser	pleased
austral	elytron	incurve	omicron	scirrhi	upsurge	canasta	greisen	podesta
autarky	elytrum	indorse	oneiric	scleral	upthrew	celesta	grossly	poussin
averred	embargo	infarct	onwards	scourer	upthrow	celeste	grouser	praiser
baldric	emperor	inferno	oratrix	scourge	upwards	ceresin	guesser	presser
begorra	empiric	inherit	orderer	scurril	utterer	chanson	hacksaw	pressup
beshrew	emporia	injurer	orderly	securer	utterly	chassis	handsaw	prussic
bestrew	endarch	innards	orphrey	senarii	valeric	chessel	handsel	pyrosis
Biafran	enderon	innerve	outcrop	senores	veneree	chiasma	handset	quassia
bistred	endorse	insured	outgrew	several	venerer	chooser	hardset	quetsch
bizarre	enforce	insurer	outgrow	shearer	ventral	choosey	headset	refusal
blurred	engorge	interim	overran	sheerly	vestral	chrisom	hearsay	refuser
botargo	enlarge	interne	overrun	sherris	veteran	christy	hoarsen	reissue
bourree	enteral	inverse	palfrey	sierran	viceroy	classes	hocused	reposal
buckram	enteric	inwards	paperer	sistrum	visored	classic	honesty	reposit
butyric	enteron	isogram	papyrus	skirret	vivaria	classis	idlesse	revisal
cabaret	enthral	isotron	parerga	slurred	wagerer	clausal	impasse	reviser
caldron	environ	jogtrot	peloria	sneerer	wallrue	coarsen	impaste	revisit
caloric	epigram	kestrel	peloric	soberly	wastrel	cockshy	impasto	ricksha
calorie	equerry	kindred	pelorus	solaria	watered	colossi	imposer	riposte
caltrap	esparto	labarum	pierrot	sororal	waterer	counsel	incised	rudesby
caltrop	etaerio	lamprey	pigiron	sparred	waverer	courser	incisor	samisen
camaron	etheric	lateral	pilgrim	sparrow	waxtree	crassly	incused	satisfy
cambrel	excerpt	layered	piperic	spheral	whirred	cresset	indusia	scepsis
cambric	excurse	lazaret	pitprop	spheric	windrow	crimson	ingesta	scissel
cameral	exedrae	legiron	pleurae	splurge	wolfram	Croesus	keelson	scissor
camorra	externe	leveret	pleural	spooner	yewtree	crossly	kenosis	Senussi
cantrip	eyebrow	liberal	pleuron	sporran	zymurgy	cruiser	khamsin	silesia
caperer	eyedrop	liberty	pomfret	spurred	Abbasid	curtsey	kinesis	skepsis
caporal	Faberge	literal	portray	spurrey	abyssal	damosel	kneesup	sorosis
caserne	federal	liturgy	poverty	squarer	accusal	deepsea	liaison	soursop
catarrh	femoral	louvred	prairie	squirmy	accused	dehisce	Liassic	splashy
cateran	figtree	loverly	Prakrit	starred	accuser	demesne	limosis	sponson
caterer	figural	lowbred	program	stearic	acrasin	deposal	looksee	sponsor
central	figured	lowbrow	puberal	stearin	advised	deposit	majesty	spousal
centred	filaria	lucarne	puberty	steerer	adviser	devisal	malison	squashy
centric	fimbria	lucerne	puggree	stirred	advisor	devisee	malmsey	squishy
centrum	firtree	lustral	puparia	stirrer	aerosol	deviser	medusae	stemson
chagrin	fleuret	lustrum	pushrod	stirrup	alyssum	devisor	medusan	stepson
charred	fleuron	malaria	pyloric	suberic	amnesia	dibasic	medusas	stetson
cheerer	floorer	mandrel	pylorus	suberin	amnesic	divisor	meiosis	sycosis
cheerio	flytrap	mandril	quadrat	suburbs	amnesty	dresser	Meissen	synesis
chevron	footrot	mantram	quadric	sudaria	anoesis	dynasty	melisma	tabasco
chirrup	foreran	mantrap	quarrel	suntrap	aphasia	ecdyses	menisci	tamasha
chloral	forerun	Masorah	queerly	sutural	aphasic	ecdysis	milksop	thirsty
chloric	Fortran	mayoral	rattrap	sutured	apheses	embassy	mimesis	thyrsus
ciboria	foxtrot	mazurka	rebirth	swearer	aphesis	embosom	mitoses	tootsie
cidaris	friarly	megaron	rectrix	synergy	aplasia	emersed	mitosis	transit
clearly	Fuehrer	menorah	recurve	tabaret	arousal	entasis	modesty	transom
coherer	fulcrum	minaret	referee	taborer	artisan	erepsin	modiste	treason
comfrey	funeral	mineral	regards	talaria	artiste	excusal	molossi	tressed
control	gambrel	minorca	regorge	tamarin	ascesis	exposal	moonset	tressel
costrel	gangrel	miserly	remarry	tangram	asepsis	exposed	morassy	trouser
coterie	gastric	mistral	remorse	tantric	askesis	exposer	Moresco	trusser
coverup	general	monarch	reserve	tantrum	atresia	exposit	Morisco	trypsin
culprit	generic	mongrel	respray	taperer	auxesis	filasse	mycoses	typeset
decorum	goitred	muskrat	resurge	taxfree	babassu	filmset	mycosis	unbosom
deforce	gomeral	myogram	retired	teatray	babysit	finesse	myiasis	unfussy
demerit	gomeril	nacarat	returns	tectrix	backsaw	floosie	nemesia	upriser
demirep	gorcrow	natural	reverie	telergy	backset	flotsam	nemesis	utensil
denarii	grogram	navarin	reverse	tendril	bagasse	focused	nonuser	vanessa
deserve	gumdrop	nephric	reversi	theorbo	bandsaw	footsie	odyssey	venison
destroy	haporth	neutral	rivered	theorem	banksia	foresaw	opossum	verismo
deterge	heparin	neutron	rosered	theurgy	batiste	foresay	opposer	vinasse
dewdrop	Homeric	nomarch	rostral	tiderip	benison	foresee	osmosis	warison
dextral	Homerid	nombril	rostrum	timbrel	bheesty	freesia	oversaw	wellset
dextran	humdrum	noniron	ruderal	tonerow	biassed	fretsaw	oversea	whimsey
dextrin	humeral	noserag	saffron	tortrix	blessed	frisson	oversee	whipsaw
diadrom	humerus	nostril	sakeret	towards	blossom	frowsty	overset	Whitsun
diagram	humoral	nostrum	samurai	towered	blouson	fuchsia	oversew	Windsor

winesap	boaster	cubital	fletton	holster	monster	punster	senator	stretto
woolsey	bobstay	cuittle	flitted	hydatid	mounter	puritan	senatus	stunted
yolksac	boletus	culotte	flitter	identic	Mountie	pyretic	shaitan	stutter
zygosis	bolster	cunette	floater	idiotic	mozetta	pyrites	shaster	styptic
zymosis	booster	curator	fluster	igniter	mulatto	pyritic	shastra	sumpter
abattis	borstal	curette	flutter	ileitis	musette	quantic	shatter	sunstar
abetted	boulter	cuvette	foretop	impetus	mycotic	quantum	sheathe	swarthy
abetter	brantle	daystar	fouette	inaptly	naphtha	quartan	shelter	swatted
abettor	brantub	debater	fracted	inciter	necktie	quarter	sheltie	swatter
abiotic	brattle	deictic	Fraktur	inditer	neritic	quartet	shifter	sweater
ablator	breathe	deistic	frantic	ineptly	neuston	quartic	shittim	sweeten
aborter	breathy	delator	fretted	inertia	nightie	quester	shooter	sweetie
abutted	bristle	demotic	fritted	inertly	nightly	questor	shorten	sweetly
abutter	bristly	devoted	fritter	invitee	Nilotic	quieten	shortie	swelter
acantha	brittle	devotee	frontal	inviter	nodated	quietly	shortly	swiftly
Achates	brittly	digital	fronton	jacktar	nonstop	quietus	shotten	swotted
acroter	builtin	dilated	frosted	janitor	notitia	quilter	shouter	symptom
adapter	builtup	dilator	fructed	jointer	nunatak	quintal	shunter	tabetic
adaptor	burette	dilutee	fruited	jointly	octette	quintan	shutter	tacitly
adeptly	burster	diluter	fruiter	jouster	odontic	quintet	shuttle	tagetes
adopter	bushtit	dilutor	frustum	jujitsu	oersted	quintic	shyster	tapetal
adultly	calotte	dimeter	gagster	Jupiter	oldster	quitted	sighted	tapetum
aerator	capital	dinette	galatea	kenotic	omental	quitter	sightly	tapster
agnatic	capitol	diopter	gametic	keratin	omentum	ratatat	simitar	taunter
alertly	capstan	dioptre	garotte	kiloton	omitted	reactor	skeeter	Telstar
allstar	carotid	docetic	gauntly	kinetic	onestep	realtor	skelter	tempter
aloetic	carotin	dogstar	gauntry	knitted	oolitic	recital	skirted	theatre
ambatch	caustic	donator	gavotte	knitter	ophitic	reciter	skirter	thistle
amentia	cavetti	doubter	gazette	knotted	opuntia	reenter	skitter	thistly
amentum	cavetto	draftee	gelatin	knotter	orbital	reentry	skittle	Tibetan
ammeter	chanter	drafter	genetic	krypton	orectic	refutal	slantly	tighten
amputee	chantry	drastic	genette	Laputan	osmotic	refuter	slatted	tightly
annates	chaotic	dratted	genitor	layette	osseter	regatta	slotted	timothy
annatta	chapter	drifter	ghastly	legatee	outstay	related	smarten	tipster
annatto	charter	drouthy	ghettos	legator	overtax	relater	smartly	toaster
anoetic	chasten	edictal	ghostly	leister	overtly	relator	smatter	tractor
aphetic	chatted	eductor	giantry	lengthy	overtop	reputed	smelter	traitor
aphotic	chattel	eidetic	glisten	levator	painter	Rhaetic	smitten	tranter
apostil	chatter	ejector	glister	licitly	palatal	ribston	smutted	treater
apostle	cheater	ekistic	glitter	lighted	paletot	ricotta	snifter	treetop
aquatic	cheetah	elastic	glottal	lighten	palette	ridotto	snorter	trental
arbiter	chested	elastin	glottis	lighter	paretic	righten	snouted	trestle
arbutus	chintzy	Eleatic	glutted	lightly	parotid	righter	solatia	trotted
arietta	chitter	elector	glutton	limited	peartly	rightly	somatic	trotter
aristae	Choctaw	electro	glyptal	limiter	phaeton	ringtaw	somitic	trustee
aristas	chortle	emitted	glyptic	linctus	phantom	risotto	sorites	truster
ascetic	chunter	emitter	gnostic	litotes	philter	riveter	Spartan	tryptic
ascites	clastic	empathy	godetia	lobster	philtre	roaster	spastic	tweeter
ascitic	clatter	enactor	grafter	locater	phratry	rocktar	spatted	twister
aseptic	clotted	entitle	grantee	lorette	piastre	roister	spattee	twitted
Asiatic	cluster	entotic	granter	lunatic	picotee	rolltop	spatter	twitter
astatic	clutter	epistle	grantor	lunette	pinetum	rooftop	spectra	twostep
auditor	clyster	equator	greaten	lyrated	pipette	rooster	spectre	unaptly
auxetic	coaltit	erectly	greatly	maestri	piratic	rosette	spelter	unbated
Avestan	coastal	erector	grifter	maestro	pivotal	rotator	spitted	unfitly
Avestic	coaster	ergates	gristle	mahatma	pivoter	rouster	spitter	unhitch
aviator	cocotte	eristic	gristly	maintop	plantar	royster	spittle	unlatch
barytes	coletit	erratic	gritted	manatee	planter	sagitta	splotch	uveitis
barytic	colitis	erratum	grottos	manitou	plaster	sainted	sporter	vaulted
bathtub	cometic	Euratom	grunter	Maratha	plastic	saintly	spotted	vaulter
beastly	comitia	evictor	gruntle	Marathi	plastid	saluter	spotter	vaunter
belated	conatus	exactly	grutten	marital	platted	sanctum	spouter	vedette
bewitch	coontie	exactor	habitat	mashtub	platter	Sanctus	spurtle	vegetal
bheetie	coulter	excited	habitue	megaton	plectra	saunter	sputter	venatic
bigoted	counter	exciter	Hamitic	meiotic	plotted	scantly	squatty	vidette
bigotry	country	exciton	hamster	messtin	plotter	scatted	squitch	visitor
biretta	courtly	excitor	hardtop	mightst	pointed	scatter	staithe	voluted
blasted	creator	faceted	haunted	militia	pointer	scented	starter	volutin
blaster	crested	fagotto	haunter	mimetic	politic	sceptic	startle	waisted
blatter	cristae	faintly	healthy	minster	pomatum	sceptre	stentor	waister
bleater	critter	fanatic	hearted	minutes	poofter	sciatic	stetted	waratah
blintze	crofter	feaster	hearten	minutia	poulter	scooter	stilted	washtub
blister	crouton	fibster	heeltap	misstep	poultry	Scottie	Stilton	wealthy
bloated	crowtoe	fighter	helotry	mitotic	praetor	scouter	stouten	webster
bloater	crustal	firstly	hepatic	mobster	prattle	scratch	stoutly	wheaten
blotted	crusted	flatten	heretic	mofette	printer	scutter	stratum	whetted
blotter	cryptal	flatter	heritor	moisten	proctor	scuttle	stratus	whetter
bluntly	cryptic	flattop	hilltop	moistly	psalter	sematic	stretch	whistle
bluster	crystal	fleetly	hipster	monitor	punctum	Semitic	stretta	whittle

```
wiretap cornual imbrute posture Tartufe inwoven screwed sprayer amildar
worsted cornuto impound potluck tempura mailvan screwer sprayey ammonal
wreathe corrupt include prelude testudo minever shipway strayer amoebae
wreathy costume incrust presume textual miniver sideway talayot amoebas
wrestle couture infauna primula texture mitzvah slipway tallyho anagram
written croquet inhouse procure through octaval someway Vandyke Ananias
zemstvo croquis inocula produce tilbury palaver sprawly vilayet anginal
zetetic culture insculp product tittupy popover strewth alcazar Anglian
zonated cumquat intrude profuse tonsure recover thalweg assizes angular
zygotic curcuma intrust purpura topfull removal thrower bedizen annular
zymotic dasyure jonquil purpure torture removed throwin blowzed antbear
account debauch jumbuck pursuer traduce remover tideway borazon anthrax
accrual debouch Kalmuck pursuit tribune revival tramway britzka anyroad
acequia default kibbutz pustule tribute reviver unbowed citizen apogean
acicula degauss kumquat racquet triduan revivor walkway damozel apparat
adjourn delouse lacquer rapture triduum samovar widowed denizen apsidal
aground demount languet rebound unbound scarves widower deutzia Arabian
aliquot denture languid recluse uncouth sheaves adnexal drizzle archway
ampoule deplume languor recount unequal shelved apraxia drizzly areaway
anchusa detrude lawsuit recruit unhouse shelves calyxes endozoa areolae
apolune diffuse leaguer redoubt unsound shrivel eutexia entozoa areolar
armfuls discuss lecture redound unstuck shriven hypoxia floozie areolas
armoury diseuse legpull rehouse untruly sleeved hypoxic frazzle aristae
asexual disgust leisure remould untruss striven indexer freezer aristas
assault dispute lettuce remount untruth striver latexes frizzle arousal
astound disrupt lingual rescuer unusual synovia murexes frizzly arrival
azimuth disturb mahound resound unwound thieves planxty genizah arsenal
banquet earmuff manhunt retouch valvula thriven pyrexia grizzle artisan
barbule encrust marquee rewound valvule twelves pyrexic grizzly asexual
bascule enthuse marquis roebuck vapours uncivil unboxed hoatzin ashtray
because entrust masquer romaunt vapoury uncover horizon         asocial
bedouin enwound measure rondure vascula unmoved metazoa         assagai
biscuit epicure mercury rorqual velours unravel acolyte mezuzah assegai
bismuth erasure misrule rupture veloute unsaved alcayde muezzin augural
bivouac espouse mixture saccule venture unwoven amboyna pretzel aurorae
bordure evacuee mollusc sacculi venturi vetiver analyse quetzal auroral
borough evolute mowburn sambuca verdure wharves analyst quizzed auroras
bouquet exclude mugwump satsuma verruca whoever anodyne quizzer austral
bravura execute multure savoury vesture archway arrayer quizzes autocar
briquet exhaust Neptune sawbuck viaduct areaway assayer seltzer Avestan
bulrush expound nervure sawdust victual beeswax bergylt sneazer axillae
caesura extrude netsuke saxtuba vincula bejewel berhyme snoozer axillar
cagoule factual noctuid scapula virgule caraway bugeyed snoozle Azilean
calculi facture noctule schmuck virtual catawba caloyer Switzer backsaw
cannula failure nocturn scopula vulture chinwag byebyes swizzle bananas
capsule falcula nonsuch scourge wafture cutaway cutaway tweezer bandeau
capture farruca nonsuit scrouge cutaway doorway carryon waltzer bandsaw
carouse feature nurture seclude akvavit embowed decrypt whizzed baseman
catsuit ferrugo obitual seizure allover embowel delayer ————    basilar
cellule ferrule obscure sensual alluvia embower dialyse abaxial batsman
censure fissure obtrude seppuku Angevin empower diptych Abelian beanbag
century fistula occlude serpula aquavit empower dryeyed abysmal beeswax
chequer fixture orotund skijump aquiver fairway embryon abyssal Belgian
cingula flexure outrush soilure arrival faraway epigyny Acadian belljar
circuit floruit outturn sojourn arriver fishway eponymy acarian bellman
circusy formula overuse spatula bedevil flyaway essayer accrual besmear
cliquey fortune oviduct specula behaver footway essoyne accusal bespeak
closure fossula parquet spicula beloved freeway fedayee Achaean bestead
cloture foxhunt pasture spicule bolivar gangway forayer Achaian bestial
coagula frenula penguin spinule cadaver gateway halcyon acrobat Biafran
coequal furcula percuss sporule caravan getaway honeyed adaxial biaxial
collude geebung perdure statued caravel halfway inlayer admiral bifilar
colours gemmule perfume stature chervil halfwit isohyet adnexal bifocal
coloury gesture perfuse statute cleaver hallway Malayan adrenal bighead
combust globule perjure stimuli datival headway martyry aeolian bilobar
commune gradual perjury stipule deliver highway metayer aeonian bimanal
commute granule permute subdual disavow imbower moneyed African bipedal
compute gravure perturb subduct duumvir parkway moneyer alcazar bipolar
concuss guayule pertuse subdued dwarves pathway oneeyed Alcoran birdman
conduce guipure picquet subfusc Elzevir periwig oophyte Alkoran bivouac
conduct hachure picture subsume enliven postwar palmyra allheal boatman
conduit Hamburg pillule succuba flivver railway pharynx allstar bobstay
confuse helluva pinguid succubi flyover renewal pieeyed almanac bogbean
confute heyduck pinnule succumb forever renewer popeyed almirah bogyman
conjure hiccupy pintuck suffuse Genevan roadway pteryla almsman bolivar
conquer hirsute planula sunburn godevil ropeway relayed alodial bondman
consult homburg plumule sunsuit greaves runaway restyle alsoran bookman
consume honours pollute tactual groover scrawly Samoyed alumnae Boolean
contuse humbuzz poseuse tarbush however scrawny sinsyne amalgam borstal
```

bowhead	cotidal	exposal	glyptal	jazzman	medusae	ortolan	quetzal	shinpad
boxseat	courlan	exurban	goahead	jemadar	medusan	ottoman	quintal	shiplap
Brahman	cranial	exuviae	godhead	jocular	medusas	outplay	quintan	shipman
brinjal	creedal	exuvial	golfbag	journal	meerkat	outstay	quondam	shipway
buckram	cristae	fabliau	gomeral	Judaean	menorah	outwear	radical	shopman
bucksaw	crowbar	fabular	gonadal	jugular	messiah	ovarian	radulae	showman
bugbear	crucial	factual	goodday	Jungian	Messias	overeat	radular	shrinal
bullbat	crucian	faculae	goodman	juryman	Mexican	overlap	railcar	sickbay
bumboat	crustal	fairway	Gordian	Kantian	mezuzah	overlay	railman	sickpay
burghal	cryptal	faraday	gradual	khaddar	miasmal	overman	railway	sidecar
burglar	crystal	faraway	grammar	kilobar	midyear	overpay	Ramadan	sideway
bushman	csardas	fascial	grandad	kinsman	milkman	overran	ratatat	sierran
buzzsaw	cubical	fastday	grandam	klipdas	milldam	oversaw	rattrap	similar
Cadmean	cubital	fathead	Grecian	kneecap	mimical	overtax	realgar	simitar
caltrap	cudbear	faucial	gremial	kneepan	mineral	ovoidal	recital	simular
cambial	cumquat	federal	greylag	kumquat	minicab	Oxonian	redcoat	skidpan
cameral	cumshaw	felspar	Grobian	kursaal	minicar	packman	redhead	slipway
capital	cupular	feminal	grogram	lacteal	minimal	paginal	refloat	slotcar
caporal	curacao	femoral	gunboat	lacunae	misdeal	pairoar	refusal	snowcap
Capsian	cutaway	fibulae	gunplay	lacunal	mishear	pajamas	refutal	snowman
capstan	cynical	fibular	gwyniad	lacunar	Mishnah	palatal	reginal	sokeman
caracal	Cyprian	fibulas	habitat	lacunas	mislead	paludal	regular	someday
caravan	czardas	figleaf	hacksaw	laminae	misplay	pampean	remblai	someway
caraway	Danelaw	figural	Halakah	laminar	misread	Pandean	removal	Sorbian
cardiac	Dantean	finical	halfway	Laotian	mistral	papadam	renewal	soroban
carinae	darshan	fireman	hallway	Laputan	mitzvah	Paphian	reposal	sororal
carinal	datival	fishway	handbag	lashkar	modular	papulae	respray	soybean
carinas	daystar	flagday	handcar	lateral	monacal	papular	retinae	spacial
carload	deadpan	flagman	handsaw	Latvian	mondial	parkway	retinal	Spartan
Catalan	decadal	flatcap	hangman	lesbian	morulae	partial	retinas	spatial
catboat	decanal	flatcar	hanuman	lethean	morular	paschal	retread	special
catenae	decimal	fleabag	hardpan	lexical	mosshag	pathway	retreat	spheral
catenas	decuman	floreat	harijan	liberal	mudflat	patrial	retrial	sporran
cateran	Delilah	flotsam	headman	liminal	muntjac	payload	revisal	spousal
cathead	deposal	fluidal	headway	lineman	muntjak	pedicab	revival	squamae
catspaw	devisal	fluvial	hearsay	lingual	musical	pelican	ringtaw	stellar
caveman	dewclaw	flyaway	heeltap	linkman	muskrat	pemican	roadman	sternal
central	dextral	flyboat	helical	Linnean	myogram	Permian	roadway	stewpan
champac	dextran	flyleaf	hellcat	lipread	myxomas	Persian	rocktar	stoical
champak	diagram	flytrap	herniae	literal	nacarat	perusal	rodsman	stopgap
chapman	digital	folkway	hernial	liveoak	nameday	phrasal	rondeau	strumae
chateau	dipnoan	footman	hernias	lobular	narwhal	pighead	ropeway	stygian
cheddar	dipolar	footpad	hessian	loculae	natural	pigmean	rorqual	subadar
cheetah	display	footway	highhat	locular	nebulae	pikeman	rosebay	subdean
chiliad	disseat	forbear	highman	logical	nebular	pilular	rostral	subdual
chinwag	diurnal	foreman	highway	longday	nebulas	pinhead	rouleau	subhead
chloral	djibbah	forepaw	hillman	loricae	neutral	pitapat	rowboat	sunbeam
Choctaw	dogstar	foreran	Hobbian	lumenal	newsman	pithead	ruderal	sunbear
chordal	domical	foresaw	hockday	luminal	nodical	pithhat	ruffian	sundial
chuddah	doorman	foresay	holiday	lunular	nodular	pivotal	runaway	sunstar
chuddar	doormat	Fortran	holmoak	lustral	nominal	plantar	Russian	suntrap
Circean	doorway	freeman	hophead	lymphad	noonday	plateau	saltcat	surcoat
clausal	drawbar	freeway	hornmad	lyncean	nosebag	pleurae	saltpan	surfman
claypan	drayman	fretsaw	hothead	lyrical	nosegay	pleural	samovar	surreal
cloacae	dustman	Frisian	humeral	macadam	noserag	pluvial	samurai	sutural
cloacal	dustpan	frogman	humoral	maculae	notepad	polecat	sandbag	swagman
clubman	earflap	frontal	hygeian	macular	nuclear	poohbah	sandbar	synodal
Cluniac	edictal	funeral	Iberian	magical	numeral	popular	sandman	tableau
clypeal	egghead	fustian	iceboat	mailbag	nunatak	portray	saphead	tabular
coastal	elegiac	gainsay	ilkaday	mailman	nuptial	postbag	satyral	tactual
coaxial	eluvial	Galahad	illegal	mailvan	nylghau	postman	saurian	taeniae
coeliac	elysian	gamebag	immoral	Malayan	nymphal	postwar	scandal	tangram
coequal	enteral	gamelan	implead	manteau	oarsman	pothead	scholar	tankcar
comical	enthral	gangway	indican	mantram	oatmeal	poundal	scleral	tapetal
Comtian	entreat	gascoal	infulae	mantrap	obitual	predial	scoriae	tapsman
conceal	epigeal	gateway	inhuman	Manxcat	ocellar	preheat	scribal	taxicab
conchae	epigean	general	initial	Manxman	octaval	preplan	seabear	taximan
congeal	epigram	Genevan	insofar	manyear	oedipal	presoak	secular	tealeaf
conical	epochal	genizah	instead	marital	oestral	program	seismal	teargas
cooncan	equinal	gentian	insular	marshal	offbeat	protean	seminal	teatray
copular	escheat	geoidal	intreat	martial	offload	puberal	seminar	tegular
copycat	escolar	getaway	Iranian	Martian	offpeak	Pullman	sensual	Telstar
cordial	estreat	gharial	irideal	Marxian	omental	pupilar	Serbian	Templar
corneal	eternal	gingham	ischial	Masorah	oppidan	puritan	Servian	tertial
cornual	etesian	glacial	isogram	matinal	optical	pygmean	several	tertian
coronae	ethical	gleeman	Italian	maximal	optimal	pyjamas	shaitan	testban
coronal	Etonian	glossal	jacamar	mayoral	orbital	Pythian	Shavian	textual
coronas	excusal	glottal	jackdaw	meatman	ordinal	quadrat	shebear	thereat
costean	exedrae	gluteal	jacktar	medical	Orphean	quartan	shellac	theriac

```
thermae wiretap bortsch finance oomiack scratch alidade outrode adviser
thermal wolfram braunch finback orifice screech already outside afeared
Tibetan woodman bullace flounce ostraca scrunch anybody ovicide affined
tideway woolfat bullock fluence ostrich seasick astride passade agnomen
tiebeam workbag burdock fluency outback secrecy avocado passado aircrew
timelag workday buttock flyback outface service ballade pentode albumen
titular workman caddice fossick outpace setback bedside peptide alkanet
tollbar yardman cadence furnace overact sferics bravado perfidy alleged
tollman yashmak cadency futtock oviduct shylock brigade pervade allover
tonneau yatagan calpack gallice oxfence silence brocade pintado allseed
topcoat yeggman caprice gimmick packice sirocco bromide precede almoner
topical yolksac carioca gorcock paddock skyjack bushido prelude althaea
torulae zooidal carrack graunch padlock sonance calando preside ambages
towboat ascribe carsick grimace pandect sonancy calends prosody ambones
towhead bilimbi cassock guanaco patency sowback carbide provide amender
tramcar catawba chalice gunlock peacock spinach cascade raggedy ammeter
tramway copaiba chocice haddock penance splotch cathode raphide amputee
trangam cordoba cogency hammock perfect squacco ceilidh rawhide ancones
trental crybaby collect hapence phonics squelch cestode regards aniseed
triduan disrobe compact hassock physics squinch charade riptide annates
trishaw earlobe concoct haycock pibroch squitch cladode rotunda annulet
trivial escribe conduce hayrick piddock statice cockade roulade another
trochal hushaby conduct hemlock pillock statics collide saccade antigen
trucial jellaba confect henpeck pinnace staunch collude sarcode apheses
trumeau lullaby connect heroics pintuck stomach commode scalade aphides
truncal marimba contact heyduck playact stretch comrade scalado apothem
tubular mastaba convect hillock pliancy subduct concede seaside apparel
Tuesday microbe convict hogback poetics subject confide seclude applied
tugboat nelumbo coppice hopsack polacca suffice corrida seconde applier
tulchan Panjabi cornice hospice pollack sundeck corrode secondi apsides
tumular placebo correct huanaco pollock surface corrody secondo aquifer
turfman Punjabi cossack hummock porrect suspect couvade spinode aquiver
tutelar redoubt cowlick icepack portico tabasco cowhide squaddy arbiter
tutenag rudesby craunch impeach potence tactics crusade subside arcaded
twankay saprobe crevice inexact potency tapioca crusado subsidy armiger
typebar sassaby currach infancy potluck tenancy custody succade arrayer
typical saxtuba cutback infarct predict terrace cyanide suicide arriver
umbonal scrubby debauch inflect preface testacy degrade testudo ascites
Umbrian shrubby debouch inflict prefect tieback deicide tetrode ashamed
unclean squabby decency infract prelacy tintack detrude thready aspirer
uncloak standby defence inspect prelect titmice dioxide topside assayer
unequal suburbs deflect invoice prepack tobacco ebbtide tornado assizes
ungulae succuba deforce jannock primacy torgoch effendi torpedo assured
unideal succubi defrock joyance privacy touraco epicede torpids assurer
unmoral syllabi defunct jumbuck produce traduce episode torsade asunder
unswear theorbo dehisce justice product traject epoxide towards atelier
unusual thereby derrick Kalmuck project trisect estrade tragedy avenger
Uralian thrombi detract kalpack protect tropics exclude tribade averred
urethan wallaby dialect killick pudency trounce explode tripody awarder
utopian whereby diptych latency putlock truancy extrude underdo babbler
uxorial wouldbe dissect lattice quetsch tussock fantods unhandy backset
Vatican abreact distich lavrock ransack unblock forbade unready baffler
vegetal abroach divorce lettuce recency unbrace forbode upgrade baloney
ventral absence dormice licence redneck unfrock gambade upwards banjoes
verglas adjunct dornick limbeck reelect unhitch gambado uranide banquet
vermian advance drydock lucency reenact unlatch gorsedd veranda banshee
vesicae afflict dunnock maffick reflect unstick grenade voivode baronet
vesical airlock durance mammock refract unstuck Haggada wayside barrier
vestral airsick earlock manjack regency unteach hydride zipcode barytes
veteran ambatch edifice mastich rejoice urgency hymnody abashed basinet
vicinal ambsace elflock mattock replace vacancy implode abdomen bayonet
victual amtrack embrace mediacy replica valance include abetted bearded
vinegar anglice emplace menisci respect valence innards abetter bedizen
virelay ardency endarch metrics restock valency intrude abjurer beechen
virtual askance enforce minorca retouch vendace inwards aborter behaver
vitular attract enhance monarch retract verdict joyride abrader beignet
walkway auspice enounce Moresco retrace verruca kalends abutted bejewel
wanigan avarice erotica Morisco rhiancy viaduct Kannada abutter belated
waratah balance errancy morocco roebuck viatica kathode accused belcher
warhead bannock essence mortice rollick warlock manmade accuser beloved
Watteau barrack eweneck mudpack romance wedlock morendo Achates bencher
weekday bawcock exotica mullock rowlock wetback nitride acrogen berried
whereas bedrock extinct nautics ruddock winnock nuclide acroter beshrew
whereat bedsock extract neglect sambuca wryneck obtrude adapter besides
whipsaw beseech faience niblick sawbuck addenda occlude adducer bestrew
wildcat bewitch fallacy nomarch schlock alameda offside adherer betaken
windbag bibcock farruca nonsuch schmuck alcaide onwards admirer betimes
winesap bionics felucca oarlock science alcalde osmunda adopter betoken
wireman bittock fetlock offence scotice alcayde outride advised between
```

```
biassed brimmed charnel colleen decider emitter flubbed goitred hobbler
bigener brimmer charred collier decoder empanel flunkey gombeen hocused
bigoted brinded charter colonel decrier empower fluster gourmet hogweed
bilboes bringer chasten comfrey deepsea emptier flutter grabbed holster
bilobed briquet chatted compeer defiler encoder flyover grabber homager
birchen brisken chattel complex definer endogen focused grafter honeyed
bistred brisket chatter conifer delayer enfiled follies grained hooklet
bitumen broaden cheapen conquer deliver engaged fondler grainer hostler
blabbed brocket cheater cornfed deluder enliven forager grandee however
blabber broider checker coroner demirep enwheel foramen granger humbles
blacken broiler cheerer coronet demoded epaulet forayer grantee hundred
bladder brooder chequer corslet denizen epithem foreleg granter hurdler
blanket brothel chessel costrel derider epithet foresee grapnel hurdles
blarney brother chested cottier devisee ergates forever grasper hurried
blasted browser chicken coulter deviser ermined forgoer grazier hustler
blaster bruiser chidden counsel devoted escapee forties greaser hypogea
blather brusher chigger counter devotee escaper founder greaten igniter
blatter buckler childer coupler diddler evacuee fracted greaves ignorer
bleater bugeyed chimney couplet dialled evacuee frapped greisen illbred
bleeder builded chipped courier dilated evangel freaked greyhen imbiber
bleeper builder chipper courser dilutee excited freezer grifter imbower
blender bullpen chitter cowheel diluter exciter freshen grilled impanel
blessed bumbler chooser cowshed dimeter exhumer fresher griller imposer
blether bungler choosey cozener dingoes exposed freshet grimmer inbreed
blinder burbler chopped crabbed diopter exposer fretted grinder incised
blinker burgher chopper cracked disobey faceted fripper grinned inciter
blister burster chowder cracker ditcher falsies frisker gripped incomer
blither burthen chuffed cragged divider fancier frisket gripper incudes
bloated burweed chugged crammed diviner farrier fritted gritted incused
bloater bustler chukker crammer doodler farther fritter Grolier indexer
blocker butcher chummed crampet dossier feaster frogged grommet indices
blooded byebyes chunnel crawler doubler feather fronded groover inditer
bloomer bygones chunter creamer doubles fedayee frosted grouper inducer
blotted bywoner chutney creeper doublet feigner fructed grouser infidel
blotter cabaret cimices cresset doubter feoffee fruited growler inhaler
blowzed cabinet circler crested dowager feoffer fruiter grubbed injurer
blubber cackler circlet cribbed drabber fiancee fuddler grubber inlayer
blucher cacumen citadel cricket drabbet fibster Fuehrer grummet insider
bluffer cadaver citizen crimper drabler fiddler fuelled grunter insured
blunder caducei civvies cringer draftee fielder fueller grutten insurer
blunger cajoler clabber crisper drafter fifteen fumbler guarded integer
blurred calices clacker critter dragged fifties funnies guardee intoner
blusher calipee claimer croaker dragnet fighter furrier guesser invader
bluster caliper clamber crochet drainer figtree further guichet invitee
boarder calomel clammed crocket dratted figured gabbler guilder inviter
boaster caloyer clanger crofter drawler filacer gagster guzzler inwoven
bobsled calumet clapped crooked dreamed filibeg galatea hackler ipomoea
boggler calyces clapper crooner dreamer filmset galilee hackney Ishmael
boloney calyxes classes cropped dredger firenew gambier haggler isohyet
bolster cambrel clatter cropper dresser firtree gambler hagweed ivories
boneset campbed clavier croquet driblet fishnet gambrel hairnet jaconet
bongoes candied cleaner crosier drifter fitchet gangrel halogen jangler
booklet canteen cleaver crowned driller fitchew gantlet hamster jellied
boomlet caperer clicker crowner drinker flagged garbler handler Jezebel
booster caramel climber crownet dripped flamfew gateleg handsel jingler
bootleg caravel clinker crozier drogher flanker geckoes handset joinder
botcher carrier clipped cruiser droplet flannel geneses hardset jointer
bottled cashier clipper cruller dropped flapped genteel harrier journey
bouchee castled cliquey crumpet dropper flapper giggler harshen jouster
boulder catcher clobber crupper drubbed flasher gillnet harslet jubilee
boulter caterer clocker crusher drudger flatlet girdler hasbeen juggler
bouncer caulker clogged crusted drugged flatten glacier hatcher jumpjet
bounden centner clogger cryogen drugget flatter gladded hatchet juncoes
bounder centred clothes cudweed drummed flecker gladden haulier juniper
bouquet cerumen clotted culices drummer fleeced gladder haunted Jupiter
bourree chaffer clubbed currier drunken fleecer glassen haunter kerogen
bowlder Chaldee clumber curtsey dryeyed fleshed glasses hayseed kestrel
bracken chamber cluster dabbler duelled flesher glazier headset kindler
bracket chamfer clutter dallier dueller fleuret gleaner hearken kindred
bragged chancel clyster damosel duramen flicker glimmer hearted kinglet
bragger changer coacher damozel dwarves flipped glisten hearten kitchen
brander channel coarsen dangler dweller flipper glister heathen knacker
brannew chanter coaster darbies earthen flitted glitter heather knapped
brawler chaplet cobbler dawdler ecdyses flitter glummer heckler knapper
brazier chapped cochlea dazzler embowed flivver glutted helices kneader
breaded chapter cockney debater embowel floater gnarled higgler kneeler
breaker charger coddler debrief embower flogged gobbler hipster knitted
breeder charley codices decibel emersed floorer goggler hitcher knitter
brevier charmer coherer decided emitted flopped goggles hoarsen knobbed
```

```
knocker metamer osselet plummet rambler salvoes shinned slubbed spoiler
knotted metayer osseter plumper rancher samisen shipped slubber spondee
knotter mettled outgrew plunder raschel Samoyed shippen slugged sponger
knurled midweek outlier plunger ratchet sampler shipper slugger spoofer
krimmer milkleg overfed plunker ratteen sandbed shirker slumber spooney
lacquer minaret oversea poacher rattler Saracen shocker slummed spoorer
lakelet minever oversee pofaced ravager satchel shogged slummer sporter
lamprey miniver oversew poinder ravined satinet shooter slurred spotted
languet minster oversew pointed reacher saunter shopped smacker spotter
lassoes minutes paddler pointer rebuker scabbed shopper smarten spouter
latchet misdeed painter polymer reciter scabies shorten smasher sprayer
latexes misdeem paisley pomfret recover scalder shotten smatter sprayey
latices misstep palaver poofter reducer scalpel shouter smeller spurner
laugher mitoses palfrey popeyed reenter scalper shrivel smelter spurred
launder mobster palsied popover referee scamper shriven smidgen spurrey
layered moisten panacea poppied refined scanned shucker smitten sputter
lazaret moither pannier porifer refiner scanner shudder smother squarer
leaflet molimen panther posteen refugee scarfed shunned smutted stabbed
leaguer moneyed panties potheen refuser scarlet shunner snagged stabber
learned moneyer paperer pouched refuter scarper shunter snapped stabler
learner mongrel parader poulter regimen scarred shutter snapper stables
leather moniker parapet pounder related scarves shyster snarler stacker
legatee monomer pardner praiser relater scatted sickbed sneaker stagger
leister monster parolee prancer relayed scatter sighted sneerer stainer
leveret moocher parquet premier remiges scauper simpler sneezer stalked
lieabed moonset parsley presser remodel scented simplex snicker stalker
lighted moorhen partlet pretzel removed schemer singlet sniffer stammel
lighten mottled partner preview remover scissel sixteen snifter stammer
lighter moulder passkey pricker reneger scoffer sixties snigger stamper
limited mounter pearled pricket renewer scolder sizzler snipped stander
limiter mourner pearler primmed rentier scomber skeeter snipper staniel
linseed mousmee peddler printer reorder scooper skegger snippet stapler
lioncel mouther pedicel prithee repaper scooter skelter snooker starlet
lipdeep muddler pennies problem repiner scorner skidded snooper starred
litotes muffler percher proceed replier scorper skilled snoozer starter
loather mumbler perigee prodded reputed scourer skillet snorkel statued
lobster murexes perplex prodder requiem scouter skimmed snorter stealer
locater murices peruser proffer rescuer scraper skimmer snouted steamer
looksee murther phellem pronged retaken screwed skinker snubbed steepen
lorimer muscled philter prophet retired screwer skinned snubber steerer
loriner mutagen piaffer propjet reviler scriber skinner snuffer stemmed
lounger muzzler pickeer propped reviser scudded skipped socager stepney
louvred mycoses pickled prosper reviver sculler skipper sofabed stepped
lowbred mynheer picotee prowler riddler scummed skippet soignee stepper
Lucifer naiades picquet psalter riffler scunner skirret soldier sterlet
luncher nankeen pieeyed puddler righten scupper skirted soliped sterned
lurcher narthex piffler puggree righter scutter skirter soother stetted
lynchet necklet pigweed puncher ringlet seaweed skitter sorites sticker
lyrated needler pikelet punster ripplet seceder skulker sounder stiffen
mahaleb neither pilsner purlieu rivered securer slabbed souther stifler
mahseer Neogaea pincher pursuer riveter seducer slabber sozzled stilted
malines nibbler pioneer purview rivulet seedbed slacken spadger stinger
malmsey niggler pitched putamen roadbed selffed slacker spancel stinker
manager nobbler pitcher puttier roaster seltzer slagged spaniel stirpes
manatee nodated pivoter puzzler rockier semiped slammed spanker stirred
manchet nominee placket pyrites rocklet senores slander spanned stirrer
mandrel nonuser plaided pyxides roedeer serried slapped spanner stocker
mangoes norther planned quaffer roister settler slasher sparger stonker
mantlet notched planner quarrel rontgen shammed slather sparred stopped
manweek notelet planter quarter rooinek shammer slatted spatted stopper
marbled numbles plaster quartet rooster shanked sledded spattee storied
marbles nymphet platted queller rootlet sharpen sleeken spatter stouten
marcher oaktree platter quester rosered sharper sleeper spawner stovies
mariner oarweed playlet quicken rotifer shaster sleeved speaker strayer
marquee obligee playpen quieten roughen shatter slender species strider
married October pleader quillet rounded shearer slicker speeder striker
martlet odoured pleased quilter roundel sheaves slidden speller striped
masquer odyssey pledgee quintet rounder shebeen slimmer spelter striven
matchet oenomel pledger quipped rouster shedder slinger spencer striver
matinee oersted pledget quitted royster shelled slinker spender strudel
maunder officer plodded quitter ruffler sheller slipped spieler stubbed
mauther oilseed plodder quizzed rumbler shelter slipper spignel studded
mayweed oldster plopped quizzer rundlet shelved slither spiller studied
mealies omitted plotted quizzes rustler shelves slobber spinner stuffer
meander oneeyed plotter rabbler saddler sherbet slogged spinney stummed
measles onestep plucker racquet sainted shereef slogger spiraea stumper
meddler opposer plugged radices sakeret shicker slopped spitted stunned
Meissen orderer plugger ragweed salicet shifter sloshed spitter stunner
merchet orphrey plumber rallier saluter shimmer slotted splicer stunted
```

```
stutter thunder udaller whacker engraft allonge hidalga seepage bruhaha
subdued tickler ulcered whangee faceoff anagoge hidalgo selvage caliche
succeed tiddler umbones wharves falloff anagogy hostage serfage capuche
suckler tiddley umpteen wheaten falsify analogy immerge seringa caroche
sumpter tiercel unarmed wheeled fortify apagoge impinge serpigo catechu
sutured tiercet unasked wheeler giraffe apanage indulge sinkage churchy
swabbed tighten unbated whether glorify apology innings skyhigh cockshy
swabber timbrel unbowed whetted gratify arraign inveigh smaragd crunchy
swagged tingler unboxed whetter handoff arrange lairage soakage delight
swagger tippler uncover whicker hayloft assuage leafage soccage diarchy
swanker tipster unhoped whidder henwife average leakage splodge draught
swanned toaster unifier whimper horrify baggage lentigo splurge drought
swapped toddler unladen whimsey indraft bandage lineage spriggy drouthy
swapper toothed unlined whinger ingraft barrage linkage springe dyarchy
swarded touched unmixed whipped jollify besiege liturgy springy earache
swarmer toucher unmoved whipper jumpoff biology lockage storage elenchi
swasher toughen unpaged whippet justify bondage longago stowage empathy
swatted tourney unquiet whirler kickoff borings lozenge strange eparchy
swatter towered unravel whirred leadoff borough luggage stringy flaught
swearer townlet unsaved whisker liftoff boscage lumbago sullage fraught
sweater trachea unscrew whiskey lignify boskage makings synergy freight
sweeper tracker unsexed whisper liquefy botargo massage syringa Frenchy
sweeten trailer untried whither magnify bottega melange syringe gnocchi
swelter trainee untuned whizzed mastiff brewage message takings gouache
swigged trainer unwoven whoever midriff brokage mileage tallage grouchy
swiller trammel upriser whoopee midwife buoyage mintage tankage healthy
swimmer tranter upsides whooper mollify burgage montage tannage heighho
swinger trapped upsweep whopper mortify cabbage moorage teenage insight
swither trapper upthrew whorled mummify cabbagy myology telergy kitschy
Switzer trawler usurper widowed mundify carnage neglige thanage lengthy
swobbed treader utterer widower mystify cartage neology theurgy Maratha
swollen treater varices wielder nigrify coinage noology through Marathi
swopped trekked vaulted wiggler nitrify collage onstage tidings naphtha
swopper trekker vaulter willies nullify college orology tillage panache
swotted tressed vaunter winglet petrify condign otology tonnage panocha
tabaret tressel veinlet wizened playoff consign outrage trilogy paunchy
tabinet triblet velamen wobbler pontiff cordage overage umbrage piranha
taborer tricker veliger woolled pontify corkage package undergo preachy
tackler trifler venerer woollen prosify cornage palings unhinge raunchy
tagetes trigger vernier woolsey putrefy corsage pannage upstage relight
talipes trimmed vetiver worrier qualify cortege parerga upsurge ricksha
taloned trimmer vilayet worsted rakeoff cottage passage urology scirrhi
tanager trinket vintner wrapped rectify courage paysage vantage sheathe
taperer triolet visaged wrapper redraft cowhage peerage ventage sketchy
tapster triplet visored wrecker restiff cranage peonage vertigo sleight
tarrier triplex vistaed wringer Russify curragh pillage vestige slouchy
tartlet tripped vittles writhen salsify derange plumage village sloughy
tattler tripper volumed written satisfy deterge plusage vintage smokeho
taunter trippet voluted ycleped sawnoff diverge pondage voltage smoochy
taxfree trochee vouchee yewtree scarify divulge pontage waftage snatchy
teacher trodden voucher yielder scorify dockage portage wastage splashy
telpher troller voyager younger scruffy drayage postage wattage squashy
templet trolley waddler younker seawife dunnage pottage windage squishy
tempter trommel wagerer zaptieh sendoff ecology presage windegg staithe
tenoner trooper wagoner zincked sheriff effulge primage wordage starchy
tentbed trotted Wahabee zonated showoff embargo prodigy yardage stenchy
tentpeg trotter waisted zymogen signify engorge protege zoology strophe
terrier trouper waister acetify skilift enlarge prurigo zymurgy swarthy
testbed trouser wakener acidify specify expunge quayage abought tallyho
thalweg trucker waltzer agraffe spinoff Faberge rampage acantha tamasha
thankee trudgen warbler airlift squiffy Falange ravings acouchy thought
thanker trumpet wastrel alewife stopoff farrago realign agrapha timothy
theorem trusser watcher alfalfa stupefy ferrugo redlegs alright tonight
thicken trustee watered amplify takeoff filings regorge anarchy tranche
thicket truster waterer bailiff Tartufe finings resurge Arapaho twitchy
thieves tumbler wattled beatify terrify fixings revenge atrophy unright
thigger tumbrel wattles caitiff testify flotage rootage attache unsight
thiller turnkey wavelet calcify tipsify flowage rummage aurochs upright
thinker tweeter waverer castoff torrefy foggage salvage bedight uptight
thinned tweezer waxtree certify versify foliage sapsago blotchy wealthy
thinner twelves wealden clarify vitrify footage sarangi bobeche wreathe
thither twigged weather crucify welloff foreign sausage borscht wreathy
thorned twilled webster damnify zincify fullage savings branchy wrought
thriven twinned weigher dandify zinkify galanga scourge breathe abattis
throned twister welcher         abridge gamboge scraggy breathy Abbasid
thrower twitted wellies distaff acreage garbage scrooge brioche abigail
thudded twitter wellset dulcify adjudge geology scrouge bronchi abiotic
thuggee twostep welsher earmuff ajutage haulage scutage broncho aboulia
thumper typeset wencher enfeoff allergy herbage sealegs brought abstain
```

```
accidie atresia chervil diploid floruit idiotic mermaid osteoid pyrexic
acclaim aurelia chindit discoid fluidic idyllic mesonic ouabain pyritic
acequia auxesis chloric disdain footsie ileitis messtin overbid pyrosis
acerbic auxetic choroid disjoin forfeit illicit metopic overdid pyrrhic
acrasin Avestic chromic distain foxtail imperil miasmic overlie pyxidia
acrylic avionic chronic docetic frantic incipit midship oxyacid quadric
actinia babysit ciboria doeskin freebie indicia milfoil pacific quantic
actinic bacchic cichlid dogskin freesia indusia militia paeonic quartic
acyclic baldric cidaris dolphin fuchsia inertia milreis paladin quassia
adenoid banksia cipolin dominie funfair ingrain mimesis palmoil quickie
adhibit bargain circuit dovekie fungoid inhabit mimetic parboil quintic
aerobic barmaid clarkia drastic galenic inherit minikin paresis racemic
agnatic barytic classic drivein gametic inhibit minutia paretic ramekin
airmail basidia classis druidic ganglia insipid mislaid parfait rapeoil
airship beatnik clastic drumlin garboil insulin mitosis parodic rarebit
akvavit bedevil clippie duckpin gastric interim mitotic parotid ratafia
albumin bedouin clupeid dustbin gelatin introit monadic parsnip rattail
alembic begonia coaltit duumvir generic invalid monodic patagia ravelin
alginic benefic coccoid dynamic genesis Islamic moonlit pelagic reclaim
alkalis benefit cockpit ecdysis genetic Jacobin moronic peloria recruit
allelic benthic codicil ectopic Geordie japonic morphia peloric rectrix
alluvia benzoic cohabit edaphic georgic javelin Mountie penguin redskin
aloetic benzoin coletit eggflip gherkin jonquil muezzin percoid refrain
amentia bheetie colitis egotrip ghillie katydid mullein periwig regalia
Amharic biennia colloid eidetic glaikit kenosis murrain pertain reposit
ammonia biscuit colonic eirenic glenoid kenotic myalgia petunia retrain
amnesia bobtail comedic ekistic gliadin keramic myalgic pfennig reverie
amnesic bohemia cometic elastic globoid keratin mycelia phallic revisit
amoebic bolshie comitia elastin Glossic khamsin mycosis phasmid Rhaetic
amyloid booksie complin Eleatic glottis kidskin mycotic phoenix rhizoid
anaemia boracic conceit Elzevir glyphic kinchin myeloid phrenic rhombic
anaemic botanic conchie embolic glyptic kinesis myiasis pigskin rockoil
android botulin conduit embroil gnathic kinetic nauplii pigtail Romanic
aneroid boudoir conidia empiric gnostic kingpin navarin pilgrim rosehip
aneurin Brahmin conjoin emporia Gobelin kinship necktie pinguid salicin
angelic brassie contain enchain godetia Kirghiz negroid pintail sandpit
Angevin breakin coontie encomia godevil Koranic nemesia piperic sangria
anionic breccia corbeil endemic godship kremlin nemesis piratic saponin
annelid brickie corsair energid gomeril laconic neozoic pissoir sapphic
anoesis brownie coterie engrail gonidia ladykin nephric placoid sarcoid
anoetic bubonic couloir engrain grannie lambkin neritic plasmic satanic
anosmia bucolic council entasis graphic languid newlaid plasmid satiric
anosmic builtin couthie enteric gremlin lanolin nightie plasmin satyric
antacid bulimia cowslip entomic griffin latakia Nilotic plastic satyrid
antefix bumpkin crampit entotic griskin lawsuit ninepin plastid sauroid
aphasia bushtit crappie entrain groupie legbail Noachic plaudit scabrid
aphasic butyric cricoid enzymic Guelfic lentoid noctuid pliskie scaglia
aphelia Byronic crinoid epizoic gumboil Liassic nomadic plumbic scaldic
aphesis caloric croquis erepsin gunship ligroin nombril polemic scepsis
aphetic calorie crowdie ergodic gymslip limosis nonskid politic sceptic
aphonia cambric cryptic ericoid hairpin limpkin nonslip polynia scholia
aphonic canakin ctenoid eristic halfwit lithoid nonsuit postfix sciarid
aphotic canikin culprit erratic Hamitic lobelia nostril potamic sciatic
aplasia canonic curtail etaerio haploid lugsail notitia poussin Scorpio
apostil Canopic curtain etheric hardhit lunatic nucleic prairie Scottie
apraxia cantrip cycloid ethmoid harelip lupulin nuclein Prakrit scrapie
aquaria capelin cystoid eugenic headpin lychnis numeric prepaid sculpin
aquatic caproic dauphin eulogia Hebraic lyingin nunship prevail scurril
aquavit captain deafaid eutexia hedonic machair obconic priapic seamaid
Aramaic carotid declaim exclaim heparin mahonia obovoid prosaic seawhip
araneid carotin deficit exhibit hepatic malacia oceanic proteid sedilia
arcadia catsuit deictic exordia heretic malaria odontic protein seedlip
archaic caustic deistic explain hexadic malefic oghamic prussic seismic
arctoid centric delimit exploit hirudin manakin oilskin psychic selenic
Armoric cepheid Delphic exposit hoatzin mandril Olympic pteroic sematic
arsenic ceramic deltaic exurbia hobnail manikin omnific ptyalin Semitic
ascarid ceresin deltoid fanatic Homeric manumit oneiric pumpkin senarii
ascaris certain demerit fanmail Homerid marquis oolitic puparia senecio
ascesis cesspit demonic fantail hominid Masonic openair purloin sequoia
ascetic cestoid demotic faradic howbeit mastoid ophitic pursuit sericin
ascidia Chablis denarii fibroid hyaloid mattoid opsonic pyaemia sexfoil
ascitic chagrin deposit fibroin hydatid maudlin opsonin pyaemic shaslik
asepsis challis despair filaria hydroid Mechlin opuntia pygmoid sheltie
aseptic chamois despoil fimbria hymenia meconic oratrix pyloric sherris
Asiatic chaotic detrain finikin hypnoid meiosis orectic pyralid shilpit
askesis chappie deutzia flaccid hypoxia meiotic organic pyralis shindig
aspirin charlie dextrin fleapit hypoxic melanic osmosis pyramid shittim
astatic chassis dibasic floosie icteric melanin osmotic pyretic shortie
asteria cheerio dimeric floozie identic melodic ossific pyrexia showbiz
```

```
sialoid thiamin alforja areally capably dewfall formula headily lumpily
sibship throwin basenji armfuls capsule diabolo fossula heavily luridly
sigmoid thummim armlike armhole cariole dingily fourale heftily lustily
silesia thyroid autarky article castile dirtily foveola hemiola lyingly
silicic tiderip bazooka asphalt casuals disable foxhole herself mamilla
sinopia tinfoil bespoke assault catcall distill fragile hexapla manacle
sirloin titanic boxlike astable cattalo dizzily frailly himself mandala
skaldic toeclip britzka atingle cattily doucely frankly hirable mandola
skepsis toenail bunraku audible catwalk dowdily frazzle holdall mangily
skidlid tonemic catlike aurally cavally drabble freckle horsily mangold
skimmia tootsie colicky aureola cedilla draggle freckly hostile manhole
skysail topsail convoke aureole cellule dribble frenula humanly manilla
sleekit topsoil cowpoke auricle cembalo drizzle freshly humidly manille
sloegin tortrix cupcake awfully cenacle drizzly friable huskily maniple
smidgin totemic dashiki axially charily drycell friarly icecold Marsala
solaria tradein dislike bacilli cheaply drysalt fribble icefall maxilla
solatia traffic droshky baggily chiefly ducally frijole ideally maxwell
solicit transit eyelike balmily childly ductile frizzle ignoble maypole
somatic travail finicky banally chorale duopoly frizzly ignobly meatfly
somitic travois forsake barbell chortle dupable fugally inanely medulla
sonship trefoil garpike barbule chuckle durable funicle inaptly menfolk
sorosis trellis godlike barilla cineole durably funnily inbuilt merrily
sparoid trenail hoecake bascule cingula duskily furcula indwell messily
spastic triacid manlike battels citable dustily fusible indwelt micelle
spathic triadic mazurka bawdily civilly dwindle fussily ineptly miracle
sphenic trophic mislike beastly cleanly eagerly fustily inertly mirkily
spheric trypsin mistake bedroll clearly earhole fuzzily infield miscall
splenic tryptic mousaka beguile clerkly earthly gabelle inkwell miserly
spongin trysail netlike Bengali closely eatable gadwall inocula misrule
spunkie tumbril netsuke benzole coagula elderly gallfly insculp missile
sputnik turdoid nutlike bergylt cockily elfbolt gaudily install mistily
squalid turmoil oatcake bicycle codable emerald gauntly inutile mixedly
standin typhoid oilcake blackly compile emptily gawkily irately modally
stannic unchain ostraka blandly condole ennoble gazelle Ismaili moistly
starlit uncivil outtake blankly condyle entitle gelidly Israeli monocle
stearic upbraid pancake bleakly console epistle gemmule jadedly monthly
stearin upstair panicky blindly consult equable gentile jaywalk moodily
steekit uraemia paprika blowfly coracle equably gestalt jazzily morally
stencil utensil partake bluffly corella equally ghastly jerkily morello
steroid uveitis provoke bluntly cornily erectly ghostly jointly Moselle
sthenic valeric ratlike bonnily corolla exactly giddily juicily movable
stickit valonia rodlike boozily cortile example gimbals jurally muddily
strigil vanadic seppuku Boswell courtly exempla gingili kabbala murkily
styloid Vaudois squeaky bouilli cowbell eyeball globule keyhole mutable
styptic Veddoid streaky boxcalf crackle eyebolt gondola kinfolk mutably
subacid velaria teacake brabble crackly eyehole gorilla knobble muzzily
subedit venatic unlucky braille crankle fadedly goutfly knobbly nacelle
suberic venefic Vandyke bramble crassly faintly grabble knowall naively
suberin ventail warlike brambly crazily falbala gracile knuckle nakedly
subjoin vermeil ziganka bransle cribble falcula grackle labella namable
subsoil vervain abubble brantle crimple falsely gradely lamella nasally
sudaria villain acerola brashly cringle fancily grandly lankily nastily
sunsuit villein acicula brattle crinkle fanfold granule lapilli nattily
surfeit vitamin acridly bravely crinkly fatally grapple largely nautili
sustain vivaria acutely brickle criollo febrile gravely laurels netball
sweetie vivific addable bricole cripple ferrule greatly legally nightly
syconia vocalic addible briefly fertile fetidly greenly legible nippily
sycosis voltaic adeptly brindle crossly fetidly gribble legibly nitrile
sylphid volutin adultly briskly crudely fictile griddle legpull noctule
synesis wagtail affable bristle cruelly fierily gristle levelly nodally
synodic warship affably bristly crumble fifthly gristly licitly noisily
synovia wassail agilely brittle crumbly finagle grizzle lightly notable
syrphid waylaid airhole brittly crumple finally grizzly likable notably
tabanid weighin alertly broadly cubicle firefly grossly lithely notedly
tabetic weirdie alienly buffalo cuckold firstly gruffly livable novella
tabloid wherein aloofly buirdly cuittle fishily grumble loathly novelle
talaria whizkid alveoli bulkily curable fissile grumbly locally nutgall
tamarin woodpie amiable bummalo cureall fistula gruntle loftily oakgall
tanghin wooloil amiably bumpily cuticle fixable guayule loosely octuple
tantric worship ampoule buyable cymbalo fixedly gunwale losable oddball
teachin xanthic ampulla cabbala cypsela fleetly gustily lousily oilwell
technic xanthin angrily cagoule dariole fleshly gutsily lovable oneself
tectrix xiphoid anomaly calculi datable flexile hallali lovably opuscle
tendril zebroid anthill calicle dazedly fluidly handily loverly orderly
terrain zetetic apetaly calycle deathly flyable happily lowlily ossicle
tetanic zygosis aphylly candela debacle flybelt harmala loyally ostiole
thallic zygotic apishly cannily decuple flyhalf harshly lucidly ourself
therein zymosis apostle cannula default foggily hastily luckily outfall
thermic zymotic arcweld capable densely foliole hatable lughole outsell
```

outsold	regally	silicle	stubble	truffle	worldly	myeloma	angling	burning
outsole	remould	silkily	stubbly	trundle	wrangle	neuroma	anguine	busking
outtalk	reptile	sillily	stumble	tumidly	wrestle	newcome	aniline	bussing
overall	rescale	sixfold	suavely	tunable	wriggle	noisome	anodyne	buttend
overfly	respell	sixthly	subtile	tunably	wriggly	oldtime	antenna	buttons
overtly	respelt	sizable	sulkily	tunicle	wrinkle	onetime	appoint	buttony
panicle	restyle	sizably	swaddle	twaddle	wrinkly	apolune	armband	cabling
panoply	retable	skiable	sweetly	twaddly	wrongly	outcome	asinine	cabrank
pantile	reticle	skiffle	swiftly	twangle	wrybill	pastime	asquint	cacanny
papally	ridable	skittle	swindle	twibill	wychelm	penname	astound	caimans
papilla	rightly	slackly	swingle	twiddle	academe	perfume	attaint	calcine
parable	rigidly	slantly	swipple	twiddly	academy	phlegmy	audient	callant
patella	risible	sleekly	swizzle	twinkle	ackemma	phoneme	augment	calling
payable	rissole	slickly	systole	twinkly	adenoma	prelims	azurine	calumny
payroll	rockily	slimily	tacitly	twofold	alchemy	presume	backing	camping
peartly	ropable	smartly	tactile	Tynwald	alltime	proximo	bagging	candent
pedicle	rosella	smokily	tadpole	ukelele	anatomy	ragtime	balcony	canning
penally	roseola	smuggle	tamable	ukulele	angioma	reclame	balding	cantina
pennill	roughly	snaffle	tangelo	unaptly	anytime	rhizome	bambini	canting
pensile	roundly	snakily	tardily	unbuild	apogamy	sarcoma	bambino	canzone
peppill	rowdily	sniffle	tastily	unbuilt	awesome	sashimi	bandana	canzoni
peptalk	royally	sniggle	tattily	unfitly	bedtime	satsuma	banking	capping
percale	rubella	snoozle	taxable	ungodly	begrime	scotoma	banning	caprine
pergola	rubeola	snowily	tenable	unmanly	beldame	seriema	banteng	carbine
perkily	ruddily	snuffle	tenably	unshell	berhyme	septime	banting	carking
petiole	rundale	snuggle	tenfold	untruly	bigname	spireme	barline	carline
pettily	rurally	soapily	tensely	upfield	bigtime	squirmy	barring	carmine
phonily	rustily	soberly	tensile	urodele	centime	sublime	basting	carping
piccolo	saccule	soggily	tentfly	usually	chiasma	subsume	bathing	carving
piebald	sacculi	solidly	tenthly	utricle	condemn	succumb	batting	caserne
pillule	saintly	soluble	tepidly	utterly	contemn	sunlamp	beading	cassino
pinball	salable	soothly	tequila	vacuole	costume	supreme	bearing	casting
pinfold	sandfly	sootily	tersely	vagally	coulomb	supremo	beating	catling
pinhole	sanicle	soppily	testfly	vaguely	coxcomb	surname	bedding	catmint
pinnule	saucily	sorrily	testily	validly	curcuma	syngamy	beeline	cayenne
piously	savable	souffle	textile	valvula	customs	teatime	begging	caymans
pistole	saveall	soundly	thickly	valvule	daytime	thalami	beguine	ceiling
pitfall	sawbill	sparely	thimble	vanilla	deplume	thrummy	belting	cervine
pithily	sawmill	sparkle	thirdly	vapidly	digamma	trigamy	belying	chalone
plainly	sayable	spatula	thistle	variola	dilemma	trireme	benzene	chicane
planula	scabble	specula	thistly	variole	diorama	tsunami	benzine	Chicano
pliable	scantly	spicily	thyself	vascula	diploma	twosome	bepaint	choline
pliably	scapple	spicula	tidally	vehicle	disfame	twotime	berline	chopine
plumply	scapula	spicule	tightly	venally	dislimn	verismo	bethink	chorine
plumule	scopula	spikily	timbale	vesicle	dodgems	wargame	betting	citrine
plushly	scrawly	spindle	timidly	vexedly	drachma	wartime	bibbing	clamant
potable	scruple	spindly	tinnily	vexilla	economy	welcome	bidding	clement
pothole	scuffle	spinule	tipsily	vincula	empyema	winsome	billing	coaming
prattle	scumble	spittle	toehold	virgule	enframe	zoogamy	biltong	coating
prickle	scuttle	sporule	tombola	visible	epitome	zoonomy	binding	cocaine
prickly	seagull	sprawly	tombolo	visibly	eponymy	zootomy	biplane	codeine
primely	seakale	spurtle	tonally	vitally	exogamy	abalone	biriani	codling
primula	seawall	spyhole	topfull	vitelli	extreme	abeyant	bitting	cogging
privily	seawolf	squails	tophole	vividly	fibroma	abiding	blatant	collins
profile	sectile	squally	tortile	vixenly	foglamp	abscond	blueing	cologne
pronely	seeable	stabile	totally	vocable	fulsome	acetone	boating	combine
prosily	seedily	staddle	trample	vocally	goddamn	adamant	bobbing	command
proudly	sequela	stagily	treacle	voluble	gourami	adenine	boiling	commend
pteryla	serpula	stalely	treacly	volubly	grandma	adjoint	bologna	comment
puerile	servile	starkly	treadle	votable	inflame	affront	bookend	commons
pugmill	sessile	stately	trehala	vowelly	irksome	agelong	booking	commune
pustule	setwall	steeple	tremble	wadable	isogamy	aground	bopping	company
queenly	sextile	steeply	trembly	waxbill	isonomy	aiblins	bottony	compend
queerly	shackle	stemple	trestle	waybill	jimjams	ailment	bowline	compony
quibble	shadily	sterile	triable	wearily	kerygma	airline	bowling	concent
quickly	shakily	sternly	trickle	weevily	leucoma	alanine	bracing	condone
quietly	shamble	stickle	trindle	weirdly	lissome	aliment	brigand	confine
rabidly	shapely	stiffly	tringle	wergild	macrame	alimony	broking	coniine
radicle	sharply	stipple	tripoli	werwolf	macrami	alumina	bromine	conning
ragbolt	sheerly	stipule	tripple	wheedle	mahatma	amarant	brucine	consent
ragdoll	shingle	stonily	trouble	whiffle	maremma	amazing	buccina	contend
rapidly	shingly	stopple	truckle	whistle	Maytime	ambient	budding	content
ratable	shoofly	stoutly		whitely	melisma	amboina	bugbane	convene
ravioli	shortly			whittle	meseems	amboyna	bugging	convent
readily	showily			windily	misname	Amerind	bumming	cooking
rebuild	shrilly			wittily	mistime	ancient	bunting	coolant
rebuilt	shuffle			womanly	mugwump	anemone	buoyant	corking
recycle	shuttle			woozily				corvina
redpoll	sightly			wordily				corvine

```
costing droving fluting hatband jutting martini outdone priming robbing
cottony dubbing flybane hatting kampong matting outgone proband rocking
cowbane ducking flyting heading karting mattins outland probang rodding
cowhand ducting fobbing hearing keeping meaning outline profane rolling
cowling dunning fogbank heating kenning mediant outrank progeny romaunt
craving duodena fogging Hellene keyring meeting outwent prolong Rommany
credent earring folding helping kidding melting oxidant propane roofing
cremona easting fondant hemione killing mending oxytone propend rotting
crimine eccrine footing hemline kissing methane packing propine rousing
cubbing echidna fopling hemming knowing midland padding propone routine
cuisine elegant fordone henbane Krishna midline padrone protend rubbing
cunning element forfend heptane lacking migrant padroni prudent ruching
cupping elevens forging heroine lagging milking pageant pruning running
curling elfland forgone herring Lallans mincing panning pudding rutting
currant emetine formant hilding lambent minuend pargana pugging sacking
current eminent fortune hipbone lamming Miocene parpend pulvini sacring
curtana emplane forwent hipping landing misdone parting pungent sagging
cutline enchant fowling hircine lantana missend parvenu punning sailing
cutting endlong foxhunt histone lapping missent passant pupping salient
cyanine enplane fugging hitting lapwing missing passing pushing salpinx
cyclone enprint fulgent hogging larceny misting patient putting saltant
cystine entrant fulmine holding lasagna mobbing patting queuing salting
czarina entwine funning holland lasagne montane Pauline quinine sapient
dabbing enwound furlong hopbind lashing mooring payment quinone sapling
damming epatant furring hopping lasting mopping peasant radiant sapping
damning epergne gabbing hormone lathing moraine pebrine ragging sardine
dapsone epicene gadding horrent latrine mordant peccant railing sarking
darling epigene gagging hosanna lawhand mordent pegging raiment savanna
darning epigone gallant housing leading morning pelting ralline scalene
dashing epigoni galling howling leaning morwong pendant ramming scoring
dawning epigyny gardant hugging legging mousing pendent rampant scranny
daylong erelong garland hulking lemming mugging pending ramsons scrawny
deadend erlking garment humming lending muggins pennine ranking sealane
dealing erodent gasring hunting lenient mumming penning rapping sealant
decking essoyne gassing hurling leonine mundane pennant rasping seapink
decline etamine gatling husband letting munting pentane rations seatang
defiant etching gearing husking leucine muraena pepping ratling seating
delaine euglena geebung hutment licking mustang peptone ratting seeming
demesne euphony Gehenna hutting lilting muttony percent reading segment
demount evening gelding hyaline lindane nabbing percine reagent seizing
dentine evident gelling hydrant linsang nagging perpend reboant sequent
deodand examine gemming hygiene lipping napping perpent rebound serpent
deplane exigent genning icerink listing nascent persona recline servant
descant explant genuine ikebana loading neoteny Petrine recount serving
descend expound geogony imagine loaning Neptune petting redound sestina
descent exscind germane impaint lobbing nervine phalanx redwing setting
despond externe getting implant lodging nesting pharynx reeding Sextans
destine eyewink gigging impound logging netting pigging regnant sextant
destiny fagging gilding imprint logline neurine pigling regrant shading
deviant failing ginning incline longing neurone pigment reliant shaving
dewpond fairing ginseng infauna looking nipping pimping remains shebang
diamond falling glaring inferno lopping nirvana pinking remnant shoeing
dibbing fanning glazing ingoing lording nodding pinning remount shoring
dickens farcing glozing inkling lotting nogging pipping repaint showing
digging fargone glycine insigne lowland nooning piquant replant siamang
diluent farming godling instant lucarne norland piscina reprint sibling
dimming fascine godsend inswing lucerne nothing piscine rescind siemens
dinning fatling golfing interne lugging noumena pitpony resound sinning
dipping fatting gosling intrant lumbang nursing pitting respond sinsyne
disband feeding gradine intwine lurdane nutpine plafond rethink sipping
discant feeling grating ironing machine nutting platane retsina sirgang
disrank felting grazing isogeny madding oakling platina retting Sistine
dissent fencing Gstring isokont madonna obscene plating returns sithens
distant fenland guanine issuant madrona ocarina playing revving sitting
distend ferment guarana iterant madrono oddment podding rewound sixaine
distent fervent guarani jabbing mahjong odorant pompano rhatany Sixtine
dittany fibbing gubbins jamming mahound offhand popping ribband skating
dogbane figging gumming jarring mailing olefine porcine ribbing skyline
dogging figment gunning jasmine malting olivine portend ridding slating
doggone filling gushing jawbone manhunt ongoing portent ridging Slovene
dogvane finding gutting jetting mankind opaline posting rifling smoking
donning finning gypping jibbing manning openend potbank rigging soaking
Dorking fishing hacking jigging mapping opening potting rimming soaring
dormant fitment halting jobbing marconi operand pouting ringent sobbing
dotting fitting hamming jogging margent operant praline ringing solvent
doyenne flaming hanging joining marking opulent prebend ripieni someone
drawing flavine hapenny jotting marline oregano present ripieno sopping
driving fleeing happing jugging Marrano orogeny pretend ripping soprani
dromond Fleming harmony juggins marring orotund prevent roaring soprano
```

```
sorbent tribune whaling buffoon dogwood foretop kiloton outcrop rumshop
sordini trident whiting bugaboo donator forsook kingdom outdoor saffron
sordino tritone wigging bulldog dovecot fourgon knockon outflow saltbox
sotting tsarina wilding bullion downbow foxtrot knowhow outfoot sandbox
soutane tubbing willing burgeon dragoon freedom kolkhoz outgrow sandboy
spacing tugging winding caisson dryshod frescos krypton outlook sandlot
sparing tunning winning caldron dudgeon frisson lampion outshot sapajou
spirant turbine wishing callbox dukedom fronton lampoon ovation sapwood
spleeny turdine witling callboy dungeon fusspot languor overtop saveloy
squinny turgent witting caltrop dyewood gadroon lardoon pageboy scallop
staging turning wording camaron eardrop galipot lection paletot schnook
stamina tutting working camelot earldom galleon legator parados scissor
statant twoline writing camphor earshot galliot legiron paradox scollop
stibine twotone yapping campion echelon galloon legroom paragon seaboot
stipend tympana yardang camwood edition gearbox legshow parasol seafood
student tympani yenning capitol eductor gemsbok levator partook searoom
styrene tympano yipping caption eidolon genitor lexicon passion section
subbing tympany zapping cardoon ejector ghettos liaison patriot semilog
subtend tyranny zebrine caribou elation girasol linkboy patroon senator
sucking tzigane zincing carrion elector glutton livebox peascod serfdom
suiting tzigany zinking carryon elision goatgod logbook pension session
sultana ululant zipping cartoon elusion godhood logwood peridot settlor
summand unbound zoogeny catalos elution gorcrow longbow phaeton shadoof
summing uncanny zoogony cathood elytron gossoon longhop phantom shallop
summons undoing abaddon caution embosom grantor lorgnon pharaoh shallot
sunning undying abandon celadon embryon griffon lowbrow picador shallow
supping unfunny abettor cession emotion grottos lycopod pidgeon shampoo
surfing unguent ablator chanson emperor grunion mailbox pierrot shippon
suspend unjoint actinon chariot emption gryphon maillot pigiron shopboy
sylvine unmeant adaptor charpoy enactor grysbok maintop pillbox signior
tabbing unsound advisor cheroot enation gudgeon malison pillion silicon
tacking unthink aerator cheviot enderon guerdon mamelon pitprop similor
tagging untwine aerosol chevron endozoa Guignol manhood platoon sjambok
tailend untying aileron chiffon enteron gumboot manihot playboy skolion
tailing unwound airdrop chignon entozoa gumdrop manitou pledgor soapbox
talking upswing airflow Chinook envelop gumshoe mansion pleuron Solomon
Tammany uptrend airglow chorion envenom gunroom marabou plosion somehow
tamping uterine alation chrisom environ gunshot markhor plumbob soupcon
tangent vaccine alcohol clarion epizoon halcyon marplot plywood soursop
tanning vagrant aleuron coinbox epsilon halidom matador polygon sparrow
tapping valiant aliquot coition equator hangdog matelot polypod sponson
tarring variant andiron complot equinox hardtop megaron pontoon sponsor
tatting varment antilog control erector haricot megaton portion squalor
taurine varmint antlion copepod erosion harpoon melilot postbox stardom
taxiing vatting apricot copilot ethanol hautboy menthol postboy station
taxying veiling apropos corncob Euratom havenot mention pothook stemson
tearing veining attaboy corydon evasion hebenon metazoa potshot stentor
tedding verbena auction crampon evictor helicon metopon praetor stepson
teeming verdant auditor crannog exactor hellbox milksop precook stetson
tegmina versant aviator creator exciton hellion million predoom stewpot
telling versine backlog crimson excitor hencoop mirador proctor Stilton
tenpins vespine ballboy crouton eyebrow heritor misknow pronaoi stridor
termini vetting balloon crowtoe eyedrop hexagon mission pronaos stuccos
terpene vibrant bandbox cubhood eyeshot hexapod mistook puccoon suasion
terrene viewing barroom cullion eyespot highboy monitor pushrod subplot
terrine violent bassoon curacoa faction hilltop monocot questor suction
thymine violone bastion curator fashion hiproof monsoon raccoon sunroof
ticking vitrine bedroom cushion feedlot horizon moorlog rainbow sunspot
tiffany volcano bellboy Cypriot feoffor hotfoot mouflon Rajpoot surgeon
timpani vulpine bellhop czardom fermion hotshot mullion rampion swallow
timpano wadding benison dashpot festoon humidor munnion reactor symptom
tinning wagging benthos daybook fiction hyperon mylodon reallot taction
tipping waiting bibelot dayroom fiefdom icefloe neuston realtor Tagalog
tithing walking billion decagon filemot icefoot neutron redwood talayot
titling walling birddog decapod filmdom iceshow newsboy relator talipot
toluene wanting blesbok delator firebox ichabod nonagon reproof tallboy
tontine warning blossom demigod firedog incisor noniron reredos tampion
tooling warrant blouson destroy fission isochor nonstop retinol tandoor
topping warring boobook develop flattop isotron nucleon reunion taproom
torment washing borazon devisor fletton Italiot nunhood revivor taproot
tormina waxwing boredom dewdrop fleuron jackpot oakwood rhabdom tearoom
torrent wearing bourbon diadrom flexion janitor obligor ribston teashop
totting weasand bourdon diction flummox jargoon octagon roadhog telamon
touring webbing bowshot dilator fluxion jibboom octopod rollmop tension
towline wedding boxroom dilutor flyblow jibdoor omicron rolltop testoon
towmond wedging boxwood disavow flybook jogtrot oneshot rooftop thereof
towmont weekend boyhood disroot fogydom jukebox opinion rotator thereon
trading westing bridoon divisor footboy keelson oration rubicon tinamou
trepang wetting Brython dogtrot footrot killjoy organon ruction tomfool
```

tompion	schappe	camorra	devilry	foundry	jobbery	norward	puckery	skyward
tonerow	schlepp	cannery	diehard	fratery	joinery	nowhere	puffery	slavery
toolbox	scrappy	canonry	dietary	froward	keyword	nummary	purport	soilure
topknot	scrimpy	capture	dioptre	futhark	knavery	nunnery	purpura	sojourn
torchon	scrumpy	carport	diptera	futhorc	laggard	nursery	purpure	sorcery
torsion	stroppy	cascara	disbark	futhork	lambert	nurture	quavery	spectra
tosspot	syncope	catarrh	discard	gallery	lancers	oakfern	quinary	spectre
toyshop	therapy	catbird	discern	gasfire	laniary	obolary	quivery	spicery
tractor	tittupy	Cathari	discerp	gathers	lantern	obscure	ragworm	spidery
traitor	towrope	Cathars	discord	gaudery	lanyard	oilbird	ragwort	spindry
transom	triceps	cattery	dishorn	gauntry	lathery	olivary	rampart	stature
treason	triumph	cautery	dispark	gemmery	laundry	onshore	rapport	steward
treetop	turnipy	cavalry	dispart	gerbera	lawlord	oosperm	rapture	subvert
trollop	unhappy	caviare	disport	gesture	lechery	oospore	rattery	subzero
tsardom	unkempt	censure	distort	giantry	lectern	oratory	rectory	succory
tuckbox	upswept	century	disturb	gilbert	lecture	orchard	reentry	summary
tuition	acquire	cerebra	dithery	gingery	leeward	ossuary	reheard	summery
tylopod	actuary	chancre	dizzard	gittern	leghorn	ostiary	remarry	sunbird
typhoon	adjourn	chantry	doddard	gizzard	legwork	outport	require	sunburn
unbosom	affaire	chicory	doddery	godward	leisure	outturn	respire	sunward
unction	airfare	chimera	dodgery	goliard	leopard	outward	restart	support
upsilon	airport	chimere	dogcart	gramary	leotard	outwore	restore	surgery
upthrow	algebra	cholera	doggery	granary	letters	outwork	retiary	suspire
venison	aliform	ciliary	drapery	grapery	library	outworn	rettery	swinery
version	allegro	cindery	dripdry	gravure	littery	overarm	revelry	syncarp
viceroy	almonry	cistern	drosera	grocery	llanero	oviform	reynard	tanagra
visitor	alphorn	cithara	dullard	gruyere	lobworm	palmary	rhodora	tanbark
vitriol	althorn	cithern	dunbird	guipure	Lollard	palmyra	rhubarb	tankard
Walloon	amatory	cittern	Dunkirk	guisard	Lombard	pampero	ribwork	tannery
warison	amphora	clivers	earmark	gullery	lottery	pandora	ribwort	tantara
warrior	anymore	closure	eastern	gunfire	lowborn	pandore	ripcord	tanyard
warthog	archery	cloture	eelworm	gunnera	lubbard	pastern	rivalry	tartare
washpot	armoire	coffers	einkorn	gunnery	lugworm	pasture	riviera	tatters
webfoot	armoury	collard	electro	gurnard	macabre	pattern	riviere	tattery
whatnot	arrears	colours	elusory	hachure	Madeira	peccary	robbery	tempera
whereof	artwork	coloury	enquire	hackery	madwort	pedlary	rockery	tempura
whereon	athwart	comfort	enquiry	haggard	maestri	peppery	roguery	terebra
whitlow	austere	compare	ensnare	halberd	maestro	perdure	rondure	ternary
widgeon	awkward	compart	ensnarl	halbert	mallard	perform	rookery	tessera
windrow	baccara	compere	ephedra	halvers	mammary	perjure	rubbers	texture
Windsor	bandore	comport	epicarp	halyard	mandora	perjury	rubbery	theatre
witloof	bastard	conacre	epicure	Hamburg	manners	perturb	rupture	tilbury
wolfdog	battery	concern	equerry	Hansard	mansard	pervert	saguaro	tindery
workbox	bedsore	concert	erasure	hauberk	manward	pessary	saltern	tinhorn
yulelog	beggary	concord	esotery	hayfork	martyry	philtre	saltire	tinware
zillion	begorra	confirm	esquire	hayward	mascara	phratry	sanders	tipcart
apocope	berserk	conform	estuary	haywire	masonry	piastre	savoury	titlark
attempt	bibbery	conjure	exocarp	hectare	masters	picture	sawwort	toggery
bagpipe	bighorn	conkers	explore	helotry	mastery	piggery	saxhorn	tonsure
cacoepy	bigotry	consort	eyesore	hennery	mattery	pillory	scenery	topiary
catalpa	biliary	contort	factory	heronry	mawworm	pincers	sceptre	torture
concept	bindery	convert	facture	hetaera	mazzard	pinfire	seabird	tottery
corrupt	bistort	cookery	failure	hetaira	measure	pinworm	seagirt	tracery
cyclops	bittern	coppery	fanfare	hickory	memoirs	piscary	sealery	tricorn
decrypt	bitters	corpora	feature	history	mercery	pismire	seamark	triform
digraph	bizarre	costard	felonry	hoggery	mercury	placard	seaport	trinary
disrupt	blowdry	country	felwort	homburg	miliary	plectra	seaward	tripery
entropy	bobbery	couture	fenfire	honours	mimicry	plenary	seaware	Tsquare
epitaph	bollard	couvert	fernery	hosiery	misfire	plumery	sectary	tuatara
ethiops	bombard	cowbird	fetters	hunkers	mixture	pochard	seizure	turbary
excerpt	bonedry	cowherd	figwort	hymnary	mockery	podagra	senhora	turnery
forceps	bonfire	culture	filbert	iceberg	moidore	polacre	sensory	tushery
galumph	bonkers	culvert	firearm	imagery	monkery	pollard	servery	tussore
gestapo	bordure	cursory	fishery	impearl	montero	poniard	shastra	tutwork
gossipy	bravery	custard	fissure	implore	mowburn	popcorn	shikari	unaware
grandpa	bravura	cutlery	fixture	inboard	mudlark	postern	shivers	unguard
hiccupy	brewery	cutworm	flexure	indoors	mugwort	posture	shivery	unheard
isotope	bribery	dastard	flowery	inkhorn	multure	potherb	showery	unicorn
isotopy	bullary	dasyure	foghorn	inquire	mummery	pottery	signary	uniform
jaloppy	bulwark	daywork	foolery	inquiry	mustard	poulard	signora	unitary
miscopy	bursary	deanery	foppery	inshore	mystery	poultry	signore	unlearn
percept	bustard	deciare	forbore	inspire	nailery	powdery	signori	unsnarl
perhaps	buttery	declare	forearm	Irishry	nectary	preform	signory	unswore
periapt	buzzard	deepfry	forgery	jaggery	nervure	prepare	silvern	unsworn
precept	caesura	deiform	forlorn	January	network	primary	silvery	upstart
preempt	caldera	denture	forward	jaybird	newborn	primero	sincere	urethra
receipt	calibre	deodara	forworn	jewelry	niggard	procure	sintery	urinary
reshape	calvary	deplore	foulard	jitters	nippers	proverb	skyborn	vampire
satrapy	camelry	dessert	foumart	jittery	nocturn	prudery	skylark	vanward

```
vapours atavism coexist dryness finesse impasse manless photism saidest
vapoury atavist cognise dualise Finnish impresa mannish phrensy Saktism
vaquero atheism coldish dualism fitness impress mannose pianism saltish
velours atheist colossi dualist fittest imprest Marxism pianist sapless
venture athirst coltish duchess Flemish impulse Marxist Pictish sarcasm
venturi atomise combust dullish florist incense matrass pietism sawdust
verdure atomism compass dulness flutist inclose mawkish pietist sawfish
vespers atomist compose dumpish flypast incrust metrist piggish Scotism
vesture autopsy compost durmast fogyish indorse midmost pigwash Scotist
victory aweless Comtism earnest fogyism ingress Midwest pinfish seabass
viscera awnless Comtist ebonise foliose inhouse mightst pinkish seafish
vulture Baalism concise echoism foolish inphase miscast planish selfish
wafture babassu concuss eclipse foppish inquest missish plenish Senussi
waggery babyish confess ecstasy fuguist intense mobbish plumose sexless
warfare baddish confuse eggcosy fulness intrust mollusc poetess shyness
warlord badmash congest egotise furbish inverse molossi poetise Siamese
waxwork badness consist egotism furioso iridise monkish poloist sickish
waymark bagasse contest egotist furnish ironist Moorish poorish Sikhism
wayward Bahaism contuse elegise gabfest itacism morassy poseuse sinless
wayworn Bahaist coolish elegist gabnash itemise moreish possess sitfast
webworm baldish copyist elitism garfish jackass mortise precast Sivaism
welfare ballast Cornish elitist garnish Jainism mudfish precise slavish
western baptise cornist ellipse gasmask jewfish mumpish premise Slavism
winkers baptism cosmism Elohism Gaulish joyless myalism premiss slowish
wintery baptist cosmist Elohist gayness Judaise mythise pretest slyness
withers bassist Coueism embassy Genoese Judaism mythist previse softish
woomera beamish couldst empress geodesy Judaist napless process soloist
yardarm bearish cowfish emprise girlish judoist nearest profess sonless
yestern because coyness enchase glimpse jujitsu Naziism profuse soonish
yoghurt bedfast cuirass enclasp globose Kaddish nebbish promise sophism
zedoary bedpost cultism enclose glucose kentish necrose propose sophist
Zingari bequest cultist encrust gnomish kermess Negress protest sottish
Zingaro biblist cupmoss endless goatish keyless netfish protist soubise
zithern biggest curiosa endmost goddess kiddish newness proviso sourish
abolish biggish currish endorse godless knavish niceish provost Spanish
abomasa bigness cutlass endwise goodish koumiss nourish prowess spinose
abreast biomass cyclist English gooiest Kurdish nunnish prudish spryest
abscess blemish cypress engross goulash kyanise nutcase publish statism
abscise boarish czarism enthuse grecise lactose oarfish puckish statist
accurst bobbish czarist entrust Grecism laicise oarless puggish stylise
acerose bombast Dadaism entwist greyish laicism obelise pugnose stylish
acquest bookish Dadaist erotism grumose Lamaism obelisk purpose stylist
actress boorish dampish espouse gutless Lamaist obverse quamash subfusc
address bossism darkish euclase gymnast lambast oculist querist subsist
adipose British decease eupepsy hagfish largess odalisk raffish success
adverse bromism declass eustasy haggish largish oddness rawness sucrose
against brutish defrost evanish hapless lawless ogreish rayless suffuse
ageless bruxism degauss excurse harness lawlist oloroso realise suggest
aggress bugloss delouse exhaust harpist laxness onanism realism sundisc
agonise bullish dentist expanse harvest leftism oneness realist sunfish
agonist bulrush depress expense hashish leftist operose recluse sunless
aimless burgess dervish express hatless legless oppress reddest sunrise
airless Burmese despise expulse hawkish legrest Orphism reddish sunwise
airmiss burnish diabase eyelash heiress lentisk outcast redness suppose
airpost caboose dialyse eyeless hellish leprosy outlast redress surbase
amongst caddish diarise eyewash heroise Lettish outmost refresh surmise
amorist calypso diarist faddish heroism license outpost regress surpass
amylase cambist diffuse faddism hipness lidless outrush rehouse Swedish
amylose canvass digress faddist Hobbism lioness overuse relapse swinish
analyse carcase dimmest fairish Hobbist lionise oxidase release synapse
analyst carcass dimmish fantasm hogfish lipless oxidise remorse tachism
anatase Carlism dimness fantast hoggish longish ozonise repress tachist
anchusa Carlist diocese fantasy hogwash loudish pachisi reprise talcose
ancress carouse diorism farmost hostess loutish palmist repulse tallish
Anglist casuist discuss Faroese hotness lowness papoose request tannish
anguish catfish disease Fascism hottest lowrise pappose reverse tarbush
animism cellist diseuse Fascist hottish lumpish parvise reversi tarnish
animist charism disgust fatness hueless maddest paydesk rhymist tartish
anodise chemise dismast fattest huffish madness peckish roguish taxless
anywise chemism dismiss fattish Hunnish mafiosi peeress rubbish teacosy
appease chemist dispose faunist hymnist mafioso peevish rumness tearose
apprise cherish diverse fauvism iciness Mahdism pelisse runless teleost
aptness Chinese dockise fauvist idlesse Mahdist pentose ruttish tempest
arabise cineast dogfish feudist idolise maidish peptise Sabaism Thomism
Arabist circusy doggish fewness illness maidism percuss sacrist Thomist
armless cirrose dogrose feyness imagism malaise perfuse saddest tigress
armrest cleanse dollish fideism imagist maltase persist saddish tigrish
artless clerisy doltish fideist immense Maltese pertuse sadness Titoism
asperse codfish donnish filasse immerse maltose pettish sagesse Titoist
```

```
toeless Zoilism christy esparto ingrate novelty rickety ululate bowlful
topless Zoilist chupati eucrite insecty nullity ricotta uncouth boxhaul
topmast ability ciliate evolute instate obesity ridotto unearth brantub
topmost absinth citrate exarate isobath obovate riposte unfaith breakup
Toryism accrete clarity excrete isolate obviate risotto unicity brimful
tourism acetate clavate execute iterate octette roseate unquote brumous
tourist acidity climate exegete jacinth oculate rosette untruth brusque
townish acolyte cocotte expiate jadeite oilbath royalty uralite buildup
traipse aconite cognate exudate Janeite omneity ruinate utility builtup
tricksy actuate collate eyebath jollity oophyte russety vacuity bulbous
tropism Adamite commute faculty kainite opacity Sabaoth vallate bureaus
tsarism adulate compete fagotto Karaite operate Sabbath valuate bureaux
tsarist agility compote falcate keynote otolith saccate valvate burnous
tubbish agitate compute falsity khanate outvote sagitta variate cacique
tundish agitato confute fatuity kibbutz overate satiate variety cadmium
Turkish alunite connate felsite kyanite ovulate satiety varsity caesium
twoness amanita connote fermata labiate oxalate sawgate vastity calamus
tychism amenity coquito ferrate lactate oxidate scutate Vedanta calcium
unblest amnesty coranto ferrety lavolta palette secrete vedette callous
unclasp andante cordate ferrite layette palmate septate veloute cambium
unclose anility cordite fidgets lemmata palpate seriate velvety candour
uncross animate cornett fidgety leucite partita serrate vibrate canthus
undress annatta cornuto filiate liberty partite Servite vibrato caracul
unfussy annatto costate flaunty librate paucity seventh vidette careful
unhorse annuity cremate flighty lignite peltate seventy viduity carious
unhouse anxiety crenate foliate limbate penalty sfumato violate cartful
unleash apatite crinite formate lineate pennate Shemite virgate caseous
unloose aplenty crudity fouette liquate perlite sigmate vitiate catchup
unroost arcuate cruelty foveate listeth permute sinuate vittate Celsius
untruss aridity culotte frailty lomenta phonate situate volante centaur
untwist arietta cuneate frigate lorette picrate Sivaite vulgate centrum
upraise artiste cunette frowsty loyalty pileate society warpath charqui
uranism athlete cuprite furcate Luddite pimento solvate weighty checkup
useless attrite curette furmety lunette pinnate spicate whereto chibouk
utilise aureate curvate furmity lyddite pipette spirits zeolite chillum
utopism avidity cuspate gadgety machete placate squatty zincite chirrup
utopist axolotl cutrate gahnite magenta planxty statute acetous chymous
vaguish azimuth cuvette galeate maggoty plicate stealth acinous cirrous
vamoose azurite cyanite gallate magmata plumate stomata agamous clamour
vampish babbitt dacoity garotte magnate podesta straits alodium cleanup
vanessa baccate Debrett gavotte magneto polenta stretta alumnus closeup
varnish Bahaite deflate gazette majesty pollute stretto alyssum clypeus
verbose barbate density gemmate mammate poverty strewth amateur coconut
veriest batiste dentate genette mammoth pravity striate amentum colobus
villose bauxite deplete genista mandate predate stylite amorous combout
vinasse beneath despite gestate mannite prelate suavity angelus conatus
violist betroth deviate giblets marlite primate sublate annicut conflux
viscose bheesty dictate Goliath marmite private sulcate annulus contour
voguish biotite dignity gradate matzoth privity sunbath antique cookout
waggish biretta dinette granita mediate probate Sunnite anurous copious
wanness bismuth diorite granite memento probity syenite anxious coverup
wannish blewits dispute gravity migrate prolate sylvite apodous crackup
warmish blighty disrate greenth miniate promote taffeta applaud cranium
waspish bornite dogeate gummite misdate pronate tallith aqueous Croesus
wayless boxkite doughty guttate mismate prorate tannate arbutus cumulus
weakish boycott dozenth haporth Moabite puberty tektite arcanum cuprous
Wendish breadth duality hastate modesty pulsate tensity arduous cupsful
wetness brevity dubiety haughty modiste pycnite tenuity armsful curious
wettest bromate dynasty hibpath mofette quality tergite autobus cyathus
wettish brucite ebonite hirsute momenta quinate termite autocue danseur
wheyish bullate ebriate Hittite mozetta quixote ternate azygous decidua
whitish burette ebriety honesty mudbath rabbity testate Bahadur decorum
whorish cahoots edacity hoplite mulatto rackety thecate baleful defocus
whoseso calcite educate Hussite muriate radiate themata baneful defraud
wigless calotte effects hyalite musette ramenta thereto baroque detinue
wildish canasta egality hydrate myomata reality thirsty bashful devalue
witless cantata elevate imamate Nahuatl rebirth thorite bateaux devious
witness cantate emanate imbrute naivete reflate thrifty bathtub direful
wolfish carroty emeriti imitate naivety regatta throaty Bauhaus doleful
wolvish cassata emicate impaste narrate regrate titrate becloud doomful
wottest caudate emirate impasto naughty regrets toccata Benelux dortour
wouldst cavetti emulate impiety Negrito replete tomenta bezique douceur
wryness cavetto Encraty implete neolith require towpath bilious driedup
Yahvist celesta enemata inanity neonate respite tribute blowgun dropout
Yahwist celeste entente indepth nervate restate trilith blowout dubious
Yiddish chapati epidote infanta nictate reunite trinity bodeful duteous
Yorkist charity epilate infante nimiety rewrite turfite boletus dutiful
Zionism chelate eremite inflate nitrate rewrote turpeth bookful eardrum
Zionist Chianti erudite ingesta nitrite rickets twelfth boozeup earplug
```

```
easeful heedful nucleus reseaux tedious deprive mildewy unfroze cascara
echinus heinous oblique residua tenuous deserve narrows ———————— cassata
eclogue helpful obloquy residue terbium devolve newmown abomasa cassava
eelpout hideous obvious restful tetanus dissave overawe aboulia catalpa
eluvium hideout occiput retinue thallus elusive peafowl acantha catawba
Elysium hindgut ocellus revalue thorium emotive pillowy acequia cedilla
elytrum holibut ochrous revenue thulium enclave putdown acerola celesta
embolus holmium octopus rhamnus thyrsus engrave rubdown acicula cerebra
emulous hoodlum odorous rhenium timeous enslave rundown ackemma chalaza
enamour hopeful oestrum rhodium toilful erosive sallowy actinia chiasma
envious hugeous oestrus rhombus touchup evasive seafowl addenda chimera
ephebus humdrum oildrum riotous trayful exclave setdown adenoma cholera
erratum humerus omentum roomful triduum festive shadowy agrapha ciboria
exergue hurtful ominous rosebud trinkum fictive sitdown alameda cingula
fadeout hydrous omnibus rosecut trismus forgave sundown alfalfa cithara
fallguy icterus onerous rostrum tritium forgive tallowy alforja clarkia
fallout igneous onymous roundup trivium furtive teagown algebra coagula
famulus impetus opossum rubadub trochus helluva uncrown alluvia cochlea
fanclub impious optimum rubious tumulus improve unknown althaea comitia
farceur incubus organum ruinous tuneful incurve willowy alumina conidia
fateful ingenue osculum ruthful turnout innerve yellowy amanita copaiba
fatigue ingroup osseous sackbut typhous involve ataraxy amboina copaiva
fatuous iridium outhaul sackful uberous inweave betwixt amboyna cordoba
fearful ischium overbuy Salique uncinus jussive cachexy amentia corella
fermium isthmus overdue sanctum uranium khedive context ammonia corolla
ferrous jacobus overrun Sanctus uranous massive epitaxy amnesia corpora
fervour jealous pabulum santour vacuous misgave pickaxe amphora corrida
fibrous jejunum pailful sarcous various misgive poleaxe ampulla corvina
firebug karakul painful sardius vicious missive pretext anaemia cremona
fistful ketchup pallium saviour vidimus observe zootaxy anchusa curacoa
flaneur kingcup papyrus seablue villous outlive acronym angioma curcuma
flareup kneesup parlour seaslug viscous pahlavi antonym annatta curiosa
flatout labarum parlous sellout wailful passive anyways anosmia curtana
flavour ladanum pasteup senatus wakeful pensive apteryx antenna cypsela
floccus ladybug paviour serious walkout plosive benzoyl aphasia czarina
foldout leafbud peasoup shakeup wallrue receive buckeye aphelia decidua
forerun leprous Pegasus shotgun washout recurve cacodyl aphonia deepsea
forkful lifeful pelorus shutout washtub relieve catseye aplasia deodara
fraenum limbous perique silenus Whitsun relievo chlamys apraxia deutzia
Fraktur limulus petasus siliqua wickiup replevy cockeye aquaria digamma
frameup linctus petrous silique wingnut reprove deadeye arcadia dilemma
fretful lineout phallus sinuous wishful reserve dogdays arietta diorama
friseur linocut piceous sistrum wistful resolve endways ascidia diploma
frustum liqueur pinetum skellum without restive fisheye asteria diptera
fulcrum lithium pipeful skilful wolfcub revolve frogeye atresia drachma
fulgour locknut piragua skinful woodcut rilievo goodbye aurelia drosera
fullout lockout pirogue skyblue workout screeve homonym aureola duodena
fulvous loculus piteous smashup wornout scrieve metonym baccara echidna
fungous lookout pitiful smeddum writeup shrieve mooneye baklava emporia
furious lustful playful snarlup yttrium stative paronym bandana empyema
fuscous lustrum polypus solanum zealous suasive pinkeye banksia encomia
gainful luteous pomatum solidus zestful survive polynya barilla endozoa
gallium macaque pompous songful zoarium tantivy shuteye basidia enemata
gallnut malleus popadum sorghum absolve tensive sockeye bazooka entozoa
gaseous manhour premium soulful abusive tussive spondyl begonia ephedra
gateaux marybud pressup speedup achieve unitive synonym begorra erotica
gibbous mashtub pronoun spinous airwave unnerve toponym biennia euglena
giltcup masseur proteus spodium amative unweave typonym biretta eulogia
glamour maximum protium spumous amusive upheave Vaishya bohemia eutexia
gleeful mimulus pullout stadium anchovy zemstvo walleye bologna exempla
gluteus mindful pulpous standup approve beknown blintze bonanza exordia
goldbug minibus punchup sternum archive bellows bonanza bottega exotica
grampus minimum punctum stickup baklava billowy cadenza bravura exurbia
grownup minimus pushful stirrup beehive bradawl capsize breccia falbala
grumous mistful pylorus stratum behoove dorhawk chalaza britzka falcula
habitue mixedup quahaug stratus believe embrown chintzy bruhaha farruca
hackbut modicum quantum stuckup bereave fernowl emblaze buccina felucca
hafnium modulus Quechua subaqua bivalve furrowy guereza bulimia fermata
haircut muonium quietus sulphur captive gallows humbuzz cabbala fibroma
halibut nacrous rancour surplus cassava goshawk mansize cadenza filaria
hamulus needful raucous surtout centavo hoedown mestiza caesura fimbria
handful nervous readout tactful commove indrawn mestizo caldera fistula
handgun niobium refocus talcous concave ingrown organza camorra formula
handout nitrous regroup         connive letdown outsize canasta fossula
hangout niveous regulus tambour copaiva lichowl scherzi candela foveola
harbour nocuous reissue tankful costive lowdown scherzo cannula freesia
harmful nonplus relique tantrum cursive lychowl squeeze cantata frenula
hateful nostrum renegue tapetum deceive marrowy tanooze cantina fuchsia
hauteur noxious repique tearful deprave meadowy trapeze carioca furcula
```

```
galanga militia sagitta vexilla caloric Homeric pyrexic Amerind chopped
galatea minorca sambuca viatica cambric hypoxic pyritic amyloid choroid
ganglia minutia sangria vincula canonic icteric pyrrhic android chuffed
Gehenna momenta sarcoma viscera Canopic identic quadric aneroid chugged
genista morphia satsuma vivaria caproic idiotic quantic aniseed chummed
gerbera mousaka savanna woomera cardiac idyllic quartic annelid cichlid
godetia mozetta saxtuba ziganka caustic Islamic quintic antacid clammed
gondola muraena scaglia bathtub centric japonic racemic anyroad clapped
gonidia myalgia scapula brantub ceramic kenotic Rhaetic applaud clipped
gorilla mycelia scholia corncob champac keramic rhombic applied clogged
grandma myeloma scopula coulomb chaotic kinetic Romanic araneid clotted
grandpa myomata scotoma coxcomb chloric Koranic sapphic arcaded clubbed
granita naphtha sedilia disturb chromic laconic satanic arctoid clupeid
guarana nemesia senhora ewelamb chronic Liassic satiric arcweld coccoid
guereza Neogaea sequela fanclub classic lunatic satyric armband collard
gunnera neuroma sequoia mahaleb clastic malefic scaldic ascarid colloid
Haggada nirvana seriema mashtub Cluniac Masonic sceptic ashamed command
harmala notitia seringa minicab coeliac meconic sciatic assured commend
helluva noumena serpula pedicab colonic meiotic seismic astound compend
hemiola novella sestina perturb comedic melanic selenic averred concord
hetaera ocarina shastra plumbob cometic melodic sematic awkward contend
hetaira opuntia signora potherb cryptic mesonic Semitic barmaid copepod
hexapla organza silesia proverb deictic metopic shellac bastard cornfed
hidalga osmunda siliqua rhubarb deistic miasmic silicic bearded costard
hosanna ostraca sinopia rubadub Delphic mimetic skaldic becloud cowbird
hymenia ostraka skimmia succumb deltaic mitotic somatic belated cowhand
hypogea oversea solaria taxicab demonic mollusc somitic beloved cowherd
hypoxia palmyra solatia washtub demotic monadic spastic berried cowshed
ikebana panacea spatula wolfcub dibasic monodic spathic bestead crabbed
impresa pandora spectra abiotic dimeric moronic sphenic biassed cracked
indicia panocha specula acerbic docetic muntjac spheric bighead cragged
indusia papilla spicula acrylic drastic myalgic splenic bigoted crammed
inertia paprika spiraea actinic druidic mycotic stannic bilobed crested
infanta parerga stamina acyclic dynamic neozoic stearic bistred cribbed
infauna pargana stomata aerobic ectopic nephric sthenic blabbed cricoid
ingesta partita stretta agnatic edaphic neritic styptic blasted crinoid
inocula patagia subaqua alembic eidetic Nilotic suberic blessed crooked
ipomoea patella succuba alginic eirenic Noachic subfusc bloated cropped
jellaba peloria sudaria allelic ekistic nomadic sundisc blooded crowned
kabbala pergola sultana almanac elastic nucleic synodic blotted crusted
Kannada persona syconia aloetic Eleatic numeric tabetic blowzed ctenoid
kerygma petunia synovia Amharic elegiac obconic tantric blurred cubhood
Krishna piragua syringa amnesic embolic oceanic technic bobsled cuckold
labella piranha taffeta amoebic empiric odontic tetanic bollard cudweed
lamella piscina talaria anaemic endemic oghamic thallic bombard custard
lantana planula tamasha angelic enteric Olympic theriac bookend cycloid
lasagna platina tanagra anionic entomic omnific thermic bottled cystoid
latakia plectra tantara anoetic entotic oneiric titanic bowhead dastard
lavolta podagra tapioca anosmic enzymic oolitic tonemic boxwood deadend
lemmata podesta tegmina aphasic epizoic ophitic totemic boyhood deafaid
leucoma polacca tempera aphetic ergodic opsonic traffic bragged decapod
lobelia polenta tempura aphonic eristic orectic triadic breaded decided
lomenta polynia tequila aphotic erratic organic trophic brigand defraud
Madeira polynya terebra aquatic etheric osmotic tryptic brimmed deltoid
madonna primula tessera Aramaic eugenic ossific valeric brinded demigod
madrona pteryla themata archaic fanatic pacific vanadic bugeyed demoded
magenta puparia toccata Armoric faradic paeonic venatic builded deodand
magmata purpura tombola arsenic fluidic paretic venefic burweed descend
mahatma pyaemia tomenta ascetic frantic parodic vivific bustard despond
mahonia pyrexia tormina ascitic futhorc pelagic vocalic buttend devoted
malacia pyxidia trachea aseptic galenic peloric voltaic buzzard dewpond
malaria quassia trehala Asiatic gametic phallic xanthic campbed dialled
mamilla Quechua tsarina astatic gastric phrenic yolksac camwood diamond
mandala ramenta tuatara auxetic generic piperic zetetic candied diehard
mandola ratafia tympana Avestic genetic piratic zygotic carload dilated
mandora regalia uraemia avionic georgic plasmic zymotic carotid diploid
manilla regatta urethra bacchic Glossic plastic abashed castled disband
Maratha replica Vaishya baldric glyphic plumbic Abbasid catbird discard
maremma residua valonia barytic glyptic polemic abetted cathead discoid
marimba retsina valvula benefic gnathic politic abscond cathood discord
Marsala rhodora vanessa benthic gnostic potamic abutted centred distend
mascara ricksha vanilla benzoic graphic priapic accused cepheid dizzard
mastaba ricotta variola bivouac Guelfic prosaic adenoid cestoid doddard
maxilla riviera vascula boracic Hamitic prussic advised chapped dogwood
mazurka rosella Vedanta botanic Hebraic psychic afeared charred dragged
medulla roseola velaria bubonic hedonic pteroic affined chatted dratted
melisma rotunda veranda bucolic hepatic pyaemic aground chested dreamed
mestiza rubella verbena butyric heretic pyloric alleged chiliad dripped
metazoa rubeola verruca Byronic hexadic pyretic allseed chipped dromond
```

```
dropped  grained  linseed  payload  retread  smutted  towered  abridge  approve
drubbed  grandad  lipread  pearled  rewound  snagged  towhead  abscise  arabise
drugged  grilled  lithoid  peascod  reynard  snapped  towmond  absence  archive
drummed  grinned  logwood  percoid  rhizoid  snipped  trapped  absolve  arcuate
dryeyed  gripped  Lollard  perpend  ribband  snouted  trekked  abubble  areolae
dryshod  gritted  Lombard  phasmid  ripcord  snubbed  tressed  abusive  aristae
duelled  grubbed  louvred  pickled  rivered  sofabed  triacid  academe  armhole
dullard  guarded  lowbred  piebald  roadbed  soliped  trimmed  accidie  armlike
dunbird  guisard  lowland  pieeyed  rosebud  sozzled  tripped  accrete  armoire
dyewood  gurnard  lubbard  piglead  rosered  spanned  trotted  acerose  arrange
egghead  gwyniad  lycopod  pigweed  rounded  sparoid  turdoid  acetate  article
elfland  haggard  lymphad  pinfold  sainted  sparred  twigged  acetone  artiste
embowed  hagweed  lyrated  pinguid  Samoyed  spatted  twilled  achieve  ascribe
emerald  halberd  mahound  pinhead  sandbed  spitted  twinned  acolyte  asinine
emersed  halyard  mallard  pitched  saphead  spotted  twitted  aconite  askance
emitted  Hansard  mangold  pithead  sapwood  spurred  twofold  acquire  asperse
energid  haploid  manhood  placard  sarcoid  squalid  tylopod  acreage  assuage
enfiled  hatband  mankind  placoid  satyrid  stabbed  Tynwald  actuate  astable
engaged  haunted  mansard  plafond  sauroid  stalked  typhoid  Adamite  astride
enwound  hayseed  manward  plaided  scabbed  starred  ulcered  addable  athlete
ericoid  hayward  marbled  planned  scabrid  statued  unarmed  addible  atingle
ermined  hearted  married  plasmid  scanned  stemmed  unasked  adenine  atomise
ethmoid  hexapod  marybud  plastid  scarfed  stepped  unbated  adipose  attache
excited  hocused  mastoid  platted  scarred  sterned  unbound  adjudge  attrite
exposed  hogweed  mattoid  pleased  scatted  steroid  unbowed  adulate  audible
expound  holland  mayweed  plodded  scented  stetted  unboxed  advance  aureate
exscind  Homerid  mazzard  plopped  sciarid  steward  unbuild  adverse  aureole
faceted  hominid  mermaid  plotted  screwed  stilted  unguard  affable  auricle
fanfold  honeyed  mettled  plugged  scudded  stipend  unheard  affaire  aurorae
fathead  hopbind  midland  plywood  scummed  stirred  unhoped  agitate  auspice
fenland  hophead  minuend  pochard  seabird  stopped  unlined  agonise  austere
fibroid  hornmad  misdeed  pofaced  seafood  storied  unmixed  agraffe  autocue
figured  hothead  mislaid  pointed  seamaid  striped  unmoved  airfare  avarice
flaccid  hundred  mislead  pollard  seaward  stubbed  unpaged  airhole  average
flagged  hurried  misread  polypod  seaweed  studded  unsaved  airline  awesome
flapped  husband  missend  poniard  seedbed  studied  unsexed  airwave  axillae
fleeced  hyaloid  moneyed  popeyed  selffed  stummed  unsound  ajutage  azurine
fleshed  hydatid  mottled  poppied  semiped  stunned  untried  alanine  azurite
flipped  hydroid  muscled  portend  serried  stunted  untuned  alcaide  baccate
flitted  hypnoid  mustard  pothead  shammed  styloid  unwound  alcalde  bagasse
flogged  icecold  myeloid  pouched  shanked  subacid  upbraid  alcayde  baggage
flopped  ichabod  negroid  poulard  shelled  subdued  upfield  alewife  bagpipe
flubbed  illbred  newlaid  prebend  shelved  subhead  uptrend  alidade  Bahaite
focused  implead  niggard  prepaid  shinned  subtend  vanward  allonge  balance
footpad  impound  noctuid  pretend  shinpad  succeed  vaulted  alltime  ballade
forfend  inboard  nodated  primmed  shipped  summand  Veddoid  alumnae  bandage
forward  inbreed  nonskid  proband  shogged  sunbird  visaged  alunite  bandore
foulard  incised  norland  proceed  shopped  sunward  visored  amative  banshee
fracted  incused  norward  prodded  shunned  suspend  vistaed  ambsace  baptise
frapped  infield  notched  pronged  sialoid  sutured  volumed  amiable  barbate
freaked  insipid  notepad  propend  sickbed  swabbed  voluted  amoebae  barbule
fretted  instead  nunhood  propped  sighted  swagged  waisted  ampoule  barline
fritted  insured  oakwood  proteid  sigmoid  swanned  warhead  amputee  baroque
frogged  invalid  oarweed  protend  sixfold  swapped  warlord  amusive  barrage
fronded  jaybird  obovoid  pushrod  skidded  swarded  watered  amylase  bascule
frosted  jellied  octopod  pygmoid  skidlid  swatted  wattled  amylose  batiste
froward  katydid  odoured  pyralid  skilled  swigged  waylaid  anagoge  bauxite
fructed  keyword  oersted  pyramid  skimmed  swobbed  wayward  analyse  because
fruited  kindred  offhand  quipped  skinned  swopped  weasand  anatase  bedside
fuelled  knapped  offload  quitted  skipped  swotted  weekend  andante  bedsore
fungoid  knitted  oilbird  quizzed  skirted  sylphid  wergild  anemone  bedtime
Galahad  knobbed  oilseed  ragweed  skyward  syrphid  wheeled  anglice  beehive
garland  knotted  omitted  ravined  slabbed  tabanid  whetted  anguine  beeline
gizzard  knurled  oneeyed  rebound  slagged  tabloid  whipped  aniline  begrime
gladded  laggard  openend  rebuild  slammed  tailend  whirred  animate  beguile
glenoid  languid  operand  redhead  slapped  taloned  whizkid  anodise  beguine
globoid  lanyard  orchard  redound  slatted  tankard  whizzed  anodyne  behoove
glutted  lawhand  orotund  redwood  sledded  tanyard  whorled  antique  beldame
gnarled  lawlord  osteoid  refined  sleeved  tenfold  widowed  anymore  believe
goahead  layered  outland  reheard  slipped  tentbed  wizened  anytime  Beltane
goatgod  leafbud  outsold  related  slogged  testbed  woolled  anywise  benzene
godhead  learned  outward  relayed  slopped  thinned  worsted  apagoge  benzine
godhood  leeward  overbid  remould  sloshed  thorned  wrapped  apanage  benzole
godsend  lentoid  overdid  removed  slotted  throned  xiphoid  apatite  bereave
godward  leopard  overfed  reputed  slubbed  thudded  ycleped  apocope  berhyme
goitred  leotard  oxyacid  rescind  slugged  thyroid  zebroid  apolune  berline
goliard  lieabed  palsied  resound  slummed  toehold  zincked  apostle  besiege
gorsedd  lighted  parotid  respond  slurred  toothed  zonated  appease  bespoke
grabbed  limited  parpend  retired  smaragd  touched  abalone  apprise  bezique
```

bheetie	capsule	cologne	cripple	dilutee	enforce	fanfare	furcate	hectare
bicycle	captive	combine	cristae	dinette	enframe	fargone	furnace	Hellene
bigname	capture	commode	crowdie	diocese	engorge	Faroese	furtive	hemione
bigtime	capuche	commove	crowtoe	dioptre	engrave	fascine	fusible	hemline
biotite	carbide	commune	crumble	diorite	enhance	fatigue	gabelle	henbane
biplane	carbine	commute	crumple	dioxide	enlarge	feature	gahnite	henwife
bivalve	carcase	compare	crusade	disable	ennoble	febrile	galeate	heptane
bizarre	carinae	compere	cubicle	disease	enounce	fedayee	galilee	herbage
blintze	cariole	compete	cuisine	diseuse	enplane	felsite	gallate	herniae
bobeche	carline	compile	cuittle	disfame	enquire	fenfire	gallice	heroine
bolshie	carmine	compose	culotte	dislike	enslave	feoffee	gambade	heroise
bondage	carnage	compote	culture	dispose	ensnare	ferrate	gamboge	hipbone
bonfire	caroche	compute	cuneate	dispute	entente	ferrite	garbage	hirable
booksie	carouse	comrade	cunette	disrate	enthuse	ferrule	garotte	hircine
bordure	cartage	conacre	cupcake	disrobe	entitle	fertile	garpike	hirsute
bornite	cascade	concave	cuprite	dissave	entwine	festive	gasfire	histone
boscage	caserne	concede	curable	diverge	epergne	fiancee	gavotte	Hittite
boskage	castile	conchae	curette	diverse	epicede	fibulae	gazelle	hoecake
bouchee	catenae	conchie	cursive	divorce	epicene	fictile	gazette	hoplite
bourree	cathode	concise	curvate	divulge	epicure	fictive	gemmate	hormone
bowline	catlike	condole	cuspate	dockage	epidote	figtree	gemmule	hospice
boxkite	catseye	condone	cuticle	dockise	epigene	filasse	genette	hostage
boxlike	caudate	conduce	cutline	dogbane	epigone	filiate	Genoese	hostile
brabble	caviare	condyle	cutrate	dogeate	epilate	finagle	gentile	Hussite
braille	cayenne	confide	cuvette	doggone	episode	finance	genuine	hyaline
bramble	celeste	confine	cyanide	dogrose	epistle	finesse	Geordie	hyalite
bransle	cellule	confuse	cyanine	dogvane	epitome	firtree	germane	hydrate
brantle	cenacle	confute	cyanite	dominie	epoxide	fisheye	gestate	hydride
brassie	censure	coniine	cyclone	dormice	equable	fissile	gesture	hygiene
brattle	centime	conjure	cystine	dovekie	erasure	fissure	ghillie	icefloe
breathe	cervine	connate	dapsone	doyenne	eremite	fixable	giraffe	idlesse
brewage	cestode	connive	dariole	drabble	erosive	fixture	glimpse	idolise
brickie	Chaldee	connote	dasyure	draftee	erudite	flavine	globose	ignoble
brickle	chalice	console	datable	draggle	escapee	flexile	globule	imagine
bricole	chalone	consume	daytime	drayage	escribe	flexure	glucose	imamate
brigade	chancre	contuse	deadeye	dribble	espouse	floosie	glycine	imbrute
brindle	chappie	convene	debacle	drizzle	esquire	floozie	godlike	imitate
brioche	charade	convoke	decease	dualise	essence	flotage	goodbye	immense
bristle	charlie	coontie	deceive	ductile	essoyne	flounce	gouache	immerge
brittle	chelate	coppice	deciare	dunnage	estrade	flowage	grabble	immerse
brocade	chemise	coracle	declare	dupable	etamine	fluence	gracile	impasse
brokage	chicane	cordage	decline	durable	euclase	flyable	grackle	impaste
bromate	chimere	cordate	decuple	durance	eucrite	flybane	gradate	impinge
bromide	Chinese	cordite	defence	dwindle	evacuee	foggage	gradine	implete
bromine	chocice	corkage	deflate	earache	evasive	foliage	grandee	implode
brownie	choline	cornage	deforce	earhole	evolute	foliate	granite	implore
brucine	chopine	cornice	degrade	earlobe	examine	foliole	grannie	improve
brucite	chorale	coronae	dehisce	eatable	example	foliose	grantee	impulse
brusque	chorine	corrode	deicide	ebbtide	exarate	footage	granule	incense
buckeye	chortle	corsage	delaine	ebonise	exclave	footsie	grapple	incline
bugbane	chuckle	cortege	delouse	ebonite	exclude	forbade	gravure	inclose
bullace	ciliate	cortile	demesne	ebriate	excrete	forbode	grecise	include
bullate	cineole	corvine	dentate	eccrine	excurse	forbore	grenade	incurve
buoyage	cirrose	costate	dentine	eclipse	execute	fordone	gribble	indorse
burette	citable	costive	denture	eclogue	exedrae	foresee	griddle	indulge
burgage	citrate	costume	deplane	edifice	exegete	forgave	grimace	infante
Burmese	citrine	coterie	deplete	educate	exergue	forgive	gristle	inflame
buyable	cladode	cottage	deplore	effulge	expanse	forgone	grizzle	inflate
cabbage	clavate	courage	deplume	egotise	expense	formate	groupie	infulae
caboose	cleanse	couthie	deprave	elegise	expiate	forsake	grumble	ingenue
cacique	climate	couture	deprive	elevate	explode	fortune	grumose	ingrate
caddice	clippie	couvade	derange	ellipse	explore	fouette	gruntle	inhouse
cadence	cloacae	cowbane	deserve	elusive	expulse	fourale	gruyere	innerve
cagoule	closure	cowhage	despise	emanate	expunge	foveate	guanine	inphase
calcine	cloture	cowhide	despite	emblaze	externe	foxhole	guardee	inquire
calcite	cocaine	cowpoke	destine	embrace	extreme	fragile	guayule	inshore
calibre	cockade	crackle	deterge	emetine	extrude	frazzle	guipure	insigne
caliche	cockeye	cranage	detinue	emicate	exudate	freckle	gummite	inspire
calicle	cocotte	crankle	detrude	emirate	exuviae	freebie	gumshoe	instate
calipee	codable	crappie	devalue	emotive	eyehole	friable	gunfire	intense
calorie	codeine	cremate	deviate	emplace	eyelike	fribble	gunwale	interne
calotte	cognate	crenate	devisee	emplane	eyesore	frigate	guttate	intrude
calycle	cognise	crevice	devolve	emprise	Faberge	frijole	habitue	intwine
cantate	coinage	cribble	devotee	emulate	facture	frizzle	hachure	inutile
canzone	collage	crimine	diabase	enchase	faculae	frogeye	hapence	inverse
capable	collate	crimple	dialyse	enclave	faience	fullage	hastate	invitee
caprice	college	cringle	diarise	enclose	failure	fulmine	hatable	invoice
caprine	collide	crinite	dictate	endorse	Falange	fulsome	haulage	involve
capsize	collude	crinkle	diffuse	endwise	falcate	funicle	haywire	inweave

```
iridise macabre multure outline perigee probate respire seablue speckle
irksome macaque mundane outlive perique procure respite seakale spectre
isolate machete muriate outpace perjure produce restate sealane spicate
isotope machine musette outrage perlite profane restive seaside spicule
itemise macrame mutable outride permute profile restore seaware spindle
iterate maculae mythise outrode pertuse profuse restyle seawife spinode
jadeite magnate nacelle outside pervade prolate resurge seclude spinose
Janeite malaise naivete outsize petiole promise retable seconde spinule
jasmine maltase namable outsole Petrine promote reticle secrete spireme
jawbone Maltese narrate outtake philtre pronate retinae sectile spittle
joyance maltose nebulae outvote phonate propane retinue seeable splodge
joyride mammate necktie outwore phoneme propine retrace seepage splurge
jubilee manacle necrose overage piastre propone reunite seizure spondee
Judaise manatee neglige overate pickaxe propose revalue selvage sporule
jussive mandate neonate overawe picotee prorate revenge septate springe
justice manhole Neptune overdue picrate protege revenue septime spunkie
kainite manille nervate overlie picture provide reverie serfage spurtle
Karaite maniple nervine oversee pileate provoke reverse seriate spyhole
kathode manlike nervure overuse pillage puerile revolve serrate squamae
keyhole manmade netlike ovicide pillule puggree rewrite service squeeze
keynote mannite netsuke ovulate pinfire pugnose rewrote servile stabile
khanate mannose neurine oxalate pinhole pulsate rhizome Servite staddle
khedive mansize neurone oxfence pinkeye purpose ridable sessile staithe
knobble marline newcome oxidase pinnace purpure riposte sextile startle
knuckle marlite nictate oxidate pinnate pustule riptide shackle statice
kyanise marmite nightie oxidise pinnule pycnite risible shamble stative
kyanite marquee nitrate oxytone pipette quayage rissole sheathe stature
labiate massage nitride ozonise pirogue quibble riviere sheltie statute
lactate massive nitrile package piscine quickie rodlike Shemite steeple
lactose matinee nitrite packice pismire quinate romance shingle stemple
lacunae maypole noctule padrone pistole quinine rondure shortie sterile
laicise Maytime noisome palette placate quinone rootage shrieve stibine
lairage measure nominee palmate platane quixote ropable shuffle stickle
laminae mediate notable palpate pledgee radiate roseate shuteye stipple
lasagne medusae novelle panache pleurae radicle rosette shuttle stipule
latrine melange nowhere pancake pliable radulae roulade Siamese stopple
lattice message nuclide pandore plicate ragtime routine sigmate storage
layette methane nurture panicle pliskie ralline ruinate signore stowage
leafage micelle nutcase pannage plosive rampage rummage silence strange
leakage microbe nutlike pantile plumage raphide rundale silicle striate
lecture midline nutpine papoose plumate rapture rupture silique strophe
legatee midwife oaktree pappose plumose ratable saccade sincere strumae
legible migrate oatcake papulae plumule ratline saccate sinkage stubble
leisure mileage obelise parable plusage rawhide saccule sinsyne stumble
leonine miniate obligee parolee poetise realise salable sinuate stylise
lettuce mintage oblique partake polacre receive Salique Sistine stylite
leucine Miocene obovate partite poleaxe reclame saltire situate styrene
leucite miracle obscene parvise pollute recline salvage Sivaite suasive
librate misdate obscure passade pondage recluse sanicle sixaine sublate
licence misdone observe passage pontage recurve saprobe skiable sublime
license misfire obtrude passive porcine recycle sarcode sizable subside
lignite misgave obverse pastime portage referee sardine skiable subsume
likable misgive obviate pasture poseuse reflate satiate skiffle subtile
limbate mislike occlude Pauline postage refugee sausage skittle succade
lindane mismate octette payable posture regorge savable skyblue sucrose
lineage misname octuple paysage potable regrate sawgate skyline suffice
lineate misrule oculate pebrine potence rehouse sayable Slovene suffuse
linkage missile offence pedicle pothole reissue scabble smuggle suicide
lionise missive offside peerage pottage rejoice scalade snaffle sulcate
liquate mistake oilcake pelisse prairie relapse scalene sniffle sullage
lissome mistime oldtime peltate praline release scapple sniggle Sunnite
livable mixture olefine penance prattle relieve sceptre snoozle sunrise
lockage Moabite olivine penname precede relique schappe snuffle sunwise
logline modiste onetime pennate precise remorse science snuggle suppose
looksee mofette onshore pennine predate renegue scoriae soakage supreme
lorette moidore onstage pensile preface repique scotice soccage surbase
loricae monocle oophyte pensive prelate replace Scottie sockeye surface
losable montage oospore pentane prelude replete scourge soignee surmise
lovable montane opaline pentode premise reprise scrapie soilure surname
lowrise mooneye operate pentose prepare reprove screeve soluble survive
lozenge moorage operose peonage presage reptile scrieve solvate suspire
lucarne moraine opuscle peptide preside repulse scrooge someone swaddle
lucerne mortice orifice peptise presume require scrouge sonance sweetie
Luddite mortise ossicle percale previse requite scruple soubise swindle
luggage morulae ostiole percine primage rescale scuffle souffle swingle
lughole Moselle outcome percine primate reserve scumble soutane swipple
lunette Mountie outdone perdure primate reshape scutage spangle swizzle
lurdane mousmee outface perfume prithee residue scutate sparkle syenite
lyddite movable outgone perfuse private resolve scuttle spattee sylvine
```

```
sylvite  tribune  vendace  debrief  bobbing  fagging  halting  lobbing  plating
synapse  tribute  ventage  distaff  boiling  failing  Hamburg  lodging  playing
syncope  trickle  venture  earmuff  booking  fairing  hamming  logging  podding
syringe  trindle  verbose  enfeoff  bootleg  falling  handbag  longing  popping
systole  tringle  verdure  faceoff  bopping  fanning  hangdog  looking  postbag
tactile  tripple  versine  falloff  bowling  farcing  hanging  lopping  posting
tadpole  trireme  vesicae  figleaf  bracing  farming  happing  lording  potting
taeniae  tritone  vesicle  flyhalf  broking  fatling  hatting  lotting  pouting
talcose  trochee  vespine  flyleaf  budding  fatting  heading  lugging  priming
tallage  trouble  vestige  handoff  bugging  feeding  hearing  lumbang  probang
tamable  trounce  vesture  herself  bulldog  feeling  heating  madding  prolong
tankage  truckle  vibrate  himself  bumming  felting  helping  mahjong  pruning
tannage  truffle  vidette  hiproof  bunting  fencing  hemming  mailbag  pudding
tannate  trundle  village  jumpoff  burning  fibbing  herring  mailing  pugging
tanooze  trustee  villose  kickoff  busking  figging  hilding  malting  punning
tartare  Tsquare  vinasse  leadoff  bussing  filibeg  hipping  manning  pupping
Tartufe  tunable  vintage  liftoff  cabling  filling  hitting  mapping  pushing
taurine  tunicle  violate  mastiff  calling  finding  hogging  marking  putting
taxable  turbine  violone  midriff  camping  finning  holding  marring  quahaug
taxfree  turdine  virgate  oneself  canning  firebug  homburg  matting  queuing
teacake  turfite  virgule  ourself  canting  firedog  hopping  meaning  ragging
tearose  tussive  viscose  playoff  capping  fishing  housing  meeting  railing
teatime  tussore  visible  pontiff  carking  fitting  howling  melting  ramming
teenage  twaddle  vitiate  rakeoff  carping  flaming  hugging  mending  ranking
tektite  twangle  vitrine  reproof  carving  fleabag  hulking  milking  rapping
tenable  twiddle  vittate  restiff  casting  fleeing  humming  milkleg  rasping
tensile  twinkle  vocable  sawnoff  catling  Fleming  hunting  mincing  ratling
tensive  twoline  voivode  seawolf  ceiling  fluting  hurling  missing  ratting
tergite  twosome  volante  sendoff  chinwag  flyting  husking  misting  reading
termite  twotime  voltage  shadoof  coaming  fobbing  hutting  mobbing  redwing
ternate  twotone  voluble  shereef  coating  fogging  iceberg  mooring  reeding
terpene  tzigane  votable  sheriff  codling  folding  ingoing  moorlog  retting
terrace  ukelele  vouchee  showoff  cogging  footing  inkling  mopping  revving
terrene  ukulele  vulgate  spinoff  conning  fopling  inswing  morning  ribbing
terrine  ululate  vulpine  stopoff  cooking  foreleg  ironing  morwong  ridding
testate  umbrage  vulture  sunroof  corking  forging  jabbing  mosshag  ridging
tetrode  unaware  wadable  takeoff  costing  fowling  jamming  mousing  rifling
textile  unbrace  waftage  tealeaf  cowling  fugging  jarring  mugging  rigging
texture  unclose  wafture  thereof  crannog  funning  jetting  mumming  rimming
thanage  unfroze  Wahabee  thyself  craving  furlong  jibbing  munting  ringing
thankee  ungulae  walleye  welloff  cubbing  furring  jigging  mustang  ripping
theatre  unhinge  wallrue  werwolf  cunning  gabbing  jobbing  nabbing  roadhog
thecate  unhorse  warfare  whereof  cupping  gadding  jogging  nagging  roaring
thermae  unhouse  wargame  witloof  curling  gagging  joining  napping  robbing
thimble  unitive  warlike  abiding  cutting  galling  jotting  nesting  rocking
thistle  unloose  wartime  agelong  dabbing  gamebag  jugging  netting  rodding
thorite  unnerve  wastage  amazing  damming  gasring  jutting  nipping  rolling
thuggee  unquote  wattage  angling  damning  gassing  kampong  nodding  roofing
thymine  unswore  waxtree  antilog  darling  gateleg  karting  nogging  rotting
tillage  untwine  wayside  backing  darning  gatling  keeping  nooning  rousing
timbale  unweave  weirdie  backlog  dashing  gearing  kenning  nosebag  rubbing
tinware  upgrade  welcome  bagging  dawning  geebung  keyring  noserag  ruching
titmice  upheave  welfare  balding  daylong  gelding  kidding  nothing  running
titrate  upraise  whangee  banking  dealing  gelling  killing  nursing  rutting
toluene  upstage  wheedle  banning  decking  gemming  kissing  nutting  sacking
tonnage  upsurge  whiffle  banteng  dibbing  genning  knowing  oakling  sacring
tonsure  uralite  whistle  banting  digging  getting  lacking  ongoing  sagging
tontine  uranide  whittle  barring  dimming  gigging  ladybug  opening  sailing
tootsie  urodele  whoopee  basting  dinning  gilding  lagging  packing  salting
tophole  uterine  windage  bathing  dipping  ginning  lamming  padding  sandbag
topside  utilise  winsome  batting  dogging  ginseng  landing  panning  sapling
torsade  utricle  woodpie  beading  donning  glaring  lapping  parting  sapping
tortile  vaccine  wordage  beanbag  Dorking  glazing  lapwing  passing  sarking
torture  vacuole  wouldbe  bearing  dotting  glozing  lashing  patting  scoring
torulae  valance  wrangle  beating  drawing  godling  lasting  pegging  seaslug
towline  valence  wreathe  bedding  driving  goldbug  lathing  pelting  seatang
towrope  vallate  wrestle  begging  droving  golfbag  leading  pending  seating
traduce  valuate  wriggle  belting  dubbing  golfing  leaning  penning  seeming
trainee  valvate  wrinkle  belying  ducking  gosling  legging  pepping  seizing
traipse  valvule  yardage  betting  ducting  grating  lemming  periwig  semilog
trample  vamoose  yewtree  bibbing  dunning  grazing  lending  petting  serving
tranche  vampire  zebrine  bidding  earplug  greylag  letting  pfennig  setting
trapeze  Vandyke  zeolite  billing  earring  Gstring  licking  pigging  shading
treacle  vantage  zincite  biltong  easting  gumming  lilting  pigling  shaving
treadle  variate  zipcode  binding  endlong  gunning  linsang  pimping  shebang
tremble  variole  bailiff  birddog  erelong  gushing  lipping  pinking  shindig
trestle  vedette  boxcalf  bitting  erlking  gutting  listing  pinning  shoeing
triable  vehicle  caitiff  blueing  etching  gypping  loading  pipping  shoring
tribade  veloute  castoff  boating  evening  hacking  loaning  pitting  showing
```

```
siamang washing cowfish knavish screech bacilli vitelli hillock seasick
sibling waxwing craunch Kurdish scrunch bambini Zingari hogback setback
sinning wearing currach largish seafish basenji airlock holmoak shaslik
sipping webbing curragh Lettish selfish Bengali airsick hopsack shylock
sirgang wedding currish listeth seventh bilimbi amtrack hummock sjambok
sitting wedging dampish longish sickish biriani artwork icepack skyjack
skating westing darkish loudish skyhigh bouilli bannock icerink skylark
slating wetting debauch loutish slavish bronchi barrack jannock sowback
smoking whaling debouch lumpish slowish caducei bawcock jaywalk sputnik
soaking whiting Delilah maidish softish calculi beatnik jumbuck Suffolk
soaring wigging dervish mammoth soonish canzoni bedrock Kalmuck sundeck
sobbing wilding digraph mannish sottish Cathari bedsock kalpack tanbark
sopping willing dimmish Masorah sourish cavetti berserk killick tieback
sotting windbag diptych mastich Spanish chapati bespeak kinfolk tintack
spacing windegg distich matzoth spinach charqui bethink lavrock titlark
sparing winding djibbah mawkish splotch Chianti bibcock legwork tussock
staging winning dogfish menorah squelch chupati bittock lentisk tutwork
subbing wishing doggish messiah squinch colossi blesbok limbeck unblock
sucking witling dollish mezuzah squitch dashiki boobook liveoak uncloak
suiting witting doltish Mishnah staunch denarii bullock logbook unfrock
summing wolfdog donnish missish stealth effendi bulwark maffick unstick
sunning wording dozenth mitzvah stomach elenchi burdock mammock unstuck
supping workbag dullish mobbish stretch emeriti buttock manjack unthink
surfing working dumpish monarch strewth epigoni cabrank manweek warlock
tabbing writing endarch monkish stylish gingili calpack mattock waxwork
tacking yapping English Moorish sunbath gnocchi carrack menfolk waymark
Tagalog yardang epitaph moreish sunfish gourami carsick midweek wedlock
tagging yenning evanish mudbath swinish guarani cassock mistook wetback
tailing yipping eyebath mudfish tallish hallali catwalk mudlark winnock
talking yulelog eyelash mumpish tallith Ismaili champak mudpack wryneck
tamping zapping eyewash nebbish tannish Israeli chibouk mullock yashmak
tanning zincing faddish neolith tarbush lapilli Chinook muntjak abaxial
tapping zinking fairish netfish tarnish macrami cossack network abigail
tarring zipping fattish niceish tartish maestri cowlick niblick abysmal
tatting abolish Finnish nomarch through mafiosi cutback nunatak abyssal
taxiing abroach Flemish nonsuch tigrish Marathi daybook oarlock accrual
taxying absinth fogyish nourish torgoch marconi daywork obelisk accusal
tearing almirah foolish nunnish townish martini defrock odalisk adaxial
tedding ambatch foppish oarfish towpath menisci derrick offpeak admiral
teeming anguish furbish ogreish toyish  molossi disbark oomiack adnexal
telling azimuth furnish oilbath trilith nauplii dispark outback adrenal
tentpeg babyish gabnash ostrich triumph nautili disrank outlook aerosol
thalweg baddish galumph otolith tubbish origami dorhawk outrank airmail
ticking badmash garfish outrush tundish pachisi dornick outtalk alcohol
timelag baldish garnish peckish Turkish padroni drydock outwork allheal
tinning beamish Gaulish peevish turpeth pahlavi Dunkirk paddock alodial
tipping bearish genizah pettish twelfth Panjabi dunnock padlock ammonal
tithing beneath girlish pharaoh uncouth pronaoi earlock partook anginal
titling beseech gnomish pibroch unearth pulvini earmark paydesk anthill
tooling betroth goatish Pictish unfaith Punjabi elflock peacock apostil
topping bewitch Goliath piggish unhitch ravioli eweneck peptalk apparel
totting biggish goodish pigwash unlatch remblai eyewink piddock apsidal
touring bismuth goulash pinfish unleash reversi fetlock pillock armsful
trading blemish graunch pinkish unteach ripieni finback pintuck arousal
trepang boarish greenth planish untruth sacculi flyback pollack arrival
tubbing bobbish greyish plenish vaguish samurai flyblow pollock arsenal
tugging bookish hagfish poohbah vampish sarangi fogbank potbank asexual
tunning boorish haggish poorish varnish sashimi forsook pothook asocial
turning borough Halakah prudish voguish scherzi fossick potluck augural
tutenag bortsch haporth publish waggish scirrhi futhark precook auroral
tutting braunch hashish puckish wannish secondi futhork prepack austral
undoing breadth hawkish puggish waratah senarii futtock presoak axolotl
undying British hellish quamash warmish Senussi gasmask putlock baleful
untying brutish hipbath quetsch warpath shikari gemsbok ransack baneful
upswing bullish hogfish raffish waspish signori gimmick redneck barbell
vatting bulrush hoggish rebirth weakish soprani gorcock restock bashful
veiling burnish hogwash reddish Wendish sordini goshawk rethink bedevil
veining caddish hottish refresh wettish stimuli grysbok ribwork bedroll
vetting catarrh huffish retouch wheyish succubi gunlock roebuck bejewel
viewing catfish Hunnish roguish whitish Swahili haddock rollick benzoyl
wadding ceilidh impeach Romansh whorish syllabi hammock rooinek bestial
wagging cheetah indepth rubbish wildish termini hassock rowlock biaxial
waiting cherish inveigh ruttish wolfish thalami hauberk ruddock bifocal
walking chuddah isobath Sabaoth wolvish thrombi haycock sawbuck bimanal
walling codfish jacinth Sabbath Yiddish timpani hayfork schlock bipedal
wanting coldish jewfish saddish zaptieh tripoli hayrick schmuck bobtail
warning coltish Kaddish saltish alveoli tsunami hemlock schnook bodeful
warring coolish kentish sawfish assagai tympani henpeck seamark bookful
warthog Cornish kiddish scratch assegai venturi heyduck seapink borstal
```

Boswell	despoil	grapnel	misdeal	ragdoll	tactful	anagram	fogyism	pianism
bowlful	devisal	gremial	mistful	rapeoil	tactual	animism	forearm	pietism
boxhaul	dewfall	Guignol	mistral	raschel	tankful	antonym	fraenum	pilgrim
bradawl	dextral	gumboil	monacal	rattail	tapetal	apothem	freedom	pinetum
brimful	digital	handful	mondial	recital	tearful	arcanum	frustum	pinworm
brinjal	direful	handsel	mongrel	redpoll	tendril	atavism	fulcrum	pomatum
brothel	distill	harmful	musical	refusal	tertial	atheism	gallium	popadum
burghal	diurnal	hateful	Nahuatl	refutal	textual	atomism	gingham	predoom
cacodyl	doleful	heedful	narwhal	reginal	thermal	Baalism	grandam	preform
calomel	domical	helical	natural	remodel	tiercel	Bahaism	Grecism	premium
cambial	doomful	helpful	needful	removal	timbrel	baptism	grogram	problem
cambrel	drycell	hernial	netball	renewal	tinfoil	barroom	gunroom	program
cameral	dutiful	hobnail	neutral	reposal	toenail	bedroom	hafnium	protium
capital	easeful	holdall	nodical	respell	toilful	blossom	halidom	punctum
capitol	edictal	hopeful	nombril	restful	tomfool	boredom	heroism	quantum
caporal	eluvial	humeral	nominal	retinal	topfull	bossism	Hobbism	quondam
caracal	embowel	humoral	nostril	retinol	topical	boxroom	holmium	ragworm
caracul	embroil	hurtful	numeral	retrial	topsail	bromism	homonym	realism
caramel	empanel	icefall	nuptial	revisal	topsoil	bruxism	hoodlum	reclaim
caravel	engrail	illegal	nutgall	revival	trammel	buckram	humdrum	requiem
careful	ensnarl	immoral	nymphal	rockoil	travail	cadmium	imagism	rhabdom
carinal	enteral	impanel	oakgall	roomful	trayful	caesium	interim	rhenium
cartful	enthral	impearl	oatmeal	rorqual	trefoil	calcium	iridium	rhodium
catcall	enwheel	imperil	obitual	rostral	trenail	cambium	ischium	rostrum
central	epigeal	indwell	octaval	roundel	trental	Carlism	isogram	Sabaism
chancel	epochal	infidel	oddball	ruderal	tressel	centrum	itacism	Saktism
channel	equinal	initial	oedipal	ruthful	trivial	charism	Jainism	sanctum
charnel	eternal	inkwell	oenomel	sackful	trochal	chemism	jejunum	sarcasm
chattel	ethanol	install	oestral	satchel	trommel	chillum	jibboom	Scotism
chervil	ethical	irideal	oilwell	satyral	trucial	chrisom	Judaism	searoom
chessel	evangel	ischial	omental	saveall	truncal	Comtism	kingdom	serfdom
chloral	excusal	Ishmael	optical	sawbill	trysail	confirm	labarum	shittim
chordal	exposal	Jezebel	optimal	sawmill	tumbrel	conform	ladanum	Sikhism
chunnel	exuvial	jonquil	orbital	scalpel	tumbril	cosmism	laicism	sistrum
citadel	eyeball	journal	ordinal	scandal	tuneful	Coueism	Lamaism	Sivaism
clausal	factual	karakul	outfall	scissel	turmoil	cranium	leftism	skellum
cloacal	fanmail	kestrel	outhaul	scleral	twibill	cultism	legroom	Slavism
clypeal	fantail	knowall	outsell	scribal	typical	cutworm	lithium	smeddum
coastal	fascial	kursaal	overall	scurril	umbonal	czardom	lobworm	solanum
coaxial	fateful	lacteal	ovoidal	seafowl	uncivil	czarism	lugworm	sophism
codicil	faucial	lacunal	paginal	seagull	unequal	Dadaism	lustrum	sorghum
coequal	fearful	lateral	pailful	seawall	unideal	dayroom	macadam	spodium
colonel	federal	legbail	painful	seismal	unmoral	declaim	Mahdism	stadium
comical	feminal	legpull	palatal	seminal	unravel	decorum	maidism	stardom
conceal	femoral	lexical	palmoil	sensual	unshell	deiform	mantram	statism
congeal	fernowl	liberal	paludal	setwall	unsnarl	diadrom	Marxism	sternum
conical	figural	lichowl	parasol	several	unusual	diagram	mawworm	stratum
control	finical	lifeful	parboil	sexfoil	utensil	diorism	maximum	sunbeam
corbeil	fistful	liminal	partial	shrinal	uxorial	dualism	metonym	symptom
cordial	flannel	lingual	paschal	shrivel	vegetal	dukedom	milldam	synonym
corneal	fluidal	lioncel	patrial	skilful	ventail	eardrum	minimum	tachism
cornual	fluvial	literal	payroll	skinful	ventral	earldom	misdeem	tangram
coronal	forkful	logical	peafowl	skysail	vermeil	echoism	modicum	tantrum
costrel	foxtail	lugsail	pedicel	snorkel	vesical	eelworm	muonium	tapetum
cotidal	fretful	lumenal	pennill	songful	vestral	egotism	myalism	taproom
council	frontal	luminal	peppill	sororal	vicinal	elitism	myogram	tearoom
counsel	funeral	lustful	perusal	soulful	victual	Elohism	Naziism	terbium
cowbell	gadwall	lustral	phrasal	spacial	virtual	eluvium	niobium	theorem
cowheel	gainful	lychowl	pigtail	spancel	vitriol	Elysium	nostrum	Thomism
cranial	gambrel	lyrical	pinball	spaniel	wagtail	elytrum	oestrum	thorium
creedal	gangrel	magical	pintail	spatial	wailful	embosom	oildrum	thulium
crucial	garboil	mandrel	pipeful	special	wakeful	envenom	omentum	thummim
crustal	gascoal	mandril	pitfall	spheral	wassail	epigram	onanism	tiebeam
cryptal	general	marital	pitiful	spignel	wastrel	epithem	oosperm	Titoism
crystal	genteel	marshal	pivotal	spondyl	waxbill	erotism	opossum	toponym
cubical	geoidal	martial	playful	spousal	waybill	erratum	optimum	Toryism
cubital	gharial	matinal	pleural	stammel	wishful	Euratom	organum	tourism
cupsful	girasol	maximal	pluvial	staniel	wistful	exclaim	Orphism	trangam
cureall	glacial	maxwell	poundal	stencil	wooloil	faddism	osculum	transom
curtail	gleeful	mayoral	predial	sternal	wrybill	fantasm	overarm	triduum
cynical	glossal	medical	pretzel	stoical	zestful	Fascism	oviform	triform
damosel	glottal	menthol	prevail	strigil	zooidal	fauvism	pabulum	trinkum
damozel	gluteal	miasmal	puberal	strudel	acclaim	fermium	pallium	tritium
datival	glyptal	milfoil	pugmill	subdual	acronym	fideism	papadam	trivium
decadal	godevil	mimical	pushful	subsoil	aliform	fiefdom	paronym	tropism
decanal	gomeral	mindful	quarrel	sundial	alodium	filmdom	perform	tsardom
decibel	gomeril	mineral	quetzal	surreal	alyssum	firearm	phantom	tsarism
decimal	gonadal	minimal	quintal	sutural	amalgam	flotsam	phellem	tychism
deposal	gradual	miscall	radical	synodal	amentum	fogydom	photism	typonym

```
unbosom blacken coarsen endogen griskin Laotian oarsman Ramadan Spartan
uniform blouson coition engrain Grobian Laputan octagon ramekin spongin
uranism blowgun colleen enliven grunion lardoon oilskin rampion sponson
uranium boatman complin enteron grutten Latvian omicron ratteen sporran
utopism bogbean Comtian entrain gryphon lectern opinion ravelin standin
webworm bogyman concern environ gudgeon lection oppidan realign station
wolfram bondman condemn epigean guerdon leghorn opsonin redskin stearin
wychelm bookman condign epizoon hairpin legiron oration refrain steepen
yardarm Boolean conjoin epsilon halcyon lesbian organon regimen stemson
yttrium borazon consign erepsin halogen letdown Orphean retaken stepson
Zionism botulin contain erosion handgun lethean ortolan retrain stetson
zoarium bounden contemn etesian hangman lexicon ottoman reunion stewpan
Zoilism bourbon cooncan Etonian hanuman liaison ouabain ribston stiffen
abaddon bourdon corydon evasion hardpan lighten outturn righten Stilton
abandon bracken costean exciton harijan ligroin outworn roadman stouten
abdomen Brahman courlan explain harpoon limpkin ovarian rodsman striven
Abelian Brahmin crampon exurban harshen lineman ovation rontgen stygian
abstain breakin crimson faction hasbeen linkman overman roughen suasion
Acadian bridoon crouton fashion headman Linnean overran rubdown subdean
acarian brisken crucian fermion headpin lorgnon overrun rubicon suberin
Achaean broaden cryogen festoon hearken lowborn Oxonian ruction subjoin
Achaian Brython cullion fibroin hearten lowdown packman ruffian suction
acrasin buffoon curtain fiction heathen lupulin paladin rundown sunburn
acrogen builtin cushion fifteen hebenon lyingin pampean Russian sundown
actinon bullion Cyprian finikin helicon lyncean Pandean saffron surfman
adjourn bullpen Dantean fireman hellion mailman Paphian salicin surgeon
aeolian bumpkin darshan fission heparin mailvan paragon saltern sustain
aeonian burgeon dauphin flagman hessian Malayan passion saltpan swagman
African burthen deadpan flatten hexagon malison pastern samisen sweeten
agnomen bushman decagon fletton highman mamelon patroon sandman swollen
aileron cacumen decuman fleuron hillman manakin pattern saponin taction
alation Cadmean denizen flexion hirudin manikin pelican Saracen tamarin
albumen caisson detrain fluxion hoarsen mansion pemican saurian tampion
albumin caldron dextran foghorn hoatzin Manxman penguin saxhorn tanghin
Alcoran camaron dextrin footman Hobbian Martian pension sculpin tapsman
aleuron campion diction foramen hoedown Marxian Permian section taximan
Alkoran canakin dipnoan foreign horizon maudlin Persian Serbian teachin
almsman canikin discern foreman hygeian meatman pertain sericin teagown
alphorn canteen disdain foreran hyperon Mechlin phaeton Servian telamon
alsoran capelin dishorn forerun Iberian medusan pidgeon session tension
althorn Capsian disjoin forlorn indican megaron pigiron setdown terrain
andiron capstan dislimn Fortran indrawn megaton pigmean shaitan tertian
aneurin captain distain forworn ingrain Meissen pigskin sharpen testban
Angevin caption doeskin fourgon ingrown melanin pikeman Shavian testoon
Anglian caravan dogskin freeman inhuman mention pillion shebeen therein
antigen cardoon dolphin freshen inkhorn messtin plasmin shipman thereon
antlion carotin doorman Frisian insulin metopon platoon shippen thiamin
apogean carrion dragoon frisson inwoven Mexican playpen shippon thicken
Arabian carryon drayman frogman Iranian milkman pleuron shopman thriven
arraign cartoon drivein fronton isotron million plosion shorten throwin
artisan Catalan drumlin fustian Italian minikin polygon shotgun Tibetan
aspirin cateran drunken gadroon Jacobin mission pontoon shotten tighten
auction caution duckpin galleon jargoon moisten popcorn showman tinhorn
Avestan caveman dudgeon galloon javelin molimen portion shriven tollman
Azilean celadon dungeon gamelan jazzman monsoon posteen sierran tompion
balloon ceresin duramen gelatin Judaean moorhen postern silicon torchon
bargain certain dustbin Genevan Jungian mouflon postman silvern torsion
baseman cerumen dustman gentian juryman mowburn potheen sirloin toughen
bassoon cession dustpan gherkin Kantian muezzin poussin sitdown tradein
bastion chagrin earthen gittern keelson mullein preplan sixteen treason
batsman chanson eastern gladden keratin mullion pronoun skidpan tricorn
bedizen chapman echelon glassen kerogen munnion protean skolion triduan
bedouin chasten edition gleeman khamsin murrain protein skyborn trodden
beechen cheapen eidolon gliadin kidskin mutagen ptyalin slacken trudgen
beknown chevron einkorn glisten kiloton mylodon puccoon sleeken trypsin
Belgian chicken elastin glutton kinchin nankeen Pullman slidden tuition
bellman chidden elation Gobelin kingpin navarin pumpkin sloegin tulchan
benison chiffon elision goddamn kinsman neuston puritan smarten turfman
benzoin chignon elusion gombeen kitchen neutron purloin smidgen typhoon
betaken chorion elution goodman kneepan newborn putamen smidgin Umbrian
betoken cipolin elysian Gordian knockon newmown putdown smitten umpteen
between Circean elytron gossoon kremlin newsman pygmean snowman unchain
Biafran cistern embrown greaten krypton ninepin Pythian sojourn unclean
bighorn cithern embryon Grecian ladykin nocturn quartan sokeman uncrown
billion citizen emotion greisen lambkin nonagon quicken Solomon unction
birchen cittern emption gremlin lampion noniron quieten Sorbian unicorn
birdman clarion enation greyhen lampoon nuclein quintan soroban unknown
bittern claypan enchain griffin lanolin nucleon raccoon soupcon unladen
bitumen clubman enderon griffon lantern oakfern railman soybean unlearn
```

```
unsworn ferrugo tremolo nonslip alcazar boulter clapper deluder fibster
unwoven furioso tympano nonstop allover bouncer clatter derider fibular
upsilon gambado underdo nunship allstar bounder clavier despair fiddler
Uralian gestapo undergo onestep almoner bowlder cleaner deviser fielder
urethan guanaco vaquero outcrop amateur bragger cleaver devisor fighter
utopian heighho verismo overlap amender brander clicker diddler filacer
Vatican hidalgo vertigo overtop amildar brawler climber dilator flaneur
velamen huanaco vibrato parsnip ammeter brazier clinker diluter flanker
venison impasto volcano pasteup angular breaker clipper dilutor flapper
vermian inferno whereto peasoup annular breeder clobber dimeter flasher
version lentigo whoseso pitprop another brevier clocker diopter flatcar
vervain llanero zemstvo pressup antbear brimmer clogger dipolar flatter
veteran longago Zingaro punchup applier bringer clumber ditcher flavour
villain lumbago airdrop rattrap aquifer broider cluster divider flecker
villein madrono airship regroup aquiver broiler clutter diviner fleecer
vitamin maestro bellhop rollmop arbiter brooder clyster divisor flesher
volutin mafioso boozeup rolltop areolar brother coacher dogstar flicker
Walloon magneto breakup rooftop armiger browser coaster donator flipper
wanigan Marrano buildup rosehip arrayer bruiser cobbler doodler flitter
warison memento builtup roundup arriver brusher coddler dortour flivver
wayworn mestizo caltrap rumshop aspirer buckler coherer dossier floater
wealden montero caltrop scallop assayer bugbear collier doubler floorer
weighin morello cantrip schlepp assurer builder compeer doubter fluster
western morendo catchup scollop asunder bumbler conifer douceur flutter
wheaten Moresco checkup seawhip atelier bungler conquer dowager flyover
wherein Morisco chirrup seedlip auditor burbler contour drabber fondler
whereon morocco cleanup shakeup autocar burgher copular drabler forager
Whitsun mulatto closeup shallop avenger burglar coroner drafter forayer
widgeon Negrito coverup shiplap aviator burster corsair drainer forbear
wireman nelumbo cowslip sibship awarder bustler cottier drawbar forever
woodman oloroso crackup skijump axillar butcher couloir drawler forgoer
woollen oregano demirep smashup babbler bywoner coulter dreamer founder
workman pampero develop snarlup baffler cackler counter dredger Fraktur
writhen passado dewdrop snowcap Bahadur cadaver coupler dresser freezer
written piccolo discerp sonship barrier cajoler courier drifter fresher
xanthin pimento driedup soursop basilar caliper courser driller fripper
yardman pintado eardrop speedup behaver caloyer cozener drinker friseur
yatagan placebo earflap standup belcher camphor cracker drogher frisker
yeggman pompano eggflip stickup belljar candour crammer dropper fritter
yestern portico egotrip stirrup bencher caperer crawler drudger fruiter
zillion primero enclasp stopgap besmear carrier creamer drummer fuddler
zithern proviso envelop stuckup bifilar cashier creator dueller Fuehrer
zymogen proximo epicarp sunlamp bigener catcher creeper duumvir fueller
agitato prurigo exocarp suntrap bilobar caterer crimper dweller fulgour
allegro relievo eyedrop syncarp bipolar caulker cringer eductor fumbler
annatto ridotto flareup teashop blabber centaur crisper ejector funfair
Arapaho rilievo flatcap tiderip bladder centner critter elector furrier
avocado ripieno flattop toeclip blaster chaffer croaker Elzevir further
bambino risotto flytrap touchup blather chamber crofter embower gabbler
botargo saguaro foglamp toyshop blatter chamfer crooner emitter gagster
bravado sapsago foretop treetop bleater changer cropper emperor gambier
broncho scalado frameup trollop bleeder chanter crosier empower gambler
buffalo scherzo giltcup twostep bleeper chapter crowbar emptier garbler
bugaboo Scorpio godship unclasp blender charger crowner enactor genitor
bummalo secondo grownup upsweep blether charmer crozier enamour giggler
bushido senecio gumdrop warship blinder charter cruiser encoder girdler
calando serpigo gunship wickiup blinker chatter cruller equator glacier
calypso sfumato gymslip winesap blister cheater crupper erector gladder
cassino shampoo hardtop wiretap blither checker crusher escaper glamour
cattalo sirocco harelip worship bloater cheddar cudbear escolar glazier
cavetto smokeho heeltap writeup blocker cheerer cupular essayer gleaner
cembalo soprano hencoop abetter bloomer chequer curator evictor glimmer
centavo sordino hilltop abettor blotter chigger currier exactor glister
cheerio squacco ingroup abjurer blubber childer dabbler exciter glitter
Chicano stretto insculp ablator blucher chipper dallier excitor glummer
coquito subzero ketchup aborter bluffer chitter dangler exhumer gobbler
coranto supremo kingcup abrader blunder chooser danseur exposer goggler
cornuto tabasco kinship abutter blunger chopper dawdler fabular grabber
criollo tallyho kneecap accuser blusher chowder daystar fancier grafter
crusado tangelo kneesup acroter bluster chuddar dazzler farceur grainer
curacao testudo lipdeep adapter boarder chukker debater farrier grammar
cymbalo theorbo longhop adaptor boaster chunter decider farther granger
diabolo thereto maintop adducer boggler circler decoder feaster granter
electro timpano mantrap adherer bolivar clabber decrier feather grantor
embargo tobacco midship admirer bolster clacker defiler feigner grasper
esparto tombolo milksop adopter booster claimer definer felspar grazier
etaerio tornado misstep adviser botcher clamber delator feoffer greaser
fagotto torpedo mixedup advisor boudoir clamour delayer feoffor grifter
farrago touraco mugwump aerator boulder clanger deliver fervour griller
```

```
grimmer knacker muzzler poulter rounder simpler sponsor tattler visitor
grinder knapper mynheer pounder rouster simular spoofer taunter vitular
gripper kneader nebular praetor royster sizzler spoorer teacher voucher
Grolier kneeler needler praiser ruffler skeeter sporter tegular voyager
groover knitter neither prancer rumbler skegger spotter telpher waddler
grouper knocker nibbler premier rustler skelter spouter Telstar wagerer
grouser knotter niggler presser saddler skimmer sprayer Templar wagoner
growler krimmer nobbler pricker saluter skinker spurner tempter waister
grubber lacquer nodular printer samovar skinner sputter tenoner wakener
grunter lacunar nonuser proctor sampler skipper squalor terrier waltzer
guesser laminar norther prodder sandbar skirter squarer thanker warbler
guilder languor nuclear proffer santour skitter stabber thigger warrior
guzzler lashkar obligor prosper saunter skulker stabler thiller watcher
hackler laugher ocellar prowler saviour slabber stacker thiller waterer
haggler launder October psalter scalder slacker stagger thinner waverer
hamster leaguer officer puddler scalper slander stainer thither weather
handcar learner oldster puncher scamper slasher stalker thrower webster
handler leather openair punster scanner slather stammer thumper weigher
harbour legator opposer pupilar scarper sleeper stamper thunder welcher
harrier leister orderer pursuer scatter slender stander tickler welsher
hatcher levator osseter puttier scauper slicker stapler tiddler wencher
haulier lighter outdoor puzzler schemer slimmer starter tingler whacker
haunter limiter outlier quaffer scholar slinger stealer tippler wheeler
hauteur liqueur outwear quarter scissor slinker steamer tipster whether
heather loather paddler queller scoffer slipper steerer titular whetter
heckler lobster painter quester scolder slither stellar toaster whicker
heritor lobular pairoar questor scomber slobber stentor toddler whidder
higgler locater palaver quilter scooper slogger stepper tollbar whimper
hipster locular pannier quitter scooter slotcar sticker toucher whinger
hitcher lorimer panther quizzer scorner slubber stifler tracker whipper
hobbler loriner paperer rabbler scorper slugger stinger tractor whirler
holster lounger papular radular scourer slumber stinker trailer whisker
homager Lucifer parader railcar scouter slummer stirrer trainer whisper
hostler luncher pardner rallier scraper smacker stocker traitor whoever
however lunular parlour rambler screwer smasher stonker tramcar whooper
humidor lurcher partner rancher scriber smatter stopper tranter whopper
hurdler machair paviour rancour sculler smeller strayer trapper whopper
hustler macular pearler rattler scunner smelter strider trawler widower
igniter mahseer peddler ravager scupper smother stridor treader wielder
ignorer manager percher reacher scutter snapper striker treater wiggler
imbiber manhour peruser reactor seabear snarler striver trekker Windsor
imbower manyear philter realgar seceder sneaker stuffer tricker wobbler
imposer marcher piaffer realtor secular sneerer stumper trifler worrier
incisor mariner picador rebuker securer sneezer stunner trigger wrapper
inciter markhor pickeer reciter seducer snicker stutter trimmer wrecker
incomer masquer piffler recover seltzer sniffer subadar tripper wringer
indexer masseur pilsner reducer seminar snifter succour troller yielder
inditer matador pilular reenter senator snigger suckler trooper younger
inducer maunder pincher refiner settler snipper sulphur trotter younker
inhaler mauther pioneer refuser settlor snooker sumpter trouper abattis
injurer meander pissoir refuter shammer snooper sunbear trouser abscess
inlayer meddler pitcher regular sharper snoozer sunstar trucker acetous
insider metamer pivoter relater shaster snorter swabber trusser Achates
insofar metayer planner relator shatter snubber swagger truster acinous
insular midyear plantar remover shearer snuffer swanker tubular actress
insurer minever planter reneger shebear socager swapper tumbler address
integer minicar plaster renewer shedder soldier swarmer tumular agamous
intoner miniver platter rentier sheller soother swasher tutelar ageless
invader minster pleader reorder shelter sounder swatter tweeter aggress
inviter mirador pledger repaper shicker souther swearer tweezer aiblins
isochor mishear pledgor repiner shifter spadger sweater twister aimless
jacamar mobster plodder replier shimmer spanker sweeper twitter airless
jacktar modular plotter rescuer shipper spanner swelter typebar airmiss
jangler moither plucker reviler shirker sparger swiller udaller alkalis
janitor moneyer plugger reviser shocker spatter swimmer uncover alumnus
jemadar moniker plumber reviver shooter spawner swinger unifier ambages
jibdoor monitor plumper revivor shopper speaker swither unswear ambones
jingler monomer plunder riddler shouter speeder Switzer upriser amoebas
jocular monster plunger riffler shucker speller swopper upstair amorous
joinder moocher plunker righter shudder spelter taborer usurper Ananias
jointer morular poacher riveter shunner spencer tabular utterer ancones
jouster moulder poinder roaster shunter spender tackler vaulter ancress
juggler mounter pointer rockier shutter spieler tambour vaunter angelus
jugular mourner polymer rocktar shyster spiller tanager veliger annates
juniper mouther poofter roedeer sidecar spinner tandoor venerer annulus
Jupiter muddler popover roister signior spitter tankcar vernier anoesis
khaddar muffler popular rooster similar splicer taperer vetiver anxious
kilobar mumbler porifer rotator similor spoiler tapster vinegar anyways
kindler murther postwar rotifer simitar sponger tarrier vintner anyways
```

```
apheses Chablis ephebus icterus mimulus pronaos spinous wetness bedight
aphesis challis ergates igneous minibus proteus spirits wharves bedpost
aphides chamois ethiops ileitis minimus prowess spumous whereas beignet
apodous chassis express illness minutes pulpous squails wigless benefit
apropos chlamys eyeless impetus mitoses pyjamas stables willies bepaint
apsides chymous falsies impious mitosis pylorus statics winkers bequest
aptness cidaris famulus impress modulus pyralis stirpes withers bergylt
aqueous cimices fantods incubus muggins pyrites stovies witless betwixt
arbutus cirrous fatness incudes murexes pyrosis straits witness bibelot
arduous civvies fatuous indices murices pyxides stratus wryness biblist
areolas classes ferrous indoors mycoses quietus stuccos zealous biggest
aristas classis fetters ingress mycosis quizzes suburbs zygosis biscuit
armfuls clivers fewness innards myiasis radices success zymosis bistort
armless clothes feyness innings myxomas ramsons summons abeyant blanket
arrears clypeus fibrous inwards nacrous rations sunless abought blatant
artless codices fibulas isthmus naiades raucous surpass abreact blowout
ascaris coffers fidgets ivories napless ravings surplus abreast bombast
ascesis colitis fifties jackass narrows rawness sycosis account boneset
ascites collins filings jacobus nautics rayless synesis accurst booklet
asepsis colobus finings jealous nebulas redlegs tactics acquest boomlet
askesis colours fitness jimjams Negress redness tagetes acrobat borscht
assizes commons fixings jitters nemesis redress takings adamant bouquet
aurochs compass floccus joyless nervous refocus talcous adhibit bowshot
auroras conatus follies juggins newness regards talipes adjoint boxseat
autobus concuss forceps juncoes nippers regress tatters adjunct boycott
auxesis confess forties kalends nitrous regrets taxless afflict bracket
aweless conkers frescos kenosis niveous regulus teargas affront briquet
awnless copious fulness kermess nocuous remains tedious against brisket
azygous coronas fulvous keyless nonplus remiges tenpins agonist brocket
badness coyness fungous kinesis noxious repress tenuous ailment brought
bananas Croesus funnies klipdas nucleus reredos tetanus airlift bullbat
banjoes croquis furious koumiss numbles retinas thallus airport bumboat
barytes csardas fuscous lacunas oarless returns thieves airpost buoyant
battels cuirass gallows Lallans obvious rhamnus thyrsus akvavit bushtit
Bauhaus culices gaseous lancers ocellus rhombus tidings aliment cabaret
bellows cumulus gathers largess ochrous rickets tigress aliquot cabinet
benthos cupmoss gayness lassoes octopus riotous timeous alkanet callant
besides cuprous geckoes latexes oddness rubbers toeless alright calumet
betimes curious geneses latices odorous rubious topless amarant cambist
bigness customs genesis laurels oestrus ruinous torpids ambient camelot
bilboes cutlass ghettos lawless ominous rumness towards amongst candent
bilious cyathus gibbous laxness omnibus runless travois amorist Carlist
biomass cyclops giblets legless oneness sadness trellis analyst carport
bionics cypress gimbals leprous onerous salvoes triceps ancient casuist
bitters czardas glasses letters onwards Sanctus trismus Anglist catboat
blewits darbies glottis lidless onymous sanders trochus animist catmint
boletus declass gluteus limbous oppress sapless tropics annicut catsuit
bongoes defocus goddess limosis osmosis sarcous tumulus annulet cellist
bonkers degauss godless limulus osseous sardius twelves apparat cesspit
borings depress goggles linctus pajamas savings twoness appoint chaplet
brumous devious grampus lioness palings scabies typhous apricot chariot
bugloss dickens greaves lipless panties scarves uberous aquavit chemist
bulbous digress grottos litotes papyrus scepsis umbones Arabist cheroot
bureaus dimness grumous loculus parados seabass uncinus armrest cheviot
burgess dingoes gubbins lowness paresis sealegs uncross asphalt chindit
burnous discuss gutless luteous parlous senatus undress asquint cineast
buttons dismiss halvers lychnis peeress senores untruss assault circlet
byebyes dodgems hamulus madness Pegasus serious upsides atavist circuit
bygones dogdays hapless makings pelorus sexless upwards atheist clamant
cahoots doubles harness malines pennies Sextans uranous athirst clement
caimans dryness hatless malleus percuss sferics useless athwart coaltit
calamus dubious heinous mangoes perhaps sheaves uveitis atomist cockpit
calends duchess heiress manless petasus shelves vacuous attaint coconut
calices dulness helices manners petrous sherris vapours attempt coexist
callous duteous hernias marbles phallus shivers varices attract cohabit
calyces dwarves heroics marquis phonics shyness various audient coletit
calyxes ecdyses hideous masters physics siemens Vaudois augment collect
canthus ecdysis hipness matrass piceous silenus velours babbitt combout
canvass echinus honours mattins pincers sinless verglas babysit combust
carcass effects hostess mealies piteous sinuous vespers backset comfort
carinas elevens hotness measles poetess sithens vicious Bahaist comment
carious embolus hueless medusas poetics sixties vidimus ballast compact
caseous empress hugeous meiosis polypus skepsis villous banquet compart
casuals emulous humbles memoirs pompous slyness viscous baptist complot
catalos endless humerus meseems possess solidus vittles baronet comport
catenas endways hunkers Messias prelims sonless wanness basinet compost
Cathars engross hurdles metrics premiss sorites wattles bassist Comtist
caymans entasis hydrous milreis process sorosis wayless bayonet conceit
Celsius envious iciness mimesis profess species wellies bedfast concent
```

concept	dimmest	feedlot	harslet	leveret	parfait	rampart	shallot	triolet
concert	discant	felwort	harvest	lineout	parquet	rapport	sherbet	triplet
concoct	disgust	ferment	hatchet	linocut	partlet	rarebit	shilpit	trippet
conduct	dismast	fervent	havenot	locknut	passant	ratatat	shutout	trisect
conduit	dispart	feudist	hayloft	lockout	patient	ratchet	singlet	trumpet
confect	disport	fideist	headset	lookout	patriot	readout	sitfast	tsarist
congest	disroot	figment	hellcat	lynchet	payment	reagent	skilift	tugboat
connect	disrupt	figwort	hideout	maddest	peasant	realist	skillet	turgent
consent	disseat	filbert	highhat	madwort	peccant	reallot	skippet	turnout
consist	dissect	filemot	hindgut	Mahdist	pendant	reboant	skirret	typeset
consort	dissent	filmset	Hobbist	maillot	pendent	rebuilt	sleekit	ululant
consult	distant	fishnet	holibut	manchet	pennant	receipt	sleight	unblest
contact	distent	fitchet	hooklet	manhunt	percent	recount	snippet	unbuilt
content	distort	fitment	horrent	manihot	percept	recruit	solicit	unguent
contest	dogcart	fittest	hotfoot	mantlet	perfect	redcoat	soloist	unjoint
context	dogtrot	flatlet	hotshot	manumit	periapt	reddest	solvent	unkempt
contort	doormat	flatout	hottest	Manxcat	peridot	redoubt	sophist	unmeant
convect	dormant	flaught	howbeit	margent	perpent	redraft	sorbent	unquiet
convent	doublet	fleapit	hutment	marplot	persist	reelect	spirant	unright
convert	dovecot	fleuret	hydrant	martlet	pervert	reenact	spryest	unroost
convict	drabbet	floreat	hymnist	Marxist	pianist	reflect	starlet	unsight
cookout	dragnet	florist	iceboat	matchet	picquet	refloat	starlit	untwist
coolant	draught	floruit	icefoot	matelot	pierrot	refract	statant	upright
copilot	driblet	flutist	illicit	mediant	pietist	regnant	statist	upstart
copycat	droplet	flybelt	imagist	meerkat	pigment	regrant	steekit	upswept
copyist	dropout	flyboat	impaint	melilot	pikelet	reliant	sterlet	uptight
cornett	drought	flypast	implant	merchet	piquant	relight	stewpot	utopist
cornist	drugget	foldout	imprest	metrist	pitapat	remnant	stickit	vagrant
coronet	drysalt	fondant	imprint	midmost	pithhat	remount	student	valiant
correct	dualist	footrot	inbuilt	Midwest	placket	repaint	stylist	variant
corrupt	durmast	forfeit	incipit	mightst	plaudit	replant	subduct	varment
corslet	earnest	formant	incrust	migrant	playact	reposit	subedit	varmint
cosmist	earshot	forwent	indraft	minaret	playlet	reprint	subject	veinlet
couldst	eelpout	foumart	indwelt	miscast	pledget	request	subplot	verdant
couplet	egotist	foxhunt	inexact	missent	plummet	respect	subsist	verdict
couvert	elegant	foxtrot	infarct	monocot	polecat	respell	subvert	veriest
crampet	elegist	fraught	inflect	moonlit	poloist	restart	suggest	versant
crampit	element	freight	inflict	moonset	pomfret	retract	sunspot	viaduct
credent	elfbolt	freshet	infract	mordant	porrect	retreat	sunsuit	vibrant
cresset	elitist	frisket	ingraft	mordent	portent	revisit	support	vilayet
cricket	Elohist	fuguist	inhabit	mudflat	potshot	rhymist	surcoat	violent
crochet	eminent	fulgent	inherit	mugwort	Prakrit	ribwort	surfeit	violist
crocket	enchant	fullout	inhibit	muskrat	precast	ringent	surtout	walkout
croquet	encrust	fusspot	inquest	mythist	precept	ringlet	suspect	warrant
crownet	endmost	gabfest	insight	nacarat	predict	ripplet	tabaret	washout
crumpet	engraft	galipot	inspect	nascent	preempt	rivulet	tabinet	washpot
culprit	enprint	gallant	instant	nearest	prefect	rocklet	tachist	wavelet
cultist	entrant	galliot	intrant	necklet	preheat	romaunt	talayot	webfoot
culvert	entreat	gallnut	intreat	neglect	prelect	rootlet	talipot	wellset
cumquat	entrust	gantlet	introit	nonsuit	present	rosecut	tangent	wettest
currant	entwist	gardant	intrust	notelet	pretest	rowboat	taproot	whatnot
current	epatant	garment	ironist	nymphet	pretext	rundlet	tartlet	whereat
cyclist	epaulet	gestalt	isohyet	occiput	prevent	sackbut	teleost	whippet
Cypriot	epithet	gilbert	isokont	oculist	pricket	sacrist	tempest	wildcat
czarist	erodent	gillnet	issuant	oddment	product	saddest	templet	winglet
Dadaist	escheat	glaikit	Italiot	odorant	project	saidest	thereat	wingnut
dashpot	estreat	gooiest	iterant	offbeat	prophet	sakeret	thicket	without
Debrett	evident	gourmet	jackpot	oneshot	propjet	salicet	Thomist	woodcut
decrypt	excerpt	grommet	jaconet	operant	protect	salient	thought	woolfat
default	exhaust	grummet	jogtrot	opulent	protest	saltant	tiercet	workout
defiant	exhibit	guichet	Judaist	osselet	protist	saltcat	tipcart	wornout
deficit	exigent	gumboot	judoist	outcast	provost	sandlot	Titoist	wottest
deflect	explant	gunboat	jumpjet	outfoot	prudent	sandpit	tonight	wouldst
defrost	exploit	gunshot	kinglet	outlast	pullout	sapient	topcoat	wrought
defunct	exposit	gymnast	kumquat	outmost	pungent	satinet	topknot	Yahvist
delight	extinct	habitat	lakelet	outport	purport	sawdust	topmast	Yahwist
delimit	extract	hackbut	Lamaist	outpost	pursuit	sawwort	topmost	yoghurt
demerit	eyebolt	haircut	lambast	outshot	quadrat	scarlet	torment	Yorkist
demount	eyeshot	hairnet	lambent	outwent	quartet	Scotist	torrent	Zionist
dentist	eyespot	halbert	lambert	overact	querist	seaboot	tosspot	Zoilist
deposit	faddist	halfwit	languet	overeat	quillet	seagirt	tourist	bandeau
descant	fadeout	halibut	latchet	overset	quintet	sealant	towboat	babassu
descent	fallout	handout	lawlist	oviduct	racquet	seaport	towmont	caribou
dessert	fantast	handset	lawsuit	oxidant	radiant	segment	townlet	catechu
detract	farmost	hangout	lazaret	pageant	ragbolt	sellout	traject	chateau
deviant	Fascist	hardhit	leaflet	paletot	ragwort	sequent	transit	fabliau
dialect	fattest	hardset	leftist	palmist	raiment	serpent	triblet	jujitsu
diarist	faunist	haricot	legrest	pandect	Rajpoot	servant	trident	manitou
diluent	fauvist	harpist	lenient	parapet	rampart	sextant	trinket	

```
manteau bureaux aplenty cabbagy crybaby estuary gallery humanly lowlily
marabou callbox apogamy cacanny cursory eupepsy gallfly humidly loyally
nylghau coinbox apology cachexy curtsey euphony gangway hushaby loyalty
parvenu complex archery cacoepy custody eustasy gateway huskily lucency
plateau conflux archway cadency cutaway exactly gaudery hymnary lucidly
purlieu equinox ardency calcify cutlery exogamy gaudily hymnody luckily
rondeau firebox areally callboy dacoity factory gauntly ideally lullaby
rouleau flummox areaway calumny damnify faculty gauntry ignobly lumpily
sapajou gateaux aridity calvary dandify fadedly gawkily ilkaday luridly
seppuku gearbox armoury camelry dazedly faintly gelidly imagery lustily
tableau hellbox ashtray cannery deanery fairway gemmery impiety lyingly
tinamou jukebox ataraxy cannily deathly fallacy geodesy inanely maggoty
tonneau livebox atrophy canonry decency fallguy geogony inanity magnify
trumeau mailbox attaboy capably deepfry falsely geology inaptly majesty
Watteau narthex aurally caraway densely falsify getaway ineptly malmsey
aircrew oratrix autarky carroty density falsity ghastly inertly mammary
airflow overtax autopsy cattery destiny fancily ghostly infancy mangily
airglow paradox avidity cattily destroy fantasy giantry inquiry marrowy
backsaw perplex awfully cautery devilry faraday giddily insecty martyry
bandsaw phalanx axially cavally diarchy faraway gingery irately masonry
beshrew pharynx baggily cavalry dietary fastday glorify Irishry mastery
bestrew phoenix balcony century dignify fatally goodday isogamy mattery
brannew pillbox ballboy certify dignity fatuity gossipy isogeny meadowy
bucksaw postbox balmily chantry dingily felonry goutfly isonomy meatfly
buzzsaw postfix baloney charily dirtily fernery gradely isotopy mediacy
catspaw rectrix banally charity disobey ferrety gramary jadedly mercery
Choctaw reseaux battery charley display fetidly granary jaggery mercury
cumshaw salpinx bawdily charpoy dithery fidgety grandly jaloppy merrily
Danelaw saltbox beastly cheaply dittany fierily grapery January messily
dewclaw sandbox beatify chicory dizzily fifthly gratify jazzily mildewy
disavow simplex beggary chiefly doddery finally gravely jerkily miliary
downbow soapbox bellboy childly dodgery finicky gravity jewelry mimicry
eyebrow tectrix bheesty chimney doggery firefly greatly jittery mirkily
firenew toolbox bibbery chintzy doorway firstly greenly jobbery miscopy
fitchew tortrix bigotry choosey doucely fishery gristly joinery miserly
flamfew triplex biliary christy doughty fishily grizzly jointly misplay
flyblow tuckbox billowy churchy dowdily fishway grocery jollify mistily
forepaw workbox bindery chutney drapery fixedly grossly jollity mixedly
foresaw ability biology ciliary dripdry flagday grouchy journey mockery
fretsaw academy blackly cindery drizzly flaunty gruffly juicily modally
gorcrow acetify blandly circusy droshky fleetly grumbly jurally modesty
hacksaw acidify blankly civilly drouthy fleshly gullery justify moistly
handsaw acidity blarney clarify duality flighty gunnery killjoy mollify
iceshow acouchy bleakly clarity dubiety flowery gunplay kitschy monkery
jackdaw acridly blighty cleanly ducally fluency gustily knavery monthly
knowhow actuary blindly clearly dulcify fluidly gutsily knobbly moodily
legshow acutely blotchy clerisy duopoly flunkey hackery lamprey morally
lockjaw adeptly blowdry clerkly durably flyaway hackney laniary morassy
longbow adultly blowfly cliquey duskily foggily halfway lankily mortify
lowbrow affably bluffly closely dustily folkway hallway larceny muddily
misknow agilely bluntly cockily dyarchy foolery handily largely mummery
outflow agility bobbery cockney dynasty footboy hapenny latency mummify
outgrew alchemy bobstay cockshy eagerly footway happily lathery mundify
outgrow alertly boloney cogency earthly foppery harmony laundry murkily
oversaw alienly bonedry colicky ebriety foresay harshly lechery mutably
oversew alimony bonnily coloury ecology forgery hastily legally muttony
preview allergy boozily comfrey economy fortify haughty legibly muzzily
purview almonry bottony company ecstasy foundry hautboy lengthy myology
rainbow aloofly brambly compony edacity frailly headily leprosy mystery
ringtaw already branchy cookery egality frailty headway levelly mystify
shallow amatory brashly coppery eggcosy frankly healthy liberty nailery
somehow amenity bravely cornily elderly fratery hearsay library naively
sparrow amiably bravery corrody elusory freckly heavily licitly naivety
swallow amnesty breathy cottony embassy freeway heftily lightly nakedly
tonerow amplify brevity country empathy Frenchy helotry lignify nameday
trishaw anagogy brewery courtly emptily freshly hennery linkboy nasally
unscrew analogy bribery crackly Encraty friarly heronry liquefy nastily
upthrew anarchy briefly crassly enquiry frizzly hiccupy lithely nattily
upthrow anatomy briskly crazily entropy frowsty hickory littery naughty
whipsaw anchovy bristly crinkly eparchy fugally highboy liturgy nectary
whitlow angrily brittly crisply epigyny funnily highway loathly neology
windrow anility broadly crossly epitaxy furmety history locally neoteny
antefix annuity buirdly crucify eponymy furmity hockday loftily newsboy
anthrax anomaly bulkily crudely equably furrowy hoggery longday nightly
apteryx anxiety bullary crudity equally fussily holiday loosely nigrify
bandbox anybody bumpily cruelly equerry fustily honesty lottery nimiety
bateaux apetaly bursary cruelty erectly fuzzily horrify lousily nippily
beeswax aphylly buttery crumbly errancy gadgety horsily lovably nitrify
Benelux apishly buttony crunchy esotery gainsay hosiery loverly nodally
```

```
noisily pessary quavery saintly silvery squeaky tentfly truancy vitally
noology petrify queenly sallowy sintery squiffy tenthly Tuesday vitrify
noonday pettily queerly salsify sixthly squinny tenuity tumidly vividly
nosegay phlegmy quickly sandboy sizably squirmy tepidly tunably vixenly
notably phonily quietly sandfly sketchy squishy ternary turbary vocally
notedly phratry quinary sassaby slackly stagily terrify turnery volubly
novelty phrensy quivery satiety slantly staidly tersely turnipy vowelly
nullify piggery rabbity satisfy slavery stalely testacy turnkey waggery
nullity pillory rabidly satrapy sleekly standby testfly tushery walkway
nummary pillowy rackety saucily slickly starchy testify twaddly wallaby
nunnery piously raggedy saveloy slimily starkly testily twankay wealthy
nursery piscary railway savoury slipway stately therapy twiddly wearily
obesity pithily rapidly scantly slouchy steeply thereby twinkly weekday
obloquy pitpony rattery scarify sloughy stenchy theurgy twitchy weevily
obolary plainly raunchy scenery smartly stepney thickly tympany weighty
odyssey planxty readily scorify smokily sternly thirdly tyranny weirdly
olivary playboy reality scraggy smoochy stiffly thirsty tzigany whereby
omneity plenary recency scranny snakily stonily thistly unaptly whimsey
opacity pliably rectify scrappy snatchy stoutly thready uncanny whiskey
oratory pliancy rectory scrawly snowily streaky thrifty unfitly whitely
orderly plumery reentry scrawny soapily stringy throaty unfunny willowy
orogeny plumply regally scrimpy soberly stroppy thrummy unfussy windily
orology plushly regency scrubby society stubbly tidally ungodly wintery
orphrey pontify remarry scruffy soggily stupefy tiddley unhandy wittily
ossuary portray replevy scrumpy solidly suavely tideway unhappy womanly
ostiary postboy respray sealery someday suavity tiffany unicity woolsey
otology potency retiary secrecy someway subsidy tightly unitary woozily
outplay pottery rettery sectary sonancy succory tilbury unlucky wordily
outstay poultry revelry seedily soothly sulkily timidly unmanly workday
overbuy poverty rhatany sensory sootily summary timothy unready worldly
overfly powdery rhiancy servery soppily summery tindery untruly wreathy
overlay pravity rickety seventy sorcery sunnily tinnily urgency wriggly
overpay preachy rightly shadily sorrily surgery tipsify urinary wrinkly
overtly prelacy rigidly shadowy soundly surlily tipsily urology wrongly
pageboy prickly rivalry shakily spangly swarthy tittupy usually yellowy
paisley primacy roadway shapely sparely sweetly toggery utility zedoary
palfrey primary robbery sharply specify swiftly tonally utterly zincify
palmary primely rockery sheerly spicery swinery topiary vacancy zinkify
panicky privacy rockily shingly spicily synergy torrefy vacuity zoogamy
panoply privily roguery shipway spidery syngamy totally vagally zoogeny
papally privity Rommany shivery spikily tacitly tottery vaguely zoogony
parkway probity rookery shoofly spindly tallboy toughly valency zoology
parsley prodigy ropeway shopboy spindry tallowy tourney validly zoonomy
passkey progeny rosebay shortly spinney Tammany tracery vapidly zootaxy
patency pronely roughly showery splashy tannery tragedy vapoury zootomy
pathway prosify roundly showily spleeny tantivy tramway variety zymurgy
paucity prosily rowdily shrilly spooney tardily treacly varsity humbuzz
paunchy prosody royally shrubby sprawly tastily trembly vastity kibbutz
peartly proudly royalty sickbay sprayey tattery tricksy velvety Kirghiz
peccary prudery rubbery sickpay spriggy tattily trigamy venally kolkhoz
pedlary puberty ruddily sideway springy teacosy trilogy versify showbiz
penally puckery rudesby sightly spurrey teatray trinary vexedly
penalty pudency runaway signary squabby telergy trinity viceroy
peppery puffery rurally signify squaddy tenably tripery victory
perfidy putrefy russety signory squally tenancy tripody viduity
perjury qualify Russify silkily squashy tensely tritely virelay
perkily quality rustily sillily squatty tensity trolley visibly
```

8 letter words

```
aardvark abeyancy abrasion absurdly accredit aciculas acrolith acturial
aardwolf abhorred abrasive abundant accuracy acidfast acrostic aculeate
aasvogel abhorrer abridger abutilon accurate acidhead acrotism Adamical
abacuses abidance abrogate abutment accursed acidosis acrylate adamitic
abattoir abjectly abruptly abuttals accustom acierage actiniae adaption
Abbaside ablation abscissa abutting aceldama acierate actinian adaptive
abbatial ablative absentee academia acentric aconitic actinias addendum
Abderite ablution absently academic acerbate aconitum actinide addition
abdicate abnegate absinthe acanthus acerbity acosmism actinism additive
abducens abnormal absolute acarpous acervate acoustic actinium adducent
abducent abomasum absolver Accadian acescent acquaint activate adductor
abductor abomasus absonant accentor achenial acrefoot actively adenitis
abelmosk aborally absorber accepter achiever acreinch activism adenoids
aberrant aborning absterge acceptor achiness acridine activist adequacy
abetment abortion abstract accident achingly acridity activity adequate
abetting abortive abstrict accolade aciculae acrimony actually adespota
abeyance abradant abstruse accoutre acicular acrolein actuator adherent
```

adhesion	aguishly	alopecia	ancestry	apically	armoured	attender	backcomb
adhesive	aigrette	alphabet	anchoret	aplastic	armourer	attested	backdate
adiantum	aiguille	alpinism	andesine	apocrine	armyworm	attester	backdoor
adjacent	airborne	alpinist	andesite	apodoses	aromatic	attestor	backdrop
adjuster	airbrake	Alsatian	androgen	apodosis	arpeggio	atticism	backfire
adjustor	airbrush	although	anecdote	apogamic	arquebus	attitude	backhand
adjutage	aircraft	altitude	anechoic	apograph	arranger	attorney	backlash
adjutant	Airedale	altruism	aneurism	apologia	arrantly	attrited	backless
adjuvant	airfield	altruist	aneurysm	apologue	arrestee	atwitter	backlist
Adlerian	airframe	alumroot	angelica	apomixis	arrester	atypical	backmost
adlibbed	airiness	alveolar	Anglican	apoplexy	arrestor	aubretia	backpack
admitted	airliner	alveolus	angstrom	apostasy	arrogant	audacity	backrest
admonish	airscrew	amadavat	anhedral	apostate	arrogate	audience	backroom
adnation	airshaft	amaranth	aniconic	apothegm	arsenate	audition	backseat
adoption	airspace	amazedly	animally	appalled	arsenide	auditive	backside
adoptive	airspeed	ambiance	animator	appanage	arsenite	auditory	backspin
adorable	airstrip	ambience	anisette	apparent	arsonist	Augustan	backstay
adorably	airtight	ambition	ankerite	appendix	arsonous	augustly	backveld
adroitly	airwoman	ambivert	ankylose	appetent	artefact	aurelian	backward
adularia	Akkadian	ambrosia	annalist	appetite	arterial	auricula	backwash
adulator	alacrity	ambulant	annotate	applause	artesian	auriform	backyard
adultery	alarmist	ambulate	announce	applepie	artfully	aurorean	Baconian
aduncate	albacore	ambusher	annually	applique	articled	auspices	bacteria
aduncous	Albanian	amenable	annulate	apposite	artifact	autacoid	Bactrian
advanced	albinism	amenably	annulled	appraise	artifice	autarchy	badinage
advisory	alburnum	American	anorexia	approach	artistic	autarkic	badlands
advocaat	alcahest	amethyst	anorexic	approval	artistry	autistic	bagpiper
advocacy	alchemic	amiantus	anorthic	apresski	asbestic	autobahn	baguette
advocate	aldehyde	amicable	anourous	apterous	asbestos	autocade	bailable
advowson	alderman	amicably	anserine	aptitude	ascender	autocrat	bailment
adynamia	Alderney	amitosis	answerer	aquacade	ascidian	autodafe	bailsman
adynamic	aleatory	amitotic	anteater	aqualung	ascidium	autodyne	bakshish
aegirine	alebench	ammoniac	antecede	aquanaut	ascocarp	autogamy	balanced
aegrotat	alehouse	ammonify	antedate	aquarist	aseptate	autogiro	balancer
aeration	aleurone	ammonite	antefixa	aquarium	asperges	autogyro	baldhead
aerially	alewives	ammonium	antelope	aquatint	asperity	autolyse	baldness
aeriform	alfresco	amnesiac	antennae	aqueduct	asphodel	automata	baldpate
aerodyne	algicide	amniotic	antennal	aquiline	asphyxia	automate	balefire
aerofoil	algidity	amoebean	antennas	araceous	aspirant	autonomy	Balinese
aerogram	alginate	amoeboid	antepost	arachnid	aspirate	autosome	balkline
aerolite	algology	amorally	anterior	Aramaean	assassin	autotomy	balladic
aerolith	Algonkin	amoretti	anteroom	Arapahoe	assemble	autotype	balladry
aerology	algorism	amoretto	anthelia	arapaima	assembly	autumnal	ballcock
aeronaut	alguazil	amortise	anthemia	arbalest	assenter	autunite	balletic
aeronomy	alienage	amperage	antheral	arbalist	assentor	avadavat	ballista
aerostat	alienate	amphibia	anthesis	arbitral	assertor	aventail	ballonet
aesthete	alienism	amphipod	anthozoa	arboreal	assessor	averment	ballroom
aestival	alienist	amphorae	antibody	arboreta	assiento	averring	ballyhoo
affected	alizarin	amphoras	antidote	arborist	assignat	aversely	ballyrag
affecter	alkahest	ampullae	antihero	Arcadian	assignee	aversion	balmoral
afferent	alkalies	amputate	antilogy	archaean	assignor	aversive	balsamic
affiance	alkalify	amusedly	antimask	archaise	assonant	aviarist	baluster
affinity	alkaline	amygdala	antimony	archaism	assonate	aviation	bambinos
affirmer	alkaloid	anabases	antinode	archaist	assorted	aviatrix	banality
afflatus	allegory	anabasis	antinomy	archduke	assuming	avidness	banausic
affluent	alleluia	anabatic	antiphon	archival	Assyrian	avifauna	bandanna
afforest	allergen	anabolic	antipode	archives	astatine	avionics	bandeaux
affright	allergic	anaconda	antipole	archness	asterisk	avowable	banderol
affusion	alleyway	anaerobe	antipope	Arcturus	asterism	avowedly	banditry
aflutter	alliance	anaglyph	antisera	arcuated	asteroid	avulsion	banditti
agaragar	allnight	anagogic	antitype	ardently	asthenia	aweather	bandsman
agedness	allocate	analcime	antlered	areolate	asthenic	axiality	bangtail
agential	allodial	analcite	antrorse	arethusa	astonied	axillary	banister
aggrieve	allodium	analecta	anyplace	argentic	astonish	axiology	banjoist
agiotage	allogamy	analogic	anything	argonaut	astragal	axletree	bankable
agitator	allopath	analogue	anywhere	arguable	astutely	Ayrshire	bankbill
agitprop	allotted	analyser	aoristic	arguably	asyndeta	babirusa	bankbook
aglimmer	allottee	analyses	apagogic	argufier	ataraxia	babouche	banknote
aglitter	allround	analysis	aperient	argument	ataraxic	babushka	bankroll
agnation	allspice	analytic	aperitif	Arianism	atheling	babyhood	bankrupt
agnostic	allusion	anapaest	aperture	arillate	Athenian	baccarat	bannered
agonised	allusive	anaphase	aphasiac	aristate	atheroma	bacchant	banneret
agraphia	alluvial	anaphora	aphelion	Armagnac	athletic	bachelor	bannerol
agrarian	alluvion	anarchic	aphicide	armament	atlantes	bacillar	banterer
agrement	alluvium	anaphore	aphorise	armature	Atlantic	bacillus	bantling
agrestic	almagest	anasarca	aphorism	armchair	atomiser	backache	banxring
agrimony	almanack	anathema	aphorist	Armenian	atremble	backbite	barathea
agrology	almighty	anatomic	apiarian	Arminian	atrocity	backbone	barbaric
agronomy	alogical	ancestor	apiarist	armorial	atropine	backchat	barbecue

barberry	bedeguar	bewilder	blastoff	bombsite	brandish	buddleia	caginess
barbette	bedimmed	bezonian	blastoid	bondmaid	brandnew	budgeree	cajolery
barbican	bedmaker	biannual	blastula	bondmans	brassage	buhlwork	cakewalk
barbital	bedplate	biassing	blatancy	bondsman	brassard	building	calabash
bareback	bedstead	biathlon	blazoner	bonefish	brassart	bulkhead	caladium
barefoot	bedstraw	bibation	blazonry	bonehead	brassica	bullcalf	calamary
bareness	bedtable	biblical	bleacher	boneless	brassily	bulldoze	calamine
bargeman	beebread	bibulous	bleakish	bonemeal	brattice	bulletin	calamint
baritone	beechnut	biconvex	blearily	boneyard	brattish	bullfrog	calamite
barkless	beeeater	bicuspid	bleeding	bonhomie	brazenly	bullhead	calamity
barnacle	beefcake	biddable	Blenheim	boniface	brazenry	bullhorn	calcanea
barndoor	beefwood	biennial	blesbuck	boniness	braziery	bullocky	calcaria
barnyard	beeswing	biennium	blessing	bonspiel	breakage	bullring	calcific
baronage	beetling	bifacial	blighter	bontebok	breaking	bullseye	calcitic
baroness	beetroot	bifocals	blimpish	bookcase	breakout	bullyboy	calcspar
baronial	befallen	bigamist	blindage	bookends	breasted	bullyoff	calctuff
barouche	befitted	bigamous	blinding	bookland	breather	bullyrag	calculus
barracks	befogged	bignonia	blinkers	booklice	breeches	bummaree	calendar
barranca	befriend	bilabial	blinking	booklore	breeding	buncombe	calender
barranco	befuddle	bilberry	blissful	bookmark	breezily	bundling	calfskin
barrator	begetter	billfold	blistery	bookpost	bregmata	bunfight	calidity
barratry	beggarly	billhead	blithely	bookrest	brethren	bungalow	califate
barrenly	beginner	billhook	blizzard	bookwork	brettese	bunghole	calipash
barrette	begirded	billiard	blockade	bookworm	brettice	bunkered	calipers
barterer	begotten	billyboy	blockage	bootjack	breveted	buntline	callable
bartizan	begrudge	billycan	blockish	bootlace	breviary	buoyancy	callgirl
baryonic	beguiler	bilobate	blondish	bootlast	brewster	Burberry	calliope
barytone	behemoth	bimanous	bloodily	bootless	Briarean	burglary	calliper
basaltic	beholden	bimbashi	bloodred	boottree	bribable	burgonet	calmness
baseball	beholder	binaural	bloomers	boracite	brickbat	Burgundy	calthrop
baseborn	bejabers	bindweed	bloomery	Bordeaux	brickred	burletta	calvados
baseless	belabour	binnacle	blooming	bordello	briefing	burnouse	calycine
baseline	believer	binomial	blossomy	borderer	brighten	burntout	calycoid
basement	belittle	bioassay	blotting	borecole	brightly	burrower	calycule
baseness	bellbird	biocidal	blowball	borehole	brimfull	bursitis	calyptra
basicity	bellbuoy	biogenic	blowfish	boringly	brimless	bushbaby	Cambrian
basidial	bellcote	biograph	blowhard	borrower	brindled	bushbuck	cameleer
basidium	bellpull	biometry	blowhole	bosseyed	brimming	bushfire	camellia
basilica	bellpush	biomorph	blowlamp	botanise	briskish	bushveld	camisade
basilisk	bellwort	bionomic	blowpipe	botanist	brisling	business	camisado
basinful	bellyful	bioplasm	blubbery	botflies	britches	bustling	camisole
basketry	beltless	bioplast	bludgeon	botryoid	britzska	busybody	camomile
bassinet	benedick	bioscope	bluebell	bottomry	broacher	busyness	campagna
basswood	benedict	biparous	bluebird	botulism	broadish	butchery	campaign
bastardy	benefice	birdbath	bluechip	botyrose	broadway	buttoner	campfire
bastille	benignly	birdcage	bluecoat	bouffant	brocaded	buttress	camphene
Batavian	Benjamin	birdcall	bluefish	boughten	brocatel	butylene	camphine
bateleur	bentwood	birdlime	blueness	bouillon	broccoli	butyrate	campsite
bathetic	benzoate	birdseed	bluenose	bouncily	brochure	buzzword	camshaft
bathotic	benzylic	birdseye	blueweed	bouncing	broidery	Byronism	Canadian
bathrobe	bequeath	birthday	blurrily	boundary	brokenly	bystreet	canaille
bathroom	berberis	bisector	blurring	bourgeon	bromelia	cabalism	canalise
battalia	berceuse	bisexual	blushful	boursier	bromidic	cabalist	canaster
battleax	bereaved	bistable	blustery	bourtree	bronchia	caballed	cancrine
baudrons	bergamot	bistoury	boarding	boutique	bronchus	cabinboy	cancroid
bauxitic	beriberi	bitchily	boastful	bouzouki	broodily	cableway	candidly
Bavarian	berliner	bitingly	boatbill	bowfront	brookite	cabochon	canister
bayadere	Bermudas	bitterly	boatdeck	bowsprit	brooklet	caboodle	cannabin
bayberry	besieger	bivalent	boathook	boxpleat	brougham	cabotage	cannabis
bdellium	beslaver	biweekly	boatload	boyishly	brouhaha	cabriole	cannibal
beadroll	besmirch	biyearly	bobbinet	bracelet	browband	cabstand	cannikin
beadsman	besotted	blabbing	bobbypin	brachial	browbeat	cachalot	cannonry
beadwork	besought	blackboy	bobbysox	brachium	browning	cachepot	cannulae
beagling	bespoken	blackcap	bobolink	brackish	brownish	cachexia	cannular
beamends	besprent	blackfly	bobwheel	bracteal	brunette	cachucha	cannulas
beanpole	bestiary	blacking	bobwhite	bractlet	brushoff	cacology	canoeing
bearable	bestowal	blackish	bodement	Bradshaw	brutally	cacomixl	canoeist
bearably	bestrewn	blackleg	bodiless	braggart	bryology	cactuses	canoness
bearings	bestride	blackout	Bodleian	bragging	bryozoan	cadastre	canonise
bearskin	bestrode	blacktie	bodyshop	braiding	bubaline	cadenced	canonist
beatific	betacism	blacktop	bodywork	brainish	buckaroo	caducean	canoodle
beautify	betatron	bladdery	Boeotian	brainpan	buckbean	caduceus	canorous
bebopper	bethesda	blahblah	bogeyman	brakeman	buckhorn	caducity	canthari
becalmed	betrayal	blamable	bohemian	brakevan	buckling	caducous	canticle
bechamel	betrayer	blamably	boldface	brancard	buckshee	caesious	cantonal
bechance	bevelled	blameful	boldness	branched	buckshot	caesural	cantoris
becoming	beveller	blandish	bollworm	brancher	buckskin	caffeine	canzonet
bedabble	beverage	blankety	bolthole	branchia	Buddhism	cagebird	capacity
bedazzle	bewigged	blastema	boltrope	brandied	Buddhist	cageling	capeline

```
capellet  catechol  champion  choragic  clearway  coercion  concerto  cooptive
capeskin  category  chancery  choragus  cleavage  coercive  concetti  coplanar
capitate  catenary  chandler  chorally  cleavers  cofactor  concetto  copperas
capitula  catenate  chapatti  chordate  clematis  cogently  conchate  copulate
caponier  cateress  chapbook  choregic  clemency  cogitate  conchoid  copybook
caponise  catering  chapelry  choregus  clerical  cognomen  conclave  copyedit
caprifig  cathedra  chaperon  choriamb  clerihew  cognosce  conclude  copyhold
capriole  catheter  chapiter  chorioid  clerkdom  cognovit  concrete  coquetry
capsicum  cathexes  chaplain  chowchow  clerkess  cogwheel  condense  coquette
capstone  cathexis  chapping  christen  cleverly  coherent  condylar  coracoid
capsular  cathodal  charcoal  christie  climatic  cohesion  conferee  cordless
captious  cathodic  charisma  Christly  clincher  cohesive  conferva  cordovan
capuchin  catholic  charlady  chromate  clinical  coiffeur  confetti  corduroy
capybara  cationic  charlock  chromite  clinking  coiffure  confider  cordwain
carabine  catsfoot  charming  chromium  clipclop  coincide  confiner  cordwood
caracara  catstail  charring  chthonic  clippers  coistrel  confines  corelate
caracole  cattleya  Chartism  chugging  clipping  cokernut  conflate  corkwing
carbolic  caudally  Chartist  chummily  cliquish  colander  conflict  corkwood
carbonic  caudated  chasseur  chumming  cliquism  coldness  confound  cornball
carbonyl  caudexes  chastely  chupatti  cloddish  coleseed  confrere  corneous
carboxyl  caudices  chastise  chupatty  clodpole  coleslaw  confront  cornetcy
carburet  caudillo  chastity  churchly  clodpoll  colewort  congener  cornetti
carcajou  cauldron  chasuble  churinga  clogging  coliform  conglobe  cornetto
carcanet  causally  chateaux  churlish  cloister  coliseum  congress  corniced
cardamom  causerie  chattily  churning  clopclop  collagen  congreve  corniche
cardamum  causeway  chatting  chutzpah  closeset  collapse  conidial  cornicle
cardigan  cautious  chaunter  ciborium  closeted  collared  conidium  cornific
cardinal  cavalier  chauntry  cicatrix  clothier  collator  coniform  cornpone
carefree  caverned  cheapish  cicerone  clothing  colleger  conjoint  coronach
careless  cavesson  checkers  ciceroni  clotting  colliery  conjugal  coronary
careworn  cavicorn  checkout  cicisbei  cloudily  collogue  conjunct  coronoid
carillon  cavilled  cheekily  cicisbeo  cloudlet  colloquy  conjurer  corporal
carinate  caviller  cheerful  cidevant  clownery  collyria  conjuror  corridor
carnally  celeriac  cheering  ciliated  clownish  colonial  conniver  corrival
carnauba  celerity  Chellean  cincture  clubbing  colonise  conoidal  corselet
carnival  celibacy  chemical  cineaste  clubfoot  colonist  conquest  corseted
Carolean  celibate  chemurgy  cinerary  clubhaul  colophon  conserve  corsetry
Caroline  cellarer  chenille  cingulum  clueless  colossal  consider  cortical
carolled  cellaret  chequers  cinnabar  clumsily  colossus  consoler  cortices
carotene  cellular  Cherokee  cinnamic  clupeoid  colubrid  conspire  corundum
carousal  cemetery  cherubic  cinnamon  clustery  columnal  constant  corvette
carousel  cenotaph  cherubim  cinquain  clypeate  columnar  construe  coryphee
carouser  Cenozoic  chessman  Circaean  coachdog  columned  consular  cosecant
carriage  centaury  chestnut  circuity  coachman  comatose  consumer  cosiness
carriole  centring  Cheyenne  circular  coaction  combings  contagia  cosmetic
carryall  centrism  chiasmus  cirriped  coactive  comeback  contango  cosmical
carryout  centrist  chiastic  cislunar  coagulum  comedian  contempt  costmary
cartload  centroid  chickpea  citation  coaldust  comedist  contents  costplus
cartouch  centuple  chiefdom  citified  coalesce  comedown  contessa  costpush
caruncle  cephalic  childbed  cityfied  coalfish  cometary  continua  costumer
caryatid  ceramics  childish  civilian  coalhole  commando  continue  cotenant
Casanova  ceramist  children  civilise  coalmine  commence  continuo  cothurni
cascabel  cercaria  chiliasm  civility  coalsack  commerce  contline  cotillon
casebook  ceratoid  chiliast  cladding  coarsely  commoner  contorno  cotquean
casemate  cerebral  chimaera  claimant  coatrack  commoney  contract  Cotswold
casement  cerebrum  chimeric  clambake  coatroom  commonly  contrail  cottager
casework  cerement  Chinaman  clammily  coauthor  communal  contrary  cottagey
cashbook  ceremony  chinchin  clamming  cobaltic  commuter  contrast  couchant
cashmere  cernuous  chipmuck  clangour  cobblers  compages  contrate  couching
cassette  cerulean  chipmunk  clannish  coccyges  compiler  contrite  couldest
castaway  cerusite  chipping  clanship  cochleae  complain  contrive  coulisse
castiron  cervelat  chirpily  clansman  cochlear  compleat  conurbia  coumarin
castrate  cervical  chirrupy  clapping  cockatoo  complete  convener  countess
castrati  cervices  chitchat  claptrap  cockboat  complice  convenor  coupling
castrato  cesspool  chivalry  claqueur  cockcrow  complier  converge  courante
casually  cetacean  chlorate  clarence  cockerel  compline  converse  coursing
casualty  chaconne  chloride  clarinet  cockeyed  composed  convexly  courtesy
catacomb  chainsaw  chlorine  classics  cockloft  composer  conveyer  courtier
catalase  chairman  chlorite  classify  cockshut  compound  conveyor  couscous
cataloes  chalazae  chlorous  clavicle  cocksure  compress  convince  cousinly
catalyse  Chaldaic  choicely  clawback  cocktail  comprise  convolve  covalent
catalyst  Chaldean  choirboy  claymore  codifier  computer  convulse  covenant
catamite  chaldron  choleric  cleancut  codpiece  conation  coolabah  coverage
catapult  chalkpit  chondrus  cleaning  codriver  conative  coolibah  coverall
cataract  chambers  chopchop  cleanser  coelomic  concasse  coolness  covering
catchall  chambray  chopping  clearcut  coenobia  conceder  coonskin  coverlet
catchfly  champers  chopsuey  clearing  coenzyme  conceive  cooption  covetous
catching
```

cowardly	crotchet	cynosure	December	denarius	diagnose	diploidy	ditherer
cowberry	croupier	Cypriote	decemvir	denature	diagonal	diplomat	dittybag
cowgrass	croupous	cypselae	decennia	denazify	diagraph	diplopia	dittybox
coworker	crowbill	Cyrenaic	decently	dendrite	diallage	dipnoous	diuresis
coxalgia	crowfoot	Cyrillic	decigram	dendroid	dialling	dipstick	diuretic
coxswain	cruciate	cysteine	decimate	denehole	dialogic	dipteral	divagate
cozenage	crucible	cystitis	decipher	deniable	dialogue	dipteran	divalent
crabbing	crucifer	cytidine	decision	denounce	dialyser	directly	divebomb
crackers	crucifix	cytology	decisive	dentalia	dialyses	director	dividend
cracking	crueller	cytosine	deckhand	dentated	dialysis	dirigism	dividivi
crackjaw	crumhorn	czaritza	declarer	denticle	dialytic	diriment	dividual
cracknel	crummock	dabchick	declasse	departed	diamante	disabuse	divinely
crackpot	crusader	dactylar	declutch	depicter	diameter	disagree	divinise
cradling	crustily	dactylic	decolour	depictor	dianthus	disallow	divinity
craftily	cruzeiro	daemonic	decorate	depilate	diapason	disarray	division
cragsman	cryogeny	daffodil	decorous	deponent	diapause	disaster	divisive
cramfull	cryolite	daftness	decouple	deportee	diaphone	disbench	divorcee
cramming	cryostat	dahabieh	decrease	depraved	diarchal	disbound	djellaba
cramoisy	cryotron	daimonic	decrepit	deprival	diarchic	disburse	Docetism
cranefly	cubature	daintily	decretal	deprived	diarrhea	disciple	Docetist
craniate	cubiform	daiquiri	decurion	depurate	diaspora	disclaim	docilely
crankily	cuboidal	dairying	dedicate	deputise	diaspore	disclose	docility
crankpin	cucumber	dairyman	deedless	deration	diastase	discount	dockland
crannied	cucurbit	dalesman	deemster	derelict	diastema	discover	dockside
crashing	culdesac	dalmatic	deeplaid	derision	diastole	discreet	dockyard
crashpad	culicine	damassin	deepness	derisive	diatomic	discrete	doctoral
cratches	culinary	damnable	deerskin	derisory	diatonic	discrown	doctrine
cravenly	culottes	damnably	defector	derivate	diatribe	diseased	document
crawfish	culpable	dampness	defender	derogate	dicacity	disendow	doddered
crayfish	culpably	dancette	deferent	derriere	dichasia	disfrock	dodderer
creakily	cultivar	dancetty	deferral	describe	dichroic	disgorge	dogberry
creamery	cultural	dandruff	deferred	deserter	dicrotic	disgrace	dogeared
creatine	cultured	dandyish	deferrer	designer	dictator	disguise	dogfaced
creation	culverin	dandyism	defiance	desirous	dicyclic	dishevel	dogfight
creative	Cumbrian	danegeld	defilade	desolate	didactic	disinter	doggedly
creatrix	cumbrous	dankness	definite	despatch	didapper	disjoint	doggerel
creature	cumulate	danseuse	deflower	despiser	didymium	disjunct	doghouse
credence	cumulous	daringly	deforest	despotic	didymous	dislodge	dogmatic
credenza	cupboard	darkling	deformed	destrier	dieldrin	disloyal	dogooder
credible	cupelled	darkness	defrayal	destruct	diereses	dismally	dogsbody
credibly	cupidity	darkroom	deftness	detached	dieresis	dismount	dogshore
credited	cupreous	darksome	degrease	detailed	diestock	disorder	dogtired
creditor	cupulate	dartrous	deionise	detainee	dietetic	dispatch	dogtooth
creeping	curarine	dastardy	dejected	detainer	diffract	dispense	dogwatch
crenated	curarise	dateless	delation	detector	diffuser	disperse	dogwhelk
crenelle	curassow	dateline	delegacy	deterred	digamist	dispirit	doldrums
creosote	curative	daughter	delegate	deterrer	digamous	displace	dolerite
crepitus	curculio	daybreak	deletion	dethrone	digester	displant	dolesome
crescent	cureless	daydream	delibate	detonate	diggings	displode	dolomite
crescive	curlicue	daylight	delicacy	detoxify	digitate	displume	doloroso
cretonne	currency	deadbeat	delicate	detrital	digitise	disposal	dolorous
crevasse	curricle	deadener	delirium	detritus	dihedral	disposer	domestic
cribbage	cursedly	deadfall	delivery	deucedly	dihybrid	dispread	domicile
cribbing	curtains	deadhead	Delphian	deuteron	dilatant	disprize	dominant
criminal	curtness	deadline	delusion	deviance	dilation	disproof	dominate
crispate	curveted	deadlock	delusive	deviancy	dilative	disprove	domineer
cristate	cushiony	deadness	delusory	deviator	dilatory	disquiet	dominion
criteria	Cushitic	deadwood	demagogy	deviling	diligent	disseise	dominoes
critical	cuspidor	deaerate	demander	devilish	dilution	disserve	donation
critique	cussedly	deafmute	demarche	devilism	diluvial	dissever	Donatism
croakily	cussword	deafness	demented	devilkin	diluvian	dissolve	Donatist
Croatian	customer	dealfish	dementia	devilled	diluvium	dissuade	donative
croceate	cuteness	deanship	demerara	deviltry	dimerism	distally	donatory
crockery	cutprice	dearness	demersal	Devonian	dimerous	distance	donought
crocoite	cutpurse	deathbed	demijohn	devotion	diminish	distaste	doomsday
crofting	cutwater	deathcap	demitted	devourer	dimmable	distinct	doomsman
cromlech	cyanogen	deathray	demiurge	devoutly	dinerout	distract	doomster
cromorna	cyanoses	debagged	demobbed	dewberry	dingdong	distrain	doorbell
cromorne	cyanosis	debarred	democrat	dewiness	dinornis	distrait	doorcase
cropping	cyanotic	debility	demolish	dewpoint	dinosaur	distress	doorknob
crossbar	cyclamen	debonair	demoness	dewyeyed	diocesan	district	doornail
crossbow	cycleway	debugged	demoniac	dextrine	dioecism	distrust	doorpost
crosscut	cyclical	debutant	demonian	dextrose	diopside	disunion	doorsill
crossing	cyclonic	decadent	demonise	dextrous	dioptase	disunite	doorstep
crosslet	cyclopes	decagram	demonism	diabasic	dioptric	disunity	doorstop
crossply	cyclosis	decanter	demotion	diabetes	dioramic	disusage	dooryard
crosstie	cylinder	deceased	demurely	diabetic	dioritic	disvalue	dopiness
crossway	cymatium	decedent	demurred	diabolic	diphenyl	ditheism	dormancy
crotched	cynicism	deceiver	demurrer	diaconal	diplogen	ditheist	dormouse

dorsally	dropping	dyslexic	eleventh	endogeny	epicycle	estuaril	exchange
dotation	dropshot	dyspnoea	elfarrow	endorsee	epidemic	esurient	excision
dotingly	dropwort	dystopia	elflocks	endorser	epidural	etcetera	excitant
dotterel	droughty	eagleowl	eligible	endostea	epifauna	eternise	exciting
douanier	drownded	earmuffs	eligibly	endozoic	epigeous	eternity	excluder
doubloon	drowsily	earnings	elkhound	endozoon	epigraph	ethereal	excursus
doubtful	drubbing	earphone	ellipses	endpaper	epilepsy	etherial	execrate
doughboy	drudgery	earpiece	ellipsis	energise	epilogue	etherise	executor
doughnut	drugging	earthnut	elliptic	enervate	epinasty	etherism	exegesis
doumpalm	druggist	easement	elongate	enfeeble	epiphany	etherist	exegetic
dourness	druidess	easiness	eloquent	enfetter	epiphyte	ethicism	exemplar
dovecote	druidism	easterly	emaciate	enfilade	episcope	ethicist	exemplum
dovetail	drumfire	eastmost	embalmer	enforcer	episemon	Ethiopic	exequies
dowdyish	drumhead	eastward	embattle	enforest	episodal	ethnarch	exercise
dowelled	drumming	ebriated	embedded	engaging	episodic	ethnical	exergual
downbeat	drummock	ecclesia	embezzle	engender	epistler	ethology	exertion
downcast	drumroll	echinate	embitter	engineer	epistyle	ethylene	exhalant
downcome	drunkard	echinoid	emblazon	enginery	epitasis	etiolate	exhorter
downfall	drupelet	echogram	embolden	engirdle	epopoeia	Etrurian	exigence
downhaul	dryclean	echoless	embolism	engramma	epyllion	Etruscan	exigency
downhill	drynurse	eclectic	embosser	engraver	equalise	eucalypt	exigible
downland	dryplate	ecliptic	embracer	enkindle	equality	eucritic	exiguity
downmost	drypoint	eclosion	embussed	enlarger	equalled	eugenics	exiguous
downpipe	drystone	ecologic	emceeing	enneagon	equation	eugenism	eximious
downpour	duchesse	economic	emendate	enormity	equinity	eugenist	existent
downtime	duckbill	ecstatic	emergent	enormous	equipage	eulachon	exlibris
downtown	duckhawk	ectoderm	emeritus	enquirer	equipped	eulogise	exocrine
downturn	duckling	ectozoon	emersion	enricher	equitant	eulogist	exogamic
downward	duckpond	edacious	emetical	enrolled	equities	eulogium	exorcise
downwind	duckweed	edentate	emigrant	ensample	equivoke	euonymin	exorcism
doxology	ductless	edgeless	emigrate	ensconce	erasable	euonymus	exorcist
doziness	duelling	edgeways	eminence	ensemble	Erastian	eupatrid	exordial
drabbler	duellist	edgewise	eminency	ensheath	erectile	eupepsia	exordium
drabness	duettist	edginess	emissary	enshrine	erection	eupeptic	exospore
dracaena	Dukhobor	editress	emission	enshroud	eremitic	euphonic	exoteric
drachmae	dulciana	educable	emissive	ensiform	erethism	euphoria	expander
drachmai	dulcimer	educated	emitting	ensigncy	erewhile	euphoric	expedite
drachmas	Dulcinea	educator	Emmental	ensilage	ergogram	euphrasy	expelled
draconic	dullness	educible	empathic	enslaver	ergotise	euphuism	expellee
dragging	dumbbell	eduction	empeople	ensphere	ergotism	euphuist	expertly
dragline	dumbhead	eelgrass	emphases	enswathe	erigeron	Eurasian	expiable
dragoman	dumbness	eeriness	emphasis	entailer	erodible	Eurocrat	expiator
dragomen	dumbshow	effector	emphatic	entangle	erogenic	European	expirant
dragonet	dumfound	efferent	employee	entellus	erotical	europium	explicit
dragsman	dumpling	efficacy	employer	enterate	errantly	eustatic	exploder
dragster	dundiver	effluent	empoison	enthalpy	errantry	eutectic	explorer
drainage	dungaree	effluvia	emporium	enthrall	eruption	eutrophy	exponent
dramatic	dungcart	effusion	empurple	enthrone	eruptive	evacuant	exporter
drammock	dunghill	effusive	empyreal	entirely	erythema	evacuate	exposure
dramshop	duodenal	eftsoons	empyrean	entirety	escalade	evadable	exserted
draughts	duodenum	egestion	emulator	entoderm	escalate	evaluate	extender
draughty	duologue	egestive	emulgent	entoptic	escallop	evanesce	extensor
drawable	durables	eggplant	emulsify	entozoic	escalope	evection	exterior
drawback	duration	eggshell	emulsion	entozoon	escapade	evenfall	external
drawtube	durative	egoistic	emulsive	entracte	escapism	evenness	extolled
drawwell	durukuli	egomania	emulsoid	entrails	escapist	evensong	extrados
dreadful	dustbowl	Egyptian	enaction	entrance	escargot	eventful	extremes
dreamful	dustcart	eighteen	enactive	entreaty	escarole	eventide	extrorse
dreamily	dustcoat	eighthly	enarched	entrench	eschalot	eventual	exultant
dreaming	dustless	eighties	encaenia	entrepot	eschewal	evermore	exuviate
drearily	dustlike	ejection	enceinte	entresol	esculent	eversion	eyeglass
drencher	dustshot	ejective	encipher	enuresis	Eskimoan	everyday	eyeliner
dressage	Dutchman	ekistics	encircle	enuretic	esoteric	everyman	eyepiece
dressing	dutiable	elatedly	enclitic	envelope	espalier	everyone	eyerhyme
dribbler	dutyfree	eldorado	enclothe	enviable	especial	everyway	eyeshade
dribblet	dutypaid	eldritch	encomion	enviably	espousal	eviction	eyesight
driftage	dwarfish	election	encomium	environs	espouser	evidence	eyestalk
driftice	dwarfism	elective	encrinal	envisage	espresso	evildoer	eyetooth
driftway	dwelling	electret	encrinic	envision	Esquimau	evilness	eyewater
drilling	dybbukim	electric	encroach	enzootic	essayist	evincive	fabliaux
drinking	dyestuff	electron	encumber	eohippus	Essenism	evitable	fabulist
dripfeed	dynamics	electrum	encyclic	eolithic	essonite	evulsion	fabulous
dripping	dynamism	elegance	endamage	ephemera	esterify	exacting	faceache
drivable	dynamist	elegancy	endanger	Ephesian	estimate	exaction	facecard
driveway	dynamite	elenchus	endemism	ephorate	Estonian	examinee	faceless
drollery	dynastic	elenctic	endermic	epiblast	estopped	examiner	facelift
drophead	dynatron	elephant	endocarp	epically	estoppel	exanthem	facepack
dropkick	dysgenic	elevated	endoderm	epicalyx	estovers	excavate	facetiae
dropleaf	dyslexia	elevator	endogamy	epicotyl	estrange	excelled	facially

facilely	feasible	filtrate	flatfoot	foamless	forensic	frapping	fumigant
facility	feasibly	fimbriae	flathead	focalise	forepart	Fraulein	fumigate
factious	feastday	finalise	flatiron	focusing	forepast	freakish	fumitory
factotum	feathery	finalism	flatling	focussed	forepeak	freakout	function
fadeaway	featured	finalist	flatmate	foetidly	foreplay	freeborn	funebral
fadeless	features	finality	flatness	fogbound	foresaid	freedman	funerary
fagoting	febrific	finedraw	flatrace	foldaway	foresail	freefall	funereal
failsafe	February	fineness	flattery	foldboat	foreseen	freehand	fungible
faineant	feckless	finespun	flattest	folderol	foreshow	freehold	funkhole
faintish	feculent	fingered	flattish	foliaged	foreside	freeload	funnyman
fairlead	fedayeen	finisher	flatware	folklore	foreskin	freeness	furbelow
fairness	federate	finitely	flatways	folkmoot	forestal	freesoil	furcated
fairyism	feeblish	finitude	flatwise	folksong	forestay	freewill	furculae
faithful	feedback	finnesko	flatworm	folktale	forested	freezeup	furcular
falcated	feedhead	firearms	flautist	follicle	forester	freezing	furfural
falchion	feedpipe	fireback	flawless	follower	forestry	fremitus	furfuran
falconer	feedtank	fireball	flaxseed	followon	foretell	frenetic	furlough
falconet	feldsher	firebird	fleabane	followup	foretime	frenulum	furriery
falconry	feldspar	fireboat	fleabite	fomenter	foretold	frenzied	furthest
falderal	felicity	firebomb	fleawort	fondling	forewarn	frequent	furuncle
fallback	felinity	firebrat	flection	fondness	forewent	frescoes	fuselage
fallfish	fellable	fireclay	fleeting	fontanel	foreword	freshman	fusiform
fallible	fellahin	firedamp	fleshfly	fontange	foreyard	freshrun	fusileer
fallibly	fellness	fireeyed	fleshpot	foodless	forgiven	fretting	fusilier
falsetto	fellowly	firehose	fletcher	foolscap	forgoing	fretwork	futilely
faltboat	felsitic	firelock	flexible	football	forklift	Freudian	futility
familial	feminine	fireopal	flexibly	footbath	formalin	fribbler	futurism
familiar	feminise	fireplug	flexuose	footfall	formally	friction	futurist
famously	feminism	fireship	flexuous	footgear	formerly	friendly	futurity
fanciful	feminist	fireside	flexural	foothill	formless	Friesian	gabbroic
fancyman	feminity	firetrap	flickery	foothold	formroom	frighten	gabbroid
fandance	fenberry	fireweed	flimflam	footless	formulae	frigidly	gableend
fandango	fencible	firewood	flimsily	footling	formulas	frijoles	gadabout
fanfaron	fenestra	firework	flincher	footmark	formwork	frillies	gadarene
fangless	feretory	firmness	flinders	footmuff	fornices	fringing	gadgetry
fanlight	fernshaw	firstaid	flintily	footnote	forrader	frippery	Gadhelic
fantasia	ferocity	fiscally	flipflap	footpace	forsaken	frisette	gadzooks
faradaic	ferreter	fishable	flipflop	footpath	forsooth	friskily	gainable
faradism	ferriage	fishball	flipping	footpost	forspeak	fritting	gainings
farcical	ferritic	fishbone	flipside	footrace	forspent	frocking	gainless
farewell	ferryman	fishbowl	floatage	footrest	forswear	frogfish	gainsaid
farflung	fervency	fishcake	flitting	footrope	forswore	frogging	galactic
farinose	fervidly	fishfarm	floating	footrule	forsworn	frogspit	galangal
farmhand	festally	fishglue	floccose	footslog	fortieth	frondage	galbanum
farmland	festival	fishhawk	floccule	footsore	fortress	frondent	galeated
farmyard	fetching	fishhook	flocculi	footstep	fortuity	frondeur	Galenism
farouche	feticide	fishless	floccose	footwear	fortyish	frondose	galenite
farriery	feudally	fishmeal	flockbed	footwork	forwards	frontage	Galilean
farthest	feverfew	fishpond	flogging	foramina	forzando	frontier	galleass
farthing	feverish	fishtail	floodlit	forborne	fosterer	frontlet	galliard
fascicle	feverous	fishwife	floodway	forcedly	fougasse	frostily	Gallican
fasciola	fewtrils	fissiped	flooring	forcefed	foulness	frosting	gallipot
fasciole	fibrilla	fistiana	floppily	forceful	founding	frothily	galloper
Fascista	fibrosis	fistical	flopping	forcible	fountain	frottage	Galloway
Fascisti	fibrotic	fistulae	florally	forcibly	fourball	froufrou	galluses
fashious	fiddling	fistular	floridly	fordable	foureyes	fructify	gallwasp
fastback	fidelity	fitfully	florigen	forebear	fourfold	fructose	galvanic
fastener	fiducial	fivefold	flotilla	forebode	fourleaf	frugally	gambados
fastfood	fiendish	fivestar	flounder	forebode	fourpart	fruitage	gambeson
fastness	fiercely	fixation	flourish	forecast	foursome	fruitbat	gambroon
fasttalk	fiftieth	fixative	flowered	foredeck	fourstar	fruitery	gamebird
fastuous	fiftyish	flabella	flowerer	foredoom	fourteen	fruitfly	gamecock
fatalism	fighting	flagella	floweret	foreedge	fourthly	fruitful	gameness
fatalist	figurant	flagging	flubbing	forefeel	foveolae	fruition	gamesome
fatality	figurine	flagpole	fluellin	forefelt	fowlpest	frumenty	gamester
fatherly	filagree	flagrant	fluently	forefoot	foxglove	frumpish	gaminess
fatigues	filament	flagship	fluepipe	foregoer	foxhound	frustule	gangland
fatstock	filariae	flambeau	fluidics	foregone	foxiness	frutices	gangling
fattener	filarial	flamenco	fluidify	forehand	foxshark	fuchsine	ganglion
faubourg	filature	flamingo	fluidise	forehead	frabjous	fuelling	gangrene
faultily	filefish	flanerie	fluidity	foreknew	fraction	fugacity	gangster
faunally	filially	flapjack	flummery	foreknow	fracture	fugitive	ganister
Faustian	filiform	flapping	fluoride	forelady	fraenula	fugleman	gantline
fauteuil	filigree	flashgun	fluorine	foreland	fragment	fullback	gantlope
favonian	Filipina	flashily	fluorite	forelock	fragrant	fullness	Ganymede
favoured	Filipino	flashing	fluttery	foremast	framesaw	fullpage	gaolbird
favourer	filmgoer	flatboat	flyblown	foremost	francium	fullsize	gapeworm
fearless	filmstar	flatfeet	flypaper	forename	Frankish	fulltime	gapingly
fearsome	filthily	flatfish	flywheel	forenoon	franklin	fumarole	garboard

gardener	ghoulish	godwards	greeting	gyratory	hardhack	hedgepig	highbrow
gardenia	giantess	gogetter	greffier	gyrostat	hardhead	hedgerow	higherup
gardyloo	giantism	Goidelic	greyfish	habanera	hardline	hedonics	highjack
garefowl	giftbook	goingson	greyness	habitant	hardness	hedonism	highland
garganey	gigantic	goitrous	gridiron	habitual	hardship	hedonist	highlows
gargoyle	gillaroo	Golconda	grievous	habitude	hardtack	heedless	highmost
garishly	gilthead	golddust	grillage	hacienda	hardware	heelball	highness
garlicky	gimcrack	goldenly	grimacer	hadronic	hardwood	heelless	highrise
garotter	gimmicky	goldfish	grimmest	haematic	harebell	Hegelian	highroad
garreted	gingerly	goldfoil	grimness	haematin	haresear	hegemony	hightail
garrison	gingival	goldleaf	grimoire	Haggadah	harikari	heighten	hightest
garrotte	gipsydom	goldmine	grindery	hairgrip	harlotry	heirless	hijacker
gaselier	gipsyism	goldrush	grinning	hairless	harmless	heirloom	hilarity
gasfired	girasole	golfclub	gripping	hairlike	harmonic	heirship	hillfort
gashouse	girlhood	golliwog	gripsack	hairline	harpseal	heliacal	hillocky
gaslight	giveaway	gonfalon	Griselda	hairworm	harridan	helicoid	hillside
gasmeter	glabella	gonidial	griseous	Halachah	harrumph	heliosis	himation
gasolene	glabrous	gonidium	grisette	halation	haruspex	heliport	hinderer
gasolier	glaciate	goodness	grisgris	haleness	hasheesh	Helladic	hindlegs
gasoline	gladdest	goodtime	grissini	halfback	hastener	hellbent	hindmost
gastight	gladding	goodwife	gritting	halfbeak	hastings	Hellenic	hinduise
gastraea	gladhand	goodwill	grizzled	halfboot	hatchery	hellfire	Hinduism
gastrula	gladioli	goodyear	groggily	halfbred	hatching	hellhole	hipflask
gasworks	gladness	goofball	grogshop	halflife	hatchway	helmeted	hipsters
gatefold	gladsome	goosegog	gromwell	halfmast	hateable	helminth	hireable
gatepost	glancing	gorgeous	groogroo	halfmoon	hatstand	helmsman	hireling
gatherer	glanders	gorgonia	grosbeak	halfnote	haulyard	helotism	hirrient
Gaullism	glandule	gormless	groschen	halfpint	haunting	helpless	Hispanic
Gaullist	glassful	gossamer	grottoes	halfsole	hausfrau	helpmate	histogen
gauntlet	glassily	gossiper	grounder	halfterm	havelock	helpmeet	historic
gavelock	glassine	gossipry	grouping	halftime	havildar	henchman	hitherto
gazogene	glaucoma	gossypol	grouting	halftone	havocked	henequen	hoarding
gazpacho	glaucous	gourmand	growling	haliotis	Hawaiian	henparty	hoarsely
gearcase	glaziery	goutweed	grubbily	halliard	hawfinch	henroost	hobbitry
gefuffle	gleaning	goutwort	grubbing	hallmark	hawkeyed	hepatica	hobbyist
gelastic	gleesome	governor	grudging	hallowed	hawklike	hepatise	hocktide
gelatine	glibness	gownsman	gruesome	halluces	hawkmoth	heptagon	hocusing
gelation	glissade	Graafian	grumbler	halteres	hawkweed	heraldic	hocussed
gelidity	glittery	grabbing	grumpily	hamartia	hawthorn	heraldry	Hogmanay
gematria	gloaming	grabbler	gruntled	hamululi	hayfield	herbaria	hogsback
geminate	globally	graceful	guacharo	handball	haymaker	herbless	hogshead
gemstone	globular	gracioso	guaiacum	handbell	haystack	Hercules	holdback
gendarme	globulin	gracious	guaranty	handbill	hazelnut	herdbook	holdfast
generate	gloomily	gradient	guardant	handbook	haziness	herdsman	holdover
generous	gloriole	graduand	guardian	handcart	headache	herdwick	holidays
genetics	glorious	graduate	Guelphic	handclap	headachy	hereaway	holiness
Genevese	glossary	Graecise	guerilla	handcuff	headband	heredity	holistic
genially	glossily	Graecism	guernsey	handfast	headfast	Hereford	hollands
genitive	glossina	graffiti	guidable	handgrip	headgear	hereunto	hollowly
geniture	glowworm	graffito	guidance	handheld	headlamp	hereupon	Holocene
genocide	gloxinia	graining	guidedog	handhold	headland	herewith	hologram
genotype	glucagon	gralloch	guideway	handicap	headless	heritage	holozoic
gentrice	glucinum	gramarye	guileful	handless	headline	hermetic	holstein
geodesic	glummest	gramatom	guiltily	handline	headlock	hernshaw	homebody
geodetic	glumness	gramercy	Gujarati	handling	headlong	heroical	homeborn
geognosy	glutting	grandame	gulfweed	handlist	headmost	herpetic	homebred
geologic	gluttony	granddad	gullable	handloom	headnote	Hertzian	homebrew
geomancy	glycerin	grandeur	gullible	handmade	headrace	hesitant	homefelt
geometer	glycerol	grandson	gulosity	handmaid	headrest	hesitate	homeland
geometry	glyceryl	granitic	gummosis	handmill	headroom	Hesperus	homeless
geophagy	glycogen	granular	gumption	handpick	headsail	hetaerae	homelike
geophone	glyconic	grapheme	gunfight	handrail	headsman	hetairai	homemade
geophyte	glyptics	graphics	gunflint	handsewn	headwind	hexagram	homesick
geoponic	gnathite	graphite	gunlayer	handsome	headword	hexapody	homespun
Georgian	gneissic	grasping	gunmetal	handwork	headwork	hexylene	hometown
geotaxis	gnomonic	grateful	gunpoint	handyman	heartily	hibernal	homeward
geraniol	goadster	gratuity	gunsmith	hangable	heatedly	hibiscus	homework
geranium	goalkick	gravamen	gunstock	hangeron	heathery	hiccough	homicide
gerbille	goalline	gravelly	gusseted	hangnail	heathhen	hickwall	hominoid
Germanic	goalpost	graviton	guttural	hangover	heavenly	hideaway	homodont
germcell	goatfish	grayling	gymkhana	haploidy	hebdomad	hidrosis	homogamy
germfree	goatherd	greasily	gymnasia	harakiri	hebetate	hidrotic	homogeny
germinal	goatling	greedily	gynandry	harangue	hebetude	hidyhole	homology
gerontic	goatmoth	greegree	gynocrat	harasser	hebraise	hielaman	homonymy
gestagen	goatskin	greenery	gynoecia	hardback	Hebraism	hierarch	homuncle
gestural	Gobelins	greenfly	gypseous	hardbake	Hebraist	hieratic	honestly
Ghanaian	godawful	greening	gypsydom	hardcase	hecatomb	highball	honeybee
ghastful	godchild	greenish	gypsyism	hardcore	hedgehog	highborn	honeydew
ghettoes	Godspeed	greenlet	gyration	hardener	hedgehop	highbred	honeypot

honorary	hydropsy	immolate	infector	intermix	isomorph	judgment	knitting
honourer	hydroski	immortal	inferior	internal	isophote	judicial	knitwear
hoodwink	hydroxyl	immunise	infernal	internee	isopleth	jugglery	knocking
hoofbeat	hygienic	immunity	inferred	Interpol	isoprene	Jugoslav	knockout
hookworm	hymenial	impacted	infilter	interred	isoptera	jugulate	knothole
hooligan	hymenium	impanate	infinite	interrex	isospory	julienne	knotting
hoosegow	hymnbook	imparity	infinity	intersex	isostasy	jumpedup	knotwork
hopeless	hyoscine	impelled	infirmly	intertie	isothere	jumpseat	knowable
Horatian	hypnoses	impeller	inflamer	interval	isotherm	jumpsuit	Kohinoor
hormonal	hypnosis	imperial	inflated	interwar	isotonic	junction	kohlrabi
hornbeam	hypnotic	imperium	inflator	inthrall	isotopic	juncture	kolinsky
hornbill	hypobole	impetigo	inflatus	intimacy	isotropy	junkshop	komitaji
hornbook	hypoderm	impishly	inflexed	intimate	issuable	junkyard	Komsomol
hornfels	hypogeal	impledge	inflight	intimism	issuance	Jurassic	korfball
hornless	hypogean	implicit	influent	intitule	isthmian	juristic	kourbash
hornpipe	hypogene	impolder	informal	intonate	Italiote	justness	kreutzer
hornrims	hypogeum	impolicy	informed	intrados	iterance	juvenile	kromesky
horntail	hypogyny	impolite	informer	intrench	ivorynut	Kaffiyeh	krumhorn
hornworm	hypothec	imponent	infrared	intrepid	jabberer	kailyard	kurtosis
hornwort	hysteria	importer	infringe	intrigue	jackaroo	kakemono	kyphosis
horologe	hysteric	imposing	infusion	intromit	jackboot	kalaazar	kyphotic
horology	ianthine	imposter	ingather	introrse	jackeroo	kamikaze	labdanum
horrible	Ibsenism	impostor	ingrowth	intruder	jackstay	Kanarese	labelled
horribly	iceblink	impotent	inguinal	intubate	Jacobean	kangaroo	labellum
horridly	icebound	imprimis	inhalant	inundate	Jacobite	Kashmiri	labially
horrific	icecream	imprison	inherent	inurbane	jacquard	katakana	lability
horsebox	icefield	improper	inhesion	invasion	jaggedly	kedgeree	labourer
horsecar	iceplant	improver	inhumane	invasive	jailbird	keelhaul	labrador
horsefly	iceskate	impudent	inimical	invected	jalousie	keelless	laburnum
horseman	icewater	impugner	iniquity	inveigle	jamboree	keenness	lacerate
hosepipe	iceyacht	impunity	initiate	inventor	janizary	keepsake	lacewing
hospital	ichorous	impurely	injector	inverted	Japanese	keeshond	lacework
hostelry	idealess	impurity	inkiness	inverter	japanned	kefuffle	lackaday
hotchpot	idealise	inaction	inkstand	investor	japhetic	keratose	laconian
hotelier	idealism	inactive	inlander	inviable	japonica	kerchief	laconism
hothouse	idealist	inasmuch	innately	inviting	jaundice	kerosene	lacrimal
hotplate	ideality	inceptor	innocent	invocate	jauntily	kerosine	lacrosse
hotpress	ideation	inchmeal	innovate	involute	Javanese	keyboard	lacrymal
hourlong	identify	inchoate	innuendo	inwardly	jealousy	keystone	lacunary
houseboy	identity	inchworm	inoculum	iodinate	Jehovist	khedival	lacunate
housedog	ideogram	incident	inositol	iodoform	jejunely	Khmerian	lacunose
housefly	ideology	incision	inquirer	iotacism	jeopardy	khuskhus	ladybird
houseful	idiolect	incisive	insanely	irenical	jeremiad	kibitzer	ladyfern
houseman	idiotism	incitant	insanity	irenicon	Jeremiah	kickback	ladyhood
housetop	idleness	incivism	inscient	Irishism	jeroboam	kickshaw	ladylike
hoverfly	idocrase	included	inscribe	Irishman	jerrican	kidglove	ladylove
howitzer	idolater	incoming	inscroll	ironbark	jerrycan	killdeer	ladyship
huckster	idolatry	increase	insecure	ironclad	jesuitic	kilogram	laically
hugeness	idoliser	increate	inserted	irongray	jesuitry	kilowatt	lakeland
huggable	idyllist	incubate	insignia	irongrey	jetblack	kindless	lallygag
Huguenot	ignition	incurred	insolate	ironical	jetplane	kindling	lamasery
hulahula	ignitron	indagate	insolent	ironside	jettison	kindness	lambaste
humanely	ignominy	indebted	insomnia	ironware	jewelled	kinesics	lambency
humanise	ignorant	indecent	insomuch	ironwood	jeweller	kinetics	lamblike
humanism	illation	Indiaman	insphere	ironwork	jiggered	kingbird	lambskin
humanist	illative	indicant	inspired	Iroquois	jingoish	kingbolt	lamellae
humanity	illfated	indicate	inspirer	irrigate	jingoism	kingcrab	lamellar
humanoid	illiquid	indicium	inspirit	irritant	jingoist	kingfish	lameness
humidify	illtimed	indigene	instable	irritate	jipijapa	kinghood	lamented
humidity	illtreat	indigent	instance	isabella	jiujitsu	kinglike	laminate
humility	illumine	indirect	instancy	isagogic	jobation	kingship	lamppost
hummocky	illusage	indocile	instinct	ischemia	jocosely	kingsize	lancelet
humorist	illusion	indolent	instruct	ischemic	jocosity	kinkajou	landarmy
humorous	illusive	inductee	insulant	Islamise	jocundly	kinsfolk	landcrab
humoured	illusory	inductor	insulate	Islamism	jodhpurs	kissable	landfall
humpback	Illyrian	indulger	insulter	Islamite	joinable	kisscurl	landform
humuncle	ilmenite	induline	insurant	islander	jointure	klephtic	landgirl
hungrily	imaginal	indurate	intaglio	isobaric	jokingly	klondike	landlady
huntress	imagines	indusium	intarsia	isocheim	jolthead	klystron	landless
huntsman	imbecile	industry	integral	isocracy	Jonathan	knackery	landline
hurtless	imitable	inedible	intended	isodicon	jongleur	knapping	landlord
hushhush	imitator	inedited	intently	isogamic	jovially	knapsack	landmark
hustings	immanent	inequity	interact	isogloss	joyfully	knapweed	landmass
hyacinth	immature	inerrant	interbed	isogonal	joyously	kneedeep	landmine
hydatoid	immersed	inertial	intercom	isogonic	joystick	kneehigh	landrail
hydranth	imminent	inexpert	intercut	isolable	jubilant	kneehole	landslip
hydrogen	immingle	infamise	interest	isolator	jubilate	kneejerk	landsman
hydromel	immobile	infamous	interior	isomeric	Judaical	knickers	langlauf
hydropic	immodest	infantry	intermit	isometry	Judaiser	knightly	Langshan

language	legalise	likeable	lodgment	lunarian	makefast	markdown	megalith
languish	legalism	likeness	lodicule	lunation	makimono	markedly	megapode
lankness	legalist	likewise	logician	luncheon	Malagasy	marketer	megawatt
lanneret	legality	limbless	logistic	lungfish	malamute	marksman	melamine
lanthorn	legatine	limekiln	logogram	lungwort	malapert	marmoset	melanism
lapboard	legation	limerick	logotype	lunulate	malaprop	marocain	melanite
lapelled	legbreak	limetwig	loiterer	luscious	malarial	maroquin	melinite
lapicide	legendry	limewash	Lollardy	lushness	malarian	marquess	mellowly
lapidary	legerity	limitary	lollipop	lustrate	malarkey	marquise	melodeon
lapidate	leggings	limonite	lollypop	lustrine	maledict	marriage	melodise
lapidify	legguard	limpidly	lomentum	lustring	malefern	married	melodist
larboard	legioned	limpness	Londoner	lustrous	malemute	marrying	membered
larcener	leisured	linchpin	loneness	lutanist	maleness	marshman	membrane
largesse	lemonade	lineally	lonesome	lutecium	maligner	martagon	mementos
larkspur	lemurine	linearly	longboat	lutenist	malignly	martello	memorial
larrikin	lemuroid	linesman	longeron	lutetium	malodour	martenot	memorise
larynges	lengthen	lingerer	longeval	Lutheran	maltreat	martinet	memsahib
larynxes	lenience	lingerie	longhair	luxation	marzipan		menarche
lashings	leniency	linguist	longhand	lychgate	maltster	mascaron	mendable
latchkey	Leninism	liniment	longhorn	lykewake	malvasia	Masorete	menhaden
lateness	Leninist	Linnaean	longness	lymphoid	Mameluke	Masoreth	menially
latently	Leninite	linoleum	longship	lymphoma	mamilla	massacre	meninges
laterite	lenitive	linstock	longsome	lynchpin	mamillar	masseter	meniscus
Latinate	lensless	lintseed	longstop	lynxeyed	mancando	masseuse	menology
latinise	lenticel	lipogram	longterm	lyophile	manciple	massicot	menstrua
Latinism	lenticle	lipomata	longtime	lyrebird	Mandaean	massless	mensural
Latinist	lepidote	lipsalve	longueur	lyricism	mandamus	masterly	menswear
latinity	leporine	lipstick	longwall	lyricist	mandarin	masthead	mentally
latitant	lethally	liquidly	longwave	lysosome	mandator	mastitis	mephitic
latitude	lethargy	liripoop	longways	lysozyme	mandible	mastodon	mephitis
latterly	lettered	listener	longwise	macaroni	Mandingo	matamata	merchant
latticed	leucitic	listless	lookeron	macaroon	mandolin	matchbox	merciful
laudable	levanter	literacy	loonybin	macerate	mandorla	matelote	mercuric
laudably	levelled	literary	loophole	machismo	mandrake	material	mergence
laudanum	leveller	literate	loosebox	mackerel	mandrill	materiel	meridian
laudator	leverage	literati	loosener	mackinaw	maneater	maternal	meringue
laughing	leviable	litharge	lopeared	maculate	manfully	matgrass	meristem
laughter	levigate	litigant	lopgrass	madapple	mangabey	matiness	meristic
launcher	levirate	litigate	lopsided	madhouse	manganic	matrices	merosome
laureate	levitate	littlego	lordless	madrigal	mangonel	matrixes	mescalin
lavalava	levulose	littling	lordling	madwoman	mangrove	matronal	Mesdames
lavation	lewdness	littoral	lordosis	Maecenas	maniacal	matronly	meshwork
lavatory	lewisite	liturgic	lordotic	maenadic	Manichee	mattress	mesially
lavender	libation	liveable	lordship	maestoso	manicure	maturate	mesmeric
laverock	libatory	liveborn	loricate	magazine	manifest	maturely	mesocarp
lavishly	libeccio	livelily	lorikeet	magdalen	manifold	maturity	mesoderm
lawcourt	libelled	livelong	lothario	magician	maniform	maverick	mesotron
lawfully	libellee	liveried	loudness	magicked	mannered	maxillae	Mesozoic
lawgiver	libeller	liverish	louvered	magister	mannerly	maximise	mesquite
lawmaker	liberate	livewire	lovebird	magmatic	mannikin	mayapple	messmate
lawyerly	libretti	lividity	loveknot	magnesia	mannitol	mayoress	messuage
laxative	libretto	lixivium	loveless	magnetic	manorial	Mayqueen	metalled
layabout	licensed	loadline	lovelily	magneton	manpower	mazarine	metallic
layshaft	licensee	loadstar	lovelock	magnific	mansized	Mazdaism	metamere
laystall	licenser	loanable	lovelorn	magnolia	mantelet	mazement	metaphor
laywoman	lichened	loanword	lovenest	maharaja	mantilla	maziness	metayage
Lazarist	lichenin	loathful	loveseat	maharani	mantissa	meagrely	metazoan
laziness	lichgate	loathing	lovesick	mahjongg	mantling	mealtime	metazoon
lazulite	licorice	lobation	lovesome	mahogany	manually	mealworm	meteoric
lazurite	liegeman	lobbyist	lovesong	Mahratta	manubria	mealybug	methanol
leadenly	lifebelt	lobeline	lovingly	Mahratti	manurial	meanness	methinks
leadless	lifeboat	loblolly	lowering	maidenly	maquette	meantime	methodic
leadsman	lifebuoy	lobotomy	lowgrade	maidhood	marabout	measured	methylic
leadwork	lifeless	lobulate	lowlevel	maieutic	marasmic	meatball	methysis
leafless	lifelike	localise	lowlying	mailable	marasmus	meatsafe	metonymy
leaflike	lifeline	localism	loyalist	mailboat	marathon	mechanic	metrical
leanness	lifelong	locality	lubberly	mailcart	marauder	meconium	mezereon
leapfrog	lifesize	locative	lubrical	mainland	maravedi	medalled	miasmata
learning	lifetime	lockable	lucidity	mainline	marbling	medallic	miasmous
leathern	lifework	lockfast	luckless	mainmast	marchesa	medially	micellar
leathery	liftable	lockknit	luculent	mainsail	marchese	mediator	microbar
leavings	ligament	lockstep	Lucullan	mainstay	marginal	medicate	microbic
lecithin	ligation	locofoco	lukewarm	maintain	margrave	medicine	microdot
lecturer	ligature	locomote	lumberer	mainyard	marigold	medieval	micrurgy
leeboard	lighting	loculate	luminant	maiolica	marinade	mediocre	midbrain
lefthand	lightish	locution	luminary	majestic	marinate	meditate	middling
leftover	ligneous	locutory	luminist	majolica	maritage	medusoid	midfield
leftward	lignitic	lodestar	luminous	majority	maritime	meekness	midlands
legalese	ligulate	lodgings	lumpfish	makebate	marjoram	meetness	midnight

midpoint	mistaken	monogram	mouseear	nacreous	neoplasm	nonrigid	obituary
midships	misthink	monoginy	moussaka	nailfile	neoprene	nonsense	objector
midwives	mistreat	monolith	mouthful	nainsook	neotenic	nonstick	oblation
mightest	mistress	monomial	moveable	nameable	neoteric	nonunion	oblatory
mightily	mistrial	monopode	moveless	namedrop	Nepalese	nonusage	obligate
migraine	mistrust	monopoly	movement	nameless	nepenthe	nonwhite	obliging
migrator	misusage	monorail	movingly	namepart	nephrite	noontide	oblivion
mildness	miswrite	monotint	mowburnt	namesake	nepotism	noontime	observer
milepost	Mithraic	monotone	muchness	nametape	nescient	normalcy	obsidian
Milesian	mitigant	monotony	mucilage	nanogram	nestling	normally	obsolete
militant	mitigate	monotype	muckluck	naphthol	neurally	Norseman	obstacle
military	mittened	monoxide	muckrake	napiform	neuritic	northern	obstruct
militate	mittimus	monsieur	muckworm	napoleon	neuritis	northing	obtainer
milkmaid	mitzvoth	monteith	mucosity	narceine	neuronal	Northman	obtected
milkweed	mnemonic	monument	mucrones	narcissi	neuronic	noseband	obturate
milkwort	mobilise	moonbeam	mudguard	narcoses	neuroses	nosecone	obtusely
millhand	mobility	mooncalf	mudstone	narcosis	neurosis	nosedive	obtusity
milliard	mobocrat	moonface	Muharram	narcotic	neurotic	nosepipe	occasion
milliary	moccasin	moonfish	mulberry	narghile	neutrino	nosering	occident
millibar	modalism	moonless	muleteer	narrator	newblown	nosiness	occluded
millieme	modalist	moonrise	mulishly	narrowly	newcomer	nosology	occlusal
milliner	modality	moonsail	mulloway	nasalise	newfound	notarial	occultly
millpond	modelled	moonshee	multeity	nasality	newlywed	notation	occupant
millrace	modeller	moonshot	multifid	nascence	newscast	notching	occupier
Miltonic	moderate	moonwort	multiped	nascency	newsheet	notebook	occurred
mimester	moderato	moorcock	multiple	natality	newspeak	notecase	ocellate
mimicked	modernly	moorfowl	multiply	natation	newsreel	noteless	ochreous
mimicker	modestly	moorings	muniment	natatory	newsroom	notional	octarchy
minacity	modifier	moorland	munition	nathless	nextdoor	notornis	octaroon
minatory	modishly	mopishly	murderer	national	niceness	noumenal	octonary
mindless	modulate	moquette	muriatic	natively	nickelic	noumenon	octoroon
minimise	Moharram	morainic	murmurer	nativism	nicknack	nouvelle	ocularly
minister	moisture	moralise	murrelet	nativist	nickname	novation	oddments
ministry	molality	moralism	murrhine	nativity	nicotian	novelise	odiously
Minoress	molarity	moralist	muscadel	naturism	nicotine	novelist	odograph
Minorite	molasses	morality	muscatel	naturist	nielloed	November	odometer
minority	molecule	moratory	muscling	naumachy	niggling	novercal	odontoid
Minotaur	molehill	Moravian	muscular	nauplius	nightcap	nowadays	Odyssean
minstrel	moleskin	morbidly	mushroom	nauseant	nighthag	nubiform	oecology
mintmark	molester	morbific	musicale	nauseate	nightjar	nubility	oeillade
minutely	Molinism	mordancy	musician	nauseous	nightowl	nubilous	oenology
minutiae	Molinist	moreover	musingly	nautical	nihilism	nucellus	oenophil
mirepoix	molossus	moresque	muskdeer	nautilus	nihilist	nuclease	oestrone
mirthful	molybdic	moribund	muskduck	navigate	nihility	nucleate	oestrous
misalign	momently	mornings	musketry	Nazarene	nimbused	nucleole	offbreak
misapply	momentum	morosely	muskrose	Nazarite	ninefold	nucleoli	offdrive
misbegot	monachal	morosity	musktree	Nazirite	ninepins	nuclidic	offender
miscarry	monadism	morpheme	muslined	neaptide	nineteen	nudeness	offering
miscegen	monandry	morphine	musquash	Nearctic	nineties	nugatory	official
mischief	monarchy	mortally	mustache	nearness	nitrogen	nuisance	offprint
miscible	monastic	mortgage	mutation	neatherd	Noachian	nullness	offshoot
miscount	monaural	mortmain	mutchkin	neatness	nobelium	numberer	offshore
misdealt	monaxial	mortuary	muteness	nebulise	nobility	numbfish	offsider
misdoing	monazite	moshavim	muticous	nebulium	nobleman	numbness	offstage
misdoubt	mondaine	mosquito	mutilate	nebulous	noblesse	numeracy	ofttimes
miserere	monetary	mossback	mutineer	neckband	nocturne	numerary	ohmmeter
misgiven	monetise	mothball	mutinous	necklace	nodalise	numerate	oilcloth
misguide	moneybag	motherly	mutterer	neckline	nodality	numerous	oilfield
misheard	moneybox	motility	mutually	necropsy	nodation	numinous	oilfired
mishmash	Mongolic	motional	mycelial	necrosis	nodosity	numskull	oiliness
Mishnaic	mongoose	motivate	mycelium	necrotic	nodulose	nuptials	oilstone
misjudge	monicker	motivity	mycetoma	nectared	nodulous	nursling	ointment
mismatch	monistic	motorail	mycology	needfire	noisette	nurturer	oiticica
misnomer	monition	motorcar	myelinic	needless	nomadise	nutarian	okeydoke
misogamy	monitive	motorial	myelitis	needment	nomadism	nutation	oldtimer
misogyny	monitory	motoring	mylonite	negation	nominate	nutbrown	oldworld
misology	monkfish	motorise	myoblast	negative	nomistic	nuthatch	oleander
misplace	MonKhmer	motorist	myogenic	negatory	nomogram	nuthouse	oleaster
misprint	monkhood	motorium	myograph	negatron	nomology	nutrient	olibanum
misprise	monkseal	motorman	myositic	negligee	nonclaim	nutshell	oligarch
misprize	monkship	motormen	myositis	Negrillo	nondairy	nymphean	oligomer
misquote	monoacid	motorway	myosotis	negroism	nonesuch	oafishly	oliphant
misshape	monocrat	mottling	myriapod	nematode	nonevent	oakapple	Olympiad
missilry	monocyte	moufflon	myriopod	nematoid	nonhuman	oakegger	Olympian
misspell	monodist	moulding	myrmidon	nenuphar	nonjuror	oatgrass	omadhaum
misspell	monogamy	mountain	mystical	NeoLatin	nonlegal	obduracy	omelette
misspend	monogeny	mounting	mystique	neomycin	nonmetal	obdurate	omission
misspent	monoglot	mournful	mythical	neonatal	nonmoral	obedient	omitting
misstate	monogony	mourning	myxomata	neophyte	nonparty	obeisant	ommateum

omnivore	orthodox	overfall	pacifist	pargeter	pederast	petaline	pinaster
omophagy	orthoepy	overfeed	padishah	parhelia	pedestal	petalled	pincenez
omoplate	oscinine	overfill	paduasoy	parhelic	pedicled	petalody	pinchers
omphalic	osculant	overfish	paganise	parietal	pedicure	petaloid	Pindaric
omphalos	osculate	overflew	paganish	parkland	pedigree	petalous	pinecone
onceover	Ossianic	overflow	paganism	parlance	pediment	petechia	pinewood
oncidium	osteitis	overfold	paginate	parlando	pedipalp	petiolar	pinkness
oncology	ostinato	overfond	pagurian	Parmesan	pedology	petioled	pinmoney
oncoming	ostracod	overgrew	painless	parodist	peduncle	petition	pinnacle
onehorse	ostracon	overgrow	paintbox	paroquet	peekaboo	petrolic	pinnated
onepiece	ostrakon	overhand	palatial	paroxysm	peelings	petronel	pinniped
onesided	otiosely	overhang	palatine	parrotry	peephole	petrosal	pinnular
onetrack	otiosity	overhaul	paleface	Parsiism	peepshow	pettifog	pinochle
onlooker	otoscope	overhead	paleness	parsonic	peerless	petulant	pinpoint
ontogeny	ottavino	overhear	palestra	partaken	Pegasean	petuntse	pinprick
ontology	outboard	overheat	palinode	parterre	pegboard	phalange	pintable
onychite	outbound	overhung	palisade	Parthian	peignoir	phantasm	pintsize
oogamous	outbrave	overjump	palliate	partible	Pekinese	phantasy	pinwheel
oogonial	outbreak	overkill	pallidly	particle	Pelagian	pharisee	pipeclay
oogonium	outburst	overlaid	pallmall	partisan	Pelasgic	pharmacy	pipefish
oologist	outcaste	overlain	palmette	partizan	pelerine	phaseout	pipeline
ooziness	outclass	overland	palmetto	partsong	pellagra	pheasant	piperack
opaquely	outdated	overleaf	palmiped	parttime	pellicle	phenolic	piperine
openable	outdoors	overleap	palmitin	pashalic	pellmell	phenylic	piquancy
opencast	outdrawn	overload	palomino	pashalik	pellucid	Philomel	pirarucu
openeyed	outfield	overlong	palpable	passable	pelorism	phlegmon	piscator
openness	outflank	overlook	palpably	passably	pembroke	phonemic	piscinae
openplan	outgoing	overlord	palterer	passbook	pemmican	phonetic	pishogue
openwork	outgrown	overmuch	paludism	passerby	penalise	phormium	pisiform
operable	outguess	overnice	pamperer	passible	penchant	phosgene	pisolite
operatic	outHerod	overpaid	pamphlet	Passover	pendency	phosphor	pitiable
operator	outhouse	overpass	pancreas	passport	pendicle	photogen	pitiably
opercula	outlawry	overpast	pandanus	password	pendular	photopia	pitiless
operetta	outlying	overplay	pandemic	pastiche	pendulum	photopic	pittance
ophidian	outmatch	overplus	pandowdy	pastille	penitent	photopsy	pitviper
oppilate	outmoded	overrate	panelled	pastoral	penknife	phrasing	pivotman
opponent	outpoint	override	pangolin	pastrami	penology	phreatic	pixieish
opposite	outrange	overripe	panicked	pastries	penstock	Phrygian	pixiness
oppugner	outreach	overrode	panmixia	pastural	pentacle	phthalic	pizzeria
opsimath	outreign	overrule	pannikin	patagium	pentagon	phthisic	placable
optative	outrider	oversail	panorama	patchily	pentroof	phthisis	placably
optician	outright	overseas	panpipes	patellae	penumbra	phyletic	placeman
optimise	outrival	overseen	pansophy	patellar	peperino	phyllary	placenta
optimism	outshine	overseer	pantheon	patentee	perceive	phyllode	placidly
optimist	outshone	oversell	pantofle	patently	perfecto	phylloid	plagiary
optional	outsider	oversewn	pantsuit	patentor	perforce	phyllome	plaguily
opulence	outsight	overshoe	papalise	paternal	perfumer	physical	plaiding
opuscula	outsmart	overshot	papalism	pathetic	perianth	physicky	plaister
opuscule	outspend	overside	papalist	pathless	pericarp	physique	planchet
oracular	outspent	oversize	paperboy	pathogen	pericope	piacular	plangent
orangery	outstare	overslip	papillae	patience	periderm	pianiste	planking
Orangism	outstrip	oversold	papillar	patronal	peridium	piassava	plankton
oratorio	outvalue	oversoul	papillon	pattypan	peridote	picaroon	planning
oratress	outvying	overstay	papistic	patulous	perigean	picayune	plantain
Orcadian	outwards	overstep	papistry	pavement	perigyny	pickerel	planulae
orchilla	outwatch	overtake	pappadom	pavilion	perilled	picketer	planular
ordainer	outweigh	overtask	papulose	pawnshop	perilous	pickings	plastery
ordinand	outworks	overtime	papulous	payphone	perilune	picklock	plastics
ordinary	ovalness	overtone	parabola	paysheet	perineal	picnicky	plastron
ordinate	ovariole	overtook	paradigm	peaceful	perineum	pictures	plateaux
ordnance	ovaritis	overture	paradise	peacocky	periodic	piddling	plateful
oreology	ovenbird	overturn	paraffin	peagreen	periotic	piecrust	platelet
organdie	ovenware	overview	paragoge	peardrop	peripety	piedmont	platform
organise	overalls	overwear	parakeet	pearlies	periplus	piercing	platinic
organism	overarch	overwind	parallax	pearling	perisher	piffling	platinum
organist	overbear	overwork	parallel	pearlite	perjurer	pigswill	platonic
orgasmic	overbook	overworn	paralyse	pearmain	perlitic	pilaster	platting
orgastic	overbore	oviposit	paramour	peasecod	permeate	pilchard	platypus
orgulous	overbusy	owlishly	paranoia	peccable	peroneal	pileated	plaudits
oriental	overcall	oxidiser	paranoid	peccancy	perorate	pilewort	playable
oriented	overcame	oximeter	paraquat	pectines	peroxide	pilferer	playback
origanum	overcast	oxpecker	parasang	pectoral	personae	piliform	playbill
original	overcoat	oxtongue	parasite	peculate	personal	pillager	playbook
ornament	overcome	oxymoron	paravane	peculiar	perspire	pillwort	playgirl
ornately	overcrop	oxytocin	parcener	pedagogy	persuade	pilosity	playgoer
ornithic	overdone	ozoniser	parclose	pedalier	pertness	pilotage	playmate
orogenic	overdose	pachalic	pardoner	pedalled	Peruvian	pilsener	playroom
orpiment	overdraw	pacifier	parental	pedantic	perverse	pimiento	playsuit
orthicon	overdrew	pacifism	parergon	pedantry	pervious	pinafore	playtime

```
pleading  polyzoan  pratique  prolapse  pugnosed  quaintly  rallying  recourse
pleasant  polyzoic  prattler  prolific  puissant  Quakerly  rallyist  recovery
pleasing  polyzoon  preacher  prolixly  pullback  qualmish  rambling  recreant
pleasure  pomander  preamble  prologue  pullover  quandary  rambutan  recreate
plebeian  pomology  precinct  prolonge  pulmonic  quandong  ramentum  rectoral
plectrum  ponderer  precious  promisee  pulpiter  quantify  ramequin  recurred
pleinair  pondweed  preclude  promiser  pulpwood  quantise  rampancy  recusant
pleonasm  pontifex  predator  promisor  pulsator  quantity  ranarian  redactor
plethora  ponytail  predella  promoter  pulvilli  quarrier  ranarium  redblind
pleurisy  poohpooh  preelect  prompter  pulvinus  quartern  ranchero  redbrick
pliantly  poorness  preexist  promptly  pumproom  quarters  ranchman  redeemer
plighted  popinjay  pregnant  promulge  puncheon  quartile  randomly  redefine
plimsoll  popishly  prehuman  pronator  punctate  quatrain  rankness  redeless
Pliocene  poppadum  prejudge  proofing  punctual  quayside  ransomer  redeploy
plodding  populace  prelatic  propense  puncture  queasily  rapacity  redesign
plopping  populate  prelease  properly  punditry  Quechuan  rapecake  redfaced
plotting  populism  premiere  property  pungency  queendom  rapeseed  redirect
plougher  populist  premolar  prophase  puniness  queening  rapidity  redistil
pluckily  populous  premorse  prophecy  punisher  queenlet  rapparee  redolent
plugging  poristic  prenatal  prophesy  punition  queerish  raptness  redouble
plumaged  porkling  prentice  propolis  punitive  quencher  raptures  redshank
plumbago  porosity  preparer  proposal  punitory  quenelle  rarefied  redshift
plumbate  porphyry  prepense  proposer  puparial  question  rareness  redshirt
plumbing  porpoise  preprint  propound  puparium  queueing  rascally  redstart
plumbism  porridge  presager  propping  pupation  quibbler  rashness  redwater
plumelet  portable  prescind  propylic  pupilage  quickset  rasorial  reedbird
plumiped  portfire  presence  prorogue  pupilary  quiddity  rataplan  reedling
plumpish  porthole  preserve  prosaism  pupillar  quidnunc  rateable  reedmace
plumular  porticos  presidio  prosaist  puppetry  quietism  ratguard  reedpipe
plurally  portiere  pressbox  prosodic  puppydog  quietist  ratifier  reedstop
plussage  portrait  pressing  prospect  puppydom  quietude  rational  reedwren
plutonic  portress  pressman  prostate  puppyfat  quillpen  ratsbane  reefknot
pluvious  position  pressure  prostyle  puppyish  quilting  ratstail  reembark
pochette  positive  prestige  protasis  purblind  quincunx  rattling  reemerge
pockmark  positron  presumer  protatic  purchase  quintain  ravelled  reemploy
podagral  posology  pretence  protease  purebred  quipping  ravenous  reexport
podagric  possible  prettify  protegee  pureness  quirkily  ravisher  referent
podiatry  possibly  prettily  protista  purfling  quisling  rawboned  referral
poetical  postcard  previous  protocol  purifier  quitrent  reabsorb  referred
poignant  postcode  priapism  protonic  puristic  quitting  reactant  refinery
pointing  postdate  prideful  protozoa  purplish  quixotic  reaction  refitted
poisoner  postfree  priedieu  protract  purpuric  quixotry  reactive  reflexed
polarise  posthorn  priestly  protrude  purpurin  quizzing  readable  refluent
polarity  postiche  priggery  provable  pursenet  quotable  readably  reforest
polemics  postlude  priggish  provably  purslane  quotient  readjust  reformed
polemise  postmark  priggism  provided  pursuant  rabbinic  reaffirm  reformer
polemist  postmill  primally  provider  purulent  rabbiter  reagency  regalism
polestar  postobit  Primates  province  purveyor  rabbitry  realness  regality
polisher  postpaid  primeval  provisor  pushball  rabidity  realtime  regelate
politely  postpone  primming  proximal  pushbike  racecard  reappear  regicide
politick  postural  primness  prudence  pushcart  racegoer  rearlamp  regiment
politico  posturer  primrose  pruinose  pushover  racemate  rearmice  regional
politics  potassic  princely  prunella  pushpull  racemise  rearmost  register
pollices  potation  princess  prunelle  pussycat  racemose  rearview  registry
pollinia  potbelly  printing  prunello  pustular  rachides  rearward  regolith
pollinic  potbound  printout  prurient  putative  rachitic  reascend  regrater
polliwog  potently  priorate  pruritic  putridly  rachitis  reasoner  regrowth
pollster  potholer  prioress  pruritus  pyelitis  racially  reassert  regulate
polluter  pothouse  priority  Prussian  pygidial  raciness  reassess  rehandle
pollywog  potlatch  prismoid  pryingly  pygidium  rackrent  reassign  rehearse
polonium  potplant  prisoner  psalmist  pygmaean  radially  reassure  rehoboam
poltfoot  potroast  prissily  psalmody  pyogenic  radiance  reawaken  reignite
poltroon  potsherd  pristine  psaltery  pyrenoid  radiancy  rebelled  reimpose
polygala  potstill  probable  psilosis  pyrexial  radiator  rebeller  reindeer
polygamy  potstone  probably  psychics  pyridine  radicant  rebellow  reinless
polygene  potterer  proceeds  psychism  pyriform  radicate  rebuttal  reinsert
polygeny  poultice  proclaim  psychist  pyroxene  raftsman  rebutted  reinsman
polyglot  poundage  procurer  pteropod  pyrrhoea  raggedly  rebutter  reinsure
polygyny  pounding  prodding  pterylae  pyrrhous  railhead  recapped  reinvest
polymath  pourable  prodigal  ptomaine  pythonic  raillery  receiver  rejecter
polypary  powdered  prodrome  ptyalism  pyxidium  railroad  recently  rejigger
polypide  powerful  producer  pubertal  quackery  rainbird  receptor  rejoicer
polypite  practice  proemial  publican  quackish  raincoat  recharge  rekindle
polypody  practise  profaner  publicly  quadrant  raindrop  recision  relation
polypoid  praecipe  profiler  puffball  quadrate  rainfall  reckless  relative
polypous  praedial  profound  puffbird  quadriga  rainwash  reckoner  relaxant
polyseme  prandial  progress  puggaree  quadroon  rainwear  recommit  releasee
polysemy  prankful  prohibit  pugilism  quaestor  rakehell  reconvey  releaser
polysomy  prankish  prolamin  pugilist  quagmire  rakishly  recorder  releasor
```

relegate	resource	ridicule	rooftree	rutilant	Sangreal	scapular	scrounge
relevant	respects	Riesling	roommate	ryegrass	sanguine	scapulas	scrubbed
reliable	response	rifeness	roothold	ryotwari	sanitary	scarcely	scrubber
reliably	respring	riffraff	rootless	sabbatic	sanitate	scarcity	scrutiny
reliance	resprung	rifleman	ropeable	sabotage	sanitise	scarfpin	scudding
reliever	restcure	rigadoon	ropewalk	saboteur	sannyasi	scarious	scullery
religion	restless	rightful	ropeyarn	saccadic	sanserif	scarless	scullion
relocate	restorer	rightist	ropiness	saccular	Sanskrit	scarring	sculptor
relucent	restrain	rigidify	rosarian	sacculus	santonin	scathing	scumming
relumine	restrict	rigidity	rosebowl	sackcoat	sapgreen	scattily	scurrile
remanent	resupine	rigorism	rosebush	sackless	sapidity	scatting	scurvily
remedial	resurvey	rigorist	rosefish	sackrace	sapience	scavenge	scutcher
remember	retailer	rigorous	roseleaf	sacraria	saponify	scenario	scutella
reminder	retainer	rimbrake	rosemary	sacredly	saponite	scenical	seaboard
remissly	retarded	rimester	roseolar	sacristy	saporous	sceptred	seaborne
remittal	retarder	ringbark	rosepink	saddlery	sapphics	schedule	seachest
remitted	retiarii	ringbolt	roseroot	Sadducee	sapphire	schemata	seacoast
remittee	reticent	ringbone	rosetree	sadistic	sapphism	scheming	seacraft
remitter	reticule	ringdove	rosewood	safeness	saraband	schiedam	seadrome
remotely	retiform	ringmain	rosiness	saffrony	sarcenet	schiller	seafarer
renderer	retinula	ringneck	rostrate	safranin	sardelle	schizoid	seafloor
renegade	retiring	ringroad	rosulate	sagacity	sardonic	schmaltz	seafront
renegado	retorted	ringside	Rotarian	sagamore	sardonyx	schnapps	seagoing
reneguer	retrench	ringtail	rotation	sageness	sargasso	scholium	seagreen
reniform	retrieve	ringwall	rotative	saginate	sarsenet	schooner	seaholly
renitent	retroact	ringworm	rotatory	sagittal	sashcord	sciagram	seahorse
renounce	retrorse	rinsings	rotenone	sailable	Sassanid	sciatica	sealable
renovate	reusable	riparian	rottenly	sailboat	satanism	scilicet	sealevel
renowned	revanche	ripeness	rotundly	sailfish	satanist	scimitar	sealskin
rentable	revealer	ritually	roturier	sailless	sateless	sciolism	sealyham
renumber	reveille	rivalled	roughage	sailorly	satiable	sciolist	seamanly
reoccupy	revelled	rivelled	roughdry	sailyard	satiably	scirocco	seamless
reorient	reveller	riverain	roughhew	sainfoin	satirise	scirrhus	seamount
repairer	revenant	riverbed	roughish	saintdom	satirist	scissile	seamouse
repartee	revenger	riverine	rouleaus	salacity	saturant	scission	seamster
repealer	reverend	riverman	rouleaux	salariat	saturate	scissors	seaonion
repeater	reverent	riverway	roulette	salaried	Saturday	sciurine	seapiece
repelled	reversal	roadbook	roundarm	saleable	saturnic	sciuroid	seaplane
repeller	reverser	roadless	rounders	saleroom	saucebox	sclereid	seapurse
repenter	reverter	roadside	roundish	Salesian	saucepan	sclerite	seaquake
repeople	revetted	roadsign	roundtop	salesman	saunders	scleroma	searcher
repetend	reviewal	roadster	rowdyish	salience	sauouari	sclerose	seascape
replacer	reviewer	roasting	rowdyism	saliency	sauropod	sclerous	seashell
replevin	reviling	roborant	royalism	salinity	Sauterne	scolding	seashore
reporter	revision	robustly	royalist	salivary	savagely	scolices	seasnail
repotted	revisory	rocaille	rubbishy	salivate	savagery	scombrid	seasnake
repousse	revivify	rockbird	rubicund	Salopian	savannah	scoopful	seasonal
reprieve	revolter	rockcake	rubidium	saltbush	savorous	scoopnet	seasoner
reprisal	revolute	rockcork	rubrical	saltless	Savoyard	scopulae	seatbelt
reproach	revolver	rockdove	rubytail	saltlick	sawbones	scopulas	seatrout
reproval	rewaking	rocketry	rucksack	saltmine	sawedged	scorcher	seawards
republic	rewarder	rockfall	rudeness	saltness	sawedoff	scornful	seawater
requital	Rhaetian	rockfish	rudiment	saltwort	sawframe	scorpion	seawrack
requiter	rhapsode	rockhewn	ruefully	salutary	sawhorse	scotfree	sebesten
rerearch	rhapsody	rocklike	ruggedly	salvable	sawtooth	scotopic	secluded
rerecord	rheology	rockling	rugosely	salvific	Saxondom	Scotsman	seconder
reremice	rheostat	rockrose	rugosity	samarium	Saxonism	scottice	secondly
rereward	rhetoric	rocksalt	rugulose	sameness	Saxonist	Scottish	secretin
rescript	rhinitis	rockweed	ruinable	samizdat	Saxonite	scourger	secretly
research	Rhinodon	rockwood	ruleless	Samoyede	sayonara	scouting	secretor
resemble	rhizopod	rockwork	Rumanian	samphire	scabbard	scrabble	sectoral
reserved	rhomboid	roentgen	Rumansch	sampling	scabious	scragend	securely
resetter	rhonchal	rogation	ruminant	sanative	scabrous	scragged	security
resettle	rhonchus	rogatory	ruminate	sanatory	scaffold	scramble	sedately
resident	rhyolite	rollcall	rummager	sanctify	scalable	scrammed	sedation
residual	rhythmic	rollneck	runabout	sanction	scalawag	scrannel	sedative
residuum	ribaldry	rolypoly	runagate	sanctity	scalepan	scraping	sederunt
resigned	ribbonry	romancer	runcible	sandarac	scallion	scrapped	sediment
resinate	ribgrass	Romanian	runnerup	sandbank	scammony	scrapper	sedition
resinify	ribosome	romanise	ruralise	sandbath	scampish	scratchy	sedulity
resinoid	ricebird	Romanism	ruralism	sandflea	scandent	scrawler	sedulous
resinous	ricercar	Romanist	ruralist	sandshoe	Scandian	screamer	seedcake
resister	richness	Romansch	rurality	sandwich	scandium	screechy	seedcase
resistor	rickrack	romantic	rushhour	sandworm	scanning	screener	seedcoat
resolute	rickshaw	rondeaux	rushlike	sandwort	scansion	screever	seedcorn
resonant	ricochet	roodbeam	rustical	sandyish	scanties	screwtop	seedfish
resonate	riddance	roodloft	rustless	saneness	scantily	scribble	seedleaf
resorcin	rideable	roofless	rutabaga	sangaree	scaphoid	scribbly	seedless
resorter	ridgeway	roofrack	ruthless	Sangrail	scapulae	scrofula	seedling

seedlobe	serially	shiftkey	sidedrum	skeletal	sloucher	snuffler	songster
seedplot	seriatim	shigella	sidehead	skeleton	slovenly	snuffles	sonobuoy
seedsman	sericite	shikaree	sidekick	skerrick	slovenry	snuggery	sonority
seedtime	serjeant	shilling	sideline	sketcher	slowdown	snugness	sonorous
segreant	serology	shimmery	sideling	skewback	slowness	soakaway	soothing
seicento	serosity	shinbone	sidelong	skewbald	slowpoke	soapbark	soothsay
seigneur	serotine	shingler	sidenote	skewness	slowworm	soapdish	sorcerer
seignior	serpulae	shingles	sidereal	skiagram	slubbing	soapless	sordidly
seignory	serranid	shinning	siderite	skidding	slugabed	soaproot	sorehead
seizable	serrated	shipload	sideroad	skilless	sluggard	soapsuds	soreness
seladang	servient	shipmate	sideshow	skilling	slugging	soapwort	sorochen
selcouth	servitor	shipment	sideslip	skimmilk	sluggish	soberise	sororate
selectee	sesamoid	shipping	sidesman	skimming	slumbery	sobriety	sorority
selector	sesterce	shipworm	sidestep	skimpily	slumming	sobstory	sorption
selenate	setscrew	shipyard	sideview	skindeep	slurring	sobstuff	sorptive
selenide	severely	shiralee	sidewalk	skinfood	sluttish	socalled	sorrower
selenite	severity	shirring	sideward	skinhead	slyboots	sociable	sortable
selenium	sewellel	shirting	sideways	skinless	smallage	sociably	soterial
selfborn	sewerage	shivaree	sidewind	skinning	smallfry	socially	souchong
selfheal	sewergas	shocking	sidewise	skipjack	smallish	societal	soulless
selfhelp	sewerrat	shoddily	siftings	skipping	smallpox	Socinian	soundbow
selfhood	sexiness	shoebill	sigmatic	skirmish	smaltite	Socratic	soundbox
selfless	sexology	shoehorn	signally	skirting	smarmily	sodalite	sounding
selflove	sextette	shoelace	signpost	skislope	smartish	sodality	sourdine
selfmade	sextuple	shoeless	silencer	skittish	smashing	sodomite	sourness
selfmate	sexually	shoetree	silently	skittles	smelling	softball	sourpuss
selfness	sforzato	shofroth	silicane	skullcap	smeltery	softboil	soutache
selfpity	shabbily	shogging	silicate	skylight	smithers	softener	southern
selfrule	shabrack	shooting	silicide	skypilot	smithery	softhead	southing
selfsame	Shabuoth	shootout	silicify	skyscape	smocking	softness	southpaw
selfsown	shadbush	shopbell	silicone	skywards	smokable	softshoe	Southron
selfwill	shaddock	shopgirl	silkworm	slabbing	smoothen	softsoap	souvenir
selvedge	shadower	shopping	sillabub	slagging	smoothie	software	sovranty
semantic	shafting	shoptalk	silphium	slagheap	smoothly	softwood	sowbread
semester	shagbark	shopworn	Silurian	slamming	smothery	soilless	spacebar
semibull	shaggily	shortage	siluroid	slangily	smoulder	soilpipe	spaceman
semidome	shagreen	shortarm	silvatic	slapbang	smudgily	solander	spacious
seminary	shagroon	shortcut	silverly	slapdash	smuggler	solanine	spadeful
seminude	shakable	shortday	similise	slapjack	smugness	solarise	spadices
semiotic	shakeout	shortish	simoniac	slapping	smuttily	solarism	spadille
Semitise	Shaktism	shothole	simonist	slashing	snackbar	solarist	spadones
Semitism	shaleoil	shoulder	simplify	slattern	snagging	solarium	spaewife
Semitist	shalloon	shouldst	simplism	Slavonic	snakepit	solation	spagyric
semitone	shallows	showbill	simulant	sleazily	snapbrim	solatium	spalpeen
semolina	shambles	showboat	simulate	sledding	snaplink	solderer	spandrel
semplice	shameful	showcard	Sinaitic	sleepily	snapnais	soldiery	spandril
sempster	shamming	showcase	sinapism	sleeping	snapping	solecism	Spaniard
senarius	shamrock	showdown	sinciput	sleidawy	snappish	solecist	spanking
senility	shanghai	showgirl	sinecure	slightly	snapshot	solemnly	spanning
sennight	shantung	showroom	sinfonia	slimmest	snatcher	soleness	spanroof
senorita	shapable	shrapnel	sinfully	slimming	snazzily	solenoid	sparable
senseful	shareout	shredded	singable	slimmish	sneakily	solfaist	sparbuoy
sensible	sharpish	shredder	singeing	slimness	sneakish	solfeggi	spardeck
sensibly	sharpset	shrewdly	singsong	slinkily	sneeshan	solidary	sparkgap
sensoria	shashlik	shrewish	singular	slipcase	sniffily	solidify	sparkish
sensuous	sheading	shrieval	sinicise	slipform	sniffler	solidity	sparkler
sentence	shealing	shrimper	sinister	slipknot	sniffles	solitary	sparklet
sentient	shedding	shrinker	sinkable	slipover	sniggler	solitude	sparling
sentinel	shedevil	shrugged	sinkhole	slippage	snippety	solleret	sparring
sentrygo	sheepdip	shrunken	sinology	slippery	snipping	solstice	sparsely
sepaloid	sheepdog	shuddery	sinophil	slipping	snipsnap	solution	sparsity
sepalous	sheepish	shuffler	sinusoid	slipring	snitcher	solvable	spathose
separate	sheepked	shunning	siphonal	sliproad	snobbery	solvency	spatting
Sephardi	sheeppen	shutdown	siphonet	slipshod	snobbish	somatism	spatular
septette	sheeprun	shutting	siphonic	slipslop	snobbism	sombrely	spavined
septfoil	sheeting	Siberian	sirenian	slithery	snogging	sombrero	speaking
septimal	sheikdom	sibilant	siriasis	slitting	snootily	sombrous	spearman
septuple	Shekinah	sibilate	sirvente	slobbery	snowball	somebody	speciate
sequelae	shelduck	Sicilian	sisterly	slobbish	snowbird	somedeal	specific
sequence	shelfful	sickener	sitarist	slobland	snowboot	somedele	specimen
seraglio	shelving	sickerly	sithence	sloeeyed	snowdrop	sometime	specious
seraphic	Shemitic	sickflag	sitology	slogging	snowfall	someways	spectral
seraphim	shepherd	sicklist	situated	sloppail	snowless	somewhat	spectrum
serenade	Sheraton	sickness	sitzbath	sloppily	snowlike	somewhen	specular
serenata	sherlock	sickroom	sixpence	slopping	snowline	somnific	speculum
serenely	Shetland	sidearms	sixpenny	slopshop	snowshoe	sonatina	speedily
serenity	shielder	sideband	sixtieth	slopwork	snubbing	songbird	speedway
serfhood	shieling	sidedish	sizeable	slothful	snuffbox	songbook	spelling
sergeant	shiftily	sidedoor	sizzling	slotting	snuffers	songless	spermary

```
sphagnum spurrier starwort stomatic stultify Sumerian swayback tackroom
sphenoid spurring stasimon stonefly stumbler summerly swearing tactical
spherics spyglass statable stopcock stumming summitry sweeping tactless
spheroid squabble statedly stopover stumpily summoner sweepnet taenioid
spherule squadron statical stoppage stunning sunbaked sweeting tafferel
sphingid squaller statuary stopping stunsail sunbathe sweetish taffrail
sphygmus squamate statured storable stuntman sunblind sweetpea tagalong
spicated squamose staylace storeman stupidly sunburnt sweetsop Tahitian
spiccato squamous staysail storeyed stuprate sunburst swelling tailback
spicebox squamule steadily stormily sturdied sundance swiftlet tailcoat
spicknel squander steading stoutish sturdily sunderer swigging tailgate
spiculae squarely stealing stowaway sturgeon sundress swimming tailings
spicular squarish stealthy strabism stylised sundried swimsuit tailless
spiculum squarson steamily straddle subacute sundries swindler tailpipe
spiffing squasher stearate straggle subagent sundrops swinging tailrace
spikelet squatted stearine straggly subahdar sunlight switchel tailspin
spillage squatter steatite straight subbasal sunproof swobbing tainture
spillway squawker stedfast strained subclass sunshade swopping takeaway
spinifex squawman steenbok strainer suberect sunshine swotting takehome
spinning squeaker steening straiten suberise sunshiny sybarite takeover
spinster squealer steepish straitly suberose sunstone sycamine takingly
spiracle squeedge steepled stramash suberous sunwards sycamore talapoin
spirally squeegee steerage stranded subfloor superadd sycomore talented
spirilla squeezer steering stranger subframe superate syconium talesman
spirited squelchy steinbok strangle subgenus superbly syenitic talisman
spiritus squibbed stellate strapoil subgroup superego syllabic tallness
spiteful squidded stellify strapped subhuman superior syllable tallyman
spitfire squiggle stellion strapper subimago superman syllabub Talmudic
spitting squiggly stemless strategy subjoint supernal syllabus tamandua
spittoon squilgee stemmata stratify sublease supertax sylphide tamanoir
spivvery squinter stemming stravaig sublunar supinate sylphine tamarack
splasher squireen stenosed streaked submerge supinely sylphish tamarind
splatter squirely stenosis streaker submerse supplant sylvatic tamarisk
splendid squirrel stenotic streamer suborder supplely symbiont tamboura
splenial squirter stepping streeted suborner supplial symbolic tameable
splenius stabbing stepwise strength suboxide supplier symmetry tameless
splinter stabling sterigma strepent subphyla supplies sympathy tameness
splitter stablish sterling Strepyan subpoena supposal symphile Tamilian
splotchy staccato sternite stretchy subprior supposed symphony tamperer
splutter staffage sternson stricken subserve suppress sympodia tandoori
spoffish staggard sternway strickle subshrub surcease symposia tangency
spoilage staggers stetting strictly subsolar surefire synapsis tangible
spoliate staghorn stibnite stridden subsonic sureness synaptic tangibly
spondaic stagnant stickful strident substage surfacer synastry tangoist
spongily stagnate stickily strigose subtitle surfbird syncline tanistry
sponsion stairrod stickjaw striking subtlety surfboat syncopal tannable
spontoon stairway stickler stringed subtonic surfduck syncytia tantalic
spookily stakenet stiffish stringer subtopia surffish syndesis tantalum
spookish stallage stigmata stripped subtotal surgical syndetic tantalus
spoonfed stallfed stilbene stripper subtract suricate syndical Tantrism
spoonful stalling stilbite strobila subulate surmisal syndrome tantrist
spoonily stallion stiletto strobile suburban surmiser synergic tapdance
sporadic stalwart stillage strobili suburbia surmount synergid tapedeck
sporozoa staminal stimulus stroller subvocal surplice syngamic tapeless
sportful stampede stingily stromata succinct surprise synonymy tapelike
sportily stancher stingray strongly succinic surround synopses tapeline
sporting stanchly stinkard strontia succinum surroyal synopsis tapestry
sportive standard stinking strophic succubae surveyor synoptic tapeworm
sporular standing stinkpot stropped succubus survival synovial taphouse
spotless standish stipites strucken suchlike survivor syntagma tapwater
spottily standoff stippler struggle suckling suspense syntonic tarboosh
spotting stanhope stipular strummed Sudanese susurrus syphilis tarlatan
spousage stannary stirring strummer sudarium suzerain syringes Tarpeian
spraints stannate stitcher strumose sudatory swabbing syrinxes tarragon
sprawler stannite stoccado strumous suddenly swagging systemic tartaric
spraygun stannous stoccata strumpet sufferer swainish systolic tartness
spreader stanzaic stockade strutted suffrage swanherd syzygial tartrate
sprigged stapelia stockcar strutter suicidal swanking taberdar Tartuffe
springal stardust stockily stubbing suitable swanlike tableaux taskwork
springer starfish stocking stubborn suitably swanmark tablecut tasselly
sprinkle stargaze stockish stubnail suitcase swanneck tableful tastebud
sprinter starkers stockist stuccoes suitings swannery tablemat tasteful
sprocket starless stockman studbook sukiyaki swanning tabletop tattered
sprucely starlike stockpot studding sullenly swanshot tabouret tattooer
spryness starling stodgily studfarm sulphate swanskin tabulate tautness
spunkily starrily stoicism studious sulphide swansong tachisme tautomer
spurgear starring stolidly studwork sulphite swapping tachiste tautonym
spurious starting stomachy stuffily sulphone swastika taciturn taverner
spurling startler stomatal stuffing sultrily swatting tackling tawdrily
```

taxation	termtime	thrasher	titanism	touching	trevally	truncate	Tychonic
taxingly	terraced	thrawart	titanite	toughish	trialist	trunnion	tympanic
taxonomy	terrapin	threader	titanium	touristy	triangle	trussing	tympanum
taxpayer	terraria	threaten	tithable	tournure	triarchy	trustful	typecast
teaboard	terrazzo	threeply	titivate	tovarish	Triassic	trustily	typeface
teabread	terrible	threeway	titmouse	towardly	triaxial	truthful	typehigh
teabreak	terribly	threnode	tittuped	towelled	tribally	tryingly	typhonic
teacaddy	terrific	threnody	tittuppy	townhall	tribasic	tsarevna	typifier
teachest	tertiary	thresher	toadfish	township	tribrach	tsaritsa	typology
teaching	tesserae	thridace	toadflax	townsman	tribunal	tsaritza	tyrannic
teacloth	tesseral	thriller	toadyish	toxaemia	trichina	tubeless	Tyrolean
teahouse	testable	thriving	toadyism	toxaemic	trichite	tubercle	tyrosine
teammate	testator	throated	toboggan	toxicant	trichoid	tuberose	Tyrrhene
teamster	testatum	throbbed	tocology	toxicity	trichome	tuberous	ubiquity
teamwork	testtube	thrombin	toepiece	trabeate	trichord	tubiform	udometer
teaparty	tetanise	thrombus	toeplate	tracheae	trickery	tubulate	ugliness
tearaway	tetchily	throstle	together	tracheal	trickily	tuckahoe	uintaite
teardrop	tetradic	throttle	toiletry	tracheid	trickish	tuckshop	ulcerate
tearduct	tetragon	thrummed	toilette	trachoma	tricorne	tumbling	ulcerous
tearless	tetrapla	thruster	toilsome	trachyte	tricycle	tumidity	ulterior
teaspoon	tetrapod	thudding	toilworn	trackage	triennia	tumorous	ultimacy
teatable	tetrarch	thuggery	tokenism	tracking	trifling	tuneable	ultimata
teatowel	Teutonic	thuggism	tokology	trackman	trifocal	tuneless	ultimate
technics	textbook	thumbpot	tolbooth	trackway	triforia	tungsten	ultraism
tectonic	texthand	thumping	tolerant	tractate	triglyph	tungstic	ultraist
teenager	textuary	thundery	tolerate	traction	trigonal	tunicate	umbonate
teething	textural	thurible	tollcall	tractive	trigraph	Tunisian	umbrella
teetotal	textured	thurifer	tolldish	tradeoff	trilling	tuppence	umbrette
teetotum	thalamic	Thursday	tollgate	traditor	trillion	tuppenny	umpirage
tegmenta	thalamus	thusness	tomahawk	traducer	trillium	Turanian	umptieth
tegument	thallium	thwacker	tomalley	tragical	trilobed	turbaned	unabated
telecast	thalloid	thwarter	tombless	tragopan	trimaran	turbidly	unaneled
telecine	thallous	thwartly	tomentum	trailnet	trimeric	turbinal	unawares
telefilm	Thanatos	thyroxin	tommybar	training	trimeter	turbofan	unbacked
telegony	thanedom	thyrsoid	tommygun	tramline	trimming	turbojet	unbarred
telegram	thankful	ticklish	tommyrot	trammels	trimness	Turcoman	unbeaten
telemark	thankyou	tickseed	tomnoddy	trampler	trioxide	turgidly	unbelief
telepath	thatcher	ticktack	tomogram	tramroad	tripeman	Turkoman	unbidden
teleport	thearchy	ticktock	tomorrow	tranquil	triplane	turmeric	unbidden
telethon	theistic	tidegate	tonality	transact	triploid	turnable	unbolted
teleview	thematic	tideland	tonedeaf	transect	tripodal	turnback	unbottle
televise	theocrat	tideless	toneless	transept	trippery	turncoat	unbridle
tellable	theodicy	tidelock	tonepoem	transfer	tripping	turncock	unbroken
telltale	theogony	tidemark	tonguing	transfix	triptych	turndown	unbuckle
telluric	theology	tidemill	tonicity	tranship	tripwire	turnings	unburied
temerity	theorise	tidewave	toolroom	transire	triskele	turnover	unburied
tempered	theorist	tidiness	toolshed	transmit	trisomic	turnpike	unbutton
temperer	therefor	tiebreak	toothful	transude	tristful	turnskin	uncalled
template	thereout	tigereye	toothily	trapball	tristich	turnsole	uncandid
temporal	thermion	tigerish	toothing	trapdoor	tritical	turnspit	uncapped
tempting	thermite	tightwad	topdress	trapezia	triumvir	turreted	uncaused
tenacity	thesauri	tilefish	topheavy	trappean	triunity	turtling	unchancy
tenacula	thespian	tillable	toplevel	trapping	trochaic	tussocky	unchaste
tenaille	thetical	tiltyard	topliner	Trappist	trochili	tutelage	unchurch
tenantry	theurgic	timbered	toplofty	traprock	trochlea	tutelary	uncially
tendence	thiamine	timeball	topnotch	trashery	trochoid	tutorage	unciform
tendency	thickety	timebomb	topology	trashily	troilite	tutoress	uncinate
tenderly	thickish	timefuse	toponymy	traumata	trollopy	tutorial	unclench
Tenebrae	thickset	timeless	topstone	traverse	trombone	twaddler	unclinch
tenement	thievery	timework	torchere	travesty	trophied	tweezers	unclothe
tenesmus	thievish	timeworn	toreador	trawlnet	tropical	twelvemo	uncoined
tenonsaw	thingamy	timidity	toreutic	treacher	trotting	twenties	uncommon
tenorite	thinking	timorous	tornadic	treadler	trottoir	twiddler	uncouple
tenotomy	thinness	timously	toroidal	treasure	troupial	twilight	uncreate
tenpence	thinnest	tincture	torpidly	treasury	trousers	twinborn	unctuous
tenpenny	thinning	tingeing	torquate	treatise	troutlet	twinkler	underact
tensible	thinnish	tininess	torridly	trecento	trouvere	twinling	underage
tentacle	thirlage	tinkerer	tortilla	treefern	truantry	twinning	underarm
tenurial	thirster	tinnitus	tortious	treefrog	truckage	twinship	underbid
teocalli	thirteen	tinplate	tortoise	treeless	trucking	twitcher	undercut
tepidity	thisness	tinselly	tortuous	treenail	truckler	twittery	underdid
teraphim	tholepin	tinsmith	torturer	trekking	trueblue	twitting	underdog
teratoma	thoraces	tinstone	totalise	trembler	trueborn	twoedged	underfur
terebene	thoracic	tintless	totality	trembles	truebred	twofaced	underlap
terebrae	thoraxes	tipstaff	totalled	trencher	truelove	twopence	underlay
terminal	thorough	tireless	totemism	trendily	trueness	twopenny	underlet
terminer	thoughts	tiresome	totemist	trephine	truistic	twopiece	underlie
terminus	thousand	titanate	totterer	trespass	trumeaux	twosided	underlip
termless	thraldom	titaness	touchily	tressure	trumpery	twotimer	underman

underpin	unseeing	utiliser	venereal	vincible	vortexes	waterway	whistler
underrun	unseemly	uvularly	Venetian	vinculum	vortical	watthour	whiteboy
undersea	unsettle	uvulitis	vengeful	vinegary	vortices	waveband	whitecap
underset	unshaped	uxorious	venially	vineyard	votaress	waveform	whitefly
undertow	unsocial	vacantly	venomous	vinosity	votarist	waveless	whitehot
underway	unsought	vacation	venosity	vinously	voteless	waviness	whitener
undraped	unsprung	vaccinal	venously	vintager	voussoir	waxberry	whiteout
undreamt	unstable	vaccinia	ventless	violable	vowelise	waxcloth	whitetie
undulant	unstably	vacuolar	venturer	violably	vowelled	waxiness	whittret
undulate	unstated	Venusian	violator	voyageur	waxlight	whizbang
unearned	unsteady	vagility	veracity	violence	vulcanic	waxworks	whizzing
uneasily	unstring	vagrancy	verandah	viperine	vulgarly	wayfarer	whizzkid
unedited	unstrung	vainness	veratrin	viperish	waesucks	waygoing	whodunit
unending	unstuffy	valanced	veratrum	viperous	waggoner	weakfish	wholehog
unerring	unsuited	valerate	verbally	virement	wagonage	weakling	whomever
unevenly	unsunned	valerian	verbatim	virginal	wagonlit	weakness	whooping
unfading	unswathe	Valhalla	verbiage	Virginia	Wahabism	weanling	whopping
unfairly	untangle	valiance	verboten	viricide	Wahabite	weaponry	whoredom
unfasten	untapped	valiancy	verdancy	viridian	wainscot	wearable	whoreson
unfetter	untaught	validate	verderer	viridity	waitress	weariful	wickedly
unfilial	untented	validity	verderor	virilism	wakeless	weaselly	wideeyed
unfitted	untether	valorise	verditer	virility	wakening	Wedgwood	wideness
unforced	unthread	valorous	verdured	virology	wakerife	weedless	wifehood
unformed	unthrift	valuable	verecund	virtuosa	waleknot	weeklong	wifeless
unfreeze	unthrone	valuably	vergence	virtuosi	Walhalla	weeviled	wifelike
unfrozen	untidily	valuator	verifier	virtuoso	walkable	weevilly	wigmaker
unfunded	untimely	valvulae	veristic	virtuous	walkaway	weldable	wildeyed
ungainly	untitled	valvular	verjuice	virulent	walkover	weldment	wildfire
unglazed	untoward	vambrace	vermouth	viscacha	Walkyrie	welladay	wildfowl
ungotten	unvalued	vampiric	vernally	visceral	wallaroo	wellaway	wildlife
ungulate	unversed	vamplate	vernicle	viscidly	walleyed	wellborn	wildness
unhinged	unvoiced	vanadate	veronica	viscount	wallfern	wellbred	wildwood
unhoused	unwanted	vanadium	verrucae	Visigoth	wallgame	welldeck	wilfully
uniaxial	unwarily	vanadous	versicle	visional	wallknot	wellhead	wiliness
unicycle	unwashed	Vandalic	vertebra	visitant	walloper	wellknit	williwaw
unifilar	unweaned	vaneless	vertexes	visually	wallower	wellnigh	windburn
unionise	unwieldy	vanguard	vertical	vitalise	wanderer	wellread	windcone
unionism	unwisdom	vanillin	vertices	vitalism	wanderoo	Wellsian	windfall
unionist	unwisely	vanisher	verticil	vitalist	wantonly	Welshman	windgall
unipolar	unwished	vanquish	vesicant	vitality	warcloud	weltered	windlass
uniquely	unwonted	vapidity	vesicate	vitellin	wardance	weregild	windless
unisonal	unwordly	vaporise	vesperal	vitellus	wardenry	werewolf	windmill
unitedly	unworthy	vaporous	vespiary	vitiable	wardress	Wesleyan	windowed
univalve	unzipped	vapourer	vestiary	vitiator	wardrobe	westerly	windpipe
universe	upheaval	varactor	vestment	vitiligo	wardroom	westward	windrose
univocal	upholder	variable	vesturer	vitreous	wardship	wetlands	windsail
unjustly	uplander	variably	vesuvian	vituline	warhorse	wetnurse	windsock
unkennel	uplifter	variance	vexation	vivacity	wariness	wettable	windward
unkindly	uppercut	varicose	vexillum	vivarium	warmness	whacking	winepalm
unkingly	uppishly	variedly	viameter	vivifier	warpaint	whapping	wineshop
unlawful	uprising	varietal	viaticum	vivisect	warplane	wharfage	wineskin
unleaded	uprooter	variform	vibrancy	vixenish	warragal	whatever	wingbeat
unlearnt	upsetter	variolar	vibrator	vizarded	warranty	whatness	wingcase
unlikely	upsprang	variorum	vibrissa	vizcacha	warrener	wheatear	wingless
unlimber	upspring	varletry	viburnum	vocalise	warrigal	wheedler	wingspan
unlinked	upsprung	vascular	vicarage	vocalism	wartweed	wheelman	winnable
unlisted	upstairs	vasculum	vicarate	vocalist	wartwort	wheezily	winnings
unloader	upstream	vasiform	vicarial	vocality	warweary	whenever	winnower
unloosen	upstroke	vastness	vicinage	vocation	warwhoop	wherever	winterly
unlovely	upthrown	vaulting	vicinity	vocative	washable	whetting	wintrily
unmanned	upthrust	vauntful	victoria	voicebox	washbowl	wheyface	wiredraw
unmarked	upwardly	vavasory	victress	voiceful	washroom	whidding	wirehair
unmeetly	uralitic	vavasour	victuals	voidable	wastable	whiffler	wireless
unmuffle	urbanely	Vedantic	Viennese	voidance	wasteful	Whiggery	wirework
unmuzzle	urbanise	vegetate	Vietcong	voidness	watchdog	Whiggish	wireworm
unopened	urbanism	vegetive	Vietminh	volatile	watchful	Whiggism	wirewove
unpaired	urbanist	vehement	viewable	volcanic	watchkey	whimbrel	wiriness
unpegged	urbanite	veilless	viewless	volcanos	watchman	whimwham	wiseacre
unperson	urbanity	velamina	vigilant	volitant	waterage	whinchat	wiseness
unpinned	urethane	velarium	vigneron	volition	waterbed	whinsill	wishbone
unplaced	urgently	velleity	vignette	volitive	waterbus	whipcord	wishwash
unreason	urochord	velocity	vigorous	volplane	watergas	whiplash	wistaria
unriddle	urostyle	velskoen	vileness	voltaism	waterice	whiplike	wisteria
unrigged	Ursuline	venality	vilifier	volution	watering	whipping	witchelm
unroofed	urticant	venation	vilipend	volvulus	waterish	whipworm	witchery
unsaddle	urticate	vendetta	villadom	vomerine	waterlog	whirring	witchety
unsealed	usefully	vendible	villager	vomitive	waterloo	whiskers	witching
unseated	usufruct	veneerer	villainy	vomitory	waterman	whiskery	withdraw
unseeded	usurious	venerate	villatic	voracity	waterski	whispery	withdrew

withheld
withhold
wizardly
wizardry
woefully
wolffish
wolfpack
wolfskin
womanise
womanish
wondrous
wontedly
woodbind
woodbine
woodchat
woodcock
woodenly
woodland
woodlark
woodlice
woodnote
woodpile
woodpulp
woodruff
woodshed
woodsman
woodwind
woodwool
woodwork
woodworm
wooldyed
woolfell
woollens
woolpack
woolsack
woolshed
woolskin
woolwork
wordbook
wordless
wordplay
workable
workaday
workfolk
workings
workless
workmate
workroom
workshop
wormcast
wormgear
wormhole
wormlike
wormseed
wormwood
worthful
worthily
wouldest
woundily
wrackful
wrangler
wrappage
wrapping
wrathful
wrathily
wreathen
wreckage
wrestler
wrestpin
wretched
wriggler
wristlet
wristpin
writable
writeoff
writings
wrongful
wrongous
wrymouth
xanthate
xanthein
xanthene
xanthine
xanthium
xanthoma
Xantippe
xenogamy
xenolith
xylocarp
xylology
xylonite
yachting
Yankeefy
yarmulka
yataghan
yeanling
yearbook
yearling
yearlong
yearning
yeastily
yellowly
yeomanly
yeomanry
yestreen
yielding
yodelled
yodeller
yoghourt
yokemate
youngest
youngish
yourself
youthful
Yugoslav
yuletide
zabaione
zamindar
zaniness
zarzuela
zealotry
zecchini
zecchino
zemindar
zenithal
zeolitic
zeppelin
zibeline
ziggurat
zinckify
zincking
zirconia
zodiacal
zoetrope
zoiatria
zombiism
zonation
zoogenic
zoolater
zoolatry
zoomancy
zoometry
zoomorph
zoonosis
zoophily
zoophyte
zoospore
zucchini
zugzwang
zwieback
zygaenid
zymology

---

aardvark
aardwolf
aasvogel
babirusa
babouche
babushka
babyhood
baccarat
bacchant
bachelor
bacillar
bacillus
backache
backbite
backbone
backchat
backcomb
backdate
backdoor
backdrop
backfire
backhand
backlash
backless
backlist
backmost
backpack
backrest
backroom
backseat
backside
backspin
backstay
backveld
backward
backwash
backyard
Baconian
bacteria
Bactrian
badinage
badlands
bagpiper
baguette
bailable
bailment
bailsman
bakshish
balanced
balancer
baldhead
baldness
baldpate
balefire
Balinese
balkline
balladic
balladry
ballcock
balletic
ballista
ballonet
ballroom
ballyhoo
ballyrag
balmoral
balsamic
baluster
bambinos
banality
banausic
bandanna
bandeaux
banderol
banditry
banditti
bandsman
bangtail
banister
banjoist
bankable
bankbill
bankbook
banknote
bankroll
bankrupt
bannered
banneret
bannerol
banterer
bantling
banxring
barathea
barbaric
barbecue
barberry
barbette
barbican
barbital
bareback
barefoot
bareness
bargeman
baritone
barkless
barnacle
barndoor
barnyard
baronage
baroness
baronial
barouche
barracks
barranca
barranco
barrator
barratry
barrenly
barrette
barterer
bartizan
baryonic
barytone
basaltic
baseball
baseborn
baseless
baseline
basement
baseness
basicity
basidial
basidium
basilica
basilisk
basinful
basketry
bassinet
basswood
bastardy
bastille
Batavian
bateleur
bathetic
bathotic
bathrobe
bathroom
battalia
battleax
baudrons
bauxitic
Bavarian
bayadere
bayberry
cabalism
cabalist
caballed
cabinboy
cableway
cabochon
caboodle
cabotage
cabriole
cabstand
cachalot
cachepot
cachexia
cachucha
cacology
cacomixl
cactuses
cadastre
cadenced
caducean
caduceus
caducity
caducous
caesious
caesural
caffeine
cagebird
cageling
caginess
cajolery
cakewalk
calabash
caladium
calamary
calamine
calamint
calamite
calamity
calcanea
calcaria
calcific
calcitic
calcspar
calctuff
calculus
calendar
calender
calfskin
calidity
califate
calipash
calipers
callable
callgirl
calliope
calliper
calmness
calthrop
calvados
calycine
calycoid
calycule
calyptra
Cambrian
cameleer
camellia
camisade
camisado
camisole
camomile
campagna
campaign
campfire
camphene
camphine
campsite
camshaft
Canadian
canaille
canalise
canaster
cancrine
cancroid
candidly
canister
cannabin
cannabis
cannibal
cannikin
cannonry
cannulae
cannular
cannulas
canoeing
canoeist
canoness
canonise
canonist
canoodle
canorous
canthari
canticle
cantonal
cantoris
canzonet
capacity
capeline
capellet
capeskin
capitate
capitula
caponier
caponise
caprifig
capriole
capsicum
capstone
capsular
captious
capuchin
capybara
carabine
caracara
caracole
carapace
carbolic
carbonic
carbonyl
carboxyl
carburet
carcajou
carcanet
cardamom
cardamum
cardigan
cardinal
carefree
careless
careworn
carillon
carinate
carnally
carnauba
carnival
Carolean
Caroline
carolled
carotene
carousal
carousel
carouser
carriage
carriole
carryall
carryout
cartload
cartouch
caruncle
caryatid
Casanova
cascabel
casebook
casemate
casement
casework
cashbook
cashmere
cassette
castaway
castiron
castrate
castrati
castrato
casually
casualty
catacomb
catalase
cataloes
catalyse
catalyst
catamite
catapult
cataract
catchall
catchfly
catching
catechol
category
catenary
catenate
cateress
catering
cathedra
catheter
cathexes
cathexis
cathodal
cathodic
catholic
cationic
catsfoot
catstail
cattleya
caudally
caudated
caudexes
caudices
caudillo
cauldron
causally
causerie
causeway
cautious
cavalier
cavatina
caverned
cavesson
cavicorn
cavilled
caviller
dabchick
dactylar
dactylic
daemonic
daffodil
daftness
dahabieh
daimonic
daintily
daiquiri
dairying
dairyman
dalesman
dalmatic
damassin
damnable
damnably
dampness
dancette
dancetty
dandruff
dandyish
dandyism
danegeld
dankness
danseuse
daringly
darkling
darkness
darkroom
darksome
dartrous
dastardy
dateless
dateline
daughter
daybreak
daydream
daylight
eagleowl
earmuffs
earnings
earphone
earpiece
earthnut
easement
easiness
easterly
eastmost
eastward
fabliaux
fabulist
fabulous
faceache
facecard
faceless
facelift
facepack
facetiae
facially
facilely
facility
factious
factotum
fadeaway
fadeless
fagoting
failsafe
faineant
faintish
fairlead
fairness
fairyism
faithful
falcated
falchion
falconer
falconet
falconry
falderal
fallback
fallfish
fallible
fallibly
falsetto
faltboat
familial
familiar
famously
fanciful
fancyman
fandance
fandango
fanfaron
fangless
fanlight
fantasia
faradaic
faradism
farcical
farewell
farflung
farinose
farmhand
farmland

farmyard	gapeworm	handclap	jabberer	landmark	Maecenas	maniacal	matronly
farouche	gapingly	handcuff	jackaroo	landmass	maenadic	Manichee	mattress
farriery	garboard	handfast	jackboot	landmine	maestoso	manicure	maturate
farthest	gardener	handgrip	jackeroo	landrail	magazine	manifest	maturely
farthing	gardenia	handheld	jackstay	landslip	magdalen	manifold	maturity
fascicle	gardyloo	handhold	Jacobean	landsman	magician	maniform	maverick
fasciola	garefowl	handicap	Jacobite	langlauf	magicked	mannered	maxillae
fasciole	garganey	handless	jacquard	Langshan	magister	mannerly	maximise
Fascista	gargoyle	handline	jaggedly	language	magmatic	mannikin	mayapple
Fascisti	garishly	handling	jailbird	languish	magnesia	mannitol	mayoress
fashious	garlicky	handlist	jalousie	lankness	magnetic	manorial	Mayqueen
fastback	garotter	handloom	jamboree	lanneret	magneton	manpower	mazarine
fastener	garreted	handmade	janizary	lanthorn	magnific	mansized	Mazdaism
fastfood	garrison	handmaid	Japanese	lapboard	magnolia	mantelet	mazement
fastness	garrotte	handmill	japanned	lapelled	maharaja	mantilla	maziness
fasttalk	gaselier	handpick	japhetic	lapicide	maharani	mantissa	nacreous
fastuous	gasfired	handrail	japonica	lapidary	mahjongg	mantling	nailfile
fatalism	gashouse	handsewn	jaundice	lapidate	mahogany	manually	nainsook
fatalist	gaslight	handsome	jauntily	lapidify	Mahratta	manubria	nameable
fatality	gasmeter	handwork	Javanese	larboard	Mahratti	manurial	namedrop
fatherly	gasolene	handyman	Kaffiyeh	larcener	maidenly	maquette	nameless
fatigues	gasolier	hangable	kailyard	largesse	maidhood	marabout	namepart
fatstock	gasoline	hangeron	kakemono	larkspur	maieutic	marasmic	namesake
fattener	gastight	hangnail	kalaazar	larrikin	mailable	marasmus	nametape
faubourg	gastraea	hangover	kamikaze	larynges	mailboat	marathon	nanogram
faultily	gastrula	harakiri	Kanarese	larynxes	mailcart	marauder	naphthol
faunally	gasworks	harangue	kangaroo	lashings	mainland	maravedi	napiform
Faustian	gatefold	harasser	Kashmiri	latchkey	mainline	marbling	napoleon
fauteuil	gatepost	hardback	katakana	lateness	mainmast	marchesa	narceine
favonian	gatherer	hardbake	labdanum	latently	mainsail	marchese	narcissi
favoured	Gaullism	hardcase	labelled	laterite	mainstay	marginal	narcoses
favourer	Gaullist	hardcore	labellum	latinise	maintain	margrave	narcosis
gabbroic	gauntlet	hardener	labially	latinise	marigold	narcotic
gabbroid	gavelock	hardhack	lability	Latinism	maiolica	marinade	narghile
gableend	gazogene	hardhead	labourer	Latinist	maiolica	marinate	narrator
gadabout	gazpacho	hardline	labrador	latinity	majestic	maritage	narrowly
gadarene	habanera	hardness	laburnum	latitant	majolica	maritime	nasalise
gadgetry	habitant	hardship	lacerate	latitude	majority	marjoram	nasality
Gadhelic	habitual	hardtack	lacewing	latterly	makebate	markdown	nascence
gadzooks	habitude	hardware	lacework	latticed	makefast	markedly	nascency
gainable	hacienda	hardwood	lackaday	laudable	Malagasy	marketer	natality
gainings	hadronic	harebell	laconian	laudably	malamute	marksman	natation
gainless	haematic	haresear	laconism	laudanum	malapert	marmoset	natatory
gainsaid	haematin	harikari	lacrimal	laudator	malaprop	marocain	nathless
galactic	Haggadah	harlotry	lacrosse	laughing	malarial	maroquin	national
galangal	hairgrip	harmless	lacrymal	laughter	malarian	marquess	natively
galbanum	hairless	harmonic	lacunary	launcher	malarkey	marquise	nativism
galeated	hairlike	harpseal	lacunate	laureate	maledict	marriage	nativist
Galenism	hairline	harridan	lacunose	lavalava	malefern	marrieds	nativity
galenite	hairworm	harrumph	ladybird	lavation	malemute	marrying	naturism
Galilean	Halachah	haruspex	ladyfern	lavatory	maleness	marshman	naturist
galleass	halation	hasheesh	ladyhood	lavender	maligner	martagon	naumachy
galliard	haleness	hastener	ladylike	laverock	malignly	martello	nauplius
Gallican	halfback	hastings	ladylove	lavishly	malinger	martenot	nauseant
gallipot	halfbeak	hatchery	ladyship	lawcourt	malodour	martinet	nauseate
galloper	halfboot	hatchery	laically	lawfully	maltreat	marzipan	nauseous
Galloway	halfbred	hatching	lakeland	lawgiver	maltster	mascaron	nautical
galluses	halflife	hatchway	lallygag	lawmaker	malvasia	Masorete	nautilus
gallwasp	halfmast	hateable	lamasery	lawyerly	Mameluke	Masoreth	navigate
galvanic	halfmoon	hatstand	lambaste	laxative	mamillae	massacre	Nazarene
gambados	halfnote	haulyard	lambency	layabout	mamillar	masseter	Nazarite
gambeson	halfpint	haunting	lamblike	layshaft	mancando	masseuse	Nazirite
gambroon	halfsole	hausfrau	lambskin	laystall	manciple	massicot	oafishly
gamebird	halfterm	havelock	lamellae	laywoman	Mandaean	massless	oakapple
gamecock	halftime	havildar	lamellar	Lazarist	mandamus	masterly	oakegger
gameness	halftone	havocked	lameness	laziness	mandarin	masthead	oatgrass
gamesome	haliotis	Hawaiian	lamented	lazulite	mandator	mastitis	pachalic
gamester	halliard	hawkeyed	laminate	lazurite	mandible	mastodon	pacifier
gaminess	hallmark	hawklike	lamppost	macaroni	Mandingo	matamata	pacifism
gangland	hallowed	hawklike	lancelet	macaroon	mandolin	matchbox	pacifist
gangling	halluces	hawkmoth	landarmy	macerate	mandorla	matelote	padishah
ganglion	halteres	hawkweed	landcrab	machismo	mandrake	material	paduasoy
gangrene	hamartia	hawthorn	landfall	mackerel	mandrill	materiel	paganise
gangster	hamululi	hayfinch	landform	mackinaw	maneater	maternal	paganish
ganister	handball	haymaker	landgirl	maculate	manfully	matgrass	paganism
gantline	handbell	haystack	landlady	madapple	mangabey	matiness	paginate
gantlope	handbill	hazelnut	landless	madhouse	manganic	matrices	pagurian
Ganymede	handbook	haziness	landline	madrigal	mangonel	matrixes	painless
gaolbird	handcart	ianthine	landlord	madwoman	mangrove	matronal	paintbox

palatial	paroxysm	rainwash	salesman	saunders	tantalum	variance	waterlog
palatine	parrotry	rainwear	salience	sauouari	tantalus	varicose	waterloo
paleface	Parsiism	rakehell	saliency	sauropod	Tantrism	variedly	waterman
paleness	parsonic	rakishly	salinity	Sauterne	tantrist	varietal	waterski
palestra	partaken	rallying	salivary	savagely	tapdance	variform	waterway
palinode	parterre	rallyist	salivate	savagery	tapedeck	variolar	watthour
palisade	Parthian	rambling	Salopian	savannah	tapeless	variorum	waveband
palliate	partible	rambutan	saltbush	savorous	tapelike	varletry	waveform
pallidly	particle	ramentum	saltless	Savoyard	tapeline	vascular	waveless
pallmall	partisan	ramequin	saltlick	sawbones	tapestry	vasculum	waviness
palmette	partizan	rampancy	saltmine	sawedged	tapeworm	vasiform	waxberry
palmetto	partsong	ranarian	saltness	sawedoff	taphouse	vastness	waxcloth
palmiped	parttime	ranarium	saltwort	sawframe	tapwater	vaulting	waxiness
palmitin	pashalic	ranchero	salutary	sawhorse	tarboosh	vauntful	waxlight
palomino	pashalik	ranchman	salvable	sawtooth	tarlatan	vavasory	waxworks
palpable	passable	randomly	salvific	saxatile	Tarpeian	vavasour	wayfarer
palpably	passably	rankness	samarium	Saxondom	tarragon	waesucks	waygoing
palterer	passbook	ransomer	sameness	Saxonism	tartaric	waggoner	xanthate
paludism	passerby	rapacity	samizdat	Saxonist	tartness	wagonage	xanthein
pamperer	passible	rapecake	Samoyede	sayonara	tartrate	wagonlit	xanthene
pamphlet	Passover	rapeseed	samphire	taberdar	Tartuffe	Wahabism	xanthine
pancreas	passport	rapidity	sampling	tableaux	taskwork	Wahabite	xanthium
pandanus	password	rapparee	sanative	tablecut	tasselly	wainscot	xanthoma
pandemic	pastiche	raptness	sanatory	tableful	tastebud	waitress	Xantippe
pandowdy	pastille	raptures	sanctify	tablemat	tasteful	wakeless	yachting
panelled	pastoral	rarefied	sanction	tabletop	tattered	wakening	Yankeefy
pangolin	pastrami	rareness	sanctity	tabouret	tattooer	wakerife	yarmulka
panicked	pastries	rascally	sandarac	tabulate	tautness	waleknot	yataghan
panmixia	pastural	rashness	sandbank	tachisme	tautomer	Walhalla	zabaione
pannikin	patagium	rasorial	sandbath	tachiste	tautonym	walkable	zamindar
panorama	patchily	rataplan	sandflea	taciturn	taverner	walkaway	zaniness
panpipes	patellae	rateable	sandshoe	tackling	tawdrily	walkover	zarzuela
pansophy	patellar	ratguard	sandwich	tackroom	taxation	Walkyrie	abacuses
pantheon	patentee	ratifier	sandworm	tactical	taxingly	wallaroo	abattoir
pantofle	patently	rational	sandwort	tactless	taxonomy	walleyed	Abbaside
pantsuit	patentor	ratsbane	sandyish	taenioid	taxpayer	wallfern	abbatial
papalise	paternal	ratstail	saneness	tafferel	vacantly	wallgame	Abderite
papalism	pathetic	rattling	sangaree	taffrail	vacation	wallknot	abdicate
papalist	pathless	ravelled	Sangrail	tagalong	vaccinal	walloper	abducens
paperboy	pathogen	ravenous	Sangreal	Tahitian	vaccinia	wallower	abducent
papillae	patience	ravisher	sanguine	tailback	vacuolar	wanderer	abductor
papillar	patronal	rawboned	sanitary	tailcoat	vagabond	wanderoo	abelmosk
papillon	pattypan	sabbatic	sanitate	tailgate	vagility	wantonly	aberrant
papistic	patulous	sabotage	sanitise	tailings	vagrancy	warcloud	abetment
papistry	pavement	saboteur	sannyasi	tailless	vainness	wardance	abetting
pappadom	pavilion	saccadic	sanserif	tailpipe	valanced	wardenry	abeyance
papulose	pawnshop	saccular	Sanskrit	tailrace	valerate	wardress	abeyancy
papulous	payphone	sacculus	santonin	tailspin	valerian	wardrobe	abhorred
parabola	paysheet	sackcoat	sapgreen	tainture	Valhalla	wardroom	abhorrer
paradigm	rabbinic	sackless	sapidity	takeaway	valiance	wardship	abidance
paradise	rabbiter	sackrace	sapience	takehome	valiancy	warhorse	abjectly
paraffin	rabbitry	sacraria	saponify	takeover	validate	wariness	ablation
paragoge	rabidity	sacredly	saponite	takingly	validity	warmness	ablative
parakeet	racecard	sacristy	saporous	talapoin	valorise	warpaint	ablution
parallax	racegoer	saddlery	sapphics	talented	valorous	warplane	abnegate
parallel	racemate	Sadducee	sapphire	talesman	valuable	warragal	abnormal
paralyse	racemise	sadistic	sapphism	talisman	valuably	warranty	abomasum
paramour	racemose	safeness	saraband	tallness	valuator	warrener	abomasus
paranoia	rachides	saffrony	sarcenet	tallyman	valvulae	warrigal	aborally
paranoid	rachitic	safranin	sardelle	Talmudic	valvular	wartweed	aborning
paraquat	rachitis	sagacity	sardonic	tamandua	vambrace	wartwort	abortion
parasang	racially	sagamore	sardonyx	tamanoir	vampiric	warweary	abortive
parasite	raciness	sageness	sargasso	tamarack	vamplate	warwhoop	abradant
paravane	rackrent	saginate	sarsenet	tamarind	vanadate	washable	abrasion
parcener	radially	sagittal	sashcord	tamarisk	vanadium	washbowl	abrasive
parclose	radiance	sailable	Sassanid	tamboura	vanadous	washroom	abridger
pardoner	radiancy	sailboat	satanism	tameable	Vandalic	wastable	abrogate
parental	radiator	sailfish	satanist	tameless	vaneless	wasteful	abruptly
parergon	radicant	sailless	sateless	tameness	vanguard	watchdog	abscissa
pargeter	radicate	sailorly	satiable	Tamilian	vanillin	watchful	absentee
parhelia	raftsman	sailyard	satiably	tamperer	vanisher	watchkey	absently
parhelic	raggedly	sainfoin	satirise	tandoori	vanquish	watchman	absinthe
parietal	railhead	saintdom	satirist	tangency	vapidity	waterage	absolute
parkland	raillery	salacity	saturant	tangible	vaporise	waterbed	absolver
parlance	railroad	salariat	saturate	tangibly	vaporous	waterbus	absonant
parlando	rainbird	salaried	Saturday	tangoist	vapourer	watergas	absorber
Parmesan	raincoat	saleable	saucebox	tannable	varactor	waterice	absterge
parodist	raindrop	saleroom	saucepan	tantalic	variable	watering	abstract
paroquet	rainfall	Salesian	saucepan		variably	waterish	abstrict

abstruse	acrylate	scarring	sculptor	idocrase	believer	cervical	delegate
absurdly	actiniae	scathing	scumming	idolater	belittle	cervices	deletion
abundant	actinian	scattily	scurrile	idolatry	bellbird	cesspool	delibate
abutilon	actinias	scatting	scurvily	idoliser	bellbuoy	cetacean	delicacy
abutment	actinide	scavenge	scutcher	idyllist	bellcote	deadbeat	delicate
abuttals	actinism	scenario	scutella	oddments	bellpull	deadener	delirium
abutting	actinium	scenical	Adamical	odiously	bellpush	deadfall	delivery
ebriated	activate	sceptred	adamitic	odograph	bellwort	deadhead	Delphian
Ibsenism	actively	schedule	adaption	odometer	bellyful	deadline	delusion
obduracy	activism	schemata	adaptive	odontoid	beltless	deadlock	delusive
obdurate	activist	scheming	addendum	Odyssean	benedick	deadness	delusory
obedient	activity	schiedam	addition	udometer	benedict	deadwood	demagogy
obeisant	actually	schiller	additive	aegirine	benefice	deaerate	demander
obituary	actuator	schizoid	adducent	aegrotat	benignly	deafmute	demarche
objector	acturial	schmaltz	adductor	aeration	Benjamin	deafness	demented
oblation	aculeate	schnapps	adenitis	aerially	bentwood	dealfish	dementia
oblatory	ecclesia	scholium	adenoids	aeriform	benzoate	deanship	demerara
obligate	echinate	schooner	adequacy	aerodyne	benzylic	dearness	demersal
obliging	echinoid	sciagram	adequate	aerofoil	bequeath	deathbed	demijohn
oblivion	echogram	sciatica	adespota	aerogram	berberis	deathcap	demitted
observer	echoless	scilicet	adherent	aerolite	berceuse	deathray	demiurge
obsidian	eclectic	scimitar	adhesion	aerolith	bereaved	debagged	demobbed
obsolete	ecliptic	sciolism	adhesive	aerology	bergamot	debarred	democrat
obstacle	eclosion	sciolist	adiantum	aeronaut	beriberi	debility	demolish
obstruct	ecologic	scirocco	adjacent	aeronomy	berliner	debonair	demoness
obtainer	economic	scirrhus	adjuster	aerostat	Bermudas	debugged	demoniac
obtected	ecstatic	scissile	adjustor	aesthete	besieger	debutant	demonian
obturate	ectoderm	scission	adjutage	aestival	beslaver	decadent	demonise
obtusely	ectozoon	scissors	adjutant	beadroll	besmirch	decagram	demonism
obtusity	iceblink	sciurine	adjuvant	beadsman	besotted	decanter	demotion
ubiquity	icebound	sciuroid	Adlerian	beadwork	besought	deceased	demurely
academia	icecream	sclereid	adlibbed	beagling	bespoken	decedent	demurred
academic	icefield	sclerite	admitted	beamends	besprent	deceiver	demurrer
acanthus	iceplant	scleroma	admonish	beanpole	bestiary	December	denarius
acarpous	iceskate	sclerose	adnation	bearable	bestowal	decemvir	denature
Accadian	icewater	sclerous	adoption	bearably	bestrewn	decennia	denazify
accentor	iceyacht	scolding	adoptive	bearings	bestride	decently	dendrite
accepter	ichorous	scolices	adorable	bearskin	bestrode	decigram	dendroid
acceptor	occasion	scombrid	adorably	beatific	betacism	decimate	denehole
accident	occident	scoopful	adroitly	beautify	betatron	decipher	deniable
accolade	occluded	scoopnet	adularia	bebopper	bethesda	decision	denounce
accoutre	occlusal	scopulae	adulator	becalmed	betrayal	decisive	dentalia
accredit	occultly	scopulas	adultery	bechamel	betrayer	deckhand	dentated
accuracy	occupant	scorcher	aduncate	bechance	bevelled	declarer	denticle
accurate	occupier	scornful	aduncous	becoming	beveller	declasse	departed
accursed	occurred	scorpion	advanced	bedabble	beverage	declutch	depicter
accustom	ocellate	scotfree	advisory	bedazzle	bewigged	decolour	depictor
aceldama	ochreous	scotopic	advocaat	bedeguar	bewilder	decorate	depilate
acentric	octarchy	Scotsman	advocacy	bedimmed	bezonian	decorous	deponent
acerbate	octaroon	scottice	advocate	bedmaker	celeriac	decouple	deportee
acerbity	octonary	Scottish	advowson	bedplate	celerity	decrease	depraved
acervate	octoroon	scourger	adynamia	bedstead	celibacy	decrepit	deprival
acescent	ocularly	scouting	adynamic	bedstraw	celibate	decretal	deprived
achenial	scabbard	scrabble	bdellium	bedtable	cellarer	decurion	depurate
achiever	scabious	scragend	edacious	beebread	cellaret	dedicate	deputise
achiness	scabrous	scragged	edentate	beechnut	cellular	deedless	deration
achingly	scaffold	scramble	edgeless	beeeater	cemetery	deemster	derelict
aciculae	scalable	scrammed	edgeways	beefcake	cenotaph	deeplaid	derision
acicular	scalawag	scrannel	edgewise	beefwood	Cenozoic	deepness	derisive
aciculas	scalepan	scraping	edginess	beeswing	centaury	deerskin	derisory
acidfast	scallion	scrapped	editress	beetling	centring	defector	derivate
acidhead	scammony	scrapper	educable	beetroot	centrism	defender	derogate
acidosis	scampish	scratchy	educated	befallen	centrist	deferent	derriere
acierage	scandent	scrawler	educator	befitted	centroid	deferral	describe
acierate	Scandian	screamer	educible	befogged	centuple	deferred	deserter
aconitic	scandium	screechy	eduction	befriend	cephalic	deferrer	designer
aconitum	scanning	screener	idealess	befuddle	ceramics	defiance	desirous
acosmism	scansion	screever	idealise	begetter	ceramist	defilade	desolate
acoustic	scanties	screwtop	idealism	beggarly	cerastes	definite	despatch
acquaint	scantily	scribble	idealist	beginner	ceratoid	deflower	despiser
acrefoot	scaphoid	scribbly	ideality	begirded	cercaria	deforest	despotic
acreinch	scapulae	scrofula	ideation	begotten	cerebral	deformed	destrier
acridine	scapular	scrounge	identify	begrudge	cerebrum	defrayal	destruct
acridity	scapulas	scrubbed	identity	beguiler	cerement	deftness	detached
acrimony	scarcely	scrubber	ideogram	behemoth	ceremony	degrease	detailed
acrolein	scarcity	scrutiny	ideology	beholden	cernuous	deionise	detainee
acrolith	scarfpin	scudding	idiolect	beholder	cerulean	dejected	detainer
acrostic	scarious	scullery	idiotism	belabour	cerusite	delation	detector
acrotism	scarless	scullion	idleness	bejabers	cervelat	delegacy	deterred

deterrer	feudally	Hebraist	jesuitry	lewdness	metaphor	oestrous	perineal
dethrone	feverfew	hecatomb	jetblack	lewisite	metayage	peaceful	perineum
detonate	feverish	hedgehog	jetplane	meagrely	metazoan	peacocky	periodic
detoxify	feverous	hedgehop	jettison	mealtime	metazoon	peagreen	periotic
detrital	fewtrils	hedgepig	jewelled	mealworm	meteoric	peardrop	peripety
detritus	gearcase	hedgerow	jeweller	mealybug	methanol	pearlies	periplus
deucedly	gefuffle	hedonics	kedgeree	meanness	methinks	pearling	perisher
deuteron	gelastic	hedonism	keelhaul	meantime	methodic	pearlite	perjurer
deviance	gelatine	hedonist	keelless	measured	methylic	pearmain	perlitic
deviancy	gelation	heedless	keenness	meatball	methysis	peasecod	permeate
deviator	gelidity	heelball	keepsake	meatsafe	metonymy	peccable	peroneal
deviling	gematria	heelless	keeshond	mechanic	metrical	peccancy	perorate
devilish	geminate	Hegelian	kefuffle	meconium	mezereon	pectines	peroxide
devilism	gemstone	hegemony	keratose	medalled	neaptide	pectoral	personae
devilkin	gendarme	heighten	kerchief	medallic	Nearctic	peculate	personal
devilled	generate	heirless	kerosene	medially	nearness	peculiar	perspire
deviltry	generous	heirloom	kerosine	mediator	neatherd	pedagogy	persuade
Devonian	genetics	heirship	keyboard	medicate	neatness	pedalier	pertness
devotion	Genevese	heliacal	keystone	medicine	nebulise	pedalled	Peruvian
devourer	genially	helicoid	leadenly	medieval	nebulium	pedantic	perverse
devoutly	genitive	heliosis	leadless	mediocre	nebulous	pedantry	pervious
dewberry	geniture	heliport	leadsman	meditate	neckband	pederast	petaline
dewiness	genocide	Helladic	leadwork	medusoid	necklace	pedestal	petalled
dewpoint	genotype	hellbent	leafless	meekness	neckline	pedicled	petalody
dewyeyed	gentrice	Hellenic	leaflike	meetness	necropsy	pedicure	petaloid
dextrine	geodesic	hellfire	leanness	megalith	necrosis	pedigree	petalous
dextrose	geodetic	hellhole	leapfrog	megapode	necrotic	pediment	petechia
dextrous	geognosy	helmeted	learning	megawatt	nectared	pedipalp	petiolar
eelgrass	geologic	helminth	leathern	melamine	needfire	pedology	petioled
eeriness	geomancy	helmsman	leathery	melanism	needless	peduncle	petition
fearless	geometer	helotism	leavings	melanite	needment	peekaboo	petrolic
fearsome	geometry	helpless	lecithin	melinite	negation	peelings	petronel
feasible	geophagy	helpmate	lecturer	mellowly	negative	peephole	petrosal
feasibly	geophone	helpmeet	leeboard	melodeon	negatory	peepshow	pettifog
feastday	geophyte	henchman	lefthand	melodise	negatron	peerless	petulant
feathery	geoponic	henequen	leftover	melodist	negligee	Pegasean	petuntse
featured	Georgian	henparty	leftward	membered	Negrillo	pegboard	reabsorb
features	geotaxis	henroost	legalese	membrane	negroism	peignoir	reactant
febrific	geraniol	hepatica	legalise	mementos	nematode	Pekinese	reaction
February	geranium	hepatise	legalism	memorial	nematoid	Pelagian	reactive
feckless	gerbille	heptagon	legalist	memorise	nenuphar	Pelasgic	readable
feculent	Germanic	heraldic	legality	memsahib	NeoLatin	pelerine	readably
fedayeen	germcell	heraldry	legatine	menarche	neomycin	pellagra	readjust
federate	germfree	herbaria	legation	mendable	neonatal	pellicle	reaffirm
feeblish	germinal	herbless	legbreak	menhaden	neophyte	pellmell	reagency
feedback	gerontic	Hercules	legendry	menially	neoplasm	pellucid	realness
feedhead	gestagen	herdbook	legerity	meninges	neoprene	pelorism	realtime
feedpipe	gestural	herdsman	leggings	meniscus	neotenic	pembroke	reappear
feedtank	headache	herdwick	legguard	menology	neoteric	pemmican	rearlamp
feldsher	headachy	hereaway	legioned	menstrua	Nepalese	penalise	rearmice
feldspar	headband	heredity	leisured	mensural	nepenthe	penchant	rearmost
felicity	headfast	Hereford	lemonade	menswear	nephrite	pendency	rearview
felinity	headgear	hereunto	lemurine	mentally	nepotism	pendicle	rearward
fellable	headlamp	hereupon	lemuroid	mephitic	nescient	pendular	reascend
fellahin	headland	herewith	lengthen	mephitis	nestling	pendulum	reasoner
fellness	headless	heritage	lenience	merchant	neurally	penitent	reassert
fellowly	headline	hermetic	leniency	merciful	neuritic	penknife	reassess
felsitic	headlock	hernshaw	Leninism	mercuric	neuritis	penology	reassign
feminine	headlong	heroical	Leninist	mergence	neuronal	penstock	reassure
feminise	headmost	herpetic	Leninite	meridian	neuronic	pentacle	reawaken
feminism	headnote	Hertzian	lenitive	meringue	neuroses	pentagon	rebelled
feminist	headrace	hesitant	lensless	meristem	neurosis	pentroof	rebeller
feminity	headrest	hesitate	lenticel	meristic	neurotic	penumbra	rebellow
fenberry	headroom	Hesperus	lenticle	merosome	neutrino	peperino	rebuttal
fencible	headsail	hetaerae	lepidote	mescalin	newblown	perceive	rebutted
fenestra	headsman	hetairai	leporine	mesdames	newcomer	perfecto	rebutter
feretory	headwind	hexagram	lethally	meshwork	newfound	perforce	recapped
fernshaw	headword	hexapody	lethargy	mesially	newlywed	perfumer	receiver
ferocity	headwork	hexylene	lettered	mesmeric	newscast	perianth	recently
ferreter	heartily	jealousy	leucitic	mesocarp	newsheet	pericarp	receptor
ferriage	heatedly	Jehovist	levanter	mesoderm	newspeak	pericope	recharge
ferritic	heathery	jejunely	levelled	mesotron	newsreel	periderm	recision
ferryman	heathhen	jeopardy	leveller	Mesozoic	newsroom	peridium	reckless
fervency	heavenly	jeremiad	leverage	mesquite	nextdoor	peridote	reckoner
fervidly	hebdomad	Jeremiah	leviable	messmate	oecology	perigean	recommit
festally	hebetate	jeroboam	levigate	messuage	oeillade	perigyny	reconvey
festival	hebetude	jerrican	levirate	metalled	oenology	perilled	recorder
fetching	hebraise	jerrycan	levitate	metallic	oenophil	perilous	recourse
feticide	Hebraism	jesuitic	levulose	metamere	oestrone	perilune	recovery

recreant	reliable	response	seashell	Semitist	teaspoon	tetrapod	weariful
recreate	reliably	respring	seashore	semitone	teatable	tetrarch	weaselly
rectoral	reliance	resprung	seasnail	semolina	teatowel	Teutonic	Wedgwood
recurred	reliever	restcure	seasnake	semplice	technics	textbook	weedless
recusant	religion	restless	seasonal	sempster	tectonic	texthand	weeklong
redactor	relocate	restorer	seasoner	senarius	teenager	textuary	weeviled
redblind	relucent	restrain	seatbelt	senility	teething	textural	weevilly
redbrick	relumine	restrict	seatrout	sennight	teetotal	textured	weldable
redeemer	remanent	resupine	seawards	senorita	teetotum	Vedantic	weldment
redefine	remedial	resurvey	seawater	senseful	tegmenta	vegetate	welladay
redeless	remember	retailer	seawrack	sensible	tegument	vegetive	wellaway
redeploy	reminder	retainer	sebesten	sensibly	telecast	vehement	wellborn
redesign	remissly	retarded	secluded	sensoria	telecine	veilless	wellbred
redfaced	remittal	retarder	seconder	sensuous	telefilm	velamina	welldeck
redirect	remitted	retiarii	secondly	sentence	telegony	velarium	wellhead
redistil	remittee	reticent	secretin	sentient	telegram	velleity	wellknit
redolent	remitter	reticule	secretly	sentinel	telemark	velocity	wellnigh
redouble	remotely	retiform	secretor	sentrygo	telepath	velskoen	wellread
redshank	renderer	retinula	sectoral	sepaloid	teleport	venality	Wellsian
redshift	renegade	retiring	securely	sepalous	telethon	venation	wellworn
redshirt	renegado	retorted	security	separate	teleview	vendetta	Welshman
redstart	reneguer	retrench	sedately	Sephardi	televise	vendible	weregild
redwater	reniform	retrieve	sedation	septette	tellable	veneerer	werewolf
reedbird	renitent	retroact	sedative	septfoil	telltale	venerate	Wesleyan
reedling	renounce	retrorse	sederunt	septimal	telluric	venereal	westerly
reedmace	renovate	reusable	sediment	septuple	temerity	Venetian	westward
reedpipe	renowned	revanche	sedition	sequelae	tempered	vengeful	wetlands
reedstop	rentable	revealer	sedulity	sequence	temperer	venially	wetnurse
reedwren	renumber	reveille	sedulous	seraglio	template	venomous	wettable
reefknot	reoccupy	revelled	seedcake	seraphic	temporal	venosity	xenogamy
reembark	reorient	reveller	seedcase	seraphim	tempting	venturer	xenolith
reemerge	repairer	revenant	seedcoat	serenade	tenacity	ventless	yeanling
reemploy	repartee	revenger	seedcorn	serenata	tenacula	venturer	yearbook
reexport	repealer	reverend	seedfish	serenely	tenaille	Venusian	yearling
referent	repeater	reverent	seedleaf	serenity	tenantry	veracity	yearlong
referral	repelled	reversal	seedless	serfhood	tendence	verandah	yearning
referred	repeller	reverser	seedling	sergeant	tendency	veratrin	yeastily
refinery	repenter	reverter	seedlobe	serially	tenderly	veratrum	yellowly
refitted	repeople	revetted	seedplot	seriatim	Tenebrae	verbally	yeomanly
reflexed	replevin	reviewal	seedsman	sericite	tenement	verbatim	yeomanry
refluent	replacer	reviewer	seedtime	serjeant	tenesmus	verbiage	yestreen
reforest	replevin	reviling	segreant	serology	tenonsaw	verboten	zealotry
reformed	reporter	revision	seicento	serosity	tenorite	verdancy	zecchini
reformer	repotted	revisory	seigneur	serotine	tenotomy	verderer	zecchino
regalism	repousse	revivify	seignior	serpulae	tenpence	verderor	zemindar
regality	reprieve	revolter	seignory	serranid	tenpenny	verditer	zenithal
regelate	reprisal	revolute	seizable	serrated	tensible	verdured	zeolitic
regicide	reproach	revolver	seladang	servient	tentacle	verecund	zeppelin
regiment	reproval	rewaking	selcouth	servitor	tenurial	vergence	affected
regional	republic	rewarder	selectee	sesamoid	teocalli	verifier	affecter
register	requital	seaboard	selector	sesterce	tepidity	veristic	afferent
registry	requiter	seaborne	selenate	setscrew	teraphim	verjuice	affiance
regolith	rerearch	seachest	selenide	severely	teratoma	vermouth	affinity
regrater	rerecord	seacoast	selenite	severity	terebene	vernally	affirmer
regrowth	reremice	seacraft	selenium	sewellel	terebrae	vernicle	afflatus
regulate	rereward	seadrome	selfborn	sewerage	terminal	veronica	affluent
rehandle	rescript	seafarer	selfheal	sewergas	terminer	verrucae	afforest
rehearse	research	seafloor	selfhelp	sewerrat	terminus	versicle	affright
rehoboam	resemble	seafront	selfhood	sexiness	termless	vertebra	affusion
reignite	reserved	seagoing	selfless	sexology	termtime	vertexes	aflutter
reimpose	resetter	seagreen	selflove	sextette	terraced	vertical	effector
reindeer	resettle	seaholly	selfmade	sextuple	terrapin	vertices	efferent
reinless	reshuffle	seahorse	selfmate	sexually	terraria	verticil	efficacy
reinsert	residual	sealable	selfness	teaboard	terrazzo	vesicant	effluent
reinsman	residuum	sealevel	selfpity	teabread	terrible	vesicate	effluvia
reinsure	resigned	sealskin	selfrule	teabreak	terribly	vesperal	effusion
reinvest	resinate	sealyham	selfsame	teacaddy	terrific	vespiary	effusive
rejecter	resinify	seamanly	selfsown	teachest	tertiary	vestiary	eftsoons
rejigger	resinoid	seamless	selfwill	teaching	tesserae	vestment	offbreak
rejoicer	resinous	seamount	selvedge	teacloth	tesseral	vesturer	offdrive
rekindle	resister	seamouse	semantic	teahouse	testable	vesuvian	offender
relation	resistor	seamster	semester	teammate	testator	vexation	offering
relative	resolute	seaonion	semibull	teamster	testatum	vexillum	official
relaxant	resonant	seapiece	semidome	teamwork	testtube	weakfish	offprint
releasee	resonate	seaplane	seminary	teaparty	tetanise	weakling	offshoot
releaser	resorcin	seapurse	seminude	tearaway	tetchily	weakness	offshore
releasor	resorter	seaquake	semiotic	teardrop	tetradic	weanling	offsider
relegate	resource	searcher	Semitise	tearduct	tetragon	weaponry	offstage
relevant	respects	seascape	Semitism	tearless	tetrapla	wearable	ofttimes

```
sforzato Chellean phantasm sheepdip shrunken thuggism airtight circuity
agaragar chemical phantasy sheepdog shuddery thumbpot airwoman circular
agedness chemurgy pharisee sheepish shuffler thumping biannual cirriped
agential chenille pharmacy sheepked shunning thundery biassing cislunar
aggrieve chequers phaseout sheeppen shutdown thurible biathlon citation
agiotage Cherokee pheasant sheeprun shutting thurifer bibation citified
agitator cherubic phenolic sheeting thalamic Thursday biblical cityfied
agitprop cherubim phenylic sheikdom thalamus thusness bibulous civilian
aglimmer chessman Philomel Shekinah thallium thwacker biconvex civilise
aglitter chestnut phlegmon shelduck thalloid thwarter bicuspid civility
agnation Cheyenne phonemic shelfful thallous thwartly biddable diabasic
agnostic chiasmus phonetic shelving Thanatos thyroxin biennial diabetes
agonised chiastic phormium Shemitic thanedom thyrsoid biennium diabetic
agraphia chickpea phosgene shepherd thankful whacking bifacial diabolic
agrarian chiefdom phosphor Sheraton thankyou whapping bifocals diaconal
agrement childbed photogen sherlock thatcher wharfage bigamist diagnose
agrestic childish photopia Shetland thearchy whatever bigamous diagonal
agrimony children photopic shielder theistic whatness bignonia diagraph
agrology chiliasm photopsy shieling thematic wheatear bilabial diallage
agronomy chiliast phrasing shiftily theocrat wheedler bilberry dialling
aguishly chimaera phreatic shiftkey theodicy wheelman billfold dialogic
egestion chimeric Phrygian shigella theogony wheezily billhead dialogue
egestive Chinaman phthalic shikaree theology whenever billhook dialyser
eggplant chinchin phthisic shilling theorise wherever billiard dialyses
eggshell chinless phthisis shimmery theorist whetting billyboy dialysis
egoistic chipmuck phyletic shinbone therefor wheyface billycan dialytic
egomania chipmunk phyllary shingler thereout whidding bilobate diamante
Egyptian chipping phyllode shingles thermion whiffler bimanous diameter
ignition chirpily phylloid shinning thermite Whiggery bimbashi dianthus
ignitron chirrupy phyllome shipload thesauri Whiggish binaural diapason
ignominy chitchat physical shipmate thespian Whiggism bindweed diapause
ignorant chivalry physicky shipment thetical whimbrel binnacle diaphone
ugliness chlorate physique shipping theurgic whimwham binomial diarchal
chaconne chloride Rhaetian shipworm thiamine whinchat bioassay diarchic
chainsaw chlorine rhapsode shipyard thickety whinsill biocidal diarrhea
chairman chlorite rhapsody shiralee thickish whipcord biogenic diaspora
chalazae chlorous rheology shirring thickset whiplash biograph diaspore
Chaldaic choicely rheostat shirting thievery whiplike biometry diastase
Chaldean choirboy rhetoric shivaree thievish whipping biomorph diastema
chaldron choleric rhinitis shocking thingamy whipworm bionomic diastole
chalkpit chondrus Rhinodon shoddily thinking whirring bioplasm diatomic
chambers chopchop rhizopod shoebill thinness whiskers bioplast diatonic
chambray chopping rhomboid shoehorn thinnest whiskery bioscope diatribe
champers chopsuey rhonchal shoelace thinning whispery biparous dicacity
champion choragic rhonchus shoeless thinnish whistler birdbath dichasia
chancery choragus rhyolite shoetree thirlage whiteboy birdcage dichroic
chandler chorally rhythmic shofroth thirster whitecap birdcall dicrotic
chapatti chordate shabbily shogging thirteen whitefly birdlime dictator
chapbook choregic shabrack shooting thisness whitehot birdseed dicyclic
chapelry choregus Shabuoth shootout tholepin whitener birdseye didactic
chaperon choriamb shadbush shopbell thoraces whiteout birthday didapper
chapiter chorioid shaddock shopgirl thoracic whitetie bisector didymium
chaplain chowchow shadower shopping thoraxes whittret bisexual didymous
chapping christen shafting shoptalk thorough whizbang bistable dieldrin
charcoal christie shagbark shopworn thoughts whizzing bistoury diereses
charisma Christly shaggily shortage thousand whizzkid bitchily dieresis
charlady chromate shagreen shortarm thraldom whodunit bitingly diestock
charlock chromite shagroon shortcut thrasher wholehog bitterly dietetic
charming chromium shakable shortday thrawart whomever bivalent diffract
charring chthonic shakeout shortish threader whooping biweekly diffuser
Chartism chugging Shaktism shothole threaten whopping biyearly digamist
Chartist chummily shaleoil shoulder threeply whoredom ciborium digamous
chasseur chumming shalloon shouldst threeway whoreson cicatrix digester
chastely chupatti shallows showbill threnode aigrette cicerone diggings
chastise chupatty shambles showboat threnody aiguille ciceroni digitate
chastity churchly shameful showcard thresher airborne cicisbei digitise
chasuble churinga shamming showcase thridace airbrake cicisbeo dihedral
chateaux churlish shamrock showdown thriller airbrush cidevant dihybrid
chattily churning shanghai showgirl thriving aircraft ciliated dilatant
chatting chutzpah shantung showroom throated Airedale cinchona dilation
chaunter Ghanaian shapable shrapnel throbbed airfield cincture dilative
chauntry ghastful shareout shredded thrombin airframe cineaste dilatory
cheapish ghettoes sharpish shredder thrombus airiness cinerary diligent
checkers ghoulish sharpset shrewdly throstle airliner cingulum dilution
checkout khedival shashlik shrewish throttle airscrew cinnabar diluvial
cheekily Khmerian sheading shrieval thrummed airshaft cinnamic diluvian
cheerful khushkus shealing shrimper thruster airspace cinnamon diluvium
cheerily ohmmeter shedding shrinker thudding airspeed cinquain dimerism
cheering phalange shedevil shrugged thuggery airstrip Circaean dimerous
```

diminish
dimmable
dinerout
dingdong
dinornis
dinosaur
diocesan
dioecism
diopside
dioptase
dioptric
dioramic
dioritic
diphenyl
diplogen
diploidy
diplomat
diplopia
dipnoous
dipstick
dipteral
dipteran
directly
director
dirigism
diriment
disabuse
disagree
disallow
disarray
disaster
disbench
disbound
disburse
disciple
disclaim
disclose
discount
discover
discreet
discrete
discrown
diseased
disendow
disfrock
disgorge
disgrace
disguise
dishevel
disinter
disjoint
disjunct
dislodge
disloyal
dismally
dismount
disorder
dispatch
dispense
disperse
dispirit
displace
displant
displode
displume
disposal
disposer
dispread
disprize
disproof
disprove
disquiet
disseise
disserve
dissever
dissolve
dissuade
distally
distance
distaste
distinct
distract
distrain
distrait
distress
district
distrust
disunion
disunite
disunity
disusage
disvalue
ditheism
ditheist
ditherer
dittybag
dittybox
diuresis
diuretic
divagate
divalent
divebomb
dividend
dividivi
dividual
divinely
divinise
divinity
division
divisive
divorcee
eighteen
eighthly
eighties
fibrilla
fibrosis
fibrotic
fiddling
fidelity
fiducial
fiendish
fiercely
fiftieth
fiftyish
fighting
figurant
figurine
filagree
filament
filariae
filarial
filature
filefish
filially
filiform
filigree
Filipina
Filipino
filmgoer
filmstar
filthily
filtrate
fimbriae
finalise
finalism
finalist
finality
finedraw
fineness
finespun
fingered
finisher
finitely
finitude
finnesko
firearms
fireback
fireball
firebird
fireboat
firebomb
firebrat
fireclay
firedamp
fireeyed
firehose
firelock
fireopal
fireplug
fireship
fireside
firetrap
fireweed
firewood
firework
firmness
firstaid
fiscally
fishable
fishball
fishbone
fishbowl
fishcake
fishfarm
fishglue
fishhawk
fishhook
fishless
fishmeal
fishpond
fishtail
fishwife
fissiped
fistiana
fistical
fistulae
fistular
fitfully
fivefold
fivestar
fixation
fixative
giantess
giantism
giftbook
gigantic
gillaroo
gilthead
gimcrack
gimmicky
gingerly
gingival
gipsydom
gipsyism
girasole
girlhood
giveaway
hibernal
hibiscus
hiccough
hickwall
hideaway
hidrosis
hidrotic
hidyhole
hielaman
hierarch
hieratic
highball
highborn
highbred
highbrow
higherup
highjack
highland
highlows
highmost
highness
highrise
highroad
hightail
hightest
hijacker
hilarity
hillfort
hillocky
hillside
himation
hinderer
hindlegs
hindmost
hinduise
Hinduism
hipflask
hipsters
hireable
hireling
hirrient
Hispanic
histogen
historic
hitherto
jiggered
jingoish
jingoism
jingoist
jipijapa
jiujitsu
kibitzer
kickback
kickshaw
kidglove
killdeer
kilogram
kilowatt
kindless
kindling
kindness
kinesics
kinetics
kingbird
kingbolt
kingcrab
kingfish
kinghood
kinglike
kingship
kingsize
kinkajou
kinsfolk
kissable
kisscurl
libation
libatory
libeccio
libelled
libellee
libeller
liberate
libretti
libretto
licensed
licensee
licenser
lichened
lichenin
lichgate
licorice
liegeman
lifebelt
lifeboat
lifebuoy
lifeless
lifelike
lifeline
lifelong
lifesize
lifetime
lifework
liftable
ligament
ligation
ligature
lighting
lightish
ligneous
lignitic
ligulate
likeable
likeness
likewise
limbless
limekiln
limerick
limetwig
limewash
limitary
limonite
limpidly
limpness
linchpin
lineally
linearly
linesman
lingerer
lingerie
linguist
liniment
Linnaean
linoleum
linstock
lintseed
lipogram
lipomata
lipsalve
lipstick
liquidly
liripoop
listener
listless
literacy
literary
literate
literati
litharge
litigant
litigate
littlego
littling
littoral
liturgic
liveable
liveborn
livelily
livelong
liveried
liverish
livewire
lividity
lixivium
miasmata
miasmous
micellar
microbar
microbic
microdot
micrurgy
midbrain
middling
midfield
midlands
midnight
midpoint
midships
midwives
mightest
mightily
migraine
migrator
mildness
milepost
Milesian
militant
military
militate
milkmaid
milkweed
milkwort
millhand
milliard
milliary
millibar
millieme
milliner
millpond
millrace
Miltonic
mimester
mimicked
mimicker
minacity
minatory
mindless
minimise
minister
ministry
Minoress
Minorite
minority
Minotaur
minstrel
mintmark
minutely
minutiae
mirepoix
mirthful
misalign
misapply
misbegot
miscarry
miscegen
mischief
miscible
miscount
misdealt
misdoing
misdoubt
miserere
misgiven
misguide
misheard
mishmash
Mishnaic
misjudge
mismatch
misnomer
misogamy
misogyny
misology
misplace
misprint
misprise
misprize
misquote
misshape
missilry
misspell
misspelt
misspend
misspent
misstate
mistaken
misthink
mistreat
mistress
mistrial
mistrust
misusage
miswrite
Mithraic
mitigant
mitigate
mittened
mittimus
mitzvoth
niceness
nickelic
nicknack
nickname
nicotian
nicotine
nielloed
niggling
nightcap
nighthag
nightjar
nightowl
nihilism
nihilist
nihility
nimbused
ninefold
ninepins
nineteen
nineties
nitrogen
oilcloth
oilfield
oilfired
oiliness
oilstone
ointment
oiticica
piacular
pianiste
piassava
picaroon
picayune
pickerel
picketer
pickings
picklock
picnicky
pictures
piddling
piecrust
piedmont
piercing
piffling
pigswill
pilaster
pilchard
pileated
pilewort
pilferer
piliform
pillager
pillwort
pilosity
pilotage
pilsener
pimiento
pinafore
pinaster
pincenez
pinchers
Pindaric
pinecone
pinewood
pinkness
pinmoney
pinnacle
pinnated
pinniped
pinnular
pinochle
pinpoint
pinprick
pintable
pintsize
pinwheel
pipeclay
pipefish
pipeline
piperack
piperine
piquancy
pirarucu
piscator
piscinae
pishogue
pisiform
pisolite
pitiable
pitiably
pitiless
pittance
pitviper
pivotman
pixieish
pixiness
pizzeria
ribaldry
ribbonry
ribgrass
ribosome
ricebird
ricercar
richness
rickrack
rickshaw
ricochet
riddance
rideable
ridgeway
ridicule
Riesling
rifeness
riffraff
rifleman
rigadoon
rightful
rightist
rigidify
rigidity
rigorism
rigorist
rigorous
rimbrake
rimester
ringbark
ringbolt
ringbone
ringdove
ringmain
ringneck
ringroad
ringside
ringtail
ringwall
ringworm
rinsings
riparian
ripeness
ritually
rivalled
rivelled
riverain
riverbed
riverine
riverman
riverway

Siberian	sirenian	victress	wildeyed	skilling	alogical	bluenose	electret
sibilant	siriasis	victuals	wildfire	skimmilk	alopecia	blueweed	electric
sibilate	sirvente	Viennese	wildfowl	skimming	alphabet	blurrily	electron
Sicilian	sisterly	Vietcong	wildlife	skimpily	alpinism	blurring	electrum
sickener	sitarist	Vietminh	wildness	skindeep	alpinist	blushful	elegance
sickerly	sithence	viewable	wildwood	skinfood	Alsatian	blustery	elegancy
sickflag	sitology	viewless	wilfully	skinhead	although	cladding	elenchus
sicklist	situated	vigilant	wiliness	skinless	altitude	claimant	elenctic
sickness	sitzbath	vigneron	williwaw	skinning	altruism	clambake	elephant
sickroom	sixpence	vignette	windburn	skipjack	altruist	clammily	elevated
sidearms	sixpenny	vigorous	windcone	skipping	alumroot	clamming	elevator
sideband	sixtieth	vileness	windfall	skirmish	alveolar	clanging	eleventh
sidedish	sizeable	vilifier	windgall	skirting	alveolus	clangour	elfarrow
sidedoor	sizzling	vilipend	windlass	skislope	blabbing	clannish	elflocks
sidedrum	ticklish	villadom	windless	skittish	blackboy	clanship	eligible
sidehead	tickseed	villager	windmill	skittles	blackcap	clansman	eligibly
sidekick	ticktack	villainy	windowed	skullcap	blackfly	clapping	elkhound
sideline	ticktock	villatic	windpipe	skylight	blacking	claptrap	ellipses
sideling	tidegate	vincible	windrose	skypilot	blackish	claqueur	ellipsis
sidelong	tideland	vinculum	windsail	skyscape	blackleg	clarence	elliptic
sidenote	tideless	vinegary	windsock	skywards	blackout	clarinet	elongate
sidereal	tidelock	vineyard	windward	alacrity	blacktie	classics	eloquent
siderite	tidemark	vinosity	winepalm	alarmist	blacktop	classify	flabella
sideroad	tidemill	vinously	wineshop	albacore	bladdery	clavicle	flagella
sideshow	tidewave	vintager	wineskin	Albanian	blahblah	clawback	flagging
sideslip	tidiness	violable	wingbeat	albinism	blamable	claymore	flagpole
sidesman	tiebreak	violably	wingcase	alburnum	blamably	cleancut	flagrant
sidestep	tigereye	violator	wingless	alcahest	blameful	cleaning	flagship
sideview	tigerish	violence	wingspan	alchemic	blandish	cleanser	flambeau
sidewalk	tightwad	viperine	winnable	aldehyde	blankety	clearcut	flamenco
sideward	tilefish	viperish	winnings	alderman	blastema	clearing	flamingo
sideways	tillable	viperous	winnower	Alderney	blastoff	clearway	flanerie
sidewind	tiltyard	virement	winterly	aleatory	blastoid	cleavage	flapjack
sidewise	timbered	virginal	wintrily	alebench	blastula	cleavers	flapping
siftings	timeball	Virginia	wiredraw	alehouse	blatancy	clematis	flashgun
sigmatic	timebomb	viricide	wirehair	aleurone	blazoner	clemency	flashily
signally	timefuse	viridian	wireless	alewives	blazonry	clerical	flashing
signpost	timeless	viridity	wirework	alfresco	bleacher	clerihew	flatboat
silencer	timework	virilism	wireworm	algicide	bleakish	clerkdom	flatfeet
silently	timeworn	virility	wirewove	algidity	blearily	clerkess	flatfish
silicane	timidity	virology	wiriness	alginate	bleeding	cleverly	flatfoot
silicate	timorous	virtuosa	wiseacre	algology	Blenheim	climatic	flathead
silicide	timously	virtuosi	wiseness	Algonkin	blesbuck	clincher	flatiron
silicify	tincture	virtuoso	wishbone	algorism	blessing	clinical	flatling
silicone	tingeing	virtuous	wishwash	alguazil	blighter	clinking	flatmate
silkworm	tininess	virulent	wistaria	alienage	blimpish	clipclop	flatness
sillabub	tinkerer	viscacha	wisteria	alienate	blindage	clippers	flatrace
silphium	tinnitus	visceral	witchelm	alienism	blinding	clipping	flattery
Silurian	tinplate	viscidly	witchery	alienist	blinkers	cliquish	flattest
siluroid	tinselly	viscount	witchety	alizarin	blinking	cliquism	flattish
silvatic	tinsmith	Visigoth	witching	alkahest	blissful	cloddish	flatware
silverly	tinstone	visional	withdraw	alkalies	blistery	clodpole	flatways
similise	tintless	visitant	withdrew	alkalify	blithely	clodpoll	flatwise
simoniac	tipstaff	visually	withheld	alkaline	blizzard	clogging	flatworm
simonist	tireless	vitalise	withhold	alkaloid	blockade	cloister	flautist
simplify	tiresome	vitalism	wizardly	allegory	blockage	clopclop	flawless
simplism	titanate	vitalist	wizardry	alleluia	blockish	closeset	flaxseed
simulant	titaness	vitality	yielding	allergen	blondish	closeted	fleabane
simulate	titanism	vitellin	zibeline	allergic	bloodily	clothier	fleabite
Sinaitic	titanite	vitellus	ziggurat	alleyway	bloodred	clothing	fleawort
sinapism	titanium	vitiable	zinckify	alliance	bloomers	clotting	flection
sinciput	tithable	vitiator	zincking	allnight	bloomery	cloudily	fleeting
sinecure	titivate	vitiligo	zirconia	allocate	blooming	cloudlet	fleshfly
sinfonia	titmouse	vitreous	djellaba	allodial	blossomy	clownery	fleshpot
sinfully	tittuped	vituline	ejection	allodium	blotting	clownish	fletcher
singable	tittuppy	vivacity	ejective	allogamy	blowball	clubbing	flexible
singeing	uintaite	vivarium	Akkadian	allopath	blowfish	clubfoot	flexibly
singsong	viameter	vivifier	ekistics	allotted	blowhard	clubhaul	flexuose
singular	viaticum	vivisect	okeydoke	allottee	blowhole	clubland	flexuous
sinicise	vibrancy	vixenish	skeletal	allround	blowlamp	clueless	flexural
sinister	vibrator	vizarded	skeleton	allspice	blowpipe	clumsily	flickery
sinkable	vibrissa	vizcacha	skerrick	allusion	blubbery	clupeoid	flimflam
sinkhole	viburnum	wickedly	sketcher	allusive	bludgeon	clustery	flimsily
sinology	vicarage	wideeyed	skewback	alluvial	bluebell	clypeate	flincher
sinophil	vicarate	wideness	skewbald	alluvion	bluebird	elatedly	flinders
sinusoid	vicarial	wifehood	skewness	alluvium	bluechip	eldorado	flintily
siphonal	vicinage	wifeless	skiagram	almagest	bluecoat	eldritch	flipflap
siphonet	vicinity	wifelike	skidding	almanack	bluefish	election	flipflop
siphonic	victoria	wigmaker	skilless	almighty	blueness	elective	flippant

flipping	glutting	plectrum	slowdown	emersion	omnivore	annotate	enfetter
flipside	gluttony	pleinair	slowness	emetical	omophagy	announce	enfilade
flitting	glycerin	pleonasm	slowpoke	emigrant	omoplate	annually	enforcer
floatage	glycerol	plethora	slowworm	emigrate	omphalic	annulate	enforest
floating	glyceryl	pleurisy	slubbing	eminence	omphalos	annulled	engaging
floccose	glycogen	pliantly	slugabed	eminency	smallage	anorexia	engender
floccule	glyconic	plighted	sluggard	emissary	smallfry	anorexic	engineer
flocculi	glyptics	plimsoll	slugging	emission	smallish	anorthic	enginery
flockbed	illation	Pliocene	sluggish	emissive	smallpox	anourous	engirdle
flogging	illative	plodding	slumbery	emitting	smaltite	anserine	engramma
floodlit	illfated	plopping	slumming	Emmental	smarmily	answerer	engraver
floodway	illiquid	plotting	slurring	empathic	smartish	anteater	enkindle
flooring	illtimed	plougher	sluttish	empeople	smashing	antecede	enlarger
floppily	illtreat	pluckily	slyboots	emphases	smelling	antedate	enneagon
flopping	illumine	plugging	ulcerate	emphasis	smeltery	antefixa	enormity
florally	illusage	plumaged	ulcerous	emphatic	smithers	antelope	enormous
floridly	illusion	plumbago	ulterior	employee	smithery	antennae	enquirer
florigen	illusive	plumbate	ultimacy	employer	smocking	antennal	enricher
flotilla	illusory	plumbing	ultimata	empoison	smokable	antennas	enrolled
flounder	Illyrian	plumbism	ultimate	emporium	smoothen	antepost	ensample
flourish	ilmenite	plumelet	ultraism	empurple	smoothie	anterior	ensconce
flowered	klephtic	plumiped	ultraist	empyreal	smoothly	anteroom	ensemble
flowerer	klondike	plumpish	amadavat	empyrean	smothery	anthelia	ensheath
floweret	klystron	plumular	amaranth	emulator	smoulder	anthemia	enshrine
flubbing	oldtimer	plurally	amazedly	emulgent	smudgily	antheral	enshroud
fluellin	oldworld	plussage	ambiance	emulsify	smuggler	anthesis	ensiform
fluently	oleander	plutonic	ambience	emulsion	smugness	anthozoa	ensigncy
fluepipe	oleaster	pluvious	ambition	emulsive	smuttily	antibody	ensilage
fluidics	olibanum	slabbing	ambivert	emulsoid	umbonate	antidote	enslaver
fluidify	oligarch	slagging	ambrosia	imaginal	umbrella	antihero	ensphere
fluidise	oligomer	slagheap	ambulant	imagines	umbrette	antilogy	enswathe
fluidity	oliphant	slamming	ambulate	imbecile	umpirage	antimask	entailer
flummery	olympiad	slangily	ambusher	imitable	umptieth	antimony	entangle
fluoride	Olympian	slapbang	amenable	imitator	anabases	antinode	entellus
fluorine	placable	slapdash	amenably	immanent	anabasis	antinomy	enterate
fluorite	placably	slapjack	American	immature	anabatic	antiphon	enthalpy
fluttery	placeman	slapping	amethyst	immersed	anabolic	antipode	enthrall
flyblown	placenta	slashing	amiantus	imminent	anaconda	antipole	enthrone
flypaper	placidly	slattern	amicable	immingle	anaerobe	antipope	entirely
flywheel	plagiary	Slavonic	amicably	immobile	anaglyph	antisera	entirety
glabella	plaguily	sleazily	amitosis	immodest	anagogic	antitype	entoderm
glabrous	plaiding	sledding	amitotic	immolate	analcime	antlered	entoptic
glaciate	plaister	sleepily	ammoniac	immortal	analcite	antrorse	entozoic
gladdest	planchet	sleeping	ammonify	immunise	analecta	anyplace	entozoon
gladding	plangent	slideway	ammonite	immunity	analects	anything	entracte
gladhand	planking	slightly	ammonium	impacted	analogic	anywhere	entrails
gladioli	plankton	slimmest	amnesiac	impanate	analogue	enaction	entrance
gladness	planning	slimming	amniotic	imparity	analyser	enactive	entreaty
gladsome	plantain	slimmish	amoebean	impelled	analyses	enarched	entrench
glancing	planulae	slimness	amoeboid	impeller	analysis	encaenia	entrepot
glanders	planular	slinkily	amorally	imperial	analytic	enceinte	entresol
glandule	plastery	slipcase	amoretti	imperium	anapaest	encipher	enuresis
glassful	plastics	slipform	amoretto	impetigo	anaphase	encircle	enuretic
glassily	plastron	slipknot	amortise	impishly	anaphora	enclitic	envelope
glassine	plateaux	slipover	amperage	impledge	anarchic	enclothe	enviable
glaucoma	plateful	slippage	amphibia	implicit	anasarca	encomion	enviably
glaucous	platelet	slippery	amphipod	impolder	anathema	encomium	environs
glaziery	platform	slipping	amphorae	impolicy	anatomic	encrinal	envisage
gleaning	platinic	slipring	amphoras	impolite	ancestor	encrinic	envision
gleesome	platinum	sliproad	ampullae	imponent	ancestry	encroach	enzootic
glibness	platonic	slipshod	amputate	importer	anchoret	encumber	gnathite
glissade	platting	slipslop	amusedly	imposing	andesine	encyclic	gneissic
glittery	platypus	slithery	amygdala	imposter	andesite	endamage	gnomonic
gloaming	plaudits	slitting	emaciate	impostor	androgen	endanger	inaction
globally	playable	slobbery	embalmer	impotent	anecdote	endemism	inactive
globular	playback	slobbish	embattle	imprimis	anechoic	endermic	inasmuch
globulin	playbill	slobland	embedded	imprison	aneurism	endocarp	inceptor
gloomily	playbook	sloeeyed	embezzle	improper	aneurysm	endoderm	inchmeal
gloriole	playgirl	slogging	embitter	improver	angelica	endogamy	inchoate
glorious	playgoer	sloppail	emblazon	impudent	Anglican	endogeny	inchworm
glossary	playmate	sloppily	embolden	impugner	angstrom	endorsee	incident
glossily	playroom	slopping	embolism	impunity	anhedral	endorser	incision
glossina	playsuit	slopshop	embosser	impurely	aniconic	endostea	incisive
glowworm	playtime	slopwork	embracer	impurity	animally	endozoic	incitant
gloxinia	pleading	slothful	embussed	omadhaum	animator	endozoon	incivism
glucagon	pleasant	slotting	emceeing	omelette	anisette	endpaper	included
glucinum	pleasing	sloucher	emendate	omission	ankerite	energise	incoming
glummest	pleasure	slovenly	emergent	omitting	ankylose	enervate	increase
glumness	plebeian	slovenry	emeritus	ommateum	annalist	enfeeble	increate

incubate	insignia	knitting	unburied	univocal	boarding	boutique	colossal
incurred	insolate	knitwear	unbutton	unjustly	boastful	bouzouki	colossus
indagate	insolent	knocking	uncalled	unkennel	boatbill	bowfront	coloured
indebted	insomnia	knockout	uncandid	unkindly	boatdeck	bowsprit	colubrid
indecent	insomuch	knothole	uncapped	unkingly	boathook	boxpleat	columnal
Indiaman	insphere	knotting	uncaused	unlawful	boatload	boyishly	columnar
indicant	inspired	knotwork	unchancy	unleaded	bobbinet	coachdog	columned
indicate	inspirer	knowable	unchaste	unlearnt	bobbypin	coachman	comatose
indicium	inspirit	mnemonic	unchurch	unlikely	bobbysox	coaction	combings
indigene	instable	onceover	uncially	unlimber	bobolink	coactive	comeback
indigent	instance	oncidium	unciform	unlinked	bobwheel	coagulum	comedian
indirect	instancy	oncology	uncinate	unlisted	bobwhite	coaldust	comedist
indocile	instinct	oncoming	unclench	unloader	bodement	coalesce	comedown
indolent	instruct	onehorse	unclinch	unloosen	bodiless	coalfish	cometary
inductee	insulant	onepiece	unclothe	unlovely	Bodleian	coalhole	commando
inductor	insulate	onesided	uncoined	unmanned	bodyshop	coalmine	commence
indulger	insulter	onetrack	uncommon	unmarked	bodywork	coalsack	commerce
induline	insurant	onlooker	uncouple	unmeetly	Boeotian	coarsely	commoner
indurate	intaglio	ontogeny	uncreate	unmuffle	bogeyman	coatrack	commoney
indusium	intarsia	ontology	unctuous	unmuzzle	bohemian	coatroom	commonly
industry	integral	onychite	underact	unopened	boldface	coauthor	communal
inedible	intended	snackbar	underage	unpaired	boldness	cobaltic	commuter
inedited	intently	snagging	underarm	unpegged	bollworm	cobblers	compages
inequity	interact	snakepit	underbid	unperson	bolthole	cobwebby	compiler
inerrant	interbed	snapbrim	undercut	unpinned	boltrope	coccyges	complain
inertial	intercom	snaplink	underdid	unplaced	bombsite	cochleae	compleat
inexpert	intercut	snappily	underdog	unreason	bondmaid	cochlear	complete
infamise	interest	snapping	underfur	unriddle	bondmans	cockatoo	complice
infamous	interior	snappish	underlap	unrigged	bondsman	cockboat	complier
infantry	intermit	snapshot	underlay	unroofed	bonefish	cockcrow	compline
infector	intermix	snatcher	underlet	unsaddle	bonehead	cockerel	composed
inferior	internal	snazzily	underlie	unsealed	boneless	cockeyed	composer
infernal	internee	sneakily	underlip	unseated	bonemeal	cockloft	compound
inferred	Interpol	sneakish	underman	unseeded	boneyard	cockshut	compress
infilter	interred	sneeshan	underpin	unseeing	bonhomie	cocksure	comprise
infinite	interrex	sniffily	underrun	unseemly	boniface	cocktail	computer
infinity	intersex	sniffler	undersea	unsettle	boniness	codifier	conation
infirmly	intertie	sniffles	underset	unshaped	bonspiel	codpiece	conative
inflamer	interval	sniggler	undertow	unsocial	bontebok	codriver	concasse
inflated	interwar	snippety	underway	unsought	bookcase	coelomic	conceder
inflator	inthrall	snipping	undraped	unsprung	bookends	coenobia	conceive
inflatus	intimacy	snipsnap	undreamt	unstable	bookland	coenzyme	concerti
inflexed	intimate	snitcher	undulant	unstably	booklice	coercion	concerto
inflight	intimism	snobbery	undulate	unstated	booklore	coercive	concetti
influent	intitule	snobbish	unearned	unsteady	bookmark	cofactor	concetto
informal	intonate	snobbism	uneasily	unstring	bookpost	cogently	conchate
informed	intrados	snogging	unedited	unstrung	bookrest	cogitate	conchoid
informer	intrench	snootily	unending	unstuffy	bookwork	cognomen	conclave
infrared	intrepid	snowball	unerring	unsuited	bookworm	cognosce	conclude
infringe	intrigue	snowbird	unevenly	unsunned	bootjack	cognovit	concrete
infusion	intromit	snowboot	unfading	unswathe	bootlace	cogwheel	condense
ingather	introrse	snowdrop	unfairly	untangle	bootlast	coherent	condylar
ingrowth	intruder	snowfall	unfasten	untapped	bootless	cohesion	conferee
inguinal	intubate	snowless	unfetter	untaught	boottree	cohesive	conferva
inhalant	inundate	snowlike	unfilial	untented	boracite	coiffeur	confetti
inherent	inurbane	snowline	unfitted	untether	Bordeaux	coiffure	confider
inhesion	invasion	snowshoe	unforced	unthread	bordello	coincide	confiner
inhumane	invasive	snubbing	unformed	unthrift	borderer	coistrel	confines
inimical	invected	snuffbox	unfreeze	unthrone	borecole	cokernut	conflate
iniquity	inveigle	snuffler	unfrozen	untidily	borehole	colander	conflict
initiate	inventor	snuffles	unfunded	untimely	boringly	coldness	confound
injector	inverted	ungainly	unglazed	untitled	borrower	coleseed	confrere
inkiness	inverter	snuggery	unglazed	untoward	bosseyed	coleslaw	confront
inkstand	investor	snugness	ungotten	unvalued	botanise	colewort	congener
inlander	inviable	unabated	ungulate	unversed	botanist	coliform	conglobe
innately	inviting	unaneled	unhinged	unvoiced	botflies	coliseum	congress
innocent	invocate	unawares	unhoused	unwanted	botryoid	collagen	congreve
innovate	involute	unbacked	uniaxial	unwarily	bottomry	collapse	conidial
innuendo	inwardly	unbarred	unicycle	unwashed	botulism	collared	conidium
inoculum	knackery	unbeaten	unifilar	unweaned	botyrose	collator	coniform
inositol	knapping	unbelief	unionise	unwieldy	bouffant	colleger	conjoint
inquirer	knapsack	unbiased	unionism	unwisdom	boughten	colliery	conjugal
insanely	knapweed	unbidden	unionist	unwisely	bouillon	collogue	conjunct
insanity	kneedeep	unbolted	unipolar	unwished	bouncily	colloquy	conjurer
inscient	kneehigh	unbottle	uniquely	unwonted	bouncing	collyria	conjuror
inscribe	kneehole	unbridle	unisonal	unwordly	boundary	colonial	conniver
inscroll	kneejerk	unbroken	unitedly	unworthy	bourgeon	colonise	conoidal
insecure	knickers	unbuckle	univalve	unzipped	boursier	colonist	conquest
inserted	knightly	unburden	universe	aoristic	bourtree	colophon	conserve

consider	cortical	dolomite	follicle	forester	goldmine	hooligan	localise
consoler	cortices	doloroso	follower	forestry	goldrush	hoosegow	localism
consomme	corundum	dolorous	followon	foretell	golfclub	hopeless	locality
conspire	corvette	domestic	followup	foretime	golliwog	Horatian	locative
constant	Corybant	domicile	fomenter	foretold	gonfalon	hormonal	lockable
construe	coryphee	dominant	fondling	forewarn	gonidial	hornbeam	lockfast
consular	cosecant	dominate	fondness	forewent	gonidium	hornbill	lockknit
consumer	cosiness	domineer	fontanel	foreword	goodness	hornbook	lockstep
contagia	cosmetic	dominion	fontange	foreyard	goodtime	hornfels	locofoco
contango	cosmical	dominoes	foodless	forgiven	goodwife	hornless	locomote
contempt	costmary	donation	foolscap	forgoing	goodwill	hornpipe	loculate
contents	costplus	Donatism	football	forklift	goodyear	hornrims	locution
contessa	costpush	Donatist	footbath	formalin	goofball	horntail	locutory
continua	costumer	donative	footfall	formally	goosegog	hornworm	lodestar
continue	cotenant	donatory	footgear	formerly	gorgeous	hornwort	lodgings
continuo	cothurni	donought	foothill	formless	gorgonia	horologe	lodgment
contline	cotillon	doomsday	foothold	formroom	gormless	horology	lodicule
contorno	cotquean	doomsman	footless	formulae	gossamer	horrible	logician
contract	Cotswold	doomster	footling	formulas	gossiper	horribly	logistic
contrail	cottager	doorbell	footmark	formwork	gossipry	horridly	logogram
contrary	cottagey	doorcase	footmuff	fornices	gossypol	horrific	logotype
contrast	couchant	doorknob	footnote	forrader	gourmand	horsebox	loiterer
contrate	couching	doornail	footpace	forsaken	goutweed	horsecar	Lollardy
contrite	couldest	doorpost	footpath	forsooth	goutwort	horsefly	lollipop
contrive	coulisse	doorsill	footpost	forspeak	governor	horseman	lollypop
conurbia	coumarin	doorstep	footrace	forspent	gownsman	hosepipe	lomentum
convener	countess	doorstop	footrest	forswear	hoarding	hospital	Londoner
convenor	coupling	dooryard	footrope	forswore	hoarsely	hostelry	loneness
converge	courante	dopiness	footrule	forsworn	hobbitry	hotchpot	lonesome
converse	coursing	dormancy	footslog	fortieth	hobbyist	hotelier	longboat
convexly	courtesy	dormouse	footsore	fortress	hocktide	hothouse	longeron
conveyer	courtier	dorsally	footstep	fortuity	hocusing	hotplate	longeval
conveyor	couscous	dotation	footwear	fortyish	hocussed	hotpress	longhair
convince	cousinly	dotingly	footwork	forwards	Hogmanay	hourlong	longhand
convolve	covalent	dotterel	foramina	forzando	hogsback	houseboy	longhorn
convulse	covenant	douanier	forborne	fosterer	hogshead	housedog	longness
cookbook	coverage	doubloon	forcedly	fougasse	holdback	housefly	longship
coolabah	coverall	doubtful	forcefed	foulness	holdfast	houseful	longsome
coolibah	covering	doughboy	forceful	founding	holdover	houseman	longstop
coolness	coverlet	doughnut	forcible	fountain	holidays	housetop	longterm
coonskin	covertly	doumpalm	forcibly	fourball	holiness	hoverfly	longtime
cooption	covetous	dourness	fordable	foureyes	holistic	howitzer	longueur
cooptive	cowardly	dovecote	fordoing	fourfold	hollands	iodinate	longwall
coplanar	cowberry	dovetail	forebear	fourleaf	hollowly	iodoform	longwave
copperas	cowgrass	dowdyish	forebode	fourpart	Holocene	iotacism	longways
copulate	coworker	dowelled	forecast	foursome	hologram	jobation	longwise
copybook	coxalgia	downbeat	foredeck	fourstar	holozoic	jocosely	lookeron
copyedit	coxswain	downcast	foredoom	fourteen	holstein	jocosity	loonybin
copyhold	cozenage	downcome	foreedge	fourthly	homebody	jocundly	loophole
coquetry	Docetism	downfall	forefeel	foveolae	homeborn	jodhpurs	loosebox
coquette	Docetist	downhaul	forefelt	fowlpest	homebred	joinable	loosener
coracoid	docilely	downhill	forefoot	foxglove	homebrew	jointure	lopeared
cordless	docility	downland	foregoer	foxhound	homefelt	jokingly	lopgrass
cordovan	dockland	downmost	foregone	foxiness	homeland	jolthead	lopsided
corduroy	dockside	downpipe	forehand	foxshark	homeless	Jonathan	lordless
cordwain	dockyard	downpour	forehead	goadster	homelike	jongleur	lordling
cordwood	doctoral	downtime	foreknew	goalkick	homemade	jovially	lordosis
corelate	doctrine	downtown	foreknow	goalline	homesick	joyfully	lordotic
corkwing	document	downturn	forelady	goalpost	homespun	joyously	lordship
corkwood	doddered	downward	foreland	goatfish	hometown	joystick	loricate
cornball	dodderer	downwind	forelock	goatherd	homeward	Kohinoor	lorikeet
corneous	dogberry	doxology	foremast	goatling	homework	kohlrabi	lothario
cornetcy	dogeared	doziness	foremost	goatmoth	homicide	kolinsky	loudness
cornetti	dogfaced	eohippus	forename	goatskin	hominoid	komitaji	louvered
cornetto	dogfight	eolithic	forenoon	Gobelins	homodont	Komsomol	lovebird
corniced	dogged	foamless	forensic	godawful	homogamy	korfball	loveknot
corniche	doggedly	focalise	forepart	godchild	homogeny	kourbash	loveless
cornicle	doghouse	focusing	forepast	Godspeed	homology	loadline	lovelily
cornific	dogmatic	focussed	forepeak	godwards	homonymy	loadstar	lovelock
cornpone	dogooder	foetidly	foreplay	gogetter	homuncle	loanable	lovelorn
coronach	dogsbody	fogbound	foresaid	Goidelic	honestly	loanword	lovenest
coronary	dogshore	foldaway	foresail	goingson	honeybee	loathful	loveseat
coronoid	dogtired	foldboat	foreseen	goitrous	honeydew	loathing	lovesick
corporal	dogtooth	folderol	foreshow	Golconda	honeypot	lobation	lovesome
corridor	dogwatch	foliaged	foreside	golddust	honorary	lobbyist	lovesong
corrival	dogwhelk	folklore	foreskin	goldenly	honourer	lobeline	lovingly
corselet	doldrums	folkmoot	forestal	goldfish	hoodwink	loblolly	lowering
corseted	dolerite	folksong	forestay	goldfoil	hoofbeat	lobotomy	lowgrade
corsetry	dolesome	folktale	forested	goldleaf	hookworm	lobulate	lowlevel

lowlying	monteith	nocturne	polemise	postmark	rosebush	solemnly	tokology
loyalist	monument	nodalise	polemist	postmill	rosefish	soleness	tolbooth
mobilise	moonbeam	nodality	polestar	postobit	roseleaf	solenoid	tolerant
mobility	mooncalf	nodation	polisher	postpaid	rosemary	solfaist	tolerate
mobocrat	moonface	nodosity	politely	postpone	roseolar	solfeggi	tollcall
moccasin	moonfish	nodulose	politick	postural	rosepink	solidary	tolldish
modalism	moonless	nodulous	politico	posturer	roseroot	solidify	tollgate
modalist	moonrise	noisette	politics	potassic	rosetree	solidity	tomahawk
modality	moonsail	nomadise	pollices	potation	rosewood	solitary	tomalley
modelled	moonshee	nomadism	pollinia	potbelly	rosiness	solitude	tombless
modeller	moonshot	nominate	pollinic	potbound	rostrate	solleret	tomentum
moderate	moonwort	nomistic	polliwog	potently	rosulate	solstice	tommybar
moderato	moorcock	nomogram	pollster	potholer	Rotarian	solution	tommygun
modernly	moorfowl	nomology	polluter	pothouse	rotation	solvable	tommyrot
modestly	moorings	nonclaim	pollywog	potlatch	rotative	solvency	tomnoddy
modifier	moorland	nondairy	polonium	potplant	rotatory	somatism	tomogram
modishly	mopishly	nonesuch	poltfoot	potroast	rotenone	sombrely	tomorrow
modulate	moquette	nonevent	poltroon	potsherd	rottenly	sombrero	tonality
Moharram	morainic	nonhuman	polygala	potstill	rotundly	sombrous	tonedeaf
moisture	moralise	nonjuror	polygamy	potstone	roturier	somebody	toneless
molality	moralism	nonlegal	polygene	potterer	roughage	somedeal	tonepoem
molarity	moralist	nonmetal	polygeny	poultice	roughdry	somedele	tonguing
molasses	morality	nonmoral	polyglot	poundage	roughhew	sometime	tonicity
molecule	moratory	nonparty	polygyny	pounding	roughish	someways	toolroom
molehill	Moravian	nonrigid	polymath	pourable	rouleaus	somewhat	toolshed
moleskin	morbidly	nonsense	polypary	powdered	rouleaux	somewhen	toothful
molester	morbific	nonstick	polypide	powerful	roulette	somnific	toothily
Molinism	mordancy	nonunion	polypite	roadbook	roundarm	sonatina	toothing
Molinist	moreover	nonusage	polypody	roadless	rounders	songbird	topdress
molossus	moresque	nonwhite	polypoid	roadside	roundish	songbook	topheavy
molybdic	moribund	noontide	polypous	roadsign	roundtop	songless	toplevel
momently	mornings	noontime	polyseme	roadster	rowdyish	songster	topliner
momentum	morosely	normalcy	polysemy	roasting	rowdyism	sonobuoy	toplofty
monachal	morosity	normally	polysomy	roborant	royalism	sonority	topnotch
monadism	morpheme	Norseman	polyzoan	robustly	royalist	sonorous	topology
monandry	morphine	northern	polyzoic	rocaille	soakaway	soothing	toponymy
monarchy	mortally	northing	polyzoon	rockbird	soapbark	soothsay	topstone
monastic	mortgage	Northman	pomander	rockcake	soapdish	sorcerer	torchere
monaural	mortmain	noseband	pomology	rockcork	soapless	sordidly	toreador
monaxial	mortuary	nosecone	ponderer	rockdove	soaproot	sorehead	toreutic
monazite	moshavim	nosedive	pondweed	rocketry	soapsuds	soreness	tornadic
mondaine	mosquito	nosepipe	pontifex	rockfall	soapwort	sorochen	toroidal
monetary	mossback	nosering	ponytail	rockfish	soberise	sororate	torpidly
monetise	mothball	nosiness	poohpooh	rockhewn	sobriety	sorority	torquate
moneybag	motherly	nosology	poorness	rocklike	sobstory	sorption	torridly
moneybox	motility	notarial	popinjay	rockling	sobstuff	sorptive	tortilla
Mongolic	motional	notation	popishly	rockrose	socalled	sorrower	tortious
mongoose	motivate	notching	poppadum	rocksalt	sociable	sortable	tortoise
monicker	motivity	notebook	populace	rockweed	sociably	soterial	tortuous
monistic	motorail	notecase	populate	rockwood	socially	souchong	torturer
monition	motorcar	noteless	populism	rockwork	societal	soulless	totalise
monitive	motorial	notional	populist	roentgen	Socinian	soundbow	totality
monitory	motoring	notornis	populous	rogation	Socratic	soundbox	totalled
monkfish	motorise	noumenal	poristic	rogatory	sodalite	sounding	totemism
MonKhmer	motorist	noumenon	porkling	rollcall	sodality	sourdine	totemist
monkhood	motorium	nouvelle	porosity	rollneck	sodomite	sourness	totterer
monkseal	motorman	novelise	porphyry	rolypoly	softball	sourpuss	touchily
monkship	motormen	novercal	porpoise	romancer	softboil	soutache	touching
monoacid	motorway	novelist	porridge	Romanian	softener	southern	toughish
monocrat	mottling	nowadays	porthole	romanise	softhead	southing	touristy
monocyte	moufflon	oogamous	porticos	Romanism	softness	southpaw	tournure
monodist	moulding	oogonial	portiere	Romanist	softshoe	Southron	tovarish
monogamy	mountain	oogonium	portrait	Romansch	softsoap	souvenir	towardly
monogeny	mounting	oologist	portress	romantic	software	sovranty	towelled
monoglot	mournful	ooziness	position	rondeaux	softwood	sowbread	townhall
monogony	mourning	pochette	positive	roodbeam	soilless	toadfish	township
monogram	mouseear	pockmark	positron	roodloft	soilpipe	toadflax	townsman
monogyny	moussaka	podagral	posology	roofless	solander	toadyish	toxaemia
monolith	mouthful	podagric	possible	roofrack	solanine	toadyism	toxaemic
monomial	moveable	podiatry	possibly	rooftree	solarise	toboggan	toxicant
monopode	moveless	poetical	postcard	roommate	solarism	tocology	toxicity
monopoly	movement	poignant	postcode	ropeable	solarist	toepiece	vocalise
monorail	movingly	pointing	postdate	ropewalk	solarium	toeplate	vocalism
monotint	mowburnt	poisoner	postfree	ropeyarn	solatium	toiletry	vocalist
monotone	Noachian	polarise	posthorn	ropiness	solderer	toilette	vocality
monotony	nobelium	polarity	postiche	rosarian	soldiery	toilsome	vocation
monotype	nobility	polemics	postlude	rosebowl	solecism	toilworn	voicebox
monoxide	nobleman				solecist	tokenism	voiceful
monsieur	noblesse						

voidable	worthily	epigeous	specious	sprinkle	squirter	brainish	crackers
voidance	wouldest	epigraph	spectral	sprinter	araceous	brainpan	cracking
voidness	woundily	epilepsy	spectrum	sprocket	arachnid	brakeman	crackjaw
volatile	yodelled	epilogue	specular	sprucely	Aramaean	brakevan	cracknel
volcanic	yodeller	epinasty	speculum	spryness	Arapahoe	brancard	crackpot
volcanos	yoghourt	epiphany	speedily	spunkily	arapaima	branched	cradling
volitant	yokemate	epiphyte	speedway	spurgear	arbalest	brancher	craftily
volition	youngest	episcope	spelling	spurious	arbalist	branchia	cragsman
volitive	youngish	episemon	spermary	spurling	arbitral	brandied	cramfull
volplane	yourself	episodal	sphagnum	spurrier	arboreal	brandish	cramming
voltaism	youthful	episodic	sphenoid	spurring	arboreta	brandnew	cramoisy
volution	zodiacal	epistler	spherics	spyglass	arborist	brassage	cranefly
volvulus	zoetrope	epistyle	spheroid	upheaval	Arcadian	brassard	craniate
vomerine	zoiatria	epitasis	spherule	upholder	archaean	brassart	crankily
vomitive	zombiism	epopoeia	sphingid	uplander	archaise	brassica	crankpin
vomitory	zonation	epyllion	sphygmus	uplifter	archaism	brassily	crannied
voracity	zoogenic	opaquely	spicated	uppercut	archaist	brattice	crashing
vortexes	zoolater	openable	spiccato	uppishly	archduke	brattish	crashpad
vortical	zoolatry	opencast	spicebox	uprising	archival	brazenly	cratches
vortices	zoomancy	openeyed	spicknel	uprooter	archives	brazenry	cravenly
votaress	zoometry	openness	spiculae	upsetter	archness	braziery	crawfish
votarist	zoomorph	openplan	spicular	upsprang	Arcturus	breakage	crayfish
voteless	zoonosis	openwork	spiculum	upspring	arcuated	breaking	creakily
voussoir	zoophily	operable	spiffing	upsprung	ardently	breakout	creamery
vowelise	zoophyte	operatic	spikelet	upstairs	areolate	breasted	creatine
vowelled	zoospore	operator	spillage	upstream	arethusa	breather	creation
voyageur	apagogic	opercula	spillway	upstroke	argentic	breeches	creative
woefully	aperient	operetta	spinifex	upthrown	argonaut	breeding	creatrix
wolffish	aperitif	ophidian	spinning	upthrust	arguable	breezily	creature
wolfpack	aperture	oppilate	spinster	upwardly	arguably	bregmata	credence
wolfskin	aphasiac	opponent	spiracle	aquacade	argufier	brethren	credenza
womanise	aphelion	opposite	spirally	aqualung	argument	brettese	credible
womanish	aphicide	oppugner	spirilla	aquanaut	Arianism	brettice	credibly
wondrous	aphorise	opsimath	spirited	aquarist	arillate	breveted	credited
wontedly	aphorism	optative	spiritus	aquarium	aristate	breviary	creditor
woodbind	aphorist	optician	spiteful	aquatint	Armagnac	brewster	creeping
woodbine	apiarian	optimise	spitfire	aqueduct	armament	Briarean	crenated
woodchat	apiarist	optimism	spitting	aquiline	armature	bribable	crenelle
woodcock	apically	optimist	spittoon	equalise	armchair	brickbat	creosote
woodenly	aplastic	optional	spivvery	equality	Armenian	brickred	crepitus
woodland	apocrine	opulence	splasher	equalled	Arminian	briefing	crescent
woodlark	apodoses	opuscula	splatter	equation	armorial	brighten	crescive
woodlice	apodosis	opuscule	splendid	equinity	armoured	brightly	cretonne
woodnote	apogamic	spacebar	splenial	equipage	armourer	brimfull	crevasse
woodpile	apograph	spaceman	splenius	equipped	armyworm	brimless	cribbage
woodpulp	apologia	spacious	splinter	equitant	aromatic	brimming	cribbing
woodruff	apologue	spadeful	splitter	equities	arpeggio	brindled	criminal
woodshed	apomixis	spadices	splotchy	equivoke	arquebus	briskish	crispate
woodsman	apoplexy	spadille	splutter	squabble	arranger	brisling	cristate
woodwind	apostasy	spadones	spoffish	squadron	arrantly	britches	criteria
woodwool	apostate	spaewife	spoilage	squaller	arrestee	britzska	critical
woodwork	apothegm	spagyric	spoliate	squamate	arrester	broacher	critique
woodworm	appalled	spalpeen	spondaic	squamose	arrestor	broadish	croakily
wooldyed	appanage	spandrel	spongily	squamous	arrogant	broadway	Croatian
woolfell	apparent	spandril	sponsion	squamule	arrogate	brocaded	croceate
woollens	appendix	Spaniard	spontoon	squander	arsenate	brocatel	crockery
woolpack	appetent	spanking	spookily	squarely	arsenide	broccoli	crocoite
woolsack	appetite	spanning	spookish	squarish	arsenite	brochure	crofting
woolshed	applause	spanroof	spoonfed	squarson	arsonist	broidery	cromlech
woolskin	applepie	sparable	spoonful	squasher	arsonous	brokenly	cromorna
woolwork	applique	sparbuoy	spoonily	squatted	artefact	bromelia	cromorne
wordbook	apposite	spardeck	sporadic	squatter	arterial	bromidic	cropping
wordless	appraise	sparkgap	sporozoa	squawker	artesian	bronchia	crossbar
wordplay	approach	sparkish	sportful	squawman	artfully	bronchus	crossbow
workable	approval	sparkler	sportily	squeaker	articled	broodily	crosscut
workaday	apresski	sparklet	sporting	squealer	artifact	brookite	crossing
workfolk	apterous	sparling	sportive	squeedge	artifice	brooklet	crosslet
workings	aptitude	sparring	sporular	squeegee	artistic	brougham	crossply
workless	ephemera	sparsely	spotless	squeezer	artistry	brouhaha	crosstie
workmate	Ephesian	sparsity	spottily	squelchy	bracelet	browband	crossway
workroom	ephorate	spathose	spotting	squibbed	brachial	browbeat	crotched
workshop	epiblast	spatting	spousage	squidded	brachium	browning	crotchet
wormcast	epically	spatular	spraints	squiggle	brackish	brownish	croupier
wormgear	epicalyx	spavined	sprawler	squiggly	bracteal	brunette	croupous
wormhole	epicotyl	speaking	spraygun	squilgee	bractlet	brushoff	crowbill
wormlike	epicycle	spearman	spreader	squinter	Bradshaw	brutally	crowfoot
wormseed	epidemic	speciate	sprigged	squireen	braggart	bryology	cruciate
wormwood	epidural	specific	springal	squirely	bragging	bryozoan	crucible
worthful	epifauna	specimen	springer	squirrel	braiding	crabbing	crucifer

crucifix	dryplate	frontage	griseous	praedial	profound	traducer	trillium
crueller	drypoint	frontier	grisette	prandial	progress	tragical	trilobed
crumhorn	drystone	frontlet	grisgris	prankful	prohibit	tragopan	trimaran
crummock	erasable	frostily	grissini	prankish	prolamin	trailnet	trimeric
crusader	Erastian	frosting	gritting	pratique	prolapse	training	trimeter
crustily	erectile	frothily	grizzled	prattler	prolific	tramline	trimming
cruzeiro	erection	frottage	groggily	preacher	prolixly	trammels	trimness
cryogeny	eremitic	froufrou	grogshop	preamble	prologue	trampler	trioxide
cryolite	erethism	fructify	gromwell	precinct	prolonge	tramroad	tripeman
cryostat	erewhile	fructose	groogroo	precious	promisee	tranquil	triplane
cryotron	ergogram	frugally	grosbeak	preclude	promiser	transact	triploid
drabbler	ergotise	fruitage	groschen	predator	promisor	transect	tripodal
drabness	ergotism	fruitbat	grottoes	predella	promoter	transept	trippery
dracaena	erigeron	fruitery	grounder	preelect	prompter	transfer	tripping
drachmae	erodible	fruitfly	grouping	preexist	promptly	transfix	triptych
drachmai	erogenic	fruitful	grouting	pregnant	promulge	tranship	tripwire
drachmas	erotical	fruition	growling	prehuman	pronator	transire	triskele
draconic	errantly	frumenty	grubbily	prejudge	proofing	transmit	trisomic
dragging	errantry	frumpish	grubbing	prelatic	propense	transude	tristful
dragline	eruption	frustule	grudging	prelease	properly	trapball	tristich
dragoman	eruptive	frutices	gruesome	premiere	property	trapdoor	tritical
dragomen	erythema	Graafian	grumbler	premolar	prophase	trapezia	triumvir
dragonet	frabjous	grabbing	grumpily	premorse	prophecy	trappean	triunity
dragsman	fraction	grabbler	gruntled	prenatal	prophesy	trapping	trochaic
dragster	fracture	graceful	irenical	prentice	propolis	Trappist	trochili
drainage	fraenula	gracioso	irenicon	preparer	proposal	traprock	trochlea
dramatic	fragment	gracious	Irishism	prepense	proposer	trashery	trochoid
drammock	fragrant	gradient	Irishman	preprint	propound	trashily	troilite
dramshop	framesaw	graduand	ironbark	presager	propping	traumata	trollopy
draughts	francium	graduate	ironclad	prescind	propylic	traverse	trombone
draughty	Frankish	Graecise	irongray	presence	prorogue	travesty	trophied
drawable	franklin	Graecism	irongrey	preserve	prosaism	trawlnet	tropical
drawback	frapping	graffiti	ironical	presidio	prosaist	treacher	trotting
drawtube	Fraulein	graffito	ironside	pressbox	prosodic	treadler	trottoir
drawwell	freakish	graining	ironware	pressing	prospect	treasure	troupial
dreadful	freakout	gralloch	ironwood	pressman	prostate	treasury	trousers
dreamful	freeborn	gramarye	ironwork	pressure	prostyle	treatise	troutlet
dreamily	freedman	gramatom	Iroquois	prestige	protasis	trecento	trouvere
dreaming	freefall	gramercy	irrigate	presumer	protatic	treefern	truantry
drearily	freehand	grandame	irritant	pretence	protease	treefrog	truckage
drencher	freehold	granddad	irritate	prettify	protegee	treeless	trucking
dressage	freeload	grandeur	kreutzer	prettily	protista	treenail	truckler
dressing	freeness	grandson	kromesky	previous	protocol	trekking	trueblue
dribbler	freesoil	granitic	krumhorn	priapism	protonic	trembler	trueborn
dribblet	freewill	granular	oracular	prideful	protozoa	trembles	truebred
driftage	freezeup	grapheme	orangery	priedieu	protract	trencher	truelove
driftice	freezing	graphics	Orangism	priestly	protrude	trendily	trueness
driftway	fremitus	graphite	oratorio	priggery	provable	trephine	truistic
drilling	frenetic	grasping	oratress	priggish	provably	trespass	trumeaux
drinking	frenulum	grateful	Orcadian	priggism	provided	tressure	trumpery
dripfeed	frenzied	gratuity	orchilla	primally	provider	trevally	truncate
dripping	frequent	gravamen	ordainer	Primates	province	trialist	trunnion
drivable	frescoes	gravelly	ordinand	primeval	provisor	triangle	trussing
driveway	freshman	graviton	ordinary	primming	proximal	triarchy	trustful
drollery	freshrun	grayling	ordinate	primness	prudence	Triassic	trustily
drophead	fretting	greasily	ordnance	primrose	pruinose	triaxial	truthful
dropkick	fretwork	greedily	oreology	princely	prunella	tribally	tryingly
dropleaf	Freudian	greegree	organdie	princess	prunelle	tribasic	uralitic
dropping	fribbler	greenery	organise	printing	prunello	tribrach	urbanely
dropshot	friction	greenfly	organism	printout	prurient	tribunal	urbanise
dropwort	friendly	greening	organist	priorate	pruritic	trichina	urbanism
droughty	Friesian	greenish	orgasmic	prioress	pruritus	trichite	urbanist
drownded	frighten	greenlet	orgastic	priority	Prussian	trichoid	urbanite
drowsily	frigidly	greeting	orgulous	prismoid	pryingly	trichome	urbanity
drubbing	frijoles	greffier	oriental	prisoner	trabeate	trichord	urethane
drudgery	frillies	greyfish	oriented	prissily	tracheae	trickery	urgently
drugging	fringing	greyness	origanum	pristine	tracheal	trickily	urochord
druggist	frippery	gridiron	original	probable	tracheid	trickish	urostyle
druidess	frisette	grievous	ornament	probably	trachoma	tricorne	Ursuline
druidism	friskily	grillage	ornately	proceeds	trachyte	triennia	urticant
drumfire	fritting	grimacer	ornithic	proclaim	trackage	triforia	urticate
drumhead	frocking	grimness	orogenic	procurer	tracking	trifling	wrackful
drumming	frogfish	grimoire	orpiment	prodding	trackman	trifocal	wrangler
drummock	frogging	grindery	orthicon	prodigal	trackway	trigonal	wrappage
drumroll	frogspit	grinning	orthodox	prodrome	tractate	triglyph	wrapping
drunkard	frondage	gripping	orthoepy	producer	traction	trigraph	wrathful
drupelet	frondent	gripsack	practice	proemial	tractive	trilling	wrathily
dryclean	frondeur	Griselda	practise	profaner	tradeoff	trillion	wreathen
drynurse	frondose		praecipe	profiler	traditor		wreckage

```
wrestler estoppel attitude statable stopcock stumming bunkered ductless
wrestpin estovers attorney statedly stopover stumpily buntline duelling
wretched estrange attrited statical stoppage stunning buoyancy duellist
wriggler estuaril atwitter statuary stopping stunsail Burberry duettist
wristlet esurient atypical statured storable stuntman burglary Dukhobor
wristpin isabella etcetera staylace storeman stupidly burgonet dulciana
writable isagogic eternise staysail storeyed stuprate Burgundy dulcimer
writeoff ischemia eternity steadily stormily sturdied burletta Dulcinea
writings ischemic ethereal steading stoutish sturdily burnouse dullness
wrongful Islamise etherial stealing stowaway sturgeon burntout dumbbell
wrongous Islamism etherise stealthy strabism stylised burrower dumbhead
wrymouth Islamite etherism steamily straddle utiliser bursitis dumbness
asbestic islander etherist stearate straggle aubretia bushbaby dumbshow
asbestos isobaric ethicism stearine straggly audacity bushbuck dumfound
ascender isocheim ethicist steatite straight audience bushfire dumpling
ascidian isocracy Ethiopic stedfast strained audition bushveld dundiver
ascidium isodicon ethnarch steenbok strainer auditive business dungaree
ascocarp isogamic ethnical steening straiten auditory bustling dungcart
aseptate isogloss ethology steepish straitly Augustan busybody dunghill
asperges isogonal ethylene steepled stramash augustly busyness duodenal
asperity isogonic etiolate steerage stranded aurelian butchery duodenum
asphodel isolable Etrurian steering stranger auricula buttoner duologue
asphyxia isolator Etruscan steinbok strangle auriform buttress durables
aspirant isomeric Italiote stellate strapoil aurorean butylene duration
aspirate isometry iterance stellify strapped auspices butyrate durative
assassin isomorph otiosely stellion strapper autacoid buzzword durukuli
assemble isophote otiosity stemless strategy autarchy cubature dustbowl
assembly isopleth otoscope stemmata stratify autarkic cubiform dustcart
assenter isoprene ottavino stemming stravaig autistic cuboidal dustcoat
assentor isoptera pteropod stenosed streaked autobahn cucumber dustless
assertor isospory pterylae stenosis streaker autocade cucurbit dustlike
assessor isostasy ptomaine stenotic streamer autocrat culdesac dustshot
assiento isothere ptyalism stepping streeted autodafe culicine Dutchman
assignat isotherm stabbing stepwise strength autodyne culinary dutiable
assignee isotonic stabling sterigma strepent autogamy culottes dutyfree
assignor isotopic stablish sterling Strepyan autogiro culpable dutypaid
assonant isotropy staccato sternite stretchy autogyro culpably eucalypt
assonate issuable staffage sternson stricken autolyse cultivar eucritic
assorted issuance staggard sternway strickle automata cultural eugenics
assuming isthmian staggers stetting strictly automate cultured eugenism
Assyrian oscinine staghorn stibnite stridden autonomy culverin eugenist
astatine osculant stagnant stickful strident autosome Cumbrian eulachon
asterisk osculate stagnate stickily strigose autotomy cumbrous eulogise
asterism Ossianic stairrod stickjaw striking autotype cumulate eulogist
asteroid osteitis stairway stickler stringed autumnal cumulous eulogium
asthenia ostinato stakenet stiffish stringer autunite cupboard euonymin
asthenic ostracod stallage stigmata stripped bubaline cupelled euonymus
astonied ostracon stallfed stilbene stripper buckaroo cupidity eupatrid
astonish ostrakon stalling stilbite strobila buckbean cupreous eupepsia
astragal psalmist stallion stiletto strobile buckhorn cupulate eupeptic
astutely psalmody stalwart stillage strobili buckling curarine euphonic
asyndeta psaltery staminal stimulus stroller buckshee curarise euphoria
escalade psilosis stampede stingily stromata buckshot curassow euphoric
escalate psychics stancher stingray strongly buckskin curative euphrasy
escallop psychism stanchly stinkard strophic Buddhism curculio euphuism
escalope psychist standard stinking strophic Buddhist cureless euphuist
escapade tsarevna standing stinkpot stropped buddleia curlicue Eurasian
escapism tsaritsa standish stipites strucken budgeree currency Eurocrat
escapist tsaritza standoff stippler struggle buhlwork curricle European
escargot usefully stanhope stipular strummed building cursedly europium
escarole usufruct stannary stirring strummer bulkhead curtains eustatic
eschalot usurious stannate stitcher strumose bullcalf curtness eutectic
eschewal ataraxia stannite stoccado strumous bulldoze curveted eutrophy
esculent ataraxic stannous stoccata strumpet bulletin cushiony fuchsine
Eskimoan atheling stanzaic stockade strutted bullfrog Cushitic fuelling
esoteric Athenian stapelia stockcar strutter bullhead cuspidor fugacity
espalier atheroma stardust stockily stubbing bullhorn cussedly fugitive
especial athletic starfish stocking stubborn bullocky cussword fugleman
espousal atlantes stargaze stockish stubnail bullring customer fullback
espouser Atlantic starkers stockist stuccoes bullseye cuteness fullness
espresso atomiser starless stockman studbook bullyboy cutprice fullpage
Esquimau atremble starlike stockpot studding bullyoff cutpurse fullsize
essayist atrocity starling stodgily studfarm bullyrag cutwater fulltime
Essenism atropine starrily stoicism studious bummaree duchesse fumarole
essonite attender starring stolidly studwork buncombe duckbill fumigant
esterify attested starting stomachy stuffily bundling duckhawk fumigate
estimate attester startler stomatal stuffing bunfight duckling fumitory
Estonian attestor starwort stomatic stultify bungalow duckpond function
estopped atticism stasimon stonefly stumbler bunghole duckweed funebral
```

funerary	hustings	murrhine	outpoint	pushbike	ruminate	sulphide	tuneless
funereal	jubilant	muscadel	outrange	pushcart	rummager	sulphite	tungsten
fungible	jubilate	muscatel	outreach	pushover	runabout	sulphone	tungstic
funkhole	Judaical	muscling	outreign	pushpull	runagate	sultrily	tunicate
funnyman	Judaiser	muscular	outrider	pussycat	runcible	Sumerian	Tunisian
furbelow	judgment	mushroom	outright	pustular	runnerup	summerly	tuppence
furcated	judicial	musicale	outrival	putative	ruralise	summitry	tuppenny
furculae	jugglery	musician	outshine	putridly	ruralism	summoner	Turanian
furcular	Jugoslav	musingly	outshone	quackery	ruralist	sunbaked	turbaned
furfural	jugulate	muskdeer	outsider	quackish	rurality	sunbathe	turbidly
furfuran	julienne	muskduck	outsight	quadrant	rushhour	sunblind	turbinal
furlough	jumpedup	musketry	outsmart	quadrate	rushlike	sunburnt	turbofan
furriery	jumpseat	muskrose	outspend	quadriga	rustical	sunburst	turbojet
furthest	jumpsuit	musktree	outspent	quadroon	rustless	sundance	Turcoman
furuncle	junction	muslined	outstare	quaestor	rutabaga	sunderer	turgidly
fuselage	juncture	musquash	outstrip	quagmire	ruthless	sundress	Turkoman
fusiform	junkshop	mustache	outvalue	quaintly	rutilant	sundried	turmeric
fusileer	junkyard	mutation	outvying	Quakerly	subacute	sundries	turnable
fusilier	Jurassic	mutchkin	outwards	qualmish	subagent	sundrops	turnback
futilely	juristic	muteness	outwatch	quandary	subahdar	sunlight	turncoat
futility	justness	muticous	outweigh	quandong	subbasal	sunproof	turncock
futurism	juvenile	mutilate	outworks	quantify	subclass	sunshade	turndown
futurist	kurtosis	mutineer	pubertal	quantise	suberect	sunshine	turnings
futurity	lubberly	mutinous	publican	quantity	suberise	sunshiny	turnover
guacharo	lubrical	mutterer	publicly	quarrier	suberose	sunstone	turnpike
guaiacum	lucidity	mutually	puffball	quartern	suberous	sunwards	turnskin
guaranty	luckless	nubiform	puffbird	quarters	subfloor	superadd	turnsole
guardant	luculent	nubility	puggaree	quartile	subframe	superate	turnspit
guardian	Lucullan	nubilous	pugilism	quatrain	subgenus	superbly	turreted
Guelphic	lukewarm	nucellus	pugilist	quayside	subgroup	superego	turtling
guerilla	lumberer	nuclease	pugnosed	queasily	subhuman	superior	tussocky
guernsey	luminant	nucleate	puissant	Quechuan	subimago	superman	tutelage
guidable	luminary	nucleole	pullback	queendom	subjoint	supernal	tutelary
guidance	luminist	nucleoli	pullover	queening	sublease	supertax	tutorage
guidedog	luminous	nuclidic	pulmonic	queenlet	sublunar	supinate	tutoress
guideway	lumpfish	nudeness	pulpiter	queerish	submerge	supinely	tutorial
guileful	lunarian	nugatory	pulpwood	quencher	submerse	supplant	vulcanic
guiltily	lunation	nuisance	pulsator	quenelle	suborder	supplely	vulgarly
Gujarati	luncheon	nullness	pulvilli	question	suborner	supplial	Yugoslav
gulfweed	lungfish	numberer	pulvinus	queueing	suboxide	supplier	yuletide
gullable	lungwort	numbfish	pumproom	quibbler	subphyla	supplies	zucchini
gullible	lunulate	numbness	puncheon	quickset	subpoena	supposal	zugzwang
gulosity	luscious	numeracy	punctate	quiddity	subprior	supposed	avadavat
gummosis	lushness	numerary	punctual	quidnunc	subserve	suppress	aventail
gumption	lustrate	numerate	puncture	quietism	subshrub	surcease	averment
gunfight	lustrine	numerous	punditry	quietist	subsolar	surefire	averring
gunflint	lustring	numinous	pungency	quietude	subsonic	sureness	aversely
gunlayer	lustrous	numskull	puniness	quillpen	substage	surfacer	aversion
gunmetal	lutanist	nuptials	punisher	quilting	subtitle	surfbird	aversive
gunpoint	lutecium	nursling	punition	quincunx	subtlety	surfboat	aviarist
gunsmith	lutenist	nurturer	punitive	quintain	subtonic	surfduck	aviation
gunstock	lutetium	nutarian	punitory	quipping	subtopia	surffish	aviatrix
gusseted	Lutheran	nutation	puparial	quirkily	subtotal	surgical	avidness
guttural	luxation	nutbrown	puparium	quisling	subtract	suricate	avifauna
huckster	muchness	nuthatch	pupation	quitrent	subulate	surmisal	avionics
hugeness	mucilage	nuthouse	pupilage	quitting	suburban	surmiser	avowable
huggable	muckluck	nutrient	pupilary	quixotic	suburbia	surmount	avowedly
Huguenot	muckrake	nutshell	pupillar	quixotry	subvocal	surplice	avulsion
hulahula	muckworm	outboard	puppetry	quizzing	succinct	surprise	evacuant
humanely	mucosity	outbound	puppydog	quotable	succinic	surround	evacuate
humanise	mucrones	outbrave	puppydom	quotient	succinum	surroyal	evadable
humanism	mudguard	outbreak	puppyfat	rubbishy	succubae	surveyor	evaluate
humanist	mudstone	outburst	puppyish	rubicund	succubus	survival	evanesce
humanity	Muharram	outcaste	purblind	rubidium	suchlike	survivor	evection
humanoid	mulberry	outclass	purchase	rubrical	suckling	suspense	evenfall
humidify	muleteer	outdated	purebred	rubytail	Sudanese	susurrus	evenness
humidity	mulishly	outdoors	pureness	rucksack	sudarium	suzerain	evensong
humility	mulloway	outdrawn	purfling	rudeness	sudatory	tubeless	eventful
hummocky	multeity	outfield	purifier	rudiment	suddenly	tubercle	eventide
humorist	multifid	outflank	puristic	ruefully	sufferer	tuberose	eventual
humorous	multiped	outgoing	purplish	ruggedly	suffrage	tuberous	evermore
humoured	multiple	outgrown	purpuric	rugosely	suicidal	tubiform	eversion
humpback	multiply	outguess	purpurin	rugosity	suitable	tubulate	everyday
humuncle	muniment	outHerod	pursenet	rugulose	suitably	tuckahoe	everyman
hungrily	munition	outhouse	purslane	ruinable	suitcase	tuckshop	everyone
huntress	murderer	outlawry	pursuant	ruleless	suitings	tumbling	everyway
huntsman	muriatic	outlying	purulent	Rumanian	sukiyaki	tumidity	eviction
hurtless	murmurer	outmatch	purveyor	Rumansch	sullenly	tumorous	evidence
hushhush	murrelet	outmoded	pushball	ruminant	sulphate	tuneable	evildoer

```
evilness overstay axiality Byronism hypogene synapsis analysis brancher
evincive overstep axillary bystreet hypogeum synaptic analytic branchia
evitable overtake axiology cyanogen hypogyny synastry anapaest brandied
evulsion overtask axletree cyanoses hypothec syncline anaphase brandish
ivorynut overtime exacting cyanosis hysteria syncopal anaphora brandnew
ovalness overtone exaction cyanotic hysteric syncytia anarchic brassage
ovariole overtook examinee cyclamen kyphosis syndesis anasarca brassard
ovaritis overture examiner cycleway kyphotic syndetic anathema brassart
ovenbird overturn exanthem cyclical lychgate syndical anatomic brassica
ovenware overview excavate cyclonic lykewake syndrome apagogic brassily
overalls overwear excelled cyclopes lymphoid synergic araceous brattice
overarch overwind exchange cyclosis lymphoma synergid arachnid brattish
overbear overwork excision cylinder lynchpin syngamic Aramaean brazenly
overbook overworn excitant cymatium lynxeyed synonymy Arapahoe brazenry
overbore oviposit exciting cynicism lyophile synopses arapaima braziery
overbusy uvularly excluder cynosure lyrebird synopsis ataraxia chaconne
overcall uvulitis excursus Cypriote lyricism synoptic ataraxic chainsaw
overcame aweather execrate cypselae lyricist synovial avadavat chairman
overcast dwarfish executor Cyrenaic lysosome syntagma beadroll chalazae
overcoat dwarfism exegesis Cyrillic lysozyme syntonic beadsman Chaldaic
overcome dwelling exegetic cysteine mycelial syphilis beadwork Chaldean
overcrop owlishly exemplar cystitis mycelium syringes beagling chaldron
overdone swabbing exemplum cytidine mycetoma syrinxes beamends chalkpit
overdose swagging exequies cytology mycology systemic beanpole chambers
overdraw swainish exercise cytosine myelinic systolic bearable chambray
overdrew swanherd exergual dybbukim myelitis syzygial bearably champers
overfall swanking exertion dyestuff mylonite Tychonic bearings champion
overfeed swanlike exhalant dynamics myoblast tympanic bearskin chancery
overfill swanmark exhorter dynamism myogenic tympanum beatific chandler
overfish swanneck exigence dynamist myograph typecast beautify chapatti
overflew swannery exigency dynamite myositic typeface biannual chapbook
overflow swanning exigible dynastic myositis typehigh biassing chapelry
overfold swanshot exiguity dynatron myosotis typhonic biathlon chaperon
overfond swanskin exiguous dysgenic myriapod typifier blabbing chapiter
overgrew swansong eximious dyslexia myriopod typology blackboy chaplain
overgrow swapping existent dyslexic myrmidon tyrannic blackcap chapping
overhand swastika exlibris dyspnoea mystical Tyrolean blackfly charcoal
overhang swatting exocrine dystopia mystique tyrosine blacking charisma
overhaul swayback exogamic eyeglass mythical Tyrrhene blackish charlady
overhead swearing exorcise eyeliner myxomata xylocarp blackleg charlock
overhear sweeping exorcism eyepiece nymphean xylology blackout charming
overheat sweepnet exorcist eyerhyme pyelitis xylonite blacktie charring
overhung sweeting exordial eyeshade pygidial zygaenid blacktop Chartism
overjump sweetish exordium eyesight pygidium zymology bladdery Chartist
overkill sweetpea exospore eyestalk pygmaean czaritza blahblah chasseur
overlaid sweetsop exoteric eyetooth pyogenic ozoniser blamable chastely
overlain swelling expander eyewater pyrenoid ──────── blamably chastise
overland swiftlet expedite gymkhana pyrexial abacuses blameful chastity
overleaf swigging expelled gymnasia pyridine abattoir blandish chasuble
overleap swimming expellee gynandry pyriform academia blankety chateaux
overload swimsuit expertly gynocrat pyroxene academic blastema chattily
overlong swindler expiable gynoecia pyrrhoea acanthus blastoff chatting
overlook swinging expiator gypseous pyrrhous acarpous blastoid chaunter
overlord switchel expirant gypsydom pythonic Adamical blastula chauntry
overmuch swobbing explicit gypsyism pyxidium adamitic blatancy cladding
overnice swooping exploder gyration ryegrass adaption blazoner claimant
overpaid swotting explorer gyratory ryotwari adaptive blazonry clambake
overpass twaddler exponent gyrostat sybarite agaragar boarding clammily
overpast tweezers exporter hyacinth sycamine alacrity boastful clamming
overplay twelvish exposure hydatoid sycamore alarmist boatbill clanging
overplus twenties exserted hydranth sycomore amadavat boatdeck clangour
overrate twiddler extender hydrogen syconium amaranth boathook clannish
override twilight extensor hydromel syenitic amazedly boatload clanship
overripe twinborn exterior hydropic syllabic anabases bracelet clansman
overrode twinkler external hydropsy syllable anabasis brachial clapping
overrule twinling extolled hydroski syllabub anabatic brachium claptrap
oversail twinning extrados hydroxyl syllabus anabolic brackish claqueur
overseas twinship extremes hygienic sylphide anaconda bracteal clarence
overseen twitcher extrorse hymenial sylphine anaerobe bractlet clarinet
overseer twittery exultant hymenium sylphish anaglyph Bradshaw classics
oversell twitting exuviate hymnbook sylvatic anagogic braggart classify
oversewn twoedged oxidiser hyoscine symbiont analcime bragging clavicle
overshoe twofaced oximeter hypnoses symbolic analcite braiding clawback
overshot twopence oxpecker hypnosis symmetry analecta brainish claymore
overside twopenny oxtongue hypnotic sympathy analects brainpan coachdog
oversize twopiece oxymoron hypobole symphile analogic brakeman coachman
overslip twosided oxytocin hypoderm symphony analogue brakevan coaction
oversold twotimer uxorious hypogeal sympodia analyser brancard coactive
oversoul zwieback Ayrshire hypogean symposia analyses branched coagulum
```

```
coaldust diarrhea flatfoot gramatom loanable playable scabrous shagroon
coalesce diaspora flathead gramercy loanword playback scaffold shakable
coalfish diaspore flatiron grandame loathful playbill scalable shakeout
coalhole diastase flatling granddad loathing playbook scalawag Shaktism
coalmine diastema flatmate grandeur meagrely playgirl scalepan shaleoil
coalsack diastole flatness grandson mealtime playgoer scallion shalloon
coarsely diatomic flatrace granitic mealworm playmate scammony shallows
coatrack diatonic flattery granular mealybug playroom scampish shambles
coatroom diatribe flattest grapheme meanness playsuit scandent shameful
coauthor drabbler flattish graphics meantime playtime Scandian shamming
crabbing drabness flatware graphite measured practice scandium shamrock
crackers dracaena flatways grasping meatball practise scanning shanghai
cracking drachmae flatwise grateful meatsafe praecipe scansion shantung
crackjaw drachmai flatworm gratuity miasmata praedial scanties shapable
cracknel drachmas flautist gravamen miasmous prandial scantily shareout
crackpot draconic flawless gravelly neaptide prankful scaphoid sharpish
cradling dragging flaxseed graviton Nearctic prankish scapulae sharpset
craftily dragline foamless grayling nearness pratique scapular shashlik
cragsman dragoman frabjous guacharo neatherd prattler scapulas slabbing
cramfull dragomen fraction guaiacum neatness psalmist scarcely slagging
cramming dragonet fracture guaranty Noachian psalmody scarcity slagheap
cramoisy dragsman fraenula guardant omadhaum psaltery scarfpin slamming
cranefly dragster fragment guardian opaquely quackery scarious slangily
craniate drainage fragrant headache oracular quackish scarless slapbang
crankily dramatic framesaw headachy orangery quadrant scarring slapdash
crankpin drammock francium headband Orangism quadrate scathing slapjack
crannied dramshop Frankish headfast oratorio quadriga scattily slapping
crashing draughts franklin headgear oratress quadroon scatting slashing
crashpad draughty frapping headlamp ovalness quaestor scavenge slattern
cratches drawable Fraulein headland ovariole quagmire seaboard Slavonic
cravenly drawback gearcase headless ovaritis quaintly seaborne smallage
crawfish drawtube Ghanaian headline peaceful Quakerly seachest smallfry
crayfish drawwell ghastful headlock peacocky qualmish seacoast smallish
cyanogen dwarfish giantess headlong peagreen quandary seacraft smallpox
cyanoses dwarfism giantism headmost peardrop quandong seadrome smaltite
cyanosis edacious glabella headnote pearlies quantify seafarer smarmily
cyanotic elatedly glabrous headrace pearling quantise seafloor smartish
czaritza emaciate glaciate headrest pearlite quantity seafront smashing
deadbeat enaction gladdest headroom pearmain quarrier seagoing snackbar
deadener enactive gladding headsail peasecod quartern seagreen snagging
deadfall enarched gladhand headsman phalange quarters seaholly snakepit
deadhead erasable gladioli headwind phantasm quartile seahorse snapbrim
deadline Erastian gladness headword phantasy quatrain sealable snaplink
deadlock evacuant gladsome headwork pharisee quayside sealevel snappily
deadness evacuate glancing heartily pharmacy reabsorb sealskin snapping
deadwood evadable glanders heatedly phaseout reactant sealyham snappish
deaerate evaluate glandule heathery piacular reaction seamanly snapshot
deafmute evanesce glassful heathhen pianiste reactive seamless snatcher
deafness exacting glassily heavenly piassava readable seamount snazzily
dealfish exaction glassine hoarding placable readably seamouse soakaway
deanship examinee glaucoma hoarsely placably readjust seamster soapbark
dearness examiner glaucous hyacinth placeman reaffirm seaonion soapdish
deathbed exanthem glaziery imaginal placenta reagency seapiece soapless
deathcap fearless gnathite imagines placidly realness seaplane soaproot
deathray fearsome goadster inaction plagiary realtime seapurse soapsuds
diabasic feasible goalkick inactive plaguily reappear seaquake soapwort
diabetes feasibly goalline inasmuch plaiding rearlamp searcher spacebar
diabetic feastday goalpost isabella plaister rearmice seascape spaceman
diabolic feathery goatfish isagogic planchet rearmost seashell spacious
diaconal featured goatherd Italiote plangent rearview seashore spadeful
diagnose features goatling jealousy planking rearward seasnail spadices
diagonal flabella goatmoth knackery plankton reascend seasnake spadille
diagraph flagella goatskin knapping planning reasoner seasonal spadones
diallage flagging Graafian knapsack plantain reassert seasoner spaewife
dialling flagpole grabbing knapweed planulae reassess seatbelt spagyric
dialogic flagrant grabbler leadenly planular reassign seatrout spalpeen
dialogue flagship graceful leadless plastery reassure seawards spandrel
dialyser flambeau gracioso leadsman plastics reawaken seawater spandril
dialyses flamenco gracious leadwork plastron Rhaetian seawrack Spaniard
dialysis flamingo gradient leafless plateaux rhapsode shabbily spanking
dialytic flanerie graduand leaflike plateful rhapsody shabrack spanning
diamante flapjack graduate leanness platelet roadbook Shabuoth spanroof
diameter flapping Graecise leapfrog platform roadless shadbush sparable
dianthus flashgun Graecism learning platinic roadside shaddock sparbuoy
diapason flashily graffiti leathern platinum roadsign shadower spardeck
diapause flashing graffito leathery platonic roadster shafting sparkgap
diaphone flatboat graining leavings platting roasting shagbark sparkish
diarchal flatfeet gralloch loadline platypus scabbard shaggily sparkler
diarchic flatfish gramarye loadstar plaudits scabious shagreen sparklet
```

```
sparling teabread tsarevna cabochon libretto suboxide ancestry cockboat
sparring teabreak tsaritsa caboodle lobation subphyla anchoret cockcrow
sparsely teacaddy tsaritza cabotage lobbyist subpoena Arcadian cockerel
sparsity teachest twaddler cabriole lobeline subprior archaean cockeyed
spathose teaching unabated cabstand loblolly subserve archaise cockloft
spatting teacloth unaneled ciborium lobotomy subshrub archaism cockshut
spatular teahouse unawares cobaltic lobulate subsolar archaist cocksure
spavined teammate uralitic cobblers lubberly subsonic archduke cocktail
stabbing teamster viameter cobwebby lubrical substage archival cucumber
stabling teamwork viaticum cubature mobilise subtitle archives cucurbit
stablish teaparty weakfish cubiform mobility subtlety archness cyclamen
staccato tearaway weakling cuboidal mobocrat subtonic Arcturus cycleway
staffage teardrop weakness dabchick nebulise subtopia arcuated cyclical
staggard tearduct weanling debagged nebulium subtotal ascender cyclonic
staggers tearless weaponry debarred nebulous subtract ascidian cyclopes
staghorn teaspoon wearable debility nobelium subulate ascidium cyclosis
stagnant teatable weariful debonair nobility suburban ascocarp dactylar
stagnate teatowel weaselly debugged nobleman suburbia baccarat dactylic
stairrod thalamic whacking debutant noblesse subvocal bacchant decadent
stairway thalamus whapping dybbukim nubiform sybarite bachelor decagram
stakenet thallium wharfage embalmer nubility taberdar bacillar decanter
stallage thalloid whatever embattle nubilous tableaux bacillus deceased
stallfed thallous whatness embedded pubertal tablecut backache decedent
stalling Thanatos wrackful embezzle publican tableful backbite deceiver
stallion thanedom wrangler embitter publicly tablemat backbone December
stalwart thankful wrappage emblazon rabbinic tabletop backchat decemvir
staminal thankyou wrapping embolden rabbiter tabouret backcomb decennia
stampede thatcher wrathful embolism rabbitry tabulate backdate decently
stancher toadfish yeanling embosser rabidity toboggan backdoor decigram
stanchly toadflax yearbook embossed rebelled tubeless backdrop decimate
standard toadyish yearling embussed rebeller tubercle backfire decipher
standing toadyism yearlong fabliaux rebellow tuberose backhand decision
standish trabeate yearning fabulist rebuttal tuberous backlash decisive
standoff tracheae yeastily fabulous rebutted tubiform backless deckhand
stanhope tracheal zealotry febrific rebutter tubulate backlist declarer
stannary tracheid February          ribaldry umbonate backmost declasse
stannate trachoma Abbaside fibrilla ribbonry umbrella backpack declutch
stannite trachyte abbatial fibrosis ribgrass umbrette backrest decolour
stannous trackage albacore fibrotic ribosome unbacked backroom decorate
stanzaic tracking Albanian gabbroic roborant unbarred backseat decorous
stapelia trackman albinism gabbroid robustly unbeaten backside decouple
stardust trackway alburnum gableend rubbishy unbelief backspin decrease
starfish tractate ambiance Gobelins rubicund unbiased backstay decrepit
stargaze traction ambience habanera rubidium unbidden backveld decretal
starkers tractive ambition habitant rubrical unbolted backward decurion
starless tradeoff ambivert habitual rubytail unbottle backwash dicacity
starlike traditor ambrosia habitude sabbatic unbridle backyard dichasia
starling traducer ambulant hebdomad sabotage unbroken Baconian dichroic
starring tragical ambulate hebetate saboteur unbuckle bacteria dicrotic
starting tragopan ambusher hebetude sebesten unburden Bactrian dictator
startler trailnet arbalest Hebraism sibilant unburied becalmed dicyclic
starwort training arbalist Hebraist sibilate urbanely bechamel Docetism
stasimon tramline arbitral hibernal soberise urbanise bechance Docetist
statable trammels arboreal hibiscus sobriety urbanism biconvex docilely
statedly trampler arboreta hobbitry sobstory urbanist bicuspid docility
statical tramroad arborist hobbyist sobstuff urbanite buckaroo dockland
statuary tranquil asbestic imbecile subacute urbanity buckbean dockside
statured transact asbestos jabberer subagent vibrancy buckhorn doctoral
staylace transect aubretia jobation subahdar vibrator buckling doctrine
staysail transept babirusa jubilant subbasal vibrissa buckshee document
swabbing transfer babouche jubilate subclass viburnum buckshot duchesse
swagging transfix babyhood kibitzer suberect zabaione buckskin duckbill
swainish tranship bebopper labdanum suberise zibeline cachalot duckhawk
swanherd transire bibation labelled suberose Accadian cachepot duckling
swanking transmit biblical labellum suberous accentor cachexia duckpond
swanlike transude bibulous labially subfloor accepter cachucha duckweed
swanmark trapball bobbinet lability subframe acceptor cacology ductless
swanneck trapdoor bobbypin labourer subgenus accident cacomixl ecclesia
swannery trappean bobbysox labrador subgroup accolade cactuses emceeing
swanning trapezia bobolink laburnum subhuman accoutre cicatrix encaenia
swanshot Trappist bobwheel libation subimago accredit cicerone enceinte
swanskin traprock bobwhite libatory subjoint accuracy ciceroni encipher
swansong trashery bubaline libeccio sublease accurate cicisbei encircle
swapping trashily cabalism libelled sublunar accursed cicisbeo enclitic
swastika traumata cabalist libellee submerge accustom coccyges enclothe
swatting traverse caballed libeller submerse alcahest cochleae encomion
swayback travesty cabinboy liberate suborder alchemic cochlear encomium
teaboard trawlnet cableway libretti suborner ancestor cockatoo encrinal
```

```
encrinic kickback nicotian rickrack Tychonic bodement indebted nudeness
encroach kickshaw nicotine rickshaw ulcerate bodiless indecent obduracy
encumber lacerate nocturne ricochet ulcerous Bodleian Indiaman obdurate
encyclic lacewing nucellus rocaille uncalled bodyshop indicant oddments
escalade lacework nuclease rockbird uncandid bodywork indicate oldtimer
escalate lackaday nucleate rockcake uncapped Buddhism indicium oldworld
escallop laconian nucleole rockcork uncaused Buddhist indigene ordainer
escalope laconism nucleoli rockdove unchancy buddleia indigent ordinand
escapade lacrimal nuclidic rocketry unchaste budgeree indirect ordinary
escapism lacrosse occasion rockfall unchurch cadastre indocile ordinate
escapist lacrymal occident rockfish uncially cadenced indolent ordnance
escargot lacunary occluded rockhewn unciform caducean inductee padishah
escarole lacunate occlusal rocklike uncinate caduceus inductor paduasoy
eschalot lacunose occultly rockling unclench caducity indulger pedagogy
eschewal lecithin occupant rockrose unclinch caducous induline pedalier
esculent lecturer occupier rocksalt unclothe cidevant indurate pedalled
etcetera licensed occurred rockweed uncoined codifier indusium pedantic
eucalypt licensee oecology rockwood uncommon codpiece industry pedantry
eucritic licenser onceover rockwork uncouple codriver iodinate pederast
excavate lichened oncidium rucksack uncreate dedicate iodoform pedestal
excelled lichenin oncology saccadic unctuous didactic jodhpurs pedicled
exchange lichgate oncoming saccular vacantly didapper Judaical pedicure
excision licorice Orcadian sacculus vacation didymium Judaiser pedigree
excitant localise orchilla sackcoat vaccinal didymous judgment pediment
exciting localism oscinine sackless vaccinia doddered judicial pedipalp
excluder locality osculant sackrace vacuolar dodderer kedgeree pedology
excursus locative osculate sacraria vicarage eldorado kidglove peduncle
faceache lockable pachalic sacredly vicarate eldritch ladybird piddling
facecard lockfast pacifier sacristy vicarial endamage ladyfern podagral
faceless lockknit pacifism secluded vicinage endanger ladyhood podagric
facelift lockstep pacifist seconder vicinity endemism ladylike podiatry
facepack locofoco peccable secondly victoria endermic ladylove radially
facetiae locomote peccancy secretin victress endocarp ladyship radiance
facially loculate pectines secretly victuals endoderm lodestar radiancy
facilely locution pectoral secretor vocalise endogamy lodgings radiator
facility locutory peculate sectoral vocalism endogeny lodgment radicant
factious lucidity peculiar securely vocalist endorsee lodicule radicate
factotum luckless picaroon security vocality endorser madapple redactor
feckless luculent picayune Sicilian vocation endostea madhouse redblind
feculent Lucullan pickerel sickener vocative endozoic madrigal redbrick
focalise lychgate picketer sickerly wickedly endozoon madwoman redeemer
focusing macaroni pickings sickflag yachting endpaper medalled redefine
focussed macaroon picklock sicklist zecchini fadeaway medallic redeless
fuchsine macerate picnicky sickness zecchino fadeless medially redeploy
hacienda machismo pictures sickroom zucchini fadeyeen mediator redesign
hecatomb mackerel pochette socalled Abderite federate medicate redfaced
hiccough mackinaw pockmark sociable abdicate fiddling medicine redirect
hickwall maculate racecard sociably abducens fidelity medieval redistil
hocktide mechanic racegoer socially abducent fiducial mediocre redolent
hocusing meconium racemate societal abductor gadabout meditate redouble
hocussed micellar racemise Socinian addendum gadarene medusoid redshank
huckster microbar racemose Socratic addition gadgetry midbrain redshift
inceptor microbic rachides succinct additive Gadhelic middling redshirt
inchmeal microdot rachitic succinic adducent gadzooks midfield redstart
inchoate micrurgy rachitis succinum adductor godawful midlands redwater
inchworm moccasin racially succubae aldehyde godchild midnight riddance
incident muchness raciness succubus alderman Godspeed midpoint rideable
incision mucilage rackrent suchlike Alderney godwards midships ridgeway
incisive muckluck recapped suckling andesine hadronic midwives ridicule
incitant muckrake receiver sycamine andesite hedgehog modalism rudeness
incivism muckworm recently sycamore androgen hedgehop modalist rudiment
included mucosity receptor syconium ardently hedgepig modality saddlery
incoming mucrones recharge syconium audacity hedgerow modelled Sadducee
increase mycelial recision tachisme audience hedonics modeller sadistic
increate mycelium reckless tachiste audition hedonism modeller sedately
incubate mycetoma reckoner taciturn auditive hedonist moderato sedation
incurred mycology recommit tackling auditory hideaway modernly sedative
ischemia nacreous reconvey tackroom badinage hidrosis modestly sederunt
ischemic neckband recorder tactical badlands hidrotic modifier sediment
jackaroo necklace recourse tactless bedabble hidyhole modishly sedition
jackboot neckline recovery technics bedazzle hydatoid modulate sedulity
jackeroo necropsy recreant tectonic bedeguar hydranth mudguard sedulous
jackstay necrosis recreate ticklish bedimmed hydrogen mudstone sidearms
Jacobean necrotic rectoral tickseed bedmaker hydromel nodalise sideband
Jacobite nectared recurred ticktack bedplate hydropic nodality sidedish
jacquard niceness recusant ticktock bedstead hydropsy nodation sidedoor
jocosely nickelic ricebird tocology bedstraw hydroski nodosity sidedrum
jocosity nicknack ricercar tuckahoe bedtable hydroxyl nodulose sidehead
jocundly nickname richness tuckshop biddable indagate nodulous sidekick
```

sideline	adespota	cherubim	electric	freakout	keelless	overhead	precious
sideling	agedness	chessman	electron	freeborn	keenness	overhear	preclude
sidelong	agential	chestnut	electrum	freedman	keepsake	overheat	predator
sidenote	aleatory	Cheyenne	elegance	freefall	keeshond	overhung	predella
sidereal	alebench	cleancut	elegancy	freehand	khedival	overjump	preelect
siderite	alehouse	cleaning	elenchus	freehold	klephtic	overkill	preexist
sideroad	aleurone	cleanser	elenctic	freeload	kneedeep	overlaid	pregnant
sideshow	alewives	clearcut	elephant	freeness	kneehigh	overlain	prehuman
sideslip	amenable	clearing	elevated	freesoil	kneehole	overland	prejudge
sidesman	amenably	clearway	elevator	freewill	kneejerk	overleaf	prelatic
sidestep	American	cleavage	eleventh	freezeup	kreutzer	overleap	prelease
sideview	amethyst	cleavers	emendate	freezing	leeboard	overload	premiere
sidewalk	anecdote	clematis	emergent	fremitus	liegeman	overlong	premolar
sideward	anechoic	clemency	emeritus	frenetic	Maecenas	overlook	premorse
sideways	aneurism	clerical	emersion	frenulum	maenadic	overlord	prenatal
sidewind	aneurysm	clerihew	emetical	frenzied	maestoso	overmuch	prentice
sidewise	aperient	clerkdom	energise	frequent	meekness	overnice	preparer
sodalite	aperitif	clerkess	enervate	frescoes	meetness	overpaid	prepense
sodality	aperture	cleverly	erectile	freshman	mnemonic	overpart	preprint
sodomite	areolate	coelomic	erection	freshrun	myelinic	overpass	presager
Sudanese	arethusa	coenobia	eremitic	fretting	myelitis	overplay	prescind
sudarium	aseptate	coenzyme	erethism	fretwork	needfire	overplus	presence
sudatory	aventail	coercion	erewhile	Freudian	needless	overrate	preserve
suddenly	averment	coercive	eternise	fuelling	needment	override	presidio
tidegate	averring	creakily	eternity	ghettoes	nielloed	overripe	pressbox
tideland	aversely	creamery	evection	gleaning	obedient	overrode	pressing
tideless	aversion	creatine	evenfall	gleesome	obeisant	overrule	pressman
tidelock	aversive	creation	evenness	gneissic	ocellate	oversail	pressure
tidemark	aweather	creative	evensong	greasily	okeydoke	overseas	prestige
tidemill	bdellium	creatrix	eventful	greedily	oleander	overseen	presumer
tidewave	beebread	creature	eventide	greegree	oleaster	overseer	pretence
tidiness	beechnut	credence	eventual	greenery	omelette	oversell	prettify
underact	beeeater	credenza	evermore	greenfly	onehorse	oversewn	prettily
underage	beefcake	credible	eversion	greening	onepiece	overshoe	previous
underarm	beefwood	credibly	everyday	greenish	onesided	overshot	pteropod
underbid	beeswing	credited	everyman	greenlet	onetrack	overside	pterylae
undercut	beetling	creditor	everyone	greeting	openable	oversize	pyelitis
underdid	beetroot	creeping	everyway	greffier	opencast	overslip	queasily
underdog	biennial	crenated	execrate	greyfish	openeyed	oversold	Quechuan
underfur	biennium	crenelle	executor	greyness	openness	oversoul	queendom
underlap	bleacher	creosote	exegesis	Guelphic	openplan	overstay	queening
underlay	bleakish	crepitus	exegetic	guerilla	openwork	overstep	queenlet
underlet	blearily	crescent	exemplar	guernsey	operable	overtake	queerish
underlie	bleeding	crescive	exemplum	haematic	operatic	overtask	quencher
underlip	Blenheim	cretonne	exequies	haematin	operator	overtime	quenelle
underman	blesbuck	crevasse	exercise	heedless	opercula	overtone	question
underpin	blessing	daemonic	exergual	heelball	operetta	overtook	queueing
underrun	Boeotian	deedless	exertion	heelless	oreology	overture	reedbird
undersea	breakage	deemster	eyeglass	hielaman	ovenbird	overturn	reedling
underset	breaking	deeplaid	eyeliner	hierarch	ovenware	overview	reedmace
undertow	breakout	deepness	eyepiece	hieratic	overalls	overwear	reedpipe
underway	breasted	deerskin	eyerhyme	iceblink	overarch	overwind	reedstop
undraped	breather	dieldrin	eyeshade	icebound	overbear	overwork	reedwren
undreamt	breeches	diereses	eyesight	icecream	overbore	overworn	reefknot
undulant	breeding	dieresis	eyestalk	icefield	overborn	peekaboo	reembark
undulate	breezily	diestock	eyetooth	iceplant	overbusy	peelings	reemerge
Vedantic	bregmata	dietetic	eyewater	iceskate	overcall	peephole	reemploy
Wedgwood	brethren	djellaba	feeblish	icewater	overcame	peepshow	reexport
wideeyed	brettese	dreadful	feedback	iceyacht	overcast	peerless	rheology
wideness	brettice	dreamful	feedhead	idealess	overcoat	pheasant	rheostat
yodelled	breveted	dreamily	feedpipe	idealise	overcome	phenolic	rhetoric
yodeller	breviary	dreaming	feedtank	idealism	overcrop	phenylic	Riesling
zodiacal	brewster	drearily	fiendish	idealist	overdone	piecrust	roentgen
abelmosk	caesious	drencher	fiercely	ideality	overdose	piedmont	ruefully
aberrant	caesural	dressage	fleabane	ideation	overdraw	piercing	ryegrass
abetment	cheapish	dressing	fleabite	identify	overdrew	pleading	scenario
abetting	checkers	duelling	fleawort	identity	overfall	pleasant	scenical
abeyance	checkout	duellist	fleeting	ideogram	overfeed	pleasing	sceptred
abeyancy	cheekily	duetting	fleshfly	ideology	overfill	pleasure	seedcake
aceldama	cheerful	dwelling	fleshpot	inedible	overfish	plebeian	seedcase
acentric	cheerily	dyestuff	fletcher	inedited	overflew	plectrum	seedcoat
acerbate	cheering	edentate	flexible	inequity	overflow	pleinair	seedcorn
acerbity	Chellean	egestion	flexibly	inerrant	overfold	pleonasm	seedfish
acervate	chemical	egestive	flexuose	inertial	overfork	plethora	seedleaf
acescent	chemurgy	ejection	flexuous	inexpert	overgrew	pleurisy	seedless
adenitis	chenille	ejective	flexural	irenical	overgrow	poetical	seedling
adenoids	chequers	election	fleysome	irenicon	overhand	preacher	seedlobe
adequacy	Cherokee	elective	foetidly	iterance	overhang	preamble	seedplot
adequate	cherubic	electret	freakish	keelhaul	overhaul	precinct	seedsman

seedtime	sterigma	weevilly	infernal	taffrail	dogtooth	legguard	regolith
sheading	sterling	wheatear	inferred	unfading	dogwatch	legioned	regrater
shealing	sternite	wheedler	infilter	unfairly	dogwhelk	ligament	regrowth
shedding	sternson	wheelman	infinite	unfasten	eagleowl	ligation	regulate
shedevil	sternway	wheezily	infinity	unfetter	edgeless	ligature	rigadoon
sheepdip	stetting	whenever	infirmly	unfilial	edgeways	lighting	rightful
sheepdog	swearing	wherever	inflamer	unfitted	edgewise	lightish	rightist
sheepish	sweeping	whetting	inflated	unforced	edginess	ligneous	rigidify
sheepked	sweepnet	wheyface	inflator	unformed	eggplant	lignitic	rigidity
sheeppen	sweeting	woefully	inflatus	unfreeze	eggshell	ligulate	rigorism
sheeprun	sweetish	wreathen	inflexed	unfrozen	eighteen	logician	rigorist
sheeting	sweetpea	wreckage	inflight	unfunded	eighthly	logistic	rigorous
sheikdom	sweetsop	wrestler	influent	wifehood	eighties	logogram	rogation
Shekinah	swelling	wrestpin	informal	wifeless	engaging	logotype	rogatory
shelduck	syenitic	wretched	informed	wifelike	engender	magazine	ruggedly
shelfful	taenioid	yielding	informer	aegirine	engineer	magdalen	rugosely
shelving	teenager	zoetrope	infrared	aegrotat	enginery	magician	rugosity
Shemitic	teething	affected	infringe	aggrieve	engirdle	magicked	rugulose
shepherd	teetotal	affecter	infusion	aigrette	engramma	magister	sagacity
Sheraton	teetotum	affiance	Kaffiyeh	aiguille	engraver	magmatic	sagamore
sherlock	thearchy	affinity	kefuffle	algicide	ergogram	magnesia	sageness
Shetland	theistic	affinity	lefthand	algidity	ergotise	magnetic	saginate
skeletal	thematic	affirmer	leftover	alginate	ergotism	magneton	sagittal
skeleton	theocrat	afflatus	leftward	algology	eugenics	magnific	segreant
skerrick	theodicy	affluent	lifebelt	Algonkin	eugenism	magnolia	sigmatic
sketcher	theogony	afforest	lifeboat	algorism	eugenist	megalith	signally
skewback	theology	affright	lifebuoy	alguazil	fagoting	megapode	signpost
skewbald	theorise	affusion	lifeless	angelica	fighting	megawatt	tagalong
skewness	theorist	alfresco	lifelike	Anglican	figurant	mightest	tegmenta
sleazily	therefor	befallen	lifeline	angstrom	figurine	mightily	tegument
sledding	thereout	befitted	lifelong	argentic	fogbound	migraine	tigereye
sleepily	thermion	befogged	lifesize	argonaut	fugacity	migrator	tigerish
sleeping	thermite	befriend	lifetime	arguable	fugitive	negation	tightwad
smelling	thesauri	befuddle	lifework	arguably	fugleman	negative	together
smeltery	thespian	bifacial	liftable	argufier	gigantic	negatory	ungainly
sneakily	thetical	bifocals	oafishly	argument	gogetter	negatron	unglazed
sneakish	theurgic	caffeine	offbreak	Augustan	Haggadah	negligee	ungotten
sneeshan	tiebreak	cofactor	offdrive	augustly	Hegelian	Negrillo	ungulate
speaking	toepiece	daffodil	offender	bagpiper	hegemony	negroism	urgently
spearman	toeplate	daftness	offering	baguette	highball	niggling	vagabond
speciate	treacher	defector	official	begetter	highborn	nightcap	vagility
specific	treadler	defender	offprint	beggarly	highbred	nighthag	vagrancy
specimen	treasure	deferent	offshoot	beginner	highbrow	nightjar	vegetate
specious	treasury	deferral	offshore	begirded	higherup	nightowl	vegetive
spectral	treatise	deferred	offsider	begotten	highjack	nugatory	vigilant
spectrum	trecento	deferrer	offstage	begrudge	highland	oogamous	vigneron
specular	treefern	defiance	piffling	beguiler	highlows	oogonial	vignette
speculum	treefrog	defilade	puffball	bigamist	highmost	oogonium	vigorous
speedily	treeless	definite	puffbird	bigamous	highness	organdie	waggoner
speedway	treenail	deflower	raftsman	bignonia	highrise	organise	wagonage
spelling	trekking	deforest	referent	bogeyman	highroad	organism	wagonlit
spermary	trembler	deformed	referral	cagebird	hightail	organist	wigmaker
steadily	trembles	defrayal	referred	cageling	hightest	orgasmic	yoghourt
steading	trencher	deftness	refinery	caginess	Hogmanay	orgastic	Yugoslav
stealing	trendily	diffract	refitted	cogently	hogsback	orgulous	ziggurat
stealthy	trephine	diffuser	reflexed	cogitate	hogshead	paganise	zugzwang
steamily	trespass	effector	refluent	cognomen	huggable	paganish	zygaenid
stearate	tressure	efferent	reforest	cognosce	Huguenot	paganism	abhorred
stearine	trevally	efficacy	reformed	cognovit	hygienic	paginate	abhorrer
steatite	tweezers	effluent	reformer	cogwheel	ingather	pagurian	achenial
stedfast	twelvemo	effluvia	rifeness	degrease	ingrowth	Pegasean	achiever
steenbok	twenties	effusion	riffraff	digamist	inguinal	pegboard	achiness
steening	unearned	effusive	rifleman	digamous	inguinal	pigswill	achingly
steepish	uneasily	elfarrow	safeness	digester	jaggedly	puggaree	adherent
steepled	unedited	elflocks	saffrony	diggings	jiggered	pugilism	adhesion
steerage	unending	enfeeble	safranin	digitate	jugglery	pugilist	adhesive
steering	unerring	enfetter	siftings	digitise	Jugoslav	pugnosed	anhedral
steinbok	unevenly	enfilade	softball	dogberry	jugulate	pygidial	aphasiac
stellate	urethane	enforcer	softboil	dogeared	legalese	pygidium	aphelion
stellify	usefully	enforest	softener	dogfaced	legalise	pygmaean	aphicide
stellion	Viennese	fiftieth	softhead	dogfight	legalism	raggedly	aphorise
stemless	Vietcong	fiftyish	softness	doggedly	legalist	regalism	aphorism
stemmata	Vietminh	gefuffle	softshoe	doggerel	legality	regality	aphorist
stemming	viewable	giftbook	softsoap	doghouse	legatine	regelate	atheling
stenosed	viewless	infamise	software	dogmatic	legation	regicide	Athenian
stenosis	waesucks	infamous	softwood	dogooder	legbreak	regiment	atheroma
stenotic	weedless	infantry	sufferer	dogsbody	legendry	regional	athletic
stepping	weeklong	infector	suffrage	dogshore	legerity	register	behemoth
stepwise	weeviled	inferior	tafferel	dogtired	leggings	registry	beholden

beholder	Wahabite	chiliasm	episcope	grissini	pliantly	sainfoin	slithery
bohemian	abidance	chiliast	episemon	gritting	plighted	saintdom	slitting
buhlwork	aciculae	chimaera	episodal	grizzled	plimsoll	sciagram	smithers
coherent	acicular	chimeric	episodic	guidable	Pliocene	sciatica	smithery
cohesion	aciculas	Chinaman	epistler	guidance	poignant	scilicet	sniffily
cohesive	acidfast	chinchin	epistyle	guidedog	pointing	scimitar	sniffler
dahabieh	acidhead	chinless	epitasis	guideway	poisoner	sciolism	sniffles
dihedral	acidosis	chipmuck	erigeron	guileful	priapism	sciolist	sniggler
dihybrid	acierage	chipmunk	etiolate	guiltily	prideful	scirocco	snippety
echinate	acierate	chipping	eviction	hairgrip	priedieu	scirrhus	snipping
echinoid	adiantum	chirpily	evidence	hairless	priestly	scissile	snipsnap
echogram	agiotage	chirrupy	evildoer	hairline	priggery	scission	snitcher
echoless	agitator	chitchat	evilness	hairnets	priggish	scissors	soilless
eohippus	agitprop	chivalry	evincive	hairworm	priggism	sciurine	soilpipe
ephemera	alienage	climatic	evitable	heighten	primally	sciuroid	spicated
Ephesian	alienate	clincher	exigence	heirless	Primates	seicento	spiccato
ephorate	alienism	clinical	exigency	heirloom	primeval	seigneur	spicebox
ethereal	alienist	clinking	exigible	heirship	primming	seignior	spicknel
etherial	alizarin	clipclop	exiguity	idiolect	primness	seignory	spiculae
etherise	amiantus	clippers	exiguous	idiotism	primrose	seizable	spicular
etherism	amicable	clipping	eximious	imitable	princely	shielder	spiculum
etherist	amicably	cliquish	existent	imitator	princess	shieling	spiffing
ethicism	amitosis	cliquism	failsafe	inimical	printing	shiftily	spikelet
ethicist	amitotic	coiffeur	faineant	iniquity	printout	shiftkey	spillage
Ethiopic	aniconic	coiffure	faintish	initiate	priorate	shigella	spillway
ethnarch	animally	coincide	fairlead	Irishism	prioress	shikaree	spinifex
ethnical	animator	coistrel	fairness	Irishman	priority	shilling	spinning
ethology	anisette	cribbage	fairyism	jailbird	prismoid	shimmery	spinster
ethylene	apiarian	cribbing	faithful	joinable	prisoner	shinbone	spiracle
exhalant	apiarist	criminal	flickery	jointure	prissily	shingler	spirally
exhorter	apically	crispate	flimflam	kailyard	pristine	shingles	spirilla
ichorous	Arianism	cristate	flimsily	knickers	psilosis	shinning	spirited
inhalant	arillate	criteria	flincher	knightly	puissant	shipload	spiritus
inherent	aristate	critical	flinders	knitting	quibbler	shipmate	spiteful
inhesion	aviarist	critique	flintily	knitwear	quickset	shipment	spitfire
inhumane	aviation	daimonic	flipflap	laically	quiddity	shipping	spitting
Jehovist	aviatrix	daintily	flipflop	leisured	quidnunc	shipworm	spittoon
Kohinoor	avidness	daiquiri	flippant	loiterer	quietism	shipyard	spivvery
kohlrabi	avifauna	dairying	flipping	maidenly	quietist	shiralee	stibnite
maharaja	avionics	dairyman	flipside	maidhood	quilling	shirring	stickful
maharani	axiality	deionise	flitches	maieutic	quillpen	shirting	stickily
mahjongg	axillary	dribbler	flitting	mailable	quilting	shivaree	stickjaw
mahogany	axiology	dribblet	fribbler	mailboat	quincunx	skiagram	stickler
Mahratta	bailable	driftage	friction	mailcart	quintain	skidding	stiffish
Mahratti	bailment	driftice	friendly	mainland	quipping	skilless	stigmata
Moharram	bailsman	driftway	Friesian	mainline	quirkily	skilling	stilbene
Muharram	blighter	drilling	frighten	mainmast	quisling	skimmilk	stilbite
nihilism	blimpish	drinking	frigidly	mainsail	quitrent	skimming	stiletto
nihilist	blindage	dripfeed	frijoles	mainstay	quitting	skimpily	stillage
nihility	blinders	dripping	frillies	maintain	quixotic	skindeep	stimulus
ochreous	blinkard	drivable	fringing	mainyard	quixotry	skinfood	stingily
ophidian	blinking	driveway	frisette	maiolica	quizzing	skinhead	stingray
rehandle	blissful	editress	friskily	moisture	railhead	skinless	stinkard
rehearse	blistery	ekistics	fritting	nailfile	raillery	skinning	stinking
rehoboam	blithely	eligible	gainable	nainsook	railroad	skipjack	stinkpot
schedule	blizzard	eligibly	gainings	noisette	rainbird	skipping	stipites
schemata	Briarean	emigrant	gainless	nuisance	raincoat	skirmish	stippler
scheming	bribable	emigrate	gainsaid	obituary	raindrop	skirting	stipular
schiedam	brickbat	eminence	glibness	odiously	rainfall	skislope	stirring
schiller	brickred	eminency	glissade	oeillade	rainwash	skittish	stitcher
schizoid	briefing	emissary	glittery	olibanum	rainwear	skittles	suicidal
schmaltz	brighten	emission	Goidelic	oligarch	reignite	slideway	suitable
schnapps	brightly	emissive	goingson	oligomer	reimpose	slightly	suitably
scholium	brimfull	emitting	goitrous	oliphant	reindeer	slimmest	suitcase
schooner	brimless	epiblast	gridiron	omission	reinless	slimming	suitings
sphagnum	brimming	epically	grievous	omitting	reinsert	slimmish	swiftlet
sphenoid	brindled	epicalyx	grillage	oriental	reinsman	slimness	swigging
spherics	briskish	epicotyl	grimacer	oriented	reinsure	slinkily	swimming
spheroid	brisling	epicycle	grimmest	origanum	reinvest	slipcase	swimsuit
spherule	britches	epidemic	grimness	original	rhinitis	slipform	swindler
sphingid	britzska	epidural	grimoire	otiosely	Rhinodon	slipknot	swinging
sphygmus	building	epifauna	grindery	otiosity	rhizopod	slipover	switchel
Tahitian	chiasmus	epigeous	grinning	oviposit	ruinable	slippage	tailback
unhinged	chiastic	epigraph	gripping	oxidiser	sailable	slippery	tailcoat
unhoused	chickpea	epilepsy	gripsack	oximeter	sailboat	slipping	tailgate
upheaval	chiefdom	epilogue	Griselda	painless	sailfish	slipring	tailings
upholder	childbed	epinasty	griseous	paintbox	sailless	sliproad	tailless
vehement	childish	epiphany	grisette	peignoir	sailorly	slipshod	tailpipe
Wahabism	children	epiphyte	grisgris	Philomel	sailyard	slipslop	tailrace

tailspin	twinship	jejunely	allround	calcitic	delibate	foldboat	hellbent
tainture	twitcher	majestic	allspice	calcspar	delicacy	folderol	Hellenic
thiamine	twittery	majolica	allusion	calctuff	delicate	foliaged	hellfire
thickety	twitting	majority	allusive	calculus	delirium	folklore	hellhole
thickish	ubiquity	objector	alluvial	calendar	delivery	folkmoot	helmeted
thickset	uniaxial	rejecter	alluvion	calender	Delphian	folksong	helminth
thievery	unicycle	rejigger	alluvium	calfskin	delusion	folktale	helmsman
thievish	unifilar	rejoicer	aplastic	calidity	delusive	follicle	helotism
thingamy	unionise	unjustly	atlantes	califate	delusory	follower	helpless
thinking	unionism	Akkadian	Atlantic	calipash	dilatant	followon	helpmate
thinness	unionist	alkahest	axletree	calipers	dilation	followup	helpmeet
thinnest	unipolar	alkalies	balanced	callable	dilative	fullback	hilarity
thinning	uniquely	alkalify	balancer	callgirl	dilatory	fullness	hillfort
thinnish	unisonal	alkaline	baldhead	calliope	diligent	fullpage	hillocky
thirlage	unitedly	alkaloid	baldness	calliper	dilution	fullsize	hillside
thirster	univalve	ankerite	baldpate	calmness	diluvial	fulltime	holdback
thirteen	universe	ankylose	balefire	calthrop	diluvian	galactic	holdfast
thisness	univocal	bakshish	Balinese	calvados	diluvium	galangal	holdover
toiletry	utiliser	cakewalk	balkline	calycine	doldrums	galbanum	holidays
toilette	vainness	cokernut	balladic	calycoid	dolerite	galeated	holiness
toilsome	veilless	Dukhobor	balladry	calycule	dolesome	Galenism	holistic
toilworn	voicebox	elkhound	ballcock	calyptra	dolomite	galenite	hollands
trialist	voiceful	enkindle	balletic	celeriac	doloroso	Galilean	hollowly
triangle	voidable	Eskimoan	ballista	celerity	dolorous	galleass	Holocene
triarchy	voidance	inkiness	ballonet	celibacy	dulciana	galliard	hologram
Triassic	voidness	inkstand	ballroom	celibate	dulcimer	Gallican	holozoic
triaxial	wainscot	jokingly	ballyhoo	cellarer	Dulcinea	gallipot	holstein
tribally	waitress	kakemono	ballyrag	cellaret	dullness	galloper	hulahula
tribasic	whidding	lakeland	balmoral	cellular	eclectic	Galloway	idleness
tribrach	whiffler	likeable	balsamic	chlorate	ecliptic	galluses	illation
tribunal	Whiggery	likeness	baluster	chloride	eclosion	gallwasp	illative
trichina	Whiggish	likewise	belabour	chlorine	eelgrass	galvanic	illfated
trichite	Whiggism	lukewarm	believer	chlorite	ellipses	gelastic	illiquid
trichoid	whimbrel	lykewake	belittle	chlorous	ellipsis	gelatine	illtimed
trichome	whimwham	makebate	bellbird	ciliated	elliptic	gelation	illtreat
trichord	whinchat	makefast	bellbuoy	colander	enlarger	gelidity	illumine
trickery	whinsill	makimono	bellcote	coldness	eolithic	gillaroo	illusage
trickily	whipcord	oakapple	bellpull	coleseed	eulachon	gilthead	illusion
trickish	whiplash	oakegger	bellpush	coleslaw	eulogise	Golconda	illusive
tricorne	whiplike	Pekinese	bellwort	colewort	eulogist	golddust	illusory
tricycle	whipping	rakehell	bellyful	coliform	eulogium	goldenly	Illyrian
triennia	whipworm	rakishly	beltless	collagen	exlibris	goldfish	inlander
trifling	whirring	rekindle	bilabial	collapse	falcated	goldfoil	Islamise
trifocal	whiskers	sukiyaki	bilberry	collared	falchion	goldleaf	Islamism
triforia	whiskery	takeaway	billfold	collared	falconer	goldmine	Islamite
triglyph	whispery	takehome	billhead	colleger	falconet	goldrush	islander
trigonal	whistler	takeover	billhook	colliery	falconry	golfclub	jalousie
trigraph	whiteboy	takingly	billiard	colloid	falderal	golliwog	jolthead
trilling	whitecap	tokenism	billyboy	collogue	fallback	gulfweed	julienne
trillion	whitefly	tokology	billycan	colloquy	fallfish	gullable	kalaazar
trillium	whitehot	unkennel	bilobate	collyria	fallible	gullible	killdeer
trilobed	whitener	unkindly	boldface	colonial	fallibly	gulosity	kilogram
trimaran	whiteout	unkingly	boldness	colonise	falsetto	Halachah	kilowatt
trimeric	whitetie	wakeless	bollworm	colonist	faltboat	halation	kolinsky
trimeter	whittret	wakening	bolthole	colophon	feldsher	haleness	lallygag
trimming	whizbang	wakerife	boltrope	colossal	feldspar	halfback	Lollardy
trimness	whizzing	yokemate	bulkhead	colossus	felicity	halfbeak	lollipop
trioxide	whizzkid	ablation	bullcalf	coloured	felinity	halfboot	lollypop
tripeman	wriggler	ablative	bulldoze	colubrid	fellable	halfbred	Malagasy
triplane	wristlet	ablution	bulletin	columnal	fellahin	halflife	malamute
triploid	wristpin	Adlerian	bullfrog	columnar	fellness	halfmast	malapert
tripodal	writable	adlibbed	bullhead	columned	fellowly	halfmoon	malaprop
trippery	writeoff	aflutter	bullhorn	culdesac	felsitic	halfnote	malarial
tripping	writings	aglimmer	bullocky	culicine	filagree	halfpint	malarian
triptych	zoiatria	aglitter	bullring	culinary	filament	halfsole	malarkey
tripwire	zwieback	allegory	bullseye	culottes	filariae	halfterm	maledict
triskele	abjectly	alleluia	bullyboy	culpable	filarial	halftime	malefern
trisomic	adjacent	alliance	bullyoff	culpably	filature	halliard	malemute
tristful	adjuster	allergen	bullyrag	cultivar	filefish	haliotis	maleness
tristich	adjustor	allergic	calabash	cultural	filially	halliard	maligner
tritical	adjutage	alleyway	caladium	cultured	filiform	hallmark	malignly
triumvir	adjutant	allnight	calamary	culverin	filigree	hallowed	malinger
triunity	adjuvant	allocate	calamine	cylinder	Filipina	halluces	malodour
twiddler	bejabers	allodial	calamint	dalesman	Filipino	halteres	maltreat
twilight	cajolery	allodium	calamite	dalmatic	filmgoer	heliacal	maltster
twinborn	dejected	allogamy	calamity	delation	filmstar	helicoid	malvasia
twinkler	Gujarati	allopath	calcanea	delegacy	filthily	heliosis	melamine
twinling	hijacker	allotted	calcaria	delegate	filtrate	heliport	melanism
twinning	injector	allottee	calcific	deletion	foldaway	Helladic	melanite

```
melinite  pelerine  reliever  solation  unlimber  wildwood  computer  gumption
mellowly  pellagra  religion  solatium  unlinked  wilfully  Cumbrian  gymkhana
melodeon  pellicle  relocate  solderer  unlisted  wiliness  cumbrous  gymnasia
melodise  pellmell  relucent  soldiery  unloader  williwaw  cumulate  hamartia
melodist  pellucid  relumine  solecism  unloosen  wolffish  cumulous  hamululi
mildness  pelorism  rollcall  solecist  unlovely  wolfpack  cymatium  himation
milepost  phlegmon  rollneck  solemnly  uplander  wolfskin  damassin  homebody
Milesian  pilaster  rolypoly  soleness  uplifter  xylocarp  damnable  homeborn
militant  pilchard  ruleless  solenoid  valanced  xylology  damnably  homebred
military  pileated  salacity  solfaist  valerate  xylonite  dampness  homebrew
militate  pilewort  salariat  solfeggi  valerian  yellowly  demagogy  homefelt
milkmaid  pilferer  salaried  solidary  Valhalla  yuletide  demander  homeland
milkweed  piliform  saleable  solidify  valiance  admitted  demarche  homeless
milkwort  pillager  saleroom  solidity  valiancy  admonish  demented  homelike
millhand  pillwort  Salesian  solitary  validate  almagest  dementia  homemade
milliard  pilosity  salesman  solitude  validity  almanack  demerara  homesick
milliary  pilotage  salience  solleret  valorise  almighty  demersal  homespun
millibar  pilsener  saliency  solstice  valorous  ammoniac  demijohn  hometown
millieme  polarise  salinity  solution  valuable  ammonify  demitted  homeward
milliner  polarity  salivary  solvable  valuably  ammonite  demiurge  homework
millpond  polemics  salivate  solvency  valuator  ammonium  demobbed  homicide
millrace  polemise  Salopian  splasher  valvulae  Armagnac  democrat  hominoid
Miltonic  polemist  saltbush  splatter  valvular  armament  demolish  homodont
molality  polestar  saltless  splendid  velamina  armature  demoness  homogamy
molarity  polisher  saltlick  splenial  velarium  armchair  demoniac  homogeny
molasses  politely  saltmine  splenius  velleity  Armenian  demonian  homology
molecule  politick  saltness  splinter  velocity  Arminian  demonise  homonymy
molehill  politico  saltwort  splitter  velskoen  armorial  demonism  homuncle
moleskin  politics  salutary  splotchy  vileness  armoured  demotion  humanely
molester  pollices  salvable  splutter  vilifier  armourer  demurely  humanise
Molinism  pollinia  salvific  sullenly  vilipend  armyworm  demurred  humanism
Molinist  pollinic  sclereid  sulphate  villadom  bambinos  demurrer  humanist
molossus  polliwog  sclerite  sulphide  villager  bimanous  dimerism  humanity
molybdic  pollster  scleroma  sulphite  villainy  bimbashi  dimerous  humanoid
mulberry  polluter  sclerose  sulphone  villatic  bombsite  diminish  humidify
muleteer  pollywog  sclerous  sultrily  volatile  bummaree  dimmable  humidity
mulishly  polonium  seladang  syllabic  volcanic  Cambrian  domestic  humility
mulloway  poltfoot  selcouth  syllable  volcanos  cameleer  domicile  hummocky
multeity  poltroon  selectee  syllabub  volitant  camellia  dominant  humorist
multifid  polygala  selector  syllabus  volition  camisade  dominate  humorous
multiped  polygamy  selenate  sylphide  volitive  camisado  domineer  humoured
multiple  polygene  selenide  sylphine  volplane  camisole  dominion  humpback
multiply  polygeny  selenite  sylphish  voltaism  camomile  dominoes  humuncle
mylonite  polyglot  selenium  sylvatic  volution  campagna  dumbbell  hymenial
nullness  polygyny  selfborn  talapoin  volvulus  campaign  dumbhead  hymenium
oblation  polymath  selfheal  talented  vulcanic  campfire  dumbness  hymnbook
oblatory  polypary  selfhelp  talesman  vulgarly  camphene  dumbshow  ilmenite
obligate  polypide  selfhood  talisman  waleknot  camphine  dumfound  immanent
obliging  polypite  selfless  tallness  Walhalla  campsite  dumpling  immature
oblivion  polypody  selflove  tallyman  walkable  camshaft  Emmental  immersed
oilcloth  polypoid  selfmade  Talmudic  walkaway  cemetery  familial  imminent
oilfield  polypous  selfmate  telecast  walkover  combings  familiar  immingle
oilfired  polyseme  selfness  telecine  Walkyrie  comatose  famously  immobile
oiliness  polysemy  selfpity  telefilm  wallaroo  comeback  feminine  immodest
oilstone  polysomy  selfrule  telegony  walleyed  comedian  feminise  immolate
onlooker  polyzoan  selfsame  telegram  wallfern  comedist  feminism  immortal
oologist  polyzoic  selfsown  telemark  wallgame  comedown  feminist  immunise
owlishly  polyzoon  selfwill  telepath  wallknot  cometary  feminity  immunity
palatial  pullback  selvedge  teleport  walloper  commando  fimbriae  jamboree
palatine  pullover  silencer  telethon  wallower  commence  fomenter  jumpedup
paleface  pulmonic  silently  teleview  weldable  commerce  fumarole  jumpseat
paleness  pulpiter  silicane  televise  weldment  commoner  fumigant  jumpsuit
palestra  pulpwood  silicate  tellable  welladay  commoney  fumigate  kamikaze
palinode  pulsator  silicide  telltale  wellaway  commonly  fumitory  Khmerian
palisade  pulvilli  silicify  telluric  wellborn  communal  gambados  komitaji
palliate  pulvinus  silicone  tilefish  wellbred  commuter  gambeson  Komsomol
pallidly  rallying  silkworm  tillable  welldeck  compages  gambroon  lamasery
pallmall  rallyist  sillabub  tiltyard  wellhead  compiler  gamebird  lambaste
palmette  relation  silphium  tolbooth  wellknit  complain  gamecock  lambency
palmetto  relative  Silurian  tolerant  wellnigh  compleat  gameness  lamblike
palmiped  relaxant  siluroid  tolerate  wellread  complete  gamesome  lambskin
palmitin  releasee  silvatic  tollcall  Wellsian  complice  gamester  lamellae
palomino  releaser  silverly  tolldish  wellworn  complier  gaminess  lamellar
palpable  relegate  solander  tollgate  Welshman  compline  gematria  lameness
palpably  relevant  solanine  ugliness  wildeyed  composed  geminate  lamented
palterer  reliable  solarise  unlawful  wildfire  composer  gemstone  laminate
paludism  reliably  solarism  unleaded  wildfowl  compound  gimcrack  lamppost
Pelagian  reliance  solarist  unlearnt  wildlife  compress  gimmicky  lemonade
Pelasgic                                 wildness  comprise  gummosis  lemurine
```

lemuroid	remitted	tamperer	bannered	cinnabar	conveyor	funnyman	honorary
limbless	remittee	temerity	banneret	cinnamic	convince	gangland	honourer
limekiln	remitter	tempered	bannerol	cinnamon	convolve	gangling	hungrily
limerick	remotely	temperer	banterer	cinquain	convulse	ganglion	huntress
limetwig	rimbrake	template	bantling	conation	cynicism	gangrene	huntsman
limewash	rimester	temporal	banxring	conative	cynosure	gangster	ianthine
limitary	romancer	tempting	benedick	concasse	dancette	ganister	ignition
limonite	Romanian	timbered	benedict	conceder	dancetty	gantline	ignitron
limpidly	romanise	timeball	benefice	conceive	dandruff	gantlope	ignominy
limpness	Romanism	timebomb	benignly	concerti	dandyish	Ganymede	ignorant
lomentum	Romanist	timefuse	Benjamin	concerto	dandyism	gendarme	innately
lumberer	Romansch	timeless	bentwood	concetti	danegeld	generate	innocent
luminant	romantic	timework	benzoate	concetto	dankness	generous	innovate
luminary	Rumanian	timeworn	benzylic	conchate	danseuse	genetics	innuendo
luminist	Rumansch	timidity	binaural	conchoid	denarius	Genevese	janizary
luminous	ruminant	timorous	bindweed	conclave	denature	genially	jingoish
lumpfish	ruminate	timously	binnacle	conclude	denazify	genitive	jingoism
lymphoid	rummager	tomahawk	binomial	concrete	dendrite	geniture	jingoist
lymphoma	samarium	tomalley	bondmaid	condense	dendroid	genocide	Jonathan
Mameluke	sameness	tombless	bondmans	condylar	denehole	genotype	jongleur
mamillae	samizdat	tomentum	bondsman	conferee	deniable	gentrice	junction
mamillar	Samoyede	tommybar	bonefish	conferva	denounce	gingerly	juncture
membered	samphire	tommygun	bonehead	confetti	dentalia	gingival	junkshop
membrane	sampling	tommyrot	boneless	confider	dentated	gonfalon	junkyard
mementos	semantic	tomnoddy	bonemeal	confiner	denticle	gonidial	Kanarese
memorial	semester	tomogram	boneyard	confines	dinerout	gonidium	kangaroo
memorise	semibull	tomorrow	bonhomie	conflate	dingdong	gunfight	kindless
memsahib	semidome	tumbling	boniface	conflict	dinornis	gunflint	kindling
mimester	seminary	tumidity	boniness	confound	dinosaur	gunlayer	kindness
mimicked	seminude	tumorous	bonspiel	confrere	donation	gunmetal	kinesics
mimicker	semiotic	tympanic	bontebok	confront	Donatism	gunpoint	kinetics
momently	Semitise	tympanum	buncombe	congener	Donatist	gunsmith	kingbird
momentum	Semitism	unmanned	bundling	conglobe	donative	gunstock	kingbolt
nameable	Semitist	unmarked	bunfight	congress	donatory	gynandry	kingcrab
namedrop	semitone	unmeetly	bungalow	congreve	donought	gynocrat	kingfish
nameless	semolina	unmuffle	bunghole	conidial	dundiver	gynoecia	kinghood
namepart	semplice	unmuzzle	bunkered	conidium	dungaree	handball	kinglike
namesake	sempster	vambrace	buntline	coniform	dungcart	handbell	kingship
nametape	similise	vampiric	Canadian	conjoint	dunghill	handbill	kingsize
nematode	simoniac	vamplate	canaille	conjugal	dynamics	handbook	kinkajou
nematoid	simonist	vomerine	canalise	conjunct	dynamism	handcart	kinsfolk
nimbused	simplify	vomitive	canaster	conjurer	dynamist	handclap	lancelet
nomadise	simplism	vomitory	cancrine	conjuror	dynamite	handcuff	landarmy
nomadism	simulant	womanise	cancroid	conniver	dynastic	handfast	landcrab
nominate	simulate	womanish	candidly	conoidal	dynatron	handgrip	landfall
nomistic	somatism	zamindar	canister	conquest	enneagon	handheld	landform
nomogram	sombrely	zemindar	cannabin	conserve	fanciful	handhold	landgirl
nomology	sombrero	zombiism	cannabis	consider	fancyman	handicap	landlady
numberer	sombrous	zymology	cannibal	consoler	fandance	handless	landless
numbfish	somebody	abnegate	cannikin	consomme	fandango	handline	landline
numbness	somedeal	abnormal	cannonry	conspire	fanfaron	handling	landlord
numeracy	somedele	adnation	cannulae	constant	fangless	handlist	landmark
numerary	sometime	agnation	cannular	construe	fanlight	handloom	landmass
numerate	someways	agnostic	cannulas	consular	fantasia	handmade	landmine
numerous	somewhat	amnesiac	canoeing	consumer	fenberry	handmaid	landrail
numinous	somewhen	amniotic	canoeist	contagia	fencible	handmill	landslip
numskull	somnific	annalist	canoness	contango	fenestra	handpick	landsman
nymphean	Sumerian	annotate	canonise	contempt	finalise	handrail	langlauf
ohmmeter	summerly	announce	canonist	contents	finalism	handsewn	Langshan
ommateum	summitry	annually	canoodle	contessa	finalist	handsome	language
pamperer	summoner	annulate	canorous	continua	finality	handwork	languish
pamphlet	symbiont	annulled	canthari	continue	finedraw	handyman	lankness
pembroke	symbolic	banality	canticle	continuo	fineness	hangable	lanneret
pemmican	symmetry	banausic	cantonal	contline	finespun	hangeron	lanthorn
pimiento	sympathy	bandanna	cantoris	contorno	fingered	hangnail	lengthen
pomander	symphile	bandeaux	canzonet	contract	finisher	hangover	lenience
pomology	symphony	banderol	cenotaph	contrail	finitely	henchman	leniency
pumproom	sympodia	banditry	Cenozoic	contrary	finitude	henequen	Leninism
rambling	symposia	banditti	centaury	contrast	finnesko	henparty	Leninist
rambutan	tamandua	bandsman	centring	contrate	fondling	henroost	Leninite
ramentum	tamanoir	bangtail	centrism	contrite	fondness	hinderer	lenitive
ramequin	tamarack	banister	centrist	contrive	fontanel	hindlegs	lensless
rampancy	tamarind	banjoist	centroid	conurbia	fontange	hindmost	lenticel
remanent	tamarisk	bankable	centuple	convener	function	hinduise	lenticle
remedial	tamboura	bankbill	cinchona	convenor	funebral	Hinduism	linchpin
remember	tameable	bankbook	cincture	converge	funerary	honestly	lineally
reminder	tameless	banknote	cineaste	converse	funereal	honeybee	linearly
remissly	tameness	bankroll	cinerary	convexly	fungible	honeydew	linesman
remittal	Tamilian	bankrupt	cingulum	conveyer	funkhole	honeypot	lingerer

lingerie	menology	nonhuman	punition	sinciput	tenderly	windrose	biograph
linguist	menstrua	nonjuror	punitive	sinecure	Tenebrae	windsail	biometry
liniment	mensural	nonlegal	punitory	sinfonia	tenement	windsock	biomorph
Linnaean	menswear	nonmetal	ranarian	sinfully	tenesmus	windward	bionomic
linoleum	mentally	nonmoral	ranarium	singable	tenonsaw	winepalm	bioplasm
linstock	minacity	nonparty	ranchero	singeing	tenorite	wineshop	bioplast
lintseed	minatory	nonrigid	ranchman	singsong	tenotomy	wineskin	bioscope
Londoner	mindless	nonsense	randomly	singular	tenpence	wingbeat	blockade
loneness	minimise	nonstick	rankness	sinicise	tenpenny	wingcase	blockage
lonesome	minister	nonunion	ransomer	sinister	tensible	wingless	blockish
longboat	ministry	nonusage	renderer	sinkable	tentacle	wingspan	blondish
longeron	Minoress	nonwhite	renegade	sinkhole	tenurial	winnable	bloodily
longeval	Minorite	oenology	renegado	sinology	tincture	winnings	bloodred
longhair	minority	oenophil	reneguer	sinophil	tingeing	winnower	bloomers
longhand	Minotaur	ointment	reniform	sinusoid	tininess	winterly	bloomery
longhorn	minstrel	omnivore	renitent	sonatina	tinkerer	wintrily	blooming
longness	mintmark	ornament	renounce	songbird	tinnitus	wondrous	blossomy
longship	minutely	ornately	renovate	songbook	tinplate	wontedly	blotting
longsome	minutiae	ornithic	renowned	songless	tinselly	xanthate	blowball
longstop	monachal	pancreas	rentable	songster	tinsmith	xanthein	blowfish
longterm	monadism	pandanus	renumber	sonobuoy	tinstone	xanthene	blowhard
longtime	monandry	pandemic	ringbark	sonority	tintless	xanthine	blowhole
longueur	monarchy	pandowdy	ringbolt	sonorous	tonality	xanthium	blowlamp
longwall	monastic	panelled	ringbone	sunbaked	tonedeaf	xanthoma	blowpipe
longwave	monaural	pangolin	ringdove	sunbathe	toneless	Xantippe	bookcase
longways	monaxial	panicked	ringmain	sunblind	tonepoem	xenogamy	bookends
longwise	monazite	panmixia	ringneck	sunburnt	tonguing	xenolith	bookland
lunarian	mondaine	pannikin	ringroad	sunburst	tonicity	Yankeefy	booklice
lunation	monetary	panorama	ringside	sundance	tuneable	zaniness	booklore
luncheon	monetise	panpipes	ringtail	sunderer	tuneless	zenithal	bookmark
lungfish	moneybag	pansophy	ringwall	sundress	tungsten	zinckify	bookpost
lungwort	moneybox	pantheon	ringworm	sundried	tungstic	zincking	bookrest
lunulate	Mongolic	pantofle	rinsings	sundries	tunicate	zonation	bookwork
lynchpin	mongoose	pantsuit	rondeaux	sundrops	Tunisian	abomasum	bookworm
lynxeyed	monicker	penalise	runabout	sunlight	uintaite	abomasus	bootjack
mancando	monistic	penchant	runagate	sunproof	vanadate	aborally	bootlace
manciple	monition	pendency	runcible	sunshade	vanadium	aborning	bootlast
Mandaean	monitive	pendicle	runnerup	sunshine	vanadous	abortion	bootless
mandamus	monitory	pendular	sanative	sunshiny	Vandalic	abortive	boottree
mandarin	monkfish	pendulum	sanatory	sunstone	vaneless	aconitic	broacher
mandator	MonKhmer	penitent	sanctify	sunwards	vanguard	aconitum	broadish
mandible	monkhood	penknife	sanction	synapsis	vanillin	acosmism	broadway
Mandingo	monkseal	penology	sanctity	synaptic	vanisher	acoustic	brocaded
mandolin	monkship	penstock	sandarac	synastry	vanquish	adoption	brocatel
mandorla	monoacid	pentacle	sandbank	syncline	venality	adoptive	broccoli
mandrake	monocrat	pentagon	sandbath	syncopal	venation	adorable	brochure
mandrill	monocyte	pentroof	sandflea	syncytia	vendetta	adorably	broidery
maneater	monodist	penumbra	sandshoe	syndesis	vendible	agonised	brokenly
manfully	monogamy	pinafore	sandwich	syndetic	veneerer	alogical	bromelia
mangabey	monogeny	pinaster	sandworm	syndical	venerate	alopecia	bromidic
manganic	monoglot	pincenez	sandwort	syndrome	venereal	amoebean	bronchia
mangonel	monogony	pinchers	sandyish	synergic	Venetian	amoeboid	bronchus
mangrove	monogram	Pindaric	saneness	synergid	vengeful	amorally	broodily
maniacal	monogyny	pinecone	sangaree	syngamic	venially	amoretti	brookite
Manichee	monolith	pinewood	Sangrail	synonymy	venomous	amoretto	brooklet
manicure	monomial	pinkness	Sangreal	synopses	venosity	amortise	brougham
manifest	monopode	pinmoney	sanguine	synopsis	venously	anorexia	brouhaha
manifold	monopoly	pinnacle	sanitary	synoptic	ventless	anorexic	browband
maniform	monorail	pinnated	sanitate	synovial	venturer	anorthic	browbeat
mannered	monotint	pinniped	sanitise	syntagma	Venusian	anourous	browning
mannerly	monotone	pinnular	sannyasi	syntonic	vincible	apocrine	brownish
mannikin	monotony	pinochle	sanserif	tandoori	vinculum	apodoses	buoyancy
mannitol	monotype	pinpoint	Sanskrit	tangency	vinegary	apodosis	choicely
manorial	monoxide	pinprick	santonin	tangible	vineyard	apogamic	choirboy
manpower	monsieur	pintable	senarius	tangibly	vinosity	apograph	choleric
mansized	monteith	pintsize	senility	tangoist	vinously	apologia	chondrus
mantelet	monument	pinwheel	sennight	tanistry	vintager	apologue	chopchop
mantilla	muniment	ponderer	senorita	tannable	wanderer	apomixis	chopping
mantissa	munition	pondweed	senseful	tantalic	wanderoo	apoplexy	chopsuey
mantling	nanogram	pontifex	sensible	tantalum	wantonly	apostasy	choragic
manually	nenuphar	ponytail	sensibly	tantalus	windburn	apostate	choragus
manubria	ninefold	puncheon	sensoria	Tantrism	windcone	apothegm	chorally
manurial	ninepins	punctate	sensuous	tantrist	windfall	aromatic	chordate
menarche	nineteen	punctual	sentence	tenacity	windgall	atomiser	choregic
mendable	nineties	puncture	sentient	tenacula	windlass	avowable	choregus
menhaden	nonclaim	punditry	sentinel	tenaille	windless	avowedly	choriamb
menially	nondairy	pungency	sentrygo	tenantry	windmill	bioassay	chorioid
meninges	nonesuch	puniness	Sinaitic	tendence	windowed	biocidal	chowchow
meniscus	nonevent	punisher	sinapism	tendency	windpipe	biogenic	cloddish

```
clodpole egoistic frostily isogonal photopic reorient slowpoke tholepin
clodpoll egomania frosting isogonic photopsy rhomboid slowworm thoraces
clogging elongate frothily isolable plodding rhonchal smocking thoracic
cloister eloquent frottage isolator plopping rhonchus smokable thoraxes
clopclop enormity froufrou isomeric plotting roodbeam smoothen thorough
closeset enormous gaolbird isometry plougher roodloft smoothie thoughts
closeted epopoeia geodesic isomorph poohpooh roofless smoothly thousand
clothier erodible geodetic isophote poorness roofrack smothery toolroom
clothing erogenic geognosy isopleth probable rooftree smoulder toolshed
clotting erotical geologic isoprene probably roommate snobbery toothful
cloudily esoteric geomancy isoptera proceeds roothold snobbish toothily
cloudlet euonymin geometer isospory proclaim rootless snobbism toothing
clownery euonymus geometry isostasy procurer ryotwari snogging trochaic
clownish exocrine geophagy isothere prodding scolding snootily trochili
cookbook exogamic geophone isotherm prodigal scolices snowball trochlea
coolabah exorcise geophyte isotonic prodrome scombrid snowbird trochoid
coolibah exorcism geoponic isotopic producer scoopful snowboot troilite
coolness exorcist Georgian isotropy proemial scoopnet snowdrop trollopy
coonskin exordial geotaxis ivorynut profaner scopulae snowfall trombone
cooption exordium ghoulish jeopardy profiler scopulas snowless trophied
cooptive exospore gloaming klondike profound scorcher snowlike tropical
croakily exoteric globally knocking progress scornful snowline trotting
Croatian floatage globular knockout prohibit scorpion snowshoe trottoir
croceate floating globulin knothole prolamin scotfree soothing troupial
crockery floccose gloomily knotting prolapse scotopic soothsay trousers
crocoite floccule gloriole knotwork prolific Scotsman spoffish troutlet
crofting flocculi glorious knowable prolixly scottice spoilage trouvere
cromlech flockbed glossary kromesky prologue Scottish spoliate twoedged
cromorna flogging glossily lookeron prolonge scourger spondaic twofaced
cromorne floodlit glossina loonybin promisee scouting spongily twopence
cropping floodway glowworm loophole promiser sforzato sponsion twopenny
crossbar flooring gloxinia loosebox promisor shocking spontoon twopiece
crossbow floppily gnomonic loosener promoter shoddily spookily twosided
crosscut flopping goodness lyophile prompter shoebill spookish twotimer
crossing florally goodtime moonbeam promptly shoehorn spoonfed udometer
crosslet floridly goodwife mooncalf promulge shoelace spoonful unopened
crossply florigen goodwill moonface pronator shoeless spoonily urochord
crosstie flotilla goodyear moonfish proofing shoetree sporadic urostyle
crossway flounder goofball moonless propense shofroth sporozoa uxorious
crotched flourish goosegog moonrise properly shogging sportful violable
crotchet flowered groggily moonsail property shooting sportily violably
croupier flowerer grogshop moonshee prophase shootout sporting violator
croupous floweret gromwell moonshot prophecy shopbell sportive violence
crowbill foodless groogroo moonwort prophesy shopgirl sporular whodunit
crowfoot foolscap grosbeak moorcock propolis shopping spotless wholehog
diocesan football groschen moorfowl proposal shoptalk spottily whomever
dioecism footbath grottoes moorings proposer shopworn spotting whooping
diopside footfall grounder moorland propound shortage spousage whopping
dioptase footgear grouping myoblast propping shortarm stoccado whoredom
dioptric foothill grouting myogenic propylic shortcut stoccata whoreson
dioramic foothold growling myograph prorogue shortday stockade woodbind
dioritic footless hoodwink myositic prosaism shortish stockcar woodbine
doomsday footling hoofbeat myositis prosaist shothole stockily woodchat
doomsman footmark hookworm myosotis prosodic shoulder stocking woodcock
doomster footmuff hooligan NeoLatin prospect shouldst stockish woodenly
doorbell footnote hoosegow neomycin prostate showbill stockist woodland
doorcase footpace hyoscine neonatal prostyle showboat stockman woodlark
doorknob footpath idocrase neophyte protasis showcard stockpot woodlice
doornail footpost idolater neoplasm protatic showcase stodgily woodnote
doorpost footrace idolatry neoprene protease showdown stoicism woodpile
doorsill footrest idoliser neotenic protegee showgirl stolidly woodpulp
doorstep footrope inoculum neoteric protista showroom stomachy woodruff
doorstop footrule inositol noontide protocol slobbery stomatal woodshed
dooryard footslog ironbark noontime protonic slobbish stomatic woodsman
drollery footsore ironclad odograph protozoa slobland stonefly woodwind
drophead footstep irongray odometer protract sloeeyed stopcock woodwool
dropkick footwear irongrey odontoid protrude slogging stopover woodwork
dropleaf footwork ironical omophagy provable sloppail stoppage woodworm
dropping frocking ironside omoplate provably sloppily stopping wooldyed
dropshot frogfish ironware orogenic provided slopping storable woolfell
dropwort frogging ironwood otoscope provider slopshop storeman woollens
droughty frogspit ironwork ozoniser province slopwork storeyed woolpack
drownded frondage Iroquois phonemic provisor slothful stormily woolsack
drowsily frondent isobaric phonetic proximal slotting stoutish woolshed
duodenal frondeur isocheim phormium ptomaine sloucher stowaway woolskin
duodenum frondose isocracy phosgene pyogenic slovenly swobbing woolwork
duologue frontage isodicon phosphor quotable slovenry swopping wrongful
ecologic frontier isogamic photogen quotient slowdown swotting wrongous
economic frontlet isogloss photopia reoccupy slowness teocalli yeomanly
```

yeomanry	depraved	hypothec	papistry	siphonet	requiter	barbican	carnauba
zeolitic	deprival	impacted	pappadom	siphonic	sequelae	barbital	carnival
zoogenic	deprived	impanate	papulose	superadd	sequence	bareback	Carolean
zoolater	depurate	imparity	papulous	superate	aardvark	barefoot	Caroline
zoolatry	deputise	impelled	peperino	superbly	aardwolf	bareness	carolled
zoomancy	diphenyl	impeller	pipeclay	superego	abradant	bargeman	carotene
zoometry	diplogen	imperial	pipefish	superior	abrasion	baritone	carousal
zoomorph	diploidy	imperium	pipeline	superman	abrasive	barkless	carousel
zoonosis	diplomat	impetigo	piperack	supernal	abridger	barnacle	carouser
zoophily	diplopia	impishly	piperine	supertax	abrogate	barndoor	carriage
zoophyte	dipnoous	impledge	popinjay	supinate	abruptly	barnyard	carriole
zoospore	dipstick	implicit	poppadum	supinely	acrefoot	baronage	carryall
alphabet	dipteral	impolder	poppadum	supplant	acreinch	baroness	carryout
alpinism	dipteran	impolicy	populace	supplely	acridine	baronial	cartload
alpinist	dopiness	impolite	populate	supplial	acridity	barouche	cartouch
amperage	empathic	imponent	populism	supplier	acrimony	barracks	caruncle
amphibia	empeople	importer	populist	supplies	acrolein	barranca	caryatid
amphipod	emphases	imposing	populous	supposal	acrolith	barranco	ceramics
amphorae	emphasis	imposter	puparial	supposed	acrostic	barrator	ceramist
amphoras	emphatic	impostor	puparium	suppress	acrotism	barratry	cerastes
ampullae	employee	impotent	pupation	syphilis	acrylate	barrenly	ceratoid
amputate	employer	imprimis	pupilage	tapdance	adroitly	barrette	cercaria
appalled	empoison	imprison	pupilary	tapedeck	aeration	barterer	cerebral
appanage	emporium	improper	pupillar	tapeless	aerially	bartizan	cerebrum
apparent	empurple	improver	puppetry	tapelike	aeriform	baryonic	cerement
appendix	empyreal	impudent	puppydog	tapeline	aerodyne	barytone	ceremony
appetent	empyrean	impugner	puppydom	tapestry	aerofoil	berberis	cernuous
appetite	espalier	impunity	puppyfat	tapeworm	aerogram	berceuse	cerulean
applause	especial	impurely	puppyish	taphouse	aerolite	bereaved	cerusite
applepie	espousal	impurity	rapacity	tapwater	aerolith	bergamot	cervelat
applique	espouser	Japanese	rapecake	tepidity	aerology	beriberi	cervical
apposite	espresso	japanned	rapeseed	tipstaff	aeronaut	berliner	cervices
appraise	eupatrid	japhetic	rapidity	topdress	aeronomy	Bermudas	christen
approach	eupepsia	japonica	rapparee	topheavy	aerostat	birdbath	christie
approval	eupeptic	jipijapa	raptness	toplevel	agraphia	birdcage	Christly
arpeggio	euphonic	kyphosis	raptures	topliner	agrarian	birdcall	chromate
asperges	euphoria	kyphotic	repairer	toplofty	agrement	birdlime	chromite
asperity	euphoric	lapboard	repartee	topnotch	agrestic	birdseed	chromium
asphodel	euphrasy	lapelled	repealer	topology	agrimony	birdseye	Circaean
asphyxia	euphuism	lapicide	repeater	toponymy	agrology	birthday	circuity
aspirant	euphuist	lapidary	repelled	topstone	agronomy	boracite	circular
aspirate	expander	lapidate	repeller	tuppence	airborne	Bordeaux	cirriped
biparous	expedite	lapidify	repenter	tuppenny	airbrake	bordello	coracoid
capacity	expelled	lepidote	repeople	typecast	airbrush	borderer	cordless
capeline	expellee	leporine	repetend	typeface	aircraft	borecole	cordovan
capellet	expertly	lipogram	replacer	typehigh	Airedale	borehole	corduroy
capeskin	expiable	lipomata	replevin	typhonic	airfield	boringly	cordwain
capitate	expiator	lipsalve	reporter	typifier	airframe	borrower	cordwood
capitula	expirant	lipstick	repotted	typology	airiness	Burberry	corelate
caponier	explicit	lopeared	repousse	umpirage	airliner	burglary	corkwing
caponise	exploder	lopgrass	reprieve	umptieth	airscrew	burgonet	corkwood
caprifig	explorer	lopsided	reprisal	unpaired	airshaft	Burgundy	cornball
capriole	exponent	mephitic	reproach	unpegged	airspace	burletta	corneous
capsicum	exporter	mephitis	reproval	unperson	airspeed	burnouse	cornetcy
capstone	exposure	mopishly	republic	unpinned	airstrip	burntout	cornetti
capsular	gapeworm	naphthol	riparian	unplaced	airtight	burrower	cornetto
captious	gapingly	napiform	ripeness	uppercut	airwoman	bursitis	corniced
capuchin	gipsydom	napoleon	ropeable	uppishly	aoristic	Byronism	corniche
capybara	gipsyism	Nepalese	ropewalk	vapidity	apresski	carabine	cornicle
cephalic	gypseous	nepenthe	ropeyarn	vaporise	arranger	caracara	cornific
coplanar	gypsydom	nephrite	ropiness	vaporous	arrantly	caracole	cornpone
copperas	gypsyism	nepotism	sapgreen	vapourer	arrestee	carapace	coronach
copulate	haploidy	nuptials	sapidity	viperine	arrester	carbolic	coronary
copybook	hepatica	omphalic	sapience	viperish	arrestor	carbonic	coronoid
copyedit	hepatise	omphalos	saponify	viperous	arrogant	carbonyl	corporal
copyhold	heptagon	oppilate	saponite	zeppelin	arrogate	carboxyl	corridor
cupboard	hipflask	opponent	saporous	acquaint	atremble	carburet	corrival
cupelled	hipsters	opposite	sapphics	arquebus	atrocity	carcajou	corselet
cupidity	hopeless	oppugner	sapphire	bequeath	atropine	carcanet	corseted
cupreous	hypnoses	orpiment	sapphism	coquetry	aurelian	cardamom	corsetry
cupulate	hypnosis	oxpecker	sepaloid	coquette	auricula	cardamum	cortical
Cypriote	hypnotic	papalise	sepalous	enquirer	auriform	cardigan	cortices
cypselae	hypobole	papalism	separate	Esquimau	aurorean	cardinal	corundum
departed	hypoderm	papalist	Sephardi	inquirer	Ayrshire	carefree	corvette
depicter	hypogeal	paperboy	septette	liquidly	barathea	careless	Corybant
depictor	hypogean	papillae	septfoil	maquette	barbaric	careworn	coryphee
depilate	hypogene	papillar	septimal	moquette	barbecue	carillon	curarine
deponent	hypogeum	papillon	septuple	piquancy	barberry	carinate	curarise
deportee	hypogyny	papistic	siphonal	requital	barbette	carnally	curassow

```
curative firebird formless harmless lordotic murrhine perineal scragged
curculio fireboat formroom harmonic lordship myriapod perineum scramble
cureless firebomb formulae harpseal loricate myriopod periodic scrammed
curlicue firebrat formulas harridan lorikeet myrmidon periotic scrannel
currency fireclay formwork harrumph lyrebird narceine peripety scraping
curricle firedamp fornices haruspex lyricism narcissi periplus scrapped
cursedly fireeyed forrader heraldic lyricist narcoses perisher scrapper
curtains firehose forsaken heraldry marabout narcosis perjurer scratchy
curtness firelock forsooth herbaria marasmic narcotic perlitic scrawler
curveted fireopal forspeak herbless marasmus narghile permeate screamer
Cyrenaic fireplug forspent Hercules marathon narrator peroneal screechy
Cyrillic fireship forswear herdbook marauder narrowly perorate screener
daringly fireside forswore herdsman maravedi normalcy peroxide screever
darkling firetrap forsworn herdwick marbling normally personae screwtop
darkness fireweed fortieth hereaway marchesa Norseman personal scribble
darkroom firewood fortress heredity marchese northern perspire scribbly
darksome firework fortuity Hereford marginal northing persuade scrofula
dartrous firmness fortyish hereunto margrave Northman pertness scrounge
deration firstaid forwards hereupon marigold nursling Peruvian scrubbed
derelict foramina forzando herewith marinade nurturer perverse scrubber
derision forborne furbelow heritage marinate parabola pervious scrutiny
derisive forcedly furcated hermetic maritage paradigm phrasing seraglio
derisory forcefed furculae hernshaw maritime paradise phreatic seraphic
derivate forceful furcular heroical marjoram paraffin Phrygian seraphim
derogate forcible furfural herpetic markdown paragoge pirarucu serenade
derriere forcibly furfuran Hertzian markedly parakeet poristic serenata
directly fordable furlough hireable marketer parallax porkling serenely
director fordoing furriery hireling marksman parallel porosity serenity
dirigism forebear furthest hirrient marmoset paralyse porphyry serfhood
diriment forebode furuncle Horatian marocain paramour porpoise sergeant
dormancy forecast garboard hormonal maroquin paranoia porridge serially
dormouse foredeck gardener hornbeam marquess paranoid portable seriatim
dorsally foredoom gardenia hornbill marquise paraquat portfire sericite
durables foreedge gardyloo hornbook marriage parasang porthole serjeant
duration forefeel garefowl hornfels marrieds parasite porticos serology
durative forefelt garganey hornless marrying paravane portiere serosity
durukuli forefoot gargoyle hornpipe marshman parcener portrait serotine
earmuffs foregoer garishly hornrims martagon parclose portress serpulae
earnings foregone garlicky horntail martello pardoner purblind serranid
earphone forehand garotter hornworm martenot parental purchase serrated
earpiece forehead garreted hornwort martinet parergon purebred servient
earthnut foreknew garrison horologe marzipan pargeter pureness servitor
ebriated foreknow garrotte horology merchant parhelia purfling shrapnel
eeriness forelady geraniol horrible merciful parhelic purifier shredded
enricher foreland geranium horribly mercuric parietal puristic shredder
enrolled forelock horridly mergence parkland purplish shrewdly
errantly foremast Germanic horrific meridian parlance purpuric shrewish
errantry foremost germcell horsebox meringue parlando purpurin shrieval
Etrurian forename germfree horsecar meristem Parmesan pursenet shrimper
Etruscan forenoon germinal horsefly meristic parodist purslane shrinker
Eurasian forensic gerontic horseman merosome paroquet pursuant shrugged
Eurocrat forepart girasole hurtless mirepoix paroxysm purulent shrunken
European forepast girlhood irrigate mirthful parrotry purveyor sirenian
europium forepeak gorgeous irritant morainic Parsiism pyrenoid siriasis
faradaic foreplay gorgonia irritate moralise parsonic pyrexial sirvente
faradism foresaid gormless jeremiad moralism partaken pyridine sorcerer
farcical foresail gyration Jeremiah moralist parterre pyriform sordidly
farewell foreseen gyratory jeroboam morality Parthian pyroxene sorehead
farflung foreshow gyrostat jerrican moratory partible pyrrhoea soreness
farinose foreside harakiri jerrycan Moravian particle pyrrhous sorochen
farmhand foreskin harangue Jurassic morbidly partisan rarefied sororate
farmland forestal harasser juristic morbific partizan rareness sorority
farmyard forestay hardback keratose mordancy partsong rerearch sorption
farouche forested hardbake kerchief moreover parttime rerecord sorptive
farriery forester hardcase kerosene moresque perceive reremice sorrower
farthest forestry hardcore kerosine moribund perfecto rereward sortable
farthing foretell hardener korfball mornings perforce ruralise spraints
feretory foretime hardhack kurtosis morosely perfumer ruralism sprawler
fernshaw foretold hardhead larboard morosity perianth ruralist spraygun
ferocity forewarn hardline larcener morpheme pericarp rurality spreader
ferreter forewent hardness largesse morphine pericope saraband sprigged
ferriage foreword hardship larkspur mortally periderm sarcenet springal
ferritic foreyard hardtack larrikin mortgage peridium sardelle springer
ferryman forgiven hardware larynges mortmain peridote sardonic sprinkle
fervency forgoing hardwood larynxes mortuary perigean sardonyx sprinter
fervidly forklift harebell liripoop murderer perigyny sargasso sprocket
firearms formalin haresear lordless muriatic perilled sarsenet sprucely
fireback formally harikari lordling murmurer perilous scrabble spryness
fireball formerly harlotry lordosis murrelet perilune scragend strabism
```

straddle	Tarpeian	turnspit	wariness	assonate	cussword	disusage	gasmeter
straggle	tarragon	turreted	warmness	assorted	customer	disvalue	gasolene
straggly	tartaric	turtling	warpaint	assuming	cysteine	dustbowl	gasolier
straight	tartness	tyrannic	warplane	Assyrian	cystitis	dustcart	gasoline
strained	tartrate	Tyrolean	warragal	auspices	dastardy	dustcoat	gastight
strainer	Tartuffe	tyrosine	warranty	basaltic	describe	dustless	gastraea
straiten	teraphim	Tyrrhene	warrener	baseball	deserter	dustlike	gastrula
straitly	teratoma	unreason	warrigal	baseborn	designer	dustshot	gasworks
stramash	terebene	unriddle	wartweed	baseless	desirous	dysgenic	gestagen
stranded	terebrae	unrigged	wartwort	baseline	desolate	dyslexia	gestural
stranger	terminal	unroofed	warweary	basement	despatch	dyslexic	gossamer
strangle	terminer	uprising	warwhoop	baseness	despiser	dyspnoea	gossiper
strapoil	terminus	uprooter	weregild	basicity	despotic	dystopia	gossipry
strapped	termless	varactor	werewolf	basidial	destrier	easement	gossypol
strapper	termtime	variable	wiredraw	basidium	destruct	easiness	gusseted
strategy	terraced	variably	wirehair	basilica	disabuse	easterly	hasheesh
stratify	terrapin	variance	wireless	basilisk	disagree	eastmost	hastener
stravaig	terraria	varicose	wirework	basinful	disallow	eastward	hastings
streaked	terrazzo	variedly	wireworm	basketry	disarray	ecstatic	hesitant
streaker	terrible	varietal	wirewove	bassinet	disaster	ensample	hesitate
streamer	terribly	variform	wiriness	basswood	disbench	ensconce	Hesperus
streeted	terrific	variolar	wordbook	bastardy	disbound	ensemble	Hispanic
strength	tertiary	variorum	wordless	bastille	disburse	ensheath	histogen
strepent	thraldom	varletry	wordplay	besieger	disciple	enshrine	historic
Strepyan	thrasher	veracity	workable	beslaver	disclaim	enshroud	hosepipe
stretchy	thrawart	verandah	workaday	besmirch	disclose	ensiform	hospital
stricken	threader	veratrin	workfolk	besotted	discount	ensigncy	hostelry
strickle	threaten	veratrum	workings	besought	discover	ensilage	hushhush
strictly	threeply	verbally	workless	bespoken	discreet	enslaver	hustings
stridden	threeway	verbatim	workmate	besprent	discrete	ensphere	hysteria
strident	threnode	verbiage	workroom	bestiary	discrown	enswathe	hysteric
strigose	threnody	verboten	workshop	bestowal	diseased	essayist	Ibsenism
striking	thresher	verdancy	wormcast	bestrewn	disendow	Essenism	insanely
stringed	thridace	verderer	wormgear	bestride	disfrock	essonite	insanity
stringer	thriller	verderor	wormhole	bestrode	disgorge	eustatic	inscient
stripped	thriving	verditer	wormlike	bisector	disgrace	exserted	inscribe
stripper	throated	verdured	wormseed	bisexual	disguise	fascicle	inscroll
strobila	throbbed	verecund	wormwood	bistable	dishevel	fasciola	insecure
strobile	thrombin	vergence	worthful	bistoury	disinter	fasciole	inserted
strobili	thrombus	verifier	worthily	bosseyed	disjoint	Fascista	insignia
stroller	throstle	veristic	yarmulka	bushbaby	disjunct	Fascisti	insolate
stromata	throttle	verjuice	zarzuela	bushbuck	dislodge	fashious	insolent
strongly	thrummed	vermouth	zirconia	bushfire	disloyal	fastback	insomnia
strontia	thruster	vernally	aasvogel	bushveld	dismally	fastener	insomuch
strophic	tireless	vernicle	abscissa	business	dismount	fastfood	insphere
stropped	tiresome	veronica	absentee	bustling	disorder	fastness	inspired
strucken	torchere	verrucae	absently	busybody	dispatch	fasttalk	inspirer
struggle	toreador	versicle	absinthe	busyness	dispense	fastuous	inspirit
strummed	toreutic	vertebra	absolute	bystreet	disperse	festally	instable
strummer	tornadic	vertexes	absolver	Casanova	dispirit	festival	instance
strumose	toroidal	vertical	absonant	cascabel	displace	fiscally	instancy
strumous	torpidly	vertices	absorber	casebook	displant	fishable	instinct
strumpet	torquate	verticil	absterge	casemate	displode	fishball	instruct
strutted	torridly	virement	abstract	casement	displume	fishbone	insulant
strutter	tortilla	virginal	abstrict	casework	disposal	fishbowl	insulate
surcease	tortious	Virginia	abstruse	cashbook	disposer	fishcake	insulter
surefire	tortoise	viricide	absurdly	cashmere	dispread	fishfarm	insurant
sureness	tortuous	viridian	aesthete	cassette	disprize	fishglue	issuable
surfacer	torturer	viridity	aestival	castaway	disproof	fishhawk	issuance
surfbird	Turanian	virilism	Alsatian	castiron	disprove	fishhook	jesuitic
surfboat	turbaned	virility	anserine	castrate	disquiet	fishless	jesuitry
surfduck	turbidly	virology	answerer	castrati	disseise	fishmeal	justness
surffish	turbinal	virtuosa	arsenate	castrato	disserve	fishpond	Kashmiri
surgical	turbofan	virtuosi	arsenide	casually	dissever	fishtail	kissable
suricate	turbojet	virtuoso	arsenite	casualty	dissolve	fishwife	kisscurl
surmisal	Turcoman	virtuous	arsonist	cesspool	dissuade	fissiped	lashings
surmiser	turgidly	virulent	arsonous	cislunar	distally	fistiana	listener
surmount	Turkoman	voracity	assassin	cosecant	distance	fistical	listless
surplice	turmeric	vortexes	assemble	cosiness	distaste	fistulae	luscious
surprise	turnable	vortical	assembly	cosmetic	distinct	fistular	lushness
surround	turnback	vortices	assenter	cosmical	distract	fosterer	lustrate
surroyal	turncoat	warcloud	assentor	costmary	distrain	fuselage	lustrine
surveyor	turncock	wardance	assertor	costplus	distrait	fusiform	lustring
survival	turndown	wardenry	assessor	costpush	distress	fusileer	lustrous
survivor	turnings	wardress	assiento	costumer	district	fusilier	lysosome
syringes	turnover	wardrobe	assignat	cushiony	distrust	gaselier	lysozyme
syrinxes	turnpike	wardroom	assignee	Cushitic	disunion	gasfired	mascaron
tarboosh	turnskin	wardship	assignor	cuspidor	disunite	gashouse	Masorete
tarlatan	turnsole	warhorse	assonant	cussedly	disunity	gaslight	Masoreth

massacre	musktree	rescript	unsocial	antennae	bathetic	detector	guttural
masseter	muslined	research	unsought	antennal	bathotic	deterred	hatchery
masseuse	musquash	resemble	unsprung	antennas	bathrobe	deterrer	hatching
massicot	mustache	reserved	unstable	antepost	bathroom	dethrone	hatchway
massless	mystical	resetter	unstably	anterior	battalia	detonate	hateable
masterly	mystique	resettle	unstated	anteroom	battleax	detoxify	hatstand
masthead	nasalise	resident	unsteady	anthelia	betacism	detrital	hetaerae
mastitis	nasality	residual	unstring	anthemia	betatron	detritus	hetairai
mastodon	nascence	residuum	unstrung	antheral	bethesda	ditheism	hitherto
mescalin	nascency	resigned	unstuffy	anthesis	betrayal	ditheist	hotchpot
mesdames	nescient	resinate	unsuited	anthozoa	betrayer	ditherer	hotelier
meshwork	nestling	resinify	unsunned	antibody	bitchily	dittybag	hothouse
mesially	noseband	resinoid	unswathe	antidote	bitingly	dittybox	hotplate
mesmeric	nosecone	resinous	upsetter	antihero	bitterly	dotation	hotpress
mesocarp	nosedive	resister	upsprang	antilogy	botanise	dotingly	intaglio
mesoderm	nosepipe	resistor	upspring	antimask	botanist	dotterel	intarsia
mesotron	nosering	resolute	upsprung	antimony	botflies	Dutchman	integral
Mesozoic	nosiness	resonant	upstairs	antinode	botryoid	dutiable	intended
mesquite	nosology	resonate	upstream	antinomy	bottomry	dutyfree	intently
messmate	observer	resorcin	upstroke	antiphon	botulism	dutypaid	interact
messuage	obsidian	resorter	Ursuline	antipode	botyrose	ectoderm	interbed
misalign	obsolete	resource	vascular	antipole	butchery	ectozoon	intercom
misapply	obstacle	respects	vasculum	antipope	buttoner	eftsoons	intercut
misbegot	obstruct	response	vasiform	antisera	buttress	entailer	interest
miscarry	oestrone	respring	vastness	antitype	butylene	entangle	interior
miscegen	oestrous	resprung	vesicant	antlered	butyrate	entellus	intermit
mischief	opsimath	restcure	vesicate	antrorse	catacomb	enterate	intermix
miscible	Ossianic	restless	vesperal	apterous	catalase	enthalpy	internal
miscount	pashalic	restorer	vespiary	aptitude	cataloes	enthrall	internee
misdealt	pashalik	restrain	vestiary	artefact	catalyse	enthrone	Interpol
misdoing	passable	restrict	vestment	arterial	catalyst	entirely	interred
misdoubt	passably	resupine	vesturer	artesian	catamite	entirety	interrex
miserere	passbook	resurvey	vesuvian	artfully	catapult	entoderm	intersex
misgiven	passerby	rosarian	viscacha	articled	cataract	entoptic	intertie
misguide	passible	rosebowl	visceral	artifact	catchall	entozoic	interval
misheard	Passover	rosebush	viscidly	artifice	catchfly	entozoon	interwar
mishmash	passport	rosefish	viscount	artistic	catching	entracte	inthrall
Mishnaic	password	roseleaf	Visigoth	artistry	catechol	entrails	intimacy
misjudge	pastiche	rosemary	visional	astatine	category	entrance	intimate
mismatch	pastille	roseolar	visitant	asterisk	catenary	entreaty	intimism
misnomer	pastoral	rosepink	visually	asterism	catenate	entrench	intitule
misogamy	pastrami	roseroot	washable	asteroid	cateress	entrepot	intonate
misogyny	pastries	rosetree	washbowl	asthenia	catering	entresol	intrados
misology	pastural	rosewood	washroom	asthenic	cathedra	esterify	intrench
misplace	piscator	rosiness	wastable	astonied	catheter	estimate	intrepid
misprint	piscinae	rostrate	wasteful	astonish	cathexes	Estonian	intrigue
misprise	pishogue	rosulate	Wesleyan	astragal	cathexis	estopped	intromit
misprize	pisiform	rushhour	westerly	astutely	cathodal	estoppel	introrse
misquote	pisolite	rushlike	westward	attender	cathodic	estovers	intruder
misshape	position	rustical	wiseacre	attested	catholic	estrange	intubate
missilry	positive	rustless	wiseness	attester	cationic	estuaril	iotacism
misspell	positron	sashcord	wishbone	attestor	catsfoot	eutectic	isthmian
misspelt	posology	Sassanid	wishwash	atticism	catstail	eutrophy	jetblack
misspend	possible	sesamoid	wistaria	attitude	cattleya	extender	jetplane
misspent	possibly	sesterce	wisteria	attorney	cetacean	extensor	jettison
misstate	postcard	sisterly	yestreen	attrited	chthonic	exterior	katakana
mistaken	postcode	suspense	actiniae	autacoid	citation	external	latchkey
misthink	postdate	susurrus	actinian	autarchy	citified	extolled	lateness
mistreat	postfree	systemic	actinias	autarkic	cityfied	extrados	latently
mistress	posthorn	systolic	actinide	autistic	cotenant	extremes	laterite
mistrial	postiche	taskwork	actinism	autobahn	cothurni	extrorse	Latinate
mistrust	postlude	tasselly	actinium	autocade	cotillon	fatalism	latinise
misusage	postmark	tastebud	activate	autocrat	cotquean	fatalist	Latinism
miswrite	postmill	tasteful	actively	autodafe	Cotswold	fatality	Latinist
moshavim	postobit	tesserae	activism	autodyne	cottager	fatherly	latinity
mosquito	postpaid	tesseral	activist	autogamy	cottagey	fatigues	latitant
mossback	postpone	testable	activity	autogiro	cuteness	fatstock	latitude
muscadel	postural	testator	actually	autogyro	cutprice	fattener	latterly
muscatel	posturer	testatum	actuator	autolyse	cutpurse	fetching	latticed
muscling	pushball	testtube	acturial	automata	cutwater	feticide	lethally
muscular	pushbike	tussocky	although	automate	cytidine	fitfully	lethargy
mushroom	pushcart	unsaddle	altitude	autonomy	cytology	futilely	lettered
musicale	pushover	unsealed	altruism	autosome	cytosine	futility	literacy
musician	pushpull	unseated	altruist	autotomy	dateless	futurism	literary
musingly	pussycat	unseeded	anteater	autotype	dateline	futurist	literate
muskdeer	pustular	unseeing	antecede	autumnal	detached	futurity	literati
muskduck	rascally	unseemly	antedate	autunite	detailed	gatefold	litharge
musketry	rashness	unsettle	antefixa	Batavian	detainee	gatepost	litigant
muskrose	rasorial	unshaped	antelope	bateleur	detainer	gatherer	litigate

littlego	natively	outshine	retailer	ultraism	aquarium	crucifix	fluttery
littling	nativism	outshone	retainer	ultraist	aquatint	crueller	fougasse
littoral	nativist	outsider	retarded	untangle	aqueduct	crumhorn	foulness
liturgic	nativity	outsight	retarder	untapped	aquiline	crummock	founding
lothario	naturism	outsmart	retiarii	untaught	avulsion	crusader	fountain
lutanist	naturist	outspend	reticent	untented	baudrons	crustily	fourball
lutecium	nitrogen	outspent	reticule	untether	bauxitic	cruzeiro	foureyes
lutenist	notarial	outstare	retiform	unthread	blubbery	daughter	fourfold
lutetium	notation	outstrip	retinula	unthrift	bludgeon	deucedly	fourleaf
Lutheran	notching	outvalue	retiring	unthrone	bluebell	deuteron	fourpart
matamata	notebook	outvying	retorted	untidily	bluebird	diuresis	foursome
matchbox	notecase	outwards	retrench	untimely	bluechip	diuretic	fourstar
matelote	noteless	outwatch	retrieve	untitled	bluecoat	douanier	fourteen
material	notional	outweigh	retroact	untoward	bluefish	doubloon	fourthly
materiel	notornis	outworks	retrorse	upthrown	blueness	doubtful	fructify
maternal	nutarian	oxtongue	ritually	upthrust	bluenose	doughboy	fructose
matgrass	nutation	patagium	Rotarian	urticant	blueweed	doughnut	frugally
matiness	nutbrown	patchily	rotation	urticate	blurrily	doumpalm	fruitage
matrices	nuthatch	patellae	rotative	vitalise	blurring	dourness	fruitbat
matrixes	nuthouse	patellar	rotatory	vitalism	blushful	drubbing	fruitery
matronal	nutrient	patentee	rotenone	vitalist	blustery	drudgery	fruitfly
matronly	nutshell	patently	rottenly	vitality	bouffant	drugging	fruitful
mattress	oatgrass	patentor	rotundly	vitellin	boughten	druggist	fruition
maturate	obtainer	paternal	roturier	vitellus	bouillon	druidess	frumenty
maturely	obtected	pathetic	rutabaga	vitiable	bouncily	druidism	frumpish
maturity	obturate	pathless	ruthless	vitiator	bouncing	drumfire	frustule
metalled	obtusely	pathogen	rutilant	vitiligo	boundary	drumhead	frutices
metallic	obtusity	patience	satanism	vitreous	bourgeon	drumming	Gaullism
metamere	octarchy	patronal	satanist	vituline	boursier	drummock	Gaullist
metaphor	octaroon	pattypan	sateless	votaress	bourtree	drumroll	gauntlet
metayage	octonary	patulous	satiable	votarist	boutique	drunkard	glucagon
metazoan	octoroon	petaline	satiably	voteless	bouzouki	drupelet	glucinum
metazoon	ofttimes	petalled	satirise	watchdog	brunette	educable	glummest
meteoric	oiticica	petalody	satirist	watchful	brushoff	educated	glumness
methanol	ontogeny	petaloid	saturant	watchkey	brutally	educator	glutting
methinks	ontology	petalous	saturate	watchman	caudally	educible	gluttony
methodic	optative	petechia	Saturday	waterage	caudated	eduction	gourmand
methylic	optician	petiolar	saturnic	waterbed	caudexes	emulator	goutweed
methysis	optimise	petioled	setscrew	waterbus	caudices	emulgent	goutwort
metonymy	optimism	petition	sitarist	watergas	caudillo	emulsify	grubbily
metrical	optimist	petrolic	sithence	waterice	cauldron	emulsion	grubbing
Mithraic	optional	petronel	sitology	watering	causally	emulsive	grudging
mitigant	orthicon	petrosal	situated	waterish	causerie	emulsoid	gruesome
mitigate	orthodox	pettifog	sitzbath	waterlog	causeway	enuresis	grumbler
mittened	orthoepy	petulant	soterial	waterloo	cautious	enuretic	grumpily
mittimus	osteitis	petuntse	tattered	waterman	chugging	equalise	gruntled
mitzvoth	ostinato	phthalic	tattooer	waterski	chummily	equality	haulyard
mothball	ostracod	phthisic	tetanise	waterway	chumming	equalled	haunting
motherly	ostracon	phthisis	tetchily	watthour	chupatti	equation	hausfrau
motility	ostrakon	pitiable	tetradic	wetlands	chupatty	equinity	hourlong
motional	ottavino	pitiably	tetragon	wetnurse	churchly	equipage	houseboy
motivate	outboard	pitiless	tetrapla	wettable	churinga	equipped	housedog
motivity	outbound	pittance	tetrapod	witchelm	churlish	equitant	housefly
motorail	outbrave	pitviper	tetrarch	witchery	churning	equities	houseful
motorcar	outbreak	potassic	titanate	witchety	chutzpah	equivoke	houseman
motorial	outburst	potation	titaness	witching	clubbing	eruption	housetop
motoring	outcaste	potbelly	titanism	withdraw	clubfoot	eruptive	inundate
motorise	outclass	potbound	titanite	withdrew	clubhaul	esurient	inurbane
motorist	outdated	potently	titanium	withheld	clubland	evulsion	jaundice
motorium	outdoors	potholer	tithable	withhold	clueless	exaltant	jauntily
motorman	outdrawn	pothouse	titivate	yataghan	clumsily	exuviate	jiujitsu
motormen	outfield	potlatch	titmouse	abundant	clupeoid	faubourg	khuskhus
motorway	outflank	potplant	tittuped	abutilon	clustery	faultily	kourbash
mottling	outgoing	potroast	tittuppy	abutment	couchant	faunally	krumhorn
mutation	outgrown	potsherd	totalise	abuttals	couching	Faustian	laudable
mutchkin	outguess	potstill	totality	abutting	couldest	fauteuil	laudably
muteness	outHerod	potstone	totalled	aculeate	coulisse	feudally	laudanum
muticous	outhouse	potterer	totemism	adularia	coumarin	flubbing	laudator
mutilate	outlawry	putative	totemist	adulator	countess	fluellin	laughing
mutineer	outlying	putridly	totterer	adultery	coupling	fluently	laughter
mutinous	outmatch	pythonic	tutelage	aduncate	courante	fluepipe	launcher
mutterer	outmoded	rataplan	tutelary	aduncous	coursing	fluidics	laureate
mutually	outpoint	rateable	tutorage	aguishly	courtesy	fluidify	leucitic
mythical	outrange	ratguard	tutoress	alumroot	courtier	fluidise	loudness
natality	outreach	ratifier	tutorial	amusedly	couscous	fluidity	louvered
natation	outreign	rational	ulterior	aquacade	cousinly	flummery	moufflon
natatory	outrider	ratsbane	ultimacy	aqualung	cruciate	fluoride	moulding
nathless	outright	ratstail	ultimata	aquanaut	crucible	fluorine	mountain
national	outrival	rattling	ultimate	aquarist	crucifer	fluorite	mounting

```
mournful  scurrile  squirely  advocacy  invected  reviewer  howitzer  foxiness
mourning  scurvily  squirrel  advocate  inveigle  reviling  inwardly  foxshark
mouseear  scutcher  squirter  advowson  inventor  revision  jewelled  hexagram
moussaka  scutella  stubbing  alveolar  inverted  revisory  jeweller  hexapody
mouthful  shuddery  stubborn  alveolus  inverter  revivify  lawcourt  hexylene
naumachy  shuffler  stubnail  Bavarian  investor  revolter  lawfully  laxative
nauplius  shunning  stuccoes  bevelled  inviable  revolute  lawgiver  lixivium
nauseant  shutdown  studbook  beveller  inviting  revolver  lawmaker  luxation
nauseate  shutting  studding  beverage  invocate  rivalled  lawyerly  maxillae
nauseous  skullcap  studfarm  bivalent  involute  rivelled  lewdness  maximise
nautical  slubbing  studious  cavalier  Javanese  riverain  lewisite  myxomata
nautilus  slugabed  studwork  cavatina  jovially  riverbed  lowering  nextdoor
neurally  sluggard  stuffily  caverned  juvenile  riverine  lowgrade  pixieish
neuritic  slugging  stuffing  cavesson  lavalava  riverman  lowlevel  pixiness
neuritis  sluggish  stultify  cavicorn  lavation  riverway  lowlying  pyxidium
neuronal  slumbery  stumbler  cavilled  lavatory  savagely  mowburnt  saxatile
neuronic  slumming  stumming  caviller  lavender  savagery  newblown  Saxondom
neuroses  slurring  stumpily  civilian  laverock  savannah  newcomer  Saxonism
neurosis  sluttish  stunning  civilise  lavishly  savorous  newfound  Saxonist
neurotic  smudgily  stunsail  civility  levanter  Savoyard  newlywed  sexiness
neutrino  smuggler  stuntman  covalent  levelled  severely  newscast  sexology
noumenal  smugness  stupidly  covenant  leveller  severity  newsheet  sextette
noumenon  smuttily  stuprate  coverage  leverage  sovranty  newspeak  sextuple
nouvelle  snubbing  sturdied  coverall  leviable  taverner  newsreel  sexually
ocularly  snuffbox  sturdily  covering  levigate  tovarish  newsroom  sixpence
opulence  snuffers  sturgeon  coverlet  levirate  unvalued  nowadays  sixpenny
opuscula  snuffler  tautness  covertly  levitate  unversed  pawnshop  sixtieth
opuscule  snuffles  tautomer  covetous  levulose  unvoiced  powdered  taxation
pluckily  snuggery  tautonym  deviance  liveable  vavasory  powerful  taxingly
plugging  snugness  Teutonic  deviancy  liveborn  vavasour  rawboned  taxonomy
plumaged  souchong  thudding  deviator  livelily  vivacity  rewaking  taxpayer
plumbago  soulless  thuggery  deviling  livelong  vivarium  rewarder  textbook
plumbate  soundbow  thuggism  devilish  liveried  vivifier  rowdyish  texthand
plumbing  soundbox  thumbpot  devilism  liverish  vivisect  rowdyism  textuary
plumbism  sounding  thumping  devilkin  livewire  waveband  sawbones  textural
plumelet  sourdine  thundery  devilled  lividity  waveform  sawedged  textured
plumiped  sourness  thurible  deviltry  lovebird  waveless  sawedoff  toxaemia
plumpish  sourpuss  thurifer  Devonian  loveknot  waviness  sawframe  toxaemic
plumular  soutache  Thursday  devotion  loveless  atwitter  sawhorse  toxicant
plurally  southern  thusness  devourer  lovelily  bewigged  sawtooth  toxicity
plussage  southing  touchily  devoutly  lovelock  bewilder  sewellel  vexation
plutonic  southpaw  touching  divagate  lovelorn  biweekly  sewerage  vexillum
pluvious  Southron  toughish  divalent  lovenest  bowfront  sewergas  vixenish
poultice  souvenir  touristy  divebomb  loveseat  bowsprit  sewerrat  waxberry
poundage  spunkily  tournure  dividend  lovesick  cowardly  sowbread  waxcloth
pounding  spurgear  truantry  dividivi  lovesome  cowberry  tawdrily  waxiness
pourable  spurious  truckage  dividual  lovesong  cowgrass  thwacker  waxlight
prudence  spurling  trucking  divinely  lovingly  coworker  thwarter  waxworks
pruinose  spurrier  truckler  divinise  maverick  dewberry  thwartly  adynamia
prunella  spurring  trueblue  divinity  moveable  dewiness  towardly  adynamic
prunelle  squabble  trueborn  division  moveless  dewpoint  towelled  amygdala
prunello  squadron  truebred  divisive  movement  dewyeyed  townhall  anyplace
prurient  squaller  truelove  divorcee  movingly  dowdyish  township  anything
pruritic  squamate  trueness  dovecote  navigate  dowelled  townsman  anywhere
pruritus  squamose  truistic  dovetail  novation  downbeat  unwanted  asyndeta
Prussian  squamous  trumeaux  envelope  novelise  downcast  unwarily  atypical
reusable  squamule  trumpery  enviable  novelist  downcome  unwashed  bayadere
roughage  squander  truncate  enviably  November  downfall  unweaned  bayberry
roughdry  squarely  trunnion  environs  novercal  downhaul  unwieldy  biyearly
roughhew  squarish  trussing  envisage  pavement  downhill  unwisdom  boyishly
roughish  squarson  trustful  envision  pavilion  downland  unwisely  bryology
rouleaus  squasher  trustily  favonian  pivotman  downmost  unwished  bryozoan
rouleaux  squatted  truthful  favoured  ravelled  downpipe  unwonted  clypeate
roulette  squatter  usufruct  favourer  ravenous  downpour  unwordly  cryogeny
roundarm  squawker  usurious  feverfew  ravisher  downtime  unworthy  cryolite
rounders  squawman  uvularly  feverish  revanche  downtown  upwardly  cryostat
roundish  squeaker  uvulitis  feverous  revealer  downturn  vowelise  cryotron
roundtop  squealer  vaulting  fivefold  reveille  downward  vowelled  daybreak
saucebox  squeedge  vauntful  fivestar  revelled  downwind  boxpleat  daydream
saucepan  squeegee  voussoir  foveolae  reveller  fewtrils  coxalgia  daylight
saunders  squeezer  wouldest  gavelock  revenant  fowlpest  coxswain  dryclean
sauouari  squelchy  woundily  giveaway  revenger  gownsman  dextrine  drynurse
sauropod  squibbed  youngest  governor  reverend  Hawaiian  dextrose  dryplate
Sauterne  squidded  youngish  havelock  reverser  hawfinch  dextrous  drypoint
scudding  squiggle  yourself  havildar  reversal  hawkeyed  doxology  drystone
scullery  squiggly  youthful  havocked  reverser  hawklike  fixation  Egyptian
scullion  squilgee  advanced  hoverfly  reverter  hawkmoth  fixative  epyllion
sculptor  squinter  advisory  invasion  revetted  hawkweed  foxglove  erythema
scumming  squireen  advocaat  invasive  reviewal  hawthorn  foxhound  flyblown
```

```
flypaper mazarine autarchy cavalier divagate floatage insanely megapode
flywheel Mazdaism autarkic cavatina divalent floating insanity megawatt
glycerin mazement aviarist ceramics donation focalise intaglio melamine
glycerol maziness aviation ceramist Donatism foramina intarsia melanism
glyceryl mezereon aviatrix cerastes Donatist freakish invasion melanite
glycogen Nazarene aweather ceratoid donative freakout invasive menarche
glyconic Nazarite axiality cetacean donatory fugacity inwardly metalled
glyptics Nazirite balanced cheapish dotation fumarole iotacism metallic
hayfield ooziness balancer chiasmus douanier gadabout Islamise metamere
haymaker pizzeria banality chiastic dreadful gadarene Islamism metaphor
haystack sizeable banausic cicatrix dreamful galactic Islamite metayage
idyllist sizzling barathea citation dreamily galangal islander metazoan
joyfully suzerain basaltic cleancut dreaming gelastic Japanese metazoon
joyously syzygial Batavian cleaning drearily gelatine japanned minacity
joystick unzipped Bavarian cleanser durables gelation Javanese minatory
keyboard vizarded bayadere clearcut duration gematria jobation misalign
keystone vizcacha becalmed clearing durative geraniol Jonathan misapply
klystron wizardly bedabble clearway dynamics geranium Judaical modalism
layabout wizardry bedazzle cleavage dynamism gigantic Judaiser modalist
layshaft ———————— befallen cleavers dynamist girasole Jurassic modality
laystall Abbaside bejabers cobaltic dynamite gleaning kalaazar Moharram
laywoman abbatial belabour cofactor dynastic gloaming Kanarese molality
loyalist ablation betacism colander dynatron godawful katakana molarity
mayapple ablative betatron comatose elfarrow Graafian keratose molasses
mayoress abradant bibation conation embalmer greasily lamasery monachal
Mayqueen abrasion bifacial conative embattle Gujarati lavalava monadism
Odyssean abrasive bigamist coracoid empathic gynandry lavation monandry
olympiad Accadian bigamous covalent encaenia gyration lavatory monarchy
Olympian adiantum bilabial cowardly endamage gyratory laxative monastic
onychite adjacent bimanous coxalgia endanger habanera layabout monaural
oxymoron adnation binaural creakily engaging Halachah Lazarist monaxial
oxytocin advanced bioassay creamery enlarger halation legalese monazite
payphone aeration biparous creatine ensample hamartia legalise morainic
paysheet agnation bivalent creation entailer harakiri legalism moralise
phyletic agraphia bleacher creative entangle harangue legalist moralism
phyllary agrarian bleakish creatrix equalise harasser legality moralist
phyllode Akkadian blearily creature equality Hawaiian legatine morality
phylloid albacore boracite croakily equalled hecatomb legation moratory
phyllome Albanian botanise Croatian equation hepatica levanter Moravian
physical alcahest botanist cubature errantly hepatise libation Muharram
physicky aleatory breakage curarine errantry heraldic libatory mutation
physique alkahest breaking curarise escalade heraldry ligament nasalise
pryingly alkalies breakout curassow escalate hetaerae ligation nasality
psychics alkaline breasted curative escallop hetairai ligature natality
psychism alkalify breather cymatium escalope hexagram lobation natation
psychist alkaloid Briarean dahabieh escapade hexapody localise natatory
ptyalism almagest broacher damassin escapism hijacker localism Nazarene
rhyolite almanack broadish debagged escapist hilarity locality Nazarite
rhythmic Alsatian broadway debarred escargot himation locative negation
royalism amiantus bubaline decadent escarole Horatian loyalist negative
royalist annalist cabalism decagram espalier hulahula lunarian negatory
sayonara aphasiac cabalist decanter essayist humanely lunation negatron
skylight apiarian caballed delation eucalypt humanise lutanist nematode
skypilot apiarist cadastre demagogy eulachon humanism luxation nematoid
skyscape aplastic calabash demander eupatrid humanist macaroni Nepalese
skywards appalled caladium demarche Eurasian humanity macaroon nodalise
slyboots appanage calamary denarius excavate humanoid madapple nodality
spyglass apparent calamine denature exhalant hydatoid magazine nodation
stylised aquacade calamint denazify expander idealess maharaja nomadise
thyroxin aqualung calamite departed faradaic idealise maharani nomadism
thyrsoid aquanaut calamity deration faradism idealism Malagasy notarial
tryingly aquarist Canadian detached fatalism idealist malamute notation
voyageur aquarium canaille detailed fatalist ideality malapert novation
wayfarer aquatint canalise detainee fatality ideation malaprop nowadays
waygoing arbalest canaster detainer fedayeen illation malarial nugatory
wrymouth arbalist capacity dicacity filagree illative malarian nutarian
bezonian Arcadian carabine didactic filament immanent malarkey nutation
buzzword Arianism caracara didapper filariae immature marabout oakapple
cozenage Armagnac caracole digamist filarial impacted marasmic oblation
doziness armament carapace digamous filature impanate marasmus oblatory
enzootic armature Casanova dilatant finalise imparity marathon obtainer
gazogene arranger catacomb dilation finalism indagate marauder occasion
gazpacho arrantly catalase dilative finalist infamise maravedi octarchy
hazelnut assassin cataloes dilatory finality infamous matamata octaroon
haziness astatine catalyse disabuse fixation infantry mayapple oleander
Lazarist atlantes catalyst disagree fixative ingather mazarine oleaster
laziness Atlantic catamite disallow fleabane inhalant medalled ommateum
lazulite audacity catapult disarray fleabite inlander medallic oogamous
lazurite autacoid cataract disaster fleawort innately megalith optative
```

Orcadian	ranarian	scrawler	stranded	unearned	zonation	fogbound	rabbinic
ordainer	ranarium	sedately	stranger	uneasily	zygaenid	forborne	rabbiter
organdie	rapacity	sedation	strangle	unfading	airborne	frabjous	rabbitry
organise	rataplan	sedative	strapoil	unfairly	airbrake	fribbler	rambling
organism	recapped	seladang	strapped	unfasten	airbrush	furbelow	rambutan
organist	redactor	semantic	strapper	ungainly	alebench	gabbroic	rawboned
orgasmic	regalism	senarius	strategy	uniaxial	anabases	gabbroid	reabsorb
orgastic	regality	sepaloid	stratify	unlawful	anabasis	galbanum	redblind
ornament	rehandle	sepalous	stravaig	unmanned	anabatic	gambados	redbrick
ornately	relation	separate	subacute	unmarked	anabolic	gambeson	ribbonry
ottavino	relative	seraglio	subagent	unpaired	bambinos	gambroon	rimbrake
paganise	relaxant	seraphic	subahdar	unsaddle	barbaric	garboard	rubbishy
paganish	remanent	seraphim	Sudanese	untangle	barbecue	gerbille	sabbatic
paganism	repairer	sesamoid	sudarium	untapped	barberry	glabella	sawbones
palatial	repartee	sheading	sudatory	untaught	barbette	glabrous	scabbard
palatine	retailer	shealing	swearing	unvalued	barbican	glibness	scabious
papalise	retainer	shrapnel	sybarite	unwanted	barbital	globally	scabrous
papalism	retarded	Sinaitic	sycamine	unwarily	bayberry	globular	seaboard
papalist	retarder	sinapism	sycamore	unwashed	beebread	globulin	seaborne
parabola	revanche	skiagram	synapsis	uplander	berberis	grabbing	shabbily
paradigm	rewaking	sleazily	synaptic	upwardly	bilberry	grabbler	shabrack
paradise	rewarder	sneakily	synastry	urbanely	bimbashi	grubbily	Shabuoth
paraffin	ribaldry	sneakish	tagalong	urbanise	blabbing	grubbing	slabbing
paragoge	rigadoon	socalled	talapoin	urbanism	blubbery	herbaria	slobbery
parakeet	riparian	sodalite	tamandua	urbanist	bobbinet	herbless	slobbish
parallax	rivalled	sodalite	tamanoir	urbanite	bobbypin	hobbitry	slobland
parallel	rocaille	sodality	tamarack	urbanity	bobbysox	hobbyist	slubbing
paralyse	rogation	solander	tamarind	vacantly	bombsite	iceblink	slyboots
paramour	rogatory	solanine	tamarisk	vacation	bribable	icebound	snobbery
paranoia	romancer	solarise	taxation	vagabond	Burberry	isabella	snobbish
paranoid	Romanian	solarism	tenacity	valanced	Cambrian	isobaric	snobbism
paraquat	romanise	solarist	tenacula	vanadate	carbolic	jabberer	snubbing
parasang	Romanism	solarium	tenaille	vanadium	carbonic	jamboree	sombrely
parasite	Romanist	solation	tenantry	vanadous	carbonyl	jetblack	sombrero
paravane	Romansch	solatium	teraphim	varactor	carboxyl	keyboard	sombrous
patagium	romantic	somatism	teratoma	vavasory	carburet	lambaste	sowbread
pedagogy	rosarian	sonatina	tetanise	vavasour	clubbing	lambency	stabbing
pedalier	Rotarian	speaking	thearchy	Vedantic	clubfoot	lamblike	stabling
pedalled	rotation	spearman	thiamine	velamina	clubhaul	lambskin	stablish
pedantic	rotative	sphagnum	thraldom	velarium	clubland	lapboard	stibnite
pedantry	rotatory	splasher	thrasher	venality	cobblers	larboard	stubbing
Pegasean	royalism	splatter	thrawart	venation	combings	leeboard	stubborn
Pelagian	royalist	spraints	thwacker	veracity	cowberry	legbreak	stubnail
Pelasgic	Rumanian	sprawler	thwarter	verandah	crabbing	limbless	subbasal
penalise	Rumansch	spraygun	thwartly	veratrin	cribbage	lobbyist	sunbaked
petaline	runabout	squabble	titanate	veratrum	cribbing	lubberly	sunbathe
petalled	runagate	squadron	titaness	vexation	Cumbrian	lumberer	sunblind
petalody	ruralise	squaller	titanism	vicarage	cumbrous	marbling	sunburnt
petaloid	ruralism	squamate	titanite	vicarate	cupboard	membered	sunburst
petalous	ruralist	squamose	titanium	vicarial	daybreak	membrane	swabbing
pheasant	rurality	squamous	tomahawk	vitalise	dewberry	midbrain	swobbing
phrasing	rutabaga	squamule	tomalley	vitalism	diabasic	misbegot	symbiont
picaroon	sagacity	squander	tonality	vitalist	diabetes	morbidly	symbolic
picayune	sagamore	squarely	totalise	vitality	diabetic	morbific	tamboura
pilaster	salacity	squarish	totality	vivacity	diabolic	mowburnt	tarboosh
pinafore	salariat	squarson	totalled	vivarium	disbench	mulberry	teaboard
pinaster	salaried	squasher	tovarish	vizarded	disbound	myoblast	teabread
pirarucu	samarium	squatted	towardly	vocalise	disburse	newblown	teabreak
pleading	sanative	squatter	toxaemia	vocalism	dogberry	nimbused	tiebreak
pleasant	sanatory	squawker	toxaemic	vocalist	doubloon	numberer	timbered
pleasing	saraband	squawman	treacher	vocality	doubtful	numbfish	tolbooth
pleasure	satanism	steadily	treadler	vocation	drabbler	numbness	tombless
pliantly	satanist	steading	treasure	vocative	drabness	nutbrown	trabeate
podagral	savagely	stealing	treasury	volatile	dribbler	offbreak	tribally
podagric	savagery	stealthy	treatise	voracity	dribblet	olibanum	tribasic
polarise	savannah	steamily	trialist	votaress	drubbing	outboard	tribrach
polarity	saxatile	stearate	triangle	votarist	dumbbell	outbound	tribunal
pomander	sciagram	stearine	triarchy	voyageur	dumbhead	outbrave	tumbling
potassic	sciatica	steatite	Triassic	Wahabism	dumbness	outbreak	turbaned
potation	scrabble	strabism	triaxial	Wahabite	dumbshow	outburst	turbidly
preacher	scragend	straddle	truantry	wheatear	dybbukim	pegboard	turbinal
preamble	scragged	straggle	Turanian	wizardly	epiblast	pembroke	turbofan
priapism	scramble	straggly	tyrannic	wizardry	faubourg	plebeian	turbojet
ptyalism	scrammed	straight	unbacked	womanise	feeblish	potbelly	unabated
puparial	scrannel	strained	unbarred	womanish	fenberry	potbound	vambrace
puparium	scraping	strainer	uncalled	wreathen	fimbriae	probable	verbally
pupation	scrapped	straiten	uncandid	yataghan	flabella	probably	verbatim
putative	scrapper	straitly	uncapped	zabaione	flubbing	purblind	verbiage
queasily	scratchy	stramash	uncaused	zoiatria	flyblown	quibbler	verboten

waxberry
zombiism
abacuses
abscissa
aciculae
acicular
aciculas
aircraft
alacrity
amicable
amicably
anaconda
anecdote
anechoic
aniconic
apically
apocrine
araceous
arachnid
armchair
baccarat
bacchant
beechnut
berceuse
biocidal
bitchily
blackboy
blackcap
blackfly
blacking
blackish
blackleg
blackout
blacktie
blacktop
blockade
blockage
blockish
bracelet
brachial
brachium
brackish
bracteal
bractlet
brickbat
brickred
brocaded
brocatel
broccoli
brochure
buncombe
butchery
calcanea
calcaria
calcific
calcitic
calcspar
calctuff
calculus
cancrine
cancroid
carcajou
carcanet
cascabel
catchall
catchfly
catching
cercaria
chaconne
checkers
checkout
chickpea
cinchona
cincture
Circaean
circuity
circular
coachdog
coachman

coaction
coactive
coccyges
concasse
conceder
conceive
concerti
concerto
concetti
concetto
conchate
conchoid
conclave
conclude
concrete
couchant
couching
crackers
cracking
crackjaw
cracknel
crackpot
croceate
crockery
crocoite
cruciate
crucible
crucifer
crucifix
curculio
dabchick
dancette
dancetty
describe
deucedly
diaconal
diocesan
disciple
disclaim
disclose
discount
discover
discreet
discrete
discrown
dracaena
drachmae
drachmai
drachmas
draconic
dryclean
dulciana
dulcimer
Dulcinea
Dutchman
edacious
educable
educated
educator
educible
eduction
ejection
ejective
election
elective
electret
electric
electron
electrum
emaciate
enaction
enactive
ensconce
epically
epicalyx
epicotyl
epicycle
erectile
erection

evacuant
evacuate
evection
eviction
exacting
exaction
execrate
executor
exocrine
falcated
falchion
falconer
falconet
falconry
fanciful
fancyman
farcical
fascicle
fasciola
fasciole
Fascista
Fascisti
fencible
fetching
fiscally
flection
flickery
floccose
floccule
flocculi
flockbed
forcedly
forcefed
forceful
forcible
forcibly
fraction
fracture
friction
frocking
fructify
fructose
function
furcated
furculae
furcular
gimcrack
glaciate
glucagon
glucinum
glycerin
glycerol
glyceryl
glycogen
glyconic
godchild
Golconda
graceful
gracioso
gracious
guacharo
hatchery
hatching
hatchway
henchman
Hercules
hiccough
hotchpot
hyacinth
icecream
idocrase
inaction
inactive
inoculum
inscient
inscribe
inscroll
isocheim
isocracy

junction
juncture
kerchief
knackery
knickers
knocking
knockout
laically
lancelet
larcener
latchkey
lawcourt
leucitic
linchpin
luncheon
luscious
lynchpin
Maecenas
mancando
manciple
marchesa
marchese
mascaron
matchbox
merchant
merciful
mercuric
mescalin
miscarry
miscegen
mischief
miscible
miscount
moccasin
muscadel
muscatel
muscling
muscular
mutchkin
narceine
narcissi
narcoses
narcosis
narcotic
nascence
nascency
nescient
newcomer
Noachian
nonclaim
notching
oilcloth
onychite
oracular
outcaste
outclass
pancreas
parcener
parclose
patchily
peaceful
peacocky
peccable
peccancy
penchant
perceive
piacular
piecrust
pilchard
pincenez
pinchers
piscator
piscinae
placable
placably
placeman
placenta
placidly
plectrum

pluckily
practice
practise
precinct
precious
preclude
proceeds
proclaim
procurer
psychics
psychism
psychist
puncheon
punctate
punctual
puncture
purchase
quackery
quackish
Quechuan
quickset
ranchero
ranchman
rascally
reactant
reaction
reactive
reoccupy
rescript
runcible
saccadic
saccular
sacculus
sanctify
sanction
sanctity
sarcenet
saucebox
saucepan
seachest
seacoast
seacraft
seicento
selcouth
shocking
sinciput
smocking
snackbar
sorcerer
souchong
spacebar
spaceman
spacious
speciate
specific
specimen
specious
spectral
spectrum
specular
speculum
spicated
spiccato
spicebox
spicknel
spiculae
spicular
spiculum
staccato
stickful
stickily
stickjaw
stickler
stoccado
stoccata
stockade
stockcar
stockily
stocking

stockish
stockist
stockman
stockpot
stuccoes
subclass
succinct
succinic
succinum
succubae
succubus
suicidal
surcease
syncline
syncopal
syncytia
teacaddy
teachest
teaching
teacloth
teocalli
tetchily
thickety
thickish
thickset
tincture
torchere
touchily
touching
tracheae
tracheal
tracheid
trachoma
trachyte
trackage
tracking
trackman
trackway
tractate
traction
tractive
trecento
trichina
trichite
trichoid
trichome
trichord
trickery
trickily
trickish
tricorne
tricycle
trochaic
trochili
trochlea
trochoid
truckage
trucking
truckler
Turcoman
unicycle
urochord
vaccinal
vaccinia
vascular
vasculum
vincible
vinculum
viscacha
visceral
viscidly
viscount
vizcacha
voicebox
voiceful
volcanic
volcanos
vulcanic
warcloud

watchdog
watchful
watchkey
watchman
waxcloth
whacking
witchelm
witchery
witchety
witching
wrackful
wreckage
zecchini
zecchino
zinckify
zincking
zirconia
zucchini
aardvark
aardwolf
abidance
academia
academic
acidfast
acidhead
acidosis
agedness
amadavat
apodoses
apodosis
avadavat
avidness
baldhead
baldness
baldpate
bandanna
bandeaux
banderol
banditry
banditti
bandsman
baudrons
beadroll
beadsman
beadwork
biddable
bindweed
birdbath
birdcage
birdcall
birdlime
birdseed
birdseye
bladdery
bludgeon
boldface
boldness
bondmaid
bondmans
bondsman
Bordeaux
bordello
borderer
Bradshaw
Buddhism
Buddhist
buddleia
bundling
candidly
cardamom
cardamum
cardigan
cardinal
caudally
caudated
caudexes
caudices
caudillo
cladding

cloddish
clodpole
clodpoll
coldness
condense
condylar
cordless
cordovan
corduroy
cordwain
cordwood
cradling
credence
credenza
credible
credibly
credited
creditor
culdesac
dandruff
dandyish
dandyism
daydream
deadbeat
deadener
deadfall
deadhead
deadline
deadlock
deadness
deadwood
deedless
dendrite
dendroid
doddered
dodderer
doldrums
dowdyish
drudgery
dundiver
duodenal
duodenum
epidemic
epidural
erodible
evadable
evidence
falderal
fandance
fandango
feedback
feedhead
feedpipe
feedtank
feldsher
feldspar
feudally
fiddling
foldaway
foldboat
folderol
fondling
fondness
foodless
fordable
fordoing
gardener
gardenia
gardyloo
gendarme
geodesic
geodetic
gladdest
gladding
gladhand
gladioli
gladness
gladsome
goadster

```
Goidelic  headwind  misdoubt  sardonic  voidance  Airedale  attester  celeriac
golddust  headword  mondaine  sardonyx  voidness  aldehyde  attestor  celerity
goldenly  headwork  mordancy  scudding  wanderer  alderman  aurelian  cemetery
goldfish  hebdomad  murderer  seadrome  wanderoo  Alderney  axletree  cerebral
goldfoil  heedless  needfire  seedcake  wardance  alienage  balefire  cerebrum
goldleaf  herdbook  needless  seedcase  wardenry  alienate  bareback  cerement
goldmine  herdsman  needment  seedcoat  wardress  alienism  barefoot  ceremony
goldrush  herdwick  nondairy  seedcorn  wardrobe  alienist  bareness  cheekily
goodness  hinderer  obedient  seedfish  wardroom  allegory  baseball  cheerful
goodtime  hindlegs  offdrive  seedleaf  wardship  alleluia  baseborn  cheerily
goodwife  hindmost  omadhaum  seedless  weedless  allergen  baseless  cheering
goodwill  hinduise  outdated  seedling  weldable  allergic  baseline  chiefdom
goodyear  Hinduism  outdoors  seedlobe  weldment  alleyway  basement  cicerone
gradient  holdback  outdrawn  seedplot  whidding  alveolar  baseness  ciceroni
graduand  holdfast  oxidiser  seedsman  whodunit  alveolus  bateleur  cidevant
graduate  holdover  pandanus  seedtime  wildeyed  amnesiac  bedeguar  cineaste
gridiron  hoodwink  pandemic  shadbush  wildfire  amoebean  beeeater  cinerary
grudging  inedible  pandowdy  shaddock  wildfowl  amoeboid  begetter  clueless
guidable  inedited  pardoner  shadower  wildlife  amperage  behemoth  cogently
guidance  isodicon  pendency  shedding  wildness  anaerobe  benedick  coherent
guidedog  khedival  pendicle  shedevil  wildwood  ancestor  benedict  cohesion
guideway  kindless  pendular  shoddily  windburn  ancestry  benefice  cohesive
handball  kindling  pendulum  shuddery  windcone  andesine  bereaved  cokernut
handbell  kindness  piddling  skidding  windfall  andesite  bevelled  coleseed
handbill  labdanum  piedmont  sledding  windgall  angelica  beveller  coleslaw
handbook  landarmy  Pindaric  slideway  windlass  anhedral  beverage  colewort
handcart  landcrab  plodding  smudgily  windless  ankerite  bisector  comeback
handclap  landfall  ponderer  solderer  windmill  anserine  bisexual  comedian
handcuff  landform  pondweed  soldiery  windowed  anteater  biweekly  comedist
handfast  landgirl  powdered  sordidly  windpipe  antecede  biyearly  comedown
handgrip  landlady  predator  spadeful  windrose  antedate  bleeding  cometary
handheld  landless  predella  spadices  windsail  antefixa  bluebell  corelate
handhold  landline  prideful  spadille  windsock  antelope  bluebird  cosecant
handicap  landlord  prodding  spadones  windward  antennae  bluechip  cotenant
handless  landmark  prodigal  stedfast  wondrous  antennal  bluecoat  covenant
handline  landmass  prodrome  stodgily  woodbind  antennas  bluefish  coverage
handling  landmine  producer  studbook  woodbine  antepost  blueness  coverall
handlist  landrail  prudence  studding  woodchat  anterior  bluenose  covering
handloom  landslip  punditry  studfarm  woodcock  anteroom  blueweed  coverlet
handmade  landsman  quadrant  studious  woodenly  aphelion  bodement  covertly
handmaid  laudable  quadrate  studwork  woodland  appendix  bogeyman  covetous
handmill  laudably  quadriga  suddenly  woodlark  appetent  bohemian  cozenage
handpick  laudanum  quadroon  sundance  woodlice  appetite  bonefish  creeping
handrail  laudator  quiddity  sunderer  woodnote  apresski  bonehead  crueller
handsewn  leadenly  quidnunc  sundress  woodpile  apterous  boneless  cupelled
handsome  leadless  randomly  sundried  woodpulp  aqueduct  bonemeal  cureless
handwork  leadsman  readable  sundries  woodruff  ardently  boneyard  cuteness
handyman  leadwork  readably  sundrops  woodshed  argentic  borecole  Cyrenaic
hardback  lewdness  readjust  syndesis  woodsman  Armenian  borehole  dalesman
hardbake  loadline  reedbird  syndetic  woodwind  arpeggio  breeches  danegeld
hardcase  loadstar  reedling  syndical  woodwool  arrestee  breeding  dateless
hardcore  Londoner  reedmace  syndrome  woodwork  arrester  breezily  dateline
hardener  lordless  reedpipe  tandoori  woodworm  arrestor  briefing  deaerate
hardhack  lordling  reedstop  tapdance  wordbook  arsenate  cadenced  deceased
hardhead  lordosis  reedwren  tawdrily  wordless  arsenide  cagebird  decedent
hardline  lordotic  renderer  tendence  wordplay  arsenite  cageling  deceiver
hardness  lordship  riddance  tendency  Abderite  artefact  cakewalk  December
hardship  loudness  roadbook  tenderly  abjectly  arterial  calendar  decemvir
hardtack  magdalen  roadless  thudding  abnegate  artesian  calender  decennia
hardware  maidenly  roadside  toadfish  absentee  asbestic  cameleer  decently
hardwood  maidhood  roadsign  toadflax  absently  asbestos  camellia  defector
headache  Mandaean  roadster  toadyish  accentor  ascender  capeline  defender
headachy  mandamus  rondeaux  toadyism  accepter  asperges  capellet  deferent
headband  mandarin  roodbeam  topdress  acceptor  asperity  capeskin  deferral
headfast  mandator  roodloft  tradeoff  achenial  assemble  carefree  deferred
headgear  mandible  rowdyish  traditor  acierage  assembly  careless  deferrer
headlamp  Mandingo  rowdyism  traducer  acierate  assenter  careworn  dejected
headland  mandolin  saddlery  twaddler  acrefoot  assentor  casebook  delegacy
headless  mandorla  Sadducee  twiddler  acreinch  assertor  casemate  delegate
headline  mandrake  sandarac  unedited  addendum  assessor  casement  deletion
headlock  mandrill  sandbank  Vandalic  adherent  asterisk  casework  demented
headlong  Mazdaism  sandbath  vendetta  adhesion  asterism  catechol  dementia
headmost  mendable  sandflea  vendible  adhesive  asteroid  category  demerara
headnote  mesdames  sandshoe  verdancy  Adlerian  atheling  catenary  demersal
headrace  middling  sandwich  verderer  affected  Athenian  catenate  denehole
headrest  mildness  sandworm  verderor  affecter  atheroma  cateress  derelict
headroom  mindless  sandwort  verditer  afferent  atremble  catering  deserter
headsail  misdealt  sandyish  verdured  agrement  attender  caverned  detector
headsman  misdoing  sardelle  voidable  agrestic  attested  cavesson  deterred
```

deterrer	farewell	foretold	hireling	kakemono	lovelorn	nonevent	queendom
digester	federate	forewarn	homebody	Khmerian	lovenest	noseband	queening
dihedral	fenestra	forewent	homeborn	kinesics	loveseat	nosecone	queenlet
dimerism	feretory	foreword	homebred	kinetics	lovesick	nosedive	queerish
dimerous	feverfew	foreyard	homebrew	kneedeep	lovesome	nosepipe	quietism
dinerout	feverish	foveolae	homefelt	kneehigh	lovesong	nosering	quietist
dioecism	feverous	fraenula	homeland	kneehole	lowering	notebook	quietude
directly	fidelity	freeborn	homeless	kneejerk	lukewarm	notecase	racecard
director	filefish	freedman	homelike	labelled	lutecium	noteless	racegoer
diseased	finedraw	freefall	homemade	labellum	lutenist	novelise	racemate
disendow	fineness	freehand	homesick	lacerate	lutetium	novelist	racemise
divebomb	finespun	freehold	homespun	lacewing	lykewake	November	racemose
Docetism	firearms	freeload	hometown	lacework	lyrebird	novercal	rakehell
Docetist	fireback	freeness	homeward	lakeland	macerate	nucellus	ramentum
dogeared	fireball	freesoil	homework	lamellae	maieutic	nudeness	ramequin
dolerite	firebird	freewill	honestly	lamellar	majestic	numeracy	rapecake
dolesome	fireboat	freezeup	honeybee	lameness	makebate	numerary	rapeseed
domestic	firebomb	freezing	honeydew	lamented	makefast	numerate	rarefied
dovecote	firebrat	friendly	honeypot	lapelled	maledict	numerous	rareness
dovetail	fireclay	Friesian	hopeless	lateness	malefern	oakegger	rateable
dowelled	firedamp	funebral	hosepipe	latently	malemute	objector	ravelled
easement	fireeyed	funerary	hoverfly	laterite	maleness	observer	ravenous
eclectic	firehose	funereal	hugeness	lavender	Mameluke	offender	rebelled
edgeless	firelock	fuselage	hymenial	laverock	maneater	offering	rebeller
edgeways	fireopal	galeated	hymenium	legendry	matelote	onceover	rebellow
edgewise	fireplug	Galenism	Ibsenism	legerity	material	oriental	receiver
effector	fireship	galenite	ilmenite	levelled	materiel	oriented	recently
efferent	fireside	gamebird	imbecile	leverage	maternal	receptor	receptor
embedded	firetrap	gamecock	immersed	libeccio	maverick	osteitis	redeemer
embezzle	fireweed	gameness	impelled	libelled	mazement	oxpecker	redefine
emceeing	firewood	gamesome	impeller	libellee	mementos	paleface	redeless
Emmental	firework	gamester	imperial	libeller	meteoric	paleness	redeploy
empeople	fivefold	gapeworm	imperium	mezereon	mezereon	palestra	redesign
enceinte	fivestar	garefowl	impetigo	liberate	micellar	panelled	referent
endemism	fleeting	gaselier	inceptor	licensed	milepost	paperboy	referral
endermic	fluellin	gatefold	indebted	licenser	Milesian	parental	referred
enfeeble	fluently	gatepost	indecent	lifebelt	mimester	parergon	regelate
enfetter	fluepipe	gavelock	infector	lifeboat	mirepoix	patellae	rehearse
engender	fomenter	generate	inferior	lifebuoy	miserere	patellar	rejecter
enneagon	forebear	generous	infernal	lifeless	modelled	patentee	releasee
ensemble	forebode	genetics	inherent	lifelike	modeller	patently	releaser
entellus	forecast	Genevese	inhesion	lifeline	moderate	patentor	releasor
enterate	foredeck	giveaway	injector	lifelong	moderato	paternal	relegate
envelope	foredoom	gleesome	insecure	lifesize	modernly	pavement	relevant
ephemera	foreedge	Gobelins	inserted	lifetime	modestly	pederast	remedial
Ephesian	forefeel	gogetter	integral	lifework	molecule	pedestal	remember
especial	forefelt	governor	intended	limekiln	molehill	pelerine	renegade
Essenism	forefoot	Graecise	intently	limerick	moleskin	peperino	renegado
esterify	foregoer	Graecism	interact	limetwig	molester	petechia	reneguer
etcetera	foregone	greedily	interbed	limewash	momently	phlegmon	repealer
ethereal	forehand	greegree	intercom	lineally	momentum	phreatic	repeater
etherial	forehead	greenery	intercut	linearly	monetary	pileated	repelled
etherise	foreknew	greenfly	interest	linesman	monetise	pilewort	repeller
etherism	foreknow	greening	interior	literacy	moneybag	pinecone	repenter
etherist	forelady	greenish	intermit	literary	moneybox	pinewood	repeople
eugenics	foreland	greenlet	intermix	literate	moreover	pipeclay	repetend
eugenism	forelock	greeting	internal	literati	moresque	pipefish	rerecord
eugenist	foremast	grievous	internee	liveable	moveable	pipeline	reremice
eupepsia	foremost	gruesome	Interpol	liveborn	moveless	piperack	rereward
eupeptic	forename	haleness	interred	livelily	movement	piperine	research
eutectic	forenoon	harebell	interrex	livelong	muleteer	polemics	resemble
excelled	forensic	haresear	intersex	liveried	muteness	polemise	reserved
expedite	forepart	hateable	intertie	liverish	mycelial	polemist	resetter
expelled	forepast	havelock	interval	livewire	mycelium	polestar	resettle
expellee	forepeak	hazelnut	interwar	lobeline	mycetoma	potently	revealer
expertly	foreplay	hebetate	invected	lodestar	nameable	powerful	reveille
exserted	foresaid	hebetude	inveigle	lomentum	namedrop	praecipe	revelled
extender	foresail	Hegelian	inventor	loneness	nameless	praedial	reveller
extensor	foreseen	hegemony	inverted	lonesome	namepart	preelect	revenant
exterior	foreshow	henequen	inverter	lopeared	namesake	preexist	revenger
external	foreside	hereaway	investor	lovebird	nametape	priedieu	reverend
faceache	forestal	heredity	jeremiad	loveknot	nepenthe	priestly	reverent
facecard	forestay	Hereford	Jeremiah	loveless	niceness	proemial	reversal
faceless	forested	hereunto	jewelled	lovelily	ninefold	pubertal	reverser
facelift	forester	hereupon	jeweller	lovelock	ninepins	purebred	reverter
facepack	forestry	herewith	Jeremiah	lovelily	nineteen	pureness	revetted
facetiae	foretell	hibernal	jewelled	lovelock	nineties	pyrenoid	Rhaetian
fadeaway	foretime	hideaway	jeweller	lovelily	nobelium	pyrexial	Rhaetian
fadeless	foretime	hireable	juvenile	lovelock	nonesuch	quaestor	ricebird

```
ricercar  shoebill  steepled  tideless  unleaded  wireless  halftone  staffage
rideable  shoehorn  steerage  tidelock  unlearnt  wirework  hawfinch  stiffish
rifeness  shoelace  steering  tidemark  unmeetly  wireworm  hayfield  stuffily
rimester  shoeless  streaked  tidemill  unpegged  wirewove  hipflask  stuffing
ripeness  shoetree  streaker  tidewave  unperson  wiseacre  hoofbeat  subfloor
rivelled  shredded  streamer  tigereye  unreason  wiseness  icefield  subframe
riverain  shredder  streeted  tigerish  unsealed  yodelled  illfated  sufferer
riverbed  shrewdly  strength  tilefish  unseated  yodeller  joyfully  suffrage
riverine  shrewish  strepent  timeball  unseeded  yokemate  Kaffiyeh  surfacer
riverman  Siberian  Strepyan  timebomb  unseeing  yuletide  korfball  surfbird
riverway  sidearms  stretchy  timefuse  unseemly  zibeline  lawfully  surfboat
ropeable  sideband  suberect  timeless  unsettle  zwieback  leafless  surfduck
ropewalk  sidedish  suberise  timework  untented  airfield  leaflike  surffish
ropeyarn  sidedoor  suberose  timeworn  untether  airframe  manfully  swiftlet
rosebowl  sidedrum  suberous  tireless  unversed  artfully  midfield  tafferel
rosebush  sidehead  Sumerian  tiresome  unweaned  avifauna  moufflon  taffrail
rosefish  sidekick  superadd  together  upheaval  beefcake  newfound  trifling
roseleaf  sideline  superate  tokenism  uppercut  beefwood  oilfield  trifocal
rosemary  sideling  superbly  tolerant  upsetter  botflies  oilfired  triforia
roseolar  sidelong  superego  tolerate  urgently  bouffant  outfield  twofaced
rosepink  sidenote  superior  tomentum  valerate  bowfront  outflank  unifilar
roseroot  sidereal  superman  tonedeaf  valerian  bunfight  perfecto  usefully
rosetree  siderite  supernal  toneless  vaneless  caffeine  perforce  usufruct
rosewood  sideroad  supertax  tonepoem  vegetate  calfskin  perfumer  wayfarer
rotenone  sideshow  surefire  toreador  vegetive  coiffeur  piffling  whiffler
rudeness  sideslip  sureness  toreutic  vehement  coiffure  pilferer  wilfully
ruleless  sidesman  suzerain  totemism  veneerer  conferee  profaner  woefully
safeness  sidestep  sweeping  totemist  venerate  conferva  profiler  wolffish
sageness  sideview  sweepnet  towelled  venereal  confetti  profound  wolfpack
saleable  sidewalk  sweeting  treefern  Venetian  confider  puffball  wolfskin
saleroom  sideward  sweetish  treefrog  verecund  confiner  puffbird  alogical
Salesian  sideways  sweetpea  treeless  vileness  confines  purfling  amygdala
salesman  sidewind  sweetsop  treenail  vinegary  conflate  reaffirm  anaglyph
sameness  sidewise  synergic  triennia  vineyard  conflict  redfaced  anagogic
saneness  silencer  synergid  trueblue  viperine  confound  reefknot  apagogic
sateless  silently  taberdar  trueborn  viperish  confrere  riffraff  apogamic
sawedged  sinecure  takeaway  truebred  viperous  confront  roofless  apograph
sawedoff  sirenian  takehome  truelove  virement  craftily  roofrack  bangtail
schedule  sizeable  takeover  trueness  vitellin  crofting  rooftree  bargeman
schemata  sleepily  talented  tubeless  vitellus  daffodil  ruefully  beagling
scheming  sleeping  talesman  tubercle  vixenish  deafmute  saffrony  beggarly
sclereid  sloeeyed  tameable  tuberose  vomerine  deafness  sawframe  bergamot
sclerite  sneeshan  tameless  tuberous  voteless  diffract  scaffold  biogenic
scleroma  soberise  tameness  tuneable  vowelise  diffuser  seafarer  biograph
sclerose  solecism  tapedeck  tuneless  vowelled  disfrock  seafloor  blighter
sclerous  solecist  tapeless  tutelage  wakeless  dogfaced  seafront  boughten
screamer  solemnly  tapelike  tutelary  wakening  dogfight  selfborn  braggart
screechy  soleness  tapeline  tweezers  wakerife  driftage  selfheal  bragging
screener  solenoid  tapestry  twoedged  waterage  driftice  selfhelp  bregmata
screwtop  somebody  tapeworm  typecast  waterbed  driftway  selfhood  brighten
sebesten  somedeal  taverner  typeface  waterbus  dumfound  selfless  brightly
sederunt  sometime  telecine  ulcerate  watergas  epifauna  selflove  budgeree
selectee  someways  telecine  ulcerous  waterice  fanfaron  selfmade  bungalow
selector  somewhat  telefilm  ulterior  watering  farflung  selfmate  bunghole
selenate  somewhen  telegony  unbeaten  waterish  fitfully  selfness  burglary
selenide  sorehead  telegram  unbelief  waterlog  furfural  selfpity  burgonet
selenite  soreness  telemark  underact  waterloo  furfuran  selfrule  Burgundy
selenium  soterial  telepath  underage  waterman  gasfired  selfsame  chugging
semester  spaewife  teleport  underarm  waterski  golfclub  selfsown  cingulum
serenade  speedily  telethon  underbid  waterway  gonfalon  selfwill  clogging
serenata  speedway  teleview  undercut  waveband  goofball  serfhood  coagulum
serenely  sphenoid  televise  underdid  waveform  graffiti  shafting  congener
serenity  spherics  temerity  underdog  waveless  graffito  shiftily  conglobe
severely  spheroid  Tenebrae  underfur  weregild  greffier  shiftkey  congress
severity  spherule  tenement  underlap  werewolf  gulfweed  shofroth  congreve
sewellel  splendid  terebene  underlay  wheedler  gunfight  shuffler  cowgrass
sewerage  splenial  terebrae  underlet  wheelman  gunflint  sinfonia  cragsman
sewergas  splenius  thievery  underlie  wheezily  halfback  sinfully  daughter
sewerrat  spreader  thievish  underlie  wideeyed  halfbeak  sniffily  diagnose
sheepdip  squeaker  threaden  underman  wifehood  halfboot  sniffler  diagonal
sheepdog  squealer  threaten  underpin  wifeless  halfbred  sniffles  diagraph
sheepish  squeedge  threeply  underrun  wifelike  halfmast  snuffers  dingdong
sheepked  squeegee  threeway  undersea  winepalm  halfmoon  snuffler  disgorge
sheeppen  squeezer  threnode  underset  wineshop  halfnote  snuffles  disgrace
sheeprun  squelchy  threnody  undertow  wineskin  halfpint  solfaist  disguise
sheeting  steenbok  thresher  underway  wiredraw  halfsole  solfeggi  doggedly
shielder  steening  tidegate  unfetter  wirehair  halfterm  spiffing  doggerel
shieling  steepish  tideland  unkennel  wirehair  halftime  spoffish  doughboy
```

doughnut	heighten	Mongolic	singular	anthelia	euphoric	methodic	suchlike
dragging	huggable	mongoose	slagging	anthemia	euphrasy	methylic	syphilis
dragline	hungrily	mudguard	slagheap	antheral	euphuism	methysis	tachisme
dragoman	imaginal	myogenic	slightly	anthesis	euphuist	mightest	tachiste
dragomen	imagines	myograph	slogging	anthozoa	exchange	mightily	taphouse
dragonet	isagogic	narghile	slugabed	archaean	fashious	misheard	teahouse
dragsman	isogamic	niggling	sluggard	archaise	fatherly	mishmash	technics
dragster	isogloss	oatgrass	slugging	archaism	fighting	Mishnaic	tightwad
drugging	isogonal	odograph	sluggish	archaist	fishable	Mithraic	tithable
druggist	isogonic	oligarch	smuggler	archduke	fishball	moshavim	topheavy
dungaree	jaggedly	oligomer	smugness	archival	fishbone	mothball	Tychonic
dungcart	jiggered	origanum	snagging	archives	fishbowl	motherly	typhonic
dunghill	jingoish	original	sniggler	archness	fishcake	muchness	unchancy
dysgenic	jingoism	orogenic	snogging	asphodel	fishfarm	mushroom	unchaste
eelgrass	jingoist	outgoing	snuggery	asphyxia	fishglue	mythical	unchurch
elegance	jongleur	outgrown	snugness	asthenia	fishhawk	naphthol	unshaped
elegancy	judgment	outguess	songbird	asthenic	fishhook	nathless	unthread
eligible	jugglery	pangolin	songbook	bachelor	fishless	nephrite	unthrift
eligibly	kangaroo	pargeter	songless	bathetic	fishmeal	nightcap	unthrone
emigrant	kedgeree	peagreen	songster	bathotic	fishpond	nighthag	upthrown
emigrate	kidglove	peignoir	spagyric	bathrobe	fishtail	nightjar	upthrust
epigeous	kingbird	plagiary	spyglass	bathroom	fishwife	nightowl	Valhalla
epigraph	kingbolt	plaguily	staggard	bechamel	foxhound	nonhuman	Walhalla
erigeron	kingcrab	plighted	staggers	bechance	fuchsine	nuthatch	warhorse
erogenic	kingfish	plugging	staghorn	bethesda	Gadhelic	nuthouse	washable
exegesis	kinghood	poignant	stagnant	blahblah	gashouse	omphalic	washbowl
exegetic	kinglike	pregnant	stagnate	bonhomie	gatherer	omphalos	washroom
exigence	kingship	priggery	stigmata	bushbaby	hasheesh	onehorse	wishbone
exigency	kingsize	priggish	subgenus	bushbuck	highball	orchilla	wishwash
exigible	knightly	priggism	subgroup	bushfire	highborn	orthicon	withdraw
exiguity	langlauf	progress	surgical	bushveld	highbred	orthodox	withdrew
exiguous	Langshan	puggaree	swagging	cachalot	highbrow	orthoepy	withheld
exogamic	language	pungency	swigging	cachepot	higherup	outHerod	withhold
eyeglass	languish	pyogenic	syngamic	cachexia	highjack	outhouse	yachting
fangless	largesse	quagmire	tangency	cachucha	highland	pachalic	yoghourt
fingered	laughing	raggedly	tangible	cashbook	highlows	parhelia	abdicate
flagella	laughter	ratguard	tangibly	cashmere	highmost	parhelic	abridger
flagging	lawgiver	reagency	tangoist	cathedra	highness	pashalic	absinthe
flagpole	leggings	reignite	thuggery	catheter	highrise	pashalik	accident
flagrant	legguard	ribgrass	thuggism	cathexes	highroad	pathetic	achiever
flagship	lengthen	ridgeway	tingeing	cathexis	hightail	pathless	achiness
flogging	liegeman	ringbark	tonguing	cathodal	hightest	pathogen	achingly
forgiven	lingerer	ringbolt	toughish	catholic	hitherto	phthalic	acridine
forgoing	lingerie	ringbone	tragical	cathodic	hothouse	phthisic	acridity
fougasse	linguist	ringdove	tragopan	cephalic	hushhush	phthisis	acrimony
foxglove	lodgings	ringmain	triglyph	chthonic	inchmeal	pishogue	actiniae
fragment	lodgment	ringneck	trigonal	cochleae	inchoate	pochette	actinian
fragrant	longboat	ringroad	trigraph	cochlear	inchworm	poohpooh	actinias
frighten	longeron	ringside	tungsten	cothurni	inthrall	potholer	actinide
frigidly	longeval	ringtail	tungstic	cushiony	ischemia	pothouse	actinism
frogfish	longhair	ringwall	turgidly	Cushitic	ischemic	prehuman	actinium
frogging	longhand	ringworm	vanguard	dethrone	isthmian	prohibit	activate
frogspit	longhorn	roughage	vengeful	dichasia	japhetic	pushball	actively
frugally	longness	roughdry	vergence	dichroic	jodhpurs	pushbike	activism
fungible	longship	roughhew	virginal	diphenyl	Kashmiri	pushcart	activist
gadgetry	longsome	roughish	Virginia	dishevel	kyphosis	pushover	activity
gangland	longstop	ruggedly	vulgarly	ditheism	kyphotic	pushpull	addition
gangling	longterm	ryegrass	waggoner	ditheist	lashings	pythonic	additive
ganglion	longtime	sangaree	waygoing	ditherer	lethally	rachides	adlibbed
gangrene	longueur	Sangrail	Wedgwood	doghouse	lethargy	rachitic	admitted
gangster	longwall	Sangreal	Whiggery	duchesse	lichened	rachitis	advisory
garganey	longwave	sanguine	Whiggish	Dukhobor	lichenin	rashness	aegirine
gargoyle	longways	sapgreen	Whiggism	eighteen	lichgate	recharge	aerially
geognosy	longwise	sargasso	wingbeat	eighthly	lighting	richness	aeriform
gingerly	lopgrass	seagoing	wingcase	eighties	lightish	rightful	affiance
gingival	lowgrade	seagreen	wingless	elkhound	litharge	rightist	affinity
gorgeous	lungfish	seigneur	wingspan	emphases	lothario	rushhour	affirmer
gorgonia	lungwort	seignior	wriggler	emphasis	lushness	rushlike	aglimmer
groggily	mangabey	seignory	ziggurat	emphatic	Lutheran	ruthless	aglitter
grogshop	manganic	sergeant	zoogenic	ensheath	lychgate	sashcord	agrimony
Haggadah	mangonel	shagbark	alchemic	enshrine	machismo	sawhorse	aguishly
hangable	mangrove	shaggily	alehouse	enshroud	madhouse	seaholly	airiness
hangeron	marginal	shagreen	alphabet	enthalpy	mechanic	seahorse	albinism
hangnail	margrave	shagroon	although	enthrall	menhaden	Sephardi	algicide
hangover	matgrass	shigella	amphibia	eschalot	mephitic	siphonal	algidity
hedgehog	meagrely	shogging	amphipod	eschewal	mephitis	siphonet	alginate
hedgehop	mergence	singable	amphorae	eschewal	meshwork	siphonic	alliance
hedgepig	misgiven	singeing	amphoras	euphonic	methanol	sithence	almighty
hedgerow	misguide	singsong	anchoret	euphoria	methinks	subhuman	alpinism

```
alpinist  bouillon  deniable  envisage  graining  lapicide  menially  oiticica
altitude  boyishly  depicter  envision  guaiacum  lapidary  meninges  omnivore
ambiance  braiding  depictor  eohippus  habitant  lapidate  meniscus  oncidium
ambience  brainish  depilate  eolithic  habitual  lapidify  meridian  ooziness
ambition  brainpan  derision  equinity  habitude  Latinate  meringue  ophidian
ambivert  broidery  derisive  equipage  hacienda  latinise  meristem  oppilate
amniotic  business  derisory  equipped  haliotis  Latinism  meristic  opsimath
antibody  cabinboy  derivate  equitant  harikari  Latinist  mesially  optician
antidote  caginess  designer  equities  havildar  latinity  militant  optimise
antihero  calidity  desirous  equivoke  haziness  latitant  military  optimism
antilogy  califate  deviance  Eskimoan  heliacal  latitude  militate  optimist
antimask  calipash  deviancy  estimate  helicoid  lavishly  mimicked  optional
antimony  calipers  deviator  ethicism  heliosis  laziness  mimicker  ordinand
antinode  camisade  deviling  ethicist  heliport  lecithin  minimise  ordinary
antinomy  camisado  devilish  Ethiopic  heritage  legioned  minister  ordinate
antiphon  camisole  devilism  excision  hesitant  lenience  ministry  ornithic
antipode  canister  devilkin  excitant  hesitate  leniency  mitigant  orpiment
antipole  capitate  devilled  exciting  hibiscus  Leninism  mitigate  oscinine
antipope  capitula  deviltry  exlibris  holidays  Leninist  mobilise  Ossianic
antisera  carillon  dewiness  expiable  holiness  Leninite  mobility  ostinato
antitype  carinate  digitate  expiator  holistic  lenitive  modifier  owlishly
aoristic  cationic  digitise  expirant  homicide  lepidote  modishly  pacifier
aphicide  cavicorn  diligent  facially  hominoid  leviable  Molinism  pacifism
aptitude  cavilled  diminish  facilely  howitzer  levigate  Molinist  pacifist
aquiline  caviller  dirigism  facility  humidify  levirate  monicker  padishah
arbitral  celibacy  diriment  familial  humidity  levitate  monistic  paginate
Arminian  celibate  disinter  familiar  humility  lewisite  monition  palinode
articled  chainsaw  dividend  farinose  hygienic  limitary  monitive  palisade
artifact  chairman  dividivi  fatigues  ignition  liniment  monitory  panicked
artifice  choicely  dividual  felicity  ignitron  liripoop  mopishly  papillae
artistic  choirboy  divinely  felinity  illiquid  litigant  moribund  papillar
artistry  christen  divinise  feminine  imminent  litigate  motility  papillon
ascidian  christie  divinity  feminise  immingle  lividity  motional  papistic
ascidium  Christly  division  feminism  impishly  lixivium  motivate  papistry
aspirant  cicisbei  divisive  feminist  incident  lodicule  motivity  parietal
aspirate  cicisbeo  docilely  feminity  incision  logician  movingly  patience
assiento  ciliated  docility  feticide  incisive  logistic  mucilage  pavilion
assignat  citified  domicile  filially  incitant  loricate  mulishly  pedicled
assignee  civilian  dominant  filiform  incivism  lorikeet  muniment  pedicure
assignor  civilise  dominate  filigree  Indiaman  lovingly  munition  pedigree
atticism  civility  domineer  Filipina  indicant  lucidity  muriatic  pediment
attitude  claimant  dominion  Filipino  indicate  luminant  musicale  pedipalp
atwitter  cloister  dominoes  finisher  indicium  luminary  musician  Pekinese
audience  codifier  dopiness  finitely  indigene  luminist  musingly  penitent
audition  cogitate  dotingly  finitude  indigent  luminous  muticous  perianth
auditive  coliform  doziness  fluidics  indirect  lyricism  mutilate  pericarp
auditory  coliseum  drainage  fluidify  infilter  lyricist  mutineer  pericope
auricula  conidial  druidess  fluidise  infinite  magician  mutinous  periderm
auriform  conidium  druidism  fluidity  infinity  magicked  myriapod  peridium
autistic  coniform  dutiable  foliaged  infirmly  magister  myriopod  peridote
babirusa  cosiness  easiness  foxiness  inkiness  makimono  napiform  perigean
bacillar  cotillon  ebriated  fruitage  insignia  maligner  national  perigyny
bacillus  cubiform  echinate  fruitbat  intimacy  malignly  natively  perilled
badinage  culicine  echinoid  fruitery  intimate  malinger  nativism  perilous
Balinese  culinary  ecliptic  fruitfly  intimism  mamillae  nativist  perilune
banister  cupidity  edginess  fruitful  intitule  mamillar  nativity  perineal
baritone  cylinder  eeriness  fruition  inviable  maniacal  navigate  perineum
basicity  cynicism  efficacy  fugitive  inviting  Manichee  Nazirite  periodic
basidial  Cyrillic  egoistic  fumigant  iodinate  manicure  nihilism  periotic
basidium  cytidine  ellipses  fumigate  irrigate  manifest  nihilist  peripety
basilica  daringly  ellipsis  fumitory  irritant  manifold  nihility  periplus
basilisk  debility  elliptic  fusiform  irritate  maniform  nobility  perisher
basinful  decigram  embitter  fusileer  janizary  marigold  nominate  petiolar
bedimmed  decimate  encipher  fusilier  jipijapa  marinade  nomistic  petioled
befitted  decipher  encircle  futilely  jokingly  marinate  nosiness  petition
beginner  decision  enfilade  futility  jovially  maritage  notional  piliform
begirded  decisive  engineer  Galilean  jubilant  maritime  nubiform  pimiento
believer  dedicate  enginery  gaminess  jubilate  matiness  nubility  pisiform
belittle  defiance  engirdle  ganister  judicial  maxillae  nubilous  pitiable
benignly  defilade  enkindle  gapingly  julienne  maximise  numinous  pitiably
beriberi  definite  enricher  garishly  juristic  maziness  oafishly  pitiless
besieger  delibate  ensiform  gelidity  kamikaze  medially  obeisant  pixieish
bewigged  delicacy  ensigncy  geminate  kibitzer  mediator  obligate  pixiness
bewilder  delicate  ensilage  genially  Kohinoor  medicate  obliging  plaiding
bitingly  delirium  entirely  genitive  kolinsky  medicine  oblivion  plaister
bodiless  delivery  entirety  geniture  komitaji  medieval  obsidian  pleinair
boniface  demijohn  enviable  gneissic  labially  mediocre  occident  podiatry
boniness  demitted  enviably  gonidial  lability  meditate  official  polisher
boringly  demiurge  environs  gonidium  laminate  melinite  oiliness  politely
```

```
politick reticent socially ugliness volitive brokenly milkwort ticklish
politico reticule societal ultimacy vomitive buckaroo monkfish tickseed
politics retiform Socinian ultimata vomitory buckbean MonKhmer ticktack
popinjay retinula solidary ultimate wariness buckhorn monkhood ticktock
popishly retiring solidify umpirage waviness buckling monkseal tinkerer
poristic reviewal solidity unbiased waxiness buckshee monkship trekking
position reviewer solitary unbidden wiliness buckshot muckluck tuckahoe
positive reviling solitude uncially wiriness buckskin muckrake tuckshop
positron revision sphingid unciform zamindar bulkhead muckworm Turkoman
pruinose revisory splinter uncinate zaniness bunkered muskdeer walkable
pryingly revivify splitter unfilial zemindar cockatoo muskduck walkaway
pugilism ridicule spoilage unfitted zenithal cockboat musketry walkover
pugilist rigidify sprigged unhinged zodiacal cockcrow muskrose Walkyrie
puniness rigidity springal unkindly banjoist cockerel musktree weakfish
punisher ropiness springer unkingly Benjamin cockeyed neckband weakling
punition rosiness sprinkle unlikely conjoint cockloft necklace weakness
punitive rubicund sprinter unlimber conjugal cockshut neckline weeklong
punitory rubidium squibbed unlinked conjunct cocksure nickelic wickedly
pupilage rudiment squidded unlisted conjurer cocktail nicknack workable
pupilary ruminant squiggle unpinned conjuror cookbook nickname workaday
pupillar ruminate squiggly unriddle disjoint corkwing parkland workfolk
purifier rutilant squilgee unrigged disjunct corkwood peekaboo workings
puristic sadistic squinter untidily frijoles dankness penknife workless
pygidial saginate squireen untimely jiujitsu darkling pickerel workmate
pygidium sagittal squirely untitled mahjongg darkness picketer workroom
pyridine salience squirrel unwieldy marjoram darkroom pickings workshop
pyriform saliency squirter unwisdom misjudge darksome picklock Yankeefy
pyxidium salinity stairrod unwisely nonjuror deckhand pinkness abelmosk
quaintly salivary stairway unwished perjurer dockland pockmark aceldama
rabidity salivate steinbok unzipped prejudge dockside porkling aculeate
racially samizdat stoicism uplifter serjeant dockyard Quakerly adularia
raciness sanitary stricken uppishly subjoint duckbill rackrent adulator
radially sanitate strickle uprising verjuice duckhawk rankness adultery
radiance sanitise strictly urticant backache duckling reckless afflatus
radiancy sapidity stridden urticate backbite duckpond reckoner airliner
radiator sapience strident vagility backbone duckweed rickrack analcime
radicant satiable strigose valiance backchat feckless rickshaw analcite
radicate satiably striking valiancy backcomb folklore rockbird analecta
rakishly satirise stringed validate backdate folkmoot rockcake analects
rapidity satirist stringer validity backdoor folksong rockcork analogic
ratifier schiedam stripped vanillin backdrop folktale rockdove analogue
rational schiller stripper vanisher backfire forklift rocketry analyser
ravisher schizoid subimago vapidity backhand funkhole rockfall analyses
recision scribble sukiyaki variable backlash gymkhana rockfish analysis
redirect scribbly supinate variably backless hawkeyed rockhewn analytic
redistil sediment supinely variance backlist hawklike rocklike Anglican
refinery sedition suricate varicose backmost hawkmoth rockling antlered
refitted semibull swainish variedly backpack hawkweed rockrose apologia
regicide semidome syringes varietal backrest hickwall rocksalt apologue
regiment seminary syrinxes variform backroom hocktide rockweed applause
regional seminude taciturn variolar backseat hookworm rockwood applepie
register semiotic Tahitian variorum backside huckster rockwork applique
registry Semitise takingly vasiform backspin jackaroo rucksack arillate
rejigger Semitism talisman venially backstay jackboot sackcoat athletic
rekindle Semitist Tamilian verifier backveld jackeroo sackless avulsion
reliable semitone tanistry veristic backward jackstay sackrace axillary
reliably senility taxingly vesicant backwash junkshop shakable badlands
reliance serially tepidity vesicate backyard junkyard shakeout bailable
reliever seriatim theistic vexillum balkline kickback Shaktism bailment
religion sericite thridace vicinage bankable kickshaw Shekinah bailsman
reminder sexiness thriller vicinity bankbill kinkajou shikaree balladic
remissly sheikdom thriving vigilant bankbook lackaday sickener balladry
remittal shrieval tidiness vilifier banknote lankness sickerly balladry
remitted shrimper timidity vilipend bankroll larkspur sickflag ballcock
remittee shrinker tininess viricide barkless lockable sicklist balletic
remitter sibilant titivate viridian barkless lockfast sickness ballista
reniform sibilate tonicity viridity basketry lockknit sickroom ballonet
renitent Sicilian toxicant virilism bookcase lockstep silkworm ballroom
resident silicane toxicity virility bookends lookeron sinkable ballyhoo
residual silicate trailnet Visigoth bookland luckless sinkhole ballyrag
residuum silicide training visional booklice mackerel smokable bdellium
resigned silicify troilite visitant booklore mackinaw snakepit bellbird
resinate silicone truistic vitiable bookmark markdown soakaway bellbuoy
resinify similise tryingly vitiator bookpost markedly spikelet bellcote
resinoid sinicise tubiform vitiligo bookrest marketer stakenet bellpull
resinous sinister tumidity vivifier bookwork marksman suckling bellpush
resister siriasis tunicate vivisect bookworm meekness tackling bellwort
resistor sociable Tunisian volitant brakeman milkmaid tackroom bellyful
retiarii sociably typifier volition brakevan milkweed taskwork berliner
```

```
beslaver declasse fuelling keelless pollster smallish trilobed biometry
biblical declutch fugleman killdeer polluter smallpox trollopy biomorph
billfold deflower fullback kohlrabi pollywog smaltite twelvemo blamable
billhead diallage fullness lallygag potlatch smelling twilight blamably
billhook dialling fullpage loblolly poultice smeltery unclench blameful
billiard dialogic fullsize Lollardy prelatic soilless unclinch blimpish
billyboy dialogue fulltime lollipop prelease soilpipe unclothe brimfull
billycan dialyser furlough lollypop prolamin solleret unglazed brimless
Bodleian dialyses gableend lowlevel prolapse soulless unplaced brimming
bollworm dialysis galleass lowlying prolific spalpeen uralitic bromelia
buhlwork dialytic galliard mailable prolixly spelling utiliser bromidic
building dieldrin Gallican mailboat prologue spillage uvularly bummaree
bullcalf diplogen gallipot mailcart prolonge spillway uvulitis calmness
bulldoze diploidy galloper mealtime psalmist spoliate varletry chambers
bulletin diplomat Galloway mealworm psalmody stallage vaulting chambray
bullfrog diplopia galluses mealybug psaltery stallfed veilless champers
bullhead dislodge gallwasp mellowly psilosis stalling velleity champion
bullhorn disloyal gaolbird midlands publican stallion villadom chemical
bullocky djellaba garlicky millhand publicly stalwart villager chemurgy
bullring drilling gaslight milliard pullback stellate villainy chimaera
bullseye drollery Gaullism milliary pullover stellify villatic chimeric
bullyboy duelling Gaullist millibar pyelitis stellion violable chummily
bullyoff duellist geologic millieme qualmish stilbene violably chumming
bullyrag dullness gillaroo milliner quillpen stilbite violator clambake
burletta duologue girlhood millpond quilting stiletto violence clammily
cableway dwelling goalkick millrace railhead stillage wallaroo clamming
callable dyslexia goalline moulding raillery stolidly walleyed clematis
callgirl dyslexic goalpost mulloway railroad stultify wallfern clemency
calliope eagleowl golliwog muslined rallying stylised wallgame climatic
calliper ecclesia gralloch myelinic rallyist sublease wallknot clumsily
cauldron ecologic grillage myelitis realness sublunar walloper commando
cellarer effluent Guelphic nailfile realtime sullenly wallower commence
cellaret effluvia guileful negligee reflexed sunlight waxlight commerce
cellular elflocks guiltily NeoLatin refluent swelling welladay commoner
chalazae emblazon gullable newlywed replacer syllabic wellaway commoney
Chaldaic employee gullible nielloed replevin syllable wellborn commonly
Chaldean employer gunlayer nobleman rifleman syllabub wellbred communal
chaldron emulator halliard noblesse rollcall syllabus welldeck commuter
chalkpit emulgent hallmark nonlegal rollneck tableaux wellhead cosmetic
Chellean emulsify hallowed nuclease rouleaus tablecut wellknit cosmical
childbed emulsion halluces nucleate rouleaux tableful wellnigh coumarin
childish emulsive haploidy nucleole roulette tablemat wellread cramfull
children emulsoid harlotry nucleoli sailable tabletop Wellsian cramming
chiliasm enclitic haulyard nuclidic sailboat tailback wellworn cramoisy
chiliast enclothe heelball nullness sailfish tailcoat Wesleyan criminal
choleric enslaver heelless occluded sailless tailgate wetlands cromlech
cislunar epilepsy Helladic occlusal sailorly tailings wholehog cromorna
coaldust epilogue hellbent ocellate sailyard tailless williwaw cromorne
coalesce epyllion Hellenic ocularly scalable tailpipe wooldyed crumhorn
coalfish evaluate hellfire oeillade scalawag tailrace woolfell crummock
coalhole evildoer hellhole omelette scalepan tailspin woollens daemonic
coalmine evilness hielaman opulence scallion tallness woolpack daimonic
coalsack evulsion hillfort outlawry scilicet tallyman woolsack dalmatic
coelomic excluder hillocky outlying scolding tarlatan woolshed deemster
collagen explicit hillside ovalness scolices tellable woolskin diamante
collapse exploder hollands palliate scullery telltale woolwork diameter
collared explorer hollowly pallidly scullion telluric wouldest dimmable
collator exultant hooligan pallmall sculptor thalamic yellowly dismally
colleger eyeliner idolater parlance sealable thalamus yielding dismount
colliery fabliaux idolatry parlando sealevel thallium zealotry dogmatic
collogue failsafe idoliser peelings sealskin thalloid zeolitic doomsday
colloquy fallback idyllist pellagra sealyham thallous zoolater doomsman
collyria fallfish impledge pellicle secluded tholepin zoolatry doomster
coolabah fallible implicit pellmell shaleoil tillable abomasum dormancy
coolibah fallibly included pellucid shalloon toiletry abomasus dormouse
coolness fanlight inflamer perlitic shallows toilette Adamical doumpalm
coplanar faultily inflated phalange shelduck toilsome adamitic dramatic
couldest fellahin inflator Philomel shelfful toilworn adamsite drammock
coulisse fellness inflatus phyletic shelving tollcall animally dramshop
curlicue fellowly inflexed phyllary shilling tolldish animator drumfire
cyclamen fellowly inflight phyllode sillabub tollgate apomixis drumhead
cycleway follicle influent phylloid skeletal toolroom Aramaean drumming
cyclical follower isolable phyllome skeleton toolshed aromatic drummock
cyclonic followon isolator pillager skilless toplevel atomiser drumroll
cyclopes followup Italiote pillwort skilling topliner balmoral earmuffs
cyclosis foolscap jailbird pollices skullcap toplofty beamends egomania
daylight foulness jealousy pollinia skylight trilling bedmaker eremitic
dealfish fowlpest kailyard pollinic smallage trillion Bermudas examinee
declarer frillies keelhaul polliwog smallfry trillium besmirch examiner
```

```
exemplar  naumachy  sigmatic  wormwood  chinchin  ethnarch  hypnotic  ovenware
exemplum  neomycin  skimmilk  wrymouth  chinless  ethnical  identify  ozoniser
eximious  nonmetal  skimming  yarmulka  chondrus  euonymin  identity  painless
farmhand  nonmoral  skimpily  yeomanly  cinnabar  euonymus  inundate  paintbox
farmland  normalcy  slamming  yeomanry  cinnamic  evanesce  irenical  pannikin
farmyard  normally  slimmest  zoomancy  cinnamon  evenfall  irenicon  pawnshop
filmgoer  noumenal  slimming  zoometry  clanging  evenness  ironbark  phantasm
filmstar  noumenon  slimmish  zoomorph  clangour  evensong  ironclad  phantasy
firmness  oddments  slimness  abundant  clannish  eventful  irongray  phenolic
flambeau  odometer  slumbery  acanthus  clanship  eventide  irongrey  phenylic
flamenco  ohmmeter  slumming  acentric  clansman  eventual  ironical  phonemic
flamingo  olympiad  staminal  aconitic  clincher  evincive  ironside  phonetic
flimflam  Olympian  stampede  aconitum  clinical  exanthem  ironware  pianiste
flimsily  outmatch  stemless  adenitis  clinking  faineant  ironwood  picnicky
flummery  outmoded  stemmata  adenoids  coenobia  faintish  ironwork  pinnacle
foamless  oximeter  stemming  aduncate  coenzyme  faunally  jaundice  pinnated
formalin  oxymoron  stimulus  aduncous  cognomen  fernshaw  jauntily  pinniped
formally  palmette  stomachy  adynamia  cognosce  fiendish  joinable  pinnular
formerly  palmetto  stomatal  adynamic  cognovit  finnesko  jointure  planchet
formless  palmiped  stomatic  agential  coincide  flanerie  keenness  plangent
formroom  palmitin  stumbler  agonised  conniver  flincher  klondike  planking
formulae  panmixia  stumming  allnight  coonskin  flinders  lanneret  plankton
formulas  Parmesan  stumpily  amenable  cornball  flintily  launcher  planning
formwork  pemmican  submerge  amenably  corneous  fornices  leanness  plantain
framesaw  permeate  submerse  asyndeta  cornetcy  founding  ligneous  planulae
fremitus  pinmoney  summerly  aventail  cornetti  fountain  lignitic  planular
frumenty  plimsoll  summitry  bannered  cornetto  francium  Linnaean  pointing
frumpish  plumaged  summoner  banneret  corniced  Frankish  loanable  poundage
gasmeter  plumbago  surmisal  bannerol  corniche  franklin  loanword  pounding
geomancy  plumbate  surmiser  barnacle  cornicle  frenetic  loonybin  prandial
geometer  plumbing  surmount  barndoor  cornific  frenulum  maenadic  prankful
geometry  plumbism  swimming  barnyard  cornpone  frenzied  magnesia  prankish
Germanic  plumelet  swimsuit  beanpole  countess  fringing  magneton  prenatal
germcell  plumiped  symmetry  biannual  cranefly  frondage  magnetic  prentice
germfree  plumpish  Talmudic  biennial  craniate  frondent  magnific  princely
germinal  plumular  teammate  biennium  crankily  frondose  magnolia  princess
gimmicky  premiere  teamster  bignonia  crankpin  frontage  mainland  printing
glummest  premolar  teamwork  binnacle  crannied  frontier  mainline  printout
glumness  premorse  tegmenta  blandish  crenated  frontlet  mainmast  pronator
gnomonic  primally  terminal  blankety  crenelle  funnyman  mainsail  prunella
gormless  Primates  terminer  blindage  cyanogen  gainable  mainstay  prunelle
gramarye  primeval  terminus  blinding  cyanosis  gainings  maintain  prunello
gramatom  primming  termless  blinkers  cyanotic  gainless  mainyard  pugnosed
gramercy  primness  termtime  blondish  daintily  gainsaid  mannered  quandary
grimacer  primrose  thematic  bouncily  damnable  gauntlet  mannerly  quandong
grimmest  promisee  thumbpot  bouncing  damnably  Ghanaian  mannikin  quantify
grimness  promiser  thumping  boundary  deanship  giantess  mannitol  quantise
grimoire  promoter  titmouse  brancard  dianthus  giantism  meanness  quantity
gromwell  prompter  tommybar  branched  dipnoous  glancing  meantime  quencher
grumbler  promptly  tommygun  brancher  downbeat  glanders  midnight  quenelle
grumpily  promulge  tommyrot  branchia  downcast  glandule  misnomer  quincunx
gummosis  ptomaine  tramline  brandied  downcome  goingson  moonbeam  quintain
gunmetal  pulmonic  trammels  brandish  downfall  gownsman  mooncalf  rainbird
haematic  pygmaean  trampler  brandnew  downhaul  grandame  moonface  raincoat
haematin  reembark  trembler  brindled  downhill  granddad  moonfish  raindrop
harmless  reemerge  trembles  bronchia  downland  grandeur  moonless  rainfall
harmonic  reemploy  trimaran  bronchus  downmost  grandson  moonrise  rainwash
haymaker  reimpose  trimeric  brunette  downpipe  granitic  moonsail  rainwear
helmeted  rhomboid  trimeter  burntout  downpour  granular  moonshee  reindeer
helminth  roommate  trimming  cannabin  downtime  grindery  moonshot  reinless
helmsman  rummager  trimness  cannabis  downtown  grinning  moonwort  reinsert
hermetic  scammony  trombone  cannikin  downturn  gruntled  mornings  reinsman
Hogmanay  scampish  trumeaux  cannonry  downward  gymnasia  mountain  reinsure
hormonal  schmaltz  trumpery  cannulae  downwind  haunting  mounting  reinvest
hummocky  scimitar  turmeric  cannular  drencher  hernshaw  nainsook  rhinitis
inimical  scombrid  udometer  cannulas  drinking  hornbeam  neonatal  Rhinodon
isomeric  scumming  vermouth  carnally  drunkard  hornbill  noontide  rhonchal
isometry  seamanly  viameter  carnauba  drynurse  hornbook  noontime  rhonchus
isomorph  seamless  warmness  carnival  earnings  hornfels  odontoid  roentgen
kromesky  seamount  warmouth  cernuous  economic  hornless  openable  roundarm
krumhorn  seamouse  whimbrel  chancery  edentate  hornpipe  opencast  rounders
lawmaker  seamster  whimwham  chandler  elenchus  hornrims  openeyed  roundish
magmatic  shambles  wigmaker  chenille  elenctic  horntail  openness  roundtop
marmoset  shameful  wormcast  Chinaman  elongate  hornworm  openplan  ruinable
mesmeric  shamming  wormgear            emendate  hornwort  openwork  runnerup
mismatch  shamrock  wormhole            eminence  hymnbook  orangery  sainfoin
mnemonic  Shemitic  wormlike            eminency  hypnoses  ordnance  saintdom
murmurer  shimmery  wormseed            epinasty  hypnosis  ovenbird  sannyasi
myrmidon                                                              saunders
```

```
scandent  swindler  youngest  autobahn  chromate  endogamy  homonymy  logogram
Scandian  swinging  youngish  autocade  chromite  endogeny  honorary  logotype
scandium  syenitic  zoonosis  autocrat  chromium  endorsee  honourer  lysosome
scanning  taenioid  abhorred  autodafe  ciborium  endorser  horologe  lysozyme
scansion  tainture  abhorrer  autodyne  colonial  endostea  horology  mahogany
scanties  tannable  abnormal  autogamy  colonise  endozoic  humorist  maiolica
scantily  teenager  abrogate  autogiro  colonist  endozoon  humorous  majolica
scenario  Thanatos  absolute  autogyro  colophon  enforcer  humoured  majority
scenical  thanedom  absolver  autolyse  colossal  enforcer  hypobole  malodour
schnapps  thankful  absonant  automata  colossus  enrolled  hypoderm  manorial
sennight  thankyou  absorber  automate  coloured  entoderm  hypogeal  marocain
shanghai  thingamy  accolade  autonomy  conoidal  entoptic  hypogean  maroquin
shantung  thinking  accoutre  autosome  coronach  entozoic  hypogene  Masorete
shinbone  thinness  acrolein  autotomy  coronary  entozoon  hypogeum  Masoreth
shingler  thinnest  acrolith  autotype  coronoid  enzootic  hypogyny  mayoress
shingles  thinning  acrostic  avionics  coworker  ephorate  hypothec  meconium
shinning  thinnish  acrotism  axiology  creosote  ergogram  ichorous  melodeon
shunning  thundery  admonish  babouche  cryogeny  ergotise  ideogram  melodise
signally  tinnitus  adroitly  Baconian  cryolite  ergotism  ideology  melodist
signpost  tomnoddy  advocaat  baronage  cryostat  espousal  idiolect  memorial
skindeep  topnotch  advocacy  baroness  cryotron  espouser  idiotism  memorise
skinfood  tornadic  advocate  baronial  cuboidal  essonite  ignominy  menology
skinhead  townhall  advowson  barouche  culottes  Estonian  ignorant  merosome
skinless  township  aerodyne  bebopper  cynosure  estopped  immobile  mesocarp
skinning  townsman  aerofoil  becoming  cytology  estoppel  immodest  mesoderm
slangily  tranquil  aerogram  befogged  cytosine  estovers  immolate  mesotron
slinkily  transact  aerolite  begotten  debonair  ethology  immortal  Mesozoic
somnific  transect  aerolith  beholden  decolour  etiolate  impolder  metonymy
soundbow  transept  aerology  beholder  decorate  eulogise  impolicy  Minoress
soundbox  transfer  aeronaut  besotted  decorous  eulogist  impolite  Minorite
sounding  transfix  aeronomy  besought  decouple  eulogium  imponent  minority
spandrel  tranship  aerostat  bezonian  deforest  Eurocrat  importer  Minotaur
spandril  transire  afforest  biconvex  deformed  European  imposing  misogamy
Spaniard  transmit  agiotage  bifocals  deionise  europium  imposter  misogyny
spanking  transude  agnostic  bilobate  demobbed  exhorter  impostor  misology
spanning  trencher  agrology  binomial  democrat  exponent  impotent  mobocrat
spanroof  trendily  agronomy  bloodily  demolish  exporter  incoming  molossus
spinifex  truncate  algology  bloodred  demoness  exposure  indocile  monoacid
spinning  trunnion  Algonkin  bloomers  demoniac  extolled  indolent  monocrat
spinster  turnable  algorism  bloomery  demonian  fagoting  informal  monocyte
spondaic  turnback  allocate  blooming  demonise  famously  informed  monodist
spongily  turncoat  allodial  bobolink  demonism  farouche  informer  monogamy
sponsion  turncock  allodium  Boeotian  demotion  favonian  innocent  monogeny
spontoon  turndown  allogamy  broodily  denounce  favoured  innovate  monoglot
spunkily  turnings  allopath  brookite  deponent  favourer  insolate  monogony
stancher  turnover  allotted  brooklet  deportee  ferocity  insolent  monogram
stanchly  turnpike  allottee  bryology  derogate  floodlit  insomnia  monogyny
standard  turnskin  ammoniac  bryozoan  desolate  floodway  insomuch  monolith
standing  turnsole  ammonify  Byronism  detonate  flooring  intonate  monomial
standish  turnspit  ammonite  cabochon  detoxify  fluoride  invocate  monopode
stanhope  twenties  annotate  caboodle  Devonian  fluorine  involute  monopoly
stannary  twinborn  announce  cabotage  devotion  fluorite  iodoform  monorail
stannate  twinkler  aphorise  cacology  devourer  garotter  Jacobean  monotint
stannite  twinling  aphorism  cacomixl  devoutly  gasolene  Jacobite  monotone
stannous  twinning  aphorist  cajolery  dinornis  gasolier  jalousie  monotony
stanzaic  twinship  apposite  camomile  dinosaur  gasoline  japonica  monotype
stenosed  unaneled  arboreal  canoeing  disorder  gazogene  Jehovist  monoxide
stenosis  unending  arboreta  canoeist  divorcee  genocide  jeroboam  morosely
stenotic  vainness  arborist  canoness  dogooder  genotype  jocosely  morosity
stingily  vauntful  areolate  canonise  dolomite  gerontic  jocosity  motorail
stingray  vernally  argonaut  canonist  doloroso  gloomily  joyously  motorcar
stinkard  vernicle  armorial  canoodle  dolorous  groogroo  Jugoslav  motorial
stinking  Viennese  armoured  canorous  donought  gulosity  kerosene  motoring
stinkpot  vigneron  armourer  caponier  doxology  gynocrat  kerosine  motorise
stonefly  wainscot  arrogant  caponise  echogram  gynoecia  kilogram  motorist
stunning  weanling  arrogate  Carolean  echoless  gyrostat  kilowatt  motorium
stunsail  wetnurse  arsonist  Caroline  eclosion  havocked  labourer  motorman
stuntman  whenever  arsonous  carotene  ectoderm  hedonics  laconian  motormen
swanherd  whinchat  ascocarp  carousal  ectozoon  hedonism  laconism  motorway
swanking  whinsill  assonant  carousel  eldorado  hedonist  lemonade  mucosity
swanlike  winnable  assonate  carouser  embolden  helotism  leporine  mycology
swanmark  winnings  assorted  cenotaph  embolism  heroical  licorice  mylonite
swanneck  winnower  astonied  Cenozoic  embosser  Holocene  limonite  myxomata
swannery  woundily  astonish  chlorate  emporium  hologram  linoleum  nanogram
swanning  wrangler  atrocity  chloride  encomion  holozoic  lipogram  napoleon
swanshot  wrongful  atropine  chlorine  encomium  homodont  lipomata  nepotism
swanskin  wrongous  attorney  chlorite  endocarp  homogamy  lobotomy  nicotian
swansong  yeanling  aurorean  chlorous  endoderm  homology  locomote  nodosity
```

nomogram	resource	strophic	venomous	composer	flopping	palpable	shopgirl
nomology	retorted	stropped	venosity	compound	flypaper	palpably	shopping
nosology	revolter	suborder	venously	compress	frapping	pamperer	shoptalk
notornis	revolute	suborner	veronica	comprise	frippery	pamphlet	shopworn
obsolete	revolver	suboxide	vigorous	computer	gazpacho	panpipes	silphium
octonary	rheology	sycomore	vinosity	cooption	geophagy	pappadom	simplify
octoroon	rheostat	syconium	vinously	cooptive	geophone	payphone	simplism
odiously	rhyolite	synonymy	virology	copperas	geophyte	peephole	sixpence
oecology	ribosome	synopses	wagonage	corporal	geoponic	peepshow	sixpenny
oenology	ricochet	synopsis	wagonlit	coupling	glyptics	pinpoint	skipjack
oenophil	rigorism	synoptic	whooping	crepitus	grapheme	pinprick	skipping
oncology	rigorist	synovial	xenogamy	cropping	graphics	plopping	skypilot
oncoming	rigorous	tabouret	xenolith	culpable	graphite	poppadum	slapbang
onlooker	roborant	taxonomy	xylocarp	culpably	gripping	porphyry	slapdash
ontogeny	rugosely	tenonsaw	xylology	cuspidor	gripsack	porpoise	slapjack
ontology	rugosity	tenorite	xylonite	cutprice	gumption	potplant	slapping
oogonial	sabotage	tenotomy	Yugoslav	cutpurse	gunpoint	preparer	slipcase
oogonium	saboteur	theocrat	zymology	dampness	harpseal	prepense	slipform
oologist	Salopian	theodicy	adaption	deeplaid	helpless	preprint	slipknot
opponent	Samoyede	theogony	adaptive	deepness	helpmate	propense	slipover
opposite	saponify	theology	adoption	Delphian	helpmeet	properly	slippage
oreology	saponite	theorise	adoptive	despatch	henparty	property	slippery
otiosely	saporous	theorist	alopecia	despiser	herpetic	prophase	slipping
otiosity	sauouari	throated	anapaest	despotic	Hesperus	prophecy	slipring
oxtongue	savorous	throbbed	anaphase	dewpoint	Hispanic	prophesy	sliproad
palomino	Savoyard	thrombin	anaphora	diapason	hospital	propolis	slipshod
panorama	Saxondom	thrombus	anyplace	diapause	hotplate	proposal	slipslop
parodist	Saxonism	throstle	apoplexy	diaphone	hotpress	proposer	sloppail
paroquet	Saxonist	throttle	Arapahoe	diopside	humpback	propound	sloppily
paroxysm	sayonara	timorous	arapaima	dioptase	iceplant	propping	slopping
pedology	scholium	timously	aseptate	dioptric	insphere	propylic	slopshop
pelorism	schooner	toboggan	atypical	dispatch	inspired	pulpiter	slopwork
penology	sciolism	tocology	auspices	dispense	inspirer	pulpwood	snapbrim
peroneal	sciolist	tokology	bagpiper	disperse	inspirit	pumproom	snaplink
perorate	scoopful	tomogram	bedplate	dispirit	isophote	puppetry	snappily
peroxide	scoopnet	tomorrow	bespoken	displace	isopleth	puppydog	snapping
pilosity	scrofula	topology	besprent	displant	isoprene	puppydom	snappish
pilotage	scrounge	toponymy	bioplasm	displode	isoptera	puppyfat	snapshot
pinochle	seaonion	toroidal	bioplast	displume	jeopardy	puppyish	snippety
pisolite	seconder	trioxide	boxpleat	disposal	jetplane	purplish	snipping
pivotman	secondly	tumorous	campagna	disposer	jumpedup	purpuric	snipsnap
pleonasm	semolina	tutorage	campaign	dispread	jumpseat	purpurin	soapbark
Pliocene	senorita	tutoress	campfire	disprize	jumpsuit	quipping	soapdish
polonium	serology	tutorial	camphene	disproof	keepsake	rampancy	soapless
pomology	serosity	typology	camphine	disprove	klephtic	rapparee	soaproot
porosity	serotine	Tyrolean	campsite	dripfeed	knapping	reappear	soapsuds
posology	sexology	tyrosine	chapatti	dripping	knapsack	respects	soapwort
priorate	shooting	umbonate	chapbook	drophead	knapweed	response	sorption
prioress	shootout	unbolted	chapelry	dropkick	lamppost	respring	sorptive
priority	simoniac	unbottle	chaperon	dropleaf	leapfrog	resprung	stapelia
proofing	simonist	uncoined	chapiter	dropping	limpidly	rhapsode	stepping
pyroxene	sinology	uncommon	chaplain	dropshot	limpness	rhapsody	stepwise
rasorial	sinophil	uncouple	chapping	dropwort	loophole	samphire	stipites
recommit	sitology	unforced	chipmuck	drupelet	lumpfish	sampling	stippler
reconvey	smoothen	unformed	chipmunk	dryplate	lymphoid	sapphics	stipular
recorder	smoothie	ungotten	chipping	drypoint	lymphoma	sapphire	stopcock
recourse	smoothly	unhoused	chopchop	dumpling	lyophile	sapphism	stopover
recovery	snootily	unionise	chopping	dyspnoea	manpower	scaphoid	stoppage
redolent	sodomite	unionism	chopsuey	earphone	midpoint	scapulae	stopping
redouble	sonobuoy	unionist	chupatti	earpiece	misplace	scapular	stupidly
reforest	sonority	unloader	chupatty	eggplant	misprint	scapulas	stuprate
reformed	sonorous	unloosen	clapping	Egyptian	misprise	sceptred	subphyla
reformer	sorochen	unlovely	claptrap	elephant	misprize	scopulae	subpoena
regolith	sororate	unroofed	clipclop	endpaper	morpheme	scopulas	subprior
rehoboam	sorority	unsocial	clippers	ensphere	morphine	seapiece	sulphate
rejoicer	splotchy	unsought	clipping	epiphany	nauplius	seaplane	sulphide
relocate	spookily	untoward	clopclop	epiphyte	neaptide	seapurse	sulphide
remotely	spookish	unvoiced	clupeoid	epopoeia	neophyte	semplice	sulphone
renounce	spoonfed	unwonted	clypeate	eruption	neoplasm	sempster	sunproof
renovate	spoonful	unwordly	codpiece	eruptive	neoprene	serpulae	supplant
renowned	spoonily	unworthy	compages	eyepiece	nonparty	shapable	supplely
reporter	sprocket	upholder	compiler	flapjack	nymphean	shepherd	supplial
repotted	strobila	uprooter	complain	flapping	offprint	shipload	supplier
repousse	strobile	valorise	compleat	flipflap	oliphant	shipmate	supplies
resolute	strobili	valorous	complete	flipflop	omophagy	shipment	supposal
resonant	stroller	vaporise	complice	flippant	omoplate	shipping	supposed
resonate	stromata	vaporous	complier	flipping	onepiece	shipworm	suppress
resorcin	strongly	vapourer	compline	flipside	outpoint	shipyard	surplice
resorter	strontia	velocity	composed	floppily	oviposit	shopbell	surprise

suspense	chequers	aversive	dairying	exorcist	hydrogen	neuronal	overrode
swapping	cinquain	barracks	dairyman	exordial	hydromel	neuronic	overrule
swopping	claqueur	barranca	dearness	exordium	hydropic	neuroses	oversail
sylphide	cliquish	barranco	decrease	extrados	hydropsy	neurosis	overseas
sylphine	cliquism	barrator	decrepit	extremes	hydroski	neurotic	overseen
sylphish	conquest	barratry	decretal	extrorse	hydroxyl	nitrogen	overseer
sympathy	cotquean	barrette	deerskin	eyerhyme	imprimis	nonrigid	oversell
symphile	daiquiri	bearable	defrayal	fairlead	imprison	nutrient	oversewn
symphony	disquiet	bearably	degrease	fairness	improper	ochreous	overshoe
sympodia	eloquent	bearings	depraved	fairyism	improver	operable	overshot
symposia	exequies	bearskin	deprival	farriery	increase	operatic	overside
tamperer	frequent	befriend	deprived	fearless	increate	operator	oversize
Tarpeian	inequity	begrudge	derriere	fearsome	inerrant	opercula	overslip
taxpayer	iniquity	betrayal	detrital	febrific	inertial	operetta	oversold
teaparty	Iroquois	betrayer	detritus	February	infrared	ostracod	oversoul
tempered	jacquard	blurrily	diarchal	ferreter	infringe	ostracon	overstay
temperer	marquess	blurring	diarchic	ferriage	ingrowth	ostrakon	overstep
template	marquise	borrower	diarrhea	ferritic	intrados	outrange	overtake
temporal	Mayqueen	botryoid	dicrotic	ferryman	intrench	outreach	overtask
tempting	mesquite	bourgeon	diereses	fibrilla	intrepid	outreign	overtime
tenpence	misquote	boursier	dieresis	fibrosis	intrigue	outrider	overtone
tenpenny	mosquito	bourtree	dioramic	fibrotic	intromit	outright	overtook
tinplate	musquash	burrower	dioritic	fiercely	introrse	outrival	overture
toepiece	opaquely	cabriole	diuresis	florally	intruder	ovariole	overturn
toeplate	seaquake	caprifig	diuretic	floridly	inurbane	ovaritis	overview
torpidly	torquate	capriole	doorbell	florigen	iterance	overalls	overwear
trapball	ubiquity	carriage	doorcase	forrader	ivorynut	overarch	overwind
trapdoor	uniquely	carriole	doorknob	fourball	jerrican	overbear	overwork
trapezia	vanquish	carryall	doornail	foureyes	jerrycan	overbook	overworn
trappean	aberrant	carryout	doorpost	fourfold	kourbash	overbore	parrotry
trapping	aborally	charcoal	doorsill	fourleaf	labrador	overbusy	patronal
Trappist	aborning	charisma	doorstep	fourpart	lacrimal	overcall	peardrop
traprock	abortion	charlady	doorstop	foursome	lacrosse	overcame	pearlies
trephine	abortive	charlock	dooryard	fourstar	lacrymal	overcast	pearling
tripeman	acarpous	charming	dourness	fourteen	larrikin	overcoat	pearlite
triplane	accredit	charring	dwarfish	fourthly	laureate	overcome	pearmain
triploid	acerbate	Chartism	dwarfism	furriery	learning	overcrop	peerless
tripodal	acerbity	Chartist	eldritch	garreted	libretti	overdone	petrolic
trippery	acervate	Cherokee	embracer	garrison	libretto	overdose	petronel
tripping	adorable	cherubic	emergent	garrotte	lubrical	overdraw	petrosal
triptych	adorably	cherubim	emeritus	gearcase	madrigal	overdrew	pharisee
tripwire	aegrotat	chirpily	emersion	Georgian	Mahratta	overfall	pharmacy
trophied	affright	chirrupy	enarched	gloriole	Mahratti	overfeed	phormium
tropical	agaragar	choragic	encrinal	glorious	marriage	overfill	piercing
tuppence	aggrieve	choragus	encrinic	gourmand	marrieds	overfish	plurally
tuppenny	aigrette	chorally	encroach	guaranty	marrying	overflew	poorness
twopence	alarmist	chordate	energise	guardant	matrices	overflow	porridge
twopenny	alfresco	choregic	enervate	guardian	matrixes	overfold	potroast
twopiece	allround	choregus	engramma	guerilla	matronal	overfond	pourable
tympanic	altruism	choriamb	engraver	guernsey	matronly	overgrew	prorogue
tympanum	altruist	chorioid	enormity	hadronic	metrical	overgrow	prurient
unipolar	amaranth	churchly	enormous	hairgrip	microbar	overhand	pruritic
unopened	ambrosia	churinga	entracte	hairless	microbic	overhang	pruritus
unsprung	American	churlish	entrails	hairlike	microdot	overhaul	pteropod
upsprang	amorally	churning	entrance	hairline	micrurgy	overhead	pterylae
upspring	amoretti	cirriped	entreaty	hairworm	migraine	overhear	putridly
upsprung	amoretto	clarence	entrench	harridan	migrator	overheat	pyrrhoea
vampiric	amortise	clarinet	entrepot	harrumph	moorcock	overhung	pyrrhous
vamplate	anarchic	clerical	entresol	heartily	moorfowl	overjump	quarrier
vesperal	androgen	clerihew	enuresis	hebraise	moorings	overkill	quartern
vespiary	anorexia	clerkdom	enuretic	Hebraism	moorland	overlaid	quarters
volplane	anorexic	clerkess	espresso	Hebraist	mournful	overlain	quartile
warpaint	anorthic	coarsely	estrange	heirless	mourning	overland	quirkily
warplane	antrorse	codriver	esurient	heirloom	mucrones	overleaf	rearlamp
weaponry	aperient	coercion	eternise	heirship	murrelet	overload	rearmice
whapping	aperitif	coercive	eternity	henroost	murrhine	overlong	rearmost
whipcord	aperture	corridor	eucritic	hierarch	nacreous	overlook	rearview
whiplash	appraise	corrival	eutrophy	hieratic	narrator	overlord	rearward
whiplike	approach	courante	evermore	hirrient	narrowly	overmuch	recreant
whipping	approval	coursing	eversion	hoarding	Nearctic	overnice	recreate
whipworm	astragal	courtesy	everyday	hoarsely	nearness	overpaid	regrater
whopping	ataraxia	courtier	everyman	horrible	necropsy	overpass	regrowth
wrappage	ataraxic	cupreous	everyone	horribly	necrosis	overpast	reorient
wrapping	attrited	currency	everyway	horridly	necrotic	overplay	reprieve
zeppelin	aubretia	curricle	exercise	horrific	Negrillo	overplus	reprisal
zoophily	averment	Cypriote	exergual	hourlong	negroism	overrate	reproach
zoophyte	averring	czaritza	exertion	hydranth	neurally	override	reproval
adequacy	aversely		exorcise		neuritic	overripe	retrench
adequate	aversion		exorcism		neuritis		retrieve

```
retroact  spurgear  uncreate  bursitis  dorsally  grosbeak  misstate  possibly
retrorse  spurious  undraped  cabstand  dressage  groschen  moisture  potsherd
rubrical  spurling  undreamt  caesious  dressing  gunsmith  monsieur  potstill
sacraria  spurrier  unerring  caesural  drystone  gunstock  mossback  potstone
sacredly  spurring  unfreeze  camshaft  dyestuff  gusseted  mouseear  presager
sacristy  stardust  unfrozen  capsicum  eftsoons  gypseous  moussaka  prescind
safranin  starfish  usurious  capstone  egestion  gypsydom  mudstone  presence
sauropod  stargaze  uxorious  capsular  egestive  gypsyism  myositic  preserve
scarcely  starkers  vagrancy  cassette  eggshell  hatstand  myositis  presidio
scarcity  starless  verrucae  catsfoot  ekistics  hausfrau  myosotis  pressbox
scarfpin  starlike  vibrancy  catstail  emissary  haystack  nauseant  pressing
scarious  starling  vibrator  causally  emission  hipsters  nauseate  pressman
scarless  starrily  vibrissa  causerie  emissive  hogsback  nauseous  pressure
scarring  starring  vitreous  causeway  episcope  hogshead  newscast  prestige
scirocco  starting  warragal  cesspool  episemon  holstein  newsheet  presumer
scirrhus  startler  warranty  chasseur  episodal  hoosegow  newspeak  prismoid
scorcher  starwort  warrener  chastely  episodic  horsebox  newsreel  prisoner
scornful  sterigma  warrigal  chastise  epistler  horsecar  newsroom  prissily
scorpion  sterling  wearable  chastity  epistyle  horsefly  noisette  pristine
scurrile  sternite  weariful  chasuble  erasable  horseman  nonsense  prosaism
scurvily  sternson  wharfage  chessman  Erastian  houseboy  nonstick  prosaist
searcher  sternway  wherever  chestnut  existent  housedog  Norseman  prosodic
secretin  stirring  whirring  classics  exospore  housefly  nuisance  prospect
secretly  storable  whoredom  classify  eyeshade  houseful  numskull  prostate
secretor  storeman  whoreson  closeset  eyesight  houseman  nursling  prostyle
segreant  storeyed  yearbook  closeted  eyestalk  housetop  nutshell  Prussian
serranid  stormily  yearling  clustery  falsetto  hyoscine  Odyssean  puissant
serrated  sturdied  yearlong  coistrel  fatstock  iceskate  offshoot  pulsator
sforzato  sturdily  yearning  conserve  Faustian  inasmuch  offshore  pursenet
shareout  sturgeon  yourself  consider  feasible  inkstand  offsider  purslane
sharpish  surround  acescent  consoler  feasibly  inositol  offstage  pursuant
sharpset  surroyal  acosmism  consomme  feastday  Irishism  oilstone  pussycat
Sheraton  tarragon  adespota  conspire  felsitic  Irishman  omission  question
sherlock  tearaway  airscrew  constant  firstaid  isospory  onesided  quisling
shiralee  teardrop  airshaft  construe  fissiped  isostasy  opuscula  ransomer
shirring  tearduct  airspace  consular  flashgun  joystick  opuscule  ratsbane
shirting  tearless  airspeed  consumer  flashily  keeshond  otoscope  ratstail
shortage  terraced  airstrip  corselet  flashing  keystone  outshine  reascend
shortarm  terrapin  allspice  corsetry  fleshfly  khuskhus  outshone  reasoner
shortcut  terraria  amusedly  corsetry  fleshpot  kinsfolk  outsider  reassert
shortday  terrazzo  anasarca  Cotswold  forsaken  kissable  outsight  reassess
shortish  terrible  angstrom  couscous  forsooth  kisscurl  outsmart  reassign
skerrick  terribly  anisette  cousinly  forspeak  klystron  outspend  reassure
skirmish  terrific  apostasy  coxswain  forspent  Komsomol  outspent  redshank
skirting  tetradic  apostate  crashing  forswear  layshaft  outstare  redshift
slurring  tetragon  aristate  crashpad  forswore  laystall  outstrip  redshirt
smarmily  tetrapla  Ayrshire  crescent  forsworn  leisured  pansophy  redstart
smartish  tetrapod  bakhshish crescive  foxshark  lensless  Parsiism  reusable
sobriety  tetrarch  balsamic  crispate  frescoes  linstock  parsonic  Riesling
Socratic  therefor  bassinet  cristate  freshman  lipsalve  passable  rinsings
sorrower  thereout  basswood  crossbar  freshrun  lipstick  passably  roasting
sourdine  thermion  bedstead  crossbow  frisette  loosebox  passbook  sanserif
sourness  thermite  bedstraw  crosscut  friskily  loosener  passerby  Sanskrit
sourpuss  thirlage  beeswing  crossing  frostily  lopsided  passible  sarsenet
sovranty  thirster  biassing  crosslet  frosting  maestoso  Passover  Sassanid
sparable  thirteen  bioscope  crossply  frustule  mansized  passport  scissile
sparbuoy  thoraces  blastema  crosstie  gemstone  marshman  password  scission
spardeck  thoracic  blastoff  crossway  ghastful  massacre  paysheet  scissors
sparkgap  thoraxes  blastoid  crusader  gipsydom  masseter  peasecod  seascape
sparkish  thorough  blastula  crustily  gipsyism  masseuse  penstock  seashell
sparkler  thurible  blesbuck  cursedly  glassful  massicot  personae  seashore
sparklet  thurifer  blessing  cussedly  glassily  massless  personal  seasnail
sparling  Thursday  blissful  cussword  glassine  measured  perspire  seasnake
sparring  thyroxin  blistery  cypselae  glissade  memsahib  persuade  seasonal
sparsely  thyrsoid  blossomy  danseuse  glossary  menstrua  phaseout  seasoner
sparsity  torridly  blushful  diaspora  glossily  mensural  phosgene  senseful
spermary  touristy  blustery  diaspore  glossina  menswear  phosphor  sensible
spiracle  tournure  boastful  diastase  Godspeed  messmate  physical  sensibly
spirally  tsarevna  bonspiel  diastema  goosegog  messuage  physicky  sensoria
spirilla  tsaritsa  bosseyed  diastole  gossamer  miasmata  physique  sensuous
spirited  tsaritza  bowsprit  diestock  gossiper  miasmous  piassava  setscrew
spiritus  turreted  brassage  dipstick  gossipry  midships  pigswill  shashlik
sporadic  Tyrrhene  brassard  disseise  gossypol  minstrel  pilsener  skislope
sporozoa  ultraism  brassart  disserve  grasping  misshape  plastery  skyscape
sportful  ultraist  brassica  dissever  Griselda  missilry  plastics  slashing
sportily  umbrella  brassily  dissolve  griseous  misspell  plastron  smashing
sporting  umbrette  briskish  dissuade  grisette  misspelt  plussage  sobstory
sportive  unbridle  brisling  dogsbody  grisgris  misspend  poisoner  sobstuff
sporular  unbroken  brushoff  dogshore  grissini  misspent  possible  solstice
```

```
stasimon  Arcturus  centuple  distinct  flatrace  halteres  masterly  pastille
subserve  arethusa  chateaux  distract  flattery  hastener  masthead  pastoral
subshrub  bacteria  chattily  distrain  flattest  hastings  mastitis  pastrami
subsolar  Bactrian  chatting  distrait  flattish  hawthorn  mastodon  pastries
subsonic  banterer  chitchat  distress  flatware  heatedly  mattress  pastural
substage  bantling  chutzpah  district  flatways  heathery  meatball  pattypan
sunshade  barterer  clothier  distrust  flatwise  heathhen  meatsafe  pectines
sunshine  bartizan  clothing  dittybag  flatworm  heptagon  meetness  pectoral
sunshiny  bastardy  clotting  dittybox  fletcher  Hertzian  mentally  pentacle
sunstone  bastille  coatrack  doctoral  flitting  histogen  Miltonic  pentagon
swastika  battalia  coatroom  doctrine  flotilla  historic  mintmark  pentroof
tasselly  battleax  contagia  dogtired  fluttery  hostelry  mirthful  pertness
teaspoon  beatific  contango  dogtooth  foetidly  huntress  mistaken  pettifog
tensible  bedtable  contempt  dotterel  fontanel  huntsman  misthink  photogen
tesserae  beetling  contents  ductless  fontange  hurtless  mistreat  photopia
tesseral  beetroot  contessa  duettist  football  hustings  mistress  photopic
thesauri  beltless  continua  dustbowl  footbath  hysteria  mistrial  photopsy
thespian  bentwood  continue  dustcart  footfall  hysteric  mistrust  pictures
thisness  bestiary  continuo  dustcoat  footgear  ianthine  mittened  pintable
thusness  bestowal  contline  dustless  foothill  illtimed  mittimus  pintsize
tinselly  bestrewn  contorno  dustlike  foothold  illtreat  monteith  pittance
tinsmith  bestride  contract  dustshot  footless  imitable  mortally  plateaux
tinstone  bestrode  contrail  dystopia  footling  imitator  mortgage  plateful
tipstaff  biathlon  contrary  earthnut  footmark  initiate  mortmain  platelet
topstone  birthday  contrast  easterly  footmuff  instable  mortuary  platform
trashery  bistable  contrate  eastmost  footnote  instance  mottling  platinic
trashily  bistoury  contrite  eastward  footpace  instancy  mouthful  platinum
trespass  bitterly  contrive  ecstatic  footpath  instinct  multeity  platonic
tressure  blatancy  cortical  editress  footpost  instruct  multifid  platting
triskele  blithely  cortices  elatedly  footrace  isothere  multiped  platypus
trisomic  blotting  costmary  emetical  footrest  isotherm  multiple  plethora
tristful  boatbill  costplus  emitting  footrope  isotonic  multiply  plotting
tristich  boatdeck  costpush  epitasis  footrule  isotopic  mustache  plutonic
trussing  boathook  costumer  erethism  footslog  isotropy  mutterer  poetical
trustful  boatload  cottager  erotical  footsore  jettison  mystical  poltfoot
trustily  bolthole  cottagey  erythema  footstep  jolthead  mystique  poltroon
tussocky  boltrope  cratches  esoteric  footwear  justness  nautical  pontifex
twosided  bontebok  cretonne  eustatic  footwork  knitting  nautilus  portable
unisonal  bootjack  criteria  evitable  fortieth  knitwear  neatherd  portfire
urostyle  bootlace  critical  exoteric  fortress  knothole  neatness  porthole
velskoen  bootlast  critique  eyetooth  fortuity  knotting  nectared  porticos
versicle  bootless  crotched  factious  fortyish  knotwork  neotenic  portiere
voussoir  boottree  crotchet  factotum  fosterer  kurtosis  neoteric  portrait
waesucks  bottomry  cultivar  faithful  fretting  lanthorn  nestling  portress
weaselly  boutique  cultural  faltboat  fretwork  latterly  neutrino  postcard
Welshman  brattice  cultured  fantasia  fritting  latticed  nextdoor  postcode
whiskers  brattish  curtains  farthest  frothily  leathern  nocturne  postdate
whiskery  brethren  curtness  farthing  frottage  leathery  northern  postfree
whispery  brettese  customer  fastback  frutices  lecturer  northing  posthorn
whistler  brettice  cysteine  fastener  furthest  lefthand  Northman  postiche
wrestler  britches  cystitis  fastfood  gantline  leftover  nuptials  postlude
wrestpin  britzska  dactylar  fastness  gantlope  leftward  nurturer  postmark
wristlet  brutally  dactylic  fasttalk  gastight  lenticel  obituary  postmill
wristpin  buntline  daftness  fastuous  gastraea  lenticle  obstacle  postobit
yeastily  bustling  dartrous  fattener  gastrula  lettered  obstruct  postpaid
zoospore  buttoner  dastardy  fauteuil  gentrice  liftable  oestrone  postpone
abattoir  buttress  deathbed  feathery  geotaxis  lintseed  oestrous  postural
abetment  bystreet  deathcap  featured  gestagen  listener  ofttimes  posturer
abetting  cactuses  deathray  features  gestural  listless  ointment  potterer
absterge  calthrop  deftness  festally  ghettoes  littlego  oldtimer  pratique
abstract  canthari  dentalia  festival  giftbook  littling  omitting  prattler
abstrict  canticle  dentated  fewtrils  gilthead  littoral  onetrack  pretence
abstruse  cantonal  denticle  fiftieth  glittery  loathful  oratorio  prettify
abutilon  cantoris  destrier  fiftyish  glutting  loathing  oratress  prettily
abutment  captious  destruct  filthily  gluttony  loiterer  oxytocin  protasis
abuttals  cartload  deuteron  filtrate  gnathite  lustrate  palterer  protatic
abutting  cartouch  dextrine  fistiana  goatfish  lustrine  pantheon  protease
aesthete  castaway  dextrose  fistical  goatherd  lustring  pantofle  protegee
aestival  castiron  dextrous  fistulae  goatling  lustrous  pantsuit  protista
agitator  castrate  diatomic  fistular  goatmoth  maltreat  partaken  protocol
agitprop  castrati  diatonic  flatboat  goatskin  maltster  parterre  protonic
airtight  castrato  diatribe  flatfeet  goitrous  mantelet  Parthian  protozoa
amethyst  cattleya  dictator  flatfish  goutweed  mantilla  partible  protract
amitosis  cautious  dietetic  flatfoot  goutwort  mantissa  particle  protrude
amitotic  centaury  dipteral  flathead  grateful  mantling  partisan  pustular
anathema  centring  dipteran  flatiron  gratuity  martagon  partizan  quatrain
anatomic  centrism  distally  flatling  gritting  martello  partsong  quitrent
anything  centrist  distance  flatmate  grottoes  martenot  parttime  quitting
apothegm  centroid  distaste  flatness  guttural  martinet  pastiche  quotable
```

```
quotient softhead Teutonic westward anourous durukuli jesuitic pleurisy
raftsman softness textbook wettable arcuated effusion jesuitry plougher
raptness softshoe texthand whatever arguable effusive jocundly populace
raptures softsoap textuary whatness arguably embussed jugulate populate
rattling software textural whetting argufier empurple kefuffle populism
rectoral softwood textured whiteboy argument encumber kreutzer populist
rentable soothing thatcher whitecap arquebus enquirer laburnum populous
restcure soothsay thetical whitefly assuming esculent lacunary purulent
restless sortable tiltyard whitehot astutely Esquimau lacunate queueing
restorer soutache tintless whitener Augustan estuaril lacunose rebuttal
restrain southern tittuped whiteout augustly Etrurian lazulite rebutted
restrict southing tittuppy whitetie autumnal Etruscan lazurite rebutter
rhetoric southpaw toothful whittret autunite excursus lemurine recurred
rhythmic Southron toothily winterly babushka fabulist lemuroid recusant
roothold spathose toothing wintrily baguette fabulous levulose regulate
rootless spatting tortilla wistaria baluster feculent ligulate relucent
rostrate spatular tortious wisteria beautify fiducial liquidly relumine
rottenly spiteful tortoise wontedly befuddle figurant liturgic renumber
rustical spitfire tortuous worthful beguiler figurine lobulate republic
rustless spitting torturer worthily bequeath flautist loculate requital
ryotwari spittoon totterer wrathful bibulous flounder locution requiter
saltbush spotless tritical wrathily bicuspid flourish locutory resupine
saltless spottily trotting wretched botulism focusing luculent resurvey
saltlick spotting trottoir writable brougham focussed Lucullan ritually
saltmine statable truthful writeoff brouhaha Fraulein lunulate robustly
saltness statedly turtling writings caducean Freudian maculate rosulate
saltwort statical twitcher xanthate caduceus froufrou manually rotundly
santonin statuary twittery xanthein caducity furuncle manubria roturier
Sauterne statured twitting xanthene caducous futurism manurial rugulose
sawtooth stetting twotimer xanthine capuchin futurist maquette salutary
scathing stitcher uintaite xanthium caruncle futurity maturate saturant
scattily subtitle umptieth xanthoma casually gefuffle maturely saturate
scatting subtlety unctuous Xantippe casualty ghoulish maturity Saturday
scotfree subtonic unitedly yestreen cerulean glaucoma medusoid saturnic
scotopic subtopia unstable youthful cerusite glaucous minutely sciurine
Scotsman subtotal unstably zoetrope chaunter grounder minutiae sciuroid
scottice subtract unstated abducens chauntry grouping misusage scourger
Scottish suitable unsteady abducent cloudily grouting modulate scouting
scutcher suitably unstring abductor cloudlet hamululi monument scrubbed
scutella suitcase unstrung ablution coauthor haruspex moquette scrubber
seatbelt suitings unstuffy abruptly colubrid hocusing mutually scrutiny
seatrout sultrily upstairs absurdly columnal hocussed naturism securely
sectoral swatting upstream accuracy columnar homuncle naturist security
sentence switchel upstroke accurate columned Huguenot nebulise sedulity
sentient swotting urethane accursed conurbia humuncle nebulium sedulous
sentinel syntagma vastness accustom copulate illumine nebulous sequelae
sentrygo syntonic ventless acoustic coquetry illusage nenuphar sequence
septette systemic venturer acquaint coquette illusion nodulose sexually
septfoil systolic vertebra actually corundum illusive nodulous shoulder
septimal tactical vertexes actuator croupier illusory nonunion shouldst
septuple tactless vertical acturial croupous immunise nonusage shrugged
sesterce tantalic vertices adducent cucumber immunity obduracy shrunken
sextette tantalum verticil adductor cucurbit impudent obdurate Silurian
sextuple tantalus vestiary adjuster cumulate impugner obturate siluroid
Shetland Tantrism vestment adjustor cumulous impunity obtusely simulant
shothole tantrist vesturer adjutage cupulate impurely obtusity simulate
shutdown tartaric viaticum adjutant debugged impurity occultly sinusoid
shutting tartness victoria adjuvant debutant incubate occupant situated
siftings tartrate victress affusion decurion incurred occupier sloucher
sisterly Tartuffe victuals aflutter delusion inductee occurred smoulder
sixtieth tastebud Vietcong aiguille delusive inductor oppugner solution
sketcher tasteful Vietminh alburnum delusory indulger orgulous splutter
skittish tattered vintager aleurone demurely induline osculant spousage
skittles tattooer virtuosa alguazil demurred indurate osculate sprucely
slattern tautness virtuosi allusion demurrer indusium paduasoy stoutish
slithery tautomer virtuoso allusive depurate industry pagurian strucken
slitting tautonym virtuous alluvial deputise infusion paludism struggle
slothful teatable voltaism alluvion dilution inguinal papulose strummed
slotting teatowel vortexes alluvium diluvial inhumane papulous strummer
sluttish tectonic vortical ambulant diluvian innuendo patulous strumose
smithers teething vortices ambulate diluvium inquirer peculate strumous
smithery teetotal waitress ambusher disunion insulant peculiar strumpet
smothery teetotum wantonly ampullae disunite insulate peduncle strutted
smuttily tentacle wartweed amputate disunity insulter penumbra strutter
snatcher tertiary wartwort aneurism disusage insurant Peruvian subulate
snitcher testable wastable aneurysm document intubate petulant suburban
softball testator wasteful annually draughts issuable petuntse suburbia
softboil testatum watthour annulate draughty issuance piquancy susurrus
softener testtube westerly annulled droughty jejunely plaudits tabulate
```

```
tegument  leavings  cogwheel  banxring  playback  actually  beeeater  contango
tenurial  louvered  crawfish  bauxitic  playbill  actuator  beggarly  coolabah
theurgic  malvasia  crowbill  flaxseed  playbook  adorable  Benjamin  coplanar
thoughts  nouvelle  crowfoot  flexible  playgirl  adorably  bereaved  cottager
thousand  outvalue  cutwater  flexibly  playgoer  adularia  bergamot  cottagey
thrummed  outvying  dogwatch  flexuose  playmate  adulator  beslaver  coumarin
thruster  perverse  dogwhelk  flexuous  playroom  adynamia  betrayal  courante
traumata  pervious  drawable  flexural  playsuit  adynamic  betrayer  crenated
triumvir  pitviper  drawback  gloxinia  playtime  aerially  biddable  crevasse
triunity  pluvious  drawtube  inexpert  polygala  affiance  bimbashi  crusader
troupial  previous  drawwell  lynxeyed  polygamy  afflatus  binnacle  culpable
trousers  provable  drownded  proximal  polygene  agaragar  bistable  culpably
troutlet  provably  drowsily  quixotic  polygeny  agitator  biyearly  curtains
trouvere  provided  enswathe  quixotry  polyglot  alguazil  blamable  cutwater
tubulate  provider  erewhile  reexport  polygyny  alizarin  blamably  cyclamen
unbuckle  province  eyewater  abeyance  polymath  alliance  blatancy  dalmatic
unburden  provisor  flawless  abeyancy  polypary  alphabet  bribable  damnable
unburied  pulvilli  flowered  acrylate  polypide  amadavat  brocaded  damnably
unbutton  pulvinus  flowerer  ankylose  polypite  amaranth  brocatel  dastardy
undulant  purveyor  floweret  armyworm  polypody  ambiance  brutally  deceased
undulate  salvable  flywheel  Assyrian  polypoid  amenable  buckaroo  declarer
unfunded  salvific  forwards  babyhood  polypous  amenably  bummaree  declasse
ungulate  scavenge  gasworks  baryonic  polyseme  amicable  bungalow  defiance
unjustly  selvedge  glowworm  barytone  polysemy  amicably  buoyancy  defrayal
unmuffle  servient  godwards  bodyshop  polysomy  amorally  cachalot  deniable
unmuzzle  servitor  growling  bodywork  polyzoan  anabases  calcanea  dentalia
unsuited  shivaree  icewater  botyrose  polyzoic  anabasis  calcaria  dentated
unsunned  silvatic  knowable  buoyancy  polyzoon  anabatic  callable  depraved
Ursuline  silverly  laywoman  busybody  ponytail  anapaest  calvados  despatch
vacuolar  sirvente  madwoman  busyness  quayside  anasarca  campagna  deviance
valuable  Slavonic  midwives  butylene  rolypoly  animally  campaign  deviancy
valuably  slovenly  miswrite  butyrate  rubytail  animator  cannabin  deviator
valuator  slovenry  nonwhite  calycine  sphygmus  annually  cannabis  diabasic
Venusian  solvable  oldworld  calycoid  spryness  anteater  carcajou  diamante
vesuvian  solvency  outwards  calycule  staylace  apically  carcanet  diapason
viburnum  souvenir  outwatch  calyptra  staysail  apogamic  cardamom  diapause
virulent  spavined  outweigh  capybara  swayback  applause  cardamum  dichasia
visually  spivvery  outworks  caryatid  syzygial  appraise  carnally  dictator
vituline  subvocal  pinwheel  Cheyenne  wheyface  Aramaean  carnauba  dimmable
volution  surveyor  reawaken  cityfied  alizarin  Arapahoe  caryatid  dioramic
aasvogel  survival  redwater  claymore  amazedly  arapaima  cascabel  diseased
breveted  survivor  seawards  copybook  benzoate  archaean  castaway  dismally
breviary  sylvatic  seawater  copyedit  benzylic  archaise  casually  dispatch
calvados  traverse  seawrack  copyhold  blazoner  archaism  casualty  distally
cervelat  travesty  showbill  Corybant  blazonry  archaist  caudally  distance
cervical  trevally  showboat  coryphee  blizzard  arcuated  caudated  distaste
cervices  unevenly  showcard  crayfish  bouzouki  arguable  causally  disvalue
chivalry  univalve  showcase  dewyeyed  brazenly  arguably  cellarer  dogeared
clavicle  universe  showdown  dicyclic  brazenry  aromatic  cellaret  dogfaced
cleverly  univocal  showgirl  didymium  braziery  astragal  centaury  dogmatic
convener  valvulae  showroom  didymous  buzzword  ataraxia  cephalic  dogwatch
convenor  valvular  skewback  dihybrid  canzonet  ataraxic  cercaria  dormancy
converge  volvulus  skewbald  dutyfree  cruzeiro  avadavat  chalazae  dorsally
converse  weeviled  skewness  dutypaid  forzando  avifauna  chapatti  dracaena
convexly  weevilly  skywards  empyreal  gadzooks  avowable  chimaera  dramatic
conveyer  airwoman  slowdown  empyrean  glaziery  baccarat  Chinaman  drawable
conveyor  alewives  slowness  encyclic  grizzled  backache  chivalry  drivable
convince  answerer  slowpoke  ethylene  marzipan  badlands  choragic  dungaree
convolve  anywhere  slowworm  Ganymede  mitzvoth  bailable  choragus  dutiable
convulse  avowable  snowball  grayling  pizzeria  balladic  chorally  ebriated
corvette  avowedly  snowbird  greyfish  quizzing  balladry  chupatti  ecstatic
cravenly  blowball  snowboot  greyness  rhizopod  balsamic  chupatty  educable
crevasse  blowfish  snowdrop  hexylene  seizable  bandanna  ciliated  educated
culverin  blowhard  snowfall  hidyhole  sitzbath  bankable  cineaste  educator
curveted  blowhole  snowless  iceyacht  sizzling  barbaric  cinnabar  egomania
disvalue  blowlamp  snowlike  Illyrian  snazzily  barnacle  cinnamic  elegance
drivable  blowpipe  snowline  ladybird  whizbang  barracks  cinnamon  elegancy
driveway  bobwheel  snowshoe  ladyfern  whizzing  barranca  Circaean  elevated
elevated  bobwhite  stowaway  ladyhood  whizzkid  barranco  clematis  elevator
elevator  brewster  sunwards  ladylike  zarzuela  barrator  climatic  emblazon
eleventh  browband  tapwater  ladylove  zugzwang  barratry  cockatoo  embracer
exuviate  browbeat  trawlnet  ladyship  ————————  bastardy  collagen  emphases
fervency  browning  unawares  larynges  abeyance  battalia  collapse  emphasis
fervidly  brownish  unswathe  larynxes  abeyancy  bearable  collared  emphatic
galvanic  chowchow  viewable  lawyerly  abidance  bearably  collator  emulator
gravamen  clawback  viewless  molybdic  abomasum  bechamel  commando  endpaper
gravelly  clownery  warweary  okeydoke  abomasus  bechance  compages  engramma
graviton  clownish  warwhoop  Phrygian  aborally  bedmaker  concasse  engraver
heavenly  cobwebby  waxworks  playable  acquaint  bedtable  contagia  enneagon
```

enslaver	gonfalon	lambaste	NeoLatin	predator	schnapps	tantalic	unswathe
enswathe	gossamer	landarmy	neonatal	prelatic	screamer	tantalum	unweaned
enthalpy	gramarye	laudable	neurally	prenatal	seafarer	tantalus	upheaval
entracte	gramatom	laudably	nondairy	preparer	sealable	tapdance	upstairs
entrails	gravamen	laudanum	nonparty	presager	seamanly	tapwater	uvularly
entrance	grimacer	laudator	normalcy	primally	seawards	tarlatan	vagrancy
enviable	guaiacum	lawmaker	normally	Primates	seawater	tarragon	Valhalla
enviably	guaranty	lethally	nuisance	probable	seizable	tartaric	valiance
epically	guidable	lethargy	nuthatch	probably	Sephardi	taxpayer	valiancy
epicalyx	guidance	leviable	obstacle	profaner	serially	teacaddy	valuable
epifauna	gullable	liftable	ocularly	prolamin	seriatim	teaparty	valuably
epinasty	gunlayer	likeable	olibanum	prolapse	serranid	tearaway	valuator
epitasis	gymnasia	lineally	oligarch	pronator	serrated	teatable	Vandalic
erasable	haematic	linearly	omphalic	prosaism	sexually	teenager	variable
eschalot	haematin	Linnaean	omphalos	prosaist	shakable	tellable	variably
estrange	Haggadah	lipsalve	openable	protasis	shapable	tentacle	variance
estuaril	hangable	litharge	operable	protatic	Sheraton	teocalli	venially
ethnarch	hateable	liveable	operatic	provable	shikaree	terraced	verbally
eustatic	haymaker	loanable	operator	provably	shiralee	terrapin	verbatim
evadable	headache	lockable	ordnance	ptomaine	shivaree	terraria	verdancy
evitable	headachy	Lollardy	origanum	puggaree	sidearms	terrazzo	vernally
exchange	hebraise	lopeared	Ossianic	pulsator	sigmatic	testable	vibrancy
exogamic	Hebraism	lothario	ostracod	pygmaean	signally	testator	vibrator
expiable	Hebraist	maenadic	ostracon	quotable	sillabub	testatum	viewable
expiator	heliacal	magdalen	ostrakon	racially	silvatic	tetradic	villadom
extrados	Helladic	magmatic	outcaste	radially	singable	tetragon	villager
eyewater	henparty	Mahratta	outdated	radiance	sinkable	tetrapla	villainy
faceache	heptagon	Mahratti	outlawry	radiancy	siriasis	tetrapod	villatic
facially	herbaria	mailable	outmatch	radiator	situated	tetrarch	vintager
fadeaway	hereaway	malvasia	outrange	rampancy	sizeable	thalamic	violable
falcated	hideaway	mancando	outvalue	rapparee	skywards	thalamus	violably
fandance	hielaman	Mandaean	outwards	rascally	slugabed	Thanatos	violator
fandango	hierarch	mandamus	outwatch	rateable	smokable	thematic	viscacha
fanfaron	hieratic	mandarin	overalls	readable	soakaway	thesauri	visually
fantasia	hireable	mandator	overarch	readably	sociable	thoraces	vitiable
faunally	Hispanic	maneater	pachalic	reawaken	sociably	thoracic	vitiator
fellable	Hogmanay	mangabey	paduasoy	recharge	socially	thoraxes	vizcacha
fellahin	hollands	manganic	palpable	redfaced	Socratic	threader	voidable
festally	huggable	maniacal	palpably	redwater	solfaist	threaten	voidance
feudally	hydranth	manually	pandanus	regrater	solvable	throated	volcanic
filially	icewater	martagon	pappadom	rehearse	sortable	tillable	volcanos
firearms	iceyacht	mascaron	parlance	releasee	soutache	tithable	voltaism
fiscally	idolater	massacre	parlando	releaser	sovranty	toreador	vulcanic
fishable	idolatry	Mazdaism	partaken	releasor	sparable	tornadic	vulgarly
florally	illfated	mechanic	pashalic	reliable	spicated	trevally	Walhalla
flypaper	imitable	medially	pashalik	reliably	spiracle	tribally	walkable
foldaway	imitator	mediator	passable	reliance	spirally	tribasic	walkaway
foliaged	Indiaman	memsahib	passably	rentable	sporadic	trimaran	wallaroo
fontanel	inflamer	mendable	peccable	repealer	spreader	tuckahoe	wardance
fontange	inflated	menhaden	peccancy	repeater	squeaker	tuneable	warpaint
fordable	inflator	menially	peekaboo	replacer	squealer	turbaned	warragal
formalin	inflatus	mentally	pellagra	rereach	statable	turnable	warranty
formally	infrared	mescalin	pentacle	research	stomachy	twofaced	washable
forrader	instable	mesdames	pentagon	retiarii	stomatal	tympanic	wastable
forsaken	instance	mesially	perianth	reusable	stomatic	tympanum	wayfarer
forwards	instancy	methanol	phalange	revealer	storable	uintaite	wearable
forzando	intrados	midlands	phreatic	riddance	stowaway	ultraism	weldable
fougasse	inviable	migraine	phthalic	rideable	streaked	ultraist	welladay
frugally	isobaric	migrator	pileated	ritually	streaker	unabated	wellaway
furcated	isogamic	miscarry	pillager	ropeable	streamer	unawares	wetlands
gainable	isolable	mismatch	Pindaric	ruinable	subbasal	unbeaten	wettable
galbanum	isolator	mistaken	pinnacle	rummager	suitable	unbiased	wigmaker
galeated	issuable	moccasin	pinnated	sabbatic	suitably	unchancy	winnable
galvanic	issuance	mondaine	pintable	saccadic	sunbaked	unchaste	wiseacre
gambados	iterance	monoacid	piquancy	sacraria	sunbathe	uncially	wistaria
garganey	jackaroo	mordancy	piscator	safranin	sundance	undraped	workable
gazpacho	jeopardy	mortally	pitiable	sailable	sunwards	unglazed	workaday
gendarme	joinable	moshavim	pitiably	saleable	surfacer	univalve	writable
genially	jovially	moveable	pittance	salvable	syllabic	unleaded	yeomanly
geomancy	kalaazar	muriatic	placable	sandarac	syllable	unlearnt	yeomanry
geotaxis	kangaroo	muscadel	placably	sangaree	syllabub	unloader	zodiacal
Germanic	kinkajou	muscatel	playable	sargasso	syllabus	unplaced	zoolater
gestagen	kissable	mustache	plumaged	Sassanid	sylvatic	unreason	zoolatry
Ghanaian	knowable	mutually	plurally	satiable	sympathy	unsealed	zoomancy
gillaroo	labdanum	myriapod	podiatry	satiably	syngamic	unseated	acerbate
giveaway	labially	nameable	poppadum	scalable	syntagma	unshaped	acerbity
globally	labrador	narrator	portable	scalawag	takeaway	unstable	adlibbed
glucagon	lackaday	naumachy	potlatch	scenario	tameable	unstably	amoebean
godwards	laically	nectared	pourable	schmaltz	tannable	unstated	amoeboid

antibody	fallback	Jacobite	scrubbed	washbowl	bronchus	enricher	lodicule
autobahn	faltboat	jailbird	scrubber	waveband	bullcalf	episcope	logician
backbite	fastback	jeroboam	seatbelt	wellborn	cabochon	especial	loricate
backbone	feedback	kickback	selfborn	wellbred	caducean	ethicism	lutecium
bankbill	fireback	kingbird	semibull	whimbrel	caduceus	ethicist	lyricism
bankbook	fireball	kingbolt	shabbily	whizbang	caducity	eulachon	lyricist
bareback	firebird	korfball	shadbush	windburn	caducous	Eurocrat	magician
baseball	fireboat	kourbash	shagbark	wingbeat	calycine	eutectic	magicked
baseborn	firebomb	ladybird	shambles	wishbone	calycoid	evincive	mailcart
bedabble	firebrat	layabout	shinbone	woodbind	calycule	exercise	Manichee
bejabers	fishball	lifebelt	shoebill	woodbine	capacity	exorcise	manicure
belabour	fishbone	lifeboat	shopbell	wordbook	capuchin	exorcism	marocain
bellbird	fishbowl	lifebuoy	showbill	yearbook	caracara	exorcist	medicate
bellbuoy	flambeau	liveborn	showboat	zwieback	caracole	facecard	medicine
beriberi	flatboat	longboat	sideband	abdicate	catacomb	felicity	mesocarp
bilabial	fleabane	lovebird	sitzbath	abducens	catechol	ferocity	mimicked
bilobate	fleabite	lyrebird	skewback	abducent	cavicorn	feticide	mimicker
birdbath	flubbing	mailboat	skewbald	abductor	cetacean	fiducial	minacity
blabbing	foldboat	makebate	slabbing	abjectly	chancery	fiercely	mobocrat
blahblah	football	manubria	slapbang	acescent	charcoal	fireclay	molecule
blesbuck	footbath	marabout	slobbery	adducent	chinchin	fishcake	monachal
blowball	forebear	meatball	slobbish	adductor	chitchat	fletcher	moniker
blubbery	forebode	molybdic	slubbing	adjacent	choicely	flincher	monocrat
bluebell	fourball	moonbeam	slumbery	aduncate	chopchop	floccose	monocyte
bluebird	freeborn	moribund	snapbrim	aduncous	chowchow	floccule	mooncalf
boatbill	fribbler	mossback	snobbery	advocaat	churchly	flocculi	moorcock
browband	fullback	mothball	snobbish	advocacy	clincher	forecast	musicale
browbeat	funebral	neckband	snobbism	advocate	clipclop	francium	musician
buckbean	gadabout	noseband	snowball	affected	clopclop	frescoes	muticous
bushbaby	gamebird	notebook	snowbird	affecter	cockcrow	fugacity	Nearctic
bushbuck	gaolbird	ovenbird	snowboot	airscrew	coercion	galactic	newscast
busybody	giftbook	overbear	snubbing	albacore	coercive	gamecock	nosecone
cagebird	goofball	overbore	soapbark	algicide	cofactor	gearcase	notecase
calabash	grabbing	overbore	softball	allocate	coincide	genocide	objector
capybara	grabbler	overbusy	softboil	analcime	coracoid	germcell	obtected
carabine	grosbeak	parabola	somebody	analcite	cosecant	glancing	official
casebook	grubbily	passbook	songbird	anarchic	couscous	glaucoma	oiticica
cashbook	grubbing	playback	songbook	antecede	cratches	glaucous	opencast
celibacy	grumbler	playbill	sonobuoy	aphicide	crescent	golfclub	opercula
celibate	halfback	playbook	sparbuoy	aquacade	crescive	Graecise	optician
cerebral	halfbeak	plumbago	squabble	articled	crotched	Graecism	opuscula
cerebrum	halfboot	plumbate	squibbed	ascocarp	crotchet	groschen	opuscule
chambers	halfbred	plumbing	stabbing	atrocity	culicine	gynocrat	otoscope
chambray	handball	plumbism	stilbene	atticism	cynicism	Halachah	overcall
chapbook	handbell	puffball	stilbite	audacity	dedicate	handcart	overcame
clambake	handbill	puffbird	strabism	auricula	defector	handclap	overcast
clawback	handbook	pullback	strobila	autacoid	dejected	handcuff	overcoat
clubbing	hardback	purebred	strobile	autocade	delicacy	hardcase	overcome
cockboat	hardbake	pushball	strobili	autocrat	delicate	hardcore	overcrop
colubrid	harebell	pushbike	stubbing	backchat	democrat	havocked	oxpecker
comeback	headband	quibbler	stubborn	backcomb	depicter	helicoid	panicked
cookbook	heelball	rainbird	studbook	ballcock	depictor	hijacker	pedicled
copybook	hellbent	ratsbane	stumbler	basicity	detached	Holocene	pedicure
cornball	herdbook	reedbird	surfbird	beefcake	detector	homicide	pericarp
Corybant	highball	reembark	surfboat	bellcote	diarchal	hyoscine	pericope
crabbing	highborn	rehoboam	swabbing	betacism	diarchic	imbecile	petechia
cribbage	highbred	republic	swayback	bifacial	dicacity	impacted	piercing
cribbing	highbrow	rhomboid	swobbing	bifocals	dicyclic	indecent	pinecone
crowbill	hogsback	ricebird	tailback	bioscope	didactic	indicant	pinochle
dahabieh	holdback	ringbark	Tenebrae	birdcage	dioecism	indicate	pipeclay
deadbeat	homebody	ringbolt	terebene	birdcall	directly	indicium	planchet
delibate	homeborn	ringbone	terebrae	bisector	director	indocile	Pliocene
demobbed	homebred	roadbook	textbook	bleacher	domicile	inductee	postcard
dihybrid	homebrew	rockbird	throbbed	bluechip	doorcase	inductor	postcode
disabuse	hoofbeat	roodbeam	thumbpot	bluecoat	dovecote	infector	praecipe
divebomb	hornbeam	rosebowl	timeball	bookcase	downcast	injector	preacher
dogsbody	hornbill	rosebush	timebomb	boracite	downcome	innocent	prescind
doorbell	hornbook	runabout	trapball	borecole	drencher	insecure	princely
downbeat	humpback	rutabaga	trembler	bouncily	dungcart	invected	princess
drabbler	hymnbook	sailboat	trembles	bouncing	dustcart	invocate	pushcart
drawback	hypobole	saltbush	trombone	brancard	dustcoat	iotacism	quencher
dribbler	immobile	sandbank	trueblue	branched	eclectic	ironclad	quincunx
dribblet	incubate	sandbath	trueborn	brancher	effector	judicial	racecard
drubbing	indebted	saraband	truebred	branchia	efficacy	kingcrab	radicant
duckbill	intubate	scabbard	turnback	breeches	elenchus	kisscurl	radicate
dumbbell	inurbane	scombrid	twinborn	britches	elenctic	landcrab	raincoat
durables	ironbark	scrabble	vagabond	broacher	enarched	lapicide	rapacity
dustbowl	jackboot	scribble	Wahabism	broccoli	encyclic	launcher	rapecake
exlibris	Jacobean	scribbly	Wahabite	bronchia	endocarp	libeccio	reascend

```
redactor  thatcher  bleeding  foredeck  peardrop  sounding  amazedly  burletta
regicide  theocrat  blindage  foredoom  periderm  sourdine  ambience  cableway
rejecter  thwacker  blinding  founding  peridium  spandrel  amoretti  cachepot
relocate  tollcall  blondish  freedman  peridote  spandril  amoretto  cachexia
relucent  tonicity  bloodily  Freudian  plaiding  spardeck  amusedly  caffeine
reoccupy  toxicant  bloodred  frondage  plaudits  speedily  analecta  canoeing
rerecord  toxicity  boarding  frondent  pleading  speedway  analects  canoeist
restcure  treacher  boatdeck  frondeur  plodding  spondaic  anisette  cassette
reticent  trencher  boundary  frondose  postdate  squadron  anorexia  cathedra
reticule  truncate  braiding  gelidity  poundage  squidded  anorexic  catheter
rhonchal  tunicate  brandied  gladdest  pounding  standard  answerer  cathexes
rhonchus  turncoat  brandish  gladding  praedial  standing  anthelia  cathexis
ricochet  turncock  brandnew  glanders  prandial  standish  anthemia  caudexes
ridicule  twitcher  breeding  glandule  priedieu  standoff  antheral  causerie
rockcake  typecast  brindled  golddust  prodding  stardust  anthesis  causeway
rockcork  unbacked  broadish  gonidial  pygidial  steadily  antlered  cervelat
rollcall  unbuckle  broadway  gonidium  pygidium  steading  applepie  chapelry
rubicund  unsocial  broidery  grandame  pyridine  straddle  araceous  chaperon
sackcoat  urticant  broodily  granddad  pyxidium  stridden  arquebus  chateaux
sagacity  urticate  building  grandeur  quandary  strident  assiento  Cheyenne
salacity  varactor  bulldoze  grandson  quandong  studding  asthenia  chimeric
sashcord  varicose  caladium  greedily  quiddity  sturdied  asthenic  choleric
scarcely  velocity  calidity  grindery  rabidity  sturdily  athletic  choregic
scarcity  veracity  Canadian  guardant  raindrop  surfduck  aubretia  choregus
scorcher  verecund  cauldron  guardian  rapidity  swindler  audience  clarence
scutcher  vesicant  Chaldaic  heredity  reindeer  tapedeck  avowedly  clemency
searcher  vesicate  Chaldean  hoarding  remedial  teardrop  bachelor  cleverly
seascape  Vietcong  chaldron  holidays  resident  tearduct  bacteria  closeset
seedcake  viricide  chandler  homodont  residual  tepidity  baguette  closeted
seedcase  vivacity  childbed  humidify  residuum  theodicy  balletic  clupeoid
seedcoat  voracity  childish  humidity  rigadoon  thridace  bandeaux  clypeate
seedcorn  whinchat  children  hypoderm  rigidify  thudding  banderol  coalesce
selectee  whipcord  chondrus  immodest  rigidity  thundery  bannered  cobwebby
selector  windcone  chordate  impudent  ringdove  timidity  banneret  cockerel
sericite  wingcase  cladding  incident  rockdove  tolldish  bannerol  cockeyed
setscrew  woodchat  cloddish  inundate  roundarm  tonedeaf  banterer  colleger
showcard  woodcock  cloudily  jaundice  rounders  trapdoor  barbecue  commence
showcase  wormcast  cloudlet  killdeer  roundish  treadler  barberry  commerce
silicane  wretched  coaldust  klondike  roundtop  trendily  barbette  conceder
silicate  xylocarp  comedian  kneedeep  rubidium  tumidity  bargeman  conceive
silicide  abradant  comedist  lapidary  sapidity  turndown  barrenly  concerti
silicify  abridger  comedown  lapidate  saunders  twaddler  barrette  concerto
silicone  abundant  conidial  lapidify  sawedged  twiddler  barterer  concetti
sinecure  Accadian  conidium  lepidote  sawedoff  twoedged  basketry  concetto
sinicise  accident  couldest  lividity  scandent  unbidden  bathetic  condense
sketcher  aceldama  cupidity  lucidity  Scandian  unending  bayberry  conferee
skyscape  acridine  cytidine  maledict  scandium  unfading  beamends  conferva
slipcase  acridity  decadent  malodour  schedule  unriddle  believer  confetti
sloucher  aerodyne  decedent  markdown  scolding  unsaddle  bequeath  congener
snatcher  Airedale  dieldrin  melodeon  scudding  untidily  berberis  conserve
snitcher  Akkadian  dihedral  melodise  seladang  validate  berceuse  contempt
solecism  algidity  dingdong  melodist  semidome  validity  besieger  contents
solecist  allodial  dividend  meridian  shaddock  vanadate  bethesda  contessa
sorochen  allodium  dividivi  mesoderm  sheading  vanadium  bilberry  convener
spiccato  amygdala  dividual  monadism  shedding  vanadous  biogenic  convenor
sprocket  anecdote  dreadful  monodist  shelduck  vapidity  biometry  converge
sprucely  anhedral  druidess  moulding  shoddily  viridian  bitterly  converse
staccato  antedate  druidism  muskdeer  showdown  viridity  biweekly  convexly
stancher  antidote  ectoderm  muskdock  shredded  welldeck  blameful  conveyer
stanchly  aqueduct  embedded  namedrop  shredder  wheedler  Bodleian  conveyor
stitcher  Arcadian  emendate  nextdoor  shuddery  whidding  bontebok  copperas
stoccado  archduke  endoderm  nomadise  shutdown  wiredraw  bookends  copyedit
stoccata  ascidian  entoderm  nomadism  sidedish  withdraw  Bordeaux  coquetry
stoicism  ascidium  evildoer  nosedive  sidedoor  withdrew  bordello  coquette
stopcock  asyndeta  exordial  nowadays  sidedrum  wooldyed  borderer  corneous
stricken  autodafe  exordium  obsidian  skidding  wouldest  bosseyed  cornetcy
strickle  autodyne  expedite  occident  skindeep  woundily  bracelet  cornetti
strictly  backdate  faradaic  okeydoke  slapdash  yielding  brakeman  cornetto
strucken  backdoor  faradism  oncidium  sledding  absterge  brakevan  corselet
stuccoes  backdrop  fiendish  ophidian  slowdown  academia  brazenly  corseted
subacute  barndoor  finedraw  Orcadian  snowdrop  academic  brazenry  corsetry
suitcase  basidial  firedamp  overdone  soapdish  accredit  breveted  corvette
suricate  basidium  flinders  overdose  solidary  achiever  brokenly  cosmetic
switchel  bayadere  floodlit  overdraw  solidify  aculeate  bromelia  cowberry
tailcoat  befuddle  floodway  overdrew  solidity  aigrette  brunette  cranefly
telecast  benedick  fluidics  paludism  somedeal  alchemic  budgeree  cravenly
telecine  benedict  fluidify  paradigm  somedele  alebench  bulletin  credence
tenacity  bladdery  fluidise  paradise  soundbow  alfresco  bunkered  credenza
tenacula  blandish  fluidity  parodist  soundbox  alopecia  Burberry  crenelle
```

criteria	epigeous	grisette	libretti	nucleate	prunella	singeing	therefor
croceate	epilepsy	guidedog	libretto	nucleole	prunelle	sirvente	thereout
cruzeiro	episemon	guideway	lichened	nucleoli	prunello	sisterly	tholepin
culdesac	erigeron	guileful	lichenin	numberer	pungency	sithence	threeply
culverin	erogenic	gunmetal	liegeman	ochreous	puppetry	sixpence	threeway
cupreous	eschewal	gusseted	ligneous	oddments	pursenet	sixpenny	timbered
currency	esoteric	gynoecia	lingerer	odometer	purveyor	skeletal	tingeing
cursedly	espresso	gypseous	lingerie	ohmmeter	pyogenic	skeleton	tinkerer
curveted	evanesce	hacienda	listener	omelette	Quakerly	slideway	tinselly
cussedly	evidence	halteres	loiterer	openeyed	quenelle	sloeeyed	toiletry
cycleway	exegesis	hangeron	longeron	operetta	queueing	slovenly	toilette
cypselae	exegetic	hardener	longeval	opulence	raggedly	slovenry	topheavy
cysteine	exigence	hasheesh	lookeron	orogenic	reagency	snakepit	toplevel
dancette	exigency	hastener	loosebox	outHerod	recreant	societal	totterer
dancetty	exoteric	hawkeyed	loosener	outreach	recreate	softener	toxaemia
danseuse	extrêmes	heatedly	louvered	outreign	redeemer	solderer	toxaemic
deadener	faineant	hedgehog	lowlevel	outweigh	reemerge	solfeggi	trabeate
decrease	falderal	hedgehop	lubberly	oximeter	reflexed	solleret	tradeoff
decrepit	falsetto	hedgepig	lumberer	palmette	reliever	solvency	trapezia
decretal	fastener	hedgerow	Lutheran	palmetto	renderer	sorcerer	traverse
degrease	fatherly	Hellenic	lynxeyed	palterer	replevin	souvenir	travesty
deucedly	fattener	helmeted	mackerel	pamperer	respects	spacebar	trecento
deuteron	fauteuil	hermetic	magnesia	pandemic	retrench	spaceman	trimeric
dewberry	fenberry	herpetic	magnetic	parcener	reviewal	spadeful	trimeter
dewyeyed	ferreter	Hesperus	magneton	pargeter	reviewer	spicebox	tripeman
diabetes	fervency	hetaerae	maidenly	parhelia	ridgeway	spikelet	trumeaux
diabetic	fingered	higherup	mannered	parhelic	rifleman	spiteful	tuppence
diameter	finnesko	hinderer	mannerly	parietal	rocketry	squeedge	tuppenny
diereses	fireeyed	hitherto	mantelet	Parmesan	rondeaux	squeegee	twopence
dieresis	flabella	hoosegow	maquette	parterre	rottenly	squeezer	twopenny
dietetic	flagella	horsebox	markedly	passerby	rouleaus	stakenet	udometer
diocesan	flamenco	horsecar	marketer	pathetic	rouleaux	stapelia	umbrella
diphenyl	flanerie	horseman	martello	peaceful	roulette	statedly	umbrette
dipteral	flowered	hostelry	martenot	peasecod	ruggedly	stiletto	unaneled
dipteran	flowerer	houseboy	masseter	pendency	runnerup	stonefly	unclench
disbench	floweret	housedog	masseuse	perceive	sacredly	storeman	uncreate
dishevel	folderol	housefly	masterly	perfecto	salience	storeyed	undreamt
dispense	forcedly	houseful	medieval	permeate	saliency	streeted	unevenly
disperse	forcefed	houseman	membered	perverse	sanserif	subgenus	unfreeze
disseise	forceful	housetop	mergence	phaseout	sapience	sublease	unitedly
disserve	foreedge	Huguenot	mesmeric	phonemic	sarcenet	submerge	universe
dissever	formerly	hygienic	misbegot	phonetic	sardelle	submerse	unmeetly
ditheism	fosterer	hysteria	miscegen	phyletic	sarsenet	subserve	unopened
ditheist	foureyes	hysteric	misdealt	pickerel	saucebox	suddenly	unseeded
ditherer	framesaw	impledge	misheard	picketer	saucepan	sufferer	unseeing
diuresis	frenetic	increase	mittened	pilferer	Sauterne	sullenly	unseemly
diuretic	frisette	increate	monteith	pilsener	scalepan	summerly	unsteady
doddered	frumenty	inflexed	moquette	pimiento	scavenge	sunderer	unwieldy
dodderer	fugleman	innuendo	motherly	pincenez	schiedam	surcease	variedly
dogberry	furbelow	intrench	mouseear	pixieish	screechy	surveyor	varietal
doggedly	gableend	intrepid	mulberry	pizzeria	screener	suspense	varletry
doggerel	gadgetry	isabella	murderer	placeman	screever	symmetry	velleity
dotterel	Gadhelic	ischemia	murrelet	placenta	secretin	syndesis	vendetta
driveway	galleass	ischemic	musketry	plateaux	secretly	syndetic	veneerer
drupelet	gambeson	isomeric	mutterer	plateful	secretor	systemic	vengeful
duchesse	gardener	isometry	myogenic	platelet	segreant	tableaux	verderer
duodenal	gardenia	jabberer	narceine	plebeian	seicento	tablecut	verderor
duodenum	garreted	jackeroo	nascence	plumelet	selvedge	tableful	vergence
dysgenic	gasmeter	jaggedly	nascency	pochette	senseful	tablemat	vertebra
dyslexia	gatherer	japhetic	nauseant	ponderer	sentence	tabletop	vertexes
dyslexic	geodesic	jiggered	nauseate	potbelly	septette	tafferel	vesperal
eagleowl	geodetic	julienne	nauseous	potterer	sequelae	tamperer	viameter
easterly	geometer	jumpedup	neotenic	powdered	sequence	tangency	vigneron
ecclesia	geometry	kedgeree	neoteric	predella	sergeant	Tarpeian	vignette
elatedly	gingerly	kromesky	nickelic	prelease	serjeant	tasselly	violence
emceeing	glabella	lambency	nobleman	prepense	sesterce	tastebud	visceral
eminence	glycerin	lancelet	noblesse	presence	sextette	tasteful	vitreous
eminency	glycerol	lanneret	noisette	preserve	shakeout	tattered	voicebox
encaenia	glyceryl	larcener	nonlegal	pretence	shaleoil	tegmenta	voiceful
enfeeble	Goidelic	largesse	nonmetal	prideful	shameful	temperer	walleyed
ensheath	goldenly	latterly	nonsense	primeval	shareout	tendence	wanderer
entreaty	goosegog	laureate	Norseman	proceeds	shedevil	tendency	wanderoo
entrench	gorgeous	lawyerly	noumenal	propense	shigella	tenderly	wardenry
entrepot	gramercy	leadenly	noumenon	properly	shrieval	tenpence	warrener
entresol	grateful	leniency	nouvelle	property	sickener	tenpenny	warweary
enuresis	gravelly	lenience		protease	sickerly	tesserae	
enuretic	Griselda	lettered	nuclease	protegee	silverly	tesseral	
epidemic	griseous			prudence		thanedom	

```
wasteful dripfeed overfeed uplifter engaging nomogram squiggly Blenheim
waxberry drumfire overfill variform ensigncy oakegger staggard blighter
weaselly dutyfree overfish vasiform ergogram obligate staggers blithely
Wesleyan dwarfish overflew verifier eulogise obliging stargaze blowhard
westerly dwarfism overflow vilifier eulogist ontogeny stingily blowhole
whatever ensiform overfold vivifier eulogium oologist stingray blushful
whenever evenfall overfond wallfern exergual oppugner stodgily boathook
wherever fallfish pacifier waveform fatigues orangery straggle bobwheel
whiteboy fastfood pacifism weakfish filagree Orangism straggly bobwhite
whitecap filefish pacifist wharfage filigree overgrew strigose bolthole
whitefly filiform paleface wheyface filmgoer overgrow struggle bonehead
whitehot fishfarm paraffin whiffler fishglue paragoge sturgeon borehole
whitener fivefold piliform wildfire flagging patagium subagent boughten
whiteout flatfeet pinafore wildfowl flogging pedagogy swagging brachial
whitetie flatfish pipefish windfall footgear pedigree swigging brachium
wholehog flatfoot pisiform wolffish foregoer Pelagian swinging brethren
whomever flimflam platform woolfell foregone perigean syzygial brighten
whoredom flipflap poltfoot workfolk fringing perigyny tailgate brightly
whoreson flipflop portfire abnegate frogging phlegmon telegony brochure
wickedly footfall postfree abrogate fumigant phosgene telegram brouhaha
wideeyed forefeel proofing aerogram fumigate Phrygian theogony brushoff
wildeyed forefelt purifier allegory gazogene plangent thingamy buckhorn
winterly forefoot pyriform allogamy Georgian playgirl thoughts Buddhism
wisteria fourfold rainfall almagest goingson playgoer thuggery Buddhist
wontedly freefall rarefied almighty greegree plougher thuggism bulkhead
woodenly frogfish ratifier Armagnac grisgris plugging tidegate bullhead
writeoff froufrou reaffirm arpeggio groggily podagral toboggan bullhorn
Yankeefy fusiform redefine arrogant groogroo podagric tollgate bunghole
zeppelin garefowl reniform arrogate grudging polygala tomogram butchery
zoogenic gatefold retiform assignat hairgrip polygamy unpegged calthrop
zoometry gefuffle rockfall assignee handgrip polygene unrigged camphene
zygaenid germfree rockfish assignor headgear polygeny vinegary camphine
acidfast goatfish rosefish autogamy hexagram polyglot Visigoth camshaft
acrefoot goldfish sailfish autogiro hologram priggery voyageur canthari
aeriform goldfoil sainfoin autogyro homogamy priggish wallgame catchall
aerofoil Graafian sandflea bedeguar homogeny priggism weregild catchfly
antefixa graffiti scaffold befogged hypogeal priggish Whiggery catching
argufier graffito scarfpin benignly hypogean racegoer Whiggish cinchona
artefact greffier scotfree bewigged hypogene rejigger Whiggism clothier
artifact greyfish scrofula bludgeon hypogeum relegate windgall clothing
artifice handfast seedfish bourgeon hypogyny religion wormgear clubhaul
auriform hausfrau septfoil braggart ideogram renegade wrangler coachdog
backfire headfast shelfful bragging impugner renegado wriggler coachman
balefire hellfire shuffler brougham indagate reneguer wrongful coalhole
barefoot Hereford sickflag callgirl indigene resigned wrongous cogwheel
benefice hillfort skinfood category indigent runagate xenogamy conchate
billfold holdfast slipform chugging insignia savagely yataghan conchoid
blowfish homefelt sniffily clanging intaglio savagery youngest copyhold
bluefish hornfels sniffler clangour integral sciagram youngish couchant
boldface iodoform sniffles clogging irongray scragend acidhead couching
bonefish kefuffle snowfall cryogeny irongrey scragged aesthete crashing
boniface kingfish snuffbox danegeld irrigate seraglio airshaft crashpad
bouffant kinsfolk snuffers debagged kilogram shaggily alcahest crumhorn
briefing ladyfern snuffler debagged landgirl shanghai aldehyde dabchick
brimfull landfall spiffing decagram levigate shingler alkahest daughter
bullfrog landform spitfire decigram lichgate shingles amethyst deadhead
bushfire leapfrog spoffish delegacy lipogram shogging anaphase deathbed
califate lockfast staffage delegate litigant shopgirl anaphora deathcap
campfire locofoco starfish demagogy litigate showgirl anathema deathray
carefree lumpfish stedfast derogate logogram shrugged anechoic deckhand
catsfoot lungfish stiffish designer lychgate skiagram antihero Delphian
chiefdom makefast studfarm diligent mahogany slagging anything denehole
citified malefern stuffily dirigism Malagasy slangily anywhere diaphone
cityfied manifest stuffily disagree maligner slogging apothegm dogshore
clubfoot manifold stuffing divagate malignly sluggard arachnid dogwhelk
coalfish maniform surefire dragging marigold slugging arethusa doughboy
codifier modifier surffish draughts misogamy sluggish armchair doughnut
coiffeur monkfish telefilm draughty misogyny smudgily Ayrshire downhaul
coiffure moonface tilefish droughty mitigant smuggler babyhood downhill
coliform moonfish timefuse drudgery mitigate snagging bacchant drachmae
coniform moorfowl toadfish drugging monogamy sniggler backhand drachmai
cramfull moufflon toadflax druggist monogeny snogging bakshish drachmas
crawfish nailfile treefern echogram monoglot snuggery baldhead drophead
crayfish napiform treefrog elongate monogony sphagnum beechnut drumhead
crowfoot needfire tubiform emergent monogram sphygmus biathlon duckhawk
cubiform ninefold typeface emulgent monogyny spongily billhead dumbhead
deadfall nubiform typifier endogamy mortgage sprigged billhook dunghill
dealfish numbfish unciform endogeny nanogram spurgear birthday Dutchman
downfall overfall unmuffle energise navigate squiggle bitchily earphone
```

earthnut	isocheim	overhaul	soothing	withheld	bunfight	cruciate	fascicle
eggshell	isophote	overhead	soothsay	withhold	bursitis	crucible	fasciola
elephant	isothere	overhear	sorehead	wormhole	cabriole	crucifer	fasciole
ensphere	isotherm	overheat	souchong	worthful	caesious	crucifix	Fascista
epiphany	jolthead	overhung	southern	worthily	calcific	cultivar	Fasciti
epiphyte	keelhaul	pamphlet	southing	wrathful	calcitic	curlicue	fashious
erethism	keeshond	pantheon	southpaw	wrathily	calliope	curricle	feasible
erewhile	kerchief	Parthian	spathose	xanthate	calliper	cushiony	feasibly
erythema	kinghood	patchily	staghorn	xanthein	canaille	cuspidor	febrific
eyerhyme	klephtic	payphone	stanhope	xanthene	candidly	cyclical	felsitic
eyeshade	kneehigh	paysheet	subahdar	xanthine	cannibal	Cypriote	fencible
faithful	kneehole	peephole	subphyla	xanthium	cannikin	cystitis	ferriage
falchion	knightly	penchant	subshrub	xanthoma	canticle	czaritza	ferritic
farmhand	knothole	pilchard	youthful	caprifig	capriole	daylight	fervidly
farthest	krumhorn	pinchers	zecchini	capriole	capsicum	deceiver	festival
farthing	ladyhood	pinwheel	zecchino	capsicum	captious	denticle	fibrilla
feathery	lanthorn	plethora	zoophily	zoophily	cardigan	deprival	fiftieth
feedhead	latchkey	plighted	zoophyte	zoophyte	cardinal	deprived	fissiped
fetching	laughing	porphyry	sunshade	zucchini	carnival	derriere	fistiana
filthily	laughter	porthole	sunshine	abscissa	carriage	despiser	fistical
firehose	layshaft	posthorn	sunshiny	abutilon	carriole	detailed	flamingo
fishhawk	leathern	potsherd	swanherd	aconitic	castiron	detainee	flatiron
fishhook	leathery	prophase	sylphide	aconitum	caudices	detainer	flexible
flashgun	lefthand	prophecy	sylphine	acreinch	caudillo	detrital	flexibly
flashily	linchpin	prophesy	sylphish	Adamical	cautious	detritus	floridly
flashing	loathful	psychics	symphile	adamitic	cervical	diggings	florigen
flathead	loathing	psychism	symphony	adenitis	cervices	dioritic	flotilla
fleshfly	longhair	psychist	takehome	adroitly	chapiter	disciple	foetidly
fleshpot	longhand	puncheon	teachest	aestival	charisma	dispirit	follicle
flywheel	longhorn	purchase	teaching	affright	chemical	distinct	forcible
foothill	loophole	pyrrhoea	teething	aggrieve	chenille	dogfight	forcibly
foothold	luncheon	pyrrhous	tetchily	agonised	chiliasm	dogtired	forgiven
forehand	lymphoid	Quechuan	texthand	aiguille	chiliast	dulciana	fornices
forehand	lymphoma	railhead	tomahawk	airfield	choriamb	dulcimer	fortieth
foxshark	lynchpin	rakehell	toothful	airliner	chorioid	Dulcinea	fremitus
freehand	lyophile	ranchero	toothily	airtight	churinga	dundiver	frigidly
freehold	maidhood	ranchman	toothing	alewives	cirriped	earnings	frutices
freshman	marchesa	redshank	torchere	allnight	clarinet	earpiece	fungible
freshrun	marchese	redshift	touchily	alogical	clavicle	edacious	furriery
frighten	marshman	redshirt	touching	American	clerical	educible	gainings
frothily	masthead	rhythmic	toughish	amphibia	clerihew	eldritch	galliard
funkhole	matchbox	rockhewn	townhall	amphipod	clinical	eligible	Gallican
furthest	merchant	roothold	tracheae	Anglican	codpiece	eligibly	gallipot
geophagy	midships	roughage	tracheal	aperient	codriver	emaciate	garlicky
geophone	millhand	roughdry	tracheid	aperitif	colliery	emeritus	garrison
geophyte	mirthful	roughhew	trachoma	apomixis	combings	emetical	gasfired
gilthead	mischief	roughish	trachyte	applique	compiler	empoison	gaslight
girlhood	misshape	rushhour	trashery	archival	confider	enceinte	gastight
gladhand	misthink	samphire	trashily	archives	confiner	enclitic	gerbille
gnathite	molehill	sapphics	trephine	atomiser	confines	encrinal	germinal
goatherd	MonKhmer	sapphire	trichina	attrited	conniver	encrinic	gimmicky
godchild	monkhood	sapphism	trichite	atypical	conoidal	enquirer	gingival
grapheme	morpheme	scaphoid	trichoid	auspices	consider	entailer	glaciate
graphics	morphine	scathing	trichome	bagpiper	continua	eremitic	gladioli
graphite	mouthful	seachest	trichord	ballista	continue	erodible	glaziery
guacharo	murrhine	seashell	trochaic	bambinos	continuo	erotical	gloriole
gymkhana	mutchkin	seashore	trochili	banditry	convince	eyeliner	glorious
handheld	narghile	selfheal	trochlea	banditti	coolibah	eyepiece	gloxinia
handhold	neatherd	selfhelp	trochoid	barbican	corniced	eyesight	glucinum
hardhack	neophyte	selfhood	trophied	barbital	corniche	fabliaux	golliwog
hardhead	newsheet	serfhood	truthful	bartizan	cornicle	factious	gossiper
hatchery	Noachian	shashlik	typehigh	bassinet	cornific	fallible	gossipry
hatching	nonwhite	shepherd	Tyrrhene	bastille	corridor	fallibly	gracioso
hatchway	northern	shoehorn	urethane	bauxitic	corrival	fanciful	gracious
hawthorn	northing	shothole	urochord	bearings	cortical	fanlight	gradient
heathery	Northman	sidehead	warwhoop	beatific	cortices	farcical	granitic
heathhen	notching	silphium	watchdog	befriend	cosmical	farriery	graviton
heighten	nutshell	sinkhole	watchful	beguiler	coulisse	eyeliner	gridiron
hellhole	nymphean	skinhead	watchkey	berliner	cousinly	eyepiece	guerilla
henchman	offshoot	slagheap	watchman	besmirch	craniate	eyesight	gullible
hidyhole	offshore	slashing	watthour	bestiary	craniate	fabliaux	gunfight
hogshead	oliphant	slightly	wellhead	biblical	credible	fabliaux	halliard
hotchpot	omadhaum	slithery	Welshman	billiard	credibly	factious	handicap
hulahula	omophagy	slothful	wifehood	biocidal	credited	fallible	harridan
hushhush	onychite	smashing	wirehair	bobbinet	creditor	fallibly	hastings
ianthine	outshine	smithers	witchelm	boutique	crepitus	fanciful	Hawaiian
insphere	outshone	smithery	witchery	braziery	criminal	fanlight	hawfinch
Irishism	overhand	smothery	witchety	breviary	critical	farcical	hayfield
Irishman	overhang	softhead	witching	bromidic	critique	farriery	helminth

heroical	mantissa	ovaritis	publican	staminal	ungainly	brooklet	spicknel
hetairai	marginal	oxidiser	publicly	stasimon	unifilar	chalkpit	spookily
hirrient	marriage	ozoniser	pulpiter	statical	unpaired	checkers	spookish
hobbitry	marrieds	palliate	pulvilli	sterigma	unsuited	checkout	spunkily
hooligan	martinet	pallidly	pulvinus	stipites	unvoiced	cheekily	starkers
horrible	marzipan	palmiped	punditry	stolidly	uralitic	chickpea	stickful
horribly	massicot	palmitin	putridly	straight	usurious	clerkdom	stickily
horridly	mastitis	panmixia	pyelitis	strained	utiliser	clerkess	stickjaw
horrific	matrices	pannikin	quotient	strainer	uvulitis	clinking	stickler
hospital	matrixes	panpipes	rabbinic	straiten	uxorious	crackers	stinkard
hustings	mephitic	Parsiism	rabbiter	straitly	vaccinal	cracking	stinking
hyacinth	mephitis	partible	rabbitry	studious	vaccinia	crackjaw	stinkpot
icefield	merciful	particle	rachides	stupidly	vampiric	cracknel	stockade
idoliser	methinks	partisan	rachitic	stylised	vendible	crackpot	stockcar
illtimed	metrical	partizan	rachitis	subtitle	verbiage	crankily	stockily
imaginal	midfield	passible	receiver	succinct	verditer	crankpin	stocking
imagines	midnight	pastiche	rejoicer	succinic	vernicle	creakily	stockish
implicit	midwives	pastille	reorient	succinum	versicle	croakily	stockist
imprimis	milliard	pectines	repairer	suicidal	vertical	crockery	stockman
imprison	milliary	peelings	reprieve	suitings	vertices	doorknob	stockpot
inedible	millibar	pellicle	reprisal	summitry	verticil	drinking	striking
inedited	millieme	pemmican	requital	sunlight	vespiary	dropkick	swanking
inflight	milliner	pendicle	requiter	surgical	vestiary	drunkard	thankful
infringe	miscible	perlitic	retailer	surmisal	viaticum	durukuli	thankyou
inguinal	misgiven	pervious	retainer	surmiser	vibrissa	flickery	thickety
inimical	missilry	pettifog	retrieve	survival	vincible	flockbed	thickish
initiate	mittimus	pharisee	reveille	survivor	virginal	foreknew	thickset
inositol	monsieur	phthisic	rhinitis	syenitic	Virginia	foreknow	thinking
inquirer	moorings	phthisis	rinsings	symbiont	viscidly	Frankish	trackage
inscient	morainic	physical	rocaille	syndical	vortical	franklin	tracking
inspired	morbidly	physicky	rubbishy	syphilis	vortices	freakish	trackman
inspirer	morbific	physique	rubrical	tachisme	warrigal	freakout	trackway
inspirit	mornings	pianiste	runcible	tachiste	waxlight	friskily	trekking
instinct	multifid	pickings	rustical	tactical	weariful	frocking	trickery
intrigue	multiped	picnicky	sacristy	taenioid	weeviled	goalkick	trickily
inveigle	multiple	pinniped	salvific	tailings	weevilly	harakiri	trickish
irenical	multiply	piscinae	scabious	tangible	williwaw	harikari	triskele
irenicon	muslined	pitviper	scarious	tangibly	winnings	iceskate	truckage
ironical	myelinic	placidly	scenical	tenaille	workings	kamikaze	trucking
isodicon	myelitis	plagiary	scilicet	tensible	writings	katakana	truckler
Italiote	myositic	platinic	scimitar	terminal	Xantippe	khuskhus	twinkler
jerrican	myositis	platinum	scolices	terminer	zabaione	knackery	unlikely
jesuitic	myrmidon	plumiped	seapiece	terminus	zeolitic	knickers	velskoen
jesuitry	mystical	pluvious	sennight	terrible	zombiism	knocking	waleknot
jettison	mystique	poetical	sensible	terribly	bootjack	knockout	wallknot
jiujitsu	mythical	pollices	sensibly	terrific	demijohn	limekiln	wellknit
Judaical	narcissi	pollinia	sentient	tertiary	flapjack	lockknit	whacking
Judaiser	nautical	pollinic	sentinel	thetical	frabjous	lorikeet	whiskers
Kaffiyeh	nautilus	polliwog	septimal	thurible	highjack	loveknot	whiskery
khedival	negligee	pontifex	servient	thurifer	jipijapa	numskull	wrackful
lacrimal	Negrillo	porridge	servitor	tinnitus	kneejerk	overkill	wreckage
larrikin	nescient	porticos	Shekinah	toepiece	overjump	parakeet	zinckify
lashings	neuritic	portiere	Shemitic	topliner	readjust	planking	zincking
latticed	neuritis	possible	siftings	toroidal	skipjack	plankton	absolute
lawgiver	nonrigid	possibly	Sinaitic	torpidly	slapjack	pluckily	absolver
leavings	nuclidic	postiche	sinciput	torridly	blackboy	prankful	accolade
leggings	nuptials	pratique	sixtieth	tortilla	blackcap	prankish	acrolein
lenticel	nutrient	precinct	skylight	tortious	blackfly	quackery	acrolith
lenticle	obedient	precious	skypilot	touristy	blacking	quackish	acrylate
leucitic	obtainer	premiere	sobriety	traditor	blackish	quickset	aerolite
lignitic	offsider	presidio	soldiery	tragical	blackleg	quirkily	aerolith
limpidly	ofttimes	previous	somnific	tritical	blackout	reefknot	aerology
liquidly	oilfield	prodigal	sordidly	tropical	blacktie	rewaking	agrology
lodgings	oilfired	profiler	spacious	tsaritsa	blacktop	Sanskrit	algology
lollipop	oldtimer	prohibit	spadices	tsaritza	blankety	sheikdom	alkalies
lopsided	onepiece	prolific	spadille	turbidly	bleakish	shocking	alkalify
lubrical	onesided	prolixly	Spaniard	turbinal	blinkers	sidekick	alkaline
luscious	orchilla	promisee	spavined	turgidly	blinking	slinkily	alkaloid
machismo	ordainer	promiser	speciate	turnings	blockade	slipknot	alleluia
mackinaw	original	promisor	specific	twilight	blockage	smocking	ambulant
madrigal	orthicon	protista	specimen	twopiece	blockish	snackbar	ambulate
magnific	osteitis	provided	specious	twosided	brackish	sneakily	ampullae
manciple	outfield	provider	spinifex	twotimer	breakage	sneakish	anaglyph
mandible	outrider	province	spirilla	umptieth	breaking	spanking	angelica
Mandingo	outright	provisor	spirited	unbridle	breakout	sparkgap	ankylose
mannikin	outrival	proximal	spiritus	unclinch	brickbat	sparkish	annalist
mannitol	outsider	prurient	spoliate	uncoined	brickred	sparkler	annulate
mansized	outsight	pruritic	spraints	unedited	briskish	sparklet	annulled
mantilla	ovariole	pruritus	spurious	unfairly	brookite	speaking	antelope

antilogy anyplace aphelion apoplexy appalled aqualung aquiline arbalest arbalist areolate arillate atheling aurelian autolyse axiality axillary axiology bacillar bacillus backlash backless backlist balkline banality bantling barkless basaltic baseless baseline basilica basilisk bateleur battleax bdellium beagling becalmed bedplate beetling befallen beholden beholder beltless bevelled beveller bewilder bibulous bioplasm bioplast birdlime bivalent blowlamp boatload bobolink bodiless boneless bookland booklice booklore bootlace bootlast bootless botflies botulism bouillon boxpleat brimless brisling bryology bubaline buckling buddleia bundling buntline burglary bustling butylene cabalism cabalist caballed

cacology cageling cajolery cameleer camellia canalise capeline capellet careless carillon Carolean Caroline carolled cartload catalase cataloes catalyse catalyst cavalier cavilled caviller cerulean chaplain charlady charlock Chellean chinless churlish civilian civilise civility clubland clueless cobaltic cobblers cochleae cochlear cockloft complain compleat complice complier compline conclave conclude conflate conflict conglobe contline copulate cordless corelate cotillon coupling covalent coxalgia cradling crueller cryolite cumulate cumulous cupelled cupulate cureless Cyrillic cytology darkling dateless dateline deadline deadlock debility decolour deedless deeplaid defilade

demolish depilate derelict desolate deviling devilish devilism devilkin devilled deviltry diallage dialling disallow disclaim disclose displace displant displode displume divalent djellaba docilely docility dockland doubloon dowelled drilling drollery dropleaf dryclean dryplate duckling ductless duelling duellist dumpling dustless dustlike echoless edgeless eggplant embalmer embolden embolism enfilade enrolled ensilage entellus envelope epiblast epyllion equalise equality equalled escalade escalope escallop esculent espalier ethology ethylene etiolate eucalypt excelled exhalant expelled expellee extolled eyeglass fabulist fabulous faceless facelift facilely

facility fadeless fairlead familial familiar fangless farflung farmland fatalism fatalist fatality fearless feckless feculent feeblish fiddling fidelity finalise finalism finalist finality firelock fishless flatling flawless fluellin flyblown focalise folklore fondling foodless footless footling forelady foreland forelock forklift formless fourleaf foxglove freeload frillies fuselage fusileer fusilier futilely futility Galilean gangland gangling ganglion gantline gantlope gaselier gasolene gasolier gasoline Gaullism Gaullist gavelock ghoulish goalline goatling Gobelins goldleaf gormless gralloch grayling grillage growling gunflint hairless hairlike hairline halflife

hamululi handless handline handling handlist handloom hardline harmless havelock havildar hawklike hazelnut headlamp headland headline headlock headlong heedless heelless Hegelian heirless heirloom helpless heraldic heraldry herbless hexylene highland highlows hindlegs hipflask hireling homeland homeless homelike homology hopeless hornless horologe horology hotelier hotplate hourlong hurtless iceblink iceplant idealess idealise idealism idealist ideality ideology idiolect idyllist immolate impelled impeller impolder impolicy impolite indolent indulger induline infilter inhalant insolate insolent insulant insulate insulter involute isogloss isopleth jetblack jetplane jewelled jeweller

jongleur jubilant jubilate jugglery jugulate keelless kidglove kindless kindling kinglike kingline labelled labellum lability ladylike ladylove lamblike lamellae lamellar landlady landless landline landlord langlauf lapelled lavalava lazulite leadless leafless leaflike legalese legalise legalism legalist legality lensless levelled leveller levulose libelled libellee libeller lifeless lifelike lifeline lifelong ligulate limbless linoleum listless littlego littling livelily livelong loadline lobeline lobulate localise localism locality loculate lordless lordling loveless lovelily lovelock lovelorn loyalist luckless Lucullan luculent lunulate maculate maiolica majolica Mameluke mamillae

mamillar mantling marbling massless matelote maxillae medalled medallic megalith menology metalled metallic micellar middling mindless misalign misology misplace mobilise mobility modalism modalist modality modelled modeller modulate molality monolith moonless moorland moralism moralist morality motility mottling moveless mucilage muckluck muscling mutilate mycelial mycelium mycology myoblast nameless napoleon nasalise nasality natality nathless nauplius nebulise nebulium nebulous necklace neckline needless neoplasm Nepalese nestling newblown nielloed niggling nihilism nihilist nihility nobelium nobility nodalise nodality nodulose nodulous nomology nonclaim noteless novelise novelist

nubility nubilous nucellus nursling obsolete occultly ocellate oecology oeillade oenology oilcloth omoplate oncology ontology oppilate oreology orgulous osculant osculate outclass outflank overlaid overlain overland overleaf overleap overload overlong overlook overlord painless panelled papalise papalism papalist papillae papillar papillon papulose papulous parallax parallel paralyse parclose parkland patellae patellar pathless patulous pavilion pearlies pearling pearlite peculate peculiar pedalier pedalled pedology peerless penalise penology perilled perilous perilune petaline petalled petalody petaloid petalous petulant phyllary phyllode phylloid phyllome picklock piddling piffling pipeline pisolite

pitiless	rustless	snowlike	tidelock	voteless	cacomixl	footmuff	myxomata
pomology	ruthless	snowline	timeless	vowelise	calamary	foramina	needment
populace	rutilant	soapless	tinplate	vowelled	calamine	foremast	November
populate	sackless	socalled	tintless	wakeless	calamint	foremost	ointment
populism	saddlery	sodalite	tireless	warcloud	calamite	fragment	oncoming
populist	sailless	sodality	tocology	warplane	calamity	Ganymede	oogamous
populous	saltless	soilless	toeplate	waveless	camomile	gloaming	opsimath
porkling	saltlick	songless	tokology	waxcloth	casemate	gloomily	optimise
posology	sampling	soulless	tomalley	weakling	casement	glummest	optimism
postlude	sateless	sparling	tombless	weanling	cashmere	goatmoth	optimist
potplant	scallion	spelling	tonality	weedless	catamite	goldmine	ornament
preclude	scarless	spillage	toneless	weeklong	ceramics	gourmand	orpiment
preelect	schiller	spillway	topology	wheelman	ceramist	grimmest	outsmart
proclaim	scholium	spoilage	totalise	whiplash	cerement	gunsmith	overmuch
ptyalism	sciolism	spotless	totality	whiplike	ceremony	halfmast	pallmall
pugilism	sciolist	spurling	totalled	wifeless	charming	halfmoon	palomino
pugilist	scullery	spyglass	towelled	wifelike	chipmuck	hallmark	paramour
pupilage	scullion	squaller	trailnet	wildlife	chipmunk	handmade	pavement
pupilary	seafloor	squelchy	tramline	windlass	chromate	handmaid	pearmain
pupillar	seamless	squilgee	trawlnet	windless	chromite	handmill	pediment
purblind	seaplane	stabling	treeless	wingless	chromium	hawkmoth	pellmell
purfling	sedulity	stablish	trialist	wireless	chummily	headmost	penumbra
purplish	sedulous	stallage	trifling	woodland	chumming	hegemony	pharmacy
purslane	seedleaf	stallfed	triglyph	woodlark	claimant	helpmate	phormium
purulent	seedless	stalling	trilling	woodlice	clammily	helpmeet	piedmont
quillpen	seedling	stallion	trillion	woollens	clamming	highmost	playmate
quisling	seedlobe	starless	trillium	wordless	claymore	hindmost	pockmark
raillery	selfless	starlike	triplane	workless	coalmine	homemade	polemics
rambling	selflove	starling	triploid	wormlike	columnal	ignominy	polemise
rattling	semolina	staylace	troilite	xenolith	columnar	illumine	polemist
ravelled	semplice	stealing	trollopy	xylology	columned	inasmuch	polymath
rearlamp	senility	stealthy	truelove	yeanling	costmary	inchmeal	postmark
rebelled	sepaloid	stellate	tubeless	yearling	cramming	incoming	postmill
rebeller	sepalous	stellify	tubulate	yearlong	creamery	infamise	preamble
rebellow	serology	stellion	tumbling	yodelled	crummock	infamous	primming
reckless	sewellel	stemless	tuneless	yodeller	cucumber	inhumane	prismoid
redblind	sexology	sterling	turtling	zibeline	deafmute	insomnia	proemial
redeless	shalloon	stillage	tutelage	zymology	December	insomuch	psalmist
redolent	shallows	stroller	tutelary	abelmosk	decemvir	intimacy	psalmody
reedling	shealing	subclass	twinling	abetment	decimate	intimate	quagmire
regalism	sherlock	subfloor	typology	abutment	didymium	intimism	qualmish
regality	Shetland	subtlety	Tyrolean	acosmism	didymous	Islamise	racemate
regelate	shielder	subulate	unbelief	acrimony	digamist	Islamism	racemise
regolith	shieling	suchlike	unbolted	aglimmer	digamous	Islamite	racemose
regulate	shilling	suckling	uncalled	agrement	diriment	isthmian	rearmice
reinless	shipload	sunblind	undulant	agrimony	document	jeremiad	rearmost
repelled	shoelace	supplant	undulate	alarmist	dolomite	Jeremiah	recommit
repeller	shoeless	supplely	unfilial	antimask	downmost	judgment	reedmace
resolute	shoulder	supplial	ungulate	antimony	drammock	kakemono	regiment
restless	shouldst	supplier	unvalued	argument	dreamful	Kashmiri	relumine
revelled	sibilant	supplies	upholder	armament	dreamily	landmark	remember
reveller	sibilate	surplice	Ursuline	assemble	dreaming	landmass	renumber
reviling	Sicilian	swanlike	vagility	assembly	drumming	landmine	reremice
revolter	sicklist	swelling	vamplate	assuming	drummock	ligament	resemble
revolute	sideline	syncline	vaneless	atremble	dynamics	liniment	ringmain
revolver	sideling	tabulate	vanillin	automata	dynamism	lipomata	roommate
rheology	sidelong	tackling	veilless	automate	dynamist	locomote	rosemary
rhyolite	similise	tactless	venality	autumnal	dynamite	lodgment	rudiment
ribaldry	simplify	tagalong	ventless	averment	easement	mainmast	sagamore
Riesling	simplism	tailless	vexillum	backmost	eastmost	makimono	saltmine
rivalled	simulant	tameless	viewless	bailment	encomion	malamute	scammony
rivelled	simulate	Tamilian	vigilant	basement	encomium	malemute	schemata
roadless	sinology	tapeless	virilism	becoming	encumber	matamata	scheming
rocklike	sitology	tapelike	virility	bedimmed	endamage	maximise	scramble
rockling	sizzling	tapeline	virology	behemoth	endemism	mazement	scrammed
roodloft	skilless	teacloth	virulent	bigamist	enormity	melamine	scumming
roofless	skilling	tearless	vitalise	bigamous	enormous	messmate	sediment
rootless	skinless	template	vitalism	binomial	ensample	metamere	selfmade
roseleaf	skislope	termless	vitalist	bloomers	ensemble	miasmata	selfmate
rosulate	skullcap	thallium	vitality	bloomery	ephemera	miasmous	sesamoid
royalism	slobland	thalloid	vitellin	blooming	Eskimoan	milkmaid	shamming
royalist	smallage	thallous	vitellus	bodement	estimate	minimise	shimmery
rugulose	smallfry	theology	vitiligo	bohemian	evermore	mintmark	shipmate
ruleless	smallish	thirlage	vituline	bondmaid	filament	mishmash	shipment
ruralise	smallpox	thraldom	vocalise	bondmans	fishmeal	monomial	shrimper
ruralism	smelling	thriller	vocalism	bonemeal	flatmate	monument	skimmilk
ruralist	smoulder	ticklish	vocalist	bookmark	flummery	mortmain	skimming
rurality	snaplink	tideland	vocality	bregmata	folkmoot	movement	skirmish
rushlike	snowless	tideless	volplane	brimming	footmark	muniment	slamming

slimmest	actinism	bezonian	decently	fellness	Ibsenism	luminary	paleness
slimming	actinium	biannual	deepness	feminine	idleness	luminist	palinode
slimmish	addendum	biconvex	defender	feminise	ilmenite	luminous	paranoia
slumming	adiantum	biennial	definite	feminism	immanent	lushness	paranoid
smarmily	admonish	biennium	deftness	feminist	imminent	lutanist	parental
sodomite	advanced	bimanous	deionise	feminity	immingle	lutenist	patentee
solemnly	aeronaut	bitingly	demander	fineness	immunise	maleness	patently
spermary	aeronomy	blueness	demented	firmness	immunity	malinger	patentor
squamate	affinity	bluenose	dementia	flatness	impanate	marinade	pedantic
squamose	agedness	boldness	demoness	flounder	imponent	marinate	pedantry
squamous	agronomy	boniness	demoniac	fluently	impunity	matiness	peduncle
squamule	airiness	boringly	demonian	fomenter	infantry	maziness	peignoir
steamily	Albanian	botanise	demonise	fondness	infinite	meanness	Pekinese
stemmata	albinism	botanist	demonism	footnote	infinity	meconium	penknife
stemming	alginate	brainish	deponent	forename	inkiness	meekness	perineal
stigmata	Algonkin	brainpan	detonate	forenoon	inlander	meetness	perineum
stormily	alienage	browning	Devonian	forensic	insanely	melanism	peroneal
stramash	alienate	brownish	dewiness	foulness	insanity	melanite	pertness
stromata	alienism	business	diagnose	foxiness	intended	melinite	petuntse
strummed	alienist	busyness	diminish	fraenula	intently	mementos	pinkness
strummer	almanack	Byronism	disendow	freeness	intonate	meninges	pixiness
strumose	alpinism	cabinboy	disinter	friendly	inventor	meringue	planning
strumous	alpinist	cadenced	disunion	fullness	iodinate	metonymy	pleinair
strumpet	amiantus	caginess	disunite	furuncle	islander	mildness	pleonasm
stumming	ammoniac	calendar	disunity	galangal	Japanese	Mishnaic	pliantly
subimago	ammonify	calender	divinely	Galenism	japanned	Molinism	poignant
swanmark	ammonite	calmness	divinise	galenite	japonica	Molinist	polonium
swimming	ammonium	canoness	divinity	gameness	Javanese	momently	pomander
sycamine	antennae	canonise	dominant	gaminess	jejunely	momentum	poorness
sycamore	antennal	canonist	dominate	gapingly	jocundly	monandry	popinjay
sycomore	antennas	caponier	domineer	geminate	jokingly	mournful	potently
teammate	antinode	caponise	dominion	geognosy	justness	mourning	pregnant
tegument	antinomy	carinate	dominoes	geraniol	juvenile	movingly	primness
telemark	appanage	caruncle	doornail	geranium	keenness	muchness	pruinose
tenement	appendix	Casanova	dopiness	gerontic	kindness	musingly	pryingly
thermion	aquanaut	catenary	dotingly	gigantic	Kohinoor	muteness	puniness
thermite	archness	catenate	douanier	gladness	kolinsky	mutineer	pureness
thiamine	ardently	chainsaw	dourness	gleaning	laconian	mutinous	pyrenoid
thrombin	argentic	chaunter	doziness	glibness	laconism	mylonite	quaintly
thrombus	argonaut	chauntry	drabness	glumness	lacunary	nearness	queendom
thrummed	Arianism	churning	drainage	goodness	lacunate	neatness	queening
tidemark	Armenian	clannish	drownded	graining	lacunose	nepenthe	queenlet
tidemill	Arminian	cleancut	dullness	greenery	lameness	niceness	quidnunc
tinsmith	arranger	cleaning	dumbness	greenfly	lamented	nicknack	raciness
totemism	arrantly	cleanser	dyspnoea	greening	laminate	nickname	ramentum
totemist	arsenate	clowness	easiness	greenish	lankness	nominate	rankness
trammels	arsenide	clownish	echinate	greenlet	larynges	nonunion	raptness
traumata	arsenite	cogently	echinoid	greyness	larynxes	nosiness	rareness
trimming	arsonist	colander	edginess	grimness	lateness	nudeness	rashness
triumvir	arsonous	coldness	eeriness	grinning	latently	nullness	ravenous
ultimacy	ascender	colonial	Emmental	grounder	Latinate	numbness	realness
ultimata	assenter	colonise	endanger	guernsey	latinise	numinous	recently
ultimate	assentor	colonist	engender	gynandry	Latinism	octonary	reconvey
uncommon	assonant	coolness	engineer	habanera	Latinist	offender	refinery
unlimber	assonate	coronach	enginery	haleness	latinity	oiliness	rehandle
untimely	astonied	coronary	enkindle	halfnote	lavender	oleander	reignite
vehement	astonish	coronoid	entangle	hangnail	laziness	oogonial	rekindle
velamina	atlantes	corundum	equinity	harangue	leanness	oogonium	remanent
venomous	Atlantic	cosiness	errantly	hardness	learning	ooziness	reminder
vestment	attender	cotenant	errantry	haziness	legendry	openness	repenter
Vietminh	autonomy	covenant	Essenism	headnote	lemonade	opponent	resinate
virement	autunite	cozenage	essonite	hedonics	Leninism	ordinand	resinify
weldment	avidness	crannied	Estonian	hedonism	Leninist	ordinary	resinoid
windmill	avionics	culinary	eternise	hedonist	Leninite	ordinate	resinous
workmate	Baconian	curtness	eternity	highness	levanter	organdie	resonant
yokemate	badinage	cuteness	eugenics	holiness	lewdness	organise	resonate
aborning	balanced	cylinder	eugenism	hominoid	licensed	organism	retinula
absentee	balancer	Cyrenaic	eugenist	homonymy	licensee	organist	revanche
absently	baldness	daftness	evenness	homuncle	licenser	oriental	revenant
absinthe	Balinese	dampness	evilness	hugeness	likeness	oriented	revenger
absonant	banknote	dankness	expander	humanely	limonite	oscinine	richness
accentor	bareness	daringly	exponent	humanise	limpness	ostinato	rifeness
achenial	baronage	darkness	extender	humanism	lomentum	overnice	ringneck
achiness	baronial	deadness	extensor	humanist	loneness	oxtongue	ripeness
achingly	baseness	deafness	fairness	humanity	longness	paganise	rollneck
actiniae	basinful	dearness	farinose	hymenial	loudness	paganish	romancer
actinian	baseness	debonair	fastness	hymenium	lovenest	paganism	Romanian
actinias	basinful	decanter	favonian	hymenial	lovingly	paganism	romanise
actinide	beginner	decennia	felinity	hymenium	luminant	paginate	Romanism

Romanist	sphingid	titanium	zamindar	Cherokee	duologue	hidrotic	misnomer
Romansch	spinning	tokenism	zaniness	chthonic	dystopia	hillocky	mnemonic
romantic	splendid	tomentum	zemindar	coelomic	ecologic	histogen	Mongolic
ropiness	splenial	toponymy	aasvogel	coenobia	economic	historic	mongoose
rosiness	splenius	tournure	acidosis	cognomen	eftsoons	holdover	moreover
rotenone	splinter	training	adenoids	cognosce	elflocks	hollowly	motional
rotundly	spoonfed	treenail	aegrotat	cognovit	elkhound	hormonal	mucrones
rudeness	spoonful	triangle	airborne	collogue	empeople	hothouse	mulloway
Rumanian	spoonily	triennia	airwoman	colloquy	employee	hummocky	myosotis
Rumansch	springal	trimness	alehouse	commoner	employer	hydrogen	myriopod
ruminant	springer	triunity	allround	commoney	enclothe	hydromel	narcoses
ruminate	sprinkle	truantry	although	commonly	encroach	hydropic	narcosis
safeness	sprinter	trueness	alveolar	composed	ensconce	hydropsy	narcotic
sageness	spryness	trunnion	alveolus	composer	enzootic	hydroski	narrowly
saginate	squander	tryingly	ambrosia	compound	epicotyl	hydroxyl	national
salinity	squinter	Turanian	amitosis	confound	epilogue	hypnoses	necropsy
saltness	stagnant	twinning	amitotic	conjoint	episodal	hypnosis	necrosis
sameness	stagnate	tyrannic	amniotic	consoler	episodic	hypnotic	necrotic
saneness	stannary	ugliness	amphorae	consomme	epopoeia	icebound	negroism
saponify	stannate	umbonate	amphoras	contorno	Ethiopic	improper	neuronal
saponite	stannite	uncandid	anabolic	convolve	euphonic	improver	neuronic
satanism	stannous	uncinate	anaconda	cordovan	euphoria	inchoate	neuroses
satanist	steenbok	unfunded	anagogic	corporal	euphoric	ingrowth	neurosis
savannah	steening	unhinged	analogic	cramoisy	eutrophy	intromit	neurotic
Saxondom	steinbok	unionise	analogue	cretonne	exploder	introrse	newcomer
Saxonism	sternite	unionism	anatomic	crocoite	explorer	isagogic	newfound
Saxonist	sternson	unionist	anchoret	cromorna	extrorse	isogonal	nitrogen
sayonara	sternway	unkennel	androgen	cromorne	eyetooth	isogonic	nonmoral
scanning	stibnite	unkindly	aniconic	cupboard	factotum	isomorph	notional
scornful	stranded	unkingly	anthozoa	customer	falconer	isotonic	nuthouse
scrannel	stranger	unlinked	antrorse	cyanogen	falconet	isotopic	oldworld
seaonion	strangle	unmanned	apagogic	cyanoses	falconry	jamboree	oligomer
seasnail	strength	unpinned	apodoses	cyanosis	faubourg	jealousy	onceover
seasnake	stringed	unsunned	apodosis	cyanotic	fellowly	jingoish	onehorse
seconder	stringer	untangle	apologia	cyclonic	fibrosis	jingoism	onlooker
secondly	strongly	untented	apologue	cyclopes	fibrotic	jingoist	optional
seigneur	strontia	unwanted	approach	cyclosis	fireopal	keyboard	oratorio
seignior	stubnail	unwonted	approval	daemonic	fogbound	Komsomol	orthodox
seignory	stunning	uplander	asphodel	daffodil	follower	kurtosis	orthoepy
selenate	Sudanese	urbanely	ballonet	daimonic	followon	kyphosis	outboard
selenide	supinate	urbanise	balmoral	deflower	followup	kyphotic	outbound
selenite	supinely	urbanism	banjoist	despotic	forborne	lacrosse	outdoors
selenium	sureness	urbanist	baryonic	dewpoint	fordoing	lapboard	outgoing
selfness	swainish	urbanite	bathotic	diabolic	forgoing	larboard	outhouse
semantic	swanneck	urbanity	benzoate	diaconal	forsooth	lawcourt	outmoded
seminary	swannery	urgently	bespoken	diagonal	foveolae	laywoman	outpoint
seminude	swanning	vacantly	bestowal	dialogic	foxhound	leeboard	outworks
serenade	syconium	vainness	bignonia	dialogue	frijoles	leftover	oviposit
serenata	synonymy	valanced	biomorph	diatomic	furlough	legioned	oxymoron
serenely	syringes	vastness	bionomic	diatonic	gadzooks	littoral	oxytocin
serenity	syrinxes	Vedantic	bistoury	dicrotic	galloper	loblolly	pandowdy
sexiness	takingly	verandah	blazoner	diplogen	Galloway	Londoner	pangolin
shinning	talented	veronica	blazonry	diploidy	garboard	lordosis	pansophy
shrinker	tallness	vicinage	bonhomie	diplomat	gargoyle	lordotic	pantofle
shrunken	tamandua	vicinity	borrower	diplopia	garrotte	madhouse	pardoner
shunning	tamanoir	Viennese	bottomry	dipnoous	gashouse	madwoman	parrotry
sickness	tameness	vileness	bouzouki	disbound	gasworks	magnolia	parsonic
sidenote	tartness	vixenish	bullocky	discount	geologic	mahjongg	Passover
silencer	tautness	voidness	buncombe	discover	geoponic	mandolin	pastoral
silently	taxingly	wagonage	burgonet	disgorge	glycogen	mandorla	pathogen
simoniac	taxonomy	wagonlit	burnouse	disjoint	glyconic	mangonel	patronal
simonist	technics	wakening	burrower	dislodge	gnomonic	manpower	peacocky
sirenian	tenantry	wariness	buttoner	disloyal	Golconda	marjoram	pectoral
skewness	tenonsaw	warmness	caboodle	dismount	gorgonia	marmoset	pegboard
skinning	tetanise	waviness	cannonry	disposal	grimoire	mastodon	perforce
slimness	thinness	waxiness	canoodle	disposer	gummosis	matronal	periodic
slowness	thinnest	weakness	cantonal	dissolve	gunpoint	matronly	periotic
smugness	thinning	wellnigh	cantoris	doctoral	hadronic	mediocre	personae
snugness	thinnish	whatness	canzonet	doghouse	haliotis	mellowly	personal
Socinian	thisness	wideness	carbolic	dogooder	hallowed	meteoric	petiolar
softness	threnode	wildness	carbonic	dogtooth	hangover	methodic	petioled
solander	threnody	wiliness	carbonyl	dormouse	haploidy	microbar	petrolic
solanine	thusness	wiriness	carboxyl	draconic	harlotry	microbic	petronel
soleness	tidiness	wiseness	cartouch	dragoman	harmonic	microdot	petrosal
solenoid	tininess	womanise	cathodal	dragomen	hebdomad	midpoint	phenolic
soreness	titanate	womanish	cathodic	dragonet	heliosis	Miltonic	Philomel
sourness	titaness	woodnote	catholic	drypoint	henroost	miscount	photogen
spanning	titanism	xylonite	cationic	Dukhobor	hiccough	misdoing	photopia
sphenoid	titanite	yearning	chaconne	dumfound	hidrosis	misdoubt	photopic

```
photopsy  seasoner  Tychonic  clippers  grasping  recapped  synaptic  Alderney
pinmoney  sectoral  typhonic  clipping  gripping  receptor  synopses  aleurone
pinpoint  selcouth  unbroken  clodpole  grouping  redeploy  synopsis  algorism
pishogue  semiotic  unclothe  clodpoll  grumpily  reedpipe  synoptic  allergen
platonic  sensoria  unfrozen  colophon  Guelphic  reemploy  tailpipe  allergic
plutonic  shadower  unipolar  conspire  halfpint  reexport  talapoin  alumroot
poisoner  sinfonia  unisonal  cornpone  handpick  reimpose  teaspoon  amperage
porpoise  siphonal  univocal  coryphee  heliport  resupine  telepath  anaerobe
postobit  siphonet  unloosen  costplus  hexapody  rolypoly  teleport  aneurism
potbound  siphonic  unroofed  costpush  hornpipe  rosepink  teraphim  aneurysm
potholer  Slavonic  uprooter  creeping  hosepipe  Salopian  thespian  ankerite
pothouse  slipover  vacuolar  crispate  inceptor  scampish  thumping  anourous
potroast  slyboots  variolar  cropping  inexpert  scoopful  tonepoem  anserine
premolar  sorrower  variorum  croupier  isospory  scoopnet  trampler  anterior
premorse  spadones  verboten  croupous  jodhpurs  scorpion  trappean  anteroom
prisoner  sporozoa  vermouth  decipher  knapping  scraping  trapping  aphorise
profound  stenosed  victoria  diaspora  lamppost  scrapped  Trappist  aphorism
prologue  stenosis  viscount  diaspore  liripoop  scrapper  trespass  aphorist
prolonge  stenotic  visional  didapper  madapple  sculptor  trippery  apiarian
promoter  stopover  waggoner  doorpost  malapert  seedplot  tripping  apiarist
propolis  subjoint  walkover  doumpalm  malaprop  selfpity  troupial  apocrine
proposal  subpoena  walloper  downpipe  mayapple  seraphic  trumpery  apograph
proposer  subsolar  wallower  downpour  megapode  seraphim  turnpike  apparent
propound  subsonic  wantonly  dripping  metaphor  sharpish  uncapped  apterous
prorogue  subtonic  warhorse  dropping  milepost  sharpset  untapped  aquarist
prosodic  subtopia  waxworks  duckpond  millpond  sheepdip  unzipped  aquarium
protocol  subtotal  waygoing  dutypaid  mirepoix  sheepdog  vilipend  arboreal
protonic  subvocal  weaponry  ecliptic  misapply  sheepish  whapping  arboreta
protozoa  summoner  windowed  ellipses  misspell  sheepked  whipping  arborist
psilosis  supposal  winnower  ellipsis  misspelt  sheeppen  whispery  armorial
pteropod  supposed  wrymouth  elliptic  misspend  sheeprun  whooping  arterial
pugnosed  surmount  yellowly  encipher  misspent  shipping  whopping  asperges
pullover  surround  yoghourt  entoptic  monopode  shopping  windpipe  asperity
pulmonic  surroyal  zealotry  eohippus  monopoly  shrapnel  winepalm  aspirant
pushover  symbolic  zirconia  equipage  namepart  signpost  wolfpack  aspirate
pythonic  sympodia  zoomorph  equipped  nenuphar  sinapism  woodpile  assertor
protozoa  symposia  zoonosis  escapade  newspeak  sinophil  woodpulp  assorted
quixotry  syncopal  abruptly  escapism  ninepins  skimpily  woolpack  Assyrian
randomly  syntonic  acarpous  escapist  nosepipe  skipping  wordplay  asterisk
ransomer  systolic  accepter  estopped  oakapple  slapping  wrappage  asterism
rational  takeover  acceptor  estoppel  occupant  sleepily  wrapping  asteroid
rawboned  tamboura  adespota  eupepsia  occupier  sleeping  zoospore  atheroma
reasoner  tandoori  agitprop  eupeptic  oenophil  slippage  henequen  attorney
reckoner  tangoist  agraphia  European  olympiad  slippery  illiquid  aurorean
rectoral  taphouse  agrarian  europium  Olympian  slipping  maroquin  autarchy
regional  tarboosh  airspeed  exemplar  openplan  sloppail  paraquat  autarkic
regrowth  tattooer  allopath  exemplum  outspend  sloppily  paroquet  averring
repeople  tautomer  allspice  exospore  outspent  slopping  ramequin  aviarist
reproach  tautonym  antepost  facepack  overpaid  slowpoke  tranquil  babirusa
reproval  teaboard  antiphon  feedpipe  overpass  snappily  Abderite  backrest
response  teahouse  antipode  Filipina  overpast  snapping  aberrant  backroom
restorer  teatowel  antipole  Filipino  overplay  snappish  abhorred  Bactrian
retroact  tectonic  antipope  fireplug  overplus  snippety  abhorrer  ballroom
retrorse  teetotal  atropine  fishpond  passport  snipping  abnormal  bankroll
rhetoric  teetotum  backpack  flagpole  pedipalp  soilpipe  absorber  bankrupt
Rhinodon  temporal  baldpate  flapping  peripety  sourpuss  abstract  banxring
rhizopod  Teutonic  beanpole  flippant  periplus  spalpeen  abstrict  bathrobe
ribbonry  thorough  bebopper  flipping  perspire  stampede  abstruse  bathroom
roseolar  thyroxin  bellpull  floppily  phosphor  steepish  absurdly  baudrons
sailorly  titmouse  bellpush  flopping  plopping  steepled  accuracy  Bavarian
santonin  tolbooth  blimpish  fluepipe  plumpish  stepping  accurate  beadroll
sardonic  tomnoddy  blowpipe  footpace  polypary  stippler  accursed  beebread
sardonyx  toplofty  bonspiel  footpath  polypide  stoppage  acierage  beetroot
sauropod  topnotch  bookpost  footpost  polypite  stopping  acierate  begirded
sawbones  tortoise  bowsprit  forepart  polypody  strapoil  acturial  besprent
sawhorse  tragopan  calipash  forepast  polypoid  strapped  adherent  bestrewn
sawtooth  tricorne  calipers  forepeak  polypous  strapper  Adlerian  bestride
schooner  trifocal  calyptra  foreplay  poohpooh  strepent  aegirine  bestrode
scirocco  triforia  carapace  forspeak  postpaid  Strepyan  afferent  beverage
scotopic  trigonal  catapult  forspent  postpone  stripped  affirmer  biograph
seaboard  trilobed  cesspool  fourpart  priapism  stripper  afforest  biparous
seaborne  tripodal  champers  fowlpest  prompter  strophic  agrarian  blearily
seacoast  trisomic  champion  frapping  promptly  stropped  airbrake  blurrily
seagoing  turbofan  chapping  frippery  propping  stumpily  airbrush  blurring
seaholly  turbojet  cheapish  frumpish  prospect  swapping  aircraft  boltrope
seahorse  Turcoman  chipping  fullpage  pushpull  sweeping  airframe  bookrest
seamount  Turkoman  chirpily  gatepost  quipping  sweepnet  alacrity  botyrose
seamouse  turnover  chopping  goalpost  rataplan  swopping  alburnum  bowfront
seasonal  tussocky  clapping  Godspeed  reappear  synapsis  alderman  Briarean
```

bullring	debarred	encircle	gimcrack	Kanarese	mistreat	panorama	reverend
buttress	decorate	endermic	glabrous	Khmerian	mistress	paperboy	reverent
butyrate	decorous	endorsee	goitrous	kohlrabi	mistrial	parergon	reversal
bystreet	decurion	endorser	goldrush	laburnum	mistrust	pastrami	reverser
Cambrian	deferent	enforcer	governor	lacerate	miswrite	pastries	reverter
cancrine	deferral	enforest	Gujarati	landrail	Mithraic	paternal	rewarder
cancroid	deferred	engirdle	hamartia	laterite	moderate	peagreen	ribgrass
canorous	deferrer	enlarger	handrail	laverock	moderato	pederast	ricercar
castrate	deforest	enshrine	headrace	Lazarist	modernly	pelerine	rickrack
castrati	deformed	enshroud	headrest	lazurite	Moharram	pelorism	riffraff
castrato	delirium	enterate	headroom	legbreak	molarity	pembroke	rigorism
cataract	demarche	enthrall	hibernal	legerity	monarchy	pentroof	rigorist
cateress	demerara	enthrone	highrise	lemurine	monorail	peperino	rigorous
catering	demersal	entirely	highroad	lemuroid	moonrise	perorate	rimbrake
caverned	demurely	entirety	hilarity	leporine	motorail	picaroon	ringroad
celeriac	demurral	environs	honorary	leverage	motorcar	piecrust	riparian
celerity	demurrer	ephorate	hornrims	levirate	motorial	pinprick	riverain
centring	denarius	epigraph	hotpress	liberate	motoring	piperack	riverbed
centrism	dendrite	escargot	hoverfly	licorice	motorise	piperine	riverine
centrist	dendroid	escarole	humorist	limerick	motorist	pirarucu	riverman
centroid	departed	esterify	humorous	literacy	motorium	playroom	riverway
chairman	deportee	ethereal	hungrily	literary	motorman	pleurisy	roborant
charring	depurate	etherial	huntress	literate	motormen	polarise	rockrose
cheerful	describe	etherise	icecream	literati	motorway	polarity	roofrack
cheerily	deserter	etherism	ichorous	liturgic	muckrake	poltroon	rosarian
cheering	desirous	etherist	idocrase	liveried	Muharram	portrait	roseroot
chirrupy	destrier	Etrurian	ignorant	liverish	mushroom	portress	rostrate
chlorate	destruct	euphrasy	illtreat	lopgrass	muskrose	powerful	Rotarian
chloride	deterred	excursus	Illyrian	lowering	myograph	preprint	roturier
chlorine	deterrer	execrate	immersed	lowgrade	naturism	primrose	ryegrass
chlorite	dethrone	exhorter	immortal	lunarian	naturist	priorate	sackrace
chlorous	dextrine	exocrine	imparity	lustrate	Nazarene	prioress	saffrony
choirboy	dextrose	expertly	imperial	lustrine	Nazarite	priority	salariat
ciborium	dextrous	expirant	imperium	lustring	Nazirite	prodrome	salaried
cicerone	diagraph	exporter	importer	lustrous	neoprene	progress	saleroom
ciceroni	diarrhea	exserted	impurely	macaroni	nephrite	protract	samarium
cinerary	diatribe	exterior	impurity	macaroon	neutrino	protrude	Sangrail
clearcut	dichroic	external	incurred	macerate	newsreel	pubertal	Sangreal
clearing	diffract	federate	indirect	maharaja	newsroom	pumproom	sapgreen
clearway	dimerism	feverfew	indurate	maharani	nosering	puparial	saporous
coatrack	dimerous	feverish	inerrant	majority	notarial	puparium	satirise
coatroom	dinerout	feverous	inferior	malarial	notornis	quadrant	satirist
coherent	dinornis	fewtrils	infernal	malarian	novercal	quadrate	saturant
cokernut	disarray	figurant	inferred	malarkey	numeracy	quadriga	saturate
compress	discreet	figurine	infirmly	maltreat	numerary	quadroon	Saturday
comprise	discrete	filariae	informal	mandrake	numerate	quarrier	saturnic
concrete	discrown	filarial	informed	mandrill	numerous	quatrain	savorous
confrere	disfrock	filtrate	informer	mangrove	nutarian	queerish	sawframe
confront	disgrace	fimbriae	inherent	manorial	nutbrown	quitrent	scabrous
congress	disorder	flagrant	inscribe	manurial	oatgrass	rackrent	scarring
congreve	dispread	flatrace	inscroll	margrave	obduracy	railroad	scirrhus
contract	disprize	flooring	inserted	Masorete	obdurate	ranarian	sciurine
contrail	disproof	flourish	instruct	Masoreth	observer	ranarium	sciuroid
contrary	disprove	fluoride	insurant	material	obstruct	rasorial	sclereid
contrast	distract	fluorine	intarsia	materiel	obturate	recorder	sclerite
contrate	distrain	fluorite	interact	maternal	occurred	recurred	scleroma
contrite	distrait	footrace	interbed	matgrass	octarchy	redbrick	sclerose
contrive	distress	footrest	intercom	mattress	octaroon	redirect	sclerous
conurbia	district	footrope	intercut	maturate	octoroon	referent	scourger
coverage	distrust	footrule	interest	maturely	odograph	referral	scurrile
coverall	divorcee	formroom	interior	maturity	oestrone	referred	seacraft
covering	doctrine	fortress	intermit	maverick	oestrous	reforest	seadrome
coverlet	doldrums	fragrant	intermix	mayoress	offbreak	reformed	seafront
covertly	dolerite	fumarole	internal	mazarine	offdrive	reformer	seagreen
cowardly	doloroso	funerary	internee	meagrely	offering	repartee	seatrout
cowgrass	dolorous	funereal	Interpol	membrane	offprint	reporter	seawrack
coworker	drearily	futurism	interred	memorial	onetrack	rescript	securely
cucurbit	drumroll	futurist	interrex	memorise	oratress	reserved	security
Cumbrian	editress	futurity	intersex	menarche	outbrave	resorcin	sederunt
cumbrous	eelgrass	gabbroic	intertie	mezereon	outbreak	resorter	selfrule
curarine	eldorado	gabbroid	interval	midbrain	outdrawn	respring	senarius
curarise	efferent	gadarene	interwar	millrace	outgrown	resprung	senorita
cutprice	elfarrow	gambroon	inthrall	Minoress	overrate	restrain	sentrygo
dandruff	emigrant	gangrene	inverted	Minorite	override	restrict	separate
darkroom	emigrate	gastraea	inverter	minority	overripe	resurvey	severely
dartrous	emporium	gastrula	inwardly	miserere	overrule	retarded	severity
daybreak	empurple	generate	isocracy	misprint	overruns	retarder	sewerage
daydream	empyreal	generous	isoprene	misprise	pagurian	retiring	sewergas
deaerate	empyrean	gentrice	isotropy	misprize	pancreas	retorted	sewerrat

```
shabrack sunproof underlap waterway blessing deanship focussed illusive
shagreen superadd underlay wellread blissful decision folksong illusory
shagroon superate underlet whirring blossomy decisive foolscap impishly
shamrock superbly underlie windrose bodyshop deemster footslog imposing
shirring superego underlip wintrily bombsite deerskin footsore imposter
shofroth superior underman wizardly bondsman delusion footstep impostor
showroom superman underpin wizardry boursier delusive foresaid incision
Siberian supernal underrun wondrous boyishly delusory foresail incisive
sickroom supertax undersea woodruff Bradshaw derision foreseen indusium
sidereal suppress underset workroom brassage derisive foreshow industry
siderite surprise undertow yestreen brassard derisory foreside infusion
sideroad susurrus underway zoetrope brassart digester foreskin inhesion
Silurian suzerain unearned Abbaside brassica dinosaur forestal invasion
siluroid swearing unerring abrasion brassily diopside forestay invasive
sitarist sybarite unforced abrasive breasted disaster forested investor
skerrick syndrome unformed accustom brewster disusage forester ironside
slipring synergic unmarked acoustic buckshee division forestry jackstay
sliproad synergid unperson acrostic buckshot divisive foursome jocosely
slurring taberdar unsprung adhesion buckskin dockside fourstar jocosity
soaproot tackroom unstring adhesive bullseye dolesome freesoil Jugoslav
soberise taffrail unstrung adjuster cadastre domestic Friesian jumpseat
solarise tailrace unthread adjustor calcspar doomsday frogspit jumpsuit
solarism tamarind unthrift advisory calfskin doomsman fuchsine junkshop
solarist tamarind unthrone aerostat camisade doomster fullsize Jurassic
solarium tamarisk unversed affusion camisado doorsill gainsaid juristic
sombrely Tantrism unwarily agnostic camisole doorstep gamesome keepsake
sombrero Tantrist unwordly agrestic campsite doorstop gamester kerosene
sombrous tartrate unworthy aguishly canaster dragsman gangster kerosine
sonority taverner uppercut allusion canister dragster ganister kickshaw
sonorous tawdrily upsprang allusive capeskin dramshop garishly kinesics
sororate teabread upspring ambusher cavesson dressage gelastic kingship
sorority teabreak upsprung amnesiac cerastes dressing girasole kingsize
soterial temerity upstream ancestor cerusite dropshot gladsome knapsack
sowbread tenorite upstroke ancestry chasseur drowsily glassful ladyship
spanroof tenurial upthrown andesine chessman dumbshow glassily lamasery
sparring thearchy upthrust andesite chiasmus dustshot glassine lambskin
spearman theorise upwardly antisera chiastic dynastic glassine landslip
spherics theorist usufruct aoristic chopsuey eclosion glissade landsman
spheroid theurgic valerate aphasiac christen effusion glossary Langshan
spherule thwarter valerian aplastic christie effusive glossily larkspur
spurrier thwartly valorise apposite Christly egoistic glossina lavishly
spurring tiebreak valorous apresski cicisbei embosser gneissic leadsman
squarely tigereye vambrace arrestee cicisbeo embussed goadster lewisite
squarish tigerish vaporise arrester clanship emersion goatskin lifesize
squarson timorous vaporous arrestor clansman emissary gownsman linesman
squireen tolerant velarium artesian classics emission greasily lintseed
squirely tolerate venerate artistic classify emissive gripsack loadstar
squirrel tomorrow venereal artistry cloister emulsify grissini lockstep
squirter toolroom viburnum asbestic clumsily emulsion grogshop lodestar
stairrod topdress vicarage asbestos coalsack emulsive gruesome logistic
stairway tovarish vicarate assassin coarsely emulsoid gulosity lonesome
starrily towardly vicarial assessor cockshut endostea gyrostat longship
starring tramroad victress attested cocksure envisage halfsole longsome
stearate traprock vigorous attester cohesion envision handsewn longstop
stearine triarchy viperine attestor cohesive Ephesian handsome lordship
steerage tribrach viperish Augustan coleseed Etruscan harasser loveseat
steering trigraph viperous augustly coleslaw Eurasian hardship lovesick
stirring tubercle vivarium autistic coliseum evensong haresear lovesome
stuprate tuberose vizarded autosome colossal eversion harpseal lovesong
suberect tuberous vomerine aversely colossus evulsion haruspex lysosome
suberise tumorous votaress aversion coonskin excision headsail magister
suberose tutorage votarist aversive coursing exposure headsman mainsail
suberous tutoress waitress avulsion cragsman failsafe heirship mainstay
subframe tutorial wakerife babushka creosote fearsome helmsman majestic
subgroup ulcerate wardress backseat crossbar feldsher herdsman maltster
suborder ulcerous wardrobe backside crossbow feldspar hernshaw marasmic
suborner ulterior wardroom backspin crosscut fenestra hibiscus marasmus
subprior umpirage washroom backstay crossing fernshaw hillside marksman
subtract unbarred waterage bailsman crosslet filmstar hoarsely meatsafe
suburban unburden waterbed baluster crossply finespun hocusing medusoid
suburbia unburied waterbus bandsman crosstie finisher hocussed meniscus
sudarium underact watergas banister crossway fireship holistic meristem
suffrage underage waterice beadsman cryostat fireside homesick meristic
sultrily underarm watering bearskin curassow fivestar homespun merosome
Sumerian underbid waterish biassing cynosure flagship honestly Milesian
sundress undercut waterlog bicuspid cytosine flaxseed huckster mimester
sundried underdid waterloo bioassay dalesman flimsily huntsman minister
sundries underdog waterman birdseed damassin flipside illusage ministry
sundrops underfur waterski birdseye darksome focusing illusion misusage
```

```
modestly pleasant seedsman Tunisian altitude Chartist doubtful filature
modishly pleasing selfsame turnskin ambition chastely dovetail finitely
molasses pleasure selfsown turnsole amortise chastise downtime finitude
moleskin plimsoll semester turnspit amputate chastity downtown firetrap
molester plussage sempster twinship angstrom chattily downturn firstaid
molossus polestar serosity tyrosine annotate chatting drawtube fishtail
monastic polisher sideshow uneasily anorthic chestnut driftage fixation
monistic pollster sideslip unfasten antitype cicatrix driftice fixative
monkseal polyseme sidesman unjustly aperture cincture driftway flattery
monkship polysemy sidestep unlisted apostasy citation drystone flattest
moonsail polysomy singsong unwashed apostate claptrap duettist flattish
moonshee popishly sinister unwisdom appetent clotting duration flautist
moonshot poristic sinusoid unwisely appetite clustery durative flection
mopishly porosity slipshod unwished aptitude coaction dyestuff fleeting
moresque potassic slipslop uppishly aquatint coactive dynatron flintily
morosely pressbox slopshop uprising arbitral coauthor edentate flitting
morosity pressing snapshot vanisher aristate cocktail eduction floatage
moussaka pressman sneeshan vavasory armature cogitate egestion floating
mucosity pressure snipsnap vavasour aseptate coistrel egestive fluttery
mulishly priestly snowshoe venosity astatine comatose Egyptian folktale
nainsook prissily soapsuds Venusian astutely cometary eighteen foretell
namesake Prussian softshoe veristic attitude conation eighthly foretime
nodosity puissant softsoap vinosity atwitter conative eighties foretold
nomistic punisher songster vivisect audition constant ejection fountain
nonesuch puristic sparsely voussoir auditive construe ejective fourteen
nonusage quaestor sparsity wainscot auditory cooption ekistics fourthly
oafishly quayside spinster wardship autotomy cooptive election fraction
obeisant queasily splasher Wellsian autotype countess elective fracture
obtusely raftsman sponsion whinsill aventail courtesy electret fretting
obtusity rakishly spousage windsail aviation courtier electric friction
occasion rapeseed squasher windsock aviatrix covetous electric fritting
Odyssean ravisher staysail wineshop aweather craftily electrum frontage
oleaster reabsorb stunsail wineskin axletree creatine embattle frontier
omission reassert swanshot wingspan bangtail creation embitter frontlet
opposite reassess swanskin wolfskin barathea creative emitting frostily
orgasmic reassign swansong woodshed baritone creatrix empathic frosting
orgastic reassure swimsuit woodsman barytone creature enaction frottage
otiosely recision synastry woolsack beautify cristate enactive fructify
otiosity recusant tailspin woolshed bedstead Croatian enfetter fructose
oversail redesign talesman woolskin bedstraw crofting eolithic fruitage
overseas redistil talisman workshop befitted crustily epistler fruitbat
overseen reedstop tanistry wormseed begetter cryotron epistyle fruitery
overseer register tapestry yourself begotten cubature equation fruitfly
oversell registry teamster Yugoslav belittle culottes equitant fruitful
oversewn reinsert tenesmus abattoir besotted curative equities fruition
overshoe reinsman theistic abbatial betatron cymatium Erastian frustule
overshot reinsure thirster abetting bibation daintily erectile fugitive
overside remissly thousand ablation blastema debutant erection fulltime
oversize resister thrasher ablative blastoff delation ergotise fumitory
overslip resistor thresher ablution blastoid deletion ergotism function
oversold revision throstle abortion blastula demitted eruption garotter
oversoul revisory thruster abortive blistery demotion eruptive gauntlet
overstay rhapsode Thursday abuttals blotting denature etcetera gelatine
overstep rhapsody thyrsoid abutting blustery deputise eupatrid gelation
owlishly rheostat tickseed acanthus boastful deration evection gematria
padishah ribosome tiresome acentric Boeotian devotion eventful gemstone
palestra rickshaw toilsome acrotism boottree dianthus eventide genetics
palisade rimester toolshed adaption bourtree diastase eventual genitive
pantsuit ringside township adaptive bracteal diastema eviction geniture
papistic roadside townsman addition bractlet diastole exacting genotype
papistry roadsign transact additive brattice diestock exaction ghastful
parasang roadster transect adjutage brattish digitate exanthem ghettoes
parasite robustly transept adjutant breather digitise excitant giantess
partsong rocksalt transfer admitted brettese dilatant exciting giantism
pawnshop rucksack transfix adnation brettice dilation exertion glittery
pedestal rugosely tranship adoption burntout dilative existent glutting
peepshow rugosity transire adoptive cabotage dilatory exultant gluttony
Pegasean sadistic transmit adultery cabstand dilution eyestalk glyptics
Pelasgic Salesian transude aeration calctuff dioptase facetiae gogetter
perisher salesman treasure aflutter capitate dioptric fagoting goodtime
pheasant sandshoe treasury agential capitula dipstick faintish greeting
phrasing scansion tressure agiotage capstone Docetism fasttalk gritting
piassava scissile Triassic aglitter carotene Docetist fatstock grottoes
pilaster scission trousers agnation catstail dotation faultily grouting
pilosity scissors truistic airstrip cavatina Donatism Faustian gruntled
pinaster Scotsman trussing aleatory cemetery Donatist feastday guiltily
pintsize sealskin tuckshop allotted cenotaph donative feedtank gumption
plaister seamster tungsten allottee ceratoid donatory feretory gunstock
playsuit sebesten tungstic Alsatian Chartism dotation fighting gyration
```

gyratory	laystall	nematoid	prostate	sceptred	squatter	vexation	communal
habitant	lecithin	nepotism	prostyle	sciatica	starting	visitant	commuter
habitual	legatine	nicotian	psaltery	scottice	startler	vocation	computer
habitude	legation	nicotine	punctate	Scottish	steatite	vocative	conjugal
halation	lengthen	nightcap	punctual	scouting	stetting	volatile	conjunct
halfterm	lenitive	nighthag	puncture	scratchy	stoutish	volitant	conjurer
halftime	levitate	nightjar	punition	scrutiny	strategy	volition	conjuror
halftone	libation	nightowl	punitive	sedately	stratify	volitive	conquest
hardtack	libatory	nineteen	punitory	sedation	stretchy	volution	consular
hatstand	lifetime	nineties	pupation	sedative	strutted	vomitive	consumer
haunting	ligation	nodation	putative	sedition	strutter	vomitory	convulse
haystack	ligature	nonstick	quantify	seedtime	stultify	wheatear	corduroy
heartily	lighting	noontide	quantise	Semitise	stuntman	whetting	costumer
hebetate	lightish	noontime	quantity	Semitism	substage	whistler	cothurni
hebetude	limetwig	notation	quartern	Semitist	sudatory	whittret	cotquean
hecatomb	limitary	novation	quarters	semitone	sunstone	wreathen	cultural
helotism	linstock	nugatory	quartile	serotine	swastika	wrestler	cultured
hepatica	lipstick	nutation	question	shafting	swatting	wrestpin	curculio
hepatise	lobation	oblation	quietism	Shaktism	sweeting	wristlet	cutpurse
heritage	lobotomy	oblatory	quietist	shantung	sweetish	wristpin	daiquiri
hesitant	locative	odontoid	quietude	sheeting	sweetpea	yachting	declutch
hesitate	locution	offstage	quilting	shiftily	sweetsop	yeastily	decouple
hightail	locutory	oilstone	quintain	shiftkey	swiftlet	yuletide	demiurge
hightest	logotype	omitting	quitting	shirting	swotting	zenithal	denounce
himation	longterm	ommateum	ratstail	shoetree	taciturn	zoiatria	devourer
hipsters	longtime	optative	reactant	shooting	Tahitian	zonation	devoutly
hocktide	lunation	ornately	reaction	shootout	tainture	abacuses	diffuser
holstein	lutetium	ornithic	reactive	shoptalk	taxation	accoutre	disburse
hometown	luxation	outstare	realtime	shortage	telethon	aciculae	disguise
Horatian	maestoso	outstrip	rebuttal	shortarm	telltale	acicular	disjunct
horntail	maintain	overtake	rebutted	shortcut	tempting	aciculas	disquiet
howitzer	marathon	overtask	rebutter	shortday	tenotomy	adequacy	dissuade
hydatoid	maritage	overtime	redstart	shortish	teratoma	adequate	donought
hypothec	maritime	overtone	refitted	shutting	termtime	affluent	drynurse
ideation	mealtime	overtook	relation	skirting	testtube	altruism	dybbukim
identify	meantime	overture	relative	skittish	thirteen	altruist	earmuffs
identity	meditate	overturn	remittal	skittles	throttle	announce	effluent
idiotism	menstrua	paintbox	remitted	slattern	ticktack	Arcturus	effluvia
ignition	mesotron	palatial	remittee	slitting	ticktock	armoured	eloquent
ignitron	mightest	palatine	remitter	slotting	tightwad	armourer	epidural
illation	mightily	parttime	remotely	sluttish	tincture	artfully	espousal
illative	militant	penitent	renitent	smaltite	tinstone	babouche	espouser
immature	military	penstock	repetend	smartish	tipstaff	banausic	euphuism
impetigo	militate	petition	repotted	smeltery	together	barouche	euphuist
impotent	minatory	phantasm	resetter	smoothen	topstone	begrudge	evacuant
inaction	Minotaur	phantasy	resettle	smoothie	tractate	Bermudas	evacuate
inactive	minstrel	pilotage	revetted	smoothly	traction	besought	evaluate
incitant	minutely	pivotman	Rhaetian	smuttily	tractive	binaural	excluder
inertial	minutiae	plantain	rightful	snootily	treatise	Burgundy	executor
ingather	misstate	plastery	rightist	sobstory	triptych	cachucha	exequies
inkstand	moisture	plastics	ringtail	sobstuff	tristful	cactuses	exiguity
innately	monetary	plastron	roasting	solation	tristich	caesural	exiguous
intitule	monetise	platting	roentgen	solarium	trotting	calculus	famously
inviting	monition	playtime	rogation	solitary	trottoir	cannulae	farouche
irritant	monitive	plectrum	rogatory	solitude	troutlet	cannular	fastuous
irritate	monitory	plotting	rooftree	solstice	trustful	cannulas	favoured
isoptera	monotint	pointing	rosetree	solution	trustily	capsular	favourer
isostasy	monotone	politely	rotation	somatism	twenties	carburet	featured
jauntily	monotony	politick	rotative	sometime	twittery	carousal	features
jobation	monotype	politico	rotatory	sonatina	twitting	carousel	February
jointure	moratory	politics	rubytail	sorption	unbottle	carouser	fistulae
Jonathan	mountain	ponytail	sabotage	sorptive	unbutton	cellular	fistular
joystick	mounting	position	saboteur	spatting	unfetter	centuple	fitfully
junction	mudstone	positive	sagittal	spectral	unfitted	cernuous	flexuose
juncture	muleteer	positron	saintdom	spectrum	ungotten	chasuble	flexuous
keratose	munition	potation	salutary	spitting	unsettle	chemurgy	flexural
keystone	musktree	potstill	sanative	spittoon	untether	chequers	formulae
kibitzer	mutation	potstone	sanatory	splatter	untitled	cherubic	formulas
kinetics	mycetoma	poultice	sanctify	splitter	upsetter	cherubim	fortuity
klystron	nametape	practice	sanction	splotchy	urostyle	cingulum	frenulum
knitting	naphthol	practise	sanctity	splutter	vacation	cinquain	frequent
knotting	natation	prattler	sanitary	spontoon	vaulting	circuity	furculae
komitaji	natatory	prentice	sanitate	sportful	vauntful	circular	furcular
kreutzer	neaptide	prestige	sanitise	sportily	vegetate	cislunar	furfural
latitant	negation	prettify	saxatile	sporting	vegetive	claqueur	furfuran
latitude	negative	prettily	scanties	sportive	venation	cliquish	galluses
lavation	negatory	printing	scantily	spottily	Venetian	cliquism	gestural
lavatory	negatron	printout	scattily	spotting	veratrin	coagulum	globular
laxative	nematode	pristine	scatting	squatted	veratrum	coloured	globulin

graduand	pinnular	tortuous	Moravian	firewood	ovenware	windward	fedayeen
graduate	plaguily	torturer	motivate	firework	overwear	wirework	ferryman
granular	planulae	traducer	motivity	fishwife	overwind	wireworm	fiftyish
gratuity	planular	tribunal	natively	flatware	overwork	wirewove	foreyard
guttural	plumular	ubiquity	nativism	flatways	overworn	wishwash	fortyish
halluces	polluter	uncaused	nativist	flatwise	password	woodwind	funnyman
harrumph	postural	unchurch	nativity	flatworm	pigswill	woodwool	gardyloo
Hercules	posturer	uncouple	nonevent	fleawort	pilewort	woodwork	gipsydom
hereunto	prehuman	unctuous	oblivion	footwear	pillwort	woodworm	gipsyism
hereupon	prejudge	unhoused	omnivore	footwork	pinewood	woolwork	goodyear
hinduise	presumer	uniquely	ottavino	forewarn	pondweed	wormwood	gossypol
Hinduism	procurer	unsought	overview	forewent	pulpwood	zugzwang	gypsydom
honourer	producer	unstuffy	paravane	foreword	rainwash	bisexual	gypsyism
humoured	promulge	untaught	Peruvian	formwork	rainwear	detoxify	handyman
included	purpuric	usefully	rearview	forswear	rearward	monaxial	haulyard
inequity	purpurin	valvulae	recovery	forswore	reedwren	monoxide	hobbyist
influent	pursuant	valvular	reinvest	forsworn	renowned	paroxysm	honeybee
iniquity	pustular	vanguard	relevant	freewill	rereward	peroxide	honeydew
inoculum	rambutan	vanquish	renovate	fretwork	ringwall	preexist	honeypot
intruder	raptures	vapourer	revivify	gallwasp	ringworm	pyrexial	ivorynut
Iroquois	ratguard	vascular	salivary	gapeworm	rockweed	pyroxene	jerrycan
jacquard	recourse	vasculum	salivate	glowworm	rockwood	relaxant	junkyard
jalousie	redouble	venously	scurvily	godawful	rockwork	suboxide	kailyard
joyfully	refluent	venturer	shelving	goodwife	ropewalk	triaxial	lacrymal
joyously	renounce	verdured	sideview	goodwill	rosewood	trioxide	lallygag
labourer	repousse	verjuice	spivvery	goutweed	ryotwari	uniaxial	lobbyist
language	resource	verrucae	stravaig	goutwort	saltwort	alleyway	lollypop
languish	ruefully	vesturer	synovial	gromwell	sandwich	analyser	loonybin
lawfully	saccular	victuals	teleview	gulfweed	sandworm	analyses	lowlying
lecturer	sacculus	vinculum	televise	hairworm	sandwort	analysis	mainyard
legguard	Sadducee	vinously	thievery	handwork	scrawler	analytic	marrying
leisured	sanguine	virtuosa	thievish	hardware	screwtop	asphyxia	mealybug
linguist	sauouari	virtuosi	thriving	hardwood	selfwill	backyard	metayage
longueur	scapulae	virtuoso	titivate	hawkweed	shipworm	ballyhoo	methylic
maieutic	scapular	virtuous	trouvere	headwind	shopworn	ballyrag	methysis
manfully	scapulas	volvulus	twelvemo	headword	shrewdly	barnyard	moneybag
marauder	scopulae	waesucks	unlovely	headwork	shrewish	bellyful	moneybox
marquess	scopulas	wetnurse	vesuvian	herdwick	sidewalk	benzylic	neomycin
marquise	scrounge	whodunit	aardwolf	herewith	sideward	billyboy	newlywed
Mayqueen	seapurse	wilfully	advowson	hickwall	sideways	billycan	outlying
measured	seaquake	woefully	armyworm	homeward	sidewind	bobbypin	outvying
mensural	secluded	yarmulka	backward	homework	sidewise	bobbysox	pattypan
mercuric	sensuous	zarzuela	backwash	hoodwink	silkworm	bogeyman	phenylic
mesquite	septuple	ziggurat	basswood	hookworm	slopwork	boneyard	picayune
messuage	serpulae	acervate	beadwork	hornworm	slowworm	botryoid	platypus
micrurgy	sextuple	activate	beefwood	hornwort	soapwort	bullyboy	pollywog
misguide	Shabuoth	activism	beeswing	inchworm	software	bullyoff	propylic
misjudge	sinfully	actively	bellwort	ironware	softwood	bullyrag	pterylae
misquote	singular	activist	bentwood	ironwood	someways	carryall	puppydog
monaural	spatular	activity	bindweed	ironwork	somewhat	carryout	puppydom
mortuary	specular	adjuvant	blueweed	kilowatt	somewhen	coccyges	puppyfat
mosquito	speculum	alluvial	bodywork	knapweed	spaewife	collyria	puppyish
mowburnt	spiculae	alluvion	bollworm	knitwear	sprawler	condylar	pussycat
mudguard	spicular	alluvium	bookwork	knotwork	squawker	dactylar	rallying
murmurer	spiculum	ambivert	bookworm	lacewing	squawman	dactylic	rallyist
muscular	sporular	backveld	buhlwork	lacework	stalwart	dairying	ropeyarn
musquash	statuary	Batavian	buzzword	leadwork	starwort	dairyman	rowdyish
nimbused	statured	bushveld	cakewalk	leftward	stepwise	dandyish	rowdyism
nocturne	stimulus	cidevant	careworn	lifework	studwork	dandyism	sailyard
nonhuman	stipular	cleavage	casework	likewise	tapeworm	dialyser	Samoyede
nonjuror	subhuman	cleavers	colewort	limewash	taskwork	dialyses	sandyish
nurturer	sublunar	delivery	cordwain	livewire	teamwork	dialysis	sannyasi
obituary	succubae	derivate	cordwood	loanword	thrawart	dialytic	Savoyard
occluded	succubus	diluvial	corkwing	longwall	tidewave	dittybag	sealyham
occlusal	sunburnt	diluvian	corkwood	longwave	timework	dittybox	shipyard
odiously	sunburst	diluvium	Cotswold	longways	timeworn	dockyard	spagyric
opaquely	tabouret	enervate	coxswain	longwise	toilworn	dooryard	spraygun
oracular	Talmudic	equivoke	cusswood	lukewarm	tripwire	dowdyish	sukiyaki
outburst	Tartuffe	estovers	deadwood	lungwort	unlawful	epicycle	syncytia
outguess	telluric	excavate	downward	lykewake	untoward	essayist	tallyman
pastural	textuary	Genevese	downwind	mealworm	wartweed	euonymin	tiltyard
pellucid	textural	grievous	drawwell	megawatt	wartwort	euonymus	toadyish
pendular	textured	incivism	dropwort	menswear	Wedgwood	everyday	toadyism
pendulum	timously	innovate	duckweed	meshwork	wellworn	everyman	tommybar
perfumer	tittuped	Jehovist	eastward	milkweed	werewolf	everyone	tommygun
perjurer	tittuppy	lixivium	edgeways	milkwort	westward	everyway	tommyrot
persuade	tonguing	maravedi	edgewise	moonwort	whimwham	fairyism	tricycle
piacular	toreutic	mitzvoth	farewell	muckworm	whipworm	fancyman	unicycle
pictures	torquate		fireweed	openwork	wildwood	farmyard	vineyard

```
Walkyrie aircraft biograph chordate desolate escalade fourball highjack
bedazzle Airedale bioplasm choriamb detonate escalate fourpart highland
blizzard airframe bioplast chromate diagraph escapade foxshark hightail
breezily airshaft birdbath cidevant diallage estimate fragrant hipflask
britzska airspace birdcage cinerary diastase etiolate freefall hogsback
bryozoan alginate birdcall cinquain diffract euphrasy freehand holdback
Cenozoic alienage blindage claimant digitate evacuant frondage holdfast
chutzpah alienate blizzard clambake dilatant evacuate frontage holidays
coenzyme allocate blockade clawback dinosaur evaluate frottage homeland
denazify allogamy blockage cleavage dioptase evenfall fruitage homemade
ectozoon allopath blowball clubhaul disclaim excavate fullback homeward
embezzle almanack blowhard clubland disgrace excitant fullpage homogamy
endozoic ambulant blowlamp clypeate displace execrate fumigant honorary
endozoon ambulate boldface coalsack displant exhalant fumigate horntail
entozoic amperage bondmaid coatrack dissuade expirant funerary hotplate
entozoon amputate bondmans cocktail distract exultant fuselage humpback
freezeup amygdala boneyard cogitate distrain exuviate gainsaid iceplant
freezing anaphase boniface comeback distrait eyeglass galleass iceskate
frenzied annotate bookcase cometary disusage eyeshade galliard idocrase
grizzled annulate bookland complain divagate eyestalk gallwasp ignorant
Hertzian antedate bookmark conchate djellaba fabliaux gangland illusage
holozoic antimask bootjack conclave dockland facecard garboard immolate
janizary anyplace bootlace conflate dockyard facepack gastraea impanate
lysozyme apograph bootlast constant dominant failsafe gearcase inchoate
magazine apostasy Bordeaux contract dominate faineant geminate incitant
Mesozoic apostate bouffant contrail doorcase fallback generate increase
metazoan appanage boundary contrary doornail faradaic geophagy increate
metazoon approach braggart contrast dooryard farmhand gimcrack incubate
monazite aquacade brancard contrate doumpalm farmland glaciate indagate
polyzoan aquanaut brassage copulate dovetail farmyard gladhand indicant
polyzoic areolate brassard cordwain downcast fastback glissade indicate
polyzoon argonaut brassart corelate downfall fasttalk glossary indurate
quizzing arillate breakage cornball downhaul February goofball inerrant
samizdat aristate bregmata coronach downland federate gourmand inhalant
schizoid armchair breviary coronary downward feedback graduand inhumane
sforzato arrogant brouhaha Corybant drainage feedtank graduate initiate
sleazily arrogate browband cosecant drawback ferriage grandame inkstand
snazzily arsenate bullcalf costmary dressage figurant grillage innovate
stanzaic artefact burglary cotenant driftage filtrate gripsack insolate
tweezers artifact bushbaby couchant drunkard fireback guacharo insulant
unmuzzle ascocarp butyrate covenant dryplate fireball guardant insulate
wheezily aseptate cabotage coverage duckhawk firedamp Gujarati insurant
whizzing aspirant cabstand coverall dulciana firstaid gymkhana interact
whizzkid aspirate cakewalk cowgrass dungcart fishball habitant inthrall
──────── assonant calabash coxswain dustcart fishcake halfback intimacy
aardvark assonate calamary cozenage dutypaid fishfarm halfmast intimate
abdicate autobahn califate craniate eastward fishhawk halliard intonate
aberrant autocade calipash cribbage echinate fishtail hallmark intubate
abnegate autodafe camisade crispate edentate fistiana handball inundate
abradant autogamy camisado cristate edgeways flagrant handcart inurbane
abrogate automata camshaft croceate eelgrass flapjack handfast invocate
absonant automate canthari cruciate efficacy flatmate handmade iodinate
abstract aventail capitate culinary eggplant flatrace handmaid ironbark
abundant axillary capybara cumulate eldorado flatware handrail ironware
abuttals bacchant caracara cupboard elephant flatways hangnail irrigate
accolade backdate carapace cupulate elongate fleabane hardback irritant
accuracy backhand carinate Cyrenaic emaciate flippant hardbake irritate
accurate backlash carriage deadfall emendate floatage hardcase isocracy
aceldama backpack carryall deaerate emigrant folktale hardhack isostasy
acerbate backward casemate debonair emigrate football hardtack jacquard
acervate backwash castrate debutant emissary footbath hardware janizary
acidfast backyard castrati decimate encroach footfall harikari jetblack
acierage badinage castrato deckhand endamage footmark hatstand jetplane
acierate baldpate catalase decorate endocarp footpace haulyard jipijapa
acrylate bandeaux cataract decrease endogamy footpath haystack jubilant
activate bangtail catchall dedicate enervate forecast headband jubilate
aculeate bareback catenary deeplaid enfilade headfast headlamp jugulate
adequacy barnyard catenate defilade ensheath forehand headlamp junkyard
adequate baronage catstail degrease ensilage forelady headland kailyard
adjutage baseball celibacy delegacy enterate foreland headrace kamikaze
adjutant bedplate celibate delegate enthrall foremast headsail katakana
adjuvant beefcake cenotaph delibate entreaty forename hebetate keelhaul
aduncate benzoate Chaldaic delicacy envisage forepart heelball keepsake
advocaat bequeath chaplain delicate ephorate forepast helpmate keyboard
advocacy bestiary charlady demerara epiblast foresaid heritage kickback
advocate beverage chateaux depilate epigraph foresail hesitant kilowatt
aeronaut bifocals chiliasm depurate epiphany forewarn hesitate knapsack
agiotage billiard chiliast derivate equipage foreyard hickwall kohlrabi
airbrake bilobate chlorate derogate equitant fountain highball komitaji
```

korfball	marinade	neoplasm	pearmain	ratguard	saturant	spermary	tertiary
kourbash	marinate	newscast	peculate	ratsbane	saturate	spiccato	texthand
lacerate	maritage	nicknack	pederast	ratstail	sauouari	spillage	textuary
lacunary	marocain	nickname	pedipalp	reactant	Savoyard	spoilage	thingamy
lacunate	marriage	nominate	pegboard	rearlamp	sawframe	spoliate	thirlage
lakeland	matamata	nonclaim	penchant	rearward	sayonara	spondaic	thousand
laminate	matgrass	nonusage	pericarp	recreant	scabbard	spousage	thrawart
landfall	maturate	noseband	permeate	recreate	schemata	spyglass	thridace
landlady	meatball	notecase	perorate	recusant	seaboard	squamate	ticktack
landmark	meatsafe	nowadays	persuade	redshank	seacoast	staccato	tidegate
landmass	medicate	nuclease	petulant	redstart	seacraft	staffage	tideland
landrail	meditate	nucleate	phantasm	reedmace	seaplane	staggard	tidemark
langlauf	megawatt	numeracy	phantasy	reembark	seaquake	stagnant	tidewave
language	membrane	numerary	pharmacy	regelate	seascape	stagnate	tiltyard
lapboard	merchant	numerate	pheasant	regulate	seasnail	stallage	timeball
lapidary	mesocarp	nuptials	phyllary	relaxant	seasnake	stalwart	tinplate
lapidate	messmate	oatgrass	piassava	relegate	seawrack	standard	tipstaff
larboard	messuage	obduracy	pilchard	relevant	seedcake	stannary	titanate
Latinate	metayage	obdurate	pilotage	relocate	seedcase	stannate	titivate
latitant	miasmata	obeisant	piperack	renegade	segreant	stanzaic	toeplate
laureate	midbrain	obituary	plagiary	renegado	seladang	stargaze	tolerant
lavalava	militant	obligate	plantain	renovate	selenate	statuary	tolerate
layshaft	military	obturate	plateaux	reproach	selfmade	staylace	tollcall
laystall	militate	occupant	playback	rereward	selfmate	staysail	tollgate
leeboard	milkmaid	ocellate	playmate	resinate	selfsame	stearate	tomahawk
lefthand	millhand	octonary	pleasant	resonant	seminary	stedfast	topheavy
leftward	milliard	odograph	pleinair	resonate	separate	steerage	torquate
legguard	milliary	oeillade	pleonasm	restrain	serenade	stellate	townhall
lemonade	millrace	offstage	plumbago	retroact	serenata	stemmata	toxicant
leverage	Minotaur	oliphant	plumbate	revenant	sergeant	stigmata	trabeate
levigate	mintmark	omadhaum	plussage	ribgrass	serjeant	stillage	trackage
levirate	misdealt	omophagy	pockmark	rickrack	sewerage	stinkard	tractate
levitate	misheard	omoplate	poignant	riffraff	sforzato	stoccado	transact
liberate	mishmash	onetrack	polygala	rimbrake	shabrack	stoccata	trapball
lichgate	Mishnaic	opencast	polygamy	ringbark	shagbark	stockade	traumata
ligulate	misogamy	oppilate	polymath	ringmain	Shetland	stoppage	treenail
limewash	misplace	opsimath	polypary	ringtail	shipmate	stramash	trespass
limitary	misshape	ordinand	ponytail	riverain	shipyard	stravaig	tribrach
lipomata	misstate	ordinary	populace	roborant	shoelace	stromata	trigraph
literacy	misusage	ordinate	populate	rockcake	shoptalk	stubnail	triplane
literary	Mithraic	osculant	portrait	rockfall	shortage	studfarm	trochaic
literate	mitigant	osculate	postcard	rockfill	shortarm	stunsail	truckage
literati	mitigate	ostinato	postdate	rocksalt	showcard	stuprate	trumeaux
litigant	moderate	outboard	postmark	rollcall	showcase	subclass	truncate
litigate	moderato	outbrave	postpaid	rondeaux	sibilant	subframe	tubulate
lobulate	modulate	outclass	potplant	roofrack	sibilate	subimago	tunicate
lockfast	monetary	outdrawn	potroast	roommate	sideband	sublease	turnback
loculate	monogamy	outflank	poundage	ropewalk	sidewalk	substage	tutelage
longhair	monorail	outreach	pregnant	ropeyarn	sideward	subtract	tutelary
longhand	mooncalf	outsmart	prelease	rosemary	sideways	subulate	tutorage
longwall	moonface	outstare	priorate	rostrate	silicane	suffrage	typecast
longwave	moonsail	ovenware	proclaim	rosulate	silicate	suitcase	typeface
longways	moorland	overcall	prophase	roughage	simulant	sukiyaki	ulcerate
lopgrass	mortgage	overcame	prostate	rouleaus	simulate	sulphate	ultimacy
loricate	mortmain	overcast	protease	rouleaux	sitzbath	sunshade	ultimata
lowgrade	mortuary	overfall	protract	roundarm	skewback	superadd	ultimate
lukewarm	mossback	overhand	puffball	rubytail	skewbald	superate	umbonate
luminant	mothball	overhang	puissant	rucksack	skipjack	supinate	umpirage
luminary	motivate	overlaid	pullback	ruminant	skyscape	supplant	uncinate
lunulate	motorail	overlain	punctate	ruminate	slapbang	surcease	uncreate
lustrate	mountain	overland	pupilage	runagate	slapdash	suricate	underact
lychgate	moussaka	overpaid	pupilary	rutabaga	slapjack	suzerain	underage
lykewake	mucilage	overpass	purchase	rutilant	slipcase	swanmark	underarm
macerate	muckrake	overrate	purslane	ryegrass	slippage	swayback	undreamt
maculate	mudguard	overrate	pursuant	ryotwari	slobland	tableaux	undulant
maharaja	musicale	overrate	pushball	sabotage	sloppail	tabulate	undulate
maharani	musquash	oversail	pushcart	sackrace	sluggard	taffrail	ungulate
mahogany	mutilate	overtake	quadrant	saginate	smallage	tailback	unsteady
mailcart	myoblast	overtask	quadrate	sailyard	snowball	tailgate	untoward
mainland	myograph	paginate	quandary	salivary	snowfall	tailrace	upsprang
mainmast	myxomata	paleface	quatrain	salivate	soapbath	tamarack	urethane
mainsail	namepart	palisade	quintain	salutary	softball	tartrate	urticant
maintain	namesake	palliate	racecard	sandbank	software	teaboard	urticate
mainyard	nametape	pallmall	racemate	sandbath	solidary	teammate	valerate
makebate	nauseant	panorama	radicant	Sangrail	solitary	telecast	validate
makefast	nauseate	parasang	radicate	sanitary	someways	telemark	vambrace
Malagasy	navigate	paravane	rainfall	sanitate	sororate	telepath	vamplate
mandrake	neckband	parkland	rainwash	sannyasi	Spaniard	telltale	vanadate
margrave	necklace	pastrami	rapecake	saraband	speciate	template	vanguard

```
vegetate  blamable  guidable  rateable  testable  corniced  meniscus  terraced
venerate  blamably  gullable  readable  throbbed  corniche  metrical  thearchy
verbiage  bontebok  gullable  readably  thrombin  cornicle  monarchy  thetical
vesicant  bribable  gullible  redouble  thrombus  cortical  monoacid  thoraces
vesicate  brickbat  hateable  reliable  thurible  cortices  motorcar  thoracic
vespiary  bullyboy  heatable  reliably  tillable  cosmical  mustache  traducer
vestiary  cabinboy  honeybee  remember  tithable  critical  mystical  tragical
vicarage  callable  horrible  rentable  tommybar  crosscut  mythical  triarchy
vicarate  cannabin  horribly  renumber  trilobed  curlicue  naumachy  tricycle
vicinage  cannabis  horsebox  resemble  tuneable  curricle  nautical  trifocal
victuals  cannibal  houseboy  reusable  turnable  cyclical  neomycin  tritical
vigilant  cascabel  huggable  rideable  underbid  deathcap  nightcap  tropical
vinegary  chasuble  imitable  riverbed  unlimber  demarche  novercal  tubercle
vineyard  cherubic  inedible  ropeable  unstable  denticle  obstacle  tussocky
visitant  cherubim  instable  ruinable  unstably  divorcee  octarchy  twofaced
volitant  childbed  interbed  runcible  valuable  dogfaced  orthicon  undercut
volplane  choirboy  inviable  sailable  valuably  elflocks  ostracod  unforced
wagonage  cicisbei  isolable  saleable  variable  embracer  ostracon  unicycle
wallgame  cicisbeo  issuable  salvable  variably  emetical  oxytocin  univocal
warplane  cinnabar  joinable  salvably  vendible  encircle  particle  unplaced
warweary  cobwebby  kissable  satiable  vertebra  enforcer  pastiche  unvoiced
waterage  coenobia  knowable  satiably  viewable  entracte  peacocky  uppercut
waveband  conurbia  laudable  saucebox  vincible  epicycle  peasecod  valanced
westward  coolabah  laudably  scalable  violable  erotical  peduncle  vernicle
wharfage  coolibah  leviable  scrabble  violably  ethnical  pellicle  verrucae
wheyface  credible  liftable  scramble  vitiable  Etruscan  pellucid  versicle
whiplash  credibly  likeable  scribble  voicebox  explicit  pemmican  vertical
whizbang  crossbar  liveable  scribbly  voidable  faceache  pendicle  vertices
windfall  crossbow  loanable  scrubbed  walkable  farcical  pentacle  verticil
windgall  crucible  lockable  scrubber  washable  farouche  perfecto  viaticum
windlass  cucumber  loonybin  sealable  wastable  fascicle  physical  viscacha
windsail  cucurbit  loosebox  seizable  waterbed  fistical  physicky  vizcacha
windward  culpable  mailable  sensible  waterbus  follicle  picnicky  vortical
winepalm  culpably  mandible  sensibly  wearable  foolscap  pinnacle  vortices
wingcase  damnable  mangabey  shapable  weldable  fornices  poetical  waesucks
wirehair  damnably  matchbox  sillabub  wettable  frutices  pollices  wainscot
wishwash  deathbed  mealybug  singable  whiteboy  furuncle  porticos  whitecap
wolfpack  December  mendable  sinkable  winnable  Gallican  postiche  wiseacre
woodland  demobbed  microbar  sizeable  workable  garlicky  producer  zodiacal
woodlark  deniable  microbic  slugabed  writable  gazpacho  protocol  absurdly
woolpack  dimmable  millibar  smokable  Adamical  gimmicky  publican  accredit
woolsack  dittybag  miscible  snackbar  advanced  grimacer  publicly  addendum
workmate  dittybox  moneybag  snuffbox  alogical  guaiacum  pussycat  amazedly
wormcast  doughboy  moneybox  sociable  alopecia  gynoecia  redfaced  amusedly
wrappage  drawable  moveable  sociably  American  halluces  rejoicer  appendix
wreckage  drivable  nameable  solvable  analecta  handicap  replacer  ascender
xanthate  Dukhobor  November  sortable  analects  headache  resorcin  asphodel
xenogamy  dutiable  openable  soundbow  Anglican  headachy  respects  attender
xylocarp  educable  operable  soundbox  atypical  heliacal  revanche  avowedly
yokemate  educible  paintbox  spacebar  auspices  heroical  ricercar  balladic
zugzwang  eligible  palpable  sparable  autarchy  hibiscus  romancer  balladry
zwieback  eligibly  palpably  spicebox  babouche  hillocky  rubrical  befuddle
absorber  encumber  paperboy  squabble  backache  homuncle  rustical  begirded
adlibbed  enfeeble  partible  squibbed  balanced  horsecar  Sadducee  begrudge
adorable  ensemble  passable  statable  balancer  hummocky  scenical  beholden
adorably  enviable  passably  steenbok  barbecue  humuncle  scilicet  beholder
alphabet  enviably  passible  steinbok  barbican  iceyacht  scirocco  Bermudas
amenable  erasable  peccable  storable  barnacle  implicit  scolices  bewilder
amenably  erodible  peekaboo  suburban  barouche  inimical  scratchy  biocidal
amicable  evadable  penumbra  suburbia  barracks  intercom  screechy  birthday
amicably  evitable  pintable  succubae  biblical  intercut  shortcut  brocaded
amphibia  exigible  pitiable  succubus  billycan  irenical  silencer  bromidic
arguable  expiable  pitiably  suitable  binnacle  irenicon  skullcap  caboodle
arguably  expiably  placable  suitably  blackcap  ironical  soutache  calendar
arquebus  fallible  placably  superbly  bullocky  isodicon  spadices  calender
assemble  feasible  playable  syllabic  cachucha  jerrican  spiracle  calvados
assembly  feasibly  portable  syllable  cadenced  jerrycan  splotchy  candidly
atremble  fellable  possible  syllabub  canticle  Judaical  squelchy  canoodle
avowable  fencible  possibly  syllabus  capsicum  latticed  statical  cathedra
bailable  fishable  postobit  tameable  caruncle  lenticel  stockcar  cathodal
bankable  flexible  pourable  tangible  caudices  lenticle  stomachy  cathodic
bearable  flexibly  preamble  tangibly  cervical  libeccio  stretchy  chiefdom
bearably  flockbed  pressbox  tannable  cervices  lubrical  subvocal  clerkdom
bedabble  forcible  probable  tastebud  chemical  maniacal  surfacer  coachdog
bedtable  forcibly  probably  teatable  clavicle  massacre  surgical  colander
biddable  fordable  prohibit  tellable  cleancut  massicot  syndical  conceder
billyboy  fruitbat  provable  tensible  clearcut  matrices  tablecut  confider
bistable  fungible  provably  terrible  clerical  mediocre  tactical  conoidal
blackboy  gainable  quotable  terribly  clinical  menarche  tentacle  consider
```

```
copyedit liquidly sordidly acrolein Blenheim clerkess document feathery
corridor lopsided splendid actively blinkers clippers dogwhelk feckless
corundum maenadic sporadic adducent blistery clownery domineer feculent
cowardly marauder spreader adherent blithely clueless doorbell fedayeen
crusader markedly squander adjacent bloomers clustery dopiness feedhead
cuboidal mastodon squeedge adultery bloomery coarsely dourness fellness
cursedly menhaden squidded aesthete blubbery cobblers downbeat fiercely
cuspidor methodic statedly afferent bludgeon cochleae doziness fiftieth
cussedly microdot stolidly affluent bluebell cochlear drabness filament
cylinder misjudge straddle afforest blueness codpiece dracaena fineness
daffodil molybdic stranded aggrieve blueweed cogwheel drawwell finitely
defender monandry stridden aggrieve blustery coherent dripfeed fireweed
demander morbidly stupidly agrement boatdeck coiffeur drollery firmness
deucedly muscadel subahdar airfield bobwheel coldness drophead fishless
disendow myrmidon suborder airiness bodement coleseed dropleaf fishmeal
dislodge nuclidic suicidal airspeed bodiless coliseum drudgery flambeau
disorder occluded sympodia alcahest boldness colliery druidess flatfeet
doggedly offender taberdar alkahest bonehead compleat drumhead flathead
dogooder offsider Talmudic almagest boneless complete dryclean flatness
doomsday oleander tamandua ambivert bonemeal compress duckweed flattery
drownded onesided teacaddy amoebean boniness concrete ductless flattest
elatedly organdie tetradic anapaest bookrest confrere dullness flawless
embedded orthodox thanedom anathema bootless congress dumbbell flaxseed
embolden outmoded thraldom antecede bourgeon congreve dumbhead flickery
engender outrider threader antihero boxpleat conquest dumbness flinders
engirdle outsider Thursday antisera bracteal coolness dustless flummery
enkindle pallidly tomnoddy anywhere braziery cordless earpiece fluttery
episodal pappadom toreador aperient brettese cosiness easement flywheel
episodic periodic tornadic apoplexy Briarean cotquean easiness foamless
everyday placidly toroidal apothegm brimless couldest echoless fondness
excluder pomander torpidly apparent broidery countess ectoderm foodless
expander poppadum torridly appetent browbeat courtesy edgeless footgear
exploder porridge towardly Aramaean buckbean covalent edginess footless
extender prejudge tripodal arbalest buddleia crackers editress footrest
extrados presidio turbidly arboreal bulkhead creamery eeriness footwear
feastday prosodic turgidly arboreta bullhead crescent efferent forebear
fervidly provided twosided archaean bullseye crockery effluent foredeck
floridly provider unbidden archness bushveld cromlech eggshell forefeel
flounder puppydog unbridle argument business cryogeny eighteen forefelt
foetidly puppydom unburden armament busyness cureless eloquent forehead
forcedly putridly uncandid astutely butchery curtness emergent forepeak
foreedge queendom underdid asyndeta buttress cuteness empyreal foreseen
forrader rachides underdog aurorean butylene daftness empyrean foretell
friendly raggedly unfunded averment bystreet dampness emulgent forewent
frigidly recorder unitedly aversely caducean danegeld endoderm formless
gambados rehandle unkindly avidness caduceus dankness endogeny forspeak
gipsydom rekindle unleaded backless caginess darkness enforest forspent
granddad reminder unloader backrest cajolery dateless engineer forswear
grounder retarded unriddle backseat calipers daybreak enginery fortieth
guidedog retarder unsaddle backveld calmness daydream ensphere fortress
gynandry rewarder unseeded bailment cameleer deadbeat entirely foulness
gypsydom Rhinodon unwisdom baldhead camphene deadhead entirety fourleaf
Haggadah ribaldry upholder baldness canoness deadness entoderm fourteen
harridan rotundly Balinese baldness careless deafness ephemera fowlpest
havildar roughdry uplander bareness Carolean dearness epopoeia foxiness
heatedly ruggedly upwardly barkless carotene decadent erythema fragment
Helladic saccadic variedly baroness casement decedent esculent Fraulein
heraldic sacredly verandah baseless cashmere deedless estovers freeness
heraldry saintdom villadom basement cateress deepness esurient freezeup
honeydew samizdat viscidly baseness cattleya deferent etcetera frequent
horridly Saturday vizarded bateleur cemetery deforest ethereal frippery
housedog Saxondom watchdog battleax cerement deftness ethylene frondent
impledge schiedam welladay bayadere cerulean delivery European frondeur
impolder secluded whoredom bedstead cetacean demoness evenness fruitery
included seconder wickedly beebread Chaldean demurely evilness fullness
inlander secondly wizardly befriend chambers deponent existent funereal
intended selvedge wizardry bejabers champers derriere exponent furriery
intrados sheepdip wontedly beltless chancery dewiness eyepiece furthest
intruder sheepdog workaday beriberi chasseur diastema faceless fusileer
inwardly sheikdom zamindar besprent chastely diligent facilely futilely
islander shielder zemindar bestrewn checkers diriment fadeless gableend
jaggedly shortday abducens billhead Chellean discreet fairlead gadarene
jocundly shoulder abducent bindweed chequers discrete fairness gainless
jumpedup shouldst abetment birdseed chimaera dispread fangless Galilean
labrador shredded abutment birdseye chinless distress farewell gameness
lackaday shredder accident bivalent choicely divalent farriery gaminess
lavender shrewdly acescent bladdery Circaean dividend farthest gangrene
legendry smoulder achiness blankety claqueur divinely fastness Ganymede
limpidly solander acidhead blastema cleavers docilely fearless gasolene
```

```
gazogene  hornfels  laziness  misspend  overfeed  rackrent  savagely  soulless
Genevese  hornless  leadless  misspent  overhead  railhead  savagery  sourness
germcell  hotpress  leafless  mistreat  overhear  raillery  scandent  southern
giantess  hugeness  leanness  mistress  overheat  rainwear  scarcely  sowbread
gilthead  humanely  leathern  monkseal  overleaf  rakehell  scarless  spalpeen
gladdest  huntress  leathery  monogeny  overleap  ranchero  sclereid  spardeck
gladness  hurtless  legalese  monsieur  overseas  rankness  scragend  sparsely
glanders  hypoderm  legbreak  monument  overseen  rapeseed  scullery  spivvery
glaziery  hypogeal  lensless  moonbeam  overseer  raptness  seachest  spotless
glibness  hypogean  lewdness  moonless  oversell  rareness  seagreen  sprucely
glittery  hypogene  lifebelt  morosely  oversewn  rashness  seamless  spryness
glummest  hypogeum  lifeless  morpheme  overwear  realness  seapiece  spurgear
glumness  icecream  ligament  mouseear  painless  reappear  seashell  squarely
goatherd  icefield  likeness  moveless  paleness  reascend  seatbelt  squireen
Godspeed  idealess  limbless  movement  pancreas  reassert  securely  squirely
goldleaf  idiolect  limpness  muchness  pantheon  reassess  sedately  staggers
goodness  idleness  liniment  muleteer  parakeet  reckless  sediment  stampede
goodyear  illtreat  Linnaean  muniment  pathless  recovery  seedleaf  starkers
gormless  immanent  linoleum  muskdeer  pavement  redeless  seedless  starless
goutweed  imminent  lintseed  muteness  paysheet  redirect  seigneur  stemless
gradient  immodest  listless  mutineer  peagreen  redolent  selfheal  stilbene
grandeur  imponent  littlego  nameless  pediment  referent  selfhelp  strategy
grapheme  impotent  lodgment  napoleon  peerless  refinery  selfless  strepent
greenery  impudent  loneness  nathless  Pegasean  refluent  selfness  strident
greyness  impurely  longness  natively  Pekinese  reforest  sentient  sturgeon
grimmest  inchmeal  longterm  Nazarene  pellmell  regiment  serenely  subagent
grimness  incident  longueur  nearness  penitent  reindeer  servient  suberect
grindery  indecent  lordless  neatherd  periderm  reinless  severely  subpoena
gromwell  indigene  lorikeet  neatness  perigean  reinsert  sexiness  subtlety
grosbeak  indigent  loudness  needless  perineal  reinvest  shagreen  Sudanese
gulfweed  indirect  loveless  needment  perineum  relucent  shepherd  sundress
habanera  indolent  lovenest  neoprene  peripety  remanent  shimmery  superego
hairless  inexpert  loveseat  Nepalese  peroneal  remotely  shipment  supinely
haleness  influent  luckless  nescient  pertness  renitent  shoeless  supplely
halfbeak  inherent  luculent  newsheet  phosgene  reorient  shopbell  suppress
halfterm  inkiness  luncheon  newspeak  pinchers  repetend  shuddery  sureness
handbell  innately  lushness  newsreel  pinkness  reprieve  sickness  swanherd
handheld  innocent  malapert  niceness  pinwheel  resident  sidehead  swanneck
handless  insanely  malefern  nineteen  pitiless  restless  sidereal  swannery
handsewn  inscient  maleness  nonevent  pixiness  reticent  sixtieth  tactless
hardhead  insolent  maltreat  northern  plangent  retrieve  skewness  tailless
hardness  insphere  Mandaean  nosiness  plastery  reverend  skilless  tallness
harebell  interest  manifest  noteless  Pliocene  reverent  skindeep  tameless
haresear  isocheim  maravedi  nudeness  politely  richness  skinhead  tameness
harmless  isopleth  marchesa  nullness  polygene  rifeness  skinless  tapedeck
harpseal  isoprene  marchese  numbness  polygeny  ringneck  slagheap  tapeless
hasheesh  isoptera  marquess  nutrient  polyseme  ripeness  slattern  tartness
hatchery  isothere  marrieds  nutshell  polysemy  roadless  slimmest  tautness
hawkweed  isotherm  Masorete  nymphean  pondweed  rockhewn  slimness  teabread
hayfield  Jacobean  Masoreth  obedient  poorness  rockweed  slippery  teabreak
haziness  Japanese  massless  obsolete  portiere  rollneck  slithery  teachest
headgear  Javanese  masthead  obtusely  portress  roodbeam  slobbery  tearless
headless  jejunely  matiness  occident  potsherd  roofless  slowness  tegument
headrest  jocosely  mattress  Odyssean  preelect  rootless  slumbery  tenement
heathery  jolthead  maturely  offbreak  premiere  ropiness  smeltery  terebene
heedless  jongleur  mayoress  oilfield  priggery  roseleaf  smithers  termless
heelless  judgment  Mayqueen  oiliness  primness  rosiness  smithery  thickety
heirless  jugglery  mazement  ointment  princely  rounders  smothery  thievery
hellbent  jumpseat  maziness  ommateum  princess  rudeness  smugness  thinness
helpless  justness  meagrely  onepiece  prioress  rudiment  snippety  thinnest
helpmeet  Kanarese  meanness  ontogeny  proceeds  rugosely  snobbery  thirteen
herbless  keelless  meekness  ooziness  progress  ruleless  snowless  thisness
hexylene  keenness  meetness  opaquely  prophecy  rustless  snuffers  thuggery
highness  kerosene  melodeon  openness  prophesy  ruthless  snuggery  thundery
hightest  killdeer  menswear  opponent  prospect  saboteur  snugness  thusness
hindlegs  kindless  mesoderm  orangery  prurient  sackless  soapless  tickseed
hipsters  kindness  metamere  oratress  psaltery  saddlery  sobriety  tideless
hirrient  knackery  mezereon  ornament  puncheon  safeness  softhead  tidiness
hoarsely  knapweed  midfield  ornately  puniness  sageness  softness  tiebreak
hogshead  kneedeep  mightest  orpiment  pureness  sailless  soilless  tigereye
holiness  kneejerk  mildness  orthoepy  purulent  saltless  soldiery  timeless
Holocene  knickers  milkweed  otiosely  pygmaean  saltness  soleness  tininess
holstein  knitwear  millieme  outbreak  pyroxene  sameness  sombrely  tintless
homefelt  ladyfern  mindless  outfield  quackery  Samoyede  sombrero  tireless
homeless  lamasery  Minoress  outguess  quartern  saneness  somedeal  titaness
homogeny  lameness  minutely  outspend  quarters  Sangreal  somedele  toepiece
hoofbeat  landless  miserere  outspent  quitrent  sapgreen  songless  tombless
hopeless  lankness  misspell  ovalness  quotient  sateless  sorehead  tonedeaf
hornbeam  lateness  misspelt  overbear  raciness  saunders  soreness  toneless
```

```
topdress whiskers mirthful analogue lallygag tetragon draughty planchet
torchere whiskery morbific androgen larynges theurgic drencher plougher
tracheae whispery mournful apagogic liturgic toboggan dropshot polisher
tracheal wideness mouthful apologia lovingly tommygun droughty popishly
tracheid wifeless multifid apologue madrigal triangle dumbshow preacher
trammels wildness pantofle arpeggio malinger tryingly dustshot punisher
transect wiliness paraffin arranger martagon twilight eighthly quencher
transept windless peaceful asperges meninges twoedged elenchus rakishly
trappean wingbeat pettifog astragal meringue unhinged empathic ravisher
trashery wingless plateful befogged midnight unkingly enarched rhonchal
treefern wireless pontifex besieger misbegot unpegged encipher rhonchus
treeless wiriness powerful besought miscegen unrigged enricher rickshaw
trickery wiseness prankful bewigged movingly unsought eolithic ricochet
trimness witchelm prideful bitingly musingly untangle eulachon roughhew
trippery witchery prolific boringly negligee untaught exanthem sandshoe
triskele witchety puppyfat bunfight nitrogen villager feldsher scirrhus
trousers withheld rightful campagna nonlegal vintager fellahin scorcher
trouvere woolfell salvific cardigan nonrigid warragal fernshaw scutcher
trueness woollens scoopful choragic oakegger warrigal finisher sealyham
trumpery wordless scornful choragus outright watergas fireship searcher
tubeless workless senseful choregic outsight waxlight flagship seraphic
tuneless wormgear shameful choregus oxtongue acanthus fletcher seraphim
tutoress wormseed shelfful coccyges parergon agraphia flincher shanghai
tweezers wouldest slothful collagen pathogen aguishly foreshow sideshow
twelvemo xanthein smallfry colleger Pelasgic almighty fourthly sinophil
twittery xanthene somnific collogue pellagra ambusher garishly sketcher
twopiece Yankeefy spadeful compages pentagon anarchic grogshop slipshod
Tyrolean yestreen specific conjugal photogen anorthic groschen slopshop
Tyrrhene youngest spinifex contagia pillager antiphon Guelphic sloucher
ugliness yourself spiteful cottager pishogue Arapahoe Halachah smoothen
umptieth zaniness spoonfed cottagey plumaged aweather hardship smoothie
unfreeze zarzuela spoonful coxalgia presager babushka heathhen smoothly
uniquely basinful sportful cyanogen prodigal backchat hedgehog snapshot
unlikely beatific stallfed daringly prologue ballyhoo hedgehop snatcher
unlovely bellyful stickful daylight prorogue barathea heirship sneeshan
unthread blackfly stonefly debagged protegee bleacher hernshaw snitcher
untimely blameful tableful debugged pryingly bluechip hypothec snowshoe
unwisely blissful Tartuffe dialogic rejigger bodyshop impishly softshoe
upstream blushful tasteful dialogue revenger boyishly ingather somewhat
urbanely boastful terrific diplogen roentgen Bradshaw Jonathan somewhen
vainness calcific thankful dogfight rummager branched junkshop sorochen
vaneless caprifig therefor donought sawedged brancher khuskhus splasher
vastness catchfly thurifer dotingly scourger branchia kickshaw squasher
vehement cheerful toothful duologue scragged breather kingship stancher
veilless cornific toplofty ecologic sennight breeches ladyship stanchly
venereal cranefly transfer endanger sewergas britches Langshan stitcher
ventless crucifer transfix enlarger shrugged broacher launcher strophic
vestment crucifix tristful enneagon skylight bronchia lavishly swanshot
victress doubtful trustful entangle solfeggi bronchus lecithin switchel
Viennese dreadful truthful epilogue sparkgap brougham lengthen telethon
viewless dreamful turbofan escargot sphingid buckshee longship teraphim
vileness earmuffs underfur eyesight spraygun buckshot lordship thatcher
vilipend eventful unlawful fanlight sprigged cabochon Manichee thoughts
virement faithful unmuffle flashgun springal capuchin marathon thrasher
virulent fanciful unroofed florigen springer catechol memsahib thresher
vivisect febrific unstuffy foliaged squeegee chinchin metaphor together
voidness feverfew vauntful galangal squiggle chitchat modishly toolshed
votaress fleshfly vengeful gapingly squiggly chopchop monachal township
voteless forcefed voiceful gaslight squilgee chowchow monkship tranship
voyageur forceful wasteful gastight sterigma churchly moonshee treacher
waitress fruitfly watchful geologic straggle clanship moonshot trencher
wakeless fruitful weariful gestagen straggly clerihew mopishly tuckahoe
wallfern gefuffle whitefly glucagon straight clincher mulishly tuckshop
wardress ghastful worthful glycogen stranger coauthor naphthol twinship
wariness glassful wrackful goosegog strangle cockshut nenuphar twitcher
warmness godawful wrathful gunfight strength colophon nighthag untether
wartweed graceful wrongful harangue stringed coryphee oafishly unwashed
waveless grateful youthful heptagon stringer cratches oenophil unwished
waviness greenfly aasvogel histogen strongly crotched ornithic uppishly
waxiness guileful abridger hooligan struggle crotchet overshoe vanisher
weakness horrific achingly hoosegow sunlight deanship overshot wardship
weedless horsefly affright hydrogen synergic decipher owlishly whimwham
weldment housefly agaragar immingle synergid detached padishah whinchat
welldeck houseful airtight indulger syntagma dianthus pawnshop whitehot
wellhead hoverfly allergen inflight syringes diarchal peepshow wholehog
wellread kefuffle allergic intrigue takingly diarchic perisher wineshop
whatness loathful allnight inveigle tarragon diarrhea petechia woodchat
wheatear magnific anagogic isagogic taxingly dramshop phosphor woodshed
Whiggery merciful analogic jokingly teenager draughts pinochle woolshed
```

workshop	alluvium	autunite	boatbill	canoeist	clubbing	cysteine	ditheist
wreathen	alpinism	averring	bobolink	canonise	clumsily	cytidine	dividivi
wretched	alpinist	aversion	bobwhite	canonist	coaction	cytosine	divinise
yataghan	Alsatian	aversive	Bodleian	capacity	coactive	dabchick	divinity
zenithal	altruism	aviarist	Boeotian	capeline	coalfish	dahabieh	division
Abbaside	altruist	aviation	bohemian	caponier	coalmine	daintily	divisive
abbatial	ambition	avionics	bombsite	caponise	codifier	daiquiri	Docetism
Abderite	ammoniac	avulsion	bonefish	carabine	coercion	dairying	Docetist
abetting	ammonify	axiality	bonspiel	Caroline	coercive	dandyish	docility
ablation	ammonite	Ayrshire	booklice	catamite	cohesion	dandyism	dockside
ablative	ammonium	backbite	boracite	catching	cohesive	darkling	doctrine
ablution	amnesiac	backfire	botanise	catering	coincide	dateline	dolerite
aborning	amortise	backlist	botanist	cavalier	colonial	deadline	dolomite
abortion	analcime	backside	botflies	cavatina	colonise	dealfish	domicile
abortive	analcite	Baconian	botulism	celeriac	colonist	debility	dominion
abrasion	andesine	Bactrian	bouncily	celerity	comedian	decision	donation
abrasive	andesite	bakshish	bouncing	centring	comedist	decisive	Donatism
abstrict	aneurism	balefire	boursier	centrism	complice	decurion	Donatist
abutting	angelica	balkline	brachial	centrist	complier	definite	donative
Accadian	ankerite	banality	brachium	ceramics	compline	deionise	doorsill
acerbity	annalist	banjoist	brackish	ceramist	comprise	delation	dotation
achenial	anserine	bankbill	bragging	cerusite	conation	deletion	douanier
acosmism	antefixa	bantling	braiding	champion	conative	delirium	dowdyish
acquaint	anterior	banxring	brainish	chapping	conceive	Delphian	downhill
acridine	anything	baronial	brandied	charming	conflict	delusion	downpipe
acridity	aphasiac	baseline	brandish	charring	conidial	delusive	downtime
acrolith	aphelion	basicity	brassica	Chartism	conidium	demolish	downwind
acrotism	aphicide	basidial	brassily	Chartist	conjoint	demoniac	dragging
actiniae	aphorise	basidium	brattice	chastise	conspire	demonian	dragline
actinian	aphorism	basilica	brattish	chastity	contline	demonise	dreamily
actinias	aphorist	basilisk	breaking	chattily	contrite	demonism	dreaming
actinide	apiarian	Batavian	breeding	chatting	contrive	demotion	drearily
actinism	apiarist	Bavarian	breezily	cheapish	cooption	denarius	dressing
actinium	apocrine	bdellium	briefing	cheekily	cooptive	denazify	driftice
activism	appetite	beagling	brimming	cheerily	corkwing	dendrite	drilling
activist	apposite	beautify	briskish	cheering	couching	deputise	drinking
activity	appraise	becoming	brisling	childish	coupling	deration	dripping
acturial	aquarist	beeswing	broadish	chipping	coursing	derelict	dropkick
adaption	aquarium	beetling	broodily	chirpily	courtier	derision	dropping
adaptive	aquatint	bellbird	brookite	chloride	covering	derisive	drowsily
addition	aquiline	benedick	browning	chlorine	crabbing	describe	drubbing
additive	arapaima	benedict	brownish	chlorite	cracking	destrier	drugging
adenoids	arbalist	benefice	bubaline	chopping	cradling	detoxify	druggist
adhesion	arborist	bestride	buckling	chromite	craftily	deviling	druidism
adhesive	Arcadian	betacism	bucolics	chromium	cramming	devilish	drumfire
Adlerian	archaise	bezonian	Buddhism	chugging	cramoisy	devilism	drumming
admonish	archaism	biassing	Buddhist	chummily	crankily	Devonian	drypoint
adnation	archaist	bibation	building	chumming	crannied	devotion	duckbill
adoption	argufier	biennial	bullring	churlish	crashing	dewpoint	duckling
adoptive	Arianism	biennium	bundling	churning	crawfish	dextrine	duelling
aegirine	Armenian	bifacial	buntline	ciborium	crayfish	dialling	duellist
aeration	Arminian	bigamist	bushfire	circuity	creakily	diatribe	duettist
aerolite	armorial	bilabial	bustling	citation	creatine	dicacity	dumpling
aerolith	arsenide	binomial	Byronism	citified	creation	didymium	dunghill
affinity	arsenite	birdlime	cabalism	cityfied	creative	digamist	duration
affusion	arsonist	bitchily	cabalist	civilian	creeping	digitise	durative
agential	arterial	blabbing	cacomixl	civilise	crescive	dilation	dustlike
agnation	artesian	blacking	caducity	civility	cribbing	dilative	dwarfish
agrarian	artifice	blackish	caffeine	cladding	croakily	dilution	dwarfism
Akkadian	ascidian	blandish	cagebird	clammily	Croatian	diluvial	dwelling
alacrity	ascidium	bleakish	cageling	clamming	crocoite	diluvian	dynamics
Albanian	asperity	blearily	caladium	clanging	crofting	diluvium	dynamism
albinism	assuming	bleeding	calamine	clannish	cropping	dimerism	dynamist
algicide	Assyrian	blessing	calamint	clapping	crossing	diminish	dynamite
algidity	astatine	blimpish	calamite	classics	croupier	dioecism	eclosion
algorism	asterisk	blinding	calamity	classify	crowbill	diopside	edgewise
alienism	asterism	blinking	calidity	cleaning	crustily	diploidy	eduction
alienist	astonied	blockish	callgirl	clearing	cruzeiro	dipstick	effusion
alkalies	atheling	blondish	calycine	clinking	cryolite	dirigism	effusive
alkalify	Athenian	bloodily	Cambrian	clipping	culicine	disguise	egestion
alkaline	atrocity	blooming	camomile	cliquish	Cumbrian	disjoint	Egyptian
allodial	atropine	blotting	campaign	cliquism	cupidity	disprize	eighties
allodium	atticism	blowfish	campfire	cloddish	curarine	disquiet	ejection
allspice	audacity	bluebird	campsite	clothier	curative	district	ejective
allusion	audition	bluefish	Canadian	clothing	curtains	disunion	ekistics
allusive	auditive	blurrily	canalise	clotting	cutprice	disunite	election
alluvial	aurelian	blurring	cancrine	cloudily	cymatium	disunity	elective
alluvion	autogiro	boarding	canoeing	clownish	cynicism	ditheism	embolism

emceeing	exorcise	flitting	Gaullist	gypsyism	ideation	kerosine	lobation	
emersion	exorcism	floating	gelatine	gyration	identify	Khmerian	lobbyist	
emission	exorcist	flogging	gelation	hairlike	identity	kindling	lobeline	
emissive	exordial	flooring	gelidity	hairline	idiotism	kinesics	localise	
emitting	exordium	floppily	genetics	halation	idyllist	kinetics	localism	
emporium	expedite	flopping	genitive	halflife	ignition	kingbird	locality	
emulsify	exterior	flourish	genocide	halfpint	ignominy	kingfish	locative	
emulsion	fabulist	flubbing	gentrice	halftime	illation	kinglike	locution	
emulsive	facelift	fluepipe	Georgian	handbill	illative	kingsize	logician	
enaction	facetiae	fluidics	geraniol	handline	illumine	klondike	longtime	
enactive	facility	fluidify	geranium	handling	illusion	knapping	longwise	
encomion	fagoting	fluidise	Ghanaian	handlist	illusive	kneehigh	lordling	
encomium	faintish	fluidity	ghoulish	handmill	Illyrian	knitting	lovebird	
endemism	fairyism	fluoride	giantism	handpick	ilmenite	knocking	lovelily	
energise	falchion	fluorine	gipsyism	haploidy	imbecile	knotting	lovesick	
engaging	fallfish	fluorite	gladding	harakiri	immobile	lability	lowering	
enormity	familial	focalise	glancing	hardline	immunise	lacewing	lowlying	
enshrine	familiar	focusing	glassily	hatching	immunity	laconian	loyalist	
entrails	faradism	fondling	glassine	haunting	imparity	laconism	lucidity	
envision	farthing	foothill	gleaning	Hawaiian	imperial	ladybird	luminist	
Ephesian	fatalism	footling	gloaming	hawklike	imperium	ladylike	lumpfish	
epyllion	fatalist	foramina	gloomily	headline	impetigo	lamblike	lunarian	
equalise	fatality	fordoing	glossily	headwind	impolicy	landgirl	lunation	
equality	faultily	foreside	glossina	heartily	impolite	landline	lungfish	
equation	Faustian	foretime	glutting	hebraise	imposing	landmine	lustrine	
equinity	favonian	forgoing	glyptics	Hebraism	impunity	languish	lustring	
equities	feeblish	forklift	gnathite	Hebraist	impurity	lapicide	lutanist	
Erastian	feedpipe	fortuity	goalkick	hedonics	inaction	lapidify	lutecium	
erectile	felicity	fortyish	goalline	hedonism	inactive	laterite	lutenist	
erection	felinity	founding	goatfish	hedonist	incision	latinise	lutetium	
erethism	feminine	fraction	goatling	Hegelian	incisive	Latinism	luxation	
erewhile	feminise	francium	Gobelins	hellfire	incivism	Latinist	lyophile	
ergotise	feminism	Frankish	godchild	helotism	incoming	latinity	lyrebird	
ergotism	feminist	frapping	goldfish	hepatica	indicium	laughing	lyricism	
eruption	feminity	freakish	goldmine	hepatise	indocile	lavation	lyricist	
eruptive	ferocity	freewill	gonidial	herdwick	induline	laxative	magazine	
escapism	fetching	freezing	gonidium	heredity	indusium	Lazarist	magician	
escapist	feticide	frenzied	goodtime	herewith	inequity	lazulite	mainline	
espalier	feverish	fretting	goodwife	Hertzian	inertial	lazurite	maiolica	
especial	fewtrils	Freudian	goodwill	highrise	infamise	leaflike	majolica	
essayist	fiddling	friction	Graafian	hilarity	inferior	learning	majority	
Essenism	fidelity	Friesian	grabbing	hillside	infinite	legalise	malarial	
essonite	fiducial	frillies	Graecise	himation	infinity	legalism	malarian	
esterify	fiendish	fringing	Graecism	hinduise	infusion	legalist	maledict	
Estonian	fiftyish	friskily	graffiti	Hinduism	inhesion	legality	mandrill	
eternise	fighting	fritting	graffito	hireling	iniquity	legatine	manorial	
eternity	figurine	frocking	graining	hoarding	insanity	legation	mantling	
etherial	filariae	frogfish	graphics	hobbyist	inscribe	legerity	manurial	
etherise	filarial	frogging	graphite	hocktide	interior	lemurine	marbling	
etherism	filefish	frontier	grasping	homelike	intimism	Leninism	maritime	
etherist	Filipina	frostily	gratuity	homesick	invasion	Leninist	marquise	
ethicism	Filipino	frosting	grayling	homicide	invasive	Leninite	marrying	
ethicist	filthily	frothily	greasily	homicide	inviting	lenitive	material	
Etrurian	fimbriae	fructify	greedily	hoodwink	iotacism	leporine	materiel	
eugenics	finalise	fruition	greening	Horatian	Irishism	lewisite	maturity	
eugenism	finalism	frumpish	greenish	hornbill	ironside	libation	maverick	
eugenist	finalist	fuchsine	greeting	hornpipe	Islamise	licorice	maximise	
eulogise	finality	fuelling	greffier	hornrims	Islamism	lifelike	mazarine	
eulogist	firebird	fugacity	greyfish	hosepipe	Islamite	lifeline	Mazdaism	
eulogium	fireside	fugitive	grimoire	hotelier	isthmian	lifesize	mealtime	
euphuism	fishwife	fullsize	grinning	humanise	Jacobite	lifetime	meantime	
euphuist	fixation	fulltime	gripping	humanism	jailbird	ligation	meconium	
Eurasian	fixative	function	grissini	humanist	japonica	lighting	medicine	
europium	flagging	fusilier	gritting	humanity	jaundice	lightish	megalith	
evection	flapping	futility	groggily	humidify	jauntily	likewise	melamine	
eventide	flashily	futurism	grouping	humidity	Jehovist	limekiln	melanism	
eversion	flashing	futurist	grouting	humility	jeremiad	limerick	melanite	
eviction	flatfish	futurity	growling	humorist	Jeremiah	limonite	melinite	
evincive	flatling	Galenism	grubbily	hungrily	jingoish	linguist	melodise	
evulsion	flattish	galenite	grubbing	hymenial	jingoism	lipstick	melodist	
exacting	flatwise	gamebird	grudging	hymenium	jingoist	littling	memorial	
exaction	flautist	gangling	grumpily	hyoscine	jobation	livelily	memorise	
excision	fleabite	ganglion	guardian	ianthine	jocosity	liveried	meridian	
exciting	flection	gantline	guiltily	Ibsenism	joystick	liverish	mesquite	
exequies	fleeting	gaolbird	gulosity	iceblink	judicial	livewire	middling	
exercise	flimsily	gaselier	gumption	idealise	junction	lividity	midpoint	
exertion	flintily	gasolier	gunflint	idealism	juvenile	lixivium	midships	
exiguity	flipping	gasoline	gunpoint	idealist	Kashmiri	loadline	mightily	
exocrine	flipside	Gaullism	gunsmith	ideality	kerchief	loathing	migraine	

Milesian	nativism	oologist	phrasing	priggism	reaffirm	rurality	seedtime
minacity	nativist	ophidian	Phrygian	primming	realtime	rushlike	seignior
minimise	nativity	opposite	piddling	printing	rearmice	sagacity	selenide
Minorite	naturism	optative	piercing	priority	rearview	sailfish	selenite
minority	naturist	optician	piffling	prissily	reassign	salacity	selenium
minutiae	nauplius	optimise	pigswill	pristine	recision	salariat	selfpity
misalign	Nazarite	optimism	pilosity	prodding	redblind	salaried	selfwill
mischief	Nazirite	optimist	pinpoint	proemial	redbrick	Salesian	Semitise
misdoing	neaptide	Orangism	pinprick	proofing	redefine	salinity	Semitism
misguide	nebulise	Orcadian	pintsize	propping	redesign	Salopian	Semitist
misprint	nebulium	organise	pipefish	prosaism	redshift	saltlick	semolina
misprise	neckline	organism	pipeline	prosaist	redshirt	saltmine	semplice
misprize	needfire	organist	piperine	Prussian	reedbird	samarium	senarius
misthink	negation	oscinine	pisolite	psalmist	reedling	samphire	senility
mistrial	negative	otiosity	pixieish	psychics	reedpipe	sampling	senorita
miswrite	negroism	ottavino	plaguily	psychism	regalism	sanative	serenity
mobilise	nephrite	outgoing	plaiding	psychist	regality	sanctify	sericite
mobility	nepotism	outlying	planking	ptomaine	regicide	sanction	serosity
modalism	nestling	outpoint	planning	ptyalism	regolith	sanctity	serotine
modalist	neutrino	outreign	plastics	puffbird	reignite	sandwich	severity
modality	nicotian	outshine	platting	pugilism	relation	sandyish	shabbily
modifier	nicotine	outvying	plaudits	pugilist	relative	sanguine	shafting
molality	niggling	outweigh	playbill	punition	religion	sanitise	shaggily
molarity	nihilism	ovenbird	playgirl	punitive	relumine	sapidity	Shaktism
molehill	nihilist	overfill	playtime	puparial	remedial	saponify	shamming
Molinism	nihility	overfish	pleading	puparium	reremice	saponite	sharpish
Molinist	ninepins	overkill	pleasing	pupation	rescript	sapphics	sheading
monadism	nineties	overnice	plebeian	puppyish	resinify	sapphire	shealing
monaxial	Noachian	override	pleurisy	purblind	respring	sapphism	shedding
monazite	nobelium	overripe	plodding	purfling	restrict	satanism	sheepish
mondaine	nobility	overside	plopping	purifier	resupine	satanist	sheeting
monetise	nodalise	oversize	plotting	purplish	retiring	satirise	shelving
monition	nodality	overtime	pluckily	pushbike	reviling	satirist	shieling
monitive	nodation	overview	plugging	putative	revision	saxatile	shiftily
monkfish	nodosity	overwind	plumbing	pygidial	revivify	Saxonism	shilling
monodist	nomadise	pacifier	plumbism	pygidium	rewaking	Saxonist	shinning
monolith	nomadism	pacifism	plumpish	pyrexial	Rhaetian	scallion	shipping
monomial	nondairy	pacifist	pointing	pyridine	rhyolite	scampish	shirring
monotint	nonstick	paganise	polarise	pyxidium	ricebird	scandium	shirting
monoxide	nonunion	paganish	polarity	quackish	Riesling	scanning	shocking
monteith	nonwhite	paganism	polemics	quadriga	rightist	scansion	shoddily
moonfish	noontide	pagurian	polemise	quagmire	rigidify	scanties	shoebill
moonrise	noontime	palatial	polemist	qualmish	rigidity	scantily	shogging
moralise	northing	palatine	politick	quantify	ringside	scantily	shooting
moralism	nosedive	palomino	politico	quantise	riparian	scarcity	shopgirl
moralist	nosepipe	paludism	politics	quantity	riverine	scarring	shopping
morality	nosering	papalise	polonium	quarrier	roadside	scathing	shortish
Moravian	notarial	papalism	polypide	quartile	roadsign	scattily	showbill
morosity	notation	papalist	polypite	quayside	roasting	scatting	showgirl
morphine	notching	paradigm	populism	queasily	rockbird	scheming	shrewish
mosquito	novation	paradise	populist	queening	rockfish	scholium	shunning
motility	novelise	parasite	porkling	queerish	rocklike	sciatica	shutting
motivity	novelist	parodist	porosity	question	rockling	sciolism	Siberian
motorial	nubility	Parsiism	porpoise	queueing	rogation	sciolist	Sicilian
motoring	numbfish	Parthian	portfire	quiddity	Romanian	sciurine	sicklist
motorise	nursling	parttime	position	quietism	romanise	sclerite	sidedish
motorist	nutarian	pastries	positive	quietist	Romanism	scolding	sidekick
motorium	nutation	patagium	postmill	quilting	Romanist	scorpion	sideline
mottling	oblation	patchily	potation	quipping	romanist	scottice	sideling
moulding	obliging	pavilion	potstill	quirkily	rosarian	scottice	siderite
mounting	oblivion	pearlies	poultice	quisling	rosefish	scottish	sideview
mourning	obsidian	pearling	pounding	quitting	rosepink	scouting	sidewind
mucosity	obtusity	pearlite	practice	quizzing	Rotarian	scraping	sidewise
multeity	occasion	peculiar	practise	rabidity	rotation	silicide
munition	occupier	pedalier	praecipe	racemise	rotative	scudding	silicify
murrhine	offdrive	Pelagian	praedial	rainbird	roturier	scullion	silphium
muscling	offering	pelerine	prandial	rallying	roughish	scumming	Silurian
musician	official	pelorism	prankish	rallyist	roundish	scurrile	similise
mutation	offprint	penalise	preexist	rambling	rowdyish	scurvily	simoniac
mycelial	oiticica	penknife	prentice	ranarian	rowdyism	seagoing	simonist
mycelium	olympiad	peperino	preprint	ranarium	royalism	seaonion	simplify
mylonite	Olympian	perceive	prescind	rapacity	royalist	seaonion	simplism
nailfile	omission	peridium	pressing	rapidity	rubidium	sedation	sinapism
narceine	omitting	peroxide	prestige	rarefied	rugosity	sedative	singeing
narghile	oncidium	perspire	prettify	rasorial	Rumanian	sedition	sinicise
nasalise	oncoming	Peruvian	prettily	ratifier	Rumanian	sedulity	sirenian
nasality	onychite	petaline	priapism	rattling	ruralise	sitarist
natality	oogonial	petition	priedieu	reaction	ruralism	seedfish	sizzling
natation	oogonium	phormium	priggish	reactive	ruralist	seedling	skerrick

```
skidding  solecist  stepping  swobbing  toothing  unseeing  vowelise  autarkic
skilling  solfaist  stepwise  swopping  tortoise  unsocial  Wahabism  bearskin
skimmilk  solidify  sterling  swotting  totalise  unstring  Wahabite  bedmaker
skimming  solidity  sternite  sybarite  totality  unthrift  wakening  bespoken
skimpily  solstice  stetting  sycamine  totemism  untidily  wakerife  biweekly
skinning  solution  stibnite  syconium  totemist  unwarily  warpaint  buckskin
skipping  somatism  stickily  sylphide  touchily  uprising  waterice  calfskin
skirmish  sometime  stiffish  sylphine  touching  upspring  watering  cannikin
skirting  sonatina  stilbite  sylphish  toughish  upstairs  waterish  capeskin
skittish  songbird  stingily  symphile  tovarish  urbanise  waygoing  Cherokee
slabbing  sonority  stinking  syncline  toxicity  urbanism  weakfish  coonskin
slagging  soothing  stirring  synovial  tracking  urbanist  weakling  coworker
slamming  sorority  stockily  syzygial  traction  urbanite  weanling  deerskin
slangily  sorption  stocking  tackling  tractive  urbanity  wellnigh  devilkin
slapping  sorptive  stockish  Tahitian  training  Ursuline  Wellsian  dybbukim
slashing  soterial  stockist  tailpipe  tramline  vacation  weregild  foreskin
sleazily  sounding  stodgily  tamarind  transire  vagility  whacking  forsaken
sledding  sourdine  stoicism  tamarisk  trapping  valerian  whapping  goatskin
sleepily  southing  stopping  Tamilian  Trappist  validity  wheezily  havocked
sleeping  spaewife  stormily  tangoist  trashily  valorise  whetting  haymaker
slimming  spanking  stoutish  Tantrism  treatise  vanadium  whidding  hijacker
slimmish  spanning  strabism  Tantrist  trekking  vanquish  Whiggish  lambskin
slinkily  sparkish  stratify  tapelike  trendily  vapidity  Whiggism  larrikin
slipping  sparling  striking  tapeline  trephine  vaporise  whinsill  latchkey
slipring  sparring  strobila  Tarpeian  trialist  vaulting  whiplike  lawmaker
slitting  sparsity  strobile  tawdrily  triaxial  vegetive  whipping  magicked
slobbish  spatting  strobili  taxation  trichina  velamina  whirring  malarkey
slogging  speaking  stubbing  teaching  trichite  velarium  whizzing  mannikin
sloppily  speedily  studding  technics  trickily  velleity  whooping  mimicked
slopping  spelling  stuffily  teething  trickish  velocity  whopping  mimicker
slotting  spherics  stuffing  telecine  trifling  venality  wifelike  mistaken
slubbing  spiffing  stultify  telefilm  trilling  venation  wildfire  moleskin
slugging  spinning  stumming  teleview  trillion  Venetian  wildlife  monicker
sluggish  spitfire  stumpily  televise  trillium  venosity  windmill  mutchkin
slumming  spitting  stunning  temerity  trimming  Venusian  windpipe  onlooker
slurring  splenial  sturdied  tempting  trioxide  veracity  wintrily  ostrakon
sluttish  splenius  sturdily  tenacity  tripping  verifier  witching  oxpecker
smallish  spoffish  suberise  tenorite  tripwire  verjuice  wolffish  panicked
smaltite  spongily  subjoint  tenurial  tristich  veronica  womanise  pannikin
smarmily  sponsion  suboxide  tepidity  triunity  vesuvian  womanish  partaken
smartish  spookily  subprior  termtime  trochili  vexation  woodbind  reawaken
smashing  spookish  suchlike  tetanise  troilite  vicarial  woodbine  sealskin
smelling  spoonily  suckling  tetchily  trophied  vicinity  woodlice  sheepked
smocking  sportily  sudarium  thallium  trotting  Vietminh  woodpile  shiftkey
smudgily  sporting  sulphide  theodicy  troupial  vilifier  woodwind  shrinker
smuttily  sportive  sulphite  theorise  trucking  villainy  wormlike  shrunken
snagging  spottily  sultrily  theorist  trunnion  vinosity  worthily  sprinkle
snaplink  spunkily  Sumerian  thermion  trussing  viperine  woundily  sprocket
snappily  spurling  sunblind  thermite  trustily  viperish  wrapping  squawker
snapping  spurring  sundried  thespian  tumbling  viricide  wrathily  squeaker
snappish  spurrier  sundries  thiamine  tumidity  viridian  xanthine  streaked
snazzily  squarish  sunshine  thickish  Tunisian  viridity  xanthium  streaker
sneakily  stabbing  sunshiny  thievish  Turanian  virilism  xenolith  stricken
sneakish  stabling  superior  thinking  turnpike  virility  xylonite  strickle
sniffily  stablish  supplial  thinning  turtling  vitalise  yachting  strucken
snipping  stalking  supplier  thinnish  tutorial  vitalism  yeanling  sunbaked
snobbish  stalling  supplies  thriving  twenties  vitalist  yearling  swanskin
snobbism  stallion  surefire  thudding  twinling  vitality  yearning  thwacker
snogging  standing  surfbird  thuggism  twinning  vitiligo  yeastily  turnskin
snootily  standish  surffish  thumping  twitting  vituline  yielding  unbacked
snowbird  stannite  surplice  ticklish  typehigh  vivacity  youngish  unbroken
snowlike  starfish  surprise  tidemill  typifier  vivarium  yuletide  unbuckle
snowline  starlike  swabbing  tigerish  tyrosine  vivifier  zecchini  unlinked
snubbing  starling  swagging  tilefish  ubiquity  vixenish  zecchino  unmarked
soapdish  starrily  swainish  timidity  uintaite  vocalise  zibeline  watchkey
soberise  starring  swanking  tingeing  ulterior  vocalism  zinckify  whizzkid
Socinian  starting  swanlike  tinsmith  ultraism  vocalist  zincking  wigmaker
sodalite  steadily  swanning  titanism  ultraist  vocality  zombiism  wineskin
sodality  steading  swapping  titanite  unbelief  vocation  zonation  wolfskin
sodomite  stealing  swastika  titanium  unburied  vocative  zoophily  woolskin
soilpipe  steamily  swatting  toadfish  uneasily  volatile  zucchini  aborally
solanine  stearine  swearing  toadyish  unending  volition  carcajou  abutilon
solarise  steatite  sweeping  toadyism  unerring  volitive  crackjaw  aciculae
solarism  steening  sweeting  tokenism  unfading  voltaism  kinkajou  acicular
solarist  steepish  sweetish  tolldish  unfilial  voltaist  nightjar  aciculas
solarium  steering  swelling  tonality  uniaxial  vomerine  popinjay  actually
solation  stellify  swigging  tonguing  unionise  vomitive  stickjaw  aerially
solatium  stellion  swimming  tonicity  unionism  voracity  turbojet  aiguille
solecism  stemming  swinging  toothily  unionist  votarist  Algonkin  alveolar
```

```
alveolus cotillon frugally methylic propolis socalled Vandalic consomme
amorally coverlet furbelow micellar propylic socially vanillin consumer
ampullae crenelle furculae missilry prunella spadille variolar contempt
anabolic crosslet furcular modelled prunelle sparkler vascular costumer
animally crueller Gadhelic modeller prunello sparklet vasculum cragsman
annually cupelled gardyloo Mongolic pterylae spatular venially customer
annulled curculio gauntlet monoglot pulvilli specular verbally cyclamen
anthelia cypselae genially mortally pupillar speculum vernally dairyman
apically Cyrillic gerbille moufflon pustular spiculum vexillum dalesman
appalled dactylar glabella murrelet queenlet spicular vinculum deformed
artfully dactylic globally muscular quenelle spiculum visually diatomic
articled dentalia globular mutually quibbler spikelet vitellin dioramic
bachelor detailed globulin nautilus racially spirally vitellus diplomat
bacillar devilled Goidelic Negrillo radially spirilla volvulus doomsman
bacillus diabolic golfclub neurally rascally sporular vowelled drachmae
bastille dicyclic gonfalon nickelic rataplan sprawler wagonlit drachmai
battalia disallow grabbler normalcy ravelled squaller Walhalla drachmas
befallen dismally granular normally rebelled squealer waterlog dragoman
beguiler dissolve gravelly nouvelle rebeller stapelia waterloo dragomen
benzylic distally greenlet nucellus rebellow startler weaselly dragsman
bevelled disvalue Griselda omphalic redeploy steepled weeviled dulcimer
beveller dorsally grizzled omphalos reemploy stickler weevilly Dutchman
biathlon dowelled grumbler openplan repealer stimulus wheedler economic
blackleg drabbler gruntled oracular repelled stippler whiffler embalmer
blahblah dribbler guerilla orchilla repeller stipular whistler endermic
bordello dribblet handclap outvalue republic stroller wilfully engramma
bouillon drupelet Hercules overalls retailer stumbler woefully epidemic
bracelet durables hostelry overflew revealer subsolar wordplay episemon
bractlet encyclic impelled overflow reveille swiftlet wrangler Esquimau
brindled enrolled impeller overplay revelled swindler wrestler euonymin
bromelia entailer inoculum overplus reveller symbolic wriggler euonymus
brooklet entellus intaglio overslip ritually syphilis wristlet everyman
brutally enthalpy ironclad pachalic rivalled systolic yarmulka exogamic
bungalow epically isabella pamphlet rivelled tantalic yodelled extremes
caballed epicalyx jewelled panelled rocaille tantalum yodeller fancyman
cachalot epistler jeweller pangolin roseolar tantalus Yugoslav ferryman
calculus equalled jovially papillae ruefully tasselly zeppelin freedman
camellia escallop joyfully papillar saccular tenaille abnormal freshman
canaille eschalot Jugoslav papillon sacculus teocalli academia fugleman
cannulae excelled labelled parallax sandflea thriller academic funnyman
cannular exemplar labellum parallel sardelle tinselly adynamia gossamer
cannulas exemplum labially parhelia scapulae toadflax adynamic gownsman
capellet expelled laically parhelic scapulas tomalley affirmer gravamen
capsular expellee lamellae pashalic scapular tortilla aglimmer handyman
carbolic extolled lamellar pashalik schiller totalled airwoman harrumph
carillon facially lancelet pastille schmaltz towelled alchemic headsman
carnally faunally landslip patellae scopulae trampler alderman hebdomad
carolled festally lapelled patellar scopulas treadler anatomic helmsman
casually feudally lawfully pedalled scrawler trembler anthemia henchman
casualty fibrilla lethally pedicled scutella trembles apogamic herdsman
catholic filially levelled pendular seaholly trevally bailsman hielaman
caudally fireclay leveller pendulum seedplot tribally balsamic horseman
caudillo fireplug libelled perilled sequelae trochlea bandsman houseman
causally fiscally libellee periplus seraglio troutlet bargeman huntsman
cavilled fishglue libeller petalled serially truckler beadsman hydromel
caviller fistulae lineally petiolar serpulae trueblue becalmed illtimed
cellular fistular lipsalve petioled sewellel twaddler bechamel imprimis
cephalic fitfully loblolly petrolic sexually twiddler bedimmed Indiaman
cervelat flabella Lucullan phenolic shambles twinkler Benjamin infirmly
chandler flagella magdalen phenylic shashlik umbrella bergamot inflamer
chapelry flimflam magnolia phthalic shigella unaneled bionomic informal
chenille flipflap mamillae piacular shingler uncalled bogeyman informed
chivalry flipflop mamillar pinnular shingles uncially bondsman informer
chorally floodlit mandolin pipeclay shiralee underlap bonhomie intermit
cingulum florally manfully planulae shuffler underlay bottomry intermix
circular flotilla mantelet planular sickflag underlet brakeman intromit
clipclop fluellin mantilla platelet sideslip underlie buncombe Irishman
clopclop footslog manually plumelet signally underlip cardamom ischemia
cloudlet foreplay martello plumular sinfully unifilar cardamum ischemic
coagulum formalin maxillae plurally singular unipolar chairman isogamic
coleslaw formally medalled polyglot skittles univalve chessman Komsomol
compiler formulae medallic potbelly skypilot unsealed chiasmus lacrimal
condylar formulas medially potholer slipslop untitled Chinaman lacrymal
consoler foveolae menially prattler smuggler unwieldy cinnamic landsman
consular franklin mentally predella sniffler usefully cinnamon laywoman
convolve frenulum mescalin premolar sniffles vacuolar clansman leadsman
convulse fribbler mesially primally sniggler Valhalla coachman liegeman
corselet frijoles metalled profiler snuffler valvulae coelomic linesman
costplus frontlet metallic promulge snuffles valvular cognomen madwoman
```

mandamus	trackman	cantonal	dragonet	hereunto	modernly	prudence	spavined
marasmic	transmit	canzonet	Dulcinea	hibernal	moorings	pulmonic	sphagnum
marasmus	tripeman	carbonic	duodenal	Hispanic	morainic	pulvinus	spicknel
marksman	trisomic	carbonyl	duodenum	Hogmanay	mordancy	pungency	spraints
marshman	Turcoman	carcanet	dysgenic	hollands	mornings	pursenet	stakenet
mesdames	Turkoman	cardinal	earnings	hormonal	motional	pyogenic	staminal
misnomer	twotimer	cationic	earthnut	Huguenot	mucrones	pythonic	strained
mittimus	uncommon	caverned	egomania	hustings	muslined	rabbinic	strainer
MonKhmer	underman	chaconne	elegance	hyacinth	myelinic	radiance	subgenus
motorman	unformed	chestnut	elegancy	hydranth	myogenic	radiancy	sublunar
motormen	unseemly	Cheyenne	eleventh	hygienic	nascence	rampancy	suborner
newcomer	watchman	chthonic	eminence	imaginal	nascency	rational	subsonic
nobleman	waterman	churinga	eminency	imagines	national	rawboned	subtonic
nonhuman	Welshman	cislunar	encaenia	impugner	neotenic	reagency	succinct
Norseman	wheelman	clarence	enceinte	infernal	neuronal	reasoner	succinic
Northman	woodsman	clarinet	encrinal	infringe	neuronic	reckoner	succinum
ofttimes	abeyance	clemency	encrinic	inguinal	nonsense	reefknot	suddenly
oldtimer	abeyancy	cokernut	ensconce	innuendo	notional	regional	suitings
oligomer	abidance	columnal	ensigncy	insignia	notornis	reliance	sullenly
orgasmic	acreinch	columnar	entrance	insomnia	noumenal	renounce	summoner
pandemic	affiance	columned	entrench	instance	noumenon	renowned	sundance
perfumer	airliner	combings	erogenic	instancy	nuisance	resigned	supernal
Philomel	alburnum	commando	estrange	instinct	obtainer	response	suspense
phlegmon	Alderney	commence	euphonic	internal	oddments	retainer	sweepnet
phonemic	alebench	commoner	evidence	internee	olibanum	retrench	syntonic
pivotman	alliance	commoney	examinee	intrench	oppugner	ribbonry	tailings
placeman	amaranth	commonly	examiner	isogonal	optional	riddance	tangency
prehuman	ambiance	communal	exchange	isogonic	opulence	rinsings	tapdance
pressman	ambience	condense	exigence	isotonic	ordainer	rottenly	tautonym
presumer	anaconda	confiner	exigency	issuance	ordnance	safranin	taverner
prolamin	aniconic	confines	external	iterance	origanum	salience	tectonic
proximal	announce	congener	eyeliner	ivorynut	original	saliency	tegmenta
raftsman	antennae	conjunct	falconer	japanned	orogenic	santonin	tendence
ranchman	antennal	contango	falconet	julienne	Ossianic	sapience	tendency
randomly	antennas	contents	falconry	labdanum	outrange	sarcenet	tenpence
ransomer	arachnid	continua	fandance	laburnum	pandanus	sardonic	tenpenny
recommit	Armagnac	continue	fandango	lambency	parcener	sardonyx	terminal
redeemer	assiento	continuo	fastener	larcener	pardoner	sarsenet	terminer
reformed	assignat	convener	fattener	lashings	parlance	Sassanid	terminus
reformer	assignee	convenor	fervency	laudanum	parlando	saturnic	Teutonic
reinsman	assignor	convince	flamenco	leadenly	parsonic	savannah	topliner
rhythmic	asthenia	coplanar	flamingo	leavings	paternal	sawbones	trailnet
rifleman	asthenic	courante	fontanel	leggings	patience	scavenge	trawlnet
riverman	attorney	cousinly	fontange	legioned	patronal	schooner	trecento
salesman	audience	cracknel	foreknew	lenience	peccancy	scoopnet	tribunal
Scotsman	autumnal	cravenly	foreknow	leniency	pectines	scrannel	triennia
scrammed	badlands	credence	forzando	lichened	peelings	screener	trigonal
screamer	ballonet	credenza	frumenty	lichenin	pendency	scrounge	tuppence
seedsman	bambinos	cretonne	gainings	listener	perianth	seamanly	tuppenny
septimal	bandanna	criminal	galbanum	lockknit	personae	seasonal	turbaned
sidesman	barranca	currency	galvanic	lodgings	personal	seasoner	turbinal
spaceman	barranco	cyclonic	gardener	Londoner	petronel	seicento	turnings
spearman	barrenly	daemonic	gardenia	loosener	phalange	sentence	twopence
specimen	baryonic	daimonic	garganey	loveknot	pickings	sentinel	twopenny
sphygmus	bassinet	deadener	geomancy	mackinaw	pilsener	sequence	Tychonic
squawman	beamends	decennia	geoponic	Maecenas	pimiento	serranid	tympanic
stasimon	bearings	defiance	Germanic	mahjongg	pincenez	Shekinah	tympanum
stockman	bechance	denounce	germinal	maidenly	pinmoney	shrapnel	typhonic
storeman	beechnut	designer	gloxinia	maligner	piquancy	sickener	tyrannic
streamer	beginner	detainee	glucinum	malignly	piscinae	siftings	unchancy
strummed	benignly	detainer	glyconic	mancando	pittance	sinfonia	unclench
strummer	berliner	deviance	gnomonic	Mandingo	placenta	siphonal	unclinch
stuntman	bignonia	deviancy	Golconda	manganic	platinic	siphonet	uncoined
subhuman	biogenic	diaconal	goldenly	mangonel	platinum	siphonic	unearned
superman	blatancy	diagonal	gorgonia	marginal	platonic	sirvente	unevenly
syngamic	blazoner	diamante	governor	martenot	plutonic	sithence	ungainly
systemic	blazonry	diatonic	guaranty	martinet	poisoner	sixpence	unisonal
tablemat	bobbinet	diggings	guidance	maternal	pollinia	sixpenny	unkennel
talesman	bookends	dinornis	hacienda	matronal	pollinic	Slavonic	unmanned
talisman	brandnew	diphenyl	hadronic	matronly	precinct	slipknot	unopened
tallyman	brazenly	disbench	hardener	mechanic	prepense	slovenly	unpinned
tautomer	brazenry	disjunct	harmonic	mergence	presence	slovenry	unsunned
tenesmus	brokenly	dispense	hastener	methanol	pretence	snipsnap	unweaned
thalamic	buoyancy	distance	hastings	methinks	prisoner	softener	vaccinal
thalamus	burgonet	distinct	hawfinch	midlands	profaner	solemnly	vaccinia
thrummed	Burgundy	doorknob	hazelnut	milliner	prolonge	solvency	vagrancy
townsman	buttoner	dormancy	heavenly	Miltonic	propense	souvenir	valiance
toxaemia	calcanea	doughnut	Hellenic	mittened	protonic	sovranty	valiancy
toxaemic	cannonry	draconic	helminth	mnemonic	province	spadones	variance

verdancy	armyworm	bullhorn	croupous	ectozoon	forelock	halftone	kinsfolk
vergence	arsonous	bullyoff	crowfoot	edacious	foremost	handbook	kneehole
vibrancy	asteroid	bunghole	crumhorn	eftsoons	forenoon	handhold	knockout
viburnum	atheroma	burntout	crummock	emulsoid	foretold	handloom	knothole
violence	auditory	busybody	cubiform	endozoic	foreword	handsome	knotwork
virginal	auriform	buzzword	cumbrous	endozoon	formroom	handwork	Kohinoor
Virginia	autacoid	cabriole	cumulous	enormous	formwork	hardcore	krumhorn
visional	autonomy	cacology	cupreous	enshroud	forsooth	hardwood	lacework
voidance	autosome	caducous	cushiony	ensiform	forswore	havelock	lacunose
volcanic	autotomy	caesious	cussword	enthrone	forsworn	hawkmoth	ladyhood
volcanos	axiology	calliope	Cypriote	entozoic	fourfold	hawthorn	ladylove
vulcanic	babyhood	calycoid	cytology	entozoon	foursome	headlock	lamppost
waggoner	backbone	camisole	darkroom	envelope	foxglove	headlong	landform
waleknot	backcomb	cancroid	darksome	environs	frabjous	headmost	landlord
wallknot	backdoor	canorous	dartrous	epigeous	freakout	headnote	lanthorn
wantonly	backmost	capriole	deadlock	episcope	freeborn	headroom	lavatory
wardance	backroom	capstone	deadwood	equivoke	freehold	headword	laverock
wardenry	ballcock	captious	decolour	escalope	freeload	headwork	layabout
warranty	ballroom	caracole	decorous	escarole	freesoil	hecatomb	leadwork
warrener	bankbook	careworn	delusory	Eskimoan	frescoes	hegemony	lemuroid
weaponry	banknote	carriole	demagogy	ethology	fretwork	heirloom	lepidote
wellknit	bankroll	carryout	demijohn	evensong	frondose	helicoid	levulose
wetlands	barefoot	cartload	dendroid	evermore	fructose	heliport	libatory
whitener	baritone	Casanova	denehole	everyone	fumarole	hellhole	lifeboat
whodunit	barndoor	casebook	derisory	evildoer	fumitory	henroost	lifelong
winnings	barytone	casework	desirous	exiguous	funkhole	herdbook	lifework
woodenly	baseborn	cashbook	dethrone	eximious	fusiform	Hereford	ligneous
workings	basswood	catacomb	dextrose	exospore	gabbroic	hexapody	linstock
writings	bathrobe	cataloes	dextrous	eyetooth	gabbroid	hidyhole	liripoop
yeomanly	bathroom	category	diagnose	fabulous	gadabout	highborn	liveborn
yeomanry	baudrons	catsfoot	diaphone	factious	gadzooks	highlows	livelong
zirconia	beadroll	cautious	diaspora	faltboat	gambroon	highmost	loanword
zoogenic	beadwork	cavicorn	diaspore	farinose	gamecock	highroad	lobotomy
zoomancy	beanpole	Cenozoic	diastole	fasciola	gamesome	hillfort	locofoco
zygaenid	beefwood	centroid	dichroic	fasciole	gantlope	hindmost	locomote
aardwolf	beetroot	ceratoid	didymous	fashious	gapeworm	holozoic	locutory
abattoir	behemoth	ceremony	diestock	fastfood	garefowl	homebody	lonesome
abelmosk	belabour	cernuous	digamous	fastuous	gatefold	homeborn	longboat
acarpous	bellcote	cesspool	dilatory	fatstock	gatepost	hometown	longhorn
acrefoot	bellwort	chapbook	dimerous	fearsome	gavelock	homework	longsome
acrimony	bentwood	charcoal	dinerout	feretory	gemstone	hominoid	loophole
adespota	bestrode	charlock	dingdong	feverous	generous	homodont	lovelock
aduncous	bibulous	checkout	dipnoous	filiform	geognosy	homology	lovelorn
advisory	bigamous	chlorous	disclose	filmgoer	geophone	hookworm	lovesome
aeriform	billfold	chorioid	discrown	fireboat	ghettoes	hornbook	lovesong
aerofoil	billhook	cicerone	disfrock	firebomb	giftbook	hornworm	luminous
aerology	bimanous	ciceroni	displode	firehose	girasole	hornwort	lungwort
aeronomy	bioscope	cinchona	disproof	firelock	girlhood	horologe	luscious
agrimony	biparous	clangour	disprove	firewood	glabrous	horology	lustrous
agrology	blackout	claymore	divebomb	firework	gladioli	hourlong	lymphoid
agronomy	blastoff	clodpole	dogsbody	fishbone	gladsome	humanoid	lymphoma
albacore	blastoid	clodpoll	dogshore	fishbowl	glaucoma	humorous	lysosome
aleatory	blossomy	clubfoot	dogtooth	fishhook	glaucous	hydatoid	macaroni
aleurone	blowhole	clupeoid	dolesome	fishpond	gleesome	hymnbook	macaroon
algology	bluecoat	coalhole	doloroso	fivefold	gloriole	hypobole	maestoso
alkaloid	bluenose	coatroom	dolorous	flagpole	glorious	ichorous	maidhood
allegory	boathook	cockboat	dominoes	flatboat	glowworm	ideology	mailboat
alumroot	boatload	cockloft	donatory	flatfoot	gluttony	illusory	makimono
amoeboid	bodywork	colewort	doorpost	flatworm	goalpost	inchworm	malodour
anaerobe	bollworm	coliform	doubloon	fleawort	goatmoth	infamous	mangrove
anaphora	bolthole	comatose	dovecote	flexuose	goitrous	inscroll	manifold
anecdote	boltrope	comedown	downcome	flexuous	goldfoil	iodoform	maniform
anechoic	booklore	conchoid	downmost	floccose	gorgeous	ironwood	marabout
ankylose	bookpost	confront	downpour	flyblown	goutwort	ironwork	marigold
anourous	bookwork	conglobe	downtown	foldboat	gracioso	Iroquois	markdown
antelope	bookworm	coniform	doxology	folklore	gracious	isogloss	matelote
antepost	borecole	cookbook	drammock	folkmoot	gralloch	isophote	mealworm
anteroom	borehole	copybook	dropwort	folksong	grallous	isospory	medusoid
antibody	botryoid	copyhold	drumroll	foothold	griseous	isotropy	megapode
antidote	botyrose	coracoid	drystone	footnote	grottoes	Italiote	menology
antilogy	bowfront	cordwood	duckpond	footpost	gruesome	jackboot	merosome
antimony	breakout	corkwood	dustbowl	footrope	gunstock	jeroboam	meshwork
antinode	broccoli	corneous	dustcoat	footsore	gypseous	kakemono	Mesozoic
antinomy	brushoff	cornpone	dustcoat	footwork	gyratory	keeshond	metazoan
antipode	bryology	coronoid	dyspnoea	forebode	hairworm	keratose	metazoon
antipole	bryozoan	Cotswold	eagleowl	foredoom	halfboot	keystone	miasmous
antipope	buckhorn	couscous	earphone	forefoot	halfmoon	kidglove	milepost
apterous	buhlwork	covetous	eastmost	foregoer	halfnote	kingbolt	milkwort
araceous	bulldoze	creosote	echinoid	foregone	halfsole	kinghood	millpond

```
minatory  ovariole  polyzoon  saltwort  sinusoid  teacloth  venomous  cirriped
mirepoix  overbook  pomology  sanatory  sitology  teamwork  Vietcong  collapse
misology  overbore  poohpooh  sandworm  skinfood  teaspoon  vigorous  crackpot
misquote  overcoat  populous  sandwort  skislope  telegony  viperous  crankpin
mitzvoth  overcome  porthole  saporous  slipform  teleport  virology  crashpad
mongoose  overdone  posology  sashcord  sliproad  tenotomy  virtuosa  crossply
monitory  overdose  postcode  savorous  slopwork  teratoma  virtuosi  cyclopes
monkhood  overfold  posthorn  sawedoff  slowdown  textbook  virtuoso  decouple
monogony  overfond  postpone  sawtooth  slowpoke  thalloid  virtuous  decrepit
monopode  overload  potstone  scabious  slowworm  thallous  Visigoth  didapper
monopoly  overlong  precious  scabrous  slyboots  theogony  vitreous  diplopia
monotone  overlook  previous  scaffold  snowboot  theology  vomitory  disciple
monotony  overlord  primrose  scammony  soaproot  thereout  voussoir  dystopia
moonwort  overrode  printout  scaphoid  soapwort  threnode  warcloud  empeople
moorcock  oversold  prismoid  scarious  sobstory  threnody  wardrobe  empurple
moorfowl  oversoul  prodrome  schizoid  softboil  thyrsoid  wardroom  endpaper
moratory  overtone  pruinose  scissors  softsoap  ticktock  wartwort  ensample
muckworm  overtook  psalmody  sciuroid  softwood  tidelock  warwhoop  entrepot
mudstone  overwork  pulpwood  scleroma  solenoid  timebomb  washbowl  eohippus
mushroom  overworn  pumproom  sclerose  sombrous  timework  washroom  epilepsy
muskrose  palinode  punitory  sclerous  somebody  timeworn  watthour  equipped
muticous  papulose  pyrenoid  seadrome  songbook  timorous  waveform  estopped
mutinous  papulous  pyriform  seafloor  sonorous  tinstone  waxcloth  estoppel
mycetoma  parabola  pyrrhoea  seafront  souchong  tiresome  Wedgwood  Ethiopic
mycology  paragoge  pyrrhous  seashore  spacious  tocology  weeklong  eutrophy
nacreous  paramour  quadroon  seatrout  spanroof  toilsome  wellborn  feldspar
nainsook  paranoia  quandong  sedulous  spathose  toilworn  wellworn  finespun
napiform  paranoid  racegoer  seedcoat  specious  tokology  werewolf  fireopal
natatory  parclose  racemose  seedcorn  sphenoid  tolbooth  whipcord  fissiped
nauseous  partsong  railroad  seedlobe  spheroid  tonepoem  whipworm  fleshpot
nebulous  passbook  raincoat  seignory  spittoon  toolroom  whiteout  flypaper
negatory  passport  ravenous  selfborn  spontoon  topology  wifehood  frogspit
nematode  password  reabsorb  selfhood  spurious  topstone  wildfowl  gallipot
nematoid  patulous  rearmost  selflove  squamose  tortious  wildwood  galloper
newblown  payphone  reexport  selfsown  squamous  tortuous  windcone  gossiper
newsroom  pedagogy  rehoboam  semidome  staghorn  trachoma  windrose  gossipry
nextdoor  pedology  reimpose  semitone  standoff  tradeoff  windsock  gossypol
nielloed  peephole  reniform  sensuous  stanhope  tramroad  wirework  haruspex
nightowl  peignoir  rerecord  sepaloid  stannous  trapdoor  wireworm  hedgepig
ninefold  pembroke  resinoid  sepalous  starwort  traprock  wirewove  hereupon
nodulose  penology  resinous  septfoil  stopcock  trichoid  wishbone  homespun
nodulous  penstock  retiform  serfhood  strapoil  trichome  withhold  honeypot
nomology  pentroof  revisory  serology  strigose  trichord  wondrous  hotchpot
nosecone  pericope  rhapsode  sesamoid  strumose  triploid  woodcock  hydropic
nosology  peridote  rhapsody  sexology  strumous  trochoid  woodnote  hydropsy
notebook  perilous  rheology  Shabuoth  stubborn  trollopy  woodwool  improper
nubiform  pervious  rhomboid  shaddock  stuccoes  trombone  woodwork  Interpol
nubilous  petalody  ribosome  shagroon  studbook  trottoir  woodworm  intrepid
nucleole  petaloid  rigadoon  shakeout  studious  trueborn  woolwork  isotopic
nucleoli  petalous  rigorous  shaleoil  studwork  truelove  wordbook  larkspur
nugatory  phaseout  ringbolt  shalloon  suberose  tuberose  workfolk  linchpin
numerous  phyllode  ringbone  shallows  suberous  tuberous  workroom  lollipop
numinous  phylloid  ringdove  shamrock  subfloor  tubiform  wormhole  lollypop
nutbrown  phyllome  ringroad  shareout  subgroup  tumorous  wormwood  lynchpin
oblatory  picaroon  ringworm  sherlock  sudatory  turncoat  writeoff  madapple
ochreous  picklock  roadbook  shinbone  sulphone  turncock  wrongous  manciple
octaroon  piedmont  rockcork  shipload  sundrops  turndown  xanthoma  marzipan
octoroon  pilewort  rockdove  shipworm  sunproof  turnsole  xylology  mayapple
odontoid  piliform  rockrose  shoehorn  sunstone  twinborn  yearbook  misapply
oecology  pillwort  rockwood  shofroth  surfboat  typology  yearlong  multiped
oenology  pinafore  rockwork  shootout  swansong  ulcerous  zabaione  multiple
oestrone  pinecone  rogatory  shopworn  sycamore  unciform  zoetrope  multiply
oestrous  pinewood  rolypoly  shothole  sycomore  unctuous  zoospore  myriapod
offshoot  pisiform  roodloft  showboat  symbiont  unthrone  zymology  myriopod
offshore  platform  roothold  showdown  symphony  upstroke  amphipod  necropsy
oilcloth  playbook  rosebowl  showroom  syndrome  upthrown  applepie  oakapple
oilstone  playgoer  roseroot  shutdown  tackroom  urochord  backspin  palmiped
okeydoke  playroom  rosewood  sickroom  taenioid  usurious  bagpiper  panpipes
omnivore  plethora  rotatory  sidedoor  tagalong  uxorious  bebopper  pansophy
oncology  plimsoll  rotenone  sidelong  tailcoat  vagabond  bicuspid  pattypan
ontology  pluvious  rugulose  sidenote  takehome  valorous  bobbypin  photopia
oogamous  poltfoot  runabout  sideroad  talapoin  vanadous  brainpan  photopic
openwork  poltroon  rushhour  signpost  tamanoir  vaporous  cachepot  photopsy
oreology  polypody  sackcoat  silicone  tandoori  varicose  calcspar  photopsy
orgulous  polypoid  saffrony  siluroid  tapeworm  variform  calliper  pinniped
otoscope  polypous  sagamore  silkworm  tarboosh  vasiform  centuple  pitviper
outdoors  polysomy  sailboat  singsong  taskwork  vavasory  chalkpit  platypus
outgrown  polyzoan  sainfoin  sinkhole  tattooer  vavasour  chickpea  plumiped
outshone  polyzoic  saleroom  sinology  taxonomy  velskoen  chutzpah  pteropod
```

quillpen	answerer	collyria	electrum	hetaerae	mannerly	podagral	snapbrim
recapped	antheral	coloured	elfarrow	hetairai	manubria	podagric	snowdrop
repeople	antlered	colubrid	enquirer	hexagram	marjoram	ponderer	solderer
rhizopod	antrorse	commerce	epidural	hierarch	mascaron	positron	solleret
saucepan	arbitral	concerti	ergogram	highbred	masterly	postfree	sorcerer
sauropod	Arcturus	concerto	erigeron	highbrow	measured	postural	Southron
scalepan	armoured	conferee	esoteric	higherup	membered	posturer	spagyric
scarfpin	armourer	conferva	estuaril	hinderer	menstrua	potterer	spandrel
schnapps	autocrat	conjurer	ethnarch	historic	mensural	powdered	spandril
scotopic	aviatrix	conjuror	eupatrid	hitherto	mercuric	premorse	spectral
scrapped	axletree	conserve	euphoria	hologram	mesmeric	preparer	spectrum
scrapper	baccarat	construe	euphoric	homebred	mesotron	preserve	squadron
septuple	backdrop	contorno	Eurocrat	homebrew	meteoric	procurer	squirrel
sextuple	bacteria	converge	exlibris	honourer	micrurgy	properly	stairrod
sheeppen	ballyrag	converse	exoteric	humoured	minstrel	property	statured
shrimper	balmoral	copperas	explorer	hysteria	miscarry	puggaree	stingray
sinciput	banderol	corduroy	extrorse	hysteric	mobocrat	purebred	submerge
smallpox	bannered	corporal	falderal	ideogram	Moharram	purpuric	submerse
snakepit	banneret	cothurni	fanfaron	ignitron	monaural	purpurin	subserve
southpaw	bannerol	coumarin	fatherly	incurred	monocrat	Quakerly	subshrub
stinkpot	banterer	cowberry	favoured	inferred	monogram	raindrop	sufferer
stockpot	barbaric	creatrix	favourer	infrared	motherly	rapparee	summerly
strapped	barberry	criteria	featured	inquirer	mowburnt	raptures	sunburnt
strapper	barterer	cromorna	features	inspired	Muharram	recharge	sunburst
stripped	bastardy	cromorne	fenberry	inspirer	mulberry	recourse	sunderer
stripper	bayberry	cryotron	filagree	inspirit	murderer	rectoral	sunwards
stropped	bedstraw	cultural	filigree	integral	murmurer	recurred	susurrus
strumpet	beggarly	cultured	finedraw	interred	musktree	reedwren	tabouret
subtopia	berberis	culverin	fingered	interrex	mutterer	reemerge	tafferel
sweetpea	besmirch	cutpurse	firearms	introrse	namedrop	referral	tamperer
syncopal	betatron	dastardy	firebrat	irongram	nanogram	referred	tartaric
tailspin	bilberry	deathray	firetrap	irongrey	nectared	rehearse	teaparty
terrapin	binaural	debarred	flanerie	isobaric	negatron	renderer	teardrop
tetrapla	biomorph	decagram	flatiron	isomeric	neoteric	repairer	telegram
tetrapod	bitterly	decigram	flexural	isomorph	nocturne	rerearch	telluric
tholepin	biyearly	declarer	flowered	jabberer	nomogram	research	tempered
threeply	bloodred	deferral	flowerer	jackaroo	nonjuror	resource	temperer
thumbpot	boottree	deferred	floweret	jackeroo	nonmoral	restorer	temporal
tittuped	borderer	deferrer	folderol	jamboree	nonparty	retiarii	temporal
tittuppy	bourtree	demiurge	forborne	jeopardy	numberer	retrorse	tenderly
tragopan	bowsprit	democrat	formerly	jiggered	nurturer	rhetoric	Tenebrae
turnspit	brethren	demurred	forwards	kangaroo	occurred	rooftree	terebrae
uncapped	brickred	demurrer	fosterer	kedgeree	ocularly	rosetree	terraria
uncouple	buckaroo	deterred	freshrun	kilogram	oilfired	runnerup	tesserae
underpin	budgeree	deterrer	froufrou	kingcrab	oldworld	sacraria	tesseral
undraped	bullfrog	deuteron	funebral	klystron	oligarch	sailorly	tetrarch
unshaped	bullyrag	devourer	furfural	labourer	onehorse	sandarac	textural
untapped	bummaree	dewberry	furfuran	landarmy	oratorio	sangaree	textured
unzipped	bunkered	dieldrin	gasfired	landcrab	outburst	sanserif	theocrat
walloper	Burberry	dihedral	gasworks	lanneret	outHerod	Sanskrit	timbered
wingspan	caesural	dihybrid	gatherer	latterly	outstrip	Sauterne	tinkerer
wrestpin	calcaria	dioptric	gematria	lawyerly	outwards	sawhorse	tommyrot
wristpin	calthrop	dipteral	gendarme	leapfrog	outworks	scenario	tomogram
Xantippe	cantoris	dipteran	germfree	lecturer	overarch	sceptred	tomorrow
applique	carburet	disagree	gestural	leisured	overcrop	sciagram	torturer
boutique	carefree	disarray	gillaroo	lethargy	overdraw	scombrid	totterer
colloquy	castiron	disburse	gingerly	lettered	overdrew	scotfree	traverse
critique	cauldron	disgorge	glycerin	linearly	overgrew	seaborne	treefrog
moresque	causerie	disperse	glycerol	lingerer	overgrow	seafarer	tricorne
mystique	cellarer	dispirit	glyceryl	lingerie	oxymoron	seahorse	triforia
physique	cellaret	disserve	godwards	lipogram	palterer	seapurse	trimaran
pratique	cercaria	ditherer	gramarye	litharge	pamperer	seawards	trimeric
abhorred	cerebral	doctoral	gramercy	littoral	parterre	sectoral	truebred
abhorrer	cerebrum	doddered	greegree	logogram	passerby	sensoria	turmeric
absterge	chaldron	dodderer	gridiron	loiterer	pastoral	Sephardi	unawares
acentric	chambray	dogberry	grisgris	Lollardy	pastural	sesterce	unbarred
adularia	chaperon	dogeared	groogroo	longeron	peardrop	setscrew	unchurch
aerogram	chemurgy	doggerel	guttural	lookeron	pectoral	sewerrat	underrun
agitprop	children	dogtired	gynocrat	lopeared	pedigree	sheeprun	unfairly
airborne	chimeric	dotterel	hairgrip	lothario	perforce	shikaree	universe
airscrew	choleric	drynurse	halfbred	louvered	perjurer	shivaree	unlearnt
airstrip	chondrus	dungaree	halteres	lubberly	perverse	shoetree	unpaired
alizarin	cicatrix	dutyfree	handgrip	lumberer	pickerel	sickerly	uvularly
amphorae	claptrap	dynatron	hangeron	Lutheran	pictures	sidearms	vampiric
amphoras	cleverly	easterly	hausfrau	mackerel	pilferer	sidedrum	vapourer
anasarca	cockcrow	echogram	hedgerow	malaprop	Pindaric	silverly	variorum
anchoret	cockerel	electret	henparty	mandarin	pizzeria	sisterly	veneerer
angstrom	coistrel	electric	herbaria	mandorla	plastron	skiagram	venturer
anhedral	collared	electron	Hesperus	mannered	plectrum	skywards	veratrin

```
veratrum contessa immersed squarson allottee brunette depictor factotum
verderce coulisse imprison stenosed amiantus bulletin deportee falcated
verderor crevasse intarsia stenosis amitotic burletta deserter falsetto
verdured culdesac intersex sternson amniotic bursitis despatch felsitic
vesperal curassow jalousie stylised amoretti cadastre despotic fenestra
vesturer cyanoses jettison subbasal amoretto calcitic detector ferreter
victoria cyanosis joyously supposal anabatic calyptra detrital ferritic
vigneron cyclosis Judaiser supposed analytic canaster detritus fibrotic
visceral damassin Jurassic surmisal ancestor canister deviator filmstar
vulgarly deceased kolinsky surmiser ancestry caryatid deviltry fivestar
Walkyrie declasse kromesky sweetsop animator cassette devoutly fluently
wallaroo demersal kurtosis symposia anisette catheter diabetes fomenter
wanderer despiser kyphosis synapsis anteater caudated diabetic footstep
wanderoo diabasic lacrosse syndesis aoristic cerastes dialytic forestal
warhorse dialyser lambaste synopses aperitif chapatti diameter forestay
waxberry dialyses largesse synopsis aplastic chapiter dicrotic forested
waxworks dialysis licensed tachisme arcuated chaunter dictator forester
wayfarer diapason licensee tachiste ardently chauntry didactic forestry
wellbred dichasia licenser tenonsaw argentic chiastic dietetic fourstar
westerly diereses lordosis thickset aromatic christen digester fremitus
wetnurse dieresis machismo timously arrantly christie dioritic frenetic
whimbrel diffuser magnesia touristy arrestee Christly directly frighten
whittret diocesan malvasia travesty arrester chupatti director frisette
winterly diseased mantissa Triassic arrestor chupatty disaster furcated
wiredraw disposal marmoset tribasic artistic ciliated disinter gadgetry
wistaria disposer methysis unbiased artistry clematis dispatch galactic
wisteria distaste moccasin uncaused asbestic climatic diuretic galeated
withdraw diuresis molasses unchaste asbestos cloister dogmatic gamester
withdrew duchesse molossus undersea assenter closeted dogwatch gangster
ziggurat ecclesia narcissi underset assentor cobaltic domestic ganister
zoiatria ellipses narcoses unhoused assertor cockatoo doomster garotter
zoomorph ellipsis narcosis unloosen assorted cofactor doorstep garreted
abacuses embosser necrosis unperson athletic cogently doorstop garrotte
abomasum embussed neuroses unreason atlantes collator dragster gasmeter
abomasus emphases neurosis unversed Atlantic commuter dramatic gelastic
abscissa emphasis nimbused utiliser attested computer dynastic geodetic
accursed empoison noblesse venously attester concetti ebriated geometer
acidosis endorsee occlusal vibrissa attestor concetto eclectic geometry
advowson endorser odiously vinously attrited confetti ecliptic gerontic
agonised entresol outcaste waterski atwitter coquetry ecstatic gigantic
alfresco enuresis oviposit whoreson aubretia coquette educated goadster
ambrosia epinasty oxidiser zoonosis Augustan cornetcy educator gogetter
amitosis epitasis ozoniser abductor augustly cornetti effector gramatom
anabases espousal paduasoy abjectly autistic cornetto egoistic granitic
anabasis espouser Parmesan abruptly backstay corseted eldritch graviton
analyser espresso partisan absentee baguette corsetry elenctic grisette
analyses eupepsia petrosal absently balletic corvette elevated gunmetal
analysis evanesce pharisee absinthe baluster cosmetic elevator gusseted
anthesis excursus phthisic accentor banditry covertly elliptic gyrostat
apodoses exegesis phthisis accepter banditti credited embattle haematic
apodosis extensor pianiste acceptor banister creditor embitter haematin
apresski famously potassic accoutre barbette crenated emeritus haliotis
assassin fantasia promisee accustom barbital crepitus Emmental hamartia
assessor Fascista promiser aconitic barrator crosstie emphatic harlotry
atomiser Fascisti promisor aconitum barratry cryostat emulator heighten
ballista fibrosis proposal acoustic barrette culottes enclitic helmeted
banausic finnesko proposer acrostic basaltic curveted enclothe hermetic
bethesda focussed protasis actuator basketry Cushitic endostea herpetic
bimbashi forensic protista adamitic bathetic cutwater enfetter hidrotic
bioassay fougasse provisor adductor bathotic cyanotic enswathe hieratic
bobbysox framesaw psilosis adenitis bauxitic cystitis entoptic hobbitry
britzska galluses pugnosed adiantum beeeater czaritza enuretic holistic
cactuses gambeson quickset adjuster befitted dalmatic enzootic honestly
carousal garrison releasee adjustor begetter dancette epicotyl hospital
carousel geodesic releaser admitted begotten dancetty eremitic housetop
carouser gneissor releasor adroitly belittle daughter errantly huckster
cavesson goingson remissly adulator besotted decanter errantry hypnotic
chainsaw grandson repousse aegrotat biometry decently eucritic icewater
charisma guernsey reprisal aerostat bisector declutch eupeptic idolater
cineaste gummosis reversal affected blacktie decretal eustatic idolatry
cleanser gymnasia reverser affecter blacktop deemster eutectic illfated
closeset harasser Romansch afflatus blighter defector executor imitator
coalesce heliosis rubbishy aflutter boughten dejected exegetic immortal
cognesce hidrosis Rumansch agitator breasted demented exhorter impacted
colossal hocussed sacristy aglitter breveted dementia expertly importer
colossus hydroski sargasso agnostic brewster demitted expiator imposter
composed hypnoses sharpset agrestic brighten dentated exporter impostor
composer hypnosis siriasis aigrette brightly departed exserted inceptor
concasse idoliser soothsay allotted brocatel depicter eyewater indebted
```

```
inductee momentum pochette roulette synoptic verboten diapause masseuse
inductor monastic podiatry roundtop tabletop verditer disabuse miscount
industry monistic polestar sabbatic talented veristic disbound misdoubt
inedited moquette pollster sadistic tanistry viameter discount mistrust
infantry muriatic polluter sagittal tapestry vibrator dismount moisture
infector muscatel poristic scimitar tapwater vignette displume molecule
infilter musketry potently screwtop tarlatan villatic distrust moribund
inflated myelitis potlatch sculptor teamster violator dividual muckluck
inflator myositic predator seamster teetotal vitiator doghouse muskduck
inflatus myositis prelatic seawater teetotum whitetie doldrums newfound
injector myosotis prenatal sebesten tenantry zealotry dormouse nonesuch
inositol narcotic priestly secretin testator zeolitic downturn numskull
inserted narrator Primates secretly testatum zoolater drawtube nuthouse
insulter Nearctic promoter secretor Thanatos zoolatry dumfound obstruct
intently necrotic prompter selectee theistic zoometry durukuli opercula
intertie NeoLatin promptly selector thematic absolute dyestuff opuscula
invected neonatal pronator semantic thirster abstruse elkhound opuscule
inventor nepenthe protatic semester threaten airbrush epifauna outbound
inverted neuritic pruritic semiotic throated alehouse eventual outhouse
inverter neuritis pruritus sempster throstle alleluia exergual overbusy
investor neurotic pubertal septette throttle allround exposure overhung
isolator noisette pulpiter seriatim thruster although farflung overjump
isometry nomistic pulsator serrated thwarter altitude fatigues overmuch
jackstay nonmetal punditry servitor thwartly aperture faubourg overrule
japhetic nuthatch puppetry sextette tinnitus applause fauteuil overture
jesuitic objector puristic Shemitic toiletry aptitude filature overturn
jesuitry obtected pyelitis Sheraton toilette aqualung finitude pantsuit
jiujitsu occultly quaestor sidestep tomentum aqueduct floccule paraquat
juristic odometer quaintly sigmatic topnotch archduke flocculi paroquet
klephtic ohmmeter quixotic silently toreutic arethusa fogbound pedicure
knightly oleaster quixotry silvatic traditor armature footmuff perilune
kyphotic omelette rabbiter Sinaitic trimeter attitude footrule picayune
lamented operatic rabbitry sinister truantry auricula foxhound piecrust
latently operator rachitic situated truistic avifauna fracture pirarucu
laudator operetta rachitis skeletal tsaritsa babirusa fraenula playsuit
laughter orgastic radiator skeleton tsaritza bankrupt frustule pleasure
leucitic oriental rambutan slightly tungsten bedeguar furlough postlude
levanter oriented ramentum societal tungstic bellbuoy gashouse potbound
libretis osteitis rebuttal Socratic turreted bellpull gastrula pothouse
libretto outdated rebutted songster udometer bellpush geniture preclude
lignitic outmatch rebutter spicated umbrette berceuse glandule pressure
loadstar outwatch recently spinster unabated biannual golddust profound
lockstep ovaritis receptor spirited unbeaten bisexual goldrush propound
lodestar overstay redactor spiritus unbolted bistoury habitual protrude
logistic overstep redistil splatter unbottle blastula habitude punctual
lomentum oximeter redwater splinter unbutton blesbuck hamululi puncture
longstop palestra reedstop splitter unclothe bouzouki handcuff pushpull
lordotic palmette refitted splutter undertow brimfull hebetude Quechuan
magister palmetto register sprinter unedited brochure henequen quidnunc
magmatic palmitin registry squatted unfasten burnouse hiccough quietude
magnetic papistic regrater squatter unfetter bushbuck hothouse quincunx
magneton papistry rejecter squinter unfitted calctuff hulahula ramequin
Mahratta parental remittal squirter ungotten calycule hushhush readjust
Mahratti pargeter remitted stealthy unjustly capitula icebound reassure
maieutic parietal remittee stenotic unlisted carnauba illiquid reinsure
mainstay parrotry remitter stiletto unmeetly cartouch immature reneguer
majestic patentee repartee stipites unseated catapult inasmuch reoccupy
maltster patently repeater stomatal unsettle centaury insecure residual
mandator patentor repenter stomatic unstated chipmeal insomuch residuum
maneater pathetic reporter straiten unsuited chipmunk instruct resolute
mannitol pedantic repotted straitly unswathe chirrupy intitule resprung
maquette pedantry requital streeted untented chopsuey involute restcure
marketer pedestal requiter strictly unwanted cincture jealousy reticule
masseter periotic resetter strontia unwonted coaldust jodhpurs retinula
mastitis perlitic resettle strutted unworthy cocksure jointure revolute
mediator petuntse resister strutter uplifter coiffure jumpsuit ridicule
mementos phonetic resistor subtitle uprooter compound juncture rosebush
mephitic phreatic resorter subtotal upsetter conclude kisscurl rubicund
mephitis phyletic retorted summitry uralitic confound latitude saltbush
meristem picketer reverter sunbathe urgently costpush lawcourt schedule
meristic pilaster revetted supertax uvulitis cramfull lifebuoy scrofula
migrator pileated revolter syenitic vacantly creature ligature seamount
mimester pinaster rheostat sylvatic valuator cubature lodicule seamouse
minister pinnated rhinitis symmetry varactor cynosure madhouse sederunt
ministry piscator rimester sympathy varietal dandruff malamute selcouth
mismatch plaister roadster synaptic varletry danseuse malemute selfrule
modestly plankton robustly synastry Vedantic deafmute Mameluke semibull
molester pliantly rocketry syncytia vendetta denature manicure seminude
momently plighted romantic syndetic verbatim destruct maroquin shadbush
```

```
shantung dundiver giveaway aldehyde chalazae ascidian buckbean cortical
shelduck effluvia golliwog amethyst embezzle assignat bulkhead cosmical
sinecure engraver guideway anaglyph emblazon Assyrian bullhead cotquean
soapsuds enslaver hallowed aneurysm howitzer astragal bullyrag crackjaw
sobstuff festival hatchway antitype kalaazar Athenian cableway cragsman
solitude forgiven hereaway autodyne kibitzer atypical caducean crashpad
sonobuoy gingival hideaway autogyro kreutzer Augustan caesural criminal
sourpuss hangover hollowly autolyse mansized aurelian calcspar critical
sparbuoy holdover ingrowth autotype partizan aurorean calendar Croatian
spherule improver interwar betrayal protozoa autocrat Cambrian crossbar
squamule interval limetwig betrayer sporozoa autumnal Canadian crossway
stardust khedival manpower bosseyed squeezer avadavat cannibal cryostat
subacute lawgiver mellowly catalyse terrazzo baccarat cannulae cuboidal
surfduck leftover motorway catalyst trapezia bacillar cannular culdesac
surmount longeval mulloway cockeyed unfrozen backchat cannulas cultivar
surround lowlevel narrowly coenzyme unglazed backseat cantonal cultural
swimsuit medieval newlywed conveyer unmuzzle backstay capsular Cumbrian
taciturn midwives outlawry conveyor ———————— Baconian cardigan cycleway
tainture misgiven pandowdy defrayal abbatial Bactrian cardinal cyclical
tamboura moreover polliwog dewyeyed abnormal bailsman carnival cypselae
taphouse moshavim pollywog disloyal Accadian baldhead Carolean dactylar
teahouse observer regrowth employee achenial ballyrag carousal dairyman
tearduct onceover reviewal employer aciculae balmoral cartload dalesman
tenacula outrival reviewer epiphyte acicular bandsman castaway daybreak
testtube Passover ridgeway epistyle aciculas barbican cathodal daydream
thesauri primeval riverway eucalypt acidhead barbital causeway deadbeat
thorough pullover scalawag eyerhyme actiniae bargeman celeriac deadhead
timefuse pushover shadower fireeyed actinian baronial cellular deathcap
tincture receiver slideway foureyes actinias bartizan cerebral deathray
titmouse reconvey soakaway gargoyle acturial basidial cerulean decagram
tournure reliever sorrower genotype Adamical Batavian cervelat decigram
tranquil replevin speedway geophyte Adlerian battleax cervical decretal
transude reproval spillway gunlayer advocaat Bavarian cetacean deferral
treasure reserved stairway hawkeyed aegrotat beadsman chainsaw defrayal
treasury resurvey sternway homonymy aerogram bedeguar chairman Delphian
tressure revolver stowaway hypogyny aerostat bedstead chalazae demersal
unsprung screever takeaway Kaffiyeh aestival bedstraw Chaldean democrat
unstrung sealevel tearaway logotype agaragar beebread chambray demoniac
unvalued shedevil teatowel lynxeyed agential Bermudas charcoal demonian
upsprung shrieval threeway lysozyme agrarian bestowal Chellean deprival
upthrust slipover tightwad metonymy airwoman betrayal chemical detrital
usufruct stopover trackway misogyny Akkadian bezonian chessman Devonian
verecund survival underway monocyte Albanian biannual Chinaman diaconal
vermouth survivor walkaway monogyny alderman biblical chitchat diagonal
viscount takeover wallower monotype alleyway biennial chutzpah diarchal
windburn toplevel waterway neophyte allodial bifacial cinnabar dihedral
woodpulp triumvir wellaway openeyed alluvial bilabial Circaean diluvial
woodruff tsarevna williwaw paralyse alogical billhead circular diluvian
wrymouth turnover windowed paroxysm Alsatian billycan cislunar diocesan
yoghourt upheaval winnower perigyny alveolar binaural civilian diplomat
absolver walkover yellowly polygyny amadavat binomial clansman dipteral
achiever whatever anorexia porphyry American biocidal claptrap dipteran
aestival whenever anorexic prostyle ammoniac bioassay clearway disarray
alewives wherever apomixis purveyor amnesiac birthday clerical disloyal
amadavat whomever asphyxia sentrygo amoebean bisexual clinical disposal
approval alleyway ataraxia sloeeyed amphorae blackcap coachman dispread
archival bestowal ataraxic storeyed amphoras blahblah cochleae dittybag
archives borrower cachexia Strepyan ampullae bluecoat cochlear dividual
avadavat broadway carboxyl subphyla Anglican boatload cockboat doctoral
believer burrower cathexes surroyal anhedral Bodleian coleslaw doomsday
bereaved cableway cathexis surveyor antennae Boeotian colonial doomsman
beslaver castaway caudexes synonymy antennal bogeyman colossal downbeat
biconvex causeway convexly taxpayer antennas bohemian columnal drachmae
brakevan clearway dyslexia thankyou antheral bondsman columnar drachmai
carnival crossway dyslexic toponymy aphasiac bonehead comedian drachmas
codriver cycleway geotaxis trachyte apiarian bonemeal communal dragoman
cognovit deflower hydroxyl triglyph approval boxpleat compleat dragsman
conniver driftway inflexed triptych Aramaean brachial condylar driftway
cordovan driveway larynxes urostyle arbitral bracteal conidial driveway
corrival eschewal matrixes walleyed arboreal Bradshaw conjugal drophead
cultivar everyway panmixia Wesleyan Arcadian brainpan conoidal dropleaf
deceiver fadeaway prolixly wideeyed archaean brakeman consular drumhead
decemvir fellowly reflexed wildeyed archival brakevan coolabah dryclean
depraved floodway syrinxes wooldyed Armagnac Briarean coolibah dumbhead
deprival foldaway thoraxes zoophyte Armenian brickbat coplanar duodenal
deprived follower thyroxin alguazil Arminian broadway copperas dustcoat
discover followon vertexes anthozoa armorial brougham cordovan Dutchman
dishevel followup vortexes bartizan arterial browbeat corporal echogram
dissever Galloway aerodyne bedazzle artesian bryozoan corrival Egyptian
```

emetical	forehead	Hertzian	laywoman	mulloway	patellae	rehoboam	sidereal
Emmental	forepeak	hetaerae	leadsman	muscular	patellar	reinsman	sideroad
empyreal	foreplay	hetairai	legbreak	musician	paternal	remedial	sidesman
empyrean	forestal	hexagram	liegeman	mycelial	patronal	remittal	Silurian
encrinal	forestay	hibernal	lifeboat	mystical	pattypan	reprisal	simoniac
Ephesian	formulae	hideaway	linesman	mythical	pectoral	reproval	singular
epidural	formulas	hielaman	Linnaean	nanogram	peculiar	requital	siphonal
episodal	forspeak	highroad	lipogram	national	pedestal	residual	sirenian
Erastian	forswear	Hogmanay	littoral	nautical	Pegasean	reversal	skeletal
ergogram	fourleaf	hogshead	loadstar	nenuphar	Pelagian	reviewal	skiagram
erotical	fourstar	hologram	lodestar	neonatal	pemmican	Rhaetian	skinhead
eschewal	foveolae	hoofbeat	logician	neuronal	pendular	rheostat	skullcap
Eskimoan	framesaw	hooligan	logogram	newspeak	perigean	rhonchal	slagheap
especial	freedman	Horatian	longboat	nicotian	perineal	ricercar	slideway
espousal	freeload	hormonal	longeval	nightcap	peroneal	rickshaw	sliproad
Esquimau	freshman	hornbeam	loveseat	nighthag	personae	ridgeway	snackbar
Estonian	Freudian	horsecar	lubrical	nightjar	personal	rifleman	sneeshan
ethereal	Friesian	horseman	Lucullan	Noachian	Peruvian	ringroad	snipsnap
etherial	fruitbat	hospital	lunarian	nobleman	petiolar	riparian	soakaway
ethnical	fugleman	houseman	Lutheran	nomogram	petrosal	riverman	societal
Etrurian	funebral	huntsman	mackinaw	nonhuman	Phrygian	riverway	Socinian
Etruscan	funereal	hymenial	madrigal	nonlegal	physical	Romanian	softhead
Eurasian	funnyman	hypogeal	madwoman	nonmetal	piacular	roodbeam	softsoap
Eurocrat	furculae	hypogean	Maecenas	nonmoral	pinnular	rosarian	somedeal
European	furcular	icecream	magician	Norseman	pipeclay	roseleaf	somewhat
eventual	furfural	ideogram	mailboat	Northman	piscinae	roseolar	soothsay
everyday	furfuran	illtreat	mainstay	notarial	pivotman	Rotarian	sorehead
everyman	galangal	Illyrian	malarial	notional	placeman	rubrical	soterial
everyway	Galilean	imaginal	malarian	noumenal	planulae	Rumanian	southpaw
exemplar	Gallican	immortal	maltreat	novercal	planular	rustical	sowbread
exergual	Galloway	imperial	mamillae	nutarian	plebeian	saccular	spacebar
exordial	Georgian	inchmeal	mamillar	nymphean	plumular	sackcoat	spaceman
external	germinal	Indiaman	Mandaean	obsidian	podagral	sagittal	sparkgap
facetiae	gestural	inertial	maniacal	occlusal	poetical	sailboat	spatular
fadeaway	Ghanaian	infernal	manorial	Odyssean	polestar	salariat	spearman
fairlead	gilthead	informal	manurial	offbreak	polyzoan	Salesian	spectral
falderal	gingival	inguinal	marginal	official	popinjay	salesman	specular
faltboat	giveaway	inimical	marjoram	olympiad	postural	Salopian	speedway
familial	globular	integral	marksman	Olympian	praedial	samizdat	spiculae
familiar	goldleaf	internal	marshman	oogonial	prandial	sandarac	spicular
fancyman	gonidial	interval	marzipan	openplan	prehuman	Sangreal	spillway
farcical	goodyear	interwar	masthead	ophidian	premolar	Saturday	splenial
Faustian	gownsman	irenical	material	optician	prenatal	saucepan	sporular
favonian	Graafian	Irishman	maternal	optional	pressman	savannah	springal
feastday	granddad	ironclad	matronal	oracular	primeval	scalawag	spurgear
feedhead	granular	irongray	maxillae	Orcadian	prodigal	scalepan	squawman
feldspar	grosbeak	ironical	medieval	oriental	proemial	Scandian	stairway
fernshaw	guardian	isogonal	memorial	original	proposal	scapulae	staminal
ferryman	guideway	isthmian	mensural	outbreak	proximal	scapular	statical
festival	gunmetal	jackstay	menswear	outrival	Prussian	scapulas	sternway
fiducial	guttural	Jacobean	meridian	overbear	pterylae	scenical	stickjaw
filariae	gynocrat	jeremiad	metazoan	overcoat	pubertal	schiedam	stingray
filarial	gyrostat	Jeremiah	metrical	overdraw	publican	sciagram	stipular
filmstar	habitual	jeroboam	micellar	overhead	punctual	scimitar	stockcar
fimbriae	Haggadah	jerrican	microbar	overhear	puparial	scopulae	stockman
finedraw	Halachah	jerrycan	Milesian	overheat	pupillar	scopulas	stomatal
fireboat	halfbeak	jolthead	millibar	overleaf	puppyfat	Scotsman	storeman
firebrat	handclap	Jonathan	minutiae	overleap	pussycat	sealyham	stowaway
fireclay	handicap	Judaical	mistreat	overload	pustular	seasonal	Strepyan
fireopal	handyman	judicial	mistrial	overplay	pygidial	sectoral	stuntman
firetrap	hardhead	Jugoslav	mobocrat	overseas	pygmaean	seedcoat	subahdar
fishmeal	hareseal	jumpseat	Moharram	overstay	pyrexial	seedleaf	subbasal
fistical	harpseal	kalaazar	monachal	overwear	Quechuan	seedsman	subhuman
fistulae	harridan	khedival	monaural	padishah	raftsman	selfheal	sublunar
fistular	hatchway	Khmerian	monaxial	pagurian	railhead	septimal	subsolar
fivestar	hausfrau	kickshaw	moneybag	palatial	railroad	sequelae	subtotal
flambeau	havildar	kilogram	monkseal	pancreas	raincoat	serpulae	suburban
flatboat	Hawaiian	kingcrab	monocrat	papillae	rainwear	sewergas	subvocal
flathead	headgear	knitwear	monogram	papillar	rambutan	sewerrat	succubae
flexural	headsman	lackaday	monomial	parallax	ranarian	shanghai	suicidal
flimflam	hebdomad	laconian	moonbeam	paraquat	ranchero	Shekinah	Sumerian
flipflap	Hegelian	lacrimal	Moravien	parental	rasorial	shipload	superman
floodway	heliacal	lacrymal	motional	parietal	rataplan	shortday	supernal
foldaway	helmsman	lallygag	motorcar	Parmesan	reappear	showboat	supertax
foldboat	henchman	lamellae	motorial	Parthian	rebuttal	shrieval	supplial
foolscap	herdsman	lamellar	motorman	partisan	regional	Siberian	supposal
footgear	hereaway	landcrab	motorway	partizan	rectoral	Sicilian	surfboat
footwear	hernshaw	landsman	mouseear	pastoral	referral	sickflag	surgical
forebear	heroical	Langshan	Muharram	pastural	regional	sidehead	surmisal

```
surroyal unifilar misdoubt conjunct forelock moorcock research triptych
survival unipolar passerby contract fullback mordancy resource tristich
syncopal unisonal seedlobe convince gamecock mossback restrict tuppence
syndical univocal testtube cornetcy gavelock muckluck retrench turnback
synovial unsocial wardrobe coronach genetics muskduck retroact turncock
syzygial unthread abeyance credence gentrice nascence rickrack twopence
taberdar upheaval abeyancy cromlech geomancy nascency riddance twopiece
tablemat upstream abidance crummock gimcrack necklace ringneck typeface
tactical vaccinal abstract currency glyptics nicknack rollneck ultimacy
Tahitian vacuolar abstrict cutprice goalkick nonesuch Romansch unchancy
tailcoat valerian accuracy dabchick gralloch nonstick roofrack unchurch
takeaway valvulae acreinch deadlock gramercy normalcy rucksack unclench
talesman valvular adequacy declutch graphics nuisance Rumansch unclinch
talisman varietal advocacy defiance gripsack numeracy sackrace underact
tallyman variolar affiance delegacy guidance nuthatch salience usufruct
Tamilian vascular airspace delicacy gunstock obduracy saliency vagrancy
tarlatan venereal alebench denounce halfback obstruct saltlick valiance
Tarpeian Venetian alfresco derelict handpick oiticica sandwich valiancy
teabread Venusian alliance despatch hardback oligarch sapience vambrace
teabreak verandah allspice destruct hardhack onepiece sapphics variance
tearaway verrucae almanack deviance hardtack onetrack sciatica verdancy
teetotal vertical ambiance deviancy havelock opulence scirocco vergence
telegram vesperal ambience diestock hawfinch ordnance scottice verjuice
temporal vesuvian anasarca diffract haystack outmatch seapiece veronica
Tenebrae vicarial angelica dipstick headlock outreach seawrack vibrancy
tenonsaw virginal announce disbench headrace outwatch semplice violence
tenurial viridian anyplace disfrock hedonics overarch sentence vivisect
terebrae visceral approach disgrace hepatica overmuch sequence voidance
terminal visional aqueduct disjunct herdwick overnice sesterce wardance
tesserae vortical artefact dispatch hierarch paleface shabrack waterice
tesseral walkaway artifact displace highjack parlance shaddock welldeck
textural warragal artifice distance hogsback patience shamrock wheyface
theocrat warrigal audience distinct holdback peccancy shelduck windsock
thespian watchman avionics distract homesick pendency sherlock wolfpack
thetical watergas backpack district humpback penstock shoelace woodcock
threeway waterman ballcock dogwatch idiolect perforce sidekick woodlice
Thursday waterway bareback dormancy impolicy pharmacy sithence woolpack
tiebreak welladay barranca drammock inasmuch picklock sixpence woolsack
tightwad wellaway barranco drawback indirect pinprick skerrick zoomancy
toadflax wellhead basilica driftice insomuch piperack skewback zwieback
toboggan wellread bechance dropkick instance piquancy skipjack Abbaside
tommygar Wellsian benedick drommack instancy pirarucu slapjack accolade
tomogram Welshman benedict dynamics instinct pittance solstice actinide
tonedeaf Wesleyan benefice earpiece instruct plastics solvency adenoids
toroidal wheatear besmirch efficacy interact playback spardeck aldehyde
townsman wheelman blatancy ekistics intimacy polemics spherics algicide
tracheae whimwham blesbuck eldritch intrench politick staylace altitude
tracheal whinchat boatdeck elegance isocracy politico stopcock anaconda
trackman whitecap boldface elegancy issuance politics suberect antecede
trackway williwaw boniface eminence iterance populace subtract antibody
tragical wingbeat booklice eminency japonica potlatch succinct antinode
tragopan wingspan bootjack encroach jaundice poultice sundance antipode
tramrod  wiredraw bootlace ensconce jetblack practice surfduck aphicide
trappean withdraw brassica ensigncy joystick precinct surplice aptitude
triaxial woodchat brattice entrance kickback preelect swanneck aquacade
tribunal woodsman brettice entrench kinesics prentice swayback arsenide
trifocal wordplay buoyancy ethnarch kinetics presence tailback attitude
trigonal workaday bushbuck eugenics knapsack pretence tailrace autocade
trimaran wormgear carapace evanesce lambency prophecy tamarack backside
tripeman yataghan cartouch evidence laverock prospect tangency badlands
tripodal Yugoslav cataract exigence lenience protract tapdance bastardy
tritical zamindar celibacy exigency leniency province tapedeck beamends
tropical zemindar ceramics eyepiece licorice prudence tearduct bestride
troupial zenithal charlock facepack limerick psychics technics bestrode
Tunisian ziggurat chipmuck fallback linstock pullback tendence bethesda
Turanian zodiacal clarence fandance lipstick pungency tendency blockade
turbinal anaerobe classics fastback literacy radiance tenpence bookends
turbofan bathrobe clawback fatstock locofoco radiancy tetrarch Burgundy
Turcoman buncombe clemency feedback lovelock rampancy theodicy busybody
Turkoman bushbaby coalesce fervency lovesick reagency thridace camisade
turncoat carnauba coalsack fireback maiolica rearmice ticktack camisado
tutorial cobwebby coatrack firelock majolica redbrick ticktock charlady
Tyrolean conglobe codpiece flamenco maledict redirect tidelock chloride
underlap describe cognosce flapjack maverick reedmace toepiece coincide
underlay diatribe comeback flatrace mergence reliance topnotch commando
underman djellaba commence fluidics millrace renounce transact conclude
underway drawtube commerce footpace mismatch reproach transect dastardy
unfilial inscribe complice footrace misplace rerearch traprock defilade
uniaxial kohlrabi conflict foredeck moonface reremice tribrach diopside
```

```
diploidy protrude anchoret blazoner chaunter crucifer disquiet estoppel
displode psalmody androgen bleacher Cherokee crueller dissever evildoer
dissuade quayside annulled blighter chickpea crusader ditherer examinee
dockside quietude answerer bloodred childbed cucumber divorcee examiner
dogsbody regicide anteater blueweed children culottes doddered exanthem
eldorado renegade antlered bobbinet chopsuey cultured dodderer excelled
enfilade renegado apodoses bobwheel christen cupelled dogeared excluder
escalade rhapsode appalled bonspiel cicisbei curveted dogfaced exequies
escapade rhapsody archives boottree cicisbeo customer doggerel exhorter
eventide ringside arcuated borderer ciliated cutwater dogooder expander
eyeshade roadside argufier borrower cirriped cyanogen dogtired expelled
feticide Samoyede armoured bosseyed citified cyanoses domineer expellee
finitude seawards armourer botflies cityfied cyclamen dominoes exploder
fireside selenide arranger boughten clarinet cyclopes doomster explorer
flipside selfmade arrestee boursier cleanser cylinder doorstep exporter
fluoride seminude arrester bourtree clerihew dahabieh dotterel exserted
forebode Sephardi articled bracelet clincher daughter douanier extender
forelady serenade ascender bractlet cloister deadener dowelled extolled
foreside silicide asperges branched closeset deathbed drabbler extremes
forwards skywards asphodel brancher closeted debagged dragomen eyeliner
forzando soapsuds assenter brandied clothier debarred dragonet eyewater
Ganymede solitude assignee brandnew cloudlet debugged dragster falcated
genocide somebody assorted breasted coccyges decanter drencher falconer
glissade stampede astonied breather cockerel deceased dribbler falconet
godwards stoccado atlantes breeches cockeyed deceiver dribblet fastener
Golconda stockade atomiser brethren codifier December dripfeed fatigues
Griselda suboxide attender breveted codriver decipher drownded fattener
habitude sulphide attested brewster cognomen declarer drupelet favoured
hacienda sunshade attester brickred cogwheel deemster duckweed favourer
handmade sunwards attorney brighten coistrel defender dulcimer featured
haploidy superadd attrited brindled colander deferred Dulcinea features
hebetude sylphide atwitter britches coleseed deferrer dundiver fedayeen
hexapody teacaddy auspices broacher collagen deflower dungaree feldsher
hillside threnode aweather brocaded collared deformed durables ferreter
hocktide threnody axletree brocatel colleger dejected dutyfree feverfew
hollands tomnoddy bagpiper brooklet coloured demander dyspnoea filagree
homebody transude balanced buckshee columned demented ebriated filigree
homemade trioxide balancer budgeree commoner demitted educated filmgoer
homicide unsteady ballonet bummaree commoney demobbed eighteen fingered
innuendo unwieldy baluster bunkered commuter demurred eighties finisher
ironside viricide banister burgonet compages demurrer electret fireeyed
jeopardy wetlands bannered burrower compiler dentated elevated fireweed
landlady yuletide banneret buttoner complier departed ellipses fissiped
lapicide aasvogel banterer bystreet composed depicter embalmer flatfeet
latitude abacuses barathea caballed composer deported embedded flaxseed
lemonade abhorred barterer cactuses computer depraved embitter fletcher
Lollardy abhorrer bassinet cadenced conceder deprived embolden flincher
lowgrade abridger bebopper calcanea conferee deserter embosser flockbed
mancando absentee becalmed calender confider designer embussed florigen
maravedi absolver bechamel calliper confiner despiser embracer flounder
marinade absorber bedimmed cameleer confines destrier emphases flowered
marrieds accepter bedmaker canaster congener detached employee flowerer
megapode accursed beeeater canister conjurer detailed employer floweret
midlands achiever befallen canzonet conniver detainee enarched flypaper
misguide adjuster befitted capellet consider detainer encipher flywheel
monopode adlibbed befogged caponier consoler deterred encumber focussed
monoxide admitted begetter carburet consumer deterrer endanger foliaged
neaptide advanced beginner carcanet convener devilled endorsee follower
nematode affected begirded carefree conveyer devourer endorser fomenter
noontide affecter begotten carolled corniced dewyeyed endostea fontanel
oeillade affirmer beguiler carousel corselet diabetes endpaper footstep
outwards aflutter beholden carouser corseted dialyser enfetter forcefed
override aglimmer beholder cascabel cortices dialyses enforcer forefeel
overrode aglitter believer cataloes coryphee diameter engender foregoer
overside agonised bereaved catheter costumer diarrhea engineer foreknew
palinode airliner berliner cathexes cottager didapper engraver foreseen
palisade airscrew besieger caudated cottagey diereses enlarger forested
pandowdy airspeed beslaver caudexes courtier diffuser enquirer forester
parlando Alderney besotted caudices coverlet digester enricher forgiven
peroxide alewives bespoken cavalier coworker diplogen enrolled fornices
persuade alkalies betrayer caverned cracknel disagree enslaver forrader
petalody allergen bevelled cavilled crannied disaster entailer forsaken
phyllode allotted beveller caviller cratches discover epistler fosterer
polypide allottee bewigged cellarer credited discreet equalled foureyes
polypody alphabet bewilder cellaret crenated diseased equipped fourteen
postcode ambusher biconvex cerastes crosslet dishevel equities frenzied
postlude anabases bindweed cervices crotched disinter espalier frescoes
preclude analyser birdseed chandler crotchet disorder espouser fribbler
proceeds analyses blackleg chapiter croupier disposer estopped frighten
```

```
frijoles honeybee lanneret milliner overdrew ponderer regrater scolices
frillies honeydew lapelled mimester overfeed pondweed reindeer scoopnet
frontier honourer larcener mimicked overflew pontifex rejecter scorcher
frontlet hotelier larynges mimicker overgrew postfree rejigger scotfree
frutices howitzer larynxes minister overseen posturer rejoicer scourger
furcated huckster latchkey minstrel overseer potholer releasee scragged
fusileer humoured latticed miscegen overstep potterer releaser scrammed
fusilier hydrogen laughter mischief overview powdered reliever scrannel
galeated hydromel launcher misgiven oxidiser prattler remember scrapped
galloper hypnoses lavender misnomer oximeter preacher reminder scrapper
galluses hypothec lawgiver mistaken oxpecker preparer remitted scrawler
gamester icewater lawmaker mittened ozoniser presager remittee screamer
gangster idolater lecturer modelled pacifier presumer remitter screener
ganister idoliser leftover modeller palmiped priedieu renderer screever
gardener illfated legioned modifier palterer Primates reneguer scrubbed
garganey illtimed leisured molasses pamperer prisoner renowned scrubber
garotter imagines lengthen molester pamphlet procurer renumber scutcher
garreted immersed lenticel monicker panelled producer repairer seafarer
gaselier impacted lettered MonKhmer panicked profaner repartee seagreen
gasfired impelled levanter moonshee panpipes profiler repealer sealevel
gasmeter impeller levelled moreover parakeet promisee repeater seamster
gasolier impolder leveller motormen parallel promiser repelled searcher
gastraea importer libelled mucrones parcener promoter repeller seasoner
gatherer imposter libellee muleteer pardoner prompter repenter seawater
gauntlet improper libeller multiped pargeter proposer replacer sebesten
geometer improver licensed murderer paroquet protegee reporter secluded
germfree impugner licensee murmurer partaken provided repotted seconder
gestagen included licenser murrelet Passover provider requiter selectee
ghettoes incurred lichened muscadel pastries puggaree reserved semester
glycogen indebted lingerer muscatel patentee pugnosed resetter sempster
goadster inductee lintseed muskdeer pathogen pullover resigned sentinel
Godspeed indulger listener musktree paysheet pulpiter resister serrated
gogetter inedited liveried muslined peagreen punisher resorter setscrew
gossamer inferred lockstep mutineer pearlies purebred restorer sewellel
gossiper infilter loiterer mutterer pectines purifier resurvey shadower
goutweed inflamer Londoner narcoses pedalier pursenet retailer shagreen
grabbler inflated loosener nectared pedalled pushover retainer shambles
gravamen inflexed lopeared negligee pedicled pyrrhoea retarded sharpset
greegree informed lopsided neuroses pedigree quarrier retarder sheepked
greenlet informer lorikeet newcomer perfumer queenlet retorted sheeppen
greffier infrared louvered newlywed perilled quencher revealer shielder
grimacer ingather lowlevel newsheet perisher quibbler revelled shiftkey
grizzled inlander lumberer newsreel perjurer quickset reveller shikaree
groschen inquirer lynxeyed nielloed petalled quillpen revenger shingler
grottoes inserted mackerel nimbused petioled rabbiter reverser shingles
grounder inspired magdalen nineteen petronel racegoer reverter shiralee
grumbler inspirer magicked nineties pharisee rachides revetted shivaree
gruntled insulter magister nitrogen Philomel ransomer reviewer shoetree
guernsey intended malarkey November photogen rapeseed revolter shoulder
gulfweed interbed maligner numberer pickerel rapparee revolver shrapnel
gunlayer internee malinger nurturer picketer raptures rewarder shredded
gusseted interred maltster oakegger pictures rarefied ricochet shredder
halfbred interrex maneater observer pilaster ratifier rimester shrimper
hallowed intersex mangabey obtainer pileated ravelled rivalled shrinker
halluces intruder mangonel obtected pilferer ravisher rivelled shrugged
halteres invected Manichee occluded pillager rawboned riverbed shrunken
hangover inverted mannered occupier pilsener rearview roadster shuffler
harasser inverter manpower occurred pinaster reasoner rockweed sickener
hardener irongrey mansized odometer pincenez reawaken roentgen sidestep
haruspex islander mantelet offender pinmoney rebelled romancer sideview
hastener jabberer marauder offsider pinnated rebeller rooftree silencer
havocked jamboree marketer ofttimes pinniped rebutted rosetree sinister
hawkeyed japanned marmoset ohmmeter pinwheel rebutter roturier siphonet
hawkweed jewelled martinet oilfired pitviper recapped roughhew situated
haymaker jeweller masseter oldtimer plaister receiver rummager sketcher
heathhen jiggered materiel oleander planchet reckoner Sadducee skindeep
heighten Judaiser matrices oleaster platelet reconvey salaried skittles
helmeted Kaffiyeh matrixes oligomer playgoer recorder sandflea slipover
helpmeet kedgeree measured onceover plighted recurred sangaree sloeeyed
henequen kerchief medalled onesided plougher redeemer sapgreen sloucher
Hercules kibitzer medaller onlooker plumaged redfaced sarcenet slugabed
highbred killdeer membered openeyed plumelet redwater sarsenet smoothen
hijacker knapweed menhaden oppugner plumiped reedwren sawbones smoulder
hinderer kneedeep meninges ordainer poisoner referred sawedoff smuggler
histogen kreutzer meristem oriented polisher refitted scanties snatcher
hocussed labelled mesdames outdated pollices reflexed sceptred sniffler
holdover labourer metalled outmoded pollster reformed schiller sniffles
homebred lamented midwives outrider polluter reformer schooner sniggler
homebrew lancelet milkweed outsider pomander register scilicet snitcher
```

snuffler	streeted	timbered	unhoused	whatever	simplify	flamingo	porridge
snuffles	stricken	tinkerer	unkennel	wheedler	sobstuff	floatage	posology
socalled	stridden	tittuped	unleaded	whenever	solidify	fontange	poundage
softener	stringed	together	unlimber	wherever	spaewife	foreedge	prejudge
solander	stringer	tomalley	unlinked	whiffler	standoff	frondage	prestige
solderer	stripped	tonepoem	unlisted	whimbrel	stellify	frontage	prolonge
solleret	stripper	toolshed	unloader	whistler	stratify	frottage	promulge
somewhen	stroller	toplevel	unloosen	whitener	stultify	fruitage	pupilage
songster	stropped	topliner	unmanned	whittret	Tartuffe	fullpage	quadriga
sorcerer	strucken	torturer	unmarked	whomever	tipstaff	furlough	reassign
sorochen	strummed	totalled	unopened	wideeyed	tradeoff	fuselage	recharge
sorrower	strummer	totterer	unpaired	wigmaker	unstuffy	gainings	redesign
spadices	strumpet	towelled	unpegged	wildeyed	unthrift	geophagy	reemerge
spadones	strutted	traducer	unpinned	windowed	wakerife	grillage	rheology
spalpeen	strutter	trailnet	unplaced	winnower	wildlife	hastings	rinsings
spandrel	stuccoes	trampler	unrigged	withdrew	woodruff	heritage	roadsign
sparkler	stumbler	transfer	unroofed	woodshed	writeoff	hiccough	roughage
sparklet	sturdied	trawlnet	unsealed	wooldyed	Yankeefy	hindlegs	rutabaga
spavined	stylised	treacher	unseated	woolshed	zinckify	homology	sabotage
specimen	suborder	treadler	unseeded	wormseed	absterge	horologe	scavenge
spicated	suborner	trembler	unshaped	wrangler	acierage	horology	scrounge
spicknel	sufferer	trembles	unstated	wreathen	adjutage	hustings	selvedge
spikelet	summoner	trencher	unsuited	wrestler	aerology	ideology	sentrygo
spinifex	sunbaked	trilobed	unsunned	wretched	agiotage	illusage	serology
spinster	sunderer	trimeter	untapped	wriggler	agrology	impetigo	sewerage
spirited	sundried	trochlea	untented	wristlet	algology	impledge	sexology
splasher	sundries	trophied	untether	yestreen	alienage	infringe	shortage
splatter	supplier	troutlet	untitled	yodelled	although	kneehigh	siftings
splinter	supplies	truckler	unvalued	yodeller	amperage	language	sinology
splitter	supposed	truebred	unversed	zoolater	antilogy	lashings	sitology
splutter	surfacer	tungsten	unvoiced	aircraft	apothegm	leavings	slippage
spoonfed	surmiser	turbaned	unwanted	airshaft	appanage	leggings	smallage
sprawler	sweepnet	turbojet	unwashed	alkalify	axiology	lethargy	solfeggi
spreader	sweetpea	turnover	unweaned	ammonify	badinage	leverage	spillage
sprigged	swiftlet	turreted	unwished	autodafe	baronage	litharge	spoilage
springer	swindler	twaddler	unwonted	beautify	bearings	littlego	spousage
sprinter	switchel	twenties	unzipped	blastoff	begrudge	lodgings	squeedge
sprocket	synopses	twiddler	upholder	brushoff	beverage	mahjongg	staffage
spurrier	syringes	twinkler	uplander	bullyoff	birdcage	Mandingo	stallage
squaller	syrinxes	twitcher	uplifter	calctuff	blindage	maritage	steerage
squander	tabouret	twoedged	uprooter	camshaft	blockage	marriage	stillage
squasher	tafferel	twofaced	upsetter	classify	brassage	menology	stoppage
squatted	takeover	twosided	utiliser	cockloft	breakage	messuage	strategy
squatter	talented	twotimer	valanced	dandruff	bryology	metayage	subimago
squawker	tamperer	typifier	vanisher	denazify	cabotage	micrurgy	submerge
squeaker	tapwater	udometer	vapourer	detoxify	cacology	misalign	substage
squealer	tattered	unabated	velskoen	dyestuff	campaign	misjudge	suffrage
squeegee	tattooer	unaneled	veneerer	earmuffs	carriage	misology	suitings
squeezer	tautomer	unawares	venturer	emulsify	chemurgy	misusage	superego
squibbed	taverner	unbacked	verboten	esterify	churinga	moorings	tailings
squidded	taxpayer	unbarred	verderer	facelift	cleavage	mornings	theology
squilgee	teamster	unbeaten	verditer	failsafe	combings	mortgage	thirlage
squinter	teatowel	unbelief	verdured	fishwife	contango	mucilage	thorough
squireen	teenager	unbiased	verifier	fluidify	converge	mycology	tocology
squirrel	teleview	unbidden	vertexes	footmuff	coverage	nomology	tokology
squirter	tempered	unbolted	vertices	forklift	cozenage	nonusage	topology
stakenet	temperer	unbroken	vesturer	fructify	cribbage	nosology	trackage
stallfed	terminer	unburden	viameter	goodwife	cytology	oecology	truckage
stancher	terraced	unburied	vilifier	halflife	demagogy	oenology	turnings
startler	textured	uncalled	villager	handcuff	demiurge	offstage	tutelage
statured	thatcher	uncapped	vintager	humidify	diallage	omophagy	tutorage
steepled	thickset	uncaused	vivifier	identify	diggings	oncology	typehigh
stenosed	thirster	uncoined	vizarded	lapidify	disgorge	ontology	typology
stickler	thirteen	underlet	vortexes	layshaft	dislodge	oreology	umpirage
stipites	thoraces	undersea	vortices	meatsafe	disusage	outrange	underage
stippler	thoraxes	underset	vowelled	penknife	doxology	outreign	verbiage
stitcher	thrasher	undraped	waggoner	prettify	drainage	outweigh	vicarage
stopover	threader	unearned	walkover	quantify	dressage	paradigm	vicinage
storeyed	threaten	unedited	walleyed	redshift	driftage	paragoge	virology
strained	thresher	unfasten	walloper	resinify	earnings	pedagogy	vitiligo
strainer	thriller	unfetter	wallower	revivify	endamage	pedology	wagonage
straiten	throated	unfitted	wanderer	riffraff	ensilage	peelings	waterage
stranded	throbbed	unforced	warrener	rigidify	envisage	penology	wellnigh
stranger	thrummed	unformed	wartweed	roodloft	equipage	phalange	wharfage
strapped	thruster	unfrozen	watchkey	sanctify	estrange	pickings	winnings
strapper	thurifer	unfunded	waterbed	saponify	ethology	pilotage	workings
streaked	thwacked	unglazed	wayfarer	sawedoff	exchange	plumbago	wrappage
streaker	thwarter	ungotten	weeviled	seacraft	fandango	plussage	wreckage
streamer	tickseed	unhinged	wellbred	silicify	ferriage	pomology	writings

xylology accredit aviatrix choragic dicrotic eutectic headsail lingerie
zymology acentric backspin choregic dicyclic exegesis hedgepig liturgic
absinthe acidosis bacteria chorioid didactic exegetic heirship lockknit
affright aconitic balladic christie dieldrin exlibris helicoid logistic
airtight acoustic balletic chthonic dieresis exogamic heliosis longhair
allnight acrolein balsamic cicatrix dietetic exoteric Helladic longship
autarchy acrostic banausic cinnamic dihybrid explicit Hellenic loonybin
autobahn adamitic bangtail cinquain dinornis fantasia heraldic lordosis
babouche adenitis barbaric clanship dioptric faradaic herbaria lordotic
backache adularia baryonic clematis dioramic fauteuil hermetic lordship
barouche adynamia basaltic climatic dioritic febrific herpetic lothario
besought adynamic bathetic clupeoid diplopia fellahin hidrosis lymphoid
bimbashi aerofoil bathotic cobaltic disclaim felsitic hidrotic lynchpin
brouhaha agnostic battalia cocktail dispirit ferritic hieratic maenadic
bunfight agraphia bauxitic coelomic distrain fibrosis hightail magmatic
cachucha agrestic bearskin coenobia distrait fibrotic Hispanic magnesia
corniche airstrip beatific cognovit diuresis fireship historic magnetic
daylight alchemic Benjamin collyria diuretic firstaid holistic magnific
demarche Algonkin benzylic colubrid dogmatic fishtail holozoic magnolia
demijohn alguazil berberis complain domestic flagship holstein maieutic
dogfight alizarin bicuspid conchoid doornail flanerie hominoid mainsail
donought alkaloid bignonia contagia dovetail floodlit horntail maintain
enclothe alleluia biogenic contrail draconic fluellin horrific majestic
enswathe allergic bionomic conurbia dramatic forensic humanoid malvasia
eutrophy alopecia blacktie coonskin dutypaid foresaid hydatoid mandarin
eyesight ambrosia blastoid copyedit dybbukim foresail hydropic mandolin
faceache amitosis Blenheim coracoid dynastic foreskin hygienic manganic
fanlight amitotic bluechip cordwain dysgenic formalin hypnosis mannikin
farouche amniotic bobbypin cornific dyslexia fountain hypnotic manubria
gaslight amoeboid bondmaid coronoid dyslexic franklin hysteria marasmic
gastight amphibia bonhomie cosmetic dystopia Fraulein hysteric marocain
gazpacho anabasis botryoid coumarin ecclesia freesoil illiquid maroquin
gunfight anabatic bowsprit coxalgia echinoid frenetic implicit mastitis
headache anabolic branchia coxswain eclectic frogspit imprimis mechanic
headachy anagogic bromelia crankpin ecliptic gabbroic insignia medallic
iceyacht analogic bromidic creatrix ecologic gabbroid insomnia medusoid
inflight analysis bronchia criteria economic Gadhelic inspirit memsahib
menarche analytic buckskin crosstie ecstatic gainsaid intaglio mephitic
midnight anarchic buddleia crucifix effluvia galactic intarsia mephitis
monarchy anatomic bulletin cucurbit egoistic galvanic intermit mercuric
mustache anechoic bursitis culverin egomania gardenia intermix meristic
naumachy aniconic cachexia curculio electric gelastic intertie mescalin
nepenthe anorexia calcaria Cushitic elenctic gematria intrepid mesmeric
octarchy anorexic calcific cyanosis ellipsis geodesic intromit Mesozoic
outright anorthic calcitic cyanotic elliptic geodetic Iroquois metallic
outsight anthelia calfskin cyclonic empathic geologic isagogic meteoric
pansophy anthemia calycoid cyclosis emphasis geoponic ischemia methodic
pastiche anthesis camellia Cyrenaic emphatic geotaxis ischemic methylic
postiche aoristic cancroid Cyrillic emulsoid Germanic isobaric methysis
revanche apagogic cannabin cystitis encaenia gerontic isocheim microbic
rubbishy aperitif cannabis dactylic enclitic gigantic isogamic midbrain
scratchy aplastic cannikin daemonic encrinic globulin isogonic milkmaid
screechy apodosis cantoris daffodil encyclic gloxinia isomeric Miltonic
sennight apogamic capeskin daimonic endermic glycerin isotonic mirepoix
skylight apologia caprifig dalmatic endozoic glyconic isotopic Mishnaic
soutache apomixis capuchin damassin entoptic gneissic jalousie Mithraic
splotchy appendix carbolic deanship entozoic gnomonic japhetic mnemonic
squelchy applepie carbonic debonair enuresis goatskin jesuitic moccasin
stealthy arachnid caryatid decemvir enuretic Goidelic jumpsuit moleskin
stomachy argentic cathexis decennia enzootic goldfoil Jurassic molybdic
straight armchair cathodic decrepit eolithic gorgonia juristic monastic
stretchy aromatic catholic deeplaid epidemic granitic kingship Mongolic
sunbathe arpeggio cationic deerskin episodic grisgris klephtic monistic
sunlight artistic catstail dementia epitasis Guelphic kurtosis monkship
sympathy asbestic causerie dendroid epopoeia gummosis kyphosis monoacid
thearchy asphyxia Cenozoic dentalia eremitic gymnasia kyphotic monorail
triarchy assassin centroid despotic erogenic gynoecia ladyship moonsail
twilight asteroid cephalic devilkin esoteric hadronic lambskin morainic
unclothe asthenia ceratoid diabasic estuaril haematic landrail morbific
unsought asthenic cercaria diabetic Ethiopic haematin landslip mortmain
unswathe ataraxia Chaldaic diabolic eucritic hairgrip larrikin moshavim
untaught ataraxic chalkpit dialogic euonymin haliotis lecithin motorail
unworthy athletic chaplain dialysis eupatrid hamartia lemuroid mountain
viscacha Atlantic cherubic dialytic eupepsia handgrip leucitic multifid
vizcacha aubretia cherubim diarchic eupeptic handmaid libeccio muriatic
waxlight autacoid chiastic diatomic euphonic handrail lichenin mutchkin
abattoir autarkic chimeric diatonic euphoria hangnail lignitic myelinic
academia autistic chinchin dichasia euphoric hardship limetwig myelitis
academic aventail choleric dichroic eustatic harmonic linchpin myogenic

```
myositic  phreatic  salvific  suburbia  turnspit  homelike  animally  bullcalf
myositis  phthalic  Sangrail  succinic  twinship  hummocky  annually  bunghole
myosotis  phthisic  sanserif  suzerain  Tychonic  hydroski  antipole  bushveld
narcosis  phthisis  Sanskrit  swanskin  tympanic  keepsake  apically  caboodle
narcotic  phyletic  santonin  swimsuit  typhonic  kinglike  ardently  cabriole
Nearctic  phylloid  sardonic  syenitic  tyrannic  klondike  arguable  cakewalk
necrosis  Pindaric  Sassanid  syllabic  uncandid  kolinsky  arguably  callable
necrotic  pizzeria  saturnic  sylvatic  underbid  kromesky  arrantly  calycule
nematoid  plantain  scaphoid  symbolic  underdid  ladylike  artfully  camisole
NeoLatin  platinic  scarfpin  sympodia  underlie  lamblike  assemble  camomile
neomycin  platonic  scenario  symposia  underlip  leaflike  assembly  canaille
neotenic  playsuit  schizoid  synapsis  underpin  lifelike  astutely  candidly
neoteric  pleinair  sciuroid  synaptic  uralitic  lykewake  atremble  canoodle
neuritic  plutonic  sclereid  syncytia  uvulitis  Mameluke  augustly  canticle
neuritis  podagric  scombrid  syndesis  vaccinia  mandrake  auricula  capitula
neuronic  pollinia  scotopic  syndetic  vampiric  methinks  aversely  capriole
neurosis  pollinic  sealskin  synergic  Vandalic  moussaka  avowable  caracole
neurotic  polypoid  seasnail  synergid  vanillin  muckrake  avowedly  carnally
nickelic  polyzoic  secretin  syngamic  Vedantic  namesake  backveld  carriole
nomistic  ponytail  semantic  synopsis  veratrin  okeydoke  bailable  carryall
nonclaim  poristic  semiotic  synoptic  verbatim  outworks  bankable  caruncle
nonrigid  portrait  sensoria  syntonic  veristic  overtake  bankbill  casually
notornis  postobit  sepaloid  syphilis  verticil  peacocky  bankroll  catapult
nuclidic  postpaid  septfoil  systemic  victoria  pembroke  barnacle  catchall
odontoid  potassic  seraglio  systolic  villatic  physicky  barrenly  catchfly
oenophil  prelatic  seraphic  taenioid  Virginia  picnicky  baseball  caudally
omphalic  presidio  seraphim  taffrail  vitellin  pushbike  bastille  caudillo
operatic  prismoid  seriatim  tailspin  volcanic  rapecake  beadroll  causally
oratorio  proclaim  serranid  talapoin  voussoir  rimbrake  beanpole  centuple
organdie  prohibit  sesamoid  Talmudic  vulcanic  rockcake  bearable  chastely
orgasmic  prolamin  shaleoil  tamanoir  wagonlit  rocklike  bearably  chasuble
orgastic  prolific  shashlik  tantalic  Walkyrie  rushlike  bedabble  chattily
ornithic  propolis  shedevil  tartaric  wardship  seaquake  bedazzle  cheekily
orogenic  propylic  sheepdip  tectonic  wellknit  seasnake  bedtable  cheerily
Ossianic  prosodic  Shemitic  telluric  whitetie  seedcake  befuddle  chenille
osteitis  protasis  sideslip  teraphim  whizzkid  slowpoke  beggarly  chirpily
outstrip  protatic  sigmatic  terrapin  whodunit  snowlike  belittle  choicely
ovaritis  protonic  siluroid  terraria  windsail  starlike  bellpull  chorally
overlaid  pruritic  silvatic  terrific  wineskin  suchlike  benignly  Christly
overlain  psilosis  Sinaitic  tetradic  wirehair  sukiyaki  biddable  chummily
overpaid  pulmonic  sinfonia  Teutonic  wistaria  swanlike  bifocals  churchly
oversail  puristic  sinophil  thalamic  wisteria  swastika  billfold  clammily
overslip  purpuric  sinusoid  thalloid  wolfskin  tapelike  binnacle  clavicle
oviposit  purpurin  siphonic  theistic  woolskin  turnpike  birdcall  cleverly
oxytocin  pyelitis  siriasis  thematic  wrestpin  tussocky  bistable  clodpole
pachalic  pyogenic  Slavonic  theurgic  wristpin  upstroke  bitchily  clodpoll
palmitin  pyrenoid  sloppail  tholepin  xanthein  waesucks  bitingly  cloudily
pandemic  pythonic  smoothie  thoracic  zeolitic  waterski  bitterly  clumsily
pangolin  quatrain  snakepit  thrombin  zeppelin  waxworks  biweekly  coalhole
panmixia  quintain  snapbrim  thyroxin  zirconia  whiplike  biyearly  coarsely
pannikin  quixotic  Socratic  thyrsoid  zoiatria  wifelike  blackfly  cogently
pantsuit  rabbinic  softboil  toreutic  zoogenic  wormlike  blamable  commonly
papistic  rachitic  solenoid  tornadic  zoonosis  yarmulka  blamably  convexly
paraffin  rachitis  somnific  township  zygaenid  aardwolf  blastula  copyhold
paranoia  ramequin  souvenir  toxaemia  komitaji  abjectly  blearily  cornball
paranoid  ratstail  spagyric  toxaemic  maharaja  aborally  blithely  cornicle
parhelia  recommit  spandril  tracheid  airbrake  abruptly  bloodily  Cotswold
parhelic  redistil  specific  tranquil  apresski  absently  blowball  cousinly
parsonic  replevin  sphenoid  transfix  archduke  absurdly  blowhole  coverall
pashalic  republic  spheroid  tranship  babushka  abuttals  bluebell  covertly
pashalik  resinoid  sphingid  transmit  barracks  achingly  blurrily  cowardly
pathetic  resorcin  splendid  trapezia  beefcake  actively  boatbill  craftily
pearmain  restrain  spondaic  treenail  bouzouki  actually  bolthole  cramfull
pedantic  retiarii  sporadic  Triassic  britzska  adorable  bordello  cranefly
peignoir  rhetoric  stanzaic  tribasic  bullocky  adorably  borecole  crankily
Pelasgic  rhinitis  stapelia  trichoid  clambake  adroitly  borehole  cravenly
pellucid  rhomboid  staysail  triennia  dustlike  aerially  boringly  creakily
periodic  rhythmic  stenosis  triforia  elflocks  aguishly  bouncily  credible
periotic  ringmain  stenotic  trimeric  equivoke  aiguille  boyishly  credibly
perlitic  ringtail  stomatic  triploid  finnesko  Airedale  brassily  crenelle
petaloid  riverain  strapoil  trisomic  fishcake  airfield  brazenly  croakily
petechia  romantic  stravaig  triumvir  gadzooks  amazedly  breezily  crossply
petrolic  rubytail  strontia  trochaic  garlicky  amenable  bribable  crowbill
phenolic  sabbatic  strophic  trochoid  gasworks  amenably  brightly  crucible
phenylic  saccadic  stubnail  trottoir  gimmicky  amicable  brimfull  crustily
phonemic  sacraria  stunsail  truistic  hairlike  amicably  broccoli  culpable
phonetic  sadistic  subsonic  tungstic  hardbake  amorally  brokenly  culpably
photopia  safranin  subtonic  turmeric  hawklike  amusedly  broodily  curricle
photopic  sainfoin  subtopia  turnskin  hillocky  amygdala  brutally  cursedly
```

cussedly	evenfall	friendly	horribly	loanable	nucleoli	postmill	rotundly
daintily	evitable	frigidly	horridly	loblolly	numskull	potbelly	ruefully
damnable	exigible	friskily	horsefly	lockable	nuptials	potently	ruggedly
damnably	expertly	frostily	housefly	lodicule	nutshell	potstill	rugosely
danegeld	expiable	frothily	hoverfly	longwall	oafishly	pourable	ruinable
daringly	eyestalk	frugally	huggable	loophole	oakapple	preamble	runcible
deadfall	facially	fruitfly	hulahula	lovelily	obstacle	predella	sacredly
decently	facilely	frustule	humanely	lubberly	obtusely	prettily	sailable
decouple	fallible	fumarole	humuncle	lovingly	occultly	priestly	sailorly
demurely	fallibly	fungible	hungrily	lyophile	ocularly	primally	saleable
denehole	famously	funkhole	hypobole	madapple	odiously	princely	salvable
deniable	farewell	furuncle	icefield	maidenly	oilfield	prissily	sardelle
denticle	fascicle	futilely	imbecile	mailable	oldworld	probable	satiable
deucedly	fasciola	gainable	imitable	malignly	opaquely	probably	satiably
devoutly	fasciole	gapingly	immingle	manciple	openable	prolixly	savagely
diastole	fasttalk	gargoyle	immobile	mandible	operable	promptly	saxatile
dimmable	fatherly	garishly	impishly	mandorla	opercula	properly	scaffold
directly	faultily	gastrula	impurely	mandrill	opuscula	prostyle	scalable
disciple	faunally	gatefold	indocile	manfully	opuscule	provable	scantily
dismally	feasible	gefuffle	inedible	manifold	orchilla	provably	scarcely
distally	feasibly	genially	infirmly	mannerly	ornately	prunella	scattily
divinely	fellable	gerbille	innately	mantilla	otiosely	prunelle	schedule
docilely	fellowly	germcell	insanely	manually	outfield	prunello	scissile
doggedly	fencible	gingerly	inscroll	marigold	ovariole	pryingly	scrabble
dogwhelk	fervidly	girasole	instable	markedly	overalls	publicly	scramble
domicile	festally	glabella	intently	martello	overcall	puffball	scribble
doorbell	feudally	gladioli	inthrall	masterly	overfall	pulvilli	scribbly
doorsill	fewtrils	glandule	intitule	matronly	overfill	pushball	scrofula
dorsally	fibrilla	glassily	inveigle	maturely	overfold	pushpull	scurrile
dotingly	fiercely	globally	inviable	mayapple	overkill	putridly	scurvily
doumpalm	filially	gloomily	inwardly	meagrely	overrule	quaintly	scutella
downfall	filthily	gloriole	isabella	meatball	oversell	Quakerly	seaholly
downhill	finitely	glossily	isolable	medially	oversold	quartile	sealable
drawable	fireball	godchild	issuable	mellowly	owlishly	queasily	seamanly
drawwell	fiscally	goldenly	jaggedly	mendable	pallidly	quenelle	seashell
dreamily	fishable	goodwill	jauntily	menially	pallmall	quirkily	seatbelt
drearily	fishball	goofball	jejunely	mentally	palpable	quotable	secondly
drivable	fitfully	gravelly	jocosely	mesially	palpably	racially	secretly
drowsily	fivefold	greasily	jocundly	midfield	pantofle	radially	securely
drumroll	flabella	greedily	joinable	mightily	parabola	raggedly	sedately
duckbill	flagella	greenfly	jokingly	minutely	partible	rainfall	seizable
dumbbell	flagpole	groggily	jovially	misapply	particle	rakehell	selfhelp
dunghill	flashily	gromwell	joyfully	miscible	passable	rakishly	selfrule
durukuli	flexible	grubbily	joyously	misdealt	passably	randomly	selfwill
dutiable	flexibly	grumpily	juvenile	misspell	passible	rascally	semibull
easterly	flimsily	guerilla	kefuffle	misspelt	pastille	rateable	sensible
educable	flintily	guidable	kingbolt	modernly	patchily	readable	sensibly
educible	floccule	guiltily	kinsfolk	modestly	patently	readably	septuple
eggshell	flocculi	gullable	kissable	modishly	peccable	recently	serenely
eighthly	floppily	gullible	kneehole	molecule	pedipalp	redouble	serially
elatedly	florally	halfsole	knightly	molehill	peduncle	rehandle	severely
eligible	floridly	handball	knothole	momently	peephole	rekindle	sextuple
eligibly	flotilla	handbill	knowable	monopoly	pellicle	reliable	sexually
embattle	fluently	handheld	korfball	mooncalf	pellmell	reliably	shabbily
embezzle	foetidly	handhold	labially	mopishly	pendicle	remissly	shaggily
empeople	folktale	landfall	laically	morbidly	pentacle	remotely	shakable
empurple	follicle	handmill	landfall	morosely	pigswill	rentable	shapable
encircle	football	hangable	latently	mortally	pinnacle	repeople	shiftily
enfeeble	footfall	harebell	latterly	mothball	pinochle	resemble	shigella
engirdle	foothill	hateable	laudable	motherly	pintable	resettle	shoddily
enkindle	foothold	hayfield	laudably	moveable	pitiable	reticule	shoebill
ensample	footrule	heartily	lavishly	movingly	pitiably	reusable	shopbell
ensemble	forcedly	heatedly	lawfully	mulishly	placable	reveille	shoptalk
entangle	forcible	heavenly	lawyerly	multiple	placably	rideable	shothole
enthrall	forcibly	heelball	laystall	multiply	placidly	ridicule	showbill
entirely	fordable	hellhole	leadenly	musicale	plaguily	ringbolt	shrewdly
entrails	forefelt	lethally	lenticle	musingly	playable	ringwall	sickerly
enviable	foretell	hidyhole	leviable	mutually	playbill	ritually	sidewalk
enviably	foretold	highball	lifebelt	nailfile	pliantly	robustly	signally
epically	formally	hireable	liftable	nameable	plimsoll	rocaille	silently
epicycle	formerly	hoarsely	likeable	narghile	pluckily	rockfall	silverly
epistyle	fourball	hollowly	limekiln	narrowly	plurally	rocksalt	sinfully
erasable	fourfold	homefelt	limpidly	natively	politely	rollcall	singable
erectile	fourthly	homuncle	lineally	Negrillo	polygala	rolypoly	sinkable
erewhile	fraenula	honestly	linearly	neurally	popishly	roothold	sinkhole
erodible	freefall	hornbill	liquidly	ninefold	portable	ropeable	sisterly
errantly	freehold	hornfels	liveable	normally	porthole	ropewalk	sizeable
escarole	freewill	horrible	livelily	nouvelle	possible	rottenly	skewbald
evadable				nucleole	possibly		skimmilk

```
skimpily  stumpily  unbridle  whitefly  gladsome  trichome  befriend  cladding
slangily  stupidly  unbuckle  wickedly  glaucoma  twelvemo  besprent  claimant
sleazily  sturdily  uncially  wilfully  gleesome  undreamt  biassing  clamming
sleepily  subphyla  uncouple  windfall  goodtime  wallgame  bivalent  clanging
slightly  subtitle  uneasily  windgall  grandame  xanthoma  blabbing  clapping
slinkily  suddenly  unevenly  windmill  grapheme  xenogamy  blacking  cleaning
sloppily  suitable  unfairly  winepalm  gruesome  abducens  bleeding  clearing
slovenly  suitably  ungainly  winnable  halftime  abducent  blessing  clinking
smarmily  sullenly  unicycle  winterly  handsome  aberrant  blinding  clipping
smokable  sultrily  uniquely  wintrily  headlamp  abetment  blinking  clogging
smoothly  summerly  unitedly  witchelm  hecatomb  abetting  blooming  clothing
smudgily  superbly  unjustly  withheld  homogamy  aborning  blotting  clotting
smuttily  supinely  unkindly  withhold  homonymy  abradant  blurring  clubbing
snappily  supplely  unkingly  wizardly  hornrims  absonant  boarding  clubland
snazzily  syllable  unlikely  woefully  landarmy  abundant  bobolink  coalmine
sneakily  symphile  unlovely  wontedly  lifetime  abutment  bodement  coherent
sniffily  takingly  unmeetly  woodenly  lobotomy  abutting  bondmans  compline
snootily  tameable  unmuffle  woodpile  lonesome  accident  bookland  compound
snowball  tangible  unmuzzle  woodpulp  longsome  acescent  bouffant  confound
snowfall  tangibly  unriddle  woolfell  longtime  acquaint  bouncing  confront
sociable  tannable  unsaddle  workable  lovesome  acridine  bowfront  conjoint
sociably  tasselly  unseemly  workfolk  lymphoma  acrimony  bragging  constant
socially  tawdrily  unsettle  wormhole  lysosome  adducent  braiding  contline
softball  taxingly  unstable  worthily  lysozyme  adherent  breaking  contorno
solemnly  teatable  unstably  woundily  machismo  adjacent  breeding  corkwing
solvable  telefilm  untangle  wrathily  maritime  adjutant  briefing  cornpone
sombrely  tellable  untidily  writable  mealtime  adjuvant  brimming  Corybant
somedele  telltale  untimely  yeastily  meantime  aegirine  brisling  cosecant
sordidly  tenacula  unwarily  yellowly  merosome  aerodyne  browband  cotenant
sortable  tenaille  unwisely  yeomanly  metonymy  afferent  browning  cothurni
spadille  tenderly  unwordly  yourself  millieme  affluent  bubaline  couchant
sparable  tensible  uppishly  zarzuela  misogamy  agrement  buckling  couching
sparsely  tentacle  upwardly  zoophily  monogamy  agrimony  building  coupling
speedily  teocalli  urbanely  aceldama  morpheme  airborne  bullring  coursing
spherule  terrible  urgently  aeronomy  mycetoma  aleurone  bundling  covalent
spiracle  terribly  urostyle  agronomy  nickname  alkaline  buntline  covenant
spirally  testable  usefully  airframe  noontime  allround  bustling  covering
spirilla  tetchily  uvularly  allogamy  overcame  ambulant  butylene  crabbing
spongily  tetrapla  vacantly  analcime  overcome  andesine  cabstand  cracking
spookily  threeply  Valhalla  anathema  overjump  anserine  caffeine  cradling
spoonily  throstle  valuable  antinomy  overtime  antimony  cageling  cramming
sportily  throttle  valuably  arapaima  panorama  anything  calamine  crashing
spottily  thurible  variable  atheroma  parttime  aperient  calamint  creatine
sprinkle  thwartly  variably  autogamy  pastrami  apocrine  calycine  creeping
sprucely  tidemill  variedly  autonomy  phyllome  apparent  campagna  crescent
spunkily  tillable  vendible  autosome  playtime  appetent  camphene  cretonne
squabble  timeball  venially  autotomy  polygamy  aqualung  camphine  cribbing
squamule  timously  venously  backcomb  polyseme  aquatint  cancrine  crofting
squarely  tinselly  verbally  birdlime  polysemy  aquiline  canoeing  cromorna
squiggle  tithable  vernally  blastema  polysomy  argument  capeline  cromorne
squiggly  tollcall  vernicle  blossomy  prodrome  armament  capstone  cropping
squirely  toothily  versicle  blowlamp  realtime  arrogant  carabine  crossing
stanchly  torpidly  victuals  catacomb  rearlamp  aspirant  Caroline  cryogeny
starrily  torridly  viewable  charisma  ribosome  assonant  carotene  culicine
statable  tortilla  vincible  choriamb  sawframe  assuming  casement  curarine
statedly  touchily  vinously  coenzyme  scleroma  astatine  catching  curtains
steadily  towardly  violable  consomme  seadrome  atheling  catering  cushiony
steamily  townhall  violably  darksome  seedtime  atropine  cavatina  cysteine
stickily  trammels  viscidly  diastema  selfsame  autodyne  centring  cytidine
stingily  trapball  visually  displume  semidome  averment  cerement  cytosine
stockily  trashily  vitiable  divebomb  sidearms  averring  ceremony  dairying
stodgily  trendily  voidable  doldrums  sometime  avifauna  chaconne  darkling
stolidly  trevally  volatile  dolesome  sterigma  bacchant  chapping  dateline
stonefly  triangle  vulgarly  downcome  subframe  backbone  charming  deadline
storable  triballa  Walhalla  downtime  syndrome  backhand  charring  debutant
stormily  trickily  walkable  endogamy  synonymy  bailment  chatting  decadent
straddle  tricycle  wantonly  engramma  syntagma  balkline  cheering  decedent
straggle  triskele  washable  erythema  tachisme  bandanna  Cheyenne  deckhand
straggly  trochili  wastable  eyerhyme  takehome  bantling  chipmunk  deferent
straitly  trustily  wearable  fearsome  taxonomy  banxring  chipping  deponent
strangle  tryingly  weaselly  firearms  tenotomy  baritone  chlorine  dethrone
strickle  tubercle  weevilly  firebomb  teratoma  barytone  chopping  deviling
strictly  tuneable  weldable  firedamp  termtime  baseline  chugging  dewpoint
strobila  turbidly  weregild  forename  thingamy  basement  chumming  dextrine
strobile  turgidly  werewolf  foretime  timebomb  baudrons  churning  dialling
strobili  turnable  westerly  foursome  tiresome  beagling  cicerone  diaphone
strongly  turnsole  wettable  fulltime  toilsome  becoming  ciceroni  dilatant
struggle  umbrella  wheezily  gamesome  toponymy  beeswing  cidevant  diligent
stuffily  unbottle  whinsill  gendarme  trachoma  beetling  cinchona  dingdong
```

```
diriment feedtank glossina indicant medicine ornament pregnant rosepink
disbound feminine glutting indigene melamine orpiment preprint rotenone
discount fetching gluttony indigent membrane oscinine prescind rubicund
disjoint fiddling goalline indolent merchant osculant pressing rudiment
dismount fighting goatling induline middling ottavino primming ruminant
displant figurant Gobelins inerrant midpoint outbound printing rutilant
divalent figurine goldmine influent migraine outflank pristine saffrony
dividend filament gourmand inhalant militant outgoing prodding saltmine
dockland Filipina grabbing inherent millhand outlying profound sampling
doctrine Filipino gradient inhumane millpond outpoint proofing sandbank
document fishbone graduand inkstand miscount outshine propound sanguine
dominant fishpond graining innocent misdoing outshone propping saraband
downland fistiana grasping inscient misogyny outspend prurient saturant
downwind flagging grayling insolent misprint outspent ptomaine Sauterne
dracaena flagrant greening insulant misspend outvying puissant scammony
dragging flapping greeting insurant misspent overdone purblind scandent
dragline flashing grinning inurbane misthink overfond purfling scanning
dreaming flatling gripping inviting mitigant overhand purslane scarring
dressing fleabane grissini irritant mondaine overhang pursuant scathing
drilling fleeting gritting isoprene monogamy overhung purulent scatting
drinking flippant grouping jetplane monogony overland pyridine scheming
dripping flipping grouting jubilant monogyny overlong pyroxene sciurine
dropping flitting growling judgment monotint overtone quadrant scolding
drubbing floating grubbing julienne monotone overwind quandong scouting
drugging flogging grudging kakemono monotony palatine queening scragend
drumming flooring guardant katakana monument palomino queueing scraping
drypoint flopping gunflint keeshond moorland parasang quidnunc scrutiny
drystone flubbing gunpoint kerosene moribund paravane quilting scudding
duckling fluorine gymkhana kerosine morphine parkland quincunx scumming
duckpond focusing habitant keystone motoring partsong quipping seaborne
duelling fogbound hairline kindling mottling pavement quisling seafront
dulciana folksong halfpint knapping moulding payphone quitrent seagoing
dumfound fondling halftone knitting mounting pearling quitting seamount
dumpling footling handline knocking mourning pediment quizzing seaplane
dwelling foramina handling knotting movement pelerine quotient sederunt
earphone forborne hardline lacewing mowburnt penchant rackrent sediment
easement fordoing hatching lakeland mudstone penitent radicant seedling
efferent foregone hatstand landline muniment peperino rallying segreant
effluent forehand haunting landmine murrhine perigyny rambling seladang
eftsoons foreland headband latitant muscling perilune ratsbane semitone
eggplant forewent headland laughing narceine petaline rattling semolina
elephant forgoing headline learning nauseant petulant reactant sentient
elkhound forspent headlong lefthand Nazarene pheasant reascend sergeant
eloquent founding headwind legatine neckband phosgene recreant serjeant
emceeing foxhound hegemony lemurine neckline phrasing recusant serotine
emergent fragment hellbent leporine needment picayune redblind servient
emigrant fragrant hesitant lifeline neoprene piddling redefine shafting
emitting frapping hexylene lifelong nescient piedmont redolent shamming
emulgent freehand highland ligament nestling piercing redshank shantung
endogeny freezing hireling lighting neutrino piffling reedling sheading
engaging frequent hirrient liniment newfound pinecone referent shealing
enshrine fretting hoarding litigant nicotine pinpoint refluent shedding
enthrone fringing hocusing littling niggling pipeline regiment sheeting
environs fritting Holocene livelong ninepins piperine relaxant shelving
epifauna frocking homeland loadline nocturne plaiding relevant Shetland
epiphany frogging homodont loathing nonevent plangent relucent shieling
equitant frondent homogeny lobeline northing planking relumine shilling
esculent frosting hoodwink lodgment noseband planning remanent shinbone
esurient fuchsine hourlong longhand nosecone platting renitent shinning
ethylene fuelling hyoscine lordling nosering pleading reorient shipment
evacuant fumigant hypogyny lovesong notching pleasant repetend shipping
evensong gableend hypopgyny lowering nursling pleasing resident shirring
everyone gadarene ianthine lowlying nutrient Pliocene resonant shirting
exacting gangland iceblink luculent obedient plodding respring shocking
excitant gangling icebound luminant obeisant plopping resprung shogging
exciting gangrene iceplant lustrine obliging plotting resupine shooting
exhalant gantline ignominy lustring occident plugging reticent shopping
existent gasoline ignorant macaroni occupant plumbing retiring shunning
exocrine gasoline illumine magazine oestrone poignant revenant shutting
expirant gazogene immanent maharani offering pointing reverend sibilant
exponent gelatine imminent mahogany offprint polygene reverent sideband
exultant gemstone imponent mainland oilstone polygeny reviling sideline
fagoting geophone imposing mainline ointment polygyny rewaking sideling
faineant gladding impotent makimono oliphant porkling Riesling sidelong
farflung gladhand impudent mantling omitting postpone ringbone sidewind
farmhand glancing incident marbling oncoming potbound riverine silicane
farmland glassine incitant marrying ontogeny potplant roasting silicone
farthing gleaning incoming mazarine opponent potstone roborant simulant
feculent gloaming indecent mazement ordinand pounding rockling singeing
```

```
singsong  stirring  tramline  whizbang  bachelor  cohesion  empoison  gossypol
sixpenny  stocking  trapping  whizzing  backdoor  collator  emulator  governor
sizzling  stopping  trekking  whooping  backdrop  colophon  emulsion  gramatom
skidding  strepent  trephine  whopping  backroom  conation  enaction  grandson
skilling  strident  trichina  windcone  ballroom  conjuror  encomion  graviton
skimming  striking  tricorne  wishbone  ballyhoo  convenor  endozoon  gridiron
skinning  stubbing  trifling  witching  bambinos  conveyor  enneagon  grogshop
skipping  studding  trilling  woodbind  banderol  cookbook  entozoon  groogroo
skirting  stuffing  trimming  woodbine  bankbook  cooption  entrepot  guidedog
slabbing  stumming  triplane  woodland  bannerol  copybook  entresol  gumption
slagging  stunning  tripping  woodwind  barefoot  corduroy  envision  gypsydom
slamming  subagent  trombone  woollens  barndoor  cordwood  episemon  gyration
slapbang  subjoint  trotting  wrapping  barrator  corkwood  epyllion  halation
slapping  subpoena  trucking  xanthene  basswood  corridor  equation  halfboot
slashing  suckling  trussing  xanthine  bathroom  cotillon  erection  halfmoon
sledding  sulphone  tsarevna  yachting  beefwood  crackpot  erigeron  handbook
sleeping  sunblind  tumbling  yeanling  beetroot  creation  eruption  handloom
slimming  sunburnt  tuppenny  yearling  bellbuoy  creditor  escallop  hangeron
slipping  sunshine  turtling  yearlong  bentwood  crossbow  escargot  hardwood
slipring  sunshiny  twinling  yearning  bergamot  crowfoot  eschalot  headroom
slitting  sunstone  twinning  yielding  betatron  cryotron  eulachon  hedgehog
slobland  supplant  twitting  zabaione  biathlon  curassow  evection  hedgehop
slogging  surmount  twopenny  zecchini  bibation  cuspidor  eversion  hedgerow
slopping  surround  tyrosine  zecchino  billhook  darkroom  eviction  heirloom
slotting  swabbing  Tyrrhene  zibeline  billyboy  deadwood  evulsion  heptagon
slubbing  swagging  undulant  zincking  bisector  decision  exaction  herdbook
slugging  swanking  unending  zucchini  blackboy  decurion  excision  hereupon
slumming  swanning  unerring  zugzwang  blacktop  defector  executor  highbrow
slurring  swansong  unfading  abductor  bludgeon  delation  exertion  himation
smashing  swapping  unlearnt  ablation  boathook  deletion  expiator  honeypot
smelling  swatting  unseeing  ablution  bobbysox  delusion  extensor  hoosegow
smocking  swearing  unsprung  abortion  bodyshop  demotion  exterior  hornbook
snagging  sweeping  unstring  abrasion  bontebok  depictor  extrados  horsebox
snaplink  sweeting  unstrung  abutilon  bouillon  deration  falchion  hotchpot
snapping  swelling  unthrone  accentor  bourgeon  derision  fanfaron  houseboy
snipping  swigging  uprising  acceptor  buckaroo  detector  fastfood  housedog
snogging  swimming  upsprang  accustom  buckshot  deuteron  firewood  housetop
snowline  swinging  upspring  acrefoot  bullfrog  deviator  fishhook  Huguenot
snubbing  swobbing  upsprung  actuator  bullyboy  devotion  fixation  hymnbook
solanine  swopping  urethane  adaption  bungalow  diapason  flatfoot  ideation
sonatina  swotting  Ursuline  addition  cabinboy  dictator  flatiron  ignition
soothing  sycamine  urticant  adductor  cabochon  dilation  flection  ignitron
souchong  sylphine  vagabond  adhesion  cachalot  dilution  fleshpot  illation
sounding  symbiont  vaulting  adjustor  cachepot  director  flipflop  illusion
sourdine  symphony  vehement  adnation  calthrop  disallow  folderol  imitator
southing  syncline  velamina  adoption  calvados  disendow  folkmoot  impostor
spanking  tackling  verecund  adulator  carcajou  disproof  followon  imprison
spanning  tagalong  vesicant  advowson  cardamom  disunion  footslog  inaction
sparling  tamarind  vestment  aeration  carillon  dittybox  foredoom  inceptor
sparring  tapeline  Vietcong  affusion  casebook  division  forefoot  incision
spatting  teaching  Vietminh  agitator  cashbook  dominion  foreknow  inductor
speaking  teething  vigilant  agitprop  castiron  donation  forenoon  infector
spelling  tegument  vilipend  agnation  catechol  doorknob  foreshow  inferior
spiffing  telecine  villainy  allusion  catsfoot  doorstop  formroom  inflator
spinning  telegony  viperine  alluvion  cauldron  dotation  fraction  infusion
spitting  tempting  virement  alumroot  cavesson  doubloon  friction  inhesion
sporting  tenement  virulent  ambition  cesspool  doughboy  froufrou  injector
spotting  tenpenny  viscount  amphipod  chaldron  dramshop  fruition  inositol
spurling  terebene  visitant  ancestor  champion  dropshot  function  intercom
spurring  texthand  vituline  angstrom  chapbook  Dukhobor  furbelow  interior
stabbing  theogony  volitant  animator  chaperon  dumbshow  gallipot  Interpol
stabling  thiamine  volplane  anterior  chiefdom  duration  gambados  intrados
stagnant  thinking  vomerine  anteroom  choirboy  dustshot  gambeson  invasion
stalling  thinning  wakening  anthozoa  chopchop  dynatron  gambroon  inventor
standing  thousand  warpaint  antiphon  chowchow  eclosion  ganglion  investor
starling  thriving  warplane  aphelion  cinnamon  ectozoon  gardyloo  irenicon
starring  thudding  watering  Arapahoe  citation  educator  garrison  ironwood
starting  thumping  waveband  arrestor  clerkdom  eduction  gelation  isodicon
steading  tideland  waygoing  asbestos  clipclop  effector  geraniol  isolator
stealing  tingeing  weakling  assentor  clopclop  effusion  giftbook  jackaroo
stearine  tinstone  weanling  assertor  clubfoot  egestion  gillaroo  jackboot
steening  tolerant  weeklong  assessor  coachdog  ejection  gipsydom  jackeroo
steering  tonguing  weldment  assignor  coaction  election  girlhood  jettison
stemming  toothing  whacking  attestor  coatroom  electron  glucagon  jobation
stepping  topstone  whapping  audition  cockatoo  elevator  glycerol  junction
sterling  touching  whetting  aversion  cockcrow  elfarrow  goingson  junkshop
stetting  toxicant  whidding  aviation  cockcrow  emblazon  golliwog  kangaroo
stilbene  tracking  whipping  avulsion  coercion  emersion  gonfalon  kinghood
stinking  training  whirring  babyhood  cofactor  emission  goosegog  kinkajou
```

klystron	objector	puppydom	soaproot	varactor	monotype	blazonry	cometary
Kohinoor	oblation	purveyor	softshoe	venation	myograph	blinkers	confrere
Komsomol	oblivion	quadroon	softwood	verderor	nametape	blistery	coniform
labrador	occasion	quaestor	solation	vexation	nosepipe	blizzard	conspire
ladyhood	octaroon	queendom	solution	vibrator	odograph	bloomers	contrary
laudator	octoroon	question	songbook	vigneron	orthoepy	bloomery	coquetry
lavation	offshoot	radiator	sonobuoy	villadom	otoscope	blowhard	coronary
leapfrog	omission	raindrop	sorption	violator	overripe	blubbery	corsetry
legation	omphalos	reaction	soundbow	vitiator	pericope	bluebird	costmary
libation	operator	rebellow	soundbox	vocation	praecipe	blustery	cowberry
lifebuoy	orthicon	receptor	Southron	voicebox	reedpipe	bodywork	crackers
ligation	orthodox	recision	spanroof	volcanos	reoccupy	bollworm	creamery
liripoop	ostracod	redactor	sparbuoy	volition	rescript	boneyard	creature
lobation	ostracon	redeploy	spicebox	volscout	schnapps	booklore	crockery
locution	ostrakon	reedstop	spittoon	wainscot	seascape	bookmark	crumhorn
lollipop	outHerod	reefknot	sponsion	waleknot	skislope	bookwork	cruzeiro
lollypop	overbook	reemploy	spontoon	wallaroo	skyscape	bookworm	cubature
longeron	overcrop	relation	sporozoa	wallknot	soilpipe	bottomry	cubiform
longstop	overflow	releasor	squadron	wanderoo	stanhope	boundary	culinary
lookeron	overgrow	religion	squarson	wardroom	sundrops	braggart	cupboard
loosebox	overlook	resistor	stairrod	warwhoop	tailpipe	brancard	cussword
loveknot	overshoe	revision	stallion	washroom	tittuppy	brassard	cynosure
lunation	overshot	Rhinodon	stasimon	transept	brassart	daiquiri
luncheon	overtook	rhizopod	steenbok	watchdog	triglyph	brazenry	delivery
luxation	oxymoron	rigadoon	steinbok	waterlog	trigraph	braziery	delusory
macaroon	paduasoy	roadbook	stellion	Wedgwood	trolloby	breviary	demerara
magneton	paintbox	rockwood	sternson	whiteboy	windpipe	brochure	denature
maidhood	pantheon	rogation	stinkpot	whitehot	Xantippe	broidery	derisory
malaprop	paperboy	roseroot	stockpot	wholehog	zoetrope	buckhorn	derriere
mandator	papillon	rosewood	studbook	whoredom	zoomorph	buhlwork	deviltry
mannitol	pappadom	rotation	sturgeon	whoreson	aardvark	bullhorn	dewberry
marathon	parergon	roundtop	subfloor	wifehood	accoutre	Burberry	diaspora
martagon	passbook	saintdom	subprior	wildwood	adultery	burglary	diaspore
martenot	patentor	saleroom	sunproof	wineshop	advisory	bushfire	dilatory
mascaron	pavilion	sanction	superior	woodwool	aeriform	butchery	dockyard
massicot	pawnshop	sandshoe	surveyor	wordbook	albacore	buzzword	dogberry
mastodon	peardrop	saucebox	survivor	workroom	aleatory	cadastre	dogshore
matchbox	peasecod	sauropod	swanshot	workshop	allegory	cagebird	donatory
mediator	peekaboo	Saxondom	sweetsop	wormwood	ambivert	cajolery	dooryard
melodeon	peepshow	scallion	tabletop	yearbook	anaphora	calamary	downturn
mementos	pentagon	scansion	tackroom	zonation	ancestry	calipers	downward
mesotron	pentroof	scission	tarragon	anaglyph	antihero	callgirl	drollery
metaphor	petition	scorpion	taxation	antelope	antisera	calyptra	dropwort
metazoon	pettifog	screwtop	teardrop	antipope	anywhere	campfire	drudgery
methanol	phlegmon	scullion	teaspoon	antitype	aperture	cannonry	drumfire
mezereon	phosphor	sculptor	telethon	apograph	armature	canthari	drunkard
microdot	picaroon	seafloor	testator	autotype	armyworm	capybara	dungcart
migrator	pinewood	seaonion	tetragon	bankrupt	artistry	caracara	dustcart
misbegot	piscator	secretor	tetrapod	biograph	ascocarp	careworn	eastward
moneybox	plankton	sedation	textbook	biomorph	auditory	casework	ectoderm
monition	plastron	sedition	Thanatos	bioscope	auriform	cashmere	emissary
monkhood	playbook	seedplot	thanedom	blowpipe	autogiro	category	endocarp
monoglot	playroom	seignior	thankyou	boltrope	autogyro	catenary	endoderm
moonshot	polliwog	selector	therefor	calliope	axillary	cathedra	enginery
moufflon	pollywog	selfhood	thermion	cenotaph	Ayrshire	cavicorn	ensiform
munition	poltfoot	serfhood	thraldom	chirrupy	backfire	cemetery	ensphere
mushroom	poltroon	servitor	thumbpot	contempt	backward	centaury	entoderm
mutation	polyglot	shagroon	tommyrot	diagraph	backyard	chambers	ephemera
myriapod	polyzoon	shalloon	tomorrow	downpipe	balefire	champers	errantry
myriopod	poohpooh	sheepdog	toolroom	enthalpy	balladry	chancery	estovers
myrmidon	porticos	sheikdom	toreador	envelope	banditry	chapelry	etcetera
nainsook	position	Sheraton	traction	epigraph	barberry	chauntry	evermore
namedrop	positron	showroom	traditor	episcope	barnyard	checkers	exospore
naphthol	potation	sickroom	trapdoor	escalope	barratry	chequers	exposure
napoleon	predator	sidedoor	treefrog	eucalypt	baseborn	chimaera	facecard
narrator	pressbox	sideshow	trillion	feedpipe	basketry	chivalry	falconry
natation	promisor	skeleton	trunnion	fluepipe	bayadere	cincture	farmyard
negation	pronator	skinfood	tuckahoe	footrope	bayberry	cinerary	farriery
negatron	protocol	skypilot	tuckshop	gantlope	beadwork	claymore	faubourg
newsroom	protozoa	slipknot	ulterior	genotype	bejabers	cleavers	feathery
nextdoor	provisor	slipshod	unbutton	harrumph	bellbird	clippers	February
nodation	pteropod	slipslop	uncommon	hornpipe	bellwort	clownery	fenberry
nonjuror	pulpwood	slopshop	underdog	hosepipe	beriberi	clustery	fenestra
nonunion	pulsator	smallpox	undertow	isomorph	bestiary	cobblers	feretory
notation	pumproom	snapshot	unperson	isotropy	bilberry	cocksure	filature
notebook	puncheon	snowboot	unreason	jipijapa	billiard	coiffure	filiform
noumenon	punition	snowdrop	unwisdom	logotype	biometry	colewort	firebird
novation	pupation	snowshoe	vacation	midships	bistoury	coliform	firework
nutation	puppydog	snuffbox	valuator	misshape	bladdery	colliery	fishfarm

```
flattery  homeborn  lovebird  pedantry  ricebird  software  tubiform  almagest
flatware  homeward  lovelorn  pedicure  ringbark  soldiery  tutelary  alpinism
flatworm  homework  lukewarm  pegboard  ringworm  solidary  tweezers  alpinist
fleawort  honorary  luminary  pellagra  rockbird  solitary  twinborn  altruism
flickery  hookworm  lungwort  penumbra  rockcork  sombrero  twittery  altruist
flinders  hornworm  lyrebird  pericarp  rocketry  songbird  unciform  amethyst
flummery  hornwort  mailcart  periderm  rockwork  southern  underarm  amortise
fluttery  hostelry  mainyard  perspire  rogatory  Spaniard  untoward  anapaest
folklore  hypoderm  malapert  phyllary  ropeyarn  spermary  upstairs  anaphase
footmark  idolatry  malefern  pilchard  rosemary  spitfire  urochord  aneurism
footsore  illusory  manicure  pilewort  rotatory  spivvery  vanguard  aneurysm
footwork  immature  maniform  piliform  roughdry  staggard  variform  ankylose
forepart  inchworm  massacre  pillwort  roundarm  staggers  varletry  annalist
forestry  industry  mealworm  pinafore  rounders  staghorn  vasiform  antepost
forewarn  inexpert  mediocre  pinchers  ryotwari  stalwart  vavasory  antimask
foreword  infantry  meshwork  pisiform  saddlery  standard  vertebra  antrorse
foreyard  insecure  mesocarp  plagiary  sagamore  stannary  vespiary  aphorise
formwork  insphere  mesoderm  plastery  sailyard  starkers  vestiary  aphorism
forswore  iodoform  metamere  platform  salivary  starwort  vinegary  aphorist
forsworn  ironbark  military  playgirl  saltwort  statuary  vineyard  apiarist
fourpart  ironware  milkwort  pleasure  salutary  stinkard  vomitory  apostasy
foxshark  ironwork  milliard  plethora  samphire  stubborn  wallfern  applause
fracture  isometry  milliary  pockmark  sanatory  studfarm  wardenry  appraise
freeborn  isoptera  minatory  podiatry  sandworm  studwork  wartwort  aquarist
fretwork  isospory  ministry  polypary  sandwort  sudatory  warweary  arbalest
frippery  isothere  mintmark  porphyry  sanitary  summitry  waveform  arbalist
fruitery  isotherm  miscarry  portfire  sapphire  surefire  waxberry  arborist
fumitory  jacquard  miserere  portiere  sashcord  surfbird  weaponry  archaise
funerary  jailbird  misheard  postcard  saunders  swanherd  wellborn  archaism
furriery  janizary  missilry  posthorn  sauouari  swanmark  wellworn  archaist
fusiform  jesuitry  moisture  postmark  savagery  swannery  westward  archness
gadgetry  jodhpurs  monandry  potsherd  Savoyard  sycamore  Whiggery  arethusa
galliard  jointure  monetary  premiere  sayonara  sycomore  whipcord  Arianism
gamebird  jugglery  monitory  pressure  scabbard  symmetry  whipworm  arsonist
gaolbird  juncture  moonwort  priggery  scissors  synastry  whiskers  asterisk
gapeworm  junkyard  moratory  psaltery  scullery  taciturn  whiskery  asterism
garboard  kailyard  mortuary  puffbird  seaboard  tainture  whispery  astonish
geniture  Kashmiri  muckworm  puncture  seashore  tamboura  wildfire  atticism
geometry  keyboard  mudguard  punditry  seedcorn  tandoori  windburn  autolyse
glanders  kingbird  mulberry  punitory  seignory  tanistry  windward  aviarist
glaziery  kisscurl  musketry  pupilary  selfborn  tapestry  wirework  avidness
glittery  knackery  namepart  puppetry  seminary  tapeworm  wireworm  babirusa
glossary  kneejerk  napiform  pushcart  shagbark  taskwork  wiseacre  backlash
glowworm  knickers  natatory  pyriform  shepherd  teaboard  witchery  backless
goatherd  knotwork  neathird  quackery  shimmery  teamwork  wizardry  backlist
gossipry  krumhorn  needfire  quagmire  shipworm  telemark  woodlark  backmost
goutwort  lacework  negatory  quandary  shipyard  teleport  woodwork  backrest
greenery  lacunary  nondairy  quartern  shoehorn  tenantry  woodworm  backwash
grimoire  ladybird  northern  quarters  shopgirl  tertiary  woolwork  bakshish
grindery  ladyfern  nubiform  quixotry  shopworn  textuary  xylocarp  baldness
guacharo  lamasery  nugatory  rabbitry  shortarm  thesauri  yeomanry  Balinese
gynandry  landform  numerary  racecard  showcard  thievery  yoghourt  banjoist
gyratory  landgirl  obituary  raillery  showgirl  thrawart  zealotry  bareness
habanera  landlord  oblatory  rainbird  shuddery  thuggery  zoolatry  barkless
hairworm  landmark  octonary  ranchero  sideward  thundery  zoometry  baroness
halfterm  lanthorn  offshore  ratguard  silkworm  tidemark  zoospore  baseless
halliard  lapboard  omnivore  reabsorb  sinecure  tiltyard  abelmosk  baseness
hallmark  lapidary  openwork  reaffirm  slattern  timework  abscissa  basilisk
handcart  larboard  orangery  rearward  slipform  timeworn  abstruse  bellpush
handwork  lavatory  ordinary  reassert  slippery  tincture  achiness  beltless
harakiri  lawcourt  outboard  reassure  slithery  toiletry  acidfast  berceuse
hardcore  leadwork  outdoors  recovery  slobbery  toilworn  acosmism  betacism
hardware  leathern  outlawry  redshirt  slopwork  torchere  acrotism  bigamist
harikari  leathery  outsmart  redstart  slovenry  tournure  actinism  bioplasm
harlotry  leeboard  outstare  reedbird  slowworm  transire  activism  bioplast
hatchery  leftward  ovenbird  reembark  sluggard  trashery  activist  blackish
haulyard  legendry  ovenware  reexport  slumbery  treasure  admonish  blandish
hawthorn  legguard  overbore  refinery  smallfry  treasury  afforest  bleakish
headwork  libatory  overlord  registry  smeltery  treefern  agedness  blimpish
headwork  lifework  overture  reinsert  smithers  tressure  airbrush  blockish
heathery  ligature  overturn  reinsure  smithery  trichord  airiness  blondish
heliport  limitary  overwork  reniform  smothery  trickery  alarmist  blowfish
hellfire  literary  palestra  rerecord  snobbery  trippery  albinism  bluefish
heraldry  livebird  papistry  rereward  snowbird  tripwire  alcahest  blueness
Hereford  livewire  parrotry  restcure  snuffers  trousers  alehouse  bluenose
highborn  loanword  parterre  retiform  snuggery  trouvere  algorism  bodiless
hillfort  locutory  passport  revisory  soapbark  truantry  alienism  boldness
hipsters  longhorn  passport  ribaldry  soapwort  trueborn  alienist  bonefish
hobbitry  longterm  password  ribbonry  sobstory  trumpery  alkahest  boneless
```

```
boniness converse doorpost farthest gladdest idiotism longness nameless
bookcase convulse dopiness fastness gladness idleness longwise narcissi
bookpost coolness dormouse fatalism glibness idocrase lopgrass nasalise
bookrest cordless dourness fatalist glummest idyllist lordless nathless
bootlast cosiness dowdyish fearless glumness immodest loudness nativism
bootless costpush downcast feckless goalpost immunise loveless nativist
botanise couldest downmost feeblish goatfish incivism lovenest naturism
botanist coulisse doziness fellness golddust increase loyalist naturist
botulism countess drabness feminise goldfish infamise luckless nearness
botyrose courtesy druggist feminism goldrush inkiness luminist neatness
brackish cowgrass druidess feminist goodness interest lumpfish nebulise
brainish cramoisy druidism feverish gormless intimism lungfish necropsy
brandish crawfish drynurse fiendish gracioso introrse lushness needless
brattish crayfish duchesse fiftyish Graecise iotacism lutanist negroism
brettese crevasse ductless filefish Graecism Irishism lutenist neoplasm
brimless curarise duellist finalise greenish Islamise lyricism Nepalese
briskish cureless duettist finalism greyfish Islamism lyricist nepotism
broadish curtness dullness finalist greyness isogloss madhouse newscast
brownish cuteness dumbness fineness grimmest isostasy maestoso niceness
Buddhism cutpurse dustless firehose grimness Japanese mainmast nihilism
Buddhist cynicism dwarfish firmness gypsyism Javanese makefast nihilist
burnouse daftness dwarfism fishless hairless jealousy Malagasy noblesse
business dampness dynamism flatfish haleness Jehovist maleness nodalise
busyness dandyish dynamist flatness halfmast jingoish manifest nodulose
buttress dandyism easiness flattest handfast jingoism mantissa nomadise
Byronism dankness eastmost flattish handless jingoist marchesa nomadism
cabalism danseuse echoless flatwise handlist jiujitsu marchese nonsense
cabalist darkness edgeless flautist hardcase justness marquess nosiness
caginess dateless edgewise flawless hardness Kanarese marquise notecase
calabash deadness edginess flexuose harmless keelless masseuse noteless
calipash deafness editress floccose hasheesh keenness massless novelise
calmness dealfish eelgrass flourish haziness keratose matgrass novelist
canalise dearness eeriness fluidise headfast kindless matiness nuclease
canoeist declasse embolism foamless headless kindness mattress nudeness
canoness decrease endemism focalise headmost kingfish maximise nullness
canonise deedless energise fondness headrest kourbash mayoress numbfish
canonist deepness enforest foodless hebraise laconism Mazdaism numbness
caponise deforest epiblast footless Hebraism lacrosse maziness nuthouse
careless deftness epilepsy footpost Hebraist lacunose meanness oatgrass
catalase degrease equalise footrest hedonism lameness meekness oiliness
catalyse deionise erethism forecast hedonist lamppost meetness onehorse
catalyst demolish ergotise foremast heedless landless melanism oologist
cateress demonese ergotism foremost heelless landmass melodise ooziness
centrism demonise escapism forepast heirless languish melodist opencast
centrist demonism escapist formless helotism lankness memorise openness
ceramist deputise espresso fortress helpless largesse mightest optimise
Chartism devilish essayist fortyish henroost lateness mildness optimism
Chartist devilism Essenism fougasse hepatise latinise milepost optimist
chastise dewiness eternise foulness herbless Latinism mindless Orangism
cheapish dextrose etherise fowlpest highmost Latinist minimise oratress
childish diagnose etherism foxiness highness Lazarist Minoress organise
chiliasm diapause etherist Frankish highrise laziness mishmash organism
chiliast diastase ethicism freakish hightest leadless misprise organist
chinless digamist ethicist freeness hindmost leafless mistress outburst
churlish digitise eugenism frogfish hinduise leanness mistrust outclass
civilise dimerism eugenist frondose Hinduism legalese mobilise outguess
clannish diminish eulogise fructose hipflask legalise modalism outhouse
clerkess dioecism eulogist frumpish hobbyist legalism modalist ovalness
cliquish dioptase euphrasy fullness holdfast legalist Molinism overbusy
cliquism dirigism euphuism furthest holiness Leninism Molinist overcast
cloddish disabuse euphuist futurism homeless Leninist monadism overdose
clownish disburse evenness futurist hopeless lensless monetise overfish
clueless disclose evilness gainless hornless levulose mongoose overpass
coaldust disguise exercise Galenism hothouse lewdness monkfish overpast
coalfish dispense exorcise galleass hotpress lifeless monodist overtask
coldness disperse exorcism gallwasp hugeness lightish moonfish pacifism
collapse disseise exorcist gameness humanise likeness moonless pacifist
colonise distress extrorse gaminess humanism likewise moonrise paganise
colonist distrust eyeglass gashouse humanist limbless moralise paganish
comatose ditheism fabulist gatepost humorist limewash moralism paganism
comedist ditheist faceless Gaullism huntress limpness moralist painless
compress divinise fadeless Gaullist hurtless linguist motorise paleness
comprise Docetism faintish gearcase hushhush listless motorist paludism
concasse Docetist fairness Genevese hydropsy liverish moveless papalise
condense doghouse fairyism geognosy Ibsenism lobbyist muchness papalism
congress doloroso fallfish ghoulish idealess localise muskrose papalist
conquest Donatism fangless giantess idealise localism musquash papulose
contessa Donatist faradism giantism idealism lockfast muteness paradise
contrast doorcase farinose gipsyism idealist loneness myoblast paralyse
```

parclose	rallyist	scampish	soulless	ticklish	voidness	allopath	castrate
parodist	rankness	scarless	sourness	tideless	voltaism	almighty	castrati
paroxysm	raptness	sciolism	sourpuss	tidiness	votaress	amaranth	castrato
Parsiism	rareness	sciolist	sparkish	tigerish	votarist	ambulate	casualty
pathless	rashness	sclerose	spathose	tilefish	voteless	ammonite	catamite
pederast	readjust	Scottish	spoffish	timefuse	vowelise	amoretti	catenate
peerless	realness	seachest	spookish	timeless	Wahabism	amoretto	celerity
Pekinese	rearmost	seacoast	spotless	tininess	waitress	amputate	celibate
pelorism	reassess	seahorse	spryness	tintless	wakeless	analcite	cerusite
penalise	reckless	seamless	spyglass	tireless	wardress	analecta	chapatti
pertness	recourse	seamouse	squamose	titaness	warhorse	analects	chastity
perverse	redeless	seapurse	squarish	titanism	wariness	andesite	chlorate
petuntse	reforest	seedcase	stablish	titmouse	warmness	anecdote	chlorite
phantasm	regalism	seedfish	standish	toadfish	waterish	anisette	chordate
phantasy	rehearse	seedless	stardust	toadyish	waveless	ankerite	chromate
photopsy	reimpose	selfless	starfish	toadyism	waviness	annotate	chromite
piecrust	reinless	selfness	starless	tokenism	waxiness	annulate	chupatti
pinkness	reinvest	Semitise	stedfast	tolldish	weakfish	antedate	chupatty
pipefish	repousse	Semitism	steepish	tombless	weakness	antidote	cineaste
pitiless	response	Semitist	stemless	toneless	weedless	apostate	circuity
pixieish	restless	sexiness	stepwise	topdress	wetnurse	appetite	civility
pixiness	retrorse	shadbush	stiffish	tortoise	whatness	apposite	clypeate
pleonasm	ribgrass	Shaktism	stockish	totalise	Whiggish	arboreta	cogitate
pleurisy	richness	sharpish	stockist	totemism	Whiggism	areolate	complete
plumbism	rifeness	sheepish	stoicism	totemist	whiplash	arillate	concerti
plumpish	rightist	shoeless	stoutish	toughish	wideness	aristate	concerto
polarise	rigorism	shortish	strabism	tovarish	wifeless	arrogate	concetti
polemise	rigorist	shouldst	stramash	Trappist	wildness	arsenate	concetto
polemist	ripeness	showcase	strigose	traverse	wiliness	arsenite	conchate
poorness	roadless	shrewish	strumose	treatise	windlass	aseptate	concrete
populism	rockfish	sicklist	subclass	treeless	windless	asperity	confetti
populist	rockrose	sickness	suberise	trespass	windrose	aspirate	conflate
porpoise	romanise	sidedish	suberose	trialist	wingcase	assiento	contents
portress	Romanism	sidewise	sublease	trickish	wingless	assonate	contrate
pothouse	Romanist	signpost	submerse	trimness	wireless	asyndeta	contrite
potroast	roofless	similise	Sudanese	trueness	wiriness	atrocity	copulate
practise	rootless	simonist	suitcase	tsaritsa	wiseness	audacity	coquette
prankish	ropiness	simplism	sunburst	tubeless	wishwash	automata	corelate
preexist	rosebush	sinapism	sundress	tuberose	wolffish	automate	cornetti
prelease	rosefish	sinicise	suppress	tuneless	womanise	autunite	cornetto
premorse	rosiness	sitarist	surcease	tutoress	womanish	axiality	corvette
prepense	roughish	skewness	sureness	typecast	wordless	backbite	courante
priapism	roundish	skilless	surffish	ugliness	workless	backdate	craniate
priggish	rowdyish	skinless	surprise	ultraism	wormcast	baguette	creosote
priggism	rowdyism	skirmish	suspense	ultraist	wouldest	baldpate	crispate
primness	royalism	skittish	swainish	unionise	youngest	ballista	cristate
primrose	royalist	slapdash	sweetish	unionism	youngish	banality	croceate
princess	rudeness	slimmest	sylphish	unionist	zaniness	banditti	crocoite
prioress	rugulose	slimmish	tactless	universe	zombiism	banknote	cruciate
progress	ruleless	slimness	tailless	upthrust	Abderite	barbette	cryolite
prolapse	ruralise	slipcase	tallness	urbanise	abdicate	barrette	cumulate
propense	ruralism	slobbish	tamarisk	urbanism	abnegate	basicity	cupidity
prophase	ruralist	slowness	tameless	urbanist	abrogate	bedplate	cupulate
prophesy	rustless	sluggish	tameness	vainness	absolute	behemoth	Cypriote
prosaism	ruthless	sluttish	tangoist	valorise	accurate	bellcote	dancette
prosaist	ryegrass	smallish	Tantrism	vaneless	acerbate	benzoate	dancetty
protease	sackless	smartish	Tantrist	vanquish	acerbity	bequeath	deaerate
pruinose	safeness	smugness	tapeless	vaporise	acervate	bilobate	deafmute
psalmist	sageness	snappish	taphouse	varicose	acierate	birdbath	debility
psychism	sailfish	sneakish	tarboosh	vastness	acridity	blankety	decimate
psychist	sailless	snobbish	tartness	veilless	acrolith	bobwhite	decorate
ptyalism	saltbush	snobbism	tautness	ventless	acrylate	bombsite	dedicate
pugilism	saltless	snowless	teachest	vibrissa	activate	boracite	definite
pugilist	saltness	snugness	teahouse	victress	activity	bregmata	delegate
puniness	sameness	soapdish	tearless	Viennese	aculeate	brookite	delibate
puppyish	sandyish	soapless	telecast	viewless	adequate	brunette	delicate
purchase	saneness	soberise	televise	vileness	adespota	burletta	dendrite
pureness	sanitise	softness	termless	viperish	aduncate	butyrate	depilate
purplish	sannyasi	soilless	tetanise	virilism	advocate	caducity	depurate
quackish	sapphism	solarise	theorise	virtuosa	aerolite	calamite	derivate
qualmish	sargasso	solarism	theorist	virtuosi	aerolith	calamity	derogate
quantise	satanism	solarist	thickish	virtuoso	aesthete	calidity	desolate
queerish	satanist	solecism	thievish	vitalise	affinity	califate	detonate
quietism	sateless	solecist	thinness	vitalism	aigrette	campsite	diamante
quietist	satirise	soleness	thinnest	vitalist	alacrity	capacity	dicacity
racemise	satirist	solfaist	thinnish	vixenish	algidity	capitate	digitate
racemose	sawhorse	somatism	thisness	vocalise	alginate	carinate	discrete
raciness	Saxonism	songless	thuggism	vocalism	alienate	casemate	distaste
rainwash	Saxonist	soreness	thusness	vocalist	allocate	cassette	disunite

```
disunity gelidity jugulate moderato plaudits serenity timidity woodnote
divagate geminate kilowatt modulate playmate sericity tinplate workmate
divinity generate lability molality plumbate serosity tinsmith wrymouth
docility geophyte lacerate molarity pochette severity titanate xanthate
dogtooth glaciate lacunate monazite polarity sextette titanite xenolith
dolerite gnathite lambaste monocyte polymath sforzato titivate xylonite
dolomite goatmoth laminate monolith polypite Shabuoth toeplate yokemate
dominate graduate lapidate monteith populate shipmate toilette zoophyte
dovecote graffiti laterite moquette porosity shofroth tolbooth abomasum
draughts graffito Latinate morality postdate sibilate tolerate abomasus
draughty graphite latinity morosity priorate sidenote tollgate acanthus
droughty gratuity laureate mosquito priority siderite tonality acarpous
dryplate grisette lazulite motility property silicate tonicity aconitum
dynamite guaranty lazurite motivate prostate simulate toplofty actinium
echinate Gujarati legality motivity protista sirvente torquate addendum
edentate gulosity legerity mucosity punctate sitzbath totality adiantum
eleventh gunsmith Leninite multeity quadrate sixtieth touristy aduncous
elongate halfnote lepidote mutilate quantity slyboots toxicity aeronaut
emaciate hawkmoth levigate mylonite quiddity smaltite trabeate afflatus
emendate headnote levirate myxomata rabidity snippety trachyte alburnum
emigrate hebetate levitate nasality racemate sobriety tractate allodium
enceinte helminth lewisite natality radicate sodalite traumata alluvium
enervate helpmate liberate nativity rapacity sodality travesty alveolus
enormity henparty libretti nauseate rapidity sodomite trecento amiantus
ensheath heredity libretto navigate recreate solidity trichite ammonium
enterate hereunto lichgate Nazarite regality sonority triunity analogue
entirety herewith ligulate Nazirite regelate sororate troilite anourous
entracte hesitate limonite neophyte regolith sorority truncate apologue
entreaty hilarity lipomata nephrite regrowth sovranty tubulate applique
ephorate hitherto literate nihility regulate sparsity tumidity apterous
epinasty hotplate literati nobility reignite speciate tunicate aquanaut
epiphyte humanity litigate nodality relegate spiccato ubiquity aquarium
equality humidity lividity nodosity relocate spoliate uintaite araceous
equinity humility lobulate noisette renovate spraints ulcerate Arcturus
escalate hyacinth locality nominate resinate squamate ultimata argonaut
essonite hydranth locomote nonparty resolute staccato ultimate arquebus
estimate iceskate loculate nonwhite resonate stagnate umbonate arsonous
eternity ideality loricate nubility respects stannate umbrette ascidium
etiolate identity lucidity nucleate revolute stannite umptieth bacillus
evacuate ilmenite lunulate numerate rhyolite stearate unchaste bandeaux
evaluate immolate lustrate obdurate rigidity steatite uncinate barbecue
excavate immunity lychgate obligate roommate stellate uncreate basidium
execrate impanate macerate obsolete rostrate stemmata undulate basinful
exiguity imparity maculate obturate rosulate sternite ungulate bateleur
expedite impolite Mahratta obtusity roulette stibnite urbanite bdellium
exuviate impunity Mahratti ocellate rugosity stigmata urbanity beechnut
eyetooth impurity majority oddments ruminate stilbite urticate belabour
facility inchoate makebate oilcloth runagate stiletto vagility bellyful
falsetto increate malamute omelette rurality stoccata valerate bibulous
Fascista incubate malemute omoplate sacristy strength validate biennium
Fascisti indagate maquette onychite sagacity stromata validity bigamous
fatality indicate marinate operetta saginate stuprate vamplate bimanous
federate indurate Masorete oppilate salacity subacute vanadate biparous
felicity inequity Masoreth opposite salinity subtlety vapidity blackout
felinity infinite matamata opsimath salivate subulate vegetate blameful
feminity infinity matelote ordinate sanctity sulphate velleity blissful
ferocity ingrowth maturate osculate sandbath sulphite velocity blushful
fidelity iniquity maturity ostinato sanitate superate venality boastful
fiftieth initiate medicate otiosity sapidity supinate vendetta Bordeaux
filtrate innovate meditate outcaste saponite suricate venerate boutique
finality insanity megalith overrate saturate sybarite venosity brachium
flatmate insolate megawatt paginate sawtooth tabulate veracity breakout
fleabite insulate melanite palliate scarcity tachiste vermouth bronchus
fluidity intimate melinite palmette schemata tailgate vesicate burntout
fluorite intonate mesquite palmetto schmaltz tartrate vicarate caduceus
footbath intubate messmate parasite sclerite teacloth vicinity caducous
footnote inundate miasmata pearlite security teammate vignette caesious
footpath invocate militate peculate sedulity teaparty vinosity caladium
forsooth involute minacity perfecto seicento tegmenta viridity calculus
fortieth iodinate Minorite perianth selcouth telepath virility canorous
fortuity irrigate minority peridote selenate temerity Visigoth capsicum
frisette irritate misquote peripety selenite template vitality captious
frumenty Islamite misstate permeate selfmate tenacity vivacity cardamum
fugacity isophote miswrite perorate selfpity tenorite vocality carryout
fumigate isopleth mitigate pianiste senility tepidity voracity cautious
futility Italiote mitzvoth pilosity senorita thermite Wahabite cerebrum
futurity Jacobite mobility pimiento separate thickety warranty cernuous
galenite jocosity modality pisolite septette thoughts waxcloth chasseur
garrotte jubilate moderate placenta serenata tidegate witchety chateaux
```

checkout	enshroud	inoculum	pandanus	shakeout	truthful	curative	duckhawk
cheerful	entellus	intercut	papulous	shameful	tuberous	decisive	dustbowl
chestnut	eohippus	intrigue	paramour	shareout	tumorous	delusive	eagleowl
chiasmus	epigeous	ivorynut	patagium	sheeprun	tympanum	derisive	fishbowl
chlorous	epilogue	jongleur	patulous	shelfful	ulcerous	dilative	fishhawk
chondrus	eulogium	jumpedup	peaceful	shootout	unctuous	disprove	flyblown
choragus	euonymus	keelhaul	pendulum	shortcut	undercut	disserve	garefowl
choregus	europium	khuskhus	peridium	sidedrum	underfur	dissolve	handsewn
chromium	eventful	knockout	perilous	sillabub	underrun	dividivi	highlows
ciborium	excursus	labdanum	perineum	silphium	unlawful	divisive	hometown
cingulum	exemplum	labellum	periplus	sinciput	uppercut	donative	markdown
clangour	exiguous	laburnum	pervious	slothful	usurious	durative	moorfowl
claqueur	eximious	langlauf	petalous	solarium	uxorious	effusive	newblown
cleancut	exordium	larkspur	phaseout	solatium	valorous	egestive	nightowl
clearcut	fabliaux	laudanum	phormium	sombrous	vanadium	ejective	nutbrown
clubhaul	fabulous	layabout	physique	sonorous	vanadous	elective	outdrawn
coagulum	factious	ligneous	pishogue	spacious	vaporous	emissive	outgrown
cockshut	factotum	linoleum	plateaux	spadeful	variorum	emulsive	oversewn
coiffeur	faithful	lixivium	plateful	specious	vasculum	enactive	rockhewn
cokernut	fanciful	loathful	platinum	spectrum	vauntful	eruptive	rosebowl
coliseum	fashious	lomentum	platypus	speculum	vavasour	evincive	selfsown
collogue	fastuous	longueur	plectrum	sphagnum	velarium	fixative	shallows
colloquy	feverous	luminous	pluvious	sphygmus	vengeful	foxglove	showdown
colossus	finespun	luscious	polonium	spiculum	venomous	fugitive	shutdown
conidium	fireplug	lustrous	polypous	spiritus	veratrum	genitive	slowdown
construe	fishglue	lutecium	poppadum	spiteful	vexillum	illative	tomahawk
continua	flashgun	lutetium	populous	splenius	viaticum	illusive	turndown
continue	flexuous	malodour	powerful	spoonful	viburnum	inactive	upthrown
continuo	followup	mandamus	prankful	sportful	vigorous	incisive	washbowl
corneous	forceful	marabout	pratique	spraygun	vinculum	invasive	wildfowl
corundum	frabjous	marasmus	precious	spurious	viperous	kidglove	antefixa
costplus	francium	mealybug	previous	squamous	virtuous	ladylove	apoplexy
couscous	freakout	meconium	prideful	stannous	vitellus	lavalava	cacomixl
covetous	freezeup	meniscus	printout	stickful	vitreous	laxative	birdseye
crepitus	fremitus	menstrua	prologue	stimulus	vivarium	lenitive	bullseye
critique	frenulum	merciful	prorogue	strumous	voiceful	lipsalve	carbonyl
crosscut	freshrun	meringue	pruritus	studious	volvulus	locative	carboxyl
croupous	frondeur	miasmous	pulvinus	suberous	voyageur	longwave	cattleya
cumbrous	fruitful	Minotaur	puparium	subgenus	warcloud	mangrove	diphenyl
cumulous	gadabout	mirthful	pygidium	subgroup	wasteful	margrave	edgeways
cupreous	galbanum	mittimus	pyrrhous	subshrub	watchful	monitive	epicalyx
curlicue	generous	molossus	pyxidium	succinum	waterbus	negative	epicotyl
cymatium	geranium	momentum	ramentum	succubus	watthour	nosedive	flatways
dartrous	ghastful	monsieur	ranarium	sudarium	weariful	offdrive	glyceryl
decolour	glabrous	moresque	ravenous	susurrus	whiteout	optative	gramarye
decorous	glassful	motorium	residuum	syconium	wondrous	outbrave	holidays
delirium	glaucous	mournful	resinous	syllabub	worthful	perceive	hydroxyl
denarius	glorious	mouthful	rhonchus	syllabus	wrackful	piassava	longways
desirous	glucinum	muticous	rightful	tableaux	wrathful	positive	nowadays
detritus	godawful	mutinous	rigorous	tablecut	wrongful	preserve	sardonyx
dextrous	goitrous	mycelium	rondeaux	tableful	wrongous	punitive	sideways
dialogue	golfclub	mystique	rouleaus	tamandua	xanthium	putative	someways
dianthus	gonidium	nacreous	rouleaux	tantalum	youthful	reactive	tautonym
didymium	gorgeous	nauplius	rubidium	tantalus	ablative	relative	tigereye
didymous	graceful	nauseous	runabout	tastebud	abortive	reprieve	bulldoze
digamous	gracious	nautilus	runnerup	tasteful	abrasive	retrieve	credenza
diluvium	grandeur	nebulium	rushhour	teetotum	adaptive	ringdove	czaritza
dimerous	grateful	nebulous	saboteur	tenesmus	additive	rockdove	disprize
dinerout	grievous	nobelium	sacculus	terminus	adhesive	rotative	fullsize
dinosaur	griseous	nodulous	samarium	testatum	adoptive	sanative	kamikaze
dipnoous	guaiacum	nubilous	saporous	thalamus	aggrieve	sedative	kingsize
disvalue	guileful	nucellus	savorous	thallium	allusive	selflove	lifesize
dolorous	gypseous	numerous	scabious	thallous	auditive	sorptive	misprize
doubtful	harangue	numinous	scabrous	thankful	aversive	sportive	oversize
doughnut	hazelnut	ochreous	scandium	thereout	Casanova	subserve	pintsize
downhaul	Hesperus	oestrous	scarious	thrombus	coactive	tidewave	stargaze
downpour	hibiscus	olibanum	scholium	timorous	coercive	topheavy	terrazzo
dreadful	higherup	omadhaun	scirrhus	tinnitus	cohesive	tractive	tsaritza
dreamful	homespun	ommateum	sclerous	titanium	conative	truelove	unfreeze
duodenum	houseful	oncidium	scoopful	tomentum	conceive	univalve	—————
duologue	humorous	oogamous	scornful	tommygun	conclave	vegetive	abscissa
earthnut	hymenium	oogonium	seatrout	toothful	conferva	vocative	academia
edacious	hypogeum	orgulous	sedulous	tortious	congreve	volitive	aceldama
electrum	ichorous	origanum	seigneur	tortuous	conserve	vomitive	adespota
elenchus	imperium	outvalue	selenium	trillium	contrive	wirewove	adularia
emeritus	indicium	overhaul	senarius	tristful	convolve	bestrewn	adynamia
emporium	indusium	overplus	senseful	trueblue	cooptive	comedown	agraphia
encomium	infamous	oversoul	sensuous	trumeaux	creative	discrown	alleluia
enormous	inflatus	oxtongue	sepalous	trustful	crescive	downtown	alopecia

ambrosia	credenza	magnesia	symposia	analogic	dialytic	granitic	neoteric
amphibia	criteria	magnolia	syncytia	analytic	diarchic	Guelphic	neuritic
amygdala	cromorna	maharaja	syntagma	anarchic	diatomic	hadronic	neuronic
anaconda	czaritza	Mahratta	tamandua	anatomic	diatonic	haematic	neurotic
analecta	decennia	maiolica	tamboura	anechoic	dichroic	harmonic	nickelic
anaphora	dementia	majolica	tegmenta	aniconic	dicrotic	Helladic	nomistic
anasarca	demerara	malvasia	tenacula	anorexic	dicyclic	Hellenic	nuclidic
anathema	dentalia	mandorla	teratoma	anorthic	didactic	heraldic	omphalic
angelica	diarrhea	mantilla	terraria	aoristic	dietetic	hermetic	operatic
anorexia	diaspora	mantissa	tetrapla	apagogic	dioptric	herpetic	orgasmic
antefixa	diastema	manubria	tortilla	aphasiac	dioramic	hidrotic	orgastic
anthelia	dichasia	marchesa	toxaemia	aplastic	dioritic	hieratic	ornithic
anthemia	diplopia	matamata	trachoma	apogamic	diuretic	Hispanic	orogenic
anthozoa	djellaba	menstrua	trapezia	argentic	dogmatic	historic	Ossianic
antisera	dracaena	miasmata	traumata	Armagnac	domestic	holistic	pachalic
apologia	dulciana	moussaka	trichina	aromatic	draconic	holozoic	pandemic
arapaima	Dulcinea	mycetoma	triennia	artistic	dramatic	horrific	papistic
arboreta	dyslexia	myxomata	triforia	asbestic	dynastic	hydropic	parhelic
arethusa	dyspnoea	oiticica	trochlea	asthenic	dysgenic	hygienic	parsonic
asphyxia	dystopia	opercula	tsarevna	ataraxic	dyslexic	hypnotic	pashalic
asthenia	ecclesia	operetta	tsaritsa	athletic	eclectic	hypothec	pathetic
asyndeta	effluvia	opuscula	tsaritza	Atlantic	ecliptic	hysteric	pedantic
ataraxia	egomania	orchilla	ultimata	autarkic	ecologic	isagogic	Pelasgic
atheroma	encaenia	palestra	umbrella	autistic	economic	ischemic	periodic
aubretia	endostea	panmixia	undersea	balladic	ecstatic	isobaric	periotic
auricula	engramma	panorama	vaccinia	balletic	egoistic	isogamic	perlitic
automata	ephemera	parabola	Valhalla	balsamic	electric	isogonic	petrolic
avifauna	epifauna	paranoia	velamina	banausic	elenctic	isomeric	phenolic
babirusa	epopoeia	parhelia	vendetta	barbaric	elliptic	isotonic	phenylic
babushka	erythema	pellagra	veronica	baryonic	empathic	isotopic	phonemic
bacteria	etcetera	penumbra	vertebra	basaltic	emphatic	japhetic	phonetic
ballista	eupepsia	petechia	vibrissa	bathetic	enclitic	jesuitic	photopic
bandanna	euphoria	photopia	victoria	bathotic	encrinic	Jurassic	phreatic
barathea	fantasia	piassava	Virginia	bauxitic	encyclic	juristic	phthalic
barranca	fasciola	pizzeria	virtuosa	beatific	endermic	klephtic	phthisic
basilica	Fascista	placenta	viscacha	benzylic	endozoic	kyphotic	phyletic
battalia	fenestra	plethora	vizcacha	biogenic	entoptic	leucitic	Pindaric
bethesda	fibrilla	pollinia	Walhalla	bionomic	entozoic	lignitic	platinic
bignonia	Filipina	polygala	wistaria	bromidic	enuretic	liturgic	platonic
blastema	fistiana	predella	wisteria	calcific	enzootic	logistic	plutonic
blastula	flabella	protista	xanthoma	calcitic	eolithic	lordotic	podagric
branchia	flagella	protozoa	yarmulka	carbolic	epidemic	maenadic	pollinic
brassica	flotilla	prunella	zarzuela	carbonic	episodic	magmatic	polyzoic
bregmata	foramina	pyrrhoea	zirconia	cathodic	eremitic	magnetic	poristic
britzska	fraenula	quadriga	zoiatria	catholic	erogenic	magnific	potassic
bromelia	gardenia	retinula	backcomb	cationic	esoteric	maieutic	prelatic
bronchia	gastraea	rutabaga	catacomb	celeriac	Ethiopic	majestic	prolific
brouhaha	gastrula	sacraria	choriamb	Cenozoic	eucritic	manganic	propylic
buddleia	gematria	sandflea	divebomb	cephalic	eupeptic	marasmic	prosodic
burletta	glabella	sayonara	doorknob	Chaldaic	euphonic	mechanic	protatic
cachexia	glaucoma	schemata	firebomb	cherubic	euphoric	medallic	protonic
cachucha	glossina	sciatica	golfclub	chiastic	eustatic	mephitic	pruritic
calcanea	gloxinia	scleroma	hecatomb	chimeric	eutectic	mercuric	pulmonic
calcaria	Golconda	scrofula	kingcrab	choleric	exegetic	meristic	puristic
calyptra	gorgonia	scutella	landcrab	choragic	exogamic	mesmeric	purpuric
camellia	Griselda	semolina	memsahib	choregic	exoteric	Mesozoic	pyogenic
campagna	guerilla	senorita	reabsorb	chthonic	faradaic	metallic	pythonic
capitula	gymkhana	sensoria	sillabub	cinnamic	febrific	meteoric	quidnunc
capybara	gymnasia	serenata	subshrub	climatic	felsitic	methodic	quixotic
caracara	gynoecia	shigella	syllabub	cobaltic	ferritic	methylic	rabbinic
carnauba	habanera	sinfonia	timebomb	coelomic	fibrotic	microbic	rachitic
Casanova	hacienda	sonatina	academic	cornific	forensic	Miltonic	republic
cathedra	hamartia	spirilla	acentric	cosmetic	frenetic	Mishnaic	rhetoric
cattleya	hepatica	sporozoa	aconitic	culdesac	gabbroic	Mithraic	rhythmic
cavatina	herbaria	stapelia	acoustic	Cushitic	Gadhelic	mnemonic	romantic
cercaria	hulahula	stemmata	acrostic	cyanotic	galactic	molybdic	sabbatic
charisma	hysteria	sterigma	adamitic	cyclonic	galvanic	monastic	saccadic
chickpea	insignia	stigmata	adynamic	Cyrenaic	gelastic	Mongolic	sadistic
chimaera	insomnia	stoccata	agnostic	Cyrillic	geodesic	monistic	salvific
churinga	intarsia	strobila	agrestic	dactylic	geodetic	morainic	sandarac
cinchona	isabella	stromata	alchemic	daemonic	geologic	morbific	sardonic
coenobia	ischemia	strontia	allergic	daimonic	geoponic	muriatic	saturnic
collyria	isoptera	subphyla	amitotic	dalmatic	Germanic	myelinic	scotopic
conferva	japonica	subpoena	amnesiac	demoniac	gerontic	myogenic	semantic
contagia	jipijapa	subtopia	amnesiac	despotic	gigantic	myositic	semiotic
contessa	katakana	suburbia	amniotic	diabasic	glyconic	narcotic	seraphic
continua	lavalava	swastika	anabatic	diabetic	gneissic	Nearctic	Shemitic
conurbia	lipomata	sweetpea	anabolic	diabolic	gnomonic	necrotic	sigmatic
coxalgia	lymphoma	sympodia	anagogic	dialogic	Goidelic	neotenic	silvatic

```
simoniac  allround  calycoid  dockland  freehand  inflexed  milliard  pinewood
Sinaitic  amoeboid  cancroid  dockyard  freehold  informed  millpond  pinnated
siphonic  amphipod  carolled  doddered  freeload  infrared  mimicked  pinniped
Slavonic  annulled  cartload  dogeared  frenzied  inkstand  misheard  plighted
Socratic  antlered  caryatid  dogfaced  furcated  inserted  misspend  plumaged
somnific  appalled  caudated  dogtired  gabbroid  inspired  mittened  plumiped
spagyric  arachnid  caverned  dooryard  gableend  intended  modelled  polypoid
specific  arcuated  cavilled  dowelled  gainsaid  interbed  monkhood  pondweed
spondaic  armoured  centroid  downland  galeated  interred  monoacid  postcard
sporadic  articled  ceratoid  downward  galliard  intrepid  moorland  postpaid
stanzaic  assorted  childbed  downwind  gamebird  invected  moribund  potbound
stenotic  asteroid  chorioid  dripfeed  gangland  inverted  mudguard  potsherd
stomatic  astonied  ciliated  drophead  gaolbird  ironclad  multifid  powdered
strophic  attested  cirriped  drownded  garboard  ironwood  multiped  prescind
subsonic  attrited  citified  drumhead  garreted  jacquard  muslined  prismoid
subtonic  autacoid  cityfied  drunkard  gasfired  jailbird  myriapod  profound
succinic  babyhood  closeted  duckpond  gatefold  japanned  myriopod  propound
syenitic  backhand  clubland  duckweed  gilthead  jeremiad  neatherd  provided
syllabic  backveld  clupeoid  dumbhead  girlhood  jewelled  neckband  pteropod
sylvatic  backward  cockeyed  dumfound  gladhand  jiggered  nectared  puffbird
symbolic  backyard  coleseed  dutypaid  goatherd  jolthead  nematoid  pugnosed
synaptic  balanced  collared  eastward  godchild  junkyard  newfound  pulpwood
syndetic  baldhead  coloured  ebriated  Godspeed  kailyard  newlywed  purblind
synergic  bannered  colubrid  echinoid  gourmand  keeshond  nielloed  purebred
syngamic  barnyard  columned  educated  goutweed  keyboard  nimbused  pyrenoid
synoptic  basswood  composed  elevated  graduand  kingbird  ninefold  racecard
syntonic  becalmed  compound  elkhound  granddad  kinghood  nonrigid  railhead
systemic  bedimmed  conchoid  embedded  grizzled  knapweed  noseband  railroad
systolic  bedstead  confound  embussed  gruntled  labelled  obtected  rainbird
Talmudic  beebread  copyhold  emulsoid  gulfweed  ladybird  occluded  rapeseed
tantalic  beefwood  coracoid  enarched  gusseted  ladyhood  occurred  rarefied
tartaric  befitted  cordwood  enrolled  halfbred  lakeland  odontoid  ratguard
tectonic  befogged  corkwood  enshroud  halliard  lamented  oilfield  ravelled
telluric  befriend  corniced  equalled  hallowed  landlord  oilfired  rawboned
terrific  begirded  coronoid  equipped  handheld  lapboard  oldworld  rearward
tetradic  bellbird  corseted  estopped  handhold  lapelled  olympiad  reascend
Teutonic  bentwood  Cotswold  eupatrid  handmaid  larboard  onesided  rebelled
thalamic  bereaved  crannied  excelled  hardhead  latticed  openeyed  rebutted
theistic  besotted  crashpad  expelled  hardwood  leeboard  ordinand  recapped
thematic  bevelled  credited  exserted  hatstand  lefthand  oriented  recurred
theurgic  bewigged  crenated  extolled  haulyard  leftward  ostracod  redblind
thoracic  bicuspid  crotched  facecard  havocked  legguard  outboard  redfaced
toreutic  billfold  cultured  fairlead  hawkeyed  legioned  outbound  redbird
tornadic  billhead  cupboard  falcated  hawkweed  leisured  outdated  referred
toxaemic  billiard  cupelled  farmhand  hayfield  lemuroid  outfield  refitted
Triassic  bindweed  curveted  farmland  headband  lettered  outHerod  reflexed
tribasic  birdseed  cussword  farmyard  headland  levelled  outmoded  reformed
trimeric  blastoid  danegeld  fastfood  headwind  libelled  outspend  remitted
trisomic  blizzard  deadhead  favoured  headword  licensed  ovenbird  renowned
trochaic  bloodred  deadwood  featured  hebdomad  lichened  overfeed  repelled
truistic  blowhard  deathbed  feedhead  helicoid  lintseed  overfold  repetend
tungstic  bluebird  debagged  fingered  helmeted  liveried  overfond  repotted
turmeric  blueweed  debarred  firebird  Hereford  loanword  overhand  rerecord
Tychonic  boatload  debugged  fireeyed  highbred  longhand  overhead  rereward
tympanic  bondmaid  deceased  fireweed  highland  lopeared  overlaid  reserved
typhonic  bonehead  deckhand  firewood  highroad  lopsided  overland  resigned
tyrannic  boneyard  deeplaid  firstaid  hocussed  louvered  overload  resinoid
uralitic  bookland  deferred  fishpond  hogshead  lovebird  overlord  retarded
vampiric  bosseyed  deformed  fissiped  homebred  lymphoid  overpaid  retorted
Vandalic  botryoid  dejected  fivefold  homeland  lynxeyed  oversold  revelled
Vedantic  brancard  demented  flathead  homeward  lyrebird  overwind  reverend
veristic  branched  demitted  flaxseed  hominoid  magicked  palmiped  revetted
villatic  brandied  demobbed  flockbed  humanoid  maidhood  panelled  rhizopod
volcanic  brassard  demurred  flowered  humoured  mainland  panicked  rhomboid
vulcanic  breasted  dendroid  focussed  hydatoid  mainyard  paranoid  ricebird
zeolitic  breveted  dentated  fogbound  icebound  manifold  parkland  ringroad
zoogenic  brickred  departed  foliaged  icefield  mannered  password  rivalled
abhorred  brindled  depraved  foothold  illfated  mansized  peasecod  rivelled
accursed  brocaded  deprived  forcefed  illiquid  marigold  pedalled  riverbed
acidhead  browband  detached  forehand  illtimed  masthead  pedicled  rockbird
adlihead  bulkhead  detailed  forehead  immersed  measured  pelludic  rockweed
admitted  bullhead  deterred  foreland  impacted  medalled  pellucid  rockwood
advanced  bunkered  devilled  foresaid  impelled  medusoid  perilled  roothold
affected  bushveld  dewyeyed  forested  included  membered  petalled  rosewood
agonised  buzzword  dihybrid  foretold  incurred  metalled  petaloid  rubicund
airfield  caballed  disbound  foreword  indebted  midfield  petioled  sailyard
airspeed  cabstand  diseased  foreyard  inedited  milkmaid  phylloid  salaried
alkaloid  cadenced  dispread  fourfold  inferred  milkweed  pilchard  saraband
allotted  cagebird  dividend  foxhound  inflated  millhand  pileated  sashcord
```

Sassanid	storeyed	unedited	wormseed	amperage	autotype	boottree	causerie
sauropod	strained	unfitted	wormwood	amphorae	autunite	boracite	celibate
Savoyard	stranded	unforced	wretched	ampullae	aversive	borecole	centuple
sawedged	strapped	unformed	yodelled	amputate	avowable	borehole	cerusite
scabbard	streaked	unfunded	zygaenid	anaerobe	axletree	botanise	chaconne
scaffold	streeted	unglazed	Abbaside	analcime	Ayrshire	botyrose	chalazae
scaphoid	stringed	unhinged	Abderite	analcite	babouche	bourtree	chastise
sceptred	stripped	unhoused	abdicate	analogue	backache	boutique	chasuble
schizoid	stropped	unleaded	abeyance	anaphase	backbite	brassage	chenille
sciuroid	strummed	unlinked	abidance	andesine	backbone	brattice	Cherokee
sclereid	strutted	unlisted	ablative	andesite	backdate	breakage	Cheyenne
scombrid	sturdied	unmanned	abnegate	anecdote	backfire	brettese	chlorate
scragend	stylised	unmarked	abortive	anisette	backside	brettice	chloride
scragged	sunbaked	unopened	abrasive	ankerite	badinage	bribable	chlorine
scrammed	sunblind	unpaired	abrogate	ankylose	baguette	brochure	chlorite
scrapped	sundried	unpegged	absentee	annotate	bailable	brookite	chordate
scrubbed	superadd	unpinned	absinthe	announce	baldpate	brunette	christie
seaboard	supposed	unplaced	absolute	annulate	balefire	bubaline	chromate
secluded	surfbird	unrigged	absterge	anserine	Balinese	buckshee	chromite
selfhood	surround	unroofed	abstruse	antecede	balkline	budgeree	cicerone
sepaloid	swanherd	unsealed	accolade	antedate	bankable	bulldoze	cincture
serfhood	synergid	unseated	accoutre	antelope	banknote	bullseye	cineaste
serranid	taenioid	unseeded	accurate	antennae	barbecue	bummaree	civilise
serrated	talented	unshaped	acerbate	antidote	barbette	buncombe	clambake
sesamoid	tamarind	unstated	acervate	antinode	baritone	bunghole	clarence
sheepked	tastebud	unsuited	aciculae	antipode	barnacle	buntline	clavicle
shepherd	tattered	unsunned	acierage	antipole	baronage	burnouse	claymore
Shetland	teaboard	untapped	acierate	antipope	barouche	bushfire	cleavage
shipload	teabread	untented	acridine	antitype	barrette	butylene	clodpole
shipyard	tempered	unthread	acrylate	antrorse	barytone	butyrate	clypeate
showcard	terraced	untitled	actiniae	anyplace	baseline	caboodle	coactive
shredded	tetrapod	untoward	actinide	anywhere	bastille	cabotage	coalesce
shrugged	texthand	unvalued	activate	aperture	bathrobe	cabriole	coalhole
sideband	textured	unversed	aculeate	aphicide	bayadere	cadastre	coalmine
sidehead	thalloid	unvoiced	adaptive	aphorise	beanpole	caffeine	cochleae
sideroad	thousand	unwanted	additive	apocrine	bearable	calamine	cocksure
sideward	throated	unwashed	adequate	apologue	bechance	calamite	codpiece
sidewind	throbbed	unweaned	adhesive	apostate	bedabble	califate	coenzyme
siluroid	thrummed	unwished	adjutage	appanage	bedazzle	callable	coercive
sinusoid	thyrsoid	unwonted	adoptive	appetite	bedplate	calliope	cogitate
situated	tickseed	unzipped	adorable	applause	bedtable	calycine	cognosce
skewbald	tideland	urochord	aduncate	applepie	beefcake	calycule	cohesive
skinfood	tightwad	vagabond	advocate	applique	befuddle	camisade	coiffure
skinhead	tiltyard	valanced	aegirine	apposite	begrudge	camisole	coincide
sliproad	timbered	vanguard	aerodyne	appraise	belittle	camomile	collapse
slipshod	tittuped	verdured	aerolite	aptitude	bellcote	campfire	collogue
slobland	toolshed	verecund	aesthete	aquacade	benefice	camphene	colonise
sloeeyed	totalled	vilipend	affiance	aquiline	benzoate	camphine	comatose
slugabed	towelled	vineyard	aggrieve	Arapahoe	berceuse	campsite	commence
sluggard	tracheid	vizarded	agiotage	archaise	bestride	canaille	commerce
snowbird	tramroad	vowelled	aigrette	archduke	bestrode	canalise	complete
socalled	trichoid	walleyed	aiguille	areolate	beverage	cancrine	complice
softhead	trichord	warcloud	airborne	arguable	biddable	cannulae	compline
softwood	trilobed	wartweed	airbrake	arillate	bilobate	canonise	comprise
solenoid	triploid	waterbed	Airedale	aristate	binnacle	canoodle	conative
songbird	trochoid	waveband	airframe	armature	bioscope	canticle	concasse
sorehead	trophied	Wedgwood	airspace	arrestee	birdcage	capeline	conceive
sowbread	truebred	weeviled	albacore	arrogate	birdlime	capitate	conchate
Spaniard	turbaned	wellbred	aldehyde	arsenate	birdseye	caponise	conclave
spavined	turreted	wellhead	alehouse	arsenide	bistable	capriole	conclude
sphenoid	twoedged	wellread	aleurone	arsenite	blacktie	capstone	concrete
spheroid	twofaced	weregild	algicide	artifice	blamable	carabine	condense
sphingid	twosided	westward	alginate	aseptate	blindage	caracole	conferee
spicated	unabated	whipcord	alienage	aspirate	blockade	carapace	conflate
spirited	unaneled	whizzkid	alienate	assemble	blockage	carefree	confrere
splendid	unbacked	wideeyed	alkaline	assignee	blowhole	carinate	conglobe
spoonfed	unbarred	wifehood	alliance	assonate	blowpipe	Caroline	congreve
sprigged	unbiased	wildeyed	allocate	astatine	bluenose	carotene	conserve
squatted	unbolted	wildwood	allottee	atremble	bobwhite	carriage	consomme
squibbed	unburied	windowed	allspice	atropine	boldface	carriole	conspire
squidded	uncalled	windward	allusive	attitude	bolthole	caruncle	construe
staggard	uncandid	withheld	altitude	audience	boltrope	casemate	continue
stairrod	uncapped	withhold	ambiance	auditive	bombsite	cashmere	contline
stallfed	uncaused	woodbind	ambience	autocade	bonhomie	cassette	contrate
standard	uncoined	woodland	ambulate	autodafe	boniface	castrate	contrite
statured	underbid	woodshed	amenable	autodyne	bookcase	catalase	contrive
steepled	underdid	woodwind	amicable	autolyse	booklice	catalyse	converge
stenosed	undraped	wooldyed	ammonite	automate	booklore	catamite	converse
stinkard	unearned	woolshed	amortise	autosome	bootlace	catenate	convince

```
convolve demarche dominate enviable filagree funkhole hardline inhumane
convulse demiurge donative envisage filariae furculae hardware initiate
cooptive demonise doorcase ephorate filature furuncle hateable innovate
copulate denature dormouse epicycle filigree fuselage hawklike inscribe
coquette dendrite dovecote epilogue filtrate gadarene headache insecure
corelate denehole downcome epiphyte fimbriae gainable headline insolate
corniche deniable downpipe episcope finalise galenite headnote insphere
cornicle denounce downtime epistyle finitude gamesome headrace instable
cornpone denticle drachmae equalise firehose gangrene hebetate instance
corvette depilate dragline equipage fireside gantline hebetude insulate
coryphee deportee drainage equivoke fishable gantlope hebraise internee
coulisse depurate drawable erasable fishbone Ganymede hellfire intertie
courante deputise drawtube erectile fishcake gargoyle hellhole intimate
coverage derisive dressage erewhile fishglue garrotte helpmate intitule
cozenage derivate driftage ergotise fishwife gashouse hepatise intonate
craniate derogate driftice erodible fistulae gasolene heritage intrigue
creatine derriere drivable eruptive fixative gasoline hesitate introrse
creative describe drumfire escalade flagpole gazogene hetaerae intubate
creature desolate drynurse escalate flanerie gearcase hexylene inundate
credence detainee dryplate escalope flatmate gefuffle hidyhole inurbane
credible dethrone drystone escapade flatrace gelatine highrise invasive
crenelle detonate duchesse escarole flatware geminate hillside inveigle
creosote deviance dungaree essonite flatwise gemstone hinduise inviable
crescive dextrine duologue estimate fleabane gendarme hireable invocate
cretonne dextrose durative estrange fleabite generate hocktide involute
crevasse diagnose dustlike eternise flexible Genevese Holocene iodinate
cribbage diallage dutiable etherise flexuose genitive homelike ironside
crispate dialogue dutyfree ethylene flipside geniture homemade ironware
cristate diamante dynamite etiolate floatage genocide homicide irrigate
critique diapause earphone eulogise floccose genotype homuncle irritate
croceate diaphone earpiece evacuate floccule gentrice honeybee Islamise
crocoite diaspore echinate evadable fluepipe geophone hornpipe Islamite
cromorne diastase edentate evaluate fluidise geophyte horologe isolable
crosstie diastole edgewise evanesce fluoride gerbille horrible isophote
cruciate diatribe educable eventide fluorine germfree hosepipe isoprene
crucible digitate educible evermore fluorite girasole hothouse isothere
cryolite digitise effusive everyone focalise glaciate hotplate issuable
cubature dilative egestive evidence folklore gladsome huggable issuance
culicine dimmable ejective evincive folktale glandule humanise Italiote
culpable diopside elective evitable follicle glassine humuncle iterance
cumulate dioptase elegance examinee fontange gleesome hyoscine Jacobite
cupulate disabuse eligible excavate footnote glissade hypobole jalousie
curarine disagree elongate exchange footpace gloriole hypogene jamboree
curarise disburse emaciate execrate footrace gnathite ianthine Japanese
curative disciple embattle exercise footrope goalline iceskate jaundice
curlicue disclose embezzle exigence footrule goldmine idealise Javanese
curricle discrete emendate exigible footsore goodtime idocrase jetplane
cutprice disgorge emigrate exocrine forborne goodwife illative joinable
cutpurse disgrace eminence exorcise forcible graduate illumine jointure
cynosure disguise emissive exospore fordable Graecise illusage jubilate
Cypriote dislodge empeople expedite forebode gramarye illusive jugulate
cypselae dispense employee expellee foreedge grandame ilmenite julienne
cysteine disperse empurple expiable foregone grapheme imbecile juncture
cytidine displace emulsive exposure forename graphite imitable juvenile
cytosine displode enactive extrorse foreside greegree immature kamikaze
damnable displume enceinte exuviate foretime grillage immingle Kanarese
dancette disprize encircle eyepiece formulae grimoire immobile kedgeree
danseuse disprove enclothe eyerhyme forswore grisette immolate keepsake
darksome disseise endamage eyeshade fougasse gruesome immunise kefuffle
dateline disserve endorsee faceache foursome guidable impanate keratose
deadline dissolve energise facetiae foveolae guidance impledge kerosene
deaerate dissuade enervate failsafe foxglove gullable impolite kerosine
deafmute distance enfeeble fallible fracture gullible inactive keystone
decimate distaste enfilade fandance frisette habitude inchoate kidglove
decisive disunite engirdle farinose frondage hairlike incisive kinglike
declasse disusage enkindle farouche frondose hairline increase kingsize
decorate disvalue ensample fascicle frontage halflife increate kissable
decouple divagate ensconce fasciole frottage halfnote incubate klondike
decrease divinise ensemble fearsome fructose halfsole indagate kneehole
dedicate divisive enshrine feasible fruitage halftime indicate knothole
defiance divorcee ensilage federate frustule halftone indigene knowable
defilade dockside ensphere feedpipe fuchsine handline indocile lacerate
definite doctrine enswathe fellable fugitive handmade inductee lacrosse
degrease doghouse entangle feminine fullpage hangable induline lacunate
deionise dogshore enterate feminise fullsize harangue indurate lacunose
delegate dolerite enthrone fencible fulltime hardback inedible ladylike
delibate dolesome entracte ferriage fumarole hardbake infamise ladylove
delicate dolomite entrance feticide fumigate hardcase infinite lambaste
delusive domicile envelope figurine fungible hardcore infringe lamblike
```

lamellae	lustrate	misprise	noisette	overtake	pintable	protegee	resolute
laminate	lustrine	misprize	nomadise	overtime	pintsize	protrude	resonate
landline	lychgate	misquote	nominate	overtone	pipeline	provable	resource
landmine	lykewake	misshape	nonsense	overture	piperine	province	response
language	lyophile	misstate	nonusage	oxtongue	piscinae	prudence	restcure
lapicide	lysosome	misusage	nonwhite	paganise	pishogue	pruinose	resupine
lapidate	lysozyme	miswrite	noontide	paginate	pisolite	prunelle	reticule
largesse	macerate	mitigate	noontime	palatine	pitiable	pterylae	retrieve
laterite	maculate	mobilise	nosecone	paleface	pittance	ptomaine	retrorse
Latinate	madapple	moderate	nosedive	palinode	placable	puggaree	reusable
latinise	madhouse	modulate	nosepipe	palisade	planulae	punctate	revanche
latitude	magazine	moisture	notecase	palliate	playable	puncture	reveille
laudable	mailable	molecule	nouvelle	palmette	playmate	punitive	revolute
laureate	mainline	monazite	novelise	palpable	playtime	pupilage	rhapsode
laxative	makebate	mondaine	nuclease	pantofle	pleasure	purchase	rhyolite
lazulite	malamute	monetise	nucleate	papalise	Pliocene	purslane	ribosome
lazurite	malemute	mongoose	nucleole	papillae	plumbate	pushbike	riddance
leaflike	Mameluke	monitive	nuisance	papulose	plussage	putative	rideable
legalese	mamillae	monocyte	numerate	paradise	pochette	pyridine	ridicule
legalise	manciple	monopode	nuthouse	paragoge	polarise	pyroxene	rimbrake
legatine	mandible	monotone	oakapple	paralyse	polemise	quadrate	ringbone
lemonade	mandrake	monotype	obdurate	parasite	polygene	quagmire	ringdove
lemurine	mangrove	monoxide	obligate	paravane	polypide	quantise	ringside
lenience	Manichee	moonface	obsolete	parclose	polypite	quartile	riverine
Leninite	manicure	moonrise	obstacle	parlance	polyseme	quayside	roadside
lenitive	maquette	moonshee	obturate	parterre	populace	quenelle	rocaille
lenticle	marchese	moquette	ocellate	partible	populate	quietude	rockcake
lepidote	margrave	moralise	oeillade	particle	porpoise	quotable	rockdove
leporine	marinade	moresque	oestrone	parttime	porridge	racemate	rocklike
leverage	marinate	morpheme	offdrive	passable	portable	racemise	rockrose
leviable	maritage	morphine	offshore	passible	portfire	racemose	romanise
levigate	maritime	mortgage	offstage	pastiche	porthole	radiance	rooftree
levirate	marquise	motivate	oilstone	pastille	portiere	radicate	roommate
levitate	marriage	motorise	okeydoke	patellae	positive	rapecake	ropeable
levulose	Masorete	moveable	omelette	patentee	possible	rapparee	rosetree
lewisite	massacre	mucilage	omnivore	patience	postcode	rateable	rostrate
libellee	masseuse	muckrake	omoplate	payphone	postdate	ratsbane	rosulate
liberate	matelote	mudstone	onehorse	pearlite	postfree	reactive	rotative
licensee	maturate	multiple	onepiece	peccable	postiche	readable	rotenone
lichgate	maxillae	murrhine	onychite	peculate	postlude	realtime	roughage
licorice	maximise	musicale	openable	pedicure	postpone	rearmice	roulette
lifelike	mayapple	muskrose	operable	pedigree	pothouse	reassure	rugulose
lifeline	mazarine	musktree	oppilate	peduncle	potstone	recharge	ruinable
lifesize	mealtime	mustache	opposite	peephole	poultice	recourse	ruminate
lifetime	meantime	mutilate	optative	Pekinese	poundage	recreate	runagate
liftable	meatsafe	mylonite	optimise	pelerine	pourable	redefine	runcible
ligature	medicate	mystique	opulence	pellicle	practice	redouble	ruralise
ligulate	medicine	nailfile	opuscule	pembroke	practise	reedmace	rushlike
likeable	mediocre	nameable	ordinate	penalise	praecipe	reedpipe	sabotage
likewise	meditate	namesake	ordnance	pendicle	pratique	reemerge	sackrace
limonite	megapode	nametape	organdie	penknife	preamble	regelate	Sadducee
lingerie	melamine	narceine	organise	pentacle	preclude	regicide	sagamore
lipsalve	melanite	narghile	oscinine	perceive	prejudge	regulate	saginate
literate	melinite	nasalise	osculate	perforce	prelease	rehandle	sailable
litharge	melodise	nascence	otoscope	pericope	premiere	rehearse	saleable
litigate	membrane	nauseate	outbrave	peridote	premorse	reignite	salience
liveable	memorise	navigate	outcaste	perilune	prentice	reimpose	salivate
livewire	menarche	Nazarene	outhouse	permeate	prepense	reinsure	saltmine
loadline	mendable	Nazarite	outrange	perorate	presence	rekindle	salvable
loanable	mergence	Nazirite	outshine	peroxide	preserve	relative	Samoyede
lobeline	meringue	neaptide	outshone	personae	pressure	releasee	samphire
lobulate	merosome	nebulise	outstare	perspire	prestige	relegate	sanative
localise	mesquite	necklace	outvalue	persuade	pretence	reliable	sandshoe
locative	messmate	neckline	ovariole	perverse	primrose	reliance	sangaree
lockable	messuage	needfire	ovenware	petaline	priorate	relocate	sanguine
locomote	metamere	negative	overbore	petuntse	pristine	relumine	sanitate
loculate	metayage	negligee	overcame	phalange	probable	remittee	sanitise
lodicule	migraine	nematode	overcome	pharisee	prodrome	renegade	sapience
logotype	militate	neophyte	overdone	phosgene	prolapse	renounce	saponite
lonesome	millieme	neoprene	overdose	phyllode	prologue	renovate	sapphire
longsome	millrace	Nepalese	overnice	phyllome	prolonge	rentable	sardelle
longtime	minimise	nepenthe	overrate	physique	promisee	repartee	satiable
longwave	Minorite	nephrite	override	pianiste	promulge	repeople	satirise
longwise	minutiae	nickname	overripe	picayune	propense	repousse	saturate
loophole	miscible	nicotine	overrode	pilotage	prophase	reprieve	Sauterne
loricate	miserere	noblesse	overrule	pinafore	prorogue	reremice	sawframe
lovesome	misguide	nocturne	overshoe	pinecone	prostate	resemble	sawhorse
lowgrade	misjudge	nodalise	overside	pinnacle	prostyle	resettle	saxatile
lunulate	misplace	nodulose	oversize	pinochle	protease	resinate	scalable

```
scapulae sidewise statable tameable trephine valvulae woodnote blessing
scavenge silicane staylace tangible tressure vambrace woodpile blinding
schedule silicate stearate tannable triangle vamplate workable blinking
scissile silicide stearine tapdance trichite vanadate workmate blooming
sciurine silicone steatite tapelike trichome vaporise wormhole blotting
sclerite similise steerage tapeline tricorne variable wormlike blurring
sclerose simulate stellate taphouse tricycle variance wrappage boarding
scopulae sinecure stepwise tartrate trioxide varicose wreckage bouncing
scotfree singable sternite Tartuffe triplane vegetate writable bragging
scottice sinicise stibnite teahouse tripwire vegetive xanthate braiding
scrabble sinkable stilbene teammate triskele vendible xanthene breaking
scramble sinkhole stilbite teatable troilite venerate xanthine breeding
scribble sirvente stillage telecine trombone verbiage Xantippe briefing
scrounge sithence stockade televise trouvere vergence xylonite brimming
scurrile sixpence stoppage tellable truckage verjuice yokemate brisling
seaborne sizeable storable telltale trueblue vernicle yuletide browning
seadrome skislope straddle template truelove verrucae zabaione buckling
seahorse skyscape straggle tenaille truncate versicle zibeline building
sealable slipcase strangle tendence tubercle vesicate zoetrope bullfrog
seamouse slippage strickle Tenebrae tuberose vicarage zoophyte bullring
seapiece slowpoke strigose tenorite tubulate vicarate zoospore bullyrag
seaplane smallage strobile tenpence tuckahoe vicinage aardwolf bundling
seapurse smaltite struggle tensible tuneable Viennese aperitif bustling
seaquake smokable strumose tentacle tunicate viewable blastoff cageling
seascape smoothie stuprate terebene tuppence vignette brushoff canoeing
seashore snowlike subacute terebrae turnable vincible bullcalf caprifig
seasnake snowline suberise termtime turnpike violable bullyoff catching
sedative snowshoe suberose terrible turnsole violence calctuff catering
seedcake soberise subframe tesserae tutelage viperine dandruff centring
seedcase sociable sublease testable tutorage viricide disproof chapping
seedlobe sodalite submerge testtube twopence vitalise dropleaf charming
seedtime sodomite submerse tetanise twopiece vitiable dyestuff charring
seizable softshoe suboxide theorise typeface vituline footmuff chatting
selectee software subserve thermite tyrosine vocalise fourleaf cheering
selenate soilpipe substage thiamine Tyrrhene vocative goldleaf chipping
selenide solanine subtitle thirlage uintaite voidable handcuff chopping
selenite solarise subulate threnode ulcerate voidance kerchief chugging
selflove solitude succubae thridace ultimate volatile langlauf chumming
selfmade solstice suchlike throstle umbonate volitive mischief churning
selfmate solvable Sudanese throttle umbrette volplane mooncalf cladding
selfrule somedele suffrage thurible umpirage vomerine overleaf clamming
selfsame sometime suitable tidegate unbottle vomitive pentroof clanging
selvedge sororate suitcase tidewave unbridle vowelise riffraff clapping
semidome sorptive sulphate tigereye unbuckle wagonage roseleaf cleaning
seminude sortable sulphide tillable unchaste Wahabite sanserif clearing
Semitise sourdine sulphite timefuse uncinate wakerife sawedoff clinking
semitone soutache sulphone tincture unclothe walkable seedleaf clipping
semplice spadille sunbathe tinplate uncouple Walkyrie sobstuff clogging
sensible spaewife sundance tinstone uncreate wallgame spanroof clothing
sentence sparable sunshade tiresome underage wardance standoff clotting
separate spathose sunshine titanate underlie wardrobe sunproof clubbing
septette speciate sunstone titanite undulate warhorse tipstaff coachdog
septuple spherule superate tithable unfreeze warplane tonedeaf corkwing
sequelae spiculae supinate titivate ungulate washable tradeoff couching
sequence spillage surcease titmouse unicycle wastable unbelief coupling
serenade spiracle surefire toepiece unionise waterage werewolf coursing
sericite spitfire suricate toeplate univalve waterice woodruff covering
serotine spoilage surplice toilette universe wearable writeoff crabbing
serpulae spoliate surprise toilsome unmuffle weldable yourself cracking
sesterce sportive suspense tolerate unmuzzle wetnurse abetting cradling
sewerage spousage swanlike tollgate unriddle wettable aborning cramming
sextette sprinkle sybarite topstone unsaddle wharfage abutting crashing
sextuple squabble sycamine torchere unsettle wheyface anything creeping
shakable squamate sycamore torquate unstable whiplike aqualung cribbing
shapable squamose sycomore tortoise unswathe whitetie assuming crofting
shikaree squamule syllable totalise untangle wifelike atheling cropping
shinbone squeedge sylphide tournure unthrone wildfire averring crossing
shipmate squeegee sylphine trabeate upstroke wildlife ballyrag dairying
shiralee squiggle symphile tracheae urbanise windcone bantling darkling
shivaree squilgee syncline trachyte urbanite windpipe banxring deviling
shoelace staffage syndrome trackage urethane windrose beagling dialling
shoetree stagnate tabulate tractate urostyle wingcase becoming dingdong
shortage stallage tachisme tractive Ursuline winnable beeswing dittybag
shothole stampede tachiste tramline urticate wirewove beetling dragging
showcase stanhope tailgate transire valerate wiseacre biassing dreaming
sibilate stannate tailpipe transude valiance womanise blabbing dressing
sideline stannite tailrace traverse validate wishbone blacking drilling
sidenote stargaze tainture treasure valorise woodbine blackleg drinking
siderite starlike takehome treatise valuable woodlice bleeding dripping
```

```
dropping hedgehog plugging skimming swanning wrapping dispatch monkfish
drubbing hedgepig plumbing skinning swansong yachting dogtooth monolith
drugging hireling pointing skipping swapping yeanling dogwatch monteith
drumming hoarding polliwog skirting swatting yearling dowdyish moonfish
duckling hocusing pollywog slabbing swearing yearlong dwarfish musquash
duelling hourlong porkling slagging sweeping yearning eldritch myograph
dumpling housedog pounding slamming sweeting yielding eleventh nonesuch
dwelling imposing pressing slapbang swelling zincking encroach numbfish
emceeing incoming primming slapping swigging zugzwang ensheath nuthatch
emitting inviting printing slashing swimming acreinch entrench odograph
engaging kindling prodding sledding swinging acrolith epigraph oilcloth
evensong knapping proofing sleeping swobbing admonish ethnarch oligarch
exacting knitting propping slimming swopping aerolith eyetooth opsimath
exciting knocking puppydog slipping swotting airbrush faintish outmatch
fagoting knotting purfling slipring tackling alebench fallfish outreach
farflung lacewing quandong slitting tagalong allopath feeblish outwatch
farthing lallygag queening slogging teaching although feverish outweigh
faubourg laughing queueing slopping teething amaranth fiendish overarch
fetching leapfrog quilting slotting tempting anaglyph fiftieth overfish
fiddling learning quipping slubbing thinking apograph fiftyish overmuch
fighting lifelong quisling slugging thinning approach filefish padishah
fireplug lighting quitting slumming thriving astonish flatfish paganish
flagging limetwig quizzing slurring thudding backlash flattish perianth
flapping littling rallying smashing thumping backwash flourish pipefish
flashing livelong rambling smelling tingeing bakshish footbath pixieish
flatling loathing rattling smocking tonguing behemoth footpath plumpish
fleeting lordling reedling snagging toothing bellpush forsooth polymath
flipping lovesong respring snapping touching bequeath fortieth poohpooh
flitting lowering resprung snipping tracking besmirch fortyish potlatch
floating lowlying retiring snogging training biograph Frankish prankish
flogging lustring reviling snubbing trapping biomorph freakish priggish
flooring mahjongg rewaking soothing treefrog birdbath frogfish puppyish
flopping mantling Riesling souchong trekking blackish frumpish purplish
flubbing marbling roasting sounding trifling blahblah furlough quackish
focusing marrying rockling southing trilling blandish ghoulish qualmish
folksong mealybug sampling spanking trimming bleakish goatfish queerish
fondling middling scalawag spanning tripping blimpish goatmoth rainwash
footling misdoing scanning sparling trotting blockish goldfish regolith
footslog moneybag scarring sparring trucking blondish goldrush regrowth
fordoing motoring scathing spatting trussing blowfish gralloch reproach
forgoing mottling scatting speaking tumbling bluefish greenish rerearch
founding moulding scheming spelling turtling bonefish greyfish research
frapping mounting scolding spiffing twinling brackish gunsmith retrench
freezing mourning scouting spinning twinning brainish Haggadah rockfish
fretting muscling scraping spitting twitting brandish Halachah Romansch
fringing nestling scudding sporting underdog brattish harrumph rosebush
fritting niggling scumming spotting unending briskish hasheesh rosefish
frocking nighthag seagoing spurling unerring broadish hawfinch roughish
frogging northing seedling spurring unfading brownish hawkmoth roundish
frosting nosering seladang stabbing unseeing calabash helminth rowdyish
fuelling notching shafting stabling unsprung calipash herewith Rumansch
gangling nursling shamming stalling unstring cartouch hiccough sailfish
gladding obliging shantung standing unstrung cenotaph hierarch saltbush
glancing offering sheading starling uprising cheapish hushhush sandbath
gleaning omitting shealing starring upsprang childish hyacinth sandwich
gloaming oncoming shedding starting upspring churlish hydranth sandyish
glutting outgoing sheepdog steading upsprung chutzpah inasmuch savannah
goatling outlying sheeting stealing vaulting clannish ingrowth sawtooth
golliwog outvying shelving steening Vietcong cliquish insomuch scampish
goosegog overhang shieling steering wakening cloddish intrench Scottish
grabbing overhung shilling stemming watchdog clownish isomorph seedfish
graining overlong shinning stepping watering coalfish isopleth selcouth
grasping parasang shipping sterling waterlog coolabah Jeremiah Shabuoth
grayling partsong shirring stetting waygoing coolibah jingoish shadbush
greening pearling shirting stinking weakling coronach Kaffiyeh sharpish
greeting pettifog shocking stirring weanling costpush kingfish sheepish
grinning phrasing shogging stocking weeklong crawfish kneehigh Shekinah
gripping piddling shooting stopping whacking crayfish kourbash shofroth
gritting piercing shopping stravaig whapping cromlech languish shortish
grouping piffling shunning striking whetting dahabieh lightish shrewish
grouting plaiding shutting stubbing whidding dandyish limewash sidedish
growling planking sickflag studding whipping dealfish liverish sitzbath
grubbing planning sideling stuffing whirring declutch lumpfish sixtieth
grudging platting sidelong stumming whizbang demolish lungfish skirmish
guidedog pleading singeing stunning whizzing despatch Masoreth skittish
handling pleasing singsong suckling wholehog devilish megalith slapdash
hatching plodding sizzling swabbing whooping diagraph mishmash slimmish
haunting plopping skidding swagging whopping diminish mismatch slobbish
headlong plotting skilling swanking witching disbench mitzvoth sluggish
```

sluttish	bouzouki	bootjack	hogsback	sandbank	antheral	clubhaul	especial
smallish	broccoli	buhlwork	holdback	seawrack	approval	cockerel	espousal
smartish	canthari	bushbuck	homesick	shabrack	arbitral	cocktail	estoppel
snappish	castrati	cakewalk	homework	shaddock	arboreal	cogwheel	estuaril
sneakish	chapatti	casebook	hoodwink	shagbark	archival	coistrel	ethereal
snobbish	chupatti	casework	hornbook	shamrock	armorial	colonial	etherial
soapdish	ciceroni	cashbook	humpback	shashlik	arterial	colossal	ethnical
sparkish	cicisbei	chapbook	hymnbook	shelduck	asphodel	columnal	evenfall
spoffish	concerti	charlock	iceblink	sherlock	astragal	communal	eventful
spookish	concetti	chipmuck	ironbark	shoptalk	atypical	conidial	eventual
squarish	confetti	chipmunk	ironwork	sidekick	autumnal	conjugal	exergual
stablish	cornetti	clawback	jetblack	sidewalk	aventail	conoidal	exordial
standish	cothurni	coalsack	joystick	skerrick	balmoral	contrail	external
starfish	daiquiri	coatrack	kickback	skewback	banderol	cornball	faithful
steepish	dividivi	comeback	kinsfolk	skimmilk	bangtail	corporal	falderal
stiffish	drachmai	cookbook	knapsack	skipjack	bankbill	corrival	familial
stockish	durukuli	copybook	kneejerk	slapjack	bankroll	cortical	fanciful
stoutish	Fascisti	crummock	knotwork	slopwork	bannerol	cosmical	farcical
stramash	flocculi	dabchick	lacework	snaplink	barbital	coverall	farewell
strength	gladioli	daybreak	landmark	soapbark	baronial	cracknel	fauteuil
surffish	graffiti	deadlock	laverock	songbook	baseball	cramfull	festival
swainish	grissini	diestock	leadwork	spardeck	basidial	criminal	fiducial
sweetish	Gujarati	dipstick	legbreak	steenbok	basinful	critical	filarial
sylphish	hamululi	disfrock	lifework	steinbok	beadroll	crowbill	fireball
tarboosh	harakiri	dogwhelk	limerick	stopcock	bechamel	cuboidal	fireopal
teacloth	harikari	drammock	linstock	studbook	bellpull	cultural	fishball
telepath	hetairai	drawback	lipstick	studwork	bellyful	cyclical	fishbowl
tetrarch	hydroski	dropkick	lovelock	surfduck	bestowal	daffodil	fishmeal
thickish	Kashmiri	drummock	lovesick	swanmark	betrayal	deadfall	fishtail
thievish	kohlrabi	duckhawk	maverick	swanneck	biannual	decretal	fistical
thinnish	komitaji	eyestalk	meshwork	swayback	biblical	deferral	flexural
thorough	libretti	facepack	mintmark	tailback	biennial	defrayal	flywheel
ticklish	literati	fallback	misthink	tamarack	bifacial	demersal	folderol
tigerish	macaroni	fastback	moorcock	tamarisk	bilabial	deprival	fontanel
tilefish	maharani	fasttalk	mossback	tapedeck	binaural	detrital	football
tinsmith	Mahratti	fatstock	muckluck	taskwork	binomial	diaconal	footfall
toadfish	maravedi	feedback	muskduck	teabreak	biocidal	diagonal	foothill
toadyish	narcissi	feedtank	nainsook	teamwork	birdcall	diarchal	forceful
tolbooth	nucleoli	firebank	newspeak	telemark	bisexual	dihedral	forefeel
tolldish	pastrami	firelock	nicknack	textbook	blameful	diluvial	foresail
topnotch	pulvilli	firework	nonstick	ticktack	blissful	diphenyl	forestal
toughish	retiarii	fishhawk	notebook	ticktock	blowball	dipteral	foretell
tovarish	ryotwari	fishhook	offbreak	tidelock	bluebell	dishevel	fourball
tribrach	sannyasi	flapjack	onetrack	tidemark	blushful	disloyal	freefall
trickish	sauouari	footmark	openwork	tiebreak	boastful	disposal	freesoil
triglyph	Sephardi	footwork	outbreak	timework	boatbill	dividual	freewill
trigraph	shanghai	foredeck	outflank	tomahawk	bobwheel	doctoral	fruitful
triptych	solfeggi	forelock	overbook	traprock	bonemeal	doggerel	funebral
tristich	strobili	forepeak	overlook	turnback	bonspiel	doorbell	funereal
typehigh	sukiyaki	formwork	overtask	turncock	brachial	doornail	furfural
umptieth	tandoori	forspeak	overtook	welldeck	bracteal	doorsill	galangal
unchurch	teocalli	foxshark	pashalik	windsock	brimfull	dotterel	garefowl
unclench	thesauri	fretwork	passbook	wirework	brocatel	doubtful	geraniol
unclinch	trochili	fullback	penstock	wolfpack	cacomixl	dovetail	germcell
vanquish	virtuosi	gamecock	picklock	woodcock	caesural	downfall	germinal
verandah	waterski	gavelock	pinprick	woodlark	callgirl	downhaul	gestural
vermouth	zecchini	giftbook	piperack	woodwork	cannibal	downhill	ghastful
Vietminh	zucchini	gimcrack	playback	woolpack	cantonal	drawwell	gingival
viperish	aardvark	goalkick	playbook	woolsack	carbonyl	dreadful	glassful
Visigoth	abelmosk	gripsack	pockmark	woolwork	carboxyl	dreamful	glycerol
vixenish	almanack	grosbeak	politick	wordbook	cardinal	drumroll	glyceryl
waterish	antimask	gunstock	postmark	workfolk	carnival	duckbill	godawful
waxcloth	asterisk	halfback	pullback	yearbook	carousal	dumbbell	goldfoil
weakfish	backpack	halfback	redbrick	zwieback	carousel	dunghill	gonidial
wellnigh	ballcock	hallmark	handbook	aasvogel	carryall	duodenal	goodwill
Whiggish	bankbook	handbook	redshank	abbatial	cascabel	dustbowl	goofball
whiplash	bareback	handpick	reembark	abnormal	catchall	eagleowl	gossypol
wishwash	basilisk	handwork	rickrack	achenial	catechol	eggshell	graceful
wolffish	beadwork	hardback	ringbark	acturial	cathodal	emetical	grateful
womanish	benedick	hardhack	ringneck	Adamical	catstail	Emmental	gromwell
wrymouth	billhook	hardtack	roadbook	aerofoil	cerebral	empyreal	guileful
xenolith	blesbuck	havelock	rockcork	aestival	cervical	encrinal	gunmetal
youngish	boatdeck	haystack	rockwork	agential	cesspool	enthrall	guttural
zoomorph	boathook	headlock	rollneck	alguazil	charcoal	entresol	habitual
amoretti	bobolink	headwork	roofrack	allodial	cheerful	epicotyl	handball
apresski	bodywork	herdbook	ropewalk	alluvial	chemical	epidural	handbell
banditti	bontebok	herdwick	rosepink	alogical	clerical	episodal	handbill
beriberi	bookmark	highjack	rucksack	anhedral	clinical	erotical	handmill
bimbashi	bookwork	hipflask	saltlick	antennal	clodpoll	eschewal	handrail

```
hangnail  methanol  pigswill  sewellel  toroidal  alienism  doumpalm  hypoderm
harebell  metrical  pinwheel  shaleoil  townhall  allodium  druidism  hypogeum
harpseal  minstrel  plateful  shameful  tracheal  alluvium  duodenum  Ibsenism
headsail  mirthful  playbill  shedevil  tragical  alpinism  dwarfism  icecream
heelball  misspell  playgirl  shelfful  tranquil  altruism  dybbukim  idealism
heliacal  mistrial  plimsoll  shoebill  trapball  ammonium  dynamism  ideogram
heroical  molehill  podagral  shopbell  treenail  aneurism  echogram  idiotism
hibernal  monachal  poetical  shopgirl  triaxial  aneurysm  ectoderm  imperium
hickwall  monaural  ponytail  showbill  tribunal  angstrom  electrum  inchworm
highball  monaxial  postmill  showgirl  trifocal  anteroom  embolism  incivism
hightail  monkseal  postural  shrapnel  trigonal  aphorism  emporium  indicium
hormonal  monomial  potstill  shrieval  tripodal  apothegm  encomium  indusium
hornbill  monorail  powerful  sidereal  tristful  aquarium  endemism  inoculum
horntail  moonsail  praedial  sinophil  tritical  archaism  endoderm  intercom
hospital  moorfowl  prandial  siphonal  tropical  Arianism  ensiform  intimism
houseful  mothball  prankful  skeletal  troupial  armyworm  entoderm  iodoform
hydromel  motional  prenatal  sloppail  trustful  ascidium  erethism  iotacism
hydroxyl  motorail  prideful  slothful  truthful  asterism  ergogram  Irishism
hymenial  motorial  primeval  snowball  turbinal  atticism  ergotism  Islamism
hypogeal  mournful  prodigal  snowfall  tutorial  auriform  escapism  isocheim
imaginal  mouthful  proemial  societal  unfilial  backroom  Essenism  isotherm
immortal  muscadel  proposal  softball  uniaxial  ballroom  etherism  jeroboam
imperial  muscatel  protocol  softboil  unisonal  basidium  ethicism  jingoism
inchmeal  mycelial  proximal  somedeal  univocal  bathroom  eugenism  kilogram
inertial  mystical  pubertal  soterial  unkennel  bdellium  eulogium  labdanum
infernal  mythical  puffball  spadeful  unlawful  betacism  euphuism  labellum
informal  naphthol  punctual  spandrel  unsocial  biennium  europium  laburnum
inguinal  national  puparial  spandril  upheaval  bioplasm  exanthem  laconism
inimical  nautical  pushball  spectral  vaccinal  Blenheim  exemplum  landform
inositol  neonatal  pushpull  spicknel  varietal  bollworm  exorcism  Latinism
inscroll  neuronal  pygidial  spiteful  vauntful  bookworm  exordium  laudanum
integral  newsreel  pyrexial  splenial  venereal  botulism  factotum  legalism
internal  nightowl  rainfall  spoonful  vengeful  brachium  fairyism  Leninism
Interpol  nonlegal  rakehell  sportful  vertical  brougham  faradism  linoleum
interval  nonmetal  rasorial  springal  verticil  Buddhism  fatalism  lipogram
inthrall  nonmoral  rational  squirrel  vesperal  Byronism  feminism  lixivium
irenical  notarial  ratstail  staminal  vicarial  cabalism  filiform  localism
ironical  notional  rebuttal  statical  virginal  caladium  finalism  logogram
isogonal  noumenal  rectoral  staysail  visceral  capsicum  fishfarm  lomentum
Judaical  novercal  redistil  stickful  visional  cardamom  flatworm  longterm
judicial  numskull  referral  stomatal  voiceful  cardamum  flimflam  lukewarm
keelhaul  nutshell  regional  strapoil  vortical  cerebrum  foredoom  lutecium
khedival  occlusal  remedial  stubnail  warragal  Chartism  formroom  lutetium
kisscurl  oenophil  remittal  stunsail  warrigal  cherubim  francium  lyricism
Komsomol  official  reprisal  subbasal  washbowl  chiefdom  frenulum  maniform
korfball  oogonial  reproval  subtotal  wasteful  chiliasm  fusiform  marjoram
lacrimal  optional  requital  subvocal  watchful  chromium  futurism  Mazdaism
lacrymal  oriental  residual  suicidal  weariful  ciborium  galbanum  mealworm
landfall  original  reversal  supernal  whimbrel  Galenism  gapeworm  meconium
landgirl  outrival  reviewal  supplial  whinsill  cingulum  gapeworm  melanism
landrail  overcall  rhonchal  supposal  wildfowl  clerkdom  Gaullism  meristem
laystall  overfall  rightful  surgical  windfall  cliquism  geranium  mesoderm
lenticel  overfill  ringtail  surmisal  windgall  coagulum  giantism  modalism
littoral  overhaul  ringwall  surroyal  windmill  coatroom  gipsydom  Moharram
loathful  overkill  rockfall  survival  windsail  coliform  gipsyism  Molinism
longeval  oversail  rollcall  switchel  woodwool  coliseum  glowworm  momentum
longwall  oversell  rosebowl  syncopal  woolfell  conidium  glucinum  monadism
lowlevel  oversoul  rubrical  syndical  worthful  coniform  gonidium  monogram
lubrical  palatial  rubytail  synovial  wrackful  corundum  Graecism  moonbeam
mackerel  pallmall  rustical  syzygial  wrathful  cubiform  gramatom  moralism
madrigal  parallel  sagittal  tableful  wrongful  cymatium  guaiacum  moshavim
mainsail  parental  Sangrail  tactical  youthful  cynicism  gypsydom  motorium
malarial  parietal  Sangreal  tafferel  zenithal  dandyism  gypsyism  muckworm
mandrill  pastoral  scenical  taffrail  zodiacal  darkroom  hairworm  Muharram
mangonel  pastural  scoopful  tasteful  abomasum  daydream  halfterm  mushroom
maniacal  paternal  scornful  teatowel  accustom  decagram  handloom  mycelium
mannitol  patronal  scrannel  teetotal  aconitum  decigram  headroom  nanogram
manorial  peaceful  sealevel  temporal  acosmism  delirium  Hebraism  napiform
manurial  pectoral  seashell  tenurial  acrotism  demonism  hedonism  nativism
marginal  pedestal  seasnail  terminal  actinism  devilism  heirloom  naturism
material  pellmell  seasonal  tesseral  actinium  didymium  helotism  nebulium
materiel  perineal  sectoral  textural  activism  diluvium  hexagram  negroism
maternal  peroneal  selfheal  thankful  addendum  dimerism  Hinduism  neoplasm
matronal  personal  selfwill  thetical  adiantum  dioecism  hologram  nepotism
meatball  petronel  semibull  tidemill  aeriform  dirigism  hookworm  newsroom
medieval  petrosal  sentinel  timeball  aerogram  disclaim  hornbeam  nihilism
memorial  Philomel  septfoil  tollcall  albinism  ditheism  hornworm  nobelium
mensural  physical  [unclear] toothful  alburnum  Docetism  humanism  nomadism
merciful  pickerel  septimal  toplevel  algorism  Donatism  hymenium  nomogram
```

```
nonclaim schiedam veratrum aversion chinchin duration Fraulein illation
nubiform scholium verbatim aviation christen Dutchman freeborn illusion
olibanum sciagram vexillum avulsion cinnamon dynatron freedman Illyrian
omadhaum sciolism viaticum backspin cinquain eclosion freshman imprison
ommateum sealyham viburnum Baconian Circaean ectozoon freshrun inaction
oncidium selenium villadom Bactrian citation eduction Freudian incision
oogonium Semitism vinculum bailsman civilian effusion friction Indiaman
optimism seraphim virilism bandsman clansman egestion Friesian infusion
Orangism seriatim vitalism barbican coachman Egyptian frighten inhesion
organism Shaktism vivarium bargeman coaction eighteen fruition invasion
origanum sheikdom vocalism bartizan coercion ejection fugleman irenicon
pacifism shipworm voltaism baseborn cognomen election function Irishman
paganism shortarm Wahabism Batavian cohesion electron funnyman isodicon
paludism showroom wardroom Bavarian collagen emblazon furfuran isthmian
papalism sickroom washroom beadsman colophon embolden Galilean Jacobean
pappadom sidedrum waveform bearskin comedian emersion Gallican jerrican
paradigm silkworm Whiggism befallen comedown emission gambeson jerrycan
paroxysm silphium whimwham begotten complain empoison gambroon jettison
Parsiism simplism whipworm beholden conation empyrean ganglion jobation
patagium sinapism whoredom Benjamin coonskin emulsion garrison Jonathan
pelorism skiagram winepalm bespoken cooption enaction gelation junction
pendulum slipform wireworm bestrewn cordovan encomion Georgian Khmerian
periderm slowworm witchelm betatron cordwain endozoon gestagen klystron
peridium snapbrim woodworm bezonian cotillon enneagon Ghanaian krumhorn
perineum snobbism workroom biathlon cotquean entozoon globulin laconian
phantasm solarism xanthium bibation coumarin envision glucagon ladyfern
phormium solarium zombiism billycan coxswain Ephesian glycerin lambskin
piliform solatium ablation bludgeon cragsman episemon glycogen landsman
pisiform solecism ablution bobbypin crankpin epyllion goatskin Langshan
platform somatism abortion Bodleian creation equation goingson lanthorn
platinum spectrum abrasion Boeotian Croatian Erastian gonfalon larrikin
playroom speculum abutilon bogeyman crumhorn erection gownsman lavation
plectrum sphagnum Accadian bohemian cryotron erigeron Graafian laywoman
pleonasm spiculum acrolein bondsman culverin eruption grandson leadsman
plumbism stoicism actinian boughten Cumbrian Eskimoan gravamen leathern
polonium strabism adaption bouillon cyanogen Estonian graviton lecithin
poppadum studfarm addition bourgeon cyclamen Etrurian gridiron legation
populism succinum adhesion brainpan dairyman Etruscan groschen lengthen
priapism sudarium Adlerian brakeman dalesman eulachon guardian libation
priggism syconium adnation brakevan damassin euonymin gumption lichenin
proclaim tackroom adoption brethren decision Eurasian gyration liegeman
prosaism tantalum advowson Briarean decurion European haematin ligation
psychism Tantrism aeration brighten deerskin evection halation limekiln
ptyalism tapeworm affusion bryozoan delation eversion halfmoon linchpin
pugilism tautonym agnation buckbean deletion everyman handsewn linesman
pumproom teetotum agrarian buckhorn Delphian eviction handyman Linnaean
puparium telefilm airwoman buckskin demijohn evulsion hangeron liveborn
puppydom telegram Akkadian bulletin demonian exaction harridan lobation
pygidium teraphim Albanian bullhorn demotion excision Hawaiian locution
pyriform testatum alderman cabochon deration exertion hawthorn logician
pyxidium thallium Algonkin caducean derision falchion headsman longeron
queendom thanedom alizarin calfskin deuteron fancyman heathhen longhorn
quietism thraldom allergen Cambrian devilkin fanfaron Hegelian lookeron
ramentum thuggism allusion campaign Devonian Faustian heighten loonybin
ranarium titanism alluvion Canadian devotion favonian helmsman lovelorn
reaffirm titanium Alsatian cannabin diapason fedayeen henchman Lucullan
regalism toadyism ambition cannikin diapason fellahin henequen lunarian
rehoboam tokenism American capeskin dieldrin ferryman heptagon lunation
reniform tomentum amoebean capuchin dilation finespun herdsman luncheon
residuum tomogram androgen cardigan dilution fixation hereupon Lutheran
retiform tonepoem Anglican careworn diluvian flashgun Hertzian luxation
rigorism toolroom antiphon carillon diocesan flatiron hielaman lynchpin
ringworm totemism aphelion Carolean diplogen flection highborn macaroon
Romanism trillium apiarian castiron dipteran florigen himation madwoman
roodbeam tubiform Aramaean cauldron discrown fluellin histogen magdalen
roundarm tympanum Arcadian cavesson distrain flyblown holstein magician
rowdyism ultraism archaean cavicorn disunion followon homeborn magneton
royalism unciform Armenian cerulean division forenoon homespun maintain
rubidium underarm Arminian cetacean dominion foreseen hometown malarian
ruralism unionism artesian chairman donation foreskin hooligan malefern
saintdom unwisdom ascidian Chaldean doomsman forewarn Horatian Mandaean
saleroom upstream assassin chaldron dotation forgiven horseman mandarin
samarium urbanism Assyrian champion doubloon formalin houseman mandolin
sandworm vanadium Athenian chaperon downtown forsaken huntsman mannikin
sapphism variform audition chaplain downturn forsworn hydrogen marathon
satanism variorum Augustan Chellean dragoman fountain hypogean markdown
Saxondom vasculum aurelian chessman dragomen fourteen ideation marksman
Saxonism vasiform aurorean children dragsman fraction ignition marocain
scandium velarium autobahn Chinaman dryclean franklin ignitron maroquin
```

```
marshman  overseen  religion  southern  turndown  concetto  trecento  pericarp
martagon  oversewn  replevin  Southron  turnskin  contango  twelvemo  raindrop
marzipan  overturn  resorcin  spaceman  twinborn  continuo  virtuoso  rearlamp
mascaron  overworn  restrain  spalpeen  Tyrolean  contorno  vitiligo  reedstop
mastodon  oxymoron  revision  spearman  unbeaten  cornetto  wallaroo  roundtop
Mayqueen  oxytocin  Rhaetian  specimen  unbidden  cruzeiro  wanderoo  runnerup
melodeon  pagurian  Rhinodon  spittoon  unbroken  curculio  waterloo  screwtop
menhaden  palmitin  rifleman  sponsion  unburden  doloroso  zecchino  selfhelp
meridian  pangolin  rigadoon  spontoon  unbutton  eldorado  agitprop  sheepdip
mescalin  pannikin  ringmain  spraygun  uncommon  espresso  airstrip  sideslip
mesotron  pantheon  riparian  squadron  underman  falsetto  ascocarp  sidestep
metazoan  papillon  riverain  squarson  underpin  fandango  backdrop  skindeep
metazoon  paraffin  riverman  squawman  underrun  Filipino  blackcap  skullcap
mezereon  parergon  roadsign  squireen  unfasten  finnesko  blacktop  slagheap
midbrain  Parmesan  rockhewn  staghorn  unfrozen  flamenco  blowlamp  slipslop
Milesian  partaken  roentgen  stallion  ungotten  flamingo  bluechip  slopshop
misalign  Parthian  rogation  stasimon  unloosen  forzando  bodyshop  snipsnap
miscegen  partisan  Romanian  stellion  unperson  gardyloo  calthrop  snowdrop
misgiven  partizan  ropeyarn  sternson  unreason  gazpacho  chopchop  softsoap
mistaken  pathogen  rosarian  stockman  upthrown  gillaroo  clanship  sparkgap
moccasin  pattypan  Rotarian  storeman  vacation  gracioso  claptrap  subgroup
moleskin  pavilion  rotation  straiten  valerian  graffito  clipclop  sweetsop
monition  peagreen  Rumanian  Strepyan  vanillin  groogroo  clopclop  tabletop
Moravian  pearmain  safranin  stricken  velskoen  guacharo  deanship  teardrop
mortmain  Pegasean  sainfoin  stridden  venation  hereunto  deathcap  township
motorman  Pelagian  Salesian  strucken  Venetian  hitherto  doorstep  tranship
motormen  pemmican  salesman  stubborn  Venusian  impetigo  doorstop  tuckshop
moufflon  pentagon  Salopian  stuntman  veratrin  innuendo  dramshop  twinship
mountain  perigean  sanction  sturgeon  verboten  intaglio  endocarp  underlap
munition  Peruvian  santonin  subhuman  vesuvian  jackaroo  escallop  underlip
musician  petition  sapgreen  suburban  vexation  jackeroo  firedamp  wardship
mutation  phlegmon  saucepan  Sumerian  vigneron  kakemono  fireship  warwhoop
mutchkin  photogen  scalepan  superman  viridian  kangaroo  firetrap  whitecap
myrmidon  Phrygian  scallion  suzerain  vitellin  libeccio  flagship  wineshop
napoleon  picaroon  Scandian  swanskin  vocation  libretto  flipflap  woodpulp
natation  pivotman  scansion  taciturn  volition  littlego  flipflop  workshop
negation  placeman  scarfpin  Tahitian  volution  locofoco  followup  xylocarp
negatron  plankton  scission  tailspin  wallfern  lothario  foolscap  abattoir
NeoLatin  plantain  scorpion  talapoin  watchman  machismo  footstep  abductor
neomycin  plastron  Scotsman  talesman  waterman  maestoso  freezeup  abhorrer
newblown  plebeian  scullion  talisman  wellborn  makimono  gallwasp  abridger
nicotian  poltroon  seagreen  tallyman  Wellsian  mancando  grogshop  absolver
nineteen  polyzoan  sealskin  Tamilian  wellworn  Mandingo  hairgrip  absorber
nitrogen  polyzoon  seaonion  tarlatan  Welshman  martello  handclap  accentor
Noachian  position  sebesten  Tarpeian  Wesleyan  moderato  handgrip  accepter
nobleman  positron  secretin  tarragon  wheelman  mosquito  handicap  acceptor
nodation  posthorn  sedation  taxation  whoreson  Negrillo  hardship  achiever
nonhuman  potation  sedition  teaspoon  windburn  neutrino  headlamp  acicular
nonunion  prehuman  seedcorn  telethon  wineskin  oratorio  hedgehop  actuator
Norseman  pressman  seedsman  terrapin  wingspan  ostinato  heirship  adductor
northern  prolamin  selfborn  tetragon  wolfskin  ottavino  higherup  adjuster
Northman  Prussian  selfsown  thermion  woodsman  palmetto  housetop  adjustor
notation  publican  shagreen  thespian  woolskin  palomino  jumpedup  adulator
noumenon  puncheon  shagroon  thirteen  wreathen  parlando  junkshop  affecter
novation  punition  shalloon  tholepin  wrestpin  peekaboo  kingship  affirmer
nutarian  pupation  sheeppen  threaten  wristpin  peperino  kneedeep  aflutter
nutation  purpurin  sheeprun  thrombin  xanthein  perfecto  ladyship  agaragar
nutbrown  pygmaean  Sheraton  thyroxin  yataghan  pimiento  landslip  agitator
nymphean  quadroon  shoehorn  timeworn  yestreen  plumbago  liripoop  aglimmer
oblation  quartern  shopworn  toboggan  zeppelin  politico  lockstep  aglitter
oblivion  quatrain  showdown  toilworn  zonation  presidio  lollipop  airliner
obsidian  Quechuan  shrunken  tommygun  alfresco  prunello  lollypop  alveolar
occasion  question  shutdown  townsman  amoretto  ranchero  longship  ambusher
octaroon  quillpen  Siberian  trackman  antihero  renegado  longstop  analyser
octoroon  quintain  Sicilian  traction  arpeggio  sargasso  lordship  ancestor
Odyssean  raftsman  sidesman  tragopan  assiento  scenario  malaprop  animator
Olympian  rambutan  Silurian  trappean  autogiro  scirocco  mesocarp  answerer
omission  ramequin  sirenian  treefern  autogyro  seicento  monkship  anteater
openplan  ranarian  skeleton  trillion  ballyhoo  sentrygo  namedrop  anterior
ophidian  ranchman  slattern  trimaran  barranco  seraglio  nightcap  argufier
optician  rataplan  slowdown  tripeman  bordello  sforzato  outstrip  armchair
Orcadian  reaction  smoothen  trueborn  buckaroo  sombrero  overcrop  armourer
orthicon  reassign  sneeshan  trunnion  camisado  spiccato  overjump  arranger
ostracon  reawaken  Socinian  tungsten  castrato  staccato  overleap  arrester
ostrakon  recision  solation  Tunisian  caudillo  stiletto  overslip  arrestor
outdrawn  redesign  solution  Turanian  cicisbeo  stoccado  overstep  ascender
outgrown  reedwren  somewhen  turbofan  cockatoo  subimago  pawnshop  assenter
outreign  reinsman  sorochen  Turcoman  commando  superego  peardrop  assentor
overlain  relation  sorption  Turkoman  concerto  terrazzo  pedipalp  assertor
```

assessor	cochlear	diameter	filmstar	impugner	millibar	petiolar	reformer
assignor	codifier	dictator	finisher	inceptor	milliner	phosphor	register
atomiser	codriver	didapper	fistular	inductor	mimester	piacular	regrater
attender	cofactor	diffuser	fivestar	indulger	mimicker	picketer	reindeer
attester	coiffeur	digester	fletcher	infector	minister	pilaster	rejecter
attestor	colander	dinosaur	flincher	inferior	Minotaur	pilferer	rejigger
atwitter	collator	director	flounder	infilter	misnomer	pillager	rejoicer
aweather	colleger	disaster	flowerer	inflamer	modeller	pilsener	releaser
bachelor	columnar	discover	flypaper	inflator	modifier	pinaster	releasor
bacillar	commoner	disinter	follower	informer	molester	pinnular	reliever
backdoor	commuter	disorder	fomenter	ingather	monicker	piscator	remember
bagpiper	compiler	disposer	footgear	injector	MonKhmer	pitviper	reminder
balancer	complier	dissever	footwear	inlander	monsieur	plaister	remitter
baluster	composer	ditherer	forebear	inquirer	moreover	planular	renderer
banister	computer	dodderer	foregoer	inspirer	motorcar	playgoer	reneguer
banterer	conceder	domineer	forester	insulter	mouseear	pleinair	renumber
barndoor	condylar	doomster	forrader	interior	muleteer	plougher	repairer
barrator	confider	douanier	forswear	interwar	murderer	plumular	repealer
barterer	confiner	downpour	fosterer	intruder	murmurer	poisoner	repeater
bateleur	congener	drabbler	fourstar	inventor	muscular	polestar	repeller
bebopper	conjurer	dragster	fribbler	inverter	muskdeer	polisher	repenter
bedeguar	conjuror	drencher	frondeur	investor	mutineer	pollster	replacer
bedmaker	conniver	dribbler	frontier	islander	mutterer	polluter	reporter
beeeater	consider	Dukhobor	furcular	isolator	narrator	pomander	requiter
begetter	consoler	dulcimer	fusileer	jabberer	nenuphar	ponderer	resetter
beginner	consular	dundiver	fusilier	jeweller	newcomer	posturer	resister
beguiler	consumer	educator	galloper	jongleur	nextdoor	potholer	resistor
beholder	convener	effector	gamester	Judaiser	nightjar	potterer	resorter
belabour	convenor	elevator	gangster	kalaazar	nonjuror	prattler	restorer
believer	conveyer	embalmer	ganister	kibitzer	November	preacher	retailer
berliner	conveyor	embitter	gardener	killdeer	numberer	predator	retainer
besieger	coplanar	embosser	garotter	knitwear	nurturer	premolar	retarder
beslaver	corridor	embracer	gaselier	Kohinoor	oakegger	preparer	revealer
betrayer	costumer	employer	gasmeter	kreutzer	objector	presager	reveller
beveller	cottager	emulator	gasolier	labourer	observer	presumer	revenger
bewilder	courtier	encipher	gatherer	labrador	obtainer	preventer	reverser
bisector	coworker	encumber	geometer	lamellar	occluder	prisoner	reverter
blazoner	creditor	endanger	globular	larcener	occupier	procurer	reviewer
bleacher	crossbar	endorser	goadster	larkspur	odometer	producer	revolter
blighter	croupier	endpaper	gogetter	laudator	offender	profaner	revolver
borderer	crucifer	enfetter	goodyear	laughter	offsider	profiler	rewarder
borrower	crueller	engender	gossamer	launcher	ohmmeter	promiser	ricercar
boursier	crusader	engineer	gossiper	lavender	oldtimer	promisor	rimester
brancher	cucumber	enlarger	governor	lawgiver	oleander	promoter	roadster
breather	cultivar	enquirer	grabbler	lawmaker	oleaster	prompter	romancer
brewster	cuspidor	enricher	grandeur	lecturer	onceover	pronator	roseolar
broacher	customer	enslaver	granular	leftover	onlooker	proposer	roturier
burrower	cutwater	entailer	greffier	levanter	operator	provider	rummager
buttoner	cylinder	epistler	grimacer	leveller	oppugner	provisor	rushhour
calcspar	dactylar	erector	grounder	libeller	oracular	pullover	saboteur
calendar	daughter	espalier	grumbler	licenser	ordainer	pulpiter	saccular
calender	deadener	espouser	gunlayer	lingerer	outrider	pulsator	scapular
calliper	debonair	evildoer	hangover	listener	outsider	punisher	schiller
cameleer	decanter	exactor	harasser	loadstar	overbear	pupillar	schooner
canaster	deceiver	examiner	hardener	lodestar	overhear	purifier	scimitar
canister	December	excluder	haresear	loiterer	overlier	purveyor	scorcher
cannular	decemvir	executor	hastener	Londoner	overseer	pushover	scourger
caponier	decipher	exemplar	havildar	longhair	overwear	pustular	scrapper
capsular	declarer	exhorter	haymaker	longueur	oxidiser	quaestor	scrawler
carouser	decolour	expander	headgear	loosener	oximeter	quarrier	screamer
catheter	deemster	expiator	hijacker	lumberer	oxpecker	quencher	screener
cavalier	defector	exploder	hinderer	magister	ozoniser	quibbler	screever
caviller	defender	explorer	holdover	makeover	pacifier	rabbiter	scrubber
cellarer	deferrer	exporter	honourer	maligner	palterer	racegoer	sculptor
cellular	deflower	extender	horsecar	malinger	pamperer	radiator	scutcher
chandler	demander	extensor	hotelier	malodour	papillar	rainwear	seafarer
chapiter	demurrer	exterior	howitzer	maltster	paramour	ransomer	seafloor
chasseur	depicter	extruder	huckster	mamillar	parcener	ratifier	seamster
chaunter	depictor	eyeliner	icewater	mandator	pargeter	ravisher	searcher
cinnabar	deserter	eyewater	idolater	maneater	Passover	reappear	seasoner
circular	designer	falconer	idoliser	manpower	patellar	reasoner	seawater
cislunar	despiser	familiar	imitator	marauder	patentor	rebeller	seconder
clangour	destrier	fastener	impeller	marketer	peculiar	rebutter	secretor
claqueur	detainer	fattener	impolder	masseter	pedalier	receiver	seigneur
cleanser	detector	favourer	importer	mediator	peignoir	reckoner	seignior
clincher	deterrer	feldsher	imposter	menswear	pendular	recorder	selector
cloister	deviator	feldspar	impostor	metaphor	perfumer	redactor	semester
clothier	devourer	ferreter	improper	microbar	perisher	redeemer	sempster
coauthor	dialyser	filmgoer	improver	migrator	perjurer	redwater	servitor

```
shadower subfloor uplifter amphoras canorous deedless exlibris gracious
shielder sublunar uprooter anabases cantoris deepness extrados graphics
shingler suborder upsetter anabasis captious deftness extremes greyness
shoulder suborner utiliser analects careless demoness eyeglass grievous
shredder subprior vacuolar analyses cataloes denarius fabulous grimness
shrimper subsolar valuator analysis caterers desirous faceless griseous
shrinker sufferer valvular anourous cathexes detritus factious grisgris
shuffler summoner vanisher antennas cathexis dewiness fadeless grottoes
sickener sunderer vapourer anthesis caudexes dextrous fairness gummosis
sidedoor superior varactor apodoses caudices diabetes fangless gypseous
silencer supplier variolar apodosis cautious dialyses fashious hairless
singular surfacer vascular apomixis ceramics dialysis fastness haleness
sinister surmiser vavasour apterous cerastes dianthus fastuous haliotis
sketcher surveyor veneerer araceous cernuous didymous fatigues halluces
slipover survivor venturer archives cervices diereses fearless halteres
sloucher swindler verderer archness chambers dieresis features handless
smoulder taberdar verderor Arcturus champers digamous feckless hardness
smuggler takeover verditer arquebus checkers diggings fellness harmless
snackbar tamanoir verifier arsonous chequers dimerous feverous hastings
snatcher tamperer vesturer asbestos chiasmus dinornis fewtrils haziness
sniffler tapwater viameter asperges chinless dipnoous fibrosis headless
sniggler tattooer vibrator atlantes chlorous distress fineness hedonics
snitcher tautomer vilifier auspices chondrus diuresis firearms heedless
snuffler taverner villager avidness choragus doldrums firmness heelless
softener taxpayer vintager avionics choregus dolorous fishless heirless
solander teamster violator bacillus classics dominoes flatness heliosis
solderer teenager vitiator backless cleavers dopiness flatways helpless
songster temperer vivifier badlands clematis dourness flawless herbless
sorcerer terminer voussoir baldness clerkess doziness flexuous Hercules
sorrower testator voyageur bambinos clippers drabness flinders Hesperus
souvenir thatcher waggoner bareness clueless drachmas fluidics hibiscus
spacebar therefor walkover barkless cobblers draughts foamless hidrosis
sparkler thirster walloper baroness coccyges druidess fondness highlows
spatular thrasher wallower barracks coldness ductless foodless highness
specular threader wanderer baseless colossus dullness footless hindlegs
spicular thresher warrener baseness combings dumbness formless hipsters
spinster thriller watthour baudrons compages durables formulas holidays
splasher thruster wayfarer beamends compress dustless fornices holiness
splatter thurifer whatever bearings confines dynamics fortress hollands
splinter thwacker wheatear bejabers congress earmuffs forwards homeless
splitter thwarter wheedler beltless contents earnings foulness hopeless
splutter tinkerer whenever berberis coolness easiness foureyes hornfels
sporular together wherever Bermudas copperas echoless foxiness hornless
sprawler tommybar whiffler bibulous cordless edacious frabjous hornrims
spreader topliner whistler bifocals corneous edgeless freeness hotpress
springer toreador whitener bigamous cortices edgeways fremitus hugeness
sprinter torturer whomever bimanous cosiness edginess frescoes humorous
spurgear totterer wigmaker biparous costplus editress frijoles huntress
spurrier traditor winnower blinkers countess eelgrass frillies hurtless
squaller traducer wirehair bloomers couscous eeriness frutices hustings
squander trampler wormgear blueness covetous eftsoons fullness hypnoses
squasher transfer wrangler bodiless cowgrass eighties gadzooks hypnosis
squatter trapdoor wrestler boldness crackers ekistics gainings ichorous
squawker treacher wriggler bondmans cratches elenchus gainless idealess
squeaker treadler yodeller boneless crepitus elflocks galleass idleness
squealer trembler zamindar boniness croupous ellipses galluses imagines
squeezer trencher zemindar bookends culottes ellipsis gambados imprimis
squinter trimeter zoolater bootless cumbrous emeritus gameness infamous
squirter triumvir abacuses botflies cumulous emphases gaminess inflatus
stancher trottoir abducens breeches cupreous emphasis gasworks inkiness
startler truckler abomasus brimless cureless enormous generous intrados
stickler turnover abuttals britches curtains entellus genetics Iroquois
stippler twaddler acanthus bronchus curtness entrails geotaxis isogloss
stipular twiddler acarpous bursitis cuteness enuresis ghettoes jodhpurs
stitcher twinkler achiness business cyanoses environs giantess justness
stockcar twitcher aciculas busyness cyanosis eohippus glabrous keelless
stopover twotimer acidosis buttress cyclopes epigeous gladness keenness
strainer typifier actinias cactuses cyclosis epitasis glanders khuskhus
stranger udometer adenitis caduceus cystitis equities glaucous kindless
strapper ulterior adenoids caducous daftness estovers glibness kindness
streaker underfur aduncous caesious dampness eugenics glorious kinesics
streamer unfetter afflatus caginess dankness euonymus glumness kinetics
stringer unifilar agedness calculus darkness evenness glyptics knickers
stripper unipolar airiness calipers dartrous evilness Gobelins kurtosis
stroller unlimber alewives calmness dateless excursus godwards kyphosis
strummer unloader alkalies calvados deadness exegesis goitrous lameness
strutter untether alveolus cannabis deafness exequies goodness landless
stumbler upholder amiantus cannulas dearness exiguous gorgeous landmass
subahdar uplander amitosis canoness decorous eximious gormless lankness
```

larynges	myosotis	pinkness	saneness	spyglass	trueness	zaniness	aviarist
larynxes	nacreous	pitiless	saporous	squamous	tubeless	zoonosis	baccarat
lashings	nameless	pixiness	sapphics	staggers	tuberous	abducent	bacchant
lateness	narcoses	plastics	sateless	stannous	tumorous	aberrant	backchat
laziness	narcosis	platypus	saunders	starkers	tuneless	abetment	backlist
leadless	nathless	plaudits	savorous	starless	turnings	abradant	backmost
leafless	nauplius	pluvious	sawbones	stemless	tutoress	absonant	backrest
leanness	nauseous	polemics	scabious	stenosis	tweezers	abstract	backseat
leavings	nautilus	politics	scabrous	stimulus	twenties	abstrict	bailment
leggings	nearness	pollices	scanties	stipites	ugliness	abundant	ballonet
lensless	neatness	polypous	scapulas	strumous	ulcerous	abutment	banjoist
lewdness	nebulous	poorness	scarious	stuccoes	unawares	accident	bankrupt
lifeless	necrosis	populous	scarless	studious	unctuous	accredit	banneret
ligneous	needless	porticos	schnapps	subclass	upstairs	acescent	barefoot
likeness	neuritis	portress	scirrhus	suberous	usurious	acidfast	basement
limbless	neuroses	precious	scissors	subgenus	uvulitis	acquaint	bassinet
limpness	neurosis	previous	sclerous	succubus	uxorious	acrefoot	beechnut
listless	niceness	Primates	scolices	suitings	vainness	activist	beetroot
lodgings	ninepins	primness	scopulas	sundress	valorous	adducent	bellwort
loneness	nineties	princess	seamless	sundries	vanadous	adherent	benedict
longness	nodulous	prioress	seawards	sundrops	vaneless	adjacent	bergamot
longways	nosiness	proceeds	sedulous	sunwards	vaporous	adjutant	besought
lopgrass	noteless	progress	seedless	supplies	vastness	adjuvant	besprent
lordless	notornis	propolis	selfless	suppress	veilless	advocaat	bigamist
lordosis	nowadays	protasis	selfness	sureness	venomous	aegrotat	bioplast
loudness	nubilous	pruritus	senarius	susurrus	ventless	aeronaut	bivalent
loveless	nucellus	psilosis	sensuous	syllabus	vertexes	aerostat	blackout
luckless	nudeness	psychics	sepalous	synapsis	vertices	afferent	bluecoat
luminous	nullness	pulvinus	sewergas	syndesis	victress	affluent	bobbinet
luscious	numbness	puniness	sexiness	synopses	victuals	afforest	bodement
lushness	numerous	pureness	shallows	synopsis	viewless	affright	bookpost
lustrous	numinous	pyelitis	shambles	syphilis	vigorous	agrement	bookrest
Maecenas	nuptials	pyrrhous	shingles	syringes	vileness	aircraft	bootlast
maleness	oatgrass	quarters	shoeless	syrinxes	viperous	airshaft	botanist
mandamus	ochreous	rachides	sickness	tactless	virtuous	airtight	bouffant
marasmus	oddments	rachitis	sidearms	tailings	vitellus	alarmist	bowfront
marquess	oestrous	raciness	sideways	tailless	vitreous	alcahest	bowsprit
marrieds	ofttimes	rankness	siftings	tallness	voidness	alienist	boxpleat
massless	oiliness	raptness	siriasis	tameless	volcanos	alkahest	bracelet
mastitis	omphalos	raptures	skewness	tameness	volvulus	allnight	bractlet
matgrass	oogamous	rareness	skilless	tantalus	vortexes	almagest	braggart
matiness	ooziness	rashness	skinless	tapeless	vortices	alphabet	brassart
matrices	openness	ravenous	skittles	tartness	votaress	alpinist	breakout
matrixes	oratress	realness	skywards	tautness	voteless	altruist	brickbat
mattress	orgulous	reassess	slimness	tearless	waesucks	alumroot	brooklet
mayoress	osteitis	redeless	slowness	technics	waitress	amadavat	browbeat
maziness	outclass	reinless	slyboots	tenesmus	wakeless	ambivert	buckshot
meanness	outdoors	redeless	smithers	terminus	wardress	ambulant	Buddhist
meekness	outguess	resinous	smugness	termless	wariness	amethyst	bunfight
meetness	outwards	respects	sniffles	thalamus	warmness	anapaest	burgonet
mementos	outworks	restless	snowless	thallous	waterbus	anchoret	burntout
meninges	ovalness	rhinitis	snuffers	Thanatos	watergas	annalist	bystreet
meniscus	ovaritis	rhonchus	snuffles	thinness	waveless	antepost	cabalist
mephitis	overalls	ribgrass	snugness	thisness	waviness	aperient	cachalot
Mesdames	overpass	richness	soapless	thoraces	waxiness	aphorist	cachepot
methinks	overplus	rifeness	soapsuds	thoraxes	waxworks	apiarist	calamint
methysis	overseas	rigorous	softness	thoughts	weakness	apparent	camshaft
miasmous	painless	rinsings	soilless	thrombus	weedless	appetent	canoeist
midlands	paleness	ripeness	soleness	thusness	wetlands	aquanaut	canonist
midships	pancreas	roadless	sombrous	tideless	whatness	aquarist	canzonet
midwives	pandanus	roofless	someways	tidiness	whiskers	aquatint	capellet
mildness	panpipes	rootless	songless	timeless	wideness	arbalest	carburet
mindless	papulous	ropiness	sonorous	timorous	wifeless	arbalist	carcanet
Minoress	pastries	rosiness	soreness	tininess	wildness	arborist	carryout
mistress	pathless	rouleaus	soulless	tinnitus	wiliness	archaist	casement
mittimus	patulous	rounders	sourness	tintless	windlass	argonaut	catalyst
molasses	pearlies	rudeness	sourpuss	tireless	windless	argument	catapult
molossus	pectines	ruleless	spacious	titaness	wingless	armament	cataract
moonless	peelings	rustless	spadices	tombless	winnings	arrogant	catsfoot
moorings	peerless	ruthless	spadones	toneless	wireless	arsonist	cellaret
mornings	perilous	ryegrass	specious	topdress	wiriness	artefact	ceramist
moveless	periplus	sacculus	spherics	tortious	wiseness	artifact	cerement
muchness	pertness	sackless	sphygmus	tortuous	wondrous	aspirant	cervelat
mucrones	pervious	safeness	spiritus	trammels	woollens	assignat	chalkpit
muteness	petalous	sageness	splenius	treeless	wordless	assonant	Chartist
muticous	phthisis	sailless	spotless	trembles	workings	autocrat	checkout
mutinous	pickings	saltless	spraints	trespass	workless	avadavat	chestnut
myelitis	pictures	saltness	spryness	trimness	writings	averment	chiliast
myositis	pinchers	sameness	spurious	trousers	wrongous		

chitchat	distrust	finalist	hesitant	Leninist	nauseant	pregnant	sailboat
cidevant	ditheist	fireboat	highmost	lifebelt	needment	preprint	salariat
claimant	divalent	firebrat	hightest	lifeboat	nescient	printout	saltwort
clarinet	Docetist	flagrant	hillfort	ligament	newscast	prohibit	samizdat
cleancut	document	flatboat	hindmost	linguist	newsheet	prosaist	sandwort
clearcut	dogfight	flatfeet	hirrient	liniment	nihilist	prospect	Sanskrit
closeset	dominant	flatfoot	hobbyist	litigant	nonevent	protract	sarcenet
cloudlet	Donatist	flattest	holdfast	lobbyist	novelist	prurient	sarsenet
clubfoot	donought	flautist	homefelt	lockfast	nutrient	psalmist	satanist
coaldust	doorpost	fleawort	homodont	lockknit	obedient	psychist	satirist
cockboat	doughnut	fleshpot	honeypot	lodgment	obeisant	pugilist	saturant
cockloft	downbeat	flippant	hoofbeat	longboat	obstruct	puissant	Saxonist
cockshut	downcast	floodlit	hornwort	lorikeet	occident	puppyfat	scandent
cognovit	downmost	floweret	hotchpot	loveknot	occupant	pursenet	scilicet
coherent	dragonet	foldboat	Huguenot	lovenest	offprint	pursuant	sciolist
cokernut	dribblet	folkmoot	humanist	loveseat	offshoot	purulent	scoopnet
colewort	dropshot	footpost	humorist	loyalist	ointment	pushcart	seachest
colonist	dropwort	footrest	iceplant	luculent	oliphant	pussycat	seacoast
comedist	druggist	forecast	iceyacht	luminant	oologist	quadrant	seacraft
compleat	drupelet	forefelt	idealist	luminist	opencast	queenlet	seafront
conflict	drypoint	forefoot	idiolect	lungwort	opponent	quickset	seamount
confront	duellist	foremast	idyllist	lutanist	optimist	quietist	seatbelt
conjoint	duettist	foremost	ignorant	lutenist	organist	quitrent	seatrout
conjunct	dungcart	forepart	illtreat	lyricist	ornament	quotient	sederunt
conquest	dustcart	forepast	immanent	mailboat	orpiment	rackrent	sediment
constant	dustcoat	forewent	imminent	mailcart	osculant	radicant	seedcoat
contempt	dustshot	forklift	immodest	mainmast	outburst	raincoat	seedplot
contract	dynamist	forspent	implicit	makefast	outpoint	rallyist	segreant
contrast	earthnut	fourpart	imponent	malapert	outright	reactant	Semitist
copyedit	easement	fowlpest	impotent	maledict	outsight	readjust	sennight
corselet	eastmost	fragment	impudent	maltreat	outsmart	rearmost	sentient
Corybant	efferent	fragrant	incident	manifest	outspent	reassert	sergeant
cosecant	effluent	freakout	incitant	mantelet	overcast	recommit	serjeant
cotenant	eggplant	frequent	indecent	marabout	overcoat	recreant	servient
couchant	electret	frogspit	indicant	marmoset	overheat	recusant	sewerrat
couldest	elephant	frondent	indigent	martenot	overpast	redirect	shakeout
covalent	eloquent	frontlet	indirect	martinet	overshot	redolent	shareout
covenant	emergent	fruitbat	indolent	massicot	oviposit	redshift	sharpset
coverlet	emigrant	fumigant	inerrant	mazement	pacifist	redshirt	shipment
crackpot	emulgent	furthest	inexpert	megawatt	pamphlet	redstart	shootout
crescent	enforest	futurist	inflight	melodist	pantsuit	reefknot	shortcut
crosscut	entrepot	gadabout	influent	merchant	papalist	reexport	shouldst
crosslet	epiblast	gallipot	inhalant	microdot	parakeet	referent	showboat
crotchet	equitant	gaslight	inherent	midnight	paraquat	refluent	sibilant
crowfoot	escapist	gastight	innocent	midpoint	parodist	reforest	sicklist
cryostat	escargot	gatepost	inscient	mightest	paroquet	regiment	signpost
cucurbit	eschalot	Gaullist	insolent	milepost	passport	reinsert	simonist
daylight	esculent	gauntlet	inspirit	militant	pavement	reinvest	simulant
deadbeat	essayist	gladdest	instinct	milkwort	paysheet	relaxant	sinciput
debutant	esurient	glummest	instruct	misbegot	pederast	relevant	siphonet
decadent	etherist	goalpost	insulant	miscount	pediment	relucent	sitarist
decedent	ethicist	golddust	insurant	misdealt	penchant	remanent	skylight
decrepit	eucalypt	goutwort	interact	misdoubt	penitent	renitent	skypilot
deferent	eugenist	gradient	intercut	misprint	petulant	reorient	slimmest
deforest	eulogist	greenlet	interest	misspelt	phaseout	rescript	slipknot
democrat	euphuist	grimmest	intermit	misspent	pheasant	resident	snakepit
deponent	Eurocrat	guardant	intromit	mistreat	piecrust	resonant	snapshot
derelict	evacuant	gunfight	irritant	mistrust	piedmont	restrict	snowboot
destruct	excitant	gunflint	ivorynut	mitigant	pilewort	reticent	soaproot
dewpoint	exhalant	gunpoint	jackboot	mobocrat	pillwort	retroact	soapwort
diffract	existent	gynocrat	Jehovist	modalist	pinpoint	revenant	solarist
digamist	exorcist	gyrostat	jingoist	Molinist	planchet	reverent	solecist
dilatant	expirant	habitant	jubilant	monocrat	plangent	rheostat	solfaist
diligent	explicit	halfboot	judgment	monodist	platelet	ricochet	solleret
dinerout	exponent	halfmast	jumpseat	monoglot	playsuit	rightist	somewhat
diplomat	exultant	halfpint	jumpsuit	monotint	pleasant	rigorist	sparklet
diriment	eyesight	handcart	kilowatt	monument	plumelet	ringbolt	spikelet
discount	fabulist	handfast	kingbolt	moonshot	poignant	roborant	sprocket
discreet	facelift	handlist	knockout	moonwort	polemist	rocksalt	stagnant
disjoint	faineant	hazelnut	lamppost	moralist	poltfoot	Romanist	stakenet
disjunct	falconet	headfast	lancelet	motorist	polyglot	roodloft	stalwart
dismount	faltboat	headmost	lanneret	movement	populist	roseroot	stardust
dispirit	fanlight	headrest	Latinist	mowburnt	portrait	royalist	starwort
displant	farthest	Hebraist	latitant	muniment	postobit	rudiment	stedfast
disquiet	fatalist	hedonist	lawcourt	murrelet	potplant	ruminant	stinkpot
distinct	feculent	heliport	layabout	myoblast	potroast	runabout	stockist
distract	feminist	hellbent	layshaft	namepart	precinct	ruralist	stockpot
distrait	figurant	helpmeet	Lazarist	nativist	preelect	rutilant	straight
district	filament	henroost	legalist	naturist	preexist	sackcoat	strepent

strident	visitant	overview	adequacy	bilberry	ceremony	cytology	errantly
strumpet	vitalist	peepshow	adorably	billyboy	chambray	daintily	errantry
subagent	vivisect	rearview	adroitly	bioassay	chancery	damnably	esterify
suberect	vocalist	rebellow	adultery	biometry	chapelry	dancetty	eternity
subjoint	volitant	rickshaw	advisory	birthday	charlady	daringly	ethology
subtract	votarist	roughhew	advocacy	bistoury	chastely	dastardy	euphrasy
succinct	wagonlit	setscrew	aerially	bitchily	chastity	deathray	eutrophy
sunburnt	wainscot	sideshow	aerology	bitingly	chattily	debility	everyday
sunburst	waleknot	sideview	aeronomy	bitterly	chauntry	decently	everyway
sunlight	wallknot	soundbow	affinity	biweekly	cheekily	delegacy	exigency
supplant	warpaint	southpaw	agrimony	biyearly	cheerily	delicacy	exiguity
surfboat	wartwort	stickjaw	agrology	blackboy	chemurgy	delivery	expertly
surmount	waxlight	teleview	agronomy	blackfly	chirpily	delusory	facially
swanshot	weldment	tenonsaw	aguishly	bladdery	chirrupy	demagogy	facilely
sweepnet	wellknit	tomorrow	alacrity	blamably	chivalry	demurely	facility
swiftlet	whinchat	undertow	Alderney	blankety	choicely	denazify	fadeaway
swimsuit	whitehot	williwaw	aleatory	blatancy	choirboy	derisory	falconry
symbiont	whiteout	wiredraw	algidity	blazonry	chopsuey	detoxify	fallibly
tablecut	whittret	withdraw	algology	blearily	chorally	deucedly	famously
tablemat	whodunit	withdrew	alkalify	blistery	chummily	deviancy	farriery
tabouret	wingbeat	appendix	allegory	blithely	chupatty	deviltry	fatality
tailcoat	woodchat	aviatrix	alleyway	bloodily	churchly	devoutly	fatherly
tangoist	wormcast	bandeaux	allogamy	bloomery	cinerary	dewberry	faultily
Tantrist	wouldest	battleax	almighty	blossomy	circuity	dicacity	faunally
teachest	wristlet	biconvex	amazedly	blubbery	civility	dilatory	feasibly
tearduct	yoghourt	bobbysox	amenably	blurrily	clammily	diploidy	feastday
tegument	youngest	Bordeaux	amicably	blustery	classify	directly	feathery
telecast	ziggurat	chateaux	ammonify	boringly	clearway	disarray	February
teleport	carcajou	cicatrix	amorally	bottomry	clemency	dismally	felicity
tenement	Esquimau	creatrix	amusedly	bouncily	cleverly	distally	felinity
theocrat	flambeau	crucifix	ancestry	boundary	disunity	fellowly
theorist	froufrou	dittybox	animally	boyishly	cloudily	divinely	feminity
thereout	hausfrau	epicalyx	annually	brassily	clownery	divinity	fenberry
thickset	jiujitsu	fabliaux	antibody	brazenly	clumsily	docilely	feretory
thinnest	kinkajou	haruspex	antilogy	brazenry	clustery	docility	ferocity
thrawart	pirarucu	horsebox	antimony	braziery	coarsely	dogberry	fervency
thumbpot	priedieu	intermix	antinomy	breezily	cobwebby	doggedly	fervidly
tolerant	thankyou	interrex	apically	breviary	cogently	dogsbody	festally
tommyrot	Jugoslav	intersex	apoplexy	brightly	colliery	donatory	feudally
totemist	Yugoslav	loosebox	apostasy	broadway	colloquy	doomsday	fidelity
toxicant	airscrew	matchbox	ardently	broidery	cometary	dormancy	fiercely
trainlet	bedstraw	mirepoix	arguably	brokenly	commoney	dorsally	filially
transact	Bradshaw	moneybox	arrantly	broodily	commonly	dotingly	filthily
transect	brandnew	orthodox	artfully	brutally	contrary	doughboy	finality
transept	bungalow	paintbox	artistry	bryology	convexly	doxology	finitely
transmit	chainsaw	parallax	asperity	bullocky	coquetry	draughty	fireclay
Trappist	chowchow	plateaux	assembly	bullyboy	corduroy	dreamily	fiscally
trawlnet	clerihew	pontifex	astutely	buoyancy	cornetcy	drearily	fitfully
trialist	cockcrow	pressbox	atrocity	Burberry	coronary	driftway	flashily
troutlet	coleslaw	quincunx	attorney	burglary	corsetry	driveway	flattery
turbojet	crackjaw	rondeaux	audacity	Burgundy	costmary	drollery	fleshfly
turncoat	crossbow	rouleaux	auditory	bushbaby	cottagey	droughty	flexibly
turnspit	curassow	sardonyx	augustly	busybody	courtesy	drowsily	flickery
twilight	disallow	saucebox	autarchy	butchery	cousinly	drudgery	flimsily
typecast	disendow	smallpox	autogamy	cabinboy	covertly	easterly	flintily
ultraist	dumbshow	snuffbox	autonomy	cableway	cowardly	efficacy	floodway
underact	elfarrow	soundbox	autotomy	cacology	cowberry	eighthly	floppily
undercut	fernshaw	spicebox	aversely	caducity	craftily	elatedly	florally
underlet	feverfew	spinifex	avowedly	cajolery	cramoisy	elegancy	floridly
underset	finedraw	supertax	axiality	calamary	cranefly	eligibly	fluently
undreamt	foreknew	tableaux	axillary	calamity	crankily	eminency	fluidify
undulant	foreknow	toadflax	axiology	calidity	cravenly	emissary	fluidity
unionist	foreshow	transfix	backstay	candidly	creakily	emulsify	flummery
unlearnt	framesaw	trumeaux	balladry	cannonry	creamery	endogamy	fluttery
unsought	furbelow	voicebox	banality	capacity	credibly	endogeny	foetidly
untaught	hedgerow	abeyancy	banditry	carnally	croakily	enginery	foldaway
unthrift	hernshaw	abjectly	barberry	castaway	crockery	enormity	forcedly
uppercut	highbrow	aborally	barratry	casually	crossply	ensigncy	forcibly
upthrust	homebrew	abruptly	barrenly	casualty	crossway	enthalpy	forelady
urbanist	honeydew	absently	basicity	catchfly	crustily	entirely	foreplay
urticant	hoosegow	absurdly	basketry	category	cryogeny	entirety	forestay
usufruct	kickshaw	accuracy	bastardy	catenary	culinary	entreaty	forestry
vehement	mackinaw	acerbity	bayberry	caudally	culpably	enviably	formally
vesicant	overdraw	achingly	bearably	causally	cupidity	epically	formerly
vestment	overdrew	acridity	beautify	causeway	currency	epilepsy	fortuity
vigilant	overflew	acrimony	beggarly	celerity	cursedly	epinasty	fourthly
virement	overflow	actively	bellbuoy	celibacy	cushiony	epiphany	friendly
virulent	overgrew	activity	benignly	cemetery	cussedly	equality	frigidly
viscount	overgrow	actually	bestiary	centaury	cycleway	equinity	frippery

friskily	hollowly	labially	ministry	oblatory	pomology	ribbonry	shimmery
frostily	homebody	lability	minority	obtusely	popinjay	ridgeway	shoddily
frothily	homogamy	lackaday	minutely	obtusity	popishly	rigidify	shortday
fructify	homogeny	lacunary	misapply	occultly	porosity	rigidity	shrewdly
frugally	homology	laically	miscarry	octarchy	porphyry	ritually	shuddery
fruitery	homonymy	lamasery	misogamy	octonary	posology	riverway	sickerly
fruitfly	honestly	lambency	misogyny	ocularly	possibly	robustly	signally
frumenty	honorary	landarmy	misology	odiously	potbelly	rocketry	silently
fugacity	horology	landlady	missilry	oecology	potently	rogatory	silicify
fumitory	horribly	lapidary	mobility	oenology	prettify	rolypoly	silverly
funerary	horridly	lapidify	modality	omophagy	prettily	rosemary	simplify
furriery	horsefly	latchkey	modernly	oncology	priestly	rotatory	sinfully
futilely	hostelry	latently	modestly	ontogeny	priggery	rottenly	sinology
futility	houseboy	latinity	modishly	ontology	primally	rotundly	sisterly
futurity	housefly	latterly	molality	opaquely	princely	roughdry	sitology
gadgetry	hoverfly	laudably	molarity	orangery	priority	rubbishy	sixpenny
Galloway	humanely	lavatory	momently	ordinary	prissily	ruefully	skimpily
gapingly	humanity	lavishly	monandry	oreology	probably	ruggedly	slangily
garganey	humidify	lawfully	monarchy	ornately	prolixly	rugosely	sleazily
garishly	humidity	lawyerly	monetary	orthoepy	promptly	rugosity	sleepily
garlicky	humility	leadenly	monitory	otiosely	properly	rurality	slideway
gelidity	hummocky	leathery	monogamy	otiosity	property	sacredly	slightly
genially	hungrily	legality	monogeny	outlawry	prophecy	sacristy	slinkily
geognosy	hydropsy	legendry	monogony	overbusy	prophesy	saddlery	slippery
geomancy	hypogyny	legerity	monogyny	overplay	provably	saffrony	slithery
geometry	ideality	leniency	monopoly	overstay	pryingly	sagacity	slobbery
geophagy	identify	lethally	monotony	owlishly	psalmody	sailorly	sloppily
gimmicky	identity	lethargy	mopishly	paduasoy	psaltery	salacity	slovenly
gingerly	ideology	libatory	morality	pallidly	publicly	saliency	slovenry
giveaway	idolatry	lifebuoy	moratory	palpably	punditry	salinity	slumbery
glassily	ignominy	limitary	morbidly	pandowdy	pungency	salivary	smallfry
glaziery	illusory	limpidly	mordancy	pansophy	punitory	salutary	smarmily
glittery	immunity	lineally	morosely	paperboy	pupilary	sanatory	smeltery
globally	imparity	linearly	morosity	papistry	puppetry	sanctify	smithery
gloomily	impishly	liquidly	mortally	parrotry	putridly	sanctity	smoothly
glossary	impolicy	literacy	mortuary	passably	quackery	sanitary	smothery
glossily	impunity	literary	motherly	passerby	quaintly	sapidity	smudgily
gluttony	impurely	livelily	motility	patchily	Quakerly	saponify	smuttily
goldenly	impurity	lividity	motivity	patently	quandary	satiably	snappily
gossipry	industry	loblolly	motorway	peacocky	quantify	Saturday	snazzily
gramercy	inequity	lobotomy	movingly	peccancy	quantity	savagely	sneakily
gratuity	infantry	locality	mucosity	pedagogy	queasily	savagery	sniffily
gravelly	infinity	locutory	mulberry	pedantry	quiddity	scammony	snippety
greasily	infirmly	Lollardy	mulishly	pedology	quirkily	scantily	snobbery
greedily	iniquity	lovelily	mulloway	pendency	quixotry	scarcely	snootily
greenery	innately	lovingly	multeity	penology	rabbitry	scarcity	snuggery
greenfly	insanely	lubberly	multiply	perigyny	rabidity	scattily	soakaway
grindery	insanity	lucidity	musingly	peripety	racially	scratchy	sobriety
groggily	instancy	luminary	musketry	petalody	radially	screechy	sobstory
grubbily	intently	mahogany	mutually	phantasy	radiancy	scribbly	sociably
grumpily	intimacy	maidenly	mycology	pharmacy	raggedly	scrutiny	socially
guaranty	inwardly	mainstay	narrowly	photopsy	raillery	scullery	sodality
guernsey	irongray	majority	nasality	phyllary	rakishly	scurvily	soldiery
guideway	irongrey	Malagasy	nascency	physicky	rampancy	seaholly	solemnly
guiltily	isocracy	malarkey	natality	picnicky	randomly	seamanly	solidary
gulosity	isometry	malignly	natatory	pilosity	rapacity	secondly	solidify
gynandry	isospory	manfully	natively	pinmoney	rapidity	secretly	solidity
gyratory	isostasy	mangabey	nativity	pipeclay	rascally	securely	solitary
haploidy	isotropy	mannerly	naumachy	piquancy	readably	security	solvency
harlotry	jackstay	manually	necropsy	pitiably	reagency	sedately	sombrely
hatchery	jaggedly	markedly	negatory	placably	recently	sedulity	somebody
hatchway	janizary	masterly	neurally	placidly	reconvey	seignory	sonobuoy
headachy	jauntily	matronly	nihility	plagiary	recovery	selfpity	sonority
heartily	jealousy	maturely	nobility	plaguily	redeploy	seminary	soothsay
heatedly	jejunely	maturity	nodality	plastery	reemploy	senility	sordidly
heathery	jeopardy	meagrely	nodosity	pleurisy	refinery	sensibly	sorority
heavenly	jesuitry	medially	nomology	pliantly	regality	serenely	sovranty
hegemony	jocosely	mellowly	nondairy	pluckily	registry	serenity	sparbuoy
henparty	jocosity	menially	nonparty	plurally	reliably	serially	sparsely
heraldry	jocundly	menology	normalcy	podiatry	remissly	serology	sparsity
hereaway	jokingly	mentally	normally	polarity	remotely	serosity	speedily
heredity	jovially	mesially	nosology	politely	reoccupy	severely	speedway
hexapody	joyfully	metonymy	nubility	polygamy	resinify	severity	spermary
hideaway	joyously	micrurgy	nugatory	polygeny	resurvey	sexology	spillway
hilarity	jugglery	mightily	numeracy	polygyny	revisory	sexually	spirally
hillocky	knackery	military	numerary	polypary	revivify	shabbily	spivvery
hoarsely	knightly	milliary	oafishly	polypody	rhapsody	shaggily	splotchy
hobbitry	kolinsky	minacity	obduracy	polysemy	rheology	shiftily	spongily
Hogmanay	kromesky	minatory	obituary	polysomy	ribaldry	shiftkey	spookily

```
spoonily strongly tearaway tomnoddy turgidly upwardly viridity witchety
sportily stuffily telegony tonality tussocky urbanely virility wizardly
spottily stultify temerity tonicity tutelary urbanity virology wizardry
sprucely stumpily tenacity toothily twittery urgently viscidly woefully
spunkily stupidly tenantry topheavy twopenny usefully visually wontedly
squarely sturdily tendency toplofty typology uvularly vitality woodenly
squelchy subtlety tenderly topology ubiquity vacantly vivacity wordplay
squiggly sudatory tenotomy toponymy ultimacy vagility vocality workaday
squirely suddenly tenpenny torpidly unchancy vagrancy vomitory worthily
stairway suitably tepidity torridly uncially valiancy voracity woundily
stanchly sullenly terribly totality underlay validity vulgarly wrathily
stannary sultrily tertiary touchily underway valuably walkaway xenogamy
starrily summerly tetchily touristy uneasily vapidity wantonly xylology
statedly summitry textuary towardly unevenly variably wardenry Yankeefy
statuary sunshiny thearchy toxicity unfairly variedly warranty yeastily
steadily superbly theodicy trackway ungainly varletry warweary yellowly
stealthy supinely theogony trashery uniquely vavasory watchkey yeomanly
steamily supplely theology trashily unitedly velleity waterway yeomanry
stellify swannery thickety travesty unjustly velocity waxberry zealotry
sternway symmetry thievery treasury unkindly venality weaponry zinckify
stickily sympathy thingamy trendily unkingly venially weaselly zoolatry
stingily symphony threeply trevally unlikely venosity weevilly zoomancy
stingray synastry threeway triarchy unlovely venously welladay zoometry
stockily synonymy threnody tribally unmeetly veracity wellaway zoophily
stodgily takeaway thuggery trickery unseemly verbally westerly zymology
stolidly takingly thundery trickily unstably verdancy wheezily pincenez
stomachy tangency Thursday trippery unsteady vernally Whiggery schmaltz
stonefly tangibly thwartly triunity unstuffy vespiary whiskery
stormily tanistry timidity trollopy untidily vestiary whispery
stowaway tapestry timously truantry untimely vibrancy whiteboy
straggly tasselly tinselly trumpery unwarily vicinity whitefly
straitly tawdrily tittuppy trustily unwieldy villainy wickedly
strategy taxingly tocology tryingly unwisely vinegary wilfully
stratify taxonomy toiletry tumidity unwordly vinosity winterly
stretchy teacaddy tokology tuppenny unworthy vinously wintrily
strictly teaparty tomalley turbidly uppishly violably witchery
```

9 letter words

```
abandoned absurdism acidophil adipocere adverbial affricate airworthy
abandonee absurdist acidulate adiposity adversary aflatoxin airyfairy
abandoner absurdity acidulent adjacency adversely aforesaid aitchbone
abasement abundance acidulous adjoining adversity Afrikaans alabaster
abashment abusively aciniform adjunctly advertent Afrikaner albatross
abatement abysmally aconitine adjutancy advertise aftercare albescent
abdicable academism acoustics adlibbing advisable afterclap albinotic
abdicator acariasis acquiesce admeasure advisably afterglow alchemise
abdominal accentual acquittal adminicle advisedly afterlife alchemist
abduction acceptant acquitted admirable advocator aftermath alcoholic
aberrance acceptive acrobatic admirably aepyornis aftermost aldehydic
aberrancy accessary acropetal admiralty aerialist afternoon aleatoric
abhorrent accession acropolis admission aeriality aftertime Alemannic
abhorring accessory acroteria admissive aerobatic afterword alertness
abidingly accidence actinozoa admitting aerobiont agapemone algarroba
abjection accipiter activator admixture aerodrome aggravate algebraic
ablatival acclaimer actualise admonitor aerograph aggregate Algonkian
ablutions acclimate actuality adnominal aerolitic aggressor Algonquin
abnegator acclivity actuarial adoptable aerometer aggrieved algorithm
abnormity accompany actuation adoration aerometry agistment alicyclic
abolisher accordant acuminate adoringly aerophyte agitation alienable
abolition according adamantly adornment aeroplane agitative alienator
abominate accordion adaptable adrenalin aerospace agnatical alignment
aborigine accretion addiction adsorbate aesthesia agonising alinement
abounding accretive addictive adsorbent aesthesis agonistic aliphatic
aboutface accusable addressee adulation aesthetic agreeable aliveness
aboutturn acellular addresser adulatory aestivate agreeably alkaloses
abradable acescence addressor adulterer aetiology agreement alkalosis
abrogator acetabula adducible adulthood affecting agriology allantois
abruption acetamide adduction adultness affection agrologic allegedly
abscissae acetifier adductive adumbrate affective agronomic allegiant
abscissas acetylate ademption advantage affianced ahistoric allegoric
absconder acetylcoA adenoidal advection affidavit ailanthus allemande
abseiling acetylene adenomata advective affiliate aimlessly alleviate
absorbent Acheulean adenosine Adventism affirmant aircooled alligator
absorbing Acheulian adeptness Adventist affixture airjacket allocable
abstainer aciculate adherence adventive afflation airminded allograph
abstinent acidifier adiabatic adventure affluence airstream allomorph
```

allopathy	anabolism	anopheles	applauder	asbestine	attrition	backspace
allophone	anabranch	anorectic	applejack	asbestous	aubergine	backstage
alloplasm	anacruses	anorthite	appliance	ascendant	aubrietia	backsword
allotment	anacrusis	anovulant	applicant	ascendent	auctorial	backtrack
allotrope	anaerobic	anoxaemia	appointee	ascension	audacious	backwards
allotropy	analeptic	anschluss	apportion	ascensive	audiology	backwater
allotting	analgesia	antarctic	appraisal	ascertain	auditable	backwoods
allowable	analgesic	antefixal	appraiser	ascetical	auditoria	bacterial
allowably	analogise	antenatal	apprehend	asclepiad	augmented	bacterise
allowance	analogist	antennary	appressed	ascospore	augmenter	bacterium
allowedly	analogous	antennule	approbate	asepalous	augmentor	bacteroid
almandine	analysand	anthelion	aquaplane	asexually	auricular	badminton
almsgiver	anamnesis	anthemion	aquarelle	ashamedly	auspicate	bagatelle
almshouse	anandrous	anthocyan	aqueously	Ashkenazi	austenite	bagginess
aloneness	anaphoric	anthology	aquilegia	ashlaring	austerely	bailiwick
alongside	anaptyxis	anthozoan	arabesque	asininity	austerity	bainmarie
aloofness	anarchism	anthracic	arabicise	askewness	autarchic	bakehouse
alpargata	anarchist	anthropic	arachnoid	asparagus	autarkist	baksheesh
alpenhorn	anatomise	anticline	aragonite	aspartate	authentic	balaclava
alterable	anatomist	anticodon	araneidal	aspectual	authoress	balalaika
altercate	ancestral	antidotal	araneidan	aspersion	authorial	balconied
alternant	anchorage	antigenic	araucaria	asphaltic	authorise	baldachin
alternate	anchoress	antiknock	arbitrage	asphaltum	authority	baldaquin
altimeter	anchorite	antimonic	arbitrary	aspirator	autoclave	baldfaced
altricial	anchorman	antinodal	arbitrate	assailant	autocracy	balefully
aluminate	anchylose	antinomic	arbitress	assaulter	autocross	balkanise
aluminise	anciently	antinovel	arboreous	assayable	autocycle	balladeer
aluminium	ancientry	antipasto	arboretum	assembler	autograft	balladist
aluminous	ancillary	antipathy	archangel	assertion	autograph	ballerina
alveolate	andantino	antiphony	archducal	assertive	autolysis	ballistae
amaryllis	andesitic	antipodal	archduchy	assiduity	autolytic	ballistic
amassment	androecia	antipodes	archenemy	assiduous	automatic	ballpoint
amauroses	androgyne	antiquary	archetype	assistant	automaton	balminess
amaurosis	androgyny	antiquate	archfiend	associate	autonomic	baltimore
amaurotic	anecdotal	antiquity	architect	assonance	autopilot	bamboozle
amazement	anecdotic	antiserum	archivist	assuasive	autoroute	banderole
amazingly	anemogram	antitoxic	archivolt	assumable	autosomal	bandicoot
amazonian	angelfish	antitoxin	arcuately	assumably	autotelic	bandoleer
ambergris	angelical	antitrade	arduously	assumpsit	autotroph	bandolero
ambiguity	angiology	antitrust	Areopagus	assurance	auxiliary	bandolier
ambiguous	angiomata	antivenin	argentine	assuredly	available	bandoline
ambitious	angleiron	antiviral	argentite	assurgent	availably	bandstand
amblyopia	anglesite	anxiously	argentous	asthmatic	avalanche	bandwagon
amblyopic	angleworm	apartheid	argillite	astraddle	aventaile	bandwidth
ambrosial	anglicise	apartment	argumenta	astrakhan	averagely	baneberry
ambulacra	anglicism	apartness	Arguseyed	astrocyte	avertible	banefully
ambulance	Anglicist	apathetic	argybargy	astrodome	avizandum	banjulele
ambuscade	anglophil	aperiodic	armadillo	astrolabe	avocation	bannister
amendable	angriness	aperitive	armigeral	astrology	avoidable	banqueter
amendment	anguished	apetalous	armillary	astronaut	avoidably	banquette
americium	angularly	aphereses	armistice	astronomy	avoidance	Bantustan
Amerindic	anhydride	apheresis	Armorican	asymmetry	avuncular	baptismal
amianthus	anhydrite	aphyllous	aromatise	asymptote	awakening	baptistry
amidships	anhydrous	apiculate	arrearage	asyndetic	awardable	barathrum
aminoacid	animalise	apishness	arrestant	asyndeton	awareness	Barbadian
amoebaean	animalism	aplanatic	arresting	atacamite	awesomely	barbarian
amoralism	animalist	apocrypha	arriviste	ataractic	awestruck	barbarise
amorality	animality	apodictic	arrogance	atavistic	awfulness	barbarism
amorously	animation	apogamous	arrowhead	atheistic	awkwardly	barbarity
amorphism	animatism	apologise	arrowroot	athematic	axiomatic	barbarous
amorphous	animistic	apologist	arrowwood	Athenaeum	Axminster	barbitone
amourette	animosity	apomictic	arrowworm	athletics	Aylesbury	barcarole
ampersand	anklebone	apophyses	arsenical	Atlantean	azeotrope	barefaced
amphibian	ankylosis	apophysis	arsenious	atmometer	azimuthal	bargainer
amphibole	ankylotic	apostolic	artemisia	atomicity	babacoote	bargepole
amphigory	annectent	apothecia	arteriole	atomistic	Babbittry	barkeeper
amphioxus	annelidan	appalling	arteritis	atonalism	babirussa	barleymow
ampleness	annotator	Appaloosa	arthritic	atonality	baboonish	barmbrack
amplifier	announcer	apparatus	arthritis	atonement	bacchanal	Barmecide
amplitude	annoyance	apparitor	arthropod	atonicity	bacchante	barnacled
amputator	annuitant	appealing	arthrosis	atrocious	bacillary	barnstorm
amusement	annularly	appellant	Arthurian	attainder	backbiter	barograph
amusingly	annulated	appellate	artichoke	attempter	backboard	barometer
amygdalin	annulling	appendage	articular	attendant	backcloth	barometry
amyloidal	annulment	appendant	artificer	attention	backcross	baronetcy
amylopsin	anomalous	appertain	artillery	attentive	backpedal	barracker
anabioses	anonymity	appetence	artlessly	attenuate	backsight	barracoon
anabiosis	anonymous	appetency	arytenoid	attractor	backslang	barracuda
anabiotic		appetiser	asafetida	attribute	backslide	barrelful

barrelled	benignity	blackbuck	bombardon	breakaway	bucktooth	Caesarist
barricade	bentonite	blackcoat	bombasine	breakdown	buckwheat	cafeteria
barricado	benzidine	blackcock	bombastic	breakeven	budgetary	cageyness
barrister	benzoline	blackdamp	bombazine	breakfast	buffaloes	cailleach
bartender	berberine	blackface	bombhappy	breakneck	buffeting	Cainozoic
bashfully	bergamask	Blackfeet	bombilate	breastpin	bughunter	cairngorm
basically	berkelium	blackfish	bombinate	breathily	buhrstone	calaboose
basilican	berserker	blackflag	bombproof	breathing	bulbously	calabrese
basipetal	beryllium	Blackfoot	bombshell	brecciate	Bulgarian	calamanco
basketful	besetment	blackgame	bombsight	breeching	bulginess	calandria
basrelief	besetting	blackhead	bondslave	breezeway	bulkiness	calcaneal
bastardly	beslobber	blackjack	bondstone	bregmatic	bulldozer	calcaneum
bastinade	besotting	blacklead	bondwoman	bretasche	bullfight	calcarate
bastinado	bespangle	blacklist	bonechina	Bretwalda	bullfinch	calcicole
bastioned	bespatter	blackmail	bonhomous	breveting	bullishly	calcifuge
bathhouse	bestially	blackness	bonniness	brevetted	bulltrout	calculate
batholite	bestirred	blackwash	boobytrap	briarroot	bullybeef	calculous
batholith	bethought	blaeberry	bookishly	briarwood	bullytree	caldarium
Bathonian	betrothal	blameable	booklouse	bricabrac	bumblebee	calendric
bathybius	betrothed	blameably	bookmaker	brickwork	bumbledon	calendula
battalion	bevelling	blameless	bookplate	brickyard	bumpiness	calenture
battening	biblicism	blandness	bookshelf	bridecake	bumptious	calibrate
battiness	biblicist	blankness	bookstall	bridesman	bundobust	calicular
battleaxe	bicameral	blaspheme	bookstand	bridewell	bunkhouse	caliology
battlecry	bicipital	blasphemy	bookstore	bridleway	buoyantly	caliphate
bawdiness	biconcave	blasthole	boomerang	briefcase	burdenous	callipers
bayoneted	bifarious	blastulae	boomslang	briefless	burlesque	callosity
beachhead	bifoliate	blastular	boondocks	briefness	burliness	callously
beachwear	bifurcate	blatantly	boorishly	brierroot	burnedout	calmative
beadledom	bigeneric	blazingly	bootblack	brierwood	burningly	calorific
beamingly	bigheaded	bleachery	bordereau	brigadier	burnisher	Calvinism
beanfeast	bilabiate	bleakness	borrowing	brigandry	burrstone	Calvinist
beanstalk	bilateral	bleareyed	boskiness	brightish	bursarial	calycinal
bearberry	bilgekeel	blessedly	bossiness	brilliant	bushcraft	camarilla
beardless	bilharzia	blindfold	botanical	brimstone	bushelful	Cambodian
beastings	bilingual	blindness	bottlefed	bringdown	bushiness	camelback
beatitude	biliously	blinkered	bottleful	briquette	bushwhack	camelhair
beauteous	bilirubin	blockader	boulevard	briskness	butadiene	Camembert
beautiful	biliteral	blockhead	boundless	bristling	butcherer	cameraman
beccafico	billabong	blockship	bounteous	Britannia	butcherly	camorrist
bedfellow	billboard	blockship	bountiful	Britannic	butterbur	campanile
bedjacket	billboard	bloodbath	bouquetin	Briticise	buttercup	campanili
bedlamite	billiards	bloodless	bourgeois	Briticism	butterfat	campanula
bedraggle	billionth	bloodlust	bowerbird	Britisher	butterfly	campchair
bedridden	billycock	bloodroot	bowlegged	brittlely	butterine	campcraft
bedsettee	billygoat	bloodshed	bowstring	broadcast	butternut	campfever
bedsitter	bimonthly	bloodshot	bowwindow	broadleaf	buttinsky	camphoric
bedspread	binocular	bloodworm	boxgirder	broadloom	buttygang	campstool
bedspring	binominal	bloodwort	boxoffice	broadness	buxomness	canalboat
beechfern	binturong	blotchily	boycotter	broadside	byproduct	cancelled
beechmast	biogenous	blowtorch	boyfriend	broadtail	bystander	cancerous
beefeater	biography	bluebeard	brachiate	broadways	caballero	candidacy
beefiness	biologist	blueberry	brachyura	broadwise	caballine	candidate
beefsteak	biometric	blueblack	bracteate	brochette	caballine	Candlemas
beekeeper	bionomics	bluegrass	bracteole	broiderer	caballing	candlenut
beemaster	biorhythm	bluepoint	Brahmanic	brokerage	cabbalism	candytuft
beeorchis	biosphere	blueprint	Brahminee	bromeliad	cabbalist	canebrake
beestings	bipartite	bluestone	Brahminic	bronchial	cablegram	canescent
befitting	bipinnate	bluffness	braincase	broomcorn	cablelaid	canesugar
befogging	birchbark	blunderer	brainless	broomrape	cabriolet	canetrash
begetting	birdbrain	bluntness	brainwash	brotherly	cachectic	canicular
beginning	birdsfoot	blushless	brainwave	brownness	cacholong	cankerous
behaviour	birdsnest	blusterer	brakeless	brummagem	caciquism	cannelure
bejabbers	birdtable	Boanerges	brakeshoe	brushfire	cacodemon	canniness
belatedly	birdwatch	boardfoot	brakesman	brushwood	cacodylic	cannonade
beleaguer	birthmark	boardroom	brambling	brushwork	cacoethes	cannoneer
belemnite	birthrate	boardwalk	branchiae	brusquely	cacophony	cannonier
bellglass	birthwort	boathouse	branchial	brutalise	cacuminal	cannulate
bellicose	bisection	boatswain	branchlet	brutalism	cadastral	canonical
bellpunch	bishopric	boattrain	brandling	brutality	cadaveric	cantabile
bellyache	bismillah	bobsleigh	brandreth	brutishly	caddisfly	cantaloup
bellyband	bitterish	bobtailed	brashness	bryophyte	cadential	cantharid
bellyflop	bivalence	bodyguard	brasserie	Brythonic	cadetship	cantharis
belvedere	bivalency	boldfaced	brassiere	buccaneer	caecilian	cantharus
bemusedly	bivariant	bolection	bratwurst	buckboard	Caenozoic	cantilena
beneficed	bivariate	boliviano	brazilnut	bucketful	caerulean	Cantonese
bengaline	bizarrely	bolometer	breadline	buckhound	Caesarean	cantorial
benighted	blackball	bolometry	breadtree	buckshish	Caesarian	canvasser
benignant	blackbird	Bolshevik	breakable	buckthorn	Caesarism	capacious

capacitor	catalepsy	certitude	chihuahua	classmate	coemption	Comintern
caparison	catalexes	cerussite	chilblain	classroom	coenobite	comitadji
capillary	catalexis	cessation	childhood	clathrate	coenobium	commander
capitally	catalogue	cetaceous	childless	clatterer	coenosarc	commandos
capitular	catalyser	chachacha	childlike	claustral	coequally	commendam
capitulum	catalyses	chaetopod	chillness	clavation	coercible	commensal
capriccio	catalysis	chafferer	chimaeric	claviform	coercibly	commenter
Capricorn	catalytic	chaffinch	Chinatown	cleanness	coeternal	commingle
capsulate	catamaran	chaingang	chinaware	cleansing	coffeecup	comminute
capsulise	catamount	chaingear	chinstrap	clearance	coffeepot	commissar
captaincy	cataplasm	chainless	chipboard	clearcole	cofferdam	committal
captivate	cataplexy	chainmail	chipolata	cleareyed	coffinite	committed
captivity	catarhine	chairlady	chiropody	clearness	cogitable	committee
carambola	catarrhal	challenge	chiselled	cleavable	cognately	commodity
carbamate	catatonia	chameleon	chiseller	clemently	cognation	commodore
carbamide	catatonic	chamomile	chisquare	clepsydra	cognisant	commonage
carbonado	catchable	champagne	chitinous	clergyman	cognition	commonlaw
carbonate	catchment	champaign	chitlings	clergymen	cognitive	commotion
carbonise	catchpole	champerty	chivalric	clerkship	coheiress	communard
carbuncle	catchpoll	champleve	chlamydes	clientage	coherence	communion
carburise	catchword	chanceful	chlorella	clientele	coherency	communise
carcinoma	catechise	chancroid	chloritic	cliffhang	coiffeuse	communism
cardboard	catechism	chancrous	chlorosis	climactic	coinsurer	communist
cardsharp	catechist	chandlery	chlorotic	climbable	colcannon	community
careerism	caterwaul	changeful	chockfull	clinician	colchicum	commutate
careerist	Catharism	chanteuse	chocolate	clinquant	colcothar	compactly
carefully	Catharist	chantilly	chokedamp	clipboard	coldshort	compactor
caretaker	catharses	chantress	choleraic	clitellum	colemouse	companion
carfuffle	catharsis	chaparral	chondrite	cloakroom	collagist	compasses
Caribbean	cathartic	chaperone	chondrule	clockwise	collation	compelled
Carmelite	cathectic	chapleted	chophouse	clockwork	colleague	compendia
carnality	cathedral	charabanc	choplogic	cloisonne	collected	competent
carnation	catoptric	character	chopstick	cloistral	collector	complaint
carnelian	cattaloes	chariness	chorister	closedown	collegial	complexly
carnitine	cattiness	charivari	chorology	closeness	collegian	complexus
carnivore	cattleman	charlatan	Christian	cloudland	collegium	compliant
carolling	Caucasian	charlotte	Christmas	cloudless	colligate	component
carpenter	causality	charmeuse	chromatic	clubbable	collimate	composite
carpentry	causation	charmless	chromatin	clubhouse	collinear	composure
carpetbag	causative	Charolais	chronical	coachwork	collision	comprador
carpeting	causeless	chartered	chronicle	coadjutor	collocate	comprisal
carpingly	cauterise	charterer	chrysalid	coadunate	collodion	comptroll
carpology	cavalcade	charwoman	chrysalis	coagulant	colloidal	comradely
carrageen	cavendish	chassepot	chthonian	coagulate	colloquia	comradery
carrefour	cavernous	chastener	churching	coalfield	collotype	concavely
carronade	cavilling	chastiser	churchman	coalition	collusion	concavity
carryover	ceanothus	chatelain	cicatrice	coalmouse	collusive	conceited
Cartesian	ceasefire	chatoyant	cicatrise	coarctate	collyrium	concentre
carthorse	ceaseless	chatterer	cigarette	coastline	colocynth	concerned
cartilage	cedarwood	chauffeur	cigarillo	coastward	colonelcy	concerted
cartogram	celandine	cheapjack	Cimmerian	coastwise	coloniser	concierge
cartology	celebrant	cheapness	cinematic	coattails	colonnade	conciliar
cartouche	celebrate	checkered	cineraria	coaxially	colophony	concisely
cartridge	celebrity	checklist	cinereous	coaxingly	colorific	concision
cartulary	celestial	checkmate	Cingalese	cobaltite	colosseum	concocter
cartwheel	cellarage	checkrein	cipollino	cobaltous	colostomy	concoctor
caryopses	celluloid	cheekbone	circadian	Cobdenism	colostrum	concordat
caryopsis	cellulose	cheerless	circinate	cobwebbed	colourful	concourse
caseation	Celticism	chelation	circuitry	cocainise	colouring	concubine
Cassandra	cementite	chelicera	circulate	cocainism	colourist	concurred
cassareep	censorial	chelonian	cirrhosis	coccidium	colourman	condenser
cassaripe	centenary	chemistry	cirripede	coccygeal	coltishly	condignly
cassation	centering	chemitype	cisalpine	cochineal	coltsfoot	condiment
casserole	centigram	chemurgic	citizenly	cochleate	colubrine	condition
cassimere	centipede	cheongsam	citizenry	cockahoop	columbary	conducive
cassoulet	centrally	chequered	citystate	Cockaigne	Columbian	conductor
cassowary	centreing	cherimoya	civically	cockatiel	columbine	condyloid
Castalian	centurion	chernozem	civiliser	cockfight	columbite	condyloma
castanets	cephalous	cherrypie	claimable	cockhorse	columbium	confabbed
castellan	cerastium	chevalier	clamantly	cockiness	columella	conferral
castigate	ceratodus	chevelure	clamorous	cockneyfy	columnist	conferred
Castilian	cerebella	chibouque	clamshell	cockroach	combatant	conferrer
Castroism	cerebrate	chicanery	clapboard	cockscomb	combative	confervae
casuarina	cerecloth	chickadee	clarifier	cocksfoot	combinate	confessor
casuistic	cerograph	chickaree	clarionet	cocoonery	comedones	confidant
casuistry	certainly	chickling	classable	coecilian	comfiture	confident
catabolic	certainty	chickweed	classical	coelomata	comforter	confiding
cataclasm	certified	chiefship	classless	coelomate	comically	configure
cataclysm	certifier	chieftain	classlist	coelostat	Cominform	confirmed

```
confirmer  copiously  courgette  crossfish  cycloidal  decapodal  demagogic
confirmor  copolymer  courtcard  crosshead  cyclopean  decapodan  demagogue
confiteor  coproduce  courteous  crosslink  cyclopian  decastere  demandant
confluent  coprolite  courtesan  crossness  cyclopses  decathlon  demanding
conformal  coprology  courtroom  crossover  cyclorama  deceitful  demarcate
conformer  copsewood  courtship  crossroad  cyclotron  decennary  demeanour
Confucian  copyright  courtyard  crossruff  cylindric  decennial  demimonde
confusion  coralline  couturier  crosstalk  cymbalist  decennium  demission
congenial  corallite  covalence  crossways  cymbidium  deception  demitasse
congeries  coralloid  covalency  crosswind  cymbiform  deceptive  demitting
congruent  corbeille  covariant  crosswise  cymophane  decidable  demiurgic
congruity  corbelled  coverable  crossword  cynically  decidedly  demobbing
congruous  corbicula  coverslip  crotchety  cyprinoid  deciduate  democracy
conically  cordelier  coverture  croustade  cystocarp  deciduous  demulcent
conjugate  cordially  covetable  crowberry  cystolith  decilitre  demurrage
connately  cordiform  cowardice  crownless  cystotomy  decillion  demurring
connation  corduroys  cowlstaff  crowsfoot  Cytherean  decimally  demystify
connature  coreopsis  coxcombry  crowsnest  cytolysis  decimator  dendritic
connected  coriander  crabbedly  crucially  cytoplasm  decimetre  denigrate
connecter  corkscrew  crackdown  cruciform  cytotoxic  decistere  denitrate
connector  cormorant  crackling  crudeness  cytotoxin  deckhouse  denitrify
connexion  cornbrash  cracksman  cruellest  czarevich  declaimer  denouncer
connivent  corncrake  craftsman  crushable  dachshund  declarant  denseness
connubial  cornelian  crampfish  crustacea  Daedalean  declinate  dentalium
conqueror  cornemuse  cranberry  cryogenic  Daedalian  declivity  dentation
conscious  cornerboy  crankcase  cryoscope  dahabiyah  declivous  dentiform
conscribe  cornerman  cranreuch  cryoscopy  dairymaid  decoction  dentistry
conscript  cornetist  crapulent  cryptical  dalliance  decollate  dentition
consensus  cornfield  crapulous  cryptogam  dalmatian  decollete  denyingly
conserver  cornflour  crashdive  cryptonym  daltonism  decomplex  deodorant
consignee  cornopean  crashland  cubbyhole  damascene  decompose  deodorise
consignor  cornsalad  crassness  cubically  damnation  decongest  deoxidise
consonant  cornstalk  craziness  cuckoldry  damnatory  decontrol  departure
consortia  cornstone  creatable  cucullate  damnedest  decorator  depasture
constable  corollary  creatress  cudgelled  damningly  decrement  dependant
constancy  coroneted  creatural  cullender  Damoclean  decretive  dependent
constrain  corporate  crediting  culminant  dancehall  decretory  depiction
constrict  corporeal  credulity  culminate  dandelion  decumbent  depictive
construct  corposant  credulous  culsdesac  dandiacal  decussate  depletion
consulage  corpulent  cremaster  cultivate  dangerous  dedicator  depletive
consulate  corpuscle  cremation  cumbrance  Dantesque  deducible  deposable
consulter  corralled  crematory  cunctator  daredevil  deduction  depositor
consultor  corrasion  crenation  cuneiform  dartboard  deductive  depravity
contactor  correctly  crenature  cunningly  Darwinian  deerberry  deprecate
contadina  corrector  crenelled  cupbearer  Darwinism  deerhound  depredate
contadino  correlate  crenulate  cupelling  Darwinist  defalcate  depressed
contagion  corrosion  crepitant  cuplichen  dashboard  defaulter  depressor
contagium  corrosive  crepitate  curbstone  dashingly  defeatism  depthbomb
container  corrugate  crepuscle  curettage  dastardly  defeatist  depthless
contemner  corrupter  crescendo  curialism  dauntless  defeature  depurator
contender  corruptly  crestless  curiosity  davenport  defection  derivable
contented  corticate  cretinism  curiously  dayschool  defective  dermatoid
continent  corticoid  cretinous  curliness  dayspring  defendant  derringdo
continual  cortisone  cricketer  curlpaper  deacidify  defensive  derringer
continuer  coruscant  criminate  currently  deaconess  deference  descended
continuum  coruscate  criminous  curricula  deadalive  deferment  describer
contralto  Corybants  crinoidal  currishly  deadlight  deferring  desecrate
contrasty  corydalis  crinoline  currycomb  deathblow  defiantly  desertion
contrived  corymbose  crippling  cursively  deathless  deficient  desiccant
contriver  coryphaei  crispness  cursorial  deathlike  definable  desiccate
contumacy  coseismal  criterion  cursorily  deathmask  definably  designate
contumely  coseismic  criticise  curstness  deathroll  deflation  designing
contusion  cosmogeny  criticism  curtilage  debagging  deflector  desirable
conundrum  cosmogony  crocodile  curvature  debarment  deflexion  desirably
convector  cosmology  croissant  curveting  debarring  defoliant  desolater
converter  cosmonaut  CroMagnon  curvetted  debatable  defoliate  desolator
convexity  cosmorama  crookback  curviform  debauched  deformity  desperado
convincer  costively  crookedly  cuspidate  debauchee  defroster  desperate
convivial  costumier  crookneck  custodial  debaucher  dehiscent  despoiler
convolute  cotangent  cropeared  custodian  debenture  dehydrate  despotism
convolved  cothurnus  croquette  customary  debugging  deinosaur  destitute
cookhouse  cotillion  crossable  customise  debutante  deistical  destroyer
cooperage  cotyledon  crossbeam  cutaneous  decadence  dejection  desuetude
cooperant  couchette  crossbill  cuticular  decadency  delftware  desultory
cooperate  coumarone  crossbred  cutinised  decagonal  delicious  detection
copacetic  countable  crossette  cutthroat  decalcify  delineate  detective
copartner  countdown  crosseyed  cuttysark  decalitre  delirious  detention
copesmate  countless  crossfade  cyanamide  decalogue  deliverer  detergent
copestone  countship  crossfire  cyclamate  decametre  deludable  determent
```

determine	dietetics	disengage	dogmatise	drummajor	ectogenic	embroider
deterrent	dietician	disentail	dogmatism	drumstick	ectomorph	embryonal
deterring	dietitian	disentomb	dogmatist	drunkenly	ectophyte	embryonic
detersion	different	disesteem	dogoodism	dryasdust	ectoplasm	embryotic
detersive	difficile	disfavour	dogshores	drysalter	ecumenism	embussing
dethroner	difficult	disfigure	dogstooth	dualistic	edelweiss	emendable
detonator	diffident	disforest	dogviolet	dubiosity	edibility	emendator
detractor	diffusely	disgracer	dolefully	dubiously	editorial	emergence
detriment	diffusion	dishcloth	doleritic	dubitable	education	emergency
detrition	diffusive	dishclout	dolomitic	duckboard	educative	eminently
detrusion	digastric	dishfaced	doltishly	ductility	Edwardian	Emmenthal
deuterate	digestion	dishonest	dominance	dulcamara	effective	emolliate
deuterium	digestive	dishonour	dominator	dulcitude	effectual	emollient
devaluate	digitalin	dishwater	dominical	dumbfound	efficient	emolument
devastate	digitalis	disinfect	Dominican	dumpiness	effluence	emotional
developer	digitally	disinfest	donnishly	dungarees	effluvial	emotively
deviation	digitated	dislocate	donothing	duodecimo	effluvium	emotivity
devilfish	dignified	dismantle	doodlebug	duodenary	effluxion	empathise
devilling	dignitary	dismember	doorframe	duplicate	effortful	empennage
devilment	dilatable	dismissal	doorplate	duplicity	effulgent	emphasise
deviously	dilatancy	disoblige	dopefiend	duralumin	eggbeater	emphysema
devisable	diligence	disorient	dorbeetle	duskiness	eglantine	empirical
devitrify	dimension	disparage	dormition	dustcover	egomaniac	emplastic
devotedly	dimidiate	disparate	dormitory	dustiness	egotistic	emptiness
dewlapped	dimissory	disparity	dosimeter	dustsheet	egregious	empyreuma
dexterity	dimorphic	dispelled	dosimetry	duteously	egression	emulation
dexterous	dimwitted	dispenser	dosshouse	dutifully	eiderdown	emulative
dextrally	dinginess	dispeople	dottiness	dynamical	eiderduck	emulously
dextrorse	diningcar	dispersal	doubleton	dynamiter	eidograph	emunctory
dharmsala	dinnerset	disperser	doubtable	dyscrasia	eightfold	enactment
diablerie	dinoceras	displease	doubtless	dysentery	eightieth	enamelled
diabolise	dinothere	disposure	doughtily	dysgenics	eightsome	enameller
diabolism	dioecious	dispraise	Doukhobor	dyspepsia	eightyish	enamoured
diabolist	Dionysiac	disputant	dowdiness	dyspeptic	eirenicon	encaustic
diachrony	Dionysian	disregard	dowelling	dysphagia	ejaculate	encephala
diachylom	dipcircle	disrelish	dowerless	dysphagic	ejectment	enchanter
diachylum	dipeptide	disrepair	downfield	dysphonia	elaborate	enchilada
diaconate	diphthong	disrepute	downgrade	dysphoria	elastomer	enchorial
diacritic	diplomacy	dissector	downright	dysphoric	elbowroom	enclosure
diactinic	diplomate	disseisin	downriver	dysplasia	eldership	encomiast
diaereses	dipswitch	dissemble	downstage	dyspnoeic	electoral	encompass
diaeresis	dipterous	dissenter	downthrow	dystrophy	electress	encounter
diagnoses	direction	dissident	downwards	dziggetai	electrify	encourage
diagnosis	directive	dissipate	draconian	eagerness	electrode	encrimson
dialectal	directory	dissocial	draftsman	ealdorman	electuary	encrinite
dialectic	directrix	dissolute	draghound	earliness	elegantly	endearing
dialogise	direfully	dissonant	dragomans	earnestly	elegiacal	endeavour
dialogism	dirigible	dissuader	dragoness	earthborn	elemental	endlessly
dialogist	dirigisme	distantly	dragonfly	earthling	elevation	endoblast
diametral	dirtiness	distemper	dragonish	earthstar	elevenses	endocrine
diametric	dirttrack	distilled	drainpipe	earthward	eliminate	endogamic
diandrous	disaccord	distiller	dramatics	earthwork	ellipsoid	endogenic
diaphragm	disaffect	distraint	dramatise	earthworm	elocution	endolymph
diaphysis	disaffirm	disturbed	dramatist	earwigged	elongated	endomixis
diarrhoea	disannual	disturber	Dravidian	easefully	elopement	endomorph
diastasis	disappear	dithyramb	drawerful	eastbound	eloquence	endophagy
diastatic	disarming	dittander	drawnwork	Eastender	elsewhere	endophyte
diastolic	disavouch	dittology	drawplate	easterner	elucidate	endoplasm
diathermy	disavowal	diurnally	drawsheet	eastwards	elusively	endoscope
diathesis	disbarred	divergent	drayhorse	easygoing	elutriate	endoscopy
diathetic	disbelief	diversely	dreamboat	eavesdrop	emaciated	endosperm
diatomite	disbranch	diversify	dreamland	ebullient	emanation	endospore
diatropic	disbudded	diversion	dreamless	eccentric	emanative	endosteal
dichasial	disburden	diversity	dreamlike	ecclesial	embarrass	endosteum
dichasium	disbursal	diverting	dresscoat	ecdysiast	embassage	endowment
dichogamy	discalced	dividable	driftsail	echolalia	embattled	endurable
dichotomy	discarder	divisible	driftweed	echovirus	embayment	endurably
dichroism	discerner	divulsion	driftwood	eclampsia	embedding	endurance
dichromat	discharge	dixieland	drinkable	eclamptic	embedment	energetic
dichromic	discoidal	dizygotic	dripstone	ecologist	embellish	energiser
dickybird	discolour	dizziness	drivelled	economics	embezzler	energumen
diclinous	discomfit	doctorate	driveller	economise	embraceor	engarland
dicrotism	discommon	doctorial	drollness	economist	embracery	Englander
dictation	discourse	doctrinal	dromedary	ecosphere	embracive	englutted
didactics	discovert	dodecagon	dropscene	ecossaise	embrangle	engraving
didelphic	discovery	dogcollar	dropscone	ecosystem	embrasure	engrosser
didrachma	discredit	doggishly	dropsical	ecritoire	embrittle	enhearten
dieselise	disembark	doglegged	drugstore	ecstasise	embrocate	enigmatic
diesinker	disembody	dogmatics	druidical	ectoblast	embroglio	enjoyable

enjoyably	eremitism	evergreen	exostosis	factional	felonious	fireirons
enjoyment	ergograph	everybody	exoticism	factitive	femineity	firelight
enlighten	ergometer	evidently	expansile	factorage	fenceless	fireplace
enrapture	ergonomic	evincible	expansion	factorial	fenestrae	firepower
enrolling	eristical	evocation	expansive	factorise	fenestral	fireproof
enrolment	erogenous	evocative	expatiate	factually	Fenianism	firestone
ensheathe	eroticism	evocatory	expectant	facundity	fenugreek	firewater
entelechy	erratical	evolution	expecting	faddiness	feoffment	fireworks
enterable	erroneous	evolutive	expedient	fairfaced	ferocious	firmament
enteritis	errorless	evolvable	expediter	faintness	ferrotype	firstborn
entertain	erstwhile	ewenecked	expellent	fairfaced	ferryboat	firstfoot
enthymeme	eruciform	exactable	expelling	fairyhood	fertilely	firsthand
entoblast	eruditely	exactment	expensive	fairyland	fertilise	firstling
entophyte	erudition	exactness	expertise	fairylike	fertility	firstrate
entourage	erythrism	examinant	expiation	fairyring	fervently	fisherman
entrammel	erythrite	exanimate	expiatory	fairytale	festinate	fishiness
entrapped	escalator	exanthema	explainer	faithcure	festively	fishplate
entrechat	escapable	exarchate	expletive	faithless	festivity	fishslice
entrecote	escheator	excavator	expletory	Falangism	festology	fishyback
entremets	escortage	exceeding	explicate	Falangist	fetichism	fissility
enucleate	esemplasy	excellent	exploiter	falciform	fetichist	fissipede
enumerate	esoterica	excelling	explosion	faldstool	fetidness	fistulous
enunciate	esoterism	excelsior	explosive	Falernian	fetishism	fittingly
enviously	esperance	excentric	expositor	fallalery	fetishist	fivepence
enwrapped	Esperanto	exceptant	expounder	falsehood	feudalise	fivepenny
enwreathe	espionage	excepting	expressly	falseness	feudalism	fixedness
enzymatic	esplanade	exception	expulsion	falsifier	feudalist	flabellum
epaenetic	espousals	exceptive	expulsive	familyman	feudality	flagellum
epaulette	Esquimaux	excerptor	expurgate	fanatical	feudatory	flageolet
ephedrine	essential	excessive	exquisite	fancyfree	fibreless	flagrance
ephemeral	establish	exchanger	exsertile	fancywork	fibriform	flagrancy
ephemerid	estaminet	exchequer	exsertion	fandangle	fibrillar	flagstaff
ephemeris	Esthonian	excipient	exservice	fandangos	fibrinoid	flagstick
ephemeron	estimable	excisable	exsiccate	fanfarade	fibrinous	flagstone
epicentre	estimator	exciseman	exsuccous	fantasied	fibroline	flakiness
epiclesis	estoppage	excitable	extempore	fantasise	fibromata	flambeaus
epicurean	estopping	excitancy	extendant	fantasist	fictional	flambeaux
epicurism	estranger	excitedly	extensile	fantastic	fideistic	flameless
epicyclic	estrapade	exclosure	extension	fantastry	fiduciary	flamingly
epidermal	estuarian	exclusion	extensity	farandole	fieldbook	flamingos
epidermic	estuarine	exclusive	extensive	farestage	fieldboot	flammable
epidermis	esuriency	excoriate	extenuate	farmhouse	fieldfare	flannelly
epidosite	eternally	excrement	externals	farmstead	fieldsman	flarepath
epigraphy	etherical	excretion	extirpate	farseeing	fieldwork	flaringly
epigynous	ethereal	excretive	extolling	fasciated	fiendlike	flashback
epilation	ethically	excretory	extolment	fascicled	fieriness	flashbulb
epileptic	Ethiopian	exculpate	extorsive	fascicule	fifteenth	flashcube
epilogist	ethmoidal	excurrent	extortion	fasciculi	figurante	flashover
epinastic	ethnarchy	excursion	extortive	fascinate	filaceous	flashtube
epiphragm	ethnicity	excursive	extractor	Fascistic	filiation	flatterer
epiphyses	ethnology	excusable	extradite	fashioner	filigreed	flatulent
epiphysis	ethylenic	excusably	extravert	fastening	fillister	flavorous
epiphytal	etiquette	execrable	extremely	fastigium	filminess	flayflint
epiphytic	etymology	execrably	extremism	fatefully	filmstrip	fleckless
epipolism	eucalypti	executant	extremist	fatheaded	filoselle	fledgling
episcopal	eucaryote	execution	extremity	fatidical	filterbed	fleetness
epistaxis	Eucharist	executive	extricate	fatigable	filtertip	fleshings
epistemic	euchology	executory	extrinsic	fattiness	filtrable	fleshless
epistoler	euclidean	executrix	extrovert	fatuously	fimbriate	fleshment
epistolic	eulogiser	exegetist	extrusion	faultless	financial	flightily
epithelia	eunuchism	exemplary	extrusive	faunistic	financier	flintlock
epithesis	eunuchoid	exemplify	exuberant	faveolate	finedrawn	flippancy
epithetic	euphemise	exemption	exuberate	favourite	fingering	floatable
epitomise	euphemism	exequatur	exudation	fawningly	fingertip	flocculus
epitomist	euphonise	exercises	exudative	fearfully	finically	floodgate
epizootic	euphonium	exfoliate	exultance	feathered	finicking	floodmark
eponymous	euphorbia	exhauster	exultancy	febricity	fioritura	floodtide
equaliser	eurhythmy	exhibitor	eyebright	febrifuge	firealarm	flophouse
equalling	eutectoid	exilement	eyeglance	feculence	fireblast	floriated
equipment	euthenics	existence	eyeopener	fecundate	firebrand	floridean
equipoise	eutherian	exodermis	eyeshadow	fecundity	firebreak	floridity
equipping	eutrophic	exogamous	eyestrain	federally	firebrick	floristic
equisetum	evaginate	exogenous	fabaceous	feedstock	firecrest	floristry
equitable	evangelic	exonerate	Fabianism	feedstuff	firedrake	floscular
equitably	evaporate	exopodite	fabricant	feelingly	firedrill	flotation
equivocal	evasively	exorciser	fabricate	feiseanna	fireeater	flouncing
equivoque	eventless	exosmosis	facecloth	felicific	fireguard	flowchart
eradicate	eventuate	exosmotic	facetious	fellowman	firehouse	flowerage
erectness	everglade	exosphere	facsimile	felicific	firehouse	flowerbed

flowering	formality	frivolous	gallicise	gentleman	glomeruli	grapevine
flowerpot	formation	frockcoat	gallicism	genuflect	gloryhole	graphemic
flowingly	formative	frogmarch	gallingly	genuinely	glossator	graphical
flowsheet	formatted	frogspawn	gallinule	geobotany	glossitis	graphitic
flowstone	formicary	frolicked	gallivant	geodesist	glowingly	grappling
fluctuant	formicate	frontally	galliwasp	geography	glucoside	graspable
fluctuate	formulaic	frontless	gallmidge	geologise	glueyness	grassland
fluecured	formulary	frontline	gallonage	geologist	glutamate	graticule
fluoresce	formulate	frontpage	gallooned	geomancer	glutinous	gratitude
fluorosis	formulise	frontward	gallopade	geomantic	glyceride	gratulate
fluorspar	fornicate	frontways	Gallophil	geometric	glycerine	gravamina
flushness	forsythia	frontwise	galloping	geometrid	glycoside	graveless
fluxional	fortalice	frostbite	gallowses	geoponics	glyptodon	gravelled
flyfisher	forthwith	frostwork	gallstone	georgette	gnathonic	graveness
flyweight	fortifier	frowardly	galvanise	geosphere	gneissoid	graveyard
focussing	fortitude	fructuate	galvanism	geostatic	gneissose	gravidity
foeticide	fortnight	fructuous	galvanist	geotropic	goalmouth	gravitate
fogginess	fortunate	frugality	gambadoes	gerfalcon	gobetween	graywacke
foliation	fortyfive	fruitcake	gambolled	geriatric	goddamned	greasegun
folkdance	forwander	fruiterer	gammadion	germander	godfather	greataunt
folkmusic	forwarder	fruitless	gammoning	germanely	godliness	greatcoat
folkweave	forwardly	fruittree	ganderism	germanise	godmother	greatness
following	fossicker	frustrate	gangboard	Germanish	godparent	Greekless
foodchain	fossilise	fruticose	gangplank	Germanise	goffering	greenback
foodstuff	fossorial	fugacious	gannister	Germanist	gogglebox	greenbelt
foolhardy	fosterage	fulfilled	gaolbreak	germanium	goingover	greeneyed
foolishly	foulbrood	fulfiller	gardening	germicide	goldbrick	greengage
foolproof	foundling	fulgently	garderobe	germinate	goldcrest	greenhorn
footboard	foundress	fulgurant	garibaldi	germplasm	goldeneye	greenness
footcloth	fourflush	fulgurate	garmented	germproof	goldenrod	greenroom
footfault	fourpence	fulgurite	garnishee	gerundial	goldfever	greensand
footlight	fourpenny	fulgurous	garniture	gerundive	goldfield	greenweed
footloose	fourscore	fullblown	garreteer	gestalten	goldfinch	greenwood
footplate	fourwheel	fullcream	garrotter	gestation	goldsinny	gregarian
footpound	foxhunter	fulldress	garrulity	gestatory	goldsmith	gregarine
footprint	fractious	fullgrown	garrulous	getatable	golflinks	Gregorian
footstalk	fraenulum	fullscale	gasconade	geyserite	goliardic	grenadier
footstall	fragility	fulminant	gasfitter	ghostlike	gomphosis	grenadine
footstool	fragrance	fulminate	gasholder	ghostword	gondolier	greybeard
foppishly	fragrancy	fulminous	gasmantle	giantlike	gongorism	greyhound
foragecap	frailness	fulsomely	gasometer	gibberish	gonophore	greywacke
forasmuch	framework	fumarolic	gaspereau	gibbosity	goodnight	griefless
forbidden	franchise	fumigator	gastraeum	gibbously	goodwives	grievance
forcefeed	francolin	fundament	gastritis	giddiness	goosander	grillroom
forceland	frangible	funebrial	gastropod	gigahertz	goosefoot	grillwork
forceless	Franglais	fungicide	gastrulae	gigantism	goosegirl	grimalkin
forcemeat	frankness	fungiform	gatecrash	giltedged	gooseherd	griminess
forcepump	franticly	funicular	gatehouse	gimmickry	gooseneck	grisaille
foreboder	fraternal	funiculus	gathering	gingerade	gooseskin	gristmill
forebrain	freeboard	funkiness	gaucherie	gingerale	goosestep	gritstone
forecaddy	freehouse	funnelled	gaudiness	ginglymus	gorblimey	groomsman
foreclose	freelance	funniness	gaugeable	ginpalace	gorgonian	grosgrain
forecourt	freeliver	furbisher	gauleiter	girandole	gorgonise	grossness
forefront	Freemason	furcation	gauntness	girlishly	gospeller	grossular
foregoing	freerange	furiously	gauziness	Girondist	gossamery	grotesque
foreigner	freerider	furnisher	gavelkind	glabellae	Gothamite	grouchily
forejudge	freestone	furniture	gawkiness	glabellar	gothicise	groundage
foreknown	freestyle	furtherer	gazehound	glacially	Gothicism	groundash
forenamed	freewheel	furtively	gazetteer	gladiator	governess	groundhog
forereach	freewoman	fusillade	gearlever	gladiolus	graceless	grounding
foreshore	freezable	fusionist	gearshift	gladstone	gracility	groundivy
foreshown	freezedry	fussiness	gearwheel	glaireous	gradation	groundnut
foresight	freighter	fustigate	gelignite	glamorise	gradatory	groundsel
forespeak	frenchify	fustiness	gemmation	glamorous	Gradgrind	grovelled
forestage	Frenchman	fuzziness	gemmology	glandered	gradually	groveller
forestall	frequence	gabardine	gemutlich	glandular	graduator	grubscrew
foretaste	frequency	gaberdine	genealogy	glaringly	grandaddy	grubstake
foretoken	freshener	gabionade	generable	glassgall	grandaunt	gruelling
forewoman	freshness	gadgeteer	generalia	glassware	grandiose	gruffness
forfeiter	fretfully	Gaeltacht	generally	glasswork	grandness	grumbling
forgather	friarbird	gainfully	generator	glasswort	grandpapa	Grundyism
forgeable	fricassee	gainsayer	genetical	gleefully	grandsire	guacamole
forgetful	fricative	galactose	genialise	glengarry	grandslam	guarantee
forgiving	frigatoon	galantine	geniality	glissandi	granitoid	guarantor
forgotten	frightful	galenical	genitival	glissando	grantable	guardbook
forlornly	frigidity	galingale	genocidal	globefish	granulate	guardedly
formalise	fritterer	gallantly	genotypic	globosity	granulite	guardrail
formalism	frivolity	gallantry	genteelly	glomerate	granulose	guardring
formalist	frivolled	galleried	gentility	glomerule	grapeshot	guardroom

guardship	halftrack	hatefully	Hercynian	hobnobber	housekeep	hypomanic
guardsman	halftruth	haughtily	hereabout	hocussing	houseleek	hyponasty
guerrilla	halieutic	haustella	hereafter	hodiernal	houseless	hypostyle
guesswork	halitosis	haustoria	heretical	hodograph	houselled	hypotaxis
guestroom	Halloween	haverings	hereunder	hodometer	housemaid	hysterics
guidebook	Hallowmas	haversack	heritable	hoggishly	housemate	hysteroid
guideline	hallstand	havocking	hermitage	Holarctic	houseroom	Icelander
guidepost	Hallstatt	hawksbill	herniated	hollyhock	housewife	Icelandic
guiderope	halophile	hawsehole	herpetoid	Hollywood	housework	iceskater
guildhall	halophyte	hawsepipe	hesitance	holocaust	howsoever	ichneumon
guildship	halothane	hazardous	hesitancy	holograph	hoydenish	ichnology
guileless	haltingly	headboard	hesitator	holophote	hubristic	ichthyoid
guillemot	hamadryad	headcloth	Hesperian	holystone	huckaback	iconology
guilloche	hamamelis	headdress	hessonite	homebound	huckstery	idealiser
guiltless	hamburger	headfirst	hetaerism	homegrown	huffiness	idealless
guitarist	hamfisted	headiness	hetairism	homemaker	hugeously	identical
gumminess	hamhanded	headlight	heterodox	homeopath	humankind	identikit
guncotton	hammerman	headliner	heteronym	homestead	humanness	ideograph
gunpowder	hammertoe	headphone	heterosis	homewards	humblebee	ideologic
gunrunner	hamstring	headpiece	heuristic	homicidal	humbugged	ideologue
gushingly	hamstrung	headscarf	hexachord	homiletic	humdinger	idiograph
gustation	handbrake	headstall	hexagonal	homogamic	humectant	idiomatic
gustative	handcraft	headstock	hexameter	homograft	humiliate	idiopathy
gustatory	handcuffs	headstone	hexaploid	homograph	hunchback	idioplasm
gustiness	handglass	headwater	hexastich	homologue	hundredth	idiotical
gutsiness	handiness	healthful	hexastyle	homonymic	Hungarian	ignescent
guttation	handiwork	healthily	Hexateuch	homophone	hunkydory	ignitable
guttering	handlebar	heartache	hibernate	homophony	hurricane	ignitible
gymnasial	handorgan	heartbeat	Hibernian	homoplasy	hurriedly	ignorable
gymnasium	handpress	heartburn	hiddenite	homopolar	hurtfully	ignoramus
gymnastic	handsdown	heartfelt	hidebound	homotaxis	husbandly	ignorance
gynaeceum	handshake	heartfree	hideously	homotonic	husbandry	iguanodon
gynocracy	handspike	hearthrug	hierarchy	homousian	huskiness	illboding
gynoecium	handstand	heartland	hieratica	homuncule	hybridise	illegally
gynophore	handwheel	heartless	hierodule	homunculi	hybridism	illegible
gyrfalcon	handywork	heartsick	hierogram	honeycomb	hybridity	illegibly
gyroplane	hangerson	heartsore	hierology	honeymoon	hydathode	illgotten
gyroscope	hankering	heartwood	highchair	honkytonk	hydraemia	illiberal
habergeon	Hanseatic	heathcock	highclass	honoraria	hydrangea	illicitly
habitable	hanselled	heathenry	highflier	honorific	hydration	illjudged
habitably	haphazard	heaviness	highflown	hoofprint	hydraulic	illogical
habituate	haplessly	heavyduty	highflyer	hopefully	hydrazine	illomened
hackamore	haplology	Hebridean	highgrade	hopscotch	hydriodic	illwisher
hackberry	happening	hectogram	highgrown	horehound	hydrocele	imageable
hackneyed	hedgingly	heedfully	highlands	horniness	hydrofoil	imageless
haematite	happiness	heelpiece	highlevel	hornstone	hydrology	imaginary
haematoid	haranguer	heftiness	highlight	hornwrack	hydrolyse	imbalance
haematoma	harbinger	hegemonic	highspeed	horologer	hydrolyte	imbecilic
haemostat	harbourer	heinously	hightoned	horologic	hydronium	imbricate
haggadist	hardboard	helically	highwater	horoscope	hydrosome	imbroglio
haggardly	hardcover	hilarious	hillbilly	horoscopy	hydroxide	imitation
hagiarchy	hardiment	heliogram	Himalayan	horseback	hydrozoan	imitative
hagiology	hardiness	heliostat	Himyarite	horsebean	hydrozoon	immanence
hagridden	hardnosed	heliotype	hindbrain	horsehair	hygienics	immanency
hailstone	hardshell	heliozoan	hindrance	horsehide	hygienist	immediacy
hailstorm	haresfoot	heliozoic	hindsight	horseless	hygrostat	immediate
hairbrush	harlequin	hellebore	hippocras	horseplay	hymnology	immensely
haircloth	harmaline	hellenise	hircosity	horsepond	hylozoism	immensity
hairgrass	harmattan	Hellenism	hirsutism	horseshoe	hymnology	immersion
hairiness	harmfully	Hellenist	hirundine	horsetail	hyperbola	immigrant
hairpiece	harmonica	hellhound	histamine	horsewhip	hyperbole	immigrate
hairshirt	harmonics	hellishly	hispidity	horsiness	hypergamy	imminence
hairslide	harmonise	helpfully	histidine	hortation	hypericum	imminency
hairspace	harmonist	Helvetian	histogeny	hortative	hyperopia	immixture
hairstyle	harmonium	hemicycle	histogram	hortatory	hyperopic	immodesty
halfbaked	harmotome	hemistich	histology	hortensia	hypethral	immolator
halfblood	harpooner	hemitrope	historian	hosteller	hyphenate	immorally
halfbound	harquebus	hemstitch	Hitlerism	hostilely	hypnoidal	immovable
halfbreed	Harrovian	hendiadys	Hitlerite	hostility	hypnology	immovably
halfcaste	harrowing	hepatitis	hitchhike	hotheaded	hypnotise	immutable
halfcrown	harshness	heptaglot	Hitlerite	hothouse	hypnotism	immutably
halfhardy	hartshorn	heptarchy	hoarfrost	Hottentot	hypnotist	impaction
halfflight	harvester	Heraclean	hoarhound	hourglass	hypoblast	impartial
halfpence	Hashemite	herbalist	hoariness	houseboat	hypocaust	impassion
halfpenny	Hashimite	herbarium	hoarstone	housebote	hypocotyl	impassive
halfprice	hastiness	herbicide	Hobbesian	housecarl	hypocrisy	impastoed
halfshell	hatchback	herbivore	hobgoblin	housecoat	hypocrite	impatiens
halfstaff	hatchling	herborise	hobnailed	houseflag	hypogeous	impatient
halftitle	hatchment	Herculean	hobnobbed	household	hypomania	impeccant

impedance	incurring	inhibitor	interject	irregular	jetstream	kitchener
impelling	incursion	inhumanly	interknit	irrigable	jewellery	kittenish
impendent	incursive	initially	interlace	irrigator	jewelweed	kittiwake
impending	incurvate	initiator	interlard	irritable	jitterbug	klinostat
imperator	indagator	injection	interleaf	irritably	jobmaster	knavishly
imperfect	indecency	injurious	interline	irruption	jockstrap	kneadable
imperious	indecorum	injustice	interlink	irruptive	jocularly	knifeedge
impetrate	indelible	innermost	interlock	isagogics	jocundity	knightage
impetuous	indelibly	innervate	interlope	isallobar	Johannine	knockdown
impiously	indemnify	innholder	interlude	ischaemia	jointress	knockknee
impleader	indemnity	innkeeper	interment	ischaemic	jollyboat	knotgrass
implement	indention	innocence	internode	ischiadic	Jordanian	knowingly
impletion	indenture	innocency	interpage	ischiatic	josshouse	knowledge
implicate	Indianise	innocuity	interplay	isinglass	jossstick	krummhorn
impliedly	indicator	innocuous	interpose	Islamitic	journeyer	Kshatriya
implosion	indiction	innovator	interpret	isobathic	joviality	kurrajong
implosive	indigence	innoxious	interring	isochrone	joylessly	kymograph
impluvium	indignant	innuendos	interrupt	isoclinal	jubilance	labelling
impolitic	indignity	inoculate	intersect	isoclinic	Judaistic	labialise
important	indigotin	inodorous	intervein	isocyclic	Judastree	labialism
importune	indispose	inorganic	intervene	isogamete	judgement	laborious
impostume	IndoAryan	inpatient	interview	isogamous	judgeship	labourite
imposture	indolence	inpouring	interwind	isogenous	judgmatic	labyrinth
impotence	indraught	inquiline	interwove	isohyetal	judiciary	laccolith
impotency	inducible	insatiate	interzone	isolation	judicious	lacerable
impounder	induction	insatiety	intestacy	isolative	juiceless	lacertian
imprecate	inductive	inscriber	intestate	isomerise	juiciness	lacertine
imprecise	indulgent	insectary	intestine	isomerism	jumpiness	lachrymal
impresari	indweller	insectile	intorsion	isomerous	Juneberry	laciniate
improbity	inebriant	insensate	intricacy	isometric	juniorate	lacrimose
impromptu	inebriate	insertion	intricate	isoniazid	juniority	lacrymose
improvise	inebriety	inservice	intrigant	isooctane	junkerdom	lactation
imprudent	ineffable	insetting	intriguer	isopodous	junkerism	ladysmock
impudence	ineffably	inshallah	intrinsic	isosceles	junketing	laevulose
impulsion	inelastic	insidious	introduce	isostatic	Junoesque	laggardly
impulsive	inelegant	insincere	introject	isotropic	juridical	lagniappe
impulsory	ineptness	insinuate	introvert	Israelite	jurywoman	lagomorph
imputable	inequable	insipidly	intrusion	issueless	justiciar	lairdship
inability	inerrable	insistent	intrusive	italicise	justifier	lallation
inamorata	inerrancy	insolence	intuition	Italicism	juvenilia	lambently
inanimate	inertness	insoluble	intuitive	itchiness	juxtapose	lamellate
inanition	inexactly	insolubly	intumesce	iteration	kaiserdom	lamellose
inaptness	infantile	insolvent	inunction	iterative	kaiserism	laminaria
inaudible	infantine	insomniac	inurement	itineracy	kaolinise	laminated
inaudibly	infatuate	inspanned	inutility	itinerant	kaolinite	lampblack
inaugural	infection	inspector	invalidly	itinerary	karabiner	lamplight
inbetween	infective	instanter	invariant	itinerate	karyotype	lampooner
inbreathe	inferable	instantly	invective	itsybitsy	katabasis	lampshade
incapable	inference	instigate	inveigler	ittybitty	katabatic	lampshell
incapably	inferring	instilled	invention	jaborandi	katabolic	lancejack
incarnate	infertile	institute	inventive	jacaranda	katharsis	lancewood
incaution	infielder	insularly	inventory	jackknife	keelivine	lancinate
incensory	infilling	insulator	inverness	jackplane	kennelled	landagent
incentive	infirmary	insurable	inversely	jacksnipe	kentledge	landaulet
inception	infirmity	insurance	inversion	jackstraw	Keplerian	landdross
inceptive	inflation	insurgent	inversive	Jacobinic	keratitis	landdrost
incessant	inflexion	integrand	invertase	jacquerie	keratosis	landgrave
incidence	inflictor	integrant	invidious	jactation	kerbstone	landloper
incipient	inflowing	integrate	inviolacy	jailbreak	kerfuffle	landowner
inclement	influence	integrity	inviolate	jambalaya	Keynesian	landscape
inclosure	influenza	intellect	invisible	jampacked	khedivial	landslide
inclusion	informant	intendant	invisibly	janissary	kibbutzim	Langobard
inclusive	infractor	intensely	involucre	janitress	kickstart	langouste
incognito	infuriate	intensify	involuted	Jansenism	kiddingly	languidly
incommode	infuscate	intension	inwrought	Jansenist	kidnapped	lankiness
incondite	infusible	intensity	ionisable	japanning	kidnapper	lanthanum
incorrect	infusoria	intensive	irascible	jargonise	kilderkin	Laodicean
incorrupt	ingenious	intention	irascibly	jarringly	killifish	lapideous
increaser	ingenuity	interbred	irksomely	jaundiced	kilocycle	Laplander
increment	ingenuous	intercede	ironbound	jaywalker	kilohertz	lapstrake
incubator	ingestion	intercept	ironmould	jazziness	kilolitre	lapstreak
inculcate	ingestive	intercity	ironsides	jealously	kilometre	larcenist
inculpate	inglenook	intercrop	ironsmith	jeeringly	kinematic	larcenous
incumbent	ingrained	interdict	ironstone	jellyfish	kingcraft	lardycake
incunable	ingrowing	interface	ironworks	jerkiness	kingdomed	largeness
incurable	inhalator	interfere	Iroquoian	jessamine	kingmaker	larghetto
incurably	inharmony	interfile	irradiant	jesuitise	kingsized	larvicide
incurious	inherence	interflow	irradiate	jesuitism	kinkiness	laryngeal
incurrent	inheritor	interfuse	irreality	jetsetter	kinswoman	lassitude

lastditch	libelling	lithesome	lowliness	Mahometan	margarite	meditator
lastingly	libellist	lithology	lowloader	maidenish	marginate	medullary
latecomer	libellous	lithopone	lowminded	mailplane	marihuana	medullate
laterally	liberally	lithotomy	lownecked	mailtrain	marijuana	megacycle
latescent	liberated	litigable	loxodrome	mainbrace	maritally	megadeath
lathering	liberator	litigious	lubricant	mainliner	marketday	megahertz
latitancy	libertine	litterbin	lubricate	mainsheet	marketing	megaphone
latterday	libidinal	litterbug	lubricity	majordomo	marlstone	megaspore
latticing	librarian	liturgics	lubricous	majorette	marmalade	mekometer
laudation	libration	liturgist	lucidness	majorship	marmoreal	melanosis
laudative	libratory	liverwort	luciferin	majuscule	marquetry	melanotic
laudatory	librettos	liveryman	luckiness	makeready	marrowfat	melaphyre
laughable	licensure	livestock	lucrative	makeshift	marshalcy	melatonin
laughably	lichenous	lividness	lucubrate	malachite	marshland	meliorate
launching	lickerish	lixiviate	ludicrous	maladroit	marshwort	meliorism
launderer	liegelord	loadstone	luftwaffe	malanders	marsupial	meliorist
laundress	lifeblood	loafsugar	lumbering	malarious	marsupium	meliority
laurelled	lifecycle	loanshark	lumberman	malathion	martially	melismata
lavaliere	lifeforce	loathsome	lumbrical	Malayalam	Martinmas	melocoton
lawgiving	lifeguard	lobectomy	lumbricus	malformed	martyrdom	melodious
lawlessly	lifesaver	lobscouse	luminance	malicious	martyrise	melodrama
lawnmower	lifesized	lobulated	lumpiness	malignant	marvelled	melomania
lazaretto	lifestyle	locatable	lumpishly	malignity	masculine	meltingly
lazybones	lifetable	locksmith	lunchtime	malleable	masochism	meltwater
lazytongs	lightfoot	locomotor	lunisolar	malleehen	masochist	mementoes
lazzarone	lightless	lodestone	lunitidal	mallemuck	masonried	memoirist
lazzaroni	lightness	lodgement	luridness	malleolar	Masoretic	memorable
leafgreen	lightning	lodgepole	lustfully	malleolus	massagist	memorably
leafmould	lightship	loftiness	lustihood	malthouse	massiness	memoranda
leafstalk	lightsome	logaoedic	lustiness	malvoisie	massively	memoriter
leakiness	lightsout	logarithm	luxuriant	mamillary	masterdom	menadione
learnable	lightwood	logically	luxuriate	mamillate	masterful	menagerie
learnedly	lightyear	logistics	luxurious	mammalian	masterkey	mendacity
leasehold	lignaloes	logogriph	lyamhound	mammalogy	masticate	Mendelian
leaselend	ligniform	logomachy	lymegrass	mammiform	matchless	Mendelism
leastways	liltingly	loincloth	lymehound	mammonish	matchlock	mendicant
leastwise	lilywhite	Lombardic	lymphatic	mammonism	matchwood	mendicity
leavening	Limburger	Londonise	lyophilic	mammonist	maternity	meningeal
lecherous	limejuice	Londonism	lyophobic	mammonite	mateyness	Mennonite
leeringly	limelight	longaeval	lyrically	Mancunian	matriarch	menopause
leewardly	limestone	longchain	lysimeter	mandarine	matricide	Menshevik
leftovers	limewater	longcoats	macaronic	mandatary	matricula	menstrual
leftwards	limitable	longeared	Maccabean	mandatory	matrimony	menstruum
legendary	limitedly	longevity	macedoine	mandoline	matronage	mentalism
legerline	limitless	longevous	macerator	manducate	matronise	mentalist
legginess	limnology	longfaced	machinate	manganate	mattamore	mentality
legionary	limonitic	longhouse	machinery	manganese	matutinal	mentation
legislate	limousine	longicorn	machinist	manganese	maulstick	mepacrine
Leicester	limpidity	longingly	machmeter	manganous	maunderer	mercaptan
leisurely	lineality	longitude	macintosh	manhandle	mausoleum	mercenary
leitmotif	lineament	longlived	macrocosm	manginess	mawkishly	mercerise
leitmotiv	linearise	Longobard	macrocyte	manhattan	maxillary	merciless
lendlease	linearity	longrange	maddening	manifesto	maximally	mercurial
lengthily	lineation	longshore	madeleine	manipular	maybeetle	mercurous
leniently	linenfold	lookalike	madrepore	mannequin	mayflower	merganser
lentiform	lineolate	looseleaf	maelstrom	mannerism	mayoralty	meropidan
leptosome	lingering	looseness	magdalena	mannerist	mayorship	merriment
lethality	lingually	lophodont	Magianism	manoeuvre	mealiness	merriness
lethargic	lingulate	loquacity	magically	manometer	meandrine	mescaline
letterbox	lintelled	lorgnette	magicking	manorseat	meandrous	mesentery
lettering	lintwhite	lotusland	magistery	mansarded	meaningly	mesmerise
leucaemia	lioncelle	loudmouth	magistral	mansionry	meanwhile	mesmerism
leucocyte	lionheart	louringly	magnalium	manslayer	meatiness	mesmerist
leucotome	lipreader	lousewort	magnesian	mansueior	mechanics	mesoblast
leucotomy	lipuation	lousiness	magnesite	manticore	mechanise	mesogloea
leukaemia	liquefier	loutishly	magnesium	mantibrae	mechanism	mesomorph
leukaemic	liquidate	loveapple	magnetics	manubrium	mechanist	mesophyll
leukocyte	liquidise	lovechild	magnetise	medallion	mediaeval	mesophyte
Levantine	liquidity	lovefeast	magnetism	manxwoman	medallist	messenger
levelling	liquorice	lovelight	magnetist	manyplies	mediately	messianic
levelness	liquorish	lovematch	magnetite	manysided	mediately	messieurs
leviathan	lispingly	loverless	magnetron	manzanita	mediation	messiness
leviratic	lissomely	lovestory	magnifico	maquisard	mediatise	metabolic
levitator	Listerism	lovetoken	magnifier	marcasite	mediative	metalline
Levitical	literally	lovingcup	magnitude	marcelled	mediatory	metalling
lexically	literatim	lowercase	maharajah	marchpane	mediatrix	metallise
liability	literator	lowerdeck	maharanee	marchpast	medicable	metalloid
libecchio	literatus	lowermost	maharishi	marestail	medically	metalwork
libellant	litheness	lowlander	mahlstick	margarine	medicinal	metameric

metaphase	minefield	monergism	motocross	nailbrush	nervously	nonviable
metaplasm	minelayer	moneybags	motorable	nakedness	nescience	normalise
meteorist	miniature	moneybill	motorbike	nameplate	Nestorian	normality
meteorite	minimally	moneywort	motorboat	nannygoat	netveined	Normanise
meteoroid	miniskirt	Mongolian	motorcade	naphthene	netwinged	Normanism
methadone	minuscule	mongolism	mouldable	napthalic	neuralgia	normative
metheglin	minutegun	Mongoloid	mountable	narcissus	neuralgic	northeast
methodise	minuteman	mongooses	mousehole	narcotine	neuration	northerly
Methodism	mirkiness	mongrelly	mousetrap	narcotise	neuroglia	northland
Methodist	mirthless	monitress	moustache	narcotism	neurology	northmost
methought	misadvise	monkeyish	mouthpart	narration	neuromata	northward
methylate	misassign	monkeyism	mouthwash	narrative	neuropath	northwest
methylene	misbecome	monkeynut	moviegoer	narratory	neutrally	Norwegian
metonymic	misbehave	monkshood	muckraker	naseberry	nevermore	nosebleed
metricate	misbelief	monobasic	mucksweat	nastiness	newlyweds	noseflute
metrician	misbeseem	monoceros	mucronate	natheless	newmarket	nosepiece
metricise	miscegene	monochord	muddiness	natrolite	newsagent	nostalgia
metricist	miscegine	monocline	muffineer	nattiness	newsflash	nostalgic
metrology	mischance	monocoque	muffinman	naturally	newshound	nostology
metronome	miscreant	monocracy	mugginess	naughtily	newsiness	notabilia
mezzanine	miscreate	monocular	mullioned	naumachia	newspaper	notedness
mezzotint	misdemean	monodical	multifoil	navelwort	newsprint	notepaper
miasmatic	misdirect	monodrama	multiform	navicular	newsstand	notionist
micaceous	misemploy	monoecism	multilane	navigable	Newtonian	notochord
micaslate	miserable	monogamic	multipara	navigator	niccolite	notoriety
microbial	miserably	monograph	multiplex	neathouse	nickelise	notorious
microchip	misesteem	monolatry	multitude	nebuliser	nickelled	nourisher
microcosm	misfeasor	monologic	mumchance	necessary	nickelous	novelette
microcyte	misgiving	monologue	mummified	necessity	nicotiana	noviciate
microfilm	misgovern	monomania	mundanely	neckcloth	nicotinic	novitiate
microgram	misguided	monomeric	mundungus	neckverse	nictation	nowhither
microlite	mishandle	monophagy	municipal	necrology	nictitate	noxiously
microlith	mishanter	monoplane	muniments	necrophil	niggardly	nucleated
micrology	misinform	monorhyme	munitions	necrotise	nightbird	nucleolus
micromesh	misleared	monostich	murderess	nectarean	nightclub	nucleonic
micropsia	mismanage	monostyle	murderous	nectarial	nightfall	nuisancer
micropyle	misoneism	monotonic	murkiness	nectarine	nightgown	nullifier
microsome	misoneist	monotreme	murmurous	nectarous	nighthawk	nullipara
microtome	mispickel	monotypic	muscadine	needfully	nightlife	nullipore
microtomy	misreckon	monsignor	muscarine	neediness	nightline	numbskull
microtone	misreport	monsoonal	muscleman	needleful	nightlong	numerable
microwave	misshapen	monstrous	muscovado	nefarious	nightmare	numerator
micturate	missioner	Montanism	muscovite	negligent	nightside	numerical
middleman	mistigris	monthling	musically	negotiant	nighttime	nummulite
midinette	mistiness	monticule	musichall	negotiate	nightwork	nuncupate
midstream	mistletoe	monzonite	musketeer	negritude	nigricant	nurseling
midsummer	mistyeyed	moodiness	muskiness	negroidal	nigritude	nursemaid
midwicket	Mithraism	moonblind	muskmelon	Negroness	nigrosine	nutriment
midwifery	Mithraist	moonlight	Mussulman	negrophil	Nilometer	nutrition
midwinter	mitigable	moonquake	mustachio	neighbour	ninepence	nutritive
migration	mitigator	moonraker	musteline	nemertean	ninepenny	nuttiness
migratory	mitraille	moonscape	mustiness	nemertine	ninetieth	nutweevil
milestone	mixedness	moonshine	mutagenic	nemophila	Nipponese	nymphalid
militancy	mnemonics	moonstone	mutilator	neodymium	nitpicker	nystagmic
milkfever	mnemonist	moraceous	mutualise	neolithic	nitratine	nystagmus
milkfloat	mobocracy	moraliser	mutualism	neologian	nitration	oakenshaw
milkiness	mockingly	moratoria	mutualist	neologise	nobiliary	oasthouse
milkshake	modelling	morbidity	mutuality	neologism	nobleness	obbligato
milktooth	moderator	mordacity	muzziness	neologist	noctiluca	obconical
millboard	modernise	mordantly	Mycenaean	neoteinia	nocturnal	obcordate
millenary	modernism	Mormonism	mycologic	neoteinic	nocuously	obedience
millennia	modernist	morphemic	mycophagy	neoterise	nodulated	obeisance
millepede	modernity	morrisman	mydriasis	neoterism	noiseless	obeseness
millepore	modillion	mortality	mydriatic	neoterist	noisiness	obfuscate
millerite	modulator	mortgagee	myelomata	nepenthes	noisomely	objectify
milligram	moistener	mortgager	myography	nephalism	nominable	objection
millinery	moistness	mortgagor	myologist	nephalist	nominally	objective
millionth	molecular	mortician	myriorama	nepheline	nominator	objurgate
millipede	molluscan	mosaicism	myrmecoid	nephelite	nomocracy	obligated
millivolt	mollymawk	mosaicist	myrobalan	nephology	nomograph	obliquely
millstone	molybdate	mosaicked	mystagogy	nephritic	nondriver	obliquity
millwheel	momentary	moschatel	mysticism	nephritis	nonentity	oblivious
milometer	momentous	mosquitos	mystifier	nephrosis	nonillion	obnoxious
Miltonian	monachism	mossagate	mythicise	Neptunian	nonjuring	obscenely
mimicking	monarchal	mossgrown	mythicism	neptunium	nonlinear	obscenity
minacious	monarchic	motheaten	mythicist	nervation	nonpareil	obscurant
mincemeat	monastery	motherwit	mythology	nervature	nonperson	obscurely
mincingly	monatomic	mothproof	myxoedema	nerveless	nonprofit	obscurity
mindfully	Mondayish	motivator	Nahuatlan	nerviness	nonsmoker	obsecrate

obsequent	oligaemia	orthoepic	overspill	panegyric	pasticcio	pensioner
obsequial	oligarchy	oscillate	overstate	panelling	pastiness	pensively
obsequies	Oligocene	oscitancy	oversteer	panellist	pastorale	pentagram
observant	oligopoly	osmometer	overstock	panhandle	pastorate	pentangle
obsession	olivenite	ossicular	overstuff	panicking	pasturage	pentarchy
obsessive	ombudsman	ossifrage	overtaken	panoplied	patchouli	Pentecost
obsolesce	ominously	ostensive	overthrew	panoramic	patchouly	penthouse
obstetric	omissible	osteoderm	overthrow	pantalets	patchwork	penultima
obstinacy	ommatidia	osteogeny	overtness	pantaloon	patellate	penumbral
obstinate	omophagia	osteology	overtones	pantheism	paternity	penurious
obtention	omophagic	osteopath	overtrain	pantheist	pathogeny	pepperbox
obtrusion	onanistic	ostracise	overtrick	pantingly	pathology	pepperpot
obtrusive	oncogenic	ostracism	overtrump	pantomime	patiently	peptonise
obturator	oncologic	Ostrogoth	overvalue	pantryman	patinated	percaline
obversely	onehanded	otherness	overwatch	pantyhose	patriarch	perceiver
obversion	onelegged	otherwise	overweary	paperback	patrician	perchance
obviation	onerously	otologist	overweigh	paperclip	patricide	percheron
obviously	onionskin	oubliette	overwhelm	papergirl	patrimony	percolate
occipital	onlicence	ourselves	overwound	paperthin	patriotic	perdition
occludent	onomastic	outbacker	overwrite	paperwork	patristic	peregrine
occlusion	onsetting	outermost	overwrote	papeterie	patrolled	perennate
occlusive	onslaught	outfitter	oviductal	papillary	patroller	perennial
occultism	ontogenic	outgiving	oviferous	papillate	patrolman	perfectly
occultist	ontologic	outgoings	oviparity	papilloma	patrology	perfector
occupancy	oogenesis	outgrowth	oviparous	papillose	patronage	perfervid
occurrent	oogenetic	outgunned	ovulation	papillote	patroness	perforate
occurring	openended	outlander	ovulatory	parabasis	patronise	performer
ocellated	openheart	outnumber	ownership	parabolic	paulownia	perfumery
ochlocrat	operation	outputted	oxidation	parachute	pauperise	perfumier
octachord	operative	outridden	oxygenate	Paraclete	pauperism	perfusion
octagonal	opercular	outrigger	oxygenise	paradisal	Pavlovian	pergunnah
octahedra	operculum	outskirts	oxygenous	paragraph	paymaster	periclase
octameter	operosely	outspoken	oysterbed	paralalia	paypacket	periclase
octastyle	operosity	outspread	oysterman	paralexia	peaceable	pericycle
octennial	ophiology	outwardly	ozocerite	paralysis	peaceably	peridotic
octillion	opinioned	outwitted	ozokerite	paralytic	peacetime	perihelia
Octobrist	opodeldoc	outworker	pacemaker	paramatta	peachblow	perilling
octopodes	opponency	ovenready	pachyderm	paramedic	pearlitic	perilymph
octostyle	opportune	overblown	packaging	parameter	pearlwort	perimeter
odalisque	opposable	overboard	packdrill	paramorph	peasantry	perimorph
oddfellow	oppressor	overborne	packhorse	paramount	peasouper	perinatal
oddjobber	oppugnant	overcheck	packtrain	paranoiac	peccantly	periodate
oddjobman	opsimathy	overcloud	paederast	paranymph	pectinate	peripatus
odontalgy	optically	overcrowd	pageantry	parapeted	peculator	periphery
odorously	optometer	overdraft	paillasse	parapodia	pecuniary	periplast
odourless	optometry	overdrawn	paillette	parasitic	pedagogic	periscope
oecologic	optophone	overdress	painfully	parataxis	pedagogue	perishing
oecumenic	opulently	overdrive	painterly	parathion	pedalling	perisperm
oenomancy	opusculum	overeaten	paintwork	parbuckle	pederasty	peristome
oenophile	orangeade	overeater	pairhorse	parcelled	pedicular	peristyle
oenophily	Orangeism	overexert	Pakistani	parcenary	pedigreed	perkiness
oesophagi	Orangeman	overflown	palaestra	parchment	pedometer	permanent
oestrogen	orangetip	overglaze	palafitte	paregoric	peepsight	permeable
offcentre	orangutan	overgraze	palankeen	parentage	peevishly	permeance
offchance	oratorial	overgrown	palanquin	parfleche	pegmatite	permitted
offcolour	oratorian	overheard	palatable	parhelion	Pekingese	permitter
offensive	orbicular	overissue	palatably	parleyvoo	Pelasgian	permutate
offertory	orchestic	overjoyed	palillogy	parlously	pellagrin	perpetual
offhanded	orchestra	overladen	Palladian	parochial	pelletise	persecute
officiant	orchidist	overleapt	palladium	parotitis	pellitory	persevere
officiate	orderbook	overlying	palladous	parquetry	pemphigus	persimmon
official	orderform	overmatch	palletise	parrakeet	pencilled	personage
officious	orderless	overnight	palliasse	parricide	penciller	personate
offscreen	ordinance	overpitch	pallidity	Parseeism	pendently	personify
offseason	organelle	overpower	palmation	parsimony	pendragon	personnel
offspring	organiser	overprice	palmipede	parsonage	pendulate	persuader
offstreet	organstop	overprint	palmistry	partially	penduline	pertinent
oilburner	organzine	overproof	palmitate	partition	pendulous	pertussis
oilcolour	orgiastic	overreach	palpation	partitive	peneplain	pervasion
oilpaints	orientate	overreact	palpebral	partridge	peneplane	pervasive
okeydokey	orificial	oversexed	palpitant	pasodoble	penetrant	perverter
oleaceous	oriflamme	overshoot	palpitate	passenger	penetrate	pessimism
olecranal	originate	oversight	palsgrave	passerine	penfriend	pessimist
olecranon	orography	oversized	paludinal	passersby	penholder	pesthouse
oleograph	orologist	overskirt	palustral	passional	peninsula	pesticide
oleoresin	orphanage	oversleep	panatella	passivate	penitence	pestilent
olfaction	Orpington	overslept	panchayat	passively	penniless	pestology
olfactive	orrisroot	overspend	pancratic	passivity	pennywort	petaurist
olfactory	orthodoxy	overspent	panderess	pastedown	penpusher	petechiae

```
petechial  pictorial  planuloid  politesse  potboiler  presbyope  profilist
petersham  picturise  plasmatic  political  potentate  presbyter  profiteer
pethidine  piecemeal  plasmodia  pollinate  potential  preschool  profusely
petiolate  piecerate  plastered  pollinium  potholing  prescient  profusion
petiolule  piecework  plasterer  pollutant  pothunter  prescribe  progestin
petroleum  pierrette  platemark  pollution  potpourri  prescript  prognoses
petrology  pietistic  platinise  polonaise  poulterer  preselect  prognosis
petticoat  piggishly  platinoid  polyamide  pouncebox  presentee  programme
pettiness  piggyback  platinous  polyandry  poundcake  presenter  projector
pettishly  piggybank  platitude  polybasic  pourboire  presently  prolamine
pettitoes  pigheaded  Platonise  polyester  pourpoint  preserver  prolapsus
petulance  pikeperch  Platonism  polygamic  poussette  preshrink  prolately
petulancy  pikestaff  Platonist  polygenic  powerboat  preshrunk  prolation
phagedena  pilferage  plausible  polygonal  powerdive  president  prolative
phagocyte  pilgarlic  plausibly  polygonum  powerless  presidial  prolepses
phalanger  pillarbox  playfully  polygraph  pozzolana  presidium  prolepsis
phalanges  pilotfish  playgroup  polyhedra  practical  pressgang  proleptic
phalanxes  pimpernel  playhouse  polymathy  practised  pressmark  prolicide
phalarope  pinchbeck  plaything  polymeric  praenomen  pressroom  prolixity
phantasma  pinchcock  pleadable  polymorph  pragmatic  pressstud  prologise
pharaonic  pineapple  pleadings  polyonymy  praiseful  presswork  prolusion
pharisaic  pinkiness  pleasance  polyphagy  pranksome  prestress  prolusory
pharyngal  pinnately  Pleiocene  polyphase  prankster  pretender  promenade
pharynges  pinnipede  plenarily  polyphone  pratingly  preterist  prominent
pharynxes  pinnulate  plenitude  polyploid  prayerful  preterite  promising
phellogen  pinstripe  plenteous  polyptych  preachify  pretermit  promotion
phenacite  pintailed  plentiful  polysemic  preachily  prettyish  promotive
phenakite  pintsized  plethoric  polysomic  preadamic  prettyism  promptbox
phenology  pipedream  pleuritic  polythene  prebendal  prevalent  pronation
phenomena  pipeorgan  plicately  polytonal  precancel  preventer  proneness
phenotype  pipestone  plication  polytypic  precative  prevision  pronghorn
pheromone  pipsqueak  plicature  polyvinyl  precatory  priceless  pronounce
philander  piquantly  ploughboy  polywater  precedent  prideless  proofread
philately  piratical  ploughman  polyzoary  preceding  primaeval  propagate
philippic  pirouette  plumbeous  pomaceous  precentor  primality  propelled
philogyny  piscatory  plumbline  pommelled  preceptor  primarily  propeller
philology  pisciform  plumdamas  pompadour  precipice  primatial  properdin
Philomela  pisolitic  plumpness  pomposity  precisely  primeness  prophetic
phlebitis  pistachio  plumulate  pompously  precisian  primipara  propionic
phonation  pistoleer  plumulose  ponderous  precision  primitive  proponent
phonatory  pistolled  plunderer  pontoneer  precocial  primordia  propriety
phonemics  pitchdark  pluralise  pontonier  precocity  princedom  proptosis
phonetics  pitchfork  pluralism  poorhouse  preconise  princekin  propylaea
phonetise  pitchpipe  pluralist  popliteal  precursor  princelet  propylene
phonetism  piteously  plurality  poppycock  predacity  principal  prorogate
phonetist  pithecoid  plusfours  poppyhead  predation  principia  prosaical
phoniness  pithiness  plushness  popularly  predative  principle  proscenia
phonogram  pitifully  plutocrat  porbeagle  predatory  printable  proscribe
phonolite  pituitary  plutonian  porcelain  predicant  printshop  prosector
phonology  pityingly  Plutonise  porcupine  predicate  priorship  prosecute
phosphate  pivotable  Plutonist  poriferal  predictor  prismatic  proselyte
phosphene  pivotally  plutonium  poriferan  predigest  privateer  prosiness
phosphide  pixilated  pneumatic  porphyria  predikant  privation  prosodist
phosphine  pizzicati  pneumonia  porringer  preemptor  privative  prostatic
phosphite  pizzicato  pneumonic  portative  preengage  privilege  prostrate
photocell  placation  pocketful  porterage  preexilic  probation  protamine
photocopy  placatory  podagrous  portfolio  prefatory  probative  protector
photogene  placeable  podginess  porticoes  preferred  probatory  proteinic
photophil  placecard  podzolise  portolano  prefigure  proboscis  protester
photopsia  placekick  poetaster  portrayal  prefixion  procedure  prothesis
phototype  placeless  poeticise  portrayer  pregnable  processed  prothetic
phrenetic  placement  poeticism  portreeve  pregnancy  processes  prothorax
phthalein  placename  poignancy  portulaca  prejudice  processor  protonema
phycology  placentae  poinciana  possessed  prelatess  proclitic  prototype
phyllopod  placental  pointduty  possessor  prelatise  proconsul  protoxide
phylogeny  placidity  pointedly  postentry  prelatism  proctitis  protozoal
physician  plainness  pointille  posterior  prelature  procreant  protozoan
physicist  plainsman  pointlace  posterity  prelector  procreate  protozoic
physicked  plainsong  pointless  posthaste  prelusion  procuracy  protozoon
phytogeny  plaintiff  pointsman  posthorse  prelusive  procuress  proveably
phytology  plaintive  poisonous  posthouse  prelusory  prodigies  Provencal
phytotomy  planarian  pokeberry  posticous  premature  prodromal  provender
phytotron  planation  pokerface  postilion  premonish  prodromic  provident
pianistic  planetary  pokerwork  postnasal  premotion  proembryo  providing
pickaback  planetoid  polariser  postnatal  prenotion  proenzyme  provision
picketing  plangency  polemical  postponed  preoccupy  profanely  provisory
picnicked  planisher  polevault  postulant  preordain  profanity  provoking
picnicker  plantable  policeman  postulate  prepotent  professed  provostry
pictogram  plantlike  politburo  potassium  prerecord  professor  proximate
```

proximity	purulency	rabbinate	rearwards	referable	repletion	retrieval
prudently	pushchair	rabbinism	reasoning	reference	replicate	retriever
prudishly	pushiness	rabbinist	rebaptise	referenda	reportage	retrocede
prurience	pushingly	rabidness	rebelling	referring	reposeful	retrodden
pruriency	pussyfoot	racehorse	rebellion	refitment	repossess	retroflex
psalmbook	pustulate	racetrack	rebidding	refitting	repotting	retroject
psalmodic	pustulous	racialism	rebukable	reflation	reprehend	retrousse
psalteria	putridity	racialist	rebutting	reflector	represent	retrovert
pseudonym	puzzolana	racketeer	recalesce	reflexion	repressor	revelator
pseudopod	pycnidium	raconteur	recapping	reflexive	reprieval	revelling
psoriasis	pyracanth	radialply	recapture	refluence	reprimand	reverence
psoriatic	pyramidal	radiantly	recension	reformism	reprobate	reversely
psychical	pyramidic	radiately	reception	reformist	reprocess	reversion
psychoses	pyramidon	radiation	receptive	refractor	reproduce	revetment
psychosis	pyrethrum	radiative	recession	refreshen	reptilian	revetting
psychotic	pyridoxin	radically	recessive	refresher	republish	revictual
ptarmigan	pyrogenic	radicular	rechauffe	refuelled	repudiate	revisable
pterosaur	pyrolater	radiocast	recherche	refulgent	repugnant	revivable
pterygium	pyrolatry	radiogram	recipient	refurbish	repulsion	revocable
pterygoid	pyrolysis	radiology	reckoning	refurnish	repulsive	revolting
Ptolemaic	pyrolytic	raffinate	reclinate	refusable	reputable	revulsion
pubescent	pyromancy	raffinose	reclusion	refutable	reputably	revulsive
publicise	pyromania	raffishly	reclusive	regardant	reputedly	rewarding
publicist	pyrometer	rafflesia	recognise	regardful	requester	rewritten
publicity	pyrometry	raincheck	recoinage	regicidal	requisite	rhapsodic
publisher	pyroscope	raincloud	recollect	regisseur	rerebrace	rheumatic
pudginess	pyroxylin	raingauge	recombine	registrar	rerelease	Rhineodon
puerility	quadratic	raininess	recommend	regretful	reremouse	rhinology
puerperal	quadrifid	rainmaker	recompose	regretted	rerunning	rhizocarp
puffadder	quadrigae	rainproof	reconcile	regularly	resalable	rhizoidal
puffiness	quadrille	rainstorm	recondite	regulator	resection	rhodamine
pugnacity	quadruman	rainwater	reconfirm	rehearsal	resentful	rhodolite
puissance	quadruped	rakehelly	reconvene	rehydrate	reserpine	rhodonite
pullulate	quadruple	rampantly	reconvert	Reichstag	reservist	rhodopsin
pulmonary	quadruply	rancidity	recording	reimburse	reservoir	rhonchial
pulmonate	Quakerdom	rancorous	recordist	reinforce	resetting	rhymester
pulpboard	Quakeress	randiness	recoverer	reinstate	reshuffle	rhythmics
pulpiness	Quakerish	randomise	recreancy	reiterate	residence	rhythmise
pulpiteer	Quakerism	ranginess	recruital	rejection	residency	rhythmist
pulpstone	quakiness	ransacker	recruiter	rejoicing	residuary	Ribbonism
pulsatile	qualified	rantingly	rectangle	rejoinder	resilient	ribosomal
pulsation	qualifier	ranunculi	rectifier	relevance	resistant	ricepaper
pulsatory	quantical	rapacious	rectitude	relevancy	resistive	riderless
pulseless	quarenden	rapidfire	rectorate	reliantly	resitting	ridgepole
pulserate	quarender	rapidness	rectorial	religiose	resoluble	ridgetile
pulverise	quarryman	raptorial	rectrices	religious	resolvent	ridiculer
pulverous	quarterly	rapturous	recumbent	reliquary	resonance	riflebird
pulvillus	quartette	rareeshow	recurrent	reliquiae	resonator	rightable
pulvinate	quartzite	rascaldom	recurring	reluctant	resorbent	righteous
pumiceous	quartzose	rascalism	recursion	reluctate	resources	righthand
pummelled	quebracho	rascality	recursive	remainder	respecter	rightness
punchball	queenhood	raspatory	recusance	remanence	responder	rightward
punchbowl	queenless	raspberry	recusancy	remeasure	restfully	rigidness
punchcard	queenlike	raspingly	redaction	remediate	restiform	rigmarole
punchline	queenpost	ratepayer	redbreast	remindful	restitute	ringfence
punctilio	queenship	rationale	redevelop	reminisce	restively	ringingly
punctuate	queerness	rationing	redhanded	remission	restraint	ringshake
pungently	quercetum	raucously	redheaded	remitment	resultant	ringsnake
punishing	querulous	raunchily	redingote	remittent	resultful	riotously
pupillage	quibbling	rauwolfia	redivivus	remitting	resumable	Ripuarian
pupillary	quickener	ravelling	redletter	remontant	resurface	riskiness
puppeteer	quicklime	ravelment	redolence	removable	resurgent	ritualise
puppyhood	quickness	ravishing	redoubted	renascent	resurrect	ritualism
purchaser	quicksand	razorback	redresser	rencontre	retaliate	ritualist
pureblood	quickstep	razorbill	reducible	rendition	retardant	rivalling
purgation	quiescent	razoredge	reductant	renewable	retention	rivalrous
purgative	quietness	razorfish	reduction	renitency	retentive	rivelling
purgatory	quillwort	reachable	reductive	renouncer	rethought	riverbank
puritanic	quinoline	reactance	redundant	renovator	retiarius	riverboat
purloiner	quintette	readdress	reediness	reparable	reticence	riverhead
purposely	quintuple	readiness	reedorgan	repayable	reticency	riverside
purposive	quirister	readymade	reeducate	repayment	reticular	riverweed
purpureal	quitclaim	realistic	reefpoint	repechage	reticulum	roadblock
purringly	quittance	reanimate	reenforce	repellant	retinitis	roadhouse
purselike	quixotism	rearguard	reentrant	repellent	retinulae	roadmetal
pursiness	quizzical	rearhorse	reexamine	repelling	retinular	roadstead
pursuable	quodlibet	rearlight	refashion	repentant	retortion	roadworks
pursuance	quotation	rearmouse	refection	repertory	retoucher	rocambole
purulence	quotidian	rearrange	refectory	replenish	retractor	rockbound

rockbrake	sacrilege	Sardinian	schoolboy	seastrand	senhorita	sgraffiti
rockdrill	sacristan	sargassos	schooling	seatangle	seniority	sgraffito
rocketeer	saddlebag	Sarmation	schoolman	seaurchin	sensation	shadberry
rockiness	saddlebow	sartorial	sciaenoid	seaworthy	sensedata	shadeless
rockplant	Sadducean	sartorius	sciagraph	sebaceous	senseless	shadetree
rocksnake	safeguard	sasquatch	sciamachy	secateurs	sensitise	shadiness
rodfisher	safetypin	sassafras	sciascopy	secernent	sensitive	shakeable
roguishly	safflower	Sassanian	sciential	secession	sensorial	shakedown
roisterer	safranine	Sassenach	scientism	seclusion	sensorium	shakerism
roodcloth	sagacious	satanical	scientist	seclusive	sensually	shakiness
roofplate	sagebrush	satellite	scintilla	secondary	sentenate	shallowly
roominess	sagegreen	satiation	scirrhous	secretage	sentience	shamanism
rootstock	sagittate	satinbird	scleritis	secretary	sentiency	shamanist
Roquefort	sailcloth	satinette	sclerosis	secretion	sentiment	shamateur
rosaceous	sailoring	satinspar	sclerotic	secretive	sentrybox	shambling
roseapple	sailorman	satinwood	scolecite	secretory	separable	shambolic
roseately	sailplane	satirical	scoliosis	sectarian	separably	shamefast
rosenoble	sainthood	saturable	scoliotic	sectility	separates	shameless
rosewater	saintlike	saturator	scombroid	sectional	separator	Shangrila
rosinweed	saintling	Saturnian	scorbutic	sectorial	Sephardic	shantyman
rostellum	saintship	saturnine	scorching	secularly	Sephardim	shapeable
rotatable	salacious	saturnism	scorebook	securable	sepiolite	shapeless
rotundity	salangane	sauceboat	scorecard	sedentary	septation	sharecrop
roughcast	saleratus	sauceless	scoredraw	sedgewren	September	sharkskin
roughhewn	salesgirl	saucerful	scorifier	seditious	septemvir	sharpener
roughneck	saleslady	sauciness	scorpioid	seduction	septenary	sharpeyed
roughness	salicetum	saunterer	Scotchman	seductive	septennia	sharpness
roughshod	salicylic	sauropoda	Scoticise	seedeater	septicity	sharpshod
Roumanian	saliently	Sauternes	scotomata	seediness	septuplet	shaveling
Roumansch	sallowish	savagedom	scoundrel	seedpearl	sepulcher	shearling
rounceval	salmonoid	savourily	scraggily	seedplant	sepulchre	sheatfish
roundelay	salpinges	saxifrage	scrambler	seemingly	sepulture	sheathing
roundhead	saltation	saxophone	scramming	segmental	sequacity	Shechinah
roundness	saltatory	scagliola	scrapbook	segregate	sequester	sheepcote
roundsman	saltglaze	scaldfish	scrapheap	seigneury	sequestra	sheepfold
roundworm	saltiness	scalefern	scrapiron	seigniory	sequinned	sheephook
rousement	saltmarsh	scalefish	scrappily	selachian	serenader	sheeplice
routinely	saltpetre	scaleleaf	scrapping	selection	sergeancy	sheepplice
routinism	saltspoon	scaleless	scrapyard	selective	serialise	sheeptick
routinist	saltwater	scalelike	scratcher	selectman	serialism	sheepwalk
rowantree	saltworks	scalemoss	scratches	selenious	serialist	sheepwash
rowdiness	salubrity	scaliness	screecher	selenitic	seriality	sheerhulk
rubberise	salvation	scallawag	screening	selfabuse	seriately	sheerlegs
rubellite	Samaritan	scallywag	screwball	selfaware	sericeous	sheerness
rubicelle	Samoyedic	scalplock	screwbolt	selfdoubt	serigraph	sheikhdom
rubricate	sanatoria	scantling	screwpile	selfdrive	serinette	shelfduck
rubrician	sanbenito	scantness	screwpine	selffaced	seriously	sheldrake
rudbeckia	sanctuary	scapegoat	screwworm	selfglory	serjeancy	shelflife
ruddiness	sandalled	scapolite	scribbler	selfimage	serjeanty	shelfmark
ruddleman	sandarach	scapulary	scrimmage	selfishly	sermonise	shelfroom
rufescent	sandblast	scarecrow	scrimpily	selfmoved	serotonin	shellback
ruffianly	sandblind	scarehead	scrimshaw	selfpride	serpentry	shellbark
ruggedise	sandcrack	scarfring	scripture	selftrust	serranoid	shellfire
ruination	sandglass	scarfskin	scrivener	Seljukian	serration	shellfish
ruinously	sandiness	scarfwise	scrollsaw	semanteme	serrefile	shellheap
rulership	sandpaper	scarifier	scrounger	semantics	serrulate	shellwork
ruminator	sandpiper	scatology	scrubbing	semaphore	serviette	shemozzle
rumrunner	sandspout	scatterer	scruffily	semblable	servilely	shewbread
runcinate	sandstone	scavenger	scrumhalf	semblably	servility	shieldbug
rushlight	sandstorm	scenarist	scrummage	semblance	servitude	shieldfem
russeting	sandtable	scenedock	scrutable	semeiotic	sessional	shillelah
Russophil	sandyacht	scentless	scrutator	semestral	sestertia	shiftless
rusticate	sangfroid	sceptical	sculpture	semibreve	setaceous	shillelah
rusticity	Sanhedrim	scheelite	scuncheon	semicolon	setsquare	shinguard
rustiness	Sanhedrin	schematic	scutcheon	semifinal	sevenfold	shininess
rustproof	sanitaria	schilling	scutellar	semifluid	seventeen	Shintoism
ruthenium	santolina	schistose	scutellum	semilunar	seventhly	Shintoist
ruthfully	santonica	schistous	scutiform	semimetal	seventies	shipboard
sabadilla	sapanwood	schlemiel	seaanchor	seminally	severable	shipcanal
sabbatise	sapheaded	schlemihl	seachange	semiology	severally	shipfever
sabbatism	sapiently	schlieren	seafaring	semiotics	severalty	shipmoney
Sabellian	sapodilla	schmaltzy	seagirdle	semiplume	severance	shipowner
saccharin	sappiness	schnauzer	sealetter	semirigid	sexennial	shipshape
sacciform	sapraemia	schnitzel	seaminess	semisolid	sexlessly	shipwreck
sacculate	sapraemic	schnorkel	seanettle	semisweet	sexlinked	shirtless
sackcloth	Saracenic	schnorrer	searching	semitonic	sextuplet	shirttail
sacrament	sarcastic	scholarly	searingly	semivowel	sexualise	shockable
sacrarium	sarcocarp	scholiast	seasoning	senescent	sexuality	shockhead
sacrifice	sarcomata	schoolbag	seasquirt	seneschal	sforzando	shoeblack

shoemaker	siltstone	slingshot	sociopath	southland	spiralled	staghound
shoeshine	silverfir	slinkweed	sodabread	southmost	spirillum	staginess
shogunate	similarly	slipcoach	sodawater	southward	spiritism	Stagirite
shootable	simpatico	slipcover	softgoods	southwest	spiritist	stagnancy
shopfloor	simpleton	slivovitz	softpedal	souwester	spiritoso	stagparty
shopfront	simplices	slopbasin	softshell	sovereign	spiritous	staidness
shoreless	simulacra	slopewise	sogginess	sovietise	spiritual	stainable
shoreline	simulacre	slothbear	soidisant	sovietism	spirituel	stainless
shoreside	simulator	Slovakian	sojourner	spaceband	spirogyra	staircase
shoreward	simulcast	Slovenian	solacious	spaceless	splashily	stairfoot
shoreweld	sincerely	slowcoach	soldierly	spaceport	splayfoot	stairhead
shortcake	sincerity	slowmatch	solemnise	spaceship	spleenful	stairwell
shortener	sinewless	sluiceway	solemnity	spacesuit	splendent	stakeboat
shortfall	singalong	slumberer	soleplate	spacetime	splendour	stalactic
shorthand	singleton	slumbrous	solfatara	spadefoot	splenetic	stalemate
shorthorn	singspiel	slushfund	solfeggio	spadework	splenitis	staleness
shortness	Sinhalese	smackeroo	solferino	spaghetti	spleuchan	Stalinism
shortstop	sinistral	smallarms	solicitor	spagyrist	splintery	Stalinist
shortterm	sinlessly	smallness	solidness	spareness	splitting	stalkeyed
shortwave	sinologue	smalltime	soliloquy	spareribs	spluttery	stalkless
shotproof	sinophile	smartness	solipsism	sparingly	spodumene	stallfeed
shottower	sinuately	smartweed	solipsist	sparkcoil	spoilsman	stalworth
shouldest	sinuation	smatterer	solitaire	sparkless	spokesman	staminate
shovelful	sinuosity	smileless	solmisate	sparkplug	spokewise	stammerer
shovelhat	sinuously	smilingly	Solomonic	spasmodic	spoliator	stampduty
shovelled	sinusitis	smokeball	Solutrean	spatially	spongebag	stampmill
shoveller	siphonage	smokebomb	Solutrian	spatulate	spongeous	stampnote
showiness	siphuncle	smokebush	solvation	speakable	spoonbeak	stanchion
showpiece	Sisyphean	smokejack	something	speakeasy	spoonbill	standpipe
showplace	situation	smokeless	sometimes	spearfish	spoonfeed	stapedial
shredding	sitzkrieg	smoketree	somewhere	spearhead	spoonmeat	starapple
shrewmice	sixfooter	smokiness	somewhile	spearmint	sporangia	starboard
shrinkage	sixteenmo	smoothish	sommelier	spearside	sporocarp	starchily
shrubbery	sixteenth	smuggling	somnolent	spearwort	sporocyst	stardrift
shrugging	skedaddle	snailfish	songcycle	specially	sporogeny	stargazer
sibilance	skeesicks	snakebird	songfully	specialty	sportsman	stargrass
sibilancy	sketchily	snakebite	songsmith	specifier	sporulate	starkness
sibylline	sketchmap	snakelike	sonneteer	speckless	spotcheck	starlight
siccative	skewwhiff	snakeroot	sonnetise	spectacle	spotlight	starshell
sickening	skiagraph	snakeskin	sonometer	spectator	spouthole	starstone
sickishly	skiamachy	snakeweed	sooterkin	speculate	spoutless	startling
sickleave	skiascopy	snakewood	soothfast	speechful	sprigging	statehood
sideboard	skijoring	snakiness	sootiness	speechify	sprightly	stateless
sideburns	skilfully	snaredrum	sophister	speedball	sprigtail	statement
sidedness	skindiver	sniggerer	sophistic	speedboat	springald	stateroom
sideissue	skinflick	snipefish	sophistry	speedster	springbok	stateside
sidelight	skinflint	snivelled	sophomore	speedwell	springily	statesman
sideritic	skingraft	sniveller	soporific	spellbind	springing	statewide
siderosis	skintight	snowberry	soppiness	spellican	springlet	stational
sideswipe	skirtings	snowblind	sopranino	spendable	sprinkler	stationer
sidetable	skirtless	snowblink	sopranist	spermatic	spritsail	statistic
sidetrack	skydiving	snowbound	sorbapple	spermatid	spurwheel	statocyst
sidewards	skyjacker	snowbroth	Sorbonist	sphagnous	sputterer	statolith
sidewheel	skyrocket	snowdrift	sorceress	spherical	squabbler	statuette
sightless	slabsided	snowfield	sorcerous	spherular	squalidly	statutory
sightseer	slabstone	snowflake	soritical	sphincter	squamosal	stauncher
sigillary	slackness	snowgoose	sorriness	sphygmoid	squarrose	staunchly
sigillate	slakeless	snowguard	sorrowful	spicebush	squashily	staymaker
sigmoidal	slanderer	snowiness	sortilege	spiciness	squatness	steadfast
signalbox	slantways	snowplant	sortition	spiculate	squatting	steamboat
signalise	slantwise	snowscape	sostenuto	spiderman	squeakily	steampipe
signalled	slaphappy	snowstorm	sottishly	spiderweb	squeamish	steamship
signaller	slapstick	snowwhite	soubrette	spikenard	squelcher	steatitic
signalman	slateclub	snubnosed	Soudanese	spikiness	squibbing	steelclad
signatory	slategrey	soapberry	soulfully	spillikin	squidding	steelhead
signature	slaughter	soapiness	soundfilm	spindling	squinancy	steelwork
signboard	slaveship	soapstone	soundhole	spindrier	squirarch	steelyard
significs	slavishly	soapworks	soundings	spindrift	squiredom	steenkirk
signorial	Slavonian	sobbingly	soundless	spineless	squirelet	steepness
signorina	Slavophil	soberness	soundness	spininess	stabilise	steersman
siliceous	sleekness	sobriquet	soundpost	spinnaker	stability	stegosaur
silicious	sleepless	sobsister	soundwave	spinneret	stableboy	stellated
silicosis	sleevenut	socialise	soupplate	spinosity	stableman	stenotype
silicotic	slenderly	socialism	soupspoon	Spinozism	stackable	stenotypy
siliquose	slickness	socialist	sourdough	Spinozist	stackroom	stepchild
silkgland	sliderule	socialite	souteneur	spinulose	stackyard	stepdance
silkiness	slightish	sociality	Southdown	spinulous	stagedoor	steradian
silliness	sliminess	sociogram	southeast	spiracula	stagehand	stercoral
siltation	slingback	sociology	southerly	spirality	staggerer	sterilise

sterility	stovepipe	sublation	supernova	syllogism	tambourin	tenaculum
sternmost	straggler	sublethal	superpose	sylphlike	tamponade	tenderise
sternness	strangely	sublimate	supersede	sylvanite	tangerine	tendinous
sternpost	strangler	sublimely	superstar	symbiosis	tanliquor	tenebrist
sternward	strangles	sublimity	supervene	symbiotic	tanpickle	tenebrous
steroidal	straphang	sublunary	supervise	symbolics	tantalate	tenseness
stevedore	strapless	submarine	supinator	symbolise	tantalise	tensility
stickwork	strappado	submaster	suppliant	symbolism	tantalite	tensional
stiffener	strapping	submental	supporter	symbolist	tapdancer	tentacled
stiffness	strapwork	submitted	supposing	symbology	tarantara	tentation
stigmatic	strapwort	subnormal	suppurate	symmetric	tarantass	tentative
stilettos	stratagem	subocular	supremacy	symphonic	tarantism	tenthrate
stillborn	strategic	subphylum	supremely	symphysis	tarantula	tentmaker
stillhunt	strawworm	subregion	surcharge	sympodial	taraxacum	tenuously
stillness	streakily	subrogate	surcingle	sympodium	tardiness	tepidness
stillroom	streaking	subscribe	surculose	symposiac	Targumist	teratogen
stiltedly	streamlet	subscript	surfacing	symposial	tarpaulin	terebinth
stimulant	streetcar	subsellia	surfboard	symposium	tarragona	terebrant
stimulate	strenuous	subsidise	surfeiter	synagogal	Tartarean	termagant
stingaree	stressful	substance	surficial	synagogue	Tartarian	terminate
stingless	stretcher	substrata	surgeoncy	synchrony	tartishly	terminism
stinkball	strewment	substrate	surliness	synclinal	Tartufian	terminist
stinkbomb	striation	subtenant	surmullet	syncopate	Tartufism	termitary
stinkhorn	striature	subtilise	surpliced	syncretic	taskforce	ternately
stinktrap	stricture	subtopian	surprisal	syncytial	Tasmanian	terramara
stinkweed	stridence	subverter	surrender	syncytium	tasselled	terramare
stinkwood	stridency	succeeder	surrogate	syndactyl	tasteless	terrarium
stintless	stringent	succentor	surveying	syndicate	tastiness	territory
stipitate	stripling	successor	suspender	synectics	tattiness	terrorise
stippling	stripping	succinate	suspensor	syneresis	tattooist	terrorism
stipulate	strobilae	succotash	suspicion	synergism	tautology	terrorist
stirabout	strobilus	succourer	sustainer	synergist	tawniness	terseness
stitchery	stromatic	succulent	susurrant	syngamous	taxidermy	tervalent
stockbook	strongarm	succursal	sutteeism	synizesis	taximeter	tessitura
stockdove	strongbox	suctorial	suturally	synodical	taxonomic	testament
stockfish	strongish	suctorian	swaddling	synoecete	taxpaying	testation
stockinet	strongyle	sudatoria	swaggerer	synonymic	teachable	testatrix
stocklist	strontium	sudorific	swangoose	synoptist	teachably	testdrive
stockpile	stropping	suffering	swansdown	synovitis	teacupful	testifier
stockroom	strouding	suffocate	swarajist	syntactic	teakettle	testimony
stockwhip	structure	suffragan	swartness	syntheses	tearfully	testiness
stockyard	struggler	suffusion	swearword	synthesis	teasingly	tetradite
stoically	strumitis	sugarbeet	sweatband	synthetic	technical	tetragram
stokehold	strumming	sugarcane	sweatmeal	syphilise	technique	tetralogy
stokehole	strutting	sugarloaf	sweatshop	syphiloid	tectonics	tetrapody
stolidity	strychnic	sugarplum	sweepback	syringeal	tectorial	tetrarchy
stolonate	studhorse	suggester	sweetcorn	systaltic	tectrices	teutonise
stomachal	studiedly	sulcation	sweetener	tablature	tediously	Teutonism
stomacher	stupefier	sulkiness	sweetmeal	tableland	tegmental	Teutonist
stomachic	stupidity	sulphonic	sweetmeat	tableleaf	tegmentum	textually
stonechat	stuporous	sulphuret	sweetness	tabletalk	tegularly	thalassic
stonecoal	stutterer	sulphuric	sweetshop	tableware	teknonymy	thaneship
stonecold	stylebook	sultanate	sweettalk	tabularly	telamones	thankless
stonecrop	styliform	sultaness	swellfish	tabulator	telegenic	thatching
stonedead	stylishly	summarily	sweptback	tacamahac	telegraph	theandric
stonedeaf	stylistic	summarise	swiftness	tachylite	telemeter	theatrics
stonefish	stylobate	summarist	swimmable	tachylyte	telemetry	theocracy
stoneless	suability	summation	swimmeret	tacitness	teleology	theocrasy
stonewall	suasively	summative	swineherd	tackiness	teleonomy	theogonic
stoneware	subaerial	summingup	swingeing	tactfully	teleostei	theologic
stonework	subagency	sumptuary	swinishly	tactician	telepathy	theologue
stonewort	subalpine	sumptuous	switchman	tactility	telephone	theomachy
stoniness	subaltern	sunbather	swivelled	tactitian	telephony	theomania
stoolball	subarctic	sunbonnet	swordcane	tactually	telephoto	theophany
stoplight	subastral	sunburned	swordfish	taeniasis	telescope	theoretic
stoppress	subatomic	sundowner	swordknot	tahsildar	televisor	theoriser
stopwatch	subbranch	sunflower	swordlike	tailboard	tellurate	theosophy
storeroom	subcaudal	sunhelmet	swordplay	taillight	tellurian	therapist
storeship	subcostal	sunlounge	swordsman	tailoress	telluride	Theravada
storiated	subdeacon	sunniness	swordtail	tailoring	tellurite	therefore
stormbelt	subdivide	sunspurge	sybaritic	tailpiece	tellurium	therefrom
stormbird	subduable	sunstroke	sycophant	taintless	tellurous	thereinto
stormcock	subduedly	sunstruck	syllabary	taioseach	telophase	thereunto
stormcone	subeditor	suntanned	syllabise	talismans	temperate	thereupon
stormless	subereous	superable	syllabism	talkathon	temporary	therewith
stormsail	subfamily	supercool	syllepses	talkative	temporise	thermally
storybook	subgenera	superfine	syllepsis	tallowish	temptable	thermidor
storyline	subjacent	superfuse	sylleptic	tallyshop	temptress	thesaurus
stoutness	subjugate	superheat	syllogise	Talmudist	tenacious	theurgist

thickener	tipstaves	traceless	tridactyl	tungstate	unchecked	unfleshed
thicketed	tiredness	traceried	tridymite	tunicated	uncinated	unfleshly
thickhead	tirewoman	tracheary	triennial	tunnelled	uncivilly	unfounded
thickknee	titillate	tracheate	triennium	tunnelnet	uncleanly	ungallant
thickness	titledeed	trachytic	trierarch	turbidity	unclothed	unguarded
thighbone	titlepage	trackless	trifacial	turbinate	unclouded	unhappily
thighboot	titration	tracksuit	trifocals	turboprop	unconcern	unharness
thingness	tittivate	tractable	trifolium	turbulent	uncounted	unhealthy
thingummy	tittlebat	tractably	triforium	Turcomans	uncouthly	unheeding
thinkable	tittuping	trademark	trigamist	turgently	uncovered	unhelpful
thinktank	tittupped	tradename	trigamous	turgidity	uncreated	unhurried
thirdhand	titularly	tradesman	trihedral	Turkomans	uncropped	unicolour
thirdrate	toadeater	tradition	trihybrid	turnabout	uncrossed	unicuspid
thirdsman	toadstone	traducian	trilinear	turnround	uncrowned	unifiable
thirstily	toadstool	tragedian	trilithon	turnstile	undamaged	uniformly
thirtieth	toastrack	trainable	trilobate	turnstone	undaunted	uniparous
thitherto	Tocharian	trainband	trilobite	turntable	undecagon	uniplanar
Thomistic	tolerable	trainload	trimerous	turpitude	undeceive	uniserial
thornback	tolerably	traitress	trimester	turquoise	undecided	unisexual
thornbill	tolerance	tramlines	trimetric	tutorship	undecimal	unisonant
thornbush	tollbooth	transcend	trimmings	twayblade	undefined	unisonous
thornless	tollhouse	transenna	trinketer	twelfthly	underbody	unitarian
thorntree	tombstone	transform	trinketry	twentieth	underbred	unitively
thoughted	tomentose	transfuse	trinomial	twentyone	underclay	univalent
thralldom	tomentous	transient	triploidy	twiceborn	undercoat	universal
thrashing	tonguelet	translate	triptyque	twicelaid	underdone	unknitted
threefold	tonguetie	transmute	triquetra	twicetold	underfelt	unknowing
threesome	tonically	transonic	trisagion	twinkling	underfoot	unlearned
threnodic	tonometer	transpire	trisector	twistable	undergird	unlimited
threshold	tonsillar	transport	triteness	twitchily	undergone	unluckily
thriftily	tonsorial	transpose	tritheism	twitterer	undergrad	unmatched
thrilling	toolhouse	transship	tritheist	twofisted	underhand	unmeaning
throatily	toothache	transumpt	triturate	twohanded	underhung	unmindful
throbbing	toothcomb	transvest	triumphal	twosuiter	underlaid	unmusical
thrombose	toothless	trapezial	triumviri	tympanist	underlain	unnamable
throttler	toothpick	trapezium	trivalent	typemetal	underline	unnatural
throughly	toothsome	trapezoid	trivially	typewrite	underling	unpegging
throwaway	toothwort	trappings	triweekly	typhlitis	undermine	unpeopled
throwback	tophamper	trattoria	trochilus	typhoidal	undermost	unplugged
throwster	topiarian	trattorie	trochleae	typically	underpaid	unplumbed
thrumming	topiarist	traumatic	trochlear	tyrannise	underpart	unpointed
thumbhole	topically	travelled	troopship	tyrannous	underpass	unpopular
thumbmark	toponymal	traveller	tropology	uintahite	underplay	unreality
thumbnail	toponymic	traversal	troublous	Uitlander	underplot	unreserve
thumbtack	torchrace	traverser	trousered	Ukrainian	underrate	unruffled
thunderer	torchsong	traycloth	trousseau	uliginous	underripe	unsavoury
Thyestean	toreutics	treachery	troutfarm	ultimatum	underseal	unsayable
thylacine	tormentil	treadmill	troutling	ultrahigh	underseas	unscathed
thyratron	tormentor	treasurer	trowelled	ululation	undersell	unselfish
thyristor	torpidity	treatable	troweller	umbellate	undershot	unsettled
thyroxine	torridity	treatment	truceless	umbellule	underside	unshackle
tidegauge	torsional	trebuchet	truculent	umberbird	undersign	unsheathe
tidewater	tortrices	trebucket	truepenny	umbilical	undersold	unsighted
tiedyeing	tortricid	treillage	trumpedup	umbilicus	undersong	unsightly
tigerlily	torturous	trematode	trumpeter	umpteenth	underspin	unskilful
tigermoth	totaliser	tremolant	truncated	unabashed	undertake	unskilled
tigerseye	totalling	tremolite	truncheon	unadopted	undertint	unsmiling
tigerwood	totempole	tremulant	trunkcall	unadorned	undertone	unsoundly
tightener	touchable	tremulous	trunkfish	unadvised	undertook	unsparing
tightness	touchdown	trenchant	trunkroad	unalloyed	undervest	unspotted
tightrope	touchhole	trepanned	trussbeam	unaltered	underwear	unstopped
tightwire	touchline	trepidant	trustdeed	unanimity	underwent	unstudied
tilestone	touchmark	trialogue	trustless	unanimous	underwing	unsuccess
timbering	touchtype	triatomic	truthless	unaptness	underwood	unsullied
timberman	touchwood	tribadism	trysquare	unashamed	undivided	untenable
timelapse	toughness	tribalism	tsarevich	unbalance	undoubted	unthought
timelimit	touristic	tribesman	tubbiness	unbeknown	undreamed	unthrifty
timeously	tournedos	tribology	tubercule	unberufen	undulated	untimeous
timepiece	tourneyer	tribunate	tubularly	unbiassed	undutiful	untouched
timesheet	towelling	tributary	tuckerbag	unblessed	unearthly	untrodden
timetable	townhouse	trichinae	tufaceous	unblinded	uneatable	untrussed
timidness	townscape	trichomic	tuitional	unblinked	unequally	untutored
timocracy	townsfolk	trichroic	tuliproot	unbounded	unethical	unusually
timpanist	toxically	trickless	tuliptree	unbraided	unfailing	unwearied
tinderbox	toxophily	tricksily	tulipwood	unbridled	unfeeling	unweeting
tinniness	trabeated	trickster	tumblebug	uncannily	unfeigned	unwelcome
tinopener	trabecula	triclinia	tumescent	unceasing	unfitness	unwilling
tinselled	traceable	triclinic	tumidness	uncertain	unfitting	unwinking
tipsiness	traceably	tricolour	tunefully	uncharted	unfledged	unwitting

unwomanly	vehemence	videotape	vulcanise	waterlily	whitebass	woodblock
unwrapped	vehicular	viewpoint	vulcanism	waterline	whitebeam	woodchuck
unwritten	veinstone	vigesimal	vulcanist	watermark	whiteface	woodcraft
unwrought	velodrome	vigilance	vulcanite	watermill	whitefish	woodiness
unzipping	velveteen	vigilante	vulgarian	waterpipe	Whitehall	woodlouse
Upanishad	vendition	vignetter	vulgarise	watershed	whitehead	woodnymph
upbraider	veneering	villagery	vulgarism	waterside	whiteness	woodwaxen
upcountry	venerable	villanage	vulgarity	waterweed	whitening	wooziness
upholster	venerably	villenage	vulnerary	waterworn	whitewash	Worcester
uplifting	venerator	villiform	vulpinism	wattmeter	whitewing	wordiness
uppercase	venereous	villosity	vulpinite	wavefront	whitewood	wordsmith
uppermost	vengeance	vimineous	vulturine	waveguide	whizzbang	workbench
uprightly	veniality	vinaceous	vulturish	wavellite	whodunnit	workhorse
upsetting	ventiduct	vindicate	vulturous	wayfaring	wholemeal	workhouse
uraninite	ventifact	violation	wackiness	waywardly	wholeness	workmanly
uranology	ventilate	violative	waggishly	wayzgoose	wholesale	workpiece
urceolate	ventrally	violently	waggonage	weakkneed	wholesome	worktable
uropygium	ventricle	violinist	Wagnerian	wealthily	whosoever	workwoman
urticaria	venturous	virescent	Wagnerite	weariless	wideawake	worldling
uselessly	veracious	Virgilian	wagonette	weariness	widowbird	worldwide
usherette	verandaed	virginals	wagonroof	wearisome	widowhood	wormeaten
usualness	veratrine	virginity	wailingly	weathered	widthways	wormwheel
usucapion	verbalise	virgulate	waistband	weatherly	widthwise	worriedly
utricular	verbalism	viricidal	waistbelt	webfooted	wieldable	worriment
utterable	verbalist	virtually	waistcoat	wedgewise	willemite	worrisome
utterance	verbicide	virtuosic	waistline	Wednesday	willingly	worrywart
utterless	verbosely	virtuosos	wakefully	weediness	willowish	worthless
uttermost	verbosity	virulence	wakerobin	weeknight	willpower	woundless
utterness	verdantly	virulency	Waldenses	weevilled	windblown	woundwort
uvarovite	verdigris	viscerate	waldgrave	wehrmacht	windbound	wrathless
uxoricide	veridical	viscidity	walkabout	weighable	windbreak	wrestling
vaccinate	veritable	viscosity	wallboard	weighbeam	windchest	wristband
vacillant	veritably	viscounty	wallcress	weightily	windhover	wristdrop
vacillate	vermicide	viscously	wallfruit	weighting	windiness	wristshot
vacuolate	vermicule	visionary	walloping	weirdness	windowbox	wrongdoer
vacuously	vermiform	visionist	wallpaper	welcoming	windproof	wrongness
vademecum	vermifuge	visitable	wallplate	welfarism	windswept	wulfenite
vagarious	vermilion	visitress	wallydrag	wellbeing	windwards	wyandotte
vagueness	verminate	visualise	Walpurgis	wellfound	wineberry	wychhazel
vainglory	verminous	vitellary	wandering	wellknown	wineglass	Wyclifite
Vaishnava	vernalise	vitelline	wapentake	welltimed	winepress	wyliecoat
valentine	vernation	vitiation	warblefly	werwolves	winestone	Xanthippe
valiantly	verrucose	vitiosity	warbonnet	westbound	winevault	xenograft
validness	verrucous	vitriform	warehouse	westering	wingchair	xenophile
vallation	versatile	vitriolic	warmonger	westerner	winningly	xenophobe
vallecula	versifier	Vitruvian	warningly	westwards	winsomely	xeromorph
valuables	versiform	vivacious	warrantee	whaleback	winterise	xerophile
valuation	versional	viverrine	warranter	whaleboat	wiredrawn	xerophily
valueless	vertebrae	vivianite	warrantor	whalebone	wiregauze	xerophyte
valveless	vertebral	vividness	wartcress	whalehead	wirephoto	xparticle
vampirism	vesicular	vizierate	washbasin	wheatmeal	wisecrack	xylograph
vandalise	vestibule	vizierial	washboard	wheedling	wishfully	xylophone
vandalism	vestigial	vocabular	washcloth	wheelbase	wistfully	yachtclub
vapidness	vestigium	vocaliser	washedout	wheelless	witchetty	yachtsman
vaporable	vestiture	vocalness	washerman	wheelwork	witchhunt	Yankeedom
vaporific	vestryman	voiceless	washhouse	wherefore	witchmeal	Yankeeism
vaporiser	vetchling	voiceover	washiness	wherefrom	withdrawn	yardstick
vapouring	vexatious	volauvent	washstand	whereinto	withering	yawningly
vapourish	vexillary	volcanism	waspishly	whereunto	witherite	yearround
Varangian	viability	volcanoes	wassailer	whereupon	withstand	yellowdog
variation	vibracula	volkslied	wasteland	wherewith	withstood	yellowish
varicella	vibraharp	volteface	wasteness	wherryman	witlessly	yesterday
variegate	vibratile	voltinism	wastepipe	whetstone	witticism	Yiddisher
variolate	vibration	voltmeter	watchable	wheyfaced	wittiness	yodelling
variolite	vibrative	volumeter	watchcase	whichever	wittingly	yohimbine
varioloid	vibratory	voluntary	watchfire	whimperer	woebegone	Yorkshire
variolous	vibrissae	volunteer	watchword	whimsical	wolfhound	youngling
variously	vicariate	vomitoria	waterbath	whinstone	wolfishly	youngness
varnisher	vicarious	voodooism	waterbuck	whipperin	wolframic	youngster
vasectomy	vicennial	voodooist	waterbutt	whipround	wolfsbane	ytterbium
vasomotor	viceregal	voracious	watercart	whipsnake	wolverene	zamindary
vassalage	vicereine	vorticism	watercool	whipstock	wolverine	zapateado
vastitude	viceroyal	vorticist	waterfall	whirligig	womanhood	zealously
vaticinal	vicesimal	vorticity	waterflea	whirlpool	womaniser	zebrawood
vectorial	viciously	vorticose	waterfowl	whirlwind	womankind	zeitgeist
Vedantist	victimise	vouchsafe	watergate	whiskered	womanlike	zemindary
veeringly	Victorian	vowelless	waterhole	whisperer	womenfolk	zestfully
vegetable	victorine	voyeurism	waterleaf	whistling	womenkind	zeugmatic
vegetably	videlicet	vulcanian	waterless	whitebait	wonderful	zibelline

zigzagged	banefully	caddisfly	cantaloup	castigate	dashboard	fasciculi
zincotype	banjulele	cadential	cantharid	Castilian	dashingly	fascinate
zinkenite	bannister	cadetship	cantharis	Castroism	dastardly	Fascistic
zirconium	banqueter	caecilian	cantharus	casuarina	dauntless	fashioner
zoiatrics	banquette	Caenozoic	cantilena	casuistic	davenport	fastening
zoogenous	Bantustan	caerulean	Cantonese	casuistry	dayschool	fastigium
zoography	baptismal	Caesarean	cantorial	catabolic	dayspring	fatefully
zoologist	baptistry	Caesarian	canvasser	cataclasm	eagerness	fatheaded
zoophagan	barathrum	Caesarism	capacious	cataclysm	ealdorman	fatidical
zoophobia	Barbadian	Caesarist	capacitor	catalepsy	earliness	fatigable
zoophytic	barbarian	cafeteria	caparison	catalexes	earnestly	fattiness
zootechny	barbarise	cageyness	capillary	catalexis	earthborn	fatuously
zootomist	barbarism	cailleach	capitally	catalogue	earthling	fatwitted
zucchetto	barbarity	Cainozoic	capitular	catalyser	earthstar	faultless
Zwinglian	barbarous	cairngorm	capitulum	catalyses	earthward	faunistic
zygomatic	barbitone	calaboose	capriccio	catalysis	earthwork	faveolate
zygospore	barcarole	calabrese	Capricorn	catalytic	earthworm	favourite
zymogenic	barefaced	calamanco	capsulate	catamaran	earwigged	fawningly
————	bargainer	calandria	capsulise	catamount	easefully	gabardine
babacoote	bargepole	calcaneal	captaincy	cataplasm	eastbound	gaberdine
Babbittry	barkeeper	calcaneum	captivate	cataplexy	Eastender	gabionade
babirussa	barleymow	calcarate	captivity	catarhine	easterner	gadgeteer
baboonish	barmbrack	calcicole	carambola	catarrhal	eastwards	Gaeltacht
bacchanal	Barmecide	calcifuge	carbamate	catatonia	easygoing	gainfully
bacchante	barnacled	calculate	carbamide	catatonic	eavesdrop	gainsayer
bacillary	barnstorm	calculous	carbonado	catchable	fabaceous	galactose
backbiter	barograph	caldarium	carbonate	catchment	Fabianism	galantine
backboard	barometer	calendric	carbonise	catchpole	fabricant	galenical
backcloth	barometry	calendula	carbuncle	catchpoll	fabricate	galingale
backcross	baronetcy	calenture	carburise	catchword	facecloth	gallantly
backpedal	barracker	calibrate	carcinoma	catechise	facetious	gallantry
backsight	barracoon	calicular	cardboard	catechism	facsimile	galleried
backslang	barracuda	caliology	cardsharp	catechist	factional	gallicise
backslide	barrelful	caliphate	careerism	Catharism	factitive	gallicism
backspace	barrelled	callipers	careerist	Catharist	factorage	gallingly
backstage	barricade	callosity	carefully	cathartic	factorial	gallinule
backsword	barricado	callously	caretaker	catharses	factorise	gallivant
backtrack	barrister	calmative	carfuffle	catharsis	factually	galliwasp
backwards	bartender	calorific	Caribbean	cathartic	facundity	gallmidge
backwater	bashfully	Calvinism	Carmelite	cathectic	faddiness	gallonage
backwoods	basically	Calvinist	carnality	cathedral	faggoting	gallooned
bacterial	basilican	calycinal	carnation	catoptric	faintness	gallopade
bacterise	basipetal	camarilla	carnelian	cattaloes	fairfaced	Gallophil
bacterium	basketful	Cambodian	carnitine	cattiness	fairyhood	galloping
bacteroid	basrelief	camelback	carnivore	cattleman	fairyland	gallowses
badminton	bastardly	camelhair	carolling	Caucasian	fairylike	gallstone
bagatelle	bastinade	Camembert	carpenter	causality	fairyring	galvanise
bagginess	bastinado	cameraman	carpentry	causation	fairytale	galvanism
bailiwick	bastioned	camorrist	carpetbag	causative	faithcure	galvanist
bainmarie	bathhouse	campanile	carpeting	causeless	faithless	gambadoes
bakehouse	batholite	campanili	carpingly	cauterise	Falangism	gambolled
baksheesh	batholith	campanula	carpology	cavalcade	Falangist	gammadion
balaclava	Bathonian	campchair	carrageen	cavendish	falciform	gammoning
balalaika	bathybius	campcraft	carrefour	cavernous	faldstool	ganderism
balconied	battalion	campfever	carronade	cavilling	Falernian	gangboard
baldachin	battening	camphoric	carryover	dachshund	fallalery	gangplank
baldaquin	battiness	campstool	Cartesian	Daedalean	falsehood	gannister
baldfaced	battleaxe	canalboat	carthorse	Daedalian	falseness	gaolbreak
balefully	battlecry	cancelled	cartilage	dahabiyah	falsifier	gardening
balkanise	bawdiness	cancerous	cartogram	dairymaid	familyman	garderobe
balladeer	bayoneted	candidacy	cartology	dalliance	fanatical	garibaldi
balladist	caballero	candidate	cartouche	dalmatian	fancyfree	garmented
ballerina	caballine	Candlemas	cartridge	daltonism	fancywork	garnishee
ballistae	caballing	candlenut	cartulary	damascene	fandangle	garniture
ballistic	cabbalism	candytuft	cartwheel	damnation	fandangos	garreteer
ballpoint	cabbalist	canebrake	caryopses	damnatory	fanfarade	garrotter
balminess	cablegram	canescent	caryopsis	damnedest	fantasied	garrulity
baltimore	cablelaid	canesugar	caseation	damningly	fantasise	garrulous
bamboozle	cabriolet	canetrash	Cassandra	Damoclean	fantasist	gasconade
banderole	cachectic	canicular	cassareep	dancehall	fantastic	gasfitter
bandicoot	cacholong	cankerous	cassaripe	dandelion	fantastry	gasholder
bandoleer	caciquism	cannelure	cassation	dandiacal	farandole	gasmantle
bandolero	cacodemon	canniness	casserole	dangerous	farestage	gasometer
bandolier	cacodylic	cannonade	cassimere	Dantesque	farmhouse	gaspereau
bandoline	cacoethes	cannoneer	cassoulet	daredevil	farmstead	gastraeum
bandstand	cacophony	cannonier	cassowary	dartboard	farseeing	gastritis
bandwagon	cacuminal	cannulate	Castalian	Darwinian	fasciated	gastropod
bandwidth	cadastral	canonical	castanets	Darwinism	fascicled	gastrulae
baneberry	cadaveric	cantabile	castellan	Darwinist	fascicule	gatecrash

gatehouse	handiwork	Jansenist	lastditch	maladroit	marshwort	paillasse
gathering	handlebar	japanning	lastingly	malanders	marsupial	paillette
gaucherie	handorgan	jargonise	latecomer	malarious	marsupium	painfully
gaudiness	handpress	jarringly	laterally	malathion	martially	painterly
gaugeable	handsdown	jaundiced	latescent	Malayalam	Martinmas	paintwork
gauleiter	handshake	jaywalker	lathering	malformed	martyrdom	pairhorse
gauntness	handspike	jazziness	latitancy	malicious	martyrise	Pakistani
gauziness	handstand	kaiserdom	latterday	malignant	marvelled	palaestra
gavelkind	handwheel	kaiserism	latticing	malignity	masculine	palafitte
gawkiness	handywork	kaolinise	laudation	malleable	masochism	palankeen
gazehound	hangerson	kaolinite	laudative	malleehen	masochist	palanquin
gazetteer	hankering	karabiner	laudatory	mallemuck	masonried	palatable
habergeon	Hanseatic	karyotype	laughable	malleolar	Masoretic	palatably
habitable	hanselled	katabasis	laughably	malleolus	massagist	palillogy
habitably	haphazard	katabatic	launching	malthouse	massiness	Palladian
habituate	haplessly	katabolic	launderer	malvoisie	massively	palladium
hackamore	haplology	katharsis	laundress	mamillary	masterdom	palladous
hackberry	happening	labelling	laurelled	mamillate	masterful	palletise
hackneyed	happiness	labialise	lavaliere	mammalian	masterkey	palliasse
haematite	haranguer	labialism	lawgiving	mammalogy	masticate	pallidity
haematoid	harbinger	laborious	lawlessly	mammiform	matchless	palmation
haematoma	harbourer	labourite	lawnmower	mammonish	matchlock	palmipede
haemostat	hardboard	labyrinth	lazaretto	mammonist	matchwood	palmistry
haggadist	hardcover	laccolith	lazybones	mammonist	maternity	palmitate
haggardly	hardihood	lacerable	lazytongs	mammonite	mateyness	palpation
hagiarchy	hardiment	lacertian	lazzarone	Mancunian	matriarch	palpebral
hagiology	hardiness	lacertine	lazzaroni	mandarine	matricide	palpitant
hagridden	hardnosed	lachrymal	macaronic	mandatary	matricula	palpitate
hailstone	hardshell	laciniate	Maccabean	mandatory	matrimony	palsgrave
hailstorm	haresfoot	lacrimose	macedoine	mandoline	matronage	paludinal
hairbrush	harlequin	lacrymose	macerator	manducate	matronise	palustral
haircloth	harmaline	lactation	machinate	maneating	mattamore	panatella
hairgrass	harmattan	ladysmock	machinery	manganate	matutinal	panchayat
hairiness	harmfully	laevulose	machinist	manganese	maulstick	pancratic
hairpiece	harmonica	laggardly	machmeter	manganite	maunderer	panderess
hairshirt	harmonics	lagniappe	macintosh	manganous	mausoleum	panegyric
hairslide	harmonise	lagomorph	macrocosm	manginess	mawkishly	panelling
hairspace	harmonist	lairdship	macrocyte	manhandle	maxillary	panellist
hairstyle	harmonium	lallation	maddening	manhattan	maximally	panhandle
halfbaked	harmotome	lambently	madeleine	Manichean	maybeetle	panicking
halfblood	harpooner	lamellate	madrepore	manifesto	mayflower	panoplied
halfbound	harquebus	lamellose	maelstrom	manipular	mayoralty	panoramic
halfbreed	Harrovian	laminaria	magdalene	manliness	mayorship	pantalets
halfcaste	harrowing	laminated	Magianism	mannequin	Nahuatlan	pantaloon
halfcrown	harshness	lampblack	magically	mannerism	nailbrush	pantheism
halfhardy	hartshorn	lamplight	magicking	mannerist	nakedness	pantheist
halfflight	harvester	lampooner	magistery	manoeuvre	nameplate	pantingly
halfpence	Hashemite	lampshade	magistral	manometer	nannygoat	pantomime
halfpenny	Hashimite	lampshell	magnalium	manorseat	naphthene	pantryman
halfprice	hastiness	lancejack	magnesian	mansarded	napthalic	pantyhose
halfshell	hatchback	lancewood	magnesite	mansionry	narcissus	paperback
halfstaff	hatchling	lancinate	magnesium	manslayer	narcotine	paperclip
halftitle	hatchment	landagent	magnetics	manticore	narcotise	papergirl
halftrack	hatefully	landaulet	magnetise	manubrium	narcotism	paperthin
halftruth	haughtily	landdross	magnetism	Manxwoman	narration	paperwork
halieutic	haustella	landdrost	magnetist	manyplies	narrative	papeterie
halitosis	haustoria	landgrave	magnetite	manysided	narratory	papillary
Halloween	haverings	landloper	magnetron	manzanita	naseberry	papillate
Hallowmas	haversack	landowner	magnifico	maquisard	nastiness	papilloma
hallstand	havocking	landscape	magnifier	marcasite	natheless	papillose
Hallstatt	hawksbill	landslide	magnitude	marcelled	natrolite	papillose
halophile	hawsehole	Langobard	maharajah	marchpane	nattiness	parabasis
halophyte	hawsepipe	langouste	maharanee	marchpast	naturally	parabolic
halothane	hazardous	languidly	maharishi	marestail	naughtily	parachute
haltingly	jaborandi	lankiness	mahlstick	margarine	naumachia	Paraclete
hamadryad	jacaranda	lanthanum	Mahometan	margarite	navelwort	paradisal
hamamelis	jackknife	Laodicean	maidenish	marginate	navicular	paragraph
hamburger	jackplane	lapideous	mailplane	marihuana	navigable	paralalia
hamfisted	jacksnipe	Laplander	mailtrain	marijuana	navigator	paralexia
hamhanded	jackstraw	lapstrake	mainbrace	maritally	oakenshaw	paralysis
hammerman	Jacobinic	lapstreak	mainliner	marketday	oasthouse	paralytic
hammertoe	jacquerie	larcenist	mainsheet	marketing	pacemaker	paramatta
hamstring	jactation	larcenous	majordomo	marlstone	pachyderm	paramedic
hamstrung	jailbreak	lardycake	majorette	marmalade	packaging	parameter
handbrake	jambalaya	largeness	majorship	marmoreal	packdrill	paramorph
handcraft	jampacked	larghetto	majuscule	marquetry	packhorse	paramount
handcuffs	janissary	larvicide	makeready	marrowfat	packtrain	paranoiac
handglass	janitress	laryngeal	makeshift	marshalcy	paederast	paranymph
handiness	Jansenism	lassitude	malachite	marshland	pageantry	parapeted

parapodia	radiantly	sagittate	satinbird	tasteless	wapentake	abjection
parasitic	radiately	sailcloth	satinette	tastiness	warblefly	ablatival
parataxis	radiation	sailoring	satinspar	tattiness	warbonnet	ablutions
parathion	radiative	sailorman	satinwood	tattooist	warehouse	abnegator
parbuckle	radically	sailplane	satirical	tautology	warmonger	abnormity
parcelled	radicular	sainthood	saturable	tawniness	warningly	abolisher
parcenary	radiocast	saintlike	saturator	taxidermy	warrantee	abolition
parchment	radiogram	saintling	Saturnian	taximeter	warranter	abominate
paregoric	radiology	saintship	saturnine	taxonomic	warrantor	aborigine
parentage	raffinate	salacious	saturnism	taxpaying	wartcress	abounding
parfleche	raffinose	salangane	sauceboat	vaccinate	washbasin	aboutface
parhelion	raffishly	saleratus	sauceless	vacillant	washboard	aboutturn
parleyvoo	rafflesia	salesgirl	saucerful	vacillate	washcloth	abradable
parlously	raincheck	saleslady	sauciness	vacuolate	washedout	abrogator
parochial	raincloud	salicetum	saunterer	vacuously	washerman	abruption
parotitis	raingauge	salicylic	sauropoda	vademecum	washhouse	abscissae
parquetry	raininess	saliently	Sauternes	vagarious	washiness	abscissas
parrakeet	rainmaker	sallowish	savagedom	vagueness	washstand	absconder
parricide	rainproof	salmonoid	savourily	vainglory	waspishly	abseiling
Parseeism	rainstorm	salpinges	saxifrage	valentine	wassailer	absorbent
parsimony	rainwater	saltation	saxophone	valiantly	wasteland	absorbing
parsonage	rakehelly	saltatory	tablature	validness	wasteness	abstainer
partially	rampantly	saltglaze	tableland	vallation	wastepipe	abstinent
partition	rancidity	saltiness	tableleaf	vallecula	watchable	absurdism
partitive	rancorous	saltmarsh	tabletalk	valuables	watchcase	absurdist
partridge	randiness	saltpetre	tableware	valuation	watchfire	absurdity
pasodoble	randomise	saltspoon	tabularly	valueless	watchword	abundance
passenger	ranginess	saltwater	tabulator	valveless	waterbath	abusively
passerine	ransacker	saltworks	tacamahac	vampirism	waterbuck	abysmally
passersby	rantingly	salubrity	tachylite	vandalise	waterbutt	ebullient
passional	ranunculi	salvation	tachylyte	vandalism	watercart	obbligato
passivate	rapacious	Samaritan	tacitness	vapidness	watercool	obconical
passively	rapidfire	Samoyedic	tackiness	vaporable	waterfall	obcordate
passivity	rapidness	sanatoria	tactfully	vaporific	waterflea	obedience
pastedown	raptorial	sanbenito	tactician	vaporiser	waterfowl	obeisance
pasticcio	rapturous	sandalled	tactility	vapouring	watergate	obeseness
pastiness	rareeshow	sandarach	tactitian	vapourish	waterhole	obfuscate
pastorale	rascaldom	sandblast	tactually	Varangian	waterleaf	objectify
pastorate	rascalism	sandblind	taeniasis	variation	waterless	objection
pasturage	rascality	sandcrack	tahsildar	varicella	waterlily	objective
patchouli	raspatory	sandglass	tailboard	variegate	waterline	objurgate
patchouly	raspberry	sandiness	taillight	variolate	watermark	obligated
patchwork	raspingly	sandpaper	tailoress	variolite	watermill	obliquely
patellate	ratepayer	sandpiper	tailoring	varioloid	waterpipe	obliquity
paternity	rationale	sandspout	tailpiece	variolous	watershed	oblivious
pathogeny	rationing	sandstone	taintless	variously	waterside	obnoxious
pathology	raucously	sandstorm	taioseach	varnisher	waterweed	obscenely
patiently	raunchily	sandtable	talkathon	vasectomy	waterworn	obscenity
patinated	rauwolfia	sandyacht	talkative	vasomotor	wattmeter	obscurant
patriarch	ravelling	sangfroid	tallowish	vassalage	wavefront	obscurely
patrician	ravelment	Sanhedrim	tallyshop	vastitude	waveguide	obscurity
patricide	ravishing	Sanhedrin	Talmudist	vaticinal	wavellite	obsecrate
patrimony	razorback	sanitaria	tambourin	wackiness	wayfaring	obsequent
patriotic	razorbill	santolina	tamponade	waggishly	waywardly	obsequial
patristic	razoredge	santonica	tangerine	waggonage	wayzgoose	obsequies
patrolled	razorfish	sapanwood	tanliquor	wagonette	Xanthippe	observant
patroller	sabadilla	sapheaded	tanpickle	wagonroof	yachtclub	obsession
patrolman	sabbatise	sapiently	tantalate	wailingly	yachtsman	obsessive
patrology	sabbatism	sapodilla	tantalise	waistband	Yankeedom	obsolesce
patronage	Sabellian	sappiness	tantalite	waistbelt	Yankeeism	obstetric
patroness	saccharin	sapraemia	tapdancer	waistcoat	yardstick	obstinacy
patronise	sacciform	sapraemic	tarantara	waistline	yawningly	obstinate
paulownia	sacculate	Saracenic	tarantass	wakefully	zamindary	obtention
pauperise	sackcloth	sarcastic	tarantism	wakerobin	zapateado	obtrusion
pauperism	sacrament	sarcocarp	tarantula	Waldenses	abandoned	obtrusive
Pavlovian	sacrarium	sarcomata	taraxacum	waldgrave	abandonee	obturator
paymaster	sacrifice	Sardinian	tardiness	walkabout	abandoner	obversely
paypacket	sacrilege	sargassos	Targumist	wallboard	abasement	obversion
rabbinate	sacristan	Sarmation	tarpaulin	wallcress	abashment	obviation
rabbinism	saddlebag	sartorial	tarragona	wallfruit	abatement	obviously
rabbinist	saddlebow	sartorius	Tartarean	walloping	abdicable	academism
rabidness	Sadducean	sasquatch	Tartarian	wallpaper	abdicator	acariasis
racehorse	safeguard	sassafras	tartishly	wallplate	abdominal	accentual
racetrack	safetypin	Sassanian	Tartufian	wallydrag	abduction	acceptant
racialism	safflower	Sassenach	Tartufism	Walpurgis	aberrance	acceptive
racialist	safranine	satanical	taskforce	wandering	aberrancy	accessary
racketeer	sagacious	satellite	Tasmanian		abhorrent	accession
raconteur	sagebrush	satiation	tasselled		abhorring	accessory
radialply	sagegreen				abidingly	accidence

```
accipiter  occupancy  scombroid  admission  beachhead  celebrate  declarant
acclaimer  occurrent  scorbutic  admissive  beachwear  celebrity  declinate
acclimate  occurring  scorching  admitting  beadledom  celestial  declivity
acclivity  ocellated  scorebook  admixture  beamingly  cellarage  declivous
accompany  ochlocrat  scorecard  admonitor  beanfeast  celluloid  decoction
accordant  octachord  scoredraw  adnominal  beanstalk  cellulose  decollate
according  octagonal  scorifier  adoptable  bearberry  Celticism  decollete
accordion  octahedra  scorpioid  adoration  beardless  cementite  decomplex
accretion  octameter  Scotchman  adoringly  beastings  censorial  decompose
accretive  octastyle  Scoticise  adornment  beatitude  centenary  decongest
accusable  octennial  scotomata  adrenalin  beauteous  centering  decontrol
acellular  octillion  scoundrel  adsorbate  beautiful  centigram  decorator
acescence  Octobrist  scraggily  adsorbent  beccafico  centipede  decrement
acetabula  octopodes  scrambler  adulation  bedfellow  centrally  decretive
acetamide  octostyle  scramming  adulatory  bedjacket  centreing  decretory
acetifier  scagliola  scrapbook  adulterer  bedlamite  centurion  decumbent
acetylate  scaldfish  scrapheap  adulthood  bedraggle  cephalous  decussate
acetylcoA  scalefern  scrapiron  adultness  bedridden  cerastium  dedicator
acetylene  scalefish  scrappily  adumbrate  bedsetter  ceratodus  deducible
Acheulean  scaleleaf  scrapping  advantage  bedsitter  cerebella  deduction
Acheulian  scaleless  scrapyard  advection  bedspread  cerebrate  deductive
aciculate  scalelike  scratcher  advective  bedspring  cerecloth  deerberry
acidifier  scalemoss  scratches  Adventism  beechfern  cerograph  deerhound
acidophil  scaliness  screecher  Adventist  beechmast  certainly  defalcate
acidulate  scallawag  screening  adventive  beefeater  certainty  defaulter
acidulent  scallywag  screwball  adventure  beefiness  certified  defeatism
acidulous  scalplock  screwbolt  adverbial  beefsteak  certifier  defeatist
aciniform  scantling  screwpile  adversary  beekeeper  certitude  defeature
aconitine  scantness  screwpine  adversely  beemaster  cerussite  defection
acoustics  scapegoat  screwworm  adversity  beeorchis  cessation  defective
acquiesce  scapolite  scribbler  advertent  beestings  cetaceous  defendant
acquittal  scapulary  scrimmage  advertise  befitting  deacidify  defensive
acquitted  scarecrow  scrimpily  advisable  befogging  deaconess  deference
acrobatic  scarehead  scrimshaw  advisably  begetting  deadalive  deferment
acropetal  scarfring  scripture  advisedly  beginning  deadlight  deferring
acropolis  scarfskin  scrivener  advocator  behaviour  deathblow  defiantly
acroteria  scarfwise  scrollsaw  edelweiss  bejabbers  deathless  deficient
actinozoa  scarifier  scrounger  edibility  belatedly  deathlike  definable
activator  scatology  scrubbing  editorial  beleaguer  deathmask  definably
actualise  scatterer  scruffily  education  belemnite  deathroll  deflation
actuality  scavenger  scrumhalf  educative  bellglass  debagging  deflector
actuarial  scenarist  scrummage  Edwardian  bellicose  debarment  deflexion
actuation  scenedock  scrutable  idealiser  bellpunch  debarring  defoliant
acuminate  scentless  scrutator  idealless  bellyache  debatable  defoliate
eccentric  sceptical  sculpture  identical  bellyband  debauched  deformity
ecclesial  scheelite  scuncheon  identikit  bellyflop  debauchee  defroster
ecdysiast  schematic  scutcheon  ideograph  belvedere  debaucher  dehiscent
echolalia  schilling  scutellar  ideologic  bemusedly  debenture  dehydrate
echovirus  schistose  scutellum  ideologue  beneficed  debugging  deinosaur
eclampsia  schistous  scutiform  idiograph  bengaline  debutante  deistical
eclamptic  schlemiel  adamantly  idiomatic  benighted  decadence  dejection
ecologist  schlemihl  adaptable  idiopathy  benignant  decadency  delftware
economics  schlieren  addiction  idioplasm  benignity  decagonal  delicious
economise  schmaltzy  addictive  odalisque  bentonite  decalcify  delineate
economist  schnauzer  addressee  oddfellow  benzidine  decalitre  delirious
ecosphere  schnitzel  addresser  oddjobber  benzoline  decalogue  deliverer
ecossaise  schnorkel  addressor  oddjobman  berberine  decametre  deludable
ecosystem  schnorrer  adducible  odontalgy  bergamask  decapodal  demagogic
ecritoire  scholarly  adduction  odorously  berkelium  decapodan  demagogue
ecstasise  scholiast  adductive  odourless  berserker  decastere  demandant
ectoblast  schoolbag  ademption  aepyornis  beryllium  decathlon  demanding
ectogenic  schoolboy  adenoidal  aerialist  besetment  deceitful  demarcate
ectomorph  schooling  adenomata  aeriality  besetting  decennary  demeanour
ectophyte  schoolman  adenosine  aerobatic  beslobber  decennial  demimonde
ectoplasm  sciaenoid  adeptness  aerobiont  besotting  decennium  demission
ecumenism  sciagraph  adherence  aerodrome  bespangle  deception  demitasse
Icelander  sciamachy  adiabatic  aerograph  bespatter  deceptive  demitting
Icelandic  sciascopy  adipocere  aerolitic  bestially  decidable  demiurgic
iceskater  sciential  adiposity  aerometer  bestirred  decidedly  demobbing
ichneumon  scientism  adjacency  aerometry  bethought  deciduate  democracy
ichnology  scientist  adjoining  aerophyte  betrothal  deciduous  demulcent
ichthyoid  scintilla  adjunctly  aeroplane  betrothed  decilitre  demurrage
iconology  scleritis  adjutancy  aerospace  bevelling  decillion  demurring
occipital  sclerosis  adlibbing  aesthesia  ceanothus  decimally  demystify
occludent  sclerotic  admeasure  aesthesis  ceasefire  decimator  dendritic
occlusion  scolecite  adminicle  aesthetic  ceaseless  decimetre  denigrate
occlusive  scoliosis  admirable  aestivate  cedarwood  decistere  denitrate
occultism  scoliotic  admirably  aetiology  celandine  deckhouse  denitrify
occultist             admiralty             celebrant  declaimer  denouncer
```

denseness	devitrify	geomantic	helpfully	leftwards	meltwater	nebuliser
dentalium	devotedly	geometric	Helvetian	legendary	mementoes	necessary
dentation	dewlapped	geometrid	hemicycle	legerline	memoirist	necessity
dentiform	dexterity	geoponics	hemistich	legginess	memorable	neckcloth
dentistry	dexterous	georgette	hemitrope	legionary	memorably	neckverse
dentition	dextrally	geosphere	hemstitch	legislate	memoranda	necrology
denyingly	dextrorse	geostatic	hendiadys	Leicester	memoriter	necrophil
deodorant	fearfully	geotropic	hepatitis	leisurely	menadione	necrotise
deodorise	feathered	gerfalcon	heptaglot	leitmotif	menagerie	nectarean
deoxidise	febricity	geriatric	heptarchy	leitmotiv	mendacity	nectarial
departure	febrifuge	germander	Heraclean	lendlease	Mendelian	nectarine
depasture	feculence	germanely	herbalist	lengthily	Mendelism	nectarous
dependant	fecundate	germanise	herbarium	leniently	mendicant	needfully
dependent	fecundity	Germanish	herbicide	lentiform	mendicity	neediness
depiction	federally	Germanism	herbivore	leptosome	meningeal	needleful
depictive	feedstock	Germanist	herborise	lethality	Mennonite	nefarious
depletion	feedstuff	germanium	Herculean	lethargic	menopause	negligent
depletive	feelingly	germicide	Hercynian	letterbox	Menshevik	negotiant
deposable	feiseanna	germinate	hereabout	lettering	menstrual	negotiate
depositor	felicific	germplasm	hereafter	leucaemia	menstruum	negritude
depravity	fellowman	germproof	heretical	leucocyte	mentalism	negroidal
deprecate	felonious	gerundial	hereunder	leucotome	mentalist	Negroness
depredate	femineity	gerundive	heritable	leucotomy	mentality	negrophil
depressed	fenceless	gestalten	hermitage	leukaemia	mentation	neighbour
depressor	fenestrae	gestation	herniated	leukaemic	mepacrine	nemertean
depthbomb	fenestral	gestatory	herpetoid	leukocyte	mercaptan	nemertine
depthless	Fenianism	getatable	hesitance	Levantine	mercenary	nemophila
depurator	fenugreek	geyserite	hesitancy	levelling	mercerise	neodymium
derivable	feoffment	headboard	hesitator	levelness	merciless	neolithic
dermatoid	ferocious	headcloth	Hesperian	leviathan	mercurial	neologian
derringdo	ferrotype	headdress	hessonite	leviratic	mercurous	neologise
derringer	ferryboat	headfirst	hetaerism	levitator	merganser	neologism
descended	fertilely	headiness	hetairism	Levitical	meropidan	neologist
describer	fertilise	headlight	heterodox	lexically	merriment	neoteinia
desecrate	fertility	headliner	heteronym	mealiness	merriness	neoteinic
desertion	fervently	headphone	heterosis	meandrine	mescaline	neoterise
desiccant	festinate	headpiece	heuristic	meandrous	mesentery	neoterism
desiccate	festively	headscarf	hexachord	meaningly	mesmerise	neoterist
designate	festivity	headstall	hexagonal	meanwhile	mesmerism	nepenthes
designing	festology	headstock	hexameter	meatiness	mesmerist	nephalism
desirable	fetichism	headstone	hexaploid	mechanics	mesoblast	nephalist
desirably	fetichist	headwater	hexastich	mechanise	mesogloea	nepheline
desolater	fetidness	healthful	hexastyle	mechanism	mesomorph	nephelite
desolator	fetishism	healthily	Hexateuch	mechanist	mesophyll	nephology
desperado	fetishist	heartache	jealously	medallion	mesophyte	nephritic
desperate	feudalise	heartbeat	jeeringly	medallist	messenger	nephritis
despoiler	feudalism	heartburn	jellyfish	mediaeval	messianic	nephrosis
despotism	feudalist	heartfelt	jerkiness	mediately	messieurs	Neptunian
destitute	feudality	heartfree	jessamine	mediation	messiness	neptunium
destroyer	feudatory	hearthrug	jesuitise	mediatise	metabolic	nervation
desuetude	gearlever	heartland	jesuitism	mediative	metalline	nervature
desultory	gearshift	heartless	jetsetter	mediatory	metalling	nerveless
detection	gearwheel	heartsick	jetstream	mediatrix	metallise	nerviness
detective	gelignite	heartsore	jewellery	medicable	metalloid	nervously
detention	gemmation	heartwood	jewelweed	medically	metalwork	nescience
detergent	gemmology	heathcock	keelivine	medicinal	metameric	Nestorian
determent	gemutlich	heathenry	kennelled	meditator	metaphase	netveined
determine	genealogy	heaviness	kentledge	medullary	metaplasm	netwinged
deterrent	generable	heavyduty	Keplerian	medullate	meteorist	neuralgia
deterring	generalia	Hebridean	keratitis	megacycle	meteorite	neuralgic
detersion	generally	hectogram	keratosis	megadeath	meteoroid	neuration
detersive	generator	hedgingly	kerbstone	megahertz	methadone	neuroglia
dethroner	genetical	heedfully	kerfuffle	megaphone	metheglin	neurology
detonator	genialise	heelpiece	Keynesian	megaspore	methodise	neuromata
detractor	geniality	heftiness	leafgreen	mekometer	Methodism	neuropath
detriment	genitival	hegemonic	leafmould	melanosis	Methodist	neutrally
detrition	genocidal	heinously	leafstalk	melanotic	methought	nevermore
detrusion	genotypic	helically	leakiness	melaphyre	methylate	newlyweds
deuterate	genteelly	heliogram	learnable	melatonin	methylene	newmarket
deuterium	gentility	heliostat	learnedly	meliorate	metonymic	newsagent
devaluate	gentleman	heliotype	leasehold	meliorism	metricate	newsflash
devastate	genuflect	heliozoan	leaselend	meliorist	metrician	newshound
developer	genuinely	heliozoic	leastways	meliority	metricise	newsiness
deviation	geobotany	hellebore	leastwise	melismata	metricist	newspaper
devilfish	geodesist	hellenise	leavening	melocoton	metrology	newsprint
devilling	geography	Hellenism	lecherous	melodious	metronome	newsstand
devilment	geologise	Hellenist	leeringly	melodrama	mezzanine	Newtonian
deviously	geologist	hellhound	leewardly	melomania	mezzotint	oecologic
devisable	geomancer	hellishly	leftovers	meltingly	neathouse	oecumenic

oenomancy	perfumier	rebelling	referring	reposeful	retrodden	selfglory
oenophile	perfusion	rebellion	refitment	repossess	retroflex	selfimage
oenophily	perfusive	rebidding	refitting	repotting	retroject	selfishly
oesophagi	pergunnah	rebukable	reflation	reprehend	retrousse	selfmoved
oestrogen	periclase	rebutting	reflector	represent	retrovert	selfpride
peaceable	pericycle	recalesce	reflexion	repressor	revelator	selftrust
peaceably	peridotic	recapping	reflexive	reprieval	revelling	Seljukian
peacetime	perihelia	recapture	refluence	reprimand	reverence	semanteme
peachblow	perilling	recension	reformism	reprobate	reversely	semantics
pearlitic	perilymph	reception	reformist	reprocess	reversion	semaphore
pearlwort	perimeter	receptive	refractor	reproduce	revetment	semblable
peasantry	perimorph	recession	refreshen	reptilian	revetting	semblably
peasouper	perinatal	recessive	refresher	republish	revictual	semblance
peccantly	periodate	rechauffe	refuelled	repudiate	revisable	semeiotic
pectinate	peripatus	recherche	refulgent	repugnant	revivable	semestral
peculator	periphery	recipient	refurbish	repulsion	revocable	semibreve
pecuniary	periplast	reckoning	refurnish	repulsive	revolting	semicolon
pedagogic	periscope	reclinate	refusable	reputable	revulsion	semifinal
pedagogue	perishing	reclusion	refutable	reputably	revulsive	semifluid
pedalling	perisperm	reclusive	regardant	reputedly	rewarding	semilunar
pederasty	peristome	recognise	regardful	requester	rewritten	semimetal
pedicular	peristyle	recoinage	regicidal	requisite	seaanchor	seminally
pedigreed	perkiness	recollect	regisseur	rerebrace	seachange	semiology
pedometer	permanent	recombine	registrar	rerelease	seafaring	semiotics
peepsight	permeable	recommend	regretful	reremouse	seagirdle	semiplume
peevishly	permeance	recompose	regretted	rerunning	sealetter	semirigid
pegmatite	permitted	reconcile	regularly	resalable	seaminess	semisolid
Pekingese	permitter	recondite	regulator	resection	seanettle	semisweet
Pelasgian	permutate	reconfirm	rehearsal	resentful	searching	semitonic
pellagrin	perpetual	reconvene	rehydrate	reserpine	searingly	semivowel
pelletise	persecute	reconvert	Reichstag	reservist	seasoning	senescent
pellitory	persevere	recording	reimburse	reservoir	seasquirt	seneschal
pemphigus	persimmon	recordist	reinforce	resetting	seastrand	senhorita
pencilled	personage	recoverer	reinstate	reshuffle	seatangle	seniority
penciller	personate	recreancy	reiterate	residence	seaurchin	sensation
pendently	personify	recruital	rejection	residency	seaworthy	sensedata
pendragon	personnel	recruiter	rejoicing	residuary	sebaceous	senseless
pendulate	persuader	rectangle	rejoinder	resilient	secateurs	sensitise
penduline	pertinent	rectifier	relevance	resistant	secernent	sensitive
pendulous	pertussis	rectitude	relevancy	resistive	secession	sensorial
peneplain	pervasion	rectorate	reliantly	resitting	seclusion	sensorium
peneplane	pervasive	rectorial	religiose	resoluble	seclusive	sensually
penetrant	perverter	rectrices	religious	resolvent	secondary	sentenate
penetrate	pessimism	recumbent	reliquary	resonance	secretage	sentience
penfriend	pessimist	recurrent	reliquiae	resonator	secretary	sentiency
penholder	pesthouse	recurring	reluctant	resorbent	secretion	sentiment
peninsula	pesticide	recursion	reluctate	resources	secretive	sentrybox
penitence	pestilent	recursive	remainder	respecter	secretory	separable
penniless	pestology	recusance	remanence	responder	sectarian	separably
pennywort	petaurist	recusancy	remeasure	restfully	sectility	separates
penpusher	petechiae	redaction	remediate	restiform	sectional	separator
pensioner	petechial	redbreast	remindful	restitute	sectorial	Sephardic
pensively	petersham	redevelop	reminisce	restively	secularly	Sephardim
pentagram	pethidine	redhanded	remission	restraint	securable	sepiolite
pentangle	petiolate	redheaded	remitment	resultant	sedentary	septation
pentarchy	petiolule	redingote	remittent	resultful	sedgewren	September
Pentecost	petroleum	redivivus	remitting	resumable	seditious	septemvir
penthouse	petrology	redletter	remontant	resurface	seduction	septenary
penultima	petticoat	redolence	removable	resurgent	seductive	septennia
penumbral	pettiness	redoubted	renascent	resurrect	seedeater	septicity
penurious	pettishly	redresser	rencontre	retaliate	seediness	septuplet
pepperbox	pettitoes	reducible	rendition	retardant	seedpearl	sepulcher
pepperpot	petulance	reductant	renewable	retention	seedplant	sepulchre
peptonise	petulancy	reduction	renitency	retentive	seemingly	sepulture
percaline	reachable	reductive	renouncer	rethought	segmental	sequacity
perceiver	reactance	redundant	renovator	retiarius	segregate	sequestra
perchance	readdress	reediness	reparable	reticence	seigneury	sequester
percheron	readiness	reedorgan	repayable	reticency	seigniory	sequinned
percolate	readymade	reeducate	repayment	reticular	selachian	serenader
perdition	realistic	reefpoint	repechage	reticulum	selection	sergeancy
peregrine	reanimate	reenforce	repellant	retinitis	selective	serialise
perennate	rearguard	reentrant	repellent	retinulae	selectman	serialism
perennial	rearhorse	reexamine	repelling	retinular	selenious	serialist
perfectly	rearlight	refashion	repentant	retortion	selenitic	seriality
perfector	rearmouse	refection	repertory	retoucher	selfabuse	seriately
perfervid	rearrange	refectory	replenish	retractor	selfaware	sericeous
perforate	rearwards	referable	repletion	retrieval	selfdoubt	serigraph
performer	reasoning	reference	replicate	retriever	selfdrive	serinette
perfumery	rebaptise	referenda	reportage	retrocede	selffaced	seriously

serjeancy	tenseness	verdigris	affective	chachacha	childlike	phoniness
serjeanty	tensility	veridical	affianced	chaetopod	chillness	phonogram
sermonise	tensional	veritable	affidavit	chafferer	chimaeric	phonolite
serotonin	tentacled	veritably	affiliate	chaffinch	Chinatown	phonology
serpentry	tentation	vermicide	affirmant	chaingang	chinaware	phosphate
serranoid	tentative	vermicule	affixture	chaingear	chinstrap	phosphene
serration	tenthrate	vermiform	afflation	chainless	chipboard	phosphide
serrefile	tentmaker	vermifuge	affluence	chainmail	chipolata	phosphine
serrulate	tenuously	vermilion	affricate	chairlady	chiropody	phosphite
serviette	tepidness	verminate	aflatoxin	challenge	chiselled	photocell
servilely	teratogen	verminous	aforesaid	chameleon	chiseller	photocopy
servility	terebinth	vernalise	Afrikaans	chamomile	chisquare	photogene
servitude	terebrant	vernation	Afrikaner	champagne	chitinous	photophil
sessional	termagant	verrucose	aftercare	champaign	chitlings	photopsia
sestertia	terminate	verrucous	afterclap	champerty	chivalric	phototype
setaceous	terminism	versatile	afterglow	champleve	chlamydes	phrenetic
setsquare	terminist	versifier	afterlife	chanceful	chlorella	phthalein
sevenfold	termitary	versiform	aftermath	chancroid	chloritic	phycology
seventeen	ternately	versional	aftermost	chancrous	chlorosis	phyllopod
seventhly	terramara	vertebrae	afternoon	chandlery	chlorotic	phylogeny
seventies	terramare	vertebral	aftertime	changeful	chockfull	physician
severable	terrarium	vesicular	afterward	chanteuse	chocolate	physicist
severally	territory	vestibule	effective	chantilly	chokedamp	physicked
severalty	terrorise	vestigial	effectual	chantress	choleraic	phytogeny
severance	terrorism	vestigium	efficient	chaparral	chondrite	phytology
sexennial	terrorist	vestiture	effluence	chaperone	chondrule	phytotomy
sexlessly	terseness	vestryman	effluvial	chapleted	chophouse	phytotron
sexlinked	tervalent	vetchling	effluvium	charabanc	choplogic	rhapsodic
sextuplet	tessitura	vexatious	effluxion	character	chopstick	rheumatic
sexualise	testament	vexillary	effortful	chariness	chorister	Rhineodon
sexuality	testation	weakkneed	effulgent	charivari	chorology	rhinology
teachable	testatrix	wealthily	offcentre	charlatan	Christian	rhizocarp
teachably	testdrive	weariless	offchance	charlotte	Christmas	rhizoidal
teacupful	testifier	weariness	offcolour	charmeuse	chromatic	rhodamine
teakettle	testimony	wearisome	offensive	charmless	chromatin	rhodolite
tearfully	testiness	weathered	offertory	Charolais	chronical	rhodonite
teasingly	tetradite	weatherly	offhanded	chartered	chronicle	rhodopsin
technical	tetragram	webfooted	officiant	charterer	chrysalid	rhonchial
technique	tetralogy	wedgewise	officiate	charwoman	chrysalis	rhymester
tectonics	tetrapody	Wednesday	officinal	chassepot	chthonian	rhythmics
tectorial	tetrarchy	weediness	officious	chastener	churching	rhythmise
tectrices	teutonism	weeknight	offscreen	chastiser	churchman	rhythmist
tediously	Teutonise	weevilled	offseason	chatelain	dharmsala	shadberry
tegmental	Teutonist	wehrmacht	offspring	chatoyant	ghostlike	shadeless
tegmentum	textually	weighable	offstreet	chatterer	ghostword	shadetree
tegularly	vectorial	weighbeam	sforzando	chauffeur	khedivial	shadiness
teknonymy	Vedantist	weightily	agapemone	cheapjack	phagedena	shakeable
telamones	veeringly	weighting	aggravate	cheapness	phagocyte	shakedown
telegenic	vegetable	weirdness	aggregate	checkered	phalanger	shakerism
telegraph	vegetably	welcoming	aggressor	checklist	phalanges	shakiness
telemeter	vehemence	welfarism	aggrieved	checkmate	phalanxes	shallowly
telemetry	vehicular	wellbeing	agistment	checkrein	phalarope	shamanism
teleology	veinstone	wellfound	agitation	cheekbone	phantasma	shamanist
telepathy	velodrome	wellknown	agitative	cheerless	pharaonic	shamateur
telephone	velveteen	welltimed	agnatical	chelation	pharisaic	shambling
telephony	vendition	werwolves	agonising	chelicera	pharyngal	shambolic
telephoto	veneering	westbound	agonistic	chelonian	pharynges	shamefast
telescope	venerable	westering	agreeable	chemistry	pharynxes	shameless
telescopy	venerably	westerner	agreeably	chemitype	phellogen	Shangrila
televisor	venerator	westwards	agreement	chemurgic	phenacite	shantyman
tellingly	venereous	xenograft	agriology	cheongsam	phenakite	shapeable
tellurate	vengeance	xenophile	agrologic	chequered	phenology	shapeless
tellurian	veniality	xenophobe	agronomic	cherimoya	phenomena	sharecrop
telluride	ventiduct	xeromorph	eggbeater	chernozem	phenotype	sharkskin
tellurite	ventifact	xerophile	eglantine	cherrypie	pheromone	sharpener
tellurium	ventilate	xerophily	egomaniac	chevalier	philander	sharpeyed
tellurous	ventrally	xerophyte	egotistic	chevelure	philately	sharpness
telophase	ventricle	yearround	egregious	chibouque	philippic	sharpshod
temperate	venturous	yellowdog	egression	chicanery	philogyny	shaveling
temporary	veracious	yellowish	ignescent	chickadee	philology	shearling
temporise	verandaed	yesterday	ignitable	chickaree	Philomela	sheatfish
temptable	veratrine	zealously	ignitible	chickling	phlebitis	sheathing
temptress	verbalise	zebrawood	ignorable	chickweed	phonation	Shechinah
tenacious	verbalism	zeitgeist	ignoramus	chiefship	phonatory	sheepcote
tenaculum	verbalist	zemindary	ignorance	chieftain	phonemics	sheepfold
tenderise	verbicide	zestfully	iguanodon	chihuahua	phonetics	sheephook
tendinous	verbosely	zeugmatic	sgraffiti	chilblain	phonetise	sheeplice
tenebrist	verbosity	affecting	sgraffito	childhood	phonetism	sheepskin
tenebrous	verdantly	affection	ahistoric	childless	phonetist	sheeptick

sheepwalk	theandric	whalehead	billionth	diaphysis	disaffirm	disturbed
sheepwash	theatrics	wheatmeal	billycock	diarrhoea	disannual	disturber
sheerhulk	theocracy	wheedling	billygoat	diastasis	disappear	dithyramb
sheerlegs	theocrasy	wheelbase	bimonthly	diastatic	disarming	dittander
sheerness	theogonic	wheelless	binocular	diastolic	disavouch	dittology
sheetbend	theologic	wheelwork	binominal	diathermy	disavowal	diurnally
sheikhdom	theologue	wherefore	binturong	diathesis	disbarred	divergent
sheldduck	theomachy	wherefrom	biogenous	diathetic	disbelief	diversely
sheldrake	theomania	whereinto	biography	diatomite	disbranch	diversify
shelflife	theophany	whereunto	biologist	diatropic	disbudded	diversion
shelfmark	theoretic	whereupon	biometric	dichasial	disburden	diversity
shelfroom	theoriser	wherewith	bionomics	dichasium	disbursal	diverting
shellback	theosophy	wherryman	biorhythm	dichogamy	discalced	dividable
shellbark	therapist	whetstone	biosphere	dichotomy	discarder	divisible
shellfire	Theravada	wheyfaced	bipartite	dichroism	discerner	divulsion
shellfish	therefore	whichever	bipinnate	dichromat	discharge	dixieland
shellheap	therefrom	whimperer	birchbark	dichromic	discoidal	dizygotic
shellwork	thereinto	whimsical	birdbrain	dickybird	discolour	dizziness
shemozzle	thereunto	whinstone	birdsfoot	diclinous	discomfit	eiderdown
shewbread	thereupon	whipperin	birdsnest	dicrotism	discommon	eiderduck
shieldbug	therewith	whipround	birdtable	dictation	discourse	eidograph
shieldfem	thermally	whipsnake	birdwatch	didactics	discovert	eightfold
shiftless	thermidor	whipstock	birthmark	didelphic	discovery	eightieth
shillelah	thesaurus	whirligig	birthrate	didrachma	discredit	eightsome
shinguard	theurgist	whirlpool	birthwort	dieselise	disembark	eightyish
shininess	thickener	whirlwind	bisection	diesinker	disembody	eirenicon
Shintoism	thicketed	whiskered	bishopric	dietetics	disengage	fibreless
Shintoist	thickknee	whisperer	bismillah	dietician	disentail	fibriform
shipboard	thickknee	whistling	bitterish	dietitian	disentomb	fibrillar
shipcanal	thickness	whitebait	bivalence	different	disesteem	fibrinoid
shipfever	thighbone	whitebass	bivalency	difficile	disfavour	fibrinous
shipmoney	thighboot	whitebeam	bivariant	difficult	disfigure	fibroline
shipowner	thingness	whiteface	bivariate	diffident	disforest	fibromata
shipshape	thingummy	whitefish	bizarrely	diffusely	disgracer	fictional
shipwreck	thinkable	Whitehall	cicatrice	diffusion	dishcloth	fideistic
shirtless	thinktank	whitehead	cicatrise	diffusive	dishclout	fiduciary
shirttail	thirdhand	whiteness	cigarette	digastric	dishfaced	fieldbook
shockable	thirdrate	whitening	cigarillo	digestion	dishonest	fieldboot
shockhead	thirdsman	whitewash	Cimmerian	digestive	dishonour	fieldfare
shoeblack	thirstily	whitewing	cinematic	digitalin	dishwater	fieldsman
shoemaker	thirtieth	whitewood	cineraria	digitalis	disinfect	fieldwork
shoeshine	thitherto	whizzbang	cinereous	digitally	disinfest	fiendlike
shogunate	Thomistic	whodunnit	Cingalese	digitated	dislocate	fieriness
shootable	thornback	wholemeal	cipollino	dignified	dismantle	fifteenth
shopfloor	thornbill	wholeness	circadian	dignitary	dismember	figurante
shopfront	thornbush	wholesale	circinate	dilatable	dismissal	filaceous
shoreless	thornless	wholesome	circuitry	dilatancy	disoblige	filiation
shoreline	thorntree	whosoever	circulate	diligence	disorient	filigreed
shoreside	thoughted	ailanthus	cirrhosis	dimension	disparage	fillister
shoreward	thralldom	aimlessly	cirripede	dimidiate	disparate	filminess
shoreweed	thrashing	aircooled	cisalpine	dimissory	disparity	filmstrip
shortcake	threefold	airjacket	citizenly	dimorphic	dispelled	filoselle
shortener	threesome	airminded	citizenry	dimwitted	dispenser	filterbed
shortfall	threnodic	airstream	citystate	dinginess	dispeople	filtertip
shorthand	threshold	airworthy	civically	diningcar	dispersal	filtrable
shorthorn	thriftily	airyfairy	civiliser	dinnerset	disperser	fimbriate
shortness	thrilling	aitchbone	diablerie	dinoceras	displease	financial
shortstop	throatily	biblicism	diabolise	dinothere	disposure	financier
shortterm	throbbing	biblicist	diabolism	dioecious	dispraise	finedrawn
shortwave	thrombose	bicameral	diabolist	Dionysiac	disputant	fingering
shotproof	throttler	bicipital	diachrony	Dionysian	disregard	fingertip
shottower	throughly	biconcave	diachylon	dipcircle	disrelish	finically
shouldest	throwaway	bicyclist	diachylum	dipeptide	disrepair	finicking
shovelful	throwback	bifarious	diaconate	diphthong	disrepute	fioritura
shovelhat	throwster	bifoliate	diacritic	diplomacy	dissector	fioriture
shovelled	thrumming	bifurcate	diactinic	diplomate	disseisin	firealarm
shoveller	thumbhole	bigeneric	diaereses	dipswitch	dissemble	fireblast
showiness	thumbmark	bigheaded	diaeresis	dipterous	dissenter	firebrand
showpiece	thumbnail	bilabiate	diagnoses	direction	dissident	firebreak
showplace	thumbtack	bilateral	diagnosis	directive	dissipate	firebrick
shredding	thunderer	bilgekeel	dialectal	directory	dissocial	firecrest
shrewmice	Thyestean	bilharzia	dialectic	directrix	dissolute	firedrake
shrinkage	thylacine	bilingual	dialogise	direfully	dissonant	firedrill
shrubbery	thyratron	biliously	dialogism	dirigible	dissuader	fireeater
shrugging	thyristor	bilirubin	dialogist	dirigisme	distantly	fireguard
thalassic	thyroxine	biliteral	diametral	dirtiness	distemper	firehouse
thaneship	whaleback	billabong	diametric	dirttrack	distilled	fireirons
thankless	whaleboat	billboard	diandrous	disaccord	distiller	firelight
thatching	whalebone	billiards	diaphragm	disaffect	distraint	fireplace

```
firepower  historian  lineament  milkshake  nicotiana  pitchfork  signorial
fireproof  hitchhike  linearise  milktooth  nicotinic  pitchpipe  signorina
firestone  Hitlerism  linearity  millboard  nictation  piteously  siliceous
firewater  Hitlerite  lineation  millenary  nictitate  pithecoid  silicious
fireworks  jitterbug  linenfold  millennia  niggardly  pithiness  silicosis
firmament  kibbutzim  lineolate  millepede  nightbird  pitifully  silicotic
firstborn  kickstart  lingering  millepore  nightclub  pituitary  siliquose
firstfoot  kiddingly  lingually  millerite  nightfall  pityingly  silkgland
firsthand  kidnapped  lingulate  milligram  nightgown  pivotable  silkiness
firstling  kidnapper  lintelled  millinery  nighthawk  pivotally  silliness
firstrate  kilderkin  lintwhite  millionth  nightlife  pixilated  siltation
fisherman  killifish  lioncelle  millipede  nightline  pizzicati  siltstone
fishiness  kilocycle  lionheart  millivolt  nightlong  pizzicato  silverfir
fishplate  kilohertz  lipreader  millstone  nightmare  Ribbonism  similarly
fishslice  kilolitre  liquation  millwheel  nightside  ribosomal  simpatico
fishyback  kilometre  liquefier  milometer  nighttime  ricepaper  simpleton
fissility  kinematic  liquidate  Miltonian  nightwork  riderless  simplices
fissipede  kingcraft  liquidise  mimicking  nigricant  ridgepole  simulacra
fistulous  kingdomed  liquidity  minacious  nigritude  ridgetile  simulacre
fittingly  kingmaker  liquorice  mincemeat  nigrosine  ridiculer  simulator
fivepence  kingsized  liquorish  mincingly  Nilometer  riflebird  simulcast
fivepenny  kinkiness  lispingly  mindfully  ninepence  rightable  sincerely
fixedness  kinswoman  lissomely  minefield  ninepenny  righteous  sincerity
giantlike  kitchener  Listerism  minelayer  ninetieth  righthand  sinewless
gibberish  kittenish  literally  miniature  Nipponese  rightness  singalong
gibbosity  kittiwake  literatim  minimally  nitpicker  rightward  singleton
gibbously  liability  literator  miniskirt  nitratine  rigidness  singspiel
giddiness  libecchio  literatus  minuscule  nitration  rigmarole  Sinhalese
gigahertz  libellant  litheness  minutegun  oilburner  ringfence  sinistral
gigantism  libelling  lithesome  minuteman  oilcolour  ringingly  sinlessly
giltedged  libellist  lithology  mirkiness  oilpaints  ringshake  sinologue
gimmickry  libellous  lithopone  mirthless  pianistic  ringsnake  sinophile
gingerade  liberally  lithotomy  misadvise  pickaback  riotously  sinuately
gingerale  liberated  litigable  misassign  picketing  Ripuarian  sinuation
ginglymus  liberator  litigious  misbecome  picnicked  riskiness  sinuosity
ginpalace  libertine  litterbin  misbehave  picnicker  ritualise  sinuously
girandole  libidinal  litterbug  misbelief  pictogram  ritualism  sinusitis
girlishly  librarian  liturgics  misbeseem  pictorial  ritualist  siphonage
Girondist  libration  liturgist  miscegene  picturise  rivalling  siphuncle
hibernate  libratory  liverwort  miscegine  piecemeal  rivalrous  Sisyphean
Hibernian  librettos  liveryman  mischance  piecerate  rivelling  situation
hiddenite  licensure  livestock  miscreant  piecework  riverbank  sitzkrieg
hidebound  lichenous  lividness  miscreate  pierrette  riverboat  sixfooter
hideously  lickerish  lixiviate  misdemean  pietistic  riverhead  sixteenmo
hierarchy  liegelord  miasmatic  misdirect  piggishly  riverside  sixteenth
hieratica  lifeblood  micaceous  misemploy  piggyback  riverweed  tidegauge
hierodule  lifecycle  micaslate  miserable  piggybank  sibilance  tidewater
hierogram  lifeforce  microbial  miserably  pigheaded  sibilancy  tiedyeing
hierology  lifeguard  microchip  misesteem  pikeperch  sibylline  tigerlily
highchair  lifesaver  microcosm  misfeasor  pikestaff  siccative  tigermoth
highclass  lifesized  microcyte  misgiving  pilferage  sickening  tigerseye
highflier  lifestyle  microfilm  misgovern  pilgarlic  sickishly  tigerwood
highflown  lifetable  microgram  misguided  pillarbox  sickleave  tightener
highflyer  lightfoot  microlite  mishandle  pilotfish  sideboard  tightness
highgrade  lightless  microlith  mishanter  pimpernel  sideburns  tightrope
highgrown  lightness  micrology  misinform  pinchbeck  sidedness  tightwire
highlands  lightning  micromesh  misleared  pinchcock  sideissue  tilestone
highlevel  lightship  micropsia  mismanage  pineapple  sidelight  timbering
highlight  lightsome  micropyle  misoneism  pinkiness  sideritic  timberman
highspeed  lightsout  microsome  misoneist  pinnately  siderosis  timelapse
hightoned  lightwood  microtome  mispickel  pinnipede  sideswipe  timelimit
highwater  lightyear  microtomy  misreckon  pinnulate  sidetable  timeously
hilarious  lignaloes  microtone  misreport  pinstripe  sidetrack  timepiece
hillbilly  ligniform  microwave  misshapen  pintailed  sidewards  timesheet
Himalayan  liltingly  micturate  missioner  pintsized  sidewheel  timetable
Himyarite  lilywhite  middleman  mistigris  pipedream  sightless  timidness
hindbrain  Limburger  midinette  mistiness  pipeorgan  sightseer  timocracy
hindrance  limejuice  midstream  mistletoe  pipestone  sigillary  timpanist
hindsight  limelight  midsummer  mistyeyed  pipsqueak  sigillate  tinderbox
hippocras  limestone  midwicket  Mithraism  piquantly  sigmoidal  tinniness
hircosity  limewater  midwifery  Mithraist  piratical  signalbox  tinopener
hirsutism  limitable  midwinter  mitigable  pirouette  signalise  tinselled
hirundine  limitedly  migration  mitigator  piscatory  signalled  tipsiness
hispidity  limitless  migratory  mitraille  pisciform  signaller  tipstaves
histamine  limnology  milestone  mixedness  pisolitic  signalman  tiredness
histidine  limonitic  militancy  niccolite  pistachio  signatory  tirewoman
histogeny  limousine  milkfever  nickelise  pistoleer  signature  titillate
histogram  limpidity  milkfloat  nickelled  pistolled  signboard  titledeed
histology  lineality  milkiness  nickelous  pitchdark  significs  titlepage
```

titration	vizierial	albatross	blacklist	clerkship	flintlock	illogical
tittivate	wideawake	albescent	blackmail	clientage	flippancy	illomened
tittlebat	widowbird	albinotic	blackness	clientele	floatable	illwisher
tittuping	widowhood	alchemise	blackwash	cliffhang	flocculus	klinostat
tittupped	widthways	alchemist	blaeberry	climactic	floodgate	oleaceous
titularly	widthwise	alcoholic	blameable	climbable	floodmark	olecranal
uintahite	wieldable	aldehydic	blameably	clinician	floodtide	olecranon
Uitlander	willemite	aleatoric	blameless	clinquant	flophouse	oleograph
viability	willingly	Alemannic	blandness	clipboard	floriated	oleoresin
vibracula	willowish	alertness	blankness	clitellum	floridean	olfaction
vibraharp	willpower	algarroba	blaspheme	cloakroom	floridity	olfactive
vibratile	windblown	algebraic	blasphemy	clockwise	floristic	olfactory
vibration	windbound	Algonkian	blasthole	clockwork	floristry	oligaemia
vibrative	windbreak	Algonquin	blastment	cloisonne	floscular	oligarchy
vibratory	windchest	algorithm	blastulae	cloistral	flotation	Oligocene
vibrissae	windhover	alicyclic	blastular	closedown	flouncing	oligopoly
vicariate	windiness	alienable	blatantly	closeness	flowchart	olivenite
vicarious	windowbox	alienator	blazingly	cloudland	flowerage	placation
vicennial	windproof	alignment	bleachery	cloudless	flowerbed	placatory
viceregal	windswept	alinement	bleakness	clubbable	flowering	placeable
vicereine	windwards	aliphatic	bleareyed	clubhouse	flowerpot	placecard
viceroyal	wineberry	aliveness	blessedly	elaborate	flowingly	placekick
vicesimal	wineglass	alkaloses	blindfold	elastomer	flowsheet	placeless
viciously	winepress	alkalosis	blindness	elbowroom	flowstone	placement
victimise	winestone	allantois	blinkered	eldership	fluctuant	placename
Victorian	winevault	allegedly	blockader	electoral	fluctuate	placentae
victorine	wingchair	allegiant	blockhead	electress	fluecured	placental
videlicet	winningly	allegoric	blockship	electrify	fluoresce	placidity
videotape	winsomely	allemande	bloodbath	electrode	fluorosis	plainness
viewpoint	winterise	alleviate	bloodless	electuary	fluorspar	plainsman
vigesimal	wiredrawn	alligator	bloodlust	elegantly	flushness	plainsong
vigilance	wiregauze	allocable	bloodroot	elegiacal	fluxional	plaintiff
vigilante	wirephoto	allograph	bloodshed	elemental	flyfisher	plaintive
vignetter	wisecrack	allomorph	bloodshot	elevation	flyweight	planarian
villagery	wishfully	allopathy	bloodworm	elevenses	glabellae	planation
villanage	wistfully	allophone	bloodwort	eliminate	glabellar	planetary
villenage	witchetty	alloplasm	blotchily	ellipsoid	glacially	planetoid
villiform	witchhunt	allotment	blowtorch	elocution	gladiator	plangency
villosity	witchmeal	allotrope	bluebeard	elongated	gladiolus	planisher
vimineous	withdrawn	allotropy	blueberry	elopement	gladstone	plantable
vinaceous	withering	allotting	blueblack	eloquence	glaireous	plantlike
vindicate	witherite	allowable	bluegrass	elsewhere	glamorise	planuloid
violation	withstand	allowably	bluepoint	elucidate	glamorous	plasmatic
violative	withstood	allowance	blueprint	elusively	glandered	plasmodia
violently	witlessly	allowedly	bluestone	elutriate	glandular	plastered
violinist	witticism	almandine	bluffness	flabellum	glaringly	plasterer
virescent	wittiness	almsgiver	blunderer	flagellum	glassgall	platemark
Virgilian	wittingly	almshouse	bluntness	flageolet	glassware	platinise
virginals	Yiddisher	aloneness	blushless	flagrance	glasswork	platinoid
virginity	zibelline	alongside	blusterer	flagrancy	glasswort	platinous
virgulate	zigzagged	aloofness	claimable	flagstaff	gleefully	platitude
viricidal	zincotype	alpargata	clamantly	flagstick	glengarry	Platonise
virtually	zinkenite	alpenhorn	clamorous	flagstone	glissandi	Platonism
virtuosic	zirconium	alterable	clamshell	flakiness	glissando	Platonist
virtuosos	ejaculate	altercate	clapboard	flambeaus	globefish	plausible
virulence	ejectment	alternant	clarifier	flambeaux	globosity	plausibly
virulency	okeydokey	alternate	clarionet	flameless	glomerate	playfully
viscerate	skedaddle	altimeter	classable	flamingly	glomerule	playgroup
viscidity	skeesicks	altricial	classical	flamingos	glomeruli	playhouse
viscosity	sketchily	aluminate	classless	flammable	gloryhole	plaything
viscounty	sketchmap	aluminise	classlist	flannelly	glossator	pleadable
viscously	skewwhiff	aluminium	classmate	flarepath	glossitis	pleadings
visionary	skiagraph	aluminous	classroom	flaringly	glowingly	pleasance
visionist	skiamachy	alveolate	clathrate	flashback	glucoside	Pleiocene
visitable	skiascopy	blackball	clatterer	flashbulb	glueyness	plenarily
visitress	skijoring	blackbird	claustral	flashcube	glutamate	plenitude
visualise	skilfully	blackbuck	clavation	flashover	glutinous	plenteous
vitellary	skindiver	blackcoat	claviform	flashtube	glyceride	plentiful
vitelline	skinflick	blackcock	cleanness	flatterer	glycerine	plethoric
vitiation	skinflint	blackdamp	cleansing	flatulent	glycoside	pleuritic
vitiosity	skingraft	blackface	clearance	flavorous	glyptodon	plicately
vitriform	skintight	Blackfeet	clearcole	flayflint	illboding	plicature
vitriolic	skirtings	blackfish	cleareyed	fleckless	illegally	ploughboy
Vitruvian	skirtless	blackflag	clearness	fledgling	illegible	ploughman
vivacious	skydiving	Blackfoot	cleavable	fleetness	illegibly	plumbeous
viverrine	skyjacker	blackgame	clemently	fleshings	illgotten	plumbline
vivianite	skyrocket	blackhead	clepsydra	fleshless	illiberal	plumdamas
vividness	Ukrainian	blackjack	clergyman	fleshment	illicitly	plumpness
vizierate	alabaster	blacklead	clergymen	flightily	illjudged	

plumulate	americium	imbricate	smartness	animalist	encourage	incarnate
plumulose	Amerindic	imbroglio	smartweed	animality	encrimson	incaution
plunderer	amianthus	imitation	smatterer	animation	encrinite	incensory
pluralise	amidships	imitative	smileless	animatism	endearing	incentive
pluralism	aminoacid	immanence	smilingly	animistic	endeavour	inception
pluralist	amoebaean	immanency	smokeball	animosity	endlessly	inceptive
plurality	amoralism	immediacy	smokebomb	anklebone	endoblast	incessant
plusfours	amorality	immediate	smokebush	ankylosis	endocrine	incidence
plushness	amorously	immensely	smokejack	ankylotic	endogamic	incipient
plutocrat	amorphism	immensity	smokeless	annectent	endogenic	inclement
plutonian	amorphous	immersion	smoketree	annelidan	endolymph	inclosure
plutonism	amourette	immigrant	smokiness	annotator	endomixis	inclusion
Plutonism	ampersand	immigrate	smoothish	announcer	endomorph	inclusive
Plutonist	amphibian	imminence	smuggling	annoyance	endophagy	incognito
plutonium	amphibole	imminency	umbellate	annuitant	endophyte	incommode
slabsided	amphigory	immixture	umbellule	annularly	endoplasm	incondite
slabstone	amphioxus	immodesty	umberbird	annulated	endoscope	incorrect
slackness	ampleness	immolator	umbilical	annulling	endoscopy	incorrupt
slakeless	amplifier	immorally	umbilicus	annulment	endosperm	increaser
slanderer	amplitude	immovable	umpteenth	anomalous	endospore	increment
slantways	amputator	immovably	anabioses	anomalure	endosteal	incubator
slantwise	amusement	immutable	anabiosis	anonymity	endosteum	inculcate
slaphappy	amusingly	immutably	anabiotic	anonymous	endowment	inculpate
slapstick	amygdalin	impaction	anabolism	anopheles	endurable	incumbent
slateclub	amyloidal	impartial	anabranch	anorectic	endurably	incunable
slategrey	amylopsin	impassion	anacruses	anorthite	endurance	incurable
slaughter	emaciated	impassive	anacrusis	anovulant	energetic	incurably
slaveship	emanation	impastoed	anaerobic	anoxaemia	energiser	incurious
slavishly	emanative	impatiens	analeptic	anschluss	energumen	incurrent
Slavonian	embarrass	impatient	analgesia	antarctic	engarland	incursion
Slavophil	embassage	impeccant	analgesic	antefixal	englutted	incursive
sleekness	embattled	impedance	analogise	antenatal	engraving	incurvate
sleepless	embayment	impelling	analogist	antennary	engrosser	indagator
sleevenut	embedding	impendent	analogous	antennule	enhearten	indecency
slenderly	embedment	impending	anamnesis	anthelion	enigmatic	indecorum
slickness	embellish	imperator	anandrous	anthemion	enjoyable	indelible
sliderule	embezzler	imperfect	anaphoric	anthocyan	enjoyably	indelibly
slightish	embraceor	imperious	anaptyxis	anthology	enjoyment	indemnify
sliminess	embracery	impetrate	anarchism	anthozoan	enlighten	indemnity
slingback	embracive	impetuous	anarchist	anthracic	enrapture	indention
slingshot	embrangle	impiously	anatomise	anthropic	enrolling	indenture
slinkweed	embrasure	impleader	anatomist	anticline	enrolment	Indianise
slipcoach	embrittle	implement	ancestral	anticodon	ensheathe	indicator
slipcover	embrocate	impletion	anchorage	antidotal	entelechy	indiction
slivovitz	embroglio	implicate	anchoress	antigenic	enterable	indigence
slopbasin	embroider	impliedly	anchorite	antiknock	enteritis	indignant
slopewise	embryonal	implosion	anchorman	antimonic	entertain	indignity
slothbear	embryonic	implosive	anchylose	antinodal	enthymeme	indigotin
Slovakian	embryotic	impluvium	anciently	antinomic	entoblast	IndoAryan
Slovenian	embussing	impolitic	ancientry	antinovel	entophyte	indolence
slowcoach	emendable	important	ancillary	antipasto	entourage	indraught
slowmatch	emendator	importune	andantino	antipathy	entrammel	inducible
sluiceway	emergence	impostume	andesitic	antiphony	entrapped	induction
slumberer	emergency	imposture	androecia	antipodal	entrechat	inductive
slumbrous	eminently	impotence	androgyne	antipodes	entrecote	indulgent
slushfund	Emmenthal	impotency	androgyny	antiquary	entremets	indweller
uliginous	emolliate	impounder	anecdotal	antiquate	enucleate	inebriant
ultimatum	emollient	imprecate	anecdotic	antiquity	enumerate	inebriate
ultrahigh	emolument	imprecise	anemogram	antiserum	enunciate	inebriety
ululation	emotional	impresari	angelfish	antitoxic	enviously	ineffable
amaryllis	emotively	improbity	angelical	antitoxin	enwrapped	ineffably
amassment	emotivity	impromptu	angiology	antitrade	enwreathe	inelastic
amauroses	empathise	improvise	angiomata	antitrust	enzymatic	inelegant
amaurosis	empennage	imprudent	angleiron	antivenin	gneissoid	ineptness
amaurotic	emphasise	impudence	anglesite	antiviral	gneissose	inequable
amazement	emphysema	impulsion	angleworm	anxiously	inability	inerrable
amazingly	empirical	impulsive	anglicise	enactment	inamorata	inerrancy
amazonian	emplastic	impulsory	anglicism	enamelled	inanimate	inertness
ambergris	empyreuma	imputable	Anglicist	enameller	inanition	infantile
ambiguity	emulation	ombudsman	anglophil	enamoured	inaptness	infantine
ambiguous	emulative	ominously	angriness	encaustic	inaudible	infatuate
ambitious	emulously	omissible	anguished	encephala	inaudibly	infection
amblyopia	emunctory	ommatidia	angularly	enchanter	inaugural	infective
amblyopic	imageable	omophagia	anhydride	enchilada	inbetween	inferable
ambrosial	imageless	omophagic	anhydrite	enchorial	inbreathe	inference
ambulacra	imaginary	smackeroo	anhydrous	enclosure	incapable	inferring
ambulance	imbalance	smallarms	animalise	encomiast	incapably	
ambuscade	imbecilic	smallness	animalism	encompass	incarnate	
amendable		smalltime		encounter		
amendment						

infertile	institute	inventive	unanimous	underwing	unsuccess	bouquetin
infielder	insularly	inventory	unaptness	underwood	unsullied	bourgeois
infilling	insulator	inverness	unashamed	undivided	untenable	bowerbird
infirmary	insurable	inversely	unbalance	undoubted	unthought	bowlegged
infirmity	insurance	inversion	unbeknown	undreamed	unthrifty	bowstring
inflation	insurgent	inversive	unbending	undulated	untimeous	bowwindow
inflexion	integrand	invertase	unberufen	undutiful	untouched	boxgirder
inflictor	integrant	invidious	unbiassed	unearthly	untrodden	boxoffice
inflowing	integrate	inviolacy	unblessed	uneatable	untrussed	boycotter
influence	integrity	inviolate	unblinded	unequally	untutored	boyfriend
influenza	intellect	invisible	unbounded	unethical	unusually	coachwork
informant	intendant	invisibly	unbraided	unfailing	unwearied	coadjutor
infractor	intensely	involucre	unbridled	unfeeling	unweeting	coadunate
infuriate	intensify	involuted	uncannily	unfeigned	unwelcome	coagulant
infuscate	intension	inwrought	unceasing	unfitness	unwilling	coagulate
infusible	intensity	knavishly	uncertain	unfitting	unwinking	coalfield
infusoria	intensive	kneadable	uncharted	unfledged	unwitting	coalition
ingenious	intention	knifeedge	unchecked	unfleshed	unwomanly	coalmouse
ingenuity	interbred	knightage	uncinated	unfleshly	unwrapped	coarctate
ingenuous	intercede	knockdown	uncivilly	unfounded	unwritten	coastline
ingestion	intercept	knockknee	uncleanly	ungallant	unwrought	coastward
ingestive	intercity	knotgrass	unclothed	unguarded	unzipping	coastwise
inglenook	intercrop	knowingly	unclouded	unhappily	Boanerges	coattails
ingrained	interdict	knowledge	unconcern	unharness	boardfoot	coaxially
ingrowing	interface	mnemonics	uncounted	unhealthy	boardroom	coaxingly
inhalator	interfere	mnemonist	uncouthly	unheeding	boardwalk	cobaltite
inharmony	interfile	onanistic	uncovered	unhelpful	boathouse	cobaltous
inherence	interflow	oncogenic	uncreated	unhurried	boatswain	Cobdenism
inheritor	interfuse	oncologic	uncropped	unicolour	boattrain	cobwebbed
inhibitor	interject	onehanded	uncrossed	unicuspid	bobsleigh	cocainise
inhumanly	interknit	onelegged	uncrowned	unifiable	bobtailed	cocainism
initially	interlace	onerously	undamaged	uniformly	bodyguard	coccidium
initiator	interlard	onionskin	undaunted	uniparous	boldfaced	coccygeal
injection	interleaf	onlicence	undecagon	uniplanar	bolection	cochineal
injurious	interline	onomastic	undeceive	uniserial	boliviano	cochleate
injustice	interlink	onsetting	undecided	unisexual	bolometer	cockahoop
innermost	interlock	onslaught	undecimal	unisonant	bolometry	Cockaigne
innervate	interlope	ontogenic	undefined	unisonous	Bolshevik	cockatiel
innholder	interlude	ontologic	underbody	unitarian	bombardon	cockfight
innkeeper	interment	pneumatic	underbred	unitively	bombasine	cockhorse
innocence	internode	pneumonia	underclay	univalent	bombastic	cockiness
innocency	interpage	pneumonic	undercoat	universal	bombazine	cockneyfy
innocuity	interplay	snailfish	underdone	unknitted	bombhappy	cockroach
innocuous	interpose	snakebird	underfelt	unknowing	bombilate	cockscomb
innovator	interpret	snakebite	underfoot	unlearned	bombinate	cocksfoot
innoxious	interring	snakelike	undergird	unlimited	bombproof	cocoonery
innuendos	interrupt	snakeroot	undergone	unluckily	bombshell	coecilian
inoculate	intersect	snakeskin	undergrad	unmatched	bombsight	coelomata
inodorous	intervein	snakeweed	underhand	unmeaning	bondslave	coelomate
inorganic	intervene	snakewood	underhung	unmindful	bondstone	coelostat
inpatient	interview	snakiness	underlaid	unmusical	bondwoman	coemption
inpouring	interwind	snaredrum	underlain	unnamable	bonechina	coenobite
inquiline	interwove	sniggerer	underline	unnatural	bonhomous	coenobium
insatiate	interzone	snipefish	underling	unpegging	bonniness	coenosarc
insatiety	intestacy	snivelled	undermine	unpeopled	boobytrap	coequally
inscriber	intestate	sniveller	undermost	unplugged	bookishly	coercible
insectary	intestine	snowberry	underpaid	unplumbed	booklouse	coercibly
insectile	intorsion	snowblind	underpart	unpointed	bookmaker	coeternal
insensate	intricacy	snowblink	underpass	unpopular	bookplate	coffeecup
insertion	intricate	snowbound	underplay	unreality	bookshelf	coffeepot
inservice	intrigant	snowbroth	underplot	unreserve	bookstall	cofferdam
insetting	intriguer	snowdrift	underrate	unruffled	bookstand	coffinite
inshallah	intrinsic	snowfield	underripe	unsavoury	bookstore	cogitable
insidious	introduce	snowflake	underseal	unsayable	boomerang	cognately
insincere	introject	snowgoose	undersell	unscathed	boomslang	cognation
insinuate	introvert	snowguard	undersell	unselfish	boondocks	cognisant
insipidly	intrusion	snowiness	undershot	unsettled	boorishly	cognition
insistent	intrusive	snowplant	undersign	unshackle	bootblack	cognitive
insolence	intuition	snowscape	undersign	unsheathe	bordereau	coheiress
insoluble	intuitive	snowstorm	undersold	unsighted	borrowing	coherence
insolubly	intumesce	snowwhite	undersong	unsightly	boskiness	coherency
insolvent	inunction	snubnosed	underspin	unskilful	bossiness	coiffeuse
insomniac	inurement	unabashed	undertake	unskilled	botanical	coinsurer
inspanned	inutility	unadopted	undertint	unsmiling	bottlefed	colcannon
inspector	invalidly	unadorned	undertone	unsoundly	bottleful	colchicum
instanter	invariant	unadvised	undertook	unsparing	boulevard	colcothar
instantly	invective	unalloyed	undervest	unspotted	boundless	coldshort
instigate	inveigler	unaltered	underwear	unstopped	bounteous	colemouse
instilled	invention	unanimity	underwent	unstudied	bountiful	collagist

collation	compelled	conserver	cornflour	dogoodism	foregoing	golflinks
colleague	compendia	consignee	cornopean	dogshores	foreigner	goliardic
collected	competent	consignor	cornsalad	dogstooth	forejudge	gomphosis
collector	complaint	consonant	cornstalk	dogviolet	foreknown	gondolier
collegial	complexly	consortia	cornstone	dolefully	forenamed	gongorism
collegian	complexus	constable	corollary	doleritic	forereach	gonophore
collegium	compliant	constancy	coroneted	dolomitic	foreshore	goodnight
colligate	component	constrain	corporate	doltishly	foreshown	goodwives
collimate	composite	constrict	corporeal	dominance	foresight	goosander
collinear	composure	construct	corposant	dominator	forespeak	goosefoot
collision	comprador	consulage	corpulent	dominical	forestage	goosegirl
collocate	comprisal	consulate	corpuscle	Dominican	forestall	gooseherd
collodion	comptroll	consulter	corralled	donnishly	foretaste	gooseneck
colloidal	comradely	consultor	corrasion	donothing	foretoken	gooseskin
colloquia	comradery	contactor	correctly	doodlebug	forewoman	goosestep
collotype	concavely	contadina	corrector	doorframe	forfeiter	gorblimey
collusion	concavity	contadino	correlate	doorplate	forgather	gorgonian
collusive	conceited	contagion	corrosion	dopefiend	forgeable	gorgonise
collyrium	concentre	contagium	corrosive	dorbeetle	forgetful	gospeller
colocynth	concerned	container	corrugate	dormition	forgiving	gossamery
colonelcy	concerted	contemner	corrupter	dormitory	forgotten	Gothamite
coloniser	concierge	contender	corruptly	dosimeter	forlornly	gothicise
colonnade	conciliar	contented	corticoid	dosimetry	formalise	Gothicism
colophony	concisely	continent	corticoid	dosshouse	formalism	governess
colorific	concision	continual	cortisone	dottiness	formalist	hoarfrost
colosseum	concocter	continuer	coruscant	doubleton	formality	hoarhound
colostomy	concoctor	continuum	coruscate	doubtable	formation	hoariness
colostrum	concordat	contralto	Corybants	doubtless	formative	hoarstone
colourful	concourse	contrasty	corydalis	doughtily	formatted	Hobbesian
colouring	concubine	contrived	corymbose	Doukhobor	formicary	hobgoblin
colourist	concurred	contriver	coryphaei	dowdiness	formicate	hobnailed
colourman	condenser	contumacy	coseismal	dowelling	formulaic	hobnobbed
coltishly	condignly	contumely	coseismic	dowerless	formulary	hobnobber
coltsfoot	condiment	contusion	cosmogeny	downfield	formulate	hocussing
colubrine	condition	conundrum	cosmogony	downgrade	formulise	hodiernal
columbary	conducive	convector	cosmology	downright	fornicate	hodograph
Columbian	conductor	converter	cosmonaut	downriver	forsythia	hodometer
columbine	condyloid	convexity	cosmorama	downstage	fortalice	hoggishly
columbite	condyloma	convincer	costively	downthrow	forthwith	Holarctic
columbium	confabbed	convivial	costumier	downwards	fortifier	hollyhock
columella	conferral	convolute	cotangent	focussing	fortitude	Hollywood
columnist	conferred	convolved	cothurnus	foeticide	fortnight	holocaust
combatant	conferrer	cookhouse	cotillion	fogginess	fortunate	holograph
combative	confervae	cooperage	cotyledon	foliation	fortyfive	holophote
combinate	confessor	cooperant	couchette	folkdance	forwander	holystone
comedones	confidant	cooperate	coumarone	folkmusic	forwarder	homebound
comfiture	confident	copacetic	countable	folkweave	forwardly	homegrown
comforter	confiding	copartner	countdown	following	fossicker	homemaker
comically	configure	copesmate	countless	foodchain	fossilise	homeopath
Cominform	confirmed	copestone	countship	foodstuff	fossorial	homestead
Comintern	confirmer	copiously	courgette	foolhardy	fosterage	homewards
comitadji	confirmor	copolymer	courtcard	foolishly	foulbrood	homicidal
commander	confiteor	coproduce	courteous	foolproof	foundling	homiletic
commandos	confluent	coprolite	courtesan	footboard	foundress	homogamic
commendam	conformal	coprology	courtroom	footcloth	fourflush	homograft
commensal	conformer	copsewood	courtship	footfault	fourpence	homograph
commenter	Confucian	copyright	courtyard	footlight	fourpenny	homologue
commingle	confusion	coralline	couturier	footloose	fourscore	homonymic
comminute	congenial	corallite	covalence	footplate	fourwheel	homophone
commissar	congeries	coralloid	covalency	footpound	foxhunter	homophony
committal	congruent	corbeille	covariant	footprint	goalmouth	homoplasy
committed	congruity	corbelled	coverable	footstalk	gadbetween	homopolar
committee	congruous	corbicula	coverslip	footstall	goddamned	homotaxis
commodity	conically	cordelier	coverture	footstool	godfather	homotonic
commodore	conjugate	cordially	covetable	foppishly	godliness	homousian
commonage	connately	cordiform	cowardice	foragecap	godmother	homuncule
commonlaw	connation	corduroys	cowlstaff	forasmuch	godparent	homunculi
commotion	connature	coreopsis	coxcombry	forbidden	goffering	honeycomb
communard	connected	coriander	doctorate	forcefeed	gogglebox	honeymoon
communion	connecter	corkscrew	doctorial	forceland	goingover	honkytonk
communise	connector	cormorant	doctrinal	forceless	goldbrick	honoraria
communism	connexion	cornbrash	dodecagon	forcemeat	goldcrest	honorific
communist	connivent	corncrake	dogcollar	forcepump	goldeneye	hoofprint
community	connubial	cornelian	doggishly	foreboder	goldenrod	hopefully
commutate	conqueror	cornemuse	doglegged	forebrain	goldfever	hopscotch
compactly	conscious	cornerboy	dogmatics	forecaddy	goldfield	horehound
compactor	conscribe	cornerman	dogmatise	foreclose	goldfinch	horniness
companion	conscript	cornetist	dogmatism	forecourt	goldsinny	hornstone
compasses	consensus	cornfield	dogmatist	forefront	goldsmith	hornwrack

horologer	Londonise	mongrelly	mousetrap	pokerface	posticous	sobsister
horologic	Londonism	monitress	moustache	pokerwork	postilion	socialise
horoscope	longaeval	monkeyish	mouthpart	polariser	postnasal	socialism
horoscopy	longchain	monkeyism	mouthwash	polemical	postnatal	socialist
horseback	longcoats	monkeynut	moviegoer	polevault	postulant	socialite
horsebean	longeared	monkshood	nobiliary	policeman	postulate	sociality
horsehair	longevity	monobasic	nobleness	politburo	potassium	sociogram
horsehide	longevous	monoceros	noctiluca	politesse	potboiler	sociology
horseless	longfaced	monochord	nocturnal	political	potentate	sociopath
horsemint	longhouse	monocline	nocuously	pollinate	potential	sodabread
horseplay	longicorn	monocoque	nodulated	pollinium	potholing	sodawater
horsepond	longingly	monocracy	noiseless	pollutant	pothunter	softgoods
horseshoe	longitude	monocular	noisiness	pollution	potpourri	softpedal
horsetail	longlived	monodical	noisomely	polonaise	poulterer	softshell
horsewhip	Longobard	monodrama	nominable	polyamide	pouncebox	sogginess
horsiness	longrange	monoecism	nominally	polyandry	poundcake	soidisant
hortation	longshore	monogamic	nominator	polybasic	pourboire	sojourner
hortative	lookalike	monograph	nomocracy	polyester	pourpoint	solacious
hortatory	looseleaf	monolatry	nomograph	polygamic	poussette	soldierly
hortensia	looseness	monologic	nondriver	polygenic	powerboat	solemnise
hosteller	lophodont	monologue	nonentity	polygonal	powerdive	solemnity
hostilely	loquacity	monomania	nonillion	polygonum	powerless	soleplate
hostility	lorgnette	monomeric	nonjuring	polygraph	pozzolana	solfatara
hotheaded	lotusland	monophagy	nonlinear	polyhedra	roadblock	solfeggio
Hottentot	loudmouth	monoplane	nonpareil	polymathy	roadhouse	solferino
hourglass	louringly	monorhyme	nonperson	polymeric	roadmetal	solicitor
houseboat	lousewort	monostich	nonprofit	polymorph	roadstead	solidness
housebote	lousiness	monostyle	nonsmoker	polyonymy	roadworks	soliloquy
housecarl	loutishly	monotonic	nonviable	polyphagy	rocambole	solipsism
housecoat	loveapple	monotreme	normalise	polyphase	rockbound	solipsist
houseflag	lovechild	monotypic	normality	polyphone	rockbrake	solitaire
household	lovefeast	monsignor	Normanise	polyphony	rockdrill	solmisate
housekeep	lovelight	monsoonal	Normanism	polyploid	rocketeer	Solomonic
houseleek	lovematch	monstrous	normative	polyptych	rockiness	Solutrean
houseless	loverless	Montanism	northeast	polysemic	rockplant	Solutrian
housellid	lovestory	monthling	northerly	polysomic	rocksnake	solvation
housemaid	lovetoken	monticule	northland	polythene	rodfisher	something
housemate	lovingcup	monzonite	northmost	polytonal	roguishly	sometimes
houseroom	lowercase	moodiness	northward	polytypic	roisterer	somewhere
housewife	lowerdeck	moonblind	northwest	polyvinyl	roodcloth	somewhile
housework	lowermost	moonlight	Norwegian	polywater	roofplate	sommelier
howsoever	lowlander	moonquake	nosebleed	polyzoary	roominess	somnolent
hoydenish	lowliness	moonraker	noseflute	pomaceous	rootstock	songcycle
ionisable	lowloader	moonscape	nosepiece	pommelled	Roquefort	songfully
jobmaster	lowminded	moonshine	nostalgia	pompadour	rosaceous	songsmith
jockstrap	lownecked	moonstone	nostalgic	pomposity	roseapple	sonneteer
jocularly	loxodrome	moraceous	nostology	pompously	roseately	sonnetise
jocundity	mobocracy	moraliser	notabilia	ponderous	rosenoble	sonometer
Johannine	mockingly	moratoria	notedness	pontoneer	rosewater	sooterkin
jointress	modelling	morbidity	notepaper	pontonier	rosinweed	soothfast
jollyboat	moderator	mordacity	notionist	poorhouse	rostellum	sootiness
Jordanian	modernise	mordantly	notochord	popliteal	rotatable	sophister
josshouse	modernism	Mormonism	notoriety	poppycock	rotundity	sophistic
jossstick	modernist	morphemic	notorious	poppyhead	roughcast	sophistry
journeyer	modernity	morrisman	nourisher	popularly	roughhewn	sophomore
joviality	modillion	mortality	novelette	porbeagle	roughneck	soporific
joylessly	modulator	mortgagee	noviciate	porcelain	roughness	soppiness
loadstone	moistener	mortgager	novitiate	porcupine	roughshod	sopranino
loafsugar	moistness	mortgagor	nowhither	poriferal	Roumanian	sopranist
loanshark	molecular	mortician	noxiously	poriferan	Roumansch	sorbapple
loathsome	molluscan	mosaicism	oogenesis	porphyria	rounceval	Sorbonist
lobectomy	mollymawk	mosaicist	oogenetic	porringer	roundelay	sorceress
lobscouse	molybdate	mosaicked	pocketful	portative	roundhead	sorcerous
lobulated	momentary	moschatel	podagrous	porterage	roundness	soritical
locatable	momentous	mosquitos	podginess	portfolio	roundsman	sorriness
locksmith	monachism	mossagate	podzolise	porticoes	roundworm	sorrowful
locomotor	monarchal	mossgrown	poetaster	portolano	rousement	sortilege
lodestone	monarchic	motheaten	poeticise	portrayal	routinely	sortition
lodgement	monastery	motherwit	poeticism	portrayer	routinism	sostenuto
lodgepole	monatomic	mothproof	poignancy	portreeve	routinist	sottishly
loftiness	Mondayish	motivator	poinciana	portulaca	rowantree	soubrette
logaoedic	monergism	motocross	pointduty	possessed	rowdiness	Soudanese
logarithm	moneybags	motorable	pointedly	possessor	soapberry	soulfully
logically	moneybill	motorbike	pointille	postentry	soapiness	soundfilm
logistics	moneywort	motorboat	pointlace	posterior	soapstone	soundhole
logogriph	Mongolian	motorcade	pointless	posterity	soapworks	soundings
logomachy	mongolism	mouldable	pointsman	posthaste	sobbingly	soundless
loincloth	Mongoloid	mountable	poisonous	posthorse	soberness	soundness
Lombardic	mongooses	mousehole	pokeberry	posthouse	sobriquet	soundpost

```
soundwave vocabular zoophagan epipolism spermatid spurwheel aromatise
soupplate vocaliser zoophobia episcopal sphagnous sputterer arrearage
soupspoon vocalness zoophytic epistaxis spherical Upanishad arrestage
sourdough voiceless zootechny epistemic spherular upbraider arresting
souteneur voiceover zootomist epistoler sphincter upcountry arriviste
Southdown volauvent apartheid epistolic sphygmoid upholster arrogance
southeast volcanism apartment epithelia spicebush uplifting arrowhead
southerly volcanoes apartness epithesis spiciness uppercase arrowroot
southland volkslied apathetic epithetic spiculate uppermost arrowwood
southmost volteface aperiodic epitomise spiderman uprightly arrowworm
southward voltinism aperitive epitomist spiderweb upsetting arsenical
southwest voltmeter apetalous epizootic spikenard xparticle arsenious
souwester volumeter aphereses eponymous spikiness aquaplane artemisia
sovereign voluntary apheresis openended spillikin aquarelle arteriole
sovietise volunteer aphyllous openheart spindling aqueously arteritis
sovietism vomitoria apiculate operation spindrier aquilegia arthritic
toadeater voodooism apishness operative spindrift equaliser arthritis
toadstone voodooist aplanatic opercular spineless equalling arthropod
toadstool voracious apocrypha operculum spininess equipment arthrosis
toastrack vorticism apodictic operosely spinnaker equipoise Arthurian
Tocharian vorticist apogamous operosity spinneret equipping artichoke
tolerable vorticity apologise ophiology spinosity equisetum articular
tolerably vorticose apologist opinioned Spinozism equitable artificer
tolerance vouchsafe apomictic opodeldoc Spinozist equitably artillery
tollbooth vowelless apophyses opponency spinulose equivocal artlessly
tollhouse voyeurism apophysis opportune spinulous equivoque arytenoid
tombstone woebegone apostolic opposable spiracula squabbler brachiate
tomentose wolfhound apothecia oppressor spirality squalidly brachyura
tomentous wolfishly appalling oppugnant spiralled squamosal bracteate
tonguelet wolframic Appaloosa opsimathy spirillum squarrose bracteole
tonguetie wolfsbane apparatus optically spiritism squashily Brahmanic
tonically wolverene apparitor optometer spiritist squatness Brahminee
tonometer wolverine appealing optometry spiritoso squatting Brahminic
tonsillar womanhood appellant optophone spiritous squeakily braincase
tonsorial womaniser appellate opulently spiritual squeamish brainless
toolhouse womankind appendage opusculum spirituel squelcher brainwash
toothache womanlike appendant spaceband spirogyra squibbing brainwave
toothcomb womenfolk appertain spaceless splashily squidding brakeless
toothless womenkind appetence spaceport splayfoot squinancy brakeshoe
toothpick wonderful appetency spaceship spleenful squirarch brakesman
toothsome woodblock appetiser spacesuit splendent squiredom brambling
toothwort woodchuck applauder spacetime splendour squirelet branchiae
tophamper woodcraft applejack spadefoot splenetic arabesque branchial
topiarian woodiness appliance spadework splenitis arabicise branchlet
topiarist woodlouse applicant spaghetti spleuchan arachnoid brandling
topically woodnymph appointee spagyrist splintery aragonite brandreth
toponymal woodwaxen apportion spareness splitting araneidal brashness
toponymic wooziness appraisal spareribs spluttery araneidan brasserie
torchrace Worcester appraiser sparingly spodumene araucaria brassiere
torchsong wordiness apprehend sparkcoil spoilsman arbitrage bratwurst
toreutics wordsmith appressed sparkless spokesman arbitrary brazilnut
tormentil workbench approbate sparkplug spokewise arbitrate breadline
tormentor workhorse epaenetic spasmodic spoliator arbitress breadtree
torpidity workhouse epaulette spatially spongebag arboreous breakable
torridity workmanly ephedrine spatulate spongeous arboretum breakaway
torsional workpiece ephemeral speakable spoonbeak archangel breakdown
tortrices worktable ephemeris speakeasy spoonbill archducal breakeven
tortricid workwoman ephemeron spearfish spoonfeed archduchy breakfast
torturous worldling ephemeron spearhead spoonmeat archenemy breakneck
totaliser worldwide epicentre spearmint sporangia archetype breastpin
totalling wormeaten epiclesis spearside sporocarp archfiend breathily
totempole wormwheel epicurean spearwort sporocyst architect breathing
touchable worriedly epicurism specially sporogeny archivist brecciate
touchdown worriment epicyclic specialty sportsman archivolt breeching
touchhole worrisome epidermal specifier sporulate arcuately breezeway
touchline worrywart epidermic speckless spotcheck arduously bregmatic
touchmark worthless epidermis spectacle spotlight Areopagus bretasche
touchtype woundless epidosite spectator spouthole argentine Bretwalda
touchwood woundwort epigraphy speculate spoutless argentite breveting
toughness yodelling epigynous speechful sprigging argentous brevetted
touristic yohimbine epilation speechify sprightly argillite briarroot
tournedos Yorkshire epileptic speedball sprigtail argumenta briarwood
tourneyer youngling epilogist speedboat springald Arguseyed bricabrac
towelling youngness epinastic speedster springbok argybargy brickwork
townhouse youngster epiphragm speedwell springily armadillo brickyard
townscape zoiatrics epiphyses spellbind springing armigeral bridecake
townsfolk zoogenous epiphysis spellican springlet armillary bridesman
toxically zoography epiphytal spendable sprinkler armistice bridewell
toxophily zoologist epiphytic spermatic spritsail Armorican bridleway
```

briefcase	crescendo	dreamless	frightful	greensand	organstop	preschool
briefless	crestless	dreamlike	frigidity	greenweed	organzine	prescient
briefness	cretinism	dresscoat	fritterer	greenwood	orgiastic	prescribe
brierroot	cretinous	driftsail	frivolity	gregarian	orientate	prescript
brierwood	cricketer	driftweed	frivolled	gregarine	orificial	preselect
brigadier	criminate	driftwood	frivolous	Gregorian	oriflamme	presentee
brigandry	criminous	drinkable	frockcoat	grenadier	originate	presenter
brightish	crinoidal	dripstone	frogmarch	grenadine	orography	presently
brilliant	crinoline	drivelled	frogspawn	greybeard	orologist	preserver
brimstone	crippling	driveller	frolicked	greyhound	orphanage	preshrink
bringdown	crispness	drollness	frontally	greywacke	Orpington	preshrunk
briquette	criterion	dromedary	frontless	griefless	orrisroot	president
briskness	criticise	dropscene	frontline	grievance	orthodoxy	presidial
bristling	criticism	dropscone	frontpage	grillroom	orthoepic	presidium
Britannia	crocodile	dropsical	frontward	grillwork	practical	pressgang
Britannic	croissant	drugstore	frontways	grimalkin	practised	pressmark
Briticise	CroMagnon	druidical	frontwise	griminess	praenomen	pressroom
Briticism	crookback	drummajor	frostbite	grisaille	pragmatic	pressstud
Britisher	crookedly	drumstick	frostwork	gristmill	praiseful	presswork
brittlely	crookneck	drunkenly	frowardly	gritstone	pranksome	prestress
broadcast	cropeared	dryasdust	fructuate	groomsman	prankster	pretender
broadleaf	croquette	drysalter	fructuous	grosgrain	pratingly	preterist
broadloom	crossable	eradicate	frugality	grossness	prayerful	preterite
broadness	crossbeam	erectness	fruitcake	grossular	prayerrug	pretermit
broadside	crossbill	eremitism	fruiterer	grotesque	preachify	prettyish
broadtail	crossbred	ergograph	fruitless	grouchily	preachily	prettyism
broadways	crossette	ergometer	fruittree	groundage	preadamic	prevalent
broadwise	crosseyed	ergonomic	frustrate	groundash	prebendal	preventer
brochette	crossfade	eristical	fruticose	groundhog	precancel	prevision
broiderer	crossfire	erogenous	graceless	grounding	precative	priceless
brokerage	crossfish	eroticism	gracility	groundivy	precatory	prideless
bromeliad	crosshead	erratical	gradation	groundnut	precedent	priestess
bronchial	crosslink	erroneous	gradatory	groundsel	preceding	primaeval
broomcorn	crossness	errorless	Gradgrind	grovelled	precentor	primality
broomrape	crossover	erstwhile	gradually	groveller	preceptor	primarily
brotherly	crossroad	eruciform	graduator	grubscrew	precipice	primatial
brownness	crossruff	eruditely	grandaddy	grubstake	precisely	primeness
brummagem	crosstalk	erudition	grandaunt	gruelling	precisian	primipara
brushfire	crossways	erythrism	grandiose	gruffness	precision	primitive
brushwood	crosswind	erythrite	grandness	grumbling	precocial	primordia
brushwork	crosswise	fractious	grandpapa	Grundyism	precocity	princedom
brusquely	crotchety	fragility	grandsire	irascible	preconise	princekin
brutalise	croustade	fragrance	grandslam	irascibly	precursor	princelet
brutalism	crowberry	fragrancy	granitoid	irksomely	predacity	principal
brutality	crownless	frailness	grantable	ironbound	predation	principia
brutishly	crowsfoot	framework	granulate	ironmould	predative	principle
bryophyte	crowsnest	franchise	granulite	ironsides	predatory	printable
Brythonic	crowsnest	francolin	granulose	ironsmith	predicant	printshop
crabbedly	crucially	frangible	grapeshot	ironstone	predicate	priorship
crackdown	cruciform	Franglais	grapevine	ironworks	predictor	prismatic
crackling	crudeness	Franglais	graphemic	Iroquoian	predigest	privateer
cracksman	cruellest	frankness	graphical	irradiant	predikant	privately
craftsman	crushable	franticly	graphitic	irradiate	preemptor	privation
crampfish	crustacea	fraternal	grappling	irreality	preengage	privative
cranberry	cryogenic	freeboard	graspable	irregular	preexilic	privilege
crankcase	cryoscope	freehouse	grassland	irrigable	prefatory	probation
cranreuch	cryoscopy	freelance	graticule	irrigator	preferred	probative
crapulent	cryptical	freeliver	gratitude	irritable	prefigure	probatory
crapulous	cryptogam	freerange	gravamina	irritably	prefixion	proboscis
crashdive	cryptonym	freerider	graveless	irruption	pregnable	procedure
crashland	draconian	freestone	gravelled	irruptive	pregnancy	procerity
crassness	draftsman	freestyle	graveness	orangeade	prelatess	processed
craziness	draghound	freewheel	graveyard	Orangeism	prelatise	processer
creatable	dragomans	freewoman	gravidity	Orangeman	prelature	processor
creatress	dragoness	freezable	gravitate	orangetip	prelector	proclitic
creatural	dragonfly	freezedry	graywacke	orangutan	prelusion	proconsul
crediting	dragonish	freighter	greasegun	oratorial	prelusive	procreant
credulity	drainpipe	frenchify	greataunt	oratorian	prelusory	procreate
credulous	dramatics	Frenchman	greatcoat	orbicular	premature	procuracy
cremaster	dramatise	frequence	greatness	orchestic	premonish	procuress
cremation	dramatist	frequency	Greekless	orchestra	premotion	prodromal
crematory	Dravidian	frequency	greenback	orchidist	prenotion	prodromic
crenation	drawerful	freshener	greenbelt	orderbook	preoccupy	proenzyme
crenature	drawnwork	freshness	greeneyed	orderform	preordain	profanely
crenelled	drawplate	fretfully	greengage	orderless	prepotent	profanity
crenulate	drawsheet	friarbird	greengage	ordinance	prerecord	professed
crepitant	drayhorse	fricassee	greenhorn	ordinance	prerecord	professor
crepitate	dreamboat	fricative	greenness	organelle	presbyope	profilist
crepuscle	dreamland	frigatoon	greenroom	organiser	presbyter	profiteer

```
profusely  prudishly  trichroic  wristband  estimator  atomicity  stammerer
profusion  prurience  trickless  wristdrop  estoppage  atomistic  stampduty
progestin  pruriency  tricksily  wristshot  estopping  atonalism  stampmill
prognoses  trabeated  trickster  wrongdoer  estranger  atonality  stampnote
prognosis  trabecula  triclinia  wrongness  estrapade  atonement  stanchion
programme  traceable  triclinic  asafetida  estuarian  atonicity  standpipe
projector  traceably  tricolour  asbestine  estuarine  atrocious  stapedial
prolamine  traceless  tridactyl  asbestous  esurience  attainder  starapple
prolapsus  traceried  tridymite  ascendant  esuriency  attempter  starboard
prolately  tracheary  triennial  ascendent  isagogics  attendant  starchily
prolation  tracheate  triennium  ascension  isallobar  attention  stardrift
prolative  trachytic  trierarch  ascensive  ischaemia  attentive  stargazer
prolepses  trackless  trifacial  ascertain  ischaemic  attenuate  stargrass
prolepsis  tracksuit  trifocals  ascetical  ischiadic  attractor  starkness
proleptic  tractable  trifolium  asclepiad  ischiatic  attribute  starlight
prolicide  tractably  triforium  ascospore  isinglass  attrition  starshell
prolixity  trademark  trigamist  asepalous  Islamitic  eternally  starstone
prologise  tradename  trigamous  asexually  isobathic  etherical  startling
prolusion  tradesman  trihedral  ashamedly  isochrone  ethically  statehood
prolusory  tradition  trihybrid  Ashkenazi  isoclinal  Ethiopian  stateless
promenade  traducian  trilinear  ashlaring  isoclinic  ethmoidal  statement
prominent  tragedian  trilithon  asininity  isocyclic  ethnarchy  stateroom
promising  trainable  trilobate  askewness  isogamete  ethnicity  stateside
promotion  trainband  trilobite  asparagus  isogamous  ethnology  statesman
promotive  trainload  trimerous  aspartate  isogenous  ethylenic  statewide
promptbox  traitress  trimester  aspectual  isohyetal  etiquette  stational
pronation  tramlines  trimetric  aspersion  isolation  etymology  stationer
proneness  transcend  trimmings  asphaltic  isolative  italicise  statistic
pronghorn  transenna  trinketer  asphaltum  isomerise  Italicism  statocyst
pronounce  transform  trinketry  aspirator  isomerism  itchiness  statolith
proofread  transfuse  trinomial  assailant  isomerous  iteration  statuette
propagate  transient  triploidy  assaulter  isometric  iterative  statutory
propelled  translate  triptyque  assayable  isoniazid  itineracy  stauncher
propeller  transmute  triquetra  assembler  isooctane  itinerant  staunchly
properdin  transonic  trisagion  assertion  isopodous  itinerary  staymaker
prophetic  transpire  trisector  assertive  isosceles  itinerate  steadfast
propionic  transport  triteness  assiduity  isostatic  itsybitsy  steamboat
proponent  transpose  tritheism  assiduous  isotropic  ittybitty  steampipe
propriety  transship  tritheist  assistant  Israelite  otherness  steamship
proptosis  transumpt  triturate  associate  issueless  otherwise  steatitic
propylaea  transvest  triumphal  assonance  Kshatriya  otologist  steelclad
propylene  trapezial  triumviri  assuasive  oscillate  ptarmigan  steelhead
prorogate  trapezium  trivalent  assumable  oscitancy  pterosaur  steelwork
prosaical  trapezoid  trivially  assumably  osmometer  pterygium  steelyard
proscenia  trappings  triweekly  assumpsit  ossicular  pterygoid  steenkirk
proscribe  trattoria  trochilus  assurance  ossifrage  Ptolemaic  steepness
prosector  trattorie  trochleae  assuredly  ostensive  stabilise  steersman
prosecute  traumatic  trochlear  assurgent  osteoderm  stability  stegosaur
proselyte  travelled  troopship  asthmatic  osteogeny  stableboy  stellated
prosiness  traveller  tropology  astraddle  osteology  stableman  stenotype
prosodist  traversal  troublous  astrakhan  osteopath  stackable  stenotypy
prostatic  traverser  trousered  astrocyte  ostracise  stackroom  stepchild
prostrate  traycloth  trousseau  astrodome  ostracism  stackyard  stepdance
protamine  treachery  troutfarm  astrolabe  Ostrogoth  stagedoor  steradian
protector  treadmill  troutling  astrology  psalmbook  stagehand  stercoral
proteinic  treasurer  trowelled  astronaut  psalmodic  staggerer  sterilise
protester  treatable  troweller  astronomy  psalteria  staghound  sterility
protestor  treatment  truceless  asymmetry  pseudonym  staginess  sternmost
prothesis  trebuchet  truculent  asymptote  pseudopod  Stagirite  sternness
prothetic  trebucket  truepenny  asyndetic  psoriasis  stagnancy  sternpost
prothorax  treillage  trumpedup  asyndeton  psoriatic  stagparty  sternward
protonema  trematode  trumpeter  escalator  psychical  staidness  steroidal
prototype  tremolant  truncated  escapable  psychoses  stainable  stevedore
protozoal  tremolite  truncheon  escheator  psychosis  stainless  stickwork
protozoan  tremulant  trunkcall  escortage  psychotic  staircase  stiffener
protozoic  tremulous  trunkfish  esemplasy  tsarevich  stairfoot  stiffness
protozoon  trenchant  trunkroad  esoterica  uselessly  stairhead  stigmatic
proveably  trepanned  trussbeam  esoterism  usherette  stairwell  stilettos
Provencal  trepidant  trustdeed  esperance  usualness  stakeboat  stillborn
provender  trialogue  trustless  Esperanto  usucapion  stalactic  stillhunt
provident  triatomic  truthless  espionage  atacamite  stalemate  stillness
providing  tribadism  trysquare  esplanade  ataractic  staleness  stillroom
provision  tribalism  uraninite  espousals  atavistic  Stalinism  stiltedly
provisory  tribesman  uranology  Esquimaux  atheistic  Stalinist  stimulant
provoking  tribology  urceolate  essential  athematic  stalkeyed  stimulate
provostry  tribunate  uropygium  establish  Athenaeum  stalkless  stingaree
proximate  tributary  urticaria  estaminet  athletics  stallfeed  stingless
proximity  trichinae  wrathless  Esthonian  Atlantean  stalworth  stinkball
prudently  trichomic  wrestling  estimable  atmometer  staminate  stinkbomb
```

stinkhorn	striature	auxiliary	curlpaper	fulminous	hurriedly	murderess
stinktrap	stricture	buccaneer	currently	fulsomely	hurtfully	murderous
stinkweed	stridence	buckboard	curricula	fumarolic	husbandly	murkiness
stinkwood	stridency	bucketful	currishly	fumigator	husbandry	murmurous
stintless	stringent	buckhound	currycomb	fundament	huskiness	muscadine
stipitate	stripling	buckshish	cursively	funebrial	jubilance	muscarine
stippling	stripping	buckthorn	cursorial	fungicide	Judaistic	muscleman
stipulate	strobilae	bucktooth	cursorily	fungiform	Judastree	muscovado
stirabout	strobilus	buckwheat	curstness	funicular	judgement	muscovite
stitchery	stromatic	budgetary	curtilage	funiculus	judgeship	musically
stockbook	strongarm	buffaloes	curvature	funkiness	judgmatic	musichall
stockdove	strongbox	buffeting	curveting	funnelled	judiciary	musketeer
stockfish	strongish	bughunter	curvetted	funniness	judicious	muskiness
stockinet	strongyle	bulbously	curviform	furbisher	juiceless	muskmelon
stocklist	strontium	Bulgarian	cuspidate	furcation	juiciness	Mussulman
stockpile	stropping	bulginess	custodial	furiously	jumpiness	mustachio
stockroom	strouding	bulkiness	custodian	furnisher	Juneberry	musteline
stockwhip	structure	bulldozer	customary	furniture	juniorate	mustiness
stockyard	struggler	bullfight	customise	furtherer	juniority	mutagenic
stoically	strumitis	bullfinch	cutaneous	furtively	junkerdom	mutilator
stokehold	strumming	bullishly	cuticular	fusillade	junkerism	mutualise
stokehole	strutting	bulltrout	cutinised	fusionist	junketing	mutualism
stolidity	strychnic	bullybeef	cutthroat	fussiness	Junoesque	mutualist
stolonate	studhorse	bullytree	cuttysark	fustigate	juridical	mutuality
stomachal	studiedly	bumblebee	dualistic	fustiness	jurywoman	muzziness
stomacher	stupefier	bumbledon	dubiosity	fuzziness	justiciar	nucleated
stomachic	stupidity	bumptious	dubiously	guacamole	justifier	nucleolus
stonechat	stuporous	bundobust	dubitable	guarantee	juvenilia	nucleonic
stonecoal	stutterer	bunkhouse	duckboard	guarantor	juxtapose	nuisancer
stonecold	stylebook	buoyantly	ductility	guardbook	kurrajong	nullifier
stonecrop	styliform	burdenous	dulcamara	guardedly	lubricant	nullipara
stonedead	stylishly	burnedout	dulcitude	guardrail	lubricate	nullipore
stonedeaf	stylistic	burningly	dumbfound	guardring	lubricity	numbskull
stonefish	stylobate	burnisher	dumpiness	guardroom	lubricous	numerable
stoneless	utricular	burrstone	dungarees	guardship	lucidness	numerator
stonewall	utterable	bursarial	duodecimo	guardsman	luciferin	numerical
stoneware	utterance	bushcraft	duodenary	guerrilla	luckiness	nummulite
stonework	utterless	bushelful	duplicate	guesswork	lucrative	nuncupate
stonewort	uttermost	bushiness	duplicity	guestroom	lucubrate	nurseling
stoniness	utterness	bushwhack	duralumin	guidebook	ludicrous	nursemaid
stoolball	ytterbium	butadiene	duskiness	guideline	luftwaffe	nutriment
stoplight	aubergine	butcherer	dustcover	guidepost	lumbering	nutrition
stoppress	aubrietia	butcherly	dustiness	guiderope	lumberman	nutritive
stopwatch	auctorial	butterbur	dustsheet	guildhall	lumbrical	nuttiness
storeroom	audacious	buttercup	duteously	guildship	lumbricus	nutweevil
storeship	audiology	butterfat	dutifully	guileless	luminance	oubliette
storiated	auditable	butterfly	eucalypti	guillemot	lumpiness	ourselves
stormbelt	auditoria	butterine	eucaryote	guilloche	lumpishly	outbacker
stormbird	augmented	butternut	Eucharist	guiltless	lunchtime	outermost
stormcock	augmenter	buttinsky	euchology	guitarist	lunisolar	outfitter
stormcone	augmentor	buttygang	euclidean	gumminess	lunitidal	outgiving
stormless	auricular	buxomness	eulogiser	guncotton	luridness	outgoings
stormsail	auspicate	cubbyhole	eunuchism	gunpowder	lustfully	outgrowth
storybook	austenite	cubically	eunuchoid	gunrunner	lustihood	outgunned
storyline	austerely	cuckoldry	euphemise	gushingly	lustiness	outlander
stoutness	austerity	cucullate	euphemism	gustation	luxuriant	outnumber
stovepipe	autarchic	cudgelled	euphonise	gustative	luxuriate	outputted
straggler	autarkist	cullender	euphonium	gustatory	luxurious	outridden
strangely	authentic	culminant	euphorbia	gustiness	muckraker	outrigger
strangler	authoress	culminate	eurhythmy	gutsiness	mucksweat	outskirts
strangles	authorial	culsdesac	eutectoid	guttation	mucronate	outspoken
straphang	authority	cumbrance	eutherian	guttering	muddiness	outspread
strapless	autoclave	cuneiform	eutrophic	hubristic	muffineer	outwardly
strappado	autocracy	cunningly	fugacious	huckaback	muffinman	outwitted
strapping	autocross	cupbearer	fulfilled	huckstery	mullioned	outworker
strapwork	autocycle	cupelling	fulfiller	huffiness	multifoil	pubescent
strapwort	autograft	cuplichen	fulgently	hugeously	multiform	publicise
stratagem	autograph	curbstone	fulgurant	humankind	multilane	publicist
strategic	autolysis	curettage	fulgurate	humanness	multipara	publicity
strawworm	autolytic	curialism	fulgurite	humblebee	multiplex	publisher
streakily	automatic	curiosity	fulgurous	humbugged	multitude	pudginess
streaking	automaton	curiously	fullblown	humdinger	mumchance	puerility
streamlet	autonomic	curbstone	fullcream	humectant	mummified	puerperal
streetcar	autopilot	curettage	fulldress	humiliate	mundanely	puffadder
strenuous	autoroute	curialism	fullgrown	hunchback	mundungus	puffiness
stressful	autosomal	curiosity	fullscale	hundredth	municipal	pugnacity
stretcher	autotelic	curiously	fulminant	Hungarian	muniments	puissance
strewment	autotroph	curliness	fulminate	hurricane	munitions	pullulate
striation						pulmonary

pulmonate	queenlike	sublunary	supervise	zucchetto	overthrow	axiomatic
pulpboard	queenpost	submarine	supinator	available	overtness	Axminster
pulpiness	queenship	submaster	suppliant	availably	overtones	exactable
pulpiteer	queerness	submental	supporter	avalanche	overtrain	exactment
pulpstone	quercetum	submitted	supposing	aventaile	overtrick	exactness
pulsatile	querulous	subnormal	suppurate	averagely	overtrump	examinant
pulsation	quibbling	subocular	supremacy	avertible	overvalue	exanimate
pulsatory	quickener	subphylum	supremely	avizandum	overwatch	exanthema
pulseless	quicklime	subregion	surcharge	avocation	overweary	exarchate
pulserate	quickness	subrogate	surcingle	avoidable	overweigh	excavator
pulverise	quicksand	subscribe	surculose	avoidably	overwhelm	exceeding
pulverous	quickstep	subscript	surfacing	avoidance	overwound	excellent
pulvillus	quiescent	subsellia	surfboard	avuncular	overwrite	excelling
pulvinate	quietness	subsidise	surfeiter	evaginate	overwrote	excelsior
pumiceous	quillwort	substance	surficial	evangelic	oviductal	excentric
pummelled	quinoline	substrata	surgeoncy	evaporate	oviferous	exceptant
punchball	quintette	substrate	surliness	evasively	oviparity	excepting
punchbowl	quintuple	subtenant	surmullet	eventless	oviparous	exception
punchcard	quirister	subtilise	surpliced	eventuate	ovulation	exceptive
punchline	quitclaim	subtopian	surprisal	everglade	ovulatory	excerptor
punctilio	quittance	subverter	surrender	evergreen	uvarovite	excessive
punctuate	quixotism	succeeder	surrogate	everybody	awakening	exchanger
pungently	quizzical	succentor	surveying	evidently	awardable	exchequer
punishing	quodlibet	successor	suspender	evincible	awareness	excipient
pupillage	quotation	succinate	suspensor	evocation	awesomely	excisable
pupillary	quotidian	succotash	suspicion	evocative	awestruck	exciseman
puppeteer	rubberise	succourer	sustainer	evocatory	awfulness	excitable
puppyhood	rubellite	succulent	susurrant	evolution	awkwardly	excitancy
purchaser	rubicelle	succursal	sutteeism	evolutive	ewenecked	excitedly
pureblood	rubricate	suctorial	suturally	evolvable	ownership	exclosure
purgation	rubrician	sudatoria	tubbiness	ovenready	swaddling	exclusion
purgative	rudbeckia	sudoheria	tubercule	overblown	swaggerer	exclusive
purgatory	ruddiness	sudorific	tubularly	overboard	swangoose	excoriate
puritanic	ruddleman	suffering	tuckerbag	overborne	swansdown	excrement
purloiner	rufescent	suffocate	tufaceous	overcheck	swarajist	excretion
purposely	ruffianly	suffragan	tuitional	overcloud	swartness	excretive
purposive	ruggedise	suffusion	tuliproot	overcrowd	swearword	excretory
purpureal	ruination	sugarbeet	tuliptree	overdraft	sweatband	exculpate
purringly	ruinously	sugarcane	tulipwood	overdrawn	sweatshop	excurrent
purselike	rulership	sugarloaf	tumblebug	overdress	sweepback	excursion
pursiness	ruminator	sugarplum	tumescent	overdrive	sweetcorn	excursive
pursuable	rumrunner	suggester	tumidness	overeaten	sweetener	excusable
pursuance	runcinate	sulcation	tunefully	overeater	sweetmeal	excusably
purulence	rushlight	sulkiness	tungstate	overexert	sweetmeat	execrable
purulency	russeting	sulphonic	tunicated	overflown	sweetness	execrably
pushchair	Russophil	sulphuret	tunnelled	overglaze	sweetshop	executant
pushiness	rusticate	sulphuric	tunnelnet	overgraze	sweettalk	execution
pushingly	rusticity	sultanate	turbidity	overgrown	swellfish	executive
pussyfoot	rustiness	sultaness	turbinate	overheard	sweptback	executory
pustulate	rustproof	summarily	turboprop	overissue	swiftness	executrix
pustulous	ruthenium	summarise	turbulent	overjoyed	swimmable	exegetist
putridity	ruthfully	summarist	Turcomans	overladen	swimmeret	exemplary
puzzolana	suability	summation	turgently	overleapt	swineherd	exemplify
quadratic	suasively	summative	turgidity	overlying	swingeing	exemption
quadrifid	subaerial	summingup	Turkomans	overmatch	swinishly	exequatur
quadrigae	subagency	sumptuary	turnabout	overnight	switchman	exercises
quadrille	subalpine	sumptuous	turnround	overpitch	swivelled	exfoliate
quadruman	subaltern	sunbather	turnstile	overpower	swordcane	exhauster
quadruped	subarctic	sunbonnet	turnstone	overprice	swordfish	exhibitor
quadruple	subastral	sunburned	turntable	overprint	swordknot	exilement
quadruply	subatomic	sundowner	turpitude	overproof	swordlike	existence
Quakerdom	subbranch	sunflower	turquoise	overreach	swordplay	exodermis
Quakeress	subcaudal	sunhelmet	tutorship	overreact	swordsman	exogamous
Quakerish	subcostal	sunlounge	vulcanian	oversexed	swordtail	exogenous
Quakerism	subdeacon	sunniness	vulcanise	overshoot	twayblade	exonerate
quakiness	subdivide	sunspurge	vulcanism	oversight	twelfthly	exopodite
qualified	subduable	sunstroke	vulcanist	oversized	twentieth	exorciser
qualifier	subduedly	sunstruck	vulcanite	overskirt	twentyone	exosmosis
quantical	subeditor	suntanned	vulgarian	oversleep	twiceborn	exosmotic
quarenden	subereous	superable	vulgarise	overslept	twicelaid	exosphere
quarender	subfamily	supercool	vulgarism	overspend	twicetold	exostosis
quarryman	subgenera	superfine	vulgarity	overspent	twinkling	exoticism
quarterly	subjacent	superfuse	vulnerary	overspill	twistable	expansile
quartette	subjugate	superheat	vulpinism	overstate	twitchily	expansion
quartzite	sublation	supernova	vulpinite	oversteer	twitterer	expansive
quartzose	sublethal	superpose	vulturine	overstock	twofisted	expatiate
quebracho	sublimate	supersede	vulturish	overstuff	twohanded	expectant
queenhood	sublimely	superstar	vulturous	overtaken	twosuiter	expecting
queenless	sublimity	supervene	wulfenite	overthrew	Zwinglian	expedient

expediter	cymophane	hypnotist	symbiotic	amaryllis	blacklist	chapleted
expellent	cynically	hypoblast	symbolics	amassment	blackmail	charabanc
expelling	cyprinoid	hypocaust	symbolise	amauroses	blackness	character
expensive	cystocarp	hypocotyl	symbolism	amaurosis	blackwash	chariness
expertise	cystolith	hypocrisy	symbolist	amaurotic	blaeberry	charivari
expiation	cystotomy	hypocrite	symbology	amazement	blameable	charlatan
expiatory	Cytherean	hypogeous	symmetric	amazingly	blameably	charlotte
explainer	cytolysis	hypomania	symphonic	amazonian	blameless	charmeuse
expletive	cytomania	hypomanic	symphysis	anabioses	blandness	charmless
expletory	cytoplasm	hyponasty	sympodial	anabiosis	blankness	Charolais
explicate	cytotoxic	hypostyle	sympodium	anabiotic	blaspheme	chartered
exploiter	cytotoxin	hypotaxis	symposiac	anabolism	blasphemy	charterer
explosion	dynamical	hysterics	symposial	anabranch	blasthole	charwoman
explosive	dynamiter	hysteroid	symposium	anacruses	blastment	chassepot
expositor	dyscrasia	kymograph	synagogal	anacrusis	blastulae	chastener
expounder	dysentery	lyamhound	synagogue	anaerobic	blastular	chastiser
expressly	dysgenics	lymegrass	synchrony	analeptic	blatantly	chatelain
expulsion	dyspepsia	lymehound	synclinal	analgesia	blazingly	chatoyant
expulsive	dyspeptic	lymphatic	syncopate	analgesic	Boanerges	chatterer
expurgate	dysphagia	lyophilic	syncretic	analogise	boardfoot	chauffeur
exquisite	dysphagic	lyophobic	syncytial	analogist	boardroom	claimable
exsertile	dysphonia	lyrically	syncytium	analogous	boardwalk	clamantly
exsertion	dysphoria	lysimeter	syndactyl	analysand	boathouse	clamorous
exservice	dysphoric	Mycenaean	syndicate	anamnesis	boatswain	clamshell
exsiccate	dysplasia	mycologic	synectics	anandrous	boattrain	clapboard
exsuccous	dyspnoeic	mycophagy	syneresis	anaphoric	brachiate	clarifier
extempore	dystrophy	mydriasis	synergism	anaptyxis	brachyura	clarionet
extendant	eyebright	mydriatic	synergist	anarchism	bracteate	classable
extensile	eyeglance	myelomata	syngamous	anarchist	bracteole	classical
extension	eyeopener	myography	synizesis	anatomise	Brahmanic	classless
extensity	eyeshadow	myologist	synodical	anatomist	Brahminee	classlist
extensive	eyestrain	myriorama	synoecete	apartheid	Brahminic	classmate
extenuate	gymnasial	myrmecoid	synonymic	apartment	braincase	classroom
externals	gymnasium	myrobalan	synoptist	apartness	brainless	clathrate
extirpate	gymnastic	mystagogy	synovitis	apathetic	brainwash	clatterer
extolling	gynaeceum	mysticism	syntactic	arabesque	brainwave	claustral
extolment	gynocracy	mystifier	syntheses	arabicise	brakeless	clavation
extorsive	gynoecium	mythicise	synthesis	arachnoid	brakeshoe	claviform
extortion	gynophore	mythicism	synthetic	aragonite	brakesman	coachwork
extortive	gyrfalcon	mythicist	syphilise	araneidal	brambling	coadjutor
extractor	gyroplane	mythology	syphiloid	araneidan	branchiae	coadunate
extradite	gyroscope	myxoedema	systaltic	asafetida	branchial	coagulant
extravert	hybridise	nymphalid	tympanist	atacamite	branchlet	coagulate
extremely	hybridism	nystagmic	typemetal	ataractic	brandling	coalfield
extremism	hybridity	nystagmus	typewrite	atavistic	brandreth	coalition
extremist	hydathode	oysterbed	typhlitis	available	brashness	coalmouse
extremity	hydraemia	oysterman	typhoidal	availably	brasserie	coarctate
extricate	hydrangea	pycnidium	typically	avalanche	brassiere	coastline
extrinsic	hydration	pyracanth	tyrannise	awakening	bratwurst	coastward
extrovert	hydraulic	pyramidal	tyrannous	awardable	brazilnut	coastwise
extrusion	hydrazine	pyramidic	wyandotte	awareness	ceanothus	coattails
extrusive	hydriodic	pyramidon	wychhazel	beachhead	ceasefire	coaxially
exuberant	hydrocele	pyrethrum	Wyclifite	beachwear	ceaseless	coaxingly
exuberate	hydrofoil	pyridoxin	wyliecoat	beadledom	chachacha	crabbedly
exudation	hydrology	pyrogenic	xylograph	beamingly	chaetopod	crackdown
exudative	hydrolyse	pyrolater	xylophone	beanfeast	chafferer	crackling
exultance	hydrolyte	pyrolatry	zygomatic	beanstalk	chaffinch	cracksman
exultancy	hydronium	pyrolysis	zygospore	bearberry	chaingang	craftsman
oxidation	hydrosome	pyrolytic	zymogenic	beardless	chaingear	crampfish
oxygenate	hydroxide	pyromancy	azeotrope	beastings	chainless	cranberry
oxygenise	hygienics	pyromania	azimuthal	beatitude	chainmail	crankcase
oxygenous	hygienist	pyrometer	czarevich	beauteous	chairlady	cranreuch
uxoricide	hygrostat	pyrometry	dziggetai	beautiful	chameleon	crapulent
Aylesbury	hylozoism	pyroscope	ozocerite	blackball	chamomile	crapulous
byproduct	hymnology	pyroxylin	ozokerite	blackbird	champagne	crashdive
bystander	hypallage	sybaritic	————————	blackbuck	champaign	crashland
Byzantine	hyperbola	sycophant		blackbuck	champaign	crassness
cyanamide	hyperbole	syllabary	abandoned	blackcoat	champerty	craziness
cyclamate	hypergamy	syllabise	abandonee	blackcock	champleve	cyanamide
cycloidal	hypericum	syllabism	abandoner	blackdamp	chanceful	czarevich
cyclopean	hyperopia	syllabled	abasement	blackface	chancroid	deacidify
cyclopian	hyperopic	syllepses	abashment	Blackfeet	chancrous	deaconess
cyclopses	hypethral	syllepsis	abatement	blackfish	chandlery	deadalive
cyclorama	hyphenate	sylleptic	academism	blackflag	changeful	deadlight
cyclotron	hypnoidal	syllogise	acariasis	Blackfoot	chanteuse	deathblow
cylindric	hypnology	syllogism	adamantly	blackgame	chantilly	deathless
cymbalist	hypnotise	sylphlike	adaptable	blackhead	chantress	deathlike
cymbidium	hypnotism	sylvanite	agapemone	blackjack	chaparral	deathmask
cymbiform	hypnotist	symbiosis	alabaster	blacklead	chaperone	deathroll

```
dharmsala  flagellum  granulite  isagogics  planetary  roadmetal  slapstick
diablerie  flageolet  granulose  isallobar  planetoid  roadstead  slateclub
diabolise  flagrance  grapeshot  italicise  plangency  roadworks  slategrey
diabolism  flagrancy  grapevine  Italicism  planisher  scagliola  slaughter
diabolist  flagstaff  graphemic  jealously  plantable  scaldfish  slaveship
diachrony  flagstick  graphical  knavishly  plantlike  scalefern  slavishly
diachylom  flagstone  graphitic  leafgreen  planuloid  scalefish  Slavonian
diachylum  flakiness  grappling  leafmould  plasmatic  scaleleaf  Slavophil
diaconate  flambeaus  graspable  leafstalk  plasmodia  scaleless  smackeroo
diacritic  flambeaux  grassland  leakiness  plastered  scalelike  smallarms
diactinic  flameless  graticule  learnable  plasterer  scalemoss  smallness
diaereses  flamingly  gratitude  learnedly  platemark  scaliness  smalltime
diaeresis  flamingos  gratulate  leasehold  platinise  scallawag  smartness
diagnoses  flammable  gravamina  leaselend  platinoid  scallywag  smartweed
diagnosis  flannelly  graveless  leastways  platinous  scalplock  smatterer
dialectal  flarepath  gravelled  leastwise  platitude  scantling  snailfish
dialectic  flaringly  graveness  leavening  Platonise  scantness  snakebird
dialogise  flashback  graveyard  liability  Platonism  scapegoat  snakebite
dialogism  flashbulb  gravidity  loadstone  Platonist  scapolite  snakelike
dialogist  flashcube  gravitate  loafsugar  plausible  scapulary  snakeroot
diametral  flashover  graywacke  loanshark  plausibly  scarecrow  snakeskin
diametric  flashtube  guacamole  loathsome  playfully  scarehead  snakeweed
diandrous  flatterer  guarantee  lyamhound  playgroup  scarfring  snakewood
diaphragm  flatulent  guarantor  mealiness  playhouse  scarfskin  snakiness
diaphysis  flavorous  guardbook  meandrine  plaything  scarfwise  snaredrum
diarrhoea  flayflint  guardedly  meandrous  practical  scarifier  soapberry
diastasis  fractious  guardrail  meaningly  practised  scatology  soapiness
diastatic  fraenulum  guardring  meanwhile  praenomen  scatterer  soapstone
diastolic  fragility  guardroom  meatiness  pragmatic  scavenger  soapworks
diathermy  fragrance  guardship  miasmatic  praiseful  seaanchor  spaceband
diathesis  fragrancy  guardsman  neathouse  pranksome  seachange  spaceless
diathetic  frailness  headboard  odalisque  prankster  seafaring  spaceport
diatomite  framework  headcloth  onanistic  pratingly  seagirdle  spaceship
diatropic  franchise  headdress  orangeade  prayerful  sealetter  spacesuit
draconian  francolin  headfirst  Orangeism  prayerrug  seaminess  spacetime
draftsman  frangible  headiness  Orangeman  psalmbook  seanettle  spadefoot
draghound  Franglais  headlight  orangetip  psalmodic  searching  spadework
dragomans  frankness  headliner  orangutan  psalteria  searingly  spaghetti
dragoness  franticly  headphone  oratorial  ptarmigan  seasoning  spagyrist
dragonfly  fraternal  headpiece  oratorian  quadratic  seasquirt  spareness
dragonish  gearlever  headscarf  peaceable  quadrifid  seastrand  spareribs
drainpipe  gearshift  headstall  peaceably  quadrigae  seatangle  sparingly
dramatics  gearwheel  headstock  peacetime  quadrille  seaurchin  sparkcoil
dramatise  giantlike  headstone  peachblow  quadruman  seaworthy  sparkless
dramatist  glabellae  headwater  pearlitic  quadruped  shadberry  sparkplug
Dravidian  glabellar  healthful  pearlwort  quadruple  shadeless  spasmodic
drawerful  glacially  healthily  peasantry  quadruply  shadetree  spatially
drawnwork  gladiator  heartache  peasouper  Quakerdom  shadiness  spatulate
drawplate  gladiolus  heartbeat  phagedena  Quakeress  shakeable  stabilise
drawsheet  gladstone  heartburn  phagocyte  Quakerish  shakedown  stability
drayhorse  glaireous  heartfelt  phalanger  Quakerism  shakerism  stableboy
dualistic  glamorise  heartfree  phalanges  quakiness  shakiness  stableman
ejaculate  glamorous  hearthrug  phalanxes  qualified  shallowly  stackable
elaborate  glandered  heartland  phalarope  qualifier  shamanism  stackroom
elastomer  glandular  heartless  phantasma  quantical  shamanist  stackyard
emaciated  glaringly  heartsick  pharaonic  quarenden  shamateur  stagedoor
emanation  glassgall  heartsore  pharisaic  quarender  shambling  stagehand
emanative  glassware  heartwood  pharyngal  quarryman  shambolic  staggerer
enactment  glasswork  heathcock  pharynges  quarterly  shamefast  staghound
enamelled  glasswort  heathenry  pharynxes  quartette  shameless  staginess
enameller  gnathonic  heaviness  pianistic  quartzite  Shangrila  Stagirite
enamoured  goalmouth  heavyduty  placation  quartzose  shantyman  stagnancy
epaenetic  graceless  hoarfrost  placatory  reachable  shapeable  stagparty
epaulette  gracility  hoarhound  placeable  reactance  shapeless  staidness
eradicate  gradation  hoariness  placecard  readdress  sharecrop  stainable
evaginate  gradatory  hoarstone  placekick  readiness  sharkskin  stainless
evangelic  Gradgrind  imageable  placeless  readymade  sharpener  staircase
evaporate  gradually  imageless  placement  realistic  sharpeyed  stairfoot
evasively  graduator  imaginary  placename  reanimate  sharpness  stairhead
exactable  grandaddy  inability  placentae  rearguard  sharpshod  stairwell
exactment  grandaunt  inamorata  placental  rearhorse  shaveling  stakeboat
exactness  grandiose  inanimate  placidity  rearlight  slabsided  stalactic
examinant  grandness  inanition  plainness  rearmouse  slabstone  stalemate
exanimate  grandpapa  inaptness  plainsman  rearrange  slackness  staleness
exanthema  grandsire  inaudible  plainsong  rearwards  slakeless  Stalinism
exarchate  grandslam  inaudibly  plaintiff  reasoning  slanderer  Stalinist
fearfully  granitoid  inaugural  plaintive  rhapsodic  slantways  stalkeyed
feathered  grantable  irascible  planarian  roadblock  slantwise  stalkless
flabellum  granulate  irascibly  planation  roadhouse  slaphappy  stallfeed
```

stalworth	trainband	arbitress	gabionade	rebukable	umbellule	backcloth
staminate	trainload	arboreous	gibberish	rebutting	umberbird	backcross
stammerer	traitress	arboretum	gibbosity	Ribbonism	umbilical	backpedal
stampduty	tramlines	asbestine	gibbously	ribosomal	umbilicus	backsight
stampmill	transcend	asbestous	gobetween	rubberise	unbalance	backslang
stampnote	transenna	aubergine	habergeon	rubellite	unbeknown	backslide
stanchion	transform	aubrietia	habitable	rubicelle	unbending	backspace
standpipe	transfuse	babacoote	habitably	rubricate	unberufen	backstage
stapedial	transient	Babbittry	habituate	rubrician	unbiassed	backsword
starapple	translate	babirussa	Hebridean	sabadilla	unblessed	backtrack
starboard	transmute	baboonish	hibernate	sabbatise	unblinded	backwards
starchily	transonic	biblicism	Hibernian	sabbatism	unbounded	backwater
stardrift	transpire	biblicist	Hobbesian	Sabellian	unbraided	backwoods
stargazer	transport	bobsleigh	hobgoblin	sebaceous	unbridled	bacterial
stargrass	transpose	bobtailed	hobnailed	sibilance	upbraider	bacterise
starkness	transship	caballero	hobnobbed	sibilancy	vibracula	bacterium
starlight	transumpt	caballine	hobnobber	sibylline	vibraharp	bacteroid
starshell	transvest	caballing	hubristic	sobbingly	vibratile	beccafico
starstone	trapezial	cabbalism	hybridise	soberness	vibration	bicameral
startling	trapezium	cabbalist	hybridism	sobriquet	vibrative	bicipital
statehood	trapezoid	cablegram	hybridity	sobsister	vibratory	biconcave
stateless	trappings	cablelaid	imbalance	subaerial	vibrissae	bicyclist
statement	trattoria	cabriolet	imbecilic	subagency	webfooted	buccaneer
stateroom	trattorie	cobaltite	imbricate	subalpine	zebrawood	buckboard
stateside	traumatic	cobaltous	imbroglio	subaltern	zibelline	bucketful
statesman	travelled	Cobdenism	inbetween	subarctic	accentual	buckhound
statewide	traveller	cobwebbed	inbreathe	subastral	acceptant	buckshish
stational	traversal	cubbyhole	jaborandi	subatomic	acceptive	buckthorn
stationer	traverser	cubically	jobmaster	subbranch	accessary	bucktooth
statistic	traycloth	debagging	jubilance	subcaudal	accession	buckwheat
statocyst	tsarevich	debarment	kibbutzim	subcostal	accessory	cachectic
statolith	twayblade	debarring	labelling	subdeacon	accidence	cacholong
statuette	unabashed	debatable	labialise	subdivide	accipiter	caciquism
statutory	unadopted	debauched	labialism	subduable	acclaimer	cacodemon
stauncher	unadorned	debauchee	laborious	subduedly	acclimate	cacodylic
staunchly	unadvised	debaucher	labourite	subeditor	acclivity	cacoethes
staymaker	unalloyed	debenture	labyrinth	subereous	accompany	cacophony
suability	unaltered	debugging	libecchio	subfamily	accordant	cacuminal
suasively	unanimity	debutante	libellant	subgenera	according	cicatrice
swaddling	unanimous	dubiosity	libelling	subjacent	accordion	cicatrise
swaggerer	unaptness	dubiously	libellist	subjugate	accretion	cocainise
swangoose	unashamed	dubitable	libellous	sublation	accretive	cocainism
swansdown	Upanishad	elbowroom	liberally	sublethal	accusable	coccidium
swarajist	uraninite	embarrass	liberated	sublimate	alchemise	coccygeal
swartness	uranology	embassage	liberator	sublimely	alchemist	cochineal
teachable	uvarovite	embattled	libertine	sublimity	alcoholic	cochleate
teachably	viability	embayment	libidinal	sublunary	ancestral	cockahoop
teacupful	weakkneed	embedding	librarian	submarine	anchorage	Cockaigne
teakettle	wealthily	embedment	libration	submaster	anchoress	cockatiel
tearfully	weariless	embellish	libratory	submental	anchorite	cockfight
teasingly	weariness	embezzler	librettos	submitted	anchorman	cockhorse
thalassic	wearisome	embraceor	lobectomy	subnormal	anchylose	cockiness
thaneship	weathered	embracery	lobscouse	subocular	anciently	cockneyfy
thankless	weatherly	embracive	lobulated	subphylum	ancientry	cockroach
thatching	whaleback	embrangle	lubricant	subregion	ancillary	cockscomb
toadeater	whaleboat	embrasure	lubricate	subrogate	archangel	cocksfoot
toadstone	whalebone	embrittle	lubricity	subscribe	archducal	cocoonery
toadstool	whalehead	embrocate	lubricous	subscript	archduchy	cuckoldry
toastrack	wrathless	embroglio	mobocracy	subsellia	archenemy	cucullate
trabeated	wyandotte	embroider	nebuliser	subsidise	archetype	cyclamate
trabecula	xparticle	embryonal	nobiliary	substance	archfiend	cycloidal
traceable	yearround	embryonic	nobleness	substrata	architect	cyclopean
traceably	zealously	embryotic	obbligato	substrate	archivist	cyclopian
traceless	albatross	embussing	ombudsman	subtenant	archivolt	cyclopses
traceried	albescent	fabaceous	orbicular	subtilise	arcuately	cyclorama
tracheary	albinotic	Fabianism	oubliette	subtopian	ascendant	cyclotron
tracheate	ambergris	fabricant	pubescent	subverter	ascendent	dachshund
trachytic	ambiguity	fabricate	publicise	sybaritic	ascension	decadence
trackless	ambiguous	febricity	publicist	tablature	ascensive	decadency
tracksuit	ambitious	febrifuge	publicity	tableland	ascertain	decagonal
tractable	amblyopia	fibreless	publisher	tableleaf	ascetical	decalcify
tractably	amblyopic	fibriform	rabbinate	tabletalk	asclepiad	decalitre
trademark	ambrosial	fibrillar	rabbinism	tableware	ascospore	decalogue
tradename	ambulacra	fibrinoid	rabbinist	tabularly	auctorial	decametre
tradesman	ambulance	fibrinous	rabidness	tabulator	bacchanal	decapodal
tradition	ambuscade	fibroline	rebaptise	tubbiness	bacchante	decapodan
traducian	arbitrage	fibromata	rebelling	tubercule	bacillary	decastere
tragedian	arbitrary	gabardine	rebellion	tubularly	backbiter	decathlon
trainable	arbitrate	gaberdine	rebidding	umbellate	backboard	deceitful

decennary	exceptant	incurious	mockingly	recapture	sickening	wackiness
decennial	excepting	incurrent	muckraker	recension	sickishly	wychhazel
decennium	exception	incurring	mucksweat	reception	sickleave	Wyclifite
deception	exceptive	incursion	mucronate	receptive	socialise	yachtclub
deceptive	excerptor	incursive	Mycenaean	recession	socialism	yachtsman
decidable	excessive	incurvate	mycologic	recessive	socialist	zucchetto
decidedly	exchanger	ischaemia	mycophagy	rechauffe	socialite	abdicable
deciduate	exchequer	ischaemic	necessary	recherche	sociality	abdicator
deciduous	excipient	ischiadic	necessity	recipient	sociogram	abdominal
decilitre	excisable	ischiatic	neckcloth	reckoning	sociology	abduction
decillion	exciseman	itchiness	neckverse	reclinate	sociopath	addiction
decimally	excitable	jacaranda	necrology	reclusion	succeeder	addictive
decimator	excitancy	jackknife	necrophil	reclusive	succentor	addressee
decimetre	excitedly	jackplane	necrotise	recognise	successor	addresser
decistere	exclosure	jacksnipe	nectarean	recoinage	succinate	addressor
deckhouse	exclusion	jackstraw	nectarial	recollect	succotash	adducible
declaimer	exclusive	Jacobinic	nectarine	recombine	succourer	adduction
declarant	excoriate	jacquerie	nectarous	recommend	succulent	adductive
declinate	excrement	jactation	niccolite	recompose	succursal	aldehydic
declivity	excretion	jockstrap	nickelise	reconcile	suctorial	andantino
declivous	excretive	jocularly	nickelled	recondite	suctorian	andesitic
decoction	excretory	jocundity	nickelous	reconfirm	sycophant	androecia
decollate	exculpate	kickstart	nicotiana	reconvene	tacamahac	androgyne
decollete	excurrent	laccolith	nicotinic	reconvert	tachylite	androgyny
decomplex	excursion	lacerable	nictation	recording	tachylyte	arduously
decompose	excursive	lacertian	nictitate	recordist	tacitness	audacious
decongest	excusable	lacertine	noctiluca	recoverer	tackiness	audiology
decontrol	excusably	lachrymal	nocturnal	recreancy	tactfully	auditable
decorator	facecloth	laciniate	nocuously	recruital	tactician	auditoria
decrement	facetious	lacrimose	nucleated	recruiter	tactility	badminton
decretive	facsimile	lacrymose	nucleolus	rectangle	tactitian	bedfellow
decretory	factional	lactation	nucleonic	rectifier	tactually	bedjacket
decumbent	factitive	lecherous	obconical	rectitude	technical	bedlamite
decussate	factorage	licensure	obcordate	rectorate	technique	bedraggle
dichasial	factorial	lichenous	occipital	rectorial	tectonics	bedridden
dichasium	factorise	lickerish	occludent	rectrices	tectorial	bedsettee
dichogamy	factually	locatable	occlusion	recumbent	tectrices	bedsitter
dichotomy	facundity	locksmith	occlusive	recurrent	Tocharian	bedspread
dichroism	feculence	locomotor	occultism	recurring	tuckerbag	bedspring
dichromat	fecundate	lucidness	occultist	recursion	uncannily	bodyguard
dichromic	fecundity	luciferin	occupancy	recursive	unceasing	budgetary
dickybird	fictional	luckiness	occurrent	recusance	uncertain	cadastral
diclinous	focussing	lucrative	occurring	recusancy	uncharted	cadaveric
dicrotism	hackamore	lucubrate	oecologic	ricepaper	unchecked	caddisfly
dictation	hackberry	macaronic	oecumenic	rocambole	uncinated	cadential
doctorate	hackneyed	Maccabean	oncogenic	rockbound	uncivilly	cadetship
doctorial	hectogram	macedoine	oncologic	rockbrake	uncleanly	cedarwood
doctrinal	hocussing	macerator	orchestic	rockdrill	unclothed	cudgelled
duckboard	huckaback	machinate	orchestra	rocketeer	unclouded	dedicator
ductility	huckstery	machinery	orchidist	rockiness	unconcern	deducible
eccentric	incapable	machinist	oscillate	rockplant	uncounted	deduction
ecclesial	incapably	machmeter	oscitancy	rocksnake	uncouthly	deductive
encaustic	incarnate	macintosh	pacemaker	saccharin	uncovered	didactics
encephala	incaution	macrocosm	pachyderm	sacciform	uncreated	didelphic
enchanter	incensory	macrocyte	packaging	sacculate	uncropped	didrachma
enchilada	incentive	mechanics	packdrill	sackcloth	uncrossed	dodecagon
enchorial	inception	mechanise	packhorse	sacrament	uncrowned	ecdysiast
enclosure	inceptive	mechanism	packtrain	sacrarium	upcountry	eiderdown
encomiast	incessant	mechanist	peccantly	sacrifice	urceolate	eiderduck
encompass	incidence	micaceous	pectinate	sacrilege	vaccinate	eidograph
encounter	incipient	micaslate	peculator	sacristan	vacillant	eldership
encourage	inclement	microbial	pecuniary	secateurs	vacillate	endearing
encrimson	inclosure	microchip	pickaback	secernent	vacuolate	endeavour
encrinite	inclusion	microcosm	picketing	secession	vacuously	endlessly
escalator	inclusive	microcyte	picnicked	seclusion	vectorial	endoblast
escapable	incognito	microfilm	picnicker	seclusive	vicariate	endocrine
escheator	incommode	microgram	pictogram	secondary	vicarious	endogamic
escortage	incondite	microlite	pictorial	secretage	vicennial	endogenic
eucalypti	incorrect	microlith	picturise	secretary	viceregal	endolymph
eucaryote	incorrupt	micrology	pocketful	secretion	vicereine	endomixis
Eucharist	increaser	micromesh	pycnidium	secretive	viceroyal	endomorph
euchology	increment	micropsia	racehorse	secretory	vicesimal	endophagy
euclidean	incubator	micropyle	racetrack	sectarian	viciously	endophyte
excavator	inculcate	microsome	racialism	sectility	victimise	endoplasm
exceeding	inculpate	microtome	racialist	sectional	Victorian	endoscope
excellent	incumbent	microtomy	racketeer	sectorial	victorine	endoscopy
excelling	incunable	microtone	raconteur	secularly	vocabular	endosperm
excelsior	incurable	microwave	recalesce	securable	vocaliser	endospore
excentric	incurably	micturate	recapping	siccative	vocalness	endosteal

endosteum	ludicrous	reduction	undertake	breakable	crenature	fiendlike
endowment	maddening	reductive	undertint	breakaway	crenelled	fieriness
endurable	madeleine	redundant	undertone	breakdown	crenulate	fleckless
endurably	madrepore	riderless	undertook	breakeven	crepitant	fledgling
endurance	medallion	ridgepole	undervest	breakfast	crepitate	fleetness
faddiness	medallist	ridgetile	underwear	breakneck	crepuscle	fleshings
federally	mediaeval	ridiculer	underwent	breastpin	crescendo	fleshless
fideistic	mediately	rodfisher	underwing	breathily	crestless	fleshment
fiduciary	mediation	rudbeckia	underwood	breathing	cretinism	foeticide
gadgeteer	mediatise	ruddiness	undivided	brecciate	cretinous	freeboard
giddiness	mediative	ruddleman	undoubted	breeching	Daedalean	freehouse
goddamned	mediatory	saddlebag	undreamed	breezeway	Daedalian	freelance
godfather	mediatrix	saddlebow	undulated	bregmatic	deerberry	freeliver
godliness	medicable	Sadducean	undutiful	bretasche	deerhound	Freemason
godmother	medically	sedentary	vademecum	Bretwalda	dieselise	freerange
godparent	medicinal	sedgewren	Vedantist	breveting	diesinker	freerider
hedgingly	meditator	seditious	videlicet	brevetted	dietetics	freestone
hiddenite	medullary	seduction	videotape	caecilian	dietician	freestyle
hidebound	medullate	seductive	wedgewise	Caenozoic	dietitian	freewheel
hideously	middleman	sideboard	Wednesday	caerulean	dreamboat	freewoman
hodiernal	midinette	sideburns	wideawake	Caesarean	dreamland	freezable
hodograph	midstream	sidedness	widowbird	Caesarian	dreamless	freezedry
hodometer	midsummer	sideissue	widowhood	Caesarism	dreamlike	freighter
hydathode	midwicket	sidelight	widthways	Caesarist	dresscoat	frenchify
hydraemia	midwifery	sideritic	widthwise	cheapjack	edelweiss	Frenchman
hydrangea	midwinter	siderosis	Yiddisher	cheapness	ejectment	frequence
hydration	modelling	sideswipe	yodelling	checkered	electoral	frequency
hydraulic	moderator	sidetable	aberrance	checklist	electress	freshener
hydrazine	modernise	sidetrack	aberrancy	checkmate	electrify	freshness
hydriodic	modernism	sidewards	acellular	checkrein	electrode	fretfully
hydrocele	modernist	sidewheel	acescence	cheekbone	electuary	Gaeltacht
hydrofoil	modernity	sodabread	acetabula	cheerless	elegantly	gleefully
hydrology	modillion	sodawater	acetamide	chelation	elegiacal	glengarry
hydrolyse	modulator	sudatoria	acetifier	chelicera	elemental	gneissoid
hydrolyte	muddiness	sudorific	acetylate	chelonian	elevation	gneissose
hydronium	mydriasis	tediously	acetylcoA	chemistry	elevenses	greasegun
hydrosome	mydriatic	tidegauge	acetylene	chemitype	emendable	greataunt
hydroxide	nodulated	tidewater	ademption	chemurgic	emendator	greatcoat
hydrozoan	oddfellow	undamaged	adenoidal	cheongsam	emergence	greatness
hydrozoon	oddjobber	undaunted	adenomata	chequered	emergency	Greekless
indagator	oddjobman	undecagon	adenosine	cherimoya	energetic	greenback
indecency	orderbook	undeceive	adeptness	chernozem	energiser	greenbelt
indecorum	orderform	undecided	aleatoric	cherrypie	energumen	greeneyed
indelible	orderless	undecimal	Alemannic	chevalier	erectness	greengage
indelibly	ordinance	undefined	alertness	chevelure	eremitism	greenhorn
indemnify	pedagogic	underbody	amendable	cleanness	esemplasy	greenness
indemnity	pedagogue	underbred	amendment	cleansing	eternally	greenroom
indention	pedalling	underclay	americium	clearance	eventless	greensand
indenture	pederasty	undercoat	Amerindic	clearcole	eventuate	greenweed
Indianise	pedicular	underdone	anecdotal	cleareyed	everglade	greenwood
indicator	pedigreed	underfelt	anecdotic	clearness	evergreen	gregarian
indiction	pedometer	underfoot	anemogram	cleavable	everybody	gregarine
indigence	podagrous	undergird	aperiodic	clemently	ewenecked	Gregorian
indignant	podginess	undergone	aperitive	clepsydra	execrable	grenadier
indignity	podzolise	undergrad	apetalous	clergyman	execrably	grenadine
indigotin	pudginess	underhand	Areopagus	clergymen	executant	greybeard
indispose	radialply	underhung	asepalous	clerkship	execution	greyhound
IndoAryan	radiantly	underlaid	asexually	coecilian	executive	greywacke
indolence	radiately	underlain	aventaile	coelomata	executory	guerrilla
indraught	radiation	underline	averagely	coelomate	executrix	guesswork
inducible	radiative	underling	avertible	coelostat	exegetist	guestroom
induction	radically	undermine	awesomely	coemption	exemplary	haematite
inductive	radicular	undermost	awestruck	coenobite	exemplify	haematoid
indulgent	radiocast	underpaid	azeotrope	coenobium	exemption	haematoma
indweller	radiogram	underpart	beechfern	coenosarc	exequatur	haemostat
Judaistic	radiology	underpass	beechmast	coequally	exercises	heedfully
Judastree	redaction	underplay	beefeater	coercible	eyebright	heelpiece
judgement	redbreast	underplot	beefiness	coercibly	eyeglance	hierarchy
judgeship	redevelop	underrate	beefsteak	coeternal	eyeopener	hieratica
judgmatic	redhanded	underripe	beekeeper	creatable	eyeshadow	hierodule
judiciary	redheaded	underseal	beemaster	creatress	eyestrain	hierogram
judicious	redingote	underseas	beeorchis	creatural	feedstock	hierology
kiddingly	redivivus	undersell	beestings	crediting	feedstuff	Icelander
kidnapped	redletter	undershot	bleachery	credulity	feelingly	Icelandic
kidnapper	redolence	underside	bleakness	credulous	fieldbook	iceskater
ladysmock	redoubted	undersign	bleareyed	cremaster	fieldboot	idealiser
lodestone	redresser	undersold	blessedly	cremation	fieldfare	idealless
lodgement	reducible	undersong	breadline	crematory	fieldsman	identical
lodgepole	reductant	underspin	breadtree	crenation	fieldwork	identikit

```
ideograph  overnight  preceptor  puerility  spectator  theurgist  defendant
ideologic  overpitch  precipice  puerperal  speculate  tiedyeing  defensive
ideologue  overpower  precisely  quebracho  speechful  treachery  deference
inebriant  overprice  precisian  queenhood  speechify  treadmill  deferment
inebriate  overprint  precision  queenless  speedball  treasurer  deferring
inebriety  overproof  precocial  queenlike  speedboat  treatable  defiantly
ineffable  overreach  precocity  queenpost  speedster  treatment  deficient
ineffably  overreact  preconise  queenship  speedwell  trebuchet  definable
inelastic  oversexed  precursor  queerness  spellbind  trebucket  definably
inelegant  overshoot  predacity  quercetum  spellican  treillage  deflation
ineptness  oversight  predation  querulous  spendable  trematode  deflector
inequable  oversized  predative  reediness  spermatic  tremolant  deflexion
inerrable  overskirt  predatory  reedorgan  spermatid  tremolite  defoliant
inerrancy  oversleep  predicant  reeducate  steadfast  tremulant  defoliate
inertness  overslept  predicate  reefpoint  steamboat  tremulous  deformity
inexactly  overspend  predictor  reenforce  steampipe  trenchant  defroster
iteration  overspent  predigest  reentrant  steamship  trepanned  different
iterative  overspill  predikant  reexamine  steatitic  trepidant  difficile
jeeringly  overstate  preemptor  rheumatic  steelclad  twelfthly  difficult
keelivine  oversteer  preengage  scenarist  steelhead  twentieth  diffident
khedivial  overstock  preexilic  scenedock  steelwork  twentyone  diffusely
kneadable  overstuff  prefatory  scentless  steelyard  unearthly  diffusion
laevulose  overtaken  preferred  sceptical  steenkirk  uneatable  diffusive
leeringly  overthrew  prefigure  seedeater  steepness  unequally  effective
leewardly  overthrow  prefixion  seediness  steersman  unethical  effectual
liegelord  overtness  pregnable  seedpearl  stegosaur  uselessly  efficient
maelstrom  overtones  pregnancy  seedplant  stellated  veeringly  effluence
mnemonics  overtrain  prejudice  seemingly  stenotype  viewpoint  effluvial
mnemonist  overtrick  prelatess  shearling  stenotypy  weediness  effluvium
myelomata  overtrump  prelatise  sheatfish  stepchild  weeknight  effluxion
needfully  overvalue  prelature  sheathing  stepdance  weevilled  effortful
neediness  overwatch  prelector  Shechinah  steradian  wheatmeal  effulgent
needleful  overweary  prelusion  sheepcote  stercoral  wheedling  exfoliate
obedience  overweigh  prelusive  sheepfold  sterilise  wheelbase  fifteenth
obeisance  overwhelm  prelusory  sheephook  sterility  wheelless  goffering
obeseness  overwound  premature  sheeplice  sternmost  wheelwork  heftiness
ocellated  overwrite  premonish  sheepskin  sternness  wherefore  huffiness
okeydokey  overwrote  premotion  sheeptick  sternpost  wherefrom  infantile
oleaceous  paederast  prenotion  sheepwalk  sternward  whereinto  infantine
olecranal  peepsight  preoccupy  sheepwash  steroidal  whereunto  infatuate
olecranon  peevishly  preordain  sheerhulk  stevedore  whereupon  infection
oleograph  phellogen  prepotent  sheerlegs  swearword  wherewith  infective
oleoresin  phenacite  prerecord  sheerness  sweatband  wherryman  inferable
onehanded  phenakite  presbyope  sheetbend  sweatshop  whetstone  inference
onelegged  phenology  presbyter  sheikhdom  sweepback  wheyfaced  inferring
onerously  phenomena  preschool  sheldduck  sweetcorn  wieldable  infertile
openended  phenotype  prescient  sheldrake  sweetener  woebegone  infielder
openheart  pheromone  prescribe  shelflife  sweetmeal  wrestling  infilling
operation  piecemeal  prescript  shelfmark  sweetmeat  affecting  infirmary
operative  piecerate  preselect  shelfroom  sweetness  affection  infirmity
opercular  piecework  presentee  shellback  sweetshop  affective  inflation
operculum  pierrette  presenter  shellbark  sweettalk  affianced  inflexion
operosely  pietistic  presently  shellfire  swellfish  affidavit  inflictor
operosity  pleadable  preserver  shellfish  sweptback  affiliate  inflowing
ovenready  pleadings  preshrink  shellheap  taeniasis  affirmant  influence
overblown  pleasance  preshrunk  shellwork  theandric  affixture  influenza
overboard  Pleiocene  president  shemozzle  theatrics  afflation  informant
overborne  plenarily  presidial  shewbread  theocracy  affluence  infractor
overcheck  plenitude  presidium  skedaddle  theocrasy  affricate  infuriate
overcloud  plenteous  pressgang  skeesicks  theogonic  awfulness  infuscate
overcrowd  plentiful  pressmark  sketchily  theologic  befitting  infusible
overdraft  plethoric  pressroom  sketchmap  theologue  befogging  infusoria
overdrawn  pleuritic  pressstud  skewwhiff  theomachy  bifarious  leftovers
overdress  pneumatic  presswork  sleekness  theomania  bifoliate  leftwards
overdrive  pneumonia  prestress  sleepless  theophany  bifurcate  lifeblood
overeaten  pneumonic  pretender  sleevenut  theoretic  buffaloes  lifecycle
overeater  poetaster  preterist  slenderly  theoriser  buffeting  lifeforce
overexert  poeticise  preterite  speakable  theosophy  cafeteria  lifeguard
overflown  poeticism  pretermit  speakeasy  therapist  coffeecup  lifesaver
overglaze  preachify  prettyish  spearfish  Theravada  coffeepot  lifesized
overgraze  preachily  prettyism  spearhead  therefore  cofferdam  lifestyle
overgrown  preadamic  prevalent  spearmint  therefrom  coffinite  lifetable
overheard  prebendal  preventer  spearside  thereinto  defalcate  loftiness
overissue  precancel  prevision  spearwort  thereunto  defaulter  luftwaffe
overjoyed  precative  pseudonym  specially  thereupon  defeatism  muffineer
overladen  precatory  pseudopod  specialty  therewith  defeatist  muffinman
overleapt  precedent  pterosaur  specifier  thermally  defeature  nefarious
overlying  preceding  pterygium  speckless  thermidor  defection  obfuscate
overmatch  precentor  pterygoid  spectacle  thesaurus  defective  offcentre
```

offchance	algorithm	gigahertz	megacycle	signatory	ethmoidal	agitation
offcolour	angelfish	gigantism	megadeath	signature	ethnarchy	agitative
offensive	angelical	gogglebox	megahertz	signboard	ethnicity	ahistoric
offertory	angiology	haggadist	megaphone	significs	ethnology	alicyclic
offhanded	angiomata	haggardly	megaspore	signorial	ethylenic	alienable
officiant	angleiron	hagiarchy	migration	signorina	exhauster	alienator
officiate	anglesite	hagiology	migratory	sogginess	exhibitor	alignment
officinal	angleworm	hagridden	mugginess	sugarbeet	ichneumon	alinement
officious	anglicise	hegemonic	negligent	sugarcane	ichnology	aliphatic
offscreen	anglicism	highchair	negotiant	sugarloaf	ichthyoid	aliveness
offseason	Anglicist	highclass	negotiate	sugarplum	inhalator	amianthus
offspring	anglophil	highflier	negritude	suggester	inharmony	amidships
offstreet	angriness	highflown	negroidal	tegmental	inherence	aminoacid
olfaction	anguished	highflyer	Negroness	tegmentum	inheritor	animalise
olfactive	angularly	highgrade	negrophil	tegularly	inhibitor	animalism
olfactory	argentine	highgrown	niggardly	tigerlily	inhumanly	animalist
puffadder	argentite	highlands	nightbird	tigermoth	Johannine	animality
puffiness	argentous	highlevel	nightclub	tigerseye	Kshatriya	animation
raffinate	argillite	highlight	nightfall	tigerwood	maharajah	animatism
raffinose	argumenta	highspeed	nightgown	tightener	maharanee	animistic
raffishly	Arguseyed	hightoned	nighthawk	tightness	maharishi	animosity
rafflesia	argybargy	highwater	nightlife	tightrope	mahlstick	apiculate
refashion	augmented	hoggishly	nightline	tightwire	Mahometan	apishness
refection	augmenter	hugeously	nightlong	ungallant	Nahuatlan	asininity
refectory	augmentor	hygienics	nightmare	unguarded	ochlocrat	avizandum
referable	bagatelle	hygienist	nightside	vagarious	ophiology	axiomatic
reference	bagginess	hygrostat	nighttime	vagueness	otherness	azimuthal
referenda	begetting	ingenious	nightwork	vegetable	otherwise	bailiwick
referring	beginning	ingenuity	nigricant	vegetably	rehearsal	bainmarie
refitment	bigeneric	ingenuous	nigritude	vigesimal	rehydrate	blindfold
refitting	bigheaded	ingestion	nigrosine	vigilance	scheelite	blindness
reflation	bughunter	ingestive	oogenesis	vigilante	schematic	blinkered
reflector	cageyness	inglenook	oogenetic	vignetter	schilling	briarroot
reflexion	cigarette	ingrained	organelle	waggishly	schistose	briarwood
reflexive	cigarillo	ingrowing	organiser	waggonage	schistous	bricabrac
refluence	cogitable	laggardly	organstop	Wagnerian	schlemiel	brickwork
reformism	cognately	lagniappe	organzine	Wagnerite	schlemihl	brickyard
reformist	cognation	lagomorph	orgiastic	wagonette	schlieren	bridecake
refractor	cognisant	legendary	pageantry	wagonroof	schmaltzy	bridesman
refreshen	cognition	legerline	pegmatite	zigzagged	schnauzer	bridewell
refresher	cognitive	legginess	piggishly	zygomatic	schnitzel	bridleway
refuelled	digastric	legionary	piggyback	zygospore	schnorkel	briefcase
refulgent	digestion	legislate	piggybank	abhorrent	schnorrer	briefless
refurbish	digestive	lightfoot	pigheaded	abhorring	scholarly	briefness
refurnish	digitalin	lightless	pugnacity	Acheulean	scholiast	brierroot
refusable	digitalis	lightness	regardant	Acheulian	schoolbag	brierwood
refutable	digitally	lightning	regardful	adherence	schoolboy	brigadier
riflebird	digitated	lightship	regicidal	anhydride	schooling	brigandry
rufescent	dignified	lightsome	regisseur	anhydrite	schoolman	brightish
ruffianly	dignitary	lightsout	registrar	anhydrous	sphagnous	brilliant
safeguard	dogcollar	lightwood	regretful	aphereses	spherical	brimstone
safetypin	doggishly	lightyear	regretted	apheresis	spherular	bringdown
safflower	doglegged	lignaloes	regularly	aphyllous	sphincter	briquette
safranine	dogmatics	ligniform	regulator	ashamedly	sphygmoid	briskness
softgoods	dogmatise	logaoedic	rightable	Ashkenazi	tahsildar	bristling
softpedal	dogmatism	logarithm	righteous	ashlaring	unhappily	Britannia
softshell	dogmatist	logically	righthand	atheistic	unharness	Britannic
suffering	dogoodism	logistics	rightness	athematic	unhealthy	Briticise
suffocate	dogshores	logogriph	rightward	Athenaeum	unheeding	Briticism
suffragan	dogstooth	logomachy	rigidness	athletics	unhelpful	Britisher
suffusion	dogviolet	magdalene	rigmarole	behaviour	unhurried	brittlely
tufaceous	eagerness	Magianism	roguishly	buhrstone	upholster	cailleach
unfailing	eggbeater	magically	ruggedise	coheiress	usherette	Cainozoic
unfeeling	eightfold	magicking	sagacious	coherence	vehemence	cairngorm
unfeigned	eightieth	magistery	sagebrush	coherency	vehicular	chibouque
unfitness	eightsome	magistral	sagegreen	dahabiyah	wehrmacht	chicanery
unfitting	eightyish	magnalium	sagittate	dehiscent	yohimbine	chickadee
unfledged	engarland	magnesian	segmental	dehydrate	abidingly	chickaree
unfleshed	Englander	magnesite	segregate	echolalia	aciculate	chickling
unfleshly	englutted	magnesium	sightless	echovirus	acidifier	chickweed
unfounded	engraving	magnetics	sightseer	enhearten	acidophil	chiefship
aggravate	engrosser	magnetise	sigillary	ephedrine	acidulate	chieftain
aggregate	ergograph	magnetism	sigillate	ephemeral	acidulent	chihuahua
aggressor	ergometer	magnetist	sigmoidal	ephemerid	acidulous	chilblain
aggrieved	ergonomic	magnetite	signalbox	ephemeris	aciniform	childhood
algarroba	faggoting	magnetron	signalise	ephemeron	adiabatic	childless
algebraic	figurante	magnifico	signalled	etherical	adipocere	childlike
Algonkian	fogginess	magnifier	signaller	ethically	adiposity	chillness
Algonquin	fugacious	magnitude	signalman	Ethiopian	agistment	chimaeric

```
Chinatown  epitomist  itinerant  primarily  shieldfem  stigmatic  trifolium
chinaware  epizootic  itinerary  primatial  shiftless  stilettos  triforium
chinstrap  eristical  itinerate  primeness  shillelah  stillborn  trigamist
chipboard  etiquette  jailbreak  primipara  shinguard  stillhunt  trigamous
chipolata  evidently  jointress  primitive  shininess  stillness  trihedral
chiropody  evincible  juiceless  primordia  Shintoism  stillroom  trihybrid
chiselled  exilement  juiciness  princedom  Shintoist  stiltedly  trilinear
chiseller  existence  kaiserdom  princekin  shipboard  stimulant  trilithon
chisquare  faintness  kaiserism  princelet  shipcanal  stimulate  trilobate
chitinous  fairfaced  klinostat  principal  shipfever  stingaree  trilobite
chitlings  fairyhood  knifeedge  principia  shipmoney  stingless  trimerous
chivalric  fairyland  knightage  principle  shipowner  stinkball  trimester
clientage  fairylike  lairdship  printable  shipshape  stinkbomb  trimetric
clientele  fairyring  Leicester  printshop  shipwreck  stinkhorn  trimmings
cliffhang  fairytale  leisurely  priorship  shirtless  stinktrap  trinketer
climactic  faithcure  leitmotif  prismatic  shirttail  stinkweed  trinketry
climbable  faithless  leitmotiv  privateer  skiagraph  stinkwood  trinomial
clinician  feiseanna  loincloth  privately  skiamachy  stintless  triploidy
clinquant  flightily  maidenish  privation  skiascopy  stipitate  triptyque
clipboard  flintlock  mailplane  privative  skijoring  stippling  triquetra
clitellum  flippancy  mailtrain  privilege  skilfully  stipulate  trisagion
coiffeuse  friarbird  mainbrace  puissance  skindiver  stirabout  trisector
coinsurer  fricassee  mainliner  quibbling  skinflick  stitchery  triteness
cricketer  fricative  mainsheet  quickener  skinflint  swiftness  tritheism
criminate  frigatoon  moistener  quicklime  skingraft  swimmable  tritheist
criminous  frightful  moistness  quickness  skintight  swimmeret  triturate
crinoidal  frigidity  nailbrush  quicksand  skirtings  swineherd  triumphal
crinoline  fritterer  neighbour  quickstep  skirtless  swingeing  triumviri
crippling  frivolity  noiseless  quiescent  slickness  swinishly  trivalent
crispness  frivolled  noisiness  quietness  sliderule  switchman  trivially
criterion  frivolous  noisomely  quillwort  slightish  swivelled  triweekly
criticise  gainfully  nuisancer  quinoline  sliminess  tailboard  tuitional
criticism  gainsayer  oligaemia  quintette  slingback  taillight  twiceborn
dairymaid  glissandi  oligarchy  quintuple  slingshot  tailoress  twicelaid
deinosaur  glissando  Oligocene  quirister  slinkweed  tailoring  twicetold
deistical  goingover  oligopoly  quitclaim  slipcoach  tailpiece  twinkling
driftsail  griefless  olivenite  quittance  slipcover  taintless  twistable
driftweed  grievance  ominously  quixotism  slivovitz  taioseach  twitchily
driftwood  grillroom  omissible  quizzical  smileless  thickener  twitterer
drinkable  grillwork  onionskin  raincheck  smilingly  thicketed  uliginous
dripstone  grimalkin  opinioned  raincloud  sniggerer  thickhead  unicolour
drivelled  griminess  orientate  raingauge  snipefish  thickknee  unicuspid
driveller  grisaille  orificial  raininess  snivelled  thickness  unifiable
dziggetai  gristmill  oriflamme  rainmaker  sniveller  thighbone  uniformly
edibility  gritstone  originate  rainproof  soidisant  thighboot  uniparous
editorial  guidebook  oviductal  rainstorm  spicebush  thingness  uniplanar
eliminate  guideline  oviferous  rainwater  spiciness  thingummy  uniserial
eminently  guidepost  oviparity  Reichstag  spiculate  thinkable  unisexual
enigmatic  guiderope  oviparous  reimburse  spiderman  thinktank  unisonant
epicentre  guildhall  oxidation  reinforce  spiderweb  thirdhand  unisonous
epiclesis  guildship  paillasse  reinstate  spikenard  thirdrate  unitarian
epicurean  guileless  paillette  reiterate  spikiness  thirdsman  unitively
epicurism  guillemot  painfully  Rhineodon  spillikin  thirstily  univalent
epicyclic  guilloche  painterly  rhinology  spindling  thirtieth  universal
epidermal  guiltless  paintwork  rhizocarp  spindrier  thitherto  vainglory
epidermic  guitarist  pairhorse  rhizoidal  spindrift  trialogue  Vaishnava
epidermis  hailstone  philander  roisterer  spineless  triatomic  veinstone
epidosite  hailstorm  philately  ruination  spininess  tribadism  voiceless
epigraphy  hairbrush  philippic  ruinously  spinnaker  tribalism  voiceover
epigynous  haircloth  philogyny  sailcloth  spinneret  tribesman  wailingly
epilation  hairgrass  philology  sailoring  spinosity  tribology  waistband
epileptic  hairiness  Philomela  sailorman  Spinozism  tribunate  waistbelt
epilogist  hairpiece  plicately  sailplane  Spinozist  tributary  waistcoat
epinastic  hairshirt  plication  sainthood  spinulose  trichinae  waistline
epiphragm  hairslide  plicature  saintlike  spinulous  trichomic  weighable
epiphyses  hairspace  poignancy  saintling  spiracula  trichroic  weighbeam
epiphysis  hairstyle  poinciana  saintship  spirality  trickless  weightily
epiphytal  heinously  pointduty  sciaenoid  spiralled  tricksily  weighting
epiphytic  idiograph  pointedly  sciagraph  spirillum  trickster  weirdness
epipolism  idiomatic  pointille  sciamachy  spiritism  triclinia  whichever
episcopal  idiopathy  pointlace  sciascopy  spiritist  triclinic  whimperer
epistaxis  idioplasm  pointless  sciential  spiritoso  tricolour  whimsical
epistemic  idiotical  pointsman  scientism  spiritous  tridactyl  whinstone
epistoler  imitation  poisonous  scientist  spiritual  tridymite  whipperin
epistolic  imitative  priceless  scintilla  spiritual  triennial  whipround
epithelia  initially  prideless  scirrhous  spirogyra  triennium  whipsnake
epithesis  initiator  priestess  seigneury  stickwork  trierarch  whipstock
epithetic  isinglass  primaeval  seigniory  stiffener  trifacial  whirligig
epitomise  itineracy  primality  shieldbug  stiffness  trifocals  whirlpool
```

```
whirlwind  aflatoxin  bullishly  colourful  fullblown  hellenise  millboard
whiskered  ailanthus  bulltrout  colouring  fullcream  Hellenism  millenary
whisperer  allantois  bullybeef  colourist  fulldress  Hellenist  millennia
whistling  allegedly  bullytree  colourman  fullgrown  hellhound  millepede
whitebait  allegiant  calaboose  coltishly  fullscale  hellishly  millepore
whitebass  allegoric  calabrese  coltsfoot  fulminant  helpfully  millerite
whitebeam  allemande  calamanco  colubrine  fulminate  Helvetian  milligram
whiteface  alleviate  calandria  columbary  fulminous  hilarious  millinery
whitefish  alligator  calcaneal  Columbian  fulsomely  hillbilly  millionth
Whitehall  allocable  calcaneum  columbine  galactose  Holarctic  millipede
whitehead  allograph  calcarate  columbite  galantine  hollyhock  millivolt
whiteness  allomorph  calcicole  columbium  galenical  Hollywood  millstone
whitening  allopathy  calcifuge  columella  galingale  holocaust  millwheel
whitewash  allophone  calculate  columnist  gallantly  holograph  milometer
whitewing  alloplasm  calculous  cullender  gallantry  holophote  Miltonian
whitewood  allotment  caldarium  culminant  galleried  holystone  molecular
whizzbang  allotrope  calendric  culminate  gallicise  hylozoism  molluscan
wristband  allotropy  calendula  culsdesac  gallicism  illboding  mollymawk
wristdrop  allotting  calenture  cultivate  gallingly  illegally  molybdate
wristshot  allowable  calibrate  cylindric  gallinule  illegible  mullioned
zeitgeist  allowably  calicular  dalliance  gallivant  illegibly  multifoil
zoiatrics  allowance  caliology  dalmatian  galliwasp  illgotten  multiform
Zwinglian  allowedly  caliphate  daltonism  gallmidge  illiberal  multilane
abjection  aplanatic  callipers  delftware  gallonage  illicitly  multipara
adjacency  Atlantean  callosity  delicious  gallooned  illjudged  multiplex
adjoining  Aylesbury  callously  delineate  gallopade  illogical  multitude
adjunctly  balaclava  calmative  delirious  Gallophil  illomened  Nilometer
adjutancy  balalaika  calorific  deliverer  galloping  illwisher  nullifier
bejabbers  balconied  Calvinism  deludable  gallowses  Islamitic  nullipara
dejection  baldachin  Calvinist  dilatable  gallstone  jellyfish  nullipore
enjoyable  baldaquin  calycinal  dilatancy  galvanise  jollyboat  obligated
enjoyably  baldfaced  celandine  diligence  galvanism  kilderkin  obliquely
enjoyment  balefully  celebrant  dolefully  galvanist  killifish  obliquity
injection  balkanise  celebrate  doleritic  gelignite  kilocycle  oblivious
injurious  balladeer  celebrity  dolomitic  giltedged  kilohertz  oilburner
injustice  balladist  celestial  doltishly  goldbrick  kilolitre  oilcolour
majordomo  ballerina  cellarage  dulcamara  goldcrest  kilometre  oilpaints
majorette  ballistae  celluloid  dulcitude  goldeneye  lallation  onlicence
majorship  ballistic  cellulose  ealdorman  goldenrod  liltingly  palaestra
majuscule  ballpoint  Celticism  eclampsia  goldfever  lilywhite  palafitte
objectify  balminess  chlamydes  eclamptic  goldfield  malachite  palankeen
objection  baltimore  chlorella  eglantine  goldfinch  maladroit  palanquin
objective  belatedly  chloritic  ellipsoid  goldsinny  malanders  palatable
objurgate  beleaguer  chlorosis  enlighten  goldsmith  malarious  palatably
rejection  belemnite  chlorotic  eulogiser  golflinks  malathion  palillogy
rejoicing  bellglass  colcannon  Falangism  goliardic  Malayalam  Palladian
rejoinder  bellicose  colchicum  Falangist  halfbaked  malformed  palladium
sojourner  bellpunch  colcothar  falciform  halfblood  malicious  palladous
alkaloses  bellyache  coldshort  faldstool  halfbound  malignant  palletise
alkalosis  bellyband  colemouse  Falernian  halfbreed  malignity  palliasse
anklebone  bellyflop  collagist  fallalery  halfcaste  malleable  pallidity
ankylosis  belvedere  collation  falsehood  halfcrown  malleehen  palmation
ankylotic  bilabiate  colleague  falseness  halfhardy  mallemuck  palmipede
askewness  bilateral  collected  falsifier  halflight  malleolar  palmistry
awkwardly  bilgekeel  collector  felicific  halfpence  malleolus  palmitate
bakehouse  bilharzia  collegial  fellowman  halfpenny  malthouse  palpation
baksheesh  bilingual  collegian  felonious  halfprice  malvoisie  palpebral
irksomely  biliously  collegium  filaceous  halfshell  melanosis  palpitant
makeready  bilirubin  colligate  filiation  halfstaff  melanotic  palpitate
makeshift  biliteral  collimate  filigreed  halftitle  melaphyre  palsgrave
mekometer  billabong  collinear  fillister  halftrack  melatonin  paludinal
nakedness  billboard  collision  filminess  halftruth  meliorate  palustral
oakenshaw  billiards  collocate  filmstrip  halieutic  meliorism  Pelasgian
Pakistani  billionth  collodion  filoselle  halitosis  meliorist  pellagrin
Pekingese  billycock  colloidal  filterbed  Halloween  meliority  pelletise
pikeperch  billygoat  colloquia  filtertip  Hallowmas  melismata  pellitory
pikestaff  boldfaced  collotype  filtrable  hallstand  melocoton  phlebitis
pokeberry  bolection  collusion  foliation  Hallstatt  melodious  pilferage
pokerface  boliviano  collusive  folkdance  halophile  melodrama  pilgarlic
pokerwork  bolometer  collyrium  folkmusic  halophyte  melomania  pillarbox
rakehelly  bolometry  colocynth  folkweave  halothane  meltingly  pilotfish
teknonymy  Bolshevik  colonelcy  following  haltingly  meltwater  polariser
unknitted  bulbously  coloniser  fulfilled  helically  milestone  polemical
unknowing  Bulgarian  colonnade  fulfiller  heliogram  militancy  polevault
wakefully  bulginess  colophony  fulgently  heliostat  milkfever  policeman
wakerobin  bulkiness  colorific  fulgurant  heliotype  milkfloat  politburo
ablatival  bulldozer  colosseum  fulgurate  heliozoan  milkiness  politesse
ablutions  bullfight  colostomy  fulgurite  heliozoic  milkshake  political
adlibbing  bullfinch  colostrum  fulgurous  hellebore  milktooth  pollinate
```

pollinium	salvation	sylphlike	vulpinite	Camembert	demanding	homuncule
pollutant	scleritis	sylvanite	vulturine	cameraman	demarcate	homunculi
pollution	sclerosis	talismans	vulturish	camorrist	demeanour	humankind
polonaise	sclerotic	talkathon	vulturous	campanile	demimonde	humanness
polyamide	selachian	talkative	Waldenses	campanili	demission	humblebee
polyandry	selection	tallowish	waldgrave	campanula	demitasse	humbugged
polybasic	selective	tallyshop	walkabout	campchair	demitting	humdinger
polyester	selectman	Talmudist	wallboard	campcraft	demiurgic	humectant
polygamic	selenious	telamones	wallcress	campfever	demobbing	humiliate
polygenic	selenitic	telegenic	wallfruit	camphoric	democracy	hymnology
polygonal	selfabuse	telegraph	walloping	campstool	demulcent	immanence
polygonum	selfaware	telemeter	wallpaper	cementite	demurrage	immanency
polygraph	selfdoubt	telemetry	wallplate	Cimmerian	demurring	immediacy
polyhedra	selfdrive	teleology	wallydrag	combatant	demystify	immediate
polymathy	selffaced	telepathy	Walpurgis	combative	dimension	immensely
polymeric	selfglory	telephone	welcoming	combinate	dimidiate	immensity
polymorph	selfimage	telephony	welfarism	comedones	dimissory	immersion
polyonymy	selfishly	telephoto	wellbeing	comfiture	dimorphic	immigrant
polyphagy	selfmoved	telescope	wellfound	comforter	dimwitted	immigrate
polyphase	selfpride	telescopy	wellknown	comically	dominance	imminence
polyphone	selftrust	televisor	welltimed	Cominform	dominator	imminency
polyphony	Seljukian	tellingly	willemite	Comintern	dominical	immixture
polyploid	siliceous	tellurate	willingly	comitadji	Dominican	immodesty
polyptych	silicious	tellurian	willowish	commander	dumbfound	immolator
polysemic	silicosis	telluride	willpower	commandos	dumpiness	immorally
polysomic	silicotic	tellurite	wolfhound	commendam	Emmenthal	immovable
polythene	siliquose	tellurium	wolfishly	commensal	familyman	immovably
polytonal	silkgland	tellurous	wolframic	commenter	femineity	immutable
polytypic	silkiness	telophase	wolfsbane	commingle	fimbriate	immutably
polyvinyl	silliness	tilestone	wolverene	comminute	fumarolic	jambalaya
polywater	siltation	tolerable	wolverine	commissar	fumigator	jampacked
polyzoary	siltstone	tolerably	wulfenite	committal	gambadoes	jumpiness
pullulate	silverfir	tolerance	wyliecoat	committed	gambolled	kymograph
pulmonary	solacious	tollbooth	xylograph	committee	gammadion	lambently
pulmonate	soldierly	tollhouse	xylophone	commodity	gammoning	lamellate
pulpboard	solemnise	tuliproot	yellowdog	commodore	gemmation	lamellose
pulpiness	solemnity	tuliptree	yellowish	commonage	gemmology	laminaria
pulpiteer	soleplate	tulipwood	admeasure	commonlaw	gemutlich	laminated
pulpstone	solfatara	unlearned	adminicle	commotion	gimmickry	lampblack
pulsatile	solfeggio	unlimited	admirable	communard	gomphosis	lamplight
pulsation	solferino	unluckily	admirably	communion	gumminess	lampooner
pulsatory	solicitor	uplifting	admiralty	communise	gymnasial	lampshade
pulseless	solidness	valentine	admission	communism	gymnasium	lampshell
pulserate	soliloquy	valiantly	admissive	communist	gymnastic	Limburger
pulverise	solipsism	validness	admitting	community	hamadryad	limejuice
pulverous	solipsist	vallation	admixture	commutate	hamamelis	limelight
pulvillus	solitaire	vallecula	admonitor	compactly	hamburger	limestone
pulvinate	solmisate	valuables	aimlessly	compactor	hamfisted	limewater
relevance	Solomonic	valuation	almandine	companion	hamhanded	limitable
relevancy	Solutrean	valueless	almsgiver	compasses	hammerman	limitedly
reliantly	Solutrian	valueless	almshouse	compelled	hammertoe	limitless
religiose	solvation	velodrome	armadillo	compendia	hamstring	limnology
religious	splashily	velveteen	armigeral	competent	hamstrung	limonitic
reliquary	splayfoot	villagery	armillary	complaint	hemicycle	limousine
reliquiae	spleenful	villanage	armistice	complexly	hemistich	limpidity
reluctant	splendent	villenage	Armorican	complexus	hemitrope	Lombardic
reluctate	splendour	villiform	atmometer	compliant	hemstitch	lumbering
rulership	splenetic	villosity	Axminster	component	Himalayan	lumberman
salacious	splenitis	volauvent	bamboozle	composite	Himyarite	lumbrical
salangane	spleuchan	volcanism	bemusedly	composure	homegrown	lumbricus
saleratus	splintery	volcanoes	bimonthly	comprador	homemaker	luminance
salesgirl	splitting	volkslied	bombardon	comprisal	homeopath	lumpiness
saleslady	spluttery	volteface	bombasine	comptroll	homestead	lumpishly
salicetum	sulcation	voltinism	bombastic	comradely	homewards	lymegrass
salicylic	sulkiness	voltmeter	bombazine	comradery	homicidal	lymehound
saliently	sulphonic	volumeter	bombhappy	cumbrance	homiletic	lymphatic
sallowish	sulphuret	voluntary	bombilate	cymbalist	homogamic	mamillary
salmonoid	sulphuric	volunteer	bombinate	cymbidium	homogamic	mamillate
salpinges	sultanate	vulcanian	bombproof	cymbiform	homograft	mammalian
saltation	sultaness	vulcanise	bombshell	cymophane	homograph	mammalogy
saltatory	syllabary	vulcanism	bombsight	damascene	homologue	mammiform
saltglaze	syllabise	vulcanist	bumblebee	damnation	homonymic	mammonish
saltiness	syllabism	vulcanite	bumbledon	damnatory	homophone	mammonism
saltmarsh	syllabled	vulgarian	bumpiness	damnedest	homophony	mammonist
saltpetre	syllepses	vulgarise	bumptious	damningly	homoplasy	mammonite
saltspoon	syllepsis	vulgarism	camarilla	Damoclean	homopolar	mementoes
saltwater	sylleptic	vulgarity	Cambodian	demagogic	homotaxis	memoirist
saltworks	syllogise	vulnerary	camelback	demagogue	homotonic	memorable
salubrity	syllogism	vulpinism	camelhair	demandant	homousian	memorably

```
memoranda  simulator  announcer  centurion  consulage  Fenianism  honorific
memoriter  simulcast  annoyance  cinematic  consulate  fenugreek  hunchback
mimicking  something  annuitant  cineraria  consulter  financial  hundredth
momentary  sometimes  annularly  cinereous  contactor  financier  Hungarian
momentous  somewhere  annulated  Cingalese  contadina  finedrawn  hunkydory
mumchance  somewhile  annulling  concavely  contadini  fingering  ignescent
mummified  sommelier  annulment  concavity  contadino  fingertip  ignitable
nameplate  somnolent  banderole  conceited  contagion  finically  ignitible
nemertean  summarily  bandicoot  concentre  contagium  finicking  ignorable
nemertine  summarise  bandoleer  concerned  container  fundament  ignoramus
nemophila  summarist  bandolero  concerted  contemner  funebrial  ignorance
nominable  summation  bandolier  concierge  contended  fungicide  innermost
nominally  summative  bandoline  conciliar  contender  fungiform  innervate
nominator  summingup  bandstand  concisely  contented  funicular  innholder
nomocracy  sumptuary  bandwagon  concision  continent  funiculus  innkeeper
nomograph  sumptuous  bandwidth  concocter  continual  funkiness  innocence
numbskull  symbiosis  baneberry  concoctor  continuer  funnelled  innocency
numerable  symbiotic  banefully  concordat  continuum  funniness  innocuity
numerator  symbolics  banjulele  concourse  contralto  ganderism  innocuous
numerical  symbolise  bannister  concubine  contrasty  gangboard  innovator
nummulite  symbolism  banqueter  concurred  contrived  gangplank  innoxious
nymphalid  symbolist  banquette  condenser  contriver  gannister  innuendos
ommatidia  symbology  Bantustan  condignly  contumacy  genealogy  ionisable
osmometer  symmetric  beneficed  condiment  contumely  generable  janissary
pemphigus  symphonic  bengaline  condition  contusion  generalia  janitress
pimpernel  symphysis  benighted  conducive  conundrum  generally  Jansenism
pomaceous  sympodial  benignant  conductor  convector  generator  Jansenist
pommelled  sympodium  benignity  condyloid  converter  genetical  Juneberry
pompadour  symposiac  bentonite  condyloma  convexity  genialise  juniorate
pomposity  symposial  benzidine  confabbed  convincer  geniality  juniority
pompously  symposium  benzoline  conferral  convivial  genitival  junkerdom
pumiceous  tambourin  binocular  conferred  convolute  genocidal  junkerism
pummelled  tamponade  binominal  conferrer  convolved  genotypic  junketing
rampantly  temperate  binturong  confervae  cunctator  genteelly  Junoesque
remainder  temporary  bondslave  confessor  cuneiform  gentility  kennelled
remanence  temporise  bondstone  confidant  cynically  gentleman  kentledge
remeasure  temptable  bondwoman  confident  dancehall  genuflect  kinematic
remediate  temptress  bonechina  confiding  dandelion  genuinely  kingcraft
remindful  timbering  bonhomous  configure  dandiacal  gingerade  kingdomed
reminisce  timberman  bonniness  confirmed  dangerous  gingerale  kingmaker
remission  timelapse  bundobust  confirmer  Dantesque  ginglymus  kingsized
remitment  timelimit  bunkhouse  confirmor  dendritic  ginpalace  kinkiness
remittent  timeously  canalboat  confiteor  denigrate  gondolier  kinswoman
remitting  timepiece  cancelled  confluent  denitrate  gongorism  lancejack
remontant  timesheet  cancerous  conformal  denitrify  gonophore  lancewood
removable  timetable  candidacy  conformer  denouncer  guncotton  lancinate
ruminator  timidness  candidate  Confucian  denseness  gunpowder  landagent
rumrunner  timocracy  Candlemas  confusion  dentalium  gunrunner  landaulet
Samaritan  timpanist  candlenut  congenial  dentation  gynaeceum  landdross
Samoyedic  tombstone  candytuft  congeries  dentiform  gynocracy  landdrost
semanteme  tomentose  canebrake  congruent  dentistry  gynoecium  landgrave
semantics  tomentous  canescent  congruity  dentition  gynophore  landloper
semaphore  tumblebug  canesugar  congruous  denyingly  handbrake  landowner
semblable  tumescent  canetrash  conically  dinginess  handcraft  landscape
semblably  tumidness  canicular  conjugate  diningcar  handcuffs  landslide
semblance  tympanist  cankerous  connately  dinnerset  handglass  Langobard
semeiotic  unmatched  cannelure  connation  dinoceras  handiness  langouste
semestral  unmeaning  canniness  connature  dinothere  handiwork  languidly
semibreve  unmindful  cannonade  connected  donnishly  handlebar  lankiness
semicolon  unmusical  cannoneer  connecter  donothing  handorgan  lanthanum
semifinal  vampirism  cannonier  connector  dungarees  handpress  lendlease
semifluid  vimineous  cannulate  connexion  dynamical  handsdown  lengthily
semilunar  vomitoria  canonical  connivent  dynamiter  handshake  leniently
semimetal  womanhood  cantabile  connubial  eunuchism  handspike  lentiform
seminally  womaniser  cantaloup  conqueror  eunuchoid  handstand  lineality
semiology  womankind  cantharid  conscious  fanatical  handwheel  lineament
semiotics  womanlike  cantharis  conscribe  fancyfree  handywork  linearise
semiplume  womenfolk  cantharus  conscript  fancywork  hangerson  linearity
semirigid  womenkind  cantilena  consensus  fandangle  hankering  lineation
semisolid  zamindary  Cantonese  conserver  fandangos  Hanseatic  linenfold
semisweet  zemindary  cantorial  consignee  fanfarade  hanselled  lineolate
semitonic  zymogenic  canvasser  consignor  fantasied  hendiadys  lingering
semivowel  abnegator  censorial  consonant  fantasise  hindbrain  lingually
similarly  abnormity  centenary  consortia  fantasist  hindrance  lingulate
simpatico  adnominal  centering  constable  fantastic  hindsight  lintelled
simpleton  agnatical  centigram  constancy  fantastry  honeycomb  lintwhite
simplices  annectent  centipede  constrain  fenceless  honeymoon  Londonise
simulacra  annelidan  centrally  constrict  fenestrae  honkytonk  Londonism
simulacre  annotator  centreing  construct  fenestral  honoraria  longaeval
```

longchain	monachism	pancratic	renouncer	sunstruck	ventrally	aromatise
longcoats	monarchal	panderess	renovator	suntanned	ventricle	atomicity
longeared	monarchic	panegyric	ringfence	synagogal	venturous	atomistic
longevity	monastery	panelling	ringingly	synagogue	vinaceous	atonalism
longevous	monatomic	panellist	ringshake	synchrony	vindicate	atonality
longfaced	Mondayish	panhandle	ringsnake	synclinal	wandering	atonement
longhouse	monergism	panicking	runcinate	syncopate	windblown	atonicity
longicorn	moneybags	panoplied	sanatoria	syncretic	windbound	avocation
longingly	moneybill	panoramic	sanbenito	syncytial	windbreak	avoidable
longitude	moneywort	pantalets	sanctuary	syncytium	windchest	avoidably
longlived	Mongolian	pantaloon	sandalled	syndactyl	windhover	avoidance
Longobard	mongolism	pantheism	sandarach	syndicate	windiness	biogenous
longrange	Mongoloid	pantheist	sandblast	synectics	windowbox	biography
longshore	mongooses	pantingly	sandblind	syneresis	windproof	biologist
lunchtime	mongrelly	pantomime	sandcrack	synergism	windswept	biometric
lunisolar	monitress	pantryman	sandglass	synergist	windwards	bionomics
lunitidal	monkeyish	pantyhose	sandiness	syngamous	wineberry	biorhythm
Mancunian	monkeyism	pencilled	sandpaper	synizesis	wineglass	biosphere
mandarine	monkeynut	penciller	sandpiper	synodical	winepress	blockader
mandatary	monkshood	pendently	sandspout	synoecete	winestone	blockhead
mandatory	monobasic	pendragon	sandstone	synonymic	winevault	blockship
mandoline	monoceros	pendulate	sandstorm	synoptist	wingchair	bloodbath
manducate	monochord	penduline	sandtable	synovitis	winningly	bloodless
maneating	monocline	pendulous	sandyacht	syntactic	winsomely	bloodlust
manganate	monocoque	peneplain	sangfroid	syntheses	winterise	bloodroot
manganese	monocracy	peneplane	Sanhedrim	synthesis	wonderful	bloodshed
manganite	monocular	penetrant	Sanhedrin	synthetic	Xanthippe	bloodshot
manganous	monodical	penetrate	sanitaria	tangerine	xenograft	bloodworm
manginess	monodrama	penfriend	santolina	tanliquor	xenophile	bloodwort
manhandle	monoecism	penholder	santonica	tanpickle	xenophobe	blotchily
manhattan	monogamic	peninsula	senescent	tantalate	Yankeedom	blowtorch
Manichean	monograph	penitence	seneschal	tantalise	Yankeeism	boobytrap
manifesto	monolatry	penniless	senhorita	tantalite	zincotype	bookishly
manipular	monologic	pennywort	seniority	tenacious	zinkenite	booklouse
manliness	monologue	penpusher	sensation	tenaculum	abolisher	bookmaker
mannequin	monomania	pensioner	sensedata	tenderise	abolition	bookplate
mannerism	monomeric	pensively	senseless	tendinous	abominate	bookshelf
mannerist	monophagy	pentagram	sensitise	tenebrist	aborigine	bookstall
manoeuvre	monoplane	pentangle	sensitive	tenebrous	abounding	bookstand
manometer	monorhyme	pentarchy	sensorial	tenseness	aboutface	bookstore
manorseat	monostich	Pentecost	sensorium	tensility	aboutturn	bcomerang
mansarded	monostyle	penthouse	sensually	tensional	aconitine	boomslang
mansionry	monotonic	penultima	sentenate	tentacled	acoustics	boondocks
manslayer	monotreme	penumbral	sentience	tentation	adoptable	boorishly
manticore	monotypic	penurious	sentiency	tentative	adoration	bootblack
manubrium	monsignor	pinchbeck	sentiment	tenthrate	adoringly	broadcast
Manxwoman	monsoonal	pinchcock	sentrybox	tentmaker	adornment	broadleaf
manyplies	monstrous	pineapple	sincerely	tenuously	aforesaid	broadloom
manysided	Montanism	pinkiness	sincerity	tinderbox	agonising	broadness
manzanita	monthling	pinnately	sinewless	tinniness	agonistic	broadside
menadione	monticule	pinnipede	singalong	tinopener	aloneness	broadtail
menagerie	monzonite	pinnulate	singleton	tinselled	alongside	broadways
mendacity	mundanely	pinstripe	singspiel	tonguelet	aloofness	broadwise
Mendelian	mundungus	pintailed	Sinhalese	tonguetie	amoebaean	brochette
Mendelism	municipal	pintsized	sinistral	tonically	amoralism	broiderer
mendicant	muniments	ponderous	sinlessly	tonometer	amorality	brokerage
mendicity	munitions	pontoneer	sinologue	tonsillar	amorously	bromeliad
meningeal	nannygoat	pontonier	sinophile	tonsorial	amorphism	bronchial
Mennonite	ninepence	punchball	sinuately	tunefully	amorphous	broomcorn
menopause	ninepenny	punchbowl	sinuation	tungstate	amourette	broomrape
Menshevik	ninetieth	punchcard	sinuosity	tunicated	anomalous	brotherly
menstrual	nondriver	punchline	sinuously	tunnelled	anomalure	brownness
menstruum	nonentity	punctilio	sinusitis	tunnelnet	anonymity	buoyantly
mentalism	nonillion	punctuate	songcycle	uintahite	anonymous	chockfull
mentalist	nonjuring	pungently	songfully	unnamable	anopheles	chocolate
mentality	nonlinear	punishing	songsmith	unnatural	anorectic	chokedamp
mentation	nonpareil	rancidity	sonneteer	vandalise	anorthite	choleraic
minacious	nonperson	rancorous	sonnetise	vandalism	anovulant	chondrite
mincemeat	nonprofit	randiness	sonometer	vendition	anoxaemia	chondrule
mincingly	nonsmoker	randomise	sunbather	veneering	apocrypha	chophouse
mindfully	nonviable	ranginess	sunbonnet	venerable	apodictic	choplogic
minefield	nuncupate	ransacker	sunburned	venerably	apogamous	chopstick
minelayer	obnoxious	rantingly	sundowner	venerator	apologise	chorister
miniature	oenomancy	ranunculi	sunflower	venereous	apologist	chorology
minimally	oenophile	renascent	sunhelmet	vengeance	apomictic	cloakroom
miniskirt	oenophily	rencontre	sunlounge	veniality	apophyses	clockwise
minuscule	ownership	rendition	sunniness	ventiduct	apophysis	clockwork
minutegun	panatella	renewable	sunspurge	ventifact	apostolic	cloisonne
minuteman	panchayat	renitency	sunstroke	ventilate	apothecia	cloistral

closedown	eroticism	geologise	kaolinise	processed	protonema	showiness
closeness	esoterica	geologist	kaolinite	processer	prototype	showpiece
cloudland	esoterism	geomancer	knockdown	processor	protozoal	showplace
cloudless	evocation	geomantic	knockknee	proclitic	protozoan	slopbasin
cookhouse	evocative	geometric	knotgrass	proconsul	protozoic	slopewise
cooperage	evocatory	geometrid	knowingly	procreant	protozoon	slothbear
cooperant	evolution	geoponics	knowledge	procreate	proveably	Slovakian
cooperate	evolutive	georgette	Laodicean	procuracy	Provencal	Slovenian
crocodile	evolvable	geosphere	lioncelle	procuress	provender	slowcoach
croissant	exodermis	geostatic	lionheart	prodromal	provident	slowmatch
CroMagnon	exogamous	geotropic	lookalike	prodromic	providing	smokeball
crookback	exogenous	ghostlike	looseleaf	proenzyme	provision	smokebomb
crookedly	exonerate	ghostword	looseness	profanely	provisory	smokebush
crookneck	exopodite	globefish	lyophilic	profanity	provoking	smokejack
cropeared	exorciser	globosity	lyophobic	professed	provostry	smokeless
croquette	exosmosis	glomerate	moodiness	professor	proximate	smoketree
crossable	exosmotic	glomerule	moonblind	profilist	proximity	smokiness
crossbeam	exosphere	glomeruli	moonlight	profiteer	psoriasis	smoothish
crossbill	exostosis	gloryhole	moonquake	profusely	psoriatic	snowberry
crossbred	exoticism	glossator	moonraker	profusion	Ptolemaic	snowblind
crossette	feoffment	glossitis	moonscape	progestin	quodlibet	snowblink
crosseyed	fioritura	glowingly	moonshine	prognoses	quotation	snowbound
crossfade	fioriture	goodnight	moonstone	prognosis	quotidian	snowbroth
crossfire	floatable	goodwives	myography	programme	rhodamine	snowdrift
crossfish	flocculus	goosander	myologist	projector	rhodolite	snowfield
crosshead	floodgate	goosefoot	neodymium	prolamine	rhodonite	snowflake
crosslink	floodmark	goosegirl	neolithic	prolapsus	rhodopsin	snowgoose
crossness	floodtide	gooseherd	neologian	prolately	rhonchial	snowguard
crossover	flophouse	gooseneck	neologise	prolation	riotously	snowiness
crossroad	floriated	gooseskin	neologism	prolative	roodcloth	snowplant
crossruff	floridean	goosestep	neologist	prolepses	roofplate	snowscape
crosstalk	floridity	groomsman	neoteinia	prolepsis	roominess	snowstorm
crossways	floristic	grosgrain	neoteinic	proleptic	rootstock	snowwhite
crosswind	floristry	grossness	neoterise	prolicide	scolecite	sooterkin
crosswise	floscular	grossular	neoterism	prolixity	scoliosis	soothfast
crossword	flotation	grotesque	neoterist	prologise	scoliotic	sootiness
crotchety	flouncing	grouchily	odontalgy	prolusion	scombroid	spodumene
croustade	flowchart	groundage	odorously	prolusory	scorbutic	spoilsman
crowberry	flowerage	groundash	odourless	promenade	scorching	spokesman
crownless	flowerbed	groundhog	omophagia	prominent	scorebook	spokewise
crowsfoot	flowering	grounding	omophagic	promising	scorecard	spoliator
crowsnest	flowerpot	groundivy	onomastic	promotion	scoredraw	spongebag
deodorant	flowingly	groundnut	opodeldoc	promotive	scorifier	spongeous
deodorise	flowsheet	groundsel	orography	promptbox	scorpioid	spoonbeak
deoxidise	flowstone	grovelled	orologist	pronation	Scotchman	spoonbill
dioecious	foodchain	groveller	otologist	proneness	Scoticise	spoonfeed
Dionysiac	foodstuff	hoofprint	ozocerite	pronghorn	scotomata	spoonmeat
Dionysian	foolhardy	iconology	ozokerite	pronounce	scoundrel	sporangía
doodlebug	foolishly	inoculate	phonation	proofread	sforzando	sporocarp
doorframe	foolproof	inodorous	phonatory	propagate	shockable	sporocyst
doorplate	footboard	inorganic	phonemics	propelled	shockhead	sporogeny
drollness	footcloth	ironbound	phonetics	propeller	shoeblack	sportsman
dromedary	footfault	ironmould	phonetise	properdin	shoemaker	sporulate
dropscene	footlight	ironsides	phonetism	prophetic	shoeshine	spotcheck
dropscone	footloose	ironsmith	phonetist	propionic	shogunate	spotlight
dropsical	footplate	ironstone	phoniness	proponent	shootable	spouthole
duodecimo	footpound	ironworks	phonogram	propriety	shopfloor	spoutless
duodenary	footprint	Iroquoian	phonolite	proptosis	shopfront	stockbook
ecologist	footstalk	isobathic	phonology	propylaea	shoreless	stockdove
economics	footstall	isochrone	phosphate	propylene	shoreline	stockfish
economise	footstool	isoclinal	phosphene	prorogate	shoreside	stockinet
economist	frockcoat	isoclinic	phosphide	prosaical	shoreward	stocklist
ecosphere	frogmarch	isocyclic	phosphine	proscenia	shoreweed	stockpile
ecossaise	frogspawn	isogamete	phosphite	proscribe	shortcake	stockroom
ecosystem	frolicked	isogamous	photocell	prosector	shortener	stockwhip
egomaniac	frontally	isogenous	photocopy	prosecute	shortfall	stockyard
egotistic	frontless	isohyetal	photogene	proselyte	shorthand	stoically
elocution	frontline	isolation	photophil	prosiness	shorthorn	stokehold
elongated	frontpage	isolative	photopsia	prosodist	shortness	stokehole
elopement	frontward	isomerise	phototype	prostatic	shortstop	stolidity
eloquence	frontways	isomerism	ploughboy	prostrate	shortterm	stolonate
emolliate	frontwise	isomerous	ploughman	protamine	shortwave	stomachal
emollient	frostbite	isometric	poorhouse	protector	shotproof	stomacher
emolument	frostwork	isoniazid	probation	proteinic	shottower	stomachic
emotional	frowardly	isooctane	probative	protester	shouldest	stonechat
emotively	gaolbreak	isopodous	probatory	protestor	shovelful	stonecoal
emotivity	geobotany	isosceles	proboscis	prothesis	shovelhat	stonecold
eponymous	geodesist	isostatic	procedure	prothetic	shovelled	stonecrop
erogenous	geography	isotropic	procerity	prothorax	shoveller	stonedead

stonedeaf	woodlouse	copartner	explosion	imprecate	repechage	supposing
stonefish	woodnymph	copesmate	explosive	imprecise	repellant	suppurate
stoneless	woodwaxen	copestone	expositor	impresari	repellent	supremacy
stonewall	wooziness	copiously	expounder	improbity	repelling	supremely
stoneware	wrongdoer	copolymer	expressly	impromptu	repentant	syphilise
stonework	wrongness	coproduce	expulsion	improvise	repertory	syphiloid
stonewort	zoogenous	coprolite	expulsive	imprudent	replenish	tapdancer
stoniness	zoography	coprology	expurgate	impudence	repletion	tepidness
stoolball	zoologist	copsewood	foppishly	impulsion	replicate	tipsiness
stoplight	zoophagan	copyright	haphazard	impulsive	reportage	tipstaves
stoppress	zoophobia	cupbearer	haplessly	impulsory	reposeful	tophamper
stopwatch	zoophytic	cupelling	haplology	imputable	repossess	topiarian
storeroom	zootechny	cuplichen	happening	inpatient	repotting	topiarist
storeship	zootomist	cyprinoid	happiness	inpouring	reprehend	topically
storiated	aepyornis	departure	hepatitis	japanning	represent	toponymal
stormbelt	alpargata	depasture	heptaglot	Keplerian	repressor	toponymic
stormbird	alpenhorn	dependant	heptarchy	lapideous	reprieval	typemetal
stormcock	ampersand	dependent	hippocras	Laplander	reprimand	typewrite
stormcone	amphibian	depiction	hopefully	lapstrake	reprobate	typhlitis
stormless	amphibole	depictive	hopscotch	lapstreak	reprocess	typhoidal
stormsail	amphigory	depletion	hypallage	leptosome	reproduce	typically
storybook	amphioxus	depletive	hyperbola	lipreader	reptilian	umpteenth
storyline	ampleness	deposable	hyperbole	lophodont	republish	unpegging
stoutness	amplifier	depositor	hypergamy	mepacrine	repudiate	unpeopled
stovepipe	amplitude	depravity	hypericum	naphthene	repugnant	unplugged
swordcane	amputator	deprecate	hyperopia	napthalic	repulsion	unplumbed
swordfish	appalling	depredate	hyperopic	nepenthes	repulsive	unpointed
swordknot	Appaloosa	depressed	hypethral	nephalism	reputable	unpopular
swordlike	apparatus	depressor	hyphenate	nephalist	reputably	uppercase
swordplay	apparitor	depthbomb	hypnoidal	nepheline	reputedly	uppermost
swordsman	appealing	depthless	hypnology	nephelite	Ripuarian	vapidness
swordtail	appellant	depurator	hypnotise	nephology	sapanwood	vaporable
Thomistic	appellate	dipcircle	hypnotism	nephritic	sapheaded	vaporific
thornback	appendage	dipeptide	hypnotist	nephritis	sapiently	vaporiser
thornbill	appendant	diphthong	hypoblast	nephrosis	sapodilla	vapouring
thornbush	appertain	diplomacy	hypocaust	Neptunian	sappiness	vapourish
thornless	appetence	diplomate	hypocotyl	neptunium	sapraemia	wapentake
thorntree	appetency	dipswitch	hypocrisy	Nipponese	sapraemic	zapateado
thoughted	appetiser	dipterous	hypocrite	opponency	separable	acquiesce
toolhouse	applauder	dopefiend	hypogeous	opportune	separably	acquittal
toothache	applejack	duplicate	hypomania	opposable	separates	acquitted
toothcomb	appliance	duplicity	hypomanic	oppressor	separator	Esquimaux
toothless	applicant	empathise	hyponasty	oppugnant	Sephardic	exquisite
toothpick	appointee	empennage	hypostyle	orphanage	Sephardim	inquiline
toothsome	apportion	emphasise	hypotaxis	Orpington	sepiolite	liquation
toothwort	appraisal	emphysema	impaction	paperback	septation	liquefier
trochilus	appraiser	empirical	impartial	paperclip	September	liquidate
trochleae	apprehend	emplastic	impassion	papergirl	septemvir	liquidise
trochlear	appressed	emptiness	impassive	paperthin	septenary	liquidity
troopship	approbate	empyreuma	impastoed	paperwork	septennia	liquorice
tropology	asparagus	esperance	impatiens	papeterie	septicity	liquorish
troublous	aspartate	Esperanto	impatient	papillary	septuplet	loquacity
trousered	aspectual	espionage	impeccant	papillate	sepulcher	maquisard
trousseau	aspersion	esplanade	impedance	papilloma	sepulchre	piquantly
troutfarm	asphaltic	espousals	impelling	papillose	sepulture	requester
troutling	asphaltum	euphemise	impendent	papillote	siphonage	requisite
trowelled	aspirator	euphemism	impending	pepperbox	siphuncle	Roquefort
troweller	baptismal	euphonise	imperator	pepperpot	sophister	sequacity
twofisted	baptistry	euphonium	imperfect	peptonise	sophistic	sequester
twohanded	bipartite	euphorbia	imperious	pipedream	sophistry	sequestra
twosuiter	bipinnate	expansile	impetrate	pipeorgan	sophomore	sequinned
uropygium	byproduct	expansion	impetuous	pipestone	soporific	abradable
uxoricide	capacious	expansive	impiously	pipsqueak	soppiness	abrogator
violation	capacitor	expatiate	impleader	popliteal	sopranino	abruption
violative	caparison	expectant	implement	poppycock	sopranist	acrobatic
violently	capillary	expecting	impletion	poppyhead	superable	acropetal
violinist	capitally	expedient	implicate	popularly	supercool	acropolis
voodooism	capitular	expediter	impliedly	pupillage	superfine	acroteria
voodooist	capitulum	expellent	implosion	pupillary	superfuse	adrenalin
whodunnit	capriccio	expelling	implosive	puppeteer	superheat	aerialist
wholemeal	Capricorn	expensive	impluvium	puppyhood	supernova	aeriality
wholeness	capsulate	expertise	impolitic	rapacious	superpose	aerobatic
wholesale	capsulise	expiation	important	rapidfire	supersede	aerobiont
wholesome	captaincy	expiatory	importune	rapidness	superstar	aerodrome
whosoever	captivate	explainer	impostume	raptorial	supervene	aerograph
woodblock	captivity	expletive	imposture	rapturous	supervise	aerolitic
woodchuck	cephalous	expletory	impotence	reparable	supinator	aerometer
woodcraft	cipollino	explicate	impotency	repayable	suppliant	aerometry
woodiness	copacetic	exploiter	impounder	repayment	supporter	aerophyte

aeroplane	burnisher	corbicula	directory	foreclose	germproof	hortation
aerospace	burrstone	cordelier	directrix	forecourt	gerundial	hortative
Afrikaans	bursarial	cordially	direfully	forefront	gerundive	hortatory
Afrikaner	carambola	cordiform	dirigible	foregoing	girandole	hortensia
agreeable	carbamate	corduroys	dirigisme	foreigner	girlishly	hurricane
agreeably	carbamide	coreopsis	dirtiness	forejudge	Girondist	hurriedly
agreement	carbonado	coriander	dirttrack	foreknown	gorblimey	hurtfully
agriology	carbonate	corkscrew	dorbeetle	forenamed	gorgonian	irradiant
agrologic	carbonise	cormorant	dormition	forereach	gorgonise	irradiate
agronomic	carbuncle	cornbrash	dormitory	foreshore	gyrfalcon	irreality
aircooled	carburise	corncrake	duralumin	foreshown	gyroplane	irregular
airjacket	carcinoma	cornelian	earliness	foresight	gyroscope	irrigable
airminded	cardboard	cornemuse	earnestly	forespeak	haranguer	irrigator
airstream	cardsharp	cornerboy	earthborn	forestage	harbinger	irritable
airworthy	careerism	cornerman	earthling	forestall	harbourer	irritably
airyfairy	careerist	cornetist	earthstar	foretaste	hardboard	irruption
arrearage	carefully	cornfield	earthward	foretoken	hardcover	irruptive
arrestant	caretaker	cornflour	earthwork	forewoman	hardihood	Israelite
arresting	carfuffle	cornopean	earthworm	forfeiter	hardiment	jargonise
arriviste	Caribbean	cornsalad	earwigged	forgather	hardiness	jarringly
arrogance	Carmelite	cornstalk	ecritoire	forgeable	hardnosed	jerkiness
arrowhead	carnality	cornstone	egregious	forgetful	hardshell	Jordanian
arrowroot	carnation	corollary	egression	forgiving	haresfoot	juridical
arrowwood	carnelian	coroneted	eirenicon	forgotten	harlequin	jurywoman
arrowworm	carnitine	corporate	enrapture	forlornly	harmaline	karabiner
atrocious	carnivore	corporeal	enrolling	formalise	harmattan	karyotype
auricular	carolling	corposant	enrolment	formalism	harmfully	keratitis
barathrum	carpenter	corpulent	erratical	formalist	harmonica	keratosis
Barbadian	carpentry	corpuscle	erroneous	formality	harmonics	kerbstone
barbarian	carpetbag	corralled	errorless	formation	harmonise	kerfuffle
barbarise	carpeting	corrasion	eurhythmy	formative	harmonist	kurrajong
barbarism	carpingly	correctly	farandole	formatted	harmonium	larcenist
barbarity	carpology	corrector	farestage	formicary	harmotome	larcenous
barbarous	carrageen	correlate	farmhouse	formicate	harpooner	lardycake
barbitone	carrefour	corrosion	farmstead	formulaic	harquebus	largeness
barcarole	carronade	corrosive	farseeing	formulary	Harrovian	larghetto
barefaced	carryover	corrugate	ferocious	formulate	harrowing	larvicide
bargainer	Cartesian	corrupter	ferrotype	formulise	harshness	laryngeal
bargepole	carthorse	corruptly	ferryboat	fornicate	hartshorn	lorgnette
barkeeper	cartilage	corticate	fertilely	forsythia	harvester	luridness
barleymow	cartogram	corticoid	fertilise	fortalice	Heraclean	lyrically
barmbrack	cartology	cortisone	fertility	forthwith	herbalist	marcasite
Barmecide	cartouche	coruscant	fervently	fortifier	herbarium	marcelled
barnacled	cartridge	coruscate	firealarm	fortitude	herbicide	marchpane
barnstorm	cartulary	Corybants	fireblast	fortnight	herbivore	marchpast
barograph	cartwheel	corydalis	firebrand	fortunate	herborise	marestail
barometer	caryopses	corymbose	firebreak	fortyfive	Herculean	margarine
barometry	caryopsis	coryphaei	firebrick	forwander	Hercynian	margarite
baronetcy	cerastium	curbstone	firecrest	forwarder	hereabout	marginate
barracker	ceratodus	curettage	firedrake	forwardly	hereafter	marihuana
barracoon	cerebella	curialism	firedrill	furbisher	heretical	marijuana
barracuda	cerebrate	curiosity	fireeater	furcation	hereunder	maritally
barrelful	cerecloth	curiously	fireguard	furiously	heritable	marketday
barrelled	cerograph	curliness	firehouse	furnisher	hermitage	marketing
barricade	certainly	curlpaper	fireirons	furniture	herniated	marlstone
barricado	certainty	currently	firelight	furtherer	herpetoid	marmalade
barrister	certified	curricula	fireplace	furtively	hircosity	marmoreal
bartender	certifier	currishly	firepower	gardening	hirsutism	marquetry
berberine	certitude	currycomb	fireproof	garderobe	hirundine	marrowfat
bergamask	cerussite	cursively	firestone	garibaldi	horehound	marshalcy
berkelium	Christian	cursorial	firewater	garmented	horniness	marshland
berserker	Christmas	cursorily	fireworks	garnishee	hornstone	marshwort
beryllium	chromatic	curstness	firmament	garniture	hornwrack	marsupial
birchbark	chromatin	curtilage	firstborn	garreteer	horologer	marsupium
birdbrain	chronical	curvature	firstfoot	garrotter	horologic	martially
birdsfoot	chronicle	curveting	firsthand	garrulity	horoscope	Martinmas
birdsnest	chrysalid	curvetted	firstling	garrulous	horoscopy	martyrdom
birdtable	chrysalis	curviform	firstrate	gerfalcon	horseback	martyrise
birdwatch	circadian	daredevil	foragecap	geriatric	horsebean	marvelled
birthmark	circinate	dartboard	forasmuch	germander	horsehair	mercaptan
birthrate	circuitry	Darwinian	forbidden	germanely	horsehide	mercenary
birthwort	circulate	Darwinism	forcefeed	germanise	horseless	mercerise
bordereau	cirrhosis	Darwinist	forceland	Germanish	horsemint	merciless
borrowing	cirripede	derivable	forceless	Germanism	horseplay	mercurial
burdenous	coralline	dermatoid	forcemeat	Germanist	horsepond	mercurous
burlesque	corallite	derringdo	forcepump	germanium	horseshoe	merganser
burliness	coralloid	derringer	foreboder	germicide	horsetail	meropidan
burnedout	corbeille	direction	forebrain	germinate	horsewhip	merriment
burningly	corbelled	directive	forecaddy	germplasm	horsiness	merriness

mirkiness	parfleche	porcupine	screwworm	streaking	thralldom	vermiform
mirthless	parhelion	poriferal	scribbler	streamlet	thrashing	vermifuge
moraceous	parleyvoo	poriferan	scrimmage	streetcar	threefold	vermilion
moraliser	parlously	porphyria	scrimpily	strenuous	threesome	verminate
moratoria	parochial	porringer	scrimshaw	stressful	threnodic	verminous
morbidity	parotitis	portative	scripture	stretcher	threshold	vernalise
mordacity	parquetry	porterage	scrivener	strewment	thriftily	vernation
mordantly	parrakeet	portfolio	scrollsaw	striation	thrilling	verrucose
Mormonism	parricide	porticoes	scrounger	striature	throatily	verrucous
morphemic	Parseeism	portolano	scrubbing	stricture	throbbing	versatile
morrisman	parsimony	portrayal	scruffily	stridence	thrombose	versifier
mortality	parsonage	portrayer	scrumhalf	stridency	throttler	versiform
mortgagee	partially	portreeve	scrummage	stringent	throughly	versional
mortgager	partition	portulaca	scrutable	stripling	throwaway	vertebrae
mortgagor	partitive	purchaser	scrutator	stripping	throwback	vertebral
mortician	partridge	pureblood	serenader	strobilae	throwster	virescent
murderess	percaline	purgation	sergeancy	strobilus	thrumming	Virgilian
murderous	perceiver	purgative	serialise	stromatic	tiredness	virginals
murkiness	perchance	purgatory	serialism	strongarm	tirewoman	virginity
murmurous	percheron	puritanic	serialist	strongbox	torchrace	virgulate
myriorama	percolate	purloiner	seriality	strongish	torchsong	viricidal
myrmecoid	perdition	purposely	seriately	strongly	toreutics	virtually
myrobalan	peregrine	purposive	sericeous	strontium	tormentil	virtuosic
narcissus	perennate	purpureal	serigraph	stropping	tormentor	virtuosos
narcotine	perennial	purringly	serinette	strouding	torpidity	virulence
narcotise	perfectly	purselike	seriously	structure	torridity	virulency
narcotism	perfector	pursiness	serjeancy	struggler	torsional	voracious
narration	perfervid	pursuable	serjeanty	strumitis	tortrices	vorticism
narrative	perforate	pursuance	sermonise	strumming	tortricid	vorticist
narratory	performer	purulence	serotonin	strutting	torturous	vorticity
nervation	perfumery	purulency	serpentry	strychnic	turbidity	vorticose
nervature	perfumier	pyracanth	serranoid	surcharge	turbinate	warblefly
nerveless	perfusion	pyramidal	serration	surcingle	turboprop	warbonnet
nerviness	perfusive	pyramidic	serrefile	surculose	turbulent	warehouse
nervously	pergunnah	pyramidon	serrulate	surfacing	Turcomans	warmonger
normalise	periclase	pyrethrum	serviette	surfboard	turgently	warningly
normality	pericycle	pyridoxin	servilely	surfeiter	turgidity	warrantee
Normanise	peridotic	pyrogenic	servility	surficial	Turkomans	warranter
Normanism	perihelia	pyrolater	servitude	surgeoncy	turnabout	warrantor
normative	perilling	pyrolatry	sgraffiti	surliness	turnround	wartcress
northeast	perilymph	pyrolysis	sgraffito	surmullet	turnstile	werwolves
northerly	perimeter	pyrolytic	shredding	surpliced	turnstone	wiredrawn
northland	perimorph	pyromancy	shrewmice	surprisal	turntable	wiregauze
northmost	perinatal	pyromania	shrinkage	surrender	turpitude	wirephoto
northward	periodate	pyrometer	shrubbery	surrogate	turquoise	Worcester
northwest	peripatus	pyrometry	shrugging	surveying	tyrannise	wordiness
Norwegian	periphery	pyroscope	sorbapple	syringeal	tyrannous	wordsmith
nurseling	periplast	pyroxylin	Sorbonist	tarantara	Ukrainian	workbench
nursemaid	periscope	rareeshow	sorceress	tarantass	unreality	workhorse
orrisroot	perishing	rerebrace	sorcerous	tarantism	unreserve	workhouse
ourselves	perisperm	rerelease	soritical	tarantula	unruffled	workmanly
parabasis	peristome	reremouse	sorriness	taraxacum	uprightly	workpiece
parabolic	peristyle	rerunning	sorrowful	tardiness	utricular	worktable
parachute	perkiness	Saracenic	sortilege	Targumist	Varangian	workwoman
Paraclete	permanent	sarcastic	sortition	tarpaulin	variation	worldling
paradisal	permeable	sarcocarp	sprigging	tarragona	varicella	worldwide
paragraph	permeance	sarcomata	sprightly	Tartarean	variegate	wormeaten
paralalia	permitted	Sardinian	sprigtail	Tartarian	variolate	wormwheel
paralexia	permitter	sargassos	springbok	tartishly	varioloid	worriedly
paralysis	permutate	Sarmation	springily	Tartufian	variolous	worriment
paralytic	perpetual	sartorial	springing	Tartufism	variously	worrisome
paramatta	persecute	sartorius	springlet	teratogen	varnisher	worrywart
paramedic	persevere	scraggily	sprinkler	terebinth	veracious	worthless
parameter	persimmon	scrambler	spritsail	terebrant	verandaed	xeromorph
paramorph	personage	scramming	straggler	termagant	veratrine	xerophile
paramount	personate	scrapbook	strangely	terminate	verbalise	xerophily
paranoiac	personify	scrapheap	strangler	terminism	verbalism	xerophyte
paranymph	personnel	scrapiron	strangles	terminist	verbalist	yardstick
parapeted	persuader	scrappily	straphang	termitary	verbicide	Yorkshire
parapodia	pertinent	scrapping	strapless	ternately	verbosely	zirconium
parasitic	pertussis	scrapyard	strappado	terramara	verbosity	abscissae
parataxis	pervasion	scratcher	strapping	terramare	verdantly	abscissas
parathion	pervasive	scratches	strapwork	terrarium	verdigris	absconder
parbuckle	perverter	screecher	strapwort	territory	veridical	abseiling
parcelled	phrenetic	screening	stratagem	terrorise	veritable	absorbent
parcenary	piratical	screwball	strategic	terrorism	veritably	absorbing
parchment	pirouette	screwbolt	strawworm	terrorist	vermicide	abstainer
paregoric	porbeagle	screwpile	strapwort	terseness	vermicule	abstinent
parentage	porcelain	screwpine	streakily	tervalent		absurdism

absurdist	cessation	dishclout	exservice	insectary	misbeseem	obsession
absurdity	cisalpine	dishfaced	exsiccate	insectile	miscegene	obsessive
adsorbate	coseismal	dishonest	exsuccous	insensate	miscegine	obsolesce
adsorbent	coseismic	dishonour	fasciated	insertion	mischance	obstetric
aesthesia	cosmogeny	dishwater	fascicled	inservice	miscreant	obstinacy
aesthesis	cosmogony	disinfect	fascicule	insetting	miscreate	obstinate
aesthetic	cosmology	disinfest	fasciculi	inshallah	misdemean	oesophagi
aestivate	cosmonaut	dislocate	fascinate	insidious	misdirect	oestrogen
anschluss	cosmorama	dismantle	Fascistic	insincere	misemploy	onsetting
arsenical	costively	dismember	fashioner	insinuate	miserable	onslaught
arsenious	costumier	dismissal	fastening	insipidly	miserably	opsimathy
assailant	cuspidate	disoblige	fastigium	insistent	misesteem	ossicular
assaulter	custodial	disorient	festinate	insolence	misfeasor	ossifrage
assayable	custodian	disparage	festively	insoluble	misgiving	oysterbed
assembler	customary	disparate	festivity	insolubly	misgovern	oysterman
assertion	customise	disparity	festology	insolvent	misguided	pasodoble
assertive	cystocarp	dispelled	fisherman	insomniac	mishandle	passenger
assiduity	cystolith	dispenser	fishiness	inpanned	mishanter	passerine
assiduous	cystotomy	dispeople	fishplate	inspector	misinform	passersby
assistant	dashboard	dispersal	fishslice	instanter	misleared	passional
associate	dashingly	disperser	fishyback	instantly	mismanage	passivate
assonance	dastardly	displease	fissility	instigate	misoneism	passively
assuasive	descended	disposure	fissipede	instilled	misoneist	passivity
assumable	describer	dispraise	fistulous	institute	mispickel	pastedown
assumably	desecrate	disputant	fossicker	insularly	misreckon	pasticcio
assumpsit	desertion	disregard	fossilise	insulator	misreport	pastiness
assurance	desiccant	disrelish	fossorial	insurable	misshapen	pastorale
assuredly	desiccate	disrepair	fosterage	insurance	missioner	pastorate
assurgent	designate	disrepute	fusillade	insurgent	mistigris	pasturage
auspicate	designing	dissector	fusionist	issueless	mistiness	pessimism
austenite	desirable	disseisin	fussiness	itsybitsy	mistletoe	pessimist
austerely	desirably	dissemble	fustigate	jessamine	mistyeyed	pesthouse
austerity	desolater	dissenter	fustiness	jesuitise	mosaicism	pesticide
bashfully	desolator	dissident	gasconade	jesuitism	mosaicist	pestilent
basically	desperado	dissipate	gasfitter	josshouse	mosaicked	pestology
basilican	desperate	dissocial	gasholder	jossstick	moschatel	piscatory
basipetal	despoiler	dissolute	gasmantle	justiciar	mosquitos	pisciform
basketful	despotism	dissonant	gasometer	justifier	mossagate	pisolitic
basrelief	destitute	dissuader	gaspereau	lassitude	mossgrown	pistachio
bastardly	destroyer	distantly	gastraeum	lastditch	muscadine	pistoleer
bastinade	desuetude	distemper	gastritis	lastingly	muscarine	pistolled
bastinado	desultory	distilled	gastropod	lispingly	muscleman	possessed
bastioned	disaccord	distiller	gastrulae	lissomely	muscovado	possessor
besetment	disaffect	distraint	gestalten	Listerism	muscovite	postentry
besetting	disaffirm	disturbed	gestation	lustfully	musically	posterior
beslobber	disannual	disturber	gestatory	lustihood	musichall	posterity
besotting	disappear	disturber	gospeller	lustiness	musketeer	posthaste
bespangle	disarming	dosimeter	gossamer	lysimeter	muskiness	posthorse
bespatter	disavouch	dosimetry	gushingly	masculine	muskmelon	posthouse
bestially	disavowal	dosshouse	gustation	masochism	Mussulman	posticous
bestirred	disbarred	duskiness	gustative	masochist	mustachio	postilion
bisection	disbelief	dustcover	gustatory	masterdom	musteline	postnasal
bishopric	disbranch	dustiness	gustiness	masterful	mustiness	postnatal
bismillah	disbudded	dustsheet	Hashemite	masterkey	mystagogy	postulant
boskiness	disburden	dyscrasia	Hashimite	masticate	mysticism	postulate
bossiness	disbursal	dysentery	hastiness	Masoretic	mystifier	pushchair
bushcraft	discalced	dysgenics	hesitance	massagist	naseberry	pushiness
bushelful	discarder	dyspepsia	hesitancy	massiness	nastiness	pushingly
bushiness	discerner	dyspeptic	hesitator	massively	nescience	pussyfoot
bushwhack	discharge	dysphagia	Hesperian	masterdom	Nestorian	pustulate
bystander	discoidal	dysphagic	hessonite	mescaline	nosebleed	pustulous
caseation	discolour	dysphonia	hispidity	mesentery	noseflute	rascaldom
Cassandra	discomfit	dysphoria	histamine	mesmerise	nosepiece	rascalism
cassareep	discommon	dysphoric	histidine	mesmerist	nostalgia	rascality
cassaripe	discourse	dysplasia	histogeny	mesoblast	nostalgic	raspatory
cassation	discovert	dyspnoeic	histogram	mesogloea	nostology	raspberry
casserole	discovery	dystrophy	histology	mesomorph	nystagmic	raspingly
cassimere	discredit	easefully	historian	mesophyll	nystagmus	resalable
cassoulet	disembark	eastbound	hosteller	mesophyll	oasthouse	resection
cassowary	disembody	Eastender	hostilely	mesophyte	obscenely	resentful
Castalian	disengage	easterner	hostility	messenger	obscenity	reserpine
castanets	disentail	eastwards	husbandly	messianic	obscurant	reservist
castellan	disentomb	easygoing	husbandry	messieurs	obscurely	reservoir
castigate	disesteem	ecstasise	huskiness	messiness	obscurity	resetting
Castilian	disfavour	elsewhere	hysterics	misadvise	obsecrate	reshuffle
Castroism	disfigure	erstwhile	hysteroid	misassign	obsequent	residence
casuarina	disforest	essential	insatiate	misbecome	obsequial	residency
casuistic	disgracer	exsertile	insatiety	misbehave	obsequies	residuary
casuistry	dishcloth	exsertion	inscriber	misbelief	observant	resilient

```
resistant  unstopped  anthozoan  autotelic  cuticular  extradite  interlope
resistive  unstudied  anthracic  autotroph  cutinised  extravert  interlude
resitting  unsuccess  anthropic  bathhouse  cutthroat  extremely  interment
resoluble  unsullied  anticline  batholite  cuttysark  extremism  internode
resolvent  upsetting  anticodon  batholith  Cytherean  extremist  interpage
resonance  vasectomy  antidotal  Bathonian  cytolysis  extremity  interplay
resonator  vasomotor  antigenic  bathybius  cytoplasm  extricate  interpose
resorbent  vassalage  antiknock  battalion  cytotoxic  extrinsic  interpret
resources  vastitude  antimonic  battening  cytotoxin  extrovert  interring
respecter  vesicular  antinodal  battiness  detection  extrusion  interrupt
responder  vestibule  antinomic  battleaxe  detective  extrusive  intersect
restfully  vestigial  antinovel  battlecry  detention  fatefully  intervein
restiform  vestigium  antipasto  bethought  detergent  fatheaded  intervene
restitute  vestiture  antipathy  betrothal  determent  fatidical  interview
restively  vestryman  antiphony  betrothed  determine  fatigable  interwind
restraint  viscerate  antipodal  bitterish  deterrent  fattiness  interwove
resultant  viscidity  antipodes  botanical  deterring  fatuously  interzone
resultful  viscosity  antiquary  bottlefed  detersion  fatwitted  intestacy
resumable  viscounty  antiquate  bottleful  detersive  fetichism  intestate
resurface  viscously  antiquity  butadiene  dethroner  fetichist  intestine
resurgent  visionary  antiserum  butcherer  detonator  fetidness  intorsion
resurrect  visionist  antitoxic  butcherly  detractor  fetishism  intricacy
riskiness  visitable  antitoxin  butterbur  detriment  fetishist  intricate
rosaceous  visitress  antitrade  buttercup  detrition  fittingly  intrigant
roseapple  visualise  antitrust  butterfat  detrusion  gatecrash  intriguer
roseately  washbasin  antivenin  butterfly  dithyramb  gatehouse  intrinsic
rosenoble  washboard  antiviral  butterine  dittander  gathering  introduce
rosewater  washcloth  artemisia  butternut  dittology  getatable  introject
rosinweed  washedout  arteriole  buttinsky  dottiness  Gothamite  introvert
rostellum  washerman  arteritis  buttygang  duteously  gothicise  intrusion
rushlight  washhouse  arthritic  catabolic  dutifully  Gothicism  intrusive
russeting  washiness  arthritis  cataclasm  ectoblast  gutsiness  intuition
Russophil  washstand  arthropod  cataclysm  ectogenic  guttation  intuitive
rusticate  waspishly  arthrosis  catalepsy  ectomorph  guttering  intumesce
rusticity  wassailer  Arthurian  catalexes  ectophyte  hatchback  ittybitty
rustiness  wasteland  artichoke  catalexis  ectoplasm  hatchling  jetsetter
rustproof  wasteness  articular  catalogue  entelechy  hatchment  jetstream
sasquatch  wastepipe  artificer  catalyser  enterable  hatefully  jitterbug
sassafras  westbound  artillery  catalyses  enteritis  hetaerism  katabasis
Sassanian  westering  artlessly  catalysis  entertain  hetairism  katabatic
Sassenach  westerner  asthmatic  catalytic  enthymeme  heterodox  katabolic
sessional  westwards  astraddle  catamaran  entoblast  heteronym  katharsis
sestertia  wisecrack  astrakhan  catamount  entophyte  heterosis  kitchener
Sisyphean  wishfully  astrocyte  cataplasm  entourage  hitchhike  kittenish
sostenuto  wistfully  astrodome  cataplexy  entrammel  Hitlerism  kittiwake
suspender  yesterday  astrolabe  catarhine  entrapped  Hitlerite  latecomer
suspensor  zestfully  astrology  catarrhal  entrechat  hotheaded  laterally
suspicion  actinozoa  astronaut  catatonia  entrecote  Hottentot  latescent
sustainer  activator  astronomy  catatonic  entremets  integrand  lathering
susurrant  actualise  attainder  catchable  establish  integrant  latitancy
systaltic  actuality  attempter  catchment  estaminet  integrate  latterday
taskforce  actuarial  attendant  catchpole  Esthonian  integrity  latticing
Tasmanian  actuation  attention  catchpoll  estimable  intellect  lethality
tasselled  aetiology  attentive  catchword  estimator  intendant  lethargic
tasteless  aftercare  attenuate  catechise  estoppage  intensely  letterbox
tastiness  afterclap  attractor  catechism  estopping  intensify  lettering
tessitura  afterglow  attribute  catechist  estranger  intension  literally
testament  afterlife  attrition  caterwaul  estrapade  intensity  literatim
testation  aftermath  autarchic  Catharism  estuarian  intensive  literator
testatrix  aftermost  autarkist  Catharist  estuarine  intention  literatus
testdrive  afternoon  authentic  catharses  eutectoid  interbred  litheness
testifier  aftertime  authoress  catharsis  euthenics  intercede  lithesome
testimony  afterword  authorial  cathartic  eutherian  intercept  lithology
testiness  aitchbone  authorise  cathectic  eutrophic  intercity  lithopone
unsavoury  alterable  authority  cathedral  extempore  intercrop  lithotomy
unsayable  altercate  autoclave  catoptric  extendant  interdict  litigable
unscathed  alternant  autocracy  cattaloes  extensile  interface  litigious
unselfish  alternate  autocross  cattiness  extension  interfere  litterbin
unsettled  altimeter  autocycle  cattleman  extensity  interfile  litterbug
unshackle  altricial  autograft  cetaceous  extensive  interflow  liturgics
unsheathe  antarctic  autograph  chthonian  extenuate  interfuse  liturgist
unsighted  antefixal  autolysis  citizenly  externals  interject  lotusland
unsightly  antenatal  autolytic  citizenry  extirpate  interknit  matchless
unskilful  antennary  automatic  citystate  extolling  interlace  matchlock
unskilled  antennule  automaton  cotangent  extolment  interlard  matchwood
unsmiling  anthelion  autonomic  cothurnus  extorsive  interleaf  maternity
unsoundly  anthemion  autopilot  cotillion  extortion  interline  mateyness
unsparing  anthocyan  autoroute  cotyledon  extortive  interlink  matriarch
unspotted  anthology  autosomal  cutaneous  extractor  interlock  matricide
```

```
matricula  obtrusion  pettiness  tetradite  witticism  crushable  fruitless
matrimony  obtrusive  pettishly  tetragram  wittiness  crustacea  fruittree
matronage  obturator  pettitoes  tetralogy  wittingly  dauntless  frustrate
matronise  octachord  petulance  tetrapody  ytterbium  deuterate  fruticose
mattamore  octagonal  petulancy  tetrarchy  abundance  deuterium  gaucherie
matutinal  octahedra  phthalein  titillate  abusively  diurnally  gaudiness
metabolic  octameter  pitchdark  titledeed  acuminate  doubleton  gaugeable
metalline  octastyle  pitchfork  titlepage  adulation  doubtable  gauleiter
metalling  octennial  pitchpipe  titration  adulatory  doubtless  gauntness
metallise  octillion  piteously  tittivate  adulterer  doughtily  gauziness
metalloid  Octobrist  pithecoid  tittlebat  adulthood  Doukhobor  glucoside
metalwork  octopodes  pithiness  tittuping  adultness  drugstore  glueyness
metameric  octostyle  pitifully  tittupped  adumbrate  druidical  glutamate
metaphase  ontogenic  pituitary  titularly  aluminate  drummajor  glutinous
metaplasm  ontologic  pityingly  totaliser  aluminise  drumstick  grubscrew
meteorist  optically  potassium  totalling  aluminium  drunkenly  grubstake
meteorite  optometer  potboiler  totempole  aluminous  ebullient  gruelling
meteoroid  optometry  potentate  tutorship  amusement  ecumenism  gruffness
methadone  optophone  potential  Uitlander  amusingly  education  grumbling
metheglin  orthodoxy  potholing  ultimatum  aquaplane  educative  Grundyism
methodise  orthoepic  pothunter  ultrahigh  aquarelle  elucidate  haughtily
Methodism  ostensive  potpourri  untenable  aqueously  elusively  haustella
Methodist  osteoderm  putridity  unthought  aquilegia  elutriate  haustoria
methought  osteogeny  ratepayer  unthrifty  avuncular  emulation  heuristic
methylate  osteology  rationale  untimeous  bluebeard  emulative  hourglass
methylene  osteopath  rationing  untouched  blueberry  emulously  houseboat
metonymic  ostracise  retaliate  untrodden  blueblack  emunctory  housebote
metricate  ostracism  retardant  untrussed  bluegrass  enucleate  housecarl
metrician  Ostrogoth  retention  untutored  bluepoint  enumerate  housecoat
metricise  outbacker  retentive  urticaria  blueprint  enunciate  houseflag
metricist  outermost  rethought  utterable  bluestone  equaliser  household
metrology  outfitter  retiarius  utterance  bluffness  equalling  housekeep
metronome  outgiving  reticence  utterless  blunderer  equipment  houseleek
Mithraism  outgoings  reticency  uttermost  bluntness  equipoise  houseless
Mithraist  outgrowth  reticular  utterness  blushless  equipping  houselled
mitigable  outgunned  reticulum  vaticinal  blusterer  equisetum  housemaid
mitigator  outlander  retinitis  vetchling  boulevard  equitable  housemate
mitraille  outnumber  retinulae  vitellary  boundless  equitably  houseroom
motheaten  outputted  retinular  vitelline  bounteous  equivocal  housewife
motherwit  outridden  retortion  vitiation  bountiful  equivoque  housework
mothproof  outrigger  retoucher  vitiosity  bouquetin  eruciform  iguanodon
motivator  outskirts  retractor  vitriform  bourgeois  eruditely  inunction
motocross  outspoken  retrieval  vitriolic  brummagem  erudition  inurement
motorable  outspread  retriever  Vitruvian  brushfire  esurience  inutility
motorbike  outwardly  retrocede  watchable  brushwood  esuriency  jaundiced
motorboat  outwitted  retrodden  watchcase  brushwork  exuberant  journeyer
motorcade  outworker  retroflex  watchfire  brusquely  exuberate  krummhorn
mutagenic  patchouli  retroject  watchword  brutalise  exudation  laudation
mutilator  patchouly  retrousse  waterbath  brutalism  exudative  laudative
mutualise  patchwork  retrovert  waterbuck  brutality  exultance  laudatory
mutualism  patellate  ritualise  waterbutt  brutishly  exultancy  laughable
mutualist  paternity  ritualism  watercart  Caucasian  faultless  laughably
mutuality  pathogeny  ritualist  watercool  causality  faunistic  launching
mythicise  pathology  rotatable  waterfall  causation  feudalise  launderer
mythicism  patiently  rotundity  waterflea  causative  feudalism  laundress
mythicist  patinated  ruthenium  waterfowl  causeless  feudalist  laurelled
mythology  patriarch  ruthfully  watergate  cauterise  feudality  leucaemia
natheless  patrician  satanical  waterhole  churching  feudatory  leucocyte
natrolite  patricide  satellite  waterleaf  churchman  fluctuant  leucotome
nattiness  patrimony  satiation  waterless  clubbable  fluctuate  leucotomy
naturally  patriotic  satinbird  waterlily  clubhouse  fluecured  leukaemia
netveined  patristic  satinette  waterline  couchette  fluoresce  leukaemic
netwinged  patrolled  satinspar  watermark  coumarone  fluorosis  leukocyte
nitpicker  patroller  satinwood  watermill  countable  fluorspar  loudmouth
nitratine  patrolman  satirical  waterpipe  countdown  flushness  louringly
nitration  patrology  saturable  watershed  countless  fluxional  lousewort
notabilia  patronage  saturator  waterside  countship  foulbrood  lousiness
notedness  patroness  Saturnian  waterweed  courgette  foundling  loutishly
notepaper  patronise  saturnine  waterworn  courtcard  foundress  maulstick
notionist  petaurist  saturnism  wattmeter  courteous  fourflush  maunderer
notochord  petechiae  setaceous  witchetty  courtesan  fourpence  mausoleum
notoriety  petechial  setsquare  witchhunt  courtroom  fourpenny  mouldable
notorious  petersham  situation  witchmeal  courtship  fourscore  mountable
nutriment  pethidine  sitzkrieg  withdrawn  courtyard  fourwheel  mousehole
nutrition  petiolate  sottishly  withering  couturier  fructuate  mousetrap
nutritive  petiolule  sutteeism  witherite  crucially  fructuous  moustache
nuttiness  petroleum  suturally  withstand  cruciform  frugality  mouthpart
nutweevil  petrology  tattiness  withstood  crudeness  fruitcake  mouthwash
obtention  petticoat  tattooist  witlessly  cruellest  fruiterer  naughtily
```

```
naumachia slumberer trunkfish fivepenny revulsion newsprint vexatious
neuralgia slumbrous trunkroad gavelkind revulsive newsstand vexillary
neuralgic slushfund trussbeam governess rivalling Newtonian abysmally
neuration smuggling trustdeed haverings rivalrous nowhither amygdalin
neuroglia snubnosed trustless haversack rivelling powerboat amyloidal
neurology soubrette truthless havocking riverbank powerdive amylopsin
neuromata Soudanese ululation invalidly riverboat powerless arytenoid
neuropath soulfully unusually invariant riverhead rewarding asymmetry
neutrally soundfilm usualness invective riverside rewritten asymptote
nourisher soundhole usucapion inveigler riverweed rowantree asyndetic
opulently soundings vouchsafe invention savagedom rowdiness asyndeton
opusculum soundless woundless inventive savourily tawniness bayoneted
ovulation soundness woundwort inventory sevenfold towelling boycotter
ovulatory soundpost youngling inverness seventeen townhouse boyfriend
paulownia soundwave youngness inversely seventhly townscape bryophyte
pauperise soupplate youngster inversion seventies townsfolk Brythonic
pauperism soupspoon zeugmatic inversive severable unwearied cryogenic
plumbeous sourdough advantage invertase severally unweeting cryoscope
plumbline souteneur advection invidious severalty unwelcome cryoscopy
plumdamas Southdown advective inviolacy severance unwilling cryptical
plumpness southeast Adventism inviolate sovereign unwinking cryptogam
plumulate southerly Adventist invisible sovietise unwitting cryptonym
plumulose southland adventive invisibly sovietism unwomanly dayschool
plunderer southmost adventure involucre vivacious unwrapped dayspring
pluralise southward adverbial involuted viverrine unwritten dryasdust
pluralism southwest adversary joviality vivianite unwrought drysalter
pluralist souwester adversely juvenilia vividness vowelless erythrism
plurality spurwheel adversity lavaliere wavefront yawningly erythrite
plusfours sputterer advertent Levantine waveguide anxiously etymology
plushness squabbler advertise levelling wavellite auxiliary flyfisher
plutocrat squalidly advisable levelness bawdiness boxgirder flyweight
plutonian squamosal advisably leviathan bowerbird boxoffice geyserite
Plutonism squarrose advisedly leviratic bowlegged buxomness glyceride
Plutonist squashily advocator levitator bowstring coxcombry glycerine
plutonium squatness alveolate Levitical bowwindow dexterity glycoside
poulterer squatting bevelling liverwort cowardice dexterous glyptodon
pouncebox squeakily bivalence liveryman cowlstaff dextrally hoydenish
poundcake squeamish bivalency livestock dewlapped dextrorse jaywalker
pourboire squelcher bivariant lividness dowdiness dixieland joylessly
pourpoint squibbing bivariate loveapple dowelling fixedness Keynesian
poussette squidding cavalcade lovechild dowerless foxhunter maybeetle
prudently squinancy cavendish lovefeast downfield hexachord mayflower
prudishly squirarch cavernous lovelight downgrade hexagonal mayoralty
prurience squiredom cavilling lovematch downright hexameter mayorship
pruriency squirelet civically loverless downriver hexaploid oxygenate
raucously studhorse civiliser lovestory downstage hexastich oxygenise
raunchily studiedly covalence lovetoken downthrow hexastyle oxygenous
rauwolfia stupefier covalency lovingcup downwards Hexateuch paymaster
roughcast stupidity covariant moviegoer Edwardian juxtapose paypacket
roughhewn stuporous coverable navelwort enwrapped lexically phycology
roughneck stutterer coverslip navicular enwreathe lixiviate phyllopod
roughness tautology coverture navigable fawningly loxodrome phylogeny
roughshod teutonise covetable navigator gawkiness luxuriant physician
Roumanian Teutonism davenport nevermore hawksbill luxuriate physicist
Roumansch Teutonist devaluate novelette hawsehole luxurious physicked
rounceval thumbhole devastate noviciate hawsepipe maxillary phytogeny
roundelay thumbmark developer novitiate howsoever maximally phytology
roundhead thumbnail deviation obversely inwrought mixedness phytotomy
roundness thumbtack devilfish obversion jewellery myxoedema phytotron
roundsman thunderer devilling obviation jewelweed noxiously psychical
roundworm touchable devilment obviously lawgiving pixilated psychoses
rousement touchdown deviously Pavlovian lawlessly saxifrage psychosis
routinely touchhole devisable pivotable lawnmower saxophone psychotic
routinism touchline devitrify pivotally lowercase sexennial rhymester
routinist touchmark devotedly ravelling lowerdeck sexlessly rhythmics
sauceboat touchtype divergent ravelment lowermost sexlinked rhythmise
sauceless touchwood diversely ravishing lowlander sextuplet rhythmist
saucerful toughness diversify revelator lowliness sexualise skydiving
sauciness touristic diversion revelling lowloader sexuality skyjacker
saunterer tournedos diversity reverence lowminded sixfooter skyrocket
sauropoda tourneyer diverting reversely lownecked sixteenmo stylebook
Sauternes truceless dividable reversion mawkishly sixteenth styliform
sculpture truculent divisible revetment newlyweds taxidermy stylishly
scuncheon truepenny divulsion revetting newmarket taximeter stylistic
scutcheon trumpedup eavesdrop revictual newsagent taxonomic stylobate
scutellar trumpeter enviously revisable newsflash taxpaying Thyestean
scutellum truncated faveolate revivable newshound textually thylacine
scutiform truncheon favourite revocable newsiness toxically thyratron
sluiceway trunkcall fivepence revolting newspaper toxophily thyristor
```

thyroxine	behaviour	cetaceous	dreamland	humanness	metalline	podagrous
trysquare	bejabbers	cheapjack	dreamless	hydathode	metalling	polariser
voyeurism	belatedly	cheapness	dreamlike	hypallage	metallise	pomaceous
wayfaring	bicameral	chlamydes	dryasdust	idealiser	metalloid	potassium
waywardly	bifarious	cicatrice	duralumin	idealless	metalwork	preachify
wayzgoose	bilabiate	cicatrise	dynamical	iguanodon	metameric	preachily
bizarrely	bilateral	cigarette	dynamiter	imbalance	metaphase	preadamic
Byzantine	bipartite	cigarillo	eclampsia	immanence	metaplasm	pyracanth
dizygotic	bivalence	cisalpine	eclamptic	immanency	micaceous	pyramidal
dizziness	bivalency	cleanness	Edwardian	impaction	micaslate	pyramidic
enzymatic	bivariant	cleansing	eglantine	impartial	minacious	pyramidon
fuzziness	bivariate	clearance	embarrass	impassion	misadvise	rapacious
gazehound	bizarrely	clearcole	embassage	impassive	misassign	rebaptise
gazetteer	bleachery	cleareyed	embattled	impastoed	monachism	recalesce
hazardous	bleakness	clearness	embayment	impatiens	monarchal	recapping
jazziness	bleareyed	cleavable	empathise	impatient	monarchic	recapture
lazaretto	botanical	cloakroom	encaustic	incapable	monastery	redaction
lazybones	breadline	cobaltite	engarland	incapably	monatomic	refashion
lazytongs	breadtree	cobaltous	enrapture	incarnate	moraceous	regardant
lazzarone	breakable	cocainise	equaliser	incaution	moraliser	regardful
lazzaroni	breakaway	cocainism	equalling	indagator	moratoria	remainder
mezzanine	breakdown	copacetic	erratical	infantile	mosaicism	remanence
mezzotint	breakeven	copartner	escalator	infantine	mosaicist	renascent
muzziness	breakfast	coralline	escapable	infatuate	mosaicked	reparable
pizzicati	breakneck	corallite	establish	inhalator	mutagenic	repayable
pizzicato	breastpin	coralloid	estaminet	inharmony	nefarious	repayment
pozzolana	breathily	cotangent	eucalypti	inpatient	notabilia	resalable
puzzolana	breathing	covalence	eucaryote	insatiate	octachord	retaliate
razorback	briarroot	covalency	excavator	insatiety	octagonal	retardant
razorbill	briarwood	covariant	exhauster	invalidly	octahedra	rewarding
razoredge	broadcast	cowardice	expansile	invariant	octameter	rivalling
razorfish	broadleaf	creatable	expansion	irradiant	octastyle	rivalrous
unzipping	broadloom	creatress	expansive	irradiate	oleaceous	rocambole
vizierate	broadness	creatural	expatiate	Islamitic	olfaction	rosaceous
vizierial	broadside	cutaneous	fabaceous	Israelite	olfactive	rotatable
———	broadtail	dahabiyah	Falangism	jacaranda	olfactory	rowantree
ablatival	broadways	damascene	Falangist	japanning	ommatidia	sabadilla
abradable	broadwise	debagging	fanatical	Johannine	organelle	sagacious
adiabatic	butadiene	debarment	farandole	Judaistic	organiser	salacious
adjacency	Byzantine	debarring	filaceous	Judastree	organstop	salangane
advantage	caballero	debatable	financial	karabiner	organzine	Samaritan
aflatoxin	caballine	debauched	financier	katabasis	palaestra	sanatoria
agnatical	caballing	debauchee	floatable	katabatic	palafitte	sapanwood
ailanthus	cadastral	debaucher	foragecap	katabolic	palankeen	Saracenic
albatross	cadaveric	decadence	forasmuch	keratitis	palanquin	satanical
aleatoric	calaboose	decadency	friarbird	keratosis	palatable	savagedom
algarroba	calabrese	decagonal	fugacious	kneadable	palatably	sciaenoid
alkaloses	calamanco	decalcify	fumarolic	Kshatriya	panatella	sciagraph
alkalosis	calandria	decalitre	gabardine	lavaliere	parabasis	sciamachy
allantois	camarilla	decalogue	galactose	lazaretto	parabolic	sciascopy
almandine	canalboat	decametre	galantine	Levantine	parachute	scraggily
alpargata	capacious	decapodal	getatable	locatable	Paraclete	scrambler
amianthus	capacitor	decapodan	gigahertz	logaoedic	paradisal	scramming
andantino	caparison	decastere	gigantism	logarithm	paragraph	scrapbook
antarctic	carambola	decathlon	girandole	macaronic	paralalia	scrapheap
aplanatic	catabolic	defalcate	greasegun	maharajah	paralexia	scrapiron
appalling	cataclasm	defaulter	greataunt	maharanee	paralysis	scrappily
Appaloosa	cataclysm	demagogic	greatcoat	maharishi	paralytic	scrapping
apparatus	catalepsy	demagogue	greatness	malachite	paramatta	scrapyard
apparitor	catalexes	demandant	gynaeceum	maladroit	paramedic	scratcher
aquaplane	catalexis	demanding	hamadryad	malanders	parameter	scratches
aquarelle	catalogue	demarcate	hamamelis	malarious	paramorph	seaanchor
armadillo	catalyser	departure	haranguer	malathion	paramount	sebaceous
ashamedly	catalyses	depasture	hazardous	Malayalam	paranoiac	secateurs
asparagus	catalysis	devaluate	hepatitis	medallion	paranymph	selachian
aspartate	catalytic	devastate	Heraclean	medallist	parapeted	semanteme
assailant	catamaran	didactics	hetaerism	megacycle	parapodia	semantics
assaulter	catamount	digastric	hetairism	megadeath	parasitic	semaphore
assayable	cataplasm	dilatable	hexachord	megahertz	parataxis	separable
Atlantean	cataplexy	dilatancy	hexagonal	megaphone	parathion	separably
attainder	catarhine	disaccord	hexameter	megaspore	pedagogic	separates
audacious	catarrhal	disaffect	hexaploid	melanosis	pedagogue	separator
autarchic	catatonia	disaffirm	hexastich	melanotic	pedalling	setaceous
autarkist	catatonic	disannual	hexastyle	melaphyre	Pelasgian	sgraffiti
babacoote	cavalcade	disappear	Hexateuch	melatonin	petaurist	sgraffito
bagatelle	cedarwood	disarming	hilarious	menadione	piratical	shearling
balaclava	celandine	disavouch	Himalayan	menagerie	pleadable	sheatfish
balalaika	cerastium	disavowal	Holarctic	mepacrine	pleadings	sheathing
barathrum	ceratodus	dreamboat	humankind	metabolic	pleasance	skiagraph

skiamachy	trialogue	Cambodian	inebriate	tribesman	brochette	diachylum
skiascopy	triatomic	carbamate	inebriety	tribology	buccaneer	diaconate
sodabread	tufaceous	carbamide	isobathic	tribunate	butcherer	diacritic
sodawater	tyrannise	carbonado	jambalaya	tributary	butcherly	diactinic
solacious	tyrannous	carbonate	kerbstone	tubbiness	caecilian	dipcircle
speakable	Ukrainian	carbonise	kibbutzim	tumblebug	calcaneal	discalced
speakeasy	unbalance	carbuncle	lambently	turbidity	calcaneum	discarder
spearfish	uncannily	carburise	liability	turbinate	calcarate	discerner
spearhead	undamaged	chibouque	Limburger	turboprop	calcicole	discharge
spearmint	undaunted	clubbable	Lombardic	turbulent	calcifuge	discoidal
spearside	unearthly	clubhouse	lumbering	unabashed	calculate	discolour
spearwort	uneatable	combatant	lumberman	verbalise	calculous	discomfit
sphagnous	unfailing	combative	lumbrical	verbalism	cancelled	discommon
splashily	ungallant	combinate	lumbricus	verbalist	cancerous	discourse
splayfoot	unhappily	corbeille	maybeetle	verbicide	carcinoma	discovert
squabbler	unharness	corbelled	misbecome	verbosely	catchable	discovery
squalidly	unmatched	corbicula	misbehave	verbosity	catchment	discredit
squamosal	unnamable	crabbedly	misbelief	viability	catchpole	dogcollar
squarrose	unnatural	cubbyhole	misbeseem	warblefly	catchpoll	draconian
squashily	unsavoury	cumbrance	morbidity	warbonnet	catchword	dulcamara
squatness	unsayable	cupbearer	numbskull	woebegone	Caucasian	dulcitude
squatting	usualness	curbstone	oilburner	abscissae	chachacha	dyscrasia
steadfast	vagarious	cymbalist	outbacker	abscissas	checkered	education
steamboat	Varangian	cymbidium	parbuckle	absconder	checklist	educative
steampipe	Vedantist	cymbiform	porbeagle	aciculate	checkmate	ejaculate
steamship	veracious	diablerie	potboiler	aircooled	checkrein	ejectment
steatitic	verandaed	diabolise	prebendal	aitchbone	chicanery	electoral
straggler	veratrine	diabolism	probation	alicyclic	chickadee	electress
strangely	vexatious	diabolist	probative	anacruses	chickaree	electrify
strangler	vicariate	disbarred	probatory	anacrusis	chickling	electrode
strangles	vicarious	disbelief	proboscis	anecdotal	chickweed	electuary
straphang	vinaceous	disbranch	quebracho	anecdotic	chockfull	elocution
strapless	vivacious	disbudden	quibbling	anschluss	chocolate	elucidate
strappado	vocabular	disburden	rabbinate	apiculate	circadian	emaciated
strapping	vocaliser	disbursal	rabbinism	apocrypha	circinate	enactment
strapwork	vocalness	dorbeetle	rabbinist	arachnoid	circuitry	enucleate
strapwort	volauvent	doubleton	redbreast	atacamite	circulate	epicentre
stratagem	voracious	doubtable	Ribbonism	avocation	clockwise	epiclesis
strategic	wheatmeal	doubtless	rubberise	bacchanal	clockwork	epicurean
strawworm	womanhood	dumbfound	rudbeckia	bacchante	coachwork	epicurism
subaerial	womaniser	edibility	sabbatism	balconied	coccidium	epicyclic
subagency	womankind	eggbeater	sabbatism	barcarole	coccygeal	erectness
subalpine	womanlike	elaborate	sanbenito	beachhead	coelacial	eruciform
subaltern	zapateado	exuberant	semblable	beachwear	colcannon	evocation
subarctic	zoiatrics	exuberate	semblably	beccafico	colchicum	evocative
subastral	alabaster	eyebright	semblance	beechfern	colcothar	evocatory
subatomic	anabioses	fimbriate	slabsided	beechmast	concavely	exactable
sudatoria	anabiosis	flabellum	slabstone	birchbark	concavity	exactment
sugarbeet	anabiotic	forbidden	snubnosed	blackball	conceited	exactness
sugarcane	anabolism	furbisher	sobbingly	blackbird	concentre	execrable
sugarloaf	anabranch	gambadoes	sorbapple	blackbuck	concerned	execrably
sugarplum	arabesque	gambolled	Sorbonist	blackcoat	concerted	executant
swearword	arabicise	geobotany	soubrette	blackcock	concierge	execution
sweatband	Babbittry	gibberish	stabilise	blackdamp	conciliar	executive
sweatshop	bamboozle	gibbosity	stability	blackface	concisely	executory
sybaritic	Barbadian	gibbously	stableboy	Blackfeet	concision	executrix
synagogal	barbarian	glabellae	stableman	blackfish	concocter	falciform
synagogue	barbarise	glabellar	suability	blackflag	concoctor	fancyfree
tacamahac	barbarism	globefish	subbranch	Blackfoot	concordat	fancywork
tarantara	barbarity	globosity	sunbather	blackgame	concourse	fasciated
tarantass	barbarous	gorblimey	sunbonnet	blackhead	concubine	fascicled
tarantism	barbitone	grubscrew	sunburned	blackjack	concurred	fascicule
tarantula	barberine	grubstake	symbiosis	blacklead	couchette	fasciculi
taraxacum	bombardon	hamburger	symbiotic	blacklist	coxcombry	fascinate
telamones	bombasine	harbinger	symbolics	blackmail	crackdown	Fascistic
tenacious	bombastic	harbourer	symbolise	blackness	crackling	fenceless
tenaculum	bombazine	herbalist	symbolism	blackwash	cracksman	fleckless
teratogen	bombhappy	herbarium	symbolist	blockader	cricketer	flocculus
theandric	bombilate	herbicide	symbology	blockhead	crocodile	fluctuant
theatrics	bombinate	herbivore	tambourin	blockship	crucially	fluctuate
thralldom	bombproof	herborise	timbering	boycotter	cruciform	forcefeed
thrashing	bombshell	Hobbesian	timberman	brachiate	cunctator	forceland
totaliser	bombsight	humblebee	tombstone	brachyura	dancehall	forceless
totalling	boobytrap	humbugged	trabeated	bracteate	deacidify	forcemeat
treachery	bulbously	husbandly	trabecula	bracteole	deaconess	forcepump
treadmill	bumblebee	husbandry	trebuchet	brecciate	descended	fractious
treasurer	bumbledon	illboding	trebucket	bricabrac	describer	fricassee
treatable	cabbalism	inability	tribadism	brickwork	diachrony	fricative
treatment	cabbalist	inebriant	tribalism	brickyard	diachylom	frockcoat

```
fructuate  narcotism  precursor  stackable  unicolour  candytuft  goldfinch
fructuous  nescience  priceless  stackroom  unicuspid  cardboard  goldsinny
furcation  niccolite  procedure  stackyard  unscathed  cardsharp  goldsmith
gasconade  nuncupate  procerity  stickwork  usucapion  coadjutor  gondolier
gaucherie  obscenely  processed  stockbook  vaccinate  coadunate  goodnight
glacially  obscenity  processer  stockdove  vetchling  Cobdenism  goodwives
glucoside  obscurant  processor  stockfish  viscerate  coldshort  gradation
glyceride  obscurely  proclitic  stockinet  viscidity  condenser  gradatory
glycerine  obscurity  proconsul  stocklist  viscosity  condignly  Gradgrind
glycoside  offcentre  procreant  stockpile  viscounty  condiment  gradually
graceless  offchance  procreate  stockroom  viscously  condition  graduator
gracility  offcolour  procuracy  stockwhip  voiceless  conducive  guidebook
guacamole  oilcolour  procuress  stockyard  voiceover  conductor  guideline
guncotton  olecranal  psychical  subcaudal  volcanism  condyloid  guidepost
hatchback  olecranon  psychoses  subcostal  volcanoes  condyloma  guiderope
hatchling  ozocerite  psychosis  succeeder  vouchsafe  cordelier  handbrake
hatchment  panchayat  psychotic  succentor  vulcanian  cordially  handcraft
Herculean  pancratic  punchball  successor  vulcanise  cordiform  handcuffs
Hercynian  parcelled  punchbowl  succinate  vulcanism  corduroys  handglass
hircosity  parcenary  punchcard  succotash  vulcanist  crediting  handiness
hitchhike  parchment  punchline  succourer  vulcanite  credulity  handiwork
hunchback  patchouli  punctilio  succulent  watchable  credulous  handlebar
inoculate  patchouly  punctuate  succursal  watchcase  crudeness  handorgan
inscriber  patchwork  purchaser  sulcation  watchfire  Daedalean  handpress
isochrone  peaceable  quickener  surcharge  watchword  Daedalian  handsdown
isoclinal  peaceably  quicklime  surcingle  welcoming  dandelion  handshake
isoclinic  peacetime  quickness  surculose  whichever  dandiacal  handspike
isocyclic  peachblow  quicksand  synchrony  witchetty  deadalive  handstand
juiceless  peccantly  quickstep  synclinal  witchhunt  deadlight  handwheel
juiciness  pencilled  rancidity  syncopate  witchmeal  dendritic  handywork
kitchener  penciller  rancorous  syncretic  Worcester  deodorant  hardboard
knockdown  percaline  rascaldom  syncytial  zincotype  deodorise  hardcover
knockknee  perceiver  rascalism  syncytium  zirconium  doodlebug  hardihood
laccolith  perchance  rascality  teachable  zucchetto  dowdiness  hardiment
lancejack  percheron  raucously  teachably  abidingly  duodecimo  hardiness
lancewood  percolate  reachable  teacupful  academism  duodenary  hardnosed
lancinate  phycology  reactance  thickener  acidifier  ealdorman  hardshell
larcenist  piecemeal  Reichstag  thicketed  acidophil  epidermal  headboard
larcenous  piecerate  rencontre  thickhead  acidulate  epidermic  headcloth
Leicester  piecework  runcinate  thickknee  acidulent  epidermis  headdress
leucaemia  pinchbeck  saccharin  thickness  acidulous  epidosite  headfirst
leucocyte  pinchcock  sacciform  torchrace  amidships  eradicate  headiness
leucotome  piscatory  sacculate  torchsong  apodictic  eruditely  headlight
leucotomy  pisciform  sanctuary  touchable  baldachin  erudition  headliner
lunchtime  pitchdark  sarcastic  touchdown  baldaquin  evidently  headphone
Maccabean  pitchfork  sarcocarp  touchhole  baldfaced  exodermis  headpiece
Mancunian  pitchpipe  sarcomata  touchline  banderole  exudation  headscarf
marcasite  placation  sauceboat  touchmark  bandicoot  exudative  headstall
marcelled  placatory  sauceless  touchtype  bandoleer  faddiness  headstock
marchpane  placeable  saucerful  touchwood  bandolero  faldstool  headstone
marchpast  placecard  sauciness  traceable  bandolier  fandangle  headwater
masculine  placekick  seachange  traceably  bandoline  fandangos  heedfully
matchless  placeless  Shechinah  traceless  bandstand  feedstock  hendiadys
matchlock  placement  shockable  traceried  bandwagon  feedstuff  hiddenite
matchwood  placename  shockhead  tracheary  bandwidth  feudalise  hindbrain
mercaptan  placentae  siccative  tracheate  bawdiness  feudalism  hindrance
mercenary  placental  sincerely  trachytic  beadledom  feudalist  hindsight
mercerise  placidity  sincerity  trackless  birdbrain  feudality  hoydenish
merciless  plicately  slackness  tracksuit  birdsfoot  feudatory  humdinger
mercurial  plication  slickness  tractable  birdsnest  fledgling  hundredth
mercurous  plicature  smackeroo  tractably  birdtable  foodchain  inodorous
mescaline  porcelain  sorceress  trichinae  birdwatch  foodstuff  Jordanian
mincemeat  porcupine  sorcerous  trichomic  boldfaced  fundament  khedivial
mincingly  practical  spaceband  trichroic  bondslave  ganderism  kiddingly
miscegene  practised  spaceless  trickless  bondstone  gardening  kilderkin
miscegine  precancel  spaceport  tricksily  bondwoman  garderobe  landagent
mischance  precative  spaceship  trickster  bordereau  gaudiness  landaulet
miscreant  precatory  spacesuit  triclinia  bridecake  geodesist  landdross
miscreate  precedent  spacetime  triclinic  bridesman  giddiness  landdrost
moschatel  preceding  specially  tricolour  bridewell  gladiator  landgrave
mumchance  precentor  specialty  trochilus  bridleway  gladiolus  landloper
muscadine  preceptor  specifier  trochleae  bundobust  gladstone  landowner
muscarine  precipice  speckless  trochlear  burdenous  goddamned  landscape
muscleman  precisely  spectacle  truceless  caddisfly  goldbrick  landslide
muscovado  precisian  spectator  truculent  caldarium  goldcrest  Laodicean
muscovite  precision  speculate  Turcomans  candidacy  goldeneye  lardycake
narcissus  precocial  spicebush  twiceborn  candidate  goldenrod  laudation
narcotine  precocity  spiciness  twicelaid  Candlemas  goldfever  laudative
narcotism  preconise  spiculate  twicetold  candlenut  goldfield  laudatory
```

```
lendlease  reeducate  unadorned  aldehydic  banefully  copestone  duteously
loadstone  rendition  unadvised  algebraic  barefaced  coreopsis  dysentery
Londonise  rhodamine  vandalise  alienable  begetting  coseismal  eagerness
Londonism  rhodolite  vandalism  alienator  beleaguer  coseismic  easefully
loudmouth  rhodonite  vendition  allegedly  belemnite  coverable  eavesdrop
maddening  rhodopsin  verdantly  allegiant  beneficed  coverslip  eccentric
magdalene  roadblock  verdigris  allegoric  besetment  coverture  effective
maidenish  roadhouse  vindicate  allemande  besetting  covetable  effectual
mandarine  roadmetal  voodooism  alleviate  bevelling  cruellest  egregious
mandatary  roadstead  voodooist  alpenhorn  bigeneric  cuneiform  egression
mandatory  roadworks  Waldenses  alterable  bisection  cupelling  eiderdown
mandoline  roodcloth  waldgrave  altercate  blaeberry  curettage  eiderduck
manducate  rowdiness  wandering  alternant  bluebeard  daredevil  eirenicon
mendacity  ruddiness  weediness  alternate  blueberry  davenport  eldership
Mendelian  ruddleman  whodunnit  alveolate  blueblack  debenture  elsewhere
Mendelism  saddlebag  windblown  ambergris  bluegrass  deceitful  embedding
mendicant  saddlebow  windbound  amoebaean  bluepoint  decennary  embedment
mendicity  Sadducean  windbreak  ampersand  blueprint  decennial  embellish
middleman  sandalled  windchest  anaerobic  bluestone  decennium  embezzler
mindfully  sandarach  windhover  ancestral  bolection  deception  Emmenthal
misdemean  sandblast  windiness  andesitic  bonechina  deceptive  empennage
misdirect  sandblind  windowbox  angelfish  bowerbird  defeatism  encephala
Mondayish  sandcrack  windproof  angelical  breeching  defeatist  endearing
moodiness  sandglass  windswept  annectent  breezeway  defeature  endeavour
mordacity  sandiness  windwards  annelidan  briefcase  defection  enhearten
mordantly  sandpaper  wonderful  antefixal  briefless  defective  entelechy
muddiness  sandpiper  woodblock  antenatal  briefness  defendant  enterable
mundanely  sandspout  woodchuck  antennary  brierroot  defensive  enteritis
mundungus  sandstone  woodcraft  antennule  brierwood  deference  entertain
murderess  sandstorm  woodiness  aphereses  cadential  deferment  epaenetic
murderous  sandtable  woodlouse  apheresis  cadetship  deferring  ephedrine
needfully  sandyacht  woodnymph  appealing  cafeteria  dejection  ephemeral
neediness  Sardinian  woodwaxen  appellant  cageyness  demeanour  ephemerid
needleful  seedeater  wordiness  appellate  calendric  dependant  ephemeris
neodymium  seediness  wordsmith  appendage  calendula  dependent  ephemeron
nondriver  seedpearl  yardstick  appendant  calenture  desecrate  esperance
obedience  seedplant  Yiddisher  appertain  camelback  desertion  Esperanto
opodeldoc  shadberry  abjection  appetence  camelhair  detection  essential
oviductal  shadeless  abnegator  appetency  Camembert  detective  etherical
oxidation  shadetree  abseiling  appetiser  cameraman  detention  eutectoid
paederast  shadiness  accentual  aqueously  canebrake  detergent  exceeding
panderast  skedaddle  acceptant  argentine  canescent  determent  excellent
pendently  skydiving  acceptive  argentite  canesugar  determine  excelling
pendragon  sliderule  accessary  argentous  canetrash  deterrent  excelsior
pendulate  soidisant  accession  arrearage  careerism  deterring  excentric
penduline  soldierly  accessory  arrestant  careerist  detersion  exceptant
pendulous  Soudanese  Acheulean  arresting  carefully  detersive  excepting
perdition  spadefoot  Acheulian  arsenical  caretaker  developer  exception
ponderous  spadework  adherence  arsenious  caseation  diaereses  exceptive
predacity  spiderman  admeasure  artemisia  catechise  diaeresis  excerptor
predation  spiderweb  adrenalin  arteriole  catechism  didelphic  excessive
predative  spodumene  advection  arteritis  catechist  digestion  expectant
predatory  studhorse  advective  asbestine  caterwaul  digestive  expecting
predicant  studiedly  Adventism  asbestous  cavendish  dimension  expedient
predicate  subdeacon  Adventist  ascendant  cavernous  dioecious  expediter
predictor  subdivide  adventive  ascendent  celebrant  dipeptide  expellent
predigest  subduable  adventure  ascension  celebrate  direction  expelling
predikant  subduedly  adverbial  ascensive  celebrity  directive  expensive
prideless  sundowner  adversary  ascertain  celestial  directory  expertise
prodromal  swaddling  adversely  ascetical  cementite  directrix  exsertile
prodromic  syndactyl  adversity  askewness  cerebella  direfully  exsertion
prudently  syndicate  advertent  aspectual  cerebrate  disembark  exservice
prudishly  tapdancer  advertise  aspersion  cerecloth  disembody  extempore
quadratic  tardiness  affecting  assembler  chaetopod  disengage  extendant
quadrifid  tenderise  affection  assertion  cheekbone  disentail  extensile
quadrigae  tendinous  affective  assertive  cheerless  disentomb  extension
quadrille  tiedyeing  aftercare  atheistic  chiefship  disesteem  extensity
quadruman  tinderbox  afterclap  athematic  chieftain  diversely  extensive
quadruped  toadeater  afterglow  Athenaeum  cinematic  diversify  extenuate
quadruply  toadstone  afterlife  attempter  cineraria  diversion  externals
quodlibet  toadstool  aftermath  attendant  cinereous  diversity  facecloth
randiness  trademark  aftermost  attention  clientage  diverting  facetious
randomise  tradename  afternoon  attentive  clientele  dodecagon  Falernian
readdress  tradesman  aftertime  attenuate  coheiress  dolefully  farestage
readiness  tradition  afterword  aubergine  coherence  doleritic  fatefully
readymade  traducian  agreeable  Aylesbury  coherency  dopefiend  faveolate
reediness  tridactyl  agreeably  bakehouse  colemouse  dowelling  federally
reedorgan  tridymite  agreement  balefully  comedones  dowerless  fenestrae
           unadopted  albescent  baneberry  copesmate             fenestral
```

fideistic	Greekless	indelibly	inveigler	lymehound	oogenetic	rareeshow
finedrawn	greenback	indemnify	invention	macedoine	orderbook	ratepayer
firealarm	greenbelt	indemnity	inventive	macerator	orderform	ravelling
fireblast	greeneyed	indention	inventory	madeleine	orderless	ravelment
firebrand	greengage	indenture	inverness	makeready	orientate	rebelling
firebreak	greenhorn	infection	inversely	makeshift	ostensive	rebellion
firebrick	greenness	infective	inversion	maneating	osteoderm	recension
firecrest	greenroom	inferable	inversive	marestail	osteogeny	reception
firedrake	greensand	inference	invertase	maternity	osteology	receptive
firedrill	greenweed	inferring	irreality	mateyness	osteopath	recession
fireeater	greenwood	infertile	irregular	mementoes	otherness	recessive
fireguard	griefless	ingenious	jewellery	mesentery	otherwise	redevelop
firehouse	grievance	ingenuity	jewelweed	meteorist	outermost	refection
fireirons	gruelling	ingenuous	Juneberry	meteorite	ownership	refectory
firelight	habergeon	ingestion	juvenilia	meteoroid	pacemaker	referable
fireplace	haresfoot	ingestive	kinematic	milestone	pageantry	reference
firepower	hatefully	inherence	labelling	minefield	panegyric	referenda
fireproof	haverings	inheritor	lacerable	minelayer	panelling	referring
firestone	haversack	injection	lacertian	misemploy	panellist	rehearsal
firewater	hegemonic	innermost	lacertine	miserable	paperback	rejection
fireworks	hereabout	innervate	lamellate	miserably	paperclip	relevance
fivepence	hereafter	insectary	lamellose	misesteem	papergirl	relevancy
fivepenny	heretical	insectile	latecomer	mixedness	paperthin	remeasure
fixedness	hereunder	insensate	laterally	modelling	paperwork	remediate
fleetness	heterodox	insertion	latescent	moderator	papeterie	renewable
fluecured	heteronym	inservice	legendary	modernise	paregoric	repechage
foreboder	heterosis	insetting	legerline	modernism	parentage	repellant
forebrain	hibernate	integrand	levelling	modernist	patellate	repellent
forecaddy	Hibernian	integrant	levelness	modernity	paternity	repelling
foreclose	hidebound	integrate	libecchio	molecular	pederasty	repentant
forecourt	hideously	integrity	libellant	momentary	peneplain	repertory
forefront	homebound	intellect	libelling	momentous	peneplane	rerebrace
foregoing	homegrown	intendant	libellist	monergism	penetrant	rerelease
foreigner	homemaker	intensely	libellous	moneybags	penetrate	reremouse
forejudge	homeopath	intensify	liberally	moneybill	peregrine	resection
foreknown	homestead	intension	liberated	moneywort	perennate	resentful
forenamed	homewards	intensity	liberator	Mycenaean	perennial	reserpine
forereach	honeycomb	intensive	libertine	nakedness	petechiae	reservist
foreshore	honeymoon	intention	licensure	nameplate	petechial	reservoir
foreshown	hopefully	interbred	lifeblood	naseberry	petersham	resetting
foresight	horehound	intercede	lifecycle	navelwort	phlebitis	retention
forespeak	hugeously	intercept	lifeforce	necessary	phrenetic	retentive
forestage	humectant	intercity	lifeguard	necessity	pikeperch	revelator
forestall	hyperbola	intercrop	lifesaver	nemertean	pikestaff	revelling
foretaste	hyperbole	interdict	lifesized	nemertine	pineapple	reverence
foretoken	hypergamy	interface	lifestyle	nepenthes	pipedream	reversely
forewoman	hypericum	interfere	lifetable	nevermore	pipeorgan	reversion
fraenulum	hyperopia	interfile	limejuice	ninepence	pipestone	revetment
freeboard	hyperopic	interflow	limelight	ninepenny	piteously	revetting
freehouse	hypethral	interfuse	limestone	ninetieth	pokeberry	ricepaper
freelance	ignescent	interject	limewater	nonentity	pokerface	riderless
freeliver	illegally	interknit	lineality	nosebleed	pokerwork	rivelling
Freemason	illegible	interlace	lineament	noseflute	polemical	riverbank
freerange	illegibly	interlard	linearise	nosepiece	polevault	riverboat
freerider	imbecilic	interleaf	linearity	notedness	potentate	riverhead
freestone	immediacy	interline	lineation	notepaper	potential	riverside
freestyle	immediate	interlink	linenfold	novelette	powerboat	riverweed
freewheel	immensely	interlock	lineolate	numerable	powerdive	roseapple
freewoman	immensity	interlope	literally	numerator	powerless	roseately
freezable	immersion	interlude	literatim	numerical	praenomen	rosenoble
freezedry	impeccant	interment	literator	oakenshaw	preemptor	rosewater
funebrial	impedance	internode	literatus	objectify	preengage	rubellite
gaberdine	impelling	interpage	liverwort	objection	preexilic	rufescent
galenical	impendent	interplay	liveryman	objective	priestess	rulership
gatecrash	impending	interpose	livestock	obsecrate	proenzyme	Sabellian
gatehouse	imperator	interpret	lobectomy	obsequial	pubescent	safeguard
gavelkind	imperfect	interring	lodestone	obsequies	pureblood	safetypin
gazehound	imperious	interrupt	loveapple	observant	pyrethrum	sagebrush
gazetteer	impetrate	intersect	lovechild	obsession	queenhood	sagegreen
genealogy	impetuous	intervein	lovefeast	obsessive	queenless	saleratus
generable	inbetween	intervene	lovelight	observive	queenlike	salesgirl
generalia	incensory	interview	lovematch	obtention	queenpost	saleslady
generally	incentive	interwind	loverless	obversely	queenship	satellite
generator	inception	interwove	lovestory	octennial	queerness	scheelite
genetical	inceptive	interzone	lovetoken	oogenesis...	quiescent	schematic
gleefully	incessant	intestacy	lowercase	lowercase	quietness	sciential
glueyness	indecency	intestate	lowerdeck	offertory	racehorse	scientism
gobetween	indecorum	intestine	lowermost	onsetting	racetrack	scientist
governess	indelible	invective	lymegrass	oogenesis	rakehelly	scleritis

```
sclerosis  speedboat  tigerseye  undervest  waterside  driftwood  raffishly
sclerotic  speedster  tigerwood  underwear  waterweed  fanfarade  rafflesia
screecher  speedwell  tilestone  underwent  waterworn  feoffment  reefpoint
screening  spherical  timelapse  underwing  wavefront  flyfisher  rodfisher
screwball  spherular  timelimit  underwood  waveguide  forfeiter  roofplate
screwbolt  spleenful  timeously  unfeeling  wavellite  fulfilled  ruffianly
screwpile  splendent  timepiece  unfeigned  wheedling  fulfiller  safflower
screwpine  splendour  timesheet  unhealthy  wheelbase  gasfitter  seafaring
screwworm  splenetic  timetable  unheeding  wheelless  gerfalcon  selfabuse
secernent  splenitis  tiredness  unhelpful  wheelwork  godfather  selfaware
secession  spleuchan  tirewoman  unlearned  wideawake  goffering  selfdoubt
sedentary  squeakily  tolerable  unmeaning  wineberry  golflinks  selfdrive
selection  squeamish  tolerably  unpegging  wineglass  gruffness  selffaced
selective  squelcher  tolerance  unpeopled  winepress  gyrfalcon  selfglory
selectman  steelclad  tomentose  unreality  winestone  halfbaked  selfimage
selenious  steelhead  tomentous  unreserve  winevault  halfblood  selfishly
selenitic  steelwork  toreutics  unselfish  wiredrawn  halfbound  selfmoved
semeiotic  steelyard  totempole  unsettled  wiregauze  halfbreed  selfpride
semestral  steenkirk  towelling  untenable  wirephoto  halfcaste  selftrust
senescent  steepness  triennial  unwearied  wisecrack  halfcrown  shiftless
seneschal  steersman  triennium  unweeting  womenfolk  halfhardy  sixfooter
serenader  streakily  trierarch  unwelcome  womenkind  halflight  solfatara
sevenfold  streaking  truepenny  uppercase  yodelling  halfpence  solfeggio
seventeen  streamlet  tubercule  uppermost  ytterbium  halfpenny  solferino
seventhly  streetcar  tumescent  upsetting  zibelline  halfprice  stiffener
seventies  strenuous  tunefully  urceolate  asafetida  halfshell  stiffness
severable  stressful  typemetal  usherette  bedfellow  halfstaff  subfamily
severally  stretcher  typewrite  utterable  beefeater  halftitle  suffering
severalty  strewment  umbellate  utterance  beefiness  halftrack  suffocate
severance  subeditor  umbellule  utterless  beefsteak  halftruth  suffragan
sexennial  subereous  umberbird  uttermost  bluffness  hamfisted  suffusion
sheepcote  superable  unbeknown  utterness  boyfriend  hoofprint  sunflower
sheepfold  supercool  unbending  vademecum  buffaloes  huffiness  surfacing
sheephook  superfine  unberufen  valentine  buffeting  ineffable  surfboard
sheeplice  superfuse  unceasing  vasectomy  carfuffle  ineffably  surfeiter
sheepskin  superheat  uncertain  vegetable  chafferer  kerfuffle  surficial
sheeptick  supernova  undecagon  vegetably  chaffinch  knifeedge  swiftness
sheepwalk  superpose  undeceive  vehemence  cliffhang  leafgreen  trifacial
sheepwash  supersede  undecided  veneering  coffeecup  leafmould  trifocals
sheerhulk  superstar  undecimal  venerable  coffeepot  leafstalk  trifolium
sheerlegs  supervene  undefined  venerably  cofferdam  loafsugar  triforium
sheerness  supervise  underbody  venerator  coffinite  malformed  twofisted
sheetbend  sweepback  underbred  venereous  coiffeuse  mayflower  unifiable
shieldbug  sweetcorn  underclay  vicennial  comfiture  misfeasor  uniformly
shieldfem  sweetener  undercoat  viceregal  comforter  muffineer  wayfaring
shoeblack  sweetmeal  underdone  vicereine  confabbed  muffinman  webfooted
shoemaker  sweetmeat  underfelt  viceroyal  conferral  oddfellow  welfarism
shoeshine  sweetness  underfoot  vicesimal  conferred  orificial  wolfhound
shredding  sweetshop  undergird  videlicet  conferrer  oriflamme  wolfishly
shrewmice  sweettalk  undergone  videotape  confervae  outfitter  wolframic
sideboard  synectics  undergrad  vigesimal  confessor  oviferous  wolfsbane
sideburns  syneresis  underhand  virescent  confidant  parfleche  wulfenite
sidedness  synergism  underhung  vitellary  confident  penfriend  alignment
sideissue  synergist  underlaid  vitelline  confiding  perfectly  amygdalin
sidelight  telegenic  underlain  viverrine  configure  perfector  apogamous
sideritic  telegraph  underline  vowelless  confirmed  perfervid  aragonite
siderosis  telemeter  underling  voyeurism  confirmer  perforate  bagginess
sideswipe  telemetry  undermine  wakefully  confirmor  performer  bargainer
sidetable  teleology  undermost  wakerobin  confiteor  perfumery  bargepole
sidetrack  telepathy  underpaid  wapentake  confluent  perfumier  bengaline
sidewards  telephone  underpart  warehouse  conformal  perfusion  bergamask
sidewheel  telephony  underpass  waterbath  conformer  perfusive  bilgekeel
sinewless  telephoto  underplay  waterbuck  Confucian  pilferage  biogenous
skeesicks  telescope  underplot  waterbutt  confusion  prefatory  biography
sleekness  telescopy  underrate  watercart  craftsman  preferred  boxgirder
sleepless  televisor  underripe  watercool  deftware   prefigure  bregmatic
sleevenut  tenebrist  underseal  waterfall  different  prefixion  brigadier
soberness  tenebrous  underseas  waterflea  difficile  profanely  brigandry
solemnise  terebinth  undersell  waterfowl  difficult  profanity  brightish
solemnity  terebrant  undershot  watergate  diffident  professed  budgetary
soleplate  threefold  underside  waterhole  diffusely  professor  Bulgarian
something  threesome  undersign  waterleaf  diffusion  profilist  bulginess
sometimes  threnodic  undersold  waterless  diffusive  profiteer  Cingalese
somewhere  threshold  undersong  waterlily  disfavour  profusely  coagulant
somewhile  Thyestean  underspin  waterline  disfigure  profusion  coagulate
sovereign  tidegauge  undertake  watermark  disforest  puffadder  congenial
speechful  tidewater  undertint  watermill  driftsail  puffiness  congeries
speechify  tigerlily  undertone  waterpipe  driftwood  raffinate  congruent
speedball  tigermoth  undertook  watershed  driftweed  raffinose  congruity
```

```
congruous  hangerson  oligarchy  surgeoncy  batholite  fisherman  mishandle
cudgelled  haughtily  Oligocene  swaggerer  batholith  fishiness  mishanter
dangerous  hedgingly  oligopoly  syngamous  Bathonian  fishplate  Mithraism
diagnoses  hobgoblin  originate  tangerine  bathybius  fishslice  Mithraist
diagnosis  hoggishly  orography  Targumist  bethought  fishyback  motheaten
dinginess  Hungarian  outgiving  thighbone  bigheaded  foxhunter  motherwit
disgracer  illgotten  outgoings  thighboot  bilharzia  gasholder  mothproof
doggishly  imageable  outgrowth  tonguelet  bishopric  gathering  mythicise
doughtily  imageless  outgunned  tonguetie  bonhomous  Gothamite  mythicism
draghound  imaginary  oxygenate  toughness  Brahmanic  gothicise  mythicist
dragomans  isagogics  oxygenise  tragedian  Brahminee  Gothicism  mythology
dragoness  isogamete  oxygenous  trigamist  Brahminic  gushingly  naphthene
dragonfly  isogamous  pergunnah  trigamous  bughunter  hamhanded  natheless
dragonish  isogenous  phagedena  tungstate  bushcraft  haphazard  nephalism
drugstore  jargonise  phagocyte  turgently  bushelful  Hashemite  nephalist
dungarees  judgement  piggishly  turgidity  bushiness  Hashimite  nepheline
dysgenics  judgeship  piggyback  uliginous  bushwhack  highchair  nephelite
dziggetai  judgmatic  piggybank  vengeance  cachectic  highclass  nephology
elegantly  kingcraft  pilgarlic  Virgilian  cacholong  highflier  nephritic
elegiacal  kingdomed  podginess  virginals  Catharism  highflown  nephritis
enigmatic  kingmaker  poignancy  virginity  Catharist  highflyer  nephrosis
epigraphy  kingsized  pragmatic  virgulate  catharses  highgrade  nightbird
epigynous  knightage  pregnable  vulgarian  catharsis  highgrown  nightclub
erogenous  laggardly  pregnancy  vulgarise  cathartic  highlands  nightfall
evaginate  Langobard  progestin  vulgarism  cathectic  highlevel  nightgown
exegetist  langouste  prognoses  vulgarity  cathedral  highlight  nighthawk
exogamous  languidly  prognosis  waggishly  cephalous  highspeed  nightlife
exogenous  largeness  programme  waggonage  chihuahua  hightoned  nightline
eyeglance  larghetto  pudginess  wedgewise  chthonian  highwater  nightlong
faggoting  laughable  pungently  weighable  cochineal  hotheaded  nightmare
fingering  laughably  purgation  weighbeam  cochleate  hyphenate  nightside
fingertip  lawgiving  purgative  weightily  cothurnus  innholder  nighttime
flagellum  legginess  purgatory  weighting  Cytherean  inshallah  nightwork
flageolet  lengthily  ranginess  wingchair  dachshund  ischaemia  nowhither
flagrance  liegelord  ridgepole  zeugmatic  dashboard  ischaemic  offhanded
flagrancy  lingering  ridgetile  zoogenous  dashingly  ischiadic  onehanded
flagstaff  lingually  ringfence  zoography  dethroner  ischiatic  orchestic
flagstick  lingulate  ringingly  alchemise  dichasial  isohyetal  orchestra
flagstone  lodgement  ringshake  alchemist  dichasium  itchiness  orchidist
flightily  lodgepole  ringsnake  amphibian  dichogamy  katharsis  orphanage
fogginess  longaeval  roughcast  amphibole  dichotomy  lachrymal  orthodoxy
forgather  longchain  roughhewn  amphigory  dichroism  lathering  orthoepic
forgeable  longcoats  roughneck  amphioxus  dichromat  lecherous  pachyderm
forgetful  longeared  roughness  anchorage  dichromic  lethality  panhandle
forgiving  longevity  roughshod  anchoress  diphthong  lethargic  parhelion
forgotten  longevous  ruggedise  anchorite  dishcloth  lichenous  pathogeny
fragility  longfaced  sangfroid  anchorman  dishclout  lightfoot  pathology
fragrance  longhouse  sargassos  anchylose  dishfaced  lightless  penholder
fragrancy  longicorn  scagliola  anthelion  dishonest  lightness  pethidine
frigatoon  longingly  seagirdle  anthemion  dishonour  lightning  phthalein
frightful  longitude  sedgewren  anthocyan  dishwater  lightship  pigheaded
frigidity  longlived  seigneury  anthology  dithyramb  lightsome  pithecoid
frogmarch  Longobard  seigniory  anthozoan  eightfold  lightsout  pithiness
frogspawn  longrange  sergeancy  anthracic  eightieth  lightwood  potholing
frugality  longshore  shogunate  anthropic  eightsome  lightyear  pothunter
fulgently  lorgnette  singalong  archangel  eightyish  litheness  pushchair
fulgurant  manganate  singleton  archducal  emphasise  lithesome  pushiness
fulgurate  manganese  singspiel  archduchy  emphysema  lithology  pushingly
fulgurite  manganite  slightish  archenemy  enchanter  lithopone  rechauffe
fulgurous  manganous  smuggling  archetype  enchilada  lithotomy  recherche
fungicide  manginess  sniggerer  archfiend  enchorial  lophodont  redhanded
fungiform  margarine  sogginess  architect  ensheathe  machinate  redheaded
gadgeteer  margarite  songcycle  archivist  enthymeme  machinery  reshuffle
gangboard  marginate  songfully  archivolt  escheator  machinist  rethought
gangplank  merganser  songsmith  arthritic  Esthonian  machmeter  rightable
gaugeable  misgiving  spaghetti  arthritis  Eucharist  manhandle  righteous
geography  misgovern  spagyrist  arthropod  euchology  manhattan  righthand
gingerade  misguided  stagedoor  arthrosis  euphemise  mechanics  rightness
gingerale  Mongolian  stagehand  Arthurian  euphemism  mechanise  rightward
ginglymus  mongolism  staggerer  asphaltic  euphonise  mechanism  rushlight
gogglebox  Mongoloid  staghound  asphaltum  euphonium  mechanist  ruthenium
gongorism  mongooses  staginess  asthmatic  euphorbia  methadone  ruthfully
gorgonian  mongrelly  Stagirite  authentic  eurhythmy  metheglin  Sanhedrim
gorgonise  mugginess  stagnancy  authoress  euthenics  methodise  Sanhedrin
gregarian  myography  stagparty  authorial  eutherian  Methodism  sapheaded
gregarine  naughtily  stegosaur  authorise  exchanger  Methodist  senhorita
Gregorian  neighbour  stigmatic  authority  exchequer  methought  Sephardic
haggadist  niggardly  subgenera  bashfully  fashioner  methylate  Sephardim
haggardly  oligaemia  suggester  bathhouse  fatheaded  methylene  sightless
```

sightseer	agriology	bilirubin	denitrate	felicific	indignant	Manichean
Sinhalese	albinotic	biliteral	denitrify	femineity	indignity	manifesto
siphonage	alligator	bipinnate	depiction	Fenianism	indigotin	manipular
siphuncle	altimeter	boliviano	depictive	fetichism	indispose	marihuana
sophister	ambiguity	braincase	derivable	fetichist	infielder	marijuana
sophistic	ambiguous	brainless	desiccant	fetidness	infilling	maritally
sophistry	ambitious	brainwash	desiccate	fetishism	infirmary	maxillary
sophomore	anciently	brainwave	designate	fetishist	infirmity	maximally
sunhelmet	ancientry	broiderer	designing	filiation	inhibitor	mediaeval
syphilise	ancillary	caciquism	desirable	filigreed	insidious	mediately
syphiloid	angiology	calibrate	desirably	finically	insincere	mediation
tachylite	angiomata	calicular	deviation	finicking	insinuate	mediatise
tachylyte	anticline	caliology	devilfish	foliation	insipidly	mediative
technical	anticodon	caliphate	devilling	frailness	insistent	mediatory
technique	antidotal	canicular	devilment	freighter	invidious	mediatrix
tightener	antigenic	capillary	deviously	fruitcake	inviolacy	medicable
tightness	antiknock	capitally	devisable	fruiterer	inviolate	medically
tightrope	antimonic	capitular	devitrify	fruitless	invisible	medicinal
tightwire	antinodal	capitulum	digitalin	fruittree	invisibly	meditator
Tocharian	antinomic	Caribbean	digitalis	fumigator	ionisable	meliorate
tophamper	antinovel	cavilling	digitally	funicular	irrigable	meliorism
trihedral	antipasto	chaingang	digitated	funiculus	irrigator	meliorist
trihybrid	antipathy	chaingear	diligence	furiously	irritable	meliority
twohanded	antiphony	chainless	dimidiate	fusillade	irritably	melismata
typhlitis	antipodal	chainmail	dimissory	fusionist	janissary	meningeal
typhoidal	antipodes	chairlady	diningcar	gabionade	janitress	midinette
uncharted	antiquary	Christian	dirigible	galingale	joviality	militancy
unchecked	antiquate	Christmas	dirigisme	garibaldi	jubilance	mimicking
unshackle	antiquity	citizenly	disinfect	gelignite	judiciary	miniature
unsheathe	antiserum	citizenry	disinfest	genialise	judicious	minimally
unthought	antitoxic	civically	dividable	geniality	juniorate	miniskirt
unthrifty	antitoxin	civiliser	divisible	genitival	juniority	misinform
washbasin	antitrade	claimable	dixieland	geriatric	juridical	mitigable
washboard	antitrust	cloisonne	dominance	glaireous	labialise	mitigator
washcloth	antivenin	cloistral	dominator	gneissoid	labialism	modillion
washedout	antiviral	cogitable	dominical	gneissose	laciniate	monitress
washerman	anxiously	comically	Dominican	goliardic	laminaria	motivator
washhouse	aquilegia	Cominform	dosimeter	habitable	laminated	moviegoer
washiness	arbitrage	Comintern	dosimetry	habitably	lapideous	municipal
washstand	arbitrary	comitadji	drainpipe	habituate	latitancy	muniments
wishfully	arbitrate	conically	druidical	hagiarchy	legionary	munitions
withdrawn	argillite	coriander	dubiosity	hagiology	legislate	musically
withering	armigeral	cotillion	dubiously	halieutic	leniently	musichall
witherite	armigeral	cotillion	dubitable	halitosis	leviathan	mutilator
withstand	armillary	croissant	dutifully	helically	leviratic	myriorama
withstood	armistice	cubically	ecritoire	heliogram	levitator	navicular
wychhazel	arriviste	curialism	efficient	heliostat	Levitical	navigable
yachtclub	artichoke	curiosity	ellipsoid	heliotype	lexically	navigator
yachtsman	articular	curiously	empirical	heliozoan	libidinal	nobiliary
abdicable	artificer	cuticular	enlighten	heliozoic	limitable	nominable
abdicator	artillery	cutinised	enviously	hemicycle	limitedly	nominally
accidence	aspirator	cylindric	equipment	hemistich	limitless	nominator
accipiter	assiduity	cynically	equipoise	hemitrope	litigable	nonillion
actinozoa	assiduous	decidable	equipping	heritable	litigious	notionist
activator	assistant	decidedly	equisetum	hesitance	lividness	noviciate
addiction	audiology	deciduate	equitable	hesitancy	lixiviate	novitiate
addictive	auditable	deciduous	equitably	hesitator	logically	noxiously
adlibbing	auditoria	decilitre	equivocal	hodiernal	logistics	obeisance
adminicle	auricular	decillion	equivoque	homicidal	lovingcup	obligated
admirable	auxiliary	decimally	espionage	homiletic	lucidness	obliquely
admirably	available	decimator	estimable	humiliate	luciferin	obliquity
admiralty	availably	decimetre	estimator	hygienics	ludicrous	oblivious
admission	avoidable	decistere	ethically	hygienist	luminance	obviation
admissive	avoidably	dedicator	Ethiopian	ignitable	lunisolar	obviously
admitting	avoidance	defiantly	excipient	ignitible	lunitidal	occipital
admixture	Axminster	deficient	excisable	illiberal	luridness	octillion
advisable	babirussa	definable	exciseman	illicitly	lyrically	officiant
advisably	bacillary	definably	excitable	immigrant	lysimeter	officiate
advisedly	basically	dehiscent	excitancy	immigrate	macintosh	officinal
aerialist	basilican	delicious	excitedly	imminence	Magianism	officious
aeriality	basipetal	delineate	exhibitor	imminency	magically	onlicence
aetiology	befitting	delirious	expiation	immixture	magicking	ophiology
affianced	beginning	deliverer	expiatory	impiously	magistery	opsimathy
affidavit	benighted	demimonde	exsiccate	incidence	magistral	optically
affiliate	benignant	demission	extirpate	incipient	malicious	orbicular
affirmant	benignity	demitasse	Fabianism	Indianise	malignant	ordinance
affixture	bicipital	demitting	familyman	indicator	malignity	orgiastic
Afrikaans	bilingual	demiurgic	fatidical	indiction	mamillary	Orpington
Afrikaner	biliously	denigrate	fatigable	indigence	mamillate	orrisroot

oscillate	recipient	semitonic	stripling	visionary	Cockaigne	ozokerite
oscitancy	redingote	semivowel	stripping	visionist	cockatiel	packaging
ossicular	redivivus	seniority	supinator	visitable	cockfight	packdrill
ossifrage	refitment	sepiolite	synizesis	visitress	cockhorse	packhorse
Pakistani	refitting	serialise	syringeal	vitiation	cockiness	packtrain
palillogy	regicidal	serialism	tacitness	vitiosity	cockneyfy	perkiness
panicking	regisseur	serialist	talismans	vivianite	cockroach	pickaback
papillary	registrar	seriality	taxidermy	vividness	cockscomb	picketing
papillate	reliantly	seriately	taximeter	vizierate	cocksfoot	pinkiness
papilloma	religiose	sericeous	tediously	vizierial	cookhouse	pocketful
papillose	religious	serigraph	tepidness	vomitoria	corkscrew	Quakerdom
papillote	reliquary	serinette	thriftily	wyliecoat	cuckoldry	Quakeress
patiently	reliquiae	seriously	thrilling	yohimbine	deckhouse	Quakerish
patinated	remindful	sheikhdom	timidness	zamindary	dickybird	Quakerism
pedicular	reminisce	shrinkage	titillate	zamindary	Doukhobor	quakiness
pedigreed	remission	sibilance	tonically	airjacket	duckboard	racketeer
Pekingese	remitment	sibilancy	topiarian	banjulele	duskiness	reckoning
peninsula	remittent	sigillary	topiarist	bedjacket	flakiness	riskiness
penitence	remitting	sigillate	topically	conjugate	folkdance	rockbound
periclase	renitency	siliceous	toxically	illjudged	folkmusic	rockbrake
pericycle	residence	silicious	trainable	nonjuring	folkweave	rockdrill
peridotic	residency	silicosis	trainband	oddjobber	funkiness	rocketeer
perihelia	residuary	silicotic	trainload	oddjobman	gawkiness	rockiness
perilling	resilient	siliquose	traitress	prejudice	hackamore	rockplant
perilymph	resistant	similarly	treillage	projector	hackberry	rocksnake
perimeter	resistive	sinistral	tuliproot	Seljukian	hackneyed	sackcloth
perimorph	resitting	sluiceway	tuliptree	serjeancy	hankering	shakeable
perinatal	retiarius	snailfish	tulipwood	serjeanty	hawksbill	shakedown
periodate	reticence	socialise	tumidness	skijoring	honkytonk	shakerism
peripatus	reticency	socialism	tunicated	skyjacker	huckaback	shakiness
periphery	reticular	socialist	typically	subjacent	huckstery	sickening
periplast	reticulum	socialite	ultimatum	subjugate	hunkydory	sickishly
periscope	retinitis	sociality	umbilical	Ashkenazi	huskiness	sickleave
perishing	retinulae	sociogram	umbilicus	awakening	innkeeper	silkgland
perisperm	retinular	sociology	unbiassed	backbiter	jackknife	silkiness
peristome	revictual	sociopath	uncinated	backboard	jackplane	slakeless
peristyle	revisable	solicitor	uncivilly	backcloth	jacksnipe	smokeball
petiolate	revivable	solidness	undivided	backcross	jackstraw	smokebomb
petiolule	ridiculer	soliloquy	unfitness	backpedal	jerkiness	smokebush
pitifully	rigidness	solipsism	unfitting	backsight	jockstrap	smokejack
pixilated	rosinweed	solipsist	unlimited	backslang	junkerdom	smokeless
plainness	rubicelle	solitaire	unmindful	backslide	junkerism	smoketree
plainsman	ruminator	soritical	unsighted	backspace	junketing	smokiness
plainsong	sagittate	sovietise	unsightly	backstage	kickstart	snakebird
plaintiff	salicetum	sovietism	untimeous	backsword	kinkiness	snakebite
plaintive	salicylic	sphincter	unwilling	backtrack	lankiness	snakelike
Pleiocene	saliently	splintery	unwinking	backwards	leakiness	snakeroot
policeman	sanitaria	splitting	unwitting	backwater	leukaemia	snakeskin
politburo	sapiently	spoilsman	unzipping	backwoods	leukaemic	snakeweed
politesse	satiation	sprigging	uplifting	balkanise	leukocyte	snakewood
political	satinbird	sprightly	uprightly	barkeeper	lickerish	snakiness
poriferal	satinette	sprigtail	urticaria	basketful	locksmith	spikenard
poriferan	satinspar	springald	utricular	beekeeper	lookalike	spikiness
praiseful	satinwood	springbok	vacillant	berkelium	luckiness	spokesman
pumiceous	satirical	springily	vacillate	bookishly	marketday	spokewise
punishing	saxifrage	springing	valiantly	booklouse	marketing	stakeboat
pupillage	schilling	springlet	validness	bookmaker	mawkishly	stakehold
pupillary	schistose	sprinkler	vapidness	bookplate	milkfever	stokehole
puritanic	schistous	spritsail	variation	bookshelf	milkfloat	sulkiness
pyridoxin	scribbler	squibbing	varicella	bookstall	milkiness	tackiness
rabidness	scrimmage	squidding	variegate	bookstand	milkshake	talkathon
racialism	scrimpily	squinancy	variolate	bookstore	milktooth	talkative
racialist	scrimshaw	squirarch	variolite	boskiness	mirkiness	taskforce
radialply	scripture	squiredom	varioloid	brakeless	mockingly	teakettle
radiantly	scrivener	squirelet	variolous	brakeshoe	monkeyish	tuckerbag
radiately	seditious	staidness	variously	brakesman	monkeyism	Turkomans
radiation	semibreve	stainable	vaticinal	brokerage	monkeynut	unskilful
radiative	semicolon	stainless	vehicular	buckboard	monkshood	unskilled
radically	semifinal	staircase	veniality	bucketful	muckraker	volkslied
radicular	semifluid	stairfoot	veridical	buckhound	mucksweat	wackiness
radiocast	semilunar	stairhead	veritable	buckshish	murkiness	walkabout
radiogram	semimetal	stairwell	veritably	buckthorn	musketeer	weakkneed
radiology	seminally	stoically	vesicular	bucktooth	muskiness	weeknight
rapidfire	semiology	striation	vexillary	buckwheat	muskmelon	workbench
rapidness	semiotics	striature	viciously	bulkiness	neckcloth	workhorse
rationale	semiplume	stricture	vigilance	bunkhouse	neckverse	workhouse
rationing	semirigid	stridence	vigilante	cankerous	nickelise	workmanly
ravishing	semisolid	stridency	vimineous	chokedamp	nickelled	workpiece
rebidding	semisweet	stringent	viricidal	cockahoop	nickelous	worktable

workwoman	brilliant	dialectal	gallantry	isolative	otologist	reflector
Yankeedom	bulldozer	dialectic	galleried	italicise	oubliette	reflexion
Yankeeism	bullfight	dialogise	gallicise	Italicism	outlander	reflexive
Yorkshire	bullfinch	dialogism	gallicism	jailbreak	ovulation	refluence
zinkenite	bullishly	dialogist	gallingly	jealously	ovulatory	replenish
abolisher	bulltrout	diclinous	gallinule	jellyfish	paillasse	repletion
abolition	bullybeef	diplomacy	gallivant	jollyboat	paillette	replicate
acclaimer	bullytree	diplomate	galliwasp	joylessly	Palladian	riflebird
acclimate	burlesque	dislocate	gallmidge	kaolinise	palladium	sailcloth
acclivity	burliness	doglegged	gallonage	kaolinite	palladous	sailoring
acellular	cablegram	drollness	gallooned	keelivine	palletise	sailorman
adulation	cablelaid	dualistic	gallopade	Keplerian	palliasse	sailplane
adulatory	cailleach	duplicate	Gallophil	killifish	pallidity	sallowish
adulterer	callipers	duplicity	galloping	lallation	parleyvoo	scaldfish
adulthood	callosity	earliness	gallowses	Laplander	parlously	scalefern
adultness	callously	ebullient	gallstone	lawlessly	paulownia	scalefish
afflation	cellarage	ecclesial	gaolbreak	lowlander	Pavlovian	scaleleaf
affluence	celluloid	ecologist	gauleiter	lowliness	pellagrin	scaleless
aimlessly	cellulose	edelweiss	geologise	lowloader	pelletise	scalelike
amblyopia	challenge	effluence	geologist	maelstrom	pellitory	scalemoss
amblyopic	chelation	effluvial	girlishly	mahlstick	phalanger	scaliness
ampleness	chelicera	effluvium	goalmouth	mailplane	phalanges	scallawag
amplifier	chelonian	effluxion	godliness	mailtrain	phalanxes	scallywag
amplitude	chilblain	emolliate	grillroom	malleable	phalarope	scalplock
amyloidal	childhood	emollient	grillwork	malleehen	phellogen	schlemiel
amylopsin	childless	emolument	guildhall	mallemuck	philander	schlemihl
analeptic	childlike	emplastic	guildship	malleolar	philately	schlieren
analgesia	chillness	emulation	guileless	malleolus	philippic	scolecite
analgesic	choleraic	emulative	guillemot	manliness	philogyny	scoliosis
analogise	coalfield	emulously	guilloche	marlstone	philology	scoliotic
analogist	coalition	enclosure	guiltless	maulstick	Philomela	sculpture
analogous	coalmouse	endlessly	hailstone	mealiness	phyllopod	sealetter
analysand	coelomata	Englander	hailstorm	millboard	phylogeny	seclusion
angleiron	coelomate	englutted	Halloween	millenary	pillarbox	seclusive
anglesite	coelostat	epilation	Hallowmas	millennia	pollinate	sexlessly
angleworm	collagist	epileptic	hallstand	millepede	pollinium	sexlinked
anglicise	collation	epilogist	Hallstatt	millepore	pollutant	shallowly
anglicism	colleague	esplanade	haplessly	millerite	pollution	sheldduck
Anglicist	collected	euclidean	haplology	milligram	popliteal	sheldrake
anglophil	collector	evolution	harlequin	millinery	poulterer	shelflife
anklebone	collegial	evolutive	healthful	millionth	prelatess	shelfmark
apologise	collegian	evolvable	healthily	millipede	prelatise	shelfroom
apologist	collegium	exclusion	heelpiece	millivolt	prelature	shellback
applauder	colligate	exclusive	hellebore	millstone	prelector	shellbark
applejack	collimate	exculpate	hellenise	millwheel	prelusion	shellfire
appliance	collinear	exilement	Hellenism	misleared	prelusive	shellfish
applicant	collision	explainer	Hellenist	molluscan	prelusory	shellheap
artlessly	collocate	expletive	hellhound	mollymawk	prolamine	shellwork
asclepiad	collodion	expletory	hellishly	mouldable	prolapsus	shillelah
ashlaring	colloidal	explicate	hillbilly	mullioned	prolately	silliness
athletics	colloquia	exploiter	Hitlerism	myelomata	prolation	sinlessly
avalanche	collotype	explosion	Hitlerite	myologist	prolative	skilfully
bailiwick	collusion	explosive	hollyhock	nailbrush	prolepses	smallarms
balladeer	collusive	exultance	Hollywood	negligent	prolepsis	smallness
balladist	collyrium	exultancy	Icelander	neolithic	proleptic	smalltime
ballerina	cowlstaff	fallalery	Icelandic	neologian	prolicide	smileless
ballistae	cullender	faultless	impleader	neologise	prolixity	smilingly
ballistic	cuplichen	feelingly	implement	neologist	prologise	soulfully
ballpoint	curliness	fellowman	impletion	newlyweds	prolusion	spellbind
barleymow	curlpaper	fieldbook	implicate	nobleness	prolusory	spellican
bedlamite	cyclamate	fieldboot	impliedly	nonlinear	psalmbook	spillikin
bellglass	cycloidal	fieldfare	implosion	nucleated	psalmodic	spoliator
bellicose	cyclopean	fieldsman	implosive	nucleolus	psalteria	stalactic
bellpunch	cyclopses	fieldwork	impluvium	nucleonic	Ptolemaic	stalemate
bellyache	cyclorama	fillister	inclement	nullifier	publicise	staleness
bellyband	cyclotron	following	inclosure	nullipara	publicist	Stalinism
bellyflop	dalliance	foolhardy	inclusion	nullipore	publicity	Stalinist
beslobber	declaimer	foolishly	inclusive	obbligato	publisher	stalkeyed
biblicism	declarant	foolproof	inelastic	occludent	pullulate	stalkless
biblicist	declinate	forlornly	inelegant	occlusion	purloiner	stallfeed
billabong	declivity	foulbrood	inflation	occlusive	qualified	stalworth
billboard	declivous	frolicked	inflexion	ocellated	qualifier	stellated
billiards	deflation	fullblown	inflictor	ochlocrat	quillwort	stilettos
billionth	deflector	fullcream	inflowing	odalisque	realistic	stillborn
billycock	deflexion	fulldress	influence	onelegged	reclinate	stillhunt
billygoat	depletion	fullgrown	influenza	onslaught	reclusion	stillness
biologist	depletive	fullscale	inglenook	opulently	reclusive	stillroom
boulevard	dewlapped	Gaeltacht	isallobar	orologist	redletter	stiltedly
bowlegged		gallantly	isolation		reflation	stolidity

```
stolonate  violative  blameably  dormitory  grimalkin  primaeval  thumbhole
stylebook  violently  blameless  dramatics  griminess  primality  thumbmark
styliform  violinist  boomerang  dramatise  grumbling  primarily  thumbnail
stylishly  wailingly  boomslang  dramatist  gumminess  primatial  thumbtack
stylistic  wallboard  brambling  dromedary  haematite  primeness  tormentil
stylobate  wallcress  brimstone  drummajor  haematoid  primipara  tormentor
sublation  wallfruit  bromeliad  drumstick  haematoma  primitive  tramlines
sublethal  walloping  brummagem  ecumenism  haemostat  primordia  trematode
sublimate  wallpaper  calmative  egomaniac  hammerman  promenade  tremolant
sublimely  wallplate  Carmelite  elemental  hammertoe  prominent  tremolite
sublimity  wallydrag  chameleon  eliminate  harmaline  promising  tremulant
sublunary  wealthily  chamomile  enamelled  harmattan  promotion  tremulous
sunlounge  wellbeing  champagne  enameller  harmfully  promotive  trimerous
surliness  wellfound  champaign  enamoured  harmonica  promptbox  trimester
swellfish  wellknown  champerty  enumerate  harmonics  pulmonary  trimetric
syllabary  welltimed  champleve  eremitism  harmonise  pulmonate  trimmings
syllabise  whaleback  chemistry  esemplasy  harmonist  pummelled  trumpedup
syllabism  whaleboat  chemitype  ethmoidal  harmonium  reimburse  trumpeter
syllabled  whalebone  chemurgic  etymology  harmotome  rhymester  unsmiling
syllepses  whalehead  chimaeric  examinant  hermitage  rigmarole  vermicide
syllepsis  wholemeal  Cimmerian  exemplary  inamorata  roominess  vermicule
sylleptic  wholeness  clamantly  exemplify  isomerise  Roumanian  vermiform
syllogise  wholesale  clamorous  exemption  isomerism  Roumansch  vermifuge
syllogism  wholesome  clamshell  farmhouse  isomerous  salmonoid  vermilion
tablature  wieldable  clemently  farmstead  isometric  Sarmation  verminate
tableland  willemite  climactic  filminess  jobmaster  schmaltzy  verminous
tableleaf  willingly  climbable  filmstrip  krummhorn  scombroid  warmonger
tabletalk  willowish  coemption  firmament  lowminded  seaminess  whimperer
tableware  willpower  commander  flambeaus  lyamhound  seemingly  whimsical
tailboard  witlessly  commandos  flambeaux  mammalian  segmental  wormeaten
taillight  worldling  commendam  flameless  mammalogy  sermonise  wormwheel
tailoress  worldwide  commensal  flamingly  mammiform  shamanism  abandoned
tailoring  Wyclifite  commenter  flamingos  mammonish  shamanist  abandonee
tailpiece  yellowdog  commingle  flammable  mammonism  shamateur  abandoner
tallowish  yellowish  comminute  formalise  mammonist  shambling  abundance
tallyshop  zealously  commissar  formalism  mammonite  shambolic  aciniform
tanliquor  zoologist  committal  formalist  marmalade  shamefast  aconitine
tellingly  abominate  committed  formality  marmoreal  shameless  adenoidal
tellurate  acuminate  committee  formation  mesmerise  shemozzle  adenomata
tellurian  adamantly  commodity  formative  mesmerism  sigmoidal  adenosine
telluride  ademption  commodore  formatted  mesmerist  sliminess  agonising
tellurite  adumbrate  commonage  formicary  mismanage  slumberer  agonistic
tellurium  airminded  commonlaw  formicate  mnemonics  slumbrous  alinement
tellurous  Alemannic  commotion  formulaic  mnemonist  solmisate  aloneness
thalassic  aluminate  communard  formulary  Mormonism  sommelier  alongside
thylacine  aluminise  communion  formulate  mummified  staminate  amendable
titledeed  aluminium  communise  formulise  murmurous  stammerer  amendment
titlepage  aluminous  communism  framework  myrmecoid  stampduty  aminoacid
tollbooth  anamnesis  communist  fulminant  naumachia  stampmill  anandrous
tollhouse  anemogram  community  fulminate  newmarket  stampnote  anonymity
toolhouse  animalise  commutate  fulminous  normalise  stimulant  anonymous
trilinear  animalism  cormorant  gammadion  normality  stimulate  araneidal
trilithon  animalist  cosmogeny  gammoning  Normanise  stomachal  araneidan
trilobate  animality  cosmogony  garmented  Normanism  stomacher  asininity
trilobite  animation  cosmology  gasmantle  normative  stomachic  asyndetic
twelfthly  animatism  cosmonaut  gemmation  nummulite  submarine  asyndeton
Uitlander  animistic  cosmorama  gemmology  onomastic  submaster  atonalism
ululation  animosity  coumarone  geomancer  palmation  submental  atonality
unalloyed  anomalous  crampfish  geomantic  palmipede  submitted  atonement
unaltered  anomalure  cremaster  geometric  palmistry  summarily  atonicity
unblessed  apomictic  cremation  geometrid  palmitate  summarise  aventaile
unblinded  aromatise  crematory  germander  paymaster  summarist  avuncular
uncleanly  asymmetry  criminate  germanely  pegmatite  summation  bainmarie
unclothed  asymptote  criminous  germanise  permeable  summative  bannister
unclouded  atomicity  CroMagnon  Germanish  permeance  summingup  barnacled
unfledged  atomistic  culminant  Germanism  permitted  surmullet  barnstorm
unfleshed  augmented  culminate  Germanist  permitter  swimmable  beanfeast
unfleshly  augmenter  dalmatian  germanium  permutate  swimmeret  beanstalk
unplugged  augmentor  dermatoid  germicide  plumbeous  symmetric  bionomics
unplumbed  azimuthal  diametral  germinate  plumbline  Talmudist  blandness
uselessly  badminton  diametric  germplasm  plumpness  Tasmanian  blankness
vallation  balminess  dismantle  germproof  plumpness  tegmental  blindfold
vallecula  barmbrack  dismember  gimmickry  plumulate  tegmentum  blindness
villagery  Barmecide  dismissal  glamorise  plumulose  termagant  blinkered
villanage  beamingly  dogmatise  glamorous  pommelled  terminate  blunderer
villenage  beemaster  dogmatism  glomerate  premature  terminism  bluntness
villiform  biometric  dogmatist  glomerule  premonish  terminist  Boanerges
villosity  bismillah  dormition  glomeruli  premotion  territary  bonniness
violation  blameable  dormition  godmother  premotion  Thomistic  boondocks
```

boundless	cranreuch	frontwise	lawnmower	picnicked	scantling	stonechat
bounteous	crenation	funnelled	lignaloes	picnicker	scantness	stonecoal
bountiful	crenature	funniness	ligniform	pinnately	scenarist	stonecold
branchiae	crenelled	furnisher	limnology	pinnipede	scenedock	stonecrop
branchial	crenulate	furniture	lioncelle	pinnulate	scentless	stonedead
branchlet	crinoidal	gainfully	lionheart	planarian	schnauzer	stonedeaf
brandling	crinoline	gainsayer	loanshark	planation	schnitzel	stonefish
brandreth	cunningly	gannister	loincloth	planetary	schnorkel	stoneless
bringdown	cyanamide	garnishee	lownecked	planetoid	schnorrer	stonewall
bronchial	damnation	garniture	magnalium	plangency	scintilla	stoneware
burnedout	damnatory	gauntness	magnesian	planisher	scuncheon	stonework
burningly	damnedest	giantlike	magnesite	plantable	seanettle	stonewort
burnisher	damningly	glandered	magnesium	plantlike	Shangrila	stoniness
Caenozoic	dauntless	glandular	magnetics	planuloid	shantyman	subnormal
Cainozoic	deinosaur	glengarry	magnetise	plenarily	shinguard	sunniness
cannelure	diandrous	goingover	magnetism	plenitude	shininess	swangoose
canniness	dignified	grandaddy	magnetist	plenteous	Shintoism	swansdown
cannonade	dignitary	grandaunt	magnetite	plentiful	Shintoist	swineherd
cannoneer	dinnerset	grandiose	magnetron	plunderer	signalbox	swingeing
cannonier	Dionysiac	grandness	magnifico	poinciana	signalise	swinishly
cannulate	Dionysian	grandpapa	magnifier	pointduty	signalled	taeniasis
carnality	donnishly	grandsire	magnitude	pointedly	signaller	taintless
carnation	downfield	grandslam	mainbrace	pointille	signalman	tawniness
carnelian	downgrade	granitoid	mainliner	pointlace	signatory	teknonymy
carnitine	downright	grantable	mainsheet	pointless	signature	ternately
carnivore	downriver	granulate	mannequin	pointsman	signboard	thaneship
ceanothus	downstage	granulite	mannerism	pouncebox	significs	thankless
chanceful	downthrow	granulose	mannerist	poundcake	signorial	thingness
chancroid	downwards	grenadier	maunderer	pranksome	signorina	thingummy
chancrous	drinkable	grenadine	meandrine	prankster	skindiver	thinkable
chandlery	drunkenly	Grundyism	meandrous	prenotion	skinflick	thinktank
changeful	earnestly	gymnasial	meaningly	princedom	skinflint	thunderer
chanteuse	economics	gymnasium	meanwhile	princekin	skingraft	tinniness
chantilly	economise	gymnastic	Mennonite	princelet	skintight	townhouse
chantress	economist	heinously	moonblind	principal	slanderer	townscape
Chinatown	elongated	herniated	moonlight	principia	slantways	townsfolk
chinaware	emanation	hobnailed	moonquake	principle	slantwise	transcend
chinstrap	emanative	hobnobbed	moonraker	printable	slenderly	transenna
chondrite	emendable	hobnobber	moonscape	printshop	slingback	transform
chondrule	emendator	horniness	moonshine	pronation	slingshot	transfuse
clinician	eminently	hornstone	mountable	proneness	slinkweed	transient
clinquant	emunctory	hornwrack	nannygoat	pronghorn	somnolent	translate
coenobite	enunciate	hymnology	odontalgy	pronounce	sonneteer	transmute
coenobium	epinastic	hypnoidal	ominously	pugnacity	sonnetise	transonic
coenosarc	eponymous	hypnology	onanistic	pycnidium	soundfilm	transpire
cognately	ethnarchy	hypnotise	openended	quantical	soundhole	transport
cognation	ethnicity	hypnotism	openheart	quinoline	soundings	transpose
cognisant	ethnology	hypnotist	opinioned	quintette	soundless	transship
cognition	evangelic	ichneumon	orangeade	quintuple	soundness	transumpt
cognitive	eventless	ichnology	Orangeism	raincheck	soundpost	transvest
coinsurer	eventuate	iconology	Orangeman	raincloud	soundwave	trenchant
connately	evincible	identical	orangetip	raingauge	spendable	trinketer
connation	ewenecked	identikit	orangutan	raininess	spindling	trinketry
connature	exanimate	inanimate	outnumber	rainmaker	spindrier	trinomial
connected	exanthema	inanition	ovenready	rainproof	spindrift	truncated
connecter	exonerate	inunction	painfully	rainstorm	spineless	truncheon
connector	faintness	ironbound	painterly	rainwater	spininess	trunkcall
connexion	faunistic	ironmould	paintwork	raunchily	spinnaker	trunkfish
connivent	fawningly	ironsides	penniless	reanimate	spinneret	trunkroad
connubial	fiendlike	ironsmith	pennywort	reenforce	spinosity	tunnelled
cornbrash	flannelly	ironstone	phantasma	reentrant	Spinozism	tunnelnet
corncrake	flintlock	ironworks	phenacite	reinforce	Spinozist	turnabout
cornelian	fornicate	isinglass	phenakite	reinstate	spinulose	turnround
cornemuse	foundling	isoniazid	phenology	Rhineodon	spinulous	turnstile
cornerboy	foundress	itineracy	phenomena	rhinology	spongebag	turnstone
cornerman	franchise	itinerant	phenotype	rhonchial	spongeous	turntable
cornetist	francolin	itinerary	phonation	rounceval	stanchion	twentieth
cornfield	frangible	itinerate	phonatory	roundelay	standpipe	twentyone
cornflour	Franglais	jaundiced	phonemics	roundhead	stenotype	twinkling
cornopean	frankness	jointress	phonetics	roundness	stenotypy	unanimity
cornsalad	franticly	kennelled	phonetism	roundsman	stingaree	unanimous
cornstalk	frenchify	Keynesian	phonetist	roundworm	stingless	unknitted
cornstone	Frenchman	kidnapped	phoniness	ruination	stinkball	unknowing
countable	frontally	kidnapper	phonogram	ruinously	stinkbomb	Upanishad
countdown	frontline	klinostat	phonolite	sainthood	stinkhorn	uraninite
countless	frontpage	lagniappe	phonology	saintlike	stinktrap	uranology
countship	frontward	launching	pianistic	saintling	stinkweed	vainglory
cranberry	frontways	launderer		saintship	stinkwood	varnisher
crankcase		laundress		saunterer	stintless	veinstone

vernalise	Areopagus	cocoonery	endophyte	honoraria	limonitic	nicotinic
vernation	Armorican	colocynth	endoplasm	honorific	limousine	Nilometer
vignetter	arrogance	colonelcy	endoscope	horologer	locomotor	nomocracy
vulnerary	arrowhead	coloniser	endoscopy	horologic	logogriph	nomograph
Wagnerian	arrowroot	colonnade	endosperm	horoscope	logomachy	notochord
Wagnerite	arrowwood	colophony	endospore	horoscopy	loxodrome	notoriety
warningly	arrowworm	colorific	endosteal	hylozoism	Mahometan	notorious
Wednesday	ascospore	colosseum	endosteum	hypoblast	majordomo	obconical
whinstone	associate	colostomy	endowment	hypocaust	majorette	obcordate
winningly	assonance	colostrum	enjoyable	hypocotyl	majorship	obnoxious
woundless	atmometer	colourful	enjoyably	hypocrisy	manoeuvre	obsolesce
woundwort	atrocious	colouring	enjoyment	hypocrite	manometer	Octobrist
wrongdoer	autoclave	colourist	enrolling	hypogeous	manorseat	octopodes
wrongness	autocracy	colourman	enrolment	hypomania	masochism	octostyle
wyandotte	autocross	copolymer	entoblast	hypomanic	masochist	oecologic
yawningly	autocycle	corollary	entophyte	hyponasty	masonried	oenomancy
youngling	autograft	coroneted	entourage	hypostyle	Masoretic	oenophile
youngness	autograph	crookback	ergograph	hypotaxis	mayoralty	oenophily
youngster	autolysis	crookedly	ergometer	ideograph	mayorship	oesophagi
Zwinglian	autolytic	crookneck	ergonomic	ideologic	mekometer	oleograph
abdominal	automatic	cryogenic	erroneous	ideologue	melocoton	oleoresin
abhorrent	automaton	cryoscope	errorless	idiograph	melodrama	oncogenic
abhorring	autonomic	cryoscopy	escortage	idiomatic	melomania	oncologic
abnormity	autopilot	cymophane	espousals	idiopathy	memoirist	onionskin
abrogator	autoroute	cytolysis	estoppage	idioplasm	memorable	ontogenic
absorbent	autosomal	cytoplasm	estopping	idiotical	memorably	ontologic
absorbing	autotelic	cytotoxic	excoriate	ignorable	memoranda	opponency
accompany	autotroph	cytotoxin	exfoliate	ignoramus	memoriter	opportune
accordant	axiomatic	Damoclean	expositor	ignorance	menopause	opposable
according	azeotrope	decoction	expounder	illogical	meropidan	optometer
accordion	baboonish	decollate	extolling	illomened	mesoblast	optometry
acrobatic	barograph	decollete	extolment	immodesty	mesogloea	optophone
acropetal	barometer	decomplex	extorsive	immolator	mesomorph	osmometer
acropolis	barometry	decompose	extortion	immorally	mesophyll	panoplied
acroteria	baronetcy	decongest	extortive	immovable	mesophyte	panoramic
adjoining	bayoneted	decontrol	eyeopener	immovably	metonymic	parochial
admonitor	beeorchis	decorator	favourite	impolitic	milometer	parotitis
adnominal	befogging	defoliant	felonious	important	misoneism	pasodoble
adsorbate	besotting	defoliate	ferocious	importune	misoneist	pedometer
adsorbent	biconcave	deformity	filoselle	impostume	mobocracy	pilotfish
advocator	bifoliate	demobbing	floodgate	imposture	monobasic	pirouette
aerobatic	bimonthly	democracy	floodmark	impotence	monoceros	pisolitic
aerobiont	binocular	denouncer	floodtide	impotency	monochord	pivotable
aerodrome	binominal	deposable	fluoresce	impounder	monocline	pivotally
aerograph	bloodbath	depositor	fluorosis	incognito	monocoque	polonaise
aerolitic	bloodless	desolater	fluorspar	incommode	monocracy	preoccupy
aerometer	bloodlust	desolator	gasometer	incondite	monocular	preordain
aerometry	bloodroot	detonator	genocidal	incorrect	monodical	priorship
aerophyte	bloodshed	devotedly	genotypic	incorrupt	monodrama	proofread
aeroplane	bloodshot	dimorphic	Girondist	IndoAryan	monoecism	pyrogenic
aerospace	bloodworm	dinoceras	gonophore	indolence	monogamic	pyrolater
agrologic	bloodwort	dinothere	groomsman	informant	monograph	pyrolatry
agronomic	bolometer	disoblige	gynocracy	innocence	monolatry	pyrolysis
alcoholic	bolometry	disorient	gynoecium	innocency	monologic	pyrolytic
Algonkian	boxoffice	dogoodism	gynophore	innocuity	monologue	pyromancy
Algonquin	broomcorn	dolomitic	gyroplane	innocuous	monomania	pyromania
algorithm	broomrape	donothing	halophile	innovator	monomeric	pyrometer
allocable	bryophyte	echolalia	halophyte	innoxious	monophagy	pyrometry
allograph	buxomness	echovirus	halothane	inpouring	monoplane	pyroscope
allomorph	cacodemon	ectoblast	havocking	insolence	monostich	pyroxylin
allopathy	cacodylic	ectogenic	hodograph	insoluble	monostyle	raconteur
allophone	cacoethes	ectomorph	hodometer	insolubly	monotonic	razorback
alloplasm	cacophony	ectoplasm	holocaust	insolvent	monotreme	razorbill
allotment	calorific	effortful	holograph	insomniac	monotypic	razoredge
allotrope	camorrist	eidograph	holophote	intorsion	motocross	razorfish
allotropy	canonical	elbowroom	homogamic	involucre	motorable	recoinage
allotting	carolling	encomiast	homograft	involuted	motorbike	recollect
allowable	catoptric	encompass	homograph	isooctane	motorboat	recombine
allowably	cerograph	encounter	homologue	jaborandi	motorcade	recommend
allowance	cheongsam	encourage	homonymic	Jacobinic	mycologic	recompose
allowedly	chlorella	endoblast	homophone	Junoesque	mycophagy	reconcile
aloofness	chloritic	endocrine	homophony	kilocycle	myrobalan	recondite
annotator	chlorosis	endogamic	homoplasy	kilohertz	myxoedema	reconfirm
announcer	chlorotic	endogenic	homopolar	kilolitre	negotiant	reconvene
annoyance	chromatic	endolymph	homotaxis	kymograph	negotiate	reconvert
appointee	chromatin	endomixis	homotonic	laborious	nemophila	recording
apportion	chronical	endomorph	homousian	labourite	nicotiana	recordist
arboreous	chronicle	endophagy		lagomorph		recoverer
arboretum	cipollino					

redolence	theomania	campchair	dropsical	palpebral	soapworks	zoophytic
redoubted	theophany	campcraft	dumpiness	palpitant	soppiness	banqueter
reformism	theoretic	campfever	dyspepsia	palpitate	soupplate	banquette
reformist	theoriser	camphoric	dyspeptic	pauperise	soupspoon	bouquetin
rejoicing	theosophy	campstool	dysphagia	pauperism	stapedial	briquette
rejoinder	throatily	carpenter	dysphagic	paypacket	stepchild	chequered
remontant	throbbing	carpentry	dysphonia	peepsight	stepdance	coequally
removable	thrombose	carpetbag	dysphoria	pemphigus	stipitate	conqueror
renouncer	throttler	carpeting	dysphoric	penpusher	stippling	croquette
renovator	throughly	carpingly	dysplasia	pepperbox	stipulate	eloquence
reportage	throwaway	carpology	dyspnoeic	pepperpot	stoplight	etiquette
reposeful	throwback	chaparral	elopement	perpetual	stoppress	exequatur
repossess	throwster	chaperone	epiphragm	pimpernel	stopwatch	frequence
repotting	timocracy	chapleted	epiphyses	pompadour	stupefier	frequency
resoluble	tinopener	chipboard	epiphysis	pomposity	stupidity	harquebus
resolvent	tonometer	chipolata	epiphytal	pompously	stuporous	inequable
resonance	toponymal	chophouse	epiphytic	poppycock	subphylum	Iroquoian
resonator	toponymic	choplogic	epipolism	poppyhead	sulphonic	jacquerie
resorbent	toxophily	chopstick	evaporate	porphyria	sulphuret	marquetry
resources	troopship	clapboard	exopodite	potpourri	sulphuric	mosquitos
retortion	tutorship	clepsydra	flippancy	prepotent	sumptuary	parquetry
retoucher	unbounded	clipboard	flophouse	propagate	sumptuous	sasquatch
revocable	unconcern	compactly	foppishly	propelled	suppliant	triquetra
revolting	uncounted	compactor	gaspereau	propeller	supporter	turquoise
ribosomal	uncouthly	companion	geoponics	properdin	supposing	unequally
Samoyedic	uncovered	compasses	ginpalace	prophetic	suppurate	aberrance
sapodilla	undoubted	compelled	glyptodon	propionic	surpliced	aberrancy
savourily	unfounded	compendia	godparent	proponent	surprisal	aborigine
saxophone	unpointed	competent	gomphosis	propriety	suspender	acariasis
scholarly	unpopular	complaint	gospeller	proptosis	suspensor	accretion
scholiast	unsoundly	complexly	grapeshot	propylaea	suspicion	accretive
schoolbag	untouched	complexus	grapevine	propylene	sweptback	addressee
schoolboy	unwomanly	compliant	graphemic	pulpboard	sylphlike	addresser
schooling	upcountry	component	graphical	pulpiness	symphonic	addressor
schoolman	upholster	composite	graphitic	pulpiteer	symphysis	adoration
scrollsaw	vaporable	composure	grappling	pulpstone	sympodial	adoringly
scrounger	vaporific	comprador	gunpowder	puppeteer	sympodium	adornment
secondary	vaporiser	comprisal	happening	puppyhood	symposiac	affricate
serotonin	vapouring	comptroll	happiness	purposely	symposial	aforesaid
shootable	vapourish	cooperage	harpooner	purposive	symposium	aggravate
sinologue	vasomotor	cooperant	helpfully	purpureal	tamponade	aggregate
sinophile	velodrome	cooperate	herpetoid	rampantly	tanpickle	aggressor
smoothish	wagonette	corporate	Hesperian	raspatory	tarpaulin	aggrieved
sojourner	wagonroof	corporeal	hippocras	raspberry	taxpaying	alertness
Solomonic	widowbird	corposant	hispidity	raspingly	temperate	altricial
sonometer	widowhood	corpulent	inaptness	respecter	temporary	amaryllis
soporific	xenograft	corpuscle	ineptness	responder	temporise	ambrosial
spoonbeak	xenophile	crapulent	inspanned	rhapsodic	temptable	americium
spoonbill	xenophobe	crapulous	inspector	salpinges	temptress	Amerindic
spoonfeed	xeromorph	crepitant	isopodous	sappiness	timpanist	amoralism
spoonmeat	xerophile	crepitate	jampacked	scapegoat	torpidity	amorality
stoolball	xerophily	crepuscle	jumpiness	scapolite	trapezial	amorously
strobilae	xerophyte	crippling	lampblack	scapulary	trapezium	amorphism
strobilus	xylograph	cropeared	lamplight	sceptical	trapezoid	amorphous
stromatic	xylophone	cryptical	lampooner	serpentry	trappings	anarchism
strongarm	zygomatic	cryptogam	lampshade	shapeable	trepanned	anarchist
strongbox	zygospore	cryptonym	lampshell	shapeless	trepidant	androecia
strongish	zymogenic	cuspidate	limpidity	shipboard	triploidy	androgyne
strongyle	adaptable	desperado	lispingly	shipcanal	triptyque	androgyny
strontium	adeptness	desperate	lumpiness	shipfever	tropology	angriness
stropping	adipocere	despoiler	lumpishly	shipmoney	turpitude	anorectic
strouding	adiposity	despotism	lymphatic	shipowner	tympanist	anorthite
subocular	adoptable	diaphragm	lyophilic	shipshape	unaptness	apartheid
sudorific	agapemone	diaphysis	lyophobic	shipwreck	uniparous	apartment
sycophant	aliphatic	disparage	mispickel	shopfloor	uniplanar	apartness
synodical	anaphoric	disparate	morphemic	shopfront	unsparing	aperiodic
synoecete	anaptyxis	disparity	Nipponese	simpatico	unspotted	aperitive
synonymic	anopheles	dispelled	nitpicker	simpleton	uropygium	appraisal
synoptist	apophyses	dispenser	nonpareil	simplices	vampirism	appraiser
synovitis	apophysis	dispeople	nonperson	slaphappy	vulpinism	apprehend
taioseach	asepalous	dispersal	nonprofit	slapstick	vulpinite	appressed
taxonomic	auspicate	disperser	nymphalid	slipcoach	Walpurgis	approbate
telophase	bespangle	displease	oilpaints	slipcover	waspishly	astraddle
theocracy	bespatter	disposure	omophagia	slopbasin	whipperin	astrakhan
theocrasy	bumpiness	dispraise	omophagic	slopewise	whipround	astrocyte
theogonic	bumptious	disputant	outputted	snipefish	whipsnake	astrodome
theologic	campanile	dripstone	oviparity	soapberry	whipstock	astrolabe
theologue	campanili	dropscene	oviparous	soapiness	zoophagan	astrology
theomachy	campanula	dropscone	palpation	soapstone	zoophobia	astronaut

```
astronomy corralled enwreathe guardrail inerrancy misreckon overproof
ataractic corrasion estranger guardring inertness misreport overreach
attractor correctly estrapade guardroom infractor mitraille overreact
attribute corrector esurience guardship ingrained morrisman oversexed
attrition correlate esuriency guardsman ingrowing mucronate overshoot
aubrietia corrosion eternally guerrilla inorganic mydriasis oversight
averagely corrosive eutrophic gunrunner intricacy mydriatic oversized
avertible corrugate everglade hagridden intricate narration overskirt
awardable corrupter evergreen hairbrush intrigant narrative oversleep
awareness corruptly everybody haircloth intriguer narratory overslept
barracker courgette exarchate hairgrass intrinsic natrolite overspend
barracoon courtcard excrement hairiness introduce necrology overspent
barracuda courteous excretion hairpiece introject necrophil overspill
barrelful courtesan excretive hairshirt introvert necrotise overstate
barrelled courtroom excretory hairslide intrusion negritude oversteer
barricade courtship exercises hairspace intrusive negroidal overstock
barricado courtyard exorciser hairstyle inurement Negroness overstuff
barrister currently expressly Harrovian inwrought negrophil overtaken
basrelief curricula extractor harrowing iteration neuralgia overthrew
bearberry currishly extradite heartache iterative neuralgic overthrow
beardless currycomb extravert heartbeat jarringly neuration overtness
bedraggle cyprinoid extremely heartburn jeeringly neuroglia overtones
bedridden czarevich extremism heartfelt journeyer neurology overtrain
betrothal dairymaid extremist heartfree kurrajong neuromata overtrick
betrothed decrement extremity hearthrug lacrimose neuropath overtrump
biorhythm decretive extricate heartland lacrymose nigricant overvalue
boardfoot decretory extrinsic heartless lairdship nigritude overwatch
boardroom deerberry extrovert heartsick laurelled nigrosine overweary
boardwalk deerhound extrusion heartsore learnable nitratine overweigh
boorishly defroster extrusive heartwood learnedly nitration overwhelm
borrowing depravity fabricant Hebridean leeringly nourisher overwound
bourgeois deprecate fabricate heuristic librarian nutriment overwrite
buhrstone depredate fairfaced hierarchy libration nutrition overwrote
burrstone depressed fairyhood hieratica libratory nutritive pairhorse
byproduct depressor fairyland hierodule librettos obtrusion parrakeet
cabriolet derringdo fairylike hierogram lipreader obtrusive parricide
caerulean derringer fairyring hierology louringly odorously patriarch
cairngorm detractor fairytale hoarfrost lubricant onerously patrician
capriccio detriment fearfully hoarhound lubricate operation patricide
Capricorn detrition febricity hoariness lubricity operative patrimony
carrageen detrusion febrifuge hoarstone lubricous opercular patriotic
carrefour dharmsala ferrotype hourglass lucrative operculum patristic
carronade diarrhoea ferryboat hubristic macrocosm operosely patrolled
carryover dicrotism fibreless hurricane macrocyte operosity patroller
charabanc didrachma fibriform hurriedly madrepore oppressor patrolman
character disregard fibrillar hybridise marrowfat ostracise patrology
chariness disrelish fibrinoid hybridism matriarch ostracism patronage
charivari disrepair fibrinous hybridity matricide Ostrogoth patroness
charlatan disrepute fibroline hydraemia matricula outridden patronise
charlotte diurnally fibromata hydrangea matrimony outrigger pearlitic
charmeuse doorframe fieriness hydration matronage overblown pearlwort
charmless doorplate fioritura hydraulic matronise overboard petroleum
Charolais embraceor fioriture hydrazine merriment overborne petrology
chartered embracery flarepath hydriodic merriness overcheck pharaonic
charterer embracive flaringly hydrocele metricate overcloud pharisaic
charwoman embrangle floriated hydrofoil metrician overcrowd pharyngal
cherimoya embrasure floridean hydrology metricise overdraft pharynges
chernozem embrittle floridity hydrolyse metricist overdrawn pharynxes
cherrypie embrocate floristic hydrolyte metrology overdress pheromone
chiropody embroglio floristry hydronium metronome overdrive pierrette
chorister embroider fourflush hydrosome microbial overeaten pluralise
chorology embryonal fourpence hydroxide microchip overeater pluralism
churching embryonic fourpenny hydrozoan microcosm overexert pluralist
churchman embryotic fourscore hydrozoon microcyte overflown plurality
cirrhosis emergence fourwheel hygrostat microfilm overglaze poorhouse
cirripede emergency garreteer imbricate microgram overgraze porringer
clarifier encrimson garrotter imbroglio microlite overgrown pourboire
clarionet encrinite garrulity imprecate microlith overheard pourpoint
clergyman energetic garrulous impresari micromesh overissue prerecord
clergymen energiser gearlever impresari micropsia overjoyed prorogate
clerkship energumen gearshift improbity microsome overladen prurience
coarctate engraving gearwheel impromptu micropyle overleapt pruriency
coercible engrosser georgette improvise microsome overlying psoriasis
coercibly entrammel glaringly imprudent microtome overmatch psoriatic
comradely entrapped gloryhole inbreathe microtomy overnight ptarmigan
comradery entrechat guarantee increaser microtone overpitch pterosaur
coproduce entrecote guarantor increment microwave overpower pterygium
coprolite entremets guardbook indraught migration overprice pterygoid
coprology enwrapped guardedly inerrable migratory overprint puerility
```

puerperal	segregate	sterilise	unbridled	blasphemy	copsewood	falsehood
purringly	serranoid	sterility	uncreated	blasthole	crashdive	falseness
putridity	serration	sternmost	uncropped	blastment	crashland	falsifier
quarenden	serrefile	sternness	uncrossed	blastulae	crassness	farseeing
quarender	serrulate	sternpost	uncrowned	blastular	crescendo	feiseanna
quarryman	sforzando	sternward	undreamed	blessedly	crestless	firstborn
quarterly	sharecrop	steroidal	untrodden	blushless	crispness	firstfoot
quartette	sharkskin	stirabout	untrussed	blusterer	crossable	firsthand
quartzite	sharpener	storeroom	unwrapped	bobsleigh	crossbeam	firstling
quartzose	sharpeyed	storeship	unwritten	Bolshevik	crossbill	firstrate
quercetum	sharpness	storiated	unwrought	bossiness	crossbred	fissility
querulous	sharpshod	stormbelt	upbraider	bowstring	crossette	fissipede
quirister	shirtless	stormbird	uvarovite	brashness	crosseyed	flashback
rearguard	shirttail	stormcock	uxoricide	brasserie	crossfade	flashbulb
rearhorse	shoreless	stormcone	veeringly	brassiere	crossfire	flashcube
rearlight	shoreline	stormless	verrucose	briskness	crossfish	flashover
rearmouse	shoreside	stormsail	verrucous	bristling	crosshead	flashtube
rearrange	shoreward	storybook	vibracula	brushfire	crosslink	fleshings
rearwards	shoreweed	storyline	vibraharp	brushwood	crossness	fleshless
recreancy	shortcake	subregion	vibratile	brushwork	crossover	fleshment
recruital	shortener	subrogate	vibration	brusquely	crossroad	floscular
recruiter	shortfall	supremacy	vibrative	bursarial	crossruff	flushness
redresser	shorthand	supremely	vibratory	caesarean	crosstalk	forsythia
refractor	shorthorn	surrender	vibrissae	caesarian	crossways	fossicker
refreshen	shortness	surrogate	vitriform	Caesarism	crosswind	fossilise
refresher	shortstop	swarajist	vitriolic	Caesarist	crosswise	fossorial
regretful	shortterm	swartness	Vitruvian	capsulate	crossword	freshener
regretted	shortwave	swordcane	warrantee	capsulise	crushable	freshness
reprehend	skirtings	swordfish	warranter	Cassandra	crustacea	frostbite
represent	skirtless	swordknot	warrantor	cassareep	culsdesac	frostwork
repressor	skyrocket	swordlike	weariless	cassaripe	cursively	frustrate
reprieval	smartness	swordplay	weariness	cassation	cursorial	fulsomely
reprimand	smartweed	swordsman	wearisome	casserole	cursorily	fussiness
reprobate	snaredrum	swordtail	wehrmacht	cassimere	curstness	geosphere
reprocess	sobriquet	tarragona	weirdness	cassoulet	dayschool	geostatic
reproduce	sopranino	tearfully	wherefore	cassowary	dayspring	geyserite
retractor	sopranist	terramara	wherefrom	causality	deistical	ghostlike
retrieval	sorriness	terramare	whereinto	causation	denseness	ghostword
retriever	sorrowful	terrarium	whereunto	causative	diastasis	glassgall
retrocede	sourdough	territory	whereupon	causeless	diastatic	glassware
retrodden	spareness	terrorise	wherewith	ceasefire	diastolic	glasswork
retroflex	spareribs	terrorism	wherryman	ceaseless	dieselise	glasswort
retroject	sparingly	terrorist	whirligig	censorial	diesinker	glissandi
retrousse	sparkcoil	tetradite	whirlpool	cessation	dipswitch	glissando
retrovert	sparkless	tetragram	whirlwind	chassepot	dissector	glossator
rewritten	sparkplug	tetralogy	worriedly	chastener	disseisin	glossitis
rubricate	spermatic	tetrapody	worriment	chastiser	dissemble	goosander
rubrician	spermatid	tetrarchy	worrisome	chiselled	dissenter	goosefoot
rumrunner	spiracula	therapist	worrywart	chiseller	dissident	goosegirl
sacrament	spirality	Theravada	xparticle	chisquare	dissipate	gooseherd
sacrarium	spiralled	therefore	yearround	classable	dissocial	gooseneck
sacrifice	spirillum	therefrom	zebrawood	classical	dissolute	gooseskin
sacrilege	spiritism	thereinto	abasement	classless	dissonant	goosestep
sacristan	spiritist	thereunto	abashment	classlist	dissuader	gossamery
safranine	spiritoso	thereupon	abusively	classmate	dogshores	graspable
sapraemia	spiritous	therewith	abysmally	classroom	dogstooth	grassland
sapraemic	spiritual	thermally	acescence	closedown	dosshouse	grisaille
sauropoda	spirituel	thermidor	agistment	closeness	dresscoat	gristmill
scarecrow	spirogyra	thirdhand	ahistoric	coastline	drysalter	grosgrain
scarehead	sporangia	thirdrate	airstream	coastward	ecosphere	grossness
scarfring	sporocarp	thirdsman	almsgiver	coastwise	ecossaise	grossular
scarfskin	sporocyst	thirstily	almshouse	conscious	ecosystem	guesswork
scarfwise	sporogeny	thirtieth	amassment	conscribe	elastomer	guestroom
scarifier	sportsman	thornback	amusement	conscript	elusively	gutsiness
scirrhous	sporulate	thornbill	amusingly	consensus	episcopal	hamstring
scorbutic	spurwheel	thornbush	apishness	conserver	epistaxis	hamstrung
scorching	starapple	thornless	apostolic	consignee	epistemic	Hanseatic
scorebook	starboard	thorntree	awesomely	consignor	epistoler	hanselled
scorecard	starchily	thyratron	awestruck	consonant	epistolic	harshness
scoredraw	stardrift	thyristor	baksheesh	consortia	eristical	haustella
scorifier	stargazer	thyroxine	beastings	constable	evasively	haustoria
scorpioid	stargrass	titration	bedsettee	constancy	existence	hawsehole
searching	starkness	torridity	bedsitter	constrain	exosmosis	hawsepipe
searingly	starlight	touristic	bedspread	constrict	exosmotic	hemstitch
secretage	starshell	tournedos	bedspring	construct	exosphere	hessonite
secretary	starstone	tourneyer	beestings	consulage	exostosis	hirsutism
secretion	startling	tsarevich	berserker	consulate	eyeshadow	hopscotch
secretive	steradian	ultrahigh	biosphere	consulter	eyestrain	horseback
secretory	stercoral	unbraided	blaspheme	consultor	facsimile	horsebean

```
horsehair  missioner  possessed  substrate  bacterial  cartwheel  daltonism
horsehide  moistener  possessor  sunspurge  bacterise  Castalian  Dantesque
horseless  moistness  poussette  sunstroke  bacterium  castanets  dartboard
horsemint  monsignor  presbyope  sunstruck  bacteroid  castellan  dastardly
horseplay  monsoonal  presbyter  tahsildar  baltimore  castigate  deathblow
horsepond  monstrous  preschool  tasselled  Bantustan  Castilian  deathless
horseshoe  mossagate  prescient  teasingly  baptismal  Castroism  deathlike
horsetail  mossgrown  prescribe  tenseness  baptistry  cattaloes  deathmask
horsewhip  mousehole  prescript  tensility  bartender  cattiness  deathroll
horsiness  mousetrap  preselect  tensional  bastardly  cattleman  dentalium
houseboat  moustache  presentee  terseness  bastinade  cauterise  dentation
housebote  Mussulman  presenter  tessitura  bastinado  Celticism  dentiform
housecarl  newsagent  presently  thesaurus  bastioned  centenary  dentistry
housecoat  newsflash  preserver  tinselled  battalion  centering  dentition
houseflag  newshound  preshrink  tipsiness  battening  centigram  depthbomb
household  newsiness  preshrunk  tipstaves  battiness  centipede  depthless
housekeep  newspaper  president  toastrack  battleaxe  centrally  destitute
houseleek  newsprint  presidial  tonsillar  battlecry  centreing  destroyer
houseless  newsstand  presidium  tonsorial  beatitude  centurion  deuterate
houselled  noiseless  pressgang  torsional  bentonite  certainly  deuterium
housemaid  noisiness  pressmark  trisagion  bestially  certainty  dexterity
housemate  noisomely  pressroom  trisector  bestirred  certified  dexterous
houseroom  nonsmoker  pressstud  trussbeam  binturong  certifier  dextrally
housewife  nuisancer  presswork  trustdeed  birthmark  certitude  dextrorse
housework  nurseling  prestress  trustless  birthrate  chatelain  diathermy
howsoever  nursemaid  prismatic  trysquare  birthwort  chatoyant  diathesis
iceskater  obeseness  prosaical  twistable  bitterish  chatterer  diathetic
irascible  offscreen  proscenia  twosuiter  blatantly  chitinous  diatomite
irascibly  offseason  proscribe  unashamed  blotchily  chitlings  diatropic
irksomely  offspring  prosector  uniserial  boathouse  clathrate  dictation
isosceles  offstreet  prosecute  unisexual  boatswain  clatterer  dietetics
isostatic  omissible  proselyte  unisonant  boattrain  clitellum  dietician
Jansenism  opusculum  prosiness  unisonous  bobtailed  coattails  dietitian
Jansenist  ourselves  prosodist  unusually  bootblack  coeternal  dipterous
jessamine  outskirts  prostatic  Vaishnava  bottlefed  coltishly  dirtiness
jetsetter  outspoken  prostrate  vassalage  bottleful  coltsfoot  dirttrack
jetstream  outspread  puissance  versatile  bratwurst  contactor  distantly
josshouse  palsgrave  pulsatile  versifier  bretasche  contadina  distemper
jossstick  Parseeism  pulsation  versiform  Bretwalda  contadino  distilled
kaiserdom  parsimony  pulsatory  versional  Britannia  contagion  distiller
kaiserism  parsonage  pulseless  waistband  Britannic  contagium  distraint
kinswoman  passenger  pulserate  waistbelt  Briticise  container  disturbed
lapstrake  passerine  purselike  waistcoat  Briticism  contemner  disturber
lapstreak  passersby  pursiness  waistline  Britisher  contender  dittander
lassitude  passional  pursuable  wassailer  brittlely  contented  dittology
leasehold  passivate  pursuance  whiskered  brotherly  continent  doctorate
leaselend  passively  pussyfoot  whisperer  brutalise  continual  doctorial
leastways  passivity  ransacker  whistling  brutalism  continuer  doctrinal
leastwise  peasantry  reasoning  whosoever  brutality  continuum  doltishly
leisurely  peasouper  roisterer  winsomely  brutishly  contralto  dottiness
lissomely  pensioner  rousement  wrestling  Brythonic  contrasty  ductility
lobscouse  pensively  russeting  wristband  butterbur  contrived  dustcover
looseleaf  persecute  Russophil  wristdrop  buttercup  contriver  dustiness
looseness  persevere  sassafras  wristshot  butterfat  contumacy  dustsheet
lousewort  persimmon  Sassanian  abatement  butterfly  contumely  dystrophy
lousiness  personage  Sassenach  abstainer  butterine  contusion  earthborn
mansarded  personate  seasoning  abstinent  butternut  corticate  earthling
mansionry  personify  seasquirt  acetabula  buttinsky  corticoid  earthstar
manslayer  personnel  seastrand  acetamide  buttygang  cortisone  earthward
marshalcy  persuader  sensation  acetifier  bystander  costively  earthwork
marshland  pessimism  sensedata  acetylate  cantabile  costumier  earthworm
marshwort  pessimist  senseless  acetylcoA  cantaloup  couturier  eastbound
marsupial  phosphate  sensitise  acetylene  cantharid  cretinism  Eastender
marsupium  phosphene  sensitive  aesthesia  cantharis  cretinous  easterner
massagist  phosphide  sensorial  aesthesis  cantharus  criterion  eastwards
massiness  phosphine  sensorium  aesthetic  cantilena  criticise  ecstasise
massively  phosphite  sensually  aestivate  Cantonese  criticism  editorial
mausoleum  physician  sessional  agitation  cantorial  crotchety  egotistic
Menshevik  physicist  setsquare  agitative  captaincy  cultivate  elutriate
menstrual  physicked  slushfund  anatomise  captivate  curtilage  emotional
menstruum  pinstripe  sobsister  anatomist  captivity  custodial  emotively
messenger  pipsqueak  spasmodic  apathetic  Cartesian  custodian  emotivity
messianic  plasmatic  suasively  apetalous  carthorse  customary  emptiness
messieurs  plasmodia  subscribe  apothecia  cartilage  customise  epithelia
messiness  plastered  subscript  arytenoid  cartogram  cutthroat  epithesis
miasmatic  plasterer  subsellia  auctorial  cartology  cuttysark  epithetic
midstream  plusfours  subsidise  austenite  cartouche  cystocarp  epitomise
midsummer  plushness  substance  austerely  cartridge  cystolith  epitomist
misshapen  poisonous  substrata  austerity  cartulary  cystotomy  eroticism
```

```
erstwhile  giltedged  lintwhite  nocturnal  platinous  restraint  Southdown
erythrism  glutamate  Listerism  northeast  platitude  rhythmics  southeast
erythrite  glutinous  litterbin  northerly  Platonise  rhythmise  southerly
esoterica  gnathonic  litterbug  northland  Platonism  rhythmist  southland
esoterism  graticule  loathsome  northmost  Platonist  riotously  southmost
exoticism  gratitude  loftiness  northward  plethoric  rootstock  southward
factional  gratulate  loutishly  northwest  plutocrat  rostellum  southwest
factitive  gritstone  luftwaffe  nostalgia  plutonian  routinely  spatially
factorage  grotesque  lustfully  nostalgic  Plutonism  routinism  spatulate
factorial  guitarist  lustihood  nostology  Plutonist  routinist  spotcheck
factorise  gustation  lustiness  nuttiness  plutonium  rusticate  spotlight
factually  gustative  malthouse  nystagmic  poetaster  rusticity  sputterer
faithcure  gustatory  manticore  nystagmus  poeticise  rustiness  statehood
faithless  gustiness  martially  oasthouse  poeticism  rustproof  stateless
fantasied  guttation  Martinmas  obstetric  pontoneer  saltation  statement
fantasise  guttering  martyrdom  obstinacy  pontonier  saltatory  stateroom
fantasist  haltingly  martyrise  obstinate  portative  saltglaze  stateside
fantastic  hartshorn  masterdom  oestrogen  porterage  saltiness  statesman
fantastry  hastiness  masterful  oratorial  portfolio  saltmarsh  statewide
fastening  heathcock  masterkey  oratorian  porticoes  saltpetre  stational
fastigium  heathenry  masticate  oysterbed  portolano  saltspoon  stationer
fattiness  hectogram  mattamore  oysterman  portrayal  saltwater  statistic
feathered  heftiness  meatiness  pantalets  portrayer  saltworks  statocyst
fertilely  heptaglot  meltingly  pantaloon  portreeve  santolina  statolith
fertilise  heptarchy  meltwater  pantheism  portulaca  santonica  statuette
fertility  histamine  mentalism  pantheist  postentry  sartorial  statutory
festinate  histidine  mentalist  pantingly  posterior  sartorius  stitchery
festively  histogeny  mentality  pantomime  posterity  Sauternes  stutterer
festivity  histogram  mentation  pantryman  posthaste  scatology  subtenant
festology  histology  micturate  pantyhose  posthorse  scatterer  subtilise
fictional  historian  Miltonian  partially  posthouse  Scotchman  subtopian
fifteenth  hortation  mirthless  partition  posticous  Scoticise  suctorial
filterbed  hortative  mistigris  partitive  postilion  scotomata  suctorian
filtertip  hortatory  mistiness  partridge  postnasal  scutcheon  sultanate
filtrable  hortensia  mistletoe  pastedown  postnatal  scutellar  sultaness
fistulous  hosteller  mistyeyed  pasticcio  postulant  scutellum  suntanned
fittingly  hostilely  Montanism  pastiness  postulate  scutiform  sustainer
flatterer  hostility  monthling  pastorale  pratingly  seatangle  sutteeism
flatulent  Hottentot  monticule  pastorate  pretender  sectarian  switchman
flotation  hurtfully  mortality  pasturage  preterist  sectility  syntactic
foeticide  hysterics  mortgagee  pectinate  preterite  sectional  syntheses
footboard  hysteroid  mortgager  pentagram  pretermit  sectorial  synthesis
footcloth  ichthyoid  mortgagor  pentangle  prettyish  sentenate  synthetic
footfault  imitation  mortician  pentarchy  prettyism  sentience  systaltic
footlight  imitative  mouthpart  Pentecost  protamine  sentiency  tactfully
footloose  initially  mouthwash  penthouse  protector  sentiment  tactician
footplate  initiator  multifoil  peptonise  proteinic  sentrybox  tactility
footpound  instanter  multiform  pertinent  protester  septation  tactitian
footprint  instantly  multilane  pertussis  protestor  September  tactually
footstalk  instigate  multipara  pesthouse  prothesis  septemvir  tantalate
footstall  instilled  multiplex  pesticide  prothetic  septenary  tantalise
footstool  institute  multitude  pestilent  prothorax  septennia  tantalite
fortalice  inutility  mustachio  pestology  protonema  septicity  Tartarean
forthwith  isotropic  musteline  petticoat  prototype  septuplet  Tartarian
fortifier  jactation  mustiness  pettiness  protozoal  sestertia  tartishly
fortitude  jitterbug  mystagogy  pettishly  protozoan  sextuplet  Tartufian
fortnight  justiciar  mysticism  pettitoes  protozoic  shotproof  Tartufism
fortunate  justifier  mystifier  photocell  protozoon  shottower  tasteless
fortyfive  juxtapose  napthalic  photocopy  pustulate  siltation  tastiness
fosterage  kentledge  nastiness  photogene  pustulous  siltstone  tattiness
fraternal  kittenish  nattiness  photophil  quitclaim  sixteenmo  tattooist
fretfully  kittiwake  neathouse  photopsia  quittance  sixteenth  tautology
fritterer  knotgrass  nectarean  phototype  quotation  sketchily  tectonics
fruticose  lactation  nectarial  phytogeny  quotidian  sketchmap  tectorial
furtherer  lanthanum  nectarine  phytology  rantingly  slateclub  tectrices
furtively  lastditch  nectarous  phytotomy  raptorial  slategrey  tentacled
fustigate  lastingly  neoteinia  phytotron  rapturous  slothbear  tentation
fustiness  latterday  neoteinic  pictogram  rectangle  smatterer  tentative
gastraeum  latticing  neoterise  pictorial  rectifier  softgoods  tenthrate
gastritis  leftovers  neoterism  picturise  rectitude  softpedal  tentmaker
gastropod  leftwards  neoterist  pietistic  rectorate  softshell  testament
gastrulae  leitmotif  Neptunian  pintailed  rectorial  sooterkin  testation
genteelly  leitmotiv  neptunium  pintsized  rectrices  soothfast  testatrix
gentility  lentiform  Nestorian  pistachio  reiterate  sootiness  testdrive
gentleman  leptosome  neutrally  pistoleer  reptilian  sortilege  testifier
geotropic  letterbox  Newtonian  pistolled  restfully  sortition  testimony
gestalten  lettering  nictation  platemark  restiform  sostenuto  testiness
gestation  liltingly  nictitate  platinise  restitute  sottishly  teutonise
gestatory  lintelled  noctiluca  platinoid  restively  souteneur  Teutonism
```

```
Teutonist  whitebeam  bifurcate  grounding  medullary  repulsion  suturally
textually  whiteface  cacuminal  groundivy  medullate  repulsive  tabularly
thatching  whitefish  casuarina  groundnut  minuscule  reputable  tabulator
thitherto  Whitehall  casuistic  groundsel  minutegun  reputably  tegularly
tittivate  whitehead  casuistry  hirundine  minuteman  reputedly  tenuously
tittlebat  whiteness  cerussite  hocussing  modulator  requester  theurgist
tittuping  whitening  chauffeur  homuncule  mutualise  requisite  thoughted
tittupped  whitewash  claustral  homunculi  mutualism  rerunning  thrumming
toothache  whitewing  cloudland  immutable  mutualist  resultant  titularly
toothcomb  whitewood  cloudless  immutably  mutuality  resultful  traumatic
toothless  widthways  colubrine  impudence  Nahuatlan  resumable  triumphal
toothpick  widthwise  columbary  impulsion  naturally  resurface  triumviri
toothsome  winterise  Columbian  impulsive  nebuliser  resurgent  troublous
toothwort  wistfully  columbine  impulsory  nocuously  resurrect  trousered
tortrices  witticism  columbite  imputable  nodulated  revulsion  trousseau
tortricid  wittiness  columbium  inaudible  obfuscate  revulsive  troutfarm
torturous  wittingly  columella  inaudibly  objurgate  rheumatic  troutling
trattoria  worthless  columnist  inaugural  obturator  Ripuarian  tubularly
trattorie  wrathless  conundrum  incubator  occultism  ritualise  undulated
triteness  Xanthippe  coruscant  inculcate  occultist  ritualism  undutiful
tritheism  yesterday  coruscate  inculpate  occupancy  ritualist  unguarded
tritheist  zeitgeist  croustade  incumbent  occurrent  roguishly  unhurried
triturate  zestfully  cucullate  incunable  occurring  Roquefort  unluckily
truthless  zootechny  debugging  incurable  odourless  rotundity  unmusical
tuitional  zootomist  debutante  incurably  oecumenic  salubrity  unruffled
twitchily  abduction  decumbent  incurious  ombudsman  saturable  unsuccess
twitterer  ablutions  decussate  incurrent  oppugnant  saturator  unsullied
uintahite  abounding  deducible  incurring  paludinal  Saturnian  untutored
umpteenth  aboutface  deduction  incursion  palustral  saturnine  vacuolate
unethical  aboutturn  deductive  incursive  peculator  saturnism  vacuously
unitarian  abruption  deludable  incurvate  pecuniary  scoundrel  vagueness
unitively  absurdism  demulcent  inducible  penultima  scrubbing  valuables
unstopped  absurdist  demurrage  induction  penumbral  scruffily  valuation
unstudied  absurdity  demurring  inductive  penurious  scrumhalf  valueless
vastitude  accusable  depurator  indulgent  petulance  scrummage  virulence
vectorial  acoustics  desuetude  infuriate  petulancy  scrutable  virulency
ventiduct  acquiesce  desultory  infuscate  piquantly  scrutator  visualise
ventifact  acquittal  divulsion  infusible  pituitary  seaurchin  volumeter
ventilate  actualise  effulgent  infusoria  plausible  secularly  voluntary
ventrally  actuality  embussing  inhumanly  plausibly  securable  volunteer
ventricle  actuarial  endurable  injurious  pleuritic  seduction  aliveness
venturous  actuarial  endurably  injustice  ploughboy  seductive  anovulant
vertebrae  actuation  endurance  innuendos  ploughman  sepulcher  atavistic
vertebral  adducible  epaulette  inquiline  pneumatic  sepulchre  belvedere
vestibule  Esquimaux  estuarian  insularly  pneumonia  sepulture  breveting
vestigial  adductive  estuarine  insulator  pneumonic  sequacity  brevetted
vestigium  adjunctly  eunuchism  insurable  popularly  sequester  Calvinism
vestiture  adjutancy  eunuchoid  insurance  pseudonym  sequestra  Calvinist
vestryman  amauroses  exculpate  insurgent  pseudopod  sequinned  canvasser
victimise  amaurosis  excurrent  intuition  purulence  sexualise  chevalier
Victorian  amaurotic  excursion  intuitive  purulency  sexuality  chevelure
victorine  ambulacra  excursive  intumesce  ranunculi  shouldest  chivalric
virtually  ambulance  excusable  irruption  rebukable  shrubbery  clavation
virtuosic  ambuscade  excusably  irruptive  rebutting  shrugging  claviform
virtuosos  amourette  expulsion  issueless  recumbent  simulacra  convector
volteface  amputator  expulsive  jesuitise  recurrent  simulacre  converter
voltinism  anguished  expurgate  jesuitism  recurring  simulator  convexity
voltmeter  angularly  exquisite  jocularly  recursion  simulcast  convincer
vorticism  annuitant  exsuccous  jocundity  recursive  sinuately  convivial
vorticist  annularly  facundity  liquation  recusance  sinuation  convolute
vorticity  annulated  fatuously  liquefier  recusancy  sinuosity  convolved
vorticose  annulling  feculence  liquidate  reducible  sinuously  curvature
vulturine  annulment  fecundate  liquidise  reductant  sinusitis  curveting
vulturish  araucaria  fecundity  liquidity  reduction  situation  curvetted
vulturous  arcuately  fenugreek  liquorice  reductive  slaughter  curviform
wartcress  arduously  fiduciary  liquorish  redundant  Solutrean  dogviolet
wasteland  argumenta  figurante  liturgics  refuelled  Solutrian  Dravidian
wasteness  Arguseyed  flouncing  liturgist  refulgent  spluttery  drivelled
wastepipe  assuasive  focussing  lobulated  refurbish  spouthole  driveller
wattmeter  assumable  gemutlich  loquacity  refurnish  spoutless  elevation
weathered  assumably  genuflect  lotusland  refusable  stauncher  elevenses
weatherly  assumpsit  genuinely  lucubrate  refutable  staunchly  fervently
westbound  assurance  gerundial  luxuriant  regularly  stoutness  flavorous
westering  assuredly  gerundive  luxuriate  regulator  structure  frivolity
westerner  assurgent  grouchily  luxurious  reluctant  struggler  frivolled
westwards  awfulness  groundage  majuscule  reluctate  strumitis  frivolous
whetstone  beauteous  groundash  manubrium  republish  strumming  galvanise
whitebait  beautiful  groundhog  maquisard  repudiate  strutting  galvanism
whitebass  bemusedly            matutinal  repugnant  susurrant  galvanist
```

```
gravamina  sylvanite  snowfield  lilywhite  wayzgoose  barnacled  causative
graveless  tervalent  snowflake  manyplies  whizzbang  barracker  cellarage
gravelled  travelled  snowgoose  manysided  wooziness  barracoon  cephalous
graveness  traveller  snowguard  molybdate  zigzagged  barracuda  certainly
graveyard  traversal  snowiness  okeydokey  ─────────  bastardly  certainty
gravidity  traverser  snowplant  pityingly  abstainer  battalion  cessation
gravitate  trivalent  snowscape  playfully  acclaimer  beccafico  chaparral
grovelled  trivially  snowstorm  playgroup  acetabula  bedjacket  charabanc
groveller  univalent  snowwhite  playhouse  acetamide  bedlamite  character
harvester  universal  souwester  plaything  actualise  bedraggle  chelation
heaviness  valveless  triweekly  polyamide  actuality  beemaster  chevalier
heavyduty  velveteen  trowelled  polyandry  actuarial  beleaguer  chicanery
Helvetian  weevilled  troweller  polybasic  actuation  bengaline  chimaeric
knavishly  wolverene  viewpoint  polyester  adamantly  bergamask  Chinatown
laevulose  wolverine  waywardly  polygamic  admeasure  bespangle  chinaware
larvicide  airworthy  werwolves  polygenic  adoration  bespatter  chivalric
leavening  awkwardly  anoxaemia  polygonal  adulation  bilharzia  Cingalese
malvoisie  blowtorch  asexually  polygonum  adulatory  billabong  circadian
marvelled  bowwindow  coaxially  polygraph  aerialist  blatantly  clamantly
nervation  brownness  coaxingly  polyhedra  aeriality  bobtailed  clavation
nervature  cobwebbed  deoxidise  polymathy  affianced  bombardon  climactic
nerveless  crowberry  fluxional  polymeric  afflation  bombasine  cockahoop
nerviness  crownless  inexactly  polymorph  aggravate  bombastic  Cockaigne
nervously  crowsfoot  Manxwoman  polyonymy  agitation  bombazine  cockatiel
netveined  crowsnest  proximate  polyphagy  agitative  bretasche  cognately
nonviable  Darwinian  proximity  polyphase  airjacket  bricabrac  cognation
olivenite  Darwinism  quixotism  polyphone  alabaster  brigadier  colcannon
peevishly  Darwinist  reexamine  polyphony  Alemannic  brigandry  collagist
pervasion  dimwitted  aepyornis  polyploid  amoralism  Britannia  collation
pervasive  drawerful  airyfairy  polyptych  amorality  Britannic  combatant
perverter  drawnwork  anhydride  polysemic  animalise  brutalise  combative
prevalent  drawplate  anhydrite  polysomic  animalism  brutalism  commander
preventer  drawsheet  anhydrous  polythene  animalist  brutality  commandos
prevision  earwigged  ankylosis  polytonal  animality  buccaneer  compactly
privateer  fatwitted  ankylotic  polytypic  animation  buffaloes  compactor
privately  flowchart  aphyllous  polyvinyl  animatism  Bulgarian  companion
privation  flowerage  argybargy  polywater  anomalous  buoyantly  compasses
privative  flowerbed  beryllium  polyzoary  anomalure  bursarial  comradely
privilege  flowering  bicyclist  prayerful  anoxaemia  bystander  comradery
proveably  flowerpot  bodyguard  prayerrug  apetalous  cabbalism  concavely
Provencal  flowingly  buoyantly  rehydrate  apogamous  cabbalist  concavity
provender  flowsheet  calycinal  sibylline  appealing  Caesarean  confabbed
provident  flowstone  caryopses  Sisyphean  applauder  Caesarian  connately
providing  flyweight  caryopsis  sphygmoid  appraisal  Caesarism  connation
provision  forwarder  chrysalid  staymaker  appraiser  Caesarist  connature
provisory  forwarder  chrysalis  strychnic  archangel  calcaneal  contactor
provoking  forwardly  citystate  traycloth  arcuately  calcaneum  contadina
provostry  frowardly  copyright  twayblade  aromatise  calcarate  contadino
pulverise  glowingly  Corybants  wheyfaced  arrearage  caldarium  contagion
pulverous  illwisher  corydalis  amazement  asepalous  calmative  contagium
pulvillus  indweller  corymbose  amazingly  ashlaring  campanile  container
pulvinate  jaywalker  coryphaei  amazonian  asphaltic  campanili  coriander
salvation  knowingly  cotyledon  avizandum  asphaltum  campanula  corralled
scavenger  knowledge  dehydrate  benzidine  assuasive  cantabile  corrasion
serviette  leewardly  demystify  benzoline  astraddle  cantaloup  coumarone
servilely  midwicket  denyingly  blazingly  astrakhan  canvasser  cremaster
servility  midwifery  dizygotic  brazilnut  atacamite  captaincy  cremation
servitude  midwinter  drayhorse  craziness  ataractic  carbamate  crematory
shaveling  netwinged  easygoing  dizziness  atonalism  carbamide  crenation
shovelful  Norwegian  ecdysiast  epizootic  atonality  carnality  crenature
shovelhat  nutweevil  empyreuma  fuzziness  attractor  carnation  CroMagnon
shovelled  outwardly  enzymatic  gauziness  avalanche  carrageen  curialism
shoveller  outwitted  ethylenic  jazziness  averagely  caseation  curvature
silverfir  outworker  flayflint  lazzarone  avizandum  Cassandra  cyanamide
slaveship  rauwolfia  graywacke  lazzaroni  avocation  cassareep  cyclamate
slavishly  seaworthy  greybeard  manzanita  awkwardly  cassaripe  cymbalist
Slavonian  shewbread  greyhound  mezzanine  baldachin  cassation  Daedalean
Slavophil  showiness  greywacke  mezzotint  baldaquin  Castalian  Daedalian
slivovitz  showpiece  Himyarite  monzonite  balkanise  castanets  dalmatian
Slovakian  showplace  holystone  muzziness  balladeer  casuarina  damnation
Slovenian  skewwhiff  itsybitsy  pizzicati  balladist  Catharism  damnatory
snivelled  slowcoach  ittybitty  pizzicato  Barbadian  Catharist  dastardly
sniveller  slowmatch  jurywoman  podzolina  barbarian  catharses  deadalive
solvation  snowberry  karyotype  pozzolana  barbarise  catharsis  declaimer
stevedore  snowblind  labyrinth  puzzolana  barbarism  cathartic  declarant
stovepipe  snowblink  ladysmock  quizzical  barbarity  cattaloes  defeatism
subverter  snowbound  laryngeal  rhizocarp  barbarous  Caucasian  defeatist
surveying  snowbroth  lazybones  rhizoidal  barcarole  causality  defeature
swivelled  snowdrift  lazytongs  sitzkrieg  bargainer  causation  defiantly
```

deflation	exudation	gravamina	jactation	mediately	operation	predacity
demeanour	exudative	gregarian	jambalaya	mediation	operative	predation
dentalium	Fabianism	gregarine	jampacked	mediatise	orgiastic	predative
dentation	fallalery	grenadier	jaywalker	mediative	orphanage	predatory
depravity	fandangle	grenadine	jessamine	mediatory	ostracise	prefatory
dermatoid	fandangos	grimalkin	jobmaster	mediatrix	ostracism	prelatess
detractor	fanfarade	grisaille	Jordanian	mendacity	outbacker	prelatise
deviation	fantasied	guacamole	joviality	mentalism	outlander	prelature
dewlapped	fantasise	guarantee	juxtapose	mentalist	outwardly	premature
dichasial	fantasist	guarantor	katharsis	mentality	oviparity	prevalent
dichasium	fantastic	guitarist	kidnapped	mentation	oviparous	primaeval
dictation	fantastry	gustation	kidnapper	mercaptan	ovulation	primality
didrachma	Fenianism	gustative	kurrajong	merganser	ovulatory	primarily
disbarred	feudalise	gustatory	labialise	mescaline	oxidation	primatial
discalced	feudalism	guttation	labialism	methadone	packaging	privateer
discarder	feudalist	gymnasial	lactation	mezzanine	pageantry	privately
disfavour	feudality	gymnasium	laggardly	migration	Palladian	privation
dismantle	feudatory	gymnastic	lallation	migratory	palladium	privative
disparage	filiation	gyrfalcon	landagent	miniature	palladous	probation
disparate	firealarm	hackamore	landaulet	mishandle	palmation	probative
disparity	firmament	haematite	Laplander	mishanter	palpation	probatory
distantly	flotation	haematoid	laudation	mismanage	panhandle	profanely
dittander	foliation	haematoma	laudative	mitraille	pantalets	profanity
dogmatics	forgather	haggadist	laudatory	Mondayish	pantaloon	prolamine
dogmatise	formalise	haggardly	lazzarone	Montanism	parrakeet	prolapsus
dogmatism	formalism	hagiarchy	lazzaroni	mordacity	paymaster	prolately
dogmatist	formalist	hamhanded	leewardly	mordantly	paypacket	prolation
dramatics	formality	haphazard	lethality	mortality	peasantry	prolative
dramatise	formation	harmaline	lethargic	mossagate	peccantly	pronation
dramatist	formative	harmattan	leucaemia	mundanely	pegmatite	propagate
drysalter	formatted	heptaglot	leukaemia	muscadine	pellagrin	prosaical
dulcamara	fortalice	heptarchy	leukaemic	muscarine	pentagram	protamine
dungarees	forwander	herbalist	leviathan	mustachio	pentangle	puffadder
ecstasise	forwarder	herbarium	librarian	mutualise	pentarchy	pugnacity
education	forwardly	hereabout	libration	mutualism	percaline	pulsatile
educative	fricassee	hereafter	libratory	mutualist	permanent	pulsation
egomaniac	fricative	hierarchy	lignaloes	mutuality	pervasion	pulsatory
elegantly	frigatoon	hieratica	lineality	mystagogy	pervasive	purgation
elevation	frowardly	Himyarite	lineament	Nahuatlan	phalanger	purgative
emanation	frugality	histamine	linearise	narration	phalanges	purgatory
emanative	fundament	hobnailed	linearity	narrative	phalanxes	quotation
embraceor	furcation	hortation	lineation	narratory	phalarope	racialism
embracery	gallantly	hortative	liquation	naumachia	pharaonic	racialist
embracive	gallantry	hortatory	Lombardic	nectarean	phenacite	radialply
embrangle	galvanise	huckaback	longaeval	nectarial	phenakite	radiantly
embrasure	galvanism	Hungarian	lookalike	nectarine	philander	radiately
emphasise	galvanist	husbandly	loquacity	nectarous	philately	radiation
emplastic	gambadoes	husbandry	loveapple	nephalism	phonation	radiative
emulation	gammadion	hydraemia	lowlander	nephalist	phonatory	rampantly
emulative	gasmantle	hydrangea	lucrative	nervation	phthalein	ransacker
enchanter	gemmation	hydration	Maccabean	nervature	pickaback	rascaldom
endearing	genealogy	hydraulic	magdalene	neuralgia	pilgarlic	rascalism
endeavour	genialise	hydrazine	Magianism	neuralgic	pillarbox	rascality
Englander	geniality	Icelander	magnalium	neuration	pineapple	raspatory
engraving	geomancer	Icelandic	mammalian	newmarket	pinnately	rechauffe
enhearten	geomantic	imitation	mammalogy	newsagent	pintailed	rectangle
entrammel	gerfalcon	imitative	mandarine	nictation	piquantly	redhanded
entrapped	geriatric	Indianise	mandatary	niggardly	piscatory	reexamine
enwrapped	germander	IndoAryan	mandatory	nitratine	pistachio	reflation
epilation	germanely	indraught	maneating	nitration	placation	refractor
epinastic	germanise	inelastic	manganate	nonpareil	placatory	rehearsal
esplanade	Germanish	inexactly	manganese	normalise	planarian	reliantly
estranger	Germanism	inflation	manganite	normality	planation	remeasure
estrapade	Germanist	infractor	manganous	Normanise	plenarily	retiarius
estuarian	germanium	ingrained	manhandle	normative	plicately	retractor
estuarine	gestalten	inshallah	manhattan	nostalgia	plication	rhodamine
ethnarchy	gestation	inspanned	mansarded	nostalgic	plicature	rigmarole
Eucharist	gestatory	instanter	manzanita	nuisancer	pluralise	Ripuarian
evocation	ginpalace	instantly	marcasite	nystagmic	pluralism	ritualise
evocative	glutamate	irreality	margarine	nystagmus	pluralist	ritualism
evocatory	goddamned	ischaemia	margarite	obviation	plurality	ritualist
exchanger	godfather	ischaemic	marmalade	offhanded	poetaster	roseapple
exogamous	godparent	isobathic	massagist	oilpaints	polyamide	roseately
expiation	goliardic	isogamete	mattamore	oligaemia	polyandry	Roumanian
expiatory	goosander	isogamous	mechanics	oligarchy	pompadour	Roumansch
explainer	gossamery	isolation	mechanise	onehanded	portative	ruination
extractor	Gothamite	isolative	mechanism	onomastic	precancel	sabbatise
extradite	gradation	iteration	mechanist	onslaught	precative	sabbatism
extravert	gradatory	iterative	mediaeval	onslaught	precatory	sacrament

```
sacrarium  stomachal  trematode  warranter  forebrain  sagebrush  anarchist
safranine  stomacher  trepanned  warrantor  foulbrood  salubrity  annectent
saltation  stomachic  tribadism  wassailer  freeboard  sandblast  anticline
saltatory  streakily  tribalism  wayfaring  fullblown  sandblind  anticodon
salvation  streaking  tridactyl  waywardly  funebrial  scombroid  araucaria
sandalled  streamlet  trifacial  welfarism  gangboard  scorbutic  artichoke
sandarach  striation  trigamist  wideawake  gaolbreak  scribbler  articular
sapraemia  striature  trigamous  zebrawood  garibaldi  scrubbing  aspectual
sapraemic  subcaudal  trisagion  zigzagged  goldbrick  semibreve  associate
sarcastic  subfamily  trivalent  acrobatic  greybeard  shadberry  atrocious
sargassos  subjacent  turnabout  adiabatic  grumbling  shambling  audacious
Sarmation  sublation  twohanded  adlibbing  hackberry  shambolic  auricular
sassafras  submarine  tympanist  adumbrate  hairbrush  shewbread  autoclave
Sassanian  submaster  uintahite  aerobatic  halfbaked  shipboard  autocracy
satiation  sulcation  Uitlander  aerobiont  halfblood  shoeblack  autocross
scenarist  sultanate  ultrahigh  algebraic  halfbound  shrubbery  autocycle
schmaltzy  sultaness  ululation  amoebaean  halfbreed  sideboard  avuncular
schnauzer  summarily  unabashed  argybargy  handbrake  sideburns  babacoote
seafaring  summarise  unbiassed  backbiter  hardboard  signboard  backcloth
seatangle  summarist  unbraided  backboard  headboard  slopbasin  backcross
sectarian  summation  unceasing  baneberry  hidebound  slumberer  balaclava
selfabuse  summative  uncharted  barmbrack  hillbilly  slumbrous  basically
selfaware  sunbather  unguarded  bearberry  hindbrain  snowberry  bicyclist
sensation  suntanned  unhealthy  bejabbers  homebound  snowblind  binocular
Sephardic  surfacing  uniparous  bilabiate  hypoblast  snowblink  bisection
Sephardim  sustainer  unitarian  billboard  illiberal  snowbound  bleachery
septation  swarajist  univalent  birdbrain  incubator  snowbroth  blotchily
sequacity  syllabary  unlearned  blaeberry  inhibitor  soapberry  bolection
serialise  syllabise  unmeaning  bluebeard  ironbound  sodabread  bonechina
serialism  syllabism  unreality  blueberry  itsybitsy  squabbler  branchiae
serialist  syllabled  unscathed  blueblack  ittybitty  squibbing  branchial
seriality  sylvanite  unshackle  bootblack  Jacobinic  starboard  branchlet
seriately  syndactyl  unsparing  brambling  jailbreak  strobilae  brecciate
serranoid  syngamous  unwearied  buckboard  Juneberry  strobilus  breeching
serration  syntactic  unwrapped  calaboose  karabiner  surfboard  bronchial
sexualise  systaltic  upbraider  calabrese  katabasis  tailboard  bushcraft
sexuality  tablature  usucapion  calibrate  katabatic  tenebrist  calicular
shamanism  talkathon  valiantly  canebrake  katabolic  tenebrous  calycinal
shamanist  talkative  vallation  cardboard  lampblack  terebinth  campchair
shamateur  tantalate  valuables  Caribbean  lazybones  terebrant  campcraft
siccative  tantalise  valuation  catabolic  lifeblood  throbbing  canicular
signalbox  tantalite  vandalise  celebrant  lucubrate  thumbhole  capacious
signalise  tapdancer  vandalism  celebrate  mainbrace  thumbmark  capacitor
signalled  tarpaulin  variation  celebrity  manubrium  thumbnail  cataclasm
signaller  tarragona  vassalage  cerebella  mesoblast  thumbtack  cataclysm
signalman  Tartarean  veniality  cerebrate  metabolic  tollbooth  catechise
signatory  Tartarian  verbalise  chilblain  millboard  troublous  catechism
signature  Tasmanian  verbalism  chipboard  molybdate  twayblade  catechist
siltation  taxpaying  verbalist  clapboard  monobasic  vocabular  cerecloth
simpatico  tentacled  verdantly  climbable  moonblind  wallboard  cetaceous
singalong  tentation  vernalise  clipboard  myrobalan  washbasin  chanceful
Sinhalese  tentative  vernation  clubbable  nailbrush  washboard  chancroid
sinuately  termagant  versatile  colubrine  naseberry  wellbeing  chancrous
sinuation  ternately  vibracula  cornbrash  nosebleed  westbound  churching
situation  terramara  vibraharp  Corybants  notabilia  windblown  churchman
skedaddle  terramare  vibratile  crabbedly  Octobrist  windbound  civically
skyjacker  terrarium  vibration  cranberry  overblown  windbreak  coarctate
Slovakian  tervalent  vibrative  crowberry  overboard  wineberry  coercible
socialise  testament  vibratory  dahabiyah  overborne  woodblock  coercibly
socialism  testation  villagery  dartboard  parabasis  workbench  colocynth
socialist  testatrix  villanage  dashboard  parabolic  abdicable  comically
socialite  tetradite  violation  deerberry  phlebitis  abdicator  conically
sociality  tetragram  violative  demobbing  plumbeous  abduction  conscious
solfatara  tetralogy  visualise  disoblige  plumbline  abjection  conscribe
solvation  tetrapody  vitiation  duckboard  pokeberry  acescence  conscript
sopranino  tetrarchy  vivianite  eastbound  polybasic  addiction  copacetic
sopranist  thalassic  volcanism  ectoblast  pourboire  addictive  corncrake
sorbapple  therapist  volcanoes  endoblast  presbyope  adducible  crescendo
Soudanese  Theravada  vulcanian  entoblast  presbyter  adduction  crotchety
spiracula  thesaurus  vulcanise  establish  pulpboard  adductive  cubically
spirality  throatily  vulcanism  exhibitor  pureblood  adjacency  cuticular
spiralled  thylacine  vulcanist  fireblast  quibbling  advection  cynically
sporangia  thyratron  vulcanite  firebrand  raspberry  advective  Damoclean
squeakily  timpanist  vulgarian  firebreak  reimburse  advocator  dayschool
squeamish  titration  vulgarise  firebrick  republish  affecting  decoction
stalactic  Tocharian  vulgarism  flambeaus  rerebrace  affection  dedicator
starapple  tophamper  vulgarity  flambeaux  roadblock  affective  deducible
steradian  topiarian  walkabout  footboard  rockbound  allocable  deduction
stirabout  topiarist  warrantee  foreboder  rockbrake  anarchism  deductive
```

defection	halfcaste	micaceous	radically	strychnic	beardless	floodmark
defective	halfcrown	mimicking	radicular	subocular	blandness	floodtide
deficient	handcraft	minacious	raincheck	subscribe	blindfold	folkdance
dejection	handcuffs	mobocracy	raincloud	subscript	blindness	foundling
delicious	hardcover	molecular	rapacious	switchman	bloodbath	foundress
democracy	havocking	monachism	raunchily	synectics	bloodless	fulldress
depiction	headcloth	monoceros	redaction	tenacious	bloodlust	glandered
depictive	helically	monochord	reducible	tenaculum	bloodroot	glandular
desecrate	hemicycle	monocline	reductant	thatching	bloodshed	grandaddy
desiccant	Heraclean	monocoque	reduction	theocracy	bloodshot	grandaunt
desiccate	hexachord	monocracy	reductive	theocrasy	bloodworm	grandiose
detection	highchair	monocular	refection	timocracy	bloodwort	grandness
detective	highclass	moraceous	refectory	tonically	blunderer	grandpapa
didactics	holocaust	motocross	regicidal	topically	boardfoot	grandsire
dinoceras	homicidal	municipal	rejection	toxically	boardroom	grandslam
dioecious	hopscotch	musically	reluctant	traycloth	boardwalk	Grundyism
direction	humectant	musichall	reluctate	treachery	boondocks	guardbook
directive	hypocaust	navicular	repechage	trenchant	boundless	guardedly
directory	hypocotyl	neckcloth	resection	truncated	brandling	guardrail
directrix	hypocrisy	nomocracy	reticence	truncheon	brandreth	guardring
disaccord	hypocrite	notochord	reticency	tufaceous	breadline	guardroom
dishcloth	illicitly	noviciate	reticular	tunicated	breadtree	guardship
dishclout	imbecilic	objectify	reticulum	twitchily	broadcast	guardsman
dodecagon	impaction	objection	revictual	typically	broadleaf	guildhall
dustcover	impeccant	objective	revocable	undecagon	broadloom	guildship
effective	indecency	obsecrate	rhonchial	undeceive	broadness	hamadryad
effectual	indecorum	octachord	ridiculer	undecided	broadside	headdress
efficient	indicator	officiant	roodcloth	undecimal	broadtail	immediacy
emunctory	indiction	officiate	rosaceous	unluckily	broadways	immediate
endocrine	inducible	officinal	rounceval	unsuccess	broadwise	immodesty
enunciate	induction	officious	rubicelle	urticaria	broiderer	impedance
episcopal	inductive	offscreen	sackcloth	utricular	bulldozer	impudence
ethically	infection	oleaceous	sagacious	varicella	butadiene	inaudible
eunuchism	infective	olfaction	sailcloth	vasectomy	cacodemon	inaudibly
eunuchoid	injection	olfactive	salacious	vaticinal	cacodylic	incidence
eutectoid	innocence	olfactory	salicetum	vehicular	chandlery	insidious
evincible	innocency	onlicence	salicylic	veracious	childhood	invidious
exarchate	innocuity	opercular	sandcrack	vesicular	childless	irradiant
exercises	innocuous	operculum	Saracenic	vinaceous	childlike	irradiate
exorciser	insectary	optically	scorching	viricidal	chondrite	jaundiced
expectant	insectile	opusculum	Scotchman	vivacious	chondrule	juridical
expecting	inunction	orbicular	scuncheon	voracious	cloudland	kingdomed
exsiccate	invective	ossicular	scutcheon	wallcress	cloudless	kneadable
exsuccous	irascible	overcheck	searching	wartcress	comedones	lairdship
fabaceous	irascibly	overcloud	sebaceous	washcloth	corydalis	landdross
facecloth	isooctane	overcrowd	seduction	windchest	culsdesac	landdrost
felicific	isosceles	panicking	seductive	wingchair	daredevil	lapideous
ferocious	judiciary	parachute	selachian	wisecrack	decadence	lastditch
fetichism	judicious	Paraclete	selection	woodchuck	decadency	launderer
fetichist	kilocycle	parochial	selective	woodcraft	decidable	laundress
fiduciary	kingcraft	pedicular	selectman	abandoned	decidedly	libidinal
filaceous	latecomer	periclase	semicolon	abandonee	deciduate	lividness
finically	launching	pericycle	sericeous	abandoner	deciduous	loxodrome
finicking	lexically	petechiae	setaceous	abradable	dehydrate	lucidness
firecrest	libecchio	petechial	shipcanal	abundance	deludable	luridness
flocculus	lifecycle	poinciana	siliceous	accidence	diandrous	macedoine
floscular	lioncelle	policeman	silicious	aerodrome	dimidiate	maladroit
flowchart	lobectomy	pomaceous	silicosis	affidavit	dividable	maunderer
fluecured	lobscouse	pouncebox	silicotic	amendable	druidical	meandrine
foodchain	logically	preachify	sketchily	amendment	embedding	meandrous
footcloth	loincloth	preachily	sketchmap	amygdalin	embedment	megadeath
forecaddy	longchain	preoccupy	slipcoach	anandrous	emendable	melodious
foreclose	longcoats	preschool	slipcover	anecdotal	emendator	melodrama
forecourt	lovechild	prescient	slowcoach	anecdotic	ephedrine	menadione
franchise	ludicrous	prescribe	sluiceway	anhydride	expedient	misadvise
francolin	lyrically	prescript	solacious	anhydrite	expediter	mixedness
frenchify	magically	princedom	solicitor	anhydrous	fatidical	monodical
Frenchman	magicking	princekin	songcycle	antidotal	fetidness	monodrama
fugacious	malachite	princelet	speechful	archducal	fieldbook	mouldable
fullcream	malicious	principal	speechify	archduchy	fieldboot	nakedness
funicular	Manichean	principia	spotcheck	armadillo	fieldfare	notedness
funiculus	masochism	principle	stanchion	assiduity	fieldsman	okeydokey
galactose	masochist	proscenia	starchily	assiduous	fieldwork	ombudsman
gatecrash	medicable	proscribe	stepchild	asyndetic	finedrawn	overdraft
genocidal	medically	pumiceous	stercoral	asyndeton	firedrake	overdrawn
goldcrest	medicinal	pushchair	stitchery	avoidable	firedrill	overdress
grouchily	megacycle	pyracanth	stoically	avoidably	fixedness	overdrive
gynocracy	melocoton	quercetum	stricture	avoidance	fjordland	packdrill
haircloth	mepacrine	quitclaim	structure	awardable	floodgate	paludinal

paradisal	taxidermy	austerely	carpetbag	cornerman	dyspeptic	flowerpot
pasodoble	tepidness	austerity	carpeting	cornetist	earnestly	flyweight
peridotic	testdrive	authentic	carrefour	correctly	Eastender	forcefeed
pipedream	thirdhand	awakening	Cartesian	corrector	easterner	forceland
pleadable	thirdrate	awareness	casserole	correlate	ecclesial	forceless
pleadings	thirdsman	bacterial	castellan	crenelled	ecumenism	forcemeat
plumdamas	thunderer	bacterise	cathectic	criterion	eggbeater	forcepump
plunderer	timidness	bacterium	cathedral	cropeared	elemental	forfeiter
poundcake	tiredness	bacteroid	causeless	crudeness	elevenses	forgeable
preadamic	treadmill	ballerina	cauterise	cudgelled	elopement	forgetful
pseudonym	tumidness	banderole	centenary	cullender	eminently	fosterage
pseudopod	validness	bargepole	centering	cupbearer	enamelled	framework
pyridoxin	vapidness	barkeeper	chameleon	currently	enameller	fraternal
rabidness	velodrome	barleymow	chaperone	curveting	endlessly	fulgently
rapidfire	veridical	Barmecide	chatelain	curvetted	ensheathe	funnelled
rapidness	vividness	barrelful	chevelure	czarevich	entrechat	gadgeteer
readdress	weirdness	barrelled	chiselled	damnedest	entrecote	galleried
rebidding	wheedling	bartender	chiseller	dancehall	entremets	ganderism
rehydrate	wieldable	basketful	chokedamp	dandelion	enumerate	gardening
remediate	wiredrawn	basrelief	choleraic	dangerous	enwreathe	garderobe
repudiate	withdrawn	battening	Cimmerian	Dantesque	epicentre	garmented
residence	worldling	bedfellow	clemently	decrement	epidermal	garreteer
residency	worldwide	bedsettee	clitellum	decretive	epidermic	gaspereau
residuary	woundless	beefeater	closedown	decretory	epidermis	gathering
rigidness	woundwort	beekeeper	closeness	deflector	epileptic	gaugeable
rockdrill	wyandotte	belvedere	Cobdenism	deprecate	erogenous	gauleiter
roundelay	abasement	berberine	cobwebbed	depredate	escheator	genteelly
roundhead	abatement	berkelium	coeternal	depressed	euphemise	geodesist
roundness	academism	berserker	coffeecup	depressor	euphemism	geometric
roundsman	accretion	bigheaded	coffeepot	descended	euthenics	geometrid
roundworm	accretive	bilgekeel	cofferdam	desperado	eutherian	geyserite
sabadilla	addressee	biogenous	colleague	desperate	evidently	gibberish
sapodilla	addresser	biometric	collected	desuetude	ewenecked	giltedged
scaldfish	addressor	bitterish	collector	deuterate	exceeding	gingerade
selfdoubt	aforesaid	blameable	collegial	deuterium	exchequer	gingerale
selfdrive	agapemone	blameably	collegian	dexterity	excrement	glabellae
shelduck	aggregate	blameless	collegium	dexterous	excretion	glabellar
sheldrake	aggressor	Boanerges	commendam	dialectal	excretive	globefish
shredding	agreeable	boomerang	commensal	dialectic	excretory	glomerate
sidedness	agreeably	bordereau	commenter	diametral	exegetist	glomerule
skindiver	agreement	boulevard	compelled	diametric	exilement	glomeruli
slanderer	aimlessly	bowlegged	compendia	dieselise	exodermis	glyceride
slenderly	alchemise	brakeless	competent	dietetics	exogenous	glycerine
snowdrift	alchemist	brakeshoe	conceited	different	exonerate	goffering
solidness	alinement	brakesman	concentre	dinnerset	expletive	goldeneye
soundfilm	aliveness	breveting	concerned	dipterous	expletory	goldenrod
soundhole	aloneness	brevetted	concerted	disbelief	expressly	goosefoot
soundings	amazement	bridecake	condenser	disrelish	extremely	goosegirl
soundless	ampleness	bridesman	conferral	disrepair	extremism	gooseherd
soundness	amusement	bridewell	conferred	disrepute	extremist	gooseneck
soundpost	analeptic	brokerage	conferrer	dissector	extremity	gooseskin
soundwave	anciently	bromeliad	confervae	disseisin	exuberant	goosestep
sourdough	ancientry	bucketful	confessor	dissemble	exuberate	gospeller
speedball	angleiron	budgetary	congenial	dissenter	falsehood	graceless
speedboat	anglesite	buffeting	congeries	distemper	falseness	grapeshot
speedster	angleworm	burdenous	connected	dixieland	farseeing	grapevine
speedwell	anklebone	burlesque	connecter	doglegged	fastening	graveless
spendable	anorectic	burnedout	connector	dorbeetle	fatheaded	gravelled
spindling	anthelion	bushelful	connexion	drawerful	feiseanna	graveness
spindrier	anthemion	butterbur	consensus	drivelled	fenceless	graveyard
spindrift	applejack	buttercup	conserver	driveller	fervently	grotesque
squidding	apprehend	butterfat	contemner	dromedary	fibreless	groveller
staidness	appressed	butterfly	contended	dysgenics	fifteenth	guidebook
standpipe	arabesque	butterine	contented	dyspepsia	filterbed	guideline
stardrift	araneidal	butternut	convector		filtertip	guidepost
steadfast	araneidan	cablegram	converter		fingering	guiderope
stepdance	archenemy	cablelaid	convexity		fingertip	guileless
stridence	archetype	cachectic	cooperage		fireeater	guttering
stridency	artlessly	cacoethes	cooperant		fisherman	gynaeceum
subeditor	arytenoid	cancelled	cooperate		flabellum	gynoecium
swaddling	asafetida	cancerous	copsewood		flagellum	halieutic
swordcane	asclepiad	cankerous	corbeille		flageolet	hammerman
swordfish	Ashkenazi	cannelure	corbelled		flameless	hammertoe
swordknot	athletics	careerism	cordelier		flarepath	hangerson
swordlike	atonement	careerist	cornelian		flowerage	hankering
swordplay	augmented	carnelian	cornemuse		flowerbed	Hanseatic
swordsman	augmenter	carpenter	cornerboy		flowering	hanselled
swordtail	augmentor	carpentry				haplessly
synodical	austenite					

happening	isomerism	magnetist	nucleated	pilferage	pulserate	scoredraw
harlequin	isomerous	magnetite	nucleolus	pimpernel	pulverise	screecher
harvester	isometric	magnetron	nucleonic	pithecoid	pulverous	screening
Hashemite	Israelite	maidenish	nurseling	placeable	pummelled	scutellar
hawsehole	issueless	malleable	nursemaid	placecard	pungently	scutellum
hawsepipe	itineracy	malleehen	nutweevil	placekick	puppeteer	sealetter
hellebore	itinerant	mallemuck	obeseness	placeless	purselike	seanettle
hellenise	itinerary	malleolar	obscenely	placement	Quakerdom	secretage
Hellenism	itinerate	malleolus	obscenity	placename	Quakeress	secretary
Hellenist	Jansenism	mannequin	obstetric	placentae	Quakerish	secretion
Helvetian	Jansenist	mannerism	oddfellow	placental	Quakerism	secretive
herpetoid	jetsetter	mannerist	offcentre	planetary	quarenden	secretory
Hesperian	jitterbug	manoeuvre	offseason	planetoid	quarender	sedgewren
hetaerism	joylessly	marcelled	olivenite	platemark	racketeer	seedeater
hiddenite	judgement	marketday	onelegged	pocketful	rareeshow	segmental
Hitlerism	judgeship	marketing	openended	polyester	recherche	segregate
Hitlerite	juiceless	marvelled	opodeldoc	pommelled	recreancy	sensedata
Hobbesian	junkerdom	masterdom	oppressor	ponderous	redheaded	senseless
hodiernal	junkerism	masterful	opulently	porbeagle	redletter	sentenate
horseback	junketing	masterkey	orchestic	porcelain	redresser	September
horsebean	Junoesque	maybeetle	orchestra	porterage	reflector	septemvir
horsehair	kaiserdom	Mendelian	ourselves	possessed	reflexion	septenary
horsehide	kaiserism	Mendelism	overeaten	possessor	reflexive	septennia
horseless	kennelled	mercenary	overeater	postentry	refreshen	sequester
horsemint	Keplerian	mercerise	overexert	posterior	refresher	sequestra
horseplay	Keynesian	mesmerise	oviferous	posterity	refuelled	sergeancy
horsepond	kilderkin	mesmerism	oxygenate	prayerful	regretful	serjeancy
horseshoe	kittenish	mesmerist	oxygenise	prayerrug	regretted	serjeanty
horsetail	knifeedge	messenger	oxygenous	prebendal	reiterate	serpentry
horsewhip	lambently	metheglin	oysterbed	precedent	replenish	serrefile
hortensia	lancejack	millenary	oysterman	preceding	repletion	sestertia
hosteller	lancewood	millennia	ozocerite	precentor	reprehend	sexlessly
hotheaded	larcenist	millepede	ozokerite	preceptor	represent	shadeless
Hottentot	larcenous	millepore	paederast	preferred	repressor	shadetree
houseboat	largeness	millerite	palaestra	prelector	requester	shakeable
housebote	lathering	mincemeat	palletise	prerecord	respecter	shakedown
housecarl	latterday	misbecome	palpebral	preselect	Rhineodon	shakerism
housecoat	laurelled	misbehave	panderess	presentee	rhymester	shamefast
houseflag	lawlessly	misbelief	parcelled	presenter	ridgepole	shameless
household	leasehold	misbeseem	parcenary	presently	ridgetile	shapeable
housekeep	leaselend	miscegene	parhelion	preserver	riflebird	shapeless
houseleek	leavening	miscegine	parleyvoo	pretender	rocketeer	sharecrop
houseless	lecherous	misdemean	Parseeism	preterist	Roquefort	shaveling
houselled	Leicester	misfeasor	passenger	preterite	rostellum	shoreless
housemaid	leniently	misleared	passerine	pretermit	rousement	shoreline
housemate	letterbox	misreckon	passersby	preventer	rubberise	shoreside
houseroom	lettering	misreport	pastedown	priceless	rudbeckia	shoreward
housewife	librettos	monkeyish	patiently	prideless	ruggedise	shoreweed
housework	lichenous	monkeyism	pauperise	primeness	russeting	shovelful
hoydenish	lickerish	monkeynut	pauperism	procedure	ruthenium	shovelhat
hygienics	liegelord	monoecism	peaceable	procerity	saliently	shovelled
hygienist	lingering	motheaten	peaceably	processed	sanbenito	shoveller
hyphenate	lintelled	motherwit	peacetime	processor	Sanhedrim	sickening
hysterics	lipreader	mousehole	pelletise	processor	Sanhedrin	silverfir
hysteroid	liquefier	mousetrap	pendently	professed	sapheaded	sincerely
ichneumon	Listerism	moviegoer	Pentecost	professor	sapiently	sincerity
imageable	litheness	murderess	pepperbox	progestin	Sassenach	sinlessly
imageless	lithesome	murderous	pepperpot	projector	sauceboat	sixteenmo
impleader	litterbug	musketeer	perceiver	prolapses	sauceless	sixteenth
implement	lodgement	musteline	perfectly	prolepsis	saucerful	slakeless
impletion	lodgepole	myrmecoid	perfector	proleptic	Sauternes	slateclub
imprecate	longcloth	myxoedema	perfervid	promenade	scalefern	slategrey
imprecise	longeared	natheless	permeable	proneness	scalefish	slaveship
impresari	longevity	neoteinia	permeance	propelled	scaleleaf	sliderule
inbreathe	longevous	neoteinic	perpetual	propeller	scaleless	slopewise
inclement	looseleaf	neoterise	persecute	properdin	scalelike	Slovenian
increaser	looseness	neoterism	persevere	prosector	scalemoss	smileless
increment	lousewort	neoterist	perverter	prosecute	scapegoat	smokeball
indweller	lownecked	nepheline	phagedena	proselyte	scarecrow	smokebomb
inelegant	lumbering	nephelite	phonemics	protector	scarehead	smokebush
infielder	lumberman	nerveless	phonetics	proteinic	scavenger	smokejack
inflexion	maddening	netveined	phonetise	protester	scenedock	smokeless
inglenook	madrepore	nickelise	phonetism	protestor	scheelite	smoketree
innkeeper	magnesian	nickelled	phonetist	proveably	schlemiel	snakebird
innuendos	magnesite	nickelous	picketing	Provencal	schlemihl	snakebite
inspector	magnesium	nobleness	piecemeal	provender	sciaenoid	snakelike
inurement	magnetics	noiseless	piecerate	prudently	scolecite	snakeroot
isogenous	magnetise	nonperson	piecework	Ptolemaic	scorebook	snakeskin
isomerise	magnetism	Norwegian	pigheaded	pulseless	scorecard	snakeweed

snakewood	subverter	triweekly	whiteness	fourflush	taskforce	eulogiser
snaredrum	succeeder	trowelled	whitening	fretfully	tearfully	evangelic
snipefish	succentor	troweller	whitewash	gainfully	thriftily	everglade
snivelled	successor	truceless	whitewing	genuflect	tunefully	evergreen
sniveller	suffering	tsarevich	whitewood	gleefully	twelfthly	fatigable
solfeggio	suggester	tuckerbag	wholemeal	goldfever	undefined	fenugreek
solferino	sunhelmet	tunnelled	wholeness	goldfield	unruffled	filigreed
sommelier	supremacy	tunnelnet	wholesale	goldfinch	uplifting	fireguard
sonneteer	supremely	turgently	wholesome	griefless	wakefully	fledgling
sonnetise	surfeiter	twiceborn	willemite	gruffness	wallfruit	foragecap
sooterkin	surgeoncy	twicelaid	winterise	harmfully	wavefront	foregoing
sorceress	surrender	twicetold	withering	hatefully	wellfound	frangible
sorcerous	surveying	umpteenth	witherite	headfirst	wheyfaced	Franglais
sostenuto	suspender	unblessed	witlessly	heedfully	wishfully	freighter
souteneur	suspensor	unchecked	woebegone	helpfully	wistfully	fullgrown
souwester	sutteeism	uncleanly	wolverene	highflier	zestfully	fumigator
sovietise	swineherd	uncreated	wolverine	highflown	abnegator	gelignite
sovietism	swivelled	undreamed	wonderful	highflyer	abrogator	georgette
spaceband	syllepses	unfeeling	Worcester	hoarfrost	aerograph	glengarry
spaceless	syllepsis	unfledged	wormeaten	hopefully	allegedly	goingover
spaceport	sylleptic	unfleshed	wulfenite	hurtfully	allegiant	Gradgrind
spaceship	symmetric	unfleshly	wyliecoat	ineffable	allegoric	grosgrain
spacesuit	synoecete	unheeding	Yankeedom	ineffably	alligator	hairgrass
spacetime	tableland	uniserial	Yankeeism	lifeforce	allograph	handglass
spadefoot	tableleaf	unisexual	yesterday	longfaced	almsgiver	hexagonal
spadework	tabletalk	universal	zinkenite	lovefeast	alongside	highgrade
spareness	tableware	unsheathe	zoogenous	luciferin	ambiguity	highgrown
spareribs	tangerine	unweeting	zootechny	lustfully	ambiguous	hodograph
spicebush	tasselled	uselessly	airyfairy	manifesto	analgesia	holograph
spiderman	tasteless	vagueness	aloofness	milkfever	analgesic	homegrown
spiderweb	teakettle	vallecula	antefixal	milkfloat	antigenic	homogamic
spikenard	tegmental	valueless	archfiend	mindfully	armigeral	homograft
spineless	tegmentum	valveless	artificer	minefield	arrogance	homograph
spleenful	temperate	variegate	baldfaced	needfully	autograft	hourglass
spokesman	tenderise	velveteen	balefully	newsflash	autograph	hypogeous
spokewise	tenseness	veneering	banefully	noseflute	baragraph	ideograph
stagedoor	terseness	vengeance	barefaced	ossifrage	befogging	idiograph
stagehand	thaneship	vertebrae	bashfully	overflown	bellglass	illegally
stakeboat	therefore	vertebral	beanfeast	painfully	benighted	illegible
stalemate	therefrom	vignetter	beneficed	palafitte	benignant	illegibly
staleness	thereinto	villenage	bluffness	pitifully	benignity	illogical
stapedial	thereunto	violently	boldfaced	playfully	bluegrass	immigrant
statehood	thereupon	viscerate	boxoffice	plusfours	bodyguard	immigrate
stateless	therewith	vizierate	briefcase	poriferal	bourgeois	inaugural
statement	threefold	vizierial	briefless	poriferan	bringdown	incognito
stateroom	threesome	voiceless	briefness	portfolio	cerograph	indagator
stateside	timbering	voiceover	bullfight	proofread	changeful	indigence
statesman	timberman	volteface	bullfinch	reenforce	clergyman	indignant
statewide	tinderbox	vulnerary	campfever	reinforce	clergymen	indignity
stevedore	tinselled	Wagnerian	carefully	restfully	courgette	indigotin
stilettos	titledeed	Wagnerite	chafferer	ringfence	cryogenic	inorganic
stokehold	titlepage	Waldenses	chaffinch	ruthfully	debagging	integrand
stokehole	toadeater	wandering	chauffeur	sangfroid	debugging	integrant
stonechat	tormentil	washedout	chiefship	saxifrage	decagonal	integrate
stonecoal	tormentor	washerman	chieftain	scarfring	demagogic	integrity
stonecold	trabeated	wasteland	cliffhang	scarfskin	demagogue	irregular
stonecrop	trabecula	wasteness	coalfield	scarfwise	denigrate	irrigable
stonedead	traceable	wastepipe	cockfight	scruffily	designate	irrigator
stonedeaf	traceably	wedgewise	coiffeuse	selffaced	designing	isinglass
stonefish	traceless	Wednesday	cornfield	semifinal	diligence	knotgrass
stoneless	traceried	westering	cornflour	semifluid	dirigible	kymograph
stonewall	trademark	westerner	direfully	sgraffiti	dirigisme	landgrave
stoneware	tradename	whaleback	disaffect	sgraffito	dizygotic	leafgreen
stonework	tradesman	whaleboat	disaffirm	shelflife	downgrade	lifeguard
stonewort	tragedian	whalebone	dishfaced	shelfmark	dziggetai	litigable
storeroom	trapezial	whalehead	dolefully	shelfroom	easygoing	litigious
storeship	trapezium	wherefore	doorframe	shipfever	ectogenic	logogriph
stovepipe	trapezoid	wherefrom	dopefiend	shopfloor	egregious	lymegrass
streetcar	travelled	whereinto	downfield	shopfront	eidograph	malignant
stupefier	traveller	whereunto	dumbfound	skilfully	elongated	malignity
stylebook	traversal	whereupon	dutifully	skinflick	emergence	menagerie
subaerial	traverser	wherewith	easefully	skinflint	emergency	mesogloea
subdeacon	tribunals	whitebait	fairfaced	snowfield	endogamic	mitigable
subgenera	trihedral	whitebass	fatefully	snowflake	endogenic	mitigator
sublethal	trimerous	whitebeam	fearfully	songfully	energetic	monogamic
submental	trimester	whiteface	feoffment	soulfully	energiser	monograph
subregion	trimetric	whitefish	flayflint	stiffener	energumen	mortgagee
subsellia	trisector	Whitehall	footfault	stiffness	enlighten	mortgager
subtenant	triteness	whitehead	forefront	tactfully	ergograph	mortgagor

```
mossgrown  stingless  brushwood  farmhouse  morphemic  roughhewn  watchcase
mutagenic  straggler  brushwork  feathered  moschatel  roughneck  watchfire
navigable  struggler  Brythonic  firehouse  mouthpart  roughness  watchword
navigator  subagency  buckhound  flashback  mouthwash  roughshod  weathered
nomograph  swaggerer  bunkhouse  flashbulb  mumchance  saccharin  weatherly
obligated  swangoose  butcherer  flashcube  napthalic  seachange  weighable
octagonal  swingeing  butcherly  flashover  naughtily  Shechinah  weighbeam
oleograph  synagogal  camphoric  flashtube  neathouse  slaphappy  weightily
oncogenic  synagogue  cantharid  fleshings  neighbour  slightish  weighting
ontogenic  telegenic  cantharis  fleshless  newshound  slothbear  whichever
oppugnant  telegraph  cantharus  fleshment  northeast  slushfund  widthways
orangeade  theogonic  carthorse  flightily  northerly  soothfast  widthwise
Orangeism  thingness  catchable  flophouse  northland  Southdown  windhover
Orangeman  thingummy  catchment  flushness  northmost  southeast  witchetty
orangetip  thoughted  catchpole  foolhardy  northward  southerly  witchhunt
orangutan  tidegauge  catchpoll  forthwith  northwest  southland  witchmeal
overglaze  unpegging  catchword  freehouse  nymphalid  southmost  wolfhound
overgraze  unsighted  chachacha  freshener  oasthouse  southward  workhorse
overgrown  unsightly  chophouse  freshness  octahedra  southwest  workhouse
palsgrave  uprightly  cirrhosis  frightful  offchance  spaghetti  worthless
panegyric  vainglory  clathrate  furtherer  omophagia  staghound  wrathless
paragraph  waldgrave  clubhouse  gatehouse  omophagic  studhorse  wychhazel
paregoric  waveguide  coachwork  gaucherie  openheart  subphylum  Xanthippe
pedagogic  wayzgoose  cockhorse  gazehound  overheard  sulphonic  zoophagan
pedagogue  wineglass  colchicum  gigahertz  packhorse  sulphuret  zoophobia
pedigreed  wiregauze  cookhouse  gnathonic  pairhorse  sulphuric  zoophytic
peregrine  wrongdoer  couchette  gomphosis  panchayat  surcharge  zucchetto
plangency  wrongness  crashdive  graphemic  pantheism  sylphlike  abidingly
playgroup  xenograft  crashland  graphical  pantheist  symphonic  abolisher
ploughboy  xylograph  crushable  graphitic  parchment  symphysis  abolition
ploughman  youngling  cutthroat  greyhound  patchouli  synchrony  abominate
podagrous  youngness  deathblow  halfhardy  patchouly  syntheses  aborigine
polygamic  youngster  deathless  harshness  patchwork  synthesis  abscissae
polygenic  zeitgeist  deathlike  hatchback  peachblow  synthetic  abscissas
polygonal  Zwinglian  deathmask  hatchling  pemphigus  teachable  abseiling
polygonum  zymogenic  deathroll  hatchment  penthouse  teachably  abstinent
polygraph  abashment  deckhouse  haughtily  perchance  tenthrate  abusively
pronghorn  aesthesia  deerhound  heathcock  percheron  thighbone  acariasis
pyrogenic  aesthesis  depthbomb  heathenry  perihelia  thighboot  acclimate
raingauge  aesthetic  depthless  hellhound  pesthouse  thitherto  acclivity
rearguard  aitchbone  diachrony  hitchhike  pinchbeck  tollhouse  acetifier
recognise  alcoholic  diachylom  hoarhound  pinchcock  toolhouse  acidifier
religiose  aldehydic  diachylum  horehound  pitchdark  toothache  aciniform
religious  aliphatic  diaphragm  hunchback  pitchfork  toothcomb  aconitine
repugnant  almshouse  diaphysis  ichthyoid  pitchpipe  toothless  acquiesce
safeguard  anaphoric  diathermy  isochrone  playhouse  toothpick  acquittal
sagegreen  anopheles  diathesis  josshouse  plethoric  toothsome  acquitted
saltglaze  anschluss  diathetic  kilohertz  plushness  toothwort  acuminate
sandglass  apathetic  discharge  kitchener  polyhedra  torchrace  adjoining
savagedom  apishness  dogshores  knightage  poorhouse  torchsong  adoringly
sciagraph  apophyses  dosshouse  lanthanum  porphyria  touchable  aestivate
scraggily  apophysis  doughtily  larghetto  posthaste  touchdown  affricate
selfglory  apothecia  Doukhobor  laughable  posthorse  touchhole  aggrieved
serigraph  arachnoid  draghound  laughably  posthouse  touchline  agonising
Shangrila  bacchanal  drayhorse  lionheart  preshrink  touchmark  agonistic
shinguard  bacchante  dysphagia  loathsome  preshrunk  touchtype  airminded
shrugging  bakehouse  dysphagic  longhouse  prophetic  touchwood  altricial
silkgland  baksheesh  dysphonia  lunchtime  prothesis  toughness  aluminate
skiagraph  bathhouse  dysphoria  lyamhound  prothetic  townhouse  aluminise
skingraft  beachhead  dysphoric  lymehound  prothorax  tracheary  aluminium
slaughter  beachwear  earthborn  lymphatic  psychical  tracheate  aluminous
slingback  beechfern  earthling  lyophilic  psychoses  trachytic  amazingly
slingshot  beechmast  earthstar  lyophobic  psychosis  trichinae  americium
smuggling  biorhythm  earthward  malthouse  psychotic  trichomic  Amerindic
sniggerer  birchbark  earthworm  marchpane  punchball  trichroic  amphibian
snowgoose  birthmark  earthworm  marchpast  punchbowl  tritheism  amphibole
snowguard  birthrate  epiphragm  marihuana  punchcard  tritheist  amphigory
softgoods  birthwort  epiphyses  marshalcy  punchline  trochilus  amphioxus
sphagnous  blushless  epiphysis  marshland  purchaser  trochleae  amplifier
sphygmoid  boathouse  epiphytal  marshwort  racehorse  trochlear  amplitude
spongebag  Bolshevik  epiphytic  matchless  rakehelly  truthless  amusingly
spongeous  bombhappy  epithelia  matchlock  reachable  unashamed  anabioses
sprigging  brachiate  epithesis  matchwood  rearhorse  unethical  anabiosis
sprightly  brachyura  epithetic  megahertz  Reichstag  Vaishnava  anabiotic
sprigtail  brashness  erythrism  Menshevik  rhythmics  vetchling  anglicise
staggerer  brightish  erythrite  mirthless  rhythmise  vouchsafe  anglicism
stargazer  brochette  eyeshadow  mischance  rhythmist  warehouse  Anglicist
stargrass  brotherly  faithcure  misshapen  roadhouse  washhouse  angriness
stingaree  brushfire  faithless  monthling  roughcast  watchable  anguished
```

animistic	burliness	concierge	derringer	fabricate	fungicide	histidine
annuitant	burningly	conciliar	destitute	facsimile	fungiform	hoariness
aperiodic	burnisher	concisely	detriment	factional	funkiness	hoggishly
aperitive	bushiness	concision	detrition	factitive	funniness	horniness
apodictic	buttinsky	condignly	diclinous	faddiness	furbisher	horsiness
apomictic	cabriolet	condiment	diesinker	falciform	furnisher	hostilely
appliance	caddisfly	condition	dietician	falsifier	furniture	hostility
applicant	caecilian	confidant	dietitian	fasciated	furtively	hubristic
appointee	calcicole	confident	difficile	fascicled	fussiness	huffiness
arabicise	calcifuge	confiding	difficult	fascicule	fustigate	humdinger
architect	callipers	configure	diffident	fasciculi	fustiness	hurricane
archivist	Calvinism	confirmed	dignified	fascinate	fuzziness	hurriedly
archivolt	Calvinist	confirmer	dignitary	Fascistic	gallicise	huskiness
asininity	candidacy	confirmor	dimwitted	fashioner	gallicism	hybridise
assailant	candidate	confiteor	dinginess	fastigium	gallingly	hybridism
atavistic	canniness	connivent	dipcircle	fattiness	gallinule	hybridity
atheistic	cantilena	consignee	dirtiness	fatwitted	gallivant	hydriodic
atomicity	capriccio	consignor	disfigure	faunistic	galliwasp	illwisher
atomistic	Capricorn	continent	dismissal	fawningly	gannister	imaginary
atonicity	captivate	continual	dissident	febricity	garnishee	imbricate
attainder	captivity	continuer	dissipate	febrifuge	garniture	implicate
attribute	carcinoma	continuum	distilled	feelingly	gasfitter	impliedly
attrition	carnitine	convincer	distiller	fertilely	gaudiness	inability
aubrietia	carnivore	convivial	dizziness	fertilise	gauziness	inanimate
auspicate	carpingly	corbicula	doggishly	fertility	gawkiness	inanition
Babbittry	cartilage	cordially	dogviolet	festinate	gentility	inflictor
badminton	cassimere	cordiform	doltishly	festively	genuinely	initially
bagginess	castigate	corticate	donnishly	festivity	germicide	initiator
bailiwick	Castilian	corticoid	dormition	fibriform	germinate	inquiline
ballistae	casuistic	cortisone	dormitory	fibrillar	giddiness	instigate
ballistic	casuistry	coseismal	dottiness	fibrinoid	gimmickry	instilled
balminess	cattiness	coseismic	dowdiness	fibrinous	girlishly	institute
baltimore	Celticism	costively	Dravidian	fictional	glacially	intricacy
bandicoot	centigram	craziness	dualistic	fideistic	gladiator	intricate
bannister	centipede	crediting	ductility	fieriness	gladiolus	intrigant
baptismal	certified	crepitant	dulcitude	fillister	glaringly	intriguer
baptistry	certifier	crepitate	dumpiness	filminess	glowingly	intrinsic
barbitone	certitude	cretinism	duplicate	fioritura	glutinous	intuition
barricade	chariness	cretinous	duplicity	fioriture	godliness	intuitive
barricado	charivari	criminate	duskiness	fireirons	gothicise	inutility
barrister	chelicera	criminous	dustiness	fishiness	Gothicism	inveigler
bastinade	chemistry	criticise	earliness	fissility	gracility	ischiadic
bastinado	chemitype	criticism	earwigged	fissipede	granitoid	ischiatic
bastioned	cherimoya	crucially	edibility	fittingly	graticule	isoniazid
battiness	chitinous	cruciform	egotistic	flakiness	gratitude	italicise
bawdiness	chorister	culminant	elegiacal	flamingly	gravidity	Italicism
beamingly	circinate	culminate	eliminate	flamingos	gravitate	itchiness
beatitude	cirripede	cultivate	elucidate	flaringly	griminess	jarringly
bedridden	clarifier	cuneiform	elusively	floriated	gumminess	jazziness
bedsitter	clarionet	cunningly	emaciated	floridean	gushingly	jeeringly
beefiness	claviform	cuplichen	embrittle	floridity	gustiness	jerkiness
bellicose	clinician	curliness	emotional	floristic	gutsiness	jesuitise
benzidine	coalition	currishly	emotivity	floristry	hagridden	jesuitism
bestially	coaxially	cursively	emptiness	flowingly	hairiness	Judaistic
bestirred	coaxingly	curtilage	enchilada	fluxional	haltingly	juiciness
biblicism	cocainise	curviform	encrimson	flyfisher	hamfisted	jumpiness
biblicist	cocainism	cuspidate	encrinite	foeticide	handiness	justiciar
billiards	coccidium	cymbidium	eradicate	fogginess	handiwork	justifier
billionth	cochineal	cymbiform	eremitism	foolishly	happiness	kaolinise
bismillah	cockiness	cyprinoid	eroticism	foppishly	harbinger	kaolinite
blazingly	coecilian	dalliance	eruciform	forbidden	hardihood	keelivine
bombilate	coffinite	damningly	eruditely	foreigner	hardiment	khedivial
bombinate	cognisant	dandiacal	erudition	forgiving	hardiness	kiddingly
bonniness	cognition	Darwinian	Esquimaux	formicary	Hashimite	killifish
bookishly	cognitive	Darwinism	esurience	formicate	hastiness	kinkiness
boorishly	coheiress	Darwinist	esuriency	fornicate	headiness	kittiwake
boskiness	colligate	dashingly	ethnicity	fortifier	heaviness	knavishly
bossiness	collimate	deacidify	euclidean	fortitude	Hebridean	knowingly
bowwindow	collinear	deceitful	evaginate	fossicker	hedgingly	lacrimose
boxgirder	collision	declinate	evasively	fossilise	heftiness	lagniappe
brazilnut	coltishly	declivity	examinant	fragility	hellishly	lancinate
Briticise	combinate	declivous	examinate	frigidity	hendiadys	lankiness
Briticism	comfiture	dentiform	exoticism	frolicked	herbicide	Laodicean
Britisher	commingle	dentistry	explicate	fruticose	herbivore	larvicide
brutishly	comminute	dentition	exquisite	fulfilled	hermitage	lassitude
bulginess	commissar	denyingly	extricate	fulfiller	herniated	lastingly
bulkiness	committal	deoxidise	extrinsic	fulminant	hetairism	latticing
bullishly	committed	derringdo	fabricant	fulminate	heuristic	lawgiving
bumpiness	committee			fulminous	hispidity	leakiness

```
leeringly  mirkiness  outfitter  plenitude  randiness  septicity  suasively
legginess  misdirect  outgiving  podginess  ranginess  sequinned  subdivide
lentiform  misgiving  outridden  poeticise  rantingly  serviette  sublimate
liability  mispickel  outrigger  poeticism  raspingly  servilely  sublimely
ligniform  missioner  outwitted  pollinate  readiness  servility  sublimity
liltingly  mistigris  overissue  pollinium  realistic  servitude  submitted
limpidity  mistiness  palliasse  popliteal  reanimate  sessional  subsidise
liquidate  mockingly  pallidity  porringer  reclinate  sexlinked  subtilise
liquidise  monsignor  palmipede  porticoes  recoinage  shadiness  succinate
liquidity  monticule  palmistry  posticous  rectifier  shakiness  sulkiness
lispingly  moodiness  palmitate  postilion  rectitude  shininess  summingup
loftiness  morbidity  palpitant  pratingly  reediness  showiness  sunniness
longicorn  morrisman  palpitate  precipice  rejoicing  sickishly  surcingle
longingly  mortician  pantingly  precisely  rejoinder  sideissue  surficial
longitude  mosaicism  parricide  precisian  remainder  significs  surliness
louringly  mosaicist  parsimony  precision  rendition  silkiness  suspicion
lousiness  mosaicked  partially  predicant  replicate  silliness  swinishly
loutishly  muddiness  partition  predicate  reprieval  skydiving  symbiosis
lowliness  muffineer  partitive  predictor  reprimand  slavishly  symbiotic
lowminded  muffinman  passional  predigest  reptilian  sliminess  syndicate
lubricant  mugginess  passivate  predikant  requisite  smilingly  syphilise
lubricate  mullioned  passively  prefigure  restiform  smokiness  syphiloid
lubricity  multifoil  passivity  prefixion  restitute  snakiness  tackiness
lubricous  multiform  pasticcio  president  restively  snowiness  tactician
luckiness  multilane  pastiness  presidial  retrieval  soapiness  tactility
lumpiness  multipara  patriarch  presidium  retriever  sobbingly  tactitian
lumpishly  multiplex  patrician  prevision  rewritten  sobriquet  taeniasis
lustihood  multitude  patricide  primipara  ringingly  sobsister  tahsildar
lustiness  mummified  patrimony  primitive  riskiness  soggingly  tanliquor
machinate  murkiness  patriotic  privilege  rockiness  soidisant  tanpickle
machinery  muskiness  patristic  profilist  rodfisher  soldierly  tardiness
machinist  mustiness  pectinate  profiteer  roguishly  solmisate  tartishly
magnifico  muzziness  peevishly  prolicide  roominess  sootiness  tastiness
magnifier  mydriasis  pellitory  prolixity  routinely  sophister  tattiness
magnitude  mydriatic  pencilled  prominent  routinism  sophistic  tawniness
mammiform  mysticism  penciller  promising  routinist  sophistry  teasingly
manginess  mystifier  penniless  propionic  rowdiness  soppiness  tellingly
manliness  mythicise  pensioner  prosiness  rubricate  sorriness  tendinous
mansionry  mythicism  pensively  provident  rubrician  sortilege  tensility
manticore  mythicist  perdition  providing  ruddiness  sortition  tensional
maquisard  narcissus  perkiness  provision  ruffianly  sottishly  terminate
marginate  nastiness  permitted  provisory  runcinate  sparingly  terminism
martially  nattiness  permitter  proximate  rusticate  spatially  terminist
Martinmas  neediness  persimmon  proximity  rusticity  specially  termitary
massiness  negligent  pertinent  prudishly  rustiness  specialty  territory
massively  negritude  pessimism  prurience  sacciform  specifier  tessitura
masticate  neolithic  pessimist  pruriency  sacrifice  spiciness  testifier
matriarch  nerviness  pesticide  psoriasis  sacrilege  spikiness  testimony
matricide  nescience  pestilent  psoriatic  sacristan  spininess  testiness
matricula  netwinged  pethidine  publicise  salpinges  spirillum  Thomistic
matrimony  newsiness  petticoat  publicist  saltiness  spiritism  thyristor
mawkishly  nictitate  pettiness  publicity  sandiness  spiritist  tinniness
mealiness  nigricant  pettishly  publisher  sappiness  spiritoso  tipsiness
meaningly  nigritude  pettitoes  pudginess  Sardinian  spiritous  tittivate
meatiness  nitpicker  pharisaic  puerility  sauciness  spiritual  tonsillar
meltingly  noctiluca  philippic  puffiness  scaliness  spirituel  torpidity
memoirist  noisiness  phoniness  pulpiness  scarifier  spoliator  torridity
mendicant  nonlinear  physician  pulpiteer  schlieren  stabilise  torsional
mendicity  nonviable  physicist  pulvillus  schnitzel  stability  touristic
merciless  nourisher  physicked  pulvinate  scoliosis  staginess  tradition
merriment  nowhither  pianistic  purringly  scoliotic  Stagirite  trepidant
merriness  nullifier  picnicked  pursiness  scorifier  Stalinism  trilinear
messianic  nullipara  picnicker  pushiness  Scoticise  Stalinist  trilithon
messieurs  nullipore  pietistic  pushingly  scutiform  staminate  trivially
messiness  nutriment  piggishly  putridity  seagirdle  stational  tubbiness
metricate  nutrition  pinkiness  pycnidium  seaminess  stationer  tuitional
metrician  nutritive  pinnipede  quakiness  searingly  statistic  turbidity
metricise  nuttiness  pisciform  qualified  sectility  sterilise  turbinate
metricist  obbligato  pithiness  qualifier  sectional  sterility  turgidity
midwicket  obedience  pituitary  quirister  seediness  stipitate  turpitude
midwifery  obstinacy  pityingly  quotidian  seemingly  stolidity  twofisted
midwinter  obstinate  pizzicati  rabbinate  selfimage  stoniness  Ukrainian
milkiness  odalisque  pizzicato  rabbinism  selfishly  storiated  uliginous
milligram  onanistic  placidity  rabbinist  semeiotic  studiedly  unanimity
millinery  opinioned  planisher  raffinate  sensitise  stupidity  unanimous
millionth  orchidist  platinise  raffinose  sensitive  styliform  unblended
millipede  orificial  platinoid  raffishly  sentience  stylishly  unbridled
millivolt  originate  platinous  raininess  sentiency  stylistic  unfailing
mincingly  oubliette  platitude  rancidity  sentiment  suability  unfeigned
```

```
unifiable  Wyclifite  pranksome  angelical  complexly  firelight  lendlease
unitively  yawningly  prankster  angularly  complexus  footlight  levelling
unknitted  Yiddisher  quickener  ankylosis  compliant  footloose  levelness
unpointed  coadjutor  quicklime  ankylotic  confluent  frailness  libellant
unskilful  forejudge  quickness  annelidan  copolymer  freelance  libelling
unskilled  limejuice  quicksand  annularly  coralline  freeliver  libellist
unsmiling  marijuana  quickstep  annulated  corallite  fusillade  libellous
unwritten  overjoyed  rebukable  annulling  coralloid  gavelkind  limelight
Upanishad  Afrikaans  sharkskin  annulment  corollary  gearlever  lobulated
uraninite  Afrikaner  sheikhdom  aphyllous  cotillion  gentleman  longlived
uxoricide  antiknock  shockable  appalling  cotyledon  ginglymus  lovelight
vaccinate  blackball  shockhead  Appaloosa  covalence  gogglebox  madeleine
vampirism  blackbird  sitzkrieg  appellant  covalency  golflinks  mainliner
varnisher  blackbuck  slackness  appellate  cruellest  gorblimey  mamillary
vastitude  blackcoat  sleekness  aquilegia  cucullate  grillroom  mamillate
veeringly  blackcock  slickness  argillite  cupelling  grillwork  manslayer
vendition  blackdamp  slinkweed  armillary  cytolysis  gruelling  maxillary
ventiduct  blackface  smackeroo  artillery  deadlight  guillemot  mayflower
ventifact  Blackfeet  sparkcoil  autolysis  decalcify  guilloche  medallion
ventilate  blackfish  sparkless  autolytic  decalitre  halflight  medallist
verbicide  blackflag  sparkplug  auxiliary  decalogue  handlebar  medullary
verdigris  Blackfoot  speakable  available  decilitre  headlight  medullate
vermicide  blackgame  speakeasy  availably  decillion  headliner  metalline
vermicule  blackhead  speckless  awfulness  decollate  highlands  metalling
vermiform  blackjack  stackable  bacillary  decollete  highlevel  metallise
vermifuge  blacklead  stackroom  balalaika  defalcate  highlight  metalloid
vermilion  blacklist  stackyard  basilican  defoliant  Himalayan  metalwork
verminate  blackmail  stalkeyed  battleaxe  defoliate  homiletic  middleman
verminous  blackness  stalkless  battlecry  demulcent  homologue  minelayer
versifier  blackwash  starkness  beadledom  desolater  horologer  mistletoe
versiform  blankness  stickwork  beryllium  desolator  horologic  modelling
versional  bleakness  stinkball  bevelling  desultory  humblebee  modillion
vestibule  blinkered  stinkbomb  bifoliate  devaluate  humiliate  modulator
vestigial  blockader  stinkhorn  bivalence  developer  hypallage  monolatry
vestigium  blockhead  stinktrap  bivalency  devilfish  idealiser  monologic
vestiture  blockship  stinkweed  bobsleigh  devilling  idealless  monologue
viability  breakable  stinkwood  booklouse  devilment  ideologic  moonlight
vibrissae  breakaway  stockbook  bottlefed  diablerie  ideologue  moraliser
victimise  breakdown  stockdove  bottleful  didelphic  imbalance  muscleman
villiform  breakeven  stockfish  bridleway  displease  immolator  mutilator
vindicate  breakfast  stockinet  brilliant  divulsion  impelling  mycologic
violinist  breakneck  stocklist  bumblebee  doodlebug  impolitic  navelwort
Virgilian  brickwork  stockpile  bumbledon  doubleton  impulsion  nebuliser
virginals  brickyard  stockroom  caballero  dowelling  impulsive  needleful
virginity  briskness  stockwhip  caballine  drollness  impulsory  nobiliary
viscidity  checkered  stockyard  caballing  duralumin  inculcate  nodulated
vitriform  checklist  thankless  cailleach  dysplasia  inculpate  nonillion
vitriolic  checkmate  thickener  camelback  ebullient  indelible  novelette
voltinism  checkrein  thicketed  camelhair  echolalia  indelibly  obsolesce
vorticism  cheekbone  thickhead  canalboat  effulgent  indolence  occultism
vorticist  chickadee  thickknee  Candlemas  embellish  indulgent  occultist
vorticity  chickaree  thickness  candlenut  emolliate  infilling  ocellated
vorticose  chickling  thinkable  capillary  emollient  inhalator  octillion
vulpinism  chickweed  thinktank  carolling  endolymph  insolence  oecologic
vulpinite  chockfull  trackless  catalepsy  enrolling  insoluble  oncologic
wackiness  clerkship  tracksuit  catalexes  enrolment  insolubly  ontologic
waggishly  cloakroom  trickless  catalexis  entelechy  insolvent  oriflamme
wailingly  clockwise  tricksily  catalogue  enucleate  insularly  oscillate
warningly  clockwork  trickster  catalyser  epaulette  insulator  overladen
washiness  crackdown  trinketer  catalyses  epiclesis  intellect  overleapt
waspishly  crackling  trinketry  catalysis  equaliser  invalidly  overlying
weariless  cracksman  trunkcall  catalytic  equalling  involucre  paillasse
weariness  crankcase  trunkfish  cattleman  escalator  involuted  paillette
wearisome  cricketer  trunkroad  cavalcade  ethylenic  isallobar  palillogy
weediness  crookback  twinkling  cavilling  eucalypti  isoclinal  panelling
weevilled  crookedly  unbeknown  challenge  excellent  isoclinic  panellist
willingly  crookneck  weakkneed  chapleted  excelling  jewellery  papillary
windiness  drinkable  wellknown  charlatan  excelsior  jewelweed  papillate
winningly  drunkenly  whiskered  charlotte  exculpate  jocularly  papilloma
witticism  fleckless  acellular  chillness  exfoliate  jubilance  papillose
wittiness  foreknown  aerolitic  chitlings  expellent  kentledge  papillote
wittingly  frankness  affiliate  choplogic  expelling  kilolitre  paralalia
wolfishly  frockcoat  agrologic  cipollino  expulsion  knowledge  paralexia
woodiness  Greekless  alkaloses  cisalpine  expulsive  labelling  paralysis
wooziness  iceskater  alkalosis  civiliser  extolling  lamellate  paralytic
wordiness  jackknife  ambulacra  cobaltite  extolment  lamellose  parfleche
worriedly  knockdown  ambulance  cobaltous  eyeglance  lamplight  patellate
worriment  knockknee  ancillary  cochleate  familyman  landloper  pearlitic
worrisome  outskirts  angelfish  complaint  feculence  lavaliere  pearlwort
```

peculator	shallowly	trialogue	bolometry	gasometer	polymeric	tonometer
pedalling	shellback	triclinia	bookmaker	goalmouth	polymorph	totempole
penultima	shellbark	triclinic	Brahmanic	groomsman	pragmatic	traumatic
perilling	shellfire	triploidy	Brahminee	hamamelis	preemptor	trimmings
perilymph	shellfish	tubularly	Brahminic	hegemonic	prismatic	triumphal
petulance	shellheap	tumblebug	bregmatic	hexameter	psalmbook	triumviri
petulancy	shellwork	typhlitis	broomcorn	hodometer	psalmodic	typemetal
phellogen	shieldbug	umbellate	broomrape	homemaker	ptarmigan	ultimatum
phyllopod	shieldfem	umbellule	brummagem	hypomania	pyramidal	undamaged
pisolitic	shillelah	umbilical	buxomness	hypomanic	pyramidic	unlimited
pixilated	shouldest	umbilicus	cacuminal	idiomatic	pyramidon	unnamable
popularly	sibilance	unalloyed	calamanco	illomened	pyromancy	untimeous
proclitic	sibilancy	unbalance	Camembert	incommode	pyromania	unwomanly
pupillage	sibylline	undulated	carambola	incumbent	pyrometer	vademecum
pupillary	sickleave	ungallant	catamaran	indemnify	pyrometry	vasomotor
purulence	sidelight	unhelpful	catamount	indemnity	rainmaker	vehemence
purulency	sigillary	uniplanar	charmeuse	inhumanly	rearmouse	voltmeter
pyrolater	sigillate	unselfish	charmless	insomniac	recombine	volumeter
pyrolatry	similarly	unsullied	chlamydes	intumesce	recommend	wattmeter
pyrolysis	simpleton	unwelcome	chromatic	ironmould	recompose	wehrmacht
pyrolytic	simplices	unwilling	chromatin	Islamitic	recumbent	workmanly
quillwort	simulacra	upholster	cinematic	judgmatic	reremouse	xeromorph
quodlibet	simulacre	usualness	claimable	kilometre	resumable	yohimbine
rafflesia	simulator	vacillant	coalmouse	kinematic	rheumatic	zeugmatic
ravelling	simulcast	vacillate	colemouse	kingmaker	roadmetal	zygomatic
ravelment	singleton	vexillary	columbary	krummhorn	rocambole	abounding
rearlight	sinologue	videlicet	Columbian	lagomorph	saltmarsh	accentual
rebelling	smallarms	vigilance	columbine	lawnmower	schematic	actinozoa
rebellion	smallness	vigilante	columbite	leafmould	sciamachy	adjunctly
recalesce	smalltime	virulence	columbium	leitmotif	scrambler	adminicle
recollect	snailfish	virulency	columella	leitmotiv	scramming	admonitor
redolence	soliloquy	vitellary	columnist	locomotor	scrimmage	adornment
refulgent	spellbind	vitelline	corymbose	logomachy	scrimpily	adrenalin
regularly	spellican	vocaliser	decametre	loudmouth	scrimshaw	advantage
regulator	spillikin	vocalness	decimally	lovematch	scrumhalf	Adventism
repellant	spoilsman	vowelless	decimator	lysimeter	scrummage	Adventist
repellent	spotlight	warblefly	decimetre	machmeter	selfmoved	adventive
repelling	squalidly	wavellite	decomplex	Mahometan	semimetal	adventure
repulsion	squelcher	wheelbase	decompose	manometer	shipmoney	agronomic
repulsive	stableboy	wheelless	decumbent	maximally	shoemaker	ailanthus
rerelease	stableman	wheelwork	demimonde	mekometer	skiamachy	albinotic
resalable	stallfeed	whirligig	dharmsala	melomania	slowmatch	Algonkian
resilient	starlight	whirlpool	disembark	mesomorph	solemnise	Algonquin
resoluble	steelclad	whirlwind	disembody	metameric	solemnity	alienable
resolvent	steelhead	woodlouse	dolomitic	miasmatic	Solomonic	alienator
resultant	steelwork	yodelling	dosimeter	milometer	sonometer	alignment
resultful	steelyard	zibelline	dosimetry	minimally	spasmodic	allantois
retaliate	stellated	abdominal	dreamboat	misemploy	spermatic	almandine
revelator	stillborn	abysmally	dreamland	monomania	spermatid	alpenhorn
revelling	stillhunt	accompany	dreamless	monomeric	squamosal	amianthus
revolting	stillness	adnominal	dreamlike	muniments	stammerer	anamnesis
revulsion	stillroom	aerometer	drummajor	muskmelon	staymaker	andantino
revulsive	stoolball	aerometry	dynamical	Nilometer	steamboat	antenatal
rivalling	stoplight	allemande	dynamiter	nonsmoker	steampipe	antennary
rivalrous	subalpine	allomorph	eclampsia	octameter	steamship	antennule
rivelling	subaltern	altimeter	eclamptic	oecumenic	stigmatic	antinodal
rubellite	sunflower	antimonic	ectomorph	oenomancy	stormbelt	antinomic
ruddleman	suppliant	argumenta	encomiast	opsimathy	stormbird	antinovel
rushlight	surpliced	artemisia	encompass	optometer	stormcock	aplanatic
Sabellian	swellfish	ashamedly	endomixis	optometry	stormcone	appendage
saddlebag	synclinal	assembler	endomorph	osmometer	stormless	appendant
saddlebow	tabularly	assumable	enigmatic	overmatch	stormsail	argentine
safflower	tabulator	assumably	enzymatic	pacemaker	stromatic	argentite
satellite	taillight	assumpsit	ephemeral	paramatta	strumitis	argentous
scagliola	tegularly	asthmatic	ephemeras	paramedic	strumming	arsenical
scallawag	theologic	asymmetry	ephemerid	parameter	swimmable	arsenious
scallywag	theologue	athematic	ephemeron	paramorph	swimmeret	ascendant
schilling	thralldom	atmometer	ergometer	paramount	tacamahac	ascendent
scholarly	thrilling	attempter	estaminet	pedometer	taximeter	ascension
scholiast	timelapse	automatic	estimable	penumbral	telamones	ascensive
scrollsaw	timelimit	automaton	estimator	perimeter	telemeter	assonance
secularly	titillate	axiomatic	exosmosis	perimorph	telemetry	Athenaeum
semblable	tittlebat	bainmarie	exosmotic	plasmatic	tentmaker	Atlantean
semblably	titularly	barometer	extempore	plasmodia	theomachy	attendant
semblance	totaliser	barometry	flammable	pneumatic	theomania	attention
semilunar	totalling	belemnite	folkmusic	pneumonia	thermally	attentive
sepulcher	towelling	bicameral	Freemason	pneumonic	thermidor	attenuate
sepulchre	tramlines	binominal	frogmarch	polemical	thrombose	autonomic
sepulture	treillage	bolometer	gallmidge	polymathy	thrumming	Axminster

baronetcy	dominance	hyponasty	onionskin	sapanwood	thornback	anemogram
bayoneted	dominator	iguanodon	oogenesis	satanical	thornbill	angiology
beginning	dominical	immanence	oogenetic	satinbird	thornbush	angiomata
biconcave	Dominican	immanency	opponency	satinette	thornless	anglophil
bigeneric	drainpipe	immensely	ordinance	satinspar	thorntree	animosity
bilingual	drawnwork	immensity	organelle	satinwood	threnodic	anthocyan
bimonthly	dysentery	imminence	organiser	sciential	tomentose	anthology
bipinnate	dyspnoeic	imminency	organstop	scientism	tomentous	anthozoan
botanical	eccentric	impendent	organzine	scientist	toponymal	anxiously
braincase	eglantine	impending	orientate	scoundrel	toponymic	apologise
brainless	eirenicon	incensory	Orpington	seaanchor	tournedos	apologist
brainwash	Emmenthal	incentive	ostensive	secondary	tourneyer	approbate
brainwave	empennage	incondite	overnight	sedentary	trainable	aqueously
brownness	epaenetic	incunable	palankeen	seigneury	trainband	aragonite
Byzantine	ergonomic	indention	palanquin	seigniory	trainload	arduously
cadential	erroneous	indenture	paranoiac	selenious	triennial	astrocyte
cairngorm	essential	infantile	paranymph	selenitic	triennium	astrodome
calandria	eternally	infantine	parentage	semanteme	tyrannise	astrolabe
calendric	excentric	ingenious	patinated	semantics	tyrannous	astrology
calendula	expansile	ingenuity	pecuniary	seminally	unbending	astronaut
calenture	expansion	ingenuous	Pekingese	serenader	uncannily	astronomy
canonical	expansive	insensate	peninsula	serinette	uncinated	auctorial
cavendish	expensive	insincere	perennate	sevenfold	unconcern	audiology
celandine	extendant	insinuate	perennial	seventeen	unmindful	authoress
cementite	extensile	intendant	perinatal	seventhly	untenable	authorial
chaingang	extension	intensely	phrenetic	seventies	unwinking	authorise
chaingear	extensity	intensify	plainness	sexennial	valentine	authority
chainless	extensive	intension	plainsman	shrinkage	Varangian	awesomely
chainmail	extenuate	intensity	plainsong	snubnosed	Vedantist	baboonish
cheongsam	facundity	intensive	plaintiff	sphincter	verandaed	balconied
chernozem	Falangism	intention	plaintive	spinnaker	vicennial	bamboozle
chronical	Falangist	invention	poignancy	spinneret	vimineous	bandoleer
chronicle	farandole	inventive	polonaise	splendent	voluntary	bandolero
cleanness	fecundate	inventory	postnasal	splendour	volunteer	bandolier
cleansing	fecundity	japanning	postnatal	splenetic	wagonette	bandoline
clientage	felonious	jocundity	potentate	splenitis	wagonroof	batholite
clientele	femineity	Johannine	potential	splintery	wapentake	batholith
cockneyfy	financial	journeyer	praenomen	spoonbeak	weeknight	Bathonian
colonelcy	financier	juvenilia	preengage	spoonbill	womanhood	bentonite
coloniser	flannelly	laciniate	pregnable	spoonfeed	womaniser	benzoline
colonnade	flouncing	laminaria	pregnancy	spoonmeat	womankind	beslobber
Cominform	forenamed	laminated	proenzyme	springald	womanlike	bethought
Comintern	fortnight	laryngeal	prognoses	springbok	womenfolk	betrothal
conundrum	fraenulum	learnable	prognosis	springily	womenkind	betrothed
coroneted	galantine	learnedly	queenhood	springing	woodnymph	biliously
cotangent	galenical	legendary	queenless	springlet	zamindary	biologist
crownless	galingale	Levantine	queenlike	sprinkler	zemindary	bionomics
cutaneous	gerundial	licensure	queenpost	squinancy	absconder	bishopric
cutinised	gerundive	limonitic	queenship	stagnancy	acidophil	bonhomous
cylindric	gigantism	linenfold	raconteur	stainable	adenoidal	borrowing
davenport	girandole	lorgnette	ranunculi	stainless	adenomata	boycotter
debenture	Girondist	lovingcup	recension	stauncher	adenosine	bulbously
decennary	goodnight	luminance	reconcile	staunchly	adipocere	bundobust
decennial	greenback	macintosh	recondite	steenkirk	adiposity	byproduct
decennium	greenbelt	malanders	reconfirm	sternmost	aepyornis	cacholong
decongest	greeneyed	masonried	reconvene	sternness	aetiology	Caenozoic
decontrol	greengage	melanosis	reconvert	sternpost	agriology	Cainozoic
defendant	greenhorn	melanotic	redingote	sternward	aircooled	caliology
defensive	greenness	mementoes	redundant	strangely	airworthy	callosity
definable	greenroom	meningeal	remanence	strangler	alveolate	callously
definably	greensand	mesentery	remindful	strangles	amazonian	Cambodian
delineate	greenweed	metonymic	reminisce	strenuous	ambrosial	cannonade
demandant	greenwood	midinette	remontant	stringent	aminoacid	cannoneer
demanding	groundage	misinform	repentant	strongarm	amorously	cannonier
dependant	groundash	misoneism	rerunning	strongbox	amyloidal	Cantonese
dependent	groundhog	misoneist	resentful	strongish	amylopsin	cantorial
detention	grounding	momentary	resonance	strongyle	anabolism	carbonado
detonator	groundivy	momentous	resonator	strontium	analogise	carbonate
diagnoses	groundnut	Mycenaean	retention	supinator	analogist	carbonise
diagnosis	groundsel	nepenthes	retentive	synonymic	analogous	carpology
dimension	hackneyed	nominable	retinitis	syringeal	anatomise	carronade
diningcar	haranguer	nominally	retinulae	tarantara	anatomist	cartogram
disannul	hardnosed	nominator	retinular	tarantass	anchorage	cartology
disengage	hirundine	nonentity	rosenoble	tarantism	anchoress	cartouche
disentail	homonymic	oakenshaw	rosinweed	tarantula	anchorite	caryopsis
disentomb	homuncle	obconical	rotundity	taxonomic	anchorman	cassoulet
disinfect	homunculi	obtention	rowantree	technical	androecia	cassowary
disinfest	humankind	octennial	ruminator	technique	androgyne	ceanothus
diurnally	humanness	offensive	salangane	theandric	androgyny	ceanothus

censorial	cyclotron	ethmoidal	harmonist	klinostat	Mongoloid	patrology
chamomile	cystocarp	ethnology	harmonium	laccolith	mongooses	patronage
Charolais	cystolith	etymology	harmotome	lampooner	monsoonal	patroness
chatoyant	cystotomy	euchology	harpooner	landowner	monzonite	patronise
chelonian	daltonism	euphonise	Harrovian	Langobard	Mormonism	paulownia
chibouque	deaconess	euphonium	harrowing	langouste	mucronate	Pavlovian
chipolata	defroster	euphorbia	hectogram	leftovers	muscovado	peasouper
chiropody	deinosaur	eutrophic	heinously	legionary	muscovite	penholder
chocolate	deodorant	evaporate	heliogram	leptosome	myelomata	peptonise
chorology	deodorise	exclosure	heliostat	leucocyte	myologist	percolate
chthonian	despoiler	exopodite	heliotype	leucotome	myriorama	perforate
clamorous	despotism	exploiter	heliozoan	leucotomy	mythology	performer
cocoonery	deviously	explosion	heliozoic	leukocyte	narcotine	periodate
coelomata	diabolise	explosive	herborise	limnology	narcotise	personage
coelomate	diabolism	extrovert	hessonite	lineolate	narcotism	personate
coelostat	diabolist	factorage	hideously	liquorice	natrolite	personify
coenobite	diaconate	factorial	hierodule	liquorish	necrology	personnel
coenobium	dialogise	factorise	hierogram	lissomely	necrophil	pestology
coenosarc	dialogism	faggoting	hierology	lithology	necrotise	petiolate
colcothar	dialogist	fatuously	hippocras	lithopone	negroidal	petiolule
collocate	diatomite	faveolate	hircosity	lithotomy	Negroness	petroleum
collodion	dichogamy	fellowman	histogeny	logaoedic	negrophil	petrology
colloidal	dichotomy	ferrotype	histogram	Londonian	negrophil	phagocyte
colloquia	dicrotism	festology	histology	Londonism	neologian	phenology
collotype	diplomacy	fibroline	historian	Longobard	neologise	phenomena
comforter	diplomate	fibromata	hobgoblin	lophodont	neologism	phenotype
commodity	discoidal	flavorous	hobnobbed	lowloader	neologist	pheromone
commodore	discolour	following	hobnobber	macrocosm	nephology	philogyny
commonage	discomfit	forgotten	homeopath	macrocyte	nervously	philology
commonlaw	discommon	forlornly	howsoever	malformed	Nestorian	Philomela
commotion	discourse	fossorial	hugeously	malvoisie	neuroglia	phonogram
component	discovert	frivolity	hydrocele	mammonism	neurology	phonolite
composite	discovery	frivolled	hydrofoil	mammonist	neuromata	phonology
composure	disforest	frivolous	hydrology	mammonist	neuropath	photocell
concocter	dishonest	fulsomely	hydrolyse	mandoline	Newtonian	photocopy
concoctor	dishonour	furiously	hydrolyte	marmoreal	niccolite	photogene
concordat	dislocate	fusionist	hydronium	marrowfat	nigrosine	photophil
concourse	disposure	gabionade	hydrosome	matronage	nocuously	photopsia
conformal	dissocial	gallonage	hydroxide	marrowfat	noisomely	phototype
conformer	dissolute	gallooned	hydrozoan	matronise	nostology	phycology
consonant	dissonant	gallopade	hydrozoon	mausoleum	notionist	phylogeny
consortia	dittology	Gallophil	hygrostat	meliorate	noxiously	phytogeny
convolute	doctorate	galloping	hymnology	meliorism	obviously	phytology
convolved	doctorial	gallowses	hypnoidal	meliorist	ochlocrat	phytotomy
copiously	dogcollar	gambolled	hypnology	meliority	oddjobber	phytotron
coproduce	dogoodism	gammoning	hypnotise	Mennonite	oddjobman	pictogram
coprolite	draconian	garrotter	hypnotism	meteorist	odorously	pictorial
coprology	dragomans	gasconade	hypnotist	meteorite	offcolour	pipeorgan
coreopsis	dragoness	gasholder	ichnology	meteoroid	oilcolour	pistoleer
cormorant	dragonfly	gemmology	iconology	methodise	Oligocene	pistolled
cornopean	dragoning	geobotany	illboding	Methodism	oligopoly	piteously
corporate	dubiosity	geologise	illgotten	Methodist	ominously	Platonise
corporeal	dubiously	geologist	imbroglio	methought	onerously	Platonism
corposant	duteously	geoponics	impiously	metrology	operosely	Platonist
corrosion	ealdorman	gibbosity	implosion	metronome	operosity	Pleiocene
corrosive	ecologist	gibbously	implosive	mezzotint	ophiology	plutocrat
cosmogeny	economics	glamorise	improbity	microbial	oratorial	plutonian
cosmogony	economise	glamorous	impromptu	microchip	oratorian	Plutonism
cosmology	economist	globosity	improvise	microcosm	orologist	Plutonist
cosmonaut	editorial	glucoside	inamorata	microcyte	orthodoxy	plutonist
cosmorama	elaborate	glycoside	inclosure	microfilm	orthoepic	podzolise
coxcombry	embrocate	godmother	inflowing	microgram	osteoderm	poisonous
crinoidal	embroglio	gondolier	ingrowing	microlite	osteogeny	polyonymy
crinoline	embroider	gongorism	innholder	microlith	osteology	pomposity
crocodile	emulously	gorgonian	inodorous	micrology	osteopath	pompously
cuckoldry	enamoured	gorgonise	introduce	micromesh	Ostrogoth	pontoneer
curiosity	enchorial	Gregorian	introject	micropsia	otologist	pontonier
curiously	enclosure	guncotton	introvert	micropyle	outgoings	portolano
cursorial	engrosser	gunpowder	inviolacy	microsome	outworker	potboiler
cursorily	enviously	haemostat	inviolate	microtome	pantomime	potholing
custodial	epidosite	hagiology	inwrought	microtomy	parlously	potpourri
custodian	epilogist	Halloween	irksomely	microtone	parsonage	pozzolana
customary	epipolism	Hallowmas	isagogics	microwave	pastorale	precocial
customise	epitomise	handorgan	isopodous	Miltonian	pastorate	precocity
cycloidal	epitomist	haplology	jargonise	misgovern	pathogeny	preconise
cyclopean	epizootic	harbourer	jealously	mnemonics	pathology	premonish
cyclopian	espionage	harmonica	juniorate	mnemonist	patrolled	premotion
cyclopses	Esthonian	harmonics	juniority	Mongolian	patroller	prenotion
cyclorama	Ethiopian	harmonise	karyotype	mongolism	patrolman	prepotent

primordia	schoolbag	symposial	viscounty	crispness	idiopathy	receptive
proboscis	schoolboy	symposium	viscously	curlpaper	idioplasm	recipient
proconsul	schooling	syncopate	visionary	cymophane	incapable	reefpoint
prologise	schoolman	tailoress	visionist	cytoplasm	incapably	ricepaper
promotion	scotomata	tailoring	vitiosity	dayspring	inception	rockplant
promotive	seasoning	tallowish	voodooism	decapodal	inceptive	roofplate
pronounce	seaworthy	tambourin	voodooist	decapodan	incipient	rustproof
proponent	sectorial	tamponade	waggonage	deception	insipidly	sailplane
prorogate	semiology	tattooist	walloping	deceptive	irruption	saltpetre
prosodist	semiotics	tautology	warbonnet	dipeptide	irruptive	sandpaper
protonema	senhorita	tectonics	warmonger	disappear	jackplane	sandpiper
prototype	seniority	tectorial	webfooted	doorplate	mailplane	saxophone
protozoal	sensorial	tediously	welcoming	drawplate	manipular	scalplock
protozoan	sensorium	teknonymy	werwolves	ecosphere	manyplies	scorpioid
protozoic	sepiolite	teleology	whosoever	ectophyte	megaphone	scrapbook
protozoon	seriously	temporary	willowish	ectoplasm	melaphyre	scrapheap
provoking	sermonise	temporise	windowbox	ellipsoid	menopause	scrapiron
provostry	shemozzle	tenuously	winsomely	encephala	meropidan	scrappily
pterosaur	shipowner	terrorise	yellowdog	endophagy	mesophyll	scrapping
pulmonary	sigmoidal	terrorism	yellowish	endophyte	mesophyte	scrapyard
pulmonate	signorial	terrorist	zealously	endoplasm	metaphase	scripture
purloiner	signorina	teutonise	zincotype	enrapture	metaplasm	sculpture
purposely	sinuosity	Teutonism	zirconium	entophyte	monophagy	seedpearl
purposive	sinuously	Teutonist	zoologist	equipment	monoplane	seedplant
puzzolana	siphonage	thyroxine	zootomist	equipoise	mothproof	selfpride
quinoline	sixfooter	timeously	abruption	equipping	mycophagy	semaphore
quixotism	skijoring	tonsorial	acceptant	escapable	nameplate	semiplume
radiocast	skyrocket	tremolant	acceptive	esemplasy	nemophila	sharpener
radiogram	Slavonian	tremolite	accipiter	estoppage	newspaper	sharpeyed
radiology	Slavophil	tribology	acropetal	estopping	newsprint	sharpness
rancorous	slivovitz	tricolour	acropolis	exceptant	ninepence	sharpshod
randomise	sociogram	trifocals	ademption	excepting	ninepenny	sheepcote
raptorial	sociology	trifolium	aerophyte	exception	nosepiece	sheepfold
rationale	sociopath	triforium	aeroplane	exceptive	notepaper	sheephook
rationing	somnolent	trilobate	allopathy	excipient	occipital	sheeplice
raucously	sophomore	trilobite	allophone	exemplary	occupancy	sheepskin
rauwolfia	Sorbonist	trinomial	alloplasm	exemplify	octopodes	sheeptick
reasoning	sorrowful	tropology	amorphism	exemption	oenophile	sheepwalk
reckoning	spinosity	turboprop	amorphous	exosphere	oenophily	sheepwash
rectorate	Spinozism	Turcomans	antipasto	eyeopener	oesophagi	shotproof
rectorial	Spinozist	Turkomans	antipathy	fireplace	offspring	showpiece
reedorgan	spirogyra	typhoidal	antiphony	firepower	optophone	showplace
rencontre	sporocarp	unadopted	antipodal	fireproof	outspoken	sinophile
reprobate	sporocyst	unadorned	antipodes	fishplate	outspread	Sisyphean
reprocess	sporogeny	unclothed	aquaplane	fivepence	overpitch	sleepless
reproduce	statocyst	unclouded	Areopagus	fivepenny	overpower	snowplant
responder	statolith	uncropped	asymptote	flippancy	overprice	softpedal
rethought	stegosaur	uncrossed	autopilot	foolproof	overprint	soleplate
retrocede	stenotype	uncrowned	backpedal	footpedal	overproof	solipsism
retrodden	stenotypy	unicolour	ballpoint	footplate	panoplied	solipsist
retroflex	steroidal	uniformly	basipetal	footpound	parapeted	soupplate
retroject	stolonate	unisonant	bedspread	footprint	parapodia	stagparty
retrousse	stuporous	unisonous	bedspring	fourpence	peneplain	stampduty
retrovert	stylobate	unknowing	bellpunch	fourpenny	peneplane	stampmill
rhinology	subcostal	unpeopled	bicipital	gangplank	peripatus	stampnote
rhizocarp	subnormal	unspotted	biosphere	geosphere	periphery	steepness
rhizoidal	subrogate	unstopped	blaspheme	germplasm	periplast	stippling
rhodolite	subtopian	unthought	blasphemy	germproof	phosphate	stoppress
rhodonite	succotash	untrodden	bluepoint	gonophore	phosphene	straphang
rhodopsin	succourer	unwrought	blueprint	grappling	phosphide	strapless
Ribbonism	suctorial	uranology	bombproof	graspable	phosphine	strappado
riotously	suctorian	urceolate	bookplate	gynophore	phosphite	strapping
ruinously	suffocate	uvarovite	bryophyte	gyroplane	pikeperch	strapwork
Russophil	sunbonnet	vacuolate	cacophony	hairpiece	plumpness	strapwort
sailoring	sundowner	vacuously	caliphate	halfpence	polyphagy	stripling
sailorman	sunlounge	variolate	cataplasm	halfpenny	polyphase	stripping
sallowish	supporter	variolite	cataplexy	halfprice	polyphone	stropping
salmonoid	supposing	varioloid	catoptric	halophile	polyphony	sunspurge
santolina	surrogate	variolous	champagne	halophyte	polyploid	sweepback
santonica	syllogise	variously	champaign	handpress	polyptych	sycophant
sarcocarp	syllogism	vectorial	champerty	headphone	pourpoint	synoptist
sarcomata	symbolics	verbosely	champleve	headpiece	promptbox	tailpiece
sartorial	symbolise	verbosity	cheapjack	heelpiece	puerperal	telepathy
sartorius	symbolism	viciously	cheapness	hexaploid	rainproof	telephone
sauropoda	symbolist	Victorian	colophony	holophote	ratepayer	telephony
scapolite	symbology	victorine	homophone	homophony	rebaptise	telephoto
scatology	sympodial	videotape	coryphaei	homoplasy	recapping	telophase
schnorkel	sympodium	villosity	crampfish	homopolar	recapture	theophany
schnorrer	symposiac	viscosity	crippling	hoofprint	reception	timepiece

tinopener	afterlife	cartridge	diatropic	fragrancy	injurious	loverless
toxophily	aftermath	Castroism	dichroism	freerange	innermost	lowercase
trappings	aftermost	catarhine	dichromat	freerider	innervate	lowerdeck
troopship	afternoon	catarrhal	dichromic	friarbird	inscriber	lowermost
truepenny	aftertime	caterwaul	dimorphic	fumarolic	insertion	lumbrical
trumpedup	afterword	cavernous	disarming	gabardine	inservice	lumbricus
trumpeter	algarroba	cedarwood	disbranch	gaberdine	insurable	luxuriant
tuliproot	algorithm	centrally	discredit	gastraeum	insurance	luxuriate
tuliptree	alpargata	centreing	disgracer	gastritis	insurgent	luxurious
tulipwood	alterable	chairlady	disorient	gastropod	interbred	macaronic
unhappily	altercate	cheerless	dispraise	gastrulae	intercede	macerator
unpopular	alternant	cherrypie	distraint	generable	intercept	maharajah
unzipping	alternate	chlorella	divergent	generalia	intercity	maharanee
viewpoint	amauroses	chloritic	diversely	generally	intercrop	maharishi
wallpaper	amaurosis	chlorosis	diversify	generator	interdict	majordomo
wallplate	amaurotic	chlorotic	diversion	geography	interface	majorette
whimperer	ambergris	cigarette	diversity	geotropic	interfere	majorship
whipperin	amourette	cigarillo	diverting	glaireous	interfile	makeready
whisperer	ampersand	cineraria	doctrinal	governess	interflow	malarious
willpower	anabranch	cinereous	doleritic	guerrilla	interfuse	manorseat
windproof	anacruses	clearance	dowerless	habergeon	interject	Masoretic
winepress	anacrusis	clearcole	downright	haverings	interknit	maternity
wirephoto	anaerobic	cleareyed	downriver	haversack	interlace	mayoralty
workpiece	antarctic	clearness	dyscrasia	hazardous	interlard	mayorship
xenophile	anthracic	cockroach	dystrophy	heterodox	interleaf	memorable
xenophobe	anthropic	coherence	eagerness	heteronym	interline	memorably
xerophile	aphereses	coherency	Edwardian	heterosis	interlink	memoranda
xerophily	apheresis	colorific	effortful	hibernate	interlock	memoriter
xerophyte	apocrypha	comprador	eiderdown	Hibernian	interlope	miscreant
xylophone	apparatus	comprisal	eiderduck	hilarious	interlude	miscreate
antiquary	apparitor	congruent	eldership	hindrance	interment	miserable
antiquate	appertain	congruity	elutriate	Holarctic	internode	miserably
antiquity	apportion	congruous	embarrass	honoraria	interpage	Mithraism
brusquely	aquarelle	contralto	empirical	honorific	interplay	Mithraist
caciquism	arboreous	contrasty	empyreuma	hundredth	interpose	moderator
chisquare	arboretum	contrived	endurable	hyperbola	interpret	modernise
clinquant	Armorican	contriver	endurably	hyperbole	interring	modernism
moonquake	arteriole	copartner	endurance	hypergamy	interrupt	modernist
obliquely	arteritis	copyright	engarland	hypericum	intersect	modernity
obliquity	arthritic	covariant	enterable	hyperopia	intervein	monarchal
obsequent	arthritis	coverable	enteritis	hyperopic	intervene	monarchic
obsequial	arthropod	coverslip	entertain	ignorable	interview	monergism
obsequies	arthrosis	coverture	epigraphy	ignoramus	interwind	mongrelly
pipsqueak	ascertain	cowardice	errorless	ignorance	interwove	monorhyme
reliquary	asparagus	cranreuch	escortage	immersion	interzone	moonraker
reliquiae	aspartate	cumbrance	esperance	immorally	intorsion	motorable
seasquirt	aspersion	debarment	Esperanto	impartial	invariant	motorbike
setsquare	aspirator	debarring	etherical	imperator	inverness	motorboat
siliquose	assertion	decorator	eucaryote	imperfect	inversely	motorcade
trysquare	assertive	deference	excerptor	imperious	inversion	muckraker
aberrance	assurance	deferment	excoriate	important	inversive	myography
aberrancy	assuredly	deferring	excurrent	importune	invertase	naturally
abhorrent	assurgent	deformity	excursion	incarnate	isotropic	nefarious
abhorring	aubergine	delirious	excursive	incorrect	jaborandi	nemertean
abnormity	autarchic	demarcate	execrable	incorrupt	jacaranda	nemertine
absorbent	autarkist	demurrage	execrably	incurable	laborious	nephritic
absorbing	autoroute	demurring	expertise	incurably	labyrinth	nephritis
absurdism	babirussa	dendritic	expurgate	incurious	lacerable	nephrosis
absurdist	beeorchis	departure	exsertile	incurrent	lacertian	neutrally
absurdity	bifarious	depurator	exsertion	incurring	lacertine	nevermore
accordant	bifurcate	describer	exservice	incursion	lachrymal	nondriver
according	bilirubin	desertion	externals	incursive	laterally	nonprofit
accordion	biography	desirable	extirpate	incurvate	lazaretto	notoriety
adherence	bipartite	desirably	extorsive	inebriant	legerline	notorious
admirable	bivariant	destroyer	extortion	inebriate	leviratic	numerable
admirably	bivariate	detergent	extortive	inebriety	liberally	numerator
admiralty	bizarrely	determent	eyebright	inerrable	liberated	numerical
adsorbate	bleareyed	determine	Falernian	inerrancy	liberator	obcordate
adsorbent	bowerbird	deterrent	federally	inferable	libertine	objurgate
adverbial	boyfriend	detering	figurante	inference	literally	observant
adversary	briarroot	detersion	filtrable	inferring	literatim	obturator
adversely	briarwood	detersive	fimbriate	infertile	literator	obversely
adversity	brierroot	dethroner	flagrance	infirmary	literatus	obversion
advertent	brierwood	dextrally	flagrancy	infirmity	liturgics	occurrent
advertise	calorific	dextrorse	fluoresce	informant	liturgist	occurring
affirmant	camarilla	diacritic	fluorosis	infuriate	liverwort	odourless
aftercare	cameraman	diaereses	fluorspar	inharmony	liveryman	oestrogen
afterclap	camorrist	diaeresis	forereach	inherence	logarithm	offertory
afterglow	caparison	diarrhoea	fragrance	inheritor	longrange	olecranal

```
olecranon  refurbish  subarctic  undersign  advisedly  cocksfoot  embussing
oleoresin  refurnish  subbranch  undersold  aerospace  coinsurer  endoscope
opportune  regardant  subereous  undersong  albescent  coldshort  endoscopy
orderbook  regardful  sudorific  underspin  amassment  colosseum  endosperm
orderform  reparable  suffragan  undertake  ambuscade  colostomy  endospore
orderless  repertory  sugarbeet  undertint  amidships  colostrum  endosteal
orography  reportage  sugarcane  undertone  ancestral  coltsfoot  endosteum
otherness  reserpine  sugarloaf  undertook  andesitic  copesmate  equisetum
otherwise  reservist  sugarplum  undervest  antiserum  copestone  excessive
outermost  reservoir  superable  underwear  Arguseyed  corkscrew  excisable
outgrowth  resorbent  supercool  underwent  armistice  cornsalad  exciseman
ovenready  restraint  superfine  underwing  arrestant  cornstalk  excusable
overreach  resurface  superfuse  underwood  arresting  cornstone  excusably
overreact  resurgent  superheat  unearthly  asbestine  coruscant  expositor
ownership  resurrect  supernova  unharness  asbestous  coruscate  faldstool
pancratic  retardant  superpose  unhurried  ascospore  cowlstaff  farestage
panoramic  retortion  supersede  unthrifty  assistant  crassness  farmstead
pantryman  reverence  superstar  uppercase  autosomal  croissant  feedstock
paperback  reversely  supervene  uppermost  Aylesbury  crossable  feedstuff
paperclip  reversion  supervise  usherette  backsight  crossbeam  fenestrae
papergirl  rewarding  surprisal  utterable  backslang  crossbill  fenestral
paperthin  riderless  susurrant  utterance  backslide  crossbred  fetishism
paperwork  riverbank  suturally  utterless  backspace  crossette  fetishist
partridge  riverboat  swearword  uttermost  backstage  crosseyed  filmstrip
paternity  riverhead  sybaritic  utterness  backsword  crossfade  filoselle
pederasty  riverside  syncretic  vagarious  bandstand  crossfire  firestone
pendragon  riverweed  syneresis  vaporable  barnstorm  crossfish  fishslice
penfriend  rulership  synergism  vaporific  beanstalk  crosshead  flagstaff
penurious  saleratus  synergist  vaporiser  beefsteak  crosslink  flagstick
petersham  Samaritan  tectrices  venerable  bemusedly  crossness  flagstone
pierrette  satirical  theoretic  venerably  birdsfoot  crossover  flowsheet
pleuritic  saturable  theoriser  venerator  birdsnest  crossroad  flowstone
pokerface  saturator  theurgist  venereous  blessedly  crossruff  focussing
pokerwork  Saturnian  tigerlily  ventrally  bluestone  crosstalk  foodstuff
polariser  saturnine  tigermoth  ventricle  boatswain  crossways  footstalk
portrayal  saturnism  tigerseye  vestryman  bombshell  crosswind  footstall
portrayer  scirrhous  tigerwood  vicariate  bombsight  crosswise  footstool
portreeve  scleritis  tolerable  vicarious  bondslave  crossword  forasmuch
powerboat  sclerosis  tolerably  viceregal  bondstone  croustade  foreshore
powerdive  sclerotic  tolerance  vicereine  bookshelf  crowsfoot  foreshown
powerless  seaurchin  tortrices  viceroyal  bookstall  crowsnest  foresight
preordain  secernent  tortricid  viverrine  bookstand  cryoscope  forespeak
priorship  securable  trierarch  wakerobin  bookstore  cryoscopy  forestage
procreant  semirigid  tubercule  waterbath  boomslang  curbstone  forestall
procreate  sentrybox  turnround  waterbuck  brasserie  dachshund  fourscore
prodromal  separable  tutorship  waterbutt  brassiere  damascene  freestone
prodromic  separably  umberbird  watercart  breastpin  decastere  freestyle
programme  separates  unberufen  watercool  brimstone  decistere  frogspawn
propriety  separator  uncertain  waterfall  buckshish  decussate  fullscale
quadratic  severable  underbody  waterflea  buhrstone  dehiscent  gainsayer
quadrifid  severally  underbred  waterfowl  burrstone  demission  gallstone
quadrigae  severalty  underclay  watergate  cadastral  demystify  gearshift
quadrille  severance  undercoat  waterhole  campstool  depasture  gladstone
quadruman  shearling  underdone  waterleaf  canescent  deposable  glassgall
quadruped  sheerhulk  underfelt  waterless  canesugar  depositor  glassware
quadruple  sheerlegs  underfoot  waterlily  cardsharp  devastate  glasswork
quadruply  sheerness  undergird  waterline  celestial  devisable  glasswort
quarryman  sideritic  undergone  watermark  cerastium  digastric  glissandi
quebracho  siderosis  undergrad  watermill  cerussite  digestion  glissando
queerness  soberness  underhand  waterpipe  chassepot  digestive  glossator
razorback  soporific  underhung  watershed  chinstrap  dimissory  glossitis
razorbill  soubrette  underlaid  waterside  chopstick  disesteem  gneissoid
razoredge  sovereign  underlain  waterweed  Christian  divisible  gneissose
razorfish  spearfish  underline  waterworn  Christmas  downstage  goldsinny
rearrange  spearhead  underling  wherryman  chrysalid  drawsheet  goldsmith
recording  spearmint  undermine  whipround  chrysalis  dresscoat  grassland
recordist  spearside  undermost  wolframic  citystate  dripstone  greasegun
rectrices  spearwort  underpaid  yearround  clamshell  dropscene  gritstone
recurrent  spherical  underpart  ytterbium  classable  dropscone  grossness
recurring  spherular  underpass  zoography  classical  dropsical  grossular
recursion  squarrose  underplay  accessary  classless  drugstore  grubscrew
recursive  squirarch  underplot  accession  classlist  drumstick  grubstake
redbreast  squiredom  underrate  accessory  classmate  dryasdust  guesswork
referable  squirelet  underripe  accusable  classroom  dustsheet  gyroscope
reference  staircase  underseal  acoustics  claustral  eavesdrop  hailstone
referenda  stairfoot  underseas  admission  clepsydra  ecdysiast  hailstorm
referring  stairhead  undersell  admissive  cloisonne  ecossaise  hairshirt
reformism  stairwell  undershot  advisable  cloistral  egression  hairslide
reformist  steersman  underside  advisably  cockscomb  embassage  hairspace
```

```
hairstyle  loanshark  pleasance  starshell  agistment  canetrash  dinothere
halfshell  locksmith  polysemic  starstone  agnatical  capitally  diphthong
halfstaff  lodestone  polysomic  stressful  ahistoric  capitular  dirttrack
hallstand  logistics  potassium  subastral  airstream  capitulum  dogstooth
Hallstatt  longshore  poussette  swansdown  albatross  caretaker  donothing
handsdown  lotusland  praiseful  taioseach  aleatoric  catatonia  doubtable
handshake  lovestory  pressgang  talismans  alertness  catatonic  doubtless
handspike  lunisolar  pressmark  telescope  allotment  ceratodus  downthrow
handstand  maelstrom  pressroom  telescopy  allotrope  chaetodon  draftsman
hardshell  magistery  pressstud  theosophy  allotropy  chaetopod  driftsail
haresfoot  magistral  presswork  thirstily  allotting  chanteuse  driftweed
hartshorn  mahlstick  priestess  thrashing  ambitious  chantilly  driftwood
hawksbill  mainsheet  pubescent  threshold  amputator  chantress  dubitable
headscarf  majuscule  puissance  Thyestean  anaptyxis  chartered  ecritoire
headstall  makeshift  pulpstone  tilestone  annotator  charterer  eightfold
headstock  manysided  punishing  timesheet  anorthite  chastener  eightieth
headstone  marestail  pyroscope  toadstone  antitoxic  chastiser  eightsome
hemistich  marlstone  quiescent  toadstool  antitoxin  chatterer  eightyish
hexastich  maulstick  rainstorm  tombstone  antitrade  cicatrice  ejectment
hexastyle  megaspore  ravishing  townscape  antitrust  cicatrise  elastomer
highspeed  melismata  recession  townsfolk  apartheid  clatterer  electoral
hindsight  micaslate  recessive  transcend  apartment  coastline  electress
hoarstone  milestone  recusance  transenna  apartness  coastward  electrify
hocussing  milkshake  recusancy  transform  apostolic  coastwise  electrode
holystone  millstone  refashion  transfuse  appetence  coattails  electuary
homestead  miniskirt  refusable  transient  appetency  cogitable  embattled
hornstone  minuscule  regisseur  translate  appetiser  comitadji  empathise
horoscope  misassign  registrar  transmute  arbitrage  comptroll  enactment
horoscopy  misesteem  reinstate  transonic  arbitrary  constable  epistaxis
huckstery  monastery  remission  transpire  arbitrate  constancy  epistemic
hypostyle  monkshood  renascent  transport  arbitress  constrain  epistoler
ignescent  monostich  reposeful  transpose  ascetical  constrict  epistolic
impassion  monostyle  repossess  transship  auditable  construct  equitable
impassive  moonscape  resistant  transumpt  auditoria  countable  equitably
impastoed  moonshine  resistive  transvest  autotelic  countdown  erectness
impostume  moonstone  revisable  treasurer  autotroph  countless  eristical
imposture  mucksweat  rhapsodic  trousered  aventaile  countship  erratical
incessant  necessary  ribosomal  trousseau  avertible  courtcard  eventless
indispose  necessity  ringshake  trussbeam  awestruck  courteous  eventuate
infuscate  newsstand  ringsnake  tumescent  azeotrope  courtesan  exactable
infusible  numbskull  roadstead  tungstate  backtrack  courtroom  exactment
infusoria  obeisance  rocksnake  turnstile  bagatelle  courtship  exactness
ingestion  obfuscate  rootstock  turnstone  barathrum  courtyard  exanthema
ingestive  obsession  rufescent  unmusical  beastings  covetable  excitable
injustice  obsessive  salesgirl  unreserve  beauteous  craftsman  excitancy
insistent  octastyle  saleslady  veinstone  beautiful  creatable  excitedly
intestacy  octostyle  saltspoon  vicesimal  beestings  creatress  existence
intestate  omissible  sandspout  vigesimal  befitting  creatural  exostosis
intestine  opposable  sandstone  virescent  begetting  crestless  expatiate
invisible  orrisroot  sandstorm  volkslied  belatedly  crustacea  exultance
invisibly  oversexed  schistose  washstand  besetment  cryptical  exultancy
ionisable  overshoot  schistous  whetstone  besetting  cryptogam  eyestrain
ironsides  oversight  sciascopy  whimsical  besotting  cryptonym  facetious
ironsmith  oversized  secession  whinstone  bilateral  cunctator  faintness
ironstone  overskirt  semestral  whipsnake  biliteral  curettage  fanatical
jacksnipe  oversleep  semisolid  whipstock  birdtable  curstness  faultless
jackstraw  overslept  semisweet  windswept  blasthole  cytotoxic  firstborn
janissary  overspend  senescent  winestone  blastment  cytotoxin  firstfoot
jockstrap  overspent  seneschal  withstand  blastulae  dauntless  firsthand
jossstick  overspill  shipshape  withstood  blastular  debatable  firstling
Judastree  overstate  shoeshine  wolfsbane  blowtorch  debutante  firstrate
kerbstone  oversteer  sideswipe  wordsmith  bluntness  decathlon  flatterer
kickstart  overstock  siltstone  yardstick  blusterer  deistical  fleetness
kingsized  overstuff  singspiel  Yorkshire  boattrain  delftware  flintlock
ladysmock  Pakistani  sinistral  zygospore  bounteous  demitasse  floatable
lampshade  palustral  sinusitis  ablatival  bountiful  demitting  fluctuant
lampshell  parasitic  skeesicks  ablutions  bowstring  denitrate  fluctuate
landscape  peepsight  skiascopy  aboutface  bracteate  denitrify  foretaste
landslide  Pelasgian  slabsided  aboutturn  bracteole  devitrify  foretoken
latescent  periscope  slabstone  acroteria  breathily  devotedly  fractious
leafstalk  perishing  slapstick  adaptable  breathing  diactinic  franticly
legislate  perisperm  snowscape  adeptness  bristling  diastasis  fritterer
lifesaver  peristome  snowstorm  adjutancy  brittlely  diastatic  frontally
lifesized  peristyle  soapstone  admitting  buckthorn  diastolic  frontless
lifestyle  pikestaff  softshell  adoptable  bucktooth  digitalis  frontline
limestone  pintsized  songsmith  adulterer  bulltrout  digitally  frontpage
livestock  pipestone  soupspoon  adulthood  bumptious  digitated  frontward
loadstone  plausible  splashily  adultness  cadetship  dilatable  frontways
loafsugar  plausibly  squashily  aflatoxin  cafeteria  dilatancy  frontwise
```

```
frostbite  impetrate  nightclub  pyrethrum  shortstop  toastrack  bughunter
frostwork  impetuous  nightfall  quantical  shortterm  tractable  caerulean
fructuate  impotence  nightgown  quarterly  shortwave  tractably  calculate
fructuous  impotency  nighthawk  quartette  shottower  traitress  calculous
fruitcake  imputable  nightlife  quartzite  sidetable  trattoria  cannulate
fruiterer  inaptness  nightline  quartzose  sidetrack  trattorie  capsulate
fruitless  inbetween  nightlong  quietness  sightless  treatable  capsulise
fruittree  ineptness  nightmare  quintette  sightseer  treatment  carbuncle
frustrate  inertness  nightside  quintuple  skintight  triatomic  carburise
Gaeltacht  infatuate  nighttime  quittance  skirtings  triptyque  carfuffle
gauntness  inpatient  nightwork  racetrack  skirtless  troutfarm  cartulary
gazetteer  insatiate  ninetieth  reactance  slantways  troutling  celluloid
gemutlich  insatiety  novitiate  rebutting  slantwise  trustdeed  cellulose
genetical  insetting  odontalgy  reentrant  smartness  trustless  centurion
genitival  irritable  offstreet  refitment  smartweed  turntable  chemurgic
genotypic  irritably  ommatidia  refitting  smatterer  twentieth  chequered
geostatic  isostatic  onsetting  refutable  smoothish  twentyone  chihuahua
getatable  janitress  oscitancy  remitment  solitaire  twistable  circuitry
ghostlike  jetstream  overtaken  remittent  Solutrean  twitterer  circulate
ghostword  jointress  overthrew  remitting  Solutrian  unaltered  coadunate
giantlike  keratitis  overthrow  renitency  something  unaptness  coagulant
glyptodon  keratosis  overtness  repotting  sometimes  undutiful  coagulate
gobetween  Kshatriya  overtones  reputable  soritical  uneatable  coequally
grantable  lapstrake  overtrain  reputably  spectacle  unfitness  collusion
greataunt  lapstreak  overtrick  reputedly  spectator  unfitting  collusive
greatcoat  latitancy  overtrump  resetting  splitting  unmatched  colourful
greatness  lazytongs  packtrain  resitting  spluttery  unnatural  colouring
gristmill  leastways  painterly  revetment  sportsman  unsettled  colourist
guestroom  leastwise  paintwork  revetting  spouthole  untutored  colourman
guiltless  lengthily  palatable  rightable  spoutless  unwitting  communard
habitable  levitator  palatably  righteous  spritsail  upsetting  communion
habitably  Levitical  panatella  righthand  sputterer  vegetable  communise
habituate  lifetable  papeterie  rightness  squatness  vegetably  communism
halftitle  lightfoot  parataxis  rightward  squatting  veratrine  communist
halftrack  lightless  parathion  roisterer  startling  veritable  community
halftruth  lightness  parotitis  rotatable  steatitic  veritably  commutate
halitosis  lightning  penetrant  safetypin  stiltedly  vexatious  concubine
halothane  lightship  penetrate  sagittate  stintless  visitable  concurred
hamstring  lightsome  penitence  sainthood  stoutness  visitress  conducive
hamstrung  lightsout  phantasma  saintlike  stratagem  vomitoria  conductor
haustella  lightwood  pilotfish  saintling  strategic  waistband  Confucian
haustoria  lightyear  pinstripe  saintship  stretcher  waistbelt  confusion
healthful  limitable  piratical  sanatoria  strutting  waistcoat  conjugate
healthily  limitedly  pivotable  sanctuary  stutterer  waistline  connubial
heartache  limitless  pivotally  sandtable  subatomic  wealthily  conqueror
heartbeat  locatable  plantable  sanitaria  substance  welltimed  consulage
heartburn  lovetoken  plantlike  saunterer  substrata  wheatmeal  consulate
heartfelt  lunitidal  plastered  scantling  substrate  whistling  consulter
heartfree  mailtrain  plasterer  scantness  sudatoria  worktable  consultor
hearthrug  malathion  plaything  scatterer  sumptuary  wrestling  contumacy
heartland  maritally  plenteous  scentless  sumptuous  wristband  contumely
heartless  matutinal  plentiful  sceptical  sunstroke  wristdrop  contusion
heartsick  meditator  pointduty  scintilla  sunstruck  wristshot  corduroys
heartsore  melatonin  pointedly  scratcher  swartness  xparticle  corpulent
heartwood  menstrual  pointille  scratches  sweatband  yachtclub  corpuscle
hemitrope  menstruum  pointlace  scrutable  sweatshop  yachtsman  corrugate
hemstitch  midstream  pointless  scrutator  sweetcorn  zapateado  corrupter
hepatitis  militancy  pointsman  seastrand  sweetener  zoiatrics  corruptly
heretical  milktooth  politburo  secateurs  sweetmeat  Acheulean  costumier
heritable  minutegun  politesse  seditious  sweetmeat  Acheulian  cothurnus
hesitance  minuteman  political  selftrust  sweetness  aciculate  couturier
hesitancy  moistener  polythene  semitonic  sweetshop  acidulate  crapulent
hesitator  moistness  polytonal  serotonin  sweettalk  acidulent  crapulous
Hexateuch  monatomic  polytypic  shantyman  sweptback  acidulous  credulity
hightoned  monitress  poulterer  sheatfish  swiftness  affluence  credulous
homotaxis  monotonic  practical  sheathing  tacitness  announcer  crenulate
homotonic  monotreme  practised  sheetbend  taintless  anovulant  crepuscle
hydathode  monotypic  prestress  shiftless  temptable  apiculate  croquette
hypethral  monstrous  prettyish  Shintoism  temptress  Arthurian  debauched
hypotaxis  moratoria  prettyism  Shintoist  teratogen  asexually  debauchee
identical  mountable  printable  shirtless  theatrics  assaulter  debaucher
identikit  moustache  printshop  shirttail  thirtieth  azimuthal  defaulter
idiotical  munitions  proptosis  shootable  throttler  banjulele  demiurgic
ignitable  naphthene  prostatic  shortcake  tightener  banqueter  denouncer
ignitible  negotiant  prostrate  shortener  tightness  banquette  detrusion
immutable  negotiate  psalteria  shortfall  tightrope  Bantustan  diffusely
immutably  nicotiana  punctilio  shorthand  tightwire  binturong  diffusion
impatiens  nicotinic  punctuate  shorthorn  timetable  bouquetin  diffusive
impatient  nightbird  puritanic  shortness  tipstaves  briquette  disbudded
```

```
disburden  inoculate  pothunter  tellurate  immovable  leftwards  bathybius
disbursal  inpouring  precursor  tellurian  immovably  lilywhite  bellyache
disputant  intrusion  prejudice  telluride  innovator  limewater  bellyband
dissuader  intrusive  prelusion  tellurite  lixiviate  lintwhite  bellyflop
disturbed  Iroquoian  prelusive  tellurium  motivator  luftwaffe  billycock
disturber  jacquerie  prelusory  tellurous  neckverse  Manxwoman  billygoat
effluence  kerfuffle  procuracy  textually  oblivious  meanwhile  boobytrap
effluvial  kibbutzim  procuress  throughly  overvalue  meltwater  bullybeef
effluvium  labourite  profusely  tittuping  polevault  millwheel  bullytree
effluxion  laevulose  profusion  tittupped  polyvinyl  overwatch  buttygang
ejaculate  languidly  prolusion  tonguelet  recoverer  overweary  cageyness
elocution  leisurely  prolusory  tonguetie  redevelop  overweigh  candytuft
eloquence  Limburger  pullulate  toreutics  redivivus  overwhelm  carryover
emolument  limousine  purpureal  torturous  relevance  overwound  coccygeal
encaustic  lingually  pursuable  traducian  relevancy  overwrite  collyrium
encounter  lingulate  pursuance  trebuchet  removable  overwrote  condyloid
encourage  Mancunian  pustulate  trebucket  renovator  polywater  condyloma
englutted  manducate  pustulous  tremulant  revivable  rainwater  cubbyhole
entourage  marquetry  querulous  tremulous  scrivener  rearwards  currycomb
epicurean  marsupial  rapturous  tribunate  semivowel  renewable  cuttysark
epicurism  marsupium  reclusion  tributary  sleevenut  roadworks  dairymaid
espousals  masculine  reclusive  triquetra  synovitis  rosewater  dickybird
etiquette  mercurial  recruital  triturate  televisor  saltwater  Dionysiac
evolution  mercurous  recruiter  truculent  unadvised  saltworks  Dionysian
evolutive  micturate  redoubted  turbulent  uncivilly  screwball  dithyramb
exclusion  midsummer  reeducate  turquoise  uncovered  screwbolt  ecosystem
exclusive  misguided  refluence  twosuiter  undivided  screwpile  embayment
executant  molluscan  renouncer  unbounded  unsavoury  screwpine  embryonal
execution  mosquitos  reshuffle  uncounted  winevault  screwworm  embryonic
executive  mundungus  resources  uncouthly  allowable  shipwreck  embryotic
executory  murmurous  retoucher  undaunted  allowably  shrewmice  emphysema
executrix  Mussulman  rumrunner  undoubted  allowance  sidewards  enjoyable
exequatur  Neptunian  sacculate  unequally  allowedly  sidewheel  enjoyably
exhauster  neptunium  Sadducean  unfounded  arrowhead  sinewless  enjoyment
expounder  nocturnal  sasquatch  unicuspid  arrowroot  skewwhiff  enthymeme
extrusion  nonjuring  savourily  unplugged  arrowwood  snowwhite  epicyclic
extrusive  nummulite  scapulary  unplumbed  arrowworm  soapworks  epigynous
factually  nuncupate  scrounger  unsoundly  askewness  sodawater  eponymous
favourite  obscurant  seclusion  unstudied  backwards  somewhere  eurhythmy
fistulous  obscurely  seclusive  untouched  backwater  somewhile  everybody
flatulent  obscurity  Seljukian  untrussed  backwoods  spurwheel  fairyhood
formulaic  obtrusion  sensually  unusually  bandwagon  stalworth  fairyland
formulary  obtrusive  septuplet  upcountry  bandwidth  stopwatch  fairylike
formulate  occludent  serrulate  vapouring  birdwatch  strawworm  fairyring
formulise  occlusion  sextuplet  vapourish  bondwoman  strewment  fairytale
fortunate  occlusive  shogunate  venturous  bratwurst  throwaway  fancyfree
foxhunter  oilburner  siphuncle  verrucose  Bretwalda  throwback  fancywork
frequence  outgunned  sojourner  verrucous  buckwheat  throwster  ferryboat
frequency  outnumber  spatulate  virgulate  bushwhack  tidewater  fishyback
fulgurant  outputted  speculate  virtually  cartwheel  tirewoman  forsythia
fulgurate  oviductal  spiculate  virtuosic  charwoman  typewrite  fortyfive
fulgurite  parbuckle  spinulose  virtuosos  dipswitch  westwards  gloryhole
fulgurous  parquetry  spinulous  Vitruvian  dishwater  widowbird  glueyness
garrulity  pasturage  spleuchan  volauvent  downwards  widowhood  handywork
garrulous  pendulate  spodumene  voyeurism  eastwards  windwards  heavyduty
gradually  penduline  sporulate  vulturine  edelweiss  woodwaxen  Hercynian
graduator  pendulous  statuette  vulturish  elbowroom  workwoman  hollyhock
granulate  penpusher  statutory  vulturous  elsewhere  wormwheel  Hollywood
granulite  perfumery  stimulant  Walpurgis  endowment  admixture  honeycomb
granulose  perfumier  stimulate  whodunnit  erstwhile  affixture  honeymoon
gratulate  perfusion  stipulate  activator  firewater  immixture  honkytonk
gunrunner  perfusive  strouding  alleviate  fireworks  innoxious  hunkydory
hamburger  pergunnah  subduable  antivenin  folkweave  obnoxious  isocyclic
harquebus  permutate  subduedly  antiviral  forewoman  preexilic  isohyetal
Herculean  persuader  subjugate  arriviste  fourwheel  pyroxylin  jellyfish
hereunder  pertussis  sublunary  behaviour  freewheel  taraxacum  jollyboat
hirsutism  petaurist  succulent  boliviano  freewoman  acetylate  lacrymose
homousian  picturise  succursal  cadaveric  gearwheel  acetylcoA  lardycake
humbugged  pinnulate  suffusion  cleavable  goodwives  acetylene  Malayalam
illjudged  pirouette  sunburned  deliverer  graywacke  alicyclic  martyrdom
impluvium  planuloid  suppurate  derivable  greywacke  amaryllis  martyrise
impounder  plumulate  surculose  disavouch  handwheel  amblyopia  mateyness
imprudent  plumulose  surmullet  disavowal  headwater  amblyopic  methylate
incaution  pollutant  tactually  echovirus  highwater  analysand  methylene
inclusion  pollution  Talmudist  equivocal  homewards  anchylose  mistyeyed
inclusive  porcupine  Targumist  equivoque  hornwrack  annoyance  mollymawk
inequable  portulaca  Tartufian  evolvable  ironworks  anonymity  moneybags
influence  postulant  Tartufism  excavator  jurywoman  anonymous  moneybill
influenza  postulate  teacupful  grievance  kinswoman  assayable  moneywort
```

```
nannygoat Afrikaans birdwatch debutante estimable greywacke ionisable
neodymium Afrikaner blameable decidable estimator grievance irrigable
newlyweds agreeable blameably decimally eternally habitable irrigator
pachyderm agreeably blockader decimator ethically habitably irritable
pantyhose airyfairy boldfaced decorator evolvable halfbaked irritably
pennywort alienable bombhappy dedicator exactable halfcaste ischiadic
pharyngal alienator bookmaker definable excavator halfhardy ischiatic
pharynges aliphatic Brahmanic definably excisable Hanseatic isoniazid
pharynxes allemande breakable deludable excitable headwater isostatic
piggyback alligator breakaway demitasse excitancy heartache jaborandi
piggybank allocable bregmatic deposable excusable helically jacaranda
poppycock allopathy Bretwalda depurator excusably hendiadys jocularly
poppyhead allowable brummagem derivable execrable heritable jubilance
propylaea allowably calamanco desirable execrably herniated judgmatic
propylene allowance cameraman desirably exequatur hesitance katabasis
pterygium alterable cantharid desolater exultance hesitancy katabatic
pterygoid ambulacra cantharis desolator exultancy hesitator kinematic
puppyhood ambulance cantharus detonator eyeglance highlands kingmaker
pussyfoot amendable capitally devisable eyeshadow highwater kneadable
readymade aminoacid caretaker dextrally factually Himalayan lacerable
repayable amoebaean catamaran diastasis fairfaced hindrance lagniappe
repayment amputator catchable diastatic fasciated holocaust laminaria
Samoyedic amygdalin centrally digitalin fatheaded homemaker laminated
sandyacht anabranch chachacha digitalis fatigable homewards lanthanum
spagyrist angularly champagne digitally federally homogamic laterally
splayfoot annotator champaign digitated feiseanna homotaxis latitancy
storybook annoyance charlatan dilatable figurante honoraria laughable
storyline annularly chickadee dilatancy filtrable hotheaded laughably
syncytial annulated chickaree disbranch finically hypocaust learnable
syncytium antenatal chihuahua discharge fireeater hypomania leftwards
tachylite anthracic chromatic disgracer firewater hypomanic leviratic
tachylyte antipasto chromatin dishfaced flagrance hyponasty levitator
tallyshop antipathy chrysalid dishwater flagrancy hypotaxis lexically
tiedyeing aplanatic chrysalis dispraise flammable iceskater liberally
tridymite apparatus cinematic dissuader flippancy idiomatic liberated
trihybrid appliance cineraria distraint floatable idiopathy liberator
unsayable araucaria civically diurnally floriated ignitable lifesaver
uropygium Areopagus claimable dividable folkdance ignorable lifetable
wallydrag argybargy classable dodecagon foolhardy ignoramus limewater
worrywart arrogance clearance dominance footfault ignorance limitable
breezeway asexually cleavable dominator forecaddy illegally lingually
citizenly asparagus climbable doubtable forenamed imageable lipreader
citizenry aspirator clubbable downwards foretaste imbalance literally
embezzler assayable coattails drinkable forgeable immolator literatim
freezable assonance coaxially drummajor fragrance immorally literator
freezedry assumable coequally dubitable fragrancy immovable literatus
hylozoism assumably cogitable dyscrasia freelance immovably litigable
polyzoary assurance colleague dysphagia Freemason immutable lobulated
quizzical asthmatic comically dysphagic freerange immutably locatable
sforzando athematic comitadji dysplasia freezable impedance logically
synizesis Athenaeum complaint eastwards frogmarch imperator logomachy
whizzbang auditable comprador echolalia frontally impleader longeared
————————— automatic conically ecossaise fumigator imputable longfaced
abdicable automaton constable eggbeater Gaeltacht inbreathe longrange
abdicator available constancy elegiacal gainsayer incapable lovematch
aberrance availably contralto elongated garibaldi incapably lowloader
aberrancy aventaile contrasty emaciated gastraeum increaser luftwaffe
abnegator avoidable cordially emendable gaugeable incubator luminance
abradable avoidably cornsalad emendator generable incunable lymphatic
abrogator avoidance Corybants endogamic generalia incurable lyrically
abundance awardable corydalis endurable generally incurably macerator
abysmally axiomatic countable endurably generator indagator magically
acariasis bacchanal coverable endurance geography indicator maharajah
accusable bacchante covetable enigmatic geostatic ineffable maharanee
acrobatic backwards creatable enjoyable getatable ineffably Malayalam
activator backwater cropeared enjoyably glacially inequable malleable
adaptable bainmarie crossable ensheathe gladiator inerrable manslayer
adiabatic balalaika crucially enterable glengarry inerrancy maritally
adjutancy baldfaced crushable enwreathe glissandi inferable marshalcy
admirable bandwagon crustacea enzymatic glissando inhalator martially
admirably barefaced cubically epigraphy glossator inhumanly matriarch
admiralty basically cumbrance epistaxis gradually initially maximally
adoptable beefeater cunctator equitable graduator initiator mayoralty
adrenalin bellyache cupbearer equitably grandaddy innovator medicable
advisable bestially curlpaper escalator grandaunt inorganic medically
advisably bigheaded cynically escapable grantable insularly meditator
advocator billiards dalliance escheator graspable insulator melomania
aerobatic biography dandiacal esperance graywacke insurable meltwater
affidavit birdtable debatable Esperanto greataunt insurance memorable
```

memorably	oscitancy	pyrolater	separable	teachably	wallpaper	disembark
memoranda	overeaten	pyrolatry	separably	tegularly	washbasin	disembody
menopause	overeater	pyromancy	separates	telepathy	watchable	dreamboat
messianic	overladen	pyromania	separator	temptable	wehrmacht	earthborn
miasmatic	overmatch	quadratic	serenader	tentmaker	weighable	everybody
militancy	overtaken	quebracho	sergeancy	textually	westwards	ferryboat
minelayer	overvalue	quittance	serjeancy	theomachy	wheyfaced	fieldbook
minimally	overwatch	radically	serjeanty	theomania	wieldable	fieldboot
mischance	pacemaker	raingauge	severable	thermally	windwards	firstborn
miserable	paillasse	rainmaker	severally	thinkable	winevault	fishyback
miserably	palatable	rainwater	severalty	throwaway	wiregauze	flashback
misfeasor	palatably	ratepayer	severance	tidegauge	wolframic	flashbulb
misleared	palliasse	reachable	sforzando	tidewater	woodwaxen	friarbird
misshapen	panchayat	reactance	shakeable	timelapse	workmanly	frostbite
Mithraism	pancratic	rearrange	shapeable	timetable	worktable	greenback
Mithraist	panoramic	rearwards	shipcanal	tipstaves	wormeaten	greenbelt
mitigable	parabasis	rebukable	shockable	titularly	wychhazel	guardbook
mitigator	paralalia	recreancy	shoemaker	toadeater	zeugmatic	guidebook
moderator	paramatta	recusance	shootable	tolerable	zoography	hatchback
modulator	parataxis	recusancy	sibilance	tolerably	zoophagan	hawksbill
monobasic	partially	redheaded	sibilancy	tolerance	zygomatic	heartbeat
monogamic	patinated	referable	sidetable	tonically	absorbent	heartburn
monolatry	patriarch	refusable	sidewards	toothache	absorbing	hellebore
monomania	peaceable	refutable	similarly	topically	acetabula	hereabout
moonraker	peaceably	regularly	simulacra	touchable	adlibbing	hobgoblin
mortgagee	peculator	regulator	simulacre	toxically	adsorbate	hobnobbed
mortgager	pederasty	relevance	simulator	trabeated	adsorbent	hobnobber
mortgagor	pendragon	relevancy	skiamachy	traceable	adverbial	horseback
moschatel	perchance	removable	slaphappy	traceably	aitchbone	horsebean
motheaten	perinatal	renewable	slopbasin	tractable	amphibian	houseboat
motivator	peripatus	renovator	slowmatch	tractably	amphibole	housebote
motorable	permeable	reparable	smallarms	trainable	anklebone	huckaback
mouldable	permeance	repayable	sodawater	traumatic	approbate	hunchback
mountable	persuader	reputable	solitaire	treatable	assembler	hyperbola
moustache	petulance	reputably	spatially	trierarch	attribute	hyperbole
muckraker	petulancy	resalable	speakable	trivially	Aylesbury	improbity
mumchance	phantasma	resonance	specially	truncated	bathybius	incumbent
musically	pigheaded	resonator	specialty	tubularly	bejabbers	interbred
mutilator	pivotable	restraint	spectacle	tunicated	bellyband	jollyboat
Mycenaean	pivotally	resumable	spectator	turntable	beslobber	Langobard
mydriasis	pixilated	revelator	spendable	twistable	billabong	Longobard
mydriatic	placeable	revisable	spermatic	typically	birchbark	Maccabean
myography	plantable	revivable	spermatid	ultimatum	blackball	microbial
myrobalan	plasmatic	revocable	spinnaker	unashamed	blackbird	moneybags
napthalic	pleadable	rheumatic	spoliator	unbalance	blackbuck	moneybill
naturally	pleasance	ricepaper	squinancy	uncinated	bloodbath	motorbike
navigable	plumdamas	rightable	squirarch	uncleanly	bowerbird	motorboat
navigator	pneumatic	rosewater	stackable	uncreated	bricabrac	neighbour
neutrally	poignancy	rotatable	stagnancy	undamaged	bullybeef	nightbird
newspaper	polevault	ruffianly	stagparty	undecagon	bundobust	oddjobber
nodulated	polonaise	ruminator	stainable	undreamed	camelback	oddjobman
nominable	polybasic	saccharin	stargazer	undulated	Camembert	orderbook
nominally	polygamic	saleratus	staymaker	uneatable	canalboat	palpebral
nominator	polymathy	saltmarsh	stellated	unequally	cantabile	paperback
nonviable	polywater	saltwater	stepdance	unifiable	carambola	peachblow
notepaper	popularly	sandpaper	stigmatic	uniplanar	Caribbean	penumbral
nucleated	porbeagle	sandtable	stingaree	unnamable	charabanc	pickaback
numerable	portrayal	sandyacht	stoically	unsayable	cheekbone	piggyback
numerator	portrayer	sanitaria	stopwatch	unsheathe	cobwebbed	piggybank
nymphalid	posthaste	sapheaded	storiated	untenable	coenobite	pinchbeck
obeisance	postnasal	sasquatch	stratagem	unusually	coenobium	politburo
obligated	postnatal	saturable	stromatic	unwomanly	columbary	powerboat
obturator	pragmatic	saturator	subbranch	urticaria	Columbian	psalmbook
occupancy	preadamic	scallawag	subdeacon	utterable	columbine	punchball
ocellated	pregnable	schematic	subduable	utterance	columbite	punchbowl
odontalgy	pregnancy	scholarly	substance	vaporable	columbium	razorback
oenomancy	printable	sciamachy	suffragan	vegetable	concubine	razorbill
offchance	prismatic	scrutable	superable	vegetably	confabbed	recombine
offseason	programme	scrutator	supinator	venerable	connubial	recumbent
olecranal	prostatic	seachange	surcharge	venerably	corymbose	redoubted
olecranon	proveably	secularly	suturally	venerator	crookback	refurbish
omophagia	psoriasis	securable	swimmable	vengeance	crossbeam	reprobate
omophagic	psoriatic	seedeater	tabularly	ventrally	crossbill	resorbent
opposable	puissance	selffaced	tabulator	veritable	crossbred	riflebird
opsimathy	purchaser	semblable	tacamahac	veritably	deathblow	riverbank
optically	puritanic	semblably	tactually	vigilance	decumbent	riverboat
ordinance	pursuable	semblance	taeniasis	vigilante	demobbing	rocambole
oriflamme	pursuance	seminally	taraxacum	virtually	depthbomb	satinbird
orography	pyracanth	sensually	teachable	visitable	dickybird	sauceboat

scorebook	whaleback	climactic	exoticism	landscape	periscope	scratcher
scrambler	whaleboat	clinician	explicate	Laodicean	persecute	scratches
scrapbook	whalebone	cockscomb	exsiccate	lardycake	pesticide	screecher
screwball	wheelbase	collected	exsuccous	larvicide	petticoat	seaanchor
screwbolt	whitebait	collector	extractor	latescent	phagocyte	seaurchin
scribbler	whitebass	collocate	extricate	leucocyte	phenacite	senescent
scrubbing	whitebeam	compactly	latticing	leukocyte	photocell	seneschal
selfabuse	whizzbang	compactor	fabricant	libecchio	photocopy	septicity
sheetbend	widowbird	concocter	fabricate	longicorn	physician	sepulcher
shellback	wolfsbane	concoctor	faithcure	loquacity	physicist	sepulchre
shellbark	wristband	conducive	fascicled	lowercase	physicked	sequacity
shrubbery	yohimbine	conductor	fascicule	lownecked	picnicked	sharecrop
slingback	ytterbium	Confucian	fasciculi	lubricant	picnicker	sheepcote
slothbear	adipocere	connected	febricity	lubricate	pinchcock	shortcake
smokeball	adjunctly	connecter	financial	lubricity	pistachio	simulcast
smokebomb	affricate	connector	financier	lubricous	pithecoid	skiascopy
smokebush	aftercare	contactor	flashcube	macrocosm	pizzicati	skyjacker
snakebird	afterclap	convector	flouncing	macrocyte	pizzicato	skyrocket
snakebite	airjacket	corbicula	foeticide	majuscule	placecard	slateclub
spaceband	albescent	corkscrew	formicary	manducate	Pleiocene	snowscape
speedball	alicyclic	correctly	formicate	manticore	plutocrat	sparkcoil
speedboat	altercate	corrector	fornicate	masticate	poeticise	spiracula
spellbind	altricial	corticate	fourscore	matricide	poeticism	spleuchan
spicebush	ambuscade	corticoid	frockcoat	matricula	poppycock	sporocarp
spoonbeak	americium	coruscant	frolicked	mendacity	porticoes	sporocyst
spoonbill	anglicise	coruscate	fruitcake	mendicant	posticous	squelcher
squabbler	anglicism	courtcard	fruticose	mendicity	poundcake	staircase
squibbing	Anglicist	crankcase	fungicide	metricate	precocial	stalactic
stakeboat	anorectic	criticise	gallicise	metrician	precocity	statocyst
steamboat	antarctic	criticism	gallicism	metricise	predacity	stauncher
stillborn	anthocyan	cryoscope	germicide	metricist	predicant	staunchly
stinkball	apodictic	cryoscopy	gimmickry	microchip	predicate	steelclad
stinkbomb	apomictic	cuplichen	gothicise	microcosm	predictor	stomachal
stirabout	applicant	curricula	Gothicism	microcyte	prelector	stomacher
stockbook	arabicise	currycomb	graticule	midwicket	preoccupy	stomachic
stoolball	astrocyte	cystocarp	greatcoat	minuscule	prerecord	stonechat
stormbelt	ataractic	damascene	grubscrew	misbecome	prolicide	stonecoal
stormbird	atomicity	debauched	gynaeceum	mispickel	prosector	stonecold
storybook	atonicity	debauchee	gynoecium	misreckon	prosecute	stonecrop
stylebook	attractor	debaucher	gyroscope	monarchal	protector	stormcock
stylobate	auspicate	decalcify	headscarf	monarchic	pubescent	stormcone
sugarbeet	autarchic	defalcate	heathcock	monoecism	publicise	stretcher
sweatband	baldachin	deflector	herbicide	monticule	publicist	subarctic
sweepback	bandicoot	dehiscent	hippocras	moonscape	publicity	subjacent
sweptback	barnacled	demarcate	Holarctic	mordacity	pugnacity	suffocate
syllabary	Barmecide	demulcent	homuncule	mortician	punchcard	sugarcane
syllabise	barracker	deprecate	homunculi	mosaicism	pyroscope	supercool
syllabism	barracoon	desiccant	honeycomb	mosaicist	quiescent	surfacing
syllabled	barracuda	desiccate	horoscope	mosaicked	radiocast	surficial
thighbone	barricade	detractor	horoscopy	motorcade	ransacker	suspicion
thighboot	barricado	dialectal	housecarl	mustachio	reconcile	sweetcorn
thornback	beeorchis	dialectic	housecoat	myrmecoid	reeducate	swordcane
thornbill	bellicose	didrachma	hurricane	mysticism	reflector	syndactyl
thornbush	biblicism	dietician	hydrocele	mythicise	refractor	syndicate
throbbing	biblicist	difficile	ignescent	mythicism	rejoicing	synoecete
thrombose	biconcave	difficult	imbricate	mythicist	renascent	syntactic
throwback	bifurcate	disaccord	impeccant	naumachia	replicate	tactician
trainband	billycock	dislocate	implicate	nightclub	reprocess	tanpickle
trihybrid	blackcoat	dissector	imprecate	nigricant	respecter	telescope
trilobate	blackcock	dissocial	imprecise	nitpicker	retoucher	telescopy
trilobite	braincase	dresscoat	inculcate	obfuscate	retractor	tentacled
trussbeam	bridecake	dropscene	inexactly	ochlocrat	retrocede	thylacine
turnabout	briefcase	dropscone	inflictor	Oligocene	rhizocarp	toothcomb
twiceborn	Briticise	duodecimo	infractor	orificial	roughcast	townscape
umberbird	Briticism	duplicate	infuscate	ostracise	rubricate	trabecula
underbody	broadcast	duplicity	insincere	ostracism	rubrician	traducian
underbred	broomcorn	embraceor	inspector	outbacker	rudbeckia	transcend
undoubted	cachectic	embracery	intercede	oviductal	rufescent	trebuchet
valuables	calcicole	embracive	intercept	paperclip	rusticate	trebucket
vertebrae	canescent	embrocate	intercity	parbuckle	rusticity	tridactyl
vertebral	capriccio	endoscope	intercrop	parricide	Sadducean	trifacial
vestibule	Capricorn	endoscopy	intricacy	pasticcio	sarcocarp	trifocals
waistband	cathectic	entrechat	intricate	patrician	scarecrow	trisector
waistbelt	cavalcade	entrecote	isocyclic	patricide	sciascopy	trunkcall
walkabout	Celticism	epicyclic	Italicism	paypacket	scolecite	tubercule
waterbath	character	eradicate	jampacked	Pentecost	scorecard	tumescent
waterbuck	chelicera	eroticism	Italicism	perfectly	Pentecost	unchecked
waterbutt	clearcole	ethnicity	jampacked	perfector	scoticise	unconcern
weighbeam		ewenecked	justiciar		Scoticise	

underclay	contadino	hybridism	rotundity	aesthesis	bounteous	crescendo
undercoat	conundrum	hybridity	ruggedise	aesthetic	bouquetin	cricketer
unmatched	coproduce	illboding	Sanhedrim	affluence	bourgeois	crookedly
unshackle	countdown	illjudged	Sanhedrin	aggrieved	bracteate	croquette
unsuccess	cowardice	impendent	scenedock	allegedly	bracteole	crossette
untouched	crackdown	impending	scoredraw	allowedly	brasserie	crosseyed
unwelcome	crashdive	imprudent	scoundrel	altimeter	breakeven	crowberry
uppercase	crocodile	incondite	secondary	amourette	breezeway	cryogenic
uxoricide	cuspidate	intendant	sensedata	analgesia	bridleway	culsdesac
vallecula	custodial	interdict	shakedown	analgesic	briquette	cutaneous
verbicide	custodian	introduce	sheldduck	anamnesis	brochette	daredevil
vermicide	cylindric	isopodous	shieldbug	androecia	broiderer	decadence
vermicule	cymbidium	jocundity	shieldfem	anopheles	brotherly	decadency
verrucose	damnedest	knockdown	shouldest	anoxaemia	bumblebee	decametre
verrucous	deacidify	legendary	shredding	antigenic	bumbledon	decidedly
vibracula	defendant	limpidity	skedaddle	antiserum	butcherer	decimetre
vindicate	demandant	liquidate	snaredrum	antivenin	butcherly	deerberry
virescent	demanding	liquidise	Southdown	apathetic	cacodemon	deference
vorticism	deoxidise	liquidity	splendent	aphereses	cadaveric	delineate
vorticist	dependant	lophodont	splendour	apheresis	cafeteria	deliverer
vorticity	dependent	lowerdeck	squidding	apothecia	cailleach	devotedly
vorticose	depredate	majordomo	stagedoor	appetence	campfever	diablerie
waistcoat	diffident	malanders	stampduty	appetency	Candlemas	diaereses
watchcase	disbudded	methadone	stapedial	aquarelle	candlenut	diaeresis
watercoat	dissident	methodise	steradian	aquilegia	catalepsy	diathermy
watercool	dogoodism	Methodism	stevedore	arboreous	catalexes	diathesis
witticism	Dravidian	Methodist	stockdove	arboretum	catalexis	diathetic
wyliecoat	dromedary	molybdate	stolidity	argumenta	cattleman	diligence
yachtclub	dryasdust	morbidity	stonedead	Arguseyed	centreing	dinoceras
zootechny	eavesdrop	muscadine	stonedeaf	armigeral	cerebella	discredit
abounding	Edwardian	myxoedema	strouding	ashamedly	cetaceous	displease
absurdism	eiderdown	obcordate	stupidity	assuredly	chafferer	doodlebug
absurdist	eiderduck	occludent	subsidise	asymmetry	challenge	dorbeetle
absurdity	elucidate	orchidist	swansdown	asyndetic	champerty	dosimeter
accordant	embedding	orthodoxy	sympodial	asyndeton	chanceful	dosimetry
according	euclidean	osteoderm	sympodium	atmometer	changeful	doubleton
accordion	exceeding	outridden	Talmudist	aubrietia	chanteuse	drunkenly
almandine	exopodite	pachyderm	tetradite	autotelic	chapleted	dziggetai
appendage	extendant	Palladian	theandric	backpedal	charmeuse	ectogenic
appendant	extradite	palladium	titledeed	bagatelle	chartered	edelweiss
ascendant	facundity	palladous	torpidity	baksheesh	charterer	effluence
ascendent	farandole	pallidity	torridity	baneberry	chassepot	eloquence
astraddle	fecundate	pastedown	touchdown	banqueter	chastener	emergence
astrodome	fecundity	periodate	tragedian	banquette	chatterer	emergency
attendant	floridean	pethidine	trepidant	barkeeper	checkered	empyreuma
balladeer	floridity	phagedena	tribadism	barometer	chequered	endogenic
balladist	forbidden	pitchdark	trihedral	barometry	chimaeric	energetic
Barbadian	frigidity	placidity	trustdeed	baronetcy	chlorella	entelechy
bedridden	gabardine	pointduty	turbidity	basipetal	cigarette	enucleate
belvedere	gaberdine	pompadour	turgidity	battleaxe	cinereous	epaenetic
benzidine	gambadoes	powerdive	unbending	battlecry	citizenly	epaulette
blackdamp	gammadion	precedent	unbridled	bayoneted	citizenry	ephemeral
breakdown	gerundial	preceding	underdone	beadledom	clatterer	ephemerid
brigadier	gerundive	prejudice	unfledged	beanfeast	cleareyed	ephemeris
bringdown	giltedged	preordain	unheeding	bearberry	cochleate	ephemeron
burnedout	girandole	president	unmindful	beauteous	cockneyfy	epiclesis
byproduct	Girondist	presidial	unstudied	beekeeper	coffeecup	epistemic
calandria	gravidity	presidium	untrodden	belatedly	coffeepot	epithelia
calendric	grenadier	procedure	ventiduct	bemusedly	coherence	epithesis
calendula	grenadine	prosodist	verandaed	bicameral	coherency	epithetic
Cambodian	groundage	provident	viscidity	bigeneric	coiffeuse	equisetum
candidacy	groundash	providing	wallydrag	bilateral	colonelcy	ergometer
candidate	groundhog	puffadder	washedout	biliteral	columella	erroneous
cathedral	grounding	putridity	wristdrop	bivalence	complexly	esurience
cavendish	groundivy	pycnidium	wrongdoer	bivalency	complexus	esuriency
celandine	groundnut	quotidian	zamindary	blaeberry	concierge	ethylenic
chokedamp	groundsel	rancidity	zemindary	bleareyed	conqueror	etiquette
circadian	haggadist	rebidding	accidence	blessedly	copacetic	evangelic
closedown	hagridden	recondite	acescence	blinkered	coroneted	exciseman
coccidium	handsdown	recording	acquiesce	bluebeard	cotyledon	excitedly
collodion	hazardous	recordist	acropetal	blueberry	couchette	existence
commodity	heavyduty	redundant	acroteria	blunderer	courgette	eyeopener
commodore	Hebridean	regardant	adherence	blusterer	courteous	fabaceous
comradely	hierodule	regardful	adjacency	bobsleigh	courtesan	farseeing
comradery	hirundine	remindful	adulterer	bolometer	covalence	feathered
confidant	hispidity	reproduce	advisedly	bolometry	covalency	feculence
confident	histidine	retardant	aerometer	Bolshevik	crabbedly	femineity
confiding	hunkydory	retrodden	aerometry	bottlefed	cranberry	fifteenth
contadina	hybridise	rewarding	aesthesia	bottleful	cranreuch	filaceous

```
filoselle  insolence  nescience  poriferan  sebaceous  taximeter  aciniform
fivepence  intumesce  Nilometer  portreeve  secateurs  telegenic  amplifier
fivepenny  ischaemia  ninepence  poulterer  seedpearl  telemeter  angelfish
flambeaus  ischaemic  ninepenny  pouncebox  seigneury  telemetry  beccafico
flambeaux  isohyetal  northeast  poussette  semimetal  theoretic  beechfern
flannelly  isosceles  northerly  praiseful  sentience  thickener  bellyflop
flatterer  jacquerie  novelette  primaeval  sentiency  thicketed  birdsfoot
fluoresce  journeyer  nutweevil  princedom  sericeous  thitherto  blackface
folkweave  Juneberry  obedience  princekin  serinette  thunderer  Blackfeet
foragecap  kentledge  obsolesce  princelet  serviette  tiedyeing  blackfish
forereach  kilohertz  octahedra  procreant  setaceous  tightener  blackflag
fourpence  kilometre  octameter  procreate  shadberry  tinopener  Blackfoot
fourpenny  kitchener  oecumenic  prophetic  sharpener  tittlebat  blindfold
freezedry  knifeedge  oleaceous  proscenia  sharpeyed  tonguelet  boardfoot
frequence  knowledge  oleoresin  prothesis  shillelah  tonguetie  boxoffice
frequency  lapideous  oligaemia  prothetic  shipfever  tonometer  breakfast
freshener  larghetto  oncogenic  prurience  shortener  tournedos  brushfire
fritterer  launderer  onlicence  pruriency  sickleave  tourneyer  calcifuge
fruiterer  lazaretto  ontogenic  psalteria  siliceous  tracheary  carfuffle
furtherer  learnedly  oogenesis  puerperal  simpleton  tracheate  carrefour
gasometer  lendlease  oogenetic  pumiceous  singleton  transenna  ceasefire
gaucherie  leucaemia  openheart  purulence  sixteenmo  trinketer  certified
gearlever  leukaemia  opponency  purulency  sixteenth  trinketry  certifier
genteelly  leukaemic  optometer  pyrogenic  slanderer  triquetra  chauffeur
gentleman  limitedly  optometry  pyrometer  sleevenut  tritheism  chockfull
georgette  lioncelle  orangeade  pyrometry  slenderly  tritheist  clarifier
gigahertz  lionheart  Orangeism  quarterly  sluiceway  triweekly  claviform
glaireous  logaoedic  Orangeman  quartette  slumberer  trousered  cocksfoot
glandered  longaeval  orangetip  quercetum  smackeroo  truepenny  coltsfoot
gogglebox  lorgnette  organelle  quickener  smatterer  trumpedup  Cominform
goldfever  lovefeast  orthoepic  quintette  sniggerer  trumpeter  cordiform
graphemic  luciferin  osmometer  rafflesia  snowberry  tufaceous  crampfish
greasegun  lysimeter  oubliette  rakehelly  soapberry  tumblebug  crossfade
greeneyed  machmeter  ovenready  raspberry  softpedal  twitterer  crossfire
greybeard  madeleine  overheard  razoredge  soldierly  typemetal  crossfish
guardedly  Mahometan  overleapt  recalesce  sonometer  umpteenth  crowsfoot
guillemot  majorette  overreach  recoverer  soubrette  unaltered  cruciform
hackberry  makeready  overreact  redbreast  southeast  uncovered  cuneiform
hackneyed  malleehen  oversexed  redevelop  southerly  undeceive  curviform
halfpence  manifesto  overweary  redolence  sovereign  unreserve  cymbiform
halfpenny  manometer  overweigh  reference  spaghetti  untimeous  dentiform
hamamelis  marquetry  paillette  referenda  speakeasy  usherette  devilfish
handlebar  Masoretic  painterly  refluence  spinneret  vademecum  dignified
harquebus  maunderer  panatella  remanence  splenetic  varicella  disaffect
haustella  maybeetle  pantheism  renitency  spongebag  vehemence  disaffirm
heathenry  mediaeval  pantheist  reposeful  spongeous  venereous  disinfect
hexameter  megadeath  papeterie  reprieval  sputterer  viceregal  disinfest
Hexateuch  megahertz  paralexia  reputedly  squiredom  vicereine  eightfold
highlevel  mekometer  paramedic  rerelease  squirelet  vimineous  eruciform
hodometer  menagerie  parameter  residence  stableboy  vinaceous  falciform
homiletic  Menshevik  parapeted  residency  stableman  virulence  falsifier
howsoever  messieurs  parfleche  reticence  staggerer  virulency  fancyfree
humblebee  metameric  parquetry  reticency  stalkeyed  voltmeter  febrifuge
hundredth  micaceous  Parseeism  retrieval  stammerer  volumeter  fibriform
hurriedly  middleman  pedometer  retriever  statuette  wagonette  fieldfare
hydraemia  midinette  penitence  reverence  stiffener  warblefly  firstfoot
hypogeous  milkfever  percheron  righteous  stiltedly  wattmeter  forcefeed
illiberal  milometer  perihelia  ringfence  strategic  weathered  fortifier
illomened  minutegun  perimeter  roadmetal  stridence  weatherly  fortyfive
immanence  minuteman  phrenetic  roisterer  stridency  wellbeing  fungiform
immanency  miscreant  pierrette  rosaceous  studiedly  whichever  globefish
imminence  miscreate  pikeperch  rounceval  stutterer  whimperer  goosefoot
imminency  misoneism  pirouette  roundelay  subagency  whipperin  haresfoot
immodesty  misoneist  plangency  rubicelle  subduedly  whiskered  heartfelt
impliedly  mistletoe  plastered  ruddleman  subereous  whisperer  heartfree
impotence  mistyeyed  plasterer  saddlebag  succeeder  whosoever  hereafter
impotency  moistener  plenteous  saddlebow  sutteeism  wineberry  houseflag
impudence  mongrelly  plumbeous  salicetum  swaggerer  witchetty  hydrofoil
incidence  monoceros  plunderer  saltpetre  sweetener  workbench  imperfect
indecency  monomeric  pointedly  Samoyedic  swimmeret  worriedly  interface
indigence  moraceous  pokeberry  sapraemia  swingeing  Yankeedom  interfere
indolence  morphemic  policeman  sapraemic  syncretic  Yankeeism  interfile
inference  muniments  politesse  Saracenic  syneresis  zapateado  interflow
influence  muscleman  polygenic  satinette  synizesis  zeitgeist  interfuse
influenza  muskmelon  polyhedra  saunterer  syntheses  zucchetto  jellyfish
inherence  mutagenic  polymeric  savagedom  synthesis  zymogenic  justifier
innkeeper  naseberry  polysemic  scatterer  synthetic  aboutface  kerfuffle
innocence  neckverse  pomaceous  schlieren  taioseach  acetifier  killifish
innocency  needleful  poriferal  scrivener  taxidermy  acidifier  lentiform
```

lightfoot	therefrom	cosmogony	neuroglia	tetragram	colophony	holophote
ligniform	threefold	cotangent	newsagent	theurgist	coryphaei	homophone
linenfold	townsfolk	CroMagnon	nightgown	throughly	crosshead	homophony
liquefier	transform	debagging	Norwegian	trisagion	crotchety	horsehair
magnifico	transfuse	debugging	nystagmic	undergird	cubbyhole	horsehide
magnifier	troutfarm	decongest	nystagmus	undergone	cymophane	household
mammiform	trunkfish	detergent	obbligato	undergrad	dachshund	hydathode
microfilm	underfelt	dialogise	objurgate	unfeigned	dancehall	hypethral
midwifery	underfoot	dialogism	onelegged	unpegging	dayschool	krummhorn
misinform	unruffled	dialogist	orologist	unplugged	decathlon	lampshade
multifoil	unselfish	dichogamy	Orpington	uropygian	diarrhoea	lampshell
multiform	ventifact	diningcar	osteogeny	Varangian	dinothere	launching
mummified	vermiform	disengage	Ostrogoth	variegate	diphthong	leasehold
mystifier	vermifuge	disfigure	otologist	verdigris	donothing	lengthily
nightfall	versifier	disregard	outrigger	vestigial	downthrow	lilywhite
nullifier	versiform	divergent	packaging	vestigium	drawsheet	lintwhite
orderform	villiform	doglegged	papergirl	villagery	dustsheet	loanshark
pilotfish	vitriform	earwigged	pathogeny	watergate	ecosphere	longchain
pisciform	volteface	ecologist	Pekingese	woebegone	ectophyte	longshore
pitchfork	watchfire	effulgent	Pelasgian	zigzagged	elsewhere	lovechild
pokerface	waterfall	embroglio	pellagrin	zoologist	empathise	lustihood
pussyfoot	waterflea	epilogist	pentagram	adulthood	encephala	mainsheet
qualified	waterfowl	expurgate	philogyny	aerophyte	endophagy	makeshift
qualifier	wherefore	Falangism	phonogram	allophone	endophyte	malachite
rapidfire	wherefrom	Falangist	photogene	alpenhorn	enlighten	malathion
razorfish	whiteface	fastigium	phylogeny	amidships	entophyte	Manichean
reconfirm	whitefish	floodgate	phytogeny	amorphism	erstwhile	masochism
rectifier	womenfolk	foreigner	pictogram	amorphous	eunuchism	masochist
reshuffle	Wyclifite	fustigate	predigest	anarchism	eunuchoid	meanwhile
restiform	aborigine	galingale	preengage	anarchist	exanthema	megaphone
resurface	afterglow	geologise	prefigure	anorthite	exarchate	melaphyre
retroflex	aggregate	geologist	pressgang	antiphony	exosphere	mesophyll
Roquefort	alpargata	glassgall	prologise	apartheid	fairyhood	mesophyte
sacciform	ambergris	goosegirl	propagate	apprehend	falsehood	metaphase
sacrifice	amphigory	greengage	prorogate	arrowhead	fetichism	milkshake
sassafras	analogise	habergeon	pterygium	artichoke	fetichist	millwheel
scaldfish	analogist	haranguer	pterygoid	barathrum	fetishism	misbehave
scalefern	analogous	hectogram	radiogram	beachhead	fetishist	monachism
scalefish	androgyne	heliogram	redingote	benighted	firsthand	monkshood
scarifier	androgyny	heptaglot	refulgent	biosphere	flowchart	monochord
scorifier	anemogram	hierogram	resurgent	blackhead	flowsheet	monophagy
scruffily	apologise	histogeny	salangane	blaspheme	foodchain	monorhyme
scutiform	apologist	histogram	salesgirl	blasphemy	foreshore	moonshine
serrefold	assurgent	humbugged	scapegoat	blasthole	foreshown	mousehole
sevenfold	aubergine	hypergamy	scraggily	bleachery	fourwheel	musichall
sgraffiti	averagely	imbroglio	segregate	blockhead	franchise	mycophagy
sgraffito	bedraggle	indulgent	shrugging	blotchily	freewheel	naphthene
shamefast	befogging	inelegant	slategrey	bombshell	freighter	nemophila
sheatfish	beleaguer	instigate	sociogram	bonechina	frenchify	nighthawk
sheepfold	bilingual	insurgent	solfeggio	bookshelf	Frenchman	notochord
shellfire	billygoat	intrigant	spirogyra	branchiae	gearshift	octachord
shellfish	biologist	intriguer	sporogeny	branchial	gearwheel	oenophile
shortfall	blackgame	inveigler	springald	branchlet	geosphere	oenophily
significs	bowlegged	isagogics	springbok	breathily	gloryhole	oesophagi
slushfund	buttygang	landagent	springily	breathing	gonophore	optophone
snailfish	cablegram	laryngeal	springing	breeching	gooseherd	overcheck
snipefish	cairngorm	liturgics	springlet	bronchial	greenhorn	overshoot
soothfast	carrageen	liturgist	straggler	bryophyte	grouchily	overthrew
soundfilm	cartogram	lovingcup	strangely	buckshish	guildhall	overthrow
spadefoot	castigate	massagist	strangler	buckthorn	gynophore	overwhelm
spearfish	centigram	meningeal	strangles	buckwheat	hairshirt	pantyhose
specifier	chaingang	metheglin	stringent	bushwhack	halfshell	parachute
splayfoot	chaingear	microgram	strongarm	cacophony	halophile	parathion
spoonfeed	cheongsam	milligram	strongbox	caliphate	halophyte	parochial
stairfoot	coccygeal	miscegine	strongish	camelhair	halothane	periphery
stallfeed	collagist	miscegine	strongyle	campchair	handshake	perishing
steadfast	collegial	mistigris	struggler	cardsharp	handwheel	petechiae
stockfish	collegian	monergism	subjugate	cartwheel	hardihood	petechial
stonefish	collegium	monsignor	subregion	catarhine	hardshell	phosphate
stupefier	colligate	mossagate	subrogate	catechise	hartshorn	phosphene
styliform	condignly	moviegoer	surrogate	catechism	hawsehole	phosphide
superfine	configure	myologist	syllogise	catechist	headphone	phosphine
superfuse	conjugate	mystagogy	syllogise	childhood	healthful	phosphite
swellfish	consignee	nannygoat	syllogism	churching	healthily	plaything
swordfish	consignor	negligent	synergism	churchman	hearthrug	ploughboy
Tartufian	contagion	neologian	synergist	clamshell	hexachord	ploughman
Tartufism	contagium	neologise	syringeal	cliffhang	highchair	polyphagy
testifier	corrugate	neologism	tarragona	cockahoop	hitchhike	polyphase
therefore	cosmogeny	neologist	termagant	coldshort	hollyhock	polyphone

polyphony	stinkhorn	angelical	chloritic	embroider	heelpiece	laborious
polythene	stitchery	angleiron	chronical	emolliate	hemstitch	labyrinth
poppyhead	stokehold	annelidan	chronicle	emollient	hepatitis	laciniate
preachify	stokehole	antefixal	cigarillo	empirical	heretical	lamplight
preachily	straphang	antiviral	circuitry	encomiast	highlight	languidly
preschool	strychnic	apparitor	civiliser	endomixis	hilarious	lastditch
pronghorn	superheat	appetiser	classical	energiser	hillbilly	lavaliere
punishing	swineherd	appraisal	coalfield	enteritis	hindsight	Levitical
puppyhood	switchman	appraiser	Cockaigne	enunciate	hobnailed	libidinal
pushchair	sycophant	araneidal	cockfight	equaliser	homicidal	lifesized
pyrethrum	telephone	araneidan	coercible	eristical	honorific	limelight
queenhood	telephony	archfiend	coercibly	erratical	humiliate	limonitic
raincheck	telephoto	armadillo	colchicum	estaminet	hypericum	litigious
raunchily	telophase	Armorican	colloidal	etherical	hypnoidal	lixiviate
ravishing	thatching	arriviste	coloniser	ethmoidal	idealiser	logarithm
refashion	theophany	arsenical	colorific	eulogiser	identical	longlived
repechage	thickhead	arsenious	compliant	evincible	identikit	lovelight
reprehend	thirdhand	artemisia	comprisal	excipient	idiotical	lumbrical
rhonchial	thoughted	arteriole	conceited	excoriate	ignitible	lumbricus
righthand	thrashing	arteritis	conscious	exercises	illegible	lunitidal
ringshake	threshold	arthritic	container	exfoliate	illegibly	luxuriant
riverhead	thumbhole	arthritis	contrived	exhibitor	illicitly	luxuriate
roughhewn	timesheet	artificer	contriver	exorciser	illogical	luxurious
roundhead	touchhole	ascetical	copyright	expatiate	imbecilic	lyophilic
sainthood	toxophily	associate	corbeille	expedient	immediacy	maharishi
saxophone	treachery	atrocious	cornfield	expediter	immediate	mainliner
scarehead	trenchant	audacious	covariant	explainer	impatiens	malarious
scirrhous	truncheon	autopilot	crinoidal	exploiter	impatient	malicious
scorching	twitchily	auxiliary	cryptical	expositor	imperious	malvoisie
Scotchman	uintahite	avertible	cutinised	eyebright	impolitic	manysided
scrapheap	ultrahigh	backbiter	cycloidal	facetious	inaudible	matutinal
scrumhalf	underhand	backsight	dahabiyah	fanatical	inaudibly	medicinal
scuncheon	underhung	bandwidth	deadlight	fatidical	incipient	melodious
scutcheon	unsighted	bargainer	decalitre	felicific	incurious	memoriter
searching	unsightly	basilican	decilitre	felonious	indelible	menadione
selachian	uprightly	beastings	declaimer	ferocious	indelibly	meropidan
semaphore	vibraharp	beautiful	deducible	fiduciary	inducible	minacious
sheathing	waterhole	beestings	deficient	fimbriate	inebriant	minefield
sheephook	wealthily	behaviour	defoliant	firelight	inebriate	misguided
sheerhulk	whalehead	beneficed	defoliate	fleshings	inebriety	mitraille
sheikhdom	Whitehall	bicipital	deistical	flyweight	infuriate	monodical
shellheap	whitehead	bifarious	delicious	footlight	infusible	moonlight
shipshape	widowhood	bifoliate	delirious	foresight	ingenious	moraliser
shockhead	windchest	bilabiate	dendritic	forfeiter	ingrained	mosquitos
shoeshine	wingchair	binominal	depositor	fortnight	inheritor	municipal
shorthand	wirephoto	bivariant	describer	fractious	inhibitor	munitions
shorthorn	witchhunt	bivariate	despoiler	frangible	injurious	nebuliser
sidewheel	womanhood	bobtailed	diacritic	franticly	innoxious	nefarious
sinophile	woodchuck	boliviano	diactinic	freeliver	inpatient	negotiant
Sisyphean	wormwheel	bombsight	dimidiate	freerider	insatiate	negotiate
sketchily	xenophile	botanical	dioecious	fugacious	insatiety	negroidal
sketchmap	xenophobe	bountiful	dipswitch	galenical	inscriber	neoteinia
skewwhiff	xerophile	boyfriend	dirigible	gallmidge	insidious	neoteinic
slaughter	xerophily	brachiate	dirigisme	gastritis	insipidly	nephritic
smoothish	xerophyte	Brahminee	discoidal	gauleiter	invalidly	nephritis
snowwhite	xylophone	Brahminic	disorient	genetical	invariant	netveined
softshell	Yorkshire	brassiere	disseisin	genitival	invidious	nicotiana
something	abdominal	brecciate	divisible	genocidal	invisible	nicotinic
somewhere	ablatival	brilliant	doctrinal	glossitis	invisibly	ninetieth
somewhile	ablutions	bullfight	doleritic	goldfield	irascible	nobiliary
soundhole	abstainer	bullfinch	dolomitic	goldfinch	irascibly	nondriver
spearhead	accipiter	bumptious	dominical	goldsinny	ironsides	nosepiece
speechful	acclaimer	butadiene	Dominican	golflinks	irradiant	notabilia
speechify	adducible	cacuminal	dopefiend	goodnight	irradiate	notoriety
splashily	adenoidal	calorific	downfield	goodwives	Islamitic	notorious
spotcheck	adminicle	calycinal	downright	gorblimey	isoclinal	noviciate
spouthole	admonitor	camarilla	downriver	grandiose	isoclinic	novitiate
sprightly	adnominal	canonical	dropsical	graphical	itsybitsy	numerical
spurwheel	aerobiont	capacious	druidical	graphitic	ittybitty	obconical
squashily	aerolitic	capacitor	dynamical	grisaille	Jacobinic	oblivious
stagehand	affiliate	caparison	dynamiter	guerrilla	jaundiced	obnoxious
stairhead	agnatical	captaincy	ebullient	hairpiece	judiciary	occipital
stanchion	algorithm	cartridge	ecdysiast	halflight	judicious	officiant
starchily	allegiant	certainly	echovirus	halftitle	juridical	officiate
starshell	alleviate	certainty	efficient	haverings	juvenilia	officinal
statehood	almsgiver	chaffinch	egregious	headfirst	karabiner	officious
steelhead	ambitious	chantilly	eightieth	headlight	keratitis	oilpaints
stepchild	amyloidal	chastiser	eirenicon	headliner	kilolitre	omissible
stillhunt	andesitic	chitlings	elutriate	headpiece	kingsized	ommatidia

```
organiser  rushlight  timelimit  knockknee  asphaltum  cannulate  corbelled
outgoings  sabadilla  timepiece  magicking  assailant  cantaloup  cordelier
outskirts  sagacious  tortrices  mimicking  assaulter  cantilena  cornelian
overnight  salacious  tortricid  miniskirt  astrolabe  capillary  cornflour
overpitch  Samaritan  totaliser  numbskull  astrology  capsulate  corollary
oversight  sandpiper  tramlines  overskirt  atonalism  capsulise  corpulent
oversized  sapodilla  transient  palankeen  atonality  Carmelite  corralled
palafitte  satanical  trappings  panicking  audiology  carnality  correlate
paludinal  satirical  trichinae  parrakeet  autoclave  carnelian  cosmology
paradisal  scagliola  triclinia  phenakite  bacillary  carolling  cotillion
parasitic  sceptical  triclinic  placekick  backcloth  carpology  countless
parotitis  scholiast  trimmings  predikant  backslang  cartilage  crackling
partridge  scintilla  trochilus  provoking  backslide  cartology  crapulent
pearlitic  scleritis  twentieth  Seljukian  balaclava  cartulary  crapulous
pecuniary  scorpioid  twosuiter  shrinkage  bandoleer  Castalian  crashland
peepsight  scrapiron  typhlitis  Slovakian  bandolero  castellan  credulity
pemphigus  seditious  typhoidal  sprinkler  bandolier  Castilian  credulous
penfriend  seigniory  umbilical  squeakily  bandoline  cataclasm  crenelled
penurious  selenious  umbilicus  steenkirk  banjulele  cataclysm  crenulate
perceiver  selenitic  unadvised  streakily  barrelful  cataplasm  crestless
phlebitis  semifinal  unbraided  streaking  barrelled  cataplexy  crinoline
pintailed  semirigid  uncivilly  swordknot  basrelief  cattaloes  crippling
pintsized  Shechinah  undecided  thickknee  batholite  causality  crosslink
piratical  showpiece  undecimal  unluckily  batholith  causeless  crownless
pisolitic  sidelight  undefined  unwinking  battalion  cavilling  cruellest
plausible  sideritic  undivided  womankind  beardless  ceaseless  cuckoldry
plausibly  sigmoidal  undutiful  womenkind  bedfellow  celluloid  cucullate
pleadings  silicious  unethical  abseiling  bellglass  cellulose  cudgelled
plentiful  simplices  unlimited  acetylate  bengaline  cephalous  cupelling
pleuritic  sinusitis  unmusical  acetylcoA  benzoline  cerecloth  curialism
poinciana  skeesicks  unthrifty  acetylene  berkelium  chainless  curtilage
pointille  skindiver  upbraider  Acheulean  beryllium  chairlady  cymbalist
polariser  skintight  vagarious  Acheulian  bevelling  chameleon  cystolith
polemical  skirtings  vaporific  aciculate  bicyclist  champleve  cytoplasm
political  slabsided  vaporiser  acidulate  bismillah  chandlery  Daedalean
polyvinyl  snowfield  vaticinal  acidulent  blacklead  charmless  Daedalian
potboiler  solacious  ventricle  acidulous  blacklist  Charolais  Damoclean
practical  solicitor  veracious  actualise  blameless  chatelain  dandelion
practised  sometimes  veridical  actuality  bloodless  checklist  dauntless
preexilic  soporific  vexatious  aerialist  bloodlust  cheerless  deadalive
prescient  soritical  vicariate  aeriality  blueblack  chevalier  deathless
principal  soundings  vicarious  aeroplane  blushless  chevelure  deathlike
principia  spellican  vicesimal  aetiology  bombilate  chickling  decillion
principle  spherical  videlicet  afterlife  bondslave  chilblain  decollate
proclitic  spillikin  vigesimal  agriology  bookplate  childless  decollete
propriety  splenitis  viricidal  alloplasm  boomslang  childlike  defaulter
prosaical  spotlight  vivacious  alveolate  bootblack  chipolata  dentalium
proteinic  squalidly  vocaliser  amaryllis  boundless  chiselled  depthless
psychical  starlight  voracious  amoralism  brainless  chiseller  devilling
ptarmigan  steatitic  wassailer  amorality  brakeless  chivalric  diabolise
punctilio  steroidal  weeknight  anabolism  brambling  chocolate  diabolism
purloiner  stockinet  welltimed  anchylose  brandling  chorology  diabolist
pyramidal  stoplight  whereinto  ancillary  brazilnut  Cingalese  dieselise
pyramidic  strobilae  whimsical  angiology  breadline  cipollino  disbelief
pyramidon  strobilus  whirligig  animalise  briefless  circulate  discalced
quadrifid  strumitis  womaniser  animalism  bristling  classless  discolour
quadrigae  subeditor  workpiece  animalist  brittlely  classlist  dishcloth
quadrille  sudorific  Xanthippe  animality  broadleaf  clitellum  dishclout
quantical  suppliant  xparticle  annulling  broadloom  cloudland  disoblige
quizzical  surfeiter  applejack  anomalous  bromeliad  cloudless  dispelled
quodlibet  surpliced  blackjack  anomalure  brutalise  coagulant  disrelish
rapacious  surprisal  cheapjack  anovulant  brutalism  coagulate  dissolute
rearlight  sustainer  interject  anschluss  brutality  coastline  distilled
recipient  sybaritic  introject  anthelion  buffaloes  coecilian  distiller
recruital  synclinal  kurrajong  anthology  bushelful  compelled  dittology
recruiter  synodical  lancejack  anticline  caballero  conciliar  dixieland
rectrices  synovitis  retroject  apetalous  caballine  condyloid  dogcollar
redivivus  taillight  smokejack  aphyllous  caballing  condyloma  doorplate
reducible  tailpiece  swarajist  apiculate  cabbalism  consulage  doubtless
regicidal  technical  Algonkian  appalling  cabbalist  consulate  dowelling
religiose  technique  astrakhan  appealing  cablelaid  consulter  dowerless
religious  tectrices  autarkist  appellant  cacholong  consultor  drawplate
remediate  televisor  bilgekeel  appellate  caecilian  convolute  dreamland
reminisce  tenacious  finicking  aquaplane  caerulean  convolved  dreamless
repudiate  terebinth  gavelkind  argillite  calculate  coprolite  dreamlike
resilient  theoriser  havocking  armillary  calculous  coprology  drivelled
retaliate  thereinto  housekeep  artillery  caliology  coralline  driveller
retinitis  thermidor  humankind  asepalous  cancelled  corallite  drysalter
rhizoidal  thirtieth  interknit  asphaltic  cannelure  coralloid  ductility
```

```
earthling  formulate  hexaploid  libellist  mutualist  penduline  quibbling
ectoblast  formulise  hierology  libellous  mutuality  pendulous  quicklime
ectoplasm  fortalice  highclass  liegelord  mythology  peneplain  quinoline
edibility  fossilise  highflier  lifeblood  nameplate  peneplane  quitclaim
ejaculate  foundling  highflown  lightless  natheless  penholder  racialism
embellish  fourflush  highflyer  lignaloes  natrolite  penniless  racialist
enamelled  fragility  histology  limitless  neckcloth  percaline  radialply
enameller  Franglais  homoplasy  limnology  necrology  percolate  radiology
enchilada  frivolity  horseless  lineality  nephalism  periclase  raincloud
endoblast  frivolled  hosteller  lineolate  nephalist  perilling  rascaldom
endoplasm  frivolous  hostilely  lingulate  nepheline  periplast  rascalism
engarland  frontless  hostility  lintelled  nephelite  pestilent  rascality
enrolling  frontline  hourglass  lithology  nephology  pestology  rauwolfia
entoblast  frugality  houseleek  loincloth  nerveless  petiolate  ravelling
epipolism  fruitless  houseless  lookalike  neuralgia  petiolule  rebelling
equalling  fulfilled  houselled  looseleaf  neuralgic  petroleum  rebellion
errorless  fulfiller  hydrology  lotusland  neurology  petrology  recollect
esemplasy  fullblown  hydrolyse  loverless  newsflash  phenology  refuelled
establish  funnelled  hydrolyte  magdalene  niccolite  philology  repellant
ethnology  fusillade  hymnology  magnalium  nickelise  phonolite  repellent
etymology  gambolled  hypallage  mailplane  nickelled  phonology  repelling
euchology  gangplank  hypnology  mamillary  nickelous  phthalein  reptilian
eventless  garrulity  hypoblast  mamillate  nightlife  phycology  republish
everglade  garrulous  ichnology  mammalian  nightline  phytology  revelling
excellent  gasholder  iconology  mammalogy  nightlong  pinnulate  rhinology
excelling  gemmology  idealless  mandoline  noctiluca  pistoleer  rhodolite
exemplary  gemutlich  idioplasm  manyplies  noiseless  pistolled  riderless
exemplify  genealogy  imageless  marcelled  nonillion  placeless  ritualise
expellent  genialise  impelling  marmalade  normalise  plantlike  ritualism
expelling  geniality  inability  marshland  normality  planuloid  ritualist
extolling  gentility  indweller  marvelled  northland  plumbline  rivalling
facecloth  genuflect  infielder  masculine  nosebleed  plumulate  rivelling
fairyland  gerfalcon  infilling  matchless  noseflute  plumulose  roadblock
fairylike  germplasm  innholder  matchlock  nostalgia  pluralise  rockplant
faithless  gestalten  inoculate  mausoleum  nostalgic  pluralism  roodcloth
fallalery  ghostlike  inquiline  maxillary  nostology  pluralist  roofplate
faultless  giantlike  inshallah  medallion  nummulite  plurality  rostellum
faveolate  ginpalace  instilled  medallist  nurseling  podzolise  rubellite
fenceless  glabellae  intellect  medullary  octillion  pointlace  Sabellian
fertilely  glabellar  interlace  medullate  oddfellow  pointless  sacculate
fertilise  gondolier  interlard  Mendelian  odourless  polyploid  sackcloth
fertility  gospeller  interleaf  Mendelism  offcolour  pommelled  sacrilege
festology  graceless  interline  mentalism  oilcolour  porcelain  sailcloth
feudalise  gracility  interlink  mentalist  ophiology  portolano  sailplane
feudalism  granulate  interlock  mentality  opodeldoc  portulaca  saintlike
feudalist  granulite  interlope  merciless  orderless  postilion  saintling
feudality  granulose  interlude  mescaline  oscillate  postulant  saleslady
fibreless  grappling  inutility  mesoblast  osteology  postulate  saltglaze
fibrillar  grassland  inviolacy  mesogloea  ourselves  potholing  sandalled
fibroline  gratulate  inviolate  metalline  overblown  powerless  sandblast
fiendlike  graveless  irreality  metalling  overcloud  pozzolana  sandblind
firealarm  gravelled  isinglass  metallise  overflown  preselect  sandglass
fireblast  Greekless  Israelite  metalloid  overglaze  prevalent  santolina
fireplace  griefless  issueless  metaplasm  oversleep  priceless  satellite
firstling  grimalkin  jackplane  methylate  overslept  prideless  sauceless
fishplate  grovelled  jambalaya  methylene  palillogy  primality  scaleleaf
fishslice  groveller  jaywalker  metrology  panelling  privilege  scaleless
fissility  gruelling  jewellery  micaslate  panellist  profilist  scalelike
fistulous  grumbling  joviality  microlite  panoplied  propelled  scalplock
flabellum  guideline  juiceless  microlith  pantalets  propeller  scantling
flagellum  guileless  kennelled  micrology  pantaloon  propylaea  scapolite
flameless  guiltless  labelling  milkfloat  papillary  propylene  scapulary
flatulent  gyrfalcon  labialise  mirthless  papillate  puerility  scatology
flayflint  gyroplane  labialism  misbelief  papilloma  pullulate  scentless
fleckless  hagiology  laccolith  modelling  papillose  pulseless  scheelite
fledgling  haircloth  laevulose  modillion  papillote  pulvillus  schilling
fleshless  hairslide  lamellate  Mongolian  Paraclete  punchline  schmaltzy
flintlock  halfblood  lamellose  mongolism  parcelled  pummelled  schoolbag
footcloth  handglass  lampblack  Mongoloid  parhelion  punchline  schoolboy
footplate  hanselled  landslide  monocline  patellate  pupillage  schooling
forceland  haplology  laurelled  monoplane  pathology  pupillary  schoolman
forceless  harmaline  leaselend  monthling  patrolled  pureblood  scrollsaw
foreclose  hatchling  legerline  moonblind  patroller  purselike  scutellar
formalise  headcloth  legislate  mortality  patrolman  pustulate  scutellum
formalism  heartland  lethality  multilane  patrology  pustulous  sectility
formalist  heartless  levelling  Mussulman  pedalling  puzzolana  seedplant
formality  Heraclean  liability  musteline  pencilled  queenless  selfglory
formulaic  herbalist  libellant  mutualise  penciller  queenlike  semifluid
formulary  Herculean  libelling  mutualism  pendulate  querulous  semiology
```

semiplume	spindling	traceless	Virgilian	blackmail	extremist	parchment
senseless	spineless	trackless	virgulate	blastment	extremity	parsimony
sepiolite	spinulose	trainload	visualise	bonhomous	facsimile	patrimony
serialise	spinulous	translate	vitellary	carbamate	feoffment	perfumery
serialism	spirality	travelled	vitelline	carbamide	fibromata	perfumier
serialist	spiralled	traveller	voiceless	cassimere	firmament	persimmon
seriality	spirillum	traycloth	volkslied	catchment	fleshment	pessimism
serrulate	sporulate	treillage	vowelless	chainmail	floodmark	pessimist
servilely	spoutless	tremolant	waistline	chamomile	forasmuch	phenomena
servility	stabilise	tremolite	wallplate	checkmate	forcemeat	pheromone
sexualise	stability	tremulant	washcloth	cherimoya	fulsomely	Philomela
sexuality	stainless	tremulous	wasteland	classmate	fundament	phonemics
shadeless	stalkless	tribalism	waterleaf	coelomata	glutamate	piecemeal
shambling	startling	tribology	waterless	coelomate	goddamned	placement
shameless	stateless	trickless	waterlily	collimate	goldsmith	platemark
shapeless	statolith	tricolour	waterline	condiment	gossamery	polyamide
shaveling	sterilise	trifolium	wavellite	contemner	Gothamite	pressmark
shearling	sterility	trivalent	weariless	contumacy	gravamina	prolamine
sheeplice	stimulant	trochleae	weevilled	contumely	gristmill	protamine
sheerlegs	stimulate	trochlear	werwolves	copesmate	guacamole	proximate
shelflife	stingless	tropology	wheedling	cornemuse	hackamore	proximity
shiftless	stintless	troublous	wheelless	costumier	hardiment	Ptolemaic
shirtless	stippling	troutling	whistling	coxcombry	Hashemite	randomise
shoeblack	stipulate	trowelled	windblown	customary	Hashimite	ravelment
shopfloor	stocklist	troweller	wineglass	customise	hatchment	readymade
shoreless	stoneless	truceless	womanlike	cyanamide	histamine	reanimate
shoreline	stormless	truculent	woodblock	cyclamate	honeymoon	recommend
shovelful	storyline	trustless	worldling	dairymaid	horsemint	reexamine
shovelhat	strapless	truthless	worthless	deathmask	housemaid	refitment
shovelled	stripling	tunnelled	woundless	debarment	housemate	reformism
shoveller	suability	tunnelnet	wrathless	decrement	implement	reformist
showplace	subsellia	turbulent	wrestling	deferment	impromptu	remitment
sibylline	subtilise	twayblade	yodelling	deformity	inanimate	repayment
sightless	succulent	twicelaid	youngling	determent	inclement	reprimand
sigillary	sugarloaf	twinkling	zibelline	determine	incommode	revetment
sigillate	sunhelmet	umbellate	Zwinglian	detriment	increment	rhodamine
signalbox	surculose	umbellule	abasement	devilment	infirmary	rhythmics
signalise	surmullet	underlaid	abashment	diatomite	infirmity	rhythmise
signalled	swaddling	underlain	abatement	diplomacy	informant	rhythmist
signaller	swivelled	underline	abnormity	diplomate	inharmony	rousement
signalman	swordlike	underling	academism	disarming	innermost	sacrament
silkgland	sylphlike	unfailing	acclimate	discomfit	interment	sarcomata
sinewless	symbolise	unfeeling	acetamide	discommon	inurement	scalemoss
singalong	symbolise	ungallant	adenomata	dismember	irksomely	schlemiel
Sinhalese	symbolism	unhealthy	adornment	dissemble	ironsmith	schlemihl
skinflick	symbolist	unicolour	affirmant	distemper	isogamete	scotomata
skinflint	symbology	univalent	aftermath	dragomans	isogamous	scramming
skirtless	syphilise	unreality	aftermost	dulcamara	jessamine	scrimmage
slakeless	syphiloid	unskilful	agapemone	economics	judgement	scrummage
sleepless	systaltic	unskilled	agistment	economise	lacrimose	selfimage
smileless	tableland	unsmiling	agreement	economist	lacrymose	sentiment
smokeless	tableleaf	unsullied	alchemise	ejectment	ladysmock	September
smuggling	tachylite	unwilling	alchemist	elopement	lineament	septemvir
snakelike	tachylyte	uranology	alignment	embayment	lissomely	shelfmark
snivelled	tactility	urceolate	alinement	embedment	locksmith	shrewmice
sniveller	tahsildar	utterless	allotment	emolument	lodgement	songsmith
snowblind	taintless	vacillant	amassment	enactment	lowermost	sophomore
snowblink	tantalate	vacillate	amazement	encrimson	mallemuck	southmost
snowflake	tantalise	vacuolate	amendment	endowment	matrimony	spearmint
snowplant	tantalite	vainglory	amusement	enjoyment	mattamore	sphygmoid
socialise	tasselled	valueless	anatomise	enrolment	melismata	spodumene
socialism	tasteless	valveless	anatomist	enthymeme	merriment	spoonmeat
socialist	tautology	vandalise	angiomata	entrammel	micromesh	squeamish
socialite	teleology	vandalism	annulment	entremets	midsummer	stalemate
sociality	tensility	variolate	anonymity	epitomise	mincemeat	stampmill
sociology	tervalent	variolite	anonymous	epitomist	misdemean	statement
soleplate	tetralogy	varioloid	anthemion	eponymous	mollymawk	sternmost
sommelier	thankless	variolous	apartment	equipment	myelomata	streamlet
somnolent	thornless	vassalage	apogamous	Esquimaux	neodymium	strewment
sortilege	thralldom	veniality	atacamite	euphemise	neuromata	strumming
soundless	thrilling	ventilate	atonement	euphemism	nevermore	subfamily
soupplate	tigerlily	verbalise	awesomely	exactmate	nightmare	sublimate
southland	tinselled	verbalism	baltimore	exanimate	noisomely	sublimely
spaceless	titillate	verbalist	bedlamite	excrement	northmost	sublimity
sparkless	tonsillar	vermilion	beechmast	exilement	nursemaid	supremacy
spatulate	toothless	vernalise	bergamask	exogamous	nutriment	supremely
speckless	totalling	vetchling	besetment	extolment	outermost	sweetmeal
speculate	touchline	vexillary	bionomics	extremely	outnumber	sweetmeat
spiculate	towelling	viability	birthmark	extremism	pantomime	syngamous

talismans	arachnoid	buxomness	contender	ecumenism	fussiness	heftiness
Targumist	aragonite	bystander	contented	egomaniac	fustiness	hellenise
terramara	archangel	cageyness	continent	elegantly	fuzziness	Hellenism
terramare	archenemy	calcaneal	continual	elemental	gabionade	Hellenist
testament	arytenoid	calcaneum	continuer	elevenses	gallantly	Hercynian
testimony	Ashkenazi	Calvinism	continuum	eliminate	gallantry	hereunder
thrumming	asininity	Calvinist	convincer	embrangle	gallingly	hessonite
thumbmark	askewness	campanile	coriander	eminently	gallinule	hibernate
tigermoth	astronaut	campanili	cosmonaut	empennage	gallonage	Hibernian
tophamper	astronomy	campanula	crassness	emptiness	galvanise	hiddenite
touchmark	attainder	canniness	craziness	enchanter	galvanism	hoariness
trademark	augmented	cannonade	cretinism	encounter	galvanist	horniness
transmute	augmenter	cannoneer	cretinous	encrinite	gammoning	horsiness
treadmill	augmentor	cannonier	criminate	Englander	gardening	hortensia
treatment	austenite	Cantonese	criminous	epicentre	garmented	Hottentot
tridymite	authentic	carbonado	crispness	epigynous	gasconade	hoydenish
trigamist	avalanche	carbonate	crookneck	erectness	gasmantle	huffiness
trigamous	avizandum	carbonise	crossness	erogenous	gaudiness	humanness
trinomial	awakening	carbuncle	crowsnest	espionage	gauntness	humdinger
Turcomans	awareness	carcinoma	crudeness	esplanade	gauziness	husbandly
Turkomans	awfulness	carpenter	cullender	Esthonian	gawkiness	husbandry
unanimity	baboonish	carpentry	culminant	estranger	gelignite	huskiness
unanimous	badminton	carpingly	culminate	euphonise	genuinely	hydrangea
undermine	bagginess	carronade	cunningly	euphonium	geomancer	hydronium
undermost	balconied	Cassandra	curliness	euthenics	geomantic	hygienics
unplumbed	balkanise	castanets	currently	evaginate	geoponics	hygienist
uppermost	balminess	cattiness	curstness	evidently	germander	hyphenate
uttermost	bartender	cavernous	cyprinoid	exactness	germanely	Icelander
victimise	bastinade	centenary	daltonism	examinant	germanise	Icelandic
watermark	bastinado	chariness	damningly	exchanger	Germanish	imaginary
watermill	Bathonian	cheapness	Darwinian	exogenous	Germanism	impounder
welcoming	battening	chelonian	Darwinism	expounder	Germanist	inaptness
wheatmeal	battiness	chicanery	Darwinist	externals	germanium	incarnate
wholemeal	bawdiness	chillness	dashingly	extrinsic	germinate	incognito
willemite	beamingly	chitinous	deaconess	Fabianism	giddiness	indemnify
winsomely	beefiness	chthonian	decennary	faddiness	glaringly	indemnity
witchmeal	beginning	circinate	decennial	faintness	glowingly	Indianise
wordsmith	belemnite	clamantly	decennium	Falernian	glueyness	indignant
worriment	benignant	cleanness	declinate	falseness	glutinous	indignity
zootomist	benignity	clearness	defiantly	fandangle	godliness	ineptness
abidingly	bentonite	clemently	demeanour	fandangos	goldeneye	inertness
abominate	bespangle	closeness	denouncer	fascinate	goldenrod	inglenook
absconder	biogenous	coadunate	denseness	fastening	goosander	innuendos
abstinent	bipinnate	coaxingly	denyingly	fattiness	gooseneck	insomniac
acuminate	birdsnest	Cobdenism	derringdo	fawningly	gorgonian	inspanned
adamantly	blackness	cocainise	derringer	feelingly	gorgonise	instanter
adeptness	blandness	cocainism	descended	Fenianism	governess	instantly
adjoining	blankness	cochineal	designate	fervently	grandness	internode
adoringly	blatantly	cockiness	designing	festinate	graveness	intrinsic
adultness	blazingly	cocoonery	diaconate	fetidness	greatness	inverness
affianced	bleakness	coffinite	diclinous	fibrinoid	greenness	isogenous
afternoon	blindness	colcannon	diesinker	fibrinous	griminess	itchiness
airminded	bluffness	collinear	dinginess	fieriness	grossness	jackknife
Alemannic	bluntness	colonnade	dirtiness	filminess	gruffness	jacksnipe
alertness	bombinate	columnist	disannual	fishiness	guarantee	Jansenism
aliveness	bonniness	combinate	dishonest	fittingly	guarantor	Jansenist
aloneness	boskiness	commander	dishonour	fixedness	gumminess	japanning
aloofness	bossiness	commandos	dismantle	flakiness	gunrunner	jargonise
alternant	bowwindow	commendam	dispenser	flamingly	gushingly	jarringly
alternate	brashness	commensal	dissenter	flamingos	gustiness	jazziness
aluminate	breakneck	commenter	dissonant	flaringly	gutsiness	jeeringly
aluminise	briefness	commingle	distantly	fleetness	hairiness	jerkiness
aluminium	brigandry	comminute	dittander	flowingly	haltingly	Johannine
aluminous	briskness	commonage	dizziness	flushness	hamhanded	Jordanian
amazingly	Britannia	commonlaw	dottiness	fogginess	handiness	juiciness
amazonian	Britannic	communard	dowdiness	foreknown	happening	jumpiness
Amerindic	broadness	communion	draconian	fortunate	happiness	kaolinise
ampleness	brownness	communise	dragoness	forwander	harbinger	kaolinite
amusingly	buccaneer	communism	dragonfly	foxhunter	hardiness	kiddingly
anciently	bughunter	communist	dragonish	frailness	harmonica	kinkiness
ancientry	bulginess	community	drollness	frankness	harmonics	kittenish
angriness	bulkiness	companion	dumpiness	freshness	harmonise	knowingly
announcer	bumpiness	compendia	duodenary	fulgently	harmonist	lambently
antennary	buoyantly	component	duskiness	fulminant	harmonium	lancinate
antennule	burdenous	concentre	dustiness	fulminate	harshness	lankiness
antiknock	burliness	condenser	dysgenics	fulminous	hastiness	Laplander
apartness	burningly	congenial	eagerness	funkiness	headiness	larcenist
apishness	bushiness	consensus	earliness	funniness	heaviness	larcenous
appointee	buttinsky	consonant	Eastender	fusionist	hedgingly	largeness

lastingly	Miltonian	parsonage	promenade	rowdiness	solemnity	terminism
leakiness	mincingly	passenger	prominent	ruddiness	solidness	terminist
leavening	mirkiness	pastiness	proneness	rumrunner	sootiness	terseness
leeringly	mishandle	paternity	proponent	runcinate	soppiness	testiness
legginess	mishanter	patiently	prosiness	rustiness	sopranino	teutonise
legionary	mismanage	patronage	protonema	ruthenium	sopranist	Teutonism
leniently	mistiness	patroness	Provencal	safranine	Sorbonist	Teutonist
levelness	mixedness	patronise	provender	saliently	sorriness	thickness
lichenous	mnemonics	peasantry	prudently	salmonoid	sostenuto	thingness
lightness	mnemonist	peccantly	pudginess	salpinges	Soudanese	thumbnail
lightning	mockingly	pectinate	puffiness	saltiness	soundness	tightness
liltingly	modernise	pendently	pulmonary	sanbenito	souteneur	timidness
lispingly	modernism	pentangle	pulmonate	sandiness	spareness	timpanist
litheness	modernist	peptonise	pulpiness	santonica	sparingly	tinniness
lividness	modernity	perennate	pulvinate	sapiently	sphagnous	tipsiness
loftiness	moistness	perennial	pungently	sappiness	spiciness	tiredness
Londonise	Montanism	pergunnah	purringly	Sardinian	spikenard	tormentil
Londonism	monzonite	perkiness	pursiness	Sassanian	spikiness	tormentor
longingly	moodiness	permanent	pushiness	Sassenach	spininess	toughness
looseness	mordantly	personage	pushingly	Saturnian	spleenful	tradename
louringly	Mormonism	personate	quakiness	saturnine	sporangia	trepanned
lousiness	mucronate	personify	quarenden	saturnism	squatness	tribunate
lowlander	muddiness	personnel	quarender	sauciness	staginess	triennial
lowliness	muffineer	pertinent	queerness	scaliness	staidness	triennium
lowminded	muffinman	pettiness	quickness	scantness	staleness	trilinear
lucidness	mugginess	phalanger	quietness	scavenger	Stalinism	triteness
luckiness	mundanely	phalanges	rabbinate	sciaenoid	Stalinist	tubbiness
lumpiness	mundungus	phalanxes	rabbinism	screening	staminate	tumidness
luridness	murkiness	pharyngal	rabbinist	scrounger	stampnote	turbinate
lustiness	muskiness	pharynges	rabidness	seaminess	starkness	turgently
machinate	mustiness	pharynxes	radiantly	searingly	steepness	twohanded
machinery	muzziness	philander	raffinate	seasoning	sternness	tympanist
machinist	nakedness	phoniness	raffinose	seatangle	stiffness	tyrannise
maddening	nastiness	pinkiness	raininess	secernent	stillness	tyrannous
Magianism	nattiness	piquantly	rampantly	seediness	stolonate	Uitlander
maidenish	neediness	pithiness	randiness	seemingly	stoniness	Ukrainian
malignant	Negroness	pityingly	ranginess	segmental	stoutness	uliginous
malignity	Neptunian	placename	rantingly	sentenate	subgenera	unaptness
mammonish	neptunium	placentae	rapidness	septenary	sublunary	unbeknown
mammonism	nerviness	placental	raspingly	septennia	submental	unblinded
mammonist	netwinged	plainness	rationale	sequinned	subtenant	unbounded
mammonite	newsiness	platinise	rationing	sermonise	succentor	uncannily
Mancunian	Newtonian	platinoid	readiness	serpentry	succinate	uncounted
manganate	Nipponese	platinous	reasoning	serranoid	sulkiness	undaunted
manganese	nobleness	Platonise	reckoning	sexennial	sultanate	unfitness
manganite	noisiness	Platonism	reclinate	sexlinked	sultaness	unfounded
manganous	nonlinear	Platonist	recognise	shadiness	summingup	unharness
manginess	Normanise	plumpness	recoinage	shakiness	sunbonnet	unisonant
manhandle	Normanism	plushness	rectangle	shamanism	sunniness	unisonous
manliness	notedness	plutonian	redhanded	shamanist	suntanned	unmeaning
manzanita	notionist	Plutonism	reediness	sharpness	supernova	unpointed
marginate	nuisancer	plutonist	refurnish	sheerness	surcingle	unsoundly
Martinmas	nuttiness	plutonium	rejoinder	shininess	surliness	upcountry
massiness	obeseness	podginess	reliantly	shogunate	surrender	uraninite
maternity	obscenely	poisonous	remainder	shortness	suspender	usualness
mateyness	obscenity	pollinate	rencontre	showiness	suspensor	utterness
matronage	obstinacy	pollinium	renouncer	sickening	swartness	vaccinate
matronise	obstinate	polyandry	replenish	sidedness	sweetness	vagueness
mealiness	octennial	polyonymy	repugnant	silkiness	swiftness	Vaishnava
meaningly	offcentre	pontoneer	rerunning	silliness	sylvanite	valiantly
meatiness	offhanded	pontonier	responder	siphonage	tacitness	validness
mechanics	olivenite	porringer	rhodonite	siphuncle	tackiness	vapidness
mechanise	onehanded	postentry	Ribbonism	slackness	tamponade	veeringly
mechanism	openended	pothunter	rightness	Slavonian	tapdancer	verdantly
mechanist	oppugnant	pratingly	rigidness	sleekness	tardiness	verminate
meltingly	opulently	prebendal	ringingly	slickness	Tasmanian	verminous
Mennonite	originate	precancel	ringsnake	sliminess	tastiness	vicennial
mercenary	orphanage	precentor	riskiness	Slovenian	tattiness	villanage
merganser	otherness	preconise	rockiness	smallness	tawniness	villenage
merriness	outgunned	premonish	rocksnake	smartness	teasingly	violently
messenger	outlander	presentee	roominess	smilingly	tectonics	violinist
messiness	overtness	presenter	roughneck	smokiness	tegmental	virginals
metronome	oxygenate	presently	roughness	snakiness	tegmentum	virginity
mezzanine	oxygenise	pretender	Roumanian	snowiness	teknonymy	visionary
midwinter	oxygenous	preventer	Roumansch	soapiness	tellingly	visionist
milkiness	pageantry	primeness	roundness	sobbingly	tendinous	vivianite
millenary	panhandle	proconsul	routinely	soberness	tenseness	vividness
millennia	pantingly	profanely	routinism	sogginess	tepidness	vocalness
millinery	parcenary	profanity	routinist	solemnise	terminate	volcanism

```
volcanoes anthropic cytotoxic footpound lazytongs patriotic Shintoist
voltinism anticodon cytotoxin foreboder leafmould pedagogic shipboard
vulcanian antidotal dartboard forecourt leitmotif pedagogue shipmoney
vulcanise antimonic dashboard foregoing leitmotiv pensioner shottower
vulcanism antinodal decagonal foretoken lifeforce penthouse sideboard
vulcanist antinomic decalogue forewoman lobscouse peridotic siderosis
vulcanite antinovel decapodal francolin locomotor perimorph signboard
vulpinism antipodal decapodan freeboard longcoats pesthouse silicosis
vulpinite antipodes deckhouse freehouse longhouse pharaonic silicotic
wackiness antitoxic deerhound freewoman loudmouth phellogen sinologue
waggonage antitoxin demagogic fumarolic lovetoken phyllopod sixfooter
wailingly aperiodic demagogue gallooned lunisolar plasmodia slipcoach
Waldenses apostolic demimonde gangboard lyamhound playhouse slipcover
warbonnet Appaloosa destroyer gastropod lymehound plethoric slowcoach
warmonger arthropod dethroner gatehouse lyophobic plusfours snowbound
warningly arthrosis developer gazehound macaronic pneumonia snowgoose
warrantee auditoria dextrorse geotropic macedoine pneumonic snubnosed
warranter autonomic diagnoses gladiolus malleolar polygonal soapworks
warrantor autoroute diagnosis glyptodon malleolus polygonum softgoods
washiness autosomal diastolic gnathonic malthouse polymorph soliloquy
wasteness babacoote diatropic goalmouth mansionry polysomic Solomonic
weakkneed backboard dichroism goingover Manxwoman polytonal sourdough
weariness backwoods dichromat gomphosis mayflower polyzoary spasmodic
weediness bakehouse dichromic greyhound melanosis poorhouse squamosal
weirdness ballpoint disavouch guilloche melanotic portfolio staghound
wellknown bamboozle disavowal halfbound melatonin posthorse stalworth
whipsnake bastioned dispeople halitosis melocoton posthouse starboard
whiteness bathhouse dizygotic hardboard mesomorph pourboire stational
whitening billboard dogshores hardcover metabolic pourpoint stationer
whodunnit billionth dogstooth hardnosed milktooth praenomen stercoral
wholeness blowtorch dogviolet harpooner millboard prodromal studhorse
willingly bluepoint dosshouse haustoria millionth prodromic subatomic
windiness boathouse Doukhobor headboard missioner prognoses sudatoria
winningly bondwoman draghound hegemonic monatomic prognosis sulphonic
wittiness booklouse drayhorse hellhound mongooses propionic sunflower
wittingly boondocks duckboard heterodox monocoque proptosis surfboard
woodiness Brythonic dumbfound heteronym monologic prothorax surgeoncy
wooziness buckboard dustcover heterosis monologue psalmodic swangoose
wordiness buckhound dysphonia hexagonal monotonic pseudonym symbiosis
wrongness bucktooth dysphoria hidebound monsoonal pseudopod symbiotic
wulfenite bulldozer dysphoric hightoned moratoria psychoses symphonic
yawningly bunkhouse dyspnoeic hoarhound mullioned psychosis synagogal
youngness cabriolet dystrophy homebound mycologic psychotic synagogue
zinkenite calaboose eastbound homologue neathouse pulpboard tailboard
zirconium camphoric easygoing homopolar nephrosis pyridoxin taskforce
zoogenous cardboard ecritoire homotonic newshound racehorse tattooist
abandoned carryover ectomorph hopscotch nonprofit rearhorse taxonomic
abandonee carthorse elastomer horehound nonsmoker rearmouse telamones
abandoner Castroism electoral horologer nucleolus reefpoint tensional
acropolis catabolic embryonal horologic nucleonic reenforce teratogen
actinozoa catalogue embryonic hydriodic oasthouse reinforce theogonic
aflatoxin catamount embryotic hylozoism octagonal reremouse theologal
agrologic catatonia emotional hyperopia octopodes rhapsodic theologue
agronomic catatonic endomorph hyperopic oecologic Rhineodon theosophy
ahistoric ceratodus episcopal hypocotyl oestrogen ribosomal threnodic
aircooled chaetopod epistoler ideologic okeydokey roadhouse tirewoman
albinotic charlotte epistolic ideologue oncologic roadworks tollbooth
alcoholic charwoman epizootic iguanodon ontologic rockbound tollhouse
aleatoric chernozem equipoise indecorum opinioned rosenoble toolhouse
alkaloses chipboard equivocal indigotin outgrowth safflower torsional
alkalosis chlorosis equivoque infusoria outspoken saltworks townhouse
allegoric chlorotic ergonomic ironbound overboard sanatoria transonic
allomorph chophouse exosmosis ironmould overborne sclerosis trattoria
almshouse choplogic exosmotic ironworks overjoyed sclerotic trattorie
amauroses cirrhosis exostosis Iroquoian overpower scoliosis trialogue
amaurosis clapboard factional isallobar overtones scoliotic triatomic
amaurotic clarionet farmhouse isotropic overwound sectional trichomic
amblyopia clipboard fashioner josshouse packhorse selfdoubt triploidy
amblyopic cloisonne fictional jurywoman pairhorse selfmoved tuitional
amphioxus clubhouse firehouse katabolic parabolic semeiotic turnround
anabioses coalmouse firepower keratosis paramorph semicolon turquoise
anabiosis cockhorse fireworks kingdomed paramount semisolid unalloyed
anabiotic cockroach flageolet kinswoman paranoiac semitonic unsavoury
anaerobic colemouse flashover lagomorph parapodia semivowel untutored
anaphoric comedones flophouse lampooner paregoric serotonin vasomotor
anecdotal cookhouse fluorosis landloper pasodoble sessional versional
anecdotic crossover fluxional latecomer passional shallowly viceroyal
ankylosis cryptogam footboard lawnmower patchouli shambolic viewpoint
ankylotic cryptonym footloose lazybones patchouly Shintoism virtuosic
```

```
virtuosos  estoppage  primipara  waterpipe  berberine  checkrein  democracy
vitriolic  estopping  prolapsus  whirlpool  berserker  chemurgic  demurrage
voiceover  estrapade  prolepses  zygospore  bestirred  choleraic  demurring
vomitoria  Ethiopian  prolepsis  Algonquin  bilharzia  chondrite  denigrate
voodooism  eutrophic  proleptic  baldaquin  binturong  chondrule  denitrate
voodooist  excerptor  queenpost  colloquia  birdbrain  cicatrice  denitrify
wakerobin  exculpate  recapping  exchequer  birthrate  cicatrise  deodorant
wallboard  extempore  recompose  harlequin  bitterish  Cimmerian  deodorise
warehouse  extirpate  reserpine  mannequin  bizarrely  clamorous  desecrate
washboard  fissipede  rhodopsin  palanquin  bloodroot  classroom  desperado
washhouse  flarepath  ridgepole  sobriquet  bluegrass  clathrate  desperate
wayzgoose  forcepump  roseapple  tanliquor  blueprint  cloakroom  deterrent
webfooted  forespeak  Russophil  abhorrent  Boanerges  coeternal  deterring
wellfound  frogspawn  saltspoon  abhorring  boardroom  cofferdam  deuterate
westbound  frontpage  sandspout  actuarial  boattrain  coheiress  deuterium
whipround  gallopade  sauropoda  adumbrate  bombardon  collyrium  devitrify
willpower  Gallophil  scrappily  aepyornis  bombproof  colourful  dexterity
windbound  galloping  scrapping  aerodrome  boomerang  colouring  dexterous
windhover  grandpapa  screwpile  aerograph  bordereau  colourist  diachrony
wolfhound  guidepost  screwpine  airstream  bowstring  colourman  diandrous
woodlouse  hairspace  scrimpily  airworthy  boxgirder  colubrine  diaphragm
workhorse  handspike  septuplet  albatross  brandreth  comforter  different
workhouse  hawsepipe  sextuplet  algarroba  briarroot  comptroll  dinnerset
workwoman  highspeed  singspiel  algebraic  brierroot  concerned  dipcircle
wyandotte  homeopath  Slavophil  allograph  brokerage  concerted  dipterous
xeromorph  horseplay  sociopath  allotrope  broomrape  concordat  dirttrack
yearround  horsepond  sorbapple  allotropy  Bulgarian  concurred  disbarred
zoophobia  inculpate  soundpost  anandrous  bulltrout  conferral  disburden
accompany  indispose  soupspoon  anchorage  bursarial  conferred  disbursal
acidophil  interpage  spaceport  anchoress  bushcraft  conferrer  discarder
aerospace  interplay  sparkplug  anchorite  butterbur  confervae  discerner
amylopsin  interpose  standpipe  anchorman  buttercup  confirmed  disforest
analeptic  interpret  starapple  anhydride  butterfat  confirmer  disparage
anglophil  juxtapose  steampipe  anhydrite  butterfly  confirmor  disparate
asclepiad  kidnapped  sternpost  anhydrous  butterine  conformal  disparity
ascospore  kidnapper  stockpile  antitrade  butternut  conformer  dispersal
assumpsit  lithopone  stovepipe  antitrust  caesarean  congeries  disperser
attempter  lodgepole  strappado  arbitrage  caesarian  conscribe  disturbed
backspace  loveapple  strapping  arbitrary  Caesarism  conscript  disturber
bargepole  madrepore  stripping  arbitrate  Caesarism  conserver  dithyramb
bishopric  marchpane  stropping  arbitress  calabrese  consortia  doctorate
callipers  marchpast  subalpine  arrearage  calcarate  constrain  doctorial
caryopses  marsupial  subtopian  arrowroot  caldarium  constrict  doorframe
caryopsis  marsupium  sugarplum  Arthurian  calibrate  construct  downgrade
catchpole  megaspore  superpose  ashlaring  camorrist  converter  drawerful
catchpoll  mercaptan  swordplay  auctorial  campcraft  cooperage  dungarees
centipede  micropsia  syllepses  austerely  cancerous  cooperant  ealdorman
chiropody  micropyle  syllepsis  austerity  canebrake  cooperate  easterner
cirripede  millepede  sylleptic  authoress  canetrash  corduroys  editorial
cisalpine  millepore  syncopate  authorial  cankerous  cormorant  eidograph
coreopsis  millipede  teacupful  authorise  cantorial  cornbrash  elaborate
cornopean  misemploy  tetrapody  authority  carburise  corncrake  elbowroom
corrupter  misreport  therapist  autocracy  careerism  cornerboy  electress
corruptly  mouthpart  titlepage  autocross  careerist  cornerman  electrify
cyclopean  multipara  tittuping  autograft  cassareep  corporate  electrode
cyclopian  multiplex  tittupped  autograph  cassaripe  corporeal  embarrass
cyclopses  necrophil  toothpick  autotroph  casserole  cosmorama  enchorial
davenport  negrophil  totempole  awestruck  casuarina  cothurnus  encourage
decomplex  neuropath  transpire  awkwardly  catarrhal  coumarone  endearing
decompose  nullipara  transport  azeotrope  Catharism  courtroom  endocrine
dewlapped  nullipore  transpose  backcross  Catharist  couturier  enhearten
didelphic  nuncupate  triumphal  backtrack  catharses  creatress  entourage
dimorphic  oligopoly  turboprop  bacterial  catharsis  criterion  enumerate
disappear  osteopath  unadopted  bacterise  cathartic  crossroad  ephedrine
disrepair  overspend  uncropped  bacterium  cauterise  crossruff  epicurean
disrepute  overspent  underpaid  bacteroid  celebrant  cursorial  epicurism
dissipate  overspill  underpart  ballerina  celebrate  cursorily  epidermal
drainpipe  palmipede  underpass  banderole  celebrity  cutthroat  epidermic
dyspepsia  perisperm  underplay  barbarian  cellarage  cyclorama  epidermis
dyspeptic  philippic  underplot  barbarise  censorial  Cytherean  epiphragm
eclampsia  photophil  unhappily  barbarism  centering  dangerous  ergograph
eclamptic  photopsia  unhelpful  barbarity  centurion  dastardly  erythrism
encompass  pineapple  unpeopled  barbarous  cerebrate  dayspring  erythrite
endosperm  pinnipede  unstopped  barcarole  cerograph  deathroll  esoterica
endospore  pitchpipe  unwrapped  barmbrack  chancroid  debarring  esoterism
entrapped  porcupine  unzipping  barograph  chancrous  declarant  estuarian
enwrapped  preceptor  usucapion  bastardly  chantress  deferring  estuarine
epileptic  precipice  walloping  bedspread  chaparral  dehydrate  ethnarchy
equipping  preemptor  wastepipe  bedspring  chaperone  demiurgic  Eucharist
```

euphorbia	godparent	incorrect	mainbrace	occurrent	ponderous	scenarist
eutherian	goffering	incorrupt	maladroit	occurring	porterage	schnorkel
evaporate	goldbrick	incurrent	malformed	Octobrist	posterior	schnorrer
evergreen	goldcrest	incurring	mandarine	offscreen	posterity	sciagraph
excurrent	goliardic	IndoAryan	mannerism	offspring	prayerful	scombroid
exodermis	gongorism	inferring	mannerist	offstreet	prayerrug	seafaring
exonerate	Gradgrind	inodorous	mansarded	oilburner	precursor	seagirdle
exuberant	greenroom	inpouring	manubrium	oleograph	preferred	seastrand
exuberate	gregarian	integrand	margarine	oligarchy	prescribe	seaworthy
eyestrain	gregarine	integrant	margarite	oratorial	prescript	sectarian
factorage	Gregorian	integrate	marmoreal	oratorian	preserver	sectorial
factorial	grillroom	integrity	martyrdom	orrisroot	preshrink	selfdrive
factorise	grosgrain	interring	martyrise	ossifrage	preshrunk	selfpride
fairyring	guardrail	interrupt	masonried	outspread	pressroom	selftrust
fanfarade	guardring	isochrone	masterdom	outwardly	prestress	semibreve
favourite	guardroom	isomerise	masterful	outworker	preterist	senhorita
fenugreek	guestroom	isomerism	masterkey	overcrowd	preterite	seniority
filigreed	guiderope	isomerous	meandrine	overdraft	pretermit	sensorial
filterbed	guitarist	itineracy	meandrous	overdrawn	primarily	sensorium
filtertip	guttering	itinerant	meliorate	overdress	primordia	Sephardic
finedrawn	gynocracy	itinerary	meliorism	overdrive	procerity	Sephardim
fingering	haggardly	itinerate	meliorist	overgraze	procuracy	serigraph
fingertip	hagiarchy	jailbreak	meliority	overgrown	procuress	sestertia
firebrand	hairbrush	janitress	melodrama	overprice	proofread	shakerism
firebreak	hairgrass	jetstream	memoirist	overprint	properdin	Shangrila
firebrick	halfbreed	jitterbug	menstrual	overproof	proscribe	sheldrake
firecrest	halfcrown	jointress	menstruum	overtrain	prostrate	shelfroom
firedrake	halfprice	juniorate	mepacrine	overtrick	pulserate	shewbread
firedrill	halftrack	juniority	mercerise	overtrump	pulverise	shipwreck
fireirons	halftruth	junkerdom	mercurial	overwrite	pulverous	shopfront
fireproof	hamadryad	junkerism	mercurous	overwrote	purpureal	shotproof
firstrate	hamburger	kaiserdom	mesmerise	oviferous	Quakerdom	sidetrack
fisherman	hammerman	kaiserism	mesmerism	oviparity	Quakeress	signorial
flavorous	hammertoe	katharsis	mesmerist	oviparous	Quakerish	signorina
flowerage	hamstring	Keplerian	meteorist	oysterbed	Quakerism	silverfir
flowerbed	hamstrung	kilderkin	meteorite	oysterman	racetrack	sincerely
flowering	handbrake	kingcraft	meteoroid	ozocerite	rainproof	sincerity
flowerpot	handcraft	knotgrass	micturate	ozokerite	rancorous	sitzkrieg
foolproof	handorgan	Kshatriya	midstream	packdrill	raptorial	skiagraph
footprint	handpress	kymograph	millerite	packtrain	rapturous	skijoring
forebrain	hangerson	labourite	misdirect	paederast	readdress	skingraft
forefront	hankering	laggardly	mobocracy	palsgrave	recherche	sliderule
forlornly	headdress	landdross	monitress	panderess	rectorate	slumbrous
forwarder	hemitrope	landdrost	monocracy	paragraph	rectorial	snakeroot
forwardly	heptarchy	landgrave	monodrama	passerine	recurrent	snowbroth
fossorial	herbarium	lapstrake	monograph	passersby	recurring	snowdrift
fosterage	herborise	lapstreak	monotreme	pastorale	reedorgan	sodabread
foulbrood	Hesperian	lathering	monstrous	pastorate	reentrant	sojourner
foundress	hetaerism	latterday	mossgrown	pasturage	referring	solferino
fraternal	hetairism	laundress	motherwit	pauperise	rehearsal	Solutrean
frowardly	hierarchy	lazzarone	mothproof	pauperism	rehydrate	Solutrian
frustrate	highgrade	lazzaroni	motocross	pedigreed	reiterate	sooterkin
fulgurant	highgrown	leafgreen	murderess	penetrant	rerebrace	sorceress
fulgurate	Himyarite	lecherous	murderous	penetrate	resources	sorcerous
fulgurite	hindbrain	leewardly	murmurous	pentarchy	resurrect	spagyrist
fulgurous	historian	leisurely	muscarine	pepperbox	retiarius	spareribs
fullcream	Hitlerism	lethargic	myriorama	pepperpot	rigmarole	spiderman
fulldress	Hitlerite	letterbox	nailbrush	peregrine	Ripuarian	spiderweb
fullgrown	hoarfrost	lettering	nectarean	perfervid	rivalrous	spindrier
funebrial	hodiernal	librarian	nectarial	perforate	rockbrake	spindrift
galleried	hodograph	lickerish	nectarine	performer	rockdrill	squarrose
ganderism	holograph	Limburger	nectarous	perverter	rubberise	stackroom
gaolbreak	homegrown	linearise	neoterise	petaurist	rustproof	Stagirite
garderobe	homograft	linearity	neoterism	phalarope	sacrarium	stardrift
gaspereau	homograph	lingering	neoterist	pictorial	sagebrush	stargrass
gatecrash	hoofprint	liquorice	Nestorian	picturise	sagegreen	stateroom
gathering	hornwrack	liquorish	newmarket	piecerate	sailoring	stillroom
germproof	houseroom	Listerism	newsprint	pilferage	sailorman	stockroom
geyserite	Hungarian	litterbin	niggardly	pilgarlic	salubrity	stoppress
gibberish	hypocrisy	litterbug	nocturnal	pillarbox	sandarach	storeroom
gingerade	hypocrite	logogriph	nomocracy	pimpernel	sandcrack	stuporous
gingerale	hysterics	Lombardic	nomograph	pinstripe	sangfroid	subaerial
glamorise	hysteroid	loxodrome	nonjuring	pipedream	sartorial	submarine
glamorous	ideograph	lucubrate	nonpareil	pipeorgan	sartorius	subnormal
glomerate	idiograph	ludicrous	nonperson	planarian	saucerful	subscribe
glomerule	immigrant	lumbering	obscurant	playgroup	Sauternes	subscript
glomeruli	immigrate	lumberman	obscurely	plenarily	savourily	substrata
glyceride	impetrate	lymegrass	obscurity	podagrous	saxifrage	substrate
glycerine	inamorata	mailtrain	obsecrate	polygraph	scarfring	subverter

```
succursal  unitarian  aforesaid  confusion  espousals  heuristic  narcissus
suctorial  universal  aggressor  contusion  excelsior  hircosity  necessary
suctorian  unlearned  agonising  corposant  excessive  Hobbesian  necessity
suffering  unsparing  agonistic  corpuscle  exclosure  hocussing  nightside
summarily  unwearied  aimlessly  corrasion  exclusion  hoggishly  nigrosine
summarise  vampirism  alabaster  corrosion  exclusive  homousian  nourisher
summarist  vapouring  alongside  corrosive  excursion  horseshoe  oakenshaw
sunburned  vapourish  ambrosial  cortisone  excursive  hubristic  obsession
sunstroke  vectorial  ampersand  coseismal  exhauster  hydrosome  obsessive
sunstruck  velodrome  analysand  coseismic  expansile  hygrostat  obtrusion
supporter  veneering  anglesite  countship  expansion  illwisher  obtrusive
suppurate  venturous  anguished  courtship  expansive  immensely  obversely
susurrant  veratrine  animistic  coverslip  expensive  immensity  obversion
synchrony  Victorian  animosity  cracksman  explosion  immersion  occlusion
tailoress  victorine  appressed  craftsman  explosive  impassion  occlusive
tailoring  viscerate  arabesque  cremaster  expressly  impassive  odalisque
tangerine  visitress  artlessly  crepuscle  expulsion  implosion  offensive
Tartarean  viverrine  ascension  croissant  expulsive  implosive  ombudsman
Tartarian  vizierate  ascensive  curiosity  exquisite  impresari  onanistic
tectorial  vizierial  aspersion  currishly  extensile  impulsion  onionskin
telegraph  voyeurism  assuasive  cuttysark  extension  impulsive  onomastic
tellurate  vulgarian  atavistic  Dantesque  extensity  impulsory  operosely
tellurian  vulgarise  atheistic  decussate  extensive  incensory  operosity
telluride  vulgarism  atomistic  defensive  extorsive  incessant  oppressor
tellurite  vulgarity  Axminster  defroster  extrusion  inclosure  orchestic
tellurium  vulnerary  ballistae  deinosaur  extrusive  inclusion  orchestra
tellurous  vulturine  ballistic  demission  fantasied  inclusive  organstop
temperate  vulturish  bannister  dentistry  fantasise  incursion  orgiastic
temporary  vulturous  Bantustan  depressed  fantasist  incursive  ostensive
temporise  Wagnerian  baptismal  depressor  fantastic  inelastic  overissue
temptress  Wagnerite  baptistry  detersion  fantastry  insensate  ownership
tenderise  wagonroof  barrister  detersive  Fascistic  intensely  palaestra
tenebrist  waldgrave  beemaster  detrusion  faunistic  intensify  palmistry
tenebrous  wallcress  blockship  dharmsala  fideistic  intension  patristic
tenthrate  wallfruit  bloodshed  dichasial  fieldsman  intensity  paymaster
terebrant  Walpurgis  bloodshot  dichasium  fillister  intensive  peevishly
terrarium  wandering  bombasine  diffusely  floristic  intersect  peninsula
terrorise  wartcress  bombastic  diffusion  floristry  intorsion  penpusher
terrorism  washerman  bookishly  diffusive  fluorspar  intrusion  perfusion
terrorist  wavefront  boorishly  dimension  flyfisher  intrusive  perfusive
testdrive  wayfaring  brakeshoe  dimissory  focussing  inversely  pertussis
tetrarchy  waywardly  brakesman  Dionysiac  foolishly  inversion  pervasion
theatrics  welfarism  bretasche  Dionysian  foppishly  inversive  pervasive
theocracy  westering  bridesman  dismissal  fricassee  janissary  petersham
theocrasy  westerner  Britisher  disposure  furbisher  jobmaster  pettishly
thirdrate  windbreak  broadside  diversely  furnisher  joylessly  pharisaic
tightrope  windproof  brutishly  diversify  gannister  Judaistic  pianistic
timbering  winepress  bullishly  diversion  garnishee  judgeship  pietistic
timberman  winterise  burlesque  diversity  geodesist  Junoesque  piggishly
timocracy  wiredrawn  burnisher  divulsion  gibbosity  Keynesian  plainsman
tinderbox  wisecrack  caddisfly  doggishly  girlishly  klinostat  plainsong
toastrack  withdrawn  cadetship  doltishly  globosity  knavishly  planisher
Tocharian  withering  callosity  donnishly  glucoside  lairdship  poetaster
tonsorial  witherite  canvasser  draftsman  glycoside  lawlessly  pointsman
topiarian  wolverene  Cartesian  driftsail  gneissoid  Leicester  polyester
topiarist  wolverine  casuistic  dualistic  gneissose  leptosome  pomposity
torchrace  wonderful  casuistry  dubiosity  gooseskin  licensure  possessed
torturous  woodcraft  Caucasian  earnestly  goosestep  lightship  possessor
traceried  xenograft  cerussite  earthstar  grandsire  lightsome  potassium
traitress  xylograph  chemistry  ecclesial  grandslam  lightsout  pranksome
traversal  yesterday  chiefship  ecosystem  grapeshot  limousine  prankster
traverser  zoiatrics  chorister  ecstasise  greensand  lithesome  precisely
trichroic  abolisher  cleansing  egotistic  groomsman  loathsome  precisian
triforium  abscissae  clerkship  egression  grotesque  loutishly  precision
trimerous  abscissas  coelostat  eightsome  guardship  lumpishly  prelusion
triturate  accessary  coenosarc  eldership  guardsman  magnesian  prelusive
trunkroad  accession  cognisant  ellipsoid  guildship  magnesite  prelusory
tuckerbag  accessory  collision  embassage  gymnasial  magnesium  pressstud
tuliproot  addressee  collusion  embrasure  gymnasium  majorship  prevision
typewrite  addresser  collusive  embussing  gymnastic  manorseat  printshop
unadorned  addressor  colosseum  emphasise  haemostat  maquisard  priorship
uncharted  adenosine  coltishly  emphysema  hamfisted  marcasite  proboscis
underrate  adiposity  commissar  emplastic  haplessly  mawkishly  processed
underripe  admeasure  compasses  encaustic  harvester  mayorship  processer
unguarded  admission  composite  enclosure  haversack  microsome  processor
unhurried  admissive  composure  endlessly  heartsick  misassign  professed
uniformly  adversary  concisely  engrosser  heartsore  misbeseem  professor
uniparous  adversely  concision  epidosite  heliostat  molluscan  profusely
uniserial  adversity  confessor  epinastic  hellishly  morrisman  profusion
```

```
progestin  slingshot  undershot  ailanthus  budgetary  crediting  disentomb
prolusion  snakeskin  underside  allantois  buffeting  cremation  disesteem
prolusory  sobsister  undersign  allotting  buhrstone  crematory  disputant
promising  soidisant  undersold  amianthus  bullytree  crenation  diverting
protester  solipsism  undersong  amplitude  burrstone  crenature  dogmatics
protestor  solipsist  underspin  ancestral  Byzantine  crepitant  dogmatise
provision  solmisate  unfleshed  andantino  cacoethes  crepitate  dogmatism
provisory  sophister  unfleshly  animation  cadastral  crosstalk  dogmatist
provostry  sophistic  unicuspid  animatism  cadential  croustade  dormition
prudishly  sophistry  untrussed  annectent  calenture  curbstone  dormitory
pterosaur  sottishly  Upanishad  annuitant  calmative  curettage  doughtily
publisher  souwester  upholster  aperitive  campstool  curvature  downstage
purposely  spaceship  uselessly  appertain  candytuft  curveting  dramatics
purposive  spacesuit  varnisher  apportion  carnation  curvetted  dramatise
queenship  spearside  verbosely  archetype  carnitine  cyclotron  dramatist
quicksand  speedster  verbosity  architect  carpetbag  cystotomy  dripstone
quickstep  spinosity  vibrissae  arcuately  carpeting  dalmatian  drugstore
quirister  spoilsman  villosity  argentine  caseation  damnation  drumstick
raffishly  spokesman  viscosity  argentite  cassation  damnatory  dulcitude
rareeshow  sportsman  vitiosity  argentous  catoptric  debenture  dysentery
realistic  spritsail  vouchsafe  armistice  causation  decastere  eccentric
recension  stateside  waggishly  aromatise  causative  deceitful  education
recession  statesman  waspishly  arrestant  ceanothus  deception  educative
recessive  statistic  watershed  arresting  celestial  deceptive  effective
reclusion  steamship  waterside  asafetida  cementite  decistere  effectual
reclusive  steersman  wearisome  asbestine  cerastium  decoction  effortful
recursion  stegosaur  Wednesday  asbestous  certitude  decontrol  eglantine
recursive  storeship  wholesale  ascertain  cessation  decretive  elevation
redresser  stormsail  wholesome  aspartate  chelation  decretory  elocution
refreshen  stressful  witlessly  aspectual  chemitype  deduction  emanation
refresher  stylishly  wolfishly  assertion  chieftain  deductive  emanative
regisseur  stylistic  Worcester  assertive  Chinatown  defeatism  embattled
Reichstag  subcostal  worrisome  assistant  chinstrap  defeatist  embrittle
remeasure  submaster  wristshot  asymptote  chopstick  defeature  Emmenthal
remission  successor  yachtsman  athletics  Christian  defection  emulation
repossess  suffusion  Yiddisher  Atlantean  Christmas  defective  emulative
represent  suggester  youngster  attention  citystate  deflation  emunctory
repressor  supersede  abduction  attentive  claustral  dejection  endosteal
repulsion  superstar  abjection  attrition  clavation  demitting  endosteum
repulsive  supposing  abolition  avocation  clientage  demystify  englutted
requester  sweatshop  aboutturn  azimuthal  clientele  dentation  enrapture
requisite  sweetshop  abruption  Babbittry  cloistral  dentition  entertain
reversely  swinishly  accentual  backstage  coalition  departure  epilation
reversion  swordsman  acceptant  bandstand  coarctate  depasture  eremitism
revulsion  symposiac  acceptive  barbitone  cobaltite  depiction  eruditely
revulsive  symposial  accretion  barnstorm  cobaltous  depictive  erudition
rhymester  symposium  accretive  basketful  cockatiel  depletion  escortage
riverside  tallyshop  aconitine  beanstalk  coemption  depletive  essential
rodfisher  tartishly  acoustics  beatitude  cognately  dermatoid  eurhythmy
roguishly  thalassic  acquittal  bedsettee  cognation  desertion  eutectoid
roughshod  thaneship  acquitted  bedsitter  cognition  despotism  evocation
roundsman  thirdsman  actuation  beefsteak  cognitive  destitute  evocative
rulership  Thomistic  addiction  befitting  colcothar  desuetude  evocatory
sacristan  threesome  addictive  begetting  collation  desultory  evolution
saintship  throwster  adduction  besetting  collotype  detection  evolutive
sarcastic  thyristor  adductive  besotting  colostomy  detective  excentric
sargassos  tigerseye  ademption  bespatter  colostrum  detention  exceptant
satinspar  toothsome  admitting  betrothal  combatant  detrition  excepting
scarfskin  torchsong  admixture  betrothed  combative  devastate  exception
scrimshaw  touristic  adoration  bimonthly  comfiture  deviation  exceptive
secession  tracksuit  adulation  biometric  Comintern  diametral  excretion
seclusion  tradesman  adulatory  bipartite  committal  diametric  excretive
seclusive  transship  advantage  bisection  committed  dichotomy  excretory
selfishly  tribesman  advection  bluestone  committee  dicrotism  executant
sequester  tricksily  advective  bolection  commotion  dictation  execution
sequestra  trickster  Adventism  bondstone  commutate  didactics  executive
sexlessly  trimester  Adventist  boobytrap  competent  dietetics  executory
sharkskin  troopship  adventive  bookstall  condition  dietitian  executrix
sharpshod  trousseau  adventure  bookstand  confiteor  digastric  exegetist
sheepskin  tutorship  advertent  bookstore  connately  digestion  exemption
shoreside  twofisted  advertise  boycotter  connation  digestive  expectant
shortstop  unabashed  affecting  breadtree  connature  dignitary  expecting
sickishly  unbiassed  affection  breastpin  copartner  dimwitted  expertise
sideissue  unblessed  affective  breveting  copestone  dipeptide  expiation
sightseer  unceasing  affixture  brevetted  cornetist  direction  expiatory
sinlessly  uncrossed  afflation  brightish  cornstalk  directive  expletive
sinuosity  underseal  aftertime  brimstone  cornstone  directory  expletory
slaveship  underseas  agitation  broadtail  coverture  directrix  exsertile
slavishly  undersell  agitative  bucketful  cowlstaff  disentail  exsertion
```

extortion	grubstake	insectary	magnetism	occultist	polyptych	remontant
extortive	guncotton	insectile	magnetist	octastyle	popliteal	rendition
exudation	gustation	insertion	magnetite	octostyle	portative	repentant
exudative	gustative	insetting	magnetron	offertory	potentate	repertory
factitive	gustatory	insistent	magnitude	olfaction	potential	repletion
faggoting	guttation	institute	mahlstick	olfactive	precative	reportage
fairytale	haematite	intention	mandatary	olfactory	precatory	repotting
faldstool	haematoid	intestacy	mandatory	onsetting	predation	resection
farestage	haematoma	intestate	maneating	operation	predative	resentful
farmstead	hailstone	intestine	manhattan	operative	predatory	resetting
fatwitted	hailstorm	intuition	marestail	opportune	prefatory	resistant
feedstock	hairstyle	intuitive	marketday	orientate	prelatess	resistive
feedstuff	halfstaff	inunction	marketing	outfitter	prelatise	resitting
fenestrae	hallstand	invective	marlstone	outputted	prelature	restitute
fenestral	Hallstatt	invention	maulstick	outwitted	premature	resultant
ferrotype	handstand	inventive	mediately	overstate	premotion	resultful
feudatory	harmattan	inventory	mediation	oversteer	prenotion	retention
filiation	harmotome	invertase	mediatise	overstock	prepotent	retentive
filmstrip	haughtily	ironstone	mediative	overstuff	priestess	retortion
fioritura	headstall	irruption	mediatory	ovulation	primatial	revetting
fioriture	headstock	irruptive	mediatrix	ovulatory	primitive	revictual
firestone	headstone	isobathic	mementoes	oxidation	privateer	revolting
flagstaff	heliotype	isolation	mentation	Pakistani	privately	rewritten
flagstick	Helvetian	isolative	mesentery	palletise	privation	ridgetile
flagstone	hemistich	isometric	mezzotint	palmation	privative	roadstead
flashtube	hermitage	isooctane	microtome	palmitate	probation	rocketeer
flightily	herpetoid	iteration	microtomy	palpation	probative	rootstock
floodtide	hexastich	iterative	microtone	palpitant	probatory	roseately
flotation	hexastyle	jackstraw	migration	palpitate	profiteer	rowantree
flowstone	hieratica	jactation	migratory	palustral	prolately	ruination
foliation	hirsutism	jesuitise	milestone	paperthin	prolation	russeting
foodstuff	hoarstone	jesuitism	millstone	parentage	prolative	sabbatise
footstalk	holystone	jetsetter	miniature	partition	promotion	sabbatism
footstall	homestead	jockstrap	misesteem	partitive	promotive	sagittate
footstool	honkytonk	jossstick	momentary	peacetime	promptbox	saltation
forestage	hornstone	Judastree	momentous	pegmatite	pronation	saltatory
forestall	horsetail	junketing	monastery	pelletise	prototype	salvation
forgather	hortation	karyotype	monostich	pellitory	pulpiteer	sandstone
forgetful	hortative	kerbstone	monostyle	penultima	pulpstone	sandstorm
forgotten	hortatory	kibbutzim	moonstone	perdition	pulsatile	Sarmation
formation	huckstery	kickstart	mousetrap	peristome	pulsation	satiation
formative	humectant	knightage	multitude	peristyle	pulsatory	schistose
formatted	hydration	lacertian	musketeer	permitted	puppeteer	schistous
forsythia	hypnotise	lacertine	Nahuatlan	permitter	purgation	schnitzel
fortitude	hypnotism	lactation	narcotine	permutate	purgative	sciential
freestone	hypnotist	lallation	narcotism	perpetual	purgatory	scientism
freestyle	hypostyle	lassitude	narcotism	pettitoes	quixotism	scientist
fricative	illgotten	laudation	narration	phenotype	quotation	scripture
frigatoon	imitation	laudative	narrative	philately	racketeer	sculpture
frightful	imitative	laudatory	narratory	phonation	raconteur	sealetter
fruittree	immixture	leafstalk	naughtily	phonatory	radiately	seanettle
furcation	impaction	leucotome	necrotise	phonetics	radiation	secretage
furniture	impartial	leucotomy	negritude	phonetise	radiative	secretary
gadgeteer	impastoed	Levantine	nemertean	phonetism	rainstorm	secretion
galactose	impletion	leviathan	nemertine	phonetist	raspatory	secretive
galantine	important	libertine	neolithic	phototype	rebaptise	secretory
gallstone	importune	libration	nepenthes	phytotomy	rebutting	sedentary
garniture	impostume	libratory	nervation	phytotron	recapture	seduction
garreteer	imposture	librettos	nervature	picketing	reception	seductive
garrotter	inanition	lifestyle	neuration	pikestaff	receptive	selection
gasfitter	incaution	limestone	newsstand	pinnately	rectitude	selective
gazetteer	incentive	lineation	nictation	pipestone	redaction	selectman
gemmation	inception	liquation	nictitate	piscatory	redletter	semanteme
geobotany	inceptive	lithotomy	nighttime	pituitary	reductant	semantics
geometric	indention	livestock	nigritude	placation	reduction	semestral
geometrid	indenture	loadstone	nitratine	placatory	reductive	semiotics
geriatric	indiction	lobectomy	nitration	plaintiff	refection	sensation
gestation	induction	lodestone	nonentity	plaintive	refectory	sensitise
gestatory	inductive	logistics	normative	planation	refitting	sensitive
gigantism	infantile	longitude	nowhither	planetary	reflation	septation
gladstone	infantine	lovestory	nutrition	planetoid	registrar	sepulture
godfather	infection	lucrative	nutritive	platitude	regretful	seriately
godmother	infective	lunchtime	objectify	plenitude	regretted	serration
gradation	infertile	macintosh	objection	plicately	reinstate	servitude
gradatory	inflation	maelstrom	objective	plication	rejection	seventeen
granitoid	ingestion	magistery	obstetric	plicature	reluctant	seventhly
gratitude	ingestive	magistral	obtention	pocketful	reluctate	seventies
gravitate	injection	magnetics	obviation	pollutant	remittent	shadetree
gritstone	injustice	magnetise	occultism	pollution	remitting	shamateur

sheeptick	teakettle	vitiation	direfully	marihuana	songfully	elusively
shirttail	tentation	voluntary	discourse	marijuana	soulfully	emotively
shortterm	tentative	volunteer	dolefully	methought	spherular	emotivity
siccative	termitary	wapentake	dubiously	mindfully	strenuous	endeavour
signatory	ternately	washstand	duralumin	molecular	subcaudal	engraving
signature	territory	weightily	duteously	monocular	subocular	evasively
siltation	tessitura	weighting	dutifully	moonquake	succourer	exservice
siltstone	testation	whetstone	easefully	navicular	sulphuret	extravert
simpatico	testatrix	whinstone	electuary	needfully	sulphuric	extrovert
sinistral	thinktank	whipstock	emulously	nervously	sumptuary	festively
sinuately	thirstily	winestone	enamoured	nocuously	sumptuous	festivity
sinuation	thorntree	withstand	energumen	noxiously	sunlounge	forgiving
situation	thriftily	withstood	enviously	obliquely	sunspurge	furtively
slabstone	throatily	yardstick	eventuate	obliquity	tactfully	gallivant
slapstick	throttler	zincotype	extenuate	obsequent	tambourin	grapevine
slightish	thumbtack	acellular	fatefully	obsequial	tarpaulin	Harrovian
smalltime	Thyestean	ambiguity	fatuously	obsequies	tearfully	herbivore
smoketree	thyratron	ambiguous	fearfully	obviously	tediously	impluvium
snowstorm	tilestone	amorously	fireguard	odorously	tenaculum	improvise
soapstone	titration	anacruses	flocculus	ominously	tenuously	incurvate
solfatara	toadstone	anacrusis	floscular	onerously	thereunto	innervate
solvation	toadstool	antiquary	fluctuant	onslaught	thereupon	inservice
sonneteer	tombstone	antiquate	fluctuate	opercular	thesaurus	insolvent
sonnetise	tomentose	antiquity	fluecured	operculum	thingummy	intervein
sortition	tomentous	anxiously	folkmusic	opusculum	timeously	intervene
sovietise	toreutics	applauder	forejudge	orangutan	transumpt	interview
sovietism	touchtype	aqueously	fraenulum	orbicular	treasurer	introvert
spacetime	tradition	archducal	fretfully	ossicular	trysquare	keelivine
spiritism	trematode	archduchy	fructuate	painfully	tunefully	khedivial
spiritist	tributary	arduously	fructuous	parlously	unberufen	lawgiving
spiritoso	trilithon	articular	funicular	peasouper	unclouded	leftovers
spiritous	trimetric	assiduity	funiculus	pedicular	unnatural	longevity
spiritual	tuliptree	assiduous	furiously	pipsqueak	unpopular	longevous
spirituel	tungstate	attenuate	gainfully	piteously	unthought	massively
splintery	turnstile	auricular	gastrulae	pitifully	unwrought	millivolt
splitting	turnstone	avuncular	gibbously	playfully	utricular	misadvise
spluttery	turpitude	babirussa	glandular	pompously	vacuously	misgiving
sprigtail	twelfthly	balefully	gleefully	potpourri	variously	misgovern
squatting	twicetold	banefully	grossular	pronounce	vehicular	muscovado
starstone	ululation	bashfully	habituate	punctuate	vesicular	muscovite
statutory	uncertain	bellpunch	halieutic	quadruman	viciously	observant
stenotype	unclothed	bethought	handcuffs	quadruped	viscounty	outgiving
stenotypy	uncouthly	biliously	harbourer	quadruple	viscously	passivate
stilettos	undertake	bilirubin	harmfully	quadruply	vocabular	passively
stinktrap	undertint	binocular	hatefully	quintuple	wakefully	passivity
stipitate	undertone	blastulae	heedfully	radicular	waveguide	Pavlovian
streetcar	undertook	blastular	heinously	raucously	whereunto	pensively
striation	unearthly	bodyguard	helpfully	rearguard	whereupon	persevere
striature	unfitting	bratwurst	hideously	rechauffe	wishfully	reconvene
stricture	unknitted	brusquely	hopefully	reimburse	wistfully	reconvert
strontium	unscathed	bulbously	hugeously	reliquary	zealously	reservist
structure	unsettled	caciquism	hurtfully	reliquiae	zestfully	reservoir
strutting	unspotted	calicular	hydraulic	residuary	abusively	resolvent
subaltern	unweeting	callously	ichneumon	resoluble	acclivity	restively
subastral	unwitting	canesugar	impetuous	restfully	aestivate	retrovert
sublation	unwritten	canicular	impiously	rethought	aggravate	skydiving
sublethal	uplifting	capitular	inaugural	reticular	archivist	slivovitz
submitted	upsetting	capitulum	indraught	reticulum	archivolt	suasively
succotash	valentine	carefully	infatuate	retinulae	boulevard	subdivide
sulcation	vallation	cartouche	ingenuity	retinular	captivate	supervene
summation	valuation	cassoulet	ingenuous	retrousse	captivity	supervise
summative	variation	chibouque	innocuity	ridiculer	carnivore	Theravada
sunbather	vasectomy	chisquare	innocuous	riotously	charivari	tittivate
sweettalk	vastitude	clinquant	insinuate	ruinously	concavely	transvest
swordtail	Vedantist	coadjutor	insoluble	ruthfully	concavity	triumviri
symmetric	veinstone	coinsurer	insolubly	safeguard	connivent	tsarevich
syncytial	velveteen	concourse	involucre	sanctuary	convivial	undervest
syncytium	vendition	confluent	involuted	schnauzer	costively	unitively
synectics	vernation	congruent	inwrought	scorbutic	cultivate	uvarovite
synoptist	versatile	congruity	irregular	seasquirt	cursively	Vitruvian
tablature	vestiture	congruous	jealously	semilunar	czarevich	volauvent
tabletalk	vibratile	copiously	landaulet	seriously	declivity	afterword
tactitian	vibration	creatural	langouste	setsquare	declivous	angleworm
talkathon	vibrative	curiously	lifeguard	shinguard	depravity	arrowwood
talkative	vibratory	cuticular	limejuice	sideburns	discovert	arrowworm
tarantara	videotape	deciduate	loafsugar	siliquose	discovery	backsword
tarantass	vignetter	deciduous	lustfully	sinuously	disfavour	bailiwick
tarantism	violation	devaluate	manipular	skilfully	effluvial	beachwear
tarantula	violative	deviously	manoeuvre	snowguard	effluvium	birthwort

```
blackwash  landowner  strawworm  diachylom  haphazard  appertain  bombinate
bloodworm  leastways  sundowner  diachylum  heliozoan  applejack  bondslave
bloodwort  leastwise  swearword  diaphysis  heliozoic  applicant  bookplate
boardwalk  lightwood  tableware  eightyish  hydrazine  approbate  bookstall
boatswain  liverwort  tallowish  endolymph  hydrozoan  aquaplane  bookstand
borrowing  lousewort  therewith  epiphyses  hydrozoon  arbitrage  boomerang
brainwash  marrowfat  tigerwood  epiphysis  interzone  arbitrary  boomslang
brainwave  marshwort  tightwire  epiphytal  organzine  arbitrate  bootblack
briarwood  matchwood  toothwort  epiphytic  proenzyme  armillary  boulevard
brickwork  metalwork  touchwood  eucalypti  protozoal  arrearage  brachiate
bridewell  microwave  tulipwood  eucaryote  protozoan  arrestant  bracteate
brierwood  moneywort  uncrowned  familyman  protozoic  ascendant  braincase
broadways  mouthwash  underwear  genotypic  protozoon  ascertain  brainwash
broadwise  mucksweat  underwent  ginglymus  quartzite  Ashkenazi  brainwave
brushwood  navelwort  underwing  graveyard  quartzose  aspartate  breakfast
brushwork  newlyweds  underwood  Grundyism  shemozzle  assailant  brecciate
cassowary  nightwork  unknowing  hemicycle  Spinozism  assistant  brickyard
catchword  northward  watchword  homonymic  Spinozist  associate  bridecake
caterwaul  northwest  waterweed  ichthyoid  trapezial  astrolabe  briefcase
cedarwood  otherwise  waterworn  kilocycle  trapezium  astronaut  brilliant
chickweed  paintwork  wedgewise  lachrymal  trapezoid  attendant  broadcast
chinaware  paperwork  wheelwork  lifecycle  ─────────  attenuate  broadtail
clockwise  patchwork  wherewith  lightyear  abominate  auspicate  broadways
clockwork  paulownia  whirlwind  liveryman  aboutface  autoclave  brokerage
coachwork  pearlwort  whitewash  megacycle  acceptant  autocracy  broomrape
coastward  pennywort  whitewing  metonymic  accessary  autograft  buckboard
coastwise  piecework  whitewood  Mondayish  acclimate  autograph  budgetary
copsewood  pokerwork  wideawake  monkeyish  accompany  auxiliary  bushcraft
crossways  presswork  widthways  monkeyism  accordant  bacillary  bushwhack
crosswind  quillwort  widthwise  monkeynut  acetylate  backboard  buttygang
crosswise  rightward  willowish  monotypic  aciculate  backslang  cablelaid
crossword  riverweed  windowbox  overlying  acidulate  backspace  cailleach
delftware  rosinweed  windswept  panegyric  acuminate  backstage  calcarate
drawnwork  roundworm  worldwide  pantryman  adenomata  backtrack  calculate
driftweed  sallowish  worrywart  paralysis  adsorbate  balaclava  calibrate
driftwood  sapanwood  woundwort  paralytic  adumbrate  bandstand  caliphate
earthward  satinwood  yellowdog  paranymph  advantage  barmbrack  camelback
earthwork  scarfwise  yellowish  parleyvoo  adversary  barograph  camelhair
earthworm  screwworm  zebrawood  pericycle  aerograph  barricade  campchair
fancywork  sedgewren  connexion  perilymph  aeroplane  barricado  campcraft
fellowman  selfaware  convexity  polytypic  aerospace  bastinade  candidacy
fieldwork  semisweet  deflexion  porphyria  aestivate  bastinado  candidate
following  sheepwalk  effluxion  presbyope  affiliate  battleaxe  canebrake
forthwith  sheepwash  hydroxide  presbyter  affirmant  beanfeast  canetrash
framework  shellwork  inflexion  prettyish  affricate  beanstalk  cannonade
frontward  shipowner  overexert  prettyism  aforesaid  beechmast  cannulate
frontways  shoreward  prefixion  pyrolysis  Afrikaans  bellglass  capillary
frontwise  shoreweed  prolixity  pyrolytic  aftercare  bellyband  capsulate
frostwork  shortwave  reflexion  pyroxylin  aftermath  benignant  captivate
galliwasp  sideswipe  reflexive  quarryman  aggravate  bergamask  carbamate
gallowses  slantways  thyroxine  safetypin  aggregate  biconcave  carbonado
ghostword  slantwise  unisexual  salicylic  algebraic  bifoliate  carbonate
glassware  slinkweed  aldehydic  scallywag  allegiant  bifurcate  cardboard
glasswork  slopewise  anaptyxis  scrapyard  alleviate  bilabiate  cardsharp
glasswort  smartweed  apocrypha  sentrybox  allograph  billboard  carronade
gobetween  snakeweed  apophyses  shantyman  alloplasm  bipinnate  cartilage
greenweed  snakewood  apophysis  songcycle  alpargata  birchbark  cartulary
greenwood  sorrowful  autocycle  stackyard  altercate  birdbrain  cassowary
grillwork  soundwave  autolysis  steelyard  alternant  birthmark  castigate
guesswork  southward  autolytic  stockyard  alternate  birthrate  cataclasm
gunpowder  southwest  barleymow  subphylum  aluminate  bivariant  cataplasm
Halloween  spadework  biorhythm  surveying  alveolate  bivariate  caterwaul
Hallowmas  spearwort  brachyura  symphysis  ambuscade  blackball  cavalcade
handiwork  speedwell  brickyard  synonymic  ampersand  blackdamp  celebrant
handywork  spokewise  cacodylic  taxpaying  analysand  blackface  celebrate
harrowing  stairwell  catalyser  toponymal  anchorage  blackgame  cellarage
heartwood  statewide  catalyses  toponymic  ancillary  blackjack  centenary
Hollywood  steelwork  catalysis  trachytic  angiomata  blackmail  cerebrate
horsewhip  sternward  catalytic  triptyque  annuitant  blackwash  cerograph
housewife  stickwork  chatoyant  twentyone  anovulant  bloodbath  chaingang
housework  stinkweed  cherrypie  vestryman  antennary  bluebeard  chainmail
inbetween  stinkwood  chlamydes  wherryman  antiquary  blueblack  chairlady
inflowing  stockwhip  clepsydra  woodnymph  antiquate  bluegrass  charabanc
ingrowing  stonewall  clergyman  zoophylic  antitrade  boardwalk  charivari
interwind  stoneware  clergymen  anthozoan  apiculate  boatswain  Charolais
interwove  stonework  colocynth  bombazine  appellant  boattrain  chatelain
jewelweed  stonewort  copolymer  Caenozoic  appellate  bodyguard  chatoyant
kittiwake  strapwork  courtyard  Cainozoic  appendage  boliviano  cheapjack
lancewood  strapwort  cytolysis  embezzler  appendant  bombilate  checkmate
```

chieftain	crookback	dixieland	extirpate	gallivant	humiliate	knotgrass
chilblain	crossfade	doctorate	extricate	galliwasp	hunchback	kymograph
chinaware	crosstalk	doorframe	exuberant	gallonage	hurricane	laciniate
chipboard	crossways	doorplate	exuberate	gallopade	hypallage	lamellate
chipolata	croustade	downgrade	eyestrain	gangboard	hypergamy	lampblack
chisquare	cucullate	downstage	fabricant	gangplank	hyphenate	lampshade
chocolate	culminant	dragomans	fabricate	gasconade	hypoblast	lancejack
chokedamp	culminate	drawplate	factorage	gatecrash	ideograph	lancinate
choleraic	cultivate	dreamland	fairyland	geobotany	idiograph	landgrave
circinate	curettage	driftsail	fairytale	germinate	idioplasm	landscape
circulate	curtilage	dromedary	fanfarade	germplasm	imaginary	Langobard
citystate	cuspidate	duckboard	farestage	gingerade	imbricate	lapstrake
clapboard	customary	dulcamara	fascinate	gingerale	immediacy	lardycake
classmate	cuttysark	duodenary	faveolate	ginpalace	immediate	leafstalk
clathrate	cyclamate	duplicate	fecundate	glassgall	immigrant	leastways
clientage	cyclorama	earthward	festinate	glassware	immigrate	legendary
cliffhang	cymophane	ecdysiast	fibromata	glomerate	impeccant	legionary
clinquant	cystocarp	ectoblast	fiduciary	glutamate	impetrate	legislate
clipboard	cytoplasm	ectoplasm	fieldfare	grandpapa	implicate	lendlease
cloudland	dairymaid	eidograph	fimbriate	granulate	important	libellant
coadunate	dancehall	ejaculate	finedrawn	grassland	imprecate	lifeguard
coagulant	dartboard	elaborate	firealarm	gratulate	impresari	lineolate
coagulate	dashboard	electuary	fireblast	graveyard	inamorata	lingulate
coarctate	deathmask	eliminate	firebrand	gravitate	inanimate	lionheart
coastward	decennary	elucidate	firedrake	greenback	incarnate	liquidate
cochleate	deciduate	elutriate	fireguard	greengage	incessant	lixiviate
cockroach	declarant	embarrass	fireplace	greensand	inculcate	loanshark
coelomata	declinate	embassage	firsthand	greybeard	inculpate	longchain
coelomate	decollate	embrocate	firstrate	grosgrain	incurvate	longcoats
coenosarc	decussate	emolliate	fishplate	groundage	indignant	Longobard
cognisant	defalcate	empennage	fishyback	groundash	inebriant	lotusland
colligate	defendant	encephala	flagstaff	grubstake	inebriate	lovefeast
collimate	defoliant	enchilada	flambeaus	guardrail	inelegant	lowercase
collocate	defoliate	encomiast	flambeaux	guildhall	infatuate	lubricant
colonnade	dehydrate	encompass	flarepath	gynocracy	infirmary	lubricate
columbary	deinosaur	encourage	flashback	gyroplane	informant	lucubrate
combatant	delftware	endoblast	floodgate	habituate	infuriate	luxuriant
combinate	delineate	endophagy	floodmark	hairgrass	infuscate	luxuriate
commonage	demandant	endoplasm	flowchart	hairspace	innervate	lymegrass
communard	demarcate	engarland	flowerage	halfstaff	inoculate	machinate
commutate	democracy	entertain	fluctuant	halftrack	insatiate	mailplane
compliant	demurrage	entoblast	fluctuate	hallstand	insectary	mailtrain
confidant	denigrate	entourage	folkweave	Hallstatt	insensate	mainbrace
conjugate	denitrate	enucleate	foodchain	halothane	insinuate	makeready
consonant	deodorant	enumerate	footboard	handbrake	instigate	malignant
constrain	dependant	enunciate	footplate	handcraft	integrand	mamillary
consulage	deprecate	epiphragm	footstalk	handglass	integrant	mamillate
consulate	deprecate	eradicate	footstall	handshake	integrate	mandatary
contumacy	desecrate	ergograph	forceland	handstand	intendant	manducate
cooperage	desiccant	escortage	forebrain	haphazard	interface	manganate
cooperant	desiccate	esemplasy	forereach	hardboard	interlace	maquisard
cooperate	designate	esplanade	forestage	hatchback	interlard	marchpane
copesmate	desperado	espousals	forestall	haversack	interpage	marchpast
cormorant	desperate	estoppage	formicary	headboard	intestacy	marestail
cornbrash	deuterate	estrapade	formicate	headscarf	intestate	marginate
corncrake	devaluate	evaginate	formulaic	headstall	intricacy	marihuana
cornstalk	devastate	evaporate	formulary	heartland	intricate	marijuana
corollary	dharmsala	eventuate	formulate	hermitage	intrigant	marmalade
corporate	dichogamy	everglade	fornicate	hibernate	invariant	marshland
corposant	dignitary	examinant	fortunate	highchair	invertase	masticate
correlate	dimidiate	exanimate	fosterage	highclass	inviolacy	matronage
corrugate	diplomacy	exarchate	Franglais	highgrade	inviolate	maxillary
corticate	diplomate	exceptant	freeboard	hindbrain	irradiant	medullary
coruscant	dirttrack	excoriate	frogspawn	hodograph	irradiate	medullate
coruscate	disembark	exculpate	frontpage	holograph	isinglass	megadeath
coryphaei	disengage	executant	frontward	homeopath	isooctane	meliorate
cosmonaut	disentail	exemplary	frontways	homograft	itineracy	melismata
cosmorama	dislocate	exfoliate	fructuate	homograph	itinerant	melodrama
courtcard	disparage	exonerate	fruitcake	homoplasy	itinerary	mendicant
courtyard	disparate	expatiate	frustrate	hornwrack	itinerate	mercenary
covariant	displease	expectant	fulgurant	horseback	jackplane	mesoblast
cowlstaff	disputant	explicate	fulgurate	horsehair	jambalaya	metaphase
crankcase	disregard	expurgate	fullscale	horsetail	janissary	metaplasm
crashland	disrepair	exsiccate	fulminant	hourglass	judiciary	methylate
crenulate	dissipate	extendant	fulminate	housecarl	juniorate	metricate
crepitant	dissonant	extenuate	fusillade	housemaid	kickstart	micaslate
crepitate	dithyramb	externals	fustigate	housemate	kingcraft	microwave
criminate			gabionade	huckaback	kittiwake	micturate
croissant			galingale	humectant	knightage	milkshake

```
millboard  overdraft  portulaca  resistant  showplace  succinate  triturate
millenary  overdrawn  postulant  resultant  shrinkage  succotash  troutfarm
misbehave  overglaze  postulate  resurface  sickleave  suffocate  trunkcall
miscreant  overgraze  potentate  retaliate  sideboard  sugarcane  trysquare
miscreate  overheard  poundcake  retardant  sidetrack  sultanate  tungstate
mismanage  overleapt  pozzolana  rhizocarp  sigillary  sumptuary  turbinate
mobocracy  overreach  predicant  righthand  sigillate  suppliant  Turcomans
mollymawk  overreact  predicate  rightward  signboard  suppurate  Turkomans
molybdate  overstate  predikant  ringshake  silkgland  supremacy  twayblade
momentary  overtrain  preengage  ringsnake  simulcast  surfboard  twicelaid
moneybags  overweary  preordain  riverbank  siphonage  surrogate  umbellate
monocracy  oxygenate  pressgang  rockbrake  skiagraph  susurrant  uncertain
monodrama  packtrain  pressmark  rockplant  skingraft  sweatband  underhand
monograph  paederast  primipara  rocksnake  slantways  sweepback  underlaid
monophagy  Pakistani  procreant  roofplate  slingback  sweettalk  underlain
monoplane  palmitate  procreate  roughcast  slipcoach  sweptback  underpaid
moonquake  palpitant  procuracy  rubricate  slowcoach  swordcane  underpart
moonscape  palpitate  promenade  runcinate  smokeball  swordtail  underpass
mossagate  palsgrave  propagate  rusticate  smokejack  syllabary  undertake
motorcade  paperback  propylaea  sacculate  snowflake  syncopate  ungallant
mouthpart  papillary  prorogate  safeguard  snowguard  syndicate  unisonant
mouthwash  papillate  prostrate  sagittate  snowplant  syndicate  uppercase
mucronate  paragraph  proximate  sailplane  snowscape  tableland  urceolate
multilane  parcenary  pterosaur  salangane  sociopath  tabletalk  vaccinate
multipara  parentage  Ptolemaic  saleslady  soidisant  tableware  vacillant
muscovado  parsonage  pullulate  saltglaze  soleplate  tailboard  vacillate
musichall  passivate  pulmonary  sanctuary  solfatara  taioseach  Vaishnava
mycophagy  pastorale  pulmonate  sandarach  solmisate  talismans  vacuolate
myelomata  pastorate  pulpboard  sandblast  soothfast  tamponade  variegate
myriorama  pasturage  pulserate  sandcrack  soundwave  tantalate  variolate
nameplate  patellate  pulvinate  sandglass  soupplate  tarantara  variolate
necessary  patronage  punchball  sarcocarp  southeast  tarantass  vassalage
negotiant  pectinate  punchcard  sarcomata  southland  telegraph  ventifact
negotiate  pecuniary  punctuate  Sassenach  southward  tellurate  ventilate
neuromata  pendulate  pupillage  saxifrage  spaceband  telophase  verandaed
neuropath  peneplain  pupillary  scapulary  spatulate  temperate  verminate
newsflash  peneplane  pushchair  scholiast  speakeasy  temporary  vexillary
newsstand  penetrant  pustulate  sciagraph  speculate  tenthrate  vibraharp
nicotiana  penetrate  puzzolana  scorecard  speedball  terebrant  vicariate
nictitate  percolate  quicksand  scotomata  spiculate  termagant  videotape
nightfall  perennate  quitclaim  scrapyard  spikenard  terminate  villanage
nighthawk  perforate  rabbinate  screwball  sporocarp  termitary  villenage
nightmare  periclase  racetrack  scrimmage  sporulate  terramara  vindicate
nigricant  periodate  radiocast  scrumhalf  sprigtail  terramare  virginals
nobiliary  periplast  raffinate  scrummage  springald  theocracy  virgulate
nomocracy  permutate  rationale  seastrand  spritsail  theocrasy  viscerate
nomograph  personage  razorback  secondary  stackyard  theophany  visionary
northeast  personate  readymade  secretage  stagehand  Theravada  vitellary
northland  petiolate  reanimate  secretary  staircase  thinktank  vizierate
northward  pharisaic  rearguard  sedentary  stalemate  thirdhand  volteface
noviciate  phosphate  reclinate  seedpearl  staminate  thirdrate  voluntary
novitiate  pickaback  recoinage  seedplant  starboard  thornbill  vouchsafe
nullipara  piecerate  rectorate  segregate  stargrass  throwback  vulnerary
nuncupate  piggyback  redbreast  selfaware  steadfast  thumbmark  waggonage
nursemaid  piggybank  reductant  selfimage  steelyard  thumbnail  waistband
obbligato  pikestaff  redundant  sensedata  stegosaur  thumbtack  waldgrave
obcordate  pilferage  reeducate  sentenate  sternward  timocracy  wallboard
obfuscate  pinnulate  reentrant  septenary  stimulant  titillate  wallplate
objurgate  pitchdark  regardant  serigraph  stimulate  titlepage  wapentake
obscurant  pituitary  rehydrate  serrulate  stinkball  tittivate  washboard
obsecrate  pizzicati  reinstate  setsquare  stipitate  toastrack  washstand
observant  pizzicato  reiterate  shamefast  stipulate  torchrace  wasteland
obstinacy  placecard  reliquary  sheepwalk  stockyard  touchmark  watchcase
obstinate  placename  reluctant  sheepwash  stolonate  townscape  waterbath
oesophagi  planetary  reluctate  sheldrake  stonewall  tracheary  watercart
officiant  platemark  remediate  shelfmark  stoneware  tracheate  waterfall
officiate  plumulate  remontant  shellback  stoolball  trademark  watergate
oleograph  poinciana  repechage  shellbark  stormsail  tradename  watermark
openheart  pointlace  repellant  shinguard  straphang  trainband  whaleback
oppugnant  pokerface  repentant  shipboard  strappado  translate  wheelbase
orangeade  pollinate  replicate  shipshape  strongarm  treillage  whipsnake
orientate  pollutant  reportage  shirttail  stylobate  tremolant  whitebait
originate  polygraph  reprimand  shoeblack  subjugate  tremulant  whitebass
orphanage  polyphagy  reprobate  shogunate  sublimate  trenchant  whiteface
oscillate  polyphase  repudiate  shoreward  sublunary  trepidant  Whitehall
ossifrage  polyzoary  repugnant  shortcake  subrogate  tribunate  whitewash
osteopath  porcelain  rerebrace  shortfall  substrata  tributary  whizzbang
ovenready  porterage  rerelease  shorthand  substrate  trifocals  wholesale
overboard  portolano  residuary  shortwave  subtenant  trilobate  wideawake
```

widthways	deludable	incurable	reachable	untenable	equivocal	skeesicks
wineglass	deposable	incurably	rebukable	utterable	eristical	skiamachy
wingchair	derivable	indelible	reducible	vaporable	erratical	songcycle
wiredrawn	describer	indelibly	referable	vegetable	etherical	soritical
wisecrack	desirable	inducible	refusable	vegetably	ethnarchy	spectacle
withdrawn	desirably	ineffable	refutable	venerable	fairfaced	spellican
withstand	devisable	ineffably	removable	venerably	fanatical	spherical
wolfsbane	dilatable	inequable	renewable	veritable	fatidical	streetcar
woodcraft	dirigible	inerrable	reparable	veritably	foragecap	subdeacon
worrywart	dismember	inferable	repayable	visitable	franticly	surpliced
wristband	dissemble	infusible	reputable	wakerobin	Gaeltacht	synodical
xenograft	disturbed	inscriber	reputably	watchable	galenical	tapdancer
xylograph	disturber	insoluble	resalable	weighable	genetical	taraxacum
zamindary	dividable	insolubly	resoluble	wieldable	geomancer	technical
zapateado	divisible	insurable	resumable	windowbox	gerfalcon	tectrices
zemindary	doodlebug	invisible	revisable	worktable	graphical	tetrarchy
abdicable	doubtable	invisibly	revivable	zoophobia	graywacke	theomachy
abradable	Doukhobor	ionisable	revocable	acetylcoA	greywacke	toothache
accusable	drinkable	irascible	rightable	adminicle	guilloche	tortrices
adaptable	dubitable	irascibly	rosenoble	affianced	gyrfalcon	tortricid
adducible	emendable	irrigable	rotatable	agnatical	hagiarchy	umbilical
admirable	endurable	irritable	saddlebag	ambulacra	heartache	umbilicus
admirably	endurably	irritably	saddlebow	aminoacid	hemicycle	unethical
adoptable	enjoyable	isallobar	sandtable	androecia	heptarchy	unmusical
advisable	enjoyably	jitterbug	saturable	angelical	heretical	vademecum
advisably	enterable	kneadable	schoolbag	announcer	hierarchy	ventricle
agreeable	equitable	lacerable	schoolboy	anthracic	hypericum	veridical
agreeably	equitably	laughable	scrutable	apothecia	identical	videlicet
alienable	escapable	laughably	securable	archducal	idiotical	wehrmacht
allocable	estimable	learnable	semblable	archduchy	illogical	wheyfaced
allowable	euphorbia	letterbox	semblably	Armorican	involucre	whimsical
allowably	evincible	lifetable	sentrybox	arsenical	jaundiced	xparticle
alterable	evolvable	limitable	separable	artificer	juridical	absconder
amendable	exactable	litigable	separably	ascetical	kilocycle	adenoidal
anaerobic	excisable	litterbin	September	autocycle	Levitical	advisedly
assayable	excitable	litterbug	severable	avalanche	lifecycle	airminded
assumable	excusable	locatable	shakeable	baldfaced	logomachy	aldehydic
assumably	excusably	lyophobic	shapeable	barefaced	longfaced	allegedly
auditable	execrable	malleable	shieldbug	basilican	lovingcup	allowedly
available	execrably	medicable	shockable	battlecry	lumbrical	Amerindic
availably	fatigable	memorable	shootable	bellyache	lumbricus	amyloidal
avertible	filterbed	memorably	sidetable	beneficed	megacycle	annelidan
avoidable	filtrable	miserable	signalbox	boldfaced	molluscan	anticodon
avoidably	flammable	miserably	speakable	boondocks	monodical	antinodal
awardable	floatable	mitigable	spendable	botanical	moustache	antipodal
beslobber	flowerbed	motorable	spongebag	bretasche	nuisancer	antipodes
bilirubin	forgeable	mouldable	springbok	buttercup	numerical	aperiodic
birdtable	frangible	mountable	stableboy	canonical	obconical	applauder
blameable	freezable	navigable	stackable	capriccio	oligarchy	araneidal
blameably	gaugeable	nominable	stainable	carbuncle	parfleche	araneidan
breakable	generable	nonviable	strongbox	cartouche	pasticcio	ashamedly
bumblebee	getatable	numerable	subduable	chachacha	pentarchy	assuredly
butterbur	gogglebox	oddjobber	superable	chronical	pericycle	astraddle
carpetbag	grantable	omissible	swimmable	chronicle	piratical	attainder
catchable	graspable	opposable	teachable	classical	polemical	avizandum
claimable	habitable	outnumber	teachably	coffeecup	political	awkwardly
classable	habitably	oysterbed	temptable	colchicum	practical	backpedal
cleavable	handlebar	palatable	thinkable	convincer	precancel	bandwidth
climbable	harquebus	palatably	timetable	corpuscle	proboscis	bartender
clubbable	heritable	pasodoble	tinderbox	crepuscle	prosaical	bastardly
cobwebbed	hobnobbed	peaceable	tittlebat	crustacea	Provencal	beadledom
coercible	hobnobber	peaceably	tolerable	cryptical	psychical	bedridden
coercibly	humblebee	pepperbox	tolerably	dandiacal	quantical	belatedly
cogitable	ignitable	permeable	touchable	deistical	quebracho	bemusedly
confabbed	ignitible	pillarbox	traceable	denouncer	quizzical	bigheaded
constable	ignorable	pivotable	traceably	diningcar	recherche	blessedly
cornerboy	illegible	placeable	tractable	dipcircle	rectrices	blockader
countable	illegibly	plantable	tractably	discalced	renouncer	bombardon
coverable	imageable	plausible	trainable	disgracer	resources	bowwindow
covetable	immovable	plausibly	treatable	dishfaced	sandyacht	boxgirder
coxcombry	immovably	pleadable	tuckerbag	dominical	satanical	brigandry
creatable	immutable	ploughboy	tumblebug	Dominican	satirical	bumbledon
crossable	immutably	pouncebox	turntable	dropsical	sceptical	bystander
crushable	imputable	pregnable	twistable	druidical	sciamachy	cartridge
debatable	inaudible	printable	uneatable	dynamical	selffaced	Cassandra
decidable	inaudibly	promptbox	unifiable	eirenicon	simplices	ceratodus
deducible	incapable	proveably	unnamable	elegiacal	simulacra	chickadee
definable	incapably	pursuable	unplumbed	empirical	simulacre	chlamydes
definably	incunable	quodlibet	unsayable	entelechy	siphuncle	clepsydra

```
cofferdam  infielder  rejoinder  alertness  bluffness  Cingalese  demulcent
colloidal  innholder  remainder  alignment  bluntness  cirripede  denseness
comitadji  innuendos  reputedly  alinement  blushless  clamshell  dependent
commander  insipidly  responder  aliveness  bombshell  classless  depthless
commandos  invalidly  retrodden  allotment  bonniness  cleanness  detergent
commendam  ironsides  rhapsodic  aloneness  bookshelf  clearness  determent
compendia  ischiadic  Rhineodon  aloofness  bordereau  clientele  deterrent
comprador  junkerdom  rhizoidal  amassment  boskiness  closeness  detriment
concordat  kaiserdom  Samoyedic  amazement  bossiness  cloudless  devilment
contender  kentledge  sapheaded  amendment  boundless  coalfield  different
coriander  knifeedge  savagedom  amoebaean  boyfriend  coccygeal  diffident
cotyledon  knowledge  seagirdle  ampleness  brainless  cochineal  diffusely
crabbedly  laggardly  Sephardic  amusement  brakeless  cockiness  dinginess
crinoidal  languidly  Sephardim  anchoress  brandreth  cocoonery  dinothere
crookedly  Laplander  serenader  angriness  brashness  cognately  dirtiness
cuckoldry  latterday  sheikhdom  annectent  brassiere  coheiress  disaffect
cullender  learnedly  sigmoidal  annulment  breakneck  collinear  disappear
cycloidal  leewardly  skedaddle  apartheid  bridewell  colosseum  discovert
dastardly  limitedly  slabsided  apartment  briefless  Comintern  discovery
decapodal  lipreader  softpedal  apartness  briefness  competent  disesteem
decapodan  logaoedic  spasmodic  apishness  briskness  component  disforest
decidedly  Lombardic  squalidly  apprehend  brittlely  comradely  dishonest
descended  lowlander  squiredom  arbitress  broadleaf  comradery  disinfect
devotedly  lowloader  steroidal  archenemy  broadness  concavely  disinfest
disbudded  lowminded  stiltedly  archfiend  brownness  concisely  disorient
disburden  lunitidal  studiedly  architect  brusquely  condiment  dissident
discarder  manhandle  subcaudal  arcuately  buccaneer  confident  divergent
discoidal  mansarded  subduedly  arrowhead  buckwheat  confiteor  diversely
discredit  manysided  succeeder  artillery  bulginess  confluent  dizziness
dissuader  marketday  surrender  ascendent  bulkiness  congruent  dopefiend
dittander  martyrdom  suspender  askewness  bullybeef  connately  dottiness
Eastender  masterdom  tahsildar  assurgent  bumpiness  connivent  doubtless
embroider  meropidan  thermidor  Athenaeum  burliness  continent  dowdiness
Englander  misguided  thralldom  Atlantean  bushiness  contumely  dowerless
ethmoidal  mishandle  threnodic  atonement  butadiene  cornfield  downfield
excitedly  negroidal  tournedos  austerely  buxomness  cornopean  dragoness
expounder  niggardly  trumpedup  authoress  caballero  corporeal  drawsheet
eyeshadow  octahedra  twohanded  averagely  caerulean  corpulent  dreamless
fatheaded  octopodes  typhoidal  awareness  caesarean  cosmogeny  driftweed
forbidden  offhanded  Uitlander  awesomely  cageyness  costively  drollness
foreboder  ommatidia  unblinded  awfulness  calabrese  cotangent  dropscene
forecaddy  onehanded  unbounded  bagginess  calcaneal  countless  dumpiness
forejudge  openended  unbraided  baksheesh  calcaneum  crapulent  dungarees
forwander  opodeldoc  unclouded  balladeer  callipers  crassness  duskiness
forwarder  outlander  undecided  balminess  Camembert  craziness  dustiness
forwardly  outridden  undivided  bandoleer  canescent  creatress  dustsheet
freerider  outwardly  unfounded  bandolero  canniness  crestless  dysentery
freezedry  overladen  unguarded  banjulele  cannoneer  crispness  dyspnoeic
frowardly  panhandle  unsoundly  battiness  cantilena  crookneck  eagerness
gallmidge  paramedic  untrodden  bawdiness  Cantonese  crossbeam  earliness
gasholder  parapodia  upbraider  beachhead  Caribbean  crosshead  ebullient
genocidal  partridge  viricidal  beachwear  carrageen  crossness  ecosphere
germander  penholder  waywardly  beardless  cartwheel  crotchety  efficient
glyptodon  persuader  Wednesday  bedspread  cassareep  crownless  effulgent
goliardic  philander  worriedly  beechfern  cassimere  crowsnest  eightieth
goosander  pigheaded  Yankeedom  beefiness  castanets  crudeness  ejectment
grandaddy  plasmodia  yellowdog  beefsteak  cataplexy  cruellest  electress
guardedly  pointedly  yesterday  bejabbers  catchment  curliness  elopement
gunpowder  polyandry  abasement  belvedere  cattiness  cursively  elsewhere
haggardly  polyhedra  abashment  besetment  causeless  curstness  elusively
hagridden  prebendal  abatement  bilgekeel  ceaseless  cyclopean  embayment
hamhanded  pretender  abhorrent  biosphere  centipede  Cytherean  embedment
hendiadys  primordia  absorbent  birdsnest  chaingear  Daedalean  embraceor
hereunder  princedom  abstinent  bizarrely  chainless  damascene  embracery
heterodox  properdin  abusively  Blackfeet  chameleon  damnedest  emollient
homicidal  provender  acetylene  blackhead  champleve  Damoclean  emolument
hotheaded  psalmodic  Acheulean  blacklead  chandlery  dauntless  emotively
hundredth  puffadder  acidulent  blackness  chantress  deaconess  emphysema
hurriedly  pyramidal  adeptness  blameless  chariness  deathless  emptiness
husbandly  pyramidic  adipocere  blandness  charmless  debarment  enactment
husbandry  pyramidon  adornment  blankness  chauffeur  decastere  endosperm
hydriodic  Quakerdom  adsorbent  blaspheme  cheapness  decistere  endosteal
hypnoidal  quarenden  adultness  blasphemy  checkrein  decollete  endosteum
Icelander  quarender  adversely  blastment  cheerless  decongest  endowment
Icelandic  rascaldom  advertent  bleachery  chelicera  decrement  enjoyment
iguanodon  razoredge  agistment  bleakness  chicanery  decumbent  enrolment
impleader  redhanded  agreement  blindness  chickweed  deferment  enthymeme
impliedly  redheaded  airstream  blockhead  childless  deficient  entremets
impounder  regicidal  albescent  bloodless  chillness  dehiscent  epicurean
```

equipment	fuzziness	horniness	largeness	mixedness	palmipede	profiteer
erectness	gadgeteer	horsebean	laryngeal	moistness	panderess	profusely
errorless	gaolbreak	horseless	latescent	monastery	pantalets	prolately
eruditely	garreteer	horsiness	laundress	monitress	Paraclete	prominent
euclidean	gaspereau	hostilely	lavaliere	monotreme	parchment	proneness
evasively	gastraeum	housekeep	leafgreen	moodiness	parrakeet	proofread
eventless	gaudiness	houseleek	leakiness	mucksweat	passively	proponent
evergreen	gauntness	houseless	leaselend	muddiness	pastiness	propriety
exactment	gauziness	huckstery	leftovers	muffineer	pathogeny	propylene
exactness	gawkiness	huffiness	legginess	mugginess	patroness	prosiness
exanthema	gazetteer	humanness	leisurely	mundanely	pedigreed	protonema
excellent	gearwheel	huskiness	levelness	murderess	Pekingese	provident
excipient	genuflect	hydrocele	lightless	murkiness	penfriend	pubescent
excrement	genuinely	idealless	lightness	musketeer	penniless	pudginess
excurrent	geosphere	ignescent	lightyear	muskiness	pensively	puffiness
exilement	germanely	imageless	limitless	mustiness	perfumery	pulpiness
exosphere	giddiness	immensely	lineament	muzziness	periphery	pulpiteer
expedient	glueyness	impatiens	lissomely	Mycenaean	perisperm	pulseless
expellent	gobetween	impatient	litheness	myxoedema	perkiness	puppeteer
extolment	godliness	impendent	lividness	nakedness	permanent	purposely
extravert	godparent	imperfect	lodgement	naphthene	persevere	purpureal
extremely	goldcrest	implement	loftiness	nastiness	pertinent	pursiness
extrovert	goldeneye	imprudent	looseleaf	natheless	pestilent	pushiness
faddiness	goldfield	inaptness	looseness	nattiness	petroleum	Quakeress
faintness	gooseherd	inbetween	lousiness	nectarean	pettiness	quakiness
faithless	gooseneck	incipient	loverless	neediness	phagedena	queenless
fallalery	gossamery	inclement	lowerdeck	negligent	phenomena	queerness
falseness	governess	incorrect	lowliness	Negroness	philately	quickness
farmstead	graceless	increment	lucidness	nemertean	Philomela	quiescent
fattiness	grandness	incumbent	luckiness	nerveless	phoniness	quietness
faultless	graveless	incurrent	lumpiness	nerviness	phosphene	rabidness
fenceless	graveness	indulgent	luridness	newlyweds	photocell	racketeer
fenugreek	greatness	inebriety	lustiness	newsagent	photogene	raconteur
feoffment	Greekless	ineptness	Maccabean	newsiness	phthalein	radiately
fertilely	greenbelt	inertness	machinery	ninetieth	phylogeny	raincheck
festively	greenness	inpatient	magdalene	Nipponese	phytogeny	raininess
fetidness	greenweed	insatiety	magistery	nobleness	piecemeal	randiness
fibreless	griefless	insincere	mainsheet	noiseless	pinchbeck	ranginess
fieriness	griminess	insistent	malanders	noisiness	pinkiness	rapidness
filigreed	grossness	insolvent	manganese	noisomely	pinnately	ravelment
filminess	gruffness	insurgent	manginess	nonlinear	pinnipede	readdress
firebreak	guileless	intellect	Manichean	nonpareil	pipedream	readiness
firecrest	guiltless	intensely	manliness	northwest	pipsqueak	recipient
firmament	gumminess	intercede	manorseat	nosebleed	pistoleer	recollect
fishiness	gustiness	intercept	marmoreal	nosepiece	pithiness	recommend
fissipede	gutsiness	interfere	massiness	notedness	placeless	reconvene
fixedness	gynaeceum	interject	massively	notoriety	placement	reconvert
flakiness	habergeon	interleaf	matchless	nutriment	plainness	recumbent
flameless	hairiness	interment	mateyness	nuttiness	Pleiocene	recurrent
flatulent	hairpiece	intersect	mausoleum	obeseness	plicately	reediness
fleckless	halfbreed	intervein	mealiness	obliquely	plumpness	refitment
fleetness	halfshell	intervene	meatiness	obscenely	plushness	refulgent
fleshless	Halloween	introject	mediately	obscurely	podginess	regisseur
fleshment	handiness	introvert	meningeal	obsequent	pointless	remitment
floridean	handpress	inurement	merciless	obversely	polythene	remittent
flowsheet	handwheel	inverness	merriment	occludent	pontoneer	renascent
flushness	happiness	inversely	merriness	occurrent	popliteal	repayment
fogginess	hardiment	irksomely	mesentery	odourless	poppyhead	repellent
forcefeed	hardiness	isogamete	messiness	offscreen	portreeve	repossess
forceless	hardshell	issueless	methylene	offstreet	powerless	reprehend
forcemeat	harshness	itchiness	micromesh	Oligocene	precedent	represent
forespeak	hastiness	jailbreak	midstream	operosely	precisely	reprocess
foundress	hatchment	janitress	midwifery	orderless	predigest	resilient
fourwheel	headdress	jazziness	milkiness	osteoderm	prelatess	resolvent
frailness	headiness	jerkiness	millepede	osteogeny	prepotent	resorbent
frankness	headpiece	jetstream	millinery	otherness	prescient	restively
freewheel	heartbeat	jewellery	millipede	outspread	preselect	resurgent
freshness	heartfelt	jewelweed	millwheel	overcheck	president	resurrect
frontless	heartless	jointress	mincemeat	overdress	prestress	retrocede
fruitless	heaviness	judgement	minefield	overexert	prevalent	retroject
fullcream	Hebridean	juiceless	mirkiness	oversleep	priceless	retrovert
fulldress	heelpiece	juiciness	mirthless	overslept	prideless	reversely
fulsomely	heftiness	jumpiness	misbeseem	overspend	priestess	revetment
fundament	Heraclean	kinkiness	miscegene	overspent	primeness	riderless
funkiness	Herculean	lampshell	misdemean	oversteer	privateer	rightness
funniness	highspeed	landagent	misdirect	overtness	privately	rigidness
furtively	histogeny	lankiness	misesteem	overwhelm	privilege	riskiness
fussiness	hoariness	Laodicean	misgovern	pachyderm	procuress	riverhead
fustiness	homestead	lapstreak	mistiness	palankeen	profanely	riverweed

roadstead	sincerely	steepness	toothless	wheelless	sorrowful	flaringly
rocketeer	sinewless	sternness	toughness	whitebeam	speechful	flowingly
rockiness	Sinhalese	stiffness	traceless	whitehead	spleenful	flyweight
roominess	sinuately	stillness	trackless	whiteness	stressful	footlight
roseately	Sisyphean	stingless	traitress	wholemeal	sudorific	foresight
rosinweed	skirtless	stinkweed	transcend	wholeness	teacupful	fortnight
roughhewn	slackness	stintless	transient	windbreak	unberufen	gallingly
roughneck	slakeless	stitchery	transvest	windchest	undutiful	giltedged
roughness	sleekness	stonedead	treachery	windiness	unhelpful	glaringly
roundhead	sleepless	stonedeaf	treatment	windswept	unmindful	glowingly
roundness	slickness	stoneless	trickless	winepress	unskilful	goodnight
rousement	sliminess	stoniness	trilinear	winsomely	unthrifty	greasegun
routinely	slinkweed	stoppress	triteness	witchmeal	vaporific	gushingly
rowdiness	slothbear	stormbelt	trivalent	wittiness	warblefly	halflight
ruddiness	smallness	stormless	trochleae	wolverene	wonderful	haltingly
rufescent	smartness	stoutness	trochlear	woodiness	abidingly	hamburger
rustiness	smartweed	strangely	trousseau	wooziness	adoringly	handorgan
sacrament	smileless	strapless	truceless	wordiness	agrologic	harbinger
sacrilege	smokeless	strewment	truculent	workpiece	amazingly	headlight
Sadducean	smokiness	stringent	truncheon	wormwheel	amusingly	hedgingly
sagegreen	snakeweed	suasively	trussbeam	worriment	aquilegia	highlight
saltiness	snakiness	subaltern	trustdeed	worthless	archangel	hindsight
sandiness	snowfield	subgenera	trustless	woundless	Areopagus	homologue
sappiness	snowiness	subjacent	truthless	wrathless	asparagus	horologer
sauceless	soapiness	sublimely	tubbiness	wrongness	backsight	horologic
sauciness	soberness	succulent	tumescent	youngness	bandwagon	humbugged
scalefern	sodabread	sugarbeet	tumidness	barrelful	beamingly	humdinger
scaleleaf	softshell	sulkiness	turbulent	basketful	bedraggle	hydrangea
scaleless	sogginess	sultaness	twentieth	beautiful	bespangle	ideologic
scaliness	solidness	sunniness	unaptness	bottlefed	bethought	ideologue
scantness	Solutrean	superheat	unconcern	bottleful	blazingly	illjudged
scarehead	somewhere	supersede	underfelt	bountiful	Boanerges	indraught
scentless	somnolent	supervene	underseal	bucketful	bombsight	inwrought
scrapheap	sonneteer	supremely	underseas	bushelful	bowlegged	jarringly
scuncheon	sootiness	surliness	undersell	butterfat	brummagem	jeeringly
scutcheon	soppiness	swartness	undervest	butterfly	bullfight	kiddingly
seaminess	sorceress	sweetmeal	underwear	caddisfly	burningly	knowingly
secernent	sorriness	sweetmeat	underwent	calorific	canesugar	lamplight
seediness	sortilege	sweetness	unfitness	carfuffle	carpingly	lastingly
semanteme	Soudanese	swiftness	unharness	chanceful	catalogue	leeringly
semibreve	soundless	swineherd	unitively	changeful	champagne	lethargic
semisweet		synoecete	univalent	colorific	chemurgic	liltingly
senescent	soutenour	syringeal	unsuccess	colourful	choplogic	Limburger
senseless	southwest	tableleaf	usualness	deceitful	coaxingly	limelight
sentiment	spaceless	tacitness	utterless	discomfit	Cockaigne	lispingly
seriately	spareness	tackiness	utterness	dragonfly	cockfight	loafsugar
servilely	sparkless	tailoress	vagueness	drawerful	colleague	longingly
seventeen	spearhead	tailpiece	validness	effortful	commingle	louringly
shadeless	speckless	taintless	valueless	felicific	copyright	lovelight
shadiness	speedwell	tardiness	valveless	forgetful	cryptogam	meaningly
shakiness	spiciness	Tartarean	vapidness	frightful	cunningly	meltingly
shamateur	spikiness	tasteless	velveteen	handcuffs	damningly	messenger
shameless	spineless	tastiness	verbosely	healthful	dashingly	methought
shapeless	spininess	tattiness	villagery	honorific	deadlight	mincingly
sharpness	splendent	tawniness	virescent	kerfuffle	decalogue	minutegun
sheerlegs	splintery	temptress	visitress	luftwaffe	demagogic	mockingly
sheerness	spluttery	tenseness	vividness	marrowfat	demagogue	monologic
sheetbend	spodumene	tepidness	vocalness	masterful	demiurgic	monologue
shellheap	spoonbeak	ternately	voiceless	needleful	denyingly	moonlight
shewbread	spoonfeed	terseness	volauvent	nonprofit	derringdo	mortgagee
shiftless	spoonmeat	tervalent	volunteer	plentiful	derringer	mortgager
shininess	sporogeny	testament	vowelless	pocketful	dodecagon	mortgagor
shipwreck	spotcheck	testiness	wackiness	praiseful	doglegged	mundungus
shirtless	spoutless	thankless	waistbelt	prayerful	downright	mycologic
shockhead	spurwheel	thickhead	wallcress	quadrifid	dysphagia	netwinged
shoreless	squatness	thickness	wartcress	rauwolfia	dysphagic	neuralgia
shoreweed	staginess	thingness	washiness	rechauffe	earwigged	neuralgic
shortness	staidness	thirtieth	wasteness	regardful	embrangle	nostalgia
shortterm	stainless	thornless	waterleaf	regretful	estranger	nostalgic
shouldest	stairhead	Thyestean	waterless	remindful	exchanger	oecologic
showiness	stairwell	tigerseye	waterweed	reposeful	eyebright	oestrogen
showpiece	staleness	tightness	weakkneed	resentful	fandangle	omophagia
shrubbery	stalkless	timepiece	weariless	reshuffle	fandangos	omophagic
sidedness	stallfeed	timesheet	weariness	resultful	fawningly	oncologic
sidewheel	starkness	timidness	weediness	saucerful	feelingly	onelegged
sightless	starshell	tinniness	weighbeam	shieldfem	firelight	onslaught
sightseer	stateless	tipsiness	weirdness	shovelful	fittingly	ontologic
silkiness	statement	tiredness	whalehead	silverfir	flamingly	outrigger
silliness	steelhead	titledeed	wheatmeal	soporific	flamingos	overnight

oversight	wittingly	lairdship	stretcher	admission	apportion	benignity
pantingly	yawningly	leviathan	stylishly	admissive	arabicise	bentonite
passenger	zigzagged	libecchio	sublethal	admitting	aragonite	benzidine
pedagogic	zoophagan	lightship	sunbather	adoration	archivist	benzoline
pedagogue	abolisher	loutishly	sweatshop	adulation	argentine	berberine
peepsight	acidophil	lumpishly	sweetshop	advection	argentite	berkelium
pemphigus	ailanthus	majorship	swinishly	advective	argillite	beryllium
pendragon	amianthus	malleehen	tacamahac	Adventism	armistice	besetting
pentangle	anglophil	mawkishly	talkathon	Adventist	aromatise	besotting
phalanger	anguished	mayorship	tallyshop	adventive	arresting	bevelling
phalanges	astrakhan	microchip	tartishly	adverbial	Arthurian	biblicism
pharyngal	autarchic	monarchal	thaneship	adversity	asafetida	biblicist
pharynges	azimuthal	monarchic	throughly	advertise	asbestine	bicyclist
phellogen	baldachin	mustachio	transship	aerialist	ascension	biologist
pipeorgan	beeorchis	naumachia	trebuchet	aeriality	ascensive	bionomics
pityingly	betrothal	necrophil	trilithon	affecting	asclepiad	bipartite
porbeagle	betrothed	negrophil	triumphal	affection	ashlaring	bisection
porringer	bimonthly	neolithic	troopship	affective	asininity	bitterish
pratingly	blockship	nepenthes	tutorship	afflation	aspersion	blackbird
ptarmigan	bloodshed	nourisher	twelfthly	afterlife	assertion	blackfish
purringly	bloodshot	nowhither	unabashed	aftertime	assertive	blacklist
pushingly	bookishly	oakenshaw	unclothed	agitation	assiduity	blotchily
quadrigae	boorishly	ownership	uncouthly	agitative	assuasive	bluepoint
rantingly	brakeshoe	paperthin	undershot	agonising	atacamite	blueprint
raspingly	Britisher	peevishly	unearthly	airyfairy	athletics	bobsleigh
rearlight	brutishly	penpusher	unfleshed	alchemise	atomicity	bolection
rectangle	bullishly	petersham	unfleshly	alchemist	atonalism	bombasine
reedorgan	burnisher	pettishly	unmatched	Algonkian	atonality	bombazine
rethought	cacoethes	photophil	unscathed	allotting	atonicity	bonechina
ringingly	cadetship	piggishly	untouched	almandine	attention	borrowing
rushlight	catarrhal	pistachio	Upanishad	alongside	attentive	bowerbird
salpinges	ceanothus	planisher	varnisher	altricial	attrition	bowstring
scavenger	chiefship	printshop	waggishly	aluminise	aubergine	boxoffice
scrounger	chihuahua	priorship	waspishly	aluminium	auctorial	brambling
searingly	clerkship	prudishly	watershed	amazonian	austenite	branchiae
seatangle	colcothar	publisher	wolfishly	ambiguity	austerity	branchial
seemingly	coltishly	queenship	wristshot	ambrosial	autarkist	brandling
semirigid	countship	raffishly	Yiddisher	americium	authorial	breadline
sidelight	courtship	rareeshow	zootechny	amidships	authorise	breathily
sinologue	cuplichen	refreshen	abduction	amoralism	authority	breathing
skintight	currishly	refresher	abhorring	amorality	aventaile	breeching
smilingly	debauched	retoucher	abjection	amorphism	avocation	breveting
sobbingly	debauchee	rodfisher	abnormity	amphibian	awakening	brigadier
solfeggio	debaucher	roguishly	abolition	amplifier	baboonish	brightish
sparingly	didelphic	roughshod	aborigine	anabolism	backslide	bristling
sporangia	didrachma	rulership	abounding	analogise	bacterial	Briticise
spotlight	dimorphic	Russophil	abruption	analogist	bacterise	Briticism
starlight	doggishly	saintship	abseiling	anarchism	bacterium	broadside
stoplight	doltishly	scratcher	absorbing	anarchist	bailiwick	broadwise
stratagem	donnishly	scratches	absurdism	anatomise	balalaika	bromeliad
strategic	eldership	screecher	absurdist	anatomist	balconied	bronchial
suffragan	Emmenthal	scrimshaw	absurdity	anchorite	balkanise	brushfire
summingup	entrechat	seaanchor	academism	andantino	balladist	brutalise
surcingle	eurhythmy	seaurchin	acceptive	angelfish	ballerina	brutalism
synagogal	eutrophic	selfishly	accession	anglesite	ballpoint	brutality
synagogue	flyfisher	seneschal	acclivity	anglicise	bandolier	buckshish
taillight	foolishly	sepulcher	according	anglicism	bandoline	buffeting
teasingly	foppishly	sepulchre	accordion	Anglicist	Barbadian	Bulgarian
tellingly	forgather	seventhly	accretion	anhydride	barbarian	bursarial
teratogen	forsythia	sharpshod	accretive	anhydrite	barbarise	butterine
theologic	furbisher	shovelhat	acetamide	animalise	barbarism	Byzantine
theologue	furnisher	sickishly	acetifier	animalism	barbarity	caballine
trialogue	Gallophil	slaveship	Acheulian	animality	basrelief	caballing
undamaged	garnishee	slavishly	acidifier	animalist	basrelief	cabbalism
undecagon	girlishly	Slavophil	aconitine	animation	batholite	cabbalist
unfledged	godfather	slingshot	acoustics	animatism	batholith	caciquism
unplugged	godmother	sottishly	actualise	animosity	Bathonian	cadential
unthought	grapeshot	spaceship	actuality	annulling	bathybius	caecilian
unwrought	groundhog	spleuchan	actuarial	anonymity	battalion	Caesarean
veeringly	guardship	squelcher	actuation	anorthite	battening	Caesarism
viceregal	guildship	stauncher	addiction	anthelion	beccafico	Caesarism
wailingly	hellishly	staunchly	addictive	anthemion	bedlamite	caldarium
Walpurgis	hoggishly	steamship	adduction	anticline	bedspring	callosity
warmonger	horseshoe	stockwhip	adductive	antiquity	befitting	calmative
warningly	horsewhip	stomachal	ademption	aperitive	befogging	Calvinism
weeknight	illwisher	stomacher	adenosine	apologise	begetting	Calvinist
whirligig	isobathic	stomachic	adiposity	apologist	beginning	Cambodian
willingly	judgeship	stonechat	adjoining	appalling	belemnite	camorrist
winningly	knavishly	storeship	adlibbing	appealing	bengaline	campanile

```
campanili  coalition  corrosion  demitting  dogmatise  eroticism  exudative
cannonier  coastline  corrosive  demobbing  dogmatism  erstwhile  Fabianism
cantabile  coastwise  costumier  demurring  dogmatist  erudition  facsimile
cantorial  coattails  cotillion  demystify  dogoodism  erythrism  factitive
capsulise  cobaltite  couturier  denitrify  donothing  erythrite  factorial
captivity  Cobdenism  cowardice  dentalium  dormition  esoterica  factorise
carbamide  cocainise  crackling  dentation  doughtily  esoterism  facundity
carbonise  cocainism  crampfish  dentition  dowelling  essential  faggoting
carburise  coccidium  crashdive  deodorise  draconian  establish  fairylike
careerism  cockatiel  crediting  deoxidise  dragonish  Esthonian  fairyring
careerist  coecilian  credulity  depiction  drainpipe  estopping  Falangism
Carmelite  coemption  cremation  depictive  dramatics  estuarian  Falangist
carnality  coenobite  crenation  depletion  dramatise  estuarine  Falernian
carnation  coenobium  cretinism  depletive  dramatist  Ethiopian  falsifier
carnelian  coffinite  crinoline  depravity  Dravidian  ethnicity  fantasied
carnitine  cognation  crippling  desertion  dreamlike  Eucharist  fantasise
carolling  cognition  criterion  designing  drumstick  eunuchoid  fantasist
carpeting  cognitive  criticise  despotism  dubiosity  euphemise  farseeing
Cartesian  collagist  criticism  detection  ductility  euphemism  fastening
caseation  collation  crocodile  detective  duodecimo  euphonise  fastigium
cassaripe  collegial  crossbill  detention  duplicity  euphonium  favourite
cassation  collegian  crossfire  determine  dysgenics  euthenics  febricity
Castalian  collegium  crossfish  deterring  earthling  eutherian  fecundity
Castilian  collision  crosslink  detersion  easygoing  evocation  femineity
Castroism  collodion  crosswind  detersive  ecclesial  evocative  Fenianism
casuarina  collusion  crosswise  detrition  ecologist  evolution  fertilise
catarhine  collusive  cupelling  detrusion  economics  evolutive  fertility
catechise  collyrium  curialism  deuterium  economise  exceeding  festivity
catechism  colouring  curiosity  deviation  economist  excelling  fetichism
catechist  colourist  cursorial  devilfish  ecossaise  excelsior  fetichist
Catharism  colubrine  cursorily  devilling  ecritoire  excepting  fetishism
Catharist  Columbian  curveting  devitrify  ecstasise  exception  fetishist
Caucasian  columbine  custodial  dexterity  ecumenism  exceptive  feudalise
causality  columbite  custodian  diabolise  edelweiss  excessive  feudalism
causation  columbium  customise  diabolism  edibility  exclusion  feudalist
causative  columnist  cyanamide  diabolist  editorial  exclusive  feudality
cauterise  combative  cyclopian  dialogise  education  excretion  fibroline
cavendish  commodity  cymbalist  dialogism  educative  excretive  fiendlike
cavilling  commotion  cymbidium  dialogist  Edwardian  excursion  filiation
ceasefire  communion  cystolith  diatomite  effective  excursive  financial
celandine  communise  czarevich  dichasial  effluvial  execution  financier
celebrity  communism  Daedalian  dichasium  effluvium  executive  fingering
celestial  communist  dalmatian  dichroism  effluxion  exegetist  finicking
Celticism  community  daltonism  dickybird  eglantine  exemplify  firebrick
cementite  companion  damnation  dicrotism  egomaniac  exemption  firedrill
censorial  complaint  dandelion  dictation  egression  exopodite  firstling
centering  composite  Darwinian  didactics  eightyish  exoticism  fishslice
centreing  concavity  Darwinism  dieselise  electrify  expansile  fissility
centurion  conciliar  Darwinist  dietetics  elevation  expansion  flagstick
cerastium  concision  dayspring  dietician  elocution  expansive  flayflint
certified  concubine  deacidify  dietitian  emanation  expecting  fledgling
certifier  condition  deadalive  difficile  emanative  expelling  flightily
cerussite  conducive  deathlike  diffusion  embedding  expensive  floodtide
cessation  confiding  debagging  diffusive  embellish  expertise  floridity
chamomile  Confucian  debarring  digestion  embracive  expiation  flotation
champaign  confusion  debugging  digestive  embussing  expletive  flouncing
checklist  congenial  decalcify  dignified  emotivity  explosion  flowering
chelation  congeries  decennial  dimension  empathise  explosive  focussing
chelonian  congruity  decennium  Dionysiac  emphasise  expulsion  foeticide
chevalier  connation  deception  Dionysian  emulation  expulsive  foliation
chickling  connexion  deceptive  dipeptide  emulative  exquisite  following
childlike  connubial  decillion  direction  enchorial  exsertile  footprint
chondrite  conscribe  declivity  directive  encrinite  exsertion  foregoing
chopstick  conscript  decoction  disaffirm  endearing  exservice  forgiving
Christian  constrict  decretive  disarming  endocrine  extensile  formalise
chthonian  contadina  deduction  disbelief  engraving  extension  formalism
churching  contadino  deductive  disoblige  enrolling  extensity  formalist
cicatrice  contagion  defeatism  disparity  ephedrine  extensive  formality
cicatrise  contagium  defeatist  dispraise  epicurism  extolling  formation
Cimmerian  contusion  defection  disrelish  epidosite  extorsive  formative
cipollino  convexity  defective  dissocial  epilation  extortion  formulise
circadian  convivial  defensive  distraint  epilogist  extortive  fortalice
cisalpine  coprolite  deferring  diversify  epipolism  extradite  forthwith
clarifier  coralline  deflation  diversion  epitomise  extremism  fortifier
classlist  corallite  deflexion  diversity  epitomist  extremist  fortyfive
clavation  cordelier  deformity  diverting  equalling  extremity  fossilise
cleansing  cornelian  dejection  divulsion  equipoise  extrusion  fossorial
clinician  cornetist  demanding  doctorial  equipping  extrusive  foundling
clockwise  corrasion  demission  dogmatics  eremitism  exudation  fragility
```

franchise	Gradgrind	hispidity	infection	jossstick	lubricity	mentalist
frenchify	grandsire	histamine	infective	joviality	lucrative	mentality
friarbird	granulite	histidine	inferring	juniority	lumbering	mentation
fricative	grapevine	historian	infertile	junkerism	lunchtime	mepacrine
frigidity	grappling	hitchhike	infilling	junketing	macedoine	mercerise
frivolity	gravamina	Hitlerism	infirmity	justiciar	machinist	mercurial
frontline	gravidity	Hitlerite	inflation	justifier	maddening	mescaline
frontwise	gregarian	Hobbesian	inflexion	kaiserism	madeleine	mesmerise
frostbite	gregarine	hocussing	inflowing	kaolinise	Magianism	mesmerism
frugality	Gregorian	homousian	ingenuity	kaolinite	magicking	mesmerist
fulgurite	grenadier	hoofprint	ingestion	keelivine	magnalium	metalline
funebrial	grenadine	horsehide	ingestive	Keplerian	magnesian	metalling
fungicide	gristmill	horsemint	ingrowing	Keynesian	magnesite	metallise
furcation	grouchily	hortation	injection	khedivial	magnesium	meteorist
fusionist	grounding	hortative	injustice	killifish	magnetics	meteorite
gabardine	groundivy	hostility	innocuity	kittenish	magnetise	methodise
gaberdine	gruelling	housewife	inpouring	Kshatriya	magnetism	Methodism
galantine	grumbling	hoydenish	inquiline	labelling	magnetist	Methodist
galleried	Grundyism	hylozoism	insectile	labialise	magnetite	metrician
gallicise	guardring	Hungarian	insertion	labialism	magnifico	metricise
gallicism	guideline	hybridise	inservice	labourite	magnifier	metricist
galloping	guitarist	hybridism	insetting	laccolith	mahlstick	mezzanine
galvanise	gustation	hybridity	insomniac	lacertian	maidenish	mezzotint
galvanism	gustative	hydration	integrity	lacertine	makeshift	microbial
galvanist	guttation	hydrazine	intensify	lactation	malachite	microfilm
gammadion	guttering	hydronium	intension	lallation	malathion	microlite
gammoning	gymnasial	hydroxide	intensity	landslide	malignity	microlith
ganderism	gymnasium	hygienics	intensive	larcenist	mammalian	migration
gardening	gynoecium	hygienist	intention	larvicide	mammonish	millerite
garrulity	haematite	hylozoism	intercity	lathering	mammonism	Miltonian
gathering	haggadist	hypnotise	interdict	latticing	mammonist	mimicking
gavelkind	hairshirt	hypnotism	interfile	laudation	mammonite	miniskirt
gearshift	hairslide	hypnotist	interline	laudative	Mancunian	misadvise
gelignite	halfprice	hypocrisy	interlink	launching	mandarine	misassign
gemmation	halophile	hypocrite	interring	lawgiving	mandoline	misbelief
gemutlich	hamstring	hysterics	interview	leastwise	maneating	miscegine
genialise	handspike	illboding	interwind	leavening	manganite	misgiving
geniality	hankering	imitation	intestine	legerline	mannerism	misoneism
gentility	happening	imitative	intorsion	lengthily	mannerist	misoneist
geodesist	harmaline	immensity	intrusion	lethality	manubrium	Mithraism
geologise	harmonica	immersion	intrusive	lettering	manyplies	Mithraist
geologist	harmonics	impaction	intuition	Levantine	manzanita	mnemonics
geoponics	harmonise	impartial	intuitive	levelling	marcasite	mnemonist
germanise	harmonist	impassion	inunction	liability	margarine	modelling
Germanish	harmonium	impassive	inutility	libelling	margarite	modernise
Germanism	Harrovian	impelling	invective	libellist	marketing	modernism
Germanist	harrowing	impending	invention	libertine	marsupial	modernist
germanium	Hashemite	impletion	inventive	librarian	marsupium	modernity
germicide	Hashimite	implosion	inversion	libration	martyrise	modillion
gerundial	hatchling	implosive	inversive	lickerish	masculine	monachism
gerundive	haughtily	impluvium	ironsmith	lightning	masochism	Mondayish
gestation	havocking	imprecise	Iroquoian	lilywhite	masochist	monergism
geyserite	hawksbill	improbity	irreality	limejuice	masonried	moneybill
ghostlike	hawsepipe	improvise	irruption	limousine	massagist	Mongolian
giantlike	healthily	impulsion	irruptive	limpidity	maternity	mongolism
gibberish	heartsick	impulsive	isagogics	lineality	matricide	monkeyish
gibbosity	hellenise	inability	isolation	linearise	matronise	monkeyism
gigantism	Hellenism	inanition	isolative	linearity	maulstick	monocline
Girondist	Hellenist	incaution	isomerise	lineation	meandrine	monoecism
glamorise	Helvetian	incentive	isomerism	lingering	meanwhile	monostich
globefish	hemistich	inception	Israelite	lintwhite	mechanics	Montanism
globosity	herbalist	inceptive	italicise	liquation	mechanise	monthling
glucoside	herbarium	inclusion	Italicism	liquefier	mechanism	monzonite
glyceride	herbicide	inclusive	iteration	liquidise	mechanist	moonblind
glycerine	herborise	incognito	iterative	liquidity	medallion	moonshine
glycoside	Hercynian	incondite	jackknife	liquorice	medallist	morbidity
goffering	Hesperian	incurring	jacksnipe	liquorish	mediation	mordacity
goldbrick	hessonite	incursion	jactation	Listerism	mediatise	Mormonism
goldsmith	hetaerism	incursive	Jansenism	liturgics	mediative	mortality
gondolier	hetairism	indemnify	Jansenist	liturgist	meliorism	mortician
gongorism	hexastich	indemnity	japanning	locksmith	meliorist	mosaicism
goosegirl	Hibernian	indention	jargonise	logistics	meliority	mosaicist
gorgonian	hiddenite	Indianise	jellyfish	logogriph	memoirist	motorbike
gorgonise	hieratica	indiction	jessamine	Londonise	mendacity	mummified
Gothamite	highflier	indignity	jesuitise	Londonism	Mendelian	muscadine
gothicise	Himyarite	induction	jesuitism	longevity	Mendelism	muscarine
Gothicism	hircosity	inductive	jocundity	lookalike	mendicity	muscovite
gracility	hirsutism	infantile	Johannine	loquacity	Mennonite	musteline
gradation	hirundine	infantine	Jordanian	lovechild	mentalism	mutualise

```
mutualism obtrusive patronise pollution publicist referring sailoring
mutualist obversion pauperise polonaise publicity refitting saintlike
mutuality obviation pauperism polyamide puerility reflation saintling
myologist occlusion Pavlovian pomposity pugnacity reflexion salesgirl
mysticism occlusive peacetime pontonier pulsatile reflexive sallowish
mystifier occultism pedalling porcupine pulsation reformism saltation
mythicise occultist pegmatite portative pulverise reformist salubrity
mythicism occurring Pelasgian posterior punchline refurbish salvation
mythicist octennial pelletise posterity punishing refurnish sanbenito
narcotine octillion penduline postilion purgation rejection sandblind
narcotise Octobrist penultima potassium purgative rejoicing santolina
narcotism oenophile peptonise potential purposive reliquiae santonica
narration oenophily percaline potholing purselike remission Sardinian
narrative offensive perdition pourboire putridity remitting Sarmation
natrolite offspring peregrine pourpoint pycnidium rendition sartorial
naughtily olfaction perennial powerdive Quakerish repelling sartorius
necessity olfactive perfumier preachify Quakerism replenish Sassanian
necrotise olivenite perfusion preachily qualified repletion satellite
nectarial onsetting perfusive precative qualifier repotting satiation
nectarine operation perilling preceding quartzite reptilian satinbird
nemertine operative perishing precipice queenlike republish Saturnian
nemophila operosity personify precisian quibbling repulsion saturnine
neodymium Orangeism pervasion precision quicklime repulsive saturnism
neologian oratorial pervasive precocial quinoline requisite savourily
neologise oratorian pessimism precocity quixotism rerunning scaldfish
neologism orchidist pessimist preconise quotation resection scalefish
neologist organzine pesticide predacity quotidian reserpine scalelike
neoterise orificial petaurist predation rabbinism reservist scantling
neoterism orologist petechiae predative rabbinist resetting scapolite
neoterist ostensive petechial prefixion racialism resistive scarfring
nephalism ostracise pethidine prejudice racialist resitting scarfwise
nephalist ostracism phenacite prelatise radiation restraint scarifier
nepheline otherwise phenakite prelusion radiative retention scenarist
nephelite otologist phonation prelusive rancidity retentive scheelite
Neptunian outgiving phonemics premonish randomise retiarius schilling
neptunium overdrive phonetics premotion rapidfire retortion schlemiel
nervation overlying phonetise prenotion raptorial revelling schlemihl
Nestorian overprice phonetism prescribe rascalism reversion schooling
neuration overprint phonetist prescript rascality revetting sciential
newsprint overskirt phonolite preshrink rationing revolting scientism
Newtonian overspill phosphide presidial raunchily revulsion scientist
niccolite overtrick phosphine presidium ravelling revulsive scolecite
nickelise overweigh phosphite preterist ravishing rewarding scorching
nictation overwrite physician preterite razorbill rhodamine scorifier
nightbird oviparity physicist prettyish razorfish rhodolite Scoticise
nightlife ovulation picketing prettyism reasoning rhodonite scraggily
nightline oxidation pictorial prevision rebaptise rhonchial scramming
nightside oxygenise picturise primality rebelling rhythmics scrappily
nighttime ozocerite pilotfish primarily rebellion rhythmise scrapping
nigrosine ozokerite pinstripe primatial rebidding rhythmist screening
nitratine packaging pitchpipe primitive rebutting Ribbonism screwpile
nitration packdrill placation privation recapping ridgetile screwpine
nonentity Palladian placekick privative recension riflebird scrimpily
nonillion palladium placidity probation reception Ripuarian scrubbing
nonjuring palletise plaintiff probative receptive ritualise scruffily
normalise pallidity plaintive procerity recession ritualism seafaring
normality palmation planarian profanity recessive ritualist searching
Normanise palpation planation profilist reckoning rivalling seasoning
Normanism panelling plantlike profusion reclusion rivelling seasquirt
normative panellist platinise prolamine reclusive riverside secession
Norwegian panicking Platonise prolation recognise rockdrill seclusion
notionist panoplied Platonism prolative recombine rotundity seclusive
nullifier pantheism Platonist prolicide reconcile Roumanian secretion
nummulite pantheist plaything prolixity recondite routinism secretive
nurseling pantomime plenarily prologise reconfirm routinist sectarian
nutrition papergirl plication prolusion recording rubberise sectility
nutritive paranoiac plumbline promising recordist rubellite sectorial
objectify parathion pluralise promotion rectifier rubrician seduction
objection parhelion pluralism promotive rectorial ruggedise seductive
objective parochial pluralist pronation recurring ruination selachian
obliquity parricide plurality proscribe recursion russeting selection
obscenity Parseeism plutonian prosodist recursive rusticity selective
obscurity partition Plutonist protamine redaction ruthenium selfdrive
obsequial partitive plutonism providing reduction sabbatise selfpride
obsequies passerine plutonium provision reductive sabbatism Seljukian
obsession passivity podzolise provoking reefpoint Sabellian semantics
obsessive paternity poeticise proximity reexamine sacrarium semiotics
obtention patrician poeticism pterygium refashion sacrifice senhorita
obtrusion patricide pollinium publicise refection safranine seniority
```

```
sensation  snailfish  statewide  sympodial  tonsorial  unpegging  volkslied
sensitise  snakebird  statolith  sympodium  toothpick  unreality  voltinism
sensitive  snakebite  steampipe  symposiac  topiarian  unselfish  voodooism
sensorial  snakelike  steenkirk  symposial  topiarist  unsmiling  voodooist
sensorium  snipefish  stepchild  symposium  toreutics  unsparing  vorticism
sepiolite  snowblind  steradian  syncytial  torpidity  unstudied  vorticist
septation  snowblink  sterilise  syncytium  torridity  unsullied  vorticity
septicity  snowdrift  sterility  synectics  totalling  unwearied  voyeurism
sequacity  snowwhite  stippling  synergism  touchline  unweeting  vulcanian
serialise  socialise  stockfish  synergist  towelling  unwilling  vulcanise
serialism  socialism  stocklist  synoptist  toxophily  unwinking  vulcanism
serialist  socialist  stockpile  syphilise  traceried  unwitting  vulcanist
seriality  socialite  stolidity  tachylite  tradition  unzipping  vulcanite
sermonise  sociality  stonefish  tactician  traducian  uplifting  vulgarian
serration  solemnise  stormbird  tactility  tragedian  upsetting  vulgarise
serrefile  solemnity  storyline  tactitian  transpire  uraninite  vulgarism
servility  solferino  stovepipe  tailoring  trapezial  uropygium  vulgarity
seventies  solipsism  strapping  talkative  trapezium  usucapion  vulpinism
sexennial  solipsist  streakily  tallowish  treadmill  uvarovite  vulpinite
sexualise  solitaire  streaking  Talmudist  tremolite  uxoricide  vulturine
sexuality  Solutrian  striation  tangerine  tribadism  valentine  vulturish
sgraffiti  solvation  stripling  tantalise  tribalism  vallation  Wagnerian
sgraffito  something  stripping  tantalite  tricksily  valuation  Wagnerite
shakerism  somewhile  strongish  tarantism  tridymite  vampirism  waistline
shamanism  sommelier  strontium  Targumist  triennial  vandalise  walloping
shamanist  songsmith  stropping  Tartarian  triennium  vandalism  wandering
shambling  sonnetise  strouding  Tartufian  trifacial  vapouring  wastepipe
Shangrila  sopranino  strumming  Tartufism  trifolium  vapourish  watchfire
shaveling  sopranist  strutting  Tasmanian  triforium  Varangian  waterlily
shearling  Sorbonist  stupefier  tattooist  trigamist  variation  waterline
sheatfish  sortition  stupidity  taxpaying  trilobite  variolite  watermill
sheathing  soundfilm  suability  tectonics  trinomial  vectorial  waterpipe
sheeplice  sovereign  subaerial  tectorial  triploidy  Vedantist  waterside
sheeptick  sovietise  subalpine  tellurian  trisagion  vendition  waveguide
shelflife  sovietism  subdivide  telluride  tritheism  veneering  wavellite
shellfire  spacetime  subfamily  tellurite  tritheist  veniality  wayfaring
shellfish  spagyrist  sublation  tellurium  triumviri  veratrine  wealthily
Shintoism  spareribs  sublimity  temporise  troutling  verbalise  wedgewise
Shintoist  spearfish  submarine  tenderise  trunkfish  verbalism  weightily
shoeshine  spearmint  subregion  tenebrist  tsarevich  verbalist  weighting
shoreline  spearside  subscribe  tensility  turbidity  verbicide  welcoming
shoreside  specifier  subscript  tentation  turgidity  verbosity  welfarism
shredding  speechify  subsidise  tentative  turnstile  vermicide  wellbeing
shrewmice  spellbind  subtilise  terminism  turquoise  vermilion  westering
shrugging  spindling  subtopian  terminist  twinkling  vernalise  wheedling
sibylline  spindrier  suctorial  terrarium  twitchily  vernation  wherewith
siccative  spindrift  suctorian  terrorise  tympanist  versatile  whirlwind
sickening  spinosity  suffering  terrorism  typewrite  versifier  whistling
sideswipe  Spinozism  suffusion  terrorist  tyrannise  vestigial  whitefish
signalise  Spinozist  sulcation  testation  uintahite  vestigium  whitening
significs  spirality  summarily  testdrive  Ukrainian  vetchling  whitewing
signorial  spiritism  summarise  testifier  ultrahigh  viability  widowbird
signorina  spiritist  summarist  tetradite  ululation  vibratile  widthwise
siltation  splashily  summation  teutonise  umberbird  vibration  willemite
simpatico  splitting  summative  Teutonism  unanimity  vibrative  willowish
sincerity  spokewise  superfine  Teutonist  unbending  vicennial  winterise
singspiel  spoonbill  supervise  thatching  uncannily  vicereine  withering
sinophile  sprigging  supposing  theatrics  unceasing  victimise  witherite
sinuation  springily  surfacing  therapist  undeceive  Victorian  witticism
sinuosity  springing  surficial  therewith  undergird  victorine  wolverine
situation  squashily  surveying  theurgist  underline  viewpoint  womankind
sitzkrieg  squatting  suspicion  thirstily  underling  villosity  womanlike
sketchily  squeakily  sutteeism  thornbill  undermine  violation  womenkind
skewwhiff  squeamish  swaddling  thrashing  underripe  violative  wordsmith
skijoring  squibbing  swarajist  thriftily  underside  violinist  worldling
skinflick  squidding  swellfish  thrilling  undersign  Virgilian  worldwide
skinflint  stabilise  swingeing  throatily  undertint  virginity  wrestling
skydiving  stability  swordfish  throbbing  underwing  viscidity  wulfenite
slantwise  Stagirite  swordlike  thrumming  unfailing  viscosity  Wyclifite
slapstick  Stalinism  syllabise  thylacine  unfeeling  visionist  xenophile
Slavonian  Stalinist  syllabism  thyroxine  unfitting  visualise  xerophile
slightish  stampmill  syllogise  tiedyeing  unhappily  vitelline  xerophily
slivovitz  stanchion  syllogism  tigerlily  unheeding  vitiation  Yankeeism
slopewise  standpipe  sylphlike  tightwire  unhurried  vitiosity  yardstick
Slovakian  stapedial  sylvanite  timbering  uniserial  Vitruvian  yellowish
Slovenian  starchily  symbolics  timpanist  unitarian  viverrine  yodelling
smalltime  stardrift  symbolise  titration  unknowing  vivianite  yohimbine
smoothish  startling  symbolism  tittuping  unluckily  vizierial  Yorkshire
smuggling  stateside  symbolist  Tocharian  unmeaning  volcanism  youngling
```

ytterbium	abysmally	corydalis	glacially	mindfully	rostellum	traveller
zeitgeist	acellular	coverslip	gladiolus	minimally	roundelay	trivially
zibelline	acropolis	crenelled	glandular	misemploy	rubicelle	trochilus
zinkenite	admiralty	crucially	gleefully	mitraille	ruthfully	trowelled
zirconium	adrenalin	cubically	gospeller	molecular	sabadilla	troweller
zoiatrics	afterclap	cudgelled	gradually	mongrelly	salicylic	tunefully
zoologist	afterglow	cuticular	grandslam	monocular	sandalled	tunnelled
zootomist	aircooled	cynically	gravelled	multiplex	sapodilla	typically
Zwinglian	alcoholic	deathblow	grisaille	musically	scintilla	unbridled
drummajor	alicyclic	decathlon	grossular	muskmelon	scrambler	uncivilly
maharajah	amaryllis	decimally	grovelled	myrobalan	scribbler	underclay
airjacket	amygdalin	decomplex	groveller	Nahuatlan	scutellar	underplay
barracker	anopheles	despoiler	guerrilla	napthalic	scutellum	underplot
bedjacket	apostolic	dextrally	hamamelis	naturally	semicolon	unequally
berserker	aquarelle	diachylom	hanselled	navicular	seminally	unpeopled
bookmaker	armadillo	diachylum	harmfully	needfully	semisolid	unpopular
caretaker	articular	diastolic	hatefully	neuroglia	sensually	unruffled
diesinker	asexually	digitalin	haustella	neutrally	septuplet	unsettled
ewenecked	assembler	digitalis	heedfully	nickelled	severally	unskilled
foretoken	auricular	digitally	helically	nightclub	severalty	unusually
fossicker	autopilot	direfully	helpfully	nominally	sextuplet	utricular
frolicked	autotelic	dispelled	heptaglot	notabilia	shambolic	valuables
gimmickry	avuncular	distilled	hillbilly	nucleolus	shillelah	varicella
gooseskin	bagatelle	distiller	hobgoblin	nymphalid	shovelled	vehicular
grimalkin	balefully	diurnally	hobnailed	oddfellow	shoveller	ventrally
halfbaked	banefully	dogcollar	homopolar	odontalgy	signalled	vesicular
homemaker	barnacled	dogviolet	hopefully	opercular	signaller	virtually
identikit	barrelled	dolefully	horseplay	operculum	skilfully	vitriolic
jampacked	bashfully	drivelled	hosteller	optically	slateclub	vocabular
jaywalker	basically	driveller	houseflag	opusculum	snivelled	wakefully
kilderkin	bedfellow	dutifully	houselled	orbicular	sniveller	wassailer
kingmaker	bellyflop	easefully	hurtfully	organelle	songfully	waterflea
lovetoken	bestially	echolalia	hydraulic	ossicular	soulfully	weevilled
lownecked	binocular	embattled	illegally	overvalue	sparkplug	wishfully
masterkey	bismillah	embezzler	imbecilic	painfully	spatially	wistfully
midwicket	blackflag	embroglio	imbroglio	panatella	specially	yachtclub
mispickel	blastulae	enamelled	immorally	paperclip	specialty	zestfully
misreckon	blastular	enameller	indweller	parabolic	spherular	acclaimer
moonraker	bobtailed	epicyclic	initially	paralalia	spiralled	agronomic
mosaicked	branchlet	epistoler	inshallah	parcelled	spirillum	anchorman
muckraker	Bretwalda	epistolic	installed	partially	springlet	anoxaemia
newmarket	cabriolet	epithelia	instilled	patrolled	sprinkler	antinomic
nitpicker	cacodylic	eternally	interflow	patroller	squabbler	autonomic
nonsmoker	calicular	ethically	interplay	peachblow	squirelet	autosomal
okeydokey	camarilla	evangelic	inveigler	pedicular	steelclad	baptismal
onionskin	cancelled	factually	irregular	pencilled	stoically	barleymow
outbacker	canicular	fascicled	isocyclic	penciller	straggler	bondwoman
outspoken	capitally	fatefully	isosceles	perihelia	strangler	brakesman
outworker	capitular	fearfully	juvenilia	pilgarlic	strangles	bridesman
overtaken	capitulum	federally	katabolic	pintailed	streamlet	cacodemon
pacemaker	carefully	fibrillar	kennelled	pistolled	strobilae	cameraman
parbuckle	cassoulet	filoselle	landaulet	pitifully	strobilus	Candlemas
paypacket	castellan	finically	laterally	pivotally	struggler	cattleman
physicked	catabolic	flabellum	laurelled	playfully	subocular	charwoman
picnicked	centrally	flagellum	lexically	pointille	subphylum	Christmas
picnicker	cerebella	flageolet	liberally	pommelled	subsellia	churchman
princekin	chantilly	flannelly	lingually	portfolio	sugarplum	clergyman
rainmaker	chiselled	flocculus	lintelled	potboiler	surmullet	clergymen
ransacker	chiseller	floscular	lioncelle	preexilic	suturally	colourman
rudbeckia	chlorella	fraenulum	literally	princelet	swivelled	confirmed
scarfskin	chrysalid	francolin	logically	propelled	swordplay	confirmer
schnorkel	chrysalis	fretfully	lunisolar	propeller	syllabled	confirmor
sexlinked	cigarillo	frivolled	lyophilic	pulvillus	tactfully	conformal
sharkskin	civically	frontally	lyrically	pummelled	tactually	conformer
sheepskin	clitellum	fulfilled	magically	punctilio	tarpaulin	copolymer
shoemaker	coaxially	fulfiller	malleolar	pyroxylin	tasselled	cornerman
skyjacker	coequally	fumarolic	malleolus	quadrille	tearfully	coseismal
skyrocket	colonelcy	funicular	Malayalam	radically	tenaculum	coseismic
snakeskin	columella	funiculus	manipular	radicular	tentacled	cracksman
sooterkin	comically	funnelled	marcelled	rakehelly	textually	craftsman
spillikin	commonlaw	gainfully	maritally	redevelop	thermally	declaimer
spinnaker	compelled	gambolled	marshalcy	refuelled	throttler	dichromat
staymaker	conically	garibaldi	martially	restfully	tinselled	dichromic
tanpickle	contralto	gastrulae	marvelled	reticular	tonguelet	discommon
tentmaker	corbeille	generalia	maximally	reticulum	tonically	draftsman
trebucket	corbelled	generally	mayoralty	retinulae	tonsillar	duralumin
triweekly	cordially	genteelly	medically	retinular	topically	ealdorman
unchecked	cornsalad	glabellae	metabolic	retroflex	toxically	elastomer
unshackle	corralled	glabellar	metheglin	ridiculer	travelled	endogamic

endolymph	polysemic	Afrikaner	dalliance	halfpence	mischance	purulence
energumen	polysomic	Alemannic	debutante	halfpenny	missioner	purulency
entrammel	praenomen	allemande	decadence	harpooner	moistener	pyracanth
epidermal	preadamic	allowance	decadency	haverings	monkeynut	pyrogenic
epidermic	pretermit	ambulance	decagonal	headliner	monomania	pyromancy
epidermis	prodromal	anabranch	deference	heathenry	monotonic	pyromania
epistemic	prodromic	annoyance	demimonde	hegemonic	monsignor	quickener
ergonomic	programme	antigenic	dethroner	hesitance	monsoonal	quittance
exciseman	quadruman	antimonic	diactinic	hesitancy	mullioned	reactance
exodermis	quarryman	antivenin	dilatancy	heteronym	mumchance	rearrange
familyman	ribosomal	appetence	diligence	hexagonal	muniments	recreancy
fellowman	roundsman	appetency	disbranch	highlands	mutagenic	recusance
fieldsman	ruddleman	appliance	discerner	hightoned	neoteinia	recusancy
fisherman	sailorman	argumenta	doctrinal	hindrance	neoteinic	redolence
forenamed	sapraemia	arrogance	dominance	hodiernal	nescience	reference
forewoman	sapraemic	assonance	drunkenly	homotonic	netveined	referenda
freewoman	schoolman	assurance	dysphonia	hypomania	nicotinic	refluence
Frenchman	Scotchman	avoidance	easterner	hypomanic	ninepence	relevance
gentleman	selectman	bacchanal	ectogenic	ignorance	ninepenny	relevancy
ginglymus	shantyman	bacchante	effluence	illomened	nocturnal	remanence
gorblimey	signalman	bargainer	eloquence	imbalance	nucleonic	renitency
graphemic	sketchmap	bastioned	embryonal	immanence	obedience	residence
groomsman	sometimes	beastings	embryonic	immanency	obeisance	residency
guardsman	spiderman	beestings	emergence	imminence	occupancy	resonance
guillemot	spoilsman	bellpunch	emergency	imminency	octagonal	reticence
Hallowmas	spokesman	billionth	emotional	impedance	oecumenic	reticency
hammerman	sportsman	binominal	endogenic	impotence	oenomancy	reverence
homogamic	stableman	bivalence	endurance	impotency	offchance	ringfence
homonymic	statesman	bivalency	esperance	impudence	officinal	ruffianly
hydraemia	steersman	Brahmanic	Esperanto	incidence	oilburner	rumrunner
ichneumon	subatomic	Brahminee	estaminet	indecency	oilpaints	Saracenic
ignoramus	subnormal	Brahminic	esurience	indigence	olecranal	Sauternes
ischaemia	sunhelmet	brazilnut	esuriency	indolence	olecranon	scrivener
ischaemic	switchman	Britannia	ethylenic	inerrancy	oncogenic	seachange
jurywoman	swordsman	Britannic	excitancy	inference	onlicence	sectional
kingdomed	synonymic	Brythonic	existence	influence	ontogenic	semblance
kinswoman	taxonomic	bullfinch	explainer	influenza	opinioned	semifinal
lachrymal	thingummy	butternut	exultance	ingrained	opponency	semilunar
latecomer	thirdsman	cacuminal	exultancy	inherence	ordinance	semitonic
leucaemia	timberman	calamanco	eyeglance	inhumanly	oscitance	sentience
leukaemia	timelimit	calycinal	eyeopener	innocence	outgoings	sentiency
leukaemic	tirewoman	candlenut	factional	innocency	outgunned	septennia
liveryman	toponymal	captaincy	fashioner	inorganic	overtones	sequinned
lumberman	toponymic	catatonia	feculence	insolence	paludinal	sergeancy
malformed	tradesman	catatonic	feiseanna	inspanned	passional	serjeancy
Manxwoman	transumpt	certainly	fictional	insurance	paulownia	serjeanty
Martinmas	triatomic	certainty	fifteenth	interknit	penitence	serotonin
metonymic	tribesman	chaffinch	figurante	isoclinal	pensioner	sessional
middleman	trichomic	challenge	fivepence	isoclinic	perchance	severance
midsummer	unashamed	chastener	fivepenny	jaborandi	pergunnah	sforzando
minuteman	undecimal	chitlings	flagrance	jacaranda	permeance	sharpener
monatomic	undreamed	citizenly	flagrancy	Jacobinic	personnel	Shechinah
monogamic	uniformly	citizenry	fleshings	jubilance	petulance	shipcanal
morphemic	vestryman	clarionet	flippancy	karabiner	petulancy	shipmoney
morrisman	vicesimal	clearance	fluxional	kitchener	pharaonic	shipowner
muffinman	vigesimal	cloisonne	folkdance	knockknee	pimpernel	shortener
muscleman	washerman	coeternal	foreigner	labyrinth	plangency	sibilance
Mussulman	welltimed	coherence	forlornly	lampooner	pleadings	sibilancy
nystagmic	wherryman	coherency	fourpence	landowner	pleasance	sixteenmo
nystagmus	wolframic	colcannon	fourpenny	lanthanum	pneumonia	sixteenth
oddjobman	woodnymph	colocynth	fragrance	latitancy	pneumonic	skirtings
oligaemia	workwoman	comedones	fragrancy	lazybones	poignancy	sleevenut
ombudsman	yachtsman	concerned	fraternal	lazytongs	polygenic	sojourner
Orangeman	abandoned	condignly	freelance	libidinal	polygonal	Solomonic
oriflamme	abandonee	consignee	freerange	longrange	polygonum	soundings
oysterman	abandoner	consignor	frequence	luminance	polytonal	squinancy
panoramic	abdominal	constancy	frequency	macaronic	polyvinyl	stagnancy
pantryman	aberrance	container	freshener	maharanee	pregnancy	stational
paranymph	aberrancy	contemner	gallooned	mainliner	pronounce	stationer
patrolman	abstainer	copartner	glissandi	mansionry	propionic	stepdance
performer	abundance	Corybants	glissando	matutinal	proscenia	stiffener
perilymph	accidence	cothurnus	gnathonic	medicinal	proteinic	stockinet
persimmon	acescence	covalence	goddamned	melatonin	prurience	stridence
plainsman	adherence	covalency	goldfinch	melomania	pruriency	stridency
ploughman	adjacency	crescendo	goldsinny	memoranda	pseudonym	strychnic
plumdamas	adjutancy	CroMagnon	golflinks	messianic	puissance	subagency
pointsman	adnominal	cryogenic	grievance	militancy	puritanic	subbranch
policeman	aepyornis	cryptonym	groundnut	millennia	purloiner	substance
polygamic	affluence	cumbrance	gunrunner	millionth	pursuance	sulphonic

```
sunbonnet  aitchbone  biogenous  cheekbone  delicious  falsehood  greenhorn
sunburned  albatross  birdsfoot  cherimoya  delirious  fancywork  greenroom
sundowner  algarroba  birthwort  childhood  demeanour  farandole  greenwood
sunlounge  allantois  blackcoat  Chinatown  dentiform  feedstock  grillroom
suntanned  allophone  blackcock  chiropody  depthbomb  felonious  grillwork
surgeoncy  allotrope  Blackfoot  chitinous  dermatoid  ferocious  gritstone
sustainer  allotropy  blasthole  chorology  desultory  ferryboat  guacamole
sweetener  alpenhorn  blindfold  cinereous  dexterous  festology  guardbook
swordknot  aluminous  bloodroot  clamorous  diachrony  feudatory  guardroom
symphonic  ambiguous  bloodworm  classroom  diandrous  fibriform  guesswork
synclinal  ambitious  bloodwort  claviform  diarrhoea  fibrinoid  guestroom
telamones  amorphous  bluestone  clearcole  dichotomy  fibrinous  guidebook
telegenic  amphibole  boardfoot  cloakroom  diclinous  fieldbook  guidepost
tensional  amphigory  boardroom  clockwork  dimissory  fieldboot  guiderope
terebinth  analogous  bombproof  closedown  dioecious  fieldwork  gustatory
theogonic  anandrous  bondstone  coachwork  diphthong  filaceous  gynophore
theomania  anchylose  bonhomous  cobaltous  dipterous  fireirons  gyroscope
thereinto  angiology  bookstore  cockahoop  directory  fireproof  hackamore
thereunto  angleworm  bounteous  cockscomb  disaccord  firestone  haematoid
thickener  anhydrous  bourgeois  cocksfoot  discolour  firstborn  haematoma
thickknee  anklebone  bracteole  coldshort  disembody  firstfoot  hagiology
tightener  anomalous  breakdown  colophony  disentomb  fistulous  hailstone
tinopener  anonymous  briarroot  colostomy  disfavour  flagstone  hailstorm
tolerance  anthology  briarwood  coltsfoot  dishcloth  flavorous  haircloth
torsional  anthozoan  brickwork  Cominform  dishclout  flintlock  halfblood
tramlines  antiknock  brierroot  commodore  dishonour  flowstone  halfcrown
transenna  antiphony  brierwood  comptroll  dittology  foolproof  handiwork
transonic  apetalous  brimstone  condyloid  dogstooth  footcloth  handsdown
trappings  aphyllous  bringdown  condyloma  dormitory  footloose  handywork
trepanned  apogamous  broadloom  congruous  drawnwork  footstool  haplology
trichinae  Appaloosa  broomcorn  conscious  dreamboat  foreclose  hardihood
triclinia  arachnoid  brushwood  copestone  dresscoat  forefront  haresfoot
triclinic  arboreous  brushwork  coprology  driftwood  foreknown  harmotome
trimmings  archivolt  buckthorn  copsewood  dripstone  foreshore  hartshorn
truepenny  argentous  bucktooth  coralloid  dropscone  foreshown  hawsehole
tuitional  arrowroot  buffaloes  cordiform  drugstore  foulbrood  hazardous
tunnelnet  arrowwood  buhrstone  corduroys  earthborn  fourscore  headcloth
umpteenth  arrowworm  bulltrout  cornflour  earthwork  fractious  headphone
unadorned  arsenious  bumptious  cornstone  earthworm  framework  headstock
unbalance  arteriole  burdenous  corticoid  egregious  freestone  headstone
uncleanly  artichoke  burnedout  cortisone  eiderdown  frigatoon  heartsore
uncrowned  arytenoid  burrstone  corymbose  eightfold  frivolous  heartwood
undefined  asbestous  cacholong  cosmogony  eightsome  frockcoat  heathcock
unfeigned  ascospore  cacophony  cosmology  elbowroom  frostwork  heliozoan
uniplanar  asepalous  Caenozoic  coumarone  electrode  fructuous  heliozoic
unlearned  assiduous  Cainozoic  countdown  ellipsoid  fruticose  hellebore
unwomanly  astrodome  cairngorm  courteous  emunctory  fugacious  hemitrope
utterance  astrology  calaboose  courtroom  endeavour  fulgurous  herbivore
vaticinal  astronomy  calcicole  crackdown  endoscope  fullblown  hereabout
vehemence  asymptote  calculous  crapulous  endoscopy  fullgrown  herpetoid
vengeance  atrocious  caliology  credulous  endospore  fulminous  hexachord
versional  audacious  campstool  crematory  entrecote  fungiform  hexaploid
vigilance  audiology  canalboat  cretinous  epigynous  galactose  hierology
vigilante  autocross  cancerous  criminous  eponymous  gallstone  highflown
virulence  autotroph  cankerous  crossroad  erogenous  gambadoes  highgrown
virulency  azeotrope  cantaloup  crossword  erroneous  garderobe  hilarious
viscounty  babacoote  capacious  crowsfoot  eruciform  garrulous  histology
warbonnet  backcloth  Capricorn  cruciform  ethnology  gemmology  hoarfrost
westerner  backcross  carambola  cryoscope  etymology  genealogy  hoarstone
whereinto  backsword  carcinoma  cryoscopy  eucaryote  germproof  hollyhock
whereunto  backwoods  carnivore  cubbyhole  euchology  gestatory  Hollywood
whodunnit  bacteroid  carpology  cuneiform. eunuchoid  ghostword  holophote
workbench  baltimore  carrefour  curbstone  eutectoid  girandole  holystone
workmanly  banderole  cartology  currycomb  everybody  gladstone  homegrown
zymogenic  bandicoot  casserole  curviform  evocatory  glaireous  homophone
ablutions  barbarous  catchpole  cutaneous  excretory  glamorous  homophony
accessory  barbitone  catchpoll  cutthroat  executory  glasswork  honeycomb
acidulous  barcarole  catchword  cymbiform  exogamous  glasswort  honeymoon
aciniform  bargepole  cattaloes  cyprinoid  exogenous  gloryhole  honkytonk
adulatory  barnstorm  cavernous  cystotomy  expiatory  glutinous  hornstone
adulthood  barracoon  cedarwood  damnatory  expletory  gneissoid  horoscope
aerobiont  beauteous  celluloid  dangerous  exsuccous  gneissose  horoscopy
aerodrome  behaviour  cellulose  davenport  extempore  gonophore  horsepond
aetiology  bellicose  cephalous  dayschool  fabaceous  goosefoot  hortatory
aftermost  bifarious  cerecloth  deathroll  facecloth  gradatory  houseboat
afternoon  billabong  cetaceous  deciduous  facetious  grandiose  housebote
afterword  billycock  chancroid  declivous  fairyhood  granitoid  housecoat
agapemone  billygoat  chancrous  decompose  falciform  granulose  household
agriology  binturong  chaperone  decretory  faldstool  greatcoat  houseroom
```

```
housework  liegelord  milktooth  oviparous  presswork  scapegoat  squarrose
hunkydory  lifeblood  millepore  ovulatory  probatory  scatology  stackroom
hydathode  lightfoot  millivolt  oxygenous  prolusory  scenedock  stagedoor
hydrofoil  lightsome  millstone  paintwork  pronghorn  schistose  stairfoot
hydrology  lightsout  minacious  palillogy  protozoal  schistous  stakeboat
hydrosome  lightwood  misbecome  palladous  protozoan  sciaenoid  stampnote
hydrozoan  lignaloes  misinform  pantaloon  protozoic  sciascopy  starstone
hydrozoon  ligniform  misreport  pantyhose  protozoon  scirrhous  statehood
hymnology  limestone  momentous  paperwork  provisory  scombroid  stateroom
hyperbola  limnology  moneywort  papilloma  psalmbook  scorebook  statutory
hyperbole  linenfold  Mongoloid  papillose  pterygoid  scorpioid  steamboat
hypnology  lithesome  monkshood  papillote  pulpstone  scrapbook  steelwork
hypogeous  lithology  monochord  parsimony  pulsatory  screwbolt  sternmost
hysteroid  lithopone  monstrous  pastedown  pulverous  screwworm  sternpost
ichnology  lithotomy  moonstone  patchwork  pumiceous  scutiform  stevedore
ichthyoid  litigious  moraceous  pathology  punchbowl  sebaceous  stickwork
iconology  liverwort  mossgrown  patrimony  puppyhood  secretory  stillborn
impastoed  livestock  mothproof  patrology  pureblood  seditious  stillroom
imperious  loadstone  motocross  pearlwort  purgatory  seigniory  stinkbomb
impetuous  loathsome  motorboat  pellitory  pussyfoot  selenious  stinkhorn
impulsory  lobectomy  mousehole  pendulous  pustulous  selfglory  stinkwood
incensory  lodestone  moviegoer  pennywort  pyroscope  semaphore  stirabout
incommode  lodgepole  multifoil  Pentecost  quartzose  semiology  stockbook
incurious  loincloth  multiform  penurious  queenhood  sericeous  stockdove
indispose  longevous  munitions  periscope  queenpost  serranoid  stockroom
ingenious  longicorn  murderous  peristome  querulous  setaceous  stokehold
ingenuous  longshore  murmurous  pestology  quillwort  sevenfold  stokehole
inglenook  lophodont  myrmecoid  petrology  radiology  shakedown  stonecoal
inharmony  lousewort  mystagogy  petticoat  raffinose  sheepcote  stonecold
injurious  lovestory  mythology  pettitoes  raincloud  sheepfold  stonework
innermost  lowermost  nannygoat  phalarope  rainproof  sheephook  stonewort
innocuous  loxodrome  narratory  phenology  rainstorm  shelfroom  storeroom
innoxious  lubricous  navelwort  pheromone  rancorous  shellwork  stormcock
inodorous  ludicrous  neckcloth  philology  rapacious  shopfloor  stormcone
insidious  lustihood  necrology  phonatory  rapturous  shopfront  storybook
interlock  luxurious  nectarous  phonology  raspatory  shorthorn  strapwork
interlope  macintosh  nefarious  photocopy  recompose  shotproof  strapwort
internode  macrocosm  neighbour  phycology  redingote  signatory  strawworm
interpose  madrepore  nephology  phytology  refectory  siliceous  strenuous
interwove  majordomo  neurology  phytotomy  religiose  silicious  stuporous
interzone  maladroit  nevermore  piecework  religious  siliquose  stylebook
inventory  malarious  nickelous  pinchcock  repertory  siltstone  styliform
invidious  malicious  nightgown  pipestone  reservoir  singalong  subereous
ironstone  mammalogy  nightlong  piscatory  restiform  skiascopy  sugarloaf
isochrone  mammiform  nightwork  pisciform  rhinology  slabstone  sumptuous
isogamous  mandatory  northmost  pitchfork  ridgepole  slumbrous  sunstroke
isogenous  manganous  nostology  pithecoid  righteous  smokebomb  supercool
isomerous  manticore  notochord  placatory  rigmarole  snakeroot  supernova
isopodous  marlstone  notorious  plainsong  rivalrous  snakewood  superpose
jollyboat  marshwort  nullipore  planetoid  riverboat  snowbroth  surculose
judicious  matchlock  oblivious  planuloid  roadblock  snowgoose  swangoose
juxtapose  matchwood  obnoxious  platinoid  rocambole  snowstorm  swansdown
kerbstone  matrimony  octachord  platinous  roodcloth  soapstone  swearword
knockdown  mattamore  offcolour  playgroup  rootstock  sociology  sweetcorn
krummhorn  meandrous  offertory  plenteous  Roquefort  softgoods  symbology
kurrajong  mediatory  officious  plumbeous  rosaceous  solacious  synchrony
laborious  megaphone  oilcolour  plumulose  roundworm  sophomore  syngamous
lacrimose  megaspore  oleaceous  podagrous  rustproof  sorcerous  syphiloid
lacrymose  melodious  olfactory  poisonous  sacciform  soundhole  tarragona
ladysmock  mementoes  oligopoly  pokerwork  sackcloth  soundpost  tautology
laevulose  menadione  ophiology  polyphone  sagacious  soupspoon  teleology
lamellose  mercurous  optophone  polyphony  sailcloth  Southdown  telephone
lancewood  mesogloea  orderbook  polyploid  sainthood  southmost  telephony
landdross  metalloid  orderform  pomaceous  salacious  spaceport  telephoto
landdrost  metalwork  orriswort  pompadour  salmonoid  spadefoot  telescope
lapideous  meteoroid  orthodoxy  ponderous  saltatory  spadework  telescopy
larcenous  methadone  osteology  poppycock  saltspoon  sparkcoil  tellurous
laudatory  metrology  Ostrogoth  porticoes  sandspout  spearwort  tenacious
lazzarone  metronome  outermost  posticous  sandstone  speedboat  tendinous
lazzaroni  micaceous  overblown  powerboat  sandstorm  sphagnous  tenebrous
leasehold  microcosm  overcloud  pranksome  sanfroid   sphenoid   territory
lecherous  micrology  overcrowd  precatory  sapanwood  sphygmoid  testimony
lentiform  microsome  overflown  predatory  satinwood  spinulose  tetralogy
leptosome  microtome  overgrown  prefatory  sauceboat  spinulous  tetrapody
leucotome  microtomy  overproof  prelusory  sauropoda  spiritoso  therefore
leucotomy  microtone  overshoot  prerecord  saxophone  spiritous  thighbone
libellous  migratory  overstock  presbyope  scagliola  splayfoot  thighboot
libratory  milestone  overwrote  preschool  scalemoss  spongeous  threefold
lichenous  milkfloat  oviferous  pressroom  scalplock  spouthole  threesome
```

threshold
thrombose
thumbhole
tigermoth
tigerwood
tightrope
tilestone
toadstone
toadstool
tollbooth
tombstone
tomentose
tomentous
toothcomb
toothsome
toothwort
torchsong
torturous
totempole
touchdown
touchhole
touchwood
townsfolk
trainload
transform
transport
transpose
trapezoid
traycloth
trematode
tremulous
tribology
trichroic
tricolour
trigamous
trimerous
tropology
troublous
trunkroad
tufaceous
tuliproot
tulipwood
turnabout
turnstone
twentyone
twiceborn
twicetold
tyrannous
uliginous
unanimous
unbeknown
underbody
undercoat
underdone
underfoot
undergone
undermost
undersold
undersong
undertone
undertook
underwood
unicolour
uniparous
unisonous
untimeous
unwelcome
uppermost
uranology
uttermost
vagarious
vainglory
varioloid
variolous
vasectomy
veinstone
velodrome
venereous
venturous
veracious
vermiform
verminous
verrucose
verrucous
versiform
vexatious
vibratory
vicarious
villiform
vimineous
vinaceous
vitriform
vivacious
volcanoes
voracious
vorticose
vulturous
wagonroof
waistcoat
walkabout
washcloth
washedout
watchword
watercool
waterfowl
waterhole
waterworn
wavefront
wayzgoose
wearisome
wellknown
whaleboat
whalebone
wheelwork
wherefore
whetstone
whinstone
whipstock
whirlpool
whitewood
wholesome
widowhood
windblown
windproof
winestone
wirephoto
withstood
woebegone
womanhood
womenfolk
woodblock
worrisome
woundwort
wrongdoer
wyliecoat
xenophobe
xylophone
zebrawood
zoogenous
zygospore
amblyopia
amblyopic
anthropic
apocrypha
arthropod
barkeeper
beekeeper
biography
bombhappy
breastpin
catalepsy
chaetopod
chassepot
cherrypie
coffeepot
curlpaper
developer
dewlapped
diatropic
dispeople
distemper
dystrophy
entrapped
enwrapped
epigraphy
episcopal
eucalypti
flowerpot
fluorspar
gastropod
genotypic
geography
geotropic
hyperopia
hyperopic
impromptu
innkeeper
isotropic
kidnapped
kidnapper
lagniappe
landloper
loveapple
misshapen
monotypic
municipal
myography
newspaper
notepaper
orography
orthoepic
peasouper
pepperpot
philippic
phyllopod
pineapple
polytypic
principal
principia
principle
pseudopod
quadruped
quadruple
quadruply
quintuple
radialply
ricepaper
roseapple
safetypin
sandpaper
sandpiper
satinspar
slaphappy
sorbapple
starapple
theosophy
thereupon
timelapse
tittupped
tophamper
uncropped
underspin
unicuspid
unstopped
unwrapped
wallpaper
whereupon
Xanthippe
zoography
arabesque
burlesque
chibouque
Dantesque
equivoque
grotesque
Junoesque
monocoque
odalisque
soliloquy
technique
triptyque
acroteria
adulterer
ahistoric
aleatoric
allegoric
allomorph
ambergris
anaphoric
ancestral
anemogram
angleiron
angularly
annularly
antiserum
antiviral
araucaria
argybargy
armigeral
auditoria
backwards
bainmarie
baneberry
barathrum
bearberry
bestirred
bicameral
bigeneric
bilateral
biliteral
billiards
biometric
bishopric
blaeberry
blinkered
blowtorch
blueberry
blunderer
blusterer
boobytrap
brasserie
bratwurst
breadtree
bricabrac
broiderer
brotherly
bullytree
butcherer
butcherly
cablegram
cadastral
cadaveric
cafeteria
calandria
calendric
camphoric
cantharid
cantharis
cantharus
carthorse
cartogram
catamaran
cathedral
catoptric
centigram
chafferer
champerty
chaparral
chartered
charterer
chatterer
checkered
chequered
chickaree
chimaeric
chinstrap
chivalric
cineraria
clatterer
claustral
cloistral
cockhorse
coinsurer
colostrum
concierge
concourse
concurred
conferral
conferred
conferrer
conqueror
conundrum
corkscrew
cranberry
creatural
cropeared
crossbred
crowberry
cupbearer
cyclotron
cylindric
decontrol
deerberry
deliverer
dextrorse
diablerie
diametral
diametric
diathermy
digastric
dinoceras
directrix
disbarred
discharge
discourse
dogshores
downthrow
downwards
drayhorse
dysphoria
dysphoric
eastwards
eavesdrop
eccentric
echovirus
ectomorph
electoral
enamoured
endomorph
ephemeral
ephemerid
ephemeris
ephemeron
excentric
executrix
fancyfree
feathered
fenestrae
fenestral
filmstrip
fireworks
flatterer
fluecured
foolhardy
fritterer
frogmarch
fruiterer
fruittree
furtherer
gaucherie
geometric
geometrid
geriatric
gigahertz
glandered
glengarry
goldenrod
grubscrew
hackberry
halfhardy
harbourer
haustoria
headfirst
heartfree
hearthrug
hectogram
heliogram
hierogram
hippocras
histogram
homewards
honoraria
hypethral
illiberal
inaugural
indecorum
infusoria
insularly
interbred
intercrop
interpret
ironworks
isometric
jackstraw
jacquerie
jockstrap
jocularly
Judastree
Juneberry
kilohertz
lagomorph
laminaria
launderer
leftwards
lifeforce
longeared
luciferin
maelstrom
magistral
magnetron
matriarch
maunderer
mediatrix
megahertz
menagerie
mesomorph
metameric
microgram
milligram
misleared
mistigris
monoceros
monomeric
moratoria
mousetrap
naseberry
neckverse
northerly
obstetric
ochlocrat
outskirts
overborne
overthrew
overthrow
packhorse
painterly
pairhorse
palpebral
palustral
panegyric
papeterie
paramorph
paregoric
patriarch
pellagrin
pentagram
penumbral
percheron
perimorph
phonogram
phytotron
pictogram
pikeperch
plastered
plasterer
plethoric
plunderer
plutocrat
pokeberry
polymeric
polymorph
popularly
poriferal
poriferan
porphyria
posthorse
potpourri
poulterer
prayerrug
preferred
prothorax
psalteria
puerperal
pyrethrum
quarterly
racehorse
radiogram
raspberry
rearhorse
rearwards
recoverer
reenforce
registrar
regularly
reimburse
reinforce
roadworks
roisterer
rowantree
saccharin
saltmarsh
saltworks
sanatoria
Sanhedrim
Sanhedrin
sanitaria
sassafras
saunterer
scarecrow
scatterer
schlieren
schnorrer
scholarly
scoredraw
scoundrel
scrapiron
secularly
sedgewren
semestral
shadberry
shadetree
sharecrop
sideburns
sidewards
similarly
sinistral
slanderer
slategrey
slenderly
slumberer
smackeroo
smallarms
smatterer

```
smoketree  whisperer  courtesan  jealously  redresser  advocator  banqueter
snaredrum  windwards  culsdesac  joylessly  rehearsal  aerobatic  banquette
sniggerer  wineberry  curiously  katabasis  reminisce  aerolitic  Bantustan
snowberry  workhorse  cutinised  katharsis  repressor  aerometer  baptistry
soapberry  wristdrop  cyclopses  keratosis  retrousse  aerometry  barometer
soapworks  xeromorph  cytolysis  langouste  rhodopsin  aesthetic  barometry
sociogram  abscissae  demitasse  lawlessly  riotously  agonistic  baronetcy
soldierly  abscissas  depressed  maharishi  Roumansch  airworthy  barrister
southerly  acariasis  depressor  malvoisie  ruinously  alabaster  basipetal
spinneret  acquiesce  deviously  manifesto  sargassos  albinotic  bayoneted
sputterer  addressee  diaereses  melanosis  sclerosis  algorithm  bedsettee
squirarch  addresser  diaeresis  merganser  scoliosis  alienator  bedsitter
staggerer  addressor  diagnoses  micropsia  scrollsaw  aliphatic  beefeater
stagparty  aesthesia  diagnosis  misfeasor  seriously  alligator  beemaster
stalworth  aesthesis  diaphysis  mongooses  sexlessly  allopathy  benighted
stammerer  aggressor  diastasis  monobasic  sideissue  altimeter  bespatter
stercoral  aimlessly  diathesis  moraliser  siderosis  amaurotic  bicipital
stingaree  alkaloses  dinnerset  mydriasis  silicosis  amourette  biorhythm
stinktrap  alkalosis  dirigisme  narcissus  sinlessly  amputator  birdwatch
stonecrop  amauroses  disbursal  nebuliser  sinuously  anabiotic  blatantly
studhorse  amaurosis  dismissal  nephrosis  slopbasin  analeptic  bolometer
stutterer  amorously  dispenser  nervously  snubnosed  anciently  bolometry
subastral  amylopsin  dispersal  nocuously  squamosal  ancientry  bombastic
succourer  anabioses  disperser  nonperson  successor  andesitic  bouquetin
sudatoria  anabiosis  disseisin  noxiously  succursal  anecdotal  boycotter
sulphuret  anacruses  dubiously  obsolesce  surprisal  anecdotic  bregmatic
sulphuric  anacrusis  duteously  obviously  suspensor  animistic  brevetted
sunspurge  analgesia  dyscrasia  odorously  syllepses  ankylotic  briquette
surcharge  analgesic  dyspepsia  offseason  syllepsis  annotator  brochette
swaggerer  anamnesis  dysplasia  oleoresin  symbiosis  annulated  bughunter
swimmeret  ankylosis  eclampsia  ominously  symphysis  anorectic  buoyantly
symmetric  antipasto  elevenses  onerously  syneresis  antarctic  cachectic
tabularly  anxiously  emulously  oogenesis  synizesis  antenatal  capacitor
tambourin  aphereses  encrimson  oppressor  syntheses  antidotal  carpenter
taskforce  apheresis  endlessly  organiser  synthesis  antipathy  carpentry
taxidermy  apophyses  energiser  overissue  taeniasis  apathetic  casuistic
tegularly  apophysis  engrosser  paillasse  tediously  aplanatic  casuistry
testatrix  appetiser  enviously  palliasse  televisor  apodictic  catalytic
tetragram  appraisal  epiclesis  parabasis  tenuously  apomictic  cathartic
theandric  appraiser  epiphyses  paradisal  thalassic  apparatus  cathectic
therefrom  appressed  epiphysis  paralysis  theoriser  apparitor  chapleted
thesaurus  aqueously  epithesis  parlously  timeously  appointee  character
thitherto  arduously  equaliser  passersby  totaliser  arboretum  charlatan
thorntree  arriviste  eulogiser  pederasty  traversal  arteritis  charlotte
thunderer  artemisia  exercises  pertussis  traverser  arthritic  chemistry
thyratron  arthrosis  exorciser  phantasma  unadvised  arthritis  chloritic
titularly  artlessly  exosmosis  photopsia  unbiassed  asphaltic  chlorotic
trattoria  assumpsit  exostosis  piteously  unblessed  asphaltum  chorister
trattorie  autolysis  expressly  polariser  uncrossed  aspirator  chromatic
treasurer  babirussa  extrinsic  politesse  universal  assaulter  chromatin
trierarch  biliously  fatuously  polybasic  untrussed  asthmatic  cigarette
trihedral  bulbously  fluoresce  pompously  uselessly  asymmetry  cinematic
trihybrid  buttinsky  fluorosis  possessed  vacuously  asyndetic  circuitry
trimetric  callously  folkmusic  possessor  vaporiser  asyndeton  clamantly
trousered  canvasser  foretaste  posthaste  variously  ataractic  clemently
tubularly  caparison  Freemason  postnasal  vibrissae  atavistic  climactic
tuliptree  caryopses  fricassee  practised  viciously  atheistic  coadjutor
turboprop  caryopsis  furiously  precursor  virtuosic  athematic  coelostat
twitterer  catalyser  gallowses  processed  virtuosos  atmometer  collected
unaltered  catalyses  gibbously  processer  viscously  atomistic  collector
uncovered  catalysis  gomphosis  processor  vocaliser  attempter  comforter
underbred  catharses  groundsel  proconsul  Waldenses  attractor  commenter
undergrad  catharsis  halfcaste  professed  washbasin  aubrietia  committal
unnatural  chastiser  halitosis  professor  witlessly  augmented  committed
unreserve  cheongsam  hangerson  prognoses  womaniser  augmenter  committee
untutored  chlorosis  haplessly  prognosis  zealously  augmentor  compactly
urticaria  cirrhosis  hardnosed  prolapsus  abdicator  authentic  compactor
verdigris  civiliser  heinously  prolepses  abnegator  autolytic  conceited
vertebrae  coloniser  heterosis  prolepsis  abrogator  automatic  concentre
vertebral  commensal  hideously  proptosis  accipiter  automaton  concerted
vomitoria  commissar  hortensia  prothesis  acquittal  axiomatic  concocter
wallydrag  compasses  hugeously  psoriasis  acrobatic  Axminster  concoctor
weathered  comprisal  hyponasty  psychoses  acropetal  Babbittry  conductor
weatherly  condenser  idealiser  psychosis  activator  backbiter  connected
westwards  confessor  immodesty  purchaser  adamantly  backwater  connecter
wherefrom  consensus  impiously  pyrolysis  adiabatic  badminton  connector
whimperer  contrasty  increaser  rafflesia  adiabatic  ballistae  consortia
whipperin  copiously  intrinsic  raucously  adjunctly  ballistic  consulter
whiskered  coreopsis  intumesce  recalesce  admonitor  bannister  consultor
```

contactor	encaustic	goosestep	larghetto	orangetip	prelector	scoliotic	
contented	enchanter	graduator	lastditch	orangutan	presbyter	scorbutic	
convector	encounter	graphitic	lazaretto	orchestic	presentee	scrutator	
converter	energetic	guarantee	Leicester	orchestra	presenter	sealetter	
copacetic	englutted	guarantor	leitmotif	organstop	presently	seanettle	
coroneted	enhearten	guncotton	leitmotiv	orgiastic	pressstud	seaworthy	
correctly	enigmatic	gymnastic	leniently	Orpington	preventer	seedeater	
corrector	enlighten	haemostat	leviratic	osmometer	prismatic	segmental	
corrupter	ensheathe	halftitle	levitator	oubliette	proclitic	selenitic	
corruptly	enteritis	halieutic	liberated	outfitter	progestin	semeiotic	
couchette	enwreathe	hamfisted	liberator	outputted	projector	semimetal	
courgette	enzymatic	hammertoe	librettos	outwitted	proleptic	separates	
cremaster	epaenetic	Hanseatic	limewater	overeaten	prophetic	separator	
cricketer	epaulette	harmattan	limonitic	overeater	prosector	sequester	
croquette	epicentre	harvester	literatim	overmatch	prostatic	sequestra	
crossette	epileptic	headwater	literator	overpitch	protector	serinette	
cunctator	epinastic	heliostat	literatus	overwatch	protester	serpentry	
currently	epiphytal	hemstitch	lobulated	oviductal	protestor	serviette	
curvetted	epiphytic	hepatitis	locomotor	pageantry	prothetic	sestertia	
decalitre	epithetic	hereafter	logarithm	paillette	provostry	shortstop	
decametre	epizootic	herniated	lorgnette	palaestra	prudently	sideritic	
decilitre	equisetum	hesitator	lovematch	palafitte	psoriatic	silicotic	
decimator	ergometer	heuristic	lymphatic	palmistry	psychotic	simpleton	
decimetre	escalator	hexameter	lysimeter	pancratic	pungently	simulator	
decorator	escheator	highwater	macerator	paralytic	pyrolater	singleton	
dedicator	estimator	hodometer	machmeter	paramatta	pyrolatry	sinusitis	
defaulter	etiquette	Holarctic	Mahometan	parameter	pyrolytic	sixfooter	
defiantly	evidently	homiletic	majorette	parapeted	pyrometer	slaughter	
deflector	excavator	hopscotch	manhattan	parasitic	pyrometry	slowmatch	
defroster	excerptor	Hottentot	manometer	parotitis	quadratic	sobsister	
dendritic	exequatur	hubristic	marquetry	parquetry	quartette	sodawater	
dentistry	exhauster	hygrostat	Masoretic	patiently	quercetum	solicitor	
depositor	exhibitor	hypocotyl	maybeetle	patinated	quickstep	sonometer	
depurator	exosmotic	iceskater	meditator	patriotic	quintette	sophister	
desolater	expediter	idiomatic	mekometer	patristic	quirister	sophistic	
desolator	exploiter	idiopathy	melanotic	paymaster	radiantly	sophistry	
detonator	expositor	illgotten	melocoton	pearlitic	rainwater	soubrette	
detractor	extractor	illicitly	meltwater	peasantry	rampantly	souwester	
diacritic	fantastic	immolator	memoriter	peccantly	realistic	spaghetti	
dialectal	fantastry	imperator	mercaptan	peculator	recruital	spectator	
dialectic	fasciated	impolitic	miasmatic	pedometer	recruiter	speedster	
diastatic	Fascistic	inbreathe	midinette	pendently	redletter	spermatic	
diathetic	fatwitted	incubator	midwinter	perfectly	redoubted	spermatid	
digitated	faunistic	indagator	milometer	perfector	reflector	sphincter	
dimwitted	fervently	indicator	mishanter	peridotic	refractor	splenetic	
dipswitch	fideistic	indigotin	mistletoe	perimeter	regretted	splenitis	
dishwater	fillister	inelastic	mitigator	perinatal	regulator	spoliator	
dismantle	filtertip	inexactly	moderator	peripatus	Reichstag	sprightly	
dissector	fingertip	inflictor	modulator	permitted	reliantly	stalactic	
dissenter	fireeater	infractor	monolatry	permitter	rencontre	statistic	
distantly	firewater	inhalator	mordantly	perverter	renovator	statuette	
dizygotic	floriated	inheritor	moschatel	phlebitis	requester	steatitic	
doleritic	floristic	inhibitor	mosquitos	phrenetic	resonator	stellated	
dolomitic	floristry	initiator	motheaten	pianistic	respecter	stigmatic	
dominator	forfeiter	innovator	motivator	pierrette	retinitis	stilettos	
dorbeetle	forgotten	inspector	mutilator	pietistic	retractor	stopwatch	
dosimeter	formatted	instanter	mydriatic	piquantly	revelator	storiated	
dosimetry	foxhunter	instantly	navigator	pirouette	rewritten	stromatic	
doubleton	freighter	insulator	nephritic	pisolitic	rheumatic	strumitis	
drysalter	fulgently	involuted	nephritis	pixilated	rhymester	stylistic	
dualistic	fumigator	irrigator	Nilometer	placentae	roadmetal	subarctic	
dynamiter	gallantly	ischiatic	nodulated	placental	rosewater	subcostal	
dyspeptic	gallantry	Islamitic	nominator	plasmatic	ruminator	subeditor	
dziggetai	gannister	isohyetal	novelette	pleuritic	sacristan	submaster	
earnestly	garmented	isostatic	nucleated	pneumatic	saleratus	submental	
earthstar	garrotter	itsybitsy	numerator	poetaster	salicetum	submitted	
eclamptic	gasfitter	ittybitty	obligated	polyester	saliently	subverter	
ecosystem	gasmantle	jetsetter	obturator	polymathy	saltpetre	succentor	
eggbeater	gasometer	jobmaster	occipital	polywater	saltwater	suggester	
egotistic	gastritis	Judaistic	ocellated	postentry	Samaritan	superstar	
elegantly	gauleiter	judgmatic	octameter	postnatal	sapiently	supinator	
elemental	generator	katabatic	offcentre	pothunter	sarcastic	supporter	
elongated	geomantic	keratitis	onanistic	poussette	sasquatch	surfeiter	
emaciated	georgette	kilolitre	onomastic	pragmatic	satinette	sybaritic	
embrittle	geostatic	kilometre	oogenetic	prankster	saturator	sylleptic	
embryotic	gestalten	kinematic	opsimathy	precentor	schematic	symbiotic	
emendator	gladiator	klinostat	optometer	preceptor	schmaltzy	syncretic	
eminently	glossator	lambently	optometry	predictor	scleritis	syndactyl	
emplastic	glossitis	laminated	opulently	preemptor	sclerotic	synovitis	

syntactic	Worcester	crossruff	hierodule	politburo	ventiduct	whichever
synthetic	wormeaten	curricula	hoarhound	poorhouse	vermicule	whosoever
systaltic	wyandotte	curvature	holocaust	posthouse	vermifuge	windhover
tabulator	youngster	dachshund	homebound	prefigure	vestibule	breakaway
taximeter	zeugmatic	debenture	homuncule	prelature	vestiture	breezeway
teakettle	zoophytic	deckhouse	homunculi	premature	vibracula	bridleway
tegmental	zucchetto	deerhound	horehound	preoccupy	wallfruit	disavowal
tegmentum	zygomatic	defeature	hypocaust	preshrunk	warehouse	firepower
telemeter	aboutturn	departure	immixture	procedure	washhouse	lawnmower
telemetry	accentual	depasture	importune	prosecute	waterbuck	mayflower
telepathy	acetabula	destitute	impostume	raingauge	waterbutt	motherwit
theoretic	admeasure	desuetude	imposture	ranunculi	wellfound	outgrowth
thicketed	admixture	difficult	inclosure	rearmouse	westbound	overpower
Thomistic	adventure	disannual	incorrupt	recapture	whipround	safflower
thoughted	affixture	disavouch	indenture	rectitude	windbound	scallawag
throwster	Algonquin	disfigure	institute	remeasure	winevault	scallywag
thyristor	almshouse	disposure	interfuse	reproduce	wiregauze	semivowel
tidewater	amplitude	disrepute	interlude	reremouse	witchhunt	shallowly
toadeater	anomalure	dissolute	interrupt	restitute	wolfhound	shottower
tonguetie	anschluss	dosshouse	intriguer	revictual	woodchuck	sluiceway
tonometer	antennule	draghound	introduce	roadhouse	woodlouse	spiderweb
tormentil	antitrust	dryasdust	ironbound	rockbound	workhouse	sunflower
tormentor	aspectual	dulcitude	ironmould	sagebrush	yearround	throwaway
touristic	attribute	dumbfound	josshouse	scripture	ablatival	willpower
trabeated	autoroute	eastbound	lassitude	sculpture	affidavit	aflatoxin
trachytic	awestruck	effectual	leafmould	secateurs	aggrieved	amphioxis
traumatic	Aylesbury	eiderduck	licensure	seigneury	almsgiver	anaptyxis
trickster	bakehouse	embrasure	lobscouse	selfabuse	antinovel	antefixal
tridactyl	baldaquin	empyreuma	longhouse	selfdoubt	Bolshevik	antitoxic
trimester	barracuda	enclosure	longitude	selftrust	breakeven	antitoxin
trinketer	bathhouse	enrapture	loudmouth	semifluid	campfever	catalexes
trinketry	beatitude	exchequer	lyamhound	semiplume	carryover	catalexis
triquetra	beleaguer	exclosure	lymehound	sepulture	confervae	complexly
trisector	bilingual	faithcure	magnitude	servitude	conserver	complexus
trumpeter	blackbuck	farmhouse	majuscule	sheerhulk	contrived	cytotoxic
truncated	bloodlust	fascicule	mallemuck	sheldduck	contriver	cytotoxin
tunicated	boathouse	fasciculi	malthouse	signature	convolved	endomixis
turgently	booklouse	febrifuge	mannequin	sliderule	crossover	epistaxis
twofisted	brachyura	feedstuff	matricula	slushfund	daredevil	homotaxis
twosuiter	buckhound	fioritura	menopause	smokebush	downriver	hypotaxis
typemetal	bundobust	fioriture	menstrual	snowbound	dustcover	oversexed
typhlitis	bunkhouse	firehouse	menstruum	sobriquet	flashover	paralexia
ultimatum	byproduct	flashbulb	messieurs	sostenuto	freeliver	parataxis
unadopted	calcifuge	flashcube	miniature	sourdough	gearlever	phalanxes
uncharted	calendula	flashtube	minuscule	spacesuit	genitival	pharynxes
uncinated	calenture	flophouse	monticule	spicebush	goingover	pyridoxin
uncounted	campanula	foodstuff	multitude	spiracula	goldfever	woodwaxen
uncreated	candytuft	footfault	nailbrush	spiritual	goodwives	aerophyte
undaunted	cannelure	footpound	neathouse	spirituel	hardcover	androgyne
undoubted	catamount	forasmuch	negritude	staghound	highlevel	androgyny
undulated	certitude	forcepump	nervature	stampduty	howsoever	anthocyan
unhealthy	chanteuse	forecourt	newshound	stillhunt	lifesaver	archetype
unknitted	charmeuse	fortitude	nigritude	striature	longaeval	Arguseyed
unlimited	chevelure	fourflush	noctiluca	stricture	longlived	astrocyte
unpointed	chockfull	freehouse	noseflute	structure	manoeuvre	bleareyed
unsheathe	chondrule	furniture	numbskull	sunstruck	mediaeval	bryophyte
unsighted	chophouse	gallinule	oasthouse	superfuse	Menshevik	cataclysm
unsightly	clubhouse	garniture	opportune	tablature	milkfever	chemitype
unspotted	coalmouse	gatehouse	overstuff	tanliquor	nondriver	cleareyed
unwritten	coiffeuse	gazehound	overtrump	tarantula	nutweevil	cockneyfy
upcountry	colemouse	glomerule	overwound	tessitura	ourselves	collotype
upholster	colloquia	glomeruli	palanquin	thornbush	parleyvoo	crosseyed
uprightly	comfiture	goalmouth	parachute	tidegauge	perceiver	dahabiyah
usherette	comminute	grandaunt	paramount	tollhouse	perfervid	destroyer
valiantly	composure	graticule	patchouli	toolhouse	preserver	ectophyte
vasomotor	configure	gratitude	patchouly	townhouse	primaeval	endophyte
venerator	connature	greataunt	peninsula	trabecula	redivivus	entophyte
verdantly	construct	greyhound	penthouse	tracksuit	reprieval	ferrotype
vignetter	continual	hairbrush	perpetual	transfuse	retrieval	freestyle
violently	continuer	halfbound	persecute	transmute	retriever	gainsayer
voltmeter	continuum	halftruth	pesthouse	tubercule	rounceval	greeneyed
volumeter	convolute	hamstring	petiolule	turnround	selfmoved	hackneyed
wagonette	cookhouse	haranguer	platitude	turpitude	septemvir	hairstyle
warrantee	coproduce	harlequin	playhouse	umbellule	shipfever	halophyte
warranter	corbicula	heartburn	plenitude	underhung	skindiver	hamadryad
warrantor	cornemuse	heavyduty	plicature	unisexual	slipcover	heliotype
wattmeter	coverture	hellhound	plusfours	unsavoury	tipstaves	hexastyle
webfooted	cranreuch	Hexateuch	pointduty	vallecula	voiceover	highflyer
witchetty	crenature	hidebound	polevault	vastitude	werwolves	Himalayan

```
hydrolyse acropetal blastulae coecilian discoidal fraternal inshallah
hydrolyte actuarial blastular coelostat dismissal freewoman insomniac
hypostyle adenoidal blockhead coeternal dispersal Frenchman interleaf
IndoAryan adnominal bondwoman cofferdam dissocial frockcoat interplay
journeyer adverbial boobytrap colcothar doctorial fullcream Iroquoian
karyotype afterclap bordereau collegial doctrinal funebrial irregular
leucocyte agnatical botanical collegian dogcollar funicular isallobar
leukocyte airstream brakesman collinear dominical galenical isoclinal
lifestyle Algonkian branchiae colloidal Dominican gaolbreak isohyetal
macrocyte altricial branchial colourman draconian gaspereau jackstraw
manslayer amazonian breakaway Columbian draftsman gastrulae jailbreak
melaphyre ambrosial breezeway commendam Dravidian genetical jetstream
mesophyll amoebaean bricabrac commensal dreamboat genitival jockstrap
mesophyte amphibian bridesman commissar dresscoat genocidal jollyboat
microcyte amyloidal bridleway committal dropsical gentleman Jordanian
micropyle ancestral broadleaf commonlaw druidical gerundial juridical
minelayer anchorman bromeliad comprisal dynamical glabellae jurywoman
mistyeyed anecdotal bronchial conciliar dziggetai glabellar justiciar
monorhyme anemogram buckwheat concordat ealdorman glandular Keplerian
monostyle angelical Bulgarian conferral earthstar gorgonian Keynesian
octastyle annelidan bursarial confervae ecclesial grandslam khedivial
octostyle antefixal butterfat conformal editorial graphical kinswoman
overjoyed antenatal cablegram Confucian Edwardian greatcoat klinostat
panchayat anthocyan cacuminal congenial effectual gregarian lacertian
peristyle anthozoan cadastral connubial effluvial Gregorian lachrymal
phagocyte antidotal cadential continual egomaniac groomsman Laodicean
phenotype antinodal caecilian convivial electoral grossular lapstreak
philogyny antipodal caerulean cornelian elegiacal guardsman laryngeal
phototype antiviral Caesarean cornerman elemental gymnasial latterday
polyonymy appraisal Caesarian cornopean embryonal haemostat leviathan
polyptych araneidal calcaneal cornsalad Emmenthal Hallowmas Levitical
portrayal araneidan calicular corporeal emotional hamadryad libidinal
portrayer archducal calycinal coseismal empirical hammerman librarian
proenzyme armigeral Cambodian courtesan enchorial handlebar lightyear
proselyte Armorican cameraman cracksman endosteal handorgan liveryman
prototype arrowhead canalboat craftsman entrechat harmattan loafsugar
ratepayer arsenical Candlemas creatural ephemeral Harrovian longaeval
sharpeyed Arthurian canesugar crinoidal epicurean heartbeat looseleaf
spirogyra articular canicular crossbeam epidermal Hebridean lumberman
sporocyst ascetical canonical crosshead epiphytal hectogram lumbrical
stalkeyed asclepiad cantorial crossroad episcopal heliogram lunisolar
statocyst aspectual capitular cryptical equivocal heliostat lunitidal
stenotype astrakhan Caribbean cryptogam eristical heliozoan Maccabean
stenotypy Atlantean carnelian culdesac  erratical Helvetian magistral
strongyle auctorial carpetbag cursorial essential Heraclean magnesian
tachylyte auricular Cartesian custodial Esthonian Herculean maharajah
teknonymy authorial cartogram custodian estuarian Hercynian Mahometan
touchtype autosomal Castalian cuticular etherical heretical Malayalam
tourneyer avuncular castellan cutthroat Ethiopian Hesperian malleolar
unalloyed azimuthal Castilian cycloidal ethmoidal hexagonal mammalian
viceroyal bacchanal catamaran cyclopean euclidean Hibernian Mancunian
xerophyte backpedal catarrhal cyclopian eutherian hierogram manhattan
zincotype bacterial cathedral Cytherean exciseman Himalayan Manichean
actinozoa ballistae cattleman Daedalean factional hippocras manipular
bamboozle Bantustan Caucasian Daedalian factorial histogram manorseat
bilharzia baptismal celestial dahabiyah Falernian historian Manxwoman
bulldozer Barbadian censorial dalmatian familyman Hobbesian marketday
chernozem barbarian centigram Damoclean fanatical hodiernal marmoreal
isoniazid basilican chaingear dandiacal farmstead homicidal marrowfat
kibbutzim basipetal chaparral Darwinian fatidical homopolar marsupial
kingsized Bathonian charlatan decagonal fellowman homousian Martinmas
lifesized beachhead charwoman decapodal fenestrae horsebean matutinal
oversized beachwear chelonian decapodan fenestral horseplay mediaeval
pintsized bedspread cheongsam decennial ferryboat houseboat medicinal
schnauzer beefsteak chinstrap deistical fibrillar housecoat Mendelian
schnitzel betrothal Christian dialectal fictional houseflag meningeal
shemozzle bicameral Christmas diametral fieldsman housemaid menstrual
stargazer bicipital chronical dichasial financial Hungarian mercaptan
wychhazel bilateral chthonian dichromat firebreak hydrozoan mercurial
————————  bilingual churchman dietician fisherman hygrostat meropidan
abdominal biliteral Cimmerian dietitian floridean hypethral metrician
ablatival billygoat circadian diningcar floscular hypnoidal microbial
abscissae binocular classical dinoceras fluorspar identical microgram
abscissas binominal claustral Dionysiac fluxional idiotical middleman
accentual bismillah clergyman Dionysian foragecap illiberal midstream
acellular blackcoat clinician disannual forcemeat illogical milkfloat
Acheulean blackflag cloistral disappear forespeak impartial milligram
Acheulian blackhead coccygeal disavowal forewoman inaugural Miltonian
acquittal blacklead cochineal disbursal fossorial IndoAryan mincemeat
```

minuteman	petechial	revictual	sluiceway	Tartarean	vicennial	awestruck
misdemean	petersham	rhizoidal	sociogram	Tartarian	viceregal	backspace
molecular	petticoat	rhonchial	sodabread	Tartufian	viceroyal	backtrack
molluscan	pharyngal	ribosomal	softpedal	Tasmanian	vicesimal	bailiwick
monarchal	phonogram	Ripuarian	Solutrean	technical	Victorian	barmbrack
Mongolian	physician	riverboat	Solutrian	tectorial	vigesimal	baronetcy
monocular	pictogram	riverhead	soritical	tegmental	Virgilian	beccafico
monodical	pictorial	roadmetal	spearhead	tellurian	viricidal	bellpunch
monsoonal	piecemeal	roadstead	speedboat	tensional	Vitruvian	billycock
morrisman	pipedream	Roumanian	spellican	tetragram	vizierial	bionomics
mortician	pipeorgan	rounceval	spherical	thickhead	vocabular	birdwatch
motorboat	pipsqueak	roundelay	spherular	thirdsman	vulcanian	bivalence
mousetrap	piratical	roundhead	spiderman	throwaway	vulgarian	bivalency
mucksweat	placentae	roundsman	spiritual	Thyestean	Wagnerian	blackbush
muffinman	placental	rubrician	spleuchan	timberman	waistcoat	blackcock
municipal	plainsman	ruddleman	spoilsman	tirewoman	wallydrag	blackface
muscleman	planarian	Sabellian	spokesman	tittlebat	washerman	blackjack
Mussulman	ploughman	sacristan	spongebag	Tocharian	waterleaf	blowtorch
Mycenaean	plumdamas	saddlebag	spoonbeak	tonsillar	Wednesday	blueblack
myrobalan	plutocrat	Sadducean	spoonmeat	tonsorial	weighbeam	bootblack
Nahuatlan	plutonian	sailorman	sportsman	topiarian	whaleboat	boxoffice
nannygoat	pointsman	Samaritan	squamosal	toponymal	whalehead	breakneck
navicular	polemical	Sardinian	stableman	torsional	wherryman	bullfinch
nectarean	policeman	sartorial	stairhead	tradesman	whimsical	bushwhack
nectarial	political	sassafras	stakeboat	traducian	whitebeam	byproduct
negroidal	polygonal	Sassanian	stapedial	tragedian	whitehead	cailleach
nemertean	polytonal	satanical	statesman	trainload	wholemeal	calamanco
neologian	popliteal	satinspar	stational	trapezial	windbreak	camelback
Neptunian	poppyhead	satirical	steamboat	traversal	witchmeal	candidacy
Nestorian	poriferal	Saturnian	steelclad	tribesman	workwoman	captaincy
Newtonian	poriferan	sauceboat	steelhead	trichinae	wyliecoat	chaffinch
nocturnal	portrayal	scaleleaf	steersman	triennial	yachtsman	cheapjack
nonlinear	postnasal	scallawag	steradian	trifacial	yesterday	chopstick
Norwegian	postnatal	scallywag	stercoral	trihedral	zoophagan	cicatrice
numerical	potential	scapegoat	steroidal	trilinear	Zwinglian	clearance
oakenshaw	powerboat	scarehead	stinktrap	trinomial	algarroba	cockroach
obconical	practical	sceptical	stomachal	triumphal	astrolabe	coherence
obsequial	prebendal	schoolbag	stonechat	trochleae	conscribe	coherency
occipital	precisian	schoolman	stonecoal	trochlear	flashcube	colonelcy
ochlocrat	precocial	sciential	stonedead	trousseau	flashtube	constancy
octagonal	presidial	scoredraw	stonedeaf	trunkroad	garderobe	constrict
octennial	primaeval	Scotchman	streetcar	trussbeam	passersby	construct
oddjobman	primatial	scrapheap	strobilae	tuckerbag	prescribe	contumacy
officinal	principal	scrimshaw	subaerial	tuitional	proscribe	coproduce
olecranal	prodromal	scrollsaw	subastral	typemetal	covalence	
ombudsman	proofread	scutellar	subcaudal	typhoidal	selfdoubt	covalency
opercular	prosaical	sectarian	subcostal	Ukrainian	spareribs	cowardice
Orangeman	prothorax	sectional	sublethal	umbilical	subscribe	cranreuch
orangutan	protozoal	sectorial	submental	undecimal	xenophobe	crookback
oratorial	protozoan	segmental	subnormal	underclay	aberrance	crookneck
oratorian	Provencal	selachian	subocular	undercoat	aberrancy	cumbrance
orbicular	psychical	selectman	subtopian	undergrad	aboutface	czarevich
orificial	ptarmigan	Seljukian	succursal	underplay	abundance	dalliance
ossicular	puerperal	semestral	suctorial	underseal	accidence	decadence
outspread	purpureal	semifinal	suctorian	underseas	acescence	decadency
oviductal	pyramidal	semilunar	suffragan	underwear	acoustics	deference
oysterman	quadrigae	semimetal	sugarloaf	unethical	acquiesce	democracy
Palladian	quadruman	seneschal	superheat	uniplanar	adherence	didactics
palpebral	quantical	sensorial	superstar	uniserial	adjacency	dietetics
paludinal	quarryman	sessional	surficial	unisexual	adjutancy	dilatancy
palustral	quizzical	sexennial	surprisal	unitarian	aerospace	diligence
panchayat	quotidian	shantyman	sweetmeal	universal	affluence	diplomacy
pantryman	radicular	Shechinah	sweetmeat	unmusical	allowance	dipswitch
paradisal	radiogram	shellheap	switchman	unnatural	ambulance	dirttrack
paranoiac	raptorial	shewbread	swordplay	unpopular	anabranch	disaffect
parochial	recruital	shillelah	swordsman	Upanishad	annoyance	disavouch
passional	rectorial	shipcanal	sympodial	utricular	antiknock	disbranch
patrician	reedorgan	shockhead	symposiac	Varangian	appetence	disinfect
patrolman	regicidal	shovelhat	symposial	vaticinal	appetency	dogmatics
Pavlovian	registrar	sigmoidal	synagogal	vectorial	applejack	dominance
pedicular	rehearsal	signalman	synclinal	vehicular	appliance	dramatics
Pelasgian	Reichstag	signorial	syncytial	veridical	architect	drumstick
pentagram	reliquiae	sinistral	synodical	versional	armistice	dysgenics
penumbral	reprieval	Sisyphean	syringeal	vertebrae	arrogance	economics
perennial	reptilian	sketchmap	tableleaf	vertebral	assonance	effluence
pergunnah	reticular	Slavonian	tacamahac	vesicular	assurance	eiderduck
perinatal	retinulae	slothbear	tactician	vestigial	athletics	eloquence
perpetual	retinular	Slovakian	tactitian	vestryman	autocracy	emergence
petechiae	retrieval	Slovenian	tahsildar	vibrissae	avoidance	emergency

```
endurance  immanence  obedience  residency  timepiece  estrapade  saleslady
esoterica  immanency  obeisance  resonance  timocracy  everglade  sauropoda
esperance  immediacy  obsolesce  resurface  toastrack  everybody  selfpride
esurience  imminence  obstinacy  resurrect  tolerance  fanfarade  servitude
esuriency  imminency  occupancy  reticence  toothpick  fissipede  sforzando
euthenics  impedance  oenomancy  reticency  torchrace  floodtide  shoreside
excitancy  imperfect  offchance  retroject  toreutics  foeticide  sidewards
existence  impotence  onlicence  reverence  trierarch  foolhardy  softgoods
exservice  impotency  opponency  rhythmics  tsarevich  forecaddy  spearside
exultance  impudence  ordinance  ringfence  unbalance  fortitude  stateside
exultancy  incidence  oscitancy  roadblock  utterance  fungicide  statewide
eyeglance  incorrect  overcheck  rootstock  vehemence  fusillade  strappado
feculence  indecency  overmatch  roughneck  vengeance  gabionade  subdivide
feedstock  indigence  overpitch  Roumansch  ventiduct  gallopade  supersede
firebrick  indolence  overprice  sacrifice  ventifact  garibaldi  tamponade
fireplace  inerrancy  overreach  sandarach  vigilance  gasconade  telluride
fishslice  inference  overreact  sandcrack  virulence  germicide  tetrapody
fishyback  influence  overstock  santonica  virulency  gingerade  Theravada
fivepence  inherence  overtrick  sasquatch  volteface  glissandi  trematode
flagrance  injustice  overwatch  Sassenach  waterbuck  glissando  triploidy
flagrancy  innocence  paperback  scalplock  whaleback  glucoside  turpitude
flagstick  innocency  patriarch  scenedock  whipstock  glyceride  twayblade
flashback  inservice  penitence  semantics  whiteface  glycoside  underbody
flintlock  insolence  perchance  semblance  wisecrack  grandaddy  underside
flippancy  insurance  permeance  semiotics  woodblock  gratitude  uxoricide
fluoresce  intellect  petulance  sentience  woodchuck  hairslide  vastitude
folkdance  interdict  petulancy  sentiency  workbench  halfhardy  verbicide
forasmuch  interface  phonemics  sergeancy  workpiece  herbicide  vermicide
forereach  interject  phonetics  serjeancy  yardstick  highgrade  waterside
fortalice  interlace  pickaback  severance  zoiatrics  highlands  waveguide
fourpence  interlock  piggyback  sheeplice  acetamide  homewards  westwards
fragrance  intersect  pikeperch  sheeptick  allemande  horsehide  windwards
fragrancy  intestacy  pinchbeck  sheldduck  alongside  hydathode  worldwide
freelance  intricacy  pinchcock  shellback  ambuscade  hydroxide  zapateado
frequence  introduce  placekick  shipwreck  amplitude  incommode  abandoned
frequency  introject  plangency  shoeblack  anhydride  intercede  abandonee
frogmarch  intumesce  pleasance  showpiece  antitrade  interlude  abandoner
gemutlich  inviolacy  poignancy  showplace  asafetida  internode  abolisher
genuflect  isagogics  pointlace  shrewmice  backslide  jaborandi  absconder
geoponics  itineracy  pokerface  sibilance  backwards  jacaranda  abstainer
ginpalace  jossstick  polyptych  sibilancy  backwoods  lampshade  accipiter
goldbrick  jubilance  poppycock  sidetrack  Barmecide  landslide  acclaimer
goldfinch  ladysmock  portulaca  significs  barracuda  larvicide  acetifier
gooseneck  lampblack  precipice  simpatico  barricade  lassitude  acidifier
greenback  lancejack  pregnancy  skinflick  barricado  leftwards  acquitted
grievance  lastditch  prejudice  slapstick  bastinade  longitude  addressee
gynocracy  latitancy  preselect  slingback  bastinado  magnitude  addresser
hairpiece  lifeforce  procuracy  slipcoach  beatitude  makeready  adulterer
hairspace  limejuice  pronounce  slowcoach  billiards  marmalade  aerometer
halfpence  liquorice  prurience  slowmatch  Bretwalda  matricide  affianced
halfprice  liturgics  pruriency  smokejack  broadside  memoranda  Afrikaner
halftrack  livestock  puissance  spotcheck  cannonade  millepede  aggrieved
harmonica  logistics  pursuance  squinancy  carbamide  millipede  aircooled
harmonics  lovematch  purulence  squirarch  carbonado  motorcade  airjacket
hatchback  lowerdeck  purulency  stagnancy  carronade  multitude  airminded
haversack  luminance  pyromancy  stepdance  cavalcade  muscovado  alabaster
headpiece  magnetics  quittance  stopwatch  centipede  negritude  alkaloses
headstock  magnifico  racetrack  stormcock  certitude  newlyweds  almsgiver
heartsick  mahlstick  raincheck  stridence  chairlady  nightside  altimeter
heathcock  mainbrace  razorback  stridency  chiropody  nigritude  amauroses
heelpiece  mallemuck  reactance  subagency  cirripede  orangeade  amplifier
hemistich  marshalcy  recalesce  subbranch  colonnade  ovenready  anabioses
hemstitch  matchlock  recollect  substance  crescendo  palmipede  anacruses
hesitance  matriarch  recreancy  sunstruck  crossfade  parricide  anguished
hesitancy  maulstick  recusance  supremacy  croustade  patricide  announcer
hexastich  mechanics  recusancy  surgeoncy  cyanamide  pesticide  annulated
Hexateuch  militancy  redolence  sweepback  demimonde  phosphide  anopheles
hieratica  mischance  reenforce  sweptback  derringdo  pinnipede  antinovel
hindrance  misdirect  reference  symbolics  desperado  platitude  antipodes
hollyhock  mnemonics  refluence  synectics  desuetude  plenitude  aphereses
hopscotch  mobocracy  reinforce  tailpiece  dipeptide  polyamide  apophyses
hornwrack  monocracy  relevance  taioseach  disembody  prolicide  appetiser
horseback  monostich  relevancy  taskforce  downgrade  promenade  applauder
huckaback  mumchance  remanence  tectonics  downwards  readymade  appointee
hunchback  nescience  reminisce  theatrics  dulcitude  rearwards  appraiser
hygienics  ninepence  renitency  theocracy  eastwards  rectitude  appressed
hysterics  noctiluca  reproduce  thornback  electrode  referenda  archangel
ignorance  nomocracy  rerebrace  throwback  enchilada  retrocede  Arguseyed
imbalance  nosepiece  residence  thumbtack  esplanade  riverside  artificer
```

assaulter	butcherer	consulter	dispenser	feathered	goldfever	innholder
assembler	bystander	container	disperser	fenugreek	gondolier	innkeeper
atmometer	cabriolet	contemner	dissenter	filigreed	goodwives	inscriber
attainder	cacoethes	contender	dissuader	fillister	goosander	inspanned
attempter	campfever	contented	distemper	filterbed	goosestep	instanter
augmented	cancelled	continuer	distilled	financier	gorblimey	instilled
augmenter	cannoneer	contrived	distiller	fireeater	gospeller	interbred
Axminster	cannonier	contriver	disturbed	firepower	gravelled	interpret
backbiter	canvasser	converter	disturber	firewater	greeneyed	interview
backwater	caretaker	convincer	dittander	flageolet	greenweed	intriguer
balconied	carpenter	convolved	doglegged	flashover	grenadier	inveigler
baldfaced	carrageen	copartner	dogshores	flatterer	groundsel	involuted
balladeer	carryover	copolymer	dogviolet	floriated	grovelled	ironsides
bandoleer	cartwheel	corbelled	dosimeter	flowerbed	groveller	isosceles
bandolier	caryopses	cordelier	downriver	flowsheet	grubscrew	jampacked
bannister	cassareep	coriander	drawsheet	fluecured	guarantee	jaundiced
banqueter	cassoulet	corkscrew	driftweed	flyfisher	gunpowder	jaywalker
barefaced	catalexes	coroneted	drivelled	forbidden	gunrunner	jetsetter
bargainer	catalyser	corralled	driveller	forcefeed	hackneyed	jewelweed
barkeeper	catalyses	corrupter	drysalter	foreboder	hagridden	jobmaster
barnacled	catharses	coryphaei	dungarees	foreigner	halfbaked	journeyer
barometer	cattaloes	costumier	dustcover	forenamed	halfbreed	Judastree
barracker	certified	couturier	dustsheet	foretoken	Halloween	justifier
barrelled	certifier	cremaster	dynamiter	forfeiter	hamburger	karabiner
barrister	chafferer	crenelled	earwigged	forgather	hamfisted	kennelled
bartender	chapleted	cricketer	Eastender	forgotten	hamhanded	kidnapped
basrelief	character	cropeared	easterner	formatted	handwheel	kidnapper
bastioned	chartered	crossbred	ecosystem	fortifier	hanselled	kingdomed
bayoneted	charterer	crosseyed	eggbeater	forwander	haranguer	kingmaker
bedjacket	chastener	crossover	elastomer	forwarder	harbinger	kingsized
bedridden	chastiser	crustacea	elevenses	fossicker	harbourer	kitchener
bedsettee	chatterer	cudgelled	elongated	fourwheel	hardcover	knockknee
bedsitter	checkered	cullender	emaciated	foxhunter	hardnosed	laminated
beefeater	chequered	cupbearer	embattled	freeliver	harpooner	lampooner
beekeeper	chernozem	cuplichen	embezzler	freerider	harvester	landaulet
beemaster	chevalier	curlpaper	embroider	freewheel	headliner	landloper
beleaguer	chickadee	curvetted	enamelled	freighter	headwater	landowner
beneficed	chickaree	cutinised	enameller	freshener	heartfree	Laplander
benighted	chickweed	cyclopses	enamoured	fricassee	hereafter	latecomer
berserker	chiselled	debauched	enchanter	fritterer	hereunder	launderer
beslobber	chiseller	debauchee	encounter	frivolled	herniated	laurelled
bespatter	chlamydes	debaucher	energiser	frolicked	hexameter	lawnmower
bestirred	chorister	declaimer	energumen	fruiterer	highflier	lazybones
betrothed	civiliser	decomplex	Englander	fruittree	highflyer	leafgreen
bigheaded	clarifier	defaulter	englutted	fulfilled	highlevel	Leicester
bilgekeel	clarionet	defroster	engrosser	fulfiller	highspeed	liberated
Blackfeet	clatterer	deliverer	enhearten	funnelled	hightoned	lifesaver
bleareyed	cleareyed	denouncer	enlighten	furbisher	hobnailed	lifesized
blinkered	clergymen	depressed	entrammel	furnisher	hobnobbed	lignaloes
blockader	cobwebbed	derringer	entrapped	furtherer	hodometer	Limburger
bloodshed	cockatiel	descended	enwrapped	gadgeteer	homemaker	limewater
blunderer	coinsurer	describer	epiphyses	gainsayer	horologer	lintelled
blusterer	collected	desolater	epistoler	galleried	hosteller	lipreader
Boanerges	coloniser	despoiler	equaliser	gallooned	hotheaded	liquefier
bobtailed	comedones	destroyer	ergometer	gallowses	housekeep	lobulated
boldfaced	comforter	dethroner	estaminet	gambadoes	houseleek	longeared
bolometer	commander	developer	estranger	gambolled	houselled	longfaced
bookmaker	commenter	dewlapped	eulogiser	gannister	howsoever	longlived
bottlefed	committed	diaereses	evergreen	garmented	humblebee	lovetoken
bowlegged	committee	diagnoses	ewenecked	garnishee	humbugged	lowlander
boxgirder	compasses	diarrhoea	exchanger	garreteer	humdinger	lowloader
boycotter	compelled	diesinker	exchequer	garrotter	hydrangea	lowminded
Brahminee	conceited	digitated	exercises	gasfitter	Icelander	lownecked
branchlet	concerned	dignified	exhauster	gasholder	iceskater	lysimeter
breadtree	condenser	dimwitted	exorciser	gasometer	idealiser	machmeter
breakeven	confabbed	dinnerset	expediter	gauleiter	illgotten	magnifier
brevetted	conferred	disbarred	explainer	gazetteer	illjudged	maharanee
brigadier	conferrer	disbelief	exploiter	gearlever	illomened	mainliner
Britisher	confirmed	disbudded	expounder	gearwheel	illwisher	mainsheet
broiderer	conformer	disburden	eyeopener	geomancer	impastoed	malformed
brummagem	congeries	discalced	fairfaced	germander	impleader	malleehen
buccaneer	connected	discarder	falsifier	gestalten	impounder	manometer
buffaloes	connecter	discerner	fancyfree	giltedged	inbetween	mansarded
bughunter	conserver	disesteem	fantasied	glandered	increaser	manslayer
bulldozer	consignee	disgracer	fasciated	gobetween	indweller	manyplies
bullybeef		dishfaced	fascicled	goddamned	infielder	manysided
bullytree		dishwater	fashioner	godfather	ingrained	marcelled
bumblebee		dismember	fatheaded	godmother		marvelled
burnisher		dispelled	fatwitted	goingover		masonried

```
masterkey optometer plunderer requester sidewheel subverter trustdeed
maunderer organiser poetaster resources sightseer succeeder tuliptree
mayflower osmometer polariser respecter signalled succourer tunicated
mekometer ourselves polyester responder signaller sugarbeet tunnelled
meltwater outbacker polywater retoucher simplices suggester tunnelnet
mementoes outfitter pommelled retriever singspiel sulphuret twitterer
memoriter outgunned pontoneer retrodden sitzkrieg sunbather twofisted
merganser outlander pontonier retroflex sixfooter sunbonnet twohanded
mesogloea outnumber porringer rewritten skindiver sunburned twosuiter
messenger outputted porticoes rhymester skyjacker sundowner Uitlander
midsummer outridden portrayer ricepaper skyrocket sunflower unabashed
midwicket outrigger possessed ridiculer slabsided sunhelmet unadopted
midwinter outspoken potboiler riverweed slanderer suntanned unadorned
milkfever outwitted pothunter rocketeer slategrey supporter unadvised
millwheel outworker poulterer rodfisher slaughter surfeiter unalloyed
milometer overeaten practised roisterer slinkweed surmullet unaltered
minelayer overeater praenomen rosewater slipcover surpliced unashamed
misbelief overjoyed prankster rosinweed slumberer surrender unberufen
misbeseem overladen precancel rowantree smartweed suspender unbiassed
misesteem overpower preferred rumrunner smatterer sustainer unblessed
misguided oversexed presbyter safflower smoketree swaggerer unblinded
mishanter oversized presentee sagegreen snakeweed sweetener unbounded
misleared oversleep presenter salpinges sniggerer swimmeret unbraided
mispickel oversteer preserver saltwater snivelled swivelled unbridled
misshapen overtaken pretender sandalled sniveller syllabled uncharted
missioner overthrew preventer sandpaper snubnosed syllepses unchecked
mistyeyed overtones princelet sandpiper sobriquet syntheses uncinated
moistener oysterbed privateer sapheaded sobsister tapdancer unclothed
mongooses pacemaker processed saunterer sodawater tasselled unclouded
moonraker palankeen processer Sauternes sojourner taximeter uncounted
moraliser panoplied professed scarifier sometimes tectrices uncovered
mortgagee parameter profiteer scatterer sommelier telamones uncreated
mortgager parapeted prognoses scavenger sonneteer telemeter uncropped
mosaicked parcelled prolepses schlemiel sonometer tentacled uncrossed
moschatel parrakeet propelled schlieren sophister tentmaker uncrowned
motheaten passenger propeller schnauzer souwester teratogen undamaged
moviegoer patinated propylaea schnitzel specifier testifier undaunted
muckraker patrolled protester schnorkel speedster theoriser undecided
muffineer patroller provender schnorrer sphincter thickener undefined
mullioned paymaster psychoses scorifier spiderweb thicketed underbred
multiplex paypacket publisher scoundrel spindrier thickknee undivided
mummified peasouper puffadder scrambler spinnaker thorntree undoubted
musketeer pedigreed pulpiteer scratcher spinneret thoughted undreamed
mystifier pedometer pummelled scratches spiralled throttler undulated
nebuliser pencilled puppeteer screecher spirituel throwster unfeigned
nepenthes penciller purchaser scribbler spoonfeed thunderer unfledged
netveined penholder purloiner scrivener springlet tidewater unfleshed
netwinged penpusher pyrolater scrounger sprinkler tightener unfounded
newmarket pensioner pyrometer sealetter spurwheel timesheet unguarded
newspaper perceiver quadruped sedgewren sputterer tinopener unhurried
nickelled performer qualified seedeater squabbler tinselled unknitted
Nilometer perfumier qualifier selffaced squelcher tipstaves unlearned
nitpicker perimeter quarenden selfmoved squirelet titledeed unlimited
nodulated permitted quarender semisweet staggerer tittupped unmatched
nondriver permitter quickener semivowel stalkeyed toadeater unpeopled
nonsmoker personnel quickstep separates stallfeed tonguelet unplugged
nosebleed persuader quirister September stammerer tonometer unplumbed
notepaper perverter quodlibet septuplet stargazer tophamper unpointed
nourisher pettitoes racketeer sepulcher stationer tortrices unruffled
nowhither phalanger rainmaker sequester stauncher totaliser unscathed
nucleated phalanges rainwater sequinned staymaker tourneyer unsettled
nuisancer phalanxes ransacker serenader stellated trabeated unsighted
nullifier pharynges ratepayer seventeen stiffener traceried unskilled
obligated pharynxes recoverer seventies stingaree tramlines unspotted
obsequies phellogen recruiter sexlinked stinkweed travelled unstopped
ocellated philander rectifier sextuplet stockinet traveller unstudied
octameter physicked rectrices shadetree stomacher traverser unsullied
octopodes picnicked redhanded sharpener storiated treasurer untouched
oddjobber picnicker redheaded sharpeyed straggler trebuchet untrodden
oestrogen pigheaded redletter shieldfem strangler trebucket untrussed
offhanded pimpernel redoubted shipfever strangles trepanned untutored
offscreen pintailed redresser shipmoney stratagem trickster unwearied
offstreet pintsized refreshen shipowner streamlet trimester unwrapped
oilburner pistoleer refresher shoemaker stretcher trinketer unwritten
okeydokey pistolled refuelled shoreweed struggler trousered upbraider
onehanded pixilated regretted shortener stupefier trowelled upholster
onelegged planisher rejoinder shottower stutterer troweller valuables
openended plastered remainder shovelled submaster trumpeter vaporiser
opinioned plasterer renouncer shoveller submitted truncated varnisher
```

velveteen	makeshift	febrifuge	preengage	firelight	aesthesia	arytenoid
verandaed	nightlife	festology	privilege	flyweight	aesthesis	ascertain
versifier	objectify	fleshings	pupillage	footlight	aesthetic	asphaltic
videlicet	overdraft	flowerage	radiology	foresight	affidavit	assumpsit
vignetter	overstuff	forejudge	raingauge	fortnight	aflatoxin	asthmatic
vocaliser	personify	forestage	razoredge	Gaeltacht	aforesaid	asyndetic
voiceover	pikestaff	fosterage	rearrange	geography	agonistic	ataractic
volcanoes	plaintiff	freerange	recoinage	goodnight	agrologic	atavistic
volkslied	preachify	frontpage	repechage	guilloche	agronomic	atheistic
voltmeter	rechauffe	gallmidge	reportage	hagiarchy	ahistoric	athematic
volumeter	shelflife	gallonage	rhinology	halflight	albinotic	atomistic
volunteer	skewwhiff	gemmology	sacrilege	headlight	alcoholic	aubrietia
Waldenses	skingraft	genealogy	saxifrage	heartache	aldehydic	auditoria
wallpaper	snowdrift	greengage	scatology	heptarchy	aleatoric	autarchic
warbonnet	speechify	groundage	scrimmage	hierarchy	Alemannic	authentic
warmonger	spindrift	hagiology	scrummage	highlight	algebraic	autolysis
warrantee	stardrift	haplology	seachange	hindsight	Algonquin	autolytic
warranter	vouchsafe	haverings	secretage	idiopathy	alicyclic	automatic
wassailer	woodcraft	hermitage	selfimage	inbreathe	aliphatic	autonomic
waterflea	xenograft	hierology	semiology	indraught	alkalosis	autotelic
watershed	advantage	histology	sheerlegs	inwrought	allantois	axiomatic
waterweed	aetiology	hydrology	shrinkage	lamplight	allegoric	bacteroid
wattmeter	agriology	hymnology	siphonage	limelight	amaryllis	bainmarie
weakkneed	anchorage	hypallage	skirtings	logarithm	amaurosis	baldachin
weathered	angiology	hypnology	sociology	logomachy	amblyopia	baldaquin
webfooted	anthology	ichnology	sortilege	lovelight	amblyopic	ballistic
weevilled	appendage	iconology	soundings	maharishi	Amerindic	beeorchis
welltimed	arbitrage	interpage	sourdough	methought	aminoacid	bigeneric
werwolves	argybargy	kentledge	sovereign	moonlight	amygdalin	bilharzia
westerner	arrearage	knifeedge	sunlounge	moustache	amylopsin	bilirubin
wheyfaced	astrology	knightage	sunspurge	myography	anabiosis	biometric
whichever	audiology	knowledge	surcharge	oligarchy	anabiotic	birdbrain
whimperer	backstage	lazytongs	symbology	onslaught	anacrusis	bishopric
whiskered	beastings	limnology	tautology	opsimathy	anaerobic	blackmail
whisperer	beestings	lithology	teleology	orography	analeptic	blockship
whosoever	bobsleigh	longrange	tetralogy	overnight	analgesia	boatswain
willpower	brokerage	mammalogy	tidegauge	oversight	analgesic	boattrain
windhover	calcifuge	matronage	titlepage	parfleche	anamnesis	Bolshevik
womaniser	caliology	metrology	trappings	peepsight	anaphoric	bombastic
woodwaxen	carpology	micrology	treillage	pentarchy	anaptyxis	bouquetin
Worcester	cartilage	misassign	tribology	polymathy	andesitic	bourgeois
wormeaten	cartology	mismanage	trimmings	quebracho	androecia	Brahmanic
wormwheel	cartridge	moneybags	tropology	rearlight	anecdotic	Brahminic
wrongdoer	cellarage	monophagy	ultrahigh	recherche	anglophil	brasserie
wychhazel	challenge	mycophagy	undersign	rethought	animistic	breastpin
Yiddisher	champaign	mystagogy	uranology	rushlight	ankylosis	bregmatic
youngster	chitlings	mythology	vassalage	sandyacht	ankylotic	Britannia
zigzagged	chorology	necrology	vermifuge	schlemihl	anoxaemia	Britannic
afterlife	clientage	nephology	villanage	sciamachy	antarctic	broadtail
autograft	commonage	neurology	villenage	seaworthy	anthracic	Brythonic
bushcraft	concierge	nostology	waggonage	sidelight	anthropic	cablelaid
campcraft	consulage	odontalgy	airworthy	skiamachy	antigenic	cachectic
candytuft	cooperage	oesophagi	algorithm	skintight	antimonic	cacodylic
cockneyfy	coprology	ophiology	allopathy	spotlight	antinomic	cadaveric
cowlstaff	cosmology	orphanage	antipathy	starlight	antigenic	cadetship
crossruff	curettage	ossifrage	apocrypha	stoplight	antimonic	Caenozoic
deacidify	curtilage	osteology	archduchy	taillight	antinomic	Cainozoic
decalcify	demurrage	outgoings	avalanche	telepathy	antitoxic	calandria
demystify	diaphragm	overweigh	backsight	tetrarchy	antitoxin	calendric
denitrify	discharge	palillogy	bellyache	theomachy	antivenin	calorific
devitrify	disengage	parentage	bethought	theosophy	apartheid	camelhair
diversify	disoblige	parsonage	biography	toothache	aperiodic	campchair
electrify	disparage	partridge	biorhythm	unhealthy	apheresis	camphoric
exemplify	dittology	pasturage	bombsight	unsheathe	aplanatic	cantharid
feedstuff	downstage	pathology	bretasche	unthought	apodictic	cantharis
flagstaff	embassage	patrology	bullfight	unwrought	apomictic	capriccio
foodstuff	empennage	patronage	cartouche	weeknight	apophysis	caryopsis
frenchify	encourage	personage	chachacha	wehrmacht	apostolic	casuistic
gearshift	endophagy	pestology	cockfight	zoography	acariasis	catabolic
halfstaff	entourage	petrology	copyright		apothecia	catalexis
handcraft	epiphragm	phenology	deadlight		acidophil	catalysis
handcuffs	escortage	philology	downright		aquilegia	catalytic
homograft	espionage	phonology	dystrophy		arachnoid	catatonia
housewife	estoppage	phycology	ensheathe		araucaria	catatonic
indemnify	ethnology	phytology	entelechy		artemisia	catharsis
intensify	etymology	pilferage	enwreathe		adiabatic	cathartic
jackknife	euchology	pleadings	epigraphy		adrenalin	cathectic
kingcraft	factorage	polyphagy	ethnarchy		aepyornis	catoptric
luftwaffe	farestage	porterage	eyebright		aerobatic	
					aerolitic	

```
celluloid  disseisin  fingertip  Icelandic  messianic  packtrain  prodromic
chainmail  dizygotic  floristic  ichthyoid  metabolic  palanquin  progestin
chancroid  doleritic  fluorosis  identikit  metalloid  pancratic  prognosis
Charolais  dolomitic  folkmusic  ideologic  metameric  panegyric  prolepsis
chatelain  driftsail  foodchain  idiomatic  meteoroid  panoramic  proleptic
checkrein  dualistic  forebrain  imbecilic  metheglin  paperclip  properdin
chemurgic  duralumin  formulaic  imbroglio  metonymic  paperthin  prophetic
cherrypie  dyscrasia  forsythia  impolitic  miasmatic  papeterie  propionic
chiefship  dyspepsia  francolin  indigotin  microchip  parabasis  proptosis
chieftain  dyspeptic  Franglais  inelastic  micropsia  parabolic  proscenia
chilblain  dysphagia  fumarolic  infusoria  millennia  paralalia  prostatic
chimaeric  dysphagic  Gallophil  inorganic  mistigris  paralexia  proteinic
chivalric  dysphonia  gastritis  interknit  monarchic  paralysis  prothesis
chloritic  dysphoria  gaucherie  intervein  monatomic  paralytic  prothetic
chlorosis  dysphoric  generalia  intrinsic  Mongoloid  paramedic  protozoic
chlorotic  dysplasia  genotypic  ischaemia  monobasic  parapodia  psalmodic
choleraic  dyspnoeic  geomantic  ischaemic  monogamic  parasitic  psalteria
choplogic  eccentric  geometric  ischiadic  monologic  parataxis  psoriasis
chromatic  echolalia  geometrid  ischiatic  monomania  paregoric  psoriatic
chromatin  eclampsia  geostatic  Islamitic  monomeric  parotitis  psychosis
chrysalid  eclamptic  geotropic  isobathic  monotonic  pasticcio  psychotic
chrysalis  ectogenic  geriatric  isoclinic  monotypic  patriotic  pterygoid
cinematic  egotistic  glossitis  isocyclic  moratoria  patristic  Ptolemaic
cineraria  eldership  gnathonic  isometric  morphemic  paulownia  punctilio
cirrhosis  ellipsoid  gneissoid  isoniazid  motherwit  pearlitic  puritanic
clerkship  embroglio  goliardic  isostatic  multifoil  pedagogic  pushchair
climactic  embryonic  gomphosis  isotropic  mustachio  pellagrin  pyramidic
colloquia  embryotic  gooseskin  Jacobinic  mutagenic  peneplain  pyridoxin
colorific  emplastic  granitoid  jacquerie  mycologic  perfervid  pyrogenic
compendia  encaustic  graphemic  Judaistic  mydriasis  peridotic  pyrolysis
condyloid  endogamic  graphitic  judgeship  mydriatic  perihelia  pyrolytic
consortia  endogenic  grimalkin  judgmatic  myrmecoid  pertussis  pyromania
constrain  endomixis  grosgrain  juvenilia  napthalic  pharaonic  pyroxylin
copacetic  energetic  guardrail  katabasis  naumachia  pharisaic  quadratic
coralloid  enigmatic  guardship  katabatic  necrophil  philippic  quadrifid
coreopsis  enteritis  guildship  katabolic  negrophil  phlebitis  queenship
corticoid  entertain  gymnastic  katharsis  neolithic  photophil  quitclaim
corydalis  enzymatic  haematoid  keratitis  neoteinia  photopsia  rafflesia
coseismic  epaenetic  halieutic  keratosis  neoteinic  phrenetic  rauwolfia
countship  ephemerid  halitosis  kibbutzim  nephritic  phthalein  realistic
courtship  ephemeris  hamamelis  kilderkin  nephritis  pianistic  reservoir
coverslip  epiclesis  Hanseatic  kinematic  nephrosis  pietistic  retinitis
cryogenic  epicyclic  harlequin  lairdship  neuralgia  pilgarlic  rhapsodic
cylindric  epidermic  haustoria  laminaria  neuralgic  pisolitic  rheumatic
cyprinoid  epidermis  hegemonic  leitmotif  neuroglia  pistachio  rhodopsin
cytolysis  epileptic  heliozoic  leitmotiv  nicotinic  pithecoid  rudbeckia
cytotoxic  epinastic  hepatitis  lethargic  nonpareil  planetoid  rulership
cytotoxin  epiphysis  herpetoid  leucaemia  nonprofit  planuloid  Russophil
dairymaid  epiphytic  heterosis  leukaemia  nostalgia  plasmatic  saccharin
daredevil  epistaxis  heuristic  leukaemic  nostalgic  plasmodia  safetypin
demagogic  epistemic  hexaploid  leviratic  notabilia  platinoid  saintship
demiurgic  epistolic  highchair  libecchio  nucleonic  plethoric  salicylic
dendritic  epithelia  hindbrain  lightship  nursemaid  pleuritic  salmonoid
dermatoid  epithesis  hobgoblin  limonitic  nutweevil  pneumatic  Samoyedic
diablerie  epithetic  Holarctic  literatim  nymphalid  pneumonia  sanatoria
diacritic  epizootic  homiletic  litterbin  nystagmic  pneumonic  sangfroid
diactinic  ergonomic  homogamic  logaoedic  obstetric  polybasic  Sanhedrim
diaeresis  ethylenic  homonymic  Lombardic  oecologic  polygamic  Sanhedrin
diagnosis  eunuchoid  homotaxis  longchain  oecumenic  polygenic  sanitaria
dialectic  euphorbia  homotonic  luciferin  oleoresin  polymeric  sapraemia
diametric  eutectoid  honoraria  lymphatic  oligaemia  polyploid  sapraemic
diaphysis  eutrophic  honorific  lyophilic  ommatidia  polysemic  Saracenic
diastasis  evangelic  horologic  lyophobic  omophagia  polysomic  sarcastic
diastatic  excentric  horsehair  macaronic  omophagic  polytypic  scarfskin
diastolic  executrix  horsetail  mailtrain  onanistic  porcelain  schematic
diathesis  exodermis  horsewhip  majorship  oncogenic  porphyria  sciaenoid
diathetic  exosmosis  hortensia  maladroit  oncologic  portfolio  scleritis
diatropic  exosmotic  housemaid  malvoisie  onionskin  pragmatic  sclerosis
dichromic  exostosis  hubristic  mannequin  onomastic  preadamic  sclerotic
didelphic  extrinsic  hydraemia  marestail  ontogenic  preexilic  scoliosis
digastric  eyestrain  hydraulic  Masoretic  ontologic  preordain  scoliotic
digitalin  fantastic  hydriodic  mayorship  oogenesis  pretermit  scombroid
digitalis  Fascistic  hydrofoil  mediatrix  oogenetic  primordia  scorbutic
dimorphic  faunistic  hyperopia  melanosis  orangetip  princekin  scorpioid
directrix  felicific  hyperopic  melanotic  orchestic  principia  seaurchin
discomfit  fibrinoid  hypomania  melatonin  orgiastic  priorship  selenitic
discredit  fideistic  hypomanic  melomania  orthoepic  prismatic  semeiotic
disentail  filmstrip  hypotaxis  menagerie  overtrain  proboscis  semifluid
disrepair  filtertip  hysteroid  Menshevik  ownership  proclitic  semirigid
```

```
semisolid  syphiloid  corncrake  allowably  breakable  corbeille  downfield
semitonic  systaltic  deathlike  allowedly  breathily  corbicula  dragonfly
Sephardic  taeniasis  dreamlike  alterable  bridewell  cordially  drinkable
Sephardim  tambourin  fairylike  amazingly  brittlely  cornfield  drunkenly
septemvir  tarpaulin  fiendlike  amendable  brotherly  cornstalk  dubiously
septennia  taxonomic  firedrake  amorously  brusquely  corpuscle  dubitable
serotonin  telegenic  fireworks  amphibole  brutishly  correctly  duteously
serranoid  testatrix  fruitcake  amusingly  bulbously  corruptly  dutifully
sestertia  thalassic  ghostlike  anciently  bullishly  costively  earnestly
shambolic  thaneship  giantlike  angularly  buoyantly  countable  easefully
sharkskin  theandric  golflinks  annularly  burningly  coverable  eightfold
sheepskin  theogonic  graywacke  antennule  butcherly  covetable  elegantly
shirttail  theologic  greywacke  anxiously  butterfly  crabbedly  elusively
sideritic  theomania  grubstake  aquarelle  caddisfly  creatable  embrangle
siderosis  theoretic  handbrake  aqueously  calcicole  crepuscle  embrittle
silicosis  Thomistic  handshake  archivolt  calendula  crocodile  emendable
silicotic  threnodic  handspike  arcuately  callously  crookedly  eminently
silverfir  thumbnail  hitchhike  arduously  camarilla  crossable  emotively
sinusitis  timelimit  ironworks  armadillo  campanile  crossbill  emulously
slaveship  tonguetie  kittiwake  arteriole  campanili  crosstalk  encephala
Slavophil  toponymic  lapstrake  artlessly  campanula  crucially  endlessly
slopbasin  tormentil  lardycake  asexually  cantabile  crushable  endurable
snakeskin  tortricid  lookalike  ashamedly  capitally  cubbyhole  endurably
solfeggio  touristic  milkshake  assayable  carambola  cubically  enjoyable
Solomonic  trachytic  moonquake  assumable  carbuncle  cunningly  enjoyably
sooterkin  tracksuit  motorbike  assumably  carefully  curiously  enterable
sophistic  transonic  plantlike  assuredly  carfuffle  currently  enviously
soporific  transship  poundcake  astraddle  carpingly  curricula  equitable
spaceship  trapezoid  purselike  auditable  casserole  currishly  equitably
spacesuit  trattoria  queenlike  austerely  catchable  cursively  erstwhile
sparkcoil  trattorie  ringshake  autocycle  catchpole  cursorily  eruditely
spasmodic  traumatic  ringsnake  available  catchpoll  cynically  escapable
spermatic  triatomic  roadworks  availably  centrally  damningly  espousals
spermatid  trichomic  rockbrake  aventaile  cerebella  dancehall  estimable
sphygmoid  trichroic  rocksnake  averagely  certainly  dashingly  eternally
spillikin  triclinia  saintlike  avertible  chamomile  dastardly  ethically
splenetic  triclinic  saltworks  avoidable  chantilly  deathroll  evasively
splenitis  trihybrid  scalelike  avoidably  chlorella  debatable  evidently
sporangia  trimetric  sheldrake  awardable  chockfull  decidable  evincible
sprigtail  troopship  shortcake  awesomely  chondrule  decidedly  evolvable
spritsail  tutorship  skeesicks  awkwardly  chronicle  decimally  exactable
stalactic  twicelaid  snakelike  bagatelle  cigarillo  deducible  excisable
statistic  typhlitis  snowflake  balefully  citizenly  defiantly  excitable
steamship  uncertain  soapworks  bamboozle  civically  definable  excitedly
steatitic  underlaid  sunstroke  banderole  claimable  definably  excusable
stigmatic  underlain  swordlike  banefully  clamantly  deludable  excusably
stockwhip  underpaid  sylphlike  banjulele  clamshell  denyingly  execrable
stomachic  underspin  undertake  barcarole  classable  deposable  execrably
storeship  unicuspid  wapentake  bargepole  clearcole  derivable  expansile
stormsail  urticaria  whipsnake  bashfully  cleavable  desirable  expressly
strategic  vaporific  wideawake  basically  clemently  desirably  exsertile
stromatic  varioloid  womanlike  bastardly  clientele  deviously  extensile
strumitis  verdigris  abdicable  beamingly  climbable  devisable  externals
strychnic  virtuosic  abidingly  beanstalk  clubbable  devotedly  extremely
stylistic  vitriolic  abradable  bedraggle  coalfield  dextrally  facsimile
subarctic  vomitoria  abusively  belatedly  coattails  dharmsala  factually
subatomic  wakerobin  abysmally  bemusedly  coaxially  difficile  fairytale
subsellia  wallfruit  accusable  bespangle  coaxingly  difficult  fandangle
sudatoria  Walpurgis  acetabula  bestially  coequally  diffusely  farandole
sudorific  washbasin  adamantly  biliously  coercible  digitally  fascicule
sulphonic  whipperin  adaptable  bimonthly  coercibly  dilatable  fasciculi
sulphuric  whirligig  adducible  birdtable  cogitable  dipcircle  fatefully
swordtail  whitebait  adjunctly  bizarrely  cognately  direfully  fatigable
sybaritic  whodunnit  adminicle  blackball  coltishly  dirigible  fatuously
syllepsis  wingchair  admirable  blameable  columella  dismantle  fawningly
sylleptic  wolframic  admirably  blameably  comically  dispeople  fearfully
symbiosis  zeugmatic  adoptable  blasthole  commingle  dissemble  federally
symbiotic  zoophobia  adoringly  blatantly  compactly  distantly  feelingly
symmetric  zoophytic  adversely  blazingly  complexly  diurnally  fertilely
symphonic  zygomatic  advisable  blessedly  comptroll  diversely  fervently
symphysis  zymogenic  advisably  blindfold  comradely  dividable  festively
syncretic  comitadji  advisedly  blotchily  concavely  divisible  filoselle
syneresis  artichoke  agreeable  boardwalk  concisely  doggishly  filtrable
synizesis  balalaika  agreeably  bombshell  condignly  dolefully  finically
synonymic  boondocks  aimlessly  bookishly  conically  doltishly  firedrill
synovitis  bridecake  alienable  bookshelf  connately  donnishly  fittingly
syntactic  buttinsky  allegedly  bookstall  constable  dorbeetle  flamingly
synthesis  canebrake  allocable  boorishly  contumely  doubtable  flammable
synthetic  childlike  allowable  bracteole  copiously  doughtily  flannelly
```

```
flaringly  hawksbill  inversely  meaningly  palatable  quarterly  scrutable
flashbulb  hawsehole  invisible  meanwhile  palatably  quintuple  seagirdle
flightily  headstall  invisibly  mediately  panatella  radialply  seanettle
floatable  healthily  ionisable  medicable  panhandle  radiantly  searingly
flowingly  heartfelt  irascible  medically  pantingly  radiately  seatangle
foolishly  hedgingly  irascibly  megacycle  parbuckle  radically  secularly
footfault  heedfully  irksomely  meltingly  parlously  raffishly  securable
footstalk  heinously  ironmould  memorable  partially  rakehelly  seemingly
footstall  helically  irrigable  memorably  pasodoble  rampantly  selfishly
foppishly  hellishly  irritable  mesophyll  passively  rantingly  semblable
forestall  helpfully  irritably  microfilm  pastorale  ranunculi  semblably
forgeable  hemicycle  jarringly  micropyle  patchouli  raspingly  seminally
forlornly  heritable  jealously  millivolt  patchouly  rationale  sensually
forwardly  hexastyle  jeeringly  mincingly  patiently  raucously  separable
frangible  hideously  jocularly  mindfully  peaceable  raunchily  separably
franticly  hierodule  joylessly  minefield  peaceably  razorbill  seriately
freestyle  hillbilly  kerfuffle  minimally  peccantly  reachable  seriously
freezable  hoggishly  kiddingly  minuscule  peevishly  rebukable  serrefile
fretfully  homuncule  kilocycle  miserable  pendently  reconcile  servilely
frontally  homunculi  knavishly  miserably  peninsula  rectangle  sevenfold
frowardly  hopefully  kneadable  mishandle  pensively  reducible  seventhly
fulgently  hostilely  knowingly  mitigable  pentangle  referable  severable
fullscale  household  lacerable  mitraille  perfectly  refusable  severally
fulsomely  hugeously  laggardly  mockingly  pericycle  refutable  sexlessly
furiously  hurriedly  lambently  moneybill  peristyle  regularly  shakeable
furtively  hurtfully  lampshell  mongrelly  permeable  reliantly  shallowly
gainfully  husbandly  languidly  monostyle  petiolule  removable  Shangrila
galingale  hydrocele  lastingly  monticule  pettishly  renewable  shapeable
gallantly  hyperbola  laterally  mordantly  philately  reparable  sheepfold
gallingly  hyperbole  laughable  motorable  Philomela  repayable  sheepwalk
gallinule  hypostyle  laughably  mouldable  photocell  reputable  sheerhulk
gasmantle  ignitable  lawlessly  mountable  piggishly  reputably  shemozzle
gaugeable  ignitible  leafmould  mousehole  pineapple  reputedly  shockable
generable  ignorable  leafstalk  mundanely  pinnately  resalable  shootable
generally  illegally  learnable  musically  piquantly  reshuffle  shortfall
genteelly  illegible  learnedly  musichall  piteously  resoluble  sickishly
genuinely  illegibly  leasehold  naturally  pitifully  restfully  sidetable
germanely  illicitly  leeringly  naughtily  pityingly  restively  similarly
getatable  imageable  leewardly  navigable  pivotable  resumable  sincerely
gibbously  immensely  leisurely  needfully  pivotally  reversely  sinlessly
gingerale  immorally  lengthily  nemophila  placeable  revisable  sinophile
girandole  immovable  leniently  nervously  plantable  revivable  sinuately
girlishly  immovably  lexically  neutrally  plausible  revocable  sinuously
glacially  immutable  liberally  niggardly  plausibly  ridgepole  siphuncle
glaringly  immutably  lifecycle  nightfall  playfully  ridgetile  skedaddle
glassgall  impiously  lifestyle  nocuously  pleadable  rightable  sketchily
gleefully  impliedly  lifetable  noisomely  plenarily  rigmarole  skilfully
glomerule  imputable  liltingly  nominable  plicately  ringingly  slavishly
glomeruli  inaudible  limitable  nominally  pointedly  riotously  slenderly
gloryhole  inaudibly  limitedly  nonviable  pointille  rocambole  sliderule
glowingly  incapable  linenfold  northerly  polevault  rockdrill  smilingly
goldfield  incapably  lingually  noxiously  pompously  roguishly  smokeball
gradually  incunable  lioncelle  numbskull  popularly  roseapple  snowfield
grantable  incurable  lispingly  numerable  porbeagle  roseately  sobbingly
graspable  incurably  lissomely  obliquely  pratingly  rosenoble  softshell
graticule  indelible  literally  obscenely  preachily  rotatable  soldierly
greenbelt  indelibly  litigable  obscurely  precisely  routinely  somewhile
grisaille  inducible  locatable  obversely  pregnable  rubicelle  songcycle
gristmill  ineffable  lodgepole  obviously  presently  ruffianly  songfully
grouchily  ineffably  logically  octastyle  primarily  ruinously  sorbapple
guacamole  inequable  longingly  octostyle  principle  ruthfully  sottishly
guardedly  inerrable  louringly  odorously  printable  sabadilla  soulfully
guerrilla  inexactly  loutishly  oenophile  privately  saliently  soundfilm
guildhall  infantile  loveapple  oenophily  profanely  sandtable  soundhole
gushingly  inferable  lovechild  oligopoly  profusely  sapiently  southerly
habitable  infertile  lumpishly  ominously  prolately  sapodilla  sparingly
habitably  infusible  lustfully  omissible  proveably  saturable  spatially
haggardly  inhumanly  lyrically  onerously  prudently  savourily  speakable
hairstyle  initially  magically  operosely  prudishly  scagliola  specially
halfshell  insectile  majuscule  opposable  pulsatile  scholarly  spectacle
halftitle  insipidly  malleable  optically  punchball  scintilla  speedball
halophile  insoluble  manhandle  opulently  pungently  scraggily  speedwell
haltingly  insolubly  maritally  organelle  purposely  scrappily  spendable
haplessly  instantly  martially  outwardly  purringly  screwball  spiracula
hardshell  insularly  massively  overspill  pursuable  screwbolt  splashily
harmfully  insurable  matricula  overwhelm  pushingly  screwpile  spoonbill
hatefully  intensely  mawkishly  packdrill  quadrille  scrimpily  spouthole
haughtily  interfile  maximally  painfully  quadruple  scruffily  sprightly
haustella  invalidly  maybeetle  painterly  quadruply  scrumhalf  springald
```

springily	touchable	viciously	exanthema	abstinent	barbitone	cisalpine
squalidly	touchhole	violently	forcepump	acceptant	battening	cleansing
squashily	townsfolk	virginals	haematoma	accompany	bedspring	cliffhang
squeakily	toxically	virtually	harmotome	accordant	befitting	clinquant
stackable	toxophily	viscously	honeycomb	according	befogging	cloisonne
stainable	trabecula	visitable	hydrosome	acetylene	begetting	cloudland
stairwell	traceable	waggishly	hypergamy	acidulent	beginning	coagulant
stampmill	traceably	wailingly	impostume	aconitine	bellyband	coastline
starapple	tractable	waistbelt	leptosome	adenosine	bengaline	Cockaigne
starchily	tractably	wakefully	leucotome	adjoining	benignant	cognisant
starshell	trainable	warblefly	leucotomy	adlibbing	benzidine	colophony
staunchly	treadmill	warningly	lightsome	admitting	benzoline	colouring
stepchild	treatable	waspishly	lithesome	adornment	berberine	colubrine
stiltedly	tricksily	watchable	lithotomy	adsorbent	besetment	columbine
stinkball	trifocals	waterfall	loathsome	advertent	besetting	combatant
stockpile	trivially	waterhole	lobectomy	aerobiont	besotting	competent
stoically	triweekly	waterlily	loxodrome	aeroplane	bevelling	complaint
stokehold	trunkcall	watermill	lunchtime	affecting	billabong	compliant
stokehole	tubercule	waywardly	majordomo	affirmant	binturong	component
stonecold	tubularly	wealthily	melodrama	Afrikaans	bivariant	concubine
stonewall	tunefully	weatherly	metronome	agapemone	blastment	condiment
stoolball	turgently	weighable	microsome	agistment	bluepoint	confidant
stormbelt	turnstile	weightily	microtome	agonising	blueprint	confident
strangely	turntable	Whitehall	microtomy	agreement	bluestone	confiding
streakily	twelfthly	wholesale	misbecome	aitchbone	boliviano	confluent
strongyle	twicetold	wieldable	monodrama	albescent	bombasine	congruent
studiedly	twistable	willingly	monorhyme	alignment	bombazine	connivent
stylishly	twitchily	winevault	monotreme	alinement	bondstone	consonant
suasively	typically	winningly	myriorama	allegiant	bonechina	contadina
subduable	umbellule	winsomely	myxoedema	allophone	bookstand	contadino
subduedly	uncannily	wishfully	nighttime	allotment	boomerang	continent
subfamily	uncivilly	wistfully	oriflamme	allotting	boomslang	cooperant
sublimely	uncleanly	witlessly	overtrump	almandine	borrowing	copestone
summarily	uncouthly	wittingly	pantomime	alternant	bowstring	coralline
superable	underfelt	wolfishly	papilloma	amassment	boyfriend	cormorant
supremely	undersell	womenfolk	peacetime	amazement	brambling	cornstone
surcingle	undersold	workmanly	penultima	amendment	brandling	corposant
suturally	unearthly	worktable	peristome	ampersand	breadline	corpulent
sweettalk	uneatable	worriedly	phantasma	amusement	breathing	cortisone
swimmable	unequally	xenophile	phytotomy	analysand	breeching	coruscant
swinishly	unfleshly	xerophile	placename	andantino	breveting	cosmogeny
tabletalk	unhappily	xerophily	polyonymy	androgyne	brilliant	cosmogony
tabularly	unifiable	xparticle	pranksome	androgyny	brimstone	cotangent
tactfully	uniformly	yawningly	proenzyme	anklebone	bristling	coumarone
tactually	unitively	zealously	programme	annectent	buckhound	covariant
tanpickle	unluckily	zestfully	protonema	annuitant	buffeting	crackling
tarantula	unnamable	aerodrome	quicklime	annulling	buhrstone	crapulent
tartishly	unsayable	aftertime	semanteme	annulment	burrstone	crashland
teachable	unshackle	archenemy	semiplume	anovulant	butadiene	crediting
teachably	unsightly	astrodome	sixteenmo	anticline	butterine	crepitant
teakettle	unsoundly	astronomy	smallarms	antiphony	buttygang	crinoline
tearfully	untenable	blackdamp	smalltime	apartment	Byzantine	crippling
teasingly	unusually	blackgame	smokebomb	appalling	caballine	croissant
tediously	unwomanly	blaspheme	spacetime	appealing	caballing	crosslink
tegularly	uprightly	blasphemy	stinkbomb	appellant	cacholong	crosswind
tellingly	uselessly	carcinoma	taxidermy	appendant	cacophony	culminant
temptable	utterable	chokedamp	teknonymy	applicant	canescent	cupelling
tenuously	vacuously	cockscomb	thingummy	apprehend	cantilena	curbstone
ternately	valiantly	colostomy	threesome	aquaplane	carnitine	curveting
textually	vallecula	condyloma	toothcomb	archfiend	carolling	cymophane
thermally	vaporable	cosmorama	toothsome	argentine	carpeting	dachshund
thinkable	varicella	currycomb	tradename	arrestant	casuarina	damascene
thirstily	variously	cyclorama	unwelcome	arresting	catamount	dayspring
thornbill	veeringly	cystotomy	vasectomy	asbestine	catarhine	debagging
threefold	vegetable	depthbomb	velodrome	ascendant	catchment	debarment
threshold	vegetably	diathermy	wearisome	ascendent	cavilling	debarring
thriftily	venerable	dichogamy	wholesome	ashlaring	celandine	debugging
throatily	venerably	dichotomy	worrisome	assailant	celebrant	declarant
throughly	ventrally	didrachma	abasement	assistant	centering	decrement
thumbhole	ventricle	dirigisme	abashment	assurgent	centreing	decumbent
tigerlily	verbosely	disentomb	abatement	atonement	chaingang	deerhound
timeously	verdantly	dithyramb	abhorrent	attendant	champagne	defendant
timetable	veritable	doorframe	abhorring	aubergine	chaperone	deferment
titularly	veritably	duodecimo	ablutions	awakening	charabanc	deferring
tolerable	vermicule	eightsome	aborigine	backslang	chatoyant	deficient
tolerably	versatile	emphysema	abounding	ballerina	cheekbone	defoliant
tonically	vestibule	empyreuma	abseiling	ballpoint	chickling	dehiscent
topically	vibracula	enthymeme	absorbent	bandoline	churching	demandant
totempole	vibratile	eurhythmy	absorbing	bandstand	cipollino	demanding

```
demitting  excurrent  greensand  inferring  madeleine  offspring  prolamine
demobbing  executant  gregarine  infilling  magdalene  Oligocene  prominent
demulcent  exilement  grenadine  inflowing  magicking  onsetting  promising
demurring  expectant  greyhound  informant  mailplane  opportune  proponent
deodorant  expecting  gritstone  ingrowing  malignant  oppugnant  propylene
dependant  expedient  grounding  inharmony  mandarine  optophone  protamine
dependent  expellent  gruelling  inpatient  mandoline  organzine  provident
desiccant  expelling  grumbling  inpouring  maneating  osteogeny  providing
designing  extendant  guardring  inquiline  marchpane  outgiving  provoking
detergent  extolling  guideline  insetting  margarine  overborne  pubescent
determent  extolment  guttering  insistent  marihuana  overlying  pulpstone
determine  exuberant  gyroplane  insolvent  marijuana  overprint  punchline
deterrent  fabricant  hailstone  insurgent  marketing  overspend  punishing
deterring  faggoting  halfbound  integrand  marlstone  overspent  puzzolana
detriment  fairyland  halfpenny  integrant  marshland  overwound  quibbling
devilling  fairyring  hallstand  intendant  masculine  packaging  quicksand
devilment  farseeing  halothane  interline  matrimony  Pakistani  quiescent
diachrony  fastening  hamstring  interlink  meandrine  palpitant  quinoline
different  feiseanna  hamstrung  interment  megaphone  panelling  rationing
diffident  feoffment  handstand  interring  menadione  panicking  ravelling
diphthong  fibroline  hankering  intervene  mendicant  paramount  ravelment
disarming  fingering  happening  interwind  mepacrine  parchment  ravishing
disorient  finicking  hardiment  interzone  merriment  parsimony  reasoning
disputant  firebrand  harmaline  intestine  mescaline  passerine  rebelling
dissident  fireirons  harrowing  intrigant  metalline  pathogeny  rebidding
dissonant  firestone  hatchling  inurement  metalling  patrimony  rebutting
distraint  firmament  hatchment  invariant  methadone  pedalling  recapping
divergent  firsthand  havocking  ironbound  methylene  penduline  recipient
diverting  firstling  headphone  ironstone  mezzanine  peneplane  reckoning
dixieland  fivepenny  headstone  irradiant  mezzotint  penetrant  recombine
donothing  flagstone  heartland  isochrone  microtone  penfriend  recommend
dopefiend  flatulent  hellhound  isooctane  milestone  percaline  reconvene
dowelling  flayflint  hidebound  itinerant  millstone  peregrine  recording
draghound  fledgling  hirundine  jackplane  mimicking  perilling  recumbent
dragomans  fleshment  histamine  japanning  miscegene  perishing  recurrent
dreamland  flouncing  histidine  jessamine  miscegine  permanent  recurring
dripstone  flowering  histogeny  Johannine  miscreant  pertinent  reductant
dropscene  flowstone  hoarhound  judgement  misgiving  pestilent  redundant
dropscone  fluctuant  hoarstone  junketing  modelling  pethidine  reefpoint
dumbfound  focussing  hocussing  keelivine  monocline  phagedena  reentrant
earthling  following  holystone  kerbstone  monoplane  phenomena  reexamine
eastbound  footpound  homebound  kurrajong  monthling  pheromone  referring
easygoing  footprint  homophone  labelling  moonblind  philogyny  refitment
ebullient  forceland  homophony  lacertine  moonshine  phosphene  refitting
efficient  forefront  honkytonk  landagent  moonstone  phosphine  refulgent
effulgent  foregoing  hoofprint  latescent  multilane  photogene  regardant
eglantine  forgiving  horehound  lathering  munitions  phylogeny  rejoicing
ejectment  foundling  hornstone  latticing  muscadine  phytogeny  reluctant
elopement  fourpenny  horsemint  launching  muscarine  picketing  remitment
embayment  freestone  horsepond  lawgiving  musteline  piggybank  remittent
embedding  frontline  humankind  lazzarone  naphthene  pipestone  remitting
embedment  fulgurant  humectant  lazzaroni  narcotine  placement  remontant
embussing  fulminant  hurricane  leaselend  nectarine  plainsong  renascent
emollient  fundament  hydrazine  leavening  negligent  plaything  repayment
emolument  gabardine  ignescent  legerline  negotiant  Pleiocene  repellant
enactment  gaberdine  illboding  lettering  nemertine  plumbline  repellent
endearing  galantine  immigrant  Levantine  nepheline  poinciana  repelling
endocrine  gallivant  impatiens  levelling  newsagent  pollutant  repentant
endowment  galloping  impatient  libellant  newshound  polyphone  repotting
engarland  gallstone  impeccant  libelling  newsprint  polyphony  reprehend
engraving  gammoning  impelling  libertine  newsstand  polythene  represent
enjoyment  gangplank  impendent  lightning  nicotiana  porcupine  reprimand
enrolling  gardening  impending  limestone  nightline  portolano  repugnant
enrolment  gathering  implement  limousine  nightlong  postulant  rerunning
ephedrine  gavelkind  important  lineament  nigricant  potholing  reserpine
equalling  gazehound  importune  lingering  nigrosine  pourpoint  resetting
equipment  geobotany  imprudent  lithopone  ninepenny  pozzolana  resilient
equipping  gladstone  incessant  loadstone  nitratine  precedent  resistant
estopping  glycerine  incipient  lodestone  nonjuring  preceding  resitting
estuarine  godparent  inclement  lodgement  northland  predicant  resolvent
exactment  goffering  increment  lophodont  nurseling  predikant  resorbent
examinant  goldsinny  incumbent  lotusland  nutriment  prepotent  restraint
exceeding  Gradgrind  incurrent  lubricant  obscurant  prescient  resultant
excellent  grandaunt  incurring  lumbering  obsequent  preshrink  resurgent
excelling  grapevine  indignant  luxuriant  observant  preshrunk  retardant
exceptant  grappling  indulgent  lyamhound  occludent  president  revelling
excepting  grassland  inebriant  lymehound  occurrent  pressgang  revetment
excipient  gravamina  inelegant  macedoine  occurring  prevalent  revetting
excrement  greataunt  infantine  maddening  officiant  procreant  revolting
```

rewarding	splendent	tombstone	wasteland	annotator	collision	diachylom
rhodamine	splitting	torchsong	waterline	anthelion	collodion	dictation
righthand	spodumene	totalling	wavefront	anthemion	collusion	diffusion
rivalling	sporogeny	touchline	wayfaring	anticodon	coltsfoot	digestion
rivelling	sprigging	towelling	weighting	apparitor	commandos	dimension
riverbank	springing	trainband	welcoming	apportion	commotion	direction
rockbound	squatting	transcend	wellbeing	arrowroot	communion	discommon
rockplant	squibbing	transenna	wellfound	arrowwood	compactor	dissector
rousement	squidding	transient	westbound	arthropod	companion	diversion
rufescent	stagehand	treatment	westering	ascension	comprador	divulsion
russeting	staghound	tremolant	whalebone	aspersion	concision	dodecagon
sacrament	starstone	tremulant	wheedling	aspirator	concoctor	dominator
safranine	startling	trenchant	whetstone	assertion	condition	dormition
sailoring	statement	trepidant	whinstone	asyndeton	conductor	doubleton
sailplane	stillhunt	trivalent	whipround	attention	confessor	Doukhobor
saintling	stimulant	troutling	whirlwind	attractor	confirmor	downthrow
salangane	stippling	truculent	whistling	attrition	confiteor	driftwood
sandblind	stormcone	truepenny	whitening	augmentor	confusion	drummajor
sandstone	storyline	tumescent	whitewing	automaton	connation	eavesdrop
santolina	straphang	turbulent	whizzbang	autopilot	connector	education
saturnine	strapping	Turcomans	windbound	avocation	connexion	effluxion
saxophone	streaking	Turkomans	winestone	badminton	conqueror	egression
scantling	strewment	turnround	witchhunt	bandicoot	consignor	eirenicon
scarfring	stringent	turnstone	withering	bandwagon	consultor	elbowroom
schilling	stripling	twentyone	withstand	barleymow	contactor	elevation
schooling	stripping	twinkling	woebegone	barracoon	contagion	elocution
scorching	stropping	unbending	wolfhound	battalion	contusion	emanation
scramming	strouding	unceasing	wolfsbane	beadledom	convector	embraceor
scrapping	strumming	underdone	wolverene	bedfellow	copsewood	emendator
screening	strutting	undergone	wolverine	bellyflop	cornerboy	emulation
screwpine	subalpine	underhand	womankind	birdsfoot	corrasion	encrimson
scrubbing	subjacent	underhung	womenkind	bisection	corrector	ephemeron
seafaring	submarine	underline	worldling	Blackfoot	corrosion	epilation
searching	subtenant	underling	worriment	bloodroot	cotillion	erudition
seasoning	succulent	undermine	wrestling	bloodshot	cotyledon	escalator
seastrand	suffering	undersong	wristband	boardfoot	courtroom	escheator
secernent	sugarcane	undertint	xylophone	boardroom	cremation	estimator
seedplant	superfine	undertone	yearround	bolection	crenation	evocation
senescent	supervene	underwent	yodelling	bombardon	criterion	evolution
sentiment	suppliant	underwing	yohimbine	bombproof	CroMagnon	excavator
shambling	supposing	unfailing	youngling	bowwindow	crowsfoot	excelsior
shaveling	surfacing	unfeeling	zibelline	brakeshoe	cunctator	exception
shearling	surveying	unfitting	zootechny	briarroot	cyclotron	excerptor
sheathing	susurrant	ungallant	abdicator	briarwood	damnation	exclusion
sheetbend	swaddling	unheading	abduction	brierroot	dandelion	excretion
shoeshine	sweatband	unheeding	abjection	brierwood	dayschool	excursion
shopfront	swingeing	univalent	abnegator	broadloom	deathblow	execution
shoreline	swordcane	unknowing	abolition	brushwood	decathlon	exemption
shorthand	sycophant	unmeaning	abrogator	bumbledon	deception	exhibitor
shredding	synchrony	unpegging	abruption	cacodemon	decillion	expansion
shrugging	tableland	unsmiling	accession	campstool	decimator	expiation
sibylline	tailoring	unsparing	accordion	capacitor	decoction	explosion
sickening	talismans	unweeting	accretion	caparison	decontrol	expositor
sideburns	tangerine	unwilling	acetylcoA	carnation	decorator	expulsion
signorina	tarragona	unwinking	actinozoa	caseation	dedicator	exsertion
silkgland	taxpaying	unwitting	activator	cassation	deduction	extension
siltstone	telephone	unzipping	actuation	causation	defection	extortion
singalong	telephony	uplifting	addiction	cedarwood	deflation	extractor
skijoring	terebrant	upsetting	addressor	centurion	deflector	extrusion
skinflint	termagant	vacillant	adduction	cessation	deflexion	exudation
skydiving	tervalent	valentine	ademption	chaetopod	dejection	eyeshadow
slabstone	testament	vapouring	admission	chameleon	demission	fairyhood
slushfund	testimony	veinstone	admonitor	chassepot	dentation	faldstool
smuggling	thatching	veneering	adoration	chelation	dentition	falsehood
snowblind	theophany	veratrine	adulation	childhood	depiction	fandangos
snowblink	thighbone	vetchling	adulthood	classroom	depletion	fieldbook
snowbound	thinktank	vicereine	advection	clavation	depositor	fieldboot
snowplant	thirdhand	victorine	advocator	cloakroom	depressor	filiation
soapstone	thrashing	viewpoint	affection	coadjutor	depurator	fireproof
soidisant	thrilling	virescent	afflation	coalition	desertion	firstfoot
solferino	throbbing	vitelline	afterglow	cockahoop	desolator	flamingos
something	thrumming	viverrine	afternoon	cocksfoot	detection	flotation
somnolent	thylacine	volauvent	aggressor	coemption	detention	flowerpot
sopranino	thyroxine	vulturine	agitation	coffeepot	detersion	foliation
southland	tiedyeing	waistband	alienator	cognation	detonator	foolproof
spaceband	tilestone	waistline	alligator	cognition	detractor	footstool
spearmint	timbering	walloping	amputator	colcannon	detrition	formation
spellbind	tittuping	wandering	angleiron	collation	detrusion	foulbrood
spindling	toadstone	washstand	animation	collector	deviation	Freemason

frigatoon	inglenook	nictation	printshop	savagedom	suspensor	autotroph
fumigator	inhalator	nitration	privation	scarecrow	suspicion	azeotrope
furcation	inheritor	nominator	probation	schoolboy	sweatshop	barograph
gammadion	inhibitor	nonillion	processor	scorebook	sweetshop	bombhappy
gastropod	initiator	nonperson	professor	scrapbook	swordknot	broomrape
gemmation	injection	numerator	profusion	scrapiron	tabulator	cassaripe
generator	innovator	nutrition	projector	scrutator	talkathon	cerograph
gerfalcon	innuendos	objection	prolation	scuncheon	tallyshop	chemitype
germproof	insertion	obsession	prolusion	scutcheon	tanliquor	collotype
gestation	inspector	obtention	promotion	seaanchor	televisor	conscript
gladiator	insulator	obtrusion	promptbox	secession	tentation	cryoscope
glossator	intension	obturator	pronation	seclusion	testation	cryoscopy
glyptodon	intention	obversion	prosector	secretion	therefrom	drainpipe
gogglebox	intercrop	obviation	protector	seduction	thereupon	ectomorph
goldenrod	interflow	occlusion	protestor	selection	thermidor	eidograph
goosefoot	intorsion	octillion	protozoon	semicolon	thighboot	endolymph
gradation	intrusion	oddfellow	provision	sensation	thralldom	endomorph
graduator	intuition	offseason	psalmbook	sentrybox	thyratron	endoscope
grapeshot	inunction	olecranon	pseudopod	separator	thyristor	endoscopy
greenroom	invention	olfaction	pulsation	septation	tigerwood	ergograph
greenwood	inversion	operation	puppyhood	serration	tinderbox	ferrotype
grillroom	irrigator	opodeldoc	pureblood	sharecrop	titration	grandpapa
groundhog	irruption	oppressor	purgation	sharpshod	toadstool	guiderope
guarantor	isolation	orderbook	pussyfoot	sheephook	tormentor	gyroscope
guardbook	iteration	organstop	pyramidon	sheikhdom	touchwood	hawsepipe
guardroom	jactation	Orpington	Quakerdom	shelfroom	tournedos	heliotype
guestroom	junkerdom	orrisroot	queenhood	shopfloor	tradition	hemitrope
guidebook	kaiserdom	overproof	quotation	shortstop	trilithon	hodograph
guillemot	lactation	overshoot	radiation	shotproof	trisagion	holograph
guncotton	lallation	overthrow	rainproof	signalbox	trisector	homograph
gustation	lancewood	ovulation	rareeshow	siltation	truncheon	horoscope
guttation	laudation	oxidation	rascaldom	simpleton	tuliproot	horoscopy
gyrfalcon	letterbox	palmation	rebellion	simulator	tulipwood	ideograph
habergeon	levitator	palpation	recension	singleton	turboprop	idiograph
halfblood	liberator	pantaloon	reception	sinuation	ululation	incorrupt
hammertoe	libration	parathion	recession	situation	undecagon	intercept
hangerson	librettos	parhelion	reclusion	slingshot	underfoot	interlope
hardihood	lifeblood	parleyvoo	recursion	smackeroo	underplot	interrupt
haresfoot	lightfoot	partition	redaction	snakeroot	undershot	jacksnipe
heartwood	lightwood	peachblow	redevelop	snakewood	undertook	karyotype
heptaglot	lineation	peculator	reduction	solicitor	underwood	kymograph
hesitator	liquation	pendragon	refashion	solvation	usucapion	lagniappe
heterodox	literator	pepperbox	refection	sortition	vallation	lagomorph
Hollywood	locomotor	pepperpot	reflation	soupspoon	valuation	landscape
honeymoon	lustihood	percheron	reflector	spadefoot	variation	logogriph
horseshoe	macerator	perdition	reflexion	spectator	vasomotor	mesomorph
hortation	maelstrom	perfector	refractor	splayfoot	vendition	monograph
Hottentot	magnetron	perfusion	regulator	spoliator	venerator	moonscape
houseroom	malathion	persimmon	rejection	springbok	vermilion	nomograph
hydration	martyrdom	pervasion	remission	squiredom	vernation	oleograph
hydrozoon	masterdom	phonation	rendition	stableboy	vibration	overleapt
ichneumon	matchwood	phyllopod	renovator	stackroom	violation	overslept
iguanodon	medallion	phytotron	repletion	stagedoor	virtuosos	paragraph
imitation	mediation	pillarbox	repressor	stairfoot	vitiation	paramorph
immersion	meditator	placation	repulsion	stanchion	wagonroof	paranymph
immolator	melocoton	planation	resection	statehood	warrantor	perilymph
impaction	mentation	plication	resonator	stateroom	watercool	perimorph
impassion	migration	ploughboy	retention	stilettos	wherefrom	periscope
imperator	misemploy	pollution	retortion	stillroom	whereupon	phalarope
impletion	misfeasor	possessor	retractor	stinkwood	whirlpool	phenotype
implosion	misreckon	posterior	revelator	stockbook	whitewood	photocopy
impulsion	mistletoe	postilion	reversion	stockroom	widowhood	phototype
inanition	mitigator	pouncebox	revulsion	stonecrop	windowbox	pinstripe
incaution	moderator	precentor	Rhineodon	storeroom	windproof	pitchpipe
inception	modillion	preceptor	roughshod	storybook	withstood	polygraph
inclusion	modulator	precision	ruination	striation	womanhood	polymorph
incubator	monkshood	precursor	ruminator	strongbox	wristdrop	preoccupy
incursion	monoceros	predation	rustproof	stylebook	wristshot	presbyope
indagator	monsignor	predictor	saddlebow	subdeacon	Yankeedom	prescript
indention	mortgagor	preemptor	sainthood	subeditor	yellowdog	prototype
indicator	mosquitos	prefixion	saltation	sublation	zebrawood	pyroscope
indiction	mothproof	prelector	saltspoon	subregion	aerograph	sciagraph
induction	motivator	prelusion	salvation	succentor	allograph	sciascopy
infection	muskmelon	premotion	sapanwood	successor	allomorph	serigraph
inflation	mutilator	prenotion	sargassos	suffusion	allotrope	shipshape
inflexion	narration	preschool	Sarmation	sulcation	allotropy	sideswipe
inflictor	navigator	pressroom	satiation	summation	amidships	skiagraph
infractor	nervation	prevision	satinwood	supercool	archetype	skiascopy
ingestion	neuration	princedom	saturator	supinator	autograph	slaphappy

snowscape	bloodworm	crematory	exosphere	hortatory	millepore	pokerwork
standpipe	bloodwort	crenature	expiatory	housecarl	millinery	politburo
steampipe	bluebeard	crossfire	expletory	housework	miniature	polyandry
stenotype	blueberry	crossword	extempore	huckstery	miniskirt	polyhedra
stenotype	bodyguard	crowberry	extravert	hunkydory	misgovern	polyzoary
stovepipe	bolometry	cruciform	extrovert	husbandry	misinform	postentry
subscript	bookstore	cuckoldry	faithcure	imaginary	misreport	potpourri
telegraph	boulevard	cuneiform	falciform	immixture	momentary	pourboire
telescope	bowerbird	curvature	fallalery	imposture	monastery	precatory
telescopy	brachyura	curviform	fancywork	impresari	moneywort	predatory
tightrope	brassiere	customary	fantastry	impulsory	monochord	prefatory
touchtype	brickwork	cuttysark	feudatory	incensory	monolatry	prefigure
townscape	brickyard	cymbiform	fibriform	inclosure	mouthpart	prelature
transumpt	brigandry	cystocarp	fiduciary	indenture	multiform	prelusory
underripe	broomcorn	damnatory	fieldfare	infirmary	multipara	premature
videotape	brushfire	dartboard	fieldwork	insectary	narratory	prerecord
wastepipe	brushwork	dashboard	fioritura	insincere	naseberry	pressmark
waterpipe	buckboard	davenport	fioriture	interfere	navelwort	presswork
windswept	buckthorn	debenture	firealarm	interlard	necessary	primipara
woodnymph	budgetary	decalitre	fireguard	introvert	nervature	probatory
Xanthippe	caballero	decametre	firstborn	inventory	nevermore	procedure
xeromorph	cairngorm	decastere	floodmark	involucre	nightbird	prolusory
xylograph	calenture	decennary	floristry	itinerary	nightmare	pronghorn
zincotype	callipers	decilitre	flowchart	janissary	nightwork	provisory
aboutturn	Camembert	decimetre	footboard	jewellery	nobiliary	provostry
accessary	cannelure	decistere	forecourt	judiciary	northward	pulmonary
accessory	capillary	decretory	foreshore	Juneberry	notochord	pulpboard
aciniform	Capricorn	deerberry	formicary	kickstart	nullipara	pulsatory
adipocere	cardboard	defeature	formulary	kilolitre	nullipore	punchcard
admeasure	cardsharp	delftware	fourscore	kilometre	octachord	pupillary
admixture	carnivore	dentiform	framework	krummhorn	octahedra	purgatory
adulatory	carpentry	dentistry	freeboard	Langobard	offcentre	pyrolatry
adventure	cartulary	departure	freezedry	laudatory	offertory	pyrometry
adversary	Cassandra	depasture	friarbird	lavaliere	olfactory	quillwort
aerometry	cassimere	desultory	frontward	leftovers	openheart	rainstorm
affixture	cassowary	dickybird	frostwork	legendary	optometry	rapidfire
aftercare	casuistry	dignitary	fungiform	legionary	orchestra	raspatory
afterword	catchword	dimissory	furniture	lentiform	orderform	raspberry
airyfairy	ceasefire	dinothere	gallantry	libratory	osteoderm	rearguard
alpenhorn	centenary	directory	gangboard	licensure	overboard	recapture
ambulacra	chandlery	disaccord	garniture	liegelord	overexert	reconfirm
amphigory	charivari	disaffirm	geosphere	lifeguard	overheard	reconvert
ancientry	chelicera	discovert	gestatory	ligniform	overskirt	refectory
ancillary	chemistry	discovery	ghostword	lionheart	overweary	reliquary
angleworm	chevelure	disembark	gimmickry	liverwort	ovulatory	remeasure
anomalure	chicanery	disfigure	glassware	loanshark	pachyderm	rencontre
antennary	chinaware	disposure	glasswork	longicorn	pageantry	repertory
antiquary	chipboard	disregard	glasswort	Longobard	paintwork	residuary
arbitrary	chisquare	dormitory	glengarry	longshore	palaestra	restiform
armillary	circuitry	dosimetry	gonophore	lousewort	palmistry	retrovert
arrowworm	citizenry	drawnwork	goosegirl	lovestory	papergirl	rhizocarp
artillery	clapboard	dromedary	gooseherd	machinery	paperwork	riflebird
ascospore	claviform	drugstore	gossamery	madrepore	papillary	rightward
asymmetry	clepsydra	duckboard	gradatory	magistery	parcenary	Roquefort
auxiliary	clipboard	dulcamara	grandsire	malanders	parquetry	roundworm
Aylesbury	clockwork	duodenary	graveyard	mamillary	patchwork	sacciform
Babbittry	coachwork	dysentery	greenhorn	mammiform	pearlwort	safeguard
bacillary	coastward	earthborn	greybeard	mandatary	peasantry	salesgirl
backboard	cocoonery	earthward	grillwork	mandatory	pecuniary	saltatory
backsword	coenosarc	earthwork	guesswork	manoeuvre	pellitory	saltpetre
baltimore	coldshort	earthworm	gustatory	mansionry	pennywort	sanctuary
bandolero	columbary	ecosphere	gynophore	manticore	perfumery	sandstorm
baneberry	comfiture	ecritoire	hackamore	maquisard	periphery	sarcocarp
baptistry	Cominform	electuary	hackberry	marquetry	perisperm	satinbird
barnstorm	Comintern	elsewhere	hailstorm	marshwort	persevere	scalefern
barometry	commodore	embracery	hairshirt	mattamore	phonatory	scapulary
battlecry	communard	embrasure	handiwork	maxillary	piecework	scorecard
bearberry	composure	emunctory	handywork	mediatory	piscatory	scrapyard
beechfern	comradery	enclosure	haphazard	medullary	pisciform	screwworm
bejabbers	concentre	endosperm	hardboard	megaspore	pitchdark	scripture
belvedere	configure	endospore	hartshorn	melaphyre	pitchfork	sculpture
billboard	connature	enrapture	headboard	mercenary	pituitary	scutiform
biosphere	cordiform	epicentre	headscarf	mesentery	placatory	seasquirt
birchbark	corollary	eruciform	heartburn	messieurs	placecard	secateurs
birthmark	courtcard	evocatory	heartsore	metalwork	planetary	secondary
birthwort	courtyard	exclosure	heathenry	midwifery	platemark	secretary
blackbird	coverture	excretory	hellebore	migratory	plicature	sedentary
blaeberry	coxcombry	executory	herbivore	millboard	plusfours	seedpearl
bleachery	cranberry	exemplary	hexachord	millenary	pokeberry	

```
seigneury sweetcorn aftermost blackfish Catharist Darwinist endoplasm
seigniory swineherd albatross blacklist cattiness dauntless entoblast
selfaware syllabary alchemise blackness causeless deaconess epicurism
selfglory tablature alchemist blackwash cauterise deathless epilogist
semaphore tableware alertness blameless cavendish deathmask epipolism
septenary tailboard aliveness blandness ceaseless deckhouse epitomise
sepulchre tarantara alloplasm blankness cellulose decompose epitomist
sepulture telemetry almshouse bleakness Celticism decongest equipoise
sequestra temporary aloneness blindness chainless defeatism erectness
serpentry termitary aloofness bloodless chanteuse defeatist eremitism
setsquare terramara aluminise bloodlust chantress demitasse eroticism
shadberry terramare amoralism bluegrass chariness denseness errorless
shelfmark territory amorphism bluffness charmeuse deodorise erythrism
shellbark tessitura ampleness bluntness charmless deoxidise esemplasy
shellfire therefore anabolism blushless cheapness depthless esoterism
shellwork thumbmark analogise boathouse checklist despotism establish
shinguard tightwire analogist bonniness cheerless devilfish Eucharist
shipboard toothwort anarchism booklouse childless dextrorse eunuchism
shoreward touchmark anarchist boskiness chillness diabolise euphemise
shorthorn tracheary anatomise bossiness chophouse diabolism euphemism
shortterm trademark anatomist boundless cicatrise diabolist euphonise
shrubbery transform anchoress braincase Cingalese dialogise eventless
sideboard transpire anchylose brainless classless dialogism exactness
sigillary transport angelfish brainwash classlist dialogist exegetist
signatory treachery anglicise brakeless cleanness dichroism exoticism
signature tributary anglicism brashness clearness dicrotism expertise
signboard trinketry Anglicist bratwurst clockwise dieselise extremism
simulacra triquetra angriness breakfast closeness dinginess extremist
simulacre triumviri animalise briefcase cloudless dirtiness Fabianism
snakebird troutfarm animalism briefless clubhouse discourse factorise
snowberry trysquare animalist briefness coalmouse disforest faddiness
snowguard twiceborn animatism brightish coastwise dishonest faintness
snowstorm umberbird anschluss briskness Cobdenism disinfest faithless
soapberry unconcern antitrust Briticise cocainise displease Falangism
solfatara undergird apartness Briticism cocainism dispraise Falangist
solitaire underpart apishness broadcast cockhorse disrelish falseness
somewhere unsavoury apologise broadness cockiness dizziness fantasise
sophistry upcountry apologist broadwise coheiress dogmatise fantasist
sophomore vainglory Appaloosa brownness coiffeuse dogmatism farmhouse
southward vermiform arabicise brutalise colemouse dogmatist fattiness
spaceport versiform arbitress brutalism collagist dogoodism faultless
spadework vestiture archivist buckshish colourist dosshouse fenceless
spearwort vexillary aromatise bulginess columnist dottiness Fenianism
spikenard vibraharp askewness bulkiness communise doubtless fertilise
spirogyra vibratory atonalism bumpiness communism dowdiness fetichism
splintery villagery autarkist bundobust communist dowerless fetichist
spluttery villiform authoress bunkhouse concourse dragoness fetidness
sporocarp visionary authorise burliness cookhouse dragonish fetishism
stackyard vitellary autocross bushiness cornbrash dramatise fetishist
starboard vitriform awareness buxomness cornemuse dramatist feudalise
statutory voluntary awfulness cabbalism cornetist drayhorse feudalism
steelwork vulnerary babirussa cabbalist corymbose dreamless feudalist
steelyard wallboard baboonish caciquism countless drollness fibreless
steenkirk washboard backcross Caesarism crampfish dryasdust fieriness
sternward watchfire bacterise Caesarist crankcase dumpiness filminess
stevedore watchword bagginess cageyness crassness duskiness fireblast
stickwork watercart bakehouse calaboose craziness dustiness firecrest
stillborn watermark baksheesh calabrese creatress eagerness firehouse
stinkhorn waterworn balkanise Calvinism crestless earliness fishiness
stitchery wheelwork balladist Calvinist cretinism ecdysiast fixedness
stockyard wherefore balminess camorrist crispness ecologist flakiness
stoneware widowbird barbarise canetrash criticise economise flameless
stonework wineberry barbarism canniness criticism economist fleckless
stonewort worrywart bathhouse Cantonese crossfish ecossaise fleetness
stormbird woundwort battiness capsulise crossness ecstasise fleshless
strapwork Yorkshire bawdiness carbonise crosswise ectoblast flophouse
strapwort zamindary beanfeast carburise crownless ectoplasm flushness
strawworm zemindary beardless careerism crowsnest ecumenism fogginess
striature zygospore beechmast careerist crudeness edelweiss footloose
stricture absurdism beefiness carthorse cruellest eightyish forceless
strongarm absurdist bellglass Castroism curialism electress foreclose
structure academism bellicose cataclasm curliness embarrass formalise
styliform actualise bergamask cataclysm curstness embellish formalism
subaltern adeptness biblicism catalepsy customise empathise formalist
subgenera adultness biblicist cataplasm cymbalist emphasise formulise
sublunary Adventism bicyclist catechise cytoplasm emptiness fossilise
sumptuary Adventist biologist catechist daltonism encomiast foundress
surfboard advertise birdsnest catechist damnedest encompass fourflush
swearword aerialist bitterish Catharism Darwinism endoblast frailness
```

franchise	handglass	jesuitise	marchpast	mutualism	patroness	pulverise
frankness	handiness	jesuitism	martyrise	mutualist	patronise	pursiness
freehouse	handpress	jointress	masochism	muzziness	pauperise	pushiness
freshness	happiness	josshouse	masochist	myologist	pauperism	Quakeress
frontless	hardiness	juiceless	massagist	mysticism	Pekingese	Quakerish
frontwise	harmonise	juiciness	massiness	mythicise	pelletise	Quakerism
fruitless	harmonist	jumpiness	matchless	mythicism	penniless	quakiness
fruticose	harshness	junkerism	mateyness	mythicist	Pentecost	quartzose
fulldress	hastiness	juxtapose	matronise	nailbrush	penthouse	queenless
funkiness	headdress	kaiserism	mealiness	nakedness	peptonise	queenpost
funniness	headfirst	kaolinise	meatiness	narcotise	periclase	queerness
fusionist	headiness	killifish	mechanise	narcotism	periplast	quickness
fussiness	heartless	kinkiness	mechanism	nastiness	perkiness	quietness
fustiness	heaviness	kittenish	mechanist	natheless	pessimism	quixotism
fuzziness	heftiness	knotgrass	medallist	nattiness	pessimist	rabbinism
galactose	hellenise	labialise	mediatise	neathouse	pesthouse	rabbinist
gallicise	Hellenism	labialism	meliorism	neckverse	petaurist	rabidness
gallicism	Hellenist	lacrimose	meliorist	necrotise	pettiness	racehorse
galliwasp	herbalist	lacrymose	memoirist	neediness	phonetise	racialism
galvanise	herborise	laevulose	Mendelism	Negroness	phonetism	racialist
galvanism	hetaerism	lamellose	menopause	neologise	phonetist	radiocast
galvanist	hetairism	landdross	mentalism	neologism	phoniness	raffinose
ganderism	highclass	landdrost	mentalist	neologist	physicist	raininess
gatecrash	hirsutism	lankiness	mercerise	neoterise	picturise	randiness
gatehouse	Hitlerism	larcenist	merciless	neoterist	pilotfish	randomise
gaudiness	hoarfrost	largeness	merriness	nephalism	pinkiness	ranginess
gauntness	hoariness	laundress	mesmerise	nephalist	pithiness	rapidness
gauziness	holocaust	leakiness	mesmerism	nerveless	placeless	rascalism
gawkiness	homoplasy	leastwise	mesmerist	nerviness	plainness	razorfish
genialise	horniness	legginess	mesoblast	newsflash	platinise	readdress
geodesist	horseless	lendlease	messiness	newsiness	Platonise	readiness
geologise	horsiness	levelness	metallise	nickelise	Platonism	rearhorse
geologist	hourglass	libellist	metaphase	Nipponese	Platonist	rearmouse
germanise	houseless	lickerish	metaplasm	nobleness	playhouse	rebaptise
Germanish	hoydenish	lightless	meteorist	noiseless	plumpness	recognise
Germanism	huffiness	lightness	methodise	noisiness	plumulose	recompose
Germanist	humanness	limitless	Methodism	normalise	pluralise	recordist
germplasm	huskiness	linearise	Methodist	Normanise	pluralism	redbreast
gibberish	hybridise	liquidise	metricise	Normanism	pluralist	reediness
giddiness	hybridism	liquorish	metricist	northeast	plushness	reformism
gigantism	hydrolyse	Listerism	microcosm	northmost	Plutonism	reformist
Girondist	hygienist	litheness	micromesh	northwest	Plutonist	refurbish
glamorise	hylozoism	liturgist	milkiness	notedness	podginess	refurnish
globefish	hypnotise	lividness	mirkiness	notionist	podzolise	reimburse
glueyness	hypnotism	lobscouse	mirthless	nuttiness	poeticise	religiose
gneissose	hypnotist	loftiness	misadvise	oasthouse	poeticism	replenish
godliness	hypoblast	Londonise	misoneism	obeseness	pointless	repossess
goldcrest	hypocaust	Londonism	misoneist	occultism	politesse	reprocess
gongorism	hypocrisy	longhouse	mistiness	occultist	polonaise	republish
gorgonise	idealless	looseness	Mithraism	Octobrist	polyphase	rerelease
gothicise	idioplasm	lousiness	Mithraist	odourless	poorhouse	reremouse
Gothicism	imageless	lovefeast	mixedness	Orangeism	posthorse	reservist
governess	imprecise	loverless	mnemonist	orchidist	posthouse	retrousse
graceless	improvise	lowercase	modernise	orderless	powerless	rhythmise
grandiose	inaptness	lowermost	modernism	orologist	preconise	rhythmist
grandness	Indianise	lowliness	modernist	ostracise	predigest	Ribbonism
granulose	indispose	lucidness	moistness	ostracism	prelatess	riderless
graveless	ineptness	luckiness	monachism	otherness	prelatise	rightness
graveness	inertness	lumpiness	Mondayish	otherwise	premonish	rigidness
greatness	innermost	luridness	monergism	otologist	prestress	riskiness
Greekless	interfuse	lustiness	mongolism	outermost	preterist	ritualise
greenness	interpose	lymegrass	monitress	overdress	prettyish	ritualism
griefless	inverness	machinist	monkeyish	overtness	prettyism	ritualist
griminess	invertase	macintosh	monkeyism	priceless	priceless	roadhouse
grossness	isinglass	macrocosm	monoecism	oxygenise	prideless	rockiness
groundash	isomerise	Magianism	Montanism	packhorse	priestess	roominess
gruffness	isomerism	magnetise	moodiness	paederast	primeness	roughcast
Grundyism	issueless	magnetism	Mormonism	paillasse	procuress	roughness
guidepost	italicise	magnetist	mosaicism	pairhorse	profilist	roundness
guileless	Italicism	maidenish	mosaicist	palletise	prologise	routinism
guiltless	itchiness	malthouse	motocross	palliasse	proneness	routinist
guitarist	itsybitsy	mammonish	mouthwash	panderess	prosiness	rowdiness
gumminess	janitress	mammonism	muddiness	panellist	prosodist	rubberise
gustiness	Jansenism	mammonist	mugginess	pantheism	publicise	ruddiness
gutsiness	Jansenist	manganese	murderess	pantheist	publicist	ruggedise
haggadist	jargonise	manginess	murkiness	pantyhose	pudginess	rustiness
hairbrush	jazziness	manliness	muskiness	papillose	puffiness	sabbatise
hairgrass	jellyfish	mannerism	mustiness	Parseeism	pulpiness	sabbatism
hairiness	jerkiness	mannerist	mutualise	pastiness	pulseless	sagebrush

```
sallowish  smileless  sternpost  teutonise  visionist  acuminate  birthrate
saltiness  smokebush  stiffness  Teutonism  visitress  adenomata  bivariate
saltmarsh  smokeless  stillness  Teutonist  visualise  adiposity  bloodbath
sandblast  smokiness  stingless  thankless  vividness  admiralty  bombilate
sandglass  smoothish  stintless  theocrasy  vocalness  adsorbate  bombinate
sandiness  snailfish  stockfish  therapist  voiceless  adumbrate  bookplate
sappiness  snakiness  stocklist  theurgist  volcanism  adversity  brachiate
saturnism  snipefish  stonefish  thickness  voltinism  aeriality  bracteate
sauceless  snowgoose  stoneless  thingness  voodooism  aerophyte  brandreth
sauciness  snowiness  stoniness  thornbush  voodooist  aestivate  brecciate
scaldfish  soapiness  stoppress  thornless  vorticism  affiliate  briquette
scalefish  soberness  stormless  thrombose  vorticist  affricate  brochette
scaleless  socialise  stoutness  tightness  vorticose  aftermath  brutality
scalemoss  socialism  strapless  timelapse  vowelless  aggravate  bryophyte
scaliness  socialist  strongish  timidness  voyeurism  aggregate  bucktooth
scantness  sogginess  studhorse  timpanist  vulcanise  alleviate  calcarate
scarfwise  solemnise  subsidise  tinniness  vulcanism  alpargata  calculate
scenarist  solidness  subtilise  tipsiness  vulcanist  altercate  calibrate
scentless  solipsism  succotash  tiredness  vulgarise  alternate  caliphate
schistose  solipsist  sulkiness  tollhouse  vulgarism  aluminate  callosity
scholiast  sonnetise  sultaness  tomentose  vulpinism  alveolate  candidate
scientism  soothfast  summarise  toolhouse  vulturish  ambiguity  cannulate
scientist  sootiness  summarist  toothless  wackiness  amorality  capsulate
Scoticise  soppiness  sunniness  topiarist  wallcress  amourette  captivate
seaminess  sopranist  superfuse  toughness  warehouse  anchorite  captivity
seediness  Sorbonist  superpose  townhouse  wartcress  angiomata  carbamate
selfabuse  sorceress  supervise  traceless  washhouse  anglesite  carbonate
selftrust  sorriness  surculose  trackless  washiness  anhydrite  Carmelite
senseless  Soudanese  surliness  traitress  wasteness  animality  carnality
sensitise  soundless  sutteeism  transfuse  watchcase  animosity  castanets
serialise  soundness  swangoose  transpose  waterless  anonymity  castigate
serialism  soundpost  swarajist  transvest  wayzgoose  anorthite  causality
serialist  southeast  swartness  tribadism  weariless  antipasto  celebrate
sermonise  southmost  sweetness  tribalism  weariness  antiquate  celebrity
sexualise  southwest  swellfish  trickless  wedgewise  antiquity  cementite
shadeless  sovietise  swiftness  trigamist  weediness  apiculate  cerebrate
shadiness  sovietism  swordfish  triteness  weirdness  appellate  cerecloth
shakerism  spaceless  syllabise  tritheism  welfarism  approbate  certainty
shakiness  spagyrist  syllabism  tritheist  wheelbase  aragonite  cerussite
shamanism  spareness  syllogise  truceless  wheelless  arbitrate  champerty
shamanist  sparkless  syllogism  trunkfish  whitebass  argentite  charlotte
shamefast  speakeasy  symbolise  trustless  whitefish  argillite  checkmate
shameless  spearfish  symbolism  truthless  whiteness  argumenta  chipolata
shapeless  speckless  symbolist  tubbiness  whitewash  arriviste  chocolate
sharpness  spicebush  synergism  tumidness  wholeness  asininity  chondrite
sheatfish  spiciness  synergist  turquoise  widthwise  aspartate  cigarette
sheepwash  spikiness  synoptist  tympanist  willowish  assiduity  circinate
sheerness  spineless  syphilise  tyrannise  windchest  associate  circulate
shellfish  spininess  tacitness  unaptness  windiness  astrocyte  citystate
shiftless  Spinozism  tackiness  undermost  wineglass  asymptote  classmate
shininess  Spinozist  tailoress  underpass  winepress  atacamite  clathrate
Shintoism  spinulose  taintless  undervest  winterise  atomicity  coadunate
Shintoist  spiritism  tallowish  unfitness  witticism  atonality  coagulate
shirtless  spiritist  Talmudist  unharness  wittiness  atonicity  coarctate
shoreless  spiritoso  tantalise  unselfish  woodiness  attenuate  cobaltite
shortness  spokewise  tarantass  unsuccess  woodlouse  attribute  cochleate
shouldest  sporocyst  tarantism  uppercase  wooziness  auspicate  coelomata
showiness  spoutless  tardiness  uppermost  wordiness  austenite  coelomate
sidedness  squarrose  Targumist  usualness  workhorse  austerity  coenobite
sightless  squatness  Tartufism  utterless  workhouse  authority  coffinite
signalise  squeamish  tasteless  uttermost  worthless  autoroute  colligate
siliquose  stabilise  tastiness  utterness  woundless  babacoote  collimate
silkiness  staginess  tattiness  vagueness  wrathless  bacchante  collocate
silliness  staidness  tattooist  validness  wrongness  backcloth  colocynth
simulcast  stainless  tawniness  valueless  Yankeeism  bandwidth  columbite
sinewless  staircase  telophase  valveless  yellowish  banquette  combinate
Sinhalese  staleness  temporise  vampirism  youngness  barbarity  comminute
skirtless  Stalinism  temptress  vandalise  zeitgeist  batholite  commodity
slackness  Stalinist  tenderise  vandalism  zoologist  batholith  community
slakeless  stalkless  tenebrist  vapidness  zootomist  bedlamite  commutate
slantwise  stargrass  tenseness  vapourish  abnormity  belemnite  composite
sleekness  starkness  tepidness  Vedantist  abominate  benignity  concavity
sleepless  stateless  terminism  verbalise  absurdity  bentonite  congruity
slickness  statocyst  terminist  verbalism  acclimate  bifoliate  conjugate
slightish  steadfast  terrorise  verbalist  acclivity  bifurcate  consulate
sliminess  steepness  terrorism  vernalise  acetylate  bilabiate  contralto
slopewise  sterilise  terrorist  verrucose  aciculate  billionth  contrasty
smallness  sternmost  terseness  victimise  acidulate  bipartite  convexity
smartness  sternness  testiness  violinist  actuality  bipinnate  convolute
```

cooperate	elucidate	frigidity	incurvate	majorette	obsecrate	procreate
copesmate	elutriate	frivolity	indemnity	malachite	obstinate	profanity
coprolite	embrocate	frostbite	indignity	malignity	officiate	prolixity
corallite	emolliate	fructuate	inebriate	mamillate	oilpaints	propagate
corporate	emotivity	frugality	inebriety	mammonite	olivenite	propriety
correlate	encrinite	frustrate	infatuate	manducate	operosity	prorogate
corrugate	endophyte	fulgurate	infirmity	manganate	orientate	prosecute
corticate	entophyte	fulgurite	infuriate	manganite	originate	proselyte
coruscate	entrecote	fulminate	infuscate	manifesto	oscillate	prostrate
Corybants	entremets	fustigate	ingenuity	manzanita	osteopath	proximate
couchette	enucleate	garrulity	innervate	marcasite	Ostrogoth	proximity
courgette	enumerate	gelignite	innocuity	margarite	oubliette	publicity
credulity	enunciate	geniality	inoculate	marginate	outgrowth	puerility
crenulate	epaulette	gentility	insatiate	masticate	outskirts	pugnacity
crepitate	epidosite	georgette	insatiety	maternity	overstate	pullulate
criminate	eradicate	germinate	insensate	mayoralty	overwrite	pulmonate
croquette	erythrite	geyserite	insinuate	medullate	overwrote	pulserate
crossette	Esperanto	gibbosity	instigate	megadeath	oviparity	pulvinate
crotchety	ethnicity	gigahertz	institute	megahertz	oxygenate	punctuate
cucullate	etiquette	globosity	integrate	meliorate	ozocerite	pustulate
culminate	eucalypti	glomerate	integrity	meliority	ozokerite	putridity
cultivate	eucaryote	glutamate	intensity	melismata	paillette	pyracanth
curiosity	evaginate	goalmouth	intercity	mendacity	palafitte	quartette
cuspidate	evaporate	goldsmith	intestate	mendicity	pallidity	quartzite
cyclamate	eventuate	Gothamite	intricate	Mennonite	palmitate	quintette
cystolith	exanimate	gracility	inutility	mentality	palpitate	rabbinate
debutante	exarchate	granulate	inviolate	mesophyte	pantalets	raffinate
deciduate	excoriate	granulite	ironsmith	meteorite	papillate	rancidity
declinate	exculpate	gratulate	irradiate	methylate	papillote	rascality
declivity	exfoliate	gravidity	irreality	metricate	parachute	reanimate
decollate	exonerate	gravitate	isogamete	micaslate	Paraclete	reclinate
decollete	exopodite	habituate	Israelite	microcyte	paramatta	recondite
decussate	expatiate	haematite	itinerate	microlite	pastorate	rectorate
defalcate	explicate	haircloth	ittybitty	microlith	patellate	redingote
defoliate	expurgate	halfcaste	jocundity	micturate	paternity	reeducate
deformity	exquisite	halftruth	joviality	midinette	pectinate	rehydrate
dehydrate	exsiccate	Hallstatt	juniorate	milktooth	pederasty	reinstate
delineate	extensity	halophyte	juniority	millerite	pegmatite	reiterate
demarcate	extenuate	Hashemite	kaolinite	millionth	pendulate	reluctate
denigrate	extirpate	Hashimite	kilohertz	miscreate	penetrate	remediate
denitrate	extradite	headcloth	labourite	modernity	percolate	replicate
depravity	extremity	heavyduty	labyrinth	molybdate	perennate	reprobate
deprecate	extricate	hessonite	laccolith	monzonite	perforate	repudiate
depredate	exuberate	hibernate	laciniate	morbidity	periodate	requisite
desecrate	fabricate	hiddenite	lamellate	mordacity	permutate	restitute
desiccate	facecloth	Himyarite	lancinate	mortality	personate	retaliate
designate	facundity	hircosity	langouste	mossagate	petiolate	rhodolite
desperate	fascinate	hispidity	larghetto	mucronate	phagocyte	rhodonite
destitute	faveolate	Hitlerite	lazaretto	muniments	phenacite	roodcloth
deuterate	favourite	holophote	legislate	muscovite	phenakite	roofplate
devaluate	febricity	homeopath	lethality	mutuality	phonolite	rotundity
devastate	fecundate	hostility	leucocyte	myelomata	phosphate	rubellite
dexterity	fecundity	housebote	leukocyte	nameplate	phosphite	rubricate
diaconate	femineity	housemate	liability	natrolite	piecerate	runcinate
diatomite	fertility	humiliate	lilywhite	necessity	pierrette	rusticate
dimidiate	festinate	hundredth	limpidity	neckcloth	pinnulate	rusticity
diplomate	festivity	hybridity	lineality	negotiate	pirouette	sacculate
dishcloth	feudality	hyphenate	linearity	nephelite	pizzicati	sackcloth
dislocate	fibromata	hypocrite	lineolate	neuromata	pizzicato	sagittate
disparate	fifteenth	hyponasty	lingulate	neuropath	placidity	sailcloth
disparity	figurante	imbricate	lintwhite	niccolite	plumulate	salubrity
disrepute	fimbriate	immediate	liquidate	nictitate	plurality	sanbenito
dissipate	firstrate	immensity	liquidity	ninetieth	pointduty	sarcomata
dissolute	fishplate	immigrate	lixiviate	nonentity	pollinate	satellite
diversity	fissility	immodesty	locksmith	normality	pomposity	satinette
doctorate	flarepath	impetrate	loincloth	noseflute	posterity	scapolite
dogstooth	floodgate	implicate	longcoats	notoriety	posthaste	scheelite
doorplate	floridity	imprecate	longevity	novelette	postulate	scolecite
drawplate	fluctuate	improbity	loquacity	noviciate	potentate	scotomata
dubiosity	footcloth	impromptu	lorgnette	novitiate	poussette	sectility
ductility	footplate	inability	loudmouth	nummulite	precocity	segregate
duplicate	foretaste	inamorata	lubricate	nuncupate	predacity	senhorita
duplicity	formality	inanimate	lubricity	obbligato	predicate	seniority
ectophyte	formicate	incarnate	lucubrate	obcordate	preterite	sensedata
edibility	formulate	incognito	luxuriate	obfuscate	primality	sentenate
eightieth	fornicate	incondite	machinate	objurgate	procerity	seriality
ejaculate	forthwith	inculcate	macrocyte	obliquity		
elaborate	fortunate	inculpate	magnesite	obscenity		
eliminate	fragility		magnetite	obscurity		

```
serinette  temperate  watergate  butternut  dipterous  impluvium  oleaceous
serjeanty  tensility  wavellite  calcaneum  discolour  incurious  operculum
serrulate  tenthrate  whereinto  calculous  disfavour  indecorum  opusculum
serviette  terebinth  whereunto  caldarium  dishclout  ingenious  overcloud
servility  terminate  wherewith  cancerous  dishonour  ingenuous  overissue
severalty  tetradite  willemite  candlenut  doodlebug  injurious  overvalue
sexuality  thereinto  wirephoto  cankerous  drawerful  innocuous  oviferous
sgraffiti  thereunto  witchetty  cantaloup  echovirus  innoxious  oviparous
sgraffito  therewith  witherite  cantharus  effluvium  inodorous  oxygenous
sheepcote  thirdrate  wordsmith  capacious  effortful  insidious  palladium
shogunate  thirtieth  wulfenite  capitulum  egregious  invidious  palladous
sigillate  thitherto  wyandotte  carrefour  endeavour  isogamous  pedagogue
sincerity  tigermoth  Wyclifite  catalogue  endosteum  isogenous  pemphigus
sinuosity  titillate  xerophyte  caterwaul  epigynous  isomerous  pendulous
sixteenth  tittivate  zinkenite  cavernous  eponymous  isopodous  penurious
slivovitz  tollbooth  zucchetto  ceanothus  equisetum  jitterbug  peripatus
snakebite  torpidity  acidulous  cephalous  equivoque  judicious  petroleum
snowbroth  torridity  ailanthus  cerastium  erogenous  Junoesque  platinous
snowwhite  tracheate  aluminium  ceratodus  erroneous  laborious  playgroup
socialite  translate  aluminous  cetaceous  Esquimaux  lanthanum  plenteous
sociality  transmute  ambiguous  chanceful  euphonium  lapideous  plentiful
sociopath  traycloth  ambitious  chancrous  exequatur  larcenous  plumbeous
solemnity  tremolite  americium  changeful  exogamous  lecherous  plutonium
soleplate  tribunate  amianthus  chauffeur  exogenous  libellous  pocketful
solmisate  tridymite  amorphous  chiboque   exsuccous  lichenous  podagrous
songsmith  trilobate  amphioxus  chihuahua  fabaceous  lightsout  poisonous
sostenuto  trilobite  analogous  chitinous  facetious  literatus  pollinium
soubrette  triturate  anandrous  cinereous  fastigium  litigious  polygonum
soupplate  tungstate  anhydrous  clamorous  felonious  litterbug  pomaceous
spaghetti  turbidity  anomalous  clitellum  ferocious  longevous  pompadour
spatulate  turbinate  anonymous  cobaltous  fibrinous  lovingcup  ponderous
specialty  turgidity  antiserum  coccidium  filaceous  lubricous  posticous
speculate  twentieth  apetalous  coenobium  fistulous  ludicrous  potassium
spiculate  typewrite  aphyllous  coffeecup  flabellum  lumbricus  praiseful
spinosity  uintahite  apogamous  colchicum  flagellum  luxurious  prayerful
spirality  umbellate  apparatus  colleague  flambeaus  magnalium  prayerrug
sporulate  umpteenth  arabesque  collegium  flambeaux  magnesium  presidium
stability  unanimity  arboreous  collyrium  flavorous  malarious  pressstud
Stagirite  underrate  arboretum  colosseum  flocculus  malicious  proconsul
stagparty  unreality  Areopagus  colostrum  forgetful  malleolus  prolapsus
stalemate  unthrifty  argentous  colourful  fractious  manganous  pterosaur
stalworth  uraninite  arsenious  columbium  fraenulum  manubrium  pterygium
staminate  urceolate  asbestous  complexus  frightful  marsupium  pulverous
stampduty  usherette  asepalous  congruous  frivolous  masterful  pulvillus
stampnote  uvarovite  asparagus  conscious  fructuous  mausoleum  pumiceous
statolith  vaccinate  asphaltum  consensus  fugacious  meandrous  pustulous
statuette  vacillate  assiduous  contagium  fulgurous  melodious  pycnidium
sterility  vacuolate  astronaut  continuum  fulminous  menstruum  pyrethrum
stimulate  variegate  Athenaeum  conundrum  funiculus  mercurous  quercetum
stipitate  variolate  atrocious  cornflour  garrulous  micaceous  querulous
stipulate  variolite  audacious  cosmonaut  gastraeum  minacious  raconteur
stolidity  veniality  avizandum  cothurnus  germanium  minutegun  raincloud
stolonate  ventilate  bacterium  courteous  ginglymus  momentous  rancorous
stupidity  verbosity  barathrum  crapulous  gladiolus  monkeynut  rapacious
stylobate  verminate  barbarous  credulous  glaireous  monocoque  rapturous
suability  viability  barrelful  cretinous  glamorous  monologue  redivivus
subjugate  vicariate  basketful  criminous  glutinous  monstrous  regardful
sublimate  vigilante  bathybius  cutaneous  greasegun  moraceous  regisseur
sublimity  villosity  beauteous  cymbidium  grotesque  mundungus  regretful
subrogate  vindicate  beautiful  dangerous  groundnut  murderous  religious
substrata  virginity  behaviour  Dantesque  gymnasium  murmurous  remindful
substrate  virgulate  berkelium  decalogue  gynaeceum  narcissus  reposeful
succinate  viscerate  beryllium  deceitful  gynoecium  nectarous  resentful
suffocate  viscidity  bifarious  decennium  harmonium  needleful  resultful
sultanate  viscosity  biogenous  deciduous  harquebus  nefarious  retiarius
suppurate  viscounty  bonhomous  declivous  hazardous  neighbour  reticulum
surrogate  vitiosity  bottleful  deinosaur  healthful  neodymium  righteous
sylvanite  vivianite  bounteous  delicious  hearthrug  neptunium  rivalrous
syncopate  vizierate  bountiful  delirious  herbarium  nickelous  rosaceous
syndicate  vorticity  brazilnut  demagogue  hereabout  nightclub  rostellum
synoecete  vulcanite  bucketful  demeanour  hilarious  notorious  ruthenium
tachylite  vulgarity  bulltrout  dentalium  homologue  nucleolus  sacrarium
tachylyte  vulpinite  bumptious  deuterium  hydronium  nystagmus  sagacious
tactility  Wagnerite  burdenous  dexterous  hypericum  oblivious  salacious
tantalate  wagonette  burlesque  diachylum  hypogeous  obnoxious  saleratus
tantalite  wallplate  burnedout  diandrous  ideologue  odalisque  salicetum
telephoto  washcloth  bushelful  dichasium  ignoramus  offcolour  sandspout
tellurate  waterbath  butterbur  diclinous  imperious  officious  sartorius
tellurite  waterbutt  buttercup  dioecious  impetuous  oilcolour  saucerful
```

```
schistous  tufaceous  digestive  portreeve  swansdown  carambola  marijuana
scirrhous  tumblebug  directive  powerdive  touchdown  carcinoma  matricula
scutellum  turnabout  educative  precative  unbeknown  Cassandra  melismata
sebaceous  tyrannous  effective  predative  waterfowl  casuarina  melodrama
seditious  uliginous  emanative  prelusive  wellknown  catatonia  melomania
selenious  ultimatum  embracive  primitive  windblown  cerebella  memoranda
sensorium  umbilicus  emulative  privative  wiredrawn  chachacha  mesogloea
sericeous  unanimous  evocative  probative  withdrawn  chelicera  micropsia
setaceous  undutiful  evolutive  prolative  battleaxe  cherimoya  millennia
shamateur  unhelpful  exceptive  promotive  cataplexy  chihuahua  monodrama
shieldbug  unicolour  excessive  purgative  orthodoxy  chipolata  monomania
shovelful  uniparous  exclusive  purposive  broadways  chlorella  moratoria
sideissue  unisonous  excretive  radiative  cherimoya  cineraria  multipara
siliceous  unmindful  excursive  receptive  corduroys  clepsydra  myelomata
silicious  unskilful  executive  recessive  crossways  coelomata  myriorama
sinologue  untimeous  expansive  reclusive  cryptonym  colloquia  myxoedema
slateclub  uropygium  expensive  recursive  frontways  columella  naumachia
sleevenut  vademecum  expletive  reductive  goldeneye  compendia  nemophila
slumbrous  vagarious  explosive  reflexive  hendiadys  condyloma  neoteinia
snaredrum  variolous  expulsive  repulsive  heteronym  consortia  neuralgia
solacious  venereous  extensive  resistive  hypocotyl  contadina  neuroglia
soliloquy  venturous  extorsive  retentive  jambalaya  corbicula  neuromata
sorcerous  veracious  extortive  revulsive  Kshatriya  cosmorama  nicotiana
sorrowful  verminous  extrusive  seclusive  leastways  crustacea  noctiluca
souteneur  verrucous  exudative  secretive  polyvinyl  curricula  nostalgia
sparkplug  vestigium  factitive  seductive  pseudonym  cyclorama  notabilia
speechful  vexatious  folkweave  selective  slantways  dharmsala  nullipara
sphagnous  vicarious  formative  selfdrive  syndactyl  diarrhoea  octahedra
spinulous  vimineous  fortyfive  semibreve  tigerseye  didrachma  oligaemia
spirillum  vinaceous  fricative  sensitive  tridactyl  dulcamara  ommatidia
spiritous  vivacious  gerundive  shortwave  widthways  dyscrasia  omophagia
spleenful  voracious  groundivy  siccative  Ashkenazi  dyspepsia  orchestra
splendour  vulturous  gustative  sickleave  influenza  dysphagia  palaestra
spongeous  walkabout  hortative  soundwave  overglaze  dysphonia  panatella
stegosaur  washedout  imitative  stockdove  overgraze  dysphoria  papilloma
stirabout  wonderful  impassive  summative  saltglaze  dysplasia  paralalia
strenuous  yachtclub  implosive  supernova  schmaltzy  echolalia  paralexia
stressful  ytterbium  impulsive  talkative  wiregauze  eclampsia  paramatta
strobilus  zirconium  incentive  tentative  ─────────  emphysema  parapodia
strontium  zoogenous  inceptive  testdrive  acetabula  empyreuma  paulownia
stuporous  acceptive  inclusive  undeceive  acetylcoA  encephala  peninsula
subereous  accretive  incursive  unreserve  acroteria  enchilada  penultima
subphylum  addictive  inductive  Vaishnava  actinozoa  epithelia  perihelia
sugarplum  adductive  infective  vibrative  adenomata  esoterica  phagedena
summingup  admissive  ingestive  violative  aesthesia  euphorbia  phantasma
sumptuous  advective  intensive  waldgrave  algarroba  exanthema  phenomena
sympodium  adventive  interwove  breakdown  alpargata  feiseanna  Philomela
symposium  affective  intrusive  bringdown  amblyopia  fibromata  photopsia
synagogue  agitative  intuitive  Chinatown  ambulacra  fioritura  plasmodia
syncytium  aperitive  invective  closedown  analgesia  forsythia  pneumonia
syngamous  ascensive  inventive  countdown  androecia  generalia  poinciana
taraxacum  assertive  inversive  crackdown  angiomata  grandpapa  polyhedra
teacupful  assuasive  irruptive  eiderdown  anoxaemia  gravamina  porphyria
technique  attentive  isolative  finedrawn  apocrypha  guerrilla  portulaca
tegmentum  autoclave  iterative  foreknown  apothecia  haematoma  pozzolana
tellurium  balaclava  landgrave  foreshown  Appaloosa  harmonica  primipara
tellurous  biconcave  laudative  frogspawn  aquilegia  haustella  primordia
tenacious  bondslave  lucrative  fullblown  araucaria  haustoria  principia
tenaculum  brainwave  mediative  fullgrown  argumenta  hieratica  propylaea
tendinous  calmative  microwave  halfcrown  artemisia  honoraria  proscenia
tenebrous  causative  misbehave  handsdown  asafetida  hortensia  protonema
terrarium  champleve  narrative  highflown  aubrietia  hydraemia  psalteria
theologue  cognitive  normative  highgrown  auditoria  hydrangea  puzzolana
thesaurus  collusive  nutritive  homegrown  babirussa  hyperbola  pyromania
tomentous  combative  objective  knockdown  balaclava  hyperopia  rafflesia
torturous  conducive  obsessive  mollymawk  balalaika  hypomania  rauwolfia
trapezium  corrosive  obtrusive  mossgrown  ballerina  inamorata  referenda
tremulous  crashdive  occlusive  nightgown  barracuda  influenza  rudbeckia
trialogue  deadalive  offensive  nighthawk  bilharzia  infusoria  sabadilla
tricolour  deceptive  olfactive  overblown  bonechina  ischaemia  sanatoria
triennium  decretive  operative  overcrowd  brachyura  jacaranda  sanitaria
trifolium  deductive  ostensive  overdrawn  Bretwalda  jambalaya  santolina
triforium  defective  overdrive  overflown  Britannia  juvenilia  santonica
trigamous  defensive  palsgrave  overgrown  cafeteria  Kshatriya  sapodilla
trimerous  depictive  partitive  pastedown  calandria  laminaria  sapraemia
triptyque  depletive  perfusive  punchbowl  calendula  leucaemia  sarcomata
trochilus  detective  pervasive  roughhewn  camarilla  leukaemia  sauropoda
troublous  detersive  plaintive  shakedown  campanula  manzanita  scagliola
trumpedup  diffusive  portative  Southdown  cantilena  marihuana  scintilla
```

```
scotomata  anecdotic  demiurgic  Holarctic  onanistic  selenitic  annulated
senhorita  animistic  dendritic  homiletic  oncogenic  semeiotic  apartheid
sensedata  ankylotic  diacritic  homogamic  oncologic  semitonic  apprehend
septennia  anorectic  diactinic  homonymic  onomastic  Sephardic  appressed
sequestra  antarctic  dialectic  homotonic  ontogenic  shambolic  arachnoid
sestertia  anthracic  diametric  honorific  ontologic  sideritic  archfiend
Shangrila  anthropic  diastatic  horologic  oogenetic  silicotic  Arguseyed
signorina  antigenic  diastolic  hubristic  opodeldoc  Solomonic  arrowhead
simulacra  antimonic  diathetic  hydraulic  orchestic  sophistic  arrowwood
solfatara  antinomic  diatropic  hydriodic  orgiastic  soporific  arthropod
spiracula  antitoxic  dichromic  hyperopic  orthoepic  spasmodic  arytenoid
spirogyra  apathetic  didelphic  hypomanic  pancratic  spermatic  asclepiad
sporangia  aperiodic  digastric  Icelandic  panegyric  splenetic  augmented
subgenera  aplanatic  dimorphic  ideologic  panoramic  stalactic  backboard
subsellia  apodictic  Dionysiac  idiomatic  parabolic  statistic  backsword
substrata  apomictic  dizygotic  imbecilic  paralytic  steatitic  bacteroid
sudatoria  apostolic  doleritic  impolitic  paramedic  stigmatic  balconied
supernova  arthritic  dolomitic  inelastic  paranoiac  stomachic  baldfaced
tarantara  asphaltic  dualistic  inorganic  parasitic  strategic  bandstand
tarantula  asthmatic  dyspeptic  insomniac  paregoric  stromatic  barefaced
tarragona  asyndetic  dysphagic  intrinsic  patriotic  strychnic  barnacled
terramara  ataractic  dysphoric  ischaemic  patristic  stylistic  barrelled
tessitura  atavistic  dyspnoeic  ischiadic  pearlitic  subarctic  bastioned
theomania  atheistic  eccentric  ischiatic  pedagogic  subatomic  bayoneted
Theravada  athematic  eclamptic  Islamitic  peridotic  sudorific  beachhead
trabecula  atomistic  ectogenic  isobathic  pharaonic  sulphonic  bedspread
transenna  autarchic  egomaniac  isoclinic  pharisaic  sulphuric  bellyband
trattoria  authentic  egotistic  isocyclic  philippic  sybaritic  beneficed
triclinia  autolytic  embryonic  isometric  phrenetic  sylleptic  benighted
triquetra  automatic  embryotic  isostatic  pianistic  symbiotic  bestirred
urticaria  autonomic  emplastic  isotropic  pietistic  symmetric  betrothed
Vaishnava  autotelic  encaustic  Jacobinic  pilgarlic  symphonic  bigheaded
vallecula  axiomatic  endogamic  Judaistic  pisolitic  symposiac  billboard
varicella  ballistic  endogenic  judgmatic  plasmatic  syncretic  blackbird
vibracula  bigeneric  energetic  katabatic  plethoric  synonymic  blackhead
vomitoria  biometric  enigmatic  katabolic  pleuritic  syntactic  blacklead
waterflea  bishopric  enzymatic  kinematic  pneumatic  synthetic  bleareyed
zoophobia  bombastic  epaenetic  lethargic  pneumonic  systaltic  blindfold
cockscomb  Brahmanic  epicyclic  leukaemic  polybasic  tacamahac  blinkered
currycomb  Brahminic  epidermic  leviratic  polygamic  taxonomic  blockhead
depthbomb  bregmatic  epileptic  limonitic  polygenic  telegenic  bloodshed
disentomb  bricabrac  epinastic  logaoedic  polymeric  thalassic  bluebeard
dithyramb  Britannic  epiphytic  Lombardic  polysemic  theandric  bobtailed
flashbulb  Brythonic  epistemic  lymphatic  polysomic  theogonic  bodyguard
honeycomb  cachectic  epistolic  lyophilic  polytypic  theologic  boldfaced
nightclub  cacodylic  epithetic  lyophobic  pragmatic  theoretic  bookstand
slateclub  cadaveric  epizootic  macaronic  preadamic  Thomistic  bottlefed
smokebomb  Caenozoic  ergonomic  Masoretic  preexilic  threnodic  boulevard
spiderweb  Cainozoic  ethylenic  melanotic  prismatic  toponymic  bowerbird
stinkbomb  calendric  eutrophic  messianic  proclitic  touristic  bowlegged
toothcomb  calorific  evangelic  metabolic  prodromic  trachytic  boyfriend
yachtclub  camphoric  excentric  metameric  proleptic  transonic  brevetted
acrobatic  casuistic  exosmotic  metonymic  prophetic  traumatic  briarwood
adiabatic  catabolic  extrinsic  miasmatic  propionic  triatomic  brickyard
aerobatic  catalytic  fantastic  monarchic  prostatic  trichomic  brierwood
aerolitic  catatonic  Fascistic  monatomic  proteinic  trichroic  bromeliad
aesthetic  cathartic  faunistic  monobasic  prothetic  triclinic  brushwood
agonistic  cathectic  felicific  monogamic  protozoic  trimetric  buckboard
agrologic  catoptric  fideistic  monologic  psalmodic  vaporific  buckhound
agronomic  charabanc  floristic  monomeric  psoriatic  virtuosic  cablelaid
ahistoric  chemurgic  folkmusic  monotonic  psychotic  vitriolic  cancelled
albinotic  chimaeric  formulaic  monotypic  Ptolemaic  wolframic  cantharid
alcoholic  chivalric  fumarolic  morphemic  puritanic  zeugmatic  cardboard
aldehydic  chloritic  genotypic  mutagenic  pyramidic  zoophytic  catchword
aleatoric  chlorotic  geomantic  mycologic  pyrogenic  zygomatic  cedarwood
Alemannic  choleraic  geometric  mydriatic  pyrolytic  zymogenic  celluloid
algebraic  choplogic  geostatic  napthalic  quadratic  abandoned  certified
alicyclic  chromatic  geotropic  neolithic  realistic  acquitted  chaetopod
aliphatic  cinematic  geriatric  neoteinic  rhapsodic  adulthood  chancroid
allegoric  climactic  gnathonic  nephritic  rheumatic  affianced  chapleted
amaurotic  coenosarc  goliardic  neuralgic  salicylic  aforesaid  chartered
amblyopic  colorific  graphemic  nicotinic  Samoyedic  afterword  checkered
Amerindic  copacetic  graphitic  nostalgic  sapraemic  aggrieved  chequered
anabiotic  coseismic  gymnastic  nucleonic  Saracenic  aircooled  chickweed
anaerobic  cryogenic  halieutic  nystagmic  sarcastic  airminded  childhood
analeptic  culsdesac  Hanseatic  obstetric  schematic  aminoacid  chipboard
analgesic  cylindric  hegemonic  oecologic  sclerotic  ampersand  chiselled
anaphoric  cytotoxic  heliozoic  oecumenic  scoliotic  analysand  chrysalid
andesitic  demagogic  heuristic  omophagic  scorbutic  anguished  clapboard
```

cleareyed	earthward	greyhound	linenfold	pedigreed	seastrand	sweatband
clipboard	earwigged	grovelled	lintelled	pencilled	selffaced	swineherd
cloudland	eastbound	hackneyed	lobulated	penfriend	selfmoved	swivelled
coalfield	eightfold	haematoid	longeared	perfervid	semifluid	syllabled
coastward	ellipsoid	halfbaked	longfaced	permitted	semirigid	syphiloid
cobwebbed	elongated	halfblood	longlived	phyllopod	semisolid	tableland
collected	emaciated	halfbound	Longobard	physicked	sequinned	tailboard
committed	embattled	halfbreed	lotusland	picnicked	serranoid	tasselled
communard	enamelled	hallstand	lovechild	pigheaded	sevenfold	tentacled
compelled	enamoured	hamadryad	lowminded	pintailed	sexlinked	thicketed
conceited	engarland	hamfisted	lownecked	pintsized	sharpeyed	thickhead
concerned	englutted	hamhanded	lustihood	pistolled	sharpshod	thirdhand
concerted	entrapped	handstand	lyamhound	pithecoid	sheepfold	thoughted
concurred	enwrapped	hanselled	lymehound	pixilated	sheetbend	threefold
condyloid	ephemerid	haphazard	malformed	placecard	shewbread	threshold
confabbed	eunuchoid	hardboard	mansarded	planetoid	shinguard	tigerwood
conferred	eutectoid	hardihood	manysided	planuloid	shipboard	tinselled
confirmed	ewenecked	hardnosed	maquisard	plastered	shockhead	titledeed
connected	fairfaced	headboard	marcelled	platinoid	shoreward	tittupped
contented	fairyhood	heartland	marshland	polyploid	shoreweed	tortricid
contrived	fairyland	heartwood	marvelled	pommelled	shorthand	touchwood
convolved	falsehood	hellhound	masonried	poppyhead	shovelled	trabeated
copsewood	fantasied	herniated	matchwood	possessed	sideboard	traceried
coralloid	farmstead	herpetoid	metalloid	practised	signalled	trainband
corbelled	fasciated	hexachord	meteoroid	preferred	signboard	trainload
cornfield	fascicled	hexaploid	millboard	prerecord	silkgland	transcend
cornsalad	fatheaded	hidebound	minefield	pressstud	slabsided	trapezoid
coroneted	fatwitted	highspeed	misguided	processed	slinkweed	travelled
corralled	feathered	hightoned	misleared	professed	slushfund	trepanned
corticoid	fibrinoid	hoarhound	mistyeyed	proofread	smartweed	trihybrid
courtcard	filigreed	hobnailed	Mongoloid	propelled	snakebird	trousered
courtyard	filterbed	hobnobbed	monkshood	pseudopod	snakeweed	trowelled
crashland	firebrand	Hollywood	monochord	pterygoid	snakewood	truncated
crenelled	fireguard	homebound	moonblind	pulpboard	snivelled	trunkroad
cropeared	firsthand	homestead	mosaicked	pummelled	snowblind	trustdeed
crossbred	floriated	horehound	mullioned	punchcard	snowbound	tulipwood
crosseyed	flowerbed	horsepond	mummified	puppyhood	snowfield	tunicated
crosshead	fluecured	hotheaded	myrmecoid	pureblood	snowguard	tunnelled
crossroad	footboard	household	netveined	quadrifid	snowyard	turnround
crosswind	footpound	houselled	netwinged	quadruped	sodabread	twicelaid
crossword	forcefeed	housemaid	newshound	qualified	southland	twicetold
cudgelled	forceland	humankind	newsstand	queenhood	southward	twofisted
curvetted	forenamed	humbugged	nickelled	quicksand	spaceband	twohanded
cutinised	formatted	hysteroid	nightbird	raincloud	spearhead	umberbird
cyprinoid	foulbrood	ichthyoid	nodulated	rearguard	spellbind	unabashed
dachshund	freeboard	illjudged	northland	recommend	spermatid	unadopted
dairymaid	friarbird	illomened	northward	redhanded	sphygmoid	unadorned
dartboard	frivolled	impastoed	nosebleed	redheaded	spikenard	unadvised
dashboard	frolicked	ingrained	notochord	redoubted	spiralled	unalloyed
debauched	frontward	inspanned	nucleated	refuelled	spoonfeed	unaltered
deerhound	fulfilled	instilled	nursemaid	regretted	springald	unashamed
depressed	funnelled	integrand	nymphalid	reprehend	stackyard	unbiassed
dermatoid	galleried	interbred	obligated	reprimand	stagehand	unblessed
descended	gallooned	interlard	ocellated	riflebird	staghound	unblinded
dewlapped	gambolled	interwind	octachord	righthand	stairhead	unbounded
dickybird	gangboard	involuted	offhanded	rightward	stalkeyed	unbraided
digitated	garmented	ironbound	onehanded	riverhead	stallfeed	unbridled
dignified	gastropod	ironmould	onelegged	riverweed	starboard	uncharted
dimwitted	gavelkind	isoniazid	openended	roadstead	statehood	unchecked
disaccord	gazehound	jampacked	opinioned	rockbound	steelclad	uncinated
disbarred	geometrid	jaundiced	outgunned	rosinweed	steelhead	unclothed
disbudded	ghostword	jewelweed	outputted	roughshod	steelyard	unclouded
discalced	giltedged	kennelled	outspread	roundhead	stellated	uncounted
dishfaced	glandered	kidnapped	outwitted	safeguard	stepchild	uncovered
dispelled	gneissoid	kingdomed	overboard	sainthood	sternward	uncreated
disregard	goddamned	kingsized	overcloud	salmonoid	stinkweed	uncropped
distilled	goldenrod	laminated	overcrowd	sandalled	stinkwood	uncrossed
disturbed	goldfield	lancewood	overheard	sandblind	stockyard	uncrowned
dixieland	gooseherd	Langobard	overjoyed	sangfroid	stokehold	undamaged
doglegged	Gradgrind	laurelled	oversexed	sapanwood	stonecold	undaunted
dopefiend	granitoid	leafmould	oversized	sapheaded	stonedead	undecided
downfield	grassland	leasehold	overspend	satinbird	storiated	undefined
draghound	gravelled	leaseland	overwound	satinwood	stormbird	underbred
dreamland	graveyard	liberated	oysterbed	scarehead	submitted	undergird
driftweed	greeneyed	liegelord	panoplied	sciaenoid	sunburned	undergrad
driftwood	greensand	lifeblood	parapeted	scombroid	suntanned	underhand
drivelled	greenweed	lifeguard	parcelled	scorecard	surfboard	underlaid
duckboard	greenwood	lifesized	patinated	scorpioid	surpliced	underpaid
dumbfound	greybeard	lightwood	patrolled	scrapyard	swearword	undersold

underwood	abradable	amendable	avalanche	bracteole	catchpole	coherence	
undivided	abscissae	amourette	aventaile	Brahminee	catechise	coiffeuse	
undoubted	abundance	amphibole	avertible	braincase	causative	colemouse	
undreamed	acceptive	amplitude	avoidable	brainwave	cauterise	colleague	
undulated	accidence	analogise	avoidance	brakeshoe	cavalcade	colligate	
unfeigned	acclimate	anatomise	awardable	branchiae	ceasefire	collimate	
unfledged	accretive	anchorage	azeotrope	brasserie	celandine	collocate	
unfleshed	accusable	anchorite	babacoote	brassiere	celebrate	collotype	
unfounded	acescence	anchylose	bacchante	breadline	cellarage	collusive	
unguarded	acetamide	androgyne	backslide	breadtree	cellulose	colonnade	
unhurried	acetylate	anglesite	backspace	breakable	cementite	colubrine	
unicuspid	acetylene	anglicise	backstage	brecciate	centipede	columbine	
unknitted	aciculate	anhydride	bacterise	bretasche	cerebrate	columbite	
unlearned	acidulate	anhydrite	bagatelle	bridecake	certitude	combative	
unlimited	aconitine	animalise	bainmarie	briefcase	cerussite	combinate	
unmatched	acquiesce	anklebone	bakehouse	brimstone	challenge	comfiture	
unpeopled	actualise	annoyance	balkanise	briquette	chamomile	commingle	
unplugged	acuminate	anomalure	ballistae	Briticise	champagne	comminute	
unplumbed	adaptable	anorthite	baltimore	broadside	champleve	committee	
unpointed	addictive	antennule	bamboozle	broadwise	chanteuse	commodore	
unruffled	addressee	anticline	banderole	brochette	chaperone	commonage	
unscathed	adducible	antiquate	bandoline	brokerage	charlotte	communise	
unsettled	adductive	antitrade	banjulele	broomrape	charmeuse	commutate	
unsighted	adenosine	aperitive	banquette	brushfire	checkmate	composite	
unskilled	adherence	apiculate	barbarise	brutalise	cheekbone	composure	
unspotted	adipocere	apologise	barbitone	bryophyte	chemitype	concentre	
unstopped	admeasure	appellate	barcarole	buhrstone	cherrypie	concierge	
unstudied	adminicle	appendage	bargepole	bullytree	chevelure	concourse	
unsullied	admirable	appetence	Barmecide	bumblebee	chibouque	concubine	
untouched	admissive	appliance	barricade	bunkhouse	chickadee	conducive	
untrussed	admixture	appointee	bastinade	burlesque	chickaree	confervae	
untutored	adoptable	approbate	bathhouse	burrstone	childlike	configure	
unwearied	adsorbate	aquaplane	batholite	butadiene	chinaware	conjugate	
unwrapped	adumbrate	aquarelle	battleaxe	butterine	chisquare	connature	
Upanishad	advantage	arabesque	beatitude	Byzantine	chocolate	conscribe	
varioloid	advective	arabicise	bedlamite	caballine	chondrite	consignee	
verandaed	adventive	aragonite	bedraggle	calaboose	chondrule	constable	
volkslied	adventure	arbitrage	bedsettee	calabrese	chophouse	consulage	
waistband	advertise	arbitrate	belemnite	calcarate	chronicle	consulate	
wallboard	advisable	archetype	bellicose	calcicole	cicatrice	convolute	
washboard	aerodrome	argentine	bellyache	calcifuge	cicatrise	cookhouse	
washstand	aerophyte	argentite	belvedere	calculate	cigarette	cooperage	
wasteland	aeroplane	argillite	bengaline	calenture	Cingalese	cooperate	
watchword	aerospace	armistice	bentonite	calibrate	circinate	copesmate	
watershed	aestivate	aromatise	benzidine	caliphate	circulate	copestone	
waterweed	affective	arrearage	benzoline	calmative	cirripede	coproduce	
weakkneed	affiliate	arriviste	berberine	campanile	cisalpine	coprolite	
weathered	affixture	arrogance	bespangle	candidate	citystate	coralline	
webfooted	affluence	arteriole	biconcave	canebrake	claimable	corallite	
weevilled	affricate	artichoke	bifoliate	cannelure	classable	corbeille	
wellfound	aftercare	asbestine	bifurcate	cannonade	classmate	corncrake	
welltimed	afterlife	ascensive	bilabiate	cannulate	clathrate	cornemuse	
westbound	aftertime	ascospore	biosphere	cantabile	clearance	cornstone	
whalehead	agapemone	aspartate	bipartite	Cantonese	clearcole	corporate	
wheyfaced	aggravate	assayable	birdtable	capsulate	cleavable	corpuscle	
whipround	aggregate	assertive	birthrate	capsulise	clientage	correlate	
whirlwind	agitative	associate	bivalence	captivate	clientele	corrosive	
whiskered	agreeable	assonance	bivariate	carbamate	climbable	corrugate	
whitehead	aitchbone	assuasive	blackface	carbamide	clockwise	corticate	
whitewood	alchemise	assumable	blackgame	carbonate	cloisonne	cortisone	
widowbird	alienable	assurance	blameable	carbonise	clubbable	coruscate	
widowhood	allemande	astraddle	blaspheme	carbuncle	clubhouse	corymbose	
windbound	alleviate	astrocyte	blasthole	carburise	coadunate	couchette	
withstand	allocable	astrodome	blastulae	Carmelite	coagulate	coumarone	
withstood	allophone	astrolabe	bluestone	carnitine	coarctate	countable	
wolfhound	allotrope	asymptote	boathouse	carnivore	coastline	courgette	
womanhood	allowable	atacamite	bombasine	carronade	coastwise	coverable	
womankind	allowance	attentive	bombazine	carthorse	cobaltite	coverture	
womenkind	almandine	attenuate	bombilate	cartilage	cocainise	covetable	
wristband	almshouse	attribute	bombinate	cartouche	cochleate	cowardice	
yearround	alongside	aubergine	bondslave	cartridge	Cockaigne	crankcase	
zebrawood	alterable	auditable	bondstone	cassarnpe	cockhorse	crashdive	
zigzagged	altercate	auspicate	booklouse	casserole	coelomate	creatable	
abandonee	alternate	austenite	bookplate	cassimere	coenobite	crenature	
abdicable	aluminate	authorise	brachiate	cassimere	coercible	crenulate	
aberrance	aluminise	autoclave	bookstore	castigate	coffinite	crepitate	
abominate	alveolate	autocycle	boxoffice	catalogue	cogitable	crepuscle	
aborigine	ambulance	autoroute	brachiate	catarhine	cognitive	criminate	
aboutface	ambuscade	available	bracteate	catchable	cognitive	criminate	

```
crinoline deposable duplicate euphonise feculence fruitcake gratitude
criticise deprecate economise evaginate fecundate fruittree gratulate
crocodile depredate ecosphere evaporate fenestrae frustrate gravitate
croquette derivable ecossaise eventuate ferrotype fruticose graywacke
crossable desecrate ecritoire everglade fertilise fulgurate greengage
crossette desiccate ecstasise evincible festinate fulgurite gregarine
crossfade designate ectophyte evocative feudalise fullscale grenadine
crossfire desirable educative evolutive fibroline fulminate greywacke
crosswise desperate effective evolvable fieldfare fungicide grievance
croustade destitute effluence exactable fiendlike furniture grisaille
crushable desuetude eglantine exanimate figurante fusillade gritstone
cryoscope detective eightsome exarchate filoselle fustigate grotesque
cubbyhole determine ejaculate exceptive filtrable gabardine groundage
cucullate detersive elaborate excessive fimbriate gaberdine grubstake
culminate deuterate electrode excisable fioriture gabionade guacamole
cultivate devaluate eliminate excitable firedrake galactose guarantee
cumbrance devastate eloquence exclosure firehouse galantine guideline
curbstone devisable elsewhere exclusive fireplace galingale guiderope
curettage dextrorse elucidate excoriate firestone gallicise guilloche
curtilage diablerie elutriate excretive firstrate gallinule gustative
curvature diabolise emanative exculpate fishplate gallmidge gynophore
cuspidate diaconate embassage excursive fishslice gallonage gyroplane
customise dialogise embracive excusable fissipede gallopade gyroscope
cyanamide diatomite embrangle execrable fivepence gallstone habitable
cyclamate dieselise embrasure executive flagrance galvanise habituate
cymophane difficile embrittle exfoliate flagstone garderobe hackamore
dalliance diffusive embrocate existence flammable garnishee haematite
damascene digestive emendable exonerate flashcube garniture hailstone
Dantesque dilatable emergence exopodite flashtube gasconade hairpiece
deadalive diligence emolliate exosphere floatable gasmantle hairslide
deathlike dimidiate empathise expansile floodgate gastrulae hairspace
debatable dinothere empennage expansive floodtide gatehouse hairstyle
debauchee dipcircle emphasise expatiate flophouse gaucherie halfcaste
debenture dipeptide emulative expensive flowerage gaugeable halfpence
debutante diplomate enclosure expertise flowstone gelignite halfprice
decadence directive encourage expletive fluctuate generable halftitle
decalitre dirigible encrinite explicate fluoresce genialise halophile
decalogue dirigisme endocrine explosive foeticide geologise halophyte
decametre discharge endophyte expulsive folkdance georgette halothane
decastere discourse endoscope expurgate folkweave geosphere hammertoe
deceptive disengage endospore exquisite footloose germanise handbrake
decidable disfigure endurable exsertile footplate germicide handshake
deciduate dislocate endurance exservice foreclose germinate handspike
decilitre dismantle enjoyable exsiccate forejudge gerundive harmaline
decimetre disoblige enrapture extempore foreshore getatable harmonise
decistere disparage ensheathe extensile forestage geyserite harmotome
deckhouse disparate enterable extensive foretaste ghostlike Hashemite
declinate dispeople enthymeme extenuate forgeable giantlike Hashimite
decollate displease entophyte extirpate formalise gingerade hawsehole
decollete disposure entourage extorsive formative gingerale hawsepipe
decompose dispraise entrecote extortive formicate ginpalace headphone
decretive disrepute enucleate extradite formulate girandole headpiece
decussate dissemble enumerate extricate formulise glabellae headstone
deducible dissipate enunciate extrusive fornicate gladstone heartache
deductive dissolute enwreathe exuberate fortalice glamorise heartfree
defalcate dividable epaulette exudative fortitude glassware heartsore
defeature divisible ephedrine exultance fortunate glomerate heelpiece
defective doctorate epicentre eyeglance fortyfive glomerule heliotype
defensive dogmatise epidosite fabricate fossilise gloryhole hellebore
deference dominance epitomise facsimile fosterage glucoside hellenise
definable doorframe equipoise factitive fourpence glutamate hemicycle
defoliate doorplate equitable factorage fourscore glyceride hemitrope
dehydrate dorbeetle equivoque factorise fragrance glycerine herbicide
delftware dosshouse eradicate fairylike franchise glycoside herbivore
delineate doubtable erstwhile fairytale frangible gneissose herborise
deludable downgrade erythrite faithcure freehouse goldeneye heritable
demagogue downstage escapable fancyfree freelance gonophore hermitage
demarcate drainpipe escortage fandangle freerange gorgonise hesitance
demimonde dramatise esperance fanfarade freestone Gothamite hessonite
demitasse drawplate espionage fantasise freestyle gothicise hexastyle
demurrage drayhorse esplanade farandole freezable grandiose hibernate
denigrate dreamlike estimable farestage frequence grandsire hiddenite
denitrate drinkable estoppage farmhouse fricassee grantable hierodule
deodorise dripstone estrapade fascicule fricative granulate highgrade
deoxidise dropscene estuarine fascinate frontline granulite Himyarite
departure dropscone esurience fatigable frontpage granulose hindrance
depasture drugstore etiquette faveolate frontwise grapevine hirundine
depictive dubitable eucaryote favourite frostbite graspable histamine
depletive dulcitude euphemise febrifuge fructuate graticule histidine
```

```
hitchhike  incunable  ironstone  libertine  margarine  modernise  numerable
Hitlerite  incurable  irradiate  licensure  margarite  molybdate  nummulite
hoarstone  incursive  irrigable  lifecycle  marginate  monocline  nuncupate
holophote  incurvate  irritable  lifeforce  marlstone  monocoque  nutritive
holystone  indelible  irruptive  lifestyle  marmalade  monologue  oasthouse
homologue  indenture  isochrone  lifetable  martyrise  monoplane  obcordate
homophone  Indianise  isogamete  lightsome  masculine  monorhyme  obedience
homuncule  indigence  isolative  lilywhite  masticate  monostyle  obeisance
hornstone  indispose  isomerise  limejuice  matricide  monotreme  obfuscate
horoscope  indolence  isooctane  limestone  matronage  monticule  objective
horsehide  inducible  Israelite  limitable  matronise  monzonite  objurgate
horseshoe  inductive  italicise  limousine  mattamore  moonquake  obsecrate
hortative  inebriate  iterative  linearise  maybeetle  moonscape  obsessive
housebote  ineffable  itinerate  lineolate  meandrine  moonshine  obsolesce
housemate  inequable  jackknife  lingulate  meanwhile  moonstone  obstinate
housewife  inerrable  jackplane  lintwhite  mechanise  mortgagee  obtrusive
humblebee  infantile  jacksnipe  lioncelle  mediatise  mossagate  occlusive
humiliate  infantine  jacquerie  liquidate  mediative  motorable  octastyle
hurricane  infatuate  jargonise  liquidise  medicable  motorbike  octostyle
hybridise  infective  jessamine  liquorice  medullate  motorcade  odalisque
hydathode  inferable  jesuitise  lithesome  megacycle  mouldable  oenophile
hydrazine  inference  Johannine  lithopone  megaphone  mountable  offcentre
hydrocele  infertile  josshouse  litigable  megaspore  mousehole  offchance
hydrolyse  influence  jubilance  lixiviate  melaphyre  moustache  offensive
hydrolyte  infuriate  Judastree  loadstone  meliorate  mucronate  officiate
hydrosome  infuscate  juniorate  loathsome  memorable  multilane  olfactive
hydroxide  infusible  Junoesque  lobscouse  menadione  multitude  Oligocene
hypallage  ingestive  juxtapose  locatable  menagerie  mumchance  olivenite
hyperbole  inherence  kaolinise  lodestone  Mennonite  muscadine  omissible
hyphenate  injustice  kaolinite  lodgepole  menopause  muscarine  onlicence
hypnotise  innervate  karyotype  Londonise  mepacrine  muscovite  operative
hypocrite  innocence  keelivine  longhouse  mercerise  musteline  opportune
hypostyle  inoculate  kentledge  longitude  mescaline  mutualise  opposable
ideologue  inquiline  kerbstone  longrange  mesmerise  mythicise  optophone
ignitable  insatiate  kerfuffle  longshore  mesophyte  nameplate  orangeade
ignitible  insectile  kilocycle  lookalike  metalline  naphthene  ordinance
ignorable  insensate  kilolitre  lorgnette  metallise  narcotine  organelle
ignorance  inservice  kilometre  loveapple  metaphase  narcotise  organzine
illegible  insincere  kittiwake  lowercase  meteorite  narrative  orientate
imageable  insinuate  kneadable  loxodrome  methadone  natrolite  oriflamme
imbalance  insolence  knifeedge  lubricate  methodise  navigable  originate
imbricate  insoluble  knightage  lucrative  methylate  neathouse  orphanage
imitative  instigate  knockknee  lucubrate  methylene  neckverse  oscillate
immanence  institute  knowledge  luftwaffe  metricate  necrotise  ossifrage
immediate  insurable  labialise  luminance  metricise  nectarine  ostensive
immigrate  insurance  labourite  lunchtime  metronome  negotiate  ostracise
imminence  integrate  lacerable  luxuriate  mezzanine  negritude  otherwise
immixture  intensive  lacertine  macedoine  micaslate  nemertine  oubliette
immovable  intercede  laciniate  machinate  microcyte  neologise  overborne
immutable  interface  lacrimose  macrocyte  microlite  neoterise  overdrive
impassive  interfere  lacrymose  madeleine  micropyle  nepheline  overglaze
impedance  interfile  laevulose  madrepore  microsome  nephelite  overgraze
impetrate  interfuse  lagniappe  magdalene  microtome  nervature  overissue
implicate  interlace  lamellate  magnesite  microtone  nescience  overprice
implosive  interline  lamellose  magnetise  microwave  nevermore  overstate
importune  interlope  lampshade  magnetite  micturate  niccolite  overvalue
impostume  interlude  lancinate  magnitude  midinette  nickelise  overwrite
imposture  internode  landgrave  maharanee  milestone  nictitate  overwrote
impotence  interpage  landscape  mailplane  milkshake  nightlife  oxygenate
imprecate  interpose  landslide  mainbrace  millepede  nightline  oxygenise
imprecise  intervene  langouste  majorette  millepore  nightmare  ozocerite
improvise  interwove  lapstrake  majuscule  millerite  nightside  ozokerite
impudence  interzone  lardycake  malachite  millipede  nighttime  packhorse
impulsive  intestate  larvicide  malleable  millstone  nigritude  paillasse
imputable  intestine  lassitude  malthouse  miniature  nigrosine  paillette
inanimate  intricate  laudative  malvoisie  minuscule  ninepence  pairhorse
inaudible  introduce  laughable  mamillate  misadvise  Nipponese  palafitte
inbreathe  intrusive  lavaliere  mammonite  misbecome  nitratine  palatable
incapable  intuitive  lazzarone  mandarine  misbehave  nominable  palletise
incarnate  intumesce  learnable  mandoline  miscegene  nonviable  palliasse
incentive  invective  leastwise  manducate  miscegine  normalise  palmipede
inceptive  inventive  legerline  manganate  mischance  Normanise  palmitate
incidence  inversive  legislate  manganese  miscreate  normative  palpitate
inclosure  invertase  lendlease  manganite  miserable  noseflute  palsgrave
inclusive  inviolate  leptosome  manhandle  mishandle  nosepiece  panhandle
incommode  invisible  leucocyte  manoeuvre  mismanage  novelette  pantomime
incondite  involucre  leucotome  manticore  mistletoe  noviciate  pantyhose
inculcate  ionisable  leukocyte  marcasite  mitigable  novitiate  papeterie
inculpate  irascible  Levantine  marchpane  mitraille  nullipore  papillate
```

papillose	phototype	principle	recapture	revisable	selfdrive	snowscape
papillote	picturise	printable	receptive	revivable	selfimage	snowwhite
parachute	piecerate	privative	recessive	revocable	selfpride	soapstone
Paraclete	pierrette	privilege	rechauffe	revulsive	semanteme	socialise
parbuckle	pilferage	probative	recherche	rhodamine	semaphore	socialite
parentage	pineapple	procedure	reclinate	rhodolite	semblable	solemnise
parfleche	pinnipede	procreate	reclusive	rhodonite	semblance	soleplate
parricide	pinnulate	proenzyme	recognise	rhythmise	semibreve	solitaire
parsonage	pinstripe	programme	recoinage	ridgepole	semiplume	solmisate
partitive	pipestone	prolamine	recombine	ridgetile	sensitise	somewhere
partridge	pirouette	prolative	recompose	rightable	sensitive	somewhile
pasodoble	pitchpipe	prolicide	reconcile	rigmarole	sentenate	songcycle
passerine	pivotable	prologise	recondite	ringfence	sentience	sonnetise
passivate	placeable	promenade	reconvene	ringshake	separable	sophomore
pastorale	placename	promotive	rectangle	ringsnake	sepiolite	sorbapple
pastorate	placentae	pronounce	rectitude	ritualise	sepulchre	sortilege
pasturage	plaintive	propagate	rectorate	riverside	sepulture	soubrette
patellate	plantable	propylene	recursive	roadhouse	serialise	Soudanese
patricide	plantlike	prorogate	recusance	rocambole	serinette	soundhole
patronage	platinise	proscribe	redingote	rockbrake	sermonise	soundwave
patronise	platitude	prosecute	redolence	rocksnake	serrefile	soupplate
pauperise	Platonise	proselyte	reducible	roofplate	serrulate	sovietise
peaceable	plausible	prostrate	reductive	roseapple	serviette	spacetime
peacetime	playhouse	protamine	reeducate	rosenoble	servitude	spatulate
pectinate	pleadable	prototype	reenforce	rotatable	setsquare	speakable
pedagogue	pleasance	proximate	reexamine	rowantree	severable	spearside
pegmatite	Pleiocene	prurience	referable	rubberise	severance	spectacle
Pekingese	plenitude	publicise	reference	rubellite	sexualise	speculate
pelletise	plicature	puissance	reflexive	rubicelle	shadetree	spendable
pendulate	plumbline	pullulate	refluence	rubricate	shakeable	spiculate
penduline	plumulate	pulmonate	refusable	ruggedise	shapeable	spinulose
peneplane	plumulose	pulpstone	refutable	runcinate	sheepcote	spodumene
penetrate	pluralise	pulsatile	rehydrate	rusticate	sheeplice	spokewise
penitence	podzolise	pulserate	reimburse	sabbatise	sheldrake	sporulate
pentangle	poeticise	pulverise	reinforce	sacculate	shelflife	spouthole
penthouse	pointille	pulvinate	reinstate	sacrifice	shellfire	squarrose
peptonise	pointlace	punchline	reiterate	sacrilege	shemozzle	stabilise
percaline	pokerface	punctuate	relevance	safranine	shipshape	stackable
perchance	politesse	pupillage	religiose	sagittate	shockable	Stagirite
percolate	pollinate	purgative	reliquiae	sailplane	shoeshine	stainable
peregrine	polonaise	purposive	reluctate	saintlike	shogunate	staircase
perennate	polyamide	purselike	remanence	salangane	shootable	stalemate
perforate	polyphase	pursuable	remeasure	saltglaze	shoreline	staminate
perfusive	polyphone	pursuance	remediate	saltpetre	shoreside	stampnote
periclase	polythene	purulence	reminisce	sandstone	shortcake	standpipe
pericycle	poorhouse	pustulate	removable	sandtable	shortwave	starapple
periodate	porbeagle	pyroscope	rencontre	satellite	showpiece	starstone
periscope	porcupine	quadrigae	renewable	satinette	showplace	stateside
peristome	portative	quadrille	reparable	saturable	shrewmice	statewide
peristyle	porterage	quadruple	repayable	saturnine	shrinkage	statuette
permeable	portreeve	quartette	repechage	saxifrage	sibilance	steampipe
permeance	posthaste	quartzite	replicate	saxophone	sibylline	stenotype
permutate	posthorse	quartzose	reportage	scalelike	siccative	stepdance
persecute	posthouse	queenlike	reprobate	scapolite	sickleave	sterilise
persevere	postulate	quicklime	reproduce	scarfwise	sideissue	stevedore
personage	potentate	quinoline	repudiate	scheelite	sideswipe	stimulate
personate	poundcake	quintette	repulsive	schistose	sidetable	stingaree
pervasive	pourboire	quintuple	reputable	scolecite	sigillate	stipitate
pesthouse	poussette	quittance	requisite	Scoticise	signalise	stipulate
pesticide	powerdive	rabbinate	rerebrace	screwpile	signature	stockdove
petechiae	pranksome	racehorse	rerelease	screwpine	siliquose	stockpile
pethidine	precative	radiative	reremouse	scrimmage	siltstone	stokehole
petiolate	precipice	raffinate	resalable	scripture	simulacre	stolonate
petiolule	preconise	raffinose	reshuffle	scrummage	Sinhalese	stoneware
petulance	predative	raingauge	residence	sculpture	sinologue	stormcone
phagocyte	predicate	randomise	resoluble	seachange	sinophile	storyline
phalarope	preengage	rapidfire	resonance	seagirdle	siphonage	stovepipe
phenacite	prefigure	rationale	resoluble	seanettle	siphuncle	striature
phenakite	pregnable	razoredge	resonance	seatangle	skedaddle	stricture
phenotype	prejudice	reachable	restitute	secretage	slabstone	stridence
pheromone	prelatise	reactance	resumable	seclusive	slantwise	strobilae
phonetise	prelature	readymade	resurface	secretage	sliderule	strongyle
phonolite	prelusive	reanimate	retaliate	secretive	slopewise	structure
phosphate	premature	rearhorse	retentive	securable	smalltime	studhorse
phosphene	presbyope	rearmouse	reticence	seductive	smoketree	stylobate
phosphide	prescribe	rearrange	retinulae	segregate	snakebite	subalpine
phosphine	presentee	rebaptise	retrocede	selective	snakelike	subdivide
phosphite	preterite	rebukable	retrousse	selfabuse	snowflake	subduable
photogene	primitive	recalesce	reverence	selfaware	snowgoose	subjugate

```
sublimate  thickknee  umbellate  viscerate  yohimbine  breathing  goffering
submarine  thighbone  umbellule  visitable  breeching  breeching  grappling
subrogate  thinkable  unbalance  visualise  zibelline  breveting  groundhog
subscribe  thirdrate  undeceive  vitelline  zincotype  bristling  grounding
subsidise  thorntree  underdone  viverrine  zinkenite  buffeting  gruelling
substance  threesome  undergone  vivianite  zygospore  buttygang  grumbling
substrate  thrombose  underline  vizierate  basrelief  caballing  guardring
subtilise  thumbhole  undermine  volteface  bombproof  cacholong  guttering
succinate  thylacine  underrate  vorticose  bookshelf  carolling  hamstring
suffocate  thyroxine  underripe  vouchsafe  broadleaf  carpetbag  hamstrung
sugarcane  tidegauge  underside  vulcanise  bullybeef  carpeting  hankering
sultanate  tigerseye  undertake  vulcanite  cowlstaff  cavilling  happening
summarise  tightrope  undertone  vulgarise  crossruff  centering  harrowing
summative  tightwire  uneatable  vulpinite  disbelief  centreing  hatchling
sunlounge  tilestone  unifiable  vulturine  feedstuff  chaingang  havocking
sunspurge  timelapse  unnamable  waggonage  fireproof  chickling  hearthrug
sunstroke  timepiece  unreserve  Wagnerite  flagstaff  churching  hocussing
superable  timetable  unsayable  wagonette  foodstuff  cleansing  houseflag
superfine  titillate  unshackle  waistline  foolproof  cliffhang  illboding
superfuse  titlepage  unsheathe  waldgrave  germproof  colouring  impelling
superpose  tittivate  untenable  wallplate  halfstaff  confiding  impending
supersede  toadstone  unwelcome  wapentake  headscarf  crackling  incurring
supervene  tolerable  uppercase  warehouse  interleaf  crediting  inferring
supervise  tolerance  uraninite  warrantee  leitmotif  crippling  infilling
suppurate  tollhouse  urceolate  washhouse  looseleaf  cupelling  inflowing
surcharge  tombstone  usherette  wastepipe  misbelief  curveting  ingrowing
surcingle  tomentose  utterable  watchable  mothproof  dayspring  inpouring
surculose  tonguetie  utterance  watchcase  overproof  debagging  insetting
surrogate  toolhouse  uvarovite  watchfire  overstuff  debarring  interring
swangoose  toothache  uxoricide  watergate  pikestaff  debugging  japanning
swimmable  toothsome  vaccinate  waterhole  plaintiff  deferring  jitterbug
swordcane  torchrace  vacillate  waterline  rainproof  demanding  junketing
swordlike  totempole  vacuolate  waterpipe  rustproof  demitting  kurrajong
syllabise  touchable  valentine  waterside  scaleleaf  demobbing  labelling
syllogise  touchhole  vandalise  waveguide  scrumhalf  demurring  lathering
sylphlike  touchline  vaporable  wavellite  shotproof  designing  latticing
sylvanite  touchtype  variegate  wayzgoose  skewwhiff  deterring  launching
symbolise  townhouse  variolate  wearisome  stonedeaf  devilling  lawgiving
synagogue  townscape  variolite  wedgewise  sugarloaf  diphthong  leavening
syncopate  traceable  vassalage  weighable  tableleaf  disarming  lettering
syndicate  tracheate  vastitude  whalebone  wagonroof  diverting  levelling
synoecete  tractable  vegetable  wheelbase  waterleaf  donothing  libelling
syphilise  tradename  vehemence  wherefore  windproof  doodlebug  lightning
tablature  trainable  veinstone  whetstone  abhorring  dowelling  lingering
tableware  transfuse  velodrome  whinstone  abounding  earthling  litterbug
tachylite  translate  venerable  whipsnake  abseiling  easygoing  lumbering
tachylyte  transmute  vengeance  whiteface  absorbing  embedding  maddening
tailpiece  transpire  ventilate  wholesale  according  embussing  magicking
talkative  transpose  ventricle  wholesome  adjoining  endearing  maneating
tamponade  trattorie  veratrine  wideawake  adlibbing  engraving  marketing
tangerine  treatable  verbalise  widthwise  admitting  enrolling  metalling
tanpickle  treillage  verbicide  wieldable  affecting  equalling  mimicking
tantalate  trematode  veritable  willemite  agonising  equipping  misgiving
tantalise  tremolite  vermicide  winestone  allotting  estopping  modelling
tantalite  trialogue  vermicule  winterise  annulling  exceeding  monthling
taskforce  tribunate  vermifuge  wiregauze  appalling  excelling  nightlong
teachable  trichinae  verminate  witherite  appealing  excepting  nonjuring
teakettle  tridymite  vernalise  woebegone  arresting  expecting  nurseling
technique  trilobate  verrucose  wolfsbane  ashlaring  expelling  occurring
telephone  trilobite  versatile  wolverene  awakening  extolling  offspring
telescope  triptyque  vertebrae  wolverine  backslang  faggoting  onsetting
tellurate  triturate  vestibule  womanlike  battening  fairyring  outgiving
telluride  trochleae  vestiture  woodlouse  bedspring  farseeing  overlying
tellurite  trysquare  vibratile  workhorse  befitting  fastening  packaging
telophase  tubercule  vibrative  workhouse  befogging  fingering  panelling
temperate  tuliptree  vibrissae  workpiece  begetting  finicking  panicking
temporise  tungstate  vicariate  worktable  beginning  firstling  pedalling
temptable  turbinate  vicereine  worldwide  besetting  fledgling  perilling
tenderise  turnstile  victimise  worrisome  besotting  flouncing  perishing
tentative  turnstone  victorine  wulfenite  bevelling  flowering  picketing
tenthrate  turntable  videotape  wyandotte  billabong  focussing  plainsong
terminate  turpitude  vigilance  Wyclifite  binturong  following  plaything
terramare  turquoise  vigilante  Xanthippe  blackflag  foregoing  potholing
terrorise  twayblade  villanage  xenophile  boomerang  forgiving  prayerrug
testdrive  twentyone  villenage  xenophobe  boomslang  foundling  preceding
tetradite  twistable  vindicate  xerophile  borrowing  galloping  pressgang
teutonise  typewrite  violative  xerophyte  bowstring  gammoning  promising
theologue  tyrannise  virgulate  xparticle  brambling  gardening  providing
therefore  uintahite  virulence  xylophone  brandling  gathering  provoking
```

punishing	strouding	baboonish	Hexateuch	roodcloth	campanili	framework
quibbling	strumming	backcloth	hodograph	Roumansch	charivari	frostwork
rationing	strutting	baksheesh	holograph	sackcloth	comitadji	gangplank
ravelling	suffering	bandwidth	homeopath	sagebrush	coryphaei	gaolbreak
ravishing	supposing	barograph	homograph	sailcloth	dziggetai	glasswork
reasoning	surfacing	batholith	hopscotch	sallowish	eucalypti	goldbrick
rebelling	surveying	bellpunch	hoydenish	saltmarsh	fasciculi	gooseneck
rebidding	swaddling	billionth	hundredth	sandarach	garibaldi	greenback
rebutting	swingeing	birdwatch	ideograph	sasquatch	glissandi	grillwork
recapping	tailoring	bismillah	idiograph	Sassenach	glomeruli	guardbook
reckoning	taxpaying	bitterish	inshallah	scaldfish	homunculi	guesswork
recording	thatching	blackfish	ironsmith	scalefish	impresari	guidebook
recurring	thrashing	blackwash	jellyfish	sciagraph	jaborandi	halftrack
referring	thrilling	bloodbath	killifish	serigraph	lazzaroni	handiwork
refitting	throbbing	blowtorch	kittenish	sheatfish	maharishi	handywork
Reichstag	thrumming	bobsleigh	kymograph	Shechinah	oesophagi	hatchback
rejoicing	tiedyeing	brainwash	labyrinth	sheepwash	Pakistani	haversack
remitting	timbering	brandreth	laccolith	shellfish	patchouli	headstock
repelling	tittuping	brightish	lagomorph	shillelah	pizzicati	heartsick
repotting	torchsong	buckshish	lastditch	sixteenth	potpourri	heathcock
rerunning	totalling	bucktooth	lickerish	skiagraph	ranunculi	hollyhock
resetting	towelling	bullfinch	liquorish	slightish	sgraffiti	honkytonk
resitting	troutling	cailleach	locksmith	slipcoach	spaghetti	hornwrack
revelling	tuckerbag	canetrash	logogriph	slowcoach	triumviri	horseback
revetting	tumblebug	cavendish	loincloth	slowmatch	antiknock	houseleek
revolting	twinkling	cerecloth	loudmouth	smokebush	applejack	housework
rewarding	unbending	cerograph	lovematch	smoothish	backtrack	huckaback
rivalling	unceasing	chaffinch	macintosh	snailfish	bailiwick	hunchback
rivelling	underhung	cockroach	maharajah	snipefish	barmbrack	inglenook
russeting	underling	colocynth	maidenish	snowbroth	beanstalk	interlink
saddlebag	undersong	cornbrash	mammonish	sociopath	beefsteak	interlock
sailoring	underwing	crampfish	matriarch	songsmith	bergamask	jailbreak
saintling	unfailing	cranreuch	megadeath	sourdough	billycock	jossstick
scallawag	unfeeling	crossfish	mesomorph	spearfish	birchbark	ladysmock
scallywag	unfitting	cystolith	microlith	spicebush	birthmark	lampblack
scantling	unheeding	czarevich	micromesh	squeamish	blackbuck	lancejack
scarfring	unknowing	dahabiyah	milktooth	squirarch	blackcock	lapstreak
schilling	unmeaning	devilfish	millionth	stalworth	blackjack	leafstalk
schoolbag	unpegging	dipswitch	Mondayish	statolith	blueblack	livestock
schooling	unsmiling	disavouch	monkeyish	stockfish	boardwalk	loanshark
scorching	unsparing	disbranch	monograph	stonefish	bootblack	lowerdeck
scramming	unweeting	dishcloth	monostich	stopwatch	breakneck	mahlstick
scrapping	unwilling	disrelish	mouthwash	strongish	brickwork	mallemuck
screening	unwinking	dogstooth	nailbrush	subbranch	brushwork	matchlock
scrubbing	unwitting	dragonish	neckcloth	succotash	bushwhack	maulstick
seafaring	unzipping	ectomorph	neuropath	swellfish	camelback	Menshevik
searching	uplifting	eidograph	newsflash	swordfish	cheapjack	metalwork
seasoning	upsetting	eightieth	ninetieth	taioseach	chopstick	mollymawk
shambling	vapouring	eightyish	nomograph	tallowish	clockwork	nighthawk
shaveling	veneering	embellish	oleograph	telegraph	coachwork	nightwork
shearling	vetchling	endolymph	osteopath	terebinth	cornstalk	orderbook
sheathing	walloping	endomorph	Ostrogoth	therewith	crookback	overcheck
shieldbug	wallydrag	ergograph	outgrowth	thirtieth	crookneck	overstock
shredding	wandering	establish	overmatch	thornbush	crosslink	overtrick
shrugging	wayfaring	facecloth	overpitch	tigermoth	crosstalk	paintwork
sickening	weighting	fifteenth	overreach	tollbooth	cuttysark	paperback
singalong	welcoming	flarepath	overwatch	traycloth	deathmask	paperwork
sitzkrieg	wellbeing	footcloth	overweigh	trierarch	dirttrack	patchwork
skijoring	westering	forasmuch	paragraph	trunkfish	disembark	pickaback
skydiving	wheedling	forereach	paramorph	tsarevich	drawnwork	piecework
smuggling	whirligig	forthwith	paranymph	twentieth	drumstick	piggyback
something	whistling	fourflush	patriarch	ultrahigh	eiderduck	piggybank
sparkplug	whitening	frogmarch	pergunnah	umpteenth	earthwork	pinchbeck
spindling	whitewing	gatecrash	perilymph	unselfish	fancywork	pinchcock
splitting	whizzbang	gemutlich	perimorph	vapourish	feedstock	pipsqueak
spongebag	withering	Germanish	pikeperch	vulturish	fenugreek	pitchdark
sprigging	worldling	gibberish	pilotfish	washcloth	fieldbook	pitchfork
springing	wrestling	globefish	polygraph	waterbath	fieldwork	placekick
squatting	yellowdog	goalmouth	polymorph	wherewith	firebreak	platemark
squibbing	yodelling	goldfinch	polyptych	whitefish	firebrick	pokerwork
squidding	youngling	goldsmith	premonish	whitewash	firebreak	poppycock
startling	aerograph	groundash	prettyish	willowish	firebrick	preshrink
stippling	aftermath	hairbrush	pyracanth	woodnymph	fishyback	preshrunk
straphang	allograph	haircloth	Quakerish	wordsmith	flagstick	pressmark
strapping	allomorph	halftruth	razorfish	workbench	flashback	presswork
streaking	anabranch	headcloth	refurbish	xeromorph	flintlock	psalmbook
stripling	angelfish	hemistich	refurnish	xylograph	floodmark	racetrack
stripping	autograph	hemstitch	replenish	yellowish	footstalk	raincheck
stropping	autotroph	hexastich	republish	Ashkenazi	forespeak	razorback

riverbank
roadblock
rootstock
roughneck
sandcrack
scalplock
scenedock
scorebook
scrapbook
sheephook
sheeptick
sheepwalk
sheerhulk
shellduck
shelfmark
shellback
shellbark
shellwork
shipwreck
shoeblack
sidetrack
skinflick
slapstick
slingback
smokejack
snowblink
spadework
spoonbeak
spotcheck
springbok
steelwork
steenkirk
stickwork
stockbook
stonework
stormcock
storybook
strapwork
stylebook
sunstruck
sweepback
sweettalk
sweptback
tabletalk
thinktank
thornback
throwback
thumbmark
thumbtack
toastrack
toothpick
touchmark
townsfolk
trademark
undertook
waterbuck
watermark
whaleback
wheelwork
whipstock
windbreak
wisecrack
womenfolk
woodblock
woodchuck
yardstick
abdominal
ablatival
accentual
acidophil
acquittal
acropetal
actuarial
adenoidal
adnominal
adverbial
agnatical
altricial
ambrosial

amyloidal
ancestral
anecdotal
angelical
anglophil
antefixal
antenatal
antidotal
antinodal
antinovel
antipodal
antiviral
appraisal
araneidal
archangel
archducal
armigeral
arsenical
ascetical
aspectual
auctorial
authorial
autosomal
azimuthal
bacchanal
backpedal
bacterial
baptismal
barrelful
basipetal
basketful
beautiful
betrothal
bicameral
bicipital
bilateral
bilgekeel
bilingual
biliteral
binominal
blackball
blackmail
bombshell
bookstall
botanical
bottleful
bountiful
branchial
bridewell
broadtail
bronchial
bucketful
bursarial
bushelful
cacuminal
cadastral
cadential
calcaneal
calycinal
campstool
canonical
cantorial
cartwheel
catarrhal
catchpoll
caterwaul
cathedral
celestial
censorial
chainmail
chanceful
changeful
chaparral
chockfull
chronical
clamshell
classical
claustral
cloistral

coccygeal
cochineal
cockatiel
coeternal
collegial
colloidal
colourful
commensal
committal
comprisal
comptroll
conferral
conformal
congenial
connubial
continual
convivial
corporeal
coseismal
creatural
crinoidal
crossbill
cryptical
cursorial
custodial
cycloidal
dancehall
dandiacal
daredevil
dayschool
deathroll
decagonal
decapodal
deceitful
decennial
decontrol
deistical
dialectal
diametral
dichasial
disannual
disavowal
disbursal
discoidal
disentail
dismissal
dispersal
dissocial
doctorial
doctrinal
dominical
drawerful
driftsail
dropsical
druidical
dynamical
ecclesial
editorial
effectual
effluvial
effortful
elegiacal
elemental
embryonal
emotional
empirical
enchorial
endosteal
entrammel
ephemeral
epidermal
episcopal
epiphytal
equivocal
eristical
erratical
essential

etherical
ethmoidal
factional
factorial
faldstool
fanatical
fatidical
fenestral
fictional
financial
firedrill
fluxional
footstall
footstool
forestall
forgetful
fossorial
fourwheel
fraternal
freewheel
frightful
funebrial
galenical
Gallophil
gearwheel
genetical
genitival
genocidal
gerundial
glassgall
goosegirl
graphical
gristmill
groundsel
guardrail
guildhall
gymnasial
halfshell
handwheel
hardshell
hawksbill
headstall
healthful
heretical
hexagonal
highlevel
hodiernal
homicidal
horsetail
housecarl
hydrofoil
hypethral
hypnoidal
hypocotyl
identical
idiotical
illiberal
illogical
impartial
inaugural
isoclinal
isohyetal
juridical
khedivial
lachrymal
lampshell
laryngeal
Levitical
libidinal
longaeval
lumbrical
lunitidal
magistral
marestail
marmoreal
marsupial
masterful
matutinal
mediaeval

medicinal
meningeal
menstrual
mercurial
mesophyll
microbial
millwheel
mispickel
monarchal
moneybill
monodical
monsoonal
moschatel
multifoil
municipal
musichall
necrophil
nectarial
needleful
negroidal
negrophil
nightfall
nocturnal
nonpareil
numbskull
numerical
nutweevil
obconical
obsequial
occipital
octagonal
octennial
officinal
olecranal
oratorial
orificial
overspill
oviductal
packdrill
palpebral
paludinal
palustral
papergirl
paradisal
parochial
passional
penumbral
perennial
perinatal
perpetual
personnel
petechial
photocell
photophil
pictorial
piecemeal
pimpernel
piratical
placental
plentiful
pocketful
polemical
political
polygonal
polytonal
polyvinyl
popliteal
poriferal
portrayal
postnasal
postnatal
potential
practical
praiseful
prayerful
prebendal
precancel
precocial

preschool
presidial
primaeval
primatial
principal
proconsul
prodromal
prosaical
protozoal
Provencal
psychical
puerperal
punchball
punchbowl
purpureal
pyramidal
quantical
quizzical
raptorial
razorbill
recruital
rectorial
regardful
regicidal
regretful
rehearsal
remindful
reposeful
resentful
resultful
retrieval
revictual
rhizoidal
rhonchial
ribosomal
roadmetal
rockdrill
rounceval
Russophil
salesgirl
sartorial
satanical
satirical
saucerful
sceptical
schlemiel
schlemihl
schnitzel
schnorkel
sciential
scoundrel
screwball
sectional
sectorial
seedpearl
segmental
semestral
semifinal
semimetal
semivowel
seneschal
sensorial
sessional
sexennial
shipcanal
shirttail
shortfall
shovelful
sidewheel
sigmoidal
signorial
singspiel
sinistral
Slavophil
smokeball
softpedal
softshell
soritical

sorrowful
sparkcoil
speechful
speedball
speedwell
spherical
spiritual
spirituel
spleenful
spoonbill
sprigtail
spritsail
spurwheel
squamosal
stairwell
stampmill
stapedial
starshell
stational
stercoral
steroidal
stinkball
stomachal
stonecoal
stonewall
stoolball
stormsail
stressful
subaerial
subastral
subcaudal
subcostal
sublethal
submental
subnormal
succursal
suctorial
supercool
surficial
surprisal
sweetmeal
swordtail
sympodial
symposial
synagogal
synclinal
syncytial
syndactyl
synodical
syringeal
teacupful
technical
tectorial
tegmental
tensional
thornbill
thumbnail
toadstool
tonsorial
toponymal
tormentil
torsional
trapezial
traversal
treadmill
tridactyl
triennial
trifacial
trihedral
trinomial
triumphal
trunkcall
tuitional
typemetal
typhoidal
umbilical
undecimal
underseal
undersell

```
undutiful  Caesarism  elbowroom  jetstream  Parseeism  spirillum  abruption
unethical  cairngorm  endoplasm  junkerdom  pauperism  spiritism  accession
unhelpful  calcaneum  endosperm  junkerism  pentagram  squiredom  accordion
uniserial  caldarium  endosteum  kaiserdom  perisperm  stackroom  accretion
unisexual  Calvinism  epicurism  kaiserism  pessimism  Stalinism  Acheulean
universal  capitulum  epiphragm  kibbutzim  petersham  stateroom  Acheulian
unmindful  careerism  epipolism  labialism  petroleum  stillroom  actuation
unmusical  cartogram  equisetum  lanthanum  phonetism  stockroom  addiction
unnatural  Castroism  eremitism  lentiform  phonogram  storeroom  adduction
unskilful  cataclasm  eroticism  ligniform  pictogram  stratagem  ademption
vaticinal  cataclysm  eruciform  Listerism  pipedream  strawworm  admission
vectorial  cataplasm  erythrism  literatim  pisciform  strongarm  adoration
veridical  catechism  esoterism  logarithm  Platonism  strontium  adrenalin
versional  Catharism  eunuchism  Londonism  pluralism  styliform  adulation
vertebral  Celticism  euphemism  macrocosm  Plutonism  subphylum  advection
vestigial  centigram  euphonium  maelstrom  plutonium  sugarplum  affection
vicennial  cerastium  exoticism  Magianism  poeticism  sutteeism  afflation
viceregal  cheongsam  extremism  magnalium  pollinium  syllabism  aflatoxin
viceroyal  chernozem  Fabianism  magnesium  polygonum  syllogism  afternoon
vicesimal  classroom  Falangism  magnetism  potassium  symbolism  agitation
vigesimal  claviform  falciform  Malayalam  presidium  sympodium  Algonkian
viricidal  clitellum  fastigium  mammiform  pressroom  symposium  Algonquin
vizierial  cloakroom  Fenianism  mammonism  prettyism  syncytium  alpenhorn
watercool  Cobdenism  fetichism  mannerism  princedom  synergism  amazonian
waterfall  cocainism  fetishism  manubrium  pseudonym  tarantism  amoebaean
waterfowl  coccidium  feudalism  marsupium  pterygium  taraxacum  amphibian
watermill  coenobium  fibriform  martyrdom  pycnidium  Tartufism  amygdalin
wheatmeal  cofferdam  firealarm  masochism  pyrethrum  tegmentum  amylopsin
whimsical  colchicum  flabellum  masterdom  Quakerdom  tellurium  anchorman
whirlpool  collegium  flagellum  mausoleum  Quakerism  tenaculum  angleiron
Whitehall  collyrium  formalism  mechanism  quercetum  terminism  animation
wholemeal  colosseum  fraenulum  meliorism  quitclaim  terrarium  annelidan
witchmeal  colostrum  fullcream  Mendelism  quixotism  terrorism  anthelion
wonderful  columbium  fungiform  menstruum  rabbinism  tetragram  anthemion
wormwheel  Cominform  gallicism  mentalism  racialism  Teutonism  anthocyan
wychhazel  commendam  galvanism  mesmerism  radiogram  therefrom  anthozoan
absurdism  communism  ganderism  metaplasm  rainstorm  thralldom  anticodon
academism  contagium  gastraeum  Methodism  rascaldom  transform  antitoxin
aciniform  continuum  Germanism  microcosm  rascalism  trapezium  antivenin
Adventism  conundrum  germanium  microfilm  reconfirm  tribadism  appertain
airstream  cordiform  germplasm  microgram  reformism  tribalism  apportion
algorithm  courtroom  gigantism  midstream  restiform  triennium  araneidan
alloplasm  cretinism  gongorism  milligram  reticulum  trifolium  Armorican
aluminium  criticism  Gothicism  misbeseem  Ribbonism  triforium  Arthurian
americium  crossbeam  grandslam  misesteem  ritualism  tritheism  ascension
amoralism  cruciform  greenroom  misinform  rostellum  troutfarm  ascertain
amorphism  cryptogam  grillroom  misoneism  roundworm  trussbeam  aspersion
anabolism  cryptonym  Grundyism  Mithraism  routinism  ultimatum  assertion
anarchism  cuneiform  guardroom  modernism  ruthenium  uropygium  astrakhan
anemogram  curialism  guestroom  monachism  sabbatism  vademecum  asyndeton
angleworm  curviform  gymnasium  monergism  sacciform  vampirism  Atlantean
anglicism  cymbidium  gynaeceum  mongolism  sacrarium  vandalism  attention
animalism  cymbiform  gynoecium  monkeyism  salicetum  verbalism  attrition
animatism  cytoplasm  hailstorm  monoecism  sandstorm  vermiform  automaton
antiserum  daltonism  harmonium  Montanism  Sanhedrim  versiform  avocation
arboretum  Darwinism  hectogram  Mormonism  saturnism  vestigium  badminton
arrowworm  decennium  heliogram  mosaicism  savagedom  villiform  baldachin
asphaltum  defeatism  Hellenism  multiform  scientism  vitriform  baldaquin
Athenaeum  dentalium  herbarium  mutualism  screwworm  volcanism  bandwagon
atonalism  dentiform  hetaerism  mysticism  scutellum  voltinism  Bantustan
avizandum  despotism  hetairism  mythicism  scutiform  voodooism  Barbadian
bacterium  diabolism  heteronym  narcotism  sensorium  vorticism  barbarian
barathrum  diachylom  hierogram  neodymium  Sephardim  voyeurism  barracoon
barbarism  diachylum  hirsutism  neologism  serialism  vulcanism  basilican
barnstorm  dialogism  histogram  neoterism  shakerism  vulgarism  Bathonian
beadledom  diaphragm  Hitlerism  nephalism  shamanism  vulpinism  battalion
berkelium  dichasium  houseroom  neptunium  sheikhdom  weighbeam  bedridden
beryllium  dichroism  hybridism  Normanism  shelfroom  welfarism  beechfern
biblicism  dichroism  hydronium  occultism  shieldfem  wherefrom  bilirubin
biorhythm  dicrotism  hylozoism  operculum  Shintoism  whitebeam  birdbrain
bloodworm  disaffirm  hypericum  opusculum  shortterm  witticism  bisection
boardroom  disesteem  hypnotism  Orangeism  snaredrum  Yankeedom  boatswain
Briticism  dogmatism  idioplasm  orderform  snowstorm  Yankeeism  boattrain
broadloom  dogoodism  impluvium  osteoderm  socialism  ytterbium  bolection
brummagem  earthworm  indecorum  ostracism  sociogram  zirconium  bombardon
brutalism  ecosystem  isomerism  overwhelm  solipsism  abduction  bondwoman
cabbalism  ectoplasm  Italicism  pachyderm  soundfilm  abjection  bouquetin
cablegram  ecumenism  Jansenism  palladium  sovietism  abolition  brakesman
caciquism  effluvium  jesuitism  pantheism  Spinozism  aboutturn  breakdown
```

```
breakeven  contagion  Edwardian  gobetween  insertion  mossgrown  peneplain
breastpin  contusion  effluxion  gooseskin  intension  motheaten  percheron
bridesman  cornelian  egression  gorgonian  intention  muffinman  perdition
bringdown  cornerman  eiderdown  gradation  intervein  muscleman  perfusion
broomcorn  cornopean  eirenicon  greasegun  intorsion  muskmelon  persimmon
buckthorn  corrasion  elevation  greenhorn  intrusion  Mussulman  pervasion
Bulgarian  corrosion  elocution  gregarian  intuition  Mycenaean  phellogen
bumbledon  cotillion  emanation  Gregorian  inunction  myrobalan  phonation
cacodemon  cotyledon  emulation  grimalkin  invention  Nahuatlan  phthalein
caecilian  countdown  encrimson  groomsman  inversion  narration  physician
caerulean  courtesan  energumen  grosgrain  Iroquoian  nectarean  phytotron
Caesarean  crackdown  enhearten  guardsman  irruption  nemertean  pipeorgan
Caesarian  cracksman  enlighten  guncotton  isolation  neologian  placation
Cambodian  craftsman  entertain  gustation  iteration  Neptunian  plainsman
cameraman  cremation  ephemeron  guttation  jactation  nervation  planarian
caparison  crenation  epicurean  gyrfalcon  Jordanian  Nestorian  planation
Capricorn  criterion  epilation  habergeon  jurywoman  neuration  plication
Caribbean  CroMagnon  erudition  hagridden  Keplerian  Newtonian  ploughman
carnation  cuplichen  Esthonian  halfcrown  Keynesian  nictation  plutonian
carnelian  custodian  estuarian  Halloween  kilderkin  nightgown  pointsman
carrageen  cyclopean  Ethiopian  hammerman  kinswoman  nitration  policeman
Cartesian  cyclopian  euclidean  handorgan  knockdown  nonillion  pollution
caseation  cyclotron  eutherian  handsdown  krummhorn  nonperson  porcelain
cassation  Cytherean  evergreen  hangerson  lacertian  Norwegian  poriferan
Castalian  cytotoxin  evocation  harlequin  lactation  nutrition  postilion
castellan  Daedalean  evolution  harmattan  lallation  objection  praenomen
Castilian  Daedalian  exception  Harrovian  Laodicean  obsession  precisian
catamaran  dalmatian  exciseman  hartshorn  laudation  obtention  precision
cattleman  damnation  exclusion  heartburn  leafgreen  obtrusion  predation
Caucasian  Damoclean. excretion  Hebridean  leviathan  obversion  prefixion
causation  dandelion  excursion  heliozoan  librarian  obviation  prelusion
centurion  Darwinian  execution  Helvetian  libration  occlusion  premotion
cessation  decapodan  exemption  Heraclean  lineation  octillion  prenotion
chameleon  decathlon  expansion  Herculean  liquation  oddjobman  preordain
champaign  deception  expiation  Hercynian  litterbin  oestrogen  prevision
charlatan  decillion  explosion  Hesperian  liveryman  offscreen  princekin
charwoman  decoction  expulsion  Hibernian  longchain  offseason  privation
chatelain  deduction  exsertion  highflown  longicorn  olecranon  probation
checkrein  defection  extension  highgrown  lovetoken  oleoresin  profusion
chelation  deflation  extortion  Himalayan  luciferin  olfaction  progestin
chelonian  deflexion  extrusion  hindbrain  lumberman  ombudsman  prolation
chieftain  dejection  exudation  historian  Maccabean  onionskin  prolusion
chilblain  demission  eyestrain  Hobbesian  magnesian  operation  promotion
Chinatown  dentation  Falernian  hobgoblin  magnetron  Orangeman  pronation
Christian  dentition  familyman  homegrown  Mahometan  orangutan  pronghorn
chromatin  depiction  fellowman  homousian  mailtrain  oratorian  properdin
chthonian  depletion  fieldsman  honeymoon  malathion  Orpington  protozoan
churchman  desertion  filiation  horsebean  malleehen  outridden  protozoon
Cimmerian  detection  finedrawn  hortation  mammalian  outspoken  provision
circadian  detention  firstborn  Hungarian  Mancunian  overblown  ptarmigan
clavation  detersion  fisherman  hydration  Manichean  overdrawn  pulsation
clergyman  detrition  floridean  hydrozoan  Manichean  overeaten  purgation
clergymen  detrusion  flotation  hydrozoon  mannequin  overflown  pyramidon
clinician  deviation  foliation  ichneumon  Manxwoman  overgrown  pyridoxin
closedown  dictation  foodchain  iguanodon  medallion  overladen  pyroxylin
coalition  dietician  forbidden  illgotten  mediation  overtaken  quadruman
coecilian  dietitian  forebrain  imitation  melatonin  overtrain  quarenden
coemption  diffusion  foreknown  immersion  melocoton  ovulation  quarryman
cognation  digestion  foreshown  impaction  Mendelian  oxidation  quotation
cognition  digitalin  foretoken  impassion  mentation  oysterman  quotidian
colcannon  dimension  forewoman  impletion  mercaptan  packtrain  radiation
collation  Dionysian  forgotten  implosion  meropidan  palankeen  rebellion
collegian  direction  formation  impulsion  metheglin  palanquin  recension
collision  disburden  francolin  inanition  metrician  Palladian  reception
collodion  discommon  Freemason  inbetween  middleman  palmation  recession
collusion  disseisin  freewoman  incaution  migration  palpation  reclusion
colourman  diversion  Frenchman  inception  Miltonian  pantaloon  recursion
Columbian  divulsion  frigatoon  inclusion  minutegun  pantryman  redaction
Comintern  dodecagon  frogspawn  incursion  minuteman  paperthin  reduction
commotion  Dominican  fullblown  indention  misassign  parathion  reedorgan
communion  dormition  fullgrown  indiction  misdemean  parhelion  refashion
companion  doubleton  furcation  indigotin  misgovern  partition  refection
concision  draconian  gammadion  IndoAryan  misreckon  pastedown  reflation
condition  draftsman  gemmation  induction  misshapen  patrician  reflexion
Confucian  Dravidian  gentleman  infection  modillion  patrolman  refreshen
confusion  duralumin  gerfalcon  inflation  molluscan  Pavlovian  rejection
connation  ealdorman  gestalten  inflexion  Mongolian  Pelasgian  remission
connexion  earthborn  gestation  ingestion  morrisman  pellagrin  rendition
constrain  education  glyptodon  injection  mortician  pendragon  repletion
```

```
reptilian  solvation  untrodden  punctilio  rulership  bandoleer  commissar
repulsion  sooterkin  unwritten  quebracho  saintship  bandolier  compactor
resection  sortition  usucapion  sanbenito  sarcocarp  bannister  comprador
retention  soupspoon  vallation  sforzando  scrapheap  banqueter  conciliar
retortion  Southdown  valuation  sgraffito  sharecrop  bargainer  concocter
retrodden  sovereign  Varangian  simpatico  shellheap  barkeeper  concoctor
reversion  spellican  variation  sixteenmo  shortstop  barometer  condenser
revulsion  spiderman  velveteen  smackeroo  sketchmap  barracker  conductor
rewritten  spillikin  vendition  solfeggio  slaveship  barrister  conferrer
Rhineodon  spleuchan  vermilion  solferino  spaceship  bartender  confessor
rhodopsin  spoilsman  vernation  sopranino  sporocarp  beachwear  confirmer
Ripuarian  spokesman  vestryman  sostenuto  steamship  bedsitter  confirmor
roughhewn  sportsman  vibration  spiritoso  stinktrap  beefeater  confiteor
Roumanian  stableman  Victorian  strappado  stockwhip  beekeeper  conformer
roundsman  stanchion  violation  telephoto  stonecrop  beemaster  connecter
rubrician  statesman  Virgilian  thereinto  storeship  behaviour  connector
ruddleman  steersman  vitiation  thereunto  summingup  beleaguer  conqueror
ruination  steradian  Vitruvian  thitherto  sweatshop  berserker  conserver
Sabellian  stillborn  vulcanian  whereinto  sweetshop  beslobber  consignor
saccharin  stinkhorn  vulgarian  whereunto  tallyshop  bespatter  consulter
sacristan  striation  Wagnerian  wirephoto  thaneship  binocular  consultor
Sadducean  subaltern  wakerobin  zapateado  transship  blastular  contactor
safetypin  subdeacon  washbasin  zucchetto  troopship  blockader  container
sagegreen  sublation  washerman  afterclap  trumpedup  blunderer  contemner
sailorman  subregion  waterworn  bellyflop  turboprop  blusterer  contender
saltation  subtopian  wellknown  blackdamp  tutorship  bolometer  continuer
saltspoon  suctorian  whereupon  blockship  vibraharp  bookmaker  contriver
salvation  suffragan  wherrywap  boobytrap  wristdrop  boxgirder  convector
Samaritan  suffusion  whipperin  buttercup  abandoner  boycotter  converter
Sanhedrin  sulcation  windblown  cadetship  abdicator  brigadier  convincer
Sardinian  summation  wiredrawn  cantaloup  abnegator  Britisher  copartner
Sarmation  suspicion  withdrawn  cardsharp  abolisher  broiderer  copolymer
Sassanian  swansdown  woodwaxen  cassareep  abrogator  buccaneer  cordelier
satiation  sweetcorn  workwoman  chiefship  absconder  bughunter  coriander
Saturnian  switchman  wormeaten  chinstrap  abstainer  bulldozer  cornflour
scalefern  swordsman  yachtsman  chokedamp  accipiter  burnisher  corrector
scarfskin  tactician  zoophagan  clerkship  acclaimer  butcherer  corrupter
schlieren  tactitian  Zwinglian  cockahoop  acellular  butterbur  costumier
schoolman  talkathon  andantino  coffeecup  acetifier  bystander  couturier
Scotchman  tambourin  antipasto  countship  acidifier  calicular  cremaster
scrapiron  tarpaulin  armadillo  courtship  activator  camelhair  cricketer
scuncheon  Tartarean  bandolero  coverslip  addresser  campchair  crossover
scutcheon  Tartarian  barricado  cystocarp  addressor  campfever  cullender
seaurchin  Tartufian  bastinado  eavesdrop  admonitor  canesugar  cunctator
secession  Tasmanian  beccafico  eldership  adulterer  cannoneer  curlpaper
seclusion  tellurian  boliviano  filmstrip  advocator  cannonier  cuticular
secretion  tentation  caballero  filtertip  aerometer  canvasser  debaucher
sectarian  teratogen  calamanco  fingertip  Afrikaner  capacitor  decimator
sedgewren  testation  capriccio  foragecap  aggressor  capitular  declaimer
seduction  thereupon  carbonado  forcepump  alabaster  caretaker  decorator
selachian  thirdsman  cigarillo  galliwasp  alienator  carpenter  dedicator
selection  Thyestean  cipollino  goosestep  alligator  carryover  deflector
selectman  thyratron  contadino  guardship  altimeter  catalyser  defroster
Seljukian  timberman  contralto  guildship  amplifier  certifier  deinosaur
semicolon  tirewoman  crescendo  horsewhip  annotator  chafferer  deliverer
sensation  titration  derringdo  housekeep  apparitor  chaingear  demeanour
septation  Tocharian  desperado  intercrop  announcer  character  denouncer
serotonin  topiarian  duodecimo  jockstrap  appetiser  charterer  depositor
serration  touchdown  embroglio  judgeship  applauder  chastener  depressor
seventeen  tradesman  Esperanto  lairdship  appraiser  chastiser  depurator
shakedown  tradition  glissando  lightship  articular  chauffeur  derringer
shantyman  traducian  imbroglio  lovingcup  artificer  chevalier  describer
sharkskin  tragedian  incognito  majorship  aspirator  chiseller  desolater
sheepskin  tribesman  larghetto  mayorship  assaulter  chorister  desolator
shorthorn  trilithon  lazaretto  microchip  assembler  civiliser  despoiler
signalman  trisagion  libecchio  mousetrap  atmometer  clarifier  destroyer
siltation  truncheon  magnifico  orangetip  attainder  clatterer  dethroner
simpleton  twiceborn  majordomo  organstop  attempter  coadjutor  detonator
singleton  Ukrainian  manifesto  oversleep  attractor  collector  detractor
sinuation  ululation  muscovado  overtrump  auricular  collinear  developer
Sisyphean  unbeknown  mustachio  ownership  augmenter  colcothar  diesinker
situation  unberufen  obbligato  paperclip  augmentor  coinsurer  dingcar
Slavonian  uncertain  parleyvoo  playgroup  auvuncular  collector  disappear
slopbasin  unconcern  pasticcio  printshop  avuncular  collinear  discarder
Slovakian  undecagon  pistachio  priorship  Axminster  coloniser  discarder
Slovenian  underlain  pizzicato  queenship  backbiter  comforter  discerner
snakeskin  undersign  politburo  quickstep  backwater  commander  discolour
Solutrean  underspin  portfolio  redevelop  backwater  commander  discolour
Solutrian  unitarian  portolano  rhizocarp  balladeer  commenter  disfavour
```

disgracer	forfeiter	iceskater	messenger	perceiver	reflector	slaughter
dishonour	forgather	idealiser	midsummer	perfector	refractor	slipcover
dishwater	fortifier	illwisher	midwinter	performer	refresher	slothbear
dismember	forwander	immolator	milkfever	perfumier	regisseur	slumberer
dispenser	forwarder	imperator	milometer	perimeter	registrar	smatterer
disperser	fossicker	impleader	minelayer	permitter	regulator	sniggerer
disrepair	foxhunter	impounder	misfeasor	persuader	rejoinder	sniveller
dissector	freeliver	increaser	mishanter	perverter	remainder	sobsister
dissenter	freerider	incubator	missioner	phalanger	renouncer	sodawater
dissuader	freighter	indagator	mitigator	philander	renovator	sojourner
distemper	freshener	indicator	moderator	picnicker	repressor	solicitor
distiller	fritterer	indweller	modulator	pistoleer	requester	sommelier
disturber	fruiterer	infielder	moistener	planisher	reservoir	sonneteer
dittander	fulfiller	inflictor	molecular	plasterer	resonator	sonometer
dogcollar	fumigator	infractor	monocular	plunderer	respecter	sophister
dominator	funicular	inhalator	monsignor	poetaster	responder	souteneur
dosimeter	furbisher	inheritor	moonraker	polariser	reticular	souwester
Doukhobor	furnisher	inhibitor	moraliser	polyester	retinular	specifier
downriver	furtherer	initiator	mortgager	polywater	retoucher	spectator
driveller	gadgeteer	innholder	mortgagor	pompadour	retractor	speedster
drummajor	gainsayer	innkeeper	motivator	pontoneer	retriever	spherular
drysalter	gannister	innovator	moviegoer	pontonier	revelator	sphincter
dustcover	garreteer	inscriber	muckraker	porringer	rhymester	spindrier
dynamiter	garrotter	inspector	muffineer	portrayer	ricepaper	spinnaker
earthstar	gasfitter	instanter	musketeer	possessor	ridiculer	splendour
Eastender	gasholder	insulator	mutilator	posterior	rocketeer	spoliator
easterner	gasometer	intriguer	mystifier	potboiler	rodfisher	sprinkler
eggbeater	gauleiter	inveigler	navicular	pothunter	roisterer	sputterer
elastomer	gazetteer	irregular	navigator	poulterer	rosewater	squabbler
embezzler	gearlever	irrigator	nebuliser	prankster	ruminator	squelcher
embraceor	generator	isallobar	neighbour	precentor	rumrunner	stagedoor
embroider	geomancer	jaywalker	newspaper	preceptor	safflower	staggerer
emendator	germander	jetsetter	Nilometer	precursor	saltwater	stammerer
enameller	glabellar	jobmaster	nitpicker	predictor	sandpaper	stargazer
enchanter	gladiator	journeyer	nominator	preemptor	sandpiper	stationer
encounter	glandular	justiciar	nondriver	prelector	satinspar	stauncher
endeavour	glossator	justifier	nonlinear	presbyter	saturator	staymaker
energiser	godfather	karabiner	nonsmoker	presenter	saunterer	stegosaur
Englander	godmother	kidnapper	notepaper	preserver	scarifier	stiffener
engrosser	goingover	kingmaker	nourisher	pretender	scatterer	stomacher
epistoler	goldfever	kitchener	nowhither	preventer	scavenger	straggler
equaliser	gondolier	lampooner	nuisancer	privateer	schnauzer	strangler
ergometer	goosander	landloper	nullifier	processer	schnorrer	streetcar
escalator	gospeller	landowner	numerator	processor	scorifier	stretcher
escheator	graduator	Laplander	obturator	professor	scrambler	struggler
estimator	grenadier	latecomer	octameter	profiteer	scratcher	stupefier
estranger	grossular	launderer	oddjobber	projector	screecher	stutterer
eulogiser	groveller	lawnmower	offcolour	propeller	scribbler	subeditor
excavator	guarantor	Leicester	oilburner	prosector	scrivener	submaster
excelsior	gunpowder	levitator	oilcolour	protector	scrounger	subocular
excerptor	gunrunner	liberator	opercular	protester	scrutator	subverter
exchanger	hamburger	lifesaver	oppressor	protestor	scutellar	succeeder
exchequer	handlebar	lightyear	optometer	provender	seaanchor	succentor
exequatur	haranguer	Limburger	orbicular	pterosaur	sealetter	successor
exhauster	harbinger	limewater	organiser	publisher	seedeater	succourer
exhibitor	harbourer	lipreader	osmometer	puffadder	semilunar	suggester
exorciser	hardcover	liquefier	ossicular	pulpiteer	separator	sunbather
expediter	harpooner	literator	outbacker	puppeteer	September	sundowner
explainer	harvester	loafsugar	outfitter	purchaser	septemvir	sunflower
exploiter	headliner	locomotor	outlander	purloiner	sepulcher	superstar
expositor	headwater	lowlander	outnumber	pushchair	sequester	supinator
expounder	hereafter	lowloader	outrigger	pyrolater	serenader	supporter
extractor	hereunder	lunisolar	outworker	pyrometer	shamateur	surfeiter
eyeopener	hesitator	lysimeter	overeater	qualifier	sharpener	surrender
falsifier	hexameter	macerator	overpower	quarender	shipfever	suspender
fashioner	highchair	machmeter	overseer	quickener	shipowner	suspensor
fibrillar	highflier	magnifier	pacemaker	quirister	shoemaker	sustainer
fillister	highflyer	mainliner	parameter	racketeer	shopfloor	swaggerer
financier	highwater	malleolar	passenger	raconteur	shortener	sweetener
fireeater	hobnobber	manipular	patroller	radicular	shottower	tabulator
firepower	hodometer	manometer	paymaster	rainmaker	shoveller	tahsildar
firewater	homemaker	manslayer	peasouper	rainwater	sightseer	tanliquor
flashover	homopolar	maunderer	peculator	ransacker	signaller	tapdancer
flatterer	horologer	mayflower	pedicular	ratepayer	silverfir	taximeter
floscular	horsehair	meditator	pedometer	recoverer	simulator	telemeter
fluorspar	hosteller	mekometer	penciller	recruiter	sixfooter	televisor
flyfisher	howsoever	meltwater	penholder	rectifier	skindiver	tentmaker
foreboder	humdinger	memoriter	penpusher	redletter	skyjacker	testifier
foreigner	Icelander	merganser	pensioner	redresser	slanderer	theoriser

```
thermidor aepyornis battiness ceratodus diaphysis felonious griminess
thickener aesthesis bawdiness cetaceous diastasis fenceless grossness
throttler Afrikaans beardless chainless diathesis ferocious gruffness
throwster ailanthus beastings chancrous diclinous fetidness guileless
thunderer albatross beauteous chantress didactics fibreless guiltless
thyristor alertness beefiness chariness dietetics fibrinous gumminess
tidewater aliveness beeorchis charmless digitalis fieriness gustiness
tightener alkaloses beestings Charolais dinginess filaceous gutsiness
tinopener alkalosis bejabbers cheapness dinoceras filminess hairgrass
toadeater allantois bellglass cheerless dioecious fireirons hairiness
tonometer aloneness bifarious childless dipterous fireworks halitosis
tonsillar aloofness billiards chillness dirtiness fishiness Hallowmas
tophamper aluminous biogenous chitinous dizziness fistulous hamamelis
tormentor amaryllis bionomics chitlings dogmatics fixedness handcuffs
totaliser amauroses blackness chlamydes dogshores flakiness handglass
tourneyer amaurosis blameless chlorosis dottiness flambeaus handiness
traveller ambergris blandness Christmas doubtless flameless handpress
traverser ambiguous blankness chrysalis dowdiness flamingos happiness
treasurer ambitious bleakness cinereous dowerless flavorous hardiness
trickster amianthus blindness cirrhosis downwards fleckless harmonics
tricolour amidships bloodless clamorous dragomans fleetness harquebus
trilinear amorphous bluegrass classless dragoness fleshings harshness
trimester amphioxus bluffness cleanness dramatics fleshless hastiness
trinketer ampleness bluntness clearness dreamless flocculus haverings
trisector anabioses blushless closeness drollness fluorosis hazardous
trochlear anabiosis Boanerges cloudless dumpiness flushness headdress
troweller anacruses bonhomous coattails dungarees fogginess headiness
trumpeter anacrusis bonniness cobaltous duskiness forceless heartless
twitterer analogous boondocks cockiness dustiness foundress heaviness
twosuiter anamnesis boskiness coheiress dysgenics fractious heftiness
Uitlander anandrous bossiness comedones eagerness frailness hendiadys
underwear anaptyxis boundless commandos earliness Franglais hepatitis
unicolour anchoress bounteous compasses eastwards frankness heterosis
uniplanar angriness bourgeois complexus echovirus freshness highclass
unpopular anhydrous brainless congeries economics frivolous highlands
upbraider ankylosis brakeless congruous edelweiss frontless hilarious
upholster anomalous brashness conscious egregious frontways hippocras
utricular anonymous briefless consensus electress fructuous hoariness
vaporiser anopheles briefness corduroys elevenses fruitless homewards
varnisher anschluss briskness coreopsis embarrass fugacious homotaxis
vasomotor antipodes broadness Corybants emptiness fulgurous horniness
vehicular apartness broadways corydalis encompass fulldress horseless
venerator apetalous brownness cothurnus endomixis fulminous horsiness
versifier aphereses buffaloes countless enteritis funiculus hourglass
vesicular apheresis bulginess courteous entremets funkiness houseless
vignetter aphyllous bulkiness crapulous ephemeris funniness huffiness
vocabular apishness bumpiness crassness epiclesis fussiness humanness
vocaliser apogamous bumptious craziness epidermis fustiness huskiness
voiceover apophyses burdenous creatress epigynous fuzziness hygienics
voltmeter apophysis burliness credulous epiphyses gallowses hypogeous
volumeter apparatus bushiness crestless epiphysis gambadoes hypotaxis
volunteer arbitress buxomness cretinous epistaxis garrulous hysterics
wallpaper arboreous cacoethes criminous epithesis gastritis idealless
warmonger Areopagus cageyness crispness eponymous gaudiness ignoramus
warranter argentous calculous crossness erectness gauntness imageless
warrantor arsenious callipers crossways erogenous gauziness impatiens
wassailer arteritis cancerous crownless erroneous gawkiness imperious
wattmeter arthritis Candlemas crudeness errorless geoponics impetuous
westerner arthrosis cankerous curliness espousals giddiness inaptness
whichever asbestous canniness curstness euthenics ginglymus incurious
whimperer asepalous cantharis cutaneous eventless gladiolus ineptness
whisperer askewness cantharus cyclopses exactness glaireous inertness
whosoever asparagus capacious cytolysis exercises glamorous ingenious
willpower assiduous caryopses dangerous exodermis glossitis ingenuous
windhover athletics caryopsis dauntless exogamous glueyness injurious
wingchair atrocious castanets deaconess exogenous glutinous innocuous
womaniser audacious catalexes deathless exosmosis godliness innoxious
Worcester authoress catalexis deciduous exostosis golflinks innuendos
wrongdoer autocross catalyses declivous exsuccous gomphosis inodorous
Yiddisher autolysis catalysis delicious externals goodwives insidious
youngster awareness catharses delirious fabaceous governess inverness
ablutions awfulness catharsis denseness facetious graceless invidious
abscissas backcross cattaloes depthless faddiness grandness ironworks
acariasis backwards cattiness dexterous faintness graveless isagogics
acidulous backwoods causeless diaereses faithless graveness isinglass
acoustics bagginess cavernous diaeresis falseness greatness isogamous
acropolis balminess ceanothus diagnoses fandangos greenness isogenous
adeptness barbarous ceaseless diagnosis fattiness greyflies isolators
adultness bathybius cephalous diandrous faultless griefless isomerous
```

```
isopodous  meatiness  otherness  pulpiness  sebaceous  speckless  tenseness
isosceles  mechanics  ourselves  pulseless  secateurs  sphagnous  tepidness
issueless  melanosis  outgoings  pulverous  seditious  spiciness  terseness
itchiness  melodious  outskirts  pulvillus  seediness  spikiness  testiness
janitress  mementoes  overdress  pumiceous  selenious  spineless  thankless
jazziness  merciless  overtness  pursiness  semantics  spininess  theatrics
jerkiness  mercurous  overtones  pushiness  semiotics  spinulous  thesaurus
jointress  merriness  oviferous  pustulous  senseless  spiritous  thickness
judicious  messieurs  oviparous  pyrolysis  separates  splenitis  thingness
juiceless  messiness  oxygenous  Quakeress  sericeous  spongeous  thornless
juiciness  micaceous  palladous  quakiness  setaceous  spoutless  tightness
jumpiness  milkiness  panderess  queenless  seventies  squatness  timidness
katabasis  minacious  pantalets  queerness  shadeless  staginess  tinniness
katharsis  mirkiness  parabasis  querulous  shadiness  staidness  tipsiness
keratitis  mirthless  paralysis  quickness  shakiness  stainless  tipstaves
keratosis  mistigris  parataxis  quietness  shameless  staleness  tiredness
kinkiness  mistiness  parotitis  rabidness  shapeless  stalkless  tomentous
knotgrass  mixedness  pastiness  raininess  sharpness  stargrass  toothless
laborious  mnemonics  patroness  rancorous  sheerlegs  starkness  toreutics
landdross  moistness  pemphigus  randiness  sheerness  stateless  tortrices
lankiness  momentous  pendulous  ranginess  shiftless  steepness  torturous
lapideous  moneybags  penniless  rapacious  shininess  sternness  toughness
larcenous  mongooses  penurious  rapidness  shirtless  stiffness  tournedos
largeness  monitress  peripatus  rapturous  shoreless  stilettos  traceless
laundress  monoceros  perkiness  readdress  shortness  stillness  trackless
lazybones  monstrous  pertussis  readiness  showiness  stingless  traitress
lazytongs  moodiness  pettiness  rearwards  sideburns  stintless  tramlines
leakiness  moraceous  pettitoes  rectrices  sidedness  stoneless  trappings
leastways  mosquitos  phalanges  redivivus  siderosis  stoniness  tremulous
lecherous  motocross  phalanxes  reediness  sidewards  stoppress  trickless
leftovers  muddiness  pharynges  religious  sightless  stormless  trifocals
leftwards  mugginess  pharynxes  repossess  significs  stoutness  trigamous
legginess  mundungus  phlebitis  reprocess  siliceous  strangles  trimerous
levelness  muniments  phonemics  resources  silicious  strapless  trimmings
libellous  munitions  phonetics  retiarius  silicosis  strenuous  triteness
librettos  murderess  phoniness  retinitis  silkiness  strobilus  trochilus
lichenous  murderous  pinkiness  rhythmics  silliness  strumitis  troublous
lightless  murkiness  pithiness  riderless  simplices  stuporous  truceless
lightness  murmurous  placeless  righteous  sinewless  subereous  trustless
lignaloes  muskiness  plainness  rightness  sinusitis  sulkiness  truthless
limitless  mustiness  platinous  rigidness  skeesicks  sultaness  tubbiness
literatus  muzziness  pleadings  riskiness  skirtings  sumptuous  tufaceous
litheness  mydriasis  plenteous  rivalrous  skirtless  sunniness  tumidness
litigious  nakedness  plumbeous  roadworks  slackness  surliness  Turcomans
liturgics  narcissus  plumdamas  rockiness  slakeless  swartness  Turkomans
lividness  nastiness  plumpness  roominess  slantways  sweetness  typhlitis
loftiness  natheless  plusfours  rosaceous  sleekness  swiftness  tyrannous
logistics  nattiness  plushness  roughness  sleepless  syllepses  uliginous
longcoats  nectarous  podagrous  roundness  slickness  syllepsis  umbilicus
longevous  neediness  podginess  rowdiness  sliminess  symbiosis  unanimous
looseness  nefarious  pointless  ruddiness  slumbrous  symbolics  unaptness
lousiness  Negroness  poisonous  rustiness  smallarms  symphysis  underpass
loverless  nepenthes  pomaceous  sagacious  smallness  synectics  underseas
lowliness  nephritis  ponderous  salacious  smartness  syneresis  unfitness
lubricous  nephrosis  porticoes  saleratus  smileless  syngamous  unharness
lucidness  nerveless  posticous  salpinges  smokeless  synizesis  uniparous
luckiness  nerviness  powerless  saltiness  smokiness  synovitis  unisonous
ludicrous  newlyweds  prelates   saltworks  snakiness  syntheses  unsuccess
lumbricus  newsiness  prestress  sandglass  snowiness  synthesis  untimeous
lumpiness  nickelous  priceless  sandiness  soapiness  tacitness  usualness
luridness  nobleness  prideless  sappiness  soapworks  tackiness  utterless
lustiness  noiseless  priestess  sargassos  soberness  tailoress  utterness
luxurious  noisiness  primeness  sartorius  softgoods  taintless  vagarious
lymegrass  notedness  proboscis  sassafras  sogginess  talismans  vagueness
magnetics  notorious  procuress  sauceless  solacious  tarantass  validness
malanders  nucleolus  prognoses  sauciness  solidness  tardiness  valuables
malarious  nuttiness  prognosis  Sauternes  sometimes  tasteless  valueless
malicious  nystagmus  prolapsus  scaleless  sootiness  tastiness  valveless
malleolus  obeseness  prolepses  scalemoss  soppiness  tattiness  vapidness
manganous  oblivious  prolepsis  scaliness  sorceress  tawniness  variolous
manginess  obnoxious  proneness  scantness  sorcerous  tectonics  venereous
manliness  obsequies  proptosis  scentless  sorriness  tectrices  venturous
manyplies  octopodes  prosiness  schistous  soundings  telamones  veracious
Martinmas  odourless  prothesis  scirrhous  soundless  tellurous  verdigris
massiness  officious  psoriasis  scleritis  soundness  temptress  verminous
matchless  oilpaints  psychoses  sclerosis  spaceless  tenacious  verrucous
mateyness  oleaceous  psychosis  scoliosis  spareness  tenacious  vexatious
mealiness  oogenesis  pudginess  scratches  spareribs  tendinous  vicarious
meandrous  orderless  puffiness  seaminess  sparkless  tenebrous  vimineous
```

```
vinaceous analogist byproduct decongest excellent haggadist inwrought
virginals anarchist cabbalist decrement exceptant hairshirt irradiant
virtuosos anatomist cabriolet decumbent excipient halflight itinerant
visitress Anglicist Caesarist defeatist excrement Hallstatt Jansenist
vivacious animalist Calvinist defendant excurrent handcraft jollyboat
vividness annectent Camembert deferment executant hardiment judgement
vocalness annuitant camorrist deficient exegetist haresfoot kickstart
voiceless annulment campcraft defoliant exilement harmonist kingcraft
volcanoes anovulant canalboat dehiscent expectant hatchment klinostat
voracious antitrust candlenut demandant expedient headfirst lamplight
vowelless apartment candytuft demulcent expellent headlight landagent
vulturous apologist canescent deodorant extendant heartbeat landaulet
wackiness appellant careerist dependant extolment heartfelt landdrost
Waldenses appendant cassoulet dependent extravert heliostat larcenist
wallcress applicant catamount desiccant extremist Hellenist latescent
Walpurgis architect catchment detergent extrovert heptaglot libellant
wartcress archivist catechist determent exuberant herbalist libellist
washiness archivolt Catharist deterrent eyebright hereabout lightfoot
wasteness arrestant celebrant detriment fabricant highlight lightsout
waterless arrowroot chassepot devilment Falangist hindsight limelight
weariless ascendant chatoyant diabolist fantasist hoarfrost lineament
weariness ascendent checklist dialogist feoffment holocaust lionheart
weediness assailant clarionet dichromat ferryboat homograft liturgist
weirdness assistant classlist different fetichist hoofprint liverwort
werwolves assumpsit clinquant difficult fetishist horsemint lodgement
westwards assurgent coagulant diffident feudalist Hottentot lophodont
wheelless astronaut cockfight dinnerset fieldboot houseboat lousewort
whitebass atonement cocksfoot disaffect fireblast housecoat lovefeast
whiteness attendant coelostat discomfit firecrest humectant lovelight
wholeness autarkist coffeepot discovert firelight hygienist lowermost
widthways autograft cognisant discredit firmament hygrostat lubricant
windiness autopilot coldshort disforest firstfoot hypnotist luxuriant
windwards backsight collagist dishclout flageolet hypoblast machinist
wineglass balladist colourist dishonest flatulent hypocaust magnetist
winepress ballpoint coltsfoot disinfect flayflint identikit mainsheet
wittiness bandicoot columnist disinfest fleshment ignescent makeshift
woodiness beanfeast combatant disorient flowchart immigrant maladroit
wooziness bedjacket communist disputant flowerpot impatient malignant
wordiness beechmast competent dissident flowsheet impeccant mammonist
worthless benignant complaint dissonant fluctuant impendent mannerist
woundless besetment compliant distraint flyweight imperfect manorseat
wrathless bethought component divergent footfault implement marchpast
wrongness biblicist concordat dogmatist footlight important marrowfat
youngness bicyclist condiment dogviolet footprint imprudent marshwort
zoiatrics billygoat confidant downright forcemeat incessant masochist
zoogenous biologist confident dramatist forecourt incipient massagist
abasement birdsfoot confluent drawsheet forefront inclement mechanist
abashment birdsnest congruent dreamboat foresight incorrect medallist
abatement birthwort connivent dresscoat formalist increment meliorist
abhorrent bivariant conscript dryasdust fortnight incumbent memoirist
absorbent blackcoat consonant dustsheet frockcoat incurrent mendicant
abstinent Blackfeet constrict ebullient fulgurant indignant mentalist
absurdist Blackfoot construct ecdysiast fulminant indraught merriment
acceptant blacklist continent ecologist fundament indulgent mesmerist
accordant blastment cooperant economist fusionist inebriant mesoblast
acidulent bloodlust copyright ectoblast Gaeltacht inelegant meteorist
adornment bloodroot cormorant efficient gallivant infestant Methodist
adsorbent bloodshot cornetist effulgent galvanist informant methought
Adventist bloodwort corposant ejectment gearshift innermost metricist
advertent bluepoint corpulent elopement genuflect inoculant mezzotint
aerialist blueprint coruscant embayment geodesist inpatient midwicket
aerobiont boardfoot cosmonaut embedment geologist insistent milkfloat
affidavit bombsight cotangent emollient Germanist insolvent millivolt
affirmant branchlet covariant emolument Girondist insurgent mincemeat
aftermost bratwurst crapulent enactment glasswort integrant miniskirt
agistment brazilnut crepitant encomiast godparent intellect miscreant
agreement breakfast croissant endoblast goldcrest intendant misdirect
airjacket briarroot crowsfoot endowment goodnight intercept misoneist
albescent brierroot crowsnest enjoyment goosefoot interdict misreport
alchemist brilliant cruellest enrolment grandaunt interknit Mithraist
alignment broadcast culminant entoblast grapeshot interment mnemonist
alinement buckwheat cutthroat entrechat greataunt interpret modernist
allegiant bullfight cymbalist epilogist greatcoat interrupt moneywort
allotment bulltrout damnedest epitomist greenbelt intersect monkeynut
alternant bundobust Darwinist equipment groundnut intrigant moonlight
amassment burnedout davenport estaminet guidepost introject mosaicist
amazement bushcraft deadlight Eucharist guillemot introvert motherwit
amendment butterfat debarment exactment guitarist inurement motorboat
amusement butternut declarant examinant haemostat invariant mouthpart
```

```
mucksweat  polevault  rockplant  starlight  tuliproot  grubscrew  amphigory
mutualist  pollutant  Roquefort  statement  tumescent  interflow  amusingly
myologist  postulant  roughcast  statocyst  tunnelnet  interview  anciently
mythicist  pourpoint  rousement  steadfast  turbulent  jackstraw  ancientry
nannygoat  powerboat  routinist  steamboat  turnabout  oakenshaw  ancillary
navelwort  precedent  rufescent  sternmost  tympanist  oddfellow  androgyny
negligent  predicant  rushlight  sternpost  undercoat  overthrew  angiology
negotiant  predigest  sacrament  stillhunt  underfelt  overthrow  angularly
neologist  predikant  sandblast  stimulant  underfoot  peachblow  animality
neoterist  prepotent  sandspout  stirabout  undermost  rareeshow  animosity
nephalist  prescient  sandyacht  stockinet  underpart  saddlebow  annularly
newmarket  prescript  sauceboat  stocklist  underplot  scarecrow  anonymity
newsagent  preselect  scapegoat  stonechat  undershot  scoredraw  antennary
newsprint  president  scenarist  stonewort  undertint  scrimshaw  anthology
nigricant  preterist  scholiast  stoplight  undervest  scrollsaw  antipathy
nonprofit  pretermit  scientist  stormbelt  underwent  decomplex  antiphony
northeast  prevalent  screwbolt  strapwort  ungallant  directrix  antiquary
northmost  princelet  seasquirt  streamlet  unisonant  Esquimaux  antiquity
northwest  procreant  secernent  strewment  univalent  executrix  anxiously
notionist  profilist  seedplant  stringent  unthought  flambeaux  appetency
nutriment  prominent  selfdoubt  subjacent  unwrought  gogglebox  aqueously
obscurant  proponent  selftrust  subscript  uppermost  heterodox  arbitrary
obsequent  prosodist  semisweet  subtenant  uttermost  letterbox  archduchy
observant  provident  senescent  succulent  vacillant  mediatrix  archenemy
occludent  pubescent  sentiment  sugarbeet  Vedantist  multiplex  arcuately
occultist  publicist  septuplet  sulphuret  ventiduct  pepperbox  arduously
occurrent  pussyfoot  serialist  summarist  ventifact  pillarbox  argybargy
ochlocrat  queenpost  sextuplet  sunbonnet  verbalist  pouncebox  armillary
Octobrist  quiescent  shamanist  sunhelmet  videlicet  promptbox  artillery
officiant  quillwort  shamefast  superheat  viewpoint  prothorax  artlessly
offstreet  quodlibet  Shintoist  suppliant  violinist  retroflex  asexually
onslaught  rabbinist  shopfront  surmullet  virescent  sentrybox  ashamedly
openheart  racialist  shouldest  susurrant  visionist  signalbox  asininity
oppugnant  radiocast  shovelhat  swarajist  volauvent  strongbox  assiduity
orchidist  ravelment  sidelight  sweetmeat  voodooist  testatrix  assumably
orologist  rearlight  simulcast  swimmeret  vorticist  tinderbox  assuredly
orrisroot  recipient  skinflint  swordknot  vulcanist  windowbox  astrology
otologist  recollect  skingraft  sycophant  waistbelt  aberrancy  astronomy
outermost  reconvert  skintight  symbolist  waistcoat  abidingly  asymmetry
overdraft  recordist  skyrocket  synergist  walkabout  abnormity  atomicity
overexert  recumbent  sleevenut  synoptist  wallfruit  absurdity  atonality
overleapt  recurrent  slingshot  taillight  warbonnet  abusively  atonicity
overnight  redbreast  snakeroot  Talmudist  washedout  abysmally  audiology
overprint  reductant  snowdrift  Targumist  waterbutt  accassary  austerely
overreact  redundant  snowplant  tattooist  watercart  accessory  austerity
overshoot  reefpoint  sobriquet  tenebrist  wavefront  acclivity  authority
oversight  reentrant  socialist  terebrant  weeknight  accompany  autocracy
overskirt  refitment  soidisant  termagant  wehrmacht  actuality  auxiliary
overslept  reformist  solipsist  terminist  whaleboat  adamantly  availably
overspent  refulgent  somnolent  terrorist  whitebait  adiposity  averagely
paederast  regardant  soothfast  tervalent  whodunnit  adjacency  avoidably
palpitant  reluctant  sopranist  testament  windchest  adjunctly  awesomely
panchayat  remitment  Sorbonist  Teutonist  windswept  adjutancy  awkwardly
panellist  remittent  soundpost  therapist  winevault  admirably  Aylesbury
pantheist  remontant  southeast  theurgist  witchhunt  admiralty  Babbittry
paramount  renascent  southmost  thighboot  woodcraft  adoringly  bacillary
parchment  repayment  southwest  timelimit  worriment  adulatory  balefully
parrakeet  repellant  spaceport  timesheet  worrywart  adversary  baneberry
paypacket  repellent  spacesuit  timpanist  woundwort  adversely  banefully
pearlwort  repentant  spadefoot  tittlebat  wristshot  adversity  baptistry
peepsight  represent  spagyrist  tonguelet  wyliecoat  advisably  barbarity
penetrant  repugnant  spearmint  toothwort  xenograft  advisedly  barometry
pennywort  reservist  spearwort  topiarist  zeitgeist  aeriality  baronetcy
Pentecost  resilient  speedboat  tracksuit  zoologist  aerometry  bashfully
pepperpot  resistant  spindrift  transient  zootomist  aetiology  basically
periplast  resolvent  spinneret  transport  bordereau  agreeably  bastardly
permanent  resorbent  Spinozist  transumpt  gaspereau  agriology  battlecry
pertinent  restraint  spiritist  transvest  impromptu  aimlessly  beamingly
pessimist  resultant  splayfoot  treatment  trousseau  airworthy  bearberry
pestilent  resurgent  splendent  trebuchet  leitmotiv  airyfairy  belatedly
petaurist  resurrect  spoonmeat  trebucket  afterglow  allegedly  bemusedly
petticoat  retardant  sporocyst  tremolant  barleymow  allopathy  benignity
phonetist  rethought  spotlight  tremulant  bedfellow  allotropy  bestially
physicist  retroject  springlet  trenchant  bowwindow  allowably  biliously
placement  retrovert  squirelet  trepidant  commonlaw  allowedly  bimonthly
Platonist  revetment  stairfoot  trigamist  corkscrew  amazingly  biography
pluralist  rhythmist  stakeboat  tritheist  deathblow  ambiguity  bivalency
plutocrat  ritualist  Stalinist  trivalent  downthrow  amorality  bizarrely
Plutonist  riverboat  stardrift  truculent  eyeshadow  amorously  blaeberry
```

```
blameably  colonelcy  depravity  etymology  fulgently  hopefully  inventory
blasphemy  colophony  desirably  euchology  fulsomely  horoscopy  inversely
blatantly  colostomy  desultory  eurhythmy  furiously  horseplay  inviolacy
blazingly  coltishly  deviously  evasively  furtively  hortatory  invisibly
bleachery  columbary  devitrify  everybody  gainfully  hostilely  irascibly
blessedly  comically  devotedly  evidently  gallantly  hostility  irksomely
blotchily  commodity  dexterity  evocatory  gallantry  huckstery  irreality
blueberry  community  dextrally  excitancy  gallingly  hugeously  irritably
bolometry  compactly  diachrony  excitedly  garrulity  hunkydory  itineracy
bombhappy  complexly  diathermy  excretory  gemmology  hurriedly  itinerary
bookishly  comradely  dichogamy  excusably  genealogy  hurtfully  itsybitsy
boorishly  comradery  dichotomy  execrably  generally  husbandly  ittybitty
breakaway  concavely  diffusely  executory  geniality  husbandry  janissary
breathily  concavity  digitally  exemplary  genteelly  hybridity  jarringly
breezeway  concisely  dignitary  exemplify  gentility  hydrology  jealously
bridleway  condignly  dilatancy  expiatory  genuinely  hymnology  jeeringly
brigandry  congruity  dimissory  expletory  geobotany  hypergamy  jewellery
brittlely  conically  diplomacy  expressly  geography  hypnology  jocularly
brotherly  connately  directory  extensity  germanely  hypocrisy  jocundity
brusquely  constancy  direfully  extremely  gestatory  hyponasty  joviality
brutality  contrasty  discovery  extremity  gibbosity  ichnology  joylessly
brutishly  contumacy  disembody  exultancy  gibbously  iconology  judiciary
budgetary  contumely  disparity  factually  gimmickry  idiopathy  Juneberry
bulbously  convexity  distantly  facundity  girlishly  illegally  juniority
bullishly  copiously  dittology  fallalery  glacially  illegibly  kiddingly
buoyantly  coprology  diurnally  fantastry  glaringly  illicitly  knavishly
burningly  cordially  diversely  fatefully  gleefully  imaginary  knowingly
butcherly  cornerboy  diversify  fatuously  glengarry  immanency  laggardly
butterfly  corollary  diversity  fawningly  globosity  immediacy  lambently
buttinsky  correctly  doggishly  fearfully  glowingly  immensely  languidly
cacophony  corruptly  dolefully  febricity  goldsinny  immensity  lastingly
caddisfly  cosmogeny  doltishly  fecundity  gorblimey  immodesty  laterally
caliology  cosmogony  donnishly  federally  gossamery  immorally  latitancy
callosity  cosmology  dormitory  feelingly  gracility  immovably  latterday
callously  costively  dosimetry  femineity  gradatory  immutably  laudatory
candidacy  covalency  doughtily  fertilely  gradually  impiously  laughably
capillary  coxcombry  dragonfly  fertility  grandaddy  impliedly  lawlessly
capitally  crabbedly  dromedary  fervently  gravidity  impotency  learnedly
captaincy  cranberry  drunkenly  festively  grouchily  improbity  leeringly
captivity  credulity  dubiosity  festivity  groundivy  impulsory  leewardly
carefully  crematory  dubiously  festology  guardedly  inability  legendary
carnality  crookedly  ductility  feudality  gushingly  inaudibly  legionary
carpentry  crotchety  duodenary  feudatory  gustatory  incapably  leisurely
carpingly  crowberry  duplicity  fiduciary  gynocracy  incensory  lengthily
carpology  crucially  duteously  finically  habitably  incurably  leniently
cartology  cryoscopy  dutifully  fissility  hackberry  indecency  lethality
cartulary  cubically  dysentery  fittingly  haggardly  indelibly  leucotomy
cassowary  cuckoldry  dystrophy  fivepenny  hagiarchy  indemnify  lexically
casuistry  cunningly  earnestly  flagrancy  hagiology  indemnity  liability
catalepsy  curiosity  easefully  flamingly  halfhardy  indignity  liberally
cataplexy  curiously  edibility  flannelly  halfpenny  indignity  libratory
causality  currently  electrify  flaringly  haltingly  inebriety  liltingly
celebrity  currishly  electuary  flightily  haplessly  ineffably  limitedly
centenary  cursively  elegantly  flippancy  haplology  inerrancy  limnology
centrally  cursorily  elusively  floridity  harmfully  inexactly  limpidity
certainly  customary  embracery  floristry  hatefully  infirmary  lineality
certainty  cynically  emergency  flowingly  haughtily  infirmity  linearity
chairlady  cystotomy  eminently  foolhardy  healthily  ingenuity  lingually
champerty  damnatory  emotively  foolishly  heathenry  inharmony  liquidity
chandlery  damningly  emotivity  foppishly  heavyduty  inhumanly  lispingly
chantilly  dashingly  emulously  forecaddy  hedgingly  initially  lissomely
chemistry  dastardly  emunctory  forlornly  heedfully  innocency  literally
chicanery  deacidify  endlessly  formality  heinously  innocuity  lithology
chiropody  decadency  endophagy  formicary  helically  insatiety  lithotomy
chorology  decalcify  endoscopy  formulary  hellishly  insectary  lobectomy
circuitry  decennary  endurably  forwardly  helpfully  insolubly  logically
citizenry  decidedly  enjoyably  fourpenny  heptarchy  instantly  logomachy
civically  decimally  entelechy  fragility  hesitancy  insularly  longevity
clamantly  declivity  enviously  fragrancy  hideously  insularly  longingly
clemently  decretory  epigraphy  franticly  hierarchy  integrity  loquacity
coaxially  deerberry  equitably  freezedry  hierology  intensely  louringly
coaxingly  defiantly  eruditely  frenchify  hillbilly  intensify  loutishly
cockneyfy  definably  esemplasy  frequency  hircosity  intensity  lovestory
cocoonery  deformity  esuriency  fretfully  hispidity  intercity  lubricity
coequally  democracy  eternally  frigidity  histogeny  interplay  lumpishly
coercibly  demystify  ethically  frivolity  histology  intestacy  lustfully
cognately  denitrify  ethnarchy  frontally  hoggishly  intricacy  lyrically
coherency  dentistry  ethnicity  frowardly  homophony  inutility  machinery
           denyingly  ethnology  frugality  homoplasy  invalidly  magically
```

```
magistery niggardly peccantly procerity saleslady smilingly tearfully
makeready ninepenny pecuniary procuracy saliently snowberry teasingly
malignity nobiliary pederasty profanely saltatory soapberry tediously
mamillary nocuously peevishly profanity salubrity sobbingly tegularly
mammalogy noisomely pellitory profusely sanctuary sociality teknonymy
mandatary nominally pendently prolately sapiently sociology telemetry
mandatory nomocracy pensively prolixity savourily soldierly teleology
mansionry nonentity pentarchy prolusory scapulary solemnity telepathy
maritally normality perfectly propriety scatology soliloquy telephony
marketday northerly perfumery proveably schmaltzy songfully telescopy
marquetry nostology periphery provisory scholarly sophistry tellingly
marshalcy notoriety personify provostry schoolboy sottishly temporary
martially noxiously pestology proximity sciamachy soulfully tensility
massively objectify petrology prudently sciascopy southerly tenuously
masterkey obliquely pettishly prudishly scraggily sparingly termitary
maternity obliquity petulancy pruriency scrappily spatially ternately
matrimony obscenely phenology publicity scrimpily speakeasy territory
mawkishly obscenity philately puerility scruffily specially testimony
maxillary obscurely philogyny pugnacity searingly specialty tetralogy
maximally obscurity philology pulmonary seaworthy speechify tetrapody
mayoralty obstinacy phonatory pulsatory secondary spinosity tetrarchy
meaningly obversely phonology pungently secretary spirality textually
mediately obviously photocopy pupillary secretory splashily theocracy
mediatory occupancy phycology purgatory sectility splintery theocrasy
medically odontalgy phylogeny purposely secularly spluttery theomachy
medullary odorously phytogeny purringly sedentary sporogeny theophany
meliority oenomancy phytology purulency seemingly sprightly theosophy
meltingly oenophily phytotomy pushingly seigneury springily thermally
memorably offertory piggishly putridity seigniory squalidly thingummy
mendacity okeydokey pinnately pyrolatry selfglory squashily thirstily
mendicity olfactory piquantly pyromancy selfishly squeakily thriftily
mentality oligarchy piscatory pyrometry semblably squinancy throatily
mercenary oligopoly piteously quadruply seminally stability throughly
mesentery ominously pitifully quarterly semiology stableboy throwaway
metrology onerously pituitary radialply seniority stagnancy tigerlily
micrology operosely pityingly radiantly sensually stagparty timeously
microtomy operosity pivotally radiately sentiency stampduty timocracy
midwifery ophiology placatory radically separably starchily titularly
migratory opponency placidity radiology septenary statutory tolerably
militancy opsimathy planetary raffishly septicity staunchly tonically
millenary optically plangency rakehelly sequacity stenotypy topically
millinery optometry plausibly rampantly sergeancy sterility torpidity
mincingly opulently playfully rancidity seriality stiltedly torridity
mindfully orography plenarily rantingly seriately stitchery toxically
minimally orthodoxy plicately rascality seriously stoically toxophily
misemploy oscitancy ploughboy raspatory serjeancy stolidity traceably
miserably osteogeny plurality raspberry serjeanty strangely tracheary
mobocracy osteology poignancy raspingly serpentry streakily tractably
mockingly outwardly pointduty raucously servilely stridency treachery
modernity ovenready pointedly raunchily servility studiedly tribology
momentary overweary pokeberry recreancy seventhly stupidity tributary
monastery oviparity polyandry recusancy severally stylishly tricksily
mongrelly ovulatory polymathy refectory severalty suability trinketry
monocracy pageantry polyonymy regularly sexlessly suasively triploidy
monolatry painfully polyphagy relevancy sexuality subagency trivially
monophagy painterly polyphony reliantly shadberry subduedly triweekly
morbidity palatably polyzoary reliquary shallowly subfamily tropology
mordacity palillogy pomposity renitency shipmoney sublimely truepenny
mordantly pallidity pompously repertory shrubbery sublimity tubularly
mortality palmistry popularly reputably sibilancy sublunary tunefully
mundanely pantingly postentry reputedly sickishly summarily turbidity
musically papillary posterity residency sigillary sumptuary turgently
mutuality parcenary pratingly residuary signatory supremacy turgidity
mycophagy parlously preachify restfully similarly supremely twelfthly
myography parquetry preachily restively sincerely surgeoncy twitchily
mystagogy parsimony precatory reticency sincerity suturally typically
mythology partially precisely reversely sinlessly swinishly unanimity
narratory passersby precocity rhinology sinuately swordplay uncannily
naseberry passively predacity ringingly sinuosity syllabary uncivilly
naturally passivity predatory riotously sinuously symbology uncleanly
naughtily patchouly prefatory roguishly sketchily synchrony uncouthly
necessary paternity pregnancy roseately skiamachy tabularly underbody
necessity pathogeny prelusory rotundity skiascopy tactfully underclay
necrology pathology preoccupy roundelay skilfully tactility underplay
needfully patiently presently routinely slaphappy tartishly unearthly
nephology patrimony primality ruffianly slategrey tautology unequally
nervously patrology primarily ruinously slavishly tautology unfleshly
neurology peaceably privately rusticity slenderly taxidermy unhappily
neutrally peasantry probatory ruthfully sluiceway teachably unhealthy
```

uniformly	vacuously	vexillary	visionary	waywardly	wolfishly	megahertz
unitively	vainglory	viability	vitellary	wealthily	workmanly	slivovitz
unluckily	valiantly	vibratory	vitiosity	weatherly	worriedly	
unreality	variously	viciously	voluntary	Wednesday	xerophily	
unsavoury	vasectomy	villagery	vorticity	weightily	yawningly	
unsightly	veeringly	villosity	vulgarity	willingly	yesterday	
unsoundly	vegetably	violently	vulnerary	wineberry	zamindary	
unthrifty	venerably	virginity	waggishly	winningly	zealously	
unusually	veniality	virtually	wailingly	winsomely	zemindary	
unwomanly	ventrally	virulency	wakefully	wishfully	zestfully	
upcountry	verbosely	viscidity	warblefly	wistfully	zoography	
uprightly	verbosity	viscosity	warningly	witchetty	zootechny	
uranology	verdantly	viscounty	waspishly	witlessly	gigahertz	
uselessly	veritably	viscously	waterlily	wittingly	kilohertz	

10 letter words

aardwolves	acceptable	adhibition	affability	allegorist	amphibious
abacterial	acceptably	adjacently	affectedly	allegretto	amphibrach
abbreviate	acceptance	adjectival	affectless	allergenic	amphictyon
abdication	acceptedly	adjudgment	affeerment	alleviator	amphigouri
abdominous	accessible	adjudicate	afferently	alliaceous	amphimacer
abducentes	accessibly	adjunction	affettuoso	alliterate	amphimixes
aberdevine	accidental	adjunctive	affiliated	allocation	amphimixis
aberrantly	accomplice	adjuration	affirmable	allocution	amphoteric
aberration	accomplish	adjuratory	affliction	allogamous	amputation
abhorrence	accordance	adjustable	afflictive	allopathic	amygdaloid
abiogenist	accoucheur	adjustment	affluently	allophonic	amylaceous
abjectness	accountant	administer	affordable	allosteric	anabaptism
abjuration	accounting	admiration	aficionado	allotropic	anabaptist
ablebodied	accredited	admiringly	Africander	alloverish	anacolutha
abnegation	accrescent	admissible	Africanise	allpurpose	anadromous
abnormally	accumulate	admittable	Africanism	allrounder	anaglyphic
abominable	accurately	admittance	Africanist	allurement	anagogical
abominably	accursedly	admittedly	Afrikander	allusively	analogical
abominator	accusation	admonition	afterbirth	almacanter	analphabet
aboriginal	accusative	admonitive	aftergrass	almondeyed	analysable
abortively	accusatory	admonitory	afterimage	almsgiving	analytical
aboveboard	accusingly	adolescent	afterlight	almucanter	anamorphic
Abrahamman	accustomed	adoptively	afterpains	alongshore	anapaestic
abrasively	acephalous	adrenaline	aftershave	alpenstock	anaplastic
abreaction	acervation	adrenergic	aftertaste	alphabetic	anaptyctic
abridgment	acetabular	adroitness	afterwards	alphameric	anarchical
abrogation	acetabulum	adsorbable	agapanthus	altarpiece	anastigmat
abruptness	achievable	adsorption	agglutinin	altazimuth	anastomose
abscission	achondrite	adsorptive	aggrandise	alteration	anastrophe
absolutely	achromatic	Adullamite	aggression	alterative	anatomical
absolution	acidimeter	adulterant	aggressive	alternance	anatropous
absolutism	acidimetry	adulterate	agitatedly	alternator	ancestress
absolutist	acidophile	adulteress	agrologist	altocumuli	anchoretic
absolutory	acoelomate	adulterine	agronomist	altogether	anchoritic
absorbable	acotyledon	adulterous	aircooling	altostrati	anchorless
absorbance	acoustical	adventurer	aircushion	altruistic	anchorring
absorbedly	acquirable	advertence	airmanship	amalgamate	anchylosis
absorbency	acquitting	advertency	alarmingly	amanuenses	anchylotic
absorption	acrobatics	advertiser	Albigenses	amanuensis	ancipitous
absorptive	acrogenous	advisement	albuminoid	amateurish	Andalusian
abstemious	acromegaly	advocation	albuminous	amateurism	andalusite
abstention	acronychal	advocatory	alchemical	ambassador	androecium
abstergent	acrophobia	aeolotropy	alcoholise	ambidexter	androgenic
abstersion	acroterion	aerenchyma	alcoholism	ambivalent	anecdotage
abstersive	acroterium	aerobatics	alcyonaria	ambulacral	anecdotist
abstinence	actinolite	aerobiosis	aldermanic	ambulacrum	anemograph
abstinency	actinozoan	aerobiotic	aldermanry	ambulation	anemometer
abstracted	actionable	aeroengine	alexanders	ambulatory	anemometry
abstracter	actionably	aerogramme	algebraist	ambushment	anemophily
abstractly	activation	aerography	algolagnia	ameliorate	aneurismal
abstractor	activeness	aerologist	algolagnic	amendatory	aneurysmal
abstrusely	adamantine	aeronautic	algologist	amercement	angiosperm
abstrusity	adaptation	aeronomist	Algonquian	amerciable	Anglistics
absurdness	adaptively	aerophobia	alienation	Amerindian	anglomania
abundantly	additional	aerostatic	alightment	amiability	anglophile
academical	addlepated	aeruginous	alimentary	ammoniacal	anglophobe
acarpelous	adenectomy	aesthetics	alkalinity	ammoniated	anglophone
acatalepsy	adequately	aesthetism	allegation	ammunition	AngloSaxon
accelerate	adherently	Aethiopian	allegiance	amoebocyte	angularity
accentuate	adhesively	aetiologic	allegorise	ampelopsis	angwantibo

animadvert	apologetic	artificial	auditorium	barbituric	Benthamite
animalcula	apophthegm	artycrafty	augustness	barcarolle	benzocaine
animalcule	apoplectic	arytaenoid	auriculate	bardolatry	benzpyrene
animatedly	aposematic	asafoetida	auriferous	barebacked	bequeathal
anisotropy	apostatise	asbestosis	auscultate	barefooted	beribboned
annalistic	apostolate	ascariasis	auspicious	bareheaded	Berkeleian
annexation	apostrophe	ascendable	austenitic	barelegged	besprinkle
annihilate	apothecary	ascendance	Australian	bargeboard	bestialise
annotation	apothecial	ascendancy	autarkical	barkentine	bestiality
annoyingly	apothecium	ascendence	autecology	barleybree	bestirring
annularity	apotheoses	ascendency	authorship	barleybroo	bestowment
annulation	apotheosis	ascendible	autochthon	barleycorn	bestridden
annunciate	apotropaic	asceticism	autocratic	Barmecidal	bestseller
anointment	apparelled	ascomycete	autodidact	barometric	betterment
anonaceous	apparently	ascribable	autoerotic	baronetage	bewitchery
anopheline	apparition	ascription	autogamous	barracouta	biannually
answerable	appealable	asexuality	autogenous	barramunda	biblically
answerably	appearance	Ashkenazim	autography	barramundi	bibliology
antagonise	appeasable	asparagine	autoimmune	barratrous	bibliopegy
antagonism	appendices	aspergilla	autologous	barrelling	bibliophil
antagonist	appendixes	asphyxiant	automation	barrenness	bibliopole
antebellum	apperceive	asphyxiate	automatise	barrenwort	bibliopoly
antecedent	appetising	aspidistra	automatism	barysphere	bibliotics
antecessor	appetitive	aspiration	automatist	basketball	bibulously
antechapel	applicable	assafetida	automobile	basketwork	bichromate
antemortem	applicably	assailable	automotive	bassethorn	bicultural
antependia	applicator	assaultive	autonomist	bassoonist	bidonville
antepenult	appointive	assemblage	autonomous	bastardise	biennially
anteriorly	appositely	assentient	autoplasty	batfowling	bigamously
antheridia	apposition	assessable	autostrada	batholitic	bighearted
anthracene	appositive	assessment	autostrade	bathometer	bigmouthed
anthracite	appreciate	asseverate	autumnally	bathymeter	bijouterie
anthracoid	apprentice	assibilate	avantgarde	bathymetry	bilgewater
anthropoid	approvable	assignable	avaricious	bathyscaph	biliverdin
antibiosis	approvably	assignment	aventurine	bathyscope	billetdoux
antibiotic	aquafortis	assimilate	averseness	batrachian	billposter
Antichrist	aquamarine	assistance	aversively	battailous	bilocation
anticipant	aquaplaner	associable	aviatrices	battledore	bimestrial
anticipate	aquiferous	assoilment	aviculture	battlement	bimetallic
anticlimax	aquilinity	assortment	avouchment	battleship	binaurally
anticlinal	aragonitic	assumption	axiologist	bawdyhouse	binoculars
antifreeze	araucarian	assumptive	azeotropic	beadlength	biochemist
antiheroic	arbalester	asteriated	babblement	Beaujolais	biodegrade
antimasque	arbalister	asteroidal	babiroussa	beautician	biodynamic
antimatter	arbitrable	astigmatic	Babylonian	beautifier	bioecology
antimonial	arbitrager	astragalus	babysitter	becomingly	biogenesis
antimonite	arbitrator	astringent	bacchantes	bedchamber	biogenetic
antinomian	arboreally	astrologer	bacchantic	bedclothes	biographer
antipathic	arborvitae	astrologic	backblocks	bedevilled	biographic
antiphonal	archaistic	astronomer	backbiting	Bedlington	biological
antipodean	archbishop	astronomic	backgammon	bedraggled	biometrics
antiproton	archdeacon	astuteness	background	beechdrops	biomorphic
antiquated	archerfish	asymmetric	backhanded	beefburger	biophysics
antiSemite	archetypal	asymptotic	backhander	beekeeping	bioscience
antisepsis	architrave	asynchrony	backsheesh	beforehand	biparietal
antiseptic	archpriest	ateleiosis	backslider	beforetime	bipartisan
antisocial	arenaceous	Athanasian	backstairs	behindhand	bipetalous
antistatic	areolation	atmosphere	backstitch	bejewelled	bipolarity
antitheism	Areopagite	atomically	backstroke	Belgravian	birdspider
antitheist	argumentum	attachable	backwardly	believable	birdstrike
antitheses	aristocrat	attachment	badderlock	belladonna	birthplace
antithesis	arithmetic	attackable	bafflement	belletrist	birthright
antithetic	Armageddon	attainable	bafflingly	bellflower	birthstone
antonymous	armigerous	attainment	balbriggan	bellringer	bisexually
aphaereses	armorially	attendance	balderdash	bellwether	bissextile
aphaeresis	armourclad	attenuated	baldheaded	bellyacher	bisulphate
aphoristic	armourless	attenuator	ballflower	bellydance	bisulphide
aphrodisia	arrestment	attornment	ballistics	bellylaugh	bisulphite
apiculture	arrhythmia	attractant	ballooning	belongings	bitchiness
aplacental	arrhythmic	attraction	balloonist	bemedalled	bitterling
apocalypse	arrogantly	attractive	balneology	bemusement	bitterness
apocarpous	arrogation	attunement	balustrade	benedicite	bitterroot
apochromat	arterially	atypically	banderilla	Benedictus	bitterwood
apocryphal	arteriolar	auctioneer	bandmaster	benefactor	bituminise
apodeictic	artfulness	audibility	banishment	beneficent	bituminous
apolaustic	arthralgia	audiometer	bankruptcy	beneficial	bivalvular
apolitical	arthralgic	audiometry	baptistery	benevolent	bivouacked
Apollinian	arthromere	audiophile	barbellate	benignancy	bizarrerie
Apollonian	articulate	auditorial	barbershop	Benthamism	blackamoor

blackberry	bootlicker	brightwork	calciferol	carmagnole	ceruminous
blackboard	bootstraps	brilliance	calcsinter	carnallite	cessionary
blackfaced	borborygmi	brilliancy	calculable	carnassial	chainsmoke
blackguard	bordereaux	Britishism	calculably	carotenoid	chairwoman
blackheart	borderland	broadcloth	calculator	carotinoid	chalcedony
Blackshirt	borderless	broadsheet	Caledonian	carpellary	chalkboard
blacksmith	borderline	broadsword	calibrator	carpetweed	chalkstone
blackthorn	Boswellian	brocatelle	caliginous	carphology	challenger
blackwater	Boswellise	brokendown	callowness	carragheen	chalybeate
bladdernut	Boswellism	brokenness	calumniate	carryingon	chamaeleon
blamefully	bothersome	bromegrass	calumnious	Carthusian	chamberpot
blancmange	botryoidal	bronchiole	calyciform	cartomancy	champignon
blanketing	bottlefeed	bronchitic	calyptrate	cartoonist	chancellor
blanquette	bottleneck	bronchitis	camelopard	cartwright	chandelier
blasphemer	bottletree	broodiness	camerlengo	caruncular	changeable
blastemata	bottomless	broodingly	camerlingo	caryatides	changeably
blastocyst	bottommost	broomstick	camouflage	cascarilla	changeless
blastoderm	bouncingly	browbeaten	campaigner	caseharden	changeling
blastomere	bourbonism	brownshirt	campestral	caseworker	changeover
blastopore	bourbonist	brownstone	camphorate	cassolette	channelise
blazonment	bowdlerise	brusquerie	canaliculi	castration	channelled
bleachable	bowdlerism	bryologist	cancellate	casualness	chaparajos
bleariness	boyishness	bubblyjock	cancelling	catabolism	chaparejos
blearyeyed	brachiator	buccinator	cancellous	catafalque	chapfallen
bleatingly	brachiopod	Buchmanism	candelabra	catalectic	chaplaincy
blepharism	brachylogy	Buchmanite	candescent	cataleptic	charactery
blindingly	brachyural	bucketshop	candidness	cataloguer	chargeable
blissfully	brachyuran	Buddhistic	candlefish	cataphract	chargehand
blistering	bradyseism	budgerigar	candletree	catarrhine	charioteer
blitheness	Brahmanism	bufflehead	candlewick	catastasis	charismata
blithering	Brahminism	buffoonery	candlewood	catburglar	charitable
blithesome	brainchild	bullethead	candyfloss	catchpenny	charitably
blitzkrieg	braininess	bullheaded	cankerworm	catechesis	Charleston
blockboard	brainpower	bullroarer	cannelloni	catechetic	charmingly
blockhouse	brainstorm	bumblingly	cannonball	catechiser	chartreuse
blockishly	brakeblock	bumpkinish	canonicals	catechumen	chartulary
bloodguilt	brakelight	bunchgrass	canonicate	categorise	chasteness
bloodhound	branchiate	bunglingly	canonicity	catenation	chatelaine
bloodiness	brandyball	burdensome	canorously	catholicon	chatoyance
bloodmoney	brandysnap	bureaucrat	cantaloupe	catholicos	chatterbox
bloodstain	brantgoose	burglarise	cantatrice	catoptrics	chattiness
bloodstock	brassiness	burramundi	canterbury	cattlegrid	chaudfroid
bloodstone	bratticing	bursarship	cantilever	causticity	chauffeuse
blottesque	brawniness	bushmaster	cantillate	cautionary	chauntress
bluebonnet	brazenness	bushranger	cantonment	cautiously	chauvinism
bluebottle	brazilwood	bustlingly	canvasback	cavalierly	chauvinist
bluecollar	breadboard	butterball	canvaswork	cavalryman	cheapishly
bluejacket	breadcrumb	butterbean	canzonetta	cavitation	cheapskate
bluepencil	breadfruit	butterfish	caoutchouc	celebrated	checkpoint
blueribbon	breadstick	buttermilk	capability	celebrator	cheekiness
bluethroat	breadstuff	butterwort	capacitate	cellophane	cheerfully
bluetongue	breakables	buttonball	capacitive	cellularly	cheeriness
bluishness	breakpoint	buttonbush	capitalise	cellulitis	cheesecake
blurringly	breakwater	buttondown	capitalism	cellulosic	cheesiness
blushingly	breastbone	buttonhole	capitalist	censorious	chelicerae
blusterous	breastwall	buttonhook	capitation	censorship	chemically
boastfully	breastwork	buttonless	Capitoline	censurable	chemisette
bobbinlace	breathable	buttonwood	capitulary	centennial	chemotaxis
bobbysocks	breathless	byelection	capitulate	centesimal	chequebook
bobbysoxer	breechless	byssaceous	cappuccino	centigrade	chersonese
boisterous	breezeless	byssinosis	capricious	centilitre	chessboard
bollweevil	breeziness	cabalistic	captiously	centillion	chevrotain
bolometric	brentgoose	cacciatore	carabineer	centimetre	chickenpox
bolshevise	bressummer	cachinnate	carabinier	centralise	chiffchaff
bolshevism	brevetting	cackhanded	caramelise	centralism	chiffonier
bolshevist	brickfield	cacodaemon	caravaneer	centralist	childbirth
bombardier	bricklayer	cacogenics	caravanned	centrality	childermas
bondholder	bridegroom	cacography	caravanner	centreback	childishly
boneheaded	bridesmaid	cacomistle	carbonnade	centrefold	childproof
bonesetter	bridgeable	cadaverous	carboxylic	centrehalf	chiliastic
boneshaker	bridgehead	caddisworm	carbuncled	centricity	chilliness
bookbinder	bridgeless	Caerphilly	carcinogen	centrifuge	chimerical
bookkeeper	bridgework	caespitose	carcinosis	centromere	chimneypot
bookmaking	bridlepath	cajolement	cardialgia	centrosome	chimpanzee
bookmarker	brigandage	cajolingly	cardiogram	cephalopod	chinagraph
bookseller	brigandine	calamander	cardiology	cerebellum	chinchilla
boondoggle	brigandism	calamitous	cardplayer	ceremonial	chiromancy
bootlegger	brigantine	calcareous	carelessly	cerography	chiselling
bootlessly	brightness	calceolate	caricature	certiorari	chivalrous

chlorinate	cloverleaf	columbaria	computator	considered	cooptation
chloroform	clownishly	comanchero	comstocker	consistent	cooptative
choiceness	clubfooted	combustion	concentric	consistory	coordinate
chokeberry	clumsiness	combustive	conception	consociate	coparcener
chondritic	Clydesdale	comedienne	conceptive	consolable	copartnery
choriambic	cnidoblast	comehither	conceptual	consonance	Copernican
Christhood	coacervate	comeliness	concerning	consonancy	copesettic
Christlike	coachbuilt	comestible	concertina	consortium	copperhead
chromatics	coachhouse	comicality	concertino	conspectus	coproducer
chromatype	coadjacent	comicopera	concession	conspiracy	coprolitic
chromosome	coagulable	commandant	concessive	conspirant	copulation
chronicity	coalbunker	commandeer	concettism	constantan	copulative
chronicler	coalescent	commandery	conchoidal	Constantia	copyholder
chronogram	coaptation	commanding	conchology	constantly	copyreader
chronology	coarseness	commandoes	conciliary	constipate	copywriter
chrysolite	coastguard	commentary	conciliate	constitute	coquettish
chrysotile	coastwards	commentate	concinnity	constraint	coradicate
chubbiness	coathanger	commercial	conclusion	constringe	coralberry
chuckerout	coatimundi	commissary	conclusive	consuetude	coralsnake
chuckwagon	cochleated	commission	conclusory	consulship	corbelling
churchgoer	cockalorum	commissure	concoction	consultant	corbiculae
churchyard	cockatrice	commitment	concoctive	consulting	cordiality
churlishly	cockchafer	committing	concordant	consultive	cordierite
cicatrices	cockneyish	commixture	concretely	consumable	cordillera
Ciceronian	cockneyism	commodious	concretion	consumedly	cordwainer
cicisbeism	cocksurely	commonable	concretise	consummate	corelation
cinchonine	codswallop	commonalty	concretism	contagious	corelative
Cinderella	coelacanth	commonness	concretist	contendent	coriaceous
cinecamera	coenobitic	commonroom	concurrent	contention	Corinthian
cinerarium	coenobytic	commonweal	concurring	contestant	corncockle
cinquefoil	coequality	communally	concussion	contextual	cornerwise
Circassian	coercively	communique	concussive	contexture	cornettist
circuitous	coetaneous	commutable	condensate	contiguity	cornflakes
circularly	coeternity	commutator	condensery	contiguous	cornflower
circulator	coexistent	compaction	condescend	continence	cornstarch
circumcise	coffeemill	comparable	condolence	contingent	cornucopia
circumflex	cogitation	comparably	conduction	continuant	coromandel
circumfuse	cogitative	comparator	conductive	continuate	coronation
circumvent	cognisable	comparison	confabbing	continuity	corporally
cismontane	cognisably	compassion	confection	continuous	corporator
cispontine	cognisance	compasssaw	conference	contortion	corporeity
Cistercian	cognominal	compatible	conferment	contortive	corpulence
citronella	cohabitant	compatibly	conferring	contraband	corpulency
clamminess	coherently	compatriot	confervoid	contrabass	corpuscule
clangorous	cohesively	compelling	confession	contractor	correction
clannishly	coincident	compendium	confidante	contradict	corrective
clarabella	colatitude	compensate	confidence	contraprop	correspond
Clarenceux	colchicine	competence	confirmand	contrarily	corrigenda
claspknife	coleoptera	competency	confiscate	contravene	corrigible
classicise	coleoptile	competitor	conflation	contribute	corrivalry
classicism	coleorhiza	complacent	confluence	contritely	corroboree
classicist	collarbeam	complainer	conformism	contrition	corrugated
classified	collarbone	complected	conformist	controlled	corrugator
classifier	collarette	complement	conformity	controller	corruption
clavichord	collarless	completely	confounded	controvert	corruptive
clavicular	collarstud	completion	confusedly	convalesce	corsetiere
clawhammer	collatable	completive	congeneric	convection	corticated
clearstory	collateral	complexion	congenital	convective	Corybantes
clementine	collection	complexity	congestion	convenable	corybantic
clerestory	collective	compliance	congestive	convenance	coryphaeus
clerically	collegiate	compliancy	conglobate	convenient	cosentient
cleverness	collembola	complicacy	congregant	convention	cosmically
clientship	collimator	complicate	congregate	conventual	cosmogonic
clingstone	collocutor	complicity	congruence	convergent	cosmopolis
clinically	colloquial	compliment	congruency	conversant	cosmoramic
clinkstone	colloquist	complotted	coniferous	conversely	costliness
clinometer	colloquium	composedly	conjecture	conversion	cottoncake
clinometry	colonially	compositor	conjointly	conveyable	cottonseed
clodhopper	colonnaded	compotator	conjugally	conveyance	cottontail
cloistered	coloration	compounder	connatural	conviction	cottonweed
closestool	coloratura	compradore	connection	convictive	cottonwood
closetplay	colossally	comprehend	connective	convincing	cottonwool
clothesbag	colourable	compressed	conniption	convoluted	couchgrass
clothespeg	colourably	compressor	connivance	convulsant	coulometry
clothespin	colourfast	compromise	conscience	convulsion	councillor
cloudberry	colourless	compulsion	consecrate	convulsive	councilman
cloudburst	colportage	compulsive	consectary	coolheaded	counselled
cloudiness	colporteur	compulsory	consensual	coolingoff	counsellor
clovehitch	colporteur	computable	consequent	cooperator	counteract

```
countryish  cryptogamy  decahedron  delicately  derogation  dictionary
countryman  cryptogram  decampment  delightful  derogatory  didactical
couplement  cryptology  decapitate  delimitate  desalinate  didgeridoo
courageous  ctenophore  decapodous  delineator  descendant  diecasting
courthouse  cuckoopint  deceivable  delinquent  descendent  dielectric
cousinhood  cuckoospit  decelerate  deliquesce  descension  diesinking
cousinship  cucullated  Decembrist  delocalise  descriptor  difference
couturiere  cuddlesome  decemviral  delphinium  desecrater  difficulty
couverture  cudgelling  deceptible  delphinoid  desecrator  diffidence
covalently  cuirassier  decigramme  deltiology  deservedly  diffusible
covariance  cultivable  decimalise  delusional  deshabille  digestible
covenanted  cultivator  decimalism  delusively  desiccator  digitalise
covenantee  culturally  decimation  demagogism  desiderata  digitately
covenanter  cumbersome  decisively  demandable  desiderate  digitation
covenantor  cumbrously  decivilise  dementedly  designator  digitiform
covetingly  cummerbund  declarable  demobilise  designedly  digression
covetously  cumulation  declassify  democratic  designment  digressive
cowcatcher  cumulative  declension  demography  desipience  dilapidate
coweringly  cumuliform  declinable  demoiselle  desirously  dilatation
cowparsley  cunctation  decolonise  demolition  desistance  dilatorily
cowpuncher  cunctative  decolorant  demonetise  desolately  dilemmatic
crackajack  curability  decolorise  demoniacal  desolation  dilettante
crackbrain  curatorial  decompound  demonology  desorption  dilettanti
cradlesong  curmudgeon  decompress  demoralise  despatcher  diligently
craftguild  curricular  decoration  demotivate  desperados  dillydally
craftiness  curriculum  decorative  demureness  despicable  diluteness
cragginess  cursedness  decorously  demurrable  despicably  diminished
cranesbill  curvaceous  decrescent  denaturant  despisable  diminuendo
craniology  curvacious  dedication  dendriform  despiteful  diminution
crankiness  curvetting  dedicative  dendrology  despiteous  diminutive
crankshaft  cuspidated  dedicatory  denegation  despondent  dimorphism
crapulence  cussedness  deductible  denigrator  desquamate  dimorphous
craquelure  custommade  deepfreeze  denominate  destructor  diningroom
crassitude  cuttlebone  deepfrozen  denotation  detachable  dinnerless
cravenness  cuttlefish  deeprooted  denotative  detachedly  diphtheria
creaminess  cuttystool  deepseated  denouement  detachment  diphtheric
creatinine  cybernetic  deerforest  densimeter  detainment  diphyletic
creatively  cyclically  deescalate  dentifrice  detectable  diphyodont
creativity  cyclograph  defacement  denudation  detergency  diplodocus
creaturely  cyclometer  defalcator  denunciate  determined  diplomatic
credential  cyclopedia  defamation  deodoriser  deterrence  dipsomania
creditable  cyclopedic  defamatory  deontology  detestable  directness
creditably  cyclostome  defeasance  deoxidiser  detestably  directoire
creepiness  cyclostyle  defeasible  department  detonation  directress
crematoria  cylindered  defeminise  dependable  detonative  disability
crenellate  cylindroid  defendable  dependably  detoxicant  disappoint
crenulated  cystoscope  defensible  dependence  detoxicate  disapprove
crepuscule  cystoscopy  defensibly  dependency  detraction  disarrange
crescentic  cytochrome  deferrable  depilation  detractive  disastrous
cretaceous  cytologist  deficiency  depilatory  Devanagari  disbarring
crewelwork  czarevitch  defilement  deplorable  devilishly  disbelieve
cribriform  daintiness  definement  deplorably  devitalise  disbudding
criminally  daisychain  definienda  deployment  devocalise  disburthen
crinolette  damageable  definitely  depolarise  devolution  discerning
crippledom  damagingly  definienda  depopulate  devotement  discharger
crispation  dampcourse  definitive  deportment  devotional  discipline
crispbread  dampingoff  definitude  depositary  devoutness  disclaimer
crisscross  dapplegrey  deflagrate  deposition  dextrality  disclosure
critically  datamation  deflection  depository  dextrously  discobolus
crocoisite  daughterly  deflective  depravedly  diabolical  discomfort
crossbench  dauphiness  deflowerer  depreciate  diachronic  discommend
crossbones  daydreamer  defoliator  depredator  diagnostic  discommode
crossbreed  dazzlement  deforciant  depressant  diagonally  discompose
crosscheck  dazzlingly  defrayable  depression  diagraphic  disconcert
crossgrain  deaconship  defrayment  depressive  dialysable  disconfirm
crosshatch  deactivate  degeneracy  deprivable  diapedesis  disconnect
crossindex  deadliness  degenerate  depuration  diapedetic  discontent
crosslight  deadweight  degradable  depurative  diaphanous  discophile
crosspatch  deaeration  degradedly  deputation  diarrhoeal  discordant
crosspiece  deathwatch  degressive  deracinate  diarrhoeic  discounter
crossrefer  debasement  dehiscence  derailleur  diastemata  discourage
crossroads  debatement  dehumanise  derailment  diathermal  discourser
crosstrees  debauchery  dehumidify  derestrict  diathermic  discoverer
crowkeeper  debilitate  dejectedly  deridingly  diatropism  discreetly
crustacean  debonairly  delaminate  derisively  dichroitic  discrepant
crustation  debouchure  delectable  derivation  dichromate  discretely
crustiness  decadently  delectably  derivative  dickcissel  discretion
cryogenics  decagramme  delegation  dermatitis  Dickensian  discursive
cryoscopic  decahedral  deliberate  dermatogen  dictatress  discussant
```

discussion	distichous	dressiness	egoistical	encystment	epigenesis
discussive	distilland	dressmaker	Egyptology	endearment	epigenetic
discutient	distillate	drivelling	eigenvalue	endemicity	epiglottal
disdainful	distillery	driverless	eighteenmo	endocrinal	epiglottic
diseconomy	distilling	droopingly	eighteenth	endodermal	epiglottis
disembogue	distinctly	drophammer	eisteddfod	endodermis	epigrapher
disembosom	distortion	drosophila	elaborator	endogamous	epigraphic
disembowel	distracted	drowsihead	elasticise	endogenous	epilimnion
disembroil	distrainer	drowsiness	elasticity	endophytic	epiphytism
disenchant	distrainor	drudgingly	elatedness	endopodite	episcopacy
disengaged	distraught	drupaceous	elderberry	endorsable	episcopate
disenthral	distressed	drysaltery	elecampane	endoscopic	episematic
disentitle	distribute	dubitation	electively	endosmosis	episodical
disentwine	distringas	dubitative	electorate	endosmotic	episternum
disenviron	disulphate	dumbledore	electrical	endothelia	epistolary
disfeature	disulphide	dumbstruck	electronic	endproduct	epistrophe
disfurnish	disutility	dumbwaiter	elementary	endstopped	epithelial
disgruntle	disyllabic	dumfounder	Eleusinian	enduringly	epithelium
disgustful	disyllable	dunderhead	elevenplus	energetics	equability
dishabille	ditriglyph	dungbeetle	eliminable	enervation	equanimity
disharmony	divagation	duniwassal	eliminator	enervative	equational
dishearten	divaricate	duodecimal	elliptical	enfacement	equatorial
dishonesty	divebomber	duodenitis	elongation	engagement	equestrian
dishwasher	divergence	duplicator	eloquently	engagingly	equilibria
disincline	divergency	durability	elucidator	engineroom	equipotent
disinherit	divestment	dustjacket	elutriator	Englishman	equitation
disjointed	divination	duumvirate	emaciation	englutting	equivalent
dislikable	divinatory	dwarfishly	emancipate	engrossing	equivocate
disloyally	divineness	dynamistic	emancipist	engulfment	eradicable
disloyalty	divisional	dysenteric	emarginate	enharmonic	eradicator
dismalness	divisively	dysgraphia	emasculate	enigmatise	erectility
dismission	divulgence	dysplastic	embalmment	enigmatist	eremitical
dismissive	doctorship	dysprosium	embankment	enjambment	erethismic
disordered	documental	dystrophic	embarkment	enjoinment	ergodicity
disorderly	doggedness	earthbound	emblazoner	enlacement	ergonomics
disownment	dogmatical	earthiness	emblazonry	enlistment	ergonomist
disparager	dogmatiser	earthlight	emblematic	enmeshment	ergosterol
disparates	dogstongue	earthquake	emblements	enormously	ericaceous
dispassion	dolomitise	earthshine	embodiment	enregister	erotically
dispatcher	dolorously	earthwards	embolismic	enrichment	erotogenic
dispelling	dominantly	eartrumpet	embonpoint	enrigiment	erotomania
dispensary	domination	earwigging	embossment	ensanguine	erubescent
dispersant	dominative	earwitness	embouchure	entailment	eructation
dispersion	donkeywork	easterling	embowelled	enterolith	eruptively
dispersive	donnybrook	Eastertide	embroidery	enterotomy	erysipelas
dispersoid	doorkeeper	ebullience	embryogeny	enterprise	escadrille
dispirited	dorsigrade	ebulliency	embryology	enthralled	escalation
dispiteous	dosimetric	ebullition	embryonate	enthusiasm	escallonia
disposable	doublebass	ecchymosis	emendation	enthusiast	escapement
dispossess	doubleness	ecchymotic	emendatory	enticement	escapology
dispraiser	doublepark	ecclesiast	emerypaper	enticingly	escarpment
disputable	doubletalk	echinoderm	emerywheel	entireness	escharotic
disputably	doubletime	ecological	emigration	entombment	escheatage
disqualify	doubtfully	economical	emigratory	entomology	escritoire
disquieten	doubtingly	economiser	emissivity	entrancing	Esculapian
disquietly	doughfaced	ectodermal	emollition	entrapment	escutcheon
disrespect	dovecolour	ectodermic	emonstrator	enumerable	espadrille
disruption	downfallen	ectogenous	empanelled	enumerator	especially
disruptive	downstairs	ecumenical	emparadise	enunciable	essayistic
dissatisfy	downstream	eczematous	empathetic	enunciator	estimation
dissection	downstroke	edentulous	emphractic	enwrapping	estimative
dissembler	downwardly	edibleness	emphractic	enzymology	eternalise
dissension	doxography	editorship	empiricism	eosinophil	eternalist
dissertate	draconites	edulcorate	empiricist	epeirogeny	ethereally
disservice	drafthorse	effaceable	employable	epentheses	ethicality
dissidence	dragonhead	effacement	employment	epenthesis	ethnically
dissilient	dragonnade	effectuate	emulsifier	epenthetic	ethnologic
dissimilar	dragontree	effeminacy	enamelling	epexegeses	ethologist
dissipated	dramatical	effeminate	enamellist	epexegesis	etiolation
dissociate	dramaturge	effervesce	enantiosis	epexegetic	eucalyptol
dissoluble	dramaturgy	effeteness	encampment	ephemerous	eucalyptus
dissolvent	drawbridge	efficacity	encasement	ephorality	eucaryotic
dissonance	drawingpin	efficiency	encashment	epiblastic	eudemonism
dissonancy	drawlingly	effloresce	encephalic	epicentral	eudemonist
dissuasion	drawstring	effortless	encephalon	epicycloid	eudiometer
dissuasive	dreadfully	effrontery	enchanting	epideictic	eudiometry
distensile	dreaminess	effulgence	encourager	epidemical	eugenicist
distension	dreamworld	effusively	encroacher	epidermoid	euhemerise
distention	dreariness	egocentric	encyclical	epigastric	euhemerism

euhemerist	experience	fancifully	fiftyfifty	floatplane	fortuitous
eulogistic	experiment	fandangoes	figuration	floatstone	fortyniner
euphonious	expertness	fantastico	figurative	flocculate	forwarding
euphuistic	expiration	fantoccini	figurehead	flocculent	forwearied
eurhythmic	expiratory	farcically	filariasis	floodlight	fosterling
Eurodollar	explicable	farfetched	filibuster	floodwater	foudroyant
Eurovision	explicitly	farsighted	filterable	floorboard	foundation
eurypterid	exploitage	fasciation	filthiness	floorcloth	founderous
euthanasia	exploitive	fascicular	filtration	floppiness	fourchette
evacuation	exportable	fasciculus	fimbriated	florentine	fourfooted
evacuative	exposition	fascinator	fingerbowl	florescent	fourhanded
evaluation	expositive	fastidious	fingerless	floriation	Fourierism
evaluative	expository	fastigiate	fingerling	floribunda	fourinhand
evanescent	expressage	fatalistic	fingermark	floridness	fourleaved
evangelise	expression	fatherhood	fingernail	florilegia	fourposter
evangelism	expressive	fatherland	fingerpost	floristics	foursquare
evangelist	expressway	fatherless	finicality	flosculous	fourstroke
evaporable	exprobrate	fatherlike	finiteness	flowergirl	fourteener
evaporator	expunction	fathership	FinnoUgric	flowerless	fourteenth
evenhanded	expurgator	fathomable	fireblight	fluffiness	fowlplague
eventually	exsanguine	fathomless	fireescape	flugelhorn	foxhunting
everglades	extemporal	fatiguable	firepolicy	flunkeydom	fractional
everliving	extendedly	faultiness	fireraiser	flunkeyism	fragmental
everyplace	extendible	favourable	firescreen	fluoridate	fragrantly
everything	extensible	favourably	firstclass	fluorinate	framboesia
everywhere	extenuator	fearlessly	firstnight	fluorotype	franchiser
evidential	exteriorly	fearnought	fishcarver	fluviatile	Franciscan
evilminded	externally	fearsomely	fisherfolk	fluxionary	Francophil
eviscerate	extinction	featherbed	fishkettle	flycatcher	frangipane
evolvement	extinctive	feathering	fishmonger	flyfishing	frangipani
exactitude	extinguish	febrifugal	fisticuffs	flyswatter	fraternise
exaggerate	extirpator	fecklessly	fitfulness	foamflower	fraternity
exaltation	extractant	federalise	fivefinger	foetidness	fratricide
examinable	extraction	federalism	fixedpoint	foliaceous	fraudulent
exasperate	extractive	federalist	flabbiness	folklorist	fraxinella
excavation	extramural	federation	flabellate	folkmemory	freakiness
excellence	extraneity	federative	flaccidity	folksiness	freakishly
excellency	extraneous	feebleness	flagellant	folksinger	freebooter
excerption	extricable	felicitate	flagellate	follicular	freedwoman
excitation	exuberance	felicitous	flagitious	fontanelle	freehanded
excitative	exulcerate	fellmonger	flagrantly	footballer	freeholder
excitatory	exultantly	fellowship	flagwaving	footbridge	freelancer
excitement	exultation	felspathic	flamboyant	footcandle	freeliving
excitingly	exultingly	femaleness	flameproof	footlights	freeloader
excogitate	exurbanite	femininely	flamingoes	footwarmer	freemartin
excrescent	exuviation	femininity	flannelled	foraminous	freesoiler
excruciate	eyeglasses	femininity	flapdoodle	forbidding	freespeech
excusatory	eyeservice	fenestella	flashboard	forcefully	freespoken
execration	eyewitness	fenestrate	flashflood	forcipated	freightage
execrative	fabricator	fertiliser	flashiness	foreboding	Frenchness
execratory	fabulously	fervidness	flashlight	forecaster	frenziedly
executable	faceharden	fescennine	flashpoint	forecastle	frequenter
exegetical	facesaving	festoonery	flatfooted	forecourse	frequently
exenterate	facileness	fetchingly	flattering	forefather	freshwater
exhalation	facilitate	fetterlock	flatulence	forefinger	friability
exhaustion	factiously	feuilleton	flatulency	foregather	fricandeau
exhaustive	factitious	feverishly	flavescent	foreground	fricasseed
exhibition	factorship	fianchetto	flavourful	forehanded	frictional
exhibitory	factualism	fibreboard	flavouring	foreignism	friendless
exhilarant	factualist	fibreglass	flawlessly	foreordain	friendlily
exhilarate	factuality	fibrillary	fleabitten	forerunner	friendship
exhumation	fadelessly	fibrillate	fleacircus	foreshadow	frigidness
exobiology	Fahrenheit	fibrillose	fleamarket	foresheets	frigorific
exorbitant	faintheart	fibrinogen	fledgeling	foreteller	frilliness
exospheric	fairground	fibrositis	fleeringly	forfeiture	fringeless
exoterical	fairhaired	fickleness	fleetingly	forgetting	friskiness
exothermal	fairleader	fictioneer	fleshiness	forgivable	fritillary
exothermic	fairminded	fictionist	fleshwound	forgivably	frivolling
exotically	fairspoken	fictitious	flexuously	formatting	frizziness
expandable	fairycycle	fiddleback	flightdeck	formidable	froghopper
expansible	faithfully	fiddlehead	flightless	formidably	frolicking
expatriate	fallacious	fiddlewood	flightpath	formlessly	frolicsome
expectance	fallingoff	fiducially	flimsiness	fornicator	frontbench
expectancy	fallowness	fieldglass	flintiness	fortepiano	frontwards
expectedly	familiarly	fieldmouse	flippantly	forthright	frostiness
expedience	famishment	fieldpiece	flirtation	fortissimi	frothiness
expediency	famousness	fieldstone	fiendishly	fortissimo	frowningly
expedition	fanaticise	fiendishly	floatboard	fortuitism	fruitarian
expendable	fanaticism	fierceness	floatingly	fortuitist	fruitfully

frutescent	geognostic	gooseflesh	groundling	hankypanky	hemipteran
fuddyduddy	geographer	goosegrass	groundmass	Hanoverian	hemisphere
fugitively	geographic	gorgeously	groundplan	Hansardise	hempnettle
fulfilling	geological	Gorgonzola	groundrent	hanselling	henceforth
fulfilment	geometrise	gormandise	groundsman	harassment	hendecagon
fuliginous	geophysics	gothically	groundwork	harbourage	henharrier
fullbodied	geoponical	governable	grovelling	hardbilled	henhearted
fullbottom	geothermal	governance	growlingly	hardbitten	henotheism
fulllength	geothermic	governess	grubbiness	hardboiled	henotheist
fumblingly	geotropism	government	grudgingly	hardfisted	heortology
fumigation	geriatrics	gracefully	gruesomely	hardhanded	heparinise
functional	geriatrist	graciosity	grumpiness	hardheaded	hepatology
funereally	germicidal	graciously	guardhouse	harelipped	heptachord
fungicidal	germinally	gradualism	guesthouse	harmlessly	heptagonal
funnelling	gerundival	gradualist	guestnight	harmonical	Heptameron
furuncular	gesundheit	graduation	guilefully	harmonious	heptameter
fusibility	ghastfully	gramicidin	guillotine	harmoniser	heptarchic
fussbudget	Ghibelline	gramineous	guiltiness	hartebeest	Heptateuch
fustanella	Gilbertian	grammarian	gunfighter	haruspices	heptatonic
futureless	gingerbeer	gramophone	gunrunning	harvestman	herbaceous
futuristic	gingersnap	granadilla	gunslinger	hauntingly	hereabouts
futurology	gingivitis	grandchild	gutturally	haustellum	hereditary
fuzzywuzzy	girlfriend	granddaddy	gymnastics	haustorium	heresiarch
gadolinite	glaciation	grandducal	gymnosophy	hawserlaid	hereticate
gadolinium	glaciology	grandmamma	gymnosperm	headcheese	heretofore
gadrooning	gladhander	grandniece	gynandrous	headhunter	hermetical
gaillardia	gladsomely	grandstand	gynocratic	headmaster	hermitcrab
gaingiving	Glagolitic	granduncle	gypsophila	headphones	heroically
galimatias	glancingly	grangerise	gyrational	headspring	heroicness
galleywest	glasscloth	grangerism	gyrocopter	headsquare	heroicomic
galliambic	glassfibre	granophyre	gyroscopic	headstream	herrenvolk
galloglass	glasshouse	granularly	habiliment	headstrong	Herrnhuter
Gallomania	glassiness	granulator	habilitate	headwaiter	hesitantly
Gallophile	glasspaper	granulitic	habitation	heartblock	hesitation
Gallophobe	glassworks	grapefruit	habitually	heartblood	hesitative
galvaniser	Glaswegian	grapesugar	hackbuteer	heartbreak	heterodont
gambolling	glauberite	graphemics	hackmatack	heartiness	heterodoxy
gamekeeper	glauconite	graphitise	haematosis	heartsease	heterodyne
gametangia	glimmering	graphology	haematuria	heartthrob	heterogamy
ganglionic	globularly	graptolite	haemolysis	heartwhole	heterogeny
gangrenous	glomerular	graspingly	haemolytic	heathendom	heterogony
gargantuan	glomerulus	grasscloth	hagiolatry	heathenise	heterology
garishness	gloominess	grassroots	hagiologic	heathenish	heteronomy
garnierite	gloriously	grasssnake	hagioscope	heathenism	heterotaxy
garnishing	glossarial	gratefully	hairraiser	heatstroke	heulandite
gasconader	glossarist	gratifying	hairspring	heavenborn	heuristics
gaslighter	glossiness	gratuitous	hairstreak	heavensent	hexahedral
gaspereaux	glossology	gravestone	hairstroke	heavenward	hexahedron
gasteropod	glottology	gravimeter	hakenkreuz	heavyarmed	hexamerous
gastrology	glumaceous	gravimetry	halberdier	hebdomadal	hexametric
gastronome	gluttonise	greasewood	halfcocked	hebetation	hibernacle
gastronomy	gluttonous	greasiness	halfdollar	Hebraistic	hierarchal
gatekeeper	glycolyses	greatniece	halflength	hectically	hierarchic
gatelegged	glycolysis	greatuncle	halfnelson	hectograph	hierocracy
gaucheness	glycosuria	GrecoRoman	halfvolley	hectolitre	hieroglyph
gaultheria	glycosuric	greediness	halfwitted	hectometre	hierograph
gauntleted	gnosticism	greedyguts	halfyearly	hedonistic	hierolatry
gelatinise	goalkeeper	greencloth	halieutics	heedlessly	hierophant
gelatinous	goaltender	greenfinch	hallelujah	heliacally	highbinder
gemination	goatsbeard	greenheart	halogenate	helianthus	highflying
gemmaceous	goatsucker	greenhouse	halogenous	Heliconian	highhanded
generalise	gobemouche	greenshank	halophytic	helicopter	highjacker
generalist	gobstopper	greenstick	hammerbeam	heliograph	highlander
generality	Godfearing	greenstone	hammerhead	heliolater	highminded
generation	goggleeyed	greenstuff	hammerless	heliolatry	highoctane
generative	goldbeater	greensward	hammerlock	heliometer	highstrung
generatrix	golddigger	gregarious	hammerpond	heliophyte	highwayman
generosity	goldenness	grenadilla	hamshackle	helioscope	Hindustani
generously	goldenseal	gressorial	handbarrow	heliotaxis	hinterland
geneticist	goldilocks	greyheaded	handedness	heliotrope	hippocampi
genialness	golfcourse	grievously	handgallop	heliotropy	Hippocrene
geniculate	goloptious	grindingly	handicraft	hellbender	hippodrome
genteelism	goluptious	grindstone	handmaiden	helminthic	hippogriff
gentilesse	goniometer	grisliness	handpicked	helplessly	hippogryph
gentlefolk	goniometry	grittiness	handselled	hemicyclic	hippomanes
gentleness	goodliness	groceteria	handsomely	hemihedral	hippophagy
geocentric	goodlooker	grogginess	handspring	hemihedron	hipsterism
geochemist	goodygoody	groundbait	handworked	hemiplegia	hirudinean
geodetical	gooseberry	groundless	hangglider	hemiplegic	histologic

histolysis	housecraft	hypotactic	impanation	incestuous	inexpiably
histolytic	houseguest	hypotenuse	impanelled	inchoately	inexplicit
historical	houselling	hypotheses	imparadise	inchoation	infallible
histrionic	houseplant	hypothesis	impartible	inchoative	infallibly
hitchhiker	houseproud	hypsometer	impartment	incidental	infamously
hithermost	housetrain	hypsometry	impassable	incinerate	infarction
hitherward	housewives	hysteresis	impassably	incipience	infatuated
hoarseness	hoverplane	hysteretic	impassible	incipiency	infeasible
hobbyhorse	hovertrain	hysterical	impassibly	incisively	infectious
hobnobbing	hucklebone	iatrogenic	impatience	incitation	infelicity
hocuspocus	hullabaloo	icebreaker	impeccable	incitement	inferiorly
hodgepodge	humaneness	ichthyosis	impeccably	incivility	infernally
hoitytoity	humanistic	iconoclasm	impeccancy	inclemency	inferrable
hokeypokey	humanities	iconolater	impediment	inclinable	infidelity
holloweyed	humbleness	iconolatry	impendence	includible	infighting
hollowness	humbuggery	iconomachy	impendency	incogitant	infiltrate
hollowware	humbugging	iconometer	impenitent	incoherent	infinitely
holography	humidifier	iconometry	imperative	incomplete	infinitive
holohedral	humoresque	iconoscope	imperially	inconstant	infinitude
holophrase	humoristic	idealistic	imperilled	incrassate	inflatable
holophytic	humorously	ideational	impersonal	incredible	inflection
holosteric	humourless	ideography	impervious	incredibly	inflective
holusbolus	humoursome	ideologist	impishness	increscent	inflexible
homebrewed	humpbacked	idiopathic	implacable	incubation	inflexibly
homecoming	hungriness	idolatress	implacably	incubative	infliction
homeliness	hurdygurdy	idolatrous	implicitly	incubatory	inflictive
homemaking	hurlyburly	ignobility	impolitely	inculcator	informally
homeopathy	husbandage	ignorantly	importable	inculpable	infraction
homiletics	husbandman	ilangilang	importance	incumbency	infrahuman
homocercal	hyaloplasm	illadvised	importuner	incunabula	infrasonic
homoeopath	hybridiser	illatively	imposingly	incurrable	infrequent
homogamous	hydraulics	illaudable	imposition	indagation	infusorial
homogenise	hydrically	illaudably	impossible	indecently	infusorian
homogenous	hydrologic	illegalise	impossibly	indecision	ingeminate
homologate	hydrolysis	illegality	imposthume	indecisive	ingestible
homologise	hydrolytic	illiteracy	impotently	indecorous	inglorious
homologous	hydromancy	illiterate	impoverish	indefinite	ingratiate
homonymous	hydrometer	illnatured	impregnant	indelicacy	ingredient
homoousian	hydrometry	illstarred	impregnate	indelicate	ingression
homophonic	hydropathy	illuminant	impresario	indexation	inhabitant
homosexual	hydrophane	illuminate	impression	indication	inhalation
homozygote	hydrophily	illuminati	impressive	indicative	inharmonic
homozygous	hydrophone	illuminism	imprimatur	indicatory	inherently
homunculus	hydrophyte	illuminist	imprinting	indictable	inheritrix
honeyeater	hydroplane	illusional	improbable	indictment	inhibition
honeyguide	hydroscope	illusively	improbably	indigenous	inhibitory
honeysweet	hydrotaxis	illusorily	improperly	indigested	inhumanely
honorarium	hygrograph	illustrate	improvable	indirectly	inhumanity
honourable	hygrometer	imaginable	improvably	indiscreet	inhumation
honourably	hygrometry	imaginably	improviser	indiscrete	inimically
honourless	hygrophyte	imbecilely	imprudence	indisposed	inimitable
hookedness	hygroscope	imbecility	impudently	indistinct	inimitably
hootenanny	hylotheism	imbibition	impudicity	inditement	iniquitous
hopelessly	hypabyssal	immaculacy	impugnable	individual	initialise
horizontal	hypaethral	immaculate	impugnment	indocility	initialled
hormonally	hypanthium	immaterial	impuissant	indolently	initiation
hornblende	hyperaemia	immaturely	impureness	Indonesian	initiative
hornedness	hyperaemic	immaturity	imputation	inducement	initiatory
hornrimmed	hyperbaric	immemorial	imputative	inductance	injunction
horologist	hyperbaton	imminently	inaccuracy	indulgence	injunctive
horoscopic	hyperbolae	immiscible	inaccurate	induration	inkslinger
horrendous	hyperbolas	immiscibly	inactivate	indurative	innateness
horridness	hyperbolic	immobilise	inactively	industrial	innerrably
horsecloth	hyperdulia	immobility	inactivity	ineducable	innocently
horsecoper	hypergolic	immoderacy	inadequacy	inefficacy	innominate
horseflesh	hypersonic	immoderate	inadequate	inelegance	innovation
horselaugh	hyphenated	immodestly	inappetent	ineligible	innovative
horseleech	hypnagogic	immolation	inapposite	ineligibly	innovatory
horsepower	hypnotiser	immoralist	inaptitude	ineloquent	innuendoes
horseshoer	hypocorism	immorality	inartistic	ineludible	innumeracy
horsewoman	hypodermal	immortally	inaugurate	ineptitude	innumerate
hospitable	hypodermic	immortelle	inbreeding	inequality	innumerous
hospitably	hypodermis	immoveable	incandesce	inevitable	inoculable
hostelling	hypogynous	immunology	incantator	inevitably	inoculator
hotblooded	hypolimnia	immurement	incapacity	inexistent	inoperable
hotchpotch	hypophyses	impairment	incasement	inexorable	inordinate
hourcircle	hypophysis	impalement	incautious	inexorably	inosculate
houseagent	hypostasis	impalpable	incendiary	inexpertly	inquietude
housebound	hypostatic	impalpably	incessancy	inexpiable	inquisitor

insaneness	intertwine	irreverent	karyoplasm	lapidarist	librettist
insanitary	intertwist	irrigation	katabolism	lapidation	licensable
insatiable	interurban	irritation	kennelling	lardydardy	licentiate
insatiably	intervener	irritative	kenspeckle	largescale	licentious
insecurely	intervenor	isentropic	keratinise	larvicidal	lieutenant
insecurity	intervolve	Ishmaelite	keratinous	laryngitic	lifegiving
inseminate	interweave	isochronal	kerchieves	laryngitis	lifejacket
insensible	interwound	isodynamic	kerseymere	lascivious	lifelessly
insensibly	interwoven	isogenetic	kerygmatic	laterality	lifesaving
insentient	interzonal	isoglossal	kettledrum	latescence	ligamental
insightful	intestinal	isolatable	keyboarder	latifundia	lighterage
insinuator	intimately	isometrics	kibbutznik	lattermost	lighterman
insipidity	intimation	isomorphic	kidnapping	laughingly	lightfaced
insistence	intimidate	isoniazide	kieselguhr	laundryman	lighthouse
insistency	intinction	isopterous	kilogramme	lauraceous	lightingup
insobriety	intolerant	isoseismal	kimberlite	laureation	lightproof
insociable	intonation	isosporous	kindliness	laurelling	likelihood
insolation	intoxicant	isothermal	kinematics	lavalliere	likeliness
insolently	intoxicate	italianate	kineticist	lavatorial	likeminded
insolvable	intramural	italianise	kingfisher	lavishment	liliaceous
insolvency	intraurban	Italianism	kingliness	lavishness	limaciform
insouciant	intrepidly	Italophile	kinnikinic	lawabiding	limeburner
inspanning	intrigante	itinerancy	knickknack	lawbreaker	limitation
inspection	intriguant	jackanapes	knifeboard	lawfulness	limitative
inspective	introducer	jackassery	knighthood	lawtennis	limitrophe
inspirator	introrsely	jackhammer	knobkerrie	lawrencium	limpidness
inspissate	introspect	jackknives	knockabout	Lawrentian	linguiform
instalment	intubation	jackrabbit	knockkneed	leadenness	linguistic
instigator	inundation	jacobinise	knopkierie	leaderless	lionhunter
instilling	inundatory	Jacobinism	knottiness	leadership	Lipizzaner
institutor	inurbanity	Jacobitism	kookaburra	leafcutter	lipography
instructor	invaginate	jaggedness	kriegspiel	leafhopper	lipomatous
instrument	invalidate	jaguarundi	Krishnaism	leafinsect	Lippizaner
insufflate	invalidism	janitorial	Krugerrand	lebensraum	lipreading
insularism	invalidity	Janusfaced	Kuomintang	lectionary	lipservice
insularity	invaluable	Japanesque	labiovelar	lederhosen	liquescent
insulation	invaluably	jardiniere	laboratory	ledgerbait	liquidator
insurgence	invariable	jargonelle	laceration	ledgerline	liquidiser
insurgency	invariably	jasperware	lacerative	lefthanded	liquidness
intactness	invariance	jauntiness	lachrymose	lefthander	lissomness
intangible	inventress	jawbreaker	lacklustre	legalistic	listlessly
intangibly	inveracity	jaywalking	laconicism	legateship	literalise
integrable	investment	Jehovistic	lacrimator	legibility	literalism
integrally	inveteracy	jejuneness	lacrymator	legislator	literalist
integrator	inveterate	jeopardise	lactescent	legitimacy	literality
integument	invigilate	jerrybuilt	lacustrine	legitimate	literarily
intendance	invigorate	jesuitical	ladderback	legitimise	literation
intendment	invincible	Jewishness	ladychapel	legitimism	literature
intenerate	invincibly	jimsonweed	ladyfinger	legitimist	lithoglyph
intentness	inviolable	jingoistic	ladykiller	leguminous	lithograph
interbreed	inviolably	jinriksha	Lamarckian	Leibnizian	lithologic
interceder	invitation	jinrikisha	Lamarckism	lemniscate	lithophane
intercross	invitatory	jobbernowl	lambrequin	lemongrass	lithophyte
interested	invitingly	jocoseness	lamentable	lengthways	lithotrity
interferer	invocation	jocularity	lamentably	lengthwise	Lithuanian
interferon	invocatory	johnnycake	lamentedly	lenticular	litigation
intergrade	involucral	Johnsonese	laminarian	lentigines	litterlout
interiorly	involucrum	johnsonian	lamination	leopardess	littleness
interleave	involution	jolterhead	Lammastide	lepidolite	liturgical
interloper	inwardness	journalese	lampoonery	leprechaun	livelihood
interlunar	iodination	journalise	lampoonist	lesbianism	liveliness
intermarry	ionisation	journalism	lanceolate	letterbomb	livingroom
intermezzi	ionosphere	journalist	landholder	letterbook	lobsterpot
intermezzo	iridaceous	journeyman	landhunger	lettercard	lobulation
internally	iridescent	joyfulness	landingnet	letterhead	lockerroom
internment	iridosmine	joyousness	landlocked	letterless	lockkeeper
internodal	Irishwoman	jubilantly	landlubber	leucocytic	lockstitch
internship	ironhanded	jubilation	landocracy	leucoplast	locomotion
interphase	ironically	judgematic	landowning	leukocytic	locomotive
interplant	ironmaster	judicatory	landscaper	levigation	locomotory
interplead	ironmonger	judicature	languisher	levitation	locustbean
interposal	ironworker	judicially	languorous	lexicology	loganberry
interposer	irradiance	juggernaut	lansquenet	lexigraphy	loganstone
interregna	irradicate	juristical	lanternfly	liberalise	loggerhead
interspace	irrational	justiciary	lanthanide	liberalism	logicality
interstate	irrelative	juvenility	lanuginose	liberalist	logistical
interstice	irrelevant	Kafkaesque	lanuginous	liberality	logography
intertidal	irreligion	kaisership	laparotomy	liberation	logorrhoea
intertrigo	irresolute	Kantianism	lapidarian	libidinous	logrolling

Lollardism	maidenlike	marshalled	meningitis	mightiness	modulation
loneliness	mainlander	marshaller	menopausal	mignonette	Mohammedan
lonesomely	mainspring	marshalsea	menstruate	migrainous	moisturise
longaevous	mainstream	marshiness	menstruous	militantly	molendinar
longhaired	maintainer	martensite	mensurable	militarily	molluscoid
longheaded	maisonette	martialism	mentorship	militarise	molluscous
longlegged	majestical	martingale	mercantile	militarism	molybdenum
longprimer	majuscular	marvelling	mercifully	militarist	monandrous
longshanks	makeweight	marvellous	meridional	militiaman	monarchial
longwinded	malacoderm	masquerade	merrymaker	millefiori	Monarchian
loosecover	malacology	Massoretic	mesenteric	millennial	monarchism
lophophore	maladapted	mastectomy	mesenteron	millennium	monarchist
lopsidedly	malapertly	masterhand	mesmeriser	millesimal	monetarily
loquacious	malapropos	masterhood	Mesolithic	millilitre	monetarism
lordliness	malcontent	masterless	mesomerism	millimetre	monetarist
lossleader	malefactor	mastermind	mesomorphy	millstream	moneymaker
lotuseater	maleficent	mastership	mesophytic	millwright	moneytaker
loudhailer	malentendu	masterwork	mesoscaphe	mimeograph	mongrelise
loungesuit	malevolent	masticable	mesosphere	mindedness	mongrelism
lovelessly	malfeasant	masticator	mesothorax	mindlessly	moniliasis
loveletter	malignance	matchboard	messianism	mineralise	moniliform
loveliness	malignancy	matchmaker	metabolise	mineralogy	monistical
lovemaking	malingerer	matchstick	metabolism	minestrone	monitorial
lovingness	malleebird	materially	metabolite	mineworker	monkeysuit
lowerclass	malleefowl	maternally	metacarpal	minimalism	monocarpic
lowpitched	mallenders	mathematic	metacarpus	minimalist	monochasia
lowprofile	malodorous	matriarchy	metacentre	ministrant	monochrome
loxodromic	Malpighian	matricidal	metagalaxy	minstrelsy	monoclinal
lubricator	Malthusian	matronhood	metalepsis	mintmaster	monoclinic
lubricious	malvaceous	matronship	metallurgy	minuscular	monocratic
luciferase	mamillated	matronymic	metamerism	minutebook	monocyclic
luciferous	manageable	maturation	metaphoric	minutehand	monoecious
lucifugous	manageably	maturative	metaphrase	minuteness	monogamist
lucubrator	management	matureness	metaphysic	miraculous	monogamous
luculently	manageress	mavourneen	metaplasia	mirthfully	monogenism
lugubrious	managerial	maxilliped	metastable	misaligned	monogynian
lukewarmly	manchineel	maximalist	metastases	misbelieve	monogynous
lumberjack	mandibular	mayblossom	metastasis	miscellany	monohybrid
lumberroom	mandragora	mayonnaise	metastatic	mischanter	monohydric
lumbersome	manfulness	meadowland	metatarsal	mischmetal	monolithic
lumberyard	mangosteen	meadowlark	metatarsus	misconduct	monologise
luminosity	maniacally	meagreness	metatheses	miscreance	monologist
luminously	Manichaean	mealbeetle	metathesis	misericord	monomaniac
lumpsucker	Manicheism	meaningful	metathetic	misfortune	monophonic
Lupercalia	manicurist	measliness	metathorax	misgivings	monopodial
lusciously	manifestly	measurable	metempiric	mishitting	monopodium
Lusitanian	manifestos	measurably	meteoritic	misjoinder	monopolise
lustration	manifoldly	measuredly	methodical	mismatched	monopolist
lustreless	manipulate	mechanical	Methuselah	mismeasure	monorhymed
lustrously	manoeuvrer	meddlesome	methylated	misnomered	monotheism
lutestring	manoeuvres	mediastina	meticulous	misogamist	monotheist
luxuriance	manometric	mediatress	metrically	misogynist	monotonous
lycopodium	manorhouse	medicament	metronomic	misogynous	monovalent
lymphocyte	manservant	medicaster	metronymic	misologist	monsignori
lymphomata	mansuetude	medication	metropolis	misprision	monstrance
lyophilise	manteltree	medicative	mettlesome	missionary	Montagnard
Lysenkoism	manucumitted	medievally	micaschist	missionise	montbretia
macadamise	manuscript	mediocrity	Michaelmas	mistakable	monumental
Maccabaean	manzanilla	meditation	microbiota	mistakenly	moonflower
macebearer	maquillage	meditative	microcline	misthought	moonshiner
maceration	maraschino	medullated	microfarad	misventure	moonstruck
machinator	marcescent	meerschaum	microfiche	miswording	mopishness
machinegun	Marcionite	megalithic	micrograph	mithridate	moralistic
mackintosh	marginalia	megalosaur	microlitic	mitigation	moratorium
macrophage	marginally	megascopic	micrometer	mitigative	morbidezza
macrospore	marginated	melancholy	micrometry	mitigatory	morbidness
maculation	margravate	Melanesian	microphone	mixedmedia	mordacious
maculature	margravine	melanistic	microphyte	mixolydian	morganatic
madreporic	marguerite	meliorator	micropylar	mizzenmast	moroseness
magistracy	Mariolater	melismatic	microscope	mizzensail	morphemics
magistrate	Mariolatry	mellowness	microscopy	mobocratic	morphinism
magnetiser	marionette	meltingpot	microseism	mockheroic	morphogeny
magnifical	marketable	membership	microspore	moderately	morphology
magnificat	markethall	membranous	middleaged	moderation	morrispike
magnifying	markettown	memorandum	middlebrow	moderatism	mosaically
Mahommedan	markswoman	menacingly	middlemost	moderniser	mosaicking
maidenhair	marquisate	mendacious	middlingly	modernness	mosasaurus
maidenhead	marrowbone	mendicancy	midmorning	modifiable	mosquitoes
maidenhood	marrowless	meningioma	midshipman	modishness	mossbunker

motherhood	nanisation	newsagency	nucivorous	oldfangled	orthoclase
motherland	nanosecond	newscaster	nucleation	oldmaidish	orthodoxly
motherless	naphthenic	newsletter	nucleonics	oleaginous	orthoepist
mothership	narcissism	newsmonger	nucleoside	oleiferous	orthogenic
motherwort	narcissist	newsreader	nucleotide	oleography	orthogonal
motionless	narcolepsy	newsvendor	nudibranch	oleraceous	orthopedic
motivation	narrowness	newsworthy	nullanulla	oligarchic	orthoptera
motiveless	nasturtium	newswriter	numberless	oligoclase	oscillator
motorcycle	natalitial	nickelling	numeration	oligopsony	oscitation
mouldboard	natatorial	nicotinism	numerology	olivaceous	osculation
mouldiness	natatorium	nidicolous	numerously	ombrometer	osculatory
mountebank	nationally	nidificate	numismatic	ommatidium	osmeterium
mournfully	nationhood	nidifugous	nunciature	omnigenous	osmiridium
mousseline	nationless	nightdress	nuptiality	omnipotent	ostensible
moustached	nationwide	nightglass	nurseryman	omniscient	ostensibly
moustachio	nativeborn	nightlight	nutcracker	omnivorous	osteoblast
Mousterian	nativeness	nightshade	nutational	omophagous	osteoclast
mouthorgan	nativistic	nightshift	nutcracker	oncogenous	osteopathy
mouthpiece	natterjack	nightshirt	nutritious	oncologist	osteophyte
movability	naturalise	nightstick	nyctalopia	oneirology	otherwhere
movelessly	naturalism	nightwatch	nyctalopic	onesidedly	otherwhile
moviemaker	naturalist	nigrescent	nyctinasty	ontologist	otherworld
mozzarella	naturopath	nihilistic	nympholept	opalescent	otioseness
muciferous	nauseating	nimbleness	oafishness	opaqueness	otterboard
mudskipper	nauseously	nincompoop	obdurately	openhanded	ottershrew
mudslinger	nautically	nineteenth	obediently	openhearth	outbalance
muffinbell	navigation	nipplewort	obfuscated	openminded	outbidding
Muhammadan	Neapolitan	nitpicking	obituarist	operculate	outerspace
Muhammedan	nebulosity	nitrochalk	objectival	operettist	outfielder
muliebrity	nebulously	nitrogroup	objectless	ophicleide	outfitting
mulishness	necrolater	noblewoman	oblateness	ophiolater	outgassing
mulligrubs	necrolatry	nodulation	obligation	ophiolatry	outgeneral
multifaced	necromancy	noisemaker	obligatory	ophiologic	outgunning
multiloquy	necrophile	nominalism	obligingly	ophthalmia	outlandish
multimedia	necrophily	nominalist	obliterate	ophthalmic	outmeasure
multiphase	necropolis	nominately	obnubilate	opinionist	outpatient
multiplier	necroscopy	nomination	obsequious	opisometer	outpouring
multipolar	nectareous	nominative	observable	oppilation	outputting
multistage	needlebath	nomography	observably	opposeless	outrageous
multivocal	needlebook	nomologist	observance	oppositely	outrightly
mumbojumbo	needlecord	nomothetic	obstetrics	opposition	outrunning
munificent	needlefish	nonaligned	obstructor	oppression	outsitting
muscularly	needlessly	nonchalant	obtainable	oppressive	outstation
musicality	needlework	noncontent	obtainment	opprobrium	outstretch
musicianly	negatively	nondrinker	obtruncate	oppugnancy	outswinger
musicology	negativism	nonferrous	obturation	optatively	outwitting
musicpaper	negativist	nonfiction	obtuseness	optimalise	ovariotomy
musicstand	negativity	nonjoinder	occasional	optimistic	overabound
musicstool	neglectful	nonlogical	occidental	optionally	overactive
muskmallow	negligence	nonnatural	occupation	oracularly	overblouse
Mussulmans	negligible	nonnuclear	occupative	orangepeel	overbought
mutability	negligibly	nonpayment	occurrence	orangewood	overburden
mutilation	negotiable	nonplaying	oceanarium	oratorical	overcharge
mutinously	negotiator	nonplussed	oceangoing	orchardist	overcommit
muttonhead	negrophile	nonstarter	oceanology	orchardman	overcooked
myasthenia	negrophobe	nonswimmer	ocellation	orchestics	overexcite
mycologist	nematocyst	nonviolent	ochlocracy	orchestral	overexpose
mycoplasma	neoclassic	noogenesis	octahedral	ordainment	overflight
mycorrhiza	neological	northbound	octahedron	ordinarily	overground
myocardium	neoplastic	northerner	octamerous	ordination	overgrowth
myological	nepenthean	northwards	octandrian	ordonnance	overhanded
myopically	nephograph	nosography	octandrous	oreography	overlander
myrtaceous	nephoscope	nosologist	octodecimo	oreologist	overlapped
mystagogic	nephralgia	nosophobia	octonarian	organicism	overlooker
mystagogue	nephridium	nostologic	octopodous	organicism	overmanned
mysterious	nephrology	notability	odiousness	organicist	overmantel
mystically	nethermost	notarially	odontalgia	organismal	overmaster
mythically	nettlerash	notchboard	odontology	orientally	overnicety
mythiciser	neurilemma	noteworthy	oecologist	originally	overpraise
mythologer	neurolemma	noticeable	oecumenism	originator	overrefine
mythologic	neuropathy	noticeably	oedematose	orneriness	overridden
mythomania	neuroplasm	notifiable	oedematous	ornateness	overriding
mythopoeia	neurotoxin	notionally	oenologist	orogenesis	overshadow
mythopoeic	neutralise	notonectal	oesophagus	orogenetic	overslaugh
myxomatous	neutralism	nourishing	officially	orographic	overspread
myxomycete	neutralist	novaculite	offlicence	orological	overstride
nailpolish	neutrality	novelistic	offputting	orological	overstrung
nambypamby	nevernever	nubiferous	offsetting	orotundity	oversubtle
namelessly	newfangled	nuciferous	oftentimes	orphanhood	oversupply

overthrown	parabiotic	patristics	perdurable	phantasmic	pictorical
overthrust	parabolise	patrolling	perdurably	phantastic	piecegoods
overtopped	paraboloid	patronymic	peremptory	phantastry	piercingly
overweight	paradisaic	patulously	perfection	pharisaism	piezometer
overwinter	paradisean	pawnbroker	perfective	pharmacist	pigeonhole
ovipositor	paradisiac	peacefully	perfidious	pharyngeal	pigeonpair
owlishness	paradisian	peacemaker	perfoliate	pheasantry	pigeonpost
oxidisable	paradoxure	peacockery	perforator	phelloderm	pigeontoed
oxygenator	paraffinic	peacockish	performing	phenacetin	pigeonwing
oysterfarm	paragnosis	pearldiver	periclinal	phenocryst	pigmentary
pacesetter	paralipsis	peashooter	pericyclic	phenomenal	pigsticker
pacifiable	paralogise	pebbledash	peridermal	phenomenon	piledriver
pacificate	paralogism	peccadillo	perigynous	phenotypic	pilgarlick
pacificism	paramecium	pectinated	perihelion	pheromonal	pilgrimage
pacificist	parametric	peculation	perilously	philatelic	piliferous
packingbox	paramnesia	peculiarly	periodical	philippina	pilliwinks
packsaddle	paranormal	pedagogics	periosteal	philippine	pillowcase
packthread	paraphrase	pedalorgan	periosteum	philistine	pillowlace
paddleboat	paraphrast	pedalpoint	peripeteia	phillumeny	pillowslip
paddyfield	paraplegia	pederastic	peripheral	philologen	pilothouse
paddywagon	paraplegic	pedestrian	peripteral	philopoena	pilotlight
paddywhack	parapodium	pediculate	periscopic	philosophe	pilotwhale
paedagogic	paraselene	pediculous	perishable	philosophy	pincerlike
paederasty	parasitism	pedicurist	perithecia	phlebotomy	pinchpenny
paediatric	parasitoid	pedimental	peritoneal	phlegmatic	pincushion
paedogogue	paratactic	pedimented	peritoneum	phlogistic	pinebeauty
paedophile	paratroops	pedologist	periwigged	phlogiston	pinecarpet
pagination	parcelling	peduncular	periwinkle	phlogopite	pinfeather
painkiller	pardonable	peerlessly	perjurious	Phoenician	pinnatifid
painlessly	pardonably	pegmatitic	permafrost	phonematic	pinnulated
paintbrush	parenchyma	pejoration	permanence	phonically	pinstriped
Palaeocene	parentally	pejorative	permanency	phonograph	piperidine
Palaeogene	parenteral	pellagrous	permeation	phonolitic	piscifauna
palaeolith	parenthood	pellicular	permeative	phonologic	pistillary
palaeotype	parimutuel	pellucidly	permission	phonometer	pistillate
Palaeozoic	parliament	pemphigoid	permissive	phosphatic	pistolling
palagonite	Parnassian	pemphigous	permitting	phosphoric	pistolshot
palatalise	paronymous	pencilling	permutable	phosphorus	pistolwhip
palatinate	paroxysmal	pendentive	pernicious	photoflood	pistonring
palimpsest	paroxytone	penetrable	pernickety	photogenic	pitchblack
palindrome	parramatta	penetrably	peroration	photograph	pitcherful
palisander	parricidal	penetralia	peroxidise	photolitho	pitchstone
palladious	parrotfish	penetrance	perpetrate	photolysis	pityriasis
pallbearer	parsonbird	penetrator	perpetuate	photolytic	pixillated
palliation	parsonical	penicillin	perpetuity	photometer	placidness
palliative	partiality	peninsular	perplexity	photometry	plagiarise
palliatory	participle	penitently	perquisite	photonasty	plagiarism
pallidness	particular	penmanship	persecutor	photophily	plagiarist
palmaceous	parturient	pennaceous	persiflage	photophore	plaguesome
palmatifid	pasquinade	pennanular	persistent	photoprint	plainchant
palmbutter	passageway	pennillion	personable	phototaxis	planchette
palmerworm	passionary	pennyroyal	personally	phototrope	planetable
PalmSunday	passionate	pennyworth	personalty	phrasebook	planetaria
paltriness	Passionist	penologist	personator	phrenology	plangently
palynology	pasteboard	penpushing	persuasion	phthisical	planigraph
Panamanian	pastellist	pensionary	persuasive	phylactery	planimeter
pancratium	pasteurise	pentachord	pertinence	phyllotaxy	planimetry
pancreatic	pasteurism	pentagonal	pertinency	phylloxera	planktonic
pancreatin	pastmaster	pentameter	perversely	phylogenic	planometer
panegyrise	pastorally	pentastich	perversion	physically	plantation
panegyrist	pastorship	pentathlon	perversity	physicking	plantlouse
pangenesis	pastrycook	pentatomic	perversive	physiocrat	plasmodesm
pangenetic	pasturable	pentatonic	pesticidal	physiology	plasmodium
panhandler	pastyfaced	pentimento	pestilence	phytogenic	plasmogamy
paniculate	patchiness	pentstemon	petiolated	phytophagy	plasmolyse
panjandrum	patentable	peppercorn	petiteness	phytotoxic	plasticise
panopticon	paternally	peppermill	petitioner	pianissimo	plasticity
pansophist	pathetical	peppermint	petroglyph	pianoforte	platelayer
pantograph	pathfinder	pepperwort	petrolatum	picaresque	playacting
pantomimic	pathogenic	percentage	petronella	picayunish	playbyplay
pantrymaid	pathologic	percentile	petulantly	piccalilli	playfellow
papaverine	patination	perception	phagedaena	piccaninny	playground
papaverous	patisserie	perceptive	phagedenic	pichiciago	playwright
paperchase	patriliny	perceptual	phagocytic	pickaninny	pleadingly
paperknife	patriarchy	perchloric	phalangeal	picketline	pleasantly
papermaker	patriciate	percipient	phallicism	pickpocket	pleasantry
papistical	patricidal	percolator	phanerogam	picnicking	pleasingly
papyrology	patrilocal	percussion	phantasise	picosecond	plebiscite
parabiosis	patriotism	percussive	phantasmal	pictograph	

plecoptera	population	precursory	primordium	propitious	puissantly
pleochroic	populistic	predacious	princeling	proportion	pulsatilla
pleonastic	populously	predecease	princeship	propounder	pulsimeter
plesiosaur	porismatic	predestine	principate	propraetor	pulsometer
pliability	pornocracy	predicable	principial	proprietor	pulveriser
pliantness	porousness	prediction	principium	propulsion	pulvinated
ploddingly	porraceous	predictive	principled	propulsive	pummelling
ploughable	portamento	predispose	prismoidal	propylaeum	punchboard
ploughland	portcullis	prednisone	prissiness	prosaicism	punchdrunk
pluckiness	portentous	preeminent	privileged	proscenium	punctation
plumassier	portliness	preemption	prizefight	prosciutto	punctually
plunderage	Portuguese	preemptive	procedural	proscriber	punctuator
plunderous	positional	preexilian	proceeding	prosecutor	punctulate
pluperfect	positively	prefecture	procession	prosilient	punishable
plutocracy	positivism	preferable	proclaimer	prosodical	punishment
plutolatry	positivist	preferably	proclivity	prospector	punitively
pneumatics	positivity	preference	procreator	prospectus	pupilarity
pocketable	possession	preferment	procrypsis	prosperity	pupiparous
pocketbook	possessive	preferring	procryptic	prosperous	purblindly
pocketsize	possessory	prefixture	proctorage	prosthesis	puristical
pockmarked	postbellum	prefrontal	proctorial	prosthetic	puritanise
podiatrist	postchaise	prefulgent	proctorise	prostitute	puritanism
poetically	postexilic	preglacial	procumbent	prostomial	purposeful
pogonology	posthumous	pregnantly	procurable	prostomium	purseproud
pogonotomy	postillion	prehensile	procurance	protanopic	pursership
poinsettia	postliminy	prehension	procurator	protection	purseseine
pointblank	postmaster	prehistory	prodigally	protective	pursuivant
pokerfaced	postmortem	prejudiced	prodigious	protectory	purtenance
polemicist	postoffice	prelatical	producible	protectrix	purulently
polemonium	postpartum	prelection	production	proteiform	purveyance
politeness	postscript	premarital	productive	proteinous	pushbutton
politician	postulator	premaxilla	profession	protensive	putatively
politicise	potability	premedical	proficient	proteolyse	putrescent
pollenosis	potamology	premonitor	profitable	protestant	putrescine
pollinator	potbellied	prepackage	profitably	prothallia	putridness
polyandric	potentiate	preparator	profitless	prothallus	puzzlement
polyanthus	potentilla	preparedly	profligacy	protophyta	pycnogonid
polyatamic	pothunting	prepayable	profligate	protophyte	pycnometer
polychaete	pouncebox	prepayment	profoundly	protoplasm	pycnostyle
polychrest	pourparler	prepensely	profundity	protoplast	pyknometer
polychrome	powderhorn	prepossess	progenitor	prototypal	pyracantha
polyclinic	powderpuff	prepotence	proglottis	prototypic	pyretology
polycyclic	powerfully	prepotency	prognathic	protracted	pyridoxine
polydactyl	powerhouse	presageful	prognostic	protractor	pyrogallol
polydipsia	pozzolanic	presbyopia	programmer	protreptic	pyrogenous
polygamist	pozzuolana	presbyopic	prohibiter	protrusile	pyrography
polygamous	practician	presbytery	prohibitor	protrusion	pyrolusite
polygenism	practising	prescience	projectile	protrusive	pyromaniac
polygenist	praecocial	prescriber	projection	proudflesh	pyromantic
polygenous	praemunire	presentday	projective	provenance	pyrometric
polygraphy	praesidium	presentive	prolicidal	proverbial	pyrophoric
polygynous	praetorial	presidency	prolocutor	providence	pyrotechny
polyhedral	praetorian	presidiary	prologuise	provincial	pyroxenite
polyhedric	pragmatise	presignify	prolongate	provisions	Pyrrhonian
polyhedron	pragmatism	pressagent	promenader	provitamin	Pyrrhonist
polyhistor	pragmatist	pressingly	promethium	provocator	pyrrhotite
polymathic	prairiedog	pressurise	prominence	proximally	pyrrhotite
polymerise	prancingly	presternum	promissory	prudential	quadrangle
polymerism	pratincole	presumable	promontory	pruriently	quadrantal
polymerous	prayerbook	presumably	promptbook	psalmodise	quadratics
Polynesian	preachment	presuppose	promptness	psalmodist	quadrature
polynomial	preadamite	pretendant	promulgate	psalterium	quadrennia
polyonymic	prearrange	pretendent	pronominal	psephology	quadriceps
polyphasic	prebendary	pretension	pronounced	pseudocarp	quadrireme
polyphonic	precarious	prettiness	pronouncer	psilocybin	quadrivial
polyploidy	precaution	prevailing	proofsheet	psittacine	quadrivium
polysemous	precedence	prevalence	propagable	psychiatry	quadrumana
polytheism	precedency	prevenancy	propaganda	psychicism	quadrumane
polytheist	preceptive	prevenient	propagator	psychicist	quadrumvir
polytocous	preceptory	prevention	propellant	psychology	quadruplet
polyvalent	precession	preventive	propellent	psychopath	quadruplex
Pomeranian	preciosity	previously	propelling	Ptolemaist	quadrupole
pomiferous	preciously	pridefully	propensity	puberulent	quaintness
pomologist	precipitin	priesthood	properness	pubescence	qualmishly
ponderable	preclusion	priestling	propertied	publishing	quantifier
pontifical	preclusive	priggishly	prophesier	puerperium	quantitive
pontifices	precocious	primevally	prophetess	puffpastry	quarantine
popularise	preconcert	primiparae	propionate	pugilistic	quarrelled
popularity	precordial	primordial	propitiate	pugnacious	quarreller

quarrender	reassemble	regretting	repurchase	revitalise	roquelaure
quartation	reassembly	regularise	reputation	revivalism	rosaniline
quarterage	rebellious	regularity	requiescat	revivalist	rosechafer
quarterday	rebuttable	regulation	reredorter	revocation	roseengine
quartering	recallable	regulative	rescission	revocatory	roselipped
quartzitic	receivable	regulatory	rescissory	revolution	rosemallow
quaternary	recentness	reichsmark	researcher	rewardable	rotational
quaternate	receptacle	reissuable	resemblant	rewardless	rotisserie
quaternion	receptible	reiterance	resentment	rhapsodise	rottenness
quaternity	rechristen	rejectable	reservedly	rhapsodist	rottweiler
quatorzain	recidivism	rejoicings	reshipment	rheologist	roughhouse
quatrefoil	recidivist	rejuvenate	resignedly	rheotropic	roughrider
queasiness	recipiency	rejuvenise	resilience	rhetorical	roundabout
quenchable	reciprocal	relational	resiliency	rheumatics	roundhouse
quenchless	recitalist	relatively	resistance	rheumatism	rouseabout
quercitron	recitation	relativise	resistible	rheumatoid	roustabout
questioner	recitative	relativism	resistless	rhinestone	rovebeetle
quickgrass	recitativo	relativist	resolutely	rhinoceros	rowanberry
quickthorn	recklessly	relativity	resolution	rhinoscope	rubberneck
quiescence	recolonise	relaxation	resolutive	rhinoscopy	rubiginous
quiescency	recommence	releasable	resolvable	rhizogenic	rubrically
quinacrine	recompense	relegation	resolvedly	rhizomorph	rubricator
quintuplet	reconciler	relentless	resonantly	rhizophore	rubythroat
quirkiness	reconsider	relevantly	resorcinol	rhodophane	rudderfish
quixotical	recordable	relievable	resorption	rhomboidal	rudderless
quizmaster	recoupment	relinquish	resorptive	rhomboidei	rudimental
rabbinical	recreantly	relishable	resounding	rhythmical	ruefulness
rabblement	recreation	relocation	respectful	ribbonfish	ruffianism
racecourse	recreative	reluctance	respecting	ribbonworm	ruggedness
Rachmanism	recrudesce	reluctancy	respective	riboflavin	ruminantly
rackrenter	rectorship	remarkable	respirable	ricinoleic	rumination
radicalise	recumbency	remarkably	respirator	rickettsia	ruminative
radicalism	recuperate	remarriage	respondent	ridgepiece	rumrunning
radication	recurrence	remediable	responsive	ridiculous	runnerbean
radiogenic	recyclable	remedially	responsory	rightangle	runthrough
radiograph	redblooded	remediless	restaurant	rightfully	rupicoline
radiologic	redcurrant	remissible	restlessly	rightwards	rupicolous
radiometer	redecorate	remissness	restorable	rigorously	Russianise
radiometry	redeemable	remittance	restrained	rinderpest	Russophile
radiopaque	redemption	remodelled	restrainer	ringfinger	Russophobe
radiophone	redemptive	remonetise	resultless	ringleader	rustically
radioscopy	redemptory	remorseful	resumption	ringmaster	ruthlessly
radiosonde	redescribe	remoteness	resumptive	ringnecked	sabbatical
ragamuffin	rediscover	remunerate	resupinate	ringtailed	sabretache
raggedness	redolently	renascence	resurgence	ripplemark	sabretooth
railroader	redundance	rencounter	retainable	riproaring	saccharate
railwayman	redundancy	renderable	reticently	ripsnorter	saccharide
rainmaking	reelection	rendezvous	reticulate	risibility	saccharify
rakishness	reeligible	renovation	retinacula	ritardando	saccharine
ramblingly	reentrance	reorganise	retirement	ritornelli	saccharoid
rampageous	referendum	repairable	retiringly	ritornello	saccharose
ramshackle	refillable	reparation	retractile	riverhorse	sacerdotal
rancidness	refinement	reparative	retraction	roadrunner	sacredness
randomness	reflection	repatriate	retractive	roadworthy	sacrificer
ranunculus	reflective	repealable	retraining	robustious	sacroiliac
rapporteur	reflexible	repeatable	retrochoir	robustness	sacrosanct
ratability	reformable	repeatedly	retrograde	rockabilly	saddleback
ratcatcher	refraction	repellance	retrogress	rockbadger	saddlefast
rationally	refractive	repellancy	retrorsely	rockbottom	saddletree
rattlehead	refractory	repellence	retrospect	rockgarden	safeblower
rattlepate	refreshing	repellency	returnable	rockhopper	safetybelt
rattletrap	refringent	repentance	reunionism	rockpigeon	sagination
ravenously	refuelling	repertoire	reunionist	rockrabbit	sagittally
ravishment	refulgence	repetiteur	revalidate	rockribbed	sailorless
razorblade	refundable	repetition	revalorise	rodfishing	salability
razorshell	refundment	repetitive	revanchism	roistering	salamander
razzmatazz	refutation	repopulate	revanchist	roisterous	salesclerk
reactivate	regalement	reportable	revealable	rollcollar	saleswoman
reactively	regardless	reportedly	revealment	rollicking	salicional
reactivity	regelation	reposition	revelation	rollingpin	salicylate
readership	regeneracy	repository	revelatory	Romanesque	salientian
reafforest	regenerate	repression	revengeful	Romanistic	saliferous
realisable	regentship	repressive	reverencer	rontgenise	salivation
reallocate	regimental	reprobance	reverently	roodscreen	sallenders
reappraise	regionally	reproducer	reversible	roofgarden	sallowness
rearmament	registered	republican	revertible	rootedness	salmagundi
reasonable	registrant	repudiator	reviewable	ropedancer	salmonella
reasonably	regression	repugnance	revilement	ropeladder	salmonleap
reasonless	regressive	repugnancy	revisional	ropewalker	salpingian

saltarello	schipperke	secularism	sensualise	shipfitter	simulative
saltcellar	schismatic	secularist	sensualism	shipmaster	simulatory
saltigrade	schizocarp	secularity	sensualist	shiprigged	sincipital
salubrious	schizogony	securement	sensuality	shipwright	sinecurism
salutarily	scholastic	secureness	sensuously	shirehorse	sinecurist
salutation	schoolable	securiform	sentential	shirtfront	sinfulness
salutatory	schoolbook	sedateness	sentiently	shirtwaist	Singhalese
samarskite	schooldays	seducement	separately	shockingly	singlefoot
sanatorium	schoolgirl	seductress	separation	shockproof	singleness
sanctifier	schoolmaam	sedulously	separatism	shoddiness	singletree
sanctimony	schoolmarm	seedpotato	separatist	shoebuckle	singularly
sanctitude	schoolmate	seedvessel	separative	shoestring	sinisterly
sandalwood	schoolroom	seemliness	separatory	shopkeeper	sinistrous
sandbagger	schooltime	seersucker	septenarii	shoplifter	sinologist
sandcastle	schoolwork	seethrough	septennial	shopsoiled	sinusoidal
sanderling	sciagraphy	segmentary	septennium	shopwalker	sisterhood
sandhopper	scientific	seguidilla	septically	shopwindow	sitophobia
sandmartin	Scillonian	seignorage	septillion	shoreleave	sixshooter
sanguinary	sciolistic	seignorial	Septuagint	shorewards	skateboard
sanguinely	scleroderm	seismicity	sepulchral	shortbread	sketchable
sanguinity	sclerotium	seismogram	sequacious	shortcrust	sketchbook
sanitarian	sclerotomy	seismology	sequential	shortdated	skewbridge
sanitarily	scoffingly	selectness	sequestrum	shortening	skiagraphy
sanitarium	scoreboard	selenodont	SerboCroat	shortlived	skibobbing
sanitation	scoresheet	selenology	sereneness	shortrange	skijumping
Sanskritic	scornfully	selfacting	sergeantcy	shouldered	skimpiness
sapiential	scorzonera	selfaction	serigraphy	shovelhead	skindiving
sappanwood	Scotswoman	selfbinder	seriocomic	shovelling	skinniness
sapphirine	Scotticise	selfcolour	serjeantcy	showerbath	skirmisher
saprogenic	Scotticism	selfdeceit	sermoniser	showjumper	skirtdance
saprophyte	scrapmetal	selfdenial	serologist	showmindow	skittishly
sarcolemma	scratchily	selfesteem	serotinous	shrewdness	skrimshank
sarcophagi	scratchwig	selffeeder	serpentine	shrewishly	skyjacking
sarcophagy	screechowl	selfglazed	serradilla	shrewmouse	skyscraper
sarcoplasm	screenings	selfguided	serviceman	shrievalty	skywriting
sargassoes	screenplay	selflessly	servomotor	shrillness	slanderous
sarmentose	screwplate	selfloving	sestertium	shrinkable	slanginess
sarmentous	screwpress	selfmotion	sestertius	shrinkwrap	slantingly
sarracenia	scribbling	selfmurder	setterwort	shrivelled	slatternly
sashwindow	scrimmager	selfparody	settlement	shroudlaid	slavetrade
satanology	scrimshank	selfpoised	seventieth	shroudless	slavocracy
satellitic	scriptoria	selfpraise	severeness	Shrovetide	Slavophile
satisfying	scriptural	selfprofit	sexagenary	shuttering	Slavophobe
saturation	scrofulous	selfraised	Sexagesima	sialagogic	sleaziness
saturnalia	scrollwork	selfregard	sexivalent	sialagogue	sleepiness
satyagraha	scrupulous	selfrising	sexlimited	sibilation	sleepyhead
satyriasis	scrutineer	selfruling	sexologist	sicklebill	sleeveless
sauerkraut	scrutinise	selfseeker	sexpartite	sickliness	sleevelink
savageness	sculptress	selfstyled	sextillion	sideboards	sleighbell
savourless	sculptural	selftaught	shabbiness	sideeffect	slenderise
sawtoothed	sculptured	selfwilled	shadowless	sideglance	slidevalve
saxicoline	scurrility	seltzogene	shagginess	siderolite	slightness
saxicolous	scurrilous	semeiology	shamefaced	siderostat	slipperily
scabrously	scurviness	semeiotics	shamefully	sidesaddle	slipstitch
scaffolder	scutellate	semestrial	shandrydan	sidestreet	slipstream
scaleboard	scyphiform	semiannual	shandygaff	sidestroke	slitpocket
scandalise	scyphozoan	semichorus	shanghaier	sidewinder	sloppiness
scandalous	seaanemone	semicircle	shantytown	siegetrain	slothfully
scansorial	seabiscuit	semidivine	sharpnosed	signalling	slowfooted
scantiness	seacaptain	semidouble	sheabutter	signwriter	slowmotion
scapegrace	sealingwax	semidrying	shearwater	silentness	slowwitted
scarabaeid	seamanlike	semifitted	sheathbill	silhouette	sluggardly
scarabaeus	seamanship	semiliquid	sheathless	silkcotton	sluggishly
scaramouch	seamstress	semilunate	sheepishly	silkscreen	sluicegate
scarceness	searchable	seminarian	sheeplouse	sillybilly	slumberful
scaredycat	searchless	seminarist	sheepshank	silverbath	slumberous
scarlatina	seaserpent	semination	sheepshead	silverfish	sluttishly
scatheless	seasonable	semiopaque	shellacked	silverside	smallscale
scathingly	seasonably	semiotical	shellmound	silverware	smallsword
scattergun	seborrhoea	semiquaver	shellproof	silverweed	smallwares
scattering	secludedly	semiuncial	shellshock	similarity	smaragdine
scattiness	secernment	semiweekly	shenanigan	similitude	smaragdite
scavengery	secondbest	semiyearly	sherardise	simoniacal	smartmoney
scenically	secondhand	senatorial	sheriffdom	simpleness	smattering
scepticism	secondment	senescence	shieldless	simplicity	smelliness
schematise	secondrate	sensedatum	shiftiness	simplifier	smockfrock
schematism	secretaire	senseorgan	shillelagh	simplistic	smokedried
schemozzle	secretaire	senseorgan	shillelagh	simulacrum	smokehouse
scherzando	secularise	sensitiser	shipbroker	simulation	smokeplant

smokeproof	Sorbonnist	splashback	stalwartly	stolidness	subculture
smokestack	sordidness	splashdown	stanchless	stomachful	subdeanery
smoothbore	sororicide	spleenwort	stanchness	stomatitis	subduction
smoothness	soubriquet	splendidly	standpoint	stomatopod	subglacial
smorrebrod	soullessly	splintbone	standstill	stomodaeum	subheading
smudginess	soundboard	splintcoal	staphyline	stoneblind	subjectify
smuttiness	soundingly	splitlevel	stargazing	stoneborer	subjection
snafflebit	soundproof	splutterer	starriness	stonebrash	subjective
snailpaced	soundtrack	spodomancy	starryeyed	stonefruit	subjugator
snailwheel	sourcebook	spoilsport	starstream	stonemason	subkingdom
snakedance	sousaphone	spokeshave	starvation	stonesnipe	subletting
snakestone	souterrain	spoliation	starveling	stopvolley	sublimable
snapdragon	southbound	spoliative	statecraft	storehouse	subliminal
snappishly	southerner	spoliatory	statically	storksbill	sublingual
sneakiness	southernly	spongecake	stationary	stormbound	submariner
sneakingly	southwards	spongewood	stationery	stormcloud	submediant
sneakthief	sowthistle	spongiform	statistics	storminess	submersion
sneeringly	spacecraft	sponginess	statoscope	stormproof	submission
sneezeweed	spacewoman	spongology	statuesque	strabismal	submissive
sneezewood	spaciously	sponsorial	statutable	strabismic	submitting
sneezewort	spadebeard	spookiness	statutably	strabismus	submontane
snickasnee	spadiceous	spoondrift	staurolite	strabotomy	subnuclear
sniffiness	spagyrical	spoonerism	stavesacre	straighten	suborbital
snivelling	spallation	sporangial	steadiness	straightly	subordinal
snobbishly	spankingly	sporangium	steakhouse	strainedly	subreption
snobocracy	sparseness	sporophore	stealthily	straitness	subroutine
snootiness	Spartacist	sporophyll	steamchest	stramonium	subscriber
snowcapped	spasticity	sporophyte	steaminess	strategist	subsection
snowgrouse	spatchcock	sportfully	steamtight	strathspey	subsellium
snowmobile	spathulate	sportiness	steeliness	stratiform	subsequent
snowplough	spatiality	sportingly	steelworks	stratocrat	subshrubby
snubbingly	speargrass	sportively	stelliform	strawberry	subsidence
snuffiness	specialise	sportswear	stenchtrap	strawboard	subsidiary
soapboiler	specialism	spotlessly	stencilled	streamless	subsistent
soapbubble	specialist	spottiness	stenciller	streamline	subspecies
soapflakes	speciality	sprightful	stenograph	streetdoor	substation
sobersided	speciation	springhalt	stentorian	streetward	substitute
sobersides	speciology	springhead	stepfather	strengthen	substratum
socialiser	speciosity	springless	stephanite	stressless	subtenancy
societally	speciously	springlike	stepladder	strictness	subterfuge
sociologic	spectacled	springtail	stepmother	stridently	subtleness
sociometry	spectacles	springtide	stepparent	stridulant	subtrahend
soddenness	spectrally	springtime	stepsister	stridulate	subvention
softbilled	speculator	springwood	stereobate	stridulous	subversion
softboiled	speechless	sprinkling	stereogram	strikingly	subversive
softfinned	speediness	sprucebeer	stereopsis	stringbean	succedanea
softheaded	speedlimit	spruceness	stereotype	stringency	successful
softspoken	speleology	spumescent	stereotypy	stringendo	succession
solacement	spellbound	spunkiness	sterigmata	stringhalt	successive
soldanella	Spencerian	spuriously	steriliser	stringless	succinctly
solecistic	Spenserian	squalidity	sternwards	striptease	succulence
solemnness	spermaceti	squamation	stertorous	Stroganoff	succulency
solenoidal	spermicide	squanderer	stewardess	stromatous	sudatorium
solicitant	sperrylite	squareness	stickiness	stronghold	suddenness
solicitous	sphalerite	squaresail	stiffening	strongroom	sufferable
solicitude	sphenodone	squaretoed	stiflebone	structural	sufferably
solidarism	sphenogram	squaretoes	stiflingly	structured	sufferance
solidarist	sphenoidal	squeezable	stigmatise	struthious	sufficient
solidarity	sphericity	squeezebox	stigmatism	strychnine	suffragist
solidstate	spheroidal	squeteague	stigmatist	strychnism	sugardaddy
solifidian	spherulite	squinteyed	stilettoes	stubbiness	sugarhouse
solitarily	spidercrab	squirarchy	stillbirth	stubbornly	sugariness
solstitial	spiderline	squirearch	stillicide	studiously	sugarmaple
solubilise	spiderwort	squirehood	stimulator	stuffiness	suggestion
solubility	spiflicate	squireling	stinginess	stumpiness	suggestive
somatology	spillikins	squireship	stingingly	stunningly	suicidally
somatotype	spinescent	stabiliser	stinkingly	stupendous	sullenness
sombreness	spiracular	stablemate	stinkstone	stupidness	sulphonate
somersault	spiraculum	stableness	stipellate	sturdiness	sulphurate
somniloquy	spiralling	stadholder	stipulator	stylistics	sulphurise
somnolence	spiritedly	staffnurse	stirrupcup	stylograph	sulphurous
somnolency	spiritless	stagbeetle	stitchwort	stypticity	sultanship
songstress	spirituous	stagecoach	stochastic	subacidity	sultriness
songthrush	spirograph	stagecraft	stockiness	subaquatic	summerlike
songwriter	spirometer	staggering	stockpiler	subaqueous	summertime
sonorously	spirometry	stagnantly	stockproof	subaverage	summitless
soothingly	spitchcock	stagnation	stockrider	subcentral	summonable
soothsayer	spitefully	stalactite	stockstill	subclavian	sunderance
sophomoric	splanchnic	stalagmite	stodginess	subcordate	sunglasses

sunparlour	swingingly	tanglement	teratogeny	threatener	torpidness
superacute	swinglebar	tankengine	teratology	threepence	torrential
superaltar	switchback	tantaliser	teratomata	threepenny	torridness
superation	switchover	tantamount	termagancy	threepiece	tortellini
superbness	swiveleyed	taperecord	terminable	threescore	tortfeasor
supercargo	swivelling	taperingly	terminably	threnodial	tortiously
superduper	swordcraft	tapestried	terminally	threnodist	tortuosity
supergiant	sworddance	tapotement	terminator	thriftless	tortuously
superhuman	swordgrass	taradiddle	termitaria	throatwort	totemistic
superiorly	swordstick	tarantella	terneplate	thromboses	touchiness
superlunar	sybaritism	tarantelle	terracotta	thrombosis	touchingly
supernally	sycophancy	tardigrade	terreplein	thrombotic	touchjudge
supernovae	syllabaria	tarmacadam	terrorless	throneless	touchpaper
superorder	syllogiser	Tartuffian	tessellate	throughout	touchstone
superpower	symbolical	Tartuffism	testaceous	throughput	tourbillon
supersonic	symboliser	taskmaster	testflight	throughway	tourmaline
superstore	symmetrise	tasselling	tetchiness	throwstick	tournament
supertonic	sympathise	tastefully	tetrachord	thruppence	tourniquet
supervisor	symphonion	tattletale	tetragonal	thumbprint	towardness
supination	symphonist	tauntingly	tetrahedra	thumbscrew	toweringly
supineness	symphylous	tauromachy	tetrameter	thumbstall	townswoman
supperless	symphyseal	tautomeric	tetramorph	thunderbox	toxication
supplanter	symphysial	tautophony	tetrapolis	thundering	toxicology
supplejack	symposiast	tawdriness	tetrarchic	thunderous	toxiphobia
supplement	synaeresis	taxability	tetrastich	thwartship	trabeation
suppleness	synaloepha	taxidancer	tetrastyle	thwartwise	trabeculae
suppletion	synanthous	taxidermal	tetterwort	tickertape	trabecular
suppletive	syncarpous	taxidermic	textualist	ticklishly	tracheated
suppletory	synchronal	taxonomist	texturally	ticpolonga	tracheitis
suppliance	synchronic	teaplanter	thalecress	tiddlywink	Tractarian
supplicant	syncopated	tearjerker	thankfully	tidewaiter	tractional
supplicate	syncopator	tearlessly	theatrical	tilthammer	trafficked
supportive	syncretise	teatrolley	theistical	timberhead	trafficker
supposable	syncretism	technetium	themselves	timberline	tragacanth
supposably	syncretist	technician	theocratic	timbertoes	tragically
supposedly	syndicator	technicist	theodicean	timberwolf	tragicomic
suppressor	synecdoche	technocrat	theodolite	timberwork	traitorous
suprarenal	synecology	technology	theogonist	timbrology	trajection
surefooted	synergetic	teenyweeny	theologian	timekeeper	trajectory
suretyship	syngenesis	teetotally	theologise	timelessly	trammelled
surfactant	synoecious	tegumental	theologist	timeliness	tramontana
surgically	synonymist	telecamera	theophanic	timesaving	tramontane
surmisable	synonymity	telecaster	theophoric	timeserver	trampoline
surplusage	synonymous	telegraphy	theopneust	timocratic	trancelike
surprising	synoptical	telemetric	theoretics	timorously	tranquilly
surrealism	synostosis	teleologic	theosopher	tinctorial	transactor
surrealist	syntagmata	teleostean	thereabout	tinselling	transcribe
survivance	synthesise	telepathic	thereafter	tirailleur	transcript
susceptive	synthesist	telephoner	thereanent	tirelessly	transducer
suspenders	synthetise	telephonic	thereunder	tiresomely	transeptal
suspension	synthetist	telescopic	thermionic	tiringroom	transferee
suspensive	syphilitic	televiewer	thermistor	titanesque	transferor
suspensoid	systematic	television	thermogram	titivation	transfuser
suspensory	systemless	televisual	thermophil	tittupping	transgress
suspicious	tabernacle	tellership	thermopile	titubation	transience
sustaining	tablecloth	telpherage	thermostat	tobogganer	transiency
sustenance	tablelinen	temperable	theurgical	tocopherol	transistor
sustention	tablespoon	temperance	thickening	toffeenose	transition
sustentive	tabularise	temperedly	thievishly	toilsomely	transitive
suzerainty	tabulation	temporally	thillhorse	tolerantly	transitory
swaggering	tachometer	temporalty	thimbleful	toleration	translator
swanmaiden	tachometry	temporiser	thimblerig	tollbridge	translucid
swanupping	tachymeter	temptation	thinkingly	tomfoolery	translunar
swarmspore	tachymetry	temptingly	thinkpiece	tomography	transmuter
swashplate	taciturnly	tenability	thirdclass	tonelessly	transplant
swaybacked	tackdriver	tenantable	thirdparty	tongueless	transposal
sweatgland	tactically	tenantless	thirteenth	tonguetied	transposer
sweatiness	tactlessly	tenderfoot	thirtyfold	toothbrush	transshape
sweatshirt	tailorbird	tenderloin	thixotropy	toothiness	transvalue
sweepingly	tailormade	tenderness	thornapple	toothpaste	transverse
sweepstake	takingness	tendinitis	thorniness	toothshell	trappiness
sweetbread	talebearer	tendrillar	thornproof	topazolite	trashiness
sweetbriar	talentless	tendrilled	thoroughly	topgallant	traumatism
sweetbrier	taleteller	tenebrific	thoughtful	topicality	travelling
sweetening	talismanic	tenebrious	thousandth	topography	travelogue
sweetheart	Talmudical	tenemental	threadbare	topologist	travertine
sweltering	tamability	tentacular	threadfish	topsyturvy	trawlerman
swimmingly	tambourine	tenterhook	threadmark	torchlight	treadboard
swinefever	tangential	tepidarium	threadworm	toroidally	treadwheel

treasonous	truculence	unattended	unemphatic	unremarked	Vaticanism
trecentist	truculency	unavailing	unemployed	unrequited	Vaticanist
tremendous	truncately	unbalanced	unendingly	unreserved	vaticinate
tremolitic	truncation	unbearable	unenviable	unresolved	vaudeville
trenchancy	trundlebed	unbearably	unequalled	unripeness	vectograph
trendiness	trustfully	unbeatable	unerringly	unrivalled	vegetarian
trepanning	trustiness	unbeatably	unevenness	unruliness	vegetation
trespasser	trustingly	unbecoming	uneventful	unscalable	vegetative
triacetate	truthfully	unbeliever	unexampled	unschooled	vehemently
triandrous	tryptophan	unbesought	unexcelled	unscramble	veldschoen
triangular	tsarevitch	unbiblical	unexpected	unscreened	velitation
tribometer	tubercular	unbiddable	unexplored	unscripted	velocipede
tribrachic	tuberculin	unblenched	unfadingly	unseasoned	velutinous
trichiasis	tuberosity	unblinking	unfairness	unselected	venational
trichinise	tubicolous	unblushing	unfaithful	unsettling	veneration
trichinous	tuffaceous	unbonneted	unfamiliar	unsociable	vengefully
trichology	tufthunter	unbrokenly	unfathered	unsociably	venialness
trichotomy	tuitionary	unbuttoned	unfeminine	unsocially	venomously
trichroism	tularaemia	unchanging	unfettered	unsporting	ventilator
trichromat	tularaemic	unchastity	unfilially	unsteadily	ventricose
trickiness	tumbledown	uncloister	unfinished	unstrained	ventriculi
trickishly	tumblerful	uncommonly	unflagging	unstressed	verandahed
triclinium	tumbleweed	uncritical	unforeseen	unsuitable	verbaliser
tricyclist	tumescence	unctuosity	unfriended	unswerving	verifiable
Tridentine	tumultuary	unctuously	unfriendly	unthinking	vermicelli
trierarchy	tumultuous	uncustomed	ungenerous	untidiness	vermicidal
triflingly	tunelessly	undefended	ungraceful	untowardly	vermicular
trifoliate	tunnelling	undeniable	ungracious	untroubled	vernacular
trifurcate	turbidness	undeniably	ungrateful	untruthful	vernissage
trigeminal	turbulence	underbelly	ungrounded	unwariness	versicular
triggerman	turbulency	underbrush	ungrudging	unwavering	vertebrate
triglyphic	turgescent	undercliff	unguentary	unwieldily	vertically
trigonally	turgidness	undercover	unhallowed	unwontedly	vesication
trilateral	turkeycock	undercroft	unhandsome	unworkable	vesicatory
trilingual	turnbuckle	underdress	unhistoric	unworthily	vesiculate
triliteral	turpentine	underfloor	unholiness	unwrinkled	vesperbell
trillionth	turtleback	underglaze	unhouseled	unyielding	vespertine
trimonthly	turtledove	underlease	uniaxially	upbraiding	vestibular
trimorphic	turtleneck	underlinen	unicameral	upbringing	vestibulum
trioecious	tutorially	underlying	unicyclist	upholstery	vestpocket
tripartite	twelvefold	underminer	uniformity	upperclass	veterinary
triphammer	twelvenote	underneath	unilateral	uppishness	vibraculum
triphthong	twelvetone	underpants	unilingual	uproarious	vibraphone
triplicate	twilighted	underproof	unilocular	upstanding	viceconsul
triplicity	twowheeler	underquote	unimproved	upwardness	vicegerent
triquetrae	tympanites	underscore	uninformed	uranometry	viceregent
triquetral	tympanitic	undersense	uninitiate	urbanology	victimiser
trisection	tympanitis	undersexed	unionistic	urethritis	Victoriana
triskelion	typescript	undershirt	unipartite	urochordal	victorious
triternate	typesetter	undershoot	uniqueness	urticarial	victualled
triturable	typewriter	undershrub	university	urtication	victualler
triturator	typicality	undersized	univocally	usefulness	videophone
triumphant	typography	underskirt	unjustness	usquebaugh	Vietnamese
triumviral	typologist	underslung	unkindness	ustulation	viewfinder
trivialise	tyrannical	understand	unknowable	usucaption	viewlessly
trivialism	Tyrrhenian	understate	unlabelled	usuriously	vigilantly
triviality	ubiquitous	understeer	unlawfully	usurpation	vignettist
trochanter	ulceration	understock	unlettered	utilisable	vigorously
trochoidal	ulcerative	understood	unlikeness	utopianism	villainage
troctolite	ulotrichan	understudy	unmannerly	uxoricidal	villainess
troglodyte	ulteriorly	undertaken	unmeasured	uxoriously	villainous
trolleybus	ultimately	undertaker	unmeetness	vaccinator	villanelle
trollopish	ultrabasic	undertrick	unmerciful	validation	villeinage
trombonist	ultrasonic	undervalue	unmorality	valleculae	vindicable
tromometer	ultrasound	underwater	unmortised	vallecular	vindicator
tropaeolum	umbellifer	underworld	unnameable	valorously	vindictive
trophology	umbilicate	underwrite	unnumbered	valvulitis	vinegarish
tropically	umbiliform	underwrote	unoccupied	vanadinite	violaceous
tropologic	umbrageous	undeserved	unofficial	vanquisher	viperiform
tropopause	umbrellaed	undesigned	unorthodox	vaporiform	viperously
tropophyte	umpireship	undesirous	unpleasant	vaporously	viraginous
Trotskyism	unabridged	undeterred	unpleasing	varicocele	virescence
Trotskyist	unaccented	undigested	unprepared	varicosity	virginally
Trotskyite	unaffected	undulation	unprovoked	variegated	virginhood
troubadour	unAmerican	undulatory	unravelled	varietally	virologist
trousseaux	unarguable	uneasiness	unreadable	variolitic	virtuality
trouvaille	unassisted	uneconomic	unredeemed	variometer	virtueless
trowelling	unassuming	unedifying	unreliable	vascularly	virtuosity
trucklebed	unattached	uneducated	unrelieved	vasoactive	virtuously

virulently	watermelon	windshield	yeastiness	barramunda	canonicate
viscerally	waterpower	windsleeve	yellowback	barramundi	canonicity
viscometer	waterproof	winebibber	yellowbird	barratrous	canorously
viscountcy	waterskier	winebottle	yellowness	barrelling	cantaloupe
visibility	waterspout	winegrower	yellowwood	barrenness	cantatrice
Visigothic	watertight	wingcollar	yesteryear	barrenwort	canterbury
visionally	waterwheel	wingfooted	yieldingly	barysphere	cantilever
visionless	waterworks	wingspread	ylangylang	basketball	cantillate
visitation	wattlebird	wintertide	yokefellow	basketwork	cantonment
visitorial	wavelength	wintertime	youngberry	bassethorn	canvasback
visualiser	waveringly	wintriness	yourselves	bassoonist	canvaswork
vitalistic	weakliness	wiredrawer	youthfully	bastardise	canzonetta
vitaminise	weakminded	wirehaired	zabaglione	batfowling	caoutchouc
vitiligate	weaponless	wirepuller	ZendAvesta	batholitic	capability
vitrescent	wearifully	wiretapper	zigzagging	bathometer	capacitate
vitriolise	weatherbox	wirewalker	zincograph	bathymeter	capacitive
vituperate	weathering	wireworker	zollverein	bathymetry	capitalise
vivandiere	weatherman	wishywashy	zoological	bathyscaph	capitalism
viviparity	weaverbird	witchcraft	zoomorphic	bathyscope	capitalist
viviparous	weedkiller	witchhazel	zoophagous	batrachian	capitation
vivisector	weightless	witchingly	zoophilous	battailous	Capitoline
viziership	weimaraner	withdrawal	zwitterion	battledore	capitulary
vocabulary	wellheeled	withdrawer	zygodactyl	battlement	capitulate
vocational	wellington	withholder	zygomorphy	battleship	cappuccino
vociferant	wellspoken	witnessbox	────────	bawdyhouse	capricious
vociferate	wellspring	wobbliness	aardwolves	cabalistic	captiously
vociferous	wellturned	woefulness	babblement	cacciatore	carabineer
voiceprint	wellwisher	wolframite	babiroussa	cachinnate	carabinier
volatilise	Welshwoman	womanishly	Babylonian	cackhanded	caramelise
volatility	wentletrap	wonderland	babysitter	cacodaemon	caravaneer
volitional	werewolves	wonderment	bacchantes	cacogenics	caravanned
volleyball	Wertherian	wonderwork	bacchantic	cacography	caravanner
voltameter	Wertherism	wondrously	backbiting	cacomistle	carbonnade
volubility	westernise	wongawonga	backblocks	cadaverous	carboxylic
volumetric	westwardly	wontedness	backgammon	caddisworm	carbuncled
voluminous	whaleshark	woodcarver	background	Caerphilly	carcinogen
voluptuary	wharfinger	woodcutter	backhanded	caespitose	carcinosis
voluptuous	whatsoever	woodenhead	backhander	cajolement	cardialgia
vomitorium	wheatstone	woodenness	backsheesh	cajolingly	cardiogram
vortically	wheelchair	woodlander	backslider	calamander	cardiology
vorticella	wheelhorse	woodpecker	backstairs	calamitous	cardplayer
vorticular	wheelhouse	woodpigeon	backstitch	calcareous	carelessly
voyageable	wheeziness	woodturner	backstroke	calceolate	caricature
vulcaniser	whensoever	woodworker	backwardly	calciferol	carmagnole
vulnerable	whereabout	woolgather	badderlock	calcsinter	carnallite
vulnerably	whipstitch	woolgrower	bafflement	calculable	carnassial
waffleiron	whirlybird	woolliness	bafflingly	calculably	carotenoid
waggonette	whiskified	woolsorter	balbriggan	calculator	carotinoid
wagonvault	whispering	wordlessly	balderdash	Caledonian	carpellary
wainwright	whitebeard	workbasket	baldheaded	calibrator	carpetweed
waistcloth	whitefaced	workingman	ballflower	caliginous	carphology
Waldensian	whitesmith	workpeople	ballistics	callowness	carragheen
wallflower	whitethorn	worldclass	ballooning	calumniate	carryingon
wallpepper	WhitMonday	worldweary	balloonist	calumnious	Carthusian
wampumpeag	WhitSunday	worshipful	balneology	calyciform	cartomancy
wanderings	wholesaler	worshipped	balustrade	calyptrate	cartoonist
wanderlust	whomsoever	worshipper	banderilla	camelopard	cartwright
wanderplug	whorehouse	worthiness	bandmaster	camerlengo	caruncular
wantonness	wickedness	worthwhile	banishment	camerlingo	caryatides
wappenshaw	wickerwork	wraparound	bankruptcy	camouflage	cascarilla
wardenship	widespread	wrathfully	baptistery	campaigner	caseharden
warmingpan	wildebeest	wrathiness	barbellate	campestral	caseworker
wassailing	wilderment	wretchedly	barbershop	camphorate	cassolette
wastefully	wilderness	wristwatch	barbituric	canaliculi	castration
wastepaper	wildfowler	wrongdoing	barcarolle	cancellate	casualness
watchfully	wilfulness	wrongfully	bardolatry	cancelling	catabolism
watchglass	willowherb	wrongously	barebacked	cancellous	catafalque
watchguard	willynilly	wunderkind	barefooted	candelabra	catalectic
watchmaker	willywilly	Wycliffite	bareheaded	candescent	cataleptic
watchtower	winceyette	Wykehamist	barelegged	candidness	cataloguer
waterborne	Winchester	xenophobia	bargeboard	candlefish	cataphract
waterbrash	windflower	xerography	barkentine	candletree	catarrhine
waterclock	windjammer	xerophytic	barleybree	candlewick	catastasis
watercraft	windowless	xiphosuran	barleybroo	candlewood	catburglar
watercress	windowpane	xylography	barleycorn	candyfloss	catchpenny
waterflood	windowseat	xylophonic	Barmecidal	cankerworm	catechesis
waterfront	windowshop	yarborough	barometric	cannelloni	catechetic
waterglass	windowsill	yardmaster	baronetage	cannonball	catechiser
wateriness	windscreen	yearningly	barracouta	canonicals	catechumen

```
categorise  fatalistic  hammerless  Lamarckian  mainlander  marshaller
catenation  fatherhood  hammerlock  Lamarckism  mainspring  marshalsea
catholicon  fatherland  hammerpond  lambrequin  mainstream  marshiness
catholicos  fatherless  hamshackle  lamentable  maintainer  martensite
catoptrics  fatherlike  handbarrow  lamentably  maisonette  martialism
cattlegrid  fathership  handedness  lamentedly  majestical  martingale
causticity  fathomable  handgallop  laminarian  majuscular  marvelling
cautionary  fathomless  handicraft  lamination  makeweight  marvellous
cautiously  fatiguable  handmaiden  Lammastide  malacoderm  masquerade
cavalierly  faultiness  handpicked  lampoonery  malacology  Massoretic
cavalryman  favourable  handselled  lampoonist  maladapted  mastectomy
cavitation  favourably  handsomely  lanceolate  malapertly  masterhand
daintiness  gadolinite  handspring  landholder  malapropos  masterhood
daisychain  gadolinium  handworked  landhunger  malcontent  masterless
damageable  gadrooning  hangglider  landingnet  malefactor  mastermind
damagingly  gaillardia  hankypanky  landlocked  maleficent  mastership
dampcourse  gaingiving  Hanoverian  landlubber  malentendu  masterwork
dampingoff  galimatias  Hansardise  landocracy  malevolent  masticable
dapplegrey  galleywest  hanselling  landowning  malfeasant  masticator
datamation  galliambic  harassment  landscaper  malignance  matchboard
daughterly  galloglass  harbourage  languisher  malignancy  matchmaker
dauphiness  Gallomania  hardbilled  languorous  malingerer  matchstick
daydreamer  Gallophile  hardbitten  lansquenet  malleebird  materially
dazzlement  Gallophobe  hardboiled  lanternfly  malleefowl  maternally
dazzlingly  galvaniser  hardfisted  lanthanide  mallenders  mathematic
earthbound  gambolling  hardhanded  lanuginose  malodorous  matriarchy
earthiness  gamekeeper  hardheaded  lanuginous  Malpighian  matricidal
earthlight  gametangia  harelipped  laparotomy  Malthusian  matronhood
earthquake  ganglionic  harmlessly  lapidarian  malvaceous  matronship
earthshine  gangrenous  harmonical  lapidarist  mamillated  matronymic
earthwards  gargantuan  harmonious  lapidation  manageable  maturation
eartrumpet  garishness  harmoniser  lardydardy  manageably  maturative
earwigging  garnierite  hartebeest  largescale  management  matureness
earwitness  garnishing  haruspices  larvicidal  manageress  mavourneen
easterling  gasconader  harvestman  laryngitic  managerial  maxilliped
Eastertide  gaslighter  hauntingly  laryngitis  manchineel  maximalist
fabricator  gaspereaux  haustellum  lascivious  mandibular  mayblossom
fabulously  gasteropod  haustorium  laterality  mandragora  mayonnaise
faceharden  gastrology  hawserlaid  latescence  manfulness  nailpolish
facesaving  gastronome  iatrogenic  latifundia  mangosteen  nambypamby
facileness  gastronomy  jackanapes  lattermost  maniacally  namelessly
facilitate  gatekeeper  jackassery  laughingly  Manichaean  nanisation
factiously  gatelegged  jackhammer  laundryman  Manicheism  nanosecond
factitious  gaucheness  jackknives  lauraceous  manicurist  naphthenic
factorship  gaultheria  jackrabbit  laureation  manifestly  narcissism
factualism  gauntleted  jacobinise  laurelling  manifestos  narcissist
factualist  habiliment  Jacobinism  lavalliere  manifoldly  narcolepsy
factuality  habilitate  Jacobitism  lavatorial  manipulate  narrowness
fadelessly  habitation  jaggedness  lavishment  manoeuvrer  nasturtium
Fahrenheit  habitually  jaguarundi  lavishness  manoeuvres  natalitial
faintheart  hackbuteer  janitorial  lawabiding  manometric  natatorial
fairground  hackmatack  Janusfaced  lawbreaker  manorhouse  natatorium
fairhaired  haematosis  Japanesque  lawfulness  manservant  nationally
fairleader  haematuria  jardiniere  lawntennis  mansuetude  nationhood
fairminded  haemolysis  jargonelle  lawrencium  manteltree  nationless
fairspoken  haemolytic  jasperware  Lawrentian  manumitted  nationwide
fairycycle  hagiolatry  jauntiness  macadamise  manuscript  nativeborn
faithfully  hagiologic  jawbreaker  Maccabaean  manzanilla  nativeness
fallacious  hagioscope  jaywalking  macebearer  maquillage  nativistic
fallingoff  hairraiser  Kafkaesque  maceration  maraschino  natterjack
fallowness  hairspring  kaisership  machinator  marcescent  naturalise
familiarly  hairstreak  Kantianism  machinegun  Marcionite  naturalism
famishment  hairstroke  karyoplasm  mackintosh  marginalia  naturalist
famousness  hakenkreuz  katabolism  macrophage  marginally  naturopath
fanaticise  halberdier  labiovelar  macrospore  marginated  nauseating
fanaticism  halfcocked  laboratory  maculation  margravate  nauseously
fancifully  halfdollar  laceration  maculature  margravine  nautically
fandangoes  halflength  lacerative  madreporic  marguerite  navigation
fantastico  halfnelson  lachrymose  magistracy  Mariolater  oafishness
fantoccini  halfvolley  lacklustre  magistrate  Mariolatry  pacesetter
farcically  halfwitted  laconicism  magnetiser  marionette  pacifiable
farfetched  halfyearly  lacrimator  magnifical  marketable  pacificate
farsighted  halieutics  lacrymator  magnificat  markethall  pacificism
fasciation  hallelujah  lactescent  magnifying  markettown  pacificist
fascicular  halogenate  lacustrine  Mahommedan  markswoman  packingbox
fasciculus  halogenous  ladderback  maidenhair  marquisate  packsaddle
fascinator  halophytic  ladychapel  maidenhead  marrowbone  packthread
fastidious  hammerbeam  ladyfinger  maidenhood  marrowless  paddleboat
fastigiate  hammerhead  ladykiller  maidenlike  marshalled  paddyfield
```

paddywagon	paraplegic	radioscopy	sandhopper	tastefully	yardmaster
paddywhack	parapodium	radiosonde	sandmartin	tattletale	zabaglione
paedagogic	paraselene	ragamuffin	sanguinary	tauntingly	abacterial
paederasty	parasitism	raggedness	sanguinely	tauromachy	abbreviate
paediatric	parasitoid	railroader	sanguinity	tautomeric	abdication
paedogogue	paratactic	railwayman	sanitarian	tautophony	abdominous
paedophile	paratroops	rainmaking	sanitarily	tawdriness	abducentes
pagination	parcelling	rakishness	sanitarium	taxability	aberdevine
painkiller	pardonable	ramblingly	sanitation	taxidancer	aberrantly
painlessly	pardonably	rampageous	Sanskritic	taxidermal	aberration
paintbrush	parenchyma	ramshackle	sapiential	taxidermic	abhorrence
Palaeocene	parentally	rancidness	sappanwood	taxonomist	abiogenist
Palaeogene	parenteral	randomness	sapphirine	vaccinator	abjectness
palaeolith	parenthood	ranunculus	saprogenic	validation	abjuration
palaeotype	parimutuel	rapporteur	saprophyte	valleculae	ablebodied
Palaeozoic	parliament	ratability	sarcolemma	vallecular	abnegation
palagonite	Parnassian	ratcatcher	sarcophagi	valorously	abnormally
palatalise	paronymous	rationally	sarcophagy	valvulitis	abominable
palatinate	paroxysmal	rattlehead	sarcoplasm	vanadinite	abominably
palimpsest	paroxytone	rattlepate	sargassoes	vanquisher	abominator
palindrome	parramatta	rattletrap	sarmentose	vaporiform	aboriginal
palisander	parricidal	ravenously	sarmentous	vaporously	abortively
palladious	parrotfish	ravishment	sarracenia	varicocele	aboveboard
pallbearer	parsonbird	razorblade	sashwindow	varicosity	Abrahamman
palliation	parsonical	razorshell	satanology	variegated	abrasively
palliative	partiality	razzmatazz	satellitic	varietally	abreaction
palliatory	participle	sabbatical	satisfying	variolitic	abridgment
pallidness	particular	sabretache	saturation	variometer	abrogation
palmaceous	parturient	sabretooth	saturnalia	vascularly	abruptness
palmatifid	pasquinade	saccharate	satyagraha	vasoactive	abscission
palmbutter	passageway	saccharide	satyriasis	Vaticanism	absolutely
palmerworm	passionary	saccharify	sauerkraut	Vaticanist	absolution
PalmSunday	passionate	saccharine	savageness	vaticinate	absolutism
paltriness	Passionist	saccharoid	savourless	vaudeville	absolutist
palynology	pasteboard	saccharose	sawtoothed	waffleiron	absolutory
Panamanian	pastellist	sacerdotal	saxicoline	waggonette	absorbable
pancratium	pasteurise	sacredness	saxicolous	wagonvault	absorbance
pancreatic	pasteurism	sacrificer	tabernacle	wainwright	absorbedly
pancreatin	pastmaster	sacroiliac	tablecloth	waistcloth	absorbency
panegyrise	pastorally	sacrosanct	tablelinen	Waldensian	absorption
panegyrist	pastorship	saddleback	tablespoon	wallflower	absorptive
pangenesis	pastrycook	saddlefast	tabularise	wallpepper	abstemious
pangenetic	pasturable	saddletree	tabulation	wampumpeag	abstention
panhandler	pastyfaced	safeblower	tachometer	wanderings	abstergent
paniculate	patchiness	safetybelt	tachometry	wanderlust	abstersion
panjandrum	patentable	sagination	tachymeter	wanderplug	abstersive
panopticon	paternally	sagittally	tachymetry	wantonness	abstinence
pansophist	pathetical	sailorless	taciturnly	wappenshaw	abstinency
pantograph	pathfinder	salability	tackdriver	wardenship	abstracted
pantomimic	pathogenic	salamander	tactically	warmingpan	abstracter
pantrymaid	pathologic	salesclerk	tactlessly	wassailing	abstractly
papaverine	patination	saleswoman	tailorbird	wastefully	abstractor
papaverous	patisserie	salicional	tailormade	wastepaper	abstrusely
paperchase	patriality	salicylate	takingness	watchfully	abstrusity
paperknife	patriarchy	salientian	talebearer	watchglass	absurdness
papermaker	patriciate	saliferous	talentless	watchguard	abundantly
papistical	patricidal	salivation	taleteller	watchmaker	ebullience
papyrology	patrilocal	sallenders	talismanic	watchtower	ebulliency
parabiosis	patriotism	sallowness	Talmudical	waterborne	ebullition
parabiotic	patristics	salmagundi	tamability	waterbrash	obdurately
parabolise	patrolling	salmonella	tambourine	waterclock	obediently
paraboloid	patronymic	salmonleap	tangential	watercraft	obfuscated
paradisaic	patulously	salpingian	tanglement	watercress	obituarist
paradisean	pawnbroker	saltarello	tankengine	waterflood	objectival
paradisiac	rabbinical	saltcellar	tantaliser	waterfront	objectless
paradisian	rabblement	saltigrade	tantamount	waterglass	oblateness
paradoxure	racecourse	salubrious	taperecord	wateriness	obligation
paraffinic	Rachmanism	salutarily	taperingly	watermelon	obligatory
paragnosis	rackrenter	salutation	tapestried	waterpower	obligingly
paralipsis	radicalise	salutatory	tapotement	waterproof	obliterate
paralogise	radicalism	samarskite	taradiddle	waterskier	obnubilate
paralogism	radication	sanatorium	tarantella	waterspout	obsequious
paramecium	radiogenic	sanctifier	tarantelle	watertight	observable
parametric	radiograph	sanctimony	tardigrade	waterwheel	observably
paramnesia	radiologic	sanctitude	tarmacadam	waterworks	observance
paranormal	radiometer	sandalwood	Tartuffian	wattlebird	obstetrics
paraphrase	radiometry	sandbagger	Tartuffism	wavelength	obstructor
paraphrast	radiopaque	sandcastle	taskmaster	waveringly	obtainable
paraplegia	radiophone	sanderling	tasselling	yarborough	obtainment

dendrology	despiteous	gentlefolk	henceforth	legitimacy	mesenteric
denegation	despondent	gentleness	hendecagon	legitimate	mesenteron
denigrator	desquamate	geocentric	henharrier	legitimise	mesmeriser
denominate	destructor	geochemist	henhearted	legitimism	Mesolithic
denotation	detachable	geodetical	henotheism	legitimist	mesomerism
denotative	detachedly	geognostic	henotheist	leguminous	mesomorphy
denouement	detachment	geographer	heortology	Leibnizian	mesophytic
densimeter	detainment	geographic	heparinise	lemniscate	mesoscaphe
dentifrice	detectable	geological	hepatical	lemongrass	mesosphere
denudation	detergency	geometrise	hepatology	lengthways	mesothorax
denunciate	determined	geophysics	heptachord	lengthwise	messianism
deodoriser	deterrence	geoponical	heptagonal	lenticular	metabolise
deontology	detestable	geothermal	Heptameron	lentigines	metabolism
deoxidiser	detestably	geothermic	heptameter	leopardess	metabolite
department	detonation	geotropism	heptarchic	lepidolite	metacarpal
dependable	detonative	geriatrics	heptateuch	leprechaun	metacarpus
dependably	detoxicant	geriatrist	heptatonic	lesbianism	metacentre
dependence	detoxicate	germicidal	herbaceous	letterbomb	metagalaxy
dependency	detraction	germinally	hereabouts	letterbook	metalepsis
depilation	detractive	gerundival	hereditary	lettercard	metallurgy
depilatory	Devanagari	gesundheit	heresiarch	letterhead	metamerism
deplorable	devilishly	headcheese	hereticate	letterless	metaphoric
deplorably	devitalise	headhunter	heretofore	leucocytic	metaphrase
deployment	devocalise	headmaster	hermetical	leucoplast	metaphysic
depolarise	devolution	headphones	hermitcrab	leukocytic	metaplasia
depopulate	devotement	headspring	heroically	levigation	metastable
deportment	devotional	headsquare	heroicness	levitation	metastases
depositary	devoutness	headstream	heroicomic	lexicology	metastasis
deposition	dextrality	headstrong	herrenvolk	lexigraphy	metastatic
depository	dextrously	headwaiter	Herrnhuter	meadowland	metatarsal
depravedly	fearlessly	heartblock	hesitantly	meadowlark	metatarsus
depreciate	fearnought	heartblood	hesitation	meagreness	metatheses
depredator	fearsomely	heartbreak	hesitative	mealbeetle	metathesis
depressant	featherbed	heartiness	heterodont	meaningful	metathetic
depression	feathering	heartsease	heterodoxy	measliness	metathorax
depressive	febrifugal	heartthrob	heterodyne	measurable	metempiric
deprivable	fecklessly	heartwhole	heterogamy	measurably	meteoritic
depuration	federalise	heathendom	heterogeny	measuredly	methodical
depurative	federalism	heathenise	heterogony	mechanical	Methuselah
deputation	federalist	heathenish	heterology	meddlesome	methylated
deracinate	federation	heathenism	heteronomy	mediastina	meticulous
derailleur	federative	heatstroke	heterotaxy	mediatress	metrically
derailment	feebleness	heavenborn	heulandite	medicament	metronomic
derestrict	felicitate	heavensent	heuristics	medicaster	metronymic
deridingly	felicitous	heavenward	hexahedral	medication	metropolis
derisively	fellmonger	heavyarmed	hexahedron	medievally	mettlesome
derivation	fellowship	hebdomadal	hexamerous	mediocrity	Neapolitan
derivative	felspathic	hebetation	hexametric	meditation	nebulosity
dermatitis	femaleness	Hebraistic	Jehovistic	meditative	nebulously
dermatogen	feminality	hectically	jejuneness	medullated	necrolater
derogation	femininely	hectograph	jeopardise	meerschaum	necrolatry
derogatory	femininity	hectolitre	jerrybuilt	megalithic	necromancy
desalinate	fenestella	hectometre	jesuitical	megalosaur	necrophile
descendant	fenestrate	hedonistic	Jewishness	megascopic	necrophily
descendent	fertiliser	heedlessly	kennelling	melancholy	necropolis
descension	fervidness	heliacally	kenspeckle	Melanesian	necroscopy
descriptor	fescennine	helianthus	keratinise	melanistic	nectareous
desecrater	festoonery	heliconian	keratinous	meliorator	needlebath
desecrator	fetchingly	helicopter	kerchieves	melismatic	needlebook
deservedly	fetterlock	heliograph	kerseymere	mellowness	needlecord
deshabille	feuilleton	heliolater	kerygmatic	meltingpot	needlefish
desiccator	feverishly	heliolatry	kettledrum	membership	needlessly
desiderata	gelatinise	heliometer	keyboarder	membranous	needlework
desiderate	gelatinous	heliophyte	leadenness	memorandum	negatively
designator	gemination	helioscope	leaderless	menacingly	negativism
designedly	gemmaceous	heliotaxis	leadership	mendacious	negativist
designment	generalise	heliotrope	leafcutter	mendicancy	negativity
desipience	generalist	heliotropy	leafhopper	meningioma	neglectful
desirously	generality	hellbender	leafinsect	meningitis	negligence
desistance	generation	helminthic	lebensraum	menopausal	negligible
desolately	generative	helplessly	lectionary	menstruate	negligibly
desolation	generatrix	hemihedral	lederhosen	menstruous	negotiable
desorption	generosity	hemihedron	ledgerbait	mentorship	negotiator
despatcher	generously	hemiplegia	ledgerline	mercantile	negrophile
desperados	geneticist	hemiplegic	lefthanded	mercifully	negrophobe
despicable	genialness	hemipteran	lefthander	meridional	nematocyst
despicably	geniculate	hemisphere	legalistic	merrymaker	neoclassic
despisable	genteelism	hempnettle	legateship		neological
despiteful	gentilesse		legibility		neoplastic

```
seignorage  septillion  tentacular  weimaraner  egoistical  chiselling
seignorial  Septuagint  tenterhook  wellheeled  Egyptology  chivalrous
seismicity  sepulchral  tepidarium  wellington  ignobility  chlorinate
seismogram  sequacious  teratogeny  wellspoken  ignorantly  chloroform
seismology  sequential  teratology  wellspring  chainsmoke  choiceness
selectness  sequestrum  teratomata  wellturned  chairwoman  chokeberry
selenodont  SerboCroat  termagancy  wellwisher  chalcedony  chondritic
selenology  sereneness  terminable  Welshwoman  chalkboard  choriambic
selfacting  sergeantcy  terminably  wentletrap  chalkstone  Christhood
selfaction  serigraphy  terminally  werewolves  challenger  Christlike
selfbinder  seriocomic  terminator  Wertherian  chalybeate  chromatics
selfcolour  serjeantcy  termitaria  Wertherism  chamaeleon  chromatype
selfdeceit  sermoniser  terneplate  westernise  chamberpot  chromosome
selfdenial  serologist  terracotta  westwardly  champignon  chronicity
selfesteem  serotinous  terreplein  xenophobia  chancellor  chronicler
selffeeder  serpentine  terrorless  xerography  chandelier  chronogram
selfglazed  serradilla  tessellate  xerophytic  changeable  chronology
selfguided  serviceman  testaceous  yearningly  changeably  chrysolite
selflessly  servomotor  testflight  yeastiness  changeless  chrysotile
selfloving  sestertium  tetchiness  yellowback  changeling  chubbiness
selfmotion  sestertius  tetrachord  yellowbird  changeover  chuckerout
selfmurder  setterwort  tetragonal  yellowness  channelise  chuckwagon
selfparody  settlement  tetrahedra  yellowwood  channelled  churchgoer
selfpoised  seventieth  tetrameter  yesteryear  chaparajos  churchyard
selfpraise  severeness  tetramorph  ZendAvesta  chaparejos  churlishly
selfprofit  sexagenary  tetrapolis  affability  chapfallen  ghastfully
selfraised  Sexagesima  tetrarchic  affectedly  chaplaincy  Ghibelline
selfregard  sexivalent  tetrastich  affectless  charactery  phagedaena
selfrising  sexlimited  tetrastyle  affeerment  chargeable  phagedenic
selfruling  sexologist  tetterwort  afferently  chargehand  phagocytic
selfseeker  sexpartite  textualist  affettuoso  charioteer  phalangeal
selfstyled  sextillion  texturally  affiliated  charismata  phallicism
selftaught  teaplanter  vectograph  affirmable  charitable  phanerogam
selfwilled  tearjerker  vegetarian  affliction  charitably  phantasise
seltzogene  tearlessly  vegetation  afflictive  Charleston  phantasmal
semeiology  teatrolley  vegetative  affluently  charmingly  phantasmic
semeiotics  technetium  vehemently  affordable  chartreuse  phantastic
semestrial  technician  veldschoen  aficionado  chartulary  phantastry
semiannual  technicist  velitation  Africander  chasteness  pharisaism
semichorus  technocrat  velocipede  Africanise  chatelaine  pharmacist
semicircle  technology  velutinous  Africanism  chatoyance  pharyngeal
semidivine  teenyweeny  venational  Africanist  chatterbox  pheasantry
semidouble  teetotally  veneration  Afrikander  chattiness  phelloderm
semidrying  tegumental  vengefully  afterbirth  chaudfroid  phenacetin
semifitted  telecamera  venialness  aftergrass  chauffeuse  phenocryst
semiliquid  telecaster  venomously  afterimage  chauntress  phenomenal
semilunate  telegraphy  ventilator  afterlight  chauvinism  phenomenon
seminarian  telemetric  ventricose  afterpains  chauvinist  phenotypic
seminarist  teleologic  ventriculi  aftershave  cheapishly  pheromonal
semination  teleostean  verandahed  aftertaste  cheapskate  philatelic
semiopaque  telepathic  verbaliser  afterwards  checkpoint  philippina
semiotical  telephoner  verifiable  effaceable  cheekiness  philippine
semiquaver  telephonic  vermicelli  effacement  cheerfully  philistine
semiuncial  telescopic  vermicidal  effectuate  cheeriness  phillumeny
semiweekly  televiewer  vermicular  effeminacy  cheesecake  philologen
semiyearly  television  vernacular  effeminate  cheesiness  philopoena
sempstress  televisual  vernissage  effervesce  chelicerae  philosophe
senatorial  tellership  versicular  effeteness  chemically  philosophy
senescence  telpherage  vertebrate  efficacity  chemisette  phlebotomy
sensedatum  temperable  vertically  efficiency  chemotaxis  phlegmatic
senseorgan  temperance  vesication  effloresce  chequebook  phlogistic
sensitiser  temperedly  vesicatory  effortless  chersonese  phlogiston
sensualise  temporally  vesiculate  effrontery  chessboard  phlogopite
sensualism  temporalty  vesperbell  effulgence  chevrotain  Phoenician
sensualist  temporiser  vespertine  effusively  chickenpox  phonematic
sensuality  temptation  vestibular  officially  chiffchaff  phonically
sensuously  temptingly  vestibulum  offlicence  chiffonier  phonograph
sentential  tenability  vestpocket  offputting  childbirth  phonolitic
sentiently  tenantable  veterinary  offsetting  childermas  phonologic
separately  tenantless  weakliness  oftentimes  childishly  phonometer
separation  tenderfoot  weakminded  agapanthus  childproof  phosphatic
separatism  tenderloin  weaponless  agglutinin  chiliastic  phosphoric
separatist  tenderness  wearifully  aggrandise  chilliness  phosphorus
separative  tendinitis  weatherbox  aggression  chimerical  photoflood
separatory  tendrillar  weathering  aggressive  chimneypot  photogenic
septenarii  tendrilled  weatherman  agitatedly  chimpanzee  photograph
septennial  tenebrific  weaverbird  agrologist  chinagraph  photolitho
septennium  tenebrious  weedkiller  agronomist  chinchilla  photolysis
septically  tenemental  weightless  egocentric  chiromancy  photolytic
```

photometer	shockproof	thoughtful	bilocation	dickcissel	discretion
photometry	shoddiness	thousandth	bimestrial	Dickensian	discursive
photonasty	shoebuckle	threadbare	bimetallic	dictatress	discussant
photophily	shoestring	threadfish	binaurally	dictionary	discussion
photophore	shopkeeper	threadmark	binoculars	didactical	discussive
photoprint	shoplifter	threadworm	biochemist	didgeridoo	discutient
phototaxis	shopsoiled	threatener	biodegrade	diecasting	disdainful
phototrope	shopwalker	threepence	biodynamic	dielectric	diseconomy
phrasebook	shopwindow	threepenny	bioecology	diesinking	disembogue
phrenology	shoreleave	threepiece	biogenesis	difference	disembosom
phthisical	shorewards	threescore	biogenetic	difficulty	disembowel
phylactery	shortbread	threnodial	biographer	diffidence	disembroil
phyllotaxy	shortcrust	threnodist	biographic	diffusible	disenchant
phylloxera	shortdated	thriftless	biological	digestible	disengaged
phylogenic	shortening	throatwort	biometrics	digitalise	disenthral
physically	shortlived	thromboses	biomorphic	digitately	disentitle
physicking	shortrange	thrombosis	biophysics	digitation	disentwine
physiocrat	shouldered	thrombotic	bioscience	digitiform	disenviron
physiology	shovelhead	throneless	biparietal	digression	disfeature
phytogenic	shovelling	throughout	bipartisan	digressive	disfurnish
phytophagy	showerbath	throughput	bipetalous	dilapidate	disgruntle
phytotoxic	showjumper	throughway	bipolarity	dilatation	disgustful
rhapsodise	showwindow	throwstick	birdspider	dilatorily	dishabille
rhapsodist	shrewdness	thruppence	birdstrike	dilemmatic	disharmony
rheologist	shrewishly	thumbprint	birthplace	dilettante	dishearten
rheotropic	shrewmouse	thumbscrew	birthright	dilettanti	dishonesty
rhetorical	shrievalty	thumbstall	birthstone	diligently	dishwasher
rheumatics	shrillness	thunderbox	bisexually	dillydally	disincline
rheumatism	shrinkable	thundering	bissextile	diluteness	disinherit
rheumatoid	shrinkwrap	thunderous	bisulphate	diminished	disjointed
rhinestone	shrivelled	thwartship	bisulphide	diminuendo	dislikable
rhinoceros	shroudlaid	thwartwise	bisulphite	diminution	disloyally
rhinoscope	shroudless	whaleshark	bitchiness	diminutive	disloyalty
rhinoscopy	Shrovetide	wharfinger	bitterling	dimorphism	dismalness
rhizogenic	shuttering	whatsoever	bitterness	dimorphous	dismission
rhizomorph	thalecress	wheatstone	bitterroot	diningroom	dismissive
rhizophore	thankfully	wheelchair	bitterwood	dinnerless	disordered
rhodophane	theatrical	wheelhorse	bituminise	diphtheria	disorderly
rhomboidal	theistical	wheelhouse	bituminous	diphtheric	disownment
rhomboidei	themselves	wheeziness	bivalvular	diphyletic	disparager
rhythmical	theocratic	whensoever	bivouacked	diphyodont	disparates
shabbiness	theodicean	whereabout	bizarrerie	diplodocus	dispassion
shadowless	theodolite	whipstitch	cicatrices	diplomatic	dispatcher
shagginess	theogonist	whirlybird	cicisbeism	dipsomania	dispelling
shamefaced	theologian	whiskified	cinchonine	directness	dispensary
shamefully	theologise	whispering	cinchonine	directoire	dispersant
shandrydan	theologist	whitebeard	Cinderella	directress	dispersion
shandygaff	theophanic	whitefaced	cinecamera	disability	dispersive
shanghaier	theophoric	whitesmith	cinerarium	disappoint	dispersoid
shantytown	theopneust	whitethorn	cinquefoil	disapprove	dispirited
sharpnosed	theoretics	WhitMonday	Circassian	disarrange	dispiteous
sheabutter	theosopher	WhitSunday	circuitous	disastrous	disposable
shearwater	thereabout	wholesaler	circularly	disbarring	dispossess
sheathbill	thereafter	whomsoever	circulator	disbelieve	dispraiser
sheathless	thereanent	whorehouse	circumcise	disbudding	disputable
sheepishly	thereunder	aircooling	circumflex	disburthen	disputably
sheeplouse	thermionic	aircushion	circumfuse	discerning	disqualify
sheepshank	thermistor	airmanship	circumvent	discharger	disquieten
sheepshead	thermogram	biannually	cismontane	discipline	disquietly
shellacked	thermophil	biblically	cispontine	disclaimer	disrespect
shellmound	thermopile	bibliology	Cistercian	disclosure	disruption
shellproof	thermostat	bibliopegy	citronella	discobolus	disruptive
shellshock	theurgical	bibliophil	diabolical	discomfort	dissatisfy
shenanigan	thickening	bibliopole	diachronic	discommend	dissection
sherardise	thievishly	bibliopoly	diagnostic	discommode	dissembler
sheriffdom	thillhorse	bibliotics	diagonally	discompose	dissension
shibboleth	thimbleful	bichromate	diagraphic	disconcert	dissertate
shieldless	thimblerig	bicultural	dialysable	disconfirm	disservice
shiftiness	thinkingly	bidonville	diapedesis	disconnect	dissidence
shillelagh	thinkpiece	biennially	diaphanous	discontent	dissilient
shipbroker	thirdclass	bigamously	diarrhoeal	discophile	dissimilar
shipfitter	thirdparty	bighearted	diarrhoeic	discordant	dissipated
shipmaster	thirteenth	bigmouthed	diastemata	discounter	dissociate
shiprigged	thirtyfold	bijouterie	diathermal	discourage	dissoluble
shipwright	thixotropy	bilgewater	diathermic	discourser	dissolvent
shirehorse	thornapple	biliverdin	diatropism	discoverer	dissonance
shirtfront	thorniness	billetdoux	dichroitic	discreetly	dissonancy
shirtwaist	thornproof	billposter	dichromate	discrepant	dissuasion
shockingly	thoroughly			discretely	dissuasive

distensile	FinnoUgric	licensable	middlebrow	nidifugous	ricinoleic
distension	fireblight	licentiate	middlemost	nightdress	rickettsia
distention	fireescape	licentious	middlingly	nightglass	ridgepiece
distichous	firepolicy	lieutenant	midmorning	nightlight	ridiculous
distilland	fireraiser	lifegiving	midshipman	nightshade	rightangle
distillate	firescreen	lifejacket	mightiness	nightshift	rightfully
distillery	firstclass	lifelessly	mignonette	nightshirt	rightwards
distilling	firstnight	lifesaving	migrainous	nightstick	rigorously
distinctly	fishcarver	ligamental	militantly	nightwatch	rinderpest
distortion	fisherfolk	lighterage	militarily	nigrescent	ringfinger
distracted	fishkettle	lighterman	militarise	nihilistic	ringleader
distrainer	fishmonger	lightfaced	militarism	nimbleness	ringmaster
distrainor	fisticuffs	lighthouse	militarist	nincompoop	ringnecked
distraught	fitfulness	lightingup	nineteenth	ringtailed	
distressed	fivefinger	lightproof	millefiori	nipplewort	ripplemark
distribute	fixedpoint	likelihood	millennial	nitpicking	riproaring
distringas	Gilbertian	likeliness	millennium	nitrochalk	ripsnorter
disulphate	gingerbeer	likeminded	millesimal	nitrogroup	risibility
disulphide	gingersnap	liliaceous	millilitre	pianissimo	ritardando
disutility	gingivitis	limaciform	millimetre	pianoforte	ritornelli
disyllabic	girlfriend	limeburner	millstream	picaresque	ritornello
disyllable	hibernacle	limitation	millwright	picayunish	riverhorse
ditriglyph	hierarchal	limitative	mimeograph	piccalilli	sialagogic
divagation	hierarchic	limitrophe	mindedness	piccaninny	sialagogue
divaricate	hierocracy	limpidness	mindlessly	pichiciago	sibilation
divebomber	hieroglyph	linguiform	mineralise	pickaninny	sicklebill
divergence	hierograph	linguistic	mineralogy	picketline	sickliness
divergency	hierolatry	lionhunter	minestrone	pickpocket	sideboards
divestment	hierophant	Lipizzaner	mineworker	picnicking	sideeffect
divination	highbinder	lipography	minimalism	picosecond	sideglance
divinatory	highflying	lipomatous	minimalist	pictograph	siderolite
divineness	highhanded	Lippizaner	ministrant	pictorial	siderostat
divisional	highjacker	lipreading	minstrelsy	piecegoods	sidesaddle
divisively	highlander	lipservice	mintmaster	piercingly	sidestreet
divulgence	highminded	liquescent	minuscular	piezometer	sidestroke
eigenvalue	highoctane	liquidator	minutebook	pigeonhole	sidewinder
eighteenmo	highstrung	liquidiser	minutehand	pigeonpair	siegetrain
eighteenth	highwayman	liquidness	minuteness	pigeonpost	signalling
eisteddfod	Hindustani	lissomness	miraculous	pigeontoed	signwriter
fianchetto	hinterland	listlessly	mirthfully	pigeonwing	silentness
fibreboard	hippocampi	literalise	misaligned	pigmentary	silhouette
fibreglass	Hippocrene	literalism	misbelieve	pigsticker	silkcotton
fibrillary	hippodrome	literalist	miscellany	piledriver	silkscreen
fibrillate	hippogriff	literality	mischanter	pilgarlick	sillybilly
fibrillose	hippogryph	literarily	mischmetal	pilgrimage	silverbath
fibrinogen	hippomanes	literation	misconduct	piliferous	silverfish
fibrositis	hippophagy	literature	miscreance	pilliwinks	silverside
fickleness	hipsterism	lithoglyph	misericord	pillowcase	silverware
fictioneer	hirudinean	lithograph	misfortune	pillowlace	silverweed
fictionist	histologic	lithologic	misgivings	pillowslip	similarity
fictitious	histolysis	lithophane	mishitting	pilothouse	similitude
fiddleback	histolytic	lithophyte	misjoinder	pilotlight	simoniacal
fiddlehead	historical	lithotrity	mismatched	pilotwhale	simpleness
fiddlewood	histrionic	Lithuanian	mismeasure	pincerlike	simplicity
fiducially	hitchhiker	litigation	misnomered	pinchpenny	simplifier
fieldglass	hithermost	litterlout	misogamist	pincushion	simplistic
fieldmouse	hitherward	littleness	misogynist	pinebeauty	simulacrum
fieldpiece	jimsonweed	liturgical	misogynous	pinecarpet	simulation
fieldstone	jingoistic	livelihood	misologist	pinfeather	simulative
fiendishly	jinricksha	liveliness	misprision	pinnatifid	simulatory
fierceness	jinrikisha	livingroom	missionary	pinnulated	sincipital
fiftyfifty	kibbutznik	micaschist	missionise	pinstriped	sinecurism
figuration	kidnapping	Michaelmas	mistakable	piperidine	sinecurist
figurative	kieselguhr	microbiota	mistakenly	piscifauna	sinfulness
figurehead	kilogramme	microcline	misthought	pistillary	Singhalese
filariasis	kimberlite	microfarad	misventure	pistillate	singlefoot
filibuster	kindliness	microfiche	miswording	pistolling	singleness
filterable	kinematics	micrograph	mithridate	pistolshot	singletree
filthiness	kineticist	microlitic	mitigation	pistolwhip	singularly
filtration	kingfisher	micrometer	mitigative	pistonring	sinisterly
fimbriated	kingliness	micrometry	mitigatory	pitchblack	sinistrous
fingerbowl	kinnikinic	microphone	mixedmedia	pitcherful	sinologist
fingerless	liberalise	microphyte	mixolydian	pitchstone	sinusoidal
fingerling	liberalism	micropylar	mizzenmast	pitilessly	sisterhood
fingermark	liberalist	microscope	mizzensail	pityriasis	sitophobia
fingernail	liberality	microscopy	nickelling	pixillated	sixshooter
fingerpost	liberation	microseism	nicotinism	ribbonfish	tickertape
finicality	libidinous	microspore	nidicolous	ribbonworm	ticklishly
finiteness	librettist	middleaged	nidificate	riboflavin	ticpolonga

tiddlywink	vitriolise	alcoholise	bleatingly	electively	flugelhorn
tidewaiter	vituperate	alcoholism	blepharism	electorate	flunkeydom
tilthammer	vivandiere	alcyonaria	blindingly	electrical	flunkeyism
timberhead	viviparity	aldermanic	blissfully	electronic	fluoridate
timberline	viviparous	aldermanry	blistering	elementary	fluorinate
timbertoes	vivisector	alexanders	blitheness	Eleusinian	fluorotype
timberwolf	viziership	algebraist	blithering	elevenplus	fluviatile
timberwork	wickedness	algolagnia	blithesome	eliminable	fluxionary
timbrology	wickerwork	algolagnic	blitzkrieg	eliminator	flycatcher
timekeeper	widespread	algologist	blockboard	elliptical	flyfishing
timelessly	wildebeest	Algonquian	blockhouse	elongation	flyswatter
timeliness	wilderment	alienation	blockishly	eloquently	glaciation
timesaving	wilderness	alightment	bloodguilt	elucidator	glaciology
timeserver	wildfowler	alimentary	bloodhound	elutriator	gladhander
timocratic	wilfulness	alkalinity	bloodiness	flabbiness	gladsomely
timorously	willowherb	allegation	bloodmoney	flabellate	Glagolitic
tinctorial	willynilly	allegiance	bloodstain	flaccidity	glancingly
tinselling	willywilly	allegorise	bloodstock	flagellant	glasscloth
tirailleur	winceyette	allegorist	bloodstone	flagellate	glassfibre
tirelessly	Winchester	allegretto	blottesque	flagitious	glasshouse
tiresomely	windflower	allergenic	bluebonnet	flagrantly	glassiness
tiringroom	windjammer	alleviator	bluebottle	flagwaving	glasspaper
titanesque	windowless	alliaceous	bluecollar	flamboyant	glassworks
titivation	windowpane	alliterate	bluejacket	flameproof	Glaswegian
tittupping	windowseat	allocation	bluepencil	flamingoes	glauberite
titubation	windowshop	allocution	blueribbon	flannelled	glauconite
vibraculum	windowsill	allogamous	bluethroat	flapdoodle	glimmering
vibraphone	windscreen	allopathic	bluetongue	flashboard	globularly
viceconsul	windshield	allophonic	bluishness	flashflood	glomerular
vicegerent	windsleeve	allosteric	blurringly	flashiness	glomerulus
viceregent	winebibber	allotropic	blushingly	flashlight	gloominess
victimiser	winebottle	alloverish	blusterous	flashpoint	gloriously
Victoriana	winegrower	allpurpose	clamminess	flatfooted	glossarial
victorious	wingcollar	allrounder	clangorous	flattering	glossarist
victualled	wingfooted	allurement	clannishly	flatulence	glossiness
victualler	wingspread	allusively	clarabella	flatulency	glossology
videophone	wintertide	almacanter	Clarenceux	flavescent	glottology
Vietnamese	wintertime	almondeyed	claspknife	flavourful	glumaceous
viewfinder	wintriness	almsgiving	classicise	flavouring	gluttonise
viewlessly	wiredrawer	almucanter	classicism	flawlessly	gluttonous
vigilantly	wirehaired	alongshore	classicist	fleabitten	glycolyses
vignettist	wirepuller	alpenstock	classified	fleacircus	glycolysis
vigorously	wiretapper	alphabetic	classifier	fleamarket	glycosuria
villainage	wirewalker	alphameric	clavichord	fledgeling	glycosuric
villainess	wireworker	altarpiece	clavicular	fleeringly	ilangilang
villainous	wishywashy	altazimuth	clawhammer	fleetingly	illadvised
villanelle	witchcraft	alteration	clearstory	fleshiness	illatively
villeinage	witchhazel	alterative	clementine	fleshwound	illaudable
vindicable	witchingly	alternance	clerestory	flexuously	illaudably
vindicator	withdrawal	alternator	clerically	flightdeck	illegalise
vindictive	withdrawer	altocumuli	cleverness	flightless	illegality
vinegarish	withholder	altogether	clientship	flightpath	illiteracy
violaceous	witnessbox	altostrati	clingstone	flimsiness	illiterate
viperiform	xiphosuran	altruistic	clinically	flintiness	illnatured
viperously	yieldingly	blackamoor	clinkstone	flippantly	illstarred
viraginous	zigzagging	blackberry	clinometer	flirtation	illuminant
virescence	zincograph	blackboard	clinometry	floatation	illuminate
virginally	skateboard	blackfaced	clodhopper	floatboard	illuminati
virginhood	sketchable	blackguard	cloistered	floatingly	illuminism
virologist	sketchbook	blackheart	closestool	floatplane	illuminist
virtuality	skewbridge	Blackshirt	closetplay	floatstone	illusional
virtueless	skiagraphy	blacksmith	clothesbag	flocculate	illusively
virtuosity	skibobbing	blackthorn	clothespeg	flocculent	illusorily
virtuously	skijumping	blackwater	clothespin	floodlight	illustrate
virulently	skimpiness	bladdernut	cloudberry	floodwater	oldfangled
viscerally	skindiving	blamefully	cloudburst	floorboard	oldmaidish
viscometer	skinniness	blancmange	cloudiness	floorcloth	oleaginous
viscountcy	skirmisher	blanketing	clovehitch	floppiness	oleiferous
visibility	skirtdance	blanquette	cloverleaf	florentine	oleography
Visigothic	skittishly	blasphemer	clownishly	florescent	oleraceous
visionally	skrimshank	blastemata	clubfooted	floriation	oligarchic
visionless	skyjacking	blastocyst	clumsiness	floribunda	oligoclase
visitation	skyscraper	blastoderm	Clydesdale	floridness	oligopsony
visitorial	skywriting	blastomere	elaborator	florilegia	olivaceous
visualiser	alarmingly	blastopore	elasticise	floristics	placidness
vitalistic	Albigenses	blazonment	elasticity	flosculous	plagiarise
vitaminise	albuminoid	bleachable	elatedness	flowergirl	plagiarism
vitiligate	albuminous	bleariness	elderberry	flowerless	plagiarist
vitrescent	alchemical	blearyeyed	elecampane	fluffiness	plaguesome

plainchant	ulotrichan	empiricist	improbable	anecdotage	antithetic
planchette	ulteriorly	employable	improbably	anecdotist	antonymous
planetable	ultimately	employment	improperly	anemograph	cnidoblast
planetaria	ultrabasic	emulsifier	improvable	anemometer	enamelling
plangently	ultrasonic	imaginable	improvably	anemometry	enamellist
planigraph	ultrasound	imaginably	improviser	anemophily	enantiosis
planimeter	ylangylang	imbecilely	imprudence	aneurismal	encampment
planimetry	amalgamate	imbecility	impudently	aneurysmal	encasement
planktonic	amanuenses	imbibition	impudicity	angiosperm	encashment
planometer	amanuensis	immaculacy	impugnable	Anglistics	encephalic
plantation	amateurish	immaculate	impugnment	anglomania	encephalon
plantlouse	amateurism	immaterial	impuissant	anglophile	enchanting
plasmodesm	ambassador	immaturely	impureness	anglophobe	encourager
plasmodium	ambidexter	immaturity	imputation	anglophone	encroacher
plasmogamy	ambivalent	immemorial	imputative	AngloSaxon	encyclical
plasmolyse	ambulacral	imminently	ombrometer	angularity	encystment
plasticise	ambulacrum	immiscible	ommatidium	angwantibo	endearment
plasticity	ambulation	immiscibly	omnigenous	animadvert	endemicity
platelayer	ambulatory	immobilise	omnipotent	animalcula	endocrinal
playacting	ambushment	immobility	omniscient	animalcule	endodermal
playbyplay	ameliorate	immoderacy	omnivorous	animatedly	endodermis
playfellow	amendatory	immoderate	omophagous	anisotropy	endogamous,
playground	amercement	immodestly	smallscale	annalistic	endogenous
playwright	amerciable	immolation	smallsword	annexation	endophytic
pleadingly	Amerindian	immoralist	smallwares	annihilate	endopodite
pleasantly	amiability	immorality	smaragdine	annotation	endorsable
pleasantry	ammoniacal	immortally	smaragdite	annoyingly	endoscopic
pleasingly	ammoniated	immortelle	smartmoney	annularity	endosmosis
plebiscite	ammunition	immoveable	smattering	annulation	endosmotic
plecoptera	amoebocyte	immunology	smelliness	annunciate	endothelia
pleochroic	ampelopsis	immurement	smockfrock	anointment	endproduct
pleonastic	amphibious	impairment	smokedried	anonaceous	endstopped
plesiosaur	amphibrach	impalement	smokehouse	anopheline	enduringly
pliability	amphictyon	impalpable	smokeplant	answerable	energetics
pliantness	amphigouri	impalpably	smokeproof	answerably	enervation
ploddingly	amphimacer	impanation	smokestack	antagonise	enervative
ploughable	amphimixes	impanelled	smoothbore	antagonism	enfacement
ploughland	amphimixis	imparadise	smoothness	antagonist	engagement
pluckiness	amphoteric	impartible	smorrebrod	antebellum	engagingly
plumassier	amputation	impartment	smudginess	antecedent	engineroom
plunderage	amygdaloid	impassable	smuttiness	antecessor	Englishman
plunderous	amylaceous	impassably	umbellifer	antechapel	englutting
pluperfect	emaciation	impassible	umbilicate	antemortem	engrossing
plutocracy	emancipate	impassibly	umbiliform	antependia	engulfment
plutolatry	emancipist	impatience	umbrageous	antepenult	enharmonic
slanderous	emarginate	impeccable	umbrellaed	anteriorly	enigmatise
slanginess	emasculate	impeccably	umpireship	antheridia	enigmatist
slantingly	embalmment	impeccancy	anabaptism	anthracene	enjambment
slatternly	embankment	impediment	anabaptist	anthracite	enjoinment
slavetrade	embarkment	impendence	anacolutha	anthracoid	enlacement
slavocracy	emblazoner	impendency	anadromous	anthropoid	enlistment
Slavophile	emblazonry	impenitent	anaglyphic	antibiosis	enmeshment
Slavophobe	emblematic	imperative	anagogical	antibiotic	enormously
sleaziness	emblements	imperially	analogical	Antichrist	enregister
sleepiness	embodiment	imperilled	analphabet	anticipant	enrichment
sleepyhead	embolismic	impersonal	analysable	anticipate	enrigment
sleeveless	embonpoint	impervious	analytical	anticlimax	ensanguine
sleevelink	embossment	impishness	anamorphic	anticlinal	entailment
sleighbell	embouchure	implacable	anapaestic	antifreeze	enterolith
slenderise	embowelled	implacably	anaplastic	antiheroic	enterotomy
slidevalve	embroidery	implicitly	anaptyctic	antimasque	enterprise
slightness	embryogeny	impolitely	anarchical	antimatter	enthralled
slipperily	embryology	importable	anastigmat	antimonial	enthusiasm
slipstitch	embryonate	importance	anastomose	antimonite	enthusiast
slipstream	emendation	importuner	anastrophe	antimonian	enticement
slitpocket	emendatory	imposingly	anatomical	antipathic	enticingly
sloppiness	emeryboard	imposition	anatropous	antiphonal	entireness
slothfully	emerypaper	impossible	ancestress	antipodean	entombment
slowfooted	emerywheel	impossibly	anchoretic	antiproton	entomology
slowmotion	emigration	imposthume	anchoritic	antiquated	entrancing
slowwitted	emigratory	impotently	anchorless	antiSemite	entrapment
sluggardly	emissivity	impoverish	anchorring	antisepsis	enumerable
sluggishly	Emmentaler	impregnant	anchylosis	antiseptic	enumerator
sluicegate	emollition	impregnate	anchylotic	antisocial	enunciable
slumberful	empanelled	impresario	ancipitous	antistatic	enunciator
slumberous	emparadise	impression	Andalusian	antitheism	enwrapping
sluttishly	empathetic	impressive	andalusite	antitheist	enzymology
ulceration	emphractic	imprimatur	androecium	antitheses	gnosticism
ulcerative	empiricism	imprinting	androgenic	antithesis	inaccuracy

cornflower	donnybrook	Fourierism	honeyeater	Lollardism	monomaniac
cornstarch	doorkeeper	fourinhand	honeyguide	loneliness	monophonic
cornucopia	dorsigrade	fourleaved	honeysweet	lonesomely	monopodial
coromandel	dosimetric	fourposter	honorarium	longaevous	monopodium
coronation	doublebass	foursquare	honourable	longhaired	monopolise
corporally	doubleness	fourstroke	honourably	longheaded	monopolist
corporator	doublepark	fourteener	honourless	longlegged	monorhymed
corporeity	doubletalk	fourteenth	hookedness	longprimer	monotheism
corpulence	doubletime	fowlplague	hootenanny	longshanks	monotheist
corpulency	doubtfully	foxhunting	hopelessly	longwinded	monotonous
corpuscule	doubtingly	goalkeeper	horizontal	loosecover	monovalent
correction	doughfaced	goaltender	hormonally	lophophore	monsignori
corrective	dovecolour	goatsbeard	hornblende	lopsidedly	monstrance
correspond	downfallen	goatsucker	hornedness	loquacious	Montagnard
corrigenda	downstairs	gobemouche	hornrimmed	lordliness	montbretia
corrigible	downstream	gobstopper	horologist	lossleader	monumental
corrivalry	downstroke	Godfearing	horoscopic	lotuseater	moonflower
corroboree	downwardly	goggleeyed	horrendous	loudhailer	moonshiner
corrugated	doxography	goldbeater	horridness	loungesuit	moonstruck
corrugator	eosinophil	golddigger	horsecloth	lovelessly	mopishness
corruption	foamflower	goldenness	horsecoper	loveletter	moralistic
corruptive	foetidness	goldenseal	horseflesh	loveliness	moratorium
corsetiere	foliaceous	goldilocks	horselaugh	lovemaking	morbidezza
corticated	folklorist	golfcourse	horseleech	lovingness	morbidness
Corybantes	folkmemory	goloptious	horsepower	lowerclass	mordacious
corybantic	folksiness	goluptious	horseshoer	lowpitched	morganatic
coryphaeus	folksinger	goniometer	horsewoman	lowprofile	moroseness
cosentient	follicular	goniometry	hospitable	loxodromic	morphemics
cosmically	fontanelle	goodliness	hospitably	mobocratic	morphinism
cosmogonic	footballer	goodlooker	hostelling	mockheroic	morphogeny
cosmopolis	footbridge	goodygoody	hotblooded	moderately	morphology
cosmoramic	footcandle	gooseberry	hotchpotch	moderation	morrispike
costliness	footlights	gooseflesh	hourcircle	moderatism	mosaically
cottoncake	footwarmer	goosegrass	houseagent	moderniser	mosaicking
cottonseed	foraminous	gorgeously	housebound	modernness	mosasaurus
cottontail	forbidding	Gorgonzola	housecraft	modifiable	mosquitoes
cottonweed	forcefully	gormandise	houseguest	modishness	mossbunker
cottonwood	forcipated	gothically	houselling	modulation	motherhood
cottonwool	foreboding	governable	houseplant	Mohammedan	motherland
couchgrass	forecaster	governance	houseproud	moisturise	motherless
coulometry	forecastle	governessy	housetrain	molendinar	mothership
councillor	forecourse	government	housewives	molluscoid	motherwort
councilman	forefather	hoarseness	hoverplane	molluscous	motionless
counselled	forefinger	hobbyhorse	hovertrain	molybdenum	motivation
counsellor	foregather	hobnobbing	iodination	monandrous	motiveless
counteract	foreground	hocuspocus	ionisation	monarchial	motorcycle
countryish	forehanded	hodgepodge	ionosphere	Monarchian	mouldboard
countryman	foreignism	hoitytoity	jobbernowl	monarchism	mouldiness
couplement	foreordain	hokeypokey	jocoseness	monarchist	mountebank
courageous	forerunner	holloweyed	jocularity	monetarily	mournfully
courthouse	foreshadow	hollowness	johnnycake	monetarism	mousseline
cousinhood	foresheets	hollowware	Johnsonese	monetarist	moustached
cousinship	foreteller	holography	johnsonian	moneymaker	moustachio
couturiere	forfeiture	holohedral	jolterhead	moneytaker	Mousterian
couverture	forgetting	holophrase	journalese	mongrelise	mouthorgan
covalently	forgivable	holophytic	journalise	mongrelism	mouthpiece
covariance	forgivably	holosteric	journalism	moniliasis	movability
covenanted	formatting	holusbolus	journalist	moniliform	movelessly
covenantee	formidable	homebrewed	journeyman	monistical	moviemaker
covenanter	formidably	homecoming	joyfulness	monitorial	mozzarella
covenantor	formlessly	homeliness	joyousness	monkeysuit	noblewoman
covetingly	fornicator	homemaking	kookaburra	monocarpic	nodulation
covetously	fortepiano	homeopathy	lobsterpot	monochasia	noisemaker
cowcatcher	forthright	homiletics	lobulation	monochrome	nominalism
coweringly	fortissima	homocercal	lockerroom	monoclinal	nominalist
cowparsley	fortissimo	homoeopath	lockkeeper	monoclinic	nominately
cowpuncher	fortuitism	homogamous	lockstitch	monocratic	nomination
doctorship	fortuitist	homogenise	locomotion	monocyclic	nominative
documental	fortuitous	homogenous	locomotive	monoecious	nomography
doggedness	fortyniner	homologate	locomotory	monogamist	nomologist
dogmatical	forwarding	homologise	locustbean	monogamous	nomothetic
dogmatiser	forwearied	homologous	loganberry	monogenism	nonaligned
dogstongue	fostering	homonymous	loganstone	monogynian	nonchalant
dolomitise	foudroyant	homoousian	loggerhead	monogynous	noncontent
dolorously	foundation	homophonic	logicality	monohybrid	nondrinker
dominantly	founderous	homosexual	logistical	monohydric	nonferrous
domination	fourchette	homozygote	logography	monolithic	nonfiction
dominative	fourfooted	homozygous	logorrhoea	monologise	nonjoinder
donkeywork	fourhanded	homunculus	logrolling	monologist	nonlogical

nonnatural	polytheist	roofgarden	sousaphone	womanishly	applicable
nonnuclear	polytocous	rootedness	souterrain	wonderland	applicably
nonpayment	polyvalent	ropedancer	southbound	wonderment	applicator
nonplaying	Pomeranian	ropeladder	southerner	wonderwork	appointive
nonplussed	pomiferous	ropewalker	southernly	wondrously	appositely
nonstarter	pomologist	roquelaure	southwards	wongawonga	apposition
nonswimmer	ponderable	rosaniline	sowthistle	wontedness	appositive
nonviolent	pontifical	rosechafer	tobogganer	woodcarver	appreciate
noogenesis	pontifices	roseengine	tocopherol	woodcutter	apprentice
northbound	popularise	roselipped	toffeenose	woodenhead	approvable
northerner	popularity	rosemallow	toilsomely	woodenness	approvably
northwards	population	rotational	tolerantly	woodlander	epeirogeny
nosography	populistic	rotisserie	toleration	woodpecker	epentheses
nosologist	populously	rottenness	tollbridge	woodpigeon	epenthesis
nosophobia	porismatic	rottweiler	tomfoolery	woodturner	epenthetic
nostologic	pornocracy	roughhouse	tomography	woodworker	epexegeses
notability	porousness	roughrider	tonelessly	woolgather	epexegesis
notarially	porraceous	roundabout	tongueless	woolgrower	epexegetic
notchboard	portamento	roundhouse	tonguetied	woolliness	ephemerous
noteworthy	portcullis	rouseabout	toothbrush	woolsorter	ephorality
noticeable	portentous	roustabout	toothiness	wordlessly	epiblastic
noticeably	portliness	rovebeetle	toothpaste	workbasket	epicentral
notifiable	Portuguese	rowanberry	toothshell	workingman	epicycloid
notionally	positional	soapboiler	topazolite	workpeople	epideictic
notonectal	positively	soapbubble	topgallant	worldclass	epidemical
nourishing	positivism	soapflakes	topicality	worldweary	epidermoid
novaculite	positivist	sobersided	topography	worshipful	epigastric
novelistic	positivity	sobersides	topologist	worshipped	epigenesis
pocketable	possession	socialiser	topsyturvy	worshipper	epigenetic
pocketbook	possessive	societally	torchlight	worthiness	epiglottal
pocketsize	possessory	sociologic	toroidally	worthwhile	epiglottic
pockmarked	postbellum	sociometry	torpidness	yokefellow	epiglottis
podiatrist	postchaise	soddenness	torrential	youngberry	epigrapher
poetically	postexilic	softbilled	torridness	yourselves	epigraphic
pogonology	posthumous	softboiled	tortellini	youthfully	epilimnion
pogonotomy	postillion	softfinned	tortfeasor	zollverein	epiphytism
poinsettia	postliminy	softheaded	tortiously	zoological	episcopacy
pointblank	postmaster	softspoken	tortuosity	zoomorphic	episcopate
pokerfaced	postmortem	solacement	tortuously	zoophagous	episematic
polemicist	postoffice	soldanella	totemistic	zoophilous	episodical
polemonium	postpartum	solecistic	touchiness	aphaereses	episternum
politeness	postscript	solemnness	touchingly	aphaeresis	epistolary
politician	postulator	solenoidal	touchjudge	aphoristic	epistrophe
politicise	potability	solicitant	touchpaper	aphrodisia	epithelial
pollenosis	potamology	solicitous	touchstone	apiculture	epithelium
pollinator	potbellied	solicitude	tourbillon	aplacental	opalescent
polyandric	potentiate	solidarism	tourmaline	apocalypse	opaqueness
polyanthus	potentilla	solidarist	tournament	apocarpous	openhanded
polyatamic	pothunting	solidarity	tourniquet	apochromat	openhearth
polychaete	pouncetbox	solidstate	towardness	apocryphal	openminded
polychrest	pourparler	solifidian	toweringly	apodeictic	operculate
polychrome	powderhorn	solitarily	townswoman	apolaustic	operettist
polyclinic	powderpuff	solstitial	toxication	apolitical	ophicleide
polycyclic	powerfully	solubilise	toxicology	Apollinian	ophiolater
polydactyl	powerhouse	solubility	toxiphobia	Apollonian	ophiolatry
polydipsia	pozzolanic	somatology	vocabulary	apologetic	ophiologic
polygamist	pozzuolana	somatotype	vocational	apophthegm	ophthalmia
polygamous	roadrunner	sombreness	vociferant	apoplectic	ophthalmic
polygenism	roadworthy	somersault	vociferate	aposematic	opinionist
polygenist	robustious	somniloquy	vociferous	apostatise	opisometer
polygenous	robustness	somnolence	voiceprint	apostolate	oppilation
polygraphy	rockabilly	somnolency	volatilise	apostrophe	opposeless
polygynous	rockbadger	songstress	volatility	apothecary	oppositely
polyhedral	rockbottom	songthrush	volitional	apothecial	opposition
polyhedric	rockgarden	songwriter	volleyball	apothecium	oppression
polyhedron	rockhopper	sonorously	voltameter	apotheoses	oppressive
polyhistor	rockpigeon	soothingly	volubility	apotheosis	opprobrium
polymathic	rockrabbit	soothsayer	volumetric	apotropaic	oppugnancy
polymerise	rockribbed	sophomoric	voluminous	apparelled	optatively
polymerism	rodfishing	Sorbonnist	voluptuary	apparently	optimalise
polymerous	roistering	sordidness	voluptuous	apparition	optimistic
Polynesian	roisterous	sororicide	vomitorium	appealable	optionally
polynomial	rollcollar	soubriquet	vortically	appearance	spacecraft
polyonymic	rollicking	soullessly	vorticella	appeasable	spacewoman
polyphasic	rollingpin	soundboard	vorticular	appendices	spaciously
polyphonic	Romanesque	soundingly	voyageable	appendixes	spadebeard
polyploidy	Romanistic	soundproof	wobbliness	apperceive	spadiceous
polysemous	rontgenise	soundtrack	woefulness	appetising	spagyrical
polytheism	roodscreen	sourcebook	wolframite	appetitive	spallation

spankingly	sporangium	architrave	brigandage	crowkeeper	freespeech
sparseness	sporophore	archpriest	brigandine	crustacean	freespoken
Spartacist	sporophyll	arenaceous	brigandism	crustation	freightage
spasticity	sporophyte	areolation	brigantine	crustiness	Frenchness
spatchcock	sportfully	Areopagite	brightness	cryogenics	frenziedly
spathulate	sportiness	argumentum	brightwork	cryoscopic	frequenter
spatiality	sportingly	aristocrat	brilliance	cryptogamy	frequently
speargrass	sportively	arithmetic	brilliancy	cryptogram	freshwater
specialise	sportswear	Armageddon	Britishism	cryptology	friability
specialism	spotlessly	armigerous	broadcloth	draconites	fricandeau
specialist	spottiness	armorially	broadsheet	drafthorse	fricasseed
speciality	sprightful	armourclad	broadsword	dragonhead	frictional
speciation	springhalt	armourless	brocatelle	dragonnade	friendless
speciology	springhead	arrestment	brokendown	dragontree	friendlily
speciosity	springless	arrhythmia	brokenness	dramatical	friendship
speciously	springlike	arrhythmic	bromegrass	dramaturge	frigidness
spectacled	springtail	arrogantly	bronchiole	dramaturgy	frigorific
spectacles	springtide	arrogation	bronchitic	drawbridge	frilliness
spectrally	springtime	arterially	bronchitis	drawingpin	fringeless
speculator	springwood	arteriolar	broodiness	drawlingly	friskiness
speechless	sprinkling	artfulness	broodingly	drawstring	fritillary
speediness	sprucebeer	arthralgia	broomstick	dreadfully	frivolling
speedlimit	spruceness	arthralgic	browbeaten	dreaminess	frizziness
speleology	spumescent	arthromere	brownshirt	dreamworld	froghopper
spellbound	spunkiness	articulate	brownstone	dreariness	frolicking
Spencerian	spuriously	artificial	brusquerie	dressiness	frolicsome
Spenserian	upbraiding	artycrafty	bryologist	dressmaker	frontbench
spermaceti	upbringing	arytaenoid	crackajack	drivelling	frontwards
spermicide	upholstery	brachiator	crackbrain	driverless	frostiness
sperrylite	upperclass	brachiopod	cradlesong	droopingly	frothiness
sphalerite	uppishness	brachylogy	craftguild	drophammer	frowningly
sphenodone	uproarious	brachyural	craftiness	drosophila	fruitarian
sphenogram	upstanding	brachyuran	cragginess	drowsihead	fruitfully
sphenoidal	upwardness	bradyseism	cranesbill	drowsiness	frutescent
sphericity	aquafortis	Brahmanism	craniology	drudgingly	gracefully
spheroidal	aquamarine	Brahminism	crankiness	drupaceous	graciosity
spherulite	aquaplaner	brainchild	crankshaft	drysaltery	graciously
spidercrab	aquiferous	braininess	crapulence	eradicable	gradualism
spiderline	aquilinity	brainpower	craquelure	eradicator	gradualist
spiderwort	equability	brainstorm	crassitude	erectility	graduation
spiflicate	equanimity	brakeblock	cravenness	eremitical	gramicidin
spillikins	equational	brakelight	creaminess	erethismic	gramineous
spinescent	equatorial	branchiate	creatinine	ergodicity	grammarian
spiracular	equestrian	brandyball	creatively	ergonomics	gramophone
spiraculum	equilibria	brandysnap	creativity	ergonomist	granadilla
spiralling	equipotent	brantgoose	creaturely	ergosterol	grandchild
spiritedly	equitation	brassiness	credential	ericaceous	granddaddy
spiritless	equivalent	bratticing	creditable	erotically	grandducal
spirituous	equivocate	brawniness	creditably	erotogenic	grandmamma
spirograph	squalidity	brazenness	creepiness	erotomania	grandniece
spirometer	squamation	brazilwood	crematoria	erubescent	grandstand
spirometry	squanderer	breadboard	crenellate	eructation	granduncle
spitchcock	squareness	breadcrumb	crenulated	eruptively	grangerise
spitefully	squaresail	breadfruit	crepuscule	erysipelas	grangerism
splanchnic	squaretoed	breadstick	crescentic	fractional	granophyre
splashback	squaretoes	breadstuff	cretaceous	fragmental	granularly
splashdown	squeezable	breakables	crewelwork	fragrantly	granulator
spleenwort	squeezebox	breakpoint	cribriform	framboesia	granulitic
splendidly	squeteague	breakwater	criminally	franchiser	grapefruit
splintbone	squinteyed	breastbone	crinolette	Franciscan	grapesugar
splintcoal	squirarchy	breastwall	crippledom	Francophil	graphemics
splitlevel	squirearch	breastwork	crispation	frangipane	graphitise
splutterer	squirehood	breathable	crispbread	frangipani	graphology
spodomancy	squireling	breathless	crisscross	fraternise	graptolite
spoilsport	squireship	breechless	critically	fraternity	graspingly
spokeshave	aragonitic	breezeless	crocoisite	fratricide	grasscloth
spoliation	araucarian	breeziness	crossbench	fraudulent	grassroots
spoliative	arbalester	brentgoose	crossbones	fraxinella	grasssnake
spoliatory	arbalister	bressummer	crossbreed	freakiness	gratefully
spongecake	arbitrable	brevetting	crosscheck	freakishly	gratifying
spongewood	arbitrager	brickfield	crossgrain	freebooter	gratuitous
spongiform	arbitrator	bricklayer	crosshatch	freedwoman	gravestone
sponginess	arboreally	bridegroom	crossindex	freehanded	gravimeter
spongology	arborvitae	bridesmaid	crosslight	freeholder	gravimetry
sponsorial	archaistic	bridgeable	crosspatch	freelancer	greasewood
spookiness	archbishop	bridgehead	crosspiece	freeliving	greasiness
spoondrift	archdeacon	bridgeless	crossrefer	freeloader	greatniece
spoonerism	archerfish	bridgework	crossroads	freemartin	greatuncle
sporangial	archetypal	bridlepath	crosstrees	freesoiler	GrecoRoman

greediness	originator	prelection	production	proteiform	travelling
greedyguts	ornamental	premarital	productive	proteinous	travelogue
greencloth	ornateness	premaxilla	profession	protensive	travertine
greenfinch	orneriness	premedical	proficient	proteolyse	trawlerman
greenheart	orogenesis	premonitor	profitable	protestant	treadboard
greenhouse	orogenetic	prepackage	profitably	prothallia	treadwheel
greenshank	orographic	preparator	profitless	prothallus	treasonous
greenstick	orological	preparedly	profligacy	protophyta	trecentist
greenstone	orotundity	prepayable	profligate	protophyte	tremendous
greenstuff	orphanhood	prepayment	profoundly	protoplasm	tremolitic
greensward	orthoclase	prepensely	profundity	protoplast	trenchancy
gregarious	orthodoxly	prepossess	progenitor	prototypal	trendiness
grenadilla	orthoepist	prepotence	proglottis	prototypic	trepanning
gressorial	orthogenic	prepotency	prognathic	protracted	trespasser
greyheaded	orthogonal	presageful	prognostic	protractor	triacetate
grievously	orthopedic	presbyopia	programmer	protreptic	triandrous
grindingly	orthoptera	presbyopic	prohibiter	protrusile	triangular
grindstone	practician	presbytery	prohibitor	protrusion	tribometer
grisliness	practising	prescience	projectile	protrusive	tribrachic
grittiness	praecocial	prescriber	projection	proudflesh	trichiasis
groceteria	praemunire	presentday	projective	provenance	trichinise
grogginess	praesidium	presentive	prolicidal	proverbial	trichinous
groundbait	praetorial	presidency	prolocutor	providence	trichology
groundless	praetorian	presidiary	prologuise	provincial	trichotomy
groundling	pragmatise	presignify	prolongate	provisions	trichroism
groundmass	pragmatism	pressagent	promenader	provitamin	trichromat
groundplan	pragmatist	pressingly	promethium	provocator	trickiness
groundrent	prairiedog	pressurise	prominence	proximally	trickishly
groundsman	prancingly	presternum	promissory	prudential	triclinium
groundwork	pratincole	presumable	promontory	pruriently	tricyclist
grovelling	prayerbook	presumably	promptbook	trabeation	Tridentine
growlingly	preachment	presuppose	promptness	trabeculae	trierarchy
grubbiness	preadamite	pretendant	promulgate	trabecular	triflingly
grudgingly	prearrange	pretendent	pronominal	tracheated	trifoliate
gruesomely	prebendary	pretension	pronounced	tracheitis	trifurcate
grumpiness	precarious	prettiness	pronouncer	Tractarian	trigeminal
iridaceous	precaution	prevailing	proofsheet	tractional	triggerman
iridescent	precedence	prevalence	propagable	trafficked	triglyphic
iridosmine	precedency	prevenancy	propaganda	trafficker	trigonally
Irishwoman	preceptive	prevenient	propagator	tragacanth	trilateral
ironhanded	preceptory	prevention	propellant	tragically	trilingual
ironically	precession	preventive	propellent	tragicomic	triliteral
ironmaster	preciosity	previously	propelling	traitorous	trillionth
ironmonger	preciously	pridefully	propensity	trajection	trimonthly
ironworker	precipitin	priesthood	properness	trajectory	trimorphic
irradiance	preclusion	priestling	propertied	trammelled	trioecious
irradicate	preclusive	priggishly	prophesier	tramontana	tripartite
irrational	precocious	primevally	prophetess	tramontane	triphammer
irrelative	preconcert	primiparae	propionate	trampoline	triphthong
irrelevant	precordial	primordial	propitiate	trancelike	triplicate
irreligion	precursory	primordium	propitious	tranquilly	triplicity
irresolute	predacious	princeling	proportion	transactor	triquetrae
irreverent	predecease	princeship	propounder	transcribe	triquetral
irrigation	predestine	principate	propraetor	transcript	trisection
irritation	predicable	principial	proprietor	transducer	triskelion
irritative	prediction	principium	propulsion	transeptal	triternate
kriegspiel	predictive	principled	propulsive	transferee	triturable
Krishnaism	predispose	prismoidal	propylaeum	transferor	triturator
Krugerrand	prednisone	prissiness	prosaicism	transfuser	triumphant
oracularly	preeminent	privileged	proscenium	transgress	triumviral
orangepeel	preemption	prizefight	prosciutto	transience	trivialise
orangewood	preemptive	procedural	proscriber	transiency	trivialism
oratorical	preexilian	proceeding	prosecutor	transistor	triviality
orchardist	prefecture	procession	prosilient	transition	trochanter
orchardman	preferable	proclaimer	prosodical	transitive	trochoidal
orchestics	preferably	proclivity	prospector	transitory	troctolite
orchestral	preference	procreator	prospectus	translator	troglodyte
ordainment	preferment	procrypsis	prosperity	translucid	trolleybus
ordinarily	preferring	procryptic	prosperous	translunar	trollopish
ordination	prefixture	proctorage	prosthesis	transmuter	trombonist
ordonnance	prefrontal	proctorial	prosthetic	transplant	tromometer
Ordovician	prefulgent	proctorise	prostitute	transposal	tropaeolum
oreography	preglacial	procumbent	prostomial	transposer	trophology
oreologist	pregnantly	procurable	prostomium	transshape	tropically
organicism	prehensile	procurance	protanopic	transvalue	tropologic
organicist	prehension	procurator	protection	transverse	tropopause
organismal	prehistory	prodigally	protective	trappiness	tropophyte
orientally	prejudiced	prodigious	protectory	trashiness	Trotskyism
originally	prelatical	producible	protectrix	traumatism	Trotskyist

Trotskyite	asymmetric	attractive	stepsister	stridulate	bullethead
troubadour	asymptotic	attunement	stereobate	stridulous	bullheaded
trousseaux	asynchrony	atypically	stereogram	strikingly	bullroarer
trouvaille	escadrille	ctenophore	stereopsis	stringbean	bumblingly
trowelling	escalation	eternalise	stereotype	stringency	bumpkinish
trucklebed	escallonia	eternalist	stereotypy	stringendo	bunchgrass
truculence	escapement	ethereally	sterigmata	stringhalt	bunglingly
truculency	escapology	ethicality	steriliser	stringless	burdensome
truncately	escarpment	ethnically	sternwards	striptease	bureaucrat
truncation	escharotic	ethnologic	stertorous	Stroganoff	burglarise
trundlebed	escheatage	ethologist	stewardess	stromatous	burramundi
trustfully	escritoire	etiolation	stickiness	stronghold	bursarship
trustiness	Esculapian	italianate	stiffening	strongroom	bushmaster
trustingly	escutcheon	italianise	stiflebone	structural	bushranger
truthfully	espadrille	Italianism	stiflingly	structured	bustlingly
tryptophan	especially	Italophile	stigmatise	struthious	butterball
uranometry	essayistic	itinerancy	stigmatism	strychnine	butterbean
urbanology	estimation	otherwhere	stigmatist	strychnism	butterfish
urethritis	estimative	otherwhile	stilettoes	stubbiness	buttermilk
urochordal	isentropic	otherworld	stillbirth	stubbornly	butterwort
urticarial	Ishmaelite	otioseness	stillicide	studiously	buttonball
urtication	isochronal	otterboard	stimulator	stuffiness	buttonbush
wraparound	isodynamic	ottershrew	stinginess	stumpiness	buttondown
wrathfully	isogenetic	Ptolemaist	stingingly	stunningly	buttonhole
wrathiness	isoglossal	stabiliser	stinkingly	stupendous	buttonhook
wretchedly	isolatable	stablemate	stinkstone	stupidness	buttonless
wristwatch	isometrics	stableness	stipellate	sturdiness	buttonwood
wrongdoing	isomorphic	stadholder	stipulator	stylistics	cuckoopint
wrongfully	isoniazide	staffnurse	stirrupcup	stylograph	cuckoospit
wrongously	isopterous	stagbeetle	stitchwort	stypticity	cucullated
asafoetida	isoseismal	stagecoach	stochastic	utilisable	cuddlesome
asbestosis	isosporous	stagecraft	stockiness	utopianism	cudgelling
ascariasis	isothermal	staggering	stockpiler	auctioneer	cuirassier
ascendable	oscillator	stagnantly	stockproof	audibility	cultivable
ascendance	oscitation	stagnation	stockrider	audiometer	cultivator
ascendancy	osculation	stalactite	stockstill	audiometry	culturally
ascendence	osculatory	stalagmite	stodginess	audiophile	cumbersome
ascendency	osmeterium	stalwartly	stolidness	auditorial	cumbrously
ascendible	osmiridium	stanchless	stomachful	auditorium	cummerbund
asceticism	ostensible	stanchness	stomatitis	augustness	cumulation
ascomycete	ostensibly	standpoint	stomatopod	auriculate	cumulative
ascribable	osteoblast	standstill	stomodaeum	auriferous	cumuliform
ascription	osteoclast	staphyline	stoneblind	auscultate	cunctation
asexuality	osteopathy	stargazing	stoneborer	auspicious	cunctative
Ashkenazim	osteophyte	starriness	stonebrash	austenitic	curability
asparagine	psalmodise	starryeyed	stonefruit	Australian	curatorial
aspergilla	psalmodist	starstream	stonemason	autarkical	curmudgeon
asphyxiant	psalterium	starvation	stonesnipe	autecology	curricular
asphyxiate	psephology	starveling	stopvolley	authorship	curriculum
aspidistra	pseudocarp	statecraft	storehouse	autochthon	cursedness
aspiration	psilocybin	statically	storksbill	autocratic	curvaceous
assafetida	psittacine	stationary	stormbound	autodidact	curvacious
assailable	psychiatry	stationery	stormcloud	autoerotic	curvetting
assaultive	psychicism	statistics	storminess	autogamous	cuspidated
assemblage	psychicist	statoscope	stormproof	autogenous	cussedness
assentient	psychology	statuesque	strabismal	autography	custommade
assessable	psychopath	statutable	strabismic	autoimmune	cuttlebone
assessment	tsarevitch	statutably	strabismus	autologous	cuttlefish
asseverate	usefulness	staurolite	strabotomy	automation	cuttystool
assibilate	usquebaugh	stavesacre	straighten	automatise	dubitation
assignable	ustulation	steadiness	straightly	automatism	dubitative
assignment	usucaption	steakhouse	strainedly	automatist	dumbledore
assimilate	usuriously	stealthily	straitness	automobile	dumbstruck
assistance	usurpation	steamchest	stramonium	automotive	dumbwaiter
associable	ateleiosis	steaminess	strategist	autonomist	dumfounder
assoilment	Athanasian	steamtight	strathspey	autonomous	dunderhead
assortment	atmosphere	steeliness	stratiform	autoplasty	dungbeetle
assumption	atomically	steelworks	stratocrat	autostrada	duniwassal
assumptive	attachable	stelliform	strawberry	autostrade	duodecimal
asteriated	attachment	stenchtrap	strawboard	autumnally	duodenitis
asteroidal	attackable	stencilled	streamless	bubblyjock	duplicator
astigmatic	attainable	stenciller	streamline	buccinator	durability
astragalus	attainment	stenograph	streetdoor	Buchmanism	dustjacket
astringent	attendance	stentorian	streetward	Buchmanite	duumvirate
astrologer	attenuated	stepfather	strengthen	bucketshop	eucalyptol
astrologic	attenuator	stephanite	stressless	budgerigar	eucalyptus
astronomer	attornment	stepladder	strictness	bufflehead	eucaryotic
astronomic	attractant	stepmother	stridently	buffoonery	eudemonism
astuteness	attraction	stepparent	stridulant	buffoonery	eudemonist

eudiometer	luciferase	outfitting	quarantine	submitting	supination
eudiometry	luciferous	outgassing	quarrelled	submontane	supineness
eugenicist	lucifugous	outgeneral	quarreller	subnuclear	supperless
euhemerise	lucubrator	outgunning	quarrender	suborbital	supplanter
euhemerism	luculently	outlandish	quartation	subordinal	supplejack
euhemerist	lugubrious	outmeasure	quarterage	subreption	supplement
eulogistic	lukewarmly	outpatient	quarterday	subroutine	suppleness
euphonious	lumberjack	outpouring	quartering	subscriber	suppletion
euphuistic	lumberroom	outputting	quartzitic	subsection	suppletive
eurhythmic	lumbersome	outrageous	quaternary	subsellium	suppletory
Eurodollar	lumberyard	outrightly	quaternate	subsequent	suppliance
Eurovision	luminosity	outrunning	quaternion	subshrubby	supplicant
eurypterid	luminously	outsitting	quaternity	subsidence	supplicate
euthanasia	lumpsucker	outstation	quatorzain	subsidiary	supportive
fuddyduddy	Lupercalia	outstretch	quatrefoil	subsistent	supposable
fugitively	lusciously	outswinger	queasiness	subspecies	supposably
fulfilling	Lusitanian	outwitting	quenchable	substation	supposedly
fulfilment	lustration	puberulent	quenchless	substitute	suppressor
fuliginous	lustreless	pubescence	quercitron	substratum	suprarenal
fullbodied	lustrously	publishing	questioner	subtenancy	surefooted
fullbottom	lutestring	puerperium	quickgrass	subterfuge	suretyship
fulllength	luxuriance	puffpastry	quickthorn	subtleness	surfactant
fumblingly	muciferous	pugilistic	quiescence	subtrahend	surgically
fumigation	mudskipper	pugnacious	quiescency	subvention	surmisable
functional	mudslinger	puissantly	quinacrine	subversion	surplusage
funereally	muffinbell	pulsatilla	quintuplet	subversive	surprising
fungicidal	Muhammadan	pulsimeter	quirkiness	succedanea	surrealism
funnelling	Muhammedan	pulsometer	quixotical	successful	surrealist
furuncular	muliebrity	pulveriser	quizmaster	succession	survivance
fusibility	mulishness	pulvinated	rubberneck	successive	susceptive
fussbudget	mulligrubs	pummelling	rubiginous	succinctly	suspenders
fustanella	multifaced	punchboard	rubrically	succulence	suspension
futureless	multiloquy	punchdrunk	rubricator	succulency	suspensive
futuristic	multimedia	punctation	rubythroat	sudatorium	suspensoid
futurology	multiphase	punctually	rudderfish	suddenness	suspensory
fuzzywuzzy	multiplier	punctuator	rudderless	sufferable	suspicious
guardhouse	multipolar	punctulate	rudimental	sufferably	sustaining
guesthouse	multistage	punishable	ruefulness	sufferance	sustenance
guestnight	multivocal	punishment	ruffianism	sufficient	sustention
guilefully	mumbojumbo	punitively	ruggedness	suffragist	sustentive
guillotine	munificent	pupilarity	ruminantly	sugardaddy	suzerainty
guiltiness	muscularly	pupiparous	rumination	sugarhouse	tubercular
gunfighter	musicality	purblindly	ruminative	sugariness	tuberculin
gunrunning	musicianly	puristical	rumrunning	sugarmaple	tuberosity
gunslinger	musicology	puritanise	runnerbean	suggestion	tubicolous
gutturally	musicpaper	puritanism	runthrough	suggestive	tuffaceous
hucklebone	musicstand	purposeful	rupicoline	suicidally	tufthunter
hullabaloo	musicstool	purseproud	rupicolous	sullenness	tuitionary
humaneness	muskmallow	pursership	Russianism	sulphonate	tularaemia
humanistic	Mussulmans	purseseine	Russophile	sulphurate	tularaemic
humanities	mutability	pursuivant	Russophobe	sulphurise	tumbledown
humbleness	mutilation	purtenance	rustically	sulphurous	tumblerful
humbuggery	mutinously	purulently	ruthlessly	sultanship	tumbleweed
humbugging	muttonhead	purveyance	subacidity	sultriness	tumescence
humidifier	nubiferous	pushbutton	subaquatic	summerlike	tumultuary
humoresque	nuciferous	putatively	subaqueous	summertime	tumultuous
humoristic	nucivorous	putrescent	subaverage	summitless	tunelessly
humorously	nucleation	putrescine	subcentral	summonable	tunnelling
humourless	nucleonics	putridness	subclavian	sunderance	turbidness
humoursome	nucleoside	puzzlement	subcordate	sunglasses	turbulence
humpbacked	nucleotide	quadrangle	subculture	sunparlour	turbulency
hungriness	nudibranch	quadrantal	subdeanery	superacute	turgescent
hurdygurdy	nullanulla	quadratics	subduction	superaltar	turgidness
hurlyburly	numberless	quadrature	subglacial	superation	turkeycock
husbandage	numeration	quadrennia	subheading	superbness	turnbuckle
husbandman	numerology	quadriceps	subjectify	supercargo	turpentine
jubilantly	numerosity	quadrireme	subjection	superduper	turtleback
jubilation	numerously	quadrivial	subjective	supergiant	turtledove
judgematic	numismatic	quadrivium	subjugator	superhuman	turtleneck
judicatory	nunciature	quadrumana	subkingdom	superiorly	tutorially
judicature	nuptiality	quadrumane	subletting	superlunar	vulcaniser
judicially	nurseryman	quadrumvir	sublimable	supernally	vulnerable
juggernaut	nutational	quadruplet	subliminal	supernovae	vulnerably
juristical	nutcracker	quadruplex	sublingual	superorder	wunderkind
justiciary	nutritious	quadrupole	submariner	superpower	avantgarde
juvenility	outbalance	quaintness	submediant	supersonic	avaricious
Kuomintang	outbidding	qualmishly	submersion	superstore	aventurine
lubricator	outerspace	quantifier	submission	supertonic	averseness
lubricious	outfielder	quantitive	submissive	supervisor	aversively

aviatrices	sweetening	exploitive	hydraulics	mythopoeia	typewriter
aviculture	sweetheart	exportable	hydrically	mythopoeic	typicality
avouchment	sweltering	exposition	hydrologic	myxomatous	typography
evacuation	swimmingly	expositive	hydrolysis	myxomycete	typologist
evacuative	swinefever	expository	hydrolytic	nyctalopia	tyrannical
evaluation	swingingly	expressage	hydromancy	nyctalopic	Tyrrhenian
evaluative	swinglebar	expression	hydrometer	nyctinasty	Wycliffite
evanescent	switchback	expressive	hydrometry	nympholept	Wykehamist
evangelise	switchover	expressway	hydropathy	oysterfarm	xylography
evangelism	swiveleyed	exprobrate	hydrophane	pycnogonid	xylophonic
evangelist	swivelling	expunction	hydrophily	pycnometer	zygodactyl
evaporable	swordcraft	expurgator	hydrophone	pycnostyle	zygomorphy
evaporator	sworddance	exsanguine	hydrophyte	pyknometer	azeotropic
evenhanded	swordgrass	extemporal	hydroplane	pyracantha	czarevitch
eventually	swordstick	extendedly	hydroscope	pyretology	──────────
everglades	twelvefold	extendible	hydrotaxis	pyridoxine	abacterial
everliving	twelvenote	extensible	hygrograph	pyrogallol	academical
everyplace	twelvetone	extenuator	hygrometer	pyrogenous	acarpelous
everything	twilighted	exteriorly	hygrometry	pyrography	acatalepsy
everywhere	twowheeler	externally	hygrophyte	pyrolusite	adamantine
evidential	zwitterion	extinction	hygroscope	pyromaniac	adaptation
evilminded	axiologist	extinctive	hylotheism	pyromantic	adaptively
eviscerate	exactitude	extinguish	hypabyssal	pyrometric	agapanthus
evolvement	exaggerate	extirpator	hypaethral	pyrophoric	alarmingly
ovariotomy	exaltation	extractant	hypanthium	pyrotechny	amalgamate
overabound	examinable	extraction	hyperaemia	pyroxenite	amanuenses
overactive	exasperate	extractive	hyperaemic	Pyrrhonian	amanuensis
overblouse	excavation	extramural	hyperbaric	Pyrrhonism	amateurish
overbought	excellence	extraneity	hyperbaton	Pyrrhonist	amateurism
overburden	excellency	extraneous	hyperbolae	pyrrhotite	anabaptism
overcharge	excerption	extricable	hyperbolas	sybaritism	anabaptist
overcommit	excitation	exuberance	hyperbolic	sycophancy	anacolutha
overcooked	excitative	exulcerate	hyperdulia	syllabaria	anadromous
overexcite	excitatory	exultantly	hypergolic	syllogiser	anaglyphic
overexpose	excitement	exultation	hypersonic	symbolical	anagogical
overflight	excitingly	exultingly	hyphenated	symboliser	analogical
overground	excogitate	exurbanite	hypnagogic	symmetrise	analphabet
overgrowth	excrescent	exuviation	hypnotiser	sympathise	analysable
overhanded	excruciate	oxidisable	hypocorism	symphonion	analytical
overlander	excusatory	oxygenator	hypodermal	symphonist	anamorphic
overlapped	execration	uxoricidal	hypodermic	symphylous	anapaestic
overlooker	execrative	uxoriously	hypodermis	symphyseal	anaplastic
overmanned	execratory	byelection	hypogynous	symphysial	anaptyctic
overmantel	executable	byssaceous	hypolimnia	symposiast	anarchical
overmaster	exegetical	byssinosis	hypophyses	synaeresis	anastigmat
overnicety	exenterate	cybernetic	hypophysis	synaloepha	anastomose
overpraise	exhalation	cyclically	hypostasis	synanthous	anastrophe
overrefine	exhaustion	cyclograph	hypostatic	syncarpous	anatomical
overridden	exhaustive	cyclometer	hypotactic	synchronal	anatropous
overriding	exhibition	cyclopedia	hypotenuse	synchronic	aragonitic
overshadow	exhibitory	cyclopedic	hypotheses	syncopated	araucarian
overslaugh	exhilarant	cyclostome	hypothesis	syncopator	asafoetida
overspread	exhilarate	cyclostyle	hypsometer	syncretise	avantgarde
overstride	exhumation	cylindered	hypsometry	syncretism	avaricious
overstrung	exobiology	cylindroid	hysteresis	syncretist	beadleship
oversubtle	exorbitant	cystoscope	hysteretic	syndicator	Beaujolais
oversupply	exospheric	cystoscopy	hysterical	synecdoche	beautician
overthrown	exoterical	cytochrome	lycopodium	synecology	beautifier
overthrust	exothermal	cytologist	lymphocyte	synergetic	biannually
overtopped	exothermic	dynamistic	lymphomata	syngenesis	blackamoor
overweight	exotically	dysenteric	lyophilise	synoecious	blackberry
overwinter	expandable	dysgraphia	Lysenkoism	synonymist	blackboard
ovipositor	expansible	dysplastic	myasthenia	synonymity	blackfaced
dwarfishly	expatriate	dysprosium	mycologist	synonymous	blackguard
owlishness	expectance	dystrophic	mycoplasma	synoptical	blackheart
swaggering	expectancy	eyeglasses	mycorrhiza	synostosis	Blackshirt
swanmaiden	expectedly	eyeservice	myocardium	syntagmata	blacksmith
swanupping	expedience	eyewitness	myological	synthesise	blackthorn
swarmspore	expediency	gymnastics	myopically	synthesist	blackwater
swashplate	expedition	gymnosophy	myrtaceous	synthetise	bladdernut
swaybacked	expendable	gymnosperm	mystagogic	synthetist	blamefully
sweatgland	experience	gynandrous	mystagogue	syphilitic	blancmange
sweatiness	experiment	gynocratic	mysterious	systematic	blanketing
sweatshirt	expertness	gypsophila	mystically	systemless	blanquette
sweepingly	expiration	gyrational	mythically	tympanites	blasphemer
sweepstake	expiratory	gyrocopter	mythiciser	tympanitic	blastemata
sweetbread	explicable	gyroscopic	mythologer	tympanitis	blastocyst
sweetbriar	explicitly	hyaloplasm	mythologic	typescript	blastoderm
sweetbrier	exploitage	hybridiser	mythomania	typesetter	blastomere

blastopore	classified	eradicable	glauconite	inactively	plasmolyse
blazonment	classifier	eradicator	goalkeeper	inactivity	plasticise
boastfully	clavichord	evacuation	goaltender	inadequacy	plasticity
brachiator	clavicular	evacuative	goatsbeard	inadequate	platelayer
brachiopod	clawhammer	evaluation	goatsucker	inappetent	playacting
brachylogy	coacervate	evaluative	gracefully	inapposite	playbyplay
brachyural	coachbuilt	evanescent	graciosity	inaptitude	playfellow
brachyuran	coachhouse	evangelise	graciously	inartistic	playground
bradyseism	coadjacent	evangelism	gradualism	inaugurate	playwright
Brahmanism	coagulable	evangelist	gradualist	italianate	practician
Brahminism	coalbunker	evaporable	graduation	italianise	practising
brainchild	coalescent	evaporator	gramicidin	Italianism	praecocial
braininess	coaptation	exactitude	gramineous	Italophile	praemunire
brainpower	coarseness	exaggerate	grammarian	leadenness	praesidium
brainstorm	coastguard	exaltation	gramophone	leaderless	praetorial
brakeblock	coastwards	examinable	granadilla	leadership	praetorian
brakelight	coathanger	exasperate	grandchild	leafcutter	pragmatise
branchiate	coatimundi	fearlessly	granddaddy	leafhopper	pragmatism
brandyball	crackajack	fearnought	grandducal	leafinsect	pragmatist
brandysnap	crackbrain	fearsomely	grandmamma	meadowland	prairiedog
brantgoose	cradlesong	featherbed	grandniece	meadowlark	prancingly
brassiness	craftguild	feathering	grandstand	meagreness	pratincole
bratticing	craftiness	fianchetto	granduncle	mealbeetle	prayerbook
brawniness	cragginess	flabbiness	grangerise	meaningful	psalmodise
brazenness	cranesbill	flabellate	grangerism	measliness	psalmodist
brazilwood	craniology	flaccidity	granophyre	measurable	psalterium
chainsmoke	crankiness	flagellant	granularly	measurably	quadrangle
chairwoman	crankshaft	flagellate	granulator	measuredly	quadrantal
chalcedony	crapulence	flagitious	granulitic	myasthenia	quadratics
chalkboard	craquelure	flagrantly	grapefruit	Neapolitan	quadrature
chalkstone	crassitude	flagwaving	grapesugar	opalescent	quadrennia
challenger	cravenness	flamboyant	graphemics	opaqueness	quadriceps
chalybeate	czarevitch	flameproof	graphitise	oracularly	quadrireme
chamaeleon	deaconship	flamingoes	graphology	orangepeel	quadrivial
chamberpot	deactivate	flannelled	graptolite	orangewood	quadrivium
champignon	deadliness	flapdoodle	graspingly	oratorical	quadrumana
chancellor	deadweight	flashboard	grasscloth	ovariotomy	quadrumane
chandelier	deaeration	flashflood	grassroots	peacefully	quadrumvir
changeable	deathwatch	flashiness	grasssnake	peacemaker	quadruplet
changeably	diabolical	flashlight	gratefully	peacockery	quadruplex
changeless	diachronic	flashpoint	gratifying	peacockish	quadrupole
changeling	diagnostic	flatfooted	gratuitous	pearldiver	quaintness
changeover	diagonally	flattering	gravestone	peashooter	qualmishly
channelise	diagraphic	flatulence	gravimeter	phagedaena	quantifier
channelled	dialysable	flatulency	gravimetry	phagedenic	quantitive
chaparajos	diapedesis	flavescent	guardhouse	phagocytic	quarantine
chaparejos	diapedetic	flavourful	headcheese	phalangeal	quarrelled
chapfallen	diaphanous	flavouring	headhunter	phallicism	quarreller
chaplaincy	diarrhoeal	flawlessly	headmaster	phanerogam	quarrender
charactery	diarrhoeic	foamflower	headphones	phantasise	quartation
chargeable	diastemata	fractional	headspring	phantasmal	quarterage
chargehand	diathermal	fragmental	headsquare	phantasmic	quarterday
charioteer	diathermic	fragrantly	headstream	phantastic	quartering
charismata	diatropism	framboesia	headstrong	phantastry	quartzitic
charitable	draconites	franchiser	headwaiter	pharisaism	quaternary
charitably	drafthorse	Franciscan	heartblock	pharmacist	quaternate
Charleston	dragonhead	Francophil	heartblood	pharyngeal	quaternion
charmingly	dragonnade	frangipane	heartbreak	pianissimo	quaternity
chartreuse	dragontree	frangipani	heartiness	pianoforte	quatorzain
chartulary	dramatical	fraternise	heartsease	placidness	quatrefoil
chasteness	dramaturge	fraternity	heartthrob	plagiarise	reactivate
chatelaine	dramaturgy	fratricide	heartwhole	plagiarism	reactively
chatoyance	drawbridge	fraudulent	heathendom	plagiarist	reactivity
chatterbox	drawingpin	fraxinella	heathenise	plaguesome	readership
chattiness	drawlingly	ghastfully	heathenish	plainchant	reafforest
chaudfroid	drawstring	glaciation	heathenism	planchette	realisable
chauffeuse	dwarfishly	glaciology	heatstroke	planetable	reallocate
chauntress	elaborator	gladhander	heavenborn	planetaria	reappraise
chauvinism	elasticise	gladsomely	heavensent	plangently	rearmament
chauvinist	elasticity	Glagolitic	heavenward	planigraph	reasonable
clamminess	elatedness	glancingly	heavyarmed	planimeter	reasonably
clangorous	emaciation	glasscloth	hoarseness	planimetry	reasonless
clannishly	emancipate	glassfibre	hyaloplasm	planktonic	reassemble
clarabella	emancipist	glasshouse	ilangilang	planometer	reassembly
Clarenceux	emarginate	glassiness	imaginable	plantation	rhapsodise
claspknife	emasculate	glasspaper	imaginably	plantlouse	rhapsodist
classicise	enamelling	glassworks	inaccuracy	plasmodesm	roadrunner
classicism	enamellist	Glaswegian	inaccurate	plasmodium	roadworthy
classicist	enantiosis	glauberite	inactivate	plasmogamy	scabrously

```
scaffolder Spartacist transferee babysitter libidinous substation
scaleboard spasticity transferor biblically librettist substitute
scandalise spatchcock transfuser bibliology lobsterpot substratum
scandalous spathulate transgress bibliopegy lobulation subtenancy
scansorial spatiality transience bibliophil lubricator subterfuge
scantiness stabiliser transiency bibliopole lubricious subtleness
scapegrace stablemate transistor bibliopoly mobocratic subtrahend
scarabaeid stableness transition bibliotics nebulosity subvention
scarabaeus stadholder transitive bibulously nebulously subversion
scaramouch staffnurse transitory bobbinlace noblewoman subversive
scarceness stagbeetle translator bobbysocks nubiferous sybaritism
scaredycat stagecoach translucid bobbysoxer ombrometer tabernacle
scarlatina stagecraft translunar bubblyjock pebbledash tablecloth
scatheless staggering transmuter cabalistic puberulent tablelinen
scathingly stagnantly transplant cybernetic pubescence tablespoon
scattergun stagnation transposal debasement publishing tabularise
scattering stalactite transposer debatement rabbinical tabulation
scattiness stalagmite transshape debauchery rabblement tobogganer
scavengery stalwartly transvalue debilitate rebellious tubercular
seaanemone stanchless transverse debonairly rebuttable tuberculin
seabiscuit stanchness trappiness debouchure ribbonfish tuberosity
seacaptain standpoint trashiness dubitation ribbonworm tubicolous
sealingwax standstill traumatism dubitative riboflavin umbellifer
seamanlike staphyline travelling embalmment robustious umbilicate
seamanship stargazing travelogue embankment robustness umbiliform
seamstress starriness travertine embarkment rubberneck umbrageous
searchable starryeyed trawlerman emblazoner rubiginous umbrellaed
searchless starstream tsarevitch emblazonry rubrically unbalanced
seaserpent starvation unabridged emblematic rubricator unbearable
seasonable starveling unaccented emblements rubythroat unbearably
seasonably statecraft unaffected embodiment sabbatical unbeatable
seasonally statically unAmerican embolismic sabretache unbeatably
shabbiness stationary unarguable embonpoint sabretooth unbecoming
shadowless stationery unassisted embossment seborrhoea unbeliever
shagginess statistics unassuming embouchure sibilation unbesought
shamefaced statoscope unattached embowelled sobersided unbiblical
shamefully statuesque unattended embroidery sobersides unbiddable
shandrydan statutable unavailing embryogeny subacidity unblenched
shandygaff statutably uranometry embryology subaquatic unblinking
shanghaier staurolite weakliness embryonate subaqueous unblushing
shantytown stavesacre weakminded fabricator subaverage unbonneted
sharpnosed swaggering weaponless fabulously subcentral unbrokenly
sialagogic swanmaiden wearifully febrifugal subclavian unbuttoned
sialagogue swanupping weatherbox fibreboard subcordate upbraiding
skateboard swanmspore weathering fibreglass subculture upbringing
slanderous swashplate weatherman fibrillary subdeanery urbanology
slanginess swaybacked weaverbird fibrillate subduction vibraculum
slantingly teaplanter whaleshark fibrillose subglacial vibraphone
slatternly tearjerker wharfinger fibrinogen subheading wobbliness
slavetrade tearlessly whatsoever fibrositis subjectify zabaglione
slavocracy teatrolley wraparound gobemouche subjection accelerate
Slavophile thalecress wrathfully gobstopper subjective accentuate
Slavophobe thankfully wrathiness habiliment subjugator acceptable
smallscale trabeation yearningly habilitate subkingdom acceptably
smallsword trabeculae yeastiness habitation subletting acceptance
smallwares trabecular ylangylang habitually sublimable acceptedly
smaragdine tracheated abbreviate hebdomadal subliminal accessible
smaragdite tracheitis Albigenses hebetation sublingual accessibly
smartmoney Tractarian albuminoid Hebraistic submariner accidental
smattering tractional albuminous hibernacle submediant accomplice
snafflebit trafficked ambassador hobbyhorse submersion accomplish
snailpaced trafficker ambidexter hobnobbing submission accordance
snailwheel tragacanth ambivalent hybridiser submissive accoucheur
snakedance tragically ambulacral imbecilely submitting accountant
snakestone tragicomic ambulacrum imbecility submontane accounting
snapdragon traitorous ambulation imbibition subnuclear accredited
snappishly trajection ambulatory inbreeding suborbital accrescent
soapboiler trajectory ambushment jobbernowl subordinal accumulate
soapbubble trammelled arbalester jubilantly subreption accurately
soapflakes tramontana arbalister jubilation subroutine accursedly
spacecraft tramontane arbitrable kibbutznik subscriber accusation
spacewoman trampoline arbitrager labiovelar subsection accusative
spaciously trancelike arbitrator laboratory subsellium accusatory
spadebeard tranquilly arboreally lebensraum subsequent accusingly
spadiceous transactor arborvitae liberalise subshrubby accustomed
spagyrical transcribe asbestosis liberalism subsidence alchemical
spallation transcript babblement liberalist subsidiary alcoholise
spankingly transducer babiroussa liberality subsistent alcoholism
sparseness transeptal Babylonian liberation subspecies alcyonaria
```

ancestress	decampment	factiously	licentious	orchestral	rockribbed
anchoretic	decapitate	factitious	lockerroom	oscillator	saccharate
anchoritic	decapodous	factorship	lockkeeper	oscitation	saccharide
anchorless	deceivable	factualism	lockstitch	osculation	saccharify
anchorring	decelerate	factualist	locomotion	osculatory	saccharine
anchylosis	Decembrist	factuality	locomotive	pacesetter	saccharoid
anchylotic	decemviral	fecklessly	locomotory	pacifiable	saccharose
ancipitous	deceptible	fickleness	locustbean	pacificate	sacerdotal
archaistic	decigramme	fictioneer	luciferase	pacificism	sacredness
archbishop	decimalise	fictionist	luciferous	pacificist	sacrificer
archdeacon	decimalism	fictitious	lucifugous	packingbox	sacroiliac
archerfish	decimation	hackbuteer	lucubrator	packsaddle	sacrosanct
archetypal	decisively	hackmatack	luculently	packthread	secernment
architrave	decivilise	hectically	lycopodium	peccadillo	secludedly
archpriest	declarable	hectograph	macadamise	pectinated	secondbest
ascariasis	declassify	hectolitre	Maccabaean	peculation	secondhand
ascendable	declension	hectometre	macebearer	peculiarly	secondment
ascendance	declinable	hocuspocus	maceration	picaresque	secondrate
ascendancy	decolonise	hucklebone	machinator	picayunish	secretaire
ascendence	decolorant	incandesce	machinegun	piccalilli	secularise
ascendency	decolorise	incasement	mackintosh	piccaninny	secularism
ascendible	decompound	incapacity	macrophage	pichiciago	secularist
asceticism	decompress	incautious	macrospore	pickaninny	secularity
ascomycete	decoration	incendiary	maculation	picketline	securement
ascribable	decorative	incessancy	maculature	pickpocket	secureness
ascription	decorously	incestuous	mechanical	picnicking	securiform
auctioneer	decrescent	inchoately	micaceous	picosecond	sicklebill
bacchantes	dichroitic	inchoation	micaschist	pictograph	sickliness
bacchantic	dichromate	inchoative	Michaelmas	pictorial	socialiser
backbiting	dickcissel	incidental	microbiota	pocketable	societally
backblocks	Dickensian	incinerate	microcline	pocketbook	sociologic
backgammon	dictatress	incipience	microfarad	pocketsize	sociometry
background	dictionary	incipiency	microfiche	pockmarked	succedanea
backhanded	doctorship	incisively	micrograph	pycnogonid	successful
backhander	documental	incitation	microlitic	pycnometer	succession
backsheesh	ecchymosis	incitement	micrometer	pycnostyle	successive
backslider	ecchymotic	incivility	micrometry	racecourse	succinctly
backstairs	ecclesiast	inclemency	microphone	rackrenter	succulence
backstitch	encampment	inclinable	microphyte	recallable	succulency
backstroke	encasement	includible	micropylar	receivable	sycophancy
backwardly	encashment	incogitant	microscope	recentness	tachometer
becomingly	encephalic	incoherent	microscopy	receptacle	tachometry
bichromate	encephalon	incomplete	microseism	receptible	tachygraph
bicultural	enchanting	inconstant	microspore	rechristen	tachymeter
buccinator	encourager	incrassate	mockheroic	recidivism	tachymetry
Buchmanism	encroacher	incredible	muciferous	recidivist	taciturnly
Buchmanite	encyclical	incredibly	mycologist	recipiency	tackdriver
bucketshop	encystment	increscent	mycoplasma	reciprocal	tactically
cacciatore	escadrille	incrustate	mycorrhiza	recitalist	tactlessly
cachinnate	escalation	incubation	necrolater	recitation	technetium
cackhanded	escallonia	incubative	necrolatry	recitative	technician
cacodaemon	escapement	incubatory	necromancy	recitativo	technicist
cacogenics	escapology	inculcator	necrophile	recklessly	technocrat
cacography	escarpment	inculpable	necrophily	recolonise	technology
cacomistle	escharotic	incumbency	necropolis	recommence	tickertape
cicatrices	escheatage	incunabula	nectareous	recompense	ticklishly
Ciceronian	escritoire	incurrable	nickelling	reconciler	ticpolonga
cicisbeism	Esculapian	jackanapes	nicotinism	reconsider	tocopherol
cochleated	escutcheon	jackassery	nuciferous	recordable	ulceration
cockalorum	eucalyptol	jackhammer	nucivorous	recoupment	ulcerative
cockatrice	eucalyptus	jackknives	nucleation	recreantly	unchanging
cockchafer	eucaryotic	jackrabbit	nucleonics	recreation	unchastity
cockneyish	excavation	jacobinise	nucleoside	recreative	uncloister
cockneyism	excellence	Jacobinism	nucleotide	recrudesce	uncommonly
cocksurely	excellency	Jacobinism	nyctalopia	rectorship	uncritical
cuckoopint	excerption	jocoseness	nyctalopic	recumbence	unctuosity
cuckoospit	excitation	jocularity	nyctinasty	recumbency	unctuously
cucullated	excitative	laceration	occasional	recuperate	uncustomed
cyclically	excitatory	lacerative	occidental	recurrence	vectograph
cyclograph	excitement	lachrymose	occupation	recyclable	viceconsul
cyclometer	excitingly	lacklustre	occupative	ricinoleic	vicegerent
cyclopedia	excogitate	laconicism	occurrence	rickettsia	viceregent
cyclopedic	excrescent	lacrimator	oecologist	rockabilly	victimiser
cyclostome	excruciate	lacrymator	oecumenism	rockbadger	Victoriana
cyclostyle	excusatory	lactescent	oncogenous	rockbottom	victorious
decadently	faceharden	lacustrine	oncologist	rockgarden	victualled
decagramme	facesaving	lectionary	orchardist	rockhopper	victualler
decahedral	facileness	licensable	orchardman	rockpigeon	vocabulary
decahedron	facilitate	licentiate	orchestics	rockrabbit	vocational

```
vociferant  Godfearing  middlemost  sedateness  ameliorate  coetaneous
vociferate  hedonistic  middlingly  seducement  amendatory  coeternity
vociferous  hodgepodge  midmorning  seductress  amercement  coexistent
wickedness  hydraulics  midshipman  sedulously  amerciable  creaminess
wickerwork  hydrically  moderately  sideboards  Amerindian  creatinine
Wycliffite  hydrologic  moderation  sideeffect  anecdotage  creatively
abdication  hydrolysis  moderatism  sideglance  anecdotist  creativity
abdominous  hydrolytic  moderniser  siderolite  anemograph  creaturely
abducentes  hydromancy  modernness  siderostat  anemometer  credential
additional  hydrometer  modifiable  sidesaddle  anemometry  creditable
addlepated  hydrometry  modishness  sidestreet  anemophily  creditably
aldermanic  hydropathy  modulation  sidestroke  aneurismal  creepiness
aldermanry  hydrophane  mudskipper  sidewinder  aneurysmal  crematoria
Andalusian  hydrophily  mudslinger  soddenness  arenaceous  crenellate
andalusite  hydrophone  nidicolous  sudatorium  areolation  crenulated
androecium  hydrophyte  nidificate  suddenness  Areopagite  crepuscule
androgenic  hydroplane  nidifugous  tiddlywink  asexuality  crescentic
audibility  hydroscope  nodulation  tidewaiter  ateleiosis  cretaceous
audiometer  hydrotaxis  nudibranch  undefended  aventurine  crewelwork
audiometry  indagation  obdurately  undeniable  averseness  ctenophore
audiophile  indecently  oedematose  undeniably  aversively  deepfreeze
auditorial  indecision  oedematous  underbelly  azeotropic  deepfrozen
auditorium  indecisive  oldfangled  underbrush  beechdrops  deeprooted
badderlock  indecorous  oldmaidish  undercliff  beefburger  deepseated
bedchamber  indefinite  ordainment  undercover  beekeeping  deerforest
bedclothes  indelicacy  ordinarily  undercroft  biennially  deescalate
bedevilled  indelicate  ordination  underdress  bleachable  diecasting
Bedlington  indexation  ordonnance  underfloor  bleariness  dielectric
bedraggled  indication  Ordovician  underglaze  blearyeyed  diesinking
bidonville  indicative  paddleboat  underlease  bleatingly  dreadfully
Buddhistic  indicatory  paddyfield  underlinen  blepharism  dreaminess
budgerigar  indictable  paddywagon  underlying  breadboard  dreamworld
cadaverous  indictment  paddywhack  underminer  breadcrumb  dreariness
caddisworm  indigenous  pedagogics  underneath  breadfruit  dressiness
codswallop  indigested  pedalorgan  underpants  breadstick  dressmaker
cuddlesome  indirectly  pedalpoint  underproof  breadstuff  edentulous
cudgelling  indiscreet  pederastic  underquote  breakables  elecampane
dedication  indiscrete  pedestrian  underscore  breakpoint  electively
dedicative  indisposed  pediculate  undersense  breakwater  electorate
dedicatory  indistinct  pediculous  undersexed  breastbone  electrical
deductible  inditement  pedicurist  undershirt  breastwall  electronic
didactical  individual  pedimental  undershoot  breastwork  elementary
didgeridoo  indocility  pedimented  undershrub  breathable  Eleusinian
elderberry  indolently  pedologist  undersized  breathless  elevenplus
endearment  Indonesian  peduncular  underskirt  breechless  emendation
endemicity  inducement  podiatrist  underslung  breezeless  emendatory
endocrinal  inductance  radicalise  understand  breeziness  emeryboard
endodermal  indulgence  radicalism  understate  brentgoose  emerypaper
endodermis  induration  radication  understeer  bressummer  emerywheel
endogamous  indurative  radiogenic  understock  brevetting  energetics
endogenous  industrial  radiograph  understood  byelection  enervation
endophytic  iodination  radiologic  understudy  Caerphilly  enervative
endopodite  judgematic  radiometer  undertaken  caespitose  epeirogeny
endorsable  judicatory  radiometry  undertaker  cheapishly  epentheses
endoscopic  judicature  radiopaque  undertrick  cheapskate  epenthesis
endosmosis  judicially  radiophone  undervalue  checkpoint  epenthetic
endosmotic  kidnapping  radioscopy  underwater  cheekiness  epexegeses
endothelia  ladderback  radiosonde  underworld  cheerfully  epexegetic
endproduct  ladychapel  redblooded  underwrite  cheeriness  erectility
endstopped  ladyfinger  redcurrant  underwrote  cheesecake  eremitical
enduringly  ladykiller  redecorate  undeserved  cheesiness  erethismic
eudemonism  lederhosen  redeemable  undesigned  chelicerae  eternalise
eudemonist  ledgerbait  redemption  undesirous  chemically  eternalist
eudiometer  ledgerline  redemptive  undeterred  chemisette  evenhanded
eudiometry  madreporic  redescribe  undigested  chemotaxis  eventually
fadelessly  meddlesome  rediscover  undulation  chequebook  everglades
federalise  mediastina  redolently  undulatory  chersonese  everliving
federalism  mediatress  redundance  videophone  chessboard  everyplace
federalist  medicament  redundancy  widespread  chevrotain  everything
federation  medicaster  ridgepiece  aberdevine  clearstory  everywhere
federative  medication  ridiculous  aberrantly  clementine  execration
fiddleback  medicative  rodfishing  aberration  clerestory  execrative
fiddlehead  medievally  rudderfish  acephalous  clerically  execratory
fiddlewood  mediocrity  rudderless  acervation  cleverness  executable
fiducially  meditation  rudimental  acetabular  coelacanth  exegetical
fuddyduddy  meditative  saddleback  acetabulum  coenobitic  exenterate
gadolinite  medullated  saddlefast  adenectomy  coenobytic  eyeglasses
gadolinium  middleaged  saddletree  adequately  coequality  eyeservice
gadrooning  middlebrow
```

eyewitness	ineligible	overwinter	premaxilla	sherardise	sweetbread
feebleness	ineligibly	paedagogic	premedical	sheriffdom	sweetbriar
fieldglass	ineloquent	paederasty	premonitor	siegetrain	sweetbrier
fieldmouse	ineludible	paediatric	prepackage	sketchable	sweetening
fieldpiece	ineptitude	paedogogue	preparator	sketchbook	sweetheart
fieldstone	inequality	paedophile	preparedly	skewbridge	sweltering
fiendishly	inevitable	peerlessly	prepayable	sleaziness	teenyweeny
fierceness	inevitably	pheasantry	prepayment	sleepiness	teetotally
fleabitten	inexistent	phelloderm	prepensely	sleepyhead	theatrical
fleacircus	inexorable	phenacetin	prepossess	sleeveless	theistical
fleamarket	inexorably	phenocryst	prepotence	sleevelink	themselves
fledgeling	inexpertly	phenomenal	prepotency	sleighbell	theocratic
fleeringly	inexpiable	phenomenon	presageful	slenderise	theodicean
fleetingly	inexpiably	phenotypic	presbyopia	smelliness	theodolite
fleshiness	inexplicit	pheromonal	presbyopic	sneakiness	theogonist
fleshwound	isentropic	piecegoods	presbytery	sneakingly	theologian
flexuously	kieselguhr	piercingly	prescience	sneakthief	theologise
foetidness	lieutenant	piezometer	prescriber	sneeringly	theologist
freakiness	meerschaum	pleadingly	presentday	sneezeweed	theophanic
freakishly	needlebath	pleasantly	presentive	sneezewood	theophoric
freebooter	needlebook	pleasantry	presidency	sneezewort	theopneust
freedwoman	needlecord	pleasingly	presidiary	speargrass	theoretics
freehanded	needlefish	plebiscite	presignify	specialise	theosopher
freeholder	needlessly	plecoptera	pressagent	specialism	thereabout
freelancer	needlework	pleochroic	pressingly	specialist	thereafter
freeliving	obediently	pleonastic	pressurise	speciality	thereanent
freeloader	oceanarium	plesiosaur	presternum	speciation	thereunder
freemartin	oceangoing	pneumatics	presumable	speciology	thermionic
freesoiler	oceanology	poetically	presumably	speciosity	thermistor
freespeech	ocellation	preachment	presuppose	speciously	thermogram
freespoken	oleaginous	preadamite	pretendant	spectacled	thermophil
freightage	oleiferous	prearrange	pretendent	spectacles	thermopile
Frenchness	oleography	prebendary	pretension	spectrally	thermostat
frenziedly	oleraceous	precarious	prettiness	speculator	theurgical
frequenter	oneirology	precaution	prevailing	speechless	treadboard
frequently	onesidedly	precedence	prevalence	speediness	treadwheel
freshwater	openhanded	precedency	prevenancy	speedlimit	treasonous
greasewood	openhearth	preceptive	prevenient	speleology	trecentist
greasiness	openminded	preceptory	prevention	spellbound	tremendous
greatniece	operculate	precession	preventive	Spencerian	tremolitic
greatuncle	operettist	preciosity	previously	Spenserian	trenchancy
GrecoRoman	oreography	preciously	psephology	spermaceti	trendiness
greediness	oreologist	precipitin	pseudocarp	spermicide	trepanning
greedyguts	overabound	preclusion	puerperium	sperrylite	trespasser
greencloth	overactive	preclusive	queasiness	steadiness	twelvefold
greenfinch	overblouse	precocious	quenchable	steakhouse	twelvenote
greenheart	overbought	preconcert	quenchless	stealthily	twelvetone
greenhouse	overburden	precordial	quercitron	steamchest	uneasiness
greenshank	overcharge	precursory	questioner	steaminess	uneconomic
greenstick	overcommit	predacious	reelection	steamtight	unedifying
greenstone	overcooked	predecease	reeligible	steeliness	uneducated
greenstuff	overexcite	predestine	reentrance	steelworks	unemphatic
greensward	overexpose	predicable	rheologist	stelliform	unemployed
gregarious	overflight	prediction	rheotropic	stenchtrap	unendingly
grenadilla	overground	predictive	rhetorical	stencilled	unenviable
gressorial	overgrowth	predispose	rheumatics	stenciller	unequalled
greyheaded	overhanded	prednisone	rheumatism	stenograph	unerringly
guesthouse	overlander	preeminent	rheumatoid	stentorian	unevenness
guestnight	overlapped	preemption	ruefulness	stepfather	uneventful
haematosis	overlooker	preemptive	scenically	stephanite	unexampled
haematuria	overmanned	preexilian	scepticism	stepladder	unexcelled
haemolysis	overmantel	prefecture	seedpotato	stepmother	unexpected
haemolytic	overmaster	preferable	seedvessel	stepparent	unexplored
heedlessly	overnicety	preferably	seemliness	stepsister	urethritis
hierarchal	overpraise	preference	seersucker	stereobate	usefulness
hierarchic	overrefine	preferment	seethrough	stereogram	Vietnamese
hierocracy	overridden	preferring	sheabutter	stereopsis	viewfinder
hieroglyph	overriding	prefixture	shearwater	stereotype	viewlessly
hierograph	overshadow	prefrontal	sheathbill	stereotypy	weedkiller
hierolatry	overslaugh	prefulgent	sheathless	sterigmata	wheatstone
hierophant	overspread	preglacial	sheepishly	steriliser	wheelchair
icebreaker	overstride	pregnantly	sheeplouse	sternwards	wheelhorse
idealistic	overstrung	prehensile	sheepshank	stertorous	wheelhouse
ideational	oversubtle	prehension	sheepshead	stewardess	wheeziness
ideography	oversupply	prehistory	shellacked	sweatgland	whensoever
ideologist	overthrown	prejudiced	shellmound	sweatiness	whereabout
ineducable	overthrust	prelatical	shellproof	sweatshirt	woefulness
inefficacy	overtopped	prelection	shellshock	sweepingly	wretchedly
inelegance	overweight	premarital	shenanigan	sweepstake	yieldingly

affability	infiltrate	waffleiron	hygrometer	pigeonpost	cohabitant
affectedly	infinitely	agglutinin	hygrometry	pigeontoed	coherently
affectless	infinitive	aggrandise	hygrophyte	pigeonwing	cohesively
affeerment	infinitude	aggression	hygroscope	pigmentary	dehiscence
afferently	inflatable	aggressive	ingeminate	pigsticker	dehumanise
affettuoso	inflection	algebraist	ingestible	pogonology	dehumidify
affiliated	inflective	algolagnia	inglorious	pogonotomy	echinoderm
affirmable	inflexible	algolagnic	ingratiate	pugilistic	enharmonic
affliction	inflexibly	algologist	ingredient	pugnacious	ephemerous
afflictive	infliction	Algonquian	ingression	ragamuffin	ephorality
affluently	inflictive	angiosperm	jaggedness	raggedness	ethereally
affordable	informally	Anglistics	jaguarundi	regalement	ethicality
bafflement	infraction	anglomania	juggernaut	regardless	ethnically
bafflingly	infrahuman	anglophile	legalistic	regelation	ethnologic
beforehand	infrasonic	anglophobe	legateship	regeneracy	ethologist
beforetime	infrequent	anglophone	legibility	regenerate	euhemerise
bufflehead	infusorial	AngloSaxon	legislator	regentship	euhemerism
buffoonery	infusorian	angularity	legitimacy	regimental	euhemerist
coffeemill	Kafkaesque	angwantibo	legitimate	regionally	exhalation
defacement	lefthanded	argumentum	legitimise	registered	exhaustion
defalcator	lefthander	augustness	legitimism	registrant	exhaustive
defamation	lifegiving	bigamously	legitimist	regression	exhibition
defamatory	lifejacket	bighearted	leguminous	regressive	exhibitory
defeasance	lifelessly	bigmouthed	ligamental	regretting	exhilarant
defeasible	lifesaving	cogitation	lighterage	regularise	exhilarate
defeminise	muffinbell	cogitative	lighterman	regularity	exhumation
defendable	oafishness	cognisable	lightfaced	regulation	Fahrenheit
defensible	obfuscated	cognisably	lighthouse	regulative	ichthyosis
defensibly	officially	cognisance	lightingup	regulatory	inhabitant
deferrable	offlicence	cognominal	lightproof	rightangle	inhalation
deficiency	offputting	degeneracy	loganberry	rightfully	inharmonic
defilement	offsetting	degenerate	loganstone	rightwards	inherently
definement	puffpastry	degradable	loggerhead	rigorously	inheritrix
definienda	referendum	degradedly	logicality	ruggedness	inhibition
definitely	refillable	degressive	logistical	sagination	inhibitory
definition	refinement	digestible	logography	sagittally	inhumanely
definitive	reflection	digitalise	logorrhoea	segmentary	inhumanity
definitude	reflective	digitately	logrolling	seguidilla	inhumation
deflagrate	reflexible	digitation	lugubrious	signalling	Ishmaelite
deflection	reformable	digitiform	magistracy	signwriter	Jehovistic
deflective	refraction	digression	magistrate	sugardaddy	johnnycake
deflowerer	refractive	digressive	magnetiser	sugarhouse	Johnsonese
defoliator	refractory	doggedness	magnifical	sugariness	johnsonian
deforciant	refreshing	dogmatical	magnificat	sugarmaple	Mahommedan
defrayable	refringent	dogmatiser	magnifying	suggestion	Mohammedan
defrayment	refuelling	dogstongue	megalithic	suggestive	Muhammadan
difference	refulgence	eigenvalue	megalosaur	tegumental	Muhammedan
difficulty	refundable	eighteenmo	megascopic	ungenerous	nihilistic
diffidence	refundment	eighteenth	mightiness	ungraceful	ochlocracy
diffusible	refutation	engagement	mignonette	ungracious	ophicleide
effaceable	ruffianism	engagingly	migrainous	ungrateful	ophiolater
effacement	safeblower	engineroom	negatively	ungrounded	ophiolatry
effectuate	safetybelt	Englishman	negativism	ungrudging	ophiologic
effeminacy	softbilled	englutting	negativist	unguentary	ophthalmia
effeminate	softboiled	engrossing	negativity	vegetarian	ophthalmic
effervesce	softfinned	engulfment	neglectful	vegetation	otherwhere
effeteness	softheaded	ergodicity	negligence	vegetative	otherwhile
efficacity	softspoken	ergonomics	negligible	vigilantly	otherworld
efficiency	sufferable	ergonomist	negligibly	vignettist	schematise
effloresce	sufferably	ergosterol	negotiable	vigorously	schematism
effortless	sufferance	eugenicist	negotiator	waggonette	schemozzle
effrontery	sufficient	figuration	negrophile	wagonvault	scherzando
effulgence	suffragist	figurative	negrophobe	zigzagging	schipperke
effusively	toffeenose	figurehead	nightdress	zygodactyl	schismatic
enfacement	tuffaceous	fugitively	nightglass	zygomorphy	schizocarp
fiftyfifty	tufthunter	goggleeyed	nightlight	abhorrence	schizogony
infallible	unfadingly	hagiolatry	nightshade	achievable	scholastic
infallibly	unfairness	hagiologic	nightshift	achondrite	schoolable
infamously	unfaithful	hagioscope	nightshirt	achromatic	schoolbook
infarction	unfamiliar	highbinder	nightstick	adherently	schooldays
infatuated	unfathered	highflying	nightwatch	adhesively	schoolgirl
infeasible	unfeminine	highhanded	nigrescent	adhibition	schoolmaam
infectious	unfettered	highjacker	organicism	aphaereses	schoolmarm
infelicity	unfilially	highlander	organicist	aphaeresis	schoolmate
inferiorly	unfinished	highminded	organismal	aphoristic	schoolroom
infernally	unflagging	highoctane	pagination	aphrodisia	schooltime
inferrable	unforeseen	highstrung	pegmatitic	Ashkenazim	schoolwork
infidelity	unfriended	highwayman	pigeonhole	Athanasian	sphalerite
infighting	unfriendly	hygrograph	pigeonpair	behindhand	sphenodone

sphenogram	clinkstone	frigidness	philistine	skijumping	tribometer
sphenoidal	clinometer	frigorific	phillumeny	skimpiness	tribrachic
sphericity	clinometry	frilliness	philologen	skindiving	trichiasis
spheroidal	cnidoblast	fringeless	philopoena	skinniness	trichinise
spherulite	coincident	friskiness	philosophe	skirmisher	trichinous
unhallowed	cribriform	fritillary	philosophy	skirtdance	trichology
unhandsome	criminally	frivolling	pliability	skittishly	trichotomy
unhistoric	crinolette	frizziness	pliantness	slidevalve	trichroism
unholiness	crippledom	gaillardia	poinsettia	slightness	trichromat
unhouseled	crispation	gaingiving	pointblank	slipperily	trickiness
upholstery	crispbread	Ghibelline	pridefully	slipstitch	trickishly
vehemently	crisscross	glimmering	priesthood	slipstream	triclinium
abiogenist	critically	grievously	priestling	slitpocket	tricyclist
acidimeter	cuirassier	grindingly	priggishly	snickasnee	Tridentine
acidimetry	daintiness	grindstone	primevally	sniffiness	trierarchy
acidophile	daisychain	grisliness	primiparae	snivelling	triflingly
aficionado	drivelling	grittiness	primordial	spidercrab	trifoliate
agitatedly	driverless	guilefully	primordium	spiderline	trifurcate
alienation	edibleness	guillotine	princeling	spiderwort	trigeminal
alightment	editorship	guiltiness	princeship	spiflicate	triggerman
alimentary	eliminable	hairraiser	principate	spillikins	triglyphic
amiability	eliminator	hairspring	principial	spinescent	trigonally
animadvert	emigration	hairstreak	principium	spiracular	trilateral
animalcula	emigratory	hairstroke	principled	spiraculum	trilingual
animalcule	emissivity	hoitytoity	prismoidal	spiralling	triliteral
animatedly	enigmatise	idiopathic	prissiness	spiritedly	trillionth
anisotropy	enigmatist	inimically	privileged	spiritless	trimonthly
apiculture	epiblastic	inimitable	prizefight	spirituous	trimorphic
aristocrat	epicentral	inimitably	psilocybin	spirograph	trioecious
arithmetic	epicycloid	iniquitous	psittacine	spirometer	tripartite
aviatrices	epideictic	initialise	puissantly	spirometry	triphammer
aviculture	epidemical	initialled	quickgrass	spitchcock	triphthong
axiologist	epidermoid	initiation	quickthorn	spitefully	triplicate
blindingly	epigastric	initiative	quiescence	stickiness	triplicity
blissfully	epigenesis	initiatory	quiescency	stiffening	triquetrae
blistering	epigenetic	iridaceous	quinacrine	stiflebone	triquetral
blitheness	epiglottal	iridescent	quintuplet	stiflingly	trisection
blithering	epiglottic	iridosmine	quirkiness	stigmatise	triskelion
blithesome	epiglottis	Irishwoman	quixotical	stigmatism	triternate
blitzkrieg	epigrapher	itinerancy	quizmaster	stigmatist	triturable
boisterous	epigraphic	kaisership	railroader	stilettoes	triturator
brickfield	epilimnion	knickknack	railwayman	stillbirth	triumphant
bricklayer	epiphytism	knifeboard	rainmaking	stillicide	triumviral
bridegroom	episcopacy	knighthood	reichsmark	stimulator	trivialise
bridesmaid	episcopate	kriegspiel	reissuable	stinginess	trivialism
bridgeable	episematic	Krishnaism	reiterance	stingingly	triviality
bridgehead	episodical	Leibnizian	rhinestone	stinkingly	tuitionary
bridgeless	episternum	maidenhair	rhinoceros	stinkstone	twilighted
bridgework	epistolary	maidenhead	rhinoscope	stipellate	ubiquitous
bridlepath	epistrophe	maidenhood	rhinoscopy	stipulator	uniaxially
brigandage	epithelial	maidenlike	rhizogenic	stirrupcup	unicameral
brigandine	epithelium	mainlander	rhizomorph	stitchwort	unicyclist
brigandism	ericaceous	mainspring	rhizophore	suicidally	uniformity
brigantine	etiolation	mainstream	roistering	swimmingly	unilateral
brightness	evidential	maintainer	roisterous	swinefever	unilingual
brightwork	evilminded	maisonette	sailorless	swingingly	unilocular
brilliance	eviscerate	moisturise	sciagraphy	swinglebar	unimproved
brilliancy	faintheart	nailpolish	scientific	switchback	uninformed
Britishism	fairground	noisemaker	Scillonian	switchover	uninitiate
chickenpox	fairhaired	obituarist	sciolistic	swiveleyed	unionistic
chiffchaff	fairleader	odiousness	seignorage	swivelling	unipartite
chiffonier	fairminded	oligarchic	seignorial	tailorbird	uniqueness
childbirth	fairspoken	oligoclase	seismicity	tailormade	university
childermas	fairycycle	oligopsony	seismogram	thickening	univocally
childishly	faithfully	olivaceous	seismology	thievishly	utilisable
childproof	flightdeck	opinionist	shibboleth	thillhorse	voiceprint
chiliastic	flightless	opisometer	shieldless	thimbleful	wainwright
chilliness	flightpath	orientally	shiftiness	thimblerig	waistcloth
chimerical	flimsiness	originally	shillelagh	thinkingly	weightless
chimneypot	flintiness	originator	shipbroker	thinkpiece	weimaraner
chimpanzee	flippantly	otioseness	shipfitter	thirdclass	whipstitch
chinagraph	flirtation	ovipositor	shipmaster	thirdparty	whirlybird
chinchilla	friability	oxidisable	shipwright	thirteenth	whiskified
chiromancy	fricandeau	painkiller	shirehorse	thirtyfold	whispering
chiselling	fricasseed	painlessly	shirtfront	thixotropy	whitebeard
chivalrous	frictional	paintbrush	shirtwaist	toilsomely	whitefaced
clientship	friendless	philatelic	skiagraphy	triacetate	whitesmith
clingstone	friendlily	philippina	skibobbing	triandrous	whitethorn
clinically	friendship	philippine		triangular	WhitMonday

WhitSunday	ballflower	coloration	galvaniser	malapropos	palmbutter
wristwatch	ballistics	coloratura	gelatinise	malcontent	palmerworm
zwitterion	ballooning	colossally	gelatinous	malefactor	PalmSunday
abjectness	balloonist	colourable	Gilbertian	maleficent	paltriness
abjuration	balneology	colourably	goldbeater	malentendu	palynology
adjacently	balustrade	colourfast	golddigger	malevolent	pellagrous
adjectival	Belgravian	colourless	goldenness	malfeasant	pellicular
adjudgment	believable	colportage	goldenseal	malignance	pellucidly
adjudicate	belladonna	colporteur	goldilocks	malignancy	phlebotomy
adjunction	belletrist	columbaria	golfcourse	malingerer	phlegmatic
adjunctive	bellflower	cultivable	goloptious	malleebird	phlogistic
adjuration	bellringer	cultivator	goluptious	malleefowl	phlogiston
adjuratory	bellwether	culturally	halberdier	mallenders	phlogopite
adjustable	bellyacher	cylindered	halfcocked	malodorous	piledriver
adjustment	bellydance	cylindroid	halfdollar	Malpighian	pilgarlick
bejewelled	bellylaugh	delaminate	halflength	Malthusian	pilgrimage
bijouterie	belongings	delectable	halfnelson	malvaceous	piliferous
cajolement	bilgewater	delectably	halfvolley	melancholy	pilliwinks
cajolingly	biliverdin	delegation	halfwitted	Melanesian	pillowcase
dejectedly	billetdoux	deliberate	halfyearly	melanistic	pillowlace
enjambment	billposter	delicately	halieutics	meliorator	pillowslip
enjoinment	bilocation	delightful	hallelujah	melismatic	pilothouse
injunction	bollweevil	delimitate	halogenate	mellowness	pilotlight
injunctive	bolometric	delineator	halogenous	meltingpot	pilotwhale
jejuneness	bolshevise	delinquent	halophytic	militantly	polemicist
majestical	bolshevism	deliquesce	heliacally	militarily	polemonium
majuscular	bolshevist	delocalise	helianthus	militarise	politeness
objectival	bullethead	delphinium	Heliconian	militarism	politician
objectless	bullheaded	delphinoid	helicopter	militarist	politicise
pejoration	bullroarer	deltiology	heliograph	militiaman	politicist
pejorative	calamander	delusional	heliolater	millefiori	pollenosis
rejectable	calamitous	delusively	heliolatry	millennial	pollinator
rejoicings	calcareous	dilapidate	heliometer	millennium	polyandric
rejuvenate	calceolate	dilatation	heliophyte	millesimal	polyanthus
rejuvenise	calciferol	dilatorily	helioscope	millilitre	polyatamic
unjustness	calcsinter	dilemmatic	heliotaxis	millimetre	polychaete
alkalinity	calculable	dilettante	heliotrope	millstream	polychrest
hakenkreuz	calculably	dilettanti	heliotropy	millwright	polychrome
hokeypokey	calculator	diligently	hellbender	molendinar	polyclinic
inkslinger	Caledonian	dillydally	helminthic	molluscoid	polycyclic
likelihood	calibrator	diluteness	helplessly	molluscous	polydactyl
likeliness	caliginous	dolomitise	holloweyed	molybdenum	polydipsia
likeminded	callowness	dolorously	hollowness	muliebrity	polygamist
lukewarmly	calumniate	elliptical	hollowware	mulishness	polygamous
makeweight	calumnious	enlacement	holography	mulligrubs	polygenism
pokerfaced	calyciform	enlistment	holohedral	multifaced	polygenist
pyknometer	calyptrate	eulogistic	holophrase	multiloquy	polygenous
rakishness	celebrated	fallacious	holophytic	multimedia	polygraphy
takingness	celebrator	fallingoff	holosteric	multiphase	polygynous
unkindness	cellophane	fallowness	holusbolus	multiplier	polyhedral
unknowable	cellularly	felicitate	hylotheism	multipolar	polyhedric
Wykehamist	cellulitis	felicitous	illadvised	multistage	polyhedron
yokefellow	cellulosic	fellmonger	illatively	multivocal	polyhistor
ablebodied	chlorinate	fellowship	illaudable	nullanulla	polymathic
allegation	chloroform	felspathic	illaudably	oblateness	polymerise
allegiance	colatitude	filariasis	illegalise	obligation	polymerism
allegorise	colchicine	filibuster	illegality	obligatory	polymerous
allegorist	coleoptera	filterable	illiteracy	obligingly	Polynesian
allegretto	coleoptile	filthiness	illiterate	obliterate	polynomial
allergenic	coleorhiza	filtration	illnatured	owlishness	polyonymic
alleviator	collarbeam	foliaceous	illstarred	Palaeocene	polyphasic
alliaceous	collarbone	folklorist	illuminant	Palaeogene	polyphonic
alliterate	collarette	folkmemory	illuminate	palaeolith	polyploidy
allocation	collarless	folksiness	illuminati	palaeotype	polysemous
allocution	collarstud	folksinger	illuminist	Palaeozoic	polytheism
allogamous	collatable	follicular	illumining	palagonite	polytheist
allopathic	collateral	fulfilling	illusional	palatalise	polytocous
allophonic	collection	fulfilment	illusively	palatinate	polyvalent
allosteric	collective	fuliginous	illusorily	palimpsest	pulsatilla
allotropic	collegiate	fullbodied	illustrate	palindrome	pulsimeter
alloverish	collembola	fullbottom	jolterhead	palisander	pulsometer
allpurpose	collimator	fulllength	kilogramme	palladious	pulveriser
allrounder	collocutor	galimatias	liliaceous	pallbearer	pulvinated
allurement	colloquial	galleywest	Lollardism	palliation	relational
allusively	colloquies	galliambic	malacoderm	palliative	relatively
aplacental	colloquium	galloglass	malacology	palliatory	relativise
balbriggan	colonially	Gallomania	maladapted	pallidness	relativism
balderdash	colonnaded	Gallophile	malapertly	palmaceous	relativist
baldheaded		Gallophobe		palmatifid	relativity
					relaxation

releasable	soldanella	volatility	comehither	cumulation	homogenous
relegation	solecistic	volitional	comeliness	cumulative	homologate
relentless	solemnness	volleyball	comestible	cumuliform	homologise
relevantly	solenoidal	voltameter	comicality	damageable	homologous
relievable	solicitant	volubility	comicopera	damagingly	homonymous
relinquish	solicitous	volumetric	commandant	dampcourse	homoousian
relishable	solicitude	voluminous	commandeer	dampingoff	homophonic
relocation	solidarism	voluptuary	commandery	demagogism	homosexual
reluctance	solidarist	voluptuous	commanding	demandable	homozygote
reluctancy	solidarity	vulcaniser	commandoes	dementedly	homozygous
rollcollar	solidstate	vulnerable	commentary	demobilise	homunculus
rollicking	solifidian	vulnerably	commentate	democratic	humaneness
rollingpin	solitarily	Waldensian	commercial	demography	humanistic
salability	solstitial	wallflower	commissary	demoiselle	humanities
salamander	solubilise	wallpepper	commission	demolition	humbleness
salesclerk	solubility	wellheeled	commissure	demonetise	humbuggery
saleswoman	splanchnic	wellington	commitment	demoniacal	humbugging
salicional	splashback	wellspoken	committing	demonology	humidifier
salicylate	splashdown	wellspring	commixture	demoralise	humoresque
salientian	spleenwort	wellturned	commodious	demotivate	humoristic
saliferous	splendidly	wellwisher	commonable	demureness	humorously
salivation	splintbone	Welshwoman	commonalty	demurrable	humourless
sallenders	splintcoal	wildebeest	commonness	diminished	humoursome
sallowness	splitlevel	wilderment	commonroom	diminuendo	humpbacked
salmagundi	splutterer	wilderness	commonweal	diminution	immaculacy
salmonella	sullenness	wildfowler	communally	diminutive	immaculate
salmonleap	sulphonate	wilfulness	communique	dimorphism	immaterial
salpingian	sulphurate	willowherb	commutable	dimorphous	immaturely
saltarello	sulphurise	willynilly	commutator	dominantly	immaturity
saltcellar	sulphurous	willywilly	compaction	domination	immemorial
saltigrade	sultanship	wolframite	comparable	dominative	imminently
salubrious	sultriness	xylography	comparably	dumbledore	immiscible
salutarily	syllabaria	xylophonic	comparator	dumbstruck	immiscibly
salutation	syllogiser	yellowback	comparison	dumbwaiter	immobilise
salutatory	talebearer	yellowbird	compassion	dumfounder	immobility
scleroderm	talentless	yellowness	compasssaw	Emmentaler	immoderacy
sclerotium	taleteller	yellowwood	compatible	enmeshment	immoderate
sclerotomy	talismanic	zollverein	compatibly	familiarly	immodestly
selectness	Talmudical	administer	compatriot	famishment	immolation
selenodont	telecamera	admiration	compelling	famousness	immoralist
selenology	telecaster	admiringly	compendium	femaleness	immorality
selfacting	telegraphy	admissible	compensate	feminality	immortally
selfaction	telemetric	admittable	competence	femininely	immortelle
selfbinder	teleologic	admittance	competency	femininity	immoveable
selfcolour	teleostean	admittedly	competitor	fimbriated	immunology
selfdeceit	telepathic	admonition	complacent	fumigation	immurement
selfdenial	telephoner	admonitive	complainer	fumblingly	jimsonweed
selfesteem	telephonic	admonitory	complected	gambolling	kimberlite
selffeeder	telescopic	almacanter	complement	gamekeeper	Lamarckian
selfglazed	televiewer	almondeyed	completely	gametangia	Lamarckism
selfguided	television	almsgiving	completion	gemination	lambrequin
selflessly	televisual	almucanter	completive	gemmaceous	lamentable
selfloving	tellership	ammoniacal	complexion	gymnastics	lamentably
selfmotion	telpherage	ammoniated	complexity	gymnosophy	lamentedly
selfmurder	tilthammer	ammunition	compliance	gymnosperm	laminarian
selfparody	tolerantly	Armageddon	compliancy	hammerbeam	lamination
selfpoised	toleration	armigerous	complicacy	hammerhead	Lammastide
selfpraise	tollbridge	armorially	complicate	hammerless	lampoonery
selfprofit	tularaemia	armourclad	complicity	hammerlock	lampoonist
selfraised	tularaemic	armourless	compliment	hammerpond	lemniscate
selfregard	unlabelled	atmosphere	complotted	hamshackle	lemongrass
selfrising	unlawfully	bemedalled	composedly	hemicyclic	limaciform
selfruling	unlettered	bemusement	compositor	hemihedral	limeburner
selfseeker	unlikeness	bimestrial	compotator	hemihedron	limitation
selfstyled	validation	bimetallic	compounder	hemiplegia	limitative
selftaught	valleculae	bombardier	compradore	hemiplegic	limitrophe
selfwilled	vallecular	bumblingly	comprehend	hemipteran	limpidness
seltzogene	valorously	bumpkinish	compressed	hemisphere	lumberjack
silentness	valvulitis	camelopard	compressor	hempnettle	lumberroom
silhouette	veldschoen	camerlengo	compromise	homebrewed	lumbersome
silkcotton	velitation	camerlingo	compulsion	homecoming	lumberyard
silkscreen	velocipede	camouflage	compulsive	homeliness	luminosity
sillybilly	velutinous	campaigner	compulsory	homemaking	luminously
silverbath	villainage	campestral	computable	homeopathy	lumpsucker
silverfish	villainess	camphorate	computator	homiletics	lymphocyte
silverside	villainous	comanchero	comstocker	homocercal	lymphomata
silverware	villanelle	combustion	cumbersome	homoeopath	mamillated
silverweed	villeinage	combustive	cumbrously	homogamous	membership
solacement	volatilise	comedienne	cummerbund	homogenise	membranous

memorandum	simoniacal	annoyingly	cinquefoil	consistent	dendrology
mimeograph	simpleness	annularity	concentric	consistory	denegation
mumbojumbo	simplicity	annulation	conception	consociate	denigrator
nambypamby	simplifier	annunciate	conceptive	consolable	denominate
namelessly	simplistic	banderilla	conceptual	consonance	denotation
nematocyst	simulacrum	bandmaster	concerning	consonancy	denotative
nimbleness	simulation	banishment	concertina	consortium	denouement
nominalism	simulative	bankruptcy	concertino	conspectus	densimeter
nominalist	simulatory	benedicite	concession	conspiracy	dentifrice
nominately	somatology	Benedictus	concessive	conspirant	denudation
nomination	somatotype	benefactor	concettism	constantan	denunciate
nominative	sombreness	beneficent	conchoidal	Constantia	diningroom
nomography	somersault	beneficial	conchology	constantly	dinnerless
nomologist	somniloquy	benevolent	conciliary	constipate	donkeywork
nomothetic	somnolence	benignancy	conciliate	constitute	donnybrook
numberless	somnolency	Benthamism	concinnity	constraint	dunderhead
numeration	summerlike	Benthamite	conclusion	constringe	dungbeetle
numerology	summertime	benzocaine	conclusive	consuetude	duniwassal
numerosity	summitless	benzpyrene	conclusory	consulship	dynamistic
numerously	summonable	binaurally	concoction	consultant	fanaticise
numismatic	symbolical	binoculars	concoctive	consulting	fanaticism
nympholept	symboliser	bondholder	concordant	consultive	fancifully
ommatidium	symmetrise	boneheaded	concretely	consumable	fandangoes
osmeterium	sympathise	bonesetter	concretion	consumedly	fantastico
osmiridium	symphonion	boneshaker	concretise	consummate	fantoccini
pemphigoid	symphonist	bunchgrass	concretist	contagious	fenestella
pemphigous	symphylous	bunglingly	concurrent	contendent	fenestrate
Pomeranian	symphyseal	canaliculi	concurring	contention	fingerbowl
pomiferous	symphysial	cancellate	concussion	contestant	fingerless
pomologist	symposiast	cancelling	concurring	contextual	fingerling
pummelling	tamability	cancellous	concussive	contexture	fingermark
ramblingly	tambourine	candelabra	condensate	contiguity	fingernail
rampageous	temperable	candescent	condensery	contiguous	fingerpost
ramshackle	temperance	candidness	condescend	continence	finicality
remarkable	temperedly	candlefish	condolence	contingent	finiteness
remarkably	temporally	candletree	conduction	continuant	FinnoUgric
remarriage	temporalty	candlewick	conductive	continuate	fontanelle
remediable	temporiser	candlewood	confabbing	continuity	functional
remedially	temptation	candyfloss	confection	continuous	funereally
remediless	temptingly	cankerworm	conference	contortion	fungicidal
remissible	timberhead	cannelloni	conferment	contortive	funnelling
remissness	timberline	cannonball	conferring	contraband	ganglionic
remittance	timbertoes	canonicals	confervoid	contrabass	gangrenous
remodelled	timberwolf	canonicate	confession	contractor	generalise
remonetise	timberwork	canonicity	confidante	contradict	generalist
remorseful	timbrology	canorously	confidence	contraprop	generality
remoteness	timekeeper	cantaloupe	confirmand	contrarily	generation
remunerate	timelessly	cantatrice	confiscate	contravene	generative
Romanesque	timeliness	canterbury	conflation	contribute	generatrix
Romanistic	timesaving	cantilever	confluence	contritely	generosity
ruminantly	timeserver	cantillate	conformism	contrition	generously
rumination	timocratic	cantonment	conformist	controlled	geneticist
ruminative	timorously	canvasback	conformity	controller	genialness
rumrunning	tomfoolery	canvaswork	confounded	controvert	geniculate
samarskite	tomography	canzonetta	confusedly	convalesce	genteelism
semeiology	tumbledown	censorious	congeneric	convection	gentilesse
semeiotics	tumblerful	censorship	congenital	convective	gentlefolk
semestrial	tumbleweed	censurable	congestion	convenable	gentleness
semiannual	tumescence	centennial	congestive	convenance	gingerbeer
semichorus	tumultuary	centesimal	conglobate	convenient	gingersnap
semicircle	tumultuous	centigrade	congregant	convention	gingivitis
semidivine	tympanites	centilitre	congregate	conventual	goniometer
semidouble	tympanitic	centillion	congruence	convergent	goniometry
semidrying	tympanitis	centimetre	congruency	conversant	gunfighter
semifitted	unmannerly	centralise	coniferous	conversely	gunrunning
semiliquid	unmeasured	centralism	conjecture	conversion	gunslinger
semilunate	unmeetness	centralist	conjointly	conveyable	gynandrous
seminarian	unmerciful	centrality	conjugally	conveyance	gynocratic
seminarist	unmorality	centreback	connatural	conviction	handbarrow
semination	unmortised	centrefold	connection	convictive	handedness
semiopaque	vomitorium	centrehalf	connective	convincing	handgallop
semiotical	wampumpeag	centricity	conniption	convoluted	handicraft
semiquaver	womanishly	centrifuge	connivance	convulsant	handmaiden
semiuncial	abnegation	centromere	conscience	convulsion	handpicked
semiweekly	abnormally	centrosome	consecrate	convulsive	handselled
semiyearly	annalistic	cinchonine	consectary	cunctation	handsomely
sempstress	annexation	Cinderella	consensual	cunctative	handspring
similarity	annihilate	cinecamera	consequent	denaturant	handworked
similitude	annotation	cinerarium	considered	dendriform	hangglider

apolaustic	clothespeg	flosculous	ironworker	proctorial	prosthetic
apolitical	clothespin	flowergirl	isochronal	proctorise	prostitute
Apollinian	cloudberry	flowerless	isodynamic	procumbent	prostomial
Apollonian	cloudburst	footballer	isogenetic	procurable	prostomium
apologetic	cloudiness	footbridge	isoglossal	procurance	protanopic
apophthegm	clovehitch	footcandle	isolatable	procurator	protection
apoplectic	cloverleaf	footlights	isometrics	prodigally	protective
aposematic	clownishly	footwarmer	isomorphic	prodigious	protectory
apostatise	coolheaded	froghopper	isoniazide	producible	protectrix
apostolate	coolingoff	frolicking	isopterous	production	proteiform
apostrophe	cooperator	frolicsome	isoseismal	productive	proteinous
apothecary	cooptation	frontbench	isosporous	profession	protensive
apothecial	cooptative	frontwards	isothermal	proficient	proteolyse
apothecium	coordinate	frostiness	jeopardise	profitable	protestant
apotheoses	crocoisite	frothiness	knobkerrie	profitably	prothallia
apotheosis	crossbench	frowningly	knockabout	profitless	prothallus
apotropaic	crossbones	geocentric	knockkneed	profligacy	protophyta
atomically	crossbreed	geochemist	knopkierie	profligate	protophyte
avouchment	crosscheck	geodetical	knottiness	profoundly	protoplasm
biochemist	crossgrain	geognostic	kookaburra	profundity	protoplast
biodegrade	crosshatch	geographer	Kuomintang	progenitor	prototypal
biodynamic	crossindex	geographic	leopardess	proglottis	prototypic
bioecology	crosslight	geological	lionhunter	prognathic	protracted
biogenesis	crosspatch	geometrise	loosecover	prognostic	protractor
biogenetic	crosspiece	geophysics	lyophilise	programmer	protreptic
biographer	crossrefer	geoponical	moonflower	prohibiter	protrusile
biographic	crossroads	geothermal	moonshiner	prohibitor	protrusion
biological	crosstrees	geothermic	moonstruck	projectile	protrusive
biometrics	crowkeeper	geotropism	myocardium	projection	proudflesh
biomorphic	deodoriser	globularly	myological	projective	provenance
biophysics	deontology	glomerular	myopically	prolicidal	proverbial
bioscience	deoxidiser	glomerulus	neoclassic	prolocutor	providence
blockboard	doorkeeper	gloominess	neological	prologuise	provincial
blockhouse	droopingly	gloriously	neoplastic	prolongate	provisions
blockishly	drophammer	glossarial	noogenesis	promenader	provitamin
bloodguilt	drosophila	glossarist	odontalgia	promethium	provocator
bloodhound	drowsihead	glossiness	odontology	prominence	proximally
bloodiness	drowsiness	glossology	omophagous	promissory	Ptolemaist
bloodmoney	duodecimal	glottology	orogenesis	promontory	reorganise
bloodstain	duodenitis	gnosticism	orogenetic	promptbook	rhodophane
bloodstock	ecological	goodliness	orographic	promptness	rhomboidal
bloodstone	economical	goodlooker	orological	promulgate	rhomboidei
blottesque	economiser	goodygoody	orotundity	pronominal	roodscreen
bookbinder	egocentric	gooseberry	Phoenician	pronounced	roofgarden
bookkeeper	egoistical	gooseflesh	phonematic	pronouncer	rootedness
bookmaking	elongation	goosegrass	phonically	proofsheet	scoffingly
bookmarker	eloquently	groceteria	phonograph	propagable	scoreboard
bookseller	emollition	grogginess	phonolitic	propaganda	scoresheet
boondoggle	enormously	groundbait	phonologic	propagator	scornfully
bootlegger	erotically	groundless	phonometer	propellant	scorzonera
bootlessly	erotogenic	groundling	phosphatic	propellent	Scotswoman
bootlicker	erotomania	groundmass	phosphoric	propelling	Scotticism
bootstraps	evolvement	groundplan	phosphorus	propensity	Scottceism
broadcloth	exobiology	groundrent	photoflood	properness	shockingly
broadsheet	exorbitant	groundsman	photogenic	propertied	shockproof
broadsword	exospheric	groundwork	photograph	prophesier	shoddiness
brocatelle	exoterical	grovelling	photolitho	prophetess	shoebuckle
brokendown	exothermal	growlingly	photolysis	propionate	shoestring
brokenness	exothermic	heortology	photolytic	propitiate	shopkeeper
bromegrass	exotically	hookedness	photometer	propitious	shoplifter
bronchiole	floatation	hootenanny	photometry	proportion	shopsoiled
bronchitic	floatboard	iconoclasm	photonasty	propounder	shopwalker
bronchitis	floatingly	iconolater	photophily	propraetor	shopwindow
broodiness	floatplane	iconolatry	photophore	proprietor	shoreleave
broodingly	floatstone	iconomachy	photoprint	propulsion	shorewards
broomstick	flocculate	iconometer	phototaxis	propulsive	shortbread
browbeaten	flocculent	iconometry	phototrope	propylaeum	shortcrust
brownshirt	floodlight	iconoscope	ploddingly	prosaicism	shortdated
brownstone	floodwater	idolatress	ploughable	proscenium	shortening
caoutchouc	floorboard	idolatrous	ploughland	prosciutto	shortlived
choiceness	floorcloth	inoculable	procedural	proscriber	shortrange
chokeberry	floppiness	inoculator	proceeding	prosecutor	shouldered
chondritic	florentine	inoperable	procession	prosilient	shovelhead
choriambic	florescent	inordinate	proclaimer	prosodical	shovelling
clodhopper	floriation	inosculate	proclivity	prospector	showerbath
cloistered	floribunda	ironhanded	procreator	prospectus	showjumper
closestool	floridness	ironically	procrypsis	prosperity	showwindow
closetplay	florilegia	ironmaster	procryptic	prosperous	sloppiness
clothesbag	floristics	ironmonger	proctorage	prosthesis	slothfully

slowfooted	thornproof	appearance	depuration	hyperbolae	imprudence
slowmotion	thoroughly	appeasable	depurative	hyperbolas	impudently
slowwitted	thoughtful	appendices	deputation	hyperbolic	impudicity
smockfrock	thousandth	appendixes	diphtheria	hyperdulia	impugnable
smokedried	toothbrush	apperceive	diphtheric	hypergolic	impugnment
smokehouse	toothiness	appetising	diphyletic	hypersonic	impuissant
smokeplant	toothpaste	appetitive	diphyodont	hyphenated	impureness
smokeproof	toothshell	applicable	diplodocus	hypnagogic	imputation
smokestack	trochanter	applicably	diplomatic	hypnotiser	imputative
smoothbore	trochoidal	applicator	dipsomania	hypocorism	Japanesque
smoothness	troctolite	appointive	duplicator	hypodermal	laparotomy
smorrebrod	troglodyte	appositely	empanelled	hypodermic	lapidarian
snobbishly	trolleybus	apposition	emparadise	hypodermis	lapidarist
snobocracy	trollopish	appositive	empathetic	hypogynous	lapidation
snootiness	trombonist	appreciate	emphractic	hypolimnia	lepidolite
snowcapped	tromometer	apprentice	empiricism	hypophyses	leprechaun
snowgrcuse	tropaeolum	approvable	empiricist	hypophysis	Lipizzaner
snowmobile	trophology	approvably	employable	hypostasis	lipography
snowplough	tropically	asparagine	employment	hypostatic	lipomatous
soothingly	tropologic	aspergilla	espadrille	hypotactic	Lippizaner
soothsayer	tropopause	asphyxiant	especially	hypotenuse	lipreading
spodomancy	tropophyte	asphyxiate	euphonious	hypotheses	lipservice
spoilsport	Trotskyism	aspidistra	euphuistic	hypothesis	lophophore
spokeshave	Trotskyist	aspiration	expandable	hypsometer	lopsidedly
spoliation	Trotskyite	baptistery	expansible	hypsometry	Lupercalia
spoliative	troubadour	biparietal	expatriate	impairment	mopishness
spoliatory	trousseaux	bipartisan	expectance	impalement	naphthenic
spongecake	trouvaille	bipetalous	expectancy	impalpable	nepenthean
spongewood	trowelling	bipolarity	expectedly	impalpably	nephograph
spongiform	twowheeler	capability	expedience	impanation	nephoscope
sponginess	ulotrichan	capacitate	expediency	impanelled	nephralgia
spongology	unoccupied	capacitive	expedition	imparadise	nephridium
sponsorial	unofficial	capitalise	expendable	impartible	nephrology
spookiness	unorthodox	capitalism	experience	impartment	nipplewort
spoondrift	urochordal	capitalist	experiment	impassable	nuptiality
spoonerism	utopianism	capitation	expertness	impassably	oppilation
sporangial	uxoricidal	Capitoline	expiration	impassible	opposeless
sporangium	uxoriously	capitulary	expiratory	impassibly	oppositely
sporophore	violaceous	capitulate	explicable	impatience	opposition
sporophyll	wholesaler	cappuccino	explicitly	impeccable	oppression
sporophyte	whomsoever	capricious	exploitage	impeccably	oppressive
sportfully	whorehouse	captiously	exploitive	impeccancy	opprobrium
sportiness	woodcarver	cephalopod	exportable	impediment	oppugnancy
sportingly	woodcutter	coparcener	exposition	impendence	orphanhood
sportively	woodenhead	copartnery	expositive	impendency	papaverine
sportswear	woodenness	Copernican	expository	impenitent	papaverous
spotlessly	woodlander	copesettic	expressage	imperative	paperchase
spottiness	woodpecker	copperhead	expression	imperially	paperknife
stochastic	woodpigeon	coproducer	expressive	imperilled	papermaker
stockiness	woodturner	coprolitic	expressway	impersonal	papistical
stockpiler	woodworker	copulation	exprobrate	impervious	papyrology
stockproof	woolgather	copulative	expunction	impishness	peppercorn
stockrider	woolgrower	copyholder	expurgator	implacable	peppermill
stockstill	woolliness	copyreader	gypsophila	implacably	peppermint
stodginess	woolsorter	copywriter	heparinise	implicitly	pepperwort
stolidness	wrongdoing	dapplegrey	hepatology	impolitely	piperidine
stomachful	wrongfully	department	heptachord	importable	popularise
stomatitis	wrongously	dependable	heptagonal	importance	popularity
stomatopod	zoological	dependably	Heptameron	importuner	population
stomodaeum	zoomorphic	dependence	heptameter	imposingly	populistic
stoneblind	zoophagous	dependency	heptarchic	imposition	populously
stoneborer	zoophilous	depilation	Heptateuch	impossible	pupilarity
stonebrash	alpenstock	depilatory	heptatonic	impossibly	pupiparous
stonefruit	alphabetic	deplorable	hippocampi	imposthume	rapporteur
stonemason	alphameric	deplorably	Hippocrene	impotently	repairable
stonesnipe	ampelopsis	deployment	hippodrome	impoverish	reparation
stopvolley	amphibious	depolarise	hippogriff	impregnant	reparative
storehouse	amphibrach	depopulate	hippogryph	impregnate	repatriate
storksbill	amphictyon	deportment	hippomanes	impresario	repealable
stormbound	amphigouri	depositary	hippophagy	impression	repeatable
stormcloud	amphimacer	deposition	hipsterism	impressive	repeatedly
storminess	amphimixes	depository	hopelessly	imprimatur	repellance
stormproof	amphimixis	depravedly	hypabyssal	imprinting	repellancy
swordcraft	amphoteric	depreciate	hypaethral	improbable	repellence
sworddance	amputation	depredator	hypanthium	improbably	repellency
swordgrass	apparelled	depressant	hyperaemia	improperly	repertoire
swordstick	apparently	depression	hyperaemic	improvable	repetiteur
thornapple	apparition	depressive	hyperbaric	improvably	repetition
thorniness	appealable	deprivable	hyperbaton	improviser	

horsewoman	narcolepsy	perihelion	pyromaniac	strabismus	threnodial
hurdygurdy	narrowness	perilously	pyromantic	strabotomy	threnodist
hurlyburly	northbound	periodical	pyrometric	straighten	thriftless
irradiance	northerner	periosteal	pyrophoric	straightly	throatwort
irradicate	northwards	periosteum	pyrotechny	strainedly	thromboses
irrational	nurseryman	peripeteia	pyroxenite	straitness	thrombosis
irrelative	parabiosis	peripheral	Pyrrhonian	stramonium	thrombotic
irrelevant	parabiotic	peripteral	Pyrrhonism	strategist	throneless
irreligion	parabolise	periscopic	Pyrrhonist	strathspey	throughout
irresolute	paraboloid	perishable	pyrrhotite	stratiform	throughput
irreverent	paradisaic	perithecia	reredorter	stratocrat	throughway
irrigation	paradisean	peritoneal	sarcolemma	strawberry	throwstick
irritation	paradisiac	peritoneum	sarcophagi	strawboard	thruppence
irritative	paradisian	periwigged	sarcophagy	streamless	tirailleur
jardiniere	paradoxure	periwinkle	sarcoplasm	streamline	tirelessly
jargonelle	paraffinic	perjurious	sargassoes	streetdoor	tiresomely
jerrybuilt	paragnosis	permafrost	sarmentose	streetward	tiringroom
juristical	paralipsis	permanence	sarmentous	strengthen	torchlight
karyoplasm	paralogise	permanency	sarracenia	stressless	toroidally
keratinise	paralogism	permeation	scrapmetal	strictness	torpidness
keratinous	paramecium	permeative	scratchily	stridently	torrential
kerchieves	parametric	permission	scratchwig	stridulant	torridness
kerseymere	paramnesia	permissive	screechowl	stridulate	tortellini
kerygmatic	paranormal	permitting	screenings	stridulous	tortfeasor
lardydardy	paraphrase	permutable	screenplay	strikingly	tortiously
largescale	paraphrast	pernicious	screwplate	stringbean	tortuosity
larvicidal	paraplegia	pernickety	screwpress	stringency	tortuously
laryngitic	paraplegic	peroration	scribbling	stringendo	turbidness
laryngitis	parapodium	peroxidise	scrimmager	stringhalt	turbulence
lordliness	paraselene	perpetrate	scrimshank	stringless	turbulency
maraschino	parasitism	perpetuate	scriptoria	striptease	turgescent
marcescent	parasitoid	perpetuity	scriptural	Stroganoff	turgidness
Marcionite	paratactic	perplexity	scrofulous	stromatous	turkeycock
marginalia	paratroops	perquisite	scrollwork	stronghold	turnbuckle
marginally	parcelling	persecutor	scrupulous	strongroom	turpentine
marginated	pardonable	persiflage	scrutineer	structural	turtleback
margravate	pardonably	persistent	scrutinise	structured	turtledove
margravine	parenchyma	personable	SerboCroat	struthious	turtleneck
marguerite	parentally	personally	sereneness	strychnine	tyrannical
Mariolater	parenteral	personally	sergeantcy	strychnism	Tyrrhenian
Mariolatry	parenthood	personator	serigraphy	surefooted	unravelled
marionette	parimutuel	persuasion	seriocomic	suretyship	unreadable
marketable	parliament	persuasive	serjeantcy	surfactant	unredeemed
markethall	Parnassian	pertinence	sermoniser	surgically	unreliable
markettown	paronymous	pertinency	serologist	surmisable	unrelieved
markswoman	paroxysmal	perversely	serotinous	surplusage	unremarked
marquisate	paroxytone	perversion	serpentine	surprising	unrequited
marrowbone	parramatta	perversity	serradilla	surrealism	unreserved
marrowless	parricidal	perversive	serviceman	surrealist	unresolved
marshalled	parrotfish	phrasebook	servomotor	survivance	unripeness
marshaller	parsonbird	phrenology	shrewdness	taradiddle	unrivalled
marshalsea	parsonical	porismatic	shrewishly	tarantella	unruliness
marshiness	partiality	pornocracy	shrewmouse	tarantelle	uproarious
martensite	participle	porousness	shrievalty	tardigrade	varicocele
martialism	particular	porraceous	shrillness	tarmacadam	varicosity
martingale	parturient	portamento	shrinkable	Tartuffian	variegated
marvelling	percentage	portcullis	shrinkwrap	Tartuffism	varietally
marvellous	percentile	portentous	shrivelled	teratogeny	variolitic
mercantile	perception	portliness	shroudlaid	teratology	variometer
mercifully	perceptive	Portuguese	shroudless	teratomata	verandahed
meridional	perceptual	purblindly	Shrovetide	termagancy	verbaliser
merrymaker	perchloric	puristical	skrimshank	terminable	verifiable
miraculous	percipient	puritanise	Sorbonnist	terminably	vermicelli
mirthfully	percolator	puritanism	sordidness	terminally	vermicidal
moralistic	percussion	purposeful	sororicide	terminator	vermicular
moratorium	percussive	purseproud	sprightful	termitaria	vernacular
morbidezza	perdurable	pursership	springhalt	terneplate	vernissage
morbidness	perdurably	purseseine	springhead	terracotta	versicular
mordacious	peremptory	pursuivant	springless	terreplein	vertebrate
morganatic	perfection	purtenance	springlike	terrorless	vertically
moroseness	perfective	purulently	springtail	threadbare	viraginous
morphemics	perfidious	purveyance	springtide	threadfish	virescence
morphinism	perfoliate	pyracantha	springtime	threadmark	virginally
morphogeny	perforator	pyretology	springwood	threadworm	virginhood
morphology	performing	pyridoxine	sprinkling	threatener	virologist
morrispike	periclinal	pyrogallol	sprucebeer	threepence	virtuality
myrtaceous	pericyclic	pyrogenous	spruceness	threepenny	virtueless
narcissism	peridermal	pyrography	strabismal	threepiece	virtuosity
narcissist	perigynous	pyrolusite	strabismic	threescore	virtuously

virulently	assumption	despiteous	dispelling	festoonery	listlessly
vortically	assumptive	despondent	dispensary	fishcarver	lossleader
vorticella	auscultate	desquamate	dispersant	fisherfolk	lusciously
vorticular	auspicious	destructor	dispersion	fishkettle	Lusitanian
wardenship	austenitic	disability	dispersive	fishmonger	lustration
warmingpan	Australian	disappoint	dispersoid	fisticuffs	lustreless
werewolves	basketball	disapprove	dispirited	fosterling	lustrously
Wertherian	basketwork	disarrange	dispiteous	fusibility	Lysenkoism
Wertherism	bassethorn	disastrous	disposable	fussbudget	masquerade
wiredrawer	bassoonist	disbarring	dispossess	fustanella	Massoretic
wirehaired	bastardise	disbelieve	dispraiser	gasconader	mastectomy
wirepuller	besprinkle	disbudding	disputable	gaslighter	masterhand
wiretapper	bestialise	disburthen	disputably	gaspereaux	masterhood
wirewalker	bestiality	discerning	disqualify	gasteropod	masterless
wireworker	bestirring	discharger	disquieten	gastrology	mastermind
wordlessly	bestowment	discipline	disquietly	gastronome	mastership
workbasket	bestridden	disclaimer	disrespect	gastronomy	masterwork
workingman	bestseller	disclosure	disruption	gesundheit	masticable
workpeople	bisexually	discobolus	disruptive	hesitantly	masticator
worldclass	bissextile	discomfort	dissatisfy	hesitation	mesenteric
worldweary	bisulphate	discommend	dissection	hesitative	mesenteron
worshipful	bisulphide	discommode	dissembler	histologic	mesmeriser
worshipped	bisulphite	discompose	dissension	histolysis	Mesolithic
worshipper	Boswellian	disconcert	dissertate	histolytic	mesomerism
worthiness	Boswellism	disconfirm	disservice	historical	mesomorphy
worthwhile	Boswellism	disconnect	dissidence	histrionic	mesophytic
xerography	bushmaster	discontent	dissilient	hospitable	mesoscaphe
xerophytic	bushranger	discophile	dissimilar	hospitably	mesosphere
yarborough	bustlingly	discordant	dissipated	hostelling	mesothorax
yardmaster	byssaceous	discounter	dissociate	husbandage	messianism
abscission	byssinosis	discourage	dissoluble	husbandman	misaligned
absolutely	cascarilla	discourser	dissolvent	hysteresis	misbelieve
absolution	caseharden	discoverer	dissonance	hysteretic	miscellany
absolutism	caseworker	discreetly	dissonancy	hysterical	mischanter
absolutist	cassolette	discrepant	dissuasion	insaneness	mischmetal
absolutory	castration	discretely	dissuasive	insanitary	misconduct
absorbable	casualness	discretion	distensile	insatiable	miscreance
absorbance	cessionary	discursive	distension	insatiably	misericord
absorbedly	cismontane	discussant	distention	insecurely	misfortune
absorbency	cispontine	discussion	distichous	insecurity	misgivings
absorption	Cistercian	discussive	distilland	inseminate	mishitting
absorptive	cosentient	discutient	distillate	insensible	misjoinder
abstemious	cosmically	disdainful	distillery	insensibly	mismatched
abstention	cosmogonic	diseconomy	distilling	insentient	mismeasure
abstergent	cosmopolis	disembogue	distinctly	insightful	misnomered
abstersion	cosmoramic	disembosom	distortion	insinuator	misogamist
abstersive	costliness	disembowel	distracted	insipidity	misogynist
abstinence	cuspidated	disembroil	distrainer	insistence	misogynous
abstinency	cussedness	disenchant	distrainor	insistency	misologist
abstracted	custommade	disengaged	distraught	insobriety	misprision
abstracter	cystoscope	disenthral	distressed	insociable	missionary
abstractly	cystoscopy	disentitle	distribute	insolation	missionise
abstractor	desalinate	disentwine	distringas	insolently	mistakable
abstrusely	descendant	disenviron	disulphate	insolvable	mistakenly
abstrusity	descendent	disfeature	disulphide	insolvency	misthought
absurdness	descension	disfurnish	disutility	insouciant	misventure
adsorbable	descriptor	disgruntle	disyllabic	inspanning	miswording
adsorption	desecrater	disgustful	disyllable	inspection	mosaically
adsorptive	desecrator	dishabille	dosimetric	inspective	mosaicking
aesthetics	deservedly	disharmony	dustjacket	inspirator	mosasaurus
aesthetism	deshabille	dishearten	dysenteric	inspissate	mosquitoes
answerable	desiccator	dishonesty	dysgraphia	instalment	mossbunker
answerably	desiderata	dishwasher	dysplastic	instigator	muscularly
assafetida	desiderate	disincline	dysprosium	instilling	musicality
assailable	designator	disinherit	dystrophic	institutor	musicianly
assaultive	designedly	disjointed	easterling	instructor	musicology
assemblage	designment	dislikable	Eastertide	instrument	musicpaper
assentient	desipience	disloyally	eisteddfod	insufflate	musicstand
assessable	desirously	disloyalty	ensanguine	insularism	musicstool
assessment	desistance	dismalness	eosinophil	insularity	muskmallow
asseverate	desolately	dismission	essayistic	insulation	Mussulmans
assibilate	desolation	dismissive	exsanguine	insurgence	mystagogic
assignable	desorption	disordered	fasciation	insurgency	mystagogue
assignment	despatcher	disorderly	fascicular	jasperware	mysterious
assimilate	desperados	disownment	fasciculus	jesuitical	mystically
assistance	despicable	disparager	fascinator	justiciary	nasturtium
associable	despicably	disparates	fastidious	lasciovius	nosography
assoilment	despisable	dispassion	fastigiate	lesbianism	nosologist
assortment	despiteful	dispatcher	fescennine	lissomness	nosophobia

nostologic	respective	viscountcy	antisocial	bitterness	enterotomy
obsequious	respirable	visibility	antistatic	bitterroot	enterprise
observable	respirator	Visigothic	antitheism	bitterwood	enthralled
observably	respondent	visionally	antitheist	bituminise	enthusiasm
observance	responsive	visionless	antitheses	bituminous	enthusiast
obstetrics	responsory	visitation	antithesis	bothersome	enticement
obstructor	restaurant	visitorial	antithetic	botryoidal	enticingly
oesophagus	restlessly	visualiser	antonymous	bottlefeed	entireness
oysterfarm	restorable	wassailing	arterially	bottleneck	entombment
pasquinade	restrained	wastefully	arteriolar	bottletree	entomology
passageway	restrainer	wastepaper	artfulness	bottomless	entrancing
passionary	resultless	westernise	arthralgia	bottommost	entrapment
passionate	resumption	westwardly	arthralgic	butterball	estimation
Passionist	resumptive	wishywashy	arthromere	butterbean	estimative
pasteboard	resupinate	yesteryear	articulate	butterfish	euthanasia
pastellist	resurgence	actinolite	artificial	buttermilk	extemporal
pasteurise	risibility	actinozoan	artycrafty	butterwort	extendedly
pasteurism	rosaniline	actionable	asteriated	buttonball	extendible
pastmaster	rosechafer	actionably	asteroidal	buttonbush	extensible
pastorally	roseengine	activation	astigmatic	buttondown	extenuator
pastorship	roselipped	activeness	astragalus	buttonhole	exteriorly
pastrycook	rosemallow	Aethiopian	astringent	buttonhook	externally
pasturable	Russianise	aetiologic	astrologer	buttonless	extinction
pastyfaced	Russophile	afterbirth	astrologic	buttonwood	extinctive
pesticidal	Russophobe	aftergrass	astronomer	catabolism	extinguish
pestilence	rustically	afterimage	astronomic	catafalque	extirpator
piscifauna	sashwindow	afterlight	astuteness	catalectic	extractant
pistillary	sestertium	afterpains	attachable	cataleptic	extraction
pistillate	sestertius	aftershave	attachment	cataloguer	extractive
pistolling	sisterhood	aftertaste	attackable	cataphract	extramural
pistolshot	susceptive	afterwards	attainable	catarrhine	extraneity
pistolwhip	suspenders	altarpiece	attainment	catastasis	extraneous
pistonring	suspension	altazimuth	attendance	catburglar	extricable
positional	suspensive	alteration	attenuated	catchpenny	fatalistic
positively	suspensoid	alterative	attenuator	catechesis	fatherhood
positivism	suspensory	alternance	attornment	catechetic	fatherland
positivist	suspicious	alternator	attractant	catechiser	fatherless
positivity	sustaining	altocumuli	attraction	catechumen	fatherlike
possession	sustenance	altogether	attractive	categorise	fathership
possessive	sustention	altostrati	attunement	catenation	fathomable
possessory	sustentive	altruistic	autarkical	catholicon	fathomless
postbellum	systematic	antagonise	autecology	catholicos	fatiguable
postchaise	systemless	antagonism	authorship	catoptrics	fetchingly
postexilic	taskmaster	antagonist	autochthon	cattlegrid	fetterlock
posthumous	tasselling	antebellum	autocratic	citronella	fitfulness
postillion	tastefully	antecedent	autodidact	cottoncake	futureless
postliminy	tessellate	antecessor	autoerotic	cottonseed	futuristic
postmaster	testaceous	antechapel	autogamous	cottontail	futurology
postmortem	testflight	antemortem	autogenous	cottonweed	gatekeeper
postoffice	unscalable	antependia	autography	cottonwood	gatelegged
postpartum	unschooled	antepenult	autoimmune	cottonwool	gothically
postscript	unscramble	anteriorly	autologous	cuttlebone	gutturally
postulator	unscreened	antheridia	automation	cuttlefish	heterodont
pushbutton	unscripted	anthracene	automatise	cuttystool	heterodoxy
rescission	unseasoned	anthracite	automatism	cytochrome	heterodyne
rescissory	unselected	anthracoid	automatist	cytologist	heterogamy
researcher	unsettling	anthropoid	automobile	datamation	heterogeny
resemblant	unsociable	antibiosis	automotive	detachable	heterogony
resentment	unsociably	antibiotic	autonomist	detachedly	heterology
reservedly	unsocially	Antichrist	autonomous	detachment	heteronomy
reshipment	unsporting	anticipant	autoplasty	detainment	heterotaxy
resignedly	unsteadily	anticipate	autostrada	detectable	hitchhiker
resilience	unstrained	anticlimax	autostrade	detergency	hithermost
resiliency	unstressed	anticlinal	autumnally	determined	hitherward
resistance	unsuitable	antifreeze	batfowling	deterrence	hotblooded
resistible	unswerving	antiheroic	batholitic	detestable	hotchpotch
resistless	upstanding	antimasque	bathometer	detestably	iatrogenic
resolutely	vascularly	antimatter	bathymeter	detonation	intactness
resolution	vasoactive	antimonial	bathymetry	detonative	intangible
resolutive	vesication	antimonite	bathyscaph	detoxicant	intangibly
resolvable	vesicatory	antimonian	bathyscope	detoxicate	integrable
resolvedly	vesiculate	antipathic	batrachian	detraction	integrally
resonantly	vesperbell	antiphonal	battailous	detractive	integrator
resorcinol	vespertine	antipodean	battledore	ditriglyph	integument
resorption	vestibular	antiproton	battlement	ectodermal	intendance
resorptive	vestibulum	antiquated	battleship	ectodermic	intendment
resounding	vestpocket	antiSemite	betterment	ectogenous	intenerate
respectful	viscerally	antisepsis	bitchiness	entailment	intentness
respecting	viscometer	antiseptic	bitterling	enterolith	interbreed

interceder	lithotrity	mythopoeia	outpouring	rottenness	witchingly
intercross	Lithuanian	mythopoeic	outputting	rottweiler	withdrawal
interested	litigation	natalitial	outrageous	ruthlessly	withdrawer
interferer	litterlout	natatorial	outrightly	satanology	withholder
interferon	littleness	natatorium	outrunning	satellitic	witnessbox
intergrade	liturgical	nationally	outsitting	satisfying	abundantly
interiorly	lotuseater	nationhood	outstation	saturation	Adullamite
interleave	lutestring	nationless	outstretch	saturnalia	adulterant
interloper	matchboard	nationwide	outswinger	satyagraha	adulterate
interlunar	matchmaker	nativeborn	outwitting	satyriasis	adulteress
intermarry	matchstick	nativeness	patchiness	setterwort	adulterine
intermezzi	materially	nativistic	patentable	settlement	adulterous
intermezzo	maternally	natterjack	paternally	sitophobia	aquafortis
internally	mathematic	naturalise	pathetical	tattletale	aquamarine
internment	matriarchy	naturalism	pathfinder	tetchiness	aquaplaner
internodal	matricidal	naturalist	pathogenic	tetrachord	aquiferous
internship	matronhood	naturopath	pathologic	tetragonal	aquilinity
interphase	matronship	nethermost	patination	tetrahedra	bluebonnet
interplant	matronymic	nettlerash	patisserie	tetrameter	bluebottle
interplead	maturation	nitpicking	patriality	tetramorph	bluecollar
interposal	maturative	nitrochalk	patriarchy	tetrapolis	bluejacket
interposer	matureness	nitrogroup	patriciate	tetrarchic	bluepencil
interregna	metabolise	notability	patricidal	tetrastich	blueribbon
interspace	metabolism	notarially	patrilocal	tetrastyle	bluethroat
interstate	metabolite	notchboard	patriotism	tetterwort	bluetongue
interstice	metacarpal	noteworthy	patristics	titanesque	bluishness
intertidal	metacarpus	noticeable	patrolling	titivation	blurringly
intertrigo	metacentre	noticeably	patronymic	tittupping	blushingly
intertwine	metagalaxy	notifiable	patulously	titubation	blusterous
intertwist	metalepsis	notionally	petiolated	totemistic	bouncingly
interurban	metallurgy	notonectal	petiteness	tutorially	bourbonism
intervener	metamerism	nutational	petitioner	ulteriorly	bourbonist
intervenor	metaphoric	nutcracker	petroglyph	ultimately	brusquerie
intervolve	metaphrase	nutritious	petrolatum	ultrabasic	causticity
interweave	metaphysic	obtainable	petronella	ultrasonic	cautionary
interwound	metaplasia	obtainment	petulantly	ultrasound	cautiously
interwoven	metastable	obtruncate	phthisical	unthinking	chubbiness
interzonal	metastases	obturation	pitchblack	untidiness	chuckerout
intestinal	metastasis	obtuseness	pitcherful	untowardly	chuckwagon
intimately	metastatic	octahedral	pitchstone	untroubled	churchgoer
intimation	metatarsal	octahedron	pitilessly	untruthful	churchyard
intimidate	metatarsus	octamerous	pityriasis	urticarial	churlishly
intinction	metatheses	octandrian	potability	urtication	clubfooted
intolerant	metathesis	octandrous	potamology	ustulation	clumsiness
intonation	metathetic	octodecimo	potbellied	Vaticanism	couchgrass
intoxicant	metathorax	octonarian	potentiate	Vaticanist	coulometry
intoxicate	metempiric	octopodous	potentilla	vaticinate	councillor
intramural	meteoritic	oftentimes	pothunting	veterinary	councilman
intraurban	methodical	ontologist	putatively	vitalistic	counselled
intrepidly	Methuselah	optatively	putrescent	vitaminise	counsellor
intrigante	methylated	optimalise	putrescine	vitiligate	counteract
intriguant	meticulous	optimistic	putridness	vitrescent	countryish
introducer	metrically	optionally	ratability	vitriolise	countryman
introrsely	metronomic	orthoclase	ratcatcher	vituperate	couplement
introspect	metronymic	orthodoxly	rationally	watchfully	courageous
intubation	metropolis	orthoepist	rattlehead	watchglass	courthouse
katabolism	mettlesome	orthogenic	rattlepate	watchguard	cousinhood
kettledrum	mithridate	orthogonal	rattletrap	watchmaker	cousinship
laterality	mitigation	orthopedic	retainable	watchtower	couturiere
latescence	mitigative	orthoptera	reticently	waterborne	couverture
latifundia	mitigatory	ostensible	reticulate	waterbrash	crustacean
lattermost	motherhood	ostensibly	retinacula	waterclock	crustation
letterbomb	motherland	osteoblast	retirement	watercraft	crustiness
letterbook	motherless	osteoclast	retiringly	watercress	daughterly
lettercard	mothership	osteopathy	retractile	waterflood	dauphiness
letterhead	motherwort	osteophyte	retraction	waterfront	doublebass
letterless	motionless	otterboard	retractive	waterglass	doubleness
literalise	motivation	ottershrew	retraining	wateriness	doublepark
literalism	motiveless	outbalance	retrochoir	watermelon	doubletalk
literalist	motorcycle	outbidding	retrograde	waterpower	doubletime
literality	mutability	outperwasp	retrogress	waterproof	doubtfully
literarily	mutilation	outfielder	retrorsely	waterskier	doubtingly
literation	mutinously	outfitting	retrospect	waterspout	doughfaced
literature	muttonhead	outgassing	returnable	watertight	drudgingly
lithoglyph	mythically	outgeneral	ritardando	waterwheel	drupaceous
lithograph	mythiciser	outgunning	ritornelli	waterworks	duumvirate
lithologic	mythologer	outlandish	ritornello	wattlebird	ebullience
lithophane	mythologic	outmeasure	rotational	witchcraft	ebulliency
lithophyte	mythomania	outpatient	rotisserie	witchhazel	ebullition

ecumenical	houseproud	sluttishly	youngberry	involucral	jawbreaker
edulcorate	housetrain	smudginess	yourselves	involucrum	Jewishness
elucidator	housewives	smuttiness	youthfully	involution	lawabiding
elutriator	inundation	snubbingly	adventurer	juvenility	lawbreaker
emulsifier	inundatory	snuffiness	advertence	lavalliere	lawfulness
enumerable	inurbanity	soubriquet	advertency	lavatorial	lawntennis
enumerator	jauntiness	soullessly	advertiser	lavishment	lawrencium
enunciable	journalese	soundboard	advisement	lavishness	Lawrentian
enunciator	journalise	soundingly	advocation	levigation	lowerclass
equability	journalism	soundproof	advocatory	levitation	lowpitched
equanimity	journalist	soundtrack	bivalvular	livelihood	lowprofile
equational	journeyman	sourcebook	bivouacked	liveliness	newfangled
equatorial	Krugerrand	sousaphone	cavalierly	livingroom	newsagency
equestrian	laughingly	souterrain	cavalryman	lovelessly	newscaster
equilibria	laundryman	southbound	cavitation	loveletter	newsletter
equipotent	lauraceous	southerner	covalently	loveliness	newsmonger
equitation	laureation	southernly	covariance	lovemaking	newsreader
equivalent	laurelling	southwards	covenanted	lovingness	newsvendor
equivocate	leucocytic	spumescent	covenantee	mavourneen	newsworthy
erubescent	leucoplast	spunkiness	covenanter	movability	newswriter
eructation	leukocytic	spuriously	covenantor	movelessly	pawnbroker
eruptively	loudhailer	squalidity	covetingly	moviemaker	powderhorn
exuberance	loungesuit	squamation	covetously	navigation	powderpuff
exulcerate	mouldboard	squanderer	Devanagari	nevernever	powerfully
exultantly	mouldiness	squareness	devilishly	novaculite	powerhouse
exultation	mountebank	squaresail	devitalise	novelistic	rewardable
exultingly	mournfully	squaretoed	devocalise	ravenously	rewardless
exurbanite	mousseline	squaretoes	devolution	ravishment	rowanberry
exuviation	moustached	squeezable	devotement	revalidate	sawtoothed
faultiness	moustachio	squeezebox	devotional	revalorise	sowthistle
feuilleton	Mousterian	squeteague	devoutness	revanchism	tawdriness
fluffiness	mouthorgan	squinteyed	divagation	revanchist	thwartship
flugelhorn	mouthpiece	squirarchy	divaricate	revealable	thwartwise
flunkeydom	nauseating	squirearch	divebomber	revealment	towardness
flunkeyism	nauseously	squirehood	divergence	revelation	toweringly
fluoridate	nautically	squireling	divergency	revelatory	townswoman
fluorinate	neurilemma	squireship	divestment	revengeful	unwariness
fluorotype	neurolemma	stubbiness	divination	reverencer	unwavering
fluviatile	neuropathy	stubbornly	divinatory	reverently	unwieldily
fluxionary	neuroplasm	studiously	divineness	reversible	unwontedly
foudroyant	neurotoxin	stuffiness	divisional	revertible	unworkable
foundation	neutralise	stumpiness	divisively	reviewable	unworthily
founderous	neutralism	stunningly	divulgence	revilement	unwrinkled
fourchette	neutralist	stupendous	dovecolour	revisional	upwardness
fourfooted	neutrality	stupidness	favourable	revitalise	dextrality
fourhanded	nourishing	sturdiness	favourably	revivalism	dextrously
Fourierism	pluckiness	tauntingly	feverishly	revivalist	doxography
fourinhand	plumassier	tauromachy	fivefinger	revocation	fixedpoint
fourleaved	plunderage	tautomeric	governable	revocatory	foxhunting
fourposter	plunderous	tautophony	governance	revolution	hexahedral
foursquare	pluperfect	thumbprint	governessy	riverhorse	hexahedron
fourstroke	plutocracy	thumbscrew	government	rovebeetle	hexamerous
fourteener	plutolatry	thumbstall	hoverplane	savageness	hexametric
fourteenth	pouncetbox	thunderbox	hovertrain	savourless	lexicology
fruitarian	pourparler	thundering	invaginate	seventieth	lexigraphy
fruitfully	prudential	thunderous	invalidate	severeness	loxodromic
frutescent	pruriently	touchiness	invalidism	vivandiere	luxuriance
gaucheness	reunionism	touchingly	invalidity	viviparity	maxilliped
gaultheria	reunionist	touchjudge	invaluable	viviparous	maximalist
gauntleted	roughhouse	touchpaper	invaluably	vivisector	mixedmedia
glumaceous	roughrider	touchstone	invariable	wavelength	mixolydian
gluttonise	roundabout	tourbillon	invariably	waveringly	myxomatous
gluttonous	roundhouse	tourmaline	invariance	bawdyhouse	myxomycete
grubbiness	rouseabout	tournament	inventress	bewitchery	pixillated
grudgingly	roustabout	tourniquet	inveracity	bowdlerise	saxicoline
gruesomely	sauerkraut	trucklebed	investment	bowdlerism	saxicolous
grumpiness	sculptress	truculence	inveteracy	cowcatcher	sexagenary
hauntingly	sculptural	truculency	inveterate	coweringly	Sexagesima
haustellum	sculptured	truncately	invigilate	cowparsley	sexivalent
haustorium	scurrility	truncation	invigorate	cowpuncher	sexlimited
heulandite	scurrilous	trundlebed	invincible	downfallen	sexologist
heuristics	scurviness	trustfully	invincibly	downstairs	sexpartite
hourcircle	scutellate	trustiness	inviolable	downstream	sextillion
houseagent	shuttering	trustingly	inviolably	downstroke	sixshooter
housebound	sluggardly	truthfully	invitation	downwardly	taxability
housecraft	sluggishly	usucaption	invitatory	enwrapping	taxidancer
houseguest	sluicegate	usuriously	invitingly	fowlplague	taxidermal
houselling	slumberful	usurpation	invocation	hawserlaid	taxidermic
houseplant	slumberous	vaudeville	invocatory	inwardness	taxonomist

```
textualist razorshell capacitive divaricate hexamerous legateship
texturally razzmatazz carabineer dreadfully hexametric ligamental
toxication suzerainty carabinier dreaminess humaneness limaciform
toxicology viziership caramelise dreamworld humanistic loganberry
toxiphobia ────────── caravaneer dreariness humanities loganstone
amygdaloid Abrahamman caravanned durability hypabyssal macadamise
amylaceous abrasively caravanner dynamistic hypaethral malacoderm
arytaenoid adjacently catabolism effaceable hypanthium malacology
asymmetric affability catafalque effacement idealistic maladapted
asymptotic alkalinity catalectic embalmment ideational malapertly
asynchrony almacanter cataleptic embankment illadvised malapropos
atypically altarpiece cataloguer embarkment illatively manageable
boyishness altazimuth cataphract empanelled illaudable manageably
bryologist ambassador catarrhine emparadise illaudably management
Clydesdale amiability catastasis empathetic immaculacy manageress
cryogenics Andalusian cavalierly encampment immaculate managerial
cryoscopic andalusite cavalryman encasement immaterial maraschino
cryptogamy annalistic cheapishly encashment immaturely megalithic
cryptogram antagonise cheapskate enfacement immaturity megalosaur
cryptology antagonism cicatrices engagement impairment megascopic
daydreamer antagonist clearstory engagingly impalement melancholy
drysaltery aphaereses cohabitant enharmonic impalpable Melanesian
Egyptology aphaeresis colatitude enjambment impalpably melanistic
erysipelas aplacental comanchero enlacement impanation menacingly
flycatcher apparelled coparcener ensanguine impanelled metabolise
flyfishing apparently copartnery entailment imparadise metabolism
flyswatter apparition coradicate equability impartible metabolite
glycolyses aquafortis coralberry equanimity impartment metacarpal
glycolysis aquamarine coralsnake equational impassable metacarpus
glycosuria aquaplaner covalently equatorial impassably metacentre
glycosuric arbalester covariance escadrille impassible metagalaxy
jaywalking arbalister creaminess escalation impassibly metalepsis
joyfulness Armageddon creatinine escallonia impatience metallurgy
joyousness ascariasis creatively escapement incandesce metamerism
keyboarder asparagine creativity escapology incantator metaphoric
mayblossom assafetida creaturely escarpment incapacity metaphrase
mayonnaise assailable curability espadrille incasement metaphysic
oxygenator assaultive curatorial essayistic incautious metaplasia
phylactery Athanasian damageable eucalyptol indagation metastable
phyllotaxy attachable damagingly eucalyptus infallible metastases
phylloxera attachment datamation eucaryotic infallibly metastasis
phylogenic attackable debasement excavation infamously metastatic
physically attainable debatement exhalation infarction metatarsal
physicking attainment debauchery exhaustion infatuated metatarsus
physiocrat autarkical decadently exhaustive inhabitant metatheses
physiology aviatrices decagramme expandable inhalation metathesis
phytogenic bigamously decahedral expansible inharmonic metathetic
phytophagy binaurally decahedron expatriate innateness metathorax
phytotoxic biparietal decampment exsanguine insaneness micaschist
psychiatry bipartisan decapitate fanaticise insanitary miraculous
psychicism bivalvular decapodous fanaticism insatiable misaligned
psychicist bizarrerie defacement fatalistic insatiably Mohammedan
psychology bleachable defalcator femaleness intactness monandrous
psychopath bleariness defamation filariasis intangible monarchial
rhythmical blearyeyed defamatory fleabitten intangibly Monarchian
scyphiform bleatingly delaminate fleacircus invaginate monarchism
scyphozoan breadboard demagogism fleamarket invalidate monarchist
skyjacking breadcrumb demandable floatation invalidism moralistic
skyscraper breadfruit denaturant floatboard invalidity moratorium
skywriting breadstick department floatingly invaluable mosaically
stylistics breadstuff deracinate floatplane invaluably mosaicking
stylograph breakables derailleur floatstone invariable mosasaurus
stypticity breakpoint derailment foraminous invariably movability
tryptophan breakwater desalinate freakiness invariance Muhammadan
unyielding breastbone detachable freakishly inwardness Muhammedan
voyageable breastwall detachedly friability irradiance mutability
bizarrerie breastwork detachment gelatinise irradicate natalitial
dazzlement breathable detainment gelatinous irrational natatorial
dazzlingly breathless Devanagari greasewood Japanesque natatorium
eczematous broadcloth didactical greasiness katabolism negatively
enzymology broadsheet dilapidate greatniece keratinise negativism
fuzzywuzzy broadsword dilatation greatuncle keratinous negativist
mizzenmast cabalistic dilatorily gynandrous Lamarckian negativity
mizzensail cadaverous disability gyrational Lamarckism nematocyst
mozzarella calamander disappoint harassment laparotomy nonaligned
pozzolanic calamitous disapprove heparinise lavalliere notability
pozzuolana canaliculi disarrange hepatology lavatorial notarially
puzzlement capability disastrous hexahedral lawabiding novaculite
razorblade capacitate divagation hexahedron legalistic nutational
```

```
oblateness  pyracantha  squaretoes  unravelled  halberdier  tribometer
obtainable  queasiness  steadiness  unwariness  harbourage  tribrachic
obtainment  ragamuffin  steakhouse  unwavering  herbaceous  tumbledown
occasional  ratability  stealthily  upwardness  hobbyhorse  tumblerful
oceanarium  recallable  steamchest  urbanology  hotblooded  tumbleweed
oceangoing  regalement  steaminess  vanadinite  humbleness  turbidness
oceanology  regardless  steamtight  venational  humbuggery  turbulence
octahedral  relational  strabismal  verandahed  humbugging  turbulency
octahedron  relatively  strabismic  viraginous  husbandage  unabridged
octamerous  relativise  strabismus  vitalistic  husbandman  verbaliser
octandrian  relativism  strabotomy  vitaminise  icebreaker  wobbliness
octandrous  relativist  straighten  vivandiere  jawbreaker  yarborough
oleaginous  relativity  straightly  vocabulary  jobbernowl  abacterial
ommatidium  relaxation  strainedly  vocational  keyboarder  abscission
optatively  remarkable  straitness  volatilise  kibbutznik  aficionado
ordainment  remarkably  stramonium  volatility  kimberlite  aircooling
organicism  remarriage  strategist  voyageable  knobkerrie  aircushion
organicist  renascence  strathspey  wheatstone  lambrequin  anacolutha
organismal  repairable  stratiform  womanishly  lawbreaker  anecdotage
ornamental  reparation  stratocrat  zabaglione  Leibnizian  anecdotist
ornateness  reparative  strawberry  anabaptism  lesbianism  apiculture
Palaeocene  repatriate  strawboard  anabaptist  lumberjack  apocalypse
Palaeogene  retainable  subacidity  babblement  lumberroom  apocarpous
palaeolith  revalidate  subaquatic  balbriggan  lumbersome  apochromat
palaeotype  revalorise  subaqueous  barbellate  lumberyard  apocryphal
Palaeozoic  revanchism  subaverage  barbershop  mayblossom  ausculate
palagonite  revanchist  sudatorium  barbituric  membership  aviculture
palatalise  rewardable  sugardaddy  bobbinlace  membranous  bacchantes
palatinate  rewardless  sugarhouse  bobbysocks  misbelieve  bacchantic
Panamanian  ritardando  sugariness  bobbysoxer  morbidezza  barcarolle
papaverine  Romanesque  sugarmaple  bombardier  morbidness  bedchamber
papaverous  Romanistic  sweatgland  borborygmi  mumbojumbo  bedclothes
parabiosis  rosaniline  sweatiness  bubblyjock  nambypamby  beechdrops
parabiotic  rotational  sweatshirt  bumblingly  nimbleness  biochemist
parabolise  rowanberry  sybaritism  carbonnade  numberless  bitchiness
paraboloid  salability  synaeresis  carboxylic  outbalance  blackamoor
paradisaic  salamander  synaloepha  carbuncled  outbidding  blackberry
paradisean  samarskite  synanthous  catburglar  pebbledash  blackboard
paradisiac  sanatorium  tamability  chubbiness  plebiscite  blackfaced
paradisian  satanology  taradiddle  clubfooted  potbellied  blackguard
paradoxure  savageness  tarantella  combustion  prebendary  blackheart
paraffinic  sciagraphy  tarantelle  combustive  purblindly  Blackshirt
paragnosis  scrapmetal  taxability  corbelling  rabbinical  blacksmith
paralipsis  scratchily  tenability  corbiculae  rabblement  blackthorn
paralogise  scratchwig  tenantable  cribriform  ramblingly  blackwater
paralogism  seaanemone  tenantless  cumbersome  redblooded  blockboard
paramecium  sedateness  teratogeny  cumbrously  ribbonfish  blockhouse
parametric  senatorial  teratology  diabolical  ribbonworm  blockishly
paramnesia  separately  teratomata  disbarring  rubberneck  brachiator
paranormal  separation  theatrical  disbelieve  sabbatical  brachiopod
paraphrase  separatism  thwartship  disbudding  scabrously  brachylogy
paraphrast  separatist  thwartwise  disburthen  seabiscuit  brachyural
paraplegia  separative  tiralliver  doublebass  SerboCroat  brachyuran
paraplegic  separatory  titanesque  doubleness  shabbiness  brickfield
parapodium  sexagenary  topazolite  doublepark  shibboleth  bricklayer
paraselene  Sexagesima  towardness  doubletalk  skibobbing  brocatelle
parasitism  sheabutter  treadboard  doubletime  snobbishly  buccinator
parasitoid  shearwater  treadwheel  doubtfully  snobocracy  bunchgrass
paratactic  sheathbill  treasonous  doubtingly  snubbingly  cacciatore
paratroops  sheathless  triacetate  dumbledore  sombreness  calcareous
pedagogics  skiagraphy  triandrous  dumbstruck  Sorbonnist  calceolate
pedalorgan  sleaziness  triangular  dumbwaiter  soubriquet  calceiferol
pedalpoint  sneakiness  tularaemia  edibleness  stabiliser  calcsinter
pheasantry  sneakingly  tularaemic  elaborator  stablemate  calculable
phrasebook  sneakthief  tyrannical  epiblastic  stableness  calculably
picaresque  solacement  unbalanced  erubescent  stubbiness  calculator
picayunish  somatology  uneasiness  exobiology  stubbornly  cancellate
pleadingly  somatotype  unfadingly  exuberance  symbolical  cancelling
pleasantly  speargrass  unfairness  feebleness  symboliser  cancellous
pleasantry  sphalerite  unfaithful  fimbriated  tambourine  carcinogen
pleasingly  splanchnic  unfamiliar  flabbiness  timberhead  carcinosis
pliability  splashback  unfathered  flabellate  timberline  cascarilla
pliantness  splashdown  unhallowed  forbidding  timbertoes  catchpenny
potability  squalidity  unhandsome  fumblingly  timberwolf  checkpoint
potamology  squamation  uniaxially  gambolling  timberwork  chickenpox
preachment  squanderer  unlabelled  Ghibelline  timbrology  chuckerout
preadamite  squareness  unlawfully  Gilbertian  trabeation  chuckwagon
prearrange  squaresail  unmannerly  globularly  trabeculae  cinchonine
putatively  squaretoed  unnameable  grubbiness  trabecular  Circassian
```

```
dendriform landlocked quadrivium windowless ancestress caseharden
dendrology landlubber quadrumana windowpane annexation caseworker
deodoriser landocracy quadrumane windowseat antebellum catechesis
disdainful landowning quadrumvir windowshop antecedent catechetic
drudgingly landscaper quadruplet windowsill antecessor catechiser
dunderhead lardydardy quadruplex windscreen antechapel catechumen
duodecimal leadenness quadrupole windshield antemortem categorise
duodenitis leaderless randomness windsleeve antependia catenation
epideictic leadership readership wonderland antepenult celebrated
epidemical lordliness renderable wonderment anteriorly celebrator
epidermoid loudhailer rendezvous wonderwork appealable cerebellum
eradicable maidenhair rhodophane wondrously appearance ceremonial
eradicator maidenhead rinderpest woodcarver appeasable cheekiness
evidential maidenhood roadrunner woodcutter appendices cheerfully
fandangoes maidenlike roadworthy woodenhead appendixes cheeriness
fiddleback mandibular roodscreen woodenness apperceive cheesecake
fiddlehead mandragora rudderfish woodlander appetising cheesiness
fiddlewood meadowland rudderless woodpecker appetitive Ciceronian
fledgeling meadowlark saddleback woodpigeon arrestment cinecamera
foudroyant meddlesome saddlefast woodturner arterially cinerarium
fuddyduddy mendacious saddletree woodworker arteriolar clientship
geodetical mendicancy sandalwood wordlessly asbestosis coherently
gladhander middleaged sandbagger wunderkind ascendable cohesively
gladsomely middlebrow sandcastle yardmaster ascendance coleoptera
goldbeater middlemost sanderling ZendAvesta ascendancy coleoptile
golddigger middlingly sandhopper abjectness ascendence coleorhiza
goldenness mindedness sandmartin ablebodied ascendency comedienne
goldenseal mindlessly seedpotato abnegation ascendible comehither
goldilocks mordacious seedvessel abreaction asceticism comeliness
goodliness needlebath shadowless accelerate aspergilla comestible
goodlooker needlebook shoddiness accentuate assemblage Copernican
goodygoody needlecord slidevalve acceptable assentient copesettic
gradualism needlefish smudginess acceptably assessable corelation
gradualist needlessly soddenness acceptance assessment corelative
graduation needlework soldanella acceptedly asseverate cosentient
grudgingly nondrinker sordidness accessible asteriated covenanted
handbarrow obediently spadebeard accessibly asteroidal covenantee
handedness oxidisable spadiceous acoelomate attendance covenanter
handgallop paddleboat spidercrab adherently attenuated covenantor
handicraft paddyfield spiderline adhesively attenuator covetingly
handmaiden paddywagon spiderwort adjectival autecology covetously
handpicked paddywhack spodomancy adrenaline barebacked coweringly
handselled paedagogic stadholder adrenergic barefooted creepiness
handsomely paederasty stodginess adventurer bareheaded cybernetic
handspring paediatric studiously advertence barelegged deaeration
handworked paedogogue subdeanery advertency bedevilled deceivable
hardbilled paedophile subduction advertiser bejewelled decelerate
hardbitten pardonable suddenness aerenchyma bemedalled Decembrist
hardboiled pardonably sunderance affectedly benedicite decemviral
hardfisted pendentive syndicator affectless Benedictus deceptible
hardhanded perdurable tardigrade affeerment benefactor defeasance
hardheaded perdurably tawdriness afferently beneficent defeasible
headcheese ploddingly tenderfoot affettuoso beneficial defeminise
headhunter ponderable tenderloin afterbirth benevolent defendable
headmaster powderhorn tenderness aftergrass bimestrial defensible
headphones powderpuff tendinitis afterimage bimetallic defensibly
headspring predacious tendrillar afterlight bioecology deferrable
headsquare predecease tendrilled afterpains bipetalous degeneracy
headstream predestine tiddlywink aftershave bisexually degenerate
headstrong predicable Tridentine aftertaste bluebonnet dejectable
headwaiter prediction unedifying afterwards bluebottle delectable
hebdomadal predictive uneducated aldermanic bluecollar delectably
heedlessly predispose vaudeville aldermanry bluejacket delegation
hendecagon prednisone veldschoen algebraist bluepencil dementedly
Hindustani pridefully vindicable alienation blueribbon denegation
hurdygurdy prodigally vindicator allegation bluethroat dependable
inadequacy prodigious vindictive allegiance bluetongue dependably
inadequate producible Waldensian allegorise boneheaded dependence
ineducable production wanderings allegorist bonesetter dependency
iridaceous productive wanderlust allegretto boneshaker derestrict
iridescent prudential wanderplug allergenic breechless desecrater
iridosmine quadrangle wardenship alleviator breezeless desecrator
isodynamic quadrantal weedkiller alpenstock breeziness deservedly
jardiniere quadratics wildebeest alteration bureaucrat detectable
kindliness quadrature wilderment alterative Caledonian detergency
ladderback quadrennia wilderness alternance camelopard determined
landholder quadriceps wildfowler alternator camerlengo deterrence
landhunger quadrireme windflower amoebocyte camerlingo detestable
landingnet quadrivial windjammer ampelopsis carelessly detestably
```

```
receptacle selenology superpower unbearable vicegerent disfurnish
receptible semeiology supersonic unbearably viceregent drafthorse
redecorate semeiotics superstore unbeatable videophone dumfounder
redeemable semestrial supertonic unbeatably vinegarish farfetched
redemption senescence supervisor unbecoming viperiform fitfulness
redemptive sereneness surefooted unbeliever viperously fluffiness
redemptory seventieth suretyship unbesought virescence flyfishing
redescribe severeness suzerainty undefended waterborne forfeiture
referendum sheepishly sweepingly undeniable waterbrash fulfilling
regelation sheeplouse sweepstake undeniably waterclock fulfilment
regeneracy sheepshank sweetbread underbelly watercraft Godfearing
regenerate sheepshead sweetbriar underbrush watercress golfcourse
regentship shieldless sweetbrier undercliff waterflood gunfighter
rejectable shoebuckle sweetening undercover waterfront halfcocked
releasable shoestring sweetheart undercroft waterglass halfdollar
relegation shrewdness synecdoche underdress wateriness halflength
relentless shrewishly synecology underfloor watermelon halfnelson
relevantly shrewmouse synergetic underglaze waterpower halfvolley
remediable sideboards tabernacle underlease waterproof halfwitted
remedially sideeffect talebearer underlinen waterskier halfyearly
remediless sideglance talentless underlying waterspout inefficacy
repealable siderolite taleteller underminer watertight joyfulness
repeatable siderostat taperecord underneath waterwheel knifeboard
repeatedly sidesaddle taperingly underpants waterworks lawfulness
repellance sidestreet tapestried underproof wavelength leafcutter
repellancy sidestroke telecamera underquote waveringly leafhopper
repellence sidewinder telecaster underscore werewolves leafinsect
repellency silentness telegraphy undersense wheelchair malfeasant
repentance sinecurism telemetric undersexed wheelhorse manfulness
repertoire sinecurist teleologic undershirt wheelhouse misfortune
repetiteur sleepiness teleostean undershoot wheeziness muffinbell
repetition sleepyhead telepathic undershrub widespread newfangled
repetitive sleeveless telephoner undersized winebibber nonferrous
reredorter sleevelink telephonic underskirt winebottle nonfiction
researcher sneeringly telescopic underslung winegrower oldfangled
resemblant sneezeweed televiewer understand wiredrawer outfielder
resentment sneezewood television understate wirehaired outfitting
reservedly sneezewort televisual understeer wirepuller perfection
revealable sobersided tenebrific understock wiretapper perfective
revealment sobersides tenebrious understood wirewalker perfidious
revelation solecistic tenemental understudy wireworker perfoliate
revelatory solemnness thievishly undertaken Wykehamist perforator
revengeful solenoidal threadbare undertaker yokefellow performing
reverencer somersault threadfish undertrick artfulness pinfeather
reverently speechless threadmark undervalue asafoetida prefecture
reversible speediness threadworm underwater bafflement preferable
revertible speedlimit threatener underworld bafflingly preferably
riverhorse sphenodone threepence underwrite batfowling preference
ropedancer sphenogram threepenny underwrote beefburger preferment
ropeladder sphenoidal threepiece undeserved bufflehead preferring
ropewalker sphericity threescore undesigned buffoonery prefixture
rosechafer spheroidal threnodial undesirous chiffchaff prefrontal
roseengine spherulite threnodist undeterred chiffonier prefulgent
roselipped spleenwort tidewaiter unfeminine coffeemill profession
rosemallow splendidly timekeeper unfettered confabbing proficient
rovebeetle squeezable timelessly ungenerous confection profitable
sacerdotal squeezebox timeliness unlettered conference profitably
safeblower squeteague timesaving unmeasured conferment profitless
safetybelt steeliness timeserver unmeetness conferring profligacy
salesclerk steelworks tirelessly unmerciful confervoid profligate
saleswoman streamless tiresomely unreadable confession profoundly
satellitic streamline tolerantly unredeemed confidante profundity
sauerkraut streetdoor toleration unreliable confidence puffpastry
schematise streetward tonelessly unrelieved confirmand reafforest
schematism strengthen totemistic unremarked confiscate rodfishing
schemozzle stressless toweringly unrequited conflation roofgarden
scherzando superacute trierarchy unreserved confluence ruefulness
scientific superaltar tubercular unresolved conformism ruffianism
scleroderm superation tuberculin unseasoned conformist scaffolder
sclerotium superbness tuberosity unselected conformity scoffingly
sclerotomy supercargo tumescence unsettling confounded selfacting
screechowl superduper tunelessly upperclass confusedly selfaction
screenings supergiant typescript vegetarian craftguild selfbinder
screenplay superhuman typesetter vegetation craftiness selfcolour
screwplate superiorly typewriter vegetative difference selfdeceit
screwpress superlunar ulceration vehemently difficulty selfdenial
secernment supernally ulcerative veneration diffidence selfesteem
selectness supernovae ulteriorly veterinary diffusible selffeeder
selenodont superorder umbellifer viceconsul disfeature selfglazed
```

```
selfguided congruence jaggedness ringnecked anchoritic fishcarver
selflessly congruency jargonelle ringtailed anchorless fisherfolk
selfloving cragginess jingoistic roughhouse anchorring fishkettle
selfmotion cudgelling judgematic roughrider anchylosis fishmonger
selfmurder daughterly juggernaut ruggedness anchylotic foxhunting
selfparody diagnostic kingfisher sanguinary antheridia gothically
selfpoised diagonally kingliness sanguinely anthracene henharrier
selfpraise diagraphic knighthood sanguinity anthracite henhearted
selfprofit didgeridoo Krugerrand sargassoes anthracoid highbinder
selfraised disgruntle languisher seignorage anthropoid highflying
selfregard disgustful languorous seignorial archaistic highhanded
selfrising doggedness largescale sergeantcy archbishop highjacker
selfruling doughfaced laughingly shagginess archdeacon highlander
selfseeker dragonhead ledgerbait siegetrain archerfish highminded
selfstyled dragonnade ledgerline Singhalese archetypal highoctane
selftaught dragontree lengthways singlefoot architrave highstrung
selfwilled dungbeetle lengthwise singleness archpriest highwayman
shiftiness dysgraphia linguiform singletree arrhythmia hithermost
sinfulness emigration linguistic singularly arrhythmic hitherward
snafflebit emigratory loggerhead slightness arthralgia hyphenated
sniffiness enigmatise longaevous sluggardly arthralgic inchoately
snuffiness enigmatist longhaired sluggishly arthromere inchoation
spiflicate epigastric longheaded songstress asphyxiant inchoative
staffnurse epigenesis longlegged songthrush asphyxiate lachrymose
stiffening epigenetic longprimer songwriter authorship lighterage
stiflebone epiglottal longshanks spagyrical batholitic lighterman
stiflingly epiglottic longwinded stagbeetle bathometer lightfaced
stuffiness epiglottis mangosteen stagecoach bathymeter lighthouse
sufferable epigrapher marginalia stagecraft bathymetry lightingup
sufferably epigraphic marginally staggering bathyscaph lightproof
sufferance exaggerate marginated stagnantly bathyscope lithoglyph
sufficient exegetical margravate stagnation bichromate lithograph
suffragist eyeglasses margravine stigmatise bighearted lithologic
surfactant fingerbowl marguerite stigmatism bothersome lithophane
toffeenose fingerless meagreness stigmatist Brahmanism lithophyte
tomfoolery fingerling misgivings subglacial Brahminism lithotrity
trafficked fingermark mongrelise suggestion Buchmanism Lithuanian
trafficker fingernail mongrelism suggestive Buchmanite lophophore
triflingly fingerpost morganatic sunglasses bushmaster machinator
trifoliate flagellant noogenesis surgically bushranger machinegun
trifurcate flagellate oligarchic swaggering cachinnate mathematic
tuffaceous flagitious oligoclase syngenesis catholicon mechanical
unaffected flagrantly oligopsony tangential catholicos methodical
uniformity flagwaving originally tanglement cephalopod Methuselah
unofficial flightdeck originator tongueless cochleated methylated
usefulness flightless orogenesis tonguetied deshabille Michaelmas
waffleiron flightpath orogenetic topgallant dichroitic mightiness
wilfulness flugelhorn orographic tragacanth dichromate mishitting
woefulness forgetting outgassing tragically diphtheria mithridate
wolframite forgivable outgeneral tragicomic diphtheric motherhood
alightment forgivably outgunning trigeminal diphyletic motherland
amygdaloid fragmental oxygenator triggerman diphyodont motherless
anaglyphic fragrantly pangenesis triglyphic dishabille mothership
anagogical frigidness pangenetic trigonally disharmony motherwort
aragonitic frigorific phagedaena troglodyte dishearten mythically
bargeboard froghopper phagedenic turgescent dishonesty mythiciser
Belgravian fungicidal phagocytic turgidness dishwasher mythologer
bilgewater ganglionic pilgarlick vengefully ecchymosis mythologic
biogenesis gangrenous pilgrimage virginally ecchymotic mythomania
biogenetic gargantuan plagiarise virginhood eighteenmo mythopoeia
biographer geognostic plagiarism waggonette eighteenth mythopoeic
biographic geographer plaguesome wingcollar emphractic naphthenic
brigandage geographic pragmatise wingfooted enchanting nephograph
brigandine gingerbeer pragmatism wingspread enthralled nephoscope
brigandism gingersnap pragmatist wongawonga enthusiasm nephralgia
brigantine gingivitis preglacial Aethiopian enthusiast nephridium
brightness Glagolitic pregnantly alchemical escharotic nephrology
brightwork goggleeyed priggishly alphabetic escheatage nethermost
budgerigar gorgeously progenitor alphameric euphonious nightdress
bunglingly Gorgonzola proglottis amphibious euphuistic nightglass
burglarise gregarious prognathic amphibrach eurhythmic nightlight
coagulable grogginess prognostic amphictyon euthanasia nightshade
congeneric hangglider programmer amphigouri fatherhood nightshift
congenital hodgepodge raggedness amphimacer fatherland nightshirt
congestion hungriness ridgepiece amphimixes fatherless nightstick
congestive imaginable ringfinger amphimixis fatherlike nightwatch
conglobate imaginably ringleader amphoteric fathership orchardist
congregant isogenetic ringmaster anchoretic fathomable orchardman
congregate isoglossal ringmaster anchoretic fathomless orchestics
```

orchestral	Afrikander	capitalise	disincline	gemination	insinuator	
orphanhood	Albigenses	capitalism	disinherit	genialness	insipidity	
orthoclase	alliaceous	capitalist	divination	geniculate	insistence	
orthodoxly	alliterate	capitation	divinatory	geriatrics	insistency	
orthoepist	ambidexter	Capitoline	divineness	geriatrist	intimately	
orthogenic	ambivalent	capitulary	divisional	goniometer	intimation	
orthogonal	ancipitous	capitulate	divisively	goniometry	intimidate	
orthopedic	angiosperm	caricature	dominantly	habiliment	intinction	
orthoptera	annihilate	cavitation	domination	habilitate	invigilate	
panhandler	anointment	chainsmoke	dominative	habitation	invigorate	
pathetical	antibiosis	chairwoman	dosimetric	habitually	invincible	
pathfinder	antibiotic	choiceness	dubitation	hagiolatry	invincibly	
pathogenic	Antichrist	Christhood	dubitative	hagiologic	inviolable	
pathologic	anticipant	Christlike	duniwassal	hagioscope	inviolably	
phthisical	anticipate	cicisbeism	echinoderm	halieutics	invitation	
pichiciago	anticlimax	cloistered	efficacity	heliacally	invitatory	
pothunting	anticlinal	cogitation	efficiency	helianthus	invitingly	
prehensile	antifreeze	cogitative	egoistical	Heliconian	iodination	
prehension	antiheroic	comicality	elliptical	helicopter	ionisation	
prehistory	antimasque	comicopera	empiricism	heliograph	irrigation	
prohibiter	antimatter	coniferous	empiricist	heliolater	irritation	
prohibitor	antimonial	coriaceous	engineroom	heliolatry	irritative	
pushbutton	antimonite	Corinthian	enlistment	heliometer	janitorial	
Rachmanism	antinomian	cylindered	enrichment	heliophyte	Jewishness	
rechristen	antipathic	cylindroid	enrigiment	helioscope	jubilantly	
reshipment	antiphonal	debilitate	enticement	heliotaxis	jubilation	
rightangle	antipodean	decigramme	enticingly	heliotrope	judicatory	
rightfully	antiproton	decimalise	entireness	heliotropy	judicature	
rightwards	antiquated	decimalism	eosinophil	hemicyclic	judicially	
ruthlessly	antiSemite	decimation	epeirogeny	hemihedral	juristical	
sashwindow	antisepsis	decisively	equilibria	hemihedron	labiovelar	
silhouette	antiseptic	decivilise	equipotent	hemiplegia	laminarian	
sophomoric	antisocial	dedication	equitation	hemiplegic	lamination	
subheading	antistatic	dedicative	equivalent	hemipteran	lapidarian	
syphilitic	antitheism	dedicatory	equivocate	hemisphere	lapidarist	
tachometer	antitheist	deficiency	estimation	hesitantly	lapidation	
tachometry	antitheses	defilement	estimative	hesitation	latifundia	
tachymeter	antithesis	definement	ethicality	hesitative	lavishment	
tachymetry	antithetic	definienda	eudiometer	homiletics	lavishness	
technetium	aquiferous	definitely	eudiometry	horizontal	legibility	
technician	aquilinity	definition	excitation	humidifier	legislator	
technicist	arbitrable	definitive	excitative	illiteracy	legitimacy	
technocrat	arbitrager	definitude	excitatory	illiterate	legitimate	
technology	arbitrator	dehiscence	excitement	imbibition	legitimise	
unchanging	armigerous	deliberate	excitingly	imminently	legitimism	
unchastity	articulate	delicately	exhibition	immiscible	legitimist	
unthinking	artificial	delightful	exhibitory	immiscibly	lepidolite	
wishywashy	aspidistra	delimitate	exhilarant	impishness	levigation	
withdrawal	aspiration	delineator	exhilarate	incidental	levitation	
withdrawer	assibilate	delinquent	expiration	incinerate	lexicology	
withholder	assignable	deliquesce	expiratory	incipience	lexigraphy	
xiphosuran	assignment	denigrator	extinction	incipiency	libidinous	
abdication	assimilate	depilation	extinctive	incisively	liliaceous	
abridgment	assistance	depilatory	extinguish	incitation	limitation	
accidental	astigmatic	deridingly	extirpator	incitement	limitative	
achievable	audibility	derisively	facileness	incivility	limitrophe	
actinolite	audiometer	derivation	facilitate	indication	Lipizzaner	
actinozoan	audiometry	derivative	familiarly	indicative	litigation	
actionable	audiophile	desiccator	famishment	indicatory	livingroom	
actionably	auditorial	desiderata	fatiguable	indictable	logicality	
activation	auditorium	desiderate	felicitate	indictment	logistical	
activeness	auriculate	designator	felicitous	indigenous	lovingness	
additional	auriferous	designedly	feminality	indigested	luciferase	
adhibition	babiroussa	designment	femininely	indirectly	luciferous	
administer	banishment	desipience	femininity	indiscreet	lucifugous	
admiration	behindhand	desirously	feuilleton	indiscrete	luminosity	
admiringly	believable	desistance	filibuster	indisposed	luminously	
admissible	benignancy	devilishly	finicality	indistinct	Lusitanian	
admittable	beribboned	devitalise	finiteness	inditement	magistracy	
admittance	bewitchery	digitalise	foliaceous	individual	magistrate	
admittedly	biliverdin	digitately	freightage	infidelity	malignance	
advisement	bluishness	digitation	fruitarian	infighting	malignancy	
aetiologic	boyishness	digitiform	fruitfully	infiltrate	malingerer	
affiliated	brainchild	diligently	fugitively	infinitely	mamillated	
affirmable	braininess	diminished	fuliginous	infinitive	maniacally	
Africander	brainpower	diminuendo	fumigation	infinitude	Manichaean	
Africanise	brainstorm	diminution	fusibility	inhibition	Manicheism	
Africanism	calibrator	diminutive	galimatias	inhibitory	manicurist	
Africanist	caliginous	diningroom	garishness	insightful	manifestly	

```
manifestos  notifiable  pixillated  ridiculous  solidarity  variegated
manifoldly  notionally  plainchant  risibility  solidstate  varietally
manipulate  nubiferous  podiatrist  rotisserie  solifidian  variolitic
Mariolater  nuciferous  politeness  rubiginous  solitarily  variometer
Mariolatry  nucivorous  politician  rudimental  splintbone  Vaticanism
marionette  nudibranch  politicise  ruminantly  splintcoal  Vaticanist
maxilliped  numismatic  pomiferous  rumination  splitlevel  vaticinate
maximalist  oafishness  porismatic  ruminative  spoilsport  velitation
mediastina  obligation  positional  rupicoline  sprightful  venialness
mediatress  obligatory  positively  rupicolous  springhalt  verifiable
medicament  obligingly  positivism  sagination  springhead  vesication
medicaster  obliterate  positivist  sagittally  springless  vesicatory
medication  occidental  positivity  salicional  springlike  vesiculate
medicative  officially  prairiedog  salicylate  springtail  vigilantly
medievally  oleiferous  pugilistic  salientian  springtide  visibility
mediocrity  omnigenous  punishable  saliferous  springtime  Visigothic
meditation  omnipotent  punishment  salivation  springwood  visionally
meditative  omniscient  punitively  sanitarian  sprinkling  visionless
meliorator  omnivorous  pupilarity  sanitarily  squinteyed  visitation
melismatic  oneirology  pupiparous  sanitarium  squirarchy  visitorial
meningioma  ophicleide  puristical  sanitation  squirearch  vitiligate
meningitis  ophiolater  puritanise  sapiential  squirehood  viviparity
meridional  ophiolatry  puritanism  satisfying  squireling  viviparous
meticulous  ophiologic  pyridoxine  saxicoline  squireship  vivisector
militantly  oppilation  quaintness  saxicolous  strictness  viziership
militarily  optimalise  radicalise  schipperke  stridently  vociferant
militarise  optimistic  radicalism  schismatic  stridulant  vociferate
militarism  optionally  radication  schizocarp  stridulate  vociferous
militarist  ordinarily  radiogenic  schizogony  stridulous  volitional
militiaman  ordination  radiograph  scribbling  strikingly  vomitorium
minimalism  oscillator  radiologic  scrimmager  stringbean  conjecture
minimalist  oscitation  radiometer  scrimshank  stringency  conjointly
ministrant  osmiridium  radiometry  scriptoria  stringendo  conjugally
mitigation  owlishness  radiopaque  scriptural  stringhalt  disjointed
mitigative  pacifiable  radiophone  semiannual  stringless  misjoinder
mitigatory  pacificate  radioscopy  semichorus  striptease  nonjoinder
modifiable  pacificism  radiosonde  semicircle  supination  panjandrum
modishness  pacificist  rakishness  semidivine  supineness  perjurious
moniliasis  pagination  rationally  semidouble  taciturnly  prejudiced
moniliform  palimpsest  ravishment  semidrying  takingness  projectile
monistical  palindrome  recidivism  semifitted  talismanic  projection
monitorial  palisander  recidivist  semiliquid  taxidancer  projective
mopishness  paniculate  recipiency  semilunate  taxidermal  serjeantcy
motionless  papistical  reciprocal  seminarian  taxidermic  skijumping
motivation  parimutuel  recitalist  seminarist  tepidarium  skyjacking
motiveless  patination  recitation  semination  theistical  subjectify
moviemaker  patisserie  recitative  semiopaque  thriftless  subjection
muciferous  pediculate  recitativo  semiotical  tiringroom  subjective
muliebrity  pediculous  rediscover  semiquaver  titivation  subjugator
mulishness  pedicurist  refillable  semiuncial  topicality  trajection
munificent  pedimental  refinement  semiweekly  toxication  trajectory
musicality  pedimented  regimental  semiyearly  toxicology  Ashkenazim
musicianly  penicillin  regionally  serigraphy  toxiphobia  backbiting
musicology  peninsular  registered  seriocomic  traitorous  backblocks
musicpaper  penitently  registrant  sexivalent  tubicolous  backgammon
musicstand  periclinal  relievable  shrievalty  typicality  background
musicstool  pericyclic  relinquish  shrillness  ultimately  backhanded
mutilation  peridermal  relishable  shrinkable  umbilicate  backhander
mutinously  perigynous  remissible  shrinkwrap  umbiliform  backsheesh
nanisation  perihelion  remissness  shrivelled  umpireship  backslider
nationally  perilously  remittance  sibilation  unbiblical  backstairs
nationhood  periodical  resignedly  similarity  unbiddable  backstitch
nationless  periosteal  resilience  similitude  undigested  backstroke
nationwide  periosteum  resiliency  sinisterly  unfilially  backwardly
nativeborn  peripeteia  resistance  sinistrous  unfinished  bankruptcy
nativeness  peripheral  resistible  skrimshank  unhistoric  barkentine
nativistic  peripteral  resistless  sleighbell  unkindness  basketball
navigation  periscopic  reticently  sluicegate  unlikeness  basketwork
nidicolous  perishable  reticulate  snailpaced  unripeness  beekeeping
nidificate  perithecia  retinacula  snailwheel  unrivalled  Berkeleian
nidifugous  peritoneal  retirement  socialiser  untidiness  bookbinder
nihilistic  peritoneum  retiringly  societally  unwieldily  bookkeeper
nominalism  periwigged  reviewable  sociologic  unyielding  bookmaking
nominalist  periwinkle  revilement  sociometry  uppishness  bookmarker
nominately  petiolated  revisional  solicitant  urticarial  bookseller
nomination  petiteness  revitalise  solicitous  urtication  brakeblock
nominative  petitioner  revivalism  solicitude  validation  brakelight
noticeable  piliferous  revivalist  solidarism  varicocele  brokendown
noticeably  pitilessly  ricinoleic  solidarist  varicosity  brokenness
```

bucketshop	spokeshave	bullethead	emblazonry	inflatable	pillowcase
cackhanded	subkingdom	bullheaded	emblematic	inflection	pillowlace
cankerworm	tackdriver	bullroarer	emblements	inflective	pillowslip
chokeberry	tankengine	byelection	emollition	inflexible	pollenosis
cockalorum	taskmaster	callowness	employable	inflexibly	pollinator
cockatrice	tickertape	cellophane	employment	infliction	prelatical
cockchafer	ticklishly	cellularly	emulsifier	inflictive	prelection
cockneyish	turkeycock	cellulitis	Englishman	inglorious	prolicidal
cockneyism	weakliness	cellulosic	englutting	isolatable	prolocutor
cocksurely	weakminded	chalcedony	epilimnion	italianate	prologuise
cuckoopint	wickedness	chalkboard	evaluation	italianise	prolongate
cuckoospit	wickerwork	chalkstone	evaluative	Italianism	psalmodise
dickcissel	workbasket	challenger	evilminded	Italophile	psalmodist
Dickensian	workingman	chalybeate	evolvement	Lollardism	psalterium
donkeywork	workpeople	chelicerae	exaltation	malleebird	psilocybin
fecklessly	addlepated	childbirth	explicable	malleefowl	Ptolemaist
fickleness	adolescent	childermas	explicitly	mallenders	publishing
folklorist	Adullamite	childishly	exploitage	mealbeetle	qualmishly
folkmemory	adulterant	childproof	exploitive	mellowness	railroader
folksiness	adulterate	chiliastic	exulcerate	millefiori	railwayman
folksinger	adulteress	chilliness	exultantly	millennial	realisable
hackbuteer	adulterine	coalbunker	exultation	millennium	reallocate
hackmatack	adulterous	coalescent	exultingly	millesimal	reelection
hankypanky	aeolotropy	coelacanth	fallacious	millilitre	reeligible
hookedness	affliction	collarbeam	fallingoff	millimetre	reflection
hucklebone	afflictive	collarbone	fallowness	millstream	reflective
jackanapes	affluently	collarette	faultiness	millwright	reflexible
jackassery	agglutinin	collarless	fellmonger	molluscoid	rollcollar
jackhammer	amalgamate	collarstud	fellowship	molluscous	rollicking
jackknives	ameliorate	collatable	fieldglass	mouldboard	rollingpin
jackrabbit	amylaceous	collateral	fieldmouse	mouldiness	sailorless
Kafkaesque	analogical	collection	fieldpiece	mulligrubs	sallenders
kookaburra	analphabet	collective	fieldstone	myological	sallowness
lacklustre	analysable	collegiate	follicular	nailpolish	scaleboard
leukocytic	analytical	collembola	fowlplague	neglectful	Scillonian
lockerroom	Anglistics	collimator	frilliness	negligence	sculptress
lockkeeper	anglomania	collocutor	frolicking	negligible	sculptural
lockstitch	anglophile	colloquial	frolicsome	negligibly	sculptured
mackintosh	anglophobe	colloquise	fullbodied	neological	sealingwax
marketable	anglophone	colloquist	fullbottom	noblewoman	secludedly
markethall	AngloSaxon	colloquium	fulllength	nonlogical	sexlimited
markettown	apolaustic	coolheaded	gaillardia	nucleation	shellacked
markswoman	apolitical	coolingoff	galleywest	nucleonics	shellmound
mockheroic	Apollinian	coulometry	galliambic	nucleoside	shellproof
monkeysuit	Apollonian	cyclically	galloglass	nucleotide	shellshock
muskmallow	apologetic	cyclograph	Gallomania	nullanulla	shillelagh
nickelling	applicable	cyclometer	Gallophile	ocellation	sialagogic
packingbox	applicably	cyclopedia	Gallophobe	ochlocracy	sialagogue
packsaddle	applicator	cyclopedic	gaslighter	offlicence	sillybilly
packthread	ateleiosis	cyclostome	gaultheria	opalescent	smallscale
pickaninny	ballflower	cyclostyle	geological	orological	smallsword
picketline	ballistics	declarable	girlfriend	outlandish	smallwares
pickpocket	ballooning	declassify	goalkeeper	palladious	smelliness
pocketable	balloonist	declension	goaltender	pallbearer	soullessly
pocketbook	barleybree	declinable	guilefully	palliation	spallation
pocketsize	barleybroo	deflagrate	guillotine	palliative	speleology
pockmarked	barleycorn	deflection	guiltiness	palliatory	spellbound
rackrenter	Bedlington	deflective	hallelujah	pallidness	spillikins
recklessly	belladonna	deflowerer	hellbender	parliament	spoliation
rickettsia	belletrist	deplorable	heulandite	pellagrous	spoliative
rockabilly	bellflower	deplorably	holloweyed	pellicular	spoliatory
rockbadger	bellringer	deployment	hollowness	pellucidly	stalactite
rockbottom	bellwether	dialysable	hollowware	phalangeal	stalagmite
rockgarden	bellyacher	dielectric	hullabaloo	phallicism	stalwartly
rockhopper	bellydance	dillydally	hurlyburly	phelloderm	stelliform
rockpigeon	bellylaugh	diplodocus	hyaloplasm	philatelic	stilettoes
rockrabbit	biblically	diplomatic	idolatress	philippina	stillbirth
rockribbed	bibliology	dislikable	idolatrous	philippine	stillicide
sicklebill	bibliopegy	disloyally	implacable	philistine	stolidness
sickliness	bibliophil	disloyalty	implacably	phillumeny	stylistics
silkcotton	bibliopole	duplicator	implicitly	philologen	stylograph
silkscreen	bibliopoly	ebullience	inclemency	philopoena	subletting
smokedried	bibliotics	ebulliency	inclinable	philosophe	sublimable
smokehouse	billetdoux	ebullition	includible	philosophy	subliminal
smokeplant	billposter	ecclesiast	inelegance	phylactery	sublingual
smokeproof	biological	ecological	ineligible	phyllotaxy	sullenness
smokestack	bollweevil	edulcorate	ineligibly	phylloxera	sweltering
snakedance	brilliance	effloresce	ineloquent	phylogenic	syllabaria
snakestone	brilliancy	emblazoner	ineludible	pilliwinks	syllogiser

```
tablecloth animalcula flamboyant primordial vermicidal counsellor
tablelinen animalcule flameproof primordium vermicular counteract
tablespoon animatedly flamingoes promenader warmingpan countryish
tailorbird asymmetric flimsiness promethium weimaraner countryman
tailormade asymptotic foamflower prominence whomsoever cranesbill
tellership atomically formatting promissory zoomorphic craniology
thalecress Barmecidal formidable promontory abundantly crankiness
thillhorse bigmouthed formidably promptbook adenectomy crankshaft
toilsomely biometrics formlessly promptness alongshore crenellate
tollbridge biomorphic framboesia promulgate amanuenses crenulated
trilateral blamefully gemmaceous pummeling amanuensis crinolette
trilingual bromegrass geometrise rhomboidal amendatory ctenophore
triliteral carmagnole germicidal rhomboidei anonaceous daintiness
trillionth chamaeleon germinally salmagundi arenaceous deontology
trolleybus chamberpot glimmering salmonella asynchrony dinnerless
trollopish champignon glomerular salmonleap avantgarde donnybrook
twelvefold chemically glomerulus sarmentose aventurine downfallen
twelvenote chemisette glumaceous sarmentous balneology downstairs
twelvetone chemotaxis gormandise seamanlike biannually downstream
twilighted chimerical gramicidin seamanship biennially downstroke
unblenched chimneypot gramineous seamstress blancmange downwardly
unblinking chimpanzee grammarian seemliness blanketing economical
unblushing cismontane gramophone segmentary blanquette economiser
uncloister clamminess grumpiness sermoniser blindingly edentulous
unflagging clementine haematosis shamefaced boondoggle elongation
unilateral clumsiness haematuria shamefully bouncingly emancipate
unilingual commandant haemolysis skimpiness branchiate emancipist
unilocular commandeer haemolytic slumberful brandyball emendation
unpleasant commandery hammerbeam slumberous brandysnap emendatory
unpleasing commanding hammerhead spumescent brentgoose enantiosis
utilisable commandoes hammerless stimulator brentgoose enunciable
valleculae commentary hammerlock stomachful bronchiole enunciator
vallecular commentate hammerpond stomatitis bronchitic epentheses
villainage commercial harmlessly stomatopod bronchitis epenthesis
villainess commissary harmonical stomodaeum cannelloni epenthetic
villainous commission harmonious stumpiness cannonball ethnically
villanelle commissure harmoniser submariner carnallite ethnologic
villeinage commitment helminthic submediant carnassial evanescent
violaceous committing hermetical submersion chancellor evangelise
volleyball commixture hermitcrab submission chandelier evangelism
wallflower commodious hormonally submissive changeable evangelist
wallpepper commonable inimically submitting changeably evenhanded
wellheeled commonalty inimitable submontane changeless eventually
wellington commonness inimitably summerlike changeling exenterate
wellspoken commonroom Ishmaelite summertime changeover faintheart
wellspring commonweal isometrics summitless channelise fianchetto
wellturned communally isomorphic summonable channelled fiendishly
wellwisher communique Kuomintang surmisable chinagraph FinnoUgric
whaleshark commutable Lammastide swimmingly chinchilla flannelled
wholesaler commutator mesmeriser symmetrise chondritic flintiness
willowherb cosmically midmorning Talmudical clangorous flunkeydom
willynilly cosmogonic mismatched tarmacadam clannishly flunkeyism
willywilly cosmopolis mismeasure termagancy clingstone fornicator
woolgather cosmoramic oldmaidish terminable clinically foundation
woolgrower crematoria outmeasure terminably clinkstone founderous
woolliness criminally palmaceous terminally clinometer franchiser
woolsorter cummerbund palmatifid terminator clinometry Franciscan
worldclass curmudgeon palmbutter termitaria coenobitic Francophil
worldweary dermatitis palmerworm themselves coenobytic frangipane
Wycliffite dermatogen PalmSunday thimbleful cognisable frangipani
yellowback dismalness pegmatitic thimblerig cognisably Frenchness
yellowbird dismission penmanship thumbprint cognisance frenziedly
yellowness dismissive permafrost thumbscrew cognominal fringeless
yellowwood dogmatical permanence thumbstall coincident frontbench
yieldingly dogmatiser permanency trammelled connatural frontwards
zollverein dramatical permeation tramontana connection funnelling
zoological dramaturge permeative tramontane connective gaingiving
abominable dramaturgy permission trampoline conniption garnierite
abominably duumvirate permissive tremendous connivance garnishing
abominator ecumenical permitting tremolitic corncockle gauntleted
adamantine elementary permutable trimonthly cornerwise glancingly
airmanship eliminable pigmentary trimorphic cornettist granadilla
alimentary eliminator plumassier trombonist cornflakes grandchild
anamorphic enamelling premarital tromometer cornflower granddaddy
anemograph enamellist premaxilla unAmerican cornstarch grandducal
anemometer enumerable premedical unemphatic cornucopia grandmamma
anemometry enumerator premonitor unemployed councillor grandniece
anemophily eremitical primevally unimproved councilman grandstand
animadvert examinable primiparae vermicelli counselled granduncle
```

```
grangerise pawnbroker scandalise transferee adroitness autonomous
grangerism pennaceous scandalous transferor adsorbable autoplasty
granophyre pennanular scansorial transfuser adsorption autostrada
granularly pennillion scantiness transgress adsorptive autostrade
granulator pennyroyal scenically transience advocation axiologist
granulitic pennyworth shandrydan transiency advocatory azeotropic
grenadilla pernicious shandygaff transistor aerobatics barometric
grindingly pernickety shanghaier transition aerobiosis baronetage
grindstone phanerogam shantytown transitive aerobiotic becomingly
gymnastics phantasise shenanigan transitory aeroengine beforehand
gymnosophy phantasmal signalling translator aerogramme beforetime
gymnosperm phantasmic signwriter translucid aerography belongings
hauntingly phantastic skindiving translunar aerologist bidonville
hobnobbing phantastry skinniness transmuter aeronautic bijouterie
hornblende phenacetin slanderous transplant aeronomist bilocation
hornedness phenocryst slanginess transposal aerophobia binoculars
hornrimmed phenomenal slantingly transposer aerostatic bipolarity
hypnagogic phenomenon slenderise transshape affordable bivouacked
hypnotiser phenotypic somniloquy transvalue agrologist bloodguilt
iconoclasm phonematic somnolence transverse agronomist bloodhound
iconolater phonically somnolency trenchancy alcoholise bloodiness
iconolatry phonograph soundboard trendiness alcoholism bloodmoney
iconomachy phonolitic soundingly truncately algolagnia bloodstain
iconometer phonologic soundproof truncation algolagnic bloodstock
iconometry phonometer soundtrack trundlebed algologist bloodstone
iconoscope pianissimo spankingly tunnelling Algonquian bolometric
ilangilang pianoforte Spencerian turnbuckle allocation broodiness
illnatured picnicking Spenserian unendingly allocution broodingly
inundation pinnatifid spinescent unenviable allogamous broomstick
inundatory pinnulated spongecake uninformed allopathic bryologist
ironhanded planchette spongewood uninitiate allophonic cacodaemon
ironically planetable spongiform unknowable allosteric cacogenics
ironmaster planetaria sponginess uranometry allotropic cacography
ironmonger plangently spongology vernacular alloverish cacomistle
ironworker planigraph sponsorial vernissage almondeyed cajolement
isentropic planimeter spunkiness vignettist altocumuli cajolingly
isoniazide planimetry stanchless vulnerable altogether camouflage
itinerancy planktonic stanchness vulnerably altostrati canonicals
jauntiness planometer standpoint wainwright ammoniacal canonicate
johnnycake plantation standstill whensoever ammoniated canonicity
Johnsonese plantlouse stenchtrap witnessbox annotation canorously
johnsonian plunderage stencilled wrongdoing annoyingly carotenoid
kennelling plunderous stenciller wrongfully antonymous carotinoid
kidnapping poinsettia stenograph wrongously aphoristic catoptrics
kinnikinic pointblank stentorian ylangylang appointive cerography
laundryman pornocracy stinginess youngberry appositely chlorinate
lawntennis pouncetbox stingingly abdominous apposition chloroform
lemniscate prancingly stinkingly abhorrence appositive chromatics
lionhunter princeling stinkstone abiogenist arboreally chromatype
loungesuit princeship stoneblind abnormally arborvitae chromosome
magnetiser principate stoneborer abrogation areolation chronicity
magnifical principial stonebrash absolutely Areopagite chronicler
magnificat principium stonefruit absolutism armorially chronogram
magnifying principled stonemason absolutist armourclad chronology
mainlander pronominal stonesnipe absolutist armourless colonially
mainspring pronounced stunningly absolutory arrogantly colonnaded
mainstream pronouncer subnuclear absorbable arrogation coloration
maintainer pugnacious swanmaiden absorbance ascomycete coloratura
meaningful pycnogonid swanupping absorbedly associable colossally
mignonette pycnometer swinefever absorbency assoilment colourable
misnomered pycnostyle swingingly absorption assortment colourably
moonflower pyknometer swinglebar absorptive atmosphere colourfast
moonshiner quantifier tauntingly accomplice attornment colourless
moonstruck quantitive teenyweeny accomplish autochthon coromandel
mountebank quenchable terneplate accordance autocratic coronation
nonnatural quenchless thankfully accoucheur autodidact cryogenics
nonnuclear quinacrine thinkingly accountant autoerotic cryoscopic
odontalgia quintuplet thinkpiece accounting autogamous cytochrome
odontology rainmaking thunderbox achondrite autogenous cytologist
openhanded reentrance thundering acrobatics autography debonairly
openhearth reunionism thunderous acrogenous autoimmune debouchure
openminded reunionist townswoman acromegaly autologous decolonise
opinionist rhinestone trancelike acronychal automation decolorant
orangepeel rhinoceros tranquilly acrophobia automatise decolorise
orangewood rhinoscope transactor acroterion automatism decompound
painkiller rhinoscopy transcribe acroterium automatist decompress
painlessly roundabout transcript admonition automobile decoration
paintbrush roundhouse transducer admonitive automotive decorative
Parnassian runnerbean transeptal admonitory autonomist decorously
```

defoliator	eulogistic	hypothesis	manoeuvrer	opposeless	rheotropic
deforciant	Eurodollar	ideography	manoeuvres	oppositely	riboflavin
delocalise	Eurovision	ideologist	manometric	opposition	rigorously
demobilise	excogitate	idiopathic	manorhouse	ordonnance	ritornelli
democratic	exportable	ignobility	mavourneen	Ordovician	ritornello
demography	exposition	ignorantly	mayonnaise	oreography	savourless
demoiselle	expositive	immobilise	memorandum	oreologist	scholastic
demolition	expository	immobility	menopausal	otioseness	schoolable
demonetise	famousness	immoderacy	Mesolithic	panopticon	schoolbook
demoniacal	favourable	immoderate	mesomerism	paronymous	schooldays
demonology	favourably	immodestly	mesomorphy	paroxysmal	schoolgirl
demoralise	floodlight	immolation	mesophytic	paroxytone	schoolmaam
demotivate	floodwater	immoralist	mesoscaphe	pedologist	schoolmarm
denominate	floorboard	immorality	mesosphere	pejoration	schoolmate
denotation	floorcloth	immortally	mesothorax	pejorative	schoolroom
denotative	fluoridate	immortelle	misogamist	penologist	schooltime
denouement	fluorinate	immoveable	misogynist	peroration	schoolwork
depolarise	fluorotype	impolitely	misogynous	peroxidise	sciolistic
depopulate	gadolinite	importable	misologist	phlogistic	scrofulous
deportment	gadolinium	importance	mixolydian	phlogiston	scrollwork
depositary	gloominess	importuner	mobocratic	phlogopite	seborrhoea
deposition	goloptious	imposingly	monocarpic	picosecond	secondbest
depository	gynocratic	imposition	monochasia	pilothouse	secondhand
derogation	gyrocopter	impossible	monochrome	pilotlight	secondment
derogatory	gyroscopic	impossibly	monoclinal	pilotwhale	secondrate
desolately	halogenate	imposthume	monoclinic	pleochroic	serologist
desolation	halogenous	impotently	monocratic	pleonastic	serotinous
desorption	halophytic	impoverish	monocyclic	pogonology	sexologist
detonation	Hanoverian	incogitant	monoecious	pogonotomy	shroudlaid
detonative	hedonistic	incoherent	monogamist	pomologist	shroudless
detoxicant	henotheism	incomplete	monogamous	porousness	Shrovetide
detoxicate	henotheist	inconstant	monogenism	proofsheet	simoniacal
devocalise	heroically	indocility	monogynian	pyrogallol	sinologist
devolution	heroicness	indolently	monogynous	pyrogenous	sitophobia
devotement	heroicomic	Indonesian	monohybrid	pyrography	smoothbore
devotional	holography	informally	monohydric	pyrolusite	smoothness
devoutness	holohedral	innocently	monolithic	pyromaniac	snootiness
dimorphism	holophrase	innominate	monologise	pyromantic	sonorously
dimorphous	holophytic	innovation	monologist	pyrometric	sororicide
disordered	holosteric	innovative	monomaniac	pyrophoric	spookiness
disorderly	homocercal	innovatory	monophonic	pyrotechny	spoondrift
disownment	homoeopath	insobriety	monopodial	pyroxenite	spoonerism
dolomitise	homogamous	insociable	monopodium	razorblade	Stroganoff
dolorously	homogenise	insolation	monopolise	razorshell	stromatous
doxography	homogenous	insolently	monopolist	recolonise	stronghold
droopingly	homologate	insolvable	monorhymed	recommence	strongroom
ectodermal	homologise	insolvency	monotheism	recompense	suborbital
ectodermic	homologous	insouciant	monotheist	reconciler	subordinal
ectogenous	homonymous	intolerant	monotonous	reconsider	sycophancy
effortless	homoousian	intonation	monovalent	recordable	synoecious
embodiment	homophonic	intoxicant	moroseness	recoupment	synonymist
embolismic	homosexual	intoxicate	motorcycle	redolently	synonymity
embonpoint	homozygote	invocation	mycologist	reformable	synonymous
embossment	homozygous	invocatory	mycoplasma	rejoicings	synoptical
embouchure	honorarium	involucral	mycorrhiza	relocation	synostosis
embowelled	honourable	involucrum	myxomatous	remodelled	tapotement
encourager	honourably	involution	myxomycete	remonetise	taxonomist
endocrinal	honourless	ionosphere	nanosecond	remorseful	theocratic
endodermal	horologist	jacobinise	negotiable	remoteness	theodicean
endodermis	horoscopic	Jacobinism	negotiator	renovation	theodolite
endogamous	humoresque	Jacobinism	nicotinism	repopulate	theogonist
endogenous	humoristic	Jehovistic	nomography	reportable	theologian
endophytic	humorously	jocoseness	nomologist	reportedly	theologise
endopodite	humourless	joyousness	nomothetic	reposition	theologist
endorsable	humoursome	kilogramme	nosography	repository	theophanic
endoscopic	hylotheism	laboratory	nosologist	resolutely	theophoric
endosmosis	hypocorism	laconicism	nosophobia	resolution	theopneust
endosmotic	hypodermal	lemongrass	notonectal	resolutive	theoretics
endothelia	hypodermic	lipography	octodecimo	resolvable	theosopher
enjoinment	hypodermis	lipomatous	octonarian	resolvedly	throatwort
entombment	hypogynous	locomotion	octopodous	resonantly	thromboses
entomology	hypolimnia	locomotive	odiousness	resorcinol	thrombosis
ephorality	hypophyses	locomotory	oecologist	resorption	thrombotic
ergodicity	hypophysis	logography	oenologist	resorptive	throneless
ergonomics	hypostasis	logorrhoea	oesophagus	resounding	throughout
ergonomist	hypostatic	loxodromic	oleography	revocation	throughput
ergosterol	hypotactic	lycopodium	oncogenous	revocatory	throughway
ethologist	hypotenuse	Mahommedan	oncologist	revolution	throwstick
etiolation	hypotheses	malodorous	ontologist	rheologist	timocratic

```
timorously  comparably  despiteful  lymphocyte  rhapsodise  symphonion
tobogganer  comparator  despiteous  lymphomata  rhapsodist  symphonist
tocopherol  comparison  despondent  lyophilise  ripplemark  symphylous
tomography  compassion  diapedesis  Malpighian  salpingian  symphyseal
topography  compasssaw  diapedetic  misprision  sappanwood  symphysial
topologist  compatible  diaphanous  morphemics  sapphirine  symposiast
toroidally  compatibly  disparager  morphinism  scapegrace  teaplanter
trioecious  compatriot  disparates  morphogeny  scepticism  telpherage
tutorially  compelling  dispassion  morphology  scyphiform  temperable
typography  compendium  dispatcher  myopically  scyphozoan  temperance
typologist  compensate  dispelling  Neapolitan  sempstress  temperedly
unbonneted  competence  dispensary  neoplastic  serpentine  temporally
uncommonly  competency  dispersant  nipplewort  sexpartite  temporalty
unforeseen  competitor  dispersion  nitpicking  shipbroker  temporiser
unholiness  complacent  dispersive  nonpayment  shipfitter  temptation
unhouseled  complainer  dispersoid  nonplaying  shipmaster  temptingly
unionistic  complected  dispirited  nonplussed  shiprigged  ticpolonga
unmorality  complement  dispiteous  nympholept  shipwright  torpidness
unmortised  completely  disposable  offputting  shopkeeper  trappiness
unsociable  completion  dispossess  omophagous  shoplifter  trepanning
unsociably  completive  dispraiser  outpatient  shopsoiled  tripartite
unsocially  complexion  disputable  outpouring  shopwalker  triphammer
untowardly  complexity  disputably  outputting  shopwindow  triphthong
unwontedly  compliance  drophammer  ovipositor  simpleness  triplicate
unworkable  compliancy  drupaceous  pemphigoid  simplicity  triplicity
unworthily  complicacy  dysplastic  pemphigous  simplifier  tropaeolum
upholstery  complicate  dysprosium  penpushing  simplistic  trophology
uproarious  complicity  Egyptology  peppercorn  slipperily  tropically
valorously  compliment  endproduct  peppermill  slipstitch  tropologic
vaporiform  complotted  epiphytism  peppermint  slipstream  tropopause
vaporously  composedly  eruptively  pepperwort  sloppiness  tropophyte
vasoactive  compositor  evaporable  perpetrate  snapdragon  tryptophan
velocipede  compotator  evaporator  perpetuate  snappishly  turpentine
venomously  compounder  flapdoodle  perpetuity  soapboiler  tympanites
vigorously  compradore  flippantly  perplexity  soapbubble  tympanitic
virologist  comprehend  floppiness  pluperfect  soapflakes  tympanitis
wagonvault  compressed  gaspereaux  prepackage  staphyline  unipartite
xenophobia  compressor  geophysics  preparator  stepfather  unsporting
xerography  compromise  geoponical  preparedly  stephanite  utopianism
xerophytic  compulsion  grapefruit  prepayable  stepladder  vesperbell
xylography  compulsive  grapesugar  prepayment  stepmother  vespertine
xylophonic  compulsory  graphemics  prepensely  stepparent  wampumpeag
zygodactyl  computable  graphitise  prepossess  stepsister  wappenshaw
zygomorphy  computator  graphology  prepotence  stipellate  weaponless
acephalous  cooperator  graptolite  prepotency  stipulator  whipstitch
adaptation  cooptation  helplessly  propagable  stopvolley  wraparound
adaptively  cooptative  hempnettle  propaganda  stupendous  zoophagous
adoptively  copperhead  hippocampi  propagator  stupidness  zoophilous
agapanthus  corporally  Hippocrene  propellant  stypticity  adequately
allpurpose  corporator  hippodrome  propellent  sulphonate  chequebook
anapaestic  corporeity  hippogriff  propelling  sulphurate  cinquefoil
anaplastic  corpulence  hippogryph  propensity  sulphurise  coequality
anaptyctic  corpulency  hippomanes  properness  sulphurous  craquelure
anopheline  corpuscule  hippophagy  propertied  sunparlour  desquamate
apophthegm  couplement  hospitable  prophesier  supperless  disqualify
apoplectic  cowparsley  hospitably  prophetess  supplanter  disquieten
atypically  cowpuncher  humpbacked  propionate  supplejack  disquietly
auspicious  crapulence  inappetent  propitiate  supplement  eloquently
besprinkle  crepuscule  inapposite  propitious  suppleness  frequenter
biophysics  crippledom  inaptitude  proportion  suppletion  frequently
blepharism  cryptogamy  ineptitude  propounder  suppletive  inequality
bumpkinish  cryptogram  inoperable  propraetor  suppletory  iniquitous
campaigner  cryptology  inspanning  proprietor  suppliance  marquisate
campestral  cuspidated  inspection  propulsion  supplicant  masquerade
camphorate  dampcourse  inspective  propulsive  supplicate  mosquitoes
cappuccino  dampingoff  inspirator  propylaeum  supportive  opaqueness
carpellary  dapplegrey  inspissate  psephology  supposable  pasquinade
carpetweed  dauphiness  isopterous  purposeful  supposably  perquisite
carphology  deepfreeze  jasperware  rampageous  supposedly  triquetrae
chaparajos  deepfrozen  jeopardise  rapporteur  suppressor  triquetral
chaparejos  deeprooted  knopkierie  reappraise  surplusage  ubiquitous
chapfallen  deepseated  lampoonery  respectful  surprising  unequalled
chaplaincy  delphinium  lampoonist  respecting  suspenders  uniqueness
cispontine  delphinoid  leopardess  respective  suspension  vanquisher
coaptation  despatcher  limpidness  respirable  suspensive  abbreviate
colportage  desperados  Lippizaner  respirator  suspensoid  aberdevine
colporteur  despicable  lowpitched  respondent  suspensory  aberrantly
compaction  despicably  lowprofile  responsive  suspicious  aberration
comparable  despisable  lumpsucker  responsory  sympathise  aboriginal
```

abortively	coordinate	exprobrate	hybridiser	lubricator	overground
acarpelous	coproducer	extractant	hydraulics	lubricious	overgrowth
accredited	coprolitic	extraction	hydrically	macrophage	overhanded
accrescent	correction	extractive	hydrologic	macrospore	overlander
acervation	corrective	extramural	hydrolysis	madreporic	overlapped
achromatic	correspond	extraneity	hydrolytic	marrowbone	overlooker
aggrandise	corrigenda	extraneous	hydromancy	marrowless	overmanned
aggression	corrigible	extricable	hydrometer	matriarchy	overmantel
aggressive	corrivalry	exurbanite	hydrometry	matricidal	overmaster
alarmingly	corroboree	fabricator	hydropathy	matronhood	overnicety
allrounder	corrugated	Fahrenheit	hydrophane	matronship	overpraise
altruistic	corrugator	fairground	hydrophily	matronymic	overrefine
amercement	corruption	fairhaired	hydrophone	meerschaum	overridden
amerciable	corruptive	fairleader	hydrophyte	merrymaker	overriding
Amerindian	courageous	fairminded	hydroplane	metrically	overshadow
anarchical	courthouse	fairspoken	hydroscope	metronomic	overslaugh
androecium	cuirassier	fairycycle	hydrotaxis	metronymic	overspread
androgenic	curricular	fearlessly	hygrograph	metropolis	overstride
aphrodisia	curriculum	fearnought	hygrometer	microbiota	overstrung
appreciate	czarevitch	fearsomely	hygrometry	microcline	oversubtle
apprentice	decrescent	febrifugal	hygrophyte	microfarad	oversupply
approvable	deerforest	fibreboard	hygroscope	microfiche	overthrown
approvably	defrayable	fibreglass	iatrogenic	micrograph	overthrust
ascribable	defrayment	fibrillary	impregnant	microlitic	overtopped
ascription	degradable	fibrillate	impregnate	micrometer	overweight
astragalus	degradedly	fibrillose	impresario	micrometry	overwinter
astringent	degressive	fibrinogen	impression	microphone	parramatta
astrologer	depravedly	fibrositis	impressive	microphyte	parricidal
astrologic	depreciate	fierceness	imprimatur	micropylar	parrotfish
astronomer	depredator	flirtation	imprinting	microscope	patriality
astronomic	depressant	florentine	improbable	microscopy	patriarchy
attractant	depression	florescent	improbably	microseism	patriciate
attraction	depressive	floriation	improperly	microspore	patricidal
attractive	deprivable	floribunda	improvable	migrainous	patrilocal
avaricious	detraction	floridness	improvably	morrispike	patriotism
averseness	detractive	florilegia	improviser	mournfully	patristics
aversively	diarrhoeal	floristics	imprudence	narrowness	patrolling
barracouta	diarrhoeic	fourchette	inartistic	necrolater	patronymic
barramunda	digression	fourfooted	inbreeding	necrolatry	pearldiver
barramundi	digressive	fourhanded	incrassate	necromancy	peerlessly
barratrous	disrespect	fourinhand	incredible	necrophile	petroglyph
barrelling	disruption	fourleaved	incredibly	necrophily	petrolatum
barrenness	disruptive	fourposter	increscent	necropolis	petronella
barrenwort	ditriglyph	foursquare	infraction	necroscopy	pharisaism
batrachian	doorkeeper	fourstroke	infrahuman	negrophile	pharmacist
bedraggled	dwarfishly	fourteener	infrasonic	negrophobe	pharyngeal
blurringly	effrontery	fourteenth	infrequent	neurilemma	pheromonal
botryoidal	emarginate	gadrooning	ingratiate	neurolemma	piercingly
bourbonism	embroidery	gloriously	ingredient	neuropathy	porraceous
bourbonist	embryogeny	guardhouse	ingression	neuroplasm	pourparler
burramundi	embryology	gunrunning	inordinate	neurotoxin	pruriently
Caerphilly	embryonate	hairraiser	intramural	nigrescent	puerperium
capricious	emeryboard	hairspring	intrahuman	nitrochalk	putrescent
carragheen	emerypaper	hairstreak	intrepidly	nitrogroup	putrescine
carryingon	emerywheel	hairstroke	intrigante	nourishing	putridness
charactery	encroacher	heartblock	intriguant	nutritious	Pyrrhonian
chargeable	energetics	heartblood	introducer	obtruncate	Pyrrhonism
chargehand	enervation	heartbreak	introrsely	oleraceous	Pyrrhonist
charioteer	enervative	heartiness	introspect	overabound	pyrrhotite
charismata	engrossing	heartsease	inurbanity	overactive	quarantine
charitable	enormously	heartthrob	jerrybuilt	overblouse	quarrelled
charitably	entrancing	heartwhole	jinricksha	overbought	quarreller
Charleston	entrapment	Hebraistic	jinrikisha	overburden	quarrender
charmingly	enwrapping	heortology	journalese	overcharge	quartation
chartreuse	escritoire	herrenvolk	journalise	overcommit	quarterage
chartulary	eternalise	Herrnhuter	journalism	overcooked	quarterday
chersonese	eternalist	heuristics	journalist	overexcite	quartering
chiromancy	everglades	hierarchal	journeyman	overexpose	quartzitic
choriambic	everliving	hierarchic	lacrimator	overflight	quercitron
churchgoer	everyplace	hierocracy	lacrymator		quirkiness
churchyard	everything	hieroglyph	lauraceous		rearmament
churlishly	everywhere	hierograph	laureation		recreantly
citronella	excrescent	hierolatry	laurelling		recreation
clarabella	excruciate	hierophant	lawrencium		recreative
Clarenceux	exorbitant	hoarseness	Lawrentian		recrudesce
clerestory	expressage	horrendous	leprechaun		refraction
clerically	expression	horridness	librettist		refractive
coarseness	expressive	hourcircle	lipreading		refractory
coercively	expressway		logrolling		refreshing

minstrelsy	presentday	subshrubby	bestowment	clothespeg	distraught
missionary	presentive	subsidence	bestridden	clothespin	distressed
missionise	presidency	subsidiary	bestseller	coathanger	distribute
moisturise	presidiary	subsistent	betterment	coatimundi	distringas
monsignori	presignify	subspecies	birthplace	coetaneous	doctorship
monstrance	pressagent	substation	birthright	coeternity	dustjacket
mossbunker	pressingly	substitute	birthstone	contagious	dystrophic
mousseline	pressurise	substratum	bitterling	contendent	earthbound
moustached	presternum	swashplate	bitterness	contention	earthiness
moustachio	presumable	tasselling	bitterroot	contestant	earthlight
Mousterian	presumably	tessellate	bitterwood	contextual	earthquake
mudskipper	presuppose	tinselling	blitheness	contexture	earthshine
mudslinger	prismoidal	topsyturvy	blithering	contiguity	earthwards
Mussulmans	prissiness	trashiness	blithesome	contiguous	eartrumpet
myasthenia	prosaicism	trespasser	blitzkrieg	continence	easterling
nauseating	proscenium	trisection	blottesque	contingent	Eastertide
nauseously	prosciutto	triskelion	bootlegger	continuant	editorship
newsagency	proscriber	trustfully	bootlessly	continuate	eisteddfod
newscaster	prosecutor	trustiness	bootlicker	continuity	elutriator
newsletter	prosilient	trustingly	bootstraps	continuous	epithelial
newsmonger	prosodical	unassisted	bottlefeed	contortion	epithelium
newsreader	prospector	unassuming	bottleneck	contortive	erethismic
newsvendor	prospectus	versicular	bottletree	contraband	erotically
newsworthy	prosperity	waistcloth	bottomless	contrabass	erotogenic
newswriter	prosperous	wassailing	bottommost	contractor	erotomania
noisemaker	prosthesis	Welshwoman	bratticing	contradict	exoterical
nonstarter	prosthetic	whiskified	Britishism	contraprop	exothermal
nonswimmer	prostitute	whispering	bustlingly	contrarily	exothermic
nurseryman	prostomial	worshipful	butterball	contravene	exotically
offsetting	prostomium	worshipped	butterbean	contribute	factiously
onesidedly	puissantly	worshipper	butterfish	contritely	factitious
opisometer	pulsatilla	wristwatch	buttermilk	contrition	factorship
outsitting	pulsimeter	yeastiness	butterwort	controlled	factualism
outstation	pulsometer	abstemious	buttonball	controller	factualist
outstretch	purseproud	abstention	buttonbush	controvert	factuality
outswinger	pursership	abstergent	buttondown	corticated	faithfully
pansophist	purseseine	abstersion	buttonhole	costliness	fantastico
parsonbird	pursuivant	abstersive	buttonhook	cottoncake	fantoccini
parsonical	questioner	abstinence	buttonless	cottonseed	fastidious
passageway	ramshackle	abstinency	buttonwood	cottontail	fastigiate
passionary	reasonable	abstracted	cantaloupe	cottonweed	featherbed
passionate	reasonably	abstracter	cantatrice	cottonwood	feathering
Passionist	reasonless	abstractly	canterbury	cottonwool	fertiliser
peashooter	reassemble	abstractor	cantilever	couturiere	festoonery
pensionary	reassembly	abstrusely	cantillate	cretaceous	fetterlock
persecutor	reissuable	abstrusity	cantonment	critically	fictioneer
persiflage	ripsnorter	acatalepsy	captiously	cultivable	fictionist
persistent	roistering	acetabular	Carthusian	cultivator	fictitious
personable	roisterous	acetabulum	cartomancy	culturally	fiftyfifty
personally	rouseabout	acotyledon	cartoonist	custommade	filterable
personalty	roustabout	aesthetics	cartwright	cuttlebone	filthiness
personator	Russianise	aesthetism	castration	cuttlefish	filtration
persuasion	Russophile	agitatedly	cattlegrid	cuttystool	fisticuffs
persuasive	Russophobe	amateurish	cautionary	cystoscope	flatfooted
phosphatic	Sanskritic	amateurism	cautiously	cystoscopy	flattering
phosphoric	seaserpent	anatomical	centennial	deathwatch	flatulence
phosphorus	seasonable	anatropous	centesimal	deltiology	flatulency
physically	seasonably	apothecary	centigrade	dentifrice	foetidness
physicking	seasonally	apothecial	centilitre	destructor	fontanelle
physiocrat	seismicity	apothecium	centillion	dextrality	footballer
physiology	seismogram	apotheoses	centimetre	dextrously	footbridge
pigsticker	seismology	apotheosis	centralise	diathermal	footcandle
pinstriped	sensedatum	apotropaic	centralism	diathermic	footlights
plasmodesm	senseorgan	arithmetic	centralist	diatropism	footwarmer
plasmodium	sensitiser	arytaenoid	centrality	dictatress	fortepiano
plasmogamy	sensualise	auctioneer	centreback	dictionary	forthright
plasmolyse	sensualism	austenitic	centrefold	distensile	fortissimi
plasticise	sensualist	Australian	centrehalf	distension	fortissimo
plasticity	sensuality	baptistery	centricity	distention	fortuitism
plesiosaur	sensuously	bastardise	centrifuge	distichous	fortuitist
possession	sixshooter	battailous	centromere	distilland	fortuitous
possessive	skyscraper	battledore	centrosome	distillate	fortyniner
possessory	solstitial	battlement	certiorari	distillery	fostering
presageful	sousaphone	battleship	chatelaine	distilling	fraternise
presbyopia	spasticity	Benthamism	chatoyance	distinctly	fraternity
presbyopic	subscriber	Benthamite	chatterbox	distortion	fratricide
presbytery	subsection	bestialise	chattiness	distracted	fritillary
prescience	subsellium	bestiality	Cistercian	distrainer	frothiness
prescriber	subsequent	bestirring	clothesbag	distrainor	

frutescent	letterbomb	pantrymaid	pretendent	settlement	tetterwort
fustanella	letterbook	partiality	pretension	sextillion	textualist
gasteropod	lettercard	participle	prettiness	shuttering	texturally
gastrology	letterhead	particular	protanopic	sisterhood	tilthammer
gastronome	letterless	parturient	protection	skateboard	tittupping
gastronomy	listlessly	pasteboard	protective	sketchable	toothbrush
genteelism	litterlout	pastellist	protectory	sketchbook	toothiness
gentilesse	littleness	pasteurise	protectrix	skittishly	toothpaste
gentlefolk	lustration	pasteurism	proteiform	slatternly	toothshell
gentleness	lustreless	pastmaster	proteinous	slitpocket	tortellini
geothermal	lustrously	pastorally	protensive	slothfully	tortfeasor
geothermic	Malthusian	pastorship	proteolyse	sluttishly	tortiously
geotropism	manteltree	pastrycook	protestant	smattering	tortuosity
glottology	martensite	pasturable	prothallia	smuttiness	tortuously
gluttonise	martialism	pastyfaced	prothallus	softbilled	triternate
gluttonous	martingale	pectinated	protophyta	softboiled	triturable
goatsbeard	mastectomy	pentachord	protophyte	softfinned	triturator
goatsucker	masterhand	pentagonal	protoplasm	softheaded	Trotskyism
gratefully	masterhood	pentameter	protoplast	softspoken	Trotskyist
gratifying	masterless	pentastich	prototypal	soothingly	Trotskyite
gratuitous	mastermind	pentathlon	prototypic	soothsayer	truthfully
grittiness	mastership	pentatomic	protracted	souterrain	tufthunter
gutturally	masterwork	pentatonic	protractor	southbound	tuitionary
hartebeest	masticable	pentimento	protreptic	southerner	turtleback
heathendom	masticator	pentstemon	protrusile	southernly	turtledove
heathenise	meltingpot	pertinence	protrusion	southwards	turtleneck
heathenish	mentorship	pertinency	protrusive	sowthistle	ulotrichan
heathenism	mettlesome	pesticidal	psittacine	spatchcock	unattached
heatstroke	mintmaster	pestilence	purtenance	spathulate	unattended
hectically	mirthfully	photoflood	quaternary	spatiality	unctuosity
hectograph	mistakable	photogenic	quaternate	spitchcock	unctuously
hectolitre	mistakenly	photograph	quaternion	spitefully	unsteadily
hectometre	misthought	photolitho	quaternity	spotlessly	unstrained
heptachord	Montagnard	photolysis	quatorzain	spottiness	unstressed
heptagonal	montbretia	photolytic	quatrefoil	statecraft	upstanding
Heptameron	mouthorgan	photometer	rattlehead	statically	urethritis
heptameter	mouthpiece	photometry	rattlepate	stationary	vectograph
heptarchic	multifaced	photonasty	rattletrap	stationery	ventilator
Heptateuch	multiloquy	photophily	rectorship	statistics	ventricose
heptatonic	multimedia	photophore	reiterance	statoscope	ventriculi
hinterland	multiphase	photoprint	restaurant	statuesque	vertebrate
histocrasis	multiplier	phototaxis	restlessly	statutable	vertically
histolysis	multipolar	phototrope	restorable	statutably	vestibular
histolytic	multistage	phytogenic	restrained	stitchwort	vestibulum
historical	multivocal	phytophagy	restrainer	subtenancy	vestpocket
histrionic	muttonhead	phytotoxic	rhetorical	subterfuge	victimiser
hoitytoity	myrtaceous	pictograph	rhythmical	subtleness	Victoriana
hootenanny	mystagogic	pictorical	rontgenise	subtrahend	victorious
hostelling	mystagogue	pistillary	rootedness	sultanship	victualled
hysteresis	mysterious	pistillate	rottenness	sultriness	victualler
hysteretic	mystically	pistolling	rottweiler	sustaining	Vietnamese
hysterical	nasturtium	pistolshot	runthrough	sustenance	virtuality
ichthyosis	natterjack	pistolwhip	rustically	sustention	virtueless
initialise	nautically	pistonring	saltarello	sustentive	virtuosity
initialled	nectareous	platelayer	saltcellar	switchback	virtuously
initiation	nettlerash	plutocracy	saltigrade	switchover	voltameter
initiative	neutralise	plutolatry	sawtoothed	syntagmata	vortically
initiatory	neutralism	poetically	scatheless	synthesise	vorticella
instalment	neutralist	pontifical	scathingly	synthesist	vorticular
instigator	neutrality	pontifices	scattergun	synthetise	wantonness
instilling	northbound	portamento	scattering	synthetist	wastefully
institutor	northerner	portcullis	scattiness	systematic	wastepaper
instructor	northwards	portentous	Scotswoman	systemless	wattlebird
instrument	nostologic	portliness	Scotticise	tactically	weatherbox
isothermal	nuptiality	Portuguese	Scotticism	tactlessly	weathering
jolterhead	nyctalopia	postbellum	scutellate	tantaliser	weatherman
justiciary	nyctalopic	postchaise	seethrough	tantamount	wentletrap
Kantianism	nyctinasty	postexilic	seltzogene	Tartuffian	Wertherian
kettledrum	obituarist	posthumous	sentential	Tartuffism	Wertherism
knottiness	obstetrics	postillion	sentiently	tastefully	westernise
lactescent	obstructor	postliminy	septenarii	tattletale	westwardly
lanternfly	ophthalmia	postmaster	septennial	tautomeric	whatsoever
lanthanide	ophthalmic	postmortem	septennium	tautophony	whitebeard
lattermost	oratorical	postoffice	septically	teatrolley	whitefaced
lectionary	orotundity	postpartum	septillion	teetotally	whitesmith
lefthanded	oysterfarm	postscript	Septuagint	tentacular	whitethorn
lefthander	paltriness	postulator	sestertium	tenterhook	WhitMonday
lenticular	pantograph	pratincole	sestertius	testaceous	WhitSunday
lentigines	pantomimic	pretendant	setterwort	testflight	wintertide

wintertime	casualness	illuminist	maturation	returnable	voluminous
wintriness	ceruminous	illusional	maturative	rheumatics	voluptuary
wontedness	chaudfroid	illusively	matureness	rheumatism	voluptuous
worthiness	chauffeuse	illusorily	medullated	rheumatoid	aboveboard
worthwhile	chauntress	illustrate	minuscular	robustious	brevetting
wrathfully	chauvinism	immunology	minutebook	robustness	canvasback
wrathiness	chauvinist	immurement	minutehand	roquelaure	canvaswork
wretchedly	cloudberry	impudently	minuteness	salubrious	chevrotain
yesteryear	cloudburst	impudicity	modulation	salutarily	chivalrous
youthfully	cloudiness	impugnable	monumental	salutation	clavichord
zwitterion	columbaria	impugnment	naturalise	salutatory	clavicular
abducentes	copulation	impuissant	naturalism	saturation	cleverness
abjuration	copulative	impureness	naturalist	saturnalia	clovehitch
abruptness	coquettish	imputation	naturopath	scrupulous	cloverleaf
absurdness	cucullated	imputative	nebulosity	scrutineer	convalesce
accumulate	cumulation	inaugurate	nebulously	scrutinise	convection
accurately	cumulative	incubation	nodulation	secularise	convective
accursedly	cumuliform	incubative	obdurately	secularism	convenable
accusation	deductible	incubatory	obfuscated	secularist	convenance
accusative	dehumanise	inculcator	obnubilate	secularity	convenient
accusatory	dehumidify	inculpable	obturation	securement	convention
accusingly	delusional	incumbency	obtuseness	secureness	conventual
accustomed	delusively	incunabula	occupation	securiform	convergent
acoustical	demureness	incurrable	occupative	seducement	conversant
acquirable	demurrable	inducement	occurrence	seductress	conversely
acquitting	denudation	inductance	oecumenism	sedulously	conversion
adjudgment	denunciate	indulgence	oppugnancy	seguidilla	conveyable
adjudicate	depuration	induration	osculation	sepulchral	conveyance
adjunction	depurative	indurative	osculatory	sequacious	conviction
adjunctive	deputation	industrial	patulously	sequential	convictive
adjuration	diluteness	infusorial	peculation	sequestrum	convincing
adjuratory	disulphate	infusorian	peculiarly	shouldered	convoluted
adjustable	disulphide	inhumanely	peduncular	simulacrum	convulsant
adjustment	disutility	inhumanity	petulantly	simulation	convulsion
aeruginous	divulgence	inhumation	ploughable	simulative	convulsive
albuminoid	documental	injunction	ploughland	simulatory	couverture
albuminous	effulgence	injunctive	pneumatics	sinusoidal	cravenness
allurement	effusively	innuendoes	popularise	solubilise	curvaceous
allusively	Eleusinian	innumeracy	popularity	solubility	curvacious
almucanter	enduringly	innumerate	population	splutterer	curvetting
ambulacral	engulfment	innumerous	populistic	sprucebeer	drivelling
ambulacrum	Esculapian	inquietude	populously	spruceness	driverless
ambulation	escutcheon	inquisitor	proudflesh	staurolite	elevenplus
ambulatory	excusatory	insufflate	pseudocarp	structural	exuviation
ambushment	exhumation	insularism	purulently	structured	fervidness
ammunition	expunction	insularity	ranunculus	struthious	flavescent
amputation	expurgator	insulation	rebuttable	tabularise	flavourful
aneurismal	fabulously	insurgence	recumbency	tabulation	flavouring
aneurysmal	fiducially	insurgency	recuperate	tegumental	fluviatile
angularity	figuration	intubation	recurrence	theurgical	frivolling
annularity	figurative	jaguarundi	redundance	thoughtful	galvaniser
annulation	figurehead	Janusfaced	redundancy	thousandth	gravestone
annunciate	fraudulent	jejuneness	refuelling	thruppence	gravimeter
araucarian	furuncular	jesuitical	refulgence	titubation	gravimetry
argumentum	futureless	jocularity	refundable	traumatism	grovelling
assumption	futuristic	lacustrine	refundment	triumphant	harvestman
assumptive	futurology	lanuginose	refutation	triumviral	heavenborn
astuteness	gerundival	languinous	regularise	troubadour	heavensent
attunement	gesundheit	leguminous	regularity	trousseaux	heavenward
augustness	glauberite	lieutenant	regulation	trouvaille	heavyarmed
autumnally	glauconite	liquescent	regulative	tumultuary	inevitable
avouchment	goluptious	liquidator	regulatory	tumultuous	inevitably
balustrade	groundbait	liquidiser	rejuvenate	unbuttoned	larvicidal
Beaujolais	groundless	liquidness	rejuvenise	uncustomed	malvaceous
beautician	groundling	liturgical	reluctance	undulation	marvelling
beautifier	groundmass	lobulation	reluctancy	undulatory	marvellous
bemusement	groundplan	locustbean	remunerate	unguentary	misventure
bequeathal	groundrent	loquacious	republican	unjustness	nonviolent
bibulously	groundsman	lotuseater	repudiator	unnumbered	olivaceous
bicultural	groundwork	lucubrator	repugnance	unruliness	perversely
bisulphate	haruspices	luculently	repugnancy	unsuitable	perversion
bisulphide	hirudinean	lugubrious	repurchase	usquebaugh	perversity
bisulphite	hocuspocus	luxuriance	reputation	ustulation	perversive
bituminise	holusbolus	maculation	requiescat	velutinous	prevailing
bituminous	homunculus	maculature	resultless	virulently	prevalence
calumniate	illuminant	majuscular	resumption	visualiser	prevenancy
calumnious	illuminate	manumitted	resumptive	vituperate	prevenient
caoutchouc	illuminati	manuscript	resupinate	volubility	prevention
caruncular	illuminism	maquillage	resurgence	volumetric	preventive

```
previously  outwitting  playbyplay  agapanthus  collarette  euthanasia
privileged  showerbath  playfellow  aggrandise  collarless  extractant
provenance  showjumper  playground  agitatedly  collarstud  extraction
proverbial  showwindow  playwright  airmanship  collatable  extractive
providence  skewbridge  polyandric  alexanders  collateral  extramural
provincial  skywriting  polyanthus  alliaceous  commandant  extraneity
provisions  slowfooted  polyatamic  alphabetic  commandeer  extraneous
provitamin  slowmotion  polychaete  alphameric  commandery  fallacious
provocator  slowwitted  polychrest  amylaceous  commanding  fandangoes
pulveriser  snowcapped  polychrome  anabaptism  commandoes  fantastico
pulvinated  snowgrouse  polyclinic  anabaptist  compaction  flycatcher
purveyance  snowmobile  polycyclic  anapaestic  comparable  foliaceous
scavengery  snowplough  polydactyl  angwantibo  comparably  fontanelle
serviceman  stewardess  polydipsia  animadvert  comparator  formatting
servomotor  trawlerman  polygamist  animalcula  comparison  forwarding
shovelhead  trowelling  polygamous  animalcule  compassion  fricandeau
shovelling  twowheeler  polygenism  animatedly  compasssaw  fricasseed
silverbath  unswerving  polygenist  anonaceous  compatible  fustanella
silverfish  viewfinder  polygenous  apocalypse  compatibly  galvaniser
silverside  viewlessly  polygraphy  apocarpous  compatriot  gargantuan
silverware  alexanders  polygynous  apolaustic  confabbing  gemmaceous
silverweed  asexuality  polyhedral  appealable  connatural  genialness
slavetrade  coexistent  polyhedric  appearance  contagious  geriatrics
slavocracy  deoxidiser  polyhedron  appeasable  convalesce  geriatrist
Slavophile  epexegeses  polyhistor  archaistic  coriaceous  glumaceous
Slavophobe  epexegesis  polymathic  arenaceous  courageous  gormandise
snivelling  epexegetic  polymerise  arytaenoid  cowcatcher  granadilla
stavesacre  flexuously  polymerism  astragalus  cowparsley  gregarious
subvention  fluxionary  polymerous  attractant  crematoria  grenadilla
subversion  fraxinella  Polynesian  attraction  cretaceous  gymnastics
subversive  inexistent  polynomial  attractive  cuirassier  haematosis
survivance  inexorable  polyonymic  barcarolle  curvaceous  haematuria
swiveleyed  inexorably  polyphasic  barracouta  curvacious  Hansardise
swivelling  inexpertly  polyphonic  barramunda  declarable  Hebraistic
travelling  inexpiable  polyploidy  barramundi  declassify  heliacally
travelogue  inexpiably  polysemous  barratrous  defeasance  helianthus
travertine  inexplicit  polytheism  bastardise  defeasible  henharrier
trivialise  proximally  polytheist  batrachian  deflagrate  heptachord
trivialism  quixotical  polytocous  battalious  defrayable  heptagonal
triviality  thixotropy  polyvalent  bedraggled  defrayment  Heptameron
unavailing  unexampled  prayerbook  belladonna  degradable  heptameter
unevenness  unexcelled  recyclable  bombardier  degradedly  heptarchic
uneventful  unexpected  rubythroat  brigandage  depravedly  Heptateuch
university  unexplored  satyagraha  brigandine  dermatitis  heptatonic
univocally  alcyonaria  satyriasis  brigandism  dermatogen  herbaceous
valvulitis  artycrafty  strychnine  brigantine  deshabille  hereabouts
weaverbird  Babylonian  strychnism  brocatelle  despatcher  heulandite
angwantibo  babysitter  swaybacked  bureaucrat  detraction  hierarchal
answerable  barysphere  benzocaine  burramundi  detractive  hierarchic
answerably  calyciform  benzpyrene  bursarship  dictatress  hullabaloo
Boswellian  calyptrate  blazonment  byssaceous  diecasting  husbandage
Boswellise  caryatides  brazenness  calcareous  disbarring  husbandman
Boswellism  chrysolite  brazilwood  campaigner  disdainful  hydraulics
brawniness  chrysotile  canzonetta  cantaloupe  dishabille  hypnagogic
browbeaten  copyholder  dazzlement  cantatrice  disharmony  idolatress
brownshirt  copyreader  dazzlingly  canvasback  dismalness  idolatrous
brownstone  copywriter  frizziness  canvaswork  disparager  illnatured
clawhammer  Corybantes  fuzzywuzzy  carmagnole  disparates  implacable
clownishly  corybantic  manzanilla  carnallite  dispassion  implacably
crewelwork  coryphaeus  mizzenmast  carnassial  dispatcher  incrassate
crowkeeper  disyllabic  mizzensail  carragheen  dissatisfy  infeasible
drawbridge  disyllable  mozzarella  caryatides  dogmatical  inflatable
drawingpin  encyclical  piezometer  cascarilla  dogmatiser  infraction
drawlingly  encystment  pozzolanic  casualness  dramatical  infrahuman
drawstring  enzymology  pozzuolana  cephalopod  dramaturge  infrasonic
drowsihead  eurypterid  prizefight  chamaeleon  dramaturgy  ingratiate
drowsiness  greyheaded  puzzlement  chaparajos  drupaceous  inspanning
earwigging  karyoplasm  quizmaster  chaparejos  drysaltery  instalment
earwitness  kerygmatic  razzmatazz  charactery  elecampane  intramural
eyewitness  ladychapel  rhizogenic  chinagraph  emblazoner  intraurban
flawlessly  ladyfinger  rhizomorph  chivalrous  emblazonry  iridaceous
flowergirl  ladykiller  rhizophore  Circassian  enchanting  Ishmaelite
flowerless  laryngitic  zigzagging  clarabella  endearment  isolatable
forwarding  laryngitis  ─────────  cockalorum  entrancing  jackanapes
forwearied  molybdenum  abreaction  cockatrice  entrapment  jackassery
frowningly  palynology  acatalepsy  coelacanth  enwrapping  jaguarundi
growlingly  papyrology  acetabular  coetaneous  epigastric  jaywalking
jaywalking  pityriasis  acetabulum  collarbeam  ericaceous  jeopardise
miswording  playacting  adamantine  collarbone  escharotic  Kafkaesque
```

```
kidnapping  phalangeal  sherardise  ungracious  drawbridge  parabolise
kookaburra  phenacetin  sialagogic  ungrateful  dungbeetle  paraboloid
Lammastide  philatelic  sialagogue  unicameral  durability   pawnbroker
lauraceous  phylactery  signalling  unilateral  equability   phlebotomy
leopardess  piccalilli  skyjacking  unipartite  exhibition   pinebeauty
liliaceous  piccaninny  smaragdine  unmeasured  exhibitory   playbyplay
Lollardism  pickaninny  smaragdite  unreadable  exorbitant   pliability
longaevous  pilgarlick  socialiser  unscalable  exurbanite   postbellum
loquacious  pinnatifid  soldanella  unseasoned  filibuster   potability
Maccabaean  playacting  sousaphone  upbraiding  fireblight   presbyopia
malvaceous  plumassier  spiracular  uproarious  flabbiness   presbyopic
maniacally  podiatrist  spiraculum  upstanding  flamboyant   presbytery
manzanilla  polyandric  spiralling  usucaption  fleabitten   pushbutton
mechanical  polyanthus  sporangial  vasoactive  footballer   ratability
mediastina  polyatamic  sporangium  venialness  footbridge   republican
mediatress  porraceous  stalactite  verbaliser  foreboding   rhomboidal
mendacious  portamento  stalagmite  vernacular  framboesia   rhomboidei
mercantile  precarious  stewardess  vibraculum  freebooter   risibility
Michaelmas  precaution  stomachful  vibraphone  friability   rockbadger
migrainous  predacious  stomatitis  villainage  fullbodied   rockbottom
mismatched  prelatical  stomatopod  villainess  fullbottom   rovebeetle
mistakable  premarital  streamless  villainous  fusibility   safeblower
mistakenly  premaxilla  streamline  villanelle  fussbudget   salability
Montagnard  prepackage  submariner  violaceous  glauberite   salubrious
mordacious  preparator  sultanship  visualiser  goldbeater   sandbagger
morganatic  preparedly  sunparlour  voltameter  grubbiness   scribbling
mozzarella  prepayable  suprarenal  vulcaniser  hackbuteer   selfbinder
myocardium  prepayment  surfactant  wassailing  handbarrow   shabbiness
myrtaceous  presageful  sustaining  weimaraner  hardbilled   sheabutter
mystagogic  prevailing  syllabaria  wongawonga  hardbitten   shibboleth
mystagogue  prevalence  sympathise  wraparound  hardboiled   shipbroker
nectareous  propagable  syncarpous  ZendAvesta  hellbender   shoebuckle
newfangled  propaganda  syntagmata  zigzagging  highbinder   sideboards
newsagency  propagator  tantaliser  ablebodied  homebrewed   skewbridge
nonnatural  prosaicism  tantamount  acrobatics  hornblende   slumberful
nonpayment  protanopic  tarmacadam  adhibition  humpbacked   slumberous
nullanulla  pugnacious  tentacular  aerobatics  hypabyssal   snobbishly
nyctalopia  pulsatilla  termagancy  aerobiosis  ignobility   snubbingly
nyctalopic  quarantine  terracotta  aerobiotic  imbibition   soapboiler
oldfangled  quinacrine  testaceous  affability  immobilise   soapbubble
oldmaidish  rampageous  tetrachord  algebraist  immobility   softbilled
oleraceous  ratcatcher  tetragonal  amiability  incubation   softboiled
oligarchic  refraction  tetrahedra  amoebocyte  incubative   solubilise
olivaceous  refractive  tetrameter  antebellum  incubatory   solubility
orchardist  refractory  tetramorph  antibiosis  inhabitant   stagbeetle
orchardman  releasable  tetrapolis  antibiotic  inhibition   strabismal
orphanhood  repealable  tetrarchic  archbishop  inhibitory   strabismic
outbalance  repeatable  tetrastich  assibilate  insobriety   strabismus
outgassing  repeatedly  tetrastyle  audibility  intubation   strabotomy
outlandish  researcher  threadbare  backbiting  inurbanity   stubbiness
outpatient  restaurant  threadfish  backblocks  jacobinise   stubbornly
outrageous  retractile  threadmark  barebacked  Jacobinism   swaybacked
overabound  retraction  threadworm  beefburger  Jacobitism   talebearer
overactive  retractive  threatener  beribboned  katabolism   tamability
paedagogic  retraining  throatwort  bluebonnet  lawabiding   taxability
palladious  revealable  topgallant  bluebottle  legibility   tenability
palmaceous  revealment  tragacanth  bookbinder  limeburner   tenebrific
palmatifid  rockabilly  trepanning  bourbonism  lucubrator   tenebrious
panhandler  sabbatical  trilateral  bourbonist  lugubrious   thimbleful
panjandrum  salmagundi  tripartite  browbeaten  macebearer   thimblerig
Parnassian  saltarello  tropaeolum  calibrator  mealbeetle   thimbleful
parramatta  sandalwood  tuffaceous  capability  metabolise   thumbscrew
passageway  sappanwood  tympanites  carabineer  metabolism   thumbstall
peccadillo  sargassoes  tympanitic  carabinier  metabolite   titubation
pegmatitic  sarracenia  tympanitis  catabolism  molybdenum   tollbridge
pellagrous  satyagraha  ultrabasic  celebrated  montbretia   tourbillon
penmanship  scarabaeid  ultrasonic  celebrator  mossbunker   trombonist
pennaceous  scarabaeus  ultrasound  cerebellum  movability   troubadour
pennanular  scaramouch  umbrageous  chamberpot  mutability   turnbuckle
pentachord  seacaptain  unavailing  chubbiness  notability   unbiblical
pentagonal  seamanlike  unbearable  coalbunker  nudibranch   unlabelled
pentameter  seamanship  unbearably  cohabitant  obnubilate   visibility
pentastich  selfacting  unbeatable  Corybantes  overblouse   vocabulary
pentathlon  selfaction  unbeatably  corybantic  overbought   volubility
pentatomic  semiannual  unchanging  curability  overburden   winebibber
pentatonic  sequacious  unchastity  deliberate  pallbearer   winebottle
permafrost  serradilla  unexampled  demobilise  palmbutter   workbasket
permanence  sexpartite  unflagging  disability  parabiosis   abdication
permanency  shenanigan  ungraceful  divebomber  parabiotic   abducentes
```

abjectness	cytochrome	geniculate	musicpaper	searchable	woodcarver
adjacently	dampcourse	glancingly	musicstand	searchless	woodcutter
adjectival	dedication	glauconite	musicstool	seducement	wretchedly
advocation	dedicative	golfcourse	newscaster	seductress	aberdevine
advocatory	dedicatory	gynocratic	nidicolous	selectness	abridgment
affectedly	deductible	gyrocopter	noticeable	selfcolour	abundantly
affectless	deescalate	halfcocked	noticeably	semichorus	accidental
Africander	defacement	headcheese	novaculite	semicircle	adjudgment
Africanise	deficiency	Heliconian	objectival	silkcotton	adjudicate
Africanism	dejectedly	helicopter	objectless	sinecurism	ambidexter
Africanist	delectable	hemicyclic	officially	sinecurist	amendatory
allocation	delectably	homecoming	operculate	sketchable	amygdaloid
allocution	delicately	homocercal	ophicleide	sketchbook	anecdotage
almacanter	delocalise	hourcircle	overcharge	skyscraper	anecdotist
almucanter	democratic	hypocorism	overcommit	sluicegate	archdeacon
altocumuli	deracinate	imbecilely	overcooked	snowcapped	aspidistra
amercement	desecrater	imbecility	paniculate	solacement	autodidact
amerciable	desecrator	immaculacy	pediculate	solecistic	bemedalled
anarchical	desiccator	immaculate	pediculous	solicitant	Benedicite
antecedent	detachable	impeccable	pedicurist	solicitous	Benedictus
antecessor	detachedly	impeccably	penicillin	solicitude	bladdernut
antechapel	detachment	impeccancy	periclinal	sourcebook	blindingly
Antichrist	detectable	inaccuracy	pericyclic	spatchcock	bloodguilt
anticipant	devocalise	inaccurate	piercingly	speechless	bloodhound
anticipate	dickcissel	indecently	pinecarpet	Spencerian	bloodiness
anticlimax	didactical	indecision	planchette	spitchcock	bloodmoney
anticlinal	directness	indecisive	pleochroic	sprucebeer	bloodstain
aplacental	directoire	indecorous	polychaete	spruceness	bloodstock
araucarian	directress	indication	polychrest	stanchless	bloodstone
articulate	diseconomy	indicative	polychrome	stanchness	boondoggle
artycrafty	dovecolour	indicatory	polyclinic	stenchtrap	brandyball
associable	edulcorate	indictable	polycyclic	stencilled	brandysnap
asynchrony	effaceable	indictment	portcullis	stenciller	breadboard
attachable	effacement	indocility	postchaise	stitchwort	breadcrumb
attachment	effectuate	inducement	pouncetbox	strictness	breadfruit
attackable	efficacity	inductance	praecocial	structural	breadstick
auriculate	efficiency	infectious	prancingly	structured	breadstuff
autecology	emancipate	innocently	preachment	strychnine	broadcloth
autochthon	emancipist	inosculate	prescience	strychnism	broadsheet
autocratic	emasculate	insecurely	prescriber	subacidity	broadsword
avouchment	encyclical	insecurity	princeling	subscriber	broodiness
bilocation	endocrinal	insociable	princeship	switchback	broodingly
binoculars	enfacement	intactness	principate	switchover	cacodaemon
bioecology	enlacement	invocation	principial	synecdoche	Caledonian
bioscience	enrichment	invocatory	principium	synecology	chandelier
blancmange	enticement	judicatory	principled	telecamera	chaudfroid
bleachable	enticingly	judicature	proscenium	telecaster	childbirth
bluecollar	enunciable	judicially	prosciutto	theocratic	childermas
bouncingly	enunciator	ladychapel	proscriber	timocratic	childishly
branchiate	episcopacy	leafcutter	pyracantha	topicality	childproof
breechless	episcopate	lexicology	quenchable	toxication	chondritic
bronchiole	especially	limaciform	quenchless	toxicology	cloudberry
bronchitic	ethicality	logicality	quercitron	trancelike	cloudburst
bronchitis	eviscerate	malacoderm	racecourse	trenchancy	cloudiness
calyciform	expectance	malacology	radicalise	triacetate	comedienne
capacitate	expectancy	Manichaean	radicalism	truncately	coordinate
capacitive	expectedly	Manicheism	radication	truncation	coradicate
caricature	exulcerate	manicurist	recyclable	tubicolous	decadently
catechesis	felicitate	medicament	redecorate	typicality	denudation
catechetic	felicitous	medicaster	rejectable	unaccented	deridingly
catechiser	fianchetto	medication	relocation	unbecoming	desiderata
catechumen	fiducially	medicative	reluctance	unexcelled	desiderate
chalcedony	fierceness	menacingly	reluctancy	unoccupied	dreadfully
chancellor	finicality	metacarpal	reticently	unsociable	ectodermal
chinchilla	fishcarver	metacarpus	reticulate	unsociably	ectodermic
choiceness	flaccidity	metacentre	revocation	unsocially	embodiment
churchgoer	fleacircus	meticulous	revocatory	urticarial	emendation
churchyard	flocculate	miraculous	ridiculous	urtication	emendatory
cinecamera	flocculent	mobocratic	rollcollar	varicocele	endodermal
cockchafer	flosculous	monocercal	rosechafer	varicosity	endodermis
coercively	footcandle	monochasia	rupicoline	Vaticanism	ergodicity
coincident	forecaster	monochrome	rupicolous	Vaticanist	escadrille
comicality	forecastle	monoclinal	salicional	velocipede	espadrille
comicopera	forecourse	monoclinic	salicylate	vesication	Eurodollar
conscience	fourchette	monocratic	saltcellar	vesicatory	expedience
corncockle	franchiser	monocyclic	sandcastle	vesiculate	expediency
councillor	Franciscan	musicality	saxicoline	viceconsul	expedition
councilman	Francophil	musicianly	saxicolous	vicecounsul	fieldglass
crescentic	Frenchness	musicology	scarceness	wingcollar	fieldmouse

fieldpiece	recidivist	abstemious	bothersome	confection	digressive
fieldstone	remediable	abstention	brakeblock	conference	dinnerless
fiendishly	remedially	abstergent	brakelight	conferment	disbelieve
fixedpoint	remediless	abstersion	brazenness	conferring	discerning
flapdoodle	remodelled	abstersive	brevetting	confervoid	disfeature
floodlight	repudiator	academical	bridegroom	confession	dishearten
floodwater	reredorter	accredited	bridesmaid	congeneric	dispelling
foundation	ropedancer	accrescent	brokendown	congenital	dispensary
founderous	roundabout	achievable	brokenness	congestion	dispersant
fraudulent	roundhouse	addlepated	bromegrass	congestive	dispersion
freedwoman	scandalise	adenectomy	bucketshop	conjecture	dispersive
golddigger	scandalous	adolescent	budgerigar	connection	dispersoid
grandchild	selfdeceit	aeroengine	bullethead	connective	disrespect
granddaddy	selfdenial	affeerment	burdensome	consecrate	dissection
grandducal	semidivine	aggression	butterball	consectary	dissembler
grandmamma	semidouble	aggressive	butterbean	consensual	dissension
grandniece	semidrying	alchemical	butterfish	consequent	dissertate
grandstand	shandrydan	alimentary	buttermilk	contendent	disservice
granduncle	shandygaff	amateurish	butterwort	contention	distensile
greediness	shoddiness	amateurism	byelection	contestant	distension
greedyguts	skindiving	answerable	calceolate	contextual	distention
grindingly	slanderous	answerably	campestral	contexture	doggedness
grindstone	slenderise	antheridia	cancellate	convection	donkeywork
guardhouse	snapdragon	aphaereses	cancelling	convective	drivelling
halfdollar	solidarism	aphaeresis	cancellous	convenable	driverless
hereditary	solidarist	apodeictic	candelabra	convenance	dunderhead
hirudinean	solidarity	aposematic	candescent	convenient	duodecimal
humidifier	solidstate	appreciate	cankerworm	convention	duodenitis
hypodermal	soundboard	apprentice	cannelloni	conventual	easterling
hypodermic	soundingly	archerfish	canterbury	convergent	Eastertide
hypodermis	soundproof	archetypal	carpellary	conversant	ecclesiast
illadvised	soundtrack	Ashkenazim	carpetweed	conversely	ecumenical
immoderacy	speediness	ateleiosis	centennial	conversion	egocentric
immoderate	speedlimit	austenitic	centesimal	conveyable	eisteddfod
immodestly	standpoint	autoerotic	chatelaine	conveyance	elatedness
impediment	standstill	badderlock	chimerical	cooperator	elementary
impudently	steadiness	balderdash	chiselling	copperhead	elevenplus
impudicity	stridently	balneology	chokeberry	coquettish	emblematic
incidental	stridulant	banderilla	Cinderella	corbelling	emblements
infidelity	stridulate	barbellate	Cistercian	cornerwise	enamelling
inordinate	stridulous	barbershop	Clarenceux	cornettist	enamellist
inundation	sturdiness	bargeboard	clementine	correction	enumerable
inundatory	swordcraft	barkentine	clerestory	corrective	enumerator
irradiance	sworddance	barleybree	cleverness	correspond	epexegeses
irradicate	swordgrass	barleybroo	closestool	corsetiere	epexegesis
lapidarian	swordstick	barleycorn	closetplay	couverture	epexegetic
lapidarist	tackdriver	Barmecidal	clovehitch	cranesbill	epicentral
lapidation	taradiddle	barrelling	cloverleaf	cravenness	epideictic
laundryman	taxidancer	barrenness	Clydesdale	credential	epidemical
lepidolite	taxidermal	barrenwort	coacervate	crenellate	epidermoid
libidinous	taxidermic	basketball	coalescent	crewelwork	epigenesis
loxodromic	tepidarium	basketwork	coeternity	cudgelling	epigenetic
macadamise	theodicean	bassethorn	coffeemill	cummerbund	episematic
maladapted	theodolite	beekeeping	collection	cursedness	erubescent
malodorous	thirdclass	believable	collective	curvetting	escheatage
meridional	thirdparty	belletrist	collegiate	cussedness	evanescent
mixedmedia	thunderbox	bequeathal	collembola	czarevitch	evidential
mouldboard	thundering	Berkeleian	commentary	declension	excrescent
mouldiness	thunderous	betterment	commentate	decrescent	exegetical
occidental	treadboard	bighearted	commercial	deflection	exoterical
octodecimo	treadwheel	bilgewater	compelling	deflective	expressage
paradisaic	trendiness	billetdoux	compendium	degressive	expression
paradisean	trundlebed	biodegrade	compensate	depreciate	expressive
paradisiac	unbiddable	biogenesis	competence	depredator	expressway
paradisian	unendingly	biogenetic	competency	depressant	eyeservice
paradoxure	unfadingly	biometrics	competitor	depression	Fahrenheit
peridermal	unredeemed	bissextile	concentric	depressive	farfetched
piledriver	untidiness	bitterling	conception	descendant	fatherhood
pleadingly	validation	bitterness	conceptive	descendent	fatherland
ploddingly	vanadinite	bitterroot	conceptual	descension	fatherless
plunderage	wiredrawer	bitterwood	concerning	desperados	fatherlike
plunderous	withdrawal	blamefully	concertina	diapedesis	fathership
polydactyl	withdrawer	bordereaux	concertino	diapedetic	fescennine
polydipsia	worldclass	borderland	concession	dielectric	fetterlock
preadamite	worldweary	borderless	concessive	difference	fibreboard
proudflesh	yieldingly	borderline	concettism	didgeridoo	fibreglass
pseudocarp	zygodactyl	Boswellian	condensate	dielectric	filterable
pyridoxine	abbreviate	Boswellise	condensery	difference	[unclear]
recidivism	aboveboard	Boswellism	condescend	digression	fingerbowl

```
fingerless hodgepodge laurelling natterjack pincerlike prudential
fingerling homoeopath lawrencium nauseating pinfeather Ptolemaist
fingermark hookedness Lawrentian nauseously planetable pulveriser
fingernail hootenanny leadenness neglectful planetaria pummelling
fingerpost hornedness leaderless nethermost platelayer purseproud
fireescape horrendous leadership nickelling pluperfect pursership
fisherfolk horsecloth ledgerbait nigrescent pocketable purseseine
flabellate horsecoper ledgerline noblewoman pocketbook purtenance
flagellant horseflesh leprechaun noisemaker pocketsize purveyance
flagellate horselaugh letterbomb nonferrous pollenosis putrescent
flameproof horseleech letterbook noogenesis ponderable putrescine
flavescent horsepower lettercard nucleation portentous quaternary
florentine horseshoer letterhead nucleonics possession quaternate
florescent horsewoman letterless nucleoside possessive quaternion
flowergirl hostelling librettist nucleotide possessory quaternity
flowerless houseagent lipreading numberless postexilic raggedness
flugelhorn housebound lipservice nurseryman potbellied readership
forcefully housecraft liquescent obstetrics powderhorn recreantly
forfeiture houseguest litterlout offsetting powderpuff recreation
forgetting houselling lockerroom opalescent prayerbook recreative
fortepiano houseplant loggerhead operettist prebendary redeemable
forwearied houseproud loosecover oppression precedence reelection
fosterling housetrain lumberjack oppressive precedency reflection
fraternise housewives lumberroom orchestics preceptive reflective
fraternity hypaethral lumbersome orchestral preceptory reflexible
frutescent hyphenated lumberyard orogenesis precession refreshing
funnelling hysteresis madreporic orogenetic predecease refuelling
galleywest hysteretic magnetiser outgeneral predestine regression
gaspereaux hysterical maidenhair outmeasure prefecture regressive
gasteropod impregnant maidenhead overexcite preferable regretting
genteelism impregnate maidenhood overexpose preferably reiterance
geocentric impresario maidenlike oxygenator preference relievable
geodetical impression malfeasant oysterfarm preferment renderable
geometrise impressive malleebird paederasty preferring rendezvous
Ghibelline inadequacy malleefowl Palaeocene prehensile repression
Gilbertian inadequate mallenders Palaeogene prehension repressive
gingerbeer inbreeding manoeuvrer palaeolith prelection respectful
gingersnap inclemency manoeuvres palaeotype premedical respecting
glomerular incredible manservant Palaeozoic prepensely respective
glomerulus incredibly manteltree palmerworm presentday reviewable
Godfearing increscent marcescent pangenesis presentive rhinestone
goldenness inelegance marketable pangenetic pretendant rickettsia
goldenseal inflection markethall parcelling pretendent ridgepiece
gooseberry inflective markettown pasteboard pretension rinderpest
gooseflesh inflexible martensite pastellist prevenancy rootedness
goosegrass inflexibly marvelling pasteurise prevenient roquelaure
gorgeously infrequent marvellous pasteurism prevention roseengine
gracefully ingredient mastectomy pathetical preventive rottenness
grapefruit ingression masterhand peacefully pridefully rouseabout
grapesugar innuendoes masterhood peacemaker primevally rubberneck
gratefully inoperable masterless pendentive prizefight rudderfish
gravestone inspection mastermind peppercorn procedural rudderless
groceteria inspective mastership peppermill proceeding ruggedness
grovelling intrepidly masterwork peppermint procession runnerbean
guilefully iridescent mathematic pepperwort profession sabretache
halberdier isogenetic medievally percentage progenitor sabretooth
halieutics isometrics membership percentile projectile sacredness
hallelujah isoseismal mesmeriser perception projection salientian
hammerbeam itinerancy millefiori perceptive projective sallenders
hammerhead jaggedness millennial perceptual promenader sanderling
hammerless jasperware millennium perfection promethium sapiential
hammerlock jobbernowl millesimal perfective propellant sarmentose
hammerpond jolterhead mindedness permeation propellent sarmentous
handedness judgematic misbelieve permeative propelling scaleboard
hanselling juggernaut miscellany perpetrate propensity scapegrace
hartebeest kaisership mismeasure perpetuate properness scaredycat
harvestman kennelling misventure perpetuity propertied scavengery
hawserlaid kerseymere mizzenmast persecutor prosecutor scoreboard
heavenborn kieselguhr mizzensail perversely protection scoresheet
heavensent kimberlite monkeysuit perversion protective screechowl
heavenward knifeboard monoecious perversity protectory screenings
henceforth Krugerrand motherhood perversive protectrix screenplay
hendecagon lactescent motherland phagedaena proteiform scutellate
henhearted ladderback motherless phagedenic proteinous seaserpent
hermetical lanceolate mothership phanerogam protensive secretaire
herrenvolk lanternfly motherwort phonematic proteolyse segmentary
hinterland largescale moviemaker picketline protestant selfesteem
hithermost lattermost muliebrity piecegoods provenance sensedatum
hitherward laureation mysterious pigmentary proverbial senseorgan
```

```
sentential  subdeanery  threescore  whitefaced  nubiferous  arrogantly
septenarii  subheading  tickertape  whitesmith  nuciferous  arrogation
septennial  subjectify  timberhead  whitethorn  oleiferous  assignable
septennium  subjection  timberline  wholesaler  overflight  assignment
sequential  subjective  timbertoes  whorehouse  pacifiable  astigmatic
sequestrum  subletting  timberwolf  wickedness  pacificate  autogamous
sergeantcy  submediant  timberwork  wickerwork  pacificism  autogenous
serjeantcy  submersion  tinselling  wildebeest  pacificist  autography
serpentine  subreption  toffeenose  wilderment  paraffinic  backgammon
sestertium  subsection  torrential  wilderness  pathfinder  background
sestertius  subsellium  tortellini  winceyette  piliferous  benignancy
setterwort  subsequent  trabeation  wintertide  playfellow  bridgeable
shamefaced  subtenancy  trabeculae  wintertime  pomiferous  bridgehead
shamefully  subterfuge  trabecular  witnessbox  proofsheet  bridgeless
shirehorse  subvention  trajection  wonderland  reafforest  bridgework
shoreleave  subversion  trajectory  wonderment  riboflavin  cacogenics
shorewards  subversive  travelling  wonderwork  ringfinger  cacography
shovelhead  succedanea  travelogue  wontedness  saliferous  caliginous
shovelling  successful  travertine  woodenhead  scaffolder  categorise
showerbath  succession  trecentist  woodenness  scoffingly  cerography
shrievalty  successive  tremendous  wunderkind  scrofulous  changeable
sideeffect  suddenness  Tridentine  yesteryear  selffeeder  changeably
siegetrain  sufferable  trigeminal  antifreeze  semifitted  changeless
silverbath  sufferably  trioecious  aquafortis  shipfitter  changeling
silverfish  sufferance  trisection  artificial  slowfooted  changeover
silverside  suggestion  triternate  assafetida  snafflebit  chargeable
silverware  suggestive  trowelling  auriferous  sniffiness  chargehand
silverweed  sullenness  tsarevitch  ballflower  snuffiness  clangorous
sisterhood  summerlike  tunnelling  barefooted  soapflakes  clingstone
skateboard  summertime  turgescent  bellflower  softfinned  cragginess
slavetrade  sunderance  turkeycock  benefactor  solifidian  cryogenics
slidevalve  supperless  turpentine  beneficent  staffnurse  damageable
smokedried  surrealism  umbrellaed  beneficial  stepfather  damagingly
smokehouse  surrealist  unAmerican  catafalque  stiffening  decagramme
smokeplant  susceptive  unblenched  chapfallen  stuffiness  decigramme
smokeproof  suspenders  unevenness  chauffeuse  surefooted  delegation
smokestack  suspension  uneventful  chiffchaff  testflight  delightful
snakedance  suspensoid  unguentary  chiffonier  thriftless  demagogism
snakestone  suspensory  university  clubfooted  tortfeasor  demography
snivelling  sustenance  unmeetness  coniferous  trafficked  denegation
societally  sustention  unpleasant  cornflakes  trafficker  denigrator
soddenness  sustentive  unpleasing  cornflower  unaffected  derogation
souterrain  swinefever  unprepared  deepfreeze  undefended  derogatory
spacecraft  swiveleyed  unsteadily  deepfrozen  uninformed  designator
spacewoman  swivelling  unswerving  deerforest  unofficial  designedly
spadebeard  symmetrise  unwieldily  downfallen  verifiable  designment
speleology  synaeresis  unyielding  dwarfishly  viewfinder  diligently
spidercrab  syngenesis  usquebaugh  fivefinger  vociferant  divagation
spiderline  synoecious  valleculae  flatfooted  vociferate  doxography
spiderwort  systematic  vallecular  foamflower  vociferous  drudgingly
spinescent  systemless  variegated  forefather  wallflower  ectogenous
spitefully  tablecloth  varietally  forefinger  wharfinger  elongation
spleenwort  tablelinen  vaudeville  fourfooted  wildfowler  emarginate
spokeshave  tablespoon  vengefully  girlfriend  windflower  endogamous
spumescent  tangential  vertebrate  hardfisted  wingfooted  endogenous
squeezable  tankengine  vesperbell  highflying  yokefellow  energetics
squeezebox  tasselling  vespertine  indefinite  abiogenist  engagement
stagecoach  tastefully  vignettist  inefficacy  abnegation  engagingly
stagecraft  tellership  villeinage  insufflate  abrogation  enregister
statecraft  temperable  viscerally  kingfisher  acrogenous  enrigment
stavesacre  temperance  vitrescent  ladyfinger  aerogramme  eulogistic
stereobate  temperedly  viziership  latifundia  aerography  evangelise
stereogram  tenderfoot  voiceprint  luciferase  aeruginous  evangelism
stereopsis  tenderloin  volleyball  luciferous  Albigenses  evangelist
stereotype  tenderness  vulnerable  lucifugous  allegation  everglades
stereotypy  tenterhook  vulnerably  malefactor  allegiance  exaggerate
stilettoes  terneplate  Waldensian  maleficent  allegorise  excogitate
stipellate  terreplein  wanderings  manifestly  allegretto  fairground
stoneblind  tessellate  wanderlust  manifestos  allogamous  fatiguable
stoneborer  tetterwort  wanderplug  manifoldly  almsgiving  fledgeling
stonebrash  thalecress  wappenshaw  modifiable  alongshore  foregather
stonefruit  thereabout  wardenship  moonflower  altogether  foreground
stonemason  thereafter  wastefully  muciferous  amalgamate  frangipane
stonesnipe  thereanent  wastepaper  munificent  antagonise  frangipani
storehouse  thereunder  weaverbird  nidificate  antagonism  freightage
streetdoor  threepence  westernise  nidifugous  antagonist  fringeless
streetward  threepenny  whaleshark  notifiable  Armageddon  fuliginous
stupendous  threepiece  whereabout              armigerous  fumigation
subcentral              whitebeard                          gaingiving
```

```
grangerise  overground  vinegarish  clothespeg  heathenise  pitchblack
grangerism  overgrowth  viraginous  clothespin  heathenish  pitcherful
grogginess  palagonite  Visigothic  coachbuilt  heathenism  pitchstone
grudgingly  panegyrise  voyageable  coachhouse  hemihedral  polyhedral
halogenate  panegyrist  winegrower  coathanger  hemihedron  polyhedric
halogenous  paragnosis  woolgather  colchicine  hexahedral  polyhedron
handgallop  pedagogics  woolgrower  comehither  hexahedron  polyhistor
hangglider  perigynous  wrongdoing  conchoidal  highhanded  posthumous
holography  phlegmatic  wrongfully  conchology  hitchhiker  prophesier
homogamous  phlogistic  wrongously  coolheaded  holohedral  prophetess
homogenise  phlogiston  xerography  copyholder  hotchpotch  prothallia
homogenous  phlogopite  xylography  couchgrass  ichthyosis  prothallus
hypogynous  plangently  ylangylang  daughterly  incoherent  psephology
ideography  playground  youngberry  dauphiness  Irishwoman  psychiatry
ilangilang  ploughable  zabaglione  deathwatch  ironhanded  psychicism
illegalise  ploughland  Abrahamman  decahedral  isochronal  psychicist
illegality  polygamist  acephalous  decahedron  isothermal  psychology
impugnable  polygamous  aesthetics  delphinium  jackhammer  psychopath
impugnment  polygenism  aesthetism  delphinoid  kerchieves  punchboard
inaugurate  polygenist  alcoholise  diachronic  knighthood  punchdrunk
incogitant  polygonous  alcoholism  diaphanous  Krishnaism  Pyrrhonian
indagation  polygraphy  alightment  diathermal  landholder  Pyrrhonism
indigenous  polygynous  annihilate  diathermic  landhunger  Pyrrhonist
indigested  priggishly  anopheline  discharger  lanthanide  pyrrhotite
infighting  pyrogallol  antiheroic  doughfaced  laughingly  ramshackle
insightful  pyrogenous  apochromat  drophammer  leafhopper  reichsmark
integrable  pyrography  apophthegm  earthbound  lefthanded  rhythmical
integrally  relegation  apothecary  earthiness  lefthander  rockhopper
integrator  reorganise  apothecial  earthlight  lionhunter  roughhouse
integument  repugnance  apothecium  earthquake  longhaired  roughrider
invaginate  repugnancy  apotheoses  earthshine  longheaded  runthrough
invigilate  resignedly  apotheosis  earthwards  loudhailer  saccharate
invigorate  rockgarden  arithmetic  epiphytism  lymphocyte  saccharide
irrigation  rontgenise  bacchantes  epithelial  lymphomata  saccharify
kerygmatic  roofgarden  bacchantic  epithelium  lyophilise  saccharine
kilogramme  rubiginous  backhanded  erethismic  Malthusian  saccharoid
kriegspiel  savageness  backhander  evenhanded  manchineel  saccharose
lanuginose  sciagraphy  baldheaded  exothermal  marshalled  sandhopper
lanuginous  selfglazed  bareheaded  exothermic  marshaller  sapphirine
levigation  selfguided  bedchamber  faceharden  marshalsea  scatheless
lexigraphy  serigraphy  beechdrops  fairhaired  marshiness  scathingly
lifegiving  sexagenary  Benthamism  faithfully  matchboard  scyphiform
lipography  Sexagesima  Benthamite  featherbed  matchmaker  scyphozoan
litigation  shagginess  biochemist  feathering  matchstick  seethrough
logography  shanghaier  biophysics  fetchingly  midshipman  Singhalese
loungesuit  sideglance  birthplace  filthiness  mirthfully  sixshooter
malignance  skiagraphy  birthright  flashboard  mischanter  slightness
malignancy  slanginess  birthstone  flashflood  mischmetal  slothfully
manageable  sleighbell  bitchiness  flashiness  misthought  softheaded
manageably  sluggardly  blepharism  flashlight  mockheroic  soothingly
management  sluggishly  blitheness  flashpoint  monohybrid  soothsayer
manageress  smudginess  blithering  fleshiness  monohydric  southbound
managerial  snowgrouse  blithesome  fleshwound  morphemics  southerner
metagalaxy  spongecake  blushingly  flightdeck  morphinism  southernly
misogamist  spongewood  bolshevise  flightless  morphogeny  southwards
misogynist  spongiform  bolshevism  flightpath  morphology  sowthistle
misogynous  sponginess  bolshevist  forehanded  mouthorgan  spathulate
mitigation  spongology  bondholder  forthright  mouthpiece  stadholder
mitigative  sprightful  boneheaded  fourhanded  nonchalant  staphyline
mitigatory  staggering  brachiator  freehanded  northbound  stephanite
monogamist  stargazing  brachiopod  freeholder  northerner  stochastic
monogamous  stinginess  brachylogy  freshwater  northwards  subshrubby
monogenism  stingingly  brachyural  froghopper  notchboard  sulphonate
monogynian  stodginess  brachyuran  frothiness  nympholept  sulphurate
monogynous  Stroganoff  brightness  gaucheness  octahedral  sulphurise
navigation  swaggering  brightwork  geochemist  octahedron  sulphurous
nomography  swingingly  Buddhistic  geophysics  omophagous  swashplate
nosography  swinglebar  bullheaded  geothermal  openhanded  symphonion
obligation  telegraphy  bunchgrass  geothermic  openhearth  symphonist
obligatory  theogonist  cackhanded  gladhander  ophthalmia  symphylous
obligingly  thoughtful  camphorate  graphemics  ophthalmic  symphyseal
oleaginous  tobogganer  carphology  graphitise  overhanded  symphysial
oleography  tomography  Carthusian  graphology  patchiness  synchronal
omnigenous  topography  caseharden  greyheaded  peashooter  synchronic
oncogenous  triggerman  catchpenny  hamshackle  pemphigoid  synthesise
oppugnancy  typography  cinchonine  hardhanded  pemphigous  synthesist
orangepeel  unarguable  clawhammer  hardheaded  perchloric  synthetise
orangewood  undigested  clodhopper  headhunter  perihelion  synthetist
oreography  vicegerent  clothesbag  heathendom  pinchpenny  telpherage
```

tetchiness aficionado choriambic detainment florilegia initialise
tilthammer ameliorate clavichord dictionary floristics initialled
toothbrush Amerindian clavicular diesinking fluviatile initiation
toothiness amphibious clerically difficulty fluxionary initiative
toothpaste amphibrach clinically diffidence flyfishing initiatory
toothshell amphictyon coatimundi discipline foetidness inquietude
torchlight amphigouri coexistent dislikable follicular inquisitor
touchiness amphimacer cognisable dismission forbidding inspirator
touchingly amphimixes cognisably dismissive forcipated inspissate
touchjudge amphimixis cognisance dispirited foreignism instigator
touchpaper Anglistics collimator dispiteous forgivable instilling
touchstone apolitical commissary dissidence forgivably institutor
tracheated applicable commission dissilient formidable intrigante
tracheitis applicably commissure dissimilar formidably intriguant
trashiness applicator commitment dissipated fornicator ironically
trichiasis appointive committing distichous fortissimi isoniazide
trichinise architrave commixture distilland fortissimo italianate
trichinous ascribable conciliary distillate Fourierism italianise
trichology ascription conciliate distillery fourinhand Italianism
trichotomy assailable concinnity distilling fraxinella jardiniere
trichroism assoilment confidante distinctly frigidness jesuitical
trichromat astringent confidence ditriglyph fritillary jinricksha
triphammer atomically confirmand dorsigrade frolicking jinrikisha
triphthong attainable confiscate drawingpin frolicsome justiciary
trochanter attainment conniption duplicator fulfilling Kantianism
trochoidal atypically connivance earwigging fulfilment kinnikinic
trophology auctioneer considered earwitness fungicidal Kuomintang
truthfully auspicious consistent eliminable galliambic lacrimator
tufthunter autoimmune consistory eliminator garnierite landingnet
twowheeler avaricious contiguity elucidator garnishing larvicidal
Tyrrhenian ballistics contiguous emaciation gaslighter lascivious
unschooled baptistery continence Englishman gentilesse leafinsect
urethritis barbituric contingent enjoinment germicidal lectionary
urochordal Bedlington continuant entailment germinally lemniscate
watchfully bestialise continuate epilimnion gingivitis lenticular
watchglass bestiality continuity eradicable glaciation lentigines
watchguard bestirring continuous eradicator glaciology lesbianism
watchmaker biblically conviction eremitical gloriously limpidness
watchtower bibliology convictive erotically goldilocks Lippizaner
weatherbox bibliopegy convincing erysipelas gothically liquidator
weathering bibliophil coolingoff escritoire graciosity liquidiser
weatherman bibliopole corbiculae ethnically graciously liquidness
weightless bibliopoly cordiality examinable gramicidin lopsidedly
wellheeled bibliotics cordierite exobiology gramineous lowpitched
Welshwoman bobbinlace cordillera exotically gratifying lubricator
Wertherian brazilwood corrigenda explicable gravimeter lubricious
Wertherism Britishism corrigible explicitly gravimetry lusciously
Winchester buccinator corrivalry extricable gunfighter machinator
wirehaired byssinosis corticated exuviation handicraft machinegun
witchcraft cacciatore cosmically eyewitness hectically mackintosh
witchhazel cachinnate cousinhood fabricator helminthic magnifical
witchingly caddisworm cousinship factiously hermitcrab magnificat
withholder calciferol craniology factitious heroically magnifying
worshipful candidness creditable fallingoff heroicness Malpighian
worshipped cantilever creditably fancifully heroicomic mandibular
worshipper cantillate criminally farcically heuristics maquillage
worthiness capricious critically farsighted horridness Marcionite
worthwhile captiously cultivable fasciation hospitable marginalia
wrathfully carcinogen cultivator fascicular hospitably marginally
wrathiness carcinosis curricular fasciculus hybridiser marginated
Wykehamist cardialgia curriculum fascinator hydrically martialism
youthfully cardiogram cuspidated fastidious imaginable martingale
zoophagous cardiology cyclically fastigiate imaginably masticable
zoophilous cautionary dampingoff febrifugal impairment masticator
abominable cautiously deceivable fertiliser implicitly matriarchy
abominably centigrade declinable fervidness imprimatur matricidal
abominator centilitre deltiology fibrillary imprinting meaningful
aboriginal centillion demoiselle fibrillate impuissant meltingpot
abscission centimetre densimeter fibrillose inclinable mendicancy
abstinence certiorari dentifrice fibrinogen ineligible mercifully
abstinency cessionary deoxidiser fictioneer ineligibly messianism
acidimeter charioteer deprivable fictionist inevitable metrically
acidimetry charismata derailleur fictitious inevitably millilitre
acquirable charitable derailment fisticuffs inexistent millimetre
acquitting charitably despicable flagitious infliction misgivings
adroitness chelicerae despicably flamingoes inflictive mishitting
Aethiopian chemically despisable floriation inimically missionary
affliction chemisette despiteful floribunda inimitable missionise
afflictive chiliastic despiteous floridness inimitably monsignori

morbidezza	perfidious	pruriently	straitness	vindicator	quickgrass
morbidness	permission	publishing	studiously	vindictive	quickthorn
morrispike	permissive	pulsimeter	stupidness	virginally	quirkiness
mosaically	permitting	pulvinated	stylistics	virginhood	Sanskritic
mosaicking	pernicious	putridness	subkingdom	vitriolise	shockingly
muffinbell	pernickety	rabbinical	sublimable	vortically	shockproof
mulligrubs	persiflage	rancidness	subliminal	vorticella	shopkeeper
multifaced	persistent	realisable	sublingual	vorticular	smockfrock
multiloquy	pertinence	receivable	submission	warmingpan	sneakiness
multimedia	pertinency	reeligible	submissive	wearifully	sneakingly
multiphase	pesticidal	refringent	submitting	wellington	sneakthief
multiplier	pestilence	rejoicings	subsidence	workingman	snickasnee
multipolar	pharisaism	repairable	subsidiary	Wycliffite	spankingly
multistage	philippina	requiescat	subsistent	Beaujolais	spookiness
multivocal	philippine	rescission	succinctly	bluejacket	spunkiness
myopically	philistine	rescissory	sufficient	coadjacent	steakhouse
mystically	phonically	reshipment	suicidally	dustjacket	stickiness
mythically	phthisical	respirable	summitless	highjacker	stinkingly
mythiciser	physically	respirator	surgically	lifejacket	stinkstone
narcissism	physicking	retainable	surmisable	showjumper	stockiness
narcissist	physiocrat	reunionism	survivance	tearjerker	stockpiler
nautically	physiology	reunionist	suspicious	windjammer	stockproof
negligence	pianissimo	rodfishing	syndicator	Afrikander	stockrider
negligible	pichiciago	rollicking	syphilitic	blackamoor	stockstill
negligibly	picnicking	rollingpin	tactically	blackberry	storksbill
neurilemma	pilliwinks	rubrically	tardigrade	blackboard	strikingly
nitpicking	piscifauna	rubricator	tendinitis	blackfaced	thankfully
nonfiction	pistillary	ruffianism	terminable	blackguard	thickening
nonviolent	pistillate	Russianise	terminably	blackheart	thinkingly
nourishing	placidness	rustically	terminally	Blackshirt	thinkpiece
nunciature	plagiarise	sacrificer	terminator	blacksmith	timekeeper
nuptiality	plagiarism	salpingian	termitaria	blackthorn	trickiness
nutritious	plagiarist	saltigrade	tirailleur	blackwater	trickishly
nyctinasty	planigraph	scenically	toroidally	blanketing	triskelion
obediently	planimeter	seabiscuit	torpidness	blockboard	trucklebed
obtainable	planimetry	sealingwax	torridness	blockhouse	unlikeness
obtainment	plebiscite	seguidilla	tortiously	blockishly	weedkiller
offlicence	plesiosaur	semeiology	tragically	bookkeeper	whiskified
onesidedly	poetically	semeiotics	tragicomic	breakables	absolutely
opinionist	pollinator	sensitiser	trilingual	breakpoint	absolution
ordainment	pontifical	sentiently	triliteral	breakwater	absolutism
originally	pontifices	septically	trivialise	brickfield	absolutist
originator	postillion	septillion	trivialism	bricklayer	absolutory
outbidding	pratincole	serviceman	triviality	bumpkinish	accelerate
outfielder	preciosity	sexlimited	tropically	chalkboard	acoelomate
outfitting	preciously	sextillion	tuitionary	chalkstone	Adullamite
outrightly	precipitin	sheriffdom	turbidness	checkpoint	aerologist
outsitting	predicable	sincipital	turgidness	cheekiness	affiliated
outwitting	prediction	somniloquy	twilighted	chickenpox	agrologist
ovariotomy	predictive	sordidness	unblinking	chuckerout	algolagnia
oxidisable	predispose	spaciously	uncritical	chuckwagon	algolagnic
packingbox	prefixture	spadiceous	unedifying	clinkstone	algologist
paediatric	prehistory	spatiality	unfairness	crackbrain	alkalinity
palliation	presidency	specialise	unfaithful	crackbrain	ambulacral
palliative	presidiary	specialism	unfriended	crankiness	ambulacrum
palliatory	presignify	specialist	unfriendly	crankshaft	ambulation
pallidness	previously	speciality	unilingual	crowkeeper	ambulatory
parliament	primiparae	speciation	uninitiate	doorkeeper	ampelopsis
parricidal	privileged	speciology	unsuitable	fishkettle	anaglyphic
partiality	prodigally	speciosity	unthinking	flunkeydom	anaplastic
participle	prodigious	speciously	unwrinkled	flunkeyism	Andalusian
particular	proficient	spiritedly	upbringing	freakiness	andalusite
passionary	profitable	spiritless	usuriously	freakishly	angularity
passionate	profitably	spirituous	utilisable	friskiness	annalistic
Passionist	profitless	spoliation	utopianism	gamekeeper	annularity
patriality	prohibiter	spoliative	uxoricidal	gatekeeper	annulation
patriarchy	prohibitor	spoliatory	uxoriously	goalkeeper	Apollinian
patriciate	prolicidal	spuriously	vaccinator	jackknives	Apollonian
patricidal	prominence	stabiliser	ventilator	knickknack	apoplectic
patrilocal	promissory	statically	vermicelli	knobkerrie	aquilinity
patriotism	propionate	stationary	vermicular	knockabout	arbalester
patristics	propitiate	stationery	vernissage	knockkneed	arbalister
pectinated	propitious	statistics	versicular	knopkierie	areolation
pellicular	prosilient	sterigmata	vertically	ladykiller	autologous
pencilling	providence	steriliser	vestibular	lockkeeper	axiologist
pennillion	provincial	stolidness	vestibulum	mudskipper	babblement
pensionary	provisions	straighten	victimiser	painkiller	Babylonian
pentimento	provitamin	straightly	vindicable	planktonic	bafflement
percipient	proximally	strainedly	vindicable	pluckiness	bafflingly

barelegged	coralsnake	fabulously	insolation	mutilation	proglottis
battledore	corelation	facileness	insolently	mycologist	pugilistic
battlement	corelative	facilitate	insolvable	namelessly	pupilarity
battleship	costliness	fadelessly	insolvency	natalitial	purblindly
beadleship	couplement	fairleader	insularism	nebulosity	purulently
bedclothes	covalently	familiarly	insularity	nebulously	puzzlement
bibulously	cradlesong	fatalistic	insulation	needlebath	pyrolusite
bicultural	cucullated	fearlessly	intolerant	needlebook	rabblement
bipolarity	cuddlesome	fecklessly	invalidate	needlecord	ramblingly
bisulphate	cumulation	feebleness	invalidism	needlefish	rattlehead
bisulphide	cumulative	femaleness	invalidity	needlessly	rattlepate
bisulphite	cumuliform	feuilleton	invaluable	needlework	rattletrap
bivalvular	cuttlebone	fickleness	invaluably	neoclassic	reallocate
bootlegger	cuttlefish	fiddleback	involucral	neoplastic	rebellious
bootlessly	cytologist	fiddlehead	involucrum	nettlerash	recallable
bootlicker	dapplegrey	fiddlewood	involution	newsletter	recklessly
bottlefeed	dazzlement	flawlessly	irrelative	nihilistic	recolonise
bottleneck	dazzlingly	folklorist	irrelevant	nimbleness	redblooded
bottletree	deadliness	footlights	irreligion	nipplewort	redolently
bowdlerise	debilitate	formlessly	isoglossal	nodulation	refillable
bowdlerism	decelerate	fourleaved	jocularity	nomologist	refulgence
bridlepath	decolonise	freelancer	jubilantly	nonaligned	regalement
brilliance	decolorant	freeliving	jubilation	nonplaying	regelation
brilliancy	decolorise	freeloader	kettledrum	nonplussed	regularise
bryologist	defalcator	frilliness	kindliness	nosologist	regularity
bubblyjock	defilement	fulllength	kingliness	novelistic	regulation
bufflehead	defoliator	fumblingly	lacklustre	ocellation	regulative
bumblingly	demolition	gadolinite	landlocked	oecologist	regulatory
bunglingly	depilation	gadolinium	landlubber	oenologist	repellance
burglarise	depilatory	gaillardia	lavalliere	oncologist	repellancy
bustlingly	depolarise	ganglionic	legalistic	ontologist	repellence
cabalistic	desalinate	gatelegged	lifelessly	oppilation	repellency
cajolement	desolately	gentlefolk	likelihood	oreologist	resilience
cajolingly	desolation	gentleness	likeliness	oscillator	resiliency
camelopard	devilishly	goggleeyed	listlessly	osculation	resolutely
canaliculi	devolution	goodliness	littleness	osculatory	resolution
candlefish	disclaimer	goodlooker	livelihood	overlander	resolutive
candletree	disclosure	grisliness	liveliness	overlapped	resolvable
candlewick	disulphate	growlingly	lobulation	overlooker	resolvedly
candlewood	disulphide	guillotine	loneliness	paddleboat	restlessly
carelessly	disyllabic	gunslinger	longlegged	painlessly	resultless
catalectic	disyllable	habiliment	lordliness	paralipsis	revalidate
cataleptic	divulgence	habilitate	lossleader	paralogise	revalorise
cataloguer	doublebass	halflength	lovelessly	paralogism	revelation
cattlegrid	doubleness	harelipped	loveletter	patulously	revelatory
cavalierly	doublepark	harmlessly	loveliness	pearldiver	revilement
cavalryman	doubletalk	heedlessly	luculently	pebbledash	revolution
challenger	doubletime	helplessly	maculation	peculation	rheologist
chaplaincy	drawlingly	highlander	maculature	peculiarly	ringleader
Charleston	dumbledore	homeliness	mainlander	pedalorgan	ripplemark
chilliness	dysplastic	homiletics	mamillated	pedalpoint	ropeladder
churlishly	ebullience	homologate	maxilliped	pedologist	roselipped
cochleated	ebulliency	homologise	mayblossom	peerlessly	ruthlessly
comeliness	ebullition	homologous	measliness	penologist	saddleback
complacent	edibleness	hopelessly	meddlesome	perilously	saddlefast
complainer	effulgence	horologist	medullated	perplexity	saddletree
complected	embalmment	hotblooded	megalithic	petulantly	satellitic
complement	embolismic	hucklebone	megalosaur	phallicism	scarlatina
completely	engulfment	humbleness	Mesolithic	phelloderm	scholastic
completion	epiblastic	hypolimnia	metalepsis	phillumeny	Scillonian
completive	epiglottal	idealistic	metallurgy	phyllotaxy	sciolistic
complexion	epiglottic	ideologist	mettlesome	phylloxera	scrollwork
complexity	epiglottis	immolation	middleaged	pitilessly	secularise
compliance	equilibria	impalement	middlebrow	pixillated	secularism
compliancy	escalation	impalpable	middlemost	pomologist	secularist
complicacy	escallonia	impalpably	middlingly	popularise	secularity
complicate	Esculapian	impolitely	mindlessly	popularity	sedulously
complicity	ethologist	inculcator	misaligned	population	seemliness
compliment	etiolation	inculpable	misologist	populistic	selflessly
complotted	eucalyptol	indelicacy	mixolydian	populously	selfloving
conclusion	eucalyptus	indelicate	modulation	portliness	semiliquid
conclusive	everliving	indolently	moniliasis	postliminy	semilunate
conclusory	excellence	indulgence	moniliform	preclusion	sepulchral
conflation	excellency	infallible	monolithic	preclusive	serologist
confluence	exhalation	infallibly	monologise	preglacial	settlement
conglobate	exhilarant	infelicity	monologist	proclaimer	sexologist
copulation	exhilarate	infiltrate	moralistic	proclivity	shellacked
copulative	eyeglasses	inhalation	movelessly	profligacy	shellmound
coralberry		inkslinger	mudslinger	profligate	shellproof

```
shellshock timeliness asymmetric ephemerous muskmallow schematise
shieldless tirelessly automation estimation myxomatous schematism
shillelagh tonelessly automatise estimative myxomycete schemozzle
shoplifter topologist automatism eudemonism newsmonger scrimmager
shouldered trawlerman automatist eudemonist octamerous scrimshank
shrillness triclinium automobile euhemerise oecumenism seismicity
sibilation triflingly automotive euhemerism oedematose seismogram
sicklebill triglyphic autumnally euhemerist oedematous seismology
sickliness trillionth bandmaster evilminded openminded selfmotion
similarity triplicate barometric exhumation optimalise selfmurder
similitude triplicity becomingly extemporal optimistic shipmaster
simpleness troglodyte bigamously fairminded ornamental skirmisher
simplicity trolleybus bituminise fellmonger overmanned skrimshank
simplifier trollopish bituminous fishmonger overmantel slowmotion
simplistic tumbledown bolometric fleamarket overmaster snowmobile
simulacrum tumblerful bookmaking folkmemory palimpsest solemnness
simulation tumbleweed bookmarker foraminous Panamanian spermaceti
simulative tumultuary Brahmanism fragmental paramecium spermicide
simulatory tumultuous Brahminism freemartin parametric squamation
singlefoot tunelessly broomstick galimatias paramnesia steamchest
singleness turtleback Buchmanism glimmering parimutuel steaminess
singletree turtledove Buchmanite gloominess pastmaster steamtight
sinologist turtleneck bushmaster gobemouche pedimental stepmother
smallscale typologist cacomistle grammarian pedimented stigmatise
smallsword umbellifer calamander hackmatack peremptory stigmatism
smallwares umbilicate calamitous handmaiden pharmacist stigmatist
smelliness umbiliform calumniate headmaster plasmodesm stormbound
snailpaced unbalanced calumnious hexamerous plasmodium stormcloud
snailwheel unbeliever caramelise hexametric plasmogamy storminess
soullessly undulation ceremonial highminded plasmolyse stormproof
spallation undulatory ceruminous homemaking pneumatics stramonium
spellbound unfilially charmingly illuminant pockmarked stromatous
sphalerite unhallowed chromatics illuminate polemicist swanmaiden
spiflicate unholiness chromatype illuminati polemonium swarmspore
spillikins unreliable chromosome illuminism polymathic swimmingly
spoilsport unrelieved clamminess illuminist polymerise taskmaster
spotlessly unruliness columbaria immemorial polymerism tegumental
squalidity unselected coromandel incomplete polymerous telemetric
stablemate upholstery creaminess incumbency postmaster tenemental
stableness ustulation datamation infamously postmortem thermionic
stealthily viewlessly decampment ingeminate potamology thermistor
steeliness vigilantly Decembrist inhumanely praemunire thermogram
steelworks virologist decemviral inhumanity pragmatise thermophil
stelliform virulently decimalise inhumation pragmatism thermopile
stepladder vitalistic decimalism innominate pragmatist thermostat
stiflebone vitiligate decimation innumeracy preeminent thromboses
stiflingly waffleiron decompound innumerate preemption thrombosis
stillbirth wattlebird decompress innumerous preemptive thrombotic
stillicide wavelength defamation inseminate prismoidal totemistic
subclavian weakliness defamatory intimately psalmodise tourmaline
subglacial wentletrap defeminise intimation psalmodist trammelled
subtleness wheelchair dehumanise intimidate pyromaniac traumatism
sunglasses wheelhorse dehumidify ironmaster pyromantic triumphant
supplanter wheelhouse delaminate ironmonger pyrometric triumviral
supplejack whirlybird delimitate kinematics qualmishly ultimately
supplement wobbliness denominate leguminous quizmaster uncommonly
suppleness woodlander dilemmatic ligamental Rachmanism unfamiliar
suppletion woolliness disembogue likeminded ragamuffin unfeminine
suppletive wordlessly disembosom lipomatous rainmaking unnameable
suppletory abdominous disembowel locomotion razzmatazz unnumbered
suppliance accomplice disembroil locomotive rearmament unremarked
supplicant accomplish documental locomotory recommence vehemently
supplicate accumulate dolomitise lovemaking recompense venomously
surplusage acromegaly dosimetric Mahommedan recumbency vitaminise
synaloepha alarmingly dreaminess manometric redemption volumetric
tabularise albuminoid dreamworld manumitted redemptory voluminous
tabulation albuminous dynamistic maximalist redemptory weakminded
tactlessly antemortem eczematous mesomerism regimental WhitMonday
tanglement antimasque effeminacy mesomorphy resemblant yardmaster
tattletale antimatter effeminate metamerism resumption zygomorphy
teaplanter antimonial encampment metempiric resumptive accentuate
tearlessly antimonite endemicity minimalism rheumatics achondrite
theologian aquamarine enigmatise minimalist rheumatism acronychal
theologise argumentum enigmatist mintmaster rheumatoid actinolite
theologist ascomycete enjambment Mohammedan ringmaster actinozoan
thillhorse assemblage enormously monomaniac rosemallow adjunction
ticklishly assimilate entombment monumental rudimental adjunctive
tiddlywink assumption entomology Muhammadan salamander administer
timelessly assumptive enzymology Muhammadan sandmartin admonition
```

aeolotropy
aetiologic
aircooling
alcyonaria
allrounder
amphoteric
anacolutha
anagogical
analogical
anamorphic
anatomical
anchoretic
anchoritic
anchorless
anchorring
androecium
androgenic
anemograph
anemometer
anemometry
anemophily
angiosperm
anglomania
anglophile
anglophobe
anglophone
AngloSaxon
anisotropy
aphrodisia
apologetic
approvable
approvably
aragonitic
asafoetida
astrologer
astrologic
astronomer
astronomic
audiometer
audiometry
audiophile
authorship
ballooning
balloonist
bardolatry
bassoonist
batfowling
batholitic
bathometer
benzocaine
bestowment
bigmouthed
biological
biomorphic
blazonment
borborygmi
bottomless
bottommost
buffoonery
buttonball
buttonbush
buttondown
buttonhole
buttonhook
buttonless
buttonwood
callowness
cannonball
cantonment
canzonetta
carbonnade
carboxylic
cartomancy
cartoonist
cassolette
catholicon
catholicos
cellophane
censorious

censorship
chatoyance
chemotaxis
chiromancy
cismontane
cispontine
citronella
clinometer
clinometry
cnidoblast
coenobitic
coenobytic
cognominal
coleoptera
coleoptile
coleorhiza
collocutor
colloquial
colloquise
colloquist
colloquium
colporteur
commodious
commonable
commonalty
commonness
commonroom
commonweal
composedly
compositor
compotator
compounder
concoction
concoctive
concordant
condolence
conformism
conformist
conformity
confounded
conjointly
consociate
consolable
consonance
consonancy
consortium
contortion
contortive
convoluted
coproducer
coprolitic
corporally
corporator
corporeity
corroboree
cosmogonic
cosmopolis
cosmoramic
cottoncake
cottonseed
cottontail
cottonweed
cottonwood
coulometry
crinolette
crocoisite
ctenophore
cuckoopint
cuckoospit
custommade
cyclograph
cyclometer
cyclopedia
cyclopedic
cyclostome
cyclostyle
cystoscope

cystoscopy
deaconship
deflowerer
deodoriser
deplorable
deplorably
deployment
despondent
diabolical
diagonally
diplodocus
diplomatic
dipsomania
discobolus
discomfort
discommend
discommode
discompose
disconcert
disconfirm
disconnect
discontent
discophile
discordant
discounter
discourage
discourser
discoverer
dishonesty
disjointed
disloyally
disloyalty
disposable
dispossess
dissociate
dissoluble
dissolvent
dissonance
dissonancy
distortion
doctorship
draconites
dragonhead
dragonnade
dragontree
drosophila
dumfounder
ecological
economical
economiser
editorship
effloresce
effrontery
elaborator
embroidery
employable
employment
encroacher
engrossing
episodical
erotogenic
erotomania
ethnologic
eudiometer
eudiometry
euphonious
evaporable
evaporator
exploitage
exploitive
exprobrate
factorship
fallowness
fantoccini
fathomable
fathomless
fellowship
festoonery
fibrositis

FinnoUgric
flavourful
flavouring
foreordain
frigorific
frivolling
gadrooning
galloglass
Gallomania
Gallophile
Gallophobe
gambolling
gasconader
geological
geoponical
Glagolitic
glycolyses
glycolysis
glycosuria
glycosuric
goniometer
goniometry
Gorgonzola
gramophone
granophyre
GrecoRoman
gymnosophy
gymnosperm
gypsophila
haemolysis
haemolytic
hagiolatry
hagiologic
hagioscope
harbourage
harmonical
harmonious
harmoniser
hebdomadal
hectograph
hectolitre
hectometre
heliograph
heliolater
heliolatry
heliometer
heliophyte
helioscope
heliotaxis
heliotrope
heliotropy
hierocracy
hieroglyph
hierograph
hierolatry
hierophant
highoctane
hippocampi
Hippocrene
hippodrome
hippogriff
hippogryph
hippomanes
hippophagy
histologic
histolysis
histolytic
historical
hobnobbing
holloweyed
hollowness
hollowware
homeopathy
homoousian
hormonally
hyaloplasm
hydrologic
hydrolysis
hydrolytic

hydromancy
hydrometer
hydrometry
hydropathy
hydrophane
hydrophily
hydrophone
hydrophyte
hydroplane
hydroscope
hydrotaxis
hygrograph
hygrometer
hygrometry
hygrophyte
hygroscope
hypnotiser
hypsometer
hypsometry
iatrogenic
iconoclasm
iconolater
iconolatry
iconomachy
iconometer
iconometry
iconoscope
improbable
improbably
improperly
improvable
improvably
improviser
inchoately
inchoation
inchoative
ineloquent
inexorable
inexorably
inglorious
introducer
introspect
inviolable
inviolably
iridosmine
isomorphic
Italophile
jargonelle
jimsonweed
jingoistic
karyoplasm
keyboarder
labiovelar
lampoonery
lampoonist
landocracy
landowning
leucocytic
leucoplast
leukocytic
lissomness
lithoglyph
lithograph
lithologic
lithophane
lithophyte
lithotrity
logrolling
lophophore
macrophage
macrospore
maisonette
malcontent
mangosteen
Mariolater
Mariolatry
marionette
marrowbone

marrowless
Massoretic
matronhood
matronship
matronymic
meadowland
meadowlark
mediocrity
meliorator
mellowness
mentorship
meteoritic
methodical
metronomic
metronymic
metropolis
microbiota
microcline
microfarad
microfiche
micrograph
microlitic
micrometer
micrometry
microphone
microphyte
micropylar
microscope
microscopy
microseism
microspore
midmorning
mignonette
mimeograph
misconduct
misfortune
misjoinder
misnomered
miswording
motionless
mumbojumbo
myological
mythologer
mythologic
mythomania
mythopoeia
mythopoeic
narcolepsy
narrowness
nationally
nationhood
nationless
nationwide
Neapolitan
necrolater
necrolatry
necromancy
necrophile
necrophily
necropolis
necroscopy
negrophile
negrophobe
neological
nephograph
nephoscope
neurolemma
neuropathy
neuroplasm
neurotoxin
nincompoop
nitrochalk
nitrogroup
noncontent
nonjoinder
nonlogical
nostologic
notionally

ochlocracy	photometry	radiosonde	spirograph	wantonness	escapology
oligoclase	photonasty	randomness	spirometer	weaponless	eurypterid
oligopsony	photophily	rapporteur	spirometry	willowherb	exasperate
ombrometer	photophore	rationally	spodomancy	windowless	exospheric
ophiolater	photoprint	reasonable	sporophore	windowpane	felspathic
ophiolatry	phototaxis	reasonably	sporophyll	windowseat	firepolicy
ophiologic	phototrope	reasonless	sporophyte	windowshop	flippantly
opisometer	phylogenic	rectorship	statoscope	windowsill	floppiness
opprobrium	phytogenic	regionally	stenograph	xiphosuran	fourposter
optionally	phytophagy	rencounter	stomodaeum	yarborough	fowlplague
oratorical	phytotoxic	reprobance	stylograph	yellowback	goloptious
orological	pianoforte	reproducer	subcordate	yellowbird	goluptious
orthoclase	pictograph	respondent	submontane	yellowness	graspingly
orthodoxly	pictorial	responsive	subroutine	yellowwood	grumpiness
orthoepist	piezometer	responsory	summonable	zincograph	halophytic
orthogenic	pigeonhole	restorable	supportive	zoological	handpicked
orthogonal	pigeonpair	retrochoir	supposable	zoomorphic	headphones
orthopedic	pigeonpost	retrograde	supposably	abruptness	hemiplegia
orthoptera	pigeontoed	retrogress	supposedly	acarpelous	hemiplegic
osteoblast	pigeonwing	retrorsely	syllogiser	acceptable	hemipteran
osteoclast	pillowcase	retrospect	symbolical	acceptably	holophrase
osteopathy	pillowlace	rhetorical	symboliser	acceptance	holophytic
osteophyte	pillowslip	rhinoceros	symposiast	acceptedly	homophonic
outpouring	pistolling	rhinoscope	syncopated	acrophobia	hypophyses
ovipositor	pistolshot	rhinoscopy	syncopator	aerophobia	hypophysis
paedogogue	pistolwhip	rhizogenic	tachometer	allopathic	idiopathic
paedophile	pistonring	rhizomorph	tachometry	allophonic	inappetent
pansophist	planometer	rhizophore	tailorbird	analphabet	inapposite
pantograph	plecoptera	rhodophane	tailormade	ancipitous	incapacity
pantomimic	plutocracy	ribbonfish	tambourine	antependia	incipience
pardonable	plutolatry	ribbonworm	tauromachy	antepenult	incipiency
pardonably	polyonymic	riproaring	tautomeric	antipathic	inexpertly
parrotfish	pornocracy	Russophile	tautophony	antiphonal	inexpiable
parsonbird	postoffice	Russophobe	teetotally	antipodean	inexpiably
parsonical	pozzolanic	sacroiliac	teleologic	antiproton	inexplicit
pastorally	precocious	sacrosanct	teleostean	aquaplaner	insipidity
pastorship	preconcert	sailorless	temporally	archpriest	isosporous
pathogenic	precordial	sallowness	temporalty	Areopagite	kenspeckle
pathologic	premonitor	salmonella	temporiser	asymptotic	longprimer
patrolling	prepossess	salmonleap	terrorless	autoplasty	lycopodium
patronymic	prepotence	saprogenic	thixotropy	benzpyrene	malapertly
peacockery	prepotency	saprophyte	thoroughly	billposter	malapropos
peacockish	primordial	sarcolemma	ticpolonga	blasphemer	manipulate
percolator	primordium	sarcophagi	tomfoolery	bluepencil	menopausal
perfoliate	profoundly	sarcophagy	tramontana	Caerphilly	mesophytic
perforator	prolocutor	sarcoplasm	tramontane	caespitose	metaphoric
performing	prologuise	sawtoothed	tremolitic	calyptrate	metaphrase
periodical	prolongate	schoolable	tribometer	cardplayer	metaphysic
periosteal	promontory	schoolbook	trifoliate	cataphract	metaplasia
periosteum	pronominal	schooldays	trigonally	catoptrics	monophonic
personable	pronounced	schoolgirl	trimonthly	champignon	monopodial
personally	pronouncer	schoolmaam	trimorphic	cheapishly	monopodium
personalty	proportion	schoolmarm	tromometer	cheapskate	monopolise
personator	propounder	schoolmate	tropologic	chimpanzee	monopolist
petiolated	prosodical	schoolroom	tropopause	claspknife	mycoplasma
petroglyph	protophyta	schooltime	tropophyte	conspectus	nailpolish
petrolatum	protophyte	schoolwork	unbrokenly	conspiracy	nosophobia
petronella	protoplasm	seasonable	uncloister	conspirant	occupation
phagocytic	protoplast	seasonably	uneconomic	coryphaeus	occupative
phenocryst	prototypal	seasonally	ungrounded	creepiness	octopodous
phenomenal	prototypic	semiopaque	uniformity	crippledom	oesophagus
phenomenon	provocator	semiotical	unilocular	crispation	omnipotent
phenotypic	psilocybin	SerboCroat	univocally	crispbread	overpraise
pheromonal	pulsometer	seriocomic	unknowable	decapitate	panopticon
philologen	purposeful	sermoniser	unprovoked	decapodous	paraphrase
philopoena	pycnogonid	servomotor	unsporting	deceptible	paraphrast
philosophe	pycnometer	shadowless	untroubled	depopulate	paraplegia
philosophy	pycnostyle	silhouette	uranometry	desipience	paraplegic
phonograph	pyknometer	skibobbing	variolitic	dilapidate	parapodium
phonolitic	quatorzain	slavocracy	variometer	disappoint	peripeteia
phonologic	quixotical	Slavophile	vectograph	disapprove	peripheral
phonometer	radiogenic	Slavophobe	Victoriana	droopingly	peripteral
photoflood	radiograph	snobocracy	victorious	elliptical	phosphatic
photogenic	radiologic	sociologic	videophone	encephalic	phosphoric
photograph	radiometer	sociometry	viscometer	encephalon	phosphorus
photolitho	radiometry	somnolence	viscountcy	endophytic	pickpocket
photolysis	radiopaque	somnolency	visionally	endopodite	polyphasic
photolytic	radiophone	sophomoric	visionless	equipotent	polyphonic
photometer	radioscopy	Sorbonnist	waggonette	escapement	polyploidy

```
postpartum  voluptuary  anthracene  comprehend  distracted  fragrantly
pourparler  voluptuous  anthracite  compressed  distrainer  fratricide
promptbook  wallpepper  anthracoid  compressor  distrainor  funereally
promptness  whispering  anthropoid  compromise  distraught  futureless
prospector  wirepuller  aphoristic  concretely  distressed  futuristic
prospectus  woodpecker  apocryphal  concretion  distribute  futurology
prosperity  woodpigeon  apotropaic  concretise  distringas  gangrenous
prosperous  workpeople  apparelled  concretism  divaricate  gastrology
puerperium  xenophobia  apparently  concretist  divergence  gastronome
puffpastry  xerophytic  apparition  congregant  divergency  gastronomy
pupiparous  xylophonic  apperceive  congregate  dolorously  generalise
pyrophoric  antiquated  arboreally  congruence  dreariness  generalist
reappraise  blanquette  arborvitae  congruency  dysgraphia  generality
receptacle  brusquerie  armorially  contraband  dysprosium  generation
receptible  deliquesce  arterially  contrabass  dystrophic  generative
recipiency  lansquenet  arteriolar  contractor  eartrumpet  generatrix
reciprocal  obsequious  arthralgia  contradict  effervesce  generosity
recuperate  semiquaver  arthralgic  contraprop  effortless  generously
repopulate  subaquatic  arthromere  contrarily  elderberry  geographer
resupinate  subaqueous  ascariasis  contravene  elutriator  geographic
rockpigeon  tranquilly  asparagine  contribute  embarkment  geotropism
schipperke  unrequited  aspergilla  contritely  emigration  governable
scrapmetal  aberrantly  aspiration  contrition  emigratory  governance
scriptoria  aberration  assortment  controlled  emparadise  governessy
scriptural  abhorrence  asteriated  controller  emphractic  government
scrupulous  abjuration  asteroidal  controvert  empiricism  hairraiser
sculptress  abnormally  attornment  coparcener  empiricist  heparinise
sculptural  absorbable  Australian  copartnery  endorsable  heterodont
sculptured  absorbance  autarkical  Copernican  endproduct  heterodoxy
seedpotato  absorbedly  babiroussa  copyreader  enduringly  heterodyne
selfparody  absorbency  balbriggan  covariance  enharmonic  heterogamy
selfpoised  absorption  bankruptcy  coweringly  enterolith  heterogeny
selfpraise  absorptive  beforehand  cribriform  enterotomy  heterogony
selfprofit  abstracted  beforetime  cumbrously  enterprise  heterology
sharpnosed  abstracter  Belgravian  cybernetic  enthralled  heteronomy
sheepishly  abstractly  bellringer  daydreamer  entireness  heterotaxy
sheeplouse  abstractor  besprinkle  deaeration  epeirogeny  hibernacle
sheepshank  abstrusely  bestridden  decoration  ephorality  histrionic
sheepshead  abstrusity  bichromate  decorative  epigrapher  honorarium
sitophobia  absurdness  biographer  decorously  epigraphic  hornrimmed
skimpiness  accordance  biographic  deeprooted  escarpment  hoverplane
sleepiness  accurately  biparietal  deferrable  ethereally  hovertrain
sleepyhead  accursedly  bipartisan  deforciant  eucaryotic  humoresque
slipperily  adherently  bizarrerie  demoralise  excerption  humoristic
slitpocket  adjuration  bleariness  demureness  execration  humorously
sloppiness  adjuratory  blearyeyed  demurrable  execrative  hungriness
snappishly  admiration  blueribbon  dendriform  execratory  hyperaemia
snowplough  admiringly  blurringly  dendrology  experience  hyperaemic
stepparent  adsorbable  bullroarer  department  experiment  hyperbaric
striptease  adsorption  bushranger  deportment  expertness  hyperbaton
stumpiness  adsorptive  camerlengo  depuration  expiration  hyperbolae
subspecies  advertence  camerlingo  depurative  expiratory  hyperbolas
sweepingly  advertency  canorously  descriptor  exportable  hyperbolic
sweepstake  advertiser  castration  deservedly  expurgator  hyperdulia
sycophancy  afferently  catarrhine  desirously  exteriorly  hypergolic
synoptical  affirmable  centralise  desorption  externally  hypersonic
telepathic  affordable  centralism  destructor  extirpator  icebreaker
telephoner  afterbirth  centralist  detergency  federalise  ignorantly
telephonic  aftergrass  centrality  determined  federalism  immoralist
theophoric  afterimage  centreback  deterrence  federalist  immorality
theophoric  afterlight  centrefold  dextrality  federation  immortally
theopneust  afterpains  centrehalf  dextrously  federative  immortelle
thruppence  aftershave  centricity  diagraphic  feverishly  immurement
tocopherol  aftertaste  centrifuge  diarrhoeal  figuration  imparadise
toxiphobia  afterwards  centromere  diarrhoeic  figurative  impartible
trampoline  aldermanic  centrosome  diatropism  figurehead  impartment
trappiness  aldermanry  chairwoman  dichroitic  filariasis  imperative
trespasser  allergenic  cheerfully  dichromate  filtration  imperially
unemphatic  allurement  cheeriness  dimorphism  fimbriated  imperilled
unemployed  altarpiece  chevrotain  dimorphous  fireraiser  impersonal
unexpected  alteration  chlorinate  disarrange  flagrantly  impervious
unexplored  alterative  chloroform  discreetly  fleeringly  importable
unimproved  alternance  Ciceronian  discrepant  floorboard  importance
unripeness  alternator  cinerarium  discretely  floorcloth  importuner
usurpation  anadromous  clearstory  discretion  fluoridate  impureness
vestpocket  anatropous  coherently  disgruntle  fluorinate  incurrable
vituperate  aneurismal  coloration  disordered  fluorotype  indirectly
viviparity  aneurysmal  coloratura  disorderly  forerunner  induration
viviparous  anteriorly  compradore  dispraiser  foudroyant  indurative
```

infarction	literarily	otterboard	reparative	squaretoed	undercliff
inferiorly	literation	ottershrew	repertoire	squaretoes	undercover
infernally	literature	outerspace	reportable	squirarchy	undercroft
inferrable	liturgical	overrefine	reportedly	squirearch	underdress
informally	logorrhoea	overridden	repurchase	squirehood	underfloor
inharmonic	lowerclass	overriding	reservedly	squireling	underglaze
inherently	lowprofile	paltriness	resorcinol	squireship	underlease
inheritrix	Lupercalia	pancratium	resorption	starriness	underlinen
innerrably	lustration	pancreatic	resorptive	starryeyed	underlying
instructor	lustreless	pancreatin	restrained	staurolite	underminer
instrument	lustrously	pantrymaid	restrainer	stirrupcup	underneath
insurgence	luxuriance	paperchase	resurgence	suborbital	underpants
insurgency	maceration	paperknife	retirement	subordinal	underproof
interbreed	mandragora	papermaker	retiringly	subtrahend	underquote
interceder	manorhouse	papyrology	returnable	suffragist	underscore
intercross	margravate	pastrycook	reverencer	sugardaddy	undersense
interested	margravine	paternally	reverently	sugarhouse	undersexed
interferer	materially	pederastic	reversible	sugariness	undershirt
interferon	maternally	pejoration	revertible	sugarmaple	undershoot
intergrade	maturation	pejorative	rewardable	sultriness	undershrub
interiorly	maturative	peroration	rewardless	superacute	undersized
interleave	matureness	picaresque	rigorously	superaltar	underskirt
interloper	meagreness	pilgrimage	ritardando	superation	underslung
interlunar	membranous	piperidine	ritornelli	superbness	understand
intermarry	memorandum	pityriasis	ritornello	supercargo	understate
intermezzi	mineralise	pokerfaced	riverhorse	superduper	understeer
intermezzo	mineralogy	Pomeranian	roadrunner	supergiant	understock
internally	miscreance	powerfully	rockrabbit	superhuman	understood
internment	misericord	powerhouse	rockribbed	superiorly	understudy
internodal	misprision	prairiedog	sacerdotal	superlunar	undertaken
internship	mithridate	prearrange	samarskite	supernally	undertaker
interphase	moderately	prefrontal	saturation	supernovae	undertrick
interplant	moderation	procreator	saturnalia	superorder	undervalue
interplead	moderatism	procrypsis	satyriasis	superpower	underwater
interposal	moderniser	procryptic	sauerkraut	supersonic	underworld
interposer	modernness	programmer	scabrously	superstore	underwrite
interregna	monarchial	propraetor	scherzando	supertonic	underwrote
interspace	Monarchian	proprietor	scleroderm	supervisor	unerringly
interstate	monarchism	protracted	sclerotium	suppressor	unforeseen
interstice	monarchist	protractor	sclerotomy	surprising	unmerciful
intertidal	mongrelise	protreptic	scurrility	suzerainty	unmorality
intertrigo	mongrelism	protrusile	scurrilous	sybaritism	unmortised
intertwine	monorhymed	protrusion	seborrhoea	syncretise	unscramble
intertwist	motorcycle	protrusive	secernment	syncretism	unscreened
interurban	mycorrhiza	puberulent	securement	syncretist	unscripted
intervener	naturalise	quadrangle	secureness	synergetic	unstrained
intervenor	naturalism	quadrantal	securiform	tabernacle	unstressed
intervolve	naturalist	quadratics	selfraised	taperecord	unwariness
interweave	naturopath	quadrature	selfregard	taperingly	unworkable
interwound	nephralgia	quadrennia	selfrising	tawdriness	unworthily
interwoven	nephridium	quadriceps	selfruling	teatrolley	upperclass
interzonal	nephrology	quadrireme	separately	tendrillar	upwardness
invariable	neutralise	quadrivial	separation	tendrilled	valorously
invariably	neutralism	quadrivium	separatism	theoretics	vaporiform
invariance	neutralist	quadrumana	separatist	theurgical	vaporously
inveracity	neutrality	quadrumane	separative	thwartship	veneration
inwardness	nevernever	quadrumvir	separatory	thwartwise	ventricose
jackrabbit	newsreader	quadruplet	severeness	timbrology	ventriculi
jawbreaker	nondrinker	quadruplex	shearwater	timorously	veterinary
laboratory	notarially	quadrupole	shiprigged	tolerantly	viceregent
laceration	numeration	quarrelled	siderolite	toleration	vigorously
lacerative	numerology	quarreller	siderostat	towardness	viperiform
lachrymose	numerosity	quarrender	skywriting	toweringly	viperously
Lamarckian	numerously	quatrefoil	smorrebrod	tribrachic	waterborne
Lamarckism	nutcracker	rackrenter	sneeringly	trierarchy	waterbrash
lambrequin	obdurately	railroader	sobersided	tubercular	waterclock
laparotomy	observable	razorblade	sobersides	tuberculin	watercraft
laterality	observably	razorshell	sombreness	tuberosity	watercress
lawbreaker	observance	rechristen	somersault	tularaemia	waterflood
lederhosen	obstructor	recordable	sonorously	tularaemic	waterfront
liberalise	obturation	recurrence	sororicide	tutorially	waterglass
liberalism	occurrence	referendum	soubriquet	ulceration	wateriness
liberalist	oneirology	reformable	speargrass	ulcerative	watermelon
liberality	orneriness	regardless	sperrylite	ulotrichan	waterpower
liberation	orographic	remarkable	sphericity	ulteriorly	waterproof
literalise	osmiridium	remarkably	spheroidal	umpireship	waterskier
literalism	otherwhere	remarriage	spherulite	unabridged	waterspout
literalist	otherwhile	remorseful	squareness	underbelly	watertight
literality	otherworld	reparation	squaresail	underbrush	waterwheel

```
waterworks  chrysolite  excusatory  imposition  oafishness  rotisserie
waveringly  chrysotile  exposition  impossible  obfuscated  salesclerk
wintriness  cicisbeism  expositive  impossibly  obtuseness  saleswoman
wolframite  classicise  expository  imposthume  occasional  satisfying
wondrously  classicism  facesaving  incasement  omniscient  scansorial
abrasively  classicist  fairspoken  incessancy  opposeless  schismatic
accessible  classified  famishment  incestuous  oppositely  Scotswoman
accessibly  classifier  fearsomely  incisively  opposition  seamstress
accusation  cloistered  fenestella  indiscreet  otioseness  seersucker
accusative  clumsiness  fenestrate  indiscrete  overshadow  selfseeker
accusatory  coarseness  firescreen  indisposed  overslaugh  selfstyled
accusingly  cocksurely  flimsiness  indistinct  overspread  semestrial
accustomed  cohesively  folksiness  industrial  overstride  sempstress
acoustical  colossally  folksinger  infusorial  overstrung  senescence
adhesively  comestible  foreshadow  infusorian  oversubtle  shoestring
adjustable  copesettic  foresheets  ingestible  oversupply  shopsoiled
adjustment  cornstarch  foursquare  insistence  owlishness  sidesaddle
admissible  counselled  fourstroke  insistency  pacesetter  sidestreet
advisement  counsellor  freesoiler  intestinal  packsaddle  sidestroke
aerostatic  crassitude  freespeech  investment  palisander  silkscreen
allosteric  crisscross  freespoken  ionisation  PalmSunday  sinisterly
allusively  crossbench  garishness  ionosphere  papistical  sinistrous
altostrati  crossbones  gladsomely  irresolute  paraselene  sinusoidal
ambassador  crossbreed  glasscloth  Janusfaced  parasitism  slipstitch
ambushment  crosscheck  glassfibre  Jewishness  parasitoid  slipstream
ancestress  crossgrain  glasshouse  jocoseness  patisserie  softspoken
antiSemite  crosshatch  glassiness  Johnsonese  pedestrian  songstress
antisepsis  crossindex  glasspaper  johnsonian  pentstemon  sparseness
antiseptic  crosslight  glassworks  juristical  periscopic  Spenserian
antisocial  crosspatch  glossarial  lacustrine  perishable  splashback
antistatic  crosspiece  glossarist  landscaper  pheasantry  splashdown
appositely  crossrefer  glossiness  latescence  phrasebook  sponsorial
apposition  crossroads  glossology  lavishment  picosecond  starstream
appositive  crosstrees  goatsbeard  lavishness  pleasantly  stepsister
arrestment  cryoscopic  goatsucker  legislator  pleasantry  stressless
asbestosis  debasement  grasscloth  lifesaving  pleasingly  synostosis
assessable  decisively  grassroots  lockstitch  poinsettia  talismanic
assessment  deepseated  grasssnake  locustbean  polysemous  tapestried
assistance  dehiscence  greasewood  logistical  porismatic  telescopic
atmosphere  delusional  greasiness  lonesomely  postscript  theistical
augustness  delusively  gressorial  longshanks  praesidium  themselves
autostrada  depositary  gruesomely  lotuseater  pressagent  theosopher
autostrade  deposition  gyroscopic  lumpsucker  pressingly  thousandth
averseness  depository  hairspring  lutestring  pressurise  timesaving
aversively  derestrict  hairstreak  magistracy  priesthood  timeserver
babysitter  derisively  hairstroke  magistrate  priestling  tiresomely
backsheesh  desistance  handselled  mainspring  prissiness  toilsomely
backslider  detestable  handsomely  mainstream  pubescence  townswoman
backstairs  detestably  handspring  majestical  puissantly  transactor
backstitch  digestible  harassment  majuscular  punishable  transcribe
backstroke  disastrous  haruspices  manuscript  punishment  transcript
balustrade  divestment  headspring  maraschino  puristical  transducer
banishment  divisional  headsquare  markswoman  queasiness  transeptal
barysphere  divisively  headstream  meerschaum  quiescence  transferee
bemusement  downstairs  headstrong  megascopic  quiescency  transferor
bestseller  downstream  heatstroke  melismatic  rakishness  transfuser
bimestrial  downstroke  hemisphere  mesoscaphe  ravishment  transgress
birdspider  drawstring  heresiarch  mesosphere  reassemble  transience
birdstrike  dressiness  highstrung  metastable  reassembly  transiency
blissfully  dressmaker  hoarseness  metastases  redescribe  transistor
bluishness  drowsihead  hocuspocus  metastasis  rediscover  transition
bonesetter  drowsiness  holosteric  metastatic  registered  transitive
boneshaker  dumbstruck  holusbolus  metaschist  registrant  transitory
bookseller  effusively  homosexual  millstream  reissuable  translator
bootstraps  egoistical  horoscopic  minestrone  relishable  translucid
boyishness  Eleusinian  hypostasis  ministrant  remissible  translunar
brassiness  embossment  hypostatic  minuscular  remissness  transmuter
breastbone  emissivity  illusional  modishness  renascence  transplant
breastwall  emulsifier  illusively  monistical  reposition  transposal
breastwork  encasement  illusorily  moonshiner  repository  transposer
bressummer  encashment  illustrate  moonstruck  resistance  transshape
calcsinter  encystment  immiscible  mopishness  resistible  transvalue
catastasis  endoscopic  immiscibly  moroseness  resistless  transverse
cheesecake  endosmosis  impassable  mosasaurus  revisional  treasonous
cheesiness  endosmotic  impassably  mousseline  rhapsodise  Trotskyism
chersonese  enlistment  impassible  mulishness  rhapsodist  Trotskyist
chessboard  enmeshment  impassibly  nanisation  robustious  Trotskyite
Christhood  equestrian  impishness  nanosecond  robustness  trousseaux
Christlike  ergosterol  imposingly  numismatic  roodscreen  tumescence
```

typescript	beautician	deactivate	fleetingly	imputation	monetarism
typesetter	beautifier	debatement	flintiness	imputative	monetarist
unassisted	bewitchery	demotivate	flirtation	inactivate	monitorial
unassuming	bimetallic	denaturant	floatation	inactively	monotheism
unbesought	bipetalous	denotation	floatboard	inactivity	monotheist
uncustomed	blastemata	denotative	floatingly	inaptitude	monotonous
undeserved	blastocyst	deontology	floatplane	inartistic	monstrance
undesigned	blastoderm	deputation	floatstone	incitation	moratorium
undesirous	blastomere	devitalise	foreteller	incitement	mountebank
uneasiness	blastopore	devotement	fourteener	inditement	moustached
unhistoric	bleatingly	devotional	fourteenth	ineptitude	moustachio
unjustness	blistering	diastemata	fractional	infatuated	Mousterian
unreserved	blottesque	digitalise	frictional	innateness	myasthenia
unresolved	bluethroat	digitately	frontbench	insatiable	naphthenic
uppishness	bluetongue	digitation	frontwards	insatiably	natatorial
veldschoen	blusterous	digitiform	frostiness	inveteracy	natatorium
virescence	boastfully	dilatation	fruitarian	inveterate	negatively
vivisector	boisterous	dilatorily	fruitfully	invitation	negativism
wellspoken	brantgoose	dilettante	fugitively	invitatory	negativist
wellspring	bratticing	dilettanti	functional	invitingly	negativity
whatsoever	breathable	diluteness	gametangia	irrational	negotiable
whensoever	breathless	diphtheria	gaultheria	irritation	negotiator
whipstitch	brentgoose	diphtheric	gauntleted	irritative	nematocyst
WhitSunday	caoutchouc	disutility	gelatinise	isentropic	nicotinism
whomsoever	capitalise	dogstongue	gelatinous	isopterous	nightdress
widespread	capitalism	doubtfully	geneticist	janitorial	nightglass
windscreen	capitalist	doubtingly	ghastfully	jauntiness	nightlight
windshield	capitation	drafthorse	glottology	keratinise	nightshade
windsleeve	Capitoline	dubitation	gluttonise	keratinous	nightshift
wingspread	capitulary	dubitative	gluttonous	kineticist	nightshirt
woolsorter	capitulate	edentulous	gnosticism	knottiness	nightstick
yourselves	carotenoid	effeteness	goaltender	lavatorial	nightwatch
abacterial	carotinoid	Egyptology	gobstopper	lawntennis	nineteenth
abortively	causticity	eighteenmo	graptolite	legateship	nomothetic
acroterion	cavitation	eighteenth	greatniece	legitimacy	nonstarter
acroterium	chartreuse	elasticise	greatuncle	legitimate	nutational
adaptation	chartulary	elasticity	grittiness	legitimise	oblateness
adaptively	chasteness	electively	guesthouse	legitimism	obliterate
additional	chatterbox	electorate	guestnight	legitimist	odontalgia
admittable	chattiness	electrical	guiltiness	lengthways	odontology
admittance	cicatrices	electronic	gyrational	lengthwise	ommatidium
admittedly	coaptation	empathetic	habitation	levitation	optatively
adoptively	coastguard	enantiosis	habitually	lieutenant	ornateness
adulterant	coastwards	endothelia	hauntingly	lighterage	oscitation
adulterate	cogitation	endstopped	haustellum	lighterman	osmeterium
adulteress	cogitative	epentheses	haustorium	lightfaced	outstation
adulterine	colatitude	epenthesis	heartblock	lighthouse	outstretch
adulterous	comstocker	epenthetic	heartblood	lightingup	overthrown
affettuoso	constantan	episternum	heartbreak	lightproof	overthrust
alliterate	Constantia	epistolary	heartiness	limitation	overtopped
allotropic	constantly	epistrophe	heartsease	limitative	packthread
amputation	constipate	equational	heartthrob	limitrophe	paintbrush
anaptyctic	constitute	equatorial	heartwhole	lobsterpot	palatalise
anastigmat	constraint	equitation	hebetation	Lusitanian	palatinate
anastomose	constringe	erectility	henotheism	maintainer	paratactic
anastrophe	cooptation	eructation	henotheist	meditation	paratroops
annotation	cooptative	eruptively	heortology	meditative	penetrable
antitheism	counteract	escutcheon	hepatology	menstruate	penetrably
antitheist	countryish	eventually	hereticate	menstruous	penetralia
antitheses	countryman	exactitude	heretofore	mesothorax	penetrance
antithesis	courthouse	exaltation	hesitantly	metatarsal	penetrator
antithetic	covetingly	excitation	hesitation	metatarsus	penitently
apostatise	covetously	excitative	hesitative	metatheses	perithecia
apostolate	craftguild	excitatory	hipsterism	metathesis	peritoneal
apostrophe	craftiness	excitement	hylotheism	metathetic	peritoneum
appetising	creatinine	excitingly	hypotactic	metathorax	petiteness
appetitive	creatively	exenterate	hypotenuse	mightiness	petitioner
arbitrable	creativity	expatriate	hypotheses	militantly	phantasise
arbitrager	creaturely	exultantly	hypothesis	militarily	phantasmal
arbitrator	crustacean	exultation	ideational	militarise	phantasmic
aristocrat	crustation	exultingly	illatively	militarism	phantastic
asceticism	crustiness	faintheart	illiteracy	militarist	phantastry
astuteness	cryptogamy	fanaticise	illiterate	militiaman	pigsticker
auditorial	cryptogram	fanaticism	illstarred	minstrelsy	pilothouse
auditorium	cryptology	faultiness	immaterial	minutebook	pilotlight
avantgarde	cunctation	finiteness	immaturely	minutehand	pilotwhale
aventurine	cunctative	firstclass	immaturity	minuteness	pinstriped
aviatrices	curatorial	firstnight	impatience	moisturise	plantation
azeotropic	daintiness	flattering	impotently	monetarily	plantlouse

plasticise	roisterous	stratiform	amanuensis	craquelure	illaudably
plasticity	rotational	stratocrat	apiculture	crenulated	imprudence
pointblank	roustabout	struthious	armourclad	crepuscule	incautious
politeness	rubythroat	stypticity	armourless	culturally	includible
politician	safetybelt	substation	artfulness	curmudgeon	ineducable
politicise	sagittally	substitute	asexuality	debauchery	ineludible
polytheism	salutarily	substratum	assaultive	debouchure	inequality
polytheist	salutation	sudatorium	auscultate	denouement	iniquitous
polytocous	salutatory	suretyship	aviculture	desquamate	inoculable
positional	sanatorium	sweatgland	bijouterie	devoutness	inoculator
positively	sanctifier	sweatiness	binaurally	diffusible	insouciant
positivism	sanctimony	sweatshirt	bivouacked	disbudding	joyfulness
positivist	sanctitude	sweetbread	calculable	disburthen	joyousness
positivity	sanitarian	sweetbriar	calculably	discursive	kibbutznik
practician	sanitarily	sweetbrier	calculator	discussant	languisher
practising	sanitarium	sweetening	camouflage	discussion	languorous
praetorial	sanitation	sweetheart	cappuccino	discussive	lawfulness
praetorian	scantiness	sweltering	carbuncled	discutient	linguiform
presternum	scattergun	taciturnly	catburglar	disfurnish	linguistic
prettiness	scattering	taleteller	cellularly	disgustful	Lithuanian
proctorage	scattiness	tapotement	cellulitis	disputable	manfulness
proctorial	scepticism	tauntingly	cellulosic	disputably	mansuetude
proctorise	Scotticise	temptation	censurable	disqualify	marguerite
prosthesis	Scotticism	temptingly	chequebook	disquieten	marquisate
prosthetic	scratchily	teratogeny	cinquefoil	disquietly	masquerade
prostitute	scratchwig	teratology	circuitous	disruption	mavourneen
prostomial	scrutineer	teratomata	circularly	disruptive	measurable
prostomium	scrutinise	theatrical	circulator	dissuasion	measurably
psalterium	sedateness	thirteenth	circumcise	dissuasive	measuredly
psittacine	selftaught	thirtyfold	circumflex	eloquently	mensurable
punctation	senatorial	tinctorial	circumfuse	embouchure	Methuselah
punctually	serotinous	Tractarian	circumvent	encourager	molluscoid
punctuator	shantytown	tractional	coagulable	englutting	molluscous
punctulate	sheathbill	traitorous	coequality	enthusiasm	mosquitoes
punitively	sheathless	troctolite	colourable	enthusiast	muscularly
puritanise	shiftiness	trustfully	colourably	euphuistic	Mussulmans
puritanism	shirtfront	trustiness	colourfast	evacuation	nasturtium
putatively	shirtwaist	trustingly	colourless	evacuative	nonnuclear
pyretology	shortbread	tryptophan	combustion	evaluation	obituarist
pyrotechny	shortcrust	unattached	combustive	evaluative	obtruncate
quantifier	shortdated	unattended	communally	excruciate	odiousness
quantitive	shortening	unbuttoned	communique	executable	offputting
quartation	shortlived	undeterred	commutable	exhaustion	opaqueness
quarterage	shortrange	unfathered	commutator	exhaustive	oracularly
quarterday	shuttering	unfettered	compulsion	factualism	orotundity
quartering	skirtdance	unlettered	compulsive	factualist	outgunning
quartzitic	skittishly	unorthodox	compulsory	factuality	outputting
questioner	slantingly	unsettling	computable	famousness	outrunning
quintuplet	slatternly	vegetarian	computator	favourable	parturient
reactivate	sluttishly	vegetation	concurrent	favourably	pasquinade
reactively	smartmoney	vegetative	concurring	fitfulness	pasturable
reactivity	smattering	velitation	concussion	flatulence	pellucidly
rebuttable	smoothbore	velutinous	concussive	flatulency	penpushing
recitalist	smoothness	venational	conduction	flexuously	percussion
recitation	smuttiness	visitation	conductive	fortuitism	percussive
recitative	snootiness	visitorial	confusedly	fortuitist	perdurable
recitativo	solitarily	vocational	conjugally	fortuitous	perdurably
reentrance	solstitial	volatilise	consuetude	foxhunting	perjurious
refutation	somatology	volatility	consulship	frequenter	permutable
relational	somatotype	volitional	consultant	frequently	perquisite
relatively	songthrush	vomitorium	consulting	globularly	persuasion
relativise	Spartacist	waistcloth	consultive	gradualism	persuasive
relativism	spasticity	wellturned	consumable	gradualist	pincushion
relativist	spectacled	wheatstone	consumedly	graduation	pinnulated
relativity	spectacles	wiretapper	consummate	granularly	plaguesome
remittance	spectrally	woodturner	convulsant	granulator	porousness
remoteness	splitlevel	wristwatch	convulsion	granulitic	Portuguese
repatriate	splutterer	yeastiness	convulsive	gratuitous	postulator
repetiteur	sportfully	zwitterion	cornucopia	gunrunning	pothunting
repetition	sportiness	accoucheur	corpulence	gutturally	pozzuolana
repetitive	sportingly	accountant	corpulency	Hindustani	precursory
reputation	sportively	accounting	corpuscule	honourable	prefulgent
revitalise	sportswear	adequately	corrugated	honourably	prejudiced
rheotropic	spottiness	affluently	corrugator	honourless	presumable
rightangle	squeteague	agglutinin	corruption	humbuggery	presumably
rightfully	stentorian	aircushion	corruptive	humbugging	presuppose
rightwards	stertorous	allpurpose	couturiere	humourless	presumbent
ringtailed	strategist	altruistic	cowpuncher	humoursome	procurable
roistering	strathspey	amanuenses	crapulence	illaudable	procurance

procurator	vanquisher	starveling	strawberry	fuzzywuzzy	accusatory
producible	vascularly	stopvolley	strawboard	goodygoody	acephalous
production	victualled	subaverage	throwstick	halfyearly	acervation
productive	victualler	televiewer	tidewaiter	hankypanky	acrobatics
profundity	virtuality	television	typewriter	heavyarmed	activation
promulgate	virtueless	televisual	unlawfully	hobbyhorse	adaptation
propulsion	virtuosity	thievishly	untowardly	hoitytoity	adequately
propulsive	virtuously	titivation	wainwright	hokeypokey	adjuration
pursuivant	wampumpeag	trouvaille	wellwisher	honeyeater	adjuratory
recoupment	wilfulness	twelvefold	werewolves	honeyguide	admiration
recrudesce	woefulness	twelvenote	westwardly	honeysweet	adrenaline
redcurrant	acervation	twelvetone	wirewalker	hurdygurdy	Adullamite
resounding	activation	unenviable	wireworker	hurlyburly	advocation
ruefulness	activeness	unravelled	woodworker	isodynamic	advocatory
rumrunning	alleviator	unrivalled	annexation	jerrybuilt	aerobatics
sanguinary	alloverish	unwavering	bisexually	lacrymator	aeronautic
sanguinely	ambivalent	zollverein	detoxicant	lardydardy	Africander
sanguinity	asseverate	aardwolves	detoxicate	merrymaker	Africanise
savourless	bedevilled	backwardly	indexation	methylated	Africanism
secludedly	benevolent	bejewelled	intoxicant	moneymaker	Africanist
semiuncial	biliverdin	bellwether	intoxicate	moneytaker	Afrikander
sensualise	cadaverous	bollweevil	paroxysmal	nambypamby	algolagnia
sensualism	caravaneer	cartwright	paroxytone	paddyfield	algolagnic
sensualist	caravanned	caseworker	peroxidise	paddywagon	alienation
sensuality	caravanner	codswallop	preexilian	paddywhack	allegation
sensuously	chauvenist	copywriter	pyroxenite	pastyfaced	allocation
Septuagint	chauvinist	cordwainer	relaxation	pennyroyal	allogamous
shroudlaid	decivilise	deadweight	uniaxially	pennyworth	allopathic
shroudless	derivation	dishwasher	acotyledon	pharyngeal	almacanter
sinfulness	derivative	disownment	analysable	picayunish	almucanter
singularly	duumvirate	downwardly	analytical	propylaeum	alteration
skijumping	enervation	dumbwaiter	anchylosis	semiyearly	alterative
speculator	enervative	duniwassal	anchylotic	sillybilly	amalgamate
statuesque	equivalent	embowelled	annoyingly	spagyrical	ambivalent
statutable	equivocate	flagwaving	arrhythmia	tachymeter	ambulacral
statutably	Eurovision	flyswatter	arrhythmic	tachymetry	ambulacrum
stimulator	evolvement	footwarmer	asphyxiant	teenyweeny	ambulation
stipulator	excavation	Glaswegian	asphyxiate	topsyturvy	ambulatory
subculture	grievously	halfwitted	bathymeter	tricyclist	amendatory
subduction	halfvolley	handworked	bathymetry	unicyclist	amputation
subjugator	Hanoverian	headwaiter	bathyscaph	willynilly	amygdaloid
subnuclear	immoveable	highwayman	bathyscope	willywilly	anaplastic
succulence	impoverish	ironworker	bawdyhouse	wishywashy	angularity
succulency	incivility	longwinded	bellyacher	altazimuth	annexation
swanupping	individual	lukewarmly	bellydance	blitzkrieg	annotation
Talmudical	innovation	makeweight	bellylaugh	breezeless	annularity
Tartuffian	innovative	millwright	biodynamic	breeziness	annulation
Tartuffism	innovatory	mineworker	bobbysocks	frenziedly	anthracene
textualist	irreverent	newsworthy	bobbysoxer	frizziness	anthracite
texturally	Jehovistic	newswriter	botryoidal	homozygote	anthracoid
throughout	malevolent	nonswimmer	bradyseism	homozygous	antimasque
throughput	monovalent	noteworthy	candyfloss	horizontal	antimatter
throughway	motivation	outswinger	carryingon	Lipizzaner	antipathic
tittupping	motiveless	overweight	chalybeate	schizocarp	apostatise
tongueless	nativeborn	overwinter	cuttystool	schizogony	aquamarine
tonguetied	nativeness	periwigged	daisychain	scorzonera	araucarian
tortuosity	nativistic	periwinkle	dialysable	seltzogene	areolation
tortuously	newsvendor	playwright	dillydally	sleaziness	Areopagite
trifurcate	nucivorous	railwayman	diphyletic	sneezeweed	arrogantly
triquetrae	omnivorous	roadworthy	diphyodont	sneezewood	arrogation
triquetral	Ordovician	ropewalker	donnybrook	sneezewort	arthralgia
triturable	papaverine	rottweiler	ecchymosis	topazolite	arthralgic
triturator	papaverous	sashwindow	ecchymotic	wheeziness	asexuality
truculence	polyvalent	screwplate	embryogeny	—————	asparagine
truculency	rejuvenate	screwpress	embryology	abdication	aspiration
turbulence	rejuvenise	selfwilled	embryonate	aberrantly	Athanasian
turbulency	relevantly	semiweekly	emeryboard	aberration	Australian
ubiquitous	renovation	shipwright	emerypaper	abjuration	autogamous
unblushing	revivalism	shopwalker	emerywheel	abnegation	automation
unctuosity	revivalist	shopwindow	epicycloid	Abrahamman	automatise
unctuously	salivation	showwindow	essayistic	abrogation	automatism
uneducated	scurviness	shrewdness	eurhythmic	abstracted	automatist
unequalled	seedvessel	shrewishly	everyplace	abstracter	bacchantes
ungrudging	sexivalent	shrewmouse	everything	abstractly	bacchantic
unhouseled	shrivelled	sidewinder	everywhere	abstractor	backgammon
uniqueness	Shrovetide	signwriter	fairycycle	abundantly	backhanded
untruthful	sleeveless	slowwitted	fiftyfifty	accurately	backhander
usefulness	sleevelink	songwriter	fortyniner	accusation	backwardly
valvulitis	starvation	stalwartly	fuddyduddy	accusative	bandmaster

barebacked	constantly	dilatation	exhilarate	hairraiser	inveracity
bedchamber	contraband	discharger	exhumation	hamshackle	invitation
Belgravian	contrabass	disclaimer	expiration	handbarrow	invitatory
bellyacher	contractor	disfeature	expiratory	handgallop	invocation
bemedalled	contradict	dishearten	exultantly	handmaiden	invocatory
benefactor	contraprop	dishwasher	exultation	hardhanded	iodination
Benthamism	contrarily	dispraiser	exurbanite	headmaster	ionisation
Benthamite	contravene	disqualify	exuviation	headwaiter	ironhanded
bequeathal	cooptation	dissuasion	eyeglasses	heavyarmed	ironmaster
bestialise	cooptative	dissuasive	faceharden	hebetation	irrelative
bestiality	copulation	distracted	facesaving	henhearted	irrigation
bighearted	copulative	distrainer	factualism	hesitantly	irritation
bilocation	cordiality	distrainor	factualist	hesitation	irritative
bimetallic	cordwainer	distraught	factuality	hesitative	isoniazide
biographer	corelation	divagation	fairhaired	highhanded	italianate
biographic	corelative	divination	fasciation	highjacker	italianise
bipetalous	coromandel	divinatory	federalise	highlander	Italianism
bipolarity	coronation	dominantly	federalism	highwayman	jackhammer
bivouacked	Corybantes	domination	federalist	homemaking	jackrabbit
blackamoor	corybantic	dominative	federation	homogamous	jocularity
blepharism	covenanted	downfallen	federative	honorarium	journalese
bluejacket	covenantee	downwardly	felspathic	houseagent	journalism
bookmaking	covenanter	drophammer	feminality	humpbacked	journalism
bookmarker	covenantor	dubitation	figuration	hyperaemia	journalist
Brahmanism	crackajack	dubitative	figurative	hyperaemic	jubilantly
breakables	crispation	dumbwaiter	filtration	hypotactic	jubilation
Buchmanism	crustacean	duniwassal	finicality	idiopathic	judicatory
Buchmanite	crustation	dustjacket	fireraiser	ignorantly	judicature
burglarise	cumulation	dysgraphia	fishcarver	illegalise	Kantianism
bushmaster	cumulative	dysplastic	flagrantly	illegality	keyboarder
bushranger	cunctation	eczematous	flagwaving	illstarred	kinematics
cacciatore	cunctative	efficacity	fleamarket	immolation	knockabout
cackhanded	datamation	elongation	flippantly	immoralist	laboratory
cacodaemon	deaeration	emaciation	flirtation	immorality	laceration
calamander	debonairly	emendation	floatation	impanation	lacerative
capitalise	decimalise	emendatory	floriation	imparadise	laminarian
capitalism	decimalism	emigration	fluviatile	imperative	lamination
capitalist	decimalist	emigratory	flyswatter	imputation	lanthanide
capitation	decoration	emparadise	footballer	imputative	lapidarian
caravaneer	decorative	emphractic	footcandle	incapacity	lapidarist
caravanned	dedication	encroacher	footwarmer	inchoately	lapidation
caravanner	dedicative	endogamous	forecaster	inchoation	laterality
cardialgia	dedicatory	enervation	forecastle	inchoative	laureation
caricature	deescalate	enervative	forefather	incitation	lefthanded
caseharden	defamation	enigmatise	foregather	incubation	lefthander
castration	defamatory	enigmatist	forehanded	incubative	lesbianism
catafalque	dehumanise	enthralled	forwearied	incubatory	levigation
catenation	delegation	ephorality	foundation	incunabula	levitation
cavitation	delicately	epiblastic	fourhanded	indagation	liberalise
centralise	delocalise	epigrapher	fragrantly	indexation	liberalism
centralism	demoralise	epigraphic	freehanded	indication	liberalist
centralist	denegation	equitation	freelancer	indicative	liberality
centrality	denotation	equivalent	freemartin	indicatory	liberation
chapfallen	denotative	eructation	fruitarian	induration	lifejacket
chaplaincy	denudation	escalation	fumigation	indurative	lifesaving
chiliastic	depilation	escheatage	gaillardia	inequality	limitation
chimpanzee	depilatory	Esculapian	galimatias	inhalation	limitative
choriambic	depolarise	estimation	galliambic	inhumanely	lipomatous
chromatics	depuration	estimative	gametangia	inhumanity	lipreading
chromatype	depurative	eternalise	gemination	inhumation	literalise
cinecamera	deputation	eternalist	generalise	initialise	literalism
cinerarium	derivation	ethicality	generalist	initialled	literalist
clawhammer	derivative	etiolation	generality	initiation	literality
coadjacent	derogation	evacuation	generation	initiative	literarily
coaptation	derogatory	evacuative	generative	initiatory	literation
coathanger	desolately	evaluation	generatrix	innovation	literature
codswallop	desolation	evaluative	geographer	innovative	Lithuanian
coequality	desquamate	evenhanded	geographic	innovatory	litigation
cogitation	detonation	exaltation	glaciation	insolation	lobulation
cogitative	detonative	excavation	gladhander	insularism	logicality
coloration	Devanagari	excitation	glossarial	insularity	longhaired
coloratura	devitalise	excitative	glossarist	insulation	loudhailer
comicality	devocalise	excitatory	Godfearing	intimately	lovemaking
complacent	dextrality	excusatory	gradualism	intimation	lukewarmly
complainer	diagraphic	execration	gradualist	intonation	Lusitanian
compradore	diaphanous	execrative	graduation	intubation	lustration
conflation	digitalise	execratory	grammarian	inundation	macadamise
constantan	digitately	exhalation	habitation	inundatory	maceration
Constantia	digitation	exhilarant	hackmatack	inurbanity	maculation

participle	respecting	transcript	cussedness	introducer	splendidly
particular	respective	tricyclist	cylindered	inwardness	spoondrift
patriciate	retractile	trioecious	cylindroid	jaggedness	squanderer
patricidal	retraction	trisection	defendable	lardydardy	stolidness
peacockery	retractive	tropically	degradable	limpidness	stomodaeum
peacockish	retrochoir	tubercular	degradedly	liquidator	stupidness
peduncular	revanchism	tuberculin	demandable	liquidiser	submediant
pellicular	revanchist	tuffaceous	deoxidiser	liquidness	subordinal
pellucidly	rhinoceros	tumescence	dependable	lopsidedly	subsidence
pennaceous	rollicking	typescript	dependably	methodical	subsidiary
pentachord	roodscreen	undercliff	dependence	mindedness	succedanea
perfection	rubrically	undercover	dependency	molendinar	sugardaddy
perfective	rubricator	undercroft	depredator	molybdenum	suicidally
periscopic	rustically	uneducated	diapedesis	monandrous	superduper
pernicious	salesclerk	ungraceful	diapedetic	morbidezza	sworddance
pernickety	sarracenia	ungracious	diffidence	morbidness	synecdoche
persecutor	scenically	unicyclist	dillydally	nightdress	Talmudical
pesticidal	scratchily	unilocular	diplodocus	octandrian	threadbare
phagocytic	scratchwig	univocally	disbudding	octandrous	threadfish
phenacetin	screechowl	unmerciful	disordered	onesidedly	threadmark
phenocryst	selfacting	upperclass	disorderly	orthodoxly	threadworm
phonically	selfaction	uxoricidal	dissidence	outbidding	toroidally
phylactery	senescence	valleculae	doggedness	palindrome	torpidness
physically	septically	vallecular	eisteddfod	palladious	torridness
physicking	sepulchral	vasoactive	elatedness	pallidness	towardness
pichiciago	sequacious	veldschoen	elucidator	pearldiver	transducer
picnicking	SerboCroat	vermicelli	episodical	peccadillo	triandrous
plainchant	seriocomic	vermicidal	expandable	perfidious	turbidness
playacting	serviceman	vermicular	expendable	periodical	turgidness
plutocracy	shortcrust	vernacular	extendedly	phagedaena	unbiddable
poetically	silkscreen	versicular	extendible	phagedenic	underdress
pornocracy	skyjacking	vertically	fastidious	placidness	ungrudging
porraceous	slavocracy	vibraculum	fervidness	precedence	unhandsome
postscript	snobocracy	vindicable	floridness	precedency	unkindness
precocious	spacecraft	vindicator	foetidness	prejudiced	unreadable
predacious	spadiceous	vindictive	forbidding	premedical	upwardness
predecease	spiracular	violaceous	formidable	presidency	verandahed
predicable	spiraculum	virescence	formidably	presidiary	vivandiere
prediction	splanchnic	vortically	friendless	procedural	wickedness
predictive	stagecoach	vorticella	friendlily	prosodical	wontedness
prefecture	stagecraft	vorticular	friendship	providence	wrongdoing
prelection	stalactite	waistcloth	frigidness	punchdrunk	abacterial
prepackage	statecraft	waterclock	fuddyduddy	putridness	abducentes
producible	statically	watercraft	gerundival	raggedness	abderdevine
production	steamchest	watercress	gesundheit	rancidness	abiogenist
productive	stomachful	wheelchair	granadilla	recordable	acarpelous
proficient	stormcloud	windscreen	granddaddy	recrudesce	accelerate
projectile	subduction	witchcraft	grandducal	redundance	accidental
projection	subjectify	worldclass	grenadilla	redundancy	acrogenous
projective	subjection	absurdness	groundbait	refundable	acromegaly
prolicidal	subjective	accordance	groundless	refundment	acroterion
prolocutor	subnuclear	accredited	groundling	regardless	acroterium
prosecutor	subsection	achondrite	groundmass	reproducer	activeness
protection	sufficient	affordable	groundplan	rewardable	adherently
protective	supercargo	almondeyed	groundrent	rewardless	adjacently
protectory	surfactant	animadvert	groundsman	ritardando	adrenergic
protectrix	surgically	aphrodisia	groundwork	rootedness	adulterant
provocator	suspicious	appendices	gynandrous	ruggedness	adulterate
psilocybin	swordcraft	appendixes	handedness	sacerdotal	adulteress
pubescence	syndicator	ascendable	hippodrome	sacredness	adulterine
pugnacious	synoecious	ascendance	hookedness	scaredycat	adulterous
quiescence	tablecloth	ascendancy	hornedness	secludedly	advisement
quiescency	tactically	ascendence	horridness	secondbest	aesthetics
quinacrine	tarmacadam	ascendency	hybridiser	secondhand	aesthetism
ranunculus	telescopic	ascendible	hyperdulia	secondment	afferently
reconciler	tentacular	attendance	illaudable	secondrate	affluently
redescribe	terracotta	beechdrops	illaudably	seguidilla	Albigenses
rediscover	testaceous	behindhand	impendence	sensedatum	alliterate
reelection	tetrachord	belladonna	impendency	serradilla	alloverish
reflection	thalecress	bellydance	imprudence	shieldless	allurement
reflective	thirdclass	candidness	incandesce	shortdated	altogether
refraction	trabeculae	commodious	incendiary	shouldered	amanuenses
refractive	trabecular	confidante	includible	shrewdness	amanuensis
refractory	tragacanth	confidence	incredible	shroudlaid	ambidexter
rejoicings	tragically	considered	incredibly	shroudless	amercement
renascence	tragicomic	coproducer	ineludible	skirtdance	anapaestic
repurchase	trajection	curmudgeon	ingredient	smokedried	androecium
resorcinol	trajectory	cursedness	intendance	snakedance	anopheline
respectful	transcribe	cuspidated	intendment	sordidness	antebellum

```
antecedent  bowdlerise  congregate  encasement  geochemist  incoherent
antecessor  bowdlerism  coniferous  endodermal  geothermal  indecently
antependia  breezeless  conspectus  endodermis  geothermic  indigenous
antepenult  bridgeable  consuetude  endogenous  Glaswegian  indigested
antiheroic  bridgehead  coolheaded  energetics  glauberite  indirectly
antiSemite  bridgeless  copesettic  enfacement  glimmering  inditement
antisepsis  bridgework  copyreader  engagement  goalkeeper  indolently
antiseptic  bridlepath  cordierite  engineroom  goaltender  Indonesian
aplacental  browbeaten  counselled  enlacement  goggleeyed  inducement
apoplectic  bufflehead  counsellor  enticement  goldbeater  inexpertly
apothecary  bullheaded  counteract  entireness  grangerise  infidelity
apothecial  cacogenics  couplement  ephemerous  grangerism  inherently
apothecium  cadaverous  covalently  episternum  graphemics  innateness
apotheoses  cajolement  cradlesong  epithelial  greasewood  innocently
apotheosis  candlefish  craquelure  epithelium  greyheaded  innumeracy
apparelled  candletree  crescentic  escapement  halflength  innumerate
apparently  candlewick  crowkeeper  ethereally  halfnelson  innumerous
aquiferous  candlewood  cryogenics  euhemerise  halfyearly  inquietude
arbalester  caramelise  cuddlesome  euhemerism  halogenate  insaneness
arboreally  carelessly  cuttlebone  euhemerist  halogenous  insolently
archdeacon  carotenoid  cuttlefish  evangelise  handselled  intenerate
argumentum  catalectic  damageable  evangelism  Hanoverian  interested
Armageddon  cataleptic  dapplegrey  evangelist  hardheaded  intolerant
armigerous  cattlegrid  daydreamer  eviscerate  harmlessly  inveteracy
arytaenoid  centreback  dazzlement  evolvement  haustellum  inveterate
asafoetida  centrefold  deadweight  exaggerate  heathendom  irrelevant
assafetida  centrehalf  debasement  exasperate  heathenise  irreverent
asseverate  cerebellum  debatement  excitement  heathenish  Ishmaelite
astuteness  chalcedony  decadently  exenterate  heathenism  isopterous
asymmetric  challenger  decahedral  exothermal  heedlessly  isothermal
attunement  chamaeleon  decahedron  exothermic  hellbender  Japanesque
auriferous  chamberpot  decelerate  exulcerate  helplessly  jawbreaker
autogenous  chancellor  deepseated  facileness  hemihedral  jejuneness
averseness  chandelier  defacement  fadelessly  hemihedron  jocoseness
babblement  changeable  defilement  fairleader  hempnettle  journeyman
bafflement  changeably  definement  fearlessly  hexahedral  Kafkaesque
baldheaded  changeless  degeneracy  featherbed  hexahedron  kenspeckle
bareheaded  changeling  degenerate  feathering  hexamerous  kettledrum
barelegged  changeover  deliberate  fecklessly  hexametric  knobkerrie
barometric  channelise  delineator  feebleness  hipsterism  lambrequin
baronetage  channelled  demonetise  femaleness  hoarseness  lawbreaker
battledore  chargeable  demureness  fickleness  holohedral  lawntennis
battlement  chargehand  denouement  fiddleback  homiletics  legateship
battleship  Charleston  desiderata  fiddlehead  homocercal  lieutenant
beadleship  chasteness  desiderate  fiddlewood  homogenise  lifelessly
beekeeping  chatterbox  devotement  fierceness  homogenous  ligamental
beforehand  cheesecake  diastemata  figurehead  homosexual  lighterage
beforetime  chequebook  diathermal  finiteness  honeyeater  lighterman
bejewelled  chickenpox  diathermic  fishkettle  hopelessly  listlessly
bellwether  childermas  diligently  flannelled  hucklebone  littleness
bemusement  chimneypot  diluteness  flattering  humaneness  lobsterpot
bestseller  choiceness  discreetly  flawlessly  humbleness  lockkeeper
biliverdin  chuckerout  discrepant  fledgeling  humoresque  longaevous
biochemist  cinquefoil  discretely  flunkeydom  hypodermal  longheaded
bladdernut  clothesbag  discretion  flunkeyism  hypodermic  longlegged
blanketing  clothespeg  distressed  folkmemory  hypodermis  lossleader
blastemata  clothespin  divineness  foreteller  hypotenuse  lotuseater
blistering  coarseness  documental  formlessly  icebreaker  loungesuit
blitheness  cochleated  doorkeeper  founderous  illiteracy  lovelessly
blithering  cockneyish  dosimetric  Fourierism  illiterate  loveletter
blithesome  cockneyism  doublebass  fourleaved  immaterial  luciferase
blottesque  coffeemill  doubleness  fourteener  imminently  luciferous
bluepencil  coherently  doublepark  fourteenth  immoderacy  luculently
blusterous  complected  doubletalk  fragmental  immoderate  lustreless
boisterous  complement  doubletime  frequenter  immodestly  macebearer
bollweevil  completely  dumbledore  frequently  immoveable  makeweight
bolometric  completion  dungbeetle  fringeless  immurement  malapertly
bolshevise  completive  ectodermal  fulllength  impalement  malleebird
bolshevism  complexion  ectodermic  funereally  impanelled  malleefowl
bolshevist  complexity  ectogenous  futureless  impotently  manageable
boneheaded  comprehend  edibleness  gamekeeper  impoverish  manageably
bonesetter  compressed  effaceable  gangrenous  impudently  management
bookkeeper  compressor  effacement  garnierite  impureness  manageress
bookseller  concretely  effeteness  gatekeeper  inappetent  managerial
bootlegger  concretion  eighteenmo  gatelegged  inbreeding  manifestly
bootlessly  concretise  eighteenth  gaucheness  incasement  manifestos
bottlefeed  concretism  eloquently  genteelism  incidental  manometric
bottleneck  concretist  embowelled  gentlefolk  incinerate  mansuetude
bottletree  congregant  empanelled  gentleness  incitement  marguerite
```

masquerade	outfielder	quarterday	sicklebill	tanglement	unscreened
matureness	overrefine	quartering	simpleness	taperecord	unselected
meagreness	overweight	quatrefoil	singlefoot	tapotement	unstressed
mealbeetle	pacesetter	rabblement	singleness	tattletale	unwavering
meddlesome	paddleboat	rackrenter	singletree	taxidermal	vehemently
Melanesian	painlessly	rattlehead	slanderous	taxidermic	vicegerent
mesomerism	pallbearer	rattlepate	slatternly	tearjerker	viceregent
metacentre	pancreatic	rattletrap	sleeveless	tearlessly	viewlessly
metalepsis	pancreatin	reassemble	sleevelink	technetium	virtueless
metamerism	papaverine	reassembly	slenderise	tegumental	virulently
mettlesome	papaverous	recklessly	slipperily	telemetric	vituperate
Michaelmas	paramecium	recuperate	sluicegate	telpherage	vivisector
middleaged	parametric	redolently	slumberful	tenemental	vociferant
middlebrow	paraselene	referendum	slumberous	themselves	vociferate
middlemost	pebbledash	refinement	smattering	theoretics	vociferous
mindlessly	pedimental	regalement	smorrebrod	thickening	volumetric
minutebook	pedimented	regeneracy	sneezeweed	thirteenth	voyageable
minutehand	peerlessly	regenerate	sneezewood	throneless	waffleiron
minuteness	penitently	regimental	sneezewort	thunderbox	wallpepper
miscreance	peridermal	rejuvenate	softheaded	thundering	wattlebird
mockheroic	perihelion	rejuvenise	solacement	thunderous	wavelength
mongrelise	peripeteia	remodelled	sombreness	timekeeper	weatherbox
mongrelism	perplexity	remonetise	soullessly	timelessly	weathering
monogenism	petiteness	remoteness	sourcebook	timeserver	weatherman
monumental	phrasebook	remunerate	southerner	tirelessly	wellheeled
moroseness	picaresque	requiescat	southernly	titanesque	wentletrap
morphemics	picosecond	restlessly	sparseness	toffeenose	Wertherian
motiveless	piliferous	reticently	Spencerian	tonelessly	Wertherism
mountebank	pinebeauty	retirement	Spenserian	tongueless	whispering
mousseline	pitcherful	reverencer	sphalerite	tonguetied	Winchester
Mousterian	pitilessly	reverently	spongecake	tortfeasor	woodpecker
movelessly	plaguesome	revilement	spongewood	tracheated	wordlessly
muciferous	plangently	ringleader	spoonerism	tracheitis	workpeople
namelessly	playfellow	ringnecked	spotlessly	trammelled	yokefellow
nanosecond	plunderage	ripplemark	sprucebeer	trancelike	yourselves
nativeborn	plunderous	roistering	spruceness	transeptal	zollverein
nativeness	poinsettia	roisterous	squareness	trawlerman	zwitterion
needlebath	politeness	Romanesque	squaresail	triacetate	blackfaced
needlebook	polygenism	rontgenise	squaretoed	triggerman	blamefully
needlecord	polygenist	rottweiler	squaretoes	triquetrae	blissfully
needlefish	polygenous	rovebeetle	squeteague	triquetral	boastfully
needlessly	polyhedral	rudimental	squirearch	triskelion	breadfruit
needlework	polyhedric	ruthlessly	squirehood	trolleybus	brickfield
nettlerash	polyhedron	saddleback	squireling	tropaeolum	calciferol
newsletter	polymerise	saddlefast	squireship	tumbledown	camouflage
newsreader	polymerism	saddletree	stablemate	tumblerful	candyfloss
newsvendor	polymerous	saliferous	stableness	tumbleweed	chaudfroid
nimbleness	Polynesian	saltcellar	stagbeetle	tunelessly	chauffeuse
nineteenth	polysemous	savageness	staggering	turtleback	cheerfully
nipplewort	pomiferous	scarceness	starveling	turtledove	dentifrice
northerner	postbellum	scatheless	statuesque	turtleneck	doubtfully
noticeable	pouncetbox	scattergun	stiffening	twelvefold	dreadfully
noticeably	presternum	scattering	stiflebone	twelvenote	engulfment
notonectal	princeling	seaanemone	strategist	twelvetone	faithfully
nubiferous	princeship	securement	stridently	twowheeler	fancifully
nuciferous	proceeding	secureness	subaverage	typesetter	febrifugal
obediently	procreator	sedateness	subspecies	Tyrrhenian	fiftyfifty
oblateness	prophesier	seducement	subtleness	umpireship	flashflood
obliterate	prophetess	seedvessel	supineness	unaccented	forcefully
obtuseness	proscenium	selfdeceit	supplejack	unaffected	fruitfully
occidental	prospector	selfdenial	supplement	unattended	ghastfully
octahedral	prospectus	selffeeder	suppleness	undefended	glassfibre
octahedron	prosperity	selflessly	suppletion	undeserved	gooseflesh
octamerous	prosperous	selfregard	suppletive	undeterred	gracefully
octodecimo	protreptic	selfseeker	suppletory	undigested	grapefruit
oecumenism	pruriently	semiweekly	suppressor	unexcelled	gratefully
oleiferous	psalterium	semiyearly	sweetening	unexpected	gratifying
omnigenous	puerperium	sentiently	sweltering	unforeseen	greenfinch
oncogenous	purulently	sereneness	syncretise	unfriended	guilefully
opaqueness	puzzlement	settlement	syncretism	unfriendly	henceforth
openhearth	pyrogenous	severeness	syncretist	ungenerous	horseflesh
opposeless	pyrometric	sexagenary	synthesise	uniqueness	insufflate
orangepeel	pyrotechny	Sexagesima	synthesist	unlabelled	interferer
orangewood	pyroxenite	shillelagh	synthetise	unlikeness	interferon
ornamental	quadrennia	shopkeeper	synthetist	unnameable	Janusfaced
ornateness	quarrelled	shortening	tactlessly	unravelled	lightfaced
orthoepist	quarreller	shrivelled	talebearer	unredeemed	magnifical
osmeterium	quarrender	Shrovetide	taleteller	unreserved	magnificat
otioseness	quarterage	shuttering		unripeness	

```
magnifying biodegrade inelegance resurgence antitheist greenhouse
mercifully biological ineligible retrograde antitheses guardhouse
microfarad blackguard ineligibly retrogress antithesis guesthouse
microfiche bloodguilt instigator revengeful antithetic halophytic
millefiori brantgoose insurgence rhizogenic asynchrony headcheese
mirthfully brentgoose insurgency salmagundi attachable headphones
mournfully bridegroom intangible saltigrade attachment henotheism
multifaced bromegrass intangibly saprogenic autochthon henotheist
paddyfield bunchgrass intergrade satyagraha avouchment Herrnhuter
paraffinic carmagnole intrigante scapegrace backsheesh hitchhiker
pastyfaced carragheen intriguant sialagogic banishment hobbyhorse
peacefully centigrade laryngitic sialagogue bawdyhouse holophrase
permafrost chinagraph laryngitis smaragdine blackheart holophytic
persiflage coastguard lemongrass smaragdite blasphemer homophonic
photoflood collegiate lentigines speargrass bleachable hylotheism
pianoforte conjugally lithoglyph spirograph blockhouse hypophyses
piscifauna contagious lithograph springhalt bloodhound hypophysis
pokerfaced contiguity liturgical springhead bluethroat hypotheses
pontifical contiguous livingroom springless bluishness hypothesis
pontifices corrigenda lovingness springlike boneshaker impishness
postoffice corrigible malingerer springtail boyishness infighting
powerfully corrugated Malpighian springtide branchiate infrahuman
pridefully corrugator meningioma springtime breathable insightful
prizefight cosmogonic meningitis springwood breathless Jewishness
proudflesh couchgrass micrograph stalagmite breechless ladychapel
rightfully courageous mimeograph stenograph bronchiole lavishment
sacrificer craftguild monsignori sterigmata bronchitic lavishness
satisfying crossgrain Montagnard straighten bronchitis lederhosen
scornfully cyclograph mulligrubs straightly Caerphilly lengthways
shamefaced deflagrate myological strengthen cataphract lengthwise
shamefully detergency mystagogic stringbean catechesis lighthouse
sheriffdom diningroom mystagogue stringency catechetic longshanks
shirtfront disengaged negligence stringendo catechiser Manichaean
sideeffect ditriglyph negligible stringhalt catechumen Manicheism
slothfully divergence negligibly stringless chinchilla manorhouse
smockfrock divergency neological stronghold churchgoer mesophytic
spitefully divulgence nephograph strongroom churchyard mesothorax
sportfully dorsigrade newsagency stylograph clovehitch metaphoric
stonefruit earwigging nightglass subjugator coachhouse metaphrase
swinefever ecological nitrogroup supergiant cockchafer metaphysic
Tartuffian effulgence nonlogical sweatgland coryphaeus metatheses
Tartuffism ensanguine oceangoing swordgrass courthouse metathesis
tastefully epexegeses orological syllogiser crosshatch metathetic
thankfully epexegesis orthogenic synergetic cytochrome metathorax
transferee epexegetic orthogonal syntagmata delightful modishness
transferor erotogenic outrageous takingness detachable monochasia
transfuser expurgator outrightly tardigrade detachedly monochrome
trustfully exsanguine paedagogic termagancy detachment monophonic
truthfully extinguish paedogogue tetragonal diarrhoeal monorhymed
underfloor farsighted pantograph theurgical diarrhoeic monotheism
unedifying fastigiate passageway throughout diphtheria monotheist
unlawfully fibreglass pathogenic throughput diphtheric moonshiner
vengefully fieldglass pellagrous throughway disinherit mopishness
wastefully foreignism pentagonal tiringroom drafthorse mulishness
watchfully galloglass petroglyph tobogganer empathetic myasthenia
waterflood gaslighter phonograph transgress encashment naphthenic
waterfront geological photogenic triangular encephalic nomothetic
wearifully goodygoody photograph twilighted encephalon nosophobia
whitefaced goosegrass phylogenic umbrageous endophytic oafishness
wrathfully gunfighter phytogenic underglaze endothelia oesophagus
wrongfully hectograph pictograph unflagging enmeshment overcharge
Wycliffite heliograph piecegoods variegated enrichment overshadow
youthfully heptagonal planigraph vectograph epentheses overthrown
aboriginal hieroglyph Portuguese watchglass epenthesis overthrust
abridgment hierograph presageful watchguard epenthetic owlishness
adjudgment hippogriff presignify waterglass exospheric packthread
aftergrass hippogryph prodigally zigzagging faintheart paraphrase
allergenic honeyguide prodigious zincograph famishment paraphrast
amphigouri houseguest prologuise zoological fianchetto peripheral
anagogical humbuggery propagable acrophobia foreshadow perishable
analogical humbugging propaganda aerophobia foresheets perithecia
androgenic hurdygurdy propagator allophonic fourchette phosphatic
anemograph hygrograph pycnogonid ambushment franchiser phosphoric
apologetic hypergolic quickgrass analphabet freightage phosphorus
aspergilla hypnagogic radiogenic anarchical Frenchness pilothouse
astragalus iatrogenic radiograph antechapel garishness planchette
avantgarde impregnant rampageous Antichrist gaultheria pleochroic
bedraggled impregnate reeligible antiphonal glasshouse ploughable
belongings indulgence refulgence antitheism greenheart ploughland
```

polychaete	windshield	autodidact	chattiness	debilitate	elutriator
polychrest	witchhazel	aversively	chauvinism	decapitate	emancipate
polychrome	wretchedly	babysitter	chauvinist	decisively	emancipist
polyphasic	xenophobia	backbiting	cheapishly	decivilise	emarginate
polyphonic	xerophytic	bafflingly	cheekiness	defeminise	embodiment
polytheism	xylophonic	balbriggan	cheeriness	deficiency	embolismic
polytheist	abdominous	battailous	cheesiness	definienda	embroidery
postchaise	abortively	beautician	childishly	definitely	emissivity
powerhouse	abrasively	beautifier	chilliness	definition	emollition
preachment	accusingly	becomingly	chlorinate	definitive	empiricism
prosthesis	adaptively	bedevilled	chronicity	definitude	empiricist
prosthetic	additional	bellringer	chronicler	defoliator	emulsifier
punishable	adhesively	benedicite	chubbiness	dehumidify	enantiosis
punishment	adhibition	Benedictus	churlishly	delaminate	endemicity
pyrophoric	adjudicate	beneficent	circuitous	delimitate	enduringly
quenchable	administer	beneficial	clamminess	delphinium	engagingly
quenchless	admiringly	besprinkle	clannishly	delphinoid	enregister
rakishness	admonition	bestridden	classicise	delusional	enrigiment
ravishment	admonitive	biennially	classicism	delusively	enticingly
relishable	admonitory	bioscience	classicist	demobilise	enunciable
riverhorse	adoptively	biparietal	classified	demolition	enunciator
rosechafer	aerobiosis	bitchiness	classifier	demoniacal	epideictic
roughhouse	aerobiotic	bituminise	cloudiness	demotivate	equability
roundhouse	aeruginous	bituminous	clownishly	dendriform	equanimity
rubythroat	affability	bleariness	clumsiness	denominate	equational
searchable	affiliated	bleatingly	coercively	depositary	equilibria
searchless	afterimage	blindingly	cohabitant	deposition	erectility
semichorus	alarmingly	blockishly	cohesively	depository	erethismic
shanghaier	albuminoid	bloodiness	coincident	deracinate	ergodicity
sheathbill	albuminous	blueribbon	colatitude	deridingly	eruptively
sheathless	alkalinity	blurringly	colchicine	derisively	especially
shirehorse	allegiance	blushingly	colonially	desalinate	essayistic
sitophobia	alleviator	bookbinder	comedienne	descriptor	eugenicist
sketchable	allusively	bootlicker	comehither	desipience	eulogistic
sketchbook	almsgiving	bouncingly	comeliness	detoxicant	euphuistic
sleighbell	altazimuth	brachiator	compliance	detoxicate	Eurovision
smokehouse	altruistic	brachiopod	compliancy	devilishly	everliving
smoothbore	amerciable	Brahminism	complicacy	devotional	evilminded
smoothness	amiability	braininess	complicate	dickcissel	exactitude
songthrush	ammoniacal	brassiness	complicity	digitiform	excitingly
spatchcock	ammoniated	bratticing	compliment	dilapidate	excogitate
speechless	ammunition	brawniness	conjointly	diminished	exhibition
spitchcock	anastigmat	breeziness	conscience	disability	exhibitory
splashback	ancipitous	brilliance	conspiracy	disdainful	exorbitant
splashdown	aneurismal	brilliancy	conspirant	disjointed	expedience
sprightful	annalistic	broodiness	constipate	disquieten	expediency
stanchless	annihilate	broodingly	constitute	disquietly	expedition
stanchness	annoyingly	Buddhistic	contribute	distribute	experience
steakhouse	anteriorly	bumblingly	contritely	distringas	experiment
stenchtrap	antibiosis	bumpkinish	contrition	disutility	exploitage
stitchwort	antibiotic	bunglingly	coordinate	divaricate	exploitive
storehouse	anticipant	bustlingly	coradicate	divisional	exposition
strathspey	anticipate	cabalistic	costliness	divisively	expositive
struthious	aphoristic	cacomistle	councillor	dolomitise	expository
strychnine	apodeictic	caespitose	councilman	doubtingly	exteriorly
strychnism	Apollinian	cajolingly	covariance	drawlingly	exultingly
sugarhouse	apparition	calamitous	covetingly	dreaminess	facilitate
superhuman	appetising	calcsinter	coweringly	dreariness	fairminded
sweetheart	appetitive	caliginous	craftiness	dressiness	familiarly
switchback	appositely	calyciform	cragginess	droopingly	fanaticise
switchover	apposition	campaigner	crankiness	drowsihead	fanaticism
sycophancy	appositive	canaliculi	crassitude	drowsiness	fatalistic
telephoner	aquilinity	canonicals	creaminess	drudgingly	faultiness
telephonic	arbalister	canonicate	creatinine	durability	felicitate
tetrahedra	archaistic	canonicity	creatively	duumvirate	felicitous
theophanic	archbishop	capability	creativity	dwarfishly	femininely
theophoric	armorially	capacitate	creepiness	dynamistic	femininity
thillhorse	arterially	capacitive	cribriform	earthiness	fetchingly
thoughtful	arteriolar	carabineer	crocoisite	ebullience	feverishly
tocopherol	artificial	carabinier	crossindex	ebulliency	fiducially
toxiphobia	ascariasis	carotinoid	crustiness	ebullition	fiendishly
trenchancy	asceticism	carryingon	cumuliform	effeminacy	filariasis
unemphatic	aspidistra	causticity	curability	effeminate	filthiness
unfathered	assibilate	cavalierly	daintiness	efficiency	fimbriated
unorthodox	assimilate	centricity	damagingly	effusively	fivefinger
uppishness	associable	centrifuge	dauphiness	elasticise	flabbiness
wheelhorse	asteriated	ceruminous	dazzlingly	elasticity	flaccidity
wheelhouse	ateleiosis	champignon	deactivate	electively	flashiness
whorehouse	audibility	charmingly	deadliness	Eleusinian	fleabitten

fleacircus	hardfisted	inhibitory	lyophilise	overriding	profligacy
fleeringly	harelipped	iniquitous	maleficent	overwinter	profligate
fleetingly	hauntingly	inkslinger	manchineel	pacifiable	proprietor
fleshiness	heartiness	innominate	manumitted	pacificate	prosaicism
flimsiness	Hebraistic	inordinate	marquisate	pacificism	prosciutto
flintiness	hedonistic	insanitary	marshiness	pacificist	prostitute
floatingly	heparinise	insatiable	materially	painkiller	proteiform
floppiness	hereditary	insatiably	measliness	palatinate	proteinous
fluffiness	heresiarch	inseminate	megalithic	paltriness	psychiatry
fluoridate	hereticate	insipidity	melanistic	parabiosis	psychicism
fluorinate	highbinder	insociable	menacingly	parabiotic	psychicist
folksiness	highminded	interiorly	meridional	paradisaic	pugilistic
folksinger	hirudinean	intimidate	Mesolithic	paradisean	punitively
footlights	histrionic	intoxicant	middlingly	paradisiac	purblindly
foraminous	homeliness	intoxicate	midshipman	paradisian	pursuivant
forefinger	hornrimmed	invaginate	mightiness	paralipsis	putatively
forfeiture	hourcircle	invalidate	migrainous	parasitism	quadriceps
fortuitism	humanistic	invalidism	militiaman	parasitoid	quadrireme
fortuitist	humanities	invalidity	misaligned	pasquinade	quadrivial
fortuitous	humidifier	invariable	misericord	patchiness	quadrivium
fractional	humoristic	invariably	misjoinder	pathfinder	qualmishly
Franciscan	hungriness	invariance	misprision	peculiarly	quantifier
frangipane	hypolimnia	invigilate	mithridate	pemphigoid	quantitive
frangipani	idealistic	invitingly	modifiable	pemphigous	queasiness
fratricide	ideational	irradiance	moniliasis	penicillin	quercitron
freakiness	ignobility	irradicate	moniliform	periwigged	questioner
freakishly	ilangilang	irrational	monolithic	periwinkle	quirkiness
freeliving	illatively	irreligion	moralistic	peroxidise	ramblingly
frenziedly	illuminant	isoseismal	morphinism	perquisite	ratability
friability	illuminate	jacobinise	mosquitoes	petitioner	reactivate
frictional	illuminati	Jacobinism	mouldiness	phallicism	reactively
frilliness	illuminism	Jacobitism	movability	phlogistic	reactivity
friskiness	illuminist	jauntiness	mudskipper	phlogiston	rechristen
frizziness	illusional	Jehovistic	mudslinger	Phoenician	recidivism
frostiness	illusively	jingoistic	munificent	piercingly	recidivist
frothiness	imbecilely	judicially	musicianly	pigsticker	recipiency
frowningly	imbecility	juvenility	mutability	pilgrimage	relational
fugitively	imbibition	keratinise	natalitial	piperidine	relatively
fuliginous	immobilise	keratinous	nativistic	pityriasis	relativise
fumblingly	immobility	kerchieves	negatively	plasticise	relativism
functional	impatience	kindliness	negativism	plasticity	relativist
fusibility	impediment	kineticist	negativist	pleadingly	relativity
futuristic	impenitent	kingfisher	negativity	pleasingly	remediable
gadolinite	imperially	kingliness	negotiable	pliability	remedially
gadolinium	imperilled	knopkierie	negotiator	ploddingly	remediless
gaingiving	impolitely	knottiness	nephridium	pluckiness	repetiteur
ganglionic	imposingly	laconicism	nicotinism	polemicist	repetition
gelatinise	imposition	ladyfinger	nidificate	politician	repetitive
gelatinous	impudicity	ladykiller	nihilistic	politicise	reposition
geneticist	inactivate	languisher	nonaligned	polydipsia	repository
glancingly	inactively	lanuginose	nondrinker	polyhistor	repudiator
glassiness	inactivity	lanuginous	nonjoinder	populistic	resilience
gloominess	inaptitude	laughingly	nonswimmer	portliness	resiliency
glossiness	inartistic	lawabiding	notability	positional	resupinate
gnosticism	incipience	legalistic	notarially	positively	retiringly
golddigger	incipiency	legibility	notifiable	positivism	retraining
goodliness	incisively	legitimacy	novelistic	positivist	revalidate
graphitise	incivility	legitimate	nutational	positivity	revisional
graspingly	incogitant	legitimise	obligingly	postliminy	ringfinger
gratuitous	indecision	legitimism	obnubilate	potability	risibility
greasiness	indecisive	legitimist	occasional	practician	rockpigeon
greediness	indefinite	leguminous	officially	practising	rockribbed
grindingly	indelicacy	Leibnizian	oldmaidish	praesidium	Romanistic
grisliness	indelicate	libidinous	oleaginous	prairiedog	rosaniline
grittiness	individual	lifegiving	ommatidium	prancingly	roselipped
grogginess	indocility	lightingup	openminded	prednisone	rotational
growlingly	inefficacy	likelihood	oppositely	preeminent	rubiginous
grubbiness	ineptitude	likeliness	opposition	preexilian	sacroiliac
grudgingly	inexpiable	likeminded	optatively	prescience	salability
grumpiness	inexpiably	limaciform	optimistic	pressingly	salicional
guiltiness	infelicity	linguiform	Ordovician	prettiness	sanctifier
gunslinger	inferiorly	linguistic	organicism	prevailing	sanctimony
gyrational	infinitely	livelihood	organicist	priggishly	sanctitude
habiliment	infinitive	liveliness	organismal	principate	sanguinary
habilitate	infinitude	loneliness	orneriness	principial	sanguinely
halfwitted	ingeminate	longwinded	osmiridium	principium	sanguinity
handpicked	inhabitant	lordliness	outswinger	principled	sapphirine
hardbilled	inheritrix	loveliness	overnicety	prissiness	sashwindow
hardbitten	inhibition	luxuriance	overridden	proclivity	satyriasis

```
scantiness  solubility  tendrilled  vanadinite  Trotskyist  compulsive
scathingly  soothingly  tetchiness  vanquisher  Trotskyite  compulsory
scattiness  sororicide  theodicean  vaporiform  unbrokenly  conciliary
scepticism  soubriquet  thermionic  vaticinate  unworkable  conciliate
sciolistic  soundingly  thermistor  velocipede  acatalepsy  condolence
scoffingly  sowthistle  thievishly  velutinous  acotyledon  consolable
Scotticise  spankingly  thinkingly  venational  aetiologic  consulship
Scotticism  spasticity  thorniness  ventricose  afterlight  consultant
scrutineer  speediness  ticklishly  ventriculi  anacolutha  consulting
scrutinise  spermicide  timeliness  verifiable  anchylosis  consultive
scurrility  sphericity  toothiness  veterinary  anchylotic  convalesce
scurrilous  spiflicate  totemistic  viewfinder  animalcula  convoluted
scurviness  spillikins  touchiness  villainage  animalcule  convulsant
scyphiform  spongiform  touchingly  villainess  anticlimax  convulsion
securiform  sponginess  tourbillon  villainous  anticlinal  convulsive
seemliness  spookiness  tourniquet  villeinage  apiculture  coprolitic
seismicity  sportiness  toweringly  viperiform  apocalypse  corbelling
selfbinder  sportingly  tractional  viraginous  appealable  cordillera
selfrising  sportively  trafficked  visibility  aquaplaner  cornflakes
selfwilled  spottiness  trafficker  vitalistic  artfulness  cornflower
semicircle  spunkiness  transience  vitaminise  assailable  corpulence
semidivine  squalidity  transiency  vitiligate  assaultive  corpulency
semifitted  starriness  transistor  vocational  assoilment  crapulence
semiliquid  steadiness  transition  volatilise  astrologer  crenellate
serotinous  steaminess  transitive  volatility  astrologic  crenulated
shabbiness  steeliness  transitory  volitional  auscultate  crewelwork
shagginess  stelliform  trappiness  volubility  autoplasty  crinolette
sheepishly  stencilled  trashiness  voluminous  aviculture  crippledom
shiftiness  stenciller  trendiness  wassailing  backblocks  crosslight
shipfitter  stepsister  trichiasis  wateriness  backslider  cucullated
shiprigged  stickiness  trichinise  waveringly  ballflower  cudgelling
shockingly  stiflingly  trichinous  weakliness  barbellate  derailleur
shoddiness  stillicide  trickiness  weakminded  bardolatry  derailment
shoplifter  stinginess  trickishly  weedkiller  barrelling  diabolical
shopwindow  stingingly  triclinium  wellwisher  batholitic  diphyletic
showwindow  stinkingly  triflingly  wharfinger  bellflower  disbelieve
shrewishly  stockiness  trillionth  wheeziness  bellylaugh  dismalness
sickliness  stodginess  triplicate  whiskified  Berkeleian  dispelling
sidewinder  storminess  triplicity  winebibber  Boswellian  dissilient
similitude  strabismal  trustiness  wintriness  Boswellise  dissoluble
simoniacal  strabismic  trustingly  witchingly  Boswellism  dissolvent
simplicity  strabismus  tutorially  wobbliness  brakelight  distilland
simplifier  stratiform  ubiquitous  womanishly  brazilwood  distillate
simplistic  strikingly  ulotrichan  woodpigeon  bricklayer  distillery
skimpiness  stubbiness  ulteriorly  woolliness  calculable  distilling
skindiving  stuffiness  umbilicate  worshipful  calculably  disyllabic
skinniness  stumpiness  umbiliform  worshipped  calculator  disyllable
skirmisher  stunningly  unabridged  worshipper  camerlengo  drivelling
skittishly  sturdiness  unassisted  worthiness  camerlingo  drysaltery
skywriting  stypticity  unavailing  wrathiness  cancellate  earthlight
slanginess  subacidity  unbeliever  yearningly  cancelling  enamelling
slantingly  substitute  uncloister  yeastiness  cancellous  enamellist
sleaziness  sugariness  undeniable  yieldingly  candelabra  encyclical
sleepiness  sultriness  undeniably  zoophilous  cannelloni  entailment
sloppiness  superiorly  undesigned  mumbojumbo  cantaloupe  escallonia
slowwitted  suppliance  undesirous  touchjudge  cantilever  ethnologic
sluggishly  supplicant  uneasiness  attackable  cantillate  everglades
sluttishly  supplicate  unendingly  autarkical  cardplayer  excellence
smelliness  surprising  unenviable  blitzkrieg  carnallite  excellency
smudginess  sustaining  unerringly  claspknife  carpellary  fertiliser
smuttiness  sweatiness  unfadingly  dislikable  cassolette  feuilleton
snappishly  sweepingly  unfamiliar  embankment  casualness  fibrillary
sneakiness  swimmingly  unfeminine  embarkment  catholicon  fibrillate
sneakingly  swingingly  unfilially  hakenkreuz  catholicos  fibrillose
sneeringly  sybaritism  unfinished  jinrikisha  cellularly  fireblight
sniffiness  tamability  unholiness  kinnikinic  cellulitis  fitfulness
snobbishly  taperingly  uniaxially  knickknack  cellulosic  flabellate
snootiness  taradiddle  unionistic  knockkneed  centilitre  flagellant
snubbingly  tauntingly  unofficial  Lysenkoism  centillion  flagellate
snuffiness  tawdriness  unreliable  mistakable  cephalopod  flashlight
softbilled  taxability  unrelieved  mistakenly  chatelaine  flatulence
softfinned  technician  unruliness  paperknife  chiselling  flatulency
solecistic  technicist  unscripted  remarkable  chivalrous  floodlight
solicitant  televiewer  unsociable  remarkably  circularly  florilegia
solicitous  television  unsociably  sauerkraut  circulator  flugelhorn
solicitude  televisual  unsocially  shrinkable  coagulable  foamflower
solifidian  temptingly  untidiness  shrinkwrap  cockalorum  fowlplague
solstitial  tenability  unwariness  sprinkling  compelling  fritillary
solubilise  tendrillar  upbraiding  Trotskyism  compulsion  frivolling
```

```
fulfilling  microlitic  propellent  symbolical  astigmatic  hydrometer
fulfilment  millilitre  propelling  symboliser  audiometer  hydrometry
funnelling  misbelieve  propulsion  syphilitic  audiometry  hygrometer
gambolling  miscellany  propulsive  tablelinen  autoimmune  hygrometry
gauntleted  monoclinal  propylaeum  tantaliser  barramunda  hypsometer
genialness  monoclinic  prosilient  tasselling  barramundi  hypsometry
gentilesse  moonflower  pummelling  teleologic  bathometer  iconomachy
Ghibelline  multiloquy  radiologic  tessellate  bathymeter  iconometer
Glagolitic  muscularly  rebellious  testflight  bathymetry  iconometry
globularly  Mussulmans  recallable  thimbleful  blancmange  imprimatur
glycolyses  mycoplasma  recyclable  thimblerig  bloodmoney  inclemency
glycolysis  mythologer  refillable  ticpolonga  bottomless  informally
goldilocks  mythologic  refuelling  tinselling  bottommost  inharmonic
granularly  narcolepsy  repealable  tirailleur  burramundi  intermarry
granulator  Neapolitan  repellance  topgallant  cartomancy  intermezzi
granulitic  necrolater  repellancy  torchlight  centimetre  intermezzo
grovelling  necrolatry  repellence  tortellini  chiromancy  intramural
haemolysis  neurilemma  repellency  translator  circumcise  judgematic
haemolytic  neurolemma  republican  translucid  circumflex  kerygmatic
hagiolatry  nickelling  revealable  translunar  circumfuse  lacrimator
hagiologic  nightlight  revealment  travelling  circumvent  lacrymator
hallelujah  nostologic  riboflavin  travelogue  clinometer  lissomness
hangglider  nyctalopia  roquelaure  tremolitic  clinometry  Mahommedan
hanselling  nyctalopic  ruefulness  trifoliate  coatimundi  matchmaker
hectolitre  ophicleide  safeblower  tropologic  cognominal  mathematic
heliolater  ophiolater  sandalwood  trowelling  collembola  melismatic
heliolatry  ophiolatry  sarcolemma  trucklebed  collimator  merrymaker
hemiplegia  ophiologic  satellitic  truculence  consumable  micrometer
hemiplegic  oracularly  schoolable  truculency  consumedly  micrometry
hierolatry  oscillator  schoolbook  trundlebed  consummate  millimetre
highflying  outbalance  schooldays  tunnelling  coulometry  mischmetal
histologic  overblouse  schoolgirl  turbulence  custommade  misnomered
histolysis  overflight  schoolmaam  turbulency  cyclometer  mixedmedia
histolytic  overslaugh  schoolmarm  umbellifer  densimeter  Mohammedan
hornblende  paraplegia  schoolmate  umbrellaed  determined  moneymaker
horselaugh  paraplegic  schoolroom  unbiblical  dilemmatic  moviemaker
horseleech  parcelling  schooltime  underlease  diplomatic  Muhammadan
hostelling  pastellist  schoolwork  underlinen  dipsomania  Muhammedan
houselling  pathologic  scrollwork  underlying  discomfort  multimedia
hydrologic  patrilocal  scutellate  unemployed  discommend  mythomania
hydrolysis  patrolling  selfglazed  unexplored  discommode  necromancy
hydrolytic  pencilling  septillion  unhallowed  discompose  nincompoop
iconolater  pennillion  sextillion  unscalable  dissembler  noisemaker
iconolatry  perchloric  sheeplouse  unwieldily  dissimilar  numismatic
inexplicit  percolator  shoreleave  unyielding  dressmaker  ombrometer
infallible  perfoliate  shortlived  usefulness  ecchymosis  opisometer
infallibly  periclinal  shovelhead  valvulitis  ecchymotic  pantomimic
inoculable  pestilence  shovelling  variolitic  economical  papermaker
inoculator  petiolated  shrillness  vascularly  economiser  parramatta
instalment  petrolatum  sideglance  venialness  elecampane  peacemaker
instilling  philologen  signalling  ventilator  embalmment  pentameter
interleave  phonolitic  sinfulness  verbaliser  emblematic  pentimento
interloper  phonologic  singularly  visualiser  emblements  phenomenal
interlunar  photolitho  snafflebit  wallflower  endosmosis  phenomenon
inviolable  photolysis  snivelling  wilfulness  endosmotic  pheromonal
inviolably  photolytic  snowplough  windflower  enharmonic  phlegmatic
jaywalking  piccalilli  soapflakes  windsleeve  epidemical  phonematic
joyfulness  pilotlight  socialiser  woefulness  epilimnion  phonometer
kennelling  pinnulated  sociologic  zabaglione  episematic  photometer
kieselguhr  pistillary  somniloquy  abnormally  erotomania  photometry
laurelling  pistillate  somnolence  abstemious  eudiometer  piezometer
lavalliere  pistolling  somnolency  academical  eudiometry  planimeter
lawfulness  pistolshot  speculator  achromatic  extramural  planimetry
legislator  pistolwhip  speedlimit  acidimeter  fathomable  planometer
lithologic  pixillated  spiralling  acidimetry  fathomless  porismatic
logrolling  plantlouse  splitlevel  affirmable  fieldmouse  portamento
mamillated  platelayer  stabiliser  alchemical  Gallomania  presumable
manfulness  plutolatry  steriliser  aldermanic  goniometer  presumably
manteltree  polyclinic  stimulator  aldermanry  goniometry  procumbent
maquillage  polyploidy  stipellate  alphameric  grandmamma  pronominal
Mariolater  postillion  stipulator  amphimacer  gravimeter  proximally
Mariolatry  postulator  subculture  amphimixes  gravimetry  Ptolemaist
marvelling  potbellied  subsellium  amphimixis  hebdomadal  pulsimeter
marvellous  pozzolanic  succulence  anatomical  hectometre  pulsometer
maxilliped  prefulgent  succulency  anemometer  heliometer  pycnometer
medullated  prevalence  superlunar  anemometry  Heptameron  pyknometer
metallurgy  privileged  swinglebar  anglomania  heptameter  radiometer
metaplasia  promulgate  swiveleyed  aposematic  hippomanes  radiometry
methylated  propellant  swivelling  arithmetic  hydromancy  randomness
```

```
recommence  Ashkenazim  consonance  euphonious  Krishnaism  oxygenator
redeemable  assignable  consonancy  euthanasia  Kuomintang  packingbox
reformable  assignment  contendent  evidential  landingnet  pangenesis
rhizomorph  astringent  contention  examinable  lawrencium  pangenetic
rhythmical  astronomer  continence  externally  Lawrentian  panhandler
scaramouch  astronomic  contingent  extraneity  leadenness  panjandrum
schismatic  attainable  continuant  extraneous  leafinsect  paragnosis
scrapmetal  attainment  continuate  Fahrenheit  machinator  paramnesia
scrimmager  attornment  continuity  fallingoff  machinegun  pardonable
servomotor  austenitic  continuous  fandangoes  mackintosh  pardonably
sexlimited  autumnally  convenable  fascinator  maidenhair  parsonbird
shellmound  barkentine  convenance  fescennine  maidenhead  parsonical
shrewmouse  barrenness  convenient  fibrinogen  maidenhood  paternally
skijumping  barrenwort  convention  firstnight  maidenlike  patronymic
smartmoney  Bedlington  conventual  flamingoes  maisonette  pectinated
sociometry  benignancy  convincing  florentine  malcontent  pendentive
sophomoric  biodynamic  coolingoff  fontanelle  malignance  penmanship
spirometer  biogenesis  Copernican  fortyniner  malignancy  pennanular
spirometry  biogenetic  cottoncake  fourinhand  mallenders  percentage
spodomancy  blazonment  cottonseed  foxhunting  manzanilla  percentile
stonemason  bobbinlace  cottontail  fraxinella  marginalia  permanence
streamless  brazenness  cottonweed  fricandeau  marginally  permanency
streamline  brigandage  cottonwood  fustanella  marginated  personable
sublimable  brigandine  cottonwool  galvaniser  marionette  personally
subliminal  brigandism  cousinhood  gargantuan  martensite  personalty
sugarmaple  brigantine  cousinship  gasconader  martingale  personator
systematic  brokendown  cowpuncher  geocentric  maternally  pertinence
systemless  brokenness  cravenness  geoponical  matronhood  pertinency
tachometer  buccinator  credential  germinally  matronship  petronella
tachometry  burdensome  criminally  goldenness  matronymic  phalangeal
tachymeter  buttonball  cybernetic  goldenseal  mayonnaise  pharyngeal
tachymetry  buttonbush  dampingoff  Gorgonzola  meaningful  photonasty
talismanic  buttondown  deaconship  gormandise  mechanical  piccaninny
tantamount  buttonhole  declension  governable  meltingpot  pickaninny
tauromachy  buttonhook  declinable  governance  mercantile  pigeonhole
tautomeric  buttonless  descendant  governessy  metronomic  pigeonpair
tetrameter  buttonwood  descendent  government  metronymic  pigeonpost
tetramorph  byssinosis  descension  gramineous  mignonette  pigeontoed
transmuter  cachinnate  designator  grandniece  millennial  pigeonwing
tribometer  calumniate  designedly  greatniece  millennium  pigmentary
trigeminal  calumnious  designment  guestnight  misconduct  pistonring
tromometer  cannonball  despondent  gunrunning  misventure  pollenosis
uncommonly  cantonment  detainment  harmonical  mizzenmast  pollinator
underminer  canzonetta  diagonally  harmonious  mizzensail  polyandric
unexampled  carbonnade  Dickensian  harmoniser  moderniser  polyanthus
unicameral  carbuncled  diesinking  heavenborn  modernness  polyonymic
uranometry  carcinogen  disconcert  heavensent  morganatic  portentous
variometer  carcinosis  disconfirm  heavenward  motionless  pothunting
victimiser  centennial  disconnect  helianthus  muffinbell  pratincole
viscometer  cismontane  discontent  helminthic  muttonhead  prebendary
voltameter  cispontine  dishonesty  herrenvolk  nationally  preconcert
wampumpeag  citronella  disownment  heulandite  nationhood  prehensile
watchmaker  Clarenceux  dispensary  hibernacle  nationless  prehension
watermelon  clementine  dissension  hootenanny  nationwide  premonitor
abominable  coetaneous  dissonance  hormonally  nevernever  prepensely
abominably  colonnaded  dissonancy  horrendous  newfangled  presentday
abominator  commandant  distensile  husbandage  noncontent  presentive
abstention  commandeer  distension  husbandman  noogenesis  pretendant
abstinence  commandery  distention  hyphenated  notionally  pretendent
abstinency  commanding  distinctly  imaginable  nullanulla  pretension
accountant  commandoes  draconites  imaginably  nyctinasty  prevenancy
accounting  commentary  dragonhead  imprinting  obtainable  prevenient
actionable  commentate  dragonnade  impugnable  obtainment  prevention
actionably  commonable  dragontree  impugnment  obtruncate  preventive
adamantine  commonalty  drawingpin  inclinable  oldfangled  profundity
aeroengine  commonness  duodenitis  infernally  oppugnancy  progenitor
agapanthus  commonroom  ecumenical  innuendoes  optionally  prolongate
aggrandise  commonweal  effrontery  inspanning  ordainment  promenader
airmanship  communally  egocentric  internally  ordonnance  prominence
alcyonaria  communique  elementary  internment  originally  promontory
alexanders  compendium  elevenplus  internodal  originator  propensity
alimentary  compensate  eliminable  internship  orogenesis  protanopic
alternance  concentric  eliminator  isodynamic  orogenetic  protensive
alternator  concinnity  enchanting  isogenetic  orotundity  provenance
Amerindian  condensate  enjoinment  jackanapes  orphanhood  provincial
angwantibo  condensery  entrancing  jackknives  outgeneral  prudential
appointive  congeneric  epicentral  jardiniere  outgunning  pulvinated
apprentice  congenital  epigenesis  jargonelle  outlandish  purtenance
aragonitic  consensual  epigenetic  jimsonweed  outrunning  quarantine
```

rabbinical	suspenders	alcoholise	camelopard	disclosure	generously
rationally	suspension	alcoholism	camphorate	diseconomy	geognostic
reasonable	suspensive	algologist	canorously	divebomber	geotropism
reasonably	suspensoid	allegorise	Capitoline	dogstongue	glaciology
reasonless	suspensory	allegorist	captiously	dolorously	gladsomely
refringent	sustenance	ameliorate	cardiogram	dovecolour	glauconite
regionally	sustention	amoebocyte	cardiology	dysprosium	gloriously
repugnance	sustentive	ampelopsis	carphology	dystrophic	glossology
repugnancy	syngenesis	anadromous	cartoonist	echinoderm	glottology
resignedly	tabernacle	anastomose	caseworker	edulcorate	gluttonise
resounding	tangential	anatropous	catabolism	Egyptology	gluttonous
respondent	tankengine	anecdotage	cataloguer	electorate	gobemouche
responsive	tendinitis	anecdotist	categorise	embryogeny	gobstopper
responsory	terminable	antagonise	cautionary	embryology	golfcourse
retainable	terminably	antagonism	cautiously	embryonate	goodlooker
returnable	terminally	antagonist	centromere	endopodite	gorgeously
ribbonfish	terminator	antemortem	centrosome	endproduct	graciosity
ribbonworm	theopneust	anthropoid	ceremonial	endstopped	graciously
ritornelli	torrential	antimonial	certiorari	enormously	graphology
ritornello	tramontana	antimonite	cessionary	enterolith	graptolite
rollingpin	tramontane	antinomian	charioteer	enterotomy	gressorial
roseengine	trecentist	antipodean	chersonese	entomology	grievously
rottenness	tremendous	antisocial	chevrotain	enzymology	gruesomely
rumrunning	trepanning	Apollonian	chiffonier	eosinophil	guillotine
salientian	Tridentine	apostolate	chloroform	epeirogeny	gyrocopter
sallenders	trigonally	apotropaic	chromosome	epiglottal	halfcocked
salmonella	trilingual	aquafortis	chronogram	epiglottic	halfdollar
salmonleap	trimonthly	aristocrat	chronology	epiglottis	halfvolley
salpingian	turpentine	arthromere	chrysolite	episcopacy	handsomely
sapiential	tympanites	asteroidal	chrysotile	episcopate	handworked
sappanwood	tympanitic	auctioneer	Ciceronian	epistolary	hardboiled
sarmentose	tympanitis	auditorial	cinchonine	equatorial	haustorium
sarmentous	tyrannical	auditorium	clangorous	equipotent	Heliconian
saturnalia	unblenched	autecology	clodhopper	equivocate	helicopter
scavengery	unblinking	autologous	clubfooted	ergonomics	heortology
screenings	unbonneted	automobile	comicopera	ergonomist	hepatology
screenplay	unchanging	automotive	complotted	escapology	heretofore
sealingwax	underneath	autonomist	compromise	ethologist	heterodont
seamanlike	uneconomic	autonomous	comstocker	eudemonism	heterodoxy
seamanship	unevenness	axiologist	conchoidal	eudemonist	heterodyne
seasonable	uneventful	babiroussa	conchology	Eurodollar	heterogamy
seasonably	unguentary	Babylonian	conglobate	exobiology	heterogeny
seasonally	unilingual	ballooning	controlled	fabulously	heterogony
secernment	unmannerly	balloonist	controller	factiously	heterology
segmentary	unthinking	balneology	controvert	fearnought	heteronomy
semiannual	unwrinkled	barefooted	copyholder	fearsomely	heterotaxy
semiuncial	upbringing	bassoonist	corncockle	fellmonger	homecoming
sentential	upstanding	Beaujolais	covetously	festoonery	homoeopath
septenarii	vaccinator	bedclothes	craniology	fictioneer	homologate
septennial	villanelle	benevolent	cryptogamy	fictionist	homologise
septennium	virginally	bibliology	cryptogram	firepolicy	homologous
sequential	virginhood	bibliopegy	cryptology	fishmonger	horizontal
sermoniser	visionally	bibliophil	cuckoopint	flamboyant	horologist
serpentine	visionless	bibliopole	cuckoospit	flapdoodle	hotblooded
sharpnosed	vulcaniser	bibliopoly	cumbrously	flatfooted	humorously
shenanigan	waggonette	bibliotics	curatorial	flexuously	hypocorism
soddenness	Waldensian	bibulously	cytologist	fluorotype	ideologist
soldanella	wantonness	bichromate	dampcourse	fluxionary	illusorily
solemnness	wappenshaw	bigamously	decapodous	folklorist	immemorial
Sorbonnist	wardenship	billposter	decolonise	foreboding	immunology
spleenwort	warmingpan	bioecology	decolorant	forecourse	inapposite
sporangial	weaponless	blastocyst	decolorise	foudroyant	indecorous
sporangium	wellington	blastoderm	decorously	fourfooted	infamously
staffnurse	willynilly	blastomere	deeprooted	fourposter	infusorial
strainedly	woodenhead	blastopore	deerforest	framboesia	infusorian
stupendous	woodenness	bluebonnet	deltiology	Francophil	invigorate
subcentral	workingman	bluebottle	demagogism	freebooter	ironmonger
subkingdom	aardwolves	bluecollar	demonology	freeholder	ironworker
sublingual	ablebodied	bluetongue	dendrology	freeloader	irresolute
submontane	acoelomate	bondholder	deontology	freesoiler	isoglossal
subtenancy	actinolite	boondoggle	desirously	froghopper	isosporous
subvention	actinozoan	botryoidal	dextrously	fullbodied	janitorial
succinctly	aerologist	bourbonism	diagnostic	fullbottom	Johnsonese
suddenness	aeronomist	bourbonist	diatropism	futurology	johnsonian
sullenness	Aethiopian	bryologist	dichroitic	gadrooning	katabolism
sultanship	aficionado	buffoonery	dichromate	gastrology	lampoonery
summonable	agrologist	bullroarer	dictionary	gastronome	lampoonist
supernally	agronomist	calceolate	dilatorily	gastronomy	lanceolate
supernovae	aircooling	Caledonian	diphyodont	generosity	landholder

landlocked	oecologist	proglottis	senseorgan	threnodist	adsorptive
languorous	oenologist	prognostic	sensuously	timbrology	afterpains
laparotomy	omnipotent	propionate	serologist	timorously	altarpiece
lavatorial	omnivorous	prostomial	sexologist	tinctorial	anabaptism
leafhopper	oncologist	prostomium	shibboleth	tiresomely	anabaptist
lectionary	oneirology	proteolyse	shopsoiled	toilsomely	anemophily
lepidolite	ontologist	psalmodise	sideboards	tomfoolery	anglophile
lexicology	opinionist	psalmodist	siderolite	topazolite	anglophobe
locomotion	oreologist	psephology	siderostat	topologist	anglophone
locomotive	ovariotomy	pseudocarp	silkcotton	tortiously	ascription
locomotory	overbought	psychology	sinologist	tortuosity	assumption
lonesomely	overcommit	psychopath	sinusoidal	tortuously	assumptive
lowprofile	overcooked	pyretology	sixshooter	toxicology	atmosphere
luminosity	overlooker	pyridoxine	slitpocket	traitorous	audiophile
luminously	overtopped	Pyrrhonian	slowfooted	trampoline	barysphere
lusciously	Palaeocene	Pyrrhonism	slowmotion	treasonous	birdspider
lustrously	Palaeogene	Pyrrhonist	snowmobile	trichology	birthplace
lycopodium	palaeolith	pyrrhotite	soapboiler	trichotomy	bisulphate
lymphocyte	palaeotype	racecourse	softboiled	trochoidal	bisulphide
lymphomata	Palaeozoic	railroader	solenoidal	troctolite	bisulphite
malacoderm	palagonite	ravenously	somatology	troglodyte	brainpower
malacology	palynology	reafforest	somatotype	trollopish	breakpoint
malevolent	papyrology	reallocate	sonorously	trombonist	catchpenny
malodorous	parabolise	recolonise	spaciously	trophology	cellophane
manifoldly	paraboloid	redblooded	speciology	tryptophan	checkpoint
Marcionite	paradoxure	redecorate	speciosity	tuberosity	childproof
mayblossom	paralogism	reredorter	speciously	tubicolous	coleoptera
megalosaur	paranormal	reunionism	speleology	tuitionary	coleoptile
mesomorphy	parapodium	reunionist	sphenodone	typologist	conception
metabolise	passionary	revalorise	sphenogram	unbecoming	conceptive
metabolism	passionate	rhapsodise	sphenoidal	unbesought	conceptual
metabolite	Passionist	rhapsodist	spheroidal	unctuosity	conniption
mineworker	patriotism	rheologist	spongology	unctuously	corruption
misologist	patulously	rhomboidal	sponsorial	uninformed	corruptive
missionary	peashooter	rhomboidei	spuriously	unresolved	cosmopolis
missionise	pedagogics	ricinoleic	stadholder	unschooled	crosspatch
misthought	pedalorgan	rigorously	stationary	urbanology	crosspiece
monitorial	pedologist	ripsnorter	stationery	urochordal	ctenophore
monologise	penologist	roadworthy	staurolite	usuriously	cyclopedia
monologist	pensionary	rockbottom	stentorian	uxoriously	cyclopedic
monopodial	perilously	rockhopper	stepmother	valorously	decampment
monopodium	peritoneal	rollcollar	stereobate	vaporously	decompound
monopolise	peritoneum	rupicoline	stereogram	varicocele	decompress
monopolist	phelloderm	rupicolous	stereopsis	varicosity	desorption
monotonous	phlebotomy	sanatorium	stereotype	venomously	dimorphism
moratorium	phlogopite	sandhopper	stereotypy	vestpocket	dimorphous
morphogeny	phlogopite	satanology	stertorous	viceconsul	disappoint
morphology	phrenology	sawtoothed	stopvolley	vigorously	disapprove
mouthorgan	phyllotaxy	saxicoline	strabotomy	viperously	discipline
musicology	phylloxera	saxicolous	stramonium	virologist	discophile
mutinously	physiocrat	scabrously	stratocrat	virtuosity	disruption
mycologist	physiology	scaffolder	stubbornly	virtuously	disruptive
nailpolish	pickpocket	scansorial	studiously	Visigothic	dissipated
natatorial	plasmodesm	schemozzle	sudatorium	visitorial	disulphate
natatorium	plasmodium	schizocarp	sulphonate	vitriolise	disulphide
naturopath	plasmogamy	schizogony	superorder	vomitorium	drosophila
nauseously	plasmolyse	Scillonian	surefooted	werewolves	embonpoint
nebulosity	plesiosaur	scleroderm	symphonion	whatsoever	emerypaper
nebulously	pogonology	sclerotium	symphonist	whensoever	encampment
nematocyst	pogonotomy	sclerotomy	synaloepha	WhitMonday	enterprise
nephrology	polemonium	scorzonera	synecology	whomsoever	entrapment
newsmonger	polynomial	scyphozoan	taxonomist	wildfowler	enwrapping
newsworthy	polytocous	sedulously	teatrolley	winebottle	erysipelas
nidicolous	pomologist	seedpotato	technocrat	wingcollar	escarpment
nomologist	populously	seignorage	technology	wingfooted	everyplace
nonviolent	postmortem	seignorial	teratogeny	wireworker	excerption
nosologist	potamology	seismogram	teratology	withholder	extemporal
noteworthy	pozzuolana	seismology	teratomata	wondrously	extirpator
nucivorous	praecocial	selenodont	theodolite	woodworker	fairspoken
nucleonics	praetorial	selenology	theogonist	woolsorter	fieldpiece
nucleoside	praetorian	selfcolour	theologian	wrongously	fixedpoint
nucleotide	preciosity	selfloving	theologise	zygomorphy	flameproof
numerology	preciously	selfmotion	theologist	absorption	flashpoint
numerosity	prefrontal	selfpoised	theosopher	absorptive	floatplane
numerously	previously	seltzogene	thermogram	accomplice	forcipated
nympholept	prismoidal	semeiology	thermophil	accomplish	fortepiano
oceanology	proctorage	semeiotics	thermopile	acidophile	freespeech
octopodous	proctorial	semidouble	thermostat	addlepated	freespoken
odontology	proctorise	senatorial	threnodial	adsorption	Gallophile

Gallophobe	osteopathy	susceptive	antiproton	coeternity	dinnerless
glasspaper	osteophyte	swanupping	aphaereses	coleorhiza	disarrange
gramophone	overspread	swashplate	aphaeresis	collarbeam	disbarring
granophyre	paedophile	syncopated	apocarpous	collarbone	disburthen
gypsophila	palimpsest	syncopator	apochromat	collarette	discerning
hairspring	pansophist	tautophony	apostrophe	collarless	discordant
handspring	pedalpoint	terneplate	appearance	collarstud	discursive
hankypanky	perception	terreplein	arbitrable	colourable	disfurnish
haruspices	perceptive	tetrapolis	arbitrager	colourably	disharmony
headspring	perceptual	thinkpiece	arbitrator	colourfast	disparager
heliophyte	percipient	thirdparty	archerfish	colourless	disparates
hemisphere	peremptory	thornproof	archpriest	colportage	dispersant
hierophant	philippina	threepence	armourclad	colporteur	dispersion
hippophagy	philippine	threepenny	armourless	commercial	dispersive
hocuspocus	philopoena	threepiece	artycrafty	comparable	dispersoid
hodgepodge	photophily	thruppence	authorship	comparably	dispirited
hokeypokey	photophore	thumbprint	autocratic	comparator	dissertate
homeopathy	photoprint	tittupping	autoerotic	comparison	disservice
horsepower	phytophagy	toothpaste	autography	concerning	distortion
hotchpotch	pinchpenny	touchpaper	aviatrices	concertina	doctorship
houseplant	plecoptera	transplant	azeotropic	concertino	doxography
houseproud	preceptive	transposal	background	concordant	drawbridge
hoverplane	preceptory	transposer	badderlock	concurrent	driverless
hyaloplasm	precipitin	triumphant	balderdash	concurring	dunderhead
hydropathy	preemption	tropopause	banderilla	conference	easterling
hydrophane	preemptive	tropophyte	barbershop	conferment	Eastertide
hydrophily	presuppose	underpants	barcarolle	conferring	editorship
hydrophone	primiparae	underproof	bastardise	confervoid	effloresce
hydrophyte	protophyta	unprepared	bestirring	confirmand	elaborator
hydroplane	protophyte	usucaption	betterment	conformism	electrical
hygrophyte	protoplasm	vibraphone	binaurally	conformist	electronic
impalpable	protoplast	videophone	biomorphic	conformity	encourager
impalpably	purseproud	voiceprint	birthright	consortium	endearment
improperly	radiopaque	wastepaper	bitterling	constraint	endocrinal
incomplete	radiophone	waterpower	bitterness	constringe	enumerable
inculpable	recompense	waterproof	bitterroot	contortion	enumerator
indisposed	recoupment	wellspoken	bitterwood	contortive	epidermoid
interphase	redemption	wellspring	bizarrerie	convergent	epistrophe
interplant	redemptive	widespread	bombardier	conversant	escadrille
interplead	redemptory	wingspread	borborygmi	conversely	escharotic
interposal	reshipment	Algonquian	bordereaux	conversion	espadrille
interposer	resorption	colloquial	borderland	cooperator	evaporable
intrepidly	resorptive	colloquise	borderless	copperhead	evaporator
ionosphere	resumption	colloquist	borderline	copywriter	exoterical
Italophile	resumptive	colloquium	bothersome	cornerwise	expatriate
karyoplasm	rhizophore	consequent	budgerigar	corporally	exuberance
kidnapping	rhodophane	delinquent	bursarship	corporator	eyeservice
leucoplast	ridgepiece	earthquake	butterball	corporeity	factorship
lightproof	Russophile	foursquare	butterbean	cosmoramic	fairground
lithophane	Russophobe	headsquare	butterfish	countryish	fatherhood
lithophyte	saprophyte	inadequacy	buttermilk	countryman	fatherland
lophophore	sarcophagi	inadequate	butterwort	couturiere	fatherless
macrophage	sarcophagy	ineloquent	cacography	couverture	fatherlike
madreporic	sarcoplasm	infrequent	calcareous	cowparsley	fathership
mainspring	schipperke	relinquish	calibrator	crossrefer	favourable
mesosphere	screwplate	subsequent	cankerworm	crossroads	favourably
metempiric	screwpress	underquote	canterbury	culturally	fetterlock
metropolis	seacaptain	abhorrence	cartwright	cumbersome	filterable
microphone	semiopaque	abstergent	cascarilla	cummerbund	fingerbowl
microphyte	shellproof	abstersion	catarrhine	decagramme	fingerless
micropylar	shockproof	abstersive	catburglar	decigramme	fingerling
mouthpiece	sincipital	acquirable	cavalryman	declarable	fingermark
multiphase	Slavophile	aerogramme	celebrated	deepfreeze	fingernail
multiplier	Slavophobe	aerography	celebrator	deepfrozen	fingerpost
multipolar	smokeplant	affeerment	censorious	deferrable	fisherfolk
musicpaper	smokeproof	algebraist	censorship	democratic	flowergirl
mythopoeia	snailpaced	allegretto	censurable	demography	flowerless
mythopoeic	softspoken	allotropic	cerography	demurrable	footbridge
nambypamby	soundproof	allpurpose	chaparajos	denigrator	foreground
necrophile	sousaphone	anamorphic	chaparejos	deodoriser	foreordain
necrophily	sporophore	anastrophe	chartreuse	deplorable	forthright
necropolis	sporophyll	anchoretic	chimerical	deplorably	forwarding
negrophile	sporophyte	anchoritic	chondritic	desecrater	fostering
negrophobe	standpoint	anchorless	cicatrices	desecrator	fraternise
neuropathy	stockpiler	anchorring	Cinderella	desperados	fraternity
neuroplasm	stockproof	answerable	Cistercian	deterrence	frigorific
oligopsony	stormproof	answerably	cleverness	diachronic	gaspereaux
orthopedic	subreption	antheridia	cloverleaf	didgeridoo	gasteropod
orthoptera	superpower	antifreeze	coacervate	difference	Gilbertian

gingerbeer	letterless	overpraise	recurrence	summerlike	weaverbird
gingersnap	lexigraphy	oysterfarm	redcurrant	summertime	weimaraner
girlfriend	limitrophe	paederasty	reentrance	sunderance	westernise
glomerular	lipography	palmerworm	reiterance	sunparlour	wickerwork
glomerulus	lipservice	paratroops	remarriage	supperless	wilderment
grassroots	litterlout	parturient	renderable	supportive	wilderness
GrecoRoman	lockerroom	pastorally	repairable	suprarenal	winegrower
gregarious	loggerhead	pastorship	repatriate	synaeresis	wintertide
gutturally	logography	pasturable	researcher	syncarpous	wintertime
gynocratic	logorrhoea	pawnbroker	respirable	synchronal	wiredrawer
halberdier	Lollardism	penetrable	respirator	synchronic	withdrawal
hammerbeam	longprimer	penetrably	restorable	tackdriver	withdrawer
hammerhead	loxodromic	penetralia	retrorsely	tailorbird	wonderland
hammerless	lucubrator	penetrance	rheotropic	tailormade	wonderment
hammerlock	lugubrious	penetrator	rhetorical	telegraphy	wonderwork
hammerpond	lumberjack	pennyroyal	rinderpest	tellership	woolgrower
Hansardise	lumberroom	peppercorn	roughrider	temperable	wraparound
hawserlaid	lumbersome	peppermill	rubberneck	temperance	wunderkind
henharrier	lumberyard	peppermint	rudderfish	temperedly	xerography
heptarchic	malapropos	pepperwort	rudderless	temporally	xylography
hierarchal	manservant	perdurable	runnerbean	temporiser	yarborough
hierarchic	Massoretic	perdurably	runthrough	tenderfoot	yesteryear
hinterland	masterhand	perforator	sailorless	tenderloin	zoomorphic
historical	masterhood	performing	saltarello	tenderness	abscission
hithermost	masterless	perjurious	salubrious	tenebrific	accessible
hitherward	mastermind	perversely	sanderling	tenebrious	accessibly
holography	mastership	perversion	Sanskritic	tenterhook	accrescent
homebrewed	masterwork	perversity	savourless	terrorless	accursedly
honourable	mavourneen	perversive	sciagraphy	tetrarchic	admissible
honourably	measurable	phanerogam	seaserpent	tetterwort	adolescent
honourless	measurably	pictorial	seborrhoea	texturally	aftershave
humoursome	measuredly	piledriver	seethrough	theatrical	aggression
hysteresis	meliorator	pilgarlick	selfpraise	theocratic	aggressive
hysteretic	membership	pincerlike	selfprofit	tickertape	aircushion
hysterical	menstruate	pinstriped	semidrying	timberhead	alongshore
ideography	menstruous	playground	serigraphy	timberline	alpenstock
impairment	mensurable	playwright	sestertium	timbertoes	ambassador
incurrable	mentorship	pluperfect	sestertius	timberwolf	analysable
inexorable	mesmeriser	polygraphy	setterwort	timberwork	angiosperm
inexorably	meteoritic	ponderable	sexpartite	timocratic	Anglistics
inferrable	midmorning	powderhorn	shandrydan	tollbridge	AngloSaxon
inglorious	millwright	powderpuff	sherardise	tomography	appeasable
innerrably	minstrelsy	prayerbook	shipbroker	topography	assessable
inoperable	misfortune	prearrange	shipwright	travertine	assessment
insobriety	miswording	precarious	shortrange	trichroism	ballistics
inspirator	mobocratic	precordial	showerbath	trichromat	baptistery
integrable	monocratic	precursory	signwriter	trifurcate	bathyscaph
integrally	monstrance	preferable	silverbath	trimorphic	bathyscope
integrator	montbretia	preferably	silverfish	tripartite	birthstone
interregna	motherhood	preference	silverside	triternate	Blackshirt
introrsely	motherland	preferment	silverware	triturable	blacksmith
isentropic	motherless	preferring	silverweed	triturator	bloodstain
isochronal	mothership	premarital	sisterhood	typewriter	bloodstock
isomorphic	motherwort	preparator	skewbridge	typography	bloodstone
itinerancy	mozzarella	preparedly	skiagraphy	unAmerican	bobbysocks
jaguarundi	mycorrhiza	prescriber	skyscraper	unbearable	bobbysoxer
jasperware	myocardium	primordial	snapdragon	unbearably	bradyseism
jeopardise	mysterious	primordium	snowgrouse	unfairness	brainstorm
jobbernowl	nasturtium	procurable	songwriter	uniformity	breadstick
jolterhead	natterjack	procurance	souterrain	unimproved	breadstuff
juggernaut	nectareous	procurator	spagyrical	unipartite	bridesmaid
kaisership	nethermost	properness	spectrally	university	Britishism
kilogramme	newswriter	propertied	spidercrab	unsporting	broadsheet
kimberlite	nomography	proportion	spiderline	unswerving	broadsword
Krugerrand	nonferrous	proscriber	spiderwort	uproarious	broomstick
ladderback	nosography	proverbial	stewardess	urethritis	brownshirt
lanternfly	nudibranch	pulveriser	stockrider	vesperbell	brownstone
lattermost	numberless	pursership	subcordate	vespertine	caddisworm
laundryman	nurseryman	pyrography	submariner	Victoriana	campestral
leaderless	occurrence	quaternary	submersion	victorious	candescent
leadership	oleography	quaternate	subscriber	viscerally	canvasback
ledgerbait	oligarchic	quaternion	subshrubby	viziership	canvaswork
ledgerline	oratorical	quaternity	substratum	vulnerable	carnassial
leopardess	orchardist	quatorzain	subterfuge	vulnerably	centesimal
letterbomb	orchardman	rapporteur	subversion	wainwright	chainsmoke
letterbook	oreography	readership	subversive	wanderings	chalkstone
lettercard	outstretch	reappraise	sufferable	wanderlust	charismata
letterhead	overground	reciprocal	sufferably	wanderplug	cheapskate
	overgrowth	rectorship	sufferance		chemisette

Circassian	engrossing	insensibly	pitchstone	stockstill	acoustical
clearstory	enthusiasm	inspissate	plebiscite	stonesnipe	acquitting
clerestory	enthusiast	interspace	plumassier	storksbill	adjectival
clingstone	epigastric	interstate	porousness	stressless	adjustable
clinkstone	erubescent	interstice	possession	stylistics	adjustment
closestool	evanescent	introspect	possessive	submission	admittable
Clydesdale	excrescent	iridescent	possessory	submissive	admittance
coalescent	exhaustion	iridosmine	precession	subsistent	admittedly
coexistent	exhaustive	jackassery	predestine	successful	adroitness
cognisable	expansible	joyousness	predispose	succession	adventurer
cognisably	expressage	kriegspiel	prehistory	successive	advertence
cognisance	expression	lactescent	prepossess	suggestion	advertency
colossally	expressive	Lammastide	procession	suggestive	advertiser
combustion	expressway	largescale	profession	supersonic	aeolotropy
combustive	extensible	lebensraum	promissory	superstore	aerostatic
commissary	famousness	lemniscate	proofsheet	supposable	affectedly
commission	fantastico	licensable	protestant	supposably	affectless
commissure	fibrositis	liquescent	provisions	supposedly	affettuoso
compassion	fieldstone	loganstone	publishing	surmisable	aftertaste
compasssaw	fireescape	macrospore	purposeful	swarmspore	agglutinin
composedly	flavescent	mangosteen	purseseine	sweatshirt	agitatedly
compositor	floatstone	marcescent	putrescent	swordstick	alightment
concession	florescent	matchstick	putrescine	symposiast	allosteric
concessive	floristics	mediastina	pycnostyle	tablespoon	altostrati
concussion	flyfishing	Methuselah	radioscopy	teleostean	amphoteric
concussive	fortissimi	microscope	radiosonde	tetrastich	analytical
condescend	fortissimo	microscopy	razorshell	tetrastyle	ancestress
confession	fricasseed	microseism	realisable	threescore	animatedly
confiscate	frutescent	microspore	reconsider	throwstick	anisotropy
confusedly	garnishing	millesimal	refreshing	thumbscrew	anointment
congestion	glycosuria	molluscoid	regression	thumbstall	antistatic
congestive	glycosuric	molluscous	regressive	toothshell	apolitical
consistent	grandstand	morrispike	reichsmark	touchstone	apophthegm
consistory	grapesugar	multistage	releasable	transshape	archetypal
contestant	grasssnake	musicstand	remissible	trousseaux	architrave
coralsnake	gravestone	musicstool	remissness	turgescent	arrestment
corpuscule	greenshank	narcissism	remorseful	ultrasonic	arrhythmia
correspond	greenstick	narcissist	repression	ultrasound	arrhythmic
cranesbill	greenstone	necroscopy	repressive	unblushing	asbestosis
crankshaft	greenstuff	nephoscope	rescission	unchastity	assentient
crepuscule	greensward	nightshade	rescissory	underscore	assistance
cuirassier	grindstone	nightshift	retrospect	undersense	assortment
cuttystool	gymnastics	nightshirt	reversible	undersexed	asymptotic
cyclostome	gymnosophy	nightstick	rhinestone	undershirt	augustness
cyclostyle	gymnosperm	nigrescent	rhinoscope	undershoot	autostrada
cystoscope	hagioscope	nourishing	rhinoscopy	undershrub	autostrade
cystoscopy	harassment	odiousness	rodfishing	undersized	backstairs
declassify	harvestman	opalescent	rotisserie	underskirt	backstitch
decrescent	heartsease	oppression	sacrosanct	underslung	backstroke
defeasance	helioscope	oppressive	samarskite	understand	balustrade
defeasible	heuristics	orchestics	sargassoes	understate	barbituric
defensible	Hindustani	orchestral	scoresheet	understeer	barratrous
defensibly	honeysweet	ostensible	scrimshank	understock	basketball
degressive	horseshoer	ostensibly	seabiscuit	understeer	basketwork
demoiselle	hydroscope	ottershace	selfesteem	understood	bassethorn
depressant	hygroscope	outerspace	sequestrum	understudy	belletrist
depression	hypersonic	outgassing	sheepshank	unhouseled	bicultural
depressive	iconoscope	ovipositor	sheepshead	unmeasured	bijouterie
despisable	impassable	oxidisable	shellshock	unseasoned	billetdoux
dialysable	impassably	Parnassian	skrimshank	upholstery	bimestrial
diecasting	impassible	patisserie	smallscale	utilisable	biometrics
diffusible	impassibly	patristics	smallsword	vernissage	bipartisan
digression	impersonal	peninsular	smokestack	vitrescent	birdstrike
digressive	impossible	penpushing	snakestone	waterskier	blackthorn
discussant	impossibly	pentastich	sobersided	waterspout	bootstraps
discussion	impresario	percussion	sobersides	whaleshark	breastbone
discussive	impression	percussive	solidstate	wheatstone	breastwall
disgustful	impressive	periosteal	somersault	whitesmith	breastwork
dismission	impuissant	periosteum	soothsayer	wholesaler	brevetting
dismissive	incessancy	permission	spinescent	witnessbox	brightness
dispassion	inconstant	permissive	spoilsport	xiphosuran	brightwork
disposable	incrassate	persistent	spokeshave	abjectness	bucketshop
dispossess	increscent	pharisaism	sportswear	abruptness	bullethead
disrespect	inexistent	philistine	spumescent	accentuate	calyptrate
earthshine	infeasible	philosophe	standstill	acceptable	cantatrice
ecclesiast	infrasonic	philosophy	statistics	acceptably	carpetweed
embossment	ingression	phthisical	statoscope	acceptance	caryatides
endorsable	inquisitor	pianissimo	stavesacre	acceptedly	catastasis
Englishman	insensible	pincushion	stinkstone	accustomed	

```
catoptrics  dissatisfy  hovertrain  mesenteron  promethium  spirituous
charitable  divestment  hydrotaxis  metastable  promptbook  splintbone
charitably  dogmatical  hypaethral  metastases  promptness  splintcoal
chauntress  dogmatiser  hypanthium  metastasis  propitiate  splutterer
chemotaxis  downstairs  hypnotiser  metastatic  propitious  squinteyed
Christhood  downstream  hypostasis  millstream  prototypal  starstream
Christlike  downstroke  hypostatic  minestrone  prototypic  statutable
clientship  dramatical  idolatress  ministrant  provitamin  statutably
cloistered  dramaturge  idolatrous  mishitting  pulsatilla  stealthily
closetplay  dramaturgy  illnatured  mismatched  puristical  steamtight
cockatrice  drawstring  illustrate  moneytaker  quaintness  stilettoes
collatable  dumbstruck  immortally  monistical  quickthorn  stomatitis
collateral  dysenteric  immortelle  moonstruck  quixotical  stomatopod
comestible  earwitness  impartible  nepenthean  ratcatcher  straitness
commitment  effectuate  impartment  neurotoxin  rebuttable  streetdoor
committing  effortless  importable  nonnatural  recentness  streetward
commutable  egoistical  importance  nutritious  receptacle  strictness
commutator  elliptical  importuner  objectival  receptible  striptease
compatible  Emmentaler  imposthume  objectless  regentship  structural
compatibly  encystment  incantator  obstetrics  registered  structured
compatriot  englutting  incautious  offputting  registrant  subletting
competence  enlistment  incestuous  offsetting  regretting  submitting
competency  equestrian  indictable  oftentimes  rejectable  summitless
competitor  eremitical  indictment  operettist  relentless  supertonic
compotator  ergosterol  indistinct  orientally  reluctance  symmetrise
computable  escritoire  inductance  outfitting  reluctancy  sympathise
computator  eurhythmic  industrial  outpatient  remittance  synanthous
concettism  eurypterid  inevitable  outputting  repeatable  synoptical
connatural  everything  inevitably  outsitting  repeatedly  synostosis
copartnery  executable  infectious  outwitting  repentance  talentless
coquettish  exegetical  infiltrate  overstride  repertoire  tapestried
Corinthian  expectance  inflatable  overstrung  reportable  tarantella
cornettist  expectancy  ingestible  palmatifid  reportedly  tarantelle
cornstarch  expectedly  ingratiate  panopticon  resentment  teetotally
corsetiere  expertness  inimitable  papistical  resistance  tenantable
cosentient  exportable  inimitably  parentally  resistible  tenantless
cowcatcher  eyewitness  insentient  parenteral  resistless  termitaria
creditable  factitious  insistence  parenthood  resultless  theistical
creditably  farfetched  insistency  parrotfish  revertible  thixotropy
crematoria  fenestella  institutor  patentable  rickettsia  threatener
crosstrees  fenestrate  intactness  pathetical  robustious  thriftless
curvetting  fictitious  intentness  pedestrian  robustness  throatwort
daughterly  flagitious  intertidal  pegmatitic  sabbatical  thwartship
deceptible  flightdeck  intertrigo  pentathlon  sabretache  thwartwise
deductible  flightless  intertwine  pentatomic  sabretooth  topsyturvy
dejectedly  flightpath  intertwist  pentatonic  sagittally  trilateral
delectable  flycatcher  intestinal  pentstemon  scientific  triliteral
delectably  forgetting  inventress  peripteral  scriptoria  triphthong
dementedly  formatting  investment  permitting  scriptural  tumultuary
department  fourstroke  isolatable  permutable  sculptress  tumultuous
deportment  geodetical  isometrics  perpetrate  sculptural  unbeatable
derestrict  geometrise  jesuitical  perpetuate  sculptured  unbeatably
dermatitis  geriatrics  juristical  perpetuity  seamstress  unbuttoned
dermatogen  geriatrist  kibbutznik  phenotypic  secretaire  uncritical
desistance  goloptious  knighthood  philatelic  seductress  uncustomed
despatcher  goluptious  lacustrine  phototaxis  selectness  undertaken
despiteful  groceteria  lamentable  phototrope  selfstyled  undertaker
despiteous  haematosis  lamentably  phytotoxic  semestrial  undertrick
detectable  haematuria  lamentedly  picketline  semiotical  unfaithful
detestable  hairstreak  librettist  pinnatifid  sempstress  unfettered
detestably  hairstroke  licentiate  planetable  sensitiser  ungrateful
devoutness  headstream  licentious  planetaria  seventieth  unhistoric
dictatress  headstrong  lithotrity  planktonic  shoestring  unilateral
didactical  heartthrob  lockstitch  pliantness  sidestreet  uninitiate
digestible  heatstroke  locustbean  pocketable  sidestroke  unjustness
dilettante  heliotaxis  logistical  pocketbook  siegetrain  unlettered
dilettanti  heliotrope  lowpitched  pocketsize  silentness  unmeetness
directness  heliotropy  lutestring  podiatrist  sinisterly  unmortised
directoire  hemipteran  magistracy  polyatamic  sinistrous  unsettling
directress  Heptateuch  magistrate  potentiate  slavetrade  unsuitable
disastrous  heptatonic  magnetiser  potentilla  slightness  untruthful
discutient  hermetical  mainstream  prelatical  slipstitch  unwontedly
disenthral  hermitcrab  majestical  prepotence  slipstream  unworthily
disentitle  highstrung  malentendu  prepotency  sneakthief  varietally
disentwine  hoitytoity  marketable  priesthood  societally  vignettist
dispatcher  holosteric  markethall  priestling  songstress  voluptuary
dispiteous  hospitable  markettown  profitable  soundtrack  voluptuous
disputable  hospitably  mediatress  profitably  spiritedly  watchtower
disputably  housetrain  mesenteric  profitless  spiritless  watertight
```

```
weightless  geniculate  pressurise  wirepuller  emerywheel  worthwhile
whipstitch  goatsucker  profoundly  woodcutter  everywhere  wristwatch
whitethorn  granduncle  pronounced  woodturner  fallowness  yellowback
absolutely  greatuncle  pronouncer  abbreviate  fellowship  yellowbird
absolution  habitually  propounder  achievable  fleshwound  yellowness
absolutism  hackbuteer  protrusile  approvable  floodwater  yellowwood
absolutist  halieutics  protrusion  approvably  freedwoman  asphyxiant
absolutory  harbourage  protrusive  arborvitae  freshwater  asphyxiate
abstrusely  headhunter  puberulent  believable  frontwards  bissextile
abstrusity  homoousian  punctually  bidonville  fuzzywuzzy  carboxylic
accumulate  hydraulics  punctuator  bivalvular  glassworks  commixture
allocution  immaculacy  punctulate  connivance  heartwhole  contextual
allrounder  immaculate  pushbutton  corrivalry  holloweyed  contexture
altocumuli  immaturely  pyrolusite  cultivable  hollowness  inflexible
amateurish  immaturity  quadrumana  cultivator  hollowware  inflexibly
amateurism  inaccuracy  quadrumane  czarevitch  horsewoman  overexcite
Andalusian  inaccurate  quadrumvir  deceivable  housewives  overexpose
andalusite  inaugurate  quadruplet  decemviral  interweave  postexilic
antiquated  infatuated  quadruplex  depravedly  interwound  prefixture
apolaustic  inosculate  quadrupole  deprivable  interwoven  premaxilla
articulate  insecurely  quintuplet  deservedly  Irishwoman  reflexible
attenuated  insecurity  ragamuffin  discoverer  landowning  acronychal
attenuator  insinuator  reissuable  disenviron  markswoman  anaglyphic
auriculate  instructor  rencounter  effervesce  marrowbone  anaptyctic
aventurine  instrument  repopulate  eigenvalue  marrowless  aneurysmal
bankruptcy  integument  resolutely  forgivable  meadowland  antonymous
beefburger  interurban  resolution  forgivably  meadowlark  apocryphal
biannually  intraurban  resolutive  gingivitis  mellowness  ascomycete
bigmouthed  invaluable  restaurant  illadvised  narrowness  barleybree
binoculars  invaluably  reticulate  impervious  nightwatch  barleybroo
bisexually  involucral  revolution  improvable  noblewoman  barleycorn
blanquette  involucrum  ridiculous  improvably  northwards  benzpyrene
bressummer  involution  roadrunner  improviser  otherwhere  biophysics
brusquerie  lacklustre  scrofulous  insolvable  otherwhile  blearyeyed
bureaucrat  landhunger  scrupulous  insolvency  otherworld  brachylogy
capitulary  landlubber  seersucker  intervener  paddywagon  brachyural
capitulate  lansquenet  selfguided  intervenor  paddywhack  brachyuran
Carthusian  latifundia  selfmurder  intervolve  pennyworth  brandyball
chartulary  leafcutter  selfruling  labiovelar  pilliwinks  brandysnap
coalbunker  limeburner  semilunate  lascivious  pillowcase  bubblyjock
cocksurely  lionhunter  semiquaver  medievally  pillowlace  chatoyance
compounder  lucifugous  sheabutter  misgivings  pillowslip  conveyable
conclusion  lumpsucker  shoebuckle  multivocal  pilotwhale  conveyance
conclusive  Malthusian  showjumper  observable  reviewable  defrayable
conclusory  manicurist  silhouette  observably  rightwards  defrayment
confluence  manipulate  sinecurism  observance  saleswoman  deployment
confounded  manoeuvrer  sinecurist  primevally  sallowness  disloyally
congruence  manoeuvres  soapbubble  receivable  Scotswoman  disloyalty
congruency  meticulous  spathulate  relievable  shadowless  donkeywork
creaturely  miraculous  spherulite  reservedly  shearwater  employable
deliquesce  moisturise  stirrupcup  resolvable  shirtwaist  employment
denaturant  mossbunker  stridulant  resolvedly  shorewards  epiphytism
depopulate  nidifugous  stridulate  shrievalty  smallwares  eucalyptol
destructor  nonplussed  stridulous  slidevalve  snailwheel  eucalyptus
devolution  novaculite  subaquatic  supervisor  southwards  eucaryotic
diminuendo  obsequious  subaqueous  survivance  spacewoman  galleywest
diminution  obstructor  subroutine  transvalue  steelworks  geophysics
diminutive  operculate  sulphurate  transverse  sternwards  greedyguts
discounter  outpouring  sulphurise  triumviral  teenyweeny  hemicyclic
discourage  overburden  sulphurous  tsarevitch  townswoman  homonymous
discourser  oversubtle  surplusage  undervalue  treadwheel  homozygote
disgruntle  oversupply  taciturnly  unprovoked  underwater  homozygous
dumfounder  palmbutter  tambourine  vaudeville  underworld  hypabyssal
eartrumpet  PalmSunday  thereunder  wagonvault  underwrite  hypogynous
edentulous  paniculate  thoroughly  ZendAvesta  underwrote  ichthyosis
emasculate  parimutuel  tranquilly  afterwards  unknowable  johnnycake
eventually  pasteurise  tufthunter  batfowling  waterwheel  kerseymere
extenuator  pasteurism  turnbuckle  bestowment  waterworks  lachrymose
fatiguable  pediculate  unarguable  bilgewater  Welshwoman  misogynist
filibuster  pediculous  unassuming  blackwater  willowherb  misogynous
FinnoUgric  pedicurist  ungrounded  breakwater  willywilly  mixolydian
flavourful  phillumeny  unoccupied  callowness  windowless  monkeysuit
flavouring  picayunish  unrequited  chairwoman  windowpane  monocyclic
flocculate  portcullis  untroubled  chuckwagon  windowseat  monogynian
flocculent  posthumous  vesiculate  coastwards  windowshop  monogynous
flosculous  praemunire  viscountcy  deathwatch  windowsill  monohybrid
forerunner  precaution  vocabulary  deflowerer  wishywashy  monohydric
fraudulent  preclusion  wellturned  dreamworld  wongawonga  myxomycete
fussbudget  preclusive  WhitSunday  earthwards  worldweary  nonpayment
```

```
panegyrise  affordable  benzocaine  compliance  designator  exportable
panegyrist  afterpains  biannually  compliancy  desistance  expurgator
pantrymaid  aftertaste  biblically  compotator  desperados  extenuator
paronymous  afterwards  biennially  computable  despicable  externally
paroxysmal  alcyonaria  bilgewater  computator  despicably  extirpator
paroxytone  aldermanic  binaurally  confidante  despisable  extricable
pastrycook  aldermanry  biodynamic  conjugally  detachable  exuberance
pericyclic  algebraist  bisexually  connivance  detectable  fabricator
perigynous  allegiance  blackfaced  consolable  detestable  fairleader
playbyplay  alleviator  blackwater  consonance  detestably  familiarly
polycyclic  alternance  blancmange  consonancy  diagonally  farcically
polygynous  alternator  bleachable  constraint  dialysable  fascinator
prepayable  ambassador  boneheaded  consumable  dilemmatic  fathomable
prepayment  amerciable  boneshaker  convenable  dilettante  fatiguable
presbyopia  ammoniacal  brachiator  convenance  dilettanti  favourable
presbyopic  ammoniated  breakwater  conveyable  dillydally  favourably
presbytery  amphimacer  breathable  conveyance  diplomatic  fiducially
procrypsis  analphabet  bricklayer  coolheaded  dipsomania  filariasis
procryptic  analysable  bridgeable  cooperator  disarrange  filterable
purveyance  anglomania  brilliance  copyreader  disengaged  fimbriated
safetybelt  AngloSaxon  brilliancy  cornflakes  dislikable  floodwater
salicylate  answerable  browbeaten  cornstarch  disloyally  forcipated
shandygaff  answerably  buccinator  corporally  disloyalty  foreshadow
shantytown  antechapel  bullheaded  corporator  disparager  forgivable
sleepyhead  antiquated  bullroarer  corrivalry  disparates  forgivably
sperrylite  antistatic  cacography  corrugated  disposable  formidable
staphyline  aposematic  calculable  corrugator  disputable  formidably
starryeyed  appealable  calculably  corticated  disputably  fornicator
suretyship  appearance  calculator  coryphaeus  dissipated  fourleaved
symphylous  appeasable  calibrator  cosmically  dissonance  fowlplague
symphyseal  applicable  candelabra  cosmoramic  dissonancy  freeloader
symphysial  applicably  cardplayer  covariance  disyllabic  freshwater
synonymist  applicator  cartomancy  creditable  disyllable  frontwards
synonymity  approvable  catastasis  creditably  doughfaced  funereally
synonymous  approvably  celebrated  crenulated  downstairs  Gallomania
thirtyfold  aquaplaner  celebrator  criminally  doxography  gasconader
tiddlywink  arbitrable  cellularly  critically  dressmaker  germinally
triglyphic  arbitrager  censurable  crosshatch  duplicator  glasspaper
turkeycock  arbitrator  cerography  crosspatch  earthwards  globularly
volleyball  arboreally  changeable  cucullated  effaceable  goldbeater
whirlybird  archdeacon  changeably  cultivable  eigenvalue  gothically
winceyette  armorially  chaparajos  cultivator  elaborator  governable
ylangylang  arterially  chargeable  culturally  eliminable  governance
emblazoner  artycrafty  charitable  cuspidated  eliminator  granddaddy
emblazonry  ascariasis  charitably  cyclically  elucidator  grandmamma
interzonal  ascendable  chatelaine  damageable  elutriator  granularly
Lipizzaner  ascendance  chatoyance  daydreamer  emblematic  granulator
Lippizaner  ascendancy  chemically  deathwatch  emerypaper  greyheaded
quartzitic  ascribable  chemotaxis  decagramme  Emmentaler  gutturally
rendezvous  Ashkenazim  chiromancy  deceivable  employable  gynocratic
scherzando  assailable  chuckwagon  decigramme  encephalic  habitually
squeezable  assessable  circularly  declarable  encephalon  hagiolatry
squeezebox  assignable  circulator  declinable  encourager  halfyearly
——————      assistance  clerically  deepseated  endorsable  hankypanky
abnormally  associable  clinically  defalcator  enumerable  hardheaded
abominable  asteriated  coagulable  defeasance  enumerator  hebdomadal
abominably  astigmatic  coastwards  defendable  enunciable  hectically
abominator  astragalus  cochleated  deferrable  enunciator  heliacally
absorbable  atomically  cockchafer  defoliator  episematic  heliolater
absorbance  attachable  coelacanth  defrayable  eradicable  heliolatry
acceptable  attackable  cognisable  degradable  eradicator  heliotaxis
acceptably  attainable  cognisably  delectable  erotically  hendecagon
acceptance  attendance  cognisance  delectably  erotomania  heresiarch
accordance  attenuated  collatable  delineator  especially  heroically
achievable  attenuator  collimator  demandable  ethereally  hibernacle
achromatic  atypically  colonially  democratic  ethnically  hierolatry
acquirable  autocratic  colonnaded  demoniacal  euthanasia  hippocampi
actionable  autography  colossally  demurrable  evaporable  hippomanes
actionably  autoplasty  colourable  denigrator  evaporator  holography
addlepated  autumnally  colourably  dependable  eventually  homeopathy
adjustable  avantgarde  columbaria  dependably  everglades  honeyeater
admittable  backstairs  commonable  deplorable  examinable  honourable
admittance  baldheaded  commonalty  deplorably  executable  honourably
adsorbable  bardolatry  communally  depredator  exotically  hootenanny
aerogramme  bareheaded  commutable  deprivable  expandable  hormonally
aerography  believable  commutator  desecrater  expectance  horselaugh
aerostatic  bellydance  comparable  desecrator  expectancy  hospitable
affiliated  bellylaugh  comparably  desiccator  expendable  hospitably
affirmable  benignancy  comparator  desiccator  explicable  hullabaloo
```

```
hydrically internally mesoscaphe overcharge prepayable resolvable
hydromancy intrigante metaplasia overpraise presumable respirable
hydropathy invaluable metastable overshadow presumably respirator
hydrotaxis invaluably metastases overslaugh prevenancy restorable
hyperbaric invariable metastasis oxidisable primevally retainable
hyperbaton invariably metastatic oxygenator primiparae returnable
hyphenated invariance methylated pacifiable procreator revealable
hypostasis inviolable metrically paddywagon procurable reviewable
hypostatic inviolably microfarad paederasty procurance rewardable
icebreaker ironically middleaged pallbearer procurator riboflavin
iconolater irradiance militiaman pancreatic prodigally rightwards
iconolatry isodynamic miscreance pancreatin profitable ringleader
iconomachy isolatable mistakable papermaker profitably ritardando
ideography itinerancy mobocratic pardonable promenader roquelaure
illaudable jackanapes modifiable pardonably propagable rosechafer
illaudably Janusfaced moneymaker parentally propaganda rubrically
imaginable jawbreaker moneytaker parramatta propagator rubricator
imaginably judgematic moniliasis pastorally propylaeum rustically
immortally judicially monochasia pasturable provenance sabretache
immoveable kerygmatic monocratic pastyfaced provitamin sacrosanct
impalpable kilogramme monstrance patentable provocator sagittally
impalpably Krishnaism morganatic paternally proximally saturnalia
impassable lacrimator mosaically peacemaker psychiatry satyriasis
impassably lacrymator moviemaker pectinated Ptolemaist scarabaeid
impeccable ladychapel Muhammadan peculiarly pulvinated scarabaeus
impeccably lamentable multifaced penetrable punctually scenically
impeccancy lamentably muscularly penetrably punctuator scherzando
imperially landscaper musicianly penetralia punishable schismatic
implacable lardydardy musicpaper penetrance purtenance schoolable
implacably lawbreaker mycoplasma penetrator purveyance sciagraphy
importable legislator myopically percolator pyrography scrimmager
importance lexigraphy mystically perdurable quenchable searchable
impresario licensable mythically perdurably radiopaque seasonable
imprimatur lightfaced mythomania perforator railroader seasonably
improbable Lipizzaner nambypamby perishable rationally seasonally
improbably lipography nationally permutable realisable secretaire
improvable Lippizaner nautically personable reappraise selfglazed
improvably liquidator necrolater personally reasonable selfpraise
impugnable logography necrolatry personalty reasonably semiopaque
incantator longheaded necromancy personator rebuttable semiquaver
incessancy longshanks negotiable petiolated recallable semiyearly
inclinable lossleader negotiator petrolatum receivable sensedatum
inculcator lotuseater neuropathy phagedaena receptacle septenarii
inculpable lubricator newsreader pharisaism recordable septically
incurrable lucubrator nightwatch phlegmatic recyclable serigraphy
indictable Lupercalia noisemaker phonematic redeemable shamefaced
inductance luxuriance nomography phonically redundance shanghaier
ineducable Maccabaean northwards phosphatic redundancy shearwater
inelegance macebearer nosography photonasty reentrance shirtwaist
inevitable machinator notarially phototaxis refillable shorewards
inevitably malignance noticeable physically reformable shortdated
inexorable malignancy noticeably pinebeauty refundable shortrange
inexorably mamillated notifiable pinnulated regionally shrievalty
inexpiable manageable notionally piscifauna reissuable shrinkable
inexpiably manageably nudibranch pityriasis reiterance sideboards
infatuated maniacally numismatic pixillated rejectable sideglance
infernally Manichaean nyctinasty planetable releasable simoniacal
inferrable marginalia obfuscated planetaria relievable singularly
inflatable marginally observable platelayer relishable sketchable
informally marginated observably ploughable reluctance skiagraphy
inimically Mariolater observance plutolatry reluctancy skirtdance
inimitable Mariolatry obtainable pocketable remarkable skyscraper
inimitably marketable oesophagus poetically remarkably slidevalve
innerrably masticable officially pokerfaced remediable smallwares
inoculable masticator oleography pollinator remedially snailpaced
inoculator matchmaker openhearth polyatamic remittance snakedance
inoperable materially ophiolater polychaete renderable snapdragon
insatiable maternally ophiolatry polygraphy repairable soapflakes
insatiably mathematic oppugnancy polyphasic repealable societally
insinuator mayonnaise optionally ponderable repeatable softheaded
insociable measurable oracularly porismatic repellance somersault
insolvable measurably ordonnance postchaise repellancy soothsayer
inspirator medievally oreography postulator repentance southwards
instigator medullated orientally pozzolanic reportable spectrally
integrable meliorator originally prearrange reprobance speculator
integrally melismatic originator predicable repudiator spodomancy
integrator mendicancy oscillator preferable repugnance squeezable
intendance mensurable osteopathy preferably repugnancy squeteague
intermarry merrymaker outbalance preparator resistance squirearch
```

```
statically  triturator  buttonball  sourcebook  cheesecake  hemicyclic
statutable  tropically  buttonbush  splashback  chronicity  heptarchic
statutably  tropopause  cannonball  splintbone  chronicler  hereticate
stavesacre  tutorially  canterbury  sprucebeer  circumcise  hermitcrab
sternwards  typography  canvasback  stereobate  Cistercian  hierarchal
stimulator  ultrabasic  centreback  stiflebone  Clarenceux  hierarchic
stipulator  unarguable  chequebook  storksbill  classicise  highjacker
stomodaeum  unbearable  collarbeam  stringbean  classicism  humpbacked
stonemason  unbearably  collarbone  switchback  classicist  hydroscope
subaquatic  unbeatable  collembola  tailorbird  coadjacent  hygroscope
subjugator  unbeatably  confabbing  thereabout  coalescent  hypotactic
sublimable  unbiddable  conglobate  threadbare  colchicine  iconoscope
substratum  undeniable  contraband  turtleback  commercial  impudicity
subtenancy  undeniably  contrabass  untroubled  complacent  incapacity
succedanea  underpants  contribute  vesperbell  complected  increscent
sufferable  undertaken  cranesbill  volleyball  complicacy  indelicacy
sufferably  undertaker  cummerbund  wattlebird  complicate  indelicate
sufferance  undervalue  cuttlebone  weaverbird  complicity  indirectly
sugardaddy  underwater  dissembler  whereabout  comstocker  inefficacy
sugarmaple  uneducated  distribute  whirlybird  condescend  infelicity
suicidally  unemphatic  doublebass  winebibber  confiscate  instructor
summonable  unenviable  equilibria  yellowback  conspectus  intoxicant
sunderance  unfilially  fiddleback  yellowbird  contractor  intoxicate
supercargo  uniaxially  fingerbowl  abstracted  convincing  inveracity
supernally  univocally  gingerbeer  abstracter  coradicate  involucral
suppliance  unknowable  groundbait  abstractly  corncockle  involucrum
supposable  unnameable  hammerbeam  abstractor  corpuscule  iridescent
supposably  unprepared  heavenborn  accrescent  cottoncake  irradiate
surgically  unreadable  hobnobbing  acronychal  cowcatcher  johnnycake
surmisable  unreliable  hucklebone  adjudicate  cowpuncher  kenspeckle
survivance  unscalable  incunabula  adolescent  crepuscule  kineticist
sustenance  unsociable  jackrabbit  ambulacral  crustacean  laconicism
sworddance  unsociably  knockabout  ambulacrum  cystoscope  lactescent
sycophancy  unsocially  ladderback  amoebocyte  cystoscopy  landlocked
syllabaria  unsuitable  landlubber  anaptyctic  decrescent  largescale
syncopated  unworkable  ledgerbait  androecium  despatcher  lawrencium
syncopator  usquebaugh  letterbomb  animalcula  destructor  lemniscate
syndicator  utilisable  letterbook  animalcule  detoxicant  lettercard
systematic  vaccinator  locustbean  anthracene  detoxicate  lifejacket
tabernacle  variegated  malleebird  anthracite  disconcert  liquescent
tactically  varietally  marrowbone  anthracoid  dispatcher  lowpitched
talebearer  vascularly  middlebrow  antisocial  distinctly  lumpsucker
talismanic  ventilator  minutebook  apodeictic  distracted  lymphocyte
tarmacadam  verandahed  monohybrid  apoplectic  divaricate  malefactor
tauromachy  verifiable  mountebank  apothecary  dustjacket  maleficent
teetotally  vertically  muffinbell  apothecial  efficacity  marcescent
telegraphy  vindicable  nativeborn  apothecium  elasticise  microscope
temperable  vindicator  needlebath  aristocrat  elasticity  microscopy
temperance  virginally  needlebook  armourclad  emphractic  misericord
temporally  viscerally  oversubtle  artificial  empiricism  mismatched
temporalty  visionally  paddleboat  asceticism  empiricist  molluscoid
tenantable  vortically  parsonbird  ascomycete  encroacher  molluscous
termagancy  voyageable  phrasebook  barebacked  endemicity  monocyclic
terminable  vulnerable  pocketbook  barleycorn  entrancing  moustached
terminably  vulnerably  prayerbook  bathyscaph  epideictic  moustachio
terminally  wagonvault  procumbent  bathyscope  equivocate  munificent
terminator  wastepaper  promptbook  beautician  ergodicity  myxomycete
termitaria  watchmaker  proverbial  bellyacher  erubescent  nanosecond
texturally  weimaraner  rockrabbit  benedicite  eugenicist  necroscopy
theocratic  whitefaced  rockribbed  Benedictus  evanescent  needlecord
theophanic  wholesaler  roundabout  benefactor  excrescent  nematocyst
thirdparty  wiredrawer  rouseabout  beneficent  fanaticise  nephoscope
timocratic  wishywashy  roustabout  beneficial  fanaticism  nidificate
tobogganer  witchhazel  runnerbean  bivouacked  fantoccini  nigrescent
tomography  withdrawal  saddleback  blastocyst  farfetched  notonectal
toothpaste  withdrawer  safetybelt  bluejacket  fireescape  nutcracker
topography  wristwatch  schoolbook  bootlicker  flavescent  obstructor
toroidally  xerography  secondbest  bratticing  florescent  obtruncate
tortfeasor  xylography  sheathbill  bureaucrat  flycatcher  octodecimo
touchpaper  automobile  showerbath  canaliculi  fratricide  oligarchic
tracheated  barleybree  sicklebill  candescent  frutescent  opalescent
tragacanth  barleybroo  silverbath  canonicals  geneticist  Ordovician
tragically  basketball  sketchbook  canonicate  gnosticism  organicism
translator  blueribbon  skibobbing  canonicity  goatsucker  organicist
transvalue  brandyball  sleighbell  cappuccino  hagioscope  overexcite
trenchancy  breakables  smoothbore  carbuncled  halfcocked  overnicety
trichiasis  breastbone  smorrebrod  catalectic  hamshackle  pacificate
trigonally  butterball  snowmobile  causticity  handpicked  pacificism
triturable  butterbean  soapbubble  centricity  helioscope  pacifist
```

```
Palaeocene  splintcoal  concordant  orchardman  acceptedly  chauffeuse
paramecium  spongecake  contendent  orotundity  accursedly  chelicerae
paratactic  spumescent  contradict  osmiridium  acidimeter  chemisette
pastrycook  statoscope  decahedral  outbidding  acidimetry  chokeberry
peppercorn  stillicide  decahedron  outlandish  acotyledon  cicisbeism
pericyclic  stratocrat  decapodous  overridden  admittedly  Cinderella
phallicism  stypticity  dehumidify  overriding  advertence  citronella
pharmacist  subglacial  descendant  packsaddle  advertency  clarabella
Phoenician  subspecies  descendent  panhandler  affectedly  clinometer
physiocrat  succinctly  despondent  panjandrum  agitatedly  clinometry
pickpocket  superacute  dilapidate  parapodium  allegretto  cloistered
picosecond  supplicant  diphyodont  pebbledash  allergenic  cloudberry
pigsticker  supplicate  disbudding  peroxidise  alliaceous  coetaneous
pillowcase  swaybacked  discordant  phelloderm  allosteric  collarette
plasticise  taperecord  dumbledore  piperidine  almondeyed  collateral
plasticity  technician  echinoderm  plasmodesm  alphabetic  comedienne
plebiscite  technicist  eisteddfod  plasmodium  alphameric  competence
polemicist  technocrat  embroidery  polyandric  amphoteric  competency
politician  tetrarchic  emparadise  polyhedral  amylaceous  composedly
politicise  theodicean  endopodite  polyhedric  anchoretic  condolence
polycyclic  threescore  endproduct  polyhedron  androgenic  conference
polydactyl  thumbscrew  flaccidity  praesidium  anemometer  confidence
polytocous  trafficked  flightdeck  prebendary  anemometry  confluence
practician  trafficker  fluoridate  precordial  animatedly  confusedly
praecocial  transactor  forbidding  pretendant  anonaceous  congeneric
pratincole  tribrachic  foreboding  pretendent  antifreeze  congruence
preconcert  trifurcate  foreordain  primordial  antitheism  congruency
preglacial  triplicate  forwarding  primordium  antitheist  conscience
prosaicism  triplicity  fricandeau  proceeding  antitheses  considered
prospector  turgescent  fullbodied  profundity  antithesis  consumedly
prospectus  turkeycock  fussbudget  psalmodise  antithetic  continence
protracted  turnbuckle  gormandise  psalmodist  aphaereses  convalesce
protractor  ulotrichan  halberdier  resounding  aphaeresis  coparcener
provincial  umbilicate  Hansardise  respondent  apologetic  coralberry
pseudocarp  unaffected  hemihedral  revalidate  apperceive  coriaceous
psittacine  unattached  hemihedron  rhapsodise  arenaceous  corporeity
psychicism  unblenched  heterodont  rhapsodist  arithmetic  corpulence
psychicist  underscore  heterodoxy  rockbadger  ascendence  corpulency
putrescent  unexpected  heterodyne  ropeladder  ascendency  corrigenda
putrescine  unofficial  heulandite  sallenders  audiometer  coulometry
pyrotechny  unselected  hexahedral  schooldays  audiometry  courageous
quadriceps  varicocele  hexahedron  scleroderm  backsheesh  crapulence
radioscopy  ventricose  holohedral  selenodont  bathometer  cretaceous
ramshackle  ventriculi  horrendous  sherardise  bathymeter  crinolette
ratcatcher  vestpocket  husbandage  sidesaddle  bathymetry  crippledom
reallocate  vitrescent  husbandman  smaragdine  Berkeleian  crossbench
researcher  vivisector  imparadise  smaragdite  bijouterie  crossrefer
retinacula  woodpecker  inbreeding  solifidian  biogenesis  crowkeeper
rhinoscope  zygodactyl  individual  sphenodone  biogenetic  curvaceous
rhinoscopy  ablebodied  innuendoes  splashdown  bioscience  cybernetic
ringnecked  aggrandise  insipidity  squalidity  biparietal  cyclometer
scepticism  alexanders  intimidate  stepladder  bizarrerie  cyclopedia
schizocarp  Amerindian  invalidate  stewardess  blackberry  cyclopedic
Scotticise  antecedent  invalidism  streetdoor  blackheart  cylindered
Scotticism  antipodean  invalidity  stupendous  blanquette  daughterly
seabiscuit  Armageddon  jeopardise  subacidity  blasphemer  deepfreeze
seersucker  autodidact  kettledrum  subcordate  blearyeyed  deficiency
seismicity  balderdash  lawabiding  subheading  bollweevil  definienda
selfdeceit  bastardise  leopardess  suspenders  bookkeeper  deflowerer
semiuncial  battledore  lipreading  taradiddle  bordereaux  degradedly
shellacked  bestridden  Lollardism  threnodial  bradyseism  dehiscence
shoebuckle  billetdoux  lycopodium  threnodist  brocatelle  dejectedly
simplicity  blastoderm  malacoderm  tremendous  brusquerie  deliquesce
simulacrum  bombardier  mallenders  troglodyte  byssaceous  dementedly
slitpocket  brigandage  misconduct  troubadour  cacodaemon  demoiselle
smallscale  brigandine  miswording  tumbledown  calcareous  densimeter
sororicide  brigandism  mithridate  turtledove  calciferol  dependence
Spartacist  brokendown  mixolydian  unabridged  camerlengo  dependency
spasticity  buttondown  monohydric  unsteadily  cantilever  depravedly
spatchcock  chalcedony  monopodial  unwieldily  canzonetta  deservedly
spectacled  Clydesdale  monopodium  unyielding  cassolette  designedly
spectacles  coincident  myocardium  upbraiding  catchpenny  desipience
spermaceti  commandant  nephridium  upstanding  catechesis  despiteful
spermicide  commandeer  octahedral  abhorrence  catechetic  despiteous
sphericity  commandery  octahedron  absorbedly  cavalierly  detachedly
spidercrab  commanding  octopodous  absorbency  centimetre  detergency
spifflicate  commandoes  oldmaidish  abstinence  chalybeate  deterrence
spinescent  compendium  ommatidium  abstinency  chaparejos  diapedesis
spitchcock  compradore  orchardist  acatalepsy  chartreuse  diapedetic
```

difference	gamekeeper	intervener	outrageous	recommence	synergetic
diffidence	gaspereaux	intervenor	outstretch	recompense	syngenesis
diminuendo	gatekeeper	interweave	palmaceous	recrudesce	tachometer
diphtheria	gaultheria	iridaceous	pangenesis	recumbency	tachometry
diphtheric	gauntleted	isogenetic	pangenetic	recurrence	tachymeter
diphyletic	gemmaceous	jargonelle	paramnesia	refulgence	tachymetry
discoverer	gentilesse	kerchieves	paraplegia	registered	tarantella
discreetly	glumaceous	knopkierie	paraplegic	remorseful	tarantelle
dishonesty	goalkeeper	labiovelar	parenteral	renascence	tautomeric
disinherit	goatsbeard	lamentedly	passageway	repeatedly	teenyweeny
disordered	goggleeyed	lansquenet	pathogenic	repellence	televiewer
disorderly	goniometer	latescence	patisserie	repellency	temperedly
dispiteous	goniometry	lauraceous	pennaceous	reportedly	testaceous
disquieten	gooseberry	liliaceous	pentameter	reservedly	tetrahedra
disquietly	governessy	lockkeeper	pentimento	resignedly	tetrameter
dissidence	gramineous	loganberry	pentstemon	resilience	theopneust
divergence	gravimeter	lopsidedly	peripheral	resiliency	thimbleful
divergency	gravimetry	machinegun	peripteral	resolvedly	thimblerig
divulgence	greenheart	Mahommedan	perithecia	resurgence	thirteenth
doorkeeper	groceteria	maisonette	permanence	revengeful	threatener
drupaceous	hartebeest	malentendu	permanency	rhinoceros	threepence
dungbeetle	headcheese	malingerer	pertinence	rhizogenic	threepenny
dysenteric	heartsease	malvaceous	pertinency	ritornelli	thruppence
ebullience	hectometre	Manicheism	pestilence	ritornello	timekeeper
ebulliency	heliometer	marionette	petronella	rotisserie	tocopherol
effervesce	hemiplegia	Massoretic	phagedenic	rovebeetle	transferee
efficiency	hemiplegic	mealbeetle	phenacetin	rowanberry	transferor
effloresce	hemipteran	measuredly	phenomenal	salmonella	transience
effulgence	henotheism	mesenteric	phenomenon	saltarello	transiency
eighteenmo	henotheist	mesenteron	philatelic	saprogenic	transverse
eighteenth	Heptameron	metatheses	phonometer	sarcolemma	tribometer
elderberry	heptameter	metathesis	photogenic	sarracenia	trilateral
emblements	Heptateuch	metathetic	photometer	schipperke	triliteral
empathetic	herbaceous	Methuselah	photometry	scrapmetal	tromometer
endothelia	holloweyed	micrometer	phylogenic	secludedly	trousseaux
epentheses	holosteric	micrometry	phytogenic	selffeeder	trucklebed
epenthesis	homebrewed	microseism	piezometer	selfseeker	truculence
epenthetic	hornblende	mignonette	pinchpenny	semiweekly	truculency
epexegeses	horseleech	millimetre	planchette	senescence	trundlebed
epexegesis	hydrometer	minstrelsy	planimeter	serviceman	tuffaceous
epexegetic	hydrometry	mischmetal	planimetry	shopkeeper	tularaemia
epigenesis	hygrometer	misnomered	planometer	shoreleave	tularaemic
epigenetic	hygrometry	mistakenly	polytheism	silhouette	tumescence
ergosterol	hylotheism	mixedmedia	polytheist	sinisterly	turbulence
ericaceous	hyperaemia	Mohammedan	porraceous	sociometry	turbulency
erotogenic	hyperaemic	molybdenum	portamento	soldanella	twowheeler
erysipelas	hypotheses	monotheism	prairiedog	somnolence	umbrageous
eudiometer	hypothesis	monotheist	precedence	somnolency	unbeliever
eudiometry	hypsometer	montbretia	precedency	spadebeard	unbonneted
eurypterid	hypsometry	morbidezza	predecease	spadiceous	unbrokenly
excellence	hysteresis	mozzarella	preference	spiritedly	underbelly
excellency	hysteretic	Muhammedan	preparedly	spirometer	underlease
exospheric	iatrogenic	multimedia	prepotence	spirometry	underneath
expectedly	iconometer	myasthenia	prepotency	splitlevel	undersense
expedience	iconometry	myrtaceous	prescience	splutterer	undersexed
expediency	immortelle	naphthenic	presageful	squanderer	unfathered
experience	impatience	narcolepsy	presidency	squeezebox	unfettered
extendedly	impendence	nectareous	prevalence	squinteyed	ungraceful
extraneity	impendency	negligence	privileged	stagbeetle	ungrateful
extraneous	improperly	neurilemma	prominence	starryeyed	unhouseled
faintheart	imprudence	neurolemma	propraetor	strainedly	unicameral
fenestella	incandesce	nevernever	proprietor	strawberry	unilateral
feuilleton	incipience	newsagency	prosthesis	stringency	unlettered
fianchetto	incipiency	nineteenth	prosthetic	stringendo	unmannerly
flatulence	inclemency	nomothetic	providence	striptease	unnumbered
flatulency	incumbency	noogenesis	pubescence	subaqueous	unredeemed
florilegia	indulgence	occurrence	pulsimeter	subsidence	unrelieved
foliaceous	insistence	offlicence	pulsometer	succulence	unscreened
fontanelle	insistency	oleraceous	purposeful	succulency	unwontedly
foresheets	insolvency	olivaceous	purseseine	suprarenal	uranometry
fourchette	insurgence	ombrometer	pycnometer	supposedly	variometer
fourteener	insurgency	onesidedly	pyknometer	sweetheart	vermicelli
fourteenth	interceder	ophicleide	quiescence	swinefever	villanelle
framboesia	interferer	opisometer	quiescency	swinglebar	violaceous
fraxinella	interferon	orogenesis	radiogenic	swiveleyed	virescence
freespeech	interleave	orogenetic	radiometer	synaeresis	viscometer
frenziedly	intermezzi	orthogenic	radiometry	synaloepha	voltameter
frontbench	intermezzo	orthopedic	rampageous		vorticella
fustanella	interregna	outgeneral	recipiency		waggonette

```
watermelon vaporiform mandragora trilingual disulphate microphyte
wellheeled viperiform martingale typologist disulphide minutehand
whatsoever whiskified meaningful unchanging dragonhead monarchial
whensoever Wycliffite meltingpot undesigned drosophila Monarchian
whitebeard abstergent misaligned unflagging drowsihead monarchism
whomsoever acromegaly misologist ungrudging dunderhead monarchist
wildebeest aeroengine monologise unilingual earthshine motherhood
winceyette aerologist monologist upbringing embouchure multiphase
windsleeve agrologist morphogeny viceregent emerywheel muttonhead
worldweary algolagnia mycologist virologist Englishman mycorrhiza
wretchedly algolagnic newfangled vitiligate escutcheon nationhood
youngberry algologist nidifugous warmingpan eurhythmic necrophile
ZendAvesta anastigmat nomologist wellington everything necrophily
archerfish Areopagite nonaligned woodpigeon everywhere negrophile
beautifier asparagine nosologist workingman Fahrenheit negrophobe
bottlefeed astringent oecologist zigzagging farsighted nepenthean
butterfish autologous oenologist zoophagous fatherhood nightshade
calyciform axiologist oldfangled accoucheur fiddlehead nightshift
candlefish balbriggan omophagous acidophile figurehead nightshirt
centrefold barelegged oncologist aerenchyma flugelhorn nitrochalk
centrifuge Bedlington ontologist aftershave flyfishing nourishing
chloroform bedraggled oreologist aircushion fourinhand orphanhood
cinquefoil boondoggle packingbox alongshore Gallophile osteophyte
circumflex bootlegger Palaeogene anemophily Gallophobe otherwhere
circumfuse bryologist paralogise anglophile garnishing otherwhile
classified campaigner paralogism anglophobe gaslighter ottershrew
classifier cardiogram pedagogics anglophone gesundheit outrightly
colourfast cataloguer pedologist apophthegm gramophone paddywhack
cribriform catburglar pemphigoid arrhythmia grandchild paedophile
cumuliform cattlegrid pemphigous arrhythmic granophyre pansophist
cuttlefish champignon penologist atmosphere greenshank paperchase
dendriform chronogram periwigged audiophile gunfighter parenchyma
digitiform churchgoer phalangeal barysphere gypsophila parenthood
discomfort congregant pharyngeal bassethorn hammerhead penpushing
disconfirm congregate plasmogamy batrachian heartthrob pentachord
emulsifier contingent pomologist beforehand heartwhole pentathlon
fisherfolk convergent prefulgent behindhand heliophyte photophily
gentlefolk coolingoff pressagent bewitchery hemisphere photophore
heretofore cryptogamy profligacy bisulphate heptachord phytophagy
humidifier cryptogram profligate bisulphide hierophant pigeonhole
limaciform curmudgeon prolongate bisulphite hippophagy pilotwhale
linguiform cytologist promulgate Blackshirt horseshoer pincushion
lowprofile dampingoff refringent blackthorn hydrophane plainchant
malleefowl dapplegrey rheologist brainchild hydrophily powderhorn
moniliform demagogism rockpigeon bridgehead hydrophone priesthood
needlefish Devanagari rollingpin Britishism hydrophyte promethium
overrefine drawingpin roseengine broadsheet hygrophyte proofsheet
oysterfarm earwigging salpingian brownshirt hypaethral protophyta
parrotfish embryogeny sandbagger bufflehead hypanthium protophyte
pluperfect epeirogeny scavengery bullethead imposthume publishing
postoffice ethologist schizogony buttonhole interphase quickthorn
proteiform fallingoff schoolgirl buttonhook ionosphere radiophone
quantifier fandangoes sealingwax caoutchouc Italophile rattlehead
quatrefoil FinnoUgric seismogram carragheen jolterhead razorshell
ragamuffin flamingoes selfregard catarrhine knighthood refreshing
ribbonfish flowergirl seltzogene cellophane leprechaun repurchase
rudderfish footlights Septuagint centrehalf letterhead retrochoir
saddlefast gatelegged serologist chargehand likelihood revanchism
sanctifier Glaswegian sexologist chiffchaff lithophane revanchist
scyphiform golddigger shandygaff Christhood lithophyte rhizophore
securiform greedyguts shiprigged clavichord livelihood rhodophane
sheriffdom heterogamy sinologist coleorhiza loggerhead rodfishing
shoplifter heterogeny sluicegate comanchero logorrhoea Russophile
sideeffect heterogony sphenogram comprehend lophophore Russophobe
silverfish homologate sporangial copperhead macrophage saprophyte
simplifier homologise sporangium Corinthian maidenhair sarcophagi
singlefoot homologous stereogram cousinhood maidenhead sarcophagy
spongiform homozygote strategist crankshaft maidenhood scoresheet
stelliform homozygous subkingdom crosscheck Malpighian scratchily
stratiform horologist sublingual ctenophore maraschino scratchwig
subterfuge houseagent suffragist daisychain markethall screechowl
Tartuffian humbuggery tankengine debauchery masterhand scrimshank
Tartuffism humbugging teratogeny debouchure masterhood seborrhoea
tenderfoot ideologist theologian dimorphism matronhood secondhand
thereafter irreligion theologise dimorphous meerschaum sepulchral
thirtyfold kieselguhr theologist discophile melancholy sheepshank
threadfish landingnet thermogram disenchant mesosphere sheepshead
twelvefold longlegged thoroughly disenthral micaschist shellshock
umbiliform lucifugous topologist distichous microphone shovelhead
```

sisterhood	analogical	complainer	epidemical	impartible	mesmeriser
skrimshank	analytical	compositor	episodical	impassible	metempiric
Slavophile	anarchical	conchoidal	eremitical	impassibly	meteoritic
Slavophobe	anatomical	conciliary	escadrille	impervious	methodical
sleepyhead	anchoritic	conciliate	espadrille	implicitly	microbiota
snailwheel	annunciate	congenital	euphonious	impossible	microfiche
sneakthief	antheridia	consociate	excruciate	impossibly	microlitic
sousaphone	anticlimax	constringe	exegetical	improviser	millefiori
splanchnic	anticlinal	contagious	exoterical	incautious	millesimal
spokeshave	aphrodisia	convenient	expansible	incendiary	millilitre
sporophore	apolitical	Copernican	expatriate	includible	millwright
sporophyll	appendices	coprolitic	explicitly	incredible	misbelieve
sporophyte	appendixes	copywriter	extendible	incredibly	misgivings
springhalt	appreciate	cordwainer	extensible	indistinct	moderniser
springhead	aragonitic	corrigible	factitious	ineligible	molendinar
squirehood	arborvitae	corsetiere	fairhaired	ineligibly	monistical
stealthily	archpriest	cosentient	fallacious	ineludible	monoclinal
steamchest	ascendible	couturiere	fastidious	inexplicit	monoclinic
stomachful	aspergilla	crosslight	fastigiate	infallible	monoecious
straighten	asphyxiant	crosspiece	fertiliser	infallibly	moonshiner
straightly	asphyxiate	curvacious	fibrositis	infeasible	mordacious
stringhalt	assentient	czarevitch	fictitious	infectious	mouthpiece
stronghold	asteroidal	deadweight	fieldpiece	inflexible	myological
subtrahend	auspicious	debonairly	fiftyfifty	inflexibly	mysterious
sweatshirt	austenitic	decemviral	fireblight	ingestible	mythiciser
sympathise	autarkical	deceptible	fireraiser	inglorious	Neapolitan
synanthous	avaricious	deductible	firstnight	ingratiate	negligible
tautophony	aviatrices	defeasible	flagitious	ingredient	negligibly
tenterhook	backslider	defensible	flashlight	inquisitor	neological
tetrachord	backstitch	deforciant	floodlight	insensible	newswriter
throughout	banderilla	denunciate	footbridge	insensibly	nightlight
throughput	Barmecidal	deodoriser	fortepiano	insentient	nonlogical
throughway	batholitic	deoxidiser	forthright	insobriety	nutritious
timberhead	belongings	depreciate	fortyniner	insouciant	objectival
toothshell	bidonville	dermatitis	franchiser	intangible	obsequious
transshape	biological	deshabille	freesoiler	intangibly	oftentimes
treadwheel	bipartisan	determined	frigorific	intertidal	omniscient
triphthong	birdspider	diabolical	fungicidal	intestinal	oratorical
triumphant	birthright	dichroitic	galvaniser	intrepidly	orological
tropophyte	botryoidal	didactical	geodetical	invincible	ostensible
twilighted	brakelight	didgeridoo	geological	invincibly	ostensibly
unblushing	branchiate	diffusible	geoponical	jackknives	outpatient
undershirt	brickfield	digestible	germicidal	jardiniere	overflight
undershoot	bronchiole	disbelieve	gerundival	jesuitical	overweight
undershrub	bronchitic	disclaimer	gingivitis	jinrikisha	ovipositor
unfaithful	bronchitis	discutient	girlfriend	juristical	paddyfield
untruthful	budgerigar	disenviron	Glagolitic	justiciary	palladious
unworthily	Caerphilly	disentitle	glassfibre	kinnikinic	palmatifid
veldschoen	calumniate	disenviron	goloptious	larvicidal	panopticon
vibraphone	calumnious	dishabille	goluptious	laryngitic	pantomimic
videophone	camerlingo	dispirited	gramicidin	laryngitis	papistical
virginhood	capricious	dispraiser	granadilla	lascivious	paraffinic
waterwheel	cartwright	dissatisfy	grandniece	lavalliere	parricidal
whaleshark	caryatides	dissilient	granulitic	lentigines	parsonical
wheelchair	cascarilla	dissimilar	greatniece	licentiate	participle
whitethorn	catechiser	dissociate	greenfinch	licentious	parturient
willowherb	catholicon	distrainer	gregarious	liquidiser	pathetical
woodenhead	catholicos	distrainor	grenadilla	liturgical	patriciate
worthwhile	cellulitis	dogmatical	guestnight	lockstitch	patricidal
abbreviate	censorious	dogmatiser	hairraiser	logistical	pearldiver
aboriginal	centesimal	draconites	handmaiden	longhaired	peccadillo
abstemious	centilitre	dramatical	hangglider	longprimer	pegmatitic
academical	chaplaincy	drawbridge	hardboiled	loquacious	pellucidly
accessible	childbirth	dumbwaiter	harmonical	loudhailer	percipient
accessibly	chimerical	duodecimal	harmonious	lubricious	perfidious
accredited	chinchilla	duodenitis	harmoniser	lugubrious	perfoliate
acoustical	chondritic	earthlight	haruspices	magnetiser	periclinal
adjectival	cicatrices	ecclesiast	headwaiter	magnifical	periodical
admissible	clovehitch	ecological	hectolitre	magnificat	perjurious
advertiser	coenobitic	economical	hermetical	maintainer	pernicious
afterbirth	cognominal	economiser	historical	majestical	pesticidal
afterlight	collegiate	ecumenical	hitchhiker	makeweight	phonolitic
agglutinin	comestible	egoistical	housewives	manzanilla	photolitho
alchemical	commodious	electrical	hybridiser	matricidal	phthisical
altarpiece	communique	elliptical	hypnotiser	maxilliped	piccalilli
amphibious	comparison	encyclical	hysterical	mechanical	piccaninny
amphimixes	compatible	endocrinal	illadvised	mendacious	pichiciago
amphimixis	compatibly	enthusiasm	immiscible	meningioma	pickaninny
anagogical	competitor	enthusiast	immiscibly	meningitis	pictorical

piledriver	Sanskritic	tidewaiter	rainmaking	breathless	demobilise
pilliwinks	satellitic	tollbridge	rollicking	breechless	demonology
pilotlight	scientific	torchlight	samarskite	breezeless	demoralise
pinnatifid	screenings	tracheitis	skyjacking	bridgeless	dendrology
pinstriped	seguidilla	tranquilly	spillikins	broadcloth	deontology
playwright	selfguided	tremolitic	unblinking	buttonless	depopulate
polyclinic	selfpoised	trifoliate	underskirt	calceolate	derailleur
pontifical	selfraised	trigeminal	unthinking	camouflage	devitalise
pontifices	semiotical	trioecious	unwrinkled	cancellate	devocalise
postexilic	sensitiser	triumviral	waterskier	cancelling	dextrality
potentiate	sequacious	trochoidal	wunderkind	cancellous	digitalise
potentilla	sermoniser	trouvaille	aardwolves	candyfloss	dinnerless
precarious	serradilla	tsarevitch	acarpelous	cannelloni	disability
precipitin	seventieth	tympanites	accomplice	cantillate	discipline
precocious	sexlimited	tympanitic	accomplish	capability	disincline
predacious	shenanigan	tympanitis	accumulate	capitalise	dispelling
prejudiced	shipwright	typewriter	acephalous	capitalism	disqualify
prelatical	shopsoiled	tyrannical	actinolite	capitalist	distilland
premarital	shortlived	umbellifer	adrenaline	Capitoline	distillate
premaxilla	signwriter	unAmerican	affability	capitulary	distillery
premedical	sillybilly	unbiblical	affectless	capitulate	distilling
premonitor	sincipital	uncritical	aircooling	caramelise	disutility
prescriber	sinusoidal	underlinen	alcoholise	cardialgia	ditriglyph
presidiary	skewbridge	underminer	alcoholism	cardiology	dovecolour
prevenient	slipstitch	undersized	ambivalent	carnallite	downfallen
prismoidal	soapboiler	ungracious	amiability	carpellary	drivelling
prizefight	sobersided	uninitiate	amygdaloid	carphology	driverless
proclaimer	sobersides	unmerciful	anchorless	catabolism	durability
prodigious	socialiser	unmortised	annihilate	catafalque	easterling
producible	softboiled	unrequited	anopheline	centillion	edentulous
proficient	solenoidal	unstrained	antebellum	centralise	effortless
progenitor	songwriter	uproarious	apostolate	centralism	Egyptology
prohibiter	spagyrical	urethritis	apparelled	centralist	emasculate
prohibitor	speedlimit	uxoricidal	armourless	centrality	embowelled
prolicidal	sphenoidal	valvulitis	arthralgia	cerebellum	embryology
pronominal	spheroidal	variolitic	arthralgic	chamaeleon	empanelled
propitiate	splendidly	vaudeville	articulate	chancellor	enamelling
propitious	stabiliser	verbaliser	asexuality	chandelier	enamellist
proscriber	steamtight	vermicidal	assemblage	changeless	enterolith
prosilient	steriliser	victimiser	assibilate	changeling	enthralled
prosodical	stillbirth	Victoriana	assimilate	channelise	entomology
provisions	stockpiler	victorious	audibility	channelled	enzymology
pugnacious	stockrider	visualiser	auriculate	chapfallen	ephorality
pulsatilla	stomatitis	vivandiere	Australian	chartulary	epicycloid
pulveriser	struthious	vulcaniser	autecology	chiselling	epistolary
puristical	subliminal	waffleiron	badderlock	Christlike	epithelial
quartzitic	submariner	wainwright	balneology	chronology	epithelium
quixotical	submediant	wanderings	barbellate	chrysolite	equability
rabbinical	suborbital	watertight	barrelling	cloverleaf	equivalent
rebellious	subordinal	whipstitch	batfowling	cnidoblast	erectility
receptible	subscriber	willynilly	battailous	codswallop	escapology
reconciler	subsidiary	willywilly	Beaujolais	coequality	eternalise
reconsider	sufficient	windshield	bedevilled	collarless	eternalist
reeligible	supergiant	wirehaired	bejewelled	colourless	ethicality
reflexible	supervisor	zabaglione	bemedalled	comicality	Eurodollar
rejoicings	suspicious	zoological	benevolent	compelling	evangelise
remarriage	suzerainty	bubblyjock	bestialise	conchology	evangelism
remissible	swanmaiden	crackajack	bestiality	controlled	evangelist
repatriate	syllogiser	lumberjack	bibliology	controller	everyplace
republican	symbolical	natterjack	bimetallic	copyholder	exobiology
resistible	symboliser	supplejack	binoculars	corbelling	factualism
resorcinol	symposiast	bookmaking	bioecology	cordiality	factualist
restrained	synoecious	cheapskate	bipetalous	cordillera	factuality
restrainer	synoptical	diesinking	birthplace	councillor	fatherland
reversible	syphilitic	frolicking	bitterling	councilman	fatherless
revertible	tablelinen	homemaking	bluecollar	counselled	fatherlike
rhetorical	tackdriver	jaywalking	bobbinlace	counsellor	fathomless
rhomboidal	Talmudical	jinricksha	bondholder	craniology	federalise
rhomboidei	tantaliser	Lamarckian	bookseller	craquelure	federalism
rhythmical	temporiser	Lamarckism	borderland	crenellate	federalist
ridgepiece	tendinitis	lovemaking	borderless	cryptology	feminality
ringtailed	tenebrific	mosaicking	borderline	cudgelling	fetterlock
robustious	tenebrious	nitpicking		curability	fibreglass
rockabilly	testflight	peacockery	Boswellian	decimalise	fibrillary
rottweiler	theatrical	peacockish	Boswellise	decimalism	fibrillate
roughrider	theistical	pernickety	Boswellism	decivilise	fibrillose
sabbatical	theurgical	physicking	bottomless	deescalate	fieldglass
sacrificer	thinkpiece	picnicking	brachylogy	delocalise	fingerless
salubrious	threepiece	prepackage	brakeblock	deltiology	fingerling

finicality	hoverplane	marshalled	osteoblast	recitalist	smokeplant
firepolicy	humourless	marshaller	osteoclast	refuelling	snivelling
firstclass	hyaloplasm	marshalsea	outfielder	regardless	softbilled
flabellate	hydraulics	martialism	painkiller	relentless	solubilise
flagellant	hydroplane	marvelling	palaeolith	remediless	solubility
flagellate	iconoclasm	marvellous	palatalise	remodelled	somatology
flannelled	ignobility	masterless	palynology	repopulate	spathulate
flashflood	ilangilang	maximalist	paniculate	resemblant	spatiality
fledgeling	illegalise	meadowland	papyrology	resistless	specialise
flightless	illegality	meadowlark	parabolise	resultless	specialism
floatplane	imbecilely	metabolise	paraboloid	reticulate	specialist
flocculate	imbecility	metabolism	paraselene	revitalise	speciality
flocculent	immaculacy	metabolite	parcelling	revivalism	speciology
floorcloth	immaculate	metagalaxy	partiality	revivalist	speechless
flosculous	immobilise	meticulous	pastellist	rewardless	speleology
flowerless	immobility	Michaelmas	patriality	ricinoleic	sperrylite
footballer	immoralist	microcline	patrolling	ridiculous	spherulite
foreteller	immorality	mineralise	pediculate	risibility	spiderline
fosterling	immunology	mineralogy	pediculous	rollcollar	spiralling
fraudulent	impanelled	minimalism	pencilling	ropewalker	spiritless
freeholder	imperilled	minimalist	penicillin	rosaniline	spongology
friability	incivility	miraculous	pennillion	rosemallow	springless
friendless	incomplete	miscellany	perihelion	rudderless	springlike
friendlily	indocility	mongrelise	persiflage	rupicoline	sprinkling
fringeless	inequality	mongrelism	petroglyph	rupicolous	squireling
fritillary	infidelity	monopolise	photoflood	sacroiliac	stadholder
frivolling	initialise	monopolist	phrenology	sailorless	stanchless
fulfilling	initialled	monovalent	physiology	salability	staphyline
funnelling	inosculate	morphology	picketline	salesclerk	starveling
fusibility	instilling	motherland	pilgarlick	salicylate	staurolite
futureless	insufflate	motherless	pillowlace	salmonleap	stencilled
futurology	interplant	motionless	pincerlike	saltcellar	stenciller
galloglass	interplead	motiveless	pistillary	sanderling	stipellate
gambolling	invigilate	mousseline	pistillate	sarcoplasm	stoneblind
gastrology	irresolute	movability	pistolling	satanology	stopvolley
generalise	Ishmaelite	multiplier	pitchblack	savourless	stormcloud
generalist	journalese	musicality	plasmolyse	saxicoline	streamless
generality	journalise	musicology	playfellow	saxicolous	streamline
geniculate	journalism	muskmallow	pliability	scaffolder	stressless
genteelism	journalist	mutability	ploughland	scandalise	stridulant
Ghibelline	juvenility	nailpolish	pogonology	scandalous	stridulate
glaciology	karyoplasm	nationless	pointblank	scatheless	stridulous
glasscloth	katabolism	naturalise	polyvalent	screwplate	stringless
glossology	kennelling	naturalism	portcullis	scribbling	subnuclear
glottology	kimberlite	naturalist	postbellum	scrofulous	subsellium
gooseflesh	ladykiller	nephralgia	postillion	scrupulous	summerlike
gradualism	lanceolate	nephrology	potability	scurrility	summitless
gradualist	landholder	neuroplasm	potamology	scurrilous	sunparlour
graphology	laterality	neutralise	potbellied	scutellate	superaltar
graptolite	laurelling	neutralism	pozzuolana	seamanlike	supperless
grasscloth	leaderless	neutralist	preexilian	searchless	surrealism
greencloth	ledgerline	neutrality	prevailing	seismology	surrealist
groundless	legibility	nickelling	priestling	selenology	swashplate
groundling	lepidolite	nidicolous	princeling	selfcolour	sweatgland
grovelling	letterless	nightglass	profitless	selfruling	swivelling
halfdollar	leucoplast	nominalism	propellant	selfwilled	symphylous
halfnelson	lexicology	nominalist	propellent	semeiology	synecology
halfvolley	liberalise	nonchalant	propelling	sensualise	systemless
hammerless	liberalism	nonnuclear	proteolyse	sensualism	tablecloth
hammerlock	liberalist	nonviolent	prothallia	sensualist	talentless
handgallop	liberality	notability	prothallus	sensuality	taleteller
handselled	literalise	novaculite	protoplasm	septillion	tamability
hanselling	literalism	numberless	protoplast	sexivalent	tasselling
hardbilled	literalist	numerology	proudflesh	sextillion	taxability
haustellum	literality	nuptiality	psephology	shadowless	teatrolley
hawserlaid	lithoglyph	nympholept	psychology	sheathless	technology
heartblock	litterlout	objectless	puberulent	shibboleth	tenability
heartblood	logicality	obnubilate	pummelling	shieldless	tenantless
heortology	logrolling	oceanology	punctulate	shillelagh	tenderloin
hepatology	lowerclass	odontalgia	pyretology	shopwalker	tendrillar
heterology	lustreless	odontology	pyrogallol	shovelling	tendrilled
hieroglyph	lyophilise	oligoclase	quarrelled	shrivelled	teratology
hinterland	maidenlike	oneirology	quarreller	shroudlaid	terneplate
honourless	malacology	operculate	quenchless	siderolite	terreplein
horsecloth	malevolent	ophthalmia	radicalise	signalling	terrorless
horseflesh	manifoldly	ophthalmic	radicalism	Singhalese	tessellate
hostelling	manipulate	opposeless	ratability	sleeveless	textualist
houselling	maquillage	optimalise	razorblade	sleevelink	themselves
houseplant	marrowless	orthoclase	reasonless	sleeveless	theodolite

thirdclass	wonderland	compliment	galliambic	preferment	acrogenous
thriftless	worldclass	compromise	geochemist	prepayment	activeness
throneless	ylangylang	conferment	gladsomely	programmer	adherently
timberline	yokefellow	confirmand	government	prostomial	adjacently
timbrology	yourselves	conformism	graphemics	prostomium	admiringly
tinselling	zoophilous	conformist	groundmass	punishment	adroitness
tirailleur	Abrahamman	conformity	gruesomely	puzzlement	aeruginous
tomfoolery	abridgment	consummate	habiliment	quadrumana	afferently
tongueless	acoelomate	couplement	handsomely	quadrumane	affluently
topazolite	adjudgment	custommade	harassment	quadrumvir	aficionado
topgallant	adjustment	dazzlement	hithermost	rabblement	Africander
topicality	Adullamite	debasement	homecoming	ravishment	Africanise
tortellini	advisement	debatement	homogamous	rearmament	Africanism
tourbillon	aeronomist	decampment	homonymous	reassemble	Africanist
tourmaline	affeerment	defacement	hornrimmed	reassembly	Afrikander
toxicology	afterimage	defilement	hypolimnia	recoupment	alarmingly
trammelled	agronomist	definement	immurement	refinement	Albigenses
trampoline	alightment	defrayment	impairment	refundment	albuminoid
trancelike	allogamous	denouement	impalement	regalement	albuminous
transplant	allurement	department	impartment	reichsmark	alkalinity
travelling	altazimuth	deployment	impediment	resentment	allrounder
trichology	altocumuli	deportment	impugnment	reshipment	almacanter
tricyclist	amalgamate	derailment	incasement	retirement	almucanter
triskelion	ambushment	designment	incitement	revealment	amanuenses
trivialise	amercement	desquamate	indictment	revilement	amanuensis
trivialism	anadromous	detachment	inditement	ripplemark	annoyingly
triviality	anastomose	detainment	inducement	sanctimony	antagonise
troctolite	anointment	devotement	instalment	schoolmaam	antagonism
trophology	antinomian	diastemata	instrument	schoolmarm	antagonist
trowelling	antiSemite	dichromate	integument	schoolmate	antependia
tubicolous	antonymous	discommend	intendment	seaanemone	antepenult
tunnelling	arrestment	discommode	internment	secernment	antimonial
typicality	arthromere	disharmony	investment	secondment	antimonite
umbrellaed	assessment	disownment	iridosmine	securement	aplacental
unavailing	assignment	divebomber	jackhammer	seducement	Apollinian
undercliff	assoilment	divestment	kerseymere	settlement	Apollonian
underfloor	assortment	drophammer	lachrymose	showjumper	apparently
underglaze	attachment	eartrumpet	lattermost	solacement	aquilinity
underslung	attainment	effacement	lavishment	stablemate	argumentum
unequalled	attornment	embalmment	legitimacy	stalagmite	arrogantly
unexcelled	attunement	embankment	legitimate	sterigmata	artfulness
unfamiliar	autogamous	embarkment	legitimise	supplement	arytaenoid
unicyclist	autoimmune	embodiment	legitimism	synonymist	astuteness
unlabelled	autonomist	embossment	legitimist	synonymity	auctioneer
unmorality	autonomous	employment	lonesomely	synonymous	augustness
unravelled	avouchment	encampment	lymphomata	syntagmata	autogenous
unresolved	babblement	encasement	macadamise	tailormade	averseness
unrivalled	backgammon	encashment	management	tanglement	Babylonian
unsettling	bafflement	encystment	mastermind	tapotement	bacchantes
upperclass	banishment	endearment	medicament	taxonomist	bacchantic
urbanology	battlement	endogamous	middlemost	telecamera	backhanded
vesiculate	bedchamber	enfacement	misogamist	teratomata	backhander
victualled	bemusement	engagement	mizzenmast	threadmark	bafflingly
victualler	Benthamism	engulfment	monogamist	tilthammer	ballooning
virtuality	Benthamite	enjambment	monogamous	tiresomely	balloonist
virtueless	bestowment	enjoinment	morphemics	toilsomely	barrenness
visibility	betterment	enlacement	Mussulmans	tournament	bassoonist
visionless	bichromate	enlistment	nethermost	triphammer	becomingly
vitriolise	biochemist	enmeshment	nonpayment	unassuming	bellringer
vocabulary	blackamoor	enrichment	nonswimmer	unbecoming	besprinkle
volatilise	blacksmith	enrigiment	obtainment	uniformity	bitchiness
volatility	blastemata	entailment	ordainment	unscramble	bitterness
volubility	blastomere	enticement	overcommit	Vietnamese	bituminise
waistcloth	blazonment	entombment	pantrymaid	whitesmith	bituminous
wanderlust	bottommost	entrapment	parliament	wilderment	bleariness
wassailing	bressummer	epidermoid	paronymous	windjammer	bleatingly
watchglass	bridesmaid	equanimity	peppermill	wolframite	blindingly
waterclock	buttermilk	ergonomics	peppermint	wonderment	blitheness
waterflood	cajolement	ergonomist	performing	Wykehamist	bloodiness
waterglass	cantonment	escapement	phillumeny	abdominous	bluebonnet
weaponless	centromere	escarpment	pilgrimage	abducentes	bluepencil
weedkiller	chainsmoke	evolvement	polygamist	aberrantly	bluetongue
weightless	charismata	excitement	polygamous	abiogenist	bluishness
werewolves	choriambic	experiment	polynomial	abjectness	blurringly
windowless	cinecamera	famishment	polysemous	abruptness	blushingly
wingcollar	clawhammer	fearsomely	posthumous	absurdness	bookbinder
wirepuller	coffeemill	fingermark	postliminy	abundantly	bottleneck
wirewalker	commitment	folkmemory	preachment	accidental	bouncingly
withholder	complement	fulfilment	preadamite	accusingly	bourbonism

bourbonist	compounder	dressiness	foreignism	heroicness	Kantianism	
boyishness	concerning	droopingly	forerunner	hesitantly	keratinise	
Brahmanism	concinnity	drowsiness	fourhanded	heteronomy	keratinous	
Brahminism	confounded	drudgingly	fragmental	highbinder	kindliness	
braininess	conjointly	dumfounder	fragrantly	highhanded	kingliness	
brassiness	constantan	earthiness	fraternise	highlander	knickknack	
brawniness	Constantia	earwitness	fraternity	highminded	knockkneed	
brazenness	constantly	ectogenous	freakiness	hirudinean	knottiness	
breeziness	coordinate	edibleness	freehanded	hoarseness	ladyfinger	
brightness	copartnery	effeminacy	freelancer	hollowness	lampoonery	
brokenness	coralsnake	effeminate	Frenchness	homeliness	lampoonist	
broodiness	coromandel	effeteness	frequenter	homogenise	landhunger	
broodingly	Corybantes	elatedness	frequently	homogenous	landowning	
Buchmanism	corybantic	Eleusinian	frigidness	hookedness	lanternfly	
Buchmanite	costliness	eloquently	frilliness	horizontal	lanthanide	
buffoonery	covalently	emarginate	friskiness	hornedness	lanuginose	
bumblingly	covenanted	embryonate	frizziness	horridness	lanuginous	
bumpkinish	covenantee	endogenous	frostiness	humaneness	latifundia	
bunglingly	covenanter	enduringly	frothiness	humbleness	laughingly	
bushranger	covenantor	engagingly	frowningly	hungriness	lavishness	
bustlingly	covetingly	enticingly	fuliginous	hypogynous	lawfulness	
cachinnate	coweringly	entireness	fulllength	hypotenuse	lawntennis	
cackhanded	craftiness	epilimnion	fumblingly	ignorantly	leadenness	
cacogenics	cragginess	eudemonism	gadolinite	illuminant	lectionary	
cajolingly	crankiness	eudemonist	gadolinium	illuminate	lefthanded	
calamander	cravenness	evenhanded	gadrooning	illuminati	lefthander	
calcsinter	creaminess	evilminded	gametangia	illuminism	leguminous	
Caledonian	creatinine	excitingly	gangrenous	illuminist	lesbianism	
caliginous	creepiness	expertness	garishness	imminently	libidinous	
callowness	crescentic	exultantly	gastronome	impishness	lieutenant	
candidness	crossindex	exultingly	gastronomy	imposingly	ligamental	
carabineer	crustiness	exurbanite	gaucheness	impotently	lightingup	
carabinier	cryogenics	eyewitness	gelatinise	impregnant	likeliness	
caravaneer	cursedness	facileness	gelatinous	impregnate	likeminded	
caravanned	cussedness	fairminded	genialness	impudently	limpidness	
caravanner	daintiness	fallowness	gentleness	impureness	lionhunter	
carbonnade	damagingly	famousness	gladhander	incidental	liquidness	
carmagnole	dauphiness	faultiness	glancingly	indecently	lissomness	
carotenoid	dazzlingly	feebleness	glassiness	indefinite	Lithuanian	
carotinoid	deadliness	fellmonger	glauconite	indigenous	littleness	
carryingon	decadently	femaleness	gloominess	indolently	liveliness	
cartoonist	decolonise	femininely	glossiness	ingeminate	loneliness	
casualness	defeminise	femininity	gluttonise	inherently	longwinded	
cautionary	dehumanise	fervidness	gluttonous	inhumanely	lordliness	
centennial	delaminate	fescennine	goaltender	inhumanity	loveliness	
ceremonial	delphinium	festoonery	goldenness	inkslinger	lovingness	
ceruminous	delphinoid	fetchingly	goodliness	innateness	luculently	
cessionary	demureness	fickleness	granduncle	innocently	Lusitanian	
challenger	denominate	fictioneer	graspingly	innominate	mainlander	
charmingly	deracinate	fictionist	grasssnake	inordinate	manchineel	
chasteness	deridingly	fierceness	greasiness	insaneness	manfulness	
chattiness	desalinate	filthiness	greatuncle	inseminate	Marcionite	
chauvinism	devoutness	fingernail	greediness	insolently	marshiness	
chauvinist	diaphanous	finiteness	grindingly	inspanning	matureness	
cheekiness	dictionary	fishmonger	grisliness	intactness	mavourneen	
cheeriness	diligently	fitfulness	grittiness	intentness	meagreness	
cheesiness	diluteness	fivefinger	grogginess	inurbanity	measliness	
chersonese	directness	flabbiness	growlingly	invaginate	mellowness	
chickenpox	discerning	flagrantly	grubbiness	invitingly	membranous	
chiffonier	disconnect	flashiness	grudgingly	inwardness	memorandum	
chilliness	discounter	fleeringly	grumpiness	ironhanded	menacingly	
chimpanzee	disdainful	fleetingly	guiltiness	ironmonger	messianism	
chlorinate	diseconomy	fleshiness	gunrunning	italianate	metacentre	
choiceness	disfurnish	flimsiness	gunslinger	italianise	middlingly	
chubbiness	disgruntle	flintiness	halflength	Italianism	midmorning	
Ciceronian	disjointed	flippantly	halogenate	jacobinise	mightiness	
cinchonine	dismalness	floatingly	halogenous	Jacobinism	migrainous	
clamminess	distringas	floppiness	handedness	jaggedness	militantly	
claspknife	divineness	floridness	hardhanded	jauntiness	millennial	
cleverness	documental	fluffiness	hauntingly	jejuneness	millennium	
cloudiness	doggedness	fluorinate	headhunter	Jewishness	mindedness	
clumsiness	dogstongue	fluxionary	heartiness	jobbernowl	minuteness	
coalbunker	dominantly	foetidness	heathendom	jocoseness	mischanter	
coarseness	doubleness	folksiness	heathenise	Johnsonese	misjoinder	
coathanger	doubtingly	folksinger	heathenish	johnsonian	misogynist	
coeternity	dragonnade	footcandle	heathenism	joyfulness	misogynous	
coherently	drawlingly	foraminous	Heliconian	joyousness	missionary	
comeliness	dreaminess	forefinger	hellbender	jubilantly	missioner	
commonness	dreariness	forehanded	heparinise	juggernaut	modernness	

```
modishness  picayunish  relevantly  simpleness  sugariness  ungrounded
monogenism  piercingly  remissness  sinfulness  sullenness  unholiness
monogynian  placidness  remoteness  singleness  sulphonate  uniqueness
monogynous  plangently  rencounter  skimpiness  sultriness  unjustness
monomaniac  pleadingly  reorganise  skinniness  superbness  unkindness
monotonous  pleasantly  resonantly  slanginess  supineness  unlikeness
monsignori  pleasantry  resupinate  slantingly  supplanter  unmeetness
Montagnard  pleasingly  reticently  sleaziness  suppleness  unripeness
monumental  pliantness  retiringly  sleepiness  sustaining  unruliness
mopishness  ploddingly  retraining  slightness  sweatiness  untidiness
morbidness  pluckiness  reunionism  sloppiness  sweepingly  unwariness
moroseness  polemonium  reunionist  smelliness  sweetening  uppishness
morphinism  politeness  reverencer  smoothness  swimmingly  upwardness
mossbunker  polygenism  reverently  smudginess  swingingly  usefulness
mouldiness  polygenist  rightangle  smuttiness  symphonion  utopianism
mudslinger  polygenous  ringfinger  sneakiness  symphonist  vanadinite
mulishness  polygynous  roadrunner  sneakingly  takingness  Vaticanism
narrowness  Pomeranian  robustness  sneeringly  taperingly  Vaticanist
nativeness  porousness  rontgenise  sniffiness  tauntingly  vaticinate
newsmonger  portliness  rootedness  snootiness  tawdriness  vehemently
newsvendor  praemunire  ropedancer  snubbingly  taxidancer  velutinous
nicotinism  prancingly  rottenness  snuffiness  teaplanter  venialness
nimbleness  preeminent  rubberneck  soddenness  tegumental  veterinary
nondrinker  prefrontal  rubiginous  softfinned  temptingly  viceconsul
nonjoinder  pregnantly  rudimental  solemnness  tenderness  viewfinder
nucleonics  presignify  ruefulness  sombreness  tenemental  vigilantly
oafishness  pressingly  ruffianism  soothingly  tetchiness  villainage
obediently  prettiness  ruggedness  Sorbonnist  theogonist  villainess
oblateness  prissiness  ruminantly  sordidness  thereanent  villainous
obligingly  profoundly  rumrunning  soundingly  thereunder  villeinage
obtuseness  promptness  Russianise  spankingly  thickening  viraginous
occidental  pronounced  sacredness  sparseness  thinkingly  virulently
odiousness  pronouncer  salamander  speediness  thorniness  viscountcy
oecumenism  properness  sallowness  sponginess  thousandth  vitaminise
oleaginous  propionate  sanguinary  spookiness  timeliness  voluminous
omnigenous  propounder  sanguinely  sportiness  toffeenose  wantonness
oncogenous  proscenium  sanguinity  sportingly  tolerantly  wateriness
opaqueness  proteinous  sashwindow  spottiness  toothiness  wavelength
openhanded  pruriently  savageness  spruceness  torpidness  waveringly
openminded  puissantly  scantiness  spunkiness  torridness  weakliness
opinionist  purblindly  scarceness  squareness  touchiness  weakminded
ornamental  puritanise  scathingly  stableness  touchingly  westernise
ornateness  puritanism  scattiness  stagnantly  towardness  wharfinger
orneriness  purulently  Scillonian  stanchness  toweringly  wheeziness
otioseness  putridness  scoffingly  starriness  trappiness  WhitMonday
outgunning  pyracantha  scorzonera  stationary  trashiness  WhitSunday
outrunning  pyrogenous  scrutineer  stationery  treasonous  wickedness
outswinger  pyromaniac  scrutinise  steadiness  trendiness  wilderness
overhanded  pyromantic  scurviness  steaminess  trepanning  wilfulness
overlander  pyroxenite  secureness  steeliness  trichinise  wintriness
overmanned  Pyrrhonian  sedateness  stephanite  trichinous  witchingly
overmantel  Pyrrhonism  seemliness  stickiness  trickiness  wobbliness
overwinter  Pyrrhonist  selectness  stiffening  triclinium  woefulness
owlishness  quadrangle  selfbinder  stiflingly  triflingly  wontedness
palagonite  quadrantal  selfdenial  stinginess  triternate  woodenness
palatinate  quadrennia  semiannual  stingingly  trochanter  woodlander
palisander  quaintness  semilunate  stinkingly  trombonist  woolliness
pallidness  quarrender  sentiently  stockiness  trustiness  worthiness
PalmSunday  quaternary  septennial  stodginess  trustingly  wrathiness
paltriness  quaternate  septennium  stolidness  tufthunter  yearningly
Panamanian  quaternion  sereneness  stonesnipe  tuitionary  yeastiness
paperknife  quaternity  sergeantcy  storminess  turbidness  yellowness
pasquinade  queasiness  serjeantcy  straitness  turgidness  yieldingly
passionary  quirkiness  serotinous  stramonium  turtleneck  aboveboard
passionate  Rachmanism  severeness  strictness  twelvenote  accustomed
Passionist  rackrenter  sexagenary  stridently  Tyrrhenian  acrophobia
patchiness  raggedness  shabbiness  strikingly  unaccented  additional
pathfinder  rakishness  shagginess  Stroganoff  unattended  aerobiosis
pedimental  ramblingly  shiftiness  strychnine  unbalanced  aerobiotic
pedimented  rancidness  shockingly  strychnism  undefended  aerophobia
penitently  randomness  shoddiness  stubbiness  undefended  aetiologic
pensionary  recentness  shopwindow  stuffiness  unendingly  allophonic
perigynous  recolonise  shortening  stumpiness  unerringly  allotropic
peritoneal  recreantly  showwindow  stunningly  unevenness  amphigouri
peritoneum  redolently  shrewdness  stupidness  unfadingly  anastrophe
periwinkle  referendum  shrillness  sturdiness  unfairness  anchylosis
petiteness  regimental  sickliness  subdeanery  unfeminine  anchylotic
petulantly  rejuvenate  sidewinder  subtleness  unfriended  anteriorly
pheasantry  rejuvenise  silentness  suddenness  unfriendly  antibiosis
```

antibiotic	disembosom	holusbolus	occasional	saleswoman	travelogue
antiphonal	disembowel	homophonic	oceangoing	salicional	treadboard
antiproton	divisional	horoscopic	ophiologic	scaleboard	trichroism
apochromat	drafthorse	horsecoper	orthodoxly	scaramouch	trichromat
apostrophe	dreamworld	horsepower	orthogonal	scoreboard	trillionth
apotheoses	earthbound	horsewoman	otherworld	Scotswoman	tropaeolum
apotheosis	ecchymosis	hotblooded	otterboard	scriptoria	tropologic
arteriolar	ecchymotic	hotchpotch	overabound	seethrough	ulteriorly
asbestosis	electronic	housebound	overblouse	selfprofit	ultrasonic
astrologer	emblazoner	hydrologic	overcooked	semichorus	ultrasound
astrologic	emblazonry	hyperbolae	overground	seriocomic	unbuttoned
astronomer	embonpoint	hyperbolas	overgrowth	servomotor	uncommonly
astronomic	emeryboard	hyperbolic	overlooker	sharpnosed	uncustomed
asymptotic	enantiosis	hypergolic	paedagogic	sheeplouse	undercover
ateleiosis	endoscopic	hypersonic	paedogogue	shellmound	underworld
autoerotic	endosmosis	hypnagogic	parabiosis	shipbroker	uneconomic
azeotropic	endosmotic	ichthyosis	parabiotic	shirehorse	unemployed
backblocks	enharmonic	ideational	paragnosis	shrewmouse	unexplored
background	epistrophe	illusional	paratroops	sialagogic	unhallowed
ballflower	equational	impersonal	pasteboard	sialagogue	unhistoric
barcarolle	escallonia	indisposed	pathologic	sitophobia	unimproved
barefooted	escharotic	inferiorly	patrilocal	sixshooter	unorthodox
bargeboard	escritoire	infrasonic	pawnbroker	skateboard	unprovoked
barracouta	ethnologic	inharmonic	peashooter	slowfooted	unschooled
bawdyhouse	eucaryotic	interiorly	pedalpoint	smartmoney	unseasoned
belladonna	extemporal	interloper	pennyroyal	smokehouse	venational
bellflower	exteriorly	internodal	pennyworth	snowgrouse	vocational
beribboned	fairground	interposal	pentagonal	snowplough	volitional
blackboard	fairspoken	interposer	pentatomic	sociologic	wallflower
blockboard	fibreboard	intervolve	pentatonic	softspoken	watchtower
blockhouse	fibrinogen	interwound	perchloric	somniloquy	waterborne
bloodhound	fieldmouse	interwoven	periscopic	sophomoric	waterpower
bloodmoney	fixedpoint	interzonal	petitioner	soundboard	waterworks
bobbysocks	flapdoodle	Irishwoman	phanerogam	southbound	wellspoken
bobbysoxer	flashboard	irrational	pheromonal	spacewoman	Welshwoman
brachiopod	flashpoint	isentropic	philologen	spellbound	wheelhorse
brainpower	flatfooted	isochronal	philopoena	stagecoach	wheelhouse
brantgoose	fleshwound	knifeboard	philosophe	standpoint	whorehouse
breadboard	floatboard	lederhosen	philosophy	steakhouse	windflower
breakpoint	floorboard	lighthouse	phonologic	steelworks	winegrower
brentgoose	foamflower	limitrophe	phosphoric	stomatopod	wingfooted
byssinosis	foreground	lithologic	phosphorus	stoneborer	wongawonga
cantaloupe	fourfooted	loosecover	phytotoxic	storehouse	woolgrower
carcinogen	fractional	loxodromic	pianoforte	stormbound	workpeople
carcinosis	freebooter	Lysenkoism	piecegoods	strawboard	wraparound
cellulosic	freedwoman	madreporic	pilothouse	sugarhouse	wrongdoing
cephalopod	freespoken	malapropos	planktonic	superiorly	xenophobia
chairwoman	frictional	manorhouse	plantlouse	supernovae	xylophonic
chalkboard	functional	markswoman	playground	superpower	yarborough
changeover	ganglionic	matchboard	pollenosis	supersonic	Aethiopian
checkpoint	gasteropod	megascopic	polyphonic	supertonic	allpurpose
chessboard	glasshouse	meridional	polyploidy	surefooted	ampelopsis
clubfooted	glassworks	mesothorax	positional	switchover	anaglyphic
coachhouse	goldilocks	metaphoric	powerhouse	synchronal	anamorphic
cockalorum	goodlooker	metathorax	presbyopia	synchronic	anatropous
cornflower	goodygoody	metronomic	presbyopic	synecdoche	angiosperm
cornucopia	grassroots	metropolis	protanopic	synostosis	anthropoid
corroboree	GrecoRoman	monophonic	punchboard	tantamount	anticipant
cosmogonic	greenhouse	moonflower	pycnogonid	teleologic	anticipate
cosmopolis	guardhouse	mouldboard	pyrophoric	telephoner	antisepsis
courthouse	guesthouse	multiloquy	questioner	telephonic	antiseptic
crematoria	gymnosophy	multipolar	radiologic	telescopic	apocarpous
crossbones	gyrational	multivocal	radiosonde	terracotta	apocryphal
crossroads	gyroscopic	mystagogic	reciprocal	tetragonal	apotropaic
cryoscopic	haematosis	mystagogue	redblooded	tetramorph	bankruptcy
decompound	hagiologic	mythologer	rediscover	tetrapolis	beekeeping
deepfrozen	headphones	mythologic	relational	theophoric	bibliopegy
deeprooted	henceforth	mythopoeia	repertoire	thermionic	bibliophil
delusional	heptagonal	mythopoeic	revisional	thillhorse	bibliopole
dermatogen	heptatonic	necropolis	rheotropic	thromboses	bibliopoly
devotional	hereabouts	neurotoxin	rhizomorph	thrombosis	biographer
diachronic	heroicomic	noblewoman	riverhorse	thrombotic	biographic
diarrhoeal	histologic	northbound	rotational	ticpolonga	biomorphic
diarrhoeic	histrionic	nosophobia	roughhouse	townswoman	blastopore
diplodocus	hobbyhorse	nostologic	roundhouse	toxiphobia	bridlepath
directoire	hocuspocus	notchboard	runthrough	tractional	camelopard
disappoint	hodgepodge	nutational	sabretooth	tragicomic	cataleptic
discobolus	hoitytoity	nyctalopia	sacerdotal	transposal	clodhopper
disembogue	hokeypokey	nyctalopic	safeblower	transposer	closetplay

```
comicopera principate ancestress clangorous euhemerist hippodrome
constipate principial anchorring cockatrice eviscerate hippogriff
contraprop principium anemograph cocksurely exaggerate hippogryph
correspond principled angularity commonroom exasperate hipsterism
cuckoopint procrypsis anisotropy compatriot exenterate holophrase
descriptor procryptic annularity concurrent exhilarant homocercal
diagraphic protreptic antemortem concurring exhilarate honorarium
diatropism psychopath Antichrist conferring exothermal hourcircle
discompose quadruplet antiheroic coniferous exothermic housecraft
discrepant quadruplex aquafortis consecrate exprobrate houseproud
disrespect quadrupole aquamarine conspiracy exulcerate housetrain
doublepark quintuplet aquiferous conspirant faceharden hovertrain
dysgraphia rattlepate araucarian contrarily featherbed hygrograph
dystrophic retrospect architrave cordierite feathering hypocorism
elecampane rinderpest armigerous couchgrass fenestrate hypodermal
elevenplus rockhopper asseverate counteract firescreen hypodermic
emancipate roselipped asynchrony crackbrain fishcarver hypodermis
emancipist sandhopper auditorial creaturely flameproof idolatress
endstopped screenplay auditorium crispbread flattering idolatrous
enwrapping seaserpent auriferous crisscross flavourful illiteracy
eosinophil skijumping autostrada crossbreed flavouring illiterate
epigrapher snowcapped autostrade crossgrain fleacircus illstarred
epigraphic spoilsport aventurine crosstrees fleamarket illusorily
episcopacy stereopsis backstroke curatorial folklorist illustrate
episcopate stirrupcup backwardly cyclograph footwarmer immaterial
Esculapian swanupping balustrade cylindroid forwearied immaturely
eucalyptol swarmspore barratrous cytochrome founderous immaturity
eucalyptus syncarpous beechdrops decelerate Fourierism immemorial
fingerpost tablespoon beefburger Decembrist fourstroke immoderacy
flightpath theosopher belletrist decolorant freemartin immoderate
Francophil thermophil benzpyrene decolorise fruitarian impoverish
frangipane thermopile bestirring decompress gaillardia inaccuracy
frangipani thornapple bighearted deerforest garnierite inaccurate
froghopper tittupping biliverdin deflagrate geometrise inaugurate
geographer transeptal bimestrial degeneracy geothermal incinerate
geographic triglyphic biodegrade degenerate geothermic incoherent
geotropism trimorphic biometrics deliberate geriatrics indecorous
gobstopper trollopish bipolarity denaturant geriatrist indiscreet
groundplan tryptophan birdstrike dentifrice glauberite indiscrete
gymnosperm unexampled bitterroot depolarise glimmering industrial
gyrocopter unoccupied bladdernut derestrict glossarial inexpertly
hammerpond unscripted blepharism desiderata glossarist infiltrate
harelipped velocipede blistering desiderate Godfearing infusorial
helicopter wallpepper blithering diathermal goosegrass innumeracy
homoeopath wampumpeag blitzkrieg diathermic grammarian innumerate
interspace wanderplug bluethroat dictatress grangerise innumerous
introspect waterspout blusterous dilatorily grangerism insecurely
isomorphic windowpane boisterous diningroom grapefruit insecurity
kidnapping wiretapper bookmarker directress gressorial insularism
kriegspiel worshipful bootstraps disapprove groundrent insularity
leafhopper worshipped bowdlerise disastrous gynandrous intenerate
macrospore worshipper bowdlerism disbarring hairspring interbreed
maladapted zoomorphic breadcrumb discharger hairstreak intercross
metalepsis lambrequin breadfruit discourage hairstroke intergrade
microspore semiliquid bridegroom discourser hakenkreuz intertrigo
midshipman soubriquet bromegrass disembroil handbarrow interurban
morrispike tourniquet bunchgrass dishearten handicraft intolerant
mudskipper abacterial burglarise donnybrook handspring intraurban
naturopath accelerate cadaverous dorsigrade handworked inventress
nincompoop achondrite calyptrate downstream Hanoverian inveteracy
orangepeel acroterion camphorate downstroke harbourage inveterate
orographic acroterium cantatrice downwardly haustorium invigorate
orthoepist adrenergic caseharden drawstring headspring ironworker
outerspace adulterate caseworker dumbstruck headstream irreverent
overexpose adulteress cataphract duumvirate headstrong isometrics
overlapped adulterine categorise ectodermal heartbreak isopterous
oversupply adulterous catoptrics ectodermic heatstroke isosporous
overtopped aeolotropy centigrade edulcorate heavyarmed isothermal
paralipsis aftergrass certiorari electorate hectograph janitorial
philippina allegorise chamberpot endodermal heliograph jocularity
philippine allegorist chatterbox endodermis heliotrope keyboarder
phlogopite alliterate chaudfroid engineroom heliotropy knobkerrie
pigeonpair alloverish chauntress enterprise henharrier Krugerrand
pigeonpost altostrati childermas ephemerous henhearted lacustrine
playbyplay amateurish childproof episternum hexamerous laminarian
polydipsia amateurism chinagraph equatorial hierocracy landocracy
powderpuff ameliorate chivalrous equestrian hierograph languorous
predispose amphibrach chuckerout euhemerise highstrung lapidarian
presuppose            cinerarium euhemerism Hippocrene
```

```
lapidarist  nubiferous  praetorian  seignorial  sudatorium  watercress
lavatorial  nuciferous  preferring  selfmurder  sulphurate  waterfront
lebensraum  nucivorous  pressurise  selfparody  sulphurise  waterproof
lemongrass  obituarist  presternum  semestrial  sulphurous  weatherbox
lighterage  obliterate  proctorage  semicircle  superorder  weathering
lighterman  obstetrics  proctorial  seminarian  swaggering  weatherman
lightproof  oceanarium  proctorise  seminarist  sweetbread  wellspring
limeburner  ochlocracy  prosperity  sempstress  sweetbriar  wellturned
literarily  octamerous  prosperous  senatorial  sweetbrier  Wertherian
lithograph  octandrian  psalterium  senseorgan  sweltering  Wertherism
lithotrity  octandrous  puerperium  SerboCroat  swordcraft  westwardly
livingroom  octonarian  punchdrunk  shellproof  swordgrass  whispering
lobsterpot  oleiferous  pupilarity  shirtfront  symmetrise  widespread
lockerroom  omnivorous  pupiparous  shockproof  tabularise  windscreen
luciferase  opprobrium  purseproud  shoestring  taciturnly  wingspread
luciferous  ordinarily  quadrireme  shortbread  tambourine  wireworker
lukewarmly  osmeterium  quarterage  shortcrust  tapestried  witchcraft
lumberroom  outpouring  quarterday  shuttering  tardigrade  woodcarver
lutestring  overburden  quartering  sidestreet  taxidermal  woodturner
magistracy  overspread  quickgrass  sidestroke  taxidermic  woodworker
magistrate  overstride  quinacrine  siegetrain  tearjerker  woolsorter
mainspring  overstrung  radiograph  silkscreen  telpherage  zincograph
mainstream  overthrown  reafforest  similarity  tepidarium  zollverein
malapertly  overthrust  recuperate  sinecurism  thalecress  zwitterion
malodorous  packthread  redcurrant  sinecurist  thixotropy  zygomorphy
manageress  paintbrush  redecorate  sinistrous  thornproof  abscission
managerial  palindrome  redescribe  slanderous  thumbprint  abstersion
manicurist  panegyrise  regeneracy  slatternly  thunderbox  abstersive
manuscript  panegyrist  regenerate  slavetrade  thundering  abstrusely
marguerite  pantograph  registrant  slavocracy  thunderous  abstrusity
masquerade  papaverine  regularise  slenderise  timeserver  administer
matriarchy  papaverous  regularity  slipperily  tinctorial  aggression
mediatress  paranormal  remunerate  slipstream  tiringroom  aggressive
mediocrity  paraphrase  reredorter  sluggardly  toothbrush  airmanship
mesomerism  paraphrast  restaurant  slumberful  Tractarian  altruistic
mesomorphy  pasteurise  retrograde  slumberous  traitorous  anapaestic
metacarpal  pasteurism  retrogress  smattering  transcribe  anaplastic
metacarpus  patriarchy  revalorise  smockfrock  transcript  Andalusian
metamerism  pedalorgan  riproaring  smokedried  transgress  andalusite
metaphrase  pedestrian  ripsnorter  smokeproof  trawlerman  aneurismal
metatarsal  pedicurist  roadworthy  snobocracy  triandrous  aneurysmal
metatarsus  pellagrous  rockgarden  solidarism  trierarchy  annalistic
micrograph  peridermal  roistering  solidarist  triggerman  antecessor
militarily  permafrost  roisterous  solidarity  tumblerful  antimasque
militarise  perpetrate  roodscreen  solitarily  typescript  aphoristic
militarism  phenocryst  rubythroat  songstress  underbrush  apolaustic
militarist  phonograph  saccharate  songthrush  undercroft  appetising
millstream  photograph  saccharide  soundproof  underdress  arbalester
mimeograph  photoprint  saccharine  soundtrack  underproof  arbalister
minestrone  phototrope  saccharify  souterrain  undertrick  archaistic
mineworker  pictograph  saccharine  southerner  underwrite  archbishop
ministrant  piliferous  saccharoid  southernly  underwrote  aspidistra
mockheroic  pinecarpet  saccharose  spacecraft  undeserved  Athanasian
moisturise  pistonring  saliferous  speargrass  undesirous  authorship
monandrous  pitcherful  saltigrade  Spencerian  undeterred  bandmaster
monetarily  plagiarise  salutarily  Spenserian  ungenerous  barbershop
monetarism  plagiarism  sanatorium  sphalerite  uninformed  battleship
monetarist  plagiarist  sandmartin  spirograph  unremarked  beadleship
monitorial  planigraph  sanitarian  sponsorial  unreserved  billposter
monocarpic  pleochroic  sanitarily  spoondrift  untowardly  biophysics
monochrome  plunderage  sanitarium  spoonerism  unwavering  blithesome
moonstruck  plunderous  sapphirine  squirarchy  urochordal  blockishly
moratorium  plutocracy  satyagraha  stagecraft  urticarial  blottesque
Mousterian  pockmarked  sauerkraut  staggering  vectograph  bootlessly
mouthorgan  podiatrist  scansorial  stalwartly  vegetarian  bothersome
muciferous  polychrest  scapegrace  starstream  vertebrate  brandysnap
muliebrity  polychrome  scattergun  statecraft  vicegerent  bucketshop
mulligrubs  polymerise  scattering  stenograph  vinegarish  Buddhistic
natatorial  polymerism  schoolroom  stentorian  visitorial  burdensome
natatorium  polymerous  screwpress  stepparent  vituperate  bursarship
nephograph  pomiferous  sculptress  stertorous  viviparity  bushmaster
nettlerash  popularise  seamstress  stockproof  viviparous  cabalistic
newsworthy  popularity  secondrate  stonebrash  vociferant  cacomistle
nightdress  pornocracy  secularise  stonefruit  vociferate  carelessly
nitrogroup  postmortem  secularism  stormproof  vociferous  carnassial
nonferrous  postpartum  secularist  strongroom  voiceprint  Carthusian
nonstarter  postscript  secularity  stubbornly  vomitorium  censorship
northerner  pourparler  seductress  stylograph  waterbrash  centrosome
noteworthy  praetorial  seignorage  subaverage  watercraft  Charleston
```

```
cheapishly dispersoid inapposite organismal pugilistic symphyseal
childishly dispossess inartistic outgassing pursership symphysial
chiliastic dissension incrassate outmeasure pyrolusite synthesise
chromosome dissuasion indecision overmaster qualmishly synthesist
churlishly dissuasive indecisive painlessly quizmaster tactlessly
Circassian distensile indigested palimpsest readership taskmaster
clannishly distension Indonesian paradisaic rechristen tearlessly
clientship distressed ingression paradisean recklessly telecaster
clothesbag doctorship inspissate paradisiac rectorship television
clothespeg duniwassal interested paradisian regentship televisual
clothespin dwarfishly internship Parnassian regression tellership
clownishly dynamistic introrsely paroxysmal regressive thermistor
collarstud dysplastic ironmaster pastmaster repression thermostat
commissary dysprosium isoglossal pastorship repressive thievishly
commission editorship isoseismal pederastic requiescat thwartship
commissure embolismic jackassery peerlessly rescission ticklishly
compassion engrossing Japanesque penmanship rescissory timelessly
compasssaw enregister Jehovistic percussion responsive tirelessly
compensate epiblastic jingoistic percussive responsory titanesque
compressed erethismic Kafkaesque permission restlessly tonelessly
compressor essayistic kaisership permissive retrorsely tortuosity
compulsion eulogistic kingfisher perquisite ringmaster totemistic
compulsive euphuistic lacklustre persuasion Romanesque transistor
compulsory Eurovision languisher persuasive Romanistic trespasser
concession expressage leadership perversely ruthlessly trickishly
concessive expression leafinsect perversion sandcastle tuberosity
conclusion expressive legalistic perversity sargassoes tunelessly
conclusive expressway legateship perversive scholastic umpireship
conclusory eyeglasses lifelessly phantasise sciolistic unassisted
concussion factorship linguistic phantasmal seamanship uncloister
concussive fadelessly listlessly phantasmic seedvessel unctuosity
condensate fatalistic loungesuit phantastic selflessly undigested
condensery fathership lovelessly phantastry selfrising unfinished
confession fearlessly lumbersome phlogistic Sexagesima unforeseen
consensual fecklessly luminosity phlogiston sheepishly unhandsome
consulship fellowship malfeasant pianissimo shipmaster unionistic
conversant feverishly Malthusian picaresque shrewishly university
conversely fiendishly manifestly pillowslip siderostat unpleasant
conversion filibuster manifestos pistolshot silverside unpleasing
convulsant flawlessly marquisate pitilessly simplistic unstressed
convulsion forecaster martensite plaguesome skirmisher vanquisher
convulsive forecastle mastership pleonastic skittishly varicosity
cottonseed formlessly matronship plesiosaur sluggishly vernissage
cousinship fortissimi mayblossom plumassier sluttishly viewlessly
cowparsley fortissimo meddlesome pocketsize snappishly virtuosity
cradlesong fourposter medicaster polyhistor snickasnee vitalistic
crocoisite Franciscan megalosaur Polynesian snobbishly viziership
cuckoospit freakishly Melanesian populistic solecistic Waldensian
cuddlesome fricasseed melanistic possession soullessly wappenshaw
cuirassier friendship membership possessive sowthistle wardenship
cumbersome frolicsome mentorship possessory speciosity wellwisher
deaconship futuristic mettlesome postmaster spotlessly Winchester
declassify generosity mindlessly practising squaresail windowseat
declension geognostic mintmaster precession squireship windowshop
degressive geophysics mismeasure preciosity statuesque windowsill
depressant gingersnap misprision preclusion stepsister witnessbox
depression goldenseal mizzensail preclusive stochastic womanishly
depressive graciosity monkeysuit precursory strabismal wordlessly
descension groundsman moralistic prednisone strabismic workbasket
devilishly hardfisted mothership prehensile strabismus yardmaster
diagnostic harmlessly movelessly prehension strathspey abdication
dickcissel headmaster namelessly prepensely submersion aberration
Dickensian heavensent narcissism prepossess submission abjuration
digression Hebraistic narcissist pretension submissive abnegation
digressive hedonistic nativistic priggishly subversion abreaction
diminished heedlessly nebulosity princeship subversive abrogation
disclosure helplessly needlessly procession successful absolutely
discursive homoousian neoclassic profession succession absolution
discussant hopelessly neoplastic prognostic successive absolutism
discussion humanistic newscaster promissory sultanship absolutist
discussive humoresque nihilistic propensity sunglasses absolutory
dishwasher humoristic nonplussed prophesier suppressor absorption
dismission humoursome novelistic propulsion suretyship absorptive
dismissive hypabyssal nucleoside propulsive surplusage abstention
dispassion idealistic numerosity protensive surprising accountant
dispensary immodestly oligopsony protrusile suspension accounting
dispersant impression oppression protrusion suspensive accurately
dispersion impressive oppressive protrusive suspensoid accusation
dispersive impuissant optimistic puffpastry suspensory accusative
```

```
accusatory  autochthon  colportage  crispation  divinatory  extinction
acervation  automation  colporteur  crustation  dolomitise  extinctive
acquitting  automatise  combustion  cumulation  domination  extractant
acrobatics  automatism  combustive  cumulative  dominative  extraction
activation  automatist  comehither  cunctation  dosimetric  extractive
adamantine  automotive  commentary  cunctative  doubletalk  exultation
adaptation  aviculture  commentate  curvetting  doubletime  exuviation
adenectomy  babysitter  committing  cuttystool  dragontree  facilitate
adequately  backbiting  commixture  cyclostome  drysaltery  fantastico
adhibition  ballistics  compaction  cyclostyle  dubitation  fasciation
adjunction  baptistery  completely  datamation  dubitative  federation
adjunctive  barkentine  completion  deaeration  Eastertide  federative
adjuration  barometric  completive  debilitate  ebullition  felicitate
adjuratory  baronetage  complotted  decapitate  eczematous  felicitous
admiration  bedclothes  concentric  decimation  effrontery  felspathic
admonition  beforetime  conception  decoration  egocentric  fieldstone
admonitive  bellwether  conceptive  decorative  elementary  figuration
admonitory  bequeathal  conceptual  dedication  elongation  figurative
adsorption  bibliotics  concertina  dedicative  emaciation  filtration
adsorptive  bigmouthed  concertino  dedicatory  emendation  fishkettle
advocation  bilocation  concettism  defamation  emendatory  fleabitten
advocatory  birthstone  concoction  defamatory  emigration  flirtation
aerobatics  bissextile  concoctive  definitely  emigratory  floatation
aesthetics  blanketing  concretely  definition  emollition  floatstone
aesthetism  bloodstain  concretion  definitive  enchanting  florentine
affliction  bloodstock  concretise  definitude  energetics  floriation
afflictive  bloodstone  concretism  deflection  enervation  floristics
agapanthus  bluebottle  concretist  deflective  enervative  fluorotype
alienation  bolometric  conduction  delegation  englutting  fluviatile
alimentary  bonesetter  conductive  delicately  enigmatise  flyswatter
allegation  bottletree  confection  delightful  enigmatist  forefather
allocation  brainstorm  conflation  delimitate  enterotomy  foregather
allocution  breadstick  congestion  demolition  epicentral  forfeiture
allopathic  breadstuff  congestive  demonetise  epigastric  forgetting
alpenstock  brevetting  conjecture  denegation  epiglottal  formatting
alteration  brigantine  connection  denotation  epiglottic  fortuitism
alterative  broomstick  connective  denotative  epiglottis  fortuitist
altogether  brownstone  conniption  denudation  epiphytism  fortuitous
ambulation  byelection  consectary  depilation  equipotent  foundation
ambulatory  cacciatore  consistent  depilatory  equitation  foxhunting
amendatory  caespitose  consistory  depositary  eructation  freightage
ammunition  calamitous  consortium  deposition  escalation  fullbottom
amphictyon  campestral  constitute  depository  escheatage  fumigation
amputation  candletree  consuetude  depuration  estimation  galimatias
anabaptism  capacitate  consultant  depurative  estimative  gargantuan
anabaptist  capacitive  consulting  deputation  etiolation  gemination
ancipitous  capitation  consultive  derivation  evacuation  generation
anecdotage  caricature  contention  derivative  evacuative  generative
anecdotist  castration  contestant  derogation  evaluation  generatrix
Anglistics  catenation  contextual  derogatory  evaluative  geocentric
angwantibo  cavitation  contexture  desolately  evidential  Gilbertian
annexation  chalkstone  contortion  desolation  exactitude  glaciation
annotation  charactery  contortive  desorption  exaltation  graduation
annulation  charioteer  contritely  detonation  excavation  grandstand
antimatter  chevrotain  contrition  detraction  excerption  graphitise
antipathic  chromatics  convection  detractive  excitation  gratuitous
apiculture  chromatype  convective  devolution  excitative  gravestone
apostatise  chrysotile  convention  diecasting  excitatory  greenstick
apparition  circuitous  conventual  dielectric  excogitate  greenstone
appetitive  cismontane  conviction  digitately  excusatory  greenstuff
appointive  cispontine  convictive  digitation  execration  grindstone
appositely  clearstory  cooptation  dilatation  execrative  guillotine
apposition  clementine  cooptative  diminution  execratory  gymnastics
appositive  clerestory  copesettic  diminutive  exhalation  habilitate
apprentice  clingstone  copulation  disburthen  exhaustion  habitation
areolation  clinkstone  copulative  discontent  exhaustive  hackbuteer
arrogation  closestool  coquettish  discretely  exhibition  hackmatack
asafoetida  coaptation  corelation  discretion  exhibitory  halfwitted
ascription  coexistent  corelative  disfeature  exhumation  halieutics
aspiration  cogitation  cornettist  disgustful  exorbitant  hardbitten
assafetida  cogitative  coronation  disruption  expedition  harvestman
assaultive  cohabitant  correction  disruptive  expiration  hebetation
assumption  colatitude  corrective  dissection  expiratory  helianthus
assumptive  coleoptera  corruption  dissertate  exploitage  helminthic
asymmetric  coleoptile  corruptive  distention  exploitive  hempnettle
attractant  collection  cottontail  distortion  exposition  hereditary
attraction  collective  couverture  distortive  expositive  hesitation
attractive  coloration  crassitude  divagation  expository  hesitative
auscultate  coloratura  credential  divination  expunction  heterotaxy
```

heuristics	invitatory	multistage	perceptual	quartation	schematise
hexametric	invocation	musicstand	peremptory	quercitron	schematism
highoctane	invocatory	musicstool	perfection	radication	schooltime
Hindustani	involution	mutilation	perfective	rapporteur	sclerotium
homiletics	iodination	myxomatous	periosteal	rattletrap	sclerotomy
humanities	ionisation	nanisation	periosteum	razzmatazz	seacaptain
idiopathic	irrelative	nasturtium	peripeteia	recitation	seedpotato
imbibition	irrigation	natalitial	permeation	recitative	segmentary
immolation	irritation	nauseating	permeative	recitativo	selfacting
impanation	irritative	navigation	permitting	recreation	selfaction
impenitent	Jacobitism	neglectful	peroration	recreative	selfesteem
imperative	jubilation	newsletter	persistent	redemption	selfmotion
impolitely	judicatory	nightstick	philistine	redemptive	semeiotics
imposition	judicature	nodulation	phlebotomy	redemptory	semifitted
imprinting	kinematics	nominately	phylactery	reelection	semination
imputation	Kuomintang	nomination	phyllotaxy	reflection	sentential
imputative	laboratory	nominative	pigeontoed	reflective	separately
inappetent	laceration	noncontent	pigmentary	refraction	separation
inaptitude	lacerative	nonfiction	pinfeather	refractive	separatism
inchoately	lamination	nucleation	pitchstone	refractory	separatist
inchoation	Lammastide	nucleotide	plantation	refutation	separative
inchoative	laparotomy	numeration	playacting	regelation	separatory
incitation	lapidation	nunciature	plecoptera	regretting	sequential
incogitant	laureation	obdurately	pneumatics	regulation	sequestrum
inconstant	Lawrentian	obligation	pogonotomy	regulative	serpentine
incubation	leafcutter	obligatory	poinsettia	regulatory	sestertium
incubative	levigation	obturation	polyanthus	relaxation	sestertius
incubatory	levitation	occupation	polymathic	relegation	sexpartite
indagation	liberation	occupative	population	relocation	shantytown
indexation	librettist	ocellation	portentous	remonetise	sheabutter
indication	limitation	oedematose	pothunting	renovation	shipfitter
indicative	limitative	oedematous	pouncetbox	reparation	Shrovetide
indicatory	lipomatous	offputting	pragmatise	reparative	sibilation
induration	literation	offsetting	pragmatism	repetiteur	silkcotton
indurative	literature	omnipotent	pragmatist	repetition	similitude
ineptitude	litigation	operettist	precaution	repetitive	simulation
inexistent	lobulation	oppilation	preceptive	reposition	simulative
infarction	locomotion	oppositely	preceptory	repository	simulatory
infighting	locomotive	opposition	predestine	reputation	singletree
infinitely	locomotory	orchestics	prediction	resolutely	skywriting
infinitive	loganstone	orchestral	predictive	resolution	slowmotion
infinitude	loveletter	ordination	preemption	resolutive	slowwitted
inflection	lustration	orthoptera	preemptive	resorption	smokestack
inflective	maceration	oscitation	prefecture	resorptive	snakestone
infliction	mackintosh	osculation	prefixture	respectful	solicitant
inflictive	maculation	osculatory	prehistory	respecting	solicitous
infraction	maculature	outfitting	prelection	respective	solicitude
inhabitant	malcontent	outputting	presbytery	resumption	solidstate
inhalation	mangosteen	outsitting	presentday	resumptive	solstitial
inheritrix	manometric	outstation	presentive	retractile	somatotype
inhibition	mansuetude	outwitting	prevention	retraction	spallation
inhibitory	manteltree	ovariotomy	preventive	retractive	speciation
inhumation	manumitted	overactive	production	revelation	spoliation
iniquitous	markettown	pacesetter	productive	revelatory	spoliative
initiation	mastectomy	paediatric	proglottis	revocation	spoliatory
initiative	matchstick	pagination	prognathic	revocatory	sprightful
initiatory	maturation	palaeotype	projectile	revolution	springtail
injunction	maturative	palliation	projection	rheumatics	springtide
injunctive	mediastina	palliative	projective	rheumatism	springtime
innovation	medication	palliatory	promontory	rheumatoid	squamation
innovative	medicative	palmbutter	propertied	rhinestone	squaretoed
innovatory	meditation	pancratium	prophetess	rickettsia	squaretoes
inquietude	meditative	parametric	proportion	rockbottom	stagnation
insanitary	megalithic	parasitism	prostitute	rumination	stalactite
insightful	mercantile	parasitoid	protection	ruminative	standstill
insolation	Mesolithic	parimutuel	protective	saddletree	starvation
inspection	misfortune	paroxytone	protectory	sagination	statistics
inspective	mishitting	patination	protectrix	salientian	stenchtrap
insulation	misventure	patriotism	protestant	salivation	stepfather
interstate	mitigation	patristics	prudential	salutation	stepmother
interstice	mitigative	peculation	punctation	salutatory	stereotype
intimately	mitigatory	pejoration	pushbutton	sanctitude	stereotypy
intimation	moderately	pejorative	pycnostyle	sanitation	stigmatise
intinction	moderation	pendentive	pyrometric	sapiential	stigmatism
intonation	moderatism	pentastich	pyrrhotite	sarmentose	stigmatist
intubation	modulation	percentage	quadratics	sarmentous	stilettoes
inundation	monolithic	percentile	quadrature	saturation	stinkstone
inundatory	mosquitoes	perception	quantitive	sawtoothed	stockstill
invitation	motivation	perceptive	quarantine	scarlatina	strabotomy

strengthen	tripartite	catechumen	graciously	prosecutor	vibraculum
stromatous	triquetrae	cautiously	grandducal	racecourse	vigorously
stylistics	triquetral	cheerfully	grapesugar	ranunculus	viperously
subcentral	trisection	clavicular	gratefully	ravenously	virtuously
subculture	truncately	cloudburst	grievously	relinquish	voluptuary
subduction	truncation	coachbuilt	guilefully	reproducer	voluptuous
subjectify	turpentine	coastguard	haematuria	rightfully	vorticular
subjection	twelvetone	coatimundi	hallelujah	rigorously	wastefully
subjective	typesetter	collocutor	headsquare	salmagundi	watchfully
subletting	ubiquitous	colloquial	Herrnhuter	scabrously	watchguard
submitting	ulceration	colloquise	homunculus	scornfully	wearifully
submontane	ulcerative	colloquist	honeyguide	scriptural	wondrously
subreption	ultimately	colloquium	houseguest	sculptural	wrathfully
subroutine	unchastity	connatural	humorously	sculptured	wrongfully
subsection	understand	consequent	hurdygurdy	sedulously	wrongously
subsistent	understate	contiguity	hurlyburly	selftaught	xiphosuran
substation	understeer	contiguous	hyperdulia	semidouble	youthfully
substitute	understock	continuant	illnatured	sensuously	aberdevine
subvention	understood	continuate	importuner	shamefully	abortively
suggestion	understudy	continuity	inadequacy	slothfully	abrasively
suggestive	undulation	continuous	inadequate	sonorously	adaptively
summertime	undulatory	convoluted	incestuous	spaciously	adhesively
superation	uneventful	coproducer	ineloquent	speciously	adoptively
superstore	unguentary	corbiculae	infamously	spiracular	allusively
supination	unipartite	covetously	infrahuman	spiraculum	almsgiving
suppletion	unsporting	craftguild	infrequent	spirituous	animadvert
suppletive	upholstery	cumbrously	institutor	spitefully	aversively
suppletory	urtication	curricular	interlunar	sportfully	Belgravian
supportive	ustulation	curriculum	intramural	spuriously	bolshevise
surfactant	usucaption	dampcourse	intriguant	staffnurse	bolshevism
susceptive	usurpation	decorously	introducer	structural	bolshevist
sustention	validation	delinquent	jaguarundi	structured	circumvent
sustentive	vasoactive	desirously	jerrybuilt	studiously	coacervate
sweepstake	vegetation	dextrously	kookaburra	subsequent	coercively
swordstick	vegetative	difficulty	lenticular	subshrubby	cohesively
sybaritism	velitation	dissoluble	luminously	superduper	confervoid
syncretise	veneration	distraught	lusciously	superhuman	contravene
syncretism	vesication	dolorously	lustrously	superlunar	controvert
syncretist	vesicatory	doubtfully	majuscular	tastefully	creatively
synthetise	vespertine	dramaturge	mandibular	tentacular	creativity
synthetist	vignettist	dramaturgy	menopausal	thankfully	deactivate
tabulation	vindictive	dreadfully	menstruate	timorously	decisively
tangential	Visigothic	earthquake	menstruous	topsyturvy	delusively
tattletale	visitation	effectuate	mercifully	tortiously	demotivate
technetium	volumetric	enormously	metallurgy	tortuously	derisively
telemetric	wentletrap	ensanguine	minuscular	touchjudge	disservice
teleostean	wheatstone	exsanguine	mirthfully	trabeculae	dissolvent
telepathic	winebottle	extinguish	misthought	trabecular	divisively
temptation	wintertide	extramural	mosasaurus	transducer	effusively
tetrastich	wintertime	fabulously	mournfully	translucid	electively
tetrastyle	woodcutter	factiously	mumbojumbo	translunar	emissivity
theoretics	woolgather	faithfully	mutinously	transmuter	eruptively
thoughtful	accentuate	fancifully	nauseously	triangular	everliving
throwstick	acetabular	fascicular	nebulously	trustfully	eyeservice
thumbstall	acetabulum	fasciculus	nonnatural	truthfully	facesaving
tickertape	adventurer	fearnought	nullanulla	tubercular	flagwaving
timbertoes	aeronautic	febrifugal	numerously	tuberculin	freeliving
titivation	affettuoso	fisticuffs	overbought	tumultuary	fugitively
titubation	Algonquian	flexuously	particular	tumultuous	gaingiving
toleration	anacolutha	floribunda	patulously	unbesought	herrenvolk
tonguetied	babiroussa	follicular	peacefully	unctuously	illatively
torrential	barbituric	forcefully	peduncular	underquote	illusively
touchstone	barramunda	forecourse	pellicular	underquote	inactivate
toxication	barramundi	foursquare	peninsular	unilocular	inactively
trabeation	bibulously	fruitfully	pennanular	unlawfully	inactivity
trajection	bicultural	fuddyduddy	perilously	unmeasured	incisively
trajectory	bigamously	furuncular	perpetuate	usuriously	irrelevant
tramontana	bivalvular	fuzzywuzzy	perpetuity	uxoriously	lifegiving
tramontane	blackguard	generously	persecutor	valleculae	lifesaving
transition	blamefully	ghastfully	populously	vallecular	lipservice
transitive	blissfully	glomerular	Portuguese	valorously	longaevous
transitory	bloodguilt	glomerulus	powerfully	vaporously	manoeuvrer
traumatism	boastfully	gloriously	preciously	vengefully	manoeuvres
travertine	brachyural	glycosuria	previously	venomously	manservant
trecentist	brachyuran	glycosuric	pridefully	vermicular	margravate
triacetate	burramundi	gobemouche	procedural	vernacular	margravine
trichotomy	canorously	golfcourse	prolocutor	versicular	negatively
Tridentine	captiously	gorgeously	prologuise	vestibular	negativism
trimonthly	caruncular	gracefully	prosciutto	vestibulum	negativist

```
negativity pistolwhip magnifying assemblage chessboard denunciate
optatively ribbonworm matronymic asseverate chevrotain depopulate
positively sandalwood mesophytic assibilate chiffchaff depositary
positivism sappanwood metaphysic assimilate chinagraph depreciate
positivist schoolwork metronymic attractant chlorinate depressant
positivity scrollwork micropylar auriculate churchyard deracinate
proclivity setterwort monorhymed auscultate cismontane desalinate
punitively shrinkwrap motorcycle autodidact Clydesdale descendant
pursuivant silverware nonplaying autostrada cnidoblast desiderata
putatively silverweed nurseryman autostrade coacervate desiderate
quadrivial smallsword patronymic balderdash coastguard desquamate
quadrivium sneezeweed phagocytic balustrade cohabitant detoxicant
reactivate sneezewood phenotypic barbellate collegiate detoxicate
reactively sneezewort photolysis bargeboard colourfast Devanagari
reactivity spiderwort photolytic baronetage colportage diastemata
recidivism spleenwort polyonymic basketball commandant dichromate
recidivist spongewood prototypal bathyscaph commentary dictionary
relatively sportswear prototypic Beaujolais commentate dilapidate
relativise springwood psilocybin beforehand commissary discordant
relativism stitchwort railwayman behindhand compensate discourage
relativist streetward satisfying bichromate complicacy discrepant
relativity tetterwort scaredycat binoculars complicate discussant
rendezvous threadworm selfstyled biodegrade conciliary disenchant
selfloving throatwort semidrying birthplace conciliate dispensary
semidivine thwartwise shandrydan bisulphate concordant dispersant
skindiving tiddlywink trolleybus blackboard condensate dissertate
sportively timberwolf Trotskyism blackguard confirmand dissociate
subclavian timberwork Trotskyist blackheart confiscate distilland
timesaving tumbleweed Trotskyite blastemata conglobate distillate
unswerving wickerwork underlying blockboard congregant disulphate
barrenwort wildfowler unedifying bloodstain congregate divaricate
basketwork wonderwork xerophytic bobbinlace consecrate dorsigrade
bitterwood yellowwood yesteryear bootstraps consectary doublebass
brazilwood ambidexter actinozoan bordereaux consociate doublepark
breastwall complexion Gorgonzola borderland conspiracy doubletalk
breastwork complexity isoniazide branchiate conspirant dragonnade
bridgework homosexual kibbutznik brandyball constipate duumvirate
brightwork paradoxure Leibnizian breadboard consultant earthquake
broadsword perplexity Palaeozoic breastwall consummate ecclesiast
butterwork phylloxera quatorzain bridesmaid contestant edulcorate
buttonwood pyridoxine schemozzle bridlepath continuant effectuate
caddisworm apocalypse scyphozoan brigandage continuate effeminacy
candlewick archetypal stargazing bromegrass contraband effeminate
candlewood borborygmi ————       bunchgrass contrabass elecampane
cankerworm carboxylic abbreviate butterball conversant electorate
canvaswork cavalryman aboveboard buttonball convulsant elementary
carpetweed chimneypot accelerate cachinnate coordinate emancipate
commonweal churchyard accentuate calceolate coradicate emarginate
cornerwise cockneyish accountant calumniate coralsnake emasculate
cottonweed cockneyism accumulate calyptrate cottoncake embryonate
cottonwood coenobytic acoelomate camelopard cottontail emeryboard
cottonwool countryish acromegaly camouflage couchgrass enthusiasm
crewelwork countryman adjudicate camphorate counteract enthusiast
disentwine endophytic adulterant cancellate crackajack episcopacy
donkeywork fairycycle adulterate cannonball crackbrain episcopate
fiddlewood flamboyant aficionado canonicals crankshaft epistolary
galleywest flunkeydom aftergrass canonicate crenellate equivocate
greasewood flunkeyism afterimage cantillate crossgrain escheatage
greensward foudroyant aftershave canvasback crossroads everyplace
groundwork glycolyses alimentary capacitate cryptogamy eviscerate
heavenward glycolysis alliterate capitulary custommade exaggerate
hitherward gratifying altostrati capitulate cyclograph exasperate
hollowware haemolysis amalgamate carbonnade daisychain excogitate
honeysweet haemolytic ameliorate carpellary deactivate excruciate
intertwine halophytic amphibrach cataphract debilitate exenterate
intertwist highflying anecdotage cautionary decapitate exhilarant
jasperware highwayman anemograph cellophane decelerate exhilarate
jimsonweed histolysis annihilate centigrade decolorant exorbitant
lengthways histolytic annunciate centreback deescalate expatriate
lengthwise holophytic anticipant centrehalf deflagrate exploitage
masterwork hydrolysis anticipate certiorari deforciant expressage
motherwort hydrolytic apostolate cessionary degeneracy exprobrate
nationwide hypophyses apothecary chalkboard degenerate extractant
needlework hypophysis apotropaic chalybeate delaminate exulcerate
nipplewort journeyman appreciate chargehand deliberate facilitate
orangewood laundryman architrave charismata delimitate faintheart
palmerworm leucocytic articulate chartulary demotivate fastigiate
pepperwort leukocytic asphyxiant cheapskate denaturate fatherland
pigeonwing lumberyard asphyxiate cheesecake denominate felicitate
```

fenestrate	hydrophane	landocracy	operculate	quadrumane	smokeplant
fibreboard	hydroplane	largescale	orthoclase	quarterage	smokestack
fibreglass	hygrograph	lebensraum	osteoblast	quaternary	snobocracy
fibrillary	iconoclasm	lectionary	osteoclast	quaternate	solicitant
fibrillate	ilangilang	ledgerbait	otterboard	quatorzain	solidstate
fiddleback	illiteracy	legitimacy	outerspace	quickgrass	soundboard
fieldglass	illiterate	legitimate	oysterfarm	radiograph	soundtrack
fingermark	illuminant	lemniscate	pacificate	rattlepate	souterrain
fingernail	illuminate	lemongrass	paddywhack	razorblade	spacecraft
fireescape	illuminati	lengthways	palatinate	razzmatazz	spadebeard
firstclass	illustrate	leprechaun	paniculate	reactivate	speargrass
flabellate	immaculacy	lettercard	pantograph	reallocate	spiflicate
flagellant	immaculate	leucoplast	pantrymaid	recuperate	spirograph
flagellate	immoderacy	licentiate	paperchase	redcurrant	splashback
flamboyant	immoderate	lieutenant	paradisaic	redecorate	spokeshave
flashboard	impregnant	lighterage	paraphrase	regeneracy	spongecake
flightpath	impregnate	lithograph	paraphrast	regenerate	springhalt
floatboard	impuissant	lithophane	pasquinade	registrant	springtail
floatplane	inaccuracy	lowerclass	passionary	reichsmark	squaresail
flocculate	inaccurate	luciferase	passionate	rejuvenate	stablemate
floorboard	inactivate	lumberjack	pasteboard	remarriage	stagecoach
fluoridate	inadequacy	lumberyard	patriciate	remunerate	stagecraft
fluorinate	inadequate	lymphomata	pebbledash	repatriate	statecraft
fluxionary	inaugurate	macrophage	pediculate	repopulate	stationary
foreordain	incendiary	magistracy	pensionary	repurchase	stenograph
fortepiano	incinerate	magistrate	percentage	resemblant	stereobate
foudroyant	incogitant	maidenhair	perfoliate	restaurant	sterigmata
fourinhand	inconstant	malfeasant	perpetrate	resupinate	stipellate
foursquare	incrassate	manipulate	perpetuate	reticulate	stonebrash
frangipane	indelicacy	manservant	persiflage	retrograde	strawboard
frangipani	indelicate	maquillage	phonograph	revalidate	streetward
freightage	inefficacy	margravate	photograph	rhodophane	stridulant
fritillary	infiltrate	markethall	phyllotaxy	ripplemark	stridulate
galloglass	ingeminate	marquisate	phytophagy	saccharate	stringhalt
gaspereaux	ingratiate	martingale	pichiciago	saddleback	striptease
geniculate	inhabitant	masquerade	pictograph	saddlefast	stylograph
goatsbeard	innominate	masterhand	pigeonpair	salicylate	subaverage
goosegrass	innumeracy	matchboard	pigmentary	saltigrade	subcordate
grandstand	innumerate	meadowland	pilgrimage	sanguinary	submediant
grasssnake	inordinate	meadowlark	pillowcase	sarcophagi	submontane
greenheart	inosculate	meerschaum	pillowlace	sarcophagy	subsidiary
greenshank	insanitary	megalosaur	pilotwhale	sarcoplasm	sulphonate
greensward	inseminate	menstruate	pistillary	satyagraha	sulphurate
groundbait	insouciant	metagalaxy	pistillate	sauerkraut	supergiant
groundmass	inspissate	metaphrase	pitchblack	scaleboard	supplejack
habilitate	insufflate	micrograph	plainchant	scapegrace	supplicant
hackmatack	intenerate	mimeograph	planigraph	schizocarp	supplicate
halogenate	intergrade	ministrant	plasmogamy	schooldays	surfactant
handicraft	interleave	minutehand	plesiosaur	schoolmarm	surplusage
harbourage	interphase	miscellany	ploughland	schoolmate	swashplate
hawserlaid	interplant	missionary	plunderage	scoreboard	sweatgland
headsquare	interspace	mithridate	plutocracy	screwplate	sweepstake
heartsease	interstate	mizzenmast	pointblank	scrimshank	sweetheart
heavenward	interweave	mizzensail	pornocracy	scutellate	switchback
hectograph	intimidate	Montagnard	potentiate	seacaptain	swordcraft
heliograph	intolerant	motherland	pozzuolana	secondhand	swordgrass
hereditary	intoxicant	mouldboard	prebendary	secondrate	symposiast
hereticate	intoxicate	mountebank	predecease	seedpotato	syntagmata
heterogamy	intriguant	multiphase	prepackage	segmentary	tailormade
heterotaxy	invaginate	multistage	presidiary	seignorage	tardigrade
hierocracy	invalidate	musicstand	pretendant	selfregard	tattletale
hierograph	inveteracy	Mussulmans	principate	semilunate	telpherage
hierophant	inveterate	natterjack	proctorage	sexagenary	teratomata
highoctane	invigilate	naturopath	profligacy	shandygaff	terneplate
Hindustani	invigorate	needlebath	profligate	sheepshank	tessellate
hinterland	irradicate	nephograph	prolongate	shillelagh	thirdclass
hippophagy	irrelevant	nettlerash	promulgate	shoreleave	threadbare
hitherward	italianate	neuroplasm	propellant	showerbath	threadmark
hollowware	jasperware	nidificate	propionate	shroudlaid	thumbstall
holophrase	johnnycake	nightglass	propitiate	siegetrain	tickertape
homoeopath	juggernaut	nightshade	protestant	silverbath	topgallant
homologate	justiciary	nitrochalk	protoplasm	silverware	tramontana
housecraft	karyoplasm	nonchalant	protoplast	skateboard	tramontane
houseplant	knickknack	notchboard	pseudocarp	skrimshank	transplant
housetrain	knifeboard	obliterate	psychopath	slavetrade	transshape
hoverplane	Krugerrand	obnubilate	punchboard	slavocracy	treadboard
hovertrain	Kuomintang	obtruncate	punctulate	sluicegate	triacetate
husbandage	ladderback	ochlocracy	pursuivant	smallscale	trifoliate
hyaloplasm	lanceolate	oligoclase	quadrumana		

```
trifurcate approvable detectable inculpable patentable sitophobia
triplicate approvably detestable incurrable penetrable sketchable
triternate arbitrable detestably indictable penetrably snafflebit
triumphant ascendable dialysable ineducable perdurable soapbubble
trousseaux ascendible diffusable ineligible perdurably squeezable
tuitionary ascribable digestible ineligibly perishable squeezebox
tumultuary assailable dislikable ineludible permutable statutable
turtleback assessable disposable inevitable personable statutably
umbilicate assignable disputable inevitably planetable sublimable
umbrellaed associable disputably inexorable ploughable subscriber
underglaze attachable dissoluble inexorably pocketable subshrubby
underlease attackable disyllabic inexpiable ponderable sufferable
underneath attainable disyllable inexpiably pouncetbox sufferably
understand bedchamber divebomber infallible predicable summonable
understate believable effaceable infallibly preferable supposable
unguentary bleachable eliminable infeasible preferably supposably
uninitiate blueribbon employable inferrable prepayable surmisable
unpleasant breathable endorsable inflatable prescriber swinglebar
upperclass bridgeable enumerable inflexible presumable temperable
vaticinate calculable enunciable inflexibly presumably tenantable
vectograph calculably eradicable ingestible procurable terminable
vernissage candelabra evaporable inimitable producible terminably
vertebrate censurable examinable inimitably profitable thunderbox
vesiculate changeable executable innerrable profitably toxiphobia
veterinary changeably expandable inoculable propagable triturable
Victoriana chargeable expansible inoperable proscriber trolleybus
villainage charitable expendable insatiable psilocybin trucklebed
villeinage charitably explicable insatiably punishable trundlebed
vitiligate chatterbox exportable insensible quenchable unarguable
vituperate choriambic extendible insensibly realisable unbearable
vocabulary clothesbag extensible insociable reasonable unbearably
vociferant coagulable extricable insolvable reasonably unbeatable
vociferate cognisable fathomable intangible reassemble unbeatably
volleyball cognisably fatiguable intangibly reassembly unbiddable
voluptuary collatable favourable integrable rebuttable undeniable
watchglass colourable favourably interurban recallable undeniably
watchguard colourably featherbed intraurban receivable unenviable
waterbrash comestible filterable invaluable receptible unknowable
watercraft commonable forgivable invaluably recordable unnameable
waterglass commutable forgivably invariable recyclable unreadable
whaleshark comparable formidable invariably redeemable unreliable
wheelchair comparably formidably invincible reeligible unscalable
whitebeard compatible galliambic invincibly refillable unscramble
windowpane compatibly glassfibre inviolable reflexible unsociable
witchcraft computable governable inviolably reformable unsociably
wonderland consolable honourable isolatable refundable unsuitable
worldclass consumable honourably jackrabbit reissuable unworkable
worldweary convenable hospitable lamentable rejectable utilisable
yellowback conveyable hospitably lamentably releasable verifiable
ylangylang corrigible illaudable landlubber relievable vindicable
zincograph creditable illaudably licensable relishable voyageable
abominable creditably imaginable manageable remarkable vulnerable
abominably cultivable imaginably manageably remarkably vulnerably
absorbable damageable immiscible marketable remediable weatherbox
acceptable deceivable immiscibly masticable remissible winebibber
acceptably deceptible immoveable measurable renderable witnessbox
accessible declarable impalpable measurably repairable xenophobia
accessibly declinable impalpably mensurable repealable academical
achievable deductible impartible metastable repeatable acoustical
acquirable defeasible impassable mistakable reportable alchemical
acrophobia defendable impassably modifiable resistible ammoniacal
actionable defensible impassible negligible resolvable amphimacer
actionably defensibly impassibly negligibly respirable anagogical
adjustable deferrable impeccable negotiable restorable analogical
admissible defrayable impeccably nosophobia retainable analytical
admittable degradable implacable noticeable returnable anarchical
adsorbable delectable implacably noticeably revealable anatomical
aerophobia delectably importable notifiable reversible apolitical
affirmable demandable impossible observable revertible appendices
affordable demurrable impossibly observably reviewable archdeacon
amerciable dependable improbable obtainable rewardable autarkical
analphabet dependably improbably ostensible rockrabbit aviatrices
analysable deplorable improvable ostensibly rockribbed backblocks
answerable deplorably improvably oxidisable schoolable biological
answerably deprivable impugnable pacifiable searchable blackfaced
appealable despicable inclinable packingbox seasonable bluepencil
appeasable despicably includible pardonable seasonably bobbysocks
applicable despisable incredible pardonably semidouble catholicon
applicably detachable incredibly pasturable shrinkable catholicos
```

```
chimerical pictorical biliverdin hotblooded sashwindow adolescent
cicatrices pokerfaced birdspider interceder scaffolder adoptively
Copernican pontifical bondholder internodal secludedly adroitness
coproducer pontifices boneheaded intertidal selfbinder adulteress
demoniacal prejudiced bookbinder intrepidly selffeeder advisement
diabolical prelatical botryoidal ironhanded selfguided affectless
didactical premedical bullheaded keyboarder selfmurder affeerment
diplodocus pronounced cackhanded lamentedly shandrydan alexanders
dogmatical pronouncer calamander landholder sheriffdom alightment
doughfaced prosodical caryatides larvicidal shopwindow allurement
dramatical puristical caseharden latifundia showwindow allusively
ecological quixotical colonnaded lefthanded sidesaddle altarpiece
economical rabbinical composedly lefthander sidewinder ambivalent
ecumenical receptacle compounder likeminded sinusoidal ambushment
egoistical reciprocal conchoidal longheaded skewbridge amercement
electrical reproducer confounded longwinded sluggardly ancestress
elliptical republican confusedly lopsidedly sobersided anchorless
encyclical requiescat consumedly lossleader sobersides angiosperm
epidemical reverencer coolheaded Mahommedan softheaded animadvert
episodical rhetorical copyholder mainlander solenoidal anointment
eremitical rhythmical copyreader manifoldly sphenoidal antecedent
exegetical ropedancer coromandel matricidal spheroidal anthracene
exoterical sabbatical crippledom measuredly spiritedly antifreeze
fairycycle sabretache crossindex memorandum splendidly antipodean
fleacircus sacrificer cyclopedia misjoinder stadholder apophthegm
Franciscan scaredycat cyclopedic mixedmedia stepladder appositely
freelancer semicircle degradedly Mohammedan stockrider archpriest
geodetical semiotical dejectedly Muhammedan strainedly armourless
geological shamefaced dementedly Muhammadan subkingdom arrestment
geoponical simoniacal depravedly multimedia sugardaddy artfulness
gobemouche snailpaced deservedly newsreader superorder arthromere
goldilocks spagyrical designedly newsvendor supposedly ascomycete
grandducal squirarchy desperados nonjoinder swanmaiden assentient
granduncle stavesacre detachedly onesidedly taradiddle assessment
greatuncle stirrupcup didgeridoo openhanded tarmacadam assignment
harmonical symbolical downwardly openminded temperedly assoilment
haruspices synecdoche drawbridge orthopedic tetrahedra assortment
hermetical synoptical dumfounder outfielder thereunder astringent
hibernacle tabernacle evenhanded overburden thousandth astuteness
historical Talmudical everglades overhanded tollbridge atmosphere
hocuspocus tauromachy evilminded overlander touchjudge attachment
homocercal taxidancer expectedly overridden trochoidal attainment
hourcircle theatrical extendedly overshadow unattended attornment
hysterical theistical faceharden packsaddle undefended attunement
iconomachy theurgical fairleader palisander unfriended auctioneer
inexplicit transducer fairminded PalmSunday unfriendly augustness
introducer translucid flapdoodle parricidal ungrounded averseness
Janusfaced trierarchy flunkeydom pathfinder unorthodox aversively
jesuitical tyrannical footbridge patricidal untowardly avouchment
juristical unAmerican footcandle pellucidly unwontedly babblement
lightfaced unbalanced forehanded pesticidal urochordal backsheesh
liturgical unbiblical foreshadow prairiedog uxoricidal bafflement
logistical uncritical fourhanded preparedly vermicidal banishment
magnifical whitefaced freehanded presentday viewfinder baptistery
magnificat zoological freeholder prismoidal weakminded barrenness
majestical absorbedly freeloader profoundly westwardly barysphere
matriarchy acceptedly frenziedly prolicidal WhitMonday battlement
mechanical accursedly fuddyduddy promenader WhitSunday bemusement
methodical acotyledon fungicidal propounder withholder beneficent
microfiche admittedly gaillardia purblindly woodlander benevolent
monistical affectedly gasconader quarrender wretchedly benzpyrene
motorcycle Africander germicidal quarterday abjectness bestowment
multifaced Afrikander gladhander railroader abortively betterment
multivocal agitatedly goaltender reconsider abrasively bewitchery
myological allrounder gramicidin redblooded abridgment bibliopegy
neological ambassador granddaddy referendum abruptness bitchiness
nonlogical animatedly greyheaded repeatedly absolutely bitterness
oratorical antependia handmaiden reportedly abstergent blastoderm
orological antheridia hangglider reservedly abstrusely blastomere
panopticon Armageddon hardhanded resignedly absurdness blazonment
papistical asteroidal hardheaded resolvedly accoucheur bleariness
parsonical backhanded heathendom rhomboidal accrescent blitheness
pastyfaced backhander hebdomadal rhomboidei accurately bloodiness
pathetical backslider hellbender ringleader activeness bluishness
patriarchy backwardly highbinder rockgarden adaptively borderless
patrilocal baldheaded highhanded roofgarden adequately bottlefeed
periodical bareheaded highlander ropelander adhesively bottleneck
perithecia Barmecidal highminded roughrider adjudgment bottomless
phthisical bestridden hodgepodge salamander adjustment boyishness
```

```
braininess  concretely  devotement  epeirogeny  genialness  impugnment
brassiness  concurrent  devoutness  equipotent  gentleness  impureness
brawniness  condensery  diarrhoeal  equivalent  gesundheit  inactively
brazenness  condescend  diarrhoeic  erubescent  gingerbeer  inappetent
breathless  conferment  dictatress  eruptively  girlfriend  incasement
breechless  consequent  digitately  escapement  gladsomely  inchoately
breezeless  consistent  diluteness  escarpment  glassiness  incisively
breeziness  contendent  dinnerless  escutcheon  gloominess  incitement
brickfield  contingent  directness  evanescent  glossiness  incoherent
bridgehead  contravene  directress  everywhere  goldenness  incomplete
bridgeless  contritely  disbelieve  evolvement  goldenseal  increscent
brightness  controvert  discommend  excitement  goodliness  indictment
broadsheet  convenient  disconcert  excrescent  gooseflesh  indiscreet
brokenness  convergent  disconnect  experiment  government  indiscrete
broodiness  conversely  discontent  expertness  grandniece  inditement
bufflehead  copartnery  discretely  eyewitness  greasiness  inducement
buffoonery  copperhead  discutient  facileness  greatniece  ineloquent
bullethead  cordillera  dismalness  Fahrenheit  greediness  inexistent
butterbean  corsetiere  disownment  fallowness  grisliness  infinitely
buttonless  coryphaeus  dispossess  famishment  grittiness  infrequent
cajolement  cosentient  disrespect  famousness  grogginess  ingredient
callowness  costliness  dissilient  fatherless  groundless  inhumanely
candescent  cottonseed  dissolvent  fathomless  groundrent  innateness
candidness  cottonweed  distillery  faultiness  grubbiness  insaneness
cantonment  couplement  divestment  fearsomely  gruesomely  insecurely
carabineer  couturiere  divineness  feebleness  grumpiness  insentient
caravaneer  craftiness  divisively  femaleness  guiltiness  insobriety
carpetweed  cragginess  doggedness  femininely  gymnosperm  instalment
carragheen  crankiness  doubleness  fervidness  habiliment  instrument
casualness  cravenness  downstream  festoonery  hackbuteer  intactness
centromere  creaminess  dragonhead  fickleness  hairstreak  integument
chamaeleon  creatively  dreaminess  fictioneer  hakenkreuz  intendment
changeless  creaturely  dreariness  fiddlehead  hammerbeam  intentness
charactery  creepiness  dressiness  fieldpiece  hammerhead  interbreed
charioteer  crispbread  driverless  fierceness  hammerless  internment
chasteness  crossbreed  drowsihead  figurehead  handedness  interplead
chattiness  crosscheck  drowsiness  filthiness  handsomely  intimately
chauntress  crosspiece  drysaltery  fingerless  harassment  introrsely
cheekiness  crosstrees  dunderhead  finiteness  hartebeest  introspect
cheeriness  crustacean  earthiness  firescreen  headcheese  inventress
cheesiness  crustiness  earwitness  fitfulness  headstream  investment
chersonese  curmudgeon  echinoderm  flabbiness  heartbreak  inwardness
chilliness  cursedness  edibleness  flashiness  heartiness  ionosphere
choiceness  cussedness  effacement  flavescent  heavensent  iridescent
chubbiness  daintiness  effeteness  fleshiness  hemisphere  irreverent
cinecamera  dauphiness  effortless  flightdeck  heroicness  jackassery
circumvent  dazzlement  effrontery  flightless  heterogeny  jaggedness
clamminess  deadliness  effusively  flimsiness  Hippocrene  jardiniere
Clarenceux  debasement  elatedness  flintiness  hirudinean  jauntiness
cleverness  debatement  electively  flocculent  hoarseness  jejuneness
cloudiness  debauchery  embalmment  floppiness  hollowness  Jewishness
cloverleaf  decampment  embankment  florescent  homeliness  jimsonweed
clumsiness  decisively  embarkment  floridness  honeysweet  jocoseness
coadjacent  decompress  embodiment  flowerless  honourless  Johnsonese
coalescent  decrescent  embossment  fluffiness  hookedness  jolterhead
coarseness  deepfreeze  embroidery  foetidness  hornedness  journalese
cocksurely  deerforest  embryogeny  folksiness  horridness  joyfulness
coercively  defacement  emerywheel  foresheets  horseflesh  joyousness
coexistent  defilement  employment  fraudulent  horseleech  kerseymere
cohesively  definement  encampment  freakiness  houseagent  kindliness
coincident  definitely  encasement  freespeech  houseguest  kingliness
coleoptera  defrayment  encashment  Frenchness  humaneness  knockkneed
collarbeam  delicately  encystment  fricandeau  humbleness  knottiness
collarless  delinquent  endearment  fricasseed  humbuggery  lactescent
colourless  delusively  enfacement  friendless  humourless  lampoonery
colporteur  demureness  engagement  frigidness  hungriness  lavalliere
comanchero  denouement  engulfment  frilliness  idolatress  lavishment
comeliness  department  enjambment  fringeless  illatively  lavishness
comicopera  deployment  enjoinment  friskiness  illusively  lawfulness
commandeer  deportment  enlacement  frizziness  imbecilely  leadenness
commandery  derailleur  enlistment  frostiness  immaturely  leaderless
commitment  derailment  enmeshment  frothiness  immurement  leafinsect
commonness  derisively  enrichment  frutescent  impairment  leopardess
commonweal  descendent  enrigiment  fugitively  impalement  letterhead
complacent  designment  entailment  fulfilment  impartment  letterless
complement  desolately  enticement  futureless  impediment  likeliness
completely  despondent  entireness  galleywest  impenitent  limpidness
compliment  detachment  entombment  garishness  impishness  liquescent
comprehend  detainment  entrapment  gaucheness  impolitely  liquidness
```

lissomness	objectless	prettiness	sacredness	slightness	summitless
littleness	oblateness	prevenient	safetybelt	slipstream	superbness
liveliness	obtainment	prissiness	sailorless	sloppiness	supineness
locustbean	obtuseness	procumbent	salesclerk	smelliness	supperless
loggerhead	odiousness	proficient	sallenders	smoothness	supplement
loneliness	omnipotent	profitless	sallowness	smudginess	suppleness
lonesomely	omniscient	promptness	salmonleap	smuttiness	suspenders
lordliness	opalescent	proofsheet	sanguinely	snailwheel	sweatiness
loveliness	opaqueness	propellent	savageness	sneakiness	sweetbread
lovingness	opposeless	properness	savourless	sneezeweed	symphyseal
lustreless	oppositely	prophetess	scantiness	sniffiness	systemless
Maccabaean	optatively	propylaeum	scarabaeid	snootiness	takingness
maidenhead	orangepeel	prosilient	scarabaeus	snuffiness	talentless
mainstream	ordainment	proudflesh	scarceness	soddenness	tanglement
malacoderm	ornateness	puberulent	scatheless	solacement	tapotement
malcontent	orneriness	punishment	scattiness	solemnness	tawdriness
maleficent	orthoptera	punitively	scavengery	sombreness	teenyweeny
malevolent	otherwhere	putatively	scleroderm	songstress	telecamera
mallenders	otioseness	putrescent	scoresheet	sordidness	teleostean
management	outpatient	putridness	scorzonera	sparseness	tenantless
manageress	overnicety	puzzlement	screwpress	speechless	tenderness
manchineel	overspread	quadriceps	scrutineer	speediness	teratogeny
manfulness	owlishness	quadrireme	sculptress	spermaceti	terreplein
mangosteen	packthread	quaintness	scurviness	spinescent	terrorless
Manichaean	paddyfield	queasiness	seamstress	spiritless	tetchiness
marcescent	Palaeocene	quenchless	searchless	sponginess	thalecress
marrowless	Palaeogene	quirkiness	seaserpent	spookiness	theodicean
marshiness	palimpsest	rabblement	secernment	sportiness	thereanent
masterless	pallidness	raggedness	secondbest	sportively	thinkpiece
matureness	paltriness	rakishness	secondment	sportswear	thorniness
mavourneen	paradisean	rancidness	securement	spottiness	threepiece
meagreness	paraselene	randomness	secureness	springhead	thriftless
measliness	parliament	rapporteur	sedateness	springless	throneless
mediatress	parturient	rattlehead	seducement	sprucebeer	timberhead
medicament	patchiness	ravishment	seductress	spruceness	timeliness
mellowness	peacockery	razorshell	seemliness	spumescent	tirailleur
mesosphere	percipient	reactively	selectness	spunkiness	tiresomely
mightiness	periosteal	reafforest	selfdeceit	squareness	toilsomely
millstream	periosteum	rearmament	selfesteem	stableness	tomfoolery
mindedness	peripeteia	reasonless	seltzogene	stanchless	tongueless
minuteness	peritoneal	recentness	sempstress	stanchness	toothiness
misbelieve	peritoneum	recoupment	separately	starriness	toothshell
moderately	pernickety	refinement	sereneness	starstream	torpidness
modernness	persistent	refringent	settlement	stationery	torridness
modishness	perversely	refundment	seventieth	steadiness	touchiness
monovalent	petiteness	regalement	severeness	steamchest	tournament
mopishness	phagedaena	regardless	sexivalent	steaminess	towardness
morbidness	phalangeal	relatively	shabbiness	steeliness	transgress
moroseness	pharyngeal	relentless	shadowless	stepparent	trappiness
morphogeny	phelloderm	remediless	shagginess	stewardess	trashiness
motherless	phillumeny	remissness	sheathless	stickiness	treadwheel
motionless	philopoena	remoteness	sheepshead	stinginess	trendiness
motiveless	phylactery	repetiteur	shibboleth	stockiness	trickiness
mouldiness	phylloxera	resentment	shieldless	stodginess	truncately
mouthpiece	placidness	reshipment	shiftiness	stolidness	trustiness
muffinbell	plasmodesm	resistless	shoddiness	stomodaeum	tumbleweed
mulishness	plecoptera	resolutely	shortbread	storminess	turbidness
munificent	pliantness	respondent	shovelhead	straitness	turgescent
muttonhead	pluckiness	resultless	shrewdness	streamless	turgidness
mythopoeia	pluperfect	retirement	shrillness	stressless	turtleneck
mythopoeic	politeness	retrogress	shroudless	strictness	ultimately
myxomycete	polychaete	retrorsely	sickliness	stringbean	underdress
narrowness	polychrest	retrospect	sideeffect	stringless	understeer
nationless	polyvalent	revealment	sidestreet	stubbiness	uneasiness
nativeness	porousness	revilement	silentness	stuffiness	unevenness
negatively	portliness	rewardless	silkscreen	stumpiness	unfairness
nepenthean	Portuguese	ricinoleic	silverweed	stupidness	unforeseen
nightdress	positively	ridgepiece	simpleness	sturdiness	unholiness
nigrescent	preachment	rinderpest	sinfulness	subdeanery	uniqueness
nimbleness	preconcert	robustness	Singhalese	subnuclear	unjustness
nominately	preeminent	rockpigeon	singleness	subsequent	unkindness
noncontent	preferment	roodscreen	skimpiness	subsistent	unlikeness
nonnuclear	prefulgent	rootedness	skinniness	subtleness	unmeetness
nonpayment	prepayment	rottenness	slanginess	subtrahend	unripeness
nonviolent	prepensely	rubberneck	sleaziness	suddenness	unruliness
numberless	prepossess	rudderless	sleepiness	sufficient	untidiness
nympholept	presbytery	ruefulness	sleepyhead	sugariness	unwariness
oafishness	pressagent	ruggedness	sleeveless	sullenness	upholstery
obdurately	pretendent	runnerbean	sleighbell	sultriness	uppishness

```
upwardness  slumberful  earthlight  obligingly  triflingly  flycatcher
usefulness  sprightful  encourager  odontalgia  tropologic  footlights
varicocele  stomachful  enduringly  oesophagus  trustingly  forefather
velocipede  successful  engagingly  ophiologic  unabridged  foregather
venialness  tenebrific  enticingly  outswinger  unbesought  Francophil
vesperbell  thimbleful  ethnologic  overbought  unendingly  freakishly
vicegerent  thoughtful  excitingly  overflight  unerringly  friendship
viceregent  tumblerful  exultingly  overweight  unfadingly  geographer
Vietnamese  umbellifer  fearnought  paddywagon  wainwright  geographic
villainess  uneventful  febrifugal  paedagogic  watertight  helianthus
virtueless  unfaithful  fellmonger  paedogogue  wavelength  helminthic
visionless  ungraceful  fetchingly  paraplegia  waveringly  heptarchic
vitrescent  ungrateful  fibrinogen  paraplegic  wharfinger  hierarchal
vivandiere  unmerciful  fireblight  pathologic  witchingly  hierarchic
wampumpeag  untruthful  firstnight  pedalorgan  yearningly  idiopathic
wantonness  worshipful  fishmonger  periwigged  yieldingly  internship
watercress  accusingly  fivefinger  phanerogam  acronychal  isomorphic
wateriness  admiringly  flashlight  philologen  agapanthus  kaisership
waterwheel  adrenergic  fleeringly  phonologic  airmanship  kingfisher
weakliness  aetiologic  fleetingly  piercingly  allopathic  languisher
weaponless  afterlight  floatingly  pilotlight  altogether  leadership
weightless  alarmingly  floodlight  playwright  anaglyphic  legateship
wheeziness  annoyingly  florilegia  pleadingly  anamorphic  lowpitched
wickedness  arbitrager  folksinger  pleasingly  antipathic  mastership
widespread  arthralgia  forefinger  ploddingly  apocryphal  matronship
wildebeest  arthralgic  forthright  prancingly  archbishop  megalithic
wilderment  astrologer  fowlplague  pressingly  authorship  membership
wilderness  astrologic  frowningly  privileged  autochthon  mentorship
wilfulness  bafflingly  fulllength  prizefight  barbershop  Mesolithic
willowherb  balbriggan  fumblingly  quadrangle  battleship  mismatched
windowless  barelegged  fussbudget  radiologic  beadleship  monolithic
windowseat  becomingly  gametangia  ramblingly  bedclothes  mothership
windscreen  beefburger  gatelegged  retiringly  bellwether  moustached
windshield  bellringer  glancingly  rightangle  bellyacher  moustachio
windsleeve  birthright  golddigger  ringfinger  bequeathal  oligarchic
wingspread  bleatingly  grapesugar  rockbadger  bibliophil  orographic
wintriness  blindingly  graspingly  sandbagger  bigmouthed  pastorship
wobbliness  bluetongue  grindingly  scathingly  biographer  penmanship
woefulness  blurringly  growlingly  scattergun  biographic  pinfeather
wonderment  blushingly  grudgingly  scoffingly  biomorphic  pistolshot
wontedness  boondoggle  guestnight  scrimmager  blockishly  pistolwhip
woodenhead  bootlegger  gunslinger  selftaught  bucketshop  polyanthus
woodenness  borborygmi  hagiologic  senseorgan  bursarship  polymathic
woodpigeon  bouncingly  halflength  shenanigan  censorship  priggishly
woolliness  brakelight  hauntingly  shiprigged  cheapishly  princeship
worthiness  broodingly  hemiplegia  shipwright  childishly  prognathic
wrathiness  budgerigar  hemiplegic  shockingly  churlishly  pursership
yeastiness  bumblingly  hendecagon  sialagogic  clannishly  pyrotechny
yellowness  bunglingly  histologic  sialagogue  clientship  qualmishly
yesteryear  bushranger  hydrologic  slantingly  clownishly  ratcatcher
zollverein  bustlingly  hypnagogic  snapdragon  comehither  readership
artycrafty  cajolingly  imposingly  sneakingly  consulship  rectorship
cockchafer  carcinogen  inkslinger  sneeringly  cousinship  regentship
crossrefer  cardialgia  interregna  snubbingly  cowcatcher  researcher
delightful  carryingon  invitingly  sociologic  cowpuncher  sawtoothed
despiteful  cartwright  ironmonger  soothingly  deaconship  seamanship
disdainful  challenger  ladyfinger  soundingly  despatcher  sheepishly
disgustful  charmingly  landhunger  spankingly  devilishly  shrewishly
eisteddfod  chuckwagon  laughingly  sportingly  diagraphic  skirmisher
fiftyfifty  coathanger  lightingup  squeteague  diminished  skittishly
fisticuffs  covetingly  lithologic  steamtight  disburthen  sluggishly
flavourful  coweringly  longlegged  stiflingly  dishwasher  sluttishly
frigorific  crosslight  machinegun  stingingly  dispatcher  snappishly
insightful  damagingly  makeweight  stinkingly  doctorship  snobbishly
lanternfly  dazzlingly  menacingly  strikingly  dwarfishly  squireship
meaningful  deadweight  middleaged  stunningly  dysgraphia  stepfather
neglectful  deridingly  middlingly  sweepingly  dystrophic  stepmother
palmatifid  dermatogen  millwright  swimmingly  editorship  strengthen
pinnatifid  discharger  misthought  swingingly  encroacher  sultanship
pitcherful  disembogue  mouthorgan  taperingly  eosinophil  suretyship
presageful  disengaged  mudslinger  tauntingly  epigrapher  telepathic
purposeful  disparager  mystagogue  teleologic  epigraphic  tellership
ragamuffin  distraught  mystagogic  temptingly  factorship  tetrarchic
remorseful  distringas  mythologer  testflight  farfetched  theosopher
respectful  dogstongue  mythologic  thinkingly  fathership  thermophil
revengeful  doubtingly  nephralgia  torchlight  fellowship  thievishly
rosechafer  drawlingly  newsmonger  touchingly  felspathic  thoroughly
scientific  droopingly  nightlight  toweringly  feverishly  thwartship
selfprofit  drudgingly  nostologic  travelogue  fiendishly  ticklishly
```

```
tribrachic  affliction  aquilinity  blithering  chauvinism  concretise
trickishly  afflictive  araucarian  blitzkrieg  chauvinist  concretism
triglyphic  Africanise  archerfish  bloodguilt  checkpoint  concretist
trimonthly  Africanism  areolation  bolshevise  chiffonier  concurring
trimorphic  Africanist  Areopagite  bolshevism  chiselling  concussion
tryptophan  afterpains  arrogation  bolshevist  Christlike  concussive
ulotrichan  aggrandise  artificial  bombardier  chromatics  conduction
umpireship  aggression  asafoetida  bookmaking  chronicity  conductive
unattached  aggressive  asceticism  borderline  chrysolite  confabbing
unblenched  agrologist  ascription  Boswellian  chrysotile  confection
unfinished  agronomist  asexuality  Boswellise  Ciceronian  conferring
vanquisher  aircooling  asparagine  Boswellism  cicisbeism  confession
verandahed  aircushion  aspiration  bourbonism  cinchonine  conflation
Visigothic  alcoholise  assafetida  bourbonist  cinerarium  conformism
viziership  alcoholism  assaultive  bowdlerise  Circassian  conformist
wappenshaw  algebraist  assumption  bowdlerism  circumcise  conformity
wardenship  algologist  assumptive  bradyseism  cispontine  congestion
wellwisher  Algonquian  Athanasian  Brahmanism  Cistercian  congestive
windowshop  alienation  attraction  Brahminism  claspknife  connection
womanishly  alkalinity  attractive  brainchild  classicise  connective
woolgather  allegation  audibility  bratticing  classicism  conniption
zoomorphic  allegorise  audiophile  breadstick  classicist  consortium
abacterial  allegorist  auditorial  breakpoint  classified  constraint
abdication  allocation  auditorium  brevetting  classifier  consulting
aberdevine  allocution  Australian  brigandine  clementine  consultive
aberration  alloverish  automation  brigandism  coachbuilt  contention
abiogenist  almsgiving  automatise  brigantine  coaptation  contiguity
abjuration  alteration  automatism  Britishism  cockatrice  continuity
ablebodied  alterative  automatist  broomstick  cockneyish  contortion
abnegation  amateurish  automobile  brownshirt  cockneyism  contortive
abreaction  amateurism  automotive  bryologist  coequality  contradict
abrogation  ambulation  autonomist  Buchmanism  coeternity  contrarily
abscission  Amerindian  aventurine  Buchmanite  coffeemill  contrition
absolution  amiability  axiologist  bumpkinish  cogitation  convection
absolutism  ammunition  Babylonian  burglarise  cogitative  convective
absolutist  amputation  backbiting  butterfish  colchicine  convention
absorption  anabaptism  backstairs  buttermilk  coleoptile  conversion
absorptive  anabaptist  ballistics  byelection  coleorhiza  conviction
abstention  anchorring  ballooning  cacogenics  collection  convictive
abstersion  Andalusian  balloonist  Caledonian  collective  convincing
abstersive  andalusite  barkentine  cancelling  colloquial  convulsion
abstrusity  androecium  barrelling  candlefish  colloquise  convulsive
accomplice  anecdotist  bassoonist  candlewick  colloquist  cooptation
accomplish  anemophily  bastardise  canonicity  colloquium  cooptative
accounting  Anglistics  batfowling  cantatrice  coloration  copulation
accusation  anglophile  batrachian  capability  combustion  copulative
accusative  angularity  beautician  capacitive  combustive  coquettish
acervation  angwantibo  beautifier  capitalise  comicality  corbelling
achondrite  annexation  beekeeping  capitalism  commanding  cordiality
acidophile  annotation  beforetime  capitalist  commercial  cordierite
acquitting  annularity  Belgravian  capitation  commission  corelation
acrobatics  annulation  belletrist  Capitoline  committing  corelative
acroterion  anopheline  benedicite  cappuccino  compaction  Corinthian
acroterium  antagonise  beneficial  carabinier  compassion  cornerwise
actinolite  antagonism  Benthamism  caramelise  compatriot  cornettist
activation  antagonist  Benthamite  carnallite  compelling  coronation
adamantine  anthracite  benzocaine  carnassial  compendium  correction
adaptation  Antichrist  Berkeleian  Carthusian  completion  corrective
adhibition  antimonial  bestialise  cartoonist  completive  corruption
adjunction  antimonite  bestiality  castration  complexion  corruptive
adjunctive  antinomian  bestirring  catabolism  complexity  countryish
adjuration  antiSemite  bibliotics  catarrhine  complicity  craftguild
admiration  antisocial  bilocation  catenation  compromise  cranesbill
admonition  antitheism  bimestrial  catoptrics  compulsion  creatinine
admonitive  antitheist  biochemist  causticity  compulsive  creativity
adrenaline  Apollinian  biometrics  cavitation  conception  credential
adsorption  Apollonian  biophysics  centennial  conceptive  crispation
adsorptive  apostatise  bipolarity  centillion  concerning  crocoisite
Adullamite  apothecial  birdstrike  centralise  concertina  crustation
adulterine  apothecium  bissextile  centralism  concertino  cryogenics
advocation  apparition  bisulphide  centralist  concession  cuckoopint
aerobatics  apperceive  bisulphite  centrality  concessive  cudgelling
aeroengine  appetising  bitterling  centricity  concettism  cuirassier
aerologist  appetitive  bituminise  ceremonial  concinnity  cumulation
aeronomist  appointive  Blackshirt  chandelier  conclusion  cumulative
aesthetics  apposition  blacksmith  changeling  conclusive  cunctation
aesthetism  appositive  blanketing  channelise  concoction  cunctative
Aethiopian  apprentice  blepharism  chatelaine  concoctive  curability
affability  aquamarine  blistering
```

```
curatorial  disappoint  engrossing  exuviation  Gallophile  hobnobbing
curvetting  disbarring  enigmatise  eyeservice  gambolling  hoitytoity
cuttlefish  disbudding  enigmatist  facesaving  garnierite  homecoming
cytologist  discerning  ensanguine  factualism  garnishing  homemaking
datamation  discipline  enterolith  factualist  gelatinise  homiletics
deaeration  disconfirm  enterprise  factuality  gemination  homogenise
Decembrist  discophile  entrancing  fanaticise  generalise  homologise
decimalise  discretion  enwrapping  fanaticism  generalist  homoousian
decimalism  discursive  ephorality  fantastico  generality  honeyguide
decimation  discussion  epilimnion  fantoccini  generation  honorarium
decivilise  discussive  epiphytism  fasciation  generative  horologist
declassify  disentwine  epithelial  fatherlike  generosity  hostelling
declension  disfurnish  epithelium  feathering  geneticist  houselling
decolonise  disincline  equability  federalise  genteelism  humanities
decolorise  dismission  equanimity  federalism  geochemist  humbugging
decoration  dismissive  equatorial  federalist  geometrise  humidifier
decorative  dispassion  equestrian  federation  geophysics  hydraulics
dedication  dispelling  equitation  federative  geotropism  hydrophily
dedicative  dispersion  erectility  feminality  geriatrics  hylotheism
defamation  dispersive  ergodicity  femininity  geriatrist  hypanthium
defeminise  disqualify  ergonomics  fescennine  Ghibelline  hypocorism
definition  disruption  ergonomist  fictionist  Gilbertian  ideologist
definitive  disruptive  eructation  figuration  glaciation  ignobility
deflection  dissection  escalation  figurative  Glaswegian  illegalise
deflective  dissension  escritoire  filtration  glauberite  illegality
degressive  disservice  Esculapian  fingerling  glauconite  illuminism
dehumanise  dissuasion  estimation  finicality  glimmering  illuminist
dehumidify  dissuasive  estimative  firepolicy  glossarial  illusorily
delegation  distensile  eternalise  fixedpoint  glossarist  imbecility
delocalise  distension  eternalist  flaccidity  gluttonise  imbibition
delphinium  distention  ethicality  flagwaving  gnosticism  immaterial
demagogism  distilling  ethologist  flashpoint  Godfearing  immaturity
demobilise  distortion  etiolation  flattering  gormandise  immemorial
demolition  disulphide  eudemonism  flavouring  graciosity  immobilise
demonetise  disutility  eudemonist  fledgeling  gradualism  immobility
demoralise  divagation  eugenicist  flirtation  gradualist  immolation
denegation  divination  euhemerise  floatation  graduation  immoralist
denotation  dolomitise  euhemerist  florentine  grammarian  immorality
denotative  domination  Eurovision  floriation  grandchild  impanation
dentifrice  dominative  evacuation  floristics  grangerise  imparadise
denudation  doubletime  evacuative  flowergirl  grangerism  imperative
depilation  downstairs  evaluation  flunkeyism  graphemics  imposition
depolarise  drawstring  evaluative  fluviatile  graphitise  impoverish
deposition  drivelling  evaluative  flyfishing  graptolite  impression
depression  drosophila  evangelise  folklorist  gratifying  impressive
depressive  dubitation  evangelism  forbidding  greenstick  imprinting
depuration  dubitative  evangelist  foreboding  gressorial  impudicity
depurative  durability  everliving  foreignism  groundling  imputation
deputation  dysprosium  everything  forgetting  grovelling  imputative
derestrict  earthshine  evidential  formatting  guillotine  inactivity
derivation  earwigging  exaltation  fortissimi  gunrunning  inapposite
derivative  easterling  excavation  fortissimo  gymnastics  inbreeding
derogation  Eastertide  excerption  fortuitism  gypsophila  incapacity
descension  ebullition  excitation  fortuitist  habitation  inchoation
desolation  efficacity  excitative  forwarding  hairspring  inchoative
desorption  elasticise  execration  forwearied  halberdier  incitation
detonation  elasticity  execrative  fosterling  halieutics  incivility
detonative  Eleusinian  exhalation  foundation  handspring  incubation
detraction  elongation  exhaustion  Fourierism  Hanoverian  incubative
detractive  emaciation  exhaustive  foxhunting  Hansardise  indagation
devitalise  emancipist  exhibition  fraternise  hanselling  indecision
devocalise  embonpoint  exhumation  fraternity  haustorium  indecisive
devolution  emendation  expedition  fratricide  headspring  indefinite
dextrality  emigration  expiration  freeliving  heathenise  indexation
diatropism  emissivity  exploitive  friability  heathenish  indication
Dickensian  emollition  exposition  friendlily  heathenism  indicative
diecasting  emparadise  expositive  frivolling  hebetation  indocility
diesinking  empiricism  expression  frolicking  Heliconian  Indonesian
digitalise  empiricist  expressive  fruitarian  henharrier  induration
digitation  emulsifier  expunction  fulfilling  henotheism  indurative
digression  enamelling  exsanguine  fullbodied  henotheist  industrial
digressive  enamellist  extinction  fumigation  heparinise  inequality
dilatation  enchanting  extinctive  funnelling  hesitation  infarction
dilatorily  endemicity  extinguish  fusibility  hesitative  infelicity
diminution  endopodite  extraction  gadolinite  heulandite  infidelity
diminutive  energetics  extractive  gadolinium  heuristics  infighting
dimorphism  enervation  extraneity  gadrooning  highflying  infinitive
directoire  enervative  exultation  gaingiving  hippogriff  inflection
disability  englutting  exurbanite  galimatias  hipsterism  inflective
```

```
infliction  kriegspiel  Malthusian  monotheism  ocellation  Parnassian
inflictive  Krishnaism  managerial  monotheist  octandrian  parrotfish
infraction  laceration  Manicheism  moratorium  octodecimo  parsonbird
infusorial  lacerative  manicurist  morphemics  octonarian  partiality
infusorian  laconicism  manuscript  morphinism  oecologist  Passionist
ingression  lacustrine  maraschino  morrispike  oecumenism  pastellist
inhalation  Lamarckian  Marcionite  mosaicking  oenologist  pasteurise
inhibition  Lamarckism  margravine  motivation  offputting  pasteurism
inhumanity  laminarian  marguerite  mousseline  offsetting  patination
inhumation  lamination  martensite  Mousterian  oldmaidish  patriality
initialise  Lammastide  martialism  movability  ommatidium  patriotism
initiation  lampoonist  marvelling  muliebrity  oncologist  patristics
initiative  landowning  mastermind  multiplier  ontologist  patrolling
injunction  lanthanide  matchstick  musicality  operettist  peacockish
injunctive  lapidarian  maturation  mutability  ophicleide  peculation
innovation  lapidarist  maturative  mutilation  opinionist  pedagogics
innovative  lapidation  maximalist  mycologist  oppilation  pedalpoint
insecurity  laterality  mayonnaise  mycorrhiza  opposition  pedestrian
insipidity  laureation  mediastina  myocardium  oppression  pedicurist
insolation  laurelling  medication  nailpolish  oppressive  pedologist
inspanning  lavatorial  medicative  nanisation  opprobrium  pejoration
inspection  lawabiding  mediocrity  narcissism  optimalise  pejorative
inspective  lawrencium  meditation  narcissist  orchardist  pencilling
instilling  Lawrentian  meditative  nasturtium  orchestics  pendentive
insularism  ledgerline  Melanesian  natalitial  ordinarily  pennillion
insularity  legibility  mercantile  natatorial  ordination  penologist
insulation  legitimise  mesomerism  natatorium  Ordovician  penpushing
interstice  legitimism  messianism  nationwide  oreologist  pentastich
intertrigo  legitimist  metabolise  naturalise  organicism  peppermill
intertwine  Leibnizian  metabolism  naturalism  organicist  peppermint
intertwist  lengthwise  metabolite  naturalist  orotundity  percentile
intimation  lepidolite  metamerism  nauseating  orthoepist  perception
intinction  lesbianism  micaschist  navigation  oscitation  perceptive
intonation  levigation  microcline  nebulosity  osculation  percussion
intubation  levitation  microseism  necrophile  osmeterium  percussive
inundation  liberalise  midmorning  necrophily  osmiridium  perfection
inurbanity  liberalism  militarily  needlefish  otherwhile  perfective
invalidism  liberalist  militarise  negativism  outbidding  performing
invalidity  liberality  militarism  negativist  outfitting  perihelion
inveracity  liberation  militarist  negativity  outgassing  permeation
invitation  librettist  millennial  negrophile  outgunning  permeative
invocation  lifegiving  millennium  nephridium  outlandish  permission
involution  lifesaving  mineralise  neutralise  outpouring  permissive
iodination  limitation  minimalism  neutralism  outputting  permitting
ionisation  limitative  minimalist  neutralist  outrunning  peroration
iridosmine  lipreading  mishitting  neutrality  outsitting  peroxidise
irrelative  lipservice  misogamist  nickelling  outstation  perpetuity
irreligion  literalise  misogynist  nicotinism  outwitting  perplexity
irrigation  literalism  misologist  nightshift  overactive  perquisite
irritation  literalist  misprision  nightshirt  overexcite  persuasion
irritative  literality  missionise  nightstick  overpraise  persuasive
Ishmaelite  literarily  miswording  nitpicking  overrefine  perversion
isometrics  literation  mitigation  nodulation  overriding  perversity
isoniazide  lithotrity  mitigative  nominalism  overstride  perversive
italianise  Lithuanian  mixolydian  nominalist  pacificism  phallicism
Italianism  litigation  moderation  nomination  pacificist  phantasise
Italophile  lobulation  moderatism  nominative  paedophile  pharisaism
jacobinise  locomotion  modulation  nomologist  pagination  pharmacist
Jacobinism  locomotive  moisturise  nonfiction  palaeolith  philippina
Jacobitism  logicality  monarchial  nonplaying  palagonite  philippine
janitorial  logrolling  Monarchian  nosologist  palatalise  philistine
jaywalking  Lollardism  monarchism  notability  palliation  phlogopite
jeopardise  lovemaking  monarchist  nourishing  palliative  Phoenician
jerrybuilt  lowprofile  monetarily  novaculite  Panamanian  photophily
jocularity  luminosity  monetarism  nucleation  pancratium  photoprint
johnsonian  Lusitanian  monetarist  nucleonics  panegyrise  physicking
journalise  lustration  mongrelise  nucleoside  panegyrist  pianissimo
journalism  lutestring  mongrelism  nucleotide  pansophist  picayunish
journalist  lycopodium  monitorial  numeration  papaverine  picketline
jubilation  lyophilise  monogamist  numerosity  paperknife  picnicking
juvenility  Lysenkoism  monogenism  nuptiality  parabolise  pigeonwing
Kantianism  macadamise  monogynian  obituarist  paradisiac  pilgarlick
katabolism  maceration  monologise  obligation  paradisian  pincerlike
kennelling  maculation  monologist  obstetrics  paralogise  pincushion
keratinise  magnifying  monomaniac  obturation  paramecium  piperidine
kidnapping  maidenlike  monopodial  occupation  paramedics  pistolling
kimberlite  mainspring  monopodium  occurrence  parapodium  pistonring
kinematics  malleebird  monopolise  oceanarium  parasitism  plagiarise
kineticist  Malpighian  monopolist  oceangoing  parcelling  plagiarism
```

plagiarist	preventive	radicalism	revocation	selfpraise	solstitial
plantation	priestling	radication	revolution	selfrising	solubilise
plasmodium	primordial	rainmaking	rhapsodise	selfruling	solubility
plasticise	primordium	ratability	rhapsodist	semeiotics	Sorbonnist
plasticity	princeling	reactivity	rheologist	semestrial	sororicide
playacting	principial	reappraise	rheumatics	semidivine	spallation
plebiscite	principium	recidivism	rheumatism	semidrying	Spartacist
pliability	proceeding	recidivist	ribbonfish	seminarian	spasticity
plumassier	procession	recitalist	riproaring	seminarist	spatiality
pneumatics	proclivity	recitation	risibility	semination	specialise
pocketsize	proctorial	recitative	rodfishing	semiuncial	specialism
podiatrist	proctorise	recitativo	roistering	senatorial	specialist
polemicist	production	recolonise	rollicking	sensualise	speciality
polemonium	productive	recreation	rontgenise	sensualism	speciation
politician	profession	recreative	rosaniline	sensualist	speciosity
politicise	profundity	redemption	roseengine	sensuality	Spencerian
polygamist	projectile	redemptive	rudderfish	sentential	Spenserian
polygenism	projection	redescribe	ruffianism	separation	spermicide
polygenist	projective	reelection	rumination	separatism	sperrylite
polymerise	prologuise	reflection	ruminative	separatist	sphalerite
polymerism	promethium	reflective	rumrunning	separative	sphericity
Polynesian	propelling	refraction	rupicoline	septennial	spherulite
polynomial	propensity	refractive	Russianise	septennium	spiderline
polyploidy	propertied	refreshing	Russophile	septillion	spillikins
polytheism	prophesier	refuelling	saccharide	Septuagint	spiralling
polytheist	proportion	refutation	saccharify	sequential	spoliation
Pomeranian	propulsion	regelation	saccharine	serologist	spoliative
pomologist	propulsive	regression	sacroiliac	serpentine	sponsorial
popularise	prosaicism	regressive	sagination	sestertium	spoondrift
popularity	proscenium	regretting	salability	sestertius	spoonerism
population	prosperity	regularise	salientian	Sexagesima	sporangial
positivism	prostomial	regularity	salivation	sexologist	sporangium
positivist	prostomium	regulation	salpingian	sexpartite	springlike
positivity	protection	regulative	salutarily	sextillion	springtide
possession	protective	rejuvenise	salutation	shanghaier	springtime
possessive	protensive	relativise	samarskite	sheathbill	sprinkling
postchaise	protrusile	relativism	sanatorium	sherardise	squalidity
postillion	protrusion	relativist	sanctifier	shirtwaist	squamation
postliminy	protrusive	relativity	sanderling	shoestring	squireling
postoffice	proverbial	relaxation	sanguinity	shortening	staggering
postscript	provincial	relegation	sanitarian	shovelling	stagnation
potability	prudential	relinquish	sanitarily	Shrovetide	stalactite
potbellied	psalmodise	relocation	sanitarium	shuttering	stalagmite
pothunting	psalmodist	remonetise	sanitation	sibilation	standpoint
practician	psalterium	renovation	sapiential	sicklebill	standstill
practising	psittacine	reorganise	sapphirine	siderolite	staphyline
praecocial	psychicism	reparation	satisfying	signalling	stargazing
praemunire	psychicist	reparative	saturation	silverfish	starvation
praesidium	Ptolemaist	repertoire	saxicoline	silverside	starveling
praetorial	publishing	repetition	scandalise	similarity	statistics
praetorian	puerperium	repetitive	scansorial	simplicity	staurolite
pragmatise	pummelling	reposition	scarlatina	simplifier	stealthily
pragmatism	punctation	repression	scattering	simulation	stentorian
pragmatist	pupilarity	repressive	scepticism	simulative	stephanite
preadamite	puritanise	reputation	schematise	sinecurism	stiffening
precaution	puritanism	rescission	schematism	sinecurist	stigmatise
preceptive	purseseine	resolution	schoolgirl	sinologist	stigmatism
precession	putrescine	resolutive	schooltime	skibobbing	stigmatist
preciosity	pyridoxine	resorption	Scillonian	skijumping	stillicide
preclusion	pyrolusite	resorptive	sclerotium	skindiving	stockstill
preclusive	pyromaniac	resounding	Scotticise	skyjacking	stoneblind
precordial	pyroxenite	respecting	Scotticism	skywriting	stonesnipe
predestine	Pyrrhonian	respective	scratchily	Slavophile	storksbill
prediction	Pyrrhonism	responsive	scribbling	sleevelink	stramonium
predictive	Pyrrhonist	resumption	scrutinise	slenderise	strategist
preemption	pyrrhotite	resumptive	scurrility	slipperily	streamline
preemptive	quadratics	retractile	seamanlike	slowmotion	strychnine
preexilian	quadrivial	retraction	secretaire	smaragdine	strychnism
preferring	quadrivium	retractive	secularise	smaragdite	stylistics
preglacial	quantifier	retraining	secularism	smattering	stypticity
prehensile	quantitive	reunionism	secularist	smokedried	subacidity
prehension	quarantine	reunionist	secularity	sneakthief	subclavian
prelection	quartation	revalorise	seignorial	snivelling	subduction
presentive	quartering	revanchism	seismicity	snowmobile	subglacial
presignify	quaternion	revanchist	selfacting	solidarism	subheading
pressurise	quaternity	revelation	selffaction	solidarist	subjectify
pretension	quinacrine	revitalise	selfdenial	solidarity	subjection
prevailing	Rachmanism	revivalism	selfloving	solifidian	subjective
prevention	radicalise	revivalist	selfmotion	solitarily	subletting

```
submersion   tepidarium   unassuming   wattlebird   pockmarked   chemically
submission   tetrastich   unavailing   weathering   ramshackle   chinchilla
submissive   textualist   unbecoming   weaverbird   ringnecked   chronicler
submitting   theodolite   unblinking   wellspring   ropewalker   Cinderella
subreption   theogonist   unblushing   Wertherian   seersucker   circumflex
subroutine   theologian   unchanging   Wertherism   selfseeker   citronella
subsection   theologise   unchastity   westernise   semiweekly   clarabella
subsellium   theologist   unctuosity   whirlybird   shellacked   clavicular
subspecies   theoretics   undercliff   whiskified   shipbroker   clerically
substation   thermopile   underlying   whispering   shoebuckle   clinically
subvention   thickening   undershirt   whitesmith   shopwalker   closetplay
subversion   threadfish   underskirt   windowsill   slitpocket   codswallop
subversive   threnodial   undertrick   wintertide   soapflakes   colonially
succession   threnodist   underwrite   wintertime   softspoken   colossally
successive   throwstick   undulation   wolframite   swaybacked   commonalty
sudatorium   thumbprint   unedifying   worthwhile   tearjerker   communally
suffragist   thundering   unfamiliar   wrongdoing   trafficked   conjugally
suggestion   thwartwise   unfeminine   wunderkind   trafficker   controlled
suggestive   tiddlywink   unflagging   Wycliffite   turnbuckle   controller
sulphurise   timberline   ungrudging   Wykehamist   undertaken   corbiculae
summerlike   timesaving   unicyclist   yellowbird   undertaker   corporally
summertime   tinctorial   uniformity   zigzagging   unprovoked   corrivalry
superation   tinselling   unipartite   zwitterion   unremarked   cosmically
supination   titivation   university   chaparajos   vestpocket   cosmopolis
suppletion   tittupping   unmorality   chaparejos   watchmaker   councillor
suppletive   titubation   unoccupied   hallelujah   wellspoken   counselled
supportive   toleration   unofficial   barebacked   wirewalker   counsellor
surprising   tonguetied   unpleasing   besprinkle   wireworker   cowparsley
surrealism   topazolite   unsettling   bivouacked   woodpecker   criminally
surrealist   topicality   unsporting   bluejacket   woodworker   critically
susceptive   topologist   unsteadily   boneshaker   workbasket   culturally
suspension   torrential   unswerving   bookmarker   abnormally   curricular
suspensive   tortellini   unthinking   bootlicker   acetabular   curriculum
sustaining   tortuosity   unwavering   caseworker   acetabulum   cyclically
sustention   tourmaline   unwieldily   coalbunker   antebellum   demoiselle
sustentive   toxication   unworthily   comstocker   apparelled   deshabille
swaggering   trabeation   unyielding   corncockle   arboreally   diagonally
swanupping   Tractarian   upbraiding   cornflakes   armorially   difficulty
sweatshirt   trajection   upbringing   dressmaker   armourclad   dillydally
sweetbriar   trampoline   upstanding   dustjacket   arterially   discobolus
sweetbrier   trancelike   urticarial   fairspoken   arteriolar   dishabille
sweetening   transcribe   urtication   fleamarket   aspergilla   disloyally
sweltering   transcript   ustulation   freespoken   astragalus   disloyalty
swivelling   transition   usucaption   goatsucker   atomically   dissembler
swordstick   transitive   usurpation   goodlooker   atypically   dissimilar
sybaritism   traumatism   utopianism   halfcocked   autumnally   doubtfully
symmetrise   travelling   validation   hamshackle   banderilla   downfallen
sympathise   travertine   vanadinite   handpicked   barcarolle   dreadfully
symphonion   trecentist   varicosity   handworked   bedevilled   eigenvalue
symphonist   trepanning   vasoactive   highjacker   bedraggled   elevenplus
symphysial   trichinise   Vaticanism   hitchhiker   bejewelled   embowelled
syncretise   trichroism   Vaticanist   hokeypokey   bemedalled   Emmentaler
syncretism   triclinium   vegetarian   humpbacked   bestseller   empanelled
syncretist   tricyclist   vegetation   icebreaker   biannually   encephalic
synonymist   Tridentine   vegetative   ironworker   biblically   encephalon
synonymity   tripartite   velitation   jawbreaker   bidonville   endothelia
synthesise   triplicity   veneration   kenspeckle   biennially   enthralled
synthesist   trisection   vesication   landlocked   bimetallic   erotically
synthetise   triskelion   vespertine   lawbreaker   binaurally   erysipelas
synthetist   trivialise   vignettist   lifejacket   bisexually   escadrille
tabularise   trivialism   vindictive   lumpsucker   bivalvular   espadrille
tabulation   triviality   vinegarish   matchmaker   blamefully   especially
tailorbird   troctolite   virologist   merrymaker   blissfully   ethereally
tamability   trollopish   virtuality   mineworker   bluecollar   ethnically
tambourine   trombonist   virtuosity   moneymaker   boastfully   Eurodollar
tangential   Trotskyism   visibility   moneytaker   bookseller   eventually
tankengine   Trotskyist   visitation   mossbunker   breakables   exotically
tapestried   Trotskyite   visitorial   moviemaker   brocatelle   externally
Tartuffian   trowelling   vitaminise   noisemaker   Caerphilly   faithfully
Tartuffism   truncation   vitriolise   nondrinker   carboxylic   fancifully
tasselling   tuberosity   viviparity   nutcracker   carbuncled   farcically
taxability   tunnelling   voiceprint   overcooked   carbuncled   fascicular
taxonomist   turpentine   volatilise   overlooker   cascarilla   fasciculus
technicist   typescript   volatility   papermaker   catburglar   fenestella
technician   typicality   volubility   pawnbroker   cerebellum   fiducially
technicist   typologist   vomitorium   peacemaker   chancellor   flannelled
television   Tyrrhenian   Waldensian   periwinkle   channelled   follicular
temptation   ulceration   wassailing   pickpocket   chapfallen   fontanelle
tenability   ulcerative   waterskier   pigsticker   cheerfully   footballer
```

```
forcefully  minuscular  rightfully  trouvaille  bressummer  ophthalmia
foreteller  mirthfully  ringtailed  trustfully  cacodaemon  ophthalmic
fraxinella  monocyclic  ritornelli  truthfully  catechumen  orchardman
freesoiler  mosaically  ritornello  tubercular  cavalryman  organismal
fruitfully  mournfully  rockabilly  tuberculin  centesimal  overcommit
funereally  mozzarella  rollcollar  tutorially  chairwoman  pantomimic
furuncular  multipolar  rosemallow  twowheeler  childermas  paranormal
fustanella  muskmallow  rottweiler  underbelly  clawhammer  paroxysmal
germinally  myopically  rubrically  undervalue  cosmoramic  patronymic
ghastfully  mystically  rustically  unequalled  councilman  pentatomic
glomerular  mythically  sagittally  unexampled  countryman  pentstemon
glomerulus  nationally  salmonella  unexcelled  daydreamer  peridermal
gothically  nautically  saltarello  unfilially  decagramme  phantasmal
gracefully  necropolis  saltcellar  unhouseled  decigramme  phantasmic
granadilla  newfangled  saturnalia  uniaxially  diathermal  polyatamic
gratefully  notarially  scenically  unilocular  diathermic  polyonymic
grenadilla  notionally  scornfully  univocally  disclaimer  proclaimer
groundplan  nullanulla  screenplay  unlabelled  drophammer  programmer
guilefully  officially  seasonally  unlawfully  duodecimal  provitamin
gutturally  oldfangled  seguidilla  unravelled  ectodermal  railwayman
habitually  optionally  selfstyled  unrivalled  ectodermic  saleswoman
halfdollar  orientally  selfwilled  unschooled  embolismic  sarcolemma
halfvolley  originally  septically  unsocially  endodermal  Scotswoman
handgallop  painkiller  serradilla  untroubled  endodermis  seriocomic
handselled  panhandler  shamefully  unwrinkled  Englishman  serviceman
hardbilled  parentally  shopsoiled  valleculae  erethismic  spacewoman
hardboiled  particular  shrievalty  vallecular  eurhythmic  speedlimit
haustellum  pastorally  shrivelled  varietally  exothermal  strabismal
hectically  paternally  sillybilly  vaudeville  exothermic  strabismic
heliacally  peacefully  slidevalve  vengefully  footwarmer  strabismus
hemicyclic  peccadillo  slothfully  vermicelli  freedwoman  superhuman
heroically  peduncular  soapboiler  vermicular  geothermal  taxidermal
holusbolus  pellicular  societally  vernacular  geothermic  taxidermic
homunculus  penetralia  softbilled  versicular  grandmamma  tilthammer
hormonally  penicillin  softboiled  vertically  GrecoRoman  townswoman
hullabaloo  peninsular  soldanella  vestibular  groundsman  tragicomic
hydrically  pennanular  spectacled  vestibulum  harvestman  trawlerman
hyperbolae  pentathlon  spectacles  vibraculum  heavyarmed  trichromat
hyperbolas  pericyclic  spectrally  victualled  heroicomic  triggerman
hyperbolic  personally  spiracular  victualler  highwayman  triphammer
hyperdulia  personalty  spiraculum  villanelle  hippocampi  tularaemia
hypergolic  petronella  spitefully  virginally  hornrimmed  tularaemic
immortally  philatelic  sportfully  viscerally  horsewoman  uncustomed
immortelle  phonically  statically  visionally  husbandman  uneconomic
impanelled  physically  stencilled  vortically  hyperaemia  uninformed
imperially  piccalilli  stenciller  vorticella  hyperaemic  unredeemed
imperilled  pillowslip  stockpiler  vorticular  hypodermal  weatherman
infernally  playbyplay  stopvolley  wanderplug  hypodermic  Welshwoman
informally  playfellow  suicidally  wastefully  hypodermis  windjammer
inimically  poetically  supernally  watchfully  infrahuman  workingman
initialled  polycyclic  surgically  watermelon  Irishwoman  abhorrence
integrally  portcullis  tactically  wearifully  isodynamic  aboriginal
internally  postbellum  taleteller  weedkiller  isoseismal  absorbance
intervolve  postexilic  tarantella  wellheeled  isothermal  absorbency
ironically  potentilla  tarantelle  wholesaler  jackhammer  abstinence
jargonelle  pourparler  tastefully  wildfowler  journeyman  abstinency
judicially  powerfully  teatrolley  willynilly  kilogramme  acceptance
labiovelar  premaxilla  teetotally  willywilly  laundryman  accordance
ladykiller  pridefully  temporally  wingcollar  lighterman  additional
lenticular  primevally  temporalty  wirepuller  longprimer  admittance
loudhailer  principled  tendrillar  wrathfully  loxodromic  advertence
Lupercalia  prodigally  tendrilled  wrongfully  lukewarmly  advertency
majuscular  prothallia  tentacular  yokefellow  markswoman  agglutinin
mandibular  prothallus  terminally  youthfully  matronymic  aldermanic
maniacally  proximally  tetrapolis  Abrahamman  metronomic  aldermanry
manzanilla  pulsatilla  texturally  accustomed  metronymic  algolagnia
marginalia  punctually  thankfully  aerogramme  Michaelmas  algolagnic
marginally  pyrogallol  toroidally  anastigmat  midshipman  allegiance
marshalled  quadruplet  tourbillon  aneurismal  militiaman  allergenic
marshaller  quadruplex  trabeculae  aneurysmal  millesimal  allophonic
materially  quarrelled  trabecular  anticlimax  monorhymed  alternance
maternally  quarreller  tragically  apochromat  mumbojumbo  androgenic
medievally  quintuplet  trammelled  arrhythmia  nambypamby  anglomania
mercifully  ranunculus  tranquilly  arrhythmic  neurilemma  anticlinal
Methuselah  rationally  transvalue  astronomer  neurolemma  antiphonal
metrically  reconciler  triangular  astronomic  noblewoman  appearance
metropolis  regionally  trigonally  backgammon  nonswimmer  aquaplaner
micropylar  remedially  tropaeolum  biodynamic  nurseryman  ascendance
minstrelsy  remodelled  tropically  blasphemer  oftentimes  ascendancy
```

ascendence	diachronic	importance	orthogenic	repellence	thruppence
ascendency	difference	importuner	orthogonal	repellency	ticpolonga
assistance	diffidence	imprudence	outbalance	repentance	tobogganer
attendance	dilettante	incessancy	overmanned	reprobance	tractional
barramunda	dilettanti	incipience	paraffinic	repugnance	tragacanth
barramundi	diminuendo	incipiency	pathogenic	repugnancy	transience
belladonna	dipsomania	inclemency	penetrance	resilience	transiency
bellydance	disarrange	incumbency	pentagonal	resiliency	translunar
belongings	dissidence	indistinct	pentatonic	resistance	trenchancy
benignancy	dissonance	inductance	pentimento	resorcinol	trigeminal
beribboned	dissonancy	indulgence	periclinal	restrained	trillionth
bioscience	distrainer	inelegance	permanence	restrainer	truculence
bladdernut	distrainor	infrasonic	permanency	resurgence	truculency
blancmange	divergence	inharmonic	pertinence	revisional	tumescence
bloodmoney	divergency	insistence	pertinency	rhizogenic	turbulence
bluebonnet	divisional	insistency	pestilence	ritardando	turbulency
brandysnap	divulgence	insolvency	petitioner	roadrunner	ultrasonic
brilliance	ebullience	insurgence	phagedenic	rotational	unbrokenly
brilliancy	ebulliency	insurgency	phenomenal	sacrosanct	unbuttoned
burramundi	efficiency	intendance	phenomenon	salicional	uncommonly
camerlengo	effulgence	interlunar	pheromonal	salmagundi	underlinen
camerlingo	eighteenmo	intervener	photogenic	saprogenic	underminer
campaigner	eighteenth	intervenor	phylogenic	sarracenia	underpants
caravanned	electronic	interzonal	phytogenic	scherzando	undersense
caravanner	emblazoner	intestinal	piccaninny	screenings	undesigned
cartomancy	emblazonry	intrigante	pickaninny	senescence	unscreened
catchpenny	emblements	invariance	pilliwinks	shortrange	unseasoned
champignon	endocrinal	irradiance	pinchpenny	sideglance	unstrained
chaplaincy	enharmonic	irrational	planktonic	skirtdance	venational
chatoyance	episternum	isochronal	polyclinic	slatternly	virescence
chiromancy	equational	itinerancy	polyphonic	smartmoney	vocational
coatimundi	erotogenic	jaguarundi	portamento	snakedance	volitional
coelacanth	erotomania	kibbutznik	positional	snickasnee	wanderings
cognisance	escallonia	kinnikinic	pozzolanic	softfinned	weimaraner
cognominal	excellence	landingnet	prearrange	somnolence	wellturned
comedienne	excellency	lansquenet	precedence	somnolency	wongawonga
competence	expectance	latescence	precedency	southerner	woodturner
competency	expectancy	lawntennis	preference	southernly	xylophonic
complainer	expedience	lentigines	prepotence	splanchnic	abdominous
compliance	expediency	limeburner	prepotency	spodomancy	absolutory
compliancy	experience	Lipizzaner	prescience	stringency	abstemious
condolence	exuberance	Lippizaner	presidency	stringendo	acarpelous
conference	flatulence	longshanks	presternum	stubbornly	acephalous
confidante	flatulency	luxuriance	prevalence	subliminal	acrogenous
confidence	floribunda	maintainer	prevenancy	submariner	actinozoan
confluence	forerunner	malentendu	procurance	subordinal	adenectomy
congruence	fortyniner	malignance	prominence	subsidence	adjuratory
congruency	fourteener	malignancy	pronominal	subtenancy	admonitory
connivance	fourteenth	mendicancy	propaganda	succedanea	adulterous
conscience	fractional	meridional	provenance	succulence	advocatory
consonance	frictional	misaligned	providence	succulency	aeolotropy
consonancy	frontbench	miscreance	pubescence	sufferance	aeruginous
constringe	functional	misgivings	purtenance	sunderance	affettuoso
continence	Gallomania	mistakenly	purveyance	superlunar	albuminoid
convenance	ganglionic	molendinar	pycnogonid	supersonic	albuminous
conveyance	gingersnap	molybdenum	quadrennia	supertonic	alliaceous
coparcener	governance	monoclinal	questioner	suppliance	allogamous
cordwainer	greenfinch	monoclinic	quiescence	suprarenal	allpurpose
corpulence	gyrational	monophonic	quiescency	survivance	alongshore
corpulency	hankypanky	monstrance	radiogenic	sustenance	alpenstock
corrigenda	headphones	moonshiner	radiosonde	suzerainty	ambulatory
cosmogonic	heptagonal	musicianly	recipiency	swordance	amendatory
covariance	heptatonic	myasthenia	recommence	sycophancy	amphibious
crapulence	hippomanes	mythomania	recompense	synchronal	amygdaloid
crossbench	histrionic	naphthenic	recumbency	synchronic	amylaceous
crossbones	homophonic	necromancy	recurrence	tablelinen	anadromous
defeasance	hootenanny	negligence	redundance	taciturnly	anastomose
deficiency	hornblende	newsagency	redundancy	talismanic	anatropous
definienda	hydromancy	nineteenth	reentrance	telephoner	ancipitous
dehiscence	hypersonic	nonaligned	refulgence	telephonic	anglophobe
delusional	hypolimnia	northerner	reiterance	temperance	anglophone
dependence	iatrogenic	nudibranch	rejoicings	termagancy	anisotropy
dependency	ideational	nutational	relational	tetragonal	anonaceous
desipience	illusional	observance	reluctance	theophanic	anthracoid
desistance	impatience	occasional	reluctancy	thermionic	anthropoid
detergency	impeccancy	occurrence	remittance	thirteenth	antiheroic
determined	impendence	offlicence	renascence	threatener	antonymous
deterrence	impendency	oppugnancy	repellance	threepence	apocarpous
devotional	impersonal	ordonnance	repellancy	threepenny	

aquiferous	cancellous	cystoscope	fingerbowl	hippodrome	lubricious
arenaceous	candlewood	cystoscopy	fingerpost	hithermost	luciferous
armigerous	candyfloss	cytochrome	fisherfolk	homogamous	lucifugous
arytaenoid	cankerworm	dampingoff	flagitious	homogenous	lugubrious
asynchrony	cannelloni	decapodous	flameproof	homologous	lumberroom
auriferous	canvaswork	dedicatory	flamingoes	homonymous	lumbersome
auspicious	caoutchouc	defamatory	flashflood	homozygote	mackintosh
autecology	capricious	delphinoid	floatstone	homozygous	macrospore
autogamous	cardiology	deltiology	floorcloth	horrendous	maidenhood
autogenous	carmagnole	demonology	flosculous	horsecloth	malacology
autologous	carotenoid	dendriform	flugelhorn	horseshoer	malleefowl
autonomous	carotinoid	dendrology	foliaceous	houseproud	malodorous
avaricious	carphology	deontology	folkmemory	hucklebone	malvaceous
backstroke	censorious	depilatory	foraminous	humoursome	mandragora
badderlock	centrefold	depository	fortuitous	hydrophone	markettown
balneology	centrosome	derogatory	founderous	hydroscope	marrowbone
barleycorn	ceruminous	despiteous	fourstroke	hygroscope	marvellous
barratrous	chainsmoke	diaphanous	frolicsome	hypogynous	mastectomy
barrenwort	chalcedony	digitiform	fuliginous	iconoscope	masterhood
basketwork	chalkstone	dimorphous	futurology	idolatrous	masterwork
bassethorn	chaudfroid	diningroom	Gallophobe	immunology	matronhood
bathyscope	chequebook	diphyodont	gangrenous	impervious	meddlesome
battailous	childproof	disapprove	gastrology	incautious	melancholy
battledore	chivalrous	disastrous	gastronome	incestuous	membranous
beechdrops	chloroform	discomfort	gastronomy	incubatory	mendacious
bibliology	Christhood	discommode	gelatinous	indecorous	meningioma
bibliopole	chromosome	discompose	gemmaceous	indicatory	menstruous
bibliopoly	chronology	diseconomy	gentlefolk	indigenous	meticulous
billetdoux	chuckerout	disembroil	glaciology	infectious	mettlesome
bioecology	churchgoer	disharmony	glasscloth	inglorious	microbiota
bipetalous	cinquefoil	dispersoid	glossology	inhibitory	microphone
birthstone	circuitous	dispiteous	glottology	iniquitous	microscope
bitterroot	clangorous	distichous	glumaceous	initiatory	microscopy
bitterwood	clavichord	divinatory	gluttonous	innovatory	microspore
bituminous	clearstory	donkeywork	goloptious	innuendoes	middlemost
blackamoor	clerestory	donnybrook	goluptious	innumerous	migrainous
blackthorn	clingstone	dovecolour	goodygoody	intercross	millefiori
blastopore	clinkstone	downstroke	Gorgonzola	inundatory	mineralogy
blithesome	closestool	drupaceous	gramineous	invitatory	minestrone
bloodstock	coetaneous	dumbledore	gramophone	invocatory	minutebook
bloodstone	collarbone	ectogenous	graphology	iridaceous	miraculous
bluethroat	collembola	eczematous	grasscloth	isopterous	misericord
blusterous	commandoes	edentulous	grassroots	isosporous	misogynous
boisterous	commodious	Egyptology	gratuitous	jobbernowl	mitigatory
bothersome	commonroom	embryology	gravestone	judicatory	mockheroic
bottommost	compradore	emendatory	greasewood	keratinous	molluscoid
brachylogy	compulsory	emigratory	greencloth	knighthood	molluscous
brainstorm	conchology	endogamous	greenstone	knockabout	monandrous
brakeblock	conclusory	endogenous	gregarious	laboratory	moniliform
brantgoose	confervoid	engineroom	grindstone	lachrymose	monochrome
brazilwood	coniferous	enterotomy	groundwork	languorous	monoecious
breastbone	consistory	entomology	gynandrous	lanuginose	monogamous
breastwork	contagious	enzymology	hagioscope	lanuginous	monogynous
brentgoose	contiguous	ephemerous	hairstroke	laparotomy	monotonous
bridegroom	continuous	epicycloid	halogenous	lascivious	monsignori
bridgework	coolingoff	epidermoid	hammerlock	lattermost	mordacious
brightwork	coriaceous	ericaceous	hammerpond	lauraceous	morphology
broadcloth	correspond	escapology	harmonious	leguminous	mosquitoes
broadsword	cottonwood	euphonious	headstrong	letterbomb	motherhood
brokendown	cottonwool	excitatory	heartblock	letterbook	motherwort
bronchiole	courageous	excusatory	heartblood	lexicology	muciferous
brownstone	cousinhood	execratory	heartwhole	libidinous	musicology
bubblyjock	cradlesong	exhibitory	heatstroke	licentious	musicstool
burdensome	craniology	exobiology	heavenborn	lightproof	myrtaceous
butterwort	cretaceous	expiratory	helioscope	likelihood	mysterious
buttondown	crewelwork	expository	heliotrope	liliaceous	myxomatous
buttonhole	cribriform	extraneous	heliotropy	limaciform	nanosecond
buttonhook	crisscross	factitious	hepatology	linguiform	nationhood
buttonwood	cryptology	fallacious	heptachord	lipomatous	nativeborn
byssaceous	ctenophore	fallingoff	herbaceous	litterlout	necroscopy
cacciatore	cuddlesome	fandangoes	heretofore	livelihood	nectareous
cadaverous	cumbersome	fastidious	herrenvolk	livingroom	needlebook
caddisworm	cumuliform	fatherhood	heterodont	lockerroom	needlecord
caespitose	curvaceous	felicitous	heterodoxy	locomotory	needlework
calamitous	curvacious	fetterlock	heterogony	loganstone	negrophobe
calcareous	cuttlebone	fibrillose	heterology	logorrhoea	nephoscope
caliginous	cuttystool	fictitious	heteronomy	longaevous	nephrology
calumnious	cyclostome	fiddlewood	heteronomy	lophophore	nethermost
calyciform	cylindroid	fieldstone	hexamerous	loquacious	nidicolous

nidifugous	piliferous	roustabout	spitchcock	toxicology	apocalypse
nincompoop	pitchstone	rubiginous	splashdown	traitorous	apostrophe
nipplewort	plaguesome	rubythroat	spleenwort	trajectory	archetypal
nitrogroup	pleochroic	rupicolous	splintbone	transitory	autography
nonferrous	plunderous	Russophobe	splintcoal	treasonous	azeotropic
nubiferous	pocketbook	sabretooth	spoilsport	tremendous	bookkeeper
nuciferous	pogonology	saccharoid	spoliatory	triandrous	brachiopod
nucivorous	pogonotomy	saccharose	spongewood	trichinous	cacography
numerology	polychrome	saliferous	spongiform	trichology	cephalopod
nutritious	polygamous	salubrious	spongology	trichotomy	cerography
obligatory	polygenous	salutatory	sporophore	trioecious	chamberpot
obsequious	polygynous	sanctimony	springwood	triphthong	chickenpox
oceanology	polymerous	sandalwood	squaretoed	trophology	chimneypot
octamerous	polysemous	sappanwood	squaretoes	troubadour	clodhopper
octandrous	polytocous	sargassoes	squirehood	tubicolous	clothespeg
octopodous	pomiferous	sarmentose	statoscope	tuffaceous	clothespin
odontology	porraceous	sarmentous	stelliform	tumbledown	cornucopia
oedematose	portentous	satanology	stertorous	tumultuous	crowkeeper
oedematous	possessory	saxicolous	stiflebone	turkeycock	cryoscopic
oleaginous	posthumous	scandalous	stilettoes	turtledove	cuckoospit
oleiferous	potamology	schizogony	stinkstone	twelvefold	demography
oleraceous	powderhorn	schoolbook	stitchwort	twelvenote	doorkeeper
oligopsony	pratincole	schoolroom	stockproof	twelvetone	doxography
olivaceous	prayerbook	schoolwork	stormcloud	ubiquitous	drawingpin
omnigenous	precarious	sclerotomy	stormproof	umbiliform	eartrumpet
omnivorous	preceptory	screechowl	strabotomy	umbrageous	emerypaper
omophagous	precocious	scrofulous	stratiform	undercroft	endoscopic
oncogenous	precursory	scrollwork	streetdoor	underfloor	endstopped
oneirology	predacious	scrupulous	stridulous	underproof	epistrophe
orangewood	predispose	scurrilous	Stroganoff	underquote	froghopper
orphanhood	prednisone	scyphiform	stromatous	underscore	gamekeeper
osculatory	prehistory	scyphozoan	stronghold	undershoot	gasteropod
outrageous	presuppose	seaanemone	strongroom	understock	gatekeeper
ovariotomy	priesthood	seborrhoea	struthious	understood	glasspaper
overexpose	prodigious	securiform	stupendous	underwrote	goalkeeper
overthrown	promissory	seismology	subaqueous	undesirous	gobstopper
paddleboat	promontory	selenodont	sulphurous	undulatory	gymnosophy
Palaeozoic	promptbook	selenology	sunparlour	ungenerous	gyroscopic
palindrome	propitious	selfcolour	superstore	ungracious	harelipped
palladious	prosperous	selfparody	suppletory	unhandsome	holography
palliatory	protectory	semeiology	suspensoid	uproarious	horoscopic
palmaceous	proteiform	separatory	suspensory	urbanology	horsecoper
palmerworm	proteinous	sequacious	suspicious	vaporiform	ideography
palynology	provisions	SerboCroat	swarmspore	veldschoen	interloper
papaverous	psephology	serotinous	symphylous	velutinous	isentropic
papyrology	psychology	setterwort	synanthous	ventricose	jackanapes
paraboloid	pugnacious	shantytown	syncarpous	vesicatory	ladychapel
parasitoid	pupiparous	shellproof	synecology	vibraphone	landscaper
paratroops	purseproud	shellshock	synoecious	victorious	leafhopper
parenthood	pyretology	shirtfront	synonymous	videophone	lexigraphy
paronymous	pyrogenous	shockproof	tablecloth	villainous	limitrophe
paroxytone	quadrupole	sidestroke	tablespoon	violaceous	lipography
pastrycook	quatrefoil	simulatory	taperecord	viperiform	lobsterpot
pediculous	quickthorn	singlefoot	tautophony	viraginous	lockkeeper
pellagrous	radiophone	sinistrous	technology	virginhood	logography
pemphigoid	radioscopy	sisterhood	tenderfoot	viviparous	malapropos
pemphigous	rampageous	sketchbook	tenderloin	vociferous	maxilliped
pennaceous	rebellious	slanderous	tenebrious	voluminous	megascopic
pentachord	redemptory	Slavophobe	tenterhook	voluptuous	meltingpot
peppercorn	refractory	slumberous	teratology	waistcloth	mesomorphy
pepperwort	regulatory	smallsword	testaceous	waterclock	mesoscaphe
peremptory	rendezvous	smockfrock	tetrachord	waterflood	metacarpal
perfidious	repository	smokeproof	tetterwort	waterfront	metacarpus
perigynous	rescissory	smoothbore	thereabout	waterproof	monocarpic
perjurious	responsory	snakestone	thirtyfold	waterspout	mudskipper
permafrost	retrochoir	sneezewood	thixotropy	wheatstone	musicpaper
pernicious	revelatory	sneezewort	thornproof	whereabout	narcolepsy
phlebotomy	revocatory	solicitous	threadworm	whitethorn	nomography
photoflood	rheumatoid	somatology	threescore	wickerwork	nosography
photophore	rhinestone	soundproof	throatwort	wonderwork	nyctalopia
phototrope	rhinoscope	sourcebook	throughout	yellowwood	nyctalopic
phrasebook	rhinoscopy	sousaphone	thunderous	zabaglione	oleography
phrenology	rhizophore	spadiceous	timbertoes	zoophagous	oreography
physiology	ribbonworm	spatchcock	timberwolf	zoophilous	overlapped
picosecond	ridiculous	speciology	timberwork	acatalepsy	oversupply
piecegoods	robustious	speleology	timbrology	aerography	overtopped
pigeonhole	roisterous	sphenodone	tiringroom	allotropic	participle
pigeonpost	roundabout	spiderwort	toffeenose	anastrophe	periscopic
pigeontoed	rouseabout	spirituous	touchstone	antechapel	phenotypic

philosophe	bicultural	FinnoUgric	octahedron	stoneborer	bibulously
philosophy	bijouterie	forecourse	openhearth	stratocrat	bigamously
pinecarpet	bizarrerie	frontwards	oracularly	strawberry	biogenesis
pinstriped	blackberry	gaultheria	orchestral	structural	bipartisan
polygraphy	bolometric	generatrix	otherworld	structured	bootlessly
presbyopia	bottletree	geocentric	ottershrew	subcentral	byssinosis
presbyopic	brachyural	glassworks	outgeneral	supercargo	canorously
protanopic	brachyuran	globularly	overcharge	superiorly	captiously
prototypal	brusquerie	glycosuria	paediatric	syllabaria	carcinosis
prototypic	bullroarer	glycosuric	pallbearer	talebearer	carelessly
pyrography	bureaucrat	golfcourse	panjandrum	tautomeric	catastasis
rheotropic	calciferol	gooseberry	parametric	technocrat	catechesis
rockhopper	campestral	granularly	parenteral	telemetric	catechiser
rollingpin	candletree	groceteria	patisserie	termitaria	cautiously
roselipped	cardiogram	haematuria	peculiarly	tetramorph	cellulosic
sandhopper	cattlegrid	halfyearly	pennyworth	theophoric	comparison
sciagraphy	cavalierly	handbarrow	perchloric	thermogram	compasssaw
serigraphy	cellularly	heartthrob	peripheral	thillhorse	compressed
shopkeeper	chelicerae	hemihedral	peripteral	thimblerig	compressor
showjumper	childbirth	hemihedron	phosphoric	thirdparty	convalesce
skiagraphy	chokeberry	hemipteran	phosphorus	thumbscrew	covetously
skyscraper	chronogram	henceforth	physiocrat	tocopherol	cumbrously
snowcapped	circularly	Heptameron	pianoforte	topsyturvy	decorously
stomatopod	cloistered	heresiarch	planetaria	transferee	deliquesce
strathspey	cloudberry	hermitcrab	polyandric	transferor	deodoriser
sugarmaple	cloudburst	hexahedral	polyhedral	transverse	deoxidiser
superduper	coastwards	hexahedron	polyhedric	trilateral	desirously
synaloepha	cockalorum	hexametric	polyhedron	triliteral	dextrously
telegraphy	collateral	hobbyhorse	primiparae	triquetrae	diapedesis
telescopic	columbaria	holohedral	procedural	triquetral	dickcissel
thornapple	concentric	holosteric	protectrix	triumviral	discourser
throughput	congeneric	hurdygurdy	pyrometric	ulteriorly	disembosom
timekeeper	connatural	hurlyburly	pyrophoric	undershrub	dishonesty
tomography	considered	hypaethral	quercitron	underworld	dispraiser
topography	contraprop	hyperbaric	racecourse	undeterred	dissatisfy
touchpaper	coralberry	illnatured	rattletrap	unexplored	distressed
typography	cornstarch	illstarred	registered	unfathered	dogmatiser
wallpepper	corroboree	impresario	rhinoceros	unfettered	dolorously
warmingpan	crematoria	improperly	rhizomorph	unhistoric	duniwassal
wastepaper	cryptogram	inferiorly	rightwards	unicameral	ecchymosis
wiretapper	cylindered	inheritrix	riverhorse	unilateral	economiser
workpeople	dampcourse	interferer	rotisserie	unlettered	effervesce
worshipped	dapplegrey	interferon	rowanberry	unmannerly	effloresce
worshipper	daughterly	interiorly	saddletree	unmeasured	enantiosis
xerography	debonairly	intermarry	schipperke	unnumbered	endosmosis
xylography	decahedral	intramural	scriptoria	unprepared	enormously
zygomorphy	decahedron	involucral	scriptural	vascularly	epentheses
antimasque	decemviral	involucrum	sculptural	volumetric	epenthesis
blottesque	deflowerer	kettledrum	sculptured	waffleiron	epexegeses
catafalque	dielectric	knobkerrie	seismogram	waterborne	epexegesis
communique	diphtheria	knopkierie	semichorus	waterworks	epigenesis
humoresque	diphtheric	kookaburra	semiyearly	wentletrap	euthanasia
Japanesque	discoverer	lardydardy	septenarii	wheelhorse	eyeglasses
Kafkaesque	disenthral	loganberry	sepulchral	wirehaired	fabulously
multiloquy	disenviron	longhaired	sequestrum	xiphosuran	factiously
picaresque	disinherit	macebearer	shirehorse	youngberry	fadelessly
radiopaque	disordered	madreporic	shorewards	advertiser	fearlessly
Romanesque	disorderly	malingerer	shouldered	aerobiosis	fecklessly
semiopaque	dosimetric	manoeuvrer	shrinkwrap	aftertaste	fertiliser
somniloquy	drafthorse	manoeuvres	sideboards	Albigenses	filariasis
statuesque	dragontree	manometric	simulacrum	amanuenses	fireraiser
titanesque	dramaturge	manteltree	singletree	amanuensis	flawlessly
adventurer	dramaturgy	mantletree	singularly	ampelopsis	flexuously
afterbirth	dreamworld	mesenteric	sinisterly	anchylosis	formlessly
afterwards	dysenteric	mesenteron	smallwares	antecessor	framboesia
alcyonaria	earthwards	mesothorax	smorrebrod	antibiosis	franchiser
allosteric	egocentric	metallurgy	sophomoric	antisepsis	galvaniser
alphameric	elderberry	metaphoric	southwards	antitheses	generously
ambulacral	epicentral	metathorax	sphenogram	antithesis	gentilesse
ambulacrum	equilibria	metempiric	spidercrab	aphaereses	gloriously
amphoteric	ergosterol	microfarad	splutterer	aphaeresis	glycolyses
anteriorly	eurypterid	middlebrow	squanderer	aphrodisia	glycolysis
aristocrat	exospheric	misnomered	squirearch	apotheoses	gorgeously
asymmetric	extemporal	monohybrid	staffnurse	apotheosis	governessy
avantgarde	exteriorly	monohydric	steelworks	asbestosis	graciously
barbituric	extramural	muscularly	stenchtrap	ascariasis	grievously
barleybree	extraneous	nonnatural	stereogram	ateleiosis	haematosis
barleybroo	fairhaired	northwards	sternwards	autoplasty	haemolysis
barometric	familiarly	octahedral	stillbirth	babiroussa	hairraiser

```
halfnelson photolysis venomously arborvitae collocutor dissipated
harmlessly photonasty verbaliser archaistic commutator distinctly
harmoniser pitilessly viceconsul argumentum comparator distracted
heedlessly pityriasis victimiser arithmetic competitor documental
helplessly pollenosis viewlessly arrogantly complected dominantly
histolysis polydipsia vigorously aspidistra complotted draconites
hopelessly polyphasic viperously asteriated compositor dumbwaiter
humorously populously virtuously astigmatic compotator dungbeetle
hybridiser preciously visualiser asymptotic computator duodenitis
hydrolysis previously vulcaniser attenuated congenital duplicator
hypabyssal procrypsis wishywashy attenuator conjointly dynamistic
hypnotiser prosthesis wondrously audiometer conspectus dysplastic
hypophyses pulveriser wordlessly audiometry constantan ecchymotic
hypophysis ravenously wrongously austenitic Constantia elaborator
hypostasis recklessly ZendAvesta autocratic constantly eliminator
hypotheses recrudesce abducentes autoerotic contractor eloquently
hypothesis restlessly aberrantly babysitter convoluted elucidator
hysteresis rickettsia abominator bacchantes cooperator elutriator
ichthyosis rigorously abstracted bacchantic copesettic emblematic
illadvised ruthlessly abstracter backstitch coprolitic empathetic
improviser satyriasis abstractly bandmaster copywriter emphractic
incandesce scabrously abstractor bankruptcy corporator endophytic
indisposed sedulously abundantly bardolatry corrugated endosmotic
infamously seedvessel accidental barefooted corrugator enregister
interposal selflessly accredited batholitic corticated enumerator
interposer selfpoised achromatic bathometer Corybantes enunciator
isoglossal selfraised acidimeter bathymeter corybantic epenthetic
jinricksha sensitiser acidimetry bathymetry coulometry epexegetic
jinrikisha sensuously addlepated Bedlington covalently epiblastic
lederhosen sermoniser adherently Benedictus covenanted epideictic
lifelessly sharpnosed adjacently benefactor covenantee epigenetic
liquidiser socialiser administer bighearted covenanter epiglottal
listlessly sonorously aerobiotic bilgewater covenantor epiglottic
lovelessly soullessly aeronautic billposter crenulated epiglottis
luminously spaciously aerostatic biogenetic crescentic episematic
lusciously speciously afferently biparietal crinolette eradicator
lustrously spotlessly affiliated blackwater crosshatch escharotic
magnetiser spuriously affluently blanquette crosspatch essayistic
marshalsea stabiliser allegretto bluebottle cucullated eucalyptol
mayblossom stereopsis alleviator bonesetter cultivator eucalyptus
menopausal steriliser almacanter brachiator cuspidated eucaryotic
mesmeriser stonemason almucanter breakwater cybernetic eudiometer
metalepsis studiously alphabetic bronchitic cyclometer eudiometry
metaphysic sunglasses alternator bronchitis czarevitch eulogistic
metaplasia supervisor altruistic browbeaten deathwatch euphuistic
metastases suppressor ambidexter buccinator decadently evaporator
metastasis syllogiser ammoniated Buddhistic deeprooted explicitly
metatarsal symboliser anacolutha bushmaster deepseated expurgator
metatarsus synaeresis anapaestic cabalistic defalcator extenuator
metatheses syngenesis anaplastic cacomistle defoliator extirpator
metathesis synostosis anaptyctic calcsinter delineator exultantly
mindlessly tactlessly anchoretic calculator democratic fabricator
moderniser tantaliser anchoritic calibrator denigrator farsighted
moniliasis tearlessly anchylotic canzonetta densimeter fascinator
monochasia temporiser anemometer cassolette depredator fatalistic
movelessly thromboses anemometry catalectic dermatitis feuilleton
mutinously thrombosis annalistic cataleptic descriptor fianchetto
mycoplasma timelessly antemortem catechetic desecrater fibrositis
mythiciser timorously antibiotic celebrated desecrator filibuster
namelessly tirelessly antimatter celebrator desiccator fimbriated
nauseously tonelessly antiproton cellulitis designator fishkettle
nebulously toothpaste antiquated centilitre destructor flagrantly
needlessly tortfeasor antiseptic centimetre diagnostic flatfooted
neoclassic tortiously antistatic Charleston diapedetic fleabitten
nonplussed tortuously antithetic chemisette dichroitic flippantly
noogenesis transfuser aphoristic chiliastic dilemmatic floodwater
numerously transposal aplacental chondritic diligently flyswatter
nyctinasty transposer apodeictic circulator diphyletic forcipated
orogenesis trespasser apolaustic clinometer diplomatic forecaster
paederasty trichiasis apologetic clinometry discounter forecastle
painlessly tunelessly apoplectic clovehitch discreetly fornicator
pangenesis ultrabasic aposematic clubfooted disentitle fourchette
parabiosis unctuously apparently cochleated disgruntle fourfooted
paragnosis unmortised applicator coenobitic dishearten fourposter
paralipsis unstressed aquafortis coenobytic disjointed fragmental
paramnesia usuriously aragonitic coherently disparates fragrantly
patulously uxoriously arbalester collarette dispirited freebooter
peerlessly valorously arbalister collarstud disquieten freemartin
perilously vaporously arbitrator collimator disquietly frequenter
```

frequently	indecently	millilitre	phantastry	quartzitic	substratum
freshwater	indigested	millimetre	pheasantry	quizmaster	succinctly
fullbottom	indirectly	mintmaster	phenacetin	rackrenter	superaltar
futuristic	indolently	mischanter	phlegmatic	radiometer	supplanter
gaslighter	inexpertly	mischmetal	phlogistic	radiometry	surefooted
gauntleted	infatuated	mobocratic	phlogiston	rechristen	syncopated
geognostic	inherently	monocratic	phonematic	recreantly	syncopator
gingivitis	innocently	montbretia	phonolitic	redolently	syndicator
Glagolitic	inoculator	monumental	phonometer	regimental	synergetic
goldbeater	inquisitor	moralistic	phosphatic	relevantly	syphilitic
goniometer	insinuator	morganatic	photolitho	rencounter	systematic
goniometry	insolently	nativistic	photolytic	repudiator	tachometer
granulator	inspirator	Neapolitan	photometer	reredorter	tachometry
granulitic	instigator	necrolater	photometry	resonantly	tachymeter
gravimeter	institutor	necrolatry	piezometer	respirator	tachymetry
gravimetry	instructor	negotiator	pinnulated	reticently	taskmaster
gunfighter	integrator	neoplastic	pixillated	reverently	teaplanter
gynocratic	interested	neuropathy	planchette	ringmaster	tegumental
gyrocopter	ironmaster	newscaster	plangently	ripsnorter	telecaster
haemolytic	isogenetic	newsletter	planimeter	roadworthy	tendinitis
hagiolatry	Jehovistic	newsworthy	planimetry	rockbottom	tenemental
halfwitted	jingoistic	newswriter	planometer	Romanistic	terminator
halophytic	jubilantly	nightwatch	pleasantly	rovebeetle	terracotta
hardbitten	judgematic	nihilistic	pleasantry	rubricator	tetrameter
hardfisted	kerygmatic	nomothetic	pleonastic	rudimental	theocratic
headhunter	lacklustre	nonstarter	plutolatry	ruminantly	thereafter
headmaster	lacrimator	noteworthy	poinsettia	sacerdotal	thermistor
headwaiter	lacrymator	notonectal	pollinator	sandcastle	thermostat
Hebraistic	laryngitic	novelistic	polydactyl	sandmartin	thrombotic
hectolitre	laryngitis	numismatic	polyhistor	Sanskritic	tidewaiter
hectometre	leafcutter	obediently	populistic	satellitic	timocratic
hedonistic	legalistic	obfuscated	porismatic	schismatic	tolerantly
helicopter	legislator	obstructor	postmaster	scholastic	totemistic
heliolater	leucocytic	occidental	postmortem	sciolistic	tracheated
heliolatry	leukocytic	ombrometer	postpartum	scrapmetal	tracheitis
heliometer	ligamental	ophiolater	postulator	semifitted	transactor
hempnettle	linguistic	ophiolatry	precipitin	sensedatum	transeptal
henhearted	lionhunter	opisometer	prefrontal	sentiently	transistor
heptameter	liquidator	optimistic	pregnantly	sergeantcy	translator
Herrnhuter	lockstitch	originator	premarital	serjeantcy	transmuter
hesitantly	lotuseater	ornamental	premonitor	servomotor	tremolitic
hierolatry	loveletter	orogenetic	preparator	sexlimited	tribometer
histolytic	lubricator	oscillator	procreator	sheabutter	triturator
holophytic	lucubrator	osteopathy	procryptic	shearwater	trochanter
homeopathy	luculently	outrightly	procurator	shipfitter	tromometer
honeyeater	machinator	outstretch	progenitor	shipmaster	tsarevitch
horizontal	maisonette	overmantel	proglottis	shoplifter	tufthunter
hotchpotch	maladapted	overmaster	prognostic	shortdated	twilighted
humanistic	malapertly	oversubtle	prohibiter	siderostat	tympanites
humoristic	malefactor	overwinter	prohibitor	signwriter	tympanitic
hydrolytic	mamillated	ovipositor	prolocutor	silhouette	tympanitis
hydrometer	manifestly	oxygenator	propagator	silkcotton	typesetter
hydrometry	manifestos	pacesetter	propraetor	simplistic	typewriter
hydropathy	manumitted	palmbutter	proprietor	sincipital	unaccented
hygrometer	marginated	pancreatic	prosciutto	sixshooter	unaffected
hygrometry	Mariolater	pancreatin	prosecutor	slipstitch	unassisted
hyperbaton	Mariolatry	pangenetic	prospector	slowfooted	unbonneted
hyphenated	marionette	parabiotic	prospectus	slowwitted	uncloister
hypostatic	Massoretic	paratactic	prosthetic	sociometry	underwater
hypotactic	masticator	parramatta	protracted	solecistic	undigested
hypsometer	mathematic	pastmaster	protractor	songwriter	uneducated
hypsometry	mealbeetle	peashooter	protreptic	sowthistle	unemphatic
hysteretic	medicaster	pectinated	provocator	speculator	unexpected
iconolater	medullated	pederastic	pruriently	spirometer	unionistic
iconolatry	melanistic	pedimental	psychiatry	spirometry	unrequited
iconometer	meliorator	pedimented	puffpastry	stagbeetle	unscripted
iconometry	melismatic	pegmatitic	pugilistic	stagnantly	unselected
idealistic	meningitis	penetrator	puissantly	stalwartly	uranometry
ignorantly	mesophytic	penitently	pulsimeter	stepsister	urethritis
imminently	metacentre	pentameter	pulsometer	stimulator	vaccinator
immodestly	metastatic	percolator	pulvinated	stipulator	valvulitis
implicitly	metathetic	perforator	punctuator	stochastic	variegated
impotently	meteoritic	persecutor	purulently	stomatitis	variolitic
imprimatur	methylated	personator	pushbutton	straighten	variometer
impudently	microlitic	petiolated	pycnometer	straightly	vehemently
inartistic	micrometer	petrolatum	pyknometer	stridently	ventilator
incantator	micrometry	petulantly	pyracantha	subaquatic	vigilantly
incidental	mignonette	phagocytic	pyromantic	subjugator	vindicator
inculcator	militantly	phantastic	quadrantal	suborbital	virulently

```
viscometer  fieldmouse  semiliquid  unreserved  petroglyph  arteriolar
viscountcy  fleshwound  sheeplouse  unresolved  phenocryst  artificial
vitalistic  foreground  shellmound  werewolves  plasmolyse  asteroidal
vivisector  forfeiture  shortcrust  whatsoever  platelayer  Athanasian
voltameter  gargantuan  shrewmouse  whensoever  proteolyse  auditorial
waggonette  glasshouse  similitude  whomsoever  protophyta  Australian
wellington  grapefruit  smokehouse  woodcarver  protophyte  autarkical
whipstitch  greedyguts  snowgrouse  yourselves  pycnostyle  Babylonian
winceyette  greenhouse  snowplough  ballflower  saprophyte  balbriggan
Winchester  greenstuff  solicitude  bellflower  somatotype  Barmecidal
winebottle  guardhouse  somersault  brainpower  soothsayer  batrachian
wingfooted  guesthouse  songthrush  cornflower  sporophyll  beautician
woodcutter  Heptateuch  soubriquet  disembowel  sporophyte  Belgravian
woolsorter  hereabouts  southbound  expressway  squinteyed  beneficial
wristwatch  highstrung  spellbound  foamflower  starryeyed  bequeathal
xerophytic  homosabula  steakhouse  homebrewed  stereotype  Berkeleian
yardmaster  horselaugh  stonefruit  horsepower  stereotypy  bicultural
zygodactyl  housebound  storehouse  moonflower  swiveleyed  bimestrial
altazimuth  hypotenuse  stormbound  overgrowth  tetrastyle  biological
altocumuli  imposthume  subculture  passageway  troglodyte  biparietal
amphigouri  inaptitude  sublingual  safeblower  tropophyte  bipartisan
animalcula  incunabula  substitute  scratchwig  unemployed  bivalvular
animalcule  individual  subterfuge  sealingwax  Ashkenazim  bluecollar
antepenult  ineptitude  sugarhouse  superpower  chimpanzee  bluethroat
apiculture  infinitude  superacute  televiewer  deepfrozen  Boswellian
autoimmune  inquietude  tantamount  throughway  fuzzywuzzy  botryoidal
aviculture  interwound  televisual  unhallowed  intermezzi  brachyural
background  irresolute  theopneust  wallflower  intermezzo  brachyuran
barracouta  judicature  toothbrush  watchtower  morbidezza  brandysnap
bawdyhouse  kieselguhr  tourniquet  waterpower  schemozzle  bridgehead
bellylaugh  lambrequin  trilingual  windflower  selfglazed  budgerigar
blockhouse  lighthouse  tropopause  winegrower  undersized  bufflehead
bloodhound  literature  ultrasound  wiredrawer  witchhazel  bullethead
breadcrumb  loungesuit  underbrush  withdrawal  ────────── bureaucrat
breadfruit  maculature  underslung  withdrawer  abacterial  butterbean
breadstuff  manorhouse  understudy  woolgrower  aboriginal  Caledonian
buttonbush  mansuetude  unilingual  amphimixes  Abrahamian  campestral
canaliculi  misconduct  usquebaugh  amphimixis  academical  cardiogram
cantaloupe  misfortune  ventriculi  AngloSaxon  accidental  carnassial
canterbury  mismeasure  wagonvault  appendixes  acetabular  Carthusian
caricature  misventure  wanderlust  bobbysoxer  acoustical  caruncular
cataloguer  monkeysuit  wheelhouse  chemotaxis  acronychal  catburglar
centrifuge  moonstruck  whorehouse  heliotaxis  actinozoan  cavalryman
chartreuse  mulligrubs  wraparound  hydrotaxis  additional  centennial
chauffeuse  northbound  yarborough  neurotoxin  adjectival  centesimal
circumfuse  nunciature  aardwolves  orthodoxly  Aethiopian  ceremonial
coachhouse  outmeasure  adjectival  phototaxis  alchemical  chairwoman
colatitude  overabound  bollweevil  phytotoxic  Algonquian  chelicerae
coloratura  overblouse  cantilever  undersexed  ambulacral  childermas
commissure  overground  changeover  aerenchyma  Amerindian  chimerical
commixture  overslaugh  fishcarver  almondeyed  ammoniacal  chronogram
conceptual  overstrung  fourleaved  amoebocyte  anagogical  Ciceronian
conjecture  overthrust  gerundival  amphictyon  analogical  Circassian
consensual  paintbrush  housewives  blastocyst  analytical  Cistercian
constitute  paradoxure  interwoven  blearyeyed  anarchical  clavicular
consuetude  parimutuel  jackknives  bricklayer  anastigmat  closetplay
contextual  perceptual  kerchieves  cardplayer  anatomical  clothesbag
contexture  pilothouse  loosecover  chromatype  Andalusian  cloverleaf
contribute  pinebeauty  nevernever  cyclostyle  aneurismal  cognominal
conventual  piscifauna  objectival  ditriglyph  aneurysmal  collarbeam
corpuscule  plantlouse  pearldiver  fluorotype  anticlimax  collateral
courthouse  playground  piledriver  goggleeyed  anticlinal  colloquial
couverture  powderpuff  quadrumvir  granophyre  antimonial  commercial
craquelure  powerhouse  rediscover  heliophyte  antinomian  commonweal
crassitude  prefecture  riboflavin  heterodyne  antiphonal  compasssaw
crepuscule  prefixture  semiquaver  hieroglyph  antipodean  conceptual
cummerbund  prostitute  shortlived  hippogryph  antisocial  conchoidal
debouchure  punchdrunk  splitlevel  holloweyed  aplacental  congenital
decompound  quadrature  supernovae  hydrophyte  apochromat  connatural
definitude  retinacula  swinefever  hygrophyte  apocryphal  consensual
disclosure  roquelaure  switchover  lithoglyph  apolitical  constantan
disfeature  roughhouse  tackdriver  lithophyte  Apollinian  contextual
distribute  roundhouse  themselves  lymphocyte  Apollonian  conventual
dumbstruck  runthrough  timeserver  microphyte  apothecial  Copernican
earthbound  sanctitude  unbeliever  nematocyst  araucarian  copperhead
embouchure  scaramouch  undercover  osteophyte  arborvitae  corbiculae
endproduct  seabiscuit  undeserved  palaeotype  archetypal  Corinthian
exactitude  seethrough  unimproved  parenchyma  aristocrat  councilman
fairground  semiannual  unrelieved  pennyroyal  armourclad  countryman
```

credential	geoponical	isoglossal	multipolar	playbyplay	scyphozoan
crispbread	geothermal	isoseismal	multivocal	politician	sealingwax
crustacean	germicidal	isothermal	muttonhead	polyhedral	seignorial
cryptogram	gerundival	janitorial	myological	Polynesian	seismogram
curatorial	Gilbertian	jesuitical	natalitial	polynomial	selfdenial
curricular	gingersnap	johnsonian	natatorial	Pomeranian	semestrial
decahedral	Glaswegian	jolterhead	Neapolitan	pontifical	semiannual
decemviral	glomerular	journeyman	neological	positional	seminarian
delusional	glossarial	juristical	nepenthean	practician	semiotical
demoniacal	goldenseal	labiovelar	noblewoman	praecocial	semiuncial
devotional	grammarian	Lamarckian	nonlogical	praetorial	senatorial
diabolical	grandducal	laminarian	nonnatural	praetorian	senseorgan
diarrhoeal	grapesugar	lapidarian	nonnuclear	precordial	sentential
diathermal	GrecoRoman	larvicidal	notonectal	preexilian	septennial
Dickensian	gressorial	laundryman	nurseryman	prefrontal	sepulchral
didactical	groundplan	lavatorial	nutational	preglacial	sequential
disenthral	groundsman	Lawrentian	objectival	prelatical	SerboCroat
dissimilar	gyrational	Leibnizian	occasional	premarital	serviceman
distringas	hairstreak	lenticular	occidental	premedical	shandrydan
divisional	halfdollar	letterhead	octahedral	presentday	sheepshead
documental	hallelujah	ligamental	octandrian	primiparae	shenanigan
dogmatical	hammerbeam	lighterman	octonarian	primordial	shortbread
downstream	hammerhead	Lithuanian	oratorical	principial	shovelhead
dragonhead	Hanoverian	liturgical	orchardman	prismoidal	shrinkwrap
dramatical	harmonical	locustbean	orchestral	procedural	siderostat
drowsihead	harvestman	loggerhead	Ordovician	proctorial	simoniacal
dunderhead	headstream	logistical	organismal	prolicidal	sincipital
duniwassal	heartbreak	Lusitanian	ornamental	pronominal	sinusoidal
duodecimal	hebdomadal	Maccabaean	orological	prosodical	sleepyhead
ecological	Heliconian	magnifical	orthogonal	prostomial	slipstream
economical	hemihedral	magnifical	outgeneral	prototypal	solenoidal
ectodermal	hemipteran	Mahommedan	overspread	proverbial	solifidian
ecumenical	heptagonal	maidenhead	packthread	provincial	solstitial
egoistical	hermetical	mainstream	paddleboat	prudential	spacewoman
electrical	hermitcrab	majestical	PalmSunday	puristical	spagyrical
Eleusinian	hexahedral	majuscular	Panamanian	pyromaniac	Spencerian
elliptical	hierarchal	Malpighian	papistical	Pyrrhonian	Spenserian
encyclical	highwayman	Malthusian	paradisean	quadrantal	sphenogram
endocrinal	hirudinean	managerial	paradisiac	quadrivial	sphenoidal
endodermal	historical	mandibular	paradisian	quarterday	spheroidal
Englishman	holohedral	Manichaean	paranormal	quixotical	spidercrab
epicentral	homocercal	markswoman	parenteral	rabbinical	spiracular
epidemical	homoousian	matricidal	Parnassian	railwayman	splintcoal
epiglottal	homosexual	mechanical	paroxysmal	rattlehead	sponsorial
episodical	horizontal	Melanesian	parricidal	rattletrap	sporangial
epithelial	horsewoman	menopausal	parsonical	reciprocal	sportswear
equational	husbandman	meridional	particular	regimental	springhead
equatorial	hypabyssal	mesothorax	passageway	relational	starstream
equestrian	hypaethral	metacarpal	pathetical	republican	stenchtrap
eremitical	hyperbolae	metatarsal	patricidal	requiescat	stentorian
erysipelas	hyperbolas	metathorax	patrilocal	revisional	stereogram
Esculapian	hypodermal	methodical	pedalorgan	rhetorical	strabismal
Eurodollar	hysterical	Methuselah	pedestrian	rhomboidal	stratocrat
evidential	ideational	Michaelmas	pedimental	rhythmical	stringbean
exegetical	illusional	microfarad	peduncular	rollcollar	structural
exoterical	immaterial	micropylar	pellicular	rotational	subcentral
exothermal	immemorial	midshipman	peninsular	rubythroat	subclavian
expressway	impersonal	militiaman	pennanular	rudimental	subglacial
extemporal	incidental	millennial	pennyroyal	runnerbean	subliminal
extramural	individual	millesimal	pentagonal	sabbatical	sublingual
fascicular	Indonesian	millstream	perceptual	sacerdotal	subnuclear
febrifugal	industrial	minuscular	periclinal	sacroiliac	suborbital
fiddlehead	infrahuman	mischmetal	peridermal	saleswoman	subordinal
figurehead	infusorial	mixolydian	periodical	salicional	superaltar
follicular	infusorian	Mohammedan	periosteal	salientian	superhuman
fractional	interlunar	molendinar	peripheral	salmonleap	superlunar
fragmental	internodal	monarchial	peripteral	salpingian	supernovae
Franciscan	interplead	Monarchian	peritoneal	saltcellar	suprarenal
freedwoman	interposal	monistical	pesticidal	sanitarian	sweetbread
fricandeau	intertidal	monitorial	phalangeal	sapiential	sweetbriar
frictional	interurban	monoclinal	phanerogam	scansorial	swinglebar
fruitarian	interzonal	monogynian	phantasmal	scaredycat	symbolical
functional	intestinal	monomaniac	pharyngeal	schoolmaam	symphyseal
fungicidal	intramural	monopodial	phenomenal	Scillonian	symphysial
furuncular	intraurban	monumental	pheromonal	Scotswoman	synchronal
galimatias	involucral	Mousterian	Phoenician	scrapmetal	synoptical
gargantuan	Irishwoman	mouthorgan	phthisical	screenplay	Talmudical
geodetical	irrational	Muhammadan	physiocrat	scriptural	tangential
geological	isochronal	Muhammadan	pictorical	sculptural	tarmacadam

Tartuffian	wentletrap	cartomancy	endproduct	introspect	pubescence
taxidermal	Wertherian	cataphract	energetics	invariance	purtenance
technician	WhitMonday	catoptrics	episcopacy	inveteracy	purveyance
technocrat	WhitSunday	centreback	ergonomics	irradiance	quadratics
tegumental	widespread	chaplaincy	everyplace	isometrics	quiescence
teleostean	windowseat	chatoyance	excellence	itinerancy	quiescency
televisual	wingcollar	chiromancy	excellency	kinematics	recipiency
tendrillar	wingspread	chromatics	expectance	knickknack	recommence
tenemental	withdrawal	clovehitch	expectancy	ladderback	recrudesce
tentacular	woodenhead	cockatrice	expedience	landocracy	recumbency
tetragonal	workingman	cognisance	expediency	latescence	recurrence
theatrical	xiphosuran	competence	experience	leafinsect	redundance
theistical	yesteryear	competency	exuberance	legitimacy	redundancy
theodicean	zoological	compliance	eyeservice	lipservice	reentrance
theologian	anglophobe	compliancy	fantastico	lockstitch	refulgence
thermogram	angwantibo	complicacy	fetterlock	lumberjack	regeneracy
thermostat	Gallophobe	condolence	fiddleback	luxuriance	reiterance
theurgical	mulligrubs	conference	fieldpiece	magistracy	reluctance
threnodial	mumbojumbo	confidence	firepolicy	malignance	reluctancy
throughway	nambypamby	confluence	flatulence	malignancy	remittance
timberhead	negrophobe	congruence	flatulency	matchstick	renascence
tinctorial	redescribe	congruency	flightdeck	mendicancy	repellance
torrential	Russophobe	connivance	floristics	misconduct	repellancy
townswoman	Slavophobe	conscience	freespeech	miscreance	repellence
trabeculae	subshrubby	consonance	frontbench	monstrance	repellency
trabecular	transcribe	consonancy	geophysics	moonstruck	repentance
Tractarian	abhorrence	conspiracy	geriatrics	morphemics	reprobance
tractional	absorbance	continence	governance	mouthpiece	repugnance
transeptal	absorbency	contradict	grandniece	natterjack	repugnancy
translunar	abstinence	convalesce	graphemics	necromancy	resilience
transposal	abstinency	convenance	greatniece	negligence	resiliency
trawlerman	acceptance	conveyance	greenfinch	newsagency	resistance
triangular	accomplice	cornstarch	greenstick	nightstick	resurgence
trichromat	accordance	corpulence	gymnastics	nightwatch	retrospect
trigeminal	acrobatics	corpulency	hackmatack	nucleonics	rheumatics
triggerman	admittance	counteract	halieutics	nudibranch	ridgepiece
trilateral	advertence	covariance	hammerlock	observance	rubberneck
trilingual	advertency	crackajack	heartblock	obstetrics	sacrosanct
triliteral	aerobatics	crapulence	Heptateuch	occurrence	saddleback
triquetrae	aesthetics	crossbench	heresiarch	ochlocracy	scapegrace
triquetral	allegiance	crosscheck	heuristics	offlicence	scaramouch
triumviral	alpenstock	crosshatch	hierocracy	oppugnancy	semeiotics
trochoidal	altarpiece	crosspatch	homiletics	orchestics	senescence
tryptophan	alternance	crosspiece	horseleech	ordonnance	sergeantcy
tubercular	amphibrach	cryogenics	hotchpotch	outbalance	serjeantcy
tyrannical	Anglistics	czarevitch	hydraulics	outerspace	shellshock
Tyrrhenian	appearance	deathwatch	hydromancy	outstretch	sideeffect
ulotrichan	apprentice	defeasance	illiteracy	paddywhack	sideglance
unAmerican	ascendance	deficiency	immaculacy	patristics	skirtdance
unbiblical	ascendancy	degeneracy	immoderacy	pedagogics	slavocracy
uncritical	ascendence	dehiscence	impatience	penetrance	slipstitch
unfamiliar	ascendency	deliquesce	impeccancy	pentastich	smockfrock
unicameral	assistance	dentifrice	impendence	permanence	smokestack
unilateral	attendance	dependence	impendency	permanency	snakedance
unilingual	autodidact	dependency	importance	pertinence	snobocracy
unilocular	backstitch	derestrict	imprudence	pertinency	somnolence
unofficial	badderlock	desipience	inaccuracy	pestilence	somnolency
urochordal	ballistics	desistance	inadequacy	pilgarlick	soundtrack
urticarial	bankruptcy	detergency	incandesce	pillowlace	spatchcock
uxoricidal	bellydance	deterrence	incessancy	pitchblack	spitchcock
valleculae	benignancy	difference	incipience	pluperfect	splashback
vallecular	bibliotics	diffidence	incipiency	plutocracy	spodomancy
vegetarian	biometrics	disconnect	inclemency	pneumatics	squirearch
venational	biophysics	disrespect	incumbency	pornocracy	stagecoach
vermicidal	bioscience	disservice	indelicacy	postoffice	statistics
vermicular	birthplace	dissidence	indistinct	precedence	stringency
vernacular	bloodstock	dissonance	inductance	precedency	stylistics
versicular	bobbinlace	dissonancy	indulgence	preference	subsidence
vestibular	bottleneck	divergence	inefficacy	prepotence	subtenancy
visitorial	brakeblock	divergency	inelegance	prepotency	succulence
vocational	breadstick	divulgence	innumeracy	prescience	succulency
volitional	brilliance	dumbstruck	insistence	presidency	sufferance
vorticular	brilliancy	ebullience	insistency	prevalence	sunderance
Waldensian	broomstick	ebulliency	insolvency	prevenancy	supplejack
wampumpeag	bubblyjock	effeminacy	insurgence	procurance	suppliance
wappenshaw	cacogenics	effervesce	insurgency	profligacy	survivance
warmingpan	candlewick	efficiency	intendance	prominence	sustenance
weatherman	cantatrice	effloresce	interspace	provenance	switchback
Welshwoman	canvasback	effulgence	interstice	providence	sworddance

swordstick	jaguarundi	antimatter	breakables	cornflakes	economiser
sycophancy	Lammastide	antiquated	breakwater	cornflower	emblazoner
temperance	lanthanide	antitheses	bressummer	coromandel	embowelled
termagancy	lardydardy	aphaereses	bricklayer	corroboree	emerypaper
tetrastich	malentendu	apotheoses	broadsheet	corrugated	emerywheel
theoretics	mansuetude	apparelled	browbeaten	corticated	Emmentaler
thinkpiece	masquerade	appendices	bullheaded	Corybantes	empanelled
threepence	nationwide	appendixes	bullroarer	cottonseed	emulsifier
threepiece	nightshade	aquaplaner	bushmaster	cottonweed	encourager
throwstick	northwards	arbalester	bushranger	counselled	encroacher
thruppence	nucleoside	arbalister	cackhanded	covenanted	endstopped
transience	nucleotide	arbitrager	calamander	covenantee	enregister
transiency	ophicleide	asteriated	calcsinter	covenanter	enthralled
trenchancy	overstride	astrologer	campaigner	cowcatcher	epentheses
truculence	pasquinade	astronomer	candletree	cowparsley	epexegeses
truculency	piecegoods	attenuated	cantilever	cowpuncher	epigrapher
tsarevitch	polyploidy	auctioneer	carabineer	crenulated	eudiometer
tumescence	propaganda	audiometer	carabinier	crossbones	evenhanded
turbulence	radiosonde	aviatrices	caravaneer	crossbreed	everglades
turbulency	razorblade	babysitter	caravanned	crossindex	evilminded
turkeycock	retrograde	bacchantes	caravanner	crossrefer	eyeglasses
turtleback	rightwards	backhanded	carbuncled	crosstrees	faceharden
turtleneck	ritardando	backhander	carcinogen	crowkeeper	fairhaired
understock	saccharide	backslider	cardplayer	cucullated	fairleader
undertrick	salmagundi	baldheaded	carpetweed	cuirassier	fairminded
virescence	saltigrade	ballflower	carragheen	cuspidated	fairspoken
viscountcy	sanctitude	bandmaster	caryatides	cyclometer	fandangoes
waterclock	scherzando	barebacked	caseharden	cylindered	farfetched
whipstitch	selfparody	barefooted	caseworker	dapplegrey	farsighted
wristwatch	shorewards	bareheaded	cataloguer	daydreamer	featherbed
yellowback	Shrovetide	barelegged	catechiser	deepfrozen	fellmonger
aficionado	sideboards	barleybree	catechumen	deeprooted	fertiliser
afterwards	silverside	bathometer	celebrated	deepseated	fibrinogen
asafoetida	similitude	bathymeter	challenger	deflowerer	fictioneer
assafetida	slavetrade	beautifier	chandelier	densimeter	filibuster
autostrada	solicitude	bedchamber	changeover	deodoriser	fimbriated
autostrade	sororicide	bedclothes	channelled	deoxidiser	fireraiser
avantgarde	southwards	bedevilled	chapfallen	dermatogen	firescreen
balustrade	spermicide	bedraggled	charioteer	desecrater	fishcarver
barramunda	springtide	beefburger	chiffonier	despatcher	fishmonger
barramundi	sternwards	bejewelled	chimpanzee	determined	fivefinger
biodegrade	stillicide	bellflower	chronicler	dickcissel	flamingoes
bisulphide	stringendo	bellringer	churchgoer	diminished	flannelled
burramundi	sugardaddy	bellwether	cicatrices	disburthen	flatfooted
carbonnade	tailormade	bemedalled	circumflex	discharger	fleabitten
centigrade	tardigrade	beribboned	classified	disclaimer	fleamarket
coastwards	understudy	bestridden	classifier	discounter	floodwater
coatimundi	velocipede	bestseller	clawhammer	discourser	flycatcher
colatitude	wintertide	bighearted	clinometer	discoverer	flyswatter
consuetude	aardwolves	bigmouthed	clodhopper	disembowel	foamflower
corrigenda	abducentes	bilgewater	cloistered	disengaged	folksinger
crassitude	ablebodied	billposter	clothespeg	dishearten	footballer
crossroads	abstracted	biographer	clubfooted	dishwasher	footwarmer
custommade	abstracter	birdspider	coalbunker	disjointed	forcipated
definienda	accredited	bivouacked	coathanger	disordered	forecaster
definitude	accustomed	blackfaced	cochleated	disparager	forefather
diminuendo	acidimeter	blackwater	cockchafer	disparates	forefinger
discommode	addlepated	blasphemer	colonnaded	dispatcher	foregather
disulphide	administer	blearyeyed	comehither	dispirited	forehanded
dorsigrade	adventurer	blitzkrieg	commandeer	dispraiser	forerunner
dragonnade	advertiser	bloodmoney	commandoes	disquieten	foreteller
earthwards	affiliated	bluebonnet	complainer	dissembler	fortyniner
Eastertide	Africander	bluejacket	complected	dissipated	forwearied
exactitude	Afrikander	bobbysoxer	complotted	distracted	fourfooted
floribunda	Albigenses	bombardier	compounder	distrainer	fourhanded
fratricide	allrounder	bondholder	compressed	distressed	fourleaved
frontwards	almacanter	boneheaded	comstocker	divebomber	fourposter
fuddyduddy	almondeyed	bonesetter	confounded	dogmatiser	fourteener
goodygoody	almucanter	boneshaker	considered	doorkeeper	franchiser
granddaddy	altogether	bookbinder	controlled	doughfaced	freebooter
honeyguide	amanuenses	bookkeeper	controller	downfallen	freehanded
hornblende	ambidexter	bookmarker	convoluted	draconical	freeholder
hurdygurdy	ammoniated	bookseller	coolheaded	dragontree	freelancer
inaptitude	amphimacer	bootlegger	coparcener	dressmaker	freeloader
ineptitude	amphimixes	bootlicker	coproducer	drophammer	freesoiler
infinitude	analphabet	bottlefeed	copyholder	dumbwaiter	freespoken
inquietude	anemometer	bottletree	copyreader	dumfounder	frequenter
intergrade	antechapel	brainpower	copywriter	dustjacket	freshwater
isoniazide	antemortem		cordwainer	eartrumpet	fricasseed

froghopper	housewives	lockkeeper	nonjoinder	proclaimer	sculptured
fullbodied	humanities	logorrhoea	nonplussed	programmer	seborrhoea
fussbudget	humidifier	longhaired	nonstarter	prohibiter	seedvessel
galvaniser	humpbacked	longheaded	nonswimmer	promenader	seersucker
gamekeeper	hybridiser	longlegged	northerner	pronounced	selfbinder
gasconader	hydrometer	longprimer	nutcracker	pronouncer	selfesteem
gaslighter	hygrometer	longwinded	obfuscated	proofsheet	selffeeder
gatekeeper	hyphenated	loosecover	oftentimes	propertied	selfglazed
gatelegged	hypnotiser	lossleader	oldfangled	prophesier	selfguided
gauntleted	hypophyses	lotuseater	ombrometer	propounder	selfmurder
geographer	hypotheses	loudhailer	openhanded	proscriber	selfpoised
gingerbeer	hypsometer	loveletter	openminded	protracted	selfraised
gladhander	icebreaker	lowpitched	ophiolater	pulsimeter	selfseeker
glasspaper	iconolater	lumpsucker	opisometer	pulsometer	selfstyled
glycolyses	iconometer	macebearer	orangepeel	pulveriser	selfwilled
goalkeeper	illadvised	magnetiser	ottershrew	pulvinated	semifitted
goaltender	illnatured	mainlander	outfielder	pycnometer	semiquaver
goatsucker	illstarred	maintainer	outswinger	pyknometer	sensitiser
gobstopper	impanelled	maladapted	overburden	quadruplet	sermoniser
goggleeyed	imperilled	malingerer	overcooked	quadruplex	sexlimited
goldbeater	importuner	mamillated	overhanded	quantifier	shamefaced
golddigger	improviser	manchineel	overlander	quarrelled	shanghaier
goniometer	indigested	mangosteen	overlapped	quarreller	sharpnosed
goodlooker	indiscreet	manoeuvrer	overlooker	quarrender	sheabutter
gravimeter	indisposed	manoeuvres	overmanned	questioner	shearwater
greyheaded	infatuated	manteltree	overmantel	quintuplet	shellacked
gunfighter	initialled	manumitted	overmaster	quizmaster	shipbroker
gunslinger	inkslinger	marginated	overridden	rackrenter	shipfitter
gyrocopter	innuendoes	Mariolater	overtopped	radiometer	shipmaster
hackbuteer	interbreed	marshalled	overwinter	railroader	shiprigged
hairraiser	interceder	marshaller	pacesetter	ratcatcher	shopkeeper
halberdier	interested	marshalsea	painkiller	rechristen	shoplifter
halfcocked	interferer	matchmaker	palisander	reconciler	shopsoiled
halfvolley	interloper	mavourneen	pallbearer	reconsider	shopwalker
halfwitted	interposer	maxilliped	palmbutter	redblooded	shortdated
handmaiden	intervener	medicaster	panhandler	rediscover	shortlived
handpicked	interwoven	medullated	papermaker	registered	shouldered
handselled	introducer	merrymaker	parimutuel	remodelled	showjumper
handworked	ironhanded	mesmeriser	pastmaster	rencounter	shrivelled
hangglider	ironmaster	metastases	pastyfaced	reproducer	sidestreet
hardbilled	ironmonger	metatheses	pathfinder	reredorter	sidewinder
hardbitten	ironworker	methylated	pawnbroker	researcher	signwriter
hardboiled	jackanapes	micrometer	peacemaker	restrained	silkscreen
hardfisted	jackhammer	middleaged	pearldiver	restrainer	silverweed
hardhanded	jackknives	mineworker	peashooter	reverencer	simplifier
hardheaded	Janusfaced	mintmaster	pectinated	rhomboidei	singletree
harelipped	jawbreaker	misaligned	pedimented	ringfinger	sixshooter
harmoniser	jimsonweed	mischanter	pentameter	ringleader	skirmisher
haruspices	kerchieves	misjoinder	periwigged	ringmaster	skyscraper
headhunter	keyboarder	mismatched	petiolated	ringnecked	slitpocket
headmaster	kingfisher	misnomered	petitioner	ringtailed	slowfooted
headphones	knockkneed	moderniser	philologen	ripsnorter	slowwitted
headwaiter	kriegspiel	moneymaker	phonometer	roadrunner	smallwares
heavyarmed	ladychapel	moneytaker	photometer	rockbadger	smartmoney
helicopter	ladyfinger	monorhymed	pickpocket	rockgarden	smokedried
heliolater	ladykiller	moonflower	piezometer	rockhopper	snailpaced
heliometer	landholder	moonshiner	pigeontoed	rockribbed	snailwheel
hellbender	landhunger	mosquitoes	pigsticker	roodscreen	sneakthief
henharrier	landingnet	mossbunker	piledriver	roofgarden	sneezeweed
henhearted	landlocked	moustached	pinecarpet	ropedancer	snickasnee
heptameter	landlubber	moviemaker	pinfeather	ropeladder	snowcapped
Herrnhuter	landscaper	mudskipper	pinnulated	ropewalker	soapboiler
highbinder	languisher	mudslinger	pinstriped	rosechafer	soapflakes
highhanded	lansquenet	multifaced	pixillated	roselipped	sobersided
highjacker	lawbreaker	multiplier	planimeter	rottweiler	sobersides
highlander	leafcutter	musicpaper	planometer	roughrider	socialiser
highminded	leafhopper	mythiciser	platelayer	sacrificer	softbilled
hippomanes	lederhosen	mythologer	plumassier	saddletree	softboiled
hitchhiker	lefthanded	necrolater	pockmarked	safeblower	softfinned
hokeypokey	lefthander	nevernever	pokerfaced	salamander	softheaded
holloweyed	lentigines	newfangled	pontifices	sanctifier	softspoken
homebrewed	lifejacket	newscaster	postmaster	sandbagger	songwriter
honeyeater	lightfaced	newsletter	postmortem	sandhopper	soothsayer
honeysweet	likeminded	newsmonger	potbellied	sargassoes	soubriquet
hornrimmed	limeburner	newsreader	pourparler	sawtoothed	southerner
horsecoper	lionhunter	newswriter	prejudiced	scaffolder	spectacled
horsepower	Lipizzaner	noisemaker	prescriber	scoresheet	spectacles
horseshoer	Lippizaner	nonaligned	principled	scrimmager	spirometer
hotblooded	liquidiser	nondrinker	privileged	scrutineer	splitlevel

```
splutterer  tracheated  unredeemed  woolsorter  escapology  spongology
sprucebeer  trafficked  unrelieved  workbasket  escheatage  subaverage
squanderer  trafficker  unremarked  worshipped  exobiology  subterfuge
squaretoed  trammelled  unrequited  worshipper  exploitage  supercargo
squaretoes  transducer  unreserved  yardmaster  expressage  surplusage
squinteyed  transferee  unresolved  yourselves  footbridge  synecology
stabiliser  transfuser  unrivalled  breadstuff  freightage  technology
stadholder  transmuter  unschooled  chiffchaff  futurology  telpherage
starryeyed  transposer  unscreened  claspknife  gastrology  teratology
stencilled  treadwheel  unscripted  coolingoff  glaciology  ticpolonga
stenciller  trespasser  unseasoned  crankshaft  glossology  timbrology
stepfather  tribometer  unselected  dampingoff  glottology  tollbridge
stepladder  triphammer  unstrained  declassify  graphology  touchjudge
stepmother  trochanter  unstressed  dehumidify  harbourage  toxicology
stepsister  tromometer  untroubled  disqualify  heortology  trichology
steriliser  trucklebed  unwrinkled  dissatisfy  hepatology  trophology
stilettoes  trundlebed  vanquisher  fallingoff  heterology  urbanology
stockpiler  tufthunter  variegated  fisticuffs  hippophagy  usquebaugh
stockrider  tumbleweed  variometer  greenstuff  hodgepodge  vernissage
stoneborer  twilighted  veldschoen  handicraft  horselaugh  villainage
stopvolley  twowheeler  verandahed  hippogriff  husbandage  villeinage
straighten  tympanites  verbaliser  housecraft  immunology  wanderings
strathspey  typesetter  vestpocket  nightshift  intertrigo  wongawonga
strengthen  typewriter  victimiser  paperknife  lexicology  yarborough
structured  umbellifer  victualled  powderpuff  lighterage  aerography
submariner  umbrellaed  victualler  presignify  macrophage  afterlight
subscriber  unabridged  viewfinder  saccharify  malacology  anacolutha
subspecies  unaccented  viscometer  shandygaff  maquillage  anastrophe
succedanea  unaffected  visualiser  spacecraft  metallurgy  apostrophe
sunglasses  unassisted  voltameter  spoondrift  mineralogy  autography
superduper  unattached  vulcaniser  stagecraft  misgivings  birthright
superorder  unattended  wallflower  statecraft  morphology  brakelight
superpower  unbalanced  wallpepper  Stroganoff  multistage  cacography
supplanter  unbeliever  wastepaper  subjectify  musicology  cartwright
surefooted  unblenched  watchmaker  swordcraft  nephrology  cerography
swanmaiden  unbonneted  watchtower  undercliff  numerology  crosslight
swaybacked  unbuttoned  waterpower  undercroft  oceanology  deadweight
sweetbrier  uncloister  waterskier  watercraft  odontology  demography
swinefever  uncustomed  waterwheel  witchcraft  oneirology  distraught
switchover  undefended  weakminded  afterimage  overcharge  doxography
swiveleyed  undercover  weedkiller  anecdotage  overslaugh  earthlight
syllogiser  underlinen  weimaraner  apophthegm  palynology  epistrophe
symboliser  underminer  wellheeled  assemblage  papyrology  fearnought
syncopated  undersexed  wellspoken  autecology  percentage  fireblight
tablelinen  undersized  wellturned  balneology  persiflage  firstnight
tachometer  understeer  wellwisher  baronetage  phrenology  flashlight
tachymeter  undertaken  werewolves  bellylaugh  physiology  floodlight
tackdriver  undertaker  wharfinger  belongings  phytophagy  forthright
talebearer  underwater  whatsoever  bibliology  pichiciago  gobemouche
taleteller  undeserved  whensoever  bibliopegy  pilgrimage  guestnight
tantaliser  undesigned  whiskified  bioecology  plunderage  gymnosophy
tapestried  undeterred  whitefaced  blancmange  pogonology  holography
taskmaster  undigested  wholesaler  brachylogy  potamology  homeopathy
taxidancer  uneducated  whomsoever  brigandage  prearrange  hydropathy
teaplanter  unemployed  wildfowler  camerlengo  prepackage  iconomachy
tearjerker  unequalled  Winchester  camerlingo  proctorage  ideography
teatrolley  unexampled  windflower  camouflage  psephology  jinricksha
telecaster  unexcelled  windjammer  cardiology  psychology  jinrikisha
telephoner  unexpected  windscreen  carphology  pyretology  kieselguhr
televiewer  unexplored  winebibber  centrifuge  quarterage  lexigraphy
temporiser  unfathered  winegrower  chronology  rejoicings  limitrophe
tendrilled  unfettered  wingfooted  colportage  remarriage  lipography
tetrameter  unfinished  wiredrawer  conchology  runthrough  logography
themselves  unforeseen  wirehaired  constringe  sarcophagi  makeweight
theosopher  unfriended  wirepuller  craniology  sarcophagy  matriarchy
thereafter  ungrounded  wiretapper  cryptology  satanology  mesomorphy
thereunder  unhallowed  wirewalker  deltiology  screenings  mesoscaphe
threatener  unhouseled  wireworker  demonology  seethrough  microfiche
thromboses  unimproved  witchhazel  dendrology  seignorage  millwright
thumbscrew  uninformed  withdrawer  deontology  seismology  misthought
tidewaiter  unlabelled  withholder  disarrange  selenology  neuropathy
tilthammer  unlettered  woodcarver  discourage  semeiology  newsworthy
timbertoes  unmeasured  woodcutter  dramaturge  shillelagh  nightlight
timekeeper  unmortised  woodlander  dramaturgy  shortrange  nomography
timeserver  unnumbered  woodpecker  drawbridge  skewbridge  nosography
tobogganer  unoccupied  woodturner  Egyptology  snowplough  noteworthy
tonguetied  unprepared  woodworker  embryology  somatology  oleography
touchpaper  unprovoked  woolgather  entomology  speciology  oreography
tourniquet  unravelled  woolgrower  enzymology  speleology  osteopathy
```

overbought	anglomania	carcinosis	dysgraphia	geocentric	inheritrix
overflight	annalistic	cardialgia	dysplastic	geognostic	internship
overweight	antependia	carotenoid	dystrophic	geographic	isentropic
patriarchy	antheridia	carotinoid	ecchymosis	geothermic	isodynamic
philosophe	anthracoid	catalectic	ecchymotic	gesundheit	isogenetic
philosophy	anthropoid	cataleptic	ectodermic	gingivitis	isomorphic
photolitho	antibiosis	catastasis	editorship	Glagolitic	jackrabbit
pilotlight	antibiotic	catechesis	egocentric	glycolysis	Jehovistic
playwright	antiheroic	catechetic	electronic	glycosuria	jingoistic
polygraphy	antipathic	cattlegrid	emblematic	glycosuric	judgematic
prizefight	antisepsis	cellulitis	embolismic	gramicidin	kaisership
pyracantha	antiseptic	cellulosic	empathetic	granulitic	kerygmatic
pyrography	antistatic	censorship	emphractic	grapefruit	kibbutznik
roadworthy	antithesis	chaudfroid	enantiosis	groceteria	kinnikinic
sabretache	antithetic	chemotaxis	encephalic	groundbait	knobkerrie
satyagraha	aphaeresis	chevrotain	endodermis	gynocratic	knopkierie
sciagraphy	aphoristic	chiliastic	endophytic	gyroscopic	lambrequin
selftaught	aphrodisia	chondritic	endoscopic	haematosis	laryngitic
serigraphy	apodeictic	choriambic	endosmosis	haematuria	laryngitis
shipwright	apolaustic	cinquefoil	endosmotic	haemolysis	latifundia
skiagraphy	apologetic	clientship	endothelia	haemolytic	lawntennis
squirarchy	apoplectic	clothespin	enharmonic	hagiologic	leadership
steamtight	aposematic	coenobitic	eosinophil	halophytic	ledgerbait
synaloepha	apotheosis	coenobytic	epenthesis	hawserlaid	legalistic
synecdoche	apotropaic	columbaria	epenthetic	Hebraistic	legateship
tauromachy	aquafortis	concentric	epexegesis	hedonistic	leucocytic
telegraphy	aragonitic	confervoid	epexegetic	heliotaxis	leukocytic
testflight	archaistic	congeneric	epicycloid	helminthic	lithologic
tomography	arithmetic	Constantia	epideictic	hemicyclic	loungesuit
topography	arrhythmia	consulship	epidermoid	hemiplegia	loxodromic
torchlight	arrhythmic	copesettic	epigastric	hemiplegic	Lupercalia
trierarchy	arthralgia	coprolitic	epigenesis	heptarchic	madreporic
typography	arthralgic	cornucopia	epigenetic	heptatonic	maidenhair
unbesought	arytaenoid	corybantic	epiglottic	heroicomic	manometric
wainwright	asbestosis	cosmogonic	epiglottis	hexametric	marginalia
watertight	ascariasis	cosmopolis	epigraphic	hierarchic	Massoretic
wishywashy	Ashkenazim	cosmoramic	episematic	histologic	mastership
xerography	astigmatic	cottontail	equilibria	histolysis	mathematic
xylography	astrologic	cousinship	erethismic	histolytic	matronship
zygomorphy	astronomic	crackbrain	erotogenic	histrionic	matronymic
achromatic	asymmetric	crematoria	erotomania	holophytic	megascopic
acrophobia	asymptotic	crescentic	escallonia	holosteric	megalithic
adrenergic	ateleiosis	crossgrain	escharotic	homophonic	melanistic
aerobiosis	austenitic	cryoscopic	essayistic	horoscopic	melismatic
aerobiotic	autocratic	cuckoospit	ethnologic	housetrain	membership
aeronautic	autoerotic	cybernetic	eucaryotic	hovertrain	meningitis
aerophobia	azeotropic	cyclopedia	eulogistic	humanistic	mentorship
aerostatic	bacchantic	cyclopedic	euphuistic	humoristic	mesenteric
aetiologic	barbituric	cylindroid	eurhythmic	hydrologic	Mesolithic
agglutinin	barometric	daisychain	eurypterid	hydrolysis	mesophytic
airmanship	batholitic	deaconship	euthanasia	hydrolytic	metalepsis
albuminoid	battleship	delphinoid	exospheric	hydrotaxis	metaphoric
alcyonaria	Beaujolais	democratic	exothermic	hyperaemia	metaphysic
aldermanic	bibliophil	dermatitis	factorship	hyperaemic	metaplasia
algolagnia	biliverdin	diachronic	Fahrenheit	hyperbaric	metastasis
algolagnic	bimetallic	diagnostic	fatalistic	hyperbolic	metastatic
allergenic	biodynamic	diagraphic	fathership	hyperdulia	metathesis
allopathic	biogenesis	diapedesis	fellowship	hypergolic	metathetic
allophonic	biogenetic	diapedetic	felspathic	hypersonic	metempiric
allosteric	biographic	diarrhoeic	fibrositis	hypnagogic	meteoritic
allotropic	biomorphic	diathermic	filariasis	hypodermic	metronomic
alphabetic	bizarrerie	dichroitic	fingernail	hypodermis	metronymic
alphameric	bloodstain	dielectric	FinnoUgric	hypolimnia	metropolis
altruistic	bluepencil	dilemmatic	florilegia	hypophysis	microlitic
amanuensis	bollweevil	diphtheria	foreordain	hypostasis	mixedmedia
ampelopsis	bolometric	diphtheric	framboesia	hypostatic	mizzensail
amphimixis	breadfruit	diphyletic	Francophil	hypotactic	mobocratic
amphoteric	bridesmaid	diplomatic	freemartin	hypothesis	mockheroic
amygdaloid	bronchitic	dipsomania	friendship	hysteresis	molluscoid
anaglyphic	bronchitis	disembroil	frigorific	hysteretic	moniliasis
anamorphic	brusquerie	disinherit	futuristic	iatrogenic	monkeysuit
anapaestic	Buddhistic	dispersoid	gaillardia	ichthyosis	monocarpic
anaplastic	bursarship	disyllabic	galliambic	idealistic	monochasia
anaptyctic	byssinosis	dosimetric	Gallomania	idiopathic	monoclinic
anchoretic	cabalistic	drawingpin	gametangia	impresario	monocratic
anchoritic	carboxylic	duodenitis	ganglionic	inartistic	monocyclic
anchylosis		dynamistic	gaultheria	inexplicit	monohybrid
anchylotic		dysenteric	generatrix	infrasonic	monohydric
androgenic				inharmonic	

monolithic	pericyclic	quatrefoil	teleologic	longshanks	appositely
monophonic	peripeteia	radiogenic	telepathic	maidenlike	approvable
montbretia	periscopic	radiologic	telephonic	morrispike	approvably
moralistic	perithecia	ragamuffin	telescopic	pilliwinks	arbitrable
morganatic	phagedenic	readership	tellership	pincerlike	arboreally
mothership	phagocytic	rectorship	tenderloin	schipperke	armorially
moustachio	phantasmic	regentship	tendinitis	seamanlike	arrogantly
multimedia	phantastic	retrochoir	tenebrific	sidestroke	arterially
myasthenia	phenacetin	rheotropic	termitaria	spongecake	ascendable
mystagogic	phenotypic	rheumatoid	terreplein	springlike	ascendible
mythologic	philatelic	rhizogenic	tetrapolis	steelworks	ascribable
mythomania	phlegmatic	riboflavin	tetrarchic	summerlike	aspergilla
mythopoeia	phlogistic	ricinoleic	theocratic	sweepstake	assailable
mythopoeic	phonematic	rickettsia	theophanic	trancelike	assessable
naphthenic	phonolitic	rockrabbit	theophoric	waterworks	assignable
nativistic	phonologic	rollingpin	thermionic	aberrantly	associable
necropolis	phosphatic	Romanistic	thermophil	abnormally	atomically
neoclassic	phosphoric	rotisserie	thimblerig	abominable	attachable
neoplastic	photogenic	saccharoid	thrombosis	abominably	attackable
nephralgia	photolysis	sandmartin	thrombotic	abortively	attainable
neurotoxin	photolytic	Sanskritic	thwartship	abrasively	atypically
nihilistic	phototaxis	saprogenic	timocratic	absolutely	audiophile
nomothetic	phylogenic	sarracenia	totemistic	absorbable	automobile
noogenesis	phytogenic	satellitic	toxiphobia	absorbedly	autumnally
nosophobia	phytotoxic	saturnalia	tracheitis	abstractly	aversively
nostologic	pigeonpair	satyriasis	tragicomic	abstrusely	backwardly
novelistic	pillowslip	scarabaeid	translucid	abundantly	bafflingly
numismatic	pinnatifid	schismatic	tremolitic	acceptable	banderilla
nyctalopia	pistolwhip	scholastic	tribrachic	acceptably	barcarolle
nyctalopic	pityriasis	scientific	trichiasis	acceptedly	basketball
odontalgia	planetaria	sciolistic	triglyphic	accessible	becomingly
oligarchic	planktonic	scratchwig	trimorphic	accessibly	believable
ophiologic	pleochroic	scriptoria	tropologic	accurately	besprinkle
ophthalmia	pleonastic	seabiscuit	tuberculin	accursedly	biannually
ophthalmic	poinsettia	seacaptain	tularaemia	accusingly	biblically
optimistic	pollenosis	seamanship	tularaemic	achievable	bibliopole
orogenesis	polyandric	selfdeceit	tympanitic	acidophile	bibliopoly
orogenetic	polyatamic	selfprofit	tympanitis	acquirable	bibulously
orographic	polyclinic	semiliquid	ultrabasic	acromegaly	bidonville
orthogenic	polycyclic	septenarii	ultrasonic	actionable	biennially
orthopedic	polydipsia	seriocomic	umpireship	actionably	bigamously
overcommit	polyhedric	shroudlaid	uneconomic	adaptively	binaurally
paedagogic	polymathic	sialagogic	unemphatic	adequately	bisexually
paediatric	polyonymic	siegetrain	unhistoric	adherently	bissextile
Palaeozoic	polyphasic	simplistic	unionistic	adhesively	blamefully
palmatifid	polyphonic	sitophobia	urethritis	adjacently	bleachable
pancreatic	populistic	snafflebit	valvulitis	adjustable	bleatingly
pancreatin	porismatic	sociologic	variolitic	admiringly	blindingly
pangenesis	portcullis	solecistic	Visigothic	admissible	blissfully
pangenetic	postexilic	sophomoric	vitalistic	admittable	blockishly
pantomimic	pozzolanic	souterrain	viziership	admittedly	bloodguilt
pantrymaid	precipitin	speedlimit	volumetric	adoptively	bluebottle
parabiosis	presbyopia	splanchnic	wardenship	adsorbable	blurringly
parabiotic	presbyopic	springtail	wheelchair	affectedly	blushingly
paraboloid	princeship	squaresail	xenophobia	afferently	boastfully
paradisaic	procrypsis	squireship	xerophytic	affirmable	boondoggle
paraffinic	procryptic	stereopsis	xylophonic	affluently	bootlessly
paragnosis	proglottis	stochastic	zollverein	affordable	bouncingly
paralipsis	prognathic	stomatitis	zoomorphic	agitatedly	brainchild
parametric	prognostic	stonefruit	backblocks	alarmingly	brandyball
paramnesia	prosthesis	strabismic	backstroke	allusively	breastwall
paraplegia	prosthetic	subaquatic	birdstrike	altocumuli	breathable
paraplegic	protanopic	sultanship	bobbysocks	amerceable	brickfield
parasitoid	protectrix	supersonic	chainsmoke	analysable	bridgeable
paratactic	prothallia	supertonic	cheesecake	anemophily	brocatelle
pastorship	prototypic	suretyship	Christlike	anglophile	bronchiole
pathogenic	protreptic	suspensoid	coralsnake	animalcula	broodingly
pathologic	provitamin	syllabaria	cottoncake	animalcule	bumblingly
patisserie	psilocybin	synaeresis	downstroke	animatedly	bunglingly
patronymic	pugilistic	synchronic	earthquake	annoyingly	bustlingly
pederastic	pursership	synergetic	fatherlike	answerable	butterball
pegmatitic	pycnogonid	syngenesis	fourstroke	answerably	buttermilk
pemphigoid	pyromantic	synostosis	glassworks	antepenult	buttonball
penetralia	pyrometric	syphilitic	goldilocks	anteriorly	buttonhole
penicillin	pyrophoric	systematic	grasssnake	apparently	cacomistle
penmanship	quadrennia	talismanic	hairstroke	appealable	Caerphilly
pentatomic	quadrumvir	tautomeric	hankypanky	appeasable	cajolingly
pentatonic	quartzitic	taxidermic	heatstroke	applicable	calculable
perchloric	quatorzain	telemetric	johnnycake	applicably	calculably

canaliculi	corrigible	dilatorily	fadelessly	gruesomely	incredible
cannonball	cosmically	diligently	fairycycle	guilefully	incredibly
canonicals	covalently	dillydally	faithfully	gutturally	inculpable
canorously	covetingly	discophile	familiarly	gypsophila	incunabula
captiously	covetously	discreetly	fancifully	habitually	incurrable
carelessly	coweringly	discretely	farcically	halfyearly	indecently
carmagnole	craftguild	disentitle	fathomable	hamshackle	indictable
cascarilla	cranesbill	disgruntle	fatiguable	handsomely	indirectly
cautiously	creatively	dishabille	favourable	harmlessly	indolently
cavalierly	creaturely	dislikable	favourably	hauntingly	ineducable
cellularly	creditable	disloyally	fearlessly	heartwhole	ineligible
censurable	creditably	disorderly	fearsomely	hectically	ineligibly
centrefold	crepuscule	disposable	fecklessly	heedlessly	ineludible
centrehalf	criminally	disputable	femininely	heliacally	inevitable
changeable	critically	disputably	fenestella	helplessly	inevitably
changeably	cultivable	disquietly	fetchingly	hempnettle	inexorable
chargeable	culturally	dissoluble	feverishly	heroically	inexorably
charitable	cumbrously	distensile	fiducially	herrenvolk	inexpertly
charitably	cyclically	distinctly	fiendishly	hesitantly	inexpiable
charmingly	cyclostyle	disyllable	filterable	hibernacle	inexpiably
cheapishly	damageable	divisively	fisherfolk	honourable	infallible
cheerfully	damagingly	dolorously	fishkettle	honourably	infallibly
chemically	daughterly	dominantly	flagrantly	hopelessly	infamously
childishly	dazzlingly	doubletalk	flapdoodle	hormonally	infeasible
chinchilla	debonairly	doubtfully	flawlessly	hospitable	inferiorly
chrysotile	decadently	doubtingly	fleeringly	hospitably	infernally
churlishly	deceivable	downwardly	fleetingly	hourcircle	inferrable
Cinderella	deceptible	drawlingly	flexuously	humorously	infinitely
circularly	decisively	dreadfully	flippantly	hurlyburly	inflatable
citronella	declarable	dreamworld	floatingly	hydrically	inflexible
clannishly	declinable	droopingly	fluviatile	hydrophily	inflexibly
clarabella	decorously	drosophila	fontanelle	ignorantly	informally
clerically	deductible	drudgingly	footcandle	illatively	ingestible
clinically	defeasible	dungbeetle	forcefully	illaudable	inherently
clownishly	defendable	dwarfishly	forecastle	illaudably	inhumanely
Clydesdale	defensible	effaceable	forgivable	illusively	inimically
coachbuilt	defensibly	effusively	forgivably	illusorily	inimitable
coagulable	deferrable	electively	formidable	imaginable	inimitably
cocksurely	definitely	eliminable	formidably	imaginably	innerrably
coercively	defrayable	eloquently	formlessly	imbecilely	innocently
coffeemill	degradable	employable	fragrantly	immaturely	inoculable
cognisable	degradedly	endorsable	fraxinella	imminently	inoperable
cognisably	dejectedly	enduringly	freakishly	immiscible	insatiable
coherently	delectable	engagingly	frenziedly	immiscibly	insatiably
cohesively	delectably	enormously	frequently	immodestly	insecurely
coleoptile	delicately	enticingly	friendlily	immortally	insensible
collatable	delusively	enumerable	frowningly	immortelle	insensibly
collembola	demandable	enunciable	fruitfully	immoveable	insociable
colonially	dementedly	eradicable	fugitively	impalpable	insolently
colossally	demoiselle	erotically	fumblingly	impalpably	insolvable
colourable	demurrable	eruptively	funereally	impartible	intangible
colourably	dependable	escadrille	fustanella	impassable	intangibly
comestible	dependably	espadrille	Gallophile	impassably	integrable
commonable	deplorable	especially	generously	impassible	integrally
communally	deplorably	ethereally	gentlefolk	impassibly	interiorly
commutable	depravedly	ethnically	germinally	impeccable	internally
comparable	deprivable	evaporable	ghastfully	impeccably	intimately
comparably	deridingly	eventually	gladsomely	imperially	intrepidly
compatible	derisively	examinable	glancingly	implacable	introrsely
compatibly	deservedly	exciting1y	globularly	implacably	invaluable
completely	deshabille	executable	gloriously	implicitly	invaluably
composedly	designedly	exotically	gorgeously	impolitely	invariable
computable	desirously	expandable	Gorgonzola	importable	invariably
concretely	desolately	expansible	gothically	imposingly	invincible
confusedly	despicable	expectedly	governable	impossible	invincibly
conjointly	despicably	expendable	gracefully	impossibly	inviolable
conjugally	despisable	explicable	graciously	impotently	inviolably
consolable	detachable	explicitly	granadilla	improbable	invitingly
constantly	detachedly	exportable	grandchild	improbably	ironically
consumable	detectable	extendedly	granduncle	improperly	isolatable
consumedly	detestable	extendible	granularly	improvable	Italophile
contrarily	detestably	extensible	graspingly	improvably	jargonelle
contritely	devilishly	exteriorly	gratefully	impudently	jerrybuilt
convenable	dextrously	externally	greatuncle	impugnable	jubilantly
conversely	diagonally	extricable	grenadilla	inactively	judicially
conveyable	dialysable	exultantly	grievously	inchoately	kenspeckle
corncockle	diffusible	exultingly	grindingly	incisively	lamentable
corporally	digestible	fabulously	growlingly	inclinable	lamentably
corpuscule	digitately	factiously	grudgingly	includible	lamentedly

lanternfly	notarially	ploddingly	regionally	semicircle	strainedly
largescale	noticeable	ploughable	reissuable	semidouble	stridently
laughingly	noticeably	pocketable	rejectable	semiweekly	strikingly
licensable	notifiable	poetically	relatively	semiyearly	stringhalt
lifelessly	notionally	ponderable	releasable	sensuously	stronghold
listlessly	nullanulla	populously	relevantly	sentiently	stubbornly
literarily	numerously	positively	relievable	separately	studiously
lonesomely	obdurately	potentilla	relishable	septically	stunningly
lopsidedly	obediently	powerfully	remarkable	serradilla	sublimable
lovelessly	obligingly	prancingly	remarkably	shamefully	succinctly
lowprofile	observable	pratincole	remediable	sheathbill	sufferable
luculently	observably	preciously	remedially	sheepishly	sufferably
lukewarmly	obtainable	predicable	remissible	shockingly	sugarmaple
luminously	officially	preferable	renderable	shoebuckle	suicidally
lusciously	onesidedly	preferably	repairable	shrewishly	summonable
lustrously	oppositely	pregnantly	repealable	shrinkable	superiorly
malapertly	optatively	prehensile	repeatable	sicklebill	supernally
manageable	optionally	premaxilla	repeatedly	sidesaddle	supposable
manageably	oracularly	preparedly	reportable	sillybilly	supposably
maniacally	ordinarily	prepayable	reportedly	singularly	supposedly
manifestly	orientally	prepensely	reservedly	sinisterly	surgically
manifoldly	originally	pressingly	resignedly	sketchable	surmisable
manzanilla	orthodoxly	presumable	resistible	skittishly	sweepingly
marginally	ostensible	presumably	resolutely	slantingly	swimmingly
marketable	ostensibly	previously	resolvable	slatternly	swingingly
markethall	otherwhile	pridefully	resolvedly	Slavophile	tabernacle
martingale	otherworld	priggishly	resonantly	sleighbell	taciturnly
masticable	outrightly	primevally	respirable	slipperily	tactically
materially	oversubtle	procurable	restlessly	slothfully	tactlessly
maternally	oversupply	prodigally	restorable	sluggardly	taperingly
mealbeetle	oxidisable	producible	retainable	sluggishly	taradiddle
measurable	pacifiable	profitable	reticently	sluttishly	tarantella
measurably	packsaddle	profitably	retinacula	smallscale	tarantelle
measuredly	paddyfield	profoundly	retiringly	snappishly	tastefully
medievally	paedophile	projectile	retractile	sneakingly	tattletale
melancholy	painlessly	propagable	retrorsely	sneeringly	tauntingly
menacingly	pardonable	protrusile	returnable	snobbishly	tearlessly
mensurable	pardonably	proximally	revealable	snowmobile	teetotally
mercantile	parentally	pruriently	reverently	snubbingly	temperable
mercifully	participle	puissantly	reversible	soapbubble	temperedly
metastable	pastorally	pulsatilla	revertible	societally	temporally
metrically	pasturable	punctually	reviewable	soldanella	temptingly
middlingly	patentable	punishable	rewardable	solitarily	tenantable
militantly	paternally	punitively	rightangle	somersault	terminable
militarily	patulously	purblindly	rightfully	sonorously	terminably
mindlessly	peacefully	purulently	rigorously	soothingly	terminally
mirthfully	peccadillo	putatively	ritornelli	soullessly	tetrastyle
mistakable	peculiarly	pycnostyle	ritornello	soundingly	texturally
mistakenly	peerlessly	quadrangle	rockabilly	southernly	thankfully
moderately	pellucidly	quadrupole	rovebeetle	sowthistle	thermopile
modifiable	penetrable	qualmishly	rubrically	spaciously	thievishly
monetarily	penetrably	quenchable	ruminantly	spankingly	thinkingly
mosaically	penitently	ramblingly	Russophile	speciously	thirtyfold
motorcycle	peppermill	ramshackle	rustically	spectrally	thornapple
mournfully	percentile	rationally	ruthlessly	spiritedly	thoroughly
movelessly	perdurable	ravenously	safetybelt	spitefully	thumbstall
mozzarella	perdurably	razorshell	sagittally	splendidly	ticklishly
muffinbell	perilously	reactively	salmonella	sporophyll	timberwolf
muscularly	perishable	realisable	saltarello	sportfully	timelessly
musicianly	periwinkle	reasonable	salutarily	sportingly	timorously
mutinously	permutable	reasonably	sandcastle	sportively	tirelessly
myopically	personable	reassemble	sanguinely	spotlessly	tiresomely
mystically	personally	reassembly	sanitarily	springhalt	toilsomely
mythically	perversely	rebuttable	scabrously	spuriously	tolerantly
namelessly	petronella	recallable	scathingly	squeezable	tonelessly
nationally	petulantly	receivable	scenically	stagbeetle	toothshell
nauseously	phonically	receptacle	schemozzle	stagnantly	toroidally
nautically	photophily	receptible	schoolable	stalwartly	tortiously
nebulously	physically	recklessly	scoffingly	standstill	tortuously
necrophile	piccalilli	recordable	scornfully	statically	touchingly
necrophily	piercingly	recreantly	scratchily	statutable	toweringly
needlessly	pigeonhole	recyclable	searchable	statutably	tragically
negatively	pilotwhale	redeemable	seasonable	stealthily	tranquilly
negligible	pitilessly	redolently	seasonably	stiflingly	trickishly
negligibly	planetable	reeligible	seasonally	stingingly	triflingly
negotiable	plangently	refillable	secludedly	stinkingly	trigonally
negrophile	pleadingly	reflexible	sedulously	stockstill	trimonthly
nitrochalk	pleasantly	reformable	seguidilla	storksbill	triturable
nominately	pleasingly	refundable	selflessly	straightly	tropically

trouvaille	vortically	pianissimo	beforehand	conferring	dispersant
truncately	vorticella	plaguesome	behindhand	confirmand	dissilient
trustfully	voyageable	plasmogamy	belladonna	congregant	dissolvent
trustingly	vulnerable	pogonotomy	bemusement	consequent	distilland
truthfully	vulnerably	polychrome	beneficent	consistent	distilling
tunelessly	wagonvault	quadrireme	benevolent	conspirant	divestment
turnbuckle	wastefully	sarcolemma	benzocaine	constraint	drawstring
tutorially	watchfully	schooltime	benzpyrene	consultant	drivelling
twelvefold	waveringly	sclerotomy	bestirring	consulting	earthbound
ulteriorly	wearifully	Sexagesima	bestowment	contendent	earthshine
ultimately	westwardly	springtime	betterment	contestant	earwigging
unarguable	willynilly	strabotomy	birthstone	contingent	easterling
unbearable	willywilly	summertime	bitterling	continuant	effacement
unbearably	windowsill	trichotomy	blanketing	contraband	elecampane
unbeatable	windshield	unhandsome	blazonment	contravene	embalmment
unbeatably	winebottle	wintertime	blistering	convenient	embankment
unbiddable	witchingly	aberdevine	blithering	convergent	embarkment
unbrokenly	womanishly	abridgment	bloodhound	conversant	embodiment
uncommonly	wondrously	abstergent	bloodstone	convincing	embonpoint
unctuously	wordlessly	accountant	bookmaking	convulsant	embossment
undeniable	workpeople	accounting	borderland	corbelling	embryogeny
undeniably	worthwhile	accrescent	borderline	correspond	employment
underbelly	wrathfully	acquitting	bratticing	cosentient	encampment
underworld	wretchedly	adamantine	breakpoint	couplement	encasement
unendingly	wrongfully	adjudgment	breastbone	cradlesong	encashment
unenviable	wrongously	adjustment	brevetting	creatinine	enchanting
unerringly	yearningly	adolescent	brigandine	cuckoopint	encystment
unfadingly	yieldingly	adrenaline	brigantine	cudgelling	endearment
unfilially	youthfully	adulterant	brownstone	cummerbund	enfacement
unfriendly	adenectomy	adulterine	cajolement	curvetting	engagement
uniaxially	aerenchyma	advisement	cancelling	cuttlebone	englutting
univocally	aerogramme	aeroengine	candescent	dazzlement	engrossing
unknowable	beforetime	affeerment	cannelloni	debasement	engulfment
unlawfully	blithesome	afterpains	cantonment	debatement	enjambment
unmannerly	borborygmi	aircooling	Capitoline	decampment	enjoinment
unnameable	bothersome	alightment	cappuccino	decolorant	enlacement
unreadable	breadcrumb	allurement	catarrhine	decompound	enlistment
unreliable	burdensome	almsgiving	catchpenny	decrescent	enmeshment
unscalable	centrosome	ambivalent	cellophane	defacement	enrichment
unscramble	chromosome	ambushment	chalcedony	defilement	enrigiment
unsociable	cryptogamy	amercement	chalkstone	definement	ensanguine
unsociably	cuddlesome	anchoring	changeling	deforciant	entailment
unsocially	cumbersome	anglophone	chargehand	defrayment	enticement
unsteadily	cyclostome	anointment	chatelaine	delinquent	entombment
unsuitable	cytochrome	anopheline	checkpoint	denaturant	entrancing
untowardly	decagramme	antecedent	chiselling	denouement	entrapment
unwieldily	decigramme	anthracene	cinchonine	department	enwrapping
unwontedly	diseconomy	anticipant	circumvent	deployment	epeirogeny
unworkable	doubletime	appetising	cismontane	deportment	equipotent
unworthily	eighteenmo	aquamarine	cispontine	depressant	equivalent
usuriously	enterotomy	arrestment	clementine	derailment	erubescent
utilisable	fortissimi	asparagine	clingstone	descendant	escapement
uxoriously	fortissimo	asphyxiant	clinkstone	descendent	escarpment
valorously	frolicsome	assentient	coadjacent	designment	evanescent
vaporously	gastronome	assessment	coalescent	despondent	everliving
varicocele	gastronomy	assignment	coexistent	detachment	everything
varietally	grandmamma	assoilment	cohabitant	detainment	evolvement
vascularly	heterogamy	assortment	coincident	detoxicant	excitement
vaudeville	heteronomy	astringent	colchicine	devotement	excrescent
vehemently	hippodrome	asynchrony	collarbone	diecasting	exhilarant
vengefully	humoursome	attachment	comedienne	diesinking	exorbitant
venomously	imposthume	attainment	commandant	diphyodont	experiment
ventriculi	kilogramme	attornment	commanding	disappoint	exsanguine
verifiable	laparotomy	attractant	commitment	disbarring	extractant
vermicelli	letterbomb	autoimmune	committing	disbudding	facesaving
vertically	lumbersome	aventurine	compelling	discerning	fairground
vesperbell	mastectomy	avouchment	complacent	discipline	famishment
viewlessly	meddlesome	babblement	complement	discommend	fantoccini
vigilantly	meningioma	backbiting	compliment	discontent	fatherland
vigorously	mettlesome	background	comprehend	discordant	feathering
villanelle	monochrome	concerning	concerning	discrepant	fescennine
vindicable	mycoplasma	bafflement	concertina	discussant	fieldstone
viperously	neurilemma	ballooning	concertino	discutient	fixedpoint
virginally	neurolemma	banishment	concordant	disenchant	flagellant
virtuously	octodecimo	barkentine	concurrent	disentwine	flagwaving
virulently	ovariotomy	barrelling	concurring	disharmony	flamboyant
viscerally	palindrome	batfowling	condescend	disincline	flashpoint
visionally	parenchyma	battlement	confabbing	disownment	
volleyball	phlebotomy	beekeeping	conferment	dispelling	

```
flattering  housebound  lovemaking  parcelling  pyrotechny  signalling
flavescent  houselling  lutestring  parliament  quadrumana  skibobbing
flavouring  houseplant  magnifying  paroxytone  quadrumane  skijumping
fledgeling  hoverplane  mainspring  parturient  quarantine  skindiving
fleshwound  hucklebone  malcontent  patrolling  quartering  skrimshank
floatplane  humbugging  maleficent  pedalpoint  quinacrine  skyjacking
floatstone  hydrophane  malevolent  pencilling  rabblement  skywriting
flocculent  hydrophone  malfeasant  penpushing  radiophone  sleevelink
florentine  hydroplane  management  peppermint  rainmaking  smaragdine
florescent  ilangilang  manservant  percipient  ravishment  smattering
flyfishing  illuminant  maraschino  performing  rearmament  smokeplant
forbidding  immurement  marcescent  permitting  recoupment  snakestone
foreboding  impairment  margravine  persistent  redcurrant  snivelling
foreground  impalement  marrowbone  phagedaena  refinement  solacement
forgetting  impartment  marvelling  philippina  refreshing  solicitant
formatting  impediment  masterhand  philippine  refringent  sousaphone
fortepiano  impenitent  mastermind  philistine  refuelling  southbound
forwarding  impregnant  meadowland  phillumeny  refundment  spellbound
fosterling  imprinting  mediastina  philopoena  regalement  sphenodone
foudroyant  impugnment  medicament  photoprint  registrant  spiderline
fourinhand  impuissant  microcline  physicking  regretting  spillikins
foxhunting  inappetent  microphone  piccaninny  resemblant  spinescent
frangipane  inbreeding  midmorning  pickaninny  resentment  spiralling
frangipani  incasement  minestrone  picketline  reshipment  splintbone
fraudulent  incitement  ministrant  picnicking  resounding  sprinkling
freeliving  incogitant  minutehand  picosecond  respecting  spumescent
frivolling  incoherent  miscellany  pigeonwing  respondent  squireling
frolicking  inconstant  misfortune  pinchpenny  restaurant  staggering
frutescent  increscent  mishitting  piperidine  retirement  standpoint
fulfilling  indictment  miswording  piscifauna  retraining  staphyline
fulfilment  inditement  monovalent  pistolling  revealment  stargazing
funnelling  inducement  morphogeny  pistonring  revilement  starveling
gadrooning  ineloquent  mosaicking  pitchstone  rhinestone  stepparent
gaingiving  inexistent  motherland  plainchant  rhodophane  stiffening
gambolling  infighting  mountebank  playacting  riproaring  stiflebone
garnishing  infrequent  mousseline  playground  rodfishing  stinkstone
Ghibelline  ingredient  munificent  ploughland  roistering  stoneblind
girlfriend  inhabitant  musicstand  pointblank  rollicking  stormbound
glimmering  insentient  Mussulmans  polyvalent  rosaniline  streamline
Godfearing  insouciant  nanosecond  postliminy  roseengine  stridulant
government  inspanning  nauseating  pothunting  rumrunning  strychnine
gramophone  instalment  nickelling  pozzuolana  rupicoline  subheading
grandstand  instilling  nigrescent  practising  saccharine  subletting
gratifying  instrument  nitpicking  preachment  sanctimony  submediant
gravestone  integument  nonchalant  predestine  sanderling  submitting
greenshank  intendment  noncontent  prednisone  sapphirine  submontane
greenstone  internment  nonpayment  preeminent  satisfying  subroutine
grindstone  interplant  nonplaying  preferment  saxicoline  subsequent
groundling  interregna  nonviolent  preferring  scarlatina  subsistent
groundrent  intertwine  northbound  prefulgent  scattering  subtrahend
grovelling  interwound  nourishing  prepayment  schizogony  sufficient
guillotine  intolerant  obtainment  pressagent  scribbling  supergiant
gunrunning  intoxicant  oceangoing  pretendant  scrimshank  supplement
habiliment  intriguant  offputting  pretendent  seaanemone  supplicant
hairspring  investment  offsetting  prevailing  seaserpent  surfactant
hammerpond  iridescent  oligopsony  prevenient  secernment  surprising
handspring  iridosmine  omnipotent  priestling  secondhand  sustaining
hanselling  irrelevant  omniscient  princeling  secondment  swaggering
harassment  irreverent  opalescent  proceeding  securement  swanupping
headspring  jaywalking  ordainment  procumbent  seducement  sweatgland
headstrong  kennelling  outbidding  proficient  selenodont  sweetening
heavensent  kidnapping  outfitting  propellant  selfacting  sweltering
heterodont  Krugerrand  outgassing  propellent  selfloving  swivelling
heterodyne  Kuomintang  outgunning  propelling  selfrising  tambourine
heterogeny  lactescent  outpatient  prosilient  selfruling  tanglement
heterogony  lacustrine  outpouring  protestant  seltzogene  tankengine
hierophant  landowning  outputting  provisions  semidivine  tantamount
highflying  laurelling  outrunning  psittacine  semidrying  tapotement
highoctane  lavishment  outsitting  puberulent  Septuagint  tasselling
highstrung  lawabiding  outwitting  publishing  serpentine  tautophony
Hindustani  ledgerline  overabound  pummelling  settlement  teenyweeny
hinterland  lieutenant  overground  punchdrunk  sexivalent  teratogeny
Hippocrene  lifegiving  overrefine  punishment  sheepshank  thereanent
hobnobbing  lifesaving  overriding  purseseine  shellmound  thickening
homecoming  lipreading  overstrung  pursuivant  shirtfront  threepenny
homemaking  liquescent  Palaeocene  putrescent  shoestring  thumbprint
hootenanny  lithophane  Palaeogene  putrescine  shortening  thundering
hostelling  loganstone  papaverine  puzzlement  shovelling  tiddlywink
houseagent  logrolling  paraselene  pyridoxine  shuttering  timberline
```

timesaving	abreaction	calculator	corelation	distrainor	gemination
tinselling	abrogation	calibrator	coronation	divagation	generation
tittupping	abscission	candlewood	corporator	divination	glaciation
topgallant	absolution	capitation	correction	domination	graduation
tortellini	absorption	carryingon	corrugator	donnybrook	granulator
touchstone	abstention	castration	corruption	dubitation	greasewood
tourmaline	abstersion	catenation	cottonwood	duplicator	habitation
tournament	abstractor	catholicon	cottonwool	ebullition	halfnelson
tramontana	accusation	catholicos	councillor	eisteddfod	handbarrow
tramontane	acervation	cavitation	counsellor	elaborator	handgallop
trampoline	acotyledon	celebrator	cousinhood	eliminator	heartblood
transplant	acroterion	centillion	covenantor	elongation	heartthrob
travelling	activation	cephalopod	crippledom	elucidator	heathendom
travertine	adaptation	chamaeleon	crispation	elutriator	hebetation
trepanning	adhibition	chamberpot	crustation	emaciation	hemihedron
Tridentine	adjunction	champignon	cultivator	emendation	hendecagon
triphthong	adjuration	chancellor	cumulation	emigration	Heptameron
triumphant	admiration	chaparajos	cunctation	emollition	hesitation
trowelling	admonition	chaparejos	curmudgeon	encephalon	hexahedron
tunnelling	adsorption	Charleston	curtystool	enervation	hullabaloo
turgescent	advocation	chatterbox	datamation	engineroom	hyperbaton
turpentine	affliction	chequebook	deaeration	enumerator	imbibition
twelvetone	aggression	chickenpox	decahedron	enunciator	immolation
ultrasound	aircushion	childproof	decimation	epilimnion	impanation
unassuming	alienation	chimneypot	declension	equitation	imposition
unavailing	allegation	Christhood	decoration	eradicator	impression
unbecoming	alleviator	chuckwagon	dedication	ergosterol	imputation
unblinking	allocation	circulator	defalcator	eructation	incantator
unblushing	allocution	closestool	defamation	escalation	inchoation
unchanging	alteration	coaptation	definition	escutcheon	incitation
underlying	alternator	codswallop	deflection	estimation	incubation
underslung	ambassador	cogitation	defoliator	etiolation	inculcator
understand	ambulation	collection	delegation	eucalyptol	indagation
unedifying	ammunition	collimator	delineator	Eurovision	indecision
unfeminine	amphictyon	collocutor	demolition	evacuation	indexation
unflagging	amputation	coloration	denegation	evaluation	indication
ungrudging	AngloSaxon	combustion	denigrator	evaporator	induration
unpleasant	annexation	commission	denotation	exaltation	infarction
unpleasing	annotation	commonroom	denudation	excavation	inflection
unsettling	annulation	commutator	depilation	excerption	infliction
unsporting	antecessor	compaction	deposition	excitation	infraction
unswerving	antiproton	comparator	depredator	execration	ingression
unthinking	apparition	comparison	depression	exhalation	inhalation
unwavering	applicator	compassion	depuration	exhaustion	inhibition
unyielding	apposition	compatriot	deputation	exhibition	inhumation
upbraiding	arbitrator	competitor	derivation	exhumation	initiation
upbringing	archbishop	completion	derogation	expedition	injunction
upstanding	archdeacon	complexion	descension	expiration	innovation
vespertine	areolation	compositor	descriptor	exposition	inoculator
vibraphone	Armageddon	compotator	desecrator	expression	inquisitor
vicegerent	arrogation	compressor	desiccator	expunction	insinuator
viceregent	ascription	compulsion	designator	expurgator	insolation
Victoriana	aspiration	computator	desolation	extenuator	inspection
videophone	assumption	conception	desorption	extinction	inspirator
vitrescent	attenuator	concession	desperados	extirpator	instigator
vociferant	attraction	conclusion	destructor	extraction	institutor
voiceprint	autochthon	concoction	detonation	exultation	instructor
wassailing	automation	concretion	detraction	exuviation	insulation
waterborne	backgammon	concussion	devolution	fabricator	integrator
waterfront	barbershop	conduction	didgeridoo	fasciation	interferon
weathering	barleybroo	confection	digitation	fascinator	intervenor
wellspring	Bedlington	confession	digression	fatherhood	intimation
wheatstone	benefactor	conflation	dilatation	federation	intinction
whispering	bilocation	congestion	diminution	feuilleton	intonation
wilderment	bitterroot	connection	diningroom	fiddlewood	intubation
windowpane	bitterwood	conniption	discretion	figuration	inundation
wonderland	blackamoor	contention	discussion	filtration	invitation
wonderment	blueribbon	contortion	disembosom	flameproof	invocation
wraparound	brachiator	contractor	disenviron	flashflood	involution
wrongdoing	brachiopod	contraprop	dismission	flirtation	iodination
wunderkind	brazilwood	contrition	dispassion	floatation	ionisation
ylangylang	bridegroom	convection	dispersion	floriation	irreligion
zabaglione	buccinator	convention	disruption	flunkeydom	irrigation
zigzagging	bucketshop	conversion	dissection	foreshadow	irritation
abdication	buttonhook	conviction	dissension	fornicator	jubilation
aberration	buttonwood	convulsion	dissuasion	foundation	knighthood
abjuration	byelection	cooperator	distension	fumigation	laceration
abnegation	cacodaemon	cooptation	distention	fullbottom	lacrimator
abominator	calciferol	copulation	distortion	gasteropod	lacrymator

```
lamination osculation prospector smorrebrod undershoot pictograph
lapidation outstation protection snapdragon understood planigraph
laureation overshadow protractor sneezewood undulation postscript
legislator ovipositor protrusion soundproof unorthodox quadriceps
letterbook oxygenator provocator sourcebook urtication radiograph
levigation packingbox punctation spallation ustulation radioscopy
levitation paddywagon punctuator speciation usucaption rhinoscope
liberation pagination pushbutton speculator usurpation rhinoscopy
lightproof palliation pyrogallol spoliation vaccinator rhizomorph
likelihood panopticon quartation spongewood validation somatotype
limitation parenthood quaternion springwood vegetation spirograph
liquidator pastrycook quercitron squamation velitation statoscope
literation patination radication squeezebox veneration stenograph
litigation peculation recitation squirehood ventilator stereotype
livelihood pejoration recreation stagnation vesication stereotypy
livingroom penetrator redemption starvation vindicator stonesnipe
lobsterpot pennillion reelection stimulator virginhood stylograph
lobulation pentathlon reflection stipulator visitation tetramorph
lockerroom pentstemon refraction stockproof vivisector thixotropy
locomotion perception refutation stomatopod waffleiron tickertape
lubricator percolator regelation stonemason waterflood transcript
lucubrator percussion regression stormproof watermelon transshape
lumberroom perfection regulation streetdoor waterproof typescript
lustration perforator relaxation strongroom weatherbox vectograph
maceration perihelion relegation subduction wellington zincograph
machinator permeation relocation subjection windowshop aboveboard
maculation permission renovation subjugator witnessbox absolutory
maidenhood peroration reparation subkingdom woodpigeon accusatory
malapropos persecutor repetition submersion yellowwood acidimetry
malefactor personator reposition submission yokefellow adjuratory
manifestos persuasion repression subreption zwitterion admonitory
masterhood perversion repudiator subsection aeolotropy advocatory
masticator phenomenon reputation substation anemograph aldermanry
matronhood phlogiston rescission subvention anisotropy alexanders
maturation photoflood resolution subversion bathyscaph alimentary
mayblossom phrasebook resorcinol succession bathyscope alongshore
medication pincushion resorption suggestion beechdrops ambulatory
meditation pistolshot respirator superation bootstraps amendatory
meliorator plantation resumption supervisor cantaloupe amphigouri
meltingpot playfellow retraction supination chinagraph anemometry
mesenteron pocketbook revelation suppletion chromatype angiosperm
middlebrow pollinator revocation suppressor cyclograph animadvert
minutebook polyhedron revolution suspension cystoscope apiculture
misprision polyhistor rhinoceros sustention cystoscopy apothecary
mitigation population rockbottom symphonion ditriglyph arthromere
moderation possession rockpigeon syncopator fireescape aspidistra
modulation postillion rosemallow syndicator fluorotype atmosphere
motherhood postulator rubricator tablespoon hagioscope audiometry
motivation pouncetbox rumination tabulation hectograph aviculture
musicstool prairiedog sagination television heliograph backstairs
muskmallow prayerbook salivation temptation helioscope baptistery
mutilation precaution salutation tenderfoot heliotrope bardolatry
nanisation precession sandalwood tenterhook heliotropy bargeboard
nationhood preclusion sanitation terminator hieroglyph barleycorn
navigation prediction sappanwood thermistor hierograph barrenwort
needlebook preemption sashwindow thornproof hippocampi barysphere
negotiator prehension saturation thunderbox hippogryph basketwork
newsvendor prelection schoolbook tiringroom hydroscope bassethorn
nincompoop premonitor schoolroom titivation hygrograph bathymetry
nodulation preparator selfaction titubation hygroscope battledore
nomination pretension selfmotion tocopherol iconoscope bewitchery
nonfiction prevention semination toleration lithoglyph binoculars
nucleation priesthood separation tortfeasor lithograph blackberry
numeration procession septillion tourbillon manuscript blackboard
obligation procreator servomotor toxication micrograph blackguard
obstructor procurator sextillion trabeation microscope blackheart
obturation production shellproof trajection microscopy Blackshirt
occupation profession sheriffdom transactor mimeograph blackthorn
ocellation progenitor shockproof transferor necroscopy blastoderm
octahedron prohibitor shopwindow transistor nephograph blastomere
oppilation projection showwindow transition nephoscope blastopore
opposition prolocutor sibilation translator nympholept blockboard
oppression promptbook silkcotton trisection palaeotype brainstorm
orangewood propagator simulation triskelion pantograph breadboard
ordination proportion singlefoot triturator paratroops breastwork
originator propraetor sisterbook truncation petroglyph bridgework
orphanhood proprietor sketchbook ulceration phonograph brightwork
oscillator propulsion slowmotion underfloor photograph broadsword
oscitation prosecutor smokeproof underproof phototrope brownshirt
```

buffoonery	discomfort	indicatory	passionary	separatory	whitethorn
butterwort	disconcert	inhibitory	pasteboard	setterwort	wickerwork
cacciatore	disconfirm	initiatory	peacockery	sexagenary	willowherb
caddisworm	disfeature	innovatory	pensionary	silverware	wonderwork
calyciform	dispensary	insanitary	pentachord	simulatory	worldweary
camelopard	distillery	intermarry	peppercorn	skateboard	yellowbird
candelabra	divinatory	inundatory	pepperwort	smallsword	youngberry
cankerworm	donkeywork	invitatory	peremptory	smoothbore	abiogenist
canterbury	doublepark	invocatory	phantastry	sneezewort	abjectness
canvaswork	downstairs	ionosphere	pheasantry	sociometry	abruptness
capitulary	drysaltery	jackassery	phelloderm	soundboard	absolutism
caricature	dumbledore	jardiniere	photometry	spadebeard	absolutist
carpellary	echinoderm	jasperware	photophore	spiderwort	absurdness
cautionary	effrontery	judicatory	phylactery	spirometry	acatalepsy
centilitre	elderberry	judicature	phylloxera	spleenwort	accomplish
centimetre	elementary	justiciary	pigmentary	spoilsport	activeness
centromere	emblazonry	kerseymere	pistillary	spoliatory	adroitness
certiorari	embouchure	knifeboard	planimetry	spongiform	adulteress
cessionary	embroidery	kookaburra	pleasantry	sporophore	aerologist
chalkboard	emendatory	laboratory	plecoptera	stationary	aeronomist
charactery	emeryboard	lacklustre	plutolatry	stationery	aesthetism
chartulary	emigratory	lampoonery	possessory	stavesacre	affectless
chessboard	epistolary	lavalliere	powderhorn	stelliform	affettuoso
chloroform	escritoire	lectionary	praemunire	stitchwort	Africanise
chokeberry	eudiometry	lettercard	prebendary	stratiform	Africanism
churchyard	everywhere	limaciform	preceptory	strawberry	Africanist
cinecamera	excitatory	linguiform	preconcert	strawboard	aftergrass
clavichord	excusatory	literature	precursory	streetward	aggrandise
clearstory	execratory	locomotory	prefecture	subculture	agrologist
clerestory	exhibitory	loganberry	prefixture	subdeanery	agronomist
clinometry	expiratory	lophophore	prehistory	subsidiary	alcoholise
cloudberry	expository	lumberyard	presbytery	superstore	alcoholism
coastguard	faintheart	macrospore	presidiary	suppletory	algebraist
coleoptera	festoonery	maculature	promissory	suspenders	algologist
coloratura	fibreboard	malacoderm	promontory	suspensory	allegorise
comanchero	fibrillary	malleebird	protectory	swarmspore	allegorist
comicopera	fingermark	mallenders	proteiform	sweatshirt	alloverish
commandery	flashboard	mandragora	pseudocarp	sweetheart	allpurpose
commentary	floatboard	Mariolatry	psychiatry	tachometry	amateurish
commissary	floorboard	masterwork	puffpastry	tachymetry	amateurism
commissure	flowergirl	matchboard	punchboard	tailorbird	anabaptism
commixture	flugelhorn	meadowlark	quadrature	taperecord	anabaptist
compradore	fluxionary	mesosphere	quaternary	telecamera	anastomose
compulsory	folkmemory	metacentre	quickthorn	tetrachord	ancestress
conciliary	forfeiture	micrometry	radiometry	tetrahedra	anchorless
conclusory	foursquare	microspore	redemptory	tetterwort	anecdotist
condensery	fritillary	millefiori	refractory	threadbare	antagonise
conjecture	glassfibre	millilitre	regulatory	threadmark	antagonism
consectary	goatsbeard	millimetre	reichsmark	threadworm	antagonist
consistory	goniometry	misericord	repertoire	threescore	Antichrist
contexture	gooseberry	mismeasure	repository	throatwort	antitheism
controvert	granophyre	missionary	rescissory	timberwork	antitheist
copartnery	gravimetry	misventure	responsory	tomfoolery	apocalypse
coralberry	greenheart	mitigatory	revelatory	trajectory	apostatise
cordillera	greensward	moniliform	revocatory	transitory	archerfish
corrivalry	groundwork	monsignori	rhizophore	treadboard	archpriest
corsetiere	gymnosperm	Montagnard	ribbonworm	tuitionary	armourless
coulometry	hagiolatry	motherwort	ripplemark	tumultuary	artfulness
couturiere	headsquare	mouldboard	roquelaure	umbiliform	asceticism
couverture	heavenborn	nativeborn	rowanberry	underscore	astuteness
craquelure	heavenward	necrolatry	salesclerk	undershirt	augustness
crewelwork	hectolitre	needlecord	sallenders	underskirt	automatise
cribriform	hectometre	needlework	salutatory	undulatory	automatism
ctenophore	heliolatry	nightshirt	sanguinary	unguentary	automatist
cumuliform	hemisphere	nipplewort	scaleboard	upholstery	autonomist
debauchery	heptachord	notchboard	scavengery	uranometry	averseness
debouchure	hereditary	nunciature	schizocarp	vaporiform	axiologist
dedicatory	heretofore	obligatory	schoolgirl	vesicatory	babiroussa
defamatory	hierolatry	ophiolatry	schoolmarm	veterinary	backsheesh
dendriform	hitherward	orthoptera	schoolwork	viperiform	balderdash
depilatory	hollowware	osculatory	scleroderm	vivandiere	balloonist
depository	humbuggery	otherwhere	scoreboard	vocabulary	barrenness
depository	hydrometry	otterboard	scorzonera	voluptuary	bassoonist
derogatory	hygrometry	outmeasure	scrollwork	watchguard	bastardise
Devanagari	hypsometry	oysterfarm	scyphiform	wattlebird	bawdyhouse
dictionary	iconolatry	palliatory	secretaire	weaverbird	belletrist
digitiform	iconometry	palmerworm	securiform	whaleshark	Benthamism
directoire	incendiary	paradoxure	segmentary	whirlybird	bestialise
disclosure	incubatory	parsonbird	selfregard	whitebeard	biochemist

bitchiness	chersonese	dictatress	fieldmouse	grogginess	Jewishness
bitterness	chilliness	digitalise	fierceness	groundless	jocoseness
bituminise	choiceness	diluteness	filthiness	groundmass	Johnsonese
blastocyst	chubbiness	dimorphism	fingerless	grubbiness	journalese
bleariness	cicisbeism	dinnerless	fingerpost	grumpiness	journalise
blepharism	circumcise	directness	finiteness	guardhouse	journalism
blitheness	circumfuse	directress	firstclass	guesthouse	journalist
blockhouse	clamminess	discompose	fitfulness	guiltiness	joyfulness
bloodiness	classicise	disfurnish	flabbiness	hammerless	joyousness
bluishness	classicism	dismalness	flashiness	handedness	Kantianism
bolshevise	classicist	dispossess	fleshiness	Hansardise	karyoplasm
bolshevism	cleverness	divineness	flightless	hartebeest	katabolism
bolshevist	cloudburst	doggedness	flimsiness	headcheese	keratinise
borderless	cloudiness	dolomitise	flintiness	heartiness	kindliness
Boswellise	clumsiness	doublebass	floppiness	heartsease	kineticist
Boswellism	cnidoblast	doubleness	floridness	heathenise	kingliness
bottomless	coachhouse	drafthorse	flowerless	heathenish	knottiness
bottommost	coarseness	dreaminess	fluffiness	heathenism	Krishnaism
bourbonism	cockneyish	dreariness	flunkeyism	henotheism	lachrymose
bourbonist	cockneyism	dressiness	foetidness	henotheist	laconicism
bowdlerise	collarless	driverless	folklorist	heparinise	Lamarckism
bowdlerism	colloquise	drowsiness	folksiness	heroicness	lampoonist
boyishness	colloquist	earthiness	forecourse	hipsterism	lanuginose
bradyseism	colourfast	earwitness	foreignism	hithermost	lapidarist
Brahmanism	colourless	ecclesiast	fortuitism	hoarseness	lattermost
Brahminism	comeliness	edibleness	fortuitist	hobbyhorse	lavishness
braininess	commonness	effeteness	Fourierism	hollowness	lawfulness
brantgoose	compromise	effortless	fraternise	holophrase	leadenness
brassiness	concettism	elasticise	freakiness	homeliness	leaderless
brawniness	concretise	elatedness	Frenchness	homogenise	legitimise
brazenness	concretism	emancipist	friendless	homologise	legitimism
breathless	concretist	emparadise	frigidness	honourless	legitimist
breechless	conformism	empiricism	frilliness	hookedness	lemongrass
breezeless	conformist	empiricist	fringeless	hornedness	lengthwise
breeziness	contrabass	enamellist	friskiness	horologist	leopardess
brentgoose	coquettish	enigmatise	frizziness	horridness	lesbianism
bridgeless	cornerwise	enigmatist	frostiness	horseflesh	letterless
brigandism	cornettist	enterprise	frothiness	houseguest	leucoplast
brightness	costliness	enthusiasm	futureless	humaneness	liberalise
Britishism	couchgrass	enthusiast	galleywest	humbleness	liberalism
brokenness	countryish	entireness	galloglass	humourless	liberalist
bromegrass	courthouse	epiphytism	garishness	hungriness	librettist
broodiness	craftiness	ergonomist	gaucheness	hyaloplasm	lighthouse
bryologist	cragginess	eternalise	gelatinise	hylotheism	likeliness
Buchmanism	crankiness	eternalist	generalise	hypocorism	limpidness
bumpkinish	cravenness	ethologist	generalist	hypotenuse	liquidness
bunchgrass	creaminess	eudemonism	geneticist	iconoclasm	lissomness
burglarise	creepiness	eudemonist	genialness	ideologist	literalise
butterfish	crisscross	eugenicist	genteelism	idolatress	literalism
buttonbush	crustiness	euhemerise	gentilesse	illegalise	literalist
buttonless	cursedness	euhemerism	gentleness	illuminism	littleness
caespitose	cussedness	euhemerist	geochemist	illuminist	liveliness
callowness	cuttlefish	evangelise	geometrise	immobilise	Lollardism
candidness	cytologist	evangelism	geotropism	immoralist	loneliness
candlefish	dampcourse	evangelist	geriatrist	imparadise	lordliness
candyfloss	dauphiness	expertness	glasshouse	impishness	loveliness
capitalise	deadliness	extinguish	glassiness	impoverish	lovingness
capitalism	Decembrist	eyewitness	glossarist	impureness	lowerclass
capitalist	decimalise	facileness	glossiness	initialise	luciferase
caramelise	decimalism	factualism	gluttonise	innateness	lustreless
cartoonist	decivilise	factualist	gnosticism	insaneness	lyophilise
casualness	decolonise	fallowness	goldenness	insularism	Lysenkoism
catabolism	decolorise	famousness	golfcourse	intactness	macadamise
categorise	decompress	fanaticise	goodliness	intentness	mackintosh
centralise	deerforest	fanaticism	gooseflesh	intercross	manageress
centralism	defeminise	fatherless	goosegrass	interphase	manfulness
centralist	dehumanise	fathomless	gormandise	intertwist	Manicheism
changeless	delocalise	faultiness	governessy	invalidism	manicurist
channelise	demagogism	federalise	gradualism	inventress	manorhouse
chartreuse	demobilise	federalism	gradualist	inwardness	marrowless
chasteness	demonetise	federalist	grangerise	italianise	marshiness
chattiness	demoralise	feebleness	grangerism	Italianism	martialism
chauffeuse	demureness	femaleness	graphitise	jacobinise	masterless
chauntress	depolarise	fervidness	greasiness	Jacobinism	matureness
chauvinism	devitalise	fibreglass	greediness	Jacobitism	maximalist
chauvinist	devocalise	fibrillose	greenhouse	jaggedness	mayonnaise
cheekiness	devoutness	fickleness	grisliness	jauntiness	meagreness
cheeriness	diatropism	fictionist	grittiness	jejuneness	measliness
cheesiness		fieldglass		jeopardise	mediatress

mellowness	nominalist	pillowcase	reasonless	secularism	specialist
mesomerism	nomologist	pilothouse	recentness	secularist	speechless
messianism	nosologist	placidness	recidivism	secureness	speediness
metabolise	numberless	plagiarise	recidivist	sedateness	spiritless
metabolism	oafishness	plagiarism	recitalist	seductress	sponginess
metamerism	obituarist	plagiarist	recolonise	seemliness	spookiness
metaphrase	objectless	plantlouse	recompense	selectness	spoonerism
micaschist	oblateness	plasmodesm	regardless	selfpraise	sportiness
microseism	obtuseness	plasmolyse	regularise	seminarist	spottiness
middlemost	odiousness	plasticise	rejuvenise	sempstress	springless
mightiness	oecologist	pliantness	relativise	sensualise	spruceness
militarise	oecumenism	pluckiness	relativism	sensualism	spunkiness
militarism	oedematose	podiatrist	relativist	sensualist	squareness
militarist	oenologist	polemicist	relentless	separatism	stableness
mindedness	oldmaidish	politeness	relinquish	separatist	staffnurse
mineralise	oligoclase	politicise	remediless	sereneness	stanchless
minimalism	oncologist	polychrest	remissness	serologist	stanchness
minimalist	ontologist	polygamist	remonetise	severeness	starriness
minstrelsy	opaqueness	polygenism	remoteness	sexologist	steadiness
minuteness	operettist	polygenist	reorganise	shabbiness	steakhouse
misogamist	opinionist	polymerise	repurchase	shadowless	steamchest
misogynist	opposeless	polymerism	resistless	shagginess	steaminess
misologist	optimalise	polytheism	resultless	sheathless	steeliness
missionise	orchardist	polytheist	retrogress	sheeplouse	stewardess
mizzenmast	oreologist	pomologist	reunionism	sherardise	stickiness
moderatism	organicism	popularise	reunionist	shieldless	stigmatise
modernness	organicist	porousness	revalorise	shiftiness	stigmatism
modishness	ornateness	portliness	revanchism	shirehorse	stigmatist
moisturise	orneriness	Portuguese	revanchist	shirtwaist	stinginess
monarchism	orthoclase	positivism	revitalise	shoddiness	stockiness
monarchist	orthoepist	positivist	revivalism	shortcrust	stodginess
monetarism	osteoblast	postchaise	revivalist	shrewdness	stolidness
monetarist	osteoclast	powerhouse	rewardless	shrewmouse	stonebrash
mongrelise	otioseness	pragmatise	rhapsodise	shrillness	storehouse
mongrelism	outlandish	pragmatism	rhapsodist	shroudless	storminess
monogamist	overblouse	pragmatist	rheologist	sickliness	straitness
monogenism	overexpose	predecease	rheumatism	silentness	strategist
monologise	overpraise	predispose	ribbonfish	silverfish	streamless
monologist	overthrust	prepossess	rinderpest	simpleness	stressless
monopolise	owlishness	pressurise	riverhorse	sinecurism	strictness
monopolist	pacificism	presuppose	robustness	sinecurist	stringless
monotheism	pacificist	prettiness	rontgenise	sinfulness	striptease
monotheist	paintbrush	prissiness	rootedness	Singhalese	strychnism
mopishness	palatalise	proctorise	rottenness	singleness	stubbiness
morbidness	palimpsest	profitless	roughhouse	sinologist	stuffiness
moroseness	pallidness	prologuise	roundhouse	skimpiness	stumpiness
morphinism	paltriness	promptness	rudderfish	skinniness	stupidness
motherless	panegyrise	properness	rudderless	slanginess	sturdiness
motionless	panegyrist	prophetess	ruefulness	sleaziness	subtleness
motiveless	pansophist	prosaicism	ruffianism	sleepiness	suddenness
mouldiness	paperchase	proteolyse	ruggedness	sleeveless	suffragist
mulishness	parabolise	protoplasm	Russianise	slenderise	sugarhouse
multiphase	paralogise	protoplast	saccharose	slightness	sugariness
mycologist	paralogism	proudflesh	sacredness	sloppiness	sullenness
nailpolish	paraphrase	psalmodise	saddlefast	smelliness	sulphurise
narcissism	paraphrast	psalmodist	sailorless	smokehouse	sultriness
narcissist	parasitism	psychicism	sallowness	smoothness	summitless
narcolepsy	parrotfish	psychicist	sarcoplasm	smudginess	superbness
narrowness	Passionist	Ptolemaist	sarmentose	smuttiness	supineness
nationless	pastellist	puritanise	savageness	sneakiness	supperless
nativeness	pasteurise	puritanism	savourless	sniffiness	suppleness
naturalise	pasteurism	putridness	scandalise	snootiness	surrealism
naturalism	patchiness	Pyrrhonism	scantiness	snowgrouse	surrealist
naturalist	patriotism	Pyrrhonist	scarceness	snuffiness	sweatiness
needlefish	peacockish	quaintness	scatheless	soddenness	swordgrass
negativism	pebbledash	queasiness	scattiness	solemnness	sybaritism
negativist	pedicurist	quenchless	scepticism	solidarism	symmetrise
nematocyst	pedologist	quickgrass	schematise	solidarist	sympathise
nethermost	penologist	quirkiness	schematism	solubilise	symphonist
nettlerash	permafrost	racecourse	Scotticise	sombreness	symposiast
neuroplasm	peroxidise	Rachmanism	Scotticism	songstress	syncretise
neutralise	petiteness	radicalise	screwpress	songthrush	syncretism
neutralism	phallicism	radicalism	scrutinise	Sorbonnist	syncretist
neutralist	phantasise	raggedness	sculptress	sordidness	synonymist
nicotinism	pharisaism	rakishness	scurviness	sparseness	synthesise
nightdress	pharmacist	rancidness	seamstress	Spartacist	synthesist
nightglass	phenocryst	randomness	searchless	speargrass	synthetise
nimbleness	picayunish	reafforest	secondbest	specialise	synthetist
nominalism	pigeonpost	reappraise	secularise	specialism	systemless

tabularise	utopianism	antiSemite	congregate	equanimity	imbecility
takingness	Vaticanism	apostolate	consecrate	equivocate	immaculate
talentless	Vaticanist	appreciate	consociate	erectility	immaturity
Tartuffism	venialness	aquilinity	constipate	ergodicity	immobility
tawdriness	ventricose	Areopagite	constitute	ethicality	immoderate
taxonomist	Vietnamese	articulate	consummate	eviscerate	immorality
technicist	vignettist	artycrafty	contiguity	exaggerate	impregnate
tenantless	villainess	ascomycete	continuate	exasperate	impudicity
tenderness	vinegarish	asexuality	continuity	excogitate	inaccurate
terrorless	virologist	asphyxiate	contribute	excruciate	inactivate
tetchiness	virtueless	asseverate	coordinate	exenterate	inactivity
textualist	visionless	assibilate	coradicate	exhilarate	inadequate
thalecress	vitaminise	assimilate	cordiality	expatriate	inapposite
theogonist	vitriolise	audibility	cordierite	exprobrate	inaugurate
theologise	volatilise	auriculate	corporeity	extraneity	incapacity
theologist	wanderlust	auscultate	creativity	exulcerate	incinerate
theopneust	wantonness	autoplasty	crenellate	exurbanite	incivility
thillhorse	watchglass	barbellate	crinolette	facilitate	incomplete
thirdclass	waterbrash	barracouta	crocoisite	factuality	incrassate
thorniness	watercress	benedicite	curability	fastigiate	indefinite
threadfish	waterglass	Benthamite	deactivate	felicitate	indelicate
threnodist	wateriness	bestiality	debilitate	feminality	indiscrete
thriftless	weakliness	bichromate	decapitate	femininity	indocility
throneless	weaponless	bipolarity	decelerate	fenestrate	inequality
thwartwise	weightless	bisulphate	deescalate	fianchetto	infelicity
timeliness	Wertherism	bisulphite	deflagrate	fibrillate	infidelity
toffeenose	westernise	blacksmith	degenerate	fiftyfifty	infiltrate
tongueless	wheelhorse	blanquette	delaminate	finicality	ingeminate
toothbrush	wheelhouse	blastemata	deliberate	flabellate	ingratiate
toothiness	wheeziness	branchiate	delimitate	flaccidity	inhumanity
topologist	whorehouse	bridlepath	demotivate	flagellate	innominate
torpidness	wickedness	broadcloth	denominate	flightpath	innumerate
torridness	wildebeest	Buchmanite	denunciate	flocculate	inordinate
touchiness	wilderness	cachinnate	depopulate	floorcloth	inosculate
towardness	wilfulness	calceolate	depreciate	fluoridate	insecurity
transgress	windowless	calumniate	deracinate	fluorinate	inseminate
transverse	wintriness	calyptrate	desalinate	footlights	insipidity
trappiness	wobbliness	camphorate	desiderata	foresheets	insobriety
trashiness	woefulness	cancellate	desiderate	fourchette	inspissate
traumatism	wontedness	canonicate	desquamate	fourteenth	insufflate
trecentist	woodenness	canonicity	detoxicate	fraternity	insularity
trendiness	woolliness	cantillate	dextrality	friability	intenerate
trichinise	worldclass	canzonetta	diastemata	fulllength	interstate
trichroism	worthiness	capability	dichromate	fusibility	intimidate
trickiness	wrathiness	capacitate	difficulty	gadolinite	intoxicate
tricyclist	Wykehamist	capitulate	dilapidate	garnierite	intrigante
trivialise	yeastiness	carnallite	dilettante	generality	inurbanity
trivialism	yellowness	cassolette	dilettanti	generosity	invaginate
trollopish	abbreviate	causticity	disability	geniculate	invalidate
trombonist	abstrusity	centrality	dishonesty	glasscloth	invalidity
tropopause	accelerate	centricity	disloyalty	glauberite	inveracity
Trotskyism	accentuate	chalybeate	dissertate	glauconite	inveterate
Trotskyist	accumulate	charismata	dissociate	graciosity	invigilate
trustiness	achondrite	cheapskate	distillate	graptolite	invigorate
turbidness	acoelomate	chemisette	distribute	grasscloth	irradicate
turgidness	actinolite	childbirth	disulphate	grassroots	irresolute
typologist	adjudicate	chlorinate	disutility	greedyguts	Ishmaelite
underbrush	Adullamite	chronicity	divaricate	greencloth	italianate
underdress	adulterate	chrysolite	durability	habilitate	jocularity
underlease	affability	coacervate	duumvirate	halflength	juvenility
undersense	afterbirth	coelacanth	edulcorate	halogenate	kimberlite
uneasiness	aftertaste	coequality	effectuate	heliophyte	lanceolate
unevenness	alkalinity	coeternity	effeminate	henceforth	laterality
unfairness	allegretto	collarette	efficacity	hereabouts	legibility
unholiness	alliterate	collegiate	eighteenth	hereticate	legitimate
unicyclist	altazimuth	comicality	elasticity	heulandite	lemniscate
uniqueness	altostrati	commentate	electorate	hoitytoity	lepidolite
unjustness	amalgamate	commonalty	emancipate	homoeopath	liberality
unkindness	ameliorate	compensate	emarginate	homologate	licentiate
unlikeness	amiability	complexity	emasculate	homozygote	literality
unmeetness	amoebocyte	complicate	emblements	horsecloth	lithophyte
unripeness	andalusite	complicity	embryonate	hydrophyte	lithotrity
unruliness	angularity	conciliate	emissivity	hygrophyte	logicality
untidiness	annihilate	concinnity	endemicity	ignobility	luminosity
unwariness	annularity	condensate	endopodite	illegality	lymphocyte
upperclass	annunciate	confidante	enterolith	illiterate	lymphomata
uppishness	anthracite	confiscate	ephorality	illuminate	magistrate
upwardness	anticipate	conformity	episcopate	illuminati	maisonette
usefulness	antimonite	conglobate	equability	illustrate	manipulate

Marcionite	preciosity	sperrylite	vaticinate	caoutchouc	fortuitous
margravate	principate	sphalerite	vertebrate	capricious	founderous
marguerite	proclivity	sphericity	vesiculate	catafalque	fowlplague
marionette	profligate	spherulite	virtuality	censorious	fuliginous
marquisate	profundity	spiflicate	virtuosity	cerebellum	gadolinium
martensite	prolongate	sporophyte	visibility	ceruminous	gangrenous
mediocrity	promulgate	squalidity	vitiligate	chivalrous	gaspereaux
menstruate	propensity	stablemate	vituperate	chuckerout	gelatinous
metabolite	propionate	stalactite	viviparity	cinerarium	gemmaceous
microbiota	propitiate	stalagmite	vociferate	circuitous	glomerulus
microphyte	prosciutto	staurolite	volatility	clangorous	glumaceous
mignonette	prosperity	stephanite	volubility	Clarenceux	gluttonous
mithridate	prostitute	stereobate	waggonette	cockalorum	goloptious
movability	protophyta	sterigmata	waistcloth	coetaneous	goluptious
muliebrity	protophyte	stillbirth	wavelength	collarstud	gramineous
musicality	psychopath	stipellate	whitesmith	colloquium	gratuitous
mutability	punctulate	stridulate	winceyette	colporteur	gregarious
myxomycete	pupilarity	stypticity	wolframite	commodious	gynandrous
naturopath	pyrolusite	subacidity	Wycliffite	communique	hakenkreuz
nebulosity	pyroxenite	subcordate	ZendAvesta	compendium	halogenous
needlebath	pyrrhotite	substitute	abdominous	coniferous	harmonious
negativity	quaternate	sulphonate	abstemious	consortium	haustellum
neutrality	quaternity	sulphurate	acarpelous	conspectus	haustorium
nidificate	ratability	superacute	accoucheur	contagious	helianthus
nineteenth	rattlepate	supplicate	acephalous	contiguous	herbaceous
notability	reactivate	suzerainty	acetabulum	continuous	hexamerous
novaculite	reactivity	swashplate	acrogenous	coriaceous	hocuspocus
numerosity	reallocate	synonymity	acroterium	coryphaeus	holusbolus
nuptiality	recuperate	syntagmata	adulterous	courageous	homogamous
nyctinasty	redecorate	tablecloth	aeruginous	cretaceous	homogenous
obliterate	regenerate	tamability	agapanthus	curriculum	homologous
obnubilate	regularity	taxability	albuminous	curvaceous	homonymous
obtruncate	rejuvenate	temporalty	alliaceous	curvacious	homozygous
openhearth	relativity	tenability	allogamous	decapodous	homunculus
operculate	remunerate	teratomata	ambulacrum	delightful	honorarium
orotundity	repatriate	terneplate	amphibious	delphinium	horrendous
osteophyte	repopulate	terracotta	amylaceous	derailleur	houseproud
overexcite	resupinate	tessellate	anadromous	despiteful	humoresque
overgrowth	reticulate	theodolite	anatropous	despiteous	hypanthium
overnicety	revalidate	thirdparty	ancipitous	diaphanous	hypogynous
pacificate	risibility	thirteenth	androecium	dimorphous	idolatrous
paederasty	sabretooth	thousandth	anonaceous	diplodocus	impervious
palaeolith	saccharate	toothpaste	antebellum	disastrous	imprimatur
palagonite	salability	topazolite	antimasque	discobolus	incautious
palatinate	salicylate	topicality	antonymous	disdainful	incestuous
paniculate	samarskite	tortuosity	apocarpous	disembogue	indecorous
parramatta	sanguinity	tragacanth	apothecium	disgustful	indigenous
partiality	saprophyte	triacetate	aquiferous	dispiteous	infectious
passionate	schoolmate	trifoliate	arenaceous	distichous	inglorious
patriality	screwplate	trifurcate	argumentum	dogstongue	iniquitous
patriciate	scurrility	trillionth	armigerous	dovecolour	innumerous
pediculate	scutellate	tripartite	astragalus	drupaceous	insightful
pennyworth	secondrate	triplicate	auditorium	dysprosium	involucrum
pentimento	secularity	triplicity	auriferous	ectogenous	iridaceous
perfoliate	seedpotato	triternate	auspicious	eczematous	isopterous
pernickety	seismicity	triviality	autogamous	edentulous	isosporous
perpetrate	semilunate	troctolite	autogenous	eigenvalue	Japanesque
perpetuate	sensuality	troglodyte	autologous	elevenplus	juggernaut
perpetuity	seventieth	tropophyte	autonomous	endogamous	Kafkaesque
perplexity	sexpartite	Trotskyite	avaricious	endogenous	keratinous
perquisite	shibboleth	tuberosity	barratrous	ephemerous	kettledrum
personalty	showerbath	twelvenote	battailous	episternum	knockabout
perversity	shrievalty	typicality	Benedictus	epithelium	languorous
phlogopite	siderolite	umbilicate	billetdoux	ericaceous	lanuginous
photonasty	silhouette	unchastity	bipetalous	eucalyptus	lascivious
pianoforte	silverbath	unctuosity	bituminous	euphonious	lauraceous
pinebeauty	similarity	underneath	bladdernut	extraneous	lawrencium
pistillate	simplicity	underpants	blottesque	factitious	lebensraum
planchette	sluicegate	underquote	bluetongue	fallacious	leguminous
plasticity	smaragdite	understate	blusterous	fasciculus	leprechaun
plebiscite	solidarity	underwrite	boisterous	fastidious	libidinous
pliability	solidstate	underwrote	bordereaux	felicitous	licentious
polychaete	solubility	uniformity	byssaceous	fictitious	lightingup
popularity	spasticity	uninitiate	cadaverous	flagitious	liliaceous
portamento	spathulate	unipartite	calamitous	flavourful	lipomatous
positivity	spatiality	university	calcareous	fleacircus	litterlout
potability	speciality	unmorality	caliginous	flosculous	longaevous
potentiate	speciosity	vanadinite	calumnious	foliaceous	loquacious
preadamite	spermaceti	varicosity	cancellous	foraminous	lubricious

luciferous	paramecium	rubiginous	travelogue	congestive	misbelieve
lucifugous	parapodium	rupicolous	treasonous	connective	mitigative
lugubrious	paronymous	saliferous	tremendous	consultive	nominative
lycopodium	pediculous	salubrious	triandrous	contortive	occupative
machinegun	pellagrous	sanatorium	trichinous	convective	oppressive
malodorous	pemphigous	sanitarium	triclinium	convictive	overactive
malvaceous	pennaceous	sarmentous	trioecious	convulsive	palliative
marvellous	perfidious	sauerkraut	trolleybus	cooptative	pejorative
meaningful	perigynous	saxicolous	tropaeolum	copulative	pendentive
meerschaum	periosteum	scandalous	troubadour	corelative	perceptive
megalosaur	peritoneum	scarabaeus	trousseaux	corrective	percussive
membranous	perjurious	scattergun	tubicolous	corruptive	perfective
memorandum	pernicious	sclerotium	tuffaceous	cumulative	permeative
mendacious	petrolatum	scrofulous	tumblerful	cunctative	permissive
menstruous	phosphorus	scrupulous	tumultuous	decorative	persuasive
metacarpus	picaresque	scurrilous	ubiquitous	dedicative	perversive
metatarsus	piliferous	selfcolour	umbrageous	definitive	possessive
meticulous	pitcherful	semichorus	undershrub	deflective	preceptive
migrainous	plasmodium	semiopaque	undervalue	degressive	preclusive
millennium	plesiosaur	sensedatum	undesirous	denotative	predictive
miraculous	plunderous	septennium	uneventful	depressive	preemptive
misogynous	polemonium	sequacious	unfaithful	depurative	presentive
molluscous	polyanthus	sequestrum	ungenerous	derivative	preventive
molybdenum	polygamous	serotinous	ungraceful	detonative	productive
monandrous	polygenous	sestertium	ungracious	detractive	projective
monoecious	polygynous	sestertius	ungrateful	digressive	propulsive
monogamous	polymerous	sialagogue	unmerciful	diminutive	protective
monogynous	polysemous	simulacrum	untruthful	disapprove	protensive
monopodium	polytocous	sinistrous	uproarious	disbelieve	protrusive
monotonous	pomiferous	slanderous	velutinous	discursive	quantitive
moratorium	porraceous	slumberful	vestibulum	discussive	recitative
mordacious	portentous	slumberous	vibraculum	dismissive	recitativo
mosasaurus	postbellum	solicitous	viceconsul	dispersive	recreative
muciferous	posthumous	somniloquy	victorious	disruptive	redemptive
multiloquy	postpartum	spadiceous	villainous	dissuasive	reflective
myocardium	praesidium	spiraculum	violaceous	dominative	refractive
myrtaceous	precarious	spirituous	viraginous	dubitative	regressive
mystagogue	precocious	sporangium	viviparous	enervative	regulative
mysterious	predacious	sprightful	vociferous	estimative	reparative
myxomatous	presageful	squeteague	voluminous	evacuative	repetitive
nasturtium	presternum	statuesque	voluptuous	evaluative	repressive
natatorium	primordium	stertorous	vomitorium	excitative	resolutive
nectareous	principium	stirrupcup	wanderplug	execrative	resorptive
neglectful	prodigious	stomachful	waterspout	exhaustive	respective
nephridium	promethium	stomodaeum	whereabout	exploitive	responsive
nidicolous	propitious	stormcloud	worshipful	expositive	resumptive
nidifugous	propylaeum	strabismus	zoophagous	expressive	retractive
nitrogroup	proscenium	stramonium	zoophilous	extinctive	ruminative
nonferrous	prospectus	stridulous	absorptive	extractive	separative
nubiferous	prosperous	stromatous	abstersive	federative	shoreleave
nuciferous	prostomium	struthious	accusative	figurative	simulative
nucivorous	proteinous	stupendous	adjunctive	generative	slidevalve
nutritious	prothallus	subaqueous	admonitive	hesitative	spokeshave
obsequious	psalterium	subsellium	adsorptive	imperative	spoliative
oceanarium	puerperium	substratum	afflictive	impressive	subjective
octamerous	pugnacious	successful	aftershave	imputative	submissive
octandrous	pupiparous	sudatorium	aggressive	inchoative	subversive
octopodous	purposeful	sulphurous	alterative	incubative	successive
oedematous	purseproud	sunparlour	apperceive	indecisive	suggestive
oesophagus	pyrogenous	suspicious	appetitive	indicative	suppletive
oleaginous	quadrivium	symphylous	appointive	indurative	supportive
oleiferous	radiopaque	synanthous	appositive	infinitive	susceptive
oleraceous	rampageous	syncarpous	architrave	inflective	suspensive
olivaceous	ranunculus	synoecious	assaultive	inflictive	sustentive
ommatidium	rapporteur	synonymous	assumptive	initiative	topsyturvy
omnigenous	rebellious	technetium	attractive	injunctive	transitive
omnivorous	referendum	tenebrious	automotive	innovative	turtledove
omophagous	remorseful	tepidarium	capacitive	inspective	ulcerative
oncogenous	rendezvous	testaceous	cogitative	interleave	vasoactive
opprobrium	repetiteur	thereabout	collective	intervolve	vegetative
osmeterium	respectful	thimbleful	combustive	interweave	vindictive
osmiridium	revengeful	thoughtful	completive	irrelative	windsleeve
outrageous	ridiculous	throughout	compulsive	irritative	brokendown
paedogogue	robustious	throughput	conceptive	lacerative	buttondown
palladious	roisterous	thunderous	concessive	limitative	fingerbowl
palmaceous	Romanesque	tirailleur	conclusive	locomotive	jobbernowl
pancratium	roundabout	titanesque	concoctive	maturative	malleefowl
panjandrum	rouseabout	traitorous	concussive	medicative	markettown
papaverous	roustabout	transvalue	conductive	meditative	overthrown

```
screechowl equilibria polydipsia anchylotic dosimetric hyperbaric
shantytown erotomania potentilla androgenic dynamistic hyperbolic
splashdown escallonia pozzuolana annalistic dysenteric hypergolic
tumbledown euthanasia premaxilla antibiotic dysplastic hypersonic
heterodoxy fenestella presbyopia antiheroic dystrophic hypnagogic
heterotaxy floribunda propaganda antipathic ecchymotic hypodermic
metagalaxy florilegia prothallia antiseptic ectodermic hypostatic
phyllotaxy framboesia protophyta antistatic egocentric hypotactic
lengthways fraxinella pulsatilla antithetic electronic hysteretic
polydactyl fustanella pyracantha aphoristic emblematic iatrogenic
schooldays gaillardia quadrennia apodeictic embolismic idealistic
zygodactyl Gallomania quadrumana apolaustic empathetic idiopathic
antifreeze gametangia retinacula apologetic emphractic inartistic
coleorhiza gaultheria rickettsia apoplectic encephalic infrasonic
deepfreeze glycosuria salmonella aposematic endophytic inharmonic
fuzzywuzzy Gorgonzola sarcolemma apotropaic endoscopic isentropic
intermezzi granadilla sarracenia aragonitic endosmotic isodynamic
intermezzo grandmamma saturnalia archaistic enharmonic isogenetic
morbidezza grenadilla satyagraha arithmetic epenthetic isomorphic
mycorrhiza groceteria scarlatina arrhythmic epexegetic Jehovistic
pocketsize gypsophila scorzonera arthralgic epiblastic jingoistic
razzmatazz haematuria scriptoria astigmatic epideictic judgematic
underglaze hemiplegia seborrhoea astrologic epigastric kerygmatic
_____  hyperaemia seguidilla astronomic epigenetic kinnikinic
acrophobia hyperdulia serradilla asymmetric epiglottic laryngitic
aerenchyma hypolimnia Sexagesima asymptotic epigraphic legalistic
aerophobia incunabula sitophobia austenitic episematic leucocytic
alcyonaria interregna soldanella autocratic erethismic leukocytic
algolagnia jinricksha sterigmata autoerotic erotogenic linguistic
anacolutha jinrikisha succedanea azeotropic escharotic lithologic
anglomania kookaburra syllabaria bacchantic essayistic loxodromic
animalcula latifundia synaloepha barbituric ethnologic madreporic
antependia logorrhoea syntagmata barometric eucaryotic manometric
antheridia Lupercalia tarantella batholitic eulogistic Massoretic
aphrodisia lymphomata telecamera bimetallic euphuistic mathematic
arrhythmia mandragora teratomata biodynamic eurhythmic matronymic
arthralgia manzanilla termitaria biogenetic exospheric megalithic
asafoetida marginalia terracotta biographic exothermic megascopic
aspergilla marshalsea tetrahedra biomorphic fatalistic melanistic
aspidistra mediastina ticpolonga bolometric felspathic melismatic
assafetida meningioma toxiphobia bronchitic FinnoUgric mesenteric
autostrada metaplasia tramontana Buddhistic frigorific Mesolithic
babiroussa microbiota tularaemia cabalistic futuristic mesophytic
banderilla mixedmedia Victoriana caoutchouc galliambic metaphoric
barracouta monochasia vorticella carboxylic ganglionic metaphysic
barramunda montbretia wongawonga catalectic geocentric metastatic
belladonna morbidezza xenophobia cataleptic geognostic metathetic
blastemata mozzarella ZendAvesta catechetic geographic metempiric
candelabra multimedia breadcrumb cellulosic geothermic meteoritic
canzonetta myasthenia heartthrob chiliastic Glagolitic metronomic
cardialgia mycoplasma hermitcrab chondritic glycosuric metronymic
cascarilla mycorrhiza letterbomb choriambic granulitic microlitic
charismata mythomania spidercrab coenobitic gynocratic mobocratic
chinchilla mythopoeia undershrub coenobytic gyroscopic mockheroic
Cinderella nephralgia willowherb concentric haemolytic monocarpic
cinecamera neurilemma achromatic congeneric hagiologic monoclinic
citronella neurolemma adrenergic copesettic halophytic monocratic
clarabella nosophobia aerobiotic coprolitic Hebraistic monocyclic
coleoptera nullanulla aeronautic corybantic hedonistic monohydric
coleorhiza nyctalopia aerostatic cosmogonic helminthic monomaniac
collembola odontalgia aetiologic cosmoramic hemicyclic monophonic
coloratura ophthalmia aldermanic crescentic hemiplegic monophonic
columbaria orthoptera algolagnic cryoscopic heptarchic moralistic
comicopera paramnesia allergenic cybernetic heptatonic morganatic
concertina paraplegia allopathic cyclopedic heroicomic mystagogic
Constantia parenchyma allophonic democratic hexametric mythologic
cordillera parramatta allosteric diachronic hierarchic mythopoeic
cornucopia penetralia allotropic diagnostic histologic naphthenic
corrigenda peripeteia alphabetic diagraphic histolytic nativistic
crematoria perithecia alphameric diapedetic histrionic neoclassic
cyclopedia petronella altruistic diarrhoeic holophytic neoplastic
definienda phagedaena amphoteric diathermic holosteric nihilistic
desiderata philippina anaglyphic dichroitic homophonic nomothetic
diastemata philopoena anamorphic dielectric horoscopic nostologic
diphtheria phylloxera anapaestic dilemmatic humanistic novelistic
dipsomania piscifauna anaplastic diphtheric humoristic numismatic
drosophila planetaria anaptyctic diphyletic hydrologic nyctalopic
dysgraphia plecoptera anchoretic diplomatic hydrolytic oligarchic
endothelia poinsettia anchoritic disyllabic hyperaemic ophiologic
```

ophthalmic	rheotropic	antiquated	confirmand	forcipated	likelihood
optimistic	rhizogenic	apparelled	confounded	foreground	likeminded
orogenetic	ricinoleic	armourclad	considered	forehanded	livelihood
orographic	Romanistic	arytaenoid	contraband	forwearied	loggerhead
orthogenic	sacroiliac	asteriated	controlled	fourfooted	longhaired
orthopedic	Sanskritic	attenuated	convoluted	fourhanded	longheaded
paedagogic	saprogenic	background	coolheaded	fourinhand	longlegged
paediatric	satellitic	backhanded	copperhead	fourleaved	longwinded
Palaeozoic	schismatic	baldheaded	correspond	freehanded	lowpitched
pancreatic	scholastic	barebacked	corrugated	fricasseed	lumberyard
pangenetic	scientific	barefooted	corticated	fullbodied	maidenhead
pantomimic	sciolistic	bareheaded	cottonseed	gasteropod	maidenhood
parabiotic	seriocomic	barelegged	cottonweed	gatelegged	maladapted
paradisaic	sialagogic	bargeboard	cottonwood	girlfriend	malleebird
paradisiac	simplistic	bedevilled	counselled	goatsbeard	mamillated
paraffinic	sociologic	bedraggled	cousinhood	goggleeyed	manumitted
parametric	solecistic	beforehand	covenanted	grandchild	marginated
paraplegic	sophomoric	behindhand	craftguild	grandstand	marshalled
paratactic	splanchnic	bejewelled	crenulated	greasewood	masterhand
pathogenic	stochastic	bemedalled	crispbread	greensward	masterhood
pathologic	strabismic	beribboned	crossbreed	greyheaded	mastermind
patronymic	subaquatic	bighearted	cucullated	halfcocked	matchboard
pederastic	supersonic	bigmouthed	cummerbund	halfwitted	matronhood
pegmatitic	supertonic	bitterwood	cuspidated	hammerhead	maxilliped
pentatomic	synchronic	bivouacked	cylindered	hammerpond	meadowland
pentatonic	synergetic	blackboard	cylindroid	handpicked	medullated
perchloric	syphilitic	blackfaced	decompound	handselled	methylated
pericyclic	systematic	blackguard	deeprooted	handworked	microfarad
periscopic	talismanic	blearyeyed	deepseated	hardbilled	middleaged
phagedenic	tautomeric	blockboard	delphinoid	hardboiled	minutehand
phagocytic	taxidermic	bloodhound	determined	hardfisted	misaligned
phantasmic	telemetric	boneheaded	diminished	hardhanded	misericord
phantastic	teleologic	borderland	discommend	hardheaded	mismatched
phenotypic	telepathic	bottlefeed	disordered	harelipped	misnomered
philatelic	telephonic	brachiopod	dispersoid	hawserlaid	molluscoid
phlegmatic	telescopic	brainchild	dispirited	heartblood	monohybrid
phlogistic	tenebrific	brazilwood	dissipated	heavenward	monorhymed
phonematic	tetrarchic	breadboard	distilland	heavyarmed	Montagnard
phonolitic	theocratic	brickfield	distracted	henhearted	motherhood
phonologic	theophanic	bridesmaid	distressed	heptachord	motherland
phosphatic	theophoric	bridgehead	doughfaced	highhanded	mouldboard
phosphoric	thermionic	broadsword	dragonhead	highminded	moustached
photogenic	thrombotic	bufflehead	dreamworld	hinterland	multifaced
photolytic	timocratic	bullethead	drowsihead	hitherward	musicstand
phylogenic	totemistic	bullheaded	dunderhead	holloweyed	muttonhead
phytogenic	tragicomic	buttonwood	earthbound	homebrewed	nanosecond
phytotoxic	tremolitic	cackhanded	eisteddfod	hornrimmed	nationhood
planktonic	tribrachic	camelopard	embowelled	hotblooded	needlecord
pleochroic	triglyphic	candlewood	emeryboard	housebound	newfangled
pleonastic	trimorphic	caravanned	empanelled	houseproud	nonaligned
polyandric	tropologic	carbuncled	endstopped	humpbacked	nonplussed
polyatamic	tularaemic	carotenoid	enthralled	hyphenated	northbound
polyclinic	tympanitic	carotinoid	epicycloid	illadvised	notchboard
polycyclic	ultrabasic	carpetweed	epidermoid	illnatured	obfuscated
polyhedric	ultrasonic	cattlegrid	eurypterid	illstarred	oldfangled
polymathic	uneconomic	celebrated	evenhanded	impanelled	openhanded
polyonymic	unemphatic	centrefold	evilminded	imperilled	openminded
polyphasic	unhistoric	cephalopod	fairground	indigested	orangewood
polyphonic	unionistic	chalkboard	fairhaired	indisposed	orphanhood
populistic	variolitic	channelled	fairminded	infatuated	otherworld
porismatic	Visigothic	chargehand	farfetched	initialled	otterboard
postexilic	vitalistic	chaudfroid	farsighted	interbreed	overabound
pozzolanic	volumetric	chessboard	fatherhood	interested	overcooked
presbyopic	xerophytic	Christhood	fatherland	interplead	overground
procryptic	xylophonic	churchyard	featherbed	interwound	overhanded
prognathic	zoomorphic	classified	fibreboard	ironhanded	overlapped
prognostic	ablebodied	clavichord	fiddlehead	jimsonweed	overmanned
prosthetic	aboveboard	cloistered	fiddlewood	jolterhead	overspread
protanopic	abstracted	clubfooted	figurehead	knifeboard	overtopped
prototypic	accredited	coastguard	fimbriated	knighthood	packthread
protreptic	accustomed	cochleated	flannelled	knockkneed	paddyfield
pugilistic	addlepated	collarstud	flashboard	landlocked	palmatifid
pyromaniac	affiliated	colonnaded	flashflood	lefthanded	pantrymaid
pyromantic	albuminoid	complected	flatfooted	lettercard	paraboloid
pyrometric	almondeyed	complotted	fleshwound	letterhead	parasitoid
pyrophoric	ammoniated	comprehend	floatboard	lightfaced	parenthood
quartzitic	amygdaloid	compressed	floorboard		parsonbird
radiogenic	anthracoid	condescend			pasteboard
radiologic	anthropoid	confervoid			pastyfaced

pectinated	smallsword	undesigned	abstinence	apostatise	bichromate
pedimented	smokedried	undeterred	accelerate	apostolate	bidonville
pemphigoid	smorrebrod	undigested	accentuate	apostrophe	bijouterie
pentachord	snailpaced	uneducated	acceptable	appealable	biodegrade
periwigged	sneezeweed	unemployed	acceptance	appearance	bioscience
petiolated	sneezewood	unequalled	accessible	appeasable	birdstrike
photoflood	snowcapped	unexampled	accomplice	apperceive	birthplace
picosecond	sobersided	unexcelled	accordance	appetitive	birthstone
pigeontoed	softbilled	unexpected	accumulate	applicable	bissextile
pinnatifid	softboiled	unexplored	accusative	appointive	bisulphate
pinnulated	softfinned	unfathered	achievable	appositive	bisulphide
pinstriped	softheaded	unfettered	achondrite	appreciate	bisulphite
pixillated	soundboard	unfinished	acidophile	apprentice	bituminise
playground	southbound	unfriended	acoelomate	approvable	bizarrerie
ploughland	spadebeard	ungrounded	acquirable	aquamarine	blancmange
pockmarked	spectacled	unhallowed	actinolite	arbitrable	blanquette
pokerfaced	spellbound	unhouseled	actionable	arborvitae	blastomere
potbellied	spongewood	unimproved	adamantine	architrave	blastopore
prejudiced	springhead	uninformed	adjudicate	Areopagite	bleachable
priesthood	springwood	unlabelled	adjunctive	arthromere	blithesome
principled	squaretoed	unlettered	adjustable	articulate	blockhouse
privileged	squinteyed	unmeasured	admissible	ascendable	bloodstone
pronounced	squirehood	unmortised	admittable	ascendance	blottesque
propertied	starryeyed	unnumbered	admittance	ascendence	bluebottle
protracted	stencilled	unoccupied	admonitive	ascendible	bluetongue
pulvinated	stomatopod	unprepared	adrenaline	ascomycete	bobbinlace
punchboard	stoneblind	unprovoked	adsorbable	ascribable	bolshevise
purseproud	stormbound	unravelled	adsorptive	asparagine	boondoggle
pycnogonid	stormcloud	unredeemed	Adullamite	asphyxiate	borderline
quarrelled	strawboard	unrelieved	adulterate	assailable	Boswellise
rattlehead	streetward	unremarked	adulterine	assaultive	bothersome
redblooded	stronghold	unrequited	advertence	assemblage	bottletree
registered	structured	unreserved	aeroengine	assessable	bowdlerise
remodelled	subtrahend	unresolved	aerogramme	asseverate	branchiate
restrained	surefooted	unrivalled	affirmable	assibilate	brantgoose
rheumatoid	suspensoid	unschooled	afflictive	assignable	breastbone
ringnecked	swaybacked	unscreened	affordable	assimilate	breathable
ringtailed	sweatgland	unscripted	Africanise	assistance	brentgoose
rockribbed	sweetbread	unseasoned	afterimage	associable	bridgeable
roselipped	swiveleyed	unselected	aftershave	assumptive	brigandage
saccharoid	syncopated	unstrained	aftertaste	atmosphere	brigandine
sandalwood	tailorbird	unstressed	aggrandise	attachable	brigantine
sappanwood	taperecord	untroubled	aggressive	attackable	brilliance
sawtoothed	tapestried	unwrinkled	alcoholise	attainable	brocatelle
scaleboard	tendrilled	variegated	allegiance	attendance	bronchiole
scarabaeid	tetrachord	verandahed	allegorise	attractive	brownstone
scoreboard	thirtyfold	victualled	alliterate	audiophile	brusquerie
sculptured	timberhead	virginhood	allpurpose	auriculate	Buchmanite
secondhand	tonguetied	watchguard	alongshore	ausculate	burdensome
selfglazed	tracheated	waterflood	altarpiece	autoimmune	burglarise
selfguided	trafficked	wattlebird	alterative	automatise	buttonhole
selfpoised	trammelled	weakminded	alternance	automobile	cacciatore
selfraised	translucid	weaverbird	amalgamate	automotive	cachinnate
selfregard	treadboard	wellheeled	ameliorate	autostrade	cacomistle
selfstyled	trucklebed	wellturned	amerciable	avantgarde	caespitose
selfwilled	trundlebed	whirlybird	amoebocyte	aventurine	calceolate
semifitted	tumbleweed	whiskified	analysable	aviculture	calculable
semiliquid	twelvefold	whitebeard	anastomose	backstroke	calumniate
sexlimited	twilighted	whitefaced	anastrophe	balustrade	calyptrate
shamefaced	ultrasound	widespread	andalusite	barbellate	camouflage
sharpnosed	umbrellaed	windshield	anecdotage	barcarolle	camphorate
sheepshead	unabridged	wingfooted	anglophile	barkentine	cancellate
shellacked	unaccented	wingspread	anglophobe	barleybree	candletree
shellmound	unaffected	wirehaired	anglophone	baronetage	canonicate
shiprigged	unassisted	wonderland	animalcule	barysphere	cantaloupe
shopsoiled	unattached	woodenhead	annihilate	bastardise	cantatrice
shortbread	unattended	worshipped	annunciate	bathyscope	cantillate
shortdated	unbalanced	wraparound	anopheline	battledore	capacitate
shortlived	unblenched	wunderkind	answerable	bawdyhouse	capacitive
shouldered	unbonneted	yellowbird	antagonise	beforetime	capitalise
shovelhead	unbuttoned	yellowwood	anthracene	believable	Capitoline
shrivelled	uncustomed	abbreviate	anthracite	bellydance	capitulate
shroudlaid	undefended	aberdevine	anticipate	benedicite	caramelise
silverweed	undersexed	abhorrence	antifreeze	Benthamite	carbonnade
sisterhood	undersized	abominable	antimasque	benzocaine	caricature
skateboard	understand	absorbable	antimonite	benzpyrene	carmagnole
sleepyhead	understood	absorbance	antiSemite	besprinkle	carnallite
slowfooted	underworld	absorptive	apiculture	bestialise	cassolette
slowwitted	undeserved	abstersive	apocalypse	bibliopole	catafalque

catarrhine	compradore	creditable	depressive	downstroke	explicable
categorise	compromise	crenellate	deprivable	drafthorse	exploitage
cellophane	compulsive	crepuscule	depurative	dragonnade	exploitive
censurable	computable	crinolette	deracinate	dragontree	exportable
centigrade	conceptive	crocoisite	derivative	dramaturge	expositive
centilitre	concessive	crosspiece	desalinate	drawbridge	expressage
centimetre	conciliate	ctenophore	deshabille	dubitative	expressive
centralise	conclusive	cuddlesome	desiderate	dumbledore	exprobrate
centrifuge	concoctive	cultivable	desipience	dungbeetle	exsanguine
centromere	concretise	cumbersome	desistance	duumvirate	extendible
centrosome	concussive	cumulative	despicable	earthquake	extensible
chainsmoke	condensate	cunctative	despisable	earthshine	extinctive
chalkstone	condolence	custommade	desquamate	Eastertide	extractive
chalybeate	conductive	cuttlebone	detachable	ebullience	extricable
changeable	conference	cyclostome	detectable	edulcorate	exuberance
channelise	confidante	cyclostyle	deterrence	effaceable	exulcerate
chargeable	confidence	cystoscope	detestable	effectuate	exurbanite
charitable	confiscate	cytochrome	detonative	effeminate	eyeservice
chartreuse	confluence	damageable	detoxicate	effervesce	facilitate
chatelaine	congestive	dampcourse	detractive	effloresce	fairycycle
chatoyance	conglobate	deactivate	devitalise	effulgence	fanaticise
chauffeuse	congregate	debilitate	devocalise	eigenvalue	fastigiate
cheapskate	congruence	debouchure	dialysable	elasticise	fatherlike
cheesecake	conjecture	decagramme	dichromate	elecampane	fathomable
chelicerae	connective	decapitate	difference	electorate	fatiguable
chemisette	connivance	deceivable	diffidence	eliminable	favourable
chersonese	conscience	decelerate	diffusible	emancipate	federalise
chimpanzee	consecrate	deceptible	digestible	emarginate	federative
chlorinate	consociate	decigramme	digitalise	emasculate	felicitate
Christlike	consolable	decimalise	digressive	embouchure	fenestrate
chromatype	consonance	decivilise	dilapidate	embryonate	fescennine
chromosome	constipate	declarable	dilettante	emparadise	fibrillate
chrysolite	constitute	declinable	diminutive	employable	fibrillose
chrysotile	constringe	decolonise	directoire	endopodite	fieldmouse
cinchonine	consuetude	decolorise	disapprove	endorsable	fieldpiece
circumcise	consultive	decorative	disarrange	enervative	fieldstone
circumfuse	consumable	deductible	disbelieve	enigmatise	figurative
cismontane	consummate	dedicative	discipline	ensanguine	filterable
cispontine	contexture	deepfreeze	disclosure	enterprise	fireescape
claspknife	continence	deescalate	discommode	enumerable	fishkettle
classicise	continuate	defeasance	discompose	enunciable	flabellate
clementine	contortive	defeasible	discophile	episcopate	flagellate
clingstone	contravene	defeminise	discourage	epistrophe	flapdoodle
clinkstone	contribute	defendable	discursive	equivocate	flatulence
Clydesdale	convalesce	defensible	discussive	eradicable	floatplane
coacervate	convective	deferrable	disembogue	escadrille	floatstone
coachhouse	convenable	definitive	disentitle	escheatage	flocculate
coagulable	convenance	definitude	disentwine	escritoire	florentine
cockatrice	conveyable	deflagrate	disfeature	espadrille	fluoridate
cogitative	conveyance	deflective	disgruntle	estimative	fluorinate
cognisable	convictive	defrayable	dishabille	eternalise	fluorotype
cognisance	convulsive	degenerate	disincline	euhemerise	fluviatile
colatitude	cooptative	degradable	dislikable	evacuative	fontanelle
colchicine	coordinate	degressive	dismissive	evaluative	footbridge
coleoptile	copulative	dehiscence	dispersive	evangelise	footcandle
collarbone	coradicate	dehumanise	disposable	evaporable	forecastle
collarette	coralsnake	delaminate	disputable	everyplace	forecourse
collatable	corbiculae	delectable	disruptive	everywhere	forfeiture
collective	cordierite	deliberate	dissertate	eviscerate	forgivable
collegiate	corelative	delimitate	disservice	exactitude	formidable
colloquise	corncockle	deliquesce	dissidence	exaggerate	fourchette
colourable	cornerwise	delocalise	dissociate	examinable	foursquare
colportage	corpulence	demandable	dissoluble	exasperate	fourstroke
combustive	corpuscule	demobilise	dissonance	excellence	fowlplague
comedienne	corrective	demoiselle	dissuasive	excitative	frangipane
comestible	corrigible	demonetise	distensile	excogitate	fraternise
commentate	corroboree	demoralise	distillate	excruciate	fratricide
commissure	corruptive	denominate	distribute	execrative	freightage
commixture	corsetiere	denotative	disulphate	executable	frolicsome
commonable	cottoncake	dentifrice	disulphide	exenterate	gadolinite
communique	courthouse	denunciate	disyllable	exhaustive	Gallophile
commutable	couturiere	dependable	divaricate	exhilarate	Gallophobe
comparable	couverture	deplorable	divergence	expandable	garnierite
compatible	covariance	depolarise	divulgence	expansible	gastronome
compensate	covenantee	depopulate	dogstongue	expatriate	gelatinise
competence	crapulence	dependence	dolomitise	expectance	generalise
completive	craquelure	depolarise	dominative	expedience	generative
compliance	crassitude	depopulate	dorsigrade	expendable	geniculate
complicate	creatinine	depreciate	doubletime	experience	gentilesse

geometrise	hydrophyte	infiltrate	journalese	measurable	offlicence
Ghibelline	hydroplane	infinitive	journalise	meddlesome	oligoclase
glassfibre	hydroscope	infinitude	judicature	medicative	operculate
glasshouse	hygrophyte	inflatable	Kafkaesque	meditative	ophicleide
glauberite	hygroscope	inflective	kenspeckle	menstruate	oppressive
glauconite	hyperbolae	inflexible	keratinise	mensurable	optimalise
gluttonise	hypotenuse	inflictive	kerseymere	mercantile	ordonnance
gobemouche	iconoscope	ingeminate	kilogramme	mesoscaphe	orthoclase
golfcourse	illaudable	ingestible	kimberlite	mesosphere	ostensible
gormandise	illegalise	ingratiate	knobkerrie	metabolise	osteophyte
governable	illiterate	inimitable	knopkierie	metabolite	otherwhere
governance	illuminate	initialise	lacerative	metacentre	otherwhile
gramophone	illustrate	initiative	lachrymose	metaphrase	outbalance
grandniece	imaginable	injunctive	lacklustre	metastable	outerspace
granduncle	immaculate	innominate	lacustrine	mettlesome	outmeasure
grangerise	immiscible	innovative	lamentable	microcline	overactive
granophyre	immobilise	innumerate	Lammastide	microfiche	overblouse
graphitise	immoderate	inoculable	lanceolate	microphone	overcharge
graptolite	immortelle	inoperable	lanthanide	microphyte	overexcite
grasssnake	immoveable	inordinate	lanuginose	microscope	overexpose
gravestone	impalpable	inosculate	largescale	microspore	overpraise
greatniece	imparadise	inquietude	latescence	mignonette	overrefine
greatuncle	impartible	insatiable	lavalliere	militarise	overstride
greenhouse	impassable	inseminate	ledgerline	millilitre	oversubtle
greenstone	impassible	insensible	legitimate	millimetre	oxidisable
grindstone	impatience	insistence	legitimise	mineralise	pacifiable
guardhouse	impeccable	insociable	lemniscate	minestrone	pacificate
guesthouse	impendence	insolvable	lengthwise	misbelieve	packsaddle
guillotine	imperative	inspective	lepidolite	miscreance	paedogogue
habilitate	implacable	inspissate	liberalise	misfortune	paedophile
hagioscope	importable	insufflate	licensable	mismeasure	Palaeocene
hairstroke	importance	insurgence	licentiate	missionise	Palaeogene
halogenate	impossible	intangible	lighterage	mistakable	palaeotype
hamshackle	imposthume	integrable	lighthouse	misventure	palagonite
Hansardise	impregnate	intendance	limitative	mithridate	palatalise
harbourage	impressive	intenerate	limitrophe	mitigative	palatinate
headcheese	improbable	intergrade	lipservice	modifiable	palindrome
headsquare	improvable	interleave	literalise	moisturise	palliative
heartsease	imprudence	interphase	literature	mongrelise	panegyrise
heartwhole	impugnable	interspace	lithophane	monochrome	paniculate
heathenise	imputative	interstate	lithophyte	monologise	papaverine
heatstroke	inaccurate	interstice	locomotive	monopolise	paperchase
hectolitre	inactivate	intertwine	loganstone	monstrance	paperknife
hectometre	inadequate	intervolve	lophophore	morrispike	parabolise
heliophyte	inapposite	interweave	lowprofile	motorcycle	paradoxure
helioscope	inaptitude	intimidate	luciferase	mousseline	paralogise
heliotrope	inaugurate	intoxicate	lumbersome	mouthpiece	paraphrase
hemisphere	incandesce	intrigante	luxuriance	multiphase	paraselene
hempnettle	inchoative	invaginate	lymphocyte	multistage	pardonable
heparinise	incinerate	invalidate	lyophilise	mystagogue	paroxytone
hereticate	incipience	invaluable	macadamise	myxomycete	participle
heretofore	inclinable	invariable	macrophage	nationwide	pasquinade
hesitative	includible	invariance	macrospore	naturalise	passionate
heterodyne	incomplete	inveterate	maculature	necrophile	pasteurise
heulandite	incrassate	invigilate	magistrate	negligence	pasturable
hibernacle	incredible	invigorate	maidenlike	negligible	patentable
highoctane	incubative	invincible	maisonette	negotiable	patisserie
Hippocrene	inculpable	inviolable	malignance	negrophile	patriciate
hippodrome	incurrable	ionosphere	manageable	negrophobe	pediculate
hobbyhorse	indecisive	iridosmine	manipulate	nephoscope	pejorative
hodgepodge	indefinite	irradiance	manorhouse	neutralise	pendentive
hollowware	indelicate	irradicate	mansuetude	nidificate	penetrable
holophrase	indicative	irrelative	manteltree	nightshade	penetrance
homogenise	indictable	irresolute	maquillage	nominative	percentage
homologate	indiscrete	irritative	Marcionite	noticeable	percentile
homologise	inductance	Ishmaelite	margravate	notifiable	perceptive
homozygote	indulgence	isolatable	margravine	novaculite	percussive
honeyguide	ineducable	isoniazide	marguerite	nucleoside	perdurable
honourable	inelegance	italianate	marionette	nucleotide	perfective
hornblende	ineligible	italianise	marketable	nunciature	perfoliate
hospitable	ineludible	Italophile	marquisate	obliterate	perishable
hourcircle	ineptitude	jacobinise	marrowbone	obnubilate	periwinkle
hoverplane	inevitable	Japanesque	martensite	observable	permanence
hucklebone	inexorable	jardiniere	martingale	observance	permeative
humoresque	inexpiable	jargonelle	masquerade	obtainable	permissive
humoursome	infallible	jasperware	masticable	obtruncate	permutable
husbandage	infeasible	jeopardise	maturative	occupative	peroxidise
hydrophane	inferrable	johnnycake	mayonnaise	occurrence	perpetrate
hydrophone		Johnsonese	mealbeetle	oedematose	perpetuate

perquisite
persiflage
personable
persuasive
pertinence
perversive
pestilence
phantasise
philippine
philistine
philosophe
phlogopite
photophore
phototrope
pianoforte
picaresque
picketline
pigeonhole
pilgrimage
pillowcase
pillowlace
pilothouse
pilotwhale
pincerlike
piperidine
pistillate
pitchstone
plagiarise
plaguesome
planchette
planetable
plantlouse
plasmodise
plasticise
plebiscite
ploughable
plunderage
pocketable
pocketsize
politicise
polychaete
polychrome
polymerise
ponderable
popularise
Portuguese
possessive
postchaise
postoffice
potentiate
powerhouse
praemunire
pragmatise
pratincole
preadamite
prearrange
precedence
preceptive
preclusive
predecease
predestine
predicable
predictive
predispose
prednisone
preemptive
prefecture
preferable
preference
prefixture
prehensile
prepackage
prepayable
prepotence
prescience
presentive
pressurise
presumable
presuppose

prevalence
preventive
primiparae
principate
proctorage
procurable
procurance
producible
productive
profitable
profligate
projectile
projective
prologuise
prolongate
prominence
promulgate
propagable
propionate
propitiate
propulsive
prostitute
protective
protensive
proteolyse
protophyte
protrusile
protrusive
provenance
providence
psalmodise
psittacine
pubescence
punctulate
punishable
puritanise
purseseine
purtenance
purveyance
putrescine
pycnostyle
pyridoxine
pyrolusite
pyroxenite
pyrrhotite
quadrangle
quadrature
quadrireme
quadrumane
quadrupole
quantitive
quarantine
quarterage
quaternate
quenchable
quiescence
quinacrine
racecourse
radicalise
radiopaque
radiophone
radiosonde
ramshackle
rattlepate
razorblade
reactivate
realisable
reallocate
reappraise
reasonable
reassemble
rebuttable
recallable
receivable
receptacle
receptible
recitative
recolonise

recommence
recompense
recordable
recreative
recrudesce
revealable
recuperate
recurrence
recyclable
redecorate
redeemable
redemptive
redescribe
redundance
reeligible
reentrance
refillable
reflective
reflexible
reformable
refractive
refulgence
refundable
regenerate
regressive
regularise
regulative
reissuable
reiterance
rejectable
rejuvenate
rejuvenise
relativise
releasable
relievable
relishable
reluctance
remarkable
remarriage
remediable
remissible
remittance
remonetise
remunerate
renascence
renderable
reorganise
repairable
reparative
repatriate
repealable
repeatable
repellance
repellence
repentance
repertoire
repetitive
repopulate
reportable
repressive
reprobance
repugnance
repurchase
resilience
resistance
resistible
resolutive
resolvable
resorptive
respective
respirable
responsive
restorable
resumptive
resupinate
resurgence
retainable
reticulate
retractile
retractive

retrograde
returnable
revalidate
revalorise
reversible
revertible
reviewable
revitalise
rewardable
rhapsodise
rhinestone
rhinoscope
rhizophore
rhodophane
ridgepiece
rightangle
riverhorse
Romanesque
rontgenise
roquelaure
rosaniline
roseengine
rotisserie
roughhouse
roundhouse
rovebeetle
ruminative
rupicoline
Russianise
Russophile
Russophobe
sabretache
saccharate
saccharide
saccharine
saccharose
saddletree
salicylate
saltigrade
samarskite
sanctitude
sandcastle
sapphirine
saprophyte
sarmentose
saxicoline
scandalise
scapegrace
schematise
schemozzle
schipperke
schoolable
schoolmate
schooltime
Scotticise
screwplate
scrutinise
scutellate
seaanemone
seamanlike
searchable
seasonable
secondrate
secretaire
secularise
seignorage
selfpraise
seltzogene
semicircle
semidivine
semidouble
semilunate
semiopaque
senescence
sensualise
separative
serpentine
sexpartite

sheeplouse
sherardise
shirehorse
shoebuckle
shoreleave
shortrange
shrewmouse
shrinkable
Shrovetide
sialagogue
sideglance
siderolite
sidesaddle
sidestroke
silhouette
silverside
silverware
similitude
simulative
Singhalese
singletree
sketchable
skewbridge
skirtdance
slavetrade
Slavophile
Slavophobe
slenderise
slidevalve
sluicegate
smallscale
smaragdine
smaragdite
smokehouse
smoothbore
snakedance
snakestone
snickasnee
snowgrouse
snowmobile
soapbubble
solicitude
solidstate
solubilise
somatotype
somnolence
sororicide
sousaphone
sowthistle
spathulate
specialise
spermicide
sperrylite
sphalerite
sphenodone
spherulite
spiderline
spiflicate
splintbone
spokeshave
spoliative
spongecake
sporophore
sporophyte
springlike
springtide
springtime
squeezable
squeteague
stablemate
staffnurse
stagbeetle
stalactite
stalagmite
staphyline
statoscope
statuesque
statutable
staurolite

stavesacre
steakhouse
stephanite
stereobate
stereotype
stiflebone
stigmatise
stillicide
stinkstone
stipellate
stonesnipe
storehouse
streamline
stridulate
striptease
strychnine
subaverage
subcordate
subculture
subjective
sublimable
submissive
submontane
subroutine
subsidence
substitute
subterfuge
subversive
successive
succulence
sufferable
sufferance
sugarhouse
sugarmaple
suggestive
sulphonate
sulphurate
sulphurise
summerlike
summertime
summonable
sunderance
superacute
supernovae
superstore
suppletive
suppliance
supplicate
supportive
supposable
surmisable
surplusage
survivance
susceptive
suspensive
sustenance
sustentive
swarmspore
swashplate
sweepstake
sworddance
symmetrise
sympathise
syncretise
synecdoche
synthesise
synthetise
tabernacle
tabularise
tailormade
tambourine
tankengine
taradiddle
tarantelle
tardigrade
tattletale
telpherage
temperable
temperance

tenantable	underwrite	powderpuff	flyfishing	overriding	thimblerig
terminable	underwrote	shandygaff	forbidding	overstrung	thundering
terneplate	unenviable	shellproof	foreboding	parcelling	timesaving
tessellate	unfeminine	shockproof	forgetting	patrolling	tinselling
tetrastyle	unhandsome	smokeproof	formatting	pencilling	tittupping
theodolite	uninitiate	sneakthief	forwarding	penpushing	travelling
theologise	unipartite	soundproof	fosterling	performing	trepanning
thermopile	unknowable	stockproof	foxhunting	permitting	triphthong
thillhorse	unnameable	stormproof	freeliving	physicking	trowelling
thinkpiece	unreadable	Stroganoff	frivolling	picnicking	tunnelling
thornapple	unreliable	thornproof	frolicking	pigeonwing	unassuming
threadbare	unscalable	timberwolf	fulfilling	pistolling	unavailing
threepence	unscramble	undercliff	funnelling	pistonring	unbecoming
threepiece	unsociable	underproof	gadrooning	playacting	unblinking
threescore	unsuitable	waterproof	gaingiving	pothunting	unblushing
thruppence	unworkable	accounting	gambolling	practising	unchanging
thwartwise	utilisable	acquitting	garnishing	prairiedog	underlying
tickertape	valleculae	aircooling	glimmering	preferring	underslung
timberline	vanadinite	almsgiving	Godfearing	prevailing	unedifying
titanesque	varicocele	anchoring	gratifying	priestling	unflagging
toffeenose	vasoactive	appetising	groundling	princeling	ungrudging
tollbridge	vaticinate	backbiting	grovelling	proceeding	unpleasing
toothpaste	vaudeville	ballooning	gunrunning	propelling	unsettling
topazolite	vegetative	barrelling	hairspring	publishing	unsporting
touchjudge	velocipede	batfowling	handspring	pummelling	unswerving
touchstone	ventricose	beekeeping	hanselling	quartering	unthinking
tourmaline	verifiable	bestirring	headspring	rainmaking	unwavering
trabeculae	vernissage	bitterling	headstrong	refreshing	unyielding
tramontane	vertebrate	blanketing	highflying	refuelling	upbraiding
trampoline	vesiculate	blistering	highstrung	regretting	upbringing
trancelike	vespertine	blithering	hobnobbing	resounding	upstanding
transcribe	vibraphone	blitzkrieg	homecoming	respecting	wampumpeag
transferee	videophone	bookmaking	homemaking	retraining	wanderplug
transience	Vietnamese	bratticing	hostelling	riproaring	wassailing
transitive	villainage	brevetting	houselling	rodfishing	weathering
transshape	villanelle	cancelling	humbugging	roistering	wellspring
transvalue	villeinage	changeling	ilangilang	rollicking	whispering
transverse	vindicable	chiselling	imprinting	rumrunning	wrongdoing
travelogue	vindictive	clothesbag	inbreeding	sanderling	ylangylang
travertine	virescence	clothespeg	infighting	satisfying	zigzagging
triacetate	vitaminise	commanding	inspanning	scattering	accomplish
trichinise	vitiligate	committing	instilling	scratchwig	afterbirth
Tridentine	vitriolise	compelling	jaywalking	scribbling	alloverish
trifoliate	vituperate	concerning	kennelling	selfacting	altazimuth
trifurcate	vivandiere	concurring	kidnapping	selfloving	amateurish
tripartite	vociferate	confabbing	Kuomintang	selfrising	amphibrach
triplicate	volatilise	conferring	landowning	selfruling	anemograph
triquetrae	voyageable	consulting	laurelling	semidrying	archerfish
triternate	vulnerable	convincing	lawabiding	shoestring	backsheesh
triturable	waggonette	corbelling	lifegiving	shortening	backstitch
trivialise	waterborne	cradlesong	lifesaving	shovelling	balderdash
troctolite	westernise	cudgelling	lipreading	shuttering	bathyscaph
troglodyte	wheatstone	curvetting	logrolling	signalling	bellylaugh
tropopause	wheelhorse	diecasting	lovemaking	skibobbing	blacksmith
tropophyte	wheelhouse	diesinking	lutestring	skijumping	bridlepath
Trotskyite	whorehouse	disbarring	magnifying	skindiving	broadcloth
trouvaille	winceyette	disbudding	mainspring	skyjacking	bumpkinish
truculence	windowpane	discerning	marvelling	skywriting	butterfish
tumescence	windsleeve	dispelling	midmorning	smattering	buttonbush
turbulence	winebottle	distilling	mishitting	snivelling	candlefish
turnbuckle	wintertide	drawstring	miswording	spiralling	childbirth
turpentine	wintertime	drivelling	mosaicking	sprinkling	chinagraph
turtledove	wolframite	earwigging	nauseating	squireling	clovehitch
twelvenote	workpeople	easterling	nickelling	staggering	cockneyish
twelvetone	worthwhile	enamelling	nitpicking	stargazing	coelacanth
ulcerative	Wycliffite	enchanting	nonplaying	starveling	coquettish
umbilicate	zabaglione	englutting	nourishing	stiffening	cornstarch
unarguable	breadstuff	engrossing	oceangoing	subheading	countryish
unbearable	centrehalf	entrancing	offputting	subletting	crossbench
unbeatable	chiffchaff	enwrapping	offsetting	submitting	crosshatch
unbiddable	childproof	everliving	outbidding	surprising	crosspatch
undeniable	cloverleaf	everything	outfitting	sustaining	cuttlefish
underglaze	coolingoff	facesaving	outgassing	swaggering	cyclograph
underlease	dampingoff	feathering	outgunning	swanupping	czarevitch
underquote	fallingoff	fingerling	outpouring	sweetening	deathwatch
underscore	flameproof	flagwaving	outputting	sweltering	disfurnish
undersense	greenstuff	flattering	outrunning	swivelling	ditriglyph
understate	hippogriff	flavouring	outsitting	tasselling	eighteenth
undervalue	lightproof	fledgeling	outwitting	thickening	enterolith

```
extinguish  shibboleth  bridgework  spitchcock  coffeemill  frictional
flightpath  shillelagh  brightwork  splashback  cognominal  functional
floorcloth  showerbath  broomstick  supplejack  collateral  fungicidal
fourteenth  silverbath  bubblyjock  switchback  colloquial  geodetical
freespeech  silverfish  buttermilk  swordstick  commercial  geological
frontbench  slipstitch  buttonhook  tenterhook  commonweal  geoponical
fulllength  snowplough  candlewick  threadmark  conceptual  geothermal
glasscloth  songthrush  canvasback  throwstick  conchoidal  germicidal
gooseflesh  spirograph  canvaswork  tiddlywink  congenital  gerundival
grasscloth  squirearch  centreback  timberwork  connatural  glossarial
greencloth  stagecoach  chequebook  turkeycock  consensual  goldenseal
greenfinch  stenograph  crackajack  turtleback  contextual  grandducal
halflength  stillbirth  crewelwork  turtleneck  conventual  gressorial
hallelujah  stonebrash  crosscheck  understock  coromandel  gyrational
heathenish  stylograph  donkeywork  undertrick  cottontail  harmonical
hectograph  tablecloth  donnybrook  waterclock  cottonwool  hebdomadal
heliograph  tetramorph  doublepark  whaleshark  cranesbill  hemihedral
henceforth  tetrastich  doubletalk  wickerwork  credential  heptagonal
Heptateuch  thirteenth  dumbstruck  wonderwork  curatorial  hermetical
heresiarch  thousandth  fetterlock  yellowback  cuttystool  hexahedral
hieroglyph  threadfish  fiddleback  abacterial  decahedral  hierarchal
hierograph  toothbrush  fingermark  aboriginal  decemviral  historical
hippogryph  tragacanth  fisherfolk  academical  delightful  holohedral
homoeopath  trillionth  flightdeck  accidental  delusional  homocercal
horsecloth  trollopish  gentlefolk  acoustical  demoniacal  homosexual
horseflesh  tsarevitch  greenshank  acronychal  despiteful  horizontal
horselaugh  underbrush  greenstick  additional  devotional  hypabyssal
horseleech  underneath  groundwork  adjectival  diabolical  hypaethral
hotchpotch  usquebaugh  hackmatack  alchemical  diarrhoeal  hypodermal
hygrograph  vectograph  hairstreak  ambulacral  diathermal  hysterical
impoverish  vinegarish  hammerlock  ammoniacal  dickcissel  ideational
lithoglyph  waistcloth  heartblock  anagogical  didactical  illusional
lithograph  waterbrash  heartbreak  analogical  disdainful  immaterial
lockstitch  wavelength  herrenvolk  analytical  disembowel  immemorial
mackintosh  whipstitch  kibbutznik  anarchical  disembroil  impersonal
Methuselah  whitesmith  knickknack  anatomical  disenthral  incidental
micrograph  wristwatch  ladderback  aneurismal  disgustful  individual
mimeograph  yarborough  letterbook  aneurysmal  divisional  industrial
nailpolish  zincograph  lumberjack  antechapel  documental  infusorial
naturopath  altocumuli  masterwork  anticlinal  dogmatical  insightful
needlebath  altostrati  matchstick  antimonial  dramatical  internodal
needlefish  amphigouri  meadowlark  antiphonal  duniwassal  interposal
nephograph  barramundi  minutebook  antisocial  duodecimal  intertidal
nettlerash  borborygmi  moonstruck  aplacental  ecological  interzonal
nightwatch  burramundi  mountebank  apocryphal  economical  intestinal
nineteenth  canaliculi  natterjack  apolitical  ectodermal  intramural
nudibranch  cannelloni  needlebook  apothecial  ecumenical  involucral
oldmaidish  certiorari  needlework  archetypal  egoistical  irrational
openhearth  coatimundi  nightstick  artificial  electrical  isochronal
outlandish  Devanagari  nitrochalk  asteroidal  elliptical  isoglossal
outstretch  dilettanti  paddywhack  auditorial  emerywheel  isoseismal
overgrowth  fantoccini  pastrycook  autarkical  encyclical  isothermal
overslaugh  fortissimi  phrasebook  Barmecidal  endocrinal  janitorial
paintbrush  frangipani  pilgarlick  basketball  endodermal  jesuitical
palaeolith  Hindustani  pitchblack  beneficial  eosinophil  jobbernowl
pantograph  hippocampi  pocketbook  bequeathal  epicentral  juristical
parrotfish  illuminati  pointblank  bibliophil  epidemical  kriegspiel
peacockish  intermezzi  prayerbook  bicultural  epiglottal  ladychapel
pebbledash  jaguarundi  promptbook  bimestrial  episodical  larvicidal
pennyworth  millefiori  punchdrunk  biological  epithelial  lavatorial
pentastich  monsignori  reichsmark  biparietal  equational  ligamental
petroglyph  piccalilli  ripplemark  bluepencil  equatorial  liturgical
phonograph  rhomboidei  rubberneck  bollweevil  eremitical  logistical
photograph  ritornelli  saddleback  botryoidal  ergosterol  magnifical
picayunish  salmagundi  salesclerk  brachyural  eucalyptol  majestical
pictograph  sarcophagi  schoolbook  brandyball  evidential  malleefowl
planigraph  septenarii  schoolwork  breastwall  exegetical  managerial
proudflesh  spermaceti  scrimshank  butterball  exoterical  manchineel
psychopath  tortellini  scrollwork  buttonball  exothermal  markethall
radiograph  ventriculi  sheepshank  calciferol  extemporal  matricidal
relinquish  vermicelli  shellshock  campestral  extramural  meaningful
rhizomorph  alpenstock  sketchbook  cannonball  febrifugal  mechanical
ribbonfish  badderlock  skrimshank  carnassial  fingerbowl  menopausal
rudderfish  basketwork  sleevelink  centennial  fingernail  meridional
runthrough  bloodstock  smockfrock  centesimal  flavourful  metacarpal
sabretooth  bottleneck  smokestack  ceremonial  flowergirl  metatarsal
scaramouch  brakeblock  soundtrack  chimerical  fractional  methodical
seethrough  breadstick  sourcebook  cinquefoil  fragmental  millennial
seventieth  breastwork  spatchcock  closestool  Francophil  millesimal
```

```
mischmetal  principial  stomachful  absolutism  empiricism  microseism
mizzensail  prismoidal  storksbill  acetabulum  engineroom  militarism
monarchial  procedural  strabismal  acroterium  enthusiasm  millennium
monistical  proctorial  structural  aesthetism  epiphytism  millstream
monitorial  prolicidal  subcentral  Africanism  episternum  minimalism
monoclinal  pronominal  subglacial  alcoholism  epithelium  moderatism
monopodial  prosodical  subliminal  amateurism  eudemonism  molybdenum
monumental  prostomial  sublingual  ambulacrum  euhemerism  monarchism
muffinbell  prototypal  suborbital  anabaptism  evangelism  monetarism
multivocal  proverbial  subordinal  androecium  factualism  mongrelism
musicstool  provincial  successful  angiosperm  fanaticism  moniliform
myological  prudential  suprarenal  antagonism  federalism  monogenism
natalitial  puristical  symbolical  antebellum  flunkeydom  monopodium
natatorial  purposeful  symphyseal  antemortem  flunkeyism  monotheism
neglectful  pyrogallol  symphysial  antitheism  foreignism  moratorium
neological  quadrantal  synchronal  apophthegm  fortuitism  morphinism
nonlogical  quadrivial  synoptical  apothecium  Fourierism  myocardium
nonnatural  quatrefoil  Talmudical  argumentum  fullbottom  narcissism
notonectal  quixotical  tangential  asceticism  gadolinium  nasturtium
nutational  rabbinical  taxidermal  Ashkenazim  genteelism  natatorium
objectival  razorshell  tegumental  auditorium  geotropism  naturalism
occasional  reciprocal  televisual  automatism  gnosticism  negativism
occidental  regimental  tenemental  Benthamism  gradualism  nephridium
octahedral  relational  tetragonal  blastoderm  grangerism  neuroplasm
orangepeel  remorseful  theatrical  blepharism  gymnosperm  neutralism
oratorical  resorcinol  theistical  bolshevism  hammerbeam  nicotinism
orchestral  respectful  thermophil  Boswellism  haustellum  nominalism
organismal  revengeful  theurgical  bourbonism  haustorium  oceanarium
ornamental  revisional  thimbleful  bowdlerism  headstream  oecumenism
orological  rhetorical  thoughtful  bradyseism  heathendom  ommatidium
orthogonal  rhomboidal  threnodial  Brahmanism  heathenism  opprobrium
outgeneral  rhythmical  thumbstall  Brahminism  henotheism  organicism
overmantel  rotational  tinctorial  brainstorm  hipsterism  osmeterium
papistical  rudimental  tocopherol  bridegroom  honorarium  osmiridium
paranormal  sabbatical  toothshell  brigandism  hyaloplasm  oysterfarm
parenteral  sacerdotal  torrential  Britishism  hylotheism  pacificism
parimutuel  salicional  tractional  Buchmanism  hypanthium  palmerworm
paroxysmal  sapiential  transeptal  caddisworm  hypocorism  pancratium
parricidal  scansorial  transposal  calyciform  iconoclasm  panjandrum
parsonical  schoolgirl  treadwheel  cankerworm  illuminism  paralogism
pathetical  scrapmetal  trigeminal  capitalism  insularism  paramecium
patricidal  screechowl  trilateral  cardiogram  invalidism  parapodium
patrilocal  scriptural  trilingual  catabolism  involucrum  parasitism
pedimental  sculptural  triliteral  centralism  Italianism  pasteurism
pennyroyal  seedvessel  triquetral  cerebellum  Jacobinism  patriotism
pentagonal  seignorial  triumviral  chauvinism  Jacobitism  periosteum
peppermill  selfdenial  trochoidal  chloroform  journalism  peritoneum
perceptual  semestrial  tumblerful  chronogram  Kantianism  petrolatum
periclinal  semiannual  tyrannical  cicisbeism  karyoplasm  phallicism
peridermal  semiotical  unbiblical  cinerarium  katabolism  phanerogam
periodical  semiuncial  uncritical  classicism  kettledrum  pharisaism
periosteal  senatorial  uneventful  cockalorum  Krishnaism  phelloderm
peripheral  sentential  unfaithful  cockneyism  laconicism  plagiarism
peripteral  septennial  ungraceful  collarbeam  Lamarckism  plasmodesm
peritoneal  sepulchral  ungrateful  colloquium  lawrencium  plasmodium
pesticidal  sequential  unicameral  commonroom  lebensraum  polemonium
phalangeal  sheathbill  unilateral  compendium  legitimism  polygenism
phantasmal  sicklebill  unilingual  concettism  lesbianism  polymerism
pharyngeal  simoniacal  unmerciful  concretism  liberalism  polytheism
phenomenal  sincipital  unofficial  conformism  limaciform  positivism
pheromonal  sinusoidal  untruthful  consortium  linguiform  postbellum
phthisical  sleighbell  urochordal  cribriform  literalism  postmortem
pictorical  slumberful  urticarial  crippledom  livingroom  postpartum
pitcherful  snailwheel  uxoricidal  cryptogram  lockerroom  praesidium
polydactyl  solenoidal  venational  cumuliform  Lollardism  pragmatism
polyhedral  solstitial  vermicidal  curriculum  lumberroom  presternum
polynomial  spagyrical  vesperbell  decimalism  lycopodium  primordium
pontifical  sphenoidal  viceconsul  delphinium  Lysenkoism  principium
positional  spheroidal  visitorial  demagogism  mainstream  promethium
praecocial  splintcoal  vocational  dendriform  malacoderm  propylaeum
praetorial  splitlevel  volitional  diatropism  Manicheism  prosaicism
precordial  sponsorial  volleyball  digitiform  martialism  proscenium
prefrontal  sporangial  waterwheel  dimorphism  mayblossom  prostomium
preglacial  sporophyll  windowsill  diningroom  meerschaum  proteiform
prelatical  sprightful  witchhazel  disconfirm  memorandum  protoplasm
premarital  springtail  withdrawal  disembosom  mesomerism  psalterium
premedical  squaresail  worshipful  downstream  messianism  psychicism
presageful  standstill  zoological  dysprosium  metabolism  puerperium
primordial  stockstill  zygodactyl  echinoderm  metamerism  puritanism
```

Pyrrhonism	Vaticanism	beautician	Copernican	emendation	hemihedron
quadrivium	vestibulum	Bedlington	copulation	emigration	hemipteran
Rachmanism	vibraculum	Belgravian	corelation	emollition	hendecagon
radicalism	viperiform	Berkeleian	Corinthian	encephalon	Heptameron
recidivism	vomitorium	bestridden	coronation	enervation	hesitation
referendum	Wertherism	biliverdin	correction	Englishman	hexahedron
relativism	abdication	bilocation	corruption	epilimnion	highwayman
reunionism	aberration	bipartisan	councilman	equestrian	hirudinean
revanchism	abjuration	blackthorn	countryman	equitation	homoousian
revivalism	abnegation	bloodstain	crackbrain	eructation	horsewoman
rheumatism	Abrahamman	blueribbon	crispation	escalation	housetrain
ribbonworm	abreaction	Boswellian	crossgrain	Esculapian	hovertrain
rockbottom	abrogation	brachyuran	crustacean	escutcheon	husbandman
ruffianism	abscission	brokendown	crustation	estimation	hyperbaton
sanatorium	absolution	browbeaten	cumulation	etiolation	imbibition
sanitarium	absorption	butterbean	cunctation	Eurovision	immolation
sarcoplasm	abstention	buttondown	curmudgeon	evacuation	impanation
scepticism	abstersion	byelection	daisychain	evaluation	imposition
schematism	accusation	cacodaemon	datamation	exaltation	impression
schoolmaam	acervation	Caledonian	deaeration	excavation	imputation
schoolmarm	acotyledon	capitation	decahedron	excerption	inchoation
schoolroom	acroterion	carcinogen	decimation	excitation	incitation
scleroderm	actinozoan	carragheen	declension	execration	incubation
sclerotium	activation	carryingon	decoration	exhalation	indagation
Scotticism	adaptation	Carthusian	dedication	exhaustion	indecision
scyphiform	adhibition	caseharden	deepfrozen	exhibition	indexation
secularism	adjunction	castration	defamation	exhumation	indication
securiform	adjuration	catechumen	definition	expedition	Indonesian
seismogram	admiration	catenation	deflection	expiration	induration
selfesteem	admonition	catholicon	delegation	exposition	infarction
sensedatum	adsorption	cavalryman	demolition	expression	inflection
sensualism	advocation	cavitation	denegation	expunction	infliction
separatism	Aethiopian	centillion	denotation	extinction	infraction
septennium	affliction	chairwoman	denudation	extraction	infrahuman
sequestrum	agglutinin	chamaeleon	depilation	exultation	infusorian
sestertium	aggression	champignon	deposition	exuviation	ingression
sheriffdom	aircushion	chapfallen	depression	faceharden	inhalation
simulacrum	Algonquian	Charleston	depuration	fairspoken	inhibition
sinecurism	alienation	chevrotain	deputation	fasciation	inhumation
slipstream	allegation	chuckwagon	derivation	federation	initiation
solidarism	allocation	Ciceronian	dermatogen	feuilleton	injunction
specialism	allocution	Circassian	derogation	fibrinogen	innovation
sphenogram	alteration	Cistercian	descension	figuration	insolation
spiraculum	ambulation	clothespin	desolation	filtration	inspection
spongiform	Amerindian	coaptation	desorption	firescreen	insulation
spoonerism	ammunition	cogitation	detonation	fleabitten	interferon
sporangium	amphictyon	collection	detraction	flirtation	interurban
starstream	amputation	coloration	devolution	floatation	interwoven
stelliform	Andalusian	combustion	Dickensian	floriation	intimation
stereogram	AngloSaxon	commission	digitation	flugelhorn	intinction
stigmatism	annexation	compaction	digression	foreordain	intonation
stomodaeum	annotation	comparison	dilatation	foundation	intraurban
stramonium	annulation	compassion	diminution	Franciscan	intubation
stratiform	antinomian	completion	disburthen	freedwoman	inundation
strongroom	antipodean	complexion	discretion	freemartin	invitation
strychnism	antiproton	compulsion	discussion	freespoken	invocation
subkingdom	Apollinian	conception	disenviron	fruitarian	involution
subsellium	Apollonian	concession	dishearten	fumigation	iodination
substratum	apparition	conclusion	dismission	gargantuan	ionisation
sudatorium	apposition	concoction	dispassion	gemination	Irishwoman
surrealism	araucarian	concretion	dispersion	generation	irreligion
sybaritism	archdeacon	concussion	disquieten	Gilbertian	irrigation
syncretism	areolation	conduction	disruption	glaciation	irritation
tarmacadam	Armageddon	confection	dissection	Glaswegian	johnsonian
Tartuffism	arrogation	confession	dissension	graduation	journeyman
technetium	ascription	conflation	dissuasion	gramicidin	jubilation
tepidarium	aspiration	congestion	distension	grammarian	laceration
thermogram	assumption	connection	distention	GrecoRoman	Lamarckian
threadworm	Athanasian	conniption	distortion	groundplan	lambrequin
tiringroom	attraction	constantan	divagation	groundsman	laminarian
traumatism	Australian	contention	divination	habitation	lamination
trichroism	autochthon	contortion	domination	halfnelson	lapidarian
triclinium	automation	contrition	downfallen	handmaiden	lapidation
trivialism	Babylonian	convection	drawingpin	Hanoverian	laundryman
tropaeolum	backgammon	convention	dubitation	hardbitten	laureation
Trotskyism	balbriggan	conversion	ebullition	harvestman	Lawrentian
umbiliform	barleycorn	conviction	Eleusinian	heavenborn	lederhosen
utopianism	bassethorn	convulsion	elongation	hebetation	Leibnizian
vaporiform	batrachian	cooptation	emaciation	Heliconian	leprechaun

```
levigation  pagination  redemption  stagnation  warmingpan  kaisership
levitation  palliation  reelection  starvation  watermelon  leadership
liberation  Panamanian  reflection  stentorian  weatherman  legateship
lighterman  pancreatin  refraction  stonemason  wellington  lightingup
limitation  panopticon  refutation  straighten  wellspoken  mastership
literation  paradisean  regelation  strengthen  Welshwoman  matronship
Lithuanian  paradisian  regression  stringbean  Wertherian  membership
litigation  Parnassian  regulation  subclavian  whitethorn  mentorship
lobulation  patination  relaxation  subduction  windscreen  mothership
locomotion  peculation  relegation  subjection  woodpigeon  nincompoop
locustbean  pedalorgan  relocation  submersion  workingman  nitrogroup
Lusitanian  pedestrian  renovation  submission  xiphosuran  pastorship
lustration  pejoration  reparation  subreption  zollverein  penmanship
Maccabaean  penicillin  repetition  subsection  zwitterion  pillowslip
maceration  pennillion  reposition  substation  affettuoso  pistolwhip
machinegun  pentathlon  repression  subvention  aficionado  princeship
maculation  pentstemon  republican  subversion  allegretto  pseudocarp
Mahommedan  peppercorn  reputation  succession  angwantibo  pursership
Malpighian  perception  rescission  suggestion  barleybroo  rattletrap
Malthusian  percussion  resolution  superation  camerlengo  readership
mangosteen  perfection  resorption  superhuman  camerlingo  rectorship
Manichaean  perihelion  resumption  supination  cappuccino  regentship
markettown  permeation  retraction  suppletion  comanchero  salmonleap
markswoman  permission  revelation  suspension  concertino  schizocarp
maturation  peroration  revocation  sustention  didgeridoo  seamanship
mavourneen  persuasion  revolution  swanmaiden  diminuendo  shrinkwrap
medication  perversion  riboflavin  symphonion  eighteenmo  squireship
meditation  phenacetin  rockgarden  tablelinen  fantastico  stenchtrap
Melanesian  phenomenon  rockpigeon  tablespoon  fianchetto  stirrupcup
mesenteron  philologen  rollingpin  tabulation  fortepiano  sultanship
midshipman  phlogiston  roodscreen  Tartuffian  fortissimo  suretyship
militiaman  Phoenician  roofgarden  technician  hullabaloo  tellership
misprision  pincushion  rumination  teleostean  impresario  thwartship
mitigation  plantation  runnerbean  television  intermezzo  umpireship
mixolydian  politician  sagination  temptation  intertrigo  viziership
moderation  polyhedron  saleswoman  tenderloin  maraschino  wardenship
modulation  Polynesian  salientian  terreplein  moustachio  wentletrap
Mohammedan  Pomeranian  salivation  theodicean  mumbojumbo  windowshop
Monarchian  population  salpingian  theologian  octodecimo  abominator
monogynian  possession  salutation  titivation  peccadillo  abstracter
motivation  postillion  sandmartin  titubation  pentimento  abstractor
Mousterian  powderhorn  sanitarian  toleration  photolitho  accoucheur
mouthorgan  practician  sanitation  tourbillon  pianissimo  acetabular
Muhammadan  praetorian  saturation  townswoman  pichiciago  acidimeter
Muhammedan  precaution  scattergun  toxication  portamento  administer
mutilation  precession  Scillonian  trabeation  prosciutto  adventurer
nanisation  precipitin  Scotswoman  Tractarian  recitativo  advertiser
nativeborn  preclusion  scyphozoan  trajection  ritardando  Africander
navigation  prediction  seacaptain  transition  ritornello  Afrikander
Neapolitan  preemption  selfaction  trawlerman  saltarello  alleviator
nepenthean  preexilian  selfmotion  triggerman  scherzando  allrounder
neurotoxin  prehension  seminarian  trisection  seedpotato  almacanter
noblewoman  prelection  semination  triskelion  stringendo  almucanter
nodulation  pretension  senseorgan  truncation  supercargo  alternator
nomination  prevention  separation  tryptophan  airmanship  altogether
nonfiction  procession  septillion  tuberculin  archbishop  ambassador
nucleation  production  serviceman  tumbledown  authorship  ambidexter
numeration  profession  sextillion  Tyrrhenian  barbershop  amphimacer
nurseryman  projection  shandrydan  ulceration  battleship  anemometer
obligation  proportion  shantytown  ulotrichan  beadleship  antecessor
obturation  propulsion  shenanigan  unAmerican  brandysnap  antimatter
occupation  protection  sibilation  underlinen  bucketshop  applicator
ocellation  protrusion  siegetrain  undertaken  bursarship  aquaplaner
octahedron  provitamin  silkcotton  undulation  censorship  arbalester
octandrian  psilocybin  silkscreen  unforeseen  clientship  arbalister
octonarian  punctation  simulation  urtication  codswallop  arbitrager
oppilation  pushbutton  slowmotion  ustulation  consulship  arbitrator
opposition  Pyrrhonian  snapdragon  usucaption  contraprop  arteriolar
oppression  quartation  softspoken  usurpation  cousinship  astrologer
orchardman  quaternion  solifidian  validation  deaconship  astronomer
ordination  quatorzain  souterrain  vegetarian  doctorship  attenuator
Ordovician  quercitron  spacewoman  vegetation  editorship  auctioneer
oscitation  quickthorn  spallation  veldschoen  factorship  audiometer
osculation  radication  speciation  velitation  fathership  babysitter
outstation  ragamuffin  Spencerian  veneration  fellowship  backhander
overburden  railwayman  Spenserian  vesication  friendship  backslider
overridden  rechristen  splashdown  visitation  gingersnap  ballflower
overthrown  recitation  spoliation  waffleiron  handgallop  bandmaster
paddywagon  recreation  squamation  Waldensian  internship  bathometer
```

bathymeter	commutator	emblazoner	gunslinger	legislator	ophiolater
beautifier	comparator	emerypaper	gyrocopter	lenticular	opisometer
bedchamber	competitor	Emmentaler	hackbuteer	limeburner	originator
beefburger	complainer	emulsifier	hairraiser	lionhunter	oscillator
bellflower	compositor	encourager	halberdier	Lipizzaner	outfielder
bellringer	compotator	encroacher	halfdollar	Lippizaner	outswinger
bellwether	compounder	enregister	hangglider	liquidator	overlander
bellyacher	compressor	enumerator	harmoniser	liquidiser	overlooker
benefactor	computator	enunciator	headhunter	lockkeeper	overmaster
bestseller	comstocker	epigrapher	headmaster	longprimer	overwinter
bilgewater	contractor	eradicator	headwaiter	loosecover	ovipositor
billposter	controller	eudiometer	helicopter	lossleader	oxygenator
biographer	cooperator	Eurodollar	heliolater	lotuseater	pacesetter
birdspider	coparcener	evaporator	heliometer	loudhailer	painkiller
bivalvular	coproducer	expurgator	hellbender	loveletter	palisander
blackamoor	copyholder	extenuator	henharrier	lubricator	pallbearer
blackwater	copyreader	extirpator	heptameter	lucubrator	palmbutter
blasphemer	copywriter	fabricator	Herrnhuter	lumpsucker	panhandler
bluecollar	cordwainer	fairleader	highbinder	macebearer	papermaker
bobbysoxer	cornflower	fascicular	highjacker	machinator	particular
bombardier	corporator	fascinator	highlander	magnetiser	pastmaster
bondholder	corrugator	fellmonger	hitchhiker	maidenhair	pathfinder
bonesetter	councillor	fertiliser	honeyeater	mainlander	pawnbroker
boneshaker	counsellor	fictioneer	horsecoper	maintainer	peacemaker
bookbinder	covenanter	filibuster	horsepower	majuscular	pearldiver
bookkeeper	covenantor	fireraiser	horseshoer	malefactor	peashooter
bookmarker	cowcatcher	fishcarver	humidifier	malingerer	peduncular
bookseller	cowpuncher	fishmonger	hybridiser	mandibular	pellicular
bootlegger	crossrefer	fivefinger	hydrometer	manoeuvrer	penetrator
bootlicker	crowkeeper	floodwater	hygrometer	Mariolater	peninsular
brachiator	cuirassier	flycatcher	hypnotiser	marshaller	pennanular
brainpower	cultivator	flyswatter	hypsometer	masticator	pentameter
breakwater	curricular	foamflower	icebreaker	matchmaker	percolator
bressummer	cyclometer	folksinger	iconolater	medicaster	perforator
bricklayer	daydreamer	follicular	iconometer	megalosaur	persecutor
buccinator	defalcator	footballer	importuner	meliorator	personator
budgerigar	deflowerer	footwarmer	imprimatur	merrymaker	petitioner
bullroarer	defoliator	forecaster	improviser	mesmeriser	phonometer
bushmaster	delineator	forefather	incantator	micrometer	photometer
bushranger	denigrator	forefinger	inculcator	micropylar	piezometer
calamander	densimeter	foregather	inkslinger	mineworker	pigeonpair
calcsinter	deodoriser	forerunner	inoculator	mintmaster	pigsticker
calculator	deoxidiser	foreteller	inquisitor	minuscular	piledriver
calibrator	depredator	fornicator	insinuator	mischanter	pinfeather
campaigner	derailleur	fortyniner	inspirator	misjoinder	planimeter
cantilever	descriptor	fourposter	instigator	moderniser	planometer
carabineer	desecrater	fourteener	institutor	molendinar	platelayer
carabinier	desecrator	franchiser	instructor	moneymaker	plesiosaur
caravaneer	desiccator	freebooter	integrator	moneytaker	plumassier
caravanner	designator	freeholder	interceder	moonflower	pollinator
cardplayer	despatcher	freelancer	interferer	moonshiner	polyhistor
caruncular	destructor	freeloader	interloper	mossbunker	postmaster
caseworker	discharger	freesoiler	interlunar	moviemaker	postulator
cataloguer	disclaimer	frequenter	interposer	mudskipper	pourparler
catburglar	discounter	freshwater	intervener	mudslinger	premonitor
catechiser	discourser	froghopper	intervenor	multiplier	preparator
celebrator	discoverer	furuncular	introducer	multipolar	prescriber
challenger	dishwasher	galvaniser	ironmaster	musicpaper	proclaimer
chancellor	disparager	gamekeeper	ironmonger	mythiciser	procreator
chandelier	dispatcher	gasconader	ironworker	mythologer	procurator
changeover	dispraiser	gaslighter	jackhammer	necrolater	progenitor
charioteer	dissembler	gatekeeper	jawbreaker	negotiator	programmer
chiffonier	dissimilar	geographer	keyboarder	nevernever	prohibiter
chronicler	distrainer	gingerbeer	kieselguhr	newscaster	prohibitor
churchgoer	distrainor	gladhander	kingfisher	newsletter	prolocutor
circulator	divebomber	glasspaper	labiovelar	newsmonger	promenader
classifier	dogmatiser	glomerular	lacrimator	newsreader	pronouncer
clavicular	doorkeeper	goalkeeper	lacrymator	newsvendor	propagator
clawhammer	dovecolour	goaltender	ladyfinger	newswriter	prophesier
clinometer	dressmaker	goatsucker	ladykiller	noisemaker	propounder
clodhopper	drophammer	gobstopper	landholder	nondrinker	propraetor
coalbunker	dumbwaiter	goldbeater	landhunger	nonjoinder	proprietor
coathanger	dumfounder	golddigger	landlubber	nonnuclear	proscriber
cockchafer	duplicator	goniometer	landscaper	nonstarter	prosecutor
collimator	economiser	goodlooker	languisher	nonswimmer	prospector
collocutor	elaborator	granulator	lawbreaker	northerner	protractor
colporteur	eliminator	grapesugar	leafcutter	nutcracker	provocator
comehither	elucidator	gravimeter	leafhopper	obstructor	pulsimeter
commandeer	elutriator	gunfighter	lefthander	ombrometer	pulsometer

pulveriser
punctuator
pycnometer
pyknometer
quadrumvir
quantifier
quarreller
quarrender
questioner
quizmaster
rackrenter
radiometer
railroader
rapporteur
ratcatcher
reconciler
reconsider
rediscover
rencounter
repetiteur
reproducer
repudiator
reredorter
researcher
respirator
restrainer
retrochoir
reverencer
ringfinger
ringleader
ringmaster
ripsnorter
roadrunner
rockbadger
rockhopper
rollcollar
ropedancer
ropeladder
ropewalker
rosechafer
rottweiler
roughrider
rubricator
sacrificer
safeblower
salamander
saltcellar
sanctifier
sandbagger
sandhopper
scaffolder
scrimmager
scrutineer
seersucker
selfbinder
selfcolour
selffeeder
selfmurder
selfseeker
semiquaver
sensitiser
sermoniser
servomotor
shanghaier
sheabutter
shearwater
shipbroker
shipfitter
shipmaster
shopkeeper
shoplifter
shopwalker
showjumper
sidewinder
signwriter
simplifier
sixshooter
skirmisher
skyscraper

soapboiler
socialiser
songwriter
soothsayer
southerner
speculator
spiracular
spirometer
splutterer
sportswear
sprucebeer
squanderer
stabiliser
stadholder
stenciller
stepfather
stepladder
stepmother
stepsister
steriliser
stimulator
stipulator
stockpiler
stockrider
stoneborer
streetdoor
subjugator
submariner
subnuclear
subscriber
sunparlour
superaltar
superduper
superlunar
superorder
superpower
supervisor
supplanter
suppressor
sweetbriar
sweetbrier
swinefever
swinglebar
switchover
syllogiser
symboliser
syncopator
syndicator
tachometer
tachymeter
tackdriver
talebearer
taleteller
tantaliser
taskmaster
taxidancer
teaplanter
tearjerker
telecaster
telephoner
televiewer
temporiser
tendrillar
tentacular
terminator
tetrameter
theosopher
thereafter
thereunder
thermistor
threatener
tidewaiter
tilthammer
timekeeper
timeserver
tirailleur
tobogganer
tortfeasor
touchpaper

trabecular
trafficker
transactor
transducer
transferor
transfuser
transistor
translator
translunar
transmuter
transposer
trespasser
triangular
tribometer
triphammer
triturator
trochanter
tromometer
troubadour
tubercular
tufthunter
twowheeler
typesetter
typewriter
umbellifer
unbeliever
uncloister
undercover
underfloor
underminer
understeer
undertaker
underwater
unfamiliar
unilocular
vaccinator
vallecular
vanquisher
variometer
ventilator
verbaliser
vermicular
vernacular
versicular
vestibular
victimiser
victualler
viewfinder
vindicator
viscometer
visualiser
vivisector
voltameter
vorticular
vulcaniser
wallflower
wallpepper
wastepaper
watchmaker
watchtower
waterpower
waterskier
weedkiller
weimaraner
wellwisher
wharfinger
wheelchair
whensoever
wholesaler
wildfowler
Winchester
windflower
windjammer
winebibber
winegrower
wingcollar
wiredrawer

wirepuller
wiretapper
wirewalker
wireworker
withdrawer
withholder
woodcarver
woodcutter
woodlander
woodpecker
woodturner
woodworker
woolgather
woolgrower
woolsorter
worshipper
yardmaster
yesteryear
aardwolves
abdominous
abducentes
abjectness
abruptness
abstemious
absurdness
acarpelous
acephalous
acrobatics
acrogenous
activeness
adroitness
adulteress
adulterous
aerobatics
aerobiosis
aeruginous
aesthetics
affectless
aftergrass
afterpains
afterwards
agapanthus
Albigenses
albuminous
alexanders
alliaceous
allogamous
amanuenses
amanuensis
ampelopsis
amphibious
amphimixes
amphimixis
amylaceous
anadromous
anatropous
ancestress
anchorless
anchylosis
ancipitous
Anglistics
anonaceous
antibiosis
antisepsis
antitheses
antithesis
antonymous
aphaereses
aphaeresis
apocarpous
apotheoses
apotheosis
appendices
appendixes
aquafortis
aquiferous
arenaceous
armigerous
armourless

artfulness
asbestosis
ascariasis
astragalus
astuteness
ateleiosis
augustness
auriferous
auspicious
autogamous
autogenous
autologous
autonomous
avaricious
averseness
aviatrices
bacchantes
backblocks
backstairs
ballistics
barratrous
barrenness
battailous
Beaujolais
bedclothes
belongings
binoculars
biogenesis
biometrics
biophysics
bipetalous
bitchiness
bitterness
bituminous
bleariness
blitheness
bloodiness
bluishness
blusterous
bobbysocks
boisterous
bootstraps
borderless
bottomless
boyishness
braininess
brassiness
brawniness
brazenness
breakables
breathless
breezeless
breeziness
bridgeless
brightness
brokenness
bromegrass
bronchitis
broodiness
bunchgrass
buttonless
byssaceous
byssinosis
cadaverous
calamitous
calcareous
caliginous
callowness
calumnious
cancellous
candidness
candyfloss
canonicals
capricious

carcinosis
caryatides
casualness
catastasis
catechesis
catholicos
catoptrics
cellulitis
censorious
ceruminous
changeless
chaparajos
chaparejos
chasteness
chattiness
chauntress
cheekiness
cheeriness
cheesiness
chemotaxis
childermas
chilliness
chivalrous
choiceness
chromatics
chubbiness
cicatrices
circuitous
clamminess
clangorous
cleverness
cloudiness
clumsiness
coarseness
coastwards
coetaneous
collarless
colourless
comeliness
commandoes
commodious
commonness
coniferous
conspectus
contagious
contiguous
continuous
contrabass
coriaceous
cornflakes
Corybantes
coryphaeus
cosmopolis
costliness
couchgrass
courageous
craftiness
cragginess
crankiness
cravenness
creaminess
creepiness
cretaceous
crisscross
crossbones
crossroads
crosstrees
crustiness
cryogenics
cursedness
curvaceous
curvacious
cussedness
dauphiness
deadliness
decapodous
decompress
demureness

porousness	satyriasis	spadiceous	synonymous	usefulness	antepenult
porraceous	savageness	sparseness	synostosis	valvulitis	Antichrist
portcullis	savourless	speargrass	systemless	velutinous	anticipant
portentous	saxicolous	spectacles	takingness	venialness	antitheist
portliness	scandalous	speechless	talentless	victorious	apochromat
posthumous	scantiness	speediness	tawdriness	villainess	archpriest
precarious	scarabaeus	spillikins	tenantless	villainous	aristocrat
precocious	scarceness	spiritless	tenderness	violaceous	arrestment
predacious	scatheless	spirituous	tendinitis	viraginous	asphyxiant
prepossess	scattiness	sponginess	tenebrious	virtueless	assentient
prettiness	schooldays	spookiness	terrorless	visionless	assessment
prissiness	screenings	sportiness	testaceous	viviparous	assignment
procrypsis	screwpress	spottiness	tetchiness	vociferous	assoilment
prodigious	scrofulous	springless	tetrapolis	voluminous	assortment
profitless	scrupulous	spruceness	thalecress	voluptuous	astringent
proglottis	sculptress	spunkiness	themselves	wanderings	attachment
promptness	scurrilous	squareness	theoretics	wantonness	attainment
properness	scurviness	squaretoes	thirdclass	watchglass	attornment
prophetess	seamstress	stableness	thorniness	watercress	attractant
propitious	searchless	stanchless	thriftless	waterglass	attunement
prospectus	secureness	stanchness	thromboses	wateriness	autodidact
prosperous	sedateness	starriness	thrombosis	waterworks	automatist
prosthesis	seductress	statistics	throneless	weakliness	autonomist
proteinous	seemliness	steadiness	thunderous	weaponless	avouchment
prothallus	selectness	steaminess	timbertoes	weightless	axiologist
provisions	semeiotics	steeliness	timeliness	werewolves	babblement
pugnacious	semichorus	steelworks	tongueless	wheeziness	bafflement
pupiparous	sempstress	stereopsis	toothiness	wickedness	balloonist
putridness	sequacious	sternwards	torpidness	wilderness	banishment
pyrogenous	sereneness	stertorous	torridness	wilfulness	barrenwort
quadratics	serotinous	stewardess	touchiness	windowless	bassoonist
quadriceps	sestertius	stickiness	towardness	wintriness	battlement
quaintness	severeness	stilettoes	tracheitis	wobbliness	belletrist
queasiness	shabbiness	stinginess	traitorous	woefulness	bemusement
quenchless	shadowless	stockiness	transgress	wontedness	beneficent
quickgrass	shagginess	stodginess	trappiness	woodenness	benevolent
quirkiness	sheathless	stolidness	trashiness	woolliness	bestowment
raggedness	shieldless	stomatitis	treasonous	worldclass	betterment
rakishness	shiftiness	storminess	tremendous	worthiness	biochemist
rampageous	shoddiness	strabismus	trendiness	wrathiness	birthright
rancidness	shorewards	straitness	triandrous	yeastiness	bitterroot
randomness	shrewdness	streamless	trichiasis	yellowness	blackheart
ranunculus	shrillness	stressless	trichinous	yourselves	Blackshirt
reasonless	shroudless	strictness	trickiness	zoophagous	bladdernut
rebellious	sickliness	stridulous	trioecious	zoophilous	blastocyst
recentness	sideboards	stringless	trolleybus	abiogenist	blazonment
regardless	silentness	stromatous	trustiness	abridgment	bloodguilt
rejoicings	simpleness	struthious	tubicolous	absolutist	bluebonnet
relentless	sinfulness	stubbiness	tuffaceous	abstergent	bluejacket
remediless	singleness	stuffiness	tumultuous	accountant	bluethroat
remissness	sinistrous	stumpiness	turbidness	accrescent	bolshevist
remoteness	skimpiness	stupendous	turgidness	adjudgment	bottommost
rendezvous	skinniness	stupidness	tympanites	adjustment	bourbonist
resistless	slanderous	sturdiness	tympanitis	adolescent	brakelight
resultless	slanginess	stylistics	ubiquitous	adulterant	breadfruit
retrogress	sleaziness	subaqueous	umbrageous	advisement	breakpoint
rewardless	sleepiness	subspecies	underdress	aerologist	broadsheet
rheumatics	sleeveless	subtleness	underpants	aeronomist	brownshirt
rhinoceros	slightness	suddenness	undesirous	affeerment	bryologist
ridiculous	sloppiness	sugariness	uneasiness	Africanist	bureaucrat
rightwards	slumberous	sullenness	unevenness	afterlight	butterwort
robustious	smallwares	sulphurous	unfairness	agrologist	cajolement
robustness	smelliness	sultriness	ungenerous	agronomist	candescent
roisterous	smoothness	summitless	ungracious	algebraist	cantonment
rootedness	smudginess	sunglasses	unholiness	algologist	capitalist
rottenness	smuttiness	superbness	uniqueness	alightment	cartoonist
rubiginous	sneakiness	supineness	unjustness	allegorist	cartwright
rudderless	sniffiness	supperless	unkindness	allurement	cataphract
ruefulness	snootiness	suppleness	unlikeness	ambivalent	centralist
ruggedness	snuffiness	suspenders	unmeetness	ambushment	chamberpot
rupicolous	soapflakes	suspicious	unripeness	amercement	chauvinist
sacredness	sobersides	sweatiness	unruliness	anabaptist	checkpoint
sailorless	soddenness	swordgrass	untidiness	analphabet	chimneypot
saliferous	solemnness	symphylous	unwariness	anastigmat	chuckerout
sallenders	solicitous	synaeresis	upperclass	anecdotist	circumvent
sallowness	sombreness	synanthous	uppishness	animadvert	classicist
salubrious	songstress	syncarpous	uproarious	anointment	cloudburst
sargassoes	sordidness	syngenesis	upwardness	antagonist	cnidoblast
sarmentous	southwards	synoecious	urethritis	antecedent	coachbuilt

coadjacent
coalescent
coexistent
cohabitant
coincident
colloquist
colourfast
commandant
commitment
compatriot
complacent
complement
compliment
concordant
concretist
concurrent
conferment
conformist
congregant
consequent
consistent
conspirant
constraint
consultant
contendent
contestant
contingent
continuant
contradict
controvert
convenient
convergent
conversant
convulsant
cornettist
cosentient
counteract
couplement
crankshaft
crosslight
cuckoopint
cuckoospit
cytologist
dazzlement
deadweight
debasement
debatement
decampment
Decembrist
decolorant
decrescent
deerforest
defacement
defilement
definement
deforciant
defrayment
delinquent
denaturant
denouement
department
deployment
deportment
depressant
derailment
derestrict
descendant
descendent
designment
despondent
detachment
detainment
detoxicant
devotement
diphyodont
disappoint
discomfort
disconcert
disconnect
discontent
discordant
discrepant
discussant
discutient
disenchant
disinherit
disownment
dispersant
disrespect
dissilient
dissolvent
distraught
divestment
dustjacket
earthlight
eartrumpet
ecclesiast
effacement
emancipist
embalmment
embankment
embarkment
embodiment
embonpoint
embossment
empiricist
employment
enamellist
encampment
encasement
encashment
encystment
endearment
endproduct
enfacement
engagement
engulfment
enigmatist
enjambment
enjoinment
enlacement
enlistment
enmeshment
enrichment
enrigiment
entailment
enthusiast
enticement
entombment
entrapment
equipotent
equivalent
ergonomist
erubescent
escapement
escarpment
eternalist
ethologist
eudemonist
eugenicist
euhemerist
evanescent
evangelist
evolvement
excitement
excrescent
exhilarant
exorbitant
experiment
extractant
factualist
Fahrenheit
faintheart
famishment
fearnought
federalist
fictionist
fingerpost
fireblight
firstnight
fixedpoint
flagellant
flamboyant
flashlight
flashpoint
flavescent
fleamarket
flocculent
floodlight
florescent
folklorist
forthright
fortuitist
foudroyant
fraudulent
frutescent
fulfilment
fussbudget
galleywest
generalist
geneticist
geochemist
geriatrist
gesundheit
glossarist
government
gradualist
grapefruit
greenheart
groundbait
groundrent
guestnight
habiliment
handicraft
harassment
hartebeest
heavensent
henotheist
heterodont
hierophant
hithermost
honeysweet
horologist
houseagent
housecraft
houseguest
houseplant
ideologist
illuminant
illuminist
immoralist
immurement
impairment
impalement
impartment
impediment
impenitent
impregnant
impugnment
impuissant
inappetent
incasement
incitement
incogitant
incoherent
inconstant
increscent
indictment
indiscreet
indistinct
inditement
inducement
ineloquent
inexistent
inexplicit
infrequent
ingredient
inhabitant
insentient
insouciant
instalment
instrument
integument
intendment
internment
interplant
intertwist
intolerant
intoxicant
intriguant
introspect
investment
iridescent
irrelevant
irreverent
jackrabbit
jerrybuilt
journalist
juggernaut
kineticist
knockabout
lactescent
lampoonist
landingnet
lansquenet
lapidarist
lattermost
lavishment
leafinsect
ledgerbait
legitimist
leucoplast
liberalist
librettist
lieutenant
lifejacket
liquescent
literalist
litterlout
lobsterpot
loungesuit
magnificat
makeweight
malcontent
maleficent
malevolent
malfeasant
management
manicurist
manservant
manuscript
marcescent
maximalist
medicament
meltingpot
micaschist
middlemost
militarist
millwright
minimalist
ministrant
misconduct
misogamist
misogynist
misologist
misthought
mizzenmast
monarchist
monetarist
monkeysuit
monogamist
monologist
monopolist
monotheist
monovalent
motherwort
munificent
mycologist
narcissist
naturalist
negativist
nematocyst
nethermost
neutralist
nightlight
nightshift
nightshirt
nigrescent
nipplewort
nominalist
nomologist
nonchalant
noncontent
nonpayment
nonviolent
nosologist
nympholept
obituarist
obtainment
oecologist
oenologist
omnipotent
omniscient
oncologist
ontologist
opalescent
operettist
opinionist
orchardist
ordainment
oreologist
organicist
orthoepist
osteoblast
osteoclast
outpatient
overbought
overcommit
overflight
overthrust
overweight
pacificist
paddleboat
palimpsest
panegyrist
pansophist
paraphrast
parliament
parturient
Passionist
pastellist
pedalpoint
pedicurist
pedologist
penologist
peppermint
pepperwort
percipient
permafrost
persistent
pharmacist
phenocryst
photoprint
physiocrat
pickpocket
pigeonpost
pilotlight
pinecarpet
pistolshot
plagiarist
plainchant
playwright
pluperfect
podiatrist
polemicist
polychrest
polygamist
polygenist
polytheist
polyvalent
pomologist
positivist
postscript
pragmatist
preachment
preconcert
preeminent
preferment
prefulgent
prepayment
pressagent
pretendant
pretendent
prevenient
prizefight
procumbent
proficient
proofsheet
propellant
propellent
prosilient
protestant
protoplast
psalmodist
psychicist
Ptolemaist
puberulent
punishment
pursuivant
putrescent
puzzlement
Pyrrhonist
quadruplet
quintuplet
rabblement
ravishment
reafforest
rearmament
recidivist
recitalist
recoupment
redcurrant
refinement
refringent
refundment
regalement
registrant
relativist
requiescat
resemblant
resentment
reshipment
respondent
restaurant
retirement
retrospect
reunionist
revanchist
revealment
revilement
revivalist
rhapsodist
rheologist
rinderpest
rockrabbit
roundabout
rouseabout
roustabout
rubythroat
sacrosanct
saddlefast
safetybelt
sauerkraut
scaredycat

```
scoresheet  swordcraft  handbarrow  afferently  brachylogy  compliancy
seabiscuit  symphonist  middlebrow  affluently  brilliancy  complicacy
seaserpent  symposiast  muskmallow  agitatedly  broodingly  complicity
secernment  syncretist  ottershrew  alarmingly  buffoonery  composedly
secondbest  synonymist  overshadow  aldermanry  bumblingly  compulsory
secondment  synthesist  playfellow  alimentary  bunglingly  conchology
secularist  synthetist  rosemallow  alkalinity  bustlingly  conciliary
securement  tanglement  sashwindow  allusively  cacography  concinnity
seducement  tantamount  shopwindow  ambulatory  Caerphilly  conclusory
selenodont  tapotement  showwindow  amendatory  cajolingly  concretely
selfdeceit  taxonomist  thumbscrew  amiability  calculably  condensery
selfprofit  technicist  wappenshaw  anemometry  canonicity  conformity
selftaught  technocrat  yokefellow  anemophily  canorously  confusedly
seminarist  tenderfoot  anticlimax  angularity  canterbury  congruency
sensualist  testflight  billetdoux  animatedly  capability  conjointly
separatist  tetterwort  bordereaux  anisotropy  capitulary  conjugally
Septuagint  textualist  chatterbox  annoyingly  captiously  consectary
SerboCroat  theogonist  chickenpox  annularity  cardiology  consistory
serologist  theologist  circumflex  answerably  carelessly  consonancy
setterwort  theopneust  Clarenceux  anteriorly  carpellary  conspiracy
settlement  thereabout  crossindex  apothecary  carphology  constantly
sexivalent  thereanent  gaspereaux  apparently  cartomancy  consumedly
sexologist  thermostat  generatrix  applicably  catchpenny  contiguity
shipwright  threnodist  inheritrix  appositely  causticity  continuity
shirtfront  throatwort  mesothorax  approvably  cautionary  contrarily
shirtwaist  throughout  metathorax  aquilinity  cautiously  contritely
shortcrust  throughput  packingbox  arboreally  cavalierly  conversely
sideeffect  thumbprint  pouncetbox  armorially  cellularly  copartnery
siderostat  topgallant  protectrix  arrogantly  centrality  coralberry
sidestreet  topologist  quadruplex  arterially  centricity  cordiality
sinecurist  torchlight  sealingwax  artycrafty  cerography  corporally
singlefoot  tournament  squeezebox  ascendancy  cessionary  corporeity
sinologist  tourniquet  thunderbox  ascendency  chalcedony  corpulency
slitpocket  transcript  trousseaux  asexuality  changeably  corrivalry
smokeplant  transplant  unorthodox  asynchrony  chaplaincy  cosmically
snafflebit  trecentist  weatherbox  atomically  charactery  coulometry
sneezewort  trichromat  witnessbox  atypically  charitably  covalently
solacement  tricyclist  aberrantly  audibility  charmingly  covetingly
solicitant  triumphant  abnormally  audiometry  chartulary  covetously
solidarist  trombonist  abominably  autecology  cheapishly  coweringly
somersault  Trotskyist  abortively  autography  cheerfully  cowparsley
Sorbonnist  turgescent  abrasively  autoplasty  chemically  craniology
soubriquet  typescript  absolutely  autumnally  childishly  creatively
spacecraft  typologist  absolutory  aversively  chiromancy  creativity
Spartacist  unbesought  absorbedly  backwardly  chokeberry  creaturely
specialist  undercroft  absorbency  bafflingly  chronicity  creditably
speedlimit  undershirt  abstinency  balneology  chronology  criminally
spiderwort  undershoot  abstractly  bankruptcy  churlishly  critically
spinescent  underskirt  abstrusely  baptistery  circularly  cryptogamy
spleenwort  unicyclist  abstrusity  bardolatry  clannishly  cryptology
spoilsport  unpleasant  abundantly  bathymetry  clearstory  culturally
spoondrift  Vaticanist  acatalepsy  becomingly  clerestory  cumbrously
springhalt  vestpocket  acceptably  benignancy  clerically  curability
spumescent  vicegerent  acceptedly  bestiality  clinically  cyclically
stagecraft  viceregent  accessibly  bewitchery  clinometry  cystoscopy
standpoint  vignettist  accurately  biannually  closetplay  damagingly
statecraft  virologist  accursedly  biblically  cloudberry  dapplegrey
steamchest  vitrescent  accusatory  bibliology  clownishly  daughterly
steamtight  vociferant  accusingly  bibliopegy  cocksurely  dazzlingly
stepparent  voiceprint  acidimetry  bibliopoly  coequality  debauchery
stigmatist  wagonvault  acromegaly  bibulously  coercively  debonairly
stitchwort  wainwright  actionably  biennially  coeternity  decadently
stonefruit  wanderlust  adaptively  bigamously  cognisably  decisively
strategist  watercraft  adenectomy  binaurally  coherently  declassify
stratocrat  waterfront  adequately  bioecology  cohesively  decorously
stridulant  waterspout  adherently  bipolarity  colonially  dedicatory
stringhalt  watertight  adhesively  bisexually  colossally  defamatory
submediant  whereabout  adjacently  blackberry  colourably  defensibly
subsequent  wildebeest  adjuratory  blamefully  comicality  deficiency
subsistent  wilderment  admiringly  bleatingly  commandery  definitely
sufficient  windowseat  admittedly  blindingly  commentary  degeneracy
suffragist  witchcraft  admonitory  blissfully  commissary  degradedly
supergiant  wonderment  adoptively  blockishly  commonalty  dehumidify
supplement  workbasket  advertency  bloodmoney  communally  dejectedly
supplicant  Wykehamist  advocatory  blurringly  comparably  delectably
surfactant  fricandeau  aeolotropy  blushingly  compatibly  delicately
surrealist  malentendu  aerography  boastfully  competency  deltiology
sweatshirt  compasssaw  affability  bootlessly  completely  delusively
sweetheart  foreshadow  affectedly  bouncingly  complexity  dementedly
```

```
demography  emblazonry  flatulency  heliotropy  impudently  invitatory
demonology  embroidery  flawlessly  helplessly  impudicity  invitingly
dendrology  embryogeny  fleeringly  heortology  inaccuracy  invocatory
deontology  embryology  fleetingly  hepatology  inactively  ironically
dependably  emendatory  flexuously  hereditary  inactivity  itinerancy
dependency  emigratory  flippantly  heroically  inadequacy  jackassery
depilatory  emissivity  floatingly  hesitantly  incapacity  jocularity
deplorably  endemicity  fluxionary  heterodoxy  incendiary  jubilantly
depositary  enduringly  folkmemory  heterogamy  incessancy  judicatory
depository  engagingly  forcefully  heterogeny  inchoately  judicially
depravedly  enormously  forgivably  heterogony  incipiency  justiciary
deridingly  enterotomy  formidably  heterology  incisively  juvenility
derisively  enticingly  formlessly  heteronomy  incivility  laboratory
derogatory  entomology  fragrantly  heterotaxy  inclemency  lamentably
deservedly  enzymology  fraternity  hierocracy  incredibly  lamentedly
designedly  epeirogeny  freakishly  hierolatry  incubatory  lampoonery
desirously  ephorality  frenziedly  hippophagy  incumbency  landocracy
desolately  episcopacy  frequently  hoitytoity  indecently  lanternfly
despicably  epistolary  friability  hokeypokey  indelicacy  laparotomy
detachedly  equability  friendlily  holography  indicatory  lardydardy
detergency  equanimity  fritillary  homeopathy  indirectly  laterality
detestably  erectility  frowningly  honourably  indocility  laughingly
devilishly  ergodicity  fruitfully  hootenanny  indolently  lectionary
dextrality  erotically  fuddyduddy  hopelessly  inefficacy  legibility
dextrously  eruptively  fugitively  hormonally  ineligibly  legitimacy
diagonally  escapology  fumblingly  hospitably  inequality  lexicology
dictionary  especially  funereally  humbuggery  inevitably  lexigraphy
difficulty  ethereally  fusibility  humorously  inexorably  liberality
digitately  ethicality  futurology  hurdygurdy  inexpertly  lifelessly
dilatorily  ethnically  fuzzywuzzy  hurlyburly  inexpiably  lipography
diligently  eudiometry  gastrology  hydrically  infallibly  listlessly
dillydally  eventually  gastronomy  hydromancy  infamously  literality
disability  excellency  generality  hydrometry  infelicity  literarily
discreetly  excitatory  generosity  hydropathy  inferiorly  lithotrity
discretely  excitingly  generously  hydrophily  infernally  locomotory
diseconomy  excusatory  germinally  hygrometry  infidelity  loganberry
disharmony  execratory  ghastfully  hypsometry  infinitely  logicality
dishonesty  exhibitory  glaciology  iconolatry  inflexibly  logography
disloyally  exobiology  gladsomely  iconomachy  informally  lonesomely
disloyalty  exotically  glancingly  iconometry  inherently  lopsidedly
disorderly  expectancy  globularly  ideography  inhibitory  lovelessly
dispensary  expectedly  gloriously  ignobility  inhumanely  luculently
disputably  expediency  glossology  ignorantly  inhumanity  lukewarmly
disqualify  expiratory  glottology  illatively  inimically  luminosity
disquietly  explicitly  goniometry  illaudably  inimitably  luminously
dissatisfy  expository  goodygoody  illegality  initiatory  lusciously
dissonancy  expressway  gooseberry  illiteracy  innerrably  lustrously
distillery  extendedly  gorgeously  illusively  innocently  magistracy
distinctly  exteriorly  gothically  illusorily  innovatory  malacology
disutility  externally  governessy  imaginably  innumeracy  malapertly
divergency  extraneity  gracefully  imbecilely  insanitary  malignancy
divinatory  exultantly  graciosity  imbecility  insatiably  manageably
divisively  exultingly  graciously  immaculacy  insecurely  maniacally
dolorously  fabulously  granddaddy  immaturely  insecurity  manifestly
dominantly  factiously  granularly  immaturity  insensibly  manifoldly
doubtfully  factuality  graphology  imminently  insipidity  marginally
doubtingly  fadelessly  graspingly  immiscibly  insistency  Mariolatry
downwardly  faithfully  gratefully  immobility  insobriety  mastectomy
doxography  familiarly  gravimetry  immoderacy  insolently  materially
dramaturgy  fancifully  grievously  immodestly  insolvency  maternally
drawlingly  farcically  grindingly  immorality  insularity  matriarchy
dreadfully  favourably  growlingly  immortally  insurgency  measurably
droopingly  fearlessly  grudgingly  immunology  intangibly  measuredly
drudgingly  fearsomely  gruesomely  impalpably  integrally  medievally
drysaltery  fecklessly  guilefully  impassably  interiorly  mediocrity
durability  feminality  gutturally  impassibly  intermarry  melancholy
dwarfishly  femininely  gymnosophy  impeccably  internally  menacingly
ebulliency  femininity  habitually  impeccancy  intimately  mendicancy
effeminacy  festoonery  hagiolatry  impendency  intrepidly  mercifully
efficacity  fetchingly  halfvolley  imperially  introrsely  mesomorphy
efficiency  feverishly  halfyearly  implacably  inundatory  metagalaxy
effrontery  fibrillary  handsomely  implicitly  inurbanity  metallurgy
effusively  fiducially  hankypanky  impolitely  invalidity  metrically
Egyptology  fiendishly  harmlessly  imposingly  invaluably  micrometry
elasticity  fiftyfifty  hauntingly  impossibly  invariably  microscopy
elderberry  finicality  hectically  impotently  inveracity  middlingly
electively  firepolicy  heedlessly  improbably  inveteracy  militantly
elementary  flaccidity  heliacally  improperly  invincibly  militarily
eloquently  flagrantly  heliolatry  improvably  inviolably  mindlessly
```

```
mineralogy ordinarily pleasantly radiometry scoffingly speleology
minstrelsy oreography pleasantry radioscopy scornfully sphericity
mirthfully orientally pleasingly ramblingly scratchily spiritedly
miscellany originally pliability ratability screenplay spirometry
missionary orotundity ploddingly rationally scurrility spitefully
mistakenly orthodoxly plutocracy ravenously seasonably splendidly
mitigatory osculatory plutolatry reactively seasonally spodomancy
moderately ostensibly poetically reactivity secludedly spoliatory
monetarily osteopathy pogonology reasonably secularity spongology
morphogeny outrightly pogonotomy reassembly sedulously sportfully
morphology ovariotomy polygraphy recipiency segmentary sportingly
mosaically overnicety polyploidy recklessly seismicity sportively
mournfully oversupply popularity recreantly seismology spotlessly
movability paederasty populously recumbency selenology spuriously
movelessly painlessly pornocracy redemptory selflessly squalidity
muliebrity palliatory positively redolently selfparody squirarchy
multiloquy PalmSunday positivity redundancy semeiology stagnantly
muscularly palynology possessory refractory semiweekly stalwartly
musicality papyrology postliminy regeneracy semiyearly statically
musicianly pardonably potability regionally sensuality stationary
musicology parentally potamology regularity sensuously stationery
mutability partiality powerfully regulatory sentiently statutably
mutinously passageway prancingly relatively separately stealthily
myopically passionary prebendary relativity separatory stereotypy
mystically pastorally precedency relevantly septically stiflingly
mythically paternally preceptory reluctancy sergeantcy stingingly
nambypamby patriality preciosity remarkably serigraphy stinkingly
namelessly patriarchy preciously remedially serjeantcy stopvolley
narcolepsy patulously precursory repeatedly sexagenary strabotomy
nationally peacefully preferably repellancy shamefully straightly
nauseously peacockery pregnantly repellency sheepishly strainedly
nautically peculiarly prehistory reportedly shockingly strathspey
nebulosity peerlessly preparedly repository shrewishly strawberry
nebulously pellucidly prepensely repugnancy shrievalty stridently
necrolatry penetrably prepotency rescissory sillybilly strikingly
necromancy penitently presbytery reservedly similarity stringency
necrophily pensionary presentday resignedly simplicity stubbornly
necroscopy perdurably presidency resiliency simulatory studiously
needlessly peremptory presidiary resolutely singularly stunningly
negatively perilously presignify resolvedly sinisterly stypticity
negativity permanency pressingly resonantly skiagraphy subacidity
negligibly pernickety presumably responsory skittishly subdeanery
nephrology perpetuity prevenancy restlessly slantingly subjectify
neuropathy perplexity previously reticently slatternly subshrubby
neutrality personally pridefully retiringly slavocracy subsidiary
newsagency personalty priggishly retrorsely slipperily subtenancy
newsworthy pertinency primevally revelatory slothfully succinctly
nominately perversely proclivity reverently sluggardly succulency
nomography perversity prodigally revocatory sluggishly sufferably
nosography petulantly profitably rhinoscopy sluttishly sugardaddy
notability phantastry profligacy rightfully smartmoney suicidally
notarially pheasantry profoundly rigorously snappishly superiorly
noteworthy phillumeny profundity risibility sneakingly supernally
noticeably philosophy promissory roadworthy sneeringly suppletory
notionally phlebotomy promontory rockabilly snobbishly supposably
numerology phonically propensity rowanberry snobocracy supposedly
numerosity photometry prosperity rubrically snubbingly surgically
numerously photonasty protectory ruminantly societally suspensory
nuptiality photophily proximally rustically sociometry suzerainty
nyctinasty phrenology pruriently ruthlessly solidarity sweepingly
obdurately phylactery psephology saccharify solitarily swimmingly
obediently phyllotaxy psychiatry sagittally solubility swingingly
obligatory physically psychology salability somatology sycophancy
obligingly physiology puffpastry salutarily somniloquy synecology
observably phytophagy puissantly salutatory somnolency synonymity
oceanology piccaninny punctually sanctimony sonorously tachometry
ochlocracy pickaninny punitively sanguinary soothingly tachymetry
odontology piercingly pupilarity sanguinely soullessly taciturnly
officially pigmentary purblindly sanguinity soundingly tactically
oleography pinchpenny purulently sanitarily southernly tactlessly
oligopsony pinebeauty putatively sarcophagy spaciously tamability
oneirology pistillary pyretology satanology spankingly taperingly
onesidedly pitilessly pyrography scabrously spasticity tastefully
ophiolatry plangently pyrotechny scathingly spatiality tauntingly
oppositely planimetry qualmishly scavengery speciality tauromachy
oppugnancy plasmogamy quarterday scenically speciology tautophony
optatively plasticity quaternary schizogony speciosity taxability
optionally playbyplay quaternity sciagraphy speciously tearlessly
oracularly pleadingly quiescency sclerotomy spectrally teatrolley
```

technology	tolerantly	tropically	unfilially	vertically	willynilly
teenyweeny	tomfoolery	truculency	unfriendly	vesicatory	willywilly
teetotally	tomography	truncately	unguentary	veterinary	wishywashy
telegraphy	tonelessly	trustfully	uniaxially	viewlessly	witchingly
temperedly	topicality	trustingly	uniformity	vigilantly	womanishly
temporally	topography	truthfully	university	vigorously	wondrously
temporalty	topsyturvy	tuberosity	univocally	viperously	wordlessly
temptingly	toroidally	tuitionary	unlawfully	virginally	worldweary
tenability	tortiously	tumultuary	unmannerly	virtuality	wrathfully
teratogeny	tortuosity	tunelessly	unmorality	virtuosity	wretchedly
teratology	tortuously	turbulency	unsociably	virtuously	wrongfully
termagancy	touchingly	tutorially	unsocially	virulently	wrongously
terminably	toweringly	typicality	unsteadily	viscerally	xerography
terminally	toxicology	typography	untowardly	viscountcy	xylography
texturally	tragically	ulteriorly	unwieldily	visibility	yearningly
thankfully	trajectory	ultimately	unwontedly	visionally	yieldingly
thievishly	tranquilly	unbearably	unworthily	viviparity	youngberry
thinkingly	transiency	unbeatably	upholstery	vocabulary	youthfully
thirdparty	transitory	unbrokenly	uranometry	volatility	zygomorphy
thixotropy	trenchancy	unchastity	urbanology	volubility	hakenkreuz
thoroughly	trichology	uncommonly	usuriously	voluptuary	razzmatazz
threepenny	trichotomy	unctuosity	uxoriously	vortically	
throughway	trickishly	unctuously	valorously	vulnerably	
ticklishly	trierarchy	undeniably	vaporously	wastefully	
timbrology	triflingly	underbelly	varicosity	watchfully	
timelessly	trigonally	understudy	varietally	waveringly	
timorously	trimonthly	undulatory	vascularly	wearifully	
tirelessly	triplicity	unendingly	vehemently	westwardly	
tiresomely	triviality	unerringly	vengefully	WhitMonday	
toilsomely	trophology	unfadingly	venomously	WhitSunday	

11 letter words

abandonment	accipitrine	adjectively	affectivity	alexandrine	amicability
Abbevillian	acclamation	adjournment	afficionado	alexandrite	amontillado
abbreviator	acclamatory	adjudgement	affiliation	algological	amorousness
abdominally	acclimation	adjudicator	affirmation	algorithmic	amorphously
abecedarian	acclimatise	adminicular	affirmative	alkalescent	amphetamine
abhorrently	acclivitous	admiralship	affirmatory	alkalimeter	amphibolite
abiogeneses	accommodate	adolescence	affranchise	alkalimetry	amphibology
abiogenesis	accompanist	adoptianism	affrication	allAmerican	amphictyony
abiogenetic	accordantly	adoptianist	affricative	allantoides	amphimictic
abiological	accordingly	adoptionism	AfroAsiatic	allegorical	amphisbaena
abiotically	accoucheuse	adoptionist	afterburner	allelomorph	amplexicaul
ablutionary	accountable	adulterator	aftereffect	alleviation	anachronism
abnormality	accountably	adumbration	agglomerate	alleviative	anachronous
abolishable	accountancy	adumbrative	agglutinate	alleviatory	anacoluthon
abolishment	accrescence	advancement	aggravation	allocatable	anacreontic
abomination	acculturate	adventuress	aggregately	allomorphic	anadiplosis
abortionist	accumulator	adventurism	aggregation	allopathist	anaesthesia
aboutsledge	accusatival	adventurist	aggregative	alphabetise	anaesthetic
aboveground	acetylation	adventurous	aggrievedly	altercation	anagnorisis
abracadabra	achievement	adverbially	agnatically	alternately	anagogously
abranchiate	achondritic	adversative	agnosticism	alternation	analogously
abridgement	achromatise	adverseness	agonisingly	alternative	anaphylaxis
absenteeism	achromatism	advertently	agonistical	altitudinal	anarchistic
absorbingly	acidifiable	advertising	agoraphobia	altocumulus	anastomoses
absorptance	acidophilic	advisedness	agoraphobic	altorilievo	anastomosis
abstentious	acidulation	Aeneolithic	agrarianism	altostratus	anastomotic
abstinently	acinaciform	aeolotropic	agriculture	amaranthine	ancientness
abstraction	acknowledge	aerobically	agrobiology	amativeness	androgynous
abstractive	acoustician	aerobiology	agrological	amazonstone	anecdotical
abstriction	acquiescent	aerodynamic	agronomical	ameliorator	anemometric
abusiveness	acquirement	aerographer	ahistorical	amenability	anencephaly
academicals	acquisition	aerological	aiguillette	amenorrhoea	anfractuous
academician	acquisitive	aeronautics	ailurophile	amentaceous	angelically
academicism	acquittance	aeronomical	ailurophobe	Americanism	angiography
acarpellous	acriflavine	aerostatics	aimlessness	Americanist	Anglicanism
acatalectic	acrimonious	aerostation	aircraftman	amethystine	AngloFrench
acaulescent	acropetally	aesthetical	airlessness	amiableness	AngloIndian
accelerando	actinometer	aestivation	airsickness	amenability	anglomaniac
accelerator	actinomyces	affectation	alabastrine	amentaceous	AngloNorman
accentually	actinomycin	affectingly	Albigensian	Americanism	anglophobia
acceptation	acumination	affectional	albuminuria	Americanist	anglophobic
acceptingly	acupuncture	affectioned	alcyonarian	amethystine	animalcular
accessorial	adenomatous	affectively	alembicated	amiableness	anisotropic
accessorise	adiaphorism		Alexandrian		annabergite
					annihilator

anniversary	arbitrageur	audibleness	bellringing	blasphemous	Britishness
annunciator	arbitrament	audiologist	Belorussian	blastogenic	brittleness
anomalistic	arbitrarily	audiometric	Benedictine	blepharitis	broadcaster
anomalously	arbitration	audiovisual	benediction	blessedness	broadleaved
anonymously	arbitrative	augmentable	benedictory	blockbuster	broadminded
antecedence	arbitratrix	Augustinian	benefaction	bloodguilty	brotherhood
antechamber	arboraceous	auricularly	beneficence	bloodlessly	brucellosis
antemundane	arborescent	Aurignacian	beneficiary	bloodstream	brusqueness
antenuptial	archaeology	austereness	beneficiate	bloodsucker	brutishness
antependium	archaeornis	autarchical	benevolence	bloodvessel	bryozoology
anteriority	archaically	autochthony	benightedly	blotchiness	bucolically
antheridium	archangelic	autoerotism	benightment	blunderbuss	buffalorobe
anthocyanin	archdiocese	autographic	benignantly	boardschool	bullbaiting
anthologise	archduchess	automatable	bereavement	Bodhisattva	bulletproof
anthologist	archdukedom	autoplastic	bergamasque	bodybuilder	bullfighter
anthracitic	Archimedean	autotrophic	bergschrund	bodyservant	bullishness
anthropical	archipelago	auxanometer	bersaglieri	bohemianism	bullterrier
anticathode	arduousness	avoirdupois	bestselling	boilermaker	bumblepuppy
anticipator	arenicolous	awesomeness	betweenmaid	bombardment	bumptiously
anticyclone	Areopagitic	awestricken	betweenness	bombilation	bureaucracy
antifouling	arglebargle	awkwardness	betweentime	bombination	burglarious
antigravity	argumentive	axiological	bewhiskered	Bonapartean	burgomaster
antiJacobin	aristocracy	azotobacter	bewitchment	Bonapartism	bushmanship
antimonious	Arminianism	babysitting	bibliolater	Bonapartist	bushwhacker
antineutron	armtwisting	bacchanalia	bibliolatry	bonbonniere	businessman
antioxidant	aromaticity	bacciferous	bibliomancy	bondservant	butcherbird
antiphonary	arraignment	bacilliform	bibliomania	bondservice	butterflies
antiphrasis	arrangement	backbencher	bibliopegic	bondwashing	butteriness
antipyretic	arrestingly	backcountry	bibliophile	bookbinding	butyraceous
antiquarian	arterialise	bactericide	bibliophily	bookinghall	byeelection
antiquation	arthrospore	balefulness	bibliopolic	bookishness	Byronically
antirrhinum	articulable	ballbearing	bibliotheca	bookkeeping	Byzantinism
antiSemitic	articulated	balletomane	bicarbonate	booklearned	Byzantinist
antistrophe	articulator	balmcricket	bicentenary	bookselling	cabbagepalm
antitypical	artillerist	BaltoSlavic	bicephalous	bookshelves	cabbagerose
antivitamin	artiodactyl	bandylegged	bicorporate	boorishness	cabbagetree
antonomasia	artlessness	banteringly	bicuspidate	bootlegging	cabbageworm
anxiousness	ascensional	baptismally	biddability	borborygmus	cabbalistic
apartmental	ascetically	barbarously	biedermeier	botanically	cacographic
aphrodisiac	ascomycetes	barbastelle	bifurcation	botheration	cacophonous
apocalyptic	aseptically	barbiturate	bilaterally	bottleglass	caddishness
Apollinaris	aspergillum	barefacedly	biliousness	bottlegreen	calceolaria
apologetics	aspergillus	barleybroth	billetsdoux	bottlenosed	calcicolous
apomorphine	aspersorium	barnstormer	billionaire	bounteously	calciferous
aponeuroses	asphyxiator	barquentine	billposting	bountifully	calcifugous
aponeurosis	assafoetida	barrelhouse	billsticker	bourgeoisie	calcination
aponeurotic	assassinate	barrelorgan	bimetallism	boutonniere	calculating
apophyllite	assemblyman	bashfulness	bimetallist	bowdleriser	calculation
aposiopesis	assentation	bashibazouk	bimillenary	boysenberry	calculative
apostleship	assertively	basipetally	bimillenium	brachiation	calefacient
apostolical	assessorial	basketchair	binocularly	brachyurous	calefactory
apostrophic	assiduously	bassethound	biochemical	bracteolate	calendrical
apotheosise	assignation	bathingsuit	biocoenoses	bradycardia	calibration
appallingly	assimilable	batholithic	biocoenosis	braggadocio	californium
apparatchik	assimilator	bathymetric	biocoenotic	Brahmanical	calisthenic
apparelling	association	bathyscaphe	biofeedback	brahmaputra	calligraphy
appealingly	associative	bathysphere	biometrical	Brahminical	callousness
appeasement	assortative	battledress	biophysical	brainlessly	calorimeter
appellation	assuagement	battlefield	bipartition	brainsickly	calorimetry
appellative	assuredness	beachcomber	biquadratic	brainteaser	calumniator
applaudable	Assyriology	bearbaiting	birdbrained	branchiopod	Calvinistic
application	astigmatism	bearishness	birdfancier	brankursine	calyptrogen
applicative	astringency	beastliness	birdwatcher	brazenfaced	camaraderie
applicatory	atheistical	beauteously	bisexuality	breadbasket	campanology
appogiatura	athleticism	beautifully	bitterapple	breadcrumbs	campanulate
appointment	atmospheric	beaverboard	bittercress	breadthways	campmeeting
appreciable	atomisation	bedevilment	bittersweet	breadthwise	canalicular
appreciably	atrabilious	bedizenment	bivouacking	breadwinner	canaliculus
appreciator	atrociously	beechmarten	blackavised	breastplate	cancellated
approbation	attemptable	befittingly	blackbeetle	breastwheel	candelabrum
approbatory	attentively	beguilement	blackbirder	breathalyse	candescence
appropriate	attenuation	beguilingly	blackcoated	breechblock	candidature
approvingly	attestation	behavioural	blackfellow	breezeblock	candleberry
approximate	attitudinal	belatedness	blackgrouse	bricklaying	candlelight
appurtenant	attractable	bellbottoms	blackmailer	bridgeboard	candlepower
aquaculture	attribution	bellfounder	blackmarket	brilliantly	candlestick
aquarellist	attributive	bellheather	bladderwort	bristletail	cannibalise
aquatically	attritional	bellicosity	blamelessly	bristleworm	cannibalism
aquiculture	audaciously	belligerent	blameworthy	bristliness	canonically

cantharides	ceroplastic	chrysarobin	cognoscible	complacence	confutative
cantharidic	certifiable	chrysoberyl	coincidence	complacency	congealable
capableness	certifiably	chrysoprase	coinheritor	complainant	congealment
capaciously	certificate	chucklehead	coinsurance	complaisant	congelation
capacitance	cesarevitch	churchgoing	coldblooded	complexness	congenerous
capillarity	cesarewitch	churchiness	coldhearted	compliantly	congenially
captainship	chaetognath	churchwoman	coleorrhiza	complicated	congressman
captionless	chafingdish	cicatricial	collaborate	complotting	congruently
captivation	chainarmour	cinnabarine	collapsible	comportment	congruously
carabiniere	chainletter	cinquecento	collectable	compositely	conjectural
carabinieri	chainsmoker	circularise	collectanea	composition	conjugality
caravanning	chainstitch	circularity	collectedly	compossible	conjugation
caravansary	chalcedonic	circulation	collectible	compotation	conjugative
carbocyclic	challenging	circulative	collenchyma	compotatory	conjunction
carbonation	chamaephyte	circulatory	colligation	compotatory	conjunctiva
carbuncular	chamberlain	circumlunar	colligative	compression	conjunctive
carburetion	chambermaid	circumpolar	collimation	compressive	conjuncture
carburetted	chameleonic	circumsolar	collinearly	comprisable	conjuration
carburetter	champertous	circumspect	collisional	comptroller	connectable
carburettor	chancellery	circumvolve	collocation	compunction	connectedly
carcinomata	chancellory	cisatlantic	collusively	compurgator	connectible
cardinalate	changefully	citizenship	colonelship	computation	connoisseur
cardiograph	channelling	cityslicker	colonialism	computerise	connotation
cardsharper	chansonnier	civilianise	colonialist	comradeship	connotative
carefulness	chanterelle	civilisable	colorimeter	comstockery	connubially
caressingly	chanticleer	clairschach	colorimetry	concatenate	conquerable
caricatural	chaotically	clairvoyant	colouration	concealable	consanguine
carminative	chaperonage	clamorously	colourblind	concealment	consciously
carnivorous	charcuterie	clandestine	colourfully	conceitedly	consecrator
Carolingian	chargesheet	clapperclaw	columbarium	conceivable	consecution
carpetsnake	charismatic	Clarencieux	columniated	conceivably	consecutive
carrageenan	charlatanry	classically	combatively	concentrate	consentient
carrageenin	chartaceous	cleanlimbed	combination	conceptacle	consequence
carriageway	chaulmoogra	cleanliness	combinative	concernment	conservable
cartography	cheerleader	cleanshaven	combinatory	concertedly	conservancy
carunculate	cheerlessly	clearheaded	combustible	concertgoer	conservator
carvelbuilt	cheesecloth	cleistogamy	comestibles	conciliator	considerate
caryopsides	cheiromancy	clericalism	comeuppance	conciseness	considering
cassiterite	chemotactic	clericalist	comfortable	concomitant	consignable
castellated	chevalglass	cliffhanger	comfortably	concordance	consignment
castigation	chiaroscuro	climacteric	comfortless	concrescent	consistence
casuistical	chickenfeed	climatology	commandment	concubinage	consistency
catachreses	chickenwire	clinometric	commemorate	concubinary	consolation
catachresis	chieftaincy	clodhopping	commendable	concubitant	consolatory
cataclysmic	childminder	closefisted	commendably	concurrence	consolidate
catadromous	chimaerical	closehauled	commendator	condemnable	consolingly
cataplectic	chinoiserie	clostridium	commensally	condensable	consonantal
catastrophe	Chippendale	clothesline	commentator	conditional	consonantly
catchphrase	chirography	clothesmoth	commination	conditioner	conspecific
catechismal	chiropodist	clothesprop	comminatory	condolatory	conspicuity
catechistic	chiropteran	cloudcastle	comminution	condominium	conspicuous
categorical	chitterling	coadunation	commiserate	condonation	conspirator
catercousin	chlorophyll	coagulation	commissural	condottiere	constellate
caterpillar	chloroplast	coalescence	committable	condottieri	consternate
catheterise	chloroprene	coarctation	commonality	conductance	constituent
catholicise	chockablock	cobblestone	commonplace	conductible	constitutor
Catholicism	choirmaster	coccidiosis	commonsense	conductress	constrictor
catholicity	chokecherry	cochinchina	communalise	condylomata	construable
catswhisker	cholesterol	cockaleekie	communalism	confabulate	constructor
cauliflower	choreograph	cockleshell	communalist	confederacy	consultancy
causatively	chorography	cockyleekie	communicant	confederate	consumerism
caustically	Christendom	coconscious	communicate	conferrable	consumingly
cavalierism	christening	codefendant	communistic	confessedly	consummator
cavedweller	christiania	codicillary	commutation	confidently	consumption
cavernously	Christianly	coeducation	commutative	confidingly	consumptive
ceaselessly	Christmassy	coefficient	compactness	confinement	containable
celebration	Christology	coessential	compaginate	confirmable	containment
celebratory	chrominance	coeternally	comparatist	confiscable	contaminant
celestially	chromoplast	coexistence	comparative	confiscator	contaminate
cellularity	chromosomal	coextension	compartment	conflagrant	contemplate
cementation	chronically	coextensive	compassable	conflagrate	contentedly
centenarian	chronograph	coffeehouse	compellable	confliction	contentious
centigramme	chronologer	coffeetable	compendious	conflictive	contentment
centreboard	chronologic	cognateness	compensator	conformable	conterminal
centrepiece	chronometer	cognitional	competently	conformably	contestable
centrifugal	chronometry	cognitively	competition	conformally	continental
centripetal	chronoscope	cognitivity	competitive	conformance	continently
cerebration	chrysalides	cognoscente	compilation	confusingly	contingence
ceremonious	chrysalises	cognoscenti	compilement	confutation	contingency

Column 1: continuable continually continuance continuator contorniate contrabasso contractile contraction contractive contractual contracture contradance contraption contrariety contrarious contrastive contretemps contributor contrivable contrivance controlling controlment controversy conurbation convenances convenience conveniency conventicle convergence convergency conversable conversance conversancy convertible convertibly conveyancer convincible convivially convocation convolution convolvulus cookgeneral cooperation cooperative coordinator coparcenary copingstone copiousness coplanarity copperplate coppersmith coralloidal corbiculate corbiesteps cordialness corecipient cornerstone cornhusking corniferous cornucopian coronagraph coronograph corporality corporately corporation corporatism corporative corporeally corpulently corpuscular correctable correctness correlation correlative corrigendum corroborant corroborate corrosively corrugation

Column 2: corruptible corruptibly corruptness coruscation cosignatory cosmetician cosmetology cosmogonist cosmography cosmologist cosmopolite costbenefit costiveness cotemporary coterminous cotoneaster cottongrass cottonmouth coulometric counselling countenance counterblow counterbond counterfeit counterfoil counterfort countermand countermark countermine countermove countermure counterpane counterpart counterplan counterplea counterplot countersign countersink countersunk counterturn countervail counterview counterwork countlessly countrified countryfied countryseat countryside countrywide courteously courtliness coxcombical crabbedness crackerjack craftswoman craniometry creationism creationist credentials credibility credulously crematorium crenellated crenulation crepitation crepuscular crestfallen criminalist criminality crimination criminative criminatory criminology criticality criticaster crocidolite crocodilian crookbacked crookedness

Column 3: crossbearer crossbowman crossgarnet crosslegged crossstitch crotcheteer cruciferous crucifixion crucigerous crunchiness crustaceous cryobiology cryosurgery cryotherapy cryptically cryptogamic cryptograph cryptomeria crystalline crystallise crystallite crystalloid ctenophoran culmination culpability cultivation cunningness cupellation cupriferous cupronickel curableness curatorship curiousness currentness currishness cursiveness cursoriness curtailment curvilineal curvilinear customarily custombuilt customhouse cybernation cybernetics cyclopaedia cyclopaedic cycloserine cyclothymia cyclothymic cylindrical cypripedium cysticercus cytogenesis cytokinesis cytological dactylogram dactylology daisycutter dangerously dauntlessly deactivator deathrattle debarkation debauchment debouchment decantation decarbonate decarbonise decarburise deceitfully deceivingly decelerator decemvirate decennially deceptively decerebrate declamation declamatory

Column 4: declaration declarative declaratory declination declivitous decollation decolletage decolourise decorticate decrepitate decrepitude decrescendo decussately decussation dedicatedly deductively deemphasise deerstalker defalcation defectively defenceless defensively deferential defibrinate deficiently definiendum deflagrator defloration defoliation deforcement deformation defraudment deglutition degradation degradingly dehydration deification deistically delectation deleterious deliciously delightedly delightsome delineation delinquency deliriously delitescent deliverable deliverance deliveryman demagnetise demagogical demagoguery demagoguism demandingly demarcation demarkation demigoddess democratise democratism demographer demographic demonolatry demonstrate demountable dendritical denigration denigratory denizenship denominator denticulate dentigerous denumerable denunciator deoxidation deoxygenate deoxyribose depauperate

Column 5: depauperise dependently deploringly depopulator deportation depravation depravement deprecation deprecative deprecatory depreciator depredation depredatory depressible deprivation depthcharge derangement dereliction dermatology desalinator descendable descendible describable description descriptive desecration desegregate desensitise deservingly desexualise desiccation desiccative desideratum designation desperadoes desperately desperation despoilment despondence despondency destination destitution destruction destructive desultorily deteriorate determinacy determinant determinate determinism determinist detestation detrainment detribalise detrimental deuteration deuterogamy Deuteronomy devaluation devastation developable development deviousness devotedness dexiotropic dexterously diachronism diacritical diadelphous diagnostics dialectally dialectical dialogistic diamagnetic diametrical diamondback diaphaneity diaphoresis diaphoretic

Column 6: diapophysis diapositive diarthrosis diastematic diastrophic diatessaron dicephalous dichogamous dichotomise dichotomist dichotomous dichromatic dicotyledon dictatorial didacticism differentia differently difficultly diffidently diffraction diffuseness diffusively digestively digitigrade dilapidated dilapidator diluvialist dimensional dimwittedly diningtable dinnerdance dinnertable dinnerwagon dinosaurian Diophantine diphtherial diphtheroid diphthongal diphycercal diplococcus diplomatise diplomatist dipsomaniac dipterocarp directional directivity directorate directorial directrices disablement disaccustom disaffected disafforest disannulled disapproval disarmament disarmingly disassemble disassembly disbandment disbeliever discalceate discardable discernible discernibly discernment discerption disciplinal discipliner discography discontinue discordance discordancy discotheque discourtesy discrepancy discussable discussible disencumber

disentangle	doctrinally	edification	enchainment	equidistant	excursively
disenthrall	documentary	edificatory	enchantment	equilateral	exdirectory
disfunction	dodecaphony	editorially	enchantress	equilibrate	executioner
disgraceful	doggishness	educability	enchiridion	equilibrist	executorial
disgruntled	dolefulness	educational	encomiastic	equilibrium	executrices
disguisedly	dollishness	effectively	encrustment	equinoctial	executrixes
disgustedly	doltishness	effectually	encumbrance	equipollent	exemplarily
disharmonic	domesticate	efficacious	encystation	equivalence	exemplarity
dishevelled	domesticity	efficiently	endearingly	equivalency	exercisable
dishonestly	domiciliary	effulgently	endemically	equivocally	exfoliation
dishonourer	domiciliate	egalitarian	endlessness	equivocator	exfoliative
disillusion	domineering	egotistical	endocardiac	eradication	exhaustible
disinclined	donnishness	egregiously	endocardial	eradicative	exhaustless
disinfector	doorknocker	einsteinium	endocardium	Erastianism	exhortation
disinterest	doublecheck	ejaculation	endometrium	ergatocracy	exhortative
disinterred	doublecross	ejaculatory	endomorphic	erotogenous	exhortatory
disjunction	doubleDutch	elaborately	endophagous	erotomaniac	existential
disjunctive	doubleedged	elaboration	endoplasmic	erratically	exogenously
disjuncture	doubleender	elaborative	endorsement	erroneously	exoneration
dislikeable	doubleentry	elastically	endoskelton	erubescence	exonerative
dislocation	doublefaced	elasticated	endothelial	erythrocyte	exorbitance
dislodgment	doublequick	elastomeric	endothelium	eschatology	exoskeletal
dismayingly	doublespeak	elbowgrease	endothermal	escheatable	exoskeleton
disobedient	doublethink	elderliness	endothermic	escheatment	exotericism
disobliging	doubtlessly	electioneer	endotrophic	esemplastic	expansional
disorganise	doughtiness	electrician	enfeoffment	esotericism	expansively
disparaging	douroucouli	electricity	enforceable	Esperantist	expansivity
disparately	downdraught	electrocute	enforcement	essentially	expatiation
dispensable	downhearted	electrolier	enfranchise	establisher	expatiative
dispersedly	downtrodden	electrology	engineering	etherealise	expatiatory
displeasure	doxographer	electrolyse	engorgement	ethereality	expectantly
disportment	draggletail	electrolyte	engrossment	ethnography	expectation
disposition	dramaturgic	electronics	enhancement	ethnologist	expectative
dispositive	drastically	electrotype	enigmatical	ethological	expectorant
disputation	draughtsman	elementally	enjambement	Etruscology	expectorate
disquieting	drawingroom	elephantine	enlargeable	etymologise	expediently
disquietude	dreadnought	elephantoid	enlargement	etymologist	expeditious
disremember	dreamlessly	elicitation	enlightened	eucalyptole	expenditure
disseminate	dresscircle	eligibility	enlivenment	Eucharistic	expensively
disseminule	dressmaking	elimination	enneahedron	euchologion	experienced
dissentient	drillmaster	eliminative	ennoblement	eudaemonism	explainable
dissepiment	dropcurtain	Elizabethan	enquiringly	eudaemonist	explanation
dissertator	dropforging	ellipsoidal	ensanguined	eudiometric	explanatory
dissimilate	drouthiness	ellipticity	enslavement	eugenically	explication
dissimulate	drunkenness	elucidation	entablature	euphemistic	explicative
dissipation	dualcontrol	elucidative	entablement	eurhythmics	explicatory
dissipative	dualpurpose	elucidatory	enterostomy	Europeanise	exploitable
dissociable	dubiousness	elusiveness	enterovirus	eurypteroid	exploration
dissolutely	dumbfounder	elutriation	enterpriser	evagination	explorative
dissolution	dundrearies	emancipator	entertainer	evanescence	exploratory
dissolvable	duniewassal	emasculator	enthralling	evangelical	explosively
dissonantly	duplication	embarkation	enthralment	evanishment	exponential
dissyllable	duplicative	embellisher	entitlement	evaporation	exportation
dissymmetry	duplicitous	emblematise	entomophily	evaporative	expostulate
distasteful	durableness	emblematist	entrainment	evasiveness	expressible
distempered	dutifulness	embowelling	entreatment	eveningstar	expropriate
distensible	dynamically	embowerment	entrustment	eventualise	expurgation
distinction	dynamometer	embraceable	enucleation	eventuality	expurgatory
distinctive	dynamometry	embracement	enumeration	everlasting	exquisitely
distinguish	dysfunction	embracingly	enumerative	evidentiary	exsiccation
distraction	dyslogistic	embrocation	enunciation	evolutional	exstipulate
distractive	earnestness	embroiderer	enunciative	exaggerator	extemporary
distressful	earpiercing	embroilment	envelopment	examination	extemporise
distribuend	earthcloset	embryologic	enviousness	exanthemata	extensional
distributor	earthenware	embryonated	environment	exarcerbate	extensively
distrustful	earthliness	emmenagogue	epeirogenic	exceedingly	extenuation
disturbance	easternmost	Emmenthaler	ephemerides	excellently	extenuatory
disunionist	ebulliently	emotionally	epidiascope	exceptional	exteriorise
dithyrambic	echosounder	emotionless	epigastrium	excessively	exteriority
dittography	eclecticism	empanelling	epigraphist	exclamation	exterminate
divergently	econometric	emperorship	epinephrine	exclamatory	externalise
diverticula	ectoblastic	empirically	epipetalous	exclusively	externalism
divestiture	ectogenesis	emplacement	episcopally	exclusivity	externality
divisionary	ectogenetic	emptyhanded	epithalamia	excoriation	extirpation
divisionism	ectomorphic	emptyheaded	epithalamic	excremental	extirpatory
divorcement	ectoplasmic	emulousness	epithelioma	excrescence	extortioner
divulgation	ectotrophic	emulsionise	epochmaking	excrescency	extractable
divulgement	ecumenicism	enarthrosis	equableness	exculpation	extradition
doctrinaire	ecumenicity	encapsulate	equiangular	exculpatory	extrapolate

extravagant	fimbriation	forgetmenot	furthersome	glassblower	gutlessness
extravagate	financially	forgettable	furtiveness	glasscutter	guttapercha
extravasate	fingerboard	forgiveness	furunculous	glassmaking	guttersnipe
extraverted	fingerglass	forlornness	fusillation	glauconitic	gutturalise
extremeness	fingerplate	formalistic	fustigation	globeflower	gutturalism
extrication	fingerprint	formational	gafftopsail	globigerina	gymnospermy
extroverted	fingerstall	formication	gainfulness	globularity	gynaecocrat
exuberantly	finicalness	formularise	gallantness	glomeration	gynaecology
eyecatching	FinnoUgrian	formulation	gallbladder	glossolalia	gypsiferous
fabrication	firecracker	fornication	galleyslave	glutinously	gyrocompass
facelifting	firefighter	forthcoming	Gallicanism	gnotobiosis	haberdasher
facetiously	fireraising	fortifiable	gallimaufry	gnotobiotic	habiliments
facsimilist	firewalking	fortnightly	Gallophobia	godchildren	habituation
factfinding	firewatcher	fortunately	gallowsbird	goddaughter	haematocele
factionally	firmamental	forwardness	gallowstree	godforsaken	haematocrit
factualness	firstfruits	foulmouthed	gametangium	godlessness	haematology
facultative	fissionable	fourflusher	gametophyte	goldbeating	haemocyanin
faddishness	fissiparity	fourpounder	gamogenesis	golddigging	haemoglobin
fairweather	fissiparous	fourwheeler	gangsterism	goldenberry	haemophilia
faithhealer	flabbergast	fractionary	gardemanger	gonfalonier	haemophilic
faithlessly	flaccidness	fractionate	garnishment	goniometric	haemoptysis
faithworthy	flagcaptain	fractionise	garrulously	goodhearted	haemorrhage
fallibility	flagellator	fractiously	gartersnake	goodlooking	haemorrhoid
Falstaffian	flagofficer	fragmentary	gaseousness	goodnatured	haemostasis
falteringly	flagwagging	Francomania	gasfittings	gormandiser	haemostatic
familiarise	flamboyance	Francophile	gastrectomy	gourmandise	haggadistic
familiarity	flamboyancy	Francophobe	gastronomic	gourmandism	haggardness
fanatically	flamboyante	francophone	gastroscope	gracelessly	Hagiographa
fanfaronade	flannelette	franctireur	gatecrasher	gracileness	hagiography
fantastical	flannelling	frankfurter	geanticline	gradational	hagiologist
farawayness	flatulently	franklinite	gegenschein	gradiometer	hagioscopic
farcicality	flauntingly	frankpledge	gemmiferous	gradualness	hairbreadth
farinaceous	flavourless	frantically	gemmiparous	GraecoRoman	hairdresser
farraginous	flavoursome	franticness	gemmologist	grammalogue	hairraising
farreaching	fleshliness	fraternally	gemmulation	grammatical	hairstyling
farthermost	flexibility	fraterniser	gendarmerie	gramophonic	hairstylist
farthingale	flightiness	fratricidal	genealogise	grandfather	hairtrigger
fasciaboard	flimflammer	fraudulence	genealogist	grandiflora	halfbinding
fasciculate	flirtatious	freebooting	generaliser	grandiosely	halfblooded
fascinating	flocculence	freehearted	generalship	grandiosity	halfhearted
fascination	floorwalker	freemasonry	generically	grandmother	halfholiday
fashionable	florescence	freethinker	genetically	grandnephew	halflanding
fashionably	floriferous	freethought	geniculated	grandparent	halfmeasure
fatefulness	florilegium	freezedried	genitivally	grangeriser	hallucinate
fatiguingly	floweriness	frenchified	genteelness	granivorous	halophilous
fatuousness	fluctuation	Frenchwoman	gentianella	granolithic	halterbreak
faultfinder	fluorescein	fretfulness	gentilitial	granophyric	Hamiltonian
faultlessly	fluorescent	friableness	gentlemanly	granularity	handbreadth
favouritism	fluoroscope	fricandeaux	gentlewoman	granulation	handfasting
fearfulness	fluoroscopy	frightfully	genuflexion	granulocyte	handgrenade
feasibility	folliculate	frigidarium	genuineness	graphically	handicapped
featheredge	fomentation	frivolously	geochemical	graphicness	handicapper
featherhead	foolishness	frontrunner	geomagnetic	grasshopper	handknitted
featherless	footpoundal	frostbitten	geometrical	gratulation	handpainted
featureless	footslogger	frothhopper	geophysical	gratulatory	handselling
fecundation	footsoldier	frowardness	geopolitics	gravedigger	handwriting
feelingness	foppishness	frowstiness	geostrophic	gravelblind	handwritten
feldspathic	foraminated	fructuation	geosyncline	gravimetric	handwrought
feloniously	foraminifer	frugivorous	geotectonic	gravitation	haphazardly
felspathoid	forbearance	fruitlessly	Germanophil	gravitative	haplessness
fenestrated	forbiddance	frustration	germination	greasepaint	haplography
fermentable	foreclosure	fulguration	germinative	greaseproof	harbourless
ferociously	foreignness	fullblooded	gerontology	greatnephew	hardhearted
ferriferous	forequarter	fullfledged	gerrymander	greengrocer	hardhitting
ferruginous	forerunning	fullhearted	gestatorial	greenkeeper	hardmouthed
festinately	foreseeable	fullmouthed	gesticulate	greenockite	hardworking
festschrift	foreshorten	fulminating	gettogether	gristliness	harebrained
fetichistic	foresighted	fulmination	ghastliness	grotesquely	harmfulness
fetishistic	forestaller	fulminatory	ghostliness	grotesquery	harmonistic
feudalistic	forestation	fulsomeness	ghostwriter	grouchiness	harpsichord
fiddlestick	forethinker	funambulate	giantpowder	groundsheet	harumscarum
fidgetiness	forethought	funambulist	gibberellin	groundwater	harvesthome
fieldcornet	foretopmast	functionary	gibbousness	grumblingly	hatefulness
fieldworker	foretopsail	functionate	gigantesque	guardedness	haughtiness
filamentary	forevermore	fundamental	gillyflower	guesstimate	haustellate
filamentous	foreverness	furnishings	gimcrackery	guilelessly	hazardously
filmography	forewarning	furtherance	gingerbread	guiltlessly	headborough
filmsetting	forfeitable	furthermore	girlishness	gullibility	headhunting
filterpaper	forgetfully	furthermost	glaringness	gurgitation	healthfully

healthiness hippopotami hydrobromic ignominious impoliticly incurvation
heartbroken hirsuteness hydrocarbon illaffected importantly incurvature
hearthstone Hispanicise hydrocyanic illbreeding importation indeciduous
heartlessly Hispanicism hydrogenate illdisposed importunate indefinable
heartsblood Hispanicist hydrogenous illfavoured importunely indefinably
heartstring histologist hydrography illhumoured importunity indehiscent
heavenwards historiated hydrologist illiberally impoundment indentation
heavyfooted historicise hydromedusa illimitable impractical independent
heavyhanded historicism hydrometeor illimitably imprecation indifferent
heavyweight historicist hydrometric illiquidity imprecatory indigestion
hebephrenia historicity hydropathic illmannered imprecisely indigestive
hebephrenic histrionics hydrophilic illogically imprecision indignantly
Hebraically histrionism hydrophobia illtempered impregnable indignation
hedgehopped hitherwards hydrophobic illuminable impregnably indirection
hedgepriest hobbledehoy hydrophytic illuminance impressible individuate
hedgeschool hoggishness hydroponics illuminator impressment indivisible
heedfulness hollandaise hydrosphere illusionism impropriate indivisibly
Hegelianism holoblastic hydrostatic illusionist impropriety IndoChinese
heinousness holographic hydrotactic illustrator improvement IndoIranian
heldentenor holothurian hydrothorax illustrious improvident indomitable
heliochrome homeopathic hydrotropic imaginarily imprudently indomitably
heliography homeostasis hygrometric imagination impuissance indorsement
heliometric homeostatic hygrophytic imaginative impulsively indubitable
heliotropic homesteader hygroscopic imbrication inadaptable indubitably
helleborine homestretch hylogenesis imitatively inadvertent inductively
Hellenistic homiletical hylozoistic immanentism inadvisable indulgently
hellishness homocentric hymenoptera immarginate inalienable industrious
helminthoid homoeopathy hymnography immediately inalienably inebriation
helpfulness homoestatic hyoscyamine immedicable inalterable inedibility
hemeralopia homogeneity hyperactive immenseness inalterably ineffective
hemianopsia homogeneous hyperbolise immenseness inanimately ineffectual
hemimorphic homogenetic hyperboloid immigration inanimation inefficient
hemipterous homogeniser hyperborean immitigable inappetence inelegantly
hemispheric homoiousian hypercharge immitigably inattention ineloquence
hepatectomy homological hypercritic immortalise inattentive ineluctable
Hepplewhite homomorphic hypermarket immortality inaugurator ineluctably
heptamerous homophonous hypermetric immoveables incalescent inequitable
heptarchist homoplastic hyperphagia immunologic incantation inequitably
Heracleidan homopterous hyperplasia impanelling incantatory inescapable
herbivorous homosporous hypersthene imparkation incarcerate inessential
hereditable homothallic hypertrophy impartation incardinate inestimable
hereinafter homozygosis hyphenation impartially incarnadine inestimably
heresiology honeybadger hypnopaedia impassioned incarnation inexactness
heretically honeymooner hypnopompic impassively incertitude inexcusable
hermeneutic honeysuckle hypoblastic impassivity incessantly inexcusably
hermeticism hooliganism hypocycloid impatiently incinerator inexistence
heroworship hopefulness hypogastric impeachable incipiently inexpedient
herpetology hornswoggle hypoglossal impeachment inclemently inexpensive
herringbone horological hypolimnion impecunious inclination infanticide
herringgull horripilate hypophyseal impedimenta inclusively infantilism
hesperidium horsecollar hypophysial impenetrate incoercible infantryman
heteroclite horsedoctor hypostatise impenitence incognisant infatuation
heteroecism horseradish hypotension impenitency incoherence inferential
heterograft hospitalise hypothecate imperfectly incoherency inferiority
heterophony hospitality hypothenuse imperforate incommodity infertility
heteroploid hospitaller hypothermia imperialise incompetent infestation
heteropolar housefather hypothesise imperialism incompliant infeudation
heterospory householder hypotyposis imperialist incongruent infiltrator
heterotaxis housekeeper hypsography imperilling incongruity infinitival
heterotroph houselights hypsometric imperilment incongruous infirmarian
heterotypic housemaster hypsophobia imperiously inconscient inflammable
hexadecimal housemother ichnography impermanent inconsonant inflammably
hexametrist housewifely ichthyology impermeable inconstancy inflexional
hibernacula housewifery ichthyornis impermeably incontinent influential
hibernation huckleberry ichthyosaur impersonate incorporate informality
Hibernicism Hudibrastic iconography impertinent incorporeal information
hideousness hugeousness iconostases imperviable incorrectly informative
hierarchism humiliation iconostasis impetration incorruptly informatory
highbrowism humiliatory icosahedral impetratory increasable infrangible
highfalutin hummingbird icosahedron impetuosity incredulity infrequence
highpitched hunchbacked identically impetuously incredulous infrequency
highpowered hundredfold ideographic impingement incremental ingathering
highranking hurriedness ideological implausible incriminate ingeniously
highstepper hurryscurry idiographic implausibly inculcation ingenuously
highwrought hurryskurry idiomorphic implemental inculpation ingrainedly
hilariously hurtfulness idiotically implication inculpatory ingratitude
Hindoostani husbandlike idolisation implicative incunabulum ingurgitate
hippocampus hyacinthine idyllically imploringly incuriosity inhabitable
Hippocratic hydraheaded ignobleness impolitical incuriously inhabitancy

```
inheritable  interactive  inventorial  kindhearted  Leibnitzian  lucratively
inheritance  interallied  investigate  kinematical  lengthiness  lucubration
inheritress  interatomic  investiture  kinesiology  lentiginous  ludicrously
initialling  interbedded  inviability  kinetograph  lepidoptera  luminescent
injudicious  intercalary  invidiously  kinetoscope  leprosarium  lumpishness
injuriously  intercalate  invigilator  kitchenette  leptodactyl  lustfulness
innavigable  intercensal  invigorator  kitchensink  lesemajesty  Lutheranism
innervation  intercepter  inviolately  kitchenware  letterpress  luxuriantly
innocuously  interceptor  involucrate  kleptomania  levelheaded  luxuriation
innoxiously  intercessor  involuntary  knavishness  leviratical  luxuriously
innumerable  interchange  involvement  knowingness  libertarian  lycanthrope
innumerably  intercostal  invultation  knownothing  liberticide  lycanthropy
innutrition  intercourse  ionospheric  knucklebone  libertinage  machicolate
inobservant  intercrural  ipecacuanha  Kulturkampf  libertinism  machination
inoculation  interdental  ipsilateral  kwashiorkor  lichenology  machinemade
inoculative  interdepend  iridescence  kymographic  lickerishly  mackerelsky
inoffensive  interesting  irksomeness  labefaction  lickspittle  macrobiotic
inofficious  interfacial  ironhearted  labiodental  lieutenancy  macrocosmic
inoperative  interfacing  ironmongery  laboriously  lifemanship  macrogamete
inopportune  interfluent  irradiation  lachrymator  ligamentary  macroscopic
inquilinous  interfusion  irradiative  lacination   ligamentous  maddeningly
inquiringly  intergrowth  irrecusable  laconically  lightfooted  madreporite
inquisition  interiorise  irrecusably  lacrimation  lighthanded  madrigalian
inquisitive  interiority  irredentism  lacrimatory  lightheaded  madrigalist
insalubrity  interjacent  irredentist  lacrimosely  lightminded  magazinegun
inscribable  interleaves  irreducible  lacrymation  lightsomely  magdalenian
inscription  interlinear  irreducibly  lacrymatory  lightweight  magisterial
inscriptive  Interlingua  irrefutable  lacrymosely  lilylivered  magisterium
inscrutable  interlining  irrefutably  lactescence  limitedness  magistratic
inscrutably  interlocker  irregularly  lactiferous  limitlessly  Maglemosian
insectarium  interlunary  irrelevance  laicisation  limnologist  magnanimity
insecticide  intermeddle  irrelevancy  lakedweller  linedrawing  magnanimous
insectifuge  intermedium  irreligious  lamellicorn  linefishing  magnificent
insectivore  intermingle  irremissive  lamelliform  linendraper  maidservant
insectology  intermitted  irremovable  lamentation  lineprinter  mailcarrier
inseminator  internalise  irremovably  lammergeier  lingeringly  maintenance
insensately  internality  irreparable  lammergeyer  linguistics  maintopmast
insensitive  internecine  irreparably  lamplighter  lionhearted  maintopsail
inseparable  internuncio  irresoluble  Lancastrian  liquefiable  maisonnette
inseparably  interosseus  irretention  lancinating  liquescence  makebelieve
insessorial  interplayed  irretentive  lancination  liquidambar  maladaptive
insidiously  interpolate  irreverence  landaulette  liquidation  maladjusted
insincerely  interpreter  irrevocable  landgrabber  lissomeness  maladroitly
insincerity  interracial  irrevocably  landgravine  literalness  malapropism
insinuation  interregnum  irruptively  landholding  lithography  malariology
insinuative  interrelate  isochronism  landingbeam  lithophytic  malediction
insipidness  interrogate  isochronous  landinggear  lithosphere  maledictory
insistently  interrupter  isoelectric  landlordism  lithotomise  malefaction
insouciance  interruptor  isogeotherm  languidness  lithotomist  maleficence
inspiration  interseptal  isometrical  larcenously  lithotripsy  malevolence
inspiratory  intersexual  isomorphism  largeminded  litigiously  malfeasance
instability  intersperse  isomorphous  laryngology  litterateur  malfunction
installment  interspinal  itacolumite  laryngotomy  lixiviation  maliciously
instigation  intertangle  ithyphallic  lastingness  loathliness  malignantly
instigative  intertribal  itinerantly  latchstring  loathsomely  malposition
instillment  intervallic  itineration  lateritious  loculicidal  malpractice
instinctive  interviewee  jabberwocky  latifundium  logarithmic  mammalogist
instinctual  interviewer  Jacobinical  latitudinal  loggerheads  managership
institution  intimidator  Jacobitical  latticework  logicalness  mandarinate
instruction  intolerable  jactitation  laudability  logographer  mandibulate
instructive  intolerably  Jansenistic  laughinggas  logographic  mandolinist
insufflator  intolerance  jargonistic  launderette  logomachist  manducation
insultingly  intractable  jauntingcar  laurustinus  longanimity  manducatory
insuperable  intractably  jealousness  lawlessness  longplaying  Manichaeism
insuperably  intravenous  jerrymander  lawmerchant  longsighted  manifestant
intagliated  intrepidity  journeywork  leapfrogged  looselimbed  manifestoes
integrality  intricately  joylessness  learnedness  loosestrife  manipulable
integration  intriguante  Judaisation  leaseholder  lophobranch  manipulator
integrative  intromitted  judgmatical  leatherback  loudmouthed  manneristic
intelligent  intromitter  judiciously  leatherhead  loudspeaker  mannishness
intemperate  introverted  jumpingbean  leatherneck  loutishness  mansardroof
intenseness  intrusively  jumpingjack  leavetaking  louverboard  mantelpiece
intensifier  intuitional  juridically  lecherously  louvreboard  mantelshelf
intensional  intuitively  justiciable  lectureship  lovableness  mantuamaker
intensively  intuitivism  justifiable  legerdemain  lowpressure  manufactory
intentional  intumescent  justifiably  legionnaire  lowreboard   manufacture
intentioned  invalidness  juvenescent  legislation  loxodromics  manumission
interactant  invectively  kickstarter  legislative  lubrication  manumitting
interaction  inventively  kilocalorie  legislature  lubricative  marcescence
```

marcescible	memorabilia	miniaturist	monstrously	neckerchief	nosographic
marchioness	memorialise	ministerial	moonlighter	necrobiosis	nosological
marconigram	memorialist	minnesinger	mooringmast	necrologist	notableness
marginalise	mendelevium	minuteglass	morbiferous	necromancer	nothingness
marginality	meningocele	mirthlessly	moribundity	necromantic	noticeboard
margraviate	menservants	misalliance	morningroom	necrophilia	notionalist
marketplace	mensuration	misanthrope	moronically	necrophilic	notoriously
marketvalue	mentholated	misanthropy	morrisdance	necropoleis	nourishment
marlinspike	mentionable	misbegotten	mortarboard	needfulness	novelettish
marquessate	meprobamate	miscarriage	mosstrooper	needlecraft	noxiousness
marqueterie	mercenarily	miscegenate	mothercraft	needlepoint	nullifidian
marquisette	merchandise	miscellanea	mothernaked	needlewoman	nulliparity
marriagebed	merchantman	mischievous	motherright	nefariously	nulliparous
marshalling	mercilessly	miscibility	motivepower	negationist	numerically
marshalship	mercurially	misconceive	mountaineer	negligently	numismatics
marshmallow	meritocracy	misconstrue	mountainous	negotiation	numismatist
martyrology	meritorious	miscreation	mountaintop	negotiatory	nuncupation
masculinely	meroblastic	misericorde	movableness	negotiatrix	nuncupative
masculinise	merogenesis	miserliness	moveability	negrophobia	nurserymaid
masculinity	Merovingian	misestimate	mudslinging	neighbourly	nutcrackers
masochistic	merryandrew	misfeasance	multangular	neologistic	nutrimental
masquerader	merrymaking	misguidance	multicolour	Neoplatonic	nutritional
massiveness	mesalliance	misguidedly	multilinear	Neotropical	nutritively
massproduce	mesoblastic	misjudgment	multinomial	nephelinite	nyctitropic
masterfully	mesomorphic	mismarriage	multiparous	nephrectomy	nyctophobia
masterpiece	messiahship	misremember	multiracial	nervelessly	nympholepsy
mastication	metacentric	misspelling	multistorey	nervousness	nymphomania
masticatory	metachrosis	mistrustful	multivalent	netherworld	oarsmanship
mastodontic	metagenesis	mithridatic	mundaneness	nettlecloth	obfuscation
mastoiditis	metagenetic	mitrailleur	municipally	neurologist	obfuscatory
matchlessly	metalloidal	mockingbird	munificence	neuropathic	objectively
matchmaking	metallurgic	moderations	murderously	neuroticism	objectivism
materialise	metalworker	modernistic	murmuration	neurotropic	objectivist
materialism	metamorphic	moisturiser	murmurously	neutraliser	objectivity
materialist	metaphysics	molecricket	musclebound	nickelplate	objurgation
materiality	metaplastic	molecularly	muscularity	nictitation	objurgatory
mathematics	metapsychic	molendinary	musculation	nightingale	obliqueness
matriarchal	metasomatic	molestation	musculature	nightmarish	obliviously
matriculate	metastasise	mollycoddle	musicalness	nightporter	obmutescent
matrilineal	meteoritics	molybdenite	muskthistle	nightwalker	obnoxiously
matrilinear	meteoroidal	momentarily	mustachioed	nigrescence	obscuration
matrimonial	meteorology	momentously	mutableness	ninnyhammer	obscureness
mawkishness	Methodistic	monarchical	muttonchops	nitrogenise	obsecration
maxillipede	methodology	monasterial	mycological	nitrogenous	observantly
McCarthyism	methylamine	monasticism	mycophagist	noctilucent	observation
meadowgrass	methylation	moneylender	mycorrhizae	noctivagant	observatory
meadowsweet	metonymical	moneymaking	mycorrhizal	noctivagous	observingly
meaningless	metoposcopy	moneymarket	myelomatous	nocturnally	obsessional
measureless	metrication	moneyspider	myocarditis	noiselessly	obsessively
measurement	Micawberish	monitorship	myrmecology	noisemaking	obsolescent
mechanician	Micawberism	monkeybread	mythography	noisomeness	obstetrical
mechanistic	micrococcal	monkeyshine	mythologise	nomadically	obstinately
mediaevally	micrococcus	monocarpous	mythologist	nomenclator	obstruction
mediastinal	microcosmic	monochasial	mythomaniac	nominatival	obstructive
mediastinum	microgamete	monochasium	mythopoeist	nomographer	obtestation
mediateness	micrography	monochromat	mythopoetic	nomographic	obtrusively
mediatorial	microgroove	monochromic	myxomatosis	nomological	obviousness
mediatrices	microlithic	monoclinous	myxomycetes	nonchalance	occipitally
medicinable	micrometric	monoculture	nailvarnish	nondelivery	occultation
medicinally	Micronesian	monogenesis	namecalling	nondescript	ochlocratic
medicolegal	microphonic	monogenetic	namedropper	nonetheless	octachordal
medievalism	microphytic	monogrammed	naphthalene	nonexistent	octagonally
medievalist	microscopic	monographer	narcoleptic	nonfeasance	octingenary
mediumistic	microsecond	monographic	narratively	nonmatching	odoriferous
megalomania	micturition	monolingual	nasofrontal	nonmetallic	odorousness
megalopolis	middleclass	monological	nationalise	nonpartisan	oecological
megatherium	middlesized	monologuise	nationalism	nonplussing	oecumenical
melancholia	millenarian	monologuist	nationalist	nonresident	oenological
melancholic	milliampere	monomorphic	nationality	nonsensical	oenophilist
melanochroi	millionaire	mononuclear	nationstate	nonsequitur	oesophageal
melanophore	millisecond	monophagous	naturalness	nonspecific	oestrogenic
melioration	mimetically	monophthong	naturopathy	nonunionist	offenceless
meliorative	mindbending	Monophysite	naughtiness	nonviolence	offensively
meliphagous	mindblowing	monopoliser	Neanderthal	nonvolatile	offhandedly
melliferous	mindfulness	monopterous	nearsighted	northeaster	officialdom
mellifluent	mindreading	Monothelite	necessarian	northwester	officialese
mellifluous	mineraliser	monozygotic	necessarily	noseyparker	officialism
melodiously	minesweeper	monseigneur	necessitate	nosographer	officiation
membraneous	miniaturise	monstrosity	necessitous	nosographer	officinally

officiously	ostracoderm	papyraceous	Pelagianism	persistence	physiologic
oilpainting	Ostrogothic	parachutist	pelargonium	persistency	phytography
oldwomanish	otherwhiles	paradisical	pellucidity	personalise	phytologist
olfactology	outbreeding	paradoxical	pendulously	personalism	phytosterol
oligochaete	outbuilding	paragrapher	penetrating	personalist	phytotomist
oligomerous	outcropping	paragraphic	penetration	personality	Pickwickian
ominousness	outdistance	paraldehyde	penetrative	personation	pictography
ommatophore	outfighting	paraleipsis	penicillate	personative	pictorially
omnifarious	outrivalled	parallactic	penicillium	personifier	picturebook
omnipotence	outspokenly	parallelism	peninsulate	perspective	picturecard
omnipresent	outstanding	parallelled	penitential	perspicuity	picturegoer
omniscience	outstripped	paramedical	pennyweight	perspicuous	picturesque
oncological	outwardness	parametrise	penological	persuadable	pieceworker
oneiromancy	ovariectomy	paramoecium	pensionable	persuasible	pietistical
onerousness	overanxious	paramorphic	pensionless	pertinacity	pigeonchest
ontogenesis	overbalance	paramountcy	pensiveness	pertinently	piggishness
ontogenetic	overbearing	paramountly	pentadactyl	perturbable	pigheadedly
ontological	overbidding	paraphraser	pentagynous	pervasively	pigsticking
opalescence	overcropped	paraplectic	pentahedron	pervertedly	pillowfight
opencircuit	overdevelop	paraselenae	pentamerous	pessimistic	pilocarpine
openhearted	overgarment	parasitical	pentandrous	pestiferous	pilotburner
openmouthed	overindulge	parasitosis	pentathlete	pestilently	pinkishness
operational	overlapping	parathyroid	pentavalent	pestologist	pinnatisect
operatively	overmanning	paratrooper	pentazocine	petitionary	pipecleaner
operculated	overmeasure	paratyphoid	Pentecostal	petrography	piperaceous
operoseness	overpayment	parentheses	pentlandite	petrologist	pipistrelle
ophidiarium	overproduce	parenthesis	penultimate	petticoated	piratically
ophiologist	overrunning	parenthetic	penuriously	pettifogger	piscatorial
opinionated	oversailing	parheliacal	peptisation	pettishness	piscivorous
opportunely	oversetting	parishioner	perambulate	phagedaenic	pitchblende
opportunism	overstepped	parochially	perceivable	phagocytise	piteousness
opportunist	overstretch	paronomasia	perceivably	phagocytose	pitifulness
opportunity	overstuffed	participant	perceptible	phalanstery	pivotbridge
opprobrious	overtopping	participate	perceptibly	phantasiast	placability
oppugnation	overweening	participial	perchlorate	phantasmata	plagiariser
optometrist	overwritten	particulate	percipience	pharisaical	plagioclase
oracularity	overwrought	partitioned	percolation	phariseeism	plagiostome
orangoutang	oviposition	partitioner	peregrinate	pharyngitis	plainspoken
orbicularly	oxygenation	partitively	perennation	phenologist	plaintively
orchestrate	oxyhydrogen	partnership	perennially	philanderer	planetarium
orchidology	oysterplant	parturition	perfectible	philatelist	planetoidal
orderliness	ozoniferous	passacaglia	perfectness	philhellene	planimetric
oreographic	ozonisation	passeriform	perforation	philologian	planisphere
oreological	ozonosphere	possibility	perforative	philologist	planoconvex
organically	pachydermal	Passiontide	performable	philosopher	plantigrade
organisable	pacifically	passivation	performance	philosophic	plasmolysis
organscreen	pacificator	passiveness	perfunctory	phonetician	plasmolytic
orientalise	packingcase	pasteuriser	pericardiac	phonography	plasterwork
orientalism	paddleboard	pastoralism	pericardial	phonologist	plasticiser
orientalist	paddlewheel	pastoralist	pericardium	phosphonium	platearmour
orientation	paederastic	pastureland	pericranial	phosphorate	plateresque
originality	paediatrics	patelliform	pericranium	phosphorism	platforming
origination	paediatrist	paternalism	perineurium	phosphorite	platinotype
originative	paedophilia	paternalist	periodicity	phosphorous	platyrrhine
ornithology	painfulness	paternoster	periodontal	photoactive	playerpiano
ornithopter	painkilling	pathologist	periostitis	photocopier	playfulness
ornithosaur	painstaking	patriarchal	peripatetic	photofinish	playingcard
orthocentre	Palaearctic	patrilineal	periphrases	photography	pleasurable
orthodontia	palaeotypic	patrimonial	periphrasis	photometric	pleasurably
orthodontic	Palestinian	patristical	perishables	photooffset	plebeianise
orthoepical	palindromic	patronising	perishingly	photoperiod	plebeianism
orthography	palmcabbage	patternshop	perispermic	photophilic	plectoptera
orthopaedic	palpability	paunchiness	peristalith	photophobia	pleinairist
orthopedics	palpitation	pawnbroking	peristalsis	photophobic	pleiotropic
orthopedist	palsgravine	peacemaking	peristaltic	photosphere	Pleistocene
orthopteran	pamphleteer	pearlescent	peristomial	phototactic	plenipotent
orthoscopic	pandemonium	pearlfisher	perithecium	phototropic	plenteously
orthotropic	panegyrical	peccability	peritonitis	phrasemaker	plentifully
oscillation	Panglossian	peccadillos	permanently	phraseogram	pleochroism
oscillatory	panhellenic	pectination	permissible	phraseology	pleomorphic
oscillogram	panicmonger	peculiarity	permissibly	phthiriasis	pleurodynia
osmotically	pantalettes	pecuniarily	permutation	phycocyanin	pliableness
ostensively	pantheistic	pedagogical	perpetrator	phycologist	plicateness
ostentation	pantomimist	pedestalled	perpetually	phylloclade	ploughshare
osteography	pantothenic	pedicellate	perpetuance	phyllotaxis	ploughstaff
osteologist	paperhanger	pediculosis	perpetuator	phylogynist	pluralistic
osteopathic	papermaking	pedological	perplexedly	physicality	plutocratic
osteophytic	paperweight	pedunculate	persecution	physiocracy	pluviometer
osteoplasty	papiermache	peevishness	perseverate	physiognomy	pneumonitis

pocketknife	prayerwheel	prickliness	prorogation	purificator	rationality
pocketmoney	preachiness	priestcraft	prosaically	puritanical	rattlebrain
pocketsized	preaudience	primaevally	prosaicness	purportedly	rattlepated
pococurante	Precambrian	primateship	prosecution	purposeless	rattlesnake
podophyllin	precautious	primatology	prosecutrix	purposively	raucousness
pointdevice	precedented	primigenial	proselytise	purpresture	raunchiness
pointedness	precedently	primiparous	proselytism	pushfulness	ravishingly
pointillism	precentress	primitively	prosenchyma	pussyfooter	reachmedown
pointillist	preceptress	primitivism	prospective	pussywillow	reactionary
pointlessly	precipitant	principally	prosthetics	pustulation	reactionist
poisonously	precipitate	privateness	prostitutor	putrescence	readability
polarimeter	precipitous	privatively	prostration	putrescible	readywitted
polarimetry	preciseness	prizewinner	protagonist	pyramidally	realignment
polarisable	preconceive	probabilism	protectoral	pyramidical	realisation
polariscope	precontract	probabilist	protectress	pyrargyrite	realpolitik
polemically	predatorily	probability	proteolysis	pyroclastic	reanimation
polevaulter	predecessor	probational	proteolytic	pyrotechnic	reapportion
policewoman	predicament	probationer	Proterozoic	Pythagorean	reappraisal
politically	predication	problematic	prothalamia	Pythagorism	rearadmiral
politicking	predicative	proceedings	prothallial	quacksalver	reassertion
pollination	predicatory	procephalic	prothallium	quadraphony	reassurance
poltergeist	predictable	prochronism	prothoracic	quadratical	reawakening
poltroonery	predictably	proconsular	protomartyr	quadrennial	rebarbative
polyandrous	predominant	procreation	protonotary	quadrennium	recalculate
polycarpous	predominate	procreative	protophytic	quadrillion	recantation
polychromic	preelection	procrustean	protractile	quadrupedal	receptacula
polycrystal	preeminence	proctorship	protraction	quaestorial	receptively
polygenesis	preexistent	procuration	protractive	qualifiable	receptivity
polygenetic	prefatorial	procuratory	protrudable	qualitative	recessional
polyglottal	prefatorily	procurement	protrusible	quarrelling	recessively
polyglottic	prefectural	prodigalise	protuberant	quarrelsome	reciprocate
polygonally	prehistoric	prodigality	provenience	quarterback	reciprocity
polygraphic	preignition	profanation	providently	quarterdeck	reclaimable
polymorphic	prejudgment	profanatory	provisional	quartertone	reclamation
polyonymous	prejudicial	profaneness	provisorily	quaternloaf	recognition
polypeptide	prelibation	professedly	provocateur	queenliness	recognitive
polyphagous	preliminary	proficiency	provocation	querulously	recognitory
polyphonous	prelusively	profiterole	provocative	questionary	recommender
polystyrene	prelusorily	profuseness	provokingly	quickchange	recommittal
polytechnic	prematurely	progenitrix	provostship	quickfiring	recondition
polyzoarium	prematurity	progeniture	proximately	quickfreeze	reconnoitre
pomegranate	premeditate	progestogen	prudishness	quickfrozen	reconstruct
pomiculture	premiership	prognathism	pruriginous	quicksilver	recoverable
pomological	premonition	prognathous	Prussianise	quickwitted	recriminate
pompousness	premonitory	progression	Prussianism	quiescently	recruitment
ponderation	prenominate	progressism	pseudograph	quilldriver	rectangular
ponderosity	preoccupied	progressist	pseudomonas	quincuncial	rectifiable
ponderously	preparation	progressive	pseudomorph	quinquennia	rectilineal
pontificals	preparative	prohibition	pseudopodia	quinquereme	rectilinear
pontificate	preparatory	prohibitive	psittacosis	quintillion	recumbently
populariser	preposition	prohibitory	psychedelia	quitchgrass	recurrently
pornography	prepositive	prolegomena	psychedelic	quizzically	redactional
porphyritic	preprandial	proletarian	psychiatric	Rabelaisian	reddishness
portability	prerogative	proletariat	psychically	racemeeting	redetermine
porterhouse	presanctify	proliferate	psychodrama	racketpress	redirection
portionless	presbyteral	proliferous	psychogenic	radicalness	rediscovery
portmanteau	presciently	prolificacy	psychograph	radioactive	redoubtable
portraitist	preselector	prolificity	psychologic	radiocarbon	redundantly
portraiture	presentable	prolocutrix	psychometry	radiography	reduplicate
positronium	presentably	prominently	psychomotor	radiolarian	reedbunting
posological	presentient	promiscuity	psychopathy	radiologist	reeducation
possibility	presentment	promiscuous	pteridology	radiometric	reedwarbler
postclassic	preservable	promisingly	pterodactyl	radiophonic	reemergence
posteriorly	pressagency	promotional	publication	raffishness	reenactment
postexilian	prestigious	promptitude	publishable	rallentando	reestablish
postglacial	prestissimo	promulgator	publishment	rancorously	referential
postnuptial	prestressed	proofreader	pulchritude	rangefinder	reflectance
postulation	presumingly	propagation	pullthrough	rapaciously	reflexively
potentially	presumption	propagative	pullulation	rapscallion	reflexology
potteringly	presumptive	prophethood	pulverulent	rapturously	reformation
pourparlers	pretendedly	prophetical	pumicestone	rarefaction	reformative
powderflask	pretentious	prophetship	punchinello	rarefactive	reformatory
powerlessly	preterhuman	prophylaxis	punctilious	Rastafarian	refrangible
practicable	preterition	propinquity	punctuality	ratatouille	refreshment
practicably	prevalently	propitiable	punctuation	rateability	refrigerant
practically	prevaricate	propitiator	pupillarity	ratiocinate	refrigerate
praetorship	preventable	proportions	purchasable	rationalise	refringency
pragmatical	preventible	proposition	pureblooded	rationalism	regardfully
prattlingly	previsional	proprietary	purgatorial	rationalist	regenerable

regenerator	respectable	rightminded	saturninely	segmentally	septenarius
regimentals	respectably	rightwinger	sauropodous	segregation	septentrion
regionalise	respiration	ringstraked	sausagemeat	segregative	septicaemia
regionalism	respiratory	riotousness	savouriness	seigneurial	septicaemic
regionalist	resplendent	ritualistic	saxophonist	seigniorage	septiferous
registrable	respondence	roadholding	scaffolding	seigniorial	septifragal
regretfully	respondency	rockcrystal	scalariform	seismically	sequestrate
regrettable	responsible	rodenticide	scalearmour	seismograph	serendipity
regrettably	responsibly	rodomontade	scaleinsect	seismometer	sericulture
regurgitate	restatement	roentgenise	scalpriform	seismometry	serigrapher
reification	restfulness	roguishness	scarabaeoid	seismoscope	seriousness
reincarnate	restitution	romanticise	scaremonger	selaginella	serological
reinsertion	restiveness	romanticism	scattergood	selectively	serpiginous
reinsurance	restoration	romanticist	scenography	selectivity	serrulation
reintegrate	restorative	ropedancing	sceptically	selfassured	sertularian
reintroduce	restriction	ropewalking	schismatise	selfcentred	serviceable
reiteration	restrictive	Rosicrucian	schistosity	selfclosing	serviceably
reiterative	restructure	rotogravure	schistosome	selfcocking	servicebook
rejoicingly	resuscitate	rottenstone	schizanthus	selfcommand	serviceline
rejuvenator	retaliation	roughfooted	scholarship	selfconceit	seventeenth
rejuvenesce	retaliative	roughlegged	scholiastic	selfcontent	seventyfold
relatedness	retaliatory	roundedness	schoolboard	selfcontrol	severalfold
relationism	retardation	rubberstamp	schoolchild	selfcreated	sexagesimal
relationist	retardative	rubefacient	schoolhouse	selfculture	sexlessness
reliability	retardatory	rubefaction	schottische	selfdefence	sexological
religionise	retentively	rubicundity	schwarmerei	selfdenying	sextodecimo
religionism	retentivity	rubrication	scientistic	selfdespair	shacklebolt
religionist	retinacular	rudimentary	scientology	selfdevoted	shacklebone
religiosity	retinaculum	ruinousness	scintillant	selfdisplay	shadowgraph
religiously	retinoscopy	rumbustious	scintillate	selfelected	shadowiness
reluctantly	retiredness	ruridecanal	scissorbill	selfevident	Shaksperean
reluctation	retraceable	Russophobia	scissortail	selffeeding	Shaksperian
remembrance	retractable	rustication	scleroderma	selffeeling	shallowness
reminiscent	retranslate	Sabbatarian	sclerometer	selffertile	shamanistic
remonstrant	retribution	sacculation	sclerophyll	selfimposed	shamelessly
remonstrate	retributive	sacramental	sclerotitis	selfinduced	shapeliness
remorseless	retributory	sacrificial	scopolamine	selfinvited	shareholder
remunerator	retrievable	saddlecloth	scorchingly	selfishness	sharepusher
renaissance	retroaction	saddlehorse	scoriaceous	selflimited	sharpwitted
renegotiate	retroactive	Sadduceeism	scorpionfly	selfloading	sheathknife
reorientate	retrocedent	safebreaker	ScotchIrish	selflocking	sheepfarmer
repartition	retroflexed	safeconduct	Scotchwoman	selfmastery	sheepmaster
repellantly	retrorocket	safecracker	scoundrelly	selfopinion	sheetanchor
repellently	revaccinate	safekeeping	scoutmaster	selfpitying	shellacking
repentantly	revaluation	safetyvalve	scragginess	selfraising	shelljacket
repetitious	revendicate	sagaciously	scrappiness	selfreliant	shelterbelt
replaceable	reverberant	Sagittarius	scratchwork	selfreproof	shelterless
replacement	reverberate	saintliness	screamingly	selfrespect	shepherdess
replenisher	reverential	saintpaulia	screwdriver	selfsealing	sheriffalty
repleteness	reversional	salaciously	scribacious	selfseeking	sheriffship
repleviable	reversioner	saleability	scrimpiness	selfservice	shiftlessly
replication	revisionary	salesladies	scriptorial	selfserving	shipbreaker
reportorial	revisionism	salinometer	scriptorium	selfstarter	shipbuilder
reposefully	revisionist	salmonberry	scruffiness	selfsterile	shirtsleeve
representer	reviviscent	salpingitis	scrumptious	selfsupport	shockheaded
repressible	rhabdomancy	saltatorial	scrutiniser	selftorture	shocktroops
repressibly	rhapsodical	saltimbanco	sculduddery	selfwinding	shoeleather
reproachful	rheological	salvageable	sculduggery	selfworship	shoplifting
reprobation	rheotropism	salvational	scuppernong	semanticist	shopsteward
reprobative	rhetorician	sandbagging	scurvygrass	semasiology	shortchange
reprobatory	rheumaticky	sandskipper	scuttlebutt	semeiotical	shortcoming
reprogramme	rhinologist	sanguinaria	scyphistoma	semidiurnal	shorthanded
reprography	rhinoscopic	sanguineous	searchingly	semiellipse	shortspoken
reprovingly	rhizanthous	sansculotte	searchlight	semimonthly	shortwinded
repudiation	rhizocarpic	Sanskritist	seasickness	semipalmate	shoulderbag
repugnantly	rhizomatous	saplessness	seborrhoeic	semiskilled	shoulderpad
repulsively	rhombohedra	saponaceous	secondarily	semitrailer	shovelboard
requirement	rhomboideus	saprobiotic	secondclass	sempiternal	showerproof
requisition	rhynchodont	saprogenous	secondrater	senatorship	showjumping
resemblance	ribbongrass	saprophytic	secondsight	sensational	showmanship
resentfully	ribvaulting	sarcomatous	secretarial	senselessly	showstopper
reservation	rickettsial	sarcophagus	secretariat	sensibility	shrinkingly
residential	ricochetted	sartorially	secretively	sensitively	shrinkproof
resignation	rifacimenti	satanically	sectionally	sensitivity	shrivelling
resiliently	rifacimento	satiability	sedentarily	sensorially	shrubbiness
resipiscent	rightangled	satinstitch	sedimentary	sententious	shutterless
resistively	righteously	satirically	seditionary	sentimental	shuttlecock
resistivity	righthanded	satisfiable	seditiously	sentinelled	sickbenefit
resourceful	righthander	saturnalian	seductively	Septembrist	sickeningly

```
sickishness  sociopathic  spifflicate  steerageway  stringybark  sunlessness
sideslipped  sockdolager  spindlelegs  steganogram  stroboscope  superabound
sidestepped  sockdologen  spindletree  stegosaurus  strongpoint  supercharge
sidewheeler  softhearted  spinelessly  stellionate  studentship  superfamily
sightlessly  softshelled  spiniferous  stencilling  studiedness  superficial
sightliness  solanaceous  Spinozistic  stenochromy  stumblingly  superficies
sightreader  soldierlike  spinsterish  stenography  stuntedness  superfluity
sightscreen  soldiership  spiraculate  stenotypist  stylisation  superfluous
sightseeing  solifluxion  spiritistic  stepbrother  stylishness  superheater
sightworthy  soliloquise  spiritlevel  stephanotis  stylography  superimpose
sigmoidally  soliloquist  spiritually  stereograph  stylopodium  superinduce
signifiable  solipsistic  spiritualty  stereometry  suasiveness  superintend
significant  solmisation  spirituelle  stereophony  subaerially  superioress
signpainter  solutionist  spirochaete  stereoscope  subarration  superiority
sillimanite  solvability  spirochetal  stereoscopy  subaudition  superjacent
silveriness  somatically  spirometric  stereotyped  subaxillary  superlative
silverplate  somatogenic  splashboard  stereotyper  subbasement  superlunary
silverpoint  somatologic  splayfooted  stereotypic  subcategory  supermarket
silversmith  somatoplasm  splendorous  sternsheets  subclinical  supernatant
silverstick  somatotonia  splenectomy  sternutator  subcontract  supernormal
simperingly  somatotonic  splenetical  stethoscope  subcontrary  superscribe
simpliciter  somewhither  spokeswoman  stethoscopy  subcortical  superscript
sincereness  somnambular  spondulicks  stevengraph  subcritical  supersedeas
sinfonietta  somniculous  spondylitis  stewardship  subcultural  supersedure
singlestick  somniferous  spongecloth  stichometry  subdivision  superstrata
singletrack  somnolently  sponsorship  stickinsect  subdominant  supersubtle
singularise  songfulness  spontaneity  stickleback  subjugation  supertanker
singularity  songsparrow  spontaneous  stiffnecked  subjunctive  supervision
sinistrally  sonofabitch  sporogenous  stiflejoint  sublimation  supervisory
sinistrorse  sophistical  sporogonium  stiltedness  sublimeness  suppliantly
sinlessness  Soroptimist  sporophytic  stimulation  sublittoral  supportable
sinological  sorrowfully  sportswoman  stimulative  submarginal  supportably
sinuousness  soteriology  sporulation  stipendiary  submergence  supposition
sittingroom  sottishness  spreadeagle  stipulation  submersible  suppositive
situational  soulfulness  springboard  stipulatory  submissible  suppository
sizableness  soundlessly  springclean  stirrupbone  submultiple  suppression
skatingrink  soupkitchen  springhouse  stirruppump  subordinate  suppressive
skeletonise  southeaster  springiness  stockbroker  subornation  suppuration
sketchiness  Southernism  squalidness  stockholder  subregional  suppurative
skilfulness  southwester  squarebuilt  stockinette  subrogation  supremacist
skulduddery  sovereignly  squarsonage  stockjobber  subscapular  supremeness
skulduggery  sovereignty  squashiness  stockmarket  subsequence  surbasement
slaughterer  spaceflight  squeakiness  stocktaking  subservient  surfboarder
slavedriver  spaceheater  squeamishly  stoicalness  subsistence  surficially
slaveholder  spacesaving  squintingly  stomachache  subspecific  surgeonfish
slavemarket  sparingness  squirearchy  stomachpump  substandard  surpassable
slavishness  sparrowbill  stadtholder  stomatology  substantial  surrebuttal
Slavonicise  sparrowhawk  stagemanage  stonecurlew  substantive  surrebutter
sleepingbag  spasmodical  stagestruck  stonecutter  substituent  surrogation
sleepingcar  spastically  stagflation  stoneground  subsumption  surveillant
sleeplessly  spathaceous  stainlessly  stonemarten  subsumptive  susceptible
sleepwalker  spatterdash  staircarpet  stonewaller  subterminal  susceptibly
sleeveboard  speakership  stakeholder  stoolpigeon  subtraction  suspenseful
slenderness  specifiable  stalactitic  storekeeper  subtractive  suspensible
sleuthhound  specificity  stalagmitic  stormcentre  subtropical  suspiration
slickenside  spectacular  stallholder  stormtroops  subumbrella  sustainable
slightingly  spectatress  stampoffice  storyteller  suburbanise  sustainment
slotmachine  spectrality  standardise  Stradivarii  suburbanite  susurration
smallholder  spectrogram  standoffish  straightcut  succedaneum  swallowable
smallminded  spectrology  standpatter  straightish  succourless  swallowdive
smilelessly  speculation  starchiness  straightway  succulently  swallowhole
smithereens  speculative  starcrossed  straitlaced  suckingfish  swallowtail
smithsonite  speechifier  starstudded  stramineous  sufficiency  swallowwort
smokescreen  speedometer  startlingly  strangeness  suffixation  swarthiness
smokingroom  spelaeology  stateliness  strangulate  suffocation  sweepstakes
smoothfaced  spellbinder  statesmanly  straphanger  suffocative  swellheaded
smorgasbord  spendthrift  statistical  strategical  suffragette  swiftfooted
snatchblock  spermaphyte  statutebook  stratocracy  suffumigate  swimbladder
snickersnee  spermatozoa  statutorily  streakiness  sugarcoated  swingletree
snowbunting  spermicidal  staunchless  streetlight  suggestible  swinishness
snowgoggles  spessartite  staunchness  strenuosity  suitability  switchblade
snowleopard  sphaeridium  staurolitic  strenuously  sulphaceous  switchboard
soapboiling  sphagnology  steadfastly  stretchable  sulphurwort  swordbearer
soberminded  spherically  steamboiler  stridulator  summariness  sybaritical
sociability  spherometer  steamroller  strikebound  summational  sycophantic
socialistic  spherulitic  steatopygia  stringboard  summerhouse  sycophantry
Socinianism  sphincteral  steelworker  stringently  summersault  syllabarium
sociologist  sphincteric  steeplebush  stringiness  sumptuosity  syllabicity
sociometric  sphygmogram  steeplejack  stringpiece  sumptuously  syllogistic
```

symbolistic	telepathise	thermometer	toxophilite	triggerfish	unbeknownst
symmetrical	telepathist	thermometry	trabeculate	trimestrial	unbelieving
sympathetic	telephonist	thermophile	tracasserie	trimorphism	unbendingly
sympathiser	teleprinter	thermoscope	tracelessly	trimorphous	unbeseeming
sympetalous	temerarious	thermotaxis	tracheotomy	Trinitarian	unboundedly
symphonious	temperament	thickheaded	trackwalker	tripetalous	unbreakable
symposiarch	temperately	thickwitted	traditional	triphibious	uncanniness
symptomatic	temperative	thimbleweed	traducement	triphyllous	uncanonical
synagogical	temperature	thingumabob	trafficator	triquetrous	uncatchable
synchromesh	tempestuous	thingumajig	trafficking	tristichous	unceasingly
synchronise	temporality	thinskinned	trafficless	trisyllabic	uncertainly
synchronism	temporarily	thirstiness	tragedienne	trisyllable	uncertainty
synchronous	tenableness	thistledown	tragicomedy	tritagonist	unchristian
synchrotron	tenaciously	thitherward	trailblazer	tritheistic	uncivilised
syncopation	tendencious	thixotropic	trainbearer	trituration	uncleanness
syndesmosis	tendentious	thoroughpin	trammelling	triumvirate	unclimbable
syndicalism	tenementary	thoroughwax	transaction	trivialness	uncluttered
syndicalist	tensibility	thoughtless	transalpine	troglodytic	uncommitted
syndication	tentaculate	thrasonical	transceiver	trophoblast	unconcealed
synergistic	tentatively	threadiness	transcriber	troposphere	unconcerned
synonymical	tenterhooks	threadpaper	transection	trothplight	uncongenial
syntactical	tentpegging	threecolour	transferred	troublesome	unconnected
synthesiser	tenuousness	threedecker	transferrer	troublously	unconscious
synthetical	tephromancy	threehanded	transfigure	trouserless	uncontested
syssarcosis	teratogenic	threelegged	transfinite	trousersuit	uncountable
systematics	teratologic	threemaster	transfixion	truculently	uncouthness
systematise	termagantly	thriftiness	transformer	truehearted	uncrushable
systematism	termination	thrillingly	transfusion	trundletail	underbidder
systematist	terminative	throatiness	transhumant	trustbuster	undercharge
tabefaction	terminology	throatlatch	transiently	trusteeship	underexpose
tabernacled	termitarium	thrombocyte	transilient	trustworthy	underground
tabletennis	terraqueous	thunderbird	translation	tryingplane	undergrowth
tacheometer	terrestrial	thunderbolt	translocate	trypanosome	underhanded
tachycardia	terricolous	thunderclap	translucent	tryptophane	undermanned
tachygraphy	terrigenous	thunderhead	translunary	tuberculate	underpinned
taciturnity	territorial	thunderless	transmarine	tuberculise	underseller
tagliatelle	tessellated	thunderpeal	transmittal	tuberculose	undersigned
tagliatelli	testability	thuriferous	transmitted	tuberculous	understated
talebearing	testatrices	thwartships	transmitter	tufthunting	undertaking
talentscout	testimonial	thyroiditis	transpadane	tumbledrier	undertenant
talkatively	tetanically	tiddlywinks	transparent	tumefaction	undervaluer
tameability	tetracyclic	tightfisted	transpierce	tunableness	underweight
tangibility	tetradactyl	tightlipped	transponder	tunefulness	underwriter
tankfarming	tetrahedral	timebargain	transporter	turbination	undeserving
tantalising	tetrahedron	timepleaser	transsexual	turbulently	undesirable
tapemachine	tetramerous	timeserving	transuranic	turgescence	undeveloped
tapemeasure	tetrapodous	timesharing	transversal	turtleshell	undisguised
taratantara	tetrarchate	titanically	trapeziform	tuttifrutti	undisturbed
tarnishable	tetravalent	Titianesque	trapezoidal	twelvemonth	undoubtedly
tarradiddle	Teutonicism	titillation	Trappistine	twelvepenny	undutifully
tastelessly	textureless	titleholder	traversable	typecasting	unemotional
tautologise	thalidomide	tittivation	treacherous	typefounder	unendurable
tautologism	thanatology	toastmaster	treacliness	typefoundry	unendurably
tautologous	thanklessly	tobacconist	treasonable	typesetting	unequivocal
tautomerism	thanksgiver	tobogganing	treasonably	typewritten	unessential
tautonymous	thankworthy	tobogganist	treecreeper	typicalness	unexploited
taxidermist	thaumatrope	toffeenosed	trelliswork	typographer	unexpressed
taxonomical	thaumaturge	togglejoint	tremblement	typographic	unfailingly
teachership	thaumaturgy	tolbutamide	tremblingly	typological	unfaltering
tearfulness	theatregoer	tonsillitis	tremulously	tyrannicide	unfashioned
tearstained	theatricals	toothbilled	trenchantly	tyrannosaur	unfeelingly
teaspoonful	thenceforth	toothpowder	trencherman	tyrannously	unfeignedly
technically	theobromine	toothsomely	trendsetter	ulotrichous	unflappable
technocracy	theocentric	topdressing	trepanation	ultramarine	unflinching
technologic	theodolitic	toploftical	trepidation	ultramodern	unforgiving
tediousness	theological	topographer	trestletree	ultrasonics	unfortunate
teenybopper	theorematic	topographic	trestlework	ultraviolet	unfurnished
teeterboard	theoretical	topological	triadically	unaccounted	ungetatable
teetotalism	theosophist	torchbearer	triangulate	unadvisedly	ungodliness
teetotaller	therapeutic	torchsinger	tribulation	unalterable	unguardedly
tegumentary	thereabouts	torticollis	tribuneship	unambiguous	unguiculate
teknonymous	theretofore	torturously	tribunicial	unanimously	unhappiness
telegrammic	therewithal	totalisator	tribunitial	unappealing	unhealthily
telegrapher	thermically	totteringly	tributarily	unashamedly	unhelpfully
telegraphic	thermionics	touchtyping	trichinosis	unassertive	unicellular
telekinesis	thermoduric	toughminded	trichomonad	unavailable	unicoloured
telekinetic	thermograph	tourbillion	tricksiness	unavoidable	unification
teleologism	thermolysis	townspeople	tricoloured	unavoidably	uniformness
teleologist	thermolytic	toxicomania	triennially	unawareness	unigeniture

unimportant	vagariously	virilescent	wellrounded	xeranthemum	calligraphy
uninhabited	valediction	virological	wellwishing	xerophilous	callousness
uninhibited	valedictory	viscountess	weltschmerz	xylocarpous	calorimeter
uninucleate	valiantness	viscousness	Wensleydale	xylographer	calorimetry
unipersonal	valleculate	visibleness	Wesleyanism	xylographic	calumniator
unipolarity	valuational	viticulture	westernmost	xylophagous	Calvinistic
unisexually	vaporimeter	vitrescence	Westminster	xylophonist	calyptrogen
universally	vaporisable	vitrifiable	wheelbarrow	yacketyyack	camaraderie
unkennelled	variability	vituperator	wheelwright	yellowbelly	campanology
unlimitedly	variational	vivaciously	whereabouts	Yugoslavian	campanulate
unmanliness	variegation	vivisection	wheresoever	zealousness	campmeeting
unmatchable	variousness	vociferance	wherewithal	zestfulness	canalicular
unmeaningly	varnishtree	vociferator	whichsoever	zincography	canaliculus
unmemorable	varsovienne	voguishness	whiffletree	zoantharian	cancellated
unmemorably	vascularise	voicelessly	whigmaleery	zoographist	candelabrum
unmitigated	vascularity	volcanicity	whimsically	zoomorphism	candescence
unnaturally	vasculiform	volcanology	whippletree	zooplankton	candidature
unnecessary	vasectomise	volitionary	whistlestop	zootechnics	candleberry
unnervingly	vasodilator	volkslieder	Whitechapel	Zoroastrian	candlelight
unobtrusive	vasopressin	voltametric	whitecollar	zygomorphic	candlepower
unorganized	vasopressor	volubleness	whiteheaded	————————	candlestick
unorthodoxy	vaticinator	volumometer	whitethroat	babysitting	cannibalise
unpalatable	vehmgericht	voluntarily	whitewasher	bacchanalia	cannibalism
unpolitical	velvetiness	voluntarism	whitherward	bacciferous	canonically
unpossessed	venatically	voluntarist	whitishness	bacilliform	cantharides
unprintable	vendibility	voodooistic	whitleather	backbencher	cantharidic
unpromising	venereology	voortrekker	Whitsuntide	backcountry	capableness
unqualified	venesection	voraciously	wholesomely	bactericide	capaciously
unquietness	venisection	vortiginous	wholesouled	balefulness	capacitance
unrealistic	ventilation	vulcanicity	whoremaster	ballbearing	capillarity
unreasoning	ventilative	vulcanology	whoremonger	balletomane	captainship
unrelenting	ventricular	waggishness	whosesoever	balmcricket	captionless
unremitting	ventriculus	wainscoting	widdershins	BaltoSlavic	captivation
unrighteous	ventriloquy	wainscotted	widowerhood	bandylegged	carabiniere
unsaturated	venturesome	waitinglist	wildcatting	banteringly	carabinieri
unselective	venturously	waitingroom	wildfowling	baptismally	caravanning
unshockable	veraciously	wakefulness	willingness	barbarously	caravansary
unshrinking	verbalistic	wappenschaw	windcheater	barbastelle	carbocyclic
unskilfully	verboseness	wapperjawed	windlestraw	barbiturate	carbonation
unsmilingly	verdantique	warmblooded	winegrowing	barefacedly	carbuncular
unsolicited	veridically	warmhearted	winetasting	barleybroth	carburetion
unsoundness	verisimilar	warrantable	winningness	barnstormer	carburetted
unsparingly	vermiculate	warrantably	winningpost	barquentine	carburetter
unspeakable	vermiculite	washability	winsomeness	barrelhouse	carburettor
unspeakably	vermination	washerwoman	winterberry	barrelorgan	carcinomata
unstoppable	verminously	washleather	wintergreen	bashfulness	cardinalate
unteachable	versatilely	waspishness	wirenetting	bashibazouk	cardiograph
unthinkable	versatility	waspwaisted	wirepulling	basipetally	cardsharper
unthinkably	verticality	wastebasket	wiretapping	basketchair	carefulness
untouchable	vertiginous	watchmaking	wisecracker	bassethound	caressingly
unusualness	vesicularly	waterbottle	wishfulness	bathingsuit	caricatural
unutterable	vespertinal	watercolour	wistfulness	batholithic	carminative
unutterably	vestigially	watercooled	witchdoctor	bathymetric	carnivorous
unvarnished	vestryclerk	watercooler	witchhunter	bathyscaphe	Carolingian
unwarranted	vesuvianite	watercourse	witenagemot	bathysphere	carpetsnake
unweetingly	vexatiously	waterlogged	witheringly	battledress	carrageenan
unwholesome	vexillology	waterskiing	withershins	battlefield	carrageenin
unwillingly	vibratility	waywardness	witlessness	cabbagepalm	carriageway
unwinkingly	vibrational	weakhearted	wolfwhistle	cabbagerose	cartography
unwittingly	vicariously	wealthiness	womanliness	cabbagetree	carunculate
Upanishadic	viceadmiral	wearilessly	wonderfully	cabbageworm	carvelbuilt
upholsterer	vicegerency	wearisomely	woodcarving	cabbalistic	caryopsides
uprightness	viceregally	weathercock	woodcutting	cacographic	cassiterite
uranography	viceroyalty	weatherwise	workability	cacophonous	castellated
urochordate	viceroyship	weatherworn	workmanlike	caddishness	castigation
urticaceous	vichyssoise	wedgeshaped	workmanship	calceolaria	casuistical
urticarious	viciousness	wedgetailed	worldbeater	calcicolous	catachreses
uselessness	vicissitude	weenybopper	worldliness	calciferous	catachresis
utilisation	victualless	weighbridge	worldlywise	calcifugous	cataclysmic
utilitarian	victualling	weightiness	worrisomely	calcination	catadromous
vacationist	vinaigrette	Weismannism	worshipable	calculating	cataplectic
vaccination	vincibility	welcomeness	worshipless	calculation	catastrophe
vacillation	vindication	welladvised	worshipping	calculative	catchphrase
vacuolation	vindicative	wellbeloved	worthlessly	calefacient	catechismal
vacuousness	vindicatory	welldefined	wreckmaster	calefactory	catechistic
vagabondage	vinedresser	wellfounded	wrongheaded	calendrical	categorical
vagabondise	viniculture	wellgroomed	xanthochroi	calibration	catercousin
vagabondism	violoncello	wellmeaning	xanthophyll	californium	caterpillar
vagabondism	viridescent	wellordered	xenophilous	calisthenic	catheterise

catholicise	gaseousness	labefaction	maladroitly	mawkishness	parenthesis
Catholicism	gasfittings	labiodental	malapropism	maxillipede	parenthetic
catholicity	gastrectomy	laboriously	malariology	nailvarnish	parheliacal
catswhisker	gastronomic	lachrymator	malediction	namecalling	parishioner
cauliflower	gastroscope	laciniation	maledictory	namedropper	parochially
causatively	gatecrasher	laconically	malefaction	naphthalene	paronomasia
caustically	haberdasher	lacrimation	maleficence	narcoleptic	participant
cavalierism	habiliments	lacrimatory	malevolence	narratively	participate
cavedweller	habituation	lacrimosely	malfeasance	nasofrontal	participial
cavernously	haematocele	lacrymation	malfunction	nationalise	particulate
dactylogram	haematocrit	lacrymatory	maliciously	nationalism	partitioned
dactylology	haematology	lacrymosely	malignantly	nationalist	partitioner
daisycutter	haemocyanin	lactescence	malposition	nationality	partitively
dangerously	haemoglobin	lactiferous	malpractice	nationstate	partnership
dauntlessly	haemophilia	laicisation	mammalogist	naturalness	parturition
earnestness	haemophilic	lakedweller	managership	naturopathy	passacaglia
earpiercing	haemoptysis	lamellicorn	mandarinate	naughtiness	passeriform
earthcloset	haemorrhage	lamelliform	mandibulate	oarsmanship	passibility
earthenware	haemorrhoid	lamentation	mandolinist	pachydermal	Passiontide
earthliness	haemostasis	lammergeier	manducation	pacifically	passivation
easternmost	haemostatic	lammergeyer	manducatory	pacificator	passiveness
fabrication	haggadistic	lamplighter	Manichaeism	packingcase	pasteuriser
facelifting	haggardness	Lancastrian	manifestant	paddleboard	pastoralism
facetiously	Hagiographa	lancinating	manifestoes	paddlewheel	pastoralist
facsimilist	hagiography	lancination	manipulable	paederastic	pastureland
factfinding	hagiologist	landaulette	manipulator	paediatrics	patelliform
factionally	hagioscopic	landgrabber	manneristic	paediatrist	paternalism
factualness	hairbreadth	landgravine	mannishness	paedophilia	paternalist
facultative	hairdresser	landholding	mansardroof	painfulness	paternoster
faddishness	hairraising	landingbeam	mantelpiece	painkilling	pathologist
fairweather	hairstyling	landinggear	mantelshelf	painstaking	patriarchal
faithhealer	hairstylist	landlordism	mantuamaker	Palaearctic	patrilineal
faithlessly	hairtrigger	languidness	manufactory	palaeotypic	patrimonial
faithworthy	halfbinding	larcenously	manufacture	Palestinian	patristical
fallibility	halfblooded	largeminded	manumission	palindromic	patronising
Falstaffian	halfhearted	laryngology	manumitting	palmcabbage	patternshop
falteringly	halfholiday	laryngotomy	marcescence	palpability	paunchiness
familiarise	halflanding	lastingness	marcescible	palpitation	pawnbroking
familiarity	halfmeasure	latchstring	marchioness	palsgravine	Rabelaisian
fanatically	hallucinate	lateritious	marconigram	pamphleteer	racemeeting
fanfaronade	halophilous	latifundium	marginalise	pandemonium	racketpress
fantastical	halterbreak	latitudinal	marginality	panegyrical	radicalness
farawayness	Hamiltonian	latticework	margraviate	Panglossian	radioactive
farcicality	handbreadth	laudability	marketplace	panhellenic	radiocarbon
farinaceous	handfasting	laughinggas	marketvalue	panicmonger	radiography
farraginous	handgrenade	launderette	marlinspike	pantalettes	radiolarian
farreaching	handicapped	laurustinus	marquessate	pantheistic	radiologist
farthermost	handicapper	lawlessness	marqueterie	pantomimist	radiometric
farthingale	handknitted	lawmerchant	marquisette	pantothenic	radiophonic
fasciaboard	handpainted	machicolate	marriagebed	paperhanger	raffishness
fasciculate	handselling	machination	marshalling	papermaking	rallentando
fascinating	handwriting	machinemade	marshalship	paperweight	rancorously
fascination	handwritten	mackerelsky	marshmallow	papiermache	rangefinder
fashionable	handwrought	macrobiotic	martyrology	papyraceous	rapaciously
fashionably	haphazardly	macrocosmic	masculinely	parachutist	rapscallion
fatefulness	haplessness	macrogamete	masculinise	paradisical	rapturously
fatiguingly	haplography	macroscopic	masculinity	paradoxical	rarefaction
fatuousness	harbourless	maddeningly	masochistic	paragrapher	rarefactive
faultfinder	hardhearted	madreporite	masquerader	paragraphic	Rastafarian
faultlessly	hardhitting	madrigalian	massiveness	paraldehyde	ratatouille
favouritism	hardmouthed	madrigalist	massproduce	paraleipsis	rateability
gafftopsail	hardworking	magazinegun	masterfully	parallactic	ratiocinate
gainfulness	harebrained	magdalenian	masterpiece	parallelism	rationalise
gallantness	harmfulness	magisterial	mastication	parallelled	rationalism
gallbladder	harmonistic	magisterium	masticatory	paramedical	rationalist
galleyslave	harpsichord	magistratic	mastodontic	parametrise	rationality
Gallicanism	harumscarum	Maglemosian	mastoiditis	paramoecium	rattlebrain
gallimaufry	harvesthome	magnanimity	matchlessly	paramorphic	rattlepated
Gallophobia	hatefulness	magnanimous	matchmaking	paramountcy	rattlesnake
gallowsbird	haughtiness	magnificent	materialise	paramountly	raucousness
gallowstree	haustellate	maidservant	materialism	paraphraser	raunchiness
gametangium	hazardously	mailcarrier	materialist	paraplectic	ravishingly
gametophyte	jabberwocky	maintenance	materiality	paraselenae	Sabbatarian
gamogenesis	Jacobinical	maintopmast	mathematics	parasitical	sacculation
gangsterism	Jacobitical	maintopsail	matriarchal	parasitosis	sacramental
gardemanger	jactitation	maisonnette	matriculate	parathyroid	sacrificial
garnishment	Jansenistic	makebelieve	matrilineal	paratrooper	saddlecloth
garrulously	jargonistic	maladaptive	matrilinear	paratyphoid	saddlehorse
gartersnake	jauntingcar	maladjusted	matrimonial	parentheses	Sadduceeism

safebreaker	vagabondise	absorptance	acquiescent	scragginess	beautifully
safeconduct	vagabondish	abstentious	acquirement	scrappiness	beaverboard
safecracker	vagabondism	abstinently	acquisition	scratchwork	bedevilment
safekeeping	vagariously	abstraction	acquisitive	screamingly	bedizenment
safetyvalve	valediction	abstractive	acquittance	screwdriver	beechmarten
sagaciously	valedictory	abstriction	acriflavine	scribacious	befittingly
Sagittarius	valiantness	abusiveness	acrimonious	scrimpiness	beguilement
saintliness	valleculate	ebulliently	acropetally	scriptorial	beguilingly
saintpaulia	valuational	obfuscation	actinometer	scriptorium	behavioural
salaciously	vaporimeter	obfuscatory	actinomyces	scruffiness	belatedness
saleability	vaporisable	objectively	actinomycin	scrumptious	bellbottoms
salesladies	variability	objectivism	acumination	scrutiniser	bellfounder
salinometer	variational	objectivist	acupuncture	sculduddery	bellheather
salmonberry	variegation	objectivity	echosounder	sculduggery	bellicosity
salpingitis	variousness	objurgation	eclecticism	scuppernong	belligerent
saltatorial	varnishtree	objurgatory	econometric	scurvygrass	bellringing
saltimbanco	varsovienne	obliqueness	ectoblastic	scuttlebutt	Belorussian
salvageable	vascularise	obliviously	ectogenesis	scyphistoma	Benedictine
salvational	vascularity	obmutescent	ectogenetic	adenomatous	benediction
sandbagging	vasculiform	obnoxiously	ectomorphic	adiaphorism	benedictory
sandskipper	vasectomise	obscuration	ectoplasmic	adjectively	benefaction
sanguinaria	vasodilator	obscureness	ectotrophic	adjournment	beneficence
sanguineous	vasopressin	obsecration	ecumenicism	adjudgement	beneficiary
sansculotte	vasopressor	observantly	ecumenicity	adjudicator	beneficiate
Sanskritist	vaticinator	observation	ichnography	adminicular	benevolence
saplessness	waggishness	observatory	ichthyology	admiralship	benightedly
saponaceous	wainscoting	observingly	ichthyornis	adolescence	benightment
saprobiotic	wainscotted	obsessional	ichthyosaur	adoptianism	benignantly
saprogenous	waitinglist	obsessively	iconography	adoptianist	bereavement
saprophytic	waitingroom	obsolescent	iconostases	adoptionism	bergamasque
sarcomatous	wakefulness	obstetrical	iconostasis	adoptionist	bergschrund
sarcophagus	wappenschaw	obstinately	icosahedral	adulterator	bersaglieri
sartorially	wapperjawed	obstruction	icosahedron	adumbration	bestselling
satanically	warmblooded	obstructive	McCarthyism	adumbrative	betweenmaid
satiability	warmhearted	obtestation	occipitally	advancement	betweenness
satinstitch	warrantable	obtrusively	occultation	adventuress	betweentime
satirically	warrantably	obviousness	ochlocratic	adventurism	bewhiskered
satisfiable	washability	academicals	octachordal	adventurist	bewitchment
saturnalian	washerwoman	academician	octagonally	adventurous	ceaselessly
saturninely	washleather	academicism	octingenary	adverbially	celebration
sauropodous	waspishness	acarpellous	scaffolding	adversative	celebratory
sausagemeat	waspwaisted	acatalectic	scalariform	adverseness	celestially
savouriness	wastebasket	acaulescent	scalearmour	advertently	cellularity
saxophonist	watchmaking	accelerando	scaleinsect	advertising	cementation
tabefaction	waterbottle	accelerator	scalpriform	advisedness	centenarian
tabernacled	watercolour	accentually	scarabaeoid	edification	centigramme
tabletennis	watercooled	acceptation	scaremonger	edificatory	centreboard
tacheometer	watercooler	acceptingly	scattergood	editorially	centrepiece
tachycardia	watercourse	accessorial	scenography	educability	centrifugal
tachygraphy	waterlogged	accessorise	sceptically	educational	centripetal
taciturnity	waterskiing	accipitrine	schismatise	identically	cerebration
tagliatelle	waywardness	acclamation	schistosity	ideographic	ceremonious
tagliatelli	xanthochroi	acclamatory	schistosome	ideological	ceroplastic
talebearing	xanthophyll	acclimation	schizanthus	idiographic	certifiable
talentscout	yacketyyack	acclimatise	scholarship	idiomorphic	certifiably
talkatively	abandonment	acclivitous	scholiastic	idiotically	certificate
tameability	Abbevillian	accommodate	schoolboard	idolisation	cesarevitch
tangibility	abbreviator	accompanist	schoolchild	idyllically	cesarewitch
tankfarming	abdominally	accordantly	schoolhouse	odoriferous	deactivator
tantalising	abecedarian	accordingly	schottische	odorousness	deathrattle
tapemachine	abhorrently	accoucheuse	schwarmerei	Aeneolithic	debarkation
tapemeasure	abiogeneses	accountable	scientistic	aeolotropic	debauchment
taratantara	abiogenesis	accountancy	scientology	aerobically	debouchment
tarnishable	abiogenetic	accountancy	scintillant	aerobiology	decantation
tarradiddle	abiological	accrescence	scintillate	aerodynamic	decarbonate
tastelessly	abiotically	acculturate	scissorbill	aerographer	decarbonise
tautologise	ablutionary	accumulator	scissortail	aerological	decarburise
tautologism	abnormality	accusatival	scleroderma	aeronautics	deceitfully
tautologous	abolishable	acetylation	sclerometer	aeronomical	deceivingly
tautomerism	abolishment	achievement	sclerophyll	aerostatics	decelerator
tautonymous	abomination	achondritic	sclerotitis	aerostation	decemvirate
taxidermist	abortionist	achromatise	scopolamine	Aesculapian	decennially
taxonomical	aboutsledge	achromatism	scorchingly	aesthetical	deceptively
vacationist	aboveground	acidifiable	scoriaceous	aestivation	decerebrate
vaccination	abracadabra	acidophilic	scorpionfly	beachcomber	declamation
vacillation	abranchiate	acidulation	ScotchIrish	bearbaiting	declamatory
vacuolation	abridgement	acinaciform	Scotchwoman	bearishness	declaration
vacuousness	absenteeism	acknowledge	scoundrelly	beastliness	declarative
vagabondage	absorbingly	acoustician	scoutmaster	beauteously	declaratory

declination	depopulator	festinately	hemispheric	melancholic	negationist
declivitous	deportation	festschrift	hepatectomy	melanochroi	negligently
decollation	depravation	fetichistic	Hepplewhite	melanophore	negotiation
decolletage	depravement	fetishistic	heptamerous	melioration	negotiatory
decolourise	deprecation	feudalistic	heptarchist	meliorative	negotiatrix
decorticate	deprecative	geanticline	Heracleidan	meliphagous	negrophobia
decrepitate	deprecatory	gegenschein	herbivorous	melliferous	neighbourly
decrepitude	depreciator	gemmiferous	hereditable	mellifluent	neologistic
decrescendo	depredation	gemmiparous	hereinafter	mellifluous	Neoplatonic
decussately	depredatory	gemmologist	heresiology	melodiously	Neotropical
decussation	depressible	gemmulation	heretically	membraneous	nephelinite
dedicatedly	deprivation	gendarmerie	hermeneutic	memorabilia	nephrectomy
deductively	depthcharge	genealogise	hermeticism	memorialise	nervelessly
deemphasise	derangement	genealogist	heroworship	memorialist	nervousness
deerstalker	dereliction	generaliser	herpetology	mendelevium	netherworld
defalcation	dermatology	generalship	herringbone	meningocele	nettlecloth
defectively	desalinator	generically	herringgull	menservants	neurologist
defenceless	descendable	genetically	hesperidium	mensuration	neuropathic
defensively	descendible	geniculated	heteroclite	mentholated	neuroticism
deferential	describable	genitivally	heteroecism	mentionable	neurotropic
defibrinate	description	genteelness	heterograft	meprobamate	neutraliser
deficiently	descriptive	gentianella	heterophony	mercenarily	oecological
definiendum	desecration	gentilitial	heteroploid	merchandise	oecumenical
deflagrator	desegregate	gentlemanly	heteropolar	merchantman	oenological
defloration	desensitise	gentlewoman	heterospory	mercilessly	oenophilist
defoliation	deservingly	genuflexion	heterotaxis	mercurially	oesophageal
deforcement	desexualise	genuineness	heterotroph	meritocracy	oestrogenic
deformation	desiccation	geochemical	heterotypic	meritorious	peacemaking
defraudment	desiccative	geomagnetic	hexadecimal	meroblastic	pearlescent
deglutition	desideratum	geometrical	hexametrist	merogenesis	pearlfisher
degradation	designation	geophysical	jealousness	Merovingian	peccability
degradingly	desperadoes	geopolitics	jerrymander	merryandrew	peccadillos
degustation	desperately	geostrophic	leapfrogged	merrymaking	pectination
dehydration	desperation	geosyncline	learnedness	mesalliance	peculiarity
deification	despoilment	geotectonic	leaseholder	mesoblastic	pecuniarily
deistically	despondence	Germanophil	leatherback	mesomorphic	pedagogical
delectation	despondency	germination	leatherhead	messiahship	pedestalled
deleterious	destination	germinative	leatherneck	metacentric	pedicellate
deliciously	destitution	gerontology	leavetaking	metachrosis	pediculosis
delightedly	destruction	gerrymander	lecherously	metagenesis	pedological
delightsome	destructive	gestatorial	lectureship	metagenetic	pedunculate
delineation	desultorily	gesticulate	legerdemain	metalloidal	peevishness
delinquency	deteriorate	gettogether	legionnaire	metallurgic	Pelagianism
deliriously	determinacy	headborough	legislation	metalworker	pelargonium
delitescent	determinant	headhunting	legislative	metamorphic	pellucidity
deliverable	determinate	healthfully	legislature	metaphysics	pendulously
deliverance	determinism	healthiness	Leibnitzian	metaplastic	penetrating
deliveryman	determinist	heartbroken	lengthiness	metapsychic	penetration
demagnetise	detestation	hearthstone	lentiginous	metasomatic	penetrative
demagogical	detrainment	heartlessly	lepidoptera	metastasise	penicillate
demagoguery	detribalise	heartsblood	leprosarium	meteoritics	penicillium
demagoguism	detrimental	heartstring	leptodactyl	meteoroidal	peninsulate
demandingly	deuteration	heavenwards	lesemajesty	meteorology	penitential
demarcation	deuterogamy	heavyfooted	letterpress	Methodistic	pennyweight
demarkation	Deuteronomy	heavyhanded	levelheaded	methodology	penological
demigoddess	devaluation	heavyweight	leviratical	methylamine	pensionable
democratise	devastation	hebephrenia	meadowgrass	methylation	pensionless
democratism	developable	hebephrenic	meadowsweet	metonymical	pensiveness
demographer	development	Hebraically	meaningless	metoposcopy	pentadactyl
demographic	deviousness	hedgehopped	measureless	metrication	pentagynous
demonolatry	devotedness	hedgepriest	measurement	Neanderthal	pentahedron
demonstrate	dexiotropic	hedgeschool	mechanician	nearsighted	pentamerous
demountable	dexterously	heedfulness	mechanistic	necessarian	pentandrous
dendritical	fearfulness	Hegelianism	mediaevally	necessarily	pentathlete
denigration	feasibility	heinousness	mediastinal	necessitate	pentavalent
denigratory	featheredge	heldentenor	mediastinum	necessitous	pentazocine
denizenship	featherhead	heliochrome	mediateness	neckerchief	Pentecostal
denominator	featherless	heliography	mediatorial	necrobiosis	pentlandite
denticulate	featureless	heliometric	mediatrices	necrologist	penultimate
dentigerous	fecundation	heliotropic	medicinable	necromancer	penuriously
denumerable	feelingness	helleborine	medicinally	necromantic	peptisation
denunciator	feldspathic	Hellenistic	medicolegal	necrophilia	perambulate
deoxidation	feloniously	hellishness	medievalism	necrophilic	perceivable
deoxygenate	felspathoid	helminthoid	medievalist	necropoleis	perceivably
deoxyribose	fenestrated	helpfulness	mediumistic	needfulness	perceptible
depauperate	fermentable	hemeralopia	megalomania	needlecraft	perceptibly
depauperise	ferociously	hemianopsia	megalopolis	needlepoint	perchlorate
dependently	ferriferous	hemimorphic	megatherium	needlewoman	percipience
deploringly	ferruginous	hemipterous	melancholia	nefariously	percolation

peregrinate	reanimation	reintroduce	restriction	selfcreated	sexagesimal
perennation	reapportion	reiteration	restrictive	selfculture	sexlessness
perennially	reappraisal	reiterative	restructure	selfdefence	sexological
perfectible	rearadmiral	rejoicingly	resuscitate	selfdenying	sextodecimo
perfectness	reassertion	rejuvenator	retaliation	selfdespair	teachership
perforation	reassurance	rejuvenesce	retaliative	selfdevoted	tearfulness
perforative	reawakening	relatedness	retaliatory	selfdisplay	tearstained
performable	rebarbative	relationism	retardation	selfelected	teaspoonful
performance	recalculate	relationist	retardative	selfevident	technically
perfunctory	recantation	reliability	retardatory	selffeeding	technocracy
pericardiac	receptacula	religionise	retentively	selffeeling	technologic
pericardial	receptively	religionism	retentivity	selffertile	tediousness
pericardium	receptivity	religionist	retinacular	selfimposed	teenybopper
pericranial	recessional	religiosity	retinaculum	selfinduced	teeterboard
pericranium	recessively	religiously	retinoscopy	selfinvited	teetotalism
perineurium	reciprocate	reluctantly	retiredness	selfishness	teetotaller
periodicity	reciprocity	reluctation	retraceable	selflimited	tegumentary
periodontal	reclaimable	remembrance	retractable	selfloading	teknonymous
periostitis	reclamation	reminiscent	retranslate	selflocking	telegrammic
peripatetic	recognition	remonstrant	retribution	selfmastery	telegrapher
periphrases	recognitive	remonstrate	retributive	selfopinion	telegraphic
periphrasis	recognitory	remorseless	retributory	selfpitying	telekinesis
perishables	recommender	remunerator	retrievable	selfraising	telekinetic
perishingly	recommittal	renaissance	retroaction	selfreliant	teleologism
perispermic	recondition	renegotiate	retroactive	selfreproof	teleologist
peristalith	reconnoitre	reorientate	retrocedent	selfrespect	telepathise
peristalsis	reconstruct	repartition	retroflexed	selfsealing	telepathist
peristaltic	recoverable	repellantly	retrorocket	selfseeking	telephonist
peristomial	recriminate	repellently	revaccinate	selfservice	teleprinter
perithecium	recruitment	repentantly	revaluation	selfserving	temerarious
peritonitis	rectangular	repetitious	revendicate	selfstarter	temperament
permanently	rectifiable	replaceable	reverberant	selfsterile	temperately
permissible	rectilineal	replacement	reverberate	selfsupport	temperative
permissibly	rectilinear	replenisher	reverential	selftorture	temperature
permutation	recumbently	repleteness	reversional	selfwinding	tempestuous
perpetrator	recurrently	repleviable	reversioner	selfworship	temporality
perpetually	redactional	replication	revisionary	semanticist	temporarily
perpetuance	reddishness	reportorial	revisionism	semasiology	tenableness
perpetuator	redetermine	reposefully	revisionist	semeiotical	tenaciously
perplexedly	redirection	representer	reviviscent	semidiurnal	tendencious
persecution	rediscovery	repressible	searchingly	semiellipse	tendentious
perseverate	redoubtable	repressibly	searchlight	semimonthly	tenementary
persistence	redundantly	reproachful	seasickness	semipalmate	tensibility
persistency	reduplicate	reprobation	seborrhoeic	semiskilled	tentaculate
personalise	reedbunting	reprobative	secondarily	semitrailer	tentatively
personalism	reeducation	reprobatory	secondclass	sempiternal	tenterhooks
personalist	reedwarbler	reprogramme	secondrater	senatorship	tentpegging
personality	reemergence	reprography	secondsight	sensational	tenuousness
personation	reenactment	reprovingly	secretarial	senselessly	tephromancy
personative	reestablish	repudiation	secretariat	sensibility	teratogenic
personifier	referential	repugnantly	secretively	sensitively	teratologic
perspective	reflectance	repulsively	sectionally	sensitivity	termagantly
perspicuity	reflexively	requirement	sedentarily	sensorially	termination
perspicuous	reflexology	requisition	sedimentary	sententious	terminative
persuadable	reformation	resemblance	seditionary	sentimental	terminology
persuasible	reformative	resentfully	seditiously	sentinelled	termitarium
pertinacity	reformatory	reservation	seductively	Septembrist	terraqueous
pertinently	refrangible	residential	segmentally	septenarius	terrestrial
perturbable	refreshment	resignation	segregation	septentrion	terricolous
pervasively	refrigerant	resiliently	segregative	septicaemia	terrigenous
pervertedly	refrigerate	resipiscent	seigneurial	septicaemic	territorial
pessimistic	refringency	resistively	seigniorage	septiferous	tessellated
pestiferous	regardfully	resistivity	seigniorial	septifragal	testability
pestilently	regenerable	resourceful	seismically	sequestrate	testatrices
pestologist	regenerator	respectable	seismograph	serendipity	testimonial
petitionary	regimentals	respectably	seismometer	sericulture	tetanically
petrography	regionalise	respiration	seismometry	serigrapher	tetracyclic
petrologist	regionalism	respiratory	seismoscope	seriousness	tetradactyl
petticoated	regionalist	resplendent	selaginella	serological	tetrahedral
pettifogger	registrable	respondence	selectively	serpiginous	tetrahedron
pettishness	regretfully	respondency	selectivity	serrulation	tetramerous
reachmedown	regrettable	responsible	selfassured	sertularian	tetrapodous
reactionary	regrettably	responsibly	selfcentred	serviceable	tetrarchate
reactionist	regurgitate	restatement	selfclosing	serviceably	tetravalent
readability	reification	restfulness	selfcocking	servicebook	Teutonicism
readywitted	reincarnate	restitution	selfcommand	serviceline	textureless
realignment	reinsertion	restiveness	selfconceit	seventeenth	vehmgericht
realisation	reinsurance	restoration	selfcontent	seventyfold	velvetiness
realpolitik	reintegrate	restorative	selfcontrol	severalfold	venatically

vendibility	affricative	chieftaincy	photophobia	showmanship	wheresoever
venereology	AfroAsiatic	childminder	photophobic	showstopper	wherewithal
venesection	afterburner	chimaerical	photosphere	shrinkingly	whichsoever
venisection	aftereffect	chinoiserie	phototactic	shrinkproof	whiffletree
ventilation	effectively	Chippendale	phototropic	shrivelling	whigmaleery
ventilative	effectually	chirography	phrasemaker	shrubbiness	whimsically
ventricular	efficacious	chiropodist	phraseogram	shutterless	whippletree
ventriculus	efficiently	chiropteran	phraseology	shuttlecock	whistlestop
ventriloquy	effulgently	chitterling	phthiriasis	thalidomide	Whitechapel
venturesome	offenceless	chlorophyll	phycocyanin	thanatology	whitecollar
venturously	offensively	chloroplast	phycologist	thanklessly	whiteheaded
veraciously	offhandedly	chloroprene	phylloclade	thanksgiver	whitethroat
verbalistic	officialdom	chockablock	phyllotaxis	thankworthy	whitewasher
verboseness	officialese	choirmaster	phylogynist	thaumatrope	whitherward
verdantique	officialism	chokecherry	physicality	thaumaturge	whitishness
veridically	officiation	cholesterol	physiocracy	thaumaturgy	whitleather
verisimilar	officinally	choreograph	physiognomy	theatregoer	Whitsuntide
vermiculate	officiously	chorography	physiologic	theatricals	wholesomely
vermiculite	agglomerate	Christendom	phytography	thenceforth	wholesouled
vermination	agglutinate	christening	phytologist	theobromine	whoremaster
verminously	aggravation	christiania	phytosterol	theocentric	whoremonger
versatilely	aggregately	Christianly	phytotomist	theodolitic	whosesoever
versatility	aggregation	Christmassy	rhabdomancy	theological	aiguillette
verticality	aggregative	Christology	rhapsodical	theorematic	ailurophile
vertiginous	aggrievedly	chrominance	rheological	theoretical	ailurophobe
vesicularly	agnatically	chromoplast	rheotropism	theosophist	aimlessness
vespertinal	agnosticism	chromosomal	rhetorician	therapeutic	aircraftman
vestigially	agonisingly	chronically	rheumaticky	thereabouts	airlessness
vestryclerk	agonistical	chronograph	rhinologist	theretofore	airsickness
vesuvianite	agoraphobia	chronologer	rhinoscopic	therewithal	bibliolater
vexatiously	agoraphobic	chronologic	rhizanthous	thermically	bibliolatry
vexillology	agrarianism	chronometer	rhizocarpic	thermionics	bibliomancy
weakhearted	agriculture	chronometry	rhizomatous	thermoduric	bibliomania
wealthiness	agrobiology	chronoscope	rhombohedra	thermograph	bibliopegic
wearilessly	agrological	chrysalides	rhomboideus	thermolysis	bibliophile
wearisomely	agronomical	chrysalises	rhynchodont	thermolytic	bibliophily
weathercock	egalitarian	chrysarobin	shacklebolt	thermometer	bibliopolic
weatherwise	egotistical	chrysoberyl	shacklebone	thermometry	bibliotheca
weatherworn	egregiously	chrysoprase	shadowgraph	thermophile	bicarbonate
wedgeshaped	ignobleness	chucklehead	shadowiness	thermoscope	bicentenary
wedgetailed	ignominious	churchgoing	Shakspearean	thermotaxis	bicephalous
weenybopper	ahistorical	churchiness	Shaksperian	thickheaded	bicorporate
weighbridge	chaetognath	churchwoman	shallowness	thickwitted	bicuspidate
weightiness	chafingdish	ghastliness	shamanistic	thimbleweed	biddability
Weismannism	chainarmour	ghostliness	shamelessly	thingumabob	biedermeier
welcomeness	chainletter	ghostwriter	shapeliness	thingumajig	bifurcation
welladvised	chainsmoker	phagedaenic	shareholder	thinskinned	bilaterally
wellbeloved	chainstitch	phagocytise	sharepusher	thirstiness	biliousness
welldefined	chalcedonic	phagocytose	sharpwitted	thistledown	billetsdoux
wellfounded	challenging	phalanstery	sheathknife	thitherward	billionaire
wellgroomed	chamaephyte	phantasiast	sheepfarmer	thixotropic	billposting
wellmeaning	chamberlain	phantasmata	sheepmaster	thoroughpin	billsticker
wellordered	chambermaid	pharisaical	sheetanchor	thoroughwax	bimetallism
wellrounded	chameleonic	phariseeism	shellacking	thoughtless	bimetallist
wellwishing	champertous	pharyngitis	shelljacket	thrasonical	bimillenary
weltschmerz	chancellery	phenologist	shelterbelt	threadiness	bimillenium
Wensleydale	chancellory	philanderer	shelterless	threadpaper	binocularly
Wesleyanism	changefully	philatelist	shepherdess	threecolour	biochemical
westernmost	channelling	philhellene	sheriffalty	threedecker	biocoenoses
Westminster	chansonnier	philologian	sheriffship	threehanded	biocoenosis
xenophilous	chanterelle	philologist	shiftlessly	threelegged	biocoenotic
xeranthemum	chanticleer	philosopher	shipbreaker	threemaster	biofeedback
xerophilous	chaotically	philosophic	shipbuilder	thriftiness	biometrical
yellowbelly	chaperonage	phonetician	shirtsleeve	throatiness	biophysical
zealousness	charcuterie	phonography	shockheaded	thrombocyte	bipartition
zestfulness	chargesheet	phonologist	shocktroops	throatlatch	biquadratic
affectation	charismatic	phosphonium	shoeleather	thrombocyte	birdbrained
affectingly	charlatanry	phosphorate	shoplifting	thunderbird	birdfancier
affectional	chartaceous	phosphorism	shopsteward	thunderbolt	birdwatcher
affectioned	chaulmoogra	phosphorite	shortchange	thunderclap	bisexuality
affectively	cheerleader	phosphorous	shorthanded	thunderhead	bitterapple
afficionado	cheerlessly	photoactive	shortspoken	thunderless	bittercress
affiliation	cheesecloth	photocopier	shortwinded	thunderpeal	bittersweet
affirmation	cheiromancy	photofinish	shoulderbag	thuriferous	bivouacking
affirmative	chemotactic	photography	shoulderpad	thwartships	cicatricial
affirmatory	chevalglass	photometric	shovelboard	thyroiditis	cinnabarine
affranchise	chiaroscuro	photooffset	showerproof	wheelbarrow	cinquecento
affrication	chickenfeed	photoperiod	showjumping	wheelwright	circularise
	chickenwire	photophilic	showerproof	whereabouts	circularity

circulation	disannulled	dissymmetry	hirsuteness	microscopic	pipistrelle
circulative	disapproval	distasteful	Hispanicise	microsecond	piratically
circulatory	disarmament	distempered	Hispanicism	micturition	piscatorial
circumlunar	disarmingly	distensible	Hispanicist	middleclass	piscivorous
circumpolar	disassemble	distinction	histologist	middlesized	pitchblende
circumsolar	disassembly	distinctive	historiated	millenarian	piteousness
circumspect	disbandment	distinguish	historicise	milliampere	pitifulness
circumvolve	disbeliever	distraction	historicism	millionaire	pivotbridge
cisatlantic	discalceate	distractive	historicist	millisecond	ribbongrass
citizenship	discardable	distressful	historicity	mimetically	ribvaulting
cityslicker	discernible	distribuend	histrionics	mindbending	rickettsial
civilianise	discernibly	distributor	histrionism	mindblowing	ricochetted
civilisable	discernment	distrustful	hitherwards	mindfulness	rifacimenti
diachronism	discerption	disturbance	kickstarter	mindreading	rifacimento
diacritical	disciplinal	disunionist	kilocalorie	mineraliser	rightangled
diadelphous	discipliner	dithyrambic	kindhearted	minesweeper	righteously
diagnostics	discography	dittography	kinematical	miniaturise	righthanded
dialectally	discontinue	divergently	kinesiology	miniaturist	righthander
dialectical	discordance	diverticula	kinetograph	ministerial	rightminded
dialogistic	discordancy	divestiture	kinetoscope	minnesinger	rightwinger
diamagnetic	discotheque	divisionary	kitchenette	minuteglass	ringstraked
diametrical	discourtesy	divisionism	kitchensink	mirthlessly	riotousness
diamondback	discrepancy	divorcement	kitchenware	misalliance	ritualistic
diaphaneity	discussable	divulgation	libertarian	misanthrope	sickbenefit
diaphoresis	discussible	divulgement	liberticide	misanthropy	sickeningly
diaphoretic	disencumber	einsteinium	libertinage	misbegotten	sickishness
diapophysis	disentangle	fiddlestick	libertinism	miscarriage	sideslipped
diapositive	disenthrall	fidgetiness	lichenology	miscegenate	sidestepped
diarthrosis	disfunction	fieldcornet	lickerishly	miscellanea	sidewheeler
diastematic	disgraceful	fieldworker	lickspittle	mischievous	sightlessly
diastrophic	disgruntled	filamentary	lieutenancy	miscibility	sightliness
diatessaron	disguisedly	filamentous	lifemanship	misconceive	sightreader
dicephalous	disgustedly	filmography	ligamentary	misconstrue	sightscreen
dichogamous	disharmonic	filmsetting	ligamentous	miscreation	sightseeing
dichotomise	dishevelled	filterpaper	lightfooted	misericorde	sightworthy
dichotomist	dishonestly	fimbriation	lighthanded	miserliness	sigmoidally
dichotomous	dishonourer	financially	lightheaded	misestimate	signifiable
dichromatic	disillusion	fingerboard	lightminded	misfeasance	significant
dicotyledon	disinclined	fingerglass	lightsomely	misguidance	signpainter
dictatorial	disinfector	fingerplate	lightweight	misguidedly	sillimanite
didacticism	disinterest	fingerprint	lilylivered	misjudgment	silveriness
differentia	disinterred	fingerstall	limitedness	mismarriage	silverplate
differently	disjunction	finicalness	limitlessly	misremember	silverpoint
difficultly	disjunctive	FinnoUgrian	limnologist	misspelling	silversmith
diffidently	disjuncture	firecracker	linedrawing	mistrustful	silverstick
diffraction	dislikeable	firefighter	linefishing	mithridatic	simperingly
diffuseness	dislocation	fireraising	linendraper	mitrailleur	simpliciter
diffusively	dislodgment	firewalking	lineprinter	nickelplate	sincereness
digestively	dismayingly	firewatcher	lingeringly	nictitation	sinfonietta
digitigrade	disobedient	firmamental	linguistics	nightingale	singlestick
dilapidated	disobliging	firstfruits	lionhearted	nightmarish	singletrack
dilapidator	disorganise	fissionable	liquefiable	nightporter	singularise
diluvialist	disparaging	fissiparity	liquescence	nightwalker	singularity
dimensional	disparately	fissiparous	liquidambar	nigrescence	sinistrally
dimwittedly	dispensable	giantpowder	liquidation	ninnyhammer	sinistrorse
diningtable	dispersedly	gibberellin	lissomeness	nitrogenise	sinlessness
dinnerdance	displeasure	gibbousness	literalness	nitrogenous	sinological
dinnertable	disportment	gigantesque	lithography	nittygritty	sinuousness
dinnerwagon	disposition	gillyflower	lithophytic	oilpainting	sittingroom
dinosaurian	dispositive	gimcrackery	lithosphere	Pickwickian	situational
Diophantine	disputation	gingerbread	lithotomise	pictography	sizableness
diphtherial	disquieting	girlishness	lithotomist	pictorially	tiddlywinks
diphtheroid	disquietude	hibernacula	lithotripsy	picturebook	tightfisted
diphthongal	disremember	hibernation	litigiously	picturecard	tightlipped
diphycercal	disseminate	Hibernicism	litterateur	picturegoer	timebargain
diplococcus	disseminule	hideousness	lixiviation	picturesque	timepleaser
diplomatise	dissentient	hierarchism	Micawberish	pieceworker	timeserving
diplomatist	dissepiment	highbrowism	Micawberism	pietistical	timesharing
dipsomaniac	dissertator	highfalutin	micrococcal	pigeonchest	titanically
dipterocarp	dissimilate	highpitched	micrococcus	piggishness	Titianesque
directional	dissimulate	highpowered	microcosmic	pigheadedly	titillation
directivity	dissipation	highranking	microgamete	pigsticking	titleholder
directorate	dissipative	highstepper	micrography	pillowfight	tittivation
directorial	dissociable	highwrought	microgroove	pilocarpine	vibratility
directrices	dissolutely	hilariously	microlithic	pilotburner	vibrational
disablement	dissolution	Hindoostani	micrometric	pinkishness	vicariously
disaccustom	dissolvable	hippocampus	Micronesian	pinnatisect	viceadmiral
disaffected	dissonantly	Hippocratic	microphonic	pipecleaner	vicegerency
disafforest	dissyllable	hippopotami	microphytic	piperaceous	viceregally

viceroyalty	alleviation	electrolyse	illustrious	ambiversion	impenetrate
viceroyship	alleviative	electrolyte	kleptomania	ameliorator	impenitence
vichyssoise	alleviatory	electronics	oldwomanish	amenability	impenitency
viciousness	allocatable	electrotype	olfactology	amenorrhoea	imperfectly
vicissitude	allomorphic	elementally	oligochaete	amentaceous	imperforate
victualless	allopathist	elephantine	oligomerous	Americanise	imperialise
victualling	alphabetise	elephantoid	placability	Americanism	imperialism
vinaigrette	altercation	elicitation	plagiariser	Americanist	imperialist
vincibility	alternately	eligibility	plagioclase	amethystine	imperilling
vindication	alternation	elimination	plagiostome	amiableness	imperilment
vindicative	alternative	eliminative	plainspoken	amicability	imperiously
vindicatory	altitudinal	Elizabethan	plaintively	amontillado	impermanent
vinedresser	altocumulus	ellipsoidal	planetarium	amorousness	impermeable
viniculture	altorelievo	ellipticity	planetoidal	amorphously	impermeably
violoncello	altorilievo	elucidation	planimetric	amphetamine	impersonate
viridescent	altostratus	elucidative	planisphere	amphibolite	impertinent
virilescent	blackavised	elucidatory	planoconvex	amphibology	imperviable
virological	blackbeetle	elusiveness	plantigrade	amphictyony	impetration
viscountess	blackbirder	elutriation	plasmolysis	amphimictic	impetratory
viscousness	blackcoated	flabbergast	plasmolytic	amphisbaena	impetuosity
visibleness	blackfellow	flaccidness	plasterwork	amplexicaul	impetuously
viticulture	blackgrouse	flagcaptain	plasticiser	emancipator	impingement
vitrescence	blackmailer	flagellator	platearmour	emasculator	implausible
vitrifiable	blackmarket	flagofficer	plateresque	embarkation	implausibly
vituperator	bladderwort	flagwagging	platinotype	embellisher	implemental
vivaciously	blamelessly	flamboyance	platyrrhine	emblematise	implication
vivisection	blameworthy	flamboyancy	playerpiano	emblematist	implicative
widdershins	blasphemous	flamboyante	playfulness	embowelling	imploringly
widowerhood	blastogenic	flannelette	playingcard	embowerment	impolitical
wildcatting	blepharitis	flannelling	pleasurable	embraceable	impoliticly
wildfowling	blessedness	flatulently	pleasurably	embracement	importantly
willingness	blockbuster	flauntingly	plebeianise	embracingly	importation
windcheater	bloodguilty	flavourless	plebeianism	embrocation	importunate
windlestraw	bloodlessly	flavoursome	plectoptera	embroiderer	importunely
winegrowing	bloodstream	fleshliness	pleinairist	embroilment	importunity
winetasting	bloodsucker	flexibility	pleiotropic	embryologic	impoundment
winningness	bloodvessel	flightiness	Pleistocene	embryonated	impractical
winningpost	blotchiness	flimflammer	plenipotent	emmenagogue	imprecation
winsomeness	blunderbuss	flirtatious	plenteously	Emmenthaler	imprecatory
winterberry	clairschach	flocculence	plentifully	emotionally	imprecisely
wintergreen	clairvoyant	floorwalker	pleochroism	emotionless	imprecision
wirenetting	clamorously	florescence	pleomorphic	empanelling	impregnable
wirepulling	clandestine	floriferous	pleurodynia	emperorship	impregnably
wiretapping	clapperclaw	florilegium	pliableness	empirically	impressible
wisecracker	Clarencieux	floweriness	plicateness	emplacement	impressment
wishfulness	classically	fluctuation	ploughshare	emptyhanded	impropriate
wistfulness	cleanlimbed	fluorescein	ploughstaff	emptyheaded	impropriety
witchdoctor	cleanliness	fluorescent	pluralistic	emulousness	improvement
witchhunter	cleanshaven	fluoroscope	plutocratic	emulsionise	improvident
witenagemot	clearheaded	fluoroscopy	pluviometer	imaginarily	imprudently
witheringly	cleistogamy	glaringness	pluviometer	imagination	impuissance
withershins	clericalism	glassblower	slaughterer	imaginative	impulsively
witlessness	clericalist	glasscutter	slavedriver	imbrication	ominousness
zincography	cliffhanger	glassmaking	slaveholder	imitatively	ommatophore
ejaculation	climacteric	glauconitic	slavemarket	immanentism	omnifarious
ejaculatory	climatology	globeflower	slavishness	immanentist	omnipotence
skatingrink	clinometric	globigerina	Slavonicise	immarginate	omnipresent
skeletonise	clodhopping	globularity	sleepingbag	immediately	omniscience
sketchiness	closefisted	glomeration	sleepingcar	immedicable	smallholder
skilfulness	closehauled	glossolalia	sleeplessly	immenseness	smallminded
skulduddery	clostridium	glutinously	sleepwalker	immigration	smilelessly
skulduggery	clothesline	illaffected	sleeveboard	immitigable	smithereens
alabastrine	clothesmoth	illbreeding	slenderness	immitigably	smithsonite
Albigensian	clothesprop	illdisposed	sleuthhound	immortalise	smokescreen
albuminuria	cloudcastle	illfavoured	slickenside	immortality	smokingroom
alcyonarian	elaborately	illhumoured	slightingly	immoveables	smoothfaced
alembicated	elaboration	illiberally	slotmachine	immunologic	smorgasbord
Alexandrian	elaborative	illimitable	ulotrichous	impanelling	anachronism
alexandrine	elastically	illimitably	ultramarine	imparkation	anachronous
alexandrite	elasticated	illiquidity	ultramodern	impartation	anacoluthon
algological	elastomeric	illmannered	ultrasonics	impartially	anacreontic
algorithmic	elbowgrease	illogically	ultraviolet	impassioned	anadiplosis
alkalescent	elderliness	illtempered	amaranthine	impassively	analogously
alkalimeter	electioneer	illuminable	amativeness	impassivity	anaphylaxis
alkalimetry	electrician	illuminance	amazonstone	impatiently	anarchistic
allAmerican	electricity	illuminator	ambiguously	impeachable	anastomoses
allantoides	electrocute	illusionism	ambitiously	impeachment	
allegorical	electrolier	illusionist	ambivalence	impecunious	
allelomorph	electrology	illustrator	ambivalency	impedimenta	

anastomosis	endorsement	incoherency	inferiority	instigation	intertangle
anastomotic	endoskelton	incommodity	infertility	instigative	intertribal
ancientness	endothelial	incompetent	infestation	instillment	intervallic
androgynous	endothelium	incompliant	infeudation	instinctive	interviewee
anecdotical	endothermal	incongruent	infiltrator	instinctual	interviewer
anemometric	endothermic	incongruity	infinitival	institution	intimidator
anencephaly	endotrophic	incongruous	infirmarian	instruction	intolerable
anfractuous	enfeoffment	inconscient	inflammable	instructive	intolerably
angelically	enforceable	inconsonant	inflammably	insufflator	intolerance
angiography	enforcement	inconstancy	inflexional	insultingly	intractable
Anglicanism	enfranchise	incontinent	influential	insuperable	intractably
AngloFrench	engineering	incorporate	informality	insuperably	intravenous
AngloIndian	engorgement	incorporeal	information	intagliated	intrepidity
anglomaniac	engrossment	incorrectly	informative	integrality	intricately
AngloNorman	enhancement	incorruptly	informatory	integration	intriguante
anglophobia	enigmatical	increasable	infrangible	integrative	intromitted
anglophobic	enjambement	incredulity	infrequence	intelligent	intromitter
animalcular	enlargeable	incredulous	infrequency	intemperate	introverted
anisotropic	enlargement	incremental	ingathering	intenseness	intrusively
annabergite	enlightened	incriminate	ingeniously	intensifier	intuitional
annihilator	enlivenment	inculcation	ingenuously	intensional	intuitively
anniversary	enneahedron	inculpation	ingrainedly	intensively	intuitivism
annunciator	ennoblement	inculpatory	ingratitude	intentional	intumescent
anomalistic	enquiringly	incunabulum	ingurgitate	intentioned	invalidness
anomalously	ensanguined	incuriosity	inhabitable	interactant	invectively
anonymously	enslavement	incuriously	inhabitancy	interaction	inventively
antecedence	entablature	incurvation	inheritable	interactive	inventorial
antechamber	entablement	incurvature	inheritance	interallied	investigate
antemundane	enterostomy	indeciduous	inheritress	interatomic	investiture
antenuptial	enterovirus	indefinable	initialling	interbedded	inviability
antependium	enterpriser	indefinably	injudicious	intercalary	invidiously
anteriority	entertainer	indehiscent	injuriously	intercalate	invigilator
antheridium	enthralling	indentation	innavigable	intercensal	invigorator
anthocyanin	enthralment	independent	innervation	intercepter	inviolately
anthologise	entitlement	indifferent	innocuously	interceptor	involucrate
anthologist	entomophily	indigestion	innoxiously	intercessor	involuntary
anthracitic	entrainment	indigestive	innumerable	interchange	involvement
anthropical	entreatment	indignantly	innumerably	intercostal	invultation
anticathode	entrustment	indignation	innutrition	intercourse	knavishness
anticipator	enucleation	indirection	inobservant	intercrural	knowingness
anticyclone	enumeration	individuate	inoculation	interdental	knownothing
antifouling	enumerative	indivisible	inoculative	interdepend	knucklebone
antigravity	enunciation	indivisibly	inoffensive	interesting	oncological
antiJacobin	enviousness	IndoChinese	inofficious	interfacial	oneiromancy
antimonious	envelopment	IndoIranian	inoperative	interfacing	onerousness
antineutron	environment	indomitable	inopportune	interfluent	ontogenesis
antioxidant	gnotobiosis	indomitably	inquilinous	interfusion	ontogenetic
antiphonary	gnotobiotic	indorsement	inquiringly	intergrowth	ontological
antiphrasis	inadaptable	indubitable	inquisition	interiorise	pneumonitis
antipyretic	inadvertent	indubitably	inquisitive	interiority	snatchblock
antiquarian	inadvisable	inductively	insalubrity	interjacent	snickersnee
antiquation	inalienable	indulgently	inscribable	interleaves	snowbunting
antirrhinum	inalienably	industrious	inscription	interlinear	snowgoggles
antiSemitic	inalterable	inebriation	inscriptive	interlingua	snowleopard
antistrophe	inalterably	inedibility	inscrutable	interlining	unaccounted
antitypical	inanimately	ineffective	inscrutably	interlocker	unadvisedly
antivitamin	inanimation	ineffectual	insectarium	intermeddle	unalterable
antonomasia	inappetence	inefficient	insecticide	intermedium	unambiguous
anxiousness	inattention	inelegantly	insectifuge	intermingle	unanimously
enarthrosis	inattentive	ineloquence	insectivore	intermitted	unappealing
encapsulate	inaugurator	ineluctable	insectology	internalise	unashamedly
enchainment	incalescent	ineluctably	inseminator	internality	unassertive
enchantment	incantation	inequitable	insensately	internecine	unavailable
enchantress	incantatory	inequitably	insensitive	internuncio	unavoidable
enchiridion	incarcerate	inescapable	inseparable	interosseus	unavoidably
encomiastic	incardinate	inessential	inseparably	interplayed	unawareness
encrustment	incarnadine	inestimable	insessorial	interpolate	unbeknownst
encumbrance	incarnation	inestimably	insidiously	interpreter	unbelieving
encystation	incertitude	inexactness	insincerely	interracial	unbendingly
endearingly	incessantly	inexcusable	insincerity	interregnum	unbeseeming
endemically	incinerator	inexcusably	insinuation	interrelate	unboundedly
endlessness	incipiently	inexistence	insinuative	interrogate	unbreakable
endocardiac	inclemently	inexpedient	insipidness	interrupter	uncanniness
endocardial	inclination	inexpensive	insistently	interruptor	uncanonical
endocardium	inclusively	infanticide	insouciance	interseptal	uncatchable
endometrium	incoercible	infantilism	inspiration	intersexual	unceasingly
endomorphic	incognisant	infantryman	inspiratory	intersperse	uncertainly
endophagous	incoherence	infatuation	instability	interspinal	uncertainty
endoplasmic		inferential	installment		unchristian

uncivilised	unmemorable	bountifully	commensally	condensable	consonantal
uncleanness	unmemorably	bourgeoisie	commentator	conditional	consonantly
unclimbable	unmitigated	boutonniere	commination	conditioner	conspecific
uncluttered	unnaturally	bowdleriser	comminatory	condolatory	conspicuity
uncommitted	unnecessary	boysenberry	comminution	condominium	conspicuous
unconcealed	unnervingly	coadunation	commiserate	condonation	conspirator
unconcerned	unobtrusive	coagulation	commissural	condottiere	constellate
uncongenial	unorganized	coalescence	committable	condottieri	consternate
unconnected	unorthodoxy	coarctation	commonality	conductance	constituent
unconscious	unpalatable	cobblestone	commonplace	conductible	constitutor
uncontested	unpolitical	coccidiosis	commonsense	conductress	constrictor
uncountable	unpossessed	cochinchina	communalise	condylomata	construable
uncouthness	unprintable	cockaleekie	communalism	confabulate	constructor
uncrushable	unpromising	cockleshell	communalist	confederacy	consultancy
underbidder	unqualified	cockyleekie	communicant	confederate	consumerism
undercharge	unquietness	coconscious	communicate	conferrable	consumingly
underexpose	unrealistic	codefendant	communistic	confessedly	consummator
underground	unreasoning	codicillary	commutation	confidently	consumption
undergrowth	unrelenting	coeducation	commutative	confidingly	consumptive
underhanded	unremitting	coefficient	compactness	confinement	containable
undermanned	unrighteous	coessential	compaginate	confirmable	containment
underpinned	unsaturated	coeternally	comparatist	confiscable	contaminant
underseller	unselective	coexistence	comparative	confiscator	contaminate
undersigned	unshockable	coextension	compartment	conflagrant	contemplate
understated	unshrinking	coextensive	compassable	conflagrate	contentedly
undertaking	unskilfully	coffeehouse	compellable	confliction	contentious
undertenant	unsmilingly	coffeetable	compendious	conflictive	contentment
undervaluer	unsolicited	cognateness	compensator	conformable	conterminal
underweight	unsoundness	cognitional	competently	conformably	contestable
underwriter	unsparingly	cognitively	competition	conformally	continental
undeserving	unspeakable	cognitivity	competitive	conformance	continently
undesirable	unspeakably	cognoscente	compilation	confusingly	contingence
undeveloped	unstoppable	cognoscenti	compilement	confutation	contingency
undisguised	unteachable	cognoscible	complacence	confutative	continuable
undisturbed	unthinkable	coincidence	complacency	congealable	continually
undoubtedly	unthinkably	coinheritor	complainant	congealment	continuance
undutifully	untouchable	coinsurance	complaisant	congelation	continuator
unemotional	unusualness	coldblooded	complexness	congenerous	contorniate
unendurable	unutterable	coldhearted	compliantly	congenially	contrabasso
unendurably	unutterably	coleorrhiza	complicated	congressman	contractile
unequivocal	unvarnished	collaborate	complotting	congruently	contraction
unessential	unwarranted	collapsible	comportment	congruously	contractive
unexploited	unweetingly	collectable	compositely	conjectural	contractual
unexpressed	unwholesome	collectanea	composition	conjugality	contracture
unfailingly	unwillingly	collectedly	compositive	conjugation	contradance
unfaltering	unwinkingly	collectible	compossible	conjugative	contraption
unfashioned	unwittingly	collenchyma	compotation	conjunction	contrariety
unfeelingly	boardschool	colligation	compotatory	conjunctiva	contrarious
unfeignedly	Bodhisattva	colligative	compression	conjunctive	contrastive
unflappable	bodybuilder	collimation	compressive	conjuncture	contretemps
unflinching	bodyservant	collinearly	comprisable	conjuration	contributor
unforgiving	bohemianism	collisional	comptroller	connectable	contrivable
unfortunate	boilermaker	collocation	compunction	connectedly	contrivance
unfurnished	bombardment	collusively	compurgator	connectible	controlling
ungetatable	bombilation	colonelship	computation	connoisseur	controlment
ungodliness	bombination	colonialism	computerise	connotation	controversy
unguardedly	Bonapartean	colonialist	comradeship	connotative	conurbation
unguiculate	Bonapartism	colorimeter	comstockery	connubially	convenances
unhappiness	Bonapartist	colorimetry	concatenate	conquerable	convenience
unhealthily	bonbonniere	colouration	concealable	consanguine	conveniency
unhelpfully	bondservant	colourblind	concealment	consciously	conventicle
unicellular	bondservice	colourfully	conceitedly	consecrator	convergence
unicoloured	bondwashing	columbarium	conceivable	consecution	convergency
unification	bookbinding	columniated	conceivably	consecutive	conversable
uniformness	bookinghall	combatively	concentrate	consentient	conversance
unigeniture	bookishness	combination	conceptacle	consequence	conversancy
unimportant	bookkeeping	combinative	concernment	conservable	convertible
uninhabited	booklearned	combinatory	concertedly	conservancy	convertibly
uninhibited	bookselling	combustible	concertgoer	conservator	conveyancer
uninucleate	bookshelves	comestibles	conciliator	considerate	convincible
unipersonal	boorishness	comeuppance	conciseness	considering	convivially
unipolarity	bootlegging	comfortable	concomitant	consignable	convocation
unisexually	borborygmus	comfortably	concordance	consignment	convolution
universally	botanically	comfortless	concrescent	consistence	convolvulus
unkennelled	botheration	commandment	concubinage	consistency	cookgeneral
unlimitedly	bottleglass	commemorate	concubinary	consolation	cooperation
unmanliness	bottlegreen	commendable	concubitant	consolatory	cooperative
unmatchable	bottlenosed	commendably	concurrence	consolidate	coordinator
unmeaningly	bounteously	commendator	condemnable	consolingly	coparcenary

anastomosis	endorsement	incoherency	inferiority	instigation	intertangle
anastomotic	endoskelton	incommodity	infertility	instigative	intertribal
ancientness	endothelial	incompetent	infestation	instillment	intervallic
androgynous	endothelium	incompliant	infeudation	instinctive	interviewee
anecdotical	endothermal	incongruent	infiltrator	instinctual	interviewer
anemometric	endothermic	incongruity	infinitival	institution	intimidator
anencephaly	endotrophic	incongruous	infirmarian	instruction	intolerable
anfractuous	enfeoffment	inconscient	inflammable	instructive	intolerably
angelically	enforceable	inconsonant	inflammably	insufflator	intolerance
angiography	enforcement	inconstancy	inflexional	insultingly	intractable
Anglicanism	enfranchise	incontinent	influential	insuperable	intractably
AngloFrench	engineering	incorporate	informality	insuperably	intravenous
AngloIndian	engorgement	incorporeal	information	intagliated	intrepidity
anglomaniac	engrossment	incorrectly	informative	integrality	intricately
AngloNorman	enhancement	incorruptly	informatory	integration	intriguante
anglophobia	enigmatical	increasable	infrangible	integrative	intromitted
anglophobic	enjambement	incredulity	infrequence	intelligent	intromitter
animalcular	enlargeable	incredulous	infrequency	intemperate	introverted
anisotropic	enlargement	incremental	ingathering	intenseness	intrusively
annabergite	enlightened	incriminate	ingeniously	intensifier	intuitional
annihilator	enlivenment	inculcation	ingenuously	intensional	intuitively
anniversary	enneahedron	inculpation	ingrainedly	intensively	intuitivism
annunciator	ennoblement	inculpatory	ingratitude	intentional	intumescent
anomalistic	enquiringly	incunabulum	ingurgitate	intentioned	invalidness
anomalously	ensanguined	incuriosity	inhabitable	interactant	invectively
anonymously	enslavement	incuriously	inhabitancy	interaction	inventively
antecedence	entablature	incurvation	inheritable	interactive	inventorial
antechamber	entablement	incurvature	inheritance	interallied	investigate
antemundane	enterostomy	indeciduous	inheritress	interatomic	investiture
antenuptial	enterovirus	indefinable	initialling	interbedded	inviability
antependium	enterpriser	indefinably	injudicious	intercalary	invidiously
anteriority	entertainer	indehiscent	injuriously	intercalate	invigilator
antheridium	enthralling	indentation	innavigable	intercensal	invigorator
anthocyanin	enthralment	independent	innervation	intercepter	inviolately
anthologise	entitlement	indifferent	innocuously	interceptor	involucrate
anthologist	entomophily	indigestion	innoxiously	intercessor	involuntary
anthracitic	entrainment	indigestive	innumerable	interchange	involvement
anthropical	entreatment	indignantly	innumerably	intercostal	invultation
anticathode	entrustment	indignation	innutrition	intercourse	knavishness
anticipator	enucleation	indirection	inobservant	intercrural	knowingness
anticyclone	enumeration	individuate	inoculation	interdental	knownothing
antifouling	enumerative	indivisible	inoculative	interdepend	knucklebone
antigravity	enunciation	indivisibly	inoffensive	interesting	oncological
antiJacobin	enunciative	IndoChinese	inofficious	interfacial	oneiromancy
antimonious	envelopment	IndoIranian	inoperative	interfacing	onerousness
antineutron	enviousness	indomitable	inopportune	interfluent	ontogenesis
antioxidant	environment	indomitably	inquilinous	interfusion	ontogenetic
antiphonary	gnotobiosis	indorsement	inquiringly	intergrowth	ontological
antiphrasis	gnotobiotic	indubitable	inquisition	interiorise	pneumonitis
antipyretic	inadaptable	indubitably	inquisitive	interiority	snatchblock
antiquarian	inadvertent	inductively	insalubrity	interjacent	snickersnee
antiquation	inadvisable	indulgently	inscribable	interleaves	snowbunting
antirrhinum	inalienable	industrious	inscription	interlinear	snowgoggles
antiSemitic	inalterable	inebriation	inscriptive	Interlingua	snowleopard
antistrophe	inanimately	inedibility	inscrutable	interlining	unaccounted
antitypical	inanimation	ineffective	inscrutably	interlocker	unadvisedly
antivitamin	inappetence	ineffectual	insectarium	interlunary	unalterable
antonomasia	inattention	inefficient	insecticide	intermeddle	unambiguous
anxiousness	inattentive	inelegantly	insectifuge	intermedium	unanimously
enarthrosis	inaugurator	ineloquence	insectivore	intermingle	unappealing
encapsulate	incalescent	ineluctable	insectology	intermitted	unashamedly
enchainment	incantation	ineluctably	inseminator	internalise	unassertive
enchantment	incantatory	inequitable	insensately	internality	unavailable
enchantress	incarcerate	inequitably	insensitive	internecine	unavoidable
enchiridion	incardinate	inescapable	inseparable	internuncio	unavoidably
encomiastic	incarnadine	inessential	inseparably	interosseus	unawareness
encrustment	incarnation	inestimable	insessorial	interplayed	unbeknownst
encumbrance	incertitude	inestimably	insidiously	interpolate	unbelieving
encystation	incessantly	inexactness	insincerely	interpreter	unbendingly
endearingly	incinerator	inexcusable	insincerity	interracial	unbeseeming
endemically	incipiently	inexcusably	insinuation	interregnum	unboundedly
endlessness	inclemently	inexistence	insinuative	interrelate	unbreakable
endocardiac	inclination	inexpedient	insipidness	interrogate	uncanniness
endocardial	inclusively	inexpensive	insistently	interrupter	uncanonical
endocardium	incoercible	infanticide	insouciance	interruptor	uncatchable
endometrium	incognisant	infantilism	inspiration	interseptal	unceasingly
endomorphic	incoherence	infantryman	inspiratory	intersexual	uncertainly
endophagous		infatuation	instability	intersperse	uncertainty
endoplasmic		inferential	installment	interspinal	unchristian

uncivilised
uncleanness
unclimbable
uncluttered
uncommitted
unconcealed
unconcerned
uncongenial
unconnected
unconscious
uncontested
uncountable
uncouthness
uncrushable
underbidder
undercharge
underexpose
underground
undergrowth
underhanded
undermanned
underpinned
underseller
undersigned
understated
undertaking
undertenant
undervaluer
underweight
underwriter
undeserving
undesirable
undeveloped
undisguised
undisturbed
undoubtedly
undutifully
unemotional
unendurable
unendurably
unequivocal
unessential
unexploited
unexpressed
unfailingly
unfaltering
unfashioned
unfeelingly
unfeignedly
unflappable
unflinching
unforgiving
unfortunate
unfurnished
ungetatable
ungodliness
unguardedly
unguiculate
unhappiness
unhealthily
unhelpfully
unicellular
unicoloured
unification
uniformness
unigeniture
unimportant
uninhabited
uninhibited
uninucleate
unipersonal
unipolarity
unisexually
universally
unkennelled
unlimitedly
unmanliness
unmatchable
unmeaningly

unmemorable
unmemorably
unmitigated
unnaturally
unnecessary
unnervingly
unobtrusive
unorganized
unorthodoxy
unpalatable
unpolitical
unpossessed
unprintable
unpromising
unqualified
unquietness
unrealistic
unreasoning
unrelenting
unremitting
unrighteous
unsaturated
unselective
unshockable
unshrinking
unskilfully
unsmilingly
unsolicited
unsoundness
unsparingly
unspeakable
unspeakably
unstoppable
unteachable
unthinkable
unthinkably
untouchable
unusualness
unutterable
unutterably
unvarnished
unwarranted
unweetingly
unwholesome
unwillingly
unwinkingly
unwittingly
boardschool
Bodhisattva
bodybuilder
bodyservant
bohemianism
boilermaker
bombardment
bombilation
bombination
Bonapartean
Bonapartism
Bonapartist
bonbonniere
bondservant
bondservice
bondwashing
bookbinding
bookinghall
bookishness
bookkeeping
booklearned
bookselling
bookshelves
boorishness
bootlegging
borborygmus
botanically
botheration
bottleglass
bottlegreen
bottlenosed
bounteously

bountifully
bourgeoisie
boutonniere
bowdleriser
boysenberry
coadunation
coagulation
coalescence
coarctation
cobblestone
coccidiosis
cochinchina
cockaleekie
cockleshell
cockyleekie
coconscious
codefendant
codicillary
coeducation
coefficient
coessential
coeternally
coexistence
coextension
coextensive
coffeehouse
coffeetable
cognateness
cognitional
cognitively
cognitivity
cognoscente
cognoscenti
cognoscible
coincidence
coinheritor
coinsurance
coldblooded
coldhearted
coleorrhiza
collaborate
collapsible
collectable
collectanea
collectedly
collectible
collenchyma
colligation
colligative
collimation
collinearly
collisional
collocation
collusively
colonelship
colonialism
colonialist
colorimeter
colorimetry
colouration
colourblind
colourfully
columbarium
columniated
combatively
combination
combinative
combinatory
combustible
comestibles
comeuppance
comfortable
comfortably
comfortless
commandment
commemorate
commendable
commendably
commendator

commensally
commentator
commination
comminatory
comminution
commiserate
commissural
committable
commonality
commonplace
commonsense
communalise
communalism
communalist
communicant
communicate
communistic
commutation
commutative
compactness
compaginate
comparatist
comparative
compartment
compassable
compellable
compendious
compensator
competently
competition
competitive
compilation
compilement
complacence
complainant
complaisant
complexness
compliantly
complicated
complotting
comportment
compositely
composition
compositive
compossible
compotation
compotatory
compression
compressive
comprisable
comptroller
compunction
compurgator
computation
computerise
comradeship
comstockery
concatenate
concealable
concealment
conceitedly
conceivable
conceivably
concentrate
conceptacle
concernment
concertedly
concertgoer
conciliator
conciseness
concomitant
concordance
concrescent
concubinage
concubinary
concurrence
condemnable

condensable
conditional
conditioner
condolatory
condominium
condonation
condottiere
condottieri
conductance
conductible
conductress
condylomata
confabulate
confederacy
confederate
conferrable
confessedly
confidently
confidingly
confinement
confirmable
confiscable
confiscator
conflagrant
conflagrate
confliction
conflictive
conformable
conformably
conformally
conformance
confusingly
confutation
confutative
congealable
congealment
congelation
congenerous
congenially
congressman
congruently
congruously
conjectural
conjugality
conjugation
conjugative
conjunction
conjunctiva
conjunctive
conjuncture
conjuration
connectable
connectedly
connectible
connoisseur
connotation
connotative
connubially
conquerable
consanguine
consciously
consecrator
consecution
consecutive
consentient
consequence
conservable
conservancy
conservator
considerate
considering
consignable
consignment
consistence
consistency
consolation
consolatory
consolidate
consolingly

consonantal
consonantly
conspecific
conspicuity
conspicuous
conspirator
constellate
consternate
constituent
constitutor
constrictor
construable
constructor
consultancy
consumerism
consumingly
consummator
consumption
consumptive
containable
containment
contaminant
contaminate
contemplate
contentedly
contentious
contentment
conterminal
contestable
continental
continently
contingence
contingency
continuable
continually
continuance
continuator
contorniate
contrabasso
contractile
contraction
contractive
contractual
contracture
contradance
contraption
contrariety
contrarious
contrastive
contretemps
contributor
contrivable
contrivance
controlling
controlment
controversy
conurbation
convenances
convenience
conveniency
conventicle
convergence
convergency
conversable
conversance
conversancy
convertible
convertibly
conveyancer
convincible
convivially
convocation
convolution
convolvulus
cookgeneral
cooperation
cooperative
coordinator
coparcenary

copingstone	countryseat	fortnightly	loggerheads	mothercraft	polycrystal
copiousness	countryside	fortunately	logicalness	mothernaked	polygenesis
coplanarity	countrywide	forwardness	logographer	motherright	polygenetic
copperplate	courteously	foulmouthed	logographic	motivepower	polyglottal
coppersmith	courtliness	fourflusher	logomachist	mountaineer	polyglottic
coralloidal	coxcombical	fourpounder	longanimity	mountainous	polygonally
corbiculate	doctrinaire	fourwheeler	longplaying	mountaintop	polygraphic
corbiesteps	doctrinally	godchildren	longsighted	movableness	polymorphic
cordialness	documentary	goddaughter	looselimbed	moveability	polyonymous
corecipient	dodecaphony	godforsaken	loosestrife	noctilucent	polypeptide
cornerstone	doggishness	godlessness	lophobranch	noctivagant	polyphagous
cornhusking	dolefulness	goldbeating	loudmouthed	noctivagous	polyphonous
corniferous	dollishness	golddigging	loudspeaker	nocturnally	polystyrene
cornucopian	doltishness	goldenberry	loutishness	noiselessly	polytechnic
coronagraph	domesticate	gonfalonier	louverboard	noisemaking	polyzoarium
coronograph	domesticity	goniometric	louvreboard	noisomeness	pomegranate
corporality	domiciliary	goodhearted	lovableness	nomadically	pomiculture
corporately	domiciliate	goodlooking	lowpressure	nomenclator	pomological
corporation	domineering	goodnatured	lowspirited	nominatival	pompousness
corporatism	donnishness	gormandiser	loxodromics	nomographer	ponderation
corporative	doorknocker	gourmandise	mockingbird	nomographic	ponderosity
corporeally	doublecheck	gourmandism	moderations	nomological	ponderously
corpulently	doublecross	hobbledehoy	modernistic	nonchalance	pontificals
corpuscular	doubleDutch	hoggishness	moisturiser	nondelivery	pontificate
correctable	doubleedged	hollandaise	molecricket	nondescript	populariser
correctness	doubleender	holoblastic	molecularly	nonetheless	pornography
correlation	doubleentry	holographic	molendinary	nonexistent	porphyritic
correlative	doublefaced	holothurian	molestation	nonfeasance	portability
corrigendum	doublequick	homeopathic	mollycoddle	nonmatching	porterhouse
corroborant	doublespeak	homeostasis	molybdenite	nonmetallic	portionless
corroborate	doublethink	homeostatic	momentarily	nonpartisan	portmanteau
corrosively	doubtlessly	homesteader	momentously	nonplussing	portraitist
corrugation	doughtiness	homestretch	monarchical	nonresident	portraiture
corruptible	douroucouli	homiletical	monasterial	nonsensical	positronium
corruptibly	downdraught	homocentric	monasticism	nonsequitur	posological
corruptness	downhearted	homoeopathy	moneylender	nonspecific	possibility
coruscation	downtrodden	homoestatic	moneymaking	nonunionist	postclassic
cosignatory	doxographer	homogeneity	moneymarket	nonviolence	posteriorly
cosmetician	folliculate	homogeneous	moneyspider	nonvolatile	postexilian
cosmetology	fomentation	homogenetic	monitorship	northeaster	postglacial
cosmogonist	foolishness	homogeniser	monkeybread	northwester	postnuptial
cosmography	footpoundal	homoiousian	monkeyshine	noseyparker	postulation
cosmologist	footslogger	homological	monocarpous	nosographer	potentially
cosmopolite	footsoldier	homomorphic	monochasial	nosographic	potteringly
costbenefit	foppishness	homophonous	monochasium	nosological	pourparlers
costiveness	foraminated	homoplastic	monochromat	notableness	powderflask
cotemporary	foraminifer	homopterous	monochromic	nothingness	powerlessly
coterminous	forbearance	homosporous	monoclinous	noticeboard	roadholding
cotoneaster	forbiddance	homothallic	monoculture	notionalist	rockcrystal
cottongrass	foreclosure	homozygosis	monogenesis	notoriously	rodenticide
cottonmouth	foreignness	honeybadger	monogenetic	nourishment	rodomontade
coulometric	forequarter	honeymooner	monogrammed	novelettish	roentgenise
counselling	forerunning	honeysuckle	monographer	noxiousness	roguishness
countenance	foreseeable	hooliganism	monographic	pocketknife	romanticise
counterblow	foreshorten	hopefulness	monolingual	pocketmoney	romanticism
counterbond	foresighted	hornswoggle	monological	pocketsized	romanticist
counterfeit	forestaller	horological	monologuise	pococurante	ropedancing
counterfoil	forestation	horripilate	monologuist	podophyllin	ropewalking
counterfort	forethinker	horsecollar	mononuclear	pointdevice	Rosicrucian
countermand	forethought	horsedoctor	monophagous	pointedness	rotogravure
countermark	foretopmast	horseradish	monophthong	pointillism	rottenstone
countermine	foretopsail	hospitalise	Monophysite	pointillist	roughfooted
countermove	forevermore	hospitality	monopoliser	pointlessly	roughlegged
countermure	foreverness	hospitaller	monopterous	poisonously	roundedness
counterpane	forewarning	housefather	Monothelite	polarimeter	soapboiling
counterpart	forfeitable	householder	monozygotic	polarimetry	soberminded
counterplan	forgetfully	housekeeper	monseigneur	polarisable	sociability
counterplea	forgetmenot	houselights	monstrosity	polariscope	socialistic
counterplot	forgettable	housemaster	monstrously	polemically	Socinianism
countersign	forgiveness	housemother	moonlighter	polevaulter	sociologist
countersink	forlornness	housewifely	mooringmast	policewoman	sociometric
countersunk	formalistic	housewifery	morbiferous	politically	sociopathic
counterturn	formational	ionospheric	moribundity	politicking	sockdolager
countervail	formication	journeywork	morningroom	pollination	sockdologen
counterview	formularise	joylessness	moronically	poltergeist	softhearted
counterwork	formulation	loathliness	morrisdance	poltroonery	softshelled
countlessly	fornication	loathsomely	mortarboard	polyandrous	solanaceous
countrified	forthcoming	loculicidal	mosstrooper	polycarpous	soldierlike
countryfied	fortifiable	logarithmic		polychromic	soldiership

solifluxion	vortiginous	operatively	sporogonium	Brahmanical	cryptomeria
soliloquise	wolfwhistle	operculated	sporophytic	brahmaputra	crystalline
soliloquist	womanliness	operoseness	sportswoman	Brahminical	crystallise
solipsistic	wonderfully	ophidiarium	sporulation	brainlessly	crystallite
solmisation	woodcarving	ophiologist	spreadeagle	brainsickly	crystalloid
solutionist	woodcutting	opinionated	springboard	brainteaser	draggletail
solvability	workability	opportunely	springclean	branchiopod	dramaturgic
somatically	workmanlike	opportunism	springhouse	brankursine	drastically
somatogenic	workmanship	opportunist	springiness	brazenfaced	draughtsman
somatologic	worldbeater	opportunity	Upanishadic	breadbasket	drawingroom
somatoplasm	worldliness	opprobrious	upholsterer	breadcrumbs	dreadnought
somatotonia	worldlywise	oppugnation	uprightness	breadthways	dreamlessly
somatotonic	worrisomely	optometrist	aquaculture	breadthwise	dresscircle
somewhither	worshipable	spaceflight	aquarellist	breadwinner	dressmaking
somnambular	worshipless	spaceheater	aquatically	breastplate	drillmaster
somniculous	worshipping	spacesaving	aquiculture	breastwheel	dropcurtain
somniferous	worthlessly	sparingness	equableness	breathalyse	dropforging
somnolently	zoantharian	sparrowbill	equiangular	breechblock	drouthiness
songfulness	zoographist	sparrowhawk	equidistant	breezeblock	drunkenness
songsparrow	zoomorphism	spasmodical	equilateral	bricklaying	eradication
sonofabitch	zooplankton	spastically	equilibrate	bridgeboard	eradicative
sophistical	zootechnics	spathaceous	equilibrist	brilliantly	Erastianism
Soroptimist	Zoroastrian	spatterdash	equilibrium	bristletail	ergatocracy
sorrowfully	apartmental	speakership	equinoctial	bristleworm	erotogenous
soteriology	aphrodisiac	specifiable	equipollent	bristliness	erotomaniac
sottishness	apocalyptic	specificity	equivalence	Britishness	erratically
soulfulness	apologetics	spectacular	equivalency	brittleness	erroneously
soundlessly	apomorphine	spectatress	equivocally	broadcaster	erubescence
soupkitchen	aponeuroses	spectrality	equivocator	broadleaved	erythrocyte
southeaster	aponeurosis	spectrogram	squalidness	broadminded	fractionary
Southernism	aponeurotic	spectrology	squarebuilt	brotherhood	fractionate
southwester	apophyllite	speculation	squarsonage	brucellosis	fractionise
sovereignly	aposiopesis	speculative	squashiness	brusqueness	fractiously
sovereignty	apostleship	speechifier	squeakiness	brutishness	fragmentary
toastmaster	apostolical	speedometer	squeamishly	bryozoology	Francomania
tobacconist	apostrophic	spelaeology	squintingly	crabbedness	Francophile
tobogganing	apotheosise	spellbinder	squirearchy	crackerjack	Francophobe
tobogganist	appallingly	spendthrift	arbitrageur	craftswoman	francophone
toffeenosed	apparatchik	spermaphyte	arbitrament	craniometry	franctireur
togglejoint	apparelling	spermatozoa	arbitrarily	creationism	frankfurter
tolbutamide	appealingly	spermicidal	arbitration	creationist	franklinite
tonsillitis	appeasement	spessartite	arbitrative	credentials	frankpledge
toothbilled	appellation	sphaeridium	arbitratrix	credibility	frantically
toothpowder	appellative	sphagnology	arboraceous	credulously	franticness
toothsomely	applaudable	spherically	arborescent	crematorium	fraternally
topdressing	application	spherometer	archaeology	crenellated	fraterniser
toploftical	applicative	spherulitic	archaeornis	crenulation	fratricidal
topographer	applicatory	sphincteral	archaically	crepitation	fraudulence
topographic	appogiatura	sphincteric	archangelic	crepuscular	freebooting
topological	appointment	sphygmogram	archdiocese	crestfallen	freehearted
torchbearer	appreciable	spifflicate	archduchess	criminalist	freemasonry
torchsinger	appreciably	spindlelegs	archdukedom	criminality	freethinker
torticollis	appreciator	spindletree	Archimedean	crimination	freethought
torturously	approbation	spinelessly	archipelago	criminative	freezedried
totalisator	approbatory	spiniferous	arduousness	criminatory	frenchified
totteringly	appropriate	Spinozistic	arenicolous	criminology	Frenchwoman
touchtyping	approvingly	spinsterish	Areopagitic	criticality	fretfulness
toughminded	approximate	spiraculate	arglebargle	criticaster	friableness
tourbillion	appurtenant	spiritistic	argumentive	crocidolite	fricandeaux
townspeople	epeirogenic	spiritlevel	aristocracy	crocodilian	frightfully
toxicomania	ephemerides	spiritually	Arminianism	crookbacked	frigidarium
toxophilite	epidiascope	spiritually	armtwisting	crookedness	frivolously
vociferance	epigastrium	spirituelle	aromaticity	crossbearer	frontrunner
vociferator	epigraphist	spirochaete	arraignment	crossbowman	frostbitten
voguishness	epinephrine	spirochetal	arrangement	crossgarnet	frothhopper
voicelessly	epipetalous	spirometric	arrestingly	crosslegged	frowardness
volcanicity	episcopally	splashboard	arterialise	crossstitch	frowstiness
volcanology	epithalamia	splayfooted	arthrospore	crotcheteer	fructuation
volitionary	epithalamic	splendorous	articulable	cruciferous	frugivorous
volkslieder	epithelioma	splenectomy	articulated	crucifixion	fruitlessly
voltametric	epochmaking	splenetical	articulator	crucigerous	frustration
volubleness	ipecacuanha	spokeswoman	artillerist	crunchiness	gracelessly
volumometer	ipsilateral	spondulicks	artiodactyl	crustaceous	gracileness
voluntarily	opalescence	spondylitis	artlessness	cryobiology	gradational
voluntarism	opencircuit	spongecloth	brachiation	cryosurgery	gradiometer
voluntarist	openhearted	sponsorship	brachyurous	cryotherapy	gradualness
voodooistic	openmouthed	spontaneity	bracteolate	cryptically	GraecoRoman
voortrekker	operational	spontaneous	bradycardia	cryptogamic	grammalogue
voraciously		sporogenous	braggadocio	cryptograph	grammatical

gramophonic	orientalise	preprandial	proletarian	trafficator	triquetrous
grandfather	orientalism	prerogative	proletariat	trafficking	tristichous
grandiflora	orientalist	presanctify	proliferate	trafficless	trisyllabic
grandiosely	orientation	presbyteral	proliferous	tragedienne	trisyllable
grandiosity	originality	presciently	prolificacy	tragicomedy	tritagonist
grandmother	origination	preselector	prolificity	trailblazer	tritheistic
grandnephew	originative	presentable	prolocutrix	trainbearer	trituration
grandparent	ornithology	presentably	prominently	trammelling	triumvirate
grangeriser	ornithopter	presentient	promiscuity	transaction	trivialness
granivorous	ornithosaur	presentment	promiscuous	transalpine	troglodytic
granolithic	orthocentre	preservable	promisingly	transceiver	trophoblast
granophyric	orthodontia	pressagency	promotional	transcriber	troposphere
granularity	orthodontic	prestigious	promptitude	transection	trothplight
granulation	orthoepical	prestissimo	promulgator	transferred	troublesome
granulocyte	orthography	prestressed	proofreader	transferrer	troublously
graphically	orthopaedic	presumingly	propagation	transfigure	trouserless
graphicness	orthopedics	presumption	propagative	transfinite	trousersuit
grasshopper	orthopedist	presumptive	prophethood	transfixion	truculently
gratulation	orthopteran	pretendedly	prophetical	transformer	truehearted
gratulatory	orthoscopic	pretentious	prophetship	transfusion	trundletail
gravedigger	orthotropic	preterhuman	prophylaxis	transhumant	trustbuster
gravelblind	practicable	preterition	propinquity	transiently	trusteeship
gravimetric	practicably	prevalently	propitiable	transilient	trustworthy
gravitation	practically	prevaricate	propitiator	translation	tryingplane
gravitative	praetorship	preventable	proportions	translocate	trypanosome
greasepaint	pragmatical	preventible	proposition	translucent	tryptophane
greaseproof	prattlingly	previsional	proprietary	translunary	uranography
greatnephew	prayerwheel	prickliness	prorogation	transmarine	urochordate
greengrocer	preachiness	priestcraft	prosaically	transmittal	urticaceous
greenkeeper	preaudience	primaevally	prosaicness	transmitted	urticarious
greenockite	Precambrian	primateship	prosecution	transmitter	wreckmaster
gristliness	precautious	primatology	prosecutrix	transpadane	wrongheaded
grotesquely	precedented	primigenial	proselytise	transparent	ascensional
grotesquery	precedently	primiparous	proselytism	transpierce	ascetically
grouchiness	precentress	primitively	prosenchyma	transponder	ascomycetes
groundsheet	preceptress	primitivism	prospective	transporter	aseptically
groundwater	precipitant	principally	prosthetics	transsexual	aspergillum
grumblingly	precipitate	privateness	prostitutor	transuranic	aspergillus
iridescence	precipitous	privatively	prostration	transversal	aspersorium
irksomeness	preciseness	prizewinner	protagonist	trapeziform	asphyxiator
ironhearted	preconceive	probabilism	protectoral	trapezoidal	assafoetida
ironmongery	precontract	probabilist	protectress	Trappistine	assassinate
irradiation	predatorily	probational	proteolysis	traversable	assemblyman
irradiative	predecessor	probationer	proteolytic	treacherous	assentation
irrecusable	predicament	problematic	Proterozoic	treacliness	assertively
irrecusably	predication	procephalic	prothalamia	treasonable	assessorial
irredentism	predicative	proceedings	prothallial	treasonably	assiduously
irredentist	predicatory	prochephalic	prothallium	treecreeper	assignation
irreducible	predictable	prochronism	prothoracic	trelliswork	assimilable
irreducibly	predictably	proconsular	protomartyr	tremblement	assimilator
irrefutable	predominant	procreation	protonotary	tremblingly	association
irrefutably	predominate	procreative	protophytic	tremulously	associative
irregularly	preelection	procrustean	protractile	trenchantly	assortative
irrelevance	preeminence	proctorship	protraction	trencherman	assuagement
irrelevancy	preexistent	procuration	protractive	trendsetter	assuredness
irreligious	prefatorial	procuratory	protrudable	trepanation	Assyriology
irremissive	prefatorily	procurement	protrusible	trepidation	astigmatism
irremovable	prefectural	prodigalise	protuberant	trestletree	astringency
irremovably	prehistoric	prodigality	provenience	trestlework	eschatology
irreparable	preignition	profanation	providently	triadically	escheatable
irreparably	prejudgment	profanatory	provisional	triangulate	escheatment
irresoluble	prejudicial	profaneness	provisorily	tribulation	esemplastic
irretention	prelibation	professedly	provocateur	tribuneship	esotericism
irretentive	preliminary	proficiency	provocation	tribunicial	Esperantist
irreverence	prelusively	profiterole	provocative	tribunitial	essentially
irrevocable	prelusorily	profuseness	provokingly	tributarily	establisher
irrevocably	prematurely	progenitrix	provostship	trichinosis	isochronism
irruptively	prematurity	progeniture	proximately	trichomonad	isochronous
oracularity	premeditate	progestogen	prudishness	tricksiness	isoelectric
orangoutang	premiership	prognathism	pruriginous	tricoloured	isogeotherm
orbicularly	premonition	prognathous	Prussianise	triennially	isometrical
orchestrate	premonitory	progression	Prussianism	triggerfish	isomorphism
orchidology	prenominate	progressism	trabeculate	trimestrial	isomorphous
orderliness	preoccupied	progressist	tracasserie	trimorphism	oscillation
oreographic	preparation	progressive	tracelessly	trimorphous	oscillatory
oreological	preparative	prohibition	tracheotomy	Trinitarian	oscillogram
organically	preparatory	prohibitive	trackwalker	tripetalous	osmotically
organisable	preposition	prohibitory	traditional	triphibious	ostensively
organscreen	prepositive	prolegomena	traducement	triphyllous	ostentation

osteography	staunchness	strenuosity	dualcontrol	Kulturkampf	purposeless
osteologist	staurolitic	strenuously	dualpurpose	lubrication	purposively
osteopathic	steadfastly	stretchable	dubiousness	lubricative	purpresture
osteophytic	steamboiler	stridulator	dumbfounder	lucratively	pushfulness
osteoplasty	steamroller	strikebound	dundrearies	lucubration	pussyfooter
ostracoderm	steatopygia	stringboard	duniewassal	ludicrously	pussywillow
Ostrogothic	steelworker	stringently	duplication	luminescent	pustulation
pseudograph	steeplebush	stringiness	duplicative	lumpishness	putrescence
pseudomonas	steeplejack	stringpiece	duplicitous	lustfulness	putrescible
pseudomorph	steerageway	stringybark	durableness	Lutheranism	quacksalver
pseudopodia	steganogram	stroboscope	dutifulness	luxuriantly	quadraphony
psittacosis	stegosaurus	strongpoint	eucalyptole	luxuriation	quadratical
psychedelia	stellionate	studentship	Eucharistic	luxuriously	quadrennial
psychedelic	stencilling	studiedness	euchologion	mudslinging	quadrennium
psychiatric	stenochromy	stumblingly	eudaemonism	multangular	quadrillion
psychically	stenography	stuntedness	eudaemonist	multicolour	quadrupedal
psychodrama	stenotypist	stylisation	eudiometric	multilinear	quaestorial
psychogenic	stepbrother	stylishness	eugenically	multinomial	qualifiable
psychograph	stephanotis	stylography	euphemistic	multiparous	qualitative
psychologic	stereograph	stylopodium	eurhythmics	multiracial	quarrelling
psychometry	stereometry	utilisation	Europeanise	multistorey	quarrelsome
psychomotor	stereophony	utilitarian	eurypteroid	multivalent	quarterback
psychopathy	stereoscope	audaciously	fulguration	mundaneness	quarterdeck
uselessness	stereoscopy	audibleness	fullblooded	municipally	quartertone
atheistical	stereotyped	audiologist	fullfledged	munificence	quaternloaf
athleticism	stereotyper	audiometric	fullhearted	murderously	queenliness
atmospheric	stereotypic	audiovisual	fullmouthed	murmuration	querulously
atomisation	sternsheets	augmentable	fulminating	murmurously	questionary
atrabilious	sternutator	Augustinian	fulmination	musclebound	quickchange
atrociously	stethoscope	auricularly	fulminatory	muscularity	quickfiring
attemptable	stethoscopy	Aurignacian	fulsomeness	musculation	quickfreeze
attentively	stevengraph	austereness	funambulate	musculature	quickfrozen
attenuation	stewardship	autarchical	funambulist	musicalness	quicksilver
attestation	stichometry	autochthony	functionary	muskthistle	quickwitted
attitudinal	stickinsect	autoerotism	functionate	mustachioed	quiescently
attractable	stickleback	autographic	fundamental	mutableness	quilldriver
attribution	stiffnecked	automatable	furnishings	muttonchops	quincuncial
attributive	stiflejoint	autoplastic	furtherance	nullifidian	quinquennia
attritional	stiltedness	autotrophic	furthermore	nulliparity	quinquereme
ctenophoran	stimulation	auxanometer	furthermost	nulliparous	quintillion
etherealise	stimulative	bucolically	furthersome	numerically	quitchgrass
ethereality	stipendiary	buffalorobe	furtiveness	numismatics	quizzically
ethnography	stipulation	bullbaiting	furunculous	numismatist	rubberstamp
ethnologist	stipulatory	bulletproof	fusillation	nuncupation	rubefacient
ethological	stirrupbone	bullfighter	fustigation	nuncupative	rubefaction
Etruscology	stirruppump	bullishness	guardedness	nurserymaid	rubicundity
etymologise	stockbroker	bullterrier	guesstimate	nutcrackers	rubrication
etymologist	stockholder	bumblepuppy	guilelessly	nutrimental	rudimentary
itacolumite	stockinette	bumptiously	guiltlessly	nutritional	ruinousness
ithyphallic	stockjobber	bureaucracy	gullibility	nutritively	rumbustious
itinerantly	stockmarket	burglarious	gurgitation	outbreeding	ruridecanal
itineration	stocktaking	burgomaster	gutlessness	outbuilding	Russophobia
otherwhiles	stoicalness	bushmanship	guttapercha	outcropping	rustication
pteridology	stomachache	bushwhacker	guttersnipe	outdistance	suasiveness
pterodactyl	stomachpump	businessman	gutturalise	outfighting	subaerially
stadtholder	stomatology	butcherbird	gutturalism	outrivalled	subarration
stagemanage	stonecurlew	butterflies	hackleberry	outspokenly	subaudition
stagestruck	stonecutter	butteriness	Hudibrastic	outstanding	subaxillary
stagflation	stoneground	butyraceous	hugeousness	outstripped	subbasement
stainlessly	stonemarten	culmination	humiliation	outwardness	subcategory
staircarpet	stonewaller	culpability	humiliatory	publication	subclinical
stakeholder	stoolpigeon	cultivation	hummingbird	publishable	subcontract
stalactitic	storekeeper	cunningness	hunchbacked	publishment	subcontrary
stalagmitic	stormcentre	cupellation	hundredfold	pulchritude	subcortical
stallholder	stormtroops	cupriferous	hurriedness	pullthrough	subcritical
stampoffice	storyteller	cupronickel	hurryscurry	pullulation	subcultural
standardise	Stradivarii	curableness	hurryskurry	pulverulent	subdivision
standoffish	straightcut	curatorship	hurtfulness	pumicestone	subdominant
standpatter	straightish	curiousness	husbandlike	punchinello	subjugation
starchiness	straightway	currentness	Judaisation	punctilious	subjunctive
starcrossed	straitlaced	cursiveness	judgmatical	punctuality	sublimation
starstudded	stramineous	cursoriness	judiciously	punctuation	sublimeness
startlingly	strangeness	curtailment	jumpingbean	pupillarity	sublittoral
stateliness	strangulate	curvilineal	jumpingjack	purchasable	submarginal
statesmanly	straphanger	curvilinear	juridically	pureblooded	submergence
statistical	strategical	customarily	justiciable	purgatorial	submersible
statutebook	stratocracy	custombuilt	justifiable	purificator	submissible
statutorily	streakiness	customhouse	justifiably	puritanical	submultiple
staunchless	streetlight		juvenescent	purportedly	subordinate

subornation	suppuration	awkwardness	explanation	hydrocarbon	nyctophobia
subregional	suppurative	kwashiorkor	explanatory	hydrocyanic	nympholepsy
subrogation	supremacist	swallowable	explication	hydrogenate	nymphomania
subscapular	supremeness	swallowdive	explicative	hydrogenous	oysterplant
subsequence	surbasement	swallowhole	explicatory	hydrography	pyramidally
subservient	surfboarder	swallowtail	exploitable	hydrologist	pyramidical
subsistence	surficially	swallowwort	exploration	hydromedusa	pyrargyrite
subspecific	surgeonfish	swarthiness	explorative	hydrometeor	pyroclastic
substandard	surpassable	sweepstakes	exploratory	hydrometric	pyrotechnic
substantial	surrebuttal	swellheaded	explosively	hydropathic	Pythagorean
substantive	surrebutter	swiftfooted	exponential	hydrophilic	Pythagorism
substituent	surrogation	swimbladder	exportation	hydrophobia	sybaritical
subsumption	surveillant	swingletree	expostulate	hydrophobic	sycophantic
subsumptive	susceptible	swinishness	expressible	hydrophytic	sycophantry
subterminal	susceptibly	switchblade	expropriate	hydroponics	syllabarium
subtraction	suspenseful	switchboard	expurgation	hydrosphere	syllabicity
subtractive	suspensible	swordbearer	expurgatory	hydrostatic	syllogistic
subtropical	suspiration	twelvemonth	exquisitely	hydrotactic	symbolistic
subumbrella	sustainable	twelvepenny	exsiccation	hydrothorax	symmetrical
suburbanise	sustainment	axiological	exstipulate	hydrotropic	sympathetic
suburbanite	susurration	exaggerator	extemporary	hygrometric	sympathiser
succedaneum	tuberculate	examination	extemporise	hygrophytic	sympetalous
succourless	tuberculise	exanthemata	extensional	hygroscopic	symphonious
succulently	tuberculose	exarcerbate	extensively	hylogenesis	symposiarch
suckingfish	tuberculous	exceedingly	extenuation	hylozoistic	symptomatic
sufficiency	tufthunting	excellently	extenuatory	hymenoptera	synagogical
suffixation	tumbledrier	exceptional	exteriorise	hymnography	synchromesh
suffocation	tumefaction	excessively	exteriority	hyoscyamine	synchronise
suffocative	tunableness	exclamation	exterminate	hyperactive	synchronism
suffragette	tunefulness	exclamatory	externalise	hyperbolise	synchronous
suffumigate	turbination	exclusively	externalism	hyperboloid	synchrotron
sugarcoated	turbulently	exclusivity	externality	hyperborean	syncopation
suggestible	turgescence	excoriation	extirpation	hypercharge	syndesmosis
suitability	turtleshell	excremental	extirpatory	hypercritic	syndicalism
sulphureous	tuttifrutti	excrescence	extortioner	hypermarket	syndicalist
sulphurwort	vulcanicity	excrescency	extractable	hypermetric	syndication
summariness	vulcanology	exculpation	extradition	hyperphagia	synergistic
summational	Yugoslavian	exculpatory	extrapolate	hyperplasia	synonymical
summerhouse	avoirdupois	excursively	extravagant	hypersthene	syntactical
summersault	evagination	exdirectory	extravagate	hypertrophy	synthesiser
sumptuosity	evanescence	executioner	extravasate	hyphenation	synthetical
sumptuously	evangelical	executorial	extraverted	hypnopaedia	syssarcosis
sunlessness	evanishment	executrices	extremeness	hypnopompic	systematics
superabound	evaporation	executrixes	extrication	hypoblastic	systematise
supercharge	evaporative	exemplarily	extroverted	hypocycloid	systematism
superfamily	evasiveness	exemplarity	exuberantly	hypogastric	systematist
superficial	eveningstar	exercisable	oxygenation	hypoglossal	typecasting
superficies	eventualise	exfoliation	oxyhydrogen	hypolimnion	typefounder
superfluity	eventuality	exfoliative	byeelection	hypophyseal	typefoundry
superfluous	everlasting	exhaustible	Byronically	hypophysial	typesetting
superheater	evidentiary	exhaustless	Byzantinism	hypostatise	typewritten
superimpose	evolutional	exhortation	Byzantinist	hypotension	typicalness
superinduce	ovariectomy	exhortative	cybernation	hypothecate	typographer
superintend	overanxious	exhortatory	cybernetics	hypothenuse	typographic
superioress	overbalance	existential	cyclopaedia	hypothermia	typological
superiority	overbearing	exogenously	cyclopaedic	hypothesise	tyrannicide
superjacent	overbidding	exoneration	cycloserine	hypotyposis	tyrannosaur
superlative	overcropped	exonerative	cyclothymia	hypsography	tyrannously
superlunary	overdevelop	exorbitance	cyclothymic	hypsometric	xylocarpous
supermarket	overgarment	exoskeletal	cylindrical	hypsophobia	xylographer
supernatant	overindulge	exoskeleton	cypripedium	kymographic	xylographic
supernormal	overlapping	exotericism	cysticercus	lycanthrope	xylophagous
superscribe	overmanning	expansional	cytogenesis	lycanthropy	xylophonist
superscript	overmeasure	expansively	cytokinesis	mycological	zygomorphic
supersedeas	overpayment	expansivity	cytological	mycophagist	azotobacter
supersedure	overproduce	expatiation	dynamically	mycorrhizae	ozoniferous
superstrata	overrunning	expatiative	dynamometer	mycorrhizal	ozonisation
supersubtle	oversailing	expatiatory	dynamometry	myelomatous	ozonosphere
supertanker	oversetting	expectantly	dysfunction	myocarditis	————————
supervision	overstepped	expectation	dyslogistic	myrmecology	abandonment
supervisory	overstretch	expectative	eyecatching	mythography	academicals
suppliantly	overstuffed	expectorant	gymnospermy	mythologise	academician
supportable	overtopping	expectorate	gynaecocrat	mythologist	academicism
supportably	overweening	expediently	gynaecology	mythomaniac	acarpellous
supposition	overwritten	expeditious	gypsiferous	mythopoeist	acatalectic
suppositive	overwrought	expenditure	gyrocompass	mythopoetic	acaulescent
suppository	oviposition	expensively	hyacinthine	myxomatosis	alabastrine
suppression	awesomeness	experienced	hydraheaded	myxomycetes	amaranthine
suppressive	awestricken	explainable	hydrobromic	nyctitropic	amativeness

amazonstone	chaulmoogra	flagellator	heartlessly	platinotype	snatchblock
anachronism	clairschach	flagofficer	heartsblood	platyrrhine	soapboiling
anachronous	clairvoyant	flagwagging	heartstring	playerpiano	spaceflight
anacoluthon	clamorously	flamboyance	heavenwards	playfulness	spaceheater
anacreontic	clandestine	flamboyancy	heavyfooted	playingcard	spacesaving
anadiplosis	clapperclaw	flamboyante	heavyhanded	practicable	sparingness
anaesthesia	Clarencieux	flannelette	heavyweight	practicably	sparrowbill
anaesthetic	classically	flannelling	hyacinthine	practically	sparrowhawk
anagnorisis	coadunation	flatulently	imaginarily	praetorship	spasmodical
analogously	coagulation	flauntingly	imagination	pragmatical	spastically
anaphylaxis	coalescence	flavourless	imaginative	prattlingly	spathaceous
anarchistic	coarctation	flavoursome	inadaptable	prayerwheel	spatterdash
anastomoses	crabbedness	fractionary	inadvertent	quacksalver	stadtholder
anastomosis	crackerjack	fractionate	inadvisable	quadraphony	stagemanage
anastomotic	craftswoman	fractionise	inalienable	quadratical	stagestruck
apartmental	craniometry	fractiously	inalienably	quadrennial	stagflation
beachcomber	deactivator	fragmentary	inalterable	quadrennium	stainlessly
bearbaiting	deathrattle	Francomania	inalterably	quadrillion	staircarpet
bearishness	diachronism	Francophile	inanimately	quadrupedal	stakeholder
beastliness	diacritical	Francophobe	inanimation	quaestorial	stalactitic
beauteously	diadelphous	francophone	inappetence	qualifiable	stalagmitic
beautifully	diagnostics	franctireur	inattention	qualitative	stallholder
beaverboard	dialectally	frankfurter	inattentive	quarrelling	stampoffice
blackavised	dialectical	franklinite	inaugurator	quarrelsome	standardise
blackbeetle	dialogistic	frankpledge	itacolumite	quarterback	standoffish
blackbirder	diamagnetic	frantically	jealousness	quarterdeck	standpatter
blackcoated	diametrical	franticness	knavishness	quartertone	starchiness
blackfellow	diamondback	fraternally	kwashiorkor	quaternloaf	starcrossed
blackgrouse	diaphaneity	fraterniser	leapfrogged	reachmedown	starstudded
blackmailer	diaphoresis	fratricidal	learnedness	reactionary	startlingly
blackmarket	diaphoretic	fraudulence	leaseholder	reactionist	stateliness
bladderwort	diapophysis	geanticline	leatherback	readability	statesmanly
blamelessly	diapositive	ghastliness	leatherhead	readywitted	statistical
blameworthy	diarthrosis	giantpowder	leatherneck	realignment	statutebook
blasphemous	diastematic	glaringness	leavetaking	realisation	statutorily
blastogenic	diastrophic	glassblower	loathliness	realpolitik	staunchless
boardschool	diatessaron	glasscutter	loathsomely	reanimation	staunchness
brachiation	draggletail	glassmaking	meadowgrass	reapportion	staurolitic
brachyurous	dramaturgic	glauconitic	meadowsweet	reappraisal	suasiveness
bracteolate	drastically	gracelessly	meaningless	rearadmiral	swallowable
bradycardia	draughtsman	gracileness	measureless	reassertion	swallowdive
braggadocio	drawingroom	gradational	measurement	reassurance	swallowhole
Brahmanical	dualcontrol	gradiometer	Neanderthal	reawakening	swallowtail
brahmaputra	dualpurpose	gradualness	nearsighted	rhabdomancy	swallowwort
Brahminical	egalitarian	GraecoRoman	opalescence	rhapsodical	swarthiness
brainlessly	ejaculation	grammalogue	oracularity	roadholding	teachership
brainsickly	ejaculatory	grammatical	orangoutang	scaffolding	tearfulness
brainteaser	elaborately	gramophonic	ovariectomy	scalariform	tearstained
branchiopod	elaboration	grandfather	peacemaking	scalearmour	teaspoonful
brankursine	elaborative	grandiflora	pearlescent	scaleinsect	thalidomide
brazenfaced	elastically	grandiosely	pearlfisher	scalpriform	thanatology
ceaselessly	elasticated	grandiosity	phagedaenic	scarabaeoid	thanklessly
chaetognath	elastomeric	grandmother	phagocytise	scaremonger	thanksgiver
chafingdish	emancipator	grandnephew	phagocytose	scattergood	thankworthy
chainarmour	emasculator	grandparent	phalanstery	searchingly	thaumatrope
chainletter	enarthrosis	grangeriser	phantasiast	searchlight	thaumaturge
chainsmoker	eradication	granivorous	phantasmata	seasickness	thaumaturgy
chainstitch	eradicative	granolithic	pharisaical	shacklebolt	toastmaster
chalcedonic	Erastianism	granophyric	phariseeism	shacklebone	trabeculate
challenging	evagination	granularity	pharyngitis	shadowgraph	tracasserie
chamaephyte	evanescence	granulation	placability	shadowiness	tracelessly
chamberlain	evangelical	granulocyte	plagiariser	Shaksperean	tracheotomy
chambermaid	evanishment	graphically	plagioclase	Shaksperian	trackwalker
chameleonic	evaporation	graphicness	plagiostome	shallowness	traditional
champertous	evaporative	grasshopper	plainspoken	shamanistic	traducement
chancellery	evasiveness	gratulation	plaintively	shamelessly	trafficator
chancellory	exaggerator	gratulatory	planetarium	shapeliness	trafficking
changefully	examination	gravedigger	planetoidal	shareholder	trafficless
channelling	exanthemata	gravelblind	planimetric	sharepusher	tragedienne
chansonnier	exarcerbate	gravimetric	planisphere	sharpwitted	tragicomedy
chanterelle	fearfulness	gravitation	planoconvex	skatingrink	trailblazer
chanticleer	feasibility	gravitative	plantigrade	slaughterer	trainbearer
chaotically	featheredge	guardedness	plasmolysis	slavedriver	trammelling
chaperonage	featherhead	headborough	plasmolytic	slaveholder	transaction
charcuterie	featherless	headhunting	plasterwork	slavemarket	transalpine
chargesheet	featureless	healthfully	plasticiser	slavishness	transceiver
charismatic	flabbergast	healthiness	platearmour	Slavonicise	transcriber
charlatanry	flaccidness	heartbroken	plateresque	smallholder	transection
chartaceous	flagcaptain	hearthstone	platforming	smallminded	transferred

```
transferrer  cabbagepalm  subdivision  ancientness  encapsulate  incunabulum
transfigure  cabbagerose  subdominant  archaeology  enchainment  incuriosity
transfinite  cabbagetree  subjugation  archaeornis  enchantment  incuriously
transfixion  cabbageworm  subjunctive  archaically  enchantress  incurvation
transformer  cabbalistic  sublimation  archangelic  enchiridion  incurvature
transfusion  cobblestone  sublimeness  archdiocese  encomiastic  Jacobinical
transhumant  cybernation  sublittoral  archduchess  encrustment  Jacobitical
transiently  cybernetics  submarginal  archdukedom  encumbrance  jactitation
transilient  debarkation  submergence  Archimedean  encystation  kickstarter
translation  debauchment  submersible  archipelago  eschatology  lachrymator
translocate  debouchment  submissible  ascensional  escheatable  laciniation
translucent  dubiousness  submultiple  ascetically  escheatment  laconically
translunary  elbowgrease  subordinate  ascomycetes  eucalyptole  lacrimation
transmarine  embarkation  subornation  bacchanalia  Eucharistic  lacrimatory
transmittal  embellisher  subregional  bacciferous  euchologion  lacrimosely
transmitted  emblematise  subrogation  bacilliform  exceedingly  lacrymation
transmitter  emblematist  subscapular  backbencher  excellently  lacrymatory
transpadane  embowelling  subsequence  backcountry  exceptional  lacrymosely
transparent  embowerment  subservient  bactericide  excessively  lactescence
transpierce  embraceable  subsistence  bicarbonate  exclamation  lactiferous
transponder  embracement  subspecific  bicentenary  exclamatory  lecherously
transporter  embracingly  substandard  bicephalous  exclusively  lectureship
transsexual  embrocation  substantial  bicorporate  exclusivity  lichenology
transuranic  embroiderer  substantive  bicuspidate  excoriation  lickerishly
transversal  embroilment  substituent  bucolically  excremental  lickspittle
trapeziform  embryologic  subsumption  cacographic  excrescence  loculicidal
trapezoidal  embryonated  subsumptive  cacophonous  excrescency  lucratively
Trappistine  fabrication  subterminal  cicatricial  exculpation  lucubration
traversable  gibberellin  subtraction  coccidiosis  exculpatory  lycanthrope
unaccounted  gibbousness  subtractive  cochinchina  exculsively  lycanthropy
unadvisedly  haberdasher  subtropical  cockaleekie  facelifting  machicolate
unalterable  habiliments  subumbrella  cockleshell  facetiously  machination
unambiguous  habituation  suburbanise  cockyleekie  facsimilist  machinemade
unanimously  hebephrenia  suburbanite  coconscious  factfinding  mackerelsky
unappealing  hebephrenic  sybaritical  cyclopaedia  factionally  macrobiotic
unashamedly  Hebraically  tabefaction  cyclopaedic  factualness  macrocosmic
unassertive  hibernacula  tabernacled  cycloserine  facultative  macrogamete
unavailable  hibernation  tabletennis  cyclothymia  fecundation  macroscopic
unavoidable  Hibernicism  tobacconist  cyclothymic  huckleberry  McCarthyism
unavoidably  hobbledehoy  tobogganing  dactylogram  incalescent  mechanician
unawareness  imbrication  tobogganist  dactylology  incantation  mechanistic
Upanishadic  jabberwocky  tuberculate  decantation  incantatory  Micawberish
uranography  labefaction  tuberculise  decarbonate  incarcerate  Micawberism
weakhearted  labiodental  tuberculose  decarbonise  incardinate  micrococcal
wealthiness  laboriously  tuberculous  decarburise  incarnadine  micrococcus
wearilessly  libertarian  unbeknownst  deceitfully  incarnation  microcosmic
wearisomely  liberticide  unbelieving  deceivingly  incertitude  microgamete
weathercock  libertinage  unbendingly  decelerator  incessantly  micrography
weatherwise  libertinism  unbeseeming  decemvirate  incinerator  microgroove
weatherworn  lubrication  unboundedly  decennially  incipiently  microlithic
zealousness  lubricative  unbreakable  deceptively  inclemently  micrometric
zoantharian  orbicularly  vibratility  decerebrate  inclination  Micronesian
Abbevillian  publication  vibrational  declamation  inclusively  microphonic
abbreviator  publishable  accelerando  declamatory  incoercible  microphytic
Albigensian  publishment  accelerator  declaration  incognisant  microscopic
albuminuria  Rabelaisian  accentually  declarative  incoherence  microsecond
ambiguously  rebarbative  acceptation  declaratory  incoherency  micturition
ambitiously  ribbongrass  acceptingly  declination  incommodity  mockingbird
ambivalence  ribvaulting  accessorial  declivitous  incompetent  mycological
ambivalency  rubberstamp  accessorise  decollation  incompliant  mycophagist
ambiversion  rubefacient  accipitrine  decolletage  incongruent  mycorrhizae
arbitrageur  rubefaction  acclamation  decolourise  incongruity  mycorrhizal
arbitrament  rubicundity  acclamatory  decorticate  incongruous  necessarian
arbitrarily  rubrication  acclimation  decrepitate  inconscient  necessarily
arbitration  Sabbatarian  acclimatise  decrepitude  inconsonant  necessitate
arbitrative  seborrhoeic  acclivitous  decrescendo  inconstancy  necessitous
arbitratrix  soberminded  accommodate  decussately  incontinent  neckerchief
arboraceous  subaerially  accompanist  decussation  incorporate  necrobiosis
arborescent  subarration  accordantly  dicephalous  incorporeal  necrologist
babysitting  subaudition  accordingly  dichogamous  incorrectly  necromancer
bibliolater  subaxillary  accoucheuse  dichotomise  incorruptly  necromantic
bibliolatry  subbasement  accountable  dichotomist  increasable  necrophilia
bibliomancy  subcategory  accountably  dichotomous  incredulity  necrophilic
bibliomania  subclinical  accountancy  dichromatic  incredulous  necropoleis
bibliopegic  subcontract  accrescence  dicotyledon  incremental  nickelplate
bibliophile  subcontrary  acculturate  dictatorial  incriminate  nictitation
bibliophily  subcortical  accumulator  doctrinaire  inculcation  noctilucent
bibliopolic  subcritical  accusatival  doctrinally  inculpation  noctivagant
bibliotheca  subcultural  alcyonarian  documentary  inculpatory  noctivagous
```

nocturnally	sickishness	dedicatedly	indorsement	underhanded	coextensive
nyctitropic	sociability	deductively	indubitable	undermanned	creationism
nyctophobia	socialistic	didacticism	indubitably	underpinned	creationist
occipitally	Socinianism	dodecaphony	inductively	underseller	credentials
occultation	sociologist	elderliness	indulgently	undersigned	credibility
oecological	sociometric	endearingly	industrious	understated	credulously
oecumenical	sociopathic	endemically	Judaisation	undertaking	crematorium
oncological	sockdolager	endlessness	judgmatical	undertenant	crenellated
orchestrate	sockdologen	endocardiac	judiciously	undervaluer	crenulation
orchidology	succedaneum	endocardial	ludicrously	underweight	crepitation
oscillation	succourless	endocardium	maddeningly	underwriter	crepuscular
oscillatory	succulently	endometrium	madreporite	undeserving	crestfallen
oscillogram	suckingfish	endomorphic	madrigalian	undesirable	ctenophoran
pachydermal	sycophantic	endophagous	madrigalist	undeveloped	deemphasise
pacifically	sycophantry	endoplasmic	mediaevally	undisguised	deerstalker
pacificator	tacheometer	endorsement	mediastinal	undisturbed	dreadnought
packingcase	tachycardia	endoskelton	mediastinum	undoubtedly	dreamlessly
peccability	tachygraphy	endothelial	mediateness	undutifully	dresscircle
peccadillos	taciturnity	endothelium	mediatorial	wedgeshaped	dressmaking
pectination	technically	endothermal	mediatrices	wedgetailed	electioneer
peculiarity	technocracy	endothermic	medicinable	widdershins	electrician
pecuniarily	technologic	endotrophic	medicinally	widowerhood	electricity
Pickwickian	uncanniness	eudaemonism	medicolegal	abecedarian	electrocute
pictography	uncanonical	eudaemonist	medievalism	acetylation	electrolier
pictorially	uncatchable	eudiometric	medievalist	adenomatous	electrology
picturebook	unceasingly	exdirectory	mediumistic	alembicated	electrolyse
picturecard	uncertainly	faddishness	middleclass	Alexandrian	electrolyte
picturegoer	uncertainty	fiddlestick	middlesized	alexandrine	electronics
picturesque	unchristian	fidgetiness	moderations	alexandrite	electrotype
pocketknife	uncivilised	godchildren	modernistic	ameliorator	elementally
pocketmoney	uncleanness	goddaughter	mudslinging	amenability	elephantine
pocketsized	unclimbable	godforsaken	oldwomanish	amenorrhoea	elephantoid
pococurante	uncluttered	godlessness	orderliness	amentaceous	epeirogenic
racemeeting	uncommitted	hedgehopped	paddleboard	Americanise	esemplastic
racketpress	unconcealed	hedgepriest	paddlewheel	Americanism	eveningstar
recalculate	unconcerned	hedgeschool	pedagogical	Americanist	eventualise
recantation	uncongenial	hideousness	pedestalled	amethystine	eventuality
receptacula	unconnected	Hudibrastic	pedicellate	anecdotical	everlasting
receptively	unconscious	hydraheaded	pediculosis	anemometric	executioner
receptivity	uncontested	hydrobromic	pedological	anencephaly	executorial
recessional	uncountable	hydrocarbon	pedunculate	arenicolous	executrices
recessively	uncouthness	hydrocyanic	podophyllin	Areopagitic	executrixes
reciprocate	uncrushable	hydrogenate	radicalness	aseptically	exemplarily
reciprocity	vacationist	hydrogenous	radioactive	awesomeness	exemplarity
reclaimable	vaccination	hydrography	radiocarbon	awestricken	exercisable
reclamation	vacillation	hydrologist	radiography	beechmarten	eyecatching
recognition	vacuolation	hydromedusa	radiolarian	biedermeier	feelingness
recognitive	vacuousness	hydrometeor	radiologist	blepharitis	fieldcornet
recognitory	vicariously	hydrometric	radiometric	blessedness	fieldwinner
recommender	viceadmiral	hydropathic	radiophonic	breadbasket	fleshliness
recommittal	vicegerency	hydrophilic	redactional	breadcrumbs	flexibility
recondition	viceregally	hydrophobia	reddishness	breadthways	freebooting
reconnoitre	viceroyalty	hydrophobic	redetermine	breadthwise	freehearted
reconstruct	viceroyship	hydrophytic	redirection	breadwinner	freemasonry
recoverable	vichyssoise	hydroponics	rediscovery	breastplate	freethinker
recriminate	viciousness	hydrosphere	redoubtable	breastwheel	freethought
recruitment	vicissitude	hydrostatic	redundantly	breathalyse	freezedried
rectangular	victualless	hydrotactic	reduplicate	breechblock	frenchified
rectifiable	victualling	hydrothorax	reenticide	breezeblock	Frenchwoman
rectilineal	vociferance	hydrotropic	rodomontade	byeelection	fretfulness
rectilinear	vociferator	indeciduous	rudimentary	cheerleader	greasepaint
recumbently	yacketyyack	indefinable	saddlecloth	cheerlessly	greaseproof
recurrently	abdominally	indefinably	saddlehorse	cheesecloth	greatnephew
rickettsial	androgynous	indehiscent	Sadduceeism	cheiromancy	greengrocer
ricochetted	arduousness	indentation	sedentarily	chemotactic	greenkeeper
rockcrystal	audaciously	independent	sedimentary	chevalglass	greenockite
sacculation	audibleness	indifferent	seditionary	cleanlimbed	guesstimate
sacramental	audiologist	indigestion	seditiously	cleanliness	haematocele
sacrificial	audiometric	indigestive	seductively	cleanshaven	haematocrit
secondarily	audiovisual	indignantly	sideslipped	clearheaded	haematology
secondclass	bedevilment	indignation	sidestepped	cleistogamy	haemocyanin
secondrater	bedizenment	indirection	sidewheeler	clericalism	haemoglobin
secondsight	biddability	individuate	tediousness	clericalist	haemophilia
secretarial	Bodhisattva	indivisible	tiddlywinks	coeducation	haemophilic
secretariat	bodybuilder	indivisibly	underbidder	coefficient	haemoptysis
secretively	bodyservant	IndoChinese	undercharge	coessential	haemorrhage
sectionally	caddishness	IndoIranian	underexpose	coeternally	haemorrhoid
sickbenefit	codefendant	indomitable	underground	coexistence	haemostasis
sickeningly	codicillary	indomitably	undergrowth	coextension	haemostatic

heedfulness	plebeianism	presumption	steerageway	unexpressed	information
hierarchism	plectoptera	presumptive	steganogram	uselessness	informative
identically	pleinairist	pretendedly	stegosaurus	weenybopper	informatory
ideographic	pleiotropic	pretentious	stellionate	wheelbarrow	infrangible
ideological	Pleistocene	preterhuman	stencilling	wheelwright	infrequence
inebriation	plenipotent	preterition	stenochromy	whereabouts	infrequency
inedibility	plenteously	prevalently	stenography	wheresoever	lifemanship
ineffective	plentifully	prevaricate	stenotypist	wherewithal	nefariously
ineffectual	pleochroism	preventable	stepbrother	wreckmaster	obfuscation
inefficient	pleomorphic	preventible	stephanotis	affectation	obfuscatory
inelegantly	pleurodynia	previsional	stereograph	affectingly	offenceless
ineloquence	pneumonitis	pseudograph	stereometry	affectional	offensively
ineluctable	preachiness	pseudomonas	stereophony	affectioned	offhandedly
ineluctably	preaudience	pseudomorph	stereoscope	affectively	officialdom
inequitable	Precambrian	pseudopodia	stereotyped	affectivity	officialese
inequitably	precautious	pteridology	stereotyper	afficionado	officialism
inescapable	precedented	pterodactyl	stereotypic	affiliation	officiation
inessential	precedently	queenliness	sternsheets	affirmation	officinally
inestimable	precentress	querulously	sternutator	affirmative	officiously
inestimably	preceptress	questionary	stethoscope	affirmatory	olfactology
inexactness	precipitant	reedbunting	stethoscopy	affranchise	raffishness
inexcusable	precipitate	reeducation	stevengraph	affrication	referential
inexcusably	precipitous	reedwarbler	stewardship	affricative	reflectance
inexistence	preciseness	reemergence	sweepstakes	anfractuous	reflexively
inexpedient	preconceive	reenactment	swellheaded	befittingly	reflexology
inexpensive	precontract	reestablish	teenybopper	bifurcation	reformation
ipecacuanha	predatorily	rheological	teeterboard	buffalorobe	reformative
kleptomania	predecessor	rheotropism	teetotalism	coffeehouse	reformatory
lieutenancy	predicament	rhetorician	teetotaller	coffeetable	refrangible
myelomatous	predication	rheumaticky	theatregoer	defalcation	refreshment
needfulness	predicative	roentgenise	theatricals	defectively	refrigerant
needlecraft	predicatory	scenography	thenceforth	defenceless	refrigerate
needlepoint	predictable	sceptically	theobromine	defensively	refringency
needlewoman	predictably	sheathknife	theocentric	deferential	rifacimenti
oneiromancy	predominant	sheepfarmer	theodolitic	defibrinate	rifacimento
onerousness	predominate	sheepmaster	theological	deficiently	safebreaker
opencircuit	preelection	sheetanchor	theorematic	definiendum	safeconduct
openhearted	preeminence	shellacking	theoretical	deflagrator	safecracker
openmouthed	preexistent	shelljacket	theosophist	defloration	safekeeping
operational	prefatorial	shelterbelt	therapeutic	defoliation	safetyvalve
operatively	prefatorily	shelterless	thereabouts	deforcement	softhearted
operculated	prefectural	shepherdess	theretofore	deformation	softshelled
operoseness	prehistoric	sheriffalty	therewithal	defraudment	sufficiency
oreographic	preignition	sheriffship	thermically	differentia	suffixation
oreological	prejudgment	skeletonise	thermionics	differently	suffocation
overanxious	prejudicial	sketchiness	thermoduric	difficultly	suffocative
overbalance	prelibation	sleepingbag	thermograph	diffidently	suffragette
overbearing	preliminary	sleepingcar	thermolysis	diffraction	suffumigate
overbidding	prelusively	sleeplessly	thermolytic	diffuseness	toffeenosed
overcropped	prelusorily	sleepwalker	thermometer	diffusively	tufthunting
overdevelop	prematurely	sleeveboard	thermometry	effectively	unfailingly
overgarment	prematurity	slenderness	thermophile	effectually	unfaltering
overindulge	premeditate	sleuthhound	thermoscope	efficacious	unfashioned
overlapping	premiership	speakership	thermotaxis	efficiently	unfeelingly
overmanning	premonition	specifiable	treacherous	effulgently	unfeignedly
overmeasure	premonitory	specificity	treacliness	enfeoffment	unflappable
overpayment	prenominate	spectacular	treasonable	enforceable	unflinching
overproduce	preoccupied	spectatress	treasonably	enforcement	unforgiving
overrunning	preparation	spectrality	treecreeper	enfranchise	unfortunate
oversailing	preparative	spectrogram	trelliswork	exfoliation	unfurnished
oversetting	preparatory	spectrology	tremblement	exfoliative	agglomerate
overstepped	preposition	speculation	tremblingly	gafftopsail	agglutinate
overstretch	prepositive	speculative	tremulously	infanticide	aggravation
overstuffed	preprandial	speechifier	trenchantly	infantilism	aggregately
overtopping	prerogative	speedometer	trencherman	infantryman	aggregation
overweening	presanctify	spelaeology	trendsetter	infatuation	aggregative
overwritten	presbyteral	spellbinder	trepanation	inferential	aggrievedly
overwrought	presciently	spendthrift	trepidation	inferiority	aiguillette
paederastic	preselector	spermaphyte	trestletree	infertility	algological
paediatrics	presentable	spermatozoa	trestlework	infestation	algorithmic
paediatrist	presentably	spermicidal	twelvemonth	infeudation	angelically
paedophilia	presentient	spessartite	twelvepenny	infiltrator	angiography
peevishness	presentment	steadfastly	unemotional	infinitival	Anglicanism
phenologist	preservable	steamboiler	unendurable	infirmarian	AngloFrench
pieceworker	pressagency	steamroller	unendurably	inflammable	AngloIndian
pietistical	prestigious	steatopygia	unequivocal	inflammably	anglomaniac
pleasurable	prestissimo	steelworker	unessential	inflexional	AngloNorman
pleasurably	prestressed	steeplebush	unexploited	influential	anglophobia
plebeianise	presumingly	steeplejack	unexploited	informality	anglophobic

arglebargle magnificent achondritic bridgeboard hairtrigger quintillion
argumentive megalomania achromatise brilliantly heinousness quitchgrass
augmentable megalopolis achromatism bristletail idiographic quizzically
Augustinian megatherium aphrodisiac bristleworm idiomorphic reification
beguilement negationist atheistical bristliness idiotically reincarnate
beguilingly negligently athleticism Britishness imitatively reinsertion
cognateness negotiation behavioural brittleness initialling reinsurance
cognitional negotiatory bohemianism chiaroscuro iridescence reintegrate
cognitively negotiatrix dehydration chickenfeed itinerantly reintroduce
cognitivity negrophobia echosounder chickenwire itineration reiteration
cognoscente nightingale enhancement chieftaincy laicisation reiterative
cognoscenti nightmarish ephemerides childminder Leibnitzian rhinologist
cognoscible nightporter etherealise chimaerical maidservant rhinoscopic
deglutition nightwalker ethereality chinoiserie mailcarrier rhizanthous
degradation nigrescence ethnography Chippendale maintenance rhizocarpic
degradingly organically ethnologist chirography maintopmast rhizomatous
degustation organisable ethological chiropodist maintopsail ruinousness
digestively organscreen exhaustible chiropteran maisonnette saintliness
digitigrade pigeonchest exhaustless chitterling moisturiser saintpaulia
doggishness piggishness exhortation cliffhanger nailvarnish scientistic
engineering pigheadedly exhortative climacteric neighbourly scientology
engorgement pigsticking exhortatory climatology noiselessly scintillant
engrossment regardfully ichnography clinometric noisemaking scintillate
ergatocracy regenerable ichthyology coincidence noisomeness scissorbill
eugenically regenerator ichthyornis coinheritor oligochaete scissortail
gegenschein regimentals ichthyosaur coinsurance oligomerous seigneurial
gigantesque regionalise inhabitable criminalist ominousness seigniorage
haggadistic regionalism inhabitancy criminality opinionated seigniorial
haggardness regionalist inheritable crimination orientalise seismically
Hagiographa registrable inheritance criminative orientalism seismograph
hagiography regretfully inheritress criminatory orientalist seismometer
hagiologist regrettable ithyphallic criminology orientation seismometry
hagioscopic regrettably ochlocratic criticality originality seismoscope
Hegelianism regurgitate ophidiarium criticaster origination shiftlessly
highbrowism rightangled ophiologist daisycutter originative shipbreaker
highfalutin righteously otherwhiles deification oviposition shipbuilder
highpitched righthanded schismatise deistically painfulness shirtsleeve
highpowered righthander schistosity drillmaster painkilling skilfulness
highranking rightminded schistosome edification painstaking slickenside
highstepper rightwinger schizanthus editorially philanderer slightingly
highwrought roguishness scholarship elicitation philatelist smilelessly
hoggishness sagaciously scholiastic eligibility philhellene smithereens
hugeousness Sagittarius schoolboard elimination philologian smithsonite
hygrometric segmentally schoolchild eliminative philologist snickersnee
hygrophytic segregation schoolhouse Elizabethan philosopher spifflicate
hygroscopic segregative schottische enigmatical philosophic spindlelegs
ingathering sightlessly schwarmerei epidiascope pliableness spindletree
ingeniously sightliness sphaeridium epigastrium plicateness spinelessly
ingenuously sightreader sphagnology epigraphist pointdevice spiniferous
ingrainedly sightscreen spherically epinephrine pointedness Spinozistic
ingratitude sightseeing spherometer epipetalous pointillism spinsterish
ingurgitate sightworthy spherulitic episcopally pointillist spiraculate
legerdemain sigmoidally sphincteral epithalamia pointlessly spiritistic
legionnaire signifiable sphincteric epithalamic poisonously spiritlevel
legislation significant sphygmogram epithelioma prickliness spiritually
legislative signpainter unhappiness evidentiary priestcraft spiritualty
legislature sugarcoated unhealthily existential primaevally spirituelle
ligamentary suggestible upholsterer fairweather primateship spirochaete
ligamentous tagliatelle vehmgericht faithhealer primatology spirochetal
lightfooted tagliatelli abiogeneses faithlessly primigenial spirometric
lighthanded tegumentary abiogenesis faithworthy primiparous stichometry
lightheaded tightfisted abiogenetic flightiness primitively stickinsect
lightminded tightlipped abiological flimflammer primitivism stickleback
lightsomely togglejoint abiotically flirtatious principally stiffnecked
lightweight ungetatable acidifiable friableness privateness stiflejoint
logarithmic ungodliness acidophilic fricandeaux privatively stiltedness
loggerheads unguardedly acidulation frightfully prizewinner stimulation
logicalness unguiculate acinaciform frigidarium psittacosis stimulative
logographer vagabondage adiaphorism frivolously quickchange stipendiary
logographic vagabondise ahistorical gainfulness quickfiring stipulation
logomachist vagabondish amiableness gristliness quickfreeze stipulatory
magazinegun vagabondism amicability guilelessly quickfrozen stirrupbone
magdalenian vagariously animalcular guiltlessly quicksilver stirruppump
magisterial voguishness anisotropic hairbreadth quickwitted suitability
magisterium waggishness aristocracy hairdresser quiescently swiftfooted
magistratic Yugoslavian axiological hairraising quilldriver swimbladder
Maglemosian zygomorphic boilermaker hairstyling quincuncial swingletree
magnanimity abhorrently bricklaying hairstylist quinquennia swinishness
magnanimous achievement   hairstylist quinquereme switchblade

switchboard	adjournment	calorimeter	folliculate	maleficence	polymorphic
thickheaded	adjudgement	calorimetry	fulguration	malevolence	polyonymous
thickwitted	adjudicator	calumniator	fullblooded	malfeasance	polypeptide
thimbleweed	enjambement	Calvinistic	fullfledged	malfunction	polyphagous
thingumabob	injudicious	calyptrogen	fullhearted	maliciously	polyphonous
thingumajig	injuriously	celebration	fullmouthed	malignantly	polystyrene
thinskinned	objectively	celebratory	fulminating	malposition	polytechnic
thirstiness	objectivism	celestially	fulmination	malpractice	polyzoarium
thistledown	objectivist	cellularity	fulminatory	melancholia	pulchritude
thitherward	objectivity	chlorophyll	fulsomeness	melancholic	pullthrough
thixotropic	objurgation	chloroplast	gallantness	melanochroi	pullulation
triadically	objurgatory	chloroprene	gallbladder	melanophore	pulverulent
triangulate	rejoicingly	coldblooded	galleyslave	melioration	rallentando
tribulation	rejuvenator	coldhearted	Gallicanism	meliorative	relatedness
tribuneship	rejuvenesce	coleorrhiza	gallimaufry	meliphagous	relationism
tribunicial	acknowledge	collaborate	Gallophobia	melliferous	relationist
tribunitial	alkalescent	collapsible	gallowsbird	mellifluent	reliability
tributarily	alkalimeter	collectable	gallowstree	mellifluous	religionise
trichinosis	alkalimetry	collectanea	gillyflower	melodiously	religionism
trichomonad	awkwardness	collectedly	goldbeating	millenarian	religionist
tricksiness	irksomeness	collectible	golddigging	milliampere	religiosity
tricoloured	lakedweller	collenchyma	goldenberry	millionaire	religiously
triennially	makebelieve	colligation	gullibility	millisecond	reluctantly
triggerfish	teknonymous	colligative	halfbinding	molecricket	reluctation
trimestrial	unkennelled	collimation	halfblooded	molecularly	salaciously
trimorphism	wakefulness	collinearly	halfhearted	molendinary	saleability
trimorphous	ablutionary	collisional	halfholiday	molestation	salesladies
Trinitarian	ailurophile	collocation	halflanding	mollycoddle	salinometer
tripetalous	ailurophobe	collusively	halfmeasure	molybdenite	salmonberry
triphibious	allAmerican	colonelship	hallucinate	multangular	salpingitis
triphyllous	allantoides	colonialism	halophilous	multicolour	saltatorial
triquetrous	allegorical	colonialist	halterbreak	multilinear	saltimbanco
tristichous	allelomorph	colorimeter	heldentenor	multinomial	salvageable
trisyllabic	alleviation	colorimetry	heliochrome	multiparous	salvational
trisyllable	alleviative	colouration	heliography	multiracial	scleroderma
tritagonist	alleviatory	colourblind	heliotropic	multistorey	sclerometer
tritheistic	allocatable	colourfully	helleborine	multivalent	sclerophyll
trituration	allomorphic	columbarium	Hellenistic	nullifidian	sclerotitis
triumvirate	allopathist	columniated	hellishness	nulliparity	selaginella
trivialness	balefulness	culmination	helminthoid	nulliparous	selectively
unicellular	ballbearing	culpability	helpfulness	obliqueness	selectivity
unicoloured	balletomane	cultivation	hilariously	obliviously	selfassured
unification	balmcricket	cylindrical	hollandaise	oilpainting	selfcentred
uniformness	BaltoSlavic	delectation	holoblastic	Palaearctic	selfclosing
unigeniture	belatedness	deleterious	holographic	palaeotypic	selfcocking
unimportant	bellbottoms	deliciously	holothurian	Palestinian	selfcommand
uninhabited	bellfounder	delightedly	hylogenesis	palindromic	selfconceit
uninhibited	bellheather	delightsome	hylozoistic	palmcabbage	selfcontent
uninucleate	bellicosity	delineation	illaffected	palpability	selfcontrol
unipersonal	belligerent	delinquency	illbreeding	palpitation	selfcreated
unipolarity	bellringing	deliriously	illdisposed	palsgravine	selfculture
unisexually	Belorussian	delitescent	illfavoured	Pelagianism	selfdefence
universally	bilaterally	deliverable	illhumoured	pelargonium	selfdenying
utilisation	biliousness	deliverance	illiberally	pellucidity	selfdespair
utilitarian	billetsdoux	deliveryman	illimitable	pillowfight	selfdevoted
voicelessly	billionaire	dilapidated	illimitably	pilocarpine	selfdisplay
wainscoting	billposting	dilapidator	illiquidity	pilotburner	selfelected
wainscotted	billsticker	diluvialist	illmannered	polarimeter	selfevident
waitinglist	bullbaiting	dolefulness	illogically	polarimetry	selffeeding
waitingroom	bulletproof	doltishness	illtempered	polarisable	selffeeling
weighbridge	bullfighter	eclecticism	illuminable	polariscope	selffertile
weightiness	bullishness	ellipsoidal	illuminance	polemically	selfimposed
Weismannism	bullterrier	ellipticity	illuminator	polevaulter	selfinduced
whichsoever	calceolaria	enlargeable	illusionism	policewoman	selfinvited
whiffletree	calcicolous	enlargement	illusionist	politically	selfishness
whigmaleery	calciferous	enlightened	illustrator	politicking	selflimited
whimsically	calcifugous	enlivenment	illustrious	pollination	selfloading
whippletree	calcination	fallibility	kilocalorie	poltroonery	selflocking
whistlestop	calculating	Falstaffian	Kulturkampf	polyandrous	selfmastery
Whitechapel	calculation	falteringly	lilylivered	polycarpous	selfopinion
whitecollar	calculative	feldspathic	maladaptive	polychromic	selfpitying
whiteheaded	calefacient	feloniously	maladjusted	polycrystal	selfraising
whitethroat	calefactory	felspathoid	maladroitly	polygenesis	selfreliant
whitewasher	calendrical	filamentary	malapropism	polygenetic	selfreproof
whitherward	calibration	filamentous	malariology	polyglottal	selfrespect
whitishness	californium	filmography	malediction	polyglottic	selfsealing
whitleather	calisthenic	filmsetting	maledictory	polygonally	selfseeking
Whitsuntide	calligraphy	filmsetting	malefaction	polygraphic	selfservice
adjectively	callousness	filterpaper	malefaction	polygraphic	selfserving

selfstarter	willingness	complaisant	homoiousian	romanticist	benightedly
selfsterile	wolfwhistle	complexness	homological	rumbustious	benightment
selfsupport	xylocarpous	compliantly	homomorphic	semanticist	benignantly
selftorture	xylographer	complicated	homophonous	semasiology	benignities
selfwinding	xylographic	complotting	homoplastic	semeiotical	binocularly
selfworship	xylophagous	comportment	homopterous	semidiurnal	Bonapartean
sillimanite	xylophonist	compositely	homosporous	semiellipse	Bonapartism
silveriness	yellowbelly	composition	homothallic	semimonthly	Bonapartist
silverplate	adminicular	compositive	homozygosis	semipalmate	bonbonniere
silverpoint	admiralship	compossible	humiliation	semiskilled	bondservant
silversmith	aimlessness	compotation	humiliatory	semitrailer	bondwashing
silverstick	Arminianism	compotatory	hummingbird	sempiternal	canalicular
solanaceous	armtwisting	compression	hymenoptera	simperingly	canaliculus
soldierlike	atmospheric	compressive	hymnography	simpliciter	cancellated
soldiership	bimetallism	comprisable	immanentism	somatically	candelabrum
solifluxion	bimetallist	comptroller	immanentist	somatogenic	candescence
soliloquise	bimillenary	compunction	immarginate	somatologic	candidature
soliloquist	bimillenium	compurgator	immediately	somatoplasm	candleberry
solipsistic	bombardment	computation	immedicable	somatotonia	candlelight
solmisation	bombilation	computerise	immenseness	somewhither	candlepower
solutionist	bombination	comradeship	immigration	somnambular	candlestick
solvability	bumblepuppy	comstockery	immitigable	somniculous	cannibalise
splashboard	bumptiously	demagnetise	immitigably	somniferous	cannibalism
splayfooted	camaraderie	demagogical	immortalise	somnolently	canonically
splendorous	campanology	demagoguery	immortality	summariness	cantharides
splenectomy	campanulate	demagoguism	immoveables	summational	cantharidic
splenetical	campmeeting	demandingly	immunologic	summerhouse	centenarian
sulphureous	cementation	demarcation	jumpingbean	summersault	centigramme
sulphurwort	combatively	demarkation	jumpingjack	sumptuosity	centreboard
syllabarium	combination	demigoddess	kymographic	sumptuously	centrepiece
syllabicity	combinative	democratise	lamellicorn	symbolistic	centrifugal
syllogistic	combinatory	democratism	lamelliform	symmetrical	centripetal
talebearing	combustible	demographer	lamentation	sympathetic	cinnabarine
talentscout	comestibles	demographic	lammergeier	sympathiser	cinquecento
talkatively	comeuppance	demonolatry	lammergeyer	sympetalous	concatenate
telegrammic	comfortable	demonstrate	lamplighter	symphonious	concealable
telegrapher	comfortably	demountable	limitedness	symposiarch	concealment
telegraphic	comfortless	dimensional	limitlessly	symptomatic	conceitedly
telekinesis	commandment	dimwittedly	limnologist	tameability	conceivable
telekinetic	commemorate	domesticate	luminescent	temerarious	conceivably
teleologism	commendable	domesticity	lumpishness	temperament	concentrate
teleologist	commendably	domiciliary	mammalogist	temperately	conceptacle
telepathise	commendator	domiciliate	membraneous	temperative	concernment
telepathist	commensally	domineering	memorabilia	temperature	concertedly
telephonist	commentator	dumbfounder	memorialise	tempestuous	concertgoer
teleprinter	commination	emmenagogue	memorialist	temporality	conciliator
tolbutamide	comminatory	Emmenthaler	mimetically	temporarily	conciseness
unlimitedly	commiserate	familiarise	momentarily	timebargain	concomitant
valediction	commissural	familiarity	momentously	timepleaser	concordance
valedictory	committable	fimbriation	namecalling	timeserving	concrescent
valiantness	commonality	fomentation	namedropper	timesharing	concubinage
valleculate	commonplace	gametangium	nomadically	tumbledrier	concubinary
valuational	commonsense	gametophyte	nomenclator	tumefaction	concubitant
velvetiness	communalise	gamogenesis	nominatival	unmanliness	concurrence
volcanicity	communalism	gemmiferous	nomographer	unmatchable	condemnable
volcanology	communalist	gemmiparous	nomographic	unmeaningly	condensable
volitionary	communicant	gemmologist	nomological	unmemorable	conditional
volkslieder	communicate	gemmulation	numerically	unmemorably	conditioner
voltametric	communistic	gimcrackery	numismatics	unmitigated	condolatory
volubleness	commutation	gymnospermy	numismatist	womanliness	condominium
volumometer	commutative	Hamiltonian	nympholepsy	abnormality	condonation
voluntarily	compactness	hemeralopia	nymphomania	Aeneolithic	condottiere
voluntarism	compaginate	hemianopsia	obmutescent	agnatically	condottieri
voluntarist	comparatist	hemimorphic	ommatophore	agnosticism	conductance
vulcanicity	comparative	hemipterous	osmotically	annabergite	conductible
vulcanology	compartment	hemispheric	pamphleteer	annihilator	conductress
welcomeness	compassable	homeopathic	pomegranate	anniversary	condylomata
welladvised	compellable	homeostasis	pomiculture	annunciator	confabulate
wellbeloved	compendious	homeostatic	pomological	bandylegged	confederacy
welldefined	compensator	homesteader	pompousness	banteringly	confederate
wellfounded	competently	homestretch	pumicestone	Benedictine	conferrable
wellgroomed	competition	homiletical	remembrance	benediction	confessedly
wellmeaning	competitive	homocentric	reminiscent	benedictory	confidently
wellordered	compilation	homoeopathy	remonstrant	benefaction	confidingly
wellrounded	compilement	homoestatic	remonstrate	beneficence	confinement
wellwishing	complacence	homogeneity	remorseless	beneficiary	confirmable
weltschmerz	complacency	homogeneous	remunerator	beneficiate	confiscable
wildcatting	complainant	homogenetic	romanticise	benevolence	confiscator
wildfowling		homogeniser	romanticism		conflagrant

conflagrate	contentedly	financially	lengthiness	Monophysite	ponderously
confliction	contentious	fingerboard	lentiginous	monopoliser	pontificals
conflictive	contentment	fingerglass	linedrawing	monopterous	pontificate
conformable	conterminal	fingerplate	linefishing	Monothelite	punchinello
conformably	contestable	fingerprint	linendraper	monozygotic	punctilious
conformally	continental	fingerstall	lineprinter	monseigneur	punctuality
conformance	continently	finicalness	lingeringly	monstrosity	punctuation
confusingly	contingence	FinnoUgrian	linguistics	monstrously	rancorously
confutation	contingency	funambulate	longanimity	mundaneness	rangefinder
confutative	continuable	funambulist	longplaying	municipally	renaissance
congealable	continually	functionary	longsighted	munificence	renegotiate
congealment	continuance	functionate	managership	ninnyhammer	ringstraked
congelation	continuator	fundamental	mandarinate	nonchalance	sandbagging
congenerous	contorniate	gangsterism	mandibulate	nondelivery	sandskipper
congenially	contrabasso	gendarmerie	mandolinist	nondescript	sanguinaria
congressman	contractile	genealogise	manducation	nonetheless	sanguineous
congruently	contraction	genealogist	manducatory	nonexistent	sansculotte
congruously	contractive	generaliser	Manichaeism	nonfeasance	Sanskritist
conjectural	contractual	generalship	manifestant	nonmatching	senatorship
conjugality	contracture	generically	manifestoes	nonmetallic	sensational
conjugation	contradance	genetically	manipulable	nonpartisan	senselessly
conjugative	contraption	geniculated	manipulator	nonplussing	sensibility
conjunction	contrariety	genitivally	manneristic	nonresident	sensitively
conjunctiva	contrarious	genteelness	mannishness	nonsensical	sensitivity
conjunctive	contrastive	gentianella	mansardroof	nonsequitur	sensorially
conjuncture	contretemps	gentilitial	mantelpiece	nonspecific	sententious
conjuration	contributor	gentlemanly	mantelshelf	nonunionist	sentimental
connectable	contrivable	gentlewoman	mantuamaker	nonviolence	sentinelled
connectedly	contrivance	genuflexion	manufactory	nonvolatile	sincereness
connectible	controlling	genuineness	manufacture	nuncupation	sinfonietta
connoisseur	controlment	gingerbread	manumission	nuncupative	singlestick
connotation	controversy	gonfalonier	manumitting	obnoxiously	singletrack
connotative	conurbation	goniometric	mendelevium	oenological	singularise
connubially	convenances	gynaecocrat	meningocele	oenophilist	singularity
conquerable	convenience	gynaecology	menservants	omnifarious	sinistrally
consanguine	conveniency	handbreadth	mensuration	omnipotence	sinistrorse
consciously	conventicle	handfasting	mentholated	omnipresent	sinlessness
consecrator	convergence	handgrenade	mentionable	omniscience	sinological
consecution	convergency	handicapped	mindbending	ornithology	sinuousness
consecutive	conversable	handicapper	mindblowing	ornithopter	songfulness
consentient	conversance	handknitted	mindfulness	ornithosaur	songsparrow
consequence	conversancy	handpainted	mindreading	pandemonium	sonofabitch
conservable	convertible	handselling	mineraliser	panegyrical	sunlessness
conservancy	convertibly	handwriting	minesweeper	Panglossian	synagogical
conservator	conveyancer	handwritten	miniaturise	panhellenic	synchromesh
considerate	convincible	handwrought	miniaturist	panicmonger	synchronise
considering	convivially	Hindoostani	ministerial	pantalettes	synchronism
consignable	convocation	honeybadger	minnesinger	pantheistic	synchronous
consignment	convolution	honeymooner	minuteglass	pantomimist	synchrotron
consistence	convolvulus	honeysuckle	monarchical	pantothenic	syncopation
consistency	cunningness	hunchbacked	monasterial	pendulously	syndesmosis
consolation	dangerously	hundredfold	monasticism	penetrating	syndicalism
consolatory	dendritical	ignobleness	moneylender	penetration	syndicalist
consolidate	denigration	ignominious	moneymaking	penetrative	syndication
consolingly	denigratory	innavigable	moneymarket	penicillate	synergistic
consonantal	denizenship	innervation	moneyspider	penicillium	synonymical
consonantly	denominator	innocuously	monitorship	peninsulate	syntactical
conspecific	denticulate	innoxiously	monkeybread	penitential	synthesiser
conspicuity	dentigerous	innumerable	monkeyshine	pennyweight	synthetical
conspicuous	denumerable	innumerably	monocarpous	penological	tangibility
conspirator	denunciator	innutrition	monochasial	pensionable	tankfarming
constellate	diningtable	ionospheric	monochasium	pensionless	tantalising
consternate	dinnerdance	Jansenistic	monochromat	pensiveness	tenableness
constituent	dinnertable	kindhearted	monochromic	pentadactyl	tenaciously
constitutor	dinnerwagon	kinematical	monoclinous	pentagynous	tendencious
constrictor	dinosaurian	kinesiology	monoculture	pentahedron	tendentious
construable	donnishness	kinetograph	monogenesis	pentamerous	tenementary
constructor	dundrearies	kinetoscope	monogenetic	pentandrous	tensibility
consultancy	duniewassal	Lancastrian	monogrammed	pentathlete	tentaculate
consumerism	dynamically	lancinating	monographer	pentavalent	tentatively
consumingly	dynamometer	lancination	monographic	pentazocine	tenterhooks
consummator	dynamometry	landaulette	monolingual	Pentecostal	tentpegging
consumption	einsteinium	landgrabber	monological	pentlandite	tenuousness
consuetude	enneahedron	landgravine	monologuise	penultimate	tonsillitis
containable	ennoblement	landholding	monologuist	penuriously	tunableness
containment	fanatically	landingbeam	monomorphic	pinkishness	tunefulness
contaminant	fanfaronade	landinggear	mononuclear	pinnatisect	unnaturally
contaminate	fantastical	landlordism	monophagous	ponderation	unnecessary
contemplate	fenestrated	languidness	monophthong	ponderosity	unnervingly

venatically
vendibility
venereology
venesection
venisection
ventilation
ventilative
ventricular
ventriculus
ventriloquy
venturesome
venturously
vinaigrette
vincibility
vindication
vindicative
vindicatory
vinedresser
viniculture
Wensleydale
windcheater
windlestraw
winegrowing
winetasting
winningness
winningpost
winsomeness
winterberry
wintergreen
wonderfully
xanthochroi
xanthophyll
xenophilous
zincography
abolishable
abolishment
abomination
abortionist
aboutsledge
aboveground
acoustician
adolescence
adoptianism
adoptianist
adoptionism
adoptionist
aeolotropic
agonisingly
agonistical
agoraphobia
agoraphobic
amontillado
amorousness
amorphously
anomalistic
anomalously
anonymously
apocalyptic
Apollinaris
apologetics
apomorphine
aponeuroses
aponeurosis
aponeurotic
apophyllite
aposiopesis
apostleship
apostolical
apostrophic
apotheosise
aromaticity
atomisation
avoirdupois
azotobacter
biochemical
biocoenoses
biocoenosis
biocoenotic
biofeedback

biometrical
biophysical
blockbuster
bloodguilty
bloodlessly
bloodstream
bloodsucker
bloodvessel
blotchiness
bookbinding
bookinghall
bookishness
bookkeeping
booklearned
bookselling
bookshelves
boorishness
bootlegging
broadcaster
broadleaved
broadminded
brotherhood
chockablock
choirmaster
chokecherry
cholesterol
choreograph
chorography
clodhopping
closefisted
closehauled
clostridium
clothesline
clothesmoth
clothesprop
cloudcastle
cookgeneral
cooperation
cooperative
coordinator
crocidolite
crocodilian
crookbacked
crookedness
crossbearer
crossbowman
crossgarnet
crosslegged
crossstitch
crotcheteer
deoxidation
deoxygenate
deoxyribose
Diophantine
doorknocker
dropcurtain
dropforging
drouthiness
econometric
egotistical
emotionally
emotionless
epochmaking
erotogenous
erotomaniac
esotericism
evolutional
exogenously
exoneration
exonerative
exorbitance
exoskeletal
exoskeleton
exotericism
flocculence
floorwalker
florescence
floriferous
florilegium

floweriness
foolishness
footpoundal
footslogger
footsoldier
frontrunner
frostbitten
frothhopper
frowardness
frowstiness
geochemical
geomagnetic
geometrical
geophysical
geopolitics
geostrophic
geosyncline
geotectonic
ghostliness
ghostwriter
globeflower
globigerina
globularity
glomeration
glossolalia
gnotobiosis
gnotobiotic
goodhearted
goodlooking
goodnatured
grotesquely
grotesquery
grouchiness
groundsheet
groundwater
hooliganism
hyoscyamine
iconography
iconostases
iconostasis
icosahedral
icosahedron
idolisation
inobservant
inoculation
inoffensive
inofficious
inoperative
inopportune
ironhearted
ironmongery
isochronism
isochronous
isoelectric
isogeotherm
isometrical
knowingness
knownothing
lionhearted
looselimbed
loosestrife
moonlighter
mooringmast
myocarditis
neologistic
Neoplatonic
Neotropical
odoriferous
odorousness
ozoniferous
ozonisation
ozonosphere
phonetician
phonography
phonologist
phosphonium

phosphorate
phosphorism
phosphorite
phosphorous
photoactive
photocopier
photofinish
photography
photometric
photooffset
photoperiod
photophilic
photophobia
photophobic
photosphere
phototactic
phototropic
ploughshare
ploughstaff
probabilism
probabilist
probability
probational
probationer
problematic
proceedings
procephalic
prochronism
proconsular
procreation
procreative
procrustean
proctorship
procuration
procuratory
procurement
prodigalise
prodigality
profanation
profanatory
profaneness
professedly
proficiency
profiterole
profuseness
progenitrix
progeniture
progestogen
prognathism
prognathous
progression
progressism
progressist
progressive
prohibition
prohibitive
prohibitory
prolegomena
proletarian
proletariat
proliferate
proliferous
prolificacy
prolificity
prolocutrix
prominently
promiscuity
promiscuous
promisingly
promotional
promptitude
promulgator
proofreader
propagation
propagative
prophethood
prophetical
prophetship
prophylaxis

propinquity
propitiable
propitiator
proportions
proposition
proprietary
prorogation
prosaically
prosaicness
prosecution
prosecutrix
proselytise
proselytism
prosenchyma
prospective
prosthetics
prostitutor
prostration
protagonist
protectoral
protectress
proteolysis
proteolytic
Proterozoic
prothalamia
prothallial
prothallium
prothoracic
protomartyr
protonotary
protophytic
protractile
protraction
protractive
protrudable
protrusible
protuberant
provenience
providently
provisional
provisorily
provocateur
provocation
provocative
provokingly
provostship
proximately
reorientate
rhombohedra
rhomboideus
riotousness
scopolamine
scorchingly
scoriaceous
scorpionfly
ScotchIrish
Scotchwoman
scoundrelly
scoutmaster
shockheaded
shocktroops
shoeleather
shoplifting
shopsteward
shortchange
shortcoming
shorthanded
shortspoken
shortwinded
shoulderbag
shoulderpad
shovelboard
showerproof
showjumping
showmanship
showstopper
slotmachine
smokescreen
smokingroom

smoothfaced
smorgasbord
snowbunting
snowgoggles
snowleopard
spokeswoman
spondulicks
spondylitis
spongecloth
sponsorship
spontaneity
spontaneous
sporogenous
sporogonium
sporophytic
sportswoman
sporulation
stockbroker
stockholder
stockinette
stockjobber
stockmarket
stocktaking
stoicalness
stomachache
stomachpump
stomatology
stonecurlew
stonecutter
stoneground
stonemarten
stonewaller
stoolpigeon
storekeeper
stormcentre
stormtroops
storyteller
swordbearer
thoroughpin
thoroughwax
thoughtless
toothbilled
toothpowder
toothsomely
troglodytic
trophoblast
troposphere
troublesome
troublously
trouserless
trousersuit
ulotrichous
unobtrusive
unorganized
unorthodoxy
urochordate
violoncello
voodooistic
voortrekker
wholesomely
wholesouled
whoremaster
whoremonger
whosesoever
woodcarving
woodcutting
wrongheaded
zoographist
zoomorphism
zooplankton
zootechnics
alphabetise
amphetamine
amphibolite
amphibology
amphictyony
amphimictic
amphisbaena

amplexicaul
appallingly
apparatchik
apparelling
appealingly
appeasement
appellation
appellative
applaudable
application
applicative
applicatory
appogiatura
appointment
appreciable
appreciably
appreciator
approbation
approbatory
appropriate
approvingly
approximate
appurtenant
aspergillum
aspergillus
aspersorium
asphyxiator
baptismally
bipartition
capableness
capaciously
capacitance
capillarity
captainship
captionless
captivation
coparcenary
copingstone
copiousness
coplanarity
copperplate
coppersmith
cupellation
cupriferous
cupronickel
cypripedium
depauperate
depauperise
dependently
deploringly
depopulator
deportation
depravation
depravement
deprecation
deprecative
deprecatory
depreciator
depredation
depredatory
depressible
deprivation
depthcharge
diphtherial
diphtheroid
diphthongal
diphycercal
diplococcus
diplomatise
diplomatist
dipsomaniac
dipterocarp
duplication
duplicative
duplicitous
empanelling
emperorship
empirically
emplacement

emptyhanded
emptyheaded
Esperantist
euphemistic
expansional
expansively
expansivity
expatiation
expatiative
expatiatory
expectantly
expectation
expectative
expectorant
expectorate
expediently
expeditious
expenditure
expensively
experienced
explainable
explanation
explanatory
explication
explicative
explicatory
exploitable
exploration
explorative
exploratory
explosively
exponential
exportation
expostulate
expressible
expropriate
expurgation
expurgatory
foppishness
gypsiferous
haphazardly
haplessness
haplography
hepatectomy
Hepplewhite
heptamerous
heptarchist
hippocampus
Hippocratic
hippopotami
hopefulness
hyperactive
hyperbolise
hyperboloid
hyperborean
hypercharge
hypercritic
hypermarket
hypermetric
hyperphagia
hyperplasia
hypersthene
hypertrophy
hyphenation
hypnopaedia
hypnopompic
hypoblastic
hypocycloid
hypogastric
hypoglossal
hypolimnion
hypophyseal
hypophysial
hypostatise
hypotension
hypothecate
hypothenuse
hypothermia
hypothesise

hypotyposis
hypsography
hypsometric
hypsophobia
impanelling
imparkation
impartation
impartially
impassioned
impassively
impassivity
impatiently
impeachable
impeachment
impecunious
impedimenta
impenetrate
impenitence
impenitency
imperfectly
imperforate
imperialise
imperialism
imperialist
imperilling
imperilment
imperiously
impermanent
impermeable
impermeably
impersonate
impertinent
imperviable
impetration
impetratory
impetuosity
impetuously
impingement
implausible
implausibly
implemental
implication
implicative
imploringly
impolitical
impoliticly
importantly
importation
importunate
importunely
importunity
impoundment
impractical
imprecation
imprecatory
imprecisely
imprecision
impregnable
impregnably
impressible
impressment
impropriate
impropriety
improvement
improvident
imprudently
impuissance
impulsively
lepidoptera
leprosarium
leptodactyl
lophobranch
meprobamate
naphthalene
nephelinite
nephrectomy
opportunely
opportunism
opportunist

opportunity
opprobrious
oppugnation
paperhanger
papermaking
paperweight
papiermache
papyraceous
peptisation
pipecleaner
piperaceous
pipistrelle
populariser
pupillarity
rapaciously
rapscallion
rapturously
repartition
repellantly
repellently
repentantly
repetitious
replaceable
replacement
replenisher
repleteness
repleviable
replication
reportorial
reposefully
representer
repressible
repressibly
reproachful
reprobation
reprobative
reprobatory
reprogramme
reprography
reprovingly
repudiation
repugnantly
repulsively
ropedancing
ropewalking
saplessness
saponaceous
saprobiotic
saprogenous
saprophytic
Septembrist
septenarius
septentrion
septicaemia
septicaemic
septiferous
septifragal
sophistical
superabound
supercharge
superfamily
superficial
superficies
superfluity
superfluous
superheater
superimpose
superinduce
superintend
superioress
superiority
superjacent
superlative
superlunary
supermarket
supernatant
supernormal
superscribe
superscript

supersedeas
supersedure
superstrata
supersubtle
supertanker
supervision
supervisory
suppliantly
supportable
supportably
supposition
suppositive
suppository
suppression
suppressive
suppuration
suppurative
supremacist
supremeness
tapemachine
tapemeasure
tephromancy
topdressing
toploftical
topographer
topographic
topological
typecasting
typefounder
typefoundry
typesetting
typewritten
typicalness
typographer
typographic
typological
unpalatable
unpolitical
unpossessed
unprintable
unpromising
vaporimeter
vaporisable
wappenschaw
wapperjawed
acquiescent
acquirement
acquisition
acquisitive
acquittance
biquadratic
enquiringly
exquisitely
inquilinous
inquiringly
inquisition
inquisitive
liquefiable
liquescence
liquidambar
liquidation
requirement
requisition
sequestrate
unqualified
unquietness
abracadabra
abranchiate
abridgement
acriflavine
acrimonious
acropetally
aerobically
aerobiology
aerodynamic
aerographer
aerological
aeronautics
aeronomical

aerostatics
aerostation
AfroAsiatic
agrarianism
agriculture
agrobiology
agrological
agronomical
aircraftman
airlessness
airsickness
arraignment
arrangement
arrestingly
atrabilious
atrociously
auricularly
Aurignacian
barbarously
barbastelle
barbiturate
barefacedly
barleybroth
barnstormer
barquentine
barrelhouse
barrelorgan
bereavement
bergamasque
bergschrund
bersaglieri
birdbrained
birdfancier
birdwatcher
borborygmus
bureaucracy
burglarious
burgomaster
Byronically
carabiniere
carabinieri
caravanning
caravansary
carbocyclic
carbonation
carbuncular
carburetion
carburetted
carburetter
carburettor
carcinomata
cardinalate
cardiograph
cardsharper
carefulness
caressingly
caricatural
carminative
carnivorous
Carolingian
carpetsnake
carrageenan
carrageenin
carriageway
cartography
carunculate
carvelbuilt
caryopsides
cerebration
ceremonious
ceroplastic
certifiable
certifiably
certificate
Christendom
christening
christiania
Christianly
Christmassy

Christology	earthcloset	gerontology	margraviate	partitioner	portability
chrominance	earthenware	gerrymander	marketplace	partitively	porterhouse
chromoplast	earthliness	girlishness	marketvalue	partnership	portionless
chromosomal	egregiously	gormandiser	marlinspike	parturition	portmanteau
chronically	erratically	gurgitation	marquessate	perambulate	portraitist
chronograph	erroneously	gyrocompass	marqueterie	perceivable	portraiture
chronologer	Etruscology	harbourless	marquisette	perceivably	purchasable
chronologic	eurhythmics	hardhearted	marriagebed	perceptible	pureblooded
chronometer	Europeanise	hardhitting	marshalling	perceptibly	purgatorial
chronometry	eurypteroid	hardmouthed	marshalship	perchlorate	purificator
chronoscope	farawayness	hardworking	marshmallow	percipience	puritanical
chrysalides	farcicality	harebrained	martyrology	percolation	purportedly
chrysalises	farinaceous	harmfulness	mercenarily	peregrinate	purposeless
chrysarobin	farraginous	harmonistic	merchandise	perennation	purposively
chrysoberyl	farreaching	harpsichord	merchantman	perennially	purpresture
chrysoprase	farthermost	harumscarum	mercilessly	perfectible	pyramidally
circularise	farthingale	harvesthome	mercurially	perfectness	pyramidical
circularity	fermentable	Heracleidan	meritocracy	perforation	pyrargyrite
circulation	ferociously	herbivorous	meritorious	perforative	pyroclastic
circulative	ferriferous	hereditable	meroblastic	performable	pyrotechnic
circulatory	ferruginous	hereinafter	merogenesis	performance	rarefaction
circumlunar	firecracker	heresiology	Merovingian	perfunctory	rarefactive
circumpolar	firefighter	heretically	merryandrew	pericardiac	ruridecanal
circumsolar	fireraising	hermeneutic	merrymaking	pericardial	sarcomatous
circumspect	firewalking	hermeticism	mirthlessly	pericardium	sarcophagus
circumvolve	firewatcher	heroworship	morbiferous	pericranial	sartorially
coralloidal	firmamental	herpetology	moribundity	pericranium	scragginess
corbiculate	firstfruits	herringbone	morningroom	perineurium	scrappiness
corbiesteps	foraminated	herringgull	moronically	periodicity	scratchwork
cordialness	foraminifer	hirsuteness	morrisdance	periodontal	screamingly
corecipient	forbearance	hornswoggle	mortarboard	periostitis	screwdriver
cornerstone	forbiddance	horological	murderously	peripatetic	scribacious
cornhusking	foreclosure	horripilate	murmuration	periphrases	scrimpiness
corniferous	foreignness	horsecollar	murmurously	periphrasis	scriptorial
cornucopian	forequarter	horsedoctor	myrmecology	perishables	scriptorium
coronagraph	forerunning	horseradish	narcoleptic	perishingly	scruffiness
coronograph	foreseeable	hurriedness	narratively	perispermic	scrumptious
corporality	foreshorten	hurryscurry	nervelessly	peristalith	scrutiniser
corporately	foresighted	hurryskurry	nervousness	peristalsis	serendipity
corporation	forestaller	hurtfulness	northeaster	peristaltic	sericulture
corporatism	forestation	irradiation	northwester	peristomial	serigrapher
corporative	forethinker	irradiative	nurserymaid	perithecium	seriousness
corporeally	forethought	irrecusable	oarsmanship	peritonitis	serological
corpulently	foretopmast	irrecusably	parachutist	permanently	serpiginous
corpuscular	foretopsail	irredentism	paradisical	permissible	serrulation
correctable	forevermore	irredentist	paradoxical	permissibly	sertularian
correctness	foreverness	irreducible	paragrapher	permutation	serviceable
correlation	forewarning	irreducibly	paragraphic	perpetrator	serviceably
correlative	forfeitable	irrefutable	paraldehyde	perpetuance	servicebook
corrigendum	forgetfully	irrefutably	paraleipsis	perpetuance	serviceline
corroborant	forgetmenot	irregularly	parallactic	perpetuator	shrinkingly
corroborate	forgettable	irrelevance	parallelism	perplexedly	shrinkproof
corrosively	forgiveness	irrelevancy	parallelled	persecution	shrivelling
corrugation	forlornness	irreligious	paramedical	perseverate	shrubbiness
corruptible	formalistic	irremissive	parametrise	persistence	Soroptimist
corruptibly	formational	irremovable	paramoecium	persistency	sorrowfully
corruptness	formication	irremovably	paramorphic	personalise	spreadeagle
coruscation	formularise	irreparable	paramountcy	personalism	springboard
curableness	formulation	irreparably	paramountly	personalist	springclean
curatorship	fornication	irresoluble	paraphraser	personality	springhouse
curiousness	forthcoming	irretention	paraplectic	personation	springiness
currentness	fortifiable	irretentive	paraselenae	personative	Stradivarii
currishness	fortnightly	irreverence	parasitical	personifier	straightcut
cursiveness	fortunately	irrevocable	parasitosis	perspective	straightish
cursoriness	forwardness	irrevocably	parathyroid	perspicuity	straightway
curtailment	furnishings	irruptively	paratrooper	perspicuous	straitlaced
curvilineal	furtherance	jargonistic	paratyphoid	persuadable	stramineous
curvilinear	furthermore	jerrymander	parentheses	persuasible	strangeness
derangement	furthermost	juridically	parenthesis	pertinacity	strangulate
dereliction	furthersome	larcenously	parenthetic	pertinently	straphanger
dermatology	furtiveness	largeminded	parheliacal	perturbable	strategical
directional	furunculous	laryngology	parishioner	pervasively	stratocracy
directivity	gardemanger	laryngotomy	parochially	pervertedly	streakiness
directorate	garnishment	marcescence	paronomasia	phrasemaker	streetlight
directorial	garrulously	marcescible	participant	phraseogram	strenuosity
directrices	gartersnake	marchioness	participate	phraseology	strenuously
durableness	Germanophil	marconigram	participial	piratically	stretchable
earnestness	germination	marginalise	particulate	pornography	stridulator
earpiercing	germinative	marginality	partitioned	porphyritic	strikebound

stringboard
stringently
stringiness
stringpiece
stringybark
stroboscope
strongpoint
surbasement
surfboarder
surficially
surgeonfish
surpassable
surrebuttal
surrebutter
surrogation
surveillant
taratantara
tarnishable
tarradiddle
teratogenic
teratologic
termagantly
termination
terminative
terminology
termitarium
terraqueous
terrestrial
terricolous
terrigenous
territorial
thrasonical
threadiness
threadpaper
threecolour
threedecker
threehanded
threelegged
threemaster
thriftiness
thrillingly
throatiness
throatlatch
thrombocyte
torchbearer
torchsinger
torticollis
torturously
turbination
turbulently
turgescence
turtleshell
tyrannicide
tyrannosaur
tyrannously
unrealistic
unreasoning
unrelenting
unremitting
unrighteous
uprightness
variability
variational
variegation
variousness
varnishtree
varsovienne
veraciously
verbalistic
verboseness
verdantique
veridically
verisimilar
vermiculate
vermiculite
vermination
verminously
versatilely
versatility

verticality
vertiginous
viridescent
virilescent
virological
voraciously
vortiginous
warmblooded
warmhearted
warrantable
warrantably
wirenetting
wirepulling
wiretapping
workability
workmanlike
workmanship
worldbeater
worldliness
worldlywise
worrisomely
worshipable
worshipless
worshipping
worthlessly
xeranthemum
xerophilous
Zoroastrian
absenteeism
absorbingly
absorptance
abstentious
abstinently
abstraction
abstractive
abstriction
Aesculapian
aesthetical
aestivation
assafoetida
assassinate
assemblyman
assentation
assertively
assessorial
assiduously
assignation
assimilable
assimilator
association
associative
assortative
assuagement
assuredness
Assyriology
austereness
bashfulness
bashibazouk
basipetally
basketchair
bassethound
bestselling
bisexuality
bushmanship
bushwhacker
businessman
cassiterite
castellated
castigation
casuistical
cesarevitch
cesarewitch
cisatlantic
cosignatory
cosmetician
cosmetology
cosmogonist
cosmography
cosmologist

cosmopolite
costbenefit
costiveness
customarily
custombuilt
customhouse
cysticercus
desalinator
descendable
descendible
describable
description
descriptive
desecration
desegregate
desensitise
deservingly
desexualise
desiccation
desiccative
desideratum
designation
desperadoes
desperately
desperation
despoilment
despondence
despondency
destination
destitution
destruction
destructive
desultorily
disablement
disaccustom
disaffected
disafforest
disannulled
disapproval
disarmament
disarmingly
disassemble
disassembly
disbandment
disbeliever
discalceate
discardable
discernible
discernibly
discernment
discerption
disciplinal
discipliner
discography
discontinue
discordance
discordancy
discotheque
discourtesy
discrepancy
discussable
discussible
disencumber
disentangle
disenthrall
disfunction
disgraceful
disgruntled
disguisedly
disgustedly
disharmonic
dishevelled
dishonestly
dishonourer
disillusion
disinclined
disinfector
disinterest
disinterred

disjunction
disjunctive
disjuncture
dislikeable
dislocation
dislodgment
dismayingly
disobedient
disobliging
disorganise
disparaging
disparately
dispensable
dispersedly
displeasure
disportment
disposition
dispositive
disputation
disquieting
disquietude
disremember
disseminate
disseminule
dissentient
dissepiment
dissertator
dissimilate
dissimulate
dissipation
dissipative
dissociable
dissolutely
dissolution
dissolvable
dissonantly
dissyllable
dissymmetry
distasteful
distempered
distensible
distinction
distinctive
distinguish
distraction
distractive
distressful
distribuend
distributor
distrustful
disturbance
disunionist
dysfunction
dyslogistic
easternmost
ensanguined
enslavement
essentially
exsiccation
exstipulate
fasciaboard
fasciculate
fascinating
fascination
fashionable
fashionably
festinately
festschrift
fissionable
fissiparity
fissiparous
fusillation
fustigation
gaseousness
gasfittings
gastrectomy
gastronomic
gastroscope
gestatorial

gesticulate
hesperidium
Hispanicise
Hispanicism
Hispanicist
histologist
historiated
historicise
historicism
historicist
historicity
histrionics
histrionism
hospitalise
hospitality
hospitaller
husbandlike
insalubrity
inscribable
inscription
inscriptive
inscrutable
inscrutably
insectarium
insecticide
insectifuge
insectivore
insectology
inseminator
insensately
insensitive
inseparable
inseparably
insessorial
insidiously
insincerely
insincerity
insinuation
insinuative
insipidness
insistently
insouciance
inspiration
inspiratory
instability
instigation
instigative
installment
instillment
instinctive
instinctual
institution
instruction
instructive
insufflator
insultingly
insuperable
insuperably
ipsilateral
justiciable
justifiable
justifiably
lastingness
lesemajesty
lissomeness
lustfulness
masculinely
masculinise
masculinity
masochistic
massiveness
massproduce
masterfully
masterpiece
mastication
masticatory
mastoiditis

mesalliance
mesoblastic
mesomorphic
messiahship
misalliance
misanthrope
misanthropy
misbegotten
miscarriage
miscegenate
miscellanea
mischievous
miscibility
misconceive
misconstrue
miscreation
misericorde
miserliness
misestimate
misfeasance
misguidance
misguidedly
misjudgment
mismarriage
misremember
misspelling
mistrustful
mosstrooper
musclebound
muscularity
musculation
musculature
musicalness
muskthistle
mustachioed
nasofrontal
noseyparker
nosographer
nosographic
nosological
obscuration
obscureness
obsecration
observantly
observation
observatory
observingly
obsessional
obsessively
obsolescent
obstetrical
obstinately
obstruction
obstructive
oesophageal
oestrogenic
oysterplant
passacaglia
passeriform
passibility
Passiontide
passivation
passiveness
pasteuriser
pastoralism
pastoralist
pastureland
pessimistic
pestiferous
pestilently
pestologist
piscatorial
piscivorous
positronium
posological
possibility
postclassic
posteriorly
postexilian

postglacial	vestigially	attitudinal	ectotrophic	interallied	lateritious
postnuptial	vestryclerk	attractable	entablature	interatomic	latifundium
postulation	vesuvianite	attribution	entablement	interbedded	latitudinal
pushfulness	viscountess	attributive	enterostomy	intercalary	latticework
pussyfooter	viscousness	attritional	enterovirus	intercalate	letterpress
pussywillow	visibleness	autarchical	enterpriser	intercensal	literalness
pustulation	washability	autochthony	entertainer	intercepter	lithography
Rastafarian	washerwoman	autoerotism	enthralling	interceptor	lithophytic
resemblance	washleather	autographic	enthralment	intercessor	lithosphere
resentfully	waspishness	automatable	entitlement	interchange	lithotomise
reservation	waspwaisted	autoplastic	entomophily	intercostal	lithotomist
residential	wastebasket	autotrophic	entrainment	intercourse	lithotripsy
resignation	Wesleyanism	bathingsuit	entreatment	intercrural	litigiously
resiliently	westernmost	batholithic	entrustment	interdental	litterateur
resipiscent	Westminster	bathymetric	establisher	interdepend	Lutheranism
resistively	wisecracker	bathyscaphe	extemporary	interesting	matchlessly
resistivity	wishfulness	bathysphere	extemporise	interfacial	matchmaking
resourceful	wistfulness	battledress	extensional	interfacing	materialise
respectable	zestfulness	battlefield	extensively	interfluent	materialism
respectably	actinometer	betweenmaid	extenuation	interfusion	materialist
respiration	actinomyces	betweenness	extenuatory	intergrowth	materiality
respiratory	actinomycin	betweentime	exteriorise	interiorise	mathematics
resplendent	afterburner	bitterapple	exteriority	interiority	matriarchal
respondence	aftereffect	bittercress	exterminate	interjacent	matriculate
respondency	altercation	bittersweet	externalise	interleaves	matrilineal
responsible	alternately	botanically	externalism	interlinear	matrilinear
responsibly	alternation	botheration	externality	Interlingua	matrimonial
restatement	alternative	bottleglass	extirpation	interlining	metacentric
restfulness	altitudinal	bottlegreen	extirpatory	interlocker	metachrosis
restitution	altocumulus	bottlenosed	extortioner	interlunary	metagenesis
restiveness	altorelievo	butcherbird	extractable	intermeddle	metagenetic
restoration	altorilievo	butterflies	extradition	intermedium	metalloidal
restorative	altostratus	butteriness	extrapolate	intermingle	metallurgic
restriction	antecedence	butyraceous	extravagant	intermitted	metalworker
restrictive	antechamber	catachreses	extravagate	internalise	metamorphic
restructure	antemundane	catachresis	extravasate	internality	metaphysics
resuscitate	antenuptial	cataclysmic	extraverted	internecine	metaplastic
Rosicrucian	antependium	catadromous	extremeness	internuncio	metapsychic
Russophobia	anteriority	cataplectic	extrication	interosseus	metasomatic
rustication	antheridium	catastrophe	extroverted	interplayed	metastasise
susceptible	anthocyanin	catchphrase	fatefulness	interpolate	meteoritics
susceptibly	anthologise	catechismal	fatiguingly	interpreter	meteoroidal
suspenseful	anthologist	catechistic	fatuousness	interracial	meteorology
suspensible	anthracitic	categorical	fetichistic	interregnum	Methodistic
suspiration	anthropical	catercousin	fetishistic	interrelate	methodology
sustainable	anticathode	caterpillar	gatecrasher	interrogate	methylamine
sustainment	anticipator	catheterise	gettogether	interrupter	methylation
susurration	anticyclone	catholicise	gutlessness	interruptor	metonymical
syssarcosis	antifouling	Catholicism	guttapercha	interseptal	metoposcopy
systematics	antigravity	catholicity	guttersnipe	intersexual	metrication
systematise	antiJacobin	catswhisker	gutturalise	intersperse	mithridatic
systematism	antimonious	citizenship	gutturalism	interspinal	mitrailleur
systematist	antineutron	cityslicker	hatefulness	intertangle	mothercraft
tastelessly	antioxidant	cotemporary	heteroclite	intertribal	mothernaked
tessellated	antiphonary	coterminous	heteroecism	intervallic	motherright
testability	antiphrasis	cotoneaster	heterograft	interviewee	motivepower
testatrices	antipyretic	cottongrass	heterophony	interviewer	mutableness
testimonial	antiquarian	cottonmouth	heteroploid	intimidator	muttonchops
unsaturated	antiquation	cytogenesis	heteropolar	intolerable	mythography
unselective	antirrhinum	cytokinesis	heterospory	intolerably	mythologise
unshockable	antiSemitic	cytological	heterotaxis	intolerance	mythologist
unshrinking	antistrophe	deteriorate	heterotroph	intractable	mythomaniac
unskilfully	antitypical	determinacy	heterotypic	intractably	mythopoeist
unsmilingly	antivitamin	determinant	hitherwards	intravenous	mythopoetic
unsolicited	antonomasia	determinate	intagliated	intrepidity	nationalise
unsoundness	arterialise	determinism	integrality	intricately	nationalism
unsparingly	arthrospore	determinist	integration	intriguante	nationalist
unspeakable	articulable	detestation	integrative	intromitted	nationality
unspeakably	articulated	detrainment	intelligent	intromitter	nationstate
unstoppable	articulator	detribalise	intemperate	introverted	naturalness
vascularise	artillerist	detrimental	intenseness	intrusively	naturopathy
vascularity	artiodactyl	dithyrambic	intensifier	intuitional	netherworld
vasculiform	artlessness	dittography	intensional	intuitively	nettlecloth
vasectomise	astigmatism	dutifulness	intensively	intuitivism	nitrogenise
vasodilator	astringency	ectoblastic	intentional	intumescent	nitrogenous
vasopressin	attemptable	ectogenesis	intentioned	kitchenette	nittygritty
vasopressor	attentively	ectogenetic	interactant	kitchensink	notableness
vesicularly	attenuation	ectomorphic	interaction	kitchenware	nothingness
vespertinal	attestation	ectoplasmic	interactive	latchstring	noticeboard

notionalist	rattlebrain	waterlogged	doubleender	loudmouthed	trustworthy
notoriously	rattlepated	waterskiing	doubleentry	loudspeaker	unusualness
nutcrackers	rattlesnake	witchdoctor	doublefaced	loutishness	unutterable
nutrimental	retaliation	witchhunter	doublequick	louverboard	unutterably
nutritional	retaliative	witenagemot	doublespeak	louvreboard	advancement
nutritively	retaliatory	witheringly	doublethink	mountaineer	adventuress
obtestation	retardation	withershins	doubtlessly	mountainous	adventurism
obtrusively	retardative	witlessness	doughtiness	mountaintop	adventurist
octachordal	retardatory	abusiveness	douroucouli	naughtiness	adventurous
octagonally	retentively	acumination	drunkenness	neurologist	adverbially
octingenary	retentivity	acupuncture	ebulliently	neuropathic	adversative
ontogenesis	retinacular	adulterator	ecumenicism	neuroticism	adverseness
ontogenetic	retinaculum	adumbration	ecumenicity	neurotropic	advertently
ontological	retinoscopy	adumbrative	educability	neutraliser	advertising
optometrist	retiredness	aquaculture	educational	nourishment	advisedness
orthocentre	retraceable	aquarellist	elucidation	paunchiness	bivouacking
orthodontia	retractable	aquatically	elucidative	pluralistic	cavalierism
orthodontic	retranslate	aquiculture	elucidatory	plutocratic	cavedweller
orthoepical	retribution	blunderbuss	elusiveness	pluviometer	cavernously
orthography	retributive	bounteously	elutriation	pourparlers	civilianise
orthopaedic	retributory	bountifully	emulousness	prudishness	civilisable
orthopedics	retrievable	bourgeoisie	emulsionise	pruriginous	devaluation
orthopedist	retroaction	boutonniere	enucleation	Prussianise	devastation
orthopteran	retroactive	brucellosis	enumeration	Prussianism	developable
orthoscopic	retrocedent	brusqueness	enumerative	raucousness	development
orthotropic	retroflexed	brutishness	enunciation	raunchiness	deviousness
ostensively	retrorocket	cauliflower	enunciative	roughfooted	devotedness
ostentation	ritualistic	causatively	equableness	roughlegged	divergently
osteography	rotogravure	caustically	equiangular	roundedness	diverticula
osteologist	rottenstone	chucklehead	equidistant	sauropodous	divestiture
osteopathic	satanically	churchgoing	equilateral	sausagemeat	divisionary
osteophytic	satiability	churchiness	equilibrate	sculduddery	divisionism
osteoplasty	satinstitch	churchwoman	equilibrist	sculduggery	divorcement
ostracoderm	satirically	coulometric	equilibrium	scuppernong	divulgation
Ostrogothic	satisfiable	counselling	equinoctial	scurvygrass	divulgement
outbreeding	saturnalian	countenance	equipollent	scuttlebutt	envelopment
outbuilding	saturninely	counterblow	equivalence	shutterless	enviousness
outcropping	sittingroom	counterbond	equivalency	shuttlecock	environment
outdistance	situational	counterfeit	equivocally	skulduddery	favouritism
outfighting	soteriology	counterfoil	equivocator	skulduggery	invalidness
outrivalled	sottishness	counterfort	erubescence	soulfulness	invectively
outspokenly	tenacically	countermand	exuberantly	soundlessly	inventively
outstanding	tetracyclic	countermark	faultfinder	soupkitchen	inventorial
outstripped	tetradactyl	countermine	faultlessly	southeaster	investigate
outwardness	tetrahedral	countermove	feudalistic	Southernism	investiture
patelliform	tetrahedron	countermure	fluctuation	southwester	inviability
paternalism	tetramerous	counterpane	fluorescein	squalidness	invidiously
paternalist	tetrapodous	counterpart	fluorescent	squarebuilt	invigilator
paternoster	tetrarchate	counterplan	fluoroscope	squarsonage	invigorator
pathologist	tetravalent	counterplea	fluoroscopy	squashiness	inviolately
patriarchal	titanically	counterplot	foulmouthed	squeakiness	involucrate
patrilineal	Titianesque	countersink	fourflusher	squeamishly	involuntary
patrimonial	titillation	countersunk	fourpounder	squintingly	involvement
patristical	titleholder	counterturn	fourwheeler	squirearchy	invultation
patronising	tittivation	countervail	fructuation	studentship	juvenescent
patternshop	totalisator	counterview	frugivorous	studiedness	levelheaded
petitionary	totteringly	counterwork	fruitlessly	stumblingly	leviratical
petrography	tuttifrutti	countlessly	frustration	stuntedness	lovableness
petrologist	ultramarine	countrified	glutinously	tautologise	movableness
petticoated	ultramodern	countryfied	gourmandise	tautologism	moveability
pettifogger	ultrasonics	countryseat	gourmandism	tautologous	novelettish
pettishness	ultraviolet	countryside	grumblingly	tautomerism	obviousness
phthiriasis	unteachable	countrywide	haughtiness	tautonymous	pivotbridge
pitchblende	unthinkable	courteously	haustellate	Teutonicism	ravishingly
piteousness	unthinkably	courtliness	housefather	thunderbird	revaccinate
pitifulness	untouchable	cruciferous	householder	thunderbolt	revaluation
potentially	urticaceous	crucifixion	housekeeper	thunderclap	revendicate
potteringly	urticarious	crucigerous	houselights	thunderhead	reverberant
putrescence	vaticinator	crunchiness	housemaster	thunderless	reverberate
putrescible	viticulture	crustaceous	housemother	thunderpeal	reverential
Pythagorean	vitrescence	dauntlessly	housewifely	thuriferous	reversional
Pythagorism	vitrifiable	deuteration	housewifery	touchtyping	reversioner
ratatouille	vituperator	deuterogamy	jauntingcar	toughminded	revisionary
rateability	watchmaking	Deuteronomy	journeywork	tourbillion	revisionism
ratiocinate	waterbottle	doublecheck	knucklebone	truculently	revisionist
rationalise	watercolour	doublecross	laudability	truehearted	reviviscent
rationalist	watercooled	doubleDutch	laughinggas	trundletail	savouriness
rationality	watercooler	doubleedged	launderette	trustbuster	seventeenth
	watercourse		laurustinus	trusteeship	seventyfold

severalfold	phylloclade	breastplate	embarkation	Judaisation	parasitosis		
sovereignly	phyllotaxis	breastwheel	empanelling	ligamentary	parathyroid		
sovereignty	phylogynist	breathalyse	encapsulate	ligamentous	paratrooper		
unvarnished	physicality	broadcaster	enhancement	logarithmic	paratyphoid		
vivaciously	physiocracy	broadleaved	enjambement	lovableness	pedagogical		
vivisection	physiognomy	broadminded	enlargeable	lycanthrope	Pelagianism		
bewhiskered	physiologic	Byzantinism	enlargement	lycanthropy	pelargonium		
bewitchment	phytography	Byzantinist	ensanguined	magazinegun	perambulate		
bowdleriser	phytologist	camaraderie	entablature	maladaptive	phrasemaker		
downdraught	phytosterol	canalicular	entablement	maladjusted	phraseogram		
downhearted	phytotomist	canaliculus	equableness	maladroitly	phraseology		
downtrodden	psychedelia	capableness	ergatocracy	malapropism	piratically		
lawlessness	psychedelic	capaciously	erratically	malariology	pleasurable		
lawmerchant	psychiatric	capacitance	establisher	managership	pleasurably		
lowpressure	psychically	carabiniere	eucalyptole	McCarthyism	pliableness		
lowspirited	psychodrama	carabinieri	eudaemonism	megalomania	polarimeter		
mawkishness	psychogenic	caravanning	eudaemonist	megalopolis	polarimetry		
pawnbroking	psychograph	caravansary	exhaustible	megatherium	polarisable		
powderflask	psychologic	catachreses	exhaustless	melancholia	polariscope		
powerlessly	psychometry	catachresis	expansional	melancholic	preachiness		
thwartships	psychomotor	cataclysmic	expansively	melanochroi	preaudience		
townspeople	psychopathy	catadromous	expansivity	melanophore	pyramidally		
unwarranted	rhynchodont	cataplectic	expatiation	mesalliance	pyramidical		
unweetingly	scyphistoma	catastrophe	expatiative	metacentric	pyrargyrite		
unwholesome	stylisation	cavalierism	expatiatory	metachrosis	rapaciously		
unwillingly	stylishness	cesarevitch	fanatically	metagenesis	ratatouille		
unwinkingly	stylography	cesarewitch	farawayness	metagenetic	rebarbative		
unwittingly	stylopodium	chiaroscuro	filamentary	metalloidal	recalculate		
anxiousness	thyroiditis	cicatricial	filamentous	metallurgic	recantation		
auxanometer	tryingplane	cisatlantic	financially	metalworker	redactional		
coxcombical	trypanosome	cleanlimbed	foraminated	metamorphic	regardfully		
dexiotropic	tryptophane	cleanliness	foraminifer	metaphysics	relatedness		
dexterously	waywardness	cleanshaven	friableness	metaplastic	relationism		
doxographer	Byzantinism	clearheaded	funambulate	metapsychic	relationist		
hexadecimal	hazardously	coparcenary	funambulist	metasomatic	renaissance		
hexametrist	sizableness	coralloidal	gigantesque	metastasise	repartition		
lixiviation	————	creationism	greasepaint	Micawberish	retaliation		
loxodromics		creationist	greaseproof	Micawberism	retaliative		
luxuriantly	abracadabra	curableness	greatnephew	misalliance	retaliatory		
luxuriation	abranchiate	curatorship	gynaecocrat	misanthrope	retardation		
luxuriously	adiaphorism	debarkation	gynaecology	misanthropy	retardative		
maxillipede	advancement	debauchment	hazardously	monarchical	retardatory		
myxomatosis	agnatically	decantation	hepatectomy	monasterial	revaccinate		
myxomycetes	agrarianism	decarbonate	Heracleidan	monasticism	revaluation		
noxiousness	alkalescent	decarbonise	hexadecimal	movableness	rifacimenti		
saxophonist	alkalimeter	decarburise	hexametrist	mutableness	rifacimento		
sexagesimal	alkalimetry	defalcation	hilariously	nefariously	romanticise		
sexlessness	allAmerican	demagnetise	illaffected	negationist	romanticism		
sexological	allantoides	demagogical	immanentism	nomadically	romanticist		
sextodecimo	amiableness	demagoguery	immanentist	notableness	sagaciously		
taxidermist	annabergite	demagoguism	immarginate	octachordal	salaciously		
taxonomical	appallingly	demandingly	impanelling	octagonally	satanically		
textureless	apparatchik	demarcation	imparkation	olfactology	scragginess		
toxicomania	apparelling	demarkation	impartation	ommatophore	scrappiness		
toxophilite	aquaculture	depauperate	impartially	organically	scratchwork		
vexatiously	aquarellist	depauperise	impassioned	organisable	selaginella		
vexillology	aquatically	derangement	impassively	organscreen	semanticist		
boysenberry	arraignment	desalinator	impassivity	Palaearctic	semasiology		
bryozoology	arrangement	devaluation	impatiently	palaeotypic	senatorship		
cryobiology	assafoetida	devastation	incalescent	parachutist	sexagesimal		
cryosurgery	assassinate	didacticism	incantation	paradisical	sheathknife		
cryotherapy	atrabilious	dilapidated	incantatory	paradoxical	sizableness		
cryptically	audaciously	dilapidator	incarcerate	paragrapher	solanaceous		
cryptogamic	autarchical	disablement	incardinate	paragraphic	somatically		
cryptograph	auxanometer	disaccustom	incarnadine	paraldehyde	somatogenic		
cryptomeria	behavioural	disaffected	incarnation	paraleipsis	somatologic		
crystalline	belatedness	disafforest	infanticide	parallactic	somatoplasm		
crystallise	bicarbonate	disannulled	infantilism	parallelism	somatotonia		
crystallite	bilaterally	disapproval	infantryman	parallelled	somatotonic		
crystalloid	bipartition	disarmament	infatuation	paramedical	speakership		
erythrocyte	Bonapartean	disarmingly	ingathering	parametrise	sphaeridium		
etymologise	Bonapartism	disassemble	inhabitable	paramoecium	sphagnology		
etymologist	Bonapartist	disassembly	inhabitancy	paramorphic	splashboard		
idyllically	botanically	dreadnought	innavigable	paramountcy	splayfooted		
joylessness	breadbasket	dreamlessly	insalubrity	paramountly	squalidness		
oxygenation	breadcrumbs	durableness	intagliated	paraphraser	squarebuilt		
oxyhydrogen	breadthways	dynamically	invalidness	paraplectic	squarsonage		
phycocyanin	breadthwise	dynamometer	irradiation	paraselenae	squashiness		
phycologist	breadwinner	dynamometry	irradiative	parasitical	steadfastly		

steamboiler	bombination	Sabbatarian	conceitedly	flaccidness	perceivably
steamroller	bonbonniere	subbasement	conceivable	flocculence	perceptible
steatopygia	borborygmus	surbasement	conceivably	fluctuation	perceptibly
Stradivarii	bumblepuppy	symbolistic	concentrate	fractionary	perchlorate
straightcut	cabbagepalm	tolbutamide	conceptacle	fractionate	percipience
straightish	cabbagerose	trabeculate	concernment	fractionise	percolation
straightway	cabbagetree	tribulation	concertedly	fractiously	phycocyanin
straitlaced	cabbageworm	tribuneship	concertgoer	fricandeaux	phycologist
stramineous	cabbalistic	tribunicial	conciliator	fructuation	pieceworker
strangeness	carbocyclic	tribunitial	conciseness	functionary	piscatorial
strangulate	carbonation	tributarily	concomitant	functionate	piscivorous
straphanger	carbuncular	tumbledrier	concordance	geochemical	pitchblende
strategical	carburetion	turbination	concrescent	gimcrackery	placability
stratocracy	carburetted	turbulently	concubinage	godchildren	plectoptera
subaerially	carburetter	unobtrusive	concubinary	gracelessly	plicateness
subarration	carburettor	verbalistic	concubitant	gracileness	practicable
subaudition	cobblestone	verboseness	concurrence	hunchbacked	practicably
subaxillary	combatively	abecedarian	coxcombical	hyacinthine	practically
sugarcoated	combination	Aesculapian	crackerjack	inoculation	Precambrian
sybaritical	combinative	aircraftman	crocidolite	inoculative	precautious
synagogical	combinatory	amicability	crocodilian	inscribable	precedented
taratantara	combustible	anachronism	cruciferous	inscription	precedently
tenableness	corbiculate	anachronous	crucifixion	inscriptive	precentress
tenaciously	corbiesteps	anacoluthon	crucigerous	inscrutable	preceptress
teratogenic	crabbedness	anacreontic	deactivator	inscrutably	precipitant
teratologic	disbandment	anecdotical	descendable	ipecacuanha	precipitate
tetanically	disbeliever	apocalyptic	descendible	isochronism	precipitous
theatregoer	doublecheck	bacchanalia	describable	isochronous	preciseness
theatricals	doublecross	bacciferous	description	itacolumite	preconceive
thrasonical	doubleDutch	beachcomber	descriptive	kitchenette	precontract
thwartships	doubleedged	beechmarten	diachronism	kitchensink	prickliness
titanically	doubleender	biochemical	diacritical	kitchenware	proceedings
tobacconist	doubleentry	biocoenoses	discalceate	knucklebone	procephalic
totalisator	doublefaced	biocoenosis	discardable	laicisation	prochronism
treacherous	doublequick	biocoenotic	discernible	Lancastrian	proconsular
treacliness	doublespeak	blackavised	discernibly	lancinating	procreation
treasonable	doublethink	blackbeetle	discernment	lancination	procreative
treasonably	doubtlessly	blackbirder	discerption	larcenously	procrustean
triadically	dumbfounder	blackcoated	disciplinal	latchstring	proctorship
triangulate	elaborately	blackfellow	discipliner	marcescence	procuration
tunableness	elaboration	blackgrouse	discography	marcescible	procuratory
tyrannicide	elaborative	blackmailer	discontinue	marchioness	procurement
tyrannosaur	erubescence	blackmarket	discordance	marconigram	psychedelia
tyrannously	exuberantly	blockbuster	discordancy	masculinely	psychedelic
uncanniness	fimbriation	brachiation	discotheque	masculinise	psychiatric
uncanonical	flabbergast	brachyurous	discourtesy	masculinity	psychically
uncatchable	forbearance	bracteolate	discrepancy	matchlessly	psychodrama
unfailingly	forbiddance	bricklaying	discussable	matchmaking	psychogenic
unfaltering	gibberellin	brucellosis	discussible	mercenarily	psychograph
unfashioned	gibbousness	butcherbird	educability	merchandise	psychologic
unhappiness	globeflower	calceolaria	educational	merchantman	psychometry
unmanliness	globigerina	calcicolous	ejaculation	mercilessly	psychomotor
unmatchable	globularity	calciferous	ejaculatory	mercurially	psychopathy
unnaturally	harbourless	calcifugous	electioneer	miscarriage	pulchritude
unpalatable	herbivorous	calcination	electrician	miscegenate	punchinello
unsaturated	hobbledehoy	calculating	electricity	miscellanea	punctilious
unvarnished	husbandlike	calculation	electrocute	mischievous	punctuality
unwarranted	illbreeding	calculative	electrolier	miscibility	punctuation
vacationist	inebriation	cancellated	electrology	misconceive	purchasable
vagabondage	inobservant	carcinomata	electrolyse	misconstrue	quacksalver
vagabondise	jabberwocky	catchphrase	electrolyte	miscreation	quickchange
vagabondish	Leibnitzian	chickenfeed	electronics	musclebound	quickfiring
vagabondism	membraneous	chickenwire	electrotype	muscularity	quickfreeze
vagariously	misbegotten	chockablock	elicitation	musculation	quickfrozen
venatically	morbiferous	chucklehead	elucidation	musculature	quicksilver
veraciously	outbreeding	circularise	elucidative	myocarditis	quickwitted
vexatiously	outbuilding	circularity	elucidatory	narcoleptic	rancorously
vicariously	plebeianise	circulation	enucleation	nonchalance	raucousness
vinaigrette	plebeianism	circulative	epochmaking	nuncupation	reachmedown
vivaciously	probabilism	circulatory	executioner	nuncupative	reactionary
voraciously	probabilist	circumlunar	executorial	nutcrackers	reactionist
womanliness	probability	circumpolar	executrices	obscuration	sacculation
xeranthemum	probational	circumsolar	executrixes	obscureness	sarcomatous
alabastrine	probationer	circumspect	eyecatching	oracularity	sarcophagus
barbarously	problematic	circumvolve	farcicality	outcropping	shacklebolt
barbastelle	rhabdomancy	coccidiosis	fasciaboard	peacemaking	shacklebone
barbiturate	ribbongrass	concatenate	fasciculate	peccability	shockheaded
bombardment	rubberstamp	concealable	fascinating	peccadillos	shocktroops
bombilation	rumbustious	concealment	fascination	perceivable	sincereness

```
slickenside  academicals  handgrenade  predicatory  Aeneolithic  cavedweller
snickersnee  academician  handicapped  predictable  affectation  cavernously
spaceflight  academicism  handicapper  predictably  affectingly  celebration
spaceheater  acidifiable  handknitted  predominant  affectional  celebratory
spacesaving  acidophilic  handpainted  predominate  affectioned  celestially
specifiable  acidulation  handselling  prodigalise  affectively  cementation
specificity  anadiplosis  handwriting  prodigality  affectivity  cerebration
spectacular  bandylegged  handwritten  prudishness  afterburner  ceremonious
spectatress  biddability  handwrought  quadraphony  aftereffect  chaetognath
spectrality  biedermeier  hardhearted  quadratical  allegorical  cheerleader
spectrogram  birdbrained  hardhitting  quadrennial  allelomorph  cheerlessly
spectrology  birdfancier  hardmouthed  quadrennium  alleviation  cheesecloth
speculation  birdwatcher  hardworking  quadrillion  alleviative  chieftaincy
speculative  bladderwort  headborough  quadrupedal  alleviatory  codefendant
stichometry  bondservant  headhunting  readability  altercation  coleorrhiza
stickinsect  bondservice  heedfulness  readywitted  alternately  comestibles
stickleback  bondwashing  heldentenor  reddishness  alternation  comeuppance
stockbroker  bowdleriser  Hindoostani  reedbunting  alternative  corecipient
stockholder  bradycardia  hundredfold  reeducation  anaesthesia  cotemporary
stockinette  bridgeboard  illdisposed  reedwarbler  anaesthetic  coterminous
stockjobber  caddishness  inadaptable  roadholding  angelically  cupellation
stockmarket  candelabrum  inadvertent  saddlecloth  antecedence  cybernation
stocktaking  candescence  inadvisable  saddlehorse  antechamber  cybernetics
subcategory  candidature  inedibility  Sadduceeism  antemundane  deceitfully
subclinical  candleberry  iridescence  sandbagging  antenuptial  deceivingly
subcontract  candlelight  kindhearted  sandskipper  antependium  decelerator
subcontrary  candlepower  landaulette  shadowgraph  anteriority  decemvirate
subcortical  candlestick  landgrabber  shadowiness  appealingly  decennially
subcritical  cardinalate  landgravine  soldierlike  appeasement  deceptively
subcultural  cardiograph  landholding  soldiership  appellation  decerebrate
succedaneum  cardsharper  landingbeam  stadtholder  appellative  defectively
succourless  clodhopping  landinggear  studentship  arrestingly  defenceless
succulently  coadunation  landlordism  studiedness  arterialise  defensively
susceptible  coeducation  laudability  subdivision  ascensional  deferential
susceptibly  coldblooded  loudmouthed  subdominant  ascetically  delectation
synchromesh  coldhearted  loudspeaker  syndesmosis  aspergillum  deleterious
synchronise  condemnable  maddeningly  syndicalism  aspergillus  dependently
synchronism  condensable  magdalenian  syndicalist  aspersorium  dereliction
synchronous  conditional  maidservant  syndication  assemblyman  desecration
synchrotron  conditioner  mandarinate  tendencious  assentation  desegregate
syncopation  condolatory  mandibulate  tendentious  assertively  desensitise
teachership  condominium  mandolinist  tiddlywinks  assessorial  deservingly
thickheaded  condonation  manducation  topdressing  atheistical  desexualise
thickwitted  condottiere  manducatory  traditional  attemptable  deteriorate
torchbearer  condottieri  meadowgrass  traducement  attentively  determinacy
torchsinger  conductance  meadowsweet  unadvisedly  attenuation  determinant
touchtyping  conductible  mendelevium  vendibility  attestation  determinate
tracasserie  conductress  middleclass  verdantique  balefulness  determinism
tracelessly  condylomata  middlesized  vindication  barefacedly  determinist
tracheotomy  cordialness  mindbending  vindicative  bedevilment  detestation
trackwalker  credentials  mindblowing  vindicatory  Benedictine  developable
trichinosis  credibility  mindfulness  voodooistic  benediction  development
trichomonad  credulously  mindreading  widdershins  benedictory  dicephalous
tricksiness  dendritical  mundaneness  wildcatting  benefaction  digestively
tricoloured  diadelphous  murderously  wildfowling  beneficence  dimensional
truculently  dundrearies  needfulness  windcheater  beneficiary  directional
unaccounted  epidiascope  needlecraft  windlestraw  beneficiate  directivity
unicellular  eradication  needlepoint  wonderfully  benevolence  directorate
unicoloured  eradicative  needlewoman  woodcarving  bereavement  directorial
urochordate  evidentiary  nondelivery  woodcutting  bicentenary  directrices
vaccination  faddishness  nondescript  Abbevillian  bicephalous  disencumber
vascularise  feldspathic  outdistance  absenteeism  bimetallism  disentangle
vascularity  feudalistic  paddleboard  accelerando  bimetallist  disenthrall
vasculiform  fiddlestick  paddlewheel  accelerator  bisexuality  divergently
vincibility  fundamental  paederastic  accentually  bohemianism  diverticula
viscountess  gardemanger  paediatrics  acceptation  breechblock  divestiture
viscousness  gendarmerie  paediatrist  acceptingly  breezeblock  dodecaphony
voicelessly  goddaughter  paedophilia  accessorial  bureaucracy  dolefulness
volcanicity  goldbeating  pandemonium  accessorise  byeelection  domesticate
volcanology  golddigging  pendulously  adjectively  calefacient  domesticity
vulcanicity  goldenberry  ponderation  adventuress  calefactory  eclecticism
vulcanology  goodhearted  ponderosity  adventurism  calendrical  effectively
watchmaking  goodlooking  ponderously  adventurist  carefulness  effectually
welcomeness  goodnatured  powderflask  adventurous  caressingly  egregiously
whichsoever  gradational  predatorily  adverbially  catechismal  elderliness
witchdoctor  gradiometer  predecessor  adversative  catechistic  embellisher
witchhunter  gradualness  predicament  adverseness  categorical  emmenagogue
wreckmaster  handbreadth  predication  advertently  catercousin  Emmenthaler
zincography  handfasting  predicative  advertising  caterpillar  emperorship
```

endearingly	genealogist	impertinent	interlunary	lineprinter	parenthesis
endemically	generaliser	imperviable	intermeddle	literalness	parenthetic
enfeoffment	generalship	impetration	intermedium	makebelieve	patelliform
enneahedron	generically	impetratory	intermingle	malediction	paternalism
enterostomy	genetically	impetuosity	intermitted	maledictory	paternalist
enterovirus	GraecoRoman	impetuously	internalise	malefaction	paternoster
enterpriser	greengrocer	incertitude	internality	maleficence	pedestalled
entertainer	greenkeeper	incessantly	internecine	malevolence	penetrating
envelopment	greenockite	indeciduous	internuncio	materialise	penetration
ephemerides	haberdasher	indefinable	interosseus	materialism	penetrative
Esperantist	harebrained	indefinably	interplayed	materialist	peregrinate
essentially	hatefulness	indehiscent	interpolate	materiality	perennation
etherealise	hebephrenia	indentation	interpreter	meteoritics	perennially
ethereality	hebephrenic	independent	interracial	meteoroidal	pigeonchest
eugenically	Hegelianism	inferential	interregnum	meteorology	pipecleaner
exceedingly	hemeralopia	inferiority	interrelate	mimetically	piperaceous
excellently	hereditable	infertility	interrogate	mineraliser	piteousness
exceptional	hereinafter	infestation	interrupter	minesweeper	polemically
excessively	heresiology	infeudation	interruptor	misericorde	polevaulter
expectantly	heretically	ingeniously	interseptal	miserliness	pomegranate
expectation	heteroclite	ingenuously	intersexual	misestimate	potentially
expectative	heteroecism	inheritable	intersperse	moderations	powerlessly
expectorant	heterograft	inheritance	interspinal	modernistic	praetorship
expectorate	heterophony	inheritress	intertangle	molecricket	preelection
expediently	heteroploid	innervation	intertribal	molecularly	preeminence
expeditious	heteropolar	insectarium	intervallic	molendinary	preexistent
expenditure	heterospory	insecticide	interviewee	molestation	priestcraft
expensively	heterotaxis	insectifuge	interviewer	momentarily	pureblooded
experienced	heterotroph	insectivore	invectively	momentously	quaestorial
extemporary	heterotypic	insectology	inventively	moneylender	queenliness
extemporise	hibernacula	inseminator	inventorial	moneymaking	quiescently
extensional	hibernation	insensately	investigate	moneymarket	Rabelaisian
extensively	Hibernicism	insensitive	investiture	moneyspider	racemeeting
extenuation	hideousness	inseparable	irrecusable	moveability	rarefaction
extenuatory	homeopathic	inseparably	irrecusably	namecalling	rarefactive
exteriorise	homeostasis	insessorial	irredentism	namedropper	rateability
exteriority	homeostatic	integrality	irredentist	necessarian	receptacula
exterminate	homesteader	integration	irreducible	necessarily	receptively
externalise	homestretch	integrative	irreducibly	necessitate	receptivity
externalism	honeybadger	intelligent	irrefutable	necessitous	recessional
externality	honeymooner	intemperate	irrefutably	nomenclator	recessively
facelifting	honeysuckle	intenseness	irregularly	nonetheless	redetermine
facetiously	hopefulness	intensifier	irrelevance	nonexistent	referential
fatefulness	hugeousness	intensional	irrelevancy	noseyparker	regenerable
fenestrated	hymenoptera	intensively	irreligious	novelettish	regenerator
firecracker	hyperactive	intentional	irremissive	numerically	remembrance
firefighter	hyperbolise	intentioned	irremovable	objectively	renegotiate
fireraising	hyperboloid	interactant	irremovably	objectivism	repellantly
firewalking	hyperborean	interaction	irreparable	objectivist	repellently
firewatcher	hypercharge	interactive	irreparably	objectivity	repentantly
fomentation	hypercritic	interallied	irresoluble	obscuration	repetitious
foreclosure	hypermarket	interatomic	irretention	observantly	resemblance
foreignness	hypermetric	interbedded	irretentive	observation	resentfully
forequarter	hyperphagia	intercalary	irreverence	observatory	reservation
forerunning	hyperplasia	intercalate	irrevocable	observingly	retentively
foreseeable	hypersthene	intercensal	irrevocably	obsessional	retentivity
foreshorten	hypertrophy	intercepter	isoelectric	obsessively	revendicate
foresighted	immediately	interceptor	juvenescent	obtestation	reverberant
forestaller	immedicable	intercessor	kinematical	offenceless	reverberate
forestation	immenseness	interchange	kinesiology	offensively	reverential
forethinker	impeachable	intercostal	kinetograph	orderliness	reversional
forethought	impeachment	intercourse	kinetoscope	orientalise	reversioner
foretopmast	impecunious	intercrural	labefaction	orientalism	rodenticide
foretopsail	impedimenta	interdental	lakedweller	orientalist	ropedancing
forevermore	impenetrate	interdepend	lamellicorn	orientation	ropewalking
foreverness	impenitence	interesting	lamelliform	ostensively	rubefacient
forewarning	impenitency	interfacial	lamentation	ostentation	rubefaction
freebooting	imperfectly	interfacing	lateritious	osteography	safebreaker
freehearted	imperforate	interfluent	legerdemain	osteologist	safeconduct
freemasonry	imperialise	interfusion	lesemajesty	osteopathic	safecracker
freethinker	imperialism	intergrowth	levelheaded	osteophytic	safekeeping
freethought	imperialist	interiorise	libertarian	osteoplasty	safetyvalve
freezedried	imperilling	interiority	liberticide	otherwhiles	saleability
gametangium	imperilment	interjacent	libertinage	Palestinian	salesladies
gametophyte	imperiously	interleaves	libertinism	panegyrical	scientistic
gaseousness	impermanent	interlinear	lifemanship	paperhanger	scientology
gatecrasher	impermeable	interlining	linedrawing	papermaking	scleroderma
gegenschein	impermeably	Interlingua	linefishing	paperweight	sclerometer
genealogise	impersonate	interlocker	linendraper	parentheses	sclerophyll

sclerotitis	tabernacled	unnecessary	dysfunction	selfrespect	fragmentary
screamingly	talebearing	unnervingly	edification	selfsealing	frightfully
screwdriver	talentscout	unrealistic	edificatory	selfseeking	frigidarium
sedentarily	tameability	unreasoning	fanfaronade	selfservice	frugivorous
selectively	tapemachine	unrelenting	forfeitable	selfserving	fulguration
selectivity	tapemeasure	unremitting	gafftopsail	selfstarter	gangsterism
semeiotical	telegrammic	unselective	gasfittings	selfsterile	gingerbread
serendipity	telegrapher	unteachable	godforsaken	selfsupport	gurgitation
seventeenth	telegraphic	unweetingly	gonfalonier	selftorture	haggadistic
seventyfold	telekinesis	valediction	halfbinding	selfwinding	haggardness
severalfold	telekinetic	valedictory	halfblooded	selfworship	haughtiness
sheepfarmer	teleologism	vasectomise	halfhearted	shiftlessly	hedgehopped
sheepmaster	teleologist	venereology	halfholiday	sinfonietta	hedgepriest
sheetanchor	telepathise	venesection	halflanding	spifflicate	hedgeschool
shoeleather	telepathist	viceadmiral	halfmeasure	stiffnecked	hoggishness
sideslipped	telephonist	vicegerency	illfavoured	stiflejoint	imaginarily
sidestepped	teleprinter	viceregally	ineffective	sufficiency	imagination
sidewheeler	temerarious	viceroyalty	ineffectual	suffixation	imaginative
sleepingbag	tenementary	viceroyship	inefficient	suffocation	isogeotherm
sleepingcar	threadiness	vinedresser	inoffensive	suffocative	jargonistic
sleeplessly	threadpaper	wakefulness	inofficious	suffragette	judgmatical
sleepwalker	threecolour	waterbottle	malfeasance	suffumigate	languidness
sleeveboard	threedecker	watercolour	malfunction	surfboarder	largeminded
soberminded	threehanded	watercooled	misfeasance	surficially	laughinggas
somewhither	threelegged	watercooler	nonfeasance	swiftfooted	lengthiness
soteriology	threemaster	watercourse	outfighting	toffeenosed	lingeringly
sovereignly	timebargain	waterlogged	perfectible	trafficator	linguistics
sovereignty	timepleaser	waterskiing	perfectness	trafficking	loggerheads
speechifier	timeserving	wheelbarrow	perforation	trafficless	longanimity
speedometer	timesharing	wheelwright	perforative	unification	longplaying
spherically	treecreeper	winegrowing	performable	uniformness	longsighted
spherometer	triennially	winetasting	performance	whiffletree	marginalise
spherulitic	truehearted	wirenetting	perfunctory	wolfwhistle	marginality
splendorous	tuberculate	wirepulling	prefatorial	anagnorisis	margraviate
splenectomy	tuberculise	wiretapping	prefatorily	bergamasque	misguidance
splenetical	tuberculose	wisecracker	prefectural	bergschrund	misguidedly
spreadeagle	tuberculous	witenagemot	profanation	braggadocio	naughtiness
squeakiness	tumefaction	biofeedback	profanatory	burglarious	neighbourly
squeamishly	tunefulness	buffalorobe	profaneness	burgomaster	oligochaete
steelworker	typecasting	chafingdish	professedly	coagulation	oligomerous
steeplebush	typefounder	cliffhanger	proficiency	congealable	originality
steeplejack	typefoundry	coefficient	profiterole	congealment	origination
steerageway	typesetting	coffeehouse	profuseness	congelation	originative
streakiness	typewritten	coffeetable	raffishness	congenerous	oxygenation
streetlight	unbeknownst	comfortable	reification	congenially	Panglossian
strenuosity	unbelieving	comfortably	scaffolding	congressman	phagedaenic
strenuously	unbendingly	comfortless	selfassured	congruently	phagocytise
stretchable	unbeseeming	confabulate	selfcentred	congruously	phagocytose
superabound	unceasingly	confederacy	selfclosing	dangerously	piggishness
supercharge	uncertainly	confederate	selfcocking	diagnostics	plagiariser
superfamily	uncertainty	conferrable	selfcommand	disgraceful	plagioclase
superficial	underbidder	confessedly	selfconceit	disgruntled	plagiostome
superficies	undercharge	confidently	selfcontent	disguisedly	pragmatical
superfluity	underexpose	confidingly	selfcontrol	disgustedly	progenitrix
superfluous	underground	confinement	selfcreated	doggishness	progeniture
superheater	undergrowth	confirmable	selfculture	doughtiness	progestogen
superimpose	underhanded	confiscable	selfdefence	draggletail	prognathism
superinduce	undermanned	confiscator	selfdenying	eligibility	prognathous
superintend	underpinned	conflagrant	selfdespair	enigmatical	progression
superioress	underseller	conflagrate	selfdevoted	epigastrium	progressism
superiority	undersigned	confliction	selfdisplay	epigraphist	progressist
superjacent	understated	conflictive	selfelected	evagination	progressive
superlative	undertaking	conformable	selfevident	exaggerator	purgatorial
superlunary	undertenant	conformably	selffeeding	exogenously	rangefinder
supermarket	undervaluer	conformally	selffeeling	fidgetiness	ringstraked
supernatant	underweight	conformance	selffertile	fingerboard	roughfooted
supernormal	underwriter	confusingly	selfimposed	fingerglass	roughlegged
superscribe	undeserving	confutation	selfinduced	fingerplate	sanguinaria
superscript	undesirable	confutative	selfinvited	fingerprint	sanguineous
supersedeas	undeveloped	craftswoman	selfishness	fingerstall	seigneurial
supersedure	unfeelingly	deification	selflimited	flagcaptain	seigniorage
superstrata	unfeignedly	differentia	selfloading	flagellator	seigniorial
supersubtle	ungetatable	differently	selflocking	flagofficer	singlestick
supertanker	unhealthily	difficultly	selfmastery	flagwagging	singletrack
supervision	unhelpfully	diffidently	selfopinion	flightiness	singularise
supervisory	unkennelled	diffraction	selfpitying	forgetfully	singularity
sweepstakes	unmeaningly	diffuseness	selfraising	forgetmenot	slightingly
synergistic	unmemorable	diffusively	selfreliant	forgettable	songfulness
tabefaction	unmemorably	disfunction	selfreproof	forgiveness	songsparrow

stagemanage	dishonourer	orthodontic	ambivalence	Christendom	equivocally
stagestruck	dithyrambic	orthoepical	ambivalency	christening	equivocator
stagflation	enchainment	orthography	ambiversion	christiania	eudiometric
steganogram	enchantment	orthopaedic	ancientness	Christianly	exdirectory
stegosaurus	enchantress	orthopedics	angiography	Christmassy	exsiccation
suggestible	enchiridion	orthopedist	annihilator	Christology	extirpation
surgeonfish	enthralling	orthopteran	anniversary	citizenship	extirpatory
tangibility	enthralment	orthoscopic	anticathode	civilianise	familiarise
togglejoint	eschatology	orthotropic	anticipator	civilisable	familiarity
toughminded	escheatable	oxyhydrogen	anticyclone	clairschach	farinaceous
tragedienne	escheatment	pachydermal	antifouling	clairvoyant	fatiguingly
tragicomedy	Eucharistic	panhellenic	antigravity	cleistogamy	fetichistic
triggerfish	euchologion	parheliacal	antiJacobin	codicillary	fetishistic
troglodytic	euphemistic	pathologist	antimonious	copingstone	finicalness
turgescence	eurhythmics	phthiriasis	antineutron	copiousness	fruitlessly
unigeniture	fashionable	pigheadedly	antioxidant	cosignatory	fusillation
waggishness	fashionably	prehistoric	antiphonary	curiousness	geniculated
wedgeshaped	haphazardly	prohibition	antiphrasis	cylindrical	genitivally
wedgetailed	highbrowism	prohibitive	antipyretic	dedicatedly	goniometric
weighbridge	highfalutin	prohibitory	antiquarian	deficiently	habiliments
weightiness	highpitched	pushfulness	antiquation	definiendum	habituation
whigmaleery	highpowered	Pythagorean	antirrhinum	deliciously	Hagiografia
zoographist	highranking	Pythagorism	antiSemitic	delightedly	hagiography
alphabetise	highstepper	rightangled	antistrophe	delightsome	hagiologist
amphetamine	highwrought	righteously	antitypical	delineation	hagioscopic
amphibolite	hitherwards	righthanded	antivitamin	delinquency	Hamiltonian
amphibology	hyphenation	righthander	anxiousness	deliriously	heliochrome
amphictyony	illhumoured	rightminded	aquiculture	deliverable	heliography
amphimictic	lachrymator	rightwinger	arbitrageur	delitescent	heliometric
amphisbaena	lecherously	sightlessly	arbitrament	deliverable	heliotropic
antheridium	lichenology	sightliness	arbitrarily	deliverance	hemianopsia
anthocyanin	lightfooted	sightreader	arbitration	deliveryman	hemimorphic
anthologise	lighthanded	sightscreen	arbitrative	demigoddess	hemipterous
anthologist	lightheaded	sightseeing	arbitratrix	denigration	hemispheric
anthracitic	lightminded	sightworthy	Arminianism	denigratory	homiletical
anthropical	lightsomely	sophistical	articulable	denizenship	Hudibrastic
archaeology	lightweight	tacheometer	articulated	desiccation	humiliation
archaeornis	lithography	tachycardia	articulator	desiccative	humiliatory
archaically	lithophytic	tachygraphy	artillerist	desideratum	illiberally
archangelic	lithosphere	technically	artiodactyl	designation	illimitable
archdiocese	lithotomise	technocracy	assiduously	deviousness	illimitably
archduchess	lithotomist	technologic	assignation	dexiotropic	illiquidity
archdukedom	lithotripsy	tephromancy	assimilable	digitigrade	immigration
Archimedean	lophobranch	tightfisted	assimilator	diningtable	immitigable
archipelago	Lutheranism	tightlipped	astigmatism	disillusion	immitigably
arthrospore	machicolate	unchristian	attitudinal	disinclined	impingement
asphyxiator	machination	unshockable	audibleness	disinfector	incinerator
bashfulness	machinemade	unshrinking	audiologist	disinterest	incipiently
bashibazouk	mathematics	unthinkable	audiometric	disinterred	indifferent
bathingsuit	mechanician	unthinkably	audiovisual	divisionary	indigestion
batholithic	mechanistic	unwholesome	auricularly	divisionism	indigestive
bathymetric	Methodistic	vichyssoise	Aurignacian	domiciliary	indignantly
bathyscaphe	methodology	washability	avoirdupois	domiciliate	indignation
bathysphere	methylamine	washerwoman	bacilliform	domineering	indirection
bewhiskered	methylation	washleather	basipetally	dubiousness	individuate
Bodhisattva	mithridatic	wishfulness	bedizenment	duniewassal	indivisible
botheration	mothercraft	witheringly	befittingly	dutifulness	indivisibly
Brahmanical	mothernaked	withershins	benightedly	efficacious	infiltrator
brahmaputra	motherright	abridgement	benightment	efficiently	infinitival
Brahminical	mythography	accipitrine	benignantly	ellipsoidal	infirmarian
bushmanship	mythologise	achievement	bewitchment	ellipticity	insidiously
bushwhacker	mythologist	acriflavine	biliousness	empirically	insincerely
catheterise	mythomaniac	acrimonious	bimillenary	engineering	insincerely
catholicise	mythopoeist	actinometer	bimillenium	enlightened	insincerity
Catholicism	mythopoetic	actinomyces	brainlessly	enlivenment	insinuation
catholicity	naphthalene	adminicular	brainsickly	entitlement	insinuative
cochinchina	nephelinite	admiralship	brainteaser	enviousness	insipidness
dichogamous	nephrectomy	advisedness	businessman	environment	insistently
dichotomise	netherworld	afficionado	calibration	epeirogenic	intimidator
dichotomist	nightingale	affiliation	californium	equiangular	inviability
dichotomous	nightmarish	affirmation	calisthenic	equidistant	invidiously
dichromatic	nightporter	affirmative	capillarity	equilateral	invigilator
diphtherial	nightwalker	affirmatory	caricatural	equilibrate	invigorator
diphtheroid	nothingness	agriculture	chainarmour	equilibrist	inviolately
diphthongal	offhandedly	Albigensian	chainletter	equilibrium	ipsilateral
diphycercal	orchestrate	altitudinal	chainsmoker	equinoctial	judiciously
disharmonic	orchidology	ambiguously	chainstitch	equipollent	juridically
dishevelled	orthocentre	ambiguously	cheiromancy	equivalence	labiodental
dishonestly	orthodontia	ambitiously	choirmaster	equivalency	laciniation
					latifundium

latitudinal
legionnaire
legislation
legislative
legislature
lepidoptera
leviratical
limitedness
limitlessly
litigiously
lixiviation
logicalness
ludicrously
luminescent
magisterial
magisterium
magistratic
maliciously
malignantly
Manichaeism
manifestant
manifestoes
manipulable
manipulator
maxillipede
mediaevally
mediastinal
mediastinum
mediateness
mediatorial
mediatrices
medicinable
medicinally
medicolegal
medievalism
medievalist
mediumistic
melioration
meliorative
meliphagous
meningocele
meritocracy
meritorious
miniaturise
miniaturist
ministerial
monitorship
moribundity
motivepower
municipally
munificence
musicalness
nationalise
nationalism
nationalist
nationality
nationstate
nominatival
noticeboard
notionalist
noxiousness
numismatics
numismatist
obliqueness
obliviously
obviousness
occipitally
octingenary
officialdom
officialese
officialism
officiation
officinally
officiously
omnifarious
omnipotence
omnipresent
omniscience
oneiromancy

ophidiarium
ophiologist
orbicularly
ornithology
ornithopter
ornithosaur
oscillation
oscillatory
oscillogram
pacifically
pacificator
palindromic
panicmonger
papiermache
parishioner
pedicellate
pediculosis
penicillate
penicillium
peninsulate
penitential
pericardiac
pericardial
pericardium
pericranial
pericranium
perineurium
periodicity
periodontal
periostitis
peripatetic
periphrases
periphrasis
perishables
perishingly
perispermic
peristalith
peristalsis
peristaltic
peristomial
perithecium
peritonitis
petitionary
pipistrelle
pitifulness
plainspoken
plaintively
pleinairist
pleiotropic
Pleistocene
policewoman
politically
politicking
pomiculture
positronium
preignition
pumicestone
pupillarity
purificator
puritanical
radicalness
radioactive
radiocarbon
radiography
radiolarian
radiologist
radiometric
radiophonic
ratiocinate
rationalise
rationalism
rationalist
rationality
ravishingly
reciprocate
reciprocity
redirection
rediscovery
regimentals

regionalise
regionalism
regionalist
registrable
reliability
religionise
religionism
religionist
religiosity
religiously
reminiscent
residential
resignation
resiliently
resipiscent
resistively
resistivity
retinacular
retinaculum
retinoscopy
retiredness
revisionary
revisionism
revisionist
reviviscent
Rosicrucian
rubicundity
rudimentary
ruridecanal
Sagittarius
salinometer
satiability
satinstitch
satirically
satisfiable
schismatise
schistosity
schistosome
schizanthus
scribacious
scrimpiness
scriptorial
scriptorium
sedimentary
seditionary
seditiously
semidiurnal
semiellipse
semimonthly
semipalmate
semiskilled
semitrailer
sericulture
serigrapher
seriousness
shrinkingly
shrinkproof
shrivelling
sinistrally
sinistrorse
sociability
socialistic
Socinianism
sociologist
sociometric
sociopathic
solifluxion
soliloquise
soliloquist
solipsistic
sphincteral
sphincteric
springboard
springclean
springhouse
springiness
squintingly
squirearchy
stainlessly

staircarpet
stoicalness
stridulator
strikebound
stringboard
stringently
stringiness
stringpiece
stringybark
taciturnity
taxidermist
tediousness
thriftiness
thrillingly
Titianesque
titillation
toxicomania
trailblazer
trainbearer
tryingplane
typicalness
uncivilised
undisguised
undisturbed
unlimitedly
unmitigated
unrighteous
unwillingly
unwinkingly
unwittingly
uprightness
urticaceous
urticarious
vacillation
valiantness
variability
variational
variegation
variousness
vaticinator
venisection
veridically
verisimilar
vesicularly
vexillology
viciousness
vicissitude
viniculture
viridescent
virilescent
visibleness
viticulture
vivisection
vociferance
vociferator
volitionary
conjectural
conjugality
conjugation
conjugative
conjunction
conjunctiva
conjuncture
conjuration
disjunctive
disjuncture
misjudgment
prejudgment
prejudicial
subjugation
subjunctive
backbencher
backcountry
basketchair
bookbinding
bookinghall
bookishness

bookkeeping
booklearned
bookselling
bookshelves
chokecherry
cockaleekie
cockleshell
cockyleekie
cookgeneral
huckleberry
kickstarter
lickerishly
lickspittle
mackerelsky
marketplace
marketvalue
mawkishness
mockingbird
monkeybread
monkeyshine
muskthistle
neckerchief
nickelplate
packingcase
Pickwickian
pinkishness
pocketknife
pocketmoney
pocketsized
racketpress
rickettsial
rockcrystal
Shaksperean
Shaksperian
sickbenefit
sickeningly
sickishness
smokescreen
smokingroom
sockdolager
sockdologen
spokeswoman
stakeholder
suckingfish
talkatively
tankfarming
unskilfully
volkslieder
weakhearted
workability
workmanlike
workmanship
yacketyyack
abolishable
abolishment
acclamation
acclamatory
acclimation
acclimatise
acclivitous
adolescence
adulterator
aeolotropic
agglomerate
agglutinate
aimlessness
airlessness
ameliorator
amplexicaul
analogously
Anglicanism
AngloFrench
AngloIndian
anglomaniac
AngloNorman
anglophobia
anglophobic
Apollinaris
apologetics

applaudable
application
applicative
applicatory
arglebargle
artlessness
athleticism
ballbearing
balletomane
barleybroth
bellbottoms
bellfounder
bellheather
bellicosity
belligerent
bellringing
bibliolater
bibliolatry
bibliomancy
bibliomania
bibliopegic
bibliophile
bibliophily
bibliopolic
bibliotheca
billetsdoux
billionaire
billposting
billsticker
boilermaker
brilliantly
bullbaiting
bulletproof
bullfighter
bullishness
bullterrier
calligraphy
callousness
cauliflower
cellularity
chalcedonic
challenging
childminder
cholesterol
coalescence
collaborate
collapsible
collectable
collectanea
collectedly
collectible
collenchyma
colligation
colligative
collimation
collinearly
collisional
collocation
collusively
coplanarity
coulometric
cyclopaedia
cyclopaedic
cycloserine
cyclothymia
cyclothymic
declamation
declamatory
declaration
declarative
declaratory
declination
declivitous
deflagrator
defloration
deglutition
deploringly
dialectally
dialectical

dialogistic	idolisation	quilldriver	utilisation	cosmography	hummingbird
diplococcus	idyllically	rallentando	utilitarian	cosmologist	illmannered
diplomatise	implausible	realignment	valleculate	cosmopolite	isometrical
diplomatist	implausibly	realisation	violoncello	crematorium	isomorphism
dislikeable	implemental	realpolitik	wealthiness	criminalist	isomorphous
dislocation	implication	reclaimable	welladvised	criminality	lammergeier
dislodgment	implicative	reclamation	wellbeloved	crimination	lammergeyer
dollishness	imploringly	reflectance	welldefined	criminative	lawmerchant
drillmaster	inalienable	reflexively	wellfounded	criminatory	mammalogist
dualcontrol	inalienably	reflexology	wellgroomed	criminology	mismarriage
dualpurpose	inalterable	replaceable	wellmeaning	culmination	murmuration
duplication	inalterably	replacement	wellordered	deemphasise	murmurously
duplicative	inclemently	replenisher	wellrounded	dermatology	myrmecology
duplicitous	inclination	repleteness	wellwishing	diamagnetic	nonmatching
dyslogistic	inclusively	repleviable	Wesleyanism	diametrical	nonmetallic
ebulliently	inelegantly	replication	wholesomely	diamondback	palmcabbage
egalitarian	ineloquence	saplessness	wholesouled	dismayingly	permanently
emblematise	ineluctable	scalariform	willingness	dramaturgic	permissible
emblematist	ineluctably	scalearmour	witlessness	ecumenicism	permissibly
emplacement	inflammable	scaleinsect	worldbeater	ecumenicity	permutation
emulousness	inflammably	scalpriform	worldliness	elementally	prematurely
emulsionise	inflexional	sculduddery	worldlywise	elimination	prematurity
endlessness	influential	sculduggery	yellowbelly	eliminative	premeditate
enslavement	jealousness	sexlessness	zealousness	enumeration	premiership
evolutional	joylessness	shallowness	abomination	enumerative	premonition
exclamation	lawlessness	shellacking	acumination	esemplastic	premonitory
exclamatory	Maglemosian	shelljacket	adumbration	etymologise	primaevally
exclusively	mailcarrier	shelterbelt	adumbrative	etymologist	primateship
exclusivity	marlinspike	shelterless	alembicated	examination	primatology
explainable	melliferous	sillimanite	anemometric	exemplarily	primigenial
explanation	mellifluent	sinlessness	animalcular	exemplarity	primiparous
explanatory	mellifluous	skeletonise	anomalistic	fermentable	primitively
explication	millenarian	skilfulness	anomalously	filmography	primitivism
explicative	milliampere	skulduddery	apomorphine	filmsetting	prominently
explicatory	millionaire	skulduggery	aromaticity	firmamental	promiscuity
exploitable	millisecond	smallholder	atomisation	flamboyance	promiscuous
exploration	mollycoddle	smallminded	augmentable	flamboyancy	promisingly
explorative	myelomatous	smilelessly	balmcricket	flamboyante	promotional
exploratory	nailvarnish	soulfulness	biometrical	flimflammer	promptitude
explosively	negligently	spelaeology	blamelessly	formalistic	promulgator
fallibility	neologistic	spellbinder	blameworthy	formational	reemergence
faultfinder	nullifidian	stalactitic	carminative	formication	rhombohedra
faultlessly	nulliparity	stalagmitic	chamaephyte	formularise	rhomboideus
feelingness	nulliparous	stallholder	chamberlain	formulation	salmonberry
fieldcornet	ochlocratic	stellionate	chambermaid	fulminating	segmentally
fieldworker	opalescence	stiltedness	chameleonic	fulmination	shamanistic
folliculate	pellucidity	stylisation	champertous	fulminatory	shamelessly
foolishness	phalanstery	stylishness	chemotactic	gemmiferous	sigmoidally
forlornness	philanderer	stylography	chimaerical	gemmiparous	solmisation
foulmouthed	philatelist	stylopodium	clamorously	gemmologist	stampoffice
fullblooded	philhellene	sublimation	climacteric	gemmulation	stimulation
fullfledged	philologian	sublimeness	climatology	geomagnetic	stimulative
fullhearted	philologist	sublittoral	commandment	geometrical	stomachache
fullmouthed	philosopher	sunlessness	commemorate	Germanophil	stomachpump
gallantness	philosophic	swallowable	commendable	germination	stomatology
gallbladder	phylloclade	swallowdive	commendably	germinative	stumblingly
galleyslave	phyllotaxis	swallowhole	commendator	glomeration	submarginal
Gallicanism	phylogynist	swallowtail	commensally	gormandiser	submergence
gallimaufry	pillowfight	swallowwort	commentator	grammalogue	submersible
Gallophobia	pollination	swellheaded	commination	grammatical	submissible
gallowsbird	prelibation	syllabarium	comminatory	gramophonic	submultiple
gallowstree	preliminary	syllabicity	comminution	grumblingly	summariness
gillyflower	prelusively	syllogistic	commiserate	haematocele	summational
girlishness	prelusorily	tabletennis	commissural	haematocrit	summerhouse
godlessness	prolegomena	tagliatelle	committable	haematology	summersault
guilelessly	proletarian	tagliatelli	commonality	haemocyanin	swimbladder
guiltlessly	proletariat	thalidomide	commonplace	haemoglobin	symmetrical
gullibility	proliferate	titleholder	commonsense	haemophilia	termagantly
gutlessness	proliferous	toploftical	communalise	haemophilic	termination
hallucinate	prolificacy	trelliswork	communalism	haemoptysis	terminative
haplessness	prolificity	twelvemonth	communalist	haemorrhage	terminology
haplography	prolocutrix	twelvepenny	communicant	haemorrhoid	termitarium
healthfully	publication	unalterable	communicate	haemostasis	thimbleweed
healthiness	publishable	uncleanness	communistic	haemostatic	trammelling
helleborine	publishment	unclimbable	commutation	harmfulness	tremblement
Hellenistic	pullthrough	uncluttered	commutative	harmonistic	tremblingly
hellishness	pullulation	unflappable	cosmetician	helminthoid	tremulously
hollandaise	qualifiable	unflinching	cosmetology	hermeneutic	trimestrial
hooliganism	qualitative	uselessness	cosmogonist	hermeticism	trimorphism

trimorphous	countermark	grandiosity	plentifully	thinskinned	acropetally
unambiguous	countermove	grandmother	pointdevice	thunderbird	adjournment
unemotional	countermure	grandnephew	pointedness	thunderbolt	aerobically
unimportant	counterpane	grandparent	pointillism	thunderclap	aerobiology
unsmilingly	counterpart	grangeriser	pointillist	thunderhead	aerodynamic
vehmgericht	counterplan	granivorous	pointlessly	thunderless	aerographer
vermiculate	counterplea	granolithic	pornography	thunderpeal	aerological
vermiculite	counterplot	granophyric	prenominate	townspeople	aeronautics
vermination	countersign	granularity	principally	transaction	aeronomical
verminously	countersink	granulation	quincuncial	transalpine	aerostatics
warmblooded	countersunk	granulocyte	quinquennia	transceiver	aerostation
warmhearted	counterturn	gymnospermy	quinquereme	transcriber	AfroAsiatic
whimsically	countervail	heinousness	quintillion	transection	agnosticism
zoomorphism	counterview	hornswoggle	raunchiness	transferred	agrobiology
abandonment	counterwork	hymnography	reanimation	transferrer	agrological
acinaciform	countlessly	hypnopaedia	reenactment	transfigure	agronomical
acknowledge	countrified	hypnopompic	reincarnate	transfinite	algorithmic
adenomatous	countryfied	ichnography	reinsertion	transfixion	algological
agonisingly	countryseat	iconography	reinsurance	transformer	allocatable
agonistical	countryside	iconostases	reintegrate	transfusion	allomorphic
amenability	countrywide	iconostasis	reintroduce	transhumant	allopathist
amenorrhoea	craniometry	identically	rhinologist	transiently	altocumulus
amentaceous	crenellated	inanimately	rhinoscopic	transilient	altorelievo
amontillado	crenulation	inanimation	rhynchodont	translation	altorilievo
anencephaly	crunchiness	ironhearted	roentgenise	translocate	altostratus
anonymously	ctenophoran	ironmongery	roundedness	translucent	antonomasia
aponeuroses	cunningness	itinerantly	ruinousness	translunary	appogiatura
aponeurosis	dauntlessly	itineration	saintliness	transmarine	appointment
aponeurotic	dinnerdance	jauntingcar	saintpaulia	transmittal	arboraceous
arenicolous	dinnertable	launderette	scenography	transmitted	arborescent
barnstormer	dinnerwagon	limnologist	scintillant	transmitter	Areopagitic
blunderbuss	donnishness	lionhearted	scintillate	transpadane	ascomycetes
bounteously	downdraught	magnanimity	signifiable	transparent	association
bountifully	downhearted	magnanimous	significant	transpierce	associative
branchiopod	downtrodden	magnificent	signpainter	transponder	assortative
brankursine	drunkenness	maintenance	slenderness	transporter	atmospheric
cannibalise	earnestness	maintopmast	somnambular	transsexual	atrociously
cannibalism	econometric	maintopsail	somniculous	transuranic	autochthony
carnivorous	emancipator	manneristic	somniferous	transversal	autoerotism
chancellery	enunciation	mannishness	somnolently	trenchantly	autographic
chancellory	enunciative	meaningless	soundlessly	trencherman	automatable
changefully	epinephrine	minnesinger	spendthrift	trendsetter	autoplastic
channelling	ethnography	moonlighter	spindlelegs	Trinitarian	autotrophic
chansonnier	ethnologist	morningroom	spindletree	trundletail	axiological
chanterelle	evanescence	mountaineer	spinelessly	unanimously	Belorussian
chanticleer	evangelical	mountainous	spiniferous	unendurable	bicorporate
chinoiserie	evanishment	mountaintop	Spinozistic	unendurably	binocularly
cinnabarine	eventualise	Neanderthal	spinsterish	uninhabited	bivouacking
clandestine	eventuality	ninnyhammer	spondulicks	uninhibited	bloodguilty
clinometric	exanthemata	ominousness	spondylitis	uninucleate	bloodlessly
cognateness	exoneration	opencircuit	spongecloth	Upanishadic	bloodstream
cognitional	exonerative	openhearted	sponsorship	uranography	bloodsucker
cognitively	FinnoUgrian	openmouthed	spontaneity	varnishtree	bloodvessel
cognitivity	flannelette	opinionated	spontaneous	wainscoting	bryozoology
cognoscente	flannelling	orangoutang	standardise	wainscotted	bucolically
cognoscenti	fornication	ozoniferous	standoffish	weenybopper	Byronically
cognoscible	Francomania	ozonisation	standpatter	winningness	cacographic
coincidence	Francophile	ozonosphere	stencilling	winningpost	cacophonous
coinheritor	Francophobe	painfulness	stenochromy	wrongheaded	calorimeter
coinsurance	francophone	painkilling	stenography	zoantharian	calorimetry
connectable	franctireur	painstaking	stenotypist	abdominally	canonically
connectedly	frankfurter	paunchiness	stonecurlew	abhorrently	Carolingian
connectible	franklinite	pawnbroking	stonecutter	abiogeneses	ceroplastic
connoisseur	frankpledge	pennyweight	stoneground	abiogenesis	chaotically
connotation	frantically	phantasiast	stonemarten	abiogenetic	chlorophyll
connotative	franticness	phantasmata	stonewaller	abiological	chloroplast
connubially	frenchified	phenologist	stuntedness	abiotically	chloroprene
cornerstone	Frenchwoman	phonetician	swingletree	abnormality	chrominance
cornhusking	frontrunner	phonography	swinishness	absorbingly	chromoplast
corniferous	furnishings	phonologist	tarnishable	absorptance	chromosomal
cornucopian	gainfulness	pinnatisect	teenybopper	accommodate	chronically
counselling	garnishment	planetarium	teknonymous	accompanist	chronograph
countenance	geanticline	planetoidal	thanatology	accordantly	chronologer
counterblow	giantpowder	planimetric	thanklessly	accordingly	chronologic
counterbond	grandfather	planisphere	thanksgiver	accoucheuse	chronometer
counterfeit	grandiflora	planoconvex	thankworthy	accountable	chronometry
counterfoil	grandiosely	plantigrade	thenceforth	accountably	chronoscope
counterfort	grandiosely	plenipotent	thingumabob	accountancy	coconscious
countermand	grandiosely	plenteously	thingumajig	achondritic	colonelship

colonialism
colonialist
colorimeter
colorimetry
colouration
colourblind
colourfully
coronagraph
coronograph
cotoneaster
crookbacked
crookedness
cryobiology
cryosurgery
cryotherapy
cytogenesis
cytokinesis
cytological
debouchment
decollation
decolletage
decolourise
decorticate
defoliation
deforcement
deformation
democratise
democratism
demographer
demographic
demonolatry
demonstrate
demountable
denominator
depopulator
deportation
devotedness
dicotyledon
dinosaurian
disobedient
disobliging
disorganise
divorcement
doxographer
echosounder
ectoblastic
ectogenesis
ectogenetic
ectomorphic
ectoplasmic
ectotrophic
elbowgrease
embowelling
embowerment
encomiastic
endocardiac
endocardial
endocardium
endometrium
endomorphic
endophagous
endoplasmic
endorsement
endoskelton
endothelial
endothelium
endothermal
endothermic
endotrophic
enforceable
enforcement
engorgement
ennoblement
entomophily
erroneously
ethological
Europeanise
excoriation
exfoliation

exfoliative
exhortation
exhortative
exhortatory
exponential
exportation
expostulate
extortioner
favouritism
feloniously
ferociously
floorwalker
fluorescein
fluorescent
fluoroscope
fluoroscopy
gamogenesis
gerontology
gyrocompass
halophilous
heroworship
holoblastic
holographic
holothurian
homocentric
homoeopathy
homoestatic
homogeneity
homogeneous
homogenetic
homogeniser
homoiousian
homological
homomorphic
homophonous
homoplastic
homopterous
homosporous
homothallic
homozygosis
horological
hylogenesis
hylozoistic
hypoblastic
hypocycloid
hypogastric
hypoglossal
hypolimnion
hypophyseal
hypophysial
hypostatise
hypotension
hypothecate
hypothenuse
hypothermia
hypothesise
hypotyposis
ideographic
ideological
idiographic
idiomorphic
idiotically
ignobleness
ignominious
illogically
immortalise
immortality
immoveables
impolitical
impoliticly
importantly
importation
importunate
importunely
importunity
impoundment
incoercible
incognisant
incoherence

incoherency
incommodity
incompetent
incompliant
incongruent
incongruity
incongruous
inconscient
inconsonant
inconstancy
incontinent
incorporate
incorporeal
incorrectly
incorruptly
IndoChinese
IndoIranian
indomitable
indomitably
indorsement
informality
information
informative
informatory
innocuously
innoxiously
insouciance
intolerable
intolerably
intolerance
involucrate
involuntary
involvement
ionospheric
Jacobinical
Jacobitical
kilocalorie
kymographic
laboriously
laconically
logographer
logographic
logomachist
loxodromics
masochistic
melodiously
memorabilia
memorialise
memorialist
meroblastic
merogenesis
Merovingian
mesoblastic
mesomorphic
metonymical
metoposcopy
monocarpous
monochasial
monochasium
monochromat
monochromic
monoclinous
monoculture
monogenesis
monogenetic
monogrammed
monographer
monographic
monolingual
monological
monologuise
monologuist
monomorphic
mononuclear
monophagous
monophthong
Monophysite
monopoliser
monopterous

Monothelite
monozygotic
moronically
mycological
mycophagist
mycorrhizae
mycorrhizal
myxomatosis
myxomycetes
nasofrontal
negotiation
negotiatory
negotiatrix
nomographer
nomographic
nomological
nosographer
nosographic
nosological
notoriously
obnoxiously
obsolescent
oecological
oenological
oenophilist
oesophageal
oncological
ontogenesis
ontogenetic
ontological
opportunely
opportunism
opportunist
opportunity
optometrist
oreographic
oreological
osmotically
parochially
paronomasia
pedological
penological
pilocarpine
pilotburner
pivotbridge
pleochroism
pleomorphic
pococurante
podophyllin
pomological
posological
preoccupied
proofreader
pyroclastic
pyrotechnic
recognition
recognitive
recognitory
recommender
recommittal
recondition
reconnoitre
reconstruct
recoverable
redoubtable
reformation
reformative
reformatory
rejoicingly
remonstrant
remonstrate
remorseless
reportorial
reposefully
resourceful
rheological
rheotropism
ricochetted
rodomontade

rotogravure
saponaceous
savouriness
saxophonist
scholarship
scholiastic
schoolboard
schoolchild
schoolhouse
schottische
seborrhoeic
secondarily
secondclass
secondrater
secondsight
serological
sexological
sinological
smoothfaced
sonofabitch
Soroptimist
stoolpigeon
stroboscope
strongpoint
subordinate
subornation
sycophantic
sycophantry
synonymical
taxonomical
theobromine
theocentric
theodolitic
theological
theorematic
theoretical
theosophist
throatiness
throatlatch
thrombocyte
tobogganing
tobogganist
topographer
topographic
topological
toxophilite
typographer
typographic
typological
unboundedly
uncommitted
unconcealed
unconcerned
uncongenial
unconnected
unconscious
uncontested
uncountable
uncouthness
undoubtedly
unforgiving
unfortunate
ungodliness
unpolitical
unpossessed
unsolicited
unsoundness
untouchable
upholsterer
vaporimeter
vaporisable
vasodilator
vasopressin
vasopressor
virological
widowerhood
xenophilous
xerophilous
xylocarpous

xylographer
xylographic
xylophagous
xylophonist
Yugoslavian
Zoroastrian
zygomorphic
acupuncture
adoptianism
adoptianist
adoptionism
adoptionist
anaphylaxis
apophyllite
aseptically
biophysical
blepharitis
bumptiously
campanology
campanulate
campmeeting
carpetsnake
chaperonage
Chippendale
clapperclaw
compactness
compaginate
comparatist
comparative
compartment
compassable
compellable
compendious
compensator
competently
competition
competitive
compilation
compilement
complacence
complacency
complainant
complaisant
complexness
compliantly
complicated
complotting
comportment
compositely
composition
compositive
compossible
compotation
compotatory
compression
compressive
comprisable
comptroller
compunction
compurgator
computation
computerise
cooperation
cooperative
copperplate
coppersmith
corporality
corporately
'corporation
corporatism
corporative
corporeally
corpulently
corpuscular
crepitation
crepuscular
cryptically
cryptogamic
cryptograph

cryptomeria	pompousness	symphonious	approbatory	doorknocker	hydrogenate
culpability	porphyritic	symposiarch	appropriate	douroucouli	hydrogenous
desperadoes	preparation	symptomatic	approvingly	embraceable	hydrography
desperately	preparative	temperament	approximate	embracement	hydrologist
desperation	preparatory	temperately	astringency	embracingly	hydromedusa
despoilment	preposition	temperative	attractable	embrocation	hydrometeor
despondence	prepositive	temperature	attribution	embroiderer	hydrometric
despondency	preprandial	tempestuous	attributive	embroilment	hydropathic
diaphaneity	propagation	temporality	attritional	embryologic	hydrophilic
diaphoresis	propagative	temporarily	barrelhouse	embryonated	hydrophobia
diaphoretic	prophethood	trapeziform	barrelorgan	enarthrosis	hydrophobic
diapophysis	prophetical	trapezoidal	bearbaiting	encrustment	hydrophytic
diapositive	prophetship	Trappistine	bearishness	enfranchise	hydroponics
Diophantine	prophylaxis	trepanation	boardschool	engrossment	hydrosphere
disparaging	propinquity	trepidation	boorishness	entrainment	hydrostatic
disparately	propitiable	tripetalous	bourgeoisie	entreatment	hydrotactic
dispensable	propitiator	triphibious	carrageenan	entrustment	hydrothorax
dispersedly	proportions	triphyllous	carrageenin	everlasting	hydrotropic
displeasure	proposition	trophoblast	carriageway	exarcerbate	hygrometric
disportment	proprietary	troposphere	charcuterie	excremental	hygrophytic
disposition	purportedly	trypanosome	chargesheet	excrescence	hygroscopic
dispositive	purposeless	tryptophane	charismatic	excrescency	imbrication
disputation	purposively	unappealing	charlatanry	exercisable	impractical
dropcurtain	purpresture	unipersonal	chartaceous	exorbitance	imprecation
dropforging	reapportion	unipolarity	chirography	expressible	imprecatory
earpiercing	reappraisal	unsparingly	chiropodist	expropriate	imprecisely
elephantine	respectable	unspeakable	chiropteran	extractable	imprecision
elephantoid	respectably	unspeakably	choreograph	extradition	impregnable
epipetalous	respiration	vespertinal	chorography	extrapolate	impregnably
evaporation	respiratory	wappenschaw	churchgoing	extravagant	impressible
evaporative	resplendent	wapperjawed	churchiness	extravagate	impressment
foppishness	respondence	waspishness	churchwoman	extravasate	impropriate
geophysical	respondency	waspwaisted	Clarencieux	extraverted	impropriety
geopolitics	responsible	whippletree	clericalism	extremeness	improvement
graphically	responsibly	zooplankton	clericalist	extrication	improvident
graphicness	rhapsodical	barquentine	coarctation	extroverted	imprudently
harpsichord	salpingitis	cinquecento	comradeship	fabrication	increasable
helpfulness	sceptically	conquerable	coordinator	fairweather	incredulity
Hepplewhite	scopolamine	disquieting	correctable	farraginous	incredulous
herpetology	scuppernong	disquietude	correctness	farreaching	incremental
hesperidium	scyphistoma	inequitable	correlation	fearfulness	incriminate
hippocampus	sempiternal	inequitably	correlative	ferriferous	infrangible
Hippocratic	serpiginous	marquessate	corrigendum	ferruginous	infrequence
hippopotami	shapeliness	marqueterie	corroborant	flirtatious	infrequency
Hispanicise	shepherdess	marquisette	corroborate	florescence	ingrainedly
Hispanicism	shipbreaker	masquerader	corrosively	floriferous	ingratitude
Hispanicist	shipbuilder	triquetrous	corrugation	florilegium	intractable
hospitalise	shoplifting	unequivocal	corruptible	fourflusher	intractably
hospitality	shopsteward	abbreviator	corruptibly	fourpounder	intravenous
hospitaller	simperingly	abortionist	corruptness	fourwheeler	intrepidity
inappetence	simpliciter	acarpellous	courteously	garrulously	intricately
inoperative	soapboiling	accrescence	courtliness	gerrymander	intriguante
inopportune	soupkitchen	achromatise	cupriferous	glaringness	intromitted
inspiration	stepbrother	achromatism	cupronickel	gourmandise	intromitter
inspiratory	stephanotis	affranchise	currentness	gourmandism	introverted
jumpingbean	stipendiary	affrication	currishness	guardedness	intrusively
jumpingjack	stipulation	affricative	cypripedium	hairbreadth	jerrymander
kleptomania	stipulatory	aggravation	decrepitate	hairdresser	journeywork
lamplighter	sulphureous	aggregately	decrepitude	hairraising	lacrimation
leapfrogged	sulphurwort	aggregation	decrescendo	hairstyling	lacrimatory
lowpressure	sumptuosity	aggregative	deerstalker	hairstylist	lacrimosely
lumpishness	sumptuously	aggrievedly	defraudment	hairtrigger	lacrymation
malposition	suppliantly	agoraphobia	degradation	heartbroken	lacrymatory
malpractice	supportable	agoraphobic	degradingly	hearthstone	lacrymosely
Neoplatonic	supportably	amaranthine	depravation	heartlessly	laurustinus
nonpartisan	supposition	Americanise	depravement	heartsblood	learnedness
nonplussing	suppositive	Americanism	deprecation	heartstring	leprosarium
nympholepsy	suppository	Americanist	deprecative	Hebraically	lubrication
nymphomania	suppression	amorousness	deprecatory	herringbone	lubricative
oilpainting	suppressive	amorphously	depreciator	herringgull	lucratively
oviposition	suppuration	anarchistic	depredation	horripilate	macrobiotic
palpability	suppurative	androgynous	depredatory	hierarchism	macrocosmic
palpitation	surpassable	anfractuous	depressible	hurriedness	macrogamete
pamphleteer	suspenseful	apartmental	deprivation	hurryscurry	macroscopic
perpetrator	suspensible	aphrodisiac	detrainment	hurryskurry	madreporite
perpetually	suspension	appreciable	detribalise	hydraheaded	madrigalian
perpetuance	sympathetic	appreciably	detrimental	hydrobromic	madrigalist
perpetuator	sympathiser	appreciator	diarthrosis	hydrocarbon	marriagebed
perplexedly	sympetalous	approbation	disremember	hydrocyanic	matriarchal

matriculate	overtopping	searchlight	tetrahedral	causatively	dissonantly
matrilineal	overweening	secretarial	tetrahedron	caustically	dissyllable
matrilinear	overwritten	secretariat	tetramerous	ceaselessly	dissymmetry
matrimonial	overwrought	secretively	tetrapodous	classically	drastically
meprobamate	patriarchal	segregation	tetrarchate	closefisted	dresscircle
merryandrew	patrilineal	segregative	tetravalent	closehauled	dressmaking
merrymaking	patrimonial	serrulation	therapeutic	clostridium	einsteinium
metrication	patristical	shareholder	thereabouts	coessential	elastically
micrococcal	patronising	sharepusher	theretofore	comstockery	elasticated
micrococcus	pearlescent	sharpwitted	therewithal	consanguine	elastomeric
microcosmic	pearlfisher	sheriffalty	thermically	consciously	elusiveness
microgamete	petrography	sheriffship	thermionics	consecrator	emasculator
micrography	petrologist	shirtsleeve	thermoduric	consecution	episcopally
microgroove	pharisaical	shortchange	thermograph	consecutive	Erastianism
microlithic	phariseeism	shortcoming	thermolysis	consentient	evasiveness
micrometric	pharyngitis	shorthanded	thermolytic	consequence	existential
Micronesian	pluralistic	shortspoken	thermometer	conservable	exoskeletal
microphonic	pourparlers	shortwinded	thermometry	conservancy	exoskeleton
microphytic	prerogative	smorgasbord	thermophile	conservator	facsimilist
microscopic	prorogation	sorrowfully	thermoscope	considerate	Falstaffian
microsecond	pruriginous	sparingness	thermotaxis	considering	feasibility
misremember	pteridology	sparrowbill	thirstiness	consignable	felspathoid
mitrailleur	pterodactyl	sparrowhawk	thoroughpin	consignment	firstfruits
mooringmast	putrescence	spermaphyte	thoroughwax	consistence	fissionable
morrisdance	putrescible	spermatozoa	thuriferous	consistency	fissiparity
narratively	quarrelling	spermicidal	thyroiditis	consolation	fissiparous
nearsighted	quarrelsome	spiraculate	tourbillion	consolatory	fleshliness
necrobiosis	quarterback	spiritistic	ultramarine	consolidate	frostbitten
necrologist	quarterdeck	spiritlevel	ultramodern	consolingly	frustration
necromancer	quartertone	spiritually	ultrasonics	consonantal	fulsomeness
necromantic	querulously	spirituelle	ultraviolet	consonantly	geostrophic
necrophilia	rearadmiral	spirituelle	unbreakable	conspecific	geosyncline
necrophilic	recriminate	spirochaete	uncrushable	conspicuity	ghastliness
necropoleis	recruitment	spirochetal	unorganized	conspicuous	ghostliness
negrophobia	refrangible	spirometric	unorthodoxy	conspirator	ghostwriter
neurologist	refreshment	sporogenous	unprintable	constellate	glassblower
neuropathic	refrigerant	sporogonium	unpromising	consternate	glasscutter
neuroticism	refrigerate	sporophytic	vibratility	constituent	glassmaking
neurotropic	refringency	sportswoman	vibrational	constitutor	glossolalia
nigrescence	regretfully	sporulation	vitrescence	constrictor	grasshopper
nitrogenise	regrettable	starchiness	vitrifiable	construable	gristliness
nitrogenous	regrettably	starcrossed	voortrekker	constructor	guesstimate
nonresident	reorientate	starstudded	warrantable	consultancy	gypsiferous
nourishment	representer	startlingly	warrantably	consumerism	haustellate
nutrimental	repressible	stereograph	wearilessly	consumingly	hirsuteness
nutritional	repressibly	stereometry	wearisomely	consummator	horsecollar
nutritively	reproachful	stereophony	whereabouts	consumption	horsedoctor
obtrusively	reprobation	stereoscope	wheresoever	consumptive	horseradish
odoriferous	reprobative	stereoscopy	wherewithal	crestfallen	housefather
odorousness	reprobatory	stereotyped	whoremaster	crossbearer	householder
onerousness	reprogramme	stereotyper	whoremonger	crossbowman	housekeeper
operational	reprography	stereotypic	worrisomely	crossgarnet	houselights
operatively	reprovingly	sternsheets	abusiveness	crosslegged	housemaster
operculated	retraceable	sternutator	ahistorical	crossstitch	housemother
operoseness	retractable	stirrupbone	airsickness	crustaceous	housewifely
opprobrious	retranslate	stirruppump	anastomoses	crystalline	housewifery
ostracoderm	retribution	storekeeper	anastomosis	crystallise	hyoscyamine
Ostrogothic	retributive	stormcentre	anastomotic	crystallite	hypsography
outrivalled	retributory	stormtroops	anisotropic	crystalloid	hypsometric
ovariectomy	retrievable	storyteller	aposiopesis	cursiveness	hypsophobia
overanxious	retroaction	subregional	apostleship	cursoriness	icosahedral
overbalance	retroactive	subrogation	apostolical	daisycutter	icosahedron
overbearing	retrocedent	supremacist	apostrophic	deistically	inescapable
overbidding	retroflexed	supremeness	aristocracy	diastematic	inessential
overcropped	retrorocket	surrebuttal	awesomeness	diastrophic	inestimable
overdevelop	rubrication	surrebutter	awestricken	dipsomaniac	inestimably
overgarment	sacramental	surrogation	bassethound	disseminate	irksomeness
overindulge	sacrificial	swarthiness	beastliness	disseminule	Jansenistic
overlapping	saprobiotic	swordbearer	bersaglieri	dissentient	kwashiorkor
overmanning	saprogenous	tarradiddle	blasphemous	dissepiment	leaseholder
overmeasure	saprophytic	tearfulness	blastogenic	dissertator	lissomeness
overpayment	sauropodous	tearstained	blessedness	dissimilate	looselimbed
overproduce	scarabaeoid	terraqueous	boysenberry	dissimulate	loosestrife
overrunning	scaremonger	terrestrial	bristletail	dissipation	lowspirited
oversailing	scorchingly	terricolous	bristleworm	dissipative	maisonnette
oversetting	scoriaceous	terrigenous	bristliness	dissociable	mansardroof
overstepped	scorpionfly	territorial	brusqueness	dissolutely	marshalling
overstretch	scurvygrass	tetracyclic	cassiterite	dissolution	marshalship
overstuffed	searchingly	tetradactyl	catswhisker	dissolvable	marshmallow

massiveness	prestissimo	versatilely	continental	egotistical	historiated
massproduce	prestressed	versatility	continently	elutriation	historicise
measureless	presumingly	Weismannism	contingence	emotionally	historicism
measurement	presumption	Wensleydale	contingency	emotionless	historicist
menservants	presumptive	whistlestop	continuable	emptyhanded	historicity
mensuration	prosaically	whosesoever	continually	emptyheaded	histrionics
messiahship	prosaicness	winsomeness	continuance	epithalamia	histrionism
misspelling	prosecution	worshipable	continuator	epithalamic	hurtfulness
moisturiser	prosecutrix	worshipless	contorniate	epithelioma	ichthyology
monseigneur	proselytise	worshipping	contrabasso	erotogenous	ichthyornis
monstrosity	proselytism	abstentious	contractile	erotomaniac	ichthyosaur
monstrously	prosenchyma	abstinently	contraction	erythrocyte	illtempered
mosstrooper	prospective	abstraction	contractive	esotericism	imitatively
mudslinging	prosthetics	abstractive	contractual	exotericism	inattention
noiselessly	prostitutor	abstriction	contracture	exstipulate	inattentive
noisemaking	prostration	acatalectic	contradance	factfinding	initialling
noisomeness	Prussianise	acetylation	contraption	factionally	instability
nonsensical	Prussianism	aesthetical	contrariety	factualness	installment
nonsequitur	pussyfooter	aestivation	contrarious	faithhealer	instigation
nonspecific	pussywillow	amativeness	contrastive	faithlessly	instigative
nurserymaid	questionary	amethystine	contretemps	faithworthy	instillment
oarsmanship	rapscallion	apotheosise	contributor	falteringly	instinctive
outspokenly	reassertion	armtwisting	contrivable	fantastical	instinctual
outstanding	reassurance	austereness	contrivance	farthermost	institution
outstripped	reestablish	azotobacter	controlling	farthingale	instruction
palsgravine	Russophobia	bactericide	controlment	featheredge	instructive
passacaglia	sansculotte	BaltoSlavic	controversy	featherhead	jactitation
passeriform	Sanskritist	banteringly	costbenefit	featherless	justiciable
passibility	sausagemeat	baptismally	costiveness	featureless	justifiable
Passiontide	scissorbill	battledress	cottongrass	festinately	justifiably
passivation	scissortail	battlefield	cottonmouth	festschrift	Kulturkampf
passiveness	seasickness	bestselling	criticality	filterpaper	lactescence
pensionable	seismically	bitterapple	criticaster	flatulently	lactiferous
pensionless	seismograph	bittercress	crotcheteer	footpoundal	lastingness
pensiveness	seismometer	bittersweet	cultivation	footslogger	latticework
persecution	seismometry	blotchiness	curtailment	footsoldier	leatherback
perseverate	seismoscope	bootlegging	customarily	forthcoming	leatherhead
persistence	sensational	bottleglass	custombuilt	fortifiable	leatherneck
persistency	senselessly	bottlegreen	customhouse	fortnightly	lectureship
personalise	sensibility	bottlenosed	cysticercus	fortunately	lentiginous
personalism	sensitively	boutonniere	dactylogram	fraternally	leptodactyl
personalist	sensitivity	Britishness	dactylology	fraterniser	letterpress
personality	sensorially	brittleness	deathrattle	fratricidal	litterateur
personation	spasmodical	brotherhood	denticulate	fretfulness	loathliness
personative	spastically	brutishness	dentigerous	frothhopper	loathsomely
personifier	spessartite	butterflies	depthcharge	furtherance	loutishness
perspective	suasiveness	butteriness	destination	furthermore	lustfulness
perspicuity	subscapular	cantharides	destitution	furthermost	mantelpiece
perspicuous	subsequence	cantharidic	destruction	furthersome	mantelshelf
persuadable	subservient	captainship	destructive	furtiveness	mantuamaker
persuasible	subsistence	captionless	deuteration	fustigation	martyrology
pessimistic	subspecific	captivation	deuterogamy	gartersnake	masterfully
phosphonium	substandard	cartography	Deuteronomy	gastrectomy	masterpiece
phosphorate	substantial	castellated	dexterously	gastronomic	mastication
phosphorism	substantive	castigation	diatessaron	gastroscope	masticatory
phosphorite	substituent	centenarian	dictatorial	genteelness	mastodontic
phosphorous	subsumptive	centigramme	dipterocarp	gentianella	mastoiditis
physicality	syssarcosis	centreboard	distasteful	gentilitial	mentholated
physiocracy	teaspoonful	centrepiece	distempered	gentlemanly	mentionable
physiognomy	tensibility	centrifugal	distensible	gentlewoman	micturition
physiologic	tessellated	centripetal	distinction	geotectonic	mirthlessly
pigsticking	certifiable	certifiable	distinctive	gestatorial	mistrustful
plasmolysis	thistledown	certifiably	distinguish	gesticulate	mortarboard
plasmolytic	toastmaster	certificate	distraction	gettogether	multangular
plasterwork	tonsillitis	chitterling	distractive	glutinously	multicolour
plasticiser	trestletree	clothesline	distressful	gnotobiosis	multilinear
poisonously	trestlework	clothesmoth	distribuend	gnotobiotic	multinomial
possibility	tristichous	clothesprop	distributor	gratulation	multiparous
presanctify	trisyllabic	coeternally	distrustful	gratulatory	multiracial
presbyteral	trisyllable	containable	disturbance	grotesquely	multistorey
presciently	trustbuster	containment	dittography	grotesquely	multivalent
preselector	trusteeship	contaminant	doctrinaire	guttapercha	mustachioed
presentable	trustworthy	contaminate	doctrinally	guttersnipe	muttonchops
presentably	unashamedly	contemplate	doltishness	gutturalise	Neotropical
presentient	unassertive	contentedly	earthcloset	gutturalism	nettlecloth
presentment	unessential	contentious	earthenware	halterbreak	neutraliser
preservable	unisexually	contentment	earthliness	heptamerous	nictitation
pressagency	unusualness	conterminal	easternmost	heptarchist	nittygritty
prestigious	varsovienne	contestable	editorially	histologist	noctilucent

noctivagant	platinotype	sectionally	totteringly	beautifully	innumerable
noctivagous	platyrrhine	sententious	tritagonist	beguilement	innumerably
nocturnally	plutocratic	sentimental	tritheistic	beguilingly	innutrition
northeaster	poltergeist	sentinelled	trituration	bicuspidate	inquilinous
northwester	poltroonery	Septembrist	trothplight	bifurcation	inquiringly
nyctitropic	pontificals	septenarius	tufthunting	biquadratic	inquisition
nyctophobia	pontificate	septentrion	turtleshell	calumniator	inquisitive
obstetrical	portability	septicaemia	tuttifrutti	carunculate	insufflator
obstinately	porterhouse	septicaemic	ulotrichous	casuistical	insultingly
obstruction	portionless	septiferous	unstoppable	chaulmoogra	insuperable
obstructive	portmanteau	septifragal	unutterable	cloudcastle	insuperably
oestrogenic	portraitist	sertularian	unutterably	columbarium	intuitional
oysterplant	portraiture	sextodecimo	ventilation	columniated	intuitively
pantalettes	postclassic	shutterless	ventilative	conurbation	intuitivism
pantheistic	posteriorly	shuttlecock	ventricular	coruscation	intumescent
pantomimist	postexilian	sittingroom	ventriculus	decussately	invultation
pantothenic	postglacial	skatingrink	ventriloquy	decussation	irruptively
participant	postnuptial	sketchiness	venturesome	deductively	lieutenancy
participate	postulation	slotmachine	venturously	degustation	liquefiable
participial	potteringly	smithereens	verticality	denumerable	liquescence
particulate	prattlingly	smithsonite	vertiginous	denunciator	liquidambar
partitioned	pretendedly	snatchblock	vestigially	desultorily	liquidation
partitioner	pretentious	softhearted	vestryclerk	diluvialist	loculicidal
partitively	preterhuman	softshelled	victualless	disunionist	lucubration
partnership	preterition	sottishness	victualling	divulgation	luxuriantly
parturition	protagonist	southeaster	voltametric	divulgement	luxuriation
pasteuriser	protectoral	Southernism	vortiginous	documentary	luxuriously
pastoralism	protectress	southwester	waitinglist	draughtsman	manufactory
pastoralist	proteolysis	spathaceous	waitingroom	drouthiness	manufacture
pastureland	proteolytic	spatterdash	wastebasket	effulgently	manumission
patternshop	Proterozoic	stateliness	weathercock	encumbrance	manumitting
pectination	prothalamia	statesmanly	weatherwise	enquiringly	minuteglass
pentadactyl	prothallial	statistical	weatherworn	Etruscology	naturalness
pentagynous	prothallium	statutebook	weltschmerz	exculpation	naturopathy
pentahedron	prothoracic	statutorily	westernmost	exculpatory	nonunionist
pentamerous	protomartyr	stethoscope	Westminster	excursively	obfuscation
pentandrous	protonotary	stethoscopy	Whitechapel	expurgation	obfuscatory
pentathlete	protophytic	subterminal	whitecollar	expurgatory	objurgation
pentavalent	protractile	subtraction	whiteheaded	exquisitely	objurgatory
pentazocine	protraction	subtractive	whitethroat	facultative	obmutescent
Pentecostal	protractive	subtropical	whitewasher	fatuousness	occultation
pentlandite	protrudable	suitability	whitherward	fecundation	oecumenical
peptisation	protrusible	sustainable	whitishness	flauntingly	oppugnation
pertinacity	protuberant	sustainment	whitleather	fraudulence	peculiarity
pertinently	psittacosis	switchblade	Whitsuntide	furunculous	pecuniarily
perturbable	pustulation	switchboard	winterberry	genuflexion	pedunculate
pestiferous	quaternloaf	syntactical	wintergreen	genuineness	penultimate
pestilently	quitchgrass	synthesiser	wistfulness	glauconitic	penuriously
pestologist	rapturously	synthetical	worthlessly	grouchiness	pleurodynia
petticoated	Rastafarian	systematics	xanthochroi	groundsheet	ploughshare
pettifogger	rattlebrain	systematise	xanthophyll	groundwater	ploughstaff
pettishness	rattlepated	systematist	zestfulness	harumscarum	pneumonitis
photoactive	rattlesnake	tantalising	zootechnics	illuminable	populariser
photocopier	rectangular	tastelessly	ablutionary	illuminance	pseudograph
photofinish	rectifiable	tautologise	aboutsledge	illuminator	pseudomonas
photography	rectilineal	tautologism	acaulescent	illusionism	pseudomorph
photometric	rectilinear	tautologous	acculturate	illusionist	pseudopodia
photooffset	reiteration	tautomerism	accumulator	illustrator	recumbently
photoperiod	reiterative	tautomerism	accusatival	illustrious	recurrently
photophilic	restatement	tautonymous	acoustician	immunologic	redundantly
photophobia	restfulness	teeterboard	acquiescent	impuissance	reduplicate
photophobic	restitution	teetotalism	acquirement	impulsively	regurgitate
photosphere	restiveness	teetotaller	acquisition	inaugurator	rejuvenator
phototactic	restoration	tentaculate	acquisitive	inculcation	rejuvenesce
phototropic	restorative	tentatively	acquittance	inculpation	reluctantly
phytography	restriction	tenterhooks	adjudgement	inculpatory	reluctation
phytologist	restrictive	testability	adjudicator	incunabulum	remunerator
phytosterol	restructure	testatrices	aiguillette	incuriosity	repudiation
phytotomist	rhetorician	testimonial	ailurophile	incuriously	repugnantly
pictography	riotousness	testimonial	ailurophobe	incurvation	repulsively
pictorially	rottenstone	Teutonicism	albuminuria	incurvature	requirement
picturebook	rustication	textureless	annunciator	indubitable	requisition
picturecard	saltatorial	thitherward	appurtenant	indubitably	resuscitate
picturegoer	saltimbanco	tittivation	arduousness	inductively	rheumaticky
picturesque	sartorially	toothbilled	argumentive	indulgently	ritualistic
pietistical	scattergood	toothpowder	assuagement	industrious	roguishness
platearmour	ScotchIrish	toothsomely	assuredness	ingurgitate	saturnalian
plateresque	Scotchwoman	torticollis	Augustinian	injudicious	saturninely
platforming	scuttlebutt	torturously	beauteously	injuriously	scoundrelly

scoutmaster	gravitation	schwarmerei	Elizabethan	comradeship	gallantness
scruffiness	gravitative	showerproof	prizewinner	concatenate	gendarmerie
scrumptious	harvesthome	showjumping	quizzically	confabulate	genealogise
scrutiniser	heavenwards	showmanship	rhizanthous	consanguine	genealogist
seductively	heavyfooted	showstopper	rhizocarpic	containable	geomagnetic
sequestrate	heavyhanded	snowbunting	rhizomatous	containment	Germanophil
shoulderbag	heavyweight	snowgoggles	———————	contaminant	gestatorial
shoulderpad	knavishness	snowleopard	acatalectic	contaminate	goddaughter
shrubbiness	leavetaking	stewardship	acclamation	coplanarity	gonfalonier
sinuousness	louverboard	unawareness	acclamatory	crematorium	gormandiser
situational	louvreboard	waywardness	acinaciform	culpability	gradational
slaughterer	nervelessly	Alexandrian	affranchise	curtailment	guttapercha
sleuthhound	nervousness	alexandrine	AfroAsiatic	declamation	haematocele
solutionist	nonviolence	alexandrite	aggravation	declamatory	haematocrit
staunchless	nonvolatile	coexistence	agoraphobia	declaration	haematology
staunchness	peevishness	coextension	agoraphobic	declarative	haggadistic
staurolitic	pervasively	coextensive	alabastrine	declaratory	haggardness
subumbrella	pervertedly	deoxidation	Alexandrian	deflagrator	haphazardly
suburbanise	pluviometer	deoxygenate	alexandrine	defraudment	Hebraically
suburbanite	prevalently	deoxyribose	alexandrite	degradation	hemianopsia
susurration	prevaricate	flexibility	alphabetise	degradingly	heptamerous
tegumentary	preventable	inexactness	amaranthine	depravation	heptarchist
tenuousness	preventible	inexcusable	amenability	depravement	hierarchism
thaumatrope	previsional	inexcusably	amicability	dermatology	Hispanicise
thaumaturge	privateness	inexistence	anfractuous	detrainment	Hispanicism
thaumaturgy	privatively	inexpedient	animalcular	diamagnetic	Hispanicist
thoughtless	provenience	inexpensive	anomalistic	dictatorial	hollandaise
triumvirate	providently	proximately	anomalously	disbandment	husbandlike
troublesome	provisional	thixotropic	apocalyptic	discalceate	hydraheaded
troublously	provisorily	unexploited	appealingly	discardable	icosahedral
trouserless	provocateur	unexpressed	appeasement	disharmonic	icosahedron
trousersuit	provocation	alcyonarian	applaudable	dismayingly	illfavoured
undutifully	provocative	Assyriology	archaeology	disparaging	illmannered
unfurnished	provokingly	babysitting	archaeornis	disparately	imitatively
unguardedly	provostship	bodybuilder	archaically	distasteful	impeachable
unguiculate	pulverulent	bodyservant	archangelic	dramaturgic	impeachment
unqualified	ribvaulting	butyraceous	aromaticity	educability	implausible
unquietness	salvageable	calyptrogen	assuagement	educational	implausibly
vacuolation	salvational	caryopsides	attractable	Elizabethan	impractical
vacuousness	serviceable	chrysalides	awkwardness	embraceable	inadaptable
valuational	serviceably	chrysalises	barbarously	embracement	inexactness
vesuvianite	servicebook	chrysarobin	barbastelle	embracingly	inflammable
vituperator	serviceline	chrysoberyl	bereavement	emplacement	inflammably
voguishness	shovelboard	chrysoprase	bergamasque	enchainment	infrangible
volubleness	silveriness	cityslicker	bersaglieri	enchantment	ingrainedly
volumometer	silverplate	dehydration	biddability	enchantress	ingratitude
voluntarily	silverpoint	encystation	biquadratic	endearingly	instability
voluntarism	silversmith	eurypteroid	bombardment	enfranchise	installment
voluntarist	silverstick	ithyphallic	buffalorobe	enneahedron	intractable
aboveground	slavedriver	laryngology	bureaucracy	enslavement	intractably
beaverboard	slaveholder	laryngotomy	cabbagepalm	entrainment	intravenous
Calvinistic	slavemarket	lilylivered	cabbagerose	epigastrium	inviability
carvelbuilt	slavishness	molybdenite	cabbagetree	equiangular	ipecacuanha
chevalglass	Slavonicise	papyraceous	cabbageworm	eschatology	Lancastrian
convenances	solvability	playerpiano	cabbalistic	Eucharistic	landaulette
convenience	stevengraph	playfulness	campanology	exclamation	laudability
conveniency	surveillant	playingcard	campanulate	exclamatory	longanimity
conventicle	traversable	polyandrous	captainship	explainable	lucratively
convergence	trivialness	polycarpous	carrageenan	explanation	magdalenian
convergency	unavailable	polychromic	carrageenin	explanatory	magnanimity
conversable	unavoidable	polycrystal	causatively	extractable	magnanimous
conversance	unavoidably	polygenesis	chamaephyte	extradition	mammalogist
conversancy	universally	polygenetic	chevalglass	extrapolate	mandarinate
convertible	velvetiness	polyglottal	chimaerical	extravagant	mansardroof
convertibly	awkwardness	polyglottic	cinnabarine	extravagate	mechanician
conveyancer	betweenmaid	polygonally	climacteric	extravasate	mechanistic
convincible	betweenness	polygraphic	climatology	extraverted	mediaevally
convivially	betweentime	polymorphic	cockaleekie	eyecatching	mediastinal
convocation	dimwittedly	polyonymous	cognateness	fanfaronade	mediastinum
convolution	drawingroom	polypeptide	collaborate	fantastical	mediateness
convolvulus	floweriness	polyphagous	collapsible	farraginous	mediatorial
curvilineal	forwardness	polyphonous	combatively	feudalistic	mediatrices
curvilinear	frowardness	polystyrene	commandment	firmamental	miniaturise
flavourless	frowstiness	polytechnic	compactness	formalistic	miniaturist
flavoursome	knowingness	polyzoarium	compaginate	formational	miscarriage
frivolously	knownothing	prayerwheel	comparatist	forwardness	mismarriage
gravedigger	oldwomanish	sphygmogram	comparative	fricandeaux	mitrailleur
gravelblind	outwardness	amazonstone	compartment	frowardness	mortarboard
gravimetric	reawakening	brazenfaced	compassable	fundamental	moveability

```
multangular  reclamation  tetrarchate  coldblooded  stumblingly  crotcheteer
mundaneness  rectangular  tetravalent  costbenefit  surfboarder  crunchiness
mustachioed  reenactment  thanatology  crabbedness  swimbladder  dedicatedly
myocarditis  refrangible  therapeutic  cryobiology  talebearing  deductively
narratively  reliability  threadiness  curableness  tenableness  defectively
nonmatching  replaceable  threadpaper  defibrinate  theobromine  deficiently
nonpartisan  replacement  throatiness  disablement  thimbleweed  delectation
offhandedly  restatement  throatlatch  disobedient  timebargain  deliciously
oilpainting  retraceable  Titianesque  disobliging  tourbillion  democratise
operational  retractable  tracasserie  durableness  tremblement  democratism
operatively  retranslate  trepanation  ectoblastic  tremblingly  desecration
ostracoderm  rhizanthous  tritagonist  ennoblement  troublesome  desiccation
outwardness  ribvaulting  trypanosome  entablature  troublously  desiccative
overanxious  ritualistic  ultramarine  entablement  tunableness  didacticism
palpability  Sabbatarian  ultramodern  equableness  unambiguous  directional
pantalettes  sacramental  ultrasonics  establisher  vagabondage  directivity
passacaglia  saleability  ultraviolet  exorbitance  vagabondise  directorate
peccability  saltatorial  unavailable  flabbergast  vagabondish  directorial
peccadillos  salvageable  unawareness  flamboyance  vagabondism  directrices
pentadactyl  salvational  unceasingly  flamboyancy  visibleness  disaccustom
pentagynous  satiability  unflappable  flamboyante  volubleness  dodecaphony
pentahedron  sausagemeat  unguardedly  freebooting  warmblooded  domiciliary
pentamerous  scalariform  unhealthily  friableness  wellbeloved  domiciliate
pentandrous  scarabaeoid  unmeaningly  fullblooded  abracadabra  dropcurtain
pentathlete  schwarmerei  unqualified  gallbladder  adjectively  dualcontrol
pentavalent  screamingly  unrealistic  goldbeating  affectation  eclecticism
pentazocine  selfassured  unreasoning  grumblingly  affectingly  effectively
permanently  sensational  unsparingly  hairbreadth  affectional  effectually
pervasively  shamanistic  unteachable  halfbinding  affectioned  efficacious
phalanstery  situational  valiantness  halfblooded  affectively  efficiently
philanderer  sociability  valuational  handbreadth  affectivity  emancipator
philatelist  socialistic  variability  harebrained  afficionado  emasculator
pinnatisect  solvability  variational  headborough  agriculture  endocardiac
piscatorial  somnambular  verbalistic  highbrowism  allocatable  endocardial
placability  spelaeology  verdantique  holoblastic  altocumulus  endocardium
plicateness  spiraculate  versatilely  Hudibrastic  anarchistic  enunciation
pluralistic  spreadeagle  versatility  hypoblastic  anencephaly  enunciative
polyandrous  squeakiness  vibratility  ignobleness  antecedence  episcopally
portability  squeamishly  vibrational  illiberally  antechamber  exacerbate
Precambrian  stalactitic  viceadmiral  indubitable  anticathode  exercisable
precautious  stalagmitic  volcanicity  indubitably  anticipator  expectantly
predatorily  steganogram  volcanology  inhabitable  anticyclone  expectation
prefatorial  stewardship  voltametric  inhabitancy  aquaculture  expectative
prefatorily  stomachache  vulcanicity  Jacobinical  aquiculture  expectorant
prematurely  stomachpump  vulcanology  Jacobitical  articulable  expectorate
prematurity  stomatology  warrantable  lovableness  articulated  exsiccation
preparation  streakiness  warrantably  lucubration  articulator  ferociously
preparative  subbasement  washability  makebelieve  association  fetichistic
preparatory  subcategory  waywardness  meroblastic  associative  finicalness
presanctify  submarginal  welladvised  mesoblastic  atrociously  firecracker
prevalently  suitability  workability  mindbending  audaciously  flaccidness
prevaricate  summariness  Zoroastrian  mindblowing  auricularly  flagcaptain
primaevally  summational  adumbration  molybdenite  autochthony  flocculence
primateship  surbasement  adumbrative  moribundity  backcountry  foreclosure
primatology  surpassable  aerobically  movableness  balmcricket  Francomania
privateness  sustainable  aerobiology  mutableness  binocularly  Francophile
privatively  sustainment  agrobiology  notableness  blotchiness  Francophobe
probabilism  syllabarium  alembicated  overbalance  branchiopod  francophone
probabilist  syllabicity  amiableness  overbearing  breechblock  franctireur
probability  sympathetic  annabergite  overbidding  capaciously  frenchified
probational  sympathiser  atrabilious  pawnbroking  capacitance  Frenchwoman
probationer  syntactical  audibleness  pliableness  caricatural  gatecrasher
profanation  syssarcosis  backbencher  presbyteral  catachreses  geniculated
profanatory  talkatively  ballbearing  pureblooded  catachresis  glauconitic
profaneness  tameability  bearbaiting  reedbunting  cataclysmic  GraecoRoman
propagation  tantalising  bellbottoms  rhombohedra  catechismal  grouchiness
propagative  tarradiddle  birdbrained  rhomboideus  catechistic  gyrocompass
prosaically  tentaculate  bodybuilder  safebreaker  chalcedonic  Heracleidan
prosaicness  tentatively  bookbinding  sandbagging  chancellery  homocentric
protagonist  termagantly  bullbaiting  scribacious  chancellory  hyoscyamine
purgatorial  terraqueous  calibration  shipbreaker  charcuterie  hypocycloid
Pythagorean  testability  capableness  shipbuilder  churchgoing  impecunious
Pythagorism  testatrices  carabiniere  shrubbiness  churchiness  indeciduous
Rastafarian  tetracyclic  carabinieri  sickbenefit  churchwoman  IndoChinese
rateability  tetradactyl  celebration  sizableness  coarctation  inductively
readability  tetrahedral  celebratory  snowbunting  codicillary  inescapable
rearadmiral  tetrahedron  cerebration  soapboiling  coincidence  inexcusable
reawakening  tetramerous  chamberlain  stepbrother  consciously  inexcusably
reclaimable  tetrapodous  chambermaid  stroboscope  corecipient  innocuously
```

insectarium	pumicestone	wisecracker	maladaptive	academician	collectedly
insecticide	pyroclastic	woodcarving	maladjusted	academicism	collectible
insectifuge	quincuncial	woodcutting	maladroitly	accrescence	collenchyma
insectivore	quitchgrass	xylocarpous	malediction	achievement	commemorate
insectology	radicalness	abandonment	maledictory	adolescence	commendable
invectively	rapaciously	abridgement	melodiously	aggregately	commendably
irrecusable	rapscallion	adjudgement	namedropper	aggregation	commendator
irrecusably	raunchiness	adjudicator	Neanderthal	aggregative	commensally
judiciously	redactional	aerodynamic	nomadically	aimlessness	commentator
kilocalorie	reincarnate	anecdotical	ophidiarium	airlessness	compellable
logicalness	reluctantly	archdiocese	overdevelop	amphetamine	compendious
ludicrously	reluctation	archduchess	paradisical	amplexicaul	compensator
mailcarrier	revaccinate	archdukedom	paradoxical	ancientness	competently
maliciously	rhynchodont	assiduously	pseudograph	antheridium	competition
Manichaeism	ricochetted	Benedictine	pseudomonas	aponeuroses	competitive
masochistic	rifacimenti	benediction	pseudomorph	aponeurosis	concealable
medicinable	rifacimento	benedictory	pseudopodia	aponeurotic	concealment
medicinally	rockcrystal	bladderwort	repudiation	appreciable	conceitedly
medicolegal	Rosicrucian	bloodguilty	residential	appreciably	conceivable
metacentric	rubicundity	bloodlessly	rhabdomancy	appreciator	conceivably
metachrosis	safeconduct	bloodstream	ropedancing	arglebargle	concentrate
molecricket	safecracker	bloodsucker	roundedness	artlessness	conceptacle
molecularly	sagaciously	bloodvessel	ruridecanal	athleticism	concernment
monocarpous	salaciously	blunderbuss	sculduddery	augmentable	concertedly
monochasial	sansculotte	boardschool	sculduggery	austereness	concertgoer
monochasium	scorchingly	breadbasket	selfdefence	autoerotism	condemnable
monochromat	ScotchIrish	breadcrumbs	selfdenying	bactericide	condensable
monochromic	Scotchwoman	breadthways	selfdespair	balletomane	confederacy
monoclinous	searchingly	breadthwise	selfdevoted	banteringly	confederate
monoculture	searchlight	breadwinner	selfdisplay	barleybroth	conferrable
municipally	seductively	broadcaster	semidiurnal	barrelhouse	confessedly
musicalness	selectively	broadleaved	skulduddery	barrelorgan	congealable
namecalling	selectivity	broadminded	skulduggery	basketchair	congealment
noticeboard	selfcentred	catadromous	slenderness	bassethound	congelation
objectively	selfclosing	cavedweller	sockdolager	beaverboard	congenerous
objectivism	selfcocking	childminder	sockdologen	betweenmaid	congenially
objectivist	selfcommand	clandestine	soundlessly	betweenness	conjectural
objectivity	selfconceit	cloudcastle	speedometer	betweentime	connectable
obsecration	selfcontent	coordinator	spendthrift	biedermeier	connectedly
octachordal	selfcontrol	dehydration	spindlelegs	billetsdoux	connectible
officialdom	selfcreated	desideratum	spindletree	biofeedback	consecrator
officialese	selfculture	downdraught	spondulicks	biometrical	consecution
officialism	sericulture	dreadnought	spondylitis	bitterapple	consecutive
officiation	sketchiness	equidistant	standardise	bittercress	consentient
officinally	snatchblock	expediently	standoffish	bittersweet	consequence
officiously	speechifier	expeditious	standpatter	blamelessly	conservable
olfactology	starchiness	fieldcornet	steadfastly	blameworthy	conservancy
opencircuit	starcrossed	fieldworker	Stradivarii	boilermaker	conservator
operculated	stencilling	fraudulence	stridulator	botheration	contemplate
orbicularly	stoicalness	golddigging	swordbearer	boysenberry	contentedly
overcropped	subscapular	grandfather	taxidermist	brazenfaced	contentious
palmcabbage	switchblade	grandiflora	theodolitic	brucellosis	contentment
panicmonger	switchboard	grandiosely	thunderbird	bulletproof	conterminal
parachutist	tenaciously	grandiosity	thunderbolt	butterflies	contestable
parochially	thenceforth	grandmother	thunderclap	butteriness	convenances
paunchiness	theocentric	grandnephew	thunderhead	calceolaria	convenience
pedicellate	tobacconist	grandparent	thunderpeal	cancellated	conveniency
pediculosis	toxicomania	guardedness	thunderpeal	candelabrum	conventicle
penicillate	treacherous	hairdresser	trendsetter	candescence	convergence
penicillium	treacliness	hereditable	triadically	carpetsnake	convergency
pericardiac	treecreeper	hexadecimal	trundletail	carvelbuilt	conversable
pericardial	trenchantly	immediately	unendurable	castellated	conversance
pericardium	trencherman	immedicable	unendurably	catheterise	conversancy
pericranial	typecasting	impedimenta	ungodliness	ceaselessly	convertible
pericranium	typicalness	injudicious	valediction	centenarian	convertibly
pilocarpine	unaccounted	insidiously	valedictory	chameleonic	conveyancer
pipecleaner	unnecessary	invidiously	vasodilator	chaperonage	cooperation
pleochroism	urticaceous	irradiation	veridically	chokecherry	cooperative
pococurante	urticarious	irradiative	vinedresser	cholesterol	copperplate
policewoman	vasectomise	irredentism	viridescent	choreograph	coppersmith
polycarpous	vaticinator	irredentist	welldefined	Clarencieux	cornerstone
polychromic	veraciously	irreducible	worldbeater	closefisted	correctable
polycrystal	vesicularly	irreducibly	worldliness	closehauled	correctness
pomiculture	viniculture	juridically	worldlywise	coalescence	correlation
postclassic	viticulture	lakedweller	abbreviator	coeternally	correlative
preachiness	vivaciously	launderette	abecedarian	coffeehouse	cosmetician
preoccupied	voraciously	lepidoptera	aboveground	coffeetable	cosmetology
presciently	wildcatting	linedrawing	abstentious	collectable	credentials
principally	windcheater	loxodromics	academicals	collectanea	crenellated

currentness
dangerously
decrepitate
decrepitude
decrescendo
deprecation
deprecative
deprecatory
depreciator
depredation
depredatory
depressible
descendable
descendible
desperadoes
desperately
desperation
deuteration
deuterogamy
Deuteronomy
dexterously
diadelphous
dialectally
dialectical
diametrical
diatessaron
differentia
differently
dinnerdance
dinnertable
dinnerwagon
dipterocarp
disbeliever
discernible
discernibly
discernment
discerption
dishevelled
dispensable
dispersedly
disremember
disseminate
disseminule
dissentient
dissepiment
dissertator
distempered
distensible
duniewassal
earnestness
easternmost
ecumenicism
ecumenicity
elementally
emblematise
emblematist
endlessness
entreatment
enumeration
enumerative
epinephrine
epipetalous
erubescence
escheatable
escheatment
esotericism
eudaemonism
eudaemonist
euphemistic
evanescence
evidentiary
exceedingly
excremental
excrescence
excrescency
exogenously
exoneration
exonerative
exotericism
expressible
extremeness
exuberantly
falteringly
farreaching
fermentable
fidgetiness
filterpaper
fingerboard
fingerglass
fingerplate
fingerprint
fingerstall
flagellator
florescence
floweriness
forbearance
forfeitable
forgetfully
forgetmenot
forgettable
fraternally
fraterniser
galleyslave
gardemanger
gartersnake
genteelness
geometrical
geotectonic
gibberellin
gingerbread
globeflower
glomeration
godlessness
goldenberry
gracelessly
gravedigger
gravelblind
grotesquely
grotesquery
guilelessly
gutlessness
guttersnipe
gynaecocrat
gynaecology
halterbreak
haplessness
harvesthome
heavenwards
hedgehopped
hedgepriest
hedgeschool
heldentenor
helleborine
Hellenistic
hermeneutic
hermeticism
herpetology
hesperidium
hitherwards
homoeopathy
homoestatic
horsecollar
horsedoctor
horseradish
housefather
householder
housekeeper
houselights
housemaster
housemother
housewifely
housewifery
hyphenation
illtempered
implemental
imprecation
imprecatory
imprecisely
imprecision
impregnable
impregnably
impressible
impressment
inclemently
incoercible
increasable
incredulity
incredulous
incremental
inelegantly
inflexional
infrequence
infrequency
inoperative
intrepidity
iridescence
isogeotherm
isometrical
itinerantly
itineration
jabberwocky
Jansenistic
joylessness
lactescence
lammergeier
lammergeyer
larcenously
largeminded
lawlessness
lawmerchant
leaseholder
leavetaking
lecherously
letterpress
lichenology
lickerishly
lingeringly
liquefiable
liquescence
litterateur
loggerheads
looselimbed
loosestrife
louverboard
Lutheranism
mackerelsky
maddeningly
madreporite
Maglemosian
malfeasance
manneristic
mantelpiece
mantelshelf
marcescence
marcescible
marketplace
marketvalue
masterfully
masterpiece
mathematics
medievalism
medievalist
mendelevium
menservants
mercenarily
millenarian
minnesinger
misbegotten
miscegenate
miscellanea
misfeasance
misremember
monkeybread
monkeyshine
monseigneur
mothercraft
mothernaked
motherright
murderously
myrmecology
neckerchief
nephelinite
nervelessly
netherworld
nickelplate
nigrescence
noiselessly
noisemaking
nondelivery
nondescript
nonfeasance
nonmetallic
nonresident
nonsensical
nonsequitur
nurserymaid
obstetrical
opalescence
orchestrate
oxygenation
oysterplant
paederastic
Palaearctic
palaeotypic
pandemonium
panhellenic
papiermache
parheliacal
passeriform
pasteuriser
patternshop
peacemaking
Pentecostal
perceivable
perceivably
perceptible
perceptibly
perfectible
perfectness
perpetrator
perpetually
perpetuance
perpetuator
persecution
perseverate
pervertedly
phagedaenic
phonetician
pieceworker
pigheadedly
planetarium
planetoidal
platearmour
plateresque
playerpiano
plebeianise
plebeianism
pocketknife
pocketmoney
pocketsized
poltergeist
ponderation
ponderosity
ponderously
porterhouse
posteriorly
postexilian
potteringly
powderflask
prayerwheel
precedented
precedently
precentress
preceptress
predecessor
prefectural
premeditate
preselector
presentable
presentably
presentient
presentment
preservable
pretendedly
pretentious
preterhuman
preterition
preventable
preventible
prizewinner
proceedings
procephalic
professedly
progenitrix
progeniture
progestogen
prolegomena
proletarian
proletariat
prosecution
prosecutrix
proselytise
proselytism
prosenchyma
protectoral
protectress
proteolysis
proteolytic
Proterozoic
provenience
pulverulent
putrescence
putrescible
quaternloaf
racketpress
rallentando
rangefinder
reemergence
reflectance
reflexively
reflexology
refreshment
regretfully
regrettable
regrettably
reiteration
reiterative
replenisher
repleteness
repleviable
representer
repressible
repressibly
respectable
respectably
rickettsial
rottenstone
rubberstamp
saplessness
scalearmour
scaleinsect
scaremonger
secretarial
secretariat
secretively
segmentally
segregation
segregative
selfelected
selfevident
semiellipse
senselessly
sententious
Septembrist
septenarius
septentrion
sequestrate
sexlessness
shamelessly
shapeliness
shareholder
sharepusher
shovelboard
showerproof
sickeningly
silveriness
silverplate
silverpoint
silversmith
silverstick
simperingly
sincereness
sinlessness
skeletonise
slavedriver
slaveholder
slavemarket
smilelessly
smokescreen
spaceflight
spaceheater
spacesaving
sphaeridium
spinelessly
spokeswoman
stagemanage
stagestruck
stakeholder
stateliness
statesmanly
stereograph
stereometry
stereophony
stereoscope
stereoscopy
stereotyped
stereotyper
stereotypic
stevengraph
stipendiary
stonecurlew
stonecutter
stoneground
stonemarten
stonewaller
storekeeper
streetlight
studentship
subaerially
submergence
submersible
subregional
subsequence
subservient
subterminal
succedaneum
suggestible
summerhouse
summersault
sunlessness
supremacist
supremeness
surgeonfish
surrebuttal
surrebutter
surveillant
susceptible
susceptibly
suspenseful
suspensible
symmetrical
sympetalous
syndesmosis
systematics

systematise	witheringly	pacifically	demigoddess	ploughshare	catchphrase
systematism	withershins	pacificator	demographer	ploughstaff	clodhopping
systematist	witlessness	painfulness	demographic	polygenesis	clothesline
tabletennis	wonderfully	pitifulness	denigration	polygenetic	clothesmoth
tacheometer	yacketyyack	platforming	denigratory	polyglottal	clothesprop
tastelessly	zootechnics	playfulness	desegregate	polyglottic	coinheritor
teeterboard	acriflavine	proofreader	designation	polygonally	coldhearted
temperament	antifouling	purificator	doxographer	polygraphic	cornhusking
temperately	assafoetida	pushfulness	draggletail	pomegranate	deathrattle
temperative	balefulness	rarefaction	draughtsman	postglacial	depthcharge
temperature	barefacedly	rarefactive	ectogenesis	preignition	diachronism
tempestuous	bashfulness	restfulness	ectogenetic	recognition	diaphaneity
tendencious	bellfounder	rubefacient	egregiously	recognitive	diaphoresis
tendentious	benefaction	rubefaction	enlightened	recognitory	diaphoretic
tenterhooks	beneficence	scaffolding	evangelical	religionise	Diophantine
terrestrial	beneficiary	scruffiness	exaggerator	religionism	doughtiness
tessellated	beneficiate	selffeeding	fatiguingly	religionist	downhearted
thereabouts	birdfancier	selffeeling	gamogenesis	religiosity	earthcloset
theretofore	bullfighter	selffertile	grangeriser	religiously	earthenware
therewithal	calefacient	skilfulness	handgrenade	renegotiate	earthliness
threecolour	calefactory	solifluxion	holographic	repugnantly	elephantine
threedecker	californium	songfulness	homogeneity	resignation	elephantoid
threehanded	carefulness	sonofabitch	homogeneous	rotogravure	epithalamia
threelegged	chieftaincy	soulfulness	homogenetic	scragginess	epithalamic
threemaster	cliffhanger	spifflicate	homogeniser	selaginella	epithelioma
titleholder	codefendant	stagflation	hylogenesis	serigrapher	epochmaking
toffeenosed	coefficient	stiffnecked	hypogastric	sexagesimal	erythrocyte
totteringly	disaffected	tabefaction	hypoglossal	slaughterer	faithhealer
trabeculate	disafforest	tankfarming	ideographic	smorgasbord	faithlessly
tracelessly	dolefulness	tearfulness	idiographic	snowgoggles	faithworthy
tragedienne	dropforging	thriftiness	illogically	sphagnology	farthermost
trapeziform	dumbfounder	trafficator	immigration	sphygmogram	farthingale
trapezoidal	dutifulness	trafficking	inaugurator	spongecloth	featheredge
traversable	factfinding	trafficless	incognisant	swingletree	featherhead
trimestrial	fatefulness	tumefaction	indigestion	synagogical	featherless
tripetalous	fearfulness	tunefulness	indigestive	telegrammic	fleshliness
turgescence	firefighter	typefounder	indignantly	telegrapher	flightiness
unbreakable	flimflammer	typefoundry	indignation	telegraphic	forthcoming
uncleanness	fourflusher	vociferance	intagliated	thingumabob	freehearted
unfeelingly	fretfulness	vociferator	integrality	thingumajig	frightfully
unicellular	fullfledged	wakefulness	integration	thoughtless	frothhopper
unigeniture	gainfulness	wellfounded	integrative	tobogganing	fullhearted
unipersonal	genuflexion	whiffletree	invigilator	tobogganist	furtherance
unisexually	handfasting	wildfowling	invigorator	topographer	furthermore
universally	harmfulness	wishfulness	irregularly	topographic	furthermost
unspeakable	hatefulness	wistfulness	kymographic	triggerfish	furthersome
unspeakably	heedfulness	zestfulness	landgrabber	typographer	geochemical
unweetingly	helpfulness	abiogeneses	landgravine	typographic	geophysical
uselessness	highfalutin	abiogenesis	litigiously	unorganized	godchildren
valleculate	hopefulness	abiogenetic	logographer	unrighteous	goodhearted
variegation	hurtfulness	aerographer	logographic	uprightness	graphically
velvetiness	illaffected	Albigensian	malignantly	vehmgericht	graphicness
vespertinal	indefinable	allegorical	managership	vicegerency	halfhearted
vitrescence	indefinably	ambiguously	merogenesis	wellgroomed	halfholiday
voicelessly	indifferent	antigravity	metagenesis	winegrowing	hardhearted
wappenschaw	ineffective	appogiatura	metagenetic	wrongheaded	hardhitting
wapperjawed	ineffectual	assignation	monogenesis	xylographer	haughtiness
washerwoman	inefficient	astigmatism	monogenetic	xylographic	headhunting
wastebasket	inoffensive	Aurignacian	monogrammed	aesthetical	hunchbacked
wedgeshaped	inofficious	autographic	monographer	amethystine	ichthyology
wedgetailed	insufflator	benightedly	monographic	anachronism	ichthyornis
Wesleyanism	irrefutable	benightment	nomographer	anachronous	ichthyosaur
westernmost	irrefutably	benignantly	nomographic	anaphylaxis	incoherence
whereabouts	labefaction	bourgeoisie	nosographer	annihilator	incoherency
wheresoever	latifundium	braggadocio	nosographic	apophyllite	indehiscent
wherewithal	leapfrogged	bridgeboard	octagonally	apotheosise	ironhearted
Whitechapel	linefishing	cacographic	ontogenesis	bacchanalia	isochronism
whitecollar	lustfulness	categorical	ontogenetic	beachcomber	isochronous
whiteheaded	malefaction	changefully	oppugnation	beechmarten	kindhearted
whitethroat	maleficence	chargesheet	orangoutang	bellheather	kitchenette
whitewasher	manifestant	cookgeneral	oreographic	biochemical	kitchensink
wholesomely	manifestoes	cosignatory	overgarment	biophysical	kitchenware
wholesouled	manufactory	cytogenesis	palsgravine	blepharitis	kwashiorkor
whoremaster	manufacture	delightedly	panegyrical	brachiation	landholding
whoremonger	mindfulness	delightsome	paragrapher	brachyurous	latchstring
whosesoever	munificence	demagnetise	paragraphic	brotherhood	laughinggas
widdershins	nasofrontal	demagogical	pedagogical	butcherbird	leatherback
winterberry	needfulness	demagoguery	Pelagianism	cantharides	leatherhead
wintergreen	omnifarious	demagoguism	peregrinate	cantharidic	leatherneck

```
lionhearted  teachership  applicatory  colligative  deoxidation  florilegium
loathliness  thitherward  appointment  collimation  deprivation  folliculate
loathsomely  toothbilled  Archimedean  collinearly  destination  foolishness
marchioness  toothpowder  archipelago  collisional  destitution  foppishness
marshalling  toothsomely  arenicolous  combination  detribalise  forbiddance
marshalship  torchbearer  arraignment  combinative  detrimental  foreignness
marshmallow  torchsinger  astringency  combinatory  difficultly  forgiveness
matchlessly  touchtyping  atheistical  commination  diffidently  formication
matchmaking  toughminded  atomisation  comminatory  dimwittedly  fornication
mentholated  tracheotomy  attribution  comminution  disciplinal  fortifiable
merchandise  trichinosis  attributive  commiserate  discipliner  frigidarium
merchantman  trichomonad  attritional  commissural  dislikeable  frugivorous
mirthlessly  triphibious  bacciferous  committable  dissimilate  fulminating
mischievous  triphyllous  baptismally  compilation  dissimulate  fulmination
naughtiness  tritheistic  barbiturate  compilement  dissipation  fulminatory
neighbourly  trophoblast  bashibazouk  conciliator  dissipative  furnishings
nonchalance  trothplight  bathingsuit  conciseness  distinction  furtiveness
northeaster  truehearted  bearishness  conditional  distinctive  fustigation
northwester  tufthunting  beguilement  conditioner  distinguish  Gallicanism
nympholepsy  unashamedly  beguilingly  confidently  doggishness  gallimaufry
nymphomania  uninhabited  bellicosity  confidingly  dollishness  garnishment
openhearted  uninhibited  belligerent  confinement  doltishness  gasfittings
pamphleteer  urochordate  bewhiskered  confirmable  donnishness  gemmiferous
pantheistic  warmhearted  bibliolater  confiscable  drawingroom  gemmiparous
perchlorate  watchmaking  bibliolatry  confiscator  duplication  gentianella
philhellene  weakhearted  bibliomancy  considerate  duplicative  gentilitial
pitchblende  weathercock  bibliomania  considering  duplicitous  genuineness
porphyritic  weatherwise  bibliopegic  consignable  earpiercing  germination
prochronism  weatherworn  bibliophile  consignment  edification  germinative
prophethood  weighbridge  bibliophily  consistence  edificatory  gesticulate
prophetical  weightiness  bibliopolic  consistency  egalitarian  girlishness
prophetship  whichsoever  bibliotheca  continental  egotistical  glaringness
prophylaxis  whitherward  billionaire  continently  elicitation  globigerina
prothalamia  witchdoctor  Bodhisattva  contingence  eligibility  glutinously
prothallial  witchhunter  bombilation  contingency  elimination  gracileness
prothallium  worshipable  bombination  continuable  eliminative  gradiometer
prothoracic  worshipless  bookinghall  continually  elucidation  granivorous
psychedelia  worshipping  bookishness  continuance  elucidative  gravimetric
psychedelic  worthlessly  boorishness  continuator  elucidatory  gravitation
psychiatric  xanthochroi  Britishness  convincible  elusiveness  gravitative
psychically  xanthophyll  brutishness  convivially  emotionally  gullibility
psychodrama  abolishable  bullishness  corbiculate  emotionless  gurgitation
psychogenic  abolishment  caddishness  corbiesteps  enchiridion  gypsiferous
psychograph  abomination  calcicolous  cordialness  enquiringly  handicapped
psychologic  abstinently  calciferous  corniferous  epidiascope  handicapper
psychometry  abusiveness  calcifugous  corrigendum  eradication  hellishness
psychomotor  acclimation  calcination  costiveness  eradicative  helminthoid
psychopathy  acclimatise  calligraphy  craniometry  evagination  herbivorous
pulchritude  acclivitous  Calvinistic  credibility  evanishment  hereinafter
punchinello  acidifiable  candidature  crepitation  evasiveness  herringbone
purchasable  acquiescent  cannibalise  criminalist  eveningstar  herringgull
reachmedown  acquirement  cannibalism  criminality  examination  hoggishness
roadholding  acquisition  captionless  crimination  explication  homoiousian
roughfooted  acquisitive  captivation  criminative  explicative  hooliganism
roughlegged  acquittance  carcinomata  criminatory  explicatory  horripilate
scyphistoma  acumination  cardinalate  criminology  exquisitely  hospitalise
shepherdess  aestivation  cardiograph  criticality  exstipulate  hospitality
slightingly  affrication  carminative  criticaster  extrication  hospitaller
smithereens  affricative  carnivorous  crocidolite  fabrication  hummingbird
smithsonite  aggrievedly  carriageway  cruciferous  facsimilist  hurriedness
softhearted  agonisingly  cassiterite  crucifixion  factionally  hyacinthine
southeaster  agonistical  castigation  crucigerous  faddishness  idolisation
Southernism  aiguillette  casuistical  culmination  fallibility  illdisposed
southwester  airsickness  cauliflower  cultivation  farcicality  imaginarily
spathaceous  amativeness  centigramme  cunningness  fasciaboard  imagination
stephanotis  ameliorator  certifiable  cupriferous  fasciculate  imaginative
stethoscope  Americanise  certifiably  currishness  fascinating  imbrication
stethoscopy  Americanism  certificate  cursiveness  fascination  implication
stichometry  Americanist  chafingdish  curvilineal  fashionable  implicative
sulphureous  amphibolite  charismatic  curvilinear  fashionably  impuissance
sulphurwort  amphibology  clericalism  cypripedium  feasibility  inalienable
symphonious  amphictyony  clericalist  cysticercus  feelingness  inalienably
synchromesh  amphimictic  coccidiosis  deceitfully  ferriferous  inanimately
synchronise  amphisbaena  cochinchina  deceivingly  festinately  inanimation
synchronism  anadiplosis  coexistence  declination  fissionable  inclination
synchronous  Anglicanism  cognitional  declivitous  fissiparity  incriminate
synchrotron  aposiopesis  cognitively  deification  fissiparous  IndoIranian
synthesiser  application  cognitivity  denticulate  flexibility  inedibility
synthetical  applicative  colligation  dentigerous  floriferous  inexistence
```

```
initialling  mooringmast  phariseeism  rectilineal  straightway  vitrifiable
inquilinous  morbiferous  phthiriasis  rectilinear  straitlaced  voguishness
inquiringly  morningroom  physicality  reddishness  studiedness  vortiginous
inquisition  morrisdance  physiocracy  refrigerant  stylisation  waggishness
inquisitive  multicolour  physiognomy  refrigerate  stylishness  waitinglist
inspiration  multilinear  physiologic  refringency  suasiveness  waitingroom
inspiratory  multinomial  pietistical  reification  subdivision  waspishness
instigation  multiparous  piggishness  rejoicingly  sublimation  wearilessly
instigative  multiracial  pinkishness  renaissance  sublimeness  wearisomely
instillment  multistorey  piscivorous  reorientate  sublittoral  whitishness
instinctive  multivalent  plagiariser  replication  submissible  willingness
instinctual  negligently  plagioclase  requirement  subsistence  winningness
institution  nictitation  plagiostome  requisition  suckingfish  winningpost
intricately  noctilucent  planimetric  respiration  sufficiency  worrisomely
intriguante  noctivagant  planisphere  respiratory  suffixation  antiJacobin
intuitional  noctivagous  platinotype  restitution  surficially  showjumping
intuitively  nonviolence  playingcard  restiveness  suspiration  blackavised
intuitivism  nothingness  plenipotent  retribution  swinishness  blackbeetle
jactitation  nourishment  pluviometer  retributive  syndicalism  blackbirder
Judaisation  nullifidian  pollination  retributory  syndicalist  blackcoated
jumpingbean  nulliparity  pontificals  retrievable  syndication  blackfellow
jumpingjack  nulliparous  pontificate  roguishness  tagliatelle  blackgrouse
justiciable  nutrimental  portionless  rubrication  tagliatelli  blackmailer
justifiable  nutritional  possibility  rustication  tangibility  blackmarket
justifiably  nutritively  precipitant  sacrificial  tarnishable  blockbuster
knavishness  nyctitropic  precipitate  salpingitis  tensibility  bookkeeping
knowingness  obstinately  precipitous  saltimbanco  termination  brankursine
lacrimation  odoriferous  preciseness  scoriaceous  terminative  bricklaying
lacrimatory  opinionated  predicament  seasickness  terminology  chickenfeed
lacrimosely  orchidology  predication  sectionally  termitarium  chickenwire
lactiferous  originality  predicative  selfimposed  terricolous  chockablock
laicisation  origination  predicatory  selfinduced  terrigenous  chucklehead
lancinating  originative  predictable  selfinvited  territorial  crackerjack
lancination  outdistance  predictably  selftalks    testimonial  crookbacked
landingbeam  outfighting  prehistoric  semeiotical  thalidomide  crookedness
landinggear  outrivalled  prelibation  sempiternal  thuriferous  cytokinesis
lastingness  ovariectomy  preliminary  sensibility  tittivation  doorknocker
latticework  overindulge  premiership  sensitively  tonsillitis  drunkenness
lentiginous  ozoniferous  previsional  sensitivity  torticollis  exoskeletal
liquidambar  ozonisation  primigenial  sentimental  traditional  exoskeleton
liquidation  packingcase  primiparous  sentinelled  tragicomedy  frankfurter
loutishness  paediatrics  primitively  septicaemia  trepidation  franklinite
lubrication  paediatrist  primitivism  septicaemic  Trinitarian  frankpledge
lubricative  palpitation  prodigalise  septiferous  trivialness  handknitted
lumpishness  participant  prodigality  septifragal  turbination  knucklebone
machicolate  participate  proficiency  serpiginous  tuttifrutti  painkilling
machination  participial  profiterole  serviceable  unanimously  prickliness
machinemade  particulate  prohibition  serviceably  unclimbable  quacksalver
madrigalian  partitioned  prohibitive  servicebook  unfailingly  quickchange
madrigalist  partitioner  prohibitory  serviceline  unfeignedly  quickfiring
magnificent  partitively  proliferate  sheriffalty  unflinching  quickfreeze
mandibulate  passibility  proliferous  sheriffship  unguiculate  quickfrozen
mannishness  Passiontide  prolificacy  sickishness  unification  quicksilver
marginalise  passivation  prolificity  signifiable  unprintable  quickwitted
marginality  passiveness  prominently  significant  unquietness  safekeeping
marlinspike  patriarchal  promiscuity  sillimanite  unskilfully  Sanskritist
marriagebed  patrilineal  promiscuous  sittingroom  unsmilingly  shacklebolt
massiveness  patrimonial  promisingly  skatingrink  unthinkable  shacklebone
mastication  patristical  propinquity  slavishness  unthinkably  shockheaded
masticatory  pectination  propitiable  smokingroom  Upanishadic  shocktroops
matriarchal  peevishness  propitiator  soldierlike  utilisation  slickenside
matriculate  pensionable  providently  soldiership  utilitarian  snickersnee
matrilineal  pensionless  provisional  solmisation  vaccination  soupkitchen
matrilinear  pensiveness  provisorily  somniculous  varnishtree  speakership
matrimonial  peptisation  proximately  somniferous  vendibility  stickinsect
mawkishness  percipience  prudishness  sophistical  ventilation  stickleback
meaningless  permissible  pruriginous  sottishness  ventilative  stockbroker
melliferous  permissibly  pteridology  sparingness  vermiculate  stockholder
mellifluent  persistence  publication  specifiable  vermiculite  stockinette
mellifluous  persistency  publishable  specificity  vermination  stockjobber
mentionable  pertinacity  publishment  spiniferous  verminously  stockmarket
mercilessly  pertinently  qualifiable  spiritistic  verticality  stocktaking
messiahship  pessimistic  qualitative  spiritlevel  vertiginous  strikebound
metrication  pestiferous  raffishness  spiritually  vestigially  telekinesis
milliampere  pestilently  realignment  spiritualty  vinaigrette  telekinetic
millionaire  petticoated  realisation  spirituelle  vincibility  thanklessly
millisecond  pettifogger  reanimation  statistical  vindication  thanksgiver
miscibility  pettishness  recriminate  straightcut  vindicative  thankworthy
mockingbird  pharisaical  rectifiable  straightish  vindicatory  thickheaded
```

thickwitted	desalinator	involvement	rattlebrain	virilescent	homomorphic
trackwalker	desultorily	invultation	rattlepated	virological	idiomorphic
tricksiness	devaluation	ipsilateral	rattlesnake	washleather	ignominious
unbeknownst	developable	irrelevance	recalculate	Wensleydale	illimitable
wreckmaster	development	irrelevancy	repellantly	wheelbarrow	illimitably
abiological	disillusion	irreligious	repellently	wheelwright	illuminable
acaulescent	displeasure	isoelectric	repulsively	whitleather	illuminance
accelerando	divulgation	lamellicorn	resiliently	windlestraw	illuminator
accelerator	divulgement	lamelliform	resplendent	zooplankton	incommodity
acculturate	doublecheck	lamplighter	retaliation	abdominally	incompetent
aerological	doublecross	landlordism	retaliative	accommodate	incompliant
affiliation	doubleDutch	levelheaded	retaliatory	accompanist	indomitable
agrological	doubleedged	lilylivered	revaluation	accumulator	indomitably
algological	doubleender	loculicidal	rheological	acrimonious	innumerable
alkalescent	doubleentry	maxillipede	saddlecloth	albuminuria	innumerably
alkalimeter	doublefaced	megalomania	saddlehorse	allAmerican	inseminator
alkalimetry	doublequick	megalopolis	scholarship	allomorphic	intemperate
allelomorph	doublespeak	mesalliance	scholiastic	antemundane	intimidator
angelically	doublethink	metalloidal	selflimited	antimonious	intumescent
Apollinaris	drillmaster	metallurgic	selfloading	argumentive	ironmongery
appallingly	ebulliently	metalworker	selflocking	ascomycetes	irremissive
appellation	effulgently	middleclass	serological	assemblyman	irremovable
appellative	embellisher	middlesized	sexological	assimilable	irremovably
artillerist	enucleation	misalliance	shallowness	assimilator	judgmatical
axiological	envelopment	monolingual	shellacking	attemptable	kinematical
bacilliform	equilateral	monological	shelljacket	automatable	lesemajesty
battledress	equilibrate	monologuise	shoeleather	bohemianism	lifemanship
battlefield	equilibrist	monologuist	shoplifting	Brahmanical	ligamentary
bimillenary	equilibrium	moonlighter	shoulderbag	brahmaputra	ligamentous
bimillenium	ethological	mudslinging	shoulderpad	Brahminical	logomachist
booklearned	eucalyptole	musclebound	simpliciter	bushmanship	loudmouthed
bootlegging	everlasting	mycological	singlestick	calumniator	manumission
bottleglass	excellently	needlecraft	singletrack	campmeeting	manumitting
bottlegreen	exculpation	needlepoint	sinological	ceremonious	mesomorphic
bottlenosed	exculpatory	needlewoman	smallholder	chrominance	metamorphic
bowdleriser	exfoliation	Neoplatonic	smallminded	chromoplast	monomorphic
brilliantly	exfoliative	nettlecloth	snowleopard	chromosomal	myxomatosis
bucolically	facelifting	nomological	soliloquise	columbarium	myxomycetes
bumblepuppy	facultative	nonplussing	soliloquist	columniated	oarsmanship
burglarious	familiarise	nosological	spellbinder	cotemporary	oecumenical
byeelection	familiarity	novelettish	squalidness	decemvirate	openmouthed
canalicular	fiddlestick	obsolescent	stallholder	denominator	optometrist
canaliculus	fusillation	occultation	steelworker	denumerable	overmanning
candleberry	gentlemanly	oecological	stellionate	documentary	overmeasure
candlelight	gentlewoman	oenological	stiflejoint	dreamlessly	paramedical
candlepower	goodlooking	oncological	stoolpigeon	dynamically	parametrise
candlestick	habiliments	ontological	subclinical	dynamometer	paramoecium
capillarity	halflanding	oreological	suppliantly	dynamometry	paramorphic
Carolingian	Hamiltonian	oscillation	swallowable	ectomorphic	paramountcy
cavalierism	Hegelianism	oscillatory	swallowdive	encomiastic	paramountly
challenging	Hepplewhite	oscillogram	swallowhole	encumbrance	perambulate
charlatanry	hobbledehoy	overlapping	swallowtail	endemically	plasmolysis
chaulmoogra	homiletical	paddleboard	swallowwort	endometrium	plasmolytic
civilianise	homological	paddlewheel	swellheaded	endomorphic	pleomorphic
civilisable	horological	Panglossian	theological	enigmatical	pneumonitis
cobblestone	huckleberry	paraldehyde	thrillingly	enjambement	polemically
cockleshell	humiliation	paraleipsis	tiddlywinks	entomophily	polymorphic
complacence	humiliatory	parallactic	titillation	ephemerides	portmanteau
complacency	hypolimnion	parallelism	togglejoint	extemporary	pragmatical
complainant	ideological	parallelled	totalisator	extemporise	preeminence
complaisant	idyllically	patelliform	trailblazer	filamentary	pyramidally
complexness	impolitical	pearlescent	trelliswork	filamentous	pyramidical
compliantly	impoliticly	pearlfisher	troglodytic	foraminated	racemeeting
complicated	impulsively	peculiarity	tumbledrier	foraminifer	recommender
complotting	incalescent	pedological	turtleshell	foulmouthed	recommittal
conflagrant	inculcation	penological	typological	fragmentary	recumbently
conflagrate	inculpation	pentlandite	unbelieving	freemasonry	regimentals
confliction	inculpatory	penultimate	unfaltering	fullmouthed	remembrance
conflictive	indulgently	perplexedly	unhelpfully	funambulate	resemblance
coralloidal	infiltrator	phylloclade	unpalatable	funambulist	rheumaticky
cupellation	insalubrity	phyllotaxis	unpolitical	gourmandise	rodomontade
cytological	insultingly	pomological	unrelenting	gourmandism	rudimentary
decelerator	intelligent	populariser	unselective	grammalogue	scrimpiness
decollation	intolerable	posological	unsolicited	grammatical	scrumptious
decolletage	intolerably	preelection	unwillingly	halfmeasure	sedimentary
decolourise	intolerance	problematic	upholsterer	hardmouthed	seismically
defalcation	invalidness	pupillarity	vacillation	harumscarum	seismograph
defoliation	involucrate	quilldriver	vexillology	hemimorphic	seismometer
dereliction	involuntary	Rabelaisian		hexametrist	seismometry

seismoscope	botanically	extensional	melancholia	secondclass	Aeneolithic
selfmastery	brainlessly	extensively	melancholic	secondrater	aeolotropic
semimonthly	brainsickly	extenuation	melanochroi	secondsight	agglomerate
showmanship	brainteaser	extenuatory	melanophore	sedentarily	alcyonarian
slotmachine	businessman	farinaceous	meningocele	seigneurial	amazonstone
spasmodical	Byronically	fecundation	metonymical	seigniorage	amenorrhoea
spermaphyte	Byzantinism	feloniously	misanthrope	seigniorial	amorousness
spermatozoa	Byzantinist	financially	misanthropy	semanticist	anacoluthon
spermicidal	calendrical	flannelette	molendinary	serendipity	analogously
steamboiler	canonically	flannelling	momentarily	seventeenth	androgynous
steamroller	carunculate	flauntingly	momentously	seventyfold	anemometric
stormcentre	cementation	fomentation	mononuclear	shrinkingly	angiography
stormtroops	chainarmour	fortnightly	moronically	shrinkproof	AngloFrench
stramineous	chainletter	furunculous	nomenclator	Socinianism	AngloIndian
subumbrella	chainsmoker	gegenschein	nominatival	solanaceous	anglomaniac
tapemachine	chainstitch	gerontology	nonunionist	sphincteral	AngloNorman
tapemeasure	channelling	gigantesque	octingenary	sphincteric	anglophobia
tegumentary	chronically	goodnatured	offenceless	splendorous	anglophobic
tenementary	chronograph	greengrocer	offensively	splenectomy	anisotropic
thaumatrope	chronologer	greenkeeper	organically	splenetical	anthocyanin
thaumaturge	chronologic	greenockite	organisable	springboard	anthologise
thaumaturgy	chronometer	groundsheet	organscreen	springclean	anthologist
thermically	chronometry	groundwater	orientalise	springhouse	antioxidant
thermionics	chronoscope	hymenoptera	orientalism	springiness	anxiousness
thermoduric	cleanlimbed	immanentism	orientalist	squintingly	aphrodisiac
thermograph	cleanliness	immanentist	orientation	stainlessly	apologetics
thermolysis	cleanshaven	immenseness	ostensively	staunchless	apomorphine
thermolytic	coconscious	immunologic	ostentation	staunchness	approbation
thermometer	colonelship	impanelling	palindromic	sternsheets	approbatory
thermometry	colonialism	impenetrate	parentheses	sternutator	appropriate
thermophile	colonialist	impenitence	parenthesis	strangeness	approvingly
thermoscope	copingstone	impenitency	parenthetic	strangulate	approximate
thermotaxis	coronagraph	impingement	paronomasia	strenuosity	arduousness
thrombocyte	coronograph	incantation	partnership	strenuously	artiodactyl
trammelling	cotoneaster	incantatory	pecuniarily	stringboard	audiologist
triumvirate	cylindrical	incinerator	pedunculate	stringently	audiometric
uncommitted	decantation	incongruent	peninsulate	stringiness	audiovisual
unlimitedly	decennially	incongruity	perennation	stringpiece	awesomeness
unmemorable	defenceless	incongruous	perennially	stringybark	azotobacter
unmemorably	defensively	inconscient	perineurium	strongpoint	BaltoSlavic
unremitting	definiendum	inconsonant	plainspoken	synonymical	batholithic
volumometer	delineation	inconstancy	plaintively	talentscout	biliousness
Weismannism	delinquency	incontinent	pleinairist	taxonomical	biocoenoses
wellmeaning	demandingly	incunabulum	postnuptial	technically	biocoenosis
Westminster	demonolatry	indentation	potentially	technocracy	biocoenotic
whigmaleery	demonstrate	infanticide	prognathism	technologic	bonbonniere
workmanlike	denunciator	infantilism	prognathous	tetanically	borborygmus
workmanship	dependently	infantryman	queenliness	titanically	boutonniere
zygomorphic	derangement	infinitival	recantation	trainbearer	burgomaster
abranchiate	desensitise	ingeniously	recondition	triangulate	callousness
absenteeism	diagnostics	ingenuously	reconnoitre	triennially	carbocyclic
accentually	dimensional	insensately	reconstruct	tryingplane	carbonation
achondritic	diningtable	insensitive	redundantly	tyrannicide	cartography
actinometer	disannulled	insincerely	regenerable	tyrannosaur	caryopsides
actinomyces	disencumber	insincerity	regenerator	tyrannously	catholicise
actinomycin	disentangle	insinuation	reminiscent	unbendingly	Catholicism
adminicular	disenthrall	insinuative	remonstrant	uncanniness	catholicity
advancement	disinclined	intenseness	remonstrate	uncanonical	chemotactic
adventuress	disinfector	intensifier	remunerator	unconcealed	chinoiserie
adventurism	disinterest	intensional	repentantly	unconcerned	chirography
adventurist	disinterred	intensively	resentfully	uncongenial	chiropodist
adventurous	disunionist	intentional	retentively	unconnected	chiropteran
aeronautics	domineering	intentioned	retentivity	unconscious	chorography
aeronomical	emmenagogue	inventively	retinacular	uncontested	clamorously
agronomical	Emmenthaler	inventorial	retinaculum	unkennelled	clinometric
allantoides	empanelling	journeywork	retinoscopy	unmanliness	cognoscente
anagnorisis	engineering	juvenescent	revendicate	unwinkingly	cognoscenti
annunciator	enhancement	knownothing	rodenticide	voluntarily	cognoscible
antenuptial	ensanguined	lacination	romanticise	voluntarism	coleorrhiza
antineutron	equinoctial	laconically	romanticism	voluntarist	collocation
antonomasia	erroneously	lamentation	romanticist	wirenetting	comfortable
Arminianism	essentially	laryngology	salinometer	witenagemot	comfortably
arrangement	eugenically	laryngotomy	saponaceous	womanliness	comfortless
ascensional	expansional	learnedness	satanically	xeranthemum	commonality
assentation	expansively	Leibnitzian	satinstitch	achromatise	commonplace
attentively	expansivity	linendraper	scientistic	achromatism	commonsense
attenuation	expenditure	luminescent	scientology	acidophilic	comportment
auxanometer	expensively	lycanthrope	scoundrelly	acknowledge	compositely
bicentenary	exponential	lycanthropy	secondarily	adenomatous	composition

compositive	discontinue	haemoptysis	itacolumite	nitrogenise	photophobia
compossible	discordance	haemorrhage	jargonistic	nitrogenous	photophobic
compotation	discordancy	haemorrhoid	jealousness	noisomeness	photosphere
compotatory	discotheque	haemostasis	labiodental	nonvolatile	phototactic
concomitant	discourtesy	haemostatic	legionnaire	notionalist	phototropic
concordance	dishonestly	Hagiographa	leprosarium	noxiousness	phycocyanin
condolatory	dishonourer	hagiography	leptodactyl	nyctophobia	phycologist
condominium	dislocation	hagiologist	limnologist	obviousness	phylogynist
condonation	dislodgment	hagioscopic	lissomeness	ochlocratic	phytography
condottiere	disportment	haplography	lithography	odorousness	phytologist
condottieri	disposition	harbourless	lithophytic	oldwomanish	phytosterol
conformable	dispositive	harmonistic	lithosphere	oligochaete	phytotomist
conformably	dissociable	heinousness	lithotomise	oligomerous	pictography
conformally	dissolutely	heliochrome	lithotomist	ominousness	pictorially
conformance	dissolution	heliography	lithotripsy	onerousness	pigeonchest
connoisseur	dissolvable	heliometric	lophobranch	operoseness	pillowfight
connotation	dissonantly	heliotropic	macrobiotic	ophiologist	piteousness
connotative	dittography	hideousness	macrocosmic	opprobrious	planoconvex
consolation	douroucouli	Hindoostani	macrogamete	orthocentre	pleiotropic
consolatory	dubiousness	hippocampus	macroscopic	orthodontia	plutocratic
consolidate	dyslogistic	Hippocratic	maisonnette	orthodontic	poisonously
consolingly	econometric	hippopotami	malposition	orthoepical	polyonymous
consonantal	editorially	histologist	mandolinist	orthography	pompousness
consonantly	elaborately	historiated	marconigram	orthopaedic	pornography
contorniate	elaboration	historicise	mastodontic	orthopedics	preconceive
convocation	elaborative	historicism	mastoiditis	orthopedist	precontract
convolution	embrocation	historicist	meadowgrass	orthopteran	predominant
convolvulus	embroiderer	historicity	meadowsweet	orthoscopic	predominate
copiousness	embroilment	homeopathic	melioration	orthotropic	premonition
corporality	emulousness	homeostasis	meliorative	osteography	premonitory
corporately	enfeoffment	homeostatic	meprobamate	osteologist	prenominate
corporation	engrossment	hugeousness	meteoritics	osteopathic	preposition
corporatism	enviousness	hydrobromic	meteoroidal	osteophytic	prepositive
corporative	erotogenous	hydrocarbon	meteorology	osteoplasty	prerogative
corporeally	erotomaniac	hydrocyanic	Methodistic	Ostrogothic	proconsular
corroborant	ethnography	hydrogenate	methodology	oviposition	prolocutrix
corroborate	ethnologist	hydrogenous	micrococcal	ozonosphere	promotional
corrosively	etymologise	hydrography	micrococcus	paedophilia	proportions
cosmogonist	etymologist	hydrologist	microcosmic	pantomimist	proposition
cosmography	euchologion	hydromedusa	microgamete	pantothenic	prorogation
cosmologist	eudiometric	hydrometeor	micrography	pastoralism	protomartyr
cosmopolite	evaporation	hydrometric	microgroove	pastoralist	protonotary
cottongrass	evaporative	hydropathic	microlithic	pathologist	protophytic
cottonmouth	exploitable	hydrophilic	micrometric	patronising	provocateur
coulometric	exploration	hydrophobia	Micronesian	percolation	provocation
coxcombical	explorative	hydrophobic	microphonic	perforation	provocative
crocodilian	exploratory	hydrophytic	microphytic	perforative	provokingly
ctenophoran	explosively	hydroponics	microscopic	performable	provostship
cupronickel	expropriate	hydrosphere	microsecond	performance	pterodactyl
curiousness	extroverted	hydrostatic	misconceive	periodicity	purportedly
cursoriness	fatuousness	hydrotactic	misconstrue	periodontal	purposeless
customarily	filmography	hydrothorax	muttonchops	periostitis	purposively
custombuilt	FinnoUgrian	hydrotropic	myelomatous	personalise	radioactive
customhouse	flagofficer	hygrometric	mythography	personalism	radiocarbon
cyclopaedia	flavourless	hygrophytic	mythologise	personalist	radiography
cyclopaedic	flavoursome	hygroscopic	mythologist	personality	radiolarian
cycloserine	forlornness	hymnography	mythomaniac	personation	radiologist
cyclothymia	frivolously	hypnopaedia	mythopoeist	personative	radiometric
cyclothymic	fulsomeness	hypnopompic	mythopoetic	personifier	radiophonic
defloration	Gallophobia	hypsography	narcoleptic	pestologist	rancorously
deploringly	gallowsbird	hypsometric	nationalise	petrography	ratiocinate
despoilment	gallowstree	hypsophobia	nationalism	petrologist	rationalise
despondence	gaseousness	ichnography	nationalist	phagocytise	rationalism
despondency	gemmologist	iconography	nationality	phagocytose	rationalist
deviousness	geopolitics	iconostases	nationstate	phenologist	rationality
dexiotropic	gettogether	iconostasis	necrobiosis	philologian	raucousness
dialogistic	gibbousness	imploringly	necrologist	philologist	regionalise
diamondback	gnotobiosis	impropriate	necromancer	philosopher	regionalism
diapophysis	gnotobiotic	impropriety	necromantic	philosophic	regionalist
diapositive	godforsaken	improvement	necrophilia	phonography	reproachful
dichogamous	goniometric	improvident	necrophilic	phonologist	reprobation
dichotomise	gramophonic	ineloquence	necropoleis	photoactive	reprobative
dichotomist	granolithic	intromitted	negrophobia	photocopier	reprobatory
dichotomous	granophyric	intromitter	neologistic	photofinish	reprogramme
diplococcus	gymnospermy	introverted	nervousness	photography	reprography
diplomatise	haemocyanin	inviolately	neurologist	photometric	reprovingly
diplomatist	haemoglobin	irksomeness	neuropathic	photooffset	respondence
dipsomaniac	haemophilia	isomorphism	neuroticism	photoperiod	respondency
discography	haemophilic	isomorphous	neurotropic	photophilic	responsible

responsibly	tautomerism	conspicuous	overpayment	xerophilous	centrifugal
restoration	tautonymous	conspirator	overproduce	xylophagous	centripetal
restorative	tediousness	deceptively	paraphraser	xylophonist	cesarevitch
retroaction	teetotalism	deemphasise	paraplectic	antiquarian	cesarewitch
retroactive	teetotaller	depopulator	peripatetic	antiquation	cheerleader
retrocedent	teknonymous	dicephalous	periphrases	brusqueness	cheerlessly
retroflexed	teleologism	dilapidated	periphrasis	forequarter	cheiromancy
retrorocket	teleologist	dilapidator	perspective	illiquidity	chiaroscuro
rhetorician	temporality	disapproval	perspicuity	obliqueness	chlorophyll
rhinologist	temporarily	dualpurpose	perspicuous	quinquennia	chloroplast
rhinoscopic	tenuousness	ectoplasmic	phosphonium	quinquereme	chloroprene
rhizocarpic	Teutonicism	ellipsoidal	phosphorate	abhorrently	choirmaster
rhizomatous	thixotropic	ellipticity	phosphorism	abnormality	clairschach
ribbongrass	thoroughpin	encapsulate	phosphorite	absorbingly	clairvoyant
riotousness	thoroughwax	endophagous	phosphorous	absorptance	clearheaded
ruinousness	thyroiditis	endoplasmic	podophyllin	abstraction	colorimeter
Russophobia	toploftical	equipollent	polypeptide	abstractive	colorimetry
salmonberry	tricoloured	esemplastic	polyphagous	abstriction	compression
saprobiotic	trimorphism	Europeanise	polyphonous	accordantly	compressive
saprogenous	trimorphous	eurypteroid	pourparlers	accordingly	comprisable
saprophytic	troposphere	exceptional	promptitude	admiralship	concrescent
sarcomatous	unavoidable	exemplarily	prospective	adverbially	congressman
sarcophagus	unavoidably	exemplarily	realpolitik	adversative	congruently
sartorially	unemotional	felspathoid	reapportion	adverseness	congruously
sauropodous	unicoloured	footpoundal	reappraisal	advertently	contrabasso
scenography	uniformness	fourpounder	receptacula	advertising	contractile
schoolboard	unipolarity	halophilous	receptively	affirmation	contraction
schoolchild	unpromising	handpainted	receptivity	affirmative	contractive
schoolhouse	unshockable	hebephrenia	reciprocate	affirmatory	contractual
scopolamine	unstoppable	hebephrenic	reciprocity	afterburner	contracture
selfopinion	unwholesome	hemipterous	reduplicate	aftereffect	contradance
sensorially	uranography	highpitched	resipiscent	agrarianism	contraption
seriousness	vacuolation	highpowered	saxophonist	ailurophile	contrariety
sextodecimo	vacuousness	homophonous	scalpriform	ailurophobe	contrarious
shadowgraph	variousness	homoplastic	scorpionfly	aircraftman	contrastive
shadowiness	varsovienne	homopterous	scrappiness	algorithmic	contretemps
sigmoidally	verboseness	hypophyseal	scriptorial	altercation	contributor
sinfonietta	viciousness	hypophysial	scriptorium	alternately	contrivable
sinuousness	violoncello	inappetence	scuppernong	alternation	contrivance
Slavonicise	viscountess	incipiently	selfpitying	alternative	controlling
sociologist	viscousness	independent	semipalmate	altorelievo	controlment
sociometric	voodooistic	inexpedient	sharpwitted	altorilievo	controversy
sociopathic	welcomeness	inexpensive	sheepfarmer	anacreontic	coparcenary
somnolently	wellordered	inopportune	sheepmaster	anteriority	coterminous
sorrowfully	winsomeness	inseparable	signpainter	anthracitic	cybernation
Spinozistic	yellowbelly	inseparably	sleepingbag	anthropical	cybernetics
spirochaete	zealousness	insipidness	sleepingcar	antirrhinum	debarkation
spirochetal	zincography	insuperable	sleeplessly	apparatchik	decarbonate
spirometric	zoomorphism	insuperably	sleepwalker	apparelling	decarbonise
sporogenous	acarpellous	irreparable	solipsistic	appurtenant	decarburise
sporogonium	acceptation	irreparably	Soroptimist	aquarellist	decerebrate
sporophytic	acceptingly	irruptively	stampoffice	arboraceous	decorticate
stegosaurus	accipitrine	ithyphallic	steeplebush	arborescent	deferential
stenochromy	acropetally	lineprinter	steeplejack	arterialise	deforcement
stenography	adiaphorism	longplaying	straphanger	arthrospore	deformation
stenotypist	allopathist	lowspirited	subspecific	aspergillum	deliriously
stylography	amorphously	malapropism	sweepstakes	aspergillus	demarcation
stylopodium	antependium	manipulable	sycophantic	aspersorium	demarkation
subcontract	antiphonary	manipulator	sycophantry	assertively	dendritical
subcontrary	antiphrasis	massproduce	teaspoonful	assortative	deportation
subcortical	antipyretic	meliphagous	telepathise	assuredness	describable
subdominant	Areopagitic	metaphysics	telepathist	Assyriology	description
subrogation	autoplastic	metaplastic	telephonist	autarchical	descriptive
succourless	basipetally	metapsychic	teleprinter	avoirdupois	deservingly
suffocation	bicephalous	metoposcopy	tentpegging	bellringing	destruction
suffocative	billposting	misspelling	timepleaser	Belorussian	destructive
supportable	blasphemous	monophagous	toxophilite	bicarbonate	deteriorate
supportably	Bonapartean	monophthong	Trappistine	bicorporate	determinacy
supposition	Bonapartism	Monophysite	unappealing	bifurcation	determinant
suppositive	Bonapartist	monopoliser	unexploited	bipartition	determinate
suppository	cacophonous	monopterous	unexpressed	butyraceous	determinism
surrogation	calyptrogen	mycophagist	unhappiness	calorimeter	determinist
syllogistic	cataplectic	nonspecific	unimportant	calorimetry	diacritical
symbolistic	ceroplastic	occipitally	vasopressin	camaraderie	dichromatic
symposiarch	champertous	oenophilist	vasopressor	catercousin	diffraction
syncopation	Chippendale	oesophageal	vituperator	caterpillar	disarmament
tautologise	clapperclaw	omnipotence	whippletree	cavernously	disarmingly
tautologism	conspecific	omnipresent	wirepulling	centreboard	disarmingly
tautologous	conspicuity	outspokenly	xenophilous	centrepiece	discrepancy

disgraceful	heterograft	inheritable	libertinage	powerlessly	stirruppump
disgruntled	heterophony	inheritance	libertinism	preprandial	subarration
disorganise	heteroploid	inheritress	literalness	procreation	subcritical
distraction	heteropolar	injuriously	logarithmic	procreative	subordinate
distractive	heterospory	innervation	louvreboard	procrustean	subornation
distressful	heterotaxis	inscribable	lowpressure	progression	subtraction
distribuend	heterotroph	inscription	luxuriantly	progressism	subtractive
distributor	heterotypic	inscriptive	luxuriation	progressist	subtropical
distrustful	hibernacula	inscrutable	luxuriously	progressive	suburbanise
divergently	hibernation	inscrutably	malariology	proprietary	suburbanite
diverticula	Hibernicism	instruction	malpractice	protractile	suffragette
divorcement	highranking	instructive	margraviate	protraction	sugarcoated
doctrinaire	hilariously	interactant	materialise	protractive	superabound
doctrinally	histrionics	interaction	materialism	protrudable	supercharge
dundrearies	histrionism	interactive	materialist	protrusible	superfamily
elderliness	hundredfold	interallied	materiality	purpresture	superficial
elutriation	hyperactive	interatomic	McCarthyism	pyrargyrite	superficies
embarkation	hyperbolise	interbedded	membraneous	quadraphony	superfluity
emperorship	hyperboloid	intercalary	memorabilia	quadratical	superfluous
empirically	hyperborean	intercalate	memorialise	quadrennial	superheater
endorsement	hypercharge	intercensal	memorialist	quadrennium	superimpose
enforceable	hypercritic	intercepter	mindreading	quadrillion	superinduce
enforcement	hypermarket	interceptor	mineraliser	quadrupedal	superintend
engorgement	hypermetric	intercessor	miscreation	quarrelling	superioress
enlargeable	hyperphagia	interchange	misericorde	quarrelsome	superiority
enlargement	hyperplasia	intercostal	miserliness	rebarbative	superjacent
enterostomy	hypersthene	intercourse	mistrustful	recurrently	superlative
enterovirus	hypertrophy	intercrural	mithridatic	redirection	superlunary
enterpriser	illbreeding	interdental	moderations	referential	supermarket
entertainer	immarginate	interdepend	modernistic	reformation	supernatant
enthralling	immortalise	interesting	monarchical	reformative	supernormal
enthralment	immortality	interfacial	mycorrhizae	reformatory	superscribe
environment	imparkation	interfacing	mycorrhizal	regardfully	superscript
epeirogenic	impartation	interfluent	naturalness	regurgitate	supersedeas
epigraphist	impartially	interfusion	naturopathy	remorseless	supersedure
Esperantist	imperfectly	intergrowth	nefariously	repartition	superstrata
etherealise	imperforate	interiorise	Neotropical	reportorial	supersubtle
ethereality	imperialise	interiority	nephrectomy	reservation	supertanker
excoriation	imperialism	interjacent	neutraliser	restriction	supervision
excursively	imperialist	interleaves	notoriously	restrictive	supervisory
exdirectory	imperilling	interlinear	numerically	restructure	suppression
exhortation	imperilment	Interlingua	nutcrackers	retardation	suppressive
exhortative	imperiously	interlining	objurgation	retardative	susurration
exhortatory	impermanent	interlocker	objurgatory	retardatory	sybaritical
experienced	impermeable	interlunary	observantly	retiredness	synergistic
exportation	impermeably	intermeddle	observation	reverberant	tabernacled
expurgation	impersonate	intermedium	observatory	reverberate	temerarious
expurgatory	impertinent	intermingle	observingly	reverential	tephromancy
exteriorise	imperviable	intermitted	obstruction	reversional	theorematic
exteriority	importantly	internalise	obstructive	reversioner	theoretical
exterminate	importation	internality	oestrogenic	satirically	thwartships
externalise	importunate	internecine	oneiromancy	saturnalian	topdressing
externalism	importunely	internuncio	opportunely	saturninely	tuberculate
externality	importunity	interosseus	opportunism	scleroderma	tuberculise
extirpation	incarcerate	interplayed	opportunist	sclerometer	tuberculose
extirpatory	incardinate	interpolate	opportunity	sclerophyll	tuberculous
extortioner	incarnadine	interpreter	orderliness	sclerotitis	ulotrichous
fimbriation	incarnation	interracial	otherwhiles	seborrhoeic	uncertainly
fireraising	incertitude	interregnum	outbreeding	selfraising	uncertainty
floorwalker	incorporate	interrelate	outcropping	selfreliant	unchristian
fluorescein	incorporeal	interrogate	overrunning	selfreproof	underbidder
fluorescent	incorrectly	interrupter	paperhanger	selfrespect	undercharge
fluoroscope	incorruptly	interruptor	papermaking	severalfold	underexpose
fluoroscopy	incuriosity	interseptal	paperweight	soberminded	underground
forerunning	incuriously	intersexual	papyraceous	soteriology	undergrowth
fratricidal	incurvation	intersperse	paternalism	sovereignly	underhanded
gastrectomy	incurvature	interspinal	paternalist	sovereignty	undermanned
gastronomic	indirection	intertangle	paternoster	sparrowbill	underpinned
gastroscope	indorsement	intertribal	pelargonium	sparrowhawk	underseller
generaliser	inebriation	intervallic	penuriously	spherically	undersigned
generalship	inferential	interviewee	piperaceous	spherometer	understated
generically	inferiority	interviewer	pleurodynia	spherulitic	undertaking
gimcrackery	infertility	laboriously	polarimeter	squarebuilt	undertenant
haberdasher	infirmarian	lachrymator	polarimetry	squarsonage	undervaluer
hairraising	informality	lateritious	polarisable	squirearchy	underweight
hazardously	information	legerdemain	polariscope	staircarpet	underwriter
hemeralopia	informative	leviratical	poltroonery	staurolitic	unforgiving
heteroclite	informatory	libertarian	portraitist	steerageway	unfortunate
heteroecism	ingurgitate	liberticide	portraiture	stirrupbone	unfurnished

unnervingly	coessential	infestation	rediscovery	transpierce	bountifully
unshrinking	coinsurance	inobservant	registrable	transponder	bracteolate
unvarnished	comestibles	insessorial	reinsertion	transporter	breathalyse
unwarranted	coruscation	insistently	reinsurance	transsexual	bristletail
vagariously	counselling	investigate	reposefully	transuranic	bristleworm
vaporimeter	crossbearer	investiture	resistively	transversal	bristliness
vaporisable	crossbowman	ionospheric	resistivity	treasonable	brittleness
venereology	crossgarnet	irresoluble	resuscitate	treasonably	bullterrier
ventricular	crosslegged	kickstarter	revisionary	trouserless	bumptiously
ventriculus	crossstitch	kinesiology	revisionism	trousersuit	caustically
ventriloquy	cryosurgery	legislation	revisionist	typesetting	chaetognath
vestryclerk	decussately	legislative	rhapsodical	unassertive	chanterelle
vicariously	decussation	legislature	ringstraked	unbeseeming	chanticleer
viceregally	deerstalker	lickspittle	salesladies	undeserving	chaotically
viceroyalty	degustation	longsighted	sandskipper	undesirable	chartaceous
viceroyship	detestation	loudspeaker	satisfiable	undisguised	chitterling
waterbottle	devastation	magisterial	schismatise	undisturbed	cicatrical
watercolour	digestively	magisterium	schistosity	unessential	cisatlantic
watercooled	dinosaurian	magistratic	schistosome	unfashioned	clostridium
watercooler	disassemble	maidservant	scissorbill	unpossessed	coextensive
watercourse	disassembly	metasomatic	scissortail	venesection	comptroller
waterlogged	divestiture	metastasise	selfsealing	venisection	comstockery
waterskiing	divisionary	minesweeper	selfseeking	verisimilar	constellate
wellrounded	divisionism	ministerial	selfservice	vicissitude	consternate
zoographist	domesticate	misestimate	selfserving	vivisection	constituent
accessorial	domesticity	molestation	selfstarter	volkslieder	constitutor
accessorise	dresscircle	monasterial	selfsterile	wainscoting	constrictor
accusatival	dressmaking	monasticism	selfsupport	wainscotted	construable
acoustician	echosounder	nearsighted	semasiology	weltschmerz	constructor
advisedness	emulsionise	necessarian	semiskilled	whimsically	countenance
aerostatics	encystation	necessarily	Shaksperean	Whitsuntide	counterblow
aerostation	endoskelton	necessitate	Shaksperian	Yugoslavian	counterbond
agnosticism	Etruscology	necessitous	shopsteward	abiotically	counterfeit
altostratus	excessively	numismatics	showstopper	ablutionary	counterfoil
anaesthesia	expostulate	numismatist	sideslipped	abortionist	counterfort
anaesthetic	feldspathic	obfuscation	sidestepped	aboutsledge	countermand
antiSemitic	fenestrated	obfuscatory	sinistrally	adoptianism	countermark
antistrophe	festschrift	obsessional	sinistrorse	adoptianist	countermine
arrestingly	fetishistic	obsessively	softshelled	adoptionism	countermove
assassinate	filmsetting	obtestation	songsparrow	adoptionist	countermure
assessorial	footslogger	omniscience	spessartine	adulterator	counterpane
atmospheric	footsoldier	oversailing	spinsterish	agnatically	counterpart
attestation	foreseeable	oversetting	splashboard	ahistorical	counterplan
Augustinian	foreshorten	overstepped	sponsorship	altitudinal	counterplea
babysitting	foresighted	overstretch	squashiness	ambitiously	counterplot
barnstormer	forestaller	overstuffed	starstudded	amentaceous	countersign
bergschrund	forestation	painstaking	tearstained	amontillado	countersink
bestselling	frowstiness	Palestinian	theosophist	anastomoses	countersunk
bicuspidate	gangsterism	paraselenae	thinskinned	anastomosis	counterturn
billsticker	glassblower	parasitical	thirstiness	anastomotic	countervail
blessedness	glasscutter	parasitosis	thrasonical	antitypical	counterview
bodyservant	glassmaking	parishioner	timeserving	apartmental	counterwork
bondservant	glossolalia	pedestalled	timesharing	apostleship	countlessly
bondservice	grasshopper	perishables	townspeople	apostolical	countrified
bookselling	greasepaint	perishingly	transaction	apostrophic	countryfied
bookshelves	greaseproof	perispermic	transalpine	aquatically	countryseat
breastplate	guesstimate	peristalith	transceiver	arbitrageur	countryside
breastwheel	hairstyling	peristalsis	transcriber	arbitrament	countrywide
calisthenic	hairstylist	peristaltic	transection	arbitrarily	courteously
cardsharper	handselling	peristomial	transferred	arbitration	courtliness
caressingly	harpsichord	phrasemaker	transferrer	arbitrative	craftswoman
catastrophe	hemispheric	phraseogram	transfigure	arbitratrix	creationism
celestially	heresiology	phraseology	transfinite	aristocracy	creationist
chansonnier	highstepper	pipistrelle	transfixion	ascetically	crestfallen
cheesecloth	homesteader	priestcraft	translation	aseptically	crustaceous
Christendom	homestretch	Prussianise	translocate	attitudinal	cryotherapy
christening	homosporous	Prussianism	translucent	autotrophic	cryptically
christiania	hornswoggle	quaestorial	translunary	awestricken	cryptogamic
Christianly	hypostatise	quiescently	transmarine	beastliness	cryptograph
Christmassy	illusionism	ravishingly	transmittal	beauteously	cryptomeria
Christology	illusionist	reassertion	transmitted	beautifully	crystalline
chrysalides	illustrator	reassurance	transmitter	befittingly	crystallise
chrysalises	illustrious	recessional	transpadane	belatedness	crystallite
chrysarobin	impassioned	recessively	transparent	bewitchment	crystalloid
chrysoberyl	impassively			bilaterally	curatorship
chrysoprase	impassivity			bimetallism	dauntlessly
cityslicker	incessantly			bimetallist	deactivator
classically	industrious			blastogenic	deistically
cleistogamy	inessential			bounteously	

deleterious	genitivally	mountainous	reactionist	stretchable	circumsolar
delitescent	geostrophic	mountaintop	redetermine	stuntedness	circumspect
devotedness	ghastliness	muskthistle	reestablish	substandard	circumvolve
diarthrosis	ghostliness	naphthalene	reintegrate	substantial	coadunation
diastematic	ghostwriter	negationist	reintroduce	substantive	coagulation
diastrophic	giantpowder	negotiation	relatedness	substituent	coeducation
dicotyledon	greatnephew	negotiatory	relationism	sumptuosity	collusively
digitigrade	gristliness	negotiatrix	relationist	sumptuously	colouration
diphtherial	guiltlessly	nightingale	repetitious	swarthiness	colourblind
diphtheroid	habituation	nightmarish	rheotropism	swiftfooted	colourfully
diphthongal	hairtrigger	nightporter	rightangled	symptomatic	combustible
doubtlessly	haustellate	nightwalker	righteously	taciturnity	comeuppance
downtrodden	healthfully	nonetheless	righthanded	taratantara	communalise
drastically	healthiness	obmutescent	righthander	teratogenic	communalism
drouthiness	heartbroken	ommatophore	rightminded	teratologic	communalist
ectotrophic	hearthstone	ornithology	rightwinger	theatregoer	communicant
einsteinium	heartlessly	ornithopter	roentgenise	theatricals	communicate
elastically	heartsblood	ornithosaur	safetyvalve	thistledown	communistic
elasticated	heartstring	osmotically	Sagittarius	tightfisted	commutation
elastomeric	hepatectomy	outstanding	saintliness	tightlipped	commutative
electioneer	heretically	outstripped	saintpaulia	toastmaster	compunction
electrician	holothurian	overtopping	scattergood	trestletree	compurgator
electricity	homothallic	parathyroid	sceptically	trestlework	computation
electrocute	hypotension	paratrooper	schottische	tristichous	computerise
electrolier	hypothecate	paratyphoid	scintillant	trustbuster	concubinage
electrology	hypothenuse	penetrating	scintillate	trusteeship	concubinary
electrolyse	hypothermia	penetration	scoutmaster	trustworthy	concubitant
electrolyte	hypothesise	penetrative	scratchwork	tryptophane	concurrence
electronics	hypotyposis	penitential	scrutiniser	unalterable	conductance
electrotype	identically	perithecium	scuttlebutt	uncatchable	conductible
enarthrosis	idiotically	peritonitis	seditionary	undutifully	conductress
endothelial	immitigable	petitionary	seditiously	ungetatable	confusingly
endothelium	immitigably	phantasiast	selftorture	unmatchable	confutation
endothermal	impatiently	phantasmata	semitrailer	unmitigated	confutative
endothermic	impetration	pigsticking	senatorship	unnaturally	conjugality
endotrophic	impetratory	pilotburner	sheathknife	unobtrusive	conjugation
entitlement	impetuosity	piratically	sheetanchor	unorthodoxy	conjugative
Erastianism	impetuously	pivotbridge	shelterbelt	unsaturated	conjunction
ergatocracy	inalterable	plantigrade	shelterless	unutterable	conjunctiva
erratically	inalterably	plasterwork	shiftlessly	unutterably	conjunctive
eventualise	inattention	plasticiser	shirtsleeve	unwittingly	conjuncture
eventuality	inattentive	plectoptera	shortchange	vacationist	conjuration
exanthemata	inestimable	plenteously	shortcoming	venatically	connubially
existential	inestimably	plentifully	shorthanded	vexatiously	conquerable
expatiation	infatuation	pointdevice	shortspoken	volitionary	consultancy
expatiative	ingathering	pointedness	shortwinded	voortrekker	consumerism
expatiatory	innutrition	pointillism	shutterless	wealthiness	consumingly
facetiously	irretention	pointillist	shuttlecock	whistlestop	consummator
Falstaffian	irretentive	pointlessly	sightlessly	winetasting	consumption
fanatically	jauntingcar	politically	sightliness	wiretapping	consumptive
faultfinder	kinetograph	politicking	sightreader	zoantharian	cornucopian
faultlessly	kinetoscope	polytechnic	sightscreen	accoucheuse	corpulently
firstfruits	kleptomania	positronium	sightseeing	accountable	corpuscular
flirtatious	latitudinal	practicable	sightworthy	accountably	corrugation
fluctuation	lengthiness	practicably	sleuthhound	accountancy	corruptible
forethinker	lieutenancy	practically	smoothfaced	acidulation	corruptibly
forethought	lightfooted	praetorship	solutionist	acupuncture	corruptness
foretopmast	lighthanded	prattlingly	somatically	adjournment	credulously
foretopsail	lightheaded	prestigious	somatogenic	Aesculapian	crenulation
fractionary	lightminded	prestissimo	somatologic	agglutinate	crepuscular
fractionate	lightsomely	prestressed	somatoplasm	barquentine	debauchment
fractionise	lightweight	proctorship	somatotonia	bivouacking	debouchment
fractiously	limitedness	prosthetics	somatotonic	calculating	deglutition
frantically	limitlessly	prostitutor	spastically	calculation	demountable
franticness	maintenance	prostration	spatterdash	calculative	depauperate
freethinker	maintopmast	psittacosis	spectacular	carbuncular	depauperise
freethought	maintopsail	pullthrough	spectatress	carburetion	diffuseness
frontrunner	megatherium	punctilious	spectrality	carburetted	diffusively
frostbitten	meritocracy	punctuality	spectrogram	carburetter	discussable
fructuation	meritorious	punctuation	spectrology	carburettor	discussible
fruitlessly	mimetically	puritanical	spontaneity	cellularity	disfunction
frustration	minuteglass	pyrotechnic	spontaneous	cinquecento	disguisedly
functionary	moisturiser	quarterback	sportswoman	circularise	disgustedly
functionate	monitorship	quarterdeck	stadtholder	circularity	disjunction
gafftopsail	Monothelite	quartertone	startlingly	circulation	disjunctive
gametangium	monstrosity	questionary	steatopygia	circulative	disjuncture
gametophyte	monstrously	quintillion	stiltedness	circulatory	disputation
geanticline	mosstrooper	ratatouille	strategical	circumlunar	disquieting
genetically	mountaineer	reactionary	stratocracy	circumpolar	disquietude

disturbance	musculation	traducement	twelvepenny	heavyhanded	bimetallist
dysfunction	musculature	tremulously	unadvisedly	heavyweight	birdfancier
ejaculation	nocturnally	tribulation	uncivilised	honeybadger	birdwatcher
ejaculatory	nuncupation	tribuneship	undeveloped	honeymooner	bivouacking
encrustment	nuncupative	tribunicial	vesuvianite	honeysuckle	blackavised
entrustment	obscuration	tribunitial	armtwisting	hurryscurry	blepharitis
evolutional	obscureness	tributarily	birdwatcher	hurryskurry	Bonapartean
exclusively	obtrusively	triquetrous	bondwashing	jerrymander	Bonapartism
exclusivity	oracularity	trituration	bushwhacker	lacrymation	Bonapartist
executioner	outbuilding	truculently	catswhisker	lacrymatory	bondwashing
executorial	parturition	turbulently	elbowgrease	lacrymosely	braggadocio
executrices	pastureland	unboundedly	embowelling	martyrology	Brahmanical
executrixes	pellucidity	uncluttered	embowerment	merryandrew	brahmaputra
exhaustible	pendulously	uncountable	fairweather	merrymaking	bullbaiting
exhaustless	perfunctory	uncouthness	farawayness	methylamine	burglarious
factualness	permutation	uncrushable	firewalking	methylation	bushmanship
favouritism	persuadable	undoubtedly	firewatcher	mollycoddle	butyraceous
featureless	persuasible	unequivocal	flagwagging	moneylender	calefacient
ferruginous	perturbable	uninucleate	forewarning	moneymaking	calefactory
flatulently	picturebook	unsoundness	fourwheeler	moneymarket	camaraderie
formularise	picturecard	untouchable	handwriting	moneyspider	cantharides
formulation	picturegoer	unusualness	handwritten	ninnyhammer	cantharidic
fortunately	picturesque	vascularise	handwrought	nittygritty	caravanning
fulguration	postulation	vascularity	hardworking	noseyparker	caravansary
garrulously	preaudience	vasculiform	heroworship	oxyhydrogen	caricatural
gemmulation	prejudgment	venturesome	highwrought	pachydermal	carriageway
globularity	prejudicial	venturously	Micawberish	pennyweight	chainarmour
gradualness	prelusively	victualless	Micawberism	pharyngitis	charlatanry
granularity	prelusorily	victualling	overweening	platyrrhine	chartaceous
granulation	presumingly	Abbevillian	overwritten	pussyfooter	chockablock
granulocyte	presumption	alleviation	overwrought	pussywillow	chrysalides
gratulation	presumptive	alleviative	Pickwickian	readywitted	chrysalises
gratulatory	procuration	alleviatory	reedwarbler	splayfooted	chrysarobin
gutturalise	procuratory	ambivalence	ropewalking	storyteller	complacence
gutturalism	procurement	ambivalency	screwdriver	tachycardia	complacency
hallucinate	profuseness	ambiversion	selfwinding	tachygraphy	complainant
hirsuteness	promulgator	anniversary	selfworship	teenybopper	complaisant
illhumoured	protuberant	antivitamin	sidewheeler	trisyllabic	concealable
impoundment	pullulation	bedevilment	somewhither	trisyllable	concealment
imprudently	pustulation	behavioural	typewritten	vichyssoise	conflagrant
inclusively	querulously	benevolence	waspwaisted	weenybopper	conflagrate
ineluctable	rapturously	caravanning	wellwishing	bedizenment	congealable
ineluctably	recruitment	caravansary	widowerhood	breezeblock	congealment
inequitable	redoubtable	deliverable	wolfwhistle	bryozoology	contrabasso
inequitably	reeducation	deliverance	bisexuality	citizenship	contractile
infeudation	resourceful	deliveryman	desexualise	denizenship	contraction
influential	rumbustious	diluvialist	innoxiously	freezedried	contractive
inoculation	sacculation	enlivenment	nonexistent	homozygosis	contractual
inoculative	Sadduceeism	equivalence	obnoxiously	hylozoistic	contracture
insouciance	sanguinaria	equivalency	preexistent	magazinegun	contradance
intrusively	sanguineous	equivocally	subaxillary	monozygotic	contraption
Kulturkampf	savouriness	equivocator	acetylation	polyzoarium	contrariety
languidness	serrulation	forevermore	anonymously	quizzically	contrarious
laurustinus	sertularian	foreverness	asphyxiator	schizanthus	contrastive
lectureship	singularise	immoveables	bandylegged	————————	cordialness
linguistics	singularity	inadvertent	bathymetric	abracadabra	coronagraph
malfunction	speculation	inadvisable	bathyscaphe	abstraction	crustaceous
manducation	speculative	individuate	bathysphere	abstractive	crystalline
manducatory	sporulation	indivisible	bradycardia	accusatival	crystallise
mantuamaker	statutebook	indivisibly	cockyleekie	admiralship	crystallite
marquessate	statutorily	innavigable	condylomata	aeronautics	crystalloid
marqueterie	stimulation	irreverence	dactylogram	aircraftman	dedicatedly
marquisette	stimulative	irrevocable	dactylology	allocatable	diaphaneity
masculinely	stipulation	irrevocably	daisycutter	allopathist	diffraction
masculinise	stipulatory	lixiviation	deoxygenate	ambivalence	dinosaurian
masculinity	subaudition	malevolence	deoxyribose	ambivalency	Diophantine
masquerader	subcultural	Merovingian	diphycercal	amentaceous	disgraceful
measureless	subjugation	motivepower	dissyllable	anthracitic	distraction
measurement	subjunctive	nailvarnish	dissymmetry	anticathode	distractive
mediumistic	submultiple	obliviously	dithyrambic	antiJacobin	dodecaphony
mensuration	subsumption	polevaulter	embryologic	apparatchik	efficacious
mercurially	subsumptive	recoverable	embryonated	arboraceous	elephantine
micturition	succulently	rejuvenator	emptyhanded	Areopagitic	elephantoid
misguidance	suffumigate	rejuvenesce	emptyheaded	automatable	emmenagogue
misguidedly	suppuration	reviviscent	eurhythmics	bacchanalia	endocardiac
misjudgment	suppurative	scurvygrass	geosyncline	barefacedly	endocardial
murmuration	textureless	shrivelling	gerrymander	bearbaiting	endocardium
murmurously	tolbutamide	sleeveboard	gillyflower	benefaction	enigmatical
muscularity	torturously	twelvemonth	heavyfooted	bimetallism	enthralling

```
enthralment mantuamaker protractile thereabouts detribalise shrubbiness
entreatment manufactory protraction timebargain educability sociability
epidiascope manufacture protractive transaction eligibility solvability
epigraphist margraviate psittacosis transalpine Elizabethan spellbinder
epithalamia marriagebed purchasable trivialness encumbrance steamboiler
epithalamic marshalling puritanical tumefaction enjambement stockbroker
equilateral marshalship quadraphony typecasting fallibility subumbrella
equivalence matriarchal quadratical typicalness feasibility suburbanise
equivalency membraneous Rabelaisian unashamedly flexibility suburbanite
escheatable memorabilia radicalness unbreakable frostbitten suitability
escheatment merchandise radioactive uncleanness funambulate surrebuttal
Esperantist merchantman rapscallion ungetatable funambulist surrebutter
everlasting merryandrew rarefaction uninhabited glassblower swordbearer
factualness messiahship rarefactive unorganized gnotobiosis syllabarium
Falstaffian milliampere reedwarbler unpalatable gnotobiotic syllabicity
farawayness mineraliser reestablish unspeakable gullibility tameability
farinaceous misfeasance reincarnate unspeakably heartbroken tangibility
farreaching moderations reproachful unusualness helleborine teenybopper
fasciaboard monocarpous retinacular urticaceous honeybadger tensibility
felspathoid mountaineer retinaculum urticarious hunchbacked testability
finicalness mountainous retroaction victualless hydrobromic thrombocyte
fireraising mountaintop retroactive victualling hyperbolise toothbilled
firewalking musicalness rheumaticky waspwaisted hyperboloid torchbearer
firewatcher myxomatosis rightangled Weismannism hyperborean trailblazer
flagcaptain nailvarnish ropedancing whereabouts inedibility trainbearer
flagwagging namecalling ropewalking whigmaleery instability trustbuster
flirtatious naturalness rubefacient wildcatting interbedded underbidder
forbearance Neoplatonic rubefaction winetasting inviability undoubtedly
forewarning neutraliser sandbagging wiretapping laudability variability
freemasonry nominatival saponaceous witenagemot lophobranch vendibility
gametangium nonchalance scalearmour woodcarving macrobiotic vincibility
generaliser nonfeasance schizanthus workmanlike mandibulate washability
generalship nutcrackers scholarship workmanship meprobamate wastebasket
gentianella oarsmanship scoriaceous xylocarpous Micawberish waterbottle
gimcrackery omnifarious scribacious zoographist Micawberism weenybopper
goodnatured outstanding selfmastery zooplankton miscibility weighbridge
gourmandise overbalance selfraising absorbingly moveability wheelbarrow
gourmandism overgarment semipalmate adverbially necrobiosis workability
gradualness overlapping severalfold afterburner neighbourly worldbeater
grammalogue overmanning sheetanchor alphabetise opprobrious abranchiate
grammatical overpayment shellacking amenability palpability accoucheuse
hairraising oversailing showmanship amicability passibility acinaciform
halflanding paediatrics signpainter amphibolite peccability advancement
handfasting paediatrist slotmachine amphibology perambulate affrication
handpainted Palaearctic smorgasbord approbation pilotburner affricative
hemeralopia palmcabbage solanaceous approbatory pitchblende airsickness
highfalutin papyraceous sonofabitch arglebargle pivotbridge altercation
highranking patriarchal spathaceous assemblyman placability Americanise
hyperactive pentlandite spectacular attribution portability Americanism
hypogastric pericardiac spectatress attributive possibility Americanist
increasable pericardial spermaphyte azotobacter prelibation amphictyony
incunabulum pericardium spermatozoa bashibazouk probabilism anfractuous
inescapable peripatetic spessartite bicarbonate probabilist Anglicanism
initialling persuadable spontaneity biddability probability annunciator
inseparable persuasible spontaneous blackbeetle prohibition anthocyanin
inseparably phantasiast standardise blackbirder prohibitive application
interactant phantasmata steerageway blockbuster prohibitory applicative
interaction photoactive stephanotis breadbasket protuberant applicatory
interactive pigheadedly stoicalness cannibalise rateability appreciable
interallied pilocarpine subscapular cannibalism readability appreciably
interatomic piperaceous substandard cinnabarine rebarbative appreciator
ipsilateral plagiariser substantial collaborate recumbently arenicolous
irreparable platearmour substantive columbarium redoubtable attractable
irreparably pleinairist subtraction concubinage reliability autarchical
judgmatical polevaulter subtractive concubinary remembrance beachcomber
kilocalorie polycarpous suffragette concubitant reprobation bellicosity
kinematical populariser superabound confabulate reprobative bergschrund
labefaction portmanteau tabefaction connubially reprobatory bewitchment
lesemajesty portraitist tagliatelle conurbation resemblance bifurcation
leviratical portraiture tagliatelli corroborant retribution blackcoated
lifemanship pourparlers tankfarming corroborate retributive bradycardia
literalness pragmatical tapemachine credibility retributory breadcrumbs
logicalness preprandial taratantara crookbacked reverberant broadcaster
logomachist pressagency telepathise crossbearer reverberate calcicolous
mailcarrier prognathism telepathist crossbowman saleability carbocyclic
maladaptive prognathous temerarious culpability saprobiotic carunculate
malefaction prothalamia thaumatrope decarbonate satiability catercousin
malfeasance prothallial thaumaturge decarbonise scarabaeoid chokecherry
malpractice prothallium thaumaturgy decarburise sensibility clericalism
```

clericalist
climacteric
cloudcastle
coeducation
collectable
collectanea
collectedly
collectible
collocation
compactness
conductance
conductible
conductress
conjectural
connectable
connectedly
connectible
consecrator
consecution
consecutive
convocation
coparcenary
corbiculate
cornucopian
correctable
correctness
coruscation
criticality
criticaster
cysticercus
daisycutter
debauchment
debouchment
defalcation
defenceless
deforcement
deification
demarcation
denticulate
denunciator
deprecation
deprecative
deprecatory
depreciator
depthcharge
desiccation
desiccative
dialectally
dialectical
difficultly
diphycercal
diplococcus
disaccustom
disencumber
disinclined
dislocation
dissociable
divorcement
dresscircle
duplication
duplicitous
duplicitous
earthcloset
edification
edificatory
embraceable
embracement
embracingly
embrocation
emplacement
enforceable
enforcement
enhancement
eradication
eradicative
Etruscology
explication
explicative
explicatory

exsiccation
extractable
extrication
fabrication
farcicality
fasciculate
festschrift
fieldcornet
financially
folliculate
formication
fornication
forthcoming
furunculous
Gallicanism
geotectonic
gesticulate
glasscutter
gynaecocrat
gynaecology
haemocyanin
hallucinate
handicapped
handicapper
heliochrome
hippocampus
Hippocratic
horsecollar
hydrocarbon
hydrocyanic
hypercharge
hypercritic
imbrication
impeachable
impeachment
implication
implicative
impractical
imprecation
imprecatory
imprecisely
imprecision
incarcerate
inculcation
ineluctable
ineluctably
inexactness
insincerely
insincerity
insouciance
intercalary
intercalate
intercensal
intercepter
interceptor
intercessor
interchange
intercostal
intercourse
intercrural
intractable
intractably
intricately
ipecacuanha
justiciable
latticework
lubrication
lubricative
machicolate
macrocosmic
manducation
manducatory
mastication
masticatory
matriculate
melancholia
melancholic
metrication
micrococcal

micrococcus
microcosmic
mollycoddle
monarchical
multicolour
mustachioed
myrmecology
nomenclator
obfuscation
obfuscatory
ochlocratic
offenceless
oligochaete
omniscience
orthocentre
ostracoderm
participant
participate
participial
particulate
passacaglia
pedunculate
pellucidity
Pentecostal
perfectible
perfectness
persecution
petticoated
phagocytise
phagocytose
photocopier
phycocyanin
physicality
planoconvex
plutocratic
predecessor
predicament
predication
predicative
predicatory
predictable
predictably
prefectural
preoccupied
proficiency
prolocutrix
prosecution
prosecutrix
protectress
provocateur
provocation
provocative
publication
quickchange
quiescently
radiocarbon
ratiocinate
recalculate
rediscovery
reeducation
reenactment
reflectance
reification
rejoicingly
replaceable
replacement
replication
respectable
respectably
resuscitate
retraceable
retractable
retrocedent
revaccinate
rhizocarpic
rubrication
rustication
Sadduceeism

scratchwork
seasickness
septicaemia
septicaemic
serviceable
serviceably
servicebook
serviceline
shortchange
shortcoming
somniculous
sphincteral
sphincteric
spiraculate
spirochaete
spirochaete
spirochetal
staircarpet
stalactitic
staunchless
staunchness
stenochromy
stomachache
stomachpump
stonecurlew
stonecutter
stormcentre
stretchable
sufficiency
suffocation
suffocative
sugarcoated
supercharge
surficially
syndicalism
syndicalist
syndication
syntactical
tachycardia
tentaculate
terricolous
tetracyclic
threecolour
tobacconist
torticollis
trabeculate
traducement
tragicomedy
transceiver
transcriber
tuberculate
tuberculise
tuberculose
tuberculous
uncatchable
unconcealed
unconcerned
undercharge
unguiculate
unification
uninucleate
unmatchable
unshockable
unteachable
untouchable
valleculate
vermiculate
vermiculite
verticality
vindication
vindicative
vindicatory
wainscoting
wainscotted
watercolour
watercooled
watercooler
watercourse
weltschmerz
Whitechapel

whitecollar
zootechnics
abecedarian
accordantly
accordingly
achondritic
aphrodisiac
artiodactyl
avoirdupois
biquadratic
calendrical
candidature
coccidiosis
comradeship
confederacy
confederate
confidently
confidingly
considerate
considering
crocidolite
crocodilian
cylindrical
degradation
degradingly
demandingly
deoxidation
dependently
depredation
depredatory
diffidently
dislodgment
elucidation
elucidative
elucidatory
exceedingly
expenditure
extradition
fecundation
forbiddance
frigidarium
gravedigger
groundsheet
groundwater
haberdasher
haggadistic
hazardously
horsedoctor
imprudently
incardinate
incredulity
incredulous
infeudation
interdental
interdepend
labiodental
legerdemain
leptodactyl
linendraper
liquidambar
liquidation
mastodontic
Methodistic
methodology
misjudgment
molendinary
molybdenite
orchidology
orthodontia
orthodontic
oxyhydrogen
pachydermal
palindromic
paraldehyde
peccadillos
pentadactyl
periodicity
periodontal
phagedaenic

pointdevice
preaudience
precedented
precedently
prejudgment
prejudicial
premeditate
providently
pteridology
pterodactyl
quilldriver
rearadmiral
recondition
redundantly
regardfully
retardation
retardative
retardatory
revendicate
scoundrelly
screwdriver
secondarily
secondclass
secondrater
secondsight
serendipity
sextodecimo
shoulderbag
shoulderpad
slavedriver
splendorous
spreadeagle
subaudition
subordinate
succedaneum
tarradiddle
tetradactyl
thalidomide
threadiness
threadpaper
threedecker
tragedienne
trepidation
unbendingly
viceadmiral
welladvised
witchdoctor
abiogenesis
abiogenetic
acarpellous
acaulescent
accelerando
accelerator
acquiescent
acropetally
adulterator
advisedness
aesthetical
aftereffect
aggrievedly
Albigensian
alkalescent
allAmerican
altorilievo
ambiversion
anacreontic
anencephaly
annabergite
anniversary
antecedence
antependium
antineutron
antiSemitic
apotheosise
apparelling
aquarellist
arborescent
archaeology

archaeornis	clothesline	doubleDutch	hepatectomy	ligamentous	polygenetic	
argumentive	clothesmoth	doubleedged	Hepplewhite	limitedness	polypeptide	
assuredness	clothesprop	doubleender	hexadecimal	lionhearted	polytechnic	
backbencher	cobblestone	doubleentry	hexametrist	louvreboard	preelection	
ballbearing	cockleshell	doublefaced	hobbledehoy	lowpressure	premiership	
barquentine	codefendant	doublequick	homiletical	luminescent	primaevally	
basipetally	coessential	doublespeak	homocentric	maidservant	problematic	
battledress	coextension	doublethink	homogeneity	maintenance	proceedings	
battlefield	coextensive	downhearted	homogeneous	makebelieve	procreation	
beauteously	coffeehouse	drunkenness	homogenetic	managership	procreative	
bedizenment	coffeetable	dundrearies	homogeniser	manifestant	progression	
belatedness	coinheritor	earpiercing	huckleberry	manifestoes	progressism	
bellheather	coldhearted	earthenware	hundredfold	marquessate	progressist	
bestselling	colonelship	ectogenesis	hurriedness	marqueterie	progressive	
betweenmaid	complexness	ectogenetic	hylogenesis	masquerader	prophethood	
betweenness	compression	einsteinium	hypotension	mediaevally	prophetical	
betweentime	compressive	embowelling	illbreeding	merogenesis	prophetship	
bilaterally	concrescent	embowerment	illiberally	metacentric	prospective	
biochemical	congressman	empanelling	immanentism	metagenesis	psychedelia	
biocoenoses	conquerable	endometrium	immanentist	metagenetic	psychedelic	
biocoenosis	conspecific	engineering	immoveables	middleclass	pumicestone	
biocoenotic	constellate	enlivenment	impanelling	middlesized	purpresture	
biofeedback	consternate	enucleation	impenetrate	mindbending	pyrotechnic	
bladderwort	contretemps	ephemerides	inadvertent	mindreading	quadrennial	
blessedness	cookgeneral	epithelioma	inalienable	minuteglass	quadrennium	
blunderbuss	corbiesteps	erroneously	inalienably	miscreation	quarrelling	
bodyservant	costbenefit	etherealise	inalterable	misspelling	quarrelsome	
bondservant	cotoneaster	ethereality	inalterably	monogenesis	quarterback	
bondservice	counselling	Europeanise	inappetence	monogenetic	quarterdeck	
bookkeeping	countenance	evangelical	inattention	motivepower	quartertone	
booklearned	counterblow	exaggerator	inattentive	musclebound	racemeeting	
bookselling	counterbond	exacerbate	incalescent	Neanderthal	rattlebrain	
bootlegging	counterfeit	exdirectory	incinerator	needlecraft	rattlepated	
bottleglass	counterfoil	existential	incoherence	needlepoint	rattlesnake	
bottlegreen	counterfort	exoskeletal	incoherency	needlewoman	reassertion	
bottlenosed	countermand	exoskeleton	independent	nephrectomy	recoverable	
bounteously	countermark	exponential	indigestion	nettlecloth	redetermine	
bourgeoisie	countermine	fairweather	indigestive	nonspecific	redirection	
bowdleriser	countermove	farthermost	indirection	northeaster	referential	
bracteolate	countermure	featheredge	ineffective	noticeboard	regenerable	
breezeblock	counterpane	featherhead	ineffectual	novelettish	regenerator	
bridgeboard	counterpart	featherless	inessential	obmutescent	regimentals	
brotherhood	counterplan	fiddlestick	inexpedient	obsolescent	reinsertion	
bullterrier	counterplea	filamentary	inexpensive	oecumenical	reintegrate	
bumblepuppy	counterplot	filamentous	inferential	ontogenesis	rejuvenator	
businessman	countersign	filmsetting	influential	ontogenetic	rejuvenesce	
butcherbird	countersink	flabbergast	innumerable	openhearted	relatedness	
byeelection	countersunk	flannelette	innumerably	optometrist	remunerator	
campmeeting	counterturn	flannelling	inobservant	orthoepical	reorientate	
candleberry	countervail	fluorescein	inoffensive	outbreeding	reposefully	
candlelight	counterview	fluorescent	insuperable	ovariectomy	residential	
candlepower	counterwork	foreseeable	insuperably	overbearing	resplendent	
candlestick	courteously	forevermore	interesting	overdevelop	retiredness	
centreboard	crabbedness	freehearted	intolerable	overmeasure	retrievable	
centrepiece	crackerjack	fragmentary	intolerably	oversetting	reverential	
cesarevitch	crookedness	freehearted	intolerance	overweening	righteously	
cesarewitch	cytogenesis	freezedried	intumescent	paddleboard	roundedness	
chalcedonic	decelerator	fullhearted	ironhearted	paddlewheel	rudimentary	
challenging	decerebrate	furtherance	irredentism	pantheistic	ruridecanal	
chamaephyte	deferential	furthermore	irredentist	paraleipsis	saddlecloth	
chamberlain	deleterious	furthermost	irrelevance	paramedical	saddlehorse	
chambermaid	delineation	furthersome	irrelevancy	parametrise	safekeeping	
champertous	delitescent	gamogenesis	irretention	paraselenae	scattergood	
chancellery	deliverable	gastrectomy	irretentive	partnership	scuppernong	
chancellory	deliveryman	genteelness	irreverence	pearlescent	sedimentary	
changefully	denizenship	gentlemanly	isoelectric	pedicellate	seigneurial	
channelling	denumerable	gentlewoman	journeywork	penitential	selfcentred	
chanterelle	desideratum	geochemical	juvenescent	perineurium	selfdefence	
chargesheet	devotedness	goldbeating	kindhearted	perplexedly	selfdenying	
cheesecloth	diastematic	goodhearted	kitchenette	perspective	selfdespair	
chickenfeed	disobedient	grangeriser	kitchensink	philhellene	selfdevoted	
chickenwire	discrepancy	greasepaint	kitchenware	phrasemaker	selffeeding	
chimaerical	displeasure	greaseproof	launderette	phraseogram	selffeeling	
Chippendale	distressful	guardedness	learnedness	phraseology	selffertile	
chitterling	documentary	halfhearted	leatherback	plasterwork	selfreliant	
cinquecento	domineering	halfmeasure	leatherhead	plenteously	selfreproof	
citizenship	doublecheck	handselling	leatherneck	pointedness	selfrespect	
clandestine	doublecheck	hardhearted	lieutenancy	policewoman	selfsealing	
clapperclaw	doublecross	haustellate	ligamentary	polygenesis	selfseeking	

selfservice	twelvepenny	imperforate	aggregation	haplography	roentgenise
selfserving	typesetting	indifferent	aggregative	heliography	salvageable
sexagesimal	unalterable	insufflator	analogously	hooliganism	saprogenous
shelterbelt	unappealing	interfacial	androgynous	hydrogenate	sausagemeat
shelterless	unassertive	interfacing	angiography	hydrogenous	scenography
shepherdess	unbeseeming	interfluent	apologetics	hydrography	scragginess
shoeleather	underexpose	interfusion	arraignment	hymnography	segregation
shrivelling	undeserving	justifiable	arrangement	hypsography	segregative
shutterless	undeveloped	justifiably	aspergillum	ichnography	serpiginous
sickbenefit	unessential	lactiferous	aspergillus	iconography	sporogenous
singlestick	unnecessary	lightfooted	assuagement	immarginate	sporogonium
singletrack	unquietness	liquefiable	belligerent	impingement	springboard
sleeveboard	unrelenting	magnificent	bersaglieri	impregnable	springclean
slenderness	unselective	melliferous	blackgrouse	impregnably	springhouse
slickenside	unutterable	mellifluent	bloodguilty	incongruent	springiness
smithereens	unutterably	mellifluous	cabbagepalm	incongruity	stalagmitic
snickersnee	vehmgericht	morbiferous	cabbagerose	incongruous	stenography
snowleopard	venereology	nullifidian	cabbagetree	indulgently	stoneground
softhearted	venesection	odoriferous	cabbageworm	inelegantly	straightcut
soldierlike	venisection	ozoniferous	calligraphy	ingurgitate	straightish
soldiership	vicegerency	pearlfisher	carrageenan	instigation	straightway
southeaster	viceregally	pestiferous	carrageenin	instigative	strangeness
Southernism	viridescent	pettifogger	cartography	intergrowth	strangulate
sovereignly	virilescent	photofinish	castigation	intriguante	stringboard
sovereignty	vituperator	pontificals	centigramme	laryngology	stringently
spatterdash	vivisection	pontificate	chirography	laryngotomy	stringiness
speakership	vociferance	proliferate	chorography	lentiginous	stringpiece
spelaeology	vociferator	proliferous	colligation	lithography	stringybark
splenectomy	warmhearted	prolificacy	colligative	macrogamete	strongpoint
splenetical	washleather	prolificity	compaginate	madrigalian	stylography
spongecloth	weakhearted	pussyfooter	conjugality	madrigalist	subjugation
squarebuilt	weathercock	qualifiable	conjugation	meningocele	subregional
squirearchy	weatherwise	quickfiring	conjugative	microgamete	subrogation
stiflejoint	weatherworn	quickfreeze	consignable	micrography	surrogation
stiltedness	wellbeloved	quickfrozen	consignment	microgroove	syllogistic
strategical	welldefined	rangefinder	copingstone	misbegotten	synergistic
strikebound	wellmeaning	Rastafarian	corrigendum	miscegenate	tachygraphy
studiedness	Wensleydale	rectifiable	corrugation	mythography	termagantly
stuntedness	whitherward	retroflexed	cosmogonist	negligently	terrigenous
subspecific	whitleather	roughfooted	cosmography	neologistic	tobogganing
suppression	widowerhood	sacrificial	crossgarnet	nitrogenise	tobogganist
suppressive	windlestraw	satisfiable	crucigerous	nitrogenous	triangulate
synthesiser	wirenetting	scruffiness	deflagrator	nittygritty	tritagonist
synthetical	acidifiable	septiferous	dentigerous	objurgation	tryingplane
talebearing	AngloFrench	septifragal	deoxygenate	objurgatory	uncongenial
tapemeasure	bacciferous	sheepfarmer	derangement	octingenary	underground
taxidermist	blackfellow	sheriffalty	dialogistic	orthography	undergrowth
teachership	calciferous	sheriffship	diamagnetic	osteography	undisguised
tegumentary	calcifugous	signifiable	dichogamous	Ostrogothic	unfeignedly
tenementary	cauliflower	significant	diningtable	outfighting	unforgiving
tentpegging	certifiable	somniferous	discography	pelargonium	uranography
thenceforth	certifiably	spaceflight	disorganise	pentagynous	variegation
theocentric	certificate	specifiable	dittography	petrography	vertiginous
theorematic	closefisted	specificity	divergently	phonography	vestigially
theoretical	corniferous	spiniferous	divulgation	photography	vinaigrette
thitherward	crestfallen	splayfooted	divulgement	phylogynist	vortiginous
thunderbird	cruciferous	steadfastly	dyslogistic	phytography	zincography
thunderbolt	crucifixion	superfamily	effulgently	pictography	adiaphorism
thunderclap	cupriferous	superficial	elbowgrease	pornography	amorphously
thunderhead	disaffected	superficies	engorgement	prerogative	anarchistic
thunderless	disafforest	superfluity	enlargeable	primigenial	antechamber
thunderpeal	disinfector	superfluous	enlargement	prodigalise	antiphonary
timeserving	enfeoffment	swiftfooted	ensanguined	prodigality	antiphrasis
toffeenosed	faultfinder	thuriferous	erotogenous	prolegomena	autochthony
togglejoint	ferriferous	tightfisted	ethnography	propagation	benightedly
topdressing	firstfruits	toploftical	expurgation	propagative	benightment
tracheotomy	flagofficer	transferred	expurgatory	prorogation	bicephalous
trammelling	floriferous	transferrer	farraginous	protagonist	blasphemous
transection	fortifiable	transfigure	ferruginous	pruriginous	blotchiness
triggerfish	frankfurter	transfinite	filmography	pyrargyrite	bookshelves
triquetrous	gemmiferous	transfixion	foreignness	Pythagorean	branchiopod
tritheistic	gillyflower	transformer	fustigation	Pythagorism	breathalyse
trouserless	globeflower	transfusion	geomagnetic	radiography	breechblock
trousersuit	grandfather	tuttifrutti	gettogether	realignment	bushwhacker
truehearted	gypsiferous	vitrifiable	globigerina	refrigerant	cacophonous
trusteeship	heavyfooted	aboveground	greengrocer	refrigerate	cardsharper
tumbledrier	housefather	abridgement	haemoglobin	regurgitate	catacheses
turtleshell	illaffected	adjudgement	Hagiographa	reprogramme	catachresis
twelvemonth	imperfectly	aggregately	hagiography	reprography	catechismal

catechistic	metachrosis	squashiness	antivitamin	connoisseur	erratically
catswhisker	metaphysics	stadtholder	Apollinaris	consciously	eugenically
churchgoing	monochasial	stakeholder	appogiatura	conspicuity	excoriation
churchiness	monochasium	stallholder	aquatically	conspicuous	exercisable
churchwoman	monochromat	starchiness	archaically	conspirator	exfoliation
clearheaded	monochromic	stockholder	archdiocese	constituent	exfoliative
cliffhanger	monophagous	straphanger	Arminianism	constitutor	exorbitance
closehauled	monophthong	superheater	armtwisting	containable	expatiation
crotcheteer	Monophysite	swarthiness	arterialise	containment	expatiative
crunchiness	Monothelite	swellheaded	ascetically	contributor	expatiatory
cryotherapy	muskthistle	switchblade	aseptically	contrivable	expediently
deemphasise	mycophagist	switchboard	assimilable	contrivance	expeditious
delightedly	naphthalene	sycophantic	assimilator	coordinator	experienced
delightsome	ninnyhammer	sycophantry	association	corecipient	explainable
diarthrosis	nonetheless	telephonist	associative	creationism	exploitable
dicephalous	octachordal	tetrahedral	Assyriology	creationist	exteriorise
diphtherial	oenophilist	tetrahedron	atrabilious	cryobiology	exteriority
diphtheroid	oesophageal	thickheaded	atrociously	cryptically	facelifting
diphthongal	ornithology	thoughtless	audaciously	curtailment	facetiously
draughtsman	ornithopter	threehanded	babysitting	cytokinesis	factfinding
drouthiness	ornithosaur	timesharing	beautifully	deactivator	familiarise
emptyhanded	paperhanger	titleholder	bedevilment	deficiently	familiarity
emptyheaded	parachutist	toxophilite	behavioural	definiendum	fanatically
enarthrosis	paraphraser	transhumant	bellringing	defoliation	farthingale
endophagous	parathyroid	treacherous	Benedictine	deistically	feloniously
endothelial	parishioner	trenchantly	benediction	deliciously	ferociously
endothelium	parochially	trencherman	benedictory	deliriously	fimbriation
endothermal	paunchiness	underhanded	beneficence	dendritical	firefighter
endothermic	pentahedron	unfashioned	beneficiary	denominator	flaccidness
enlightened	periphrases	unorthodoxy	beneficiate	dereliction	foraminated
enneahedron	periphrasis	unrighteous	bohemianism	desalinator	foraminifer
exanthemata	perishables	uprightness	bookbinding	describable	foresighted
faithhealer	perishingly	wealthiness	botanically	description	forfeitable
fetichistic	perithecium	whiteheaded	bountifully	descriptive	fortnightly
fetishistic	phosphonium	windcheater	brachiation	despoilment	fractionary
foreshorten	phosphorate	witchhunter	Brahminical	deteriorate	fractionate
forethinker	phosphorism	wolfwhistle	brilliantly	detrainment	fractionise
forethought	phosphorite	wrongheaded	bucolically	diacritical	fractiously
fourwheeler	phosphorous	xenophilous	bullfighter	digitigrade	frantically
freethinker	pleochroism	xerophilous	bumptiously	dilapidated	franticness
freethought	ploughshare	xylophagous	Byronically	dilapidator	fratricidal
frenchified	ploughstaff	xylophonist	calorimeter	diluvialist	functionary
Frenchwoman	podophyllin	zoantharian	calorimetry	disguisedly	functionate
frothhopper	polychromic	Abbevillian	canalicular	disquieting	geanticline
grasshopper	polyphagous	abdominally	canaliculus	disquietude	generically
grouchiness	polyphonous	abiotically	canonically	distribuend	genetically
halophilous	preachiness	ablutionary	capaciously	distributor	genitivally
healthfully	prosthetics	abortionist	capacitance	disunionist	godchildren
healthiness	pullthrough	abstriction	captainship	divisionary	golddigging
hearthstone	quitchgrass	accipitrine	carabiniere	divisionism	grandiflora
heavyhanded	raunchiness	adjudicator	carabinieri	doctrinaire	grandiosely
hebephrenia	ravishingly	adminicular	Carolingian	doctrinally	grandiosity
hebephrenic	rhynchodont	adoptianism	caustically	domiciliary	graphically
hedgehopped	ricochetted	adoptianist	cavalierism	domiciliate	graphicness
holothurian	righthanded	adoptionism	centrifugal	drastically	habiliments
homophonous	righthander	adoptionist	centripetal	dynamically	halfbinding
homothallic	saxophonist	aerobically	chanticleer	ebulliently	hardhitting
householder	scorchingly	aerobiology	chaotically	efficiently	harpsichord
hydraheaded	ScotchIrish	afficionado	chinoiserie	egregiously	Hebraically
hypophyseal	Scotchwoman	affiliation	chrominance	elastically	Hegelianism
hypophysial	searchingly	agnatically	chronically	elasticated	hereditable
hypothecate	searchlight	agrarianism	civilianise	electioneer	heresiology
hypothenuse	shareholder	agrobiology	civilisable	elutriation	heretically
hypothermia	sheathknife	albuminuria	classically	emancipator	highpitched
hypothesise	shockheaded	alembicated	codicillary	embroiderer	hilariously
icosahedral	shorthanded	algorithmic	coefficient	embroilment	histrionics
icosahedron	sidewheeler	alkalimeter	coincidence	empirically	histrionism
IndoChinese	sketchiness	alkalimetry	colonialism	emulsionise	humiliation
ingathering	slaughterer	alleviation	colonialist	enchainment	humiliatory
ithyphallic	slaveholder	alleviative	colorimeter	encomiastic	hypolimnion
leaseholder	sleuthhound	alleviatory	colorimetry	endemically	identically
lengthiness	smallholder	altorilievo	compliantly	entrainment	idiotically
levelheaded	smoothfaced	ambitiously	complicated	enunciation	idyllically
lighthanded	snatchblock	amontillado	comprisable	enunciative	ignominious
lightheaded	softshelled	angelically	conceitedly	equidistant	illimitable
Manichaeism	somewhither	AngloIndian	conceivable	equilibrate	illimitably
masochistic	spaceheater	annihilator	conceivably	equilibrist	illogically
megatherium	speechifier	anteriority	confliction	equilibrium	illuminable
meliphagous	splashboard	anticipator	conflictive	Erastianism	illuminance

```
illuminator  laconically  osmotically  resipiscent  thyroiditis  shrinkproof
illusionism  lamplighter  outbuilding  restriction  titanically  squeakiness
illusionist  languidness  overbidding  restrictive  totalisator  storekeeper
immediately  lateritious  pacifically  retaliation  tourbillion  streakiness
immedicable  laughinggas  pacificator  retaliative  trafficator  thinskinned
immitigable  Leibnitzian  painkilling  retaliatory  trafficking  unwinkingly
immitigably  lilylivered  paradisical  revisionary  trafficless  acatalectic
impatiently  linefishing  parasitical  revisionism  transiently  acetylation
impedimenta  linguistics  parasitosis  revisionist  transilient  acidulation
impenitence  litigiously  peculiarity  reviviscent  Trappistine  acriflavine
impenitency  lixiviation  pecuniarily  rifacimenti  trelliswork  Aeneolithic
imperialise  loculicidal  Pelagianism  rifacimento  triadically  Aesculapian
imperialism  logarithmic  penicillate  sagaciously  trichinosis  aiguillette
imperialist  longsighted  penicillium  salaciously  triphibious  amiableness
imperilling  lowspirited  penuriously  sanguinaria  tristichous  anacoluthon
imperilment  luxuriantly  perceivable  sanguineous  ulotrichous  animalcular
imperiously  luxuriation  perceivably  satanically  unadvisedly  anomalistic
impolitical  luxuriously  perspicuity  satirically  unambiguous  anomalously
impoliticly  magazinegun  perspicuous  scaleinsect  unavailable  anthologise
inadvisable  malariology  petitionary  sceptically  unavoidable  anthologist
incipiently  malediction  Pickwickian  scholiastic  unavoidably  apocalyptic
incuriosity  maledictory  pigsticking  scintillant  unbelieving  apostleship
incuriously  maleficence  piratically  scintillate  unchristian  appallingly
indeciduous  maliciously  plantigrade  scorpionfly  uncivilised  appealingly
indefinable  manumission  plasticiser  scrutiniser  undesirable  appellation
indefinably  manumitting  plebeianise  scyphistoma  undutifully  appellative
indehiscent  marchioness  plebeianism  seditionary  unequivocal  artillerist
individuate  marquisette  plentifully  seditiously  uninhibited  audibleness
indivisible  mastoiditis  pointillism  seigniorage  unlimitedly  audiologist
indivisibly  materialise  pointillist  seigniorial  unmitigated  autoplastic
indomitable  materialism  polarimeter  seismically  unpolitical  bacilliform
indomitably  materialist  polarimetry  selaginella  unremitting  bandylegged
indubitable  materiality  polarisable  selfdisplay  unshrinking  barrelhouse
indubitably  medicinable  polariscope  selflimited  unsolicited  barrelorgan
inebriation  medicinally  polemically  selfpitying  vacationist  batholithic
inefficient  melodiously  politically  selfwinding  vagariously  beastliness
inequitable  memorialise  politicking  semasiology  valediction  beguilement
inequitably  memorialist  practicable  semidiurnal  valedictory  beguilingly
inestimable  Merovingian  practicably  shoplifting  vaporimeter  bimillenary
inestimably  mimetically  practically  sigmoidally  vaporisable  bimillenium
inferiority  mischievous  preeminence  simpliciter  vasodilator  blamelessly
infinitival  misericorde  preexistent  sleepingbag  vaticinator  bloodlessly
ingeniously  misguidance  presciently  sleepingcar  venatically  bombilation
ingrainedly  misguidedly  prestigious  Socinianism  ventricular  brainlessly
inhabitable  mithridatic  prestissimo  solutionist  ventriculus  bricklaying
inhabitancy  mitrailleur  principally  somatically  ventriloquy  bristletail
inheritable  monolingual  proprietary  soteriology  veraciously  bristleworm
inheritance  monseigneur  prosaically  soupkitchen  veridically  bristliness
inheritress  moonlighter  prosaicness  spastically  verisimilar  brittleness
injudicious  moronically  prostitutor  spermicidal  vesuvianite  broadleaved
injuriously  mudslinging  Prussianise  spherically  vexatiously  brucellosis
innavigable  municipally  Prussianism  squalidness  vicariously  buffalorobe
innoxiously  munificence  psychiatric  stellionate  vivaciously  cabbalistic
inofficious  nearsighted  psychically  stencilling  volitionary  calculating
inscribable  nefariously  punchinello  stickinsect  voraciously  calculation
inscription  negationist  punctilious  stockinette  wellwishing  calculative
inscriptive  negotiation  purificator  Stradivarii  Westminster  cancellated
inseminator  negotiatory  pyramidally  stramineous  whimsically  candelabrum
insidiously  negotiatrix  pyramidical  subaxillary  worshipable  capableness
insipidness  nightingale  quadrillion  subclinical  worshipless  capillarity
interiorise  nomadically  questionary  subcritical  worshipping  carvelbuilt
interiority  nonexistent  quintillion  substituent  interjacent  castellated
intimidator  nonunionist  quizzically  superimpose  maladjusted  cataclysmic
invalidness  notoriously  rapaciously  superinduce  shelljacket  cataplectic
invidiously  numerically  reactionary  superintend  stockjobber  catholicise
invigilator  obliviously  reactionist  superioress  superjacent  Catholicism
irradiation  obnoxiously  reclaimable  superiority  debarkation  catholicity
irradiative  occipitally  recruitment  suppliantly  demarkation  ceaselessly
irreligious  officialdom  relationism  surveillant  dislikeable  cellularity
irremissive  officialese  relationist  sustainable  embarkation  ceroplastic
Jacobinical  officialism  religionise  sustainment  endoskelton  chainletter
Jacobitical  officiation  religionism  sybaritical  greenkeeper  chameleonic
jauntingcar  officinally  religionist  technically  housekeeper  cheerleader
judiciously  officiously  religiosity  telekinesis  imparkation  cheerlessly
juridically  oilpainting  religiously  telekinetic  provokingly  chevalglass
kinesiology  opencircuit  reminiscent  tenaciously  reawakening  chucklehead
kwashiorkor  ophidiarium  repetitious  tetanically  sandskipper  circularise
laboriously  organically  repudiation  thermically  semiskilled  circularity
lacination   organisable  resiliently  thermionics  shrinkingly  circulation
```

circulative	exemplarity	legislative	pestologist	spindlelegs	vacuolation
circulatory	faithlessly	legislature	petrologist	spindletree	vascularise
cisatlantic	faultlessly	limitlessly	phenologist	spinelessly	vascularity
cityslicker	feudalistic	limnologist	philologian	sporulation	vasculiform
cleanlimbed	flagellator	loathliness	philologist	stagflation	ventilation
cleanliness	flatulently	longplaying	phonologist	stainlessly	ventilative
coagulation	fleshliness	looselimbed	phycologist	startlingly	verbalistic
cockaleekie	flimflammer	lovableness	phytologist	stateliness	vexillology
cockyleekie	florilegium	magdalenian	pipecleaner	steeplebush	visibleness
coldblooded	footslogger	mammalogist	pliableness	steeplejack	voicelessly
compellable	foreclosure	mandolinist	pluralistic	stickleback	volkslieder
compilation	formalistic	mantelpiece	pointlessly	stimulation	volubleness
compilement	formularise	mantelshelf	polyglottal	stimulative	warmblooded
conciliator	formulation	masculinely	polyglottic	stipulation	waterlogged
condolatory	fourflusher	masculinise	postclassic	stipulatory	wearilessly
condylomata	franklinite	masculinity	postglacial	stumblingly	whiffletree
congelation	friableness	matchlessly	postulation	subcultural	whippletree
consolation	frivolously	matrilineal	powerlessly	submultiple	whistlestop
consolatory	fruitlessly	matrilinear	prattlingly	succulently	womanliness
consolidate	fullblooded	maxillipede	preselector	superlative	worldliness
consolingly	fullfledged	mendelevium	prevalently	superlunary	worldlywise
consultancy	fusillation	mercilessly	prickliness	swimbladder	worthlessly
convolution	gallbladder	meroblastic	promulgator	swingletree	Yugoslavian
convolvulus	garrulously	mesalliance	proselytise	symbolistic	abnormality
coralloidal	gemmologist	mesoblastic	proselytism	tantalising	academicals
corpulently	gemmulation	metalloidal	pullulation	tastelessly	academician
correlation	genealogise	metallurgic	pupillarity	tautologise	academicism
correlative	genealogist	metaplastic	pureblooded	tautologism	acclamation
cosmologist	gentilitial	methylamine	pustulation	tautologous	acclamatory
countlessly	genuflexion	methylation	pyroclastic	teleologist	acclimation
courtliness	geopolitics	microlithic	queenliness	teleologist	acclimatise
credulously	ghastliness	mindblowing	querulously	tenableness	accommodate
crenellated	ghostliness	mirthlessly	radiolarian	tessellated	achromatise
crenulation	globularity	misalliance	radiologist	thanklessly	achromatism
crosslegged	gonfalonier	miscellanea	rectilineal	thimbleweed	adenomatous
cupellation	gracelessly	miserliness	rectilinear	thistledown	affirmation
curableness	gracileness	moneylender	reduplicate	threelegged	affirmative
curvilineal	granolithic	monoclinous	repellantly	thrillingly	affirmatory
curvilinear	granularity	movableness	repellently	tightlipped	agglomerate
dactylogram	granulation	multilinear	rhinologist	timepleaser	amphimictic
dactylology	granulocyte	muscularity	ritualistic	titillation	anemometric
dauntlessly	gratulation	musculation	roughlegged	tonsillitis	anglomaniac
decollation	gratulatory	musculature	sacculation	tracelessly	anonymously
decolletage	gravelblind	mutableness	saintliness	translation	apartmental
diadelphous	gristliness	mythologise	salesladies	translocate	Archimedean
disablement	grumblingly	mythologist	schoolboard	translucent	astigmatism
disbeliever	guilelessly	narcoleptic	schoolchild	translunary	audiometric
discalceate	guiltlessly	necrologist	schoolhouse	treacliness	awesomeness
disillusion	hagiologist	nephelinite	scopolamine	tremblement	bathymetric
disobliging	halfblooded	nervelessly	scuttlebutt	tremblingly	beechmarten
dissolutely	heartlessly	neurologist	selfclosing	tremulously	bergamasque
dissolution	Heracleidan	nickelplate	selfelected	trestletree	blackmailer
dissolvable	histologist	noctilucent	semiellipse	trestlework	blackmarket
dissyllable	holoblastic	noiselessly	senselessly	tribulation	broadminded
doubtlessly	homoplastic	nondelivery	serrulation	tricoloured	burgomaster
draggletail	houselights	nonvolatile	sertularian	trisyllabic	chaulmoogra
dreamlessly	hydrologist	notableness	shacklebolt	trisyllable	childminder
durableness	hypoblastic	ophiologist	shacklebone	troublesome	choirmaster
earthliness	hypoglossal	oracularity	shamelessly	troublously	circumlunar
ectoblastic	ignobleness	orderliness	shapeliness	truculently	circumpolar
ectoplasmic	inoculation	oscillation	shiftlessly	trundletail	circumsolar
ejaculation	inoculative	oscillatory	shovelboard	tunableness	circumspect
ejaculatory	inquilinous	oscillogram	shuttlecock	turbulently	circumvolve
elderliness	installment	osteologist	sideslipped	unexploited	clinometric
embellisher	instillment	pamphleteer	sightlessly	unfailingly	collimation
endoplasmic	intagliated	panhellenic	sightliness	unfeelingly	commemorate
ennoblement	intelligent	pantalettes	singularise	ungodliness	concomitant
entablature	interleaves	parallactic	singularity	unhealthily	condemnable
entablement	interlinear	parallelism	sizableness	unicellular	condominium
entitlement	Interlingua	parallelled	sleeplessly	unicoloured	consumerism
equableness	interlining	paraplectic	smilelessly	unipolarity	consumingly
esemplastic	interlocker	parheliacal	socialistic	unmanliness	consummator
establisher	interlunary	patelliform	sociologist	unqualified	consumption
ethnologist	inviolately	pathologist	solifluxion	unrealistic	consumptive
etymologise	itacolumite	patrilineal	somnolently	unskilfully	contaminant
etymologist	knucklebone	pendulously	soundlessly	unsmilingly	contaminate
euchologion	lamellicorn	perchlorate	speculation	unwholesome	contemplate
excellently	lamelliform	percolation	speculative	unwillingly	coterminous
exemplarily	legislation	pestilently	spifflicate	vacillation	coulometric

coxcombical	informality	scaremonger	assignation	continuator	fricandeaux
customarily	information	schismatise	astringency	convenances	fulminating
custombuilt	informative	scoutmaster	augmentable	convenience	fulmination
customhouse	informatory	screamingly	Aurignacian	conveniency	fulminatory
declamation	intermeddle	selfimposed	bathingsuit	conventicle	gallantness
declamatory	intermedium	sentimental	benignantly	convincible	genuineness
deformation	intermingle	Septembrist	bombination	coplanarity	geosyncline
determinacy	intermitted	sheepmaster	bonbonniere	cosignatory	Germanophil
determinant	intromitted	sillimanite	bookinghall	cottongrass	germination
determinate	intromitter	slavemarket	boutonniere	cottonmouth	germinative
determinism	irksomeness	smallminded	boysenberry	credentials	glaringness
determinist	jerrymander	soberminded	brazenfaced	criminalist	glutinously
detrimental	lacrimation	sociometric	calcination	criminality	goldenberry
diplomatise	lacrimatory	somnambular	calumniator	crimination	gormandiser
diplomatist	lacrimosely	sphygmogram	campanology	criminative	grandnephew
dipsomaniac	lacrymation	spirometric	campanulate	criminatory	greatnephew
disarmament	lacrymatory	squeamishly	carbonation	criminology	handknitted
disarmingly	lacrymosely	stagemanage	carbuncular	culmination	harmonistic
disremember	largeminded	stockmarket	carcinomata	cunningness	heavenwards
disseminate	lightminded	stonemarten	cardinalate	cupronickel	heldentenor
disseminule	lissomeness	subdominant	carminative	currentness	Hellenistic
dissimilate	Maglemosian	sublimation	cavernously	cybernation	helminthoid
dissimulate	marshmallow	sublimeness	centenarian	cybernetics	hemianopsia
dissymmetry	matchmaking	subsumption	chafingdish	decennially	hereinafter
distempered	mathematics	subsumptive	Clarencieux	declination	hermeneutic
dressmaking	matrimonial	suffumigate	coadunation	demagnetise	herringbone
drillmaster	mediumistic	supermarket	cochinchina	demountable	herringgull
econometric	merrymaking	supremacist	collenchyma	descendable	hibernacula
emblematise	micrometric	supremeness	collinearly	descendible	hibernation
emblematist	misremember	systematics	columniated	designation	Hibernicism
epochmaking	moneymaking	systematise	combination	despondence	Hispanicise
erotomaniac	moneymarket	systematist	combinative	despondency	Hispanicism
eudaemonism	myelomatous	tautomerism	combinatory	destination	Hispanicist
eudaemonist	mythomaniac	testimonial	commandment	diamondback	hollandaise
eudiometric	necromancer	tetramerous	commendable	disannulled	hummingbird
euphemistic	necromantic	threemaster	commendably	disbandment	husbandlike
exclamation	nightmarish	toastmaster	commendator	discontinue	hyacinthine
exclamatory	noisemaking	toughminded	commensally	disfunction	hyphenation
excremental	noisomeness	transmarine	commentator	dishonestly	illmannered
exterminate	numismatics	transmittal	commination	dishonourer	imaginarily
extremeness	numismatist	transmitted	comminatory	disjunction	imagination
facsimilist	nutrimental	transmitter	comminution	disjunctive	imaginative
firmamental	oldwomanish	ultramarine	commonality	disjuncture	impoundment
fulsomeness	oligomerous	ultramodern	commonplace	dispensable	incarnadine
fundamental	pandemonium	unanimously	commonsense	dissentient	incarnation
gallimaufry	panicmonger	unclimbable	communalise	dissonantly	inclination
gardemanger	pantomimist	uncommitted	communalism	distensible	incognisant
gerrymander	papermaking	undermanned	communalist	distinction	indignantly
glassmaking	patrimonial	unpromising	communicant	distinctive	indignation
goniometric	peacemaking	voltametric	communicate	distinguish	infrangible
grandmother	pentamerous	watchmaking	communistic	doorknocker	instinctive
gravimetric	pessimistic	welcomeness	compendious	drawingroom	instinctual
heliometric	photometric	whoremaster	compensator	dreadnought	internalise
heptamerous	planimetric	whoremonger	compunction	dysfunction	internality
honeymooner	Precambrian	winsomeness	concentrate	ecumenicism	internecine
housemaster	predominant	wreckmaster	condensable	ecumenicity	internuncio
housemother	predominate	abomination	condonation	elementally	Jansenistic
hydromedusa	preliminary	abstentious	confinement	elimination	jargonistic
hydrometeor	prenominate	abstinently	congenerous	eliminative	jumpingbean
hydrometric	presumingly	accountable	congenially	enchantment	jumpingjack
hygrometric	presumption	accountably	conjunction	enchantress	knowingness
hypermarket	presumptive	accountancy	conjunctiva	enfranchise	lancinating
hypermetric	protomartyr	acumination	conjunctive	equiangular	lancination
hypsometric	proximately	acupuncture	conjuncture	evagination	landingbeam
illhumoured	radiometric	affranchise	consanguine	eveningstar	landinggear
illtempered	reachmedown	alcyonarian	consentient	evidentiary	larcenously
impermanent	reanimation	Alexandrian	consonantal	examination	lastingness
impermeable	reclamation	alexandrine	consonantly	exogenously	legionnaire
impermeably	recommender	alexandrite	contentedly	explanation	lichenology
implemental	recommittal	alternately	contentious	explanatory	longanimity
inanimately	recriminate	alternation	contentment	externalise	machination
inanimation	reformation	alternative	continental	externalism	machinemade
inclemently	reformative	amaranthine	continently	externality	maddeningly
incommodity	reformatory	amazonstone	contingence	fascinating	magnanimity
incremental	rhizomatous	ancientness	contingency	fascination	magnanimous
incriminate	rightminded	AngloNorman	continuable	feelingness	maisonnette
infirmarian	sacramental	appointment	continually	fermentable	malfunction
inflammable	saltimbanco	archangelic	continuance	festinately	malignantly
inflammably	sarcomatous			fortunately	marconigram

```
marginalise  preventable  terminative  auxanometer  emotionless  ironmongery
marginality  preventible  terminology  axiological  emperorship  irremovable
marlinspike  proconsular  Teutonicism  backcountry  endomorphic  irremovably
meaningless  profanation  Titianesque  bellbottoms  enterostomy  irresoluble
mechanician  profanatory  trepanation  bellfounder  enterovirus  irrevocable
mechanistic  profaneness  tribuneship  benevolence  entomophily  irrevocably
mercenarily  progenitrix  tribunicial  bibliolater  envelopment  isogeotherm
Micronesian  progeniture  tribunitial  bibliolatry  environment  kinetograph
millenarian  prominently  triennially  bibliomancy  epeirogenic  kinetoscope
misconceive  propinquity  trypanosome  bibliomania  episcopally  kleptomania
misconstrue  prosenchyma  turbination  bibliopegic  equinoctial  knownothing
mockingbird  protonotary  tyrannicide  bibliophile  equipollent  landholding
modernistic  provenience  tyrannosaur  bibliophily  equivocally  landlordism
mooringmast  rallentando  tyrannously  bibliopolic  equivocator  lepidoptera
morningroom  rationalise  unbeknownst  bibliotheca  ergatocracy  loudmouthed
multangular  rationalism  unboundedly  billionaire  ethological  maintopmast
multinomial  rationalist  uncanniness  billposting  factionally  maintopsail
mundaneness  rationality  unconnected  blastogenic  fashionable  malevolence
muttonchops  recognition  uncountable  bryozoology  fashionably  medicolegal
nationalise  recognitive  unflinching  calceolaria  fissionable  megalomania
nationalism  recognitory  unfurnished  californium  flamboyance  megalopolis
nationalist  reconnoitre  unigeniture  captionless  flamboyancy  melanochroi
nationality  rectangular  unkennelled  cardiograph  flamboyante  melanophore
nationstate  refrangible  unmeaningly  categorical  fluoroscope  mentholated
nonsensical  refringency  unprintable  ceremonious  fluoroscopy  mentionable
nothingness  regionalise  unsoundness  chaetognath  footpoundal  meritocracy
notionalist  regionalism  unthinkable  chansonnier  footsoldier  meritorious
obstinately  regionalist  unthinkably  cheiromancy  foretopmast  mesomorphic
offhandedly  replenisher  unvarnished  chiaroscuro  foretopsail  metamorphic
oppugnation  repugnantly  vaccination  chlorophyll  foulmouthed  metasomatic
originality  resignation  valiantness  chloroplast  fourpounder  metoposcopy
origination  respondence  verdantique  chloroprene  Francomania  millionaire
originative  respondency  vermination  choreograph  Francophile  monitorship
overanxious  responsible  verminously  chromoplast  Francophobe  monological
overindulge  responsibly  violoncello  chromosomal  francophone  monologuise
oxygenation  retranslate  volcanicity  chronograph  freebooting  monologuist
packingcase  rhizanthous  volcanology  chronologer  fullmouthed  monomorphic
paternalism  ribbongrass  vulcanicity  chronologic  gafftopsail  monopoliser
paternalist  rottenstone  vulcanology  chronometer  gametophyte  mycological
paternoster  salmonberry  waitinglist  chronometry  gastronomic  naturopathy
patronising  salpingitis  waitingroom  chronoscope  gastroscope  Neotropical
pectination  saturnalian  wappenschaw  chrysoberyl  glauconitic  nomological
pentandrous  saturninely  warrantable  chrysoprase  glossolalia  nonviolence
perennation  segmentally  warrantably  clodhopping  goodlooking  nosological
perennially  selfinduced  willingness  complotting  gradiometer  nympholepsy
perfunctory  selfinvited  winningness  comstockery  GraecoRoman  nymphomania
permanently  sententious  winningpost  controlling  greenockite  octagonally
personalise  sentinelled  abandonment  controlment  gyrocompass  oecological
personalism  septenarius  abiological  controversy  halfholiday  oenological
personalist  septentrion  acrimonious  coronagraph  hardmouthed  oestrogenic
personality  shamanistic  actinometer  craniometry  hardworking  ommatophore
personation  sickeningly  actinomyces  cryptogamic  headborough  omnipotence
personative  sinfonietta  actinomycin  cryptograph  hemimorphic  oncological
personifier  sittingroom  aerological  cryptomeria  heroworship  oneiromancy
pertinacity  skatingrink  aeronomical  cytological  heteroclite  ontological
pertinently  Slavonicise  agrological  decolourise  heteroecism  openmouthed
phalanstery  smokingroom  agronomical  demagogical  heterograft  opinionated
pharyngitis  sparingness  ailurophile  demagoguery  heterophony  orangoutang
philanderer  sphagnology  ailurophobe  demagoguism  heteroploid  oreological
pigeonchest  steganogram  algological  demigoddess  heteropolar  outcropping
platinotype  stevengraph  allegorical  demonolatry  heterospory  outspokenly
playingcard  stiffnecked  allelomorph  developable  heterotaxis  overtopping
poisonously  stipendiary  allomorphic  development  heterotroph  palaeotypic
pollination  studentship  ameliorator  diagnostics  heterotypic  Panglossian
polyandrous  subcontract  anagnorisis  diaphoresis  highpowered  paradoxical
polyonymous  subcontrary  anastomoses  diaphoretic  Hindoostani  paramoecium
precentress  subjunctive  anastomosis  dichromatic  homoeopathy  paramorphic
preconceive  subornation  anastomotic  dropforging  homoiousian  paramountcy
precontract  suckingfish  anecdotical  dualcontrol  homological  paramountly
preignition  supernatant  anthropical  dumbfounder  homomorphic  paronomasia
premonition  supernormal  antifouling  dynamometer  horological  Passiontide
premonitory  suspenseful  antimonious  dynamometry  hylozoistic  pedagogical
presanctify  suspensible  antonomasia  echosounder  hymenoptera  pedological
presentable  tabernacled  aposiopesis  ectomorphic  ideological  penological
presentably  tautonymous  apostolical  elastomeric  idiomorphic  pensionable
presentient  teknonymous  aristocracy  embryologic  immunologic  pensionless
presentment  tendencious  arthrospore  embryonated  inopportune  peritonitis
pretendedly  tendentious  assafoetida  emotionally  interosseus  photooffset
pretentious  termination                            invigorator  phylloclade
```

phyllotaxis	snowgoggles	unimportant	gramophonic	precipitant	banteringly
physiocracy	soapboiling	unmemorable	grandparent	precipitate	barbarously
physiognomy	sockdolager	unmemorably	granophyric	precipitous	beaverboard
physiologic	sockdologen	urochordate	guttapercha	primiparous	biedermeier
plagioclase	soliloquise	vagabondage	haemophilia	procephalic	birdbrained
plagiostome	soliloquist	vagabondise	haemophilic	protophytic	bitterapple
plasmolysis	somatogenic	vagabondish	haemoptysis	radiophonic	bittercress
plasmolytic	somatologic	vagabondism	hedgepriest	Russophobia	bittersweet
platforming	somatoplasm	viceroyalty	hemispheric	saintpaulia	boilermaker
plectoptera	somatotonia	viceroyship	hippopotami	saprophytic	bombardment
pleomorphic	somatotonic	virological	homeopathic	sarcophagus	borborygmus
pleurodynia	sparrowbill	volumometer	homosporous	sauropodous	botheration
pluviometer	sparrowhawk	voodooistic	horripilate	scrappiness	butterflies
pneumonitis	spasmodical	wellfounded	hydropathic	scrimpiness	butteriness
poltroonery	speedometer	wellrounded	hydrophilic	scrumptious	cacographic
polygonally	spherometer	wildfowling	hydrophobia	selfopinion	calibration
polymorphic	sponsorship	xanthochroi	hydrophobic	Shaksperean	carburetion
polyzoarium	stampoffice	xanthophyll	hydrophytic	Shaksperian	carburetted
pomological	standoffish	zygomorphic	hydroponics	sharepusher	carburetter
portionless	staurolitic	absorptance	hygrophytic	sociopathic	carburettor
posological	steatopygia	accompanist	hyperphagia	songsparrow	catadromous
praetorship	stereograph	acidophilic	hyperplasia	sporophytic	celebration
proctorship	stereometry	agoraphilia	hypnopaedia	standpatter	celebratory
proteolysis	stereophony	agoraphobic	hypnopompic	stoolpigeon	cerebration
proteolytic	stereoscope	anadiplosis	hypsophobia	stylopodium	chaperonage
prothoracic	stereoscopy	anglophobia	impropriate	susceptible	cicatricial
pseudograph	stereotyped	anglophobic	impropriety	susceptibly	clamorously
pseudomonas	stereotyper	appropriate	inadaptable	syncopation	clostridium
pseudomorph	stereotypic	archipelago	incompetent	tetrapodous	coeternally
pseudopodia	stethoscope	atmospheric	incompliant	therapeutic	coleorrhiza
psychodrama	stethoscopy	attemptable	incorporate	toothpowder	colouration
psychogenic	stichometry	bicorporate	incorporeal	townspeople	colourblind
psychograph	stratocracy	bicuspidate	inculpation	transpadane	colourfully
psychologic	stroboscope	caryopsides	inculpatory	transparent	comfortable
psychometry	subtropical	catchphrase	intemperate	transpierce	comfortably
psychomotor	surfboarder	caterpillar	interplayed	transponder	comfortless
psychopathy	surgeonfish	chiropodist	interpolate	transporter	comparatist
ratatouille	swallowable	chiropteran	interpreter	trothplight	comparative
realpolitik	swallowdive	collapsible	intrepidity	underpinned	compartment
reapportion	swallowhole	comeuppance	ionospheric	unflappable	comportment
renegotiate	swallowtail	conceptacle	lickspittle	unhappiness	comptroller
retinoscopy	swallowwort	corruptible	lithophytic	unhelpfully	compurgator
rhabdomancy	symphonious	corruptibly	loudspeaker	unstoppable	concernment
rhapsodical	symptomatic	corruptness	madreporite	consequence	concertedly
rheological	synagogical	cosmopolite	microphonic	delinquency	concertgoer
rhombohedra	tacheometer	cotemporary	microphytic	ineloquence	concordance
rhomboideus	taxonomical	ctenophoran	multiparous	infrequence	concurrence
roadholding	teaspoonful	cyclopaedia	mythopoeist	infrequency	conferrable
rodomontade	technocracy	cyclopaedic	mythopoetic	nonsequitur	confirmable
safeconduct	technologic	cypripedium	necrophilia	subsequence	conformable
salinometer	tephromancy	decrepitate	necrophilic	terraqueous	conformably
scaffolding	teratogenic	decrepitude	necropoleis	abhorrently	conformally
scissorbill	teratologic	depauperate	negrophilic	acquirement	conformance
scissortail	theodolitic	depauperise	neuropathic	adjournment	conjuration
scleroderma	theological	diapophysis	nightporter	adumbration	conservable
sclerometer	theosophist	disapproval	noseyparker	adumbrative	conservancy
sclerophyll	thermoduric	disciplinal	nulliparity	aerographer	conservator
sclerotitis	thermograph	discipliner	nulliparous	amenorrhoea	constrictor
sectionally	thermolysis	dissepiment	nuncupation	anachronism	construable
seismograph	thermolytic	dissipation	nuncupative	anachronous	constructor
seismometer	thermometer	dissipative	nyctophobia	antheridium	conterminal
seismometry	thermometry	enterpriser	orthopaedic	antigravity	contorniate
seismoscope	thermophile	epinephrine	orthopedics	antirrhinum	convergence
selfcocking	thermoscope	exculpation	orthopedist	apomorphine	conversable
selfcommand	thermotaxis	exculpatory	orthopteran	apostrophic	conversably
selfconceit	thrasonical	expropriate	osteopathic	arbitrageur	conversance
selfcontent	topological	exstipulate	osteophytic	arbitrament	conversancy
selfcontrol	toxicomania	extemporary	osteoplasty	arbitrarily	convertible
selfloading	treasonable	extemporise	paedophilia	arbitration	convertibly
selflocking	treasonably	extirpation	perceptible	arbitrative	cooperation
selftorture	trichomonad	extirpatory	perceptibly	arbitratrix	cooperative
selfworship	troglodytic	extrapolate	percipience	austereness	copperplate
semeiotical	trophoblast	feldspathic	perispermic	autoerotism	coppersmith
semimonthly	tryptophane	fissiparity	photoperiod	autographic	cornerstone
senatorship	typefounder	fissiparous	photophilic	autotrophic	corporality
serological	typefoundry	frankpledge	photophobia	awestricken	corporately
sexological	typological	Gallophobia	photophobic	awkwardness	corporation
shallowness	unaccounted	gemmiparous	plenipotent	bactericide	corporatism
sinological	uncanonical	giantpowder	preceptress	balmcricket	corporative

corporeally	erythrocyte	IndoIranian	motherright	preparative	subservient
countrified	esotericism	innutrition	multiracial	preparatory	subterminal
countryfied	Eucharistic	inoperative	murderously	preservable	summariness
countryseat	evaporation	inquiringly	murmuration	prestressed	summerhouse
countryside	evaporative	inspiration	murmurously	preterhuman	summersault
countrywide	exoneration	inspiratory	mycorrhizae	preterition	supportable
cursoriness	exonerative	integrality	mycorrhizal	prevaricate	supportably
dangerously	exotericism	integration	myocarditis	prochronism	suppuration
deathrattle	exploration	integrative	namedropper	procuration	suppurative
declaration	explorative	interracial	nasofrontal	procuratory	suspiration
declarative	exploratory	interregnum	neckerchief	procurement	susurration
declaratory	exuberantly	interrelate	netherworld	proofreader	synchromesh
defibrinate	falteringly	interrogate	nocturnally	proportions	synchronise
defloration	fanfaronade	interrupter	nomographer	prostration	synchronism
dehydration	favouritism	interruptor	nomographic	Proterozoic	synchronous
democratise	featureless	isochronism	nonpartisan	pulchritude	synchrotron
democratism	filterpaper	isochronous	nosographer	pulverulent	syssarcosis
demographer	fingerboard	isomorphism	nosographic	purportedly	teeterboard
demographic	fingerglass	isomorphous	nurserymaid	quaternloaf	telegrammic
denigration	fingerplate	itinerantly	obscuration	rancorously	telegrapher
denigratory	fingerprint	itineration	obscureness	rapturously	telegraphic
deoxyribose	fingerstall	jabberwocky	obsecration	reappraisal	teleprinter
deploringly	firecracker	Kulturkampf	omnipresent	reciprocate	temperament
desecration	floweriness	kymographic	oreographic	reciprocity	temperately
desegregate	forlornness	lammergeier	outstripped	recurrently	temperative
desperadoes	forwardness	lammergeyer	outwardness	reemergence	temperature
desperately	fraternally	landgrabber	overcropped	reintroduce	temporality
desperation	fraterniser	landgravine	overproduce	reiteration	temporarily
deuteration	frontrunner	lawmerchant	overwritten	reiterative	tenterhooks
deuterogamy	frowardness	leapfrogged	overwrought	requirement	tetrarchate
Deuteronomy	frustration	lecherously	oysterplant	resourceful	textureless
dexterously	fulguration	lectureship	paederastic	respiration	theatregoer
diachronism	gartersnake	letterpress	palsgravine	respiratory	theatricals
diastrophic	gatecrasher	lickerishly	papiermache	restoration	theobromine
differentia	gendarmerie	linedrawing	paragrapher	restorative	topographer
differently	geostrophic	lineprinter	paragraphic	retrorocket	topographic
dinnerdance	gibberellin	lingeringly	paratrooper	rheotropism	tortuously
dinnertable	gingerbread	litterateur	parturition	rhetorician	totteringly
dinnerwagon	glomeration	loggerheads	passeriform	rockcrystal	traversable
dipterocarp	godforsaken	logographer	pastoralism	Rosicrucian	treecreeper
discardable	guttersnipe	logographic	pastoralist	rotogravure	trimorphism
discernible	gutturalise	louverboard	pastureland	rubberstamp	trimorphous
discernibly	gutturalism	loxodromics	patternshop	safebreaker	trituration
discernment	haemorrhage	lucubration	pawnbroking	safecracker	typewritten
discerption	haemorrhoid	ludicrously	penetrating	Sanskritist	typographer
discordance	haggardness	Lutheranism	penetration	sartorially	typographic
discordancy	hairbreadth	mackerelsky	penetrative	savouriness	unawareness
disharmonic	hairdresser	maladroitly	peregrinate	scalariform	unexpressed
disparaging	hairtrigger	malapropism	perforation	scalpriform	unguardedly
disparately	halterbreak	mandarinate	perforative	schwarmerei	uniformness
dispersedly	handbreadth	manneristic	performable	seborrhoeic	unipersonal
disportment	handgrenade	mansardroof	performance	selfcreated	universally
dissertator	handwriting	martyrology	pericranial	semitrailer	unobtrusive
disturbance	handwritten	massproduce	pericranium	sensorially	unsparingly
dithyrambic	handwrought	masterfully	perturbable	serigrapher	unwarranted
downdraught	harebrained	masterpiece	pervertedly	shipbreaker	vasopressin
downtrodden	heptarchist	measureless	phthiriasis	showerproof	vasopressor
doxographer	hesperidium	measurement	pictorially	sightreader	venturesome
easternmost	hierarchism	melioration	picturebook	silveriness	venturously
ectotrophic	highbrowism	meliorative	picturecard	silverplate	vespertinal
editorially	highwrought	menservants	picturegoer	silverpoint	vinedresser
elaborately	historiated	mensuration	picturesque	silversmith	voortrekker
elaboration	historicise	mercurially	platereuse	silverstick	wapperjawed
elaborative	historicism	meteoritics	platyrrhine	simperingly	washerwoman
electrician	historicist	meteoroidal	playerpiano	sincereness	waywardness
electricity	historicity	meteorology	poltergeist	spectrality	wellgroomed
electrocute	hitherwards	micturition	polycrystal	spectrogram	wellordered
electrolier	holographic	miscarriage	polygraphic	spectrology	westernmost
electrology	horseradish	mismarriage	pomegranate	sphaeridium	widdershins
electrolyse	Hudibrastic	molecricket	ponderation	starcrossed	winegrowing
electrolyte	ideographic	monogrammed	ponderosity	steamroller	winterberry
electronics	idiographic	monographer	ponderously	stepbrother	wintergreen
electrotype	immigration	monographic	porterhouse	stewardship	wisecracker
enchiridion	impetration	monstrosity	positronium	subaxially	witheringly
endearingly	impetratory	monstrously	posteriorly	subarration	withershins
endotrophic	imploringly	mortarboard	potteringly	subcortical	wonderfully
enquiringly	incoercible	mosstrooper	powderflask	submarginal	xylographer
enumeration	incorrectly	mothercraft	prayerwheel	submergence	xylographic
enumerative	incorruptly	mothernaked	preparation	submersible	zoomorphism

abolishable	craftswoman	heartsblood	minnesinger	reddishness	ultrasonics
abolishment	crepuscular	heartstring	moneyspider	refreshment	unceasingly
aboutsledge	crossstitch	hedgeschool	morrisdance	remonstrant	unconscious
accessorial	currishness	hellishness	multistorey	remonstrate	uncrushable
accessorise	cycloserine	hoggishness	necessarian	remorseless	underseller
accrescence	decrescendo	homeostasis	necessarily	renaissance	undersigned
acquisition	decussately	homeostatic	necessitate	representer	understated
acquisitive	decussation	homoestatic	necessitous	repressible	unpossessed
adolescence	defensively	honeysuckle	nigrescence	repressibly	unreasoning
adversative	demonstrate	hurryscurry	nondescript	repulsively	Upanishadic
adverseness	depressible	hurryskurry	nonresident	requisition	upholsterer
AfroAsiatic	desensitise	hydrosphere	nourishment	reversional	uselessness
agonisingly	diapositive	hydrostatic	obsessional	reversioner	utilisation
agonistical	diatessaron	hygroscopic	obsessively	rhinoscopic	varnishtree
aimlessness	diffuseness	hypersthene	obtrusively	roguishness	verboseness
airlessness	diffusively	iconostases	offensively	rumbustious	vichyssoise
alabastrine	dimensional	iconostasis	opalescence	saplessness	vicissitude
amphisbaena	disassemble	idolisation	operoseness	satinstitch	vitrescence
appeasement	disassembly	illdisposed	orchestrate	selfassured	voguishness
artlessness	discussable	immenseness	organscreen	selfishness	waggishness
ascensional	discussible	impassioned	orthoscopic	sequestrate	waspishness
aspersorium	disgustedly	impassively	ostensively	sexlessness	waterskiing
assassinate	disposition	impassivity	outdistance	shirtsleeve	wearisomely
assessorial	dispositive	impersonate	oviposition	shortspoken	wedgeshaped
atheistical	distasteful	impressible	ozonisation	sickishness	wheresoever
atomisation	doggishness	impressment	ozonosphere	sightscreen	whichsoever
BaltoSlavic	dollishness	impuissance	patristical	sightseeing	whitishness
baptismally	doltishness	impulsively	peevishness	sinlessness	wholesomely
barbastelle	donnishness	incessantly	peninsulate	slavishness	wholesouled
bathyscaphe	earnestness	inclusively	peptisation	smithsonite	whosesoever
bathysphere	egotistical	inconscient	periostitis	smokescreen	witlessness
bearishness	ellipsoidal	inconsonant	permissible	solipsistic	worrisomely
bewhiskered	encapsulate	inconstancy	permissibly	solmisation	Zoroastrian
bloodstream	encrustment	indorsement	persistence	sophistical	absenteeism
bloodsucker	endlessness	inexistence	persistency	sottishness	accentually
boardschool	endorsement	inquisition	pervasively	spacesaving	acceptation
Bodhisattva	engrossment	inquisitive	pettishness	spokeswoman	acceptingly
bookishness	entrustment	insensately	pharisaical	sportswoman	acculturate
boorishness	epigastrium	insensitive	phariseeism	squarsonage	acoustician
brainsickly	erubescence	insessorial	philosopher	stagestruck	acquittance
Britishness	evanescence	intenseness	philosophic	statesmanly	adjectively
brutishness	evanishment	intensifier	photosphere	statistical	adventuress
bullishness	excessively	intensional	phytosterol	stegosaurus	adventurism
caddishness	exclusively	intensively	pietistical	sternsheets	adventurist
candescence	exclusivity	interseptal	piggishness	stylisation	adventurous
caressingly	excrescence	intersexual	pinkishness	stylishness	advertently
casuistical	excrescency	intersperse	plainspoken	subbasement	advertising
chainsmoker	excursively	interspinal	planisphere	submissible	aeolotropic
chainstitch	exhaustible	intrusively	preciseness	subsistence	aerostatics
charismatic	exhaustless	iridescence	prehistoric	suggestible	aerostation
cholesterol	expansional	joylessness	prelusively	sunlessness	affectation
clairschach	expansively	Judaisation	prelusorily	superscribe	affectingly
cleanshaven	expansivity	knavishness	preposition	superscript	affectional
coalescence	expensively	lactescence	prepositive	supersedeas	affectioned
coconscious	explosively	laicisation	previsional	supersedure	affectively
coexistence	expressible	Lancastrian	professedly	superstrata	affectivity
cognoscente	exquisitely	latchstring	profuseness	supersubtle	agglutinate
cognoscenti	extensional	laurustinus	progestogen	supposition	agnosticism
cognoscible	extensively	lawlessness	promiscuity	suppositive	allantoides
collisional	faddishness	leprosarium	promiscuous	suppository	altostratus
collusively	fantastical	lightsomely	promisingly	surbasement	amphetamine
combustible	florescence	liquescence	proposition	surpassable	anaesthesia
commiserate	foolishness	lithosphere	provisional	sweepstakes	anaesthetic
commissural	foppishness	loathsomely	provisorily	swinishness	anisotropic
compassable	furnishings	loosestrife	provostship	symposiarch	antistrophe
compositely	garnishment	loutishness	prudishness	syndesmosis	appurtenant
composition	gegenschein	lumpishness	publishable	tarnishable	aromaticity
compositive	girlishness	macroscopic	publishment	tempestuous	arrestingly
compossible	godlessness	malposition	purposeless	terrestrial	assentation
conciseness	grotesquely	mannishness	purposively	thanksgiver	assertively
confessedly	grotesquery	marcescence	putrescence	toothsomely	assortative
confiscable	gutlessness	marcescible	putrescible	torchsinger	athleticism
confiscator	gymnospermy	mawkishness	quacksalver	tracasserie	attentively
confusingly	haemostasis	mediastinal	quicksilver	transsexual	attestation
consistence	haemostatic	mediastinum	raffishness	trendsetter	attritional
consistency	hagioscopic	metapsychic	realisation	tricksiness	Augustinian
contestable	haplessness	microscopic	recessional	trimestrial	balletomane
corpuscular	harumscarum	microsecond	recessively	troposphere	barbiturate
corrosively	harvesthome	millisecond	reconstruct	turgescence	barnstormer

basketchair	destitution	gasfittings	investigate	parenthesis	restatement
bassethound	desultorily	geometrical	investiture	parenthetic	restitution
befittingly	detestation	gerontology	invultation	partitioned	retentively
bicentenary	devastation	gestatorial	irruptively	partitioner	retentivity
billetsdoux	dexiotropic	gigantesque	isometrical	partitively	rickettsial
billsticker	diametrical	gradational	jactitation	pedestalled	ringstraked
biometrical	dichotomise	gravitation	kickstarter	pentathlete	rodenticide
bipartition	dichotomist	gravitative	lamentation	penultimate	romanticise
brainteaser	dichotomous	guesstimate	leavetaking	peristalith	romanticism
breadthways	dictatorial	gurgitation	libertarian	peristalsis	romanticist
breadthwise	didacticism	haematocele	liberticide	peristaltic	Sabbatarian
breastplate	digestively	haematocrit	libertinage	peristomial	Sagittarius
breastwheel	dimwittedly	haematology	libertinism	permutation	saltatorial
bulletproof	directional	hairstyling	lithotomise	perpetrator	salvational
Byzantinism	directivity	hairstylist	lithotomist	perpetually	schistosity
Byzantinist	directorate	Hamiltonian	lithotripsy	perpetuance	schistosome
calisthenic	directorial	haughtiness	lucratively	perpetuator	schottische
calyptrogen	directrices	heliotropic	lycanthrope	philatelist	scientistic
carpetsnake	discotheque	hemipterous	lycanthropy	phonetician	scientology
cassiterite	disentangle	hermeticism	magisterial	phototactic	scriptorial
catastrophe	disenthrall	herpetology	magisterium	phototropic	scriptorium
catheterise	disinterest	highstepper	magistratic	phytotomist	secretarial
causatively	disinterred	hirsuteness	marketplace	pinnatisect	secretariat
celestially	disputation	homesteader	marketvalue	pipistrelle	secretively
cementation	diverticula	homestretch	McCarthyism	piscatorial	sedentarily
chemotactic	divestiture	homopterous	mediateness	plaintively	seductively
chieftaincy	domesticate	hospitalise	mediatorial	planetarium	selectively
Christendom	domesticity	hospitality	mediatrices	planetoidal	selectivity
christening	doughtiness	hospitaller	metastasise	pleiotropic	selfstarter
christiania	dramaturgic	hydrotactic	miniaturise	Pleistocene	selfsterile
Christianly	eclecticism	hydrothorax	miniaturist	plicateness	semanticist
Christmassy	educational	hydrotropic	ministerial	pocketknife	sempiternal
Christology	effectively	hypertrophy	misanthrope	pocketmoney	sensational
cleistogamy	effectually	hypostatise	misanthropy	pocketsized	sensitively
climatology	egalitarian	illustrator	misestimate	polystyrene	sensitivity
coarctation	elicitation	illustrious	molestation	potentially	seventeenth
cognateness	ellipticity	imitatively	momentarily	predatorily	seventyfold
cognitional	Emmenthaler	immortalise	momentously	prefatorial	shocktroops
cognitively	encystation	immortality	monasterial	prefatorily	shopsteward
cognitivity	entertainer	impartation	monasticism	prematurely	showstopper
combatively	epipetalous	impartially	monopterous	prematurity	sidestepped
comestibles	eschatology	impertinent	narratively	priestcraft	sinistrally
committable	essentially	importantly	naughtiness	primateship	sinistrorse
commutation	eurhythmics	importation	neuroticism	primatology	situational
commutative	eurypteroid	importunate	neurotropic	primitively	skeletonise
competently	evolutional	importunely	nictitation	primitivism	slightingly
competition	exceptional	importunity	nonmatching	privateness	Soroptimist
competitive	executioner	incantation	nonmetallic	privatively	spendthrift
compotation	executorial	incantatory	nutritional	probational	spinsterish
compotatory	executrices	incertitude	nutritively	probationer	spiritistic
computation	executrixes	incontinent	nyctitropic	profiterole	spiritlevel
computerise	exhortation	indentation	objectively	proletarian	spiritually
concatenate	exhortative	inductively	objectivism	proletariat	spiritualty
conditional	exhortatory	industrious	objectivist	promotional	spirituelle
conditioner	expectantly	infanticide	objectivity	promptitude	squintingly
condottiere	expectation	infantilism	obstetrical	propitiable	starstudded
condottieri	expectative	infantryman	obtestation	propitiator	statutebook
confutation	expectorant	infertility	occultation	purgatorial	statutorily
confutative	expectorate	infestation	olfactology	quaestorial	stenotypist
connotation	exportation	infiltrator	operational	qualitative	stocktaking
connotative	expostulate	ingratitude	operatively	racketpress	stomatology
cosmetician	extortioner	insectarium	opportunely	recantation	stormtroops
cosmetology	eyecatching	insecticide	opportunism	receptacula	storyteller
crematorium	facultative	insectifuge	opportunist	receptively	straitlaced
crepitation	fenestrated	insectivore	opportunity	receptivity	streetlight
cyclothymia	fidgetiness	insectology	orientalise	redactional	subcategory
cyclothymic	flauntingly	insistently	orientalism	registrable	sublittoral
decantation	flightiness	institution	orientalist	regretfully	summational
deceitfully	fomentation	insultingly	orientation	regrettable	supertanker
deceptively	forestaller	intentional	orthotropic	regrettably	symmetrical
decorticate	forestation	intentioned	ostentation	reluctantly	sympathetic
deductively	forgetfully	intertangle	overstepped	reluctation	sympathiser
deerstalker	forgetmenot	intertribal	overstretch	repartition	sympetalous
defectively	forgettable	intuitional	overstuffed	repentantly	tabletennis
deglutition	formational	intuitively	painstaking	repleteness	talentscout
degustation	franctireur	intuitivism	Palestinian	reportorial	talkatively
delectation	frightfully	invectively	palpitation	resentfully	tearstained
deportation	frowstiness	inventively	pantothenic	resistively	teetotalism
dermatology	gangsterism	inventorial	parentheses	resistivity	teetotaller

```
tentatively binocularly infatuation rubicundity cursiveness ghostwriter
termitarium bisexuality ingenuously ruinousness deceivingly heavyweight
territorial bodybuilder innocuously sansculotte decemvirate hornswoggle
testatrices brankursine insalubrity sculduddery declivitous housewifely
thanatology brusqueness inscrutable sculduggery depravation housewifery
theretofore bureaucracy inscrutably selfculture depravement lakedweller
thirstiness callousness insinuation selfsupport deprivation lightweight
thixotropic carefulness insinuative sericulture deservingly meadowgrass
thriftiness charcuterie instruction seriousness dishevelled meadowsweet
throatiness coinsurance instructive shipbuilder elusiveness metalworker
throatlatch congruently involucrate showjumping enslavement minesweeper
thwartships congruously involuntary sinuousness evasiveness nightwalker
tolbutamide copiousness irrecusable skilfulness extravagant northwester
touchtyping cornhusking irrecusably skulduddery extravagate otherwhiles
traditional cryosurgery irreducible skulduggery extravasate paperweight
tributarily curiousness irreducibly snowbunting extraverted pennyweight
Trinitarian defraudment irrefutable songfulness extroverted pieceworker
tripetalous depopulator irrefutably soulfulness forgiveness pillowfight
uncertainly desexualise irregularly spherulitic frugivorous prizewinner
uncertainty destruction jealousness spondulicks furtiveness pussywillow
uncluttered destructive landaulette sternutator granivorous quickwitted
uncontested devaluation latifundium stirrupbone herbivorous readywitted
uncouthness deviousness latitudinal stirruppump illfavoured rightwinger
undertaking discourtesy lustfulness strenuosity imperviable shadowgraph
undertenant disgruntled manipulable strenuously improvement shadowiness
undisturbed distrustful manipulator stridulator improvident sharpwitted
unemotional dolefulness mindfulness succourless incurvation shortwinded
unfaltering douroucouli mistrustful sulphureous incurvature sightworthy
unfortunate dropcurtain moisturiser sulphurwort innervation sleepwalker
unweetingly dualpurpose molecularly sumptuosity intervallic sorrowfully
unwittingly dubiousness monoculture sumptuously interviewee southwester
utilitarian dutifulness mononuclear taciturnity interviewer steelworker
valuational emasculator moribundity tearfulness intravenous stonewaller
variational emulousness needfulness tediousness introverted thankworthy
vasectomise enviousness nervousness tenuousness involvement therewithal
velvetiness eventualise nonplussing thingumabob massiveness thickwitted
versatilely eventuality noxiousness thingumajig medievalism trackwalker
versatility extenuation obliqueness thoroughpin medievalist trustworthy
vibratility extenuatory obstruction thoroughwax multivalent underweight
vibrational fatefulness obstructive transuranic noctivagant underwriter
voluntarily fatiguingly obviousness tufthunting noctivagous wheelwright
voluntarism fatuousness odorousness tunefulness observantly wherewithal
voluntarist fearfulness ominousness unendurable observation whitewasher
wedgetailed FinnoUgrian onerousness unendurably observatory yellowbelly
weightiness flavourless operculated unnaturally observingly amplexicaul
whitethroat flavoursome orbicularly unsaturated outrivalled antioxidant
xeranthemum flocculence overrunning vacuousness passivation approximate
yacketyyack fluctuation painfulness variousness passiveness asphyxiator
accumulator forequarter pasteuriser vesicularly pensiveness inflexional
agriculture forerunning pediculosis viciousness pentavalent postexilian
altitudinal fraudulence piteousness viniculture perseverate reflexively
altocumulus fretfulness pitifulness viscountess piscivorous reflexology
ambiguously fructuation playfulness viscousness repleviable suffixation
amorousness gainfulness pleasurable viticulture reprovingly unisexually
antemundane gaseousness pleasurably wakefulness reservation aerodynamic
antenuptial geniculated pococurante Whitsuntide restiveness amethystine
antiquarian gibbousness pomiculture wirepulling selfevident anaphylaxis
antiquation goddaughter pompousness wishfulness suasiveness anticyclone
anxiousness habituation postnuptial wistfulness subdivision antipyretic
aponeuroses harbourless precautious woodcutting supervision antitypical
aponeurosis harmfulness procrustean zealousness supervisory apophyllite
aponeurotic hatefulness protrudable zestfulness tetravalent ascomycetes
applaudable headhunting protrusible abbreviator tittivation barleybroth
aquaculture heedfulness punctuality abusiveness transversal biophysical
aquiculture heinousness punctuation acclivitous triumirate brachyurous
archduchess helpfulness pushfulness achievement ultraviolet conveyancer
archdukedom hideousness quadrupedal aestivation undervaluer dicotyledon
arduousness hopefulness quincuncial aggravation unnervingly dismayingly
articulable hugeousness quinquennia amativeness varsovienne eucalyptole
articulated hurtfulness quinquereme approvingly acknowledge galleyslave
articulator illiquidity raucousness audiovisual blameworthy geophysical
assiduously impecunious reassurance bereavement breadwinner homozygosis
attenuation impetuosity reedbunting bloodvessel cavedweller hyoscyamine
attitudinal impetuously reinsurance captivation duniewassal hypocycloid
auricularly implausible restfulness carnivorous faithworthy hypotyposis
balefulness implausibly restructure clairvoyant fieldworker ichthyology
bashfulness inaugurator revaluation convivially floorwalker ichthyornis
Belorussian inexcusable ribvaulting costiveness gallowsbird ichthyosaur
biliousness inexcusably riotousness cultivation gallowstree lachrymator
```

```
metonymical antiquarian celebratory corporative devaluation exclamation
monkeybread antiquation cellularity correlation devastation exclamatory
monkeyshine appellation cementation correlative dicephalous excoriation
monozygotic appellative centenarian corrugation dichogamous exculpation
myxomycetes application cerebration coruscation diluvialist exculpatory
panegyrical applicative ceroplastic cosignatory diplomatise exemplarily
paratyphoid applicatory chemotactic cotoneaster diplomatist exemplarity
porphyritic appogiatura chieftaincy crenulation dipsomaniac exfoliation
presbyteral approbation choirmaster crepitation disarmament exfoliative
prophylaxis approbatory cinnabarine crestfallen disentangle exhortation
safetyvalve arbitrageur circularise criminalist dislocation exhortative
scurvygrass arbitrament circularity criminality disorganise exhortatory
spondylitis arbitrarily circulation crimination disparaging exoneration
synonymical arbitration circulative criminative disparately exonerative
tiddlywinks arbitrative circulatory criminatory displeasure expatiation
triphyllous arbitratrix cisatlantic criticality disputation expatiative
vestryclerk arglebargle civilianise criticaster dissipation expatiatory
Wesleyanism Arminianism clericalism crookbacked dissipative expectantly
haphazardly arterialise clericalist crossgarnet dissonantly expectation
pentazocine artiodactyl cliffhanger culmination dithyrambic expectative
Spinozistic assentation closehauled cultivation divulgation explanation
trapeziform assignation cloudcastle cupellation downdraught explanatory
trapezoidal association coadunation customarily downhearted explication
─────────── associative coagulation cybernation doxographer explicative
abecedarian assortative coarctation cyclopaedia dressmaking explicatory
abnormality astigmatism coeducation cyclopaedic drillmaster exploration
abomination atomisation coldhearted deathrattle dundrearies explorative
acceptation attenuation colligation debarkation duniewassal exploratory
acclamation attestation colligative decantation duplication exportation
acclamatory Aurignacian collimation declamation duplicative expurgation
acclimation autographic collocation declamatory ectoblastic expurgatory
acclimatise autoplastic colonialism declaration ectoplasmic exsiccation
accompanist azotobacter colonialist declarative edification extenuation
accordantly ballbearing colouration declaratory edificatory extenuatory
acetylation bashibazouk columbarium declination egalitarian externalise
achromatise beechmarten combination decollation ejaculation externalism
achromatism bellheather combinative decussately ejaculatory externality
acidulation benignantly combinatory decussation elaborately extirpation
acriflavine bergamasque commination deemphasise elaboration extirpatory
acumination bicephalous comminatory deerstalker elaborative extravagant
adenomatous bifurcation commonality defalcation elicitation extravagate
adoptianism birdbrained communalise defloration elimination extravasate
adoptianist bisexuality communalism defoliation eliminative extrication
adumbration bitterapple communalist deformation elucidation exuberantly
adumbrative blackmailer commutation degradation elucidative fabrication
adversative blackmarket commutative degustation elucidatory facultative
aerographer Bodhisattva comparatist dehydration elutriation fairweather
aerostatics bohemianism comparative deification embarkation familiarise
aerostation bombilation compilation delectation emblematise familiarity
Aesculapian bombination compliantly delineation emblematist farcicality
aestivation booklearned compotation demarcation embrocation fascinating
affectation botheration compotatory demarkation emptyhanded fascination
affiliation brachiation computation democratise encomiastic fecundation
affirmation bradycardia condolatory democratism encystation feldspathic
affirmative breadbasket condonation demographer endophagous festinately
affirmatory breathalyse confutation demographic endoplasmic fimbriation
affrication bricklaying confutative denigration entablature firecracker
affricative brilliantly congelation denigratory entertainer fissiparity
aggravation broadcaster conjugality deoxidation enucleation fissiparous
aggregately burgomaster conjugation deportation enumeration flimflammer
aggregation bushwhacker conjugative depravation enumerative floorwalker
aggregative cacographic conjuration deprecation enunciation fluctuation
agrarianism calcination connotation deprecative enunciative fomentation
alcyonarian calculating connotative deprecatory epipetalous forequarter
alleviation calculation consolation depredation epochmaking forestaller
alleviative calculative consolatory depredatory eradication forestation
alleviatory calibration consonantal deprivation eradicative formication
altercation candelabrum consonantly desecration Erastianism formularise
alternately candidature conurbation desexualise erotomaniac formulation
alternation cannibalise convenances desiccation esemplastic fornication
alternative cannibalism conveyancer desiccative etherealise fortunately
Americanise capillarity convocation designation ethereality freehearted
Americanism captivation cooperation desperadoes Europeanise frigidarium
Americanism carbonation cooperative desperately evagination fructuation
amphetamine cardinalate coplanarity desperation evaporation frustration
Anglicanism cardsharper corporality destination evaporative fulguration
anglomaniac carminative corporately detestation eventualise fullhearted
antechamber castigation corporation detribalise eventuality fulminating
antigravity celebration corporatism deuteration examination fulmination
```

fulminatory	immortalise	jerrymander	miscreation	orientalise	predication
fusillation	immortality	Judaisation	molestation	orientalism	predicative
fustigation	immoveables	kickstarter	momentarily	orientalist	predicatory
gallbladder	imparkation	kindhearted	moneymaking	orientation	prelibation
Gallicanism	impartation	kymographic	moneymarket	originality	preparation
gallimaufry	imperialise	laciniation	monochasial	origination	preparative
gardemanger	imperialism	lacrimation	monochasium	originative	preparatory
gatecrasher	imperialist	lacrimatory	monogrammed	orthopaedic	prerogative
gemmiparous	impermanent	lacrymation	monographer	oscillation	primiparous
gemmulation	impetration	lacrymatory	monographic	oscillatory	procreation
germination	impetratory	laicisation	monophagous	ostentation	procreative
germinative	implication	lamentation	multiparous	osteopathic	procuration
gerrymander	implicative	lancinating	multiracial	outrivalled	procuratory
glassmaking	importantly	lancination	multivalent	overbearing	prodigalise
globularity	importation	landgrabber	murmuration	overmeasure	prodigality
glomeration	imprecation	landgravine	muscularity	oxygenation	profanation
goldbeating	imprecatory	leavetaking	musculation	ozonisation	profanatory
goodhearted	inanimately	legislation	musculature	paederastic	proletarian
grandfather	inanimation	legislative	mycophagist	painstaking	proletariat
grandparent	incantation	legislature	myelomatous	palpitation	propagation
granularity	incantatory	leprosarium	mythomaniac	palsgravine	propagative
granulation	incarnadine	leptodactyl	naphthalene	paperhanger	prorogation
gratulation	incarnation	libertarian	nationalise	papermaking	prostration
gratulatory	incessantly	lighthanded	nationalism	paragrapher	protomartyr
gravitation	inclination	linedrawing	nationalist	paragraphic	provocateur
gravitative	inculcation	lionhearted	nationality	parallactic	provocation
gurgitation	inculpation	liquidambar	necessarian	passacaglia	provocative
gutturalise	inculpatory	liquidation	necessarily	passivation	proximately
gutturalism	incurvation	litterateur	necromancer	pastoralism	Prussianise
haberdasher	incurvature	lixiviation	necromantic	pastoralist	Prussianism
habituation	indentation	logographer	negotiation	paternalism	psychiatric
halfhearted	indignantly	logographic	negotiatory	paternalist	pterodactyl
halfmeasure	indignation	longplaying	negotiatrix	peacemaking	publication
handicapped	IndoIranian	lubrication	neuropathic	pectination	pullulation
handicapper	inebriation	lubricative	nictitation	peculiarity	punctuality
haphazardly	inelegantly	lucubration	nightmarish	pecuniarily	punctuation
hardhearted	infatuation	Lutheranism	nightwalker	pedestalled	pupillarity
harebrained	infestation	luxuriantly	ninnyhammer	Pelagianism	pustulation
heavyhanded	infeudation	luxuriation	noctivagant	penetrating	pyroclastic
Hegelianism	infirmarian	machination	noctivagous	penetration	quacksalver
hereinafter	informality	macrogamete	noisemaking	penetrative	qualitative
hibernacula	information	madrigalian	nomographer	pentadactyl	radiocarbon
hibernation	informative	madrigalist	nomographic	pentavalent	radiolarian
hippocampus	informatory	malignantly	nonmetallic	peptisation	Rastafarian
holoblastic	innervation	manducation	nonvolatile	percolation	rationalise
holographic	inoculation	manducatory	northeaster	perennation	rationalism
homeopathic	inoculative	Manichaeism	noseparker	perforation	rationalist
homoplastic	inoperative	marginalise	nosographer	perforative	rationality
homothallic	insectarium	marginality	nosographic	pericranial	realisation
honeybadger	insensately	marshmallow	notionalist	pericranium	reanimation
hooliganism	insinuation	mastication	nulliparity	perishables	reappraisal
horseradish	insinuative	masticatory	nulliparous	peristalith	rebarbative
hospitalise	inspiration	matchmaking	numismatics	peristalsis	recantation
hospitality	inspiratory	materialise	numismatist	peristaltic	receptacula
hospitaller	instigation	materialism	nuncupation	permutation	reclamation
housefather	instigative	materialist	nuncupative	personalise	redundantly
housemaster	integrality	materiality	obfuscation	personalism	reeducation
Hudibrastic	integration	mathematics	obfuscatory	personalist	reformation
humiliation	integrative	medievalism	objurgation	personality	reformative
humiliatory	intercalary	medievalist	objurgatory	personation	reformatory
hunchbacked	intercalate	melioration	obscuration	personative	regionalise
hydrocarbon	interfacial	meliorative	obsecration	pertinacity	regionalism
hydropathic	interfacing	meliphagous	observantly	phagedaenic	regionalist
hydrotactic	interjacent	memorialise	observation	pharisaical	reification
hyoscyamine	internalise	memorialist	observatory	phototactic	reiteration
hypermarket	internality	mensuration	obstinately	physicality	reiterative
hyphenation	interracial	meprobamate	obtestation	planetarium	reluctantly
hypnopaedia	intertangle	mercenarily	occultation	plebeianise	reluctation
hypoblastic	intervallic	meroblastic	oesophageal	plebeianism	repellantly
hypostatise	intricately	merrymaking	officialdom	pollination	repentantly
ideographic	inviolately	mesoblastic	officialese	polygraphic	replication
idiographic	invultation	metaplastic	officialism	polyphagous	reprobation
idolisation	ironhearted	metastasise	officiation	polyzoarium	reprobative
imaginarily	irradiation	methylamine	oldwomanish	pomegranate	reprobatory
imagination	irradiative	methylation	openhearted	ponderation	repudiation
imaginative	ithyphallic	metrication	ophidiarium	postclassic	repugnantly
imbrication	itinerantly	microgamete	oppugnation	postglacial	reservation
immediately	itineration	millenarian	oracularity	postulation	resignation
immigration	jactitation	mindreading	oreographic	predicament	respiration

respiratory stocktaking transpadane custombuilt aquatically deistically
restoration stonemarten transparent decerebrate arboraceous dereliction
restorative stonewaller trenchantly describable archaically destruction
retaliation straphanger trepanation distribuend archduchess destructive
retaliative stylisation trepidation distributor aristocracy diffraction
retaliatory subarration tribulation disturbance ascetically discalceate
retardation subjugation tributarily equilibrate ascomycetes disfunction
retardative sublimation Trinitarian equilibrist aseptically disgraceful
retardatory subornation tripetalous equilibrium barefacedly disjunction
revaluation subrogation trituration fasciaboard basketchair disjunctive
rhizocarpic suburbanise truehearted fingerboard bathyscaphe disjuncture
rhizomatous suburbanite turbination gingerbread Benedictine distinction
righthanded succedaneum typographer goldenberry benediction distinctive
righthander suffixation typographic gravelblind benedictory distraction
rotogravure suffocation ultramarine halterbreak benefaction distractive
rubrication suffocative unappealing heartsblood beneficence doublecheck
rustication superfamily uncertainly huckleberry beneficiary doublecross
Sabbatarian superjacent uncertainty incunabulum beneficiate douroucouli
sacculation superlative underhanded insalubrity bittercress drastically
safecracker supermarket undermanned inscribable bivouacking dynamically
Sagittarius supernatant undertaking louverboard boardschool dysfunction
saintpaulia supertanker undervaluer louverboard botanically efficacious
salesladies suppliantly unification memorabilia bucolically elastically
sarcomatous suppuration unipolarity monkeybread bureaucracy elasticated
saturnalian suppurative unwarranted mortarboard butyraceous empirically
scarabaeoid supremacist utilisation musclebound byeelection endemically
schismatise surfboarder utilitarian noticeboard Byronically enfranchise
scholiastic surrogation vaccination paddleboard calefacient equinoctial
scopolamine suspiration vacillation palmcabbage calefactory equivocally
scoutmaster susurration vacuolation perturbable canalicular equivocator
secondarily swimbladder variegation Precambrian canaliculus ergatocracy
secretarial sycophantic vascularise rattlebrain candescence erratically
secretariat sycophantry vascularity reestablish canonically erubescence
sedentarily syllabarium ventilation salmonberry carbuncular eugenically
segregation sympetalous ventilative saltimbanco caustically evanescence
segregative syncopation vermination schoolboard chanticleer excrescence
selfloading syndicalism verticality Septembrist chaotically excrescency
selfsealing syndicalist vesuvianite shovelboard chartaceous exdirectory
selfstarter syndication vindication sleeveboard cheesecloth eyecatching
semitrailer systematics vindicative snatchblock chronically fanatically
septenarius systematise vindicatory somnambular cinquecento farinaceous
septicaemia systematism voluntarily sonofabitch clairschach farreaching
septicaemic systematist voluntarism splashboard Clarencieux florescence
serigrapher tabernacled voluntarist springboard classically frantically
serrulation tachycardia warmhearted squarebuilt coalescence franticness
sertularian talebearing washleather strikebound cochinchina fratricidal
sheepfarmer tapemeasure wastebasket stringboard coconscious gastrectomy
sheepmaster tearstained watchmaking superabound coefficient geanticline
shelljacket teetotalism weakhearted switchblade cognoscente gegenschein
shoeleather teetotaller wedgetailed switchboard cognoscenti generically
shorthanded telegrammic wellmeaning teeterboard cognoscible genetically
sillimanite telegrapher Wesleyanism thereabouts collenchyma geosyncline
singularise telegraphic wheelbarrow triphibious complacence gimcrackery
singularity temperament whitewasher trophoblast complacency graphically
slavemarket temperately whitleather unclimbable complicated graphicness
sleepwalker temperative whoremaster uninhabited compunction greenockite
Socinianism temperature wisecracker uninhibited comstockery hagioscopic
sociopathic temporality wreckmaster whereabouts confiscable harpsichord
softhearted temporarily xylographer winterberry confiscator harumscarum
solmisation termagantly xylographic yellowbelly confliction Hebraically
songsparrow termination xylophagous abiotically conflictive hedgeschool
southeaster terminative Yugoslavian abstraction conjunction hepatectomy
spacesaving termitarium zoantharian abstractive conjunctiva heptandrist
spectrality tetradactyl amphisbaena abstriction conjunctive heretically
speculation tetravalent barleybroth accrescence conjuncture heteroclite
speculative threehanded beaverboard acupuncture conspecific hexadecimal
sporulation threemaster boysenberry adjudicator conspicuity hierarchism
squirearchy timesharing breechblock adminicular conspicuous hurryscurry
stagemanage titillation breezeblock adolescence contractile hygroscopic
stagflation tittivation bridgeboard aerobically contraction hyperactive
staircarpet toastmaster candleberry affranchise contractive hypocycloid
standpatter tobogganing carvelbuilt agnatically contractual identically
steadfastly tobogganist centreboard alembicated contracture idiotically
stegosaurus tolbutamide chockablock amentaceous convincible idyllically
stimulation topographer chrysoberyl angelically corpuscular illogically
stimulative topographic colourblind animalcular crepuscular immedicable
stipulation trackwalker contrabasso anthracitic crustaceous incoercible
stipulatory translation contributor anticyclone cryptically inconscient
stockmarket transmarine coxcombical antiJacobin decrescendo indirection

ineffective	physiocracy	stratocracy	despondence	stewardship	carburetion
ineffectual	Pickwickian	subjunctive	despondency	stiltedness	carburetted
inefficient	pigeonchest	subspecific	devotedness	stipendiary	carburetter
injudicious	pigsticking	subtraction	diamondback	studiedness	carburettor
inofficious	piperaceous	subtractive	dilapidated	stuntedness	carrageenan
instinctive	piratically	superscribe	dilapidator	carrageenan	carrageenin
instinctual	plagioclase	superscript	dinnerdance	thermoduric	cassiterite
instruction	plasticiser	syssarcosis	disbandment	thyroiditis	cataplectic
instructive	polemically	tabefaction	discardable	troglodytic	catheterise
interactant	politically	tapemachine	discordance	tumbledrier	cavalierism
interaction	politicking	technically	discordancy	unavoidable	cavedweller
interactive	polytechnic	technocracy	disobedient	unavoidably	ceaselessly
involucrate	practicable	tendencious	doubleDutch	unboundedly	chainletter
iridescence	practicably	tetanically	embroiderer	unguardedly	chameleonic
irreducible	practically	tetrarchate	flaccidness	wellordered	cheerleader
irreducibly	preconceive	thermically	forbiddance	waywardness	cheerlessly
irrevocable	preelection	titanically	forwardness	abhorrently	Christendom
irrevocably	presanctify	trafficator	freezedried	abridgement	christening
isoelectric	priestcraft	trafficking	fricandeaux	absenteeism	chucklehead
juridically	promiscuity	trafficless	frowardness	abstinently	clearheaded
labefaction	promiscuous	transaction	gormandiser	abusiveness	clinometric
laconically	prosaically	transection	guardedness	acatalectic	cockaleekie
lactescence	prosaicness	triadically	haggardness	achievement	cockyleekie
lawmerchant	prosenchyma	tristichous	hobbledehoy	acquirement	cognateness
liquescence	prospective	tumefaction	hollandaise	adjudgement	collinearly
loculicidal	protractile	turgescence	hundredfold	advancement	commiserate
logomachist	protraction	ulotrichous	hurriedness	adverseness	competently
macroscopic	protractive	unconscious	husbandlike	advertently	compilement
malediction	psittacosis	unflinching	impoundment	agglomerate	computerise
maledictory	psychically	unselective	indeciduous	alphabetise	comradeship
malefaction	purificator	unsolicited	individuate	amativeness	concatenate
maleficence	putrescence	urticaceous	inexpedient	amiableness	conciseness
malfunction	putrescible	valediction	insipidness	anemometric	confederacy
malpractice	pyrotechnic	valedictory	intimidator	apartmental	confederate
manufactory	quizzically	venatically	invalidness	apologetics	confidently
manufacture	radioactive	venesection	languidness	apostleship	confinement
marcescence	rarefaction	venisection	latitudinal	appeasement	congenerous
marcescible	rarefactive	ventricular	learnedness	appurtenant	congruently
melanochroi	redirection	ventriculus	limitedness	Archimedean	considerate
meritocracy	reproachful	veridically	mansardroof	archipelago	considering
microscopic	resourceful	vestryclerk	mastoiditis	arrangement	consumerism
middleclass	restriction	violoncello	misguidance	artillerist	continental
mimetically	restrictive	vitrescence	misguidedly	assafoetida	continently
misconceive	restructure	vivisection	mithridatic	assuagement	coparcenary
misericorde	retinacular	whimsically	morrisdance	audibleness	corniferous
mononuclear	retinaculum	xanthochroi	myocarditis	audiometric	corporeally
moronically	retroaction	abracadabra	offhandedly	austereness	corpulently
mothercraft	retroactive	advisedness	outwardness	awesomeness	corrigendum
munificence	rhinoscopic	Alexandrian	overbidding	bacciferous	costiveness
muttonchops	rubefacient	alexandrine	overindulge	bandylegged	coulometric
myxomycetes	rubefaction	alexandrite	paramedical	bathymetric	countlessly
neckerchief	ruridecanal	altitudinal	pentandrous	beguilement	crossbearer
needlecraft	saddlecloth	antecedence	persuadable	belligerent	crosslegged
nephrectomy	saponaceous	applaudable	philanderer	bereavement	crotcheteer
nettlecloth	satanically	assuredness	pigheadedly	bicentenary	cruciferous
nigrescence	satirically	attitudinal	pleurodynia	bimillenary	crucigerous
nomadically	sceptically	awkwardness	pointedness	bimillenium	cryotherapy
nondescript	schoolchild	battledress	polyandrous	blackbeetle	cupriferous
nonmatching	scoriaceous	belatedness	pretendedly	blackfellow	curableness
nonspecific	scribacious	biofeedback	proceedings	blamelessly	cursiveness
numerically	secondclass	blessedness	protrudable	blasphemous	cybernetics
nutcrackers	seismically	bombardment	psychedelia	bloodlessly	cycloserine
obstruction	selfcocking	braggadocio	psychedelic	bloodvessel	cypripedium
obstructive	selflocking	camaraderie	psychodrama	bookkeeping	cysticercus
opalescence	shellacking	chalcedonic	pyramidally	bookshelves	dauntlessly
organically	sightscreen	coincidence	pyramidical	brainlessly	decolletage
organscreen	simpliciter	commandment	relatedness	brainteaser	defenceless
orthoscopic	slotmachine	commendable	respondence	bristletail	deficiently
osmotically	smokescreen	commendably	respondency	bristleworm	definiendum
ovariectomy	solanaceous	commendator	retiredness	brittleness	deforcement
pacifically	somatically	compendious	rhapsodical	broadleaved	demagnetise
pacificator	spastically	concordance	roundedness	brusqueness	dentigerous
papyraceous	spathaceous	contradance	scleroderma	cabbagepalm	deoxygenate
perfunctory	spectacular	crabbedness	sculduddery	cabbagerose	depauperate
perspective	spermicidal	crookedness	selfinduced	cabbagetree	depauperise
perspicuity	spherically	defraudment	sigmoidally	cabbageworm	dependently
perspicuous	splenectomy	demigoddess	skulduddery	calciferous	depravement
photoactive	spongecloth	descendable	spasmodical	campmeeting	derangement
phylloclade	springclean	descendible	squalidness	capableness	desegregate

```
detrimental  firmamental  incompetent  mutableness  profuseness  sightreader
differentia  flatulently  incorrectly  narcoleptic  proliferate  sightseeing
differently  floriferous  incremental  negligently  proliferous  sincereness
diffidently  florilegium  indifferent  nervelessly  prominently  sizableness
diffuseness  foreseeable  indorsement  nitrogenise  proofreader  sleeplessly
diphtherial  forgiveness  indulgently  nitrogenous  proprietary  smilelessly
diphtheroid  fourwheeler  ingathering  noiselessly  prosthetics  sociometric
diphycercal  friableness  insincerely  noisomeness  protuberant  softshelled
disablement  fruitlessly  insincerity  nonetheless  providently  somniferous
disaffected  fullfledged  insistently  northwester  purposeless  somnolently
disassemble  fulsomeness  intemperate  notableness  quiescently  soundlessly
disassembly  fundamental  intenseness  nutrimental  quinquennia  southwester
dishevelled  furtiveness  interbedded  obliqueness  quinquereme  spaceheater
dishonestly  gangsterism  intercensal  obscureness  racemeeting  spindlelegs
disinfector  gemmiferous  intercepter  octingenary  radiometric  spindletree
disinterest  genuflexion  interceptor  odoriferous  reachmedown  spinelessly
disinterred  genuineness  intercessor  offenceless  reawakening  spiniferous
dislikeable  gettogether  interdental  oligomerous  recommender  spinsterish
disquieting  gibberellin  interdepend  omnipresent  recumbently  spirometric
disquietude  gigantesque  interleaves  operoseness  recurrently  sporogenous
disremember  globigerina  intermeddle  orthocentre  refrigerant  spreadeagle
divergently  goniometric  intermedium  orthopedics  refrigerate  stainlessly
divorcement  gracelessly  internecine  orthopedist  remorseless  statutebook
divulgement  gracileness  interregnum  outbreeding  repellently  steeplebush
domineering  grandnephew  interrelate  overstepped  replaceable  steeplejack
doubleedged  gravimetric  interseptal  overweening  replacement  stickleback
doubleender  greatnephew  intersexual  ozoniferous  repleteness  stiffnecked
doubleentry  greenkeeper  intravenous  pachydermal  representer  storekeeper
doubtlessly  guilelessly  introverted  pamphleteer  requirement  stormcentre
draggletail  guiltlessly  involvement  pantalettes  resiliently  storyteller
dreamlessly  guttapercha  irksomeness  paperweight  restatement  strangeness
durableness  gypsiferous  knucklebone  paraldehyde  restiveness  stringently
ebulliently  hairbreadth  labiodental  parallelism  retraceable  suasiveness
econometric  hairdresser  lactiferous  paralleled   retrocedent  subbasement
efficiently  handbreadth  lakedweller  paramoecium  reverberant  subcategory
effulgently  handgrenade  latticework  paraplectic  reverberate  sublimeness
Elizabethan  heartlessly  lectureship  passiveness  ricochetted  succulently
elusiveness  heavyweight  legerdemain  pastureland  roentgenise  superheater
embraceable  heliometric  levelheaded  pennyweight  roughlegged  supersedeas
embracement  hemipterous  lightheaded  pensiveness  sacramental  supersedure
emplacement  heptamerous  lightweight  pentahedron  Sadduceeism  supremeness
emptyheaded  Heracleidan  limitlessly  pentamerous  safebreaker  surbasement
endorsement  hermeneutic  lissomeness  perispermic  safekeeping  swellheaded
endoskelton  heteroecism  loudspeaker  perithecium  salvageable  swingletree
endothelial  highstepper  lovableness  permanently  saprogenous  swordbearer
endothelium  hirsuteness  machinemade  perseverate  sausagemeat  tabletennis
endothermal  homesteader  mackerelsky  pertinently  scuttlebutt  tastelessly
endothermic  homopterous  magdalenian  pestiferous  selfcreated  tautomerism
enforceable  housekeeper  magisterial  pestilently  selfelected  tenableness
enforcement  hydraheaded  magisterium  phariseeism  selffeeding  terrigenous
engineering  hydrogenate  massiveness  philatelist  selffeeling  tetrahedral
engorgement  hydrogenous  matchlessly  photometric  selfseeking  tetrahedron
enhancement  hydromedusa  measureless  photoperiod  selfsterile  tetramerous
enjambement  hydrometeor  measurement  picturebook  sempiternal  textureless
enlargeable  hydrometric  mediateness  picturecard  senselessly  thanklessly
enlargement  hygrometric  megatherium  picturegoer  sentimental  theatregoer
enneahedron  hypermetric  melliferous  picturesque  sentinelled  therapeutic
ennoblement  hypothecate  mendelevium  pipecleaner  septiferous  thickheaded
enslavement  hypothenuse  mercilessly  planimetric  serviceable  thimbleweed
entablement  hypothermia  Micawberish  plateresque  serviceably  thistledown
entitlement  hypothesise  Micawberism  pliableness  servicebook  threedecker
equableness  hypsometric  micrometric  plicateness  serviceline  threelegged
erotogenous  icosahedral  Micronesian  pointdevice  seventeenth  thuriferous
eudiometric  icosahedron  microsecond  pointlessly  sextodecimo  timepleaser
eurypteroid  ignobleness  millisecond  powerlessly  shacklebolt  Titianesque
evasiveness  illaffected  minesweeper  precedented  shacklebone  torchbearer
exanthemata  illbreeding  ministerial  precedently  Shaksperean  townspeople
excellently  immenseness  mirthlessly  preciseness  Shaksperian  tracelessly
excremental  impatiently  miscegenate  predecessor  shamelessly  traducement
expediently  imperfectly  mischievous  presciently  shiftlessly  trainbearer
experienced  impermeable  misremember  preselector  shipbreaker  transceiver
extraverted  impermeably  molybdenite  prestressed  shockheaded  transferred
extremeness  impingement  monasterial  prevalently  shopsteward  transferrer
extroverted  implemental  moneylender  primateship  shoulderbag  transiently
faithhealer  improvement  monopterous  primigenial  shoulderpad  transsexual
faithlessly  imprudently  Monothelite  privateness  shuttlecock  transversal
faultlessly  incarcerate  morbiferous  procurement  sidestepped  treacherous
featureless  incipiently  movableness  profaneness  sidewheeler  treecreeper
ferriferous  inclemently  mundaneness  profiterole  sightlessly  tremblement
```

```
trencherman  sheriffship  ideological  skatingrink  dollishness  porterhouse
trendsetter  shoplifting  immitigable  skulduggery  doltishness  preterhuman
trestletree  smoothfaced  immitigably  smokingroom  donnishness  procephalic
trestlework  sorrowfully  infrangible  snowgoggles  Emmenthaler  protophytic
tribuneship  stampoffice  innavigable  somatogenic  epinephrine  prudishness
troublesome  standoffish  irreligious  sparingness  eurhythmics  publishable
truculently  thenceforth  jumpingbean  steerageway  evanishment  publishment
trundletail  undutifully  jumpingjack  stereograph  faddishness  quickchange
trusteeship  unhelpfully  kinetograph  stevengraph  festschrift  radiophonic
tunableness  unskilfully  knowingness  strategical  foolishness  raffishness
turbulently  welldefined  lammergeier  submarginal  foppishness  reddishness
unawareness  wonderfully  lammergeyer  submergence  furnishings  refreshment
unbelieving  abiological  lamplighter  suckingfish  Gallophobia  rhombohedra
unbeseeming  aerological  landingbeam  suffragette  garnishment  roguishness
unconcealed  agrological  landinggear  synagogical  girlishness  Russophobia
unconcerned  algological  lastingness  tentpegging  gramophonic  saddlehorse
uncongenial  archangelic  longsighted  teratogenic  granophyric  saprophytic
unconnected  Areopagitic  marriagebed  thanksgiver  haemophilia  sarcophagus
uncontested  astringency  meadowgrass  theological  haemophilic  schoolhouse
underseller  axiological  meaningless  thermograph  heliochrome  scratchwork
undertenant  bathingsuit  minuteglass  thoroughpin  hellishness  seborrhoeic
underweight  blastogenic  misjudgment  thoroughwax  hemispheric  selfishness
unexpressed  bookinghall  mockingbird  topological  hoggishness  shortchange
unfaltering  bootlegging  monological  typological  hydrophilic  sickishness
unkennelled  bottleglass  monologuise  unambiguous  hydrophobia  slavishness
unpossessed  bottlegreen  monologuist  unmitigated  hydrophobic  sleuthhound
unwholesome  bullfighter  monozygotic  viceregally  hydrophytic  sottishness
vasopressin  cardiograph  monseigneur  virological  hydrothorax  spendthrift
vasopressor  carriageway  moonlighter  waitinglist  hygrophytic  spirochaete
venturesome  chaetognath  mooringmast  waitingroom  hypercharge  spirochetal
verboseness  chafingdish  morningroom  willingness  hyperphagia  sporophytic
vinedresser  chevalglass  multangular  winningness  hypsophobia  springhouse
visibleness  choreograph  mycological  winningpost  impeachable  staunchless
voicelessly  chronograph  nearsighted  wintergreen  impeachment  staunchness
voltametric  churchgoing  nomological  witenagemot  interchange  stenochromy
volubleness  compurgator  nosological  abolishable  ionospheric  sternsheets
voortrekker  conflagrant  nothingness  abolishment  knavishness  stomachache
wearilessly  conflagrate  oecological  abranchiate  lithophytic  stomachpump
welcomeness  consanguine  oenological  accoucheuse  loggerheads  straightcut
whiffletree  contingence  oestrogenic  acidophilic  loutishness  straightish
whippletree  contingency  oncological  agoraphobia  lumpishness  straightway
whistlestop  convergence  ontological  agoraphobic  lycanthrope  stretchable
whiteheaded  convergency  oreological  anaesthesia  lycanthropy  stylishness
windcheater  coronagraph  packingcase  anaesthetic  mannishness  summerhouse
winsomeness  coronograph  pedagogical  anglophobia  mawkishness  supercharge
worldbeater  cottongrass  pedological  anglophobic  McCarthyism  swinishness
worthlessly  cryptogamic  penological  antirrhinum  melancholia  sympathetic
wrongheaded  cryptograph  pharyngitis  atmospheric  melancholic  sympathiser
aftereffect  cunningness  physiognomy  autarchical  messiahship  tarnishable
aircraftman  cytological  plantigrade  barrelhouse  microphonic  tenterhooks
battlefield  demagogical  playingcard  bassethound  microphytic  uncatchable
beautifully  demagoguery  poltergeist  bearishness  misanthrope  uncouthness
bountifully  demagoguism  pomological  bergschrund  misanthropy  uncrushable
brazenfaced  digitigrade  posological  bewitchment  monarchical  undercharge
butterflies  dislodgment  prejudgment  bookishness  mustachioed  unmatchable
centrifugal  distinguish  pressagency  boorishness  mycorrhizae  unteachable
changefully  drawingroom  prestigious  breadthways  mycorrhizal  untouchable
colourfully  emmenagogue  promulgator  breadthwise  necrophilia  Upanishadic
deceitfully  epeirogenic  pseudograph  Britishness  necrophilic  varnishtree
doublefaced  equiangular  psychogenic  brutishness  negrophobia  voguishness
enfeoffment  ethological  psychograph  bullishness  nourishment  waggishness
facelifting  eveningstar  quitchgrass  caddishness  nyctophobia  waspishness
Falstaffian  feelingness  rectangular  calisthenic  oligochaete  wedgeshaped
flagofficer  fingerglass  reemergence  catchphrase  osteophytic  weltschmerz
forgetfully  FinnoUgrian  refrangible  chokecherry  otherwhiles  Whitechapel
frightfully  firefighter  refringency  cleanshaven  outfighting  whitethroat
grandiflora  flagwagging  reintegrate  coffeehouse  paedophilia  whitishness
healthfully  foresighted  rheological  ctenophoran  pantothenic  xeranthemum
masterfully  fortnightly  ribbongrass  currishness  parentheses  zootechnics
photooffset  glaringness  salpingitis  customhouse  parenthesis  abbreviator
pillowfight  goddaughter  sandbagging  cyclothymia  parenthetic  absorbingly
plentifully  golddigging  sculduggery  cyclothymic  peevishness  academicals
powderflask  herringbone  scurvygrass  debauchment  pentathlete  academician
regardfully  herringgull  seismograph  debouchment  pettishness  academicism
regretfully  heterograft  serological  depthcharge  photophilic  acceptingly
reposefully  homological  sexological  diapophysis  photophobia  acclivitous
resentfully  homozygosis  shadowgraph  discotheque  photophobic  accordingly
selfdefence  horological  sinological  disenthrall  piggishness  acidifiable
sheriffalty  hummingbird  sittingroom  doggishness  pinkishness  acinaciform
```

```
acoustician  catholicise  decorticate  excursively  historicise  justiciable
acquisition  Catholicism  decrepitate  executioner  historicism  justifiable
acquisitive  catholicity  decrepitude  exotericism  historicist  justifiably
adjectively  catswhisker  deductively  expansional  historicity  lamellicorn
adverbially  causatively  defectively  expansively  horripilate  lamelliform
advertising  celestially  defensively  expansivity  houselights  largeminded
Aeneolithic  certifiable  defibrinate  expenditure  housewifely  laudability
affectingly  certifiably  deglutition  expensively  housewifery  lengthiness
affectional  certificate  degradingly  explosively  hylozoistic  lentiginous
affectioned  childminder  demandingly  exquisitely  illiquidity  liberticide
affectively  christiania  denunciator  extensional  imitatively  libertinage
affectivity  Christianly  deoxyribose  extensively  immarginate  libertinism
AfroAsiatic  churchiness  deploringly  exterminate  impartially  lickerishly
agglutinate  cicatricial  depreciator  extortioner  impassioned  lickspittle
agnosticism  cityslicker  desensitise  extradition  impassively  lightminded
agonisingly  cleanlimbed  deservingly  facsimilist  impassivity  lineprinter
amenability  cleanliness  determinacy  fallibility  impertinent  lingeringly
amicability  closefisted  determinant  falteringly  imperviable  liquefiable
amphimictic  clostridium  determinate  farraginous  imploringly  loathliness
amplexicaul  coccidiosis  determinism  fatiguingly  imprecisely  longanimity
anarchistic  cognitional  determinist  faultfinder  imprecision  looselimbed
annunciator  cognitively  dialogistic  favouritism  improvident  lucratively
anomalistic  cognitivity  diapositive  feasibility  impulsively  macrobiotic
antheridium  collisional  didacticism  ferruginous  incardinate  maddeningly
antioxidant  collusively  diffusively  fetichistic  incertitude  magnanimity
aphrodisiac  columniated  digestively  fetishistic  inclusively  magnanimous
appallingly  combatively  dimensional  feudalistic  incognisant  magnificent
appealingly  comestibles  directional  fidgetiness  incontinent  malposition
appreciable  communicant  directivity  financially  incriminate  mandarinate
appreciably  communicate  disarmingly  fireraising  IndoChinese  mandolinist
appreciator  communistic  disbeliever  flauntingly  inductively  manneristic
approvingly  compaginate  dismayingly  fleshliness  inedibility  marconigram
approximate  competition  disobliging  flexibility  infanticide  masculinely
aromaticity  competitive  disposition  flightiness  infantilism  masculinise
arrestingly  complainant  dispositive  floweriness  infertility  masculinity
ascensional  complaisant  disseminate  forethinker  inflexional  masochistic
aspergillum  compositely  disseminule  formalistic  ingratitude  matrilineal
aspergillus  composition  dissepiment  formational  ingurgitate  matrilinear
asphyxiator  compositive  dissimilate  fortifiable  innutrition  maxillipede
assassinate  conciliator  dissociable  franctireur  inquilinous  mechanician
assertively  concomitant  diverticula  franklinite  inquiringly  mechanistic
athleticism  concubinage  divestiture  freethinker  inquisition  mediumistic
attentively  concubinary  domesticate  frenchified  inquisitive  mercurially
attritional  concubitant  domesticity  frostbitten  insecticide  mesalliance
audiovisual  conditional  doughtiness  frowstiness  insectifuge  meteoritics
Augustinian  conditioner  dresscircle  gentilitial  insectivore  Methodistic
awestricken  condominium  drouthiness  geopolitics  insensitive  microlithic
bacilliform  confidingly  duplicitous  ghastliness  insouciance  micturition
bactericide  confusingly  dyslogistic  ghostliness  instability  minnesinger
balmcricket  congenially  earthliness  gnotobiosis  insultingly  misalliance
banteringly  connubially  eclecticism  gnotobiotic  intagliated  miscibility
batholithic  consolidate  ecumenicism  gradational  intelligent  miserliness
bearbaiting  consolingly  ecumenicity  granolithic  intensifier  misestimate
beastliness  constrictor  editorially  gravedigger  intensional  modernistic
befittingly  consumingly  educability  gristliness  intensively  molecricket
beguilingly  contaminant  educational  grouchiness  intentional  molendinary
bicuspidate  contaminate  effectively  grumblingly  intentioned  monasticism
biddability  convenience  einsteinium  guesstimate  interlinear  monoclinous
billsticker  conveniency  elderliness  gullibility  Interlingua  mountaineer
bipartition  convivially  electrician  haggadistic  interlining  mountainous
blackbirder  corrosively  electricity  hairraising  intermingle  mountaintop
blotchiness  cosmetician  eligibility  hairtrigger  intermitted  moveability
bodybuilder  coterminous  ellipticity  hallucinate  interviewee  multilinear
brainsickly  countrified  embellisher  halophilous  interviewer  muskthistle
branchiopod  courtliness  embracingly  handknitted  intrepidity  narratively
breadwinner  credibility  enchiridion  handpainted  intromitted  naughtiness
bristliness  crocodilian  endearingly  handwriting  intromitter  necessitate
broadminded  crucifixion  enquiringly  handwritten  intrusively  necessitous
bullbaiting  crunchiness  esotericism  harmonistic  intuitional  necrobiosis
butteriness  culpability  essentially  haughtiness  intuitively  neologistic
Byzantinism  cupronickel  establisher  healthiness  intuitivism  nephelinite
Byzantinist  cursoriness  Eucharistic  Hellenistic  invectively  neuroticism
cabbalistic  curvilineal  euphemistic  hermeticism  inventively  nondelivery
calumniator  curvilinear  evolutional  hesperidium  investigate  nonresident
Calvinistic  deceivingly  exceedingly  Hibernicism  investiture  nullifidian
caressingly  decemvirate  exceptional  Hispanicise  inviability  nutritional
catechismal  decennially  excessively  Hispanicism  irruptively  nutritively
catechistic  deceptively  exclusively  Hispanicist  Jansenistic  objectively
caterpillar  declivitous  exclusivity  historiated  jargonistic  objectivism
```

objectivist	prejudicial	reprovingly	sketchiness	tightlipped	waspwaisted
objectivity	preliminary	repulsively	Slavonicise	toothbilled	wealthiness
observingly	prelusively	requisition	slightingly	torchsinger	weightiness
obsessional	premeditate	resistively	smallminded	totteringly	wherewithal
obsessively	premonition	resistivity	soapboiling	toughminded	witheringly
obtrusively	premonitory	resuscitate	soberminded	toxophilite	wolfwhistle
oenophilist	prenominate	retentively	sociability	traditional	womanliness
offensively	preposition	retentivity	socialistic	tragedienne	workability
omniscience	prepositive	revaccinate	solipsistic	transfigure	worldliness
operational	presumingly	revendicate	solvability	transfinite	xenophilous
operatively	preterition	reversional	somewhither	transfixion	xerophilous
orderliness	prevaricate	reversioner	Soroptimist	transmittal	lesemajesty
ostensively	previsional	rhetorician	sovereignly	transmitted	stiflejoint
outstripped	prickliness	rhomboideus	sovereignty	transmitter	togglejoint
oversailing	primitively	rightminded	specifiable	transpierce	wapperjawed
overwritten	primitivism	rightwinger	specificity	trapeziform	airsickness
oviposition	privatively	ritualistic	speechifier	treacliness	archdukedom
Palestinian	prizewinner	rodenticide	spellbinder	tremblingly	bewhiskered
palpability	probabilism	romanticise	sphaeridium	tribunicial	hurryskurry
pantheistic	probabilist	romanticism	spifflicate	tribunitial	Kulturkampf
pantomimist	probability	romanticist	Spinozistic	tricksiness	outspokenly
paraleipsis	probational	sacrificial	spiritistic	triennially	pocketknife
parheliacal	probationer	saintliness	springiness	tritheistic	seasickness
parishioner	proficiency	saleability	squashiness	triumvirate	sheathknife
parochially	progenitrix	salvational	squeakiness	typewritten	unbreakable
participant	progeniture	sandskipper	squeamishly	tyrannicide	unshockable
participate	prohibition	Sanskritist	squintingly	ultraviolet	unspeakable
participial	prohibitive	saprobiotic	starchiness	unbendingly	unspeakably
partitioned	prohibitory	sartorially	startlingly	uncanniness	unthinkable
partitioner	prolificacy	satiability	stateliness	unceasingly	unthinkably
partitively	prolificity	satisfiable	stoolpigeon	uncommitted	waterskiing
parturition	promisingly	saturninely	streakiness	underbidder	Abbevillian
passeriform	promotional	savouriness	stringiness	underpinned	aboutsledge
passibility	promptitude	scalariform	stumblingly	undersigned	acarpellous
patelliform	propitiable	scalpriform	subaerially	unemotional	accumulator
patrilineal	propitiator	schottische	subaudition	unfailingly	acknowledge
patronising	proposition	scientistic	subdivision	unfashioned	admiralship
paunchiness	provenience	scorchingly	subdominant	unfeelingly	agriculture
pearlfisher	provisional	ScotchIrish	subordinate	unforgiving	aiguillette
peccability	provokingly	scragginess	subregional	unfurnished	altorelievo
peccadillos	pruriginous	scrappiness	sufficiency	ungodliness	altorilievo
pellucidity	pulchritude	screamingly	suffumigate	unhappiness	ambivalence
penultimate	purposively	scrimpiness	suitability	unigeniture	ambivalency
percipience	pussywillow	scruffiness	summariness	unmanliness	amontillado
peregrinate	qualifiable	searchingly	summational	unmeaningly	anadiplosis
perennially	queenliness	secretively	superficial	unnervingly	anaphylaxis
periodicity	quickfiring	seductively	superficies	unpromising	annihilator
perishingly	quicksilver	selectively	supervision	unqualified	apophyllite
personifier	quickwitted	selectivity	supervisory	unrealistic	apostolical
pervasively	Rabelaisian	selfevident	supposition	unsmilingly	apparelling
pessimistic	rangefinder	selfopinion	suppositive	unsparingly	aquaculture
phonetician	rateability	selfraising	suppository	unvarnished	aquarellist
photofinish	ratiocinate	semanticist	surficially	unweetingly	aquiculture
phthiriasis	raunchiness	semiskilled	swarthiness	unwillingly	articulable
pictorially	ravishingly	sensational	syllabicity	unwinkingly	articulated
pinnatisect	readability	sensibility	syllogistic	unwittingly	articulator
placability	readywitted	sensitively	symbolistic	valuational	assemblyman
plaintively	receptively	sensitivity	symposiarch	variability	assimilable
pleinairist	receptivity	sensorially	synergistic	variational	assimilator
pluralistic	recessional	serendipity	talkatively	varsovienne	atrabilious
pontificals	recessively	serpiginous	tameability	vasculiform	auricularly
pontificate	recognition	shadowiness	tangibility	velvetiness	balefulness
portability	recognitive	shamanistic	tantalising	vendibility	BaltoSlavic
portraitist	recognitory	shapeliness	tarradiddle	verbalistic	bashfulness
portraiture	recommittal	sharpwitted	teleprinter	versatilely	bedevilment
possibility	recondition	shipbuilder	tensibility	versatility	benevolence
posteriorly	recriminate	shortwinded	tentatively	vertiginous	bersaglieri
postexilian	rectifiable	shrinkingly	testability	vestigially	bestselling
potentially	rectilineal	shrubbiness	Teutonicism	vibratility	bibliolater
potteringly	rectilinear	sickeningly	theatricals	vibrational	bibliolatry
prattlingly	redactional	sideslipped	therewithal	vicissitude	bimetallism
preachiness	reduplicate	sightliness	thickwitted	vincibility	bimetallist
preaudience	reflexively	signifiable	thinskinned	vitrifiable	binocularly
precipitant	regurgitate	significant	thirstiness	volcanicity	bookselling
precipitate	rejoicingly	signpainter	threadiness	volkslieder	brucellosis
precipitous	reliability	silveriness	thriftiness	voodooistic	calceolaria
predominant	repartition	simperingly	thrillingly	vortiginous	cancellated
predominate	replenisher	sinfonietta	throatiness	vulcanicity	candlelight
preignition	repleviable	situational	tightfisted	washability	carefulness

castellated	godchildren	pitchblende	trisyllabic	gradiometer	adjournment
cauliflower	gradualness	pitifulness	trisyllable	gyrocompass	aerodynamic
chancellery	grammalogue	plasmolysis	trivialness	habiliments	Albigensian
chancellory	haemoglobin	plasmolytic	trothplight	hypolimnion	albuminuria
channelling	halfholiday	playfulness	tunefulness	impedimenta	AngloIndian
chronologer	handselling	pointillism	typicalness	inestimable	antemundane
chronologic	harmfulness	pointillist	unavailable	inestimably	antependium
chrysalides	hatefulness	pomiculture	uncivilised	inflammable	antimonious
chrysalises	haustellate	prophylaxis	undeveloped	inflammably	Apollinaris
circumlunar	heedfulness	proteolysis	unicellular	kleptomania	argumentive
codicillary	helpfulness	proteolytic	uninucleate	lachrymator	arraignment
colonelship	hemeralopia	prothalamia	unusualness	mantuamaker	bacchanalia
compellable	highfalutin	prothallial	vasodilator	megalomania	backbencher
concealable	hopefulness	prothallium	ventriloquy	metasomatic	barquentine
concealment	hurtfulness	psychologic	vesicularly	metonymical	bedizenment
congealable	hyperplasia	punctilious	victualless	milliampere	bellringing
congealment	immunologic	pushfulness	victualling	nymphomania	betweenmaid
constellate	impanelling	quadrillion	viniculture	oneiromancy	betweenness
controlling	imperilling	quarrelling	viticulture	papiermache	betweentime
controlment	imperilment	quarrelsome	wakefulness	paronomasia	billionaire
cordialness	incompliant	quintillion	wellbeloved	performable	biocoenoses
counselling	initialling	radicalness	whigmaleery	performance	biocoenosis
crenellated	installment	rapscallion	wirepulling	phrasemaker	biocoenotic
crystallise	instillment	realpolitik	wishfulness	pluviometer	birdfancier
crystallise	insufflator	resemblance	wistfulness	pocketmoney	bonbonniere
crystallite	interallied	restfulness	zestfulness	polarimeter	bookbinding
crystalloid	interfluent	retroflexed	actinometer	polarimetry	bottlenosed
curtailment	interplayed	ribvaulting	actinomyces	problematic	boutonniere
demonolatry	invigilator	roadholding	actinomycin	pseudomonas	Brahmanical
depopulator	irregularly	ropewalking	aeronomical	pseudomorph	Brahminical
despoilment	irresoluble	sansculotte	agronomical	psychometry	bushmanship
dicotyledon	kilocalorie	scaffolding	alkalimeter	psychomotor	captainless
disciplinal	landaulette	scintillant	alkalimetry	rearadmiral	captionless
discipliner	landholding	scintillate	allelomorph	reclaimable	carabiniere
disinclined	literalness	searchlight	altocumulus	rhabdomancy	carabinieri
dissyllable	logicalness	selfculture	anastomoses	rifacimenti	caravanning
dolefulness	lustfulness	selfreliant	anastomosis	rifacimento	caravansary
domiciliary	makebelieve	semiellipse	anastomotic	salinometer	Carolingian
domiciliate	malevolence	semipalmate	antiSemitic	schwarmerei	ceremonious
dutifulness	manipulable	sericulture	antonomasia	sclerometer	challenging
earthcloset	manipulator	severalfold	auxanometer	seismometer	chansonnier
emasculator	marshalling	shirtsleeve	baptismally	seismometry	chickenfeed
embowelling	marshalship	shrivelling	bibliomancy	selfcommand	chickenwire
embroilment	medicolegal	skilfulness	bibliomania	selflimited	Chippendale
embryologic	mellifluent	sockdolager	biedermeier	showjumping	chrominance
empanelling	mellifluous	sockdologen	biochemical	speedometer	citizenship
enthralling	mentholated	somatologic	boilermaker	spherometer	codefendant
enthralment	mindfulness	songfulness	calorimeter	stalagmitic	coessential
epithalamia	mineraliser	soulfulness	calorimetry	statesmanly	coeternally
epithalamic	miscellanea	spaceflight	chainsmoker	stereometry	coextension
epithelioma	misspelling	spherulitic	charismatic	stichometry	coextensive
equipollent	mitrailleur	spiritlevel	cheiromancy	subterminal	concernment
equivalence	molecularly	spondulicks	Christmassy	superimpose	condemnable
equivalency	monoculture	spondylitis	chronometer	symptomatic	consignable
evangelical	monopoliser	staurolitic	chronometry	syndesmosis	consignment
exoskeletal	musicalness	stencilling	colorimeter	synonymical	containable
exoskeleton	namecalling	stoicalness	colorimetry	tacheometer	containment
factualness	naturalness	straitlaced	confirmable	taxonomical	contorniate
fatefulness	needfulness	streetlight	conformable	tephromancy	cookgeneral
fearfulness	neutraliser	stridulator	conformably	theorematic	coordinator
finicalness	nomenclator	subaxillary	conformally	thermometer	costbenefit
firewalking	nonchalance	superfluity	conformance	thermometry	countenance
flagellator	nonviolence	superfluous	consummator	thingumabob	cytogenesis
flannelette	nympholepsy	surveillant	conterminal	thingumajig	cytokinesis
flannelling	operculated	tearfulness	cottonmouth	toxicomania	deferential
flocculence	orbicularly	technologic	craniometry	trichomonad	denizenship
footsoldier	osteoplasty	teratologic	cryptomeria	twelvemonth	denominator
frankpledge	outbuilding	tessellated	diastematic	unashamedly	desalinator
fraudulence	overbalance	theodolitic	dichromatic	uniformness	detrainment
fretfulness	painfulness	thermolysis	disharmonic	vaporimeter	diamagnetic
gainfulness	painkilling	thermolytic	dissymmetry	verisimilar	diaphaneity
generaliser	panhellenic	throatlatch	dynamometer	viceadmiral	Diophantine
generalship	paraselenae	tonsillitis	dynamometry	volumometer	discernible
geniculated	pedicellate	tourbillion	elastomeric	abandonment	discernibly
genteelness	pediculosis	trailblazer	forgetmenot	abdominally	discernment
gillyflower	penicillate	trammelling	Francomania	abiogeneses	disgruntled
glassblower	penicillium	transalpine	gendarmerie	abiogenesis	doctrinaire
globeflower	philhellene	transilient	gentlemanly	abiogenetic	doctrinally
glossolalia	physiologic	triphyllous	geochemical	acrimonious	documentary

drunkenness ironmongery rejuvenesce workmanship climatology eudaemonism
dualcontrol irredentism reorientate zooplankton coldblooded eudaemonist
earthenware irredentist residential ablutionary collaborate executorial
easternmost irretention resplendent abortionist commemorate exogenously
ectogenesis irretentive reverential accessorial comptroller expectorant
ectogenetic Jacobinical rightangled accessorise condylomata expectorate
elephantine jauntingcar rodomontade accommodate congruously extemporary
elephantoid kitchenette ropedancing adiaphorism consciously extemporise
embryonated kitchensink rubicundity adoptionism coralloidal exteriorise
emotionally kitchenware rudimentary adoptionist cornucopian exteriority
emotionless latifundium safeconduct aerobiology corroborant extrapolate
enchainment laughinggas sanguinaria afficionado corroborate facetiously
enlivenment legionnaire sanguineous agrobiology cosmetology faithworthy
entrainment lieutenancy scaleinsect allantoides cosmogonist fanfaronade
environment lifemanship schizanthus ambiguously cosmologist feloniously
Esperantist ligamentary scrutiniser ambitiously cosmopolite ferociously
existential ligamentous sectionally amorphously cotemporary fieldcornet
explainable magazinegun sedimentary amphibolite courteously fieldworker
exponential maintenance selaginella amphibology creationism footslogger
factfinding maisonnette selfcentred anachronism creationist foreclosure
factionally medicinable selfconceit anachronous credulously foreshorten
farthingale medicinally selfcontent anacreontic crematorium forethought
fashionable membraneous selfcontrol analogously criminology forthcoming
fashionably mentionable selfdenying AngloNorman crocidolite fractionary
filamentary merchandise selfwinding anomalously crossbowman fractionate
filamentous merchantman semimonthly anonymously cryobiology fractionise
fissionable merogenesis sheetanchor anteriority dactylogram fractiously
foraminated Merovingian showmanship anthologise dactylology freebooting
foraminifer merryandrew sickbenefit anthologist dangerously freethought
foreignness metacentric sleepingbag antiphonary decarbonate frivolously
forerunning metagenesis sleepingcar apostrophic decarbonise frothhopper
forlornness metagenetic slickenside apotheosise deliciously frugivorous
fragmentary millionaire snowbunting archaeology deliriously fullblooded
fraternally mindbending spontaneity archaeornis dermatology functionary
fraterniser monogenesis spontaneous archdiocese desultorily functionate
gametangium monogenetic stephanotis arenicolous deteriorate garrulously
gamogenesis monolingual stickinsect aspersorium deuterogamy gemmologist
gastronomic moribundity stockinette assessorial Deuteronomy genealogise
gentianella mothernaked stramineous assiduously dexterously genealogist
geomagnetic mudslinging subclinical atrociously diachronism geostrophic
glauconitic nightingale substandard audaciously diastrophic Germanophil
gourmandise nocturnally substantial audiologist dichotomise gerontology
gourmandism oarsmanship substantive autoerotism dichotomist gestatorial
halfbinding octagonally superinduce autotrophic dichotomous giantpowder
halflanding oecumenical superintend balletomane dictatorial glutinously
headhunting officinally surgeonfish barbarously diphthongal gonfalonier
highranking oilpainting sustainable barnstormer diplococcus goodlooking
homocentric ontogenesis sustainment barrelorgan dipterocarp grandiosely
homogeneity ontogenetic symphonious beachcomber directorate grandiosity
homogeneous opinionated taratantara beauteously directorial grandmother
homogenetic outstanding tegumentary behavioural disafforest granivorous
homogeniser overmanning telekinesis bellicosity dishonourer granulocyte
hylogenesis overrunning telekinetic bicarbonate disunionist grasshopper
hypotension Passiontide tenementary bicorporate divisionary gynaecocrat
ignominious patternshop theocentric blackcoated divisionism gynaecology
illmannered penitential thrasonical blameworthy doorknocker haematocele
illuminable pensionable toffeenosed bounteously downtrodden haematocrit
illuminance pensionless treasonable bourgeoisie dreadnought haematology
illuminator pentlandite treasonably bracteolate ectotrophic hagiologist
immanentism peritonitis trichinosis bryozoology egregiously halfblooded
immanentist pneumonitis tufthunting buffalorobe electioneer Hamiltonian
impecunious polygenesis uncanonical bumptiously electrocute handwrought
impregnable polygenetic uncleanness cacophonous electrolier hazardously
impregnably polygonally unessential calcicolous electrolyse heavyfooted
inalienable portionless unfeignedly campanology electrolyte hedgehopped
inalienably portmanteau unorganized capaciously electronics helleborine
inattention preeminence unrelenting carcinomata electrotype hemianopsia
inattentive preprandial unshrinking carnivorous ellipsoidal heresiology
indefinable punchinello vagabondage catadromous emulsionise herpetology
indefinably puritanical vagabondise catercousin endotrophic highbrowism
independent quadrennial vagabondish cavernously erroneously highwrought
inessential quadrennium vagabondism chaperonage erythrocyte hilariously
inexpensive quaternloaf vaticinator chaulmoogra eschatology hippopotami
inferential quincuncial viscountess chiropodist ethnologist histologist
influential realignment Weismannism Christology etymologise histrionics
ingrainedly reedbunting westernmost clairvoyant etymologist histrionism
inoffensive referential Westminster clamorously euchologion homophonous
inseminator regimentals Whitsuntide cleistogamy   homosporous
involuntary rejuvenator workmanlike

honeymooner	malapropism	periodontal	religiously	tautologise	whichsoever
hornswoggle	malariology	peristomial	reportorial	tautologism	whitecollar
horsecollar	maliciously	pestologist	retrorocket	tautologous	wholesomely
horsedoctor	mammalogist	petitionary	revisionary	teaspoonful	wholesouled
householder	marchioness	petrologist	revisionism	teenybopper	whoremonger
housemother	martyrology	petticoated	revisionist	teleologism	whosesoever
hydrologist	massproduce	pettifogger	rheotropism	teleologist	winegrowing
hydroponics	mastodontic	phenologist	rhinologist	telephonist	witchdoctor
hyperbolise	matrimonial	philologian	rhynchodont	tenaciously	worrisomely
hyperboloid	mediatorial	philologist	righteously	terminology	xylophonist
hyperborean	melodiously	philosopher	roughfooted	terricolous	ailurophile
hypnopompic	meningocele	philosophic	sagaciously	territorial	ailurophobe
hypoglossal	metalloidal	phonologist	salaciously	testimonial	anencephaly
ichthyology	metalworker	phosphonium	saltatorial	tetrapodous	antenuptial
ichthyornis	meteoroidal	phosphorate	sauropodous	thalidomide	anthropical
ichthyosaur	meteorology	phosphorism	saxophonist	thanatology	anticipator
illfavoured	methodology	phosphorite	scaremonger	thankworthy	antitypical
illhumoured	micrococcal	phosphorous	schistosity	theobromine	apomorphine
illusionism	micrococcus	photocopier	schistosome	theretofore	aposiopesis
illusionist	microcosmic	phraseogram	scientology	therminics	bathysphere
imperforate	mindblowing	phraseology	scorpionfly	threecolour	bibliopegic
imperiously	misbegotten	phycologist	scriptorial	thrombocyte	bibliophile
impersonate	mollycoddle	phytologist	scriptorium	titleholder	bibliophily
impetuosity	momentously	phytotomist	seditionary	tobacconist	bibliopolic
impetuously	monstrosity	pieceworker	seditiously	toothpowder	brahmaputra
incommodity	monstrously	piscatorial	seigniorage	toothsomely	breastplate
inconsonant	mosstrooper	piscivorous	seigniorial	torticollis	bulletproof
incorporate	multicolour	planetoidal	selfclosing	torturously	bumblepuppy
incorporeal	multinomial	planoconvex	semasiology	tracheotomy	candlepower
incuriosity	murderously	platinotype	shareholder	tragicomedy	centrepiece
incuriously	murmurously	Pleistocene	shortcoming	transformer	centripetal
inferiority	myrmecology	plenipotent	showstopper	translocate	chamaephyte
ingeniously	mythologise	plenteously	sightworthy	transponder	chlorophyll
ingenuously	mythologist	poisonously	skeletonise	transporter	chloroplast
injuriously	mythopoeist	poltroonery	slaveholder	trapezoidal	chloroprene
innocuously	mythopoetic	polyglottal	smallholder	tremulously	chromoplast
innoxiously	namedropper	polyglottic	smithsonite	tricoloured	chrysoprase
insectology	nasofrontal	polyphonous	snowleopard	tritagonist	circumpolar
insessorial	necrologist	ponderosity	sociologist	troublously	clodhopping
insidiously	necropoleis	ponderously	solutionist	trustworthy	comeuppance
intercostal	nefariously	positronium	soteriology	trypanosome	commonplace
intercourse	negationist	predatorily	spectrogram	tyrannosaur	consumption
interiorise	neighbourly	prefatorial	spectrology	tyrannously	consumptive
interiority	neurologist	prefatorily	spelaeology	ultramodern	contemplate
interlocker	nightporter	prelusorily	sphagnology	ultrasonics	contraption
interpolate	nonunionist	primatology	sphygmogram	unanimously	copperplate
interrogate	notoriously	prochronism	splayfooted	unbeknownst	corecipient
inventorial	obliviously	prolegomena	splendorous	unexploited	description
invidiously	obnoxiously	protagonist	sporogonium	unicoloured	descriptive
isochronism	octachordal	Proterozoic	squarsonage	unorthodoxy	developable
isochronous	officiously	protonotary	stadtholder	unreasoning	development
judiciously	olfactology	provisorily	stakeholder	vacationist	diadelphous
kinesiology	ophiologist	pteridology	stallholder	vagariously	discerption
kwashiorkor	orchidology	pureblooded	starcrossed	vasectomise	discrepancy
laboriously	ornithology	purgatorial	statutorily	venereology	distempered
lacrimosely	ornithopter	pussyfooter	steamboiler	venturously	dodecaphony
lacrymosely	ornithosaur	Pythagorean	steamroller	veraciously	emancipator
larcenously	orthodontia	Pythagorism	steelworker	verminously	entomophily
laryngology	orthodontic	quaestorial	steganogram	vexatiously	envelopment
laryngotomy	oscillogram	querulously	stellionate	vexillology	epigraphist
leapfrogged	osteologist	questionary	stepbrother	vicariously	episcopally
leaseholder	ostracoderm	radiologist	stockholder	vivaciously	eucalyptole
lecherously	Ostrogothic	rancorously	stockjobber	volcanology	filterpaper
lichenology	overcropped	rapaciously	stomatology	volitionary	fingerplate
lightfooted	overproduce	rapturously	strenuosity	voraciously	fingerprint
lightsomely	overwrought	reactionary	strenuously	vulcanology	flagcaptain
limnologist	pandemonium	reactionist	stylopodium	wainscoting	foretopmast
lithologist	panicmonger	reciprocate	sugarcoated	wainscotted	foretopsail
lithotomist	paratrooper	reciprocity	sumptuosity	warmblooded	Francophile
litigiously	paternoster	reconnoitre	sumptuously	waterbottle	Francophobe
loathsomely	pathologist	rediscovery	superioress	watercolour	francophone
loxodromics	patrimonial	reflexology	superiority	watercooled	gafftopsail
ludicrously	pawnbroking	reintroduce	supernormal	watercooler	gametophyte
luxuriously	pelargonium	relationism	swiftfooted	watercourse	greasepaint
machicolate	pendulously	relationist	synchromesh	waterlogged	greaseproof
macrocosmic	pentazocine	religionise	synchronise	wearisomely	gymnospermy
madreporite	Pentecostal	religionism	synchronism	weenybopper	heterophony
Maglemosian	penuriously	religionist	synchronous	wellgroomed	heteroploid
maladroitly	perchlorate	religiosity	synchrotron	wheresoever	heteropolar

homoeopathy	trimorphism	centigramme	endocardial	infantryman	pericardiac
hydrosphere	trimorphous	chainarmour	endocardium	infiltrator	pericardial
hymenoptera	troposphere	chamberlain	endomorphic	innumerable	pericardium
hypotyposis	tryingplane	chambermaid	enterpriser	innumerably	periphrases
illdisposed	tryptophane	champertous	ephemerides	inobservant	periphrasis
illtempered	twelvepenny	chanterelle	ethnography	inopportune	perpetrator
inescapable	unflappable	chimaerical	exaggerator	inseparable	petrography
inscription	unstoppable	chirography	exarcerbate	inseparably	phonography
inscriptive	wiretapping	chitterling	executrices	insuperable	photography
intersperse	worshipable	chorography	executrixes	insuperably	phototropic
interspinal	worshipless	chrysarobin	expropriate	intercrural	phytography
isomorphism	worshipping	clapperclaw	farthermost	intergrowth	pictography
isomorphous	xanthophyll	coinheritor	featheredge	interpreter	pilocarpine
lepidoptera	zoographist	coinsurance	featherhead	intertribal	pipistrelle
letterpress	zoomorphism	coleorrhiza	featherless	intolerable	pivotbridge
lithosphere	doublequick	concurrence	fenestrated	intolerably	plagiariser
maintopmast	grotesquely	conferrable	filmography	intolerance	plasterwork
maintopsail	grotesquery	conquerable	firstfruits	invigorator	platearmour
maladaptive	propinquity	consecrator	flabbergast	irreparable	platforming
mantelpiece	soliloquise	conspirator	flavourless	irreparably	platyrrhine
marketplace	soliloquist	consternate	flavoursome	irreverence	pleasurable
masterpiece	aboveground	contrariety	forbearance	isometrical	pleasurably
megalopolis	accelerando	contrarious	forevermore	landlordism	pleiotropic
melanophore	accelerator	cosmography	foreverness	launderette	pleochroism
moneyspider	achondritic	counterblow	forewarning	leatherback	pleomorphic
motivepower	adulterator	counterbond	furtherance	leatherhead	plutocratic
municipally	aeolotropic	counterfeit	furthermore	leatherneck	pococurante
naturopathy	ahistorical	counterfoil	furthermost	linendraper	polycarpous
needlepoint	allAmerican	counterfort	furthersome	lithography	polychromic
Neotropical	allegorical	countermand	geometrical	lithotripsy	polymorphic
nickelplate	allomorphic	countermark	ghostwriter	lophobranch	populariser
ommatophore	altostratus	countermine	GraecoRoman	lowspirited	pornography
orthoepical	ambiversion	countermove	grangeriser	magistratic	porphyritic
outcropping	ameliorator	countermure	greengrocer	maidservant	pourparlers
overlapping	amenorrhoea	counterpane	haemorrhage	mailcarrier	praetorship
overtopping	anagnorisis	counterpart	haemorrhoid	managership	premiership
oysterplant	angiography	counterplan	Hagiographa	masquerader	proctorship
ozonosphere	AngloFrench	counterplea	hagiography	matriarchal	prothoracic
paratyphoid	anisotropic	counterplot	haplography	mediatrices	pullthrough
photosphere	annabergite	countersign	harbourless	meritorious	quarterback
plainspoken	anniversary	countersink	hardworking	mesomorphic	quarterdeck
planisphere	antiphrasis	countersunk	headborough	metachrosis	quartertone
playerpiano	antipyretic	counterturn	heartbroken	metamorphic	quickfreeze
plectoptera	antistrophe	countervail	hebephrenia	micrography	quickfrozen
polypeptide	aponeuroses	counterview	hebephrenic	microgroove	quilldriver
postnuptial	aponeurosis	counterwork	hedgepriest	miscarriage	radiography
presumption	aponeurotic	crackerjack	heliography	mismarriage	reapportion
presumptive	appropriate	cryosurgery	heliotropic	moisturiser	reassertion
principally	bilaterally	curatorship	hemimorphic	monitorship	reassurance
pseudopodia	biometrical	cylindrical	heroworship	monocarpous	recoverable
psychopathy	biquadratic	decelerator	Hippocratic	monochromat	redetermine
quadraphony	blackgrouse	deflagrator	homestretch	monochromic	reedwarbler
quadrupedal	bladderwort	deleterious	homomorphic	monomorphic	regenerable
racketpress	blepharitis	deliverable	hydrobromic	motherright	regenerator
rattlepated	blunderbuss	deliverance	hydrography	mythography	registrable
sclerophyll	bodyservant	deliveryman	hydrotropic	nailvarnish	reincarnate
selfimposed	Bonapartean	denumerable	hymnography	Neanderthal	reinsertion
selfreproof	Bonapartism	desideratum	hypercritic	neurotropic	reinsurance
selfsupport	Bonapartist	dexiotropic	hypertrophy	nittygritty	remembrance
shortspoken	bondservant	diametrical	hypsography	nyctitropic	remunerator
showerproof	bondservice	diaphoresis	ichnography	obstetrical	reprogramme
shrinkproof	bowdleriser	diaphoretic	iconography	ochlocratic	reprography
silverplate	brankursine	diarthrosis	idiomorphic	omnifarious	ringstraked
silverpoint	breadcrumbs	directrices	illiberally	opencircuit	scalearmour
somatoplasm	brotherhood	disapproval	illustrator	opprobrious	scattergood
spermaphyte	bullterrier	discography	illustrious	orthography	scenography
steatopygia	burglarious	discourtesy	impropriate	orthotropic	scholarship
stereophony	butcherbird	dittography	impropriety	osteography	scissorbill
stirrupbone	calendrical	dropcurtain	inadvertent	overgarment	scissortail
stirruppump	californium	dropforging	inalterable	overstretch	scoundrelly
stringpiece	calligraphy	dualpurpose	inalterably	oxyhydrogen	screwdriver
strongpoint	calyptrogen	earpiercing	inaugurator	Palaearctic	scuppernong
subscapular	cantharides	ectomorphic	incinerator	palindromic	secondrater
subsumption	cantharidic	elbowgrease	incoherence	panegyrical	selffertile
subsumptive	cartography	embowerment	incoherency	paramorphic	selfservice
subtropical	catachreses	emperorship	incongruent	paraphraser	selfserving
theosophist	catachresis	enarthrosis	incongruity	partnership	selftorture
thermophile	catastrophe	encumbrance	incongruous	pasteuriser	selfworship
threadpaper	categorical	endocardiac	industrious	patriarchal	senatorship

septifragal	weatherwise	diagnostics	linguistics	scyphistoma	algorithmic
shelterbelt	weatherworn	diatessaron	lowpressure	secondsight	allocatable
shelterless	weighbridge	discussable	luminescent	seismoscope	allopathist
shepherdess	wheelwright	discussible	malfeasance	selfassured	amaranthine
shocktroops	whitherward	disguisedly	manifestant	selfdespair	amphictyony
shutterless	widowerhood	dispensable	manifestoes	selfdisplay	ancientness
sinistrally	woodcarving	dispersedly	mantelshelf	selfmastery	anecdotical
sinistrorse	xylocarpous	distensible	manumission	selfrespect	anfractuous
slavedriver	zincography	distressful	marlinspike	seriousness	anticathode
slenderness	zygomorphic	distrustful	marquessate	sexagesimal	antivitamin
smithereens	acaulescent	doublespeak	marquisette	sexlessness	apparatchik
snickersnee	acquiescent	dubiousness	meadowsweet	silversmith	appointment
soldierlike	aimlessness	emulousness	metoposcopy	silverstick	atheistical
soldiership	airlessness	endlessness	middlesized	singlestick	attemptable
Southernism	alkalescent	engrossment	misconstrue	sinlessness	attractable
spatterdash	amazonstone	enterostomy	misfeasance	sinuousness	augmentable
speakership	amethystine	enviousness	mistrustful	smorgasbord	autochthony
spessartite	amorousness	epidiascope	monkeyshine	stereoscope	automatable
sponsorship	anxiousness	equidistant	nationstate	stereoscopy	babysitting
standardise	arborescent	everlasting	nervousness	stethoscope	barbastelle
stenography	arduousness	exercisable	nonexistent	stethoscopy	basipetally
stockbroker	armtwisting	expressible	nonfeasance	stroboscope	bellbottoms
stoneground	arthrospore	fatuousness	nonplussing	submersible	benightedly
stormtroops	artlessness	fiddlestick	nonsensical	submissible	benightment
stylography	Belorussian	fingerstall	noxiousness	summersault	bibliotheca
subumbrella	biliousness	fluorescein	obmutescent	sunlessness	birdwatcher
succourless	billetsdoux	fluorescent	obsolescent	suppression	bloodstream
sulphureous	billposting	fluoroscope	obviousness	suppressive	capacitance
sulphurwort	biophysical	fluoroscopy	odorousness	surpassable	caricatural
symmetrical	bittersweet	freemasonry	ominousness	suspenseful	casuistical
tachygraphy	bondwashing	galleyslave	onerousness	suspensible	chainstitch
taciturnity	businessman	gallowsbird	organisable	synthesiser	charcuterie
tankfarming	callousness	gallowstree	Panglossian	talentscout	charlatanry
taxidermist	candlestick	gartersnake	paradisical	tediousness	chiropteran
teachership	carpetsnake	gaseousness	pearlescent	tenuousness	cholesterol
temerarious	caryopsides	gastroscope	permissible	thermoscope	climacteric
testatrices	chargesheet	geophysical	permissibly	thwartships	coexistence
thitherward	chiaroscuro	gibbousness	persuasible	topdressing	coffeetable
thixotropic	chinoiserie	godforsaken	phalanstery	totalisator	collectable
thunderbird	chromosomal	godlessness	phantasiast	tracasserie	collectanea
thunderbolt	chronoscope	groundsheet	phantasmata	Trappistine	collectedly
thunderclap	circumsolar	gutlessness	piteousness	traversable	collectible
thunderhead	circumspect	guttersnipe	plagiostome	trelliswork	combustible
thunderless	civilisable	handfasting	ploughshare	turtleshell	comfortable
thunderpeal	clandestine	haplessness	ploughstaff	typecasting	comfortably
timebargain	clothesline	hearthstone	pocketsized	unadvisedly	comfortless
timeserving	clothesmoth	heinousness	polarisable	unchristian	commentator
transcriber	clothesprop	heterospory	polariscope	unipersonal	committable
transuranic	cobblestone	hideousness	pompousness	universally	compactness
triggerfish	cockleshell	Hindoostani	preexistent	unnecessary	compartment
trouserless	collapsible	hugeousness	prestissimo	uselessness	complotting
trousersuit	commensally	hypogastric	proconsular	vacuousness	comportment
tuttifrutti	commissural	implausible	procrustean	vaporisable	conceitedly
unalterable	commonsense	implausibly	professedly	variousness	concentrate
unassertive	compassable	impressible	progression	vichyssoise	conceptacle
underground	compensator	impressment	progressism	viciousness	concertedly
undergrowth	compossible	impuissance	progressist	viridescent	concertgoer
underwriter	compression	inadvisable	progressive	virilescent	condottiere
undeserving	compressive	incalescent	protrusible	viscousness	condottieri
undesirable	comprisable	increasable	pumicestone	wappenschaw	conductance
unendurable	concrescent	indehiscent	purchasable	wellwishing	conductible
unendurably	condensable	indigestion	purpresture	widdershins	conductress
unimportant	confessedly	indigestive	rattlesnake	windlestraw	conjectural
unmemorable	congressman	indivisible	raucousness	winetasting	connectable
unmemorably	connoisseur	indivisibly	reminiscent	withershins	connectedly
unnaturally	contrastive	inexcusable	renaissance	witlessness	connectible
unsaturated	conversable	inexcusably	repressible	zealousness	consentient
unutterable	conversance	interesting	repressibly	absorptance	consistence
unutterably	conversancy	interosseus	resipiscent	abstentious	consistency
uranography	copingstone	intumescent	responsible	accipitrine	constituent
urochordate	copiousness	irrecusable	responsibly	accountable	constitutor
urticarious	coppersmith	irrecusably	retinoscopy	accountably	consultancy
vehmgericht	corbiesteps	irremissive	retranslate	accountancy	contentedly
vicegerency	cornerstone	jealousness	reviviscent	accusatival	contentious
vinaigrette	cornhusking	joylessness	riotousness	acquittance	contentment
vituperator	curiousness	juvenescent	rottenstone	acropetally	contestable
vociferance	delitescent	kinetoscope	rubberstamp	aesthetical	contretemps
vociferator	depressible	lawlessness	ruinousness	agonistical	conventicle
weathercock	deviousness	linefishing	saplessness	alabastrine	convertible

convertibly	homeostatic	parasitical	spectatress	aeronautics	infrequence
correctable	homiletical	parasitosis	spermatozoa	afterburner	infrequency
correctness	homoestatic	patristical	sphincteral	anacoluthon	institution
corruptible	hyacinthine	perceptible	sphincteric	antifouling	interfusion
corruptibly	hydrostatic	perceptibly	splenetical	antineutron	interlunary
corruptness	hypersthene	perfectible	stagestruck	attribution	internuncio
credentials	iconostases	perfectness	stalactitic	attributive	interrupter
crossstitch	iconostasis	periostitis	statistical	avoirdupois	interruptor
currentness	illimitable	peripatetic	stereotyped	backcountry	intriguante
dedicatedly	illimitably	persistence	stereotyper	barbiturate	ipecacuanha
delightedly	impenetrate	persistency	stereotypic	bellfounder	itacolumite
delightsome	impenitence	pervertedly	sternutator	blockbuster	loudmouthed
demonstrate	impenitency	phyllotaxis	studentship	bloodguilty	maladjusted
demountable	impolitical	phytosterol	subcontract	bloodsucker	mandibulate
dendritical	impoliticly	pietistical	subcontrary	brachyurous	matriculate
diacritical	impractical	pragmatical	subcortical	calcifugous	metallurgic
dialectally	inadaptable	precautious	subcritical	campanulate	miniaturise
dialectical	inappetence	precentress	subcultural	carunculate	miniaturist
dimwittedly	inconstancy	preceptress	sublittoral	comminution	noctilucent
diningtable	indomitable	precontract	submultiple	confabulate	nonsequitur
dinnertable	indomitably	predictable	subsistence	consecution	openmouthed
discontinue	indubitable	predictably	substituent	consecutive	opportunely
disgustedly	indubitably	prefectural	suggestible	consequence	opportunism
disportment	ineluctable	prehistoric	superstrata	construable	opportunist
dissentient	ineluctably	presbyteral	supportable	constructor	opportunity
dissertator	inequitable	presentable	supportably	continuable	orangoutang
distasteful	inequitably	presentably	susceptible	continually	overstuffed
doublethink	inexactness	presentient	susceptibly	continuance	parachutist
draughtsman	inexistence	presentment	sweepstakes	continuator	paramountcy
earnestness	infinitival	pretentious	sybaritical	convolution	paramountly
egotistical	inhabitable	preventable	syntactical	corbiculate	particulate
elementally	inhabitancy	preventible	synthetical	daisycutter	pedunculate
enchantment	inheritable	progestogen	tagliatelle	decarburise	peninsulate
enchantress	inheritress	prognathism	tagliatelli	decolourise	perambulate
encrustment	inscrutable	prognathous	telepathise	delinquency	perineurium
endometrium	inscrutably	prophethood	telepathist	denticulate	perpetually
enigmatical	interatomic	prophetical	tempestuous	destitution	perpetuance
enlightened	intractable	prophetship	tendentious	difficultly	perpetuator
entreatment	intractably	proportions	terrestrial	dinosaurian	persecution
entrustment	ipsilateral	prostitutor	thaumatrope	disaccustom	pilotburner
epigastrium	irrefutable	protectoral	thaumaturge	disannulled	polevaulter
equilateral	irrefutably	protectress	thaumaturgy	disencumber	prematurely
escheatable	isogeotherm	provostship	theoretical	disillusion	prematurity
escheatment	Jacobitical	purportedly	thermotaxis	dissimulate	preoccupied
evidentiary	judgmatical	quadratical	thoughtless	dissolutely	prolocutrix
exhaustible	kinematical	rallentando	toploftical	dissolution	prosecution
exhaustless	knownothing	reconstruct	trimestrial	dramaturgic	prosecutrix
exorbitance	Lancastrian	recruitment	triquetrous	dumbfounder	pulverulent
expeditious	latchstring	redoubtable	typesetting	echosounder	ratatouille
exploitable	lateritious	reenactment	uncluttered	effectually	recalculate
extractable	laurustinus	reflectance	uncountable	encapsulate	restitution
fantastical	Leibnitzian	regrettable	understated	ensanguined	retribution
felspathoid	leviratical	regrettably	undoubtedly	expostulate	retributive
fermentable	logarithmic	remonstrant	ungetatable	exstipulate	retributory
filmsetting	loosestrife	remonstrate	unhealthily	fasciculate	Rosicrucian
firewatcher	manumitting	renegotiate	unlimitedly	folliculate	seigneurial
flirtatious	marqueterie	repetitious	unpalatable	footpoundal	semidiurnal
forfeitable	mediastinal	respectable	unpolitical	foulmouthed	sharepusher
forgettable	mediastinum	respectably	unprintable	fourflusher	solifluxion
gallantness	moderations	retractable	unquietness	fourpounder	somniculous
gasfittings	monophthong	rheumaticky	unremitting	frankfurter	spiraculate
geotectonic	monophthong	rhizanthous	unrighteous	frontrunner	spiritually
goodnatured	multistorey	rickettsial	upholsterer	fullmouthed	spiritualty
grammatical	myxomatosis	rumbustious	uprightness	funambulate	spirituelle
haemoptysis	Neoplatonic	satinstitch	valiantness	funambulist	starstudded
haemostasis	nominatival	sclerotitis	verdantique	furunculous	stonecurlew
haemostatic	nonpartisan	scrumptious	vespertinal	gesticulate	stonecutter
hardhitting	novelettish	segmentally	warrantable	glasscutter	strangulate
harvesthome	occipitally	selfpitying	warrantably	hardmouthed	subsequence
heartstring	omnipotence	semeiotical	wildcatting	holothurian	superlunary
heldentenor	optometrist	sententious	wirenetting	homoiousian	supersubtle
helminthoid	orchestrate	septentrion	woodcutting	honeysuckle	surrebuttal
hereditable	orthopteran	sequestrate	Zoroastrian	importunate	surrebutter
heterotaxis	outdistance	singletrack	accentually	importunely	tentaculate
heterotroph	oversetting	slaughterer	acculturate	importunity	terraqueous
heterotypic	paediatrics	somatotonia	adventuress	incorruptly	trabeculate
hexametrist	paediatrist	somatotonic	adventurism	incredulity	transfusion
highpitched	palaeotypic	sophistical	adventurist	incredulous	transhumant
homeostasis	parametrise	soupkitchen	adventurous	ineloquence	translucent

translunary	Scotchwoman	accelerator	castellated	continuance	empirically
triangulate	shallowness	accentually	caustically	continuator	emptyheaded
trustbuster	sparrowbill	accountable	celestially	contrabasso	encumbrance
tuberculate	sparrowhawk	accountably	centigramme	contradance	endemically
tuberculise	spokeswoman	accountancy	certifiable	contrivable	enforceable
tuberculose	sportswoman	accumulator	certifiably	contrivance	enlargeable
tuberculous	swallowable	acidifiable	chaotically	conversable	episcopally
typefounder	swallowdive	acquittance	charismatic	conversance	epithalamia
typefoundry	swallowhole	acropetally	charlatanry	conversancy	epithalamic
unaccounted	swallowtail	adjudicator	cheerleader	convivially	equivocally
undisguised	swallowwort	adulterator	cheiromancy	coordinator	equivocator
undisturbed	tiddlywinks	adverbially	chirography	corporeally	erratically
unfortunate	washerwoman	aerobically	chorography	correctable	escheatable
unguiculate	wildfowling	aerodynamic	christiania	cosmography	essentially
unisexually	complexness	AfroAsiatic	Christianly	countenance	ethnography
unobtrusive	overanxious	agnatically	Christmassy	crenellated	eugenically
valleculate	paradoxical	alembicated	chrominance	crossbearer	exaggerator
vermiculate	perplexedly	allocatable	chronically	cryptically	exercisable
vermiculite	underexpose	altostratus	civilisable	cryptogamic	exorbitance
wellfounded	androgynous	ameliorator	classically	deactivator	explainable
wellrounded	anthocyanin	amphisbaena	cleanshaven	decelerator	exploitable
witchhunter	apocalyptic	anaphylaxis	clearheaded	decennially	extractable
aggrievedly	borborygmus	angelically	coeternally	deflagrator	factionally
blackavised	carbocyclic	angiography	coffeetable	deistically	faithhealer
cesarevitch	cataclysmic	annihilator	coinsurance	deliverable	fanatically
circumvolve	countryfied	annunciator	collectable	deliverance	fashionable
conceivable	countryseat	anthocyanin	collectanea	demonolatry	fashionably
conceivably	countryside	anticipator	collinearly	demountable	fenestrated
conservable	countrywide	antiphrasis	columniated	denominator	fermentable
conservancy	farawayness	antivitamin	comeuppance	denumerable	filmography
conservator	flamboyance	antonomasia	comfortable	denunciator	filterpaper
contrivable	flamboyancy	Apollinaris	comfortably	depopulator	financially
contrivance	flamboyante	applaudable	commendable	depreciator	fissionable
controversy	haemocyanin	appreciable	commendably	depthcharge	flagellator
convolvulus	hairstyling	appreciably	commendator	desalinator	flamboyance
deactivator	hairstylist	appreciator	commensally	descendable	flamboyancy
dissolvable	hydrocyanic	aquatically	commentator	describable	flamboyante
enterovirus	hypophyseal	archaically	committable	desideratum	foraminated
genitivally	hypophysial	articulable	compassable	developable	forbearance
irrelevance	journeywork	articulated	compellable	dialectally	forbiddance
irrelevancy	metaphysics	articulator	compensator	diastematic	foreseeable
irremovable	metapsychic	ascetically	complicated	diatessaron	forfeitable
irremovably	Monophysite	aseptically	comprisable	dichromatic	forgettable
lilylivered	nurserymaid	asphyxiator	compurgator	dilapidated	fortifiable
margraviate	overpayment	assimilable	concealable	dilapidator	Francomania
marketvalue	parathyroid	assimilator	conceivable	diningtable	frantically
mediaevally	pentagynous	attemptable	conceivably	dinnerdance	fraternally
menservants	phagocytise	attractable	conceptacle	dinnertable	furtherance
overdevelop	phagocytose	augmentable	conciliator	dinnerwagon	generically
perceivable	phycocyanin	auricularly	concordance	discardable	genetically
perceivably	phylogynist	automatable	condemnable	discography	geniculated
preservable	podophyllin	bacchanalia	condensable	discordance	genitivally
primaevally	polycrystal	BaltoSlavic	conductance	discordancy	gentlemanly
retrievable	polyonymous	baptismally	conferrable	discrepancy	glossolalia
safetyvalve	polystyrene	basipetally	confirmable	discussable	godforsaken
selfdevoted	proselytise	bathyscaphe	confiscable	dislikeable	graphically
selfinvited	proselytism	bibliolater	confiscator	dispensable	greasepaint
Stradivarii	pyrargyrite	bibliolatry	conformable	dissertator	groundwater
subservient	rockcrystal	bibliomancy	conformably	dissociable	haemocyanin
unequivocal	seventyfold	bibliomania	conformally	dissolvable	haemostasis
welladvised	stenotypist	bilaterally	conformance	dissyllable	haemostatic
breastwheel	stringybark	billionaire	congealable	disturbance	Hagiographa
cesarewitch	tautonymous	binocularly	congenially	dittography	hagiography
churchwoman	teknonymous	biquadratic	connectable	doctrinaire	hairbreadth
craftswoman	tetracyclic	blackcoated	connubially	doctrinally	handbreadth
dinnerwagon	touchtyping	boilermaker	conquerable	doublefaced	haplography
Frenchwoman	viceroyalty	botanically	consecrator	drastically	harumscarum
gentlewoman	viceroyship	brainteaser	conservable	dynamically	heavenwards
groundwater	Wensleydale	brazenfaced	conservancy	editorially	Hebraically
heavenwards	worldlywise	broadleaved	conservator	effectually	heliography
Hepplewhite	yacketyyack	bucolically	consignable	elastically	hereditable
highpowered	————	Byronically	conspirator	elasticated	heretically
hitherwards	abbreviator	calceolaria	construable	elementally	heterotaxis
jabberwocky	abdominally	calligraphy	consultancy	emancipator	Hippocratic
needlewoman	abiotically	calumniator	consummator	emasculator	historiated
netherworld	abolishable	cancellated	containable	embraceable	hitherwards
paddlewheel	abracadabra	canonically	contestable	embryonated	hollandaise
policewoman	absorptance	capacitance	continuable	Emmenthaler	homeostasis
prayerwheel	accelerando	cartography	continually	emotionally	homeostatic

homesteader	insouciance	mythography	primaevally	sightreader	uncrushable
homoeopathy	insufflator	naturopathy	principally	sigmoidally	undercharge
homoestatic	insuperable	nocturnally	problematic	signifiable	understated
hydraheaded	insuperably	nomadically	procephalic	sinistrally	undesirable
hydrocyanic	intagliated	nomenclator	promulgator	smoothfaced	unendurable
hydrography	interchange	nonchalance	proofreader	sockdolager	unendurably
hydrostatic	interleaves	nonfeasance	prophylaxis	somatically	unflappable
hymnography	interplayed	numerically	propitiable	spaceheater	ungetatable
hypercharge	intimidator	nymphomania	propitiator	spastically	unisexually
hyperphagia	intolerable	occipitally	prosaically	specifiable	universally
hyperplasia	intolerably	ochlocratic	prothalamia	spherically	unmatchable
hypsography	intolerance	octagonally	prothoracic	spiritually	unmemorable
ichnography	intractable	officinally	protrudable	spiritualty	unmemorably
iconography	intractably	oligochaete	psychically	spirochaete	unmitigated
iconostases	intriguante	oneiromancy	psychopathy	spreadeagle	unnaturally
iconostasis	invigilator	operculated	publishable	statesmanly	unpalatable
identically	invigorator	opinionated	purchasable	stenography	unprintable
idiotically	ipecacuanha	orbicularly	purificator	sternutator	unsaturated
idyllically	irrecusable	organically	pyramidally	stomachache	unshockable
illiberally	irrecusably	organisable	qualifiable	Stradivarii	unspeakable
illimitable	irrefutable	orthography	quickchange	straitlaced	unspeakably
illimitably	irrefutably	osmotically	quizzically	stretchable	unstoppable
illogically	irregularly	osteography	radiography	stridulator	unteachable
illuminable	irrelevance	osteoplasty	rallentando	stylography	unthinkable
illuminance	irrelevancy	outdistance	rattlepated	subaerially	unthinkably
illuminator	irremovable	overbalance	reassurance	sugarcoated	untouchable
illustrator	irremovably	pacifically	reclaimable	summersault	unutterable
immedicable	irreparable	pacificator	recoverable	supercharge	unutterably
immitigable	irreparably	papiermache	rectifiable	superheater	Upanishadic
immitigably	irrevocable	paraphraser	redoubtable	supportable	uranography
impartially	irrevocably	parheliacal	reflectance	supportably	vaporisable
impeachable	juridically	parochially	regenerable	surficially	vasodilator
impermeable	justiciable	paronomasia	regenerator	surpassable	vaticinator
impermeably	justifiable	pensionable	registrable	sustainable	venatically
imperviable	justifiably	perceivable	regrettable	swallowable	veridically
impregnable	kleptomania	perceivably	regrettably	sweepstakes	vesicularly
impregnably	Kulturkampf	perennially	reinsurance	swellheaded	vestigially
impuissance	lachrymator	performable	rejuvenator	swordbearer	viceregally
inadaptable	laconically	performance	remembrance	symposiarch	viceroyalty
inadvisable	legionnaire	periphrases	remunerator	symptomatic	vitrifiable
inalienable	levelheaded	periphrasis	renaissance	tachygraphy	vituperator
inalienably	lieutenancy	perpetrator	replaceable	tarnishable	vociferance
inalterable	lightheaded	perpetually	repleviable	technically	vociferator
inalterably	linendraper	perpetuance	reprogramme	tephromancy	wapperjawed
inaugurator	liquefiable	perpetuator	reprography	tessellated	warrantable
incinerator	lithography	persuadable	resemblance	tetanically	warrantably
inconstancy	lophobranch	perturbable	respectable	theorematic	wedgeshaped
increasable	loudspeaker	petrography	respectably	thermically	whimsically
indefinable	magistratic	petticoated	retraceable	thermotaxis	Whitechapel
indefinably	maintenance	phonography	retractable	thickheaded	whiteheaded
indomitable	malfeasance	photography	retrievable	thingumabob	windcheater
indomitably	manipulable	phrasemaker	rhabdomancy	thingumajig	worldbeater
indubitable	manipulator	phthiriasis	ringstraked	threadpaper	worshipable
indubitably	mantuamaker	phycocyanin	ruridecanal	throatlatch	wrongheaded
ineluctable	marketvalue	phyllotaxis	safebreaker	timepleaser	zincography
ineluctably	masquerader	phytography	safetyvalve	titanically	biofeedback
inequitable	mediaevally	pictography	saltimbanco	torchbearer	blunderbuss
inequitably	medicinable	pictorially	salvageable	totalisator	butcherbird
inescapable	medicinally	pipecleaner	sanguinaria	toxicomania	candelabrum
inestimable	megalomania	piratically	sarcophagus	trafficator	comestibles
inestimably	menservants	pleasurable	sartorially	trailblazer	counterblow
inexcusable	mentholated	pleasurably	satanically	trainbearer	counterbond
inexcusably	mentionable	plutocratic	satirically	transuranic	deoxyribose
infiltrator	mercurially	pococurante	satisfiable	traversable	diamondback
inflammable	mesalliance	polarisable	scenography	treasonable	exarcerbate
inflammably	metasomatic	polemically	sceptically	treasonably	gallowsbird
inhabitable	micrography	politically	secondrater	triadically	herringbone
inhabitancy	millionaire	polygonally	sectionally	triennially	hummingbird
inheritable	mimetically	pornography	segmentally	trisyllabic	immoveables
inheritance	misalliance	potentially	seismically	trisyllable	jumpingbean
innavigable	miscellanea	practicable	selfcreated	unalterable	knucklebone
innumerable	misfeasance	practicably	sensorially	unavailable	landgrabber
innumerably	misguidance	practically	septifragal	unavoidable	landingbeam
inscribable	mithridatic	predictable	serviceable	unavoidably	leatherback
inscrutable	molecularly	predictably	serviceably	unbreakable	mockingbird
inscrutably	moronically	presentable	sheriffalty	uncatchable	palmcabbage
inseminator	morrisdance	presentably	shipbreaker	unclimbable	perishables
inseparable	mothernaked	preservable	shockheaded	unconcealed	picturebook
inseparably	municipally	preventable	shortchange	uncountable	quarterback

reedwarbler	eclecticism	parallactic	translocate	outbreeding	antipyretic
scissorbill	ecumenicism	paramoecium	translucent	outbuilding	aposiopesis
scuttlebutt	ecumenicity	paraplectic	tribunicial	outstanding	arboraceous
servicebook	electrician	patriarchal	tyrannicide	overbidding	archangelic
shacklebolt	electricity	pearlescent	unconnected	overproduce	archdukedom
shacklebone	electrocute	pentadactyl	viridescent	pellucidity	ascomycetes
shelterbelt	ellipticity	pentazocine	virilescent	pentahedron	astringency
smorgasbord	epidiascope	periodicity	volcanicity	pentlandite	atmospheric
sparrowbill	erythrocyte	perithecium	vulcanicity	pericardiac	auxanometer
statutebook	esotericism	pertinacity	wappenschaw	pericardial	barbastelle
steeplebush	exotericism	phonetician	weathercock	pericardium	barefacedly
stickleback	firecracker	phototactic	wisecracker	preprandial	beneficence
stirrupbone	firewatcher	picturecard	witchdoctor	quarterdeck	benevolence
stockjobber	fluorescein	playingcard	accommodate	reachmedown	benightedly
stringybark	fluorescent	Pleistocene	AngloIndian	reintroduce	bewhiskered
supersubtle	fluoroscope	polariscope	antemundane	resplendent	bibliopegic
thunderbird	fluoroscopy	pontificals	antependium	retrocedent	biedermeier
thunderbolt	gastroscope	pontificate	antheridium	rhomboideus	blackbeetle
academicals	granulocyte	postglacial	antioxidant	rhynchodont	blastogenic
academician	gynaecocrat	prejudicial	Archimedean	roadholding	boysenberry
academicism	haematocele	preselector	bicuspidate	rubicundity	butyraceous
acatalectic	haematocrit	prevaricate	billetsdoux	safeconduct	calisthenic
acaulescent	hermeticism	prolificacy	bookbinding	salesladies	calorimeter
acoustician	heteroecism	prolificity	chafingdish	sauropodous	calorimetry
acquiescent	hibernacula	pterodactyl	Chippendale	scaffolding	camaraderie
agnosticism	Hibernicism	quincuncial	chiropodist	sculduddery	candescence
alkalescent	highpitched	receptacula	clostridium	selfevident	candleberry
amphimictic	Hispanicise	reciprocate	codefendant	selffeeding	carrageenan
amplexicaul	Hispanicism	reciprocity	consolidate	selfloading	carrageenin
apparatchik	Hispanicist	reduplicate	cypripedium	selfwinding	carriageway
arborescent	historicise	reminiscent	demigoddess	shepherdess	catachreses
archdiocese	historicism	resipiscent	desperadoes	skulduddery	catachresis
aromaticity	historicist	retinoscopy	doubleedged	spatterdash	centripetal
artiodactyl	historicity	retrorocket	downtrodden	sphaeridium	chanterelle
athleticism	honeysuckle	reviviscent	enchiridion	standardise	charcuterie
Aurignacian	horsedoctor	rhetorician	endocardiac	starstudded	chartaceous
awestricken	hunchbacked	rodenticide	endocardial	stylopodium	chinoiserie
azotobacter	hydrotactic	romanticise	endocardium	substandard	chiropteran
backbencher	hypothecate	romanticism	enneahedron	superinduce	chokecherry
bactericide	illaffected	romanticist	factfinding	supersedeas	cholesterol
balmcricket	imperfectly	ropedancing	footsoldier	supersedure	chronometer
billsticker	incalescent	Rosicrucian	fullfledged	swallowdive	chronometry
birdfancier	incorrectly	sacrificial	gallbladder	swimbladder	chrysoberyl
birdwatcher	indehiscent	safecracker	godchildren	tarradiddle	cinquecento
bloodsucker	infanticide	seismoscope	gourmandise	tetrahedral	climacteric
brainsickly	insecticide	selfconceit	gourmandism	tetrahedron	coalescence
bushwhacker	interfacial	selfelected	halfbinding	tetrapodous	cockaleekie
carbocyclic	interfacing	semanticist	halflanding	thistledown	cockyleekie
cataplectic	interjacent	sextodecimo	hesperidium	transpadane	coexistence
catholicise	interlocker	sheetanchor	honeybadger	ultramodern	cognoscente
Catholicism	internecine	shelljacket	horseradish	underbidder	cognoscenti
catholicity	interracial	shuttlecock	hydromedusa	unorthodoxy	coincidence
certificate	intumescent	significant	icosahedral	urochordate	collectedly
chemotactic	juvenescent	Slavonicise	icosahedron	vagabondage	colorimeter
chiaroscuro	kinetoscope	soupkitchen	illbreeding	vagabondise	colorimetry
chronoscope	lamellicorn	specificity	illiquidity	vagabondish	commonsense
cicatricial	leptodactyl	spifflicate	improvident	vagabondism	complacence
cityslicker	liberticide	stereoscope	incarnadine	Wensleydale	complacency
clapperclaw	luminescent	stereoscopy	incommodity	abiogeneses	conceitedly
communicant	magnificent	stethoscope	independent	abiogenesis	concertedly
communicate	matriarchal	stethoscopy	interbedded	abiogenetic	concurrence
concrescent	mechanician	stiffnecked	intermeddle	aboutsledge	confessedly
constrictor	meningocele	stroboscope	intermedium	accrescence	connectedly
constructor	metapsychic	superficial	intrepidity	acknowledge	consequence
cosmetician	metoposcopy	superficies	landholding	actinometer	consistence
crookbacked	micrococcal	superjacent	landlordism	adolescence	consistency
cupronickel	micrococcus	supremacist	latifundium	aggrievedly	contentedly
decorticate	microsecond	syllabicity	massproduce	aiguillette	contingence
delitescent	millisecond	tabernacled	merchandise	alkalimeter	contingency
didacticism	molecricket	talentscout	merryandrew	alkalimetry	contretemps
diplococcus	monasticism	tetracyclic	mindbending	ambivalence	controversy
dipterocarp	multiracial	tetradactyl	mindreading	ambivalency	convenience
disaffected	neuroticism	Teutonicism	mollycoddle	amentaceous	conveniency
disinfector	noctilucent	theatricals	moribundity	anaesthesia	convergence
diverticula	obmutescent	thermoscope	nonresident	anaesthetic	convergency
domesticate	obsolescent	threedecker	nullifidian	AngloFrench	cookgeneral
domesticity	opencircuit	thrombocyte	orthopedics	antecedence	costbenefit
doorknocker	packingcase	thunderclap	orthopedist		craniometry
earpiercing	Palaearctic		ostracoderm		crustaceous

cryptomeria	illtempered	persistency	spontaneity	lamelliform	marconigram
cyclopaedia	impedimenta	pervertedly	spontaneous	overstuffed	meliphagous
cyclopaedic	impenitence	phagedaenic	steerageway	passeriform	Merovingian
cytogenesis	impenitency	phariseeism	stereometry	patelliform	monolingual
cytokinesis	inappetence	philanderer	sternsheets	personifier	monophagous
decrescendo	incoherence	phytosterol	stichometry	photooffset	mudslinging
dedicatedly	incoherency	pigheadedly	stockinette	scalariform	mycophagist
delightedly	ineloquence	piperaceous	storekeeper	scalpriform	mythologise
delinquency	inexistence	pipistrelle	stramineous	seventyfold	mythologist
despondence	infrequence	pitchblende	submergence	severalfold	necrologist
despondency	infrequency	pluviometer	subsequence	speechifier	neurologist
diamagnetic	ingrainedly	polarimeter	subsistence	stampoffice	nightingale
diaphaneity	interpreter	polarimetry	subumbrella	standoffish	noctivagant
diaphoresis	intersperse	poltergeist	sufficiency	suckingfish	noctivagous
diaphoretic	interviewee	polygenesis	suffragette	surgeonfish	oesophageal
dicotyledon	interviewer	polygenetic	sulphureous	theretofore	ophiologist
dimwittedly	ionospheric	preaudience	suspenseful	trapeziform	oscillogram
disbeliever	ipsilateral	preconceive	sympathetic	triggerfish	osteologist
discalceate	iridescence	preeminence	tacheometer	unqualified	passacaglia
discotheque	irreverence	presbyteral	tagliatelle	vasculiform	pathologist
disgraceful	kitchenette	pressagency	tagliatelli	annabergite	pestologist
disguisedly	lactescence	pretendedly	telekinesis	anthologise	petrologist
disgustedly	lammergeier	professedly	telekinetic	anthologist	pettifogger
dispersedly	lammergeyer	proficiency	teratogenic	arbitrageur	phenologist
dissymmetry	landaulette	provenience	terraqueous	audiologist	philologian
distasteful	launderette	psychedelia	thermometer	bandylegged	philologist
distempered	lesemajesty	psychedelic	thermometry	bellringing	phonologist
dynamometer	lilylivered	psychogenic	tracasserie	bootlegging	phraseogram
dynamometry	liquescence	psychometry	tragedienne	borborygmus	phycologist
ectogenesis	loggerheads	punchinello	transpierce	calcifugous	phytologist
ectogenetic	magazinegun	purportedly	treecreeper	Carolingian	picturegoer
elastomeric	maisonnette	putrescence	turgescence	challenging	polyphagous
elbowgrease	maleficence	quadrupedal	twelvepenny	cleistogamy	radiologist
embroiderer	malevolence	quickfreeze	unadvisedly	concertgoer	rhinologist
enlightened	Manichaeism	reemergence	unashamedly	cosmologist	rightangled
epeirogenic	marcescence	refringency	unboundedly	crosslegged	roughlegged
equilateral	marqueterie	rejuvenesce	uncluttered	cryosurgery	sandbagging
equivalence	marquisette	resourceful	undoubtedly	dactylogram	scattergood
equivalency	marriagebed	respondence	unfeignedly	desegregate	sculduggery
erubescence	medicolegal	respondency	unguardedly	deuterogamy	skulduggery
evanescence	membraneous	retroflexed	uninucleate	disobliging	sleepingbag
excrescence	merogenesis	rhombohedra	unlimitedly	disparaging	sleepingcar
excrescency	metagenesis	rifacimenti	unrighteous	dropforging	snowgoggles
exoskeletal	metagenetic	rifacimento	upholsterer	endophagous	sociologist
exoskeleton	minesweeper	Sadduceeism	urticaceous	ethnologist	sovereignly
farinaceous	misconceive	salinometer	vaporimeter	etymologise	sovereignty
featheredge	misguidedly	salmonberry	varsovienne	etymologist	spectrogram
flannelette	monogenesis	sanguineous	vicegerency	euchologion	sphygmogram
flocculence	monogenetic	saponaceous	vinaigrette	extravagant	steganogram
florescence	munificence	scarabaeoid	violoncello	extravagate	stoolpigeon
forgetmenot	mythopoeist	schwarmerei	vitrescence	farthingale	subcategory
fourwheeler	mythopoetic	scleroderma	volkslieder	flabbergast	suffumigate
frankpledge	myxomycetes	sclerometer	volumometer	flagwagging	tautologise
fraudulence	nigrescence	scoriaceous	wellordered	florilegium	tautologism
fricandeaux	nonviolence	scoundrelly	wheresoever	footslogger	tautologous
gamogenesis	nympholepsy	seismometer	whichsoever	gametangium	teleologism
gendarmerie	oestrogenic	seismometry	whigmaleery	gemmologist	teleologist
gentianella	offhandedly	selaginella	whosesoever	genealogise	tentpegging
geomagnetic	omnipotence	selfdefence	winterberry	genealogist	theatregoer
goldenberry	omniscience	septicaemia	witenagemot	golddigging	threelegged
gradiometer	ontogenesis	septicaemic	xeranthemum	gravedigger	timebargain
greenkeeper	ontogenetic	seventeenth	yellowbelly	hagiologist	transfigure
gymnospermy	opalescence	shirtsleeve	acinaciform	hairtrigger	undersigned
habiliments	orthopaedic	sickbenefit	aftereffect	herringgull	waterlogged
hebephrenia	orthopteran	sidewheeler	bacilliform	histologist	xylophagous
hebephrenic	outspokenly	sightseeing	chickenfeed	hornswoggle	affranchise
heldentenor	overdevelop	sinfonietta	counterfeit	houselights	ailurophile
hemispheric	overstretch	slaughterer	counterfoil	hydrologist	ailurophobe
highpowered	panhellenic	smithereens	counterfort	intelligent	algorithmic
hobbledehoy	pantothenic	solanaceous	countrified	interregnum	allopathist
homestretch	papyraceous	somatogenic	countryfied	interrogate	amaranthine
homogeneity	paraselenae	spathaceous	Falstaffian	investigate	amenorrhoea
homogeneous	parentheses	speedometer	frenchified	ironmongery	anencephaly
homogenetic	parenthesis	spherometer	hereinafter	jauntingcar	anticathode
housekeeper	parenthetic	sphincteral	housewifely	landinggear	apomorphine
huckleberry	percipience	sphincteric	housewifery	laughinggas	archduchess
hylogenesis	peripatetic	spiritlevel	hundredfold	leapfrogged	autochthony
hypnopaedia	perplexedly	spirituelle	insectifuge	limnologist	basketchair
illmannered	persistence	spirochetal	intensifier	mammalogist	bathysphere

bibliophile	photosphere	appropriate	deleterious	impractical	oecumenical
bibliophily	pigeonchest	Areopagitic	demagogical	impressible	oenological
bibliotheca	planisphere	atheistical	dendritical	impropriate	omnifarious
boardschool	platyrrhine	atrabilious	depressible	impropriety	oncological
bondwashing	ploughshare	attitudinal	descendible	incoercible	ontological
bookinghall	polytechnic	autarchical	diacritical	incompliant	opprobrious
breastwheel	prayerwheel	axiological	dialectical	inconscient	oreological
brotherhood	prognathism	battlefield	diametrical	indivisible	orthoepical
bullfighter	prognathous	beneficiary	directrices	indivisibly	otherwhiles
chamaephyte	prophethood	beneficiate	discernible	industrious	overanxious
chargesheet	prosenchyma	bersaglieri	discernibly	inefficient	paedophilia
chlorophyll	pyrotechnic	biochemical	disciplinal	inexpedient	panegyrical
chucklehead	quadraphony	biometrical	discipliner	infinitival	paperweight
clairschach	reproachful	biophysical	discontinue	infrangible	paradisical
cochinchina	rhizanthous	birdbrained	discussible	injudicious	paradoxical
cockleshell	schoolchild	blackavised	disinclined	inofficious	paramedical
coleorrhiza	sclerophyll	blackmailer	disobedient	interspinal	parasitical
collenchyma	slotmachine	blepharitis	dissentient	intertribal	pasteuriser
diadelphous	sparrowhawk	bloodguilty	distensible	irreducible	patristical
dodecaphony	spermaphyte	bonbonniere	domiciliary	irreducibly	pedagogical
doublecheck	stereophony	bourgeoisie	domiciliate	irreligious	pedological
doublethink	swallowhole	boutonniere	efficacious	isometrical	pennyweight
enfranchise	tapemachine	bowdleriser	egotistical	Jacobinical	penological
entomophily	telepathise	Brahmanical	ellipsoidal	Jacobitical	perceptible
epigraphist	telepathist	Brahminical	enigmatical	judgmatical	perceptibly
eyecatching	tetrarchate	burglarious	ensanguined	kinematical	perfectible
farreaching	theosophist	calefacient	enterovirus	lateritious	periostitis
featherhead	thermophile	calendrical	enterpriser	latitudinal	peritonitis
felspathoid	thoroughpin	candlelight	entertainer	laurustinus	permissible
firefighter	thoroughwax	cantharides	ephemerides	leviratical	permissibly
foresighted	thunderhead	cantharidic	epithelioma	lightweight	persuasible
fortnightly	thwartships	carabiniere	ethological	lithotripsy	phantasiast
Francophile	trimorphism	carabinieri	evangelical	loculicidal	pharisaical
Francophobe	trimorphous	caryopsides	evidentiary	lowspirited	pharyngitis
francophone	tristichous	casuistical	executrices	makebelieve	photophilic
gametophyte	troposphere	categorical	executrixes	maladroitly	pietistical
gegenschein	tryptophane	centrepiece	exhaustible	mantelpiece	pillowfight
goddaughter	turtleshell	ceremonious	expeditious	marcescible	pivotbridge
groundsheet	ulotrichous	cesarevitch	expressible	margraviate	plagiariser
haemorrhage	unflinching	cesarewitch	expropriate	masterpiece	planetoidal
haemorrhoid	unhealthily	chainstitch	fantastical	mastoiditis	plasticiser
harpsichord	wellwishing	chieftaincy	flagofficer	mediastinal	playerpiano
harvesthome	widdershins	chimaerical	flirtatious	mediastinum	pneumonitis
hedgeschool	widowerhood	chrysalides	foraminifer	mediatrices	pocketsized
helminthoid	withershins	chrysalises	fraterniser	memorabilia	pomological
Hepplewhite	xanthochroi	Clarencieux	fratricidal	meritorious	populariser
heptarchist	xanthophyll	coconscious	furnishings	metalloidal	porphyritic
heterophony	zoographist	coefficient	gasfittings	meteoroidal	posological
hierarchism	zoomorphism	cognoscible	generaliser	metonymical	pragmatical
hyacinthine	abiological	coinheritor	geochemical	middlesized	precautious
hydrosphere	abranchiate	collapsible	geometrical	mineraliser	presentient
hypersthene	abstentious	collectible	geophysical	miscarriage	prestigious
isogeotherm	accusatival	combustible	ghostwriter	mismarriage	pretentious
isomorphism	achondritic	compendious	glauconitic	moderations	preventible
isomorphous	acidophilic	compossible	gormandiser	moisturiser	proceedings
knownothing	acrimonious	condottiere	grammatical	monarchical	prophetical
lamplighter	aerological	condottieri	grangeriser	moneyspider	proportions
lawmerchant	aeronomical	conductible	haemophilia	monological	protrusible
leatherhead	aesthetical	connectible	haemophilic	monopoliser	punctilious
linefishing	agonistical	consentient	halfholiday	monopoliser	puritanical
lithosphere	agrological	conspecific	harebrained	mustachioed	putrescible
logarithmic	agronomical	contentious	heavyweight	mycological	pyramidical
logomachist	ahistorical	conterminal	hedgepriest	mycorrhizae	quadratical
longsighted	algological	contorniate	Heracleidan	mycorrhizal	quilldriver
mantelshelf	allAmerican	contrariety	hexadecimal	myocarditis	ratatouille
melanochroi	allantoides	contrarious	homiletical	necrophilia	realpolitik
melanophore	allegorical	conventicle	homogeniser	necrophilic	reappraisal
monkeyshine	altitudinal	convertible	homological	Neotropical	rearadmiral
monophthong	altorelievo	convertibly	horological	neutraliser	reconnoitre
moonlighter	altorilievo	convincible	hydrophilic	nittygritty	refrangible
muttonchops	anagnorisis	coralloidal	hypercritic	nominatival	renegotiate
nearsighted	anecdotical	corecipient	ideological	nomological	repetitious
neckerchief	anthracitic	corruptible	ignominious	nonpartisan	repressible
nonmatching	anthropical	corruptibly	illustrious	nonsensical	repressibly
ommatophore	antimonious	coxcombical	impecunious	nonsequitur	responsible
ozonosphere	antirrhinum	credentials	implausible	nonspecific	responsibly
paddlewheel	antiSemitic	crossstitch	implausibly	nosological	rhapsodical
paraldehyde	antitypical	cylindrical	impolitical	obstetrical	rheological
paratyphoid	apostolical	cytological	impoliticly	oecological	rheumaticky

```
rubefacient  tonsillitis  acarpellous  controlling  funambulate  marginality
rumbustious  toploftical  aerobiology  copperplate  funambulist  marketplace
salpingitis  topological  agrobiology  corbiculate  furunculous  marshalling
satinstitch  transceiver  amenability  corporality  galleyslave  marshmallow
sclerotitis  transcriber  amicability  cosmetology  geanticline  martyrology
screwdriver  transilient  amontillado  cosmopolite  geosyncline  materialise
scribacious  trapezoidal  amphibolite  counselling  gerontology  materialism
scrumptious  triphibious  amphibology  credibility  gesticulate  materialist
scrutiniser  trothplight  anticyclone  crestfallen  gibberellin  materiality
searchlight  typological  antifouling  criminalist  grandiflora  matriculate
secondsight  uncanonical  apophyllite  criminality  gravelblind  meaningless
selfinvited  uncertainly  apparelling  criminology  gullibility  measureless
selflimited  uncertainty  aquarellist  criticality  gutturalise  medievalism
selfreliant  uncivilised  archaeology  crocidolite  gutturalism  medievalist
semeiotical  unconscious  archipelago  crocodilian  gynaecology  memorialise
semiellipse  underweight  arenicolous  cryobiology  haematology  memorialist
semitrailer  underwriter  arterialise  crystalline  hairstyling  meteorology
sententious  undisguised  aspergillum  crystallise  hairstylist  methodology
serological  unexploited  aspergillus  crystallite  halophilous  middleclass
sexagesimal  uninhabited  Assyriology  crystalloid  handselling  minuteglass
sexological  uninhibited  bestselling  culpability  harbourless  miscibility
simpliciter  unorganized  bicephalous  dactylology  haustellate  misspelling
sinological  unpolitical  biddability  deerstalker  heartsblood  mitrailleur
slavedriver  unsolicited  bimetallism  defenceless  heresiology  mononuclear
sonofabitch  urticarious  bimetallist  denticulate  herpetology  Monothelite
sophistical  vehmgericht  bisexuality  dermatology  heteroclite  moveability
spaceflight  verdantique  blackfellow  desexualise  heteroploid  multicolour
spasmodical  verisimilar  bodybuilder  detribalise  homothallic  multivalent
spermicidal  vespertinal  bookselling  dicephalous  horripilate  myrmecology
spherulitic  viceadmiral  bookshelves  difficultly  horsecollar  namecalling
splenetical  virological  bottleglass  diluvialist  hospitalise  naphthalene
spondulicks  waterskiing  bracteolate  disannulled  hospitality  nationalise
spondylitis  wedgetailed  breastplate  dishevelled  hospitaller  nationalism
stalactitic  weighbridge  breathalyse  dissimilate  householder  nationalist
stalagmitic  welladvised  breechblock  dissimulate  husbandlike  nationality
statistical  welldefined  breezeblock  educability  hyperbolise  necropoleis
staurolitic  wheelwright  bryozoology  electrolier  hyperboloid  nettlecloth
steamboiler  crackerjack  butterflies  electrology  hypocycloid  nickelplate
stipendiary  jumpingjack  calcicolous  electrolyse  ichthyology  nightwalker
strategical  steeplejack  campanology  electrolyte  immortalise  nonetheless
streetlight  bivouacking  campanulate  eligibility  immortality  nonmetallic
stringpiece  comstockery  cannibalise  embowelling  impanelling  notionalist
subclinical  cornhusking  cannibalism  emotionless  imperialise  oenophilist
subcortical  dressmaking  captionless  empanelling  imperialism  offenceless
subcritical  epochmaking  cardinalate  encapsulate  imperialist  officialdom
submarginal  firewalking  carunculate  endoskelton  imperilling  officialese
submersible  gimcrackery  caterpillar  endothelial  incredulity  officialism
submissible  glassmaking  cavedweller  endothelium  incredulous  olfactology
submultiple  goodlooking  chamberlain  enthralling  inedibility  orchidology
subservient  greenockite  chancellery  epipetalous  infantilism  orientalise
subspecific  hardworking  chancellory  equipollent  infertility  orientalism
subterminal  highranking  channelling  eschatology  informality  orientalist
subtropical  leavetaking  chanticleer  etherealise  initialling  originality
suggestible  matchmaking  cheesecloth  ethereality  insectology  ornithology
susceptible  merrymaking  chevalglass  Etruscology  instability  outrivalled
susceptibly  moneymaking  chitterling  eventualise  integrality  oversailing
suspensible  noisemaking  chloroplast  eventuality  interallied  oysterplant
sybaritical  nutcrackers  chockablock  exhaustless  intercalary  painkilling
symmetrical  painstaking  Christology  expostulate  intercalate  palpability
sympathiser  papermaking  chromoplast  exstipulate  internalise  parallelism
symphonious  pawnbroking  clericalism  externalise  internality  parallelled
synagogical  peacemaking  clericalist  externalism  interpolate  particulate
synonymical  Pickwickian  climatology  externality  interrelate  passibility
syntactical  pigsticking  clothesline  extrapolate  intervallic  pastoralism
synthesiser  politicking  codicillary  facsimilist  inviability  pastoralist
synthetical  ropewalking  colonialism  fallibility  ithyphallic  pastureland
taxonomical  selfcocking  colonialist  farcicality  kinesiology  paternalism
tearstained  selflocking  colourblind  fasciculate  lakedweller  paternalist
temerarious  selfseeking  comfortless  feasibility  laryngology  peccability
tendencious  shellacking  commonality  featherless  laudability  peccadillos
tendentious  stocktaking  commonplace  featureless  leaseholder  pedestalled
testatrices  trafficking  communalise  fingerglass  lichenology  pedicellate
thanksgiver  undertaking  communalism  fingerplate  machicolate  pedunculate
theodolitic  unshrinking  communalist  flannelling  mackerelsky  penicillate
theological  voortrekker  comptroller  flavourless  madrigalist  penicillium
theoretical  watchmaking  confabulate  flexibility  madrigalist  peninsulate
thrasonical  zooplankton  conjugality  floorwalker  malariology  pensionless
thyroiditis  Abbevillian  constellate  folliculate  mandibulate  pentathlete
tiddlywinks  abnormality  contemplate  forestalle   marginalise  pentavalent
```

perambulate	shutterless	unguiculate	countermark	impressment	tolbutamide
peristalith	silverplate	unkennelled	countermine	improvement	toothsomely
peristalsis	slaveholder	valleculate	countermove	indorsement	traducement
peristaltic	sleepwalker	variability	countermure	installment	tragicomedy
personalise	smallholder	vendibility	curtailment	instillment	transhumant
personalism	snatchblock	venereology	debauchment	involvement	tremblement
personalist	soapboiling	vermiculate	debouchment	itacolumite	unbeseeming
personality	sociability	vermiculite	deforcement	legerdemain	vasectomise
philatelist	softshelled	versatilely	defraudment	lightsomely	wearisomely
philhellene	soldierlike	versatility	depravement	liquidambar	weltschmerz
phraseology	solvability	verticality	derangement	lithotomise	westernmost
phylloclade	somatoplasm	vestryclerk	despoilment	lithotomist	wholesomely
physicality	somniculous	vexillology	detrainment	loathsomely	worrisomely
placability	soteriology	vibratility	development	longanimity	abhorrently
plagioclase	spectrality	victualless	dichogamous	looselimbed	ablutionary
podophyllin	spectrology	victualling	dichotomise	loxodromics	abortionist
pointilism	spelaeology	vincibility	dichotomist	machinemade	absorbingly
pointillist	sphagnology	volcanology	dichotomous	macrogamete	abstinently
polevaulter	spindlelegs	vulcanology	disablement	magnanimity	abusiveness
portability	spiraculate	waitinglist	disarmament	magnaninous	acceptingly
portionless	spongecloth	washability	disassemble	maintopmast	accompanist
possibility	springclean	watercolour	disassembly	measurement	accordantly
postexilian	stadtholder	whitecollar	disbandment	meprobamate	accordingly
pourparlers	stakeholder	wildfowling	discernment	methylamine	adoptianism
powderflask	stallholder	wirepulling	disencumber	microgamete	adoptianist
primatology	staunchless	workability	dislodgment	misestimate	adoptionism
probabilism	steamroller	workmanlike	disportment	misjudgment	adoptionist
probabilist	stencilling	worshipless	disremember	misremember	adverseness
probability	stockholder	xenophilous	dissepiment	monogrammed	advertently
prodigalise	stomatology	xerophilous	dithyrambic	mooringmast	advisedness
prodigality	stonewaller	abandonment	divorcement	multinomial	affectingly
prothallial	storyteller	abolishment	divulgement	ninnyhammer	afficionado
prothallium	strangulate	abridgement	easternmost	nourishment	agglutinate
pteridology	subaxillary	achievement	embowerment	nurserymaid	agonisingly
pulverulent	succourless	acquirement	embracement	overgarment	agrarianism
punctuality	suitability	adjournment	embroilment	overpayment	aimlessness
purposeless	surveillant	adjudgement	emplacement	pantomimist	airlessness
pussywillow	switchblade	advancement	enchainment	penultimate	airsickness
quacksalver	sympetalous	amphetamine	enchantment	peristomial	amativeness
quadrillion	syndicalism	antechamber	encrustment	phantasmata	Americanise
quarrelling	syndicalist	appeasement	endorsement	phytotomist	Americanism
quaternloaf	tameability	appointment	enfeoffment	platearmour	Americanist
quicksilver	tangibility	approximate	enforcement	platforming	amiableness
quintillion	teetotalism	arbitrament	engorgement	polyonymous	amorousness
rapscallion	teetotaller	arraignment	engrossment	predicament	anachronism
rateability	temporality	arrangement	enhancement	prejudgment	anachronous
rationalise	tensibility	assuagement	enjambement	presentment	anacreontic
rationalism	tentaculate	balletomane	enlargement	procurement	ancientness
rationalist	terminology	beachcomber	enlivenment	prolegomena	androgynous
rationality	terricolous	bedevilment	ennoblement	publishment	Anglicanism
readability	testability	bedizenment	enslavement	realignment	anglomaniac
recalculate	tetravalent	beguilement	entablement	recruitment	antiphonary
reestablish	textureless	benightment	enthralment	redetermine	anxiousness
reflexology	thanatology	bereavement	entitlement	reenactment	apartmental
regionalise	thoughtless	betweenmaid	entrainment	refreshment	appallingly
regionalism	threecolour	bewitchment	entreatment	replacement	appealingly
regionalist	thunderless	blasphemous	entrustment	requirement	approvingly
reliability	titleholder	bombardment	envelopment	restatement	appurtenant
remorseless	toothbilled	carcinomata	environment	sausagemeat	arduousness
retranslate	torticollis	catadromous	escheatment	scalemailer	Arminianism
saddlecloth	tourbillion	chainarmour	eurhythmics	scopolamine	arrestingly
saleability	toxophilite	chambermaid	evanishment	selfcommand	artlessness
satiability	trabeculate	cleanlimbed	exanthemata	semipalmate	assassinate
saturnalian	trackwalker	clothesmoth	farthermost	shortcoming	assuredness
scientology	trafficless	commandment	flimflammer	silversmith	audibleness
scintillant	trammelling	compartment	foretopmast	Soroptimist	Augustinian
scintillate	triangulate	compilement	forevermore	subbasement	austereness
secondclass	tripetalous	comportment	forthcoming	superfamily	awesomeness
selffeeling	triphyllous	concealment	furthermore	surbasement	awkwardness
selfsealing	trophoblast	concernment	furthermost	sustainment	backcountry
semasiology	trouserless	condylomata	garnishment	synchromesh	balefulness
semiskilled	tryingplane	confinement	guesstimate	tankfarming	banteringly
sensibility	tuberculate	congealment	hippocampus	tautonymous	bashfulness
sentinelled	tuberculise	consignment	hyoscyamine	taxidermist	bearishness
serviceline	tuberculose	containment	hypnopompic	teknonymous	beastliness
shareholder	tuberculous	contentment	impeachment	telegrammic	befittingly
shelterless	unappealing	controlment	imperilment	temperament	beguilingly
shipbuilder	underseller	coppersmith	impingement	thalidomide	belatedness
shrivelling	undervaluer	countermand	impoundment	theobromine	bellfounder

benignantly	costiveness	electronics	Gallicanism	indignantly	molendinary
betweenness	coterminous	elusiveness	gardemanger	IndoChinese	molybdenite
bicarbonate	courtliness	embracingly	gartersnake	IndoIranian	moneylender
bicentenary	crabbedness	emptyhanded	gaseousness	indulgently	monoclinous
biliousness	creationism	emulousness	genteelness	inelegantly	monseigneur
bimillenary	creationist	emulsionise	genuineness	inexactness	mountaineer
bimillenium	crookedness	endearingly	gerrymander	inquilinous	mountainous
blessedness	crunchiness	endlessness	ghastliness	inquiringly	mountaintop
blotchiness	cunningness	enquiringly	ghostliness	insipidness	movableness
bohemianism	curableness	enviousness	gibbousness	insistently	multilinear
bookishness	curiousness	equableness	girlishness	insultingly	mundaneness
boorishness	currentness	Erastianism	glaringness	intenseness	musicalness
breadwinner	currishness	erotogenous	godlessness	intercensal	mutableness
brilliantly	cursiveness	erotomaniac	gonfalonier	interdental	mythomaniac
bristliness	cursoriness	eudaemonism	gracileness	interlinear	nailvarnish
Britishness	curvilineal	eudaemonist	gradualness	Interlingua	nasofrontal
brittleness	curvilinear	Europeanise	graphicness	interlining	naturalness
broadminded	decarbonate	evasiveness	gristliness	interlunary	naughtiness
brusqueness	decarbonise	exceedingly	grouchiness	intermingle	necromancer
brutishness	deceivingly	excellently	grumblingly	internuncio	necromantic
bullishness	defibrinate	excremental	guardedness	intertangle	needfulness
butteriness	deficiently	expectantly	gutlessness	intravenous	negationist
Byzantinism	definiendum	expediently	guttersnipe	invalidness	negligently
Byzantinist	degradingly	experienced	haggardness	irksomeness	nephelinite
cacophonous	demandingly	exterminate	hallucinate	isochronism	nervousness
caddishness	deoxygenate	extremeness	Hamiltonian	isochronous	nitrogenise
californium	dependently	exuberantly	handgrenade	itinerantly	nitrogenous
callousness	deploringly	factualness	handpainted	jealousness	noisomeness
capableness	deservingly	faddishness	haplessness	jerrymander	nonunionist
caravanning	determinacy	falteringly	harmfulness	joylessness	notableness
carefulness	determinant	fanfaronade	hatefulness	knavishness	nothingness
caressingly	determinate	farawayness	haughtiness	knowingness	noxiousness
carpetsnake	determinism	farraginous	healthiness	labiodental	nutrimental
chaetognath	determinist	fatefulness	heavyhanded	languidness	obliqueness
chansonnier	detrimental	fatiguingly	heedfulness	largeminded	obscureness
chaperonage	Deuteronomy	fatuousness	Hegelianism	lastingness	observantly
childminder	deviousness	faultfinder	heinousness	lawlessness	observingly
Christendom	devotedness	fearfulness	hellishness	learnedness	obviousness
christening	diachronism	feelingness	helpfulness	leatherneck	octingenary
churchiness	differentia	ferruginous	hideousness	lengthiness	odorousness
cisatlantic	differently	fidgetiness	hirsuteness	lentiginous	oldwomanish
civilianise	diffidently	finicalness	histrionics	libertinage	ominousness
cleanliness	diffuseness	firmamental	histrionism	libertinism	onerousness
cliffhanger	diphthongal	flaccidness	hoggishness	lighthanded	operoseness
cognateness	dipsomaniac	flatulently	homophonous	lightminded	opportunely
compactness	disarmingly	flauntingly	hooliganism	limitedness	opportunism
compaginate	disentangle	fleshliness	hopefulness	lineprinter	opportunist
competently	dismayingly	flightiness	hugeousness	lingeringly	opportunity
complainant	disorganise	floweriness	hurriedness	lissomeness	orderliness
complexness	disseminate	foolishness	hurtfulness	literalness	orthocentre
compliantly	disseminule	footpoundal	hydrogenate	loathliness	orthodontia
concatenate	dissonantly	foppishness	hydrogenous	logicalness	orthodontic
conciseness	disunionist	foreignness	hydroponics	loutishness	outwardness
concubinage	divergently	forerunning	hypolimnion	lovableness	overmanning
concubinary	divisionary	forethinker	hypothenuse	lumpishness	overrunning
condominium	divisionism	foreverness	ignobleness	lustfulness	overweening
confidently	doggishness	forewarning	illusionism	Lutheranism	painfulness
confidingly	dolefulness	forgiveness	illusionist	luxuriantly	Palestinian
confusingly	dollishness	forlornness	immarginate	maddeningly	pandemonium
congruently	doltishness	forwardness	immenseness	magdalenian	panicmonger
consolingly	donnishness	fourpounder	impatiently	malignantly	paperhanger
consonantal	doubleender	fractionary	impermanent	mandarinate	paramountcy
consonantly	doubleentry	fractionate	impersonate	mandolinist	paramountly
consternate	doughtiness	fractionise	impertinent	mannishness	passiveness
consumingly	drouthiness	franklinite	implemental	marchioness	patrilineal
contaminant	drunkenness	franticness	imploringly	masculinely	patrimonial
contaminate	dubiousness	freethinker	importantly	masculinise	paunchiness
continental	dumbfounder	fretfulness	importunate	masculinity	peevishness
continently	durableness	friableness	importunely	massiveness	Pelagianism
convenances	dutifulness	frontrunner	importunity	mastodontic	pelargonium
conveyancer	earnestness	frowardness	imprudently	matrilineal	pensiveness
coparcenary	earthliness	frowstiness	incardinate	matrilinear	pentagynous
copiousness	ebulliently	fulsomeness	incessantly	matrimonial	peregrinate
cordialness	echosounder	functionary	incipiently	mawkishness	perfectness
corpulently	efficiently	functionate	inclemently	mediateness	pericranial
correctness	effulgently	fundamental	inconsonant	mindfulness	pericranium
corrigendum	einsteinium	furtiveness	incontinent	minnesinger	periodontal
corruptness	elderliness	gainfulness	incremental	miscegenate	perishingly
cosmogonist	electioneer	gallantness	incriminate	miserliness	permanently

pertinently	reddishness	skeletonise	thirstiness	waggishness	circumvolve
pestilently	redundantly	sketchiness	threadiness	wakefulness	coccidiosis
petitionary	reincarnate	skilfulness	threehanded	waspishness	coffeehouse
pettishness	rejoicingly	slavishness	thriftiness	waywardness	cognitional
phosphonium	relatedness	slenderness	thrillingly	wealthiness	coldblooded
photofinish	relationism	slightingly	throatiness	weightiness	collisional
phylogynist	relationist	smallminded	tobacconist	Weismannism	conditional
physiognomy	religionise	smithsonite	tobogganing	welcomeness	conditioner
piggishness	religionism	soberminded	tobogganist	wellfounded	cottonmouth
pinkishness	religionist	Socinianism	torchsinger	wellmeaning	craftswoman
piteousness	reluctantly	solutionist	totteringly	wellrounded	ctenophoran
pitifulness	repellantly	somnolently	toughminded	Wesleyanism	customhouse
planoconvex	repellently	songfulness	transfinite	whitishness	dexiotropic
playfulness	repentantly	sottishness	transiently	whoremonger	diarthrosis
plebeianise	repleteness	soulfulness	translunary	willingness	dimensional
plebeianism	representer	Southernism	transponder	winningness	directional
pliableness	reprovingly	sparingness	treacliness	winsomeness	disapproval
plicateness	repugnantly	spellbinder	tremblingly	wishfulness	disharmonic
pocketknife	resiliently	sporogenous	trenchantly	wistfulness	douroucouli
pointedness	restfulness	sporogonium	tricksiness	witchhunter	earthcloset
poltroonery	restiveness	springiness	tritagonist	witheringly	educational
polyphonous	retiredness	squalidness	trivialness	witlessness	embryologic
pomegranate	revaccinate	squarsonage	truculently	womanliness	emmenagogue
pompousness	revisionary	squashiness	tunableness	worldliness	enarthrosis
positronium	revisionism	squeakiness	tunefulness	xylophonist	evolutional
potteringly	revisionist	squintingly	turbulently	zealousness	exceptional
prattlingly	righthanded	stagemanage	typefounder	zestfulness	executioner
preachiness	righthander	starchiness	typefoundry	zootechnics	expansional
precedented	rightminded	startlingly	typicalness	aboveground	extensional
precedently	rightwinger	stateliness	ultrasonics	aeolotropic	extortioner
preciseness	riotousness	staunchness	unaccounted	affectional	fasciaboard
predominant	roentgenise	stellionate	unawareness	affectioned	fingerboard
predominate	roguishness	stiltedness	unbendingly	agoraphobia	formational
preliminary	roundedness	stoicalness	uncanniness	agoraphobic	freemasonry
prenominate	ruinousness	stormcentre	unceasingly	allelomorph	Frenchwoman
presciently	sacramental	strangeness	uncleanness	anadiplosis	fullblooded
presumingly	saintliness	straphanger	uncongenial	anastomoses	Gallophobia
prevalently	saplessness	streakiness	uncouthness	anastomosis	gastronomic
prickliness	saprogenous	stringently	underhanded	anastomotic	gentlewoman
primigenial	saturninely	stringiness	undermanned	anglophobia	geotectonic
privateness	savouriness	studiedness	underpinned	anglophobic	gillyflower
prizewinner	saxophonist	stumblingly	undertenant	anisotropic	glassblower
prochronism	scaremonger	stuntedness	unfailingly	antiJacobin	globeflower
profaneness	scorchingly	stylishness	unfeelingly	antistrophe	gnotobiosis
profuseness	scorpionfly	suasiveness	unfortunate	aponeuroses	gnotobiotic
prominently	scragginess	subdominant	ungodliness	aponeurosis	gradational
promisingly	scrappiness	sublimeness	unhappiness	aponeurotic	GraecoRoman
prosaicness	screamingly	subordinate	uniformness	ascensional	grammalogue
protagonist	scrimpiness	suburbanise	unmanliness	attritional	gramophonic
providently	scruffiness	suburbanite	unmeaningly	barrelhouse	greengrocer
provokingly	scuppernong	succedaneum	unnervingly	bassethound	haemoglobin
prudishness	searchingly	succulently	unquietness	beaverboard	hagioscopic
pruriginous	seasickness	summariness	unreasoning	bibliopolic	halfblooded
Prussianise	seditionary	sunlessness	unsmilingly	biocoenoses	headborough
Prussianism	selfishness	superlunary	unsoundness	biocoenosis	heartbroken
pushfulness	selfopinion	supertanker	unsparingly	biocoenotic	heavyfooted
quadrennial	sentimental	suppliantly	unusualness	blackgrouse	heliotropic
quadrennium	seriousness	supremeness	unwarranted	bottlenosed	hemeralopia
queenliness	serpiginous	swarthiness	unweetingly	braggadocio	heteropolar
questionary	sexlessness	swinishness	unwillingly	branchiopod	homozygosis
quiescently	shadowiness	sycophantic	unwinkingly	bridgeboard	honeymooner
quinquennia	shallowness	sycophantry	unwittingly	brucellosis	hydrobromic
radicalness	shapeliness	synchronise	uprightness	calyptrogen	hydrophobia
raffishness	sheathknife	synchronism	uselessness	candlepower	hydrophobic
rangefinder	shorthanded	synchronous	vacationist	catastrophe	hydrothorax
ratiocinate	shortwinded	tabletennis	vacuousness	cauliflower	hydrotropic
rattlesnake	shrinkingly	taciturnity	valiantness	centreboard	hygroscopic
raucousness	shrubbiness	tearfulness	variousness	chainsmoker	hypertrophy
raunchiness	sickeningly	teaspoonful	velvetiness	chalcedonic	hypotyposis
ravishingly	sickishness	tediousness	verboseness	chameleonic	hypsophobia
reactionary	sightliness	telephonist	vertiginous	chaulmoogra	illdisposed
reactionist	signpainter	teleprinter	vesuvianite	chromosomal	immunologic
reawakening	sillimanite	tenableness	viciousness	chronologer	impassioned
recommender	silveriness	tenuousness	viscousness	chronologic	inflexional
recriminate	simperingly	termagantly	visibleness	chrysarobin	intensional
rectilineal	sincereness	terrigenous	voguishness	churchgoing	intentional
rectilinear	sinlessness	testimonial	volitionary	churchwoman	intentioned
recumbently	sinuousness	thermionics	volubleness	circumpolar	interatomic
recurrently	sizableness	thinskinned	vortiginous	circumsolar	intergrowth

intuitional	radiophonic	ventriloquy	monographic	adventurous	coronagraph
jabberwocky	recessional	vibrational	monomorphic	afterburner	coronograph
kilocalorie	redactional	vichyssoise	namedropper	agglomerate	corroborant
lightfooted	reversional	warmblooded	narcoleptic	alabastrine	corroborate
louverboard	reversioner	washerwoman	nomographer	alcyonarian	cotemporary
louvreboard	rhinoscopic	watercooled	nomographic	Alexandrian	cottongrass
macrobiotic	roughfooted	watercooler	nosographer	alexandrine	crematorium
macroscopic	Russophobia	wellbeloved	nosographic	alexandrite	crossgarnet
megalopolis	saddlehorse	wellgroomed	oreographic	AngloNorman	cruciferous
melancholia	salvational	whereabouts	ornithopter	anteriority	crucigerous
melancholic	sansculotte	aerographer	outcropping	antiquarian	cryotherapy
metachrosis	saprobiotic	Aesculapian	outstripped	arbitrarily	cryptograph
microgroove	schoolboard	allomorphic	overcropped	archaeornis	cupriferous
microphonic	schoolhouse	apocalyptic	overlapping	arglebargle	customarily
microscopic	Scotchwoman	apostrophic	overstepped	aristocracy	cycloserine
misericorde	seborrhoeic	arthrospore	overtopping	artillerist	cysticercus
monochromat	selfdevoted	autographic	paragrapher	aspersorium	decarburise
monochromic	selfimposed	autotrophic	paragraphic	assessorial	decemvirate
monozygotic	sensational	avoirdupois	paraleipsis	bacciferous	decerebrate
mortarboard	shocktroops	bitterapple	paramorphic	ballbearing	decolourise
mosstrooper	shortspoken	bookkeeping	participant	barbiturate	demonstrate
motivepower	shovelboard	cabbagepalm	participate	barleybroth	dentigerous
multistorey	silverpoint	cacographic	participial	barnstormer	depauperate
musclebound	sinistrorse	circumspect	philosopher	barrelorgan	depauperise
myxomatosis	situational	clodhopping	philosophic	battledress	desultorily
necrobiosis	sleeveboard	clothesprop	photocopier	beechmarten	deteriorate
needlepoint	sleuthhound	cornucopian	pilocarpine	belligerent	dictatorial
needlewoman	sockdologen	counterpane	pleomorphic	bergschrund	digitigrade
negrophobia	somatologic	counterpart	polycarpous	bicorporate	dinosaurian
Neoplatonic	somatotonia	counterplan	polygraphic	bittercress	diphtherial
netherworld	somatotonic	counterplea	polymorphic	blackbirder	diphtheroid
neurotropic	spermatozoa	counterplot	preoccupied	blackmarket	diphycercal
noticeboard	splashboard	demographer	rheotropism	blameworthy	directorate
nutritional	splayfooted	demographic	safekeeping	bloodstream	directorial
nyctitropic	spokeswoman	diastrophic	sandskipper	booklearned	disafforest
nyctophobia	sportswoman	doublespeak	selfdespair	bottlegreen	disenthrall
obsessional	springboard	doxographer	selfdisplay	brachyurous	disinterest
operational	springhouse	dualpurpose	selfrespect	bradycardia	disinterred
orthoscopic	stephanotis	ectomorphic	selfsupport	buffalorobe	domineering
orthotropic	stiflejoint	ectotrophic	serendipity	bulletproof	doublecross
oxyhydrogen	stockbroker	endomorphic	serigrapher	bullterrier	downhearted
paddleboard	stoneground	endotrophic	showjumping	bureaucracy	dramaturgic
palindromic	stormtroops	frothhopper	showstopper	cabbagerose	drawingroom
parasitosis	strikebound	geostrophic	sideslipped	calciferous	dresscircle
paratrooper	stringboard	Germanophil	sidestepped	capillarity	dundrearies
parishioner	strongpoint	grandnephew	snowleopard	cardiograph	egalitarian
partitioned	sublittoral	grasshopper	stenotypist	cardsharper	enchantress
partitioner	subregional	greatnephew	stirruppump	carnivorous	endometrium
pediculosis	summational	gyrocompass	stomachpump	cassiterite	endothermal
photophobia	summerhouse	handicapped	superimpose	catchphrase	endothermic
photophobic	superabound	handicapper	teenybopper	catheterise	engineering
phototropic	swiftfooted	hedgehopped	telegrapher	cavalierism	epigastrium
physiologic	switchboard	hemianopsia	telegraphic	cellularity	epinephrine
plainspoken	syndesmosis	hemimorphic	thunderpeal	centenarian	equilibrate
pleiotropic	syssarcosis	heterospory	tightlipped	chloroprene	equilibrist
pleochroism	technologic	highstepper	topographer	choreograph	equilibrium
pocketmoney	teeterboard	holographic	topographic	chronograph	ergatocracy
policewoman	tenterhooks	homomorphic	touchtyping	chrysoprase	eurypteroid
polychromic	teratologic	ideographic	transalpine	cinnabarine	executorial
porterhouse	thenceforth	idiographic	typographer	circularise	exemplarily
posteriorly	thereabouts	idiomorphic	typographic	circularity	exemplarity
prehistoric	thixotropic	incorruptly	underexpose	coldhearted	expectorant
previsional	toffeenosed	intercepter	weenybopper	collaborate	expectorate
probational	togglejoint	interceptor	winningpost	columbarium	extemporary
probationer	townspeople	interdepend	wiretapping	commemorate	extemporise
progestogen	traditional	interrupter	worshipping	commiserate	exteriorise
promotional	trichinosis	interruptor	xylocarpous	computerise	exteriority
protectoral	trichomonad	interseptal	xylographer	concentrate	extraverted
provisional	twelvemonth	kymographic	xylographic	conductress	extroverted
pseudomonas	ultraviolet	logographer	zygomorphic	confederacy	faithworthy
pseudomorph	underground	logographic	abecedarian	confederate	familiarise
pseudopodia	undergrowth	malapropism	accessorial	conflagrant	familiarity
psittacosis	undeveloped	marlinspike	accessorise	conflagrate	ferriferous
psychologic	unemotional	maxillipede	accipitrine	congenerous	festschrift
psychomotor	unequivocal	mesomorphic	acculturate	considerate	fieldcornet
pullthrough	unfashioned	metamorphic	adiaphorism	considering	fieldworker
pureblooded	unipersonal	milliampere	adventuress	consumerism	fingerprint
pussyfooter	valuational	monocarpous	adventurism	coplanarity	FinnoUgrian
quickfrozen	variational	monographer	adventurist	corniferous	fissiparity

```
fissiparous  libertarian  piscivorous  septiferous  triumvirate  countlessly
floriferous  lionhearted  planetarium  sequestrate  truehearted  countryseat
forequarter  loosestrife  plantigrade  sertularian  trustworthy  countryside
foreshorten  lycanthrope  pleinairist  shadowgraph  tumbledrier  criticaster
formularise  lycanthropy  polyandrous  Shaksperean  ultramarine  curatorship
franctireur  madreporite  polystyrene  Shaksperian  unconcerned  dauntlessly
frankfurter  magisterial  polyzoarium  sheepfarmer  undisturbed  deemphasise
freehearted  magisterium  Precambrian  shoulderbag  unfaltering  delightsome
freezedried  mailcarrier  precentress  shoulderpad  unipolarity  denizenship
frigidarium  mansardroof  preceptress  showerproof  utilitarian  dialogistic
frugivorous  meadowgrass  precontract  shrinkproof  vascularise  disaccustom
fullhearted  mediatorial  predatorily  sightscreen  vascularity  dishonestly
gangsterism  megatherium  prefatorial  sightworthy  voluntarily  disillusion
gemmiferous  melliferous  prefatorily  singletrack  voluntarism  displeasure
gemmiparous  mercenarily  prelusorily  singularise  voluntarist  distressful
gestatorial  meritocracy  prematurely  singularity  waitingroom  doubtlessly
gingerbread  metallurgic  prematurity  sittingroom  warmhearted  draughtsman
globigerina  metalworker  priestcraft  skatingrink  weakhearted  dreamlessly
globularity  Micawberish  primiparous  slavemarket  wheelbarrow  drillmaster
goodhearted  Micawberism  profiterole  smokescreen  whitethroat  duniewassal
grandparent  millenarian  proletarian  smokingroom  wintergreen  dyslogistic
granivorous  miniaturise  proletariat  softhearted  zoantharian  ectoblastic
granularity  miniaturist  proliferate  somniferous  Zoroastrian  ectoplasmic
greaseproof  ministerial  proliferous  songsparrow  admiralship  embellisher
guttapercha  misanthrope  protectress  spectatress  advertising  emperorship
gypsiferous  misanthropy  protomartyr  spendthrift  Albigensian  encomiastic
halfhearted  momentarily  protuberant  spiniferous  ambiversion  endoplasmic
halterbreak  monasterial  provisorily  spinsterish  anarchistic  esemplastic
haphazardly  moneymarket  pseudograph  splendorous  anniversary  establisher
hardhearted  monkeybread  psychodrama  squirearchy  anomalistic  Eucharistic
heartstring  monopterous  psychograph  stagestruck  aphrodisiac  euphemistic
heliochrome  morbiferous  pupillarity  staircarpet  apostleship  eveningstar
helleborine  morningroom  purgatorial  statutorily  apotheosise  extravasate
hemipterous  mothercraft  pyrargyrite  steelworker  audiovisual  faithlessly
heptamerous  multiparous  Pythagorean  stenochromy  autoplastic  faultlessly
herbivorous  muscularity  Pythagorism  stereograph  bathingsuit  fetichistic
heterograft  necessarian  quaestorial  stevengraph  bellicosity  fetishistic
heterotroph  necessarily  quickfiring  stockmarket  Belorussian  feudalistic
hexametrist  needlecraft  quinquereme  stonecurlew  bergamasque  fireraising
holothurian  nightmarish  quitchgrass  stonemarten  blamelessly  flavoursome
homopterous  nightporter  racketpress  stratocracy  blockbuster  foreclosure
homosporous  nondescript  radiocarbon  subcontract  bloodlessly  foretopsail
hydrocarbon  noseyparker  radiolarian  subcontrary  bloodvessel  formalistic
hyperborean  nulliparity  Rastafarian  superioress  brainlessly  fourflusher
hypermarket  nulliparous  rattlebrain  superiority  brankursine  fruitlessly
hypothermia  octachordal  reconstruct  supermarket  breadbasket  furthersome
ichthyornis  odoriferous  refrigerant  supernormal  broadcaster  gafftopsail
imaginarily  oligomerous  refrigerate  superscribe  burgomaster  gatecrasher
impenetrate  openhearted  reintegrate  superscript  bushmanship  generalship
imperforate  ophidiarium  remonstrant  superstrata  businessman  gigantesque
incarcerate  optometrist  remonstrate  surfboarder  cabbalistic  gracelessly
incorporate  oracularity  reportorial  syllabarium  Calvinistic  grandiosely
incorporeal  orchestrate  reverberant  tachycardia  captainship  grandiosity
indifferent  organscreen  reverberate  talebearing  caravansary  guilelessly
inferiority  overbearing  rhizocarpic  tautomerism  cataclysmic  guiltlessly
infirmarian  ozoniferous  ribbongrass  technocracy  catechismal  haberdasher
ingathering  pachydermal  Sabbatarian  temporarily  catechistic  haggadistic
inheritress  paediatrics  Sagittarius  termitarium  catswhisker  hairdresser
insalubrity  paediatrist  saltatorial  terrestrial  ceaselessly  hairraising
insectarium  parametrise  ScotchIrish  territorial  ceroplastic  halfmeasure
insessorial  parathyroid  scriptorial  tetramerous  cheerlessly  harmonistic
insincerely  peculiarity  scriptorium  thankworthy  choirmaster  heartlessly
insincerity  pecuniarily  scurvygrass  thaumatrope  citizenship  Hellenistic
intemperate  pentamerous  secondarily  thermograph  closefisted  heroworship
interiorise  pentandrous  secretarial  thuriferous  cloudcastle  holoblastic
interiority  perchlorate  secretariat  timesharing  coextension  homoiousian
introverted  perineurium  sedentarily  transferred  coextensive  homoplastic
inventorial  perispermic  seigneurial  transferrer  colonelship  housemaster
involucrate  perseverate  seigniorage  transformer  communistic  Hudibrastic
ironhearted  pestiferous  seigniorial  transmarine  complaisant  hylozoistic
kickstarter  phosphorate  seismograph  transparent  compression  hypoblastic
kindhearted  phosphorism  selfreproof  transporter  compressive  hypoglossal
kinetograph  phosphorous  selfstarter  transversal  comradeship  hypophyseal
kwashiorkor  phosphorous  selfsterile  treacherous  congressman  hypophysial
lactiferous  photoperiod  semidiurnal  trencherman  connoisseur  hypotension
Lancastrian  physiocracy  sempiternal  tributarily  cotoneaster  hypothesise
latchstring  pieceworker  Septembrist  trimestrial  countersign  ichthyosaur
leprosarium  pilotburner  septenarius  Trinitarian  countersink  impetuosity
letterpress  piscatorial  septentrion  triquetrous  countersunk  imprecisely
```

imprecision	powerlessly	thanklessly	aggravation	calculating	consolation
incognisant	praetorship	threemaster	aggregately	calculation	consolatory
incuriosity	predecessor	tightfisted	aggregation	calculative	consumption
inexpensive	premiership	Titianesque	aggregative	calefactory	consumptive
inoffensive	prestissimo	toastmaster	agriculture	calibration	contractile
intercessor	prestressed	topdressing	aircraftman	campmeeting	contraction
intercostal	primateship	tracelessly	alleviation	candidature	contractive
interfusion	proctorship	transfusion	alleviative	candlestick	contractual
interosseus	progression	tribuneship	alleviatory	captivation	contracture
irremissive	progressism	tritheistic	alphabetise	carbonation	contraption
Jansenistic	progressist	troublesome	altercation	carburetion	contrastive
jargonistic	progressive	trousersuit	alternately	carburetted	conurbation
kitchensink	prophetship	trustbuster	alternation	carburetter	convocation
lacrimosely	provostship	trusteeship	alternative	carburettor	convolution
lacrymosely	pyroclastic	trypanosome	amazonstone	carminative	cooperation
lectureship	quarrelsome	tyrannosaur	amethystine	castigation	cooperative
lickerishly	Rabelaisian	uncontested	anacoluthon	celebration	copingstone
lifemanship	religiosity	unexpressed	anemometric	celebratory	corbiesteps
limitlessly	replenisher	unfurnished	antenuptial	cementation	cornerstone
lowpressure	rickettsial	unnecessary	antineutron	cerebration	corporately
macrocosmic	ritualistic	unobtrusive	antiquation	chainletter	corporation
Maglemosian	rockcrystal	unpossessed	apologetics	champertous	corporatism
maintopsail	scaleinsect	unpromising	appellation	circulation	corporative
maladjusted	schistosity	unrealistic	appellative	circulative	correlation
managership	schistosome	unvarnished	application	circulatory	correlative
manneristic	scholarship	unwholesome	applicative	clandestine	corrugation
manumission	scholiastic	vasopressin	applicatory	clinometric	coruscation
marquessate	schottische	vasopressor	appogiatura	coadunation	cosignatory
marshalship	scientistic	venturesome	approbation	coagulation	coulometric
masochistic	scoutmaster	verbalistic	approbatory	coarctation	counterturn
matchlessly	selfclosing	viceroyship	aquaculture	cobblestone	crenulation
mechanistic	selfraising	vinedresser	aquiculture	coeducation	crepitation
mediumistic	selfworship	voicelessly	arbitration	coessential	crimination
mercilessly	senatorship	voodooistic	arbitrative	colligation	criminative
meroblastic	senselessly	waspwaisted	arbitratrix	colligative	criminatory
mesoblastic	shamanistic	wastebasket	argumentive	collimation	crotcheteer
messiahship	shamelessly	wearilessly	armtwisting	collocation	culmination
metaphysics	sharepusher	Westminster	assafoetida	colouration	cultivation
metaplastic	sheepmaster	whistlestop	assentation	combination	cupellation
metastasise	sheriffship	whitewasher	assignation	combinative	cybernation
Methodistic	shiftlessly	whoremaster	association	combinatory	cybernetics
microcosmic	showmanship	wolfwhistle	associative	commination	daisycutter
Micronesian	sightlessly	workmanship	assortative	comminatory	deathrattle
mirthlessly	sleeplessly	worthlessly	astigmatism	comminution	debarkation
modernistic	slickenside	wreckmaster	atomisation	commutation	decantation
monitorship	smilelessly	abomination	attenuation	commutative	declamation
monochasial	snickersnee	abstraction	attestation	comparatist	declamatory
monochasium	socialistic	abstractive	attribution	comparative	declaration
Monophysite	soldiership	abstriction	attributive	competition	declarative
monstrosity	solipsistic	acceptation	audiometric	competitive	declaratory
muskthistle	soundlessly	acclamation	autoerotism	compilation	declination
neologistic	southeaster	acclamatory	babysitting	complotting	declivitous
nervelessly	southwester	acclimation	barquentine	compositely	decollation
noiselessly	speakership	acclimatise	batholithic	composition	decolletage
nonplussing	spinelessly	acclivitous	bathymetric	compositive	decrepitate
northeaster	Spinozistic	acetylation	bearbaiting	compotation	decrepitude
northwester	spiritistic	achromatise	bellbottoms	compotatory	decussately
oarsmanship	sponsorship	achromatism	bellheather	compunction	decussation
omnipresent	squeamishly	acidulation	Benedictine	computation	defalcation
ornithosaur	stainlessly	acquisition	benediction	concomitant	deferential
overmeasure	starcrossed	acquisitive	benedictory	concubitant	defloration
paederastic	steadfastly	acumination	benefaction	condolatory	defoliation
Panglossian	stewardship	acupuncture	betweentime	condonation	deformation
pantheistic	stickinsect	adenomatous	bifurcation	confliction	deglutition
partnership	strenuosity	adumbration	billposting	conflictive	degradation
paternoster	studentship	adumbrative	bipartition	confutation	degustation
patronising	subdivision	adversative	Bodhisattva	confutative	dehydration
patternshop	sumptuosity	Aeneolithic	bombilation	congelation	deification
pearlfisher	supervision	aeronautics	bombination	conjugation	delectation
Pentecostal	supervisory	aerostatics	Bonapartean	conjugative	delineation
pessimistic	suppression	aerostation	Bonapartism	conjunction	demagnetise
picturesque	suppressive	aestivation	Bonapartist	conjunctiva	demarcation
pinnatisect	syllogistic	affectation	botheration	conjunctive	demarkation
plateresque	symbolistic	affiliation	brachiation	conjuncture	democratise
pluralistic	synergistic	affirmation	bristletail	conjuration	democratism
pointlessly	tantalising	affirmative	bullbaiting	connotation	denigration
polycrystal	tapemeasure	affirmatory	byeelection	connotative	denigratory
ponderosity	tastelessly	affrication	cabbagetree	consecution	deoxidation
postclassic	teachership	affricative	calcination	consecutive	deportation

depravation	elucidation	filamentary	idolisation	interactive	mistrustful
deprecation	elucidative	filamentous	imagination	interesting	molestation
deprecative	elucidatory	filmsetting	imaginative	intermitted	monoculture
deprecatory	elutriation	fimbriation	imbrication	intricately	murmuration
depredation	embarkation	fingerstall	immanentism	intromitted	musculation
depredatory	emblematise	flagcaptain	immanentist	intromitter	musculature
deprivation	emblematist	fluctuation	immediately	investiture	myelomatous
dereliction	embrocation	fomentation	immigration	inviolately	nationstate
description	encystation	forestation	imparkation	involuntary	Neanderthal
descriptive	entablature	formication	impartation	invultation	necessitate
desecration	enterostomy	formulation	impetration	irradiation	necessitous
desensitise	enucleation	fornication	impetratory	irradiative	negotiation
desiccation	enumeration	fortunately	implication	irredentism	negotiatory
desiccative	enumerative	foulmouthed	implicative	irredentist	negotiatrix
designation	enunciation	fragmentary	importation	irretention	nephrectomy
desperately	enunciative	freebooting	imprecation	irretentive	neuropathic
desperation	equidistant	frostbitten	imprecatory	isoelectric	nictitation
destination	equinoctial	fructuation	inadvertent	itineration	nonexistent
destitution	eradication	frustration	inanimately	jactitation	nonvolatile
destruction	eradicative	fulguration	inanimation	Judaisation	novelettish
destructive	Esperantist	fullmouthed	inattention	labefaction	numismatics
detestation	eucalyptole	fulminating	inattentive	laciniation	numismatist
deuteration	eudiometric	fulmination	incantation	lacrimation	nuncupation
devaluation	evagination	fulminatory	incantatory	lacrimatory	nuncupative
devastation	evaporation	fusillation	incarnation	lacrymation	obfuscation
diagnostics	evaporative	fustigation	incertitude	lacrymatory	obfuscatory
diapositive	everlasting	gallowstree	inclination	laicisation	objurgation
diffraction	examination	gastrectomy	incompetent	lamentation	objurgatory
Diophantine	exclamation	gemmulation	inculcation	lancinating	obscuration
diplomatise	exclamatory	gentilitial	inculpation	lancination	obsecration
diplomatist	excoriation	geopolitics	inculpatory	laryngotomy	observation
discerption	exculpation	germination	incurvation	legislation	observatory
discourtesy	exculpatory	germinative	incurvature	legislative	obstinately
disfunction	exdirectory	gettogether	indentation	legislature	obstruction
disgruntled	exfoliation	glasscutter	indigestion	lepidoptera	obstructive
disjunction	exfoliative	glomeration	indigestive	lickspittle	obtestation
disjunctive	exhortation	goldbeating	indignation	ligamentary	occultation
disjuncture	exhortative	goniometric	indirection	ligamentous	officiation
dislocation	exhortatory	grandfather	inebriation	linguistics	oilpainting
disparately	existential	grandmother	ineffective	liquidation	openmouthed
disposition	exoneration	granolithic	ineffectual	litterateur	oppugnation
dispositive	exonerative	granulation	inessential	lixiviation	orangoutang
disputation	expatiation	gratulation	infatuation	loudmouthed	orientation
disquieting	expatiative	gratulatory	inferential	lubrication	origination
disquietude	expatiatory	gravimetric	infestation	lubricative	originative
dissipation	expectation	gravitation	infeudation	lucubration	oscillation
dissipative	expectative	gravitative	influential	luxuriation	oscillatory
dissolutely	expenditure	gurgitation	information	machination	ostentation
dissolution	explanation	habituation	informative	maladaptive	osteopathic
distinction	explanatory	handfasting	informatory	malediction	Ostrogothic
distinctive	explication	handknitted	ingratitude	maledictory	outfighting
distraction	explicative	handwriting	ingurgitate	malefaction	ovariectomy
distractive	explicatory	handwritten	innervation	malfunction	oversetting
distrustful	exploration	hardhitting	innutrition	malposition	overwritten
divestiture	exploratory	hardmouthed	inoculation	malpractice	oviposition
divulgation	exponential	headhunting	inoculative	manducation	oxygenation
documentary	exportation	hearthstone	inoperative	manducatory	ozonisation
draggletail	expurgation	heliometric	inopportune	manifestant	palpitation
dropcurtain	expurgatory	hepatectomy	inquisition	manifestoes	pamphleteer
dualcontrol	exquisitely	hibernation	inquisitive	manufactory	pantalettes
duplication	exsiccation	Hindoostani	inscription	manufacture	parachutist
duplicative	extenuation	hippopotami	inscriptive	manumitting	parturition
duplicitous	extenuatory	homeopathic	insensately	mastication	Passiontide
dysfunction	extirpation	homocentric	insensitive	masticatory	passivation
econometric	extirpatory	housefather	insinuation	mathematics	pectination
edification	extradition	housemother	insinuative	melioration	penetrating
edificatory	extrication	humiliation	inspiration	meliorative	penetration
ejaculation	fabrication	humiliatory	inspiratory	mensuration	penetrative
ejaculatory	facelifting	hydrometeor	instigation	merchantman	penitential
elaborately	facultative	hydrometric	instigative	metacentric	peptisation
elaboration	fairweather	hydropathic	instinctive	meteoritics	percolation
elaborative	fascinating	hygrometric	instinctual	methylation	perennation
electrotype	fascination	hymenoptera	institution	metrication	perforation
elephantine	favouritism	hyperactive	instruction	microlithic	perforative
elephantoid	fecundation	hypermetric	instructive	micrometric	perfunctory
elicitation	feldspathic	hyphenation	integration	micturition	permutation
elimination	festinately	hypogastric	integrative	misbegotten	persecution
eliminative	fiddlestick	hypostatise	interactant	misconstrue	personation
Elizabethan		hypsometric	interaction	miscreation	personative

perspective	proximately	ricochetted	suppuration	viniculture	dexterously
phagocytise	psychiatric	rodomontade	suppurative	viscountess	dishonourer
phagocytose	publication	rottenstone	surrebuttal	viticulture	distinguish
phalanstery	pulchritude	rubberstamp	surrebutter	vivisection	distribuend
photoactive	pullulation	rubefaction	surrogation	voltametric	distributor
photometric	pumicestone	rubrication	suspiration	wainscoting	doubleDutch
plagiostome	punctuation	rudimentary	susurration	wainscotted	doublequick
planimetric	purpresture	rustication	swallowtail	washleather	downdraught
platinotype	pustulation	sacculation	swingletree	waterbottle	dreadnought
plectoptera	qualitative	Sanskritist	synchrotron	wherewithal	egregiously
plenipotent	quartertone	sarcomatous	syncopation	whiffletree	equiangular
ploughstaff	quickwitted	schismatise	syndication	whippletree	erroneously
pollination	racemeeting	schizanthus	systematics	whitleather	exogenously
polyglottal	radioactive	scissortail	systematise	Whitsuntide	facetiously
polyglottic	radiometric	scyphistoma	systematism	wildcatting	feloniously
polypeptide	rarefaction	sedimentary	systematist	windlestraw	ferociously
pomiculture	rarefactive	segregation	tabefaction	winetasting	firstfruits
ponderation	readywitted	segregative	taratantara	wirenetting	forethought
portmanteau	realisation	selfcentred	tegumentary	woodcutting	forgetfully
portraitist	reanimation	selfcontent	temperately	adminicular	fractiously
portraiture	reapportion	selfcontrol	temperature	albuminuria	freethought
postnuptial	reassertion	selfculture	temperature	altocumulus	frightfully
postulation	rebarbative	selffertile	tenementary	ambiguously	frivolously
precipitant	recantation	selfmastery	termination	ambitiously	gallimaufry
precipitate	reclamation	selftorture	terminative	amorphously	garrulously
precipitous	recognition	semimonthly	theocentric	analogously	glutinously
predication	recognitive	sericulture	therewithal	anfractuous	goodnatured
predicative	recognitory	serrulation	thickwitted	animalcular	grotesquely
predicatory	recommittal	sharpwitted	titillation	anomalously	grotesquery
preelection	recondition	shoeleather	tittivation	anonymously	handwrought
preexistent	redirection	shoplifting	tracheotomy	assiduously	hazardously
preignition	reedbunting	silverstick	transaction	atrociously	healthfully
prelibation	reeducation	singlestick	transection	audaciously	hermeneutic
premeditate	referential	snowbunting	translation	barbarously	highfalutin
premonition	reformation	sociometric	transmittal	beauteously	highwrought
premonitory	reformative	sociopathic	transmitted	beautifully	hilariously
preparation	reformatory	solmisation	transmitter	behavioural	hurryscurry
preparative	regimentals	somewhither	Trappistine	bounteously	hurryskurry
preparatory	regurgitate	speculation	trendsetter	bountifully	illfavoured
preposition	reification	speculative	trepanation	brahmaputra	illhumoured
prepositive	reinsertion	spessartite	trepidation	breadcrumbs	imperiously
prerogative	reiteration	spindletree	trestletree	bumblepuppy	impetuously
presanctify	reiterative	spirometric	tribulation	bumptiously	incongruent
presumption	reluctation	splenectomy	tribunitial	canalicular	incongruity
presumptive	reorientate	sporulation	trituration	canaliculus	incongruous
preterition	repartition	stagflation	trundletail	capaciously	incunabulum
procreation	replication	standpatter	tufthunting	carbuncular	incuriously
procreative	reprobation	stepbrother	tumefaction	caricatural	indeciduous
procrustean	reprobative	stimulation	turbination	carvelbuilt	individuate
procuration	reprobatory	stimulative	typecasting	catercousin	ingeniously
procuratory	repudiation	stipulation	typesetting	cavernously	ingenuously
profanation	requisition	stipulatory	typewritten	centrifugal	injuriously
profanatory	reservation	stonecutter	unassertive	changefully	innocuously
progenitrix	residential	straightcut	unchristian	circumlunar	innoxiously
progeniture	resignation	straightish	uncommitted	clamorously	insidiously
prohibition	respiration	straightway	unessential	closehauled	intercourse
prohibitive	respiratory	stylisation	unification	colourfully	intercrural
prohibitory	restitution	subarration	unigeniture	commissural	interfluent
prolocutrix	restoration	subaudition	unimportant	congruously	invidiously
promptitude	restorative	subjugation	unrelenting	conjectural	irresoluble
propagation	restriction	subjunctive	unremitting	consanguine	judiciously
propagative	restrictive	sublimation	unselective	consciously	laboriously
proposition	restructure	subornation	utilisation	conspicuity	larcenously
proprietary	resuscitate	subrogation	vaccination	conspicuous	lecherously
prorogation	retaliation	substantial	vacillation	constituent	litigiously
prosecution	retaliative	substantive	vacuolation	constitutor	ludicrously
prosecutrix	retaliatory	subsumption	valediction	contributor	luxuriously
proselytise	retardation	subsumptive	valedictory	convolvulus	maliciously
proselytism	retardative	subtraction	variegation	corpuscular	masterfully
prospective	retardatory	subtractive	varnishtree	courteously	mellifluent
prosthetics	retribution	suffixation	venesection	credulously	mellifluous
prostration	retributive	suffocation	venisection	crepuscular	melodiously
protonotary	retributory	suffocative	ventilation	custombuilt	momentously
protractile	retroaction	superintend	ventilative	dangerously	monologuise
protraction	retroactive	superlative	vermination	deceitfully	monologuist
protractive	revaluation	supernatant	vicissitude	deliciously	monstrously
provocateur	reverential	supposition	vindication	deliriously	multangular
provocation	rhizomatous	suppositive	vindicative	demagoguery	murderously
provocative	ribvaulting	suppository	vindicatory	demagoguism	murmurously

```
nefariously veraciously plaintively assemblyman bracteolate cryptograph
neighbourly verminously pointdevice bricklaying breadthways decarbonate
notoriously vexatiously prelusively clairvoyant breastplate decemvirate
obliviously vicariously primitively cyclothymia bridgeboard decerebrate
obnoxiously vivaciously primitivism cyclothymic bristletail decolletage
officiously voraciously privatively deliveryman bureaucracy decorticate
overindulge watercourse purposively diapophysis cabbagepalm decrepitate
overwrought wholesouled receptively granophyric campanulate defibrinate
pendulously wonderfully receptivity haemoptysis caravansary demonstrate
penuriously acriflavine recessively heterotypic carcinomata denticulate
perspicuity adjectively rediscovery hydrophytic cardinalate deoxygenate
perspicuous affectively reflexively hygrophytic cardiograph depauperate
plenteously affectivity repulsively infantryman carpetsnake desegregate
plentifully antigravity resistively lithophytic carunculate deteriorate
poisonously assertively resistivity longplaying catchphrase determinacy
ponderously attentively retentively McCarthyism centreboard determinant
prefectural bodyservant retentivity microphytic certificate determinate
preterhuman bondservant rotogravure osteophytic chaetognath deuterogamy
proconsular bondservice secretively palaeotypic chamberlain diamondback
promiscuity causatively seductively plasmolysis chambermaid digitigrade
promiscuous cognitively selectively plasmolytic chaperonage dipterocarp
propinquity cognitivity selectivity pleurodynia chevalglass directorate
prostitutor collusively selfservice proteolysis Chippendale discalceate
querulously combatively selfserving proteolytic chloroplast disenthrall
rancorously corrosively sensitively protophytic choreograph disseminate
rapaciously countervail sensitivity saprophytic chromoplast dissimilate
rapturously counterview spacesaving selfdenying chronograph dissimulate
rectangular deceptively talkatively selfpitying chrysoprase divisionary
regardfully deductively tentatively sporophytic clairschach documentary
regretfully defectively timeserving steatopygia clairvoyant domesticate
religiously defensively unbelieving stereotyped cleistogamy domiciliary
reposefully diffusively undeserving stereotyper codefendant domiciliate
resentfully digestively unforgiving stereotypic codicillary draggletail
retinacular directivity woodcarving thermolysis collaborate dropcurtain
retinaculum effectively Yugoslavian thermolytic commemorate earthenware
righteously excessively bittersweet troglodytic commiserate elbowgrease
sagaciously exclusively bladderwort yacketyyack commonplace encapsulate
saintpaulia exclusivity breadthways bashibazouk communicant equidistant
salaciously excursively breadthwise Leibnitzian communicate equilibrate
seditiously expansively bristleworm Proterozoic compaginate ergatocracy
selfassured expansivity cabbageworm ─────────── complainant evidentiary
selfinduced expensively chickenwire ablutionary complaisant exanthemata
soliloquise explosively counterwork abranchiate concatenate exarcerbate
soliloquist extensively countrywide academicals concentrate expectorant
somnambular imitatively crossbowman accommodate concomitant expectorate
sorrowfully impassively earthenware acculturate concubinage expostulate
spectacular impassivity giantpowder afficionado concubinary expropriate
squarebuilt impulsively highbrowism agglomerate concubitant exstipulate
stegosaurus inclusively journeywork agglutinate condylomata extemporary
strenuously inductively kitchenware amontillado confabulate exterminate
subcultural inobservant latticework amplexicaul confederacy extrapolate
subscapular insectivore linedrawing anencephaly confederate extravagant
substituent intensively meadowsweet anniversary conflagrant extravagate
sumptuously intrusively mindblowing antemundane conflagrate extravasate
superfluity intuitively plasterwork antioxidant considerate fanfaronade
superfluous intuitivism scratchwork antiphonary consolidate farthingale
tempestuous invectively shopsteward appropriate constellate fasciaboard
tenaciously inventively sulphurwort approximate consternate fasciculate
thaumaturge irruptively swallowwort appurtenant contaminant filamentary
thaumaturgy landgravine thimbleweed archipelago contaminate fingerboard
therapeutic lucratively thitherward aristocracy contemplate fingerglass
thermoduric maidservant toothpowder assassinate contorniate fingerplate
torturously mendelevium trelliswork balletomane coparcenary fingerstall
tremulously mischievous trestlework barbiturate copperplate flabbergast
tricoloured narratively unbeknownst basketchair corbiculate flagcaptain
troublously nondelivery weatherwise beaverboard coronagraph folliculate
tuttifrutti nutritively weatherworn beneficiary coronograph foretopmast
tyrannously objectively whitherward beneficiate corroborant foretopsail
unambiguous objectivism winegrowing betweenmaid corroborate fractionary
unanimously objectivist worldlywise bicarbonate cotemporary fractionate
undutifully objectivity crucifixion bicentenary cottongrass fragmentary
unhelpfully obsessively genuflexion bicorporate countermand fricandeaux
unicellular obtrusively intersexual bicuspidate countermark funambulate
unicoloured offensively solifluxion bimillenary counterpane functionary
unskilfully operatively transfixion biofeedback counterpart functionate
vagariously ostensively transsexual bodyservant countervail gafftopsail
ventricular palsgravine actinomyces bondservant crackerjack galleyslave
ventriculus partitively actinomycin bookinghall credentials gartersnake
venturously pervasively amphictyony bottleglass cryotherapy gesticulate
```

guesstimate	nickelplate	remonstrate	thitherward	confiscable	impermeable
gyrocompass	nightingale	renegotiate	timebargain	conformable	impermeably
haemorrhage	noctivagant	reorientate	trabeculate	conformably	imperviable
hallucinate	noticeboard	resuscitate	transhumant	congealable	implausible
handgrenade	nurserymaid	retranslate	translocate	connectable	implausibly
haustellate	octingenary	revaccinate	translunary	connectible	impregnable
heterograft	orangoutang	revendicate	transpadane	conquerable	impregnably
Hindoostani	orchestrate	reverberant	triangulate	conservable	impressible
hippopotami	ornithosaur	reverberate	triumvirate	consignable	inadaptable
horripilate	oysterplant	revisionary	trophoblast	construable	inadvisable
hydrogenate	packingcase	ribbongrass	trundletail	containable	inalienable
hypothecate	paddleboard	rodomontade	tryingplane	contestable	inalienably
ichthyosaur	palmcabbage	rubberstamp	tryptophane	continuable	inalterable
immarginate	participant	rudimentary	tuberculate	contrivable	inalterably
impenetrate	participate	schoolboard	tyrannosaur	conversable	incoercible
imperforate	particulate	scintillant	undertenant	convertible	increasable
impersonate	pastureland	scintillate	unfortunate	convertibly	indefinable
importunate	pedicellate	scissortail	unguiculate	convincible	indefinably
impropriate	pedunculate	scurvygrass	unimportant	correctable	indivisible
incarcerate	penicillate	secondclass	uninucleate	corruptible	indivisibly
incardinate	peninsulate	sedimentary	unnecessary	corruptibly	indomitable
incognisant	penultimate	seditionary	urochordate	deliverable	indomitably
incompliant	perambulate	seigniorage	vagabondage	demountable	indubitable
inconsonant	perchlorate	seismograph	valleculate	denumerable	indubitably
incorporate	peregrinate	selfcommand	vermiculate	depressible	ineluctable
incriminate	perseverate	selfdespair	volitionary	descendable	ineluctably
individuate	petitionary	selfreliant	Wensleydale	descendible	inequitable
ingurgitate	phantasiast	semipalmate	whitherward	describable	inequitably
inobservant	phantasmata	sequestrate	yacketyyack	developable	inescapable
intemperate	phosphorate	shadowgraph	abolishable	diningtable	inestimable
interactant	phylloclade	shopsteward	abracadabra	dinnertable	inestimably
intercalary	physiocracy	shovelboard	accountable	disassemble	inexcusable
intercalate	picturecard	significant	accountably	disassembly	inexcusably
interlunary	plagioclase	silverplate	acidifiable	discardable	inflammable
interpolate	plantigrade	singletrack	agoraphobia	discernible	inflammably
interrelate	playerpiano	sleeveboard	agoraphobic	discernibly	infrangible
interrogate	playingcard	snowleopard	allocatable	discussable	inheritable
investigate	ploughshare	somatoplasm	anglophobia	discussible	innavigable
involucrate	ploughstaff	sparrowhawk	anglophobic	disencumber	innumerable
involuntary	pomegranate	spatterdash	antechamber	dislikeable	inscribable
jumpingjack	pontificals	spifflicate	antiJacobin	dispensable	inscrutable
kinetograph	pontificate	spiraculate	applaudable	disremember	inscrutably
kitchenware	powderflask	splashboard	appreciable	dissociable	inseparable
lawmerchant	precipitant	springboard	appreciably	dissolvable	inseparably
leatherback	precipitate	squarsonage	articulable	dissyllable	insuperable
legerdemain	precontract	stagemanage	assimilable	distensible	insuperably
libertinage	predominant	steeplejack	attemptable	dithyrambic	intertribal
ligamentary	predominate	stellionate	attractable	embraceable	intolerable
loggerheads	preliminary	stereograph	augmentable	enforceable	intolerably
louverboard	premeditate	stevengraph	automatable	enlargeable	intractable
louvreboard	prenominate	stickleback	beachcomber	escheatable	intractably
machicolate	prevaricate	stipendiary	certifiable	exercisable	irrecusable
machinemade	priestcraft	strangulate	certifiably	exhaustible	irrecusably
maidservant	proliferate	stratocracy	chrysarobin	explainable	irreducible
maintopmast	prolificacy	stringboard	civilisable	exploitable	irreducibly
maintopsail	proprietary	stringybark	cleanlimbed	expressible	irrefutable
mandarinate	protonotary	subaxillary	coffeetable	extractable	irrefutably
mandibulate	protuberant	subcontract	cognoscible	fashionable	irremovable
manifestant	pseudograph	subcontrary	collapsible	fashionably	irremovably
margraviate	psychodrama	subdominant	collectable	fermentable	irreparable
marketplace	psychograph	subordinate	collectible	fissionable	irreparably
marquessate	quarterback	substandard	combustible	foreseeable	irresoluble
matriculate	questionary	suffumigate	comfortable	forfeitable	irrevocable
meadowgrass	quitchgrass	superlunary	comfortably	forgettable	irrevocably
meprobamate	ratiocinate	supernatant	commendable	fortifiable	justiciable
meritocracy	rattlebrain	superstrata	commendably	Gallophobia	justifiable
middleclass	rattlesnake	surveillant	committable	haemoglobin	justifiably
minuteglass	reactionary	swallowtail	compassable	hereditable	landgrabber
miscarriage	recalculate	switchblade	compellable	hydrocarbon	liquefiable
miscegenate	reciprocate	switchboard	compossible	hydrophobia	liquidambar
misestimate	recriminate	taratantara	comprisable	hydrophobic	looselimbed
mismarriage	reduplicate	technocracy	concealable	hypsophobia	manipulable
molendinary	refrigerant	teeterboard	conceivable	illimitable	marcescible
mooringmast	refrigerate	tegumentary	conceivably	illimitably	marriagebed
mortarboard	regimentals	tenementary	condemnable	illuminable	medicinable
mothercraft	regurgitate	tentaculate	condensable	immedicable	mentionable
nationstate	reincarnate	tetrarchate	conductible	immitigable	medicinable
necessitate	reintegrate	theatricals	conferrable	immitigably	mentionable
needlecraft	remonstrant	thermograph	confirmable	impeachable	misremember

negrophobia	tarnishable	cylindrical	prophetical	cyclopaedic	shipbuilder
nyctophobia	thingumabob	cysticercus	prothoracic	dedicatedly	shockheaded
organisable	transcriber	cytological	puritanical	definiendum	shorthanded
pensionable	traversable	demagogical	pyramidical	delightedly	shortwinded
perceivable	treasonable	dendritical	quadratical	dicotyledon	sightreader
perceivably	treasonably	diacritical	rhapsodical	dimwittedly	slaveholder
perceptible	trisyllabic	dialectical	rheological	disguisedly	smallholder
perceptibly	trisyllable	diametrical	rheumaticky	disgustedly	smallminded
perfectible	unalterable	diphycercal	schottische	dispersedly	soberminded
performable	unavailable	diplococcus	selfinduced	doubleender	spellbinder
permissible	unavoidable	directrices	semeiotical	downtrodden	spermicidal
permissibly	unavoidably	doublefaced	serological	dumbfounder	stadtholder
persuadable	unbreakable	dresscircle	sexological	echosounder	stakeholder
persuasible	uncatchable	egotistical	sinological	ellipsoidal	stallholder
perturbable	unclimbable	enigmatical	sleepingcar	emptyhanded	starstudded
photophobia	uncountable	ethological	smoothfaced	emptyheaded	stockholder
photophobic	uncrushable	evangelical	sophistical	ephemerides	surfboarder
pleasurable	undesirable	executrices	spasmodical	faultfinder	swellheaded
pleasurably	undisturbed	experienced	splenetical	featheredge	swimbladder
polarisable	unendurable	fantastical	spondulicks	footpoundal	tachycardia
practicable	unendurably	flagofficer	squirearchy	fourpounder	tarradiddle
practicably	unflappable	geochemical	statistical	frankpledge	thickheaded
predictable	ungetatable	geometrical	stomachache	fratricidal	threehanded
predictably	unmatchable	geophysical	straightcut	fullblooded	titleholder
presentable	unmemorable	grammatical	straitlaced	gallbladder	toothpowder
presentably	unmemorably	greengrocer	strategical	gerrymander	toughminded
preservable	unpalatable	guttapercha	subclinical	giantpowder	transponder
preventable	unprintable	homiletical	subcortical	hairbreadth	trapezoidal
preventible	unshockable	homological	subcritical	halfblooded	typefounder
propitiable	unspeakable	horological	subtropical	halfholiday	typefoundry
protrudable	unspeakably	ideological	sybaritical	handbreadth	unadvisedly
protrusible	unstoppable	impolitical	symmetrical	haphazardly	unashamedly
publishable	unteachable	impoliticly	synagogical	heavyhanded	unboundedly
purchasable	unthinkable	impractical	synonymical	Heracleidan	underbidder
putrescible	unthinkably	internuncio	syntactical	homesteader	underhanded
qualifiable	untouchable	isometrical	synthetical	householder	undoubtedly
radiocarbon	unutterable	jabberwocky	taxonomical	hydraheaded	unfeignedly
reclaimable	unutterably	Jacobinical	testatrices	hypnopaedia	unguardedly
recoverable	vaporisable	Jacobitical	theological	ingrainedly	unlimitedly
rectifiable	vitrifiable	jauntingcar	theoretical	interbedded	Upanishadic
redoubtable	warrantable	judgmatical	thrasonical	intermeddle	volkslieder
refrangible	warrantably	kinematical	toploftical	jerrymander	warmblooded
regenerable	worshipable	leviratical	topological	largeminded	weighbridge
registrable	abiological	mediatrices	typological	leaseholder	wellfounded
regrettable	actinomyces	metonymical	uncanonical	levelheaded	wellrounded
regrettably	actinomycin	micrococcal	unequivocal	lighthanded	whiteheaded
replaceable	aerological	micrococcus	unpolitical	lightheaded	wrongheaded
repleviable	aeronomical	monarchical	vehmgericht	lightminded	abandonment
repressible	aesthetical	monological	virological	loculicidal	abolishment
repressibly	agonistical	mycological	aboutsledge	masquerader	abridgement
respectable	agrological	necromancer	acknowledge	metalloidal	abusiveness
respectably	agronomical	Neotropical	aggrievedly	meteoroidal	acaulescent
responsible	ahistorical	nomological	allantoides	misguidedly	achievement
responsibly	algological	nonsensical	archdukedom	mollycoddle	acquiescent
retraceable	allAmerican	nosological	barefacedly	moneylender	acquirement
retractable	allegorical	obstetrical	bellfounder	moneyspider	adjectively
retrievable	anecdotical	oecological	benightedly	octachordal	adjournment
Russophobia	anthropical	oecumenical	blackbirder	offhandedly	adjudgement
salvageable	antitypical	oenological	bodybuilder	officialdom	advancement
satisfiable	apostolical	oncological	bradycardia	orthopaedic	adventuress
serviceable	atheistical	ontological	broadminded	perplexedly	adverseness
serviceably	autarchical	oreological	cantharides	pervertedly	advisedness
shoulderbag	axiological	orthoepical	cantharidic	pigheadedly	affectively
signifiable	biochemical	panegyrical	caryopsides	pivotbridge	aftereffect
sleepingbag	biometrical	papiermache	cheerleader	planetoidal	aggregately
specifiable	biophysical	paradisical	childminder	pretendedly	aimlessness
stockjobber	braggadocio	paradoxical	Christendom	professedly	airlessness
stretchable	Brahmanical	paramedical	chrysalides	proofreader	airsickness
submersible	Brahminical	parasitical	clearheaded	pseudopodia	alkalescent
submissible	brazenfaced	parheliacal	coldblooded	pureblooded	alternately
suggestible	calendrical	patristical	collectedly	purportedly	altorelievo
supportable	casuistical	pedagogical	conceitedly	quadrupedal	altorilievo
supportably	categorical	pedological	concertedly	rangefinder	amativeness
surpassable	chimaerical	penological	confessedly	recommender	amiableness
susceptible	conceptacle	pharisaical	connectedly	rhombohedra	amorousness
susceptibly	convenances	pietistical	contentedly	righthanded	amphisbaena
suspensible	conventicle	pomological	coralloidal	righthander	ancientness
sustainable	conveyancer	posological	corrigendum	rightminded	anxiousness
swallowable	coxcombical	pragmatical	cyclopaedia	shareholder	appeasement

appointment	coefficient	diffuseness	exhaustless	hedgepriest	irksomeness
arbitrageur	cognateness	diffusively	expansively	heedfulness	ironmongery
arbitrament	cognitively	digestively	expensively	heinousness	irruptively
arborescent	collusively	disablement	explosively	hellishness	isogeotherm
archdiocese	combatively	disafforest	exquisitely	helpfulness	jealousness
archduchess	comfortless	disarmament	extensively	hideousness	joylessness
Archimedean	commandment	disbandment	extremeness	hirsuteness	jumpingbean
arduousness	compactness	discernment	factualness	hoggishness	juvenescent
arraignment	compartment	discourtesy	faddishness	hopefulness	knavishness
arrangement	compilement	disinterest	farawayness	housewifely	knowingness
artlessness	complexness	dislodgment	fatefulness	housewifery	lacrimosely
assertively	comportment	disobedient	fatuousness	hugeousness	lacrymosely
assuagement	compositely	disparately	fearfulness	hurriedness	landingbeam
assuredness	comstockery	disportment	featherhead	hurtfulness	landinggear
attentively	concealment	dissentient	featherless	hydrometeor	languidness
audibleness	concernment	dissepiment	featureless	hydrosphere	lastingness
austereness	conciseness	dissolutely	feelingness	hymenoptera	lawlessness
awesomeness	concrescent	distribuend	festinately	hyperborean	learnedness
awkwardness	condottiere	divorcement	fidgetiness	hypersthene	leatherhead
balefulness	condottieri	divulgement	finicalness	hypophyseal	leatherneck
bashfulness	conductress	doggishness	flaccidness	ignobleness	lengthiness
bathysphere	confinement	dolefulness	flavourless	imitatively	lepidoptera
battledress	congealment	dollishness	fleshliness	immediately	letterpress
battlefield	connoisseur	doltishness	flightiness	immenseness	lightsomely
bearishness	consentient	donnishness	floweriness	impassively	limitedness
beastliness	consignment	doublecheck	fluorescein	impeachment	lissomeness
bedevilment	constituent	doublespeak	fluorescent	imperilment	literalness
bedizenment	containment	doughtiness	foolishness	impermanent	lithosphere
beguilement	contentment	drouthiness	foppishness	impertinent	litterateur
belatedness	contrariety	drunkenness	foreignness	impingement	loathliness
belligerent	controlment	dubiousness	foreverness	importunely	loathsomely
benightment	copiousness	durableness	forgiveness	impoundment	logicalness
bereavement	corbiesteps	dutifulness	forlornness	imprecisely	loutishness
bersaglieri	cordialness	earnestness	fortunately	impressment	lovableness
betweenness	corecipient	earthliness	forwardness	impropriety	lucratively
bewitchment	corporately	effectively	franctireur	improvement	luminescent
bibliotheca	correctness	elaborately	franticness	improvident	lumpishness
biliousness	corrosively	elderliness	fretfulness	impulsively	lustfulness
bittercress	corruptness	electioneer	friableness	inadvertent	macrogamete
bittersweet	costiveness	elusiveness	frowardness	inanimately	magnificent
blessedness	counterfeit	embowerment	frowstiness	incalescent	makebelieve
bloodstream	countryseat	embracement	fulsomeness	inclusively	mannishness
blotchiness	courtliness	embroilment	furtiveness	incompetent	mantelpiece
bombardment	crabbedness	emotionless	gainfulness	incongruent	mantelshelf
Bonapartean	crookedness	emplacement	gallantness	inconscient	marchioness
bonbonniere	crotcheteer	emulousness	garnishment	incontinent	masculinely
bookishness	crunchiness	enchainment	gaseousness	incorporeal	massiveness
boorishness	cryosurgery	enchantment	gegenschein	indehiscent	masterpiece
bottlegreen	cunningness	enchantress	genteelness	independent	matrilineal
boutonniere	curableness	encrustment	genuineness	indifferent	matrilinear
breastwheel	curiousness	endlessness	ghastliness	IndoChinese	mawkishness
bristliness	currentness	endorsement	ghostliness	indorsement	maxillipede
Britishness	currishness	enfeoffment	gibbousness	inductively	meadowsweet
brittleness	cursiveness	enforcement	gimcrackery	inefficient	meaningless
brusqueness	cursoriness	engorgement	gingerbread	inexactness	measureless
brutishness	curtailment	engrossment	girlishness	inexpedient	measurement
bullishness	curvilineal	enjambement	glaringness	inheritress	mediateness
butteriness	curvilinear	enhancement	godlessness	insatiately	mellifluent
caddishness	debauchment	enlargement	gracileness	insincerely	meningocele
calefacient	debouchment	enlivenment	gradualness	insipidness	microgamete
callousness	deceptively	ennoblement	grandiosely	installment	milliampere
capableness	decussately	enslavement	grandparent	instillment	mindfulness
captionless	deductively	entablement	graphicness	intelligent	miserliness
carabiniere	defectively	enthralment	gristliness	intenseness	misjudgment
carabinieri	defenceless	entitlement	grotesquely	intensively	mitrailleur
carefulness	defensively	entrainment	grotesquery	interdepend	monkeybread
causatively	deforcement	entreatment	grouchiness	interfluent	mononuclear
centrepiece	defraudment	entrustment	groundsheet	interjacent	monseigneur
chancellery	delitescent	envelopment	guardedness	interlinear	mountaineer
chanticleer	demagoguery	enviousness	gutlessness	interosseus	movableness
chargesheet	demigoddess	environment	haematocele	intricately	multilinear
chickenfeed	depravement	equableness	haggardness	intrusively	multivalent
chloroprene	derangement	equipollent	halterbreak	intuitively	mundaneness
chucklehead	desperately	escheatment	haplessness	invalidness	musicalness
churchiness	despoilment	evanishment	harbourless	invectively	mutableness
circumspect	detrainment	evasiveness	harmfulness	inventively	naphthalene
Clarencieux	development	excessively	hatefulness	inviolately	narratively
cleanliness	deviousness	exclusively	haughtiness	inviolately	naturalness
cockleshell	devotedness	excursively	healthiness	involvement	naughtiness

```
necropoleis  polystyrene  ruinousness  stuntedness  victualless  crosslegged
needfulness  pompousness  saintliness  stylishness  viridescent  deceivingly
nervousness  portionless  saplessness  suasiveness  virilescent  degradingly
noctilucent  portmanteau  saturninely  subbasement  viscountess  demandingly
noisomeness  pourparlers  sausagemeat  sublimeness  viscousness  deploringly
nondelivery  prayerwheel  savouriness  subservient  visibleness  deservingly
nonetheless  preachiness  scaleinsect  substituent  voguishness  dinnerwagon
nonexistent  precentress  scragginess  succedaneum  volubleness  diphthongal
nonresident  preceptress  scrappiness  succourless  waggishness  disarmingly
notableness  preciseness  scrimpiness  summariness  wakefulness  disentangle
nothingness  predicament  scruffiness  sunlessness  waspishness  dismayingly
nourishment  preexistent  sculduddery  superintend  waywardness  doubleedged
noxiousness  prejudgment  sculduggery  superioress  wealthiness  downdraught
nutcrackers  prelusively  seasickness  superjacent  wearisomely  dramaturgic
nutritively  prematurely  seborrhoeic  supersedeas  weightiness  dreadnought
objectively  presentient  secretively  supremeness  welcomeness  embracingly
obliqueness  presentment  seductively  surbasement  weltschmerz  embryologic
obmutescent  prickliness  selectively  sustainment  whigmaleery  emmenagogue
obscureness  primitively  selfconceit  swarthiness  whitishness  endearingly
obsessively  privateness  selfcontent  swinishness  wholesomely  enquiringly
obsolescent  privatively  selfevident  synchromesh  willingness  exceedingly
obstinately  procrustean  selfishness  talkatively  winningness  falteringly
obtrusively  procurement  selfmastery  tearfulness  winsomeness  fatiguingly
obviousness  profaneness  selfrespect  tediousness  wintergreen  flauntingly
odorousness  profuseness  sensitively  temperament  wishfulness  footslogger
oesophageal  prolegomena  seriousness  temperately  wistfulness  forethought
offenceless  prosaicness  sexlessness  tenableness  witlessness  freethought
offensively  protectress  shadowiness  tentatively  womanliness  fullfledged
officialese  provocateur  Shaksperean  tenuousness  worldliness  gardemanger
oligochaete  proximately  shallowness  tetravalent  worrisomely  grammalogue
ominousness  prudishness  shapeliness  textureless  worshipless  gravedigger
omnipresent  publishment  shelterbelt  thimbleweed  zealousness  grumblingly
onerousness  pulverulent  shelterless  thirstiness  zestfulness  hairtrigger
operatively  purposeless  shepherdess  thoughtless  conspecific  handwrought
operoseness  purposively  shirtsleeve  threadiness  costbenefit  heavyweight
opportunely  pushfulness  shrubbiness  thriftiness  disgraceful  highwrought
orderliness  Pythagorean  shutterless  throatiness  distasteful  honeybadger
organscreen  quarterdeck  sickishness  thunderhead  distressful  hornswoggle
ostensively  queenliness  sightliness  thunderless  distrustful  hyperphagia
ostracoderm  quickfreeze  sightscreen  thunderpeal  foraminifer  immunologic
outwardness  quinquereme  silveriness  toothsomely  gallimaufry  imploringly
overgarment  racketpress  sincereness  traducement  mistrustful  inquiringly
overpayment  radicalness  sinlessness  trafficless  nonspecific  insultingly
ozonosphere  raffishness  sinuousness  tragicomedy  overstuffed  Interlingua
paddlewheel  raucousness  sizableness  transilient  reproachful  intermingle
painfulness  raunchiness  sketchiness  translucent  resourceful  intertangle
pamphleteer  realignment  skilfulness  transparent  scorpionfly  laughinggas
partitively  receptively  skulduddery  treacliness  sickbenefit  leapfrogged
passiveness  recessively  skulduggery  tremblement  subspecific  lightweight
patrilineal  recruitment  slavishness  tricksiness  suspenseful  lingeringly
paunchiness  rectilineal  slenderness  trivialness  teaspoonful  maddeningly
pearlescent  rectilinear  smithereens  troposphere  absorbingly  magazinegun
peevishness  reddishness  smokescreen  trouserless  acceptingly  medicolegal
pensionless  rediscovery  songfulness  tunableness  accordingly  metallurgic
pensiveness  reenactment  sottishness  tunefulness  affectingly  minnesinger
pentathlete  reflexively  soulfulness  turtleshell  agonisingly  motherright
pentavalent  refreshment  sparingness  typicalness  appallingly  observingly
perfectness  relatedness  spectatress  ultramodern  appealingly  overwrought
pervasively  reminiscent  spindlelegs  unawareness  approvingly  oxyhydrogen
pettishness  remorseless  spirochaete  uncanniness  arglebargle  panicmonger
phalanstery  replacement  springclean  uncleanness  arrestingly  paperhanger
philhellene  repleteness  springiness  uncouthness  bandylegged  paperweight
photosphere  repulsively  squalidness  ungodliness  banteringly  pennyweight
pigeonchest  requirement  squashiness  unhappiness  barrelorgan  perishingly
piggishness  resipiscent  squeakiness  uniformness  befittingly  pettifogger
pinkishness  resistively  starchiness  unmanliness  beguilingly  physiologic
pinnatisect  resplendent  stateliness  unquietness  bibliopegic  pillowfight
piteousness  restatement  staunchless  unsoundness  calyptrogen  potteringly
pitifulness  restfulness  staunchness  unusualness  candlelight  prattlingly
plaintively  restiveness  sternsheets  uprightness  caressingly  presumingly
planisphere  retentively  stickinsect  uselessness  centrifugal  progestogen
playfulness  retiredness  stiltedness  vacuousness  chaulmoogra  promisingly
plectoptera  retrocedent  stoicalness  valiantness  chronologer  provokingly
Pleistocene  reviviscent  stoolpigeon  variousness  chronologic  psychologic
plenipotent  rhomboideus  strangeness  velvetiness  cliffhanger  ravishingly
pliableness  riotousness  streakiness  verboseness  confidingly  rejoicingly
plicateness  roguishness  stringiness  versatilely  confusingly  reprovingly
pointedness  roundedness  stringpiece  vestryclerk  consolingly  rightwinger
poltroonery  rubefacient  studiedness  viciousness  consumingly  roughlegged
```

sarcophagus	endomorphic	primateship	adoptionism	arbitrative	calculative
scaremonger	endotrophic	proctorship	adoptionist	argumentive	calibration
scorchingly	establisher	prophetship	adumbration	Arminianism	californium
screamingly	fairweather	provostship	adumbrative	armtwisting	campmeeting
searchingly	feldspathic	replenisher	adventurism	aromaticity	candlestick
searchlight	firewatcher	schizanthus	adventurist	arterialise	cannibalise
secondsight	foulmouthed	scholarship	adversative	artillerist	cannibalism
septifragal	fourflusher	selfworship	advertising	aspersorium	capillarity
shrinkingly	fullmouthed	semimonthly	aeronautics	assafoetida	captivation
sickeningly	gatecrasher	senatorship	aerostatics	assentation	caravanning
simperingly	generalship	serigrapher	aerostation	assessorial	carbonation
slightingly	geostrophic	sharepusher	Aesculapian	assignation	carburetion
sockdolager	Germanophil	sheetanchor	aestivation	association	carminative
sockdologen	gettogether	sheriffship	affectation	associative	Carolingian
somatologic	grandfather	shoeleather	affectivity	assortative	carvelbuilt
spaceflight	grandmother	showmanship	affiliation	astigmatism	cassiterite
spreadeagle	grandnephew	sociopathic	affirmation	athleticism	castigation
squintingly	granolithic	soldiership	affirmative	atomisation	catheterise
startlingly	greatnephew	somewhither	affranchise	attenuation	catholicise
steatopygia	haberdasher	soupkitchen	affrication	attestation	Catholicism
straphanger	hardmouthed	speakership	affricative	attribution	catholicity
streetlight	hemimorphic	sponsorship	aggravation	attributive	cavalierism
stumblingly	heroworship	squeamishly	aggregation	audiologist	celebration
technologic	highpitched	stepbrother	aggregative	Augustinian	cellularity
teratologic	hobbledehoy	stewardship	agnosticism	Aurignacian	cementation
threelegged	holographic	studentship	agrarianism	autoerotism	centenarian
thrillingly	homeopathic	teachership	ailurophile	babysitting	cerebration
torchsinger	homomorphic	telegrapher	alabastrine	bactericide	chafingdish
totteringly	housefather	telegraphic	Albigensian	ballbearing	challenging
tremblingly	houselights	therewithal	alcyonarian	barquentine	channelling
trothplight	housemother	topographer	Alexandrian	bearbaiting	chansonnier
unbendingly	hydropathic	topographic	alexandrine	bellicosity	chickenwire
unceasingly	ideographic	tribuneship	alexandrite	bellringing	chiropodist
underweight	idiographic	trusteeship	alleviation	Belorussian	chitterling
unfailingly	idiomorphic	typographer	alleviative	Benedictine	christening
unfeelingly	kymographic	typographic	allopathist	benediction	churchgoing
unmeaningly	lectureship	unfurnished	alphabetise	benefaction	cicatricial
unnervingly	lickerishly	unvarnished	altercation	bestselling	cinnabarine
unsmilingly	lifemanship	viceroyship	alternation	betweentime	circularise
unsparingly	logographer	wappenschaw	alternative	bibliophile	circularity
unweetingly	logographic	washleather	amaranthine	bibliophily	circulation
unwillingly	loudmouthed	wherewithal	ambiversion	biddability	circulative
unwinkingly	managership	whitewasher	amenability	biedermeier	civilianise
unwittingly	marshalship	whitleather	Americanise	bifurcation	clandestine
waterlogged	matriarchal	workmanship	Americanism	billionaire	clericalism
wheelwright	mesomorphic	xylographer	Americanist	billposting	clericalist
whoremonger	messiahship	xylographic	amethystine	bimetallism	clodhopping
witheringly	metamorphic	zygomorphic	amicability	bimetallist	clostridium
admiralship	metapsychic	Abbevillian	amphetamine	bimillenium	clothesline
Aeneolithic	microlithic	abecedarian	amphibolite	bipartition	coadunation
aerographer	monitorship	abnormality	anachronism	birdfancier	coagulation
allomorphic	monographer	abomination	Anglicanism	bisexuality	coarctation
anacoluthon	monographic	abortionist	AngloIndian	bivouacking	cochinchina
apostleship	monomorphic	absenteeism	anglomaniac	bohemianism	coeducation
apostrophic	Neanderthal	abstraction	annabergite	bombilation	coessential
apparatchik	neuropathic	abstractive	antenuptial	bombination	coextension
autographic	nomographer	abstriction	antependium	Bonapartism	coextensive
autotrophic	nomographic	academician	anteriority	Bonapartist	cognitivity
backbencher	nosographer	academicism	antheridium	bondservice	coleorrhiza
batholithic	nosographic	acceptation	anthologise	bondwashing	colligation
bellheather	oarsmanship	accessorial	anthologist	bookbinding	colligative
birdwatcher	openmouthed	accessorise	antifouling	bookkeeping	collimation
bushmanship	oreographic	accipitrine	antigravity	bookselling	collocation
cacographic	osteopathic	acclamation	antiquarian	bootlegging	colonialism
captainship	Ostrogothic	acclimation	antiquation	botheration	colonialist
citizenship	paragrapher	acclimatise	aphrodisiac	brachiation	colouration
colonelship	paragraphic	accompanist	apologetics	brankursine	colourblind
comradeship	paramorphic	acetylation	apomorphine	breadthwise	columbarium
curatorship	partnership	achromatise	apophyllite	bricklaying	combination
demographer	patriarchal	achromatism	apotheosise	bullbaiting	combinative
demographic	patternshop	acidulation	apparelling	bullterrier	commination
denizenship	pearlfisher	acoustician	appellation	butcherbird	comminution
diastrophic	philosopher	acquisition	appellative	butterflies	commonality
doxographer	philosophic	acquisitive	application	byeelection	communalise
ectomorphic	pleomorphic	acriflavine	applicative	Byzantinism	communalist
ectotrophic	polygraphic	acumination	approbation	Byzantinist	commutation
Elizabethan	polymorphic	adiaphorism	aquarellist	calcination	commutative
embellisher	praetorship	adoptianism	arbitrarily	calculating	comparatist
emperorship	premiership	adoptianist	arbitration	calculation	comparatist

```
comparative  crepitation  detribalise  elucidative  exploration  gemmulation
competition  criminalist  deuteration  elutriation  explorative  genealogise
competitive  criminality  devaluation  embarkation  exponential  genealogist
compilation  crimination  devastation  emblematise  exportation  gentilitial
complotting  criminative  diachronism  emblematist  expurgation  genuflexion
composition  criticality  diagnostics  embowelling  exsiccation  geopolitics
compositive  crocidolite  diaphaneity  embrocation  extemporise  geosyncline
compotation  crocodilian  diapositive  empanelling  extenuation  germination
compression  crucifixion  dichotomise  emulsionise  exteriorise  germinative
compressive  crystalline  dichotomist  enchiridion  exteriority  gestatorial
compunction  crystallise  dictatorial  encystation  externalise  glassmaking
computation  crystallite  didacticism  endocardiac  externalism  globigerina
computerise  culmination  diffraction  endocardial  externality  globularity
condominium  culpability  diluvialist  endocardium  extirpation  glomeration
condonation  cultivation  dinosaurian  endometrium  extradition  goldbeating
confliction  cupellation  Diophantine  endothelial  extrication  golddigging
conflictive  customarily  diphtherial  endothelium  eyecatching  gonfalonier
confutation  custombuilt  diplomatise  enfranchise  fabrication  goodlooking
confutative  cybernation  diplomatist  engineering  facelifting  gourmandise
congelation  cybernetics  dipsomaniac  enthralling  facsimilist  gourmandism
conjugality  cycloserine  directivity  entomophily  factfinding  grandiosity
conjugation  cypripedium  directorial  enucleation  facultative  granularity
conjugative  debarkation  discerption  enumeration  fallibility  granulation
conjunction  decantation  disfunction  enumerative  Falstaffian  gratulation
conjunctiva  decarbonise  disillusion  enunciation  familiarise  gravelblind
conjuration  decarburise  disjunction  enunciative  familiarity  gravitation
connotation  declamation  disjunctive  epigastrium  farcicality  gravitative
connotative  declaration  dislocation  epigraphist  farreaching  greasepaint
consanguine  declarative  disobliging  epinephrine  fascinating  greenockite
consecution  declination  disorganise  epochmaking  fascination  gullibility
consecutive  decollation  disparaging  equilibrist  favouritism  gurgitation
considering  decolourise  disposition  equilibrium  feasibility  guttersnipe
consolation  decussation  dispositive  equinoctial  fecundation  gutturalise
conspicuity  deemphasise  disputation  eradication  festschrift  gutturalism
consumerism  defalcation  disquieting  eradicative  fiddlestick  habituation
consumption  deferential  dissipation  Erastianism  filmsetting  hagiologist
consumptive  defloration  dissipative  erotomaniac  fimbriation  hairraising
contractile  defoliation  dissolution  esotericism  fingerprint  hairstyling
contraction  deformation  distinction  Esperantist  FinnoUgrian  hairstylist
contractive  deglutition  distinctive  etherealise  fireraising  halfbinding
contraption  degradation  distinguish  ethereality  firewalking  halflanding
contrastive  degustation  distraction  ethnologist  firstfruits  Hamiltonian
controlling  dehydration  distractive  etymologise  fissiparity  handfasting
conurbation  deification  disunionist  etymologist  flagwagging  handselling
convocation  delectation  divisionism  euchologion  flannelling  handwriting
convolution  delineation  divulgation  eudaemonism  flexibility  hardhitting
cooperation  demagnetise  doctrinaire  eudaemonist  florilegium  hardworking
cooperative  demagoguism  domesticity  eurhythmics  fluctuation  headhunting
coplanarity  demarcation  domineering  Europeanise  fomentation  heartstring
coppersmith  demarkation  doublequick  evagination  footsoldier  Hegelianism
cornhusking  democratise  doublethink  evaporation  forerunning  helleborine
cornucopian  democratism  dressmaking  evaporative  forestation  Hepplewhite
corporality  denigration  dropforging  eventualise  forewarning  heptarchist
corporation  deoxidation  dundrearies  eventuality  formication  hermeticism
corporatism  depauperise  duplication  everlasting  formularise  hesperidium
corporative  deportation  duplicative  examination  formulation  heteroclite
correlation  depravation  dysfunction  exclamation  fornication  heteroecism
correlative  deprecation  earpiercing  exclusivity  forthcoming  hexametrist
corrugation  deprecative  eclecticism  excoriation  fractionise  hibernation
coruscation  depredation  ecumenicism  exculpation  Francophile  Hibernicism
cosmetician  deprivation  ecumenicity  executorial  franklinite  hierarchism
cosmogonist  dereliction  edification  exemplarily  freebooting  highbrowism
cosmologist  description  educability  exemplarity  freezedried  highranking
cosmopolite  descriptive  egalitarian  exfoliation  frenchified  Hispanicise
counselling  desecration  einsteinium  exfoliative  frigidarium  Hispanicism
countermine  desensitise  ejaculation  exhortation  fructuation  Hispanicist
countersign  desexualise  elaboration  exhortative  frustration  histologist
countersink  desiccation  elaborative  existential  fulguration  historicise
counterview  desiccative  electrician  exoneration  fulminating  historicism
countrified  designation  electricity  exonerative  fulmination  historicist
countryfied  desperation  electrolier  exotericism  funambulist  historicity
countryside  destination  electronics  expansivity  fusillation  histrionics
countrywide  destitution  elephantine  expatiation  fustigation  histrionism
creationism  destruction  elicitation  expatiative  Gallicanism  hollandaise
creationist  destructive  eligibility  expectation  gallowsbird  holothurian
credibility  desultorily  elimination  expectative  gametangium  homogeneity
crematorium  determinism  eliminative  explanation  gangsterism  homoiousian
crenulation  determinist  ellipticity  explication  geanticline  hooliganism
             detestation  elucidation  explicative  gemmologist  horseradish
```

hospitalise	infeudation	lammergeier	megatherium	nitrogenise	pantomimist
hospitality	infirmarian	Lancastrian	melioration	noisemaking	papermaking
humiliation	influential	lancinating	meliorative	nondescript	parachutist
hummingbird	informality	lancination	memorialise	nonmatching	parallelism
husbandlike	information	landgravine	memorialist	nonplussing	parametrise
hyacinthine	informative	landholding	mendelevium	nonunionist	paramoecium
hydrologist	ingathering	landlordism	mensuration	nonvolatile	participial
hydroponics	initialling	latchstring	mercenarily	notionalist	parturition
hyoscyamine	innervation	latifundium	merchandise	novelettish	passibility
hyperactive	innutrition	laudability	Merovingian	nullifidian	Passiontide
hyperbolise	inoculation	leavetaking	merrymaking	nulliparity	passivation
hyphenation	inoculative	legionnaire	metaphysics	numismatics	pastoralism
hypolimnion	inoffensive	legislation	metastasise	numismatist	pastoralist
hypophysial	inoperative	legislative	meteoritics	nuncupation	paternalism
hypostatise	inquisition	Leibnitzian	methylamine	nuncupative	paternalist
hypotension	inquisitive	leprosarium	methylation	obfuscation	pathologist
hypothesise	insalubrity	libertarian	metrication	objectivism	patrimonial
idolisation	inscription	liberticide	Micawberish	objectivist	patronising
illbreeding	inscriptive	libertinism	Micawberism	objectivity	pawnbroking
illiquidity	insectarium	limnologist	Micronesian	objurgation	peacemaking
illusionism	insecticide	linedrawing	micturition	obscuration	peccability
illusionist	insensitive	linefishing	millenarian	obsecration	pectination
imaginarily	insessorial	linguistics	millionaire	observation	peculiarity
imagination	insincerity	liquidation	mindbending	obstruction	pecuniarily
imaginative	insinuation	lithotomise	mindblowing	obstructive	Pelagianism
imbrication	insinuative	lithotomist	mindreading	obtestation	pelargonium
immanentism	inspiration	lixiviation	miniaturise	occultation	pellucidity
immanentist	instability	logomachist	miniaturist	oenophilist	penetrating
immigration	instigation	longanimity	ministerial	officialism	penetration
immortalise	instigative	longplaying	miscibility	officiation	penetrative
immortality	instinctive	loosestrife	misconceive	oilpainting	penicillium
impanelling	institution	loxodromics	miscreation	oldwomanish	penitential
imparkation	instruction	lubrication	misspelling	ophidiarium	pentazocine
impartation	instructive	lubricative	mockingbird	ophiologist	pentlandite
impassivity	integrality	lucubration	molestation	opportunism	peptisation
imperialise	integration	Lutheranism	molybdenite	opportunist	percolation
imperialism	integrative	luxuriation	momentarily	opportunity	perennation
imperialist	intensifier	machination	monasterial	oppugnation	perforation
imperilling	interaction	madreporite	monasticism	optometrist	perforative
impetration	interactive	madrigalian	moneymaking	oracularity	pericardiac
impetuosity	interallied	madrigalist	monkeyshine	orientalise	pericardial
implication	interesting	magdalenian	monochasial	orientalism	pericardium
implicative	interfacial	magisterial	monochasium	orientalist	pericranial
importation	interfacing	magisterium	monologuise	orientation	pericranium
importunity	interfusion	Maglemosian	monologuist	originality	perineurium
imprecation	interiorise	magnanimity	Monophysite	origination	periodicity
imprecision	interiority	mailcarrier	Monothelite	originative	peristalith
inanimation	interlining	maladaptive	monstrosity	orthopedics	peristomial
inattention	intermedium	malapropism	moribundity	orthopedist	perithecium
inattentive	internalise	malediction	moveability	oscillation	permutation
incantation	internality	malefaction	mudslinging	ostentation	persecution
incarnadine	internecine	malfunction	multinomial	osteologist	personalise
incarnation	interracial	malposition	multiracial	outbreeding	personalism
inclination	intrepidity	malpractice	murmuration	outbuilding	personalist
incommodity	intuitivism	mammalogist	muscularity	outcropping	personality
incongruity	inventorial	mandolinist	musculation	outfighting	personation
incredulity	inviability	manducation	mycophagist	outstanding	personative
inculcation	invultation	Manichaeism	mythologise	overbearing	personifier
inculpation	irradiation	manumission	mythologist	overbidding	perspective
incuriosity	irradiative	manumitting	mythomaniac	overlapping	perspicuity
incurvation	irredentism	marginalise	mythopoeist	overmanning	pertinacity
indentation	irredentist	marginality	nailvarnish	overrunning	pestologist
indigestion	irremissive	marlinspike	namecalling	oversailing	petrologist
indigestive	irretention	marshalling	nationalise	oversetting	phagocytise
indignation	irretentive	masculinise	nationalism	overtopping	phariseeism
indirection	isochronism	masculinity	nationalist	overweening	phenologist
IndoIranian	isomorphism	mastication	nationality	oviposition	philatelist
inebriation	itacolumite	matchmaking	necessarian	oxygenation	philologian
inedibility	itineration	materialise	necessarily	ozonisation	philologist
ineffective	jactitation	materialism	neckerchief	paediatrics	phonetician
inessential	Judaisation	materialist	necrologist	paediatrist	phonologist
inexpensive	kitchensink	materiality	needlepoint	painkilling	phosphonium
infanticide	knownothing	mathematics	negationist	painstaking	phosphorism
infantilism	labefaction	matrimonial	negotiation	Palestinian	phosphorite
infatuation	laciniation	McCarthyism	nephelinite	palpability	photoactive
inferential	lacrimation	mechanician	neurologist	palpitation	photocopier
inferiority	lacrymation	mediatorial	neuroticism	palsgravine	photofinish
infertility	laicisation	medievalism	nictitation	pandemonium	photoperiod
infestation	lamentation	medievalist	nightmarish	Panglossian	phycologist

phylogynist	prohibitive	referential	saxophonist	solvability	syllabicity
physicality	proletarian	reformation	scaffolding	Soroptimist	synchronise
phytologist	proletariat	reformative	schismatise	Southernism	synchronism
phytotomist	prolificity	regionalise	schistosity	spacesaving	syncopation
Pickwickian	promiscuity	regionalism	schoolchild	sparrowbill	syndicalism
pigsticking	propagation	regionalist	scissorbill	specificity	syndicalist
pilocarpine	propagative	reification	scopolamine	spectrality	syndication
piscatorial	propinquity	reinsertion	ScotchIrish	speculation	systematics
placability	proposition	reiteration	scriptorial	speculative	systematise
planetarium	prorogation	reiterative	scriptorium	speechifier	systematism
platforming	prosecution	relationism	secondarily	spendthrift	systematist
platyrrhine	proselytise	relationist	secretarial	spessartite	tabefaction
plebeianise	proselytism	reliability	secretariat	sphaeridium	taciturnity
plebeianism	prospective	religionise	sedentarily	spinsterish	talebearing
pleinairist	prosthetics	religionist	segregation	spontaneity	tameability
pleochroism	prostration	religiosity	segregative	sporogonium	tangibility
pocketknife	protagonist	reluctation	seigneurial	sporulation	tankfarming
pointdevice	prothallial	repartition	seigniorial	squarebuilt	tantalising
pointillism	prothallium	replication	selectivity	stagflation	tapemachine
pointillist	protractile	reportorial	selfclosing	stampoffice	tautologise
politicking	protraction	reprobation	selfcocking	standardise	tautologism
pollination	protractive	reprobative	selfdenying	standoffish	tautomerism
poltergeist	provisorily	repudiation	selffeeding	statutorily	taxidermist
polypeptide	provocation	requisition	selffeeling	stencilling	teetotalism
polyzoarium	provocative	reservation	selffertile	stenotypist	teleologism
ponderation	Prussianise	residential	selfloading	stiflejoint	teleologist
ponderosity	Prussianism	resignation	selflocking	stimulation	telepathise
portability	publication	resistivity	selfopinion	stimulative	telepathist
portraitist	pullulation	respiration	selfpitying	stipulation	telephonist
positronium	punctuality	restitution	selfraising	stocktaking	temperative
possibility	punctuation	restoration	selfsealing	straightish	temporality
postexilian	pupillarity	restorative	selfseeking	strenuosity	temporarily
postglacial	purgatorial	restriction	selfservice	strongpoint	tensibility
postnuptial	pustulation	restrictive	selfserving	stylisation	tentpegging
postulation	pyrargyrite	retaliation	selfsterile	stylopodium	termination
Precambrian	Pythagorism	retaliative	selfwinding	subarration	terminative
preconceive	quadrennial	retardation	semanticist	subaudition	termitarium
predatorily	quadrennium	retardative	sensibility	subdivision	terrestrial
predication	quadrillion	retentivity	sensitivity	subjugation	territorial
predicative	quaestorial	retribution	Septembrist	subjunctive	testability
preelection	qualitative	retributive	septenarius	sublimation	testimonial
prefatorial	quarrelling	retroaction	septentrion	subornation	Teutonicism
prefatorily	quickfiring	retroactive	serendipity	subrogation	thalidomide
preignition	quincuncial	revaluation	serrulation	substantial	theobromine
prejudicial	quintillion	reverential	sertularian	substantive	theosophist
prelibation	Rabelaisian	revisionism	serviceline	subsumption	thermionics
prelusorily	racemeeting	revisionist	sextodecimo	subsumptive	thermophile
prematurity	radioactive	rheotropism	Shaksperian	subtraction	thunderbird
premonition	radiolarian	rhetorician	sheathknife	subtractive	thwartships
preoccupied	radiologist	rhinologist	shellacking	suburbanise	timeserving
preparation	rapscallion	ribvaulting	shoplifting	suburbanite	timesharing
preparative	rarefaction	rickettsial	shortcoming	suckingfish	titillation
preposition	rarefactive	roadholding	showjumping	suffixation	tittivation
prepositive	Rastafarian	rodenticide	shrivelling	suffocation	tobacconist
preprandial	rateability	roentgenise	sightseeing	suffocative	tobogganing
prerogative	rationalise	romanticise	sillimanite	suitability	tobogganist
presanctify	rationalism	romanticism	silverpoint	sumptuosity	togglejoint
prestissimo	rationalist	romanticist	silversmith	superfamily	tolbutamide
presumption	rationality	ropedancing	silverstick	superficial	topdressing
presumptive	reactionist	ropewalking	singlestick	superficies	touchtyping
preterition	readability	Rosicrucian	singularise	superfluity	tourbillion
primigenial	realisation	rubefaction	singularity	superiority	toxophilite
primitivism	reanimation	rubicundity	skatingrink	superlative	trafficking
probabilism	reapportion	rubrication	skeletonise	superscribe	trammelling
probabilist	reassertion	rustication	Slavonicise	superscript	transaction
probability	reawakening	Sabbatarian	slickenside	supervision	transalpine
prochronism	rebarbative	sacculation	slotmachine	supposition	transection
procreation	recantation	sacrificial	smithsonite	suppositive	transfinite
procreative	receptivity	Sadduceeism	snowbunting	suppression	transfixion
procuration	reciprocity	safekeeping	soapboiling	suppressive	transfusion
prodigalise	reclamation	Sagittarius	sociability	suppuration	translation
prodigality	recognition	saleability	Socinianism	suppurative	transmarine
profanation	recognitive	salesladies	sociologist	supremacist	Trappistine
prognathism	recondition	saltatorial	soldierlike	surgeonfish	trepanation
progression	redetermine	sandbagging	solifluxion	surrogation	trepidation
progressism	redirection	Sanskritist	soliloquise	suspiration	tribulation
progressist	reedbunting	satiability	soliloquist	susurration	tribunicial
progressive	reeducation	saturnalian	solmisation	swallowdive	tribunitial
prohibition	reestablish	saxophonist	solutionist	syllabarium	tributarily

```
triggerfish  watchmaking  slavemarket  counterblow  memorabilia  sentinelled
trimestrial  waterskiing  sleepwalker  counterplan  mercurially  sheriffalty
trimorphism  weatherwise  steelworker  counterplea  mimetically  sidewheeler
Trinitarian  Weismannism  stiffnecked  counterplot  moronically  sigmoidally
tritagonist  wellmeaning  stockbroker  crepuscular  multangular  sinistrally
trituration  wellwishing  stockmarket  crestfallen  municipally  snowgoggles
tuberculise  Wesleyanism  supermarket  cryptically  necrophilia  softshelled
tufthunting  Whitsuntide  supertanker  deceitfully  necrophilic  somatically
tumbledrier  widdershins  sweepstakes  decennially  nocturnally  somnambular
tumefaction  wildcatting  threedecker  deistically  nomadically  sorrowfully
turbination  wildfowling  trackwalker  dialectally  nonmetallic  spastically
typecasting  winegrowing  voortrekker  disannulled  numerically  spectacular
typesetting  winetasting  wastebasket  disgruntled  occipitally  spherically
tyrannicide  wirenetting  wisecracker  dishevelled  octagonally  spiritually
ultramarine  wirepulling  abdominally  doctrinally  officinally  spirituelle
ultrasonics  wiretapping  abiotically  drastically  organically  spirituelle
unappealing  withershins  accentually  dynamically  osmotically  steamboiler
unassertive  woodcarving  acidophilic  editorially  otherwhiles  steamroller
unbelieving  woodcutting  acropetally  effectually  outrivalled  stonecurlew
unbeseeming  workability  adminicular  elastically  overdevelop  stonewaller
unchristian  workmanlike  adverbially  elementally  overindulge  storyteller
uncongenial  worldlywise  aerobically  Emmenthaler  pacifically  subaerially
undertaking  worshipping  agnatically  emotionally  paedophilia  subscapular
undeserving  xylophonist  altocumulus  empirically  parallelled  subumbrella
unessential  Yugoslavian  angelically  endemically  parochially  surficially
unfaltering  zoantharian  animalcular  episcopally  passacaglia  tabernacled
unflinching  zoographist  aquatically  equiangular  peccadillos  tagliatelle
unforgiving  zoomorphism  archaically  equivocally  pedestalled  tagliatelli
unhealthily  zootechnics  archangelic  erratically  perennially  technically
unification  Zoroastrian  ascetically  essentially  perishables  teetotaller
unipolarity  thingumajig  aseptically  eugenically  perpetually  tetanically
unobtrusive  awestricken  aspergillum  factionally  photophilic  tetracyclic
unpromising  balmcricket  aspergillus  faithhealer  pictorially  thermically
unqualified  billsticker  bacchanalia  fanatically  pipistrelle  thunderclap
unreasoning  blackmarket  baptismally  financially  piratically  titanically
unrelenting  bloodsucker  barbastelle  forestaller  plentifully  toothbilled
unremitting  boilermaker  basipetally  forgetfully  podophyllin  torticollis
unselective  brainsickly  beautifully  fourwheeler  polemically  triadically
unshrinking  breadbasket  bibliopolic  frantically  politically  triennially
utilisation  bushwhacker  bilaterally  fraternally  polygonally  ultraviolet
utilitarian  catswhisker  blackfellow  frightfully  potentially  unconcealed
vacationist  chainsmoker  blackmailer  generically  practically  underseller
vaccination  cityslicker  bloodguilty  genetically  primaevally  undutifully
vacillation  cockaleekie  botanically  genitivally  principally  unhelpfully
vacuolation  cockyleekie  bountifully  gentianella  procephalic  unicellular
vagabondise  crookbacked  bucolically  gibberellin  proconsular  unisexually
vagabondish  cupronickel  Byronically  glossolalia  prosaically  universally
vagabondism  deerstalker  canalicular  graphically  psychedelia  unkennelled
valediction  doorknocker  canaliculus  haemophilia  psychedelic  unnaturally
variability  fieldworker  canonically  haemophilic  psychically  unskilfully
variegation  firecracker  carbocyclic  healthfully  punchinello  venatically
vascularise  floorwalker  carbuncular  Hebraically  pussywillow  ventricular
vascularity  forethinker  caterpillar  heretically  pyramidally  ventriculus
vasectomise  freethinker  caustically  heteropolar  quizzically  veridically
vendibility  godforsaken  cavedweller  homothallic  ratatouille  verisimilar
venesection  heartbroken  celestially  horsecollar  rectangular  vestigially
venisection  honeysuckle  changefully  hospitaller  reedwarbler  viceregally
ventilation  hunchbacked  chanterelle  hydrophilic  regardfully  viceroyalty
ventilative  hypermarket  chaotically  identically  regretfully  violoncello
vermiculite  interlocker  chronically  idiotically  reposefully  watercooled
vermination  kwashiorkor  circumpolar  idyllically  resentfully  watercooler
versatility  loudspeaker  circumsolar  illiberally  retinacular  wedgetailed
verticality  mantuamaker  circumvolve  illogically  retinaculum  whimsically
vesuvianite  metalworker  clapperclaw  immoveables  rightangled  whitecollar
vibratility  molecricket  classically  impartially  safetyvalve  wholesouled
vichyssoise  moneymarket  closehauled  incunabulum  saintpaulia  wonderfully
victualling  mothernaked  coeternally  intervallic  sartorially  yellowbelly
vincibility  nightwalker  colourfully  ithyphallic  satanically  aerodynamic
vindication  noseyparker  comestibles  juridically  satirically  aircraftman
vindicative  phrasemaker  commensally  laconically  sceptically  algorithmic
vivisection  pieceworker  comptroller  lakedweller  scoundrelly  AngloNorman
volcanicity  plainspoken  conformally  marketvalue  sectionally  antivitamin
voluntarily  retrorocket  congenially  marshmallow  segmentally  assemblyman
voluntarism  ringstraked  connubially  masterfully  seismically  barnstormer
voluntarist  safebreaker  continually  mediaevally  selaginella  borborygmus
vulcanicity  safecracker  convivially  medicinally  selfdisplay  breadcrumbs
wainscoting  shelljacket  convolvulus  megalopolis  semiskilled  businessman
waitinglist  shipbreaker  corporeally  melancholia  semitrailer  cataclysmic
washability  shortspoken  corpuscular  melancholic  sensorially  catechismal
```

centigramme	astringency	disinclined	iridescence	putrescence	vociferance
chromosomal	attitudinal	disturbance	irrelevance	pyrotechnic	welldefined
churchwoman	attritional	educational	irrelevancy	quickchange	abstentious
congressman	beneficence	encumbrance	irreverence	quinquennia	acarpellous
contretemps	benevolence	enlightened	kleptomania	radiophonic	acclamatory
craftswoman	bibliomancy	ensanguined	lactescence	rallentando	acclivitous
crossbowman	bibliomania	entertainer	latitudinal	reassurance	acinaciform
cryptogamic	birdbrained	epeirogenic	laurustinus	recessional	acrimonious
cyclothymia	blastogenic	equivalence	lieutenancy	redactional	adenomatous
cyclothymic	booklearned	equivalency	liquescence	reemergence	adventurous
deliveryman	breadwinner	erubescence	lophobranch	reflectance	aerobiology
draughtsman	calisthenic	evanescence	maintenance	refringency	affirmatory
ectoplasmic	candescence	evolutional	maleficence	reinsurance	agrobiology
endoplasmic	capacitance	exceptional	malevolence	remembrance	ailurophobe
endothermal	carrageenan	excrescence	malfeasance	renaissance	alleviatory
endothermic	carrageenin	excrescency	marcescence	resemblance	amazonstone
epithalamia	chalcedonic	executioner	mediastinal	respondence	amenorrhoea
epithalamic	chameleonic	exorbitance	mediastinum	respondency	amentaceous
flimflammer	charlatanry	expansional	megalomania	reversional	amphibology
Frenchwoman	cheiromancy	extensional	menservants	reversioner	amphictyony
gastronomic	chieftaincy	extortioner	mesalliance	rhabdomancy	anachronous
gentlewoman	christiania	fieldcornet	microphonic	rifacimenti	androgynous
GraecoRoman	Christianly	flamboyance	misalliance	rifacimento	anfractuous
hexadecimal	chrominance	flamboyancy	miscellanea	ruridecanal	anticathode
hydrobromic	cinquecento	flamboyante	misfeasance	saltimbanco	anticyclone
hypothermia	circumlunar	flocculence	misguidance	salvational	antimonious
infantryman	coalescence	florescence	morrisdance	selfdefence	applicatory
interatomic	coexistence	forbearance	munificence	semidiurnal	approbatory
Kulturkampf	cognitional	forbiddance	Neoplatonic	sempiternal	arboraceous
logarithmic	cognoscente	forgetmenot	nigrescence	sensational	archaeology
macrocosmic	cognoscenti	formational	nonchalance	seventeenth	arenicolous
merchantman	coincidence	Francomania	nonfeasance	shortchange	arthrospore
microcosmic	coinsurance	fraudulence	nonviolence	situational	Assyriology
monochromat	collectanea	freemasonry	nutritional	snickersnee	atrabilious
monochromic	collisional	frontrunner	nymphomania	somatogenic	autochthony
monogrammed	comeuppance	furnishings	obsessional	somatotonia	avoirdupois
needlewoman	commonsense	furtherance	oestrogenic	somatotonic	bacciferous
ninnyhammer	complacence	gasfittings	omnipotence	sovereignly	bacilliform
pachydermal	complacency	gentlemanly	omniscience	sovereignty	barleybroth
palindromic	concordance	geotectonic	oneiromancy	statesmanly	bashibazouk
perispermic	concurrence	gradational	opalescence	submarginal	bellbottoms
policewoman	conditional	gramophonic	operational	submergence	benedictory
polychromic	conditioner	habiliments	outdistance	subregional	bicephalous
preterhuman	conductance	haemocyanin	outspokenly	subsequence	billetsdoux
prothalamia	conformance	harebrained	overbalance	subsistence	bladderwort
reprogramme	consequence	hebephrenia	panhellenic	subterminal	blasphemous
Scotchwoman	conservancy	hebephrenic	pantothenic	sufficiency	boardschool
septicaemia	consistence	heldentenor	paraselenae	summational	brachyurous
septicaemic	consistency	honeymooner	parishioner	tabletennis	breechblock
sexagesimal	consultancy	hydrocyanic	partitioned	tearstained	breezeblock
sheepfarmer	conterminal	ichthyornis	partitioner	tephromancy	bristleworm
spokeswoman	contingence	illuminance	percipience	teratogenic	brotherhood
sportswoman	contingency	impassioned	performance	thinskinned	bryozoology
supernormal	continuance	impedimenta	perpetuance	tiddlywinks	buffalorobe
telegrammic	contradance	impenitence	persistence	toxicomania	bulletproof
transformer	contrivance	impenitency	persistency	traditional	burglarious
trencherman	convenience	impuissance	phagedaenic	tragedienne	butyraceous
washerwoman	conveniency	inappetence	phycocyanin	transuranic	cabbagerose
wellgroomed	convergence	incoherence	pilotburner	trichomonad	cabbageworm
witenagemot	convergency	incoherency	pipecleaner	turgescence	cacophonous
xeranthemum	conversance	inconstancy	pitchblende	twelvemonth	calcicolous
absorptance	conversancy	ineloquence	pleurodynia	twelvepenny	calciferous
accelerando	countenance	inexistence	pocketmoney	unbeknownst	calcifugous
accountancy	crossgarnet	inflexional	pococurante	uncertainly	calefactory
accrescence	decrescendo	infrequence	polytechnic	uncertainty	campanology
acquittance	delinquency	infrequency	preaudience	unconcerned	carnivorous
adolescence	deliverance	inhabitancy	preeminence	undermanned	catadromous
affectional	despondence	inheritance	pressagency	underpinned	celebratory
affectioned	despondency	insouciance	previsional	undersigned	ceremonious
afterburner	dimensional	intensional	prizewinner	unemotional	chainarmour
altitudinal	dinnerdance	intentional	probational	unfashioned	champertous
ambivalence	directional	intentioned	probationer	unipersonal	chancellory
ambivalency	disciplinal	interchange	proceedings	valuational	chartaceous
AngloFrench	discipliner	interregnum	proficiency	variational	cheesecloth
antecedence	discontinue	interspinal	promotional	varsovienne	chockablock
anthocyanin	discordance	intolerance	provenience	vespertinal	Christology
antirrhinum	discordancy	intriguante	provisional	vibrational	chronoscope
archaeornis	discrepancy	intuitional	pseudomonas	vicegerency	circulatory
ascensional	disharmonic	ipecacuanha	psychogenic	vitrescence	climatology

clothesmoth	expeditious	inculpatory	objurgatory	retributory	swallowhole
cobblestone	explanatory	indeciduous	observatory	rhizanthous	swallowwort
coconscious	explicatory	industrious	odoriferous	rhizomatous	sympetalous
combinatory	exploratory	informatory	olfactology	rhynchodont	symphonious
comminatory	expurgatory	injudicious	oligomerous	rottenstone	synchronous
compendious	extenuatory	inofficious	ommatophore	rumbustious	talentscout
compotatory	extirpatory	inquilinous	omnifarious	saddlecloth	tautologous
concertgoer	farinaceous	insectivore	opprobrious	sanguineous	tautonymous
condolatory	farraginous	insectology	orchidology	saponaceous	teknonymous
congenerous	farthermost	inspiratory	ornithology	saprogenous	temerarious
consolatory	felspathoid	intravenous	oscillatory	sarcomatous	tempestuous
conspicuous	ferriferous	irreligious	ovariectomy	sauropodous	tendencious
contentious	ferruginous	isochronous	overanxious	scalariform	tendentious
contrarious	filamentous	isomorphous	ozoniferous	scalearmour	tenterhooks
copingstone	fissiparous	journeywork	papyraceous	scarabaeoid	terminology
cornerstone	flavoursome	kinesiology	parathyroid	scattergood	terraqueous
corniferous	flirtatious	kinetoscope	paratyphoid	schistosome	terricolous
cosignatory	floriferous	knucklebone	passeriform	scientology	terrigenous
cosmetology	fluoroscope	lacrimatory	patelliform	scoriaceous	tetramerous
coterminous	fluoroscopy	lacrymatory	pentagynous	scratchwork	tetrapodous
counterbond	forevermore	lactiferous	pentamerous	scribacious	thanatology
counterfoil	Francophobe	lamellicorn	pentandrous	scrumptious	thaumatrope
counterfort	francophone	lamelliform	perfunctory	scuppernong	theatregoer
countermove	frugivorous	laryngology	perspicuous	scyphistoma	theretofore
counterwork	fulminatory	laryngotomy	pestiferous	seismoscope	thermoscope
criminatory	furthermore	lateritious	phagocytose	selfreproof	thistledown
criminology	furthermost	latticework	phosphorous	selfsupport	threecolour
cruciferous	furthersome	lentiginous	phraseology	semasiology	thunderbolt
crucigerous	furunculous	lichenology	physiognomy	sententious	thuriferous
crustaceous	gastrectomy	ligamentous	picturebook	septiferous	tracheotomy
cryobiology	gastroscope	lycanthrope	picturegoer	serpiginous	trapeziform
crystalloid	gemmiferous	lycanthropy	piperaceous	servicebook	treacherous
cupriferous	gemmiparous	magnanimous	piscivorous	seventyfold	trelliswork
dactylology	gerontology	malariology	plagiostome	severalfold	trestlework
declamatory	grandiflora	maledictory	plasterwork	shacklebolt	trimorphous
declaratory	granivorous	manducatory	platearmour	shacklebone	tripetalous
declivitous	gratulatory	manifestoes	polariscope	shocktroops	triphibious
deleterious	greaseproof	mansardroof	polyandrous	showerproof	triphyllous
delightsome	gynaecology	manufactory	polycarpous	shrinkproof	triquetrous
denigratory	gypsiferous	martyrology	polyonymous	shuttlecock	tristichous
dentigerous	haematology	masticatory	polyphagous	sittingroom	troublesome
deoxyribose	haemorrhoid	melanophore	polyphonous	smokingroom	trypanosome
deprecatory	halophilous	meliphagous	precautious	smorgasbord	tuberculose
depredatory	harpsichord	melliferous	precipitous	snatchblock	tuberculous
dermatology	harvesthome	mellifluous	predicatory	solanaceous	ulotrichous
desperadoes	hearthstone	membraneous	premonitory	somniculous	unambiguous
Deuteronomy	heartsblood	meritorious	preparatory	somniferous	unconscious
diadelphous	hedgeschool	meteorology	prestigious	soteriology	underexpose
dicephalous	heliochrome	methodology	pretentious	spathaceous	unorthodoxy
dichogamous	helminthoid	metoposcopy	primatology	spectrology	unrighteous
dichotomous	hemipterous	microgroove	primiparous	spelaeology	unwholesome
diphtheroid	hepatectomy	microsecond	procuratory	sphagnology	urticaceous
dodecaphony	herbivorous	millisecond	profanatory	spiniferous	urticarious
doublecross	heresiology	misanthrope	profiterole	splendorous	valedictory
drawingroom	herpetology	misanthropy	prognathous	splenectomy	vasculiform
dualpurpose	herringbone	mischievous	prohibitory	spongecloth	venereology
duplicitous	heterophony	moderations	proliferous	spontaneous	venturesome
easternmost	heteroploid	monocarpous	promiscuous	sporogenous	vertiginous
edificatory	heterospory	monoclinous	prophethood	statutebook	vexillology
efficacious	heterotroph	monophagous	proportions	stenochromy	vindicatory
ejaculatory	homogeneous	monophthong	Proterozoic	stereophony	volcanology
electrology	homophonous	monopterous	pruriginous	stereoscope	vortiginous
elephantoid	homopterous	morbiferous	pteridology	stereoscopy	vulcanology
elucidatory	homosporous	morningroom	pumicestone	stethoscope	waitingroom
endophagous	humiliatory	mountainous	punctilious	stethoscopy	watercolour
enterostomy	hundredfold	multicolour	quadraphony	stipulatory	weathercock
epidiascope	hydrogenous	multiparous	quarrelsome	stirrupbone	weatherworn
epipetalous	hyperboloid	mustachioed	quartertone	stomatology	westernmost
epithelioma	hypocycloid	muttonchops	quaternloaf	stormtroops	whitethroat
erotogenous	ichthyology	myelomatous	reachmedown	stramineous	widowerhood
eschatology	ignominious	myrmecology	recognitory	stroboscope	winningpost
Etruscology	illustrious	necessitous	reflexology	subcategory	xenophilous
eucalyptole	impecunious	negotiatory	reformatory	sulphureous	xerophilous
eurypteroid	impetratory	nephrectomy	repetitious	sulphurwort	xylocarpous
exclamatory	imprecatory	nettlecloth	reprobatory	superfluous	xylophagous
exculpatory	incantatory	nitrogenous	respiratory	superimpose	aeolotropic
exdirectory	incongruous	noctivagous	retaliatory	supervisory	angiography
exhortatory	incredulous	nulliparous	retardatory	suppository	anisotropic
expatiatory	incredulous	obfuscatory	retinoscopy	suppository	antistrophe

bathyscaphe	semiellipse	dualcontrol	prosecutrix	antonomasia	haemoptysis
bitterapple	shoulderpad	econometric	protectoral	aponeuroses	haemostasis
branchiopod	showstopper	elastomeric	pseudomorph	aponeurosis	hairdresser
bumblepuppy	sideslipped	embroiderer	psychiatric	aposiopesis	hazardously
calligraphy	sidestepped	enneahedron	radiometric	assiduously	heartlessly
cardsharper	staircarpet	enterovirus	rearadmiral	atrociously	hemianopsia
cartography	stenography	equilateral	saddlehorse	audaciously	hilariously
catastrophe	stereotyped	eudiometric	salmonberry	barbarously	homeostasis
chirography	stereotyper	gallowstree	sanguinaria	beauteously	homogeniser
chorography	stereotypic	gendarmerie	schwarmerei	biocoenoses	homozygosis
cosmography	storekeeper	godchildren	scleroderma	biocoenosis	hylogenesis
dexiotropic	stylography	goldenberry	selfassured	blackavised	hyperplasia
discography	submultiple	goniometric	selfcentred	blamelessly	hypoglossal
dittography	tachygraphy	goodnatured	selfcontrol	bloodlessly	hypotyposis
ethnography	teenybopper	granophyric	sinistrorse	bloodvessel	iconostases
filmography	thixotropic	gravimetric	slaughterer	bottlenosed	iconostasis
filterpaper	thoroughpin	gymnospermy	sociometric	bounteously	illdisposed
frothhopper	threadpaper	gynaecocrat	songsparrow	bourgeoisie	imperiously
grasshopper	tightlipped	haematocrit	spectrogram	bowdleriser	impetuously
greenkeeper	townspeople	harumscarum	sphincteral	brainlessly	incuriously
Hagiographa	treecreeper	heavenwards	sphincteric	brainteaser	ingeniously
hagiography	undeveloped	heliometric	sphygmogram	brucellosis	ingenuously
hagioscopic	uranography	hemispheric	spindletree	bumptiously	injuriously
handicapped	wedgeshaped	highpowered	spirometric	capaciously	innocuously
handicapper	weenybopper	hitherwards	steganogram	catachreses	innoxiously
haplography	Whitechapel	homocentric	stegosaurus	catachresis	insidiously
hedgehopped	zincography	huckleberry	Stradivarii	catercousin	intercensal
heliography	bergamasque	hurryscurry	subcultural	cavernously	intercessor
heliotropic	discotheque	hurryskurry	sublittoral	ceaselessly	invidiously
hemeralopia	gigantesque	hydrometric	supercharge	cheerlessly	judiciously
heterotypic	picturesque	hydrothorax	swingletree	Christmassy	laboriously
highstepper	plateresque	hygrometric	swordbearer	chrysalises	larcenously
hippocampus	Titianesque	hypercharge	symposiarch	clamorously	lecherously
housekeeper	ventriloquy	hypermetric	synchrotron	coccidiosis	lesemajesty
hydrography	verdantique	hypogastric	tetrahedral	congruously	limitlessly
hydrotropic	albuminuria	hypsometric	tetrahedron	consciously	litigiously
hygroscopic	allelomorph	icosahedral	thaumaturge	contrabasso	ludicrously
hymnography	anemometric	icosahedron	thaumaturgy	countlessly	luxuriously
hypertrophy	antineutron	illfavoured	thenceforth	courteously	mackerelsky
hypnopompic	Apollinaris	illhumoured	theocentric	credulously	maliciously
hypsography	arbitratrix	illmannered	thermoduric	cytogenesis	matchlessly
ichnography	atmospheric	illtempered	torchbearer	cytokinesis	melodiously
iconography	audiometric	intercourse	tracasserie	dangerously	mercilessly
linendraper	auricularly	intercrural	trainbearer	dauntlessly	merogenesis
lithography	bathymetric	intersperse	transferred	deliciously	metachrosis
lithotripsy	behavioural	ionospheric	transferrer	deliriously	metagenesis
macroscopic	bewhiskered	ipsilateral	transpierce	dexterously	mineraliser
micrography	binocularly	irregularly	trestletree	diaphoresis	mirthlessly
microscopic	boysenberry	isoelectric	tricoloured	diapophysis	moisturiser
minesweeper	cabbagetree	kilocalorie	uncluttered	diarthrosis	momentously
mosstrooper	calceolaria	lilylivered	undercharge	doubtlessly	monogenesis
mythography	camaraderie	marconigram	unicoloured	dreamlessly	monopoliser
namedropper	candelabrum	marqueterie	upholsterer	duniewassal	monstrously
neurotropic	candleberry	melanochroi	varnishtree	earthcloset	murderously
nyctitropic	caricatural	merryandrew	vesicularly	ectogenesis	murmurously
nympholepsy	charcuterie	metacentric	viceadmiral	egregiously	myxomatosis
orthography	chinoiserie	micrometric	voltametric	enarthrosis	necrobiosis
orthoscopic	chiropteran	misconstrue	watercourse	enterpriser	nefariously
orthotropic	chokecherry	misericorde	wellordered	erroneously	nervelessly
osteography	cholesterol	molecularly	wheelbarrow	exogenously	neutraliser
outstripped	chrysoberyl	multistorey	whiffletree	facetiously	noiselessly
overcropped	climacteric	negotiatrix	whippletree	faithlessly	nonpartisan
overstepped	clinometric	neighbourly	windlestraw	faultlessly	notoriously
palaeotypic	clothesprop	netherworld	winterberry	feloniously	obliviously
paratrooper	collinearly	orbicularly	xanthochroi	ferociously	obnoxiously
petrography	commissural	orthopteran	abiogeneses	fractiously	officiously
phonography	conjectural	oscillogram	abiogenesis	fraterniser	ontogenesis
photography	controversy	pentahedron	ambiguously	frivolously	osteoplasty
phototropic	cookgeneral	philanderer	anadiplosis	fruitlessly	paraleipsis
phytography	coulometric	photometric	amorphously	gamogenesis	paraphraser
pictography	crossbearer	phraseogram	anadiplosis	garrulously	parasitosis
pleiotropic	cryptomeria	phytosterol	anagnorisis	generaliser	parentheses
pornography	ctenophoran	planimetric	analogously	glutinously	parenthesis
radiography	dactylogram	posteriorly	anastomoses	gnotobiosis	paronomasia
reprography	depthcharge	prefectural	anastomosis	gormandiser	pasteuriser
rhinoscopic	diatessaron	prehistoric	anomalously	gracelessly	pediculosis
rhizocarpic	dishonourer	presbyteral	anonymously	grangeriser	pendulously
sandskipper	disinterred	progenitrix	anonymously	guilelessly	penuriously
scenography	distempered	prolocutrix	antiphrasis	guiltlessly	periphrases

periphrasis	wearilessly	centripetal	dishonestly	heavyfooted	lionhearted
peristalsis	welladvised	ceroplastic	disinfector	Hellenistic	lithophytic
photooffset	worthlessly	cesarevitch	dissertator	hereinafter	longsighted
phthiriasis	abbreviator	cesarewitch	dissonantly	hermeneutic	lowspirited
plagiariser	abhorrently	chainletter	dissymmetry	highfalutin	luxuriantly
plasmolysis	abiogenetic	chainstitch	distributor	Hippocratic	macrobiotic
plasticiser	abstinently	charismatic	divergently	historiated	magistratic
plenteously	acatalectic	chemotactic	doubleDutch	holoblastic	maisonnette
pointlessly	accelerator	choirmaster	doubleentry	homeostatic	maladjusted
poisonously	accordantly	chronometer	downhearted	homestretch	maladroitly
polygenesis	accumulator	chronometry	drillmaster	homoeopathy	malignantly
ponderously	achondritic	cisatlantic	dynamometer	homoestatic	manipulator
populariser	actinometer	closefisted	dynamometry	homogenetic	manneristic
postclassic	adjudicator	cloudcastle	dyslogistic	homoplastic	marquisette
powerlessly	adulterator	coinheritor	ebulliently	horsedoctor	masochistic
predecessor	advertently	coldhearted	ectoblastic	housemaster	mastodontic
prestressed	AfroAsiatic	colorimeter	ectogenetic	hydrophytic	mastoiditis
proteolysis	aiguillette	colorimetry	efficiently	hydrostatic	mechanistic
psittacosis	alembicated	columniated	effulgently	hydrotactic	mediumistic
querulously	alkalimeter	commendator	elasticated	hygrophytic	mentholated
rancorously	alkalimetry	commentator	emancipator	hylozoistic	meroblastic
rapaciously	altostratus	communistic	emasculator	hypercritic	mesoblastic
rapturously	ameliorator	compensator	embryonated	hypoblastic	metagenetic
reappraisal	amphimictic	competently	encomiastic	illaffected	metaplastic
rejuvenesce	anacreontic	compliantly	endoskelton	illuminator	metasomatic
religiously	anaesthetic	complicated	equivocator	illustrator	Methodistic
righteously	anarchistic	compurgator	esemplastic	impatiently	microphytic
sagaciously	anastomotic	conciliator	Eucharistic	imperfectly	misbegotten
salaciously	annihilator	confidently	euphemistic	implemental	mithridatic
scrutiniser	annunciator	confiscator	eveningstar	importantly	modernistic
seditiously	anomalistic	congruently	exaggerator	imprudently	monogenetic
selfimposed	anthracitic	consecrator	excellently	inaugurator	monozygotic
senselessly	anticipator	conservator	excremental	incessantly	moonlighter
shamelessly	antipyretic	consonantal	exoskeletal	incinerator	mountaintop
shiftlessly	antiSemitic	consonantly	exoskeleton	incipiently	muskthistle
sightlessly	apartmental	conspirator	expectantly	inclemently	myocarditis
sleeplessly	apocalyptic	constitutor	expediently	incorrectly	mythopoetic
smilelessly	aponeurotic	constrictor	extraverted	incorruptly	myxomycetes
soundlessly	appreciator	constructor	extroverted	incremental	narcoleptic
spinelessly	Areopagitic	consummator	exuberantly	indignantly	nasofrontal
stainlessly	articulated	continental	faithworthy	indulgently	naturopathy
starcrossed	articulator	continently	fenestrated	inelegantly	nearsighted
strenuously	artiodactyl	continuator	fetichistic	infiltrator	necromantic
sumptuously	ascomycetes	contributor	fetishistic	inseminator	negligently
sympathiser	asphyxiator	coordinator	feudalistic	insistently	neologistic
syndesmosis	assimilator	corpulently	firefighter	insufflator	nightporter
synthesiser	autoplastic	cotoneaster	firmamental	intagliated	nittygritty
syssarcosis	auxanometer	craniometry	flagellator	intercepter	nomenclator
tastelessly	azotobacter	crenellated	flannelette	interceptor	nonsequitur
telekinesis	backcountry	criticaster	flatulently	intercostal	northeaster
tenaciously	beechmarten	crossstitch	foraminated	interdental	northwester
thanklessly	benignantly	daisycutter	forequarter	intermitted	nutrimental
thermolysis	bibliolater	deactivator	foreshorten	interpreter	observantly
timepleaser	bibliolatry	deathrattle	foresighted	interrupter	ochlocratic
toffeenosed	biocoenotic	decelerator	formalistic	interruptor	ontogenetic
torturously	biquadratic	deficiently	fortnightly	interseptal	openhearted
tracelessly	blackbeetle	deflagrator	frankfurter	intimidator	operculated
transversal	blackcoated	demonolatry	freehearted	intromitted	opinionated
tremulously	blameworthy	denominator	frostbitten	intromitter	ornithopter
trichinosis	blepharitis	denunciator	fullhearted	introverted	orthocentre
troublously	blockbuster	dependently	fundamental	invigilator	orthodontia
tyrannously	Bodhisattva	depopulator	geniculated	invigorator	orthodontic
unanimously	brahmaputra	depreciator	geomagnetic	ironhearted	osteophytic
uncivilised	brilliantly	desalinator	ghostwriter	itinerantly	overstretch
undisguised	broadcaster	desideratum	glasscutter	Jansenistic	overwritten
unexpressed	bullfighter	detrimental	glauconitic	jargonistic	paederastic
unpossessed	burgomaster	dialogistic	gnotobiotic	kickstarter	Palaearctic
vagariously	cabbalistic	diamagnetic	goddaughter	kitchenette	pantalettes
vasopressin	calorimeter	diaphoretic	goodhearted	labiodental	pantheistic
vasopressor	calorimetry	diastematic	gradiometer	lachrymator	parallactic
venturously	calumniator	dichromatic	groundwater	lamplighter	paramountcy
veraciously	Calvinistic	differentia	haemostatic	landaulette	paramountly
verminously	cancellated	differently	haggadistic	launderette	paraplectic
vexatiously	carburetted	difficultly	halfhearted	leptodactyl	parenthetic
vicariously	carburetter	diffidently	handknitted	lickspittle	paternoster
vinedresser	carburettor	dilapidated	handpainted	lightfooted	pentadactyl
vivaciously	castellated	dilapidator	handwritten	lineprinter	Pentecostal
voicelessly	cataplectic	disaccustom	hardhearted	harmonistic	periodontal
voraciously	catechistic	disaffected	harmonistic		

```
periostitis  scientistic  thermolytic  blunderbuss  superabound  xanthophyll
peripatetic  sclerometer  thermometer  candidature  superinduce  middlesized
peristaltic  sclerotitis  thermometry  chiaroscuro  supersedure  mycorrhizae
peritonitis  scoutmaster  thickwitted  coffeehouse  tapemeasure  mycorrhizal
permanently  secondrater  threemaster  conjuncture  temperature  pocketsized
perpetrator  seismometer  throatlatch  contractual  thereabouts  quickfrozen
perpetuator  seismometry  thyroiditis  contracture  transfigure  spermatozoa
pertinently  selfcreated  tightfisted  cottonmouth  transsexual  trailblazer
pessimistic  selfdevoted  toastmaster  countermure  trousersuit  unorganized
pestilently  selfelected  tonsillitis  countersunk  underground  ───────────
petticoated  selfinvited  totalisator  counterturn  undervaluer  Abbevillian
pharyngitis  selflimited  trafficator  customhouse  unigeniture  abecedarian
phototactic  selfstarter  transiently  decrepitude  vicissitude  abiological
plasmolytic  sentimental  transmittal  disjuncture  viniculture  academician
pluralistic  shamanistic  transmitted  displeasure  viticulture  accessorial
plutocratic  sharpwitted  transmitter  disquietude  whereabouts  accusatival
pluviometer  sheepmaster  transporter  disseminule  accusatival  acoustician
pneumonitis  sightworthy  trenchantly  diverticula  BaltoSlavic  adminicular
polarimeter  signpainter  trendsetter  divestiture  bookshelves  aerological
polarimetry  simpliciter  tritheistic  douroucouli  broadleaved  aeronomical
polevaulter  sinfonietta  troglodytic  electrocute  cleanshaven  Aesculapian
polycrystal  socialistic  truculently  entablature  disapproval  aesthetical
polygenetic  softhearted  truehearted  expenditure  disbeliever  affectional
polyglottal  solipsistic  trustbuster  foreclosure  infinitival  agonistical
polyglottic  somnolently  trustworthy  halfmeasure  interleaves  agrological
porphyritic  sonofabitch  turbulently  headborough  nominatival  agronomical
precedented  southeaster  tuttifrutti  herringgull  planoconvex  ahistorical
precedently  southwester  typewritten  hibernacula  quacksalver  aircraftman
presciently  spaceheater  unaccounted  hydromedusa  quicksilver  Albigensian
preselector  speedometer  uncommitted  hypothenuse  quilldriver  alcyonarian
prevalently  spherometer  unconnected  incertitude  screwdriver  Alexandrian
problematic  spherulitic  uncontested  incurvature  slavedriver  algological
prominently  Spinozistic  understated  ineffectual  spiritlevel  allAmerican
promulgator  spiritistic  underwriter  ingratitude  thanksgiver  allegorical
propitiator  spirochetal  unexploited  inopportune  transceiver  altitudinal
prostitutor  splayfooted  uninhabited  insectifuge  wellbeloved  anecdotical
proteolytic  spondylitis  uninhibited  instinctual  wheresoever  AngloIndian
protomartyr  sporophytic  unmitigated  intersexual  whichsoever  anglomaniac
protophytic  stalactitic  unrealistic  investiture  whosesoever  AngloNorman
providently  stalagmitic  unsaturated  legislature  candlepower  animalcular
psychometry  standpatter  unsolicited  lowpressure  carriageway  antenuptial
psychomotor  staurolitic  unwarranted  manufacture  cauliflower  anthropical
psychopathy  steadfastly  vaporimeter  massproduce  gillyflower  antiquarian
pterodactyl  stephanotis  vasodilator  monoculture  glassblower  antitypical
purificator  stereometry  vaticinator  monolingual  globeflower  apartmental
pussyfooter  sternutator  verbalistic  musclebound  intergrowth  aphrodisiac
pyroclastic  stichometry  vinaigrette  musculature  interviewee  apostolical
quickwitted  stockinette  vituperator  opencircuit  interviewer  Archimedean
quiescently  stonecutter  vociferator  overmeasure  motivepower  ascensional
rattlepated  stonemarten  volumometer  overproduce  steerageway  assemblyman
readywitted  stormcentre  voodooistic  pomiculture  straightway  assessorial
realpolitik  stridulator  wainscotted  porterhouse  thoroughwax  atheistical
recommittal  stringently  warmhearted  portraiture  undergrowth  attitudinal
reconnoitre  succulently  waspwaisted  progeniture  wapperjawed  attritional
recumbently  suffragette  waterbottle  promptitude  anaphylaxis  audiovisual
recurrently  sugarcoated  weakhearted  pulchritude  executrixes  Augustinian
redundantly  superheater  Westminster  pullthrough  heterotaxis  Aurignacian
regenerator  supersubtle  whistlestop  purpresture  phyllotaxis  autarchical
rejuvenator  suppliantly  whoremaster  receptacula  prophylaxis  axiological
reluctantly  surrebuttal  windcheater  reconstruct  retroflexed  barrelorgan
remunerator  surrebutter  witchdoctor  reintroduce  thermotaxis  behavioural
repellantly  swiftfooted  witchhunter  restructure  breathalyse  Belorussian
repellently  sycophantic  wolfwhistle  rotogravure  chamaephyte  biochemical
repentantly  sycophantry  worldbeater  safeconduct  chlorophyll  biometrical
representer  syllogistic  wreckmaster  schoolhouse  collenchyma  biophysical
repugnantly  symbolistic  zooplankton  scuttlebutt  electrolyse  bloodstream
resiliently  sympathetic  aboveground  selfculture  electrolyte  Bonapartean
ricochetted  symptomatic  accoucheuse  selftorture  electrotype  Brahmanical
ritualistic  synergistic  acupuncture  sericulture  erythrocyte  Brahminical
rockcrystal  tacheometer  agriculture  sleuthhound  gametophyte  businessman
roughfooted  telekinetic  appogiatura  springhouse  granulocyte  calendrical
sacramental  teleprinter  aquaculture  stagestruck  interplayed  canalicular
salinometer  termagantly  aquiculture  steeplebush  lammergeyer  carbuncular
salpingitis  tessellated  audiovisual  stirruppump  paraldehyde  caricatural
sansculotte  tetradactyl  barrelhouse  stomachpump  platinotype  Carolingian
saprobiotic  thankworthy  bassethound  stoneground  prosenchyma  carrageenan
saprophytic  theodolitic  bathingsuit  strikebound  sclerophyll  carriageway
satinstitch  theorematic  bergschrund  summerhouse  spermaphyte  casuistical
scholiastic  therapeutic  blackgrouse  summersault  thrombocyte  catechismal
```

categorical	equinoctial	interseptal	octachordal	quadratical	strategical
caterpillar	erotomaniac	intersexual	oecological	quadrennial	subclinical
centenarian	ethological	interspinal	oecumenical	quadrupedal	subcortical
centrifugal	evangelical	intertribal	oenological	quaestorial	subcritical
centripetal	eveningstar	intuitional	oesophageal	quaternloaf	subcultural
chimaerical	evolutional	inventorial	oncological	quincuncial	sublittoral
chiropteran	exceptional	ipsilateral	ontological	Rabelaisian	submarginal
chromosomal	excremental	isometrical	operational	radiolarian	subregional
chucklehead	executorial	Jacobinical	oreological	Rastafarian	subscapular
churchwoman	existential	Jacobitical	orthoepical	reappraisal	substantial
cicatricial	exoskeletal	jauntingcar	orthopteran	rearadmiral	subterminal
circumlunar	expansional	judgmatical	oscillogram	recessional	subtropical
circumpolar	exponential	jumpingbean	pachydermal	recommittal	summational
circumsolar	extensional	kinematical	Palestinian	rectangular	superficial
clapperclaw	Falstaffian	labiodental	panegyrical	rectilineal	supernormal
coessential	fantastical	Lancastrian	Panglossian	rectilinear	supersedeas
cognitional	featherhead	landingbeam	paradisical	redactional	surrebuttal
collisional	FinnoUgrian	landinggear	paradoxical	referential	sybaritical
commissural	firmamental	latitudinal	paramedical	reportorial	symmetrical
conditional	footpoundal	laughinggas	paraselenae	residential	synagogical
congressman	formational	leatherhead	parasitical	retinacular	synonymical
conjectural	fratricidal	Leibnitzian	parheliacal	reverential	syntactical
consonantal	Frenchwoman	leviratical	participial	reversional	synthetical
conterminal	fundamental	libertarian	patriarchal	rhapsodical	taxonomical
continental	gentilitial	liquidambar	patrilineal	rheological	terrestrial
contractual	gentlewoman	loculicidal	patrimonial	rhetorician	territorial
cookgeneral	geochemical	madrigalian	patristical	rickettsial	testimonial
coralloidal	geometrical	magdalenian	pedagogical	rockcrystal	tetrahedral
cornucopian	geophysical	magisterial	pedological	Rosicrucian	theological
corpuscular	gestatorial	Maglemosian	penitential	ruridecanal	theoretical
cosmetician	gingerbread	marconigram	penological	Sabbatarian	therewithal
counterplan	gradational	matriarchal	Pentecostal	sacramental	thoroughwax
countryseat	GraecoRoman	matrilineal	pericardiac	sacrificial	thrasonical
coxcombical	grammatical	matrilineal	pericardial	saltatorial	thunderclap
craftswoman	gynaecocrat	matrimonial	pericranial	salvational	thunderhead
crepuscular	halfholiday	mechanician	periodontal	saturnalian	thunderpeal
crocodilian	halterbreak	mediastinal	peristomial	sausagemeat	toploftical
crossbowman	Hamiltonian	mediatorial	pharisaical	Scotchwoman	topological
ctenophoran	Heracleidan	medicolegal	philologian	scriptorial	traditional
curvilineal	heteropolar	merchantman	phonetician	secretarial	transmittal
curvilinear	hexadecimal	Merovingian	phraseogram	secretariat	transsexual
cylindrical	holothurian	metalloidal	Pickwickian	seigneurial	transversal
cytological	homiletical	meteoroidal	pietistical	seigniorial	trapezoidal
dactylogram	homoiousian	metonymical	piscatorial	selfdisplay	trencherman
deferential	homological	micrococcal	planetoidal	semeiotical	tribunicial
deliveryman	horological	Micronesian	policewoman	semidiurnal	tribunitial
demagogical	horsecollar	millenarian	polycrystal	sempiternal	trichomonad
dendritical	hydrothorax	ministerial	polyglottal	sensational	trimestrial
detrimental	hyperborean	monarchical	pomological	sentimental	Trinitarian
diacritical	hypoglossal	monasterial	portmanteau	septifragal	typological
dialectical	hypophyseal	monkeybread	posological	serological	uncanonical
diametrical	hypophysial	monochasial	postexilian	sertularian	unchristian
dictatorial	icosahedral	monochromat	postglacial	sexagesimal	uncongenial
dimensional	ideological	monolingual	postnuptial	sexological	unemotional
dinosaurian	implemental	monological	pragmatical	Shaksperean	unequivocal
diphtherial	impolitical	mononuclear	Precambrian	Shaksperian	unessential
diphthongal	impractical	multangular	prefatorial	shoulderbag	unicellular
diphycercal	incorporeal	multilinear	prefectural	shoulderpad	unipersonal
dipsomaniac	incremental	multinomial	prejudicial	sinological	unpolitical
directional	IndoIranian	multiracial	preprandial	situational	utilitarian
directorial	ineffectual	mycological	presbyteral	sleepingbag	valuational
disapproval	inessential	mycorrhizae	preterhuman	sleepingcar	variational
disciplinal	infantryman	mycorrhizal	previsional	somnambular	ventricular
doublespeak	inferential	mythomaniac	primigenial	sophistical	verisimilar
draughtsman	infinitival	nasofrontal	probational	spasmodical	vespertinal
duniewassal	infirmarian	Neanderthal	proconsular	spectacular	vibrational
educational	inflexional	necessarian	procrustean	spectrogram	viceadmiral
egalitarian	influential	needlewoman	proletarian	spermicidal	virological
egotistical	insessorial	Neotropical	proletariat	sphincteral	wappenschaw
electrician	instinctual	nominatival	promotional	sphygmogram	washerwoman
Elizabethan	intensional	nomological	prophetical	spirochetal	wherewithal
ellipsoidal	intentional	nonpartisan	protectoral	splenetical	whitecollar
endocardiac	intercensal	nonsensical	prothallial	spokeswoman	whitethroat
endocardial	intercostal	nosological	provisional	sportswoman	windlestraw
endothelial	intercrural	nullifidian	pseudomonas	springclean	Yugoslavian
enigmatical	interdental	nutrimental	purgatorial	statistical	zoantharian
equiangular	interfacial	nutritional	puritanical	steerageway	Zoroastrian
equilateral	interlinear	obsessional	pyramidical	steganogram	ailurophobe
	interracial	obstetrical	Pythagorean	straightway	breadcrumbs

buffalorobe	diamondback	misguidance	systematics	barnstormer	collectanea
Francophobe	dinnerdance	morrisdance	technocracy	beachcomber	colorimeter
superscribe	discordance	munificence	tephromancy	beechmarten	columniated
absorptance	discordancy	nigrescence	thermionics	bellfounder	comestibles
accountancy	discrepancy	nonchalance	throatlatch	bellheather	complicated
accrescence	disturbance	nonfeasance	transpierce	bewhiskered	comptroller
acquittance	doublecheck	nonviolence	turgescence	bibliolater	concertgoer
adolescence	doubleDutch	numismatics	ultrasonics	biedermeier	conditioner
aeronautics	doublequick	omnipotence	vicegerency	billsticker	convenances
aerostatics	electronics	oneiromancy	vitrescence	biocoenoses	conveyancer
aftereffect	encumbrance	opalescence	vociferance	birdbrained	cotoneaster
ambivalence	equivalence	orthopedics	weathercock	birdfancier	counterplea
ambivalency	equivalency	outdistance	yacketyyack	birdwatcher	counterview
AngloFrench	ergatocracy	overbalance	zootechnics	bittersweet	countrified
antecedence	erubescence	overproduce	accelerando	blackavised	countryfied
apologetics	eurhythmics	overstretch	afficionado	blackbirder	crenellated
aristocracy	evanescence	paediatrics	amontillado	blackcoated	crestfallen
astringency	excrescence	paramountcy	anticathode	blackmailer	criticaster
beneficence	excrescency	percipience	assafoetida	blackmarket	crookbacked
benevolence	exorbitance	performance	bactericide	blockbuster	crossbearer
bibliomancy	fiddlestick	perpetuance	countryside	bloodsucker	crossgarnet
bibliotheca	flamboyance	persistence	countrywide	bloodvessel	crosslegged
biofeedback	flamboyancy	persistency	decrepitude	bodybuilder	crotcheteer
bondservice	flocculence	physiocracy	decrescendo	boilermaker	cupronickel
breechblock	florescence	pinnatisect	digitigrade	booklearned	daisycutter
breezeblock	forbearance	pointdevice	disquietude	bookshelves	deerstalker
bureaucracy	forbiddance	preaudience	fanfaronade	bottlegreen	demographer
candescence	fraudulence	precontract	handgrenade	bottlenosed	desperadoes
candlestick	furtherance	preeminence	heavenwards	bowdleriser	dilapidated
capacitance	geopolitics	pressagency	hitherwards	brainteaser	directrices
centrepiece	histrionics	proficiency	incertitude	brazenfaced	disaffected
cesarevitch	homestretch	prolificacy	infanticide	breadbasket	disannulled
cesarewitch	hydroponics	prosthetics	ingratitude	breadwinner	disbeliever
chainstitch	illuminance	provenience	insecticide	breastwheel	discipliner
cheiromancy	impenitence	putrescence	liberticide	broadcaster	disencumber
chieftaincy	impenitency	quarterback	loggerheads	broadleaved	disgruntled
chockablock	impuissance	quarterdeck	machinemade	broadminded	dishevelled
chrominance	inappetence	reassurance	maxillipede	bullfighter	dishonourer
circumspect	incoherence	reconstruct	misericorde	bullterrier	disinclined
clairschach	incoherency	reemergence	paraldehyde	burgomaster	disinterred
coalescence	inconstancy	reflectance	Passiontide	bushwhacker	disremember
coexistence	ineloquence	refringency	phylloclade	butterflies	distempered
coincidence	inexistence	reinsurance	pitchblende	cabbagetree	doorknocker
coinsurance	infrequence	reintroduce	plantigrade	calorimeter	doubleedged
comeuppance	infrequency	rejuvenesce	polypeptide	calyptrogen	doubleender
commonplace	inhabitancy	remembrance	promptitude	cancellated	doublefaced
complacence	inheritance	renaissance	pulchritude	candlepower	downhearted
complacency	insouciance	resemblance	rallentando	cantharides	downtrodden
concordance	intolerance	respondence	rodenticide	carburetted	doxographer
concurrence	iridescence	respondency	rodomontade	carburetter	drillmaster
conductance	irrelevance	rhabdomancy	slickenside	cardsharper	dumbfounder
confederacy	irrelevancy	safeconduct	switchblade	caryopsides	dundrearies
conformance	irreverence	saltimbanco	thalidomide	castellated	dynamometer
consequence	jumpingjack	satinstitch	tolbutamide	catachreses	earthcloset
conservancy	lactescence	scaleinsect	tragicomedy	catswhisker	echosounder
consistence	leatherback	selfdefence	tyrannicide	cauliflower	elasticated
consistency	leatherneck	selfrespect	vicissitude	cavedweller	electioneer
consultancy	lieutenancy	selfservice	Whitsuntide	chainletter	electrolier
contingence	linguistics	shuttlecock	abiogeneses	chainsmoker	embellisher
contingency	liquescence	silverstick	actinometer	chansonnier	embroiderer
continuance	lophobranch	singlestick	actinomyces	chanticleer	embryonated
contradance	loxodromics	singletrack	aerographer	chargesheet	Emmenthaler
contrivance	maintenance	snatchblock	affectioned	cheerleader	emptyhanded
convenience	maleficence	sonofabitch	afterburner	chickenfeed	emptyheaded
conveniency	malevolence	stagestruck	alembicated	childminder	enlightened
convergence	malfeasance	stampoffice	alkalimeter	choirmaster	ensanguined
convergency	malpractice	steeplejack	allantoides	chronologer	enterpriser
conversance	mantelpiece	stickinsect	amenorrhoea	chronometer	entertainer
conversancy	marcescence	stickleback	anastomoses	chrysalides	ephemerides
countenance	marketplace	stratocracy	antechamber	chrysalises	establisher
crackerjack	massproduce	stringpiece	aponeuroses	cityslicker	executioner
crossstitch	masterpiece	subcontract	articulated	cleanlimbed	executrices
cybernetics	mathematics	submergence	ascomycetes	cleanshaven	executrixes
delinquency	meritocracy	subsequence	auxanometer	clearheaded	experienced
deliverance	mesalliance	subsistence	awestricken	cliffhanger	extortioner
despondence	metaphysics	sufficiency	azotobacter	closefisted	extraverted
despondency	meteoritics	superinduce	backbencher	closehauled	extroverted
determinacy	misalliance	symposiarch	balmcricket	coldblooded	fairweather
diagnostics	misfeasance		bandylegged	coldhearted	faithhealer

faultfinder	handwritten	mailcarrier	perishables	selfstarter	straphanger
fenestrated	hardhearted	maladjusted	personifier	semiskilled	sugarcoated
fieldcornet	hardmouthed	manifestoes	petticoated	semitrailer	superficies
fieldworker	harebrained	mantuamaker	pettifogger	sentinelled	superheater
filterpaper	heartbroken	marriagebed	philanderer	serigrapher	supermarket
firecracker	heavyfooted	masquerader	philosopher	shareholder	supertanker
firefighter	heavyhanded	meadowsweet	photocopier	sharepusher	surfboarder
firewatcher	hedgehopped	mediatrices	photooffset	sharpwitted	surrebutter
flagofficer	hereinafter	mentholated	phrasemaker	sheepfarmer	sweepstakes
flimflammer	highpitched	merryandrew	picturegoer	sheepmaster	swellheaded
floorwalker	highpowered	metalworker	pieceworker	shelljacket	swiftfooted
footslogger	highstepper	middlesized	pilotburner	shipbreaker	swimbladder
footsoldier	historiated	mineraliser	pipecleaner	shipbuilder	swingletree
foraminated	homesteader	minesweeper	plagiariser	shockheaded	swordbearer
foraminifer	homogeniser	minnesinger	plainspoken	shoeleather	sympathiser
forequarter	honeybadger	miscellanea	planoconvex	shorthanded	synthesiser
foreshorten	honeymooner	misremember	plasticiser	shortspoken	tabernacled
foresighted	hospitaller	moisturiser	pluviometer	shortwinded	tacheometer
forestaller	housefather	molecricket	pocketmoney	showstopper	tearstained
forethinker	householder	moneylender	pocketsized	sideslipped	teenybopper
foulmouthed	housekeeper	moneymarket	polarimeter	sidestepped	teetotaller
fourflusher	housemaster	moneyspider	polevaulter	sidewheeler	telegrapher
fourpounder	housemother	monogrammed	populariser	sightreader	teleprinter
fourwheeler	hunchbacked	monographer	prayerwheel	sightscreen	tessellated
frankfurter	hydraheaded	monopoliser	precedented	signpainter	testatrices
fraterniser	hypermarket	moonlighter	preoccupied	simpliciter	thanksgiver
freehearted	iconostases	mosstrooper	prestressed	slaughterer	theatregoer
freethinker	illaffected	mothernaked	prizewinner	slavedriver	thermometer
freezedried	illdisposed	motivepower	probationer	slaveholder	thickheaded
frenchified	illfavoured	mountaineer	progestogen	slavemarket	thickwitted
frontrunner	illhumoured	multistorey	proofreader	sleepwalker	thimbleweed
frostbitten	illmannered	mustachioed	pureblooded	smallholder	thinskinned
frothhopper	illtempered	myxomycetes	pussyfooter	smallminded	threadpaper
fullblooded	immoveables	namedropper	quacksalver	smokescreen	threedecker
fullfledged	impassioned	nearsighted	quickfrozen	smoothfaced	threehanded
fullhearted	intagliated	neckerchief	quicksilver	snickersnee	threelegged
fullmouthed	intensifier	necromancer	quickwitted	snowgoggles	threemaster
gallbladder	intentioned	neutraliser	quilldriver	soberminded	tightfisted
gallowstree	interallied	nightporter	rangefinder	sockdolager	tightlipped
gardemanger	interbedded	nightwalker	rattlepated	sockdologen	timepleaser
gatecrasher	intercepter	ninnyhammer	readywitted	softhearted	titleholder
generaliser	interleaves	nomographer	recommender	softshelled	toastmaster
geniculated	interlocker	northeaster	reedwarbler	somewhither	toffeenosed
gerrymander	intermitted	northwester	replenisher	soupkitchen	toothbilled
gettogether	interplayed	noseyparker	represented	southeaster	toothpowder
ghostwriter	interpreter	nosographer	retroflexed	southwester	topographer
giantpowder	interrupter	openhearted	retrorocket	spaceheater	torchbearer
gillyflower	interviewee	openmouthed	reversioner	speechifier	torchsinger
glassblower	interviewer	operculated	ricochetted	speedometer	toughminded
glasscutter	intromitted	opinionated	rightangled	spellbinder	trackwalker
globeflower	intromitter	organscreen	righthanded	spherometer	trailblazer
godchildren	introverted	ornithopter	rightminded	spindletree	trainbearer
goddaughter	ironhearted	otherwhiles	rightwinger	spiritlevel	transceiver
godforsaken	jerrymander	outrivalled	ringstraked	splayfooted	transcriber
gonfalonier	kickstarter	outstripped	roughfooted	stadtholder	transferred
goodhearted	kindhearted	overcropped	roughlegged	staircarpet	transferrer
goodnatured	lakedweller	overstepped	safebreaker	stakeholder	transformer
gormandiser	lammergeier	overstuffed	safecracker	stallholder	transmitted
gradiometer	lammergeyer	overwritten	salesladies	standpatter	transmitter
grandfather	lamplighter	oxyhydrogen	salinometer	starcrossed	transponder
grandmother	landgrabber	paddlewheel	sandskipper	starstudded	transporter
grandnephew	largeminded	pamphleteer	scaremonger	steamboiler	treecreeper
grangeriser	leapfrogged	panicmonger	schwarmerei	steamroller	trendsetter
grasshopper	leaseholder	pantalettes	sclerometer	steelworker	trestletree
gravedigger	levelheaded	paperhanger	scoutmaster	stepbrother	tricoloured
greatnephew	lightfooted	paragrapher	screwdriver	stereotyped	truehearted
greengrocer	lighthanded	parallelled	scrutiniser	stiffnecked	trustbuster
greenkeeper	lightheaded	paraphraser	secondrater	stockbroker	tumbledrier
groundsheet	lightminded	paratrooper	seismometer	stockholder	typefounder
groundwater	lilylivered	parentheses	selfassured	stockjobber	typewritten
haberdasher	linendraper	parishioner	selfcentred	stockmarket	typographer
hairdresser	lineprinter	partitioned	selfcreated	stonecurlew	ultraviolet
hairtrigger	lionhearted	partitioner	selfdevoted	stonecutter	unaccounted
halfblooded	logographer	pasteuriser	selfimposed	stonemason	uncivilised
halfhearted	longsighted	paternoster	selfinduced	stonewaller	uncluttered
handicapped	looselimbed	pearlfisher	selfinvited	storekeeper	uncommitted
handicapper	loudmouthed	pedestalled	selflimited	storyteller	unconcealed
handknitted	loudspeaker	periphrases		straitlaced	unconcerned
handpainted	lowspirited				unconnected

```
uncontested  heterograft  soteriology  schottische  bathingsuit  diarthrosis
underbidder  loosestrife  spectrology  searchlight  batholithic  diastematic
underhanded  mothercraft  spelaeology  secondsight  bathymetric  diastrophic
undermanned  needlecraft  sphagnology  sightworthy  betweenmaid  dichromatic
underpinned  ploughstaff  spindlelegs  spaceflight  bibliomania  differentia
underseller  pocketknife  squarsonage  squirearchy  bibliopegic  diphtheroid
undersigned  presanctify  stagemanage  stenography  bibliopolic  disharmonic
understated  priestcraft  stomatology  stomachache  biocoenosis  dithyrambic
undervaluer  sheathknife  supercharge  streetlight  biocoenotic  draggletail
underwriter  spendthrift  terminology  stylography  biquadratic  dramaturgic
undeveloped  aboutsledge  thanatology  tachygraphy  blastogenic  dropcurtain
undisguised  acknowledge  thaumaturge  thankworthy  blepharitis  dyslogistic
undisturbed  aerobiology  thaumaturgy  trothplight  bourgeoisie  econometric
unexploited  agrobiology  undercharge  trustworthy  bradycardia  ectoblastic
unexpressed  amphibology  vagabondage  underweight  braggadocio  ectogenesis
unfashioned  archaeology  venereology  uranography  bristletail  ectogenetic
unfurnished  archipelago  vexillology  vehmgericht  brucellosis  ectomorphic
unicoloured  Assyriology  volcanology  wheelwright  bushmanship  ectoplasmic
uninhabited  bryozoology  vulcanology  zincography  cabbalistic  ectotrophic
uninhibited  campanology  weighbridge  abiogenesis  cacographic  elastomeric
unkennelled  chaperonage  angiography  abiogenetic  calceolaria  elephantoid
unmitigated  Christology  antistrophe  acatalectic  calisthenic  embryologic
unorganized  climatology  bathyscaphe  achondritic  Calvinistic  emperorship
unpossessed  concubinage  blameworthy  acidophilic  camaraderie  enarthrosis
unqualified  cosmetology  calligraphy  actinomycin  cantharidic  encomiastic
unsaturated  countersign  candlelight  admiralship  captainship  endomorphic
unsolicited  criminology  cartography  Aeneolithic  carbocyclic  endoplasmic
unvarnished  cryobiology  catastrophe  aeolotropic  carrageenin  endothermic
unwarranted  dactylology  chirography  aerodynamic  catachresis  endotrophic
upholsterer  decolletage  chorography  AfroAsiatic  cataclysmic  epeirogenic
vaporimeter  depthcharge  cosmography  agoraphobia  cataplectic  epithalamia
varnishtree  dermatology  discography  agoraphobic  catechistic  epithalamic
vinedresser  electrology  dittography  albuminuria  catercousin  esemplastic
volkslieder  eschatology  downdraught  algorithmic  ceroplastic  Eucharistic
volumometer  Etruscology  dreadnought  allomorphic  chalcedonic  eudiometric
voortrekker  featheredge  ethnography  amphimictic  chamberlain  euphemistic
wainscotted  frankpledge  faithworthy  anacreontic  chambermaid  eurypteroid
wapperjawed  furnishings  filmography  anadiplosis  chameleonic  feldspathic
warmblooded  gasfittings  forethought  anaesthesia  charcuterie  felspathoid
warmhearted  gerontology  freethought  anaesthetic  charismatic  fetichistic
washleather  gynaecology  guttapercha  anagnorisis  chemotactic  fetishistic
waspwaisted  haematology  Hagiographa  anaphylaxis  chinoiserie  feudalistic
wastebasket  haemorrhage  hagiography  anarchistic  christiania  flagcaptain
watercooled  headborough  handwrought  anastomosis  chronologic  fluorescein
watercooler  heresiology  haplography  anastomotic  chrysarobin  foretopsail
waterlogged  herpetology  heavyweight  anemometric  cisatlantic  formalistic
weakhearted  hypercharge  heliography  anglophobia  citizenship  Francomania
wedgeshaped  ichthyology  highwrought  anglophobic  climacteric  gafftopsail
wedgetailed  insectifuge  homoeopathy  anisotropic  clinometric  Gallophobia
weenybopper  insectology  hydrography  anomalistic  coccidiosis  gamogenesis
welladvised  interchange  hymnography  anthocyanin  cockaleekie  gastronomic
wellbeloved  kinesiology  hypertrophy  anthracitic  cockyleekie  gegenschein
welldefined  laryngology  hypsography  antiJacobin  colonelship  gendarmerie
wellfounded  libertinage  ichnography  antiphrasis  communistic  generalship
wellgroomed  lichenology  iconography  antipyretic  comradeship  geomagnetic
wellordered  malariology  ipecacuanha  antiSemitic  conspecific  geostrophic
wellrounded  martyrology  lightweight  antivitamin  costbenefit  geotectonic
Westminster  meteorology  lithography  antonomasia  coulometric  Germanophil
wheresoever  methodology  micrography  apocalyptic  counterfeit  gibberellin
whichsoever  miscarriage  motherright  Apollinaris  counterfoil  glauconitic
whiffletree  mismarriage  mythography  aponeurosis  countervail  glossolalia
whippletree  myrmecology  naturopathy  aponeurotic  cryptogamic  gnotobiosis
Whitechapel  olfactology  orthography  aposiopesis  cryptomeria  gnotobiotic
whiteheaded  orchidology  osteography  apostleship  crystalloid  goniometric
whitewasher  ornithology  overwrought  apostrophic  curatorship  gramophonic
whitleather  overindulge  paperweight  apparatchik  cyclopaedia  granolithic
wholesouled  palmcabbage  papiermache  arbitratrix  cyclopaedic  granophyric
whoremaster  phraseology  pennyweight  archaeornis  cyclothymia  gravimetric
whoremonger  pivotbridge  petrography  archangelic  cyclothymic  haematocrit
whosesoever  primatology  phonography  Areopagitic  cytogenesis  haemocyanin
windcheater  proceedings  photography  atmospheric  cytokinesis  haemoglobin
wintergreen  pteridology  phytography  audiometric  demographic  haemophilia
wisecracker  pullthrough  pictography  autographic  denizenship  haemophilic
witchhunter  quickchange  pillowfight  autoplastic  dexiotropic  haemoptysis
worldbeater  reflexology  pornography  autotrophic  dialogistic  haemorrhoid
wreckmaster  scientology  psychopathy  avoirdupois  diamagnetic  haemostasis
wrongheaded  seigniorage  radiography  bacchanalia  diaphoresis  haemostatic
xylographer  semasiology  reprography  BaltoSlavic  diaphoretic  haggadistic
festschrift  shortchange  scenography  basketchair  diapophysis  hagioscopic
```

harmonistic	legerdemain	oestrogenic	problematic	stewardship	absorbingly
hebephrenia	lifemanship	ontogenesis	procephalic	Stradivarii	abstinently
hebephrenic	lithophytic	ontogenetic	proctorship	studentship	academicals
heliometric	logarithmic	opencircuit	progenitrix	subspecific	accentually
heliotropic	logographic	oreographic	prolocutrix	swallowtail	acceptingly
Hellenistic	macrobiotic	orthodontia	prophetship	sycophantic	accordantly
helminthoid	macrocosmic	orthodontic	prophylaxis	syllogistic	accordingly
hemeralopia	macroscopic	orthopaedic	prosecutrix	symbolistic	accountable
hemianopsia	magistratic	orthoscopic	proteolysis	sympathetic	accountably
hemimorphic	maintopsail	orthotropic	proteolytic	symptomatic	acidifiable
hemispheric	managership	osteopathic	Proterozoic	syndesmosis	acropetally
hermeneutic	manneristic	osteophytic	prothalamia	synergistic	adjectively
heroworship	marqueterie	Ostrogothic	prothoracic	syssarcosis	adverbially
heteroploid	marshalship	paederastic	protophytic	tabletennis	advertently
heterotaxis	masochistic	paedophilia	provostship	tachycardia	aerobically
heterotypic	mastodontic	Palaearctic	pseudopodia	teachership	affectingly
highfalutin	mastoiditis	palaeotypic	psittacosis	technologic	affectively
Hippocratic	mechanistic	palindromic	psychedelia	telegrammic	aggregately
holoblastic	mediumistic	panhellenic	psychedelic	telegraphic	aggrievedly
holographic	megalomania	pantheistic	psychiatric	telekinesis	agnatically
homeopathic	megalopolis	pantothenic	psychogenic	telekinetic	agonisingly
homeostasis	melancholia	paragraphic	psychologic	teratogenic	ailurophile
homeostatic	melancholic	paraleipsis	pyroclastic	teratologic	allocatable
homocentric	memorabilia	parallactic	pyrotechnic	tetracyclic	alternately
homoestatic	meroblastic	paramorphic	quinquennia	theocentric	ambiguously
homogenetic	merogenesis	paraplectic	radiometric	theodolitic	ambitiously
homomorphic	mesoblastic	parasitosis	radiophonic	theorematic	amorphously
homoplastic	mesomorphic	parathyroid	rattlebrain	therapeutic	analogously
homothallic	messiahship	paratyphoid	realpolitik	thermoduric	anencephaly
homozygosis	metacentric	parenthesis	rhinoscopic	thermolysis	angelically
Hudibrastic	metachrosis	parenthetic	rhizocarpic	thermolytic	anomalously
hydrobromic	metagenesis	paronomasia	ritualistic	thermotaxis	anonymously
hydrocyanic	metagenetic	partnership	Russophobia	thingumajig	appallingly
hydrometric	metallurgic	passacaglia	saintpaulia	thixotropic	appealingly
hydropathic	metamorphic	pediculosis	salpingitis	thoroughpin	applaudable
hydrophilic	metaplastic	periostitis	sanguinaria	thyroiditis	appreciable
hydrophobia	metapsychic	peripatetic	saprobiotic	timebargain	appreciably
hydrophobic	metasomatic	periphrasis	saprophytic	tonsillitis	approvingly
hydrophytic	Methodistic	perispermic	scarabaeoid	topographic	aquatically
hydrostatic	microcosmic	peristalsis	scholarship	torticollis	archaically
hydrotactic	microlithic	peristaltic	scholiastic	toxicomania	arglebargle
hydrotropic	micrometric	peritonitis	scientistic	tracasserie	arrestingly
hygrometric	microphonic	pessimistic	scissortail	transuranic	articulable
hygrophytic	microphytic	phagedaenic	sclerotitis	tribuneship	ascetically
hygroscopic	microscopic	pharyngitis	seborrhoeic	trichinosis	aseptically
hylogenesis	mithridatic	philosophic	selfconceit	trisyllabic	assertively
hylozoistic	modernistic	photometric	selfdespair	tritheistic	assiduously
hyperboloid	monitorship	photophilic	selfworship	troglodytic	assimilable
hypercritic	monochromic	photophobia	senatorship	trousersuit	atrociously
hypermetric	monogenesis	photophobic	septicaemia	trundletail	attemptable
hyperphagia	monogenetic	phototactic	septicaemic	trusteeship	attentively
hyperplasia	monographic	phototropic	shamanistic	typographic	attractable
hypnopaedia	monomorphic	phthiriasis	sheriffship	unrealistic	audaciously
hypnopompic	monozygotic	phycocyanin	showmanship	Upanishadic	augmentable
hypoblastic	myocarditis	phyllotaxis	sickbenefit	vasopressin	auricularly
hypocycloid	mythopoetic	physiologic	socialistic	verbalistic	automatable
hypogastric	myxomatosis	planimetric	sociometric	viceroyship	banteringly
hypothermia	narcoleptic	plasmolysis	sociopathic	voltametric	baptismally
hypotyposis	necrobiosis	plasmolytic	soldiership	voodooistic	barbarously
hypsometric	necromantic	pleiotropic	solipsistic	workmanship	barbastelle
hypsophobia	necrophilia	pleomorphic	somatogenic	xylographic	barefacedly
ichthyornis	necrophilic	pleurodynia	somatologic	zygomorphic	basipetally
iconostasis	necropoleis	pluralistic	somatotonia		battlefield
ideographic	negotiatrix	plutocratic	somatotonic		beauteously
idiographic	negrophobia	pneumonitis	speakership		beautifully
idiomorphic	neologistic	podophyllin	spherulitic		befittingly
immunologic	Neoplatonic	polychromic	sphincteric		beguilingly
interatomic	neuropathic	polygenesis	Spinozistic		benightedly
internuncio	neurotropic	polygenetic	spiritistic		benignantly
intervallic	nomographic	polyglottic	spirometric		bibliophile
ionospheric	nonmetallic	polygraphic	spondylitis		bibliophily
isoelectric	nonspecific	polymorphic	sponsorship		bilaterally
ithyphallic	nosographic	polytechnic	sporophytic		binocularly
Jansenistic	nurserymaid	porphyritic	stalactitic		bitterapple
jargonistic	nyctitropic	postclassic	stalagmitic		blackbeetle
kilocalorie	nyctophobia	praetorship	staurolitic		blamelessly
kleptomania	nymphomania	prehistoric	steatopygia		bloodlessly
kymographic	oarsmanship	premiership	stephanotis		abioticaly
lectureship	ochlocratic	primateship	stereotypic		bookinghall

botanically	congealable	difficultly	expectantly	illogically	innumerable
bounteously	congenially	diffidently	expediently	illuminable	innumerably
bountifully	congruently	diffusively	expensively	imaginarily	inquiringly
brainlessly	congruously	digestively	explainable	imitatively	inscribable
brainsickly	connectable	dimwittedly	exploitable	immediately	inscrutable
brilliantly	connectedly	diningtable	explosively	immedicable	inscrutably
bucolically	connectible	dinnertable	expressible	immitigable	insensately
bumptiously	connubially	disarmingly	exquisitely	immitigably	inseparable
Byronically	conquerable	disassemble	extensively	impartially	inseparably
cabbagepalm	consciously	disassembly	extractable	impassively	insidiously
canonically	conservable	discardable	exuberantly	impatiently	insincerely
capaciously	consignable	discernible	facetiously	impeachable	insistently
caressingly	consolingly	discernibly	factionally	imperfectly	insultingly
carvelbuilt	consonantly	discussable	faithlessly	imperiously	insuperable
causatively	construable	discussible	falteringly	impermeable	insuperably
caustically	consumingly	disentangle	fanatically	impermeably	intensively
cavernously	containable	disenthrall	farthingale	imperviable	intermeddle
ceaselessly	contentedly	disguisedly	fashionable	impetuously	intermingle
celestially	contestable	disgustedly	fashionably	implausible	intertangle
certifiable	continently	dishonestly	fatiguingly	implausibly	intolerable
certifiably	continuable	dislikeable	faultlessly	imploringly	intolerably
changefully	continually	dismayingly	feloniously	impoliticly	intractable
chanterelle	contractile	disparately	fermentable	importantly	intractably
chaotically	contrivable	dispensable	ferociously	importunely	intricately
cheerlessly	conventicle	dispersedly	festinately	imprecisely	intrusively
Chippendale	conversable	disseminule	financially	impregnable	intuitively
chlorophyll	convertible	dissociable	fingerstall	impregnably	invectively
Christianly	convertibly	dissolutely	fissionable	impressible	inventively
chronically	convincible	dissolvable	flatulently	imprudently	invidiously
civilisable	convivially	dissonantly	flauntingly	impulsively	inviolately
clamorously	corporately	dissyllable	foreseeable	inadaptable	irrecusable
classically	corporeally	distensible	forfeitable	inadvisable	irrecusably
cloudcastle	corpulently	divergently	forgetfully	inalienable	irreducible
cockleshell	correctable	diverticula	forgettable	inalienably	irreducibly
coeternally	corrosively	doctrinally	fortifiable	inalterable	irrefutable
coffeetable	corruptible	doubtlessly	fortnightly	inalterably	irrefutably
cognitively	corruptibly	douroucouli	fortunately	inanimately	irregularly
cognoscible	countlessly	drastically	fractiously	incessantly	irremovable
collapsible	courteously	dreamlessly	Francophile	incipiently	irremovably
collectable	credentials	dresscircle	frantically	inclemently	irreparable
collectedly	credulously	dynamically	fraternally	inclusively	irreparably
collectible	cryptically	ebulliently	frightfully	incoercible	irresoluble
collinearly	customarily	editorially	frivolously	incorrectly	irrevocable
collusively	custombuilt	effectively	fruitlessly	incorruptly	irrevocably
colourfully	dangerously	effectually	garrulously	increasable	irruptively
combatively	dauntlessly	efficiently	generically	incuriously	itinerantly
combustible	deathrattle	effulgently	genetically	indefinable	judiciously
comfortable	deceitfully	egregiously	genitivally	indefinably	juridically
comfortably	deceivingly	elaborately	gentianella	indignantly	justiciable
commendable	decennially	elastically	gentlemanly	indivisible	justifiable
commendably	deceptively	elementally	glutinously	indivisibly	justifiably
commensally	decussately	embraceable	gracelessly	indomitable	laboriously
committable	dedicatedly	embracingly	grandiosely	indomitably	laconically
compassable	deductively	emotionally	graphically	indubitable	lacrimosely
compellable	defectively	empirically	grotesquely	indubitably	lacrymosely
competently	defensively	endearingly	grumblingly	inductively	larcenously
compliantly	deficiently	endemically	guilelessly	indulgently	lecherously
compositely	degradingly	enforceable	guiltlessly	inelegantly	lickerishly
compossible	deistically	enlargeable	haematocele	ineluctable	lickspittle
comprisable	deliciously	enquiringly	haphazardly	ineluctably	lightsomely
concealable	delightedly	entomophily	hazardously	inequitable	limitlessly
conceitedly	deliriously	episcopally	healthfully	inequitably	lingeringly
conceivable	deliverable	equivocally	heartlessly	inescapable	liquefiable
conceivably	demandingly	erratically	Hebraically	inestimable	litigiously
conceptacle	demountable	erroneously	hereditable	inestimably	loathsomely
concertedly	denumerable	escheatable	heretically	inexcusable	lucratively
condemnable	dependently	essentially	herringgull	inexcusably	ludicrously
condensable	deploringly	eucalyptole	hibernacula	inflammable	luxuriantly
conductible	depressible	eugenically	hilariously	inflammably	luxuriously
conferrable	descendable	exceedingly	honeysuckle	infrangible	maddeningly
confessedly	descendible	excellently	hornswoggle	ingeniously	maladroitly
confidently	describable	excessively	housewifely	ingenuously	maliciously
confidingly	deservingly	exclusively	hundredfold	ingrainedly	malignantly
confirmable	desperately	excursively	identically	inhabitable	manipulable
confiscable	desultorily	exemplarily	idiotically	inheritable	mantelshelf
conformable	developable	exercisable	idyllically	injuriously	marcescible
conformably	dexterously	exhaustible	illiberally	innavigable	masculinely
conformally	dialectally	exogenously	illimitable	innocuously	masterfully
confusingly	differently	expansively	illimitably	innoxiously	matchlessly

mediaevally	perplexedly	rancorously	semimonthly	tentatively	unthinkable
medicinable	persuadable	rapaciously	senselessly	termagantly	unthinkably
medicinally	persuasible	rapturously	sensitively	tetanically	untouchable
melodiously	pertinently	ratatouille	sensorially	thanklessly	unutterable
meningocele	perturbable	ravishingly	serviceable	theatricals	unutterably
mentionable	pervasively	receptacula	serviceably	thermically	unweetingly
mercenarily	pervertedly	receptively	seventyfold	thermophile	unwillingly
mercilessly	pestilently	recessively	severalfold	thrillingly	unwinkingly
mercurially	pictorially	reclaimable	shacklebolt	thunderbolt	unwittingly
mimetically	pigheadedly	recoverable	shamelessly	titanically	vagariously
mirthlessly	pipistrelle	rectifiable	shelterbelt	toothsomely	vaporisable
misguidedly	piratically	recumbently	shiftlessly	torturously	venatically
molecularly	plaintively	recurrently	shrinkingly	totteringly	venturously
mollycoddle	pleasurable	redoubtable	sickeningly	townspeople	veraciously
momentarily	pleasurably	redundantly	sightlessly	tracelessly	veridically
momentously	plenteously	reflexively	sigmoidally	transiently	verminously
monstrously	plentifully	refrangible	signifiable	traversable	versatilely
moronically	pointlessly	regardfully	simperingly	treasonable	vesicularly
municipally	poisonously	regenerable	sinistrally	treasonably	vestigially
murderously	polarisable	regimentals	sleeplessly	tremblingly	vexatiously
murmurously	polemically	registrable	slightingly	tremulously	vicariously
muskthistle	politically	regretfully	smilelessly	trenchantly	viceregally
narratively	polygonally	regrettable	somatically	triadically	violoncello
necessarily	ponderously	regrettably	somnolently	tributarily	vitrifiable
nefariously	pontificals	rejoicingly	sorrowfully	triennially	vivaciously
negligently	posteriorly	religiously	soundlessly	trisyllable	voicelessly
neighbourly	potentially	reluctantly	sovereignly	troublously	voluntarily
nervelessly	potteringly	repellantly	sparrowbill	truculently	voraciously
netherworld	powerlessly	repellently	spasticably	turbulently	warrantable
nightingale	practicable	repentantly	specifiable	turtleshell	warrantably
nocturnally	practicably	replaceable	spherically	tyrannously	waterbottle
noiselessly	practically	repleviable	spinelessly	unadvisedly	wearilessly
nomadically	prattlingly	reposefully	spiritually	unalterable	wearisomely
nonvolatile	precedently	repressible	spirituelle	unanimously	Wensleydale
notoriously	predatorily	repressibly	spreadeagle	unashamedly	whimsically
numerically	predictable	reprovingly	squarebuilt	unavailable	wholesomely
nutritively	predictably	repugnantly	squeamishly	unavoidable	witheringly
objectively	prefatorily	repulsively	squintingly	unavoidably	wolfwhistle
obliviously	prelusively	resentfully	stainlessly	unbendingly	wonderfully
obnoxiously	prelusorily	resiliently	startlingly	unboundedly	worrisomely
observantly	prematurely	resistively	statesmanly	unbreakable	worshipable
observingly	presciently	respectable	statutorily	uncatchable	worthlessly
obsessively	presentable	respectably	steadfastly	unceasingly	xanthophyll
obstinately	presentably	responsible	strenuously	uncertainly	yellowbelly
obtrusively	preservable	responsibly	stretchable	unclimbable	bellbottoms
occipitally	presumingly	retentively	stringently	uncountable	betweentime
octagonally	pretendedly	retraceable	stumblingly	uncrushable	centigramme
offensively	prevalently	retractable	subaerially	undesirable	cleistogamy
offhandedly	preventable	retrievable	submersible	undoubtedly	collenchyma
officinally	preventible	righteously	submissible	undutifully	delightsome
officiously	primaevally	sagaciously	submultiple	unendurable	deuterogamy
operatively	primitively	salaciously	subumbrella	unendurably	Deuteronomy
opportunely	principally	salvageable	succulently	unfailingly	enterostomy
orbicularly	privatively	sartorially	suggestible	unfeelingly	epithelioma
organically	professedly	satanically	summersault	unfeignedly	flavoursome
organisable	profiterole	satirically	sumptuously	unflappable	furthersome
osmotically	prominently	satisfiable	superfamily	ungetatable	gastrectomy
ostensively	promisingly	saturninely	supersubtle	unguardedly	gymnospermy
outspokenly	propitiable	sceptically	suppliantly	unhealthily	harvesthome
pacifically	prosaically	schoolchild	supportable	unhelpfully	heliochrome
paramountly	protractile	scissorbill	supportably	unisexually	hepatectomy
parochially	protrudable	sclerophyll	surficially	universally	hippopotami
partitively	protrusible	scorchingly	surpassable	unlimitedly	laryngotomy
pecuniarily	providently	scorpionfly	susceptible	unmatchable	nephrectomy
pendulously	provisorily	scoundrelly	susceptibly	unmeaningly	ovariectomy
pensionable	provokingly	screamingly	suspensible	unmemorable	physiognomy
penuriously	proximately	searchingly	sustainable	unmemorably	plagiostome
perceivable	psychically	secondarily	swallowable	unnaturally	prestissimo
perceivably	publishable	secretively	swallowhole	unnervingly	prosenchyma
perceptible	punchinello	sectionally	tagliatelle	unpalatable	psychodrama
perceptibly	purchasable	sedentarily	tagliatelli	unprintable	quarrelsome
perennially	purportedly	seditiously	talkatively	unshockable	quinquereme
perfectible	purposively	seductively	tarnishable	unskilfully	reprogramme
performable	putrescible	segmentally	tarradiddle	unsmilingly	rubberstamp
perishingly	pyramidally	seismically	tastelessly	unsparingly	schistosome
permanently	qualifiable	selaginella	technically	unspeakable	scleroderma
permissible	querulously	selectively	temperately	unspeakably	scyphistoma
permissibly	quiescently	selffertile	temporarily	unstoppable	sextodecimo
perpetually	quizzically	selfsterile	tenaciously	unteachable	splenectomy

stenochromy	campmeeting	disportment	grandparent	linefishing	Pleistocene
stirruppump	caravanning	disquieting	gravelblind	longplaying	plenipotent
stomachpump	challenging	dissentient	greasepaint	luminescent	politicking
tracheotomy	channelling	dissepiment	hairraising	magnificent	polystyrene
troublesome	chitterling	distribuend	hairstyling	maidservant	precipitant
trypanosome	chloroprene	divorcement	halfbinding	manifestant	predicament
unwholesome	christening	divulgement	halflanding	manumitting	predominant
venturesome	churchgoing	dodecaphony	handfasting	marshalling	preexistent
abandonment	cinnabarine	domineering	handselling	matchmaking	prejudgment
abolishment	clairvoyant	doublethink	handwriting	measurement	presentient
aboveground	clandestine	dressmaking	hardhitting	mellifluent	presentment
abridgement	clodhopping	dropforging	hardworking	merrymaking	procurement
acaulescent	clothesline	earpiercing	headhunting	methylamine	prolegomena
accipitrine	cobblestone	elephantine	hearthstone	microsecond	proportions
achievement	cochinchina	embowelling	heartstring	millisecond	protuberant
acquiescent	codefendant	embowerment	helleborine	mindbending	publishment
acquirement	coefficient	embracement	herringbone	mindblowing	pulverulent
acriflavine	colourblind	embroilment	heterophony	mindreading	pumicestone
adjournment	commandment	empanelling	highranking	misjudgment	quadraphony
adjudgement	communicant	emplacement	Hindoostani	misspelling	quarrelling
advancement	compartment	enchainment	hyacinthine	moderations	quartertone
advertising	compilement	enchantment	hyoscyamine	moneymaking	quickfiring
alabastrine	complainant	encrustment	hypersthene	monkeyshine	racemeeting
alexandrine	complaisant	endorsement	illbreeding	monophthong	realignment
alkalescent	complotting	enfeoffment	impanelling	mudslinging	reawakening
amaranthine	comportment	enforcement	impeachment	multivalent	recruitment
amazonstone	concealment	engineering	imperilling	musclebound	redetermine
amethystine	concernment	engorgement	imperilment	namecalling	reedbunting
amphetamine	concomitant	engrossment	impermanent	naphthalene	reenactment
amphictyony	concrescent	enhancement	impertinent	needlepoint	refreshment
amphisbaena	concubitant	enjambement	impingement	noctilucent	refrigerant
antemundane	confinement	enlargement	impoundment	noctivagant	reminiscent
anticyclone	conflagrant	enlivenment	impressment	noisemaking	remonstrant
antifouling	congealment	ennoblement	improvement	nonexistent	replacement
antioxidant	consanguine	enslavement	improvident	nonmatching	requirement
apomorphine	consentient	entablement	inadvertent	nonplussing	resipiscent
apparelling	considering	enthralling	incalescent	nonresident	resplendent
appeasement	consignment	enthralment	incarnadine	nourishment	restatement
appointment	constituent	entitlement	incognisant	obmutescent	retrocedent
appurtenant	containment	entrainment	incompetent	obsolescent	reverberant
arbitrament	contaminant	entreatment	incompliant	oilpainting	reviviscent
arborescent	contentment	entrustment	incongruent	omnipresent	rhynchodont
armtwisting	controlling	envelopment	inconscient	orangoutang	ribvaulting
arraignment	controlment	environment	inconsonant	outbreeding	roadholding
arrangement	copingstone	epinephrine	incontinent	outbuilding	ropedancing
assuagement	corecipient	epochmaking	indehiscent	outcropping	ropewalking
autochthony	cornerstone	equidistant	independent	outfighting	rottenstone
babysitting	cornhusking	equipollent	indifferent	outstanding	rubefacient
ballbearing	corroborant	escheatment	indorsement	overbearing	safekeeping
balletomane	counselling	evanishment	inefficient	overbidding	sandbagging
barquentine	counterbond	everlasting	inexpedient	overgarment	scaffolding
bassethound	countermand	expectorant	ingathering	overlapping	scintillant
bearbaiting	countermine	extravagant	initialling	overmanning	scopolamine
bedevilment	counterpane	eyecatching	inobservant	overpayment	scuppernong
bedizenment	countersink	facelifting	inopportune	overrunning	selfclosing
beguilement	countersunk	factfinding	installment	oversailing	selfcocking
belligerent	crystalline	farreaching	instilment	oversetting	selfcommand
bellringing	curtailment	fascinating	intelligent	overtopping	selfcontent
Benedictine	cycloserine	filmsetting	interactant	overweening	selfdenying
benightment	debauchment	fingerprint	interdepend	oysterplant	selfevident
bereavement	debouchment	fireraising	interesting	painkilling	selffeeding
bergschrund	deforcement	firewalking	interfacing	painstaking	selffeeling
bestselling	defraudment	flagwagging	interfluent	palsgravine	selfloading
bewitchment	delitescent	flannelling	interjacent	papermaking	selfflocking
billposting	depravement	fluorescent	interlining	participant	selfpitying
bivouacking	derangement	forerunning	internecine	pastureland	selfraising
bodyservant	despoilment	forewarning	intumescent	patronising	selfreliant
bombardment	determinant	forthcoming	involvement	pawnbroking	selfsealing
bondservant	detrainment	francophone	juvenescent	peacemaking	selfseeking
bondwashing	development	freebooting	kitchensink	pearlescent	selfserving
bookbinding	Diophantine	fulminating	knownothing	penetrating	selfwinding
bookkeeping	disablement	garnishment	knucklebone	pentavalent	serviceline
bookselling	disarmament	geanticline	lancinating	pentazocine	shacklebone
bootlegging	disbandment	geosyncline	landgravine	philhellene	shellacking
brankursine	discernment	glassmaking	landholding	pigsticking	shoplifting
bricklaying	dislodgment	globigerina	latchstring	pilocarpine	shortcoming
bullbaiting	disobedient	goldbeating	lawmerchant	platforming	showjumping
calculating	disobliging	golddigging	leavetaking	platyrrhine	shrivelling
calefacient	disparaging	goodlooking	linedrawing	playerpiano	sightseeing

significant	victualling	botheration	coruscation	divulgation	heldentenor
silverpoint	viridescent	brachiation	counterblow	drawingroom	hibernation
skatingrink	virilescent	branchiopod	counterplot	dualcontrol	hobbledehoy
sleuthhound	wainscoting	brotherhood	crenulation	duplication	horsedoctor
slotmachine	watchmaking	bulletproof	crepitation	dysfunction	humiliation
smithereens	waterskiing	byeelection	crimination	edification	hydrocarbon
snowbunting	wellmeaning	calcination	crucifixion	ejaculation	hydrometeor
soapboiling	wellwishing	calculation	culmination	elaboration	hyphenation
spacesaving	widdershins	calibration	cultivation	elicitation	hypolimnion
stencilling	wildcatting	calumniator	cupellation	elimination	hypotension
stereophony	wildfowling	captivation	cybernation	elucidation	icosahedron
stiflejoint	winegrowing	carbonation	deactivator	elutriation	idolisation
stirrupbone	winetasting	carburetion	debarkation	emancipator	illuminator
stocktaking	wirenetting	carburettor	decantation	emasculator	illustrator
stoneground	wirepulling	castigation	decelerator	embarkation	imagination
strikebound	wiretapping	celebration	declamation	embrocation	imbrication
strongpoint	withershins	cementation	declaration	enchiridion	immigration
subbasement	woodcarving	cerebration	declination	encystation	imparkation
subdominant	woodcutting	cholesterol	decollation	endoskelton	impartation
subservient	worshipping	Christendom	decussation	enneahedron	impetration
substituent	abbreviator	circulation	defalcation	enucleation	implication
superabound	abomination	clothesprop	deflagrator	enumeration	importation
superintend	abstraction	coadunation	defloration	enunciation	imprecation
superjacent	abstriction	coagulation	defoliation	equivocator	imprecision
supernatant	accelerator	coarctation	deformation	eradication	inanimation
surbasement	acceptation	coeducation	deglutition	euchologion	inattention
surveillant	acclamation	coextension	degradation	evagination	inaugurator
sustainment	acclimation	coinheritor	degustation	evaporation	incantation
talebearing	accumulator	colligation	dehydration	exaggerator	incarnation
tankfarming	acetylation	collimation	deification	examination	incinerator
tantalising	acidulation	collocation	delectation	exclamation	inclination
tapemachine	acquisition	colouration	delineation	excoriation	inculcation
temperament	acumination	combination	demarcation	exculpation	inculpation
tentpegging	adjudicator	commendator	demarkation	exfoliation	incurvation
tetravalent	adulterator	commentator	denigration	exhortation	indentation
theobromine	adumbration	commination	denominator	exoneration	indigestion
timeserving	aerostation	comminution	denunciator	exoskeleton	indignation
timesharing	aestivation	commutation	deoxidation	expatiation	indirection
tobogganing	affectation	compensator	depopulator	expectation	inebriation
togglejoint	affiliation	competition	deportation	explanation	infatuation
topdressing	affirmation	compilation	depravation	explication	infestation
touchtyping	affrication	composition	deprecation	exploration	infeudation
traducement	aggravation	compotation	depreciator	exportation	infiltrator
trafficking	aggregation	compression	depredation	expurgation	information
tragedienne	alleviation	compunction	deprivation	exsiccation	innervation
trammelling	altercation	compurgator	dereliction	extenuation	innutrition
transalpine	alternation	computation	desalinator	extirpation	inoculation
transhumant	ambiversion	conciliator	description	extradition	inquisition
transilient	ameliorator	condonation	desecration	extrication	inscription
translucent	anacoluthon	confiscator	desiccation	fabrication	inseminator
transmarine	annihilator	confliction	designation	fascination	insinuation
transpadane	annunciator	confutation	desperation	fecundation	inspiration
transparent	anticipator	congelation	destination	fimbriation	instigation
Trappistine	antineutron	conjugation	destitution	flagellator	institution
tremblement	antiquation	conjunction	destruction	fluctuation	instruction
tryingplane	appellation	conjuration	detestation	fomentation	insufflator
tryptophane	application	connotation	deuteration	forestation	integration
tufthunting	appreciator	consecrator	devaluation	forgetmenot	interaction
twelvepenny	approbation	consecution	devastation	formication	interceptor
typecasting	arbitration	conservator	diatessaron	formulation	intercessor
typesetting	archdukedom	consolation	dicotyledon	fornication	interfusion
ultramarine	articulator	conspirator	diffraction	fructuation	interruptor
unappealing	asphyxiator	constitutor	dilapidator	frustration	intimidator
unbelieving	assentation	constrictor	dinnerwagon	fulguration	invigilator
unbeseeming	assignation	constructor	disaccustom	fulmination	invigorator
underground	assimilator	consummator	discerption	fusillation	invultation
undertaking	association	consumption	disfunction	fustigation	irradiation
undertenant	atomisation	continuator	disillusion	gemmulation	irretention
undeserving	attenuation	contraction	disinfector	genuflexion	itineration
unfaltering	attestation	contraption	disjunction	germination	jactitation
unflinching	attribution	contributor	dislocation	glomeration	Judaisation
unforgiving	benediction	conurbation	disposition	granulation	kwashiorkor
unimportant	benefaction	convocation	disputation	gratulation	labefaction
unpromising	bifurcation	convolution	dissertator	gravitation	lachrymator
unreasoning	bipartition	cooperation	dissipation	greaseproof	laciniation
unrelenting	blackfellow	coordinator	dissolution	gurgitation	lacrimation
unremitting	boardschool	corporation	distinction	habituation	lacrymation
unshrinking	bombilation	correlation	distraction	heartsblood	laicisation
varsovienne	bombination	corrugation	distributor	hedgeschool	lamentation

```
lancination  preelection  selfreproof  vituperator  arthrospore  domiciliary
legislation  preignition  septentrion  vivisection  bacilliform  doubleentry
liquidation  prelibation  serrulation  vociferator  backcountry  dynamometry
lixiviation  premonition  servicebook  waitingroom  bathysphere  earthenware
lubrication  preparation  sheetanchor  wheelbarrow  beaverboard  edificatory
lucubration  preposition  showerproof  whistlestop  benedictory  ejaculatory
luxuriation  preselector  shrinkproof  widowerhood  beneficiary  elucidatory
machination  presumption  sittingroom  witchdoctor  bersaglieri  entablature
malediction  preterition  smokingroom  witenagemot  bibliolatry  evidentiary
malefaction  procreation  solifluxion  xanthochroi  bicentenary  exclamatory
malfunction  procuration  solmisation  zooplankton  billionaire  exculpatory
malposition  profanation  songsparrow  allelomorph  bimillenary  exdirectory
manducation  progression  speculation  bumblepuppy  bladderwort  exhortatory
manipulator  prohibition  spermatozoa  cardiograph  bonbonniere  expatiatory
mansardroof  promulgator  sporulation  choreograph  boutonniere  expenditure
manumission  propagation  stagflation  chronograph  boysenberry  explanatory
marshmallow  prophethood  statutebook  chronoscope  brahmaputra  explicatory
mastication  propitiator  sternutator  contretemps  bridgeboard  exploratory
melanochroi  proposition  stimulation  corbiesteps  bristleworm  expurgatory
melioration  prorogation  stipulation  coronagraph  butcherbird  extemporary
mensuration  prosecution  stoolpigeon  coronograph  cabbageworm  extenuatory
methylation  prostitutor  stridulator  cryotherapy  calefactory  extirpatory
metrication  prostration  stylisation  cryptograph  calorimetry  fasciaboard
micturition  protraction  subarration  electrotype  candidature  filamentary
miscreation  provocation  subaudition  epidiascope  candleberry  fingerboard
molestation  psychomotor  subdivision  fluoroscope  carabiniere  foreclosure
morningroom  publication  subjugation  fluoroscopy  carabinieri  forevermore
mountaintop  pullulation  sublimation  gastroscope  caravansary  fractionary
murmuration  punctuation  subornation  guttersnipe  celebratory  fragmentary
musculation  purificator  subrogation  heterotroph  centreboard  freemasonry
negotiation  pussywillow  subsumption  kinetograph  chancellery  fulminatory
nictitation  pustulation  subtraction  kinetoscope  chancellory  functionary
nomenclator  quadrillion  suffixation  Kulturkampf  charlatanry  furthermore
nuncupation  quintillion  suffocation  lycanthrope  chaulmoogra  gallimaufry
obfuscation  radiocarbon  supervision  lycanthropy  chiaroscuro  gallowsbird
objurgation  rapscallion  supposition  metoposcopy  chickenwire  gimcrackery
obscuration  rarefaction  suppression  misanthrope  chokecherry  goldenberry
obsecration  realisation  suppuration  misanthropy  chronometry  grandiflora
observation  reanimation  surrogation  muttonchops  circulatory  gratulatory
obstruction  reapportion  suspiration  nondescript  codicillary  grotesquery
obtestation  reassertion  susurration  platinotype  colorimetry  halfmeasure
occultation  recantation  synchrotron  polariscope  combinatory  harpsichord
officialdom  reclamation  syncopation  pseudograph  comminatory  heterospory
officiation  recognition  syndication  pseudomorph  compotatory  housewifery
oppugnation  recondition  tabefaction  psychograph  comstockery  huckleberry
orientation  redirection  termination  retinoscopy  concubinary  humiliatory
origination  reeducation  tetrahedron  seismograph  condolatory  hummingbird
oscillation  reformation  thingumabob  seismoscope  condottiere  hurryscurry
ostentation  regenerator  titillation  shadowgraph  condottieri  hurryskurry
overdevelop  reification  tittivation  shocktroops  conjuncture  hydrosphere
oviposition  reinsertion  totalisator  stereograph  consolatory  hymenoptera
oxygenation  reiteration  tourbillion  stereoscope  contracture  impetratory
ozonisation  rejuvenator  trafficator  stereoscopy  coparcenary  imprecatory
pacificator  reluctation  transaction  stethoscope  cosignatory  incantatory
palpitation  remunerator  transection  stethoscopy  cotemporary  inculpatory
parturition  repartition  transfixion  stevengraph  counterfort  incurvature
passivation  replication  transfusion  stormtroops  countermark  informatory
patternshop  reprobation  translation  stroboscope  countermure  insectivore
peccadillos  repudiation  trepanation  superscript  counterpart  inspiratory
pectination  requisition  trepidation  thaumatrope  counterturn  intercalary
penetration  reservation  tribulation  thermograph  counterwork  interlunary
pentahedron  resignation  trituration  thermoscope  craniometry  investiture
peptisation  respiration  tumefaction  thwartships  criminatory  involuntary
percolation  restitution  turbination  ablutionary  cryosurgery  ironmongery
perennation  restoration  unification  abracadabra  declamatory  isogeotherm
perforation  restriction  utilisation  acclamatory  declaratory  journeywork
permutation  retaliation  vaccination  acinaciform  demagoguery  kitchenware
perpetrator  retardation  vacillation  acupuncture  demonolatry  lacrimatory
perpetuator  retribution  vacuolation  affirmatory  denigratory  lacrymatory
persecution  retroaction  valediction  agriculture  deprecatory  lamellicorn
personation  revaluation  variegation  alkalimetry  depredatory  lamelliform
photoperiod  rubefaction  vasodilator  alleviative  dipterocarp  latticework
phytosterol  rubrication  vasopressor  anniversary  disjuncture  legionnaire
picturebook  rustication  vaticinator  antiphonary  displeasure  legislature
pollination  sacculation  venesection  applicatory  dissymmetry  lepidoptera
ponderation  scattergood  venisection  appogiatura  divestiture  ligamentary
postulation  segregation  ventilation  approbatory  divisionary  lithosphere
predecessor  selfcontrol  vermination  aquaculture  doctrinaire  louverboard
predication  selfopinion  vindication  aquiculture  documentary  louvreboard
```

lowpressure	sculduddery	achromatism	butteriness	demigoddess	extremeness
maledictory	sculduggery	adiaphorism	Byzantinism	democratise	facsimilist
manducatory	sedimentary	adoptianism	Byzantinist	democratism	factualness
manufactory	seditionary	adoptianist	cabbagerose	deoxyribose	faddishness
manufacture	seismometry	adoptionism	caddishness	depauperise	familiarise
masticatory	selfculture	adoptionist	callousness	desensitise	farawayness
melanophore	selfmastery	adventuress	cannibalise	desexualise	farthermost
milliampere	selfsupport	adventurism	cannibalism	determinism	fatefulness
millionaire	selftorture	adventurist	capableness	determinist	fatuousness
mockingbird	sericulture	adverseness	captionless	detribalise	favouritism
molendinary	shopsteward	advisedness	carefulness	deviousness	fearfulness
monoculture	shovelboard	affranchise	catchphrase	devotedness	featherless
mortarboard	skulduddery	agnosticism	catheterise	diachronism	featureless
musculature	skulduggery	agrarianism	catholicise	dichotomise	feelingness
negotiatory	sleeveboard	aimlessness	Catholicism	dichotomist	fidgetiness
nondelivery	smorgasbord	airlessness	cavalierism	didacticism	fingerglass
noticeboard	snowleopard	airsickness	chafingdish	diffuseness	finicalness
nutcrackers	splashboard	allopathist	chevalglass	diluvialist	flabbergast
obfuscatory	springboard	alphabetise	chiropodist	diplomatise	flaccidness
objurgatory	stereometry	amativeness	chloroplast	diplomatist	flavourless
observatory	stichometry	Americanise	Christmassy	disafforest	fleshliness
octingenary	stipendiary	Americanism	chromoplast	discourtesy	flightiness
ommatophore	stipulatory	Americanist	chrysoprase	disinterest	floweriness
orthocentre	stormcentre	amiableness	churchiness	disorganise	foolishness
oscillatory	stringboard	amorousness	circularise	distinguish	foppishness
ostracoderm	stringybark	anachronism	civilianise	disunionist	foreignness
overmeasure	subaxillary	ancientness	cleanliness	divisionism	foretopmast
ozonosphere	subcategory	Anglicanism	clericalism	doggishness	foreverness
paddleboard	subcontrary	anthologise	clericalist	dolefulness	forgiveness
passeriform	substandard	anthologist	coffeehouse	dollishness	forlornness
patelliform	sulphurwort	anxiousness	cognateness	doltishness	formularise
perfunctory	superlunary	apotheosise	colonialism	donnishness	forwardness
petitionary	supersedure	aquarellist	colonialist	doublecross	fractionise
phalanstery	supervisory	archdiocese	comfortless	doughtiness	franticness
photosphere	suppository	archduchess	commonsense	drouthiness	fretfulness
picturecard	swallowwort	arduousness	communalise	drunkenness	friableness
planisphere	switchboard	Arminianism	communalism	dualpurpose	frowardness
plasterwork	sycophantry	arterialise	communalist	dubiousness	frowstiness
playingcard	tapemeasure	artillerist	compactness	durableness	fulsomeness
plectoptera	taratantara	artlessness	comparatist	dutifulness	funambulist
ploughshare	teeterboard	assuredness	complexness	earnestness	furthermost
polarimetry	tegumentary	astigmatism	computerise	earthliness	furtiveness
poltroonery	temperature	athleticism	conciseness	easternmost	gainfulness
pomiculture	tenementary	audibleness	conductress	eclecticism	gallantness
portraiture	theretofore	audiologist	consumerism	ecumenicism	Gallicanism
pourparlers	thermometry	austereness	contrabasso	elbowgrease	gangsterism
predicatory	thitherward	autoerotism	controversy	elderliness	gaseousness
preliminary	thunderbird	awesomeness	copiousness	electrolyse	gemmologist
premonitory	transfigure	awkwardness	cordialness	elusiveness	genealogise
preparatory	translunary	balefulness	corporatism	emblematise	genealogist
procuratory	trapeziform	barrelhouse	correctness	emblematist	genteelness
profanatory	trelliswork	bashfulness	corruptness	emotionless	genuineness
progeniture	trestlework	battledress	cosmogonist	emulousness	ghastliness
prohibitory	troposphere	bearishness	cosmologist	emulsionise	ghostliness
proprietary	typefoundry	beastliness	costiveness	enchantress	gibbousness
protonotary	ultramodern	belatedness	cottongrass	endlessness	girlishness
psychometry	unigeniture	betweenness	courtliness	enfranchise	glaringness
purpresture	unnecessary	biliousness	crabbedness	enviousness	godlessness
questionary	valedictory	bimetallism	creationism	epigraphist	gourmandise
reactionary	vasculiform	bimetallist	creationist	equableness	gourmandism
recognitory	vestryclerk	bittercress	criminalist	equilibrist	gracileness
reconnoitre	vindicatory	blackgrouse	crookedness	Erastianism	gradualness
rediscovery	viniculture	blessedness	crunchiness	esotericism	graphicness
reformatory	viticulture	blotchiness	crystallise	Esperantist	gristliness
reprobatory	volitionary	blunderbuss	cunningness	etherealise	grouchiness
respiratory	weatherworn	bohemianism	curableness	ethnologist	guardedness
restructure	weltschmerz	Bonapartism	curiousness	etymologise	gutlessness
retaliatory	whigmaleery	Bonapartist	currentness	etymologist	gutturalise
retardatory	whitherward	bookishness	currishness	eudaemonism	gutturalism
retributory	winterberry	boorishness	cursiveness	eudaemonist	gyrocompass
revisionary	abortionist	bottleglass	cursoriness	Europeanise	haggardness
rhombohedra	absenteeism	breadthwise	customhouse	evasiveness	hagiologist
rotogravure	abusiveness	breathalyse	decarbonise	eventualise	hairstylist
rudimentary	academicism	bristliness	decarburise	exhaustless	haplessness
salmonberry	accessorise	Britishness	decolourise	exotericism	harbourless
scalariform	acclimatise	brittleness	deemphasise	extemporise	harmfulness
scalpriform	accompanist	brusqueness	defenceless	exteriorise	hatefulness
schoolboard	accoucheuse	brutishness	demagnetise	externalise	haughtiness
scratchwork	achromatise	bullishness	demagoguism	externalism	healthiness

hedgepriest	lissomeness	novelettish	pliableness	saddlehorse	studiedness
heedfulness	literalness	noxiousness	plicateness	Sadduceeism	stuntedness
Hegelianism	lithotomise	numismatist	pointedness	saintliness	stylishness
heinousness	lithotomist	nympholepsy	pointillism	Sanskritist	suasiveness
hellishness	lithotripsy	objectivism	pointillist	saplessness	sublimeness
helpfulness	loathliness	objectivist	poltergeist	savouriness	suburbanise
heptarchist	logicalness	obliqueness	pompousness	saxophonist	succourless
hermeticism	logomachist	obscureness	porterhouse	schismatise	suckingfish
heteroecism	loutishness	obviousness	portionless	schoolhouse	summariness
hexametrist	lovableness	odorousness	portraitist	ScotchIrish	summerhouse
Hibernicism	lumpishness	oenophilist	powderflask	scragginess	sunlessness
hideousness	lustfulness	offenceless	preachiness	scrappiness	superimpose
hierarchism	Lutheranism	officialese	precentress	scrimpiness	superioress
highbrowism	madrigalist	officialism	preceptress	scruffiness	supremacist
hirsuteness	maintopmast	oldwomanish	preciseness	scurvygrass	supremeness
Hispanicise	malapropism	ominousness	prickliness	seasickness	surgeonfish
Hispanicism	mammalogist	onerousness	primitivism	secondclass	swarthiness
Hispanicist	mandolinist	operoseness	privateness	selfishness	swinishness
histologist	Manichaeism	ophiologist	probabilism	semanticist	synchromesh
historicise	mannishness	opportunism	probabilist	semiellipse	synchronise
historicism	marchioness	opportunist	prochronism	Septembrist	synchronism
historicist	marginalise	optometrist	prodigalise	seriousness	syndicalism
histrionism	masculinise	orderliness	profaneness	sexlessness	syndicalist
hoggishness	massiveness	orientalise	profuseness	shadowiness	systematise
hollandaise	materialise	orientalism	prognathism	shallowness	systematism
hooliganism	materialism	orientalist	progressism	shapeliness	systematist
hopefulness	materialist	orthopedist	progressist	shelterless	tautologise
horseradish	mawkishness	osteologist	prosaicness	shepherdess	tautologism
hospitalise	McCarthyism	outwardness	proselytise	shrubbiness	tautomerism
hugeousness	meadowgrass	packingcase	proselytism	shutterless	taxidermist
hurriedness	meaningless	paediatrist	protagonist	sickishness	tearfulness
hurtfulness	measureless	painfulness	protectress	sightliness	tediousness
hydrologist	mediateness	pantomimist	prudishness	silveriness	teetotalism
hydromedusa	medievalism	parachutist	Prussianise	sincereness	teleologism
hyperbolise	medievalist	parallelism	Prussianism	singularise	teleologist
hypostatise	memorialise	parametrise	purposeless	sinistrorse	telepathise
hypothenuse	memorialist	passiveness	pushfulness	sinlessness	telepathist
hypothesise	merchandise	pastoralism	Pythagorism	sinuousness	telephonist
ignobleness	metastasise	pastoralist	queenliness	sizableness	tenableness
illusionism	Micawberism	paternalism	quitchgrass	skeletonise	tenuousness
illusionist	Micawberish	paternalist	racketpress	sketchiness	Teutonicism
immanentism	middleclass	pathologist	radicalness	skilfulness	textureless
immanentist	mindfulness	paunchiness	radiologist	slavishness	theosophist
immenseness	miniaturise	peevishness	raffishness	Slavonicise	thirstiness
immortalise	miniaturist	Pelagianism	rationalise	slenderness	thoughtless
imperialise	minuteglass	pensionless	rationalism	Socinianism	threadiness
imperialism	miserliness	pensiveness	rationalist	sociologist	thriftiness
imperialist	monasticism	perfectness	raucousness	soliloquise	throatiness
IndoChinese	monologuise	personalise	raunchiness	soliloquist	thunderless
inexactness	monologuist	personalism	reactionist	solutionist	tobacconist
infantilism	mooringmast	personalist	reddishness	somatoplasm	tobogganist
inheritress	movableness	pestologist	reestablish	songfulness	trafficless
insipidness	mundaneness	petrologist	regionalise	Soroptimist	treacliness
intenseness	musicalness	pettishness	regionalism	sottishness	tricksiness
intercourse	mutableness	phagocytise	regionalist	soulfulness	triggerfish
interiorise	mycophagist	phagocytose	relatedness	Southernism	trimorphism
internalise	mythologise	phantasiast	relationism	sparingness	tritagonist
intersperse	mythologist	phariseeism	relationist	spatterdash	trivialness
intuitivism	mythopoeist	phenologist	religionise	spectatress	trophoblast
invalidness	nailvarnish	philatelist	religionism	spinsterish	trouserless
irksomeness	nationalise	philologist	religionist	springhouse	tuberculise
irredentism	nationalism	phonologist	remorseless	springiness	tuberculose
irredentist	nationalist	phosphorism	repleteness	squalidness	tunableness
isochronism	naturalness	photofinish	restfulness	squashiness	tunefulness
isomorphism	naughtiness	phycologist	restiveness	squeakiness	typicalness
jealousness	necrologist	phylogynist	retiredness	standardise	unawareness
joylessness	needfulness	phytologist	revisionism	standoffish	unbeknownst
knavishness	negationist	phytotomist	revisionist	starchiness	uncanniness
knowingness	nervousness	pigeonchest	rheotropism	stateliness	uncleanness
landlordism	neurologist	piggishness	rhinologist	staunchless	uncouthness
languidness	neuroticism	pinkishness	ribbongrass	staunchness	underexpose
lastingness	nightmarish	piteousness	riotousness	steeplebush	ungodliness
lawlessness	nitrogenise	pitifulness	roentgenise	stenotypist	unhappiness
learnedness	noisomeness	plagioclase	roguishness	stiltedness	uniformness
lengthiness	nonetheless	playfulness	romanticise	stoicalness	unmanliness
letterpress	nonunionist	plebeianise	romanticism	straightish	unquietness
libertinism	notableness	plebeianism	romanticist	strangeness	unsoundness
limitedness	nothingness	pleinairist	roundedness	streakiness	unusualness
limnologist	notionalist	pleochroism	ruinousness	stringiness	uprightness

uselessness	biddability	domesticate	importunity	oracularity	rifacimenti
vacationist	bisexuality	domesticity	impropriate	orchestrate	rifacimento
vacuousness	bloodguilty	domiciliate	impropriety	originality	rubicundity
vagabondise	bracteolate	ecumenicity	incarcerate	osteoplasty	saddlecloth
vagabondish	breastplate	educability	incardinate	palpability	saleability
vagabondism	campanulate	electricity	incommodity	participate	sansculotte
valiantness	capillarity	electrocute	incongruity	particulate	satiability
variousness	carcinomata	electrolyte	incorporate	passibility	schistosity
vascularise	cardinalate	eligibility	incredulity	peccability	scintillate
vasectomise	carunculate	ellipticity	incriminate	peculiarity	scuttlebutt
velvetiness	cassiterite	encapsulate	incuriosity	pedicellate	selectivity
verboseness	catholicity	equilibrate	individuate	pedunculate	semipalmate
vichyssoise	cellularity	erythrocyte	inedibility	pellucidity	sensibility
viciousness	certificate	ethereality	inferiority	penicillate	sensitivity
victualless	chaetognath	eventuality	infertility	peninsulate	sequestrate
viscountess	chamaephyte	exanthemata	informality	pentathlete	serendipity
viscousness	cheesecloth	exarcerbate	ingurgitate	pentlandite	seventeenth
visibleness	cinquecento	exclusivity	insalubrity	penultimate	sheriffalty
voguishness	circularity	exemplarity	insincerity	perambulate	sillimanite
volubleness	clothesmoth	expansivity	instability	perchlorate	silverplate
voluntarism	cognitivity	expectorate	integrality	peregrinate	silversmith
voluntarist	cognoscente	expostulate	intemperate	periodicity	sinfonietta
waggishness	cognoscenti	expropriate	intercalate	peristalith	singularity
waitinglist	collaborate	exstipulate	intergrowth	perseverate	smithsonite
wakefulness	commemorate	exteriority	interiority	personality	sociability
waspishness	commiserate	exterminate	internality	perspicuity	solvability
watercourse	commonality	externality	interpolate	pertinacity	sovereignty
waywardness	communicate	extrapolate	interrelate	phantasmata	specificity
wealthiness	compaginate	extravagate	interrogate	phosphorate	spectrality
weatherwise	concatenate	extravasate	intrepidity	phosphorite	spermaphyte
weightiness	concentrate	fallibility	intriguante	physicality	spessartite
Weismannism	condylomata	familiarity	investigate	placability	spifflicate
welcomeness	confabulate	farcicality	inviability	pococurante	spiraculate
Wesleyanism	confederate	fasciculate	involucrate	pomegranate	spiritualty
westernmost	conflagrate	feasibility	itacolumite	ponderosity	spirochaete
whitishness	conjugality	fingerplate	kitchenette	pontificate	spongecloth
willingness	considerate	firstfruits	landaulette	portability	spontaneity
winningness	consolidate	fissiparity	laudability	possibility	stellionate
winningpost	conspicuity	flamboyante	launderette	precipitate	sternsheets
winsomeness	constellate	flannelette	lesemajesty	predominate	stockinette
wishfulness	consternate	flexibility	longanimity	prematurity	strangulate
wistfulness	contaminate	folliculate	machicolate	premeditate	strenuosity
witlessness	contemplate	fractionate	macrogamete	prenominate	subordinate
womanliness	contorniate	franklinite	madreporite	prevaricate	suburbanite
worldliness	contrariety	funambulate	magnanimity	probability	suffragette
worldlywise	coplanarity	functionate	maisonnette	prodigality	suffumigate
worshipless	copperplate	gametophyte	mandarinate	proliferate	suitability
xylophonist	coppersmith	gesticulate	mandibulate	prolificity	sumptuosity
zealousness	corbiculate	globularity	marginality	promiscuity	superfluity
zestfulness	corporality	grandiosity	margraviate	propinquity	superiority
zoographist	corroborate	granularity	marquessate	punctuality	superstrata
zoomorphism	cosmopolite	granulocyte	marquisette	pupillarity	syllabicity
abnormality	cottonmouth	greenockite	masculinity	pyrargyrite	taciturnity
abranchiate	credibility	guesstimate	materiality	rateability	tameability
accommodate	criminality	gullibility	matriculate	ratiocinate	tangibility
acculturate	criticality	habiliments	menservants	rationality	temporality
affectivity	crocidolite	hairbreadth	meprobamate	readability	tensibility
agglomerate	crystallite	hallucinate	microgamete	recalculate	tentaculate
agglutinate	culpability	handbreadth	miscegenate	receptivity	testability
aiguillette	decarbonate	haustellate	miscibility	reciprocate	tetrarchate
alexandrite	decemvirate	Hepplewhite	misestimate	reciprocity	thenceforth
amenability	decerebrate	heteroclite	molybdenite	recriminate	thereabouts
amicability	decorticate	historicity	Monophysite	reduplicate	thrombocyte
amphibolite	decrepitate	homogeneity	Monothelite	refrigerate	toxophilite
annabergite	defibrinate	horripilate	monstrosity	regurgitate	trabeculate
anteriority	demonstrate	hospitality	moribundity	reincarnate	transfinite
antigravity	denticulate	houselights	moveability	reintegrate	translocate
apophyllite	deoxygenate	hydrogenate	muscularity	reliability	triangulate
appropriate	depauperate	hypothecate	nationality	religiosity	triumvirate
approximate	desegregate	illiquidity	nationstate	remonstrate	tuberculate
aromaticity	deteriorate	immarginate	necessitate	renegotiate	tuttifrutti
assassinate	determinate	immortality	nephelinite	reorientate	twelvemonth
barbiturate	diaphaneity	impassivity	nettlecloth	resistivity	uncertainty
barleybroth	directivity	impedimenta	nickelplate	resuscitate	undergrowth
bellicosity	directorate	impenetrate	nittygritty	retentivity	unfortunate
beneficiate	discalceate	imperforate	nulliparity	retranslate	unguiculate
bicarbonate	disseminate	impersonate	objectivity	revaccinate	uninucleate
bicorporate	dissimilate	impetuosity	oligochaete	revendicate	unipolarity
bicuspidate	dissimulate	importunate	opportunity	reverberate	urochordate

valleculate	corrigendum	indeciduous	picturesque	tempestuous	cooperative
variability	coterminous	industrious	piperaceous	tendencious	corporative
vascularity	crematorium	injudicious	piscivorous	tendentious	correlative
vendibility	cruciferous	inofficious	planetarium	termitarium	countermove
vermiculate	crucigerous	inquilinous	platearmour	terraqueous	criminative
vermiculite	crustaceous	insectarium	plateresque	terricolous	declarative
versatility	cupriferous	Interlingua	polyandrous	terrigenous	deprecative
verticality	cypripedium	intermedium	polycarpous	tetramerous	descriptive
vesuvianite	cysticercus	interosseus	polyonymous	tetrapodous	desiccative
vibratility	declivitous	interregnum	polyphagous	threecolour	destructive
viceroyalty	definiendum	intravenous	polyphonous	thuriferous	diapositive
vinaigrette	deleterious	irreligious	polyzoarium	Titianesque	disjunctive
vincibility	dentigerous	isochronous	positronium	treacherous	dispositive
volcanicity	desideratum	isomorphous	precautious	trimorphous	distinctive
vulcanicity	diadelphous	lactiferous	precipitous	tripetalous	distractive
washability	dicephalous	lateritious	prestigious	triphibious	duplicative
whereabouts	dichogamous	latifundium	pretentious	triphyllous	elaborative
workability	dichotomous	laurustinus	primiparous	triquetrous	eliminative
abstentious	diplococcus	lentiginous	prognathous	tristichous	elucidative
acarpellous	discontinue	leprosarium	proliferous	tuberculous	enumerative
acclivitous	discotheque	ligamentous	promiscuous	tyrannosaur	enunciative
acrimonious	disgraceful	litterateur	prothallium	ulotrichous	eradicative
adenomatous	distasteful	magazinegun	provocateur	unambiguous	evaporative
adventurous	distressful	magisterium	pruriginous	unconscious	exfoliative
altocumulus	distrustful	magnanimous	punctilious	unrighteous	exhortative
altostratus	duplicitous	marketvalue	quadrennium	urticaceous	exonerative
amentaceous	efficacious	mediastinum	repetitious	urticarious	expatiative
amplexicaul	einsteinium	megatherium	reproachful	ventriculus	expectative
anachronous	emmenagogue	meliphagous	resourceful	ventriloquy	explicative
androgynous	endocardium	melliferous	retinaculum	verdantique	explorative
anfractuous	endometrium	mellifluous	rhizanthous	vertiginous	facultative
antependium	endophagous	membraneous	rhizomatous	vortiginous	galleyslave
antheridium	endothelium	mendelevium	rhomboideus	watercolour	germinative
antimonious	enterovirus	meritorious	rumbustious	xenophilous	gravitative
antirrhinum	epigastrium	micrococcus	Sagittarius	xeranthemum	hyperactive
arbitrageur	epipetalous	mischievous	sanguineous	xerophilous	imaginative
arboraceous	equilibrium	misconstrue	saponaceous	xylocarpous	implicative
arenicolous	erotogenous	mistrustful	saprogenous	xylophagous	inattentive
aspergillum	expeditious	mitrailleur	sarcomatous	abstractive	indigestive
aspergillus	farinaceous	monocarpous	sarcophagus	acquisitive	ineffective
aspersorium	farraginous	monochasium	sauropodous	adumbrative	inexpensive
atrabilious	ferriferous	monoclinous	scalearmour	adversative	inoculative
bacciferous	ferruginous	monophagous	schizanthus	affirmative	inoffensive
bashibazouk	filamentous	monopterous	scoriaceous	affricative	inquisitive
bergamasque	fissiparous	monseigneur	scribacious	aggregative	inscriptive
bicephalous	flirtatious	morbiferous	scriptorium	alleviative	insensitive
billetsdoux	floriferous	mountainous	scrumptious	alternative	insinuative
bimillenium	florilegium	multicolour	sententious	altorelievo	instigative
blasphemous	franctireur	multiparous	septenarius	altorilievo	instinctive
borborygmus	fricandeaux	myelomatous	septiferous	appellative	instructive
brachyurous	frigidarium	necessitous	serpiginous	applicative	integrative
burglarious	frugivorous	nitrogenous	solanaceous	arbitrative	interactive
butyraceous	furunculous	noctivagous	somniculous	argumentive	irradiative
cacophonous	gametangium	nonsequitur	somniferous	associative	irremissive
calcicolous	gemmiferous	nulliparous	spathaceous	assortative	irretentive
calciferous	gemmiparous	odoriferous	sphaeridium	attributive	legislative
calcifugous	gigantesque	oligomerous	spiniferous	Bodhisattva	lubricative
californium	grammalogue	omnifarious	splendorous	calculative	makebelieve
canaliculus	granivorous	ophidiarium	spontaneous	carminative	maladaptive
candelabrum	gypsiferous	opprobrious	sporogenous	circulative	meliorative
carnivorous	halophilous	ornithosaur	sporogonium	circumvolve	microgroove
catadromous	harumscarum	overanxious	stegosaurus	coextensive	misconceive
ceremonious	hemipterous	ozoniferous	straightcut	colligative	meliorative
chainarmour	heptamerous	pandemonium	stramineous	combinative	microgroove
champertous	herbivorous	papyraceous	stylopodium	commutative	misconceive
chartaceous	hesperidium	paramoecium	succedaneum	comparative	nuncupative
Clarencieux	hippocampus	pelargonium	sulphureous	competitive	obstructive
clostridium	homogeneous	penicillium	superfluous	compositive	originative
coconscious	homophonous	pentagynous	suspenseful	compressive	penetrative
columbarium	homopterous	pentamerous	syllabarium	conflictive	perforative
compendious	homosporous	pentandrous	sympetalous	confutative	personative
condominium	hydrogenous	pericardium	symphonious	conjugative	perspective
congenerous	ichthyosaur	pericranium	synchronous	conjunctiva	photoactive
connoisseur	ignominious	perineurium	talentscout	conjunctive	preconceive
conspicuous	illustrious	perithecium	tautologous	connotative	predicative
contentious	impecunious	perspicuous	tautonymous	consecutive	preparative
contrarious	incongruous	pestiferous	teaspoonful	consumptive	prepositive
convolvulus	incredulous	phosphonium	teknonymous	contractive	prerogative
corniferous	incunabulum	phosphorous	temerarious	contrastive	presumptive

procreative	coleorrhiza	taratantara	disharmonic	hylozoistic	osteophytic
progressive	collectanea	toxicomania	dithyrambic	hypercritic	Ostrogothic
prohibitive	collenchyma	thingumabob	dramaturgic	hypermetric	paederastic
propagative	condylomata	abiogenetic	dyslogistic	hypnopompic	Palaearctic
prospective	conjunctiva	acatalectic	econometric	hypoblastic	palaeotypic
protractive	counterplea	achondritic	ectoblastic	hypogastric	palindromic
provocative	cryptomeria	acidophilic	ectogenetic	hypsometric	panhellenic
qualitative	cyclopaedia	Aeneolithic	ectomorphic	ideographic	pantheistic
radioactive	cyclothymia	aeolotropic	ectoplasmic	idiographic	pantothenic
rarefactive	differentia	aerodynamic	ectotrophic	idiomorphic	paragraphic
rebarbative	diverticula	AfroAsiatic	elastomeric	immunologic	parallactic
recognitive	epithalamia	agoraphobic	embryologic	interatomic	paramorphic
reformative	epithelioma	algorithmic	encomiastic	intervallic	paraplectic
reiterative	exanthemata	allomorphic	endocardiac	ionospheric	parenthetic
reprobative	Francomania	amphimictic	endomorphic	isoelectric	pericardiac
restorative	Gallophobia	anacreontic	endoplasmic	ithyphallic	peripatetic
restrictive	gentianella	anaesthetic	endothermic	Jansenistic	perispermic
retaliative	globigerina	anarchistic	endotrophic	jargonistic	peristaltic
retardative	glossolalia	anastomotic	epeirogenic	kymographic	pessimistic
retributive	grandiflora	anemometric	epithalamic	lithophytic	phagedaenic
retroactive	guttapercha	anglomaniac	erotomaniac	logarithmic	philosophic
safetyvalve	haemophilia	anglophobic	esemplastic	logographic	photometric
segregative	Hagiographa	anisotropic	Eucharistic	macrobiotic	photophilic
shirtsleeve	hebephrenia	anomalistic	eudiometric	macrocosmic	photophobic
speculative	hemeralopia	anthracitic	euphemistic	macroscopic	phototactic
stimulative	hemianopsia	antipyretic	feldspathic	magistratic	phototropic
subjunctive	hibernacula	antiSemitic	fetichistic	manneristic	physiologic
substantive	hydromedusa	aphrodisiac	fetishistic	masochistic	planimetric
subsumptive	hydrophobia	apocalyptic	feudalistic	mastodontic	plasmolytic
subtractive	hymenoptera	aponeurotic	formalistic	mechanistic	pleiotropic
suffocative	hyperphagia	apostrophic	gastronomic	mediumistic	pleomorphic
superlative	hyperplasia	archangelic	geomagnetic	melancholic	pluralistic
suppositive	hypnopaedia	Areopagitic	geostrophic	meroblastic	plutocratic
suppressive	hypothermia	atmospheric	geotectonic	mesoblastic	polychromic
suppurative	hypsophobia	audiometric	glauconitic	mesomorphic	polygenetic
swallowdive	impedimenta	autographic	gnotobiotic	metacentric	polyglottic
temperative	Interlingua	autoplastic	goniometric	metagenetic	polygraphic
terminative	ipecacuanha	autotrophic	gramophonic	metallurgic	polymorphic
unassertive	kleptomania	BaltoSlavic	granolithic	metamorphic	polytechnic
unobtrusive	lepidoptera	batholithic	granophyric	metaplastic	porphyritic
unselective	megalomania	bathymetric	gravimetric	metapsychic	postclassic
ventilative	melancholia	bibliopegic	haemophilic	metasomatic	prehistoric
vindicative	memorabilia	bibliopolic	haemostatic	Methodistic	problematic
reachmedown	miscellanea	biocoenotic	haggadistic	microcosmic	procephalic
sparrowhawk	necrophilia	biquadratic	hagioscopic	microlithic	proteolytic
thistledown	negrophobia	blastogenic	harmonistic	micrometric	Proterozoic
unorthodoxy	nyctophobia	cabbalistic	hebephrenic	microphonic	prothoracic
artiodactyl	nymphomania	cacographic	heliometric	microphytic	protophytic
breadthways	orthodontia	calisthenic	heliotropic	microscopic	psychedelic
chrysoberyl	paedophilia	Calvinistic	Hellenistic	mithridatic	psychiatric
leptodactyl	paronomasia	cantharidic	hemimorphic	modernistic	psychogenic
pentadactyl	passacaglia	carbocyclic	hemispheric	monochromic	psychologic
protomartyr	phantasmata	cataclysmic	hermeneutic	monogenetic	pyroclastic
pterodactyl	photophobia	cataplectic	heterotypic	monographic	pyrotechnic
tetradactyl	plectoptera	catechistic	Hippocratic	monomorphic	radiometric
coleorrhiza	pleurodynia	ceroplastic	holoblastic	monozygotic	radiophonic
quickfreeze	prolegomena	chalcedonic	holographic	mythomaniac	rhinoscopic
———————————	prosenchyma	chameleonic	homeopathic	mythopoetic	rhizocarpic
abracadabra	prothalamia	charismatic	homeostatic	narcoleptic	ritualistic
agoraphobia	pseudopodia	chemotactic	homocentric	necromantic	saprobiotic
albuminuria	psychedelia	chronologic	homoeostatic	necrophilic	saprophytic
amenorrhoea	psychodrama	cisatlantic	homogenetic	neologistic	scholiastic
amphisbaena	quinquennia	climacteric	homomorphic	Neoplatonic	scientistic
anaesthesia	receptacula	clinometric	homoplastic	neuropathic	seborrhoeic
anglophobia	rhombohedra	communistic	homothallic	neurotropic	septicaemic
antonomasia	Russophobia	conspecific	Hudibrastic	nomographic	shamanistic
appoggiatura	saintpaulia	coulometric	hydrobromic	nonmetallic	socialistic
assafoetida	sanguinaria	cryptogamic	hydrocyanic	nonspecific	sociometric
bacchanalia	scleroderma	cyclopaedic	hydrometric	nosographic	sociopathic
bibliomania	scyphistoma	cyclothymic	hydropathic	nyctitropic	solipsistic
bibliotheca	selaginella	demographic	hydrophilic	ochlocratic	somatogenic
Bodhisattva	septicaemia	dexiotropic	hydrophobic	oestrogenic	somatologic
bradycardia	sinfonietta	dialogistic	hydrophytic	ontogenetic	somatotonic
brahmaputra	somatotonia	diamagnetic	hydrostatic	oreographic	spherulitic
calceolaria	spermatozoa	diaphoretic	hydrotactic	orthodontic	sphincteric
carcinomata	steatopygia	diastematic	hydrotropic	orthopaedic	Spinozistic
chaulmoogra	subumbrella	diastrophic	hygrometric	orthoscopic	spiritistic
christiania	superstrata	dichromatic	hygrophytic	orthotropic	spirometric
cochinchina	tachycardia	dipsomaniac	hygroscopic	osteopathic	sporophytic

stalactitic	countrified	illhumoured	rightangled	transmitted	adolescence
stalagmitic	countryfied	illmannered	righthanded	trichomonad	adumbrative
staurolitic	crenellated	illtempered	rightminded	tricoloured	adversative
stereotypic	crookbacked	impassioned	ringstraked	truehearted	affirmative
subspecific	crosslegged	intagliated	roughfooted	unaccounted	affranchise
sycophantic	crystalloid	intentioned	roughlegged	uncivilised	affricative
syllogistic	dilapidated	interallied	scarabaeoid	uncluttered	agglomerate
symbolistic	diphtheroid	interbedded	scattergood	uncommitted	agglutinate
sympathetic	disaffected	interdepend	schoolboard	unconcealed	aggregative
symptomatic	disannulled	intermitted	schoolchild	unconcerned	agriculture
synergistic	disgruntled	interplayed	selfassured	unconnected	aiguillette
technologic	dishevelled	intromitted	selfcentred	uncontested	ailurophile
telegrammic	disinclined	introverted	selfcommand	underground	ailurophobe
telegraphic	disinterred	ironhearted	selfcreated	underhanded	alabastrine
telekinetic	distempered	kindhearted	selfdevoted	undermanned	alexandrine
teratogenic	distribuend	largeminded	selfelected	underpinned	alexandrite
teratologic	doubleedged	leapfrogged	selfimposed	undersigned	alleviative
tetracyclic	doublefaced	leatherhead	selfinduced	understated	allocatable
theocentric	downhearted	levelheaded	selfinvited	undeveloped	alphabetise
theodolitic	elasticated	lightfooted	selflimited	undisguised	alternative
theorematic	elephantoid	lighthanded	semiskilled	undisturbed	amaranthine
therapeutic	embryonated	lightheaded	sentinelled	unexploited	amazonstone
thermoduric	emptyhanded	lightminded	seventyfold	unexpressed	ambivalence
thermolytic	emptyheaded	lilylivered	severalfold	unfashioned	Americanise
thixotropic	enlightened	lionhearted	sharpwitted	unfurnished	amethystine
topographic	ensanguined	longsighted	shockheaded	unicoloured	amphetamine
transuranic	eurypteroid	looselimbed	shopsteward	uninhabited	amphibolite
trisyllabic	experienced	loudmouthed	shorthanded	uninhibited	annabergite
tritheistic	extraverted	louverboard	shortwinded	unkennelled	antecedence
troglodytic	extroverted	louvreboard	shoulderpad	unmitigated	antemundane
typographic	fasciaboard	lowspirited	shovelboard	unorganized	anthologise
unrealistic	featherhead	maladjusted	sideslipped	unpossessed	anticathode
Upanishadic	felspathoid	marriagebed	sidestepped	unqualified	anticyclone
verbalistic	fenestrated	mentholated	sleeveboard	unsaturated	antistrophe
voltametric	fingerboard	microsecond	sleuthhound	unsolicited	apomorphine
voodooistic	foraminated	middlesized	smallminded	unvarnished	apophyllite
xylographic	foresighted	millisecond	smoothfaced	unwarranted	apotheosise
zygomorphic	foulmouthed	mockingbird	smorgasbord	wainscotted	appellative
aboveground	freehearted	monkeybread	snowleopard	wapperjawed	applaudable
affectioned	freezedried	monogrammed	soberminded	warmblooded	applicative
alembicated	frenchified	mortarboard	softhearted	warmhearted	appreciable
articulated	fullblooded	mothernaked	softshelled	waspwaisted	appropriate
bandylegged	fullfledged	musclebound	splashboard	watercooled	approximate
bassethound	fullhearted	mustachioed	splayfooted	waterlogged	aquaculture
battlefield	fullmouthed	nearsighted	springboard	weakhearted	aquiculture
beaverboard	gallowsbird	netherworld	starcrossed	wedgeshaped	arbitrative
bergschrund	geniculated	noticeboard	starstudded	wedgetailed	archdiocese
betweenmaid	gingerbread	nurserymaid	stereotyped	welladvised	arglebargle
bewhiskered	goodhearted	openhearted	stiffnecked	wellbeloved	argumentive
birdbrained	goodnatured	openmouthed	stoneground	welldefined	arterialise
blackavised	gravelblind	operculated	straitlaced	wellfounded	arthrospore
blackcoated	haemorrhoid	opinionated	strikebound	wellgroomed	articulable
booklearned	halfblooded	outrivalled	stringboard	wellordered	assassinate
bottlenosed	halfhearted	outstripped	substandard	wellrounded	assimilable
branchiopod	handicapped	overcropped	sugarcoated	whiteheaded	associative
brazenfaced	handknitted	overstepped	superabound	whitherward	assortative
bridgeboard	handpainted	overstuffed	superintend	wholesouled	attemptable
broadleaved	hardhearted	paddleboard	swellheaded	widowerhood	attractable
broadminded	hardmouthed	parallelled	swiftfooted	wrongheaded	attributive
brotherhood	harebrained	parathyroid	switchboard	abolishable	augmentable
butcherbird	harpsichord	paratyphoid	tabernacled	aboutsledge	automatable
cancellated	heartsblood	partitioned	tearstained	abranchiate	bactericide
carburetted	heavyfooted	pastureland	teeterboard	absorptance	balletomane
castellated	heavyhanded	pedestalled	tessellated	abstractive	barbastelle
centreboard	hedgehopped	petticoated	thickheaded	accessorise	barbiturate
chambermaid	helminthoid	photoperiod	thickwitted	accipitrine	barquentine
chickenfeed	heteroploid	picturecard	thimbleweed	acclimatise	barrelhouse
chucklehead	highpitched	playingcard	thinskinned	accommodate	bathyscaphe
cleanlimbed	highpowered	pocketsized	thitherward	accoucheuse	bathysphere
clearheaded	historiated	precedented	threehanded	accountable	Benedictine
closefisted	hummingbird	preoccupied	threelegged	accrescence	beneficence
closehauled	hunchbacked	prestressed	thunderbird	acculturate	beneficiate
coldblooded	hundredfold	prophethood	thunderhead	achromatise	benevolence
coldhearted	hydraheaded	pureblooded	tightfisted	acidifiable	bergamasque
colourblind	hyperboloid	quickwitted	tightlipped	acknowledge	betweentime
columniated	hypocycloid	rattlepated	toffeenosed	acquisitive	bibliophile
complicated	illaffected	readywitted	toothbilled	acquittance	bicarbonate
counterbond	illdisposed	retroflexed	toughminded	acriflavine	bicorporate
countermand	illfavoured	ricochetted	transferred	acupuncture	bicuspidate

billionaire
bitterapple
blackbeetle
blackgrouse
bonbonniere
bondservice
bourgeoisie
boutonniere
bracteolate
brankursine
breadthwise
breastplate
breathalyse
buffalorobe
cabbagerose
cabbagetree
calculative
camaraderie
campanulate
candescence
candidature
cannibalise
capacitance
carabiniere
cardinalate
carminative
carpetsnake
carunculate
cassiterite
catastrophe
catchphrase
catheterise
catholicise
centigramme
centrepiece
certifiable
certificate
chamaephyte
chanterelle
chaperonage
charcuterie
chickenwire
chinoiserie
Chippendale
chloroprene
chrominance
chronoscope
chrysoprase
cinnabarine
circularise
circulative
circumvolve
civilianise
civilisable
clandestine
clothesline
cloudcastle
coalescence
cobblestone
cockaleekie
cockyleekie
coexistence
coextensive
coffeehouse
coffeetable
cognoscente
cognoscible
coincidence
coinsurance
collaborate
collapsible
collectable
collectible
colligative
combinative
combustible
comeuppance
comfortable
commemorate

commendable
commiserate
committable
commonplace
commonsense
communalise
communicate
commutative
compaginate
comparative
compassable
compellable
competitive
complacence
compositive
compossible
compressive
comprisable
computerise
concatenate
concealable
conceivable
concentrate
conceptacle
concordance
concubinage
concurrence
condemnable
condensable
condottiere
conductance
conductible
confabulate
confederate
conferrable
confirmable
confiscable
conflagrate
conflictive
conformable
conformance
confutative
congealable
conjugative
conjunctive
conjuncture
connectable
connectible
connotative
conquerable
consanguine
consecutive
consequence
conservable
considerate
consignable
consistence
consolidate
constellate
consternate
construable
consumptive
containable
contaminate
contemplate
contestable
contingence
continuable
continuance
contorniate
contractile
contractive
contracture
contradance
contrastive
contrivable
contrivance
convenience
conventicle

convergence
conversable
conversance
convertible
convincible
cooperative
copingstone
copperplate
corbiculate
cornerstone
corporative
correctable
correlative
corroborate
cosmopolite
countenance
countermine
countermove
countermure
counterpane
countryside
countrywide
criminative
crocidolite
crystalline
crystallise
crystallite
customhouse
cycloserine
deathrattle
decarbonate
decarbonise
decarburise
decerebrate
declarative
decolletage
decolourise
decorticate
decrepitate
decrepitude
deemphasise
defibrinate
delightsome
deliverable
deliverance
demagnetise
democratise
demonstrate
demountable
denticulate
denumerable
deoxygenate
deoxyribose
depauperate
depauperise
deprecative
depressible
descendable
descendible
describable
descriptive
desegregate
desensitise
desexualise
desiccative
despondence
destructive
deteriorate
determinate
detribalise
developable
diapositive
dichotomise
digitigrade
diningtable
dinnerdance

dinnertable
Diophantine
diplomatise
directorate
disassemble
discalceate
discardable
discernible
discontinue
discordance
discotheque
discussable
discussible
disentangle
disjunctive
disjuncture
dislikeable
disorganise
dispensable
displeasure
dispositive
disquietude
disseminate
disseminule
dissimilate
dissimulate
dissipative
dissociable
dissolvable
dissyllable
distensible
distinctive
distractive
disturbance
divestiture
doctrinaire
domesticate
domiciliate
dresscircle
dualpurpose
duplicative
earthenware
elaborative
elbowgrease
electrocute
electrolyse
electrolyte
electrotype
elephantine
eliminative
elucidative
emblematise
embraceable
emmenagogue
emulsionise
encapsulate
encumbrance
enforceable
enfranchise
enlargeable
entablature
enumerative
enunciative
epidiascope
epinephrine
equilibrate
equivalence
eradicative
erubescence
erythrocyte
escheatable
etherealise
etymologise
eucalyptole
Europeanise
evanescence
evaporative
eventualise
exarcerbate

excrescence
exercisable
exfoliative
exhaustible
exhortative
exonerative
exorbitance
expatiative
expectative
expectorate
expenditure
explainable
explicative
exploitable
explorative
expostulate
expressible
expropriate
exstipulate
extemporise
exteriorise
exterminate
externalise
extractable
extrapolate
extravagate
extravasate
facultative
familiarise
fanfaronade
farthingale
fasciculate
fashionable
featheredge
fermentable
fingerplate
fissionable
flamboyance
flamboyante
flannelette
flavoursome
flocculence
florescence
fluoroscope
folliculate
forbearance
forbiddance
foreclosure
foreseeable
forevermore
forfeitable
forgettable
formularise
fortifiable
fractionate
fractionise
Francophile
Francophobe
francophone
franklinite
frankpledge
fraudulence
funambulate
functionate
furtherance
furthermore
furthersome
galleyslave
gallowstree
gametophyte
gartersnake
gastroscope
geanticline
gendarmerie
genealogise
geosyncline
germinative
gesticulate
gigantesque

gourmandise
grammalogue
granulocyte
gravitative
greenockite
guesstimate
guttersnipe
gutturalise
haematocele
haemorrhage
halfmeasure
hallucinate
handgrenade
harvesthome
haustellate
hearthstone
heliochrome
helleborine
Hepplewhite
hereditable
herringbone
heteroclite
Hispanicise
historicise
hollandaise
honeysuckle
hornswoggle
horripilate
hospitalise
husbandlike
hyacinthine
hydrogenate
hydrosphere
hyoscyamine
hyperactive
hyperbolise
hypercharge
hypersthene
hypostatise
hypothecate
hypothenuse
hypothesise
illimitable
illuminable
illuminance
imaginative
immarginate
immedicable
immitigable
immortalise
impeachable
impenetrate
impenitence
imperforate
imperialise
impermeable
impersonate
imperviable
implausible
implicative
importunate
impregnable
impressible
impropriate
impuissance
inadaptable
inadvisable
inalienable
inalterable
inappetence
inattentive
incarcerate
incardinate
incarnadine
incertitude
incoercible
incoherence
incorporate
increasable

```
incriminate  irremissive  milliampere  perambulate  progressive  responsible
incurvature  irremovable  millionaire  perceivable  prohibitive  restorative
indefinable  irreparable  miniaturise  perceptible  proliferate  restrictive
indigestive  irresoluble  misalliance  perchlorate  promptitude  restructure
individuate  irretentive  misanthrope  percipience  propagative  resuscitate
indivisible  irreverence  miscarriage  peregrinate  propitiable  retaliative
IndoChinese  irrevocable  miscegenate  perfectible  proselytise  retardative
indomitable  itacolumite  misconceive  perforative  prospective  retraceable
indubitable  justiciable  misconstrue  performable  protractile  retractable
ineffective  justifiable  misericorde  performance  protractive  retranslate
ineloquence  kilocalorie  misestimate  permissible  protrudable  retributive
ineluctable  kinetoscope  misfeasance  perpetuance  protrusible  retrievable
inequitable  kitchenette  misguidance  perseverate  provenience  retroactive
inescapable  kitchenware  mismarriage  persistence  provocative  revaccinate
inestimable  knucklebone  mollycoddle  personalise  Prussianise  revendicate
inexcusable  lactescence  molybdenite  personative  publishable  reverberate
inexistence  landaulette  monkeyshine  perspective  pulchritude  rodenticide
inexpensive  landgravine  monoculture  persuadable  pumicestone  rodomontade
infanticide  launderette  monologuise  persuasible  purchasable  roentgenise
inflammable  legionnaire  Monophysite  perturbable  purpresture  romanticise
informative  legislative  Monothelite  phagocytise  putrescence  rotogravure
infrangible  legislature  morrisdance  phagocytose  putrescible  rottenstone
infrequence  liberticide  munificence  philhellene  pyrargyrite  saddlehorse
ingratitude  libertinage  musculature  phosphorate  qualifiable  safetyvalve
ingurgitate  lickspittle  muskthistle  phosphorite  qualitative  salvageable
inhabitable  liquefiable  mycorrhizae  photoactive  quarrelsome  sansculotte
inheritable  liquescence  mythologise  photosphere  quartertone  satisfiable
inheritance  lithosphere  naphthalene  phylloclade  quickchange  schismatise
innavigable  lithotomise  nationalise  picturesque  quickfreeze  schistosome
innumerable  loosestrife  nationstate  pilocarpine  quinquereme  schoolhouse
inoculative  lowpressure  necessitate  pipistrelle  radioactive  schottische
inoffensive  lubricative  nephelinite  pitchblende  rarefactive  scintillate
inoperative  lycanthrope  nickelplate  pivotbridge  ratatouille  scopolamine
inopportune  machicolate  nightingale  plagioclase  ratiocinate  segregative
inquisitive  machinemade  nigrescence  plagiostome  rationalise  seigniorage
inscribable  macrogamete  nitrogenise  planisphere  rattlesnake  seismoscope
inscriptive  madreporite  nonchalance  plantigrade  reassurance  selfculture
inscrutable  maintenance  nonfeasance  plateresque  rebarbative  selfdefence
insecticide  maisonnette  nonviolence  platinotype  recalculate  selffertile
insectifuge  makebelieve  nonvolatile  platyrrhine  reciprocate  selfservice
insectivore  maladaptive  nuncupative  pleasurable  reclaimable  selfsterile
insensitive  maleficence  obstructive  plebeianise  recognitive  selftorture
inseparable  malevolence  officialese  Pleistocene  reconnoitre  semiellipse
insinuative  malfeasance  oligochaete  ploughshare  recoverable  semipalmate
insouciance  malpractice  ommatophore  pocketknife  recriminate  sequestrate
instigative  mandarinate  omnipotence  pococurante  rectifiable  sericulture
instinctive  mandibulate  omniscience  pointdevice  redetermine  serviceable
instructive  manipulable  opalescence  polarisable  redoubtable  serviceline
insuperable  mantelpiece  orchestrate  polariscope  reduplicate  shacklebone
integrative  manufacture  organisable  polypeptide  reemergence  sheathknife
intemperate  marcescence  orientalise  polystyrene  reflectance  shirtsleeve
interactive  marcescible  originative  pomegranate  reformative  shortchange
intercalate  marginalise  orthocentre  pomiculture  refrangible  signifiable
interchange  margraviate  outdistance  pontificate  refrigerate  sillimanite
intercourse  marketplace  overbalance  porterhouse  regenerable  silverplate
interiorise  marketvalue  overindulge  portraiture  regionalise  singularise
intermeddle  marlinspike  overmeasure  practicable  registrable  sinistrorse
intermingle  marquessate  overproduce  preaudience  regrettable  skeletonise
internalise  marqueterie  ozonosphere  precipitate  regurgitate  Slavonicise
internecine  marquisette  packingcase  preconceive  reincarnate  slickenside
interpolate  masculinise  palmcabbage  predicative  reinsurance  slotmachine
interrelate  massproduce  palsgravine  predictable  reintegrate  smithsonite
interrogate  masterpiece  papiermache  predominate  reintroduce  snickersnee
intersperse  materialise  paraldehyde  preeminence  reiterative  soldierlike
intertangle  matriculate  parametrise  premeditate  rejuvenesce  soliloquise
interviewee  maxillipede  paraselenae  prenominate  religionise  specifiable
intolerable  medicinable  participate  preparative  remembrance  speculative
intolerance  melanophore  particulate  prepositive  remonstrate  spermaphyte
intractable  meliorative  Passiontide  prerogative  renaissance  spessartite
intriguante  memorialise  pedicellate  presentable  renegotiate  spifflicate
investigate  meningocele  pedunculate  preservable  reorientate  spindletree
investiture  mentionable  penetrative  presumptive  replaceable  spiraculate
involucrate  meprobamate  penicillate  prevaricate  repleviable  spirituelle
iridescence  merchandise  peninsulate  preventable  repressible  spirochaete
irradiative  mesalliance  pensionable  preventible  reprobative  spreadeagle
irrecusable  metastasise  pentathlete  procreative  reprogramme  springhouse
irreducible  methylamine  pentazocine  prodigalise  resemblance  squarsonage
irrefutable  microgamete  pentlandite  profiterole  respectable  stagemanage
irrelevance  microgroove  penultimate  progeniture  respondence  stampoffice
```

standardise	tragedienne	viticulture	fireraising	pigsticking	winetasting
stellionate	transalpine	vitrescence	firewalking	platforming	wirenetting
stereoscope	transfigure	vitrifiable	flagwagging	politicking	wirepulling
stethoscope	transfinite	vociferance	flannelling	quarrelling	wiretapping
stimulative	translocate	warrantable	forerunning	quickfiring	woodcarving
stirrupbone	transmarine	waterbottle	forewarning	racemeeting	woodcutting
stockinette	transpadane	watercourse	forthcoming	reawakening	worshipping
stomachache	transpierce	weatherwise	freebooting	reedbunting	allelomorph
stormcentre	Trappistine	weighbridge	fulminating	ribvaulting	AngloFrench
strangulate	traversable	Wensleydale	glassmaking	roadholding	barleybroth
stretchable	treasonable	whiffletree	goldbeating	ropedancing	cardiograph
stringpiece	trestletree	whippletree	golddigging	ropewalking	cesarevitch
stroboscope	triangulate	Whitsuntide	goodlooking	safekeeping	cesarewitch
subjunctive	trisyllable	wolfwhistle	hairraising	sandbagging	chaetognath
submergence	triumvirate	workmanlike	hairstyling	scaffolding	chafingdish
submersible	troposphere	worldlywise	halfbinding	scuppernong	chainstitch
submissible	troublesome	worshipable	halflanding	selfclosing	cheesecloth
submultiple	tryingplane	bulletproof	handfasting	selfcocking	choreograph
subordinate	trypanosome	greaseproof	handselling	selfdenying	chronograph
subsequence	tryptophane	Kulturkampf	handwriting	selffeeding	clairschach
subsistence	tuberculate	mansardroof	hardhitting	selffeeling	clothesmoth
substantive	tuberculise	mantelshelf	hardworking	selfloading	coppersmith
subsumptive	tuberculose	neckerchief	headhunting	selflocking	coronagraph
subtractive	turgescence	ploughstaff	heartstring	selfpitying	coronograph
suburbanise	tyrannicide	quaternloaf	highranking	selfraising	cottonmouth
suburbanite	ultramarine	selfreproof	illbreeding	selfsealing	crossstitch
suffocative	unalterable	showerproof	impanelling	selfseeking	cryptograph
suffragette	unassertive	shrinkproof	imperilling	selfserving	distinguish
suffumigate	unavailable	advertising	ingathering	selfwinding	doubleDutch
suggestible	unbreakable	antifouling	initialling	shellacking	hairbreadth
summerhouse	uncatchable	apparelling	interesting	shoplifting	handbreadth
supercharge	unclimbable	armtwisting	interfacing	shortcoming	headborough
superimpose	uncountable	babysitting	interlining	shoulderbag	heterotroph
superinduce	uncrushable	ballbearing	knownothing	showjumping	homestretch
superlative	undercharge	bearbaiting	lancinating	shrivelling	horseradish
superscribe	underexpose	bellringing	landholding	sightseeing	intergrowth
supersedure	undesirable	bestselling	latchstring	sleepingbag	kinetograph
supersubtle	unendurable	billposting	leavetaking	snowbunting	lophobranch
supportable	unflappable	bivouacking	linedrawing	soapboiling	Micawberish
suppositive	unfortunate	bondwashing	linefishing	spacesaving	nailvarnish
suppressive	ungetatable	bookbinding	longplaying	stencilling	nettlecloth
suppurative	unguiculate	bookkeeping	manumitting	stocktaking	nightmarish
surpassable	unigeniture	bookselling	marshalling	talebearing	novelettish
susceptible	uninucleate	bootlegging	matchmaking	tankfarming	oldwomanish
suspensible	unmatchable	bricklaying	merrymaking	tantalising	overstretch
sustainable	unmemorable	bullbaiting	mindbending	tentpegging	peristalith
swallowable	unobtrusive	calculating	mindblowing	thingumajig	photofinish
swallowdive	unpalatable	campmeeting	mindreading	timeserving	pseudograph
swallowhole	unprintable	caravanning	misspelling	timesharing	pseudomorph
swingletree	unselective	challenging	moneymaking	tobogganing	psychograph
switchblade	unshockable	channelling	monophthong	topdressing	pullthrough
synchronise	unspeakable	chitterling	mudslinging	touchtyping	reestablish
systematise	unstoppable	christening	namecalling	trafficking	saddlecloth
tagliatelle	unteachable	clodhopping	noisemaking	trammelling	satinstitch
tapemachine	unthinkable	complotting	nonmatching	typecasting	ScotchIrish
tapemeasure	untouchable	considering	nonplussing	typesetting	seismograph
tarnishable	unutterable	controlling	oilpainting	unappealing	seventeenth
tarradiddle	unwholesome	cornhusking	orangoutang	unbelieving	shadowgraph
tautologise	urochordate	counselling	outbreeding	unbeseeming	silversmith
telepathise	vagabondage	disobliging	outbuilding	undertaking	sonofabitch
temperature	vagabondise	disparaging	outcropping	undeserving	spatterdash
temperature	valleculate	disquieting	outfighting	unfaltering	spinsterish
tentaculate	vaporisable	domineering	outstanding	unflinching	spongecloth
terminative	varnishtree	dressmaking	overbearing	unforgiving	standoffish
tetrarchate	varsovienne	dropforging	overbidding	unpromising	steeplebush
thalidomide	vascularise	earpiercing	overlapping	unreasoning	stereograph
thaumatrope	vasectomise	embowelling	overmanning	unrelenting	stevengraph
thaumaturge	ventilative	empanelling	overrunning	straightish	suckingfish
theobromine	venturesome	engineering	oversailing	unremitting	surgeonfish
theretofore	verdantique	enthralling	oversetting	unshrinking	symposiarch
thermophile	vermiculate	epochmaking	overtopping	victualling	synchromesh
thermoscope	vermiculite	everlasting	overweening	wainscoting	thenceforth
thrombocyte	vesuvianite	eyecatching	painkilling	watchmaking	thermograph
Titianesque	vichyssoise	facelifting	painstaking	waterskiing	throatlatch
tolbutamide	vicissitude	factfinding	papermaking	wellmeaning	triggerfish
townspeople	vinaigrette	farreaching	patronising	wellwishing	twelvemonth
toxophilite	vindicative	fascinating	pawnbroking	wildcatting	undergrowth
trabeculate	viniculture	filmsetting	peacemaking	wildfowling	vagabondish
tracasserie			penetrating	winegrowing	

bersaglieri	anecdotical	distrustful	ipsilateral	phytosterol	sphincteral
carabinieri	antenuptial	draggletail	isometrical	pietistical	spiritlevel
cognoscenti	anthropical	dualcontrol	Jacobinical	piscatorial	spirochetal
condottieri	antitypical	duniewassal	Jacobitical	planetoidal	splenetical
douroucouli	apartmental	educational	judgmatical	polycrystal	statistical
Hindoostani	apostolical	egotistical	kinematical	polyglottal	strategical
hippopotami	artiodactyl	ellipsoidal	labiodental	pomological	subclinical
melanochroi	ascensional	endocardial	latitudinal	posological	subcortical
rifacimenti	assessorial	endothelial	leptodactyl	postglacial	subcritical
schwarmerei	atheistical	endothermal	leviratical	postnuptial	subcultural
Stradivarii	attitudinal	enigmatical	loculicidal	pragmatical	sublittoral
tagliatelli	attritional	equilateral	magisterial	prayerwheel	submarginal
tuttifrutti	audiovisual	equinoctial	maintopsail	prefatorial	subregional
xanthochroi	autarchical	ethological	matriarchal	prefectural	substantial
apparatchik	axiological	evangelical	matrilineal	prejudicial	subterminal
bashibazouk	behavioural	evolutional	matrimonial	preprandial	subtropical
biofeedback	biochemical	exceptional	mediastinal	presbyteral	summational
breechblock	biometrical	excremental	mediatorial	previsional	superficial
breezeblock	biophysical	executorial	medicolegal	primigenial	supernormal
candlestick	bloodvessel	existential	metalloidal	probational	surrebuttal
chockablock	boardschool	exoskeletal	meteoroidal	promotional	suspenseful
countermark	bookinghall	expansional	metonymical	prophetical	swallowtail
countersink	Brahmanical	exponential	micrococcal	protectoral	sybaritical
countersunk	Brahminical	extensional	ministerial	prothallial	symmetrical
counterwork	breastwheel	fantastical	mistrustful	provisional	synagogical
crackerjack	bristletail	fingerstall	monarchical	pterodactyl	synonymical
diamondback	calendrical	firmamental	monasterial	purgatorial	syntactical
doublecheck	caricatural	footpoundal	monochasial	puritanical	synthetical
doublequick	casuistical	foretopsail	monolingual	pyramidical	taxonomical
doublespeak	catechismal	formational	monological	quadratical	teaspoonful
doublethink	categorical	fratricidal	multinomial	quadrennial	terrestrial
fiddlestick	centrifugal	fundamental	multiracial	quadrupedal	territorial
halterbreak	centripetal	gafftopsail	mycological	quaestorial	testimonial
journeywork	chimaerical	gentilitial	mycorrhizal	quincuncial	tetradactyl
jumpingjack	chlorophyll	geochemical	nasofrontal	reappraisal	tetrahedral
kitchensink	cholesterol	geometrical	Neanderthal	rearadmiral	theological
latticework	chromosomal	geophysical	Neotropical	recessional	theoretical
leatherback	chrysoberyl	Germanophil	nominatival	recommittal	therewithal
leatherneck	cicatricial	gestatorial	nomological	rectilineal	thrasonical
picturebook	cockleshell	gradational	nonsensical	redactional	thunderpeal
plasterwork	coessential	grammatical	nosological	referential	toploftical
powderflask	cognitional	hedgeschool	nutrimental	reportorial	topological
quarterback	collisional	herringgull	nutritional	reproachful	traditional
quarterdeck	commissural	hexadecimal	obsessional	residential	transmittal
realpolitik	conditional	homiletical	obstetrical	resourceful	transsexual
scratchwork	conjectural	homological	octachordal	reverential	transversal
servicebook	consonantal	horological	oecological	reversional	trapezoidal
shuttlecock	conterminal	hypoglossal	oecumenical	rhapsodical	tribunicial
silverstick	continental	hypophyseal	oenological	rheological	tribunitial
singlestick	contractual	hypophysial	oesophageal	rickettsial	trimestrial
singletrack	cookgeneral	icosahedral	oncological	rockcrystal	trundletail
skatingrink	coralloidal	ideological	ontological	ruridecanal	turtleshell
snatchblock	counterfoil	implemental	operational	sacramental	typological
sparrowhawk	countervail	impolitical	oreological	sacrificial	uncanonical
stagestruck	coxcombical	impractical	orthoepical	saltatorial	uncongenial
statutebook	cupronickel	incorporeal	pachydermal	salvational	unemotional
steeplejack	curvilineal	incremental	paddlewheel	scissorbill	unequivocal
stickleback	cylindrical	ineffectual	panegyrical	scissortail	unessential
stringybark	cytological	inessential	paradisical	sclerophyll	unipersonal
trelliswork	deferential	inferential	paradoxical	scriptorial	unpolitical
trestlework	demagogical	infinitival	paramedical	secretarial	valuational
vestryclerk	dendritical	inflexional	parasitical	seigneurial	variational
weathercock	detrimental	influential	parheliacal	seigniorial	vespertinal
yacketyyak	diacritical	insessorial	participial	selfcontrol	vibrational
abiological	dialectical	instinctual	patriarchal	semeiotical	viceadmiral
accessorial	diametrical	intensional	patrilineal	semidiurnal	virological
accusatival	dictatorial	intentional	patrimonial	sempiternal	wherewithal
aerological	dimensional	intercansal	patristical	sensational	Whitechapel
aeronomical	diphtherial	intercostal	pedagogical	sentimental	xanthophyll
aesthetical	diphthongal	intercrural	pedological	septifragal	absenteeism
affectional	diphycercal	interdental	penitential	serological	academicism
agonistical	directional	interfacial	penological	sexagesimal	achromatism
agrological	directorial	interracial	pentadactyl	sexological	acinaciform
agronomical	disapproval	interseptal	Pentecostal	sinological	adiaphorism
ahistorical	disciplinal	intersexual	pericardial	situational	adoptianism
algological	disenthrall	interspinal	pericranial	sophistical	adoptionism
allegorical	disgraceful	intertribal	periodontal	sparrowbill	adventurism
altitudinal	distasteful	intuitional	peristomial	spasmodical	agnosticism
amplexicaul	distressful	inventorial	pharisaical	spermicidal	agrarianism

Americanism	hierarchism	progressism	allAmerican	commutation	desiccation
anachronism	highbrowism	proselytism	alleviation	competition	designation
Anglicanism	Hispanicism	prothallium	altercation	compilation	desperation
antependium	historicism	Prussianism	alternation	composition	destination
antheridium	histrionism	Pythagorism	ambiversion	compotation	destitution
antirrhinum	hooliganism	quadrennium	anacoluthon	compression	destruction
archdukedom	illusionism	rationalism	AngloIndian	compunction	detestation
Arminianism	immanentism	regionalism	AngloNorman	computation	deuteration
aspergillum	imperialism	relationism	anthocyanin	condonation	devaluation
aspersorium	incunabulum	religionism	antiJacobin	confliction	devastation
astigmatism	infantilism	retinaculum	antineutron	confutation	diatessaron
athleticism	insectarium	revisionism	antiquarian	congelation	dicotyledon
autoerotism	intermedium	rheotropism	antiquation	congressman	diffraction
bacilliform	interregnum	romanticism	antivitamin	conjugation	dinnerwagon
bimetallism	intuitivism	Sadduceeism	appellation	conjunction	dinosaurian
bimillenium	irredentism	scalariform	application	conjuration	discerption
bloodstream	isochronism	scalpriform	approbation	connotation	disfunction
bohemianism	isogeotherm	scriptorium	arbitration	consecution	disillusion
Bonapartism	isomorphism	sittingroom	Archimedean	consolation	disjunction
bristleworm	lamelliform	smokingroom	assemblyman	consumption	dislocation
Byzantinism	landingbeam	Socinianism	assentation	contraction	disposition
cabbagepalm	landlordism	somatoplasm	assignation	contraption	disputation
cabbageworm	latifundism	Southernism	association	conurbation	dissipation
californium	leprosarium	spectrogram	atomisation	convocation	dissolution
candelabrum	libertinism	sphaeridium	attenuation	convolution	distinction
cannibalism	Lutheranism	sphygmogram	attestation	cooperation	distraction
Catholicism	magisterium	sporogonium	attribution	cornucopian	divulgation
cavalierism	malapropism	steganogram	Augustinian	corporation	downtrodden
Christendom	Manichaeism	stylopodium	Aurignacian	correlation	draughtsman
clericalism	marconigram	succedaneum	awestricken	corrugation	dropcurtain
clostridium	materialism	syllabarium	barrelorgan	coruscation	duplication
colonialism	McCarthyism	synchronism	beechmarten	cosmetician	dysfunction
columbarium	mediastinum	syndicalism	Belorussian	counterplan	edification
communalism	medievalism	systematism	benediction	countersign	egalitarian
condominium	megatherium	tautologism	benefaction	counterturn	ejaculation
consumerism	mendelevium	tautomerism	bifurcation	craftswoman	elaboration
corporatism	Micawberism	teetotalism	bipartition	crenulation	electrician
corrigendum	monasticism	teleologism	bombilation	crepitation	elicitation
creationism	monochasium	termitarium	bombination	crestfallen	elimination
crematorium	morningroom	Teutonicism	Bonapartean	crimination	Elizabethan
cypripedium	nationalism	trapeziform	botheration	crocodilian	elucidation
dactylogram	neuroticism	trimorphism	bottlegreen	crossbowman	elutriation
definiendum	objectivism	vagabondism	brachiation	crucifixion	embarkation
demagoguism	officialdom	vasculiform	businessman	ctenophoran	embrocation
democratism	officialism	voluntarism	byeelection	culmination	enchiridion
desideratum	ophidiarium	waitingroom	calcination	cultivation	encystation
determinism	opportunism	Weismannism	calculation	cupellation	endoskelton
diachronism	orientalism	Wesleyanism	calibration	cybernation	enneahedron
didacticism	oscillogram	xeranthemum	calyptrogen	debarkation	enucleation
disaccustom	ostracoderm	zoomorphism	captivation	decantation	enumeration
divisionism	pandemonium	Abbevillian	carbonation	declamation	enunciation
drawingroom	parallelism	abecedarian	carburetion	declaration	eradication
eclecticism	paramoecium	abomination	Carolingian	declination	euchologion
ecumenicism	passeriform	abstraction	carrageenan	decollation	evagination
einsteinium	pastoralism	abstriction	carrageenin	decussation	evaporation
endocardium	patelliform	academician	castigation	defalcation	examination
endometrium	paternalism	acceptation	catercousin	defloration	exclamation
endothelium	Pelagianism	acclamation	celebration	defoliation	excoriation
epigastrium	pelargonium	acclimation	cementation	deformation	exculpation
equilibrium	penicillium	acetylation	centenarian	deglutition	exfoliation
Erastianism	pericardium	acidulation	cerebration	degradation	exhortation
esotericism	pericranium	acoustician	chamberlain	degustation	exoneration
eudaemonism	perineurium	acquisition	chiropteran	dehydration	exoskeleton
exotericism	perithecium	actinomycin	chrysarobin	deification	expatiation
externalism	personalism	acumination	churchwoman	delectation	expectation
favouritism	phariseeism	adumbration	circulation	delineation	explanation
florilegium	phosphonium	aerostation	cleanshaven	deliveryman	explication
frigidarium	phosphorism	Aesculapian	coadunation	demarcation	exploration
Gallicanism	phraseogram	aestivation	coagulation	demarkation	exportation
gametangium	planetarium	affectation	coarctation	denigration	expurgation
gangsterism	plebeianism	affiliation	coeducation	deoxidation	exsiccation
gourmandism	pleochroism	affirmation	coextension	deportation	extenuation
gutturalism	pointillism	affrication	colligation	depravation	extirpation
harumscarum	polyzoarium	aggravation	collimation	deprecation	extradition
Hegelianism	positronium	aggregation	collocation	depredation	extrication
hermeticism	primitivism	aircraftman	colouration	deprivation	fabrication
hesperidium	probabilism	Albigensian	combination	dereliction	Falstaffian
heteroecism	prochronism	alcyonarian	commination	description	fascination
Hibernicism	prognathism	Alexandrian	comminution	desecration	fecundation

fimbriation	infeudation	observation	radiolarian	subtraction	violoncello
FinnoUgrian	infirmarian	obstruction	rapscallion	suffixation	admiralship
flagcaptain	information	obtestation	rarefaction	suffocation	apostleship
fluctuation	innervation	occultation	Rastafarian	supervision	bushmanship
fluorescein	innutrition	officiation	rattlebrain	supposition	captainship
fomentation	inoculation	oppugnation	reachmedown	suppression	citizenship
foreshorten	inquisition	organscreen	realisation	suppuration	clothesprop
forestation	inscription	orientation	reanimation	surrogation	colonelship
formication	insinuation	origination	reapportion	suspiration	comradeship
formulation	inspiration	orthopteran	reassertion	susurration	curatorship
fornication	instigation	oscillation	recantation	synchrotron	denizenship
Frenchwoman	institution	ostentation	reclamation	syncopation	dipterocarp
frostbitten	instruction	overwritten	recognition	syndication	emperorship
fructuation	integration	oviposition	recondition	tabefaction	generalship
frustration	interaction	oxygenation	redirection	termination	heroworship
fulguration	interfusion	oxyhydrogen	reeducation	tetrahedron	lectureship
fulmination	invultation	ozonisation	reformation	thistledown	lifemanship
fusillation	irradiation	Palestinian	reification	thoroughpin	managership
fustigation	irretention	palpitation	reinsertion	timebargain	marshalship
gegenschein	itineration	Panglossian	reiteration	titillation	messiahship
gemmulation	jactitation	parturition	reluctation	tittivation	monitorship
gentlewoman	Judaisation	passivation	repartition	tourbillion	mountaintop
genuflexion	jumpingbean	pectination	replication	transaction	oarsmanship
germination	labefaction	penetration	reprobation	transection	overdevelop
gibberellin	laciniation	pentahedron	repudiation	transfixion	partnership
glomeration	lacrimation	peptisation	requisition	transfusion	patternshop
godchildren	lacrymation	percolation	reservation	translation	praetorship
godforsaken	laicisation	perennation	resignation	trencherman	premiership
GraecoRoman	lamellicorn	perforation	respiration	trepanation	primateship
granulation	lamentation	permutation	restitution	trepidation	proctorship
gratulation	Lancastrian	persecution	restoration	tribulation	prophetship
gravitation	lancination	personation	restriction	Trinitarian	provostship
gurgitation	legerdemain	philologian	retaliation	trituration	rubberstamp
habituation	legislation	phonetician	retardation	tumefaction	scholarship
haemocyanin	Leibnitzian	phycocyanin	retribution	turbination	selfworship
haemoglobin	libertarian	Pickwickian	retroaction	typewritten	senatorship
Hamiltonian	liquidation	plainspoken	revaluation	ultramodern	sheriffship
handwritten	lixiviation	podophyllin	rhetorician	unchristian	showmanship
heartbroken	lubrication	policewoman	Rosicrucian	unification	soldiership
Heracleidan	lucubration	pollination	rubefaction	utilisation	speakership
hibernation	luxuriation	ponderation	rubrication	utilitarian	sponsorship
highfalutin	machination	postexilian	rustication	vaccination	stewardship
holothurian	madrigalian	postulation	Sabbatarian	vacillation	stirruppump
homoiousian	magazinegun	Precambrian	sacculation	vacuolation	stomachpump
humiliation	magdalenian	predication	saturnalian	valediction	studentship
hydrocarbon	Maglemosian	preelection	Scotchwoman	variegation	teachership
hyperborean	malediction	preignition	segregation	vasopressin	thunderclap
hyphenation	malefaction	prelibation	selfopinion	venesection	tribuneship
hypolimnion	malfunction	premonition	septentrion	venisection	trusteeship
hypotension	malposition	preparation	serrulation	ventilation	viceroyship
icosahedron	manducation	preposition	sertularian	vermination	whistlestop
idolisation	manumission	presumption	Shaksperean	vindication	workmanship
imagination	mastication	preterhuman	Shaksperian	vivisection	abbreviator
imbrication	mechanician	preterition	shortspoken	washerwoman	accelerator
immigration	melioration	procreation	sightscreen	weatherworn	accumulator
imparkation	mensuration	procrustean	smokescreen	wintergreen	actinometer
impartation	merchantman	procuration	sockdologen	Yugoslavian	adjudicator
impetration	Merovingian	profanation	solifluxion	zoantharian	adminicular
implication	methylation	progestogen	solmisation	zooplankton	adulterator
importation	metrication	progression	soupkitchen	Zoroastrian	aerographer
imprecation	Micronesian	prohibition	speculation	accelerando	afterburner
imprecision	micturition	proletarian	spokeswoman	afficionado	alkalimeter
inanimation	millenarian	propagation	sportswoman	altorelievo	ameliorator
inattention	misbegotten	proposition	sporulation	altorilievo	animalcular
incantation	miscreation	prorogation	springclean	amontillado	annihilator
incarnation	molestation	prosecution	stagflation	archipelago	annunciator
inclination	murmuration	prostration	stimulation	braggadocio	antechamber
inculcation	musculation	protraction	stipulation	chiaroscuro	anticipator
inculpation	necessarian	provocation	stonemarten	cinquecento	appreciator
incurvation	needlewoman	publication	stoolpigeon	contrabasso	arbitrageur
indentation	negotiation	pullulation	stylisation	decrescendo	articulator
indigestion	nictitation	punctuation	subarration	internuncio	asphyxiator
indignation	nonpartisan	pustulation	subaudition	playerpiano	assimilator
indirection	nullifidian	Pythagorean	subdivision	prestissimo	auxanometer
IndoIranian	nuncupation	quadrillion	subjugation	punchinello	azotobacter
inebriation	obfuscation	quickfrozen	sublimation	rallentando	backbencher
infantryman	objurgation	quintillion	subornation	rifacimento	barnstormer
infatuation	obscuration	Rabelaisian	subrogation	saltimbanco	basketchair
infestation	obsecration	radiocarbon	subsumption	sextodecimo	beachcomber

bellfounder	deactivator	glasscutter	matrilinear	purificator	stonewaller
bellheather	decelerator	globeflower	metalworker	pussyfooter	storekeeper
bibliolater	deerstalker	goddaughter	mineraliser	quacksalver	storyteller
biedermeier	deflagrator	gonfalonier	minesweeper	quicksilver	straphanger
billsticker	demographer	gormandiser	minnesinger	quilldriver	stridulator
birdfancier	denominator	gradiometer	misremember	rangefinder	subscapular
birdwatcher	denunciator	grandfather	mitrailleur	recommender	superheater
blackbirder	depopulator	grandmother	moisturiser	rectangular	supertanker
blackmailer	depreciator	grangeriser	moneylender	rectilinear	surrebutter
blockbuster	desalinator	grasshopper	moneyspider	reedwarbler	swimbladder
bloodsucker	dilapidator	gravedigger	monographer	regenerator	swordbearer
bodybuilder	disbeliever	greengrocer	mononuclear	rejuvenator	sympathiser
boilermaker	discipliner	greenkeeper	monopoliser	remunerator	synthesiser
bowdleriser	disencumber	groundwater	monseigneur	replenisher	tacheometer
brainteaser	dishonourer	haberdasher	moonlighter	representer	teenybopper
breadwinner	disinfector	hairdresser	mosstrooper	retinacular	teetotaller
broadcaster	disremember	hairtrigger	motivepower	reversioner	telegrapher
bullfighter	dissertator	handicapper	mountaineer	righthander	teleprinter
bullterrier	distributor	heldentenor	multangular	rightwinger	telegrapher
burgomaster	doorknocker	hereinafter	multicolour	safebreaker	thanksgiver
bushwhacker	doubleender	heteropolar	multilinear	safecracker	theatregoer
calorimeter	doxographer	highstepper	namedropper	salinometer	thermometer
calumniator	drillmaster	homesteader	necromancer	sandskipper	threadpaper
canalicular	dumbfounder	homogeniser	neutraliser	scalearmour	threecolour
candlepower	dynamometer	honeybadger	nightporter	scaremonger	threedecker
carbuncular	echosounder	honeymooner	nightwalker	sclerometer	threemaster
carburetter	electioneer	horsecollar	ninnyhammer	scoutmaster	timepleaser
carburettor	electrolier	horsedoctor	nomenclator	screwdriver	titleholder
cardsharper	emancipator	hospitaller	nomographer	scrutiniser	toastmaster
caterpillar	emasculator	housefather	nonsequitur	secondrater	toothpowder
catswhisker	embellisher	householder	northeaster	seismometer	topographer
cauliflower	embroiderer	housekeeper	northwester	selfdespair	torchbearer
cavedweller	Emmenthaler	housemaster	noseyparker	selfstarter	torchsinger
chainarmour	enterpriser	housemother	nosographer	semitrailer	totalisator
chainletter	entertainer	hydrometeor	ornithopter	serigrapher	trackwalker
chainsmoker	equiangular	ichthyosaur	ornithosaur	shareholder	trafficator
chansonnier	equivocator	illuminator	pacificator	sharepusher	trailblazer
chanticleer	establisher	illustrator	pamphleteer	sheepfarmer	trainbearer
cheerleader	eveningstar	inaugurator	panicmonger	sheepmaster	transceiver
childminder	exaggerator	incinerator	paperhanger	sheetanchor	transcriber
choirmaster	executioner	infiltrator	paragrapher	shipbreaker	transferrer
chronologer	extortioner	inseminator	paraphraser	shipbuilder	transformer
chronometer	fairweather	insufflator	paratrooper	shoeleather	transmitter
circumlunar	faithhealer	intensifier	parishioner	showstopper	transponder
circumpolar	faultfinder	intercepter	partitioner	sidewheeler	transporter
circumsolar	fieldworker	interceptor	pasteuriser	sightreader	treecreeper
cityslicker	filterpaper	intercessor	paternoster	signpainter	trendsetter
cliffhanger	firecracker	interlinear	pearlfisher	simpliciter	trustbuster
coinheritor	firefighter	interlocker	perpetrator	slaughterer	tumbledrier
colorimeter	firewatcher	interpreter	perpetuator	slavedriver	typefounder
commendator	flagellator	interrupter	personifier	slaveholder	typographer
commentator	flagofficer	interruptor	pettifogger	sleepingcar	tyrannosaur
compensator	flimflammer	interviewer	philanderer	sleepwalker	underbidder
comptroller	floorwalker	intimidator	philosopher	smallholder	underseller
compurgator	footslogger	intromitter	photocopier	sockdolager	undervaluer
concertgoer	footsoldier	invigilator	phrasemaker	somewhither	underwriter
conciliator	foraminifer	invigorator	picturegoer	somnambular	unicellular
conditioner	forequarter	jauntingcar	pieceworker	southeaster	upholsterer
confiscator	forestaller	jerrymander	pilotburner	southwester	vaporimeter
connoisseur	forethinker	kickstarter	pipecleaner	spaceheater	vasodilator
consecrator	fourflusher	kwashiorkor	plagiariser	spectacular	vasopressor
conservator	fourpounder	lachrymator	plasticiser	speechifier	vaticinator
conspirator	fourwheeler	lakedweller	platearmour	speedometer	ventricular
constitutor	franctireur	lammergeier	pluviometer	spellbinder	verisimilar
constrictor	frankfurter	lammergeyer	polarimeter	spherometer	vinedresser
constructor	fraterniser	lamplighter	polevaulter	stadtholder	vituperator
consummator	freethinker	landgrabber	popother	stakeholder	vociferator
continuator	frontrunner	landinggear	predecessor	stallholder	volkslieder
contributor	frothhopper	leaseholder	preselector	standpatter	volumometer
conveyancer	gallbladder	linendraper	prizewinner	steamboiler	voortrekker
coordinator	gardemanger	lineprinter	probationer	steamroller	washleather
corpuscular	gatecrasher	liquidambar	proconsular	steelworker	watercolour
cotoneaster	generaliser	litterateur	promulgator	stepbrother	watercooler
crepuscular	gerrymander	logographer	proofreader	stereotyper	weenybopper
criticaster	gettogether	loudspeaker	propitiator	sternutator	Westminster
crossbearer	ghostwriter	mailcarrier	prostitutor	stockbroker	wheresoever
crotcheteer	giantpowder	manipulator	protomartyr	stockholder	whichsoever
curvilinear	gillyflower	mantuamaker	provocateur	stockjobber	whitecollar
daisycutter	glassblower	masquerader	psychomotor	stonecutter	whitewasher

```
whitleather  biliousness  crabbedness  faddishness  healthiness  loathliness
whoremaster  biocoenoses  credentials  farawayness  heavenwards  loggerheads
whoremonger  biocoenosis  crookedness  farinaceous  heedfulness  logicalness
whosesoever  bittercress  cruciferous  farraginous  heinousness  loutishness
windcheater  blasphemous  crucigerous  fatefulness  hellishness  lovableness
wisecracker  blepharitis  crunchiness  fatuousness  helpfulness  loxodromics
witchdoctor  blessedness  crustaceous  fearfulness  hemipterous  lumpishness
witchhunter  blotchiness  cunningness  featherless  heptamerous  lustfulness
worldbeater  blunderbuss  cupriferous  featureless  herbivorous  magnanimous
wreckmaster  bookishness  curableness  feelingness  heterotaxis  manifestoes
xylographer  bookshelves  curiousness  ferriferous  hideousness  mannishness
abiogeneses  boorishness  currentness  ferruginous  hippocampus  marchioness
abiogenesis  borborygmus  currishness  fidgetiness  hirsuteness  massiveness
abstentious  bottleglass  cursiveness  filamentous  histrionics  mastoiditis
abusiveness  brachyurous  cursoriness  fingerglass  hitherwards  mathematics
academicals  breadcrumbs  cybernetics  finicalness  hoggishness  mawkishness
acarpellous  breadthways  cysticercus  firstfruits  homeostasis  meadowgrass
acclivitous  bristliness  cytogenesis  fissiparous  homogeneous  meaningless
acrimonious  Britishness  cytokinesis  flaccidness  homophonous  measureless
actinomyces  brittleness  declivitous  flavourless  homopterous  mediateness
adenomatous  brucellosis  defenceless  fleshliness  homosporous  mediatrices
adventuress  brusqueness  deleterious  flightiness  homozygosis  megalopolis
adventurous  brutishness  demigoddess  flirtatious  hopefulness  meliphagous
adverseness  bullishness  dentigerous  floriferous  houselights  melliferous
advisedness  burglarious  desperadoes  floweriness  hugeousness  mellifluous
aeronautics  butterflies  deviousness  foolishness  hurriedness  membraneous
aerostatics  butteriness  devotedness  foppishness  hurtfulness  menservants
aimlessness  butyraceous  diadelphous  foreignness  hydrogenous  meritorious
airlessness  cacophonous  diagnostics  foreverness  hydroponics  merogenesis
airsickness  caddishness  diaphoresis  forgiveness  hylogenesis  metachrosis
allantoides  calcicolous  diapophysis  forlornness  hypotyposis  metagenesis
altocumulus  calciferous  diarthrosis  forwardness  ichthyornis  metaphysics
altostratus  calcifugous  dicephalous  franticness  iconostases  meteoritics
amativeness  callousness  dichogamous  fretfulness  iconostasis  micrococcus
amentaceous  canaliculus  dichotomous  friableness  ignobleness  middleclass
amiableness  cantharides  diffuseness  frowardness  ignominious  mindfulness
amorousness  capableness  diplococcus  frowstiness  illustrious  minuteglass
anachronous  captionless  directrices  frugivorous  immenseness  mischievous
anadiplosis  carefulness  doggishness  fulsomeness  immoveables  miserliness
anagnorisis  carnivorous  dolefulness  furnishings  impecunious  moderations
anaphylaxis  caryopsides  dollishness  furtiveness  incongruous  monocarpous
anastomoses  catachreses  doltishness  furunculous  incredulous  monoclinous
anastomosis  catachresis  donnishness  gainfulness  indeciduous  monogenesis
ancientness  catadromous  doublecross  gallantness  industrious  monophagous
androgynous  ceremonious  doughtiness  gamogenesis  inexactness  monopterous
anfractuous  champertous  drouthiness  gaseousness  inheritress  morbiferous
antimonious  chartaceous  drunkenness  gasfittings  injudicious  mountainous
antiphrasis  chevalglass  dubiousness  gemmiferous  inofficious  movableness
anxiousness  chrysalides  dundrearies  gemmiparous  inquilinous  multiparous
Apollinaris  chrysalises  duplicitous  genteelness  insipidness  mundaneness
apologetics  churchiness  durableness  genuineness  intenseness  musicalness
aponeuroses  cleanliness  dutifulness  geopolitics  interleaves  mutableness
aponeurosis  coccidiosis  earnestness  ghastliness  interosseus  muttonchops
aposiopesis  coconscious  earthliness  ghostliness  intravenous  myelomatous
arboraceous  cognateness  ectogenesis  gibbousness  invalidness  myocarditis
archaeornis  comestibles  efficacious  girlishness  irksomeness  myxomatosis
archduchess  comfortless  elderliness  glaringness  irreligious  myxomycetes
arduousness  compactness  electronics  gnotobiosis  isochronous  naturalness
arenicolous  compendious  elusiveness  godlessness  isomorphous  naughtiness
artlessness  complexness  emotionless  gracileness  jealousness  necessitous
ascomycetes  conciseness  emulousness  gradualness  joylessness  necrobiosis
aspergillus  conductress  enarthrosis  granivorous  knavishness  necropoleis
assuredness  congenerous  enchantress  graphicness  knowingness  needfulness
atrabilious  conspicuous  endlessness  gristliness  lactiferous  nervousness
audibleness  contentious  endophagous  grouchiness  languidness  nitrogenous
austereness  contrarious  enterovirus  guardedness  lastingness  noctivagous
avoirdupois  contretemps  enviousness  gutlessness  lateritious  noisomeness
awesomeness  convenances  ephemerides  gypsiferous  laughinggas  nonetheless
awkwardness  convolvulus  epipetalous  gyrocompass  laurustinus  notableness
bacciferous  copiousness  equableness  habiliments  lawlessness  nothingness
balefulness  corbiesteps  erotogenous  haemoptysis  learnedness  noxiousness
bashfulness  cordialness  eurhythmics  haemostasis  lengthiness  nulliparous
battledress  corniferous  evasiveness  haggardness  lentiginous  numismatics
bearishness  correctness  executrices  halophilous  letterpress  nutcrackers
beastliness  corruptness  executrixes  haplessness  ligamentous  obliqueness
belatedness  costiveness  exhaustless  harbourless  limitedness  obscureness
bellbottoms  coterminous  expeditious  harmfulness  linguistics  obviousness
betweenness  cottongrass  extremeness  hatefulness  lissomeness  odoriferous
bicephalous  courtliness  factualness  haughtiness  literalness  odorousness
```

offenceless	proceedings	shepherdess	teknonymous	viscountess	bombardment
oligomerous	profaneness	shocktroops	telekinesis	viscousness	Bonapartist
ominousness	profuseness	shrubbiness	temerarious	visibleness	bondservant
omnifarious	prognathous	shutterless	tempestuous	voguishness	breadbasket
onerousness	proliferous	sickishness	tenableness	volubleness	Byzantinist
ontogenesis	promiscuous	sightliness	tendencious	vortiginous	calefacient
operoseness	prophylaxis	silveriness	tendentious	waggishness	candlelight
opprobrious	proportions	sincereness	tenterhooks	wakefulness	carvelbuilt
orderliness	prosaicness	sinlessness	tenuousness	waspishness	chargesheet
orthopedics	prosthetics	sinuousness	terraqueous	waywardness	chiropodist
otherwhiles	protectress	sizableness	terricolous	wealthiness	chloroplast
outwardness	proteolysis	sketchiness	terrigenous	weightiness	chromoplast
overanxious	prudishness	skilfulness	testatrices	welcomeness	circumspect
ozoniferous	pruriginous	slavishness	tetramerous	whereabouts	clairvoyant
paediatrics	pseudomonas	slenderness	tetrapodous	whitishness	clericalist
painfulness	psittacosis	smithereens	textureless	widdershins	codefendant
pantalettes	punctilious	snowgoggles	thereabouts	willingness	coefficient
papyraceous	purposeless	solanaceous	thermionics	winningness	colonialist
paraleipsis	pushfulness	somniculous	thermolysis	winsomeness	commandment
parasitosis	queenliness	somniferous	thermotaxis	wishfulness	communalist
parentheses	quitchgrass	songfulness	thirstiness	wistfulness	communicant
parenthesis	racketpress	sottishness	thoughtless	withershins	comparatist
passiveness	radicalness	soulfulness	threadiness	witlessness	compartment
paunchiness	raffishness	sparingness	thriftiness	womanliness	compilement
peccadillos	raucousness	spathaceous	throatiness	worldliness	complainant
pediculosis	raunchiness	spectatress	thunderless	worshipless	complaisant
peevishness	reddishness	spindlelegs	thuriferous	xenophilous	comportment
pensionless	regimentals	spiniferous	thwartships	xerophilous	concealment
pensiveness	relatedness	splendorous	thyroiditis	xylocarpous	concernment
pentagynous	remorseless	spondulicks	tiddlywinks	xylophagous	concomitant
pentamerous	repetitious	spondylitis	tonsillitis	zealousness	concrescent
pentandrous	repleteness	spontaneous	torticollis	zestfulness	concubitant
perfectness	restfulness	sporogenous	trafficless	zootechnics	confinement
periostitis	restiveness	springiness	treacherous	abandonment	conflagrant
periphrases	retiredness	squalidness	treacliness	abolishment	congealment
periphrasis	rhizanthous	squashiness	trichinosis	abortionist	consentient
perishables	rhizomatous	squeakiness	tricksiness	abridgement	consignment
peristalsis	rhomboideus	starchiness	trimorphous	acaulescent	constituent
peritonitis	ribbongrass	stateliness	tripetalous	accompanist	containment
perspicuous	riotousness	staunchless	triphibious	achievement	contaminant
pestiferous	roguishness	staunchness	triphyllous	acquiescent	contentment
pettishness	roundedness	stegosaurus	triquetrous	acquirement	controlment
pharyngitis	ruinousness	stephanotis	tristichous	adjournment	corecipient
phosphorous	rumbustious	sternsheets	trivialness	adjudgement	corroborant
phthiriasis	Sagittarius	stiltedness	trouserless	adoptianist	cosmogonist
phyllotaxis	saintliness	stoicalness	tuberculous	adoptionist	cosmologist
piggishness	salesladies	stormtroops	tunableness	advancement	costbenefit
pinkishness	salpingitis	stramineous	tunefulness	adventurist	counterfeit
piperaceous	sanguineous	strangeness	typicalness	aftereffect	counterfort
piscivorous	saplessness	streakiness	ulotrichous	alkalescent	counterpart
piteousness	saponaceous	stringiness	ultrasonics	allopathist	counterplot
pitifulness	saprogenous	studiedness	unambiguous	Americanist	countryseat
plasmolysis	sarcomatous	stuntedness	unawareness	anthologist	creationist
playfulness	sarcophagus	stylishness	uncanniness	antioxidant	criminalist
pliableness	sauropodous	suasiveness	uncleanness	appeasement	crossgarnet
plicateness	savouriness	sublimeness	unconscious	appointment	curtailment
pneumonitis	schizanthus	succourless	uncouthness	appurtenant	custombuilt
pointedness	sclerotitis	sulphureous	ungodliness	aquarellist	debauchment
polyandrous	scoriaceous	summariness	unhappiness	arbitrament	debouchment
polycarpous	scragginess	sunlessness	uniformness	arborescent	deforcement
polygenesis	scrappiness	superficies	unmanliness	arraignment	defraudment
polyonymous	scribacious	superfluous	unquietness	arrangement	delitescent
polyphagous	scrimpiness	superioress	unrighteous	artillerist	depravement
polyphonous	scruffiness	supersedeas	unsoundness	assuagement	derangement
pompousness	scrumptious	supremeness	unusualness	audiologist	despoilment
pontificals	scurvygrass	swarthiness	uprightness	balmcricket	determinant
portionless	seasickness	sweepstakes	urticaceous	bathingsuit	determinist
pourparlers	secondclass	swinishness	urticarious	bedevilment	detrainment
preachiness	selfishness	sympetalous	uselessness	bedizenment	development
precautious	sententious	symphonious	vacuousness	beguilement	dichotomist
precentress	septenarius	synchronous	valiantness	belligerent	diluvialist
preceptress	septiferous	syndesmosis	variousness	benightment	diplomatist
precipitous	seriousness	syssarcosis	velvetiness	bereavement	disablement
preciseness	serpiginous	systematics	ventriculus	bewitchment	disafforest
prestigious	sexlessness	tabletennis	verboseness	bimetallist	disarmament
pretentious	shadowiness	tautologous	vertiginous	bittersweet	disbandment
prickliness	shallowness	tautonymous	viciousness	blackmarket	discernment
primiparous	shapeliness	tearfulness	victualless	bladderwort	disinterest
privateness	shelterless	tediousness	victualless	bodyservant	dislodgment

disobedient	highwrought	needlepoint	reactionist	surveillant	accentually
disportment	Hispanicist	negationist	realignment	sustainment	acceptingly
dissentient	histologist	neurologist	reconstruct	swallowwort	acclamatory
dissepiment	historicist	noctilucent	recruitment	syndicalist	accordantly
disunionist	hydrologist	noctivagant	reenactment	systematist	accordingly
divorcement	hypermarket	nondescript	refreshment	talentscout	accountably
divulgement	illusionist	nonexistent	refrigerant	taxidermist	accountancy
downdraught	immanentist	nonresident	regionalist	teleologist	acropetally
dreadnought	impeachment	nonunionist	relationist	telepathist	adjectively
earthcloset	imperialist	notionalist	religionist	telephonist	adverbially
easternmost	imperilment	nourishment	reminiscent	temperament	advertently
emblematist	impermanent	numismatist	remonstrant	tetravalent	aerobically
embowerment	impertinent	objectivist	replacement	theosophist	aerobiology
embracement	impingement	obmutescent	requirement	thunderbolt	affectingly
embroilment	impoundment	obsolescent	resipiscent	tobacconist	affectively
emplacement	impressment	oenophilist	resplendent	tobogganist	affectivity
enchainment	improvement	omnipresent	restatement	togglejoint	affirmatory
enchantment	improvident	opencircuit	retrocedent	traducement	aggregately
encrustment	inadvertent	ophiologist	retrorocket	transhumant	aggrievedly
endorsement	incalescent	opportunist	reverberant	transilient	agnatically
enfeoffment	incognisant	optometrist	revisionist	translucent	agonisingly
enforcement	incompetent	orientalist	reviviscent	transparent	agrobiology
engorgement	incompliant	orthopedist	rhinologist	tremblement	alkalimetry
engrossment	incongruent	osteologist	rhynchodont	tritagonist	alleviatory
enhancement	inconscient	overgarment	romanticist	trophoblast	alternately
enjambement	inconsonant	overpayment	rubefacient	trothplight	ambiguously
enlargement	incontinent	overwrought	safeconduct	trousersuit	ambitiously
enlivenment	indehiscent	oysterplant	Sanskritist	ultraviolet	ambivalency
ennoblement	independent	paediatrist	sausagemeat	unbeknownst	amenability
enslavement	indifferent	pantomimist	saxophonist	undertenant	amicability
entablement	indorsement	paperweight	scaleinsect	underweight	amorphously
enthralment	inefficient	parachutist	scintillant	unimportant	amphibology
entitlement	inexpedient	participant	scuttlebutt	vacationist	amphictyony
entrainment	inobservant	pastoralist	searchlight	vehmgericht	analogously
entreatment	installment	paternalist	secondsight	viridescent	anencephaly
entrustment	instillment	pathologist	secretariat	virilescent	angelically
envelopment	intelligent	pearlescent	selfconceit	voluntarist	angiography
environment	interactant	pennyweight	selfcontent	waitinglist	anniversary
epigraphist	interfluent	pentavalent	selfevident	wastebasket	anomalously
equidistant	interjacent	personalist	selfreliant	westernmost	anonymously
equilibrist	intumescent	pestologist	selfrespect	wheelwright	anteriority
equipollent	involvement	petrologist	selfsupport	whitethroat	antigravity
escheatment	irredentist	phantasiast	semanticist	winningpost	antiphonary
Esperantist	juvenescent	phenologist	Septembrist	witenagemot	appallingly
ethnologist	lawmerchant	philatelist	shacklebolt	xylophonist	appealingly
etymologist	lightweight	philologist	shelljacket	zoographist	applicatory
eudaemonist	limnologist	phonologist	shelterbelt	portmanteau	appreciably
evanishment	lithotomist	photooffset	sickbenefit	blackfellow	approbatory
expectorant	logomachist	phycologist	significant	clapperclaw	approvingly
extravagant	luminescent	phylogynist	silverpoint	counterblow	aquatically
facsimilist	madrigalist	phytologist	slavemarket	counterview	arbitrarily
farthermost	magnificent	phytotomist	sociologist	grandnephew	archaeology
festschrift	maidservant	pigeonchest	soliloquist	greatnephew	archaically
fieldcornet	maintopmast	pillowfight	solutionist	marshmallow	aristocracy
fingerprint	mammalogist	pinnatisect	Soroptimist	merryandrew	aromaticity
flabbergast	mandolinist	pleinairist	spaceflight	pussywillow	arrestingly
fluorescent	manifestant	plenipotent	spendthrift	songsparrow	ascetically
forethought	materialist	pointillist	squarebuilt	stonecurlew	aseptically
foretopmast	meadowsweet	poltergeist	staircarpet	wappenschaw	assertively
forgetmenot	measurement	portraitist	stenotypist	wheelbarrow	assiduously
freethought	medievalist	precipitant	stickinsect	windlestraw	Assyriology
funambulist	mellifluent	precontract	stiflejoint	arbitratrix	astringency
furthermost	memorialist	predicament	stockmarket	billetsdoux	atrociously
garnishment	miniaturist	predominant	straightcut	Clarencieux	attentively
gemmologist	misjudgment	preexistent	streetlight	fricandeaux	audaciously
genealogist	molecricket	prejudgment	strongpoint	hydrothorax	auricularly
grandparent	moneymarket	presentient	subbasement	negotiatrix	autochthony
greasepaint	monochromat	presentment	subcontract	planoconvex	backcountry
groundsheet	monologuist	priestcraft	subdominant	progenitrix	banteringly
gynaecocrat	mooringmast	probabilist	subservient	prolocutrix	baptismally
haematocrit	mothercraft	procurement	substituent	prosecutrix	barbarously
hagiologist	motherright	progressist	sulphurwort	thoroughwax	barefacedly
hairstylist	multivalent	proletariat	summersault	abdominally	basipetally
handwrought	mycophagist	protagonist	superjacent	abhorrently	beauteously
heavyweight	mythologist	protuberant	supermarket	abiotically	beautifully
hedgepriest	mythopoeist	publishment	supernatant	ablutionary	befittingly
heptarchist	nationalist	pulverulent	superscript	abnormality	beguilingly
heterograft	necrologist	radiologist	supremacist	absorbingly	bellicosity
hexametrist	needlecraft	rationalist	surbasement	abstinently	benedictory

beneficiary	colorimetry	customarily	ecumenicity	familiarity	homogeneity
benightedly	colourfully	dactylology	edificatory	fanatically	hospitality
benignantly	combatively	dangerously	editorially	farcicality	housewifely
bibliolatry	combinatory	dauntlessly	educability	fashionably	housewifery
bibliomancy	comfortably	deceitfully	effectively	fatiguingly	huckleberry
bibliophily	commendably	deceivingly	effectually	faultlessly	humiliatory
bicentenary	commensally	decennially	efficiently	feasibility	hurryscurry
biddability	comminatory	deceptively	effulgently	feloniously	hurryskurry
bilaterally	commonality	declamatory	egregiously	ferociously	hydrography
bimillenary	competently	declaratory	ejaculatory	festinately	hymnography
binocularly	complacency	decussately	elaborately	filamentary	hypertrophy
bisexuality	compliantly	dedicatedly	elastically	filmography	hypsography
blamelessly	compositely	deductively	electricity	financially	ichnography
blameworthy	compotatory	defectively	electrology	fissiparity	ichthyology
bloodguilty	comstockery	defensively	elementally	flamboyancy	iconography
bloodlessly	conceitedly	deficiently	eligibility	flatulently	identically
botanically	conceivably	degradingly	ellipticity	flauntingly	idiotically
bounteously	concertedly	deistically	elucidatory	flexibility	idyllically
bountifully	concubinary	deliciously	embracingly	fluoroscopy	illiberally
boysenberry	condolatory	delightedly	emotionally	forgetfully	illimitably
brainlessly	confederacy	delinquency	empirically	fortnightly	illiquidity
brainsickly	confessedly	deliriously	endearingly	fortunately	illogically
brilliantly	confidently	demagoguery	endemically	fractionary	imaginarily
bryozoology	confidingly	demandingly	enquiringly	fractiously	imitatively
bucolically	conformably	demonolatry	enterostomy	fragmentary	immediately
bumblepuppy	conformally	denigratory	entomophily	frantically	immitigably
bumptiously	confusingly	dependently	episcopally	fraternally	immortality
bureaucracy	congenially	deploringly	equivalency	freemasonry	impartially
Byronically	congruently	deprecatory	equivocally	frightfully	impassively
calefactory	congruously	depredatory	ergatocracy	frivolously	impassivity
calligraphy	conjugality	dermatology	erratically	fruitlessly	impatiently
calorimetry	connectedly	deservingly	erroneously	fulminatory	impenitency
campanology	connubially	desperately	eschatology	functionary	imperfectly
candleberry	consciously	despondency	essentially	gallimaufry	imperiously
canonically	conservancy	desultorily	ethereality	garrulously	impermeably
capaciously	consistency	determinacy	ethnography	gastrectomy	impetratory
capillarity	consolatory	deuterogamy	Etruscology	generically	impetuosity
caravansary	consolingly	Deuteronomy	eugenically	genetically	impetuously
caressingly	consonantly	dexterously	eventuality	genitivally	implausibly
carriageway	conspicuity	dialectally	evidentiary	gentlemanly	imploringly
cartography	consultancy	diaphaneity	exceedingly	gerontology	impoliticly
catholicity	consumingly	differently	excellently	gimcrackery	importantly
causatively	contentedly	difficultly	excessively	globularity	importunely
caustically	continently	diffidently	exclamatory	glutinously	importunity
cavernously	contingency	diffusively	exclusively	goldenberry	imprecatory
ceaselessly	continually	digestively	exclusivity	gracelessly	imprecisely
celebratory	contrariety	dimwittedly	excrescency	grandiosely	impregnably
celestially	controversy	directivity	exculpatory	grandiosity	impropriety
cellularity	conveniency	disarmingly	excursively	granularity	imprudently
certifiably	convergency	disassembly	exdirectory	graphically	impulsively
chancellery	conversancy	discernibly	exemplarily	gratulatory	inalienably
chancellory	convertibly	discography	exemplarity	grotesquely	inalterably
changefully	convivially	discordancy	exhortatory	grotesquery	inanimately
chaotically	coparcenary	discourtesy	exogenously	grumblingly	incantatory
charlatanry	coplanarity	discrepancy	expansively	guilelessly	incessantly
cheerlessly	corporality	disguisedly	expansivity	guiltlessly	incipiently
cheiromancy	corporately	disgustedly	expatiatory	gullibility	inclemently
chieftaincy	corporeally	dishonestly	expectantly	gymnospermy	inclusively
chirography	corpulently	dismayingly	expediently	gynaecology	incoherency
chokecherry	corrosively	disparately	expensively	haematology	incommodity
chorography	corruptibly	dispersedly	explanatory	hagiography	incongruity
Christianly	cosignatory	dissolutely	explicatory	halfholiday	inconstancy
Christmassy	cosmetology	dissonantly	exploratory	haphazardly	incorrectly
Christology	cosmography	dissymmetry	explosively	haplography	incorruptly
chronically	cotemporary	dittography	expurgatory	hazardously	incredulity
chronometry	countlessly	divergently	exquisitely	healthfully	inculpatory
circularity	courteously	divisionary	extemporary	heartlessly	incuriosity
circulatory	craniatory	doctrinally	extensively	Hebraically	incuriously
clamorously	credibility	documentary	extenuatory	heliography	indefinably
classically	credulously	dodecaphony	exteriority	hepatectomy	indignantly
cleistogamy	criminality	domesticity	externality	heresiology	indivisibly
climatology	criminatory	domiciliary	extirpatory	heretically	indomitably
codicillary	criminology	doubleentry	exuberantly	herpetology	indubitably
coeternally	criticality	doubtlessly	facetiously	heteronomy	inductively
cognitively	cryobiology	drastically	factionally	heterospory	indulgently
cognitivity	cryosurgery	dreamlessly	faithlessly	hilariously	inedibility
collectedly	cryotherapy	dynamically	faithworthy	historicity	inelegantly
collinearly	cryptically	dynamometry	fallibility	hobbledehoy	ineluctably
collusively	culpability	ebulliently	falteringly	homoeopathy	inequitably

inestimably	ligamentary	notoriously	phraseology	psychometry	satiability
inexcusably	lightsomely	nulliparity	physicality	psychopathy	satirically
inferiority	limitlessly	numerically	physiocracy	pteridology	saturninely
infertility	lingeringly	nutritively	physiognomy	punctuality	scenography
inflammably	lithography	nympholepsy	phytography	pupillarity	sceptically
informality	lithotripsy	obfuscatory	pictography	purportedly	schistosity
informatory	litigiously	objectively	pictorially	purposively	scientology
infrequency	loathsomely	objectivity	pigheadedly	pyramidally	scorchingly
ingeniously	longanimity	objurgatory	piratically	quadraphony	scorpionfly
ingenuously	lucratively	obliviously	placability	querulously	scoundrelly
ingrainedly	ludicrously	obnoxiously	plaintively	questionary	screamingly
inhabitancy	luxuriantly	observantly	pleasurably	quiescently	sculduddery
injuriously	luxuriously	observatory	plenteously	quizzically	sculduggery
innocuously	lycanthropy	observingly	plentifully	radiography	searchingly
innoxiously	mackerelsky	obsessively	pocketmoney	rancorously	secondarily
innumerably	maddeningly	obstinately	pointlessly	rapaciously	secretively
inquiringly	magnanimity	obtrusively	poisonously	rapturously	sectionally
insalubrity	maladroitly	occipitally	polarimetry	rateability	sedentarily
inscrutably	malariology	octagonally	polemically	rationality	sedimentary
insectology	maledictory	octingenary	politically	ravishingly	seditionary
insensately	maliciously	offensively	poltroonery	reactionary	seditiously
inseparably	malignantly	offhandedly	polygonally	readability	seductively
insidiously	manducatory	officinally	ponderosity	receptively	segmentally
insincerely	manufactory	officiously	ponderously	receptivity	seismically
insincerity	marginality	olfactology	pornography	recessively	seismometry
insistently	martyrology	oneiromancy	portability	reciprocity	selectively
inspiratory	masculinely	operatively	possibility	recognitory	selectivity
instability	masculinity	opportunely	posteriorly	recumbently	selfdisplay
insultingly	masterfully	opportunity	potentially	recurrently	selfmastery
insuperably	masticatory	oracularity	potteringly	rediscovery	semasiology
integrality	matchlessly	orbicularly	powerlessly	redundantly	semimonthly
intensively	materiality	orchidology	practicably	reflexively	senselessly
intercalary	mediaevally	organically	practically	reflexology	sensibility
interiority	medicinally	originality	prattlingly	reformatory	sensitively
interlunary	melodiously	ornithology	precedently	refringency	sensitivity
internality	mercenarily	orthography	predatorily	regardfully	sensorially
intolerably	mercilessly	oscillatory	predicatory	regretfully	serendipity
intractable	mercurially	osmotically	predictably	regrettably	serviceably
intrepidity	meritocracy	ostensively	prefatorily	rejoicingly	shamelessly
intricately	meteorology	osteography	preliminary	reliability	sheriffalty
intrusively	methodology	osteoplasty	prelusively	religiosity	shiftlessly
intuitively	metoposcopy	outspokenly	prelusorily	religiously	shrinkingly
invectively	micrography	ovariectomy	prematurely	reluctantly	sickeningly
inventively	mimetically	pacifically	prematurity	repellantly	sightlessly
inviability	mirthlessly	palpability	premonitory	repellently	sightworthy
invidiously	misanthropy	paramountcy	preparatory	repentantly	sigmoidally
inviolately	miscibility	paramountly	presanctify	reposefully	simperingly
involuntary	misguidedly	parochially	presciently	repressibly	singularity
ironmongery	molecularly	partitively	presentably	reprobatory	sinistrally
irrecusably	molendinary	passibility	pressagency	reprography	skulduddery
irreducibly	momentarily	peccability	presumingly	reprovingly	skulduggery
irrefutably	momentously	peculiarity	pretendedly	repugnantly	sleeplessly
irregularly	monstrosity	pecuniarily	prevalently	repulsively	slightingly
irrelevancy	monstrously	pellucidity	primaevally	resentfully	smilelessly
irremovably	moribundity	pendulously	primatology	resiliently	sociability
irreparably	moronically	penuriously	primitively	resistively	solvability
irrevocably	moveability	perceivably	principally	resistivity	somatically
irruptively	multistorey	perceptibly	privatively	respectably	somnolently
itinerantly	municipally	perennially	probability	respiratory	sorrowfully
jabberwocky	murderously	perfunctory	procuratory	respondency	soteriology
judiciously	murmurously	periodicity	prodigality	responsibly	soundlessly
juridically	muscularity	perishingly	profanatory	retaliatory	sovereignly
justifiably	myrmecology	permanently	professedly	retardatory	sovereignty
kinesiology	mythography	permissibly	proficiency	retentively	spastically
laboriously	narratively	perpetually	prohibitory	retentivity	specificity
laconically	nationality	perplexedly	prolificacy	retinoscopy	spectrality
lacrimatory	naturopathy	persistency	prolificity	retributory	spectrology
lacrimosely	necessarily	personality	prominently	revisionary	spelaeology
lacrymatory	nefariously	perspicuity	promiscuity	rhabdomancy	sphagnology
lacrymosely	negligently	pertinacity	promisingly	rheumaticky	spherically
larcenously	negotiatory	pertinently	propinquity	righteously	spinelessly
laryngology	neighbourly	pervasively	proprietary	rubicundity	spiritually
laryngotomy	nephrectomy	pervertedly	prosaically	rudimentary	spiritualty
laudability	nervelessly	pestilently	protonotary	sagaciously	splenectomy
lecherously	nittygritty	petitionary	providently	salaciously	spontaneity
lesemajesty	nocturnally	petrography	provisorily	saleability	squeamishly
lichenology	noiselessly	phalanstery	provokingly	salmonberry	squintingly
lickerishly	nomadically	phonography	proximately	sartorially	squirearchy
lieutenancy	nondelivery	photography	psychically	satanically	stainlessly

```
startlingly superiority thankworthy unboundedly uranography voraciously
statesmanly superlunary thaumaturgy unceasingly vagariously vulcanicity
statutorily supervisory thermically uncertainly valedictory vulcanology
steadfastly suppliantly thermometry uncertainty variability warrantably
steerageway supportably thrillingly undoubtedly vascularity washability
stenochromy suppository titanically undutifully venatically wearilessly
stenography surficially toothsomely unendurably vendibility wearisomely
stereometry susceptibly torturously unfailingly venereology whigmaleery
stereophony sycophantry totteringly unfeelingly ventriloquy whimsically
stereoscopy syllabicity tracelessly unfeignedly venturously wholesomely
stethoscopy tachygraphy tracheotomy unguardedly veraciously winterberry
stichometry taciturnity tragicomedy unhealthily veridically witheringly
stipendiary talkatively transiently unhelpfully verminously wonderfully
stipulatory tameability translunary unipolarity versatilely workability
stomatology tangibility treasonably unisexually versatility worrisomely
straightway tastelessly tremblingly universally verticality worthlessly
stratocracy technically tremulously unlimitedly vesicularly yellowbelly
strenuosity technocracy trenchantly unmeaningly vestigially zincography
strenuously tegumentary triadically unmemorably vexatiously weltschmerz
stringently temperately tributarily unnaturally vexillology
stumblingly temporality triennially unnecessary vibratility
stylography temporarily troublously unnervingly vicariously
subaerially tenaciously truculently unorthodoxy vicegerency
subaxillary tenementary trustworthy unskilfully viceregally
subcategory tensibility turbulently unsmilingly viceroyalty
subcontrary tentatively twelvepenny unsparingly vincibility
succulently tephromancy typefoundry unspeakably vindicatory
sufficiency termagantly tyrannously unthinkably vivaciously
suitability terminology unadvisedly unutterably voicelessly
sumptuosity testability unanimously unweetingly volcanicity
sumptuously tetanically unashamedly unwillingly volcanology
superfamily thanatology unavoidably unwinkingly volitionary
superfluity thanklessly unbendingly unwittingly voluntarily
```

12 letter words

```
abbreviation acoustically aggressively anaerobiosis antineutrino
abolitionary acquaintance agranulocyte anaesthetise antiparticle
abolitionism acquiescence agribusiness anaesthetist antipathetic
abolitionist acronychally agricultural anagogically antiperiodic
aboriginally actinomycete ailurophobia anagrammatic antiphonally
abortiveness adaptability aircondition analogically antirachitic
abrasiveness adaptiveness aircraftsman analphabetic antiSemitism
absentminded additionally alexipharmic analytically antistrophic
absoluteness adequateness Alhambresque anamorphosis antithetical
absolutistic adhesiveness alimentation anaphylactic aperiodicity
absorptional adjectivally alimentative anastigmatic apiculturist
absorptivity adjudication alkalescence anathematise apochromatic
absquatulate adjudicatory alliteration anatomically apolitically
abstemiously adjudicatory alliterative anecdotalist apostolicism
abstractable administrant allomorphism anemographic apostolicity
abstractedly administrate allusiveness anemophilous apostrophise
abstractness admonishment alphabetical angiocarpous apothegmatic
abstruseness adorableness alphamerical annihilation apparatchiki
academically adscititious alphanumeric annihilative apparatchiks
acaulescence adulteration alterability announcement apparentness
acceleration adulterously altitudinous annunciation apparitional
accelerative advantageous amalgamation anotherguess appendectomy
accentuation adventitious amalgamative antagonistic appendicitis
acciaccatura advisability amateurishly antecedently appendicular
accidentally aerodynamics ambassadress antediluvian apperception
accommodator aeroembolism ambidextrous anteprandial apperceptive
accompanyist aeronautical ambivalently anthelmintic appetisingly
accomplished aeroneurosis amelioration anthropogeny appositeness
accordionist aerosiderite ameliorative anthropoidal appositional
accouchement aesthetician amenableness anthropology appraisement
accoutrement aestheticism amentiferous antiaircraft appraisingly
accretionary aetiological amicableness anticipation appreciation
accumulation affectedness amitotically anticipative appreciative
accumulative affectionate amortisation anticipatory appreciatory
accurateness aforethought amphibiously anticlerical apprehension
accursedness AfroAmerican amphibrachic anticyclonic apprehensive
accusatively afterthought amphictyonic antigenicity approachable
accusatorial agamogenesis amphisbaenic antigropelos appropriable
acetabularia agamogenetic amphitheatre antimacassar appropriator
acetaldehyde agentgeneral amphitropous antimagnetic appurtenance
achlamydeous agglutinogen amygdaloidal antimalarial aquicultural
```

arborescence	balletomania	blisteringly	calycoideous	cheeseparing
arborisation	ballottement	blithesomely	camiknickers	cheirography
archdeaconry	banderillero	blockbusting	campfollower	chemotherapy
archdiocesan	bantamweight	bloodbrother	campodeiform	chequerboard
archetypally	barbarically	bloodletting	canaliculate	cherubically
archetypical	barometrical	bloodstained	canalisation	chesterfield
archipelagic	baselessness	bloodthirsty	cancellation	chieftainess
architecture	basidiospore	bloodyminded	candleholder	childbearing
argillaceous	bassorelievo	bluestocking	canonisation	childishness
aristocratic	bassorilievo	blunderingly	canorousness	chimneypiece
Aristotelean	bathypelagic	blusteringly	Cantabrigian	chiropractic
Aristotelian	battleground	boastfulness	cantankerous	chiropractor
arithmetical	battlemented	bobbydazzler	cantharidian	chitterlings
aromatically	beachcombing	bodybuilding	cantillation	chivalrously
aromaticness	beatifically	bodysnatcher	capercaillie	chlorination
arrhythmical	bedazzlement	bodystocking	capercailzie	chocolatebox
articulately	beggarliness	boisterously	capitalistic	chondriosome
articulation	behaviourism	bombdisposal	capitulation	choreography
articulatory	behaviourist	bonnetmonkey	capriciously	chorographic
artificially	belittlement	bonnyclabber	captiousness	chorological
artilleryman	bellbottomed	boogiewoogie	caravansarai	chrematistic
artistically	belletristic	bookingclerk	caravanserai	chrestomathy
asphyxiation	belligerence	booklearning	carbohydrate	Christianise
assassinator	belligerency	bootlessness	carbonaceous	Christianity
assibilation	bellylanding	borosilicate	carburetting	Christolatry
assimilation	benefactress	bottlewasher	carcinogenic	Christophory
assimilative	beneficently	boulevardier	cardcarrying	chromaticism
assimilatory	beneficially	bowcompasses	cardinalship	chromaticity
astonishment	benevolently	brachydactyl	cardiography	chromatogram
astoundingly	benzaldehyde	brackishness	cardiologist	chromatology
astringently	bequeathment	brainstormer	carelessness	chromatopsia
astrological	berzelianite	brainwashing	caricaturist	chromosphere
astronautics	beseechingly	brambleberry	carillonneur	chronography
astronomical	bespectacled	brassbounder	Carlovingian	chronologise
astrophysics	bewilderedly	brassrubbing	carpetbagger	chronologist
asymmetrical	bewilderment	breakthrough	carpetknight	chronometric
asynchronism	bewitchingly	breaststroke	carragheenin	churchianity
asynchronous	bibliography	breastsummer	carriageable	churchwarden
atheromatous	bibliologist	breathalyser	Cartesianism	churlishness
athletically	bibliomaniac	breathlessly	cartographer	cinematheque
atmospherics	bibliopegist	breathtaking	cartographic	circuitously
attitudinise	bibliophilic	breechloader	cartological	circumcision
attorneyship	bibliopolist	brickfielder	cashandcarry	circumfluent
attractively	bibliothecae	brilliantine	catachrestic	circumfusion
attributable	bicentennial	brinkmanship	catamountain	circumjacent
augmentation	bilateralism	brokenwinded	cataphoresis	circumscribe
augmentative	bilharziasis	bronchoscope	catastrophic	circumstance
auscultation	bilharziosis	broncobuster	catechetical	cirrocumulus
auscultatory	bilingualism	brontosaurus	caterwauling	cirrostratus
auspiciously	billingsgate	buccaneering	catholically	civilisation
Australasian	billsticking	buccaneerish	catilinarian	clairaudient
authenticate	biochemistry	buffalograss	cattlelifter	clairvoyance
authenticity	biocoenology	bulletheaded	cautiousness	clangorously
autocatalyse	bioecologist	bullfighting	cementitious	clannishness
autochthones	biogeography	bullheadedly	censoriously	clapperboard
autodidactic	biographical	bureaucratic	centesimally	clarinettist
autoimmunity	biologically	burglarproof	centrespread	classicalism
automaticity	biometrician	burningglass	centrosphere	classicalist
automobilist	biophysicist	businesslike	centuplicate	classicality
automorphism	bioscientist	butterflynut	ceremonially	classifiable
autonomously	biosynthesis	buttermuslin	chairmanship	clatteringly
availability	biosynthetic	butterscotch	chalcolithic	claudication
avantgardism	birdsnesting	Byelorussian	chalcopyrite	clavicembalo
avantgardist	birdwatching	cabbagewhite	championship	clearsighted
avariciously	birefringent	cabinetmaker	chancemedley	cleistogamic
avitaminoses	blabbermouth	cachinnation	chaplainship	cliffhanging
avitaminosis	blackbirding	cachinnatory	characterise	clinkerbuilt
bacchanalian	blackcurrant	calamitously	charlatanism	closecropped
bachelorhood	blackguardly	calcareously	charnelhouse	closegrained
bachelorship	bladderwrack	calculatedly	charterhouse	closemouthed
backbreaking	blamableness	calisthenics	charterparty	clotheshorse
backpedalled	blamefulness	calligrapher	chastisement	clothespress
backslapping	blandishment	calligraphic	chauvinistic	clownishness
backwardness	blastfurnace	callisthenic	checkerberry	coacervation
backwoodsman	blastosphere	calorescence	checkerboard	coachbuilder
bactericidal	blastulation	calorimetric	cheerfulness	coalitionist
bacteriology	blatherskite	calumniation	cheeseburger	cockfighting
bacteriostat	bletherskate	calumniatory	cheesecutter	cocksureness
balladmonger	blissfulness	calumniously	cheesemonger	codification

coelenterate	conceptually	constructive	counterclaim	decomposable
coenobitical	conchiferous	consultation	counterforce	decompressor
coenobytical	conchologist	consultative	counterlight	decongestant
coerciveness	conciliation	consummately	countermarch	decongestion
coetaneously	conciliative	consummation	counterplead	decongestive
cohabitation	conciliatory	consummative	counterpoint	deconsecrate
cohesiveness	conclusively	consummatory	counterpoise	decontrolled
coincidental	concomitance	contagionist	counterproof	decoratively
coincidently	concordantly	contagiously	counterscarp	decorousness
coldshoulder	concrescence	containerise	countershaft	decreasingly
coleopterist	concreteness	contemplator	countertenor	deescalation
coleopterous	concubitancy	contemporary	countrydance	definiteness
collaborator	concupiscent	contemporise	countrywoman	definitively
collaterally	concurrently	contemptible	courageously	deflagration
collectively	condemnation	contemptibly	courtmartial	deflationary
collectivise	condemnatory	contemptuous	courtplaster	deflationist
collectivism	condensation	conterminous	cousingerman	defraudation
collectivist	conductivity	contestation	covetousness	degenerately
collectivity	conduplicate	contextually	cowardliness	degeneration
collegialism	confabulator	contiguously	crackbrained	degenerative
collegiality	confectioner	contingently	craftbrother	deionisation
collegiately	conferential	continuation	craniologist	dejectedness
collinearity	confessional	continuative	crashlanding	delamination
colloquially	confidential	continuously	creativeness	deliberately
collywobbles	confirmation	contractable	creepycrawly	deliberation
colonisation	confirmative	contractedly	crenellation	deliberative
coloquintida	confirmatory	contractible	criticalness	delicatessen
colorimetric	confiscation	contradictor	crossbedding	delightfully
colourlessly	confiscatory	contrapuntal	crossbencher	delimitation
columniation	conformation	contrariness	crossbuttock	delinquently
combinations	confoundedly	contrariwise	crosscountry	deliquescent
comfortingly	Confucianism	contribution	crosscurrent	delitescence
commandingly	confusedness	contributive	crossexamine	delusiveness
commemorator	congeniality	contributory	crossgrained	demilitarise
commencement	congenitally	contriteness	crossheading	demimondaine
commendation	conglobation	contrivement	crossingover	demineralise
commendatory	conglomerate	controllable	crosspurpose	demodulation
commensalism	conglutinate	contumacious	crosssection	demoniacally
commensalist	congratulant	contumelious	cryptanalyst	demonstrable
commensurate	congratulate	convalescent	cryptogamous	demonstrably
commentation	congregation	convectional	cryptography	demonstrator
commercially	conidiophore	conveniently	cryptologist	denaturalise
commiserator	conidiospore	conventicler	crystalgazer	denaturation
commissarial	conjunctival	conventional	cuckingstool	denomination
commissariat	connaturally	conversation	cuckooflower	denominative
commissioner	connectional	conveyancing	culpableness	denouncement
committeeman	connectively	convincement	cultivatable	densitometer
commodiously	conningtower	convincingly	cumbersomely	denticulated
commonwealth	connubiality	conviviality	cumbrousness	dentilingual
communicable	conquistador	convulsively	cumulatively	denuclearise
communicably	conscionable	coordinately	cumulocirrus	denunciation
communicator	conscription	coordination	cumulonimbus	denunciative
companionate	consecration	coordinative	cuprammonium	denunciatory
companionway	consecratory	copolymerise	curlingirons	deontologist
compatriotic	consensually	copulatively	curlingtongs	departmental
compellation	consentience	coquettishly	curmudgeonly	depoliticise
compensation	consentingly	corelatively	curvicaudate	depopulation
compensative	consequently	corespondent	curvicostate	depravedness
compensatory	conservation	corporeality	curvifoliate	depreciation
complacently	conservatism	correctional	curvirostral	depreciatory
complaisance	conservative	correctitude	customshouse	depressingly
complemental	conservatory	correctively	cynocephalus	deputisation
completeness	considerable	corroborator	cytogenetics	deracination
complexional	considerably	cosmetically	Czechoslovak	derisiveness
complexioned	consignation	cosmogonical	deactivation	derivational
complication	consistently	cosmographer	deambulatory	derivatively
composedness	consistorial	cosmographic	debilitation	dermatophyte
compoundable	consociation	cosmological	debonairness	derogatorily
compressible	consolidator	cosmopolitan	decaffeinate	desalination
compulsively	conspiration	cosmopolitic	decalescence	desideration
compulsivity	constabulary	costermonger	decapitation	desiderative
compulsorily	constipation	cottonocracy	decasyllabic	desirability
compunctious	constituency	cotyledonary	decasyllable	desirousness
compurgation	constitution	cotyledonous	deceleration	desolateness
compurgatory	constitutive	councilwoman	decentralise	despairingly
concelebrant	constriction	countenancer	decipherable	despitefully
concelebrate	constrictive	counteragent	decipherment	despoliation
concentrator	constringent	counterblast	decisiveness	despondently
conceptional	construction	countercheck	declinometer	despotically

desquamation	discountable	divisiveness	elucubration	equilibrator
desquamative	discouraging	dodecahedral	emancipation	equipollence
desquamatory	discourteous	dodecahedron	emargination	equipollency
dessertspoon	discoverable	dodecaphonic	emasculation	equiprobable
destructible	discoverture	dogmatically	emasculatory	equitability
desulphurise	discreetness	dolorousness	embattlement	equivalently
detachedness	discreteness	domestically	embezzlement	equivocation
determinable	discretional	domesticator	embitterment	equivocatory
determinably	discriminant	dorsiventral	emblazonment	eruptiveness
determinedly	discriminate	doubleacting	emblematical	erythematous
dethronement	discursively	doubledealer	embranchment	erythroblast
detoxication	disdainfully	doubledecked	embryologist	erythromycin
detumescence	disembarrass	doubledecker	emotionalise	escapologist
Deuteronomic	disenchanter	doublelocked	emotionalism	escutcheoned
deviationism	disendowment	doubtfulness	emotionalist	esoterically
deviationist	disestablish	dovecoloured	emotionality	espagnolette
dextrousness	disfranchise	downwardness	emphatically	essentiality
diabolically	disgorgement	dramatically	empoisonment	estrangement
diageotropic	disguisement	dramaturgist	empressement	etherisation
diagrammatic	disgustfully	draughtboard	emulsifiable	ethnocentric
dialectician	disgustingly	draughthorse	enantiomorph	ethnographer
dialectology	disharmonise	drawingboard	encephalitic	ethnographic
diamagnetism	dishevelment	drawingpaper	encephalitis	ethnological
diamonddrill	disincentive	dreadfulness	enchantingly	etymological
diamondfield	disinfectant	dressinggown	encirclement	etymologicon
diaphanously	disinfection	droughtiness	enclitically	euhemeristic
diastrophism	disinflation	dubitatively	encroachment	eunuchoidism
diathermancy	disingenuous	duckingstool	encrustation	euphonically
diatomaceous	disintegrate	dunderheaded	encumberment	euphoniously
diatonically	disinterment	duraluminium	encumbrancer	EuroAmerican
dibranchiate	disjointedly	dwarfishness	encyclopedia	evanescently
dichromatism	dislodgement	dynamometric	encyclopedic	evangelistic
dictatorship	disobedience	dynastically	endamagement	eveningdress
didactically	disorientate	earsplitting	endangerment	evidentially
dietetically	dispensation	earthshaking	endermically	evisceration
differentiae	dispensatory	eavesdropped	endocarditis	evolutionary
differential	dispiritedly	eavesdropper	endometritis	evolutionism
digressional	displaceable	eccentricity	endoparasite	evolutionist
digressively	displacement	ecclesiastic	endoskeletal	exacerbation
dilapidation	displeasedly	ecclesiology	enfeeblement	exaggeration
dilatability	dispossessor	echinococcus	enginedriver	exaggerative
dilatoriness	disputatious	echolocation	enginetuning	exaggeratory
dilettantish	disquisition	echosounding	Englishwoman	exasperation
dilettantism	disregardful	eclectically	enormousness	exchangeable
diminishable	disreputable	ecologically	enshrinement	excitability
diminishment	disreputably	econometrics	enswathement	exclusionary
diminutively	dissatisfied	economically	entanglement	exclusionism
dinnerjacket	disseminator	ecstatically	enterprising	exclusionist
diphtheritic	dissentingly	ectoparasite	entertaining	excogitation
diphthongise	dissertation	editorialise	enthronement	excogitative
directorship	disseverance	editorialist	enthusiastic	excruciating
disaccharide	disseverment	educationist	entomologise	excruciation
disadvantage	dissimilarly	edulcoration	entomologist	excursionist
disaffection	dissimulator	effectuality	entrammelled	executorship
disaffiliate	dissocialise	effectuation	entrancement	exegetically
disagreeable	dissociation	effeminately	entreatingly	exenteration
disagreeably	dissociative	effervescent	entrenchment	exercitation
disagreement	dissuasively	efflorescent	entrepreneur	exhaustively
disallowance	dissymmetric	effortlessly	enviableness	exhibitioner
disambiguate	distemperate	effusiveness	envisagement	exhilaration
disannulling	distillation	Egyptologist	enzymologist	exhilarative
disannulment	distillatory	elasmobranch	epexegetical	exiguousness
disassociate	distinctness	electrically	ephemerality	exophthalmic
disastrously	distortional	electrolysis	epicureanism	exophthalmos
disbursement	distractedly	electrolytic	epicycloidal	exophthalmus
discerningly	distrainable	electrometer	epidemically	exorbitantly
discerptible	distrainment	electronvolt	epidemiology	exospherical
discipleship	distributary	electroplate	epigrammatic	exoterically
disciplinary	distribution	electroscope	epiphenomena	expansionary
disclamation	distributive	electroshock	episcopalian	expansionism
discographer	disturbingly	electrotonus	episodically	expansionist
discomfiture	divarication	electrotyper	epistemology	expatriation
discommodity	diversionary	electrotypes	epithalamion	expediential
discomposure	diversionist	eleemosynary	epithalamium	experiential
disconnected	diverticular	elementalism	equalisation	experimental
disconnexion	diverticulum	elementarily	equalitarian	experimenter
disconsolate	divertimenti	elliptically	equationally	explantation
discontented	divertimento	elocutionary	equestrienne	explicitness
discordantly	divisibility	elocutionist	equidistance	exploitation

exploitative	finalisation	gamesmanship	griseofulvin	henceforward
expressional	firefighting	gamesomeness	grossularite	henotheistic
expressively	firstnighter	gametophytic	grotesquerie	heortologist
expressivity	flabelliform	gamopetalous	groundcherry	heraldically
exprobration	flagellation	gamophyllous	groundlessly	hereditament
exsanguinate	flagellatory	gamosepalous	grovellingly	hereditarily
exsanguinous	flagitiously	ganglionated	gruesomeness	hereinbefore
exsufflicate	flamboyantly	gasification	guaranteeing	heritability
extensometer	flamethrower	gastronomist	guardianship	hermeneutics
exterminable	flammability	gastropodous	guestchamber	hermetically
exterminator	flatteringly	geanticlinal	guilefulness	heroicalness
extinguisher	flavoprotein	genealogical	gymnosophist	heroicomical
extortionary	flickeringly	generousness	gynaecocracy	herpetologic
extortionate	flocculation	genuflection	gyromagnetic	hesitatingly
extracranial	floodlighted	geochemistry	haberdashery	hesperididia
extraditable	floriculture	geographical	habilitation	heterocercal
extralimital	fluidisation	geologically	habitability	heterocyclic
extramarital	fluorescence	geomagnetism	habitforming	heteroecious
extramundane	fluoridation	geometrician	habitualness	heterogamous
extraneously	fluorination	geophysicist	haematoblast	heterogenous
extrasensory	fluorocarbon	geopolitical	haematolysis	heterologous
extraspecial	focalisation	geosynclinal	haematoxylon	heteromerous
extrauterine	folliculated	geotectonics	haemophiliac	heteronomous
extravagance	footplateman	geriatrician	haemopoiesis	heterophylly
extravagancy	foraminifera	Germanophile	haemorrhagic	heterosexual
extravaganza	forbiddingly	Germanophobe	hagiographer	heterozygote
extraversion	forcefulness	gerontocracy	hagiographic	heterozygous
extroversion	forcibleness	gesellschaft	hagiological	hibernaculum
exulceration	forebodement	gesticulator	hairdressing	hierarchical
fabulousness	forebodingly	ghoulishness	hairsbreadth	hieroglyphic
facelessness	forensically	gigantically	hairsplitter	hierographer
facilitation	foresightful	glaciologist	halftimbered	hierophantic
factionalism	forestalment	gladiatorial	hallucinogen	highcoloured
factiousness	formaldehyde	gladsomeness	hallucinosis	highfaluting
factitiously	formlessness	glassblowing	halogenation	highhandedly
fainthearted	forthrightly	glaucescence	halterbroken	highlystrung
faintishness	fortuitously	glaucomatous	handicapping	highpressure
faithfulness	fostermother	glitteringly	handkerchief	highsounding
faithhealing	foundationer	globetrotter	handsbreadth	highspirited
falcongentil	fountainhead	glockenspiel	handsomeness	highstepping
falcongentle	fractionally	gloriousness	happenstance	hindquarters
fallaciously	fractionator	glossography	hardfavoured	hippocentaur
fancifulness	FrancoGerman	glossologist	hardfeatured	hippopotamus
fantasticate	frangibility	gluttonously	hardstanding	hirepurchase
fantasticism	frankincense	glycogenesis	harlequinade	histogenesis
farmsteading	fraudulently	glycoprotein	harmlessness	histogenetic
farsightedly	freakishness	glyphography	harmonically	histological
fastidiously	freestanding	glyptography	harmoniously	historically
fatherfigure	freeswimming	gobbledegook	harquebusier	holidaymaker
fatherliness	freethinking	gobbledygook	headmistress	homeomorphic
faultfinding	freewheeling	gonadotropic	headquarters	homeopathist
fearlessness	freightliner	gonadotropin	headshrinker	homesickness
fearsomeness	frenchpolish	goodhumoured	heartburning	homoeopathic
featherbrain	frenetically	goodtempered	heartrending	homoeostasis
featheriness	frequentness	goosepimples	heartstrings	homologation
fecklessness	fricasseeing	gorgeousness	heartwarming	homomorphism
feebleminded	frictionless	governmental	heathenishly	homomorphous
feldspathoid	friendliness	governorship	heavenliness	homonymously
felicitation	frontbencher	gracefulness	heavyhearted	homosexually
felicitously	frontiersman	graciousness	hebdomadally	homothallism
feminineness	frontispiece	grallatorial	hebetudinous	honeybuzzard
feminisation	fructiferous	graminaceous	hectographic	hoodmanblind
fenestration	fructivorous	grammaticise	hedgehopping	hopelessness
fermentation	fruitfulness	grammolecule	heedlessness	horizontally
fermentative	fugitiveness	gramnegative	heliocentric	horrendously
ferrugineous	fuliginosity	grampositive	heliographer	horribleness
fertilisable	fullyfledged	granodiorite	heliographic	horrifically
feverishness	functionally	graphologist	heliogravure	horrorstruck
fibrillation	functionless	graspingness	heliolatrous	horsebreaker
fibrinolysin	furfuraceous	gratefulness	heliotherapy	horsemanship
fictionalise	furunculosis	gratifyingly	heliotropism	horsetrading
fictitiously	futilitarian	gratuitously	hellgrammite	horsewhipped
fiddlefaddle	futurologist	graveclothes	helplessness	horticulture
fiddlesticks	galactogogue	gravelelling	hemerocallis	housebreaker
fieldglasses	galligaskins	greathearted	hemichordate	housekeeping
fiendishness	gallinaceous	greengrocery	hemimorphism	housetrained
figuratively	galvanically	greenishness	hemimorphite	housewarming
filibusterer	galvanometer	gregariously	hemiparasite	hubblebubble
filtrability	galvanoscope	grievousness	hemispheroid	hucklebacked

huggermugger	illtreatment	incapability	indistinctly	intelligible
humanisation	illumination	incapacitate	indivertible	intelligibly
humanitarian	illuminative	incatenation	indivertibly	intemperance
humification	illusiveness	incautiously	individually	inteneration
humorousness	illusoriness	incendiarism	indoctrinate	interbedding
humptydumpty	illustration	incestuously	IndoEuropean	interception
hybridisable	illustrative	incidentally	IndoGermanic	intercession
hydatidiform	immaculately	incineration	industrially	intercessory
hydrochloric	immaterially	incisiveness	ineffaceable	interchanger
hydrodynamic	immatureness	inclinometer	ineffaceably	interconnect
hydrofluoric	immeasurable	incognisable	inefficiency	intercropped
hydrographer	immeasurably	incognisance	inelasticity	intercurrent
hydrographic	immemorially	incognitable	ineradicable	intercutting
hydrokinetic	immensurable	incoherently	ineradicably	interdiction
hydrological	immethodical	incommodious	inescutcheon	interdictive
hydrolysable	immoderately	incommutable	inexactitude	interdictory
hydromedusae	immoderation	incommutably	inexpedience	interdigital
hydromedusan	immovability	incomparable	inexpediency	interestedly
hydrophilous	immunisation	incomparably	inexperience	interfemoral
hydroquinone	immunologist	incompatible	inexpertness	interference
hydrostatics	immutability	incompatibly	inexplicable	interglacial
hydrotherapy	impartiality	incompetence	inexplicably	interjection
hydrothermal	impedimental	incompetency	inexpressive	interjectory
hydrotropism	impenetrable	incompletely	inexpugnable	interlobular
hygienically	impenetrably	incompliance	inexpugnably	interlocutor
hygrophilous	impenitently	incomputable	inextensible	intermeddler
hymenopteran	imperatively	inconcinnity	inextricable	intermediacy
hymnographer	imperatorial	inconclusive	inextricably	intermediary
hyperacidity	imperceptive	inconformity	infanticidal	intermediate
hyperbolical	impercipient	inconsequent	infectiously	interminable
hyperplastic	imperfection	inconsistent	infelicitous	interminably
hyperpyretic	imperfective	inconsolable	infiniteness	intermission
hyperpyrexia	imperishable	inconsolably	infinitively	intermittent
hypersthenia	imperishably	inconsonance	inflammation	intermitting
hypersthenic	impermanence	inconstantly	inflammatory	intermixture
hypertension	impermanency	inconsumable	inflationary	intermundane
hypertensive	impersonally	inconsumably	inflationism	internuclear
hyperthermia	impersonator	incontiguous	inflationist	internuncial
hypertrophic	impertinence	incontinence	inflectional	interoceanic
hypnogenesis	impertinency	incontinency	infrequently	interoceptor
hypnogenetic	imperviously	inconvenient	infringement	interpellate
hypnotherapy	impetiginous	incoordinate	infundibular	interpleader
hypnotically	implantation	incorporated	infusibility	interpolator
hypnotisable	implicitness	incorporator	ingloriously	interpretive
hypochlorite	impoliteness	incorporeity	ingratiating	interrelated
hypochondria	imponderable	incorrigible	inhabitation	interrogator
hypocoristic	imponderably	incorrigibly	inharmonious	interruption
hypocritical	impoverished	incorruption	inhospitable	interruptive
hypogastrium	impregnation	increasingly	inhospitably	intersection
hypognathous	impressively	incrustation	iniquitously	interservice
hypophrygian	imprisonment	incurability	innutritious	interspinous
hypostatical	impropriator	indebtedness	inobservance	interstellar
hyposulphite	improvidence	indecisively	inoccupation	interstitial
hypothalamic	improvisator	indeclinable	inoperculate	intertexture
hypothalamus	imputability	indecorously	inordinately	intervenient
hypothecator	imputatively	indefeasible	inosculation	intervention
hypothetical	inaccessible	indefeasibly	insalubrious	intervocalic
hysterectomy	inaccessibly	indefectible	insecticidal	interwreathe
hysterically	inaccurately	indefensible	insemination	intimidation
hysteromania	inactivation	indefensibly	insolubilise	intimidatory
ichthyocolla	inadequately	indefinitely	insolubility	intolerantly
ichthyolatry	inadmissible	indehiscence	inspectorate	intoxication
ichthyophagy	inadmissibly	indelibility	inspectorial	intracardiac
iconoclastic	inadvertence	indelicately	inspissation	intracranial
iconographer	inadvertency	independence	installation	intramundane
idealisation	inappeasable	independency	instauration	intransigent
ideationally	inapplicable	indicatively	instillation	intransitive
identifiable	inapplicably	indifference	instructress	intrauterine
idiosyncrasy	inappositely	indifferency	instrumental	intrenchment
idiothermous	inarticulate	indigenously	insufferable	intriguingly
idolatrously	inartificial	indigestible	insufferably	introduction
illadvisedly	inaudibility	indirectness	insufficient	introductory
illegibility	inauguration	indiscipline	insufflation	introjection
illegitimacy	inauguratory	indiscreetly	insurrection	intromission
illegitimate	inauspicious	indiscretion	integumental	intromittent
illiberality	incalculable	indisputable	intellection	intromitting
illiterately	incalculably	indisputably	intellective	introversion
illnaturedly	incalescence	indissoluble	intellectual	introversive
illogicality	incandescent	indissolubly	intelligence	introvertive

intrusionist	kremlinology	lovelessness	menstruation	mispronounce
intuitionism	laboursaving	lovelornness	mercantilism	misquotation
intuitionist	labyrinthian	LowChurchman	mercantilist	misrepresent
intumescence	labyrinthine	lugubriously	merchantable	misselthrush
intussuscept	lachrymation	lukewarmness	mercifulness	misstatement
invagination	lachrymatory	lumberjacket	mercurialise	mistakenness
invalidation	lachrymosely	luminescence	mercurialism	mistranslate
inveiglement	lacininiated	luminiferous	meretricious	mistreatment
invertebrate	laisserfaire	luminousness	meridionally	mistressship
investigator	laissezaller	lusciousness	meristematic	mithridatise
inveterately	laissezfaire	lycanthropic	merrythought	mithridatism
invigilation	lakedwelling	machicolated	mesocephalic	mitochondria
invigoration	landingcraft	macrocephaly	mesothoracic	mitrailleuse
invisibility	landingfield	macropterous	messeigneurs	mnemotechnic
involutional	landingstage	mademoiselle	metachronism	mobilisation
invulnerable	landingstrip	magistrature	metagalactic	moderateness
invulnerably	landlubberly	magnetically	metalanguage	modification
irascibility	languishment	magnetisable	metallically	modificatory
irrationally	languorously	magnetograph	metallophone	moistureless
irredeemable	lanternjawed	magnetometer	metallurgist	molecularity
irredeemably	lanternslide	magnifically	metalworking	monadelphous
irreflective	largehearted	magnificence	metamorphism	monastically
irreformable	laryngoscope	magniloquent	metamorphose	monetisation
irrefragable	laryngoscopy	maidenliness	metaphorical	moneychanger
irrefragably	lasciviously	maidenstakes	metaphrastic	moneygrubber
irregardless	laterisation	maintainable	metaphysical	moneyspinner
irregularity	laticiferous	majestically	metapsychics	monitorially
irrelatively	latinisation	majorgeneral	metasomatism	monkeyflower
irrelevantly	latitudinous	malacologist	metathetical	monkeyjacket
irremediable	laudableness	malapertness	metathoracic	monkeypuzzle
irremediably	laureateship	malcontented	meteorically	monkeywrench
irremissible	leapfrogging	malevolently	meteorograph	monochromate
irrepealable	leathercloth	malformation	methodically	monodramatic
irreprovable	ledgertackle	malleability	meticulously	monofilament
irresistible	lefthandedly	malnutrition	metrological	monographist
irresistibly	legalisation	maltreatment	metropolitan	monomaniacal
irresolutely	legitimately	malversation	mezzorelievo	monometallic
irresolution	legitimation	mangelwurzel	mezzosoprano	monomorphous
irresolvable	legitimatise	Manicheanism	microanalyst	monopetalous
irrespective	lepidopteran	manifoldness	microbiology	monophyletic
irrespirable	leucocytosis	manipulation	microcapsule	Monophysitic
irresponsive	leukocytosis	manipulative	microcephaly	monopodially
irreverently	levorotation	manipulatory	microcircuit	monopolistic
irreversible	levorotatory	mannerliness	microclimate	monostichous
irreversibly	lexicography	manoeuvrable	microcopying	monostrophic
irritability	lexicologist	manometrical	microcrystal	monosyllabic
irritatingly	liberalistic	mansionhouse	micrographer	monosyllable
Ishmaelitish	libidinously	manslaughter	microphysics	monotheistic
isochromatic	licentiously	manufacturer	microscopist	monotonously
isochronally	licketysplit	Marcionitism	microseismic	monumentally
isodiametric	lifelessness	marketgarden	microsurgery	moralisation
isolationism	lighthearted	marketsquare	middleweight	mordaciously
isolationist	limnological	marksmanship	militaristic	morningdress
isothermally	linguistical	marlinespike	millesimally	morphallaxis
jerrybuilder	liquefacient	marriageable	milliammeter	morphologist
jesuitically	liquefaction	Marseillaise	mindlessness	morrisdancer
jetpropelled	listlessness	marshharrier	minedetector	mosstrooping
journalistic	literariness	marvellously	mineralogist	motherfigure
judgematical	lithographer	mastersinger	minicomputer	motherliness
jurisconsult	lithographic	masterstroke	minimisation	mothertongue
jurisdiction	lithological	masterswitch	ministration	motivational
jurisprudent	lithospheric	mastigophora	ministrative	motorcyclist
juvenescence	lithotritist	materialness	miraculously	motorisation
kaleidoscope	liturgically	mathematical	mirthfulness	mountainside
karyokinesis	liturgiology	matriarchate	misadventure	mournfulness
katzenjammer	Liverpudlian	maximisation	misalignment	mourningband
Keynesianism	liverystable	mealymouthed	misanthropic	mourningring
kilowatthour	localisation	meaningfully	misapprehend	mouthbreeder
kinaesthesia	lodginghouse	mechanically	misbehaviour	moveableness
kinaesthesis	logistically	mediaevalism	miscalculate	movelessness
kinaesthetic	lonesomeness	mediaevalist	miscellanist	mucilaginous
kindergarten	longdistance	meditatively	misdemeanant	muddleheaded
kinnikinnick	longitudinal	meetinghouse	misdemeanour	mulligatawny
kirschwasser	longshoreman	megalomaniac	misdirection	multicentral
kissingcrust	longstanding	melancholiac	miseducation	multidentate
kleptomaniac	longwindedly	melanochroic	misinterpret	multifarious
klipspringer	lopsidedness	melodramatic	misjudgement	multiflorous
knighterrant	loquaciously	meltingpoint	misknowledge	multifoliate
knightliness	loungelizard	mendaciously	misplacement	multiformity

multilateral	neurosurgery	odontologist	overestimate	peasepudding
multilingual	neurotically	officeholder	overexertion	peccadilloes
multiloquous	nevertheless	offscourings	overexposure	pedantically
multinuclear	newfashioned	oldfashioned	overlordship	pedicellaria
multipartite	Newfoundland	oligarchical	overniceness	pedunculated
multipliable	newspaperman	omnipotently	overpersuade	peerlessness
multiplicand	nicotinamide	omnipresence	overpowering	pejoratively
multiplicate	nidification	omnisciently	overpressure	pellucidness
multiplicity	nightclothes	omnivorously	overreaction	penalisation
multipurpose	nimbostratus	oncorhynchus	oversimplify	penitentiary
multistoried	niminypiminy	oneirocritic	overstepping	pennypincher
multivalence	nitrobenzene	onesidedness	oxyacetylene	pennywhistle
multiversity	noctambulant	oneupmanship	pacification	peradventure
multungulate	noctambulism	onomatopoeia	pacificatory	perambulator
municipalise	noctambulist	onomatopoeic	paedobaptism	perceptively
municipality	noctambulous	openhandedly	paedogenesis	perceptivity
munificently	noctilucence	openmindedly	paedogenetic	perceptually
musicianship	nomenclative	operatically	paedomorphic	percussively
musicologist	nomenclature	ophiophagous	painlessness	percutaneous
mutinousness	nominalistic	opinionative	palaeobotany	peregrinator
muttonheaded	nonagenarian	opisthograph	palaeography	peremptorily
muzzleloader	nonalignment	opisthotonos	Palaeolithic	perfectively
myrmecophily	nonchalantly	opposability	palatability	perfervidity
mysteriously	noncombatant	oppositeness	paletteknife	perfidiously
mystifyingly	noncommittal	oppositional	palingenesia	perfoliation
mythographer	noncomplying	oppressively	palingenesis	performative
mythological	nonconductor	optimisation	palingenetic	pericarditis
mythologiser	nonconformer	orbicularity	Palladianism	perilousness
nailscissors	noneffective	orchestrator	palynologist	periodically
namedropping	nonefficient	orchidaceous	panchromatic	periodontics
namelessness	nonessential	ordinariness	pancreatitis	periodontist
nanoplankton	noneuclidean	organgrinder	panhellenism	periostracum
narcissistic	nonexistence	organisation	panification	peripherally
narcotically	nonflammable	organography	pantechnicon	periphrastic
narrowminded	nonflowering	organoleptic	pantisocracy	perispomenon
naturalistic	nonidentical	orienteering	pantographic	peristeronic
naturopathic	nonobjective	ornamentally	papyrologist	peristomatic
nauseatingly	nonresidence	ornithomancy	paraboloidal	perjuriously
nauseousness	nonresistant	ornithoscopy	paradigmatic	permanganate
navigability	noradrenalin	orographical	paradisaical	permeability
navigational	northeastern	orthodontics	paradisiacal	permissively
nebulisation	northernmost	orthodontist	paraesthesia	permittivity
nebulousness	Northumbrian	orthogenesis	paragraphist	perniciously
necrographer	northwestern	orthogenetic	parallelling	pernoctation
necrological	notification	orthographer	paralysation	peroxidation
necrophagous	novelisation	orthographic	paramagnetic	perpetration
necrophiliac	numerologist	orthopaedics	parametrical	perpetuation
necrophilism	numerousness	orthopaedist	paramilitary	perplexingly
necrophilous	nutritionist	orthopterist	paramorphism	perseverance
needlessness	nutritiously	orthopteroid	paranormally	persistently
negativeness	nychthemeral	orthopterous	paraphrastic	perspicacity
negativistic	nychthemeron	orthotropism	parasiticide	perspiration
neglectfully	nyctitropism	orthotropous	parasitology	perspiratory
negotiatress	nympholeptic	oscillograph	paratactical	persuasively
negrophilism	nymphomaniac	oscilloscope	parenthesise	pertinacious
negrophilist	obdurateness	ossification	parisyllabic	perturbation
neighbouring	obedientiary	ostentatious	parkinsonism	perturbative
neoclassical	oblanceolate	osteogenesis	parochialise	perverseness
neoDarwinian	obligatorily	osteological	parochialism	perviousness
neoDarwinism	obligingness	osteomalacia	parochiality	pestilential
neoDarwinist	obliteration	osteoplastic	paronomastic	pestological
Neohellenism	obliterative	osteoporosis	parsimonious	petrifaction
neonomianism	obmutescence	otherworldly	participator	petrographer
Neoplatonism	obnubilation	outdatedness	particularly	petrographic
Neoplatonist	obscurantism	outlandishly	partisanship	petrological
nephanalysis	obscurantist	outmanoeuvre	partitionist	pettifoggery
nephelometer	obsequiously	outpensioner	pasqueflower	pettifogging
nephelometry	obsolescence	outrageously	passepartout	phagocytosis
nephrologist	obsoleteness	outrivalling	passionately	phagocytotic
nerveracking	obstetrician	outstretched	passionfruit	phanerogamic
Nestorianism	obstreperous	outstripping	pathetically	pharmaceutic
neurasthenia	occasionally	outwardbound	pathogenesis	pharmacology
neurasthenic	occidentally	overabundant	pathogenetic	phenological
neuroanatomy	occupational	overachiever	pathological	phenomenally
neurobiology	oceanography	overactivity	patriarchate	phenotypical
neurological	oceanologist	overcautious	patternmaker	philadelphus
neuropterous	octogenarian	overcritical	patulousness	philanthropist
neuroscience	octosyllabic	overcropping	peacefulness	philanthropy
neurosurgeon	octosyllable	overemphasis	pearlescence	philharmonic

philhellenic	plumbaginous	precociously	proconsulate	psychologist
philistinism	plumbiferous	precognition	prodigiously	psychometric
phillumenist	plummerblock	precognitive	productively	psychopathic
philodendron	pluriliteral	precondition	productivity	psychosexual
philological	pluviometric	preconscious	professional	psychotropic
philosophise	pneumaticity	predesignate	professorate	psychrometer
phlebotomise	pneumatology	predestinate	professoress	psychrometry
phlebotomist	pneumothorax	predetermine	professorial	pteridophyte
phonasthenia	poikilotherm	predictively	proficiently	pteridosperm
phonemically	pointilliste	predigestion	profiteering	pterodactyle
phonetically	polarimetric	predilection	profligately	publicspirit
phonographer	polarisation	predominance	profoundness	puerperally
phonographic	polarography	predominancy	progenitress	pugnaciously
phonological	policyholder	preeminently	progesterone	pulverisable
phosphoresce	polychaetous	preestablish	proglottides	pumpernickel
photochromic	polychromous	preexistence	programmable	punchingball
photofission	polyethylene	prefabricate	programmatic	purblindness
photogeology	polyglottism	prefectorial	projectional	purification
photographer	polyhistoric	preferential	projectively	purificatory
photographic	polymorphism	preformation	prolegomenon	purposebuilt
photogravure	polymorphous	preformative	prolifically	purposefully
photokinesis	polyneuritic	prehensility	prolificness	pursestrings
photokinetic	polyneuritis	prehistorian	prolongation	putrefaction
photomontage	polypetalous	prelapsarian	promulgation	putrefactive
photophilous	polyphyletic	premaxillary	pronominally	pyroelectric
photosetting	polysepalous	premeditated	pronouncedly	pyroligneous
photospheric	polysyllabic	premeditator	proofreading	pyromaniacal
phototropism	polysyllable	premenstrual	propaedeutic	pyromorphite
phrasemonger	polytheistic	prenticeship	propagandise	pyrotechnics
phraseograph	polytonality	preoccupancy	propagandism	pyrotechnist
phreatophyte	polyurethane	preparedness	propagandist	Quadragesima
phrenologist	pontifically	preponderant	prophylactic	quadrangular
phycological	pontificator	preponderate	propitiation	quadraphonic
phycomycetes	poorspirited	preposterous	propitiatory	quadriennium
phyllotactic	populousness	prerequisite	propitiously	quadrinomial
phylogenesis	porcelainise	presbyterate	proportional	quadriplegia
phylogenetic	porcelainous	presbyterial	proportioned	quadriplegic
physiognomic	porcellanous	Presbyterian	proprietress	quadrivalent
physiography	pornographer	prescription	proscription	quadrumanous
physiologist	pornographic	prescriptive	proscriptive	quaestorship
phytogenesis	portentously	preselection	prosectorial	qualmishness
phytogenetic	portmanteaus	preselective	prosecutable	quantifiable
phytographer	portmanteaux	presentation	proselytiser	quantisation
phytological	positiveness	presentative	prosodically	quantitative
phytophagous	positivistic	presentiment	prosopopoeia	quaquaversal
pickerelweed	possessively	preservation	prosperously	quarterbound
pictographic	postdiluvian	preservative	prostitution	quarterfinal
pigeonbreast	postdoctoral	presidential	protactinium	quarterstaff
pigmentation	posteriority	presumptuous	protectively	quattrocento
pilotballoon	postgraduate	pretermitted	protectorate	questionable
pinfeathered	posthumously	prevailingly	protensively	questionably
pisciculture	postmeridian	prevaricator	protestation	questionless
pitcherplant	postmistress	preventative	prothalamion	quinquennial
pitiableness	postponement	preventively	prothalamium	quinquennium
pitilessness	postposition	previousness	prothonotary	quintessence
pitterpatter	postpositive	pricecutting	protistology	quixotically
placesetting	postprandial	pridefulness	protohistory	quizzicality
plainclothed	potentiality	priestliness	protoplasmic	rabbinically
plainclothes	practicality	priestridden	protoplastic	rabblerouser
plaindealing	practitioner	priggishness	prototypical	racemisation
planetesimal	pragmatistic	primigravida	protozoology	racketeering
planetstruck	praiseworthy	primogenital	protrusively	radiobiology
planispheric	pralltriller	primogenitor	protuberance	radioelement
planoconcave	praseodymium	primordially	proudhearted	radiographer
plasterboard	precancelled	princeliness	proverbially	radiographic
platonically	precariously	principality	providential	radioisotope
Plattdeutsch	precedential	printability	provincially	radiological
plausibility	preceptorial	privatdocent	provisionary	radionuclide
playingfield	precessional	privatdozent	prudentially	radiophonics
pleasantness	prechristian	privateering	psephologist	radiotherapy
pleasingness	preciousness	prizefighter	pseudocyesis	rambunctious
pleasureless	precipitable	prizewinning	pseudonymity	ramification
plebiscitary	precipitance	probationary	pseudonymous	rapprochment
plecopterous	precipitancy	proboscidean	pseudopodium	ratification
plectognathi	precipitator	proboscidian	psychiatrist	ratiocinator
pleiotropism	precisianism	procathedral	psychoactive	rattleheaded
plenipotence	precisionist	processional	psychography	ravenousness
pleomorphism	preclassical	proclamation	psychologise	razzledazzle
plesiosaurus	preclusively	proclamatory	psychologism	reactivation

reactiveness	remunerative	rhynchophora	scintigraphy	selfsameness
readableness	remuneratory	rhythmically	scintillator	selfstarting
readjustment	renegotiable	ribonuclease	sclerenchyma	selfviolence
reallocation	renouncement	ricochetting	scornfulness	sellingplate
reappearance	renunciation	ridiculously	scorpionfish	semantically
reassessment	renunciative	rightfulness	scoundreldom	semiannually
reassignment	renunciatory	rigorousness	scoundrelism	semibasement
reassuringly	reoccupation	risorgimento	scouringrush	semicircular
rebelliously	repatriation	robustiously	scraperboard	semicylinder
recalcitrant	repercussion	rollingstock	scratchiness	semidarkness
recalcitrate	repercussive	romanisation	screenwriter	semideponent
recalescence	repetitional	romantically	scrimshanker	semidetached
recapitulate	repetitively	rontgenogram	scripturally	semidiameter
receivership	repossession	rontgenology	scriptwriter	semidomestic
receptaculum	reprehension	rootlessness	scrobiculate	semifinalist
receptionist	reprehensive	rosecoloured	scrupulosity	semifinished
recessionary	repressively	rumbletumble	scrupulously	semiliterate
rechargeable	reproachable	ruminatively	sculpturally	seminiferous
reciprocally	reproachless	runningboard	scurrilously	semiofficial
reciprocator	reproducible	ruralisation	scutellation	semiological
recklessness	reproduction	ruthlessness	secessionism	semiparasite
recognisable	reproductive	sabretoothed	secessionist	semiprecious
recognisably	reprographic	saccharinity	seclusionist	semitropical
recognisance	reservedness	saccharoidal	secondstring	sempiternity
recollection	resettlement	sacerdotally	sectarianise	sensibleness
recollective	residentiary	sacrilegious	sectarianism	sensitometer
recommitment	residentship	saddlebacked	sectionalism	sensualistic
reconcilable	resignedness	sadistically	secularistic	sensuousness
reconstitute	resiniferous	safecracking	sedgewarbler	sententially
reconversion	resipiscence	salamandrian	sedulousness	separability
reconveyance	resistlessly	salamandrine	segmentation	separateness
recreational	resoluteness	salamandroid	seismography	septennially
recrudescent	resolvedness	salesmanship	seismologist	septilateral
recuperation	resoundingly	salmonladder	seismometric	septuagenary
recuperative	respectfully	salpiglossis	seismoscopic	Septuagesima
redecoration	respectively	salubriously	selenography	Septuagintal
redemptioner	resplendence	salutariness	selenologist	sepulchrally
Redemptorist	resplendency	salutational	selfabsorbed	sequaciously
redeployment	responsively	salutiferous	selfactivity	sequentially
redintegrate	responsorial	salvationism	selfaffected	sequestrator
redistribute	restaurateur	salvationist	selfanalysis	seraphically
reducibility	restlessness	Samaritanism	selfapplause	sergeantfish
reductionism	restrainable	sandyachting	selfapproval	sergeantship
reductionist	restrainedly	sanguinarily	selfbegotten	sericultural
reflationary	restrictedly	sanguineness	selfbetrayal	serjeantship
reflectional	resupination	sanguinolent	selfcatering	serpentiform
reflectively	resurrection	sansculottic	selfcoloured	serpentinely
reflectivity	resuscitator	saponifiable	selfcomposed	serviceberry
refractivity	reticulately	saprophagous	selfcontempt	servicecourt
refractorily	reticulation	sarcomatosis	selfcritical	servicewoman
refreshingly	reticulocyte	sarcophagous	selfdeceived	servitorship
refreshments	retiringness	sardonically	selfdeceiver	servocontrol
refrigerator	retractation	sarrusophone	selfdelusion	sesquialtera
regardlessly	retractility	satisfaction	selfdestruct	sexagenarian
regeneration	retrenchment	satisfactory	selfdevotion	sexcentenary
regenerative	retrocedence	satisfyingly	selfdirected	shadowboxing
regimentally	retrocession	scabbardfish	selfdistrust	Shakspereana
registration	retrocessive	scabrousness	selfdoubting	Shaksperiana
regressively	retroflexion	scandalously	selfeducated	shamateurism
rehabilitate	retropulsion	Scandinavian	selfeffacing	shamefacedly
reinvestment	retroversion	scareheading	selfelective	shamefulness
reinvigorate	reunionistic	scarificator	selfemployed	sharecropper
rejectamenta	revelational	scatological	selfevidence	sharpshooter
rejuvenation	revengefully	scatterbrain	selfexistent	sharpsighted
relationally	reverberator	scatteringly	selfflattery	shatterproof
relationship	reversionary	scenepainter	selfhypnosis	sheepishness
relativeness	revictualled	sceneshifter	selfidentity	sheepshearer
relativistic	revivalistic	scenographic	selfignition	shillyshally
relentlessly	reviviscence	schismatical	selfinterest	shipbuilding
reliableness	rhetorically	schizogonous	selfinvolved	shirtwaister
rememberable	rheumatology	schizomycete	selflessness	shootingiron
remembrancer	rhinocerotic	schizophrene	selflimiting	shortchanger
remilitarise	rhinological	schizophthymia	selfluminous	shortcircuit
reminiscence	rhizocarpous	schizothymia	selfmurderer	shortpitched
remonstrance	rhizogenetic	schizothymic	selfpleasing	shortsighted
remonstrator	rhizophagous	schoolfellow	selfportrait	shortsleeved
remorsefully	rhododendron	schoolleaver	selfreliance	shortstaffed
removability	rhombohedral	schoolmaster	selfreproach	shoulderbelt
remuneration	rhombohedron	schorlaceous	selfrighting	shoulderknot

shouldernote	southernmost	stepdaughter	suberisation	susceptivity
shrewishness	southernwood	stereochromy	subinfeudate	suspensively
shuffleboard	southwestern	stereography	subjectively	suspiciously
sideslipping	spaciousness	stereoisomer	subjectivise	sustentation
sidestepping	sparkingplug	stereometric	subjectivism	sustentative
sidewhiskers	sparrowgrass	stereophonic	subjectivist	swaggeringly
sightreading	speakingtube	stereopticon	subjectivity	swaggerstick
significance	specialistic	stereoscopic	sublapsarian	swainishness
significancy	specifically	sterlingness	submaxillary	swashbuckler
silicicolous	specificness	sternutation	subminiature	sweepingness
siliciferous	speciousness	sternutative	submissively	sweetishness
silverglance	specktioneer	sternutatory	subnormality	swimmingbath
silviculture	spectrograph	sternwheeler	subsaturated	swimmingbell
simoniacally	spectrometer	stertorously	subscription	swimmingpool
simpleminded	spectrometry	stethoscopic	subsequently	swizzlestick
simultaneity	spectroscope	stichomythia	subservience	sycophantish
simultaneous	spectroscopy	stichomythic	subserviency	syllabically
Sinanthropus	speechlessly	stilboestrol	subsidiarily	sylviculture
singleacting	speedboating	stillhunting	subsonically	symbolically
singledecker	speleologist	stockbreeder	substantiate	synaesthesia
singlehanded	spermaphytic	stockbroking	substantival	synaesthetic
singleminded	spermathecal	stockingless	substitution	synarthrosis
singleseater	spermatocyte	stockjobbery	substitutive	synchronical
sinistrality	spermatozoid	stockjobbing	substruction	synchroniser
sinistrorsal	spermatozoon	stockraising	substructure	syncretistic
sinusoidally	spermogonium	stoneboiling	subtemperate	syndactylism
siphonophore	spheroidally	stonecutting	subterranean	syndactylous
siphonostele	sphragistics	stonedresser	subthreshold	syndetically
skateboarder	sphygmograph	stonemasonry	subversively	synonymously
skippingrope	spidermonkey	stonyhearted	succedaneous	synoptically
skittishness	spiegeleisen	stormtrooper	successfully	systematical
skrimshanker	spinsterhood	stouthearted	successional	systematiser
skullduggery	spiritedness	Stradivarius	successively	systemically
skunkcabbage	spiritlessly	straightaway	succinctness	taberdarship
slanderously	spiritualise	straightbred	sudoriferous	tabernacular
slaughterous	spiritualism	straightedge	sufficiently	tachygrapher
slaveholding	spiritualist	straightener	suggestively	tachygraphic
sledgehammer	spirituality	straightness	suitableness	tactlessness
sleepingpill	spitefulness	straitjacket	sulphonamide	tamelessness
sleepwalking	splendidness	stranglehold	sulphonation	tangentially
slipcarriage	spokesperson	straticulate	sulphuration	tangibleness
slipperiness	sporadically	stratigraphy	sulphuretted	taperecorder
slothfulness	sporogenesis	stratosphere	superannuate	taskmistress
slovenliness	sportfulness	streetwalker	supercharger	tastefulness
sluggishness	sportiveness	strengthener	superciliary	tautological
sluttishness	spotlessness	strengthless	supercilious	taxcollector
smallclothes	sprightfully	streptococci	supereminent	teachability
smallholding	spuriousness	streptomycin	supererogate	tearlessness
snaggletooth	squarerigged	stridulation	superhighway	technicality
snakecharmer	squattocracy	strikingness	superhumanly	technicolour
snapfastener	squirrelcage	stringcourse	supermundane	technocratic
snappishness	squirreltail	strobilation	supernaculum	technologist
snarlingiron	stablishment	stroboscopic	supernatural	tectonically
snobbishness	staffofficer	strongminded	superposable	teensyweensy
sociableness	staffsurgeon	strongylosis	supersedence	teetertotter
sociological	stagemanager	strontianite	supersensory	telaesthesia
sociometrist	staggeringly	strophanthin	supersession	telaesthetic
Socratically	Stakhanovism	structurally	superstition	telegraphese
sodafountain	Stakhanovite	strychninism	superstratum	telegraphist
softpedalled	stalactiform	stubbornness	supervenient	teleological
solarisation	stalwartness	studdingsail	supervention	televisional
solicitation	stammeringly	studiousness	supplemental	temptability
solicitously	standardbred	stupefacient	supplementer	teratologist
solifluction	standingroom	stupefaction	supplicantly	teratomatous
solitariness	stanniferous	stupefactive	supplication	tercentenary
somatopleure	starspangled	stupendously	supplicatory	terebinthine
somnambulant	stationhouse	stutteringly	suppositious	tergiversate
somnambulate	stationwagon	stylographic	suppressible	terribleness
somnambulism	statistician	subalternate	supramundane	terrifically
somnambulist	statuesquely	subalternity	supraorbital	terrifyingly
somniloquism	stealthiness	subapostolic	surefootedly	terrorstruck
somniloquist	steatopygous	subarrhation	surmountable	tessellation
sonorousness	steeplechase	subcelestial	surprisingly	testamentary
sophisticate	steganograph	subcommittee	surrealistic	testosterone
soporiferous	stellenbosch	subconscious	surrejoinder	testudineous
sorbefacient	stelliferous	subcontinent	surroundings	tetrachordal
soullessness	stenographer	subcutaneous	surveillance	tetragonally
soundingline	stenographic	subdivisible	surveyorship	tetrahedrite
southeastern	stepchildren	subeditorial	survivorship	tetramorphic

Teutonically	traditionary	truthfulness	unencumbered	usufructuary
thankfulness	traditionist	tuberculated	uneventfully	usuriousness
thanksgiving	traducianism	tuberculosis	unexpectedly	uxoriousness
thaumaturgic	traducianist	tumultuously	unfaithfully	vainglorious
theanthropic	tragicomical	tunelessness	unfamiliarly	Valenciennes
theatregoing	trainspotter	turbellarian	unfathomable	valetudinary
theatrically	traitorously	turriculated	unfavourable	valorisation
theistically	trampolinist	turtlenecked	unfavourably	valuableness
thematically	tranquillise	twentyfourmo	unflattering	vanquishable
theocratical	tranquillity	twitteringly	unfrequented	vanquishment
theoretician	transcendent	typefounding	ungainliness	vantagepoint
theosophical	transduction	typification	ungovernable	vaporisation
therapeutics	transferable	tyrannically	ungracefully	vaporousness
therapeutist	transference	tyrannicidal	ungraciously	variableness
thereinafter	transferring	ubiquitarian	ungratefully	varicoloured
thermocouple	transformism	ubiquitously	unhesitating	vasodilation
thermography	transformist	ultramontane	unhistorical	vasodilatory
thermolabile	transfusible	ultramundane	unifoliolate	vaticination
thermometric	transgressor	umbrageously	unilaterally	vauntcourier
thermophilic	transhipment	unacceptable	unimaginable	vegetatively
thermoscopic	transhumance	unaccustomed	unimaginably	venepuncture
thermosphere	transiliency	unaffectedly	unimportance	venerability
thermostable	transitional	unambivalent	uninterested	vengefulness
thermostatic	transitively	unanswerable	unionisation	venipuncture
thermotactic	transitivity	unapologetic	unisexuality	venomousness
thermotropic	transitorily	unappeasable	unitarianism	ventripotent
thickskinned	translatable	unappetising	universalise	veridicality
thickskulled	translucence	unassailable	universalism	verification
thievishness	translucency	unassumingly	universalist	verificatory
thimbleberry	transmigrant	unattractive	universality	vermiculated
thirdborough	transmigrate	unauthorised	unkindliness	vernacularly
thitherwards	transmission	unbecomingly	unlawfulness	vertebration
thoroughbass	transmissive	unbelievable	unlikelihood	verticalness
thoroughbred	transmitting	unbelievably	unlikeliness	verticillate
thoroughfare	transmogrify	unblinkingly	unloveliness	vesiculation
thoroughness	transmontane	unblushingly	unmanageable	veterinarian
thoughtfully	transmutable	unbrokenness	unmercifully	vibraphonist
thousandfold	transoceanic	uncalculated	unmistakable	vicargeneral
threequarter	transpacific	uncelebrated	unmistakably	vicechairman
threewheeler	transparency	unchangeable	unofficially	Victorianism
thriftlessly	transpirable	unchangeably	unparalleled	victoriously
throughstone	transplanter	uncharitable	unpleasantly	vigorousness
thundercloud	transpontine	uncharitably	unpopularity	vilification
thunderingly	transposable	unchivalrous	unprejudiced	villainously
thunderously	transshipped	unclassified	unpretending	vindictively
thunderstone	transudation	uncomeatable	unprincipled	vinification
thunderstorm	transudatory	uncommercial	unprofitable	viridescence
ticklishness	transversely	uncommonness	unprofitably	virtuosoship
tightmouthed	transvestism	unconformity	unpronounced	virtuousness
timehonoured	transvestite	unconsidered	unreasonable	viscerotonic
timelessness	tremendously	unconstraint	unreasonably	viscosimeter
timorousness	trephination	uncontrolled	unrecognised	viscountship
tintinnabula	trestletable	unconvincing	unregenerate	visitational
tirelessness	triangularly	uncritically	unrepeatable	visitatorial
tiresomeness	tricentenary	unctuousness	unreservedly	vitalisation
tittletattle	trichologist	undemocratic	unresponsive	vitiligation
toastingfork	trichotomise	underachieve	unrestrained	vitreousness
togetherness	trichotomous	underbidding	unscientific	vitrifaction
toggleswitch	trichromatic	underclothes	unscriptural	vituperation
toilsomeness	trickishness	undercoating	unscrupulous	vituperative
tolerability	tridactylous	undercurrent	unsearchable	vituperatory
tonelessness	trifurcation	undercutting	unseasonable	vivification
toploftiness	triggerhappy	underdevelop	unsegregated	viviparously
topsyturvily	triglyphical	undergarment	unsteadiness	vocabularian
torrefaction	trigonometry	underinsured	unstructured	vocalisation
torrentially	trinomialism	underletting	unsuccessful	vociferation
Torricellian	tripartitely	undermanning	unthinkingly	vociferously
tortuousness	tripartition	underpinning	unthoughtful	voidableness
totalisation	triphthongal	underrunning	untimeliness	volatileness
totalitarian	triplication	undersetting	untowardness	volcanically
touchingness	triumphantly	understaffed	untruthfully	volitionally
towardliness	trochanteric	undersurface	unwieldiness	volumetrical
toxicologist	troglodytism	undertenancy	unwontedness	voluminosity
toxicophobia	trophallaxis	underwritten	unworldiness	voluminously
traceability	tropological	undetermined	unworthiness	voluntaryism
trachomatous	tropospheric	undiplomatic	unyieldingly	voluntaryist
tractability	troublemaker	uneconomical	uproariously	voluptuosity
tradescantia	trumpetshell	unemployable	urbanisation	voluptuously
tradespeople	trustfulness	unemployment	urbanologist	vomiturition

wainscotting	bantamweight	earsplitting	katzenjammer	masterstroke
waistcoating	barbarically	earthshaking	laboursaving	masterswitch
walkietalkie	barometrical	eavesdropped	labyrinthian	mastigophora
wallpainting	baselessness	eavesdropper	labyrinthine	materialness
wallydraigle	basidiospore	fabulousness	lachrymation	mathematical
warehouseman	bassorelievo	facelessness	lachrymatory	matriarchate
wastefulness	bassorilievo	facilitation	lachrymosely	maximisation
watchfulness	bathypelagic	factionalism	lacininiated	nailscissors
watermanship	battleground	factiousness	laisserfaire	namedropping
weatherboard	battlemented	factitiously	laissezaller	namelessness
weatherbound	cabbagewhite	fainthearted	laissezfaire	nanoplankton
weatherglass	cabinetmaker	faintishness	lakedwelling	narcissistic
weatherhouse	cachinnation	faithfulness	landingcraft	narcotically
weatherproof	cachinnatory	faithhealing	landingfield	narrowminded
welldisposed	calamitously	falcongentil	landingstage	naturalistic
wellfavoured	calcareously	falcongentle	landingstrip	naturopathic
wellgrounded	calculatedly	fallaciously	landlubberly	nauseatingly
Wellingtonia	calisthenics	fancifulness	languishment	nauseousness
welterweight	calligrapher	fantasticate	languorously	navigability
whencesoever	calligraphic	fantasticism	lanternjawed	navigational
wherethrough	callisthenic	farmsteading	lanternslide	pacification
whigmaleerie	calorescence	farsightedly	largehearted	pacificatory
whimperingly	calorimetric	fastidiously	laryngoscope	paedobaptism
whimsicality	calumniation	fatherfigure	laryngoscopy	paedogenesis
whippoorwill	calumniatory	fatherliness	lasciviously	paedogenetic
whisperingly	calumniously	faultfinding	laterisation	paedomorphic
whitelivered	calycoideous	galactogogue	laticiferous	painlessness
whitewashing	camiknickers	galligaskins	latinisation	palaeobotany
whitherwards	campfollower	gallinaceous	latitudinous	palaeography
wholehearted	campodeiform	galvanically	laudableness	Palaeolithic
whortleberry	canaliculate	galvanometer	laureateship	palatability
wicketkeeper	canalisation	galvanoscope	machicolated	paletteknife
williewaught	cancellation	gamesmanship	macrocephaly	palingenesia
windingsheet	candleholder	gamesomeness	macropterous	palingenesis
wineglassful	canonisation	gametophytic	mademoiselle	palingenetic
winklepicker	canorousness	gamopetalous	magistrature	Palladianism
winterbourne	Cantabrigian	gamophyllous	magnetically	palynologist
wollastonite	cantankerous	gamosepalous	magnetisable	panchromatic
womanishness	cantharidian	ganglionated	magnetograph	pancreatitis
wonderstruck	cantillation	gasification	magnetometer	panhellenism
wonderworker	capercaillie	gastronomist	magnifically	panification
wondrousness	capercailzie	gastropodous	magnificence	pantechnicon
woodengraver	capitalistic	haberdashery	magniloquent	pantisocracy
woodenheaded	capitulation	habilitation	maidenliness	pantographic
woolgatherer	capriciously	habitability	maidenstakes	papyrologist
woollyheaded	captiousness	habitforming	maintainable	paraboloidal
workableness	caravansarai	habitualness	majestically	paradigmatic
workingclass	caravanserai	haematoblast	majorgeneral	paradisaical
worshipfully	carbohydrate	haematolysis	malacologist	paradisiacal
wrathfulness	carbonaceous	haematoxylon	malapertness	paraesthesia
wretchedness	carburetting	haemophiliac	malcontented	paragraphist
wrongfulness	carcinogenic	haemopoiesis	malevolently	parallelling
wunderkinder	cardcarrying	haemorrhagic	malformation	paralysation
xanthochroia	cardinalship	hagiographer	malleability	paramagnetic
xiphisternum	cardiography	hagiographic	malnutrition	parametrical
YankeeDoodle	cardiologist	hagiological	maltreatment	paramilitary
yellowhammer	carelessness	hairdressing	malversation	paramorphism
youngberries	caricaturist	hairsbreadth	mangelwurzel	paranormally
youthfulness	carillonneur	hairsplitter	Manicheanism	paraphrastic
zoogeography	Carlovingian	halftimbered	manifoldness	parasiticide
zygapophysis	carpetbagger	hallucinogen	manipulation	parasitology
zygomorphism	carpetknight	hallucinosis	manipulative	paratactical
zygomorphous	carragheenin	halogenation	manipulatory	parenthesise
————————————	carriageable	halterbroken	mannerliness	parisyllabic
bacchanalian	Cartesianism	handicapping	manoeuvrable	parkinsonism
bachelorhood	cartographer	handkerchief	manometrical	parochialise
bachelorship	cartographic	handsbreadth	mansionhouse	parochialism
backbreaking	cartological	handsomeness	manslaughter	parochiality
backpedalled	cashandcarry	happenstance	manufacturer	paronomastic
backslapping	catachrestic	hardfavoured	Marcionitism	parsimonious
backwardness	catamountain	hardfeatured	marketgarden	participator
backwoodsman	cataphoresis	hardstanding	marketsquare	particularly
bactericidal	catastrophic	harlequinade	marksmanship	partisanship
bacteriology	catechetical	harmlessness	marlinespike	partitionist
bacteriostat	caterwauling	harmonically	marriageable	pasqueflower
balladmonger	catholically	harmoniously	Marseillaise	passepartout
balletomania	catilinarian	harquebusier	marshharrier	passionately
ballottement	cattlelifter	kaleidoscope	marvellously	passionfruit
banderillero	cautiousness	karyokinesis	mastersinger	pathetically

pathogenesis	valorisation	accusatorial	adequateness	decisiveness
pathogenetic	valuableness	acetabularia	adhesiveness	declinometer
pathological	vanquishable	acetaldehyde	adjectivally	decomposable
patriarchate	vanquishment	achlamydeous	adjudication	decompressor
patternmaker	vantagepoint	acoustically	adjudicative	decongestant
patulousness	vaporisation	acquaintance	adjudicatory	decongestion
rabbinically	vaporousness	acquiescence	administrant	decongestive
rabblerouser	variableness	acronychally	administrate	deconsecrate
racemisation	varicoloured	actinomycete	admonishment	decontrolled
racketeering	vasodilation	eccentricity	adorableness	decoratively
radiobiology	vasodilatory	ecclesiastic	adscititious	decorousness
radioelement	vaticination	ecclesiology	adulteration	decreasingly
radiographer	vauntcourier	echinococcus	adulterously	deescalation
radiographic	wainscotting	echolocation	advantageous	definiteness
radioisotope	waistcoating	echosounding	adventitious	definitively
radiological	walkietalkie	eclectically	advisability	deflagration
radionuclide	wallpainting	ecologically	editorialise	deflationary
radiophonics	wallydraigle	econometrics	editorialist	deflationist
radiotherapy	warehouseman	economically	educationist	defraudation
rambunctious	wastefulness	ecstatically	edulcoration	degenerately
ramification	watchfulness	ectoparasite	idealisation	degeneration
rapprochment	watermanship	ichthyocolla	ideationally	degenerative
ratification	xanthochroia	ichthyolatry	identifiable	deionisation
ratiocinator	YankeeDoodle	ichthyophagy	idiosyncrasy	dejectedness
rattleheaded	abbreviation	iconoclastic	idiothermous	delamination
ravenousness	abolitionary	iconographer	idolatrously	deliberately
razzledazzle	abolitionism	occasionally	odontologist	deliberation
sabretoothed	abolitionist	occidentally	aerodynamics	deliberative
saccharinity	aboriginally	occupational	aeroembolism	delicatessen
saccharoidal	abortiveness	oceanography	aeronautical	delightfully
sacerdotally	abrasiveness	oceanologist	aeroneurosis	delimitation
sacrilegious	absentminded	octogenarian	aerosiderite	delinquently
saddlebacked	absoluteness	octosyllabic	aesthetician	deliquescent
sadistically	absolutistic	octosyllable	aestheticism	delitescence
safecracking	absorptional	scabbardfish	aetiological	delusiveness
salamandrian	absorptivity	scabrousness	beachcombing	demilitarise
salamandrine	absquatulate	scandalously	beatifically	demimondaine
salamandroid	abstemiously	Scandinavian	bedazzlement	demineralise
salesmanship	abstractable	scareheading	beggarliness	demodulation
salmonladder	abstractedly	scarificator	behaviourism	demoniacally
salpiglossis	abstractness	scatological	behaviourist	demonstrable
salubriously	abstruseness	scatterbrain	belittlement	demonstrably
salutariness	obdurateness	scatteringly	bellbottomed	demonstrator
salutational	obedientiary	scenepainter	belletristic	denaturalise
salutiferous	oblanceolate	sceneshifter	belligerence	denaturation
salvationism	obligatorily	scenographic	belligerency	denomination
salvationist	obligingness	schismatical	bellylanding	denominative
Samaritanism	obliteration	schizogonous	benefactress	denouncement
sandyachting	obliterative	schizomycete	beneficently	densitometer
sanguinarily	obmutescence	schizophrene	beneficially	denticulated
sanguineness	obnubilation	schizothymia	benevolently	dentilingual
sanguinolent	obscurantism	schizothymic	benzaldehyde	denuclearise
sansculottic	obscurantist	schoolfellow	bequeathment	denunciation
saponifiable	obsequiously	schoolleaver	berzelianite	denunciative
saprophagous	obsolescence	schoolmaster	beseechingly	denunciatory
sarcomatosis	obsoleteness	schorlaceous	bespectacled	deontologist
sarcophagous	obstetrician	scintigraphy	bewilderedly	departmental
sardonically	obstreperous	scintillator	bewilderment	depoliticise
sarrusophone	ubiquitarian	sclerenchyma	bewitchingly	depopulation
sarsaparilla	ubiquitously	scornfulness	cementitious	depravedness
satisfaction	academically	scorpionfish	censoriously	depreciation
satisfactory	acaulescence	scoundreldom	centesimally	depreciatory
satisfyingly	acceleration	scoundrelism	centrespread	depressingly
taberdarship	accelerative	scouringrush	centrosphere	deputisation
tabernacular	accentuation	scraperboard	centuplicate	deracination
tachygrapher	acciaccatura	scratchiness	ceremonially	derisiveness
tachygraphic	accidentally	screenwriter	deactivation	derivational
tactlessness	accommodator	scrimshanker	deambulatory	derivatively
tamelessness	accompanyist	scripturally	debilitation	dermatophyte
tangentially	accomplished	scriptwriter	debonairness	derogatorily
tangibleness	accordionist	scrobiculate	decaffeinate	desalination
taperecorder	accouchement	scrupulosity	decalescence	desideration
taskmistress	accoutrement	scrupulously	decapitation	desiderative
tastefulness	accretionary	sculpturally	decasyllabic	desirability
tautological	accumulation	scurrilously	decasyllable	desirousness
taxcollector	accumulative	scutellation	deceleration	desolateness
vainglorious	accurateness	adaptability	decentralise	despairingly
Valenciennes	accursedness	adaptiveness	decipherable	despitefully
valetudinary	accusatively	additionally	decipherment	despoliation

despondently	hemerocallis	metachronism	penitentiary	recklessness
despotically	hemichordate	metagalactic	pennypincher	recognisable
desquamation	hemimorphism	metalanguage	pennywhistle	recognisably
desquamative	hemimorphite	metallically	peradventure	recognisance
desquamatory	hemiparasite	metallophone	perambulator	recollection
dessertspoon	hemispheroid	metallurgist	perceptively	recollective
destructible	henceforward	metalworking	perceptivity	recommitment
desulphurise	henotheistic	metamorphism	perceptually	reconcilable
detachedness	heortologist	metamorphose	percussively	reconstitute
determinable	heraldically	metaphorical	percutaneous	reconversion
determinably	hereditament	metaphrastic	peregrinator	reconveyance
determinedly	hereditarily	metaphysical	peremptorily	recreational
dethronement	hereinbefore	metapsychics	perfectively	recrudescent
detoxication	heritability	metasomatism	perfervidity	recuperation
detumescence	hermeneutics	metathetical	perfidiously	recuperative
Deuteronomic	hermetically	metathoracic	perfoliation	redecoration
deviationism	heroicalness	meteorically	performative	redemptioner
deviationist	heroicomical	meteorograph	pericarditis	Redemptorist
dextrousness	herpetologic	methodically	perilousness	redeployment
fearlessness	hesitatingly	meticulously	periodically	redintegrate
fearsomeness	hesperididia	metrological	periodontics	redistribute
featherbrain	heterocercal	metropolitan	periodontist	reducibility
featheriness	heterocyclic	mezzorelievo	periostracum	reductionism
fecklessness	heteroecious	mezzosoprano	peripherally	reductionist
feebleminded	heterogamous	nebulisation	periphrastic	reflationary
feldspathoid	heterogenous	nebulousness	perispomenon	reflectional
felicitation	heterologous	necrographer	peristeronic	reflectively
felicitously	heteromerous	necrological	peristomatic	reflectivity
feminineness	heteronomous	necrophagous	perjuriously	refractivity
feminisation	heterophylly	necrophiliac	permanganate	refractorily
fenestration	heterosexual	necrophilism	permeability	refreshingly
fermentation	heterozygote	necrophilous	permissively	refreshments
fermentative	heterozygous	needlessness	permittivity	refrigerator
ferrugineous	jerrybuilder	negativeness	perniciously	regardlessly
fertilisable	jesuitically	negativistic	pernoctation	regeneration
feverishness	jetpropelled	neglectfully	peroxidation	regenerative
geanticlinal	Keynesianism	negotiatress	perpetration	regimentally
genealogical	leapfrogging	negrophilism	perpetuation	registration
generousness	leathercloth	negrophilist	perplexingly	regressively
genuflection	ledgertackle	neighbouring	perseverance	rehabilitate
geochemistry	lefthandedly	neoclassical	persistently	reinvestment
geographical	legalisation	neoDarwinian	perspicacity	reinvigorate
geologically	legitimately	neoDarwinism	perspiration	rejectamenta
geomagnetism	legitimation	neoDarwinist	perspiratory	rejuvenation
geometrician	legitimatise	Neohellenism	persuasively	relationally
geophysicist	lepidopteran	neonomianism	pertinacious	relationship
geopolitical	leucocytosis	Neoplatonism	perturbation	relativeness
geosynclinal	leukocytosis	Neoplatonist	perturbative	relativistic
geotectonics	levorotation	nephanalysis	perverseness	relentlessly
geriatrician	levorotatory	nephelometer	perviousness	reliableness
Germanophile	lexicography	nephelometry	pestilential	rememberable
Germanophobe	lexicologist	nephrologist	pestological	remembrancer
gerontocracy	mealymouthed	nerveracking	petrifaction	reminiscence
gesellschaft	meaningfully	Nestorianism	petrographer	remonstrance
gesticulator	mechanically	neurasthenia	petrographic	remonstrator
headmistress	mediaevalism	neurasthenic	petrological	remorsefully
headquarters	mediaevalist	neuroanatomy	pettifoggery	removability
headshrinker	meditatively	neurobiology	pettifogging	remuneration
heartburning	meetinghouse	neurological	reactivation	remunerative
heartrending	megalomaniac	neuropterous	reactiveness	remuneratory
heartstrings	melancholiac	neuroscience	readableness	renegotiable
heartwarming	melanochroic	neurosurgeon	readjustment	renouncement
heathenishly	melodramatic	neurosurgery	reallocation	renunciation
heavenliness	meltingpoint	neurotically	reappearance	renunciative
heavyhearted	mendaciously	nevertheless	reassessment	renunciatory
hebdomadally	menstruation	newfashioned	reassignment	reoccupation
hebetudinous	mercantilism	Newfoundland	reassuringly	repatriation
hectographic	mercantilist	newspaperman	rebelliously	repercussion
hedgehopping	merchantable	peacefulness	recalcitrant	repercussive
heedlessness	mercifulness	pearlescence	recalcitrate	repetitional
heliocentric	mercurialise	peasepudding	recalescence	repetitively
heliographer	mercurialism	peccadilloes	recapitulate	repossession
heliographic	meretricious	pedantically	receivership	reprehension
heliogravure	meridionally	pedicellaria	receptaculum	reprehensive
heliolatrous	meristematic	pedunculated	receptionist	repressively
heliotherapy	merrythought	peerlessness	recessionary	reproachable
heliotropism	mesocephalic	pejoratively	rechargeable	reproachless
hellgrammite	mesothoracic	pellucidness	reciprocally	reproducible
helplessness	messeigneurs	penalisation	reciprocator	

reproduction	selfdeceived	servitorship	officeholder	philanthrope
reproductive	selfdeceiver	servocontrol	offscourings	philanthropy
reprographic	selfdelusion	sesquialtera	agamogenesis	philharmonic
reservedness	selfdestruct	sexagenarian	agamogenetic	philhellenic
resettlement	selfdevotion	sexcentenary	agentgeneral	philistinism
residentiary	selfdirected	teachability	agglutinogen	phillumenist
residentship	selfdistrust	tearlessness	aggressively	philodendron
resignedness	selfdoubting	technicality	agranulocyte	philological
resiniferous	selfeducated	technicolour	agribusiness	philosophise
resipiscence	selfeffacing	technocratic	agricultural	phlebotomise
resistlessly	selfelective	technologist	Egyptologist	phlebotomist
resoluteness	selfemployed	tectonically	chairmanship	phonasthenia
resolvedness	selfevidence	teensyweensy	chalcolithic	phonemically
resoundingly	selfexistent	teetertotter	chalcopyrite	phonetically
respectfully	selfflattery	telaesthesia	championship	phonographer
respectively	selfhypnosis	telaesthetic	chancemedley	phonographic
resplendence	selfidentity	telegraphese	chaplainship	phonological
resplendency	selfignition	telegraphist	characterise	phosphoresce
responsively	selfinterest	teleological	charlatanism	photochromic
responsorial	selfinvolved	televisional	charnelhouse	photofission
restaurateur	selflessness	temptability	charterhouse	photogeology
restlessness	selflimiting	teratologist	charterparty	photographer
restrainable	selfluminous	teratomatous	chastisement	photographic
restrainedly	selfmurderer	tercentenary	chauvinistic	photogravure
restrictedly	selfpleasing	terebinthine	checkerberry	photokinesis
resupination	selfportrait	tergiversate	checkerboard	photokinetic
resurrection	selfreliance	terribleness	cheerfulness	photomontage
resuscitator	selfreproach	terrifically	cheeseburger	photophilous
reticulately	selfrighting	terrifyingly	cheesecutter	photosetting
reticulation	selfsameness	terrorstruck	cheesemonger	photospheric
reticulocyte	selfstarting	tessellation	cheeseparing	phototropism
retiringness	selfviolence	testamentary	cheirography	phrasemonger
retractation	sellingplate	testosterone	chemotherapy	phraseograph
retractility	semantically	testudineous	chequerboard	phreatophyte
retrenchment	semiannually	tetrachordal	cherubically	phrenologist
retrocedence	semibasement	tetragonally	chesterfield	phycological
retrocession	semicircular	tetrahedrite	chieftainess	phycomycetes
retrocessive	semicylinder	tetramorphic	childbearing	phyllotactic
retroflexion	semidarkness	Teutonically	childishness	phylogenesis
retropulsion	semideponent	vegetatively	chimneypiece	phylogenetic
retroversion	semidetached	venepuncture	chiropractic	physiognomic
reunionistic	semidiameter	venerability	chiropractor	physiography
revelational	semidomestic	vengefulness	chitterlings	physiologist
revengefully	semifinalist	venipuncture	chivalrously	phytogenesis
reverberator	semifinished	venomousness	chlorination	phytogenetic
reversionary	semiliterate	ventripotent	chocolatebox	phytographer
revictualled	seminiferous	veridicality	chondriosome	phytological
revivalistic	semiofficial	verification	choreography	phytophagous
reviviscence	semiological	verificatory	chorographic	rhetorically
secessionism	semiparasite	vermiculated	chorological	rheumatology
secessionist	semiprecious	vernacularly	chrematistic	rhinocerotic
seclusionist	semitropical	vertebration	chrestomathy	rhinological
secondstring	sempiternity	verticalness	Christianise	rhizocarpous
sectarianise	sensibleness	verticillate	Christianity	rhizogenetic
sectarianism	sensitometer	vesiculation	Christolatry	rhizophagous
sectionalism	sensualistic	veterinarian	Christophany	rhododendron
secularistic	sensuousness	weatherboard	chromaticism	rhombohedral
sedgewarbler	sententially	weatherbound	chromaticity	rhombohedron
sedulousness	separability	weatherglass	chromatogram	rhynchophora
segmentation	separateness	weatherhouse	chromatology	rhythmically
seismography	septennially	weatherproof	chromatopsia	shadowboxing
seismologist	septilateral	welldisposed	chromosphere	Shakspereana
seismometric	septuagenary	wellfavoured	chronography	Shaksperiana
seismoscopic	Septuagesima	wellgrounded	chronologise	shamateurism
selenography	Septuagintal	Wellingtonia	chronologist	shamefacedly
selenologist	sepulchrally	welterweight	chronometric	shamefulness
selfabsorbed	sequaciously	yellowhammer	churchianity	sharecropper
selfactivity	sequentially	affectedness	churchwarden	sharpshooter
selfaffected	sequestrator	affectionate	churlishness	sharpsighted
selfanalysis	seraphically	aforethought	ghoulishness	shatterproof
selfapplause	sergeantfish	afterthought	phagocytosis	sheepishness
selfapproval	sergeantship	effectuality	phagocytotic	sheepshearer
selfbegotten	sericultural	effectuation	phanerogamic	shillyshally
selfbetrayal	serjeantship	effeminately	pharmaceutic	shipbuilding
selfcatering	serpentiform	effervescent	pharmacology	shirtwaister
selfcoloured	serpentinely	efflorescent	phenological	shootingiron
selfcomposed	serviceberry	effortlessly	phenomenally	shortchanger
selfcontempt	servicecourt	effusiveness	phenotypical	shortcircuit
selfcritical	servicewoman		philadelphus	shortpitched

shortsighted	bilharziosis	discipleship	distributary	microbiology
shortsleeved	bilingualism	disciplinary	distribution	microcapsule
shortstaffed	billingsgate	disclamation	distributive	microcephaly
shoulderbelt	billsticking	discographer	disturbingly	microcircuit
shoulderknot	biochemistry	discomfiture	divarication	microclimate
shouldernote	biocoenology	discommodity	diversionary	microcopying
shrewishness	bioecologist	discomposure	diversionist	microcrystal
shuffleboard	biogeography	disconnected	diverticular	micrographer
thankfulness	biographical	disconnexion	diverticulum	microphysics
thanksgiving	biologically	disconsolate	divertimenti	microscopist
thaumaturgic	biometrician	discontented	divertimento	microseismic
theanthropic	biophysicist	discordantly	divisibility	microsurgery
theatregoing	bioscientist	discountable	divisiveness	middleweight
theatrically	biosynthesis	discouraging	fibrillation	militaristic
theistically	biosynthetic	discourteous	fibrinolysin	millesimally
thematically	birdsnesting	discoverable	fictionalise	milliammeter
theocratical	birdwatching	discoverture	fictitiously	mindlessness
theoretician	birefringent	discreetness	fiddlefaddle	minedetector
theosophical	cinematheque	discreteness	fiddlesticks	mineralogist
therapeutics	circuitously	discretional	fieldglasses	minicomputer
therapeutist	circumcision	discriminant	fiendishness	minimisation
thereinafter	circumfluent	discriminate	figuratively	ministration
thermocouple	circumfusion	discursively	filibusterer	ministrative
thermography	circumjacent	disdainfully	filtrability	miraculously
thermolabile	circumscribe	disembarrass	finalisation	mirthfulness
thermometric	circumstance	disenchanter	firefighting	misadventure
thermophilic	cirrocumulus	disendowment	firstnighter	misalignment
thermoscopic	cirrostratus	disestablish	gigantically	misanthropic
thermosphere	civilisation	disfranchise	hibernaculum	misapprehend
thermostable	diabolically	disgorgement	hierarchical	misbehaviour
thermostatic	diageotropic	disguisement	hieroglyphic	miscalculate
thermotactic	diagrammatic	disgustfully	hierographer	miscellanist
thermotropic	dialectician	disgustingly	hierophantic	misdemeanant
thickskinned	dialectology	disharmonise	highcoloured	misdemeanour
thickskulled	diamagnetism	dishevelment	highfaluting	misdirection
thievishness	diamonddrill	disincentive	highhandedly	miseducation
thimbleberry	diamondfield	disinfectant	highlystrung	misinterpret
thirdborough	diaphanously	disinfection	highpressure	misknowledge
thitherwards	diastrophism	disinflation	highsounding	misplacement
thoroughbass	diathermancy	disingenuous	highspirited	mispronounce
thoroughbred	diatomaceous	disintegrate	highstepping	misquotation
thoroughfare	diatonically	disinterment	hindquarters	misrepresent
thoroughness	dibranchiate	disjointedly	hippocentaur	misselthrush
thoughtfully	dichromatism	dislodgement	hippopotamus	misstatement
thousandfold	dictatorship	disobedience	hirepurchase	mistakenness
threequarter	didactically	disorientate	histogenesis	mistranslate
threewheeler	dietetically	dispensation	histogenetic	mistreatment
thriftlessly	differentiae	dispensatory	histological	mistressship
throughstone	differential	dispiritedly	historically	mithridatise
thundercloud	digressional	displaceable	kilowatthour	mithridatism
thunderingly	digressively	displacement	kinaesthesia	mitochondria
thunderously	dilapidation	displeasedly	kinaesthesis	mitrailleuse
thunderstone	dilatability	dispossessor	kinaesthetic	nicotinamide
thunderstorm	dilatoriness	disputatious	kindergarten	nidification
whencesoever	dilettantish	disquisition	kinnikinnick	nightclothes
wherethrough	dilettantism	disregardful	kirschwasser	nimbostratus
whigmaleerie	diminishable	disreputable	kissingcrust	niminypiminy
whimperingly	diminishment	disreputably	liberalistic	nitrobenzene
whimsicality	diminutively	dissatisfied	libidinously	pickerelweed
whippoorwill	dinnerjacket	disseminator	licentiously	pictographic
whisperingly	diphtheritic	dissentingly	licketysplit	pigeonbreast
whitelivered	diphthongise	dissertation	lifelessness	pigmentation
whitewashing	directorship	disseverance	lighthearted	pilotballoon
whitherwards	disaccharide	disseverment	limnological	pinfeathered
wholehearted	disadvantage	dissimilarly	linguistical	pisciculture
whortleberry	disaffection	dissimulator	liquefacient	pitcherplant
ailurophobia	disaffiliate	dissocialise	liquefaction	pitiableness
aircondition	disagreeable	dissociation	listlessness	pitilessness
aircraftsman	disagreeably	dissociative	literariness	pitterpatter
bibliography	disagreement	dissuasively	lithographer	ribonuclease
bibliologist	disallowance	dissymmetric	lithographic	ricochetting
bibliomaniac	disambiguate	distemperate	lithological	ridiculously
bibliopegist	disannulling	distillation	lithospheric	rightfulness
bibliophilic	disannulment	distillatory	lithotritist	rigorousness
bibliopolist	disassociate	distinctness	liturgiology	risorgimento
bibliothecae	disastrously	distortional	liverypudlian	sideslipping
bicentennial	disbursement	distractedly	Liverpudlian	sidestepping
bilateralism	discerningly	distrainable	liverystable	sidewhiskers
bilharziasis	discerptible	distrainment	microanalyst	sidewhiskers

sightreading	allusiveness	flammability	sledgehammer	impersonally
significance	alphabetical	flatteringly	sleepingpill	impersonator
significancy	alphamerical	flavoprotein	sleepwalking	impertinence
silicicolous	alphanumeric	flickeringly	slipcarriage	impertinency
siliciferous	alterability	flocculation	slipperiness	imperviously
silverglance	altitudinous	floodlighted	slothfulness	impetiginous
silviculture	blabbermouth	floriculture	slovenliness	implantation
simoniacally	blackbirding	fluidisation	sluggishness	implicitness
simpleminded	blackcurrant	fluorescence	sluttishness	impoliteness
simultaneity	blackguardly	fluoridation	ultramontane	imponderable
simultaneous	bladderwrack	fluorination	ultramundane	imponderably
Sinanthropus	blamableness	fluorocarbon	amalgamation	impoverished
singleacting	blamefulness	glaciologist	amalgamative	impregnation
singledecker	blandishment	gladiatorial	amateurishly	impressively
singlehanded	blastfurnace	gladsomeness	ambassadress	imprisonment
singleminded	blastosphere	glassblowing	ambidextrous	impropriator
singleseater	blastulation	glaucescence	ambivalently	improvidence
sinistrality	blatherskite	glaucomatous	amelioration	improvisator
sinistrorsal	bletherskate	glitteringly	ameliorative	imputability
sinusoidally	blissfulness	globetrotter	amenableness	imputatively
siphonophore	blisteringly	glockenspiel	amentiferous	omnipotently
siphonostele	blithesomely	gloriousness	amicableness	omnipresence
ticklishness	blockbusting	glossography	amitotically	omnisciently
tightmouthed	bloodbrother	glossologist	amortisation	omnivorously
timehonoured	bloodletting	gluttonously	amphibiously	smallclothes
timelessness	bloodstained	glycogenesis	amphibrachic	smallholding
timorousness	bloodthirsty	glycoprotein	amphictyonic	umbrageously
tintinnabula	bloodyminded	glyphography	amphisbaenic	anaerobiosis
tirelessness	bluestocking	glyptography	amphitheatre	anaesthetise
tiresomeness	blunderingly	illadvisedly	amphitropous	anaesthetist
tittletattle	blusteringly	illegibility	amygdaloidal	anagogically
vibraphonist	clairaudient	illegitimacy	emancipation	anagrammatic
vicargeneral	clairvoyance	illegitimate	emargination	analogically
vicechairman	clangorously	illiberality	emasculation	analphabetic
Victorianism	clannishness	illiterately	emasculatory	analytically
victoriously	clapperboard	illnaturedly	embattlement	anamorphosis
vigorousness	clarinettist	illogicality	embezzlement	anaphylactic
vilification	classicalism	illtreatment	embitterment	anastigmatic
villainously	classicalist	illumination	emblazonment	anathematise
vindictively	classicality	illuminative	emblematical	anatomically
vinification	classifiable	illusiveness	embranchment	anecdotalist
viridescence	clatteringly	illusoriness	embryologist	anemographic
virtuosoship	claudication	illustration	emotionalise	anemophilous
virtuousness	clavicembalo	illustrative	emotionalism	angiocarpous
viscerotonic	clearsighted	kleptomaniac	emotionalist	annihilation
viscosimeter	cleistogamic	klipspringer	emotionality	annihilative
viscountship	cliffhanging	oldfashioned	emphatically	announcement
visitational	clinkerbuilt	oligarchical	empoisonment	annunciation
visitatorial	closecropped	placesetting	empressement	anotherguess
vitalisation	closegrained	plainclothed	emulsifiable	antagonistic
vitiligation	closemouthed	plainclothes	immaculately	antecedently
vitreousness	clotheshorse	plaindealing	immaterially	antediluvian
vitrifaction	clothespress	planetesimal	immatureness	anteprandial
vituperation	clownishness	planetstruck	immeasurable	anthelmintic
vituperative	elasmobranch	planispheric	immeasurably	anthropogeny
vituperatory	electrically	planoconcave	immemorially	anthropoidal
vivification	electrolysis	plasterboard	immensurable	anthropology
viviparously	electrolytic	platonically	immethodical	antiaircraft
wicketkeeper	electrometer	Plattdeutsch	immoderately	anticipation
williewaught	electronvolt	plausibility	immoderation	anticipative
windingsheet	electroplate	playingfield	immovability	anticipatory
wineglassful	electroscope	pleasantness	immunisation	anticlerical
winklepicker	electroshock	pleasingness	immunologist	anticyclonic
winterbourne	electrotonic	pleasureless	immutability	antigenicity
xiphisternum	electrotonus	plebiscitary	impartiality	antigropelos
skateboarder	electrotyper	plecopterous	impedimental	antimacassar
skippingrope	eleemosynary	plectognathi	impenetrable	antimagnetic
skittishness	elementalism	pleiotropism	impenetrably	antimalarial
skrimshanker	elementarily	plenipotence	impenitently	antineutrino
skullduggery	elliptically	pleomorphism	imperatively	antiparticle
skunkcabbage	elocutionary	plesiosaurus	imperatorial	antipathetic
alexipharmic	elocutionist	plumbaginous	imperceptive	antiperiodic
Alhambresque	elucubration	plumbiferous	impercipient	antiphonally
alimentation	flabelliform	plummerblock	imperfection	antirachitic
alimentative	flagellation	pluriliteral	imperfective	antiSemitism
alkalescence	flagellatory	pluviometric	imperishable	antistrophic
alliteration	flagitiously	slanderously	imperishably	antithetical
alliterative	flamboyantly	slaughterous	impermanence	enantiomorph
allomorphism	flamethrower	slaveholding	impermanency	encephalitic

encephalitis	incomparable	inexpediency	interestedly	knighterrant
enchantingly	incomparably	inexperience	interfemoral	knightliness
encirclement	incompatible	inexpertness	interference	mnemotechnic
enclitically	incompatibly	inexplicable	interglacial	oncorhynchus
encroachment	incompetence	inexplicably	interjection	oneirocritic
encrustation	incompetency	inexpressive	interjectory	onesidedness
encumberment	incompletely	inexpugnable	interlobular	oneupmanship
encumbrancer	incompliance	inexpugnably	interlocutor	onomatopoeia
encyclopedia	incomputable	inextensible	intermeddler	onomatopoeic
encyclopedic	inconcinnity	inextricable	intermediacy	pneumaticity
endamagement	inconclusive	inextricably	intermediary	pneumatology
endangerment	inconformity	infanticidal	intermediate	pneumothorax
endermically	inconsequent	infectiously	interminable	snaggletooth
endocarditis	inconsistent	infelicitous	interminably	snakecharmer
endometritis	inconsolable	infiniteness	intermission	snapfastener
endoparasite	inconsolably	infinitively	intermittent	snappishness
endoskeletal	inconsonance	inflammation	intermitting	snarlingiron
enfeeblement	inconstantly	inflammatory	intermixture	snobbishness
enginedriver	inconsumable	inflationary	intermundane	unacceptable
enginetuning	inconsumably	inflationism	internuclear	unaccustomed
Englishwoman	incontiguous	inflationist	internuncial	unaffectedly
enormousness	incontinence	inflectional	interoceanic	unambivalent
enshrinement	incontinency	infrequently	interoceptor	unanswerable
enswathement	inconvenient	infringement	interpellate	unapologetic
entanglement	incoordinate	infundibular	interpleader	unappeasable
enterprising	incorporated	infusibility	interpolator	unappetising
entertaining	incorporator	ingloriously	interpretive	unassailable
enthronement	incorporeity	ingratiating	interrelated	unassumingly
enthusiastic	incorrigible	inhabitation	interrogator	unattractive
entomologise	incorrigibly	inharmonious	interruption	unauthorised
entomologist	incorruption	inhospitable	interruptive	unbecomingly
entrammelled	increasingly	inhospitably	intersection	unbelievable
entrancement	incrustation	iniquitously	interservice	unbelievably
entreatingly	incurability	innutritious	interspinous	unblinkingly
entrenchment	indebtedness	inobservance	interstellar	unblushingly
entrepreneur	indecisively	inoccupation	interstitial	unbrokenness
enviableness	indeclinable	inoperculate	intertexture	uncalculated
envisagement	indecorously	inordinately	intervenient	uncelebrated
enzymologist	indefeasible	inosculation	intervention	unchangeable
inaccessible	indefeasibly	insalubrious	intervocalic	unchangeably
inaccessibly	indefectible	insecticidal	interwreathe	uncharitable
inaccurately	indefensible	insemination	intimidation	uncharitably
inactivation	indefensibly	insolubilise	intimidatory	unchivalrous
inadequately	indefinitely	insolubility	intolerantly	unclassified
inadmissible	indehiscence	inspectorate	intoxication	uncomeatable
inadmissibly	indelibility	inspectorial	intracardiac	uncommercial
inadvertence	indelicately	inspissation	intracranial	uncommonness
inadvertency	independence	installation	intramundane	unconformity
inappeasable	independency	instauration	intransigent	unconsidered
inapplicable	indicatively	instillation	intransitive	unconstraint
inapplicably	indifference	instructress	intrauterine	uncontrolled
inappositely	indifferency	instrumental	intrenchment	unconvincing
inarticulate	indigenously	insufferable	intriguingly	uncritically
inartificial	indigestible	insufferably	introduction	unctuousness
inaudibility	indirectness	insufficient	introductory	undemocratic
inauguration	indiscipline	insufflation	introjection	underachieve
inauguratory	indiscreetly	insurrection	intromission	underbidding
inauspicious	indiscretion	integumental	intromittent	underclothes
incalculable	indisputable	intellection	intromitting	undercoating
incalculably	indisputably	intellective	introversion	undercurrent
incalescence	indissoluble	intellectual	introversive	undercutting
incandescent	indissolubly	intelligence	introvertive	underdevelop
incapability	indistinctly	intelligible	intrusionist	undergarment
incapacitate	indivertible	intelligibly	intuitionism	underinsured
incatenation	indivertibly	intemperance	intuitionist	underletting
incautiously	individually	inteneration	intumescence	undermanning
incendiarism	indoctrinate	interbedding	intussuscept	underpinning
incestuously	IndoEuropean	interception	invagination	underrunning
incidentally	IndoGermanic	intercession	invalidation	undersetting
incineration	industrially	intercessory	inveiglement	understaffed
incisiveness	ineffaceable	interchanger	invertebrate	undersurface
inclinometer	ineffaceably	interconnect	investigator	undertenancy
incognisable	inefficiency	intercropped	inveterately	underwritten
incognisance	inelasticity	intercurrent	invigilation	undetermined
incognitable	ineradicable	intercutting	invigoration	undiplomatic
incoherently	ineradicably	interdiction	invisibility	uneconomical
incommodious	inescutcheon	interdictive	involutional	unemployable
incommutable	inexactitude	interdictory	invulnerable	unemployment
incommutably	inexpedience	interdigital	invulnerably	unencumbered

uneventfully	bodystocking	complaisance	conservative	correctitude
unexpectedly	boisterously	complemental	conservatory	correctively
unfaithfully	bombdisposal	completeness	considerable	corroborator
unfamiliarly	bonnetmonkey	complexional	considerably	cosmetically
unfathomable	bonnyclabber	complexioned	consignation	cosmogonical
unfavourable	boogiewoogie	complication	consistently	cosmographer
unfavourably	bookingclerk	composedness	consistorial	cosmographic
unflattering	booklearning	compoundable	consociation	cosmological
unfrequented	bootlessness	compressible	consolidator	cosmopolitan
ungainliness	borosilicate	compulsively	conspiration	cosmopolitic
ungovernable	bottlewasher	compulsivity	constabulary	costermonger
ungracefully	boulevardier	compulsorily	constipation	cottonocracy
ungraciously	bowcompasses	compunctious	constituency	cotyledonary
ungratefully	coacervation	compurgation	constitution	cotyledonous
unhesitating	coachbuilder	compurgatory	constitutive	councilwoman
unhistorical	coalitionist	concelebrant	constriction	countenancer
unifoliolate	cockfighting	concelebrate	constrictive	counteragent
unilaterally	cocksureness	concentrator	constringent	counterblast
unimaginable	codification	conceptional	construction	countercheck
unimaginably	coelenterate	conceptually	constructive	counterclaim
unimportance	coenobitical	conchiferous	consultation	counterforce
uninterested	coenobytical	conchologist	consultative	counterlight
unionisation	coerciveness	conciliation	consummately	countermarch
unisexuality	coetaneously	conciliative	consummation	counterplead
unitarianism	cohabitation	conciliatory	consummative	counterpoint
universalise	cohesiveness	conclusively	consummatory	counterpoise
universalism	coincidental	concomitance	contagionist	counterproof
universalist	coincidently	concordantly	contagiously	counterscarp
universality	coldshoulder	concrescence	containerise	countershaft
unkindliness	coleopterist	concreteness	contemplator	countertenor
unlawfulness	coleopterous	concubitancy	contemporary	countrydance
unlikelihood	collaborator	concupiscent	contemporise	countrywoman
unlikeliness	collaterally	concurrently	contemptible	courageously
unloveliness	collectively	condemnation	contemptibly	courtmartial
unmanageable	collectivise	condemnatory	contemptuous	courtplaster
unmercifully	collectivism	condensation	conterminous	cousingerman
unmistakable	collectivist	conductivity	contestation	covetousness
unmistakably	collectivity	conduplicate	contextually	cowardliness
unofficially	collegialism	confabulator	contiguously	dodecahedral
unparalleled	collegiality	confectioner	contingently	dodecahedron
unpleasantly	collegiately	conferential	continuation	dodecaphonic
unpopularity	collinearity	confessional	continuative	dogmatically
unprejudiced	colloquially	confidential	continuously	dolorousness
unpretending	collywobbles	confirmation	contractable	domestically
unprincipled	colonisation	confirmative	contractedly	domesticator
unprofitable	coloquintida	confirmatory	contractible	dorsiventral
unprofitably	colorimetric	confiscation	contradictor	doubleacting
unpronounced	colourlessly	confiscatory	contrapuntal	doubledealer
unreasonable	columniation	conformation	contrariness	doubledecked
unreasonably	combinations	confoundedly	contrariwise	doubledecker
unrecognised	comfortingly	Confucianism	contribution	doublelocked
unregenerate	commandingly	confusedness	contributive	doubtfulness
unrepeatable	commemorator	congeniality	contributory	dovecoloured
unreservedly	commencement	congenitally	contrivement	downwardness
unresponsive	commendation	conglobation	contriteness	focalisation
unrestrained	commendatory	conglomerate	controllable	folliculated
unscientific	commensalism	conglutinate	contumacious	footplateman
unscriptural	commensalist	congratulant	contumelious	foraminifera
unscrupulous	commensurate	congratulate	convalescent	forbiddingly
unsearchable	commentation	congregation	convectional	forcefulness
unseasonable	commercially	conidiophore	conveniently	forcibleness
unsegregated	commiserator	conidiospore	conventicler	forebodement
unsteadiness	commissarial	conjunctival	conventional	forebodingly
unstructured	commissariat	connaturally	conversation	forensically
unsuccessful	commissioner	connectional	conveyancing	foresightful
unthinkingly	committeeman	connectively	convincement	forestalment
unthoughtful	commodiously	conningtower	convincingly	formaldehyde
untimeliness	commonwealth	connubiality	conviviality	formlessness
untowardness	communicable	conquistador	convulsively	forthrightly
untruthfully	communicably	conscionable	coordinately	fortuitously
unwieldiness	communicator	conscription	coordination	fostermother
unwontedness	companionate	consecration	coordinative	foundationer
unworthiness	companionway	consecratory	copolymerise	fountainhead
unyieldingly	compatriotic	consensually	copulatively	gobbledegook
boastfulness	compellation	consentience	corespondent	gobbledygook
bobbydazzler	compensation	consentingly	corelatively	gonadotropic
bodybuilding	compensative	consequently	coquettishly	gonadotropin
bodysnatcher	compensatory	conservation	corporeality	goodhumoured
	complacently	conservatism	correctional	goodtempered

goosepimples	monostrophic	polysyllable	totalisation	epithalamion
gorgeousness	monosyllabic	polytheistic	totalitarian	epithalamium
governmental	monosyllable	polytonality	touchingness	openhandedly
governorship	monotheistic	polyurethane	towardliness	openmindedly
holidaymaker	monotonously	pontifically	toxicologist	operatically
homeomorphic	monumentally	pontificator	toxicophobia	ophiophagous
homeopathist	moralisation	poorspirited	vocabularian	opinionative
homesickness	mordaciously	populousness	vocalisation	opisthograph
homoeopathic	morningdress	porcelainise	vociferation	opisthotonos
homoeostasis	morphallaxis	porcelainous	vociferously	opposability
homologation	morphologist	porcellanous	voidableness	oppositeness
homomorphism	morrisdancer	pornographer	volatileness	oppositional
homomorphous	mosstrooping	pornographic	volcanically	oppressively
homonymously	motherfigure	portentously	volitionally	optimisation
homosexually	motherliness	portmanteaus	volumetrical	spaciousness
homothallism	mothertongue	portmanteaux	voluminosity	sparkingplug
honeybuzzard	motivational	positiveness	voluminously	sparrowgrass
hoodmanblind	motorcyclist	positivistic	voluntaryism	speakingtube
hopelessness	motorisation	possessively	voluntaryist	specialistic
horizontally	mountainside	postdiluvian	voluptuosity	specifically
horrendously	mournfulness	postdoctoral	voluptuously	specificness
horribleness	mourningband	posteriority	vomiturition	speciousness
horrifically	mourningring	postgraduate	wollastonite	specktioneer
horrorstruck	mouthbreeder	posthumously	womanishness	spectrograph
horsebreaker	moveableness	postmeridian	wonderstruck	spectrometer
horsemanship	movelessness	postmistress	wonderworker	spectrometry
horsetrading	noctambulant	postponement	wondrousness	spectroscope
horsewhipped	noctambulism	postposition	woodengraver	spectroscopy
horticulture	noctambulist	postpositive	woodenheaded	speechlessly
housebreaker	noctambulous	postprandial	woolgatherer	speedboating
housekeeping	noctilucence	potentiality	woollyheaded	speleologist
housetrained	nomenclative	robustiously	workableness	spermaphytic
housewarming	nomenclature	rollingstock	workingclass	spermathecal
journalistic	nominalistic	romanisation	worshipfully	spermatocyte
localisation	nonagenarian	romantically	youngberries	spermatozoid
lodginghouse	nonalignment	rontgenogram	youthfulness	spermatozoon
logistically	nonchalantly	rontgenology	zoogeography	spermogonium
lonesomeness	noncombatant	rootlessness	aperiodicity	spheroidally
longdistance	noncommittal	rosecoloured	apiculturist	sphragistics
longitudinal	noncomplying	sociableness	apochromatic	sphygmograph
longshoreman	nonconductor	sociological	apolitically	spidermonkey
longstanding	nonconformer	sociometrist	apostolicism	spiegeleisen
longwindedly	noneffective	Socratically	apostolicity	spinsterhood
lopsidedness	nonefficient	sodafountain	apostrophise	spiritedness
loquaciously	nonessential	softpedalled	apothegmatic	spiritlessly
loungelizard	noneuclidean	solarisation	apparatchiki	spiritualise
lovelessness	nonexistence	solicitation	apparatchiks	spiritualism
lovelornness	nonflammable	solicitously	apparentness	spiritualist
LowChurchman	nonflowering	solifluction	apparitional	spirituality
mobilisation	nonidentical	solitariness	appendectomy	spitefulness
moderateness	nonobjective	somatopleure	appendicitis	splendidness
modification	nonresidence	somnambulant	appendicular	spokesperson
modificatory	nonresistant	somnambulate	apperception	sporadically
moistureless	noradrenalin	somnambulism	apperceptive	sporogenesis
molecularity	northeastern	somnambulist	appetisingly	sportfulness
monadelphous	northernmost	somniloquism	appositeness	sportiveness
monastically	Northumbrian	somniloquist	appositional	spotlessness
monetisation	northwestern	sonorousness	appraisement	sprightfully
moneychanger	notification	sophisticate	appraisingly	spuriousness
moneygrubber	novelisation	soporiferous	appreciation	uproariously
moneyspinner	poikilotherm	sorbefacient	appreciative	aquicultural
monitorially	pointilliste	soullessness	appreciatory	equalisation
monkeyflower	polarimetric	soundingline	apprehension	equalitarian
monkeyjacket	polarisation	southeastern	apprehensive	equationally
monkeypuzzle	polarography	southernmost	approachable	equestrienne
monkeywrench	policyholder	southernwood	appropriable	equidistance
monochromate	polychaetous	southwestern	appropriator	equilibrator
monodramatic	polychromous	toastingfork	appurtenance	equipollence
monofilament	polyethylene	togetherness	epexegetical	equipollency
monographist	polyglottism	toggleswitch	ephemerality	equiprobable
monomaniacal	polyhistoric	toilsomeness	epicureanism	equitability
monometallic	polymorphism	tolerability	epicycloidal	equivalently
monomorphous	polymorphous	tonelessness	epidemically	equivocation
monopetalous	polyneuritic	toploftiness	epidemiology	equivocatory
monophyletic	polyneuritis	topsyturvily	epigrammatic	squarerigged
Monophysitic	polypetalous	torrefaction	epiphenomena	squattocracy
monopodially	polyphyletic	torrentially	episcopalian	squirrelcage
monopolistic	polysepalous	Torricellian	episodically	squirreltail
monostichous	polysyllabic	tortuousness	epistemology	arborescence

arborisation	fractionally	irreversibly	prenticeship	propagandise
archdeaconry	fractionator	irritability	preoccupancy	propagandism
archdiocesan	FrancoGerman	irritatingly	preparedness	propagandist
archetypally	frangibility	kremlinology	preponderant	prophylactic
archetypical	frankincense	orbicularity	preponderate	propitiation
archipelagic	fraudulently	orchestrator	preposterous	propitiatory
architecture	freakishness	orchidaceous	prerequisite	propitiously
argillaceous	freestanding	ordinariness	presbyterate	proportional
aristocratic	freeswimming	organgrinder	presbyterial	proportioned
Aristotelean	freethinking	organisation	Presbyterian	proprietress
Aristotelian	freewheeling	organography	prescription	proscription
arithmetical	freightliner	organoleptic	prescriptive	proscriptive
aromatically	frenchpolish	orienteering	preselection	prosectorial
aromaticness	frenetically	ornamentally	preselective	prosecutable
arrhythmical	frequentness	ornithomancy	presentation	proselytiser
articulately	fricasseeing	ornithoscopy	presentative	prosodically
articulation	frictionless	orographical	presentiment	prosopopoeia
articulatory	friendliness	orthodontics	preservation	prosperously
artificially	frontbencher	orthodontist	preservative	prostitution
artilleryman	frontiersman	orthogenesis	presidential	protactinium
artistically	frontispiece	orthogenetic	presumptuous	protectively
brachydactyl	fructiferous	orthographer	pretermitted	protectorate
brackishness	fructivorous	orthographic	prevailingly	protensively
brainstormer	fruitfulness	orthopaedics	prevaricator	protestation
brainwashing	gracefulness	orthopaedist	preventative	prothalamion
brambleberry	graciousness	orthopterist	preventively	prothalamium
brassbounder	grallatorial	orthopteroid	previousness	prothonotary
brassrubbing	graminaceous	orthopterous	pricecutting	protistology
breakthrough	grammaticise	orthotropism	pridefulness	protohistory
breaststroke	grammolecule	orthotropous	priestliness	protoplasmic
breastsummer	gramnegative	practicality	priestridden	protoplastic
breathalyser	grampositive	practitioner	priggishness	prototypical
breathlessly	granodiorite	pragmatistic	primigravida	protozoology
breathtaking	graphologist	praiseworthy	primogenital	protrusively
breechloader	graspingness	pralltriller	primogenitor	protuberance
brickfielder	gratefulness	praseodymium	primordially	proudhearted
brilliantine	gratifyingly	precancelled	princeliness	proverbially
brinkmanship	gratuitously	precariously	principality	providential
brokenwinded	graveclothes	precedential	printability	provincially
bronchoscope	gravelelling	preceptorial	privatdocent	provisionary
broncobuster	greathearted	precessional	privatdozent	prudentially
brontosaurus	greengrocery	prechristian	privateering	traceability
crackbrained	greenishness	preciousness	prizefighter	trachomatous
craftbrother	gregariously	precipitable	prizewinning	tractability
craniologist	grievousness	precipitance	probationary	tradescantia
crashlanding	griseofulvin	precipitancy	proboscidean	tradespeople
creativeness	grossularite	precipitator	proboscidian	traditionary
creepycrawly	grotesquerie	precisianism	procathedral	traditionist
crenellation	groundcherry	precisionist	processional	traducianism
criticalness	groundlessly	preclassical	proclamation	traducianist
crossbedding	grovellingly	preclusively	proclamatory	tragicomical
crossbencher	gruesomeness	precociously	proconsulate	trainspotter
crossbuttock	irascibility	precognition	prodigiously	traitorously
crosscountry	irrationally	precognitive	productively	trampolinist
crosscurrent	irredeemable	precondition	productivity	tranquillise
crossexamine	irredeemably	preconscious	professional	tranquillity
crossgrained	irreflective	predesignate	professorate	transcendent
crossheading	irreformable	predestinate	professoress	transduction
crossingover	irrefragable	predetermine	professorial	transferable
crosspurpose	irrefragably	predictively	proficiently	transference
crosssection	irregardless	predigestion	profiteering	transferring
cryptanalyst	irregularity	predilection	profligately	transformism
cryptogamous	irrelatively	predominance	profoundness	transformist
cryptography	irrelevantly	predominancy	progenitress	transfusible
cryptologist	irremediable	preestablish	progesterone	transgressor
crystalgazer	irremediably	preexistence	proglottides	transhipment
dramatically	irremissible	prefabricate	programmable	transhumance
dramaturgist	irrepealable	prefectorial	programmatic	transiliency
draughtboard	irreprovable	preferential	projectional	transitional
draughthorse	irresistible	preformation	projectively	transitively
drawingboard	irresistibly	preformative	prolegomenon	transitivity
drawingpaper	irresolutely	prehensility	prolifically	transitorily
dreadfulness	irresolution	prehistorian	prolificness	translatable
dressinggown	irresolvable	prehistoric	prolongation	translucence
droughtiness	irrespective	prelapsarian	promulgation	translucency
eruptiveness	irrespirable	premaxillary	pronominally	transmigrant
erythematous	irresponsive	premeditated	pronouncedly	transmigrate
erythroblast	irreverently	premeditator	proofreading	transmission
erythromycin	irreversible	premenstrual	propaedeutic	transmissive

transmitting	isolationist	stereometric	autonomously	multifarious
transmogrify	isothermally	stereophonic	buccaneering	multiflorous
transmontane	oscillograph	stereopticon	buccaneerish	multifoliate
transmutable	oscilloscope	stereoscopic	buffalograss	multiformity
transoceanic	ossification	sterlingness	bulletheaded	multilateral
transpacific	ostentatious	sternutation	bullfighting	multilingual
transparency	osteogenesis	sternutative	bullheadedly	multiloquous
transpirable	osteological	sternutatory	bureaucratic	multinuclear
transplanter	osteomalacia	sternwheeler	burglarproof	multipartite
transpontine	osteoplastic	stertorously	burningglass	multipliable
transposable	osteoporosis	stethoscopic	businesslike	multiplicand
transshipped	psephologist	stichomythia	butterflynut	multiplicate
transudation	pseudocyesis	stichomythic	buttermuslin	multiplicity
transudatory	pseudonymity	stilboestrol	butterscotch	multipurpose
transversely	pseudonymous	stillhunting	cuckingstool	multistoried
transvestism	pseudopodium	stockbreeder	cuckooflower	multivalence
transvestite	psychiatrist	stockbroking	culpableness	multiversity
tremendously	psychoactive	stockingless	cultivatable	multungulate
trephination	psychography	stockjobbery	cumbersomely	municipalise
trestletable	psychologise	stockjobbing	cumbrousness	municipality
triangularly	psychologist	stockraising	cumulatively	munificently
tricentenary	psychometric	stoneboiling	cumulocirrus	musicianship
trichologist	psychopathic	stonecutting	cumulonimbus	musicologist
trichotomise	psychosexual	stonedresser	cuprammonium	mutinousness
trichotomous	psychotropic	stonemasonry	curlingirons	muttonheaded
trichromatic	psychrometer	stonyhearted	curlingtongs	muzzleloader
trickishness	psychrometry	stormtrooper	curmudgeonly	numerologist
tridactylous	usufructuary	stouthearted	curvicaudate	numerousness
trifurcation	usuriousness	Stradivarius	curvicostate	nutritionist
triggerhappy	atheromatous	straightaway	curvifoliate	nutritiously
triglyphical	athletically	straightbred	curvirostral	outdatedness
trigonometry	atmospherics	straightedge	customshouse	outlandishly
trinomialism	attitudinise	straightener	dubitatively	outmanoeuvre
tripartitely	attorneyship	straightness	duckingstool	outpensioner
tripartition	attractively	straitjacket	dunderheaded	outrageously
triphthongal	attributable	stranglehold	duraluminium	outrivalling
triplication	etherisation	straticulate	euhemeristic	outstretched
triumphantly	ethnocentric	stratigraphy	eunuchoidism	outstripping
trochanteric	ethnographer	stratosphere	euphonically	outwardbound
troglodytism	ethnographic	streetwalker	euphoniously	publicspirit
trophallaxis	ethnological	strengthener	EuroAmerican	puerperrally
tropological	etymological	strengthless	fugitiveness	pugnaciously
tropospheric	etymologicon	streptococci	fuliginosity	pulverisable
troublemaker	otherworldly	streptomycin	fullyfledged	pumpernickel
trumpetshell	pteridophyte	stridulation	functionally	punchingball
trustfulness	pteridosperm	strikingness	functionless	purblindness
truthfulness	pterodactyle	stringcourse	furfuraceous	purification
urbanisation	stablishment	strobilation	furunculosis	purificatory
urbanologist	staffofficer	stroboscopic	futilitarian	purposebuilt
wrathfulness	staffsurgeon	strongminded	futurologist	purposefully
wretchedness	stagemanager	strongylosis	guaranteeing	pursestrings
wrongfulness	staggeringly	strontianite	guardianship	putrefaction
asphyxiation	Stakhanovism	strophanthin	guestchamber	putrefactive
assassinator	Stakhanovite	structurally	guilefulness	Quadragesima
assibilation	stalactiform	strychninism	hubblebubble	quadrangular
assimilation	stalwartness	stubbornness	hucklebacked	quadraphonic
assimilative	stammeringly	studdingsail	huggermugger	quadriennium
assimilatory	standardbred	studiousness	humanisation	quadrinomial
astonishment	standingroom	stupefacient	humanitarian	quadriplegia
astoundingly	stanniferous	stupefaction	humification	quadriplegic
astringently	starspangled	stupefactive	humorousness	quadrivalent
astrological	stationhouse	stupendously	humptydumpty	quadrumanous
astronautics	stationwagon	stutteringly	judgematical	quaestorship
astronomical	statistician	stylographic	jurisconsult	qualmishness
astrophysics	statuesquely	augmentation	jurisdiction	quantifiable
asymmetrical	stealthiness	augmentative	jurisprudent	quantisation
asynchronism	steatopygous	auscultation	juvenescence	quantitative
asynchronous	steeplechase	auscultatory	lugubriously	quaquaversal
escapologist	steganograph	auspiciously	lukewarmness	quarterbound
escutcheoned	stellenbosch	Australasian	lumberjacket	quarterfinal
esoterically	stelliferous	authenticate	luminescence	quarterstaff
espagnolette	stenographer	authenticity	luminiferous	quattrocento
essentiality	stenographic	autocatalyse	luminousness	questionable
estrangement	stepchildren	autochthones	lusciousness	questionably
Ishmaelitish	stepdaughter	autodidactic	mucilaginous	questionless
isochromatic	stereochromy	autoimmunity	muddleheaded	quinquennial
isochronally	stereography	automaticity	mulligatawny	quinquennium
isodiametric	stereoisomer	automobilist	multicentral	quintessence
isolationism		automorphism	multidentate	quixotically

quizzicality
rumbletumble
ruminatively
runningboard
ruralisation
ruthlessness
subalternate
subalternity
subapostolic
subarrhation
subcelestial
subcommittee
subconscious
subcontinent
subcutaneous
subdivisible
subeditorial
suberisation
subinfeudate
subjectively
subjectivise
subjectivism
subjectivist
subjectivity
sublapsarian
submaxillary
subminiature
submissively
subnormality
subsaturated
subscription
subsequently
subservience
subserviency
subsidiarily
subsonically
substantiate
substantival
substitution
substitutive
substruction
substructure
subtemperate
subterranean
subthreshold
subversively
succedaneous
successfully
successional
successively
succinctness
sudoriferous
sufficiently
suggestively
suitableness
sulphonamide
sulphonation
sulphuration
sulphuretted
superannuate
supercharger
superciliary
supercilious
supereminent
supererogate
superhighway
superhumanly
supermundane
supernaculum
supernatural
superposable
supersedence
supersensory
supersession
superstition
superstratum
supervenient
supervention
supplemental

supplementer
supplicantly
supplication
supplicatory
suppositious
suppressible
supramundane
supraorbital
surefootedly
surmountable
surprisingly
surrealistic
surrejoinder
surroundings
surveillance
surveyorship
survivorship
susceptivity
suspensively
suspiciously
sustentation
sustentative
tuberculated
tuberculosis
tumultuously
tunelessness
turbellarian
turriculated
turtlenecked
wunderkinder
availability
avantgardism
avantgardist
avariciously
avitaminoses
avitaminosis
evanescently
evangelistic
eveningdress
evidentially
evisceration
evolutionary
evolutionism
evolutionist
overabundant
overachiever
overactivity
overcautious
overcropping
overemphasis
overestimate
overexertion
overexposure
overlordship
overniceness
overpersuade
overpowering
overpressure
overreaction
oversimplify
overstepping
dwarfishness
swaggeringly
swaggerstick
swainishness
swashbuckler
sweepingness
sweetishness
swimmingbath
swimmingbell
swimmingpool
swizzlestick
twentyfourmo
twitteringly
exacerbation
exaggeration
exaggerative
exaggeratory

exasperation
exchangeable
excitability
exclusionary
exclusionism
exclusionist
excogitation
excogitative
excruciating
excruciation
excursionist
executorship
exegetically
exenteration
exercitation
exhaustively
exhibitioner
exhilaration
exhilarative
exiguousness
exophthalmic
exophthalmos
exophthalmus
exorbitantly
exospherical
exoterically
expansionary
expansionism
expansionist
expatriation
expediential
experiential
experimental
experimenter
explantation
explicitness
exploitation
exploitative
expressional
expressively
expressivity
exprobration
exsanguinate
exsanguinous
exsufflicate
extensometer
exterminable
exterminator
extinguisher
extortionary
extortionate
extracranial
extraditable
extralimital
extramarital
extramundane
extraneously
extrasensory
extraspecial
extrauterine
extravagance
extravagancy
extravaganza
extraversion
extroversion
exulceration
oxyacetylene
uxoriousness
Byelorussian
cynocephalus
cytogenetics
dynamometric
dynastically
gymnosophist
gynaecocracy
gyromagnetic
hybridisable
hydatidiform
hydrochloric

hydrodynamic
hydrofluoric
hydrographer
hydrographic
hydrokinetic
hydrological
hydrolysable
hydromedusae
hydromedusan
hydrophilous
hydroquinone
hydrostatics
hydrotherapy
hydrothermal
hydrotropism
hygienically
hygrophilous
hymenopteran
hymnographer
hyperacidity
hyperbolical
hyperplastic
hyperpyretic
hyperpyrexia
hypersthenia
hypersthenic
hypertension
hypertensive
hyperthermia
hypertrophic
hypnogenesis
hypnogenetic
hypnotherapy
hypnotically
hypnotisable
hypochlorite
hypochondria
hypocoristic
hypocritical
hypogastrium
hypognathous
hypophrygian
hypostatical
hyposulphite
hypothalamic
hypothalamus
hypothecator
hypothetical
hysterectomy
hysterically
hysteromania
lycanthropic
myrmecophily
mysteriously
mystifyingly
mythographer
mythological
mythologiser
nychthemeral
nychthemeron
nyctitropism
nympholeptic
nymphomaniac
pyroelectric
pyroligneous
pyromaniacal
pyromorphite
pyrotechnics
pyrotechnist
sycophantish
syllabically
sylviculture
symbolically
synaesthesia
synaesthetic
synarthrosis
synchronical
synchroniser
syncretistic

syndactylism
syndactylous
syndetically
synonymously
synoptically
systematical
systematiser
systemically
typefounding
typification
tyrannically
tyrannicidal
zygapophysis
zygomorphism
zygomorphous
Czechoslovak
─────────────
academically
acaulescence
adaptability
adaptiveness
agamogenesis
agamogenetic
amalgamation
amalgamative
amateurishly
anaerobiosis
anaesthetise
anaesthetist
anagogically
anagrammatic
analogically
analphabetic
analytically
anamorphosis
anaphylactic
anastigmatic
anathematise
anatomically
availability
avantgardism
avantgardist
avariciously
beachcombing
beatifically
blabbermouth
blackbirding
blackcurrant
blackguardly
bladderwrack
blamableness
blamefulness
blandishment
blastfurnace
blastosphere
blastulation
blatherskite
boastfulness
brachydactyl
brackishness
brainstormer
brainwashing
brambleberry
brassbounder
brassrubbing
chairmanship
chalcolithic
chalcopyrite
championship
chancemedley
chaplainship
characterise
charlatanism
charnelhouse
charterhouse
charterparty
chastisement
chauvinistic
clairaudient

```
clairvoyance glaucomatous praseodymium statuesquely weatherbound
clangorously gracefulness Quadragesima swaggeringly weatherglass
clannishness graciousness quadrangular swaggerstick weatherhouse
clapperboard grallatorial quadraphonic swainishness weatherproof
clarinettist graminaceous quadriennium swashbuckler wrathfulness
classicalism grammaticise quadrinomial teachability abbreviation
classicalist grammolecule quadriplegia tearlessness ambassadress
classicality gramnegative quadriplegic thankfulness ambidextrous
classifiable grampositive quadrivalent thanksgiving ambivalently
clatteringly granodiorite quadrumanous thaumaturgic arborescence
claudication graphologist quaestorship toastingfork arborisation
clavicembalo graspingness qualmishness traceability bibliography
coacervation gratefulness quantifiable trachomatous bibliologist
coachbuilder gratifyingly quantisation tractability bibliomaniac
coalitionist gratuitously quantitative tradescantia bibliopegist
crackbrained graveclothes quaquaversal tradespeople bibliophilic
craftbrother gravelelling quarterbound traditionary bibliopolist
craniologist guaranteeing quarterfinal traditionist bibliothecae
crashlanding guardianship quarterstaff traducianism bobbydazzler
deactivation headmistress quattrocento traducianist cabbagewhite
deambulatory headquarters reactivation tragicomical cabinetmaker
diabolically headshrinker reactiveness trainspotter debilitation
diageotropic heartburning readableness traitorously debonairness
diagrammatic heartrending readjustment trampolinist dibranchiate
dialectician heartstrings reallocation tranquillise dubitatively
dialectology heartwarming reappearance tranquillity embattlement
diamagnetism heathenishly reassessment transcendent embezzlement
diamonddrill heavenliness reassignment transduction embitterment
diamondfield heavyhearted reassuringly transferable emblazonment
diaphanously inaccessible scabbardfish transference emblematical
diastrophism inaccessibly scabrousness transferring embranchment
diathermancy inaccurately scandalously transformism embryologist
diatomaceous inactivation Scandinavian transformist fabulousness
diatonically inadequately scareheading transfusible fibrillation
dramatically inadmissible scarificator transgressor fibrinolysin
dramaturgist inadmissibly scatological transhipment gobbledegook
draughtboard inadvertence scatterbrain transhumance gobbledygook
draughthorse inadvertency scatteringly transiliency haberdashery
drawingboard inappeasable shadowboxing transitional habilitation
drawingpaper inapplicable Shakspereana transitively habitability
dwarfishness inapplicably Shaksperiana transitivity habitforming
elasmobranch inappositely shamateurism transitorily habitualness
emancipation inarticulate shamefacedly translatable hebdomadally
emargination inartificial shamefulness translucence hebetudinous
emasculation inaudibility sharecropper translucency hibernaculum
emasculatory inauguration sharpshooter transmigrant hubblebubble
enantiomorph inauguratory sharpsighted transmigrate hybridisable
evanescently inauspicious shatterproof transmission laboursaving
evangelistic irascibility skateboarder transmissive labyrinthian
exacerbation leapfrogging slanderously transmitting labyrinthine
exaggeration leathercloth slaughterous transmogrify liberalistic
exaggerative mealymouthed slaveholding transmontane libidinously
exaggeratory meaningfully smallclothes transmutable mobilisation
exasperation peacefulness smallholding transoceanic nebulisation
fearlessness pearlescence snaggletooth transpacific nebulousness
fearsomeness peasepudding snakecharmer transparency orbicularity
featherbrain phagocytosis snapfastener transpirable publicspirit
featheriness phagocytotic snappishness transplanter rabbinically
flabelliform phanerogamic snarlingiron transpontine rabblerouser
flagellation pharmaceutic spaciousness transposable rebelliously
flagellatory pharmacology sparkingplug transshipped ribonuclease
flagitiously placesetting sparrowgrass transudation robustiously
flamboyantly plainclothed stablishment transudatory sabretoothed
flamethrower plainclothes staffofficer transversely subalternate
flammability plaindealing staffsurgeon transvestism subalternity
flatteringly planetesimal stagemanager transvestite subapostolic
flavoprotein planetstruck staggeringly unacceptable subarrhation
fractionally planispheric Stakhanovism unaccustomed subcelestial
fractionator planoconcave Stakhanovite unaffectedly subcommittee
FrancoGerman plasterboard stalactiform unambivalent subconscious
frangibility platonically stalwartness unanswerable subcontinent
frankincense Plattdeutsch stammeringly unapologetic subcutaneous
fraudulently plausibility standardbred unappeasable subdivisible
geanticlinal playingfield standingroom unappetising subeditorial
glaciologist practicality stanniferous unassailable suberisation
gladiatorial practitioner starspangled unassumingly subinfeudate
gladsomeness pragmatistic stationhouse unattractive subjectively
glassblowing praiseworthy stationwagon unauthorised subjectivise
glaucescence pralltriller statistician weatherboard subjectivism
```

```
subjectivist  cocksureness  incognisance  nychthemeron  uncharitable
subjectivity  cuckingstool  incognitable  nyctitropism  uncharitably
sublapsarian  cuckooflower  incoherently  occasionally  unchivalrous
submaxillary  decaffeinate  incommodious  occidentally  unclassified
subminiature  decalescence  incommutable  occupational  uncomeatable
submissively  decapitation  incommutably  oncorhynchus  uncommercial
subnormality  decasyllabic  incomparable  orchestrator  uncommonness
subsaturated  decasyllable  incomparably  orchidaceous  unconformity
subscription  deceleration  incompatible  oscillograph  unconsidered
subsequently  decentralise  incompatibly  oscilloscope  unconstraint
subservience  decipherable  incompetence  pacification  uncontrolled
subserviency  decipherment  incompetency  pacificatory  unconvincing
subsidiarily  decisiveness  incompletely  peccadilloes  uncritically
subsonically  declinometer  incompliance  pickerelweed  unctuousness
substantiate  decomposable  incomputable  pictographic  vicargeneral
substantival  decompressor  inconcinnity  racemisation  vicechairman
substitution  decongestant  inconclusive  racketeering  Victorianism
substitutive  decongestion  inconformity  recalcitrant  victoriously
substruction  decongestive  inconsequent  recalcitrate  vocabularian
substructure  deconsecrate  inconsistent  recalescence  vocalisation
subtemperate  decontrolled  inconsolable  recapitulate  vociferation
subterranean  decoratively  inconsolably  receivership  vociferously
subthreshold  decorousness  inconsonance  receptaculum  wicketkeeper
subversively  decreasingly  inconstantly  receptionist  additionally
taberdarship  dichromatism  inconsumable  recessionary  bedazzlement
tabernacular  dictatorship  inconsumably  rechargeable  bodybuilding
tuberculated  duckingstool  incontiguous  reciprocally  bodysnatcher
tuberculosis  eccentricity  incontinence  reciprocator  bodystocking
umbrageously  ecclesiastic  incontinency  recklessness  codification
unbecomingly  ecclesiology  inconvenient  recognisable  didactically
unbelievable  encephalitic  incoordinate  recognisably  dodecahedral
unbelievably  encephalitis  incorporated  recognisance  dodecahedron
unblinkingly  enchantingly  incorporator  recollection  dodecaphonic
unblushingly  encirclement  incorporeity  recollective  endamagement
unbrokenness  enclitically  incorrigible  recommitment  endangerment
urbanisation  encroachment  incorrigibly  reconcilable  endermically
urbanologist  encrustation  incorruption  reconstitute  endocarditis
vibraphonist  encumberment  increasingly  reconversion  endometritis
acceleration  encumbrancer  incrustation  reconveyance  endoparasite
accelerative  encyclopedia  incurability  recreational  endoskeletal
accentuation  encyclopedic  lachrymation  recrudescent  fiddlefaddle
acciaccatura  escapologist  lachrymatory  recuperation  fiddlesticks
accidentally  escutcheoned  lachrymosely  recuperative  hedgehopping
accommodator  exchangeable  lacininiated  ricochetting  hydatidiform
accompanyist  excitability  licentiously  saccharinity  hydrochloric
accomplished  exclusionary  licketysplit  saccharoidal  hydrodynamic
accordionist  exclusionism  localisation  sacerdotally  hydrofluoric
accouchement  exclusionist  lycanthropic  sacrilegious  hydrographer
accoutrement  excogitation  machicolated  secessionism  hydrographic
accretionary  excogitative  macrocephaly  secessionist  hydrokinetic
accumulation  excruciating  macropterous  seclusionist  hydrological
accumulative  excruciation  mechanically  secondstring  hydrolysable
accurateness  excursionist  microanalyst  sectarianise  hydromedusae
accursedness  facelessness  microbiology  sectarianism  hydromedusan
accusatively  facilitation  microcapsule  sectionalise  hydrophilous
accusatorial  factionalism  microcephaly  secularistic  hydroquinone
archdeaconry  factiousness  microcircuit  sociableness  hydrostatics
archdiocesan  factitiously  microclimate  sociological  hydrotherapy
archetypally  fecklessness  microcopying  sociometrist  hydrothermal
archetypical  fictionalise  microcrystal  Socratically  hydrotropism
archipelagic  fictitiously  micrographer  succedaneous  indebtedness
architecture  focalisation  microphysics  successfully  indecisively
bacchanalian  hectographic  microscopist  successional  indeclinable
bachelorhood  hucklebacked  microseismic  successively  indecorously
bachelorship  incalculable  microsurgery  succinctness  indefeasible
backbreaking  incalculably  mucilaginous  sycophantish  indefeasibly
backpedalled  incalescence  necrographer  tachygrapher  indefectible
backslapping  incandescent  necrological  tachygraphic  indefensible
backwardness  incapability  necrophagous  tactlessness  indefensibly
backwoodsman  incapacitate  necrophiliac  technicality  indefinitely
bactericidal  incatenation  necrophilism  technicolour  indehiscence
bacteriology  incautiously  necrophilous  technocratic  indelibility
bacteriostat  incendiarism  nicotinamide  technologist  indelicately
bicentennial  incestuously  noctambulant  tectonically  independence
buccaneering  incidentally  noctambulism  ticklishness  independency
buccaneerish  incineration  noctambulist  uncalculated  indicatively
cachinnation  incisiveness  noctambulous  uncelebrated  indifference
cachinnatory  inclinometer  noctilucence  unchangeable  indifferency
cockfighting  incognisable  nychthemeral  unchangeably  indigenously
```

indigestible	understaffed	freestanding	paedobaptism	presentative
indirectness	undersurface	freeswimming	paedogenesis	presentiment
indiscipline	undertenancy	freethinking	paedogenetic	preservation
indiscreetly	underwritten	freewheeling	paedomorphic	preservative
indiscretion	undetermined	freightliner	peerlessness	presidential
indisputable	undiplomatic	frenchpolish	phenological	presumptuous
indisputably	acetabularia	frenetically	phenomenally	pretermitted
indissoluble	acetaldehyde	frequentness	phenotypical	prevailingly
indissolubly	adequateness	greathearted	pleasantness	prevaricator
indistinctly	agentgeneral	greengrocery	pleasingness	preventative
indivertible	alexipharmic	greenishness	pleasureless	preventively
indivertibly	amelioration	gregariously	plebiscitary	previousness
individually	ameliorative	guestchamber	plecopterous	psephologist
indoctrinate	amenableness	haematoblast	plectognathi	pseudocyesis
IndoEuropean	amentiferous	haematolysis	pleiotropism	pseudonymity
IndoGermanic	anecdotalist	haematoxylon	plenipotence	pseudonymous
industrially	anemographic	haemophiliac	pleomorphism	pseudopodium
judgematical	anemophilous	haemopoiesis	plesiosaurus	pteridophyte
ledgertackle	aperiodicity	haemorrhagic	pneumaticity	pteridosperm
lodginghouse	bletherskate	heedlessness	pneumatology	pterodactyle
mademoiselle	breakthrough	hierarchical	pneumothorax	puerperrally
mediaevalism	breaststroke	hieroglyphic	precancelled	questionable
mediaevalist	breastsummer	hierographer	precariously	questionably
meditatively	breathalyser	hierophantic	precedential	questionless
middleweight	breathlessly	idealisation	preceptorial	rhetorically
moderateness	breathtaking	ideationally	precessional	rheumatology
modification	breechloader	identifiable	prechristian	scenepainter
modificatory	Byelorussian	ineffaceable	preciousness	sceneshifter
muddleheaded	checkerberry	ineffaceably	precipitable	scenographic
nidification	checkerboard	inefficiency	precipitance	sheepishness
obdurateness	cheerfulness	inelasticity	precipitancy	sheepshearer
oldfashioned	cheeseburger	ineradicable	precipitator	sledgehammer
ordinariness	cheesecutter	ineradicably	precisianism	sleepingpill
pedantically	cheesemonger	inescutcheon	precisionist	sleepwalking
pedicellaria	cheeseparing	inexactitude	preclassical	speakingtube
pedunculated	cheirography	inexpedience	preclusively	specialistic
radiobiology	chemotherapy	inexpediency	precociously	specifically
radioelement	chequerboard	inexperience	precognition	specificness
radiographer	cherubically	inexpertness	precognitive	speciousness
radiographic	chesterfield	inexplicable	precondition	specktioneer
radioisotope	clearsighted	inexplicably	preconscious	spectrograph
radiological	cleistogamic	inexpressive	predesignate	spectrometer
radionuclide	coelenterate	inexpugnable	predestinate	spectrometry
radiophonics	coenobitical	inexpugnably	predetermine	spectroscope
radiotherapy	coenobytical	inextensible	predictively	spectroscopy
redecoration	coerciveness	inextricable	predigestion	speechlessly
redemptioner	coetaneously	inextricably	predilection	speedboating
Redemptorist	creativeness	kleptomaniac	predominance	speleologist
redeployment	creepycrawly	kremlinology	predominancy	spermaphytic
redintegrate	crenellation	meetinghouse	preeminently	spermathecal
redistribute	Czechoslovak	mnemotechnic	preestablish	spermatocyte
reducibility	deescalation	needlessness	preexistence	spermatozoid
reductionism	dietetically	obedientiary	prefabricate	spermatozoon
reductionist	dreadfulness	oceanography	prefectorial	spermogonium
ridiculously	dressinggown	oceanologist	preferential	stealthiness
saddlebacked	electrically	oneirocritic	preformation	steatopygous
sadistically	electrolysis	onesidedness	preformative	steeplechase
sedgewarbler	electrolytic	oneupmanship	prehensility	steganograph
sedulousness	electrometer	openhandedly	prehistorian	stellenbosch
sideslipping	electronvolt	openmindedly	prelapsarian	stelliferous
sidestepping	electroplate	operatically	premaxillary	stenographer
sidewhiskers	electroscope	overabundant	premeditated	stenographic
sodafountain	electroshock	overachiever	premeditator	stepchildren
sudoriferous	electrotonic	overactivity	premenstrual	stepdaughter
undemocratic	electrotonus	overcautious	prenticeship	stereochromy
underachieve	electrotyper	overcritical	preoccupancy	stereography
underbidding	eleemosynary	overcropping	preparedness	stereoisomer
underclothes	elementalism	overemphasis	preponderant	stereometric
undercoating	elementarily	overestimate	preponderate	stereophonic
undercurrent	epexegetical	overexertion	preposterous	stereopticon
undercutting	eveningdress	overexposure	prerequisite	stereoscopic
underdevelop	executorship	overlordship	presbyterate	sterlingness
undergarment	exegetically	overniceness	presbyterial	sternutation
underinsured	exenteration	overpersuade	Presbyterian	sternutative
underletting	exercitation	overpowering	prescription	sternutatory
undermanning	feebleminded	overpressure	prescriptive	sternwheeler
underpinning	fieldglasses	overreaction	preselection	stertorously
underrunning	fiendishness	oversimplify	preselective	stethoscopic
undersetting	freakishness	overstepping	presentation	sweepingness

sweetishness	reflectivity	pigmentation	amicableness	opisthotonos
teensyweensy	refractivity	pugnaciously	amitotically	orienteering
teetertotter	refractorily	regardlessly	apiculturist	painlessness
theanthropic	refreshingly	regeneration	aristocratic	philadelphus
theatregoing	refreshments	regenerative	Aristotelean	philanthrope
theatrically	refrigerator	regimentally	Aristotelian	philanthropy
theistically	safecracking	registration	arithmetical	philharmonic
thematically	softpedalled	regressively	avitaminoses	philhellenic
theocratical	sufficiently	rightfulness	avitaminosis	philistinism
theoretician	unfaithfully	rigorousness	blissfulness	phillumenist
theosophical	unfamiliarly	segmentation	blisteringly	philodendron
therapeutics	unfathomable	sightreading	blithesomely	philological
therapeutist	unfavourable	significance	boisterously	philosophise
thereinafter	unfavourably	significancy	brickfielder	poikilotherm
thermocouple	unflattering	suggestively	brilliantine	pointilliste
thermography	unfrequented	tightmouthed	brinkmanship	pricecutting
thermolabile	agglutinogen	togetherness	chieftainess	pridefulness
thermometric	aggressively	toggleswitch	childbearing	priestliness
thermophilic	angiocarpous	ungainliness	childishness	priestridden
thermoscopic	argillaceous	ungovernable	chimneypiece	priggishness
thermosphere	augmentation	ungracefully	chiropractic	primigravida
thermostable	augmentative	ungraciously	chiropractor	primogenital
thermostatic	beggarliness	ungratefully	chitterlings	primogenitor
thermotactic	degenerately	vegetatively	chivalrously	primordially
thermotropic	degeneration	vigorousness	cliffhanging	princeliness
tremendously	degenerative	zygapophysis	clinkerbuilt	principality
trephination	digressional	zygomorphism	coincidental	printability
trestletable	digressively	zygomorphous	coincidently	privatdocent
twentyfourmo	dogmatically	achlamydeous	criticalness	privatdozent
uneconomical	enginedriver	adhesiveness	deionisation	privateering
unemployable	enginetuning	Alhambresque	editorialise	prizefighter
unemployment	Englishwoman	atheromatous	editorialist	prizewinning
unencumbered	figuratively	athletically	epicureanism	quinquennial
uneventfully	fugitiveness	behaviourism	epicycloidal	quinquennium
unexpectedly	gigantically	behaviourist	epidemically	quintessence
whencesoever	hagiographer	cohabitation	epidemiology	quixotically
wherethrough	hagiographic	cohesiveness	epigrammatic	quizzicality
wretchedness	hagiological	echinococcus	epiphenomena	reinvestment
affectedness	highcoloured	echolocation	episcopalian	reinvigorate
affectionate	highfaluting	echosounding	episodically	rhinocerotic
buffalograss	highhandedly	ephemerality	epistemology	rhinological
definiteness	highlystrung	etherisation	epithalamion	rhizocarpous
definitively	highpressure	ethnocentric	epithalamium	rhizogenetic
deflagration	highsounding	ethnographer	evidentially	rhizophagous
deflationary	highspirited	ethnographic	evisceration	scintigraphy
deflationist	highstepping	ethnological	exiguousness	scintillator
defraudation	huggermugger	euhemeristic	fainthearted	seismography
differentiae	hygienically	exhaustively	faintishness	seismologist
differential	hygrophilous	exhibitioner	faithfulness	seismometric
effectuality	ingloriously	exhilaration	faithhealing	seismoscopic
effectuation	ingratiating	exhilarative	flickeringly	shillyshally
effeminately	legalisation	ichthyocolla	fricasseeing	shipbuilding
effervescent	legitimately	ichthyolatry	frictionless	shirtwaister
efflorescent	legitimation	ichthyophagy	friendliness	skippingrope
effortlessly	legitimatise	inhabitation	glitteringly	skittishness
effusiveness	lighthearted	inharmonious	grievousness	slipcarriage
enfeeblement	logistically	inhospitable	griseofulvin	slipperiness
infanticidal	lugubriously	inhospitably	guilefulness	spidermonkey
infectiously	magistrature	Ishmaelitish	hairdressing	spiegeleisen
infelicitous	magnetically	ophiophagous	hairsbreadth	spinsterhood
infiniteness	magnetisable	otherworldly	hairsplitter	spiritedness
infinitively	magnetograph	rehabilitate	idiosyncrasy	spiritlessly
inflammation	magnetometer	schismatical	idiothermous	spiritualise
inflammatory	magnifically	schizogonous	iniquitously	spiritualism
inflationary	magnificence	schizomycete	klipspringer	spiritualist
inflationism	magniloquent	schizophrene	knighterrant	spirituality
inflationist	megalomaniac	schizothymia	knightliness	spitefulness
inflectional	negativeness	schizothymic	laisserfaire	stichomythia
infrequently	negativistic	schoolfellow	laissezaller	stichomythic
infringement	neglectfully	schoolleaver	laissezfaire	stilboestrol
infundibular	negotiatress	schoolmaster	maidenliness	stillhunting
infusibility	negrophilism	schorlaceous	maidenstakes	suitableness
lefthandedly	negrophilist	spheroidally	maintainable	swimmingbath
lifelessness	nightclothes	sphragistics	moistureless	swimmingbell
officeholder	organgrinder	sphygmograph	nailscissors	swimmingpool
offscourings	organisation	unhesitating	neighbouring	swizzlestick
reflationary	organography	unhistorical	oligarchical	thickskinned
reflectional	organoleptic	alimentation	opinionative	thickskulled
reflectively	pigeonbreast	alimentative	opisthograph	thievishness

thimbleberry	bilharziasis	galvanometer	Palaeolithic	selfelective
thirdborough	bilharziosis	galvanoscope	palatability	selfemployed
thitherwards	bilingualism	halftimbered	paletteknife	selfevidence
toilsomeness	billingsgate	hallucinogen	palingenesia	selfexistent
triangularly	billsticking	hallucinosis	palingenesis	selfflattery
tricentenary	bulletheaded	halogenation	palingenetic	selfhypnosis
trichologist	bullfighting	halterbroken	Palladianism	selfidentity
trichotomise	bullheadedly	heliocentric	palynologist	selfignition
trichotomous	calamitously	heliographer	pellucidness	selfinterest
trichromatic	calcareously	heliographic	phlebotomise	selfinvolved
trickishness	calculatedly	heliogravure	phlebotomist	selflessness
tridactylous	calisthenics	heliolatrous	pilotballoon	selflimiting
trifurcation	calligrapher	heliotherapy	polarimetric	selfluminous
triggerhappy	calligraphic	heliotropism	polarisation	selfmurderer
triglyphical	callisthenic	hellgrammite	polarography	selfpleasing
trigonometry	calorescence	helplessness	policyholder	selfportrait
trinomialism	calorimetric	holidaymaker	polychaetous	selfreliance
tripartitely	calumniation	illadvisedly	polychromous	selfreproach
tripartition	calumniatory	illegibility	polyethylene	selfrighting
triphthongal	calumniously	illegitimacy	polyglottism	selfsameness
triplication	calycoideous	illegitimate	polyhistoric	selfstarting
triumphantly	chlorination	illiberality	polymorphism	selfviolence
twitteringly	coldshoulder	illiterately	polymorphous	sellingplate
ubiquitarian	coleopterist	illnaturedly	polyneuritic	silicicolous
ubiquitously	coleopterous	illogicality	polyneuritis	siliciferous
unifoliolate	collaborator	illtreatment	polypetalous	silverglance
unilaterally	collaterally	illumination	polyphyletic	silviculture
unimaginable	collectively	illuminative	polysepalous	solarisation
unimaginably	collectivise	illusiveness	polysyllabic	solicitation
unimportance	collectivism	illusoriness	polysyllable	solicitously
uninterested	collectivist	illustration	polytheistic	solifluction
unionisation	collectivity	illustrative	polytonality	solitariness
unisexuality	collegialism	kaleidoscope	polyurethane	splendidness
unitarianism	collegiality	kilowatthour	pulverisable	sulphonamide
universalise	collegiately	malacologist	relationally	sulphonation
universalism	collinearity	malapertness	relationship	sulphuration
universalist	colloquially	malcontented	relativeness	sulphuretted
universality	collywobbles	malevolently	relativistic	syllabically
vainglorious	colonisation	malformation	relentlessly	sylviculture
voidableness	coloquintida	malleability	reliableness	telaesthesia
wainscotting	colorimetric	malnutrition	rollingstock	telaesthetic
waistcoating	colourlessly	maltreatment	salamandrian	telegraphese
whigmaleerie	columniation	malversation	salamandrine	telegraphist
whimperingly	culpableness	melancholiac	salamandroid	teleological
whimsicality	cultivatable	melanochroic	salmonladder	televisional
whippoorwill	delamination	melodramatic	salpiglossis	tolerability
whisperingly	deliberately	meltingpoint	salubriously	unlawfulness
whitelivered	deliberation	militaristic	salutariness	unlikelihood
whitewashing	deliberative	millesimally	salutational	unlikeliness
whitherwards	delicatessen	milliammeter	salutiferous	unloveliness
adjectivally	delightfully	molecularity	salvationism	Valenciennes
adjudication	delimitation	mulligatawny	salvationist	valetudinary
adjudicative	delinquently	multicentral	sclerenchyma	valorisation
adjudicatory	deliquescent	multidentate	selenography	valuableness
dejectedness	delitescence	multifarious	selenologist	vilification
majestically	delusiveness	multiflorous	selfabsorbed	villainously
majorgeneral	dilapidation	multifoliate	selfactivity	volatileness
pejoratively	dilatability	multiformity	selfaffected	volcanically
rejectamenta	dilatoriness	multilateral	selfanalysis	volitionally
rejuvenation	dilettantish	multilingual	selfapplause	volumetrical
alkalescence	dilettantism	multiloquous	selfapproval	voluminosity
lakedwelling	dolorousness	multinuclear	selfbegotten	voluminously
lukewarmness	eclectically	multipartite	selfbetrayal	voluntaryism
unkindliness	elliptically	multipliable	selfcatering	voluntaryist
ailurophobia	falcongentil	multiplicand	selfcoloured	voluptuosity
alliteration	falcongentle	multiplicate	selfcomposed	voluptuously
alliterative	fallaciously	multiplicity	selfcontempt	walkietalkie
allomorphism	feldspathoid	multipurpose	selfcritical	wallpainting
allusiveness	felicitation	multistoried	selfdeceived	wallydraigle
balladmonger	felicitously	multivalence	selfdeceiver	welldisposed
balletomania	filibusterer	multiversity	selfdelusion	wellfavoured
ballottement	filtrability	multungulate	selfdestruct	wellgrounded
belittlement	folliculated	oblanceolate	selfdevotion	Wellingtonia
bellbottomed	fuliginosity	obligatorily	selfdirected	welterweight
belletristic	fullyfledged	obligingness	selfdistrust	williewaught
belligerence	galactogogue	obliteration	selfdoubting	wollastonite
belligerency	galligaskins	obliterative	selfeducated	yellowhammer
bellylanding	gallinaceous	palaeobotany	selfeffacing	administrant
bilateralism	galvanically	palaeography	selfeffacing	administrate

admonishment	hemerocallis	semidarkness	concomitance	contagionist
atmospherics	hemichordate	semideponent	concordantly	contagiously
bombdisposal	hemimorphism	semidetached	concrescence	containerise
camiknickers	hemimorphite	semidiameter	concreteness	contemplator
campfollower	hemiparasite	semidomestic	concubitancy	contemporary
campodeiform	hemispheroid	semifinalist	concupiscent	contemporise
cementitious	homeomorphic	semifinished	concurrently	contemptible
combinations	homeopathist	semiliterate	condemnation	contemptibly
comfortingly	homesickness	seminiferous	condemnatory	contemptuous
commandingly	homoeopathic	semiofficial	condensation	conterminous
commemorator	homoeostasis	semiological	conductivity	contestation
commencement	homologation	semiparasite	conduplicate	contextually
commendation	homomorphism	semiprecious	confabulator	contiguously
commendatory	homomorphous	semitropical	confectioner	contingently
commensalism	homonymously	sempiternity	conferential	continuation
commensalist	homosexually	simoniacally	confessional	continuative
commensurate	homothallism	simpleminded	confidential	continuously
commentation	humanisation	simultaneity	confirmation	contractable
commercially	humanitarian	simultaneous	confirmative	contractedly
commiserator	humification	somatopleure	confirmatory	contractible
commissarial	humorousness	somnambulant	confiscation	contradictor
commissariat	humptydumpty	somnambulate	confiscatory	contrapuntal
commissioner	hymenopteran	somnambulism	conformation	contrariness
committeeman	hymnographer	somnambulist	confoundedly	contrariwise
commodiously	immaculately	somniloquism	Confucianism	contribution
commonwealth	immaterially	somniloquist	confusedness	contributive
communicable	immatureness	symbolically	congeniality	contributory
communicably	immeasurable	tamelessness	congenitally	contriteness
communicator	immeasurably	temptability	conglobation	contrivement
companionate	immemorially	timehonoured	conglomerate	controllable
companionway	immensurable	timelessness	conglutinate	contumacious
compatriotic	immethodical	timorousness	congratulant	contumelious
compellation	immoderately	tumultuously	congratulate	convalescent
compensation	immoderation	unmanageable	congregation	convectional
compensative	immovability	unmercifully	conidiophore	conveniently
compensatory	immunisation	unmistakable	conidiospore	conventicler
complacently	immunologist	unmistakably	conjunctival	conventional
complaisance	immutability	vomiturition	connaturally	conversation
complemental	limnological	womanishness	connectional	conveyancing
completeness	lumberjacket	annihilation	connectively	convincement
complexional	luminescence	annihilative	conningtower	convincingly
complexioned	luminiferous	announcement	connubiality	conviviality
complication	luminousness	annunciation	conquistador	convulsively
composedness	namedropping	banderillero	conscionable	cynocephalus
compoundable	namelessness	bantamweight	conscription	denaturalise
compressible	nimbostratus	benefactress	consecration	denaturation
compulsively	niminypiminy	beneficently	consecratory	denomination
compulsivity	nomenclative	beneficially	consensually	denominative
compulsorily	nomenclature	benevolently	consentience	denouncement
compunctious	nominalistic	benzaldehyde	consentingly	densitometer
compurgation	numerologist	bonnetmonkey	consequently	denticulated
compurgatory	numerousness	bonnyclabber	conservation	dentilingual
cumbersomely	nympholeptic	canaliculate	conservatism	denuclearise
cumbrousness	nymphomaniac	canalisation	conservative	denunciation
cumulatively	obmutescence	cancellation	conservatory	denunciative
cumulocirrus	pumpernickel	candleholder	considerable	denunciatory
cumulonimbus	rambunctious	canonisation	considerably	dinnerjacket
demilitarise	ramification	canorousness	consignation	dunderheaded
demimondaine	rememberable	Cantabrigian	consistently	dynamometric
demineralise	remembrancer	cantankerous	consistorial	dynastically
demodulation	remilitarise	cantharidian	consociation	eunuchoidism
demoniacally	reminiscence	cantillation	consolidator	fancifulness
demonstrable	remonstrance	censoriously	conspiration	fantasticate
demonstrably	remonstrator	centesimally	constabulary	fantasticism
demonstrator	remorsefully	centrespread	constipation	fenestration
diminishable	removability	centrosphere	constituency	finalisation
diminishment	remuneration	centuplicate	constitution	functionally
diminutively	remunerative	cinematheque	constitutive	functionless
domestically	remuneratory	concelebrant	constriction	ganglionated
domesticator	romanisation	concelebrate	constrictive	genealogical
feminineness	romantically	concentrator	constringent	generousness
feminisation	rumbletumble	conceptional	construction	genuflection
gamesmanship	ruminatively	conceptually	constructive	gonadotropic
gamesomeness	Samaritanism	conchiferous	consultation	gonadotropin
gametophytic	semantically	conchologist	consultative	gynaecocracy
gamopetalous	semiannually	conciliation	consummately	handicapping
gamophyllous	semibasement	conciliative	consummation	handkerchief
gamosepalous	semicircular	conciliatory	consummative	handsbreadth
gymnosophist	semicylinder	conclusively	consummatory	handsomeness

```
henceforward munificently syndactylous closegrained inordinately
henotheistic nanoplankton syndetically closemouthed inosculation
hindquarters nonagenarian synonymously clotheshorse isochromatic
honeybuzzard nonalignment synoptically clothespress isochronally
innutritious nonchalantly tangentially clownishness isodiametric
kinaesthesia noncombatant tangibleness coordinately isolationism
kinaesthesis noncommittal tintinnabula coordination isolationist
kinaesthetic noncomplying tonelessness coordinative isothermally
kindergarten nonconductor tunelessness crossbedding neoclassical
kinnikinnick nonconformer vanquishable crossbencher neoDarwinian
landingcraft noneffective vanquishment crossbuttock neoDarwinism
landingfield nonefficient vantagepoint crosscountry neoDarwinist
landingstage nonessential venepuncture crosscurrent Neohellenism
landingstrip noneuclidean venerability crossexamine neonomianism
landlubberly nonexistence vengefulness crossgrained Neoplatonism
languishment nonflammable venipuncture crossheading Neoplatonist
languorously nonflowering venomousness crossingover odontologist
lanternjawed nonidentical ventripotent crosspurpose onomatopoeia
lanternslide nonobjective vindictively crosssection onomatopoeic
linguistical nonresidence vinification deontologist orographical
lonesomeness nonresistant windingsheet droughtiness phonasthenia
longdistance obnubilation wineglassful ecologically phonemically
longitudinal omnipotently winklepicker econometrics phonetically
longshoreman omnipresence winterbourne economically phonographer
longstanding omnisciently wonderstruck elocutionary phonographic
longwindedly omnivorously wonderworker elocutionist phonological
mangelwurzel ornamentally wondrousness emotionalise phosphoresce
Manicheanism ornithomancy wunderkinder emotionalism photochromic
manifoldness ornithoscopy xanthochroia emotionalist photofission
manipulation panchromatic YankeeDoodle emotionality photogeology
manipulative pancreatitis abolitionary enormousness photographer
manipulatory panhellenism abolitionism esoterically photographic
mannerliness panification abolitionist evolutionary photogravure
manoeuvrable pantechnicon aboriginally evolutionism photokinesis
manometrical pantisocracy abortiveness evolutionist photokinetic
mansionhouse pantographic acoustically exophthalmic photomontage
manslaughter penalisation adorableness exophthalmos photophilous
manufacturer penitentiary aforethought exophthalmus photosetting
mendaciously pennypincher amortisation exorbitantly photospheric
menstruation pennywhistle anotherguess exospherical phototropism
mindlessness pinfeathered apochromatic exoterically poorspirited
minedetector pontifically apolitically flocculation probationary
mineralogist pontificator apostolicism floodlighted proboscidean
minicomputer punchingball apostolicity floriculture proboscidian
minimisation renegotiable apostrophise footplateman procathedral
ministration renouncement apothegmatic frontbencher processional
ministrative renunciation aromatically frontiersman proclamation
monadelphous renunciative aromaticness frontispiece proclamatory
monastically renunciatory biochemistry geochemistry proconsulate
monetisation rontgenogram biocoenology geographical prodigiously
moneychanger rontgenology bioecologist geologically productively
moneygrubber runningboard biogeography geomagnetism productivity
moneyspinner sandyachting biographical geometrician professional
monitorially sanguinarily biologically geophysicist professorate
monkeyflower sanguineness biometrician geopolitical professoress
monkeyjacket sanguinolent biophysicist geosynclinal professorial
monkeypuzzle sansculottic bioscientist geotectonics proficiently
monkeywrench sensibleness biosynthesis ghoulishness profiteering
monochromate sensitometer biosynthetic globetrotter profligately
monodramatic sensualistic blockbusting glockenspiel profoundness
monofilament sensuousness bloodbrother gloriousness progenitress
monographist sententially bloodletting glossography progesterone
monomaniacal Sinanthropus bloodstained glossologist proglottides
monometallic singleacting bloodthirsty goodhumoured programmable
monomorphous singledecker bloodyminded goodtempered programmatic
monopetalous singlehanded boogiewoogie goosepimples projectional
monophyletic singleminded bookingclerk grossularite projectively
Monophysitic singleseater booklearning grotesquerie prolegomenon
monopodially sinistrality bootlessness groundcherry prolifically
monopolistic sinistrorsal brokenwinded groundlessly prolificness
monostichous sinusoidally bronchoscope grovellingly prolongation
monostrophic sonorousness broncobuster heortologist promulgation
monosyllabic synaesthesia brontosaurus hoodmanblind pronominally
monosyllable synaesthetic chocolatebox iconoclastic pronouncedly
monotheistic synarthrosis chondriosome iconographer proofreading
monotonously synchronical choreography idolatrously propaedeutic
monumentally synchroniser chorographic inobservance propagandise
municipalise syncretistic chorological inoccupation propagandism
municipality syndactylism closecropped inoperculate propagandist
```

prophylactic	thoroughbass	euphoniously	imprisonment	typefounding
propitiation	thoroughbred	expansionary	impropriator	typification
propitiatory	thoroughfare	expansionism	improvidence	unparalleled
propitiously	thoroughness	expansionist	improvisator	unpleasantly
proportional	thoughtfully	expatriation	imputability	unpopularity
proportioned	thousandfold	expediential	imputatively	unprejudiced
proprietress	trochanteric	experiential	lepidopteran	unpretending
proscription	troglodytism	experimental	lopsidedness	unprincipled
proscriptive	trophallaxis	experimenter	nephanalysis	unprofitable
prosectorial	tropological	explantation	nephelometer	unprofitably
prosecutable	tropospheric	explicitness	nephelometry	unpronounced
proselytiser	troublemaker	exploitation	nephrologist	vaporisation
prosodically	unofficially	exploitative	opposability	vaporousness
prosopopoeia	uxoriousness	expressional	oppositeness	xiphisternum
prosperously	wholeheaded	expressively	oppositional	acquaintance
prostitution	whortleberry	expressivity	oppressively	acquiescence
protactinium	woodengraver	exprobration	papyrologist	bequeathment
protectively	woodenheaded	happenstance	populousness	coquettishly
protectorate	woolgatherer	hippocentaur	rapprochment	liquefacient
protensively	woollyheaded	hippopotamus	repatriation	liquefaction
protestation	wrongfulness	hopelessness	repercussion	loquaciously
prothalamion	zoogeography	hyperacidity	repercussive	sequaciously
prothalamium	alphabetical	hyperbolical	repetitional	sequentially
prothonotary	alphamerical	hyperplastic	repetitively	sequestrator
protistology	alphanumeric	hyperpyretic	repossession	abrasiveness
protohistory	amphibiously	hyperpyrexia	reprehension	acronychally
protoplasmic	amphibrachic	hypersthenia	reprehensive	aerodynamics
protoplastic	amphictyonic	hypersthenic	repressively	aeroembolism
prototypical	amphisbaenic	hypertension	reproachable	aeronautical
protozoology	amphitheatre	hypertensive	reproachless	aeroneurosis
protrusively	amphitropous	hyperthermia	reproducible	aerosiderite
protuberance	apparatchiki	hypertrophic	reproduction	AfroAmerican
proudhearted	apparatchiks	hypnogenesis	reproductive	agranulocyte
proverbially	apparentness	hypnogenetic	reprographic	agribusiness
providential	apparitional	hypnotherapy	saponifiable	agricultural
provincially	appendectomy	hypnotically	saprophagous	aircondition
provisionary	appendicitis	hypnotisable	separability	aircraftsman
reoccupation	appendicular	hypochlorite	separateness	arrhythmical
rhododendron	apperception	hypochondria	septennially	barbarically
rhombohedral	apperceptive	hypocoristic	septilateral	barometrical
rhombohedron	appetisingly	hypocritical	septuagenary	berzelianite
rootlessness	appositeness	hypogastrium	Septuagesima	birdsnesting
scornfulness	appositional	hypognathous	Septuagintal	birdwatching
scorpionfish	appraisement	hypophrygian	sepulchrally	birefringent
scoundreldom	appraisingly	hypostatical	siphonophore	borosilicate
scouringrush	appreciation	hyposulphite	siphonostele	bureaucratic
shootingiron	appreciative	hypothalamic	sophisticate	burglarproof
shortchanger	appreciatory	hypothalamus	soporiferous	burningglass
shortcircuit	apprehension	hypothecator	superannuate	caravansarai
shortpitched	apprehensive	hypothetical	supercharger	caravanserai
shortsighted	approachable	impartiality	superciliary	carbohydrate
shortsleeved	appropriable	impedimental	supercilious	carbonaceous
shortstaffed	appropriator	impenetrable	supereminent	carburetting
shoulderbelt	asphyxiation	impenetrably	supererogate	carcinogenic
shoulderknot	capercaillie	impenitently	superhighway	cardcarrying
shouldernote	capercailzie	imperatively	superhumanly	cardinalship
slothfulness	capitalistic	imperatorial	supermundane	cardiography
slovenliness	capitulation	imperceptive	supernaculum	cardiologist
snobbishness	capriciously	impercipient	supernatural	carelessness
spokesperson	captiousness	imperfection	superposable	caricaturist
sporadically	copolymerise	imperfective	supersedence	carillonneur
sporogenesis	copulatively	imperishable	supersensory	Carlovingian
sportfulness	cuprammonium	imperishably	supersession	carpetbagger
sportiveness	departmental	impermanence	superstition	carpetknight
spotlessness	depoliticise	impermanency	superstratum	carragheenin
stockbreeder	depopulation	impersonally	supervenient	carriageable
stockbroking	depravedness	impersonator	supervention	Cartesianism
stockingless	depreciation	impertinence	supplemental	cartographer
stockjobbery	depreciatory	impertinency	supplementer	cartographic
stockjobbing	depressingly	imperviously	supplicantly	cartological
stockraising	deputisation	impetiginous	supplication	ceremonially
stoneboiling	diphtheritic	implicitness	supplicatory	chrematistic
stonecutting	diphthongise	impoliteness	suppositious	chrestomathy
stonedresser	emphatically	imponderable	suppressible	Christianise
stonemasonry	empoisonment	imponderably	supramundane	Christianity
stonyhearted	empressement	impoverished	supraorbital	Christolatry
stormtrooper	espagnolette	impregnation	taperecorder	Christophany
stouthearted	euphonically	impressively	toploftiness	chromaticism
			topsyturvily	chromaticity

chromatogram	harquebusier	miraculously	peroxidation	stratigraphy
chromatology	heraldically	mirthfulness	perpetration	stratosphere
chromatopsia	hereditament	moralisation	perpetuation	streetwalker
chromosphere	hereditarily	mordaciously	perplexingly	strengthener
chronography	hereinbefore	morningdress	perseverance	strengthless
chronologise	heritability	morphallaxis	persistently	streptococci
chronologist	hermeneutics	morphologist	perspicacity	streptomycin
chronometric	hermetically	morrisdancer	perspiration	stridulation
circuitously	heroicalness	myrmecophily	perspiratory	strikingness
circumcision	heroicomical	narcissistic	persuasively	stringcourse
circumfluent	herpetologic	narcotically	pertinacious	strobilation
circumfusion	hirepurchase	narrowminded	perturbation	stroboscopic
circumjacent	horizontally	nerveracking	perturbative	strongminded
circumscribe	horrendously	noradrenalin	perverseness	strongylosis
circumstance	horribleness	northeastern	perviousness	strontianite
cirrocumulus	horrifically	northernmost	phrasemonger	strophanthin
cirrostratus	horrorstruck	Northumbrian	phraseograph	structurally
corelatively	horsebreaker	northwestern	phreatophyte	strychninism
corespondent	horsemanship	paraboloidal	phrenologist	surefootedly
corporeality	horsetrading	paradigmatic	porcelainise	surmountable
correctional	horsewhipped	paradisaical	porcelainous	surprisingly
correctitude	horticulture	paradisiacal	porcellanous	surrealistic
correctively	irrationally	paraesthesia	pornographer	surrejoinder
corroborator	irredeemable	paragraphist	pornographic	surroundings
curlingirons	irredeemably	parallelling	portentously	surveillance
curlingtongs	irreflective	paralysation	portmanteaus	surveyorship
curmudgeonly	irreformable	paramagnetic	portmanteaux	survivorship
curvicaudate	irrefragable	parametrical	purblindness	teratologist
curvicostate	irrefragably	paramilitary	purification	teratomatous
curvifoliate	irregardless	paramorphism	purificatory	tercentenary
curvirostral	irregularity	paranormally	purposebuilt	terebinthine
deracination	irrelatively	paraphrastic	purposefully	tergiversate
derisiveness	irrelevantly	parasiticide	pursestrings	terribleness
derivational	irremediable	parasitology	pyroelectric	terrifically
derivatively	irremediably	paratactical	pyroligneous	terrifyingly
dermatophyte	irremissible	parenthesise	pyromaniacal	terrorstruck
derogatorily	irrepealable	parisyllabic	pyromorphite	threequarter
directorship	irreprovable	parkinsonism	pyrotechnics	threewheeler
dorsiventral	irresistible	parochialise	pyrotechnist	thriftlessly
duraluminium	irresistibly	parochialism	ruralisation	throughstone
earsplitting	irresolutely	parochiality	sarcomatosis	tirelessness
earthshaking	irresolution	paronomastic	sarcophagous	tiresomeness
EuroAmerican	irresolvable	parsimonious	sardonically	torrefaction
farmsteading	irrespective	participator	sarrusophone	torrentially
farsightedly	irrespirable	particularly	sarsaparilla	Torricellian
fermentation	irresponsive	partisanship	scraperboard	tortuousness
fermentative	irreverently	partitionist	scratchiness	turbellarian
ferrugineous	irreversible	peradventure	screenwriter	turriculated
fertilisable	irreversibly	perambulator	scrimshanker	turtlenecked
firefighting	irritability	perceptively	scripturally	tyrannically
firstnighter	irritatingly	perceptivity	scriptwriter	tyrannicidal
foraminifera	jerrybuilder	perceptually	scrobiculate	unreasonable
forbiddingly	jurisconsult	percussively	scrupulosity	unreasonably
forcefulness	jurisdiction	percutaneous	scrupulously	unrecognised
forcibleness	jurisprudent	peregrinator	seraphically	unregenerate
forebodement	karyokinesis	peremptorily	sergeantfish	unrepeatable
forebodingly	kirschwasser	perfectively	sergeantship	unreservedly
forensically	largehearted	perfervidity	sericultural	unresponsive
foresightful	laryngoscope	perfidiously	serjeantship	unrestrained
forestalment	laryngoscopy	perfoliation	serpentiform	uproariously
formaldehyde	Marcionitism	performative	serpentinely	variableness
formlessness	marketgarden	pericarditis	serviceberry	varicoloured
forthrightly	marketsquare	perilousness	servicecourt	veridicality
fortuitously	marksmanship	periodically	servicewoman	verification
furfuraceous	marlinespike	periodontics	servitorship	verificatory
furunculosis	marriageable	periodontist	servocontrol	vermiculated
geriatrician	Marseillaise	periostracum	shrewishness	vernacularly
Germanophile	marshharrier	peripherally	skrimshanker	vertebration
Germanophobe	marvellously	periphrastic	sorbefacient	verticalness
gerontocracy	mercantilism	perispomenon	sprightfully	verticillate
gorgeousness	mercantilist	peristeronic	Stradivarius	viridescence
gyromagnetic	mercifulness	peristomatic	straightaway	virtuosoship
hardfavoured	mercurialise	perjuriously	straightbred	virtuousness
hardfeatured	mercurialism	permanganate	straightedge	warehouseman
hardstanding	meretricious	permeability	straightener	workableness
harlequinade	meridionally	permissively	straightness	workingclass
harmlessness	meristematic	permittivity	straitjacket	worshipfully
harmonically	merrythought	perniciously	stranglehold	absentminded
harmoniously		pernoctation	straticulate	absoluteness

absolutistic	disconnexion	exsanguinate	obscurantism	unsuccessful
absorptional	disconsolate	exsanguinous	obscurantist	vasodilation
absorptivity	discontented	exsufflicate	obsequiously	vasodilatory
absquatulate	discordantly	fastidiously	obsolescence	vesiculation
abstemiously	discountable	fostermother	obsoleteness	viscerotonic
abstractable	discouraging	gasification	obstetrician	viscosimeter
abstractedly	discourteous	gastronomist	obstreperous	viscountship
abstractness	discoverable	gastropodous	ossification	visitational
abstruseness	discoverture	gesellschaft	pasqueflower	visitatorial
adscititious	discreetness	gesticulator	passepartout	wastefulness
aesthetician	discreteness	hesitatingly	passionately	actinomycete
aestheticism	discretional	hesperididia	passionfruit	aetiological
assassinator	discriminant	histogenesis	pestilential	afterthought
assibilation	discriminate	histogenetic	pestological	alterability
assimilation	discursively	histological	pisciculture	altitudinous
assimilative	disdainfully	historically	positiveness	antagonistic
assimilatory	disembarrass	hysterectomy	positivistic	antecedently
auscultation	disenchanter	hysterically	possessively	antediluvian
auscultatory	disendowment	hysteromania	postdiluvian	anteprandial
auspiciously	disestablish	insalubrious	postdoctoral	anthelmintic
Australasian	disfranchise	insecticidal	posteriority	anthropogeny
baselessness	disgorgement	insemination	postgraduate	anthropoidal
basidiospore	disguisement	insolubilise	posthumously	anthropology
bassorelievo	disgustfully	insolubility	postmeridian	antiaircraft
bassorilievo	disgustingly	inspectorate	postmistress	anticipation
beseechingly	disharmonise	inspectorial	postponement	anticipative
bespectacled	dishevelment	inspissation	postposition	anticipatory
businesslike	disincentive	installation	postpositive	anticlerical
cashandcarry	disinfectant	instauration	postprandial	anticyclonic
cosmetically	disinfection	instillation	reservedness	antigenicity
cosmogonical	disinflation	instructress	resettlement	antigropelos
cosmographer	disingenuous	instrumental	residentiary	antimacassar
cosmographic	disintegrate	insufferable	residentship	antimagnetic
cosmological	disinterment	insufferably	resignedness	antimalarial
cosmopolitan	disjointedly	insufficient	resiniferous	antineutrino
cosmopolitic	dislodgement	insufflation	resipiscence	antiparticle
costermonger	disobedience	insurrection	resistlessly	antipathetic
customshouse	disorientate	jesuitically	resoluteness	antiperiodic
desalination	dispensation	kissingcrust	resolvedness	antiphonally
desideration	dispensatory	lasciviously	resoundingly	antirachitic
desiderative	dispiritedly	listlessness	respectfully	antiSemitism
desirability	displaceable	lusciousness	respectively	antistrophic
desirousness	displacement	mastersinger	resplendence	antithetical
desolateness	displeasedly	masterstroke	resplendency	articulately
despairingly	dispossessor	masterswitch	responsively	articulation
despitefully	disputatious	mastigophora	responsorial	articulatory
despoliation	disquisition	mesocephalic	restaurateur	artificially
despondently	disregardful	mesothoracic	restlessness	artilleryman
despotically	disreputable	messeigneurs	restrainable	artistically
desquamation	disreputably	misadventure	restrainedly	astonishment
desquamative	dissatisfied	misalignment	restrictedly	astoundingly
desquamatory	disseminator	misanthropic	resupination	astringently
dessertspoon	dissentingly	misapprehend	resurrection	astrological
destructible	dissertation	misbehaviour	resuscitator	astronautics
desulphurise	disseverance	miscalculate	risorgimento	astronomical
disaccharide	disseverment	miscellanist	rosecoloured	astrophysics
disadvantage	dissimilarly	misdemeanant	sesquialtera	attitudinise
disaffection	dissimulator	misdemeanour	susceptivity	attorneyship
disaffiliate	dissocialise	misdirection	suspensively	attractively
disagreeable	dissociation	miseducation	suspiciously	attributable
disagreeably	dissociative	misinterpret	sustentation	authenticate
disagreement	dissuasively	misjudgement	sustentative	authenticity
disallowance	dissymmetric	misknowledge	systematical	autocatalyse
disambiguate	distemperate	misplacement	systematiser	autochthones
disannulling	distillation	mispronounce	systemically	autodidactic
disannulment	distillatory	misquotation	taskmistress	autoimmunity
disassociate	distinctness	misrepresent	tastefulness	automaticity
disastrously	distortional	misselthrush	tessellation	automobilist
disbursement	distractedly	misstatement	testamentary	automorphism
discerningly	distrainable	mistakenness	testosterone	autonomously
discerptible	distrainment	mistranslate	testudineous	bathypelagic
discipleship	distributary	mistreatment	unscientific	battleground
disciplinary	distribution	mistressship	unscriptural	battlemented
disclamation	distributive	mosstrooping	unscrupulous	bottlewasher
discographer	disturbingly	musicianship	unsearchable	butterflynut
discomfiture	ecstatically	musicologist	unseasonable	buttermuslin
discommodity	enshrinement	mysteriously	unsegregated	butterscotch
discomposure	enswathement	mystifyingly	unsteadiness	catachrestic
disconnected	essentiality	Nestorianism	unstructured	catamountain

cataphoresis	intercession	katzenjammer	osteomalacia	aquicultural
catastrophic	intercessory	laterisation	osteoplastic	bluestocking
catechetical	interchanger	laticiferous	osteoporosis	blunderingly
caterwauling	interconnect	latinisation	outdatedness	blusteringly
catholically	intercropped	latitudinous	outlandishly	boulevardier
catilinarian	intercurrent	literariness	outmanoeuvre	cautiousness
cattlelifter	intercutting	lithographer	outpensioner	churchianity
cottonocracy	interdiction	lithographic	outrageously	churchwarden
cotyledonary	interdictive	lithological	outrivalling	churlishness
cotyledonous	interdictory	lithospheric	outstretched	councilwoman
cytogenetics	interdigital	lithotritist	outstripping	countenancer
detachedness	interestedly	liturgically	outwardbound	counteragent
determinable	interfemoral	liturgiology	pathetically	counterblast
determinably	interference	materialness	pathogenesis	countercheck
determinedly	interglacial	mathematical	pathogenetic	counterclaim
dethronement	interjection	matriarchate	pathological	counterforce
detoxication	interjectory	metachronism	patriarchate	counterlight
detumescence	interlobular	metagalactic	patternmaker	countermarch
ectoparasite	interlocutor	metalanguage	patulousness	counterplead
entanglement	intermeddler	metallically	petrifaction	counterpoint
enterprising	intermediacy	metallophone	petrographer	counterpoise
entertaining	intermediary	metallurgist	petrographic	counterproof
enthronement	intermediate	metalworking	petrological	counterscarp
enthusiastic	interminable	metamorphism	pettifoggery	countershaft
entomologise	interminably	metamorphose	pettifogging	countertenor
entomologist	intermission	metaphorical	pitcherplant	countrydance
entrammelled	intermittent	metaphrastic	pitiableness	countrywoman
entrancement	intermitting	metaphysical	pitilessness	courageously
entreatingly	intermixture	metapsychics	pitterpatter	courtmartial
entrenchment	intermundane	metasomatism	potentiality	courtplaster
entrepreneur	internuclear	metathetical	putrefaction	cousingerman
estrangement	internuncial	metathoracic	putrefactive	Deuteronomic
extensometer	interoceanic	meteorically	ratification	doubleacting
exterminable	interoceptor	meteorograph	ratiocinator	doubledealer
exterminator	interpellate	methodically	rattleheaded	doubledecked
extinguisher	interpleader	meticulously	reticulately	doubledecker
extortionary	interpolator	metrological	reticulation	doublelocked
extortionate	interpretive	metropolitan	reticulocyte	doubtfulness
extracranial	interrelated	mithridatise	retiringness	educationist
extraditable	interrogator	mithridatism	retractation	edulcoration
extralimital	interruption	mitochondria	retractility	elucubration
extramarital	interruptive	mitrailleuse	retrenchment	emulsifiable
extramundane	intersection	motherfigure	retrocedence	equalisation
extraneously	interservice	motherliness	retrocession	equalitarian
extrasensory	interspinous	mothertongue	retrocessive	equationally
extraspecial	interstellar	motivational	retroflexion	equestrienne
extrauterine	interstitial	motorcyclist	retropulsion	equidistance
extravagance	intertexture	motorisation	retroversion	equilibrator
extravagancy	intervenient	mutinousness	ruthlessness	equipollence
extravaganza	intervention	muttonheaded	satisfaction	equipollency
extraversion	intervocalic	mythographer	satisfactory	equiprobable
extroversion	interwreathe	mythological	satisfyingly	equitability
fatherfigure	intimidation	mythologiser	tetrachordal	equivalently
fatherliness	intimidatory	naturalistic	tetragonally	equivocation
futilitarian	intolerantly	naturopathic	tetrahedrite	equivocatory
futurologist	intoxication	nitrobenzene	tetramorphic	eruptiveness
heterocercal	intracardiac	notification	tittletattle	exulceration
heterocyclic	intracranial	nutritionist	totalisation	faultfinding
heteroecious	intramundane	nutritiously	totalitarian	fluidisation
heterogamous	intransigent	octogenarian	ultramontane	fluorescence
heterogenous	intransitive	octosyllabic	ultramundane	fluoridation
heterologous	intrauterine	octosyllable	unthinkingly	fluorination
heteromerous	intrenchment	optimisation	unthoughtful	fluorocarbon
heteronomous	intriguingly	orthodontics	untimeliness	foundationer
heterophylly	introduction	orthodontist	untowardness	fountainhead
heterosexual	introductory	orthogenesis	untruthfully	fructiferous
heterozygote	introjection	orthogenetic	vaticination	fructivorous
heterozygous	intromission	orthographer	veterinarian	fruitfulness
integumental	intromittent	orthographic	vitaligation	gluttonously
intellection	intromitting	orthographis	vitiligation	gruesomeness
intellective	introversion	orthopaedics	vitreousness	housebreaker
intellectual	introversive	orthopaedist	vitrifaction	housekeeping
intelligence	introvertive	orthopteroid	vituperation	housetrained
intelligible	intrusionist	orthopterous	vituperative	housewarming
intelligibly	intuitionism	orthotropism	vituperatory	journalistic
intemperance	intuitionist	orthotropous	watchfulness	laudableness
inteneration	intumescence	ostentatious	watermanship	laureateship
interbedding	intussuscept	osteogenesis	adulteration	leucocytosis
interception	jetpropelled	osteological	adulterously	leukocytosis

```
loungelizard diverticulum cryptologist catastrophic incandescent
mountainside divertimenti crystalgazer clearsighted incapability
mournfulness divertimento Egyptologist cohabitation incapacitate
mourningband divisibility erythematous cowardliness incatenation
mourningring divisiveness erythroblast creativeness incautiously
mouthbreeder dovecoloured erythromycin decaffeinate infanticidal
nauseatingly eavesdropped etymological decalescence inhabitation
nauseousness eavesdropper etymologicon decapitation inharmonious
neurasthenia enviableness glycogenesis decasyllabic insalubrious
neurasthenic envisagement glycoprotein decasyllable invagination
neuroanatomy feverishness glyphography delamination invalidation
neurobiology governmental glyptography denaturalise irrationally
neurological governorship Keynesianism denaturation kinaesthesia
neuropterous invagination oxyacetylene departmental kinaesthesis
neuroscience invalidation phycological deracination kinaesthetic
neurosurgeon inveiglement phycomycetes desalination legalisation
neurosurgery invertebrate phyllotactic detachedness localisation
neurotically investigator phylogenesis didactically lycanthropic
plumbaginous inveterately phylogenetic dilapidation malacologist
plumbiferous invigilation physiognomic dilatability malapertness
plummerblock invigoration physiography dilatoriness megalomaniac
pluriliteral invisibility physiologist disaccharide melancholiac
pluviometric involutional phytogenesis disadvantage melanochroic
prudentially invulnerable phytogenetic disaffection metachronism
reunionistic invulnerably phytographer disaffiliate metagalactic
sculpturally juvenescence phytological disagreeable metalanguage
scurrilously levorotation phytophagous disagreeably metallically
scutellation levorotatory psychiatrist disagreement metallophone
shuffleboard Liverpudlian psychoactive disallowance metallurgist
skullduggery liverystable psychography disambiguate metalworking
skunkcabbage lovelessness psychologise disannulling metamorphism
sluggishness lovelornness psychologism disannulment metamorphose
sluttishness moveableness psychologist disassociate metaphorical
soullessness movelessness psychometric disastrously metaphrastic
soundingline navigability psychopathic divarication metaphysical
southeastern navigational psychosexual dreadfulness metapsychics
southernmost nevertheless psychotropic duraluminium metasomatism
southernwood novelisation psychrometer dynamometric metathetical
southwestern ravenousness psychrometry dynastically metathoracic
spuriousness revelational rhynchophora embattlement miraculously
squarerigged revengefully rhythmically endamagement misadventure
squattocracy reverberator stylographic endangerment misalignment
squirrelcage reversionary unyieldingly entanglement misanthropic
squirreltail revictualled enzymologist equalisation misapprehend
stubbornness revivalistic mezzorelievo equalitarian monadelphous
studdingsail reviviscence mezzosoprano equationally monastically
studiousness vivification muzzleloader escapologist moralisation
stupefacient viviparously razzledazzle espagnolette negativeness
stupefaction bewilderedly ──────────── exhaustively negativistic
stupefactive bewilderment abrasiveness expansionary nonagenarian
stupendously bewitchingly advantageous expansionism nonalignment
stutteringly bowcompasses agranulocyte expansionist noradrenalin
tautological cowardliness Alhambresque expatriation oblanceolate
Teutonically downwardness alkalescence exsanguinate occasionally
thundercloud LowChurchman ambassadress exsanguinous oceanography
thunderingly newfashioned antagonistic finalisation oceanologist
thunderously Newfoundland apparatchiki focalisation organgrinder
thunderstone newspaperman apparatchiks foraminifera organisation
thunderstorm towardliness apparentness freakishness organography
touchingness unwieldiness apparitional galactogogue organoleptic
trumpetshell unwontedness assassinator gigantically ornamentally
trustfulness unworldiness bedazzlement gonadotropic oxyacetylene
truthfulness unworthiness behaviourism gonadotropin palaeobotany
usufructuary dextrousness behaviourist greathearted palaeography
usuriousness lexicography bilateralism gynaecocracy Palaeolithic
vauntcourier lexicologist breakthrough heraldically palatability
youngberries maximisation breaststroke humanisation paraboloidal
youthfulness sexagenarian breastsummer humanitarian paradigmatic
advantageous sexcentenary breathalyser hydatidiform paradisaical
adventitious taxcollector breathlessly idealisation paradisiacal
advisability toxicologist breathtaking ideationally paraesthesia
civilisation toxicophobia calamitously illadvisedly paragraphist
covetousness amygdaloidal canaliculate immaculately parallelling
deviationism asymmetrical canalisation immaterially paralysation
deviationist asynchronism caravansarai immatureness paramagnetic
divarication asynchronous caravanserai impartiality parametrical
diversionary cryptanalyst catachrestic incalculable paramilitary
diversionist cryptogamous catamountain incalculably paramorphism
diverticular cryptography cataphoresis incalescence paranormally
```

subconscious	hindquarters	vindictively	directorship	heteroecious
subcontinent	hoodmanblind	voidableness	disembarrass	heterogamous
subcutaneous	inadequately	windingsheet	disenchanter	heterogenous
succedaneous	inadmissible	wonderstruck	disendowment	heterologous
successfully	inadmissibly	wonderworker	disestablish	heteromerous
successional	inadvertence	wondrousness	diversionary	heteronomous
successively	inadvertency	woodengraver	diversionist	heterophylly
succinctness	isodiametric	woodenheaded	diverticular	heterosexual
susceptivity	kindergarten	wunderkinder	diverticulum	heterozygote
synchronical	landingcraft	absentminded	divertimenti	heterozygous
synchroniser	landingfield	acceleration	divertimento	hibernaculum
syncretistic	landingstage	accelerative	dodecahedral	hirepurchase
taxcollector	landingstrip	accentuation	dodecahedron	homeomorphic
teachability	landlubberly	adhesiveness	dodecaphonic	homeopathist
tercentenary	laudableness	adjectivally	domestically	homesickness
thickskinned	maidenliness	adventitious	domesticator	honeybuzzard
thickskulled	maidenstakes	affectedness	dovecoloured	hopelessness
touchingness	mendaciously	affectionate	eavesdropped	hymenopteran
traceability	middleweight	afterthought	eavesdropper	hyperacidity
trachomatous	mindlessness	alterability	eccentricity	hyperbolical
tractability	misdemeanant	anaerobiosis	eclectically	hyperplastic
tricentenary	misdemeanour	anaesthetise	effectuality	hyperpyretic
trichologist	misdirection	anaesthetist	effectuation	hyperpyrexia
trichotomise	mordaciously	antecedently	effeminately	hypersthenia
trichotomous	muddleheaded	antediluvian	effervescent	hypersthenic
trichromatic	neoDarwinian	anteprandial	eleemosynary	hypertension
trickishness	neoDarwinism	appendectomy	embezzlement	hypertensive
trochanteric	neoDarwinist	appendicitis	encephalitic	hyperthermia
unacceptable	obedientiary	appendicular	encephalitis	hypertrophic
unaccustomed	outdatedness	apperception	endermically	illegibility
uneconomical	paedobaptism	apperceptive	enfeeblement	illegitimacy
unscientific	paedogenesis	appetisingly	enterprising	illegitimate
unscriptural	paedogenetic	atheromatous	entertaining	immeasurable
unscrupulous	paedomorphic	baselessness	ephemerality	immeasurably
viscerotonic	predesignate	benefactress	equestrienne	immemorially
viscosimeter	predestinate	beneficently	essentiality	immensurable
viscountship	predetermine	beneficially	etherisation	immethodical
volcanically	predictively	benevolently	euhemeristic	impedimental
watchfulness	predigestion	beseechingly	expediential	impenetrable
academically	predilection	bicentennial	experiential	impenetrably
banderillero	predominance	bioecologist	experimental	impenitently
birdsnesting	predominancy	birefringent	experimenter	imperatively
birdwatching	pridefulness	bluestocking	extensometer	imperatorial
bladderwrack	prodigiously	breechloader	exterminable	imperceptive
candleholder	productively	bureaucratic	exterminator	impercipient
cardcarrying	productivity	capercaillie	facelessness	imperfection
cardinalship	prudentially	capercailzie	fenestration	imperfective
cardiography	Quadragesima	carelessness	feverishness	imperishable
cardiologist	quadrangular	catechetical	firefighting	imperishably
coldshoulder	quadraphonic	caterwauling	forebodement	impermanence
condemnation	quadriennium	cementitious	forebodingly	impermanency
condemnatory	quadrinomial	ceremonially	forensically	impersonally
condensation	quadriplegia	cheeseburger	foresightful	impersonator
conductivity	quadriplegic	cheesecutter	forestalment	impertinence
conduplicate	quadrivalent	cheesemonger	freestanding	impertinency
disdainfully	quadrumanous	cheeseparing	freeswimming	imperviously
dunderheaded	readableness	chieftainess	freethinking	impetiginous
epidemically	readjustment	chrematistic	freewheeling	incendiarism
epidemiology	rhododendron	chrestomathy	friendliness	incestuously
evidentially	saddlebacked	cinematheque	gamesmanship	indebtedness
feldspathoid	sandyachting	cohesiveness	gamesomeness	indecisively
fiddlefaddle	sardonically	coleopterist	gametophytic	indeclinable
fiddlesticks	shadowboxing	coleopterous	genealogical	indecorously
gladiatorial	sledgehammer	corelatively	generousness	indefeasible
gladsomeness	spidermonkey	corespondent	gesellschaft	indefeasibly
goodhumoured	studdingsail	covetousness	governmental	indefectible
goodtempered	studiousness	creepycrawly	governorship	indefensible
handicapping	subdivisible	deceleration	greengrocery	indefensibly
handkerchief	syndactylism	decentralise	greenishness	indefinitely
handsbreadth	syndactylous	degenerately	grievousness	indehiscence
handsomeness	syndetically	degeneration	gruesomeness	indelibility
hardfavoured	tradescantia	degenerative	haberdashery	indelicately
hardfeatured	tradespeople	dejectedness	hebetudinous	independence
hardstanding	traditionary	determinable	hemerocallis	independency
headmistress	traditionist	determinably	hereditament	infectiously
headquarters	traducianism	determinedly	hereditarily	infelicitous
headshrinker	traducianist	dilettantish	hereinbefore	insecticidal
hebdomadally	tridactylous	dilettantism	heterocercal	insemination
heedlessness			heterocyclic	integumental

intellection	irrepealable	preexistence	superstratum	confabulator
intellective	irreprovable	priestliness	supervenient	confectioner
intellectual	irresistible	priestridden	supervention	conferential
intelligence	irresistibly	quaestorship	surefootedly	confessional
intelligible	irresolutely	racemisation	sweepingness	confidential
intelligibly	irresolution	ravenousness	sweetishness	confirmation
intemperance	irresolvable	rebelliously	taberdarship	confirmative
inteneration	irrespective	receivership	tabernacular	confirmatory
interbedding	irrespirable	receptaculum	tamelessness	confiscation
interception	irresponsive	receptionist	taperecorder	confiscatory
intercession	irreverently	recessionary	telegraphese	conformation
intercessory	irreversible	redecoration	telegraphist	confoundedly
interchanger	irreversibly	redemptioner	teleological	Confucianism
interconnect	juvenescence	Redemptorist	televisional	confusedness
intercropped	kaleidoscope	redeployment	terebinthine	craftbrother
intercurrent	lakedwelling	regeneration	thievishness	differentiae
intercutting	laterisation	regenerative	threequarter	differential
interdiction	liberalistic	rejectamenta	threewheeler	disfranchise
interdictive	licentiously	relentlessly	timehonoured	furfuraceous
interdictory	lifelessness	rememberable	timelessness	halftimbered
interdigital	literariness	remembrancer	tirelessness	ineffaceable
interestedly	Liverpudlian	renegotiable	tiresomeness	ineffaceably
interfemoral	liverystable	repercussion	togetherness	inefficiency
interference	lonesomeness	repercussive	tolerability	malformation
interglacial	lovelessness	repetitional	tonelessness	newfashioned
interjection	lovelornness	repetitively	tuberculated	Newfoundland
interjectory	lukewarmness	reservedness	tuberculosis	nonflammable
interlobular	mademoiselle	resettlement	tunelessness	nonflowering
interlocutor	majestically	revelational	typefounding	oldfashioned
intermeddler	malevolently	revengefully	unbecomingly	perfectively
intermediacy	materialness	reverberator	unbelievable	perfervidity
intermediary	meretricious	reversionary	unbelievably	perfidiously
intermediate	meteorically	rosecoloured	uncelebrated	perfoliation
interminable	meteorograph	sacerdotally	undemocratic	performative
interminably	minedetector	safecracking	underachieve	pinfeathered
intermission	mineralogist	salesmanship	underbidding	prefabricate
intermittent	miseducation	sclerenchyma	underclothes	prefectorial
intermitting	moderateness	screenwriter	undercoating	preferential
intermixture	molecularity	secessionism	undercurrent	preformation
intermundane	monetisation	secessionist	undercutting	preformative
internuclear	moneychanger	selenography	underdevelop	professional
internuncial	moneygrubber	selenologist	undergarment	professorate
interoceanic	moneyspinner	sheepishness	underinsured	professoress
interoceptor	moveableness	sheepshearer	underletting	professorial
interpellate	movelessness	shrewishness	undermanning	proficiently
interpleader	namedropping	sideslipping	underpinning	profiteering
interpolator	namelessness	sidestepping	underrunning	profligately
interpretive	nevertheless	sidewhiskers	undersetting	profoundness
interrelated	nomenclative	sleepingpill	understaffed	selfabsorbed
interrogator	nomenclature	sleepwalking	undersurface	selfactivity
interruption	noneffective	speechlessly	undertenancy	selfaffected
interruptive	nonefficient	speedboating	underwritten	selfanalysis
intersection	nonessential	spheroidally	undetermined	selfapplause
interservice	noneuclidean	spiegeleisen	unhesitating	selfapproval
interspinous	nonexistence	splendidness	unmercifully	selfbegotten
interstellar	novelisation	steeplechase	unreasonable	selfbetrayal
interstitial	numerologist	streetwalker	unreasonably	selfcatering
intertexture	numerousness	strengthener	unrecognised	selfcoloured
intervenient	obsequiously	strengthless	unregenerate	selfcomposed
intervention	orienteering	streptococci	unrepeatable	selfcontempt
intervocalic	ostentatious	streptomycin	unreservedly	selfcritical
interwreathe	osteogenesis	subeditorial	unresponsive	selfdeceived
inveiglement	osteological	suberisation	unrestrained	selfdeceiver
invertebrate	osteomalacia	superannuate	unsearchable	selfdelusion
investigator	osteoplastic	supercharger	unseasonable	selfdestruct
inveterately	osteoporosis	superciliary	unsegregated	selfdevotion
irredeemable	otherworldly	supercilious	Valenciennes	selfdirected
irredeemably	paletteknife	supereminent	valetudinary	selfdistrust
irreflective	parenthesise	supererogate	vegetatively	selfdoubting
irreformable	peregrinator	superhighway	venepuncture	selfeducated
irrefragable	peremptorily	superhumanly	venerability	selfeffacing
irrefragably	phlebotomise	supermundane	veterinarian	selfelective
irregardless	phlebotomist	supernaculum	vicechairman	selfemployed
irregularity	phreatophyte	supernatural	warehouseman	selfevidence
irrelatively	phrenologist	superposable	watermanship	selfexistent
irrelevantly	pigeonbreast	supersedence	wineglassful	selfflattery
irremediable	potentiality	supersensory	buffalograss	selfhypnosis
irremediably	preeminently	supersession	cliffhanging	selfidentity
irremissible	preestablish	superstition	comfortingly	selfignition

selfinterest	phagocytotic	enshrinement	technologist	chairmanship
selfinvolved	pragmatistic	enthronement	tightmouthed	cheirography
selflessness	priggishness	enthusiastic	unchangeable	Christianise
selflimiting	progenitress	euphonically	unchangeably	Christianity
selfluminous	progesterone	euphoniously	uncharitable	Christolatry
selfmurderer	proglottides	exchangeable	uncharitably	Christophany
selfpleasing	programmable	fatherfigure	unchivalrous	civilisation
selfportrait	programmatic	fatherliness	unthinkingly	clairaudient
selfreliance	sanguinarily	highcoloured	unthoughtful	clairvoyance
selfreproach	sanguineness	highfaluting	xiphisternum	cleistogamic
selfrighting	sanguinolent	highhandedly	acciaccatura	codification
selfsameness	sedgewarbler	highlystrung	accidentally	conidiophore
selfstarting	sergeantfish	highpressure	actinomycete	conidiospore
selfviolence	sergeantship	highsounding	additionally	debilitation
shuffleboard	singleacting	highspirited	administrant	decipherable
staffofficer	singledecker	highstepping	administrate	decipherment
staffsurgeon	singlehanded	lachrymation	advisability	decisiveness
sufficiently	singleminded	lachrymatory	aetiological	definiteness
trifurcation	singleseater	lachrymosely	agribusiness	definitively
unaffectedly	sluggishness	lighthearted	agricultural	deliberately
unifoliolate	snaggletooth	lithographer	alliteration	deliberation
unofficially	stagemanager	lithographic	alliterative	deliberative
usufructuary	staggeringly	lithological	altitudinous	delicatessen
amygdaloidal	steganograph	lithospheric	ambidextrous	delightfully
anagogically	suggestively	lithotritist	ambivalently	delimitation
anagrammatic	swaggeringly	machicolated	angiocarpous	delinquently
beggarliness	swaggerstick	mathematical	annihilation	deliquescence
biogeography	tangentially	mechanically	annihilative	delitescence
biographical	tangibleness	methodically	antiaircraft	demilitarise
boogiewoogie	tergiversate	mithridatise	anticipation	demimondaine
burglarproof	toggleswitch	mithridatism	anticipative	demineralise
congeniality	tragicomical	motherfigure	anticipatory	derisiveness
congenitally	triggerhappy	motherliness	anticlerical	derivational
conglobation	triglyphical	mothertongue	anticyclonic	derivatively
conglomerate	trigonometry	mythographer	antigenicity	desideration
conglutinate	troglodytism	mythological	antigropelos	desiderative
congratulant	vengefulness	mythologiser	antimacassar	desirability
congratulate	whigmaleerie	Neohellenism	antimagnetic	desirousness
congregation	zoogeography	nephanalysis	antimalarial	deviationism
diageotropic	alphabetical	nephelometer	antineutrino	deviationist
diagrammatic	alphamerical	nephelometry	antiparticle	diminishable
disgorgement	alphanumeric	nephrologist	antipathetic	diminishment
disguisement	amphibiously	nightclothes	antiperiodic	diminutively
disgustfully	amphibrachic	nychthemeral	antiphonally	disincentive
disgustingly	amphictyonic	nychthemeron	antirachitic	disinfectant
epigrammatic	amphisbaenic	orchestrator	antiSemitism	disinfection
exaggeration	amphitheatre	orchidaceous	antistrophic	disinflation
exaggerative	amphitropous	orthodontics	antithetical	disingenuous
exaggeratory	anthelmintic	orthodontist	aquicultural	disintegrate
exegetically	anthropogeny	orthogenesis	argillaceous	disinterment
exiguousness	anthropoidal	orthogenetic	articulately	divisibility
flagellation	anthropology	orthographer	articulation	divisiveness
flagellatory	archdeaconry	orthographic	articulatory	dubitatively
flagitiously	archdiocesan	orthopaedics	artificially	echinococcus
ganglionated	archetypally	orthopaedist	artilleryman	elliptically
geographical	archetypical	orthopterist	artistically	embitterment
gorgeousness	archipelagic	orthopteroid	assibilation	encirclement
gregariously	architecture	orthopterous	assimilation	enginedriver
hedgehopping	arrhythmical	orthotropism	assimilative	enginetuning
huggermugger	asphyxiation	orthotropous	assimilatory	enviableness
judgematical	authenticate	panhellenism	attitudinise	envisagement
knighterrant	authenticity	pathetically	availability	equidistance
knightliness	bachelorhood	pathogenesis	basidiospore	equilibrator
languishment	bachelorship	pathogenetic	belittlement	equipollence
languorously	bathypelagic	pathological	bewilderedly	equipollency
largehearted	bilharziasis	prehensility	bewilderment	equiprobable
ledgertackle	bilharziosis	prehistorian	bewitchingly	equitability
linguistical	cachinnation	rechargeable	bilingualism	equivalently
lodginghouse	cachinnatory	rightfulness	brainstormer	equivocation
longdistance	cashandcarry	ruthlessness	brainwashing	equivocatory
longitudinal	catholically	sightreading	businesslike	excitability
longshoreman	dethronement	siphonophore	cabinetmaker	exhibitioner
longstanding	dichromatism	siphonostele	calisthenics	exhilaration
longwindedly	diphtheritic	sophisticate	camiknickers	exhilarative
mangelwurzel	diphthongise	tachygrapher	capitalistic	extinguisher
neighbouring	disharmonise	tachygraphic	capitulation	facilitation
oligarchical	dishevelment	technicality	caricaturist	feliciation
orographical	emphatically	technicolour	carillonneur	felicitously
phagocytosis	enchantingly	technocratic	catilinarian	feminineness

feminisation	libidinously	periphrastic	semiological	bookingclerk
filibusterer	logistically	perispomenon	semiparasite	booklearning
fluidisation	luminescence	peristeronic	semiprecious	brokenwinded
freightliner	luminiferous	peristomatic	semitropical	cockfighting
fruitfulness	luminousness	pitiableness	sericultural	cocksureness
fugitiveness	magistrature	pitilessness	silicicolous	cuckingstool
fuliginosity	Manicheanism	plainclothed	siliciferous	cuckooflower
futilitarian	manifoldness	plainclothes	sinistrality	duckingstool
gasification	manipulation	plaindealing	sinistrorsal	fecklessness
geriatrician	manipulative	pleiotropism	skrimshanker	hucklebacked
habilitation	manipulatory	policyholder	sociableness	leukocytosis
habitability	maximisation	positiveness	sociological	licketysplit
habitforming	mediaevalism	positivistic	sociometrist	marketgarden
habitualness	mediaevalist	praiseworthy	solicitation	marketsquare
hagiographer	meditatively	purification	solicitously	marksmanship
hagiographic	meridionally	purificatory	solifluction	misknowledge
hagiological	meristematic	radiobiology	solitariness	monkeyflower
heliocentric	meticulously	radioelement	sprightfully	monkeyjacket
heliographer	militaristic	radiographer	squirrelcage	monkeypuzzle
heliographic	minicomputer	radiographic	squirreltail	monkeywrench
heliogravure	minimisation	radioisotope	stridulation	parkinsonism
heliolatrous	ministration	radiological	strikingness	pickerelweed
heliotherapy	ministrative	radionuclide	stringcourse	poikilotherm
heliotropism	misinterpret	radiophonics	subinfeudate	racketeering
hemichordate	mobilisation	radiotherapy	swainishness	recklessness
hemimorphism	modification	ramification	theistically	Shakspereana
hemimorphite	modificatory	ratification	thriftlessly	Shaksperiana
hemiparasite	monitorially	ratiocinator	toxicologist	snakecharmer
hemispheroid	motivational	reciprocally	toxicophobia	spokesperson
heritability	mucilaginous	reciprocator	trainspotter	Stakhanovism
hesitatingly	municipalise	redintegrate	traitorously	Stakhanovite
holidaymaker	municipality	redistribute	typification	taskmistress
horizontally	munificently	regimentally	undiplomatic	ticklishness
humification	musicianship	registration	unhistorical	walkietalkie
hygienically	musicologist	reliableness	unkindliness	wicketkeeper
illiberality	mutinousness	remilitarise	unlikelihood	winklepicker
illiterately	navigability	reminiscence	unlikeliness	workableness
incidentally	navigational	residentiary	unmistakable	workingclass
incineration	nidification	residentship	unmistakably	YankeeDoodle
incisiveness	niminypiminy	resignedness	untimeliness	abolitionary
indicatively	nominalistic	resiniferous	unwieldiness	abolitionism
indifference	nonidentical	resipiscence	unyieldingly	abolitionist
indifferency	notification	resistlessly	variableness	achlamydeous
indigenously	obligatorily	reticulately	varicoloured	adulteration
indigestible	obligingness	reticulation	vaticination	adulterously
indirectness	obliteration	reticulocyte	venipuncture	agglutinogen
indiscipline	obliterative	retiringness	veridicality	amalgamation
indiscreetly	occidentally	revictualled	verification	amalgamative
indiscretion	officeholder	revivalistic	verificatory	amelioration
indisputable	omnipotently	reviviscence	vesiculation	ameliorative
indisputably	omnipresence	ridiculously	vilification	analogically
indissoluble	omnisciently	ruminatively	vinification	analphabetic
indissolubly	omnivorously	sadistically	viridescence	analytically
indistinctly	oneirocritic	satisfaction	visitational	apolitically
indivertible	ophiophagous	satisfactory	visitatorial	athletically
indivertibly	optimisation	satisfyingly	vitiligation	balladmonger
individually	orbicularity	schismatical	vivification	balletomania
infiniteness	ordinariness	schizogonous	viviparously	ballottement
infinitively	ornithomancy	schizomycete	vociferation	bellbottomed
intimidation	ornithoscopy	schizophrene	vociferously	belletristic
intimidatory	oscillograph	schizothymia	volitionally	belligerence
invigilation	oscilloscope	schizothymic	vomiturition	belligerency
invigoration	ossification	scrimshanker	conjunctival	bellylanding
invisibility	pacification	scripturally	disjointedly	bibliography
irritability	pacificatory	scriptwriter	misjudgement	bibliologist
irritatingly	palingenesia	semiannually	perjuriously	bibliomaniac
jurisconsult	palingenesis	semibasement	projectional	bibliopegist
jurisdiction	palingenetic	semicircular	projectively	bibliophilic
jurisprudent	panification	semicylinder	serjeantship	bibliopolist
lacininiated	parisyllabic	semidarkness	subjectively	bibliothecae
laticiferous	pedicellaria	semideponent	subjectivise	billingsgate
latinisation	penitentiary	semidetached	subjectivism	billsticking
latitudinous	pericarditis	semidiameter	subjectivist	biologically
legitimately	perilousness	semidomestic	subjectivity	boulevardier
legitimation	periodically	semifinalist	backbreaking	brilliantine
legitimatise	periodontics	semifinished	backpedalled	bulletheaded
lepidopteran	periodontist	semiliterate	backslapping	bullfighting
lexicography	periostracum	seminiferous	backwardness	bullheadedly
lexicologist	peripherally	semiofficial	backwoodsman	Byelorussian

calligrapher	isolationism	agamogenesis	haemophiliac	clangorously
calligraphic	isolationist	agamogenetic	haemopoiesis	clannishness
callisthenic	malleability	alimentation	haemorrhagic	clinkerbuilt
Carlovingian	marlinespike	alimentative	harmlessness	coenobitical
chalcolithic	mealymouthed	anamorphosis	harmonically	coenobytical
chalcopyrite	millesimally	anemographic	harmoniously	coincidental
childbearing	milliammeter	anemophilous	hermeneutics	coincidently
childishness	mulligatawny	aromatically	hermetically	connaturally
coalitionism	nailscissors	aromaticness	Ishmaelitish	connectional
coelenterate	neglectfully	asymmetrical	kremlinology	connectively
collaborator	outlandishly	augmentation	mnemotechnic	conningtower
collaterally	Palladianism	augmentative	myrmecophily	connubiality
collectively	pellucidness	biometrician	onomatopoeia	councilwoman
collectivise	philadelphus	blamableness	onomatopoeic	countenancer
collectivism	philanthrope	blamefulness	outmanoeuvre	counteragent
collectivist	philanthropy	brambleberry	permanganate	counterblast
collectivity	philharmonic	championship	permeability	countercheck
collegialism	philhellenic	chemotherapy	permissively	counterclaim
collegiality	philistinism	chimneypiece	permittivity	counterforce
collegiately	phillumenist	commandingly	pigmentation	counterlight
collinearity	philodendron	commemorator	plumbaginous	countermarch
colloquially	philological	commencement	plumbiferous	counterplead
collywobbles	philosophise	commendation	plummerblock	counterpoint
curlingirons	phyllotactic	commendatory	premaxillary	counterpoise
curlingtongs	phylogenesis	commensalism	premeditated	counterproof
declinometer	phylogenetic	commensalist	premeditator	counterscarp
deflagration	pralltriller	commensurate	premenstrual	countershaft
deflationary	prelapsarian	commentation	primigravida	countertenor
deflationist	prolegomenon	commercially	primogenital	countrydance
dialectician	prolifically	commiserator	primogenitor	countrywoman
dialectology	prolificness	commissarial	primordially	craniologist
dislodgement	prolongation	commissariat	promulgation	crenellation
ecclesiastic	publicspirit	commissioner	rhombohedral	deontologist
ecclesiology	qualmishness	committeeman	rhombohedron	dinnerjacket
ecologically	reallocation	commodiously	salmonladder	downwardness
edulcoration	reflationary	commonwealth	segmentation	econometrics
efflorescent	reflectional	communicable	shamateurism	economically
emblazonment	reflectively	communicably	shamefacedly	emancipation
emblematical	reflectivity	communicator	shamefulness	enantiomorph
emulsifiable	rollingstock	cosmetically	stammeringly	ethnocentric
enclitically	sculpturally	cosmogonical	submaxillary	ethnographer
Englishwoman	seclusionist	cosmographer	subminiature	ethnographic
evolutionary	sellingplate	cosmographic	submissively	ethnological
evolutionism	shillyshally	cosmological	surmountable	evanescently
evolutionist	skullduggery	cosmopolitan	swimmingbath	evangelistic
exclusionary	smallclothes	cosmopolitic	swimmingbell	eveningdress
exclusionism	smallholding	curmudgeonly	swimmingpool	exenteration
exclusionist	soullessness	deambulatory	thematically	fainthearted
explantation	speleologist	dermatophyte	thimbleberry	faintishness
explicitness	stalactiform	diamagnetism	trampolinist	fiendishness
exploitation	stalwartness	diamonddrill	tremendously	foundationer
exploitative	stellenbosch	diamondfield	trumpetshell	fountainhead
exulceration	stelliferous	dogmatically	unambivalent	FrancoGerman
fallaciously	stilboestrol	dramatically	unemployable	frangibility
faultfinding	stillhunting	dramaturgist	unemployment	frankincense
fieldglasses	stylographic	elementalism	unimaginable	frenchpolish
folliculated	sublapsarian	elementarily	unimaginably	frenetically
fullyfledged	syllabically	etymological	unimportance	frontbencher
galligaskins	toilsomeness	etymologicon	vermiculated	frontiersman
gallinaceous	toploftiness	farmsteading	whimperingly	frontispiece
geologically	unblinkingly	fermentation	whimsicality	geanticlinal
grallatorial	unblushingly	fermentative	agentgeneral	granodiorite
guilefulness	unclassified	flamboyantly	amenableness	gymnosophist
hallucinogen	unflattering	flamethrower	amentiferous	hymnographer
hallucinosis	unilaterally	flammability	asynchronism	hypnogenesis
harlequinade	unpleasantly	formaldehyde	asynchronous	hypnogenetic
hellgrammite	villainously	formlessness	avantgardism	hypnotherapy
idolatrously	wallpainting	geomagnetism	avantgardist	hypnotically
implantation	wallydraigle	geometrician	blandishment	hypnotisable
implicitness	welldisposed	Germanophile	blunderingly	iconoclastic
inclinometer	wellfavoured	Germanophobe	bonnetmonkey	iconographer
inelasticity	wellgrounded	graminaceous	bonnyclabber	identifiable
inflammation	Wellingtonia	grammaticise	brinkmanship	illnaturedly
inflammatory	wholehearted	grammolecule	bronchoscope	Keynesianism
inflationary	williewaught	gramnegative	broncobuster	kinnikinnick
inflationism	wollastonite	grampositive	brontosaurus	limnological
inflationist	woolgatherer	haematoblast	burningglass	loungelizard
inflectional	woollyheaded	haematolysis	chancemedley	magnetically
ingloriously	yellowhammer	haematoxylon	chondriosome	magnetisable

magnetograph	standingroom	accordionist	derogatorily	incompetence
magnetometer	stanniferous	accouchement	desolateness	incompetency
magnifically	stenographer	accoutrement	detoxication	incompletely
magnificence	stenographic	acronychally	disobedience	incompliance
magniloquent	stoneboiling	admonishment	disorientate	incomputable
maintainable	stonecutting	aerodynamics	dolorousness	inconcinnity
malnutrition	stonedresser	aeroembolism	echolocation	inconclusive
mannerliness	stonemasonry	aeronautical	echosounding	inconformity
meaningfully	stonyhearted	aeroneurosis	ectoparasite	inconsequent
morningdress	subnormality	aerosiderite	effortlessly	inconsistent
mountainside	teensyweensy	AfroAmerican	empoisonment	inconsolable
neonomianism	thankfulness	allomorphism	endocarditis	inconsolably
odontologist	thanksgiving	announcement	endometritis	inconsonance
openhandedly	thundercloud	appositeness	endoparasite	inconstantly
openmindedly	thunderingly	appositional	endoskeletal	inconsumable
opinionative	thunderously	arborescence	entomologise	inconsumably
painlessness	thunderstone	arborisation	entomologist	incontiguous
pennypincher	thunderstorm	astonishment	EuroAmerican	incontinence
pennywhistle	tranquillise	astoundingly	excogitation	incontinency
perniciously	tranquillity	atmospherics	excogitative	inconvenient
pernoctation	transcendent	attorneyship	extortionary	incoordinate
phanerogamic	transduction	autocatalyse	extortionate	incorporated
phenological	transferable	autochthones	floodlighted	incorporator
phenomenally	transference	autodidactic	fluorescence	incorporeity
phenotypical	transferring	autoimmunity	fluoridation	incorrigible
phonasthenia	transformism	automaticity	fluorination	incorrigibly
phonemically	transformist	automobilist	fluorocarbon	incorruption
phonetically	transfusible	automorphism	gamopetalous	indoctrinate
phonographer	transgressor	autonomously	gamophyllous	IndoEuropean
phonographic	transhipment	barometrical	gamosepalous	IndoGermanic
phonological	transhumance	bloodbrother	gerontocracy	inhospitable
planetesimal	transiliency	bloodletting	gyromagnetic	inhospitably
planetstruck	transitional	bloodstained	halogenation	insolubilise
planispheric	transitively	bloodthirsty	henotheistic	insolubility
planoconcave	transitivity	bloodyminded	heroicalness	intolerantly
plenipotence	transitorily	borosilicate	heroicomical	intoxication
pointilliste	translatable	calorescence	homoeopathic	involutional
pornographer	translucence	calorimetric	homoeostasis	kilowatthour
pornographic	translucency	canonisation	homologation	laboursaving
prenticeship	transmigrant	canorousness	homomorphism	levorotation
princeliness	transmigrate	chlorination	homomorphous	levorotatory
principality	transmission	chromaticism	homonymously	majorgeneral
printability	transmissive	chromaticity	homosexually	manoeuvrable
pronominally	transmitting	chromatogram	homothallism	manometrical
pronouncedly	transmogrify	chromatology	humorousness	melodramatic
pugnaciously	transmontane	chromatopsia	hypochlorite	mesocephalic
quantifiable	transmutable	chromosphere	hypochondria	mesothoracic
quantisation	transoceanic	chronography	hypocoristic	mitochondria
quantitative	transpacific	chronologise	hypocritical	monochromate
quinquennial	transparency	chronologist	hypogastrium	monodramatic
quinquennium	transpirable	chronometric	hypognathous	monofilament
quintessence	transplanter	colonisation	hypophrygian	monographist
reinvestment	transpontine	coloquintida	hypostatical	monomaniacal
reinvigorate	transposable	colorimetric	hyposulphite	monometallic
reunionistic	transshipped	colourlessly	hypothalamic	monomorphous
rhinocerotic	transudation	copolymerise	hypothalamus	monopetalous
rhinological	transudatory	cynocephalus	hypothecator	monophyletic
rhynchophora	transversely	cytogenetics	hypothetical	Monophysitic
runningboard	transvestism	debonairness	idiosyncrasy	monopodially
scandalously	trinomialism	decomposable	idiothermous	monopolistic
Scandinavian	twentyfourmo	decompressor	illogicality	monostichous
scenepainter	unanswerable	decongestant	immoderately	monostrophic
sceneshifter	unencumbered	decongestion	immoderation	monosyllabic
scenographic	uninterested	decongestive	immovability	monosyllable
scintigraphy	vainglorious	deconsecrate	impoliteness	monotheistic
scintillator	vauntcourier	decontrolled	imponderable	monotonously
significance	vernacularly	decoratively	imponderably	motorcyclist
significancy	wainscotting	decorousness	impoverished	motorisation
skunkcabbage	whencesoever	deionisation	incognisable	nanoplankton
slanderously	wrongfulness	demodulation	incognisance	negotiatress
somnambulant	youngberries	demoniacally	incognitable	nicotinamide
somnambulate	absoluteness	demonstrable	incoherently	nonobjective
somnambulism	absolutistic	demonstrably	incommodious	obsolescence
somnambulist	absorptional	demonstrator	incommutable	obsoleteness
somniloquism	absorptivity	denomination	incommutably	octogenarian
somniloquist	accommodator	denominative	incomparable	octosyllabic
soundingline	accompanyist	denouncement	incomparably	octosyllable
spinsterhood	accomplished	depoliticise	incompatible	oncorhynchus
standardbred		depopulation	incompatibly	opposability

oppositeness	untowardness	graphologist	sulphuretted	chiropractic
oppositional	unwontedness	happenstance	supplemental	chiropractor
parochialise	unworldiness	helplessness	supplementer	choreography
parochialism	unworthiness	herpetologic	supplicantly	chorographic
parochiality	uproariously	hesperididia	supplication	chorological
paronomastic	valorisation	hippocentaur	supplicatory	churchianity
pejoratively	vaporisation	hippopotamus	suppositious	churchwarden
peroxidation	vaporousness	humptydumpty	suppressible	churlishness
pilotballoon	vasodilation	inappeasable	surprisingly	cirrocumulus
pleomorphism	vasodilatory	inapplicable	suspensively	cirrostratus
preoccupancy	venomousness	inapplicably	suspiciously	clarinettist
proofreading	vigorousness	inappositely	temptability	coerciveness
pyroelectric	zygomorphism	inoperculate	trephination	coordinately
pyroligneous	zygomorphous	inspectorate	tripartitely	coordination
pyromaniacal	adaptability	inspectorial	tripartition	coordinative
pyromorphite	adaptiveness	inspissation	triphthongal	correctional
pyrotechnics	anaphylactic	jetpropelled	triplication	correctitude
pyrotechnist	auspiciously	kleptomaniac	trophallaxis	correctively
recognisable	bespectacled	klipspringer	tropological	corroborator
recognisably	biophysicist	leapfrogging	tropospheric	courageously
recognisance	campfollower	misplacement	unapologetic	courtmartial
recollection	campodeiform	mispronounce	unappeasable	courtplaster
recollective	carpetbagger	morphallaxis	unappetising	cuprammonium
recommitment	carpetknight	morphologist	whippoorwill	decreasingly
reconcilable	chaplainship	Neoplatonism	absquatulate	defraudation
reconstitute	clapperboard	Neoplatonist	adequateness	depravedness
reconversion	companionate	nympholeptic	chequerboard	depreciation
reconveyance	companionway	nymphomaniac	conquistador	depreciatory
remonstrance	compatriotic	outpensioner	desquamation	depressingly
remonstrator	compellation	perpetration	desquamative	dibranchiate
remorsefully	compensation	perpetuation	desquamatory	digressional
removability	compensative	perplexingly	disquisition	digressively
renouncement	compensatory	preparedness	frequentness	disregardful
repossession	complacently	preponderant	harquebusier	disreputable
resoluteness	complaisance	preponderate	iniquitously	disreputably
resolvedness	complemental	preposterous	misquotation	dwarfishness
resoundingly	completeness	propaedeutic	pasqueflower	emargination
ribonuclease	complexional	propagandise	quaquaversal	embranchment
ricochetting	complexioned	propagandism	sesquialtera	embryologist
rigorousness	complication	propagandist	ubiquitarian	empressement
risorgimento	composedness	prophylactic	ubiquitously	encroachment
saponifiable	compoundable	propitiation	vanquishable	encrustation
schoolfellow	compressible	propitiatory	vanquishment	enormousness
schoolleaver	compulsively	propitiously	abbreviation	entrammelled
schoolmaster	compulsivity	proportional	aboriginally	entrancement
schorlaceous	compulsorily	proportioned	abortiveness	entreatingly
scrobiculate	compunctious	proprietress	accretionary	entrenchment
secondstring	compurgation	psephologist	adorableness	entrepreneur
shootingiron	compurgatory	pumpernickel	aforethought	estrangement
simoniacally	corporeality	purposebuilt	aggressively	excruciating
sonorousness	cryptanalyst	purposefully	amortisation	excruciation
soporiferous	cryptogamous	rapprochment	aperiodicity	exercitation
strobilation	cryptography	reappearance	appraisement	exorbitantly
stroboscopic	cryptologist	respectfully	appraisingly	expressional
strongminded	culpableness	respectively	appreciation	expressively
strongylosis	despairingly	resplendence	appreciative	expressivity
strontianite	despitefully	resplendency	appreciatory	exprobration
strophanthin	despoliation	responsively	apprehension	extracranial
sudoriferous	despondently	responsorial	apprehensive	extraditable
sycophantish	despotically	salpiglossis	approachable	extralimital
synonymously	diaphanously	sempiternity	appropriable	extramarital
synoptically	dispensation	serpentiform	appropriator	extramundane
theocratical	dispensatory	serpentinely	astringently	extraneously
theoretician	dispiritedly	shipbuilding	astrological	extrasensory
theosophical	displaceable	simpleminded	astronautics	extraspecial
throughstone	displacement	skippingrope	astronomical	extrauterine
timorousness	displeasedly	slipcarriage	astrophysics	extravagance
uncomeatable	dispossessor	slipperiness	attractively	extravagancy
uncommercial	disputatious	snapfastener	attributable	extravaganza
uncommonness	Egyptologist	snappishness	avariciously	extraversion
unconformity	epiphenomena	stepchildren	capriciously	extroversion
unconsidered	eruptiveness	stepdaughter	carragheenin	fearlessness
unconstraint	exophthalmic	stupefacient	carriageable	fearsomeness
uncontrolled	exophthalmos	stupefaction	characterise	ferrugineous
unconvincing	exophthalmus	stupefactive	charlatanism	fibrillation
ungovernable	geophysicist	stupendously	charnelhouse	fibrinolysin
unionisation	geopolitical	sulphonamide	charterhouse	floriculture
unloveliness	glyphography	sulphonation	charterparty	gloriousness
unpopularity	glyptography	sulphuration	cherubically	guaranteeing

guardianship	microanalyst	pterodactyle	stereophonic	bioscientist
hairdressing	microbiology	puerperrally	stereopticon	biosynthesis
hairsbreadth	microcapsule	putrefaction	stereoscopic	biosynthetic
hairsplitter	microcephaly	putrefactive	sterlingness	blastfurnace
heartburning	microcircuit	quarterbound	sternutation	blastosphere
heartrending	microclimate	quarterfinal	sternutative	blastulation
heartstrings	microcopying	quarterstaff	sternutatory	blissfulness
heartwarming	microcrystal	recreational	sternwheeler	blisteringly
heortologist	micrographer	recrudescent	stertorously	blusteringly
hierarchical	microphysics	refractivity	stormtrooper	boastfulness
hieroglyphic	microscopist	refractorily	supramundane	boisterously
hierographer	microseismic	refreshingly	supraorbital	brassbounder
hierophantic	microsurgery	refreshments	surrealistic	brassrubbing
horrendously	misrepresent	refrigerator	surrejoinder	censoriously
horribleness	mitrailleuse	regressively	surroundings	chastisement
horrifically	morrisdancer	reprehension	tearlessness	chesterfield
horrorstruck	mournfulness	reprehensive	terribleness	classicalism
hybridisable	mourningband	repressively	terrifically	classicalist
hydrochloric	mourningring	reproachable	terrifyingly	classicality
hydrodynamic	narrowminded	reproachless	terrorstruck	classifiable
hydrofluoric	necrographer	reproducible	tetrachordal	closecropped
hydrographer	necrological	reproduction	tetragonally	closegrained
hydrographic	necrophagous	reproductive	tetrahedrite	closemouthed
hydrokinetic	necrophiliac	reprographic	tetramorphic	conscionable
hydrological	necrophilism	retractation	therapeutics	conscription
hydrolysable	necrophilous	retractility	therapeutist	consecration
hydromedusae	negrophilism	retrenchment	thereinafter	consecratory
hydromedusan	negrophilist	retrocedence	thermocouple	consensually
hydrophilous	neurasthenia	retrocession	thermography	consentience
hydroquinone	neurasthenic	retrocessive	thermolabile	consentingly
hydrostatics	neuroanatomy	retroflexion	thermometric	consequently
hydrotherapy	neurobiology	retropulsion	thermophilic	conservation
hydrothermal	neurological	retroversion	thermoscopic	conservatism
hydrotropism	neuropterous	sabretoothed	thermosphere	conservative
hygrophilous	neuroscience	sacrilegious	thermostable	conservatory
impregnation	neurosurgeon	saprophagous	thermostatic	considerable
impressively	neurosurgery	sarrusophone	thermotactic	considerably
imprisonment	neurotically	scareheading	thermotropic	consignation
impropriator	nitrobenzene	scarificator	thirdborough	consistently
improvidence	nonresidence	scornfulness	thoroughbass	consistorial
improvisator	nonresistant	scorpionfish	thoroughbred	consociation
inarticulate	nutritionist	scurrilously	thoroughfare	consolidator
inartificial	nutritiously	sharecropper	thoroughness	conspiration
increasingly	operatically	sharpshooter	torrefaction	constabulary
incrustation	oppressively	sharpsighted	torrentially	constipation
ineradicable	outrageously	shirtwaister	Torricellian	constituency
ineradicably	outrivalling	shortchanger	turriculated	constitution
infrequently	overabundant	shortcircuit	ultramontane	constitutive
infringement	overachiever	shortpitched	ultramundane	constriction
ingratiating	overactivity	shortsighted	umbrageously	constrictive
inordinately	overcautious	shortsleeved	unbrokenness	constringent
intracardiac	overcritical	shortstaffed	uncritically	construction
intracranial	overcropping	snarlingiron	unfrequented	constructive
intramundane	overemphasis	Socratically	ungracefully	consultation
intransigent	overestimate	sparkingplug	ungraciously	consultative
intransitive	overexertion	sparrowgrass	ungratefully	consummately
intrauterine	overexposure	spermaphytic	unprejudiced	consummation
intrenchment	overlordship	spermathecal	unpretending	consummative
intriguingly	overniceness	spermatocyte	unprincipled	consummatory
introduction	overpersuade	spermatozoid	unprofitable	cousingerman
introductory	overpowering	spermatozoon	unprofitably	crashlanding
introjection	overpressure	spermogonium	unpronounced	crossbedding
intromission	overreaction	sphragistics	untruthfully	crossbencher
intromittent	oversimplify	spiritedness	usuriousness	crossbuttock
intromitting	overstepping	spiritlessly	uxoriousness	crosscountry
introversion	patriarchate	spiritualise	vibraphonist	crosscurrent
introvertive	pearlescence	spiritualism	vitreousness	crossexamine
intrusionist	peerlessness	spiritualist	vitrifaction	crossgrained
jerrybuilder	petrifaction	spirituality	wherethrough	crossheading
journalistic	petrographer	sporadically	whortleberry	crossingover
laureateship	petrographic	sporogenesis	anastigmatic	crosspurpose
macrocephaly	petrological	sportfulness	apostolicism	crosssection
macropterous	pharmaceutic	sportiveness	apostolicity	crystalgazer
marriageable	pharmacology	spuriousness	apostrophise	deescalation
matriarchate	pluriliteral	starspangled	aristocratic	densitometer
merrythought	poorspirited	stereochromy	Aristotelean	dessertspoon
metrological	prerequisite	stereography	Aristotelian	diastrophism
metropolitan	pteridophyte	stereoisomer	bassorelievo	dissatisfied
	pteridosperm	stereometric	bassorilievo	disseminator

dissentingly
dissertation
disseverance
disseverment
dissimilarly
dissimulator
dissocialise
dissociation
dissociative
dissuasively
dissymmetric
dorsiventral
dressinggown
earsplitting
elasmobranch
emasculation
emasculatory
episcopalian
episodically
epistemology
evisceration
exasperation
exospherical
farsightedly
firstnighter
geosynclinal
glassblowing
glossography
glossologist
goosepimples
graspingness
griseofulvin
grossularite
guestchamber
horsebreaker
horsemanship
horsetrading
horsewhipped
housebreaker
housekeeping
housetrained
housewarming
inescutcheon
inosculation
irascibility
kirschwasser
kissingcrust
laisserfaire
laissezelais
laissezfaire
lopsidedness
mansionhouse
manslaughter
Marseillaise
marshharrier
menstruation
messeigneurs
misselthrush
misstatement
moistureless
mosstrooping
nauseatingly
nauseousness
newspaperman
offscourings
onesidedness
opisthograph
opisthotonos
outstretched
outstripping
parsimonious
passepartout
passionately
passionfruit
peasepudding
perseverance
persistently
perspicacity
perspiration

perspiratory
persuasively
phosphoresce
physiognomic
physiography
physiologist
plasterboard
plesiosaurus
possessively
praseodymium
presbyterate
presbyterial
Presbyterian
prescription
prescriptive
preselection
preselective
presentation
presentative
presentiment
preservation
preservative
presidential
presumptuous
proscription
proscriptive
prosectorial
prosecutable
proselytiser
prosodically
prosopopoeia
prosperously
prostitution
pursestrings
questionable
questionably
questionless
reassessment
reassignment
reassuringly
sansculottic
sarsaparilla
seismography
seismologist
seismometric
seismoscopic
sensibleness
sensitometer
sensualistic
sensuousness
subsaturated
subscription
subsequently
subservience
subserviency
subsidiarily
subsonically
substantiate
substantival
substitution
substitutive
substruction
substructure
swashbuckler
tessellation
toastingfork
topsyturvily
trestletable
trustfulness
unassailable
unassumingly
unisexuality
waistcoating
whisperingly
worshipfully
abstemiously
abstractable
abstractedly
abstractness

abstruseness
acetabularia
acetaldehyde
aesthetician
aestheticism
amateurishly
amitotically
anathematise
anatomically
anotherguess
apothegmatic
arithmetical
Australasian
avitaminoses
avitaminosis
bactericidal
bacteriology
bacteriostat
bantamweight
battleground
battlemented
beatifically
blatherskite
bletherskate
blithesomely
bootlessness
bottlewasher
butterflynut
buttermuslin
butterscotch
Cantabrigian
cantankerous
cantharidian
cantillation
captiousness
Cartesianism
cartographer
cartographic
cartological
cattlelifter
cautiousness
centesimally
centrespread
centrosphere
centuplicate
chitterlings
clatteringly
clotheshorse
clothespress
coetaneously
contagionist
contagiously
containerise
contemplator
contemporary
contemporise
contemptible
contemptibly
contemptuous
conterminous
contestation
contextually
contiguously
contingently
continuation
continuative
continuously
contractable
contractedly
contractible
contradictor
contrapuntal
contrariness
contrariwise
contribution
contributive
contributory
contriteness
contrivement

controllable
contumacious
contumelious
costermonger
cottonocracy
criticalness
cultivatable
customshouse
denticulated
dentilingual
destructible
Deuteronomic
dextrousness
diathermancy
diatomaceous
diatonically
dictatorship
dietetically
distemperate
distillation
distillatory
distinctness
distortional
distractedly
distrainable
distrainment
distributary
distribution
distributive
disturbingly
earthshaking
ecstatically
editorialise
editorialist
emotionalise
emotionalism
emotionalist
emotionality
epithalamion
epithalamium
erythematous
erythroblast
erythromycin
esoterically
exoterically
factionalism
factiousness
factitiously
faithfulness
faithhealing
fantasticate
fantasticism
fastidiously
featherbrain
featheriness
fertilisable
fictionalise
fictitiously
filtrability
flatteringly
footplateman
forthrightly
fortuitously
fostermother
gastronomist
gastropodous
geotectonics
gesticulator
glitteringly
gluttonously
gratefulness
gratifyingly
gratuitously
grotesquerie
halterbroken
heathenishly
hectographic
histogenesis
histogenetic

histological
historically
horticulture
hysterectomy
hysterically
hysteromania
ichthyocolla
ichthyolatry
ichthyophagy
illtreatment
installation
instauration
instillation
instructress
instrumental
isothermally
lanternjawed
lanternslide
leathercloth
lefthandedly
listlessness
maltreatment
mastersinger
masterstroke
masterswitch
mastigophora
meetinghouse
meltingpoint
mirthfulness
mistakenness
mistranslate
mistreatment
mistressship
mouthbreeder
multicentral
multidentate
multifarious
multiflorous
multifoliate
multiformity
multilateral
multilingual
multiloquous
multinuclear
multipartite
multipliable
multiplicand
multiplicate
multiplicity
multipurpose
multistoried
multivalence
multiversity
multungulate
muttonheaded
mysteriously
mystifyingly
Nestorianism
noctambulant
noctambulism
noctambulist
noctambulous
noctilucence
northeastern
northernmost
Northumbrian
northwestern
nyctitropism
obstetrician
obstreperous
pantechnicon
pantisocracy
pantographic
participator
particularly
partisanship
partitionist
patternmaker
pertinacious

perturbation	sectionalism	acaulescence	insufferably	stouthearted
perturbative	sententially	accumulation	insufficient	structurally
pestilential	septennially	accumulative	insufflation	thaumaturgic
pestological	septilateral	accurateness	insurrection	thoughtfully
pettifoggery	septuagenary	accursedness	intuitionism	thousandfold
pettifogging	Septuagesima	accusatively	intuitionist	triumphantly
photochromic	Septuagintal	accusatorial	intumescence	troublemaker
photofission	shatterproof	acoustically	intussuscept	tumultuously
photogeology	skateboarder	acquaintance	invulnerable	unauthorised
photographer	skittishness	acquiescence	invulnerably	unsuccessful
photographic	slothfulness	adjudication	jesuitically	valuableness
photogravure	sluttishness	adjudicative	liquefacient	vituperation
photokinesis	softpedalled	adjudicatory	liquefaction	vituperative
photokinetic	southeastern	ailurophobia	liturgically	vituperatory
photomontage	southernmost	allusiveness	liturgiology	volumetrical
photophilous	southernwood	annunciation	loquaciously	voluminosity
photosetting	southwestern	appurtenance	lugubriously	voluminously
photospheric	spitefulness	bequeathment	manufacturer	voluntaryism
phototropism	spotlessness	calumniation	monumentally	voluntaryist
phytogenesis	stationhouse	calumniatory	naturalistic	voluptuosity
phytogenetic	stationwagon	calumniously	naturopathic	voluptuously
phytographer	statistician	chauvinistic	nebulisation	chivalrously
phytological	statuesquely	claudication	nebulousness	clavicembalo
phytophagous	stethoscopic	columniation	obdurateness	convalescent
pictographic	stutteringly	copulatively	obmutescence	convectional
pitterpatter	subtemperate	coquettishly	obnubilation	conveniently
platonically	subterranean	cumulatively	occupational	conventicler
Plattdeutsch	subthreshold	cumulocirrus	oneupmanship	conventional
pontifically	suitableness	cumulonimbus	patulousness	conversation
pontificator	sustentation	delusiveness	pedunculated	conveyancing
portentously	sustentative	denuclearise	plausibility	convincement
portmanteaus	systematical	denunciation	pneumaticity	convincingly
portmanteaux	systematiser	denunciative	pneumatology	conviviality
postdiluvian	systemically	denunciatory	pneumothorax	convulsively
postdoctoral	tactlessness	deputisation	populousness	curvicaudate
posteriority	tastefulness	desulphurise	proudhearted	curvicostate
postgraduate	tautological	detumescence	pseudocyesis	curvifoliate
posthumously	tectonically	draughtboard	pseudonymity	curvirostral
postmeridian	teetertotter	draughthorse	pseudonymous	flavoprotein
postmistress	testamentary	droughtiness	pseudopodium	galvanically
postponement	testosterone	effusiveness	recuperation	galvanometer
postposition	testudineous	encumberment	recuperative	galvanoscope
postpositive	Teutonically	encumbrancer	reducibility	graveclothes
postprandial	thitherwards	escutcheoned	reductionism	gravelelling
pretermitted	tintinnabula	eunuchoidism	reductionist	grovellingly
protactinium	tittletattle	excursionist	rejuvenation	heavenliness
protectively	tortuousness	exsufflicate	remuneration	heavyhearted
protectorate	truthfulness	fabulousness	remunerative	malversation
protensively	turtlenecked	figuratively	remuneratory	marvellously
protestation	twitteringly	fraudulently	renunciation	nerveracking
prothalamion	unattractive	furunculosis	renunciative	perverseness
prothalamium	unctuousness	futurologist	renunciatory	perviousness
prothonotary	unitarianism	genuflection	resupination	pluviometric
protistology	unsteadiness	ghoulishness	resurrection	prevailingly
protohistory	unstructured	glaucescence	resuscitator	prevaricator
protoplasmic	vantagepoint	glaucomatous	rheumatology	preventative
protoplastic	ventripotent	groundcherry	robustiously	preventively
prototypical	vertebration	groundlessly	salubriously	previousness
protozoology	verticalness	illumination	salutariness	privatdocent
protrusively	verticillate	illuminative	salutational	privatdozent
protuberance	Victorianism	illusiveness	salutiferous	privateering
quattrocento	victoriously	illusoriness	scoundreldom	proverbially
rattleheaded	virtuosoship	illustration	scoundrelism	providential
restaurateur	virtuousness	illustrative	scouringrush	provincially
restlessness	wastefulness	immunisation	scrupulosity	provisionary
restrainable	weatherboard	immunologist	scrupulously	pulverisable
restrainedly	weatherbound	immutability	secularistic	salvationism
restrictedly	weatherglass	imputability	sedulousness	salvationist
rhetorically	weatherhouse	imputatively	sepulchrally	serviceberry
rhythmically	weatherproof	inaudibility	sequaciously	servicecourt
rontgenogram	welterweight	inauguration	sequentially	servicewoman
rontgenology	whitelivered	inauguratory	sequestrator	servitorship
rootlessness	whitewashing	inauspicious	shoulderbelt	servocontrol
scatological	whitherwards	incurability	shoulderknot	silverglance
scatterbrain	winterbourne	industrially	shouldernote	silviculture
scatteringly	wrathfulness	infundibular	simultaneity	slaveholding
scutellation	wretchedness	infusibility	simultaneous	slovenliness
sectarianise	xanthochroia	innutritious	sinusoidally	subversively
sectarianism	youthfulness	insufferable	slaughterous	surveillance

surveyorship	swizzlestick	embranchment	mitrailleuse	Socratically
survivorship	————	emphatically	mordaciously	somnambulant
sylviculture	acciaccatura	enchantingly	moveableness	somnambulate
uneventfully	acetabularia	enswathement	neoDarwinian	somnambulism
universalise	acetaldehyde	entrammelled	neoDarwinism	somnambulist
universalism	achlamydeous	entrancement	neoDarwinist	sphragistics
universalist	acquaintance	enviableness	nephanalysis	sporadically
universality	adorableness	estrangement	neurasthenia	stalactiform
clownishness	AfroAmerican	EuroAmerican	neurasthenic	steganograph
drawingboard	alphabetical	exchangeable	newfashioned	sublapsarian
drawingpaper	alphamerical	explantation	noctambulant	submaxillary
enswathement	alphanumeric	extracranial	noctambulism	subsaturated
outwardbound	amenableness	extraditable	noctambulist	suitableness
alexipharmic	amicableness	extralimital	noctambulous	supramundane
epexegetical	antiaircraft	extramarital	oldfashioned	supraorbital
inexactitude	appraisement	extramundane	oligarchical	syllabically
inexpedience	appraisingly	extraneously	onomatopoeia	syndactylism
inexpediency	aromatically	extrasensory	onomatopoeic	syndactylous
inexperience	aromaticness	extraspecial	operatically	testamentary
inexpertness	attractively	extrauterine	outdatedness	tetrachordal
inexplicable	avitaminoses	extravagance	outlandishly	tetragonally
inexplicably	avitaminosis	extravagancy	outmanoeuvre	tetrahedrite
inexpressive	balladmonger	extravaganza	outrageously	tetramorphic
inexpugnable	bantamweight	extraversion	outwardbound	thematically
inexpugnably	barbarically	fallaciously	overabundant	therapeutics
inextensible	beggarliness	fantasticate	overachiever	therapeutist
inextricable	benzaldehyde	fantasticism	overactivity	tridactylous
inextricably	bilharziasis	formaldehyde	Palladianism	tripartitely
quixotically	bilharziosis	fricasseeing	peccadilloes	tripartition
unexpectedly	blamableness	galvanically	permanganate	ultramontane
bodybuilding	buccaneering	galvanometer	philadelphus	ultramundane
bodysnatcher	buccaneerish	galvanoscope	philanthrope	umbrageously
bodystocking	buffalograss	genealogical	philanthropy	unchangeable
calycoideous	bureaucratic	geomagnetism	phonasthenia	unchangeably
cotyledonary	cabbagewhite	geriatrician	phreatophyte	uncharitable
cotyledonous	calcareously	Germanophile	pitiableness	uncharitably
encyclopedia	Cantabrigian	Germanophobe	precancelled	unclassified
encyclopedic	cantankerous	gregariously	precariously	unflattering
enzymologist	carragheenin	guaranteeing	prefabricate	ungracefully
karyokinesis	cashandcarry	haematoblast	prelapsarian	ungraciously
labyrinthian	characterise	haematolysis	premaxillary	ungratefully
labyrinthine	chivalrously	haematoxylon	preparedness	unilaterally
laryngoscope	coetaneously	hierarchical	prevailingly	unimaginable
laryngoscopy	collaborator	idolatrously	prevaricator	unimaginably
palynologist	collaterally	illnaturedly	privatdocent	unitarianism
papyrologist	commandingly	immeasurable	privatdozent	unreasonable
playingfield	companionate	immeasurably	privateering	unreasonably
polychaetous	companionway	implantation	probationary	unsearchable
polychromous	compatriotic	inelasticity	procathedral	unseasonable
polyethylene	confabulator	ineradicable	propaedeutic	uproariously
polyglottism	connaturally	ineradicably	propagandise	valuableness
polyhistoric	contagionist	inexactitude	propagandism	vantagepoint
polymorphism	contagiously	inflammation	propagandist	variableness
polymorphous	containerise	inflammatory	protactinium	vernacularly
polyneuritic	convalescent	inflationary	pugnaciously	vibraphonist
polyneuritis	courageously	inflationism	readableness	villainously
polypetalous	culpableness	inflationist	rechargeable	voidableness
polyphyletic	cuprammonium	ingratiating	reflationary	volcanically
polysepalous	deflagration	installation	refractivity	wollastonite
polysyllabic	deflationary	instauration	refractorily	workableness
polysyllable	deflationist	intracardiac	reliableness	agribusiness
polytheistic	defraudation	intracranial	restaurateur	assibilation
polytonality	depravedness	intramundane	retractation	backbreaking
polyurethane	dermatophyte	intransigent	retractility	bellbottomed
sphygmograph	despairingly	intransitive	salvationism	blabbermouth
strychninism	deviationism	intrauterine	salvationist	bodybuilding
benzaldehyde	deviationist	Ishmaelitish	sarsaparilla	brambleberry
berzelianite	diamagnetism	isolationism	sectarianise	cohabitation
katzenjammer	dibranchiate	isolationist	sectarianism	deambulatory
mezzorelievo	dictatorship	laudableness	selfabsorbed	deliberately
mezzosoprano	disdainfully	loquaciously	selfactivity	deliberation
muzzleloader	disharmonise	mechanically	selfaffected	deliberative
prizefighter	dissatisfied	mediaevalism	selfanalysis	disobedience
prizewinning	dogmatically	mediaevalist	selfapplause	exhibitioner
quizzicality	dramatically	mendaciously	selfapproval	exorbitantly
razzledazzle	dramaturgist	mercantilism	semiannually	filibusterer
rhizocarpous	ecstatically	mercantilist	sequaciously	flamboyantly
rhizogenetic	educationist	miscalculate	shamateurism	forebodement
rhizophagous	emblazonment	mistakenness	sociableness	forebodingly

illiberality	detachedness	parochiality	bloodstained	selfdistrust
indebtedness	didactically	pedicellaria	bloodthirsty	selfdoubting
inhabitation	directorship	pericarditis	bloodyminded	semidarkness
lugubriously	disaccharide	policyholder	blunderingly	semideponent
nonobjective	dodecahedral	polychaetous	bombdisposal	semidetached
obnubilation	dodecahedron	polychromous	childbearing	semidiameter
paraboloidal	dodecaphonic	preoccupancy	childishness	semidomestic
phlebotomise	dovecoloured	prescription	chondriosome	slanderously
phlebotomist	eclectically	prescriptive	claudication	soundingline
plumbaginous	edulcoration	princeliness	conidiophore	speedboating
plumbiferous	effectuality	principality	conidiospore	standardbred
presbyterate	effectuation	proscription	coordinately	standingroom
presbyterial	emancipation	proscriptive	coordination	stepdaughter
Presbyterian	emasculation	redecoration	coordinative	Stradivarius
rehabilitate	emasculatory	reducibility	demodulation	stridulation
rhombohedral	encyclopedia	reductionism	desideration	studdingsail
rhombohedron	encyclopedic	reductionist	desiderative	subeditorial
salubriously	endocarditis	rejectamenta	disadvantage	thirdborough
scabbardfish	episcopalian	reoccupation	dreadfulness	thundercloud
scrobiculate	eunuchoidism	reticulately	equidistance	thunderingly
selfbegotten	evisceration	reticulation	expediential	thunderously
selfbetrayal	exercitation	reticulocyte	fieldglasses	thunderstone
semibasement	exulceration	revictualled	fiendishness	thunderstorm
shipbuilding	felicitation	rhynchophora	floodlighted	vasodilation
snobbishness	felicitously	ricochetting	fluidisation	vasodilatory
stilboestrol	flocculation	ridiculously	foundationer	veridicality
strobilation	FrancoGerman	rosecoloured	fraudulently	viridescence
stroboscopic	frenchpolish	safecracking	gonadotropic	welldisposed
stubbornness	galactogogue	sansculottic	gonadotropin	abbreviation
terebinthine	glaucescence	selfcatering	guardianship	abstemiously
thimbleberry	glaucomatous	selfcoloured	hairdressing	academically
troublemaker	hemichordate	selfcomposed	hereditament	accretionary
unambivalent	highcoloured	selfcontempt	hereditarily	aeroembolism
vocabularian	hypochlorite	selfcritical	holidaymaker	aforethought
adjectivally	hypochondria	semicircular	illadvisedly	aggressively
affectedness	hypocoristic	semicylinder	immoderately	alimentation
affectionate	hypocritical	sericultural	immoderation	alimentative
agricultural	immaculately	silicicolous	impedimental	amateurishly
antecedently	inaccessible	siliciferous	inaudibility	anthelmintic
anticipation	inaccessibly	slipcarriage	incidentally	appreciation
anticipative	inaccurately	solicitation	inordinately	appreciative
anticipatory	indecisively	solicitously	irredeemable	appreciatory
anticlerical	indeclinable	speechlessly	irredeemably	apprehension
anticyclonic	indecorously	stepchildren	lakedwelling	apprehensive
aquicultural	indicatively	structurally	lepidopteran	archetypally
articulately	indoctrinate	strychninism	libidinously	archetypical
articulation	inescutcheon	subscription	longdistance	athletically
articulatory	infectiously	theocratical	melodramatic	augmentation
asynchronism	inoccupation	toxicologist	meridionally	augmentative
asynchronous	inosculation	toxicophobia	minedetector	authenticate
autocatalyse	insecticidal	unacceptable	misadventure	authenticity
autochthones	irascibility	unaccustomed	miseducation	bachelorhood
bioecologist	kirschwasser	unbecomingly	monadelphous	bachelorship
bioscientist	laticiferous	unencumbered	monodramatic	bactericidal
breechloader	lexicography	unrecognised	namedropping	bacteriology
bronchoscope	lexicologist	unsuccessful	nonidentical	bacteriostat
broncobuster	malacologist	varicoloured	noradrenalin	balletomania
calycoideous	Manicheanism	vaticination	occidentally	banderillero
cardcarrying	mesocephalic	vesiculation	paradigmatic	belletristic
caricaturist	metachronism	vicechairman	paradisaical	bequeathment
catachrestic	meticulously	whencesoever	paradisiacal	berzelianite
catechetical	minicomputer	wretchedness	peradventure	beseechingly
chalcolithic	miraculously	accidentally	postdiluvian	bespectacled
chalcopyrite	mitochondria	adjudication	postdoctoral	biogeography
chancemedley	molecularity	adjudicative	proudhearted	biometrician
churchianism	monochromate	adjudicatory	pseudocyesis	blamefulness
churchwarden	municipalise	aerodynamics	pseudonymity	bonnetmonkey
coerciveness	municipality	ambidextrous	pseudonymous	boulevardier
coincidental	musicianship	amygdaloidal	pseudopodium	brokenwinded
coincidently	musicologist	anecdotalist	residentiary	bulletheaded
conscionable	officeholder	antediluvian	residentship	butterflynut
conscription	offscourings	archdeaconry	scandalously	buttermuslin
councilwoman	orbicularity	archdiocesan	Scandinavian	butterscotch
cynocephalus	overcautious	autodidactic	selfdeceived	cancellation
deescalation	overcritical	basidiospore	selfdeceiver	carpetbagger
dejectedness	overcropping	bladderwrack	selfdelusion	carpetknight
delicatessen	oxyacetylene	blandishment	selfdestruct	Cartesianism
denuclearise	parochialise	bloodbrother	selfdevotion	centesimally
deracination	parochialism	bloodletting	selfdirected	choreography

closecropped
closegrained
closemouthed
coacervation
coelenterate
collectively
collectivise
collectivism
collectivist
collectivity
collegialism
collegiality
collegiately
commemorator
commencement
commendation
commendatory
commensalism
commensalist
commensurate
commentation
commercially
compellation
compensation
compensative
compensatory
concelebrant
concelebrate
concentrator
conceptional
conceptually
condemnation
condemnatory
condensation
confectioner
conferential
confessional
congeniality
congenitally
connectional
connectively
consecration
consecratory
consensually
consentience
consentingly
consequently
conservation
conservatism
conservative
conservatory
contemplator
contemporary
contemporise
contemptible
contemptibly
contemptuous
conterminous
contestation
contextually
convectional
conveniently
conventicler
conventional
conversation
conveyancing
coquettishly
correctional
correctitude
correctively
cosmetically
costermonger
crenellation
cumbersomely
decreasingly
depreciation
depreciatory
depressingly
dessertspoon

Deuteronomic
diageotropic
dialectician
dialectology
dietetically
differentiae
differential
digressional
digressively
dinnerjacket
discerningly
discerptible
dishevelment
dispensation
dispensatory
disregardful
disreputable
disreputably
disseminator
dissentingly
dissertation
disseverance
disseverment
distemperate
dunderheaded
ecclesiastic
ecclesiology
elementalism
elementarily
emblematical
empressement
enfeeblement
entreatingly
entrenchment
entrepreneur
epexegetical
epidemically
epidemiology
esoterically
evanescently
evidentially
exacerbation
exegetically
exoterically
expressional
expressively
expressivity
fatherfigure
fatherliness
fermentation
fermentative
flabelliform
flagellation
flagellatory
flamethrower
forcefulness
fostermother
frenetically
geometrician
geotectonics
globetrotter
goosepimples
gorgeousness
gracefulness
gratefulness
graveclothes
gravelelling
griseofulvin
grotesquerie
grovellingly
guilefulness
gynaecocracy
halterbroken
happenstance
harlequinade
heavenliness
hedgehopping
henceforward
hermeneutics

hermetically
herpetologic
hesperididia
homoeopathic
homoeostasis
horrendously
horsebreaker
horsemanship
horsetrading
horsewhipped
housebreaker
housekeeping
housetrained
housewarming
huggermugger
hygienically
hysterectomy
hysterically
hysteromania
impregnation
impressively
inadequately
increasingly
IndoEuropean
inflectional
infrequently
inoperculate
inspectorate
inspectorial
intrenchment
judgematical
katzenjammer
Keynesianism
kinaesthesia
kinaesthesis
kinaesthetic
kindergarten
lanternjawed
lanternslide
largehearted
laureateship
ledgertackle
licketysplit
liquefacient
liquefaction
lumberjacket
magnetically
magnetisable
magnetograph
magnetometer
maidenliness
maidenstakes
malleability
malversation
mangelwurzel
mannerliness
manoeuvrable
marketgarden
marketsquare
Marseillaise
marvellously
mastersinger
masterstroke
masterswitch
mathematical
messeigneurs
millesimally
misbehaviour
miscellanist
misdemeanant
misdemeanour
misrepresent
misselthrush
monkeyflower
monkeyjacket
monkeypuzzle
monkeywrench
motherfigure
motherliness

mothertongue
myrmecophily
mysteriously
nauseatingly
nauseousness
neglectfully
Neohellenism
nephelometer
nephelometry
nerveracking
nonresidence
nonresistant
obstetrician
oppressively
orchestrator
outpensioner
overemphasis
overestimate
overexertion
overexposure
palaeobotany
palaeography
Palaeolithic
panhellenism
pantechnicon
paraesthesia
passepartout
pathetically
patternmaker
peacefulness
peasepudding
perceptively
perceptivity
perceptually
perfectively
perfervidity
permeability
perpetration
perpetuation
perseverance
perverseness
phanerogamic
phonemically
phonetically
pickerelweed
pinfeathered
pitterpatter
placesetting
planetesimal
planetstruck
polyethylene
porcelainise
porcelainous
porcellanous
portentously
possessively
posteriority
praseodymium
precedential
preceptorial
precessional
predesignate
predestinate
predetermine
prefectorial
preferential
prehensility
premeditated
premeditator
premenstrual
prerequisite
preselection
preselective
presentation
presentative
presentiment
preservation
preservative

pretermitted
preventative
preventively
pricecutting
pridefulness
prizefighter
prizewinning
processional
professional
professorate
professoress
professorial
progenitress
progesterone
projectional
projectively
prolegomenon
prosectorial
prosecutable
proselytiser
protectively
protectorate
protensively
protestation
proverbially
prudentially
pulverisable
pumpernickel
pursestrings
putrefaction
putrefactive
pyroelectric
racketeering
recreational
reflectional
reflectively
reflectivity
refreshingly
refreshments
regressively
reprehension
reprehensive
repressively
respectfully
respectively
retrenchment
sabretoothed
scareheading
scenepainter
sceneshifter
screenwriter
scutellation
sedgewarbler
segmentation
selfeducated
selfeffacing
selfelective
selfemployed
selfevidence
selfexistent
sententially
septennially
sequentially
sequestrator
sergeantfish
sergeantship
serjeantship
serpentiform
serpentinely
sexcentenary
shamefacedly
shamefulness
sharecropper
silverglance
skateboarder
slaveholding
slovenliness
snakecharmer
sorbefacient

speleologist	unpretending	panification	monographist	exophthalmos
spidermonkey	unsteadiness	proofreading	navigability	exophthalmus
spitefulness	unwieldiness	purification	navigational	faithfulness
spokesperson	unyieldingly	purificatory	nonagenarian	faithhealing
stagemanager	vengefulness	ramification	obligatorily	featherbrain
stereochromy	vertebration	ratification	obliginess	featheriness
stereography	viscerotonic	selfflattery	octogenarian	forthrightly
stereoisomer	vitreousness	semifinalist	paragraphist	geochemistry
stereometric	wastefulness	semifinished	peregrinator	geophysicist
stereophonic	welterweight	shuffleboard	polyglottism	glyphography
stereopticon	wherethrough	snapfastener	postgraduate	goodhumoured
stereoscopic	whitelivered	sodafountain	priggishness	graphologist
stoneboiling	whitewashing	solifluction	recognisable	heathenishly
stonecutting	wholehearted	staffofficer	recognisably	highhandedly
stonedresser	wicketkeeper	staffsurgeon	recognisance	ichthyocolla
stonemasonry	winterbourne	surefootedly	renegotiable	ichthyolatry
streetwalker	wonderstruck	thriftlessly	resignedness	ichthyophagy
stupefacient	wonderworker	typefounding	rontgenogram	incoherently
stupefaction	woodengraver	typification	rontgenology	indehiscence
stupefactive	woodenheaded	unaffectedly	sexagenarian	isochromatic
stupendously	wunderkinder	unofficially	slaughterous	isochronally
subcelestial	YankeeDoodle	verification	sledgehammer	isothermally
subjectively	zoogeography	verificatory	sluggishness	knighterrant
subjectivise	artificially	vilification	snaggletooth	knightliness
subjectivism	benefactress	vinification	sphygmograph	leathercloth
subjectivist	beneficently	vivification	spiegeleisen	lefthandedly
subjectivity	beneficially	vociferation	sprightfully	LowChurchman
subsequently	birefringent	vociferously	staggeringly	marshharrier
subservience	bullfighting	wellfavoured	swaggeringly	merchantable
subserviency	campfollower	amalgamation	swaggerstick	mirthfulness
subtemperate	chieftainess	amalgamative	telegraphese	morphallaxis
subterranean	cliffhanging	antagonistic	telegraphist	morphologist
subversively	cockfighting	antigenicity	thoughtfully	mouthbreeder
succedaneous	codification	antigropelos	triggerhappy	neighbouring
successfully	decaffeinate	clangorously	unregenerate	nonchalantly
successional	disaffection	cytogenetics	unsegregated	northeastern
successively	disaffiliate	delightfully	vainglorious	northernmost
suggestively	dwarfishness	derogatorily	wellgrounded	Northumbrian
surrealistic	exsufflicate	disagreeable	wineglassful	northwestern
surrejoinder	firefighting	disagreeably	woolgatherer	nympholeptic
surveillance	gasification	disagreement	wrongfulness	nymphomaniac
surveyorship	genuflection	draughtboard	youngberries	openhandedly
susceptively	hardfavoured	draughthorse	aesthetician	panchromatic
suspensively	hardfeatured	droughtiness	aestheticism	philharmonic
sustentation	highfaluting	emargination	anaphylactic	philhellenic
sustentative	humification	espagnolette	anathematise	pitcherplant
synaesthesia	indefeasible	evangelistic	annihilation	polyhistoric
synaesthetic	indefeasibly	exaggeration	annihilative	posthumously
syndetically	indefectible	exaggerative	anotherguess	prechristian
systematical	indefensible	exaggeratory	apochromatic	prophylactic
systematiser	indefensibly	excogitation	apothegmatic	prothalamion
systemically	indefinitely	excogitative	arithmetical	prothalamium
tangentially	indifference	frangibility	bacchanalian	prothonotary
tastefulness	indifferency	freightliner	beachcombing	psephologist
teetertotter	ineffaceable	fuliginosity	biochemistry	psychiatrist
telaesthesia	ineffaceably	halogenation	biophysicist	psychoactive
telaesthetic	inefficiency	hellgrammite	blatherskite	psychography
tercentenary	insufferable	hypogastrium	bletherskate	psychologise
tessellation	insufferably	hypognathous	blithesomely	psychologism
thereinafter	insufficient	illegibility	brachydactyl	psychologist
threequarter	insufflation	illegitimacy	bullheadedly	psychometric
threewheeler	irreflective	illegitimate	cantharidian	psychopathic
torrefaction	irreformable	illogicality	clotheshorse	psychosexual
torrentially	irrefragable	inauguration	clothespress	psychotropic
traceability	irrefragably	inauguratory	coachbuilder	psychrometer
tradescantia	leapfrogging	incognisable	conchiferous	psychrometry
tradespeople	manifoldness	incognisance	conchologist	punchingball
tremendously	manufacturer	incognitable	crashlanding	rhythmically
tricentenary	modification	indigenously	Czechoslovak	saccharinity
turbellarian	modificatory	indigestible	diaphanously	saccharoidal
uneventfully	monofilament	IndoGermanic	diathermancy	selfhypnosis
unfrequented	munificently	integumental	earthshaking	slothfulness
unisexuality	nidification	invagination	epiphenomena	southeastern
universalise	noneffective	invigilation	epithalamion	southernmost
universalism	nonefficient	invigoration	epithalamium	southernwood
universalist	notification	irregardless	erythematous	southwestern
universality	ossification	irregularity	erythroblast	Stakhanovism
unpleasantly	pacification	loungelizard	erythromycin	Stakhanovite
unprejudiced	pacificatory	metagalactic	exophthalmic	stethoscopic

stichomythia	cantillation	factionalism	multiflorous	profiteering
stichomythic	capriciously	factiousness	multifoliate	prolifically
subthreshold	captiousness	factitiously	multiformity	prolificness
sulphonamide	carcinogenic	fancifulness	multilateral	propitiation
sulphonation	cardinalship	farsightedly	multilingual	propitiatory
sulphuration	cardiography	fastidiously	multiloquous	propitiously
sulphuretted	cardiologist	fertilisable	multinuclear	protistology
swashbuckler	carriageable	fibrillation	multipartite	providential
synchronical	cautiousness	fibrinolysin	multipliable	provincially
synchroniser	clarinettist	fictionalise	multiplicand	provisionary
teachability	clavicembalo	fictitiously	multiplicate	pteridophyte
thitherwards	coalitionist	flagitiously	multiplicity	pteridosperm
timehonoured	collinearity	floriculture	multipurpose	publicspirit
touchingness	combinations	folliculated	multistoried	rabbinically
trachomatous	commiserator	forbiddingly	multivalence	receivership
trephination	commissarial	forcibleness	multiversity	refrigerator
trichologist	commissariat	galligaskins	mystifyingly	reunionistic
trichotomise	commissioner	gallinaceous	narcissistic	rollingstock
trichotomous	committeeman	gesticulator	noctilucence	runningboard
trichromatic	conciliation	glaciologist	nutritionist	sacrilegious
triphthongal	conciliative	gladiatorial	nutritiously	salpiglossis
trochanteric	conciliatory	gloriousness	nyctitropism	scarificator
trophallaxis	confidential	graciousness	obedientiary	sectionalism
truthfulness	confirmation	graminaceous	onesidedness	selfidentity
warehouseman	confirmative	gratifyingly	opinionative	selfignition
watchfulness	confirmatory	handicapping	orchidaceous	selfinterest
weatherboard	confiscation	hereinbefore	outrivalling	selfinvolved
weatherbound	confiscatory	heroicalness	pantisocracy	sellingplate
weatherglass	conningtower	heroicomical	parkinsonism	sempiternity
weatherhouse	considerable	horribleness	parsimonious	sensibleness
weatherproof	considerably	horrifically	participator	sensitometer
whitherwards	consignation	horticulture	particularly	septilateral
worshipfully	consistently	hybridisable	partisanship	serviceberry
wrathfulness	consistorial	implicitness	partitionist	servicecourt
xanthochroia	contiguously	imprisonment	passionately	servicewoman
youthfulness	contingently	inclinometer	passionfruit	servitorship
abolitionary	continuation	infringement	patriarchate	significance
abolitionism	continuative	inspissation	perfidiously	significancy
abolitionist	continuously	instillation	permissively	silviculture
aboriginally	convincement	intriguingly	permittivity	somniloquism
acquiescence	convincingly	intuitionism	perniciously	somniloquist
adscititious	conviviality	intuitionist	persistently	sophisticate
alexipharmic	cousingerman	inveiglement	pertinacious	spaciousness
amelioration	craniologist	isodiametric	perviousness	specialistic
ameliorative	criticalness	jesuitically	pestilential	specifically
amphibiously	cuckingstool	kaleidoscope	petrifaction	specificness
amphibrachic	cultivatable	kinnikinnick	pettifoggery	speciousness
amphictyonic	curlingirons	kissingcrust	pettifogging	spiritedness
amphisbaenic	curlingtongs	landingcraft	philistinism	spiritlessly
amphitheatre	curvicaudate	landingfield	physiognomic	spiritualise
amphitropous	curvicostate	landingstage	physiography	spiritualism
aperiodicity	curvifoliate	landingstrip	physiologist	spiritualist
apolitically	curvirostral	lasciviously	pisciculture	spirituality
archipelagic	declinometer	lodginghouse	planispheric	spuriousness
architecture	densitometer	longitudinal	playingfield	stationhouse
astringently	denticulated	lopsidedness	plebiscitary	stationwagon
attributable	dentilingual	lusciousness	plenipotence	statistician
auspiciously	despitefully	machicolated	plesiosaurus	straightaway
autoimmunity	discipleship	magnifically	pluriliteral	straightbred
avariciously	disciplinary	magnificence	pluviometric	straightedge
beatifically	dispiritedly	magniloquent	poikilotherm	straightener
belligerence	dissimilarly	mansionhouse	pontifically	straightness
belligerency	dissimulator	Marcionitism	pontificator	straitjacket
bibliography	distillation	marlinespike	preciousness	studiousness
bibliologist	distillatory	marriageable	precipitable	subdivisible
bibliomaniac	distinctness	mastigophora	precipitance	subminiature
bibliopegist	dorsiventral	matriarchate	precipitancy	submissively
bibliophilic	drawingboard	meaningfully	precipitator	subsidiarily
bibliopolist	drawingpaper	meetinghouse	precisianism	succinctness
bibliothecae	duckingstool	meltingpoint	precisionist	sufficiently
billingsgate	emotionalise	mercifulness	predictively	survivorship
boogiewoogie	emotionalism	milliammeter	predigestion	suspiciously
bookingclerk	emotionalist	misdirection	predilection	sylviculture
burningglass	emotionality	morningdress	prehistorian	tangibleness
cachinnation	empoisonment	morrisdancer	presidential	tergiversate
cachinnatory	enclitically	mulligatawny	previousness	terribleness
calligrapher	Englishwoman	multicentral	primigravida	terrifically
calligraphic	eveningdress	multidentate	prodigiously	terrifyingly
callisthenic	explicitness	multifarious	proficiently	tintinnabula

Torricellian	bottlewasher	helplessness	perilousness	ticklishness
traditionary	brilliantine	heraldically	perplexingly	timelessness
traditionist	burglarproof	highlystrung	phillumenist	tirelessness
tragicomical	canaliculate	homologation	phyllotactic	tittletattle
turriculated	canalisation	hopelessness	pitilessness	toggleswitch
unblinkingly	candleholder	hubblebubble	populousness	tonelessness
unchivalrous	carelessness	hucklebacked	pralltriller	totalisation
uncritically	carillonneur	idealisation	preclassical	totalitarian
unfaithfully	catilinarian	impoliteness	preclusively	triglyphical
ungainliness	cattlelifter	incalculable	proclamation	triplication
unprincipled	chaplainship	incalculably	proclamatory	troglodytism
unscientific	charlatanism	incalescence	profligately	tumultuously
unthinkingly	churlishness	indelibility	proglottides	tunelessness
usuriousness	civilisation	indelicately	purblindness	turtlenecked
uxoriousness	complacently	infelicitous	pyroligneous	unbelievable
vermiculated	complaisance	insalubrious	rabblerouser	unbelievably
verticalness	complemental	insolubilise	rattleheaded	uncalculated
verticillate	completeness	insolubility	razzledazzle	uncelebrated
vindictively	complexional	intellection	reallocation	vitalisation
vitrifaction	complexioned	intellective	rebelliously	vitiligation
walkietalkie	complication	intellectual	recalcitrant	vocalisation
Wellingtonia	conclusively	intelligence	recalcitrate	winklepicker
williewaught	conglobation	intelligible	recalescence	woollyheaded
windingsheet	conglomerate	intelligibly	recklessness	accommodator
workingclass	conglutinate	intolerantly	recollection	accompanyist
xiphisternum	copolymerise	invalidation	recollective	accomplished
readjustment	copulatively	involutional	remilitarise	accumulation
blackbirding	corelatively	invulnerable	resoluteness	accumulative
blackcurrant	cotyledonary	invulnerably	resolvedness	Alhambresque
blackguardly	cotyledonous	irrelatively	resplendence	allomorphism
blockbusting	cumulatively	irrelevantly	resplendency	antimacassar
brackishness	cumulocirrus	kremlinology	restlessness	antimagnetic
breakthrough	cumulonimbus	landlubberly	revelational	antimalarial
brickfielder	debilitation	legalisation	rootlessness	assimilation
brinkmanship	decalescence	lifelessness	rumbletumble	assimilative
camiknickers	deceleration	listlessness	ruralisation	assimilatory
checkerberry	demilitarise	localisation	ruthlessness	asymmetrical
checkerboard	depoliticise	lovelessness	saddlebacked	automaticity
clinkerbuilt	desalination	lovelornness	secularistic	automobilist
crackbrained	desolateness	manslaughter	sedulousness	automorphism
flickeringly	desulphurise	megalomaniac	selflessness	barometrical
frankincense	disallowance	metalanguage	selflimiting	calamitously
freakishness	disclamation	metallically	selfluminous	calumniation
glockenspiel	displaceable	metallophone	semiliterate	calumniatory
handkerchief	displacement	metallurgist	sepulchrally	calumniously
skunkcabbage	displeasedly	metalworking	shillyshally	catamountain
sparkingplug	doubleacting	middleweight	shoulderbelt	ceremonially
speakingtube	doubledealer	mindlessness	shoulderknot	chrematistic
specktioneer	doubledecked	misalignment	shouldernote	chromaticism
stockbreeder	doubledecker	misplacement	simpleminded	chromaticity
stockbroking	doublelocked	mobilisation	simultaneity	chromatogram
stockingless	duraluminium	moralisation	simultaneous	chromatology
stockjobbery	echolocation	movelessness	singleacting	chromatopsia
stockjobbing	equalisation	mucilaginous	singledecker	chromosphere
stockraising	equalitarian	muddleheaded	singlehanded	cinematheque
strikingness	equilibrator	muzzleloader	singleminded	columniation
thankfulness	exhilaration	namelessness	singleseater	decomposable
thanksgiving	exhilarative	nebulisation	skullduggery	decompressor
thickskinned	fabulousness	nebulousness	smallclothes	delamination
thickskulled	facelessness	needlessness	smallholding	delimitation
trickishness	facilitation	neoclassical	snarlingiron	demimondaine
unlikelihood	fearlessness	Neoplatonism	soullessness	denomination
unlikeliness	fecklessness	Neoplatonist	spotlessness	denominative
absoluteness	feebleminded	nonalignment	stablishment	detumescence
absolutistic	fiddlefaddle	nonflammable	stealthiness	disambiguate
acaulescence	fiddlesticks	nonflowering	stellenbosch	disembarrass
acceleration	finalisation	novelisation	stelliferous	dynamometric
accelerative	focalisation	obsolescence	sterlingness	effeminately
alkalescence	formlessness	obsoleteness	stillhunting	elasmobranch
argillaceous	futilitarian	oscillograph	subalternate	eleemosynary
artilleryman	ganglionated	oscilloscope	subalternity	encumberment
availability	gesellschaft	overlordship	supplemental	encumbrancer
baselessness	ghoulishness	painlessness	supplementer	endamagement
battleground	gobbledegook	parallelling	supplicantly	endometritis
battlemented	gobbledygook	paralysation	supplication	enormousness
bewilderedly	grallatorial	patulousness	supplicatory	entomologise
bewilderment	habilitation	pearlescence	tactlessness	entomologist
booklearning	harmlessness	peerlessness	tamelessness	enzymologist
bootlessness	heedlessness	penalisation	tearlessness	ephemerality

euhemeristic	rememberable	chimneypiece	impenitently	reconstitute
flammability	remembrancer	chronography	imponderable	reconversion
foraminifera	rheumatology	chronologise	imponderably	reconveyance
grammaticise	salamandrian	chronologist	incandescent	redintegrate
grammolecule	salamandrine	chronometric	incendiarism	regeneration
gyromagnetic	salamandroid	clannishness	incineration	regenerative
headmistress	scrimshanker	clownishness	inconcinnity	relentlessly
hemimorphism	seismography	colonisation	inconclusive	reminiscence
hemimorphite	seismologist	debonairness	inconformity	remonstrance
homomorphism	seismometric	decentralise	inconsequent	remonstrator
homomorphous	seismoscopic	decongestant	inconsistent	remuneration
hoodmanblind	selfmurderer	decongestion	inconsolable	remunerative
illumination	skrimshanker	decongestive	inconsolably	remuneratory
illuminative	spermaphytic	deconsecrate	inconsonance	renunciation
immemorially	spermathecal	decontrolled	inconstantly	renunciative
inadmissible	spermatocyte	definiteness	inconsumable	renunciatory
inadmissibly	spermatozoid	definitively	inconsumably	resiniferous
incommodious	spermatozoon	degenerately	incontiguous	revengefully
incommutable	spermogonium	degeneration	incontinence	ribonuclease
incommutably	stammeringly	degenerative	incontinency	romanisation
incomparable	stormtrooper	deionisation	inconvenient	romantically
incomparably	swimmingbath	delinquently	infanticidal	ruminatively
incompatible	swimmingbell	demineralise	infiniteness	saponifiable
incompatibly	swimmingpool	demoniacally	infinitively	scornfulness
incompetence	taskmistress	demonstrable	infundibular	scoundreldom
incompetency	thaumaturgic	demonstrably	inteneration	scoundrelism
incompletely	thermocouple	demonstrator	journalistic	secondstring
incompliance	thermography	denunciation	juvenescence	selenography
incomputable	thermolabile	denunciative	lacininiated	selenologist
insemination	thermometric	denunciatory	laryngoscope	semantically
intemperance	thermophilic	diminishable	laryngoscopy	seminiferous
intimidation	thermoscopic	diminishment	latinisation	simoniacally
intimidatory	thermosphere	diminutively	licentiously	Sinanthropus
intumescence	thermostable	disannulling	luminescence	splendidness
irremediable	thermostatic	disannulment	luminiferous	stanniferous
irremediably	thermotactic	disenchanter	luminousness	sternutation
irremissible	thermotropic	disendowment	lycanthropic	sternutative
mademoiselle	triumphantly	disincentive	melancholiac	sternutatory
manometrical	uncomeatable	disinfectant	melanochroic	sternwheeler
maximisation	uncommercial	disinfection	misanthropic	stranglehold
metamorphism	uncommonness	disinflation	misinterpret	strengthener
metamorphose	undemocratic	disingenuous	misknowledge	strengthless
minimisation	unfamiliarly	disintegrate	mournfulness	stringcourse
monomaniacal	untimeliness	disinterment	mourningband	strongminded
monometallic	venomousness	eccentricity	mourningring	strongylosis
monomorphous	volumetrical	echinococcus	mutinousness	strontianite
monumentally	voluminosity	endangerment	niminypiminy	subinfeudate
openmindedly	voluminously	enginedriver	nomenclative	swainishness
optimisation	whigmaleerie	enginetuning	nomenclature	synonymously
ornamentally	zygomorphism	entanglement	nominalistic	technicality
paramagnetic	zygomorphous	essentiality	oblanceolate	technicolour
parametrical	absentminded	expansionary	oceanography	technocratic
paramilitary	accentuation	expansionism	oceanologist	technologist
paramorphism	acronychally	expansionist	ordinariness	theanthropic
perambulator	actinomycete	exsanguinate	organgrinder	trainspotter
peremptorily	administrant	exsanguinous	organisation	triangularly
pharmaceutic	administrate	extensometer	organography	tyrannically
pharmacology	admonishment	extinguisher	organoleptic	tyrannicidal
pleomorphism	advantageous	feminineness	orienteering	unconformity
plummerblock	adventitious	feminisation	ostentatious	unconsidered
pneumaticity	aeronautical	forensically	overniceness	unconstraint
pneumatology	aeroneurosis	friendliness	palingenesia	uncontrolled
pneumothorax	agranulocyte	furunculosis	palingenesis	unconvincing
polymorphism	annunciation	gerontocracy	palingenetic	unionisation
polymorphous	antineutrino	gigantically	palynologist	unkindliness
portmanteaus	appendectomy	gramnegative	paranormally	unmanageable
portmanteaux	appendicitis	greengrocery	parenthesise	unwontedness
postmeridian	appendicular	greenishness	paronomastic	urbanisation
postmistress	astonishment	groundcherry	pedantically	urbanologist
pragmatistic	autonomously	groundlessly	pedunculated	Valenciennes
preeminently	bicentennial	homonymously	phrenologist	voluntaryism
pyromaniacal	bilingualism	humanisation	plainclothed	voluntaryist
pyromorphite	brainstormer	humanitarian	plainclothes	womanishness
qualmishness	brainwashing	hymenopteran	plaindealing	aetiological
racemisation	businesslike	immensurable	polyneuritic	agamogenesis
recommitment	cabinetmaker	immunisation	polyneuritis	agamogenetic
redemptioner	canonisation	immunologist	potentiality	aircondition
Redemptorist	cementitious	impenetrable	ravenousness	amitotically
regimentally	charnelhouse	impenetrably	reconcilable	anagogically

analogically	discontented	hydrological	negrophilism	photosetting
anamorphosis	discordantly	hydrolysable	negrophilist	photospheric
anatomically	discountable	hydromedusae	neonomianism	phototropism
anemographic	discouraging	hydromedusan	Nestorianism	phycological
anemophilous	discourteous	hydrophilous	neuroanatomy	phycomycetes
angiocarpous	discoverable	hydroquinone	neurobiology	phylogenesis
approachable	discoverture	hydrostatics	neurological	phylogenetic
appropriable	disgorgement	hydrotherapy	neuropterous	phytogenesis
appropriator	disjointedly	hydrothermal	neuroscience	phytogenetic
astrological	dislodgement	hydrotropism	neurosurgeon	phytographer
astronautics	dispossessor	hygrophilous	neurosurgery	phytological
astronomical	dissocialise	hymnographer	neurotically	phytophagous
astrophysics	dissociation	hypnogenesis	Newfoundland	pictographic
ballottement	dissociative	hypnogenetic	nimbostratus	pigeonbreast
bassorelievo	distortional	hypnotherapy	nitrobenzene	planoconcave
bassorilievo	ecologically	hypnotically	noncombatant	platonically
biocoenology	econometrics	hypnotisable	noncommittal	plecopterous
biologically	economically	iconoclastic	noncomplying	pleiotropism
bowcompasses	editorialise	iconographer	nonconductor	pornographer
Byelorussian	editorialist	impropriator	nonconformer	pornographic
campodeiform	efflorescent	improvidence	ophiophagous	precociously
carbohydrate	encroachment	improvisator	orthodontics	precognition
carbonaceous	episodically	incoordinate	orthodontist	precognitive
Carlovingian	ethnocentric	ingloriously	orthogenesis	precondition
cartographer	ethnographer	introduction	orthogenetic	preconscious
cartographic	ethnographic	introductory	orthographer	predominance
cartological	ethnological	introjection	orthographic	predominancy
catholically	etymological	intromission	orthopaedics	preformation
censoriously	etymologicon	intromittent	orthopaedist	preformative
chemotherapy	euphonically	intromitting	orthopterist	preponderant
chiropractic	euphoniously	introversion	orthopteroid	preponderate
chiropractor	exploitation	introversive	orthopterous	preposterous
chocolatebox	exploitative	introvertive	orthotropism	primogenital
chorographic	exprobration	karyokinesis	orthotropous	primogenitor
chorological	extroversion	leucocytosis	osteogenesis	primordially
cirrocumulus	falcongentil	leukocytosis	osteological	proboscidean
cirrostratus	falcongentle	limnological	osteomalacia	proboscidian
coenobitical	flavoprotein	lithographer	osteoplastic	proconsulate
coenobytical	geologically	lithographic	osteoporosis	profoundness
coleopterist	geopolitical	lithospheric	paedobaptism	prolongation
coleopterous	glycogenesis	lithotritist	paedogenesis	pronominally
colloquially	glycoprotein	macrocephaly	paedogenetic	pronouncedly
comfortingly	granodiorite	macropterous	paedomorphic	proportional
commodiously	gymnosophist	malcontented	pantographic	proportioned
commonwealth	haemophiliac	malformation	pathogenesis	prosodically
composedness	haemopoiesis	meteorically	pathogenetic	prosopopoeia
compoundable	haemorrhagic	meteorograph	pathological	protohistory
concomitance	hagiographer	methodically	perfoliation	protoplasmic
concordantly	hagiographic	metrological	performative	protoplastic
conformation	hagiological	metropolitan	periodically	prototypical
confoundedly	harmonically	mezzorelievo	periodontics	protozoology
consociation	harmoniously	mezzosoprano	periodontist	pterodactyle
consolidator	hebdomadally	microanalyst	periostracum	purposebuilt
corporeality	hectographic	microbiology	pernoctation	purposefully
corroborator	heliocentric	microcapsule	pestological	quixotically
cosmogonical	heliographer	microcephaly	petrographer	radiobiology
cosmographer	heliographic	microcircuit	petrographic	radioelement
cosmographic	heliogravure	microclimate	petrological	radiographer
cosmological	heliolatrous	microcopying	phagocytosis	radiographic
cosmopolitan	heliotherapy	microcrystal	phagocytotic	radioisotope
cosmopolitic	heliotropism	micrographer	phenological	radiological
cottonocracy	hieroglyphic	microphysics	phenomenally	radionuclide
cuckooflower	hierographer	microscopist	phenotypical	radiophonics
customshouse	hierophantic	microseismic	philodendron	radiotherapy
despoliation	hippocentaur	microsurgery	philological	ratiocinator
despondently	hippopotamus	mnemotechnic	philosophise	reproachable
despotically	histogenesis	muttonheaded	phonographer	reproachless
diabolically	histogenetic	mythographer	phonographic	reproducible
diamonddrill	histological	mythological	phonological	reproduction
diamondfield	historically	mythologiser	photochromic	reproductive
diatomaceous	homeomorphic	narcotically	photofission	reprographic
diatonically	homeopathist	narrowminded	photogeology	responsively
discographer	horrorstruck	necrographer	photographer	responsorial
discomfiture	hydrochloric	necrological	photographic	retrocedence
discommodity	hydrodynamic	necrophagous	photogravure	retrocession
discomposure	hydrofluoric	necrophiliac	photokinesis	retrocessive
disconnected	hydrographer	necrophilism	photokinetic	retroflexion
disconnexion	hydrographic	necrophilous	photomontage	retropulsion
disconsolate	hydrokinetic		photophilous	retroversion

```
rhetorically decapitation postpositive absorptivity diagrammatic
rhinocerotic decipherable postprandial abstractable dichromatism
rhinological decipherment prosperously abstractedly discreetness
rhizocarpous depopulation puerperrally abstractness discreteness
rhizogenetic dilapidation reappearance abstruseness discretional
rhizophagous earsplitting recapitulate accordionist discriminant
rhododendron ectoparasite receptaculum accurateness discriminate
salmonladder elliptically receptionist accursedness disfranchise
saprophagous encephalitic reciprocally afterthought disorientate
sarcomatosis encephalitis reciprocator ailurophobia distractedly
sarcophagous endoparasite recuperation aircraftsman distrainable
sardonically equipollence recuperative alterability distrainment
scatological equipollency redeployment anaerobiosis distributary
scenographic equiprobable resipiscence anagrammatic distribution
schoolfellow escapologist resupination anthropogeny distributive
schoolleaver exasperation scorpionfish anthropoidal divarication
schoolmaster exospherical scraperboard anthropology diversionary
semiofficial footplateman scripturally antirachitic diversionist
semiological gamopetalous scriptwriter apparatchiki diverticular
servocontrol gamophyllous scrupulosity apparatchiks diverticulum
shadowboxing grampositive scrupulously apparentness divertimenti
siphonophore graspingness sculpturally apparitional divertimento
siphonostele hemiparasite selfpleasing apperception dolorousness
sociological highpressure selfportrait apperceptive effervescent
sociometrist hirepurchase semiparasite appurtenance effortlessly
sporogenesis hypophrygian semiprecious arborescence encirclement
stenographer inappeasable seraphically arborisation endermically
stenographic inapplicable sharpshooter atheromatous enshrinement
stylographic inapplicably sharpsighted attorneyship enterprising
subcommittee inappositely sheepishness Australasian entertaining
subconscious incapability sheepshearer biographical enthronement
subcontinent incapacitate skippingrope calorescence epigrammatic
subnormality independence sleepingpill calorimetric etherisation
subsonically independency sleepwalking canorousness excursionist
suppositious inexpedience slipperiness capercaillie experiential
surmountable inexpediency snappishness capercailzie experimental
surroundings inexperience softpedalled caterwauling experimenter
symbolically inexpertness steeplechase centrespread exterminable
tautological inexplicable streptococci centrosphere exterminator
taxcollector inexplicably streptomycin chairmanship extortionary
tectonically inexpressive strophanthin cheerfulness extortionate
teleological inexpugnable subapostolic cheirography feverishness
terrorstruck inexpugnably sweepingness chlorination figuratively
testosterone irrepealable sycophantish clairaudient filtrability
Teutonically irreprovable synoptically clairvoyance fluorescence
thoroughbass malapertness trampolinist clearsighted fluoridation
thoroughbred manipulation trumpetshell colorimetric fluorination
thoroughfare manipulative unappeasable compressible fluorocarbon
thoroughness manipulatory unappetising concrescence futurologist
toploftiness metaphorical undiplomatic concreteness gastronomist
trigonometry metaphrastic unemployable congratulant gastropodous
trinomialism metaphysical unemployment congratulate generousness
tropological metapsychics unexpectedly congregation geographical
tropospheric misapprehend unimportance contractable governmental
unapologetic monopetalous unpopularity contractedly governorship
unbrokenness monophyletic unrepeatable contractible haberdashery
uneconomical Monophysitic venepuncture contradictor hemerocallis
unifoliolate monopodially venipuncture contrapuntal heterocercal
unprofitable monopolistic vituperation contrariness heterocyclic
unprofitably nanoplankton vituperative contrariwise heteroecious
unpronounced newspaperman vituperatory contribution heterogamous
unthoughtful occupational viviparously contributive heterogenous
Victorianism omnipotently voluptuosity contributory heterologous
victoriously omnipresence voluptuously contriteness heteromerous
viscosimeter oneupmanship wallpainting contrivement heteronomous
viscountship overpersuade whimperingly controllable heterophylly
yellowhammer overpowering whippoorwill cowardliness heterosexual
analphabetic overpressure whisperingly cumbrousness heterozygote
anteprandial paraphrastic zygapophysis decoratively heterozygous
antiparticle peripherally coloquintida decorousness hibernaculum
antipathetic periphrastic deliquescent departmental humorousness
antiperiodic perspicacity headquarters desirability hyperacidity
antiphonally perspiration hindquarters desirousness hyperbolical
backpedalled perspiratory obsequiously destructible hyperplastic
cataphoresis phosphoresce quinquennial determinable hyperpyretic
championship polypetalous quinquennium determinably hyperpyrexia
clapperboard polyphyletic tranquillise determinedly hypersthenia
conspiration postponement tranquillity dethronement hypersthenic
creepycrawly postposition absorptional dextrousness hypertension
```

hypertensive	interstellar	reverberator	unscriptural	decisiveness
hyperthermia	interstitial	reversionary	unscrupulous	delusiveness
hypertrophic	intertexture	rigorousness	unstructured	derisiveness
illtreatment	intervenient	risorgimento	unworldiness	disassociate
impartiality	intervention	sacerdotally	unworthiness	disastrously
imperatively	intervocalic	Samaritanism	usufructuary	disestablish
imperatorial	interwreathe	scabrousness	valorisation	divisibility
imperceptive	invertebrate	schorlaceous	vaporisation	divisiveness
impercipient	jetpropelled	sclerenchyma	vaporousness	domestically
imperfection	labyrinthian	scouringrush	venerability	domesticator
imperfective	labyrinthine	scurrilously	ventripotent	dressinggown
imperishable	lachrymation	selfreliance	veterinarian	dynastically
imperishably	lachrymatory	selfreproach	vicargeneral	eavesdropped
impermanence	lachrymosely	selfrighting	vigorousness	eavesdropper
impermanency	laterisation	separability	watermanship	echosounding
impersonally	levorotation	separateness	wondrousness	effusiveness
impersonator	levorotatory	solarisation	abrasiveness	emulsifiable
impertinence	liberalistic	sonorousness	accusatively	endoskeletal
impertinency	literariness	soporiferous	accusatorial	envisagement
imperviously	liturgically	sparrowgrass	acoustically	equestrienne
incorporated	liturgiology	spheroidally	adhesiveness	farmsteading
incorporator	Liverpudlian	squarerigged	advisability	fearsomeness
incorporeity	liverystable	squirrelcage	aerosiderite	feldspathoid
incorrigible	majorgeneral	squirreltail	allusiveness	fenestration
incorrigibly	maltreatment	subarrhation	ambassadress	foresightful
incorruption	materialness	suberisation	anaesthetise	forestalment
incurability	mineralogist	sudoriferous	anaesthetist	freestanding
indirectness	mispronounce	superannuate	antiSemitism	freeswimming
inharmonious	mistranslate	supercharger	antistrophic	gamesmanship
instructress	mistreatment	superciliary	appositeness	gamesomeness
instrumental	mistressship	supercilious	appositional	gamosepalous
insurrection	mithridatise	supereminent	artistically	gladsomeness
interbedding	mithridatism	supererogate	assassinator	glassblowing
interception	moderateness	superhighway	atmospherics	glossography
intercession	motorcyclist	superhumanly	backslapping	glossologist
intercessory	motorisation	supermundane	billsticking	grossularite
interchanger	naturalistic	supernaculum	birdsnesting	gruesomeness
interconnect	naturopathic	supernatural	blissfulness	hairsbreadth
intercropped	nephrologist	superposable	bluestocking	hairsplitter
intercurrent	nevertheless	supersedence	bodysnatcher	handsbreadth
intercutting	numerologist	supersensory	bodystocking	handsomeness
interdiction	numerousness	supersession	borosilicate	hardstanding
interdictive	obdurateness	superstition	brassbounder	headshrinker
interdictory	obstreperous	superstratum	brassrubbing	hemispheroid
interdigital	oncorhynchus	supervenient	breaststroke	highsounding
interestedly	oneirocritic	supervention	breastsummer	highspirited
interfemoral	orographical	suppressible	calisthenics	highstepping
interference	otherworldly	surprisingly	catastrophic	homesickness
interglacial	overreaction	synarthrosis	cheeseburger	homosexually
interjection	pancreatitis	syncretistic	cheesecutter	hypostatical
interjectory	papyrologist	taberdarship	cheesemonger	hyposulphite
interlobular	pejoratively	tabernacular	cheeseparing	idiosyncrasy
interlocutor	polarimetric	taperecorder	chrestomathy	illusiveness
intermeddler	polarisation	theoretician	Christianise	illusioriness
intermediacy	polarography	timorousness	Christianity	illustration
intermediary	programmable	tolerability	Christolatry	illustrative
intermediate	programmatic	towardliness	Christophany	inauspicious
interminable	proprietress	tuberculated	classicalism	incestuously
interminably	protrusively	tuberculosis	classicalist	incisiveness
intermission	Quadragesima	underachieve	classicality	indiscipline
intermittent	quadrangular	underbidding	classifiable	indiscreetly
intermitting	quadraphonic	underclothes	cleistogamic	indiscretion
intermixture	quadriennium	undercoating	cocksureness	indisputable
intermundane	quadrinomial	undercurrent	cohesiveness	indisputably
internuclear	quadriplegia	undercutting	coldshoulder	indissoluble
internuncial	quadriplegic	underdevelop	corespondent	indissolubly
interoceanic	quadrivalent	undergarment	crossbedding	indistinctly
interoceptor	quadrumanous	underinsured	crossbencher	industrially
interpellate	rapprochment	underletting	crossbuttock	infusibility
interpleader	regardlessly	undermanning	crosscountry	inhospitable
interpolator	remorsefully	underpinning	crosscurrent	inhospitably
interpretive	repercussion	underrunning	crossexamine	inobservance
interrelated	repercussive	undersetting	crossgrained	intussuscept
interrogator	reservedness	understaffed	crossheading	investigator
interruption	restrainable	undersurface	crossingover	invisibility
interruptive	restrainedly	undertenancy	crosspurpose	irresistible
intersection	restrictedly	underwritten	crosssection	irresistibly
interservice	resurrection	unmercifully	decasyllabic	irresolutely
interspinous	retiringness	unparalleled	decasyllable	irresolution

irresolvable	Shakspereana	anastigmatic	dilatoriness	idiothermous
irrespective	Shaksperiana	antithetical	dilettantish	illiterately
irrespirable	sideslipping	apostolicism	dilettantism	immaterially
irresponsive	sidestepping	apostolicity	diphtheritic	immatureness
jurisconsult	sinistrality	apostrophise	diphthongise	immethodical
jurisdiction	sinistrorsal	appetisingly	doubtfulness	immutability
jurisprudent	sinusoidally	aristocratic	dubitatively	impetiginous
klipspringer	spinsterhood	Aristotelean	Egyptologist	imputability
laisserfaire	starspangled	Aristotelian	electrically	imputatively
laissezaller	teensyweensy	attitudinise	electrolysis	inactivation
laissezfaire	theistically	avantgardism	electrolytic	inarticulate
logistically	theosophical	avantgardist	electrometer	inartificial
lonesomeness	thousandfold	belittlement	electronvolt	incatenation
longshoreman	tiresomeness	bewitchingly	electroplate	inextensible
longstanding	toilsomeness	bilateralism	electroscope	inextricable
magistrature	transcendent	blastfurnace	electroshock	inextricably
majestically	transduction	blastosphere	electrotonic	innutritious
marksmanship	transferable	blastulation	electrotonus	inveterately
meristematic	transference	blisteringly	electrotyper	irrationally
metasomatism	transferring	blusteringly	embattlement	irritability
ministration	transformism	boastfulness	embitterment	irritatingly
ministrative	transformist	boisterously	enantiomorph	kleptomaniac
monastically	transfusible	breathalyser	epistemology	latitudinous
monostichous	transgressor	breathlessly	equationally	legitimately
monostrophic	transhipment	breathtaking	equitability	legitimation
monosyllabic	transhumance	brontosaurus	eruptiveness	legitimatise
monosyllable	transiliency	capitalistic	escutcheoned	lighthearted
nailscissors	transitional	capitulation	excitability	maintainable
nonessential	transitively	charterhouse	exenteration	meditatively
occasionally	transitivity	charterparty	expatriation	menstruation
octosyllabic	transitorily	chastisement	fainthearted	meretricious
octosyllable	translatable	chesterfield	faintishness	mesothoracic
omnisciently	translucence	chitterlings	faultfinding	metathetical
opposability	translucency	clatteringly	firstnighter	metathoracic
oppositeness	transmigrant	constabulary	flatteringly	militaristic
oppositional	transmigrate	constipation	fountainhead	misstatement
oversimplify	transmission	constituency	fractionally	moistureless
overstepping	transmissive	constitution	fractionator	monetisation
parasiticide	transmitting	constitutive	freethinking	monitorially
parasitology	transmogrify	constriction	frictionless	monotheistic
parisyllabic	transmontane	constrictive	frontbencher	monotonously
perispomenon	transmutable	constringent	frontiersman	mosstrooping
peristeronic	transoceanic	construction	frontispiece	mountainside
peristomatic	transpacific	constructive	fructiferous	negativeness
phrasemonger	transparency	countenancer	fructivorous	negativistic
phraseograph	transpirable	counteragent	fruitfulness	negotiatress
plausibility	transplanter	counterblast	fugitiveness	nicotinamide
pleasantness	transpontine	countercheck	functionally	nightclothes
pleasingness	transposable	counterclaim	functionless	nychthemeral
pleasureless	transshipped	counterforce	gametophytic	nychthemeron
polysepalous	transudation	counterlight	geanticlinal	obliteration
polysyllabic	transudatory	countermarch	glitteringly	obliterative
polysyllable	transversely	counterplead	gluttonously	obmutescence
poorspirited	transvestism	counterpoint	glyptography	odontologist
praiseworthy	transvestite	counterpoise	goodtempered	opisthograph
preestablish	unanswerable	counterproof	greathearted	opisthotonos
priestliness	unassailable	counterscarp	guestchamber	ornithomancy
priestridden	unassumingly	countershaft	habitability	ornithoscopy
quaestorship	unhesitating	countertenor	habitforming	outstretched
reassessment	unhistorical	countrydance	habitualness	outstripping
reassignment	unmistakable	countrywoman	halftimbered	palatability
reassuringly	unmistakably	courtmartial	heartburning	paletteknife
recessionary	unreservedly	courtplaster	heartrending	paractactical
redistribute	unresponsive	covetousness	heartstrings	penitentiary
registration	unrestrained	craftbrother	heartwarming	pilotballoon
repossession	wainscotting	creativeness	hebetudinous	plasterboard
resistlessly	whimsicality	cryptanalyst	henotheistic	Plattdeutsch
resuscitator	abortiveness	cryptogamous	heortologist	plectognathi
robustiously	adaptability	cryptography	heritability	pointilliste
sadistically	adaptiveness	cryptologist	hesitatingly	polytheistic
salesmanship	additionally	crystalgazer	homothallism	polytonality
satisfaction	adulteration	deactivation	humptydumpty	positiveness
satisfactory	adulterously	delitescence	hydatidiform	positivistic
satisfyingly	agentgeneral	denaturalise	hypothalamic	practicality
schismatical	alliteration	denaturation	hypothalamus	practitioner
secessionism	alliterative	deontologist	hypothecator	prenticeship
secessionist	altitudinous	deputisation	hypothetical	printability
selfsameness	amentiferous	diastrophism	ideationally	prostitution
selfstarting	amortisation	dilatability	identifiable	pyrotechnics

pyrotechnist	trustfulness	disputatious	throughstone	bonnyclabber
quantifiable	twentyfourmo	disquisition	tortuousness	collywobbles
quantisation	twitteringly	dissuasively	traducianism	dissymmetric
quantitative	unattractive	disturbingly	traducianist	embryologist
quarterbound	unauthorised	elocutionary	trifurcation	epicycloidal
quarterfinal	undetermined	elocutionist	ubiquitarian	fullyfledged
quarterstaff	unfathomable	elucubration	ubiquitously	geosynclinal
quattrocento	uninterested	encrustation	unblushingly	heavyhearted
questionable	valetudinary	enthusiastic	unctuousness	honeybuzzard
questionably	vauntcourier	epicureanism	untruthfully	jerrybuilder
questionless	vegetatively	evolutionary	vanquishable	mealymouthed
quintessence	visitational	evolutionism	vanquishment	merrythought
reactivation	visitatorial	evolutionist	virtuosoship	moneychanger
reactiveness	volatileness	exclusionary	virtuousness	moneygrubber
relationally	volitionally	exclusionism	ambivalently	moneyspinner
relationship	vomiturition	exclusionist	behaviourism	pennypincher
relativeness	waistcoating	excruciating	behaviourist	pennywhistle
relativistic	whortleberry	excruciation	benevolently	sandyachting
repatriation	absquatulate	executorship	caravansarai	stonyhearted
repetitional	accouchement	exhaustively	caravanserai	tachygrapher
repetitively	accoutrement	exiguousness	chauvinistic	tachygraphic
resettlement	adequateness	ferrugineous	derivational	topsyturvily
rightfulness	agglutinogen	fortuitously	derivatively	wallydraigle
salutariness	announcement	frequentness	equivalently	bedazzlement
salutational	apiculturist	furfuraceous	equivocation	embezzlement
salutiferous	astoundingly	gratuitously	equivocatory	horizontally
scatterbrain	auscultation	hallucinogen	grievousness	quizzicality
scatteringly	auscultatory	hallucinosis	immovability	schizogonous
scintigraphy	calculatedly	harquebusier	impoverished	schizomycete
scintillator	carburetting	incautiously	inadvertence	schizophrene
scratchiness	centuplicate	incrustation	inadvertency	schizothymia
semitropical	chequerboard	iniquitously	indivertible	schizothymic
shatterproof	cherubically	intrusionist	indivertibly	swizzlestick
shirtwaister	circuitously	laboursaving	individually	————————————
shootingiron	circumcision	languishment	irreverently	absquatulate
shortchanger	circumfluent	languorously	irreversible	abstractable
shortcircuit	circumfusion	linguistical	irreversibly	abstractedly
shortpitched	circumjacent	malnutrition	malevolently	abstractness
shortsighted	circumscribe	mercurialise	motivational	accurateness
shortsleeved	circumstance	mercurialism	omnivorously	accusatively
shortstaffed	colourlessly	misjudgement	reinvestment	accusatorial
sightreading	communicable	misquotation	reinvigorate	adaptability
skittishness	communicably	multungulate	rejuvenation	adequateness
sluttishness	communicator	noneuclidean	removability	advisability
solitariness	compulsively	obscurantism	revivalistic	aeronautical
somatopleure	compulsivity	obscurantist	reviviscence	aircraftsman
spectrograph	compulsorily	pasqueflower	selfviolence	alterability
spectrometer	compunctious	pellucidness	televisional	amalgamation
spectrometry	compurgation	percussively	thievishness	amalgamative
spectroscope	compurgatory	percutaneous	unfavourable	ambivalently
spectroscopy	concubitancy	perjuriously	unfavourably	amygdaloidal
sportfulness	concupiscent	persuasively	ungovernable	anagrammatic
sportiveness	concurrently	perturbation	unloveliness	antimacassar
squattocracy	conductivity	perturbative	backwardness	antimagnetic
steatopygous	conduplicate	polyurethane	backwoodsman	antimalarial
stertorously	Confucianism	presumptuous	birdwatching	antiparticle
stouthearted	confusedness	productively	downwardness	antipathetic
straticulate	conjunctival	productivity	freewheeling	antirachitic
stratigraphy	connubiality	promulgation	kilowatthour	apparatchiki
stratosphere	conquistador	protuberance	longwindedly	apparatchiks
stutteringly	consultation	quaquaversal	lukewarmness	approachable
substantiate	consultative	rambunctious	shrewishness	Australasian
substantival	consummately	recrudescent	sidewhiskers	autocatalyse
substitution	consummation	renouncement	stalwartness	automaticity
substitutive	consummative	resoundingly	unlawfulness	availability
substruction	consummatory	sanguinarily	untowardness	bacchanalian
substructure	contumacious	sanguineness	detoxication	backwardness
sweetishness	contumelious	sanguinolent	intoxication	benefactress
temptability	convulsively	sarrusophone	nonexistence	bequeathment
teratologist	curmudgeonly	seclusionist	peroxidation	biographical
teratomatous	denouncement	sensualistic	preexistence	birdwatching
theatregoing	desquamation	sensuousness	analytically	burglarproof
theatrically	desquamative	septuagenary	arrhythmical	cantharidian
tightmouthed	desquamatory	Septuagesima	asphyxiation	capitalistic
toastingfork	disbursement	Septuagintal	bathypelagic	caravansarai
togetherness	discursively	sesquialtera	bellylanding	caravanserai
tractability	disguisement	statuesquely	biosynthesis	cardcarrying
traitorously	disgustfully	subcutaneous	biosynthetic	caricaturist
trestletable	disgustingly	testudineous	bobbydazzler	carriageable

chaplainship	grammaticise	orographical	Stakhanovite	horribleness
charlatanism	gyromagnetic	overcautious	stalwartness	horsebreaker
chrematistic	habitability	palatability	standardbred	housebreaker
chromaticism	hardfavoured	paramagnetic	stepdaughter	hyperbolical
chromaticity	hemiparasite	paratactical	substantiate	interbedding
chromatogram	heritability	pejoratively	substantival	jerrybuilder
chromatology	hesitatingly	pericarditis	superannuate	laudableness
chromatopsia	highfaluting	permeability	surrealistic	microbiology
cinematheque	highhandedly	persuasively	teachability	mouthbreeder
clairaudient	holidaymaker	pharmaceutic	temptability	moveableness
complacently	hoodmanblind	pharmacology	thaumaturgic	neighbouring
complaisance	hyperacidity	philharmonic	thousandfold	neurobiology
congratulant	hypogastrium	pinfeathered	tolerability	nitrobenzene
congratulate	immovability	pleasantness	traceability	overabundant
constabulary	immutability	plumbaginous	tractability	paedobaptism
contractable	imperatively	pneumaticity	trochanteric	perambulator
contractedly	imperatorial	pneumatology	trophallaxis	pilotballoon
contractible	imputability	portmanteaus	unassailable	pitiableness
contradictor	imputatively	portmanteaux	underachieve	prefabricate
contrapuntal	incapability	pragmatistic	unmanageable	protuberance
contrariness	incapacitate	preclassical	unparalleled	radiobiology
contrariwise	increasingly	printability	unpleasantly	readableness
copulatively	incurability	proclamation	unsteadiness	reliableness
corelatively	indicatively	proclamatory	untowardness	rememberable
cryptanalyst	ineffaceable	programmable	vegetatively	remembrancer
crystalgazer	ineffaceably	programmatic	venerability	reverberator
cumulatively	irregardless	prothalamion	visitational	selfabsorbed
debonairness	irrelatively	prothalamium	visitatorial	sensibleness
decoratively	irritability	pyromaniacal	viviparously	skateboarder
decreasingly	irritatingly	Quadragesima	wallpainting	sociableness
deescalation	isodiametric	quadrangular	wellfavoured	speedboating
delicatessen	journalistic	whigmaleerie	stockbreeder
derivational	kilowatthour	quadraphonic	woolgatherer	stockbroking
derivatively	laureateship	quaquaversal	acetabularia	stoneboiling
derogatorily	lefthandedly	recreational	adorableness	suitableness
desirability	liberalistic	removability	Alhambresque	swashbuckler
desolateness	literariness	reproachable	alphabetical	syllabically
desquamation	lukewarmness	reproachless	amenableness	tangibleness
desquamative	maintainable	restrainable	amicableness	terribleness
desquamatory	malleability	restrainedly	amphibiously	thirdborough
diagrammatic	manslaughter	revelational	amphibrachic	underbidding
diaphanously	manufacturer	revivalistic	attributable	valuableness
dilatability	marriageable	rheumatology	blackbirding	variableness
disclamation	matriarchate	ruminatively	blamableness	vertebration
disfranchise	meditatively	saccharinity	blockbusting	voidableness
displaceable	merchantable	saccharoidal	bloodbrother	workableness
displacement	metagalactic	salamandrian	brassbounder	youngberries
dissuasively	metalanguage	salamandrine	Cantabrigian	acciaccatura
distractedly	microanalyst	salamandroid	cherubically	accouchement
distrainable	militaristic	salutariness	childbearing	amphictyonic
distrainment	milliammeter	salutational	coachbuilder	angiocarpous
dodecahedral	mineralogist	sandyachting	coenobitical	annunciation
dodecahedron	misplacement	scabbardfish	coenobytical	apperception
dodecaphonic	misstatement	scandalously	collaborator	apperceptive
downwardness	mistranslate	secularistic	concubitancy	appreciation
dubitatively	moderateness	selfcatering	confabulator	appreciative
ectoparasite	monomaniacal	selfsameness	connubiality	appreciatory
encroachment	morphallaxis	semibasement	corroborator	attractively
endamagement	motivational	semidarkness	crackbrained	auspiciously
endocarditis	mountainside	semiparasite	craftbrother	avariciously
endoparasite	mucilaginous	sensualistic	crossbedding	beachcombing
entreatingly	naturalistic	separability	crossbencher	beseechingly
envisagement	nauseatingly	separateness	crossbuttock	bespectacled
epigrammatic	navigability	septuagenary	culpableness	bewitchingly
epithalamion	navigational	Septuagesima	disambiguate	blackcurrant
epithalamium	neoclassical	Septuagintal	disembarrass	bonnyclabber
equitability	Neoplatonism	sergeantfish	elucubration	capercaillie
equivalently	Neoplatonist	sergeantship	encumberment	capercailzie
excitability	neuroanatomy	serjeantship	encumbrancer	capriciously
exhilaration	newspaperman	slipcarriage	enfeeblement	characterise
exhilarative	nominalistic	snapfastener	enviableness	cirrocumulus
figuratively	nonchalantly	solitariness	exprobration	clavicembalo
filtrability	nonflammable	specialistic	forcibleness	closecropped
flammability	obdurateness	spermaphytic	frontbencher	collectively
foundationer	obligatorily	spermathecal	glassblowing	collectivise
fountainhead	occupational	spermatocyte	hairsbreadth	collectivism
geographical	openhandedly	spermatozoid	handsbreadth	collectivist
gladiatorial	opposability	spermatozoon	heartburning	collectivity
grallatorial	ordinariness	Stakhanovism	honeybuzzard	conductivity

confectioner	intracardiac	resuscitator	cowardliness	subsidiarily
Confucianism	intracranial	retractation	curmudgeonly	succedaneous
connectional	jurisconsult	retractility	disendowment	taberdarship
connectively	leucocytosis	retrocedence	dislodgement	testudineous
consecration	leukocytosis	retrocession	eavesdropped	towardliness
consecratory	loquaciously	retrocessive	eavesdropper	transduction
consociation	machicolated	rhinocerotic	episodically	underdevelop
convectional	macrocephaly	rhizocarpous	extraditable	unkindliness
correctional	melancholiac	scratchiness	fastidiously	wallydraigle
correctitude	mendaciously	selfactivity	forbiddingly	acaulescence
correctively	microcapsule	sepulchrally	friendliness	acceleration
criticalness	microcephaly	sequaciously	granodiorite	accelerative
crosscountry	microcircuit	serviceberry	groundcherry	accidentally
crosscurrent	microclimate	servicecourt	groundlessly	acquiescence
curvicaudate	microcopying	servicewoman	haberdashery	adulteration
curvicostate	microcrystal	servocontrol	heraldically	adulterously
denticulated	moneychanger	sharecropper	hybridisable	aeroneurosis
denunciation	mordaciously	shortchanger	hydrodynamic	aesthetician
denunciative	motorcyclist	shortcircuit	imponderable	aestheticism
denunciatory	multicentral	silviculture	imponderably	alkalescence
depreciation	myrmecophily	skunkcabbage	incandescent	alliteration
depreciatory	nailscissors	smallclothes	incendiarism	alliterative
dialectician	neglectfully	snakecharmer	ineradicable	ambidextrous
dialectology	nightclothes	stalactiform	ineradicably	anathematise
disaccharide	nomenclative	stonecutting	infundibular	anotherguess
disenchanter	nomenclature	subjectively	interdiction	antecedently
disincentive	noneuclidean	subjectivise	interdictive	antigenicity
dissocialise	oblanceolate	subjectivism	interdictory	antineutrino
dissociation	omnisciently	subjectivist	interdigital	antiperiodic
dissociative	overachiever	subjectivity	introduction	antiSemitism
encirclement	overactivity	sufficiently	introductory	apothegmatic
epicycloidal	pantechnicon	supercharger	jurisdiction	apparentness
escutcheoned	participator	superciliary	kaleidoscope	arborescence
ethnocentric	particularly	supercilious	lopsidedness	archdeaconry
excruciating	pedunculated	suspiciously	methodically	asymmetrical
excruciation	pellucidness	sylviculture	misjudgement	backpedalled
explicitness	perfectively	syndactylism	multidentate	barometrical
extracranial	perniciously	syndactylous	onesidedness	baselessness
fallaciously	pernoctation	tetrachordal	orchidaceous	battleground
floriculture	phagocytosis	Torricellian	orthodontics	battlemented
folliculated	phagocytotic	traducianism	orthodontist	bilateralism
furunculosis	photochromic	traducianist	Palladianism	biochemistry
geotectonics	pisciculture	tragicomical	peccadilloes	biocoenology
gesticulator	plainclothed	transcendent	perfidiously	blabbermouth
graveclothes	plainclothes	tridactylous	periodically	bladderwrack
guestchamber	planoconcave	tuberculated	periodontics	blatherskite
gynaecocracy	precociously	tuberculosis	periodontist	bletherskate
hallucinogen	predictively	turriculated	philadelphus	blisteringly
hallucinosis	prefectorial	uncalculated	philodendron	blithesomely
handicapping	preoccupancy	underclothes	plaindealing	blunderingly
heliocentric	pricecutting	undercoating	Plattdeutsch	blusteringly
heroicalness	productively	undercurrent	precedential	boisterously
heroicomical	productivity	undercutting	premeditated	boogiewoogie
hippocentaur	proficiently	ungracefully	premeditator	booklearning
horticulture	projectional	ungraciously	presidential	bootlessness
hydrochloric	projectively	unmercifully	prosodically	bottlewasher
iconoclastic	prosectorial	unsuccessful	providential	bullheadedly
imperceptive	prosecutable	Valenciennes	pteridophyte	businesslike
impercipient	protactinium	vauntcourier	pteridosperm	cabinetmaker
implicitness	protectively	vermiculated	pterodactyle	calorescence
incalculable	protectorate	vernacularly	recrudescent	candleholder
incalculably	publicspirit	verticalness	regardlessly	carelessness
inconcinnity	pugnaciously	verticillate	reproducible	cattlelifter
inconclusive	ratiocinator	vindictively	reproduction	centrespread
indiscipline	recalcitrant	wainscotting	reproductive	chancemedley
indiscreetly	recalcitrate	waistcoating	rhododendron	charnelhouse
indiscretion	reconcilable	accordionist	sacerdotally	charterhouse
inexactitude	reflectional	appendectomy	scoundreldom	charterparty
inflectional	reflectively	appendicitis	scoundrelism	checkerberry
inspectorate	reflectivity	appendicular	secondstring	checkerboard
inspectorial	refractivity	balladmonger	selfeducated	cheeseburger
interception	refractorily	bewilderedly	selfidentity	cheesecutter
intercession	renunciation	bewilderment	shoulderbelt	cheesemonger
intercessory	renunciative	bobbydazzler	shoulderknot	cheeseparing
interchanger	renunciatory	campodeiform	shouldernote	chequerboard
interconnect	repercussion	commodiously	skullduggery	chesterfield
intercropped	repercussive	confidential	splendidness	chimneypiece
intercurrent	respectfully	considerable	sporadically	chitterlings
intercutting	respectively	considerably	stonedresser	clapperboard

clatteringly	fiddlesticks	irreversibly	quarterbound	swaggerstick
clinkerbuilt	flatteringly	Ishmaelitish	quarterfinal	syncretistic
clotheshorse	flickeringly	isothermally	quarterstaff	tactlessness
clothespress	fluorescence	juvenescence	quintessence	tamelessness
complemental	formlessness	laisserfaire	rabblerouser	taperecorder
completeness	frequentness	laissezaller	radioelement	tearlessness
complexional	gamopetalous	laissezfaire	rattleheaded	theoretician
complexioned	gamosepalous	leathercloth	razzledazzle	thitherwards
compressible	geochemistry	lifelessness	reappearance	thundercloud
concrescence	glaucescence	listlessness	reassessment	thunderingly
concreteness	glitteringly	loungelizard	recalescence	thunderously
congregation	glockenspiel	lovelessness	recklessness	thunderstone
cotyledonary	gobbledegook	luminescence	recuperation	thunderstorm
cotyledonous	gobbledygook	malapertness	recuperative	timelessness
countenancer	goodtempered	maltreatment	regeneration	tirelessness
counteragent	gramnegative	manometrical	regenerative	tittletattle
counterblast	halogenation	mediaevalism	regimentally	toggleswitch
countercheck	handkerchief	mediaevalist	reinvestment	tonelessness
counterclaim	hardfeatured	mesocephalic	rejuvenation	triggerhappy
counterforce	harmlessness	middleweight	remuneration	trumpetshell
counterlight	harquebusier	mindlessness	remunerative	tunelessness
countermarch	heathenishly	minedetector	remuneratory	turtlenecked
counterplead	heedlessness	mistreatment	residentiary	twitteringly
counterpoint	helplessness	mistressship	residentship	unacceptable
counterpoise	homosexually	monadelphous	resplendence	unaffectedly
counterproof	hopelessness	monometallic	resplendency	unappeasable
counterscarp	hubblebubble	monopetalous	restlessness	unappetising
countershaft	hucklebacked	monumentally	rontgenogram	uncelebrated
countertenor	illiberality	movelessness	rontgenology	uncomeatable
crossexamine	illiterately	muddleheaded	rootlessness	undetermined
cynocephalus	illtreatment	muzzleloader	rumbletumble	unexpectedly
cytogenetics	immaterially	namelessness	ruthlessness	ungovernable
decalescence	immoderately	needlessness	saddlebacked	uninterested
deceleration	immoderation	nonagenarian	scatterbrain	unlikelihood
degenerately	impenetrable	nonidentical	scatteringly	unlikeliness
degeneration	impenetrably	northeastern	sclerenchyma	unloveliness
degenerative	impoverished	northernmost	scraperboard	unregenerate
deliberately	inaccessible	obedientiary	selfbegotten	unrepeatable
deliberation	inaccessibly	obliteration	selfbetrayal	unreservedly
deliberative	inadvertence	obliterative	selfdeceived	unscientific
delitescence	inadvertency	obmutescence	selfdeceiver	untimeliness
demineralise	inappeasable	obsolescence	selfdelusion	viridescence
desideration	incalescence	obsoleteness	selfdestruct	vituperation
desiderative	incatenation	obstreperous	selfdevotion	vituperative
detumescence	incidentally	occidentally	selflessness	vituperatory
diathermancy	incineration	octogenarian	selfreliance	vociferation
discreetness	incoherently	officeholder	selfreproach	vociferously
discreteness	indefeasible	ornamentally	semideponent	volumetrical
discretional	indefeasibly	overpersuade	semidetached	walkietalkie
disobedience	indefectible	overreaction	sexagenarian	weatherboard
displeasedly	indefensible	oxyacetylene	shatterproof	weatherbound
doubleacting	indefensibly	painlessness	simpleminded	weatherglass
doubledealer	independence	pancreatitis	singleacting	weatherhouse
doubledecked	independency	parametrical	singledecker	weatherproof
doubledecker	indigenously	pasqueflower	singlehanded	whencesoever
doublelocked	indigestible	pearlescence	singleminded	whimperingly
endometritis	indirectness	pedicellaria	singleseater	whisperingly
enginedriver	indivertible	peerlessness	slanderously	whitherwards
enginetuning	indivertibly	penitentiary	sledgehammer	williewaught
ephemerality	IndoGermanic	perplexingly	slipperiness	winklepicker
epiphenomena	inexpediency	philhellenic	softpedalled	YankeeDoodle
epistemology	inexpedience	phrasemonger	soullessness	beatifically
erythematous	inexperience	phraseograph	southeastern	blamefulness
euhemeristic	inexpertness	pitcherplant	southernmost	blastfurnace
evangelistic	inextensible	pitilessness	southernwood	blissfulness
evisceration	inobservance	plasterboard	spiegeleisen	boastfulness
exaggeration	inteneration	plummerblock	spotlessness	brickfielder
exaggerative	interestedly	polyneuritic	squarerigged	cheerfulness
exaggeratory	intolerantly	polyneuritis	staggeringly	curvifoliate
exasperation	intumescence	polypetalous	stammeringly	decaffeinate
exenteration	inveterately	polysepalous	statuesquely	disaffection
exulceration	irredeemable	postmeridian	stellenbosch	disaffiliate
facelessness	irredeemably	praiseworthy	stutteringly	disinfectant
fearlessness	irrelevantly	princeliness	supereminent	disinfection
featherbrain	irremediable	propaedeutic	supererogate	disinflation
featheriness	irremediably	prosperously	supplemental	doubtfulness
fecklessness	irrepealable	puerperrally	supplementer	dreadfulness
feebleminded	irreverently	pyrotechnics	suppressible	exsufflicate
fiddlefaddle	irreversible	pyrotechnist	swaggeringly	faithfulness

fancifulness	toploftiness	greengrocery	reprographic	heavyhearted
faultfinding	torrefaction	hagiographer	revengefully	hedgehopping
forcefulness	transferable	hagiographic	rhizogenetic	hemichordate
fruitfulness	transference	hectographic	risorgimento	henotheistic
fullyfledged	transferring	heliographer	salpiglossis	homothallism
gracefulness	transformism	heliographic	scenographic	hypochlorite
gratefulness	transformist	heliogravure	selfignition	hypochondria
gratifyingly	transfusible	hieroglyphic	sphragistics	hypophrygian
guilefulness	trustfulness	hierographer	sporogenesis	hypothalamic
habitforming	truthfulness	histogenesis	stenographer	hypothalamus
henceforward	unconformity	histogenetic	stenographic	hypothecator
horrifically	unlawfulness	hydrographer	straightaway	hypothetical
hydrofluoric	unprofitable	hydrographic	straightbred	idiothermous
imperfection	unprofitably	hymnographer	straightedge	immethodical
imperfective	vengefulness	hypnogenesis	straightener	kirschwasser
inconformity	vitrifaction	hypnogenetic	straightness	largehearted
indifference	wastefulness	iconographer	stranglehold	lighthearted
indifferency	watchfulness	impregnation	strengthener	longshoreman
insufferable	wrathfulness	interglacial	strengthless	Manicheanism
insufferably	wrongfulness	intriguingly	stringcourse	marshharrier
insufficient	youthfulness	inveiglement	strongminded	mesothoracic
insufflation	aboriginally	laryngoscope	strongylosis	metachronism
interfemoral	agamogenesis	laryngoscopy	stylographic	metaphorical
interference	agamogenetic	lithographer	tachygrapher	metaphrastic
liquefacient	agentgeneral	lithographic	tachygraphic	metaphysical
liquefaction	anagogically	liturgically	tetragonally	metatheatical
magnifically	analogically	liturgiology	throughstone	metathoracic
magnificence	anemographic	majorgeneral	transgressor	misbehaviour
mercifulness	avantgardism	mastigophora	triangularly	mitochondria
mirthfulness	avantgardist	micrographer	umbrageously	monochromate
mournfulness	belligerence	moneygrubber	undergarment	monophyletic
multifarious	belligerency	mulligatawny	unimaginable	Monophysitic
multiflorous	bilingualism	mythographer	unimaginably	monotheistic
multifoliate	biologically	necrographer	vantagepoint	nychthemeral
multiformity	blackguardly	organgrinder	vicargeneral	nychthemeron
mystifyingly	cabbagewhite	orthogenesis	analphabetic	oncorhynchus
noneffective	calligrapher	orthogenetic	antiphonally	opisthograph
nonefficient	calligraphic	orthographer	antithetical	opisthotonos
peacefulness	carragheenin	orthographic	apprehension	ornithomancy
petrifaction	cartographer	osteogenesis	apprehensive	ornithoscopy
pettifoggery	cartographic	outrageously	asynchronism	paraphrastic
pettifogging	chorographic	paedogenesis	asynchronous	parochialise
photofission	closegrained	paedogenetic	autochthones	parochialism
pontifically	collegialism	palingenesia	breathalyser	parochiality
pontificator	collegiality	palingenesis	breathlessly	peripherally
pridefulness	collegiately	palingenetic	breathtaking	periphrastic
prizefighter	consignation	pantographic	breechloader	phosphoresce
prolifically	contagionist	pathogenesis	bronchoscope	polychaetous
prolificness	contagiously	pathogenetic	carbohydrate	polychromous
putrefaction	contiguously	petrographer	catachrestic	polyphyletic
putrefactive	cosmogonical	petrographic	cataphoresis	polytheistic
retroflexion	cosmographer	phonographer	catechetical	protohistory
rightfulness	cosmographic	phonographic	churchianity	proudhearted
satisfaction	courageously	photogeology	churchwarden	reprehension
satisfactory	crossgrained	photographer	cliffhanging	reprehensive
satisfyingly	decongestant	photographic	coldshoulder	rhynchophora
scarificator	decongestion	photogravure	crossheading	ricochetting
scornfulness	decongestive	phylogenesis	decipherable	scareheading
selfaffected	deflagration	phylogenetic	decipherment	seraphically
selfeffacing	diamagnetism	phytogenesis	delightfully	sidewhiskers
semiofficial	discographer	phytogenetic	detachedness	slaughterous
shamefacedly	disingenuous	phytographer	diphtheritic	slaveholding
shamefulness	disregardful	pictographic	diphthongise	smallholding
significance	ecologically	pornographer	draughtboard	speechlessly
significancy	endangerment	pornographic	draughthorse	sprightfully
slothfulness	entanglement	precognition	draughtiness	stepchildren
sorbefacient	epexegetical	precognitive	encephalitic	stillhunting
specifically	ethnographer	predigestion	encephalitis	stonyhearted
specificness	ethnographic	primigravida	eunuchoidism	stouthearted
spitefulness	exsanguinate	primogenital	exospherical	strophanthin
sportfulness	exsanguinous	primogenitor	fainthearted	strychninism
stupefacient	extinguisher	prodigiously	faithhealing	superhighway
stupefaction	farsightedly	prolegomenon	freethinking	superhumanly
stupefactive	ferrugineous	propagandise	freewheeling	sycophantish
subinfeudate	fieldglasses	propagandism	freightliner	tetrahedrite
tastefulness	galligaskins	propagandist	frenchpolish	thoughtfully
terrifically	geologically	radiographer	gamophyllous	togetherness
terrifyingly	geomagnetism	radiographic	greathearted	transhipment
thankfulness	glycogenesis	refrigerator	headshrinker	transhumance

```
unauthorised   coerciveness   equidistance   imperishably   negativeness
unfathomable   cohabitation   equilibrator   impetiginous   negativistic
vicechairman   cohesiveness   eruptiveness   impoliteness   negotiatress
wholehearted   coincidental   etherisation   inactivation   nicotinamide
wretchedness   coincidently   excogitation   inadmissible   nidification
abortiveness   colonisation   excogitative   inadmissibly   nonalignment
abrasiveness   colorimetric   exercitation   inarticulate   nonexistence
acquaintance   complication   exhibitioner   inartificial   notification
adaptiveness   conchiferous   exorbitantly   inaudibility   novelisation
additionally   conidiophore   expediential   incisiveness   obligingness
adhesiveness   conidiospore   experiential   indecisively   obnubilation
adjudication   conquistador   experimental   indefinitely   occasionally
adjudicative   conscionable   experimenter   indehiscence   openmindedly
adjudicatory   conspiration   exploitation   indelibility   oppositeness
administrant   constipation   exploitative   indelicately   oppositional
administrate   constituency   facilitation   individually   optimisation
admonishment   constitution   faintishness   inefficiency   organisation
aerosiderite   constitutive   felicitation   infelicitous   ossification
allusiveness   containerise   felicitously   infiniteness   overniceness
amentiferous   contribution   feminineness   infinitively   oversimplify
amortisation   contributive   feminisation   infusibility   pacification
anastigmatic   contributory   feverishness   inhabitation   pacificatory
annihilation   contriteness   fiendishness   iniquitously   panification
annihilative   contrivement   finalisation   inordinately   paradigmatic
antediluvian   coordinately   firefighting   insemination   paradisaical
antiaircraft   coordination   fluidisation   intimidation   paradisiacal
anticipation   coordinative   fluoridation   intimidatory   paramilitary
anticipative   councilwoman   fluorination   intoxication   parasiticide
anticipatory   creativeness   focalisation   invagination   parasitology
apparitional   crossingover   foraminifera   invalidation   penalisation
appetisingly   deactivation   foresightful   invigilation   peroxidation
appositeness   debilitation   fortuitously   invisibility   perspicacity
appositional   decapitation   fractionally   irascibility   perspiration
appraisement   decisiveness   fractionator   irrationally   perspiratory
appraisingly   definiteness   frangibility   irremissible   plausibility
arborisation   definitively   frankincense   irresistible   pleasingness
archdiocesan   deionisation   freakishness   irresistibly   plumbiferous
artificially   delamination   frictionless   kremlinology   pointilliste
assibilation   delimitation   frontiersman   labyrinthian   polarimetric
assimilation   delusiveness   frontispiece   labyrinthine   polarisation
assimilative   demilitarise   fructiferous   lacininiated   polyhistoric
assimilatory   demoniacally   fructivorous   languishment   positiveness
astonishment   denomination   fugitiveness   laterisation   positivistic
autodidactic   denominative   fuliginosity   laticiferous   postdiluvian
basidiospore   depoliticise   functionally   latinisation   postmistress
behaviourism   deputisation   functionless   legalisation   practicality
behaviourist   deracination   futilitarian   legitimately   practitioner
beneficently   derisiveness   ganglionated   legitimation   preeminently
beneficially   desalination   gasification   legitimatise   preexistence
bioscientist   despairingly   geanticlinal   libidinously   prenticeship
blandishment   detoxication   ghoulishness   linguistical   prevailingly
bombdisposal   dilapidation   graspingness   localisation   priggishness
borosilicate   diminishable   gratuitously   longdistance   principality
brackishness   diminishment   greenishness   longwindedly   profligately
brilliantine  discriminant   guardianship   luminiferous   proprietress
bullfighting   discriminate   habilitation   Marseillaise   prostitution
calamitously   disdainfully   halftimbered   materialness   psychiatrist
calorimetric   disguisement   headmistress   maximisation   punchingball
canaliculate   disjointedly   hereditament   meridionally   purblindness
canalisation   disorientate   hereditarily   messeigneurs   purification
canonisation   disquisition   homesickness   minimisation   purificatory
catilinarian   distributary   humanisation   misalignment   pyroligneous
championship   distribution   humanitarian   mithridatise   quadriennium
chastisement   distributive   humification   mithridatism   quadrinomial
chauvinistic   divarication   hydatidiform   mitrailleuse   quadriplegia
childishness   divisibility   idealisation   mobilisation   quadriplegic
chlorination   divisiveness   ideationally   modification   quadrivalent
churlishness   dressinggown   identifiable   modificatory   qualmishness
circuitously   dwarfishness   illegibility   monetisation   quantifiable
civilisation   effeminately   illegitimacy   monofilament   quantisation
clannishness   effusiveness   illegitimate   moralisation   quantitative
classicalism   emancipation   illogicality   motorisation   questionable
classicalist   emargination   illumination   mourningband   questionably
classicality   emulsifiable   illuminative   mourningring   questionless
classifiable   enantiomorph   illusiveness   municipalise   quizzicality
claudication   enshrinement   immunisation   municipality   racemisation
clownishness   equalisation   impedimental   munificently   radioisotope
cockfighting   equalitarian   impenitently   musicianship   ramification
codification   equationally   imperishable   nebulisation   ratification
```

reactivation	strikingness	interjection	flagellation	preselective
reactiveness	strobilation	interjectory	flagellatory	promulgation
reassignment	studdingsail	introjection	floodlighted	proselytiser
recapitulate	subeditorial	nonobjective	footplateman	pyroelectric
reducibility	suberisation	stockjobbery	formaldehyde	radiological
rehabilitate	substitution	stockjobbing	genealogical	rebelliously
reinvigorate	substitutive	surrejoinder	genuflection	recollection
relationally	sudoriferous	unprejudiced	geopolitical	recollective
relationship	supplicantly	endoskeletal	gesellschaft	redeployment
relativeness	supplication	housekeeping	gravelelling	rhinological
relativistic	supplicatory	hydrokinetic	grovellingly	sacrilegious
remilitarise	surprisingly	karyokinesis	hagiological	scatological
reminiscence	surveillance	kinnikinnick	heliolatrous	schoolfellow
repetitional	swainishness	mistakenness	histological	schoolleaver
repetitively	sweepingness	photokinesis	hydrological	schoolmaster
resiniferous	sweetishness	photokinetic	hydrolysable	schorlaceous
resipiscence	swimmingbath	unbrokenness	inapplicable	scutellation
restrictedly	swimmingbell	acetaldehyde	inapplicably	selfelective
resupination	swimmingpool	aetiological	indeclinable	selfflattery
retiringness	taskmistress	anthelmintic	inexplicable	selfpleasing
reviviscence	technicality	anticlerical	inexplicably	semiological
romanisation	technicolour	apiculturist	installation	septilateral
ruralisation	televisional	argillaceous	instillation	shuffleboard
salutiferous	terebinthine	artilleryman	intellection	sideslipping
Samaritanism	thereinafter	astrological	intellective	snaggletooth
sanguinarily	thievishness	auscultation	intellectual	sociological
sanguineness	ticklishness	auscultatory	intelligence	solifluction
sanguinolent	toastingfork	bachelorhood	intelligible	somniloquism
saponifiable	totalisation	bachelorship	intelligibly	somniloquist
Scandinavian	totalitarian	backslapping	interlobular	steeplechase
scintigraphy	touchingness	bellylanding	interlocutor	subcelestial
scintillator	transiliency	benzaldehyde	irreflective	swizzlestick
scorpionfish	transitional	berzelianite	limnological	symbolically
scouringrush	transitively	bloodletting	lithological	tautological
scrobiculate	transitivity	brambleberry	magniloquent	taxcollector
scurrilously	transitorily	buffalograss	mangelwurzel	teleological
selfdirected	trephination	calculatedly	marvellously	tessellation
selfdistrust	trickishness	cancellation	metallically	thimbleberry
selflimiting	triplication	cantillation	metallophone	translatable
selffrighting	typification	carillonneur	metallurgist	translucence
selfviolence	ubiquitarian	cartological	metrological	translucency
semicircular	ubiquitously	catholically	miscalculate	trestletable
semidiameter	unambivalent	chivalrously	miscellanist	tropological
semifinalist	unbelievable	chocolatebox	misselthrush	troublemaker
semifinished	unbelievably	chorological	multilateral	turbellarian
semiliterate	underinsured	compellation	multilingual	unapologetic
seminiferous	unfamiliarly	compulsively	multiloquous	underletting
sesquialtera	unhesitating	compulsivity	mythological	undiplomatic
sheepishness	unionisation	compulsorily	mythologiser	unemployable
shootingiron	unofficially	concelebrant	nanoplankton	unemployment
shrewishness	unscriptural	concelebrate	necrological	unifoliolate
silicicolous	urbanisation	conciliation	Neohellenism	unwieldiness
siliciferous	valorisation	conciliative	nephelometer	unworldiness
simoniacally	vanquishable	conciliatory	nephelometry	unyieldingly
skippingrope	vanquishment	consolidator	neurological	vainglorious
skittishness	vaporisation	consultation	noctilucence	whitelivered
sleepingpill	vasodilation	consultative	oscillograph	whortleberry
sluggishness	vasodilatory	convalescent	oscilloscope	wineglassful
sluttishness	vaticination	convulsively	osteological	abstemiously
snappishness	ventripotent	cosmological	panhellenism	academically
snarlingiron	veridicality	crashlanding	parallelling	accommodator
snobbishness	verification	crenellation	pathological	achlamydeous
solarisation	verificatory	dentilingual	perfoliation	aeroembolism
solicitation	veterinarian	denuclearise	pestilential	AfroAmerican
solicitously	vilification	despoliation	pestological	alphamerical
soporiferous	villainously	diabolically	petrological	anatomically
soundingline	vinification	disallowance	phenological	arithmetical
sparkingplug	vitalisation	distillation	philological	autoimmunity
speakingtube	vitiligation	distillatory	phonological	avitaminoses
sportiveness	vivification	earsplitting	phycological	avitaminosis
stablishment	vocalisation	encyclopedia	phytological	bantamweight
standingroom	volatileness	encyclopedic	pluriliteral	bowcompasses
stanniferous	volitionally	ethnological	poikilotherm	brinkmanship
stelliferous	voluminosity	etymological	polyglottism	chairmanship
sterlingness	voluminously	etymologicon	porcelainise	circumcision
stockingless	welldisposed	extralimital	porcelainous	circumfluent
Stradivarius	whimsicality	fertilisable	porcellanous	circumfusion
straticulate	womanishness	fibrillation	predilection	circumjacent
stratigraphy	worshipfully	flabelliform	preselection	circumscribe

```
circumstance misdemeanour bodysnatcher dissentingly multungulate
closemouthed neonomianism bookingclerk distinctness muttonheaded
commemorator noctambulant brokenwinded drawingboard nephanalysis
concomitance noctambulism buccaneering drawingpaper nonconductor
condemnation noctambulist buccaneerish duckingstool nonconformer
condemnatory noctambulous burningglass elementalism outlandishly
consummately noncombatant cachinnation elementarily outmanoeuvre
consummation noncommittal cachinnatory embranchment outpensioner
consummative noncomplying calumniation enchantingly parkinsonism
consummatory oneupmanship calumniatory entrancement permanganate
contemplator osteomalacia calumniously entrenchment pertinacious
contemporary overemphasis camiknickers espagnolette philanthrope
contemporise paedomorphic cantankerous estrangement philanthropy
contemptible parsimonious carbonaceous euphonically pigeonbreast
contemptibly phenomenally carcinogenic euphoniously pigmentation
contemptuous phonemically cardinalship eveningdress platonically
contumacious photomontage cashandcarry evidentially playingfield
contumelious phycomycetes clarinettist exchangeable portentously
courtmartial predominance coelenterate explantation precancelled
cuprammonium predominancy coetaneously extraneously precondition
customshouse presumptuous collinearity falcongentil preconscious
determinable pronominally columniation falcongentle prehensility
determinably recommitment combinations fermentation premenstrual
determinedly rhythmically commandingly fermentative preponderant
diatomaceous salesmanship commencement fibrinolysin preponderate
discomfiture sarcomatosis commendation firstnighter presentation
discommodity schismatical commendatory gallinaceous presentative
discomposure selfemployed commensalism galvanically presentiment
disseminator sociometrist commensalist galvanometer preventative
dissimilarly somnambulant commensurate galvanoscope preventively
dissimulator somnambulate commentation geosynclinal proconsulate
dissymmetric somnambulism commonwealth Germanophile progenitress
distemperate somnambulist communicable Germanophobe prolongation
econometrics sphygmograph communicably governmental protensively
economically stagemanager communicator governorship provincially
emblematical stonemasonry companionate graminaceous prudentially
endermically subcommittee companionway guaranteeing rabbinically
entrammelled subtemperate compensation happenstance radionuclide
epidemically supermundane compensative harmonically rambunctious
epidemiology supramundane compensatory harmoniously recognisable
EuroAmerican systematical compunctious heavenliness recognisably
exterminable systematiser concentrator hereinbefore recognisance
exterminator systemically condensation hermeneutics renouncement
extramarital testamentary congeniality hibernaculum resignedness
extramundane tetramorphic congenitally horrendously resoundingly
gamesmanship tightmouthed conjunctival hygienically responsively
hebdomadally transmigrant conningtower hypognathous responsorial
homeomorphic transmigrate consensually implantation retrenchment
horsemanship transmission consentience inclinometer rollingstock
hydromedusae transmissive consentingly incognisable runningboard
hydromedusan transmitting contingently incognisance salmonladder
impermanence transmogrify continuation incognitable sardonically
impermanency transmontane continuative infringement screenwriter
incommodious transmutable continuously internuclear segmentation
incommutable trinomialism conveniently internuncial selfanalysis
incommutably ultramontane conventicler intransigent selfinterest
inflammation ultramundane conventional intransitive selfinvolved
inflammatory uncommercial convincement intrenchment sellingplate
inharmonious uncommonness convincingly invulnerable semiannually
intermeddler undermanning cottonocracy invulnerably sententially
intermediacy watermanship cousingerman katzenjammer septennially
intermediary aircondition cuckingstool kissingcrust sequentially
intermediate alimentation curlingirons landingcraft serpentiform
interminable alimentative curlingtongs landingfield serpentinely
interminably alphanumeric declinometer landingstage sexcentenary
intermission announcement denouncement landingstrip siphonophore
intermittent astoundingly despondently lodginghouse siphonostele
intermitting astringently diamonddrill maidenliness slovenliness
intermixture astronautics diamondfield maidenstakes steganograph
intermundane astronomical diatonically malcontented stupendously
intramundane attorneyship dibranchiate marlinespike subconscious
intromission augmentation disannulling meaningfully subcontinent
intromittent augmentative disannulment mechanically subminiature
intromitting authenticate disconnected meetinghouse subsonically
judgematical authenticity disconnexion meltingpoint succinctness
marksmanship billingsgate disconsolate mercantilism supernaculum
mathematical biosynthesis discontented mercantilist supernatural
mealymouthed biosynthetic dispensation morningdress suspensively
misdemeanant birdsnesting dispensatory multinuclear sustentation
```

sustentative	chronography	glyptography	monomorphous	psychopathic
tabernacular	chronologise	gonadotropic	monopodially	psychosexual
tangentially	chronologist	gonadotropin	monopolistic	psychotropic
tectonically	chronometric	gorgeousness	monotonously	pyromorphite
tercentenary	clangorously	graciousness	morphologist	rapprochment
Teutonically	conchologist	grammolecule	musicologist	ravenousness
tintinnabula	conglobation	grampositive	mutinousness	reallocation
torrentially	conglomerate	graphologist	naturopathic	redecoration
tremendously	controllable	grievousness	nauseousness	renegotiable
tricentenary	covetousness	griseofulvin	nebulousness	reunionistic
trigonometry	craniologist	gruesomeness	nephrologist	rhombohedral
tyrannically	cryptogamous	handsomeness	nonflowering	rhombohedron
tyrannicidal	cryptography	hemerocallis	numerologist	rigorousness
unblinkingly	cryptologist	hemimorphism	numerousness	rosecoloured
unchangeable	cuckooflower	hemimorphite	nympholeptic	scabrousness
unchangeably	cumbrousness	heortologist	nymphomaniac	schizogonous
uneconomical	cumulocirrus	heterocercal	oceanography	schizomycete
uneventfully	cumulonimbus	heterocyclic	oceanologist	schizophrene
ungainliness	Czechoslovak	heteroecious	odontologist	schizothymia
unprincipled	decorousness	heterogamous	offscourings	schizothymic
unpronounced	demimondaine	heterogenous	omnipotently	sectionalism
unthinkingly	deontologist	heterologous	omnivorously	sedulousness
volcanically	desirousness	heteromerous	oneirocritic	seismography
Wellingtonia	dethronement	heteronomous	opinionative	seismologist
windingsheet	dextrousness	heterophylly	organography	seismometric
woodengraver	diageotropic	heterosexual	organoleptic	seismoscopic
woodenheaded	dichromatism	heterozygote	overlordship	selenography
workingclass	dilatoriness	heterozygous	overpowering	selenologist
actinomycete	dolorousness	highcoloured	palaeobotany	selfcoloured
ailurophobia	dovecoloured	highsounding	palaeography	selfcomposed
allomorphism	dynamometric	homoeopathic	Palaeolithic	selfcontempt
amelioration	echinococcus	homoeostasis	palynologist	selfdoubting
ameliorative	echolocation	homologation	papyrologist	selfportrait
anaerobiosis	echosounding	homomorphism	paraboloidal	semidomestic
anecdotalist	edulcoration	homomorphous	paramorphism	sensuousness
antagonistic	Egyptologist	horizontally	paranormally	sinusoidally
anthropogeny	elasmobranch	humorousness	paronomastic	sodafountain
anthropoidal	eleemosynary	hymenopteran	passionately	somatopleure
anthropology	embryologist	hypocoristic	passionfruit	sonorousness
aperiodicity	emotionalise	illusoriness	patulousness	spaciousness
apostolicism	emotionalism	immemorially	perilousness	sparrowgrass
apostolicity	emotionalist	immunologist	perviousness	speciousness
aristocratic	emotionality	inappositely	phlebotomise	speleologist
Aristotelean	enormousness	indecorously	phlebotomist	spermogonium
Aristotelian	enthronement	interoceanic	phrenologist	spheroidally
atheromatous	entomologise	interoceptor	phyllotactic	spuriousness
automobilist	entomologist	invigoration	physiognomic	staffofficer
automorphism	enzymologist	irreformable	physiography	stationhouse
autonomously	episcopalian	irresolutely	physiologist	stationwagon
backwoodsman	equipollence	irresolution	plectognathi	steatopygous
bellbottomed	equipollency	irresolvable	pleomorphism	stereochromy
benevolently	equivocation	jetpropelled	plesiosaurus	stereography
bibliography	equivocatory	kleptomaniac	pluviometric	stereoisomer
bibliologist	escapologist	languorously	pneumothorax	stereometric
bibliomaniac	exiguousness	lepidopteran	polarography	stereophonic
bibliopegist	fabulousness	levorotation	polymorphism	stereopticon
bibliophilic	factionalism	levorotatory	polymorphous	stereoscopic
bibliopolist	factiousness	lexicography	polytonality	stertorously
bibliothecae	fearsomeness	lexicologist	populousness	stethoscopic
bioecologist	fictionalise	lonesomeness	postdoctoral	stichomythia
biogeography	flamboyantly	lovelornness	postponement	stichomythic
blastosphere	fluorocarbon	luminousness	postposition	stilboestrol
broncobuster	forebodement	lusciousness	postpositive	stratosphere
brontosaurus	forebodingly	mademoiselle	praseodymium	stroboscopic
calycoideous	FrancoGerman	malacologist	preciousness	stubbornness
campfollower	futurologist	malevolently	previousness	studiousness
canorousness	gamesomeness	manifoldness	proglottides	subapostolic
captiousness	gametophytic	mansionhouse	prothonotary	sulphonamide
cardiography	gastronomist	Marcionitism	psephologist	sulphonation
cardiologist	gastropodous	megalomaniac	pseudocyesis	supraorbital
catamountain	generousness	melanochroic	pseudonymity	surefootedly
cautiousness	glaciologist	metamorphism	pseudonymous	technocratic
centrosphere	gladsomeness	metamorphose	pseudopodium	technologist
ceremonially	glaucomatous	metasomatism	psychoactive	teratologist
chalcolithic	gloriousness	minicomputer	psychography	teratomatous
chalcopyrite	glossography	misknowledge	psychologise	theosophical
cheirography	glossologist	mispronounce	psychologism	thermocouple
choreography	gluttonously	misquotation	psychologist	thermography
chromosphere	glyphography	monitorially	psychometric	thermolabile

thermometric	disciplinary	pennypincher	butterflynut	exacerbation
thermophilic	disreputable	perceptively	buttermuslin	exoterically
thermoscopic	disreputably	perceptivity	butterscotch	expatriation
thermosphere	enterprising	perceptually	Byelorussian	fatherfigure
thermostable	entrepreneur	peremptorily	calcareously	fatherliness
thermostatic	feldspathoid	perispomenon	carburetting	forthrightly
thermotactic	flavoprotein	photophilous	censoriously	fostermother
thermotropic	glycoprotein	phytophagous	chondriosome	furfuraceous
timehonoured	goosepimples	plecopterous	coacervation	gregariously
timorousness	haemophiliac	plenipotence	colourlessly	haemorrhagic
tiresomeness	haemopoiesis	poorspirited	comfortingly	hairdressing
toilsomeness	hairsplitter	preceptorial	commercially	halterbroken
tortuousness	hemispheroid	precipitable	compurgation	heartrending
toxicologist	hierophantic	precipitance	compurgatory	hellgrammite
toxicophobia	highspirited	precipitancy	concordantly	hesperididia
trachomatous	hippopotamus	precipitator	concurrently	hierarchical
traitorously	homeopathist	prelapsarian	conferential	highpressure
trampolinist	hydrophilous	prosopopoeia	confirmation	historically
transoceanic	hygrophilous	protoplasmic	confirmative	horrorstruck
trichologist	hyperplastic	protoplastic	confirmatory	huggermugger
trichotomise	hyperpyretic	radiophonics	conformation	hypocritical
trichotomous	hyperpyrexia	redemptioner	conscription	hysterectomy
troglodytism	impropriator	Redemptorist	conservation	hysterically
typefounding	inauspicious	retropulsion	conservatism	hysteromania
unbecomingly	incomparable	rhizophagous	conservative	incoordinate
unctuousness	incomparably	saprophagous	conservatory	incorrigible
undemocratic	incompatible	sarcophagous	constriction	incorrigibly
unfavourable	incompatibly	sarsaparilla	constrictive	incorruption
unfavourably	incompetence	scenepainter	constringent	inexpressive
unimportance	incompetency	selfapplause	construction	inextricable
unrecognised	incompletely	selfapproval	constructive	inextricably
urbanologist	incompliance	Shakspereana	conterminous	ingloriously
usuriousness	incomputable	Shaksperiana	conversation	innutritious
uxoriousness	incorporated	shortpitched	corporeality	inoperculate
vaporousness	incorporator	starspangled	costermonger	insurrection
varicoloured	incorporeity	sublapsarian	countrydance	interrelated
venomousness	indisputable	superposable	countrywoman	interrogator
vigorousness	indisputably	susceptivity	cumbersomely	interruption
virtuosoship	inhospitable	therapeutics	curvirostral	interruptive
virtuousness	inhospitably	therapeutist	dessertspoon	irrefragable
vitreousness	intemperance	transpacific	Deuteronomic	irrefragably
warehouseman	interpellate	transparency	diastrophism	irreprovable
whippoorwill	interpleader	transpirable	differentiae	isochromatic
wondrousness	interpolator	transplanter	differential	isochronally
xanthochroia	interpretive	transpontine	dinnerjacket	kindergarten
zoogeography	irrespective	transposable	disagreeable	laboursaving
zygapophysis	irrespirable	triumphantly	disagreeably	lanternjawed
zygomorphism	irresponsive	underpinning	disagreement	lanternslide
zygomorphous	jurisprudent	unresponsive	disbursement	leapfrogging
absorptional	klipspringer	vibraphonist	discerningly	ledgertackle
absorptivity	Liverpudlian	colloquially	discerptible	lugubriously
accompanyist	macropterous	consequently	discordantly	lumberjacket
accomplished	metropolitan	delinquently	discursively	malformation
alexipharmic	microphysics	harlequinade	disgorgement	malversation
anemophilous	misapprehend	hydroquinone	disharmonise	mannerliness
appropriable	misrepresent	inadequately	dispiritedly	mastersinger
appropriator	multipartite	infrequently	dissertation	masterstroke
archipelagic	multipliable	prerequisite	distortional	masterswitch
astrophysics	multiplicand	subsequently	disturbingly	melodramatic
atmospherics	multiplicate	threequarter	dunderheaded	menstruation
bathypelagic	multiplicity	unfrequented	editorialise	mercurialise
centuplicate	multipurpose	anamorphosis	editorialist	mercurialism
chiropractic	necrophagous	anteprandial	efflorescent	meretricious
chiropractor	necrophiliac	antigropelos	electrically	meteorically
coleopterist	necrophilism	apochromatic	electrolysis	meteorograph
coleopterous	necrophilous	apostrophise	electrolytic	mezzorelievo
conceptional	negrophilism	backbreaking	electrometer	misdirection
conceptually	negrophilist	bactericidal	electronvolt	monodramatic
concupiscent	neuropterous	bacteriology	electroplate	monographist
conduplicate	ophiophagous	bacteriostat	electroscope	mosstrooping
corespondent	orthopaedics	banderillero	electroshock	motherfigure
cosmopolitan	orthopaedist	barbarically	electrotonic	motherliness
cosmopolitic	orthopterist	bassorelievo	electrotonus	mothertongue
courtplaster	orthopteroid	bassorilievo	epicureanism	mysteriously
crosspurpose	osteoplastic	beggarliness	equiprobable	namedropping
decomposable	osteoporosis	bilharziasis	erythroblast	neoDarwinian
decompressor	passepartout	bilharziosis	erythromycin	neoDarwinism
desulphurise	peasepudding	birefringent	esoterically	neoDarwinist
discipleship		brassrubbing		nerveracking

Nestorianism	subscription	diversionist	neurosurgeon	successional
noradrenalin	subservience	earthshaking	neurosurgery	successively
obscurantism	subserviency	ecclesiastic	newfashioned	suggestively
obscurantist	substruction	ecclesiology	nimbostratus	supersedence
oligarchical	substructure	empoisonment	nonessential	supersensory
omnipresence	subterranean	empressement	nonresidence	supersession
outstretched	subthreshold	encrustation	nonresistant	superstition
outstripping	subversively	Englishwoman	oldfashioned	superstratum
outwardbound	synchronical	enthusiastic	oppressively	suppositious
overcritical	synchroniser	evanescently	orchestrator	synaesthesia
overcropping	teetertotter	exclusionary	overestimate	synaesthetic
overpressure	telegraphese	exclusionism	pantisocracy	telaesthesia
panchromatic	telegraphist	exclusionist	paraesthesia	telaesthetic
paragraphist	terrorstruck	excursionist	partisanship	testosterone
patternmaker	theatregoing	exhaustively	percussively	thanksgiving
peregrinator	theatrically	expansionary	periostracum	thickskinned
perfervidity	theocratical	expansionism	permissively	thickskulled
performative	trichromatic	expansionist	persistently	tradescantia
perjuriously	trifurcation	expressional	philistinism	tradespeople
perturbation	tripartitely	expressively	philosophise	trainspotter
perturbative	tripartition	expressivity	phonasthenia	transshipped
perverseness	unattractive	extensometer	photosetting	tropospheric
phanerogamic	uncharitable	extrasensory	photospheric	unblushingly
pickerelweed	uncharitably	extraspecial	placesetting	unclassified
pitterpatter	underrunning	fantasticate	planispheric	unconsidered
polyurethane	unitarianism	fantasticism	plebiscitary	unconstraint
posteriority	universalise	forensically	possessively	undersetting
postgraduate	universalism	fricasseeing	precessional	understaffed
postprandial	universalist	grotesquerie	precisianism	undersurface
precariously	universality	gymnosophist	precisionist	unreasonable
prechristian	unsearchable	heartstrings	predesignate	unreasonably
preferential	unsegregated	hydrostatics	predestinate	unseasonable
preformation	uproariously	hypersthenia	prehistorian	viscosimeter
preformative	Victorianism	hypersthenic	preposterous	wollastonite
preparedness	victoriously	immeasurable	proboscidean	xiphisternum
prescription	viscerotonic	immeasurably	proboscidian	abolitionary
prescriptive	wellgrounded	immensurable	processional	abolitionism
preservation	welterweight	impersonally	professional	abolitionist
preservative	winterbourne	impersonator	professorate	absentminded
pretermitted	wonderstruck	imprisonment	professoress	accentuation
prevaricator	wonderworker	inconsequent	professorial	accoutrement
primordially	wunderkinder	inconsistent	progesterone	accretionary
proofreading	accursedness	inconsolable	protestation	acoustically
proportional	aggressively	inconsolably	protistology	adjectivally
proportioned	ambassadress	inconsonance	provisionary	adscititious
proscription	amphisbaenic	inconstantly	purposebuilt	advantageous
proscriptive	assassinator	inconsumable	purposefully	adventitious
proverbially	bloodstained	inconsumably	pursestrings	affectedness
psychrometer	brainstormer	incrustation	recessionary	affectionate
psychrometry	callisthenic	indissoluble	reconstitute	aforethought
pulverisable	Cartesianism	indissolubly	refreshingly	afterthought
pumpernickel	centesimally	inelasticity	refreshments	agglutinogen
quattrocento	cirrostratus	inspissation	regressively	amitotically
rechargeable	clearsighted	intersection	remonstrance	amphitheatre
reciprocally	commiserator	interservice	remonstrator	amphitropous
reciprocator	commissarial	interspinous	remorsefully	anaesthetise
repatriation	commissariat	interstellar	repossession	anaesthetist
resurrection	commissioner	interstitial	repressively	analytically
rhetorically	composedness	intrusionist	reversionary	antistrophic
safecracking	confessional	intussuscept	sarrusophone	apolitically
salubriously	confiscation	Keynesianism	sceneshifter	appurtenance
sectarianise	confiscatory	kinaesthesia	scrimshanker	archetypally
sectarianism	confusedness	kinaesthesis	secessionism	archetypical
selfcritical	consistently	kinaesthetic	secessionist	architecture
semiprecious	consistorial	lithospheric	seclusionist	aromatically
semitropical	contestation	metapsychics	sequestrator	aromaticness
sightreading	crosssection	mezzosoprano	sharpshooter	arrhythmical
silverglance	deconsecrate	microscopist	sharpsighted	artistically
spectrograph	demonstrable	microseismic	sheepshearer	athletically
spectrometer	demonstrably	microsurgery	shortsighted	balletomania
spectrometry	demonstrator	millesimally	shortsleeved	ballottement
spectroscope	depressingly	moneyspinner	shortstaffed	belittlement
spectroscopy	digressional	morrisdancer	skrimshanker	belletristic
spidermonkey	digressively	multistoried	sophisticate	bicentennial
squirrelcage	disassociate	narcissistic	spokesperson	billsticking
squirreltail	disgustfully	neurasthenia	staffsurgeon	biometrician
stockraising	disgustingly	neurasthenic	statistician	bloodthirsty
subarrhation	dispossessor	neuroscience	submissively	bluestocking
subnormality	diversionary		successfully	bodystocking

bonnetmonkey	evolutionist	licketysplit	radiotherapy	unpretending
breakthrough	executorship	lithotritist	receptaculum	unrestrained
breaststroke	exegetically	logistically	receptionist	untruthfully
breastsummer	exophthalmic	longitudinal	redintegrate	unwontedness
bulletheaded	exophthalmos	longstanding	redistribute	unworthiness
calisthenics	exophthalmus	lycanthropic	reductionism	voluntaryism
carpetbagger	extortionary	magistrature	reductionist	voluntaryist
carpetknight	extortionate	magnetically	reflationary	voluptuosity
catastrophic	factitiously	magnetisable	registration	voluptuously
cementitious	farmsteading	magnetograph	rejectamenta	wherethrough
chemotherapy	fenestration	magnetometer	relentlessly	wicketkeeper
chieftainess	fictitiously	majestically	resettlement	absoluteness
chrestomathy	flagitiously	malnutrition	resistlessly	absolutistic
Christianise	flamethrower	marketgarden	revictualled	abstruseness
Christianity	forestalment	marketsquare	robustiously	accumulation
Christolatry	freestanding	meristematic	romantically	accumulative
Christophany	frenetically	merrythought	sabretoothed	agranulocyte
cleistogamic	galactogogue	ministration	sadistically	agribusiness
coalitionist	geometrician	ministrative	salvationism	agricultural
collaterally	geriatrician	misanthropic	salvationist	altitudinous
committeeman	gerontocracy	misinterpret	scripturally	amateurishly
compatriotic	gigantically	mnemotechnic	scriptwriter	aquicultural
connaturally	globetrotter	monastically	sculpturally	articulately
coquettishly	haematoblast	monostichous	selfstarting	articulation
cosmetically	haematolysis	monostrophic	semantically	articulatory
decentralise	haematoxylon	narcotically	sempiternity	attitudinise
decontrolled	hardstanding	neurotically	sensitometer	blastulation
deflationary	heliotherapy	nevertheless	servitorship	bodybuilding
deflationist	heliotropism	nutritionist	shamateurism	bureaucratic
dejectedness	hermetically	nutritiously	sidestepping	capitulation
densitometer	herpetologic	nyctitropism	simultaneity	cocksureness
departmental	highstepping	obstetrician	simultaneous	coloquintida
dermatophyte	horsetrading	onomatopoeia	Sinanthropus	compoundable
despitefully	housetrained	onomatopoeic	sinistrality	conclusively
despotically	hydrotherapy	operatically	sinistrorsal	confoundedly
deviationism	hydrothermal	orienteering	Socratically	conglutinate
deviationist	hydrotropism	orthotropism	specktioneer	deambulatory
dictatorship	hypertension	orthotropous	spinsterhood	defraudation
didactically	hypertensive	ostentatious	spiritedness	deliquescent
dietetically	hyperthermia	outdatedness	spiritlessly	demodulation
dilettantish	hypertrophic	overstepping	spiritualise	denaturalise
dilettantism	hypnotherapy	paletteknife	spiritualism	denaturation
directorship	hypnotically	parenthesise	spiritualist	depopulation
disastrously	hypnotisable	partitionist	spirituality	destructible
disestablish	hypostatical	pathetically	squattocracy	diminutively
disintegrate	idolatrously	pedantically	stealthiness	discountable
disinterment	illnaturedly	percutaneous	stormtrooper	discouraging
disputatious	illustration	peristeronic	straitjacket	discourteous
dissatisfied	illustrative	peristomatic	streetwalker	duraluminium
diverticular	impartiality	permittivity	streptococci	emasculation
diverticulum	impertinence	perpetration	streptomycin	emasculatory
divertimenti	impertinency	perpetuation	strontianite	extrauterine
divertimento	incautiously	phenotypical	structurally	filibusterer
dogmatically	incestuously	phonetically	subalternate	flocculation
domestically	incontiguous	phototropism	subalternity	fraudulently
domesticator	incontinence	phreatophyte	subcutaneous	goodhumoured
dramatically	incontinency	planetesimal	subsaturated	grossularite
dramaturgist	indebtedness	planetstruck	synarthrosis	habitualness
dynastically	indistinctly	pleiotropism	syndetically	headquarters
eccentricity	indoctrinate	polyethylene	synoptically	hebetudinous
eclectically	industrially	potentiality	theanthropic	hindquarters
ecstatically	infanticidal	pralltriller	theistically	hirepurchase
educationist	infectiously	predetermine	thematically	hyposulphite
effectuality	inflationary	preestablish	thriftlessly	immaculately
effectuation	inflationism	priestliness	topsyturvily	immatureness
effortlessly	inflationist	priestridden	traditionary	inaccurately
elliptically	ingratiating	privatdocent	traditionist	inauguration
elocutionary	insecticidal	privatdozent	triphthongal	inauguratory
elocutionist	intertexture	privateering	tumultuously	IndoEuropean
embattlement	intuitionism	probationary	uncontrolled	inescutcheon
embitterment	intuitionist	procathedral	uncritically	inexpugnable
emphatically	invertebrate	profiteering	undertenancy	inexpugnably
enclitically	investigator	propitiation	unfaithfully	inoccupation
enswathement	isolationism	propitiatory	unflattering	inosculation
entertaining	isolationist	propitiously	ungratefully	insalubrious
equestrienne	jesuitically	prototypical	unhistorical	insolubilise
essentiality	knighterrant	quaestorship	unilaterally	insolubility
evolutionary	knightliness	quixotically	unmistakable	instauration
evolutionism	licentiously	racketeering	unmistakably	instructress

instrumental	abbreviation	whitewashing	bobbydazzler	impermanency
integumental	boulevardier	yellowhammer	bodysnatcher	inappeasable
intrauterine	Carlovingian	asphyxiation	booklearning	incomparable
involutional	clairvoyance	contextually	boulevardier	incomparably
irregularity	conviviality	overexertion	brainwashing	incompatible
landlubberly	cultivatable	overexposure	breathalyser	incompatibly
latitudinous	depravedness	premaxillary	brilliantine	indefeasible
LowChurchman	disadvantage	selfexistent	brinkmanship	indefeasibly
manipulation	discoverable	submaxillary	bullheadedly	intracardiac
manipulative	discoverture	unisexuality	calculatedly	irrefragable
manipulatory	dishevelment	acronychally	capercaillie	irrefragably
manoeuvrable	disseverance	aerodynamics	capercailzie	irrepealable
meticulously	disseverment	anaphylactic	carbonaceous	judgematical
miraculously	dorsiventral	anticyclonic	cardinalship	liquefacient
miseducation	effervescent	biophysicist	caterwauling	liquefaction
moistureless	extravagance	bloodyminded	chairmanship	longstanding
molecularity	extravagancy	brachydactyl	chieftainess	maltreatment
Newfoundland	extravaganza	conveyancing	chocolatebox	marksmanship
Northumbrian	extraversion	copolymerise	cliffhanging	marshharrier
obsequiously	extroversion	creepycrawly	combinations	materialness
orbicularity	illadvisedly	decasyllabic	contumacious	mathematical
phillumenist	imperviously	decasyllable	conveyancing	melodramatic
pleasureless	improvidence	geophysicist	courtmartial	microcapsule
posthumously	improvisator	highlystrung	crashlanding	misbehaviour
preclusively	inconvenient	homonymously	criticalness	mistreatment
profoundness	intervenient	humptydumpty	cultivatable	monodramatic
pronouncedly	intervention	ichthyocolla	curvicaudate	monographist
protrusively	intervocalic	ichthyolatry	demoniacally	mulligatawny
quadrumanous	introversion	ichthyophagy	diatomaceous	multifarious
quinquennial	introversive	idiosyncrasy	dilettantish	multilateral
quinquennium	introvertive	lachrymation	dilettantism	multipartite
readjustment	lasciviously	lachrymatory	disadvantage	multivalence
reassuringly	misadventure	lachrymosely	disembarrass	musicianship
reoccupation	multivalence	liverystable	disestablish	nanoplankton
resoluteness	multiversity	monkeyflower	displeasedly	negotiatress
restaurateur	outrivalling	monkeyjacket	disputatious	nephanalysis
reticulately	peradventure	monkeypuzzle	disregardful	nerveracking
reticulation	perseverance	monkeywrench	doubleacting	northeastern
reticulocyte	receivership	monosyllabic	emblematical	obscurantism
ribonuclease	reconversion	monosyllable	encephalitic	obscurantist
ridiculously	reconveyance	niminypiminy	encephalitis	oneupmanship
sansculottic	reservedness	octosyllabic	entertaining	orchidaceous
scrupulosity	resolvedness	octosyllable	extramarital	orthopaedics
scrupulously	retroversion	paralysation	extravagance	orthopaedist
selfluminous	selfevidence	parisyllabic	extravagancy	ostentatious
selfmurderer	subdivisible	policyholder	extravaganza	osteomalacia
sericultural	supervenient	polysyllabic	feldspathoid	outrivalling
shipbuilding	supervention	polysyllable	footplateman	overreaction
sternutation	survivorship	presbyterate	forestalment	paedobaptism
sternutative	tergiversate	presbyterial	freestanding	pancreatitis
sternutatory	transversely	Presbyterian	furfuraceous	paragraphist
stridulation	transvestism	prophylactic	galligaskins	partisanship
sulphuration	transvestite	selfhypnosis	gallinaceous	passepartout
sulphuretted	unchivalrous	semicylinder	gamesmanship	percutaneous
surmountable	unconvincing	shillyshally	graminaceous	pertinacious
surroundings	brainwashing	surveyorship	guardianship	petrifaction
thoroughbass	caterwauling	synonymously	haberdashery	pilotballoon
thoroughbred	collywobbles	teensyweensy	habitualness	polychaetous
thoroughfare	freeswimming	triglyphical	handicapping	porcelainise
thoroughness	heartwarming	twentyfourmo	hardfeatured	porcelainous
tranquillise	horsewhipped	woollyheaded	hardstanding	postgraduate
tranquillity	housewarming	bedazzlement	headquarters	postprandial
transudation	interwreathe	embezzlement	heartwarming	preestablish
transudatory	lakedwelling	emblazonment	hebdomadally	propagandise
unaccustomed	metalworking	protozoology	heliolatrous	propagandism
unassumingly	narrowminded	——————————	hellgrammite	propagandist
unencumbered	northwestern	accompanyist	heroicalness	psychiatrist
unpopularity	otherworldly	advantageous	hibernaculum	psychoactive
unscrupulous	pennywhistle	ambassadress	hindquarters	pterodactyle
unstructured	prizewinning	analphabetic	homeopathist	putrefaction
unthoughtful	sedgewarbler	angiocarpous	homothallism	putrefactive
usufructuary	shadowboxing	anteprandial	horsemanship	reappearance
valetudinary	shirtwaister	archdeaconry	housewarming	receptaculum
venepuncture	sleepwalking	argillaceous	hypognathous	rejectamenta
venipuncture	southwestern	astronautics	hypostatical	rhizocarpous
vesiculation	sternwheeler	avantgardism	hypothalamic	safecracking
viscountship	threewheeler	avantgardist	hypothalamus	salesmanship
vocabularian	unanswerable	backslapping	illtreatment	sarcomatosis
vomiturition	underwritten	bellylanding	impermanence	sarsaparilla

satisfaction	desirability	adjudicatory	intoxication	unstructured
satisfactory	dilatability	announcement	intrenchment	usufructuary
scenepainter	distributary	anticyclonic	manufacturer	veridicality
schismatical	distribution	antimacassar	melanochroic	verification
schorlaceous	distributive	antirachitic	microscopist	verificatory
sedgewarbler	disturbingly	approachable	miscalculate	vilification
selfanalysis	divisibility	aristocratic	miseducation	vinification
selfflattery	elasmobranch	artificially	misplacement	vivification
selfstarting	equilibrator	benefactress	modification	whimsicality
semidiameter	equitability	beneficently	modificatory	xanthochroia
septilateral	exacerbation	beneficially	munificently	acetaldehyde
sesquialtera	excitability	bureaucratic	neuroscience	aerosiderite
shamefacedly	filtrability	canaliculate	nidification	aircondition
shirtwaister	flammability	cheesecutter	notification	altitudinous
simoniacally	frangibility	circumcision	oligarchical	antecedently
simultaneity	habitability	classicalism	oneirocritic	aperiodicity
simultaneous	halterbroken	classicalist	ossification	astoundingly
singleacting	harquebusier	classicality	overniceness	attitudinise
skunkcabbage	hereinbefore	claudication	pacification	autodidactic
sleepwalking	heritability	codification	pacificatory	backpedalled
sorbefacient	hubblebubble	commencement	panification	benzaldehyde
southeastern	hucklebacked	commercially	paratactical	brachydactyl,
stagemanager	illegibility	complacently	perspicacity	cashandcarry
starspangled	immovability	complication	pharmaceutic	coincidental
stockraising	immutability	compunctious	pharmacology	coincidently
stonemasonry	imputability	confiscation	plebiscitary	commandingly
strophanthin	inaudibility	confiscatory	postdoctoral	commendation
stupefacient	incapability	conjunctival	practicality	commendatory
stupefaction	incurability	contractable	precancelled	concordantly
stupefactive	indelibility	contractedly	prenticeship	contradictor
subcutaneous	infusibility	contractible	proboscidean	cotyledonary
succedaneous	insalubrious	convincement	proboscidian	cotyledonous
supernaculum	insolubilise	convincingly	provincially	defraudation
supernatural	insolubility	creepycrawly	pseudocyesis	despondently
sycophantish	invisibility	cumulocirrus	purification	diamonddrill
systematical	irascibility	denouncement	purificatory	diamondfield
systematiser	irritability	destructible	pyrotechnics	dilapidation
taberdarship	landlubberly	detoxication	pyrotechnist	discordantly
tabernacular	malleability	dibranchiate	quizzicality	disobedience
telegraphese	navigability	displaceable	rambunctious	doubledealer
telegraphist	noctambulant	displacement	ramification	doubledecked
theocratical	noctambulism	distinctness	rapprochment	doubledecker
torrefaction	noctambulist	distractedly	ratification	enginedriver
translatable	noctambulous	divarication	reallocation	fluoridation
transpacific	noncombatant	echinococcus	renouncement	forbiddingly
transparency	opposability	echolocation	reproachable	forebodement
unappeasable	palaeobotany	embranchment	reproachless	forebodingly
unattractive	palatability	encroachment	restrictedly	formaldehyde
unchivalrous	permeability	entrancement	retrenchment	gobbledegook
uncomeatable	perturbation	entrenchment	ribonuclease	gobbledygook
undergarment	perturbative	equivocation	sandyachting	hebetudinous
undermanning	pigeonbreast	equivocatory	scrobiculate	horrendously
unmistakable	plausibility	evanescently	selfdeceived	humptydumpty
unmistakably	printability	fluorocarbon	selfdeceiver	hydatidiform
unrepeatable	proverbially	gasification	silicicolous	incoordinate
verticalness	reducibility	geanticlinal	stereochromy	individually
vicechairman	removability	geosynclinal	straticulate	inexpedience
vitrifaction	saddlebacked	groundcherry	stringcourse	inexpediency
voluntaryism	separability	hemerocallis	succinctness	intimidation
voluntaryist	shadowboxing	heterocercal	supplicantly	intimidatory
watermanship	somnambulant	heterocyclic	supplication	invalidation
whitewashing	somnambulate	hierarchical	supplicatory	irremediable
wineglassful	somnambulism	homesickness	taperecorder	irremediably
adaptability	somnambulist	humification	technicality	latitudinous
advisability	teachability	hyperacidity	technicolour	mithridatise
aeroembolism	temptability	illogicality	technocratic	mithridatism
alterability	tolerability	inarticulate	thermocouple	monopodially
amphisbaenic	traceability	incapacitate	tradescantia	morrisdancer
anaerobiosis	tractability	indefectible	transoceanic	nonconductor
automobilist	uncelebrated	indelicately	trifurcation	outlandishly
availability	venerability	indirectness	triplication	outwardbound
broncobuster	winterbourne	ineffaceable	typification	peroxidation
carpetbagger	abstractable	ineffaceably	unaffectedly	praseodymium
cheeseburger	abstractedly	inefficiency	undemocratic	precondition
conglobation	abstractness	infelicitous	underachieve	preponderant
constabulary	acciaccatura	inoperculate	unexpectedly	preponderate
contribution	acronychally	instructress	unofficially	primordially
contributive	adjudication	interoceanic	unprincipled	privatdocent
contributory	adjudicative	interoceptor	unsearchable	privatdozent

propaedeutic	decaffeinate	hypnogenesis	multicentral	receivership
razzledazzle	decipherable	hypnogenetic	multidentate	recollection
resoundingly	decipherment	hypothecator	multiversity	recollective
singledecker	decongestant	hypothetical	nitrobenzene	reconversion
softpedalled	decongestion	hysterectomy	noneffective	reconveyance
stupendously	decongestive	idiothermous	nonessential	recrudescent
transudation	deconsecrate	imperceptive	nonobjective	redintegrate
transudatory	dejectedness	imperfection	noradrenalin	refrigerator
tremendously	deliquescent	imperfective	northwestern	rememberable
troglodytism	denuclearise	imponderable	nychthemeral	remorsefully
unsteadiness	depravedness	imponderably	nychthemeron	repossession
unwieldiness	despitefully	incandescent	oblanceolate	reprehension
unworldiness	detachedness	incompetence	omnipresence	reprehensive
unyieldingly	differentiae	incompetency	onesidedness	reservedness
valetudinary	differential	inconsequent	orienteering	resignedness
YankeeDoodle	diphtheritic	inconvenient	orthogenesis	resolvedness
accursedness	disaffection	indebtedness	orthogenetic	resurrection
affectedness	disagreeable	indifference	osteogenesis	retrocedence
AfroAmerican	disagreeably	indifferency	outdatedness	retrocession
agamogenesis	disagreement	inexpressive	outrageously	retrocessive
agamogenetic	discoverable	insufferable	outstretched	retroversion
agentgeneral	discoverture	insufferably	overexertion	revengefully
alphabetical	discreetness	insurrection	overpressure	reverberator
alphamerical	dishevelment	intellection	overstepping	rhinocerotic
anticlerical	disincentive	intellective	paedogenesis	rhizogenetic
antithetical	disinfectant	intellectual	paedogenetic	rhododendron
appendectomy	disinfection	intemperance	paletteknife	ricochetting
apperception	disingenuous	interbedding	palingenesia	sacrilegious
apperceptive	disintegrate	interception	palingenesis	scareheading
apprehension	disinterment	intercession	palingenetic	selfelective
apprehensive	disorientate	intercessory	parallelling	selfidentity
appurtenance	disseverance	interfemoral	pathogenesis	selfpleasing
archipelagic	disseverment	interference	pathogenetic	semiprecious
architecture	dorsiventral	interjection	peradventure	sempiternity
arithmetical	econometrics	interjectory	peripherally	serviceberry
artilleryman	effervescent	intermeddler	peristeronic	servicecourt
attorneyship	efflorescent	intermediacy	perseverance	servicewoman
backbreaking	embitterment	intermediary	pestilential	Shakspereana
bassorelievo	encumberment	intermediate	phenomenally	Shaksperiana
bathypelagic	endangerment	interpellate	philadelphus	shamateurism
belligerence	endoskeletal	interrelated	philodendron	shoulderbelt
belligerency	epexegetical	intersection	photogeology	shoulderknot
bewilderedly	epicureanism	interservice	photosetting	shouldernote
bewilderment	ethnocentric	intertexture	phylogenesis	shuffleboard
bicentennial	EuroAmerican	intervenient	phylogenetic	sidestepping
bioscientist	exospherical	intervention	phytogenesis	sightreading
birdsnesting	expediential	introjection	phytogenetic	snaggletooth
bloodletting	experiential	introversion	pickerelweed	sociometrist
brambleberry	extraneously	introversive	placesetting	southwestern
buccaneering	extrasensory	introvertive	plaindealing	spinsterhood
buccaneerish	extraversion	invertebrate	planetesimal	spiritedness
cabbagewhite	extroversion	invulnerable	Plattdeutsch	sporogenesis
calcareously	fainthearted	invulnerably	polytheistic	squirrelcage
campodeiform	faithhealing	irredeemable	polyurethane	squirreltail
carburetting	farmsteading	irredeemably	precedential	steeplechase
catechetical	freewheeling	irreflective	predetermine	stilboestrol
childbearing	frontbencher	irrespective	predigestion	stonyhearted
clarinettist	frontiersman	knighterrant	predilection	stouthearted
clavicembalo	genuflection	lakedwelling	preferential	subalternate
coetaneously	glycogenesis	largehearted	preparedness	subalternity
collaterally	gravelelling	lighthearted	preselection	subcelestial
collinearity	greathearted	lopsidedness	preselective	subinfeudate
commiserator	hairdressing	macrocephaly	presidential	subthreshold
composedness	heartrending	majorgeneral	primogenital	supersedence
concelebrant	heavyhearted	Manicheanism	primogenitor	supersensory
concelebrate	heliocentric	marlinespike	privateering	supersession
conferential	henotheistic	meristematic	profiteering	supervenient
confidential	hermeneutics	metathetical	proofreading	supervention
confusedness	heteroecious	mezzorelievo	proprietress	swizzlestick
considerable	highpressure	microcephaly	protuberance	tergiversate
considerably	highstepping	microseismic	proudhearted	testamentary
contumelious	hippocentaur	misadventure	providential	tetrahedrite
convalescent	histogenesis	misdemeanant	purposebuilt	theatregoing
corporeality	histogenetic	misdemeanour	purposefully	therapeutics
courageously	housekeeping	misdirection	pyroelectric	therapeutist
crossbedding	hydromedusae	misinterpret	quadriennium	thimbleberry
crossbencher	hydromedusan	mistakenness	quinquennial	togetherness
crossheading	hypertension	mnemotechnic	quinquennium	Torricellian
crosssection	hypertensive	monotheistic	racketeering	transcendent

transferable	bullfighting	profligately	heliotherapy	triumphantly
transference	burningglass	prolongation	hemispheroid	unblushingly
transferring	cardiography	promulgation	hierophantic	unfaithfully
transversely	carriageable	psychography	horsewhipped	untruthfully
transvestism	cheirography	pyroligneous	hydrochloric	unworthiness
transvestite	choreography	Quadragesima	hydrophilous	vibraphonist
trestletable	chronography	reassignment	hydrotherapy	wherethrough
troublemaker	cockfighting	rechargeable	hydrothermal	woodenheaded
umbrageously	compurgation	reinvigorate	hygrophilous	woollyheaded
unanswerable	compurgatory	rollingstock	hyperthermia	yellowhammer
unbelievable	congregation	runningboard	hypnotherapy	abbreviation
unbelievably	conningtower	schizogonous	interchanger	abolitionary
unbrokenness	contingently	scintigraphy	lycanthropic	abolitionism
uncommercial	cousingerman	seismography	melancholiac	abolitionist
underdevelop	cryptogamous	selenography	merrythought	aboriginally
underletting	cryptography	selfbegotten	microphysics	abstemiously
undersetting	cuckingstool	selfrighting	misanthropic	academically
undertenancy	curlingirons	sellingplate	moneychanger	accordionist
ungracefully	curlingtongs	septuagenary	muddleheaded	accretionary
ungratefully	curmudgeonly	Septuagesima	muttonheaded	acoustically
unilaterally	disgorgement	Septuagintal	necrophagous	adjectivally
unpretending	dislodgement	silverglance	necrophiliac	adscititious
unsegregated	drawingboard	spermogonium	necrophilism	adventitious
unsuccessful	drawingpaper	stereography	necrophilous	affectionate
unwontedness	duckingstool	stratigraphy	negrophilism	agglutinogen
vantagepoint	endamagement	thanksgiving	negrophilist	amitotically
vicargeneral	envisagement	thermography	nevertheless	amphibiously
wholehearted	estrangement	thoroughbass	newfashioned	anagogically
whortleberry	eveningdress	thoroughbred	officeholder	analogically
wretchedness	exchangeable	thoroughfare	oldfashioned	analytically
youngberries	falcongentil	thoroughness	ophiophagous	anatomically
aircraftsman	falcongentle	unchangeable	overachiever	annunciation
amentiferous	firefighting	unchangeably	pantechnicon	apolitically
butterflynut	foresightful	unmanageable	parenthesise	appendicitis
circumfluent	FrancoGerman	unrecognised	pennywhistle	appendicular
circumfusion	glossography	unthoughtful	photochromic	appreciation
classifiable	glyphography	vitiligation	photophilous	appreciative
conchiferous	glyptography	Wellingtonia	phytophagous	appreciatory
cuckooflower	gramnegative	windingsheet	policyholder	aromatically
discomfiture	gyromagnetic	woodengraver	polyethylene	aromaticness
emulsifiable	heterogamous	workingclass	procathedral	artistically
fatherfigure	heterogenous	zoogeography	radiophonics	asphyxiation
fiddlefaddle	homologation	accouchement	radiotherapy	assassinator
fructiferous	impetiginous	aforethought	rattleheaded	athletically
griseofulvin	inexpugnable	afterthought	refreshingly	auspiciously
identifiable	inexpugnably	alexipharmic	refreshments	avariciously
inartificial	infringement	amphitheatre	rhizophagous	avitaminoses
laticiferous	kindergarten	anaesthetise	rhombohedral	avitaminosis
luminiferous	kissingcrust	anaesthetist	rhombohedron	bactericidal
monkeyflower	landingcraft	anemophilous	saprophagous	bacteriology
motherfigure	landingfield	arrhythmical	sarcophagous	bacteriostat
nonconformer	landingstage	astrophysics	sceneshifter	banderillero
pasqueflower	landingstrip	atmospherics	scratchiness	barbarically
plumbiferous	lexicography	beseechingly	scrimshanker	bassorilievo
quantifiable	lodginghouse	bewitchingly	sepulchrally	beatifically
resiniferous	marketgarden	bloodthirsty	sharpshooter	berzelianite
salutiferous	marriageable	breakthrough	sheepshearer	billsticking
saponifiable	meaningfully	bulletheaded	shortchanger	biologically
schoolfellow	meetinghouse	calisthenics	Sinanthropus	birefringent
selfaffected	meltingpoint	candleholder	singlehanded	blackbirding
selfeffacing	messeigneurs	carragheenin	skrimshanker	bodybuilding
seminiferous	misalignment	chemotherapy	sledgehammer	brickfielder
semiofficial	misjudgement	desulphurise	snakecharmer	calumniation
siliciferous	morningdress	disaccharide	stealthiness	calumniatory
soporiferous	mucilaginous	disenchanter	sternwheeler	calumniously
staffofficer	multungulate	dodecahedral	straightaway	calycoideous
stanniferous	nonalignment	dodecahedron	straightbred	camiknickers
stelliferous	oceanography	dunderheaded	straightedge	capriciously
sudoriferous	organography	earthshaking	straightener	Carlovingian
twentyfourmo	palaeography	Englishwoman	straightness	Cartesianism
anastigmatic	paradigmatic	enswathement	subarrhation	catholically
antimagnetic	paramagnetic	escutcheoned	supercharger	cementitious
apothegmatic	permanganate	exophthalmic	synarthrosis	censoriously
astringently	physiognomic	exophthalmos	tetrachordal	centesimally
battleground	physiography	exophthalmus	theanthropic	chaplainship
bibliography	playingfield	farsightedly	threewheeler	cherubically
billingsgate	plectognathi	flamethrower	throughstone	chondriosome
biogeography	plumbaginous	guestchamber	transshipped	Christianise
bookingclerk	polarography	haemophiliac	triphthongal	Christianity

churchianity	earsplitting	horrifically	karyokinesis	precariously
clearsighted	ecclesiastic	hybridisable	Keynesianism	prechristian
coalitionist	ecclesiology	hydrokinetic	kinnikinnick	precipitable
coenobitical	eclectically	hygienically	lasciviously	precipitance
collegialism	ecologically	hypnotically	licentiously	precipitancy
collegiality	economically	hypnotisable	liturgically	precipitator
collegiately	ecstatically	hypocritical	liturgiology	precisianism
coloquintida	editorialise	hysterically	logistically	precisionist
columniation	editorialist	illadvisedly	loquaciously	precociously
commodiously	educationist	impartiality	lugubriously	predesignate
communicable	electrically	impercipient	mademoiselle	predominance
communicably	elliptically	impertinence	magnetically	predominancy
communicator	elocutionary	impertinency	magnetisable	premaxillary
companionate	elocutionist	imperviously	magnifically	premeditated
companionway	emphatically	implicitness	magnificence	premeditator
complaisance	enclitically	improvidence	maintainable	prescription
conciliation	endermically	improvisator	majestically	prescriptive
conciliative	enthusiastic	inapplicable	mechanically	prevaricator
conciliatory	epidemically	inapplicably	mendaciously	prizefighter
concomitance	epidemiology	inauspicious	mercurialise	prizewinning
concubitancy	episodically	incautiously	mercurialism	probationary
concupiscent	esoterically	incendiarism	meretricious	prodigiously
Confucianism	essentiality	incognisable	metallically	proficiently
congeniality	euphonically	incognisance	meteorically	progenitress
congenitally	euphoniously	incognitable	methodically	prolifically
connubiality	evolutionary	inconcinnity	microbiology	prolificness
conscription	evolutionism	inconsistent	microcircuit	pronominally
consociation	evolutionist	incontiguous	millesimally	propitiation
consolidator	exclusionary	incontinence	monastically	propitiatory
constriction	exclusionism	incontinency	monostichous	propitiously
constrictive	exclusionist	incorrigible	mordaciously	proscription
constringent	excruciating	incorrigibly	mountainside	proscriptive
contagionist	excruciation	indeclinable	multilingual	prosodically
contagiously	excursionist	indiscipline	mysteriously	protohistory
conveniently	exegetically	indistinctly	nailscissors	provisionary
conviviality	exoterically	ineradicable	narcotically	pugnaciously
cosmetically	expansionary	ineradicably	neonomianism	pulverisable
debonairness	expansionism	inexplicable	Nestorianism	quixotically
deflationary	expansionist	inexplicably	neurobiology	rabbinically
deflationist	expatriation	inextricable	neurotically	radiobiology
dentilingual	explicitness	inextricably	nonefficient	ratiocinator
denunciation	exterminable	infanticidal	nonresidence	rebelliously
denunciative	exterminator	infectiously	nonresistant	recalcitrant
denunciatory	extortionary	inflationary	nutritionist	recalcitrate
depreciation	extortionate	inflationism	nutritiously	receptionist
depreciatory	extraditable	inflationist	obsequiously	recessionary
despoliation	explicitness	infundibular	omnisciently	recognisable
despotically	factitiously	ingloriously	operatically	recognisably
determinable	fallaciously	ingratiating	overcritical	recognisance
determinably	fastidiously	inhospitable	Palladianism	recommitment
determinedly	faultfinding	inhospitably	parochialise	reconcilable
deviationary	ferrugineous	innutritious	parochialism	reductionism
deviationist	fertilisable	insecticidal	parochiality	reductionist
diabolically	fictitiously	insufficient	participator	reflationary
diatonically	firstnighter	intelligence	partitionist	renunciation
didactically	flagitiously	intelligible	pathetically	renunciative
dietetically	floodlighted	intelligibly	peccadilloes	renunciatory
disaffiliate	forensically	interdiction	pedantically	repatriation
disambiguate	forthrightly	interdictive	pellucidness	restrainable
dispiritedly	fountainhead	interdictory	pennypincher	restrainedly
dissatisfied	freeswimming	interdigital	peregrinator	resuscitator
disseminator	freethinking	interminable	perfidiously	reversionary
dissimilarly	frenetically	interminably	perfoliation	rhetorically
dissocialise	galvanically	intermission	periodically	rhythmically
dissociation	geologically	intermittent	perjuriously	risorgimento
dissociative	geopolitical	intermitting	perniciously	robustiously
distrainable	gigantically	intermixture	phonemically	romantically
distrainment	goosepimples	intromission	phonetically	sadistically
diversionary	granodiorite	intromittent	photofission	salubriously
diversionist	gregariously	intromitting	photokinesis	salvationism
diverticular	hallucinogen	intrusionist	photokinetic	salvationist
diverticulum	hallucinosis	intuitionism	platonically	sardonically
divertimenti	harmonically	intuitionist	pluriliteral	scarificator
divertimento	harmoniously	investigator	pontifically	secessionism
dogmatically	heraldically	irrespirable	pontificator	secessionist
domestically	hermetically	isolationism	poorspirited	seclusionist
domesticator	hesperididia	isolationist	posteriority	sectarianise
dramatically	highspirited	jesuitically	potentiality	sectarianism
dynastically	historically	jurisdiction		selfcritical

selfevidence	unmercifully	conduplicate	hyposulphite	Palaeolithic
selfexistent	unprofitable	controllable	iconoclastic	palynologist
semantically	unprofitably	councilwoman	immaculately	panhellenism
sequaciously	uproariously	courtplaster	immunologist	papyrologist
seraphically	Valenciennes	cowardliness	incompletely	paraboloidal
sharpsighted	verticillate	craniologist	incompliance	paramilitary
shipbuilding	Victorianism	crenellation	inconclusive	parisyllabic
shortcircuit	victoriously	cryptologist	inosculation	pedicellaria
shortpitched	viscosimeter	crystalgazer	installation	philhellenic
shortsighted	volcanically	culpableness	instillation	phrenologist
sideslipping	wallpainting	deambulatory	insufflation	physiologist
sidewhiskers	whitelivered	decasyllabic	interglacial	pitiableness
significance	circumjacent	decasyllable	interpleader	plainclothed
significancy	dinnerjacket	deescalation	inveiglement	plainclothes
sinusoidally	katzenjammer	demodulation	invigilation	pointilliste
Socratically	lumberjacket	deontologist	irregularity	polysyllabic
specifically	monkeyjacket	depopulation	irresolutely	polysyllable
specificness	straitjacket	discipleship	irresolution	porcellanous
specktioneer	cantankerous	disciplinary	irresolvable	postdiluvian
spheroidally	carpetknight	disinflation	Ishmaelitish	prevailingly
sphragistics	thickskinned	distillation	journalistic	priestliness
splendidness	thickskulled	distillatory	knightliness	princeliness
sporadically	unblinkingly	doublelocked	laudableness	prophylactic
stepchildren	unthinkingly	dovecoloured	lexicologist	prothalamion
stereoisomer	wicketkeeper	effortlessly	liberalistic	prothalamium
strontianite	wunderkinder	emasculation	loungelizard	protoplasmic
subdivisible	accomplished	emasculatory	maidenliness	protoplastic
submaxillary	accumulation	embattlement	malacologist	psephologist
subminiature	accumulative	embezzlement	malevolently	psychologise
subscription	adorableness	embryologist	manifoldness	psychologism
subsidiarily	agranulocyte	encirclement	manipulation	psychologist
subsonically	agricultural	enfeeblement	manipulative	radioelement
sufficiently	ambivalently	entanglement	manipulatory	readableness
superciliary	amenableness	entomologise	mannerliness	regardlessly
supercilious	amicableness	entomologist	Marseillaise	rehabilitate
superhighway	amygdaloidal	enviableness	marvellously	relentlessly
suppositious	anaphylactic	enzymologist	metagalactic	reliableness
suspiciously	annihilation	epicycloidal	meticulously	resettlement
syllabically	annihilative	epithalamion	microclimate	resistlessly
symbolically	antediluvian	epithalamium	mineralogist	reticulately
syndetically	antimalarial	equipollence	miraculously	reticulation
synoptically	apostolicism	equipollency	miscellanist	reticulocyte
systemically	apostolicity	equivalently	mitrailleuse	retroflexion
tectonically	aquicultural	escapologist	molecularity	revivalistic
terrifically	articulately	evangelistic	monadelphous	ridiculously
testudineous	articulation	exsufflicate	monofilament	rosecoloured
Teutonically	articulatory	fatherliness	monopolistic	salmonladder
theatrically	assibilation	fibrillation	monosyllabic	salpiglossis
theistically	assimilation	fieldglasses	monosyllable	sansculottic
thematically	assimilative	flabelliform	morphallaxis	scandalously
traditionary	assimilatory	flagellation	morphologist	schoolleaver
traditionist	Australasian	flagellatory	motherliness	scintillator
traducianism	bedazzlement	flocculation	moveableness	scrupulosity
traducianist	beggarliness	forcibleness	multiflorous	scrupulously
tranquillise	belittlement	fraudulently	multipliable	scurrilously
tranquillity	benevolently	friendliness	multiplicand	scutellation
transhipment	bibliologist	fullyfledged	multiplicate	seismologist
transmigrant	bioecologist	futurologist	multiplicity	selenologist
transmigrate	blamableness	glaciologist	musicologist	selfcoloured
transmission	blastulation	glassblowing	muzzleloader	selfdelusion
transmissive	bonnyclabber	glossologist	naturalistic	selfreliance
transmitting	borosilicate	grammecule	Neohellenism	semicylinder
transpirable	breathlessly	graphologist	nephrologist	sensibleness
trinomialism	breechloader	graveclothes	nightclothes	sensualistic
tyrannically	campfollower	grossularite	nomenclative	sericultural
tyrannicidal	cancellation	groundlessly	nomenclature	shortsleeved
unassailable	cantillation	grovellingly	nominalistic	slovenliness
uncharitable	capitalistic	hairsplitter	nonchalantly	smallclothes
uncharitably	capitulation	heavenliness	noneuclidean	sociableness
unconsidered	cardiologist	heortologist	numerologist	specialistic
unconvincing	cattlelifter	heterologous	nympholeptic	speechlessly
uncritically	centuplicate	hieroglyphic	obnubilation	speleologist
underbidding	chalcolithic	highcoloured	oceanologist	spiegeleisen
underpinning	charnelhouse	highfaluting	octosyllabic	spiritlessly
ungraciously	chronologise	horribleness	octosyllable	stranglehold
unifoliolate	chronologist	hydrofluoric	odontologist	stridulation
unimaginable	colourlessly	hyperplastic	orbicularity	strobilation
unimaginably	compellation	hypochlorite	organoleptic	suitableness
unitarianism	conchologist		osteoplastic	surrealistic

surveillance	desquamatory	selfluminous	epiphenomena	postponement
tangibleness	diagrammatic	selfsameness	factionalism	precognition
taxcollector	dichromatism	semidomestic	feminineness	precognitive
technologist	disclamation	simpleminded	fictionalise	preeminently
teratologist	discommodity	singleminded	fluorination	profoundness
terribleness	discriminant	spidermonkey	foraminifera	pronouncedly
tessellation	discriminate	stereometric	frankincense	prothonotary
thermolabile	disharmonise	stichomythia	frequentness	pseudonymity
thriftlessly	dissymmetric	stichomythic	fuliginosity	pseudonymous
towardliness	duraluminium	strongminded	gastronomist	pumpernickel
toxicologist	dynamometric	subcommittee	geomagnetism	punchingball
trampolinist	entrammelled	subnormality	glockenspiel	purblindness
transiliency	epigrammatic	supereminent	gluttonously	pyromaniacal
transplanter	epistemology	supplemental	graspingness	quadrangular
trichologist	erythematous	supplementer	halogenation	quadrinomial
trophallaxis	experimental	synonymously	heathenishly	regimentally
turbellarian	experimenter	teratomatous	heteronomous	rejuvenation
underclothes	fearsomeness	thermometric	highhandedly	residentiary
unfamiliarly	feebleminded	tiresomeness	hoodmanblind	residentship
ungainliness	fostermother	toilsomeness	horizontally	resplendence
unkindliness	gamesomeness	trachomatous	idiosyncrasy	resplendency
unlikelihood	geochemistry	unassumingly	illumination	resupination
unlikeliness	gladsomeness	unbecomingly	illuminative	retiringness
unloveliness	glaucomatous	unencumbered	impregnation	reunionistic
unparalleled	goodhumoured	accidentally	incatenation	rontgenogram
unpopularity	goodtempered	acquaintance	incidentally	rontgenology
untimeliness	governmental	aerodynamics	indefensible	salamandrian
urbanologist	gruesomeness	antagonistic	indefensibly	salamandrine
valuableness	halftimbered	antigenicity	indefinitely	salamandroid
variableness	handsomeness	apparentness	independence	sanguinarily
varicoloured	heteromerous	bacchanalian	independency	sanguineness
vasodilation	homonymously	biocoenology	indigenously	sanguinolent
vasodilatory	huggermugger	cachinnation	inextensible	Scandinavian
vesiculation	impedimental	cachinnatory	inordinately	sclerenchyma
vocabularian	inflammation	caravansarai	insemination	scouringrush
voidableness	inflammatory	caravanserai	invagination	sectionalism
volatileness	instrumental	catilinarian	kremlinology	selfcontempt
whigmaleerie	integumental	ceremonially	labyrinthian	selfignition
workableness	isodiametric	chauvinistic	labyrinthine	semiannually
absentminded	kleptomaniac	chlorination	lacininiated	semifinalist
actinomycete	lachrymation	compoundable	lanternjawed	semifinished
amalgamation	lachrymatory	condemnation	lanternslide	septennially
amalgamative	lachrymosely	condemnatory	lefthandedly	sergeantfish
anagrammatic	legitimately	confoundedly	libidinously	sergeantship
anathematise	legitimation	consignation	longwindedly	serjeantship
anthelmintic	legitimatise	containerise	mansionhouse	sexagenarian
antiSemitism	lonesomeness	coordinately	Marcionitism	shootingiron
atheromatous	malformation	coordination	merchantable	skippingrope
autoimmunity	megalomaniac	coordinative	metalanguage	sleepingpill
autonomously	metasomatism	countenancer	microanalyst	snarlingiron
balladmonger	milliammeter	crossingover	mispronounce	soundingline
battlemented	minicomputer	cryptanalyst	mistranslate	sparkingplug
bibliomaniac	narrowminded	cumulonimbus	monomaniacal	speakingtube
biochemistry	noncommittal	cytogenetics	monotonously	Stakhanovism
bloodyminded	nonflammable	delamination	monumentally	Stakhanovite
bonnetmonkey	Northumbrian	demimondaine	mourningband	standingroom
buttermuslin	nymphomaniac	denomination	mourningring	stationhouse
calorimetric	oversimplify	denominative	neuroanatomy	stationwagon
chancemedley	paronomastic	deracination	Newfoundland	stellenbosch
cheesemonger	performative	desalination	nicotinamide	sterlingness
chronometric	phillumenist	dethronement	nonagenarian	stockingless
colorimetric	phrasemonger	diamagnetism	nonidentical	strikingness
complemental	pluviometric	diaphanously	obedientiary	strychninism
confirmation	polarimetric	discerningly	obligingness	studdingsail
confirmative	posthumously	disconnected	occidentally	substantiate
confirmatory	preformation	disconnexion	octogenarian	substantival
conformation	preformative	discountable	openhandedly	sulphonamide
conglomerate	pretermitted	disdainfully	openmindedly	sulphonation
consummately	proclamation	disfranchise	opinionative	superannuate
consummation	proclamatory	disjointedly	ornamentally	surmountable
consummative	programmable	dressinggown	passionately	surroundings
consummatory	programmatic	effeminately	passionfruit	sweepingness
conterminous	psychometric	emargination	patternmaker	swimmingbath
copolymerise	quadrumanous	emotionalise	penitentiary	swimmingbell
costermonger	schizomycete	emotionalism	pleasantness	swimmingpool
cuprammonium	schoolmaster	emotionalist	pleasingness	terebinthine
departmental	seismometric	emotionality	polytonality	thereinafter
desquamation	selfcomposed	enshrinement	portmanteaus	thousandfold
desquamative	selflimiting	enthronement	portmanteaux	timehonoured

tintinnabula	disallowance	incorporator	peristomatic	synchroniser
toastingfork	disassociate	incorporeity	pestological	tautological
touchingness	disendowment	indissoluble	petrological	teleological
trephination	electrolysis	indissolubly	pettifoggery	tetragonally
trochanteric	electrolytic	inharmonious	pettifogging	tetramorphic
turtlenecked	electrometer	interconnect	phanerogamic	thirdborough
underinsured	electronvolt	interlobular	phenological	tightmouthed
unregenerate	electroplate	interlocutor	philological	tragicomical
unscientific	electroscope	interpolator	philosophise	transformism
vaticination	electroshock	interrogator	phonological	transformist
venepuncture	electrotonic	intervocalic	phosphoresce	transmogrify
venipuncture	electrotonus	irrationally	photomontage	transmontane
veterinarian	electrotyper	irreprovable	phraseograph	transpontine
villainously	emblazonment	irresponsive	phreatophyte	transposable
viscountship	empoisonment	isochromatic	phycological	trichromatic
voluminosity	enantiomorph	isochronally	phytological	trigonometry
voluminously	encyclopedia	jurisconsult	planoconcave	tropological
accommodator	encyclopedic	kaleidoscope	plenipotence	ultramontane
additionally	equationally	laryngoscope	poikilotherm	unapologetic
aetiological	equiprobable	laryngoscopy	polyglottism	unauthorised
antigropelos	erythroblast	leapfrogging	prolegomenon	uncommonness
antiphonally	erythromycin	limnological	prosopopoeia	unconformity
apochromatic	espagnolette	lithological	protozoology	undercoating
apostrophise	ethnological	longshoreman	psychrometer	undiplomatic
archdiocesan	etymological	machicolated	psychrometry	uneconomical
astrological	etymologicon	magnetograph	pteridophyte	unemployable
astronomical	eunuchoidism	magnetometer	pteridosperm	unemployment
bachelorhood	executorship	magniloquent	quaestorship	unfathomable
bachelorship	extensometer	mastigophora	quattrocento	unhistorical
backwoodsman	fibrinolysin	mealymouthed	questionable	unpronounced
balletomania	fractionally	meridionally	questionably	unreasonable
basidiospore	fractionator	mesothoracic	questionless	unreasonably
beachcombing	frictionless	metallophone	radiological	unresponsive
behaviourism	functionally	metalworking	reciprocally	unseasonable
behaviourist	functionless	metaphorical	reciprocator	vainglorious
bluestocking	galactogogue	metathoracic	redeployment	vauntcourier
bodystocking	galvanometer	meteorograph	relationally	viscerotonic
brassbounder	galvanoscope	metrological	relationship	volitionally
bronchoscope	ganglionated	metropolitan	rhinological	wainscotting
buffalograss	genealogical	mezzosoprano	rhynchophora	waistcoating
carcinogenic	Germanophile	microcopying	sabretoothed	wellgrounded
carillonneur	Germanophobe	mitochondria	sacerdotally	whippoorwill
cartological	gerontocracy	mosstrooping	sarrusophone	ailurophobia
cataphoresis	governorship	multifoliate	scatological	anamorphosis
championship	gymnosophist	multiformity	scorpionfish	anthropogeny
chorological	gynaecocracy	multiloquous	selfviolence	anthropoidal
chrestomathy	habitforming	myrmecophily	semiological	anthropology
Christolatry	haematoblast	mythological	semitropical	anticipation
Christophany	haematolysis	mythologiser	sensitometer	anticipative
clairvoyance	haematoxylon	namedropping	servitorship	anticipatory
cleistogamic	haemopoiesis	necrological	servocontrol	bibliopegist
closemouthed	hagiological	neighbouring	siphonophore	bibliophilic
coldshoulder	hedgehopping	nephelometer	siphonostele	bibliopolist
collaborator	hemichordate	nephelometry	skateboarder	biographical
collywobbles	henceforward	neurological	slaveholding	bowcompasses
commemorator	heroicomical	occasionally	smallholding	chalcopyrite
conidiophore	herpetologic	onomatopoeia	sociological	cheeseparing
conidiospore	hippopotamus	onomatopoeic	somniloquism	constipation
conscionable	histological	opisthograph	somniloquist	contemplator
corespondent	homeomorphic	opisthotonos	spectrograph	contemporary
corroborator	hydrological	ornithomancy	spectrometer	contemporise
cosmogonical	hyperbolical	ornithoscopy	spectrometry	contemptible
cosmological	hypochondria	orthodontics	spectroscope	contemptibly
cosmopolitan	hysteromania	orthodontist	spectroscopy	contemptuous
cosmopolitic	ichthyocolla	oscillograph	speedboating	contrapuntal
cottonocracy	ichthyolatry	oscilloscope	sphygmograph	cynocephalus
crosscountry	ichthyophagy	osteological	squattocracy	discerptible
curvicostate	ideationally	osteoporosis	steganograph	discomposure
curvifoliate	immethodical	otherworldly	stockjobbery	distemperate
curvirostral	impersonally	outmanoeuvre	stockjobbing	dodecaphonic
declinometer	impersonator	overcropping	stoneboiling	emancipation
decomposable	imprisonment	paedomorphic	streptococci	episcopalian
densitometer	inclinometer	panchromatic	streptomycin	extraspecial
dermatophyte	incommodious	pantisocracy	superposable	frenchpolish
Deuteronomic	inconformity	parsimonious	surefootedly	gametophytic
diastrophism	inconsolable	pathological	surrejoinder	gamosepalous
dictatorship	inconsolably	periodontics	surveyorship	gastropodous
diphthongise	inconsonance	periodontist	survivorship	geographical
directorship	incorporated	perispomenon	synchronical	heterophylly

homoeopathic	antiperiodic	degenerately	housebreaker	militaristic
hymenopteran	antistrophic	degeneration	housetrained	ministration
inoccupation	appropriable	degenerative	hydrographer	ministrative
interspinous	appropriator	deliberately	hydrographic	misapprehend
jetpropelled	asynchronism	deliberation	hydrotropism	misrepresent
lepidopteran	asynchronous	deliberative	hymnographer	moistureless
lithospheric	automorphism	demineralise	hypertrophic	moneygrubber
mesocephalic	backwardness	denaturalise	hypocoristic	monitorially
moneyspinner	belletristic	denaturation	hypophrygian	monochromate
monkeypuzzle	bilateralism	desideration	iconographer	monomorphous
municipalise	biometrician	desiderative	idolatrously	monostrophic
municipality	blabbermouth	despairingly	illiberality	mouthbreeder
naturopathic	bladderwrack	diathermancy	illiterately	mythographer
newspaperman	blatherskite	dilatoriness	illusoriness	necrographer
niminypiminy	bletherskate	disastrously	illustration	northernmost
noncomplying	blisteringly	discographer	illustrative	nyctitropism
obstreperous	bloodbrother	discouraging	immaterially	obliteration
orographical	blunderingly	discourteous	immatureness	obliterative
overemphasis	blusteringly	downwardness	immemorially	obstetrician
overexposure	boisterously	eavesdropped	immoderately	omnivorously
photospheric	burglarproof	eavesdropper	immoderation	ordinariness
pitterpatter	calligrapher	eccentricity	impoverished	organgrinder
planispheric	calligraphic	ectoparasite	impropriator	orthographer
polysepalous	Cantabrigian	edulcoration	inaccurately	orthographic
presumptuous	cantharidian	elucubration	inadvertence	orthotropism
principality	cardcarrying	encumbrancer	inadvertency	orthotropous
pseudopodium	cartographer	endocarditis	inauguration	overlordship
psychopathic	cartographic	endoparasite	inauguratory	overpersuade
quadraphonic	catachrestic	enterprising	incineration	pantographic
quadriplegia	catastrophic	entrepreneur	incoherently	paramorphism
quadriplegic	charterhouse	ephemerality	indecorously	paranormally
reoccupation	charterparty	equestrienne	indiscreetly	paraphrastic
schizophrene	checkerberry	ethnographer	indiscretion	patriarchate
selfapplause	checkerboard	ethnographic	indivertible	pericarditis
selfapproval	chequerboard	euhemeristic	indivertibly	periphrastic
selfemployed	chesterfield	evisceration	indoctrinate	perpetration
selfhypnosis	chiropractic	exaggeration	IndoEuropean	perspiration
selfreproach	chiropractor	exaggerative	IndoGermanic	perspiratory
semideponent	chitterlings	exaggeratory	industrially	petrographer
somatopleure	chivalrously	exasperation	inexperience	petrographic
spermaphytic	chorographic	exenteration	inexpertness	philharmonic
spokesperson	clangorously	exhilaration	inobservance	phonographer
steatopygous	clapperboard	exhilarative	instauration	phonographic
stereophonic	clatteringly	exprobation	inteneration	photographer
stereopticon	clinkerbuilt	extracranial	intercropped	photographic
subtemperate	closecropped	exulceration	interpretive	photogravure
theosophical	closegrained	featherbrain	interwreathe	phototropism
thermophilic	cocksureness	featheriness	intolerantly	phytographer
toxicophobia	compatriotic	fenestration	intracranial	pictographic
tradespeople	concurrently	flatteringly	inveterately	pitcherplant
trainspotter	consecration	flavoprotein	invigoration	plasterboard
triglyphical	consecratory	flickeringly	irreformable	pleasureless
tropospheric	conspiration	geometrician	irregardless	pleiotropism
unacceptable	contrariness	geriatrician	irreverently	pleomorphism
unscriptural	contrariwise	glitteringly	irreversible	plummerblock
unscrupulous	cosmographer	globetrotter	irreversibly	polychromous
ventripotent	cosmographic	glycoprotein	isothermally	polymorphism
winklepicker	counteragent	greengrocery	jurisprudent	polymorphous
worshipfully	counterblast	haemorrhagic	klipspringer	pornographer
zygapophysis	countercheck	hagiographer	laisserfaire	pornographic
grotesquerie	counterclaim	hagiographic	languorously	postmeridian
acceleration	counterforce	hairsbreadth	leathercloth	pralltriller
accelerative	counterlight	handkerchief	literariness	prefabricate
accoutrement	countermarch	handsbreadth	lithographer	priestridden
adulteration	counterplead	headshrinker	lithographic	primigravida
adulterously	counterpoint	hectographic	lithotritist	prosperously
Alhambresque	counterpoise	heliographer	lovelornness	puerperrally
alliteration	counterproof	heliographic	LowChurchman	pyromorphite
alliterative	counterscarp	heliogravure	lukewarmness	quarterbound
allomorphism	countershaft	heliotropism	magistrature	quarterfinal
amateurishly	countertenor	hemimorphism	malapertness	quarterstaff
amelioration	crackbrained	hemimorphite	malnutrition	rabblerouser
ameliorative	craftbrother	hemiparasite	matriarchate	radiographer
amphibrachic	crossgrained	hierographer	metachronism	radiographic
amphitropous	deceleration	hirepurchase	metamorphism	reassuringly
anemographic	decentralise	homomorphism	metamorphose	recuperation
anotherguess	decompressor	homomorphous	metaphrastic	recuperative
antiaircraft	decontrolled	horsebreaker	microcrystal	redecoration
antiparticle	deflagration	horsetrading	micrographer	redistribute

regeneration	vertebration	conclusively	impressively	postmistress
regenerative	vituperation	concrescence	inaccessible	postposition
registration	vituperative	condensation	inaccessibly	postpositive
remembrancer	vituperatory	confessional	inadmissible	precessional
remuneration	viviparously	conquistador	inadmissibly	preclassical
remunerative	vociferation	consensually	inappositely	preclusively
remuneratory	vociferously	conversation	incalescence	preconscious
reprographic	vomiturition	convulsively	increasingly	preexistence
restaurateur	wallydraigle	cumbersomely	indecisively	prehensility
saccharinity	weatherboard	customshouse	indehiscence	prelapsarian
saccharoidal	weatherbound	Czechoslovak	indigestible	premenstrual
salutariness	weatherglass	decalescence	inspissation	priggishness
scabbardfish	weatherhouse	decreasingly	interestedly	processional
scatterbrain	weatherproof	deionisation	intransigent	proconsulate
scatteringly	whimperingly	delitescence	intransitive	professional
scenographic	whisperingly	depressingly	intumescence	professorate
scoundreldom	whitherwards	deputisation	irremissible	professoress
scoundrelism	zygomorphism	detumescence	irresistible	professorial
scraperboard	zygomorphous	digressional	irresistibly	protensively
secularistic	abstruseness	digressively	juvenescence	protrusively
selfdirected	acaulescence	diminishable	laboursaving	psychosexual
selfmurderer	acquiescence	diminishment	languishment	publicspirit
selfportrait	administrant	disbursement	laterisation	qualmishness
semicircular	administrate	disconsolate	latinisation	quantisation
semidarkness	admonishment	discursively	legalisation	quintessence
semiparasite	aggressively	disguisement	lifelessness	racemisation
sharecropper	agribusiness	dispensation	linguistical	radioisotope
shatterproof	alkalescence	dispensatory	listlessness	readjustment
sinistrality	amortisation	dispossessor	liverystable	reassessment
sinistrorsal	appetisingly	disquisition	localisation	recalescence
slanderously	appraisement	dissuasively	longdistance	recklessness
slipcarriage	appraisingly	dwarfishness	lovelessness	regressively
slipperiness	arborescence	eleemosynary	luminescence	reinvestment
solitariness	arborisation	empressement	maidenstakes	reminiscence
southernmost	astonishment	equalisation	malversation	repressively
southernwood	baselessness	equidistance	marketsquare	resipiscence
squarerigged	biophysicist	etherisation	mastersinger	responsively
staggeringly	blandishment	expressional	masterstroke	responsorial
stalwartness	blastosphere	expressively	masterswitch	restlessness
stammeringly	blithesomely	expressivity	maximisation	reviviscence
standardbred	bombdisposal	facelessness	mindlessness	romanisation
stenographer	bootlessness	faintishness	minimisation	rootlessness
stenographic	brackishness	fearlessness	mistressship	ruralisation
stertorously	breaststroke	fecklessness	mobilisation	ruthlessness
stockbreeder	breastsummer	feminisation	monetisation	secondstring
stockbroking	brontosaurus	feverishness	moralisation	seismoscopic
stonedresser	businesslike	fiddlesticks	motorisation	selfabsorbed
stormtrooper	butterscotch	fiendishness	movelessness	selfdestruct
stubbornness	calorescence	filibusterer	namelessness	selfdistrust
stutteringly	canalisation	finalisation	narcissistic	selflessness
stylographic	canonisation	fluidisation	nebulisation	semibasement
subterranean	carelessness	fluorescence	needlessness	sheepishness
sulphuration	centrespread	focalisation	neoclassical	shillyshally
sulphuretted	centrosphere	formlessness	nonexistence	shrewishness
supererogate	chastisement	freakishness	novelisation	singleseater
supraorbital	childishness	fricasseeing	obmutescence	skittishness
swaggeringly	chromosphere	frontispiece	obsolescence	sluggishness
swaggerstick	churlishness	geophysicist	oppressively	sluttishness
tachygrapher	circumscribe	gesellschaft	optimisation	snapfastener
tachygraphic	circumstance	ghoulishness	organisation	snappishness
thitherwards	civilisation	glaucescence	outpensioner	snobbishness
thundercloud	clannishness	grampositive	painlessness	solarisation
thunderingly	clotheshorse	greenishness	paradisaical	soullessness
thunderously	clothespress	happenstance	paradisiacal	spotlessness
thunderstone	clownishness	harmlessness	paralysation	stablishment
thunderstorm	colonisation	headmistress	parkinsonism	statuesquely
traitorously	commensalism	heedlessness	pearlescence	stereoscopic
transgressor	commensalist	helplessness	peerlessness	stethoscopic
triggerhappy	commensurate	heterosexual	penalisation	stratosphere
twitteringly	commissarial	highlystrung	percussively	stroboscopic
uncontrolled	commissariat	homoeostasis	permissively	subapostolic
underwritten	commissioner	hopelessness	persuasively	subconscious
undetermined	compensation	horrorstruck	perverseness	suberisation
ungovernable	compensative	humanisation	pitilessness	sublapsarian
unimportance	compensatory	hypogastrium	planetstruck	submissively
uninterested	compressible	idealisation	plesiosaurus	subversively
unreservedly	compulsively	immunisation	polarisation	successfully
unrestrained	compulsivity	imperishable	polyhistoric	successional
untowardness	compulsorily	imperishably	possessively	successively

suppressible	automaticity	delicatessen	illegitimate	pejoratively
surprisingly	ballottement	delightfully	impenetrable	perceptively
suspensively	barometrical	delimitation	impenetrably	perceptivity
swainishness	bellbottomed	demilitarise	impenitently	perceptually
sweetishness	bequeathment	demonstrable	imperatively	peremptorily
tactlessness	bespectacled	demonstrably	imperatorial	perfectively
tamelessness	bibliothecae	demonstrator	implantation	periostracum
taskmistress	biosynthesis	depoliticise	impoliteness	permittivity
tearlessness	biosynthetic	derivational	imputatively	pernoctation
televisional	birdwatching	derivatively	inconstantly	persistently
terrorstruck	bloodstained	derogatorily	incrustation	philanthrope
thermoscopic	brainstormer	desolateness	indicatively	philanthropy
thermosphere	breathtaking	dessertspoon	inelasticity	philistinism
thermostable	cabinetmaker	diageotropic	inescutcheon	phlebotomise
thermostatic	calamitously	dialectician	inexactitude	phlebotomist
thievishness	callisthenic	dialectology	infiniteness	phonasthenia
ticklishness	caricaturist	diminutively	infinitively	phyllotactic
timelessness	characterise	discontented	inflectional	pigmentation
tirelessness	charlatanism	discreteness	inhabitation	pinfeathered
toggleswitch	chrematistic	discretional	iniquitously	plecopterous
tonelessness	chromaticism	disgustfully	inspectorate	pneumaticity
totalisation	chromaticity	disgustingly	inspectorial	pneumatology
trickishness	chromatogram	dissentingly	interstellar	pneumothorax
tunelessness	chromatology	dissertation	interstitial	polypetalous
unaccustomed	chromatopsia	distortional	intrauterine	portentously
unclassified	cinematheque	draughtboard	involutional	practitioner
unionisation	circuitously	draughthorse	irrelatively	pragmatistic
universalise	cirrostratus	droughtiness	irritatingly	preceptorial
universalism	coelenterate	dubitatively	kilowatthour	predestinate
universalist	cohabitation	elementalism	kinaesthesia	predictively
universality	coleopterist	elementarily	kinaesthesis	prefectorial
unpleasantly	coleopterous	enchantingly	kinaesthetic	prehistorian
urbanisation	collectively	encrustation	laureateship	preposterous
valorisation	collectivise	endometritis	ledgertackle	presbyterate
vanquishable	collectivism	enginetuning	levorotation	presbyterial
vanquishment	collectivist	entreatingly	levorotatory	Presbyterian
vaporisation	collectivity	equalitarian	macropterous	presentation
viridescence	comfortingly	evidentially	malcontented	presentative
virtuosoship	commentation	excogitation	manometrical	presentiment
vitalisation	committeeman	excogitative	meditatively	preventative
vocalisation	completeness	exercitation	mercantilism	preventively
welldisposed	concentrator	exhaustively	mercantilist	productively
whencesoever	conceptional	exhibitioner	minedetector	productivity
womanishness	conceptually	exorbitantly	misquotation	progesterone
wonderstruck	concreteness	explantation	misselthrush	proglottides
absoluteness	conductivity	exploitation	misstatement	projectional
absolutistic	confectioner	exploitative	moderateness	projectively
absorptional	conglutinate	extrauterine	monometallic	proportional
absorptivity	congratulant	facilitation	monopetalous	proportioned
absquatulate	congratulate	fantasticate	mothertongue	prosectorial
accurateness	connectional	fantasticism	motivational	prostitution
accusatively	connectively	felicitation	multistoried	protactinium
accusatorial	consentience	felicitously	nauseatingly	protectively
adequateness	consentingly	fermentation	navigational	protectorate
aesthetician	consistently	fermentative	neglectfully	protestation
aestheticism	consistorial	figuratively	Neoplatonism	protistology
alimentation	constituency	fortuitously	Neoplatonist	prudentially
alimentative	constitution	foundationer	neurasthenia	psychotropic
amphictyonic	constitutive	freightliner	neurasthenic	pursestrings
anecdotalist	consultation	futilitarian	neuropterous	quantitative
antipathetic	consultative	gamopetalous	nimbostratus	recapitulate
apiculturist	contestation	geotectonics	obdurateness	reconstitute
apparatchiki	contextually	gladiatorial	obligatorily	recreational
apparatchiks	contriteness	gonadotropic	obsoleteness	redemptioner
apparitional	convectional	gonadotropin	occupational	Redemptorist
appositeness	conventicler	grallatorial	omnipotently	reflectional
appositional	conventional	grammaticise	oppositeness	reflectively
Aristotelean	copulatively	gratuitously	oppositional	reflectivity
Aristotelian	coquettishly	guaranteeing	orchestrator	refractivity
asymmetrical	corelatively	habilitation	orthopterist	refractorily
attractively	correctional	heartstrings	orthopteroid	remilitarise
augmentation	correctitude	hereditament	orthopterous	remonstrance
augmentative	correctively	hereditarily	overactivity	remonstrator
auscultation	cumulatively	hesitatingly	overestimate	renegotiable
auscultatory	debilitation	humanitarian	oxyacetylene	repetitional
authenticate	decapitation	hydrostatics	paraesthesia	repetitively
authenticity	decoratively	hypersthenia	parametrical	resoluteness
autocatalyse	definiteness	hypersthenic	parasiticide	respectfully
autochthones	definitively	illegitimacy	parasitology	respectively

```
retractation  transitorily  echosounding  nebulousness  thankfulness
retractility  tricentenary  effectuality  neurosurgeon  threequarter
revelational  trichotomise  effectuation  neurosurgery  timorousness
rheumatology  trichotomous  enormousness  noctilucence  topsyturvily
rumbletumble  tridactylous  exiguousness  numerousness  tortuousness
ruminatively  tripartitely  exsanguinate  offscourings  transduction
salutational  tripartition  exsanguinous  overabundant  transfusible
Samaritanism  trumpetshell  extinguisher  overcautious  transhumance
schizothymia  ubiquitarian  extramundane  particularly  translucence
schizothymic  ubiquitously  fabulousness  patulousness  translucency
segmentation  unappetising  factiousness  peacefulness  transmutable
selfactivity  unconstraint  faithfulness  peasepudding  triangularly
selfbetrayal  understaffed  fancifulness  pedunculated  trustfulness
selfcatering  uneventfully  floriculture  perambulator  truthfulness
selfinterest  unflattering  folliculated  perilousness  tuberculated
semidetached  unhesitating  forcefulness  perpetuation  tuberculosis
semiliterate  vegetatively  fruitfulness  perviousness  tumultuously
sententially  vindictively  furunculosis  pisciculture  turriculated
separateness  visitational  generousness  polyneuritic  typefounding
sequentially  visitatorial  gesticulator  polyneuritis  ultramundane
sequestrator  volumetrical  gloriousness  populousness  uncalculated
serpentiform  walkietalkie  gorgeousness  preciousness  unctuousness
serpentinely  wollastonite  gracefulness  preoccupancy  undercurrent
sexcentenary  woolgatherer  graciousness  prerequisite  undercutting
shortstaffed  xiphisternum  gratefulness  previousness  underrunning
slaughterous  accentuation  grievousness  pricecutting  undersurface
solicitation  acetabularia  guilefulness  pridefulness  unfavourable
solicitously  aeronautical  harlequinade  prosecutable  unfavourably
sophisticate  aeroneurosis  heartburning  radionuclide  unfrequented
spermathecal  alphanumeric  highsounding  ravenousness  unisexuality
spermatocyte  antineutrino  honeybuzzard  repercussion  unlawfulness
spermatozoid  attributable  horticulture  repercussive  unprejudiced
spermatozoon  bilingualism  humorousness  reproducible  usuriousness
sprightfully  blackcurrant  hydroquinone  reproduction  uxoriousness
stalactiform  blackguardly  illnaturedly  reproductive  vaporousness
statistician  blamefulness  immeasurable  retropulsion  vengefulness
sternutation  blastfurnace  immeasurably  revictualled  venomousness
sternutative  blissfulness  immensurable  rightfulness  vermiculated
sternutatory  blockbusting  inadequately  rigorousness  vernacularly
strengthener  boastfulness  incalculable  scabrousness  vigorousness
strengthless  brassrubbing  incalculably  scornfulness  virtuousness
subcontinent  Byelorussian  incestuously  scripturally  vitreousness
subeditorial  canorousness  incommutable  sculpturally  voluptuosity
subjectively  captiousness  incommutably  sedulousness  voluptuously
subjectivise  catamountain  incomputable  selfdoubting  warehouseman
subjectivism  cautiousness  inconsumable  selfeducated  wastefulness
subjectivist  cheerfulness  inconsumably  sensuousness  watchfulness
subjectivity  cirrocumulus  incorruption  shamefulness  wondrousness
substitution  clairaudient  indisputable  silviculture  wrathfulness
substitutive  coachbuilder  indisputably  skullduggery  wrongfulness
suggestively  colloquially  infrequently  slothfulness  youthfulness
superstition  confabulator  intercurrent  sodafountain  abortiveness
superstratum  connaturally  intercutting  solifluction  abrasiveness
susceptivity  consequently  intermundane  sonorousness  adaptiveness
sustentation  construction  internuclear  spaciousness  adhesiveness
sustentative  constructive  internuncial  speciousness  allusiveness
synaesthesia  contiguously  interruption  spiritualise  coacervation
synaesthetic  continuation  interruptive  spiritualism  coerciveness
syncretistic  continuative  intramundane  spiritualist  cohesiveness
syndactylism  continuously  intriguingly  spirituality  conservation
syndactylous  covetousness  introduction  spitefulness  conservatism
tangentially  crossbuttock  introductory  sportfulness  conservative
teetertotter  crosscurrent  intussuscept  spuriousness  conservatory
telaesthesia  crosspurpose  jerrybuilder  staffsurgeon  contrivement
telaesthetic  cumbrousness  Liverpudlian  stepdaughter  creativeness
tercentenary  decorousness  longitudinal  stillhunting  deactivation
testosterone  delinquently  luminousness  stonecutting  decisiveness
thaumaturgic  denticulated  lusciousness  structurally  delusiveness
theoretician  desirousness  manslaughter  studiousness  derisiveness
thermotactic  dextrousness  menstruation  subsaturated  divisiveness
thermotropic  disannulling  mercifulness  subsequently  effusiveness
thoughtfully  disannulment  metallurgist  substruction  eruptiveness
tittletattle  disreputable  microsurgery  substructure  fructivorous
toploftiness  disreputably  mirthfulness  superhumanly  fugitiveness
torrentially  dissimulator  mournfulness  supermundane  hardfavoured
totalitarian  dolorousness  multinuclear  supramundane  illusiveness
transitional  doubtfulness  multipurpose  swashbuckler  inactivation
transitively  dramaturgist  mutinousness  sylviculture  incisiveness
transitivity  dreadfulness  nauseousness  tastefulness  irrelevantly
```

manoeuvrable	mystifyingly	bespectacled	confirmatory	deracination
mediaevalism	oncorhynchus	bibliomaniac	confiscation	desalination
mediaevalist	phagocytosis	bilateralism	confiscatory	desideration
negativeness	phagocytotic	bilingualism	conformation	desiderative
negativistic	phenotypical	blackguardly	Confucianism	despoliation
perfervidity	phycomycetes	blastulation	congeniality	desquamation
positiveness	polyphyletic	bloodstained	conglobation	desquamative
positivistic	proselytiser	bonnyclabber	congregation	desquamatory
preservation	prototypical	bottlewasher	connubiality	detoxication
preservative	satisfyingly	bowcompasses	consecration	dichromatism
quadrivalent	strongylosis	brachydactyl	consecratory	dilapidation
quaquaversal	terrifyingly	breathtaking	conservation	dinnerjacket
reactivation	bilharziasis	brontosaurus	conservatism	disaccharide
reactiveness	bilharziosis	cachinnation	conservative	disclamation
relativeness	heterozygote	cachinnatory	conservatory	discographer
relativistic	heterozygous	calligrapher	consignation	discordantly
selfdevotion	laissezaller	calligraphic	consociation	discouraging
selfinvolved	laissezfaire	calumniation	conspiration	disenchanter
sportiveness	————————————	calumniatory	constipation	disinflation
Stradivarius	abbreviation	canalisation	consultation	dispensation
subservience	acceleration	cancellation	consultative	dispensatory
subserviency	accelerative	canonisation	consummately	dissertation
unambivalent	accentuation	cantillation	consummation	dissocialise
wellfavoured	acciaccatura	capitulation	consummative	dissociation
bantamweight	accumulation	carpetbagger	consummatory	dissociative
boogiewoogie	accumulative	Cartesianism	contestation	distillation
bottlewasher	adjudication	cartographer	continuation	distillatory
brokenwinded	adjudicative	cartographic	continuative	divarication
churchwarden	adjudicatory	catilinarian	conversation	earthshaking
commonwealth	adulteration	charlatanism	conviviality	ecclesiastic
kirschwasser	aerodynamics	cheeseparing	coordinately	echolocation
mangelwurzel	alexipharmic	childbearing	coordination	ectoparasite
middleweight	alimentation	chiropractic	coordinative	editorialise
misknowledge	alimentative	chiropractor	corporeality	editorialist
monkeywrench	alliteration	chlorination	cosmographer	edulcoration
neoDarwinian	alliterative	chorographic	cosmographic	effectuality
neoDarwinism	amalgamation	Christianise	countenancer	effectuation
neoDarwinist	amalgamative	Christianity	counteragent	effeminately
nonflowering	amelioration	churchianity	courtplaster	elementalism
overpowering	ameliorative	churchwarden	crackbrained	elementarily
praiseworthy	amortisation	circumjacent	crenellation	elucubration
screenwriter	amphibrachic	civilisation	crossexamine	emancipation
scriptwriter	amphisbaenic	classicalism	crossgrained	emargination
sparrowgrass	anaphylactic	classicalist	crossheading	emasculation
streetwalker	anathematise	classicality	cryptanalyst	emasculatory
teensweensy	anecdotalist	claudication	cryptogamous	emotionalise
welterweight	anemographic	closegrained	deactivation	emotionalism
williewaught	annihilation	coacervation	deambulatory	emotionalist
wonderworker	annihilative	codification	debilitation	emotionality
ambidextrous	annunciation	cohabitation	decapitation	encrustation
complexional	anticipation	collegialism	deceleration	encumbrancer
complexioned	anticipative	collegiality	decentralise	endoparasite
crossexamine	anticipatory	collegiately	deescalation	enthusiastic
homosexually	antimacassar	collinearity	deflagration	ephemerality
perplexingly	antimalarial	colonisation	defraudation	epicureanism
achlamydeous	appreciation	columniation	degenerately	episcopalian
archetypally	appreciative	commendation	degeneration	epithalamion
archetypical	appreciatory	commendatory	degenerative	epithalamium
carbohydrate	arborisation	commensalism	deionisation	equalisation
chimneypiece	articulately	commensalist	delamination	equalitarian
coenobytical	articulation	commentation	deliberately	equivocation
countrydance	articulatory	commissarial	deliberation	equivocatory
countrywoman	asphyxiation	commissariat	deliberative	erythematous
flamboyantly	assibilation	compellation	delimitation	essentiality
gamophyllous	assimilation	compensation	demilitarise	etherisation
gratifyingly	assimilative	compensative	demineralise	ethnographer
holidaymaker	assimilatory	compensatory	demodulation	ethnographic
hydrodynamic	atheromatous	complication	denaturalise	evisceration
hydrolysable	augmentation	compurgation	denaturation	exacerbation
hyperpyretic	augmentative	compurgatory	denomination	exaggeration
hyperpyrexia	auscultation	conciliation	denominative	exaggerative
leucocytosis	auscultatory	conciliative	denuclearise	exaggeratory
leukocytosis	Australasian	conciliatory	denunciation	exasperation
licketysplit	autocatalyse	concordantly	denunciative	excogitation
metaphysical	autodidactic	condemnation	denunciatory	excogitative
metapsychics	bacchanalian	condemnatory	depopulation	excruciating
monophyletic	backbreaking	condensation	depreciation	excruciation
Monophysitic	backpedalled	confirmation	depreciatory	exenteration
motorcyclist	berzelianite	confirmatory	deputisation	exercitation

exhilaration	illiterately	Manicheanism	paralysation	racemisation
exhilarative	illogicality	manipulation	paraphrastic	radiographer
exophthalmic	illumination	manipulative	parochialise	radiographic
exophthalmos	illuminative	manipulatory	parochialism	ramification
exophthalmus	illustration	marketgarden	parochiality	ratification
exorbitantly	illustrative	maximisation	paronomastic	razzledazzle
expatriation	immaculately	mediaevalism	passionately	reactivation
explantation	immoderately	mediaevalist	penalisation	reallocation
exploitation	immoderation	megalomaniac	perfoliation	recuperation
exploitative	immunisation	menstruation	performative	recuperative
exprobration	impartiality	mercurialise	periphrastic	redecoration
extracranial	implantation	mercurialism	permanganate	regeneration
exulceration	impregnation	metagalactic	pernoctation	regenerative
facilitation	inaccurately	metaphrastic	peroxidation	registration
factionalism	inactivation	metasomatism	perpetration	rejuvenation
fainthearted	inadequately	microanalyst	perpetuation	remembrancer
faithhealing	inauguration	micrographer	perspicacity	remilitarise
farmsteading	inauguratory	minimisation	perspiration	remuneration
felicitation	incatenation	ministration	perspiratory	remunerative
feminisation	incendiarism	ministrative	perturbation	remuneratory
fenestration	incineration	miscellanist	perturbative	renunciation
fermentation	inconstantly	misdemeanant	petrographer	renunciative
fermentative	incrustation	misdemeanour	petrographic	renunciatory
fibrillation	indelicately	miseducation	phonographer	reoccupation
fictionalise	inflammation	misquotation	phonographic	repatriation
fiddlefaddle	inflammatory	mithridatise	photographer	reprographic
fieldglasses	ingratiating	mithridatism	photographic	restaurateur
finalisation	inhabitation	mobilisation	photogravure	resupination
flagellation	inoccupation	modification	phyllotactic	reticulately
flagellatory	inordinately	modificatory	phytographer	reticulation
flamboyantly	inosculation	molecularity	phytophagous	retractation
flocculation	insemination	monetisation	pictographic	revictualled
fluidisation	inspissation	moneychanger	pigmentation	rhizophagous
fluoridation	installation	monkeyjacket	pitterpatter	romanisation
fluorination	instauration	monofilament	plaindealing	ruralisation
fluorocarbon	instillation	monometallic	plesiosaurus	saddlebacked
focalisation	insufflation	monopetalous	polarisation	salmonladder
futilitarian	inteneration	moralisation	polypetalous	Samaritanism
gamopetalous	interchanger	morrisdancer	polysepalous	sanguinarily
gamosepalous	interglacial	motorisation	polytonality	saprophagous
gasification	intimidation	municipalise	porcellanous	sarcophagous
glaucomatous	intimidatory	municipality	pornographer	Scandinavian
gramnegative	intolerantly	mythographer	pornographic	scareheading
greathearted	intoxication	naturopathic	potentiality	scenographic
grossularite	intracranial	nebulisation	practicality	schoolmaster
guestchamber	invagination	necrographer	precisianism	scrimshanker
habilitation	invalidation	necrophagous	preformation	scutellation
hagiographer	inveterately	neonomianism	preformative	sectarianise
hagiographic	invigilation	Nestorianism	prelapsarian	sectarianism
halogenation	invigoration	neuroanatomy	presentation	sectionalism
heavyhearted	irregularity	nicotinamide	presentative	segmentation
hectographic	irrelevantly	nidification	preservation	selfeffacing
heliographer	katzenjammer	nomenclative	preservative	selfpleasing
heliographic	Keynesianism	nomenclature	preventative	semidetached
heliogravure	kindergarten	nonagenarian	primigravida	semifinalist
hemerocallis	kirschwasser	nonchalantly	principality	semiparasite
hemiparasite	kleptomaniac	noncombatant	proclamation	sexagenarian
hereditament	laboursaving	notification	proclamatory	shortchanger
hereditarily	lachrymation	novelisation	profligately	shortstaffed
heterogamous	lachrymatory	nymphomaniac	prolongation	sightreading
hierographer	laissezaller	obliteration	promulgation	singlehanded
hierophantic	largehearted	obliterative	proofreading	sinistrality
homoeopathic	laterisation	obnubilation	prophylactic	skateboarder
homologation	latinisation	octogenarian	propitiation	skrimshanker
horsetrading	ledgertackle	ophiophagous	propitiatory	sledgehammer
housetrained	legalisation	opinionative	protestation	snakecharmer
hucklebacked	legitimately	optimisation	prothalamion	softpedalled
humanisation	legitimation	orbicularity	prothalamium	solarisation
humanitarian	legitimatise	organisation	protoplasmic	solicitation
humification	levorotation	orthographer	protoplastic	speedboating
hydrographer	levorotatory	orthographic	proudhearted	spiritualise
hydrographic	lighthearted	ossification	psychopathic	spiritualism
hydrostatics	lithographer	osteoplastic	purification	spiritualist
hymnographer	lithographic	pacification	purificatory	spirituality
hyperplastic	localisation	pacificatory	quadrivalent	stenographer
iconoclastic	lumberjacket	Palladianism	quadrumanous	stenographic
iconographer	magistrature	panification	quantisation	sternutation
idealisation	malformation	pantographic	quantitative	sternutative
illiberality	malversation	paradisaical	quizzicality	sternutatory

stonyhearted	Victorianism	apparatchiki	episodically	liquefaction
stouthearted	vilification	apparatchiks	esoterically	liturgically
Stradivarius	vinification	appendectomy	euphonically	logistically
straitjacket	vitalisation	appendicitis	exegetically	LowChurchman
streetwalker	vitiligation	appendicular	exoterically	luminescence
stridulation	vituperation	arborescence	fluorescence	magnetically
strobilation	vituperative	archdeaconry	forensically	magnifically
strontianite	vituperatory	archdiocesan	frankincense	magnificence
stylographic	vivification	architecture	frenetically	majestically
subarrhation	vocabularian	argillaceous	furfuraceous	matriarchate
suberisation	vocalisation	aromatically	gallinaceous	mechanically
sublapsarian	vociferation	aromaticness	galvanically	meretricious
subminiature	waistcoating	artistically	genuflection	metallically
subnormality	walkietalkie	athletically	geologically	metapsychics
subsidiarily	wallydraigle	bactericidal	gerontocracy	meteorically
subterranean	whimsicality	barbarically	gesellschaft	methodically
sulphonamide	wholehearted	beatifically	gigantically	misdirection
sulphonation	williewaught	billsticking	glaucescence	mnemotechnic
sulphuration	yellowhammer	biologically	graminaceous	monastically
supercharger	analphabetic	birdwatching	gynaecocracy	monostichous
supplicantly	brambleberry	bluestocking	handkerchief	motorcyclist
supplication	brassrubbing	bodystocking	harmonically	multinuclear
supplicatory	checkerberry	bookingclerk	heraldically	narcotically
sustentation	checkerboard	butterscotch	hermetically	nerveracking
sustentative	chequerboard	calorescence	heteroecious	neurotically
tachygrapher	clapperboard	camiknickers	hibernaculum	noctilucence
tachygraphic	clinkerbuilt	carbonaceous	hirepurchase	noneffective
technicality	collywobbles	cashandcarry	historically	nonefficient
teratomatous	concelebrant	catholically	horrifically	nonobjective
tessellation	concelebrate	cherubically	hygienically	obmutescence
thereinafter	counterblast	circumscribe	hypnotically	obsolescence
thermolabile	disestablish	communicable	hypothecator	operatically
thermotactic	draughtboard	communicably	hysterectomy	orchidaceous
threequarter	drawingboard	communicator	hysterically	overreaction
tintinnabula	equiprobable	concrescence	ichthyocolla	pantisocracy
tittletattle	erythroblast	constriction	idiosyncrasy	pathetically
totalisation	featherbrain	constrictive	imperfection	patriarchate
totalitarian	haematoblast	construction	imperfective	pearlescence
trachomatous	halftimbered	constructive	inapplicable	pedantically
tradescantia	hoodmanblind	contumacious	inapplicably	periodically
traducianism	infundibular	cosmetically	inauspicious	pertinacious
traducianist	interlobular	cottonocracy	incalescence	petrifaction
transplanter	invertebrate	countercheck	indehiscence	phonemically
transudation	landlubberly	counterclaim	ineradicable	phonetically
transudatory	Northumbrian	crosssection	ineradicably	phycomycetes
trephination	outwardbound	decalescence	inescutcheon	platonically
trifurcation	plasterboard	deconsecrate	inexplicable	pontifically
trinomialism	plummerblock	delitescence	inexplicably	pontificator
triplication	preestablish	demoniacally	inextricable	preconscious
triumphantly	purposebuilt	despotically	inextricably	predilection
turbellarian	quarterbound	detumescence	infanticidal	preselection
typification	runningboard	diabolically	insecticidal	preselective
ubiquitarian	scatterbrain	diatomaceous	insufficient	prevaricator
unambivalent	scraperboard	diatonically	insurrection	prolifically
undercoating	selfdoubting	didactically	intellection	prolificness
understaffed	serviceberry	dietetically	intellective	pronouncedly
unhesitating	shuffleboard	disaffection	intellectual	prosodically
unionisation	skunkcabbage	disassociate	interdiction	psychoactive
unisexuality	stellenbosch	disfranchise	interdictive	pterodactyle
unitarianism	stockjobbery	disinfectant	interdictory	putrefaction
universalise	stockjobbing	disinfection	interjection	putrefactive
universalism	supraorbital	diverticular	interjectory	pyroelectric
universalist	thimbleberry	diverticulum	interlocutor	quattrocento
universality	unencumbered	dogmatically	internuclear	quixotically
unpleasantly	weatherboard	domestically	intersection	rabbinically
unpopularity	weatherbound	domesticator	intervocalic	radionuclide
unrestrained	whortleberry	doubleacting	introduction	recalescence
urbanisation	academically	dramatically	introductory	receptaculum
valorisation	acaulescence	dynastically	introjection	reciprocally
vaporisation	acoustically	eclectically	intumescence	reciprocator
vasodilation	acquiescence	ecologically	irreflective	recollection
vasodilatory	alkalescence	economically	irrespective	recollective
vaticination	amitotically	ecstatically	jesuitically	reminiscence
veridicality	anagogically	electrically	jurisdiction	reproducible
verification	analogically	elliptically	juvenescence	reproduction
verificatory	analytically	emphatically	kissingcrust	reproductive
vertebration	anatomically	enclitically	landingcraft	resipiscence
vesiculation	antiaircraft	endermically	leathercloth	resurrection
veterinarian	apolitically	epidemically	liquefacient	reviviscence

rhetorically	backwardness	thousandfold	conchiferous	experimental
rhythmically	backwoodsman	unconsidered	concreteness	experimenter
romantically	bullheadedly	underbidding	concurrently	extraspecial
sadistically	calycoideous	unprejudiced	conglomerate	extrauterine
safecracking	carbohydrate	untowardness	consequently	falcongentil
sardonically	clairaudient	unwontedness	consistently	falcongentle
satisfaction	composedness	wretchedness	containerise	fearsomeness
satisfactory	compoundable	abortiveness	contingently	feminineness
scarificator	confoundedly	abrasiveness	contriteness	forcibleness
schorlaceous	confusedness	absoluteness	contrivement	forebodement
sclerenchyma	consolidator	abstruseness	conveniently	formaldehyde
seismoscopic	countrydance	accouchement	convincement	FrancoGerman
selfeducated	crossbedding	accoutrement	copolymerise	fraudulently
selfelective	dejectedness	accurateness	cousingerman	freewheeling
semantically	demimondaine	acetaldehyde	creativeness	fricasseeing
semicircular	depravedness	adaptiveness	culpableness	fructiferous
semiprecious	detachedness	adequateness	curmudgeonly	fugitiveness
seraphically	diamonddrill	adhesiveness	cytogenetics	fullyfledged
servicecourt	downwardness	adorableness	decisiveness	gamesomeness
shamefacedly	endocarditis	aerosiderite	decompressor	geomagnetism
significance	eveningdress	Alhambresque	definiteness	gladsomeness
significancy	hebdomadally	allusiveness	delicatessen	gobbledegook
simoniacally	hesperididia	ambivalently	delinquently	governmental
singleacting	highhandedly	amenableness	delusiveness	grammolecule
Socratically	hydromedusae	amentiferous	denouncement	groundlessly
solifluction	hydromedusan	amicableness	departmental	gruesomeness
sorbefacient	immethodical	amphitheatre	derisiveness	guaranteeing
specifically	improvidence	anaesthetise	desolateness	hairsbreadth
specificness	incommodious	anaesthetist	despondently	handsbreadth
sporadically	indebtedness	announcement	dethronement	handsomeness
squattocracy	independence	antecedently	diamagnetism	heliotherapy
steeplechase	independency	appositeness	disagreeable	hemispheroid
stereoscopic	interbedding	appraisement	disagreeably	hereinbefore
stethoscopic	intermeddler	Aristotelean	disagreement	heterocercal
streptococci	intermediacy	Aristotelian	disbursement	heterogenous
stroboscopic	intermediary	astringently	discipleship	heteromerous
stupefacient	intermediate	atmospherics	disconnected	heterosexual
stupefaction	irregardless	ballottement	disconnexion	horribleness
stupefactive	lefthandedly	bantamweight	discontented	horsebreaker
subconscious	Liverpudlian	battlemented	discreteness	housebreaker
subsonically	longitudinal	bedazzlement	disgorgement	housekeeping
substruction	longwindedly	belittlement	disguisement	hydrotherapy
substructure	lopsidedness	beneficently	dislodgement	hydrothermal
supernaculum	manifoldness	benevolently	displaceable	hyperthermia
swashbuckler	morningdress	benzaldehyde	displacement	hypnotherapy
syllabically	Newfoundland	bibliopegist	dispossessor	illusiveness
symbolically	nonresidence	blamableness	dissymmetric	immatureness
syndetically	onesidedness	breathlessly	distemperate	impedimental
synoptically	openhandedly	brickfielder	divisiveness	impenitently
systemically	openmindedly	buccaneering	dodecahedral	impoliteness
tabernacular	outdatedness	buccaneerish	dodecahedron	incisiveness
tectonically	overlordship	bulletheaded	doubledealer	incoherently
terrifically	peasepudding	calisthenics	doubledecked	incompletely
Teutonically	pellucidness	calorimetric	doubledecker	indiscreetly
theatrically	pericarditis	cantankerous	dunderheaded	indiscretion
theistically	postgraduate	carragheenin	dynamometric	ineffaceable
thematically	preparedness	carriageable	effortlessly	ineffaceably
thermoscopic	profoundness	catachrestic	effusiveness	infiniteness
thundercloud	purblindness	chancemedley	embattlement	infrequently
torrefaction	reservedness	characterise	embezzlement	infringement
transduction	resignedness	chastisement	empressement	instrumental
translucence	resolvedness	chemotherapy	encirclement	integumental
translucency	resplendence	chronometric	endamagement	interoceanic
transpacific	resplendency	cocksureness	enfeeblement	interoceptor
tyrannically	retrocedence	coelenterate	enshrinement	interpleader
tyrannicidal	salamandrian	coerciveness	enswathement	interpretive
unattractive	salamandrine	cohesiveness	entanglement	interstellar
uncritically	salamandroid	coincidental	enthronement	interwreathe
venepuncture	scabbardfish	coincidently	entrammelled	intrauterine
venipuncture	selfevidence	coleopterist	entrancement	inveiglement
viridescence	selfmurderer	coleopterous	entrepreneur	irreverently
vitrifaction	sinusoidally	colorimetric	enviableness	isodiametric
volcanically	spheroidally	colourlessly	envisagement	jetpropelled
workingclass	spiritedness	commencement	equivalently	laticiferous
accommodator	splendidness	committeeman	eruptiveness	laudableness
accursedness	standardbred	commonwealth	escutcheoned	laureateship
achlamydeous	supersedence	complacently	estrangement	lonesomeness
affectedness	surroundings	complemental	evanescently	luminiferous
ambassadress	tetrahedrite	completeness	exchangeable	macropterous

malcontented readableness tricentenary graspingness superhighway
malevolently rechargeable turtlenecked hagiological sweepingness
marriageable regardlessly unchangeable histological swimmingbath
middleweight relativeness unchangeably hydrological swimmingbell
minedetector relentlessly unflattering incontiguous swimmingpool
misapprehend reliableness unfrequented incorrigible tautological
misjudgement renouncement uninterested incorrigibly teleological
misplacement resettlement unmanageable intelligence theatregoing
misrepresent resiniferous unregenerate intelligible toastingfork
misstatement resistlessly Valenciennes intelligibly touchingness
moderateness resoluteness valuableness interdigital transmigrant
moistureless retroflexion variableness interrogator transmigrate
mouthbreeder rhombohedral voidableness investigator transmogrify
moveableness rhombohedron volatileness irrefragable tropological
muddleheaded salutiferous welterweight irrefragably unapologetic
munificently sanguineness whigmaleerie leapfrogging unsegregated
muttonheaded schoolfellow wicketkeeper limnological weatherglass
negativeness schoolleaver woodenheaded lithological acronychally
Neohellenism scoundreldom woollyheaded magnetograph admonishment
neuropterous scoundrelism workableness manslaughter ailurophobia
nevertheless seismometric xiphisternum metalanguage anamorphosis
newspaperman selfaffected chesterfield meteorograph antipathetic
nonflowering selfcatering counterforce metrological antirachitic
nympholeptic selfdeceived delightfully mourningband approachable
obdurateness selfdeceiver despitefully mourningring astonishment
obsoleteness selfdirected diamondfield mythological autochthones
obstreperous selfinterest disdainfully mythologiser bequeathment
omnipotently selfsameness disgustfully necrological bibliophilic
omnisciently semibasement laisserfaire neurological bibliothecae
oppositeness semidomestic laissezfaire obligingness biographical
organoleptic semiliterate landingfield opisthograph biosynthesis
orienteering seminiferous meaningfully oscillograph biosynthetic
orthopaedics sensibleness neglectfully osteological blandishment
orthopaedist separateness passionfruit pathological brackishness
orthopterist septuagenary playingfield pestological bullfighting
orthopteroid Septuagesima purposefully petrological callisthenic
orthopterous sexcentenary quarterfinal pettifoggery charnelhouse
outmanoeuvre sheepshearer remorsefully pettifogging charterhouse
overniceness shortsleeved respectfully phanerogamic childishness
overpowering siliciferous revengefully phenological churlishness
panhellenism singledecker sprightfully philological cinematheque
parenthesise singleseater staffofficer phonological clannishness
persistently slaughteress successfully phraseograph clotheshorse
perverseness sociableness thoughtfully phycological clownishness
pharmaceutic soporiferous uneventfully phytological cockfighting
phillumenist speechlessly unfaithfully pleasingness customshouse
pitiableness spiegeleisen ungracefully predesignate cynocephalus
pleasureless spiritlessly ungratefully prizefighter dibranchiate
plecopterous spokesperson unmercifully punchingball diminishable
plumbiferous sportiveness untruthfully quadrangular diminishment
pluviometric stanniferous worshipfully radiological dodecaphonic
polarimetric stelliferous advantageous redintegrate draughthorse
polychaetous stereometric aetiological retiringness dwarfishness
positiveness sternwheeler anotherguess rhinological embranchment
postponement stockbreeder astrological sacrilegious encroachment
precancelled stonedresser buffalograss scatological entrenchment
preeminently stranglehold burningglass scouringrush faintishness
prenticeship subsequently carcinogenic semiological feverishness
preponderant subtemperate cartological sharpsighted fiendishness
preponderate sudoriferous chorological shootingiron firefighting
preposterous sufficiently clearsighted shortsighted foresightful
presbyterate suitableness cleistogamic skippingrope freakishness
presbyterial sulphuretted cosmological skullduggery gametophytic
Presbyterian supplemental crossingover sleepingpill geographical
privateering supplementer crystalgazer snarlingiron ghoulishness
procathedral tangibleness disambiguate sociological greenishness
proficiently taxcollector disintegrate soundingline groundcherry
profiteering teensyweensy dressinggown sparkingplug haemorrhagic
progesterone tercentenary ethnological sparrowgrass heterophylly
propaedeutic terribleness etymological speakingtube hierarchical
psychometric testosterone etymologicon spectrograph hypersthenia
psychosexual thermometric extravagance sphygmograph hypersthenic
Quadragesima threewheeler extravagancy standingroom imperishable
quaquaversal thriftlessly extravaganza steganograph imperishably
racketeering tiresomeness firstnighter stepdaughter intrenchment
radioelement toilsomeness floodlighted sterlingness kinaesthesia
radiotherapy tradespeople forthrightly stockingless kinaesthesis
rattleheaded transgressor galactogogue strikingness kinaesthetic
reactiveness transoceanic genealogical studdingsail languishment

lithospheric	absentminded	collectivism	emulsifiable	impressively
lodginghouse	absolutistic	collectivist	enchantingly	impropriator
mansionhouse	absorptional	collectivity	enterprising	imputability
meetinghouse	absorptivity	colloquially	entertaining	imputatively
melanochroic	accomplished	comfortingly	entreatingly	inappositely
mesocephalic	accusatively	commandingly	equestrienne	inartificial
misselthrush	adaptability	commercially	equitability	inaudibility
neurasthenia	advisability	commissioner	euhemeristic	incapability
neurasthenic	aesthetician	compatriotic	eunuchoidism	incapacitate
oligarchical	aestheticism	complexional	evangelistic	incompliance
orographical	aggressively	complexioned	evidentially	incoordinate
overemphasis	agribusiness	compulsively	excitability	increasingly
paraesthesia	aircondition	compulsivity	exhaustively	incurability
philanthrope	alterability	conceptional	exhibitioner	indecisively
philanthropy	altitudinous	conclusively	expressional	indefinitely
phonasthenia	amateurishly	conductivity	expressively	indelibility
photospheric	anaerobiosis	conduplicate	expressivity	indicatively
pinfeathered	anemophilous	confectioner	exsanguinate	indoctrinate
planispheric	antagonistic	confessional	exsanguinous	industrially
pneumothorax	anthelmintic	conglutinate	exsufflicate	inefficiency
priggishness	antigenicity	connectional	extinguisher	inelasticity
pyrotechnics	antiperiodic	connectively	fantasticate	inexactitude
pyrotechnist	antiSemitism	consentience	fantasticism	inexpedience
quadraphonic	aperiodicity	consentingly	fatherfigure	inexpediency
qualmishness	apostolicism	conterminous	fatherliness	inexperience
rapprochment	apostolicity	contradictor	featheriness	infelicitous
reproachable	apparitional	contrariness	feebleminded	infinitively
reproachless	appetisingly	contrariwise	figuratively	inflectional
retrenchment	appositional	convectional	filtrability	infusibility
sandyachting	appraisingly	conventicler	flabelliform	insolubilise
schizophrene	appropriable	conventional	flammability	insolubility
schizothymia	appropriator	convincingly	flatteringly	interspinous
schizothymic	artificially	convulsively	flickeringly	interstitial
selfrighting	astoundingly	copulatively	foraminifera	intransigent
sheepishness	attitudinise	coquettishly	forbiddingly	intransitive
shillyshally	attractively	corelatively	forebodingly	intriguingly
shrewishness	authenticate	correctional	foundationer	invisibility
skittishness	authenticity	correctitude	frangibility	involutional
sluggishness	automaticity	correctively	friendliness	irascibility
sluttishness	automobilist	cowardliness	geochemistry	irrelatively
snappishness	availability	cumulatively	geometrician	irremediable
snobbishness	beggarliness	cumulocirrus	geophysicist	irremediably
spermaphytic	belletristic	cumulonimbus	geriatrician	irritability
spermathecal	beneficially	curlingirons	glitteringly	irritatingly
stablishment	beseechingly	decaffeinate	grammaticise	Ishmaelitish
stationhouse	bewitchingly	decoratively	grampositive	jerrybuilder
stereochromy	bilharziasis	decreasingly	gratifyingly	journalistic
stereophonic	bilharziosis	definitively	grovellingly	klipspringer
strengthener	biochemistry	depoliticise	habitability	knightliness
strengthless	biometrician	depressingly	haemophiliac	lacininiated
swainishness	biophysicist	derivational	haemopoiesis	latitudinous
sweetishness	blisteringly	derivatively	hairsplitter	liberalistic
synaesthesia	bloodthirsty	desirability	harlequinade	literariness
synaesthetic	bloodyminded	despairingly	headshrinker	lithotritist
telaesthesia	blunderingly	dialectician	heathenishly	loungelizard
telaesthetic	blusteringly	digressional	heavenliness	maidenliness
theosophical	borosilicate	digressively	hebetudinous	malleability
thermophilic	brokenwinded	dilatability	henotheistic	malnutrition
thievishness	campodeiform	dilatoriness	heritability	mannerliness
thoroughbass	Cantabrigian	diminutively	hesitatingly	Marcionitism
thoroughbred	cantharidian	discerningly	horsewhipped	mastersinger
thoroughfare	capercaillie	disciplinary	hydatidiform	meditatively
thoroughness	capercailzie	discomfiture	hydrophilous	mercantilism
ticklishness	capitalistic	discretional	hydroquinone	mercantilist
toxicophobia	cattlelifter	discriminant	hygrophilous	microclimate
trickishness	centuplicate	discriminate	hyperacidity	microseismic
triggerhappy	ceremonially	discursively	hypocoristic	militaristic
triglyphical	chalcolithic	disgustingly	identifiable	moneyspinner
tropospheric	chauvinistic	disobedience	illegibility	monitorially
underachieve	chieftainess	disquisition	illegitimacy	monomaniacal
unsearchable	chrematistic	dissentingly	illegitimate	monopodially
unthoughtful	chromaticism	dissuasively	illusoriness	monopolistic
vanquishable	chromaticity	distortional	immaterially	monotheistic
vanquishment	circumcision	disturbingly	immemorially	motherfigure
weatherhouse	classifiable	divisibility	immovability	motherliness
womanishness	clatteringly	droughtiness	immutability	motivational
woolgatherer	coachbuilder	dubitatively	imperatively	mucilaginous
xanthochroia	collectively	duraluminium	impetiginous	multipliable
zygapophysis	collectivise	eccentricity	impoverished	multiplicand

multiplicate prehensility septennially ungainliness espagnolette
multiplicity prerequisite Septuagintal unkindliness faithfulness
mystifyingly presentiment sequentially unlikelihood fancifulness
narcissistic pretermitted serpentiform unlikeliness fibrinolysin
narrowminded prevailingly serpentinely unloveliness floriculture
naturalistic preventively shirtwaister unofficially folliculated
nauseatingly priestliness simpleminded unprincipled forcefulness
navigability priestridden singleminded unsteadiness forestalment
navigational primordially slipperiness unthinkingly freightliner
necrophiliac princeliness slovenliness untimeliness fruitfulness
necrophilism printability solitariness unwieldiness furunculosis
necrophilous proboscidean sophisticate unworldiness gamophyllous
negativistic proboscidian specialistic unworthiness geanticlinal
negrophilism processional squarerigged unyieldingly geosynclinal
negrophilist productively staggeringly valetudinary gesticulator
neoDarwinian productivity stalactiform vegetatively gracefulness
neoDarwinism professional stammeringly venerability gratefulness
neoDarwinist projectional statistician vicechairman gravelelling
neuroscience projectively stealthiness vindictively guilefulness
newfashioned proportional stockraising visitational habitualness
niminypiminy proportioned stoneboiling vomiturition haematolysis
nominalistic protactinium strongminded whimperingly heroicalness
noncommittal protectively strychninism whisperingly herpetologic
noneuclidean protensively stutteringly winklepicker homothallism
obstetrician protrusively subcommittee wunderkinder horticulture
occupational proverbially subcontinent lanternjawed hydrochloric
oldfashioned provincially subjectively homesickness hyperbolical
opposability prudentially subjectivise paletteknife hypothalamic
oppositional pumpernickel subjectivism semidarkness hypothalamus
oppressively pyromaniacal subjectivist unmistakable ichthyolatry
ordinariness quantifiable subjectivity unmistakably incalculable
organgrinder reassuringly submissively acetabularia incalculably
outlandishly reconstitute subservience anticyclonic inconsolable
outpensioner recreational subserviency archipelagic inconsolably
overachiever redemptioner subversively banderillero indissoluble
overactivity redistribute successional bassorelievo indissolubly
overestimate reducibility successively bassorilievo interpellate
Palaeolithic reflectional suggestively bathypelagic interpolator
palatability reflectively supereminent blamefulness interrelated
paradisiacal reflectivity superstition blissfulness irrepealable
paramilitary refractivity surprisingly boastfulness lakedwelling
parasiticide refreshingly surrealistic bodybuilding machicolated
pejoratively regressively surrejoinder breathalyser Marseillaise
pennywhistle rehabilitate susceptivity butterflynut materialness
perceptively relativistic suspensively campfollower mercifulness
perceptivity removability swaggeringly cardinalship metropolitan
percussively renegotiable syncretistic cheerfulness mezzorelievo
perfectively repetitional tangentially chitterlings mirthfulness
perfervidity repetitively teachability Christolatry misknowledge
permeability repressively televisional circumfluent mitrailleuse
permissively resoundingly temptability confabulator monkeyflower
permittivity respectively terrifyingly contemplator monophyletic
perplexingly responsively thanksgiving controllable monosyllabic
persuasively retractility theoretician contumelious monosyllable
philistinism reunionistic thickskinned cosmopolitan morphallaxis
photophilous revelational thunderingly cosmopolitic mournfulness
plausibility revivalistic tolerability counterlight multifoliate
plebiscitary ruminatively toploftiness criticalness multivalence
plumbaginous saccharinity torrentially cuckooflower nephanalysis
pneumaticity salutariness towardliness curvifoliate noncomplying
polytheistic salutational traceability Czechoslovak octosyllabic
porcelainise saponifiable tractability decasyllabic octosyllable
porcelainous satisfyingly trampolinist decasyllable osteomalacia
positivistic scatteringly transiliency denticulated outrivalling
possessively scenepainter transitional disaffiliate parallelling
postmeridian sceneshifter transitively disannulling parisyllabic
postposition scratchiness transitivity disannulment particularly
postpositive secularistic transshipped dishevelment pasqueflower
practitioner selfactivity tripartitely dissimilarly peacefulness
pragmatistic selfignition tripartition dissimulator peccadilloes
pralltriller selflimiting twitteringly doubtfulness pedicellaria
precessional selfluminous unappetising dreadfulness pedunculated
preclusively selfreliance unassumingly electrolysis perambulator
precognition semicylinder unbecomingly electrolytic philadelphus
precognitive semifinished unblinkingly encephalitic philhellenic
precondition semiofficial unblushingly encephalitis pickerelweed
predestinate sensualistic unclassified endoskeletal pilotballoon
predictively sententially underwritten equipollence pisciculture
prefabricate separability unfamiliarly equipollency pointilliste

```
polyphyletic  clavicembalo  agamogenetic  glycogenesis  orthodontics
polysyllabic  countermarch  agentgeneral  guardianship  orthodontist
polysyllable  declinometer  agglutinogen  gyromagnetic  orthogenesis
premaxillary  densitometer  anteprandial  hallucinogen  orthogenetic
pridefulness  diagrammatic  antimagnetic  hallucinosis  osteogenesis
quadriplegia  diathermancy  antiphonally  hardstanding  overabundant
quadriplegic  divertimenti  apprehension  heartrending  paedogenesis
reconcilable  divertimento  apprehensive  heliocentric  paedogenetic
retropulsion  electrometer  appurtenance  highsounding  palingenesia
ribonuclease  enantiomorph  assassinator  hippocentaur  palingenesis
rightfulness  epigrammatic  avitaminoses  histogenesis  palingenetic
scintillator  erythromycin  avitaminosis  histogenetic  pantechnicon
scornfulness  extensometer  bellylanding  horsemanship  paramagnetic
selfanalysis  extralimital  bicentennial  hydrodynamic  parsimonious
selfapplause  freeswimming  bioscientist  hydrokinetic  partisanship
selfemployed  galvanometer  birefringent  hypertension  pathogenesis
selfviolence  goosepimples  brilliantine  hypertensive  pathogenetic
sesquialtera  hellgrammite  brinkmanship  hypnogenesis  pennypincher
shamefulness  heroicomical  carillonneur  hypnogenetic  peradventure
shipbuilding  holidaymaker  Carlovingian  hypochondria  percutaneous
silverglance  hysteromania  carpetknight  ideationally  peregrinator
silviculture  inclinometer  catamountain  impermanence  periodontics
slaveholding  inconsumable  chairmanship  impermanency  periodontist
sleepwalking  inconsumably  championship  impersonally  pestilential
slothfulness  IndoGermanic  chaplainship  impersonator  phenomenally
smallholding  interfemoral  cliffhanging  impertinence  philodendron
somatopleure  irredeemable  coloquintida  impertinency  photokinesis
spitefulness  irredeemably  conferential  imprisonment  photokinetic
sportfulness  irreformable  confidential  inconcinnity  photomontage
squirrelcage  isochromatic  conscionable  inconsonance  phylogenesis
squirreltail  isothermally  constringent  incontinence  phylogenetic
stepchildren  lukewarmness  conveyancing  incontinency  physiognomic
strongylosis  magnetometer  corespondent  inconvenient  phytogenesis
submaxillary  melodramatic  cosmogonical  indeclinable  phytogenetic
superciliary  meristematic  crashlanding  indistinctly  planoconcave
supercilious  millesimally  crossbencher  inexpugnable  plectognathi
surveillance  milliammeter  dentilingual  inexpugnably  postprandial
sylviculture  monodramatic  determinable  inharmonious  precedential
tastefulness  nephelometer  determinably  interconnect  predominance
thankfulness  nephelometry  determinedly  interminable  predominancy
Torricellian  nonflammable  Deuteronomic  interminably  preferential
tranquillise  nychthemeral  differentiae  intermundane  presidential
tranquillity  nychthemeron  differential  internuncial  primogenital
triangularly  ornithomancy  dilettantish  intervenient  primogenitor
trophallaxis  panchromatic  dilettantism  intervention  prizewinning
trustfulness  paradigmatic  diphthongise  intramundane  pronominally
truthfulness  paranormally  disadvantage  irrationally  propagandise
tuberculated  patternmaker  disincentive  irresponsive  propagandism
tuberculosis  perispomenon  disingenuous  isochronally  propagandist
turriculated  peristomatic  disorientate  jurisconsult  providential
unassailable  philharmonic  disseminator  karyokinesis  pyroligneous
uncalculated  programmable  distrainable  kinnikinnick  quadriennium
unchivalrous  programmatic  distrainment  longstanding  questionable
unlawfulness  prolegomenon  dorsiventral  lovelornness  questionably
unparalleled  psychrometer  echosounding  maintainable  questionless
vengefulness  psychrometry  electronvolt  majorgeneral  quinquennial
vermiculated  refreshments  emblazonment  marksmanship  quinquennium
vernacularly  rejectamenta  empoisonment  meridionally  ratiocinator
verticalness  risorgimento  equationally  messeigneurs  reassignment
verticillate  semidiameter  ethnocentric  misadventure  relationally
wastefulness  sensitometer  expediential  misalignment  relationship
watchfulness  spectrometer  experiential  mistakenness  reprehension
wrathfulness  spectrometry  exterminable  mitochondria  reprehensive
wrongfulness  streptomycin  exterminator  mountainside  restrainable
youthfulness  superhumanly  extramundane  multicentral  restrainedly
alphanumeric  tragicomical  extrasensory  multidentate  rhizogenetic
anagrammatic  transhumance  faultfinding  multilingual  rhododendron
anastigmatic  trichromatic  ferrugineous  musicianship  salesmanship
apochromatic  trigonometry  fountainhead  nanoplankton  scorpionfish
apothegmatic  troublemaker  fractionally  nitrobenzene  selfhypnosis
arrhythmical  undetermined  fractionator  nonalignment  selfidentity
astronomical  undiplomatic  freestanding  nonessential  servocontrol
balletomania  uneconomical  freethinking  noradrenalin  simultaneity
beachcombing  unfathomable  frictionless  northernmost  simultaneous
blabbermouth  viscosimeter  frontbencher  obscurantism  sodafountain
cabinetmaker  aboriginally  functionally  obscurantist  southernmost
centesimally  accompanyist  functionless  occasionally  southernwood
chrestomathy  additionally  gamesmanship  oncorhynchus  sporogenesis
cirrocumulus  agamogenesis  ganglionated  oneupmanship  stagemanager
```

```
starspangled  bonnetmonkey  epistemology  intuitionist  pleiotropism
stillhunting  boogiewoogie  escapologist  isolationism  pneumatology
strophanthin  brainstormer  euphoniously  isolationist  policyholder
stubbornness  breechloader  evolutionary  kremlinology  polychromous
subcutaneous  calamitously  evolutionism  lachrymosely  portentously
succedaneous  calcareously  evolutionist  languorously  posteriority
superannuate  calumniously  exclusionary  lasciviously  posthumously
supermundane  candleholder  exclusionism  lexicologist  praiseworthy
supersensory  capriciously  exclusionist  libidinously  precariously
supervenient  cardiologist  excursionist  licentiously  preceptorial
supervention  catastrophic  expansionary  liturgiology  precisionist
supramundane  censoriously  expansionism  loquaciously  precociously
sycophantish  cheesemonger  expansionist  lugubriously  prefectorial
synchronical  chivalrously  extortionary  malacologist  prehistorian
synchroniser  chondriosome  extortionate  marvellously  privatdocent
testamentary  chromatogram  extraneously  melancholiac  privatdozent
testudineous  chromatology  factitiously  mendaciously  probationary
tetragonally  chromatopsia  fallaciously  merrythought  prodigiously
transcendent  chronologise  fastidiously  metachronism  professorate
transmontane  chronologist  felicitously  meticulously  professoress
transpontine  circuitously  fictitiously  microbiology  professorial
typefounding  clangorously  flagitiously  microscopist  propitiously
ultramontane  closecropped  flavoprotein  mineralogist  prosectorial
ultramundane  coalitionist  fortuitously  miraculously  prosperously
unbrokenness  coetaneously  fostermother  mispronounce  protectorate
uncommonness  commodiously  frenchpolish  monochromate  prothonotary
unconvincing  companionate  fructivorous  monostrophic  protistology
undermanning  companionway  fuliginosity  monotonously  protozoology
underpinning  compulsorily  futurologist  mordaciously  provisionary
underrunning  conchologist  gastronomist  morphologist  psephologist
undertenancy  consistorial  gastropodous  mosstrooping  pseudopodium
ungovernable  contagionist  geotectonics  mothertongue  psychologise
unimaginable  contagiously  glaciologist  multiflorous  psychologism
unimaginably  contemporary  gladiatorial  multistoried  psychologist
unpretending  contemporise  glassblowing  musicologist  pugnaciously
unreasonable  contiguously  globetrotter  muzzleloader  quadrinomial
unreasonably  continuously  glossologist  mysteriously  rabblerouser
unrecognised  costermonger  gluttonously  Neoplatonism  radiobiology
unresponsive  cotyledonary  glycoprotein  Neoplatonist  radioisotope
unseasonable  cotyledonous  goodhumoured  nephrologist  radiophonics
vicargeneral  courageously  grallatorial  neurobiology  rebelliously
volitionally  craftbrother  granodiorite  nightclothes  receptionist
wallpainting  craniologist  graphologist  nonconformer  recessionary
watermanship  cryptologist  gratuitously  numerologist  Redemptorist
abolitionary  cumbersomely  graveclothes  nutritionist  reductionism
abolitionism  cuprammonium  greengrocery  nutritiously  reductionist
abolitionist  decontrolled  gregariously  nyctitropism  reflationary
abstemiously  deflationary  hardfavoured  oblanceolate  refractorily
accordionist  deflationist  harmoniously  obligatorily  reinvigorate
accretionary  deontologist  heliotropism  obsequiously  responsorial
accusatorial  derogatorily  heortologist  oceanologist  reticulocyte
adulterously  deviationism  heterologous  odontologist  reversionary
aeroembolism  deviationist  heteronomous  officeholder  rheumatology
affectionate  dialectology  highcoloured  omnivorously  ridiculously
aforethought  diaphanously  homonymously  orthotropism  robustiously
afterthought  disastrously  horrendously  orthotropous  rontgenogram
agranulocyte  discommodity  hydrotropism  outrageously  rontgenology
amphibiously  discomposure  hypertrophic  overexposure  rosecoloured
amphitropous  disconsolate  hypochlorite  palaeobotany  sabretoothed
amygdaloidal  disharmonise  idolatrously  palynologist  saccharoidal
anthropogeny  diversionary  immunologist  papyrologist  salpiglossis
anthropoidal  diversionist  imperatorial  paraboloidal  salubriously
anthropology  doublelocked  imperviously  parasitology  salvationism
antistrophic  dovecoloured  incautiously  parkinsonism  salvationist
asynchronism  eavesdropped  incestuously  partitionist  sanguinolent
asynchronous  eavesdropper  indecorously  peremptorily  sansculottic
auspiciously  ecclesiology  indigenously  perfidiously  scandalously
autonomously  echinococcus  IndoEuropean  perjuriously  schizogonous
avariciously  educationist  infectiously  perniciously  scrupulosity
bacteriology  Egyptologist  inflationary  pharmacology  scrupulously
bacteriostat  elocutionary  inflationism  phlebotomise  scurrilously
balladmonger  elocutionist  inflationist  phlebotomist  secessionism
bibliologist  embryologist  ingloriously  photogeology  secessionist
bibliopolist  entomologise  iniquitously  phototropism  seclusionist
biocoenology  entomologist  inspectorate  phrasemonger  seismologist
bioecologist  enzymologist  inspectorial  phrenologist  selenologist
blithesomely  epicycloidal  intercropped  physiologist  selfabsorbed
bloodbrother  epidemiology  intrusionist  plainclothed  selfbegotten
boisterously  epiphenomena  intuitionism  plainclothes  selfcoloured
```

selfdevotion	allomorphism	philosophise	commemorator	incorporeity
selfinvolved	antigropelos	phreatophyte	commiserator	indifference
semideponent	apostrophise	pitcherplant	concentrator	indifferency
sequaciously	apperception	pleomorphism	connaturally	insalubrious
shadowboxing	apperceptive	polymorphism	considerable	insufferable
sharecropper	archetypally	polymorphous	considerably	insufferably
sharpshooter	archetypical	preoccupancy	corroborator	intemperance
silicicolous	automorphism	prescription	courtmartial	intercurrent
sinistrorsal	backslapping	prescriptive	creepycrawly	interference
slanderously	blastosphere	proscription	crosscurrent	interservice
smallclothes	bombdisposal	proscriptive	crosspurpose	intracardiac
solicitously	burglarproof	prosopopoeia	cryptography	introversion
specktioneer	centrespread	prototypical	debonairness	introversive
speleologist	centrosphere	pteridophyte	decipherable	introvertive
spermatocyte	charterparty	publicspirit	decipherment	invulnerable
spermatozoid	chimneypiece	pyromorphite	demonstrable	invulnerably
spermatozoon	Christophany	rhynchophora	demonstrably	irrespirable
spermogonium	chromosphere	sarrusophone	demonstrator	knighterrant
spidermonkey	clothespress	selfcomposed	diageotropic	lexicography
Stakhanovism	conidiophore	sellingplate	dictatorship	longshoreman
Stakhanovite	conscription	semitropical	diphtheritic	lycanthropic
stertorously	counterplead	shatterproof	directorship	manoeuvrable
stockbroking	counterpoint	sideslipping	discoverable	manometrical
stormtrooper	counterpoise	sidestepping	discoverture	marshharrier
stringcourse	counterproof	siphonophore	disembarrass	mesothoracic
stupendously	dermatophyte	stratosphere	disinterment	metallurgist
subeditorial	diastrophism	subscription	disregardful	metalworking
supererogate	drawingpaper	telegraphese	disseverance	metaphorical
suspiciously	electroplate	telegraphist	disseverment	metathoracic
synonymously	encyclopedia	thermosphere	dramaturgist	microcircuit
taperecorder	encyclopedic	transhipment	elasmobranch	microsurgery
technicolour	frontispiece	vantagepoint	embitterment	misanthropic
technologist	Germanophile	weatherproof	encumberment	misinterpret
teetertotter	Germanophobe	welldisposed	endangerment	monkeywrench
teratologist	goodtempered	zygomorphism	endometritis	multifarious
tetrachordal	gymnosophist	zygomorphous	enginedriver	multiformity
thermocouple	handicapping	inconsequent	equilibrator	multipartite
thunderously	hedgehopping	magniloquent	EuroAmerican	multipurpose
timehonoured	hemimorphism	marketsquare	executorship	multiversity
toxicologist	hemimorphite	multiloquous	exospherical	neurosurgeon
traditionary	highstepping	somniloquism	extramarital	neurosurgery
traditionist	homomorphism	somniloquist	extraversion	nimbostratus
trainspotter	homomorphous	statuesquely	extroversion	oceanography
traitorously	hyposulphite	aeroneurosis	flamethrower	offscourings
transitorily	ichthyophagy	AfroAmerican	frontiersman	oneirocritic
tremendously	imperceptive	alphamerical	glossography	orchestrator
trichologist	impercipient	angiocarpous	glyphography	organography
trichotomise	incorruption	anticlerical	glyptography	osteoporosis
trichotomous	indiscipline	aristocratic	gonadotropic	otherworldly
triphthongal	interception	artilleryman	gonadotropin	overexertion
tumultuously	interruption	asymmetrical	governorship	paedomorphic
twentyfourmo	interruptive	avantgardism	habitforming	palaeography
ubiquitously	macrocephaly	avantgardist	halterbroken	parametrical
umbrageously	mastigophora	bachelorhood	headquarters	passepartout
uncontrolled	meltingpoint	bachelorship	heartburning	periostracum
underclothes	metallophone	barometrical	heartstrings	peripherally
ungraciously	metamorphism	battleground	heartwarming	peristeronic
unifoliolate	metamorphose	belligerence	hemichordate	perseverance
uproariously	mezzosoprano	belligerency	henceforward	phosphoresce
urbanologist	microcapsule	bewilderedly	highspirited	photochromic
varicoloured	microcephaly	bewilderment	hindquarters	physiography
ventripotent	microcopying	bibliography	homeomorphic	pigeonbreast
vibraphonist	minicomputer	biogeography	housewarming	polarography
victoriously	monadelphous	blackbirding	hyperpyretic	polyneuritic
villainously	monographist	blackcurrant	hyperpyrexia	polyneuritis
virtuosoship	monomorphous	blastfurnace	idiothermous	poorspirited
visitatorial	myrmecophily	booklearning	illnaturedly	predetermine
viviparously	namedropping	boulevardier	immeasurable	protuberance
vociferously	onomatopoeia	breakthrough	immeasurably	psychography
voluminosity	onomatopoeic	bureaucratic	immensurable	psychotropic
voluminously	outstripping	cardcarrying	impenetrable	puerperally
voluptuosity	overcropping	cardiography	impenetrably	pursestrings
voluptuously	oversimplify	cataphoresis	imponderable	quaestorship
wellfavoured	overstepping	cheirography	imponderably	reappearance
whencesoever	paedobaptism	choreography	incomparable	receivership
winterbourne	paragraphist	chronography	incomparably	reconversion
wollastonite	paramorphism	cirrostratus	inconformity	refrigerator
wonderworker	participator	collaborator	incorporated	rememberable
YankeeDoodle	phenotypical	collaterally	incorporator	remonstrance

remonstrator
retroversion
reverberator
rhinocerotic
rhizocarpous
sarsaparilla
scintigraphy
screenwriter
scripturally
scriptwriter
sculpturally
sedgewarbler
seismography
selenography
selfapproval
selfbetrayal
selfreproach
selfstarting
sempiternity
sepulchrally
sequestrator
servitorship
Shakspereana
Shaksperiana
shortcircuit
shoulderbelt
shoulderknot
shouldernote
Sinanthropus
slipcarriage
spinsterhood
staffsurgeon
stereography
stratigraphy
structurally
subalternate
subalternity
subsaturated
superstratum
surveyorship
survivorship
synarthrosis
taberdarship
technocratic
tergiversate
tetramorphic
theanthropic
thermography
thermotropic
thirdborough
togetherness
topsyturvily
transferable
transference
transferring
transformism
transformist
transparency
transpirable
transversely
unanswerable
unauthorised
uncelebrated
uncommercial
unconformity
unconstraint
undemocratic
undercurrent
undergarment
undersurface
unfavourable
unfavourably
unhistorical
unilaterally
vainglorious
volumetrical
voluntaryism
voluntaryist
wherethrough

whippoorwill
woodengraver
youngberries
zoogeography
baselessness
basidiospore
billingsgate
birdsnesting
blatherskite
bletherskate
blockbusting
bootlessness
brainwashing
bronchoscope
businesslike
Byelorussian
canorousness
captiousness
caravansarai
caravanserai
carelessness
cautiousness
complaisance
compressible
concupiscent
conidiospore
convalescent
counterscarp
countershaft
covetousness
cuckingstool
cumbrousness
curvicostate
curvirostral
decomposable
decongestant
decongestion
decongestive
decorousness
deliquescent
desirousness
dessertspoon
dextrousness
displeasedly
dissatisfied
dolorousness
duckingstool
effervescent
efflorescent
electroscope
electroshock
enormousness
exiguousness
fabulousness
facelessness
factiousness
fearlessness
fecklessness
fertilisable
formlessness
galligaskins
galvanoscope
generousness
glockenspiel
gloriousness
gorgeousness
graciousness
grievousness
haberdashery
hairdressing
harmlessness
heedlessness
helplessness
highpressure
hopelessness
humorousness
hybridisable
hydrolysable
hypnotisable

illadvisedly
improvisator
inaccessible
inaccessibly
inadmissible
inadmissibly
inappeasable
incandescent
incognisable
incognisance
inconsistent
indefeasible
indefeasibly
indefensible
indefensibly
inexpressive
inextensible
intercession
intercessory
intermission
intromission
intussuscept
irremissible
irreversible
irreversibly
kaleidoscope
landingstage
landingstrip
lanternslide
laryngoscope
laryngoscopy
licketysplit
lifelessness
listlessness
lovelessness
luminousness
lusciousness
mademoiselle
magnetisable
marlinespike
metaphysical
mindlessness
mistranslate
mistressship
Monophysitic
movelessness
mutinousness
nailscissors
namelessness
nauseousness
nebulousness
needlessness
neoclassical
nonresistant
northeastern
northwestern
numerousness
omnipresence
ornithoscopy
oscilloscope
overpersuade
overpressure
painlessness
patulousness
peerlessness
perilousness
perviousness
photofission
pitilessness
planetesimal
populousness
prechristian
preciousness
preclassical
predigestion
previousness
protohistory
pteridosperm
pulverisable

quarterstaff
quintessence
ravenousness
reassessment
recklessness
recognisable
recognisably
recognisance
recrudescent
repercussion
repercussive
repossession
restlessness
retrocession
retrocessive
rigorousness
rollingstock
rootlessness
ruthlessness
scabrousness
sedulousness
selfexistent
selflessness
sensuousness
sidewhiskers
siphonostele
sonorousness
soullessness
southeastern
southwestern
spaciousness
speciousness
spectroscope
spectroscopy
sphragistics
spotlessness
spuriousness
stereoisomer
stilboestrol
stonemasonry
studiousness
subcelestial
subdivisible
subthreshold
superposable
supersession
suppressible
swaggerstick
swizzlestick
tactlessness
tamelessness
tearlessness
throughstone
thunderstone
thunderstorm
timelessness
timorousness
tirelessness
tonelessness
tortuousness
transfusible
transmission
transmissive
transposable
transvestism
transvestite
trumpetshell
tunelessness
unappeasable
unctuousness
underinsured
unsuccessful
usuriousness
uxoriousness
vaporousness
venomousness
vigorousness
virtuousness
vitreousness

warehouseman
whitewashing
windingsheet
wineglassful
wondrousness
abstractable
abstractedly
abstractness
accidentally
acquaintance
administrant
administrate
adscititious
adventitious
aeronautical
agricultural
aircraftsman
alphabetical
ambidextrous
antineutrino
antiparticle
antithetical
apparentness
aquicultural
arithmetical
attributable
bellbottomed
benefactress
bloodletting
bodysnatcher
breaststroke
calculatedly
carburetting
catechetical
cementitious
chocolatebox
circumstance
clarinettist
coenobitical
coenobytical
combinations
compunctious
concomitance
concubitancy
congenitally
conjunctival
conningtower
conquistador
contemptible
contemptibly
contemptuous
contractable
contractedly
contractible
countertenor
crossbuttock
cultivatable
curlingtongs
destructible
discountable
discourteous
discreetness
disjointedly
dispiritedly
disputatious
disreputable
disreputably
distinctness
distractedly
earsplitting
econometrics
electrotonic
electrotonus
electrotyper
emblematical
epexegetical
equidistance
explicitness

extraditable	negotiatress	stonecutting	contrapuntal	cabbagewhite
farsightedly	nonexistence	straightaway	contribution	councilwoman
feldspathoid	nonidentical	straightbred	contributive	countrywoman
fiddlesticks	obedientiary	straightedge	contributory	disallowance
filibusterer	occidentally	straightener	crosscountry	disendowment
footplateman	opisthotonos	straightness	curvicaudate	Englishwoman
frequentness	ornamentally	subapostolic	desulphurise	masterswitch
geopolitical	ostentatious	substantiate	distributary	servicewoman
happenstance	outstretched	substantival	distribution	stationwagon
hardfeatured	overcautious	succinctness	distributive	thitherwards
headmistress	overcritical	supernatural	enginetuning	toggleswitch
heliolatrous	pancreatitis	suppositious	griseofulvin	whitherwards
highlystrung	paratactical	surefootedly	grotesquerie	haematoxylon
hippopotamus	penitentiary	surmountable	harquebusier	intermixture
homeopathist	phagocytosis	systematical	hermeneutics	intertexture
homoeostasis	phagocytotic	systematiser	highfaluting	actinomycete
horizontally	photosetting	taskmistress	homosexually	amphictyonic
horrorstruck	placesetting	terebinthine	hubblebubble	astrophysics
hymenopteran	planetstruck	terrorstruck	huggermugger	attorneyship
hypocritical	pleasantness	theocratical	humptydumpty	chalcopyrite
hypogastrium	plenipotence	thermostable	hydrofluoric	clairvoyance
hypognathous	pluriliteral	thermostatic	inarticulate	eleemosynary
hypostatical	poikilotherm	translatable	inconclusive	gobbledygook
hypothetical	polyglottism	transmitting	individually	heterocyclic
illtreatment	polyhistoric	transmutable	inoperculate	heterozygote
implicitness	polyurethane	trestletable	irresolutely	heterozygous
inadvertence	portmanteaus	trochanteric	irresolution	hieroglyphic
inadvertency	portmanteaux	unacceptable	jurisprudent	hypophrygian
incidentally	postdoctoral	unaccustomed	mangelwurzel	microcrystal
incognitable	postmistress	unaffectedly	mealymouthed	microphysics
incommutable	precipitable	uncharitable	miscalculate	oxyacetylene
incommutably	precipitance	uncharitably	moneygrubber	polyethylene
incompatible	precipitancy	uncomeatable	monkeypuzzle	praseodymium
incompatibly	precipitator	undercutting	multungulate	pseudocyesis
incompetence	preexistence	underletting	neighbouring	pseudonymity
incompetency	premeditated	undersetting	noctambulant	pseudonymous
incomputable	premeditator	unexpectedly	noctambulism	reconveyance
indefectible	premenstrual	unimportance	noctambulist	redeployment
indigestible	presumptuous	unprofitable	noctambulous	schizomycete
indirectness	pricecutting	unprofitably	nonconductor	steatopygous
indisputable	progenitress	unrepeatable	perceptually	stichomythia
indisputably	proglottides	unscientific	Plattdeutsch	stichomythic
indivertible	proprietress	unscriptural	postdiluvian	syndactylism
indivertibly	prosecutable	unstructured	proconsulate	syndactylous
inexpertness	proselytiser	usufructuary	prostitution	tridactylous
inhospitable	psychiatrist	viscerotonic	recapitulate	troglodytism
inhospitably	rambunctious	viscountship	rumbletumble	unemployable
innutritious	readjustment	wainscotting	scrobiculate	unemployment
instructress	recalcitrant	Wellingtonia	selfdelusion	bobbydazzler
intercutting	recalcitrate	wonderstruck	semiannually	honeybuzzard
interestedly	recommitment	absquatulate	shamateurism	—————
intermittent	regimentally	antediluvian	somnambulant	aboriginally
intermitting	reinvestment	apiculturist	somnambulate	abstractable
intromittent	residentiary	astronautics	somnambulism	academically
intromitting	residentship	autoimmunity	somnambulist	accidentally
irresistible	restrictedly	behaviourism	straticulate	accommodator
irresistibly	resuscitator	behaviourist	subinfeudate	acetabularia
judgematical	ricochetting	brassbounder	substitution	acoustically
kilowatthour	sacerdotally	breastsummer	substitutive	acquaintance
labyrinthian	sarcomatosis	broncobuster	thaumaturgic	acronychally
labyrinthine	schismatical	buttermuslin	therapeutics	additionally
lepidopteran	secondstring	canaliculate	therapeutist	adjectivally
leucocytosis	selfcontempt	caricaturist	thickskulled	amitotically
leukocytosis	selfcritical	caterwauling	tightmouthed	amphitheatre
linguistical	selfdestruct	cheeseburger	unpronounced	anagogically
liverystable	selfdistrust	cheesecutter	unscrupulous	anagrammatic
longdistance	selfflattery	circumfusion	vauntcourier	analogically
maidenstakes	selfportrait	closemouthed	wellgrounded	analytically
malapertness	septilateral	coldshoulder	adjectivally	anastigmatic
maltreatment	sergeantfish	commensurate	inobservance	anatomically
manufacturer	sergeantship	conceptually	irreprovable	antiphonally
masterstroke	sericultural	congratulant	irresolvable	apochromatic
mathematical	serjeantship	congratulate	misbehaviour	apolitically
merchantable	shortpitched	consensually	unbelievable	apothegmatic
metathetical	snaggletooth	constabulary	unbelievably	approachable
mistreatment	snapfastener	constituency	underdevelop	appropriable
monumentally	sociometrist	constitution	unreservedly	appropriator
mulligatawny	stalwartness	constitutive	whitelivered	appurtenance
multilateral	stereopticon	contextually	bladderwrack	archetypally

archipelagic decasyllable geologically industrially monomaniacal
aristocratic decipherable gesticulator ineffaceable monopodially
aromatically decomposable gigantically ineffaceably monosyllabic
artificially demimondaine glossography ineradicable monosyllable
artistically demoniacally glyphography ineradicably monumentally
assassinator demonstrable glyptography inexplicable morphallaxis
athletically demonstrably haemorrhagic inexplicably muddleheaded
attributable demonstrator hairsbreadth inexpugnable mulligatawny
balletomania denticulated handsbreadth inexpugnably multipliable
barbarically despotically happenstance inextricable muttonheaded
bathypelagic determinable harmonically inextricably muzzleloader
beatifically determinably hebdomadally inhospitable narcotically
beneficially diabolically heraldically inhospitably neurotically
bibliography diagrammatic hermetically inobservance nimbostratus
bilharziasis diathermancy hippopotamus insufferable nonflammable
biogeography diatonically historically insufferably noradrenalin
biologically didactically holidaymaker intemperance occasionally
breechloader dietetically homoeostasis interminable occidentally
bulletheaded diminishable homosexually interminably oceanography
bureaucratic disagreeable horizontally interoceanic octosyllabic
cabinetmaker disagreeably horrifically interpleader octosyllable
caravansarai disallowance horsebreaker interpolator operatically
cardiography discountable housebreaker interrelated orchestrator
carriageable discoverable hybridisable interrogator organography
cashandcarry displaceable hydrodynamic intervocalic ornamentally
catholically disreputable hydrolysable interwreathe ornithomancy
centesimally disreputably hygienically investigator osteomalacia
ceremonially disseminator hypnotically invulnerable overemphasis
charterparty disseverance hypnotisable invulnerably palaeography
cheirography dissimilarly hypothalamic irrationally panchromatic
cherubically dissimulator hypothalamus irredeemable paradigmatic
choreography distrainable hypothecator irredeemably paradisiacal
chrestomathy dogmatically hysterically irreformable paranormally
Christolatry domestically hysteromania irrefragable parisyllabic
chronography domesticator ichthyolatry irrefragably participator
circumstance doubledealer ideationally irremediable particularly
cirrostratus dramatically identifiable irremediably pathetically
clairvoyance drawingpaper immaterially irrepealable patternmaker
classifiable dunderheaded immeasurable irreprovable pedantically
cleistogamic dynastically immeasurably irresolvable pedicellaria
collaborator eclectically immemorially irrespirable pedunculated
collaterally ecologically immensurable isochromatic perambulator
colloquially economically impenetrable isochronally perceptually
commemorator ecstatically impenetrably isothermally peregrinator
commercially elasmobranch imperishable jesuitically periodically
commiserator electrically imperishably lacininiated periostracum
commonwealth elliptically impersonally laisserfaire peripherally
communicable emphatically impersonator laissezfaire peristomatic
communicably emulsifiable imponderable lanternjawed perseverance
communicator enclitically imponderably lexicography phanerogamic
complaisance endermically impropriator liturgically phenomenally
compoundable epidemically improvisator liverystable phonemically
concentrator epigrammatic inappeasable logistically phonetically
conceptually episodically inapplicable longdistance physiography
concomitance equationally inapplicably machicolated platonically
concubitancy equidistance incalculable magnetically plectognathi
confabulator equilibrator incalculably magnetisable polarography
congenitally equiprobable incidentally magnifically polysyllabic
connaturally esoterically incognisable maidenstakes polysyllable
conquistador euphonically incognisance maintainable pontifically
conscionable evidentially incognitable majestically pontificator
consensually exchangeable incommutable manoeuvrable precipitable
considerable exegetically incommutably marriageable precipitance
considerably exoterically incomparable Marseillaise precipitancy
consolidator exterminable incomparably mechanically precipitator
contemplator exterminator incompliance melodramatic predominance
contextually extraditable incomputable merchantable predominancy
contractable extravagance inconsolable meridionally premeditated
controllable extravagancy inconsolably meristematic premeditator
corroborator extravaganza inconsonance mesocephalic preoccupancy
cosmetically fertilisable inconsumable mesothoracic prevaricator
countermarch folliculated inconsumably metallically primordially
countrydance forensically incorporated metathoracic programmable
creepycrawly fractionally incorporator meteorically programmatic
cryptography fractionator indeclinable methodically prolifically
crystalgazer frenetically indisputable millesimally pronominally
cultivatable functionally indisputably monastically prosecutable
cynocephalus galvanically individually monitorially prosodically
decasyllabic ganglionated IndoGermanic monodramatic protuberance

proverbially	subsaturated	unsearchable	eccentricity	winklepicker
provincially	subsonically	unseasonable	echinococcus	anteprandial
prudentially	superhumanly	unsegregated	effervescent	avantgardism
psychography	superposable	vanquishable	efflorescent	avantgardist
puerperrally	superstratum	vermiculated	electroscope	bellylanding
pulverisable	surmountable	vernacularly	exsufflicate	blackbirding
pyromaniacal	surveillance	volcanically	extraspecial	bodybuilding
quantifiable	syllabically	volitionally	fantasticate	boulevardier
questionable	symbolically	whitherwards	fantasticism	cantharidian
questionably	syndetically	woodengraver	frontbencher	chancemedley
quixotically	synoptically	woodenheaded	galvanoscope	corespondent
rabbinically	systemically	woollyheaded	geometrician	crashlanding
ratiocinator	tangentially	zoogeography	geophysicist	crossbedding
rattleheaded	technocratic	beachcombing	geriatrician	crossheading
reappearance	tectonically	bonnyclabber	grammaticise	curvicaudate
rechargeable	terrifically	brassrubbing	grammolecule	discommodity
reciprocally	tetragonally	clavicembalo	greengrocery	disregardful
reciprocator	Teutonically	collywobbles	heterocyclic	dodecahedral
recognisable	theatrically	hubblebubble	hucklebacked	dodecahedron
recognisably	theistically	moneygrubber	inartificial	echosounding
recognisance	thematically	mourningband	incandescent	eunuchoidism
reconcilable	thermography	punchingball	indistinctly	extramundane
reconveyance	thermostable	redistribute	inelasticity	farmsteading
refrigerator	thermostatic	sedgewarbler	interglacial	faultfinding
regimentally	thitherwards	shoulderbelt	internuncial	fiddlefaddle
relationally	torrentially	skunkcabbage	intussuscept	freestanding
rememberable	transferable	standardbred	kaleidoscope	fullyfledged
remonstrance	transhumance	stockjobbery	laryngoscope	gastropodous
remonstrator	translatable	stockjobbing	laryngoscopy	hardstanding
renegotiable	transmutable	straightbred	ledgertackle	heartrending
reproachable	transoceanic	swimmingbath	lumberjacket	hemichordate
restrainable	transpirable	swimmingbell	metagalactic	highsounding
resuscitator	transposable	thermolabile	microcircuit	horsetrading
reverberator	trestletable	thoroughbass	minedetector	hyperacidity
rhetorically	triangularly	thoroughbred	monkeyjacket	hypochondria
rhythmically	trichromatic	tintinnabula	multiplicand	interbedding
romantically	triggerhappy	actinomycete	multiplicate	intermeddler
sacerdotally	trophallaxis	aesthetician	multiplicity	intermundane
sadistically	troublemaker	aestheticism	nonconductor	intracardiac
saponifiable	tuberculated	agranulocyte	obstetrician	intramundane
sardonically	turriculated	amphibrachic	oncorhynchus	jurisprudent
scarificator	tyrannically	anaphylactic	ornithoscopy	longstanding
schoolleaver	unacceptable	antigenicity	oscilloscope	mitochondria
scintigraphy	unanswerable	aperiodicity	outstretched	noneuclidean
scintillator	unappeasable	apostolicism	parasiticide	orthopaedics
scripturally	unassailable	apostolicity	pennypincher	orthopaedist
sculpturally	unbelievable	authenticate	perspicacity	overabundant
seismography	unbelievably	authenticity	phyllotactic	peasepudding
selenography	uncalculated	autodidactic	planoconcave	perfervidity
selfapplause	uncelebrated	automaticity	pneumaticity	philodendron
selfbetrayal	unchangeable	bespectacled	prefabricate	postmeridian
selfeducated	unchangeably	biometrician	privatdocent	postprandial
selfreliance	uncharitable	biophysicist	prophylactic	priestridden
semantically	uncharitably	bodysnatcher	pumpernickel	proboscidean
semiannually	uncomeatable	borosilicate	recrudescent	proboscidian
sententially	unconstraint	brachydactyl	reticulocyte	procathedral
septennially	uncritically	bronchoscope	saddlebacked	proofreading
sepulchrally	undemocratic	centuplicate	schizomycete	propagandise
sequentially	undertenancy	chiropractic	selfaffected	propagandism
sequestrator	undiplomatic	chiropractor	selfdirected	propagandist
seraphically	unemployable	chromaticism	selfeffacing	pseudopodium
sheepshearer	unfamiliarly	chromaticity	semidetached	rhododendron
shillyshally	unfathomable	circumjacent	semiofficial	rhombohedral
significance	unfavourable	concupiscent	shortcircuit	rhombohedron
significancy	unfavourably	conduplicate	shortpitched	salmonladder
silverglance	ungovernable	contradictor	singledecker	scareheading
simoniacally	unilaterally	convalescent	sophisticate	shipbuilding
singleseater	unimaginable	conventicler	spectroscope	sightreading
sinusoidally	unimaginably	conveyancing	spectroscopy	slaveholding
Socratically	unimportance	counterscarp	spermatocyte	smallholding
specifically	unmanageable	crossbencher	squirrelcage	stepchildren
spheroidally	unmistakable	deliquescent	statistician	subinfeudate
sporadically	unmistakably	depoliticise	straitjacket	supermundane
stagemanager	unofficially	dialectician	taxcollector	supramundane
stationwagon	unprofitable	dinnerjacket	theoretician	transcendent
stereography	unprofitably	disconnected	thermotactic	typefounding
straightaway	unreasonable	doubledecked	turtlenecked	ultramundane
stratigraphy	unreasonably	doubledecker	uncommercial	underbidding
structurally	unrepeatable	doublelocked	unconvincing	unpretending

```
abstractedly glaucescence neurasthenic sensitometer undersurface
acaulescence glycogenesis neuroscience septilateral anthropogeny
achlamydeous goodtempered noctilucence serviceberry bibliologist
acquiescence graminaceous nonexistence Shakspereana bibliopegist
advantageous grotesquerie nonresidence shamefacedly billingsgate
agamogenesis groundcherry nychthemeral shortsleeved bioecologist
agamogenetic guaranteeing nychthemeron simultaneity birefringent
agentgeneral gyromagnetic obmutescence simultaneous Cantabrigian
alkalescence haemopoiesis obsolescence snapfastener cardiologist
alphanumeric halftimbered omnipresence somatopleure Carlovingian
amphisbaenic highhandedly openhandedly spectrometer carpetbagger
analphabetic histogenesis openmindedly spectrometry chromatogram
antigropelos histogenetic orchidaceous spermathecal chronologise
antimagnetic hydrokinetic orthogenesis sporogenesis chronologist
antipathetic hymenopteran orthogenetic sternwheeler cliffhanging
arborescence hyperpyretic osteogenesis stockbreeder conchologist
archdiocesan hyperpyrexia overachiever straightedge constringent
argillaceous hypersthenia paedogenesis straightener counteragent
belligerence hypersthenic paedogenetic strengthener craniologist
belligerency hypnogenesis palingenesia subcutaneous cryptologist
bewilderedly hypnogenetic palingenesis subservience dentilingual
bibliothecae illadvisedly palingenetic subserviency deontologist
biosynthesis illnaturedly paraesthesia succedaneous diphthongise
biosynthetic impermanence paramagnetic supersedence discouraging
brambleberry impermanency pathogenesis surefootedly dramaturgist
bullheadedly impertinence pathogenetic synaesthesia dressinggown
calculatedly impertinency pearlescence synaesthetic Egyptologist
callisthenic improvidence percutaneous teensyweensy embryologist
calorescence inadvertence perispomenon telaesthesia entomologise
calycoideous inadvertency philhellenic telaesthetic entomologist
caravanserai incalescence phonasthenia testudineous enzymologist
carbonaceous inclinometer phosphoresce thimbleberry escapologist
carcinogenic incompetence photokinesis threewheeler fatherfigure
carragheenin incompetency photokinetic transference futurologist
cataphoresis incontinence photospheric transiliency glaciologist
checkerberry incontinency phycomycetes translucence glossologist
chocolatebox incorporeity phylogenesis translucency gobbledegook
cinematheque indehiscence phylogenetic transparency gobbledygook
committeeman independence phytogenesis trigonometry graphologist
concrescence independency phytogenetic trochanteric heortologist
confoundedly indifference pigeonbreast tropospheric heterologous
consentience indifferency pinfeathered unaffectedly heterozygote
constituency indiscreetly planispheric unapologetic heterozygous
contractedly inefficiency plenipotence unconsidered huggermugger
countertenor inexpedience pluriliteral underdevelop hypophrygian
decalescence inexpediency polyphyletic unencumbered immunologist
declinometer inexperience portmanteaus unexpectedly intransigent
delitescence intelligence portmanteaux unparalleled leapfrogging
densitometer interestedly preexistence unreservedly lexicologist
determinedly interference prolegomenon vicargeneral malacologist
detumescence intumescence pronouncedly viridescence metallurgist
diatomaceous juvenescence pseudocyesis viscosimeter microsurgery
discourteous karyokinesis psychrometer warehouseman mineralogist
disjointedly kinaesthesia psychrometry whencesoever morphologist
disobedience kinaesthesis pyroligneous whigmaleerie motherfigure
dispiritedly kinaesthetic quadriplegia whitelivered multilingual
displeasedly landlubberly quadriplegic whortleberry musicologist
distractedly lefthandedly quattrocento wicketkeeper necrophagous
divertimenti lepidopteran quintessence woolgatherer nephrologist
divertimento lithospheric recalescence campodeiform neurosurgeon
electrometer longshoreman refreshments cattlelifter neurosurgery
encyclopedia longwindedly rejectamenta dissatisfied numerologist
encyclopedic luminescence reminiscence flabelliform oceanologist
endoskeletal mademoiselle resipiscence foraminifera odontologist
equestrienne magnetometer resplendence hereinbefore ophiophagous
equipollence magnificence resplendency hydatidiform palynologist
equipollency majorgeneral restrainedly scabbardfish papyrologist
espagnolette messeigneurs restrictedly sceneshifter pettifoggery
extensometer milliammeter retrocedence scorpionfish pettifogging
farsightedly misknowledge reviviscence sergeantfish phrenologist
ferruginous mitrailleuse rhizogenous serpentiform physiologist
filibusterer monkeywrench ribonuclease shortstaffed phytophagous
fluorescence monophyletic risorgimento stalactiform psephologist
footplateman mouthbreeder schorlaceous thereinafter psychologise
frankincense multilateral selfcontempt thoroughfare psychologism
fricasseeing multivalence selfevidence thousandfold psychologist
furfuraceous nephelometer selfmurderer toastingfork rhizophagous
gallinaceous nephelometry selfviolence unclassified rontgenogram
galvanometer neurasthenia semidiameter understaffed saprophagous
```

```
sarcophagous  myrmecophily  compunctious  indivertible  playingfield
seismologist  paragraphist  conjunctival  indivertibly  pointilliste
selenologist  paramorphism  contemptible  inextensible  polyneuritic
skullduggery  patriarchate  contemptibly  infanticidal  polyneuritis
speleologist  philosophise  contractible  inharmonious  poorspirited
squarerigged  phreatophyte  contumacious  innutritious  preclassical
staffsurgeon  pleomorphism  contumelious  insalubrious  preconscious
starspangled  poikilotherm  cosmogonical  insecticidal  primogenital
steatopygous  polymorphism  cosmological  insufficient  primogenitor
supererogate  polymorphous  cosmopolitan  intelligible  proglottides
technologist  polyurethane  cosmopolitic  intelligibly  proselytiser
teratologist  prizefighter  counterlight  interdigital  prototypical
toxicologist  pteridophyte  crackbrained  intermediacy  publicspirit
trichologist  pyromorphite  crossgrained  intermediary  pursestrings
urbanologist  rhynchophora  curvifoliate  intermediate  quarterfinal
acetaldehyde  sarrusophone  destructible  intervenient  radiological
allomorphism  sclerenchyma  diamondfield  irremissible  rambunctious
apostrophise  sharpsighted  dibranchiate  irresistible  reproducible
apparatchiki  shortsighted  diphtheritic  irresistibly  residentiary
apparatchiks  siphonophore  disaffiliate  irreversible  rhinological
automorphism  spinsterhood  disassociate  irreversibly  saccharoidal
bachelorhood  steeplechase  discerptible  judgematical  sacrilegious
benzaldehyde  stepdaughter  disputatious  landingfield  sarsaparilla
birdwatching  stranglehold  emblematical  limnological  scatological
blastosphere  stratosphere  encephalitic  linguistical  schismatical
brainwashing  subthreshold  encephalitis  liquefacient  screenwriter
cabbagewhite  superhighway  endocarditis  lithological  scriptwriter
centrosphere  telegraphese  endometritis  longitudinal  selfcritical
Christophany  telegraphist  enginedriver  manometrical  selfdeceived
chromosphere  terebinthine  epexegetical  masterswitch  selfdeceiver
clearsighted  thermosphere  epicycloidal  mathematical  semiological
conidiophore  trumpetshell  ethnological  meretricious  semiprecious
countercheck  unlikelihood  etymological  metaphorical  semitropical
countershaft  whitewashing  etymologicon  metaphysical  Shaksperiana
dermatophyte  windingsheet  EuroAmerican  metathetical  shootingiron
diastrophism  zygomorphism  exospherical  metrological  slipcarriage
disfranchise  zygomorphous  extralimital  metropolitan  snarlingiron
electroshock  adscititious  extramarital  mezzorelievo  sociological
feldspathoid  adventitious  fiddlesticks  middleweight  sorbefacient
firstnighter  aeronautical  freightliner  misbehaviour  spiegeleisen
floodlighted  aetiological  frontispiece  Monophysitic  staffofficer
formaldehyde  AfroAmerican  geanticlinal  multifarious  stereopticon
forthrightly  alphabetical  genealogical  multifoliate  stupefacient
fountainhead  alphamerical  geographical  mythological  subconscious
Germanophile  amygdaloidal  geopolitical  mythologiser  subdivisible
Germanophobe  anthropoidal  geosynclinal  necrological  substantiate
gesellschaft  anticlerical  hagiological  neoclassical  substantival
gymnosophist  antiparticle  heartstrings  neurological  superciliary
haberdashery  antirachitic  heroicomical  nonefficient  supercilious
handkerchief  antithetical  hesperididia  nonidentical  supervenient
hemimorphism  appendicitis  heteroecious  obedientiary  suppositious
hemimorphite  archetypical  hierarchical  offscourings  suppressible
hirepurchase  arithmetical  highspirited  oligarchical  supraorbital
homeopathist  arrhythmical  histological  oneirocritic  surroundings
homomorphism  astrological  housetrained  orographical  synchronical
homomorphous  astronomical  hydrological  ostentatious  synchroniser
hypognathous  asymmetrical  hyperbolical  osteological  systematical
hyposulphite  bactericidal  hypocritical  overcautious  systematiser
ichthyophagy  bantamweight  hypostatical  overcritical  tautological
inescutcheon  barometrical  hypothetical  pancreatitis  teleological
kilowatthour  bassorelievo  immethodical  pantechnicon  theocratical
labyrinthian  bassorilievo  impercipient  paraboloidal  theosophical
labyrinthine  bibliophilic  inaccessible  paradisaical  thermophilic
LowChurchman  biographical  inaccessibly  parametrical  toggleswitch
macrocephaly  bloodstained  inadmissible  paratactical  tragicomical
manslaughter  carpetknight  inadmissibly  parsimonious  transfusible
mastigophora  cartological  inauspicious  pathological  transpacific
matriarchate  catechetical  incommodious  penitentiary  triglyphical
metallophone  cementitious  incompatible  pericarditis  tropological
metamorphism  chesterfield  incompatibly  pertinacious  tyrannicidal
metamorphose  chimneypiece  inconvenient  pestological  unauthorised
metapsychics  chitterlings  incorrigible  petrological  underachieve
microcephaly  chorological  incorrigibly  phenological  undetermined
misapprehend  clairaudient  indefeasible  phenotypical  uneconomical
mnemotechnic  closegrained  indefeasibly  philological  unhistorical
monadelphous  coenobitical  indefectible  phonological  unprejudiced
monographist  coenobytical  indefensible  phycological  unrecognised
monomorphous  combinations  indefensibly  phytological  unrestrained
monostichous  compressible  indigestible  planetesimal  unscientific
```

vainglorious desirability jetpropelled printability accoutrement
volumetrical dialectology kremlinology proconsulate admonishment
wallydraigle dilatability laissezaller protistology aerodynamics
welterweight disannulling lakedwelling protozoology announcement
backbreaking disconsolate lanternslide quadrivalent appraisement
billsticking disestablish leathercloth questionless astonishment
blatherskite dissocialise liturgiology quizzicality ballottement
bletherskate divisibility Liverpudlian radiobiology bedazzlement
bluestocking ecclesiology malleability radionuclide belittlement
bodystocking editorialise mediaevalism recapitulate bequeathment
breathtaking editorialist mediaevalist reducibility bewilderment
camiknickers effectuality melancholiac removability blandishment
earthshaking electroplate mercantilism reproachless blithesomely
freethinking elementalism mercantilist retractility breastsummer
galligaskins emotionalise mercurialise revictualled chastisement
metalworking emotionalism mercurialism rheumatology commencement
nanoplankton emotionalist microanalyst rontgenology contrivement
nerveracking emotionality microbiology sanguinolent convincement
safecracking entrammelled miscalculate schoolfellow crossexamine
shoulderknot ephemerality mistranslate scoundreldom cryptogamous
sidewhiskers epidemiology moistureless scoundrelism cumbersomely
sleepwalking episcopalian monometallic scrobiculate cumulonimbus
stockbroking epistemology monopetalous sectionalism decipherment
swashbuckler equitability motorcyclist selfinvolved denouncement
absquatulate erythroblast multinuclear sellingplate dethronement
adaptability essentiality multungulate semifinalist diminishment
advisability excitability municipalise separability disagreement
aeroembolism exophthalmic municipality silicicolous disannulment
alterability exophthalmos navigability sinistrality disbursement
anecdotalist exophthalmus necrophiliac softpedalled disendowment
anemophilous factionalism necrophilism somnambulant disgorgement
anthropology faithhealing necrophilous somnambulate disguisement
Aristotelean fictionalise negrophilism somnambulism dishevelment
Aristotelian filtrability negrophilist somnambulist disinterment
autocatalyse flammability neurobiology soundingline dislodgement
automobilist frangibility nevertheless spiritualise displacement
availability freewheeling Newfoundland spiritualism disseverment
bacchanalian frenchpolish noctambulant spiritualist distrainment
backpedalled frictionless noctambulism spirituality embattlement
bacteriology functionless noctambulist stockingless embezzlement
banderillero gamopetalous noctambulous stoneboiling embitterment
bibliopolist gamophyllous oblanceolate straticulate emblazonment
bilateralism gamosepalous officeholder streetwalker embranchment
bilingualism gravelelling opposability strengthless empoisonment
biocoenology griseofulvin otherworldly submaxillary empressement
bookingclerk habitability outrivalling subnormality encirclement
brickfielder haematoblast oversimplify syndactylism encroachment
burningglass haemophiliac oxyacetylene syndactylous encumberment
businesslike hemerocallis palatability teachability endamagement
canaliculate heritability parallelling technicality endangerment
candleholder homothallism parasitology technicolour enfeeblement
capercaillie hoodmanblind parochialise temptability enshrinement
capercailzie hydrophilism parochialism thickskulled enswathement
caterwauling hygrophilous parochiality thundercloud entanglement
chromatology illegibility peccadilloes tolerability enthronement
classicalism illiberality permeability Torricellian entrancement
classicalist illogicality pharmacology traceability entrenchment
classicality immovability photogeology tractability envisagement
coachbuilder immutability photophilous tranquillise epiphenomena
coldshoulder impartiality pilotballoon tranquillity epithalamion
collegialism imputability pitcherplant tridactylous epithalamium
collegiality inarticulate plaindealing trinomialism estrangement
commensalism inaudibility plausibility unambivalent forebodement
commensalist incapability pleasureless uncontrolled forestalment
congeniality incurability plummerblock unifoliolate freeswimming
congratulant indelibility pneumatology unisexuality gastronomist
congratulate indiscipline policyholder universalise guestchamber
connubiality infusibility polyethylene universalism habitforming
constabulary inoperculate polypetalous universalist heartwarming
conviviality insolubilise polysepalous universality hellgrammite
corporeality insolubility polytonality unscrupulous hereditament
counterblast internuclear potentiality venerability heterogamous
counterclaim interpellate practicality veridicality heteronomous
counterplead interstellar pralltriller verticillate housewarming
cryptanalyst invisibility precancelled walkietalkie humptydumpty
decentralise irascibility preestablish weatherglass idiothermous
decontrolled irregardless prehensility whimsicality illegitimacy
demineralise irritability premaxillary workingclass illegitimate
denaturalise jerrybuilder principality accouchement illtreatment

imprisonment	affectionate	composedness	effusiveness	gratefulness
inconformity	agribusiness	concordantly	eleemosynary	gratifyingly
infringement	allusiveness	concreteness	elocutionary	greenishness
intrenchment	altitudinous	concurrently	elocutionist	grievousness
inveiglement	ambivalently	Confucianism	enchantingly	grovellingly
katzenjammer	amenableness	confusedness	encumbrancer	gruesomeness
languishment	amicableness	conglutinate	enginetuning	guilefulness
maltreatment	antecedently	consentingly	enormousness	habitualness
microclimate	anthelmintic	consequently	entertaining	handsomeness
misalignment	apparentness	consistently	entreatingly	harlequinade
misjudgement	appetisingly	contagionist	entrepreneur	harmlessness
misplacement	appositeness	conterminous	enviableness	headshrinker
misstatement	appraisingly	contingently	epicureanism	heartburning
mistreatment	aromaticness	contrapuntal	equivalently	heavenliness
monochromate	astoundingly	contrariness	eruptiveness	hebetudinous
monofilament	astringently	contriteness	evanescently	heedlessness
multiformity	asynchronism	conveniently	evolutionary	helplessness
nicotinamide	asynchronous	convincingly	evolutionism	heroicalness
niminypiminy	attitudinise	costermonger	evolutionist	hesitatingly
nonalignment	autoimmunity	cotyledonary	exclusionary	heterogenous
northernmost	backwardness	cotyledonous	exclusionism	hierophantic
overestimate	balladmonger	countenancer	exclusionist	homesickness
phlebotomise	baselessness	covetousness	excursionist	hopelessness
phlebotomist	battlemented	cowardliness	exiguousness	horribleness
polychromous	beggarliness	creativeness	exorbitantly	humorousness
postponement	beneficently	criticalness	expansionary	hydroquinone
praseodymium	benevolently	crosscountry	expansionism	illusiveness
predetermine	berzelianite	culpableness	expansionist	illusoriness
presentiment	beseechingly	cumbrousness	experimental	immatureness
prothalamion	bewitchingly	cuprammonium	experimenter	impedimental
prothalamium	bibliomaniac	debonairness	explicitness	impenitently
pseudonymity	bicentennial	decaffeinate	exsanguinate	impetiginous
pseudonymous	blamableness	decisiveness	exsanguinous	implicitness
quadrinomial	blamefulness	decorousness	extortionary	impoliteness
radioelement	blastfurnace	decreasingly	extortionate	incisiveness
rapprochment	blissfulness	definiteness	extracranial	incoherently
readjustment	blisteringly	deflationary	fabulousness	inconcinnity
reassessment	bloodyminded	deflationist	facelessness	inconstantly
reassignment	blunderingly	dejectedness	factiousness	incoordinate
recommitment	blusteringly	delinquently	faintishness	increasingly
redeployment	boastfulness	delusiveness	faithfulness	indebtedness
reinvestment	bonnetmonkey	departmental	falcongentil	indirectness
renouncement	booklearning	depravedness	falcongentle	indoctrinate
resettlement	bootlessness	depressingly	fancifulness	inexpertness
retrenchment	brackishness	derisiveness	fatherliness	infiniteness
rumbletumble	brassbounder	desirousness	fearlessness	inflationary
semibasement	brokenwinded	desolateness	fearsomeness	inflationism
sledgehammer	calisthenics	despairingly	featheriness	inflationist
southernmost	canorousness	despondently	fecklessness	infrequently
stablishment	captiousness	detachedness	feebleminded	instrumental
sulphonamide	carelessness	deviationism	feminineness	integumental
transformism	carillonneur	deviationist	feverishness	interchanger
transformist	Cartesianism	dextrousness	fiendishness	interconnect
transhipment	cautiousness	dilatoriness	flamboyantly	interspinous
trichotomise	charlatanism	discerningly	flatteringly	intolerantly
trichotomous	cheerfulness	disciplinary	flickeringly	intracranial
unconformity	cheesemonger	discontented	forbiddingly	intriguingly
undergarment	chieftainess	discordantly	forcefulness	intrusionist
unemployment	childishness	discreetness	forcibleness	intuitionism
vanquishment	Christianise	discreteness	forebodingly	intuitionist
yellowhammer	Christianity	discriminant	formlessness	irrelevantly
abolitionary	churchianity	discriminate	fraudulently	irreverently
abolitionism	churlishness	disenchanter	freakishness	irritatingly
abolitionist	clannishness	disgustingly	frequentness	isolationism
abortiveness	clatteringly	disharmonise	friendliness	isolationist
abrasiveness	clownishness	dissentingly	fruitfulness	Keynesianism
absentminded	coalitionist	distinctness	fugitiveness	kinnikinnick
absoluteness	cocksureness	disturbingly	gamesomeness	kleptomaniac
abstractness	coerciveness	diversionary	generousness	klipspringer
abstruseness	cohesiveness	diversionist	geotectonics	knightliness
accordionist	coincidental	divisiveness	ghoulishness	latitudinous
accretionary	coincidently	dolorousness	gladsomeness	laudableness
accurateness	comfortingly	doubtfulness	glitteringly	lifelessness
accursedness	commandingly	downwardness	gloriousness	listlessness
adaptiveness	companionate	dreadfulness	gorgeousness	literariness
adequateness	companionway	droughtiness	governmental	lonesomeness
adhesiveness	complacently	duraluminium	gracefulness	lopsidedness
adorableness	complemental	dwarfishness	graciousness	lovelessness
affectedness	completeness	educationist	graspingness	lovelornness

```
lukewarmness  perviousness  schizogonous  supereminent  uxoriousness
luminousness  philistinism  scornfulness  supplemental  Valenciennes
lusciousness  phillumenist  scratchiness  supplementer  valetudinary
maidenliness  phrasemonger  scrimshanker  supplicantly  valuableness
malapertness  pitiableness  secessionism  surprisingly  vaporousness
malcontented  pitilessness  secessionist  surrejoinder  variableness
malevolently  pleasantness  seclusionist  swaggeringly  vengefulness
Manicheanism  pleasingness  sectarianise  swainishness  venomousness
manifoldness  plumbaginous  sectarianism  sweepingness  verticalness
mannerliness  populousness  sedulousness  sweetishness  vibraphonist
mastersinger  porcelainise  selflessness  tactlessness  Victorianism
materialness  porcelainous  selfluminous  tamelessness  vigorousness
megalomaniac  porcellanous  selfsameness  tangibleness  virtuousness
mercifulness  positiveness  semicylinder  tastefulness  vitreousness
metachronism  preciousness  semidarkness  tearlessness  voidableness
mindlessness  precisianism  semideponent  tercentenary  volatileness
mirthfulness  precisionist  sempiternity  terribleness  wastefulness
miscellanist  predesignate  sensibleness  terrifyingly  watchfulness
misdemeanant  predestinate  sensuousness  thankfulness  wellgrounded
misdemeanour  preeminently  separateness  thickskinned  whimperingly
mistakenness  preparedness  septuagenary  thievishness  whisperingly
moderateness  prevailingly  Septuagintal  thoroughness  wollastonite
moneychanger  previousness  serpentinely  thunderingly  womanishness
moneyspinner  pridefulness  sexcentenary  ticklishness  wondrousness
morrisdancer  priestliness  shamefulness  timelessness  workableness
motherliness  priggishness  sheepishness  timorousness  wrathfulness
mothertongue  princeliness  shortchanger  tirelessness  wretchedness
mournfulness  prizewinning  shouldernote  tiresomeness  wrongfulness
moveableness  probationary  shrewishness  togetherness  wunderkinder
movelessness  proficiently  simpleminded  toilsomeness  youthfulness
mucilaginous  profoundness  singlehanded  tonelessness  absorptional
munificently  prolificness  singleminded  toploftiness  aeroneurosis
mutinousness  protactinium  skittishness  tortuousness  agglutinogen
mystifyingly  provisionary  skrimshanker  touchingness  ailurophobia
namelessness  purblindness  slipperiness  towardliness  amphictyonic
narrowminded  pyrotechnics  slothfulness  tradescantia  anaerobiosis
nauseatingly  pyrotechnist  slovenliness  traditionary  anamorphosis
nauseousness  quadriennium  sluggishness  traditionist  anticyclonic
nebulousness  quadrumanous  sluttishness  traducianism  antiperiodic
needlessness  qualmishness  snappishness  traducianist  apparitional
negativeness  quinquennial  snobbishness  trampolinist  appositional
neoDarwinian  quinquennium  sociableness  transplanter  archdeaconry
neoDarwinism  radiophonics  solitariness  tricentenary  autochthones
neoDarwinist  ravenousness  sonorousness  trickishness  avitaminoses
Neohellenism  reactiveness  soullessness  triphthongal  avitaminosis
neonomianism  readableness  spaciousness  triumphantly  battleground
Neoplatonism  reassuringly  specificness  trustfulness  bellbottomed
Neoplatonist  receptionist  speciousness  truthfulness  bilharziosis
Nestorianism  recessionary  specktioneer  tunelessness  blabbermouth
nonchalantly  recklessness  spermogonium  twitteringly  bombdisposal
numerousness  reductionism  spidermonkey  unassumingly  boogiewoogie
nutritionist  reductionist  spiritedness  unbecomingly  breakthrough
nymphomaniac  reflationary  spitefulness  unblinkingly  butterscotch
obdurateness  refreshingly  splendidness  unblushingly  campfollower
obligingness  relativeness  sportfulness  unbrokenness  charnelhouse
obsoleteness  reliableness  sportiveness  uncommonness  charterhouse
omnipotently  remembrancer  spotlessness  unctuousness  checkerboard
omnisciently  reservedness  spuriousness  undermanning  chequerboard
onesidedness  resignedness  staggeringly  underpinning  clapperboard
oppositeness  resoluteness  stalwartness  underrunning  clotheshorse
ordinariness  resolvedness  stammeringly  unfrequented  commissioner
organgrinder  resoundingly  stealthiness  ungainliness  compatriotic
outdatedness  restlessness  sterlingness  unitarianism  complexional
overniceness  retiringness  straightness  unkindliness  complexioned
painlessness  reversionary  strikingness  unlawfulness  conceptional
paletteknife  rightfulness  strongminded  unlikeliness  confectioner
Palladianism  rigorousness  strontianite  unloveliness  confessional
panhellenism  rootlessness  strychninism  unpleasantly  connectional
parkinsonism  ruthlessness  stubbornness  unpronounced  conningtower
partitionist  saccharinity  studiousness  unsteadiness  convectional
patulousness  salutariness  stutteringly  unthinkingly  conventional
peacefulness  salvationism  subalternate  untimeliness  correctional
peerlessness  salvationist  subalternity  untowardness  councilwoman
pellucidness  Samaritanism  subcontinent  unwieldiness  counterforce
perilousness  sanguineness  subsequently  unwontedness  counterpoint
permanganate  satisfyingly  subterranean  unworldiness  counterpoise
perplexingly  scabrousness  succinctness  unworthiness  countrywoman
persistently  scatteringly  sufficiently  unyieldingly  crossingover
perverseness  scenepainter  suitableness  usuriousness  cuckooflower
```

curlingtongs	quarterbound	eavesdropper	stylographic	distemperate
curmudgeonly	recreational	ethnographer	swimmingpool	econometrics
customshouse	redemptioner	ethnographic	tachygrapher	elementarily
Czechoslovak	reflectional	glockenspiel	tachygraphic	equalitarian
derivational	repetitional	goosepimples	tetramorphic	eveningdress
Deuteronomic	revelational	hagiographer	transshipped	extrauterine
diageotropic	rhinocerotic	hagiographic	unprincipled	fainthearted
digressional	runningboard	handicapping	accusatorial	featherbrain
discretional	salutational	hectographic	administrant	fluorocarbon
distortional	sarcomatosis	hedgehopping	administrate	FrancoGerman
dodecaphonic	scraperboard	heliographer	aerosiderite	fructiferous
draughtboard	seismoscopic	heliographic	alexipharmic	fructivorous
draughthorse	selfapproval	heliotropism	ambassadress	futilitarian
drawingboard	selfcomposed	hieroglyphic	ambidextrous	gerontocracy
electrotonic	selfemployed	hierographer	amentiferous	gladiatorial
electrotonus	selfhypnosis	highstepping	antiaircraft	grallatorial
enantiomorph	selfreproach	homeomorphic	antimalarial	granodiorite
Englishwoman	servicecourt	horsewhipped	antineutrino	greathearted
escutcheoned	servicewoman	housekeeping	apiculturist	grossularite
exhibitioner	sharpshooter	hydrographer	atmospherics	gynaecocracy
expressional	shuffleboard	hydrographic	behaviourism	headmistress
flamethrower	Sinanthropus	hydrotropism	behaviourist	heavyhearted
foundationer	snaggletooth	hymnographer	benefactress	heliolatrous
furunculosis	stationhouse	hypertrophic	blackcurrant	heliotherapy
galactogogue	stellenbosch	iconographer	blackguardly	hemispheroid
gonadotropic	stereoisomer	IndoEuropean	bladderwrack	hereditarily
gonadotropin	stereophonic	intercropped	bloodthirsty	heterocercal
hallucinogen	stereoscopic	interceptor	brainstormer	heteromerous
hallucinosis	stethoscopic	licketysplit	breaststroke	highlystrung
halterbroken	stonemasonry	lithographer	buccaneering	horrorstruck
herpetologic	stormtrooper	lithographic	buccaneerish	humanitarian
hydrochloric	streptococci	marlinespike	buffalograss	hydrotherapy
hydrofluoric	stroboscopic	micrographer	burglarproof	hydrothermal
ichthyocolla	strongylosis	microscopist	cantankerous	hyperthermia
inflectional	subapostolic	misinterpret	carbohydrate	hypnotherapy
interfemoral	successional	monostrophic	caricaturist	hypochlorite
involutional	synarthrosis	mosstrooping	catilinarian	hypogastrium
leucocytosis	televisional	multipurpose	centrespread	idiosyncrasy
leukocytosis	theanthropic	mythographer	chalcopyrite	imperatorial
lodginghouse	theatregoing	namedropping	characterise	incendiarism
lycanthropic	thermoscopic	necrographer	cheeseburger	inspectorate
mansionhouse	thermotropic	nyctitropism	cheeseparing	inspectorial
meetinghouse	thirdborough	nympholeptic	chemotherapy	instructress
meltingpoint	toxicophobia	organoleptic	childbearing	intercurrent
misanthropic	tradespeople	orthographer	churchwarden	intrauterine
monkeyflower	transitional	orthographic	circumscribe	invertebrate
motivational	tuberculosis	orthotropism	clothespress	irregularity
navigational	unaccustomed	orthotropous	coelenterate	kindergarten
newfashioned	vantagepoint	outstripping	coleopterist	kissingcrust
occupational	viscerotonic	overcropping	coleopterous	knighterrant
oldfashioned	visitational	overstepping	collinearity	landingcraft
onomatopoeia	weatherboard	paedomorphic	commensurate	largehearted
onomatopoeic	weatherbound	pantographic	commissarial	laticiferous
opisthotonos	weatherhouse	petrographer	commissariat	lighthearted
oppositional	welldisposed	petrographic	compulsorily	luminiferous
osteoporosis	Wellingtonia	philadelphus	concelebrant	macropterous
outpensioner	wherethrough	phonographer	concelebrate	magnetograph
outwardbound	YankeeDoodle	phonographic	conchiferous	mangelwurzel
pasqueflower	amphitropous	photographer	conglomerate	marketgarden
peristeronic	anemographic	photographic	consistorial	marshharrier
phagocytosis	angiocarpous	phototropism	containerise	masterstroke
phagocytotic	antistrophic	phytographer	contemporary	melanochroic
philharmonic	backslapping	pictographic	contemporise	meteorograph
photochromic	basidiospore	pleiotropism	copolymerise	mezzosoprano
physiognomic	calligrapher	pornographer	cottonocracy	misselthrush
plasterboard	calligraphic	pornographic	counterproof	molecularity
pneumothorax	cartographer	pteridosperm	cousingerman	morningdress
polyhistoric	cartographic	radiographer	crosscurrent	mourningring
postdoctoral	catastrophic	radiographic	cumulocirrus	multiflorous
practitioner	chorographic	reprographic	curlingirons	multistoried
precessional	chromatopsia	rhizocarpous	deconsecrate	negotiatress
processional	closecropped	scenographic	demilitarise	neighbouring
professional	conidiospore	sharecropper	denuclearise	neuropterous
projectional	cosmographer	sideslipping	derogatorily	newspaperman
proportional	cosmographic	sidestepping	desulphurise	nonagenarian
proportioned	crosspurpose	sleepingpill	diamonddrill	nonconformer
prosopopoeia	dessertspoon	sparkingplug	disaccharide	nonflowering
psychotropic	discographer	stenographer	disembarrass	Northumbrian
quadraphonic	eavesdropped	stenographic	disintegrate	obligatorily

obstreperous	skateboarder	broncobuster	militaristic	surveyorship
octogenarian	skippingrope	buttermuslin	misrepresent	survivorship
opisthograph	slaughterous	Byelorussian	mistressship	syncretistic
orbicularity	snakecharmer	capitalistic	monopolistic	taberdarship
orienteering	sociometrist	cardinalship	monotheistic	tergiversate
orthopterist	soporiferous	catachrestic	mountainside	thriftlessly
orthopteroid	sparrowgrass	chairmanship	multiversity	transgressor
orthopterous	spectrograph	championship	musicianship	transmission
oscillograph	sphygmograph	chaplainship	nailscissors	transmissive
overpowering	spokesperson	chauvinistic	narcissistic	transversely
pantisocracy	squattocracy	chondriosome	naturalistic	unappetising
passionfruit	standingroom	chrematistic	negativistic	uninterested
peremptorily	stanniferous	circumcision	nominalistic	unresponsive
philanthrope	steganograph	circumfusion	oneupmanship	unsuccessful
philanthropy	stelliferous	colourlessly	osteoplastic	virtuosoship
phraseograph	stereochromy	coquettishly	outlandishly	viscountship
planetstruck	stonyhearted	courtplaster	overexposure	voluminosity
plecopterous	stouthearted	decompressor	overlordship	voluptuosity
plumbiferous	Stradivarius	delicatessen	overpressure	watermanship
posteriority	subeditorial	dictatorship	paraphrastic	wineglassful
postmistress	sublapsarian	directorship	parenthesise	abbreviation
praiseworthy	subsidiarily	discipleship	paronomastic	acceleration
preceptorial	subtemperate	discomposure	partisanship	accelerative
prefectorial	sudoriferous	dispossessor	pennywhistle	accentuation
prehistorian	supercharger	ecclesiastic	periphrastic	acciaccatura
prelapsarian	taperecorder	ectoparasite	photofission	accumulation
premenstrual	taskmistress	effortlessly	polytheistic	accumulative
preponderant	terrorstruck	endoparasite	positivistic	adjudication
preponderate	testosterone	enterprising	pragmatistic	adjudicative
preposterous	tetrachordal	enthusiastic	prenticeship	adjudicatory
presbyterate	tetrahedrite	euhemeristic	prerequisite	adulteration
presbyterial	thaumaturgic	evangelistic	protoplasmic	aircondition
Presbyterian	threequarter	executorship	protoplastic	alimentation
privateering	totalitarian	extinguisher	Quadragesima	alimentative
professorate	transferring	extrasensory	quaestorship	alliteration
professoress	transitorily	extraversion	receivership	alliterative
professorial	transmigrant	extroversion	reconversion	amalgamation
profiteering	transmigrate	fieldglasses	regardlessly	amalgamative
progenitress	transmogrify	frontiersman	relationship	amelioration
progesterone	turbellarian	fuliginosity	relativistic	ameliorative
proprietress	ubiquitarian	gamesmanship	relentlessly	amortisation
prosectorial	unchivalrous	geochemistry	repercussion	anaesthetise
protectorate	undercurrent	governorship	repercussive	anaesthetist
proudhearted	unflattering	groundlessly	repossession	anathematise
psychiatrist	unpopularity	guardianship	reprehension	annihilation
quaquaversal	unregenerate	hairdressing	reprehensive	annihilative
racketeering	vauntcourier	harquebusier	residentship	annunciation
radiotherapy	veterinarian	heathenishly	resistlessly	anticipation
recalcitrant	vicechairman	hemiparasite	retrocession	anticipative
recalcitrate	visitatorial	henotheistic	retrocessive	anticipatory
Redemptorist	vocabularian	highpressure	retropulsion	antiSemitism
redintegrate	weatherproof	horsemanship	retroversion	appendectomy
refractorily	wholehearted	hyperplastic	reunionistic	apperception
reinvigorate	wonderstruck	hypertension	revivalistic	apperceptive
remilitarise	wonderworker	hypertensive	salesmanship	appreciation
resiniferous	xanthochroia	hypocoristic	salpiglossis	appreciative
responsorial	xiphisternum	iconoclastic	schoolmaster	appreciatory
salamandrian	youngberries	impoverished	scrupulosity	arborisation
salamandrine	absolutistic	inconclusive	secularistic	architecture
salamandroid	accomplished	inexpressive	selfdelusion	articulately
salutiferous	aircraftsman	intercession	selfpleasing	articulation
sanguinarily	Alhambresque	intercessory	semidomestic	articulatory
scatterbrain	amateurishly	intermission	semifinalist	asphyxiation
schizophrene	antagonistic	intromission	semiparasite	assibilation
scouringrush	antimacassar	introversion	sensualistic	assimilation
secondstring	apprehension	introversive	Septuagesima	assimilative
selfabsorbed	apprehensive	irresponsive	sergeantship	assimilatory
selfcatering	astrophysics	journalistic	serjeantship	astronautics
selfdestruct	attorneyship	jurisconsult	servitorship	atheromatous
selfdistrust	Australasian	kirschwasser	shirtwaister	augmentation
selfinterest	bachelorship	lachrymosely	specialistic	augmentative
selfportrait	backwoodsman	laureateship	speechlessly	auscultation
semiliterate	bacteriostat	liberalistic	spiritlessly	auscultatory
seminiferous	belletristic	marksmanship	stockraising	bioscientist
sexagenarian	biochemistry	metaphrastic	stonedresser	birdsnesting
shamateurism	bottlewasher	microcapsule	studdingsail	blastulation
shatterproof	bowcompasses	microcrystal	supersensory	blockbusting
siliciferous	breathlessly	microphysics	supersession	bloodbrother
sinistrorsal	brinkmanship	microseismic	surrealistic	bloodletting

brilliantine	consummatory	dispensatory	globetrotter	intermittent
bullfighting	contestation	disquisition	glycoprotein	intermitting
cachinnation	continuation	dissertation	gramnegative	intermixture
cachinnatory	continuative	dissociation	grampositive	interpretive
calorimetric	contribution	dissociative	graveclothes	interruption
calumniation	contributive	dissymmetric	habilitation	interruptive
calumniatory	contributory	distillation	hairsplitter	intersection
canalisation	conversation	distillatory	halogenation	interstitial
cancellation	coordinately	distributary	headquarters	intertexture
canonisation	coordination	distribution	heliocentric	intervention
cantillation	coordinative	distributive	hermeneutics	intimidation
capitulation	correctitude	divarication	highfaluting	intimidatory
carburetting	courtmartial	dorsiventral	hindquarters	intoxication
catamountain	craftbrother	doubleacting	hippocentaur	intransitive
chalcolithic	crenellation	duckingstool	homoeopathic	introduction
cheesecutter	crossbuttock	dynamometric	homologation	introductory
chlorination	crosssection	earsplitting	horticulture	introjection
chronometric	cuckingstool	echolocation	humanisation	intromittent
civilisation	curvicostate	edulcoration	humification	intromitting
clarinettist	curvirostral	effectuation	hydrostatics	introvertive
claudication	cytogenetics	effeminately	hysterectomy	invagination
closemouthed	deactivation	elucubration	idealisation	invalidation
coacervation	deambulatory	emancipation	illiterately	inveterately
cockfighting	debilitation	emargination	illumination	invigilation
codification	decapitation	emasculation	illuminative	invigoration
cohabitation	deceleration	emasculatory	illustration	irreflective
collegiately	decongestant	encrustation	illustrative	irresolutely
colonisation	decongestion	equalisation	immaculately	irresolution
coloquintida	decongestive	equivocation	immoderately	irrespective
colorimetric	deescalation	equivocatory	immoderation	Ishmaelitish
columniation	deflagration	erythematous	immunisation	isodiametric
commendation	defraudation	etherisation	imperceptive	jurisdiction
commendatory	degenerately	ethnocentric	imperfection	lachrymation
commentation	degeneration	evisceration	imperfective	lachrymatory
compellation	degenerative	exacerbation	implantation	landingstage
compensation	deionisation	exaggeration	impregnation	landingstrip
compensative	delamination	exaggerative	inaccurately	laterisation
compensatory	deliberately	exaggeratory	inactivation	latinisation
complication	deliberation	exasperation	inadequately	legalisation
compurgation	deliberative	excogitation	inappositely	legitimately
compurgatory	delimitation	excogitative	inauguration	legitimation
conciliation	demodulation	excruciating	inauguratory	legitimatise
conciliative	denaturation	excruciation	incapacitate	levorotation
conciliatory	denomination	exenteration	incatenation	levorotatory
condemnation	denominative	exercitation	incineration	liquefaction
condemnatory	denunciation	exhilaration	incompletely	lithotritist
condensation	denunciative	exhilarative	inconsistent	localisation
conferential	denunciatory	expatriation	incorruption	magistrature
confidential	depopulation	expediential	incrustation	malformation
confirmation	depreciation	experiential	indefinitely	malnutrition
confirmative	depreciatory	explantation	indelicately	malversation
confirmatory	deputisation	exploitation	indiscretion	manipulation
confiscation	deracination	exploitative	inexactitude	manipulative
confiscatory	desalination	exprobration	infelicitous	manipulatory
conformation	desideration	exulceration	inflammation	Marcionitism
conglobation	desiderative	facilitation	inflammatory	maximisation
congregation	despoliation	felicitation	ingratiating	mealymouthed
conscription	desquamation	feminisation	inhabitation	menstruation
consecration	desquamative	fenestration	inoccupation	metasomatism
consecratory	desquamatory	fermentation	inordinately	minimisation
conservation	detoxication	fermentative	inosculation	ministration
conservatism	diamagnetism	fibrillation	insemination	ministrative
conservative	dichromatism	finalisation	inspissation	misadventure
conservatory	differentiae	firefighting	installation	misdirection
consignation	differential	flagellation	instauration	miseducation
consociation	dilapidation	flagellatory	instillation	misquotation
conspiration	dilettantish	flavoprotein	insufflation	mithridatise
constipation	dilettantism	flocculation	insurrection	mithridatism
constitution	disadvantage	floriculture	intellection	mobilisation
constitutive	disaffection	fluidisation	intellective	modification
constriction	disclamation	fluoridation	intellectual	modificatory
constrictive	discomfiture	fluorination	inteneration	monetisation
construction	discoverture	focalisation	interception	moralisation
constructive	disincentive	foresightful	intercutting	motorisation
consultation	disinfectant	fostermother	interdiction	multicentral
consultative	disinfection	gasification	interdictive	multidentate
consummately	disinflation	genuflection	interdictory	multipartite
consummation	disorientate	geomagnetism	interjection	naturopathic
consummative	dispensation	glaucomatous	interjectory	nebulisation

neuroanatomy	preformation	sansculottic	thunderstorm	censoriously
nidification	preformative	satisfaction	tightmouthed	chivalrously
nightclothes	prescription	satisfactory	tittletattle	circuitously
nomenclative	prescriptive	scutellation	torrefaction	circumfluent
nomenclature	preselection	segmentation	totalisation	cirrocumulus
noncombatant	preselective	seismometric	trachomatous	clangorously
noncommittal	presentation	selfbegotten	trainspotter	clinkerbuilt
noneffective	presentative	selfdevotion	transduction	coetaneously
nonessential	preservation	selfdoubting	transmitting	commodiously
nonobjective	preservative	selfelective	transmontane	contagiously
nonresistant	presidential	selfexistent	transpontine	contemptuous
northeastern	pretermitted	selfflattery	transudation	contiguously
northwestern	preventative	selfidentity	transudatory	continuously
notification	pricecutting	selfignition	transvestism	courageously
novelisation	proclamation	selflimiting	transvestite	delightfully
obliteration	proclamatory	selfrighting	trephination	despitefully
obliterative	profligately	selfstarting	trifurcation	diaphanously
obnubilation	prolongation	servocontrol	tripartitely	disambiguate
obscurantism	promulgation	sesquialtera	tripartition	disastrously
obscurantist	propitiation	silviculture	triplication	disdainfully
opinionative	propitiatory	singleacting	troglodytism	disgustfully
optimisation	proscription	siphonostele	typification	disingenuous
organisation	proscriptive	smallclothes	ultramontane	diverticular
orthodontics	prostitution	sodafountain	unattractive	diverticulum
orthodontist	protestation	solarisation	underclothes	dovecoloured
ossification	prothonotary	solicitation	undercoating	euphoniously
overexertion	protohistory	solifluction	undercutting	extraneously
overreaction	providential	southeastern	underletting	factitiously
pacification	psychoactive	southwestern	undersetting	fallaciously
pacificatory	psychometric	speakingtube	underwritten	fastidiously
paedobaptism	psychopathic	speedboating	unhesitating	felicitously
palaeobotany	pterodactyle	sphragistics	unionisation	fictitiously
Palaeolithic	purification	squirreltail	unthoughtful	flagitiously
panification	purificatory	stereometric	urbanisation	fortuitously
paralysation	putrefaction	sternutation	valorisation	gluttonously
paramilitary	putrefactive	sternutative	vaporisation	goodhumoured
passepartout	pyroelectric	sternutatory	vasodilation	gratuitously
passionately	quantisation	stichomythia	vasodilatory	gregariously
penalisation	quantitative	stichomythic	vaticination	hardfavoured
peradventure	quarterstaff	stilboestrol	venepuncture	hardfeatured
perfoliation	racemisation	stillhunting	venipuncture	harmoniously
performative	radioisotope	stonecutting	ventripotent	hibernaculum
periodontics	ramification	stridulation	verification	highcoloured
periodontist	ratification	strobilation	verificatory	homonymously
pernoctation	reactivation	strophanthin	vertebration	horrendously
peroxidation	reallocation	stupefaction	vesiculation	hydromedusae
perpetration	recollection	stupefactive	vilification	hydromedusan
perpetuation	recollective	subarrhation	vinification	idolatrously
perspiration	reconstitute	subcelestial	vitalisation	imperviously
perspiratory	recuperation	subcommittee	vitiligation	incautiously
perturbation	recuperative	suberisation	vitrifaction	incestuously
perturbative	redecoration	subminiature	vituperation	inconsequent
pestilential	regeneration	subscription	vituperative	incontiguous
petrifaction	regenerative	substitution	vituperatory	indecorously
photomontage	registration	substitutive	vivification	indigenously
photosetting	rehabilitate	substruction	vocalisation	indissoluble
pigmentation	rejuvenation	substructure	vociferation	indissolubly
pisciculture	remuneration	sulphonation	vomiturition	infectiously
pitterpatter	remunerative	sulphuration	wainscotting	infundibular
placesetting	remuneratory	sulphuretted	waistcoating	ingloriously
plainclothed	renunciation	superstition	wallpainting	iniquitously
plainclothes	renunciative	supervention	abstemiously	interlobular
Plattdeutsch	renunciatory	supplication	adulterously	interlocutor
plebiscitary	reoccupation	supplicatory	aforethought	languorously
pluviometric	repatriation	sustentation	afterthought	lasciviously
polarimetric	reproduction	sustentative	agricultural	libidinously
polarisation	reproductive	swaggerstick	amphibiously	licentiously
polychaetous	restaurateur	swizzlestick	anotherguess	loquaciously
polyglottism	resupination	sycophantish	appendicular	lugubriously
postposition	resurrection	sylviculture	aquicultural	magniloquent
postpositive	reticulately	teetertotter	auspiciously	manufacturer
precedential	reticulation	teratomatous	autonomously	marketsquare
prechristian	retractation	tessellation	avariciously	marvellously
precognition	ricochetting	testamentary	boisterously	meaningfully
precognitive	rollingstock	therapeutics	brontosaurus	mendaciously
precondition	romanisation	therapeutist	calamitously	merrythought
predigestion	ruralisation	thermometric	calcareously	metalanguage
predilection	sabretoothed	throughstone	calumniously	meticulously
preferential	sandyachting	thunderstone	capriciously	minicomputer

miraculously	ungraciously	primigravida	razzledazzle	expansionary
mispronounce	ungratefully	productively	spermatozoid	exsanguinate
monotonously	unmercifully	productivity	spermatozoon	exsufflicate
mordaciously	unscriptural	projectively	————————	extortionary
multiloquous	unstructured	protectively	abolitionary	extortionate
mysteriously	untruthfully	protensively	absquatulate	extramundane
neglectfully	uproariously	protrusively	accretionary	fantasticate
nutritiously	usufructuary	reflectively	administrant	featherbrain
obsequiously	varicoloured	reflectivity	administrate	gerontocracy
omnivorously	victoriously	refractivity	affectionate	gesellschaft
outmanoeuvre	villainously	regressively	antiaircraft	gynaecocracy
outrageously	viviparously	repetitively	authenticate	haematoblast
overpersuade	vociferously	repressively	billingsgate	harlequinade
perfidiously	voluminously	responsively	blackcurrant	heliotherapy
perjuriously	voluptuously	ruminatively	bladderwrack	hemichordate
perniciously	wellfavoured	Scandinavian	blastfurnace	henceforward
pharmaceutic	williewaught	selfactivity	bletherskate	hippocentaur
plesiosaurus	winterbourne	Stakhanovism	borosilicate	hirepurchase
portentously	worshipfully	Stakhanovite	buffalograss	honeybuzzard
postgraduate	absorptivity	subjectively	burningglass	hydrotherapy
posthumously	accusatively	subjectivise	canaliculate	hypnotherapy
precariously	aggressively	subjectivism	carbohydrate	ichthyophagy
precociously	antediluvian	subjectivist	catamountain	idiosyncrasy
presumptuous	attractively	subjectivity	centuplicate	illegitimacy
prodigiously	collectively	submissively	checkerboard	illegitimate
propaedeutic	collectivise	subversively	chemotherapy	inarticulate
propitiously	collectivism	successively	chequerboard	incapacitate
prosperously	collectivist	suggestively	Christophany	incoordinate
pugnaciously	collectivity	susceptivity	clapperboard	indoctrinate
purposebuilt	compulsively	suspensively	clavicembalo	inflationary
purposefully	compulsivity	thanksgiving	coelenterate	inoperculate
quadrangular	conclusively	topsyturvily	commensurate	inspectorate
rabblerouser	conductivity	transitively	companionate	intermediacy
rebelliously	connectively	transitivity	concelebrant	intermediary
receptaculum	convulsively	vegetatively	concelebrate	intermediate
remorsefully	copulatively	vindictively	conduplicate	intermundane
respectfully	corelatively	conglomerate	interpellate	
respectfully	corelatively	contrariwise	conglomerate	interpellate
revengefully	correctively	contrariwise	conglutinate	intramundane
ridiculously	cumulatively	glassblowing	congratulant	invertebrate
robustiously	decoratively	henceforward	congratulate	knighterrant
rosecoloured	definitively	pickerelweed	constabulary	landingcraft
salubriously	derivatively	southernwood	contemporary	landingstage
scandalously	digressively	whippoorwill	cottonocracy	loungelizard
scrupulously	diminutively	disconnexion	cotyledonary	macrocephaly
scurrilously	discursively	heterosexual	counterblast	magnetograph
selfcoloured	dissuasively	psychosexual	counterclaim	marketsquare
semicircular	dubitatively	retroflexion	counterscarp	matriarchate
sequaciously	electronvolt	shadowboxing	countershaft	metalanguage
sericultural	exhaustively	accompanyist	curvicaudate	meteorograph
slanderously	expressively	artilleryman	curvicostate	mezzosoprano
solicitously	expressivity	breathalyser	curvifoliate	microcephaly
somniloquism	figuratively	butterflynut	decaffeinate	microclimate
somniloquist	heliogravure	cardcarrying	decongestant	miscalculate
sprightfully	imperatively	electrolysis	deconsecrate	misdemeanant
statuesquely	impressively	electrolytic	deflationary	mistranslate
stertorously	imputatively	electrotyper	dibranchiate	monochromate
stringcourse	indecisively	erythromycin	disadvantage	mourningband
stupendously	indicatively	fibrinolysin	disaffiliate	multidentate
successfully	infinitively	gametophytic	disambiguate	multifoliate
superannuate	interservice	haematolysis	disassociate	multiplicand
supernaculum	irrelatively	haematoxylon	disciplinary	multiplicate
supernatural	laboursaving	heterophylly	disconsolate	multungulate
suspiciously	meditatively	microcopying	discriminant	Newfoundland
synonymously	oppressively	nephanalysis	discriminate	noctambulant
tabernacular	overactivity	noncombatant		
tabernacular	overactivity	noncombatant	disembarrass	noncombatant
thermocouple	pejoratively	schizothymia	disinfectant	nonresistant
thoughtfully	perceptively	schizothymic	disintegrate	obedientiary
thunderously	perceptivity	selfanalysis	disorientate	oblanceolate
timehonoured	percussively	spermaphytic	distemperate	opisthograph
traitorously	perfectively	streptomycin	distributary	oscillograph
tremendously	permissively	voluntaryism	diversionary	overabundant
tumultuously	permittivity	voluntaryist	draughtboard	overestimate
twentyfourmo	persuasively	zygapophysis	drawingboard	overpersuade
ubiquitously	photogravure	bobbydazzler	electroplate	palaeobotany
umbrageously	possessively	honeybuzzard	eleemosynary	pantisocracy
underinsured	postdiluvian	loungelizard	elocutionary	paramilitary
uneventfully	preclusively	monkeypuzzle	erythroblast	patriarchate
unfaithfully	predictively	nitrobenzene	evolutionary	penitentiary
ungracefully	preventively	privatdozent	exclusionary	permanganate

photomontage	tergiversate	impenetrably	liverystable	AfroAmerican
phraseograph	testamentary	imperishable	magnetisable	alphabetical
pigeonbreast	thoroughbass	imperishably	maintainable	alphamerical
pitcherplant	thoroughfare	imponderable	manoeuvrable	anticlerical
planoconcave	traditionary	imponderably	marriageable	antiparticle
plasterboard	transmigrant	inaccessible	merchantable	antithetical
plebiscitary	transmigrate	inaccessibly	moneygrubber	archetypical
polyurethane	transmontane	inadmissible	monosyllabic	arithmetical
portmanteaus	tricentenary	inadmissibly	monosyllable	arrhythmical
portmanteaux	ultramontane	inappeasable	multipliable	astrological
postgraduate	ultramundane	inapplicable	nonflammable	astronomical
predesignate	undersurface	inapplicably	octosyllabic	asymmetrical
predestinate	unifoliolate	incalculable	octosyllable	barometrical
prefabricate	unregenerate	incalculably	parisyllabic	bibliothecae
premaxillary	usufructuary	incognisable	polysyllabic	biographical
preponderant	valetudinary	incognitable	polysyllable	cartological
preponderate	verticillate	incommutable	precipitable	catechetical
presbyterate	weatherboard	incommutably	programmable	chorological
probationary	weatherglass	incomparable	prosecutable	coenobitical
proconsulate	workingclass	incomparably	pulverisable	coenobytical
professorate	abstractable	incompatible	quantifiable	cosmogonical
protectorate	ailurophobia	incompatibly	questionable	cosmological
prothonotary	approachable	incomputable	questionably	countenancer
provisionary	appropriable	inconsolable	rechargeable	echinococcus
punchingball	attributable	inconsolably	recognisable	emblematical
quarterstaff	bonnyclabber	inconsumable	recognisably	encumbrancer
radiotherapy	carriageable	inconsumably	reconcilable	epexegetical
recalcitrant	chocolatebox	incorrigible	rememberable	erythromycin
recalcitrate	classifiable	incorrigibly	renegotiable	ethnological
recapitulate	communicable	indeclinable	reproachable	etymological
recessionary	communicably	indefeasible	reproducible	etymologicon
redintegrate	compoundable	indefeasibly	restrainable	EuroAmerican
reflationary	compressible	indefectible	rumbletumble	exospherical
rehabilitate	conscionable	indefensible	saponifiable	fiddlesticks
reinvigorate	considerable	indefensibly	selfabsorbed	genealogical
residentiary	considerably	indigestible	subdivisible	geographical
reversionary	contemptible	indisputable	superposable	geopolitical
ribonuclease	contemptibly	indisputably	suppressible	hagiological
runningboard	contractable	indissoluble	surmountable	heroicomical
scatterbrain	contractible	indissolubly	thermostable	heterocercal
scraperboard	controllable	indivertible	toxicophobia	hierarchical
scrobiculate	cultivatable	indivertibly	transferable	histological
selfportrait	cumulonimbus	ineffaceable	transfusible	hydrological
selfreproach	decasyllabic	ineffaceably	translatable	hyperbolical
sellingplate	decasyllable	ineradicable	transmutable	hypocritical
semiliterate	decipherable	ineradicably	transpirable	hypostatical
septuagenary	decomposable	inexplicable	transposable	hypothetical
sexcentenary	demonstrable	inexplicably	trestletable	immethodical
Shakspereana	demonstrably	inexpugnable	unacceptable	judgematical
Shaksperiana	destructible	inexpugnably	unanswerable	limnological
shuffleboard	determinable	inextensible	unappeasable	linguistical
skunkcabbage	determinably	inextricable	unassailable	lithological
slipcarriage	diminishable	inextricably	unbelievable	manometrical
sodafountain	disagreeable	inhospitable	unbelievably	mathematical
somnambulant	disagreeably	inhospitably	unchangeable	mesothoracic
somnambulate	discerptible	insufferable	unchangeably	metaphorical
sophisticate	discountable	insufferably	uncharitable	metaphysical
sparrowgrass	discoverable	intelligible	uncharitably	metathetical
spectrograph	displaceable	intelligibly	uncomeatable	metathoracic
sphygmograph	disreputable	interminable	unemployable	metrological
squattocracy	disreputably	interminably	unfathomable	monomaniacal
squirrelcage	distrainable	invulnerable	unfavourable	morrisdancer
squirreltail	emulsifiable	invulnerably	unfavourably	mythological
steeplechase	equiprobable	irredeemable	ungovernable	necrological
steganograph	exchangeable	irredeemably	unimaginable	neoclassical
straticulate	exterminable	irreformable	unimaginably	neurological
studdingsail	extraditable	irrefragable	unmanageable	nonidentical
subalternate	fertilisable	irrefragably	unmistakable	oligarchical
subinfeudate	fluorocarbon	irremediable	unmistakably	orographical
submaxillary	guestchamber	irremediably	unprofitable	osteological
substantiate	hubblebubble	irremissible	unprofitably	osteomalacia
subtemperate	hybridisable	irrepealable	unreasonable	overcritical
superannuate	hydrolysable	irreprovable	unreasonably	pantechnicon
superciliary	hypnotisable	irresistible	unrepeatable	paradisaical
supererogate	identifiable	irresistibly	unsearchable	paradisiacal
supermundane	immeasurable	irresolvable	unseasonable	parametrical
supramundane	immeasurably	irrespirable	vanquishable	paratactical
swimmingbath	immensurable	irreversible	aeronautical	pathological
tercentenary	impenetrable	irreversibly	aetiological	periostracum

```
pestological illnaturedly apparentness correctively endangerment
petrological infanticidal appositeness counteragent enfeeblement
phenological insecticidal appraisement countercheck enormousness
phenotypical interestedly Aristotelean counterplead enshrinement
philological interpleader aromaticness covetousness enswathement
phonological jerrybuilder articulately cowardliness entanglement
phycological lefthandedly astonishment creativeness enthronement
phytological longwindedly attractively criticalness entrancement
preclassical marketgarden backwardness crosscurrent entrenchment
prototypical misknowledge ballottement culpableness entrepreneur
pyromaniacal mouthbreeder banderillero cumbersomely enviableness
radiological muddleheaded baselessness cumbrousness envisagement
remembrancer muttonheaded bassorelievo cumulatively epiphenomena
rhinological muzzleloader bassorilievo debonairness eruptiveness
scatological narrowminded bedazzlement decipherment estrangement
schismatical officeholder beggarliness decisiveness eveningdress
selfcritical openhandedly belittlement decoratively exhaustively
semiological openmindedly benefactress decorousness exiguousness
semitropical organgrinder bequeathment definiteness explicitness
sociological otherworldly bewilderment definitively expressively
spermathecal paraboloidal birefringent degenerately fabulousness
staffofficer policyholder blamableness dejectedness facelessness
stereopticon priestridden blamefulness deliberately factiousness
streptococci proglottides blandishment deliquescent faintishness
streptomycin pronouncedly blastosphere delusiveness faithfulness
synchronical rattleheaded blissfulness denouncement fancifulness
systematical restrainedly blithesomely depravedness fatherliness
tautological restrictedly boastfulness derisiveness fearlessness
teleological saccharoidal bookingclerk derivatively fearsomeness
theocratical salmonladder bootlessness desirousness featheriness
theosophical scoundreldom brackishness desolateness fecklessness
tragicomical semicylinder camiknickers detachedness feminineness
triglyphical shamefacedly canorousness dethronement feverishness
tropological simpleminded captiousness dextrousness fiendishness
uneconomical singlehanded carelessness diamondfield figuratively
unhistorical singleminded carillonneur digressively flavoprotein
unprejudiced skateboarder cautiousness dilatoriness foraminifera
unpronounced stockbreeder centrespread diminishment forcefulness
volumetrical straightedge centrosphere diminutively forcibleness
absentminded strongminded chastisement disagreement forebodement
abstractedly surefootedly cheerfulness disannulment forestalment
amygdaloidal surrejoinder chesterfield disbursement formlessness
anthropoidal taperecorder chieftainess discreetness fountainhead
antiperiodic tetrachordal childishness discreteness freakishness
bactericidal tyrannicidal chimneypiece discursively frequentness
bewilderedly unaffectedly chromosphere disendowment frictionless
blackguardly unexpectedly churlishness disgorgement friendliness
bloodyminded unreservedly circumfluent disguisement frontispiece
brassbounder wellgrounded circumjacent dishevelment fruitfulness
breechloader woodenheaded clairaudient disinterment fugitiveness
brickfielder woollyheaded clannishness dislodgement functionless
brokenwinded wunderkinder clothespress displacement gamesomeness
bulletheaded YankeeDoodle clownishness disseverment generousness
bullheadedly abortiveness cocksureness dissuasively ghoulishness
calculatedly abrasiveness coerciveness distinctness gladsomeness
candleholder absoluteness cohesiveness distrainment gloriousness
churchwarden abstractness collectively divisiveness glycoprotein
coachbuilder abstruseness collegiately dolorousness gorgeousness
coldshoulder accouchement commencement doubtfulness gracefulness
confoundedly accoutrement completeness downwardness graciousness
conquistador accurateness composedness dreadfulness graspingness
contractedly accursedness compulsively droughtiness gratefulness
determinedly accusatively conclusively dubitatively greengrocery
disjointedly actinomycete concreteness dwarfishness greenishness
dispiritedly adaptiveness concupiscent effeminately grievousness
displeasedly adequateness confusedness effervescent gruesomeness
distractedly adhesiveness connectively efflorescent guilefulness
dunderheaded admonishment constringent effusiveness haberdashery
encyclopedia adorableness consummately embattlement habitualness
encyclopedic affectedness contrariness embezzlement handsomeness
epicycloidal aggressively contriteness embitterment harmlessness
farsightedly agribusiness contrivement emblazonment headmistress
feebleminded allusiveness convalescent embranchment headquarters
fiddlefaddle ambassadress convincement empoisonment heavenliness
hairsbreadth amenableness convulsively empressement heedlessness
handsbreadth amicableness coordinately encirclement helplessness
hesperididia announcement copulatively encroachment hereditament
highhandedly anotherguess corelatively encumberment heroicalness
illadvisedly anthropogeny corespondent endamagement hindquarters
```

```
homesickness   mannerliness   populousness   schizophrene   sweetishness
hopelessness   materialness   positiveness   scornfulness   swimmingbell
horribleness   meditatively   possessively   scratchiness   tactlessness
humorousness   mercifulness   postmistress   sedulousness   tamelessness
illiterately   mezzorelievo   postponement   selfexistent   tangibleness
illtreatment   microsurgery   preciousness   selfflattery   taskmistress
illusiveness   mindlessness   preclusively   selfinterest   tastefulness
illusoriness   mirthfulness   predictively   selflessness   tearlessness
immaculately   misalignment   preparedness   selfsameness   telegraphese
immatureness   misapprehend   presentiment   semibasement   terribleness
immoderately   misjudgement   preventively   semidarkness   thankfulness
imperatively   misplacement   previousness   semideponent   thermosphere
impercipient   misrepresent   pridefulness   sensibleness   thievishness
implicitness   misstatement   priestliness   sensuousness   thoroughness
impoliteness   mistakenness   priggishness   separateness   ticklishness
impressively   mistreatment   princeliness   serpentinely   timelessness
imprisonment   moderateness   privatdocent   sesquialtera   timorousness
imputatively   moistureless   privatdozent   shamefulness   tirelessness
inaccurately   monofilament   proboscidean   sheepishness   tiresomeness
inadequately   morningdress   productively   shoulderbelt   togetherness
inappositely   motherliness   professoress   shrewishness   toilsomeness
incandescent   mournfulness   profligately   sidewhiskers   tonelessness
incisiveness   moveableness   profoundness   siphonostele   toploftiness
incompletely   movelessness   progenitress   skittishness   tortuousness
inconsequent   multinuclear   projectively   skullduggery   touchingness
inconsistent   mutinousness   prolificness   slipperiness   towardliness
inconvenient   namelessness   proprietress   slothfulness   transcendent
indebtedness   nauseousness   prosopopoeia   slovenliness   transhipment
indecisively   nebulousness   protectively   sluggishness   transitively
indefinitely   needlessness   protensively   sluttishness   transversely
indelicately   negativeness   protrusively   snappishness   trickishness
indicatively   negotiatress   pteridosperm   snobbishness   tripartitely
indirectness   neurosurgeon   purblindness   sociableness   trumpetshell
IndoEuropean   neurosurgery   quadrivalent   solitariness   trustfulness
inescutcheon   nevertheless   qualmishness   sonorousness   truthfulness
inexpertness   nitrobenzene   questionless   sorbefacient   tunelessness
infiniteness   nonalignment   radioelement   soullessness   unambivalent
infinitively   nonefficient   rapprochment   southeastern   unbrokenness
infringement   noneuclidean   ravenousness   southwestern   uncommonness
inordinately   northeastern   reactiveness   spaciousness   unctuousness
instructress   northwestern   readableness   specificness   underachieve
insufficient   numerousness   readjustment   speciousness   undercurrent
interconnect   obdurateness   reassessment   specktioneer   undergarment
intercurrent   obligingness   reassignment   spiritedness   unemployment
intermittent   obsoleteness   recklessness   spitefulness   ungainliness
internuclear   onesidedness   recommitment   splendidness   unkindliness
intervenient   onomatopoeia   recrudescent   sportfulness   unlawfulness
intransigent   onomatopoeic   redeployment   sportiveness   unlikeliness
intrenchment   oppositeness   reflectively   spotlessness   unloveliness
intromittent   oppressively   regressively   spuriousness   unsteadiness
intussuscept   ordinariness   reinvestment   stablishment   untimeliness
inveiglement   outdatedness   relativeness   staffsurgeon   untowardness
inveterately   overniceness   reliableness   stalwartness   unwieldiness
irregardless   oxyacetylene   renouncement   statuesquely   unwontedness
irrelatively   painlessness   repetitively   stealthiness   unworldiness
irresolutely   passionately   repressively   sterlingness   unworthiness
jurisprudent   patulousness   reproachless   stockingless   usuriousness
knightliness   peacefulness   reservedness   stockjobbery   uxoriousness
lachrymosely   peerlessness   resettlement   straightness   valuableness
landingfield   pejoratively   resignedness   stratosphere   vanquishment
languishment   pellucidness   resoluteness   strengthless   vaporousness
laudableness   perceptively   resolvedness   strikingness   variableness
legitimately   percussively   respectively   stubbornness   vegetatively
lifelessness   perfectively   responsively   studiousness   vengefulness
liquefacient   perilousness   restaurateur   stupefacient   venomousness
listlessness   permissively   restlessness   subcontinent   ventripotent
literariness   persuasively   reticulately   subjectively   verticalness
lonesomeness   perverseness   retiringness   submissively   vigorousness
lopsidedness   perviousness   retrenchment   subterranean   vindictively
lovelessness   pettifoggery   rightfulness   subversively   virtuousness
lovelornness   pickerelweed   rigorousness   successively   vitreousness
lukewarmness   pitiableness   rootlessness   succinctness   voidableness
luminousness   pitilessness   ruminatively   suggestively   volatileness
lusciousness   playingfield   ruthlessness   suitableness   wastefulness
magniloquent   pleasantness   salutariness   supereminent   watchfulness
maidenliness   pleasingness   sanguineness   supervenient   windingsheet
malapertness   pleasureless   sanguinolent   suspensively   womanishness
maltreatment   poikilotherm   scabrousness   swainishness   wondrousness
manifoldness   polyethylene   schizomycete   sweepingness   workableness
```

wrathfulness	quadriplegic	heliographic	tachygraphic	atmospherics
wretchedness	reassuringly	hieroglyphic	tetramorphic	attitudinise
wrongfulness	refreshingly	hierographer	tightmouthed	augmentation
youthfulness	resoundingly	homeomorphic	underclothes	augmentative
disregardful	satisfyingly	homoeopathic	virtuosoship	auscultation
foresightful	scatteringly	horsemanship	viscountship	Australasian
shortstaffed	shortchanger	hydrographer	watermanship	authenticity
transpacific	squarerigged	hydrographic	abbreviation	autoimmunity
understaffed	stagemanager	hymnographer	abolitionism	automaticity
unscientific	staggeringly	hypertrophic	abolitionist	automobilist
unsuccessful	stammeringly	iconographer	absorptivity	automorphism
unthoughtful	stationwagon	impoverished	acceleration	availability
wineglassful	stutteringly	laureateship	accelerative	avantgardism
aforethought	supercharger	lithographer	accentuation	avantgardist
afterthought	surprisingly	lithographic	accompanyist	bacchanalian
agglutinogen	swaggeringly	marksmanship	accordionist	backbreaking
appetisingly	terrifyingly	mealymouthed	accumulation	backslapping
appraisingly	thaumaturgic	micrographer	accumulative	beachcombing
archipelagic	thunderingly	mistressship	accusatorial	behaviourism
astoundingly	triphthongal	monostrophic	adaptability	behaviourist
balladmonger	twitteringly	musicianship	adjudication	bellylanding
bantamweight	unassumingly	mythographer	adjudicative	berzelianite
bathypelagic	unbecomingly	naturopathic	adulteration	bibliologist
beseechingly	unblinkingly	necrographer	advisability	bibliomaniac
bewitchingly	unblushingly	nightclothes	aerodynamics	bibliopegist
blisteringly	unthinkingly	oncorhynchus	aeroembolism	bibliopolist
blunderingly	unyieldingly	oneupmanship	aerosiderite	bicentennial
blusteringly	wallydraigle	orthographer	aesthetician	bilateralism
boogiewoogie	welterweight	orthographic	aestheticism	bilingualism
carpetbagger	whimperingly	outlandishly	aircondition	billsticking
carpetknight	whisperingly	outstretched	alimentation	bioecologist
cheeseburger	williewaught	overlordship	alimentative	biometrician
cheesemonger	accomplished	paedomorphic	alliteration	biophysicist
clatteringly	amateurishly	Palaeolithic	alliterative	bioscientist
comfortingly	amphibrachic	pantographic	allomorphism	birdsnesting
commandingly	anemographic	partisanship	alterability	birdwatching
consentingly	antistrophic	pennypincher	amalgamation	blackbirding
convincingly	attorneyship	petrographer	amalgamative	blastulation
costermonger	bachelorship	petrographic	amelioration	blatherskite
counterlight	bloodbrother	philadelphus	ameliorative	blockbusting
decreasingly	bodysnatcher	phonographer	amortisation	bloodletting
depressingly	bottlewasher	phonographic	anaesthetise	bluestocking
despairingly	brinkmanship	photographer	anaesthetist	bodybuilding
discerningly	calligrapher	photographic	anathematise	bodystocking
disgustingly	calligraphic	phytographer	anecdotalist	booklearning
dissentingly	cardinalship	pictographic	annihilation	boulevardier
disturbingly	cartographer	plainclothed	annihilative	brainwashing
enchantingly	cartographic	plainclothes	annunciation	brassrubbing
entreatingly	catastrophic	pornographer	antediluvian	breathtaking
flatteringly	chairmanship	pornographic	anteprandial	brilliantine
flickeringly	chalcolithic	prenticeship	anticipation	buccaneering
forbiddingly	championship	psychopathic	anticipative	buccaneerish
forebodingly	chaplainship	quaestorship	antigenicity	bullfighting
fullyfledged	chorographic	radiographer	antimalarial	businesslike
galactogogue	closemouthed	radiographic	antineutrino	Byelorussian
glitteringly	coquettishly	receivership	antiSemitism	cabbagewhite
gratifyingly	cosmographer	relationship	aperiodicity	cachinnation
grovellingly	cosmographic	reprographic	apiculturist	calisthenics
haemorrhagic	craftbrother	residentship	apostolicism	calumniation
hallucinogen	crossbencher	sabretoothed	apostolicity	canalisation
herpetologic	dictatorship	salesmanship	apostrophise	cancellation
hesitatingly	directorship	scenographic	apparatchiki	canonisation
huggermugger	discipleship	semidetached	apparatchiks	Cantabrigian
increasingly	discographer	semifinished	apperception	cantharidian
interchanger	ethnographer	sergeantship	apperceptive	cantillation
intriguingly	ethnographic	serjeantship	appreciation	capitulation
irritatingly	executorship	servitorship	appreciative	carburetting
klipspringer	extinguisher	shortpitched	apprehension	cardcarrying
mastersinger	fostermother	smallclothes	apprehensive	cardiologist
merrythought	frontbencher	stenographer	arborisation	caricaturist
middleweight	gamesmanship	stenographic	Aristotelian	Carlovingian
moneychanger	governorship	stichomythia	articulation	Cartesianism
mothertongue	graveclothes	stichomythic	asphyxiation	caterwauling
mystifyingly	guardianship	strophanthin	assibilation	catilinarian
nauseatingly	hagiographer	stylographic	assimilation	chalcopyrite
perplexingly	hagiographic	surveyorship	assimilative	characterise
phrasemonger	heathenishly	survivorship	astronautics	charlatanism
prevailingly	hectographic	taberdarship	astrophysics	cheeseparing
quadriplegia	heliographer	tachygrapher	asynchronism	childbearing

chlorination	construction	detoxication	epicureanism	futurologist
Christianise	constructive	deviationism	episcopalian	galligaskins
Christianity	consultation	deviationist	epithalamion	gasification
chromaticism	consultative	dialectician	epithalamium	gastronomist
chromaticity	consummation	diamagnetism	equalisation	genuflection
chronologise	consummative	diamonddrill	equalitarian	geomagnetism
chronologist	contagionist	diastrophism	equitability	geometrician
churchianity	containerise	dichromatism	equivocation	geophysicist
circumcision	contemporise	differentiae	escapologist	geotectonics
circumfusion	contestation	differential	essentiality	geriatrician
circumscribe	continuation	dilapidation	etherisation	Germanophile
civilisation	continuative	dilatability	eunuchoidism	glaciologist
clarinettist	contrariwise	dilettantish	evisceration	gladiatorial
classicalism	contribution	dilettantism	evolutionism	glassblowing
classicalist	contributive	diphthongise	evolutionist	glockenspiel
classicality	conversation	disaccharide	exacerbation	glossologist
claudication	conveyancing	disaffection	exaggeration	grallatorial
cliffhanging	conviviality	disannulling	exaggerative	grammaticise
clinkerbuilt	coordination	disclamation	exasperation	gramnegative
coacervation	coordinative	discommodity	excitability	grampositive
coalitionist	copolymerise	disconnexion	exclusionism	granodiorite
cockfighting	corporeality	discouraging	exclusionist	graphologist
codification	counterpoint	disestablish	excogitation	gravelelling
cohabitation	counterpoise	disfranchise	excogitative	grossularite
coleopterist	courtmartial	disharmonise	excruciating	guaranteeing
collectivise	craniologist	disincentive	excruciation	gymnosophist
collectivism	crashlanding	disinfection	excursionist	habilitation
collectivist	crenellation	disinflation	exenteration	habitability
collectivity	crossbedding	dispensation	exercitation	habitforming
collegialism	crossexamine	disquisition	exhilaration	haemophiliac
collegiality	crossheading	dissertation	exhilarative	hairdressing
collinearity	crosssection	dissocialise	expansionism	halogenation
colonisation	cryptologist	dissociation	expansionist	handicapping
coloquintida	cuprammonium	dissociative	expatriation	handkerchief
columniation	cytogenetics	distillation	expediential	hardstanding
commendation	deactivation	distribution	experiential	harquebusier
commensalism	debilitation	distributive	explantation	heartburning
commensalist	decapitation	divarication	exploitation	heartrending
commentation	deceleration	diversionist	exploitative	heartwarming
commissarial	decentralise	divisibility	expressivity	hedgehopping
commissariat	decongestion	doubleacting	exprobration	heliotropism
compellation	decongestive	dramaturgist	extracranial	hellgrammite
compensation	deescalation	duraluminium	extraspecial	hemimorphism
compensative	deflagration	earsplitting	extrauterine	hemimorphite
complication	deflationist	earthshaking	extraversion	hemiparasite
compulsivity	defraudation	eccentricity	extroversion	heortologist
compulsorily	degeneration	echolocation	exulceration	hereditarily
compurgation	degenerative	echosounding	facilitation	heritability
conchologist	deionisation	econometrics	factionalism	hermeneutics
conciliation	delamination	ectoparasite	faithhealing	highfaluting
conciliative	deliberation	editorialise	fantasticism	highsounding
condemnation	deliberative	editorialist	farmsteading	highstepping
condensation	delimitation	educationist	faultfinding	homeopathist
conductivity	demilitarise	edulcoration	felicitation	homologation
conferential	demimondaine	effectuality	feminisation	homomorphism
confidential	demineralise	effectuation	fenestration	homothallism
confirmation	demodulation	Egyptologist	fermentation	hoodmanblind
confirmative	denaturalise	elementalism	fermentative	horsetrading
confiscation	denaturation	elementarily	fibrillation	housekeeping
conformation	denomination	elocutionist	fictionalise	housewarming
Confucianism	denominative	elucubration	filtrability	humanisation
congeniality	denuclearise	emancipation	finalisation	humanitarian
conglobation	denunciation	emargination	firefighting	humification
congregation	denunciative	emasculation	flagellation	hydrostatics
connubiality	deontologist	embryologist	flammability	hydrotropism
conscription	depoliticise	emotionalise	flocculation	hyperacidity
consecration	depopulation	emotionalism	fluidisation	hypertension
conservation	depreciation	emotionalist	fluoridation	hypertensive
conservatism	deputisation	emotionality	fluorination	hypochlorite
conservative	deracination	encrustation	focalisation	hypogastrium
consignation	derogatorily	endoparasite	frangibility	hypophrygian
consistorial	desalination	enginetuning	freestanding	hyposulphite
consociation	desideration	enterprising	freeswimming	idealisation
conspiration	desiderative	entertaining	freethinking	illegibility
constipation	desirability	entomologise	freewheeling	illogicality
constitution	despoliation	entomologist	frenchpolish	illumination
constitutive	desquamation	enzymologist	fricasseeing	illuminative
constriction	desquamative	ephemerality	fuliginosity	illustration
constrictive	desulphurise		futilitarian	

illustrative	introduction	microcopying	octogenarian	plausibility
immoderation	introjection	microphysics	odontologist	pleiotropism
immovability	intromission	microscopist	opinionative	pleomorphism
immunisation	intromitting	mineralogist	opposability	pneumaticity
immunologist	introversion	minimisation	optimisation	polarisation
immutability	introversive	ministration	orbicularity	polyglottism
impartiality	introvertive	ministrative	organisation	polymorphism
imperatorial	intrusionist	miscellanist	orienteering	polytonality
imperceptive	intuitionism	misdirection	orthodontics	porcelainise
imperfection	intuitionist	miseducation	orthodontist	postdiluvian
imperfective	invagination	misquotation	orthopaedics	posteriority
implantation	invalidation	mithridatise	orthopaedist	postmeridian
impregnation	invigilation	mithridatism	orthopterist	postposition
imputability	invigoration	mobilisation	orthotropism	postpositive
inactivation	invisibility	modification	ossification	postprandial
inartificial	irascibility	molecularity	outrivalling	potentiality
inaudibility	irreflective	monetisation	outstripping	practicality
inauguration	irregularity	monographist	overactivity	praseodymium
incapability	irresolution	moralisation	overcropping	precedential
incatenation	irrespective	morphologist	overexertion	preceptorial
incendiarism	irresponsive	mosstrooping	overpowering	prechristian
incineration	irritability	motorcyclist	overreaction	precisianism
inconcinnity	Ishmaelitish	motorisation	oversimplify	precisionist
inconclusive	isolationism	mountainside	overstepping	precognition
inconformity	isolationist	mourningring	pacification	precognitive
incorporeity	jurisdiction	multiformity	paedobaptism	precondition
incorruption	Keynesianism	multipartite	palatability	predetermine
incrustation	kinnikinnick	multiplicity	paletteknife	predigestion
incurability	kleptomaniac	multistoried	Palladianism	predilection
indelibility	laboursaving	multiversity	palynologist	preestablish
indiscipline	labyrinthian	municipalise	panhellenism	prefectorial
indiscretion	labyrinthine	municipality	panification	preferential
inelasticity	lachrymation	musicologist	papyrologist	preformation
inexpressive	laisserfaire	myrmecophily	paragraphist	preformative
inflammation	laissezfaire	namedropping	parallelling	prehensility
inflationism	lakedwelling	navigability	paralysation	prehistorian
inflationist	lanternslide	nebulisation	paramorphism	prelapsarian
infusibility	laterisation	necrophiliac	parasiticide	prerequisite
ingratiating	latinisation	necrophilism	parenthesise	presbyterial
inhabitation	leapfrogging	negrophilism	parkinsonism	Presbyterian
inoccupation	legalisation	negrophilist	parochialise	prescription
inosculation	legitimation	neighbouring	parochialism	prescriptive
insemination	legitimatise	neoDarwinian	parochiality	preselection
insolubilise	levorotation	neoDarwinism	partitionist	preselective
insolubility	lexicologist	neoDarwinist	peasepudding	presentation
inspectorial	liquefaction	Neohellenism	penalisation	presentative
inspissation	lithotritist	neonomianism	perceptivity	preservation
installation	Liverpudlian	Neoplatonism	peremptorily	preservative
instauration	localisation	Neoplatonist	perfervidity	presidential
instillation	longstanding	nephrologist	perfoliation	preventative
insufflation	malacologist	nerveracking	performative	pricecutting
insurrection	malformation	Nestorianism	periodontics	primigravida
intellection	malleability	nicotinamide	periodontist	principality
intellective	malnutrition	nidification	permeability	printability
inteneration	malversation	niminypiminy	permittivity	privateering
interbedding	Manicheanism	noctambulism	pernoctation	prizewinning
interception	manipulation	noctambulist	peroxidation	proboscidian
intercession	manipulative	nomenclative	perpetration	proclamation
intercutting	Marcionitism	nonagenarian	perpetuation	productivity
interdiction	marlinespike	noncomplying	perspicacity	professorial
interdictive	Marseillaise	noneffective	perspiration	profiteering
interglacial	marshharrier	nonessential	perturbation	prolongation
interjection	maximisation	nonflowering	perturbative	promulgation
intermission	mediaevalism	nonobjective	pestilential	proofreading
intermitting	mediaevalist	Northumbrian	petrifaction	propagandise
internuncial	megalomaniac	notification	pettifogging	propagandism
interpretive	melancholiac	novelisation	philistinism	propagandist
interruption	meltingpoint	numerologist	phillumenist	propitiation
interruptive	menstruation	nutritionist	philosophise	proscription
intersection	mercantilism	nyctitropism	phlebotomise	proscriptive
interservice	mercantilist	nymphomaniac	phlebotomist	prosectorial
interstitial	mercurialise	obligatorily	photofission	prostitution
intervention	mercurialism	obliteration	photosetting	protactinium
intimidation	metachronism	obliterative	phototropism	protestation
intoxication	metallurgist	obnubilation	phrenologist	prothalamion
intracardiac	metalworking	obscurantism	physiologist	prothalamium
intracranial	metamorphism	obscurantist	pigmentation	providential
intransitive	metapsychics	obstetrician	placesetting	psephologist
intrauterine	metasomatism	oceanologist	plaindealing	pseudonymity

pseudopodium	salamandrine	sternutative	transitorily	voluptuosity
psychiatrist	salvationism	stillhunting	transmission	vomiturition
psychoactive	salvationist	stockbroking	transmissive	wainscotting
psychologise	Samaritanism	stockjobbing	transmitting	waistcoating
psychologism	sandyachting	stockraising	transmogrify	wallpainting
psychologist	sanguinarily	stoneboiling	transpontine	whimsicality
purification	satisfaction	stonecutting	transudation	whippoorwill
purposebuilt	scabbardfish	Stradivarius	transvestism	whitewashing
putrefaction	Scandinavian	stridulation	transvestite	wollastonite
putrefactive	scareheading	strobilation	trephination	youngberries
pyromorphite	scorpionfish	strontianite	trichologist	zygomorphism
pyrotechnics	scoundrelism	strychninism	trichotomise	bonnetmonkey
pyrotechnist	scrupulosity	stupefaction	trifurcation	cabinetmaker
Quadragesima	scutellation	stupefactive	trinomialism	dinnerjacket
quadriennium	secessionism	subalternity	tripartition	doubledecked
quadrinomial	secessionist	subarrhation	triplication	doubledecker
quantisation	seclusionist	subcelestial	troglodytism	doublelocked
quantitative	secondstring	subeditorial	turbellarian	halterbroken
quinquennial	sectarianise	suberisation	typefounding	headshrinker
quinquennium	sectarianism	subjectivise	typification	holidaymaker
quizzicality	sectionalism	subjectivism	ubiquitarian	horsebreaker
racemisation	segmentation	subjectivist	unappetising	housebreaker
racketeering	seismologist	subjectivity	unattractive	hucklebacked
radionuclide	selenologist	sublapsarian	unclassified	ledgertackle
radiophonics	selfactivity	subnormality	uncommercial	lumberjacket
ramification	selfcatering	subscription	unconformity	maidenstakes
ratification	selfdelusion	subsidiarily	unconstraint	monkeyjacket
reactivation	selfdevotion	substitution	unconvincing	patternmaker
reallocation	selfdoubting	substitutive	underbidding	pumpernickel
receptionist	selfeffacing	substruction	undercoating	saddlebacked
recollection	selfelective	sulphonamide	undercutting	scrimshanker
recollective	selfidentity	sulphonation	underletting	singledecker
reconversion	selfignition	sulphuration	undermanning	skrimshanker
recuperation	selflimiting	supersession	underpinning	spidermonkey
recuperative	selfpleasing	superstition	underrunning	straitjacket
redecoration	selffrighting	supervention	undersetting	streetwalker
Redemptorist	selfstarting	supplication	unflattering	troublemaker
reducibility	semifinalist	susceptivity	unhesitating	turtlenecked
reductionism	semiofficial	sustentation	unionisation	walkietalkie
reductionist	semiparasite	sustentative	unisexuality	winklepicker
reflectivity	sempiternity	swaggerstick	unitarianism	wonderworker
refractivity	separability	swizzlestick	universalise	aboriginally
refractorily	Septuagesima	sycophantish	universalism	academically
regeneration	sergeantfish	syndactylism	universalist	accidentally
regenerative	sexagenarian	teachability	universality	acoustically
registration	shadowboxing	technicality	unpopularity	acronychally
rejuvenation	shamateurism	technologist	unpretending	additionally
remilitarise	shipbuilding	telegraphist	unresponsive	adjectivally
removability	sideslipping	temptability	urbanisation	amitotically
remuneration	sidestepping	teratologist	urbanologist	anagogically
remunerative	sightreading	terebinthine	valorisation	analogically
renunciation	simultaneity	tessellation	vantagepoint	analytically
renunciative	singleacting	tetrahedrite	vaporisation	anatomically
reoccupation	sinistrality	thanksgiving	vasodilation	antigropelos
repatriation	slaveholding	theatregoing	vaticination	antiphonally
repercussion	sleepingpill	theoretician	vauntcourier	apolitically
repercussive	sleepwalking	therapeutics	venerability	appendicular
repossession	smallholding	therapeutist	veridicality	archetypally
reprehension	sociometrist	thermolabile	verification	aromatically
reprehensive	solarisation	tolerability	vertebration	artificially
reproduction	solicitation	topsyturvily	vesiculation	artistically
reproductive	solifluction	torrefaction	veterinarian	athletically
responsorial	somnambulism	Torricellian	vibraphonist	backpedalled
resupination	somnambulist	totalisation	Victorianism	barbarically
resurrection	somniloquism	totalitarian	vilification	beatifically
reticulation	somniloquist	toxicologist	vinification	beneficially
retractation	soundingline	traceability	visitatorial	bespectacled
retractility	speedboating	tractability	vitalisation	bibliophilic
retrocession	speleologist	traditionist	vitiligation	biologically
retrocessive	spermogonium	traducianism	vitrifaction	bobbydazzler
retroflexion	sphragistics	traducianist	vituperation	buttermuslin
retropulsion	spiritualise	trampolinist	vituperative	capercaillie
retroversion	spiritualism	tranquillise	vivification	catholically
ricochetting	spiritualist	tranquillity	vocabularian	centesimally
romanisation	spirituality	transduction	vocalisation	ceremonially
ruralisation	Stakhanovism	transferring	vociferation	chancemedley
saccharinity	Stakhanovite	transformism	voluminosity	cherubically
safecracking	statistician	transformist	voluntaryism	cirrocumulus
salamandrian	sternutation	transitivity	voluntaryist	collaterally

colloquially	industrially	sarsaparilla	Deuteronomic	countertenor
collywobbles	infundibular	schoolfellow	Englishwoman	countrydance
commercially	interlobular	scripturally	exophthalmic	crackbrained
commonwealth	intermeddler	sculpturally	exophthalmos	crossgrained
conceptually	interstellar	sedgewarbler	exophthalmus	curlingtongs
congenitally	intervocalic	semantically	footplateman	curmudgeonly
connaturally	irrationally	semiannually	FrancoGerman	decalescence
consensually	isochronally	semicircular	frontiersman	delitescence
contextually	isothermally	sententially	hippopotamus	derivational
conventicler	jesuitically	septennially	hydrodynamic	detumescence
cosmetically	jetpropelled	sepulchrally	hydrothermal	diathermancy
cynocephalus	laissezaller	sequentially	hyperthermia	digressional
decontrolled	licketysplit	seraphically	hypothalamic	disallowance
delightfully	liturgically	shillyshally	hypothalamus	discretional
demoniacally	logistically	simoniacally	katzenjammer	disobedience
despitefully	mademoiselle	sinusoidally	longshoreman	disseverance
despotically	magnetically	Socratically	LowChurchman	distortional
diabolically	magnifically	softpedalled	microseismic	divertimenti
diatonically	majestically	sparkingplug	newspaperman	divertimento
didactically	meaningfully	specifically	nonconformer	dodecaphonic
dietetically	mechanically	spheroidally	phanerogamic	elasmobranch
disdainfully	meridionally	sporadically	photochromic	electrotonic
disgustfully	mesocephalic	sprightfully	physiognomic	electrotonus
diverticular	metallically	starspangled	planetesimal	equestrienne
diverticulum	meteorically	sternwheeler	protoplasmic	equidistance
dogmatically	methodically	structurally	schizothymia	equipollence
domestically	millesimally	subapostolic	schizothymic	equipollency
doubledealer	monastically	subsonically	selfcontempt	escutcheoned
dramatically	monitorially	successfully	servicewoman	exhibitioner
dynastically	monometallic	supernaculum	sledgehammer	expressional
eclectically	monopodially	swashbuckler	snakecharmer	extravagance
ecologically	monumentally	syllabically	stereoisomer	extravagancy
economically	narcotically	symbolically	unaccustomed	extravaganza
ecstatically	neglectfully	syndetically	vicechairman	fluorescence
electrically	neurotically	synoptically	warehouseman	foundationer
elliptically	noradrenalin	systemically	yellowhammer	frankincense
emphatically	occasionally	tabernacular	absorptional	freightliner
enclitically	occidentally	tangentially	acaulescence	geanticlinal
endermically	operatically	tectonically	acquaintance	geosynclinal
entrammelled	ornamentally	terrifically	acquiescence	glaucescence
epidemically	paranormally	tetragonally	alkalescence	happenstance
episodically	pathetically	Teutonically	amphictyonic	heartstrings
equationally	pedantically	theatrically	amphisbaenic	housetrained
esoterically	perceptually	theistically	anticyclonic	hypersthenia
euphonically	periodically	thematically	apparitional	hypersthenic
evidentially	peripherally	thermophilic	appositional	hysteromania
exegetically	phenomenally	thickskulled	appurtenance	impermanence
exoterically	phonemically	thoughtfully	arborescence	impermanency
forensically	phonetically	threewheeler	archdeaconry	impertinence
fractionally	platonically	torrentially	autochthones	impertinency
frenetically	pontifically	tyrannically	balletomania	improvidence
functionally	pralltriller	uncontrolled	belligerence	inadvertence
galvanically	precancelled	uncritically	belligerency	inadvertency
geologically	primordially	underdevelop	bloodstained	incalescence
gigantically	prolifically	uneventfully	butterflynut	incognisance
goosepimples	pronominally	unfaithfully	callisthenic	incompetence
haematoxylon	prosodically	ungracefully	calorescence	incompetency
harmonically	proverbially	ungratefully	carcinogenic	incompliance
hebdomadally	provincially	unilaterally	carragheenin	inconsonance
hemerocallis	prudentially	unmercifully	chitterlings	incontinence
heraldically	puerperally	unofficially	circumstance	incontinency
hermetically	purposefully	unparalleled	clairvoyance	indehiscence
heterocyclic	quadrangular	unprincipled	closegrained	independence
heterophylly	quixotically	untruthfully	commissioner	independency
hibernaculum	rabbinically	volcanically	complaisance	indifference
historically	receptaculum	volitionally	complexional	indifferency
homosexually	reciprocally	worshipfully	complexioned	IndoGermanic
horizontally	regimentally	aircraftsman	conceptional	inefficiency
horrifically	relationally	alexipharmic	concomitance	inexpedience
hygienically	remorsefully	artilleryman	concrescence	inexpediency
hypnotically	respectfully	backwoodsman	concubitancy	inexperience
hysterically	revengefully	bellbottomed	confectioner	inflectional
ichthyocolla	revictualled	brainstormer	confessional	inobservance
ideationally	rhetorically	breastsummer	connectional	intelligence
immaterially	rhythmically	cleistogamic	consentience	intemperance
immemorially	romantically	committeeman	constituency	interference
impersonally	sacerdotally	councilwoman	convectional	interoceanic
incidentally	sadistically	countrywoman	conventional	intumescence
individually	sardonically	cousingerman	correctional	involutional

juvenescence selfviolence compunctious heterozygous passepartout
longdistance shoulderknot compurgatory homomorphous peccadilloes
longitudinal significance conchiferous hydatidiform percutaneous
luminescence significancy conciliatory hydrophilous perspiratory
magnificence silverglance condemnatory hydroquinone pertinacious
mispronounce snapfastener confirmatory hygrophilous pharmacology
mnemotechnic stereophonic confiscatory hypognathous philanthrope
moneyspinner stonemasonry conidiophore hysterectomy philanthropy
monkeywrench straightener conidiospore idiothermous photogeology
motivational strengthener consecratory impetiginous photophilous
multivalence subservience conservatory inauguratory phytophagous
navigational subserviency consummatory inauspicious pilotballoon
neurasthenia successional contemptuous incommodious plecopterous
neurasthenic superhumanly conterminous incontiguous plumbaginous
neuroscience supersedence contributory infelicitous plumbiferous
newfashioned surroundings contumacious inflammatory plummerblock
noctilucence surveillance contumelious inharmonious pneumatology
nonexistence teensyweensy cotyledonous innutritious polychaetous
nonresidence televisional counterproof insalubrious polychromous
obmutescence thickskinned crossbuttock intercessory polymorphous
obsolescence transference crosspurpose interdictory polypetalous
occupational transhumance cryptogamous interjectory polysepalous
offscourings transiliency cuckingstool interspinous porcelainous
oldfashioned transitional curlingirons intimidatory porcellanous
omnipresence translucence deambulatory introductory preconscious
opisthotonos translucency denunciatory kaleidoscope preposterous
oppositional transoceanic depreciatory kilowatthour presumptuous
ornithomancy transparency desquamatory kremlinology proclamatory
outpensioner undertenancy dessertspoon lachrymatory progesterone
pearlescence undetermined dialectology laryngoscope propitiatory
perispomenon unimportance diatomaceous laryngoscopy protistology
peristeronic unrestrained discourteous laticiferous protohistory
perseverance Valenciennes disingenuous latitudinous protozoology
philharmonic viridescence dispensatory leathercloth pseudonymous
philhellenic viscerotonic disputatious levorotatory purificatory
phonasthenia visitational distillatory liturgiology pyroligneous
plenipotence Wellingtonia dressinggown luminiferous quadrumanous
practitioner xiphisternum duckingstool macropterous radiobiology
precessional achlamydeous ecclesiology manipulatory radioisotope
precipitance adjudicatory electronvolt masterstroke rambunctious
precipitancy adscititious electroscope mastigophora remuneratory
predominance advantageous electroshock melanochroic renunciatory
predominancy adventitious emasculatory meretricious resiniferous
preexistence altitudinous epidemiology metallophone rheumatology
preoccupancy ambidextrous epistemology metamorphose rhizocarpous
processional amentiferous equivocatory microbiology rhizophagous
professional amphitropous erythematous misbehaviour rhynchophora
projectional anemophilous exaggeratory misdemeanour rollingstock
prolegomenon angiocarpous exsanguinous modificatory rontgenology
proportional anthropology extrasensory monadelphous sacrilegious
proportioned anticipatory feldspathoid monomorphous salamandroid
protuberance appendectomy ferrugineous monopetalous salutiferous
pursestrings appreciatory flabelliform monostichous saprophagous
quadraphonic argillaceous flagellatory mucilaginous sarcophagous
quarterfinal articulatory fructiferous multifarious sarrusophone
quattrocento assimilatory fructivorous multiflorous satisfactory
quintessence asynchronous furfuraceous multiloquous schizogonous
reappearance atheromatous gallinaceous multipurpose schorlaceous
recalescence auscultatory galvanoscope nailscissors selfluminous
recognisance bachelorhood gamopetalous necrophagous seminiferous
reconveyance bacteriology gamophyllous necrophilous semiprecious
recreational basidiospore gamosepalous neuroanatomy serpentiform
redemptioner biocoenology gastropodous neurobiology shatterproof
reflectional breaststroke Germanophobe neuropterous shouldernote
refreshments bronchoscope glaucomatous noctambulous silicicolous
rejectamenta burglarproof gobbledegook northernmost siliciferous
reminiscence cachinnatory gobbledygook obstreperous simultaneous
remonstrance calumniatory graminaceous ophiophagous siphonophore
repetitional calycoideous hebetudinous orchidaceous skippingrope
resipiscence campodeiform heliolatrous ornithoscopy slaughterous
resplendence cantankerous hemispheroid orthopteroid snaggletooth
resplendency carbonaceous hereinbefore orthopterous soporiferous
retrocedence cementitious heteroecious orthotropous southernmost
revelational chondriosome heterogamous oscilloscope southernwood
reviviscence chromatology heterogenous ostentatious spectroscope
risorgimento coleopterous heterologous overcautious spectroscopy
salutational combinations heteromerous pacificatory spermatozoid
selfevidence commendatory heteronomous parasitology spermatozoon
selfreliance compensatory heterozygote parsimonious spinsterhood

stalactiform	Sinanthropus	pedicellaria	biosynthesis	lugubriously
standingroom	stereography	philodendron	bloodthirsty	marvellously
stanniferous	stereoscopic	photospheric	boisterously	mendaciously
steatopygous	stethoscopic	pinfeathered	bombdisposal	meticulously
stelliferous	stormtrooper	planispheric	bowcompasses	miraculously
stereochromy	stratigraphy	plesiosaurus	breathalyser	monotonously
sternutatory	stroboscopic	pluriliteral	breathlessly	mordaciously
stranglehold	theanthropic	pluviometric	calamitously	mysteriously
subconscious	thermocouple	pneumothorax	calcareously	mythologiser
subcutaneous	thermography	polarimetric	calumniously	nephanalysis
subthreshold	thermoscopic	polyhistoric	capriciously	nutritiously
succedaneous	thermotropic	postdoctoral	cataphoresis	obsequiously
sudoriferous	tradespeople	procathedral	censoriously	omnivorously
supercilious	transshipped	psychometric	chivalrously	orthogenesis
supersensory	triggerhappy	publicspirit	chromatopsia	osteogenesis
supplicatory	wicketkeeper	pyroelectric	circuitously	osteoporosis
supposititious	zoogeography	rhododendron	clangorously	outrageously
swimmingpool	Alhambresque	rhombohedral	coetaneously	overemphasis
syndactylous	cinematheque	rhombohedron	colourlessly	paedogenesis
technicolour	acetabularia	rontgenogram	commodiously	palingenesia
teratomatous	agentgeneral	rosecoloured	contagiously	palingenesis
testosterone	agricultural	seismometric	contiguously	paraesthesia
testudineous	alphanumeric	selfcoloured	continuously	pathogenesis
thousandfold	aquicultural	selfmurderer	courageously	perfidiously
throughstone	brambleberry	septilateral	decompressor	perjuriously
thundercloud	brontosaurus	sericultural	delicatessen	perniciously
thunderstone	calorimetric	serviceberry	diaphanously	phagocytosis
thunderstorm	caravansarai	servocontrol	disastrously	phosphoresce
toastingfork	caravanserai	sheepshearer	dispossessor	photokinesis
trachomatous	cashandcarry	shootingiron	effortlessly	phylogenesis
transudatory	charterparty	snarlingiron	electrolysis	phytogenesis
trichotomous	checkerberry	standardbred	euphoniously	Plattdeutsch
tridactylous	chromatogram	stepchildren	extraneously	pointilliste
unchivalrous	chronometric	stereometric	factitiously	portentously
unlikelihood	clotheshorse	stilboestrol	fallaciously	posthumously
unscrupulous	colorimetric	straightbred	fastidiously	precariously
vainglorious	counterforce	stringcourse	felicitously	precociously
vasodilatory	countermarch	supernatural	fibrinolysin	prodigiously
verificatory	cumulocirrus	thermometric	fictitiously	propitiously
vituperatory	curvirostral	thimbleberry	fieldglasses	proselytiser
weatherproof	dissimilarly	thitherwards	flagitiously	prosperously
xanthochroia	dissymmetric	thoroughbred	fortuitously	pseudocyesis
zygomorphous	dodecahedral	timehonoured	furunculosis	pugnaciously
bibliography	dodecahedron	triangularly	gluttonously	quaquaversal
biogeography	dorsiventral	trochanteric	glycogenesis	rabblerouser
cardiography	dovecoloured	tropospheric	gratuitously	rebelliously
cheirography	draughthorse	twentyfourmo	gregariously	regardlessly
choreography	dynamometric	unconsidered	groundlessly	relentlessly
chronography	enantiomorph	underinsured	haematolysis	resistlessly
closecropped	ethnocentric	unencumbered	haemopoiesis	ridiculously
cryptography	filibusterer	unfamiliarly	hallucinosis	robustiously
diageotropic	goodhumoured	unscriptural	harmoniously	salpiglossis
drawingpaper	goodtempered	unstructured	histogenesis	salubriously
eavesdropped	grotesquerie	varicoloured	homoeostasis	sarcomatosis
eavesdropper	groundcherry	vernacularly	homonymously	scandalously
electrotyper	halftimbered	vicargeneral	horrendously	scrupulously
glossography	hardfavoured	wellfavoured	hydromedusae	scurrilously
glyphography	hardfeatured	whigmaleerie	hydromedusan	selfanalysis
glyptography	heliocentric	whitelivered	hypnogenesis	selfcomposed
gonadotropic	highcoloured	whitherwards	idolatrously	selfhypnosis
gonadotropin	hydrochloric	whortleberry	imperviously	sequaciously
horsewhipped	hydrofluoric	winterbourne	incautiously	sinistrorsal
humptydumpty	hymenopteran	woolgatherer	incestuously	slanderously
intercropped	hypochondria	abstemiously	indecorously	solicitously
lexicography	interfemoral	adulterously	indigenously	speechlessly
lycanthropic	isodiametric	aeroneurosis	infectiously	spiegeleisen
misanthropic	landingstrip	agamogenesis	ingloriously	spiritlessly
oceanography	landlubberly	amphibiously	iniquitously	spokesperson
organography	lepidopteran	anaerobiosis	karyokinesis	sporogenesis
palaeography	lithospheric	anamorphosis	kinaesthesia	stellenbosch
physiography	majorgeneral	antimacassar	kinaesthesis	stertorously
polarography	manufacturer	archdiocesan	kirschwasser	stonedresser
psychography	misinterpret	auspiciously	languorously	strongylosis
psychotropic	mitochondria	autonomously	lasciviously	stupendously
scintigraphy	multicentral	avariciously	leucocytosis	suspiciously
seismography	multilateral	avitaminoses	leukocytosis	synaesthesia
seismoscopic	nychthemeral	avitaminosis	libidinously	synarthrosis
selenography	nychthemeron	bilharziasis	licentiously	synchroniser
sharecropper	particularly	bilharziosis	loquaciously	synonymously

systematiser	concordantly	histogenetic	oneirocritic	selfbegotten
telaesthesia	concurrently	hydrokinetic	orchestrator	selfdirected
thriftlessly	confabulator	hyperplastic	organoleptic	selfeducated
thunderously	consequently	hyperpyretic	orthogenetic	semidiameter
traitorously	consistently	hypnogenetic	osteoplastic	semidomestic
transgressor	consolidator	hypocoristic	paedogenetic	sensitometer
tremendously	contemplator	hypothecator	palingenetic	sensualistic
tuberculosis	contingently	ichthyolatry	panchromatic	Septuagintal
tumultuously	contradictor	iconoclastic	pancreatitis	sequestrator
ubiquitously	contrapuntal	impedimental	paradigmatic	sharpshooter
umbrageously	conveniently	impenitently	paramagnetic	sharpsighted
unauthorised	corroborator	impersonator	paraphrastic	shirtwaister
ungraciously	cosmopolitan	impropriator	paronomastic	shortsighted
unrecognised	cosmopolitic	improvisator	participator	singleseater
uproariously	courtplaster	inclinometer	pathogenetic	specialistic
victoriously	crosscountry	incoherently	pedunculated	spectrometer
villainously	declinometer	inconstantly	pennywhistle	spectrometry
viviparously	delinquently	incorporated	perambulator	spermaphytic
vociferously	demonstrator	incorporator	peregrinator	stepdaughter
voluminously	densitometer	indiscreetly	pericarditis	stonyhearted
voluptuously	denticulated	indistinctly	periphrastic	stouthearted
welldisposed	departmental	infrequently	peristomatic	subcommittee
zygapophysis	despondently	instrumental	persistently	subsaturated
absolutistic	diagrammatic	integumental	phagocytotic	subsequently
accommodator	diphtheritic	interdigital	pharmaceutic	sufficiently
agamogenetic	disconnected	interlocutor	photokinetic	sulphuretted
ambivalently	discontented	interoceptor	phycomycetes	superstratum
amphitheatre	discordantly	interpolator	phyllotactic	supplemental
anagrammatic	disenchanter	interrelated	phylogenetic	supplementer
analphabetic	disseminator	interrogator	phytogenetic	supplicantly
anaphylactic	dissimulator	interwreathe	pitterpatter	supraorbital
anastigmatic	domesticator	intolerantly	plectognathi	surrealistic
antagonistic	ecclesiastic	investigator	polyneuritic	synaesthetic
antecedently	electrolytic	irrelevantly	polyneuritis	syncretistic
anthelmintic	electrometer	irreverently	polyphyletic	taxcollector
antimagnetic	encephalitic	isochromatic	polytheistic	technocratic
antipathetic	encephalitis	journalistic	pontificator	teetertotter
antirachitic	endocarditis	kinaesthetic	poorspirited	telaesthetic
apochromatic	endometritis	kindergarten	positivistic	thereinafter
apothegmatic	endoskeletal	laciniiated	pragmatistic	thermostatic
appendicitis	enthusiastic	largehearted	praiseworthy	thermotactic
appropriator	epigrammatic	liberalistic	precipitator	threequarter
aristocratic	equilibrator	lighthearted	preeminently	tittletattle
assassinator	equivalently	machicolated	premeditated	toggleswitch
astringently	espagnolette	magnetometer	premeditator	tradescantia
autodidactic	euhemeristic	malcontented	pretermitted	trainspotter
bacteriostat	evanescently	malevolently	prevaricator	transplanter
battlemented	evangelistic	manslaughter	primogenital	trichromatic
belletristic	exorbitantly	masterswitch	primogeniter	trigonometry
beneficently	experimental	melodramatic	prizefighter	triumphantly
benevolently	experimenter	meristematic	proficiently	tuberculated
biochemistry	extensometer	metagalactic	programmatic	turriculated
biosynthetic	exterminator	metaphrastic	propaedeutic	unapologetic
brachydactyl	extralimital	metropolitan	prophylactic	uncalculated
broncobuster	extramarital	microcrystal	protoplastic	uncelebrated
bureaucratic	fainthearted	militaristic	proudhearted	undemocratic
butterscotch	falcongentil	milliammeter	psychrometer	underwritten
capitalistic	falcongentle	minedetector	psychrometry	undiplomatic
catachrestic	firstnighter	minicomputer	ratiocinator	unfrequented
cattlelifter	flamboyantly	monodramatic	reciprocator	uninterested
chauvinistic	floodlighted	monophyletic	refrigerator	unpleasantly
cheesecutter	folliculated	Monophysitic	relativistic	unsegregated
chiropractic	forthrightly	monopolistic	remonstrator	vermiculated
chiropractor	fractionator	monotheistic	resuscitator	viscosimeter
chrematistic	fraudulently	munificently	reunionistic	wholehearted
chrestomathy	galvanometer	nanoplankton	reverberator	acciaccatura
Christolatry	gametophytic	narcissistic	revivalistic	architecture
cirrostratus	ganglionated	naturalistic	rhinocerotic	battleground
clearsighted	geochemistry	negativistic	rhizogenetic	blabbermouth
coincidental	gesticulator	nephelometer	sansculottic	breakthrough
coincidently	globetrotter	nephelometry	scarificator	charnelhouse
collaborator	governmental	nimbostratus	scenepainter	charterhouse
commemorator	greathearted	nominalistic	sceneshifter	correctitude
commiserator	gyromagnetic	noncommittal	schoolmaster	customshouse
communicator	hairsplitter	nonconductor	scintillator	dentilingual
compatriotic	heavyhearted	nympholeptic	screenwriter	discomfiture
complacently	henotheistic	omnipotently	scriptwriter	discomposure
complemental	hierophantic	omnisciently	secularistic	discoverture
concentrator	highspirited	omnisciently	selfaffected	fatherfigure

floriculture	companionway	biometrician	futilitarian	multilingual
grammolecule	conningtower	bombdisposal	geanticlinal	multinuclear
heliogravure	creepycrawly	Byelorussian	genealogical	mythological
heterosexual	cuckooflower	Cantabrigian	geographical	navigational
highlystrung	flamethrower	cantharidian	geometrician	necrological
highpressure	lanternjawed	caravansarai	geopolitical	necrophiliac
horrorstruck	monkeyflower	caravanserai	geosynclinal	neoclassical
horticulture	mulligatawny	Carlovingian	geriatrician	neoDarwinian
inexactitude	pasqueflower	cartological	gladiatorial	neurological
intellectual	straightaway	catechetical	governmental	newspaperman
intermixture	superhighway	catilinarian	grallatorial	nonagenarian
intertexture	hyperpyrexia	centrespread	haemophiliac	noncommittal
jurisconsult	morphallaxis	chorological	hagiological	nonessential
kissingcrust	trophallaxis	chromatogram	heroicomical	noneuclidean
lodginghouse	acetaldehyde	coenobitical	heterocercal	nonidentical
magistrature	agranulocyte	coenobytical	heterosexual	Northumbrian
mansionhouse	autocatalyse	coincidental	hierarchical	nychthemeral
meetinghouse	benzaldehyde	commissarial	histological	nymphomaniac
messeigneurs	cryptanalyst	commissariat	humanitarian	obstetrician
microcapsule	dermatophyte	committeeman	hydrological	occupational
microcircuit	formaldehyde	companionway	hydromedusae	octogenarian
misadventure	microanalyst	complemental	hydromedusan	oligarchical
misselthrush	phreatophyte	complexional	hydrothermal	oppositional
mitrailleuse	pteridophyte	conceptional	hymenopteran	orographical
motherfigure	pterodactyle	conferential	hyperbolical	osteological
multilingual	reticulocyte	confessional	hypocritical	overcritical
nomenclature	sclerenchyma	confidential	hypophrygian	paraboloidal
outwardbound	selfbetrayal	conjunctival	hypostatical	paradisaical
overexposure	selfemployed	connectional	hypothetical	paradisiacal
overpressure	spermatocyte	consistorial	immethodical	parametrical
passionfruit	capercailzie	contrapuntal	impedimental	paratactical
peradventure	crystalgazer	convectional	imperatorial	pathological
photogravure	mangelwurzel	conventional	inartificial	pestilential
pisciculture	monkeypuzzle	correctional	IndoEuropean	pestological
planetstruck	razzledazzle	cosmogonical	infanticidal	petrological
premenstrual	————	cosmological	inflectional	phenological
psychosexual	absorptional	cosmopolitan	infundibular	phenotypical
quarterbound	accusatorial	councilwoman	insecticidal	philological
reconstitute	aeronautical	counterplead	inspectorial	phonological
redistribute	aesthetician	countrywoman	instrumental	phycological
scouringrush	aetiological	courtmartial	integumental	phytological
selfapplause	AfroAmerican	cousingerman	intellectual	planetesimal
selfdestruct	agentgeneral	curvirostral	interdigital	pluriliteral
selfdistrust	agricultural	Czechoslovak	interfemoral	pneumothorax
servicecourt	aircraftsman	dentilingual	interglacial	postdiluvian
shortcircuit	alphabetical	departmental	interlobular	postdoctoral
silviculture	alphamerical	derivational	internuclear	postmeridian
somatopleure	amygdaloidal	dialectician	internuncial	postprandial
speakingtube	antediluvian	differentiae	interstellar	precedential
stationhouse	anteprandial	differential	interstitial	preceptorial
subminiature	anthropoidal	digressional	intracardiac	precessional
substructure	anticlerical	discretional	intracranial	prechristian
sylviculture	antimacassar	distortional	involutional	preclassical
terrorstruck	antimalarial	diverticular	judgematical	prefectorial
thirdborough	antithetical	dodecahedral	kleptomaniac	preferential
tintinnabula	apparitional	dorsiventral	labyrinthian	prehistorian
venepuncture	appendicular	emblematical	lepidopteran	prelapsarian
venipuncture	appositional	endoskeletal	limnological	premenstrual
weatherboard	aquicultural	epexegetical	linguistical	presbyterial
weatherhouse	archdiocesan	epicycloidal	lithological	Presbyterian
wherethrough	archetypical	episcopalian	Liverpudlian	presidential
wonderstruck	Aristotelean	equalitarian	longitudinal	primogenital
conjunctival	Aristotelian	ethnological	longshoreman	proboscidean
crossingover	arithmetical	etymological	LowChurchman	proboscidian
Czechoslovak	arrhythmical	EuroAmerican	majorgeneral	procathedral
enginedriver	artilleryman	exospherical	manometrical	processional
griseofulvin	astrological	expediential	mathematical	professional
outmanoeuvre	astronomical	experiential	megalomaniac	professorial
overachiever	asymmetrical	experimental	melancholiac	projectional
schoolleaver	Australasian	expressional	metaphorical	proportional
selfapproval	bacchanalian	extracranial	metaphysical	prosectorial
selfdeceived	backwoodsman	extralimital	metathetical	prototypical
selfdeceiver	bactericidal	extramarital	metrological	providential
selfinvolved	bacteriostat	extraspecial	metropolitan	psychosexual
shortsleeved	barometrical	footplateman	microcrystal	pyromaniacal
substantival	bibliomaniac	monomaniacal	quadrangular
whencesoever	bibliothecae	fountainhead	motivational	quadrinomial
woodengraver	bicentennial	FrancoGerman	multicentral	quaquaversal
campfollower	biographical	frontiersman	multilateral	quarterfinal

quinquennial	acquaintance	inexpedience	swaggerstick	coachbuilder
radiological	acquiescence	inexpediency	swizzlestick	coldshoulder
recreational	aerodynamics	inexperience	terrorstruck	collywobbles
reflectional	alkalescence	inobservance	therapeutics	commissioner
repetitional	appurtenance	intelligence	toggleswitch	complexioned
responsorial	arborescence	intemperance	transference	confectioner
revelational	astronautics	interconnect	transhumance	conningtower
rhinological	astrophysics	interference	transiliency	conventicler
rhombohedral	atmospherics	intermediacy	translucence	cosmographer
rontgenogram	belligerence	interservice	translucency	costermonger
saccharoidal	belligerency	intumescence	transparency	countenancer
salamandrian	bladderwrack	juvenescence	undersurface	courtplaster
salutational	blastfurnace	kinnikinnick	undertenancy	crackbrained
Scandinavian	butterscotch	longdistance	unimportance	craftbrother
scatological	calisthenics	luminescence	viridescence	crossbencher
schismatical	calorescence	magnificence	wonderstruck	crossgrained
selfapproval	chimneypiece	masterswitch	acetaldehyde	crossingover
selfbetrayal	circumstance	metapsychics	benzaldehyde	crystalgazer
selfcritical	clairvoyance	microphysics	coloquintida	cuckooflower
semicircular	complaisance	mispronounce	correctitude	declinometer
semiofficial	concomitance	monkeywrench	disaccharide	decontrolled
semiological	concrescence	multivalence	formaldehyde	delicatessen
semitropical	concubitancy	neuroscience	harlequinade	densitometer
septilateral	consentience	noctilucence	inexactitude	denticulated
Septuagintal	constituency	nonexistence	lanternslide	dinnerjacket
sericultural	cottonocracy	nonresidence	mountainside	discographer
servicewoman	countercheck	obmutescence	nicotinamide	disconnected
sexagenarian	counterforce	obsolescence	overpersuade	discontented
sinistrorsal	countermarch	omnipresence	parasiticide	disenchanter
sociological	countrydance	ornithomancy	primigravida	dissatisfied
spermathecal	crossbuttock	orthodontics	radionuclide	doubledealer
statistician	cytogenetics	orthopaedics	sulphonamide	doubledecked
straightaway	decalescence	pantisocracy	thitherwards	doubledecker
subcelestial	delitescence	pearlescence	whitherwards	doublelocked
subeditorial	detumescence	periodontics	absentminded	dovecoloured
sublapsarian	diathermancy	perseverance	accomplished	drawingpaper
substantival	disallowance	phosphoresce	agglutinogen	dunderheaded
subterranean	disobedience	planetstruck	autochthones	eavesdropped
successional	disseverance	Plattdeutsch	avitaminoses	eavesdropper
superhighway	econometrics	plenipotence	backpedalled	electrometer
supernatural	elasmobranch	plummerblock	balladmonger	electrotyper
supplemental	electroshock	precipitance	battlemented	encumbrancer
supraorbital	equidistance	precipitancy	bellbottomed	enginedriver
synchronical	equipollence	predominance	bespectacled	entrammelled
systematical	equipollency	predominancy	bloodbrother	escutcheoned
tabernacular	extravagance	preexistence	bloodstained	ethnographer
tautological	extravagancy	preoccupancy	bloodyminded	exhibitioner
teleological	fluorescence	preponderance	bobbydazzler	experimenter
televisional	frontispiece	protuberance	bodysnatcher	extensometer
tetrachordal	geotectonics	pyrotechnics	bonnetmonkey	extinguisher
theocratical	gerontocracy	quintessence	bonnyclabber	fainthearted
theoretician	glaucescence	radiophonics	bottlewasher	feebleminded
theosophical	gynaecocracy	reappearance	boulevardier	fieldglasses
Torricellian	happenstance	recalescence	bowcompasses	filibusterer
totalitarian	hermeneutics	reconveyance	brainstormer	firstnighter
tragicomical	horrorstruck	reminiscence	brassbounder	flamethrower
transitional	hydrostatics	remonstrance	breastsummer	floodlighted
triglyphical	illegitimacy	resipiscence	breathalyser	folliculated
triphthongal	impermanence	resplendence	breechloader	fostermother
tropological	impermanency	resplendency	brickfielder	foundationer
turbellarian	impertinence	retrocedence	brokenwinded	freightliner
tyrannicidal	impertinency	reviviscence	broncobuster	frontbencher
ubiquitarian	improvidence	rollingstock	bulletheaded	fullyfledged
uncommercial	inadvertence	selfdestruct	cabinetmaker	galvanometer
uneconomical	inadvertency	selfevidence	calligrapher	ganglionated
unhistorical	incalescence	selfreliance	campfollower	globetrotter
unscriptural	incognisance	selfreproach	candleholder	glockenspiel
veterinarian	incompetence	selfviolence	carpetbagger	goodhumoured
vicargeneral	incompetency	significance	cartographer	goodtempered
vicechairman	incompliance	significancy	cattlelifter	goosepimples
visitational	inconsonance	silverglance	chancemedley	graveclothes
visitatorial	incontinence	sphragistics	cheeseburger	greathearted
vocabularian	incontinency	squattocracy	cheesecutter	guestchamber
volumetrical	indehiscence	stellenbosch	cheesemonger	hagiographer
warehouseman	independence	streptococci	churchwarden	hairsplitter
circumscribe	independency	subservience	clearsighted	halftimbered
Germanophobe	indifference	subserviency	closecropped	hallucinogen
speakingtube	indifferency	supersedence	closegrained	halterbroken
acaulescence	inefficiency	surveillance	closemouthed	handkerchief

hardfavoured	outstretched	simpleminded	unparalleled	afterthought
hardfeatured	overachiever	singledecker	unprejudiced	bantamweight
harquebusier	pasqueflower	singlehanded	unprincipled	bibliography
headshrinker	patternmaker	singleminded	unpronounced	biogeography
heavyhearted	peccadilloes	singleseater	unrecognised	cardiography
heliographer	pedunculated	skateboarder	unrestrained	carpetknight
hierographer	pennypincher	skrimshanker	unsegregated	cheirography
highcoloured	petrographer	sledgehammer	unstructured	choreography
highspirited	phonographer	smallclothes	Valenciennes	chrestomathy
holidaymaker	photographer	snakecharmer	varicoloured	chronography
horsebreaker	phrasemonger	snapfastener	vauntcourier	counterlight
horsewhipped	phycomycetes	softpedalled	vermiculated	cryptography
housebreaker	phytographer	specktioneer	viscosimeter	glossography
housetrained	pickerelweed	spectrometer	welldisposed	glyphography
hucklebacked	pinfeathered	spidermonkey	wellfavoured	glyptography
huggermugger	pitterpatter	spiegeleisen	wellgrounded	interwreathe
hydrographer	plainclothed	squarerigged	whencesoever	lexicography
hymnographer	plainclothes	staffofficer	whitelivered	merrythought
iconographer	policyholder	stagemanager	wholehearted	middleweight
impoverished	poorspirited	standardbred	wicketkeeper	oceanography
inclinometer	pornographer	starspangled	windingsheet	organography
incorporated	practitioner	stenographer	winklepicker	palaeography
interchanger	pralltriller	stepchildren	wonderworker	physiography
intercropped	precancelled	stepdaughter	woodengraver	plectognathi
intermeddler	premeditated	stereoisomer	woodenheaded	polarography
interpleader	pretermitted	sternwheeler	woolgatherer	praiseworthy
interrelated	priestridden	stockbreeder	woollyheaded	psychography
jerrybuilder	prizefighter	stonedresser	wunderkinder	scintigraphy
jetpropelled	proglottides	stonyhearted	yellowhammer	seismography
katzenjammer	proportioned	stormtrooper	youngberries	selenography
kindergarten	proselytiser	stouthearted	antiaircraft	stereography
kirschwasser	proudhearted	straightbred	countershaft	stratigraphy
klipspringer	psychrometer	straightener	gesellschaft	thermography
laciniated	pumpernickel	straitjacket	landingcraft	welterweight
laissezaller	rabblerouser	streetwalker	oversimplify	williewaught
lanternjawed	radiographer	strengthener	paletteknife	zoogeography
largehearted	rattleheaded	strongminded	quarterstaff	absolutistic
lighthearted	redemptioner	subcommittee	transmogrify	acetabularia
lithographer	remembrancer	subsaturated	anthropology	aeroneurosis
lumberjacket	revictualled	sulphuretted	bacteriology	agamogenesis
machicolated	rosecoloured	supercharger	biocoenology	agamogenetic
magnetometer	sabretoothed	supplementer	breakthrough	ailurophobia
maidenstakes	saddlebacked	surrejoinder	chitterlings	alexipharmic
malcontented	salmonladder	swashbuckler	chromatology	alphanumeric
mangelwurzel	scenepainter	synchroniser	curlingtongs	amphibrachic
manslaughter	sceneshifter	systematiser	dialectology	amphictyonic
manufacturer	schoolleaver	tachygrapher	disadvantage	amphisbaenic
marketgarden	schoolmaster	taperecorder	ecclesiology	anaerobiosis
marshharrier	screenwriter	teetertotter	epidemiology	anagrammatic
mastersinger	scrimshanker	thereinafter	epistemology	analphabetic
mealymouthed	scriptwriter	thickskinned	heartstrings	anamorphosis
micrographer	sedgewarbler	thickskulled	ichthyophagy	anaphylactic
milliammeter	selfabsorbed	thoroughbred	kremlinology	anastigmatic
minicomputer	selfaffected	threequarter	landingstage	anemographic
misinterpret	selfbegotten	threewheeler	liturgiology	antagonistic
moneychanger	selfcoloured	tightmouthed	metalanguage	anthelmintic
moneygrubber	selfcomposed	timehonoured	microbiology	anticyclonic
moneyspinner	selfdeceived	trainspotter	misknowledge	antimagnetic
monkeyflower	selfdeceiver	transplanter	neurobiology	antipathetic
monkeyjacket	selfdirected	transshipped	offscourings	antiperiodic
morrisdancer	selfeducated	troublemaker	parasitology	antirachitic
mouthbreeder	selfemployed	tuberculated	pharmacology	antistrophic
muddleheaded	selfinvolved	turriculated	photogeology	apochromatic
multistoried	selfmurderer	turtlenecked	photomontage	apothegmatic
muttonheaded	semicylinder	unaccustomed	pneumatology	appendicitis
muzzleloader	semidetached	unauthorised	protistology	archipelagic
mythographer	semidiameter	uncalculated	protozoology	aristocratic
mythologiser	semifinished	uncelebrated	pursestrings	attorneyship
narrowminded	sensitometer	unclassified	radiobiology	autodidactic
necrographer	sharecropper	unconsidered	rheumatology	avitaminosis
nephelometer	sharpshooter	uncontrolled	rontgenology	bachelorship
newfashioned	sharpsighted	underclothes	skunkcabbage	balletomania
nightclothes	sheepshearer	underinsured	slipcarriage	bathypelagic
nonconformer	shirtwaister	understaffed	squirrelcage	belletristic
officeholder	shortchanger	underwritten	straightedge	bibliophilic
oldfashioned	shortpitched	undetermined	surroundings	bilharziasis
organgrinder	shortsighted	unencumbered	thirdborough	bilharziosis
orthographer	shortsleeved	unfrequented	wherethrough	biosynthesis
outpensioner	shortstaffed	uninterested	aforethought	biosynthetic

boogiewoogie	guardianship	monometallic	phytogenetic	studdingsail
brinkmanship	gyromagnetic	monophyletic	pictographic	stylographic
bureaucratic	haematolysis	Monophysitic	planispheric	subapostolic
buttermuslin	haemopoiesis	monopolistic	pluviometric	surrealistic
calligraphic	haemorrhagic	monostrophic	polarimetric	surveyorship
callisthenic	hagiographic	monosyllabic	polyhistoric	survivorship
calorimetric	hallucinosis	monotheistic	polyneuritic	synaesthesia
capercaillie	hectographic	morphallaxis	polyneuritis	synaesthetic
capercailzie	heliocentric	musicianship	polyphyletic	synarthrosis
capitalistic	heliographic	narcissistic	polysyllabic	syncretistic
carcinogenic	hemerocallis	naturalistic	polytheistic	taberdarship
cardinalship	hemispheroid	naturopathic	pornographic	tachygraphic
carragheenin	henotheistic	negativistic	positivistic	technocratic
cartographic	herpetologic	nephanalysis	pragmatistic	telaesthesia
catachrestic	hesperididia	neurasthenia	prenticeship	telaesthetic
catamountain	heterocyclic	neurasthenic	programmatic	tetramorphic
cataphoresis	hieroglyphic	nominalistic	propaedeutic	thaumaturgic
catastrophic	hierophantic	noradrenalin	prophylactic	theanthropic
chairmanship	histogenesis	nympholeptic	prosopopoeia	thermometric
chalcolithic	histogenetic	octosyllabic	protoplasmic	thermophilic
championship	homeomorphic	oneirocritic	protoplastic	thermoscopic
chaplainship	homoeopathic	oneupmanship	pseudocyesis	thermostatic
chauvinistic	homoeostasis	onomatopoeia	psychometric	thermotactic
chiropractic	horsemanship	onomatopoeic	psychopathic	thermotropic
chorographic	hydrochloric	organoleptic	psychotropic	toxicophobia
chrematistic	hydrodynamic	orthogenesis	publicspirit	tradescantia
chromatopsia	hydrofluoric	orthogenetic	pyroelectric	transoceanic
chronometric	hydrographic	orthographic	quadraphonic	transpacific
cleistogamic	hydrokinetic	orthopteroid	quadriplegia	trichromatic
colorimetric	hyperplastic	osteogenesis	quadriplegic	trochanteric
compatriotic	hyperpyretic	osteomalacia	quaestorship	trophallaxis
cosmographic	hyperpyrexia	osteoplastic	radiographic	tropospheric
cosmopolitic	hypersthenia	osteoporosis	receivership	tuberculosis
counterclaim	hypersthenic	overemphasis	relationship	unapologetic
decasyllabic	hyperthermia	overlordship	relativistic	undemocratic
Deuteronomic	hypertrophic	paedogenesis	reprographic	undiplomatic
diageotropic	hypnogenesis	paedogenetic	residentship	virtuosoship
diagrammatic	hypnogenetic	paedomorphic	reunionistic	viscerotonic
dictatorship	hypochondria	Palaeolithic	revivalistic	viscountship
diphtheritic	hypocoristic	palingenesia	rhinocerotic	walkietalkie
directorship	hypothalamic	palingenesis	rhizogenetic	watermanship
discipleship	hysteromania	palingenetic	salamandroid	Wellingtonia
dissymmetric	iconoclastic	panchromatic	salesmanship	whigmaleerie
dodecaphonic	IndoGermanic	pancreatitis	salpiglossis	xanthochroia
dynamometric	interoceanic	pantographic	sansculottic	zygapophysis
ecclesiastic	intervocalic	paradigmatic	sarcomatosis	apparatchiki
electrolysis	isochromatic	paraesthesia	scatterbrain	apparatchiks
electrolytic	isodiametric	paramagnetic	scenographic	breaststroke
electrotonic	journalistic	paraphrastic	schizothymia	businesslike
encephalitic	karyokinesis	parisyllabic	schizothymic	fiddlesticks
encephalitis	kinaesthesia	paronomastic	secularistic	marlinespike
encyclopedia	kinaesthesis	partisanship	seismometric	masterstroke
encyclopedic	kinaesthetic	passionfruit	seismoscopic	aboriginally
endocarditis	landingstrip	pathogenesis	selfanalysis	abstemiously
endometritis	laureateship	pathogenetic	selfhypnosis	abstractable
enthusiastic	leucocytosis	pedicellaria	selfportrait	abstractedly
epigrammatic	leukocytosis	pericarditis	semidomestic	academically
erythromycin	liberalistic	periphrastic	sensualistic	accidentally
ethnocentric	licketysplit	peristeronic	sergeantship	accusatively
ethnographic	lithographic	peristomatic	serjeantship	acoustically
euhemeristic	lithospheric	petrographic	servitorship	acronychally
evangelistic	lycanthropic	phagocytosis	shortcircuit	additionally
executorship	marksmanship	phagocytotic	sodafountain	adjectivally
exophthalmic	melanochroic	phanerogamic	specialistic	adulterously
falcongentil	melodramatic	pharmaceutic	spermaphytic	aggressively
featherbrain	meristematic	philharmonic	spermatozoid	amateurishly
feldspathoid	mesocephalic	philhellenic	sporogenesis	ambivalently
fibrinolysin	mesothoracic	phonasthenia	squirreltail	amitotically
flavoprotein	metagalactic	phonographic	stenographic	amphibiously
furunculosis	metaphrastic	photochromic	stereometric	anagogically
gamesmanship	metathoracic	photogenesis	stereophonic	analogically
gametophytic	microcircuit	photokinesis	stereoscopic	analytically
glycogenesis	microseismic	photokinetic	stethoscopic	anatomically
glycoprotein	militaristic	photospheric	stichomythia	antecedently
gonadotropic	misanthropic	phyllotactic	stichomythic	antiparticle
gonadotropin	mistressship	phylogenesis	streptomycin	antiphonally
governorship	mitochondria	phylogenetic	stroboscopic	apolitically
griseofulvin	mnemotechnic	physiognomic	strongylosis	appetisingly
grotesquerie	monodramatic	phytogenesis	strophanthin	

appraisingly	consensually	disjointedly	glitteringly	incompatible
approachable	consentingly	dispiritedly	gluttonously	incompatibly
appropriable	consequently	displaceable	grammolecule	incompletely
archetypally	considerable	displeasedly	gratifyingly	incomputable
aromatically	considerably	disreputable	gratuitously	inconsolable
articulately	consistently	disreputably	gregariously	inconsolably
artificially	consummately	dissentingly	groundlessly	inconstantly
artistically	contagiously	dissimilarly	grovellingly	inconsumable
astoundingly	contemptible	dissuasively	harmonically	inconsumably
astringently	contemptibly	distractedly	harmoniously	incorrigible
athletically	contextually	distrainable	heathenishly	incorrigibly
attractively	contiguously	disturbingly	hebdomadally	increasingly
attributable	contingently	dogmatically	heraldically	indecisively
auspiciously	continuously	domestically	hereditarily	indeclinable
autonomously	contractable	dramatically	hermetically	indecorously
avariciously	contractedly	dubitatively	hesitatingly	indefeasible
barbarically	contractible	dynastically	heterophylly	indefeasibly
beatifically	controllable	eclectically	highhandedly	indefectible
beneficently	conveniently	ecologically	historically	indefensible
beneficially	convincingly	economically	homonymously	indefensibly
benevolently	convulsively	ecstatically	homosexually	indefinitely
beseechingly	coordinately	effeminately	horizontally	indelicately
bewilderedly	copulatively	effortlessly	horrendously	indicatively
bewitchingly	coquettishly	electrically	horrifically	indigenously
biologically	corelatively	electronvolt	hubblebubble	indigestible
blackguardly	correctively	elementarily	hybridisable	indiscreetly
blisteringly	cosmetically	elliptically	hydrolysable	indisputable
blithesomely	courageously	emphatically	hygienically	indisputably
blunderingly	creepycrawly	emulsifiable	hypnotically	indissoluble
blusteringly	cultivatable	enchantingly	hypnotisable	indissolubly
boisterously	cumbersomely	enclitically	hysterically	indistinctly
breathlessly	cumulatively	endermically	ichthyocolla	indivertible
bullheadedly	curmudgeonly	entreatingly	ideationally	indivertibly
calamitously	decasyllable	epidemically	identifiable	individually
calcareously	decipherable	episodically	idolatrously	industrially
calculatedly	decomposable	equationally	illadvisedly	ineffaceable
calumniously	decoratively	equiprobable	illiterately	ineffaceably
capriciously	decreasingly	equivalently	illnaturedly	ineradicable
carriageable	definitively	esoterically	immaculately	ineradicably
catholically	degenerately	euphonically	immaterially	inexplicable
censoriously	deliberately	euphoniously	immeasurable	inexplicably
centesimally	delightfully	evanescently	immeasurably	inexpugnable
ceremonially	delinquently	evidentially	immemorially	inexpugnably
cherubically	demoniacally	exchangeable	immensurable	inextensible
chesterfield	demonstrable	exegetically	immoderately	inextricable
chivalrously	demonstrably	exhaustively	impenetrable	inextricably
circuitously	depressingly	exorbitantly	impenetrably	infectiously
clangorously	derivatively	exoterically	impenitently	infinitively
classifiable	derogatorily	expressively	imperatively	infrequently
clatteringly	despairingly	exterminable	imperishable	ingloriously
clavicembalo	despitefully	extraditable	imperishably	inhospitable
clinkerbuilt	despondently	extraneously	impersonally	inhospitably
coetaneously	despotically	factitiously	imperviously	iniquitously
coincidently	destructible	falcongentle	imponderable	inordinately
collaterally	determinable	fallaciously	imponderably	insufferable
collectively	determinably	farsightedly	impressively	insufferably
collegiately	determinedly	fastidiously	imputatively	intelligible
colloquially	diabolically	felicitously	inaccessible	intelligibly
colourlessly	diamonddrill	fertilisable	inaccessibly	interestedly
comfortingly	diamondfield	fictitiously	inaccurately	interminable
commandingly	diaphanously	fiddlefaddle	inadequately	interminably
commercially	diatonically	figuratively	inadmissible	intolerantly
commodiously	didactically	flagitiously	inadmissibly	intriguingly
communicable	dietetically	flamboyantly	inappeasable	inveterately
communicably	digressively	flatteringly	inapplicable	invulnerable
complacently	diminishable	flickeringly	inapplicably	invulnerably
compoundable	diminutively	forbiddingly	inappositely	irrationally
compressible	disagreeable	forebodingly	incalculable	irredeemable
compulsively	disagreeably	forensically	incalculably	irredeemably
compulsorily	disastrously	forthrightly	incautiously	irreformable
conceptually	discerningly	fortuitously	incestuously	irrefragable
conclusively	discerptible	fractionally	incidentally	irrefragably
concordantly	discordantly	fraudulently	incognisable	irrelatively
concurrently	discountable	frenetically	incognitable	irrelevantly
confoundedly	discoverable	functionally	incoherently	irremediable
congenitally	discursively	galvanically	incommutable	irremediably
connaturally	disdainfully	geologically	incommutably	irremissible
connectively	disgustfully	Germanophile	incomparable	irrepealable
conscionable	disgustingly	gigantically	incomparably	irreprovable

irresistible	omnipotently	questionably	spiritlessly	twitteringly
irresistibly	omnisciently	quixotically	sporadically	tyrannically
irresolutely	omnivorously	rabbinically	sprightfully	ubiquitously
irresolvable	openhandedly	razzledazzle	staggeringly	umbrageously
irrespirable	openmindedly	reassuringly	stammeringly	unacceptable
irreverently	operatically	rebelliously	statuesquely	unaffectedly
irreversible	oppressively	rechargeable	stertorously	unanswerable
irreversibly	ornamentally	reciprocally	stranglehold	unappeasable
irritatingly	otherworldly	recognisable	structurally	unassailable
isochronally	outlandishly	recognisably	stupendously	unassumingly
isothermally	outrageously	reconcilable	stutteringly	unbecomingly
jesuitically	paranormally	reflectively	subdivisible	unbelievable
jurisconsult	particularly	refractorily	subjectively	unbelievably
lachrymosely	passionately	refreshingly	submissively	unblinkingly
landingfield	pathetically	regardlessly	subsequently	unblushingly
landlubberly	pedantically	regimentally	subsidiarily	unchangeable
languorously	pejoratively	regressively	subsonically	unchangeably
lasciviously	pennywhistle	relationally	subthreshold	uncharitable
ledgertackle	perceptively	relentlessly	subversively	uncharitably
lefthandedly	perceptually	rememberable	successfully	uncomeatable
legitimately	percussively	remorsefully	successively	uncritically
libidinously	peremptorily	renegotiable	sufficiently	unemployable
licentiously	perfectively	repetitively	suggestively	uneventfully
liturgically	perfidiously	repressively	superhumanly	unexpectedly
liverystable	periodically	reproachable	superposable	unfaithfully
logistically	peripherally	reproducible	supplicantly	unfamiliarly
longwindedly	perjuriously	resistlessly	suppressible	unfathomable
loquaciously	permissively	resoundingly	surefootedly	unfavourable
lugubriously	perniciously	respectfully	surmountable	unfavourably
macrocephaly	perplexingly	respectively	surprisingly	ungovernable
mademoiselle	persistently	responsively	suspensively	ungracefully
magnetically	persuasively	restrainable	suspiciously	ungraciously
magnetisable	phenomenally	restrainedly	swaggeringly	ungratefully
magnifically	phonemically	restrictedly	swimmingbell	unilaterally
maintainable	phonetically	reticulately	syllabically	unimaginable
majestically	platonically	revengefully	symbolically	unimaginably
malevolently	playingfield	rhetorically	syndetically	unmanageable
manoeuvrable	polysyllable	rhythmically	synonymously	unmercifully
marriageable	pontifically	ridiculously	synoptically	unmistakable
marvellously	portentously	robustiously	systemically	unmistakably
meaningfully	possessively	romantically	tangentially	unofficially
mechanically	posthumously	rumbletumble	tectonically	unpleasantly
meditatively	precariously	ruminatively	terrifically	unprofitable
mendaciously	precipitable	sacerdotally	terrifyingly	unprofitably
merchantable	preclusively	sadistically	tetragonally	unreasonable
meridionally	precociously	salubriously	Teutonically	unreasonably
metallically	predictively	sanguinarily	theatrically	unrepeatable
meteorically	preeminently	saponifiable	theistically	unreservedly
methodically	prevailingly	sardonically	thematically	unsearchable
meticulously	preventively	sarsaparilla	thermocouple	unseasonable
microcapsule	primordially	satisfyingly	thermolabile	unthinkingly
microcephaly	prodigiously	scandalously	thermostable	untruthfully
millesimally	productively	scatteringly	thoughtfully	unyieldingly
miraculously	proficiently	scripturally	thousandfold	uproariously
monastically	profligately	scrupulously	thriftlessly	vanquishable
monitorially	programmable	sculpturally	thunderingly	vegetatively
monkeypuzzle	projectively	scurrilously	thunderously	vernacularly
monopodially	prolifically	semantically	tintinnabula	victoriously
monosyllable	pronominally	semiannually	tittletattle	villainously
monotonously	pronouncedly	sententially	topsyturvily	vindictively
monumentally	propitiously	septennially	torrentially	viviparously
mordaciously	prosecutable	sepulchrally	tradespeople	vociferously
multipliable	prosodically	sequaciously	traitorously	volcanically
munificently	prosperously	sequentially	transferable	volitionally
myrmecophily	protectively	seraphically	transfusible	voluminously
mysteriously	protensively	serpentinely	transitively	voluptuously
mystifyingly	protrusively	shamefacedly	transitorily	wallydraigle
narcotically	proverbially	shillyshally	translatable	whimperingly
nauseatingly	provincially	shoulderbelt	transmutable	whippoorwill
neglectfully	prudentially	simoniacally	transpirable	whisperingly
neurotically	pterodactyle	sinusoidally	transposable	worshipfully
nonchalantly	puerperrally	siphonostele	transversely	YankeeDoodle
nonflammable	pugnaciously	slanderously	tremendously	appendectomy
nutritiously	pulverisable	sleepingpill	trestletable	chondriosome
obligatorily	punchingball	Socratically	triangularly	hysterectomy
obsequiously	purposebuilt	solicitously	tripartitely	neuroanatomy
occasionally	purposefully	specifically	triumphantly	Quadragesima
occidentally	quantifiable	speechlessly	trumpetshell	sclerenchyma
octosyllable	questionable	spheroidally	tumultuously	Septuagesima

stereochromy	disannulling	horsetrading	overstepping	stoneboiling
twentyfourmo	disannulment	housekeeping	oxyacetylene	stonecutting
accouchement	disbursement	housewarming	palaeobotany	stupefacient
accoutrement	discouraging	hydroquinone	parallelling	subcontinent
administrant	discriminant	illtreatment	peasepudding	supereminent
admonishment	disendowment	impercipient	pettifogging	supermundane
announcement	disgorgement	imprisonment	photosetting	supervenient
anthropogeny	disguisement	incandescent	pitcherplant	supramundane
antineutrino	dishevelment	inconsequent	placesetting	terebinthine
appraisement	disinfectant	inconsistent	plaindealing	testosterone
astonishment	disinterment	inconvenient	polyethylene	thanksgiving
backbreaking	dislodgement	indiscipline	polyurethane	theatregoing
backslapping	displacement	infringement	postponement	throughstone
ballottement	disseverment	ingratiating	predetermine	thunderstone
battleground	distrainment	insufficient	preponderant	transcendent
beachcombing	doubleacting	interbedding	presentiment	transferring
bedazzlement	earsplitting	intercurrent	pricecutting	transhipment
belittlement	earthshaking	intercutting	privatdocent	transmigrant
bellylanding	echosounding	intermittent	privatdozent	transmitting
bequeathment	effervescent	intermitting	privateering	transmontane
bewilderment	efflorescent	intermundane	prizewinning	transpontine
billsticking	embattlement	intervenient	profiteering	typefounding
birdsnesting	embezzlement	intramundane	progesterone	ultramontane
birdwatching	embitterment	intransigent	proofreading	ultramundane
birefringent	emblazonment	intrauterine	quadrivalent	unambivalent
blackbirding	embranchment	intrenchment	quarterbound	unappetising
blackcurrant	empoisonment	intromittent	racketeering	unconstraint
blandishment	empressement	intromitting	radioelement	unconvincing
blockbusting	encirclement	inveiglement	rapprochment	underbidding
bloodletting	encroachment	jurisprudent	readjustment	undercoating
bluestocking	encumberment	knighterrant	reassessment	undercurrent
bodybuilding	endamagement	laboursaving	reassignment	undercutting
bodystocking	endangerment	labyrinthine	recalcitrant	undergarment
booklearning	enfeeblement	lakedwelling	recommitment	underletting
brainwashing	enginetuning	languishment	recrudescent	undermanning
brassrubbing	enshrinement	leapfrogging	redeployment	underpinning
breathtaking	enswathement	liquefacient	reinvestment	underrunning
brilliantine	entanglement	longstanding	renouncement	undersetting
buccaneering	enterprising	magniloquent	resettlement	unemployment
bullfighting	entertaining	maltreatment	retrenchment	unflattering
carburetting	enthronement	meltingpoint	ricochetting	unhesitating
cardcarrying	entrancement	metallophone	safecracking	unpretending
caterwauling	entrenchment	metalworking	salamandrine	vanquishment
chastisement	envisagement	mezzosoprano	sandyachting	vantagepoint
cheeseparing	epiphenomena	microcopying	sanguinolent	ventripotent
childbearing	equestrienne	misalignment	sarrusophone	wainscotting
Christophany	estrangement	misapprehend	scareheading	waistcoating
circumfluent	excruciating	misdemeanant	schizophrene	wallpainting
circumjacent	extramundane	misjudgement	secondstring	weatherbound
clairaudient	extrauterine	misplacement	selfcatering	whitewashing
cliffhanging	faithhealing	misrepresent	selfdoubting	winterbourne
cockfighting	farmsteading	misstatement	selfeffacing	abbreviation
combinations	faultfinding	mistreatment	selfexistent	acceleration
commencement	firefighting	monofilament	selflimiting	accentuation
concelebrant	forebodement	mosstrooping	selfpleasing	accommodator
concupiscent	forestalment	mourningband	selfrighting	accumulation
congratulant	freestanding	mourningring	selfstarting	adjudication
constringent	freeswimming	mulligatawny	semibasement	adulteration
contrivement	freethinking	multiplicand	semideponent	aircondition
convalescent	freewheeling	namedropping	shadowboxing	alimentation
conveyancing	fricasseeing	neighbouring	Shakspereana	alliteration
convincement	galligaskins	nerveracking	Shaksperiana	amalgamation
corespondent	glassblowing	Newfoundland	shipbuilding	amelioration
counteragent	gravelelling	niminypiminy	sideslipping	amortisation
counterpoint	guaranteeing	nitrobenzene	sidestepping	annihilation
crashlanding	habitforming	noctambulant	sightreading	annunciation
crossbedding	hairdressing	nonalignment	singleacting	anticipation
crosscurrent	handicapping	noncombatant	slaveholding	antigropelos
crossexamine	hardstanding	noncomplying	sleepwalking	apperception
crossheading	heartburning	nonefficient	smallholding	appreciation
curlingirons	heartrending	nonflowering	somnambulant	apprehension
decipherment	heartwarming	nonresistant	sorbefacient	appropriator
decongestant	hedgehopping	orienteering	soundingline	arborisation
deliquescent	hereditament	outrivalling	speedboating	articulation
demimondaine	highfaluting	outstripping	stablishment	asphyxiation
denouncement	highlystrung	outwardbound	stillhunting	assassinator
dethronement	highsounding	overabundant	stockbroking	assibilation
diminishment	highstepping	overcropping	stockjobbing	assimilation
disagreement	hoodmanblind	overpowering	stockraising	augmentation

auscultation	degeneration	flocculation	laterisation	prolegomenon
bachelorhood	deionisation	fluidisation	latinisation	prolongation
blastulation	delamination	fluoridation	legalisation	promulgation
burglarproof	deliberation	fluorination	legitimation	propitiation
cachinnation	delimitation	fluorocarbon	levorotation	proscription
calumniation	demodulation	focalisation	liquefaction	prostitution
canalisation	demonstrator	fractionator	localisation	protestation
cancellation	denaturation	gasification	malformation	prothalamion
canonisation	denomination	genuflection	malnutrition	purification
cantillation	denunciation	gesticulator	malversation	putrefaction
capitulation	depopulation	gobbledegook	manipulation	quantisation
chiropractor	depreciation	gobbledygook	maximisation	racemisation
chlorination	deputisation	habilitation	menstruation	ramification
chocolatebox	deracination	haematoxylon	minedetector	ratification
circumcision	desalination	halogenation	minimisation	ratiocinator
circumfusion	desideration	homologation	ministration	reactivation
civilisation	despoliation	humanisation	misdirection	reallocation
claudication	desquamation	humification	miseducation	reciprocator
coacervation	dessertspoon	hypertension	misquotation	recollection
codification	detoxication	hypothecator	mobilisation	reconversion
cohabitation	dilapidation	idealisation	modification	recuperation
collaborator	disaffection	illumination	monetisation	redecoration
colonisation	disclamation	illustration	moralisation	refrigerator
columniation	disconnexion	immoderation	motorisation	regeneration
commemorator	disinfection	immunisation	nanoplankton	registration
commendation	disinflation	imperfection	nebulisation	rejuvenation
commentation	dispensation	impersonator	neurosurgeon	remonstrator
commiserator	dispossessor	implantation	nidification	remuneration
communicator	disquisition	impregnation	nonconductor	renunciation
compellation	disseminator	impropriator	notification	reoccupation
compensation	dissertation	improvisator	novelisation	repatriation
complication	dissimulator	inactivation	nychthemeron	repercussion
compurgation	dissociation	inauguration	obliteration	repossession
concentrator	distillation	incatenation	obnubilation	reprehension
conciliation	distribution	incineration	opisthotonos	reproduction
condemnation	divarication	incorporator	optimisation	resupination
condensation	dodecahedron	incorruption	orchestrator	resurrection
confabulator	domesticator	incrustation	organisation	resuscitator
confirmation	duckingstool	indiscretion	ossification	reticulation
confiscation	echolocation	inescutcheon	overexertion	retractation
conformation	edulcoration	inflammation	overreaction	retrocession
conglobation	effectuation	inhabitation	pacification	retroflexion
congregation	elucubration	inoccupation	panification	retropulsion
conquistador	emancipation	inosculation	pantechnicon	retroversion
conscription	emargination	insemination	paralysation	reverberator
consecration	emasculation	inspissation	participator	rhododendron
conservation	encrustation	installation	penalisation	rhombohedron
consignation	epithalamion	instauration	perambulator	romanisation
consociation	equalisation	instillation	peregrinator	ruralisation
consolidator	equilibrator	insufflation	perfoliation	satisfaction
conspiration	equivocation	insurrection	perispomenon	scarificator
constipation	etherisation	intellection	pernoctation	schoolfellow
constitution	etymologicon	inteneration	peroxidation	scintillator
constriction	evisceration	interception	perpetration	scoundreldom
construction	exacerbation	intercession	perpetuation	scutellation
consultation	exaggeration	interdiction	perspiration	segmentation
consummation	exasperation	interjection	perturbation	selfdelusion
contemplator	excogitation	interlocutor	petrifaction	selfdevotion
contestation	excruciation	intermission	philodendron	selfignition
continuation	exenteration	interoceptor	photofission	sequestrator
contradictor	exercitation	interpolator	pigmentation	servocontrol
contribution	exhilaration	interrogator	pilotballoon	shatterproof
conversation	exophthalmos	interruption	polarisation	shootingiron
coordination	expatriation	intersection	pontificator	shoulderknot
corroborator	explantation	intervention	postposition	snarlingiron
counterproof	exploitation	intimidation	precipitator	solarisation
countertenor	exprobration	intoxication	precognition	solicitation
crenellation	exterminator	introduction	precondition	solifluction
crosssection	extraversion	introjection	predigestion	southernwood
cuckingstool	extroversion	intromission	predilection	spermatozoon
deactivation	exulceration	introversion	preformation	spinsterhood
debilitation	facilitation	invagination	premeditator	spokesperson
decapitation	felicitation	invalidation	prescription	staffsurgeon
deceleration	feminisation	investigator	preselection	standingroom
decompressor	fenestration	invigilation	presentation	stationwagon
decongestion	fermentation	invigoration	preservation	stereopticon
deescalation	fibrillation	irresolution	prevaricator	sternutation
deflagration	finalisation	jurisdiction	primogenitor	stilboestrol
defraudation	flagellation	lachrymation	proclamation	stridulation

strobilation	steganograph	foraminifera	satisfactory	antiSemitism
stupefaction	triggerhappy	geochemistry	scraperboard	apiculturist
subarrhation	abolitionary	greengrocery	selfflattery	apostolicism
suberisation	acciaccatura	groundcherry	septuagenary	apostrophise
subscription	accretionary	haberdashery	serpentiform	apparentness
substitution	adjudicatory	headquarters	serviceberry	appositeness
substruction	amphitheatre	heliogravure	servicecourt	aromaticness
sulphonation	anticipatory	henceforward	sesquialtera	asynchronism
sulphuration	appreciatory	hereinbefore	sexcentenary	attitudinise
supersession	archdeaconry	highpressure	shuffleboard	autocatalyse
superstition	architecture	hindquarters	sidewhiskers	automobilist
supervention	articulatory	honeybuzzard	silviculture	automorphism
supplication	assimilatory	horticulture	siphonophore	avantgardism
sustentation	auscultatory	hydatidiform	skullduggery	avantgardist
swimmingpool	banderillero	ichthyolatry	somatopleure	backwardness
taxcollector	basidiospore	inauguratory	southeastern	baselessness
tessellation	biochemistry	inflammatory	southwestern	beggarliness
torrefaction	blastosphere	inflationary	spectrometry	behaviourism
totalisation	bookingclerk	intercessory	stalactiform	behaviourist
transduction	brambleberry	interdictory	sternutatory	benefactress
transgressor	cachinnatory	interjectory	stockjobbery	bibliologist
transmission	calumniatory	intermediary	stonemasonry	bibliopegist
transudation	camiknickers	intermixture	stratosphere	bibliopolist
trephination	campodeiform	intertexture	submaxillary	bilateralism
trifurcation	cashandcarry	intimidatory	subminiature	bilingualism
tripartition	centrosphere	introductory	substructure	bioecologist
triplication	checkerberry	lachrymatory	superciliary	biophysicist
typification	checkerboard	laisserfaire	supersensory	bioscientist
underdevelop	chequerboard	laissezfaire	supplicatory	blamableness
unionisation	Christolatry	levorotatory	sylviculture	blamefulness
unlikelihood	chromosphere	loungelizard	tercentenary	blissfulness
urbanisation	clapperboard	magistrature	testamentary	boastfulness
valorisation	commendatory	manipulatory	thermosphere	bootlessness
vaporisation	compensatory	marketsquare	thimbleberry	brackishness
vasodilation	compurgatory	mastigophora	thoroughfare	buccaneerish
vaticination	conciliatory	messeigneurs	thunderstorm	buffalograss
verification	condemnatory	microsurgery	toastingfork	burningglass
vertebration	confirmatory	misadventure	traditionary	canorousness
vesiculation	confiscatory	modificatory	transudatory	captiousness
vilification	conidiophore	motherfigure	tricentenary	cardiologist
vinification	conidiospore	nailscissors	trigonometry	carelessness
vitalisation	consecratory	nephelometry	usufructuary	caricaturist
vitiligation	conservatory	neurosurgery	valetudinary	Cartesianism
vitrifaction	constabulary	nomenclature	vasodilatory	cautiousness
vituperation	consummatory	northeastern	venepuncture	characterise
vivification	contemporary	northwestern	venipuncture	charlatanism
vocalisation	contributory	obedientiary	verificatory	charnelhouse
vociferation	cotyledonary	outmanoeuvre	vituperatory	charterhouse
vomiturition	counterscarp	overexposure	weatherboard	cheerfulness
weatherproof	crosscountry	overpressure	whortleberry	chieftainess
bronchoscope	deambulatory	pacificatory	abolitionism	childishness
chemotherapy	deflationary	paramilitary	abolitionist	Christianise
electroscope	denunciatory	penitentiary	abortiveness	chromaticism
enantiomorph	depreciatory	peradventure	abrasiveness	chronologise
galvanoscope	desquamatory	perspiratory	absoluteness	chronologist
heliotherapy	disciplinary	pettifoggery	abstractness	churlishness
hydrotherapy	discomfiture	photogravure	abstruseness	clannishness
hypnotherapy	discomposure	pisciculture	accompanyist	clarinettist
intussuscept	discoverture	plasterboard	accordionist	classicalism
kaleidoscope	dispensatory	plebiscitary	accurateness	classicalist
laryngoscope	distillatory	poikilotherm	accursedness	clotheshorse
laryngoscopy	distributory	premaxillary	adaptiveness	clothespress
magnetograph	diversionary	probationary	adequateness	clownishness
meteorograph	draughtboard	proclamatory	adhesiveness	coalitionist
opisthograph	drawingboard	propitiatory	adorableness	cocksureness
ornithoscopy	eleemosynary	prothonotary	aeroembolism	coerciveness
oscillograph	elocutionary	protohistory	aestheticism	cohesiveness
oscilloscope	emasculatory	provisionary	affectedness	coleopterist
philanthrope	equivocatory	psychrometry	agribusiness	collectivise
philanthropy	evolutionary	pteridosperm	allomorphism	collectivism
phraseograph	exaggeratory	purificatory	allusiveness	collectivist
radioisotope	exclusionary	recessionary	ambassadress	collegialism
radiotherapy	expansionary	reflationary	amenableness	commensalism
selfcontempt	extortionary	remuneratory	amicableness	commensalist
skippingrope	extrasensory	renunciatory	anaesthetise	completeness
spectrograph	fatherfigure	residentiary	anaesthetist	composedness
spectroscope	flabelliform	reversionary	anathematise	conchologist
spectroscopy	flagellatory	rhynchophora	anecdotalist	concreteness
sphygmograph	floriculture	runningboard	anotherguess	Confucianism

confusedness	emotionalism	heavenliness	metamorphose	parochialism
conservatism	emotionalist	heedlessness	metasomatism	partitionist
contagionism	enormousness	heliotropism	microanalyst	patulousness
containerise	entomologise	helplessness	microscopist	peacefulness
contemporise	entomologist	hemimorphism	mindlessness	peerlessness
contrariness	enviableness	heortologist	mineralogist	pellucidness
contrariwise	enzymologist	heroicalness	mirthfulness	perilousness
contriteness	epicureanism	hirepurchase	miscellanist	periodontist
copolymerise	eruptiveness	homeopathist	misselthrush	perverseness
counterblast	erythroblast	homesickness	mistakenness	perviousness
counterpoise	escapologist	homomorphism	mithridatise	philistinism
covetousness	eunuchoidism	homothallism	mithridatism	phillumenist
cowardliness	eveningdress	hopelessness	mitrailleuse	philosophise
craniologist	evolutionism	horribleness	moderateness	phlebotomise
creativeness	evolutionist	humorousness	moistureless	phlebotomist
criticalness	exclusionism	hydrotropism	monographist	phototropism
crosspurpose	exclusionist	idiosyncrasy	morningdress	phrenologist
cryptanalyst	excursionist	illusiveness	morphologist	physiologist
cryptologist	exiguousness	illusoriness	motherliness	pigeonbreast
culpableness	expansionism	immatureness	motorcyclist	pitiableness
cumbrousness	expansionist	immunologist	mournfulness	pitilessness
customshouse	explicitness	implicitness	moveableness	pleasantness
debonairness	fabulousness	impoliteness	movelessness	pleasingness
decentralise	facelessness	incendiarism	multipurpose	pleasureless
decisiveness	factionalism	incisiveness	municipalise	pleiotropism
decorousness	factiousness	indebtedness	musicologist	pleomorphism
definiteness	faintishness	indirectness	mutinousness	polyglottism
deflationist	faithfulness	inexpertness	namelessness	polymorphism
dejectedness	fancifulness	infiniteness	nauseousness	populousness
delusiveness	fantasticism	inflationism	nebulousness	porcelainise
demilitarise	fatherliness	inflationist	necrophilism	positiveness
demineralise	fearlessness	insolubilise	needlessness	postmistress
denaturalise	fearsomeness	instructress	negativeness	preciousness
denuclearise	featheriness	intrusionist	negotiatress	precisianism
deontologist	fecklessness	intuitionism	negrophilism	precisionist
depoliticise	feminineness	intuitionist	negrophilist	preestablish
depravedness	feverishness	irregardless	neoDarwinism	preparedness
derisiveness	fictionalise	Ishmaelitish	neoDarwinist	previousness
desirousness	fiendishness	isolationism	Neohellenism	pridefulness
desolateness	forcefulness	isolationist	neonomianism	priestliness
desulphurise	forcibleness	Keynesianism	Neoplatonism	priggishness
detachedness	formlessness	kissingcrust	Neoplatonist	princeliness
deviationism	frankincense	knightliness	nephrologist	professoress
deviationist	freakishness	laudableness	Nestorianism	profoundness
dextrousness	frenchpolish	legitimatise	nevertheless	progenitress
diamagnetism	frequentness	lexicologist	noctambulism	prolificness
diastrophism	frictionless	lifelessness	noctambulist	propagandise
dichromatism	friendliness	listlessness	northernmost	propagandism
dilatoriness	fruitfulness	literariness	numerologist	propagandist
dilettantish	fugitiveness	lithotritist	numerousness	proprietress
dilettantism	functionless	lodginghouse	nutritionist	psephologist
diphthongise	futurologist	lonesomeness	nyctitropism	psychiatrist
discreetness	gamesomeness	lopsidedness	obdurateness	psychologise
discreteness	gastronomist	lovelessness	obligingness	psychologism
disembarrass	generousness	lovelornness	obscurantism	psychologist
disestablish	geomagnetism	lukewarmness	obscurantist	purblindness
disfranchise	geophysicist	luminousness	obsoleteness	pyrotechnist
disharmonise	ghoulishness	lusciousness	oceanologist	qualmishness
dissocialise	glaciologist	maidenliness	odontologist	questionless
distinctness	gladsomeness	malacologist	onesidedness	ravenousness
diversionist	gloriousness	malapertness	oppositeness	reactiveness
divisiveness	glossologist	Manicheanism	ordinariness	readableness
dolorousness	gorgeousness	manifoldness	orthodontist	receptionist
doubtfulness	gracefulness	mannerliness	orthopaedist	recklessness
downwardness	graciousness	mansionhouse	orthopterist	Redemptorist
dramaturgist	grammaticise	Marcionitism	orthotropism	reductionism
draughthorse	graphologist	Marseillaise	outdatedness	reductionist
dreadfulness	graspingness	materialness	overniceness	relativeness
droughtiness	gratefulness	mediaevalism	paedobaptism	reliableness
dwarfishness	greenishness	mediaevalist	painlessness	remilitarise
editorialise	grievousness	meetinghouse	Palladianism	reproachless
editorialist	gruesomeness	mercantilism	palynologist	reservedness
educationist	guilefulness	mercantilist	panhellenism	resignedness
effusiveness	gymnosophist	mercifulness	papyrologist	resoluteness
Egyptologist	habitualness	mercurialise	paragraphist	resolvedness
elementalism	haematoblast	mercurialism	paramorphism	restlessness
elocutionist	handsomeness	metachronism	parenthesise	retiringness
embryologist	harmlessness	metallurgist	parkinsonism	ribonuclease
emotionalise	headmistress	metamorphism	parochialise	rightfulness

rigorousness	straightness	unwontedness	conduplicate	incorporeity
rootlessness	strengthless	unworldiness	congeniality	incurability
ruthlessness	strikingness	unworthiness	conglomerate	indelibility
salutariness	stringcourse	urbanologist	conglutinate	indoctrinate
salvationism	strychninism	usuriousness	congratulate	inelasticity
salvationist	stubbornness	uxoriousness	connubiality	infusibility
Samaritanism	studiousness	valuableness	conviviality	inoperculate
sanguineness	subjectivise	vaporousness	corporeality	insolubility
scabbardfish	subjectivism	variableness	curvicaudate	inspectorate
scabrousness	subjectivist	vengefulness	curvicostate	intermediate
scornfulness	succinctness	venomousness	curvifoliate	interpellate
scorpionfish	suitableness	verticalness	decaffeinate	invertebrate
scoundrelism	swainishness	vibraphonist	deconsecrate	invisibility
scouringrush	sweepingness	Victorianism	dermatophyte	irascibility
scratchiness	sweetishness	vigorousness	desirability	irregularity
secessionism	sycophantish	virtuousness	dibranchiate	irritability
secessionist	syndactylism	vitreousness	dilatability	leathercloth
seclusionist	tactlessness	voidableness	disaffiliate	malleability
sectarianise	tamelessness	volatileness	disambiguate	matriarchate
sectarianism	tangibleness	voluntaryism	disassociate	microclimate
sectionalism	taskmistress	voluntaryist	discommodity	miscalculate
sedulousness	tastefulness	wastefulness	disconsolate	mistranslate
seismologist	tearlessness	watchfulness	discriminate	molecularity
selenologist	technologist	weatherglass	disintegrate	monochromate
selfapplause	teensyweensy	weatherhouse	disorientate	multidentate
selfdistrust	telegraphese	womanishness	distemperate	multifoliate
selfinterest	telegraphist	wondrousness	divertimenti	multiformity
selflessness	teratologist	workableness	divertimento	multipartite
selfsameness	terribleness	workingclass	divisibility	multiplicate
semidarkness	thankfulness	wrathfulness	eccentricity	multiplicity
semifinalist	therapeutist	wretchedness	ectoparasite	multiversity
sensibleness	thievishness	wrongfulness	effectuality	multungulate
sensuousness	thoroughbass	youthfulness	electroplate	municipality
separateness	thoroughness	zygomorphism	emotionality	navigability
sergeantfish	ticklishness	absorptivity	endoparasite	oblanceolate
shamateurism	timelessness	absquatulate	ephemerality	opposability
shamefulness	timorousness	actinomycete	equitability	orbicularity
sheepishness	tirelessness	adaptability	espagnolette	overactivity
shrewishness	tiresomeness	administrate	essentiality	overestimate
skittishness	togetherness	advisability	excitability	palatability
slipperiness	toilsomeness	aerosiderite	expressivity	parochiality
slothfulness	tonelessness	affectionate	exsanguinate	patriarchate
slovenliness	toploftiness	agranulocyte	exsufflicate	perceptivity
sluggishness	tortuousness	alterability	extortionate	perfervidity
sluttishness	touchingness	antigenicity	fantasticate	permanganate
snappishness	towardliness	aperiodicity	filtrability	permeability
snobbishness	toxicologist	apostolicity	flammability	permittivity
sociableness	traditionist	authenticate	frangibility	perspicacity
sociometrist	traducianism	authenticity	fuliginosity	phreatophyte
solitariness	traducianist	autoimmunity	granodiorite	plausibility
somnambulism	trampolinist	automaticity	grossularite	pneumaticity
somnambulist	tranquillise	availability	habitability	pointilliste
somniloquism	transformism	berzelianite	hairsbreadth	polytonality
somniloquist	transformist	billingsgate	handsbreadth	posteriority
sonorousness	transvestism	blabbermouth	hellgrammite	postgraduate
soullessness	trichologist	blatherskite	hemichordate	potentiality
southernmost	trichotomise	bletherskate	hemimorphite	practicality
spaciousness	trickishness	bloodthirsty	hemiparasite	predesignate
sparrowgrass	trinomialism	borosilicate	heritability	predestinate
specificness	troglodytism	cabbagewhite	heterozygote	prefabricate
speciousness	trustfulness	canaliculate	humptydumpty	prehensility
speleologist	truthfulness	carbohydrate	hyperacidity	preponderate
spiritedness	tunelessness	centuplicate	hypochlorite	prerequisite
spiritualise	unbrokenness	chalcopyrite	hyposulphite	presbyterate
spiritualism	uncommonness	charterparty	illegibility	principality
spiritualist	unctuousness	Christianity	illegitimate	printability
spitefulness	ungainliness	chromaticity	illiberality	proconsulate
splendidness	unitarianism	churchianity	illogicality	productivity
sportfulness	universalise	classicality	immovability	professorate
sportiveness	universalism	coelenterate	immutability	protectorate
spotlessness	universalist	collectivity	impartiality	pseudonymity
spuriousness	unkindliness	collegiality	imputability	pteridophyte
Stakhanovism	unlawfulness	collinearity	inarticulate	pyromorphite
stalwartness	unlikeliness	commensurate	inaudibility	quattrocento
stationhouse	unloveliness	commonwealth	incapability	quizzicality
stealthiness	unsteadiness	companionate	incapacitate	recalcitrate
steeplechase	untimeliness	compulsivity	inconcinnity	recapitulate
sterlingness	untowardness	concelebrate	inconformity	reconstitute
stockingless	unwieldiness	conductivity	incoordinate	redintegrate

redistribute
reducibility
reflectivity
refractivity
refreshments
rehabilitate
reinvigorate
rejectamenta
removability
reticulocyte
retractility
risorgimento
saccharinity
schizomycete
scrobiculate
scrupulosity
selfactivity
selfidentity
sellingplate
semiliterate
semiparasite
sempiternity
separability
shouldernote
simultaneity
sinistrality
snaggletooth
somnambulate
sophisticate
spermatocyte
spirituality
Stakhanovite
straticulate
strontianite
subalternate
subalternity
subinfeudate
subjectivity
subnormality
substantiate
subtemperate
superannuate
supererogate
susceptivity
swimmingbath
teachability
technicality
temptability
tergiversate
tetrahedrite
tolerability
traceability
tractability
tranquillity
transitivity
transmigrate
transvestite
unconformity
unifoliolate
unisexuality
universality
unpopularity
unregenerate
venerability
veridicality
verticillate
voluminosity
voluptuosity
whimsicality
wollastonite
achlamydeous
adscititious
advantageous
adventitious
Alhambresque
altitudinous
ambidextrous
amentiferous
amphitropous

anemophilous
angiocarpous
argillaceous
asynchronous
atheromatous
brontosaurus
butterflynut
calycoideous
cantankerous
carbonaceous
carillonneur
cementitious
cinematheque
cirrocumulus
cirrostratus
coleopterous
compunctious
conchiferous
contemptuous
conterminous
contumacious
contumelious
cotyledonous
cryptogamous
cumulocirrus
cumulonimbus
cuprammonium
cynocephalus
diatomaceous
discourteous
disingenuous
disputatious
disregardful
diverticulum
duraluminium
echinococcus
electrotonus
entrepreneur
epithalamium
erythematous
exophthalmus
exsanguinous
ferrugineous
foresightful
fructiferous
fructivorous
furfuraceous
galactogogue
gallinaceous
gamopetalous
gamophyllous
gamosepalous
gastropodous
glaucomatous
graminaceous
hebetudinous
heliolatrous
heteroecious
heterogamous
heterogenous
heterologous
heteromerous
heteronomous
heterozygous
hibernaculum
hippocentaur
hippopotamus
homomorphous
hydrophilous
hygrophilous
hypogastrium
hypognathous
hypothalamus
idiothermous
impetiginous
inauspicious
incommodious
incontiguous
infelicitous

inharmonious
innutritious
insalubrious
interspinous
kilowatthour
laticiferous
latitudinous
luminiferous
macropterous
meretricious
misbehaviour
misdemeanour
monadelphous
monomorphous
monopetalous
monostichous
mothertongue
mucilaginous
multifarious
multiflorous
multiloquous
necrophagous
necrophilous
neuropterous
nimbostratus
noctambulous
obstreperous
oncorhynchus
ophiophagous
orchidaceous
orthopterous
orthotropous
ostentatious
overcautious
parsimonious
passepartout
percutaneous
periostracum
pertinacious
philadelphus
photophilous
phytophagous
plecopterous
plesiosaurus
plumbaginous
plumbiferous
polychaetous
polychromous
polymorphous
polypetalous
polysepalous
porcelainous
porcellanous
portmanteaus
portmanteaux
praseodymium
preconscious
preposterous
presumptuous
protactinium
prothalamium
pseudonymous
pseudopodium
pyroligneous
quadriennium
quadrumanous
quinquennium
rambunctious
receptaculum
resiniferous
restaurateur
rhizocarpous
rhizophagous
sacrilegious
salutiferous
saprophagous
sarcophagous
schizogonous
schorlaceous

selfluminous
seminiferous
semiprecious
silicicolous
siliciferous
simultaneous
Sinanthropus
slaughterous
soporiferous
sparkingplug
spermogonium
stanniferous
steatopygous
stelliferous
Stradivarius
subconscious
subcutaneous
succedaneous
sudoriferous
supercilious
supernaculum
superstratum
suppositious
syndactylous
technicolour
teratomatous
testudineous
thundercloud
trachomatous
trichotomous
tridactylous
unchivalrous
unscrupulous
unsuccessful
unthoughtful
vainglorious
wineglassful
xiphisternum
zygomorphous
accelerative
accumulative
adjudicative
alimentative
alliterative
amalgamative
ameliorative
annihilative
anticipative
apperceptive
appreciative
apprehensive
assimilative
augmentative
bassorelievo
bassorilievo
compensative
conciliative
confirmative
conservative
constitutive
constrictive
constructive
consultative
consummative
continuative
contributive
coordinative
decongestive
————————
degenerative
deliberative
denominative
denunciative
desiderative
desquamative
disincentive
dissociative
distributive
exaggerative
excogitative

exhilarative
exploitative
fermentative
gramnegative
grampositive
hypertensive
illuminative
illustrative
imperceptive
imperfective
inconclusive
inexpressive
intellective
interdictive
interpretive
interruptive
intransitive
introversive
introvertive
irreflective
irrespective
irresponsive
manipulative
mezzorelievo
ministrative
nomenclative
noneffective
nonobjective
obliterative
opinionative
performative
perturbative
planoconcave
postpositive
precognitive
preformative
prescriptive
preselective
presentative
preservative
preventative
proscriptive
psychoactive
putrefactive
quantitative
recollective
recuperative
regenerative
remunerative
renunciative
repercussive
reprehensive
reproductive
retrocessive
selfelective
sternutative
stupefactive
substitutive
sustentative
transmissive
unattractive
underachieve
unresponsive
vituperative
dressinggown
brachydactyl
extravaganza
————————
acciaccatura
acetabularia
ailurophobia
balletomania
chromatopsia
coloquintida
encyclopedia
epiphenomena
extravaganza
foraminifera
hesperididia

hyperpyrexia	chorographic	metaphrastic	psychotropic	crossgrained
hypersthenia	chrematistic	metathoracic	pyroelectric	decontrolled
hyperthermia	chronometric	microseismic	quadraphonic	denticulated
hypochondria	cleistogamic	militaristic	quadriplegic	diamondfield
hysteromania	colorimetric	misanthropic	radiographic	disconnected
ichthyocolla	compatriotic	mnemotechnic	relativistic	discontented
kinaesthesia	cosmographic	monodramatic	reprographic	dissatisfied
mastigophora	cosmopolitic	monometallic	reunionistic	doubledecked
mitochondria	decasyllabic	monophyletic	revivalistic	doublelocked
neurasthenia	Deuteronomic	Monophysitic	rhinocerotic	dovecoloured
onomatopoeia	diageotropic	monopolistic	rhizogenetic	draughtboard
osteomalacia	diagrammatic	monostrophic	sansculottic	drawingboard
palingenesia	diphtheritic	monosyllabic	scenographic	dunderheaded
paraesthesia	dissymmetric	monotheistic	schizothymic	eavesdropped
pedicellaria	dodecaphonic	narcissistic	secularistic	entrammelled
phonasthenia	dynamometric	naturalistic	seismometric	escutcheoned
primigravida	ecclesiastic	naturopathic	seismoscopic	fainthearted
prosopopoeia	electrolytic	necrophiliac	semidomestic	feebleminded
Quadragesima	electrotonic	negativistic	sensualistic	feldspathoid
quadriplegia	encephalitic	neurasthenic	specialistic	floodlighted
rejectamenta	encyclopedic	nominalistic	spermaphytic	folliculated
rhynchophora	enthusiastic	nympholeptic	stenographic	fountainhead
sarsaparilla	epigrammatic	nymphomaniac	stereometric	fullyfledged
schizothymia	ethnocentric	octosyllabic	stereophonic	ganglionated
sclerenchyma	ethnographic	oneirocritic	stereoscopic	goodhumoured
Septuagesima	euhemeristic	onomatopoeic	stethoscopic	goodtempered
sesquialtera	evangelistic	organoleptic	stichomythic	greathearted
Shakspereana	exophthalmic	orthogenetic	stroboscopic	halftimbered
Shaksperiana	gametophytic	orthographic	stylographic	hardfavoured
stichomythia	gonadotropic	osteoplastic	subapostolic	hardfeatured
synaesthesia	gyromagnetic	paedogenetic	surrealistic	heavyhearted
telaesthesia	haemophiliac	paedomorphic	synaesthetic	hemispheroid
tintinnabula	haemorrhagic	Palaeolithic	syncretistic	henceforward
toxicophobia	hagiographic	palingenetic	tachygraphic	highcoloured
tradescantia	hectographic	panchromatic	technocratic	highspirited
Wellingtonia	heliocentric	pantographic	telaesthetic	honeybuzzard
xanthochroia	heliographic	paradigmatic	tetramorphic	hoodmanblind
absolutistic	henotheistic	paramagnetic	thaumaturgic	horsewhipped
agamogenetic	herpetologic	paraphrastic	theanthropic	housetrained
alexipharmic	heterocyclic	parisyllabic	thermometric	hucklebacked
alphanumeric	hieroglyphic	paronomastic	thermophilic	impoverished
amphibrachic	hierophantic	pathogenetic	thermoscopic	incorporated
amphictyonic	histogenetic	periphrastic	thermostatic	intercropped
amphisbaenic	homeomorphic	peristeronic	thermotactic	interrelated
anagrammatic	homoeopathic	peristomatic	thermotropic	jetpropelled
analphabetic	hydrochloric	petrographic	transoceanic	laciniated
anaphylactic	hydrodynamic	phagocytotic	transpacific	landingfield
anastigmatic	hydrofluoric	phanerogamic	trichromatic	lanternjawed
anemographic	hydrographic	pharmaceutic	trochanteric	largehearted
antagonistic	hydrokinetic	philharmonic	tropospheric	lighthearted
anthelmintic	hyperplastic	philhellenic	unapologetic	loungelizard
anticyclonic	hyperpyretic	phonographic	undemocratic	machicolated
antimagnetic	hypersthenic	photochromic	undiplomatic	malcontented
antipathetic	hypertrophic	photographic	unscientific	mealymouthed
antiperiodic	hypnogenetic	photokinetic	viscerotonic	misapprehend
antirachitic	hypocoristic	photospheric	absentminded	mourningband
antistrophic	hypothalamic	phyllotactic	accomplished	muddleheaded
apochromatic	iconoclastic	phylogenetic	bachelorhood	multiplicand
apothegmatic	IndoGermanic	physiognomic	backpedalled	multistoried
archipelagic	interoceanic	phytogenetic	battleground	muttonheaded
aristocratic	intervocalic	pictographic	battlemented	narrowminded
autodidactic	intracardiac	planispheric	bellbottomed	newfashioned
bathypelagic	isochromatic	pluviometric	bespectacled	Newfoundland
belletristic	isodiametric	polarimetric	bloodstained	oldfashioned
bibliomaniac	journalistic	polyhistoric	bloodyminded	orthopteroid
bibliophilic	kinaesthetic	polyneuritic	brokenwinded	outstretched
biosynthetic	kleptomaniac	polyphyletic	bulletheaded	outwardbound
bureaucratic	liberalistic	polysyllabic	centrespread	pedunculated
calligraphic	lithographic	polytheistic	checkerboard	pickerelweed
callisthenic	lithospheric	pornographic	chequerboard	pinfeathered
calorimetric	lycanthropic	positivistic	chesterfield	plainclothed
capitalistic	megalomaniac	pragmatistic	clapperboard	plasterboard
carcinogenic	melancholiac	programmatic	clearsighted	playingfield
cartographic	melanochroic	propaedeutic	closecropped	poorspirited
catachrestic	melodramatic	prophylactic	closegrained	precancelled
catastrophic	meristematic	protoplasmic	closemouthed	premeditated
chalcolithic	mesocephalic	protoplastic	complexioned	pretermitted
chauvinistic	mesothoracic	psychometric	counterplead	proportioned
chiropractic	metagalactic	psychopathic	crackbrained	proudhearted

quarterbound	weatherboard	chimneypiece	denuclearise	formaldehyde
rattleheaded	weatherbound	chondriosome	denunciative	frankincense
revictualled	welldisposed	Christianise	depoliticise	frontispiece
rosecoloured	wellfavoured	chromosphere	dermatophyte	galactogogue
runningboard	wellgrounded	chronologise	desiderative	galvanoscope
sabretoothed	whitelivered	cinematheque	desquamative	Germanophile
saddlebacked	wholehearted	circumscribe	destructible	Germanophobe
salamandroid	woodenheaded	circumstance	desulphurise	glaucescence
scraperboard	woollyheaded	clairvoyance	determinable	grammaticise
selfabsorbed	absquatulate	classifiable	detumescence	grammolecule
selfaffected	abstractable	clotheshorse	dibranchiate	gramnegative
selfcoloured	acaulescence	coelenterate	differentiae	grampositive
selfcomposed	accelerative	collectivise	diminishable	granodiorite
selfdeceived	accumulative	commensurate	diphthongise	grossularite
selfdirected	acetaldehyde	communicable	disaccharide	grotesquerie
selfeducated	acquaintance	companionate	disadvantage	happenstance
selfemployed	acquiescence	compensative	disaffiliate	harlequinade
selfinvolved	actinomycete	complaisance	disagreeable	heliogravure
semidetached	adjudicative	compoundable	disallowance	hellgrammite
semifinished	administrate	compressible	disambiguate	hemichordate
sharpsighted	aerosiderite	concelebrate	disassociate	hemimorphite
shortpitched	affectionate	conciliative	discerptible	hemiparasite
shortsighted	agranulocyte	concomitance	discomfiture	hereinbefore
shortsleeved	Alhambresque	concrescence	discomposure	heterozygote
shortstaffed	alimentative	conduplicate	disconsolate	highpressure
shuffleboard	alkalescence	confirmative	discountable	hirepurchase
simpleminded	alliterative	conglomerate	discoverable	horticulture
singlehanded	amalgamative	conglutinate	discoverture	hubblebubble
singleminded	ameliorative	congratulate	discriminate	hybridisable
softpedalled	amphitheatre	conidiophore	disfranchise	hydrolysable
southernwood	anaesthetise	conidiospore	disharmonise	hydromedusae
spermatozoid	anathematise	conscionable	disincentive	hydroquinone
spinsterhood	annihilative	consentience	disintegrate	hypertensive
squarerigged	anticipative	conservative	disobedience	hypnotisable
standardbred	antiparticle	considerable	disorientate	hypochlorite
starspangled	apostrophise	constitutive	displaceable	hyposulphite
stonyhearted	apperceptive	constrictive	disreputable	identifiable
stouthearted	appreciative	constructive	disseverance	illegitimate
straightbred	apprehensive	consultative	dissocialise	illuminative
stranglehold	approachable	consummative	dissociative	illustrative
strongminded	appropriable	containerise	distemperate	immeasurable
subsaturated	appurtenance	contemporise	distrainable	immensurable
subthreshold	arborescence	contemptible	distributive	impenetrable
sulphuretted	architecture	continuative	draughthorse	imperceptive
thickskinned	assimilative	contractable	ectoparasite	imperfective
thickskulled	attitudinise	contractible	editorialise	imperishable
thoroughbred	attributable	contrariwise	electroplate	impermanence
thousandfold	augmentative	contributive	electroscope	impertinence
thundercloud	authenticate	controllable	emotionalise	imponderable
tightmouthed	autocatalyse	coordinative	emulsifiable	improvidence
timehonoured	basidiospore	copolymerise	endoparasite	inaccessible
transshipped	belligerence	correctitude	entomologise	inadmissible
tuberculated	benzaldehyde	counterforce	equestrienne	inadvertence
turriculated	berzelianite	counterpoise	equidistance	inappeasable
turtlenecked	bibliothecae	countrydance	equipollence	inapplicable
unaccustomed	billingsgate	crossexamine	equiprobable	inarticulate
unauthorised	blastfurnace	crosspurpose	espagnolette	incalculable
uncalculated	blastosphere	cultivatable	exaggerative	incalescence
uncelebrated	blatherskite	curvicaudate	exchangeable	incapacitate
unclassified	bletherskate	curvicostate	excogitative	incognisable
unconsidered	boogiewoogie	curvifoliate	exhilarative	incognisance
uncontrolled	borosilicate	customshouse	exploitative	incognitable
underinsured	breaststroke	decaffeinate	exsanguinate	inconclusive
understaffed	brilliantine	decalescence	exsufflicate	inconsolable
undetermined	bronchoscope	decasyllable	exterminable	inconsonance
unencumbered	businesslike	decentralise	extortionate	inconsumable
unfrequented	cabbagewhite	decipherable	extraditable	incontinence
uninterested	calorescence	decomposable	extramundane	incoordinate
unlikelihood	canaliculate	decongestive	extrauterine	incorrigible
unparalleled	capercaillie	deconsecrate	extravagance	indeclinable
unprejudiced	capercailzie	degenerative	falcongentle	indefeasible
unprincipled	carbohydrate	deliberative	fantasticate	indefectible
unpronounced	carriageable	delitescence	fatherfigure	indefensible
unrecognised	centrosphere	demilitarise	fermentative	incoordinate
unrestrained	centuplicate	demimondaine	fertilisable	incorrigible
unsegregated	chalcopyrite	demineralise	fictionalise	indeclinable
unstructured	characterise	demonstrable	fiddlefaddle	indefeasible
varicoloured	charnelhouse	denaturalise	floriculture	indefectible
vermiculated	charterhouse	denominative	fluorescence	indefensible

indehiscence	magnetisable	perturbative	remonstrance	supramundane
independence	magnificence	philanthrope	remunerative	surmountable
indifference	maintainable	philosophise	renegotiable	surveillance
indigestible	manipulative	phlebotomise	renunciative	sustentative
indiscipline	manoeuvrable	phosphoresce	repercussive	sylviculture
indisputable	mansionhouse	photogravure	reprehensive	telegraphese
indissoluble	marketsquare	photomontage	reproachable	terebinthine
indivertible	marlinespike	phreatophyte	reproducible	tergiversate
indoctrinate	marriageable	pisciculture	reproductive	testosterone
ineffaceable	Marseillaise	planoconcave	resipiscence	tetrahedrite
ineradicable	masterstroke	plenipotence	resplendence	thermocouple
inexactitude	matriarchate	pointilliste	restrainable	thermolabile
inexpedience	meetinghouse	polyethylene	reticulocyte	thermosphere
inexperience	merchantable	polysyllable	retrocedence	thermostable
inexplicable	mercurialise	polyurethane	retrocessive	thoroughfare
inexpressive	metalanguage	porcelainise	reviviscence	throughstone
inexpugnable	metallophone	postgraduate	ribonuclease	thunderstone
inextensible	metamorphose	postpositive	rumbletumble	tittletattle
inextricable	microcapsule	precipitable	salamandrine	tradespeople
inhospitable	microclimate	precipitance	saponifiable	tranquillise
inobservance	ministrative	precognitive	sarrusophone	transferable
inoperculate	misadventure	predesignate	schizomycete	transference
insolubilise	miscalculate	predestinate	schizophrene	transfusible
inspectorate	misknowledge	predetermine	scrobiculate	transhumance
insufferable	mispronounce	predominance	sectarianise	translatable
intellective	mistranslate	preexistence	selfapplause	translucence
intelligence	mithridatise	prefabricate	selfelective	transmigrate
intelligible	mitrailleuse	preformative	selfevidence	transmissive
intemperance	monkeypuzzle	preponderate	selfreliance	transmontane
interdictive	monochromate	prerequisite	selfviolence	transmutable
interference	monosyllable	presbyterate	sellingplate	transpirable
intermediate	motherfigure	prescriptive	semiliterate	transpontine
interminable	mothertongue	preselective	semiparasite	transposable
intermixture	mountainside	presentative	shouldernote	transvestite
intermundane	multidentate	preservative	significance	trestletable
interpellate	multifoliate	preventative	silverglance	trichotomise
interpretive	multipartite	proconsulate	silviculture	ultramontane
interruptive	multipliable	professorate	siphonophore	ultramundane
interservice	multiplicate	progesterone	siphonostele	unacceptable
intertexture	multipurpose	programmable	skippingrope	unanswerable
interwreathe	multivalence	propagandise	skunkcabbage	unappeasable
intramundane	multungulate	proscriptive	slipcarriage	unassailable
intransitive	municipalise	prosecutable	somatopleure	unattractive
intrauterine	neuroscience	protectorate	somnambulate	unbelievable
introversive	nicotinamide	protuberance	sophisticate	unchangeable
introvertive	nitrobenzene	psychoactive	soundingline	uncharitable
intumescence	noctilucence	psychologise	speakingtube	uncomeatable
invertebrate	nomenclative	pteridophyte	spectroscope	underachieve
invulnerable	nomenclature	pterodactyle	spermatocyte	undersurface
irredeemable	noneffective	pulverisable	spiritualise	unemployable
irreflective	nonexistence	putrefactive	squirrelcage	unfathomable
irreformable	nonflammable	pyromorphite	Stakhanovite	unfavourable
irrefragable	nonobjective	quantifiable	stationhouse	ungovernable
irremediable	nonresidence	quantitative	steeplechase	unifoliolate
irremissible	oblanceolate	questionable	sternutative	unimaginable
irrepealable	obliterative	quintessence	straightedge	unimportance
irreprovable	obmutescence	radioisotope	straticulate	universalise
irresistible	obsolescence	radionuclide	stratosphere	unmanageable
irresolvable	octosyllable	razzledazzle	stringcourse	unmistakable
irrespective	omnipresence	reappearance	strontianite	unprofitable
irrespirable	opinionative	recalcitrate	stupefactive	unreasonable
irresponsive	oscilloscope	recalescence	subalternate	unregenerate
irreversible	outmanoeuvre	recapitulate	subcommittee	unrepeatable
juvenescence	overestimate	rechargeable	subdivisible	unresponsive
kaleidoscope	overexposure	recognisable	subinfeudate	unsearchable
labyrinthine	overpersuade	recognisance	subjectivise	unseasonable
laisserfaire	overpressure	recollective	subminiature	vanquishable
laissezfaire	oxyacetylene	reconcilable	subservience	venepuncture
landingstage	paletteknife	reconstitute	substantiate	venipuncture
lanternslide	parasiticide	reconveyance	substitutive	verticillate
laryngoscope	parenthesise	recuperative	substructure	viridescence
ledgertackle	parochialise	redintegrate	subtemperate	vituperative
legitimatise	patriarchate	redistribute	sulphonamide	walkietalkie
liverystable	pearlescence	regenerative	superannuate	wallydraigle
lodginghouse	pennywhistle	rehabilitate	supererogate	weatherhouse
longdistance	peradventure	reinvigorate	supermundane	whigmaleerie
luminescence	performative	rememberable	superposable	winterbourne
mademoiselle	permanganate	remilitarise	supersedence	wollastonite
magistrature	perseverance	reminiscence	suppressible	YankeeDoodle

burglarproof	lakedwelling	wallpainting	antithetical	hagiological
counterproof	leapfrogging	whitewashing	apparitional	heroicomical
handkerchief	longstanding	blabbermouth	appositional	heterocercal
quarterstaff	metalworking	breakthrough	aquicultural	heterosexual
shatterproof	microcopying	buccaneerish	archetypical	hierarchical
weatherproof	mosstrooping	butterscotch	arithmetical	histological
backbreaking	mourningring	commonwealth	arrhythmical	hydrological
backslapping	namedropping	countermarch	astrological	hydrothermal
beachcombing	neighbouring	dilettantish	astronomical	hyperbolical
bellylanding	nerveracking	disestablish	asymmetrical	hypocritical
billsticking	noncomplying	elasmobranch	bactericidal	hypostatical
birdsnesting	nonflowering	enantiomorph	barometrical	hypothetical
birdwatching	orienteering	frenchpolish	bicentennial	immethodical
blackbirding	outrivalling	hairsbreadth	biographical	impedimental
blockbusting	outstripping	handsbreadth	bombdisposal	imperatorial
bloodletting	overcropping	Ishmaelitish	brachydactyl	inartificial
bluestocking	overpowering	leathercloth	cartological	infanticidal
bodybuilding	overstepping	magnetograph	catechetical	inflectional
bodystocking	parallelling	masterswitch	chorological	insecticidal
booklearning	peasepudding	meteorograph	coenobitical	inspectorial
brainwashing	pettifogging	misselthrush	coenobytical	instrumental
brassrubbing	photosetting	monkeywrench	coincidental	integumental
breathtaking	placesetting	oscillograph	commissarial	intellectual
buccaneering	plaindealing	phraseograph	complemental	interdigital
bullfighting	pricecutting	Plattdeutsch	complexional	interfemoral
carburetting	privateering	preestablish	conceptional	interglacial
cardcarrying	prizewinning	scabbardfish	conferential	internuncial
caterwauling	profiteering	scorpionfish	confessional	interstitial
cheeseparing	proofreading	scouringrush	confidential	intracranial
childbearing	racketeering	selfreproach	conjunctival	involutional
cliffhanging	ricochetting	sergeantfish	connectional	judgematical
cockfighting	safecracking	snaggletooth	consistorial	limnological
conveyancing	sandyachting	spectrograph	contrapuntal	linguistical
crashlanding	scareheading	sphygmograph	convectional	lithological
crossbedding	secondstring	steganograph	conventional	longitudinal
crossheading	selfcatering	stellenbosch	correctional	majorgeneral
disannulling	selfdoubting	swimmingbath	cosmogonical	mangelwurzel
discouraging	selfeffacing	sycophantish	cosmological	manometrical
doubleacting	selflimiting	thirdborough	courtmartial	mathematical
earsplitting	selfpleasing	toggleswitch	cuckingstool	metaphorical
earthshaking	selfrighting	wherethrough	curvirostral	metaphysical
echosounding	selfstarting	apparatchiki	dentilingual	metathetical
enginetuning	shadowboxing	caravansarai	departmental	metrological
enterprising	shipbuilding	caravanserai	derivational	microcrystal
entertaining	sideslipping	divertimenti	diamonddrill	monomaniacal
excruciating	sidestepping	plectognathi	differential	motivational
faithhealing	sightreading	streptococci	digressional	multicentral
farmsteading	singleacting	bladderwrack	discretional	multilateral
faultfinding	slaveholding	bookingclerk	disregardful	multilingual
firefighting	sleepwalking	countercheck	distortional	mythological
freestanding	smallholding	crossbuttock	dodecahedral	navigational
freeswimming	sparkingplug	Czechoslovak	dorsiventral	necrological
freethinking	speedboating	electroshock	duckingstool	neoclassical
freewheeling	stillhunting	gobbledegook	emblematical	neurological
fricasseeing	stockbroking	gobbledygook	endoskeletal	noncommittal
glassblowing	stockjobbing	horrorstruck	epexegetical	nonessential
gravelelling	stockraising	kinnikinnick	epicycloidal	nonidentical
guaranteeing	stoneboiling	planetstruck	ethnological	nychthemeral
habitforming	stonecutting	plummerblock	etymological	occupational
hairdressing	thanksgiving	rollingstock	exospherical	oligarchical
handicapping	theatregoing	swaggerstick	expediential	oppositional
hardstanding	transferring	swizzlestick	experiential	orographical
heartburning	transmitting	terrorstruck	experimental	osteological
heartrending	typefounding	toastingfork	expressional	overcritical
heartwarming	unappetising	wonderstruck	extracranial	paraboloidal
hedgehopping	unconvincing	absorptional	extralimital	paradisaical
highfaluting	underbidding	accusatorial	extramarital	paradisiacal
highlystrung	undercoating	aeronautical	extraspecial	parametrical
highsounding	undercutting	aetiological	falcongentil	paratactical
highstepping	underletting	agentgeneral	foresightful	pathological
horsetrading	undermanning	agricultural	geanticlinal	pestilential
housekeeping	underpinning	alphabetical	genealogical	pestological
housewarming	underrunning	alphamerical	geographical	petrological
ingratiating	undersetting	amygdaloidal	geopolitical	phenological
interbedding	unflattering	anteprandial	geosynclinal	phenotypical
intercutting	unhesitating	anthropoidal	gladiatorial	philological
intermitting	unpretending	anticlerical	glockenspiel	phonological
intromitting	wainscotting	antimalarial	governmental	phycological
laboursaving	waistcoating	antimalarial	grallatorial	phytological

planetesimal	triglyphical	metachronism	adjudication	consignation
pluriliteral	triphthongal	metamorphism	adulteration	consociation
postdoctoral	tropological	metasomatism	aesthetician	conspiration
postprandial	trumpetshell	mithridatism	AfroAmerican	constipation
precedential	tyrannicidal	necrophilism	agglutinogen	constitution
preceptorial	uncommercial	negrophilism	aircondition	constriction
precessional	uneconomical	neoDarwinism	aircraftsman	construction
preclassical	unhistorical	Neohellenism	alimentation	consultation
prefectorial	unscriptural	neonomianism	alliteration	consummation
preferential	unsuccessful	Neoplatonism	amalgamation	contestation
premenstrual	unthoughtful	Nestorianism	amelioration	continuation
presbyterial	vicargeneral	noctambulism	amortisation	contribution
presidential	visitational	nyctitropism	annihilation	conversation
primogenital	visitatorial	obscurantism	annunciation	coordination
procathedral	volumetrical	orthotropism	antediluvian	cosmopolitan
processional	whippoorwill	paedobaptism	anticipation	councilwoman
professional	wineglassful	Palladianism	apperception	countrywoman
professorial	abolitionism	panhellenism	appreciation	cousingerman
projectional	aeroembolism	paramorphism	apprehension	crenellation
proportional	aestheticism	parkinsonism	arborisation	crosssection
prosectorial	allomorphism	parochialism	archdiocesan	deactivation
prototypical	antiSemitism	periostracum	Aristotelean	debilitation
providential	apostolicism	philistinism	Aristotelian	decapitation
psychosexual	asynchronism	phototropism	articulation	deceleration
pumpernickel	automorphism	pleiotropism	artilleryman	decongestion
punchingball	avantgardism	pleomorphism	assibilation	deescalation
pyromaniacal	behaviourism	poikilotherm	assimilation	deflagration
quadrinomial	bilateralism	polyglottism	augmentation	defraudation
quaquaversal	bilingualism	polymorphism	auscultation	degeneration
quarterfinal	campodeiform	praseodymium	Australasian	deionisation
quinquennial	Cartesianism	precisianism	bacchanalian	delamination
radiological	charlatanism	propagandism	backwoodsman	deliberation
recreational	chromaticism	protactinium	biometrician	delicatessen
reflectional	chromatogram	prothalamium	blastulation	delimitation
repetitional	classicalism	pseudopodium	buttermuslin	demodulation
responsorial	collectivism	psychologism	Byelorussian	denaturation
revelational	collegialism	pteridosperm	cachinnation	denomination
rhinological	commensalism	quadriennium	calumniation	denunciation
rhombohedral	Confucianism	quinquennium	canalisation	depopulation
saccharoidal	conservatism	receptaculum	cancellation	depreciation
salutational	counterclaim	reductionism	canonisation	deputisation
scatological	cuprammonium	rontgenogram	Cantabrigian	deracination
schismatical	deviationism	salvationism	cantharidian	desalination
selfapproval	diamagnetism	Samaritanism	cantillation	desideration
selfbetrayal	diastrophism	scoundreldom	capitulation	despoliation
selfcritical	dichromatism	scoundrelism	Carlovingian	desquamation
semiofficial	dilettantism	secessionism	carragheenin	dessertspoon
semiological	diverticulum	sectarianism	catamountain	detoxication
semitropical	duraluminium	sectionalism	catilinarian	dialectician
septilateral	elementalism	serpentiform	chlorination	dilapidation
Septuagintal	emotionalism	shamateurism	churchwarden	disaffection
sericultural	epicureanism	somnambulism	circumcision	disclamation
servocontrol	epithalamium	somniloquism	circumfusion	disconnexion
sinistrorsal	eunuchoidism	spermogonium	civilisation	disinfection
sleepingpill	evolutionism	spiritualism	claudication	disinflation
sociological	exclusionism	Stakhanovism	coacervation	dispensation
spermathecal	expansionism	stalactiform	codification	disquisition
squirreltail	factionalism	standingroom	cohabitation	dissertation
stilboestrol	fantasticism	strychninism	colonisation	dissociation
studdingsail	flabelliform	subjectivism	columniation	distillation
subcelestial	geomagnetism	supernaculum	commendation	distribution
subeditorial	heliotropism	superstratum	commentation	divarication
substantival	hemimorphism	syndactylism	committeeman	dodecahedron
successional	hibernaculum	thunderstorm	compellation	dressinggown
supernatural	homomorphism	traducianism	compensation	echolocation
supplemental	homothallism	transformism	complication	edulcoration
supraorbital	hydatidiform	transvestism	compurgation	effectuation
swimmingbell	hydrotropism	trinomialism	conciliation	elucubration
swimmingpool	hypogastrium	troglodytism	condemnation	emancipation
synchronical	incendiarism	unitarianism	condensation	emargination
systematical	inflationism	universalism	confirmation	emasculation
tautological	intuitionism	Victorianism	confiscation	encrustation
teleological	isolationism	voluntaryism	conformation	Englishwoman
televisional	Keynesianism	xiphisternum	conglobation	episcopalian
tetrachordal	Manicheanism	zygomorphism	congregation	epithalamion
theocratical	Marcionitism	abbreviation	conscription	equalisation
theosophical	mediaevalism	acceleration	consecration	equalitarian
tragicomical	mercantilism	accentuation	consecration	equivocation
transitional	mercurialism	accumulation	conservation	erythromycin

etherisation	inoccupation	obnubilation	resurrection	vaporisation
etymologicon	inosculation	obstetrician	reticulation	vasodilation
EuroAmerican	insemination	octogenarian	retractation	vaticination
evisceration	inspissation	optimisation	retrocession	verification
exacerbation	installation	organisation	retroflexion	vertebration
exaggeration	instauration	ossification	retropulsion	vesiculation
exasperation	instillation	overexertion	retroversion	veterinarian
excogitation	insufflation	overreaction	rhododendron	vicechairman
excruciation	insurrection	pacification	rhombohedron	vilification
exenteration	intellection	panification	romanisation	vinification
exercitation	inteneration	pantechnicon	ruralisation	vitalisation
exhilaration	interception	paralysation	salamandrian	vitiligation
expatriation	intercession	penalisation	satisfaction	vitrifaction
explantation	interdiction	perfoliation	Scandinavian	vituperation
exploitation	interjection	perispomenon	scatterbrain	vivification
exprobration	intermission	pernoctation	scutellation	vocabularian
extraversion	interruption	peroxidation	segmentation	vocalisation
extroversion	intersection	perpetration	selfbegotten	vociferation
exulceration	intervention	perpetuation	selfdelusion	vomiturition
facilitation	intimidation	perspiration	selfdevotion	warehouseman
featherbrain	intoxication	perturbation	selfignition	antineutrino
felicitation	introduction	petrifaction	servicewoman	banderillero
feminisation	introjection	philodendron	sexagenarian	bassorelievo
fenestration	intromission	photofission	shootingiron	bassorilievo
fermentation	introversion	pigmentation	snarlingiron	clavicembalo
fibrillation	invagination	pilotballoon	sodafountain	divertimento
fibrinolysin	invalidation	polarisation	solarisation	mezzorelievo
finalisation	invigilation	postdiluvian	solicitation	mezzosoprano
flagellation	invigoration	postmeridian	solifluction	quattrocento
flavoprotein	irresolution	postposition	southeastern	risorgimento
flocculation	jurisdiction	prechristian	southwestern	twentyfourmo
fluidisation	kindergarten	precognition	spermatozoon	attorneyship
fluoridation	labyrinthian	precondition	spiegeleisen	bachelorship
fluorination	lachrymation	predigestion	spokesperson	brinkmanship
fluorocarbon	laterisation	predilection	staffsurgeon	cardinalship
focalisation	latinisation	preformation	stationwagon	chairmanship
footplateman	legalisation	prehistorian	statistician	championship
FrancoGerman	legitimation	prelapsarian	stepchildren	chaplainship
frontiersman	lepidopteran	Presbyterian	stereopticon	counterscarp
futilitarian	levorotation	prescription	sternutation	dictatorship
gasification	liquefaction	preselection	streptomycin	directorship
genuflection	Liverpudlian	presentation	stridulation	discipleship
geometrician	localisation	preservation	strobilation	executorship
geriatrician	longshoreman	priestridden	strophanthin	gamesmanship
glycoprotein	LowChurchman	proboscidean	stupefaction	governorship
gonadotropin	malformation	proboscidian	subarrhation	guardianship
griseofulvin	malnutrition	proclamation	suberisation	horsemanship
habilitation	malversation	prolegomenon	sublapsarian	landingstrip
haematoxylon	manipulation	prolongation	subscription	laureateship
hallucinogen	marketgarden	promulgation	substitution	marksmanship
halogenation	maximisation	propitiation	substruction	mistressship
halterbroken	menstruation	proscription	subterranean	musicianship
homologation	metropolitan	prostitution	sulphonation	oneupmanship
humanisation	minimisation	protestation	sulphuration	overlordship
humanitarian	ministration	prothalamion	supersession	partisanship
humification	misdirection	purification	superstition	prenticeship
hydromedusan	miseducation	putrefaction	supervention	quaestorship
hymenopteran	misquotation	quantisation	supplication	receivership
hypertension	mobilisation	racemisation	sustentation	relationship
hypophrygian	modification	ramification	tessellation	residentship
idealisation	monetisation	ratification	theoretician	salesmanship
illumination	moralisation	reactivation	torrefaction	sergeantship
illustration	motorisation	reallocation	Torricellian	serjeantship
immoderation	nanoplankton	recollection	totalisation	servitorship
immunisation	nebulisation	reconversion	totalitarian	surveyorship
imperfection	neoDarwinian	recuperation	transduction	survivorship
implantation	neurosurgeon	redecoration	transmission	taberdarship
impregnation	newspaperman	regeneration	transudation	underdevelop
inactivation	nidification	registration	trephination	virtuosoship
inauguration	nonagenarian	rejuvenation	trifurcation	viscountship
incatenation	noneuclidean	remuneration	tripartition	watermanship
incineration	noradrenalin	renunciation	triplication	accommodator
incorruption	northeastern	reoccupation	turbellarian	antimacassar
incrustation	Northumbrian	repatriation	typification	appendicular
indiscretion	northwestern	repercussion	ubiquitarian	appropriator
IndoEuropean	notification	repossession	underwritten	assassinator
inescutcheon	novelisation	reprehension	unionisation	balladmonger
inflammation	nychthemeron	reproduction	urbanisation	bloodbrother
inhabitation	obliteration	resupination	valorisation	bobbydazzler

bodysnatcher	flamethrower	overachiever	streetwalker	backwardness
bonnyclabber	fostermother	participator	strengthener	baselessness
bottlewasher	foundationer	pasqueflower	supercharger	beggarliness
boulevardier	fractionator	patternmaker	supplementer	benefactress
brainstormer	freightliner	pennypincher	surrejoinder	bilharziasis
brassbounder	frontbencher	perambulator	swashbuckler	bilharziosis
breastsummer	galvanometer	peregrinator	synchroniser	biosynthesis
breathalyser	gesticulator	petrographer	systematiser	blamableness
breechloader	globetrotter	phonographer	tabernacular	blamefulness
brickfielder	guestchamber	photographer	tachygrapher	blissfulness
broncobuster	hagiographer	phrasemonger	taperecorder	boastfulness
cabinetmaker	hairsplitter	phytographer	taxcollector	bootlessness
calligrapher	harquebusier	pitterpatter	technicolour	bowcompasses
campfollower	headshrinker	policyholder	teetertotter	brackishness
candleholder	heliographer	pontificator	thereinafter	brontosaurus
carillonneur	hierographer	pornographer	threequarter	buffalograss
carpetbagger	hippocentaur	practitioner	threewheeler	burningglass
cartographer	holidaymaker	pralltriller	trainspotter	calisthenics
cattlelifter	horsebreaker	precipitator	transgressor	calycoideous
cheeseburger	housebreaker	premeditator	transplanter	camiknickers
cheesecutter	huggermugger	prevaricator	troublemaker	canorousness
cheesemonger	hydrographer	primogenitor	vauntcourier	cantankerous
chiropractor	hymnographer	prizefighter	viscosimeter	captiousness
coachbuilder	hypothecator	proselytiser	whencesoever	carbonaceous
coldshoulder	iconographer	psychrometer	wicketkeeper	carelessness
collaborator	impersonator	quadrangular	winklepicker	cataphoresis
commemorator	impropriator	rabblerouser	wonderworker	cautiousness
commiserator	improvisator	radiographer	woodengraver	cementitious
commissioner	inclinometer	ratiocinator	woolgatherer	cheerfulness
communicator	incorporator	reciprocator	wunderkinder	chieftainess
concentrator	infundibular	redemptioner	yellowhammer	childishness
confabulator	interchanger	refrigerator	abortiveness	chitterlings
confectioner	interlobular	remembrancer	abrasiveness	churlishness
conningtower	interlocutor	remonstrator	absoluteness	cirrocumulus
conquistador	intermeddler	restaurateur	abstractness	cirrostratus
consolidator	internuclear	resuscitator	abstruseness	clannishness
contemplator	interoceptor	reverberator	accurateness	clothespress
contradictor	interpleader	salmonladder	accursedness	clownishness
conventicler	interpolator	scarificator	achlamydeous	cocksureness
corroborator	interrogator	scenepainter	adaptiveness	coerciveness
cosmographer	interstellar	sceneshifter	adequateness	cohesiveness
costermonger	investigator	schoolleaver	adhesiveness	coleopterous
countenancer	jerrybuilder	schoolmaster	adorableness	collywobbles
countertenor	katzenjammer	scintillator	adscititious	combinations
courtplaster	kilowatthour	screenwriter	advantageous	completeness
craftbrother	kirschwasser	scrimshanker	adventitious	composedness
crossbencher	klipspringer	scriptwriter	aerodynamics	compunctious
crossingover	laissezaller	sedgewarbler	aeroneurosis	conchiferous
crystalgazer	lithographer	selfdeceiver	affectedness	concreteness
cuckooflower	magnetometer	selfmurderer	agamogenesis	confusedness
declinometer	manslaughter	semicircular	agribusiness	contemptuous
decompressor	manufacturer	semicylinder	allusiveness	conterminous
demonstrator	marshharrier	semidiameter	altitudinous	contrariness
densitometer	mastersinger	sensitometer	ambassadress	contriteness
discographer	micrographer	sequestrator	ambidextrous	contumacious
disenchanter	milliammeter	sharecropper	amenableness	contumelious
dispossessor	minedetector	sharpshooter	amentiferous	cotyledonous
disseminator	minicomputer	sheepshearer	amicableness	covetousness
dissimulator	misbehaviour	shirtwaister	amphitropous	cowardliness
diverticular	misdemeanour	shortchanger	anaerobiosis	creativeness
domesticator	moneychanger	singledecker	anamorphosis	criticalness
doubledealer	moneygrubber	singleseater	anemophilous	cryptogamous
doublelocker	moneyspinner	skateboarder	angiocarpous	cumbrousness
drawingpaper	monkeyflower	skrimshanker	anotherguess	cumulocirrus
eavesdropper	morrisdancer	sledgehammer	antigropelos	cumulonimbus
electrometer	mouthbreeder	snakecharmer	apparatchiks	curlingirons
electrotyper	multinuclear	snapfastener	apparentness	curlingtongs
encumbrancer	muzzleloader	specktioneer	appendicitis	cynocephalus
enginedriver	mythographer	spectrometer	appositeness	cytogenetics
entrepreneur	mythologiser	staffofficer	argillaceous	debonairness
equilibrator	necrographer	stagemanager	aromaticness	decisiveness
ethnographer	nephelometer	stenographer	astronautics	decorousness
exhibitioner	nonconductor	stepdaughter	astrophysics	dejectedness
experimenter	nonconformer	stereoisomer	asynchronous	definiteness
extensometer	officeholder	sternwheeler	atheromatous	dejectedness
exterminator	orchestrator	stockbreeder	atmospherics	delusiveness
extinguisher	organgrinder	stonedresser	autochthones	depravedness
filibusterer	orthographer	stormtrooper	avitaminoses	derisiveness
firstnighter	outpensioner	straightener	avitaminosis	desirousness

desolateness	glaucomatous	laticiferous	orthopterous	quadrumanous
detachedness	gloriousness	latitudinous	orthotropous	qualmishness
dextrousness	glycogenesis	laudableness	ostentatious	questionless
diatomaceous	goosepimples	leucocytosis	osteogenesis	radiophonics
dilatoriness	gorgeousness	leukocytosis	osteoporosis	rambunctious
discourteous	gracefulness	lifelessness	outdatedness	ravenousness
discreetness	graciousness	listlessness	overcautious	reactiveness
discreteness	graminaceous	literariness	overemphasis	readableness
disembarrass	graspingness	lonesomeness	overniceness	recklessness
disingenuous	gratefulness	lopsidedness	paedogenesis	refreshments
disputatious	graveclothes	lovelessness	painlessness	relativeness
distinctness	greenishness	lovelornness	palingenesis	reliableness
divisiveness	grievousness	lukewarmness	pancreatitis	reproachless
dolorousness	gruesomeness	luminiferous	parsimonious	reservedness
doubtfulness	guilefulness	luminousness	pathogenesis	resignedness
downwardness	habitualness	lusciousness	patulousness	resiniferous
dreadfulness	haematolysis	macropterous	peacefulness	resoluteness
droughtiness	haemopoiesis	maidenliness	peccadilloes	resolvedness
dwarfishness	hallucinosis	maidenstakes	peerlessness	restlessness
echinococcus	handsomeness	malapertness	pellucidness	retiringness
econometrics	harmlessness	manifoldness	percutaneous	rhizocarpous
effusiveness	headmistress	mannerliness	pericarditis	rhizophagous
electrolysis	headquarters	mercifulness	perilousness	rigorousness
electrotonus	heartstrings	meretricious	periodontics	rootlessness
encephalitis	heavenliness	messeigneurs	pertinacious	ruthlessness
endocarditis	hebetudinous	metapsychics	perverseness	sacrilegious
endometritis	heedlessness	microphysics	perviousness	salpiglossis
enormousness	heliolatrous	mindlessness	phagocytosis	salutariness
enviableness	helplessness	mirthfulness	philadelphus	salutiferous
eruptiveness	hemerocallis	mistakenness	photokinesis	sanguineness
erythematous	hermeneutics	moderateness	photophilous	saprophagous
eveningdress	heroicalness	moistureless	phycomycetes	sarcomatosis
exiguousness	heteroecious	monadelphous	phylogenesis	sarcophagous
exophthalmos	heterogamous	monomorphous	phytogenesis	scabrousness
exophthalmus	heterogenous	monopetalous	phytophagous	schizogonous
explicitness	heterologous	monostichous	pitiableness	schorlaceous
exsanguinous	heteromerous	morningdress	pitilessness	scornfulness
fabulousness	heteronomous	morphallaxis	plainclothes	scratchiness
facelessness	heterozygous	motherliness	pleasantness	sedulousness
factiousness	hindquarters	mournfulness	pleasingness	selfanalysis
faintishness	hippopotamus	moveableness	pleasureless	selfhypnosis
faithfulness	histogenesis	movelessness	plecopterous	selflessness
fancifulness	homesickness	mucilaginous	plesiosaurus	selfluminous
fatherliness	homoeostasis	multifarious	plumbaginous	selfsameness
fearlessness	homomorphous	multiflorous	plumbiferous	semidarkness
fearsomeness	hopelessness	multiloquous	polychaetous	seminiferous
featheriness	horribleness	mutinousness	polychromous	semiprecious
fecklessness	humorousness	nailscissors	polymorphous	sensibleness
feminineness	hydrophilous	namelessness	polyneuritis	sensuousness
ferrugineous	hydrostatics	nauseousness	polypetalous	separateness
feverishness	hygrophilous	nebulousness	polysepalous	shamefulness
fiddlesticks	hypnogenesis	necrophagous	populousness	sheepishness
fieldglasses	hypognathous	necrophilous	porcelainous	shrewishness
fiendishness	hypothalamus	needlessness	porcellanous	sidewhiskers
forcefulness	idiothermous	negativeness	portmanteaus	silicicolous
forcibleness	illusiveness	negotiatress	positiveness	siliciferous
formlessness	illusoriness	nephanalysis	postmistress	simultaneous
freakishness	immatureness	neuropterous	preciousness	Sinanthropus
frequentness	impetiginous	nevertheless	preconscious	skittishness
frictionless	implicitness	nightclothes	preparedness	slaughterous
friendliness	impoliteness	nimbostratus	preposterous	slipperiness
fructiferous	inauspicious	noctambulous	presumptuous	slothfulness
fructivorous	incisiveness	numerousness	previousness	slovenliness
fruitfulness	incommodious	obdurateness	pridefulness	sluggishness
fugitiveness	incontiguous	obligingness	priestliness	sluttishness
functionless	indebtedness	obsoleteness	priggishness	smallclothes
furfuraceous	indirectness	offscourings	princeliness	snappishness
furunculosis	inexpertness	obstreperous	professoress	snobbishness
galligaskins	infelicitous	oncorhynchus	profoundness	sociableness
gallinaceous	infiniteness	onesidedness	progenitress	solitariness
gamesomeness	inharmonious	ophiophagous	proglottides	sonorousness
gamopetalous	innutritious	opisthotonos	prolificness	soporiferous
gamophyllous	insalubrious	oppositeness	proprietress	soullessness
gamosepalous	instructress	orchidaceous	pseudocyesis	spaciousness
gastropodous	interspinous	ordinariness	pseudonymous	sparrowgrass
generousness	irregardless	orthodontics	purblindness	specificness
geotectonics	karyokinesis	orthogenesis	pursestrings	speciousness
ghoulishness	kinaesthesis	orthopaedics	pyroligneous	speciousness
gladsomeness	knightliness	orthopaedics	pyrotechnics	sphragistics

spiritedness	unlawfulness	carpetknight	endamagement	mineralogist
spitefulness	unlikeliness	chastisement	endangerment	misalignment
splendidness	unloveliness	chronologist	enfeeblement	miscellanist
sporogenesis	unscrupulous	circumfluent	enshrinement	misdemeanant
sportfulness	unsteadiness	circumjacent	enswathement	misinterpret
sportiveness	untimeliness	clairaudient	entanglement	misjudgement
spotlessness	untowardness	clarinettist	enthronement	misplacement
spuriousness	unwieldiness	classicalist	entomologist	misrepresent
stalwartness	unwontedness	clinkerbuilt	entrancement	misstatement
stanniferous	unworldiness	coalitionist	entrenchment	mistreatment
stealthiness	unworthiness	coleopterist	envisagement	monkeyjacket
steatopygous	usuriousness	collectivist	enzymologist	monofilament
stelliferous	uxoriousness	commencement	erythroblast	monographist
sterlingness	vainglorious	commensalist	escapologist	morphologist
stockingless	Valenciennes	commissariat	estrangement	motorcyclist
Stradivarius	valuableness	concelebrant	evolutionist	musicologist
straightness	vaporousness	conchologist	exclusionist	negrophilist
strengthless	variableness	concupiscent	excursionist	neoDarwinist
strikingness	vengefulness	congratulant	expansionist	Neoplatonist
strongylosis	venomousness	constringent	forebodement	nephrologist
stubbornness	verticalness	contagionist	forestalment	noctambulant
studiousness	vigorousness	contrivement	futurologist	noctambulist
subconscious	virtuousness	convalescent	gastronomist	nonalignment
subcutaneous	vitreousness	convincement	geophysicist	noncombatant
succedaneous	voidableness	corespondent	gesellschaft	nonefficient
succinctness	volatileness	counteragent	glaciologist	nonresistant
sudoriferous	wastefulness	counterblast	glossologist	northernmost
suitableness	watchfulness	counterlight	graphologist	numerologist
supercilious	weatherglass	counterpoint	gymnosophist	nutritionist
suppositious	whitherwards	countershaft	haematoblast	obscurantist
surroundings	womanishness	craniologist	heortologist	oceanologist
swainishness	wondrousness	crosscurrent	hereditament	odontologist
sweepingness	workableness	cryptanalyst	homeopathist	orthodontist
sweetishness	workingclass	cryptologist	illtreatment	orthopaedist
synarthrosis	wrathfulness	decipherment	immunologist	orthopterist
syndactylous	wretchedness	decongestant	impercipient	overabundant
tactlessness	wrongfulness	deflationist	imprisonment	palynologist
tamelessness	youngberries	deliquescent	incandescent	papyrologist
tangibleness	youthfulness	denouncement	inconsequent	paragraphist
taskmistress	zygapophysis	deontologist	inconsistent	partitionist
tastefulness	zygomorphous	dethronement	inconvenient	passepartout
tearlessness	abolitionist	deviationist	inflationist	passionfruit
teratomatous	accompanyist	diminishment	infringement	periodontist
terribleness	accordionist	dinnerjacket	insufficient	phillumenist
testudineous	accouchement	disagreement	interconnect	phlebotomist
thankfulness	accoutrement	disannulment	intercurrent	phrenologist
therapeutics	administrant	disbursement	intermittent	physiologist
thievishness	admonishment	discriminant	intervenient	pigeonbreast
thitherwards	aforethought	disendowment	intransigent	pitcherplant
thoroughbass	afterthought	disgorgement	intrenchment	postponement
thoroughness	anaesthetist	disguisement	intromittent	precisionist
ticklishness	anecdotalist	dishevelment	intrusionist	preponderant
timelessness	announcement	disinfectant	intuitionist	presentiment
timorousness	antiaircraft	disinterment	intussuscept	privatdocent
tirelessness	apiculturist	dislodgement	inveiglement	privatdozent
tiresomeness	appraisement	displacement	isolationist	propagandist
togetherness	astonishment	disseverment	jurisconsult	psephologist
toilsomeness	automobilist	distrainment	jurisprudent	psychiatrist
tonelessness	avantgardist	diversionist	kissingcrust	psychologist
toploftiness	bacteriostat	dramaturgist	knighterrant	publicspirit
tortuousness	ballottement	editorialist	landingcraft	purposebuilt
touchingness	bantamweight	educationist	languishment	pyrotechnist
towardliness	bedazzlement	effervescent	lexicologist	quadrivalent
trachomatous	behaviourist	efflorescent	licketysplit	radioelement
trichotomous	belittlement	Egyptologist	liquefacient	rapprochment
trickishness	bequeathment	electronvolt	lithotritist	readjustment
tridactylous	bewilderment	elocutionist	lumberjacket	reassessment
trophallaxis	bibliologist	embattlement	magniloquent	reassignment
trustfulness	bibliopegist	embezzlement	malacologist	recalcitrant
truthfulness	bibliopolist	embitterment	maltreatment	receptionist
tuberculosis	bioecologist	emblazonment	mediaevalist	recommitment
tunelessness	biophysicist	embranchment	meltingpoint	recrudescent
unbrokenness	bioscientist	embryologist	mercantilist	Redemptorist
unchivalrous	birefringent	emotionalist	merrythought	redeployment
uncommonness	blackcurrant	empoisonment	metallurgist	reductionist
unctuousness	blandishment	empressement	microanalyst	reinvestment
underclothes	butterflynut	encirclement	microcircuit	renouncement
ungainliness	cardiologist	encroachment	microscopist	resettlement
unkindliness	caricaturist	encumberment	middleweight	retrenchment

salvationist	adjectivally	capriciously	contemptibly	distillatory
sanguinolent	adjudicatory	cardiography	contextually	distractedly
secessionist	adulterously	cashandcarry	contiguously	distributary
seclusionist	advisability	catholically	contingently	disturbingly
seismologist	aggressively	censoriously	continuously	diversionary
selenologist	alterability	centesimally	contractedly	divisibility
selfcontempt	amateurishly	ceremonially	contributory	dogmatically
selfdestruct	ambivalently	chancemedley	conveniently	domestically
selfdistrust	amitotically	charterparty	convincingly	dramatically
selfexistent	amphibiously	checkerberry	conviviality	dubitatively
selfinterest	anagogically	cheirography	convulsively	dynastically
selfportrait	analogically	chemotherapy	coordinately	eccentricity
semibasement	analytically	cherubically	copulatively	ecclesiology
semideponent	anatomically	chivalrously	coquettishly	eclectically
semifinalist	antecedently	choreography	corelatively	ecologically
servicecourt	anthropogeny	chrestomathy	corporeality	economically
shortcircuit	anthropology	Christianity	correctively	ecstatically
shoulderbelt	anticipatory	Christolatry	cosmetically	effectuality
shoulderknot	antigenicity	Christophany	cottonocracy	effeminately
sociometrist	antiphonally	chromaticity	cotyledonary	effortlessly
somnambulant	aperiodicity	chromatology	courageously	electrically
somnambulist	apolitically	chronography	creepycrawly	eleemosynary
somniloquist	apostolicity	churchianity	crosscountry	elementarily
sorbefacient	appendectomy	circuitously	cryptography	elliptically
southernmost	appetisingly	clangorously	cumbersomely	elocutionary
speleologist	appraisingly	classicality	cumulatively	emasculatory
spiritualist	appreciatory	clatteringly	curmudgeonly	emotionality
stablishment	archdeaconry	coetaneously	deambulatory	emphatically
straitjacket	archetypally	coincidently	decoratively	enchantingly
stupefacient	aromatically	collaterally	decreasingly	enclitically
subcontinent	articulately	collectively	definitively	endermically
subjectivist	articulatory	collectivity	deflationary	entreatingly
supereminent	artificially	collegiality	degenerately	ephemerality
supervenient	artistically	collegiately	deliberately	epidemically
technologist	assimilatory	collinearity	delightfully	epidemiology
telegraphist	astoundingly	colloquially	delinquently	episodically
teratologist	astringently	colourlessly	demoniacally	epistemology
therapeutist	athletically	comfortingly	demonstrably	equationally
toxicologist	attractively	commandingly	denunciatory	equipollency
traditionist	auscultatory	commendatory	depreciatory	equitability
traducianist	auspiciously	commercially	depressingly	equivalently
trampolinist	authenticity	commodiously	derivatively	equivocatory
transcendent	autoimmunity	communicably	derogatorily	esoterically
transformist	automaticity	companionway	desirability	essentiality
transhipment	autonomously	compensatory	despairingly	euphonically
transmigrant	availability	complacently	despitefully	euphoniously
trichologist	avariciously	compulsively	despondently	evanescently
unambivalent	bacteriology	compulsivity	despotically	evidentially
unconstraint	barbarically	compulsorily	desquamatory	evolutionary
undercurrent	beatifically	compurgatory	determinably	exaggeratory
undergarment	belligerency	conceptually	determinedly	excitability
unemployment	beneficently	conciliatory	diabolically	exclusionary
universalist	beneficially	conclusively	dialectology	exegetically
urbanologist	benevolently	concordantly	diaphanously	exhaustively
vanquishment	beseechingly	concubitancy	diathermancy	exorbitantly
vantagepoint	bewilderedly	concurrently	diatonically	expansionary
ventripotent	bewitchingly	condemnatory	didactically	exoterically
vibraphonist	bibliography	conductivity	dietetically	expressively
voluntaryist	biochemistry	confirmatory	digressively	expressivity
welterweight	biocoenology	confiscatory	dilatability	extortionary
williewaught	biogeography	confoundedly	diminutively	extraneously
windingsheet	biologically	congeniality	disagreeably	extrasensory
schoolfellow	blackguardly	congenitally	disastrously	extravagancy
chocolatebox	blisteringly	connaturally	discerningly	factitiously
pneumothorax	blithesomely	connectively	disciplinary	fallaciously
portmanteaux	bloodthirsty	connubiality	discommodity	farsightedly
abolitionary	blunderingly	consecratory	discordantly	fastidiously
aboriginally	blusteringly	consensually	discursively	felicitously
absorptivity	boisterously	consentingly	disdainfully	fictitiously
abstemiously	bonnetmonkey	consequently	disgustfully	figuratively
abstractedly	brambleberry	conservatory	disgustingly	filtrability
academically	breathlessly	considerably	disjointedly	flagellatory
accidentally	bullheadedly	consistently	dispensatory	flagitiously
accretionary	cachinnatory	constabulary	dispiritedly	flamboyantly
accusatively	calamitously	constituency	displeasedly	flammability
acoustically	calcareously	consummately	disreputably	flatteringly
acronychally	calculatedly	consummatory	dissentingly	flickeringly
adaptability	calumniatory	contagiously	dissimilarly	forbiddingly
additionally	calumniously	contemporary	dissuasively	forebodingly

forensically	impermanency	interestedly	multiformity	pettifoggery
forthrightly	impersonally	interjectory	multiplicity	pharmacology
fortuitously	impertinency	intermediacy	multiversity	phenomenally
fractionally	imperviously	intermediary	municipality	philanthropy
frangibility	imponderably	interminably	munificently	phonemically
fraudulently	impressively	intimidatory	myrmecophily	phonetically
frenetically	imputability	intolerantly	mysteriously	photogeology
fuliginosity	imputatively	intriguingly	mystifyingly	physiography
functionally	inaccessibly	introductory	narcotically	platonically
galvanically	inaccurately	inveterately	nauseatingly	plausibility
geochemistry	inadequately	invisibility	navigability	plebiscitary
geologically	inadmissibly	invulnerably	neglectfully	pneumaticity
gerontocracy	inadvertency	irascibility	nephelometry	pneumatology
gigantically	inapplicably	irrationally	neuroanatomy	polarography
glitteringly	inappositely	irredeemably	neurobiology	polytonality
glossography	inaudibility	irrefragably	neurosurgery	pontifically
gluttonously	inauguratory	irrelatively	neurotically	portentously
glyphography	incalculably	irrelevantly	niminypiminy	possessively
glyptography	incapability	irremediably	nonchalantly	posteriority
gratifyingly	incautiously	irresistibly	nutritiously	posthumously
gratuitously	incestuously	irresolutely	obedientiary	potentiality
greengrocery	incidentally	irreverently	obligatorily	practicality
gregariously	incoherently	irreversibly	obsequiously	praiseworthy
groundcherry	incommutably	irritability	occasionally	precariously
groundlessly	incomparably	irritatingly	occidentally	precipitancy
grovellingly	incompatibly	isochronally	oceanography	preclusively
gynaecocracy	incompetency	isothermally	omnipotently	precociously
haberdashery	incompletely	jesuitically	omnisciently	predictively
habitability	inconcinnity	kremlinology	omnivorously	predominancy
harmonically	inconformity	lachrymatory	openhandedly	preeminently
harmoniously	inconsolably	lachrymosely	openmindedly	prehensility
heathenishly	inconstantly	landlubberly	operatically	premaxillary
hebdomadally	inconsumably	languorously	opposability	preoccupancy
heliotherapy	incontinency	laryngoscopy	oppressively	prevailingly
heraldically	incorporeity	lasciviously	orbicularity	preventively
hereditarily	incorrigibly	lefthandedly	organography	primordially
heritability	increasingly	legitimately	ornamentally	principality
hermetically	incurability	levorotatory	ornithomancy	printability
hesitatingly	indecisively	lexicography	ornithoscopy	probationary
heterophylly	indecorously	libidinously	otherworldly	proclamatory
highhandedly	indefeasibly	licentiously	outlandishly	prodigiously
historically	indefensibly	liturgically	outrageously	productively
homonymously	indefinitely	liturgiology	overactivity	productivity
homosexually	indelibility	logistically	oversimplify	proficiently
horizontally	indelicately	longwindedly	pacificatory	profligately
horrendously	independency	loquaciously	palaeobotany	projectively
horrifically	indicatively	lugubriously	palaeography	prolifically
humptydumpty	indifferency	macrocephaly	palatability	pronominally
hydrotherapy	indigenously	magnetically	pantisocracy	pronouncedly
hygienically	indiscreetly	magnifically	paramilitary	propitiatory
hyperacidity	indisputably	majestically	paranormally	propitiously
hypnotherapy	indissolubly	malevolently	parasitology	prosodically
hypnotically	indistinctly	malleability	parochiality	prosperously
hysterectomy	indivertibly	manipulatory	particularly	protectively
hysterically	individually	marvellously	passionately	protensively
ichthyolatry	industrially	meaningfully	pathetically	prothonotary
ichthyophagy	ineffaceably	mechanically	pedantically	protistology
ideationally	inefficiency	meditatively	pejoratively	protohistory
idiosyncrasy	inelasticity	mendaciously	penitentiary	protozoology
idolatrously	ineradicably	meridionally	perceptively	protrusively
illadvisedly	inexpediency	metallically	perceptivity	proverbially
illegibility	inexplicably	meteorically	perceptually	provincially
illegitimacy	inexpugnably	methodically	percussively	provisionary
illiberality	inextricably	meticulously	peremptorily	prudentially
illiterately	infectiously	microbiology	perfectively	pseudonymity
illnaturedly	infinitively	microcephaly	perfervidity	psychography
illogicality	inflammatory	microsurgery	perfidiously	psychrometry
immaculately	inflationary	millesimally	periodically	puerperally
immaterially	infrequently	miraculously	peripherally	pugnaciously
immeasurably	infusibility	modificatory	perjuriously	purificatory
immemorially	ingloriously	molecularity	permeability	purposefully
immoderately	inhospitably	monastically	permissively	questionably
immovability	iniquitously	monitorially	permittivity	quixotically
immutability	inordinately	monopodially	perniciously	quizzicality
impartiality	insolubility	monotonously	perplexingly	rabbinically
impenetrably	insufferably	monumentally	persistently	radiobiology
impenitently	intelligibly	mordaciously	perspicacity	radiotherapy
imperatively	intercessory	mulligatawny	perspiratory	reassuringly
imperishably	interdictory	mulligatawny	persuasively	rebelliously

recessionary scrupulosity straightaway thimbleberry unimaginably
reciprocally scrupulously stratigraphy thoughtfully unisexuality
recognisably sculpturally structurally thriftlessly universality
reducibility scurrilously stupendously thunderingly unmercifully
reflationary seismography stutteringly thunderously unmistakably
reflectively selenography subalternity tolerability unofficially
reflectivity selfactivity subjectively topsyturvily unpleasantly
refractivity selfflattery subjectivity torrentially unpopularity
refractorily selfidentity submaxillary traceability unprofitably
refreshingly semantically submissively tractability unreasonably
regardlessly semiannually subnormality traditionary unreservedly
regimentally sempiternity subsequently traitorously unthinkingly
regressively sententially subserviency tranquillity untruthfully
relationally separability subsidiarily transiliency unyieldingly
relentlessly septennially subsonically transitively uproariously
remorsefully septuagenary subversively transitivity usufructuary
removability sepulchrally successfully transitorily valetudinary
remuneratory sequaciously successively translucency vasodilatory
renunciatory sequentially sufficiently transmogrify vegetatively
repetitively seraphically suggestively transparency venerability
repressively serpentinely superciliary transudatory veridicality
residentiary serviceberry superhighway transversely verificatory
resistlessly sexcentenary superhumanly tremendously vernacularly
resoundingly shamefacedly supersensory triangularly victoriously
respectfully shillyshally supplicantly tricentenary villainously
respectively significancy supplicatory triggerhappy vindictively
resplendency simoniacally surefootedly trigonometry vituperatory
responsively simultaneity surprisingly tripartitely viviparously
restrainedly sinistrality susceptivity triumphantly vociferously
restrictedly sinusoidally suspensively tumultuously volcanically
reticulately skullduggery suspiciously twitteringly volitionally
retractility slanderously swaggeringly tyrannically voluminosity
revengefully Socratically syllabically ubiquitously voluminously
reversionary solicitously symbolically umbrageously voluptuosity
rhetorically specifically syndetically unaffectedly voluptuously
rheumatology spectrometry synonymously unassumingly whimperingly
rhythmically spectroscopy synoptically unbecomingly whimsicality
ridiculously speechlessly systemically unbelievably whisperingly
robustiously spheroidally tangentially unblinkingly whortleberry
romantically spidermonkey teachability unblushingly worshipfully
rontgenology spiritlessly technicality unchangeably zoogeography
ruminatively spirituality tectonically uncharitably
saccharinity sporadically teensyweensy unconformity
sacerdotally sprightfully temptability uncritically
sadistically squattocracy tercentenary undertenancy
salubriously staggeringly terrifically uneventfully
sanguinarily stammeringly terrifyingly unexpectedly
sardonically statuesquely testamentary unfaithfully
satisfactory stereochromy tetragonally unfamiliarly
satisfyingly stereography theatrically unfavourably
scandalously sternutatory theistically ungracefully
scatteringly stertorously thematically ungraciously
scintigraphy stockjobbery thematically ungratefully
scripturally stonemasonry thermography unilaterally

13 letter words

abiologically achromaticity adventurously aircraftwoman anachronistic
abortifacient acidification adversatively airworthiness anachronously
absorbability acotyledonous advertisement alcoholically anaerobically
abstractional acquiescently advisableness alcoholometer anagrammatise
accelerometer acquiescingly aerodynamical alcoholometry anagrammatism
acceptability acrimoniously aesthetically algebraically analogousness
accessibility acrobatically affectionless allegorically anaphrodisiac
accidentalism acrylonitrile affenpinscher allelomorphic anfractuosity
accidentprone actinomorphic affirmatively alternatively angiospermous
acclimatation actinomycetes afforestation aluminiferous anglicisation
accommodating actinomycosis affreightment aluminisation AngloAmerican
accommodation actualisation aggiornamento ambassadorial AngloCatholic
accommodative adiabatically agglomeration ambidexterity animadversion
accompaniment admeasurement agglomerative ambidexterous animalisation
accoutrements administrable agglutination ambiguousness annexationist
accreditation administrator agglutinative ambitiousness anomalistical
acculturation admirableness aggravatingly amniocentesis anomalousness
acculturative admissibility agonistically amorphousness anonymousness
acetification admonishingly agreeableness amphiprostyle answerability
acetylcholine adventuresome agriculturist amplification anthelminthic

anthropogenic	autocatalytic	brotherliness	circumvallate	conceptualism
anthropometry	autocephalous	brutalisation	circumvention	conceptualist
anthropopathy	autochthonism	bumptiousness	clairaudience	concertmaster
anthropophagi	autochthonous	bureaucratise	clandestinely	concessionary
anthropophagy	autoeroticism	burglariously	clarification	conchological
anthroposophy	automatically	businesswoman	clearheadedly	concomitantly
Antichristian	autonomically	butterfingers	clearinghouse	concretionary
anticlimactic	availableness	butterflyfish	cleistogamous	concupiscence
anticlockwise	axiomatically	buttonthrough	climactically	concupiscible
anticoagulant	baccalaureate	cabinetmaking	climatologist	condescension
antihistamine	backformation	cacographical	climbingframe	conditionally
antilogarithm	backpedalling	calcification	closedcircuit	conduciveness
antinomianism	backscratcher	calculatingly	clothesbasket	conductorship
antipersonnel	backwardation	calligraphist	coagulability	condylomatous
antiscorbutic	bacteriolysis	callisthenics	coarsegrained	confabulation
apathetically	bacteriolytic	Calvinistical	cobelligerent	confabulatory
apheliotropic	bacteriophage	campanologist	coeducational	confectionary
apocalyptical	balkanisation	camphoraceous	coenaesthesis	confectionery
appellatively	balsamiferous	canaliculated	coldbloodedly	confederation
applicability	BaltoSlavonic	candlelighter	coldheartedly	confederative
applicatively	bamboozlement	candlesnuffer	collaboration	confessionary
apportionment	barbarisation	cannibalistic	collaborative	confidingness
apprehensible	barbarousness	capaciousness	collaterality	configuration
appropriately	barefacedness	caprification	colleagueship	conflagration
appropriation	barrelchested	carboniferous	collectedness	conflictingly
appropriative	basidiomycete	carbonisation	collectorship	confraternity
approximately	bathymetrical	carcinomatous	collieshangie	confrontation
approximation	battlecruiser	cardiographer	colloquialism	conglomeratic
approximative	beatification	carnivorously	colourfulness	congratulator
arbitrariness	beauteousness	cartilaginous	combativeness	congressional
arbitrational	beleaguerment	catechisation	combinatorial	congresswoman
arboriculture	belleslettres	categorically	commandership	congruousness
archaeologist	belligerently	cauterisation	commemoration	conjecturable
archaeopteryx	beneficiation	centreforward	commemorative	conjecturally
archbishopric	Berkeleianism	centrifugally	commemoratory	conjugateness
archdeaconate	betweenwhiles	centripetally	commensurable	conjugational
archidiaconal	bewilderingly	cephalothorax	commensurably	conjunctional
archimandrite	bibliographer	cerebrospinal	commercialise	conjunctively
architectonic	bibliographic	ceremonialism	commercialism	connaturality
architectural	bibliolatrist	ceremonialist	commercialist	connectedness
argentiferous	bibliolatrous	ceremoniously	commiseration	consanguinity
argumentation	bibliological	certification	commiserative	conscientious
argumentative	bibliophilism	certificatory	communication	consciousness
arithmetician	bibliophilist	chalcoography	communicative	consecutively
aromatisation	bildungsroman	challengeable	communicatory	consenescence
arthritically	biodegradable	challengingly	communisation	consentaneity
artificiality	bioenergetics	changeability	communitarian	consentaneous
ascertainable	biogeographer	changefulness	commutability	consequential
ascertainment	biotechnology	characterless	compagination	conservatoire
assassination	birefringence	chateaubriand	companionable	considerately
assertiveness	blackguardism	cheerlessness	companionably	consideration
asseveration	blameableness	chemoreceptor	companionless	consolidation
assiduousness	blamelessness	chieftainship	companionship	consolidative
associateship	blanketflower	chinkerinchee	comparability	consolidatory
associativity	blasphemously	chlamydomonas	comparatively	conspicuously
Assyriologist	blastogenesis	chlamydospore	compartmental	constellation
asthenosphere	bloodboltered	choreographer	compassionate	constellatory
asthmatically	bloodcurdling	choreographic	compatibility	consternation
astonishingly	bloodlessness	chrematistics	compendiously	constrainable
astronautical	bloodrelation	Christmastide	competitively	constrainedly
astrophysical	Bloomsburyite	Christmastime	complainingly	constructable
atheistically	boardinghouse	chromatically	complaisantly	constructible
atlantosaurus	bombastically	chromatograph	complementary	consumptively
atmospherical	bookingoffice	chromatolytic	complexedness	containership
atomistically	bouillabaisse	chromatophore	complicatedly	contamination
atrociousness	boundlessness	chromospheric	complimentary	contaminative
attainability	bounteousness	chronographic	compositeness	contemplation
attentiveness	bountifulness	chronological	compositional	contemplative
attributively	boustrophedon	chrysanthemum	comprehension	contentedness
auctioneering	brachycephaly	chuckleheaded	comprehensive	contentiously
audaciousness	brachydactyly	churchmanship	compressional	continentally
Australianism	brachypterous	cicatrisation	computational	contortionist
authentically	brainlessness	cinematically	concatenation	contrabandist
authenticator	brainstorming	cinematograph	concavoconvex	contrabassoon
authorisation	breechloading	cinquecentist	conceitedness	contraception
authoritarian	brilliantness	circumambient	concentration	contraceptive
authoritative	broadmindedly	circumference	concentrative	contractility
autobiography	broadspectrum	circumfluence	concentricity	contractually
autocatalysis	brokenhearted	circumspectly	conceptualise	contradiction

contradictory	deciduousness	disarticulate	eccentrically	excitableness
contrafagotto	declaratively	disciplinable	ecumenicalism	exclusiveness
contrapuntist	decomposition	discoloration	educationally	excommunicate
contrariously	decompression	discommodious	effectiveness	excrescential
contravention	decontaminate	disconcerting	effervescence	excursiveness
controversial	decontrolling	disconcertion	effervescency	excusableness
convalescence	decortication	disconformity	efficaciously	exemplariness
conventionary	decrepitation	disconnection	efflorescence	exhibitionism
conversazione	deductibility	discontinuity	egocentricity	exhibitionist
conversazioni	defeasibility	discontinuous	egregiousness	existentially
convertiplane	defectiveness	discreditable	elaborateness	expansibility
convexoconvex	defencelessly	discreditably	electioneerer	expansiveness
convocational	defensibility	discretionary	electrocution	expectoration
convulsionary	deferentially	discriminator	electrologist	expeditionary
cooperatively	defervescence	disembodiment	electromagnet	expeditiously
copartnership	defibrination	disengagement	electrometric	expensiveness
coreligionist	deforestation	disfigurement	electromotive	explanatorily
cornification	deformational	disgracefully	electrophorus	explorational
corporativism	degranulation	disharmonious	electroscopic	explosiveness
correlatively	deipnosophist	dishonourable	electrostatic	exponentially
correlativity	deleteriously	dishonourably	electrovalent	expostulation
correspondent	deliciousness	disintegrator	elephantiasis	expostulatory
corresponsive	deliquescence	disinterested	embarrassment	expressionism
corrigibility	deliriousness	disinvestment	embellishment	expressionist
corroboration	dematerialise	disjunctively	embranglement	expropriation
corroborative	demonstration	dismantlement	embrittlement	expurgatorial
corroboratory	demonstrative	dismemberment	embryogenesis	exquisiteness
corrosiveness	demythologise	disobediently	embryological	extemporarily
corruptionist	denationalise	disparagement	emphysematous	extensibility
corticotropic	dendritically	disparagingly	encapsulation	extensionally
corticotropin	denticulation	disparateness	encephalogram	extensiveness
cosmopolitise	deodorisation	dispassionate	encompassment	extermination
cosmopolitism	deontological	displantation	encouragement	exterminatory
costeffective	dependability	disposability	encouragingly	exteroceptive
cottonpicking	depersonalise	dispossession	encyclopaedia	exterritorial
counteraction	deprecatingly	dispraisingly	encyclopaedic	extracellular
counteractive	derequisition	disproportion	encyclopedism	extragalactic
counterattack	derestriction	disrespectful	encyclopedist	extrajudicial
counterchange	dermatologist	dissemblingly	endocrinology	extraordinary
countercharge	descriptively	dissemination	energetically	extraphysical
counterfeiter	desegregation	disseminative	enigmatically	extrapolation
counterstroke	desirableness	disseveration	enjoyableness	extratropical
counterweight	desperateness	dissimilarity	enlightenment	extravagantly
countinghouse	destructively	dissimilation	entertainment	extravasation
courteousness	destructivity	dissimilitude	entomological	extravascular
courtsmartial	desultoriness	dissimulation	entomophagous	extrinsically
crackerbarrel	deterioration	dissolubility	entomophilous	facetiousness
craftsmanship	deteriorative	dissoluteness	entomostracan	facultatively
craniological	determinately	dissymetrical	environmental	faithlessness
credulousness	determination	distastefully	epeirogenesis	falsification
criminalistic	determinative	distinctively	epigrammatise	fantastically
criminologist	deterministic	distinguished	epigrammatist	fasciculation
crosscultural	detrimentally	distressfully	epiphenomenal	fascinatingly
crossgartered	deuteragonist	distressingly	epiphenomenon	Fascistically
crosshatching	Deuteronomist	distributable	equestrianism	faultlessness
crosspurposes	devastatingly	distrustfully	equidistantly	featherheaded
crossquestion	developmental	divertisement	equilibration	featherstitch
cruiserweight	devolutionary	doctrinairism	equiponderant	featherweight
cryobiologist	devolutionist	documentalist	equiponderate	felicitations
cryptanalysis	dexterousness	documentation	equipotential	feloniousness
cryptanalytic	diageotropism	dodecaphonist	equivocalness	ferociousness
cryptographer	diagnostician	domestication	erroneousness	ferrimagnetic
cryptographic	diagrammatise	domiciliation	eschatologist	ferroconcrete
cryptological	dialectically	doublecrosser	eschscholtzia	ferroelectric
crystalgazing	diametrically	doubledealing	essentialness	ferromagnetic
crystallinity	diaphragmatic	doubleglazing	establishment	fertilisation
curvilinearly	diathermanous	doublejointed	ethnocentrism	festschriften
customariness	dichlamydeous	doubletongued	Eucharistical	feudalisation
cyberneticist	dichotomously	doubtlessness	evangelically	feuilletonism
cylindrically	dictatorially	draftsmanship	everlastingly	feuilletonist
cytochemistry	differentiate	draggletailed	evocativeness	fibrovascular
daguerreotype	diffusiveness	dramatisation	examinational	filterability
dangerousness	digestibility	dramaturgical	examinatorial	fissiparously
dastardliness	dimensionally	dreamlessness	exanthematous	flagellantism
dauntlessness	dimensionless	dressimprover	exasperatedly	flirtatiously
deathlessness	disadvantaged	dressingtable	exceptionable	floricultural
deceitfulness	disaffectedly	dulcification	exceptionably	floristically
deceptiveness	disaffirmance	dysfunctional	exceptionally	flourishingly
decerebration	disappearance	eavesdropping	excessiveness	followthrough

foolhardiness	gravitational	hydrosulphide	impulsiveness	ineligibility
foraminiferal	greensickness	hydrosulphite	inadvertently	inevitability
foreknowledge	grotesqueness	hydroxylamine	inanimateness	inexhaustible
forementioned	gubernatorial	hymenopterous	inappreciable	inexhaustibly
foresightedly	guilelessness	hyperboloidal	inappreciably	inexorability
forgetfulness	guiltlessness	hypercritical	inappropriate	inexpediently
formalisation	gymnastically	hypermetrical	inattentively	inexpensively
formidability	gymnospermous	hypermetropia	incandescence	inexperienced
formulisation	gynaecocratic	hypermetropic	incarceration	inexpressible
fortification	gynaecologist	hyperphysical	incardination	inexpressibly
fortississimo	gynandromorph	hypertrophied	inclusiveness	infallibilism
fortunateness	habitableness	hypnoanalysis	incombustible	infallibilist
fortunehunter	haematologist	hypnotisation	incommunicado	infallibility
fortuneteller	hairsplitting	hypochondriac	incompetently	infeasibility
fossiliferous	halfheartedly	hypoglycaemia	inconceivable	inferentially
fossilisation	halfsovereign	hypothecation	inconceivably	infinitesimal
fractionalise	hallucination	ichthyography	incondensable	inflexibility
fractionation	hallucinative	ichthyologist	incongruously	inflexionless
fractiousness	hallucinatory	ichthyosaurus	inconsecutive	inflorescence
fragmentarily	haphazardness	identicalness	inconsequence	influentially
fragmentation	harbourmaster	ideographical	inconsiderate	informational
freeselection	hardheartedly	ideologically	inconsistence	informatively
frequentation	harmonisation	idiomatically	inconsistency	infundibulate
frequentative	hazardousness	idiosyncratic	inconspicuous	infuriatingly
frighteningly	healthfulness	ignominiously	incontestable	ingeniousness
frightfulness	heartbreaking	illogicalness	incontestably	ingenuousness
frivolousness	heartlessness	illustriously	incontinently	ingurgitation
frontogenesis	heartsickness	imaginatively	inconvenience	inhospitality
fruitlessness	heebiejeebies	imitativeness	inconveniency	injudiciously
frustratingly	helminthiasis	immarcescible	inconvertible	injuriousness
fullfashioned	helminthology	immaterialise	inconvertibly	innocuousness
funambulation	helterskelter	immaterialism	inconvincible	innoxiousness
functionalism	hemicellulose	immaterialist	incorporation	inoffensively
functionalist	hemiparasitic	immateriality	incorporative	inopportunely
fundamentally	hemispherical	immediateness	incorporeally	inorganically
galactosaemia	heptasyllabic	immiscibility	incorrectness	inquisitional
galvanisation	hermaphrodite	immovableness	incorruptible	inquisitively
gametogenesis	hermeneutical	immunological	incorruptibly	inquisitorial
garnetiferous	herpetologist	immunotherapy	incorruptness	insatiability
garrulousness	heterogeneity	immutableness	incredibility	inscriptional
gasteropodous	heterogeneous	impalpability	incredulously	insectivorous
gastrocnemius	heterogenesis	impartibility	incrementally	insensateness
gastroenteric	heteromorphic	impassability	incriminatory	insensibility
gastrological	heteromorphic	impassibility	incurableness	insensitively
gastronomical	heteropterous	impassiveness	incuriousness	insensitivity
generalisable	heterosporous	impeccability	indefatigable	insidiousness
generalissimo	heterothallic	impecuniosity	indefatigably	insignificant
gentlemanlike	heterotrophic	impenetration	independently	insinuatingly
geocentricism	hilariousness	imperceptible	indescribable	insociability
geochronology	histrionicism	imperceptibly	indescribably	insolubleness
geometrically	hocuspocussed	impercipience	indeterminacy	inspectorship
geomorphology	hollowhearted	imperfectness	indeterminate	inspirational
geostationary	homeomorphism	imperialistic	indeterminism	instantaneity
geotropically	homoeomorphic	imperiousness	indeterminist	instantaneous
germanisation	homoeopathist	impermissible	indifferently	instinctively
gerontocratic	homogeneously	impersonalise	indiscernible	institutional
gerontologist	homoiothermal	impersonality	indiscernibly	instructional
gesticulation	homoiothermic	impersonation	indispensable	instructively
gesticulative	homosexuality	impertinently	indispensably	insubordinate
gesticulatory	honorifically	imperturbable	indisposition	insubstantial
glaciological	horizontality	imperturbably	indissociable	insufficience
glamorisation	horripilation	impetuousness	indistinctive	insufficiency
globetrotting	horsechestnut	implacability	individualise	insupportable
glorification	horsewhipping	implicatively	individualism	insupportably
glossographer	horticultural	impolitically	individualist	insusceptible
glutinousness	housebreaking	imponderables	individuality	intangibility
gonadotrophic	hundredweight	importunately	individuation	integumentary
gonadotrophin	hybridisation	impossibility	indoctrinator	intelligencer
goniometrical	hydraulically	impracticable	inductiveness	intelligently
goodnaturedly	hydrocephalic	impracticably	industrialise	intemperately
gracelessness	hydrocephalus	impractically	industrialism	intensiveness
graminivorous	hydrochloride	impressionism	industrialist	intentionally
grammatically	hydrocracking	impressionist	industriously	intercalation
granddaughter	hydrodynamics	improbability	ineducability	intercellular
grandfatherly	hydroelectric	impropriation	ineffableness	intercolonial
grandiloquent	hydrogenation	improvability	ineffectively	intercolumnar
grandmotherly	hydromedusoid	improvidently	ineffectually	intercropping
graphological	hydrometrical	improvisation	inefficacious	intercultural
gratification	hydrostatical	improvisatory	inefficiently	intercurrence

interdentally irritableness macrocephalic microorganism necessitously
interdigitate isochronously macromolecule microphyllous nectariferous
interestingly isomerisation Maginotminded microscopical nefariousness
intergalactic isometrically magisterially microtonality negligibility
interjectural isostatically magnanimously millefeuilles negotiability
interlacement italicisation magnetisation millennialism neighbourhood
interlocution jerrybuilding magnetomotive millionairess nemathelminth
interlocutory jiggerypokery magnetosphere mineralogical neoclassicism
interlocutrix jollification magnification ministerially neoclassicist
intermarriage judgeadvocate magnificently mirthlessness neoplasticism
intermediator judgmatically magniloquence misanthropist nephelometric
intermittence judiciousness malacological miscegenation nervelessness
international jurisprudence malacostracan miscellaneous neurastheniac
interoceptive justification maladaptation mischievously neurovascular
interosculate justificative maladjustment miscomprehend nickeliferous
interparietal justificatory maladminister misconception niggardliness
interpellator juxtaposition maladroitness miserableness nightmarishly
interpersonal kaleidoscopic malariologist misgovernment nightwatchman
interpolation kapellmeister maliciousness mismanagement nitrification
interpolative Kidderminster malleableness mistrustfully nitrobacteria
interposition kinematically Malthusianism mistrustingly nitrocompound
interpretable kinematograph mammaliferous misunderstand noiselessness
interpretress knickerbocker manageability misunderstood nomenclatural
interpunction knowledgeable manganiferous mitochondrion nonaggression
interrelation knowledgeably mangoldwurzel mnemotechnics nonappearance
interrogation knuckleduster Manichaeanism moderatorship nonattendance
interrogative laboriousness manifestation modernisation noncollegiate
interrogatory lackadaisical manifestative Mohammedanism noncompliance
interruptible laevorotation manipulatable mollification nonconducting
interspecific laevorotatory manneristical momentariness nonconforming
interspersion laissezpasser martyrisation momentousness nonconformism
interstratify lamellibranch martyrologist Monarchianism nonconformist
intertropical lancecorporal masculineness moneygrubbing nonconformity
intraarterial lancesergeant masterfulness monochromatic nondeductable
intracellular landownership materfamilias monocotyledon nonfigurative
intramuscular languishingly materialistic monodactylous nonforfeiting
intransigeant laryngoscopic mathematician monogrammatic nonfulfilment
intransigence laughableness matriculation monometallism nongovernment
intrapersonal laughingstock matrilineally monometallist nonproductive
intravenously leadpoisoning meadowsaffron monomolecular nonresistance
intricateness leatherjacket mechanisation mononucleosis nonreturnable
intrinsically lecherousness mediatisation monophthongal nonsensically
introgression legislatively mediterranean Monophysitism normalisation
introspection legislatorial megacephalous monosyllabism northeasterly
introspective leishmaniasis megasporangia monosymmetric northeastward
introversible leisureliness meistersinger Monotheletism northwesterly
intrusiveness lepidopterist mellifluously monotrematous northwestward
intuitiveness lepidopterous melodiousness monstrousness nostalgically
invariability leptocephalic melodramatics monumentalise notoriousness
inventiveness leptospirosis melodramatise morphogenesis nucleoprotein
inventorially lethargically melodramatist morphogenetic nullification
investigation letterperfect membranaceous morphological numerological
investigative levelcrossing mensurability mortification numismatology
investigatory lexicographer mercenariness mothercountry nutritionally
invidiousness lexicographic mercerisation mouldingboard objectionable
invincibility liberationist merchandising mountainously objectionably
inviolability librarianship mercilessness mountebankery objectiveness
inviolateness lickerishness meritoriously mourningcloak objectivistic
invisibleness liebfraumilch mesencephalon mourningpaper obliviousness
involuntarily lifepreserver mesmerisation mouthwatering obnoxiousness
irrationalise lightfingered metagrobolise Muhammadanism observational
irrationalism lightheadedly metalliferous multicellular obsessiveness
irrationalist lightmindedly metallisation multicoloured obstinateness
irrationality lightsomeness metallography multinational obstructively
irreclaimable lignification metallurgical multinucleate obtrusiveness
irreclaimably limitlessness metamorphoses multiplicable occasionalism
irrecoverable lineengraving metamorphosis multitudinous occasionalist
irrecoverably linseywoolsey metaphosphate mummification occasionality
irrefrangible litigiousness metaphysician musicological occidentalise
irreligionist loathsomeness metastability mutagenically Occidentalism
irreligiously longsuffering meteorologist mutualisation Occidentalist
irreplaceable lucrativeness Methodistical myrmecologist oceanographer
irrepressible ludicrousness metonymically mystification oceanographic
irrepressibly luxuriousness metrification naphthylamine ochlocratical
irresponsible macaronically microanalysis nationalistic octocentenary
irresponsibly Machiavellian microcephalic navigableness odontoglossum
irretrievable machicolation micrococcocci nearsightedly odontological
irretrievably machinegunner microdetector necessitarian odoriferously
irreverential mackerelshark micronutrient necessitation oecologically

offensiveness	parasynthetic	photochromics	precentorship	prolegomenous
offhandedness	parenthetical	photochromism	precipitantly	proliferation
officiousness	parliamentary	photoelectric	precipitately	proliferative
oleomargarine	parthenocarpy	photoelectron	precipitation	proliferously
omnicompetent	participation	photoemission	precipitative	prolification
onomatopoetic	participative	photoemissive	precipitously	promiscuously
ontogenically	participatory	photoperiodic	preconception	pronounceable
ontologically	particoloured	photopositive	predatoriness	pronouncement
openheartedly	particularise	photoreceptor	predestinator	pronunciation
operativeness	particularism	phraseologist	predicability	proparoxytone
ophthalmology	particularist	phreatophytic	predicamental	prophetically
opinionatedly	particularity	phrenetically	predicatively	proportionate
opisthobranch	partridgewood	phrenological	predominantly	propositional
opportuneness	passementerie	phycoerythrin	predomination	proprietorial
opportunistic	passionflower	phyllophagous	preengagement	proprioceptor
oppositionist	paterfamilias	physiognomist	preengineered	prosopography
opprobriously	paternalistic	physiographer	prefatorially	prospectively
orangeblossom	pathogenicity	physiographic	preferability	prostaglandin
orchestration	pathognomonic	physiological	prefiguration	prosthodontia
oreographical	patriotically	physiotherapy	prefigurative	protectionism
organogenesis	patronisingly	phytoplankton	prefigurement	protectionist
organotherapy	peaceableness	picturepalace	prehistorical	protectorship
ornamentation	pedagogically	picturesquely	prejudicially	proteinaceous
ornithologist	pedestrianise	piezoelectric	preliminarily	Protestantism
orthocephalic	pedestrianism	pigeonchested	prematureness	protohistoric
orthognathism	pendulousness	pigeonhearted	premeditation	protonotarial
orthognathous	penetrability	pigeonlivered	premeditative	protuberantly
osteomyelitis	penetratingly	pigheadedness	premillennial	provincialise
ostreiculture	penetratively	piscicultural	premonitorily	provincialism
outgeneralled	penitentially	plaintiveness	preoccupation	provincialist
outspokenness	Pennsylvanian	planimetrical	preordainment	provinciality
outstandingly	pennyfarthing	platiniferous	preordination	provisionally
overabundance	pennypinching	platitudinise	preparatively	prudentialism
overbearingly	penuriousness	platitudinous	preparatorily	prudentialist
overconfident	peptonisation	platyhelminth	preponderance	prudentiality
overcredulous	perambulation	plausibleness	preponderancy	pseudoarchaic
overelaborate	perambulatory	plenitudinous	prepositional	pseudomorphic
overemphasise	percussionist	plenteousness	prepossessing	pseudoscience
overindulgent	perdurability	plentifulness	prepossession	psilanthropic
overpopulated	peregrination	plethorically	prepreference	psychasthenia
overqualified	perfectionism	pluralisation	PreRaphaelite	psychoanalyse
oversensitive	perfectionist	pluripresence	prescientific	psychoanalyst
overstatement	perfunctorily	pneumatically	presidentship	psychodynamic
oversubscribe	perichondrial	pneumatolysis	prestigiously	psychogenesis
overvaluation	perichondrium	pneumatolytic	presumptively	psychogenetic
ovoviviparous	periodisation	pneumatometer	pretentiously	psychokinesis
owneroccupier	perishability	pneumatophore	pretermission	psychokinetic
oystercatcher	perissodactyl	pneumogastric	pretermitting	psychological
paddlesteamer	permutability	pneumonectomy	preternatural	psychometrics
paediatrician	perpendicular	pococurantism	prevarication	psychometrist
paedomorphism	perseveration	pointillistic	pricelessness	psychophysics
painstakingly	perspectively	pointlessness	primigravidae	psychosomatic
painterliness	perspicacious	polarographic	primitiveness	psychosurgery
palaeographer	perspicuously	poliomyelitis	primogenitary	psychotherapy
palaeographic	pervasiveness	polliniferous	primogenitive	psychrometric
palaeontology	pestiferously	polyadelphous	primogeniture	pteridologist
palaeozoology	petrification	polycarbonate	primordiality	pulverisation
palatableness	petrochemical	polychromatic	principalship	punctiliously
palletisation	petroliferous	polycotyledon	prismatically	puritanically
palynological	phalansterian	polydactylous	prizefighting	purposelessly
panegyrically	phanerogamous	polyhistorian	probationally	purposiveness
panicstricken	pharisaically	polypropylene	problematical	pusillanimity
pantagruelian	pharmaceutics	polysynthesis	processionary	pusillanimous
pantagruelism	pharmaceutist	polysynthetic	processionist	pyrheliometer
pantagruelist	pharmacologic	ponderability	proconsulship	pyrimethamine
pantheistical	pharmacopoeia	ponderousness	procrastinate	pyrotechnical
pantisocratic	phenomenalise	pontification	procuratorial	quadragesimal
papaveraceous	phenomenalism	porcellaneous	professoriate	quadrennially
paperhangings	phenomenalist	postclassical	professorship	quadricipital
papillomatous	phenomenology	postcommunion	profitability	quadrilateral
parabolically	phenylalanine	postoperative	profitsharing	quadrillionth
paradoxically	philanthropic	postulational	progenitorial	quadripartite
parallelogram	philhellenism	potentiometer	prognosticate	quadrumvirate
paramagnetism	philhellenist	powerlessness	progressional	quadruplicate
paranormality	philosophical	practicalness	progressively	quadruplicity
paraphernalia	philosophiser	pragmatically	progressivism	qualification
parasitically	phonautograph	prairieoyster	prohibitively	qualificatory
parasiticidal	phosphoretted	prayermeeting	projectionist	qualitatively
parasynthesis	photochemical	precautionary	prolegomenary	quarrelsomely

quartermaster	remorselessly	sarcastically	selfexistence	shoulderstrap
quartziferous	removableness	scandalmonger	selffertility	sicklefeather
querulousness	renegotiation	scarification	selfforgetful	sidesplitting
questioningly	reorientation	schadenfreude	selfgenerated	sightlessness
questionnaire	repetitionary	schematically	selfgoverning	signalisation
quicktempered	repetitiously	schizocarpous	selfimportant	significantly
quickwittedly	replenishment	schizogenesis	selfinduction	signification
quincentenary	reprehensible	schizophrenia	selfindulgent	significative
quincuncially	reprehensibly	schizophrenic	selfinflicted	silvertongued
quingentenary	representable	scholarliness	selfinsurance	singlehearted
quinquagenary	reproachfully	scholasticism	selfknowledge	skateboarding
Quinquagesima	reproachingly	schoolteacher	selfopinioned	slangingmatch
quinquevalent	republicanise	scientologist	selfpityingly	sleeplessness
quintillionth	republicanism	scintillating	selfpollinate	smellingsalts
quintuplicate	republication	scintillation	selfpossessed	smokelessness
radioactivity	repulsiveness	scleroprotein	selfpropelled	smoothingiron
radiolocation	requisiteness	scolopendrium	selfrecording	sniftingvalve
radiotelegram	resentfulness	scorbutically	selfregarding	snowblindness
randomisation	resistibility	scorification	selfreproving	sobermindness
rapaciousness	resolvability	scorpiongrass	selfrepugnant	socialisation
rapturousness	resourcefully	scrapmerchant	selfrestraint	sociocultural
ratiocination	resplendently	scripturalism	selfrevealing	socioeconomic
ratiocinative	restoratively	scripturalist	selfrighteous	softpedalling
rationalistic	restrictively	scrumptiously	selfsacrifice	solderingiron
rattlebrained	resuscitation	sculpturesque	selfsatisfied	solemnisation
reaffirmation	resuscitative	searchwarrant	selfslaughter	solicitorship
realistically	retentiveness	seaworthiness	selfsterility	solidungulate
rearcommodore	retranslation	secondariness	selfsufficing	somatological
rearrangement	retroactively	secretarybird	selfsupported	somnambulator
recalcitrance	retroactivity	secretaryship	selfsurrender	somniloquence
receptibility	retrogression	secretiveness	selfsustained	sophistically
receptiveness	retrogressive	sedentariness	selftormentor	sophisticated
recessiveness	retrospection	sedimentation	semeiological	sorrowfulness
reciprocality	retrospective	seditiousness	semiautomatic	soulsearching
reciprocation	revaccination	seductiveness	semibarbarian	soundingboard
reciprocative	revelationist	seismographer	semibarbarism	southeasterly
recombination	revendication	seismographic	semicivilised	southeastward
recommendable	reverberation	seismological	semiconductor	southwesterly
recomposition	reverberative	selectiveness	semiconscious	southwestward
reconcilement	reverberatory	selenocentric	semilogarithm	sovietologist
reconsolidate	reverentially	selenographer	semiparasitic	spasmodically
reconstructor	reversibility	selenographic	semipermanent	specification
recrimination	revolutionary	selenological	semipermeable	spectacularly
recriminative	revolutionise	selfabasement	semiporcelain	spectrography
recriminatory	revolutionism	selfaddressed	sensationally	spectrometric
recrudescence	revolutionist	selfadjusting	senselessness	spectroscopic
recrystallise	rhadamanthine	selfappointed	sensitisation	speculatively
rectangularly	RhaetoRomanic	selfapproving	sensitiveness	spelaeologist
rectification	rhapsodically	selfasserting	sententiously	speleological
rectilinearly	rheumatically	selfassertion	sentimentally	Spencerianism
redescription	rhodochrosite	selfassertive	separableness	spermatoblast
redevelopment	righteousness	selfassurance	separationist	spermatogenic
reduplication	righthandedly	selfassuredly	septentrional	spermatophore
reduplicative	ritualisation	selfawareness	sequentiality	spermatophyte
reembarkation	roentgenogram	selfcentredly	sequestration	spheroidicity
reexamination	roentgenology	selfcollected	SerboCroatian	sphygmography
referentially	rollercoaster	selfcommunion	serendipitous	spindlelegged
reflexibility	rontgenoscopy	selfconceited	sergeantmajor	spindleshanks
reforestation	rudimentarily	selfcondemned	serialisation	spinelessness
reformability	runningstitch	selfconfessed	sericulturist	spinninghouse
reformational	Russification	selfconfident	seriousminded	spinningwheel
refractometer	sabrerattling	selfconscious	serologically	spiritualness
refrigeration	saccharimeter	selfconsuming	sesquiplicate	splendiferous
regardfulness	saccharimetry	selfcontained	sewingmachine	splenetically
regimentation	saccharometer	selfcontented	shabbygenteel	spontaneously
regretfulness	sacerdotalise	selfconvicted	Shakespearean	sportsmanlike
regurgitation	sacerdotalism	selfcriticism	Shakespearian	sportsmanship
reimbursement	sacerdotalist	selfdeceiving	shamelessness	sprightliness
reincarnation	sacramentally	selfdeception	shapelessness	sprocketwheel
reinforcement	sacrificially	selfdeceptive	sharecropping	squandermania
reinstatement	sacrosanctity	selfdefeating	sharpshooting	squarebashing
reintegration	sadomasochism	selfdependent	sheepshearing	squeamishness
reinvigorator	sadomasochist	selfdirecting	shiftlessness	squeezability
rejuvenescent	sagaciousness	selfdirection	shockabsorber	stabilisation
religiousness	salaciousness	selfdiscovery	shootingbrake	stainlessness
reminiscently	salmonellosis	selfdispraise	shootingrange	stalkinghorse
remonstrantly	sanctimonious	selfeducation	shootingstick	staminiferous
remonstration	sanitationist	selfevidently	shorttempered	standoffishly
remonstrative	sansculottism	selfexecuting	shoulderblade	statelessness

statesmanlike	superposition	thermochemist	tremulousness	unimpassioned
statesmanship	supersaturate	thermodynamic	triangularity	unimpeachable
stationmaster	supersensible	thermogenesis	triangulation	uninformative
statistically	superstitious	thermonuclear	tributariness	unintelligent
steadfastness	supersubtlety	thermophilous	tricentennial	unintentional
steeplechaser	supervenience	thermoplastic	trichromatism	uninterrupted
steppingstone	supplantation	thermosetting	trigonometric	unmeaningness
stercoraceous	supplementary	thermotropism	triliteralism	unmentionable
stereographic	suppositional	thigmotropism	tritheistical	unnaturalness
stereoscopist	supranational	thimblerigged	troglodytical	unnecessarily
sterilisation	surreptitious	thimblerigger	troublesomely	unobtrusively
sternforemost	surrogateship	thoroughbrace	troublousness	unprecedented
stickingplace	swallowtailed	thoroughgoing	trustworthily	unpredictable
stigmatically	swashbuckling	thoroughpaced	tuberculation	unpretentious
stirpiculture	Swedenborgian	thoughtlessly	turkeygobbler	unpromisingly
stoichiometry	swordsmanship	thoughtreader	typographical	unputdownable
stoloniferous	syllabication	thrasonically	typologically	unqualifiedly
stomatologist	symbiotically	threateningly	tyrannosaurus	unquestioning
strangulation	symbolisation	threecornered	umbelliferous	unrelentingly
strategically	symmetrically	threequarters	unaccompanied	unremittingly
stratigraphic	symphonically	thremmatology	unaccountable	unrighteously
stratocumulus	symphoniously	thrillingness	unaccountably	unselfishness
stratospheric	synallagmatic	thundershower	unadulterated	unsociability
strawcoloured	synchronistic	thunderstruck	unambiguously	unsubstantial
streetwalking	synchronously	thurification	unanimousness	unsuitability
strenuousness	syntactically	tiddledywinks	unanticipated	unsymmetrical
streptococcal	synthetically	timeconsuming	unarticulated	untrustworthy
streptococcus	tablespoonful	tintinnabular	unbelievingly	unwarrantable
strikebreaker	tachistoscope	tintinnabulum	unceremonious	unwarrantably
structuralism	talkativeness	titillatingly	uncertainness	unwholesomely
structuralist	tantalisation	toastmistress	uncircumcised	unwillingness
structureless	tantalisingly	tolerableness	uncleanliness	vacillatingly
stylistically	taperecording	tonguelashing	uncomfortable	valuelessness
subcontractor	tastelessness	tonguetwister	uncomfortably	vantageground
subeditorship	tautologously	tonsillectomy	uncompetitive	vapourishness
subirrigation	taxonomically	toothsomeness	uncomplaining	vegetarianism
sublieutenant	teachableness	topographical	uncomplicated	venerableness
submachinegun	technicalness	topologically	unconceivable	venereologist
subordinately	technological	topsyturvydom	unconcernedly	ventriloquial
subordination	telegrammatic	tortoiseshell	unconditional	ventriloquise
subordinative	telencephalon	toxicological	unconditioned	ventriloquism
subpostmaster	teleportation	toxoplasmosis	unconformable	ventriloquist
subreptitious	telerecording	traceableness	unconquerable	venturesomely
subsaturation	televisionary	tractableness	unconsciously	venturousness
subsequential	temerariously	Tractarianism	unconstrained	veraciousness
subserviently	temperamental	traditionally	uncoordinated	verbalisation
substantially	temperateness	tranquilliser	underachiever	verbigeration
substantively	tempestuously	transatlantic	undercarriage	verifiability
substantivise	temporalities	transcendence	underclothing	verisimilarly
substitutable	temporariness	transcendency	undereducated	vermiculation
substructural	temporisation	transcription	underemphasis	vernacularise
subternatural	tenaciousness	transcriptive	underemployed	vernacularity
subterraneous	tendentiously	transformable	underestimate	vernalisation
subtilisation	tenderhearted	transgression	underexposure	versicoloured
subversionary	tentativeness	transgressive	undergraduate	versification
suffocatingly	teratological	transistorise	underhandedly	vertiginously
suffraganship	tercentennial	transitionary	understanding	vexatiousness
suffumigation	tergiversator	translational	understrapper	vicariousness
sulphureously	terminability	transliterate	underwhelming	viceadmiralty
summarisation	terminational	translocation	undisciplined	vicepresident
sumptuousness	terminatively	translucently	unearthliness	victimisation
superabundant	terpsichorean	translucidity	unemotionally	villeggiatura
superaddition	terrestrially	transmigrator	unenlightened	viniculturist
superannuable	territorially	transmissible	unequivocally	violoncellist
supercalender	terrorisation	transmittable	unestablished	visionariness
supercritical	testification	transmutation	unexceptional	visualisation
superdominant	tetrasyllable	transmutative	unfamiliarity	viticulturist
supereminence	thalassocracy	transnational	unfashionable	vitrification
superfamilies	thanklessness	transparently	unfashionably	vivaciousness
superfetation	thaumaturgist	transpiration	unfeelingness	vivisectional
superficially	theanthropism	transpiratory	unflinchingly	vocationalism
superfluidity	theatricalise	transportable	unforgettable	voicelessness
superfluously	theatricalism	transposition	unforgettably	volatilisable
superhumanity	theatricality	transshipment	unforthcoming	volcanologist
superlatively	thenceforward	transshipping	unfortunately	volumenometer
supernational	theologically	transversally	ungrammatical	voluntariness
supernumerary	theoretically	traumatically	unhealthiness	voluntaristic
superordinate	thereinbefore	treacherously	unicameralism	voluntaristic
superphysical	theriomorphic	treasurership	unicameralist	voraciousness

vouchsafement	facetiousness	manifestative	saccharimetry	ichthyologist
vulcanisation	facultatively	manipulatable	saccharometer	ichthyosaurus
vulcanologist	faithlessness	manneristical	sacerdotalise	occasionalism
vulgarisation	falsification	martyrisation	sacerdotalism	occasionalist
vulnerability	fantastically	martyrologist	sacerdotalist	occasionality
waterproofing	fasciculation	masculineness	sacramentally	occidentalise
wearisomeness	fascinatingly	masterfulness	sacrificially	Occidentalism
weatherbeaten	Fascistically	materfamilias	sacrosanctity	Occidentalist
wellapPointed	faultlessness	materialistic	sadomasochism	oceanographer
wheelerdealer	galactosaemia	mathematician	sadomasochist	oceanographic
whimsicalness	galvanisation	matriculation	sagaciousness	ochlocratical
whithersoever	gametogenesis	matrilineally	salaciousness	octocentenary
wholesomeness	garnetiferous	naphthylamine	salmonellosis	scandalmonger
windowshopper	garrulousness	nationalistic	sanctimonious	scarification
winterberries	gasteropodous	navigableness	sanitationist	schadenfreude
wonderfulness	gastrocnemius	paddlesteamer	sansculottism	schematically
wonderworking	gastroenteric	paediatrician	sarcastically	schizocarpous
woodengraving	gastrological	paedomorphism	tablespoonful	schizogenesis
woolgathering	gastronomical	painstakingly	tachistoscope	schizophrenia
worldlyminded	habitableness	painterliness	talkativeness	schizophrenic
worrisomeness	haematologist	palaeographer	tantalisation	scholarliness
worthlessness	hairsplitting	palaeographic	tantalisingly	scholasticism
wrongheadedly	halfheartedly	palaeontology	taperecording	schoolteacher
xanthochroism	halfsovereign	palaeozoology	tastelessness	scientologist
xylographical	hallucination	palatableness	tautologously	scintillating
Zarathustrian	hallucinative	palletisation	taxonomically	scintillation
zinjanthropus	hallucinatory	palynological	vacillatingly	scleroprotein
zoogeographer	haphazardness	panegyrically	valuelessness	scolopendrium
zoogeographic	harbourmaster	panicstricken	vantageground	scorbutically
zygodactylous	hardheartedly	pantagruelian	vapourishness	scorification
	harmonisation	pantagruelism	waterproofing	scorpiongrass
baccalaureate	hazardousness	pantagruelist	xanthochroism	scrapmerchant
backformation	kaleidoscopic	pantheistical	Zarathustrian	scripturalism
backpedalling	kapellmeister	pantisocratic	abiologically	scripturalist
backscratcher	laboriousness	papaveraceous	abortifacient	scrumptiously
backwardation	lackadaisical	paperhangings	absorbability	sculpturesque
bacteriolysis	laevorotation	papillomatous	abstractional	adiabatically
bacteriolytic	laevorotatory	parabolically	objectionable	admeasurement
bacteriophage	laissezpasser	paradoxically	objectionably	administrable
balkanisation	lamellibranch	parallelogram	objectiveness	administrator
balsamiferous	lancecorporal	paramagnetism	objectivistic	admirableness
BaltoSlavonic	lancesergeant	paranormality	obliviousness	admissibility
bamboozlement	landownership	paraphernalia	obnoxiousness	admonishingly
barbarisation	languishingly	parasitically	observational	adventuresome
barbarousness	laryngoscopic	parasiticidal	obsessiveness	adventurously
barefacedness	laughableness	parasynthesis	obstinateness	adversatively
barrelchested	laughingstock	parasynthetic	obstructively	advertisement
basidiomycete	macaronically	parenthetical	obtrusiveness	advisableness
bathymetrical	Machiavellian	parliamentary	accelerometer	educationally
battlecruiser	machicolation	parthenocarpy	acceptability	identicalness
cabinetmaking	machinegunner	participation	accessibility	ideographical
cacographical	mackerelshark	participative	accidentalism	ideologically
calcification	macrocephalic	participatory	accidentprone	idiomatically
calculatingly	macromolecule	particoloured	acclimatation	idiosyncratic
calligraphist	Maginotminded	particularise	accommodating	odontoglossum
callisthenics	magisterially	particularism	accommodation	odontological
Calvinistical	magnanimously	particularist	accommodative	odoriferously
campanologist	magnetisation	particularity	accompaniment	aerodynamical
camphoraceous	magnetomotive	partridgewood	accoutrements	aesthetically
canaliculated	magnetosphere	passementerie	accreditation	beatification
candlelighter	magnification	passionflower	acculturation	beauteousness
candlesnuffer	magnificently	paterfamilias	acculturative	beleaguerment
cannibalistic	magniloquence	paternalistic	acetification	belleslettres
capaciousness	malacological	pathogenicity	acetylcholine	belligerently
caprification	malacostracan	pathognomonic	achromaticity	beneficiation
carboniferous	maladaptation	patriotically	acidification	Berkeleianism
carbonisation	maladjustment	patronisingly	acotyledonous	betweenwhiles
carcinomatous	maladminister	radioactivity	acquiescently	bewilderingly
cardiographer	maladroitness	radiolocation	acquiescingly	centreforward
carnivorously	malariologist	radiotelegram	acrimoniously	centrifugally
cartilaginous	maliciousness	randomisation	acrobatically	centripetally
catechisation	malleableness	rapaciousness	acrylonitrile	cephalothorax
categorically	Malthusianism	rapturousness	actinomorphic	cerebrospinal
cauterisation	mammaliferous	ratiocination	actinomycetes	ceremonialism
daguerreotype	manageability	ratiocinative	actinomycosis	ceremonialist
dangerousness	manganiferous	rationalistic	actualisation	ceremoniously
dastardliness	mangoldwurzel	rattlebrained	eccentrically	certification
dauntlessness	Manichaeanism	sabrerattling	ecumenicalism	certificatory
eavesdropping	manifestation	saccharimeter	ichthyography	deathlessness

deceitfulness	generalissimo	metallography	recommendable	reverberation
deceptiveness	gentlemanlike	metallurgical	recomposition	reverberative
decerebration	geocentricism	metamorphoses	reconcilement	reverberatory
deciduousness	geochronology	metamorphosis	reconsolidate	reverentially
declaratively	geometrically	metaphosphate	reconstructor	reversibility
decomposition	geomorphology	metaphysician	recrimination	revolutionary
decompression	geostationary	metastability	recriminative	revolutionise
decontaminate	geotropically	meteorologist	recriminatory	revolutionism
decontrolling	germanisation	Methodistical	recrudescence	revolutionist
decortication	gerontocratic	metonymically	recrystallise	searchwarrant
decrepitation	gerontologist	metrification	rectangularly	seaworthiness
deductibility	gesticulation	nearsightedly	rectification	secondariness
defeasibility	gesticulative	necessitarian	rectilinearly	secretarybird
defectiveness	gesticulatory	necessitation	redescription	secretaryship
defencelessly	healthfulness	necessitously	redevelopment	secretiveness
defensibility	heartbreaking	nectariferous	reduplication	sedentariness
deferentially	heartlessness	negligibility	reduplicative	sedimentation
defervescence	heartsickness	negotiability	reembarkation	seditiousness
defibrination	heebiejeebies	neighbourhood	reexamination	seductiveness
deforestation	helminthiasis	nemathelminth	referentially	seismographer
deformational	helminthology	neoclassicism	reflexibility	seismographic
degranulation	helterskelter	neoclassicist	reforestation	seismological
deipnosophist	hemicellulose	neoplasticism	reformability	selectiveness
deleteriously	hemiparasitic	nephelometric	reformational	selenocentric
deliciousness	hemispherical	nervelessness	refractometer	selenographer
deliquescence	heptasyllabic	neurastheniac	refrigeration	selenographic
deliriousness	hermaphrodite	neurovascular	regardfulness	selenological
dematerialise	hermeneutical	oecologically	regimentation	selfabasement
demonstration	herpetologist	peaceableness	regretfulness	selfaddressed
demonstrative	heterogeneity	pedagogically	regurgitation	selfadjusting
demythologise	heterogeneous	pedestrianise	reimbursement	selfappointed
denationalise	heterogenesis	pedestrianism	reincarnation	selfapproving
dendritically	heterogenetic	pendulousness	reinforcement	selfasserting
denticulation	heteromorphic	penetrability	reinstatement	selfassertion
deodorisation	heteropterous	penetratingly	reintegration	selfassertive
deontological	heterosporous	penetratively	reinvigorator	selfassurance
dependability	heterothallic	penitentially	rejuvenescent	selfassuredly
depersonalise	heterotrophic	Pennsylvanian	religiousness	selfawareness
deprecatingly	jerrybuilding	pennyfarthing	reminiscently	selfcentredly
derequisition	leadpoisoning	pennypinching	remonstrantly	selfcollected
derestriction	leatherjacket	penuriousness	remonstration	selfcommunion
dermatologist	lecherousness	peptonisation	remonstrative	selfconceited
descriptively	legislatively	perambulation	remorselessly	selfcondemned
desegregation	legislatorial	perambulatory	removableness	selfconfessed
desirableness	leishmaniasis	percussionist	renegotiation	selfconfident
desperateness	leisureliness	perdurability	reorientation	selfconscious
destructively	lepidopterist	peregrination	repetitionary	selfconsuming
destructivity	lepidopterous	perfectionism	repetitiously	selfcontained
desultoriness	leptocephalic	perfectionist	replenishment	selfcontented
deterioration	leptospirosis	perichondrial	reprehensible	selfconvicted
deteriorative	lethargically	perichondrium	reprehensibly	selfcriticism
determinately	letterperfect	periodisation	representable	selfdeceiving
determination	levelcrossing	perishability	reproachfully	selfdeception
determinative	lexicographer	perissodactyl	reproachingly	selfdeceptive
deterministic	lexicographic	perpendicular	republicanise	selfdefeating
detrimentally	meadowsaffron	perseveration	republicanism	selfdependent
deuteragonist	mechanisation	perspectively	republication	selfdirecting
Deuteronomist	mediatisation	perspicacious	repulsiveness	selfdirection
devastatingly	mediterranean	perspicuously	requisiteness	selfdiscovery
developmental	megacephalous	pervasiveness	resentfulness	selfdispraise
devolutionary	megasporangia	pestiferously	resistibility	selfeducation
devolutionist	meistersinger	petrification	resolvability	selfevidently
dexterousness	mellifluously	petrochemical	resourcefully	selfexecuting
featherheaded	melodiousness	petroliferous	resplendently	selfexistence
featherstitch	melodramatics	reaffirmation	restoratively	selffertility
featherweight	melodramatise	realistically	restrictively	selfforgetful
felicitations	melodramatist	rearcommodore	resuscitation	selfgenerated
feloniousness	membranaceous	rearrangement	resuscitative	selfgoverning
ferociousness	mensurability	recalcitrance	retentiveness	selfimportant
ferrimagnetic	mercenariness	receptibility	retranslation	selfinduction
ferroconcrete	mercerisation	receptiveness	retroactively	selfindulgent
ferroelectric	merchandising	recessiveness	retroactivity	selfinflicted
ferromagnetic	mercilessness	reciprocality	retrogression	selfinsurance
fertilisation	meritoriously	reciprocation	retrogressive	selfknowledge
festschriften	mesencephalon	reciprocative	retrospection	selfopinioned
feudalisation	mesmerisation	recombination	retrospective	selfpityingly
feuilletonism	metagrobolise		revaccination	selfpollinate
feuilletonist	metalliferous		revelationist	selfpossessed
generalisable	metallisation		revendication	selfpropelled

selfrecording	vegetarianism	phalansterian	thermoplastic	discreditably
selfregarding	venerableness	phanerogamous	thermosetting	discretionary
selfreproving	venereologist	pharisaically	thermotropism	discriminator
selfrepugnant	ventriloquial	pharmaceutics	thigmotropism	disembodiment
selfrestraint	ventriloquise	pharmaceutist	thimblerigged	disengagement
selfrevealing	ventriloquism	pharmacologic	thimblerigger	disfigurement
selfrighteous	ventriloquist	pharmacopoeia	thoroughbrace	disgracefully
selfsacrifice	venturesomely	phenomenalise	thoroughgoing	disharmonious
selfsatisfied	venturousness	phenomenalism	thoroughpaced	dishonourable
selfslaughter	veraciousness	phenomenalist	thoughtlessly	dishonourably
selfsterility	verbalisation	phenomenology	thoughtreader	disintegrator
selfsufficing	verbigeration	phenylalanine	thrasonically	disinterested
selfsupported	verifiability	philanthropic	threateningly	disinvestment
selfsurrender	verisimilarly	philhellenism	threecornered	disjunctively
selfsustained	vermiculation	philhellenist	threequarters	dismantlement
selftormentor	vernacularise	philosophical	thremmatology	dismemberment
semeiological	vernacularism	philosophiser	thrillingness	disobediently
semiautomatic	vernalisation	phonautograph	thundershower	disparagement
semibarbarian	versicoloured	phosphoretted	thunderstruck	disparagingly
semibarbarism	versification	photochemical	thurification	disparateness
semicivilised	vertiginously	photochromics	wheelerdealer	dispassionate
semiconductor	vexatiousness	photochromism	whimsicalness	displantation
semiconscious	wearisomeness	photoelectric	whithersoever	disposability
semilogarithm	weatherbeaten	photoelectron	wholesomeness	dispossession
semiparasitic	wellapPointed	photoemission	aircraftwoman	dispraisingly
semipermanent	affectionless	photoemissive	airworthiness	disproportion
semipermeable	affenpinscher	photoperiodic	bibliographer	disrespectful
semiporcelain	affirmatively	photopositive	bibliographic	dissemblingly
sensationally	afforestation	photoreceptor	bibliolatrist	dissemination
senselessness	affreightment	phraseologist	bibliolatrous	disseminative
sensitisation	effectiveness	phreatophytic	bibliological	disseveration
sensitiveness	effervescence	phrenetically	bibliophilism	dissimilarity
sententiously	effervescency	phrenological	bibliophilist	dissimilation
sentimentally	efficaciously	phycoerythrin	bildungsroman	dissimilitude
separableness	efflorescence	phyllophagous	biodegradable	dissimulation
separationist	offensiveness	physiognomist	bioenergetics	dissolubility
septentrional	offhandedness	physiographer	biogeographer	dissoluteness
sequentiality	officiousness	physiographic	biotechnology	dissymetrical
sequestration	aggiornamento	physiological	birefringence	distastefully
SerboCroatian	agglomeration	physiotherapy	cicatrisation	distinctively
serendipitous	agglomerative	phytoplankton	cinematically	distinguished
sergeantmajor	agglutination	rhadamanthine	cinematograph	distressfully
serialisation	agglutinative	RhaetoRomanic	cinquecentist	distressingly
sericulturist	aggravatingly	rhapsodically	circumambient	distributable
seriousminded	agonistically	rheumatically	circumference	distrustfully
serologically	agreeableness	rhodochrosite	circumfluence	divertisement
sesquiplicate	agriculturist	shabbygenteel	circumspectly	fibrovascular
sewingmachine	egocentricity	Shakespearean	circumvallate	filterability
teachableness	egregiousness	Shakespearian	circumvention	fissiparously
technicalness	ignominiously	shamelessness	diageotropism	hilariousness
technological	chalcoography	shapelessness	diagnostician	histrionicism
telegrammatic	challengeable	sharecropping	diagrammatise	jiggerypokery
telencephalon	challengingly	sharpshooting	dialectically	Kidderminster
teleportation	changeability	sheepshearing	diametrically	kinematically
telerecording	changefulness	shiftlessness	diaphragmatic	kinematograph
televisionary	characterless	shockabsorber	diathermanous	liberationist
temerariously	chateaubriand	shootingbrake	dichlamydeous	librarianship
temperamental	cheerlessness	shootingrange	dichotomously	lickerishness
temperateness	chemoreceptor	shootingstick	dictatorially	liebfraumilch
tempestuously	chieftainship	shorttempered	differentiate	lifepreserver
temporalities	chinkerinchee	shoulderblade	diffusiveness	lightfingered
temporariness	chlamydomonas	shoulderstrap	digestibility	lightheadedly
temporisation	chlamydospore	thalassocracy	dimensionally	lightmindedly
tenaciousness	choreographer	thanklessness	dimensionless	lightsomeness
tendentiously	choreographic	theanthropism	disadvantaged	lignification
tenderhearted	chrematistics	theatricalise	disaffectedly	limitlessness
tentativeness	Christmastide	theatricalism	disaffirmance	lineengraving
teratological	Christmastime	theatricality	disappearance	linseywoolsey
tercentennial	chromatically	thenceforward	disarticulate	litigiousness
tergiversator	chromatograph	theologically	disciplinable	microanalysis
terminability	chromatolytic	theoretically	discoloration	microcephalic
terminational	chromatophore	thereinbefore	discommodious	micrococcocci
terminatively	chromospheric	theriomorphic	disconcerting	microdetector
terpsichorean	chronographic	thermochemist	disconcertion	micronutrient
terrestrially	chronological	thermodynamic	disconformity	microorganism
territorially	chrysanthemum	thermogenesis	disconnection	microphyllous
terrorisation	chuckleheaded	thermonuclear	discontinuity	microscopical
testification	churchmanship	thermophilous	discontinuous	microtonality
tetrasyllable			discreditable	millefeuilles

millennialism	blamelessness	immarcescible	anthropophagi	indescribable
millionairess	blanketflower	immaterialise	anthropophagy	indescribably
mineralogical	blasphemously	immaterialism	anthroposophy	indeterminacy
ministerially	blastogenesis	immaterialist	Antichristian	indeterminate
mirthlessness	bloodboltered	immateriality	anticlimactic	indeterminism
misanthropist	bloodcurdling	immediateness	anticlockwise	indeterminist
miscegenation	bloodlessness	immiscibility	anticoagulant	indifferently
miscellaneous	bloodrelation	immovableness	antihistamine	indiscernible
mischievously	Bloomsburyite	immunological	antilogarithm	indiscernibly
miscomprehend	clairaudience	immunotherapy	antinomianism	indispensable
misconception	clandestinely	immutableness	antipersonnel	indispensably
miserableness	clarification	impalpability	antiscorbutic	indisposition
misgovernment	clearheadedly	impartibility	encapsulation	indissociable
mismanagement	clearinghouse	impassability	encephalogram	indistinctive
mistrustfully	cleistogamous	impassibility	encompassment	individualise
mistrustingly	climactically	impassiveness	encouragement	individualism
misunderstand	climatologist	impeccability	encouragingly	individualist
misunderstood	climbingframe	impecuniosity	encyclopaedia	individuality
mitochondrion	closedcircuit	impenetration	encyclopaedic	individuation
nickeliferous	clothesbasket	imperceptible	encyclopedism	indoctrinator
niggardliness	elaborateness	imperceptibly	encyclopedist	inductiveness
nightmarishly	electioneerer	impercipience	endocrinology	industrialise
nightwatchman	electrocution	imperfectness	energetically	industrialism
nitrification	electrologist	imperialistic	enigmatically	industrialist
nitrobacteria	electromagnet	imperiousness	enjoyableness	industriously
nitrocompound	electrometric	impermissible	enlightenment	ineducability
picturepalace	electromotive	impersonalise	entertainment	ineffableness
picturesquely	electrophorus	impersonality	entomological	ineffectively
piezoelectric	electroscopic	impersonation	entomophagous	ineffectually
pigeonchested	electrostatic	impertinently	entomophilous	inefficacious
pigeonhearted	electrovalent	imperturbable	entomostracan	inefficiently
pigeonlivered	elephantiasis	imperturbably	environmental	ineligibility
pigheadedness	flagellantism	impetuousness	inadvertently	inevitability
piscicultural	flirtatiously	implacability	inanimateness	inexhaustible
righteousness	floricultural	implicatively	inappreciable	inexhaustibly
righthandedly	floristically	impolitically	inappreciably	inexorability
ritualisation	flourishingly	imponderables	inappropriate	inexpediently
sicklefeather	glaciological	importunately	inattentively	inexpensively
sidesplitting	glamorisation	impossibility	incandescence	inexperienced
sightlessness	globetrotting	impracticable	incarceration	inexpressible
signalisation	glorification	impracticably	incardination	inexpressibly
significantly	glossographer	impractically	inclusiveness	infallibilism
signification	glutinousness	impressionism	incombustible	infallibilist
significative	illogicalness	impressionist	incommunicado	infallibility
silvertongued	illustriously	improbability	incompetently	infeasibility
singlehearted	oleomargarine	impropriation	inconceivable	inferentially
tiddledywinks	plaintiveness	improvability	inconceivably	infinitesimal
timeconsuming	planimetrical	improvidently	incondensable	inflexibility
tintinnabular	platiniferous	improvisation	incongruously	inflexionless
tintinnabulum	platitudinise	improvisatory	inconsecutive	inflorescence
titillatingly	platitudinous	impulsiveness	inconsequence	influentially
vicariousness	platyhelminth	omnicompetent	inconsiderate	informational
viceadmiralty	plausibleness	smellingsalts	inconsistence	informatively
vicepresident	plenitudinous	smokelessness	inconsistency	infundibulate
victimisation	plenteousness	smoothingiron	inconspicuous	infuriatingly
villeggiatura	plentifulness	umbelliferous	incontestable	ingeniousness
viniculturist	plethorically	anachronistic	incontestably	ingenuousness
violoncellist	pluralisation	anachronously	incontinently	ingurgitation
visionariness	pluripresence	anaerobically	inconvenience	inhospitality
visualisation	slangingmatch	anagrammatise	inconveniency	injudiciously
viticulturist	sleeplessness	anagrammatism	inconvertible	injuriousness
vitrification	ambassadorial	analogousness	inconvertibly	innocuousness
vivaciousness	ambidexterity	anaphrodisiac	inconvincible	innoxiousness
vivisectional	ambidexterous	anfractuosity	incorporation	inoffensively
windowshopper	ambiguousness	angiospermous	incorporative	inopportunely
winterberries	ambitiousness	anglicisation	incorporeally	inorganically
zinjanthropus	amniocentesis	AngloAmerican	incorrectness	inquisitional
skateboarding	amorphousness	AngloCatholic	incorruptible	inquisitively
alcoholically	amphiprostyle	animadversion	incorruptibly	inquisitorial
alcoholometer	amplification	animalisation	incorruptness	insatiability
alcoholommetry	embarrassment	annexationist	incredibility	inscriptional
algebraically	embellishment	anomalistical	incredulously	insectivorous
allegorically	embranglement	anomalousness	incrementally	insensateness
allelomorphic	embrittlement	anonymousness	incriminatory	insensibility
alternatively	embryogenesis	answerability	incurableness	insensitively
aluminiferous	embryological	anthelminthic	incuriousness	insensitivity
aluminisation	emphysematous	anthropogenic	indefatigable	insidiousness
blackguardism	imaginatively	anthropometry	indefatigably	insignificant
blameableness	imitativeness	anthropopathy	independently	insinuatingly

insociability	invariability	unfeelingness	communicative	consecutively
insolubleness	inventiveness	unflinchingly	communicatory	consenescence
inspectorship	inventorially	unforgettable	communisation	consentaneity
inspirational	investigation	unforgettably	communitarian	consentaneous
instantaneity	investigative	unforthcoming	commutability	consequential
instantaneous	investigatory	unfortunately	compagination	conservatoire
instinctively	invidiousness	ungrammatical	companionable	considerately
institutional	invincibility	unhealthiness	companionably	consideration
instructional	inviolability	unicameralism	companionless	consolidation
instructively	inviolateness	unicameralist	companionship	consolidative
insubordinate	involuntarily	unimpassioned	comparability	consolidatory
insubstantial	knickerbocker	unimpeachable	comparatively	conspicuously
insufficience	knowledgeable	uninformative	compartmental	constellation
insufficiency	knowledgeably	unintelligent	compassionate	constellatory
insupportable	knuckleduster	unintentional	compatibility	consternation
insupportably	mnemotechnics	uninterrupted	compendiously	constrainable
insusceptible	onomatopoetic	unmeaningness	competitively	constrainedly
intangibility	ontogenically	unmentionable	complainingly	constructable
integumentary	ontologically	unnaturalness	complaisantly	constructible
intelligencer	pneumatically	unnecessarily	complementary	containership
intelligently	pneumatolysis	unobtrusively	complexedness	contamination
intemperately	pneumatolytic	unprecedented	complicatedly	contaminative
intensiveness	pneumatometer	unpredictable	complimentary	contemplation
intentionally	pneumatophore	unpretentious	compositeness	contemplative
intercalation	pneumatophore	unpromisingly	compositional	contentedness
intercellular	pneumogastric	unputdownable	comprehension	contentiously
intercolonial	pneumonectomy	unqualifiedly	comprehensive	continentally
intercolumnar	sniftingvalve	unquestioning	compressional	contortionist
intercropping	snowblindness	unrelentingly	computational	contrabandist
intercultural	unaccompanied	unremittingly	concatenation	contrabassoon
intercurrence	unaccountable	unrighteously	concavoconvex	contraception
interdentally	unaccountably	unselfishness	conceitedness	contraceptive
interdigitate	unadulterated	unsociability	concentration	contractility
interestingly	unambiguously	unsubstantial	concentrative	contractually
intergalactic	unanimousness	unsuitability	concentricity	contradiction
interjectural	unanticipated	unsymmetrical	conceptualise	contradictory
interlacement	unarticulated	untrustworthy	conceptualism	contrafagotto
interlocution	unbelievingly	unwarrantable	conceptualist	contrapuntist
interlocutory	unceremonious	unwarrantably	concertmaster	contrariously
interlocutrix	uncertainness	unwholesomely	conchological	contravention
intermarriage	uncircumcised	unwillingness	concomitantly	controversial
intermediator	uncleanliness	boardinghouse	concretionary	convalescence
intermittence	uncomfortable	bombastically	concupiscence	conventionary
international	uncomfortably	bookingoffice	concupiscible	conversazione
interoceptive	uncompetitive	bouillabaisse	condescension	conversazioni
interosculate	uncomplaining	boundlessness	conditionally	convertiplane
interparietal	uncomplicated	bounteousness	conduciveness	convexoconvex
interpellator	unconceivable	boustrophedon	conductorship	convocational
interpersonal	unconcernedly	coagulability	condylomatous	convulsionary
interpolation	unconditional	confabulation	confabulation	cooperatively
interpolative	unconditioned	coarsegrained	confabulatory	copartnership
interposition	unconformable	cobelligerent	confectionary	coreligionist
interpretable	unconquerable	coeducational	confectionery	cornification
interpretress	unconsciously	coenaesthesis	confederation	corporativism
interpunction	unconstrained	coldbloodedly	confederative	correlatively
interrelation	uncoordinated	coldheartedly	confessionary	correlativity
interrogation	underachiever	collaboration	confidingness	correspondent
interrogative	undercarriage	collaborative	configuration	corresponsive
interrogatory	underclothing	collaterality	conflagration	corrigibility
interruptible	undereducated	colleagueship	conflictingly	corroboration
interspecific	underemphasis	collectedness	confraternity	corroborative
interspersion	underemployed	collectorship	confrontation	corroboratory
interstratify	underestimate	collieshangie	conglomeratic	corrosiveness
intertropical	underexposure	colloquialism	congressional	corruptionist
intraarterial	undergraduate	colourfulness	congresswoman	corticotropic
intracellular	underhandedly	combativeness	congruousness	corticotropin
intramuscular	understanding	combinatorial	conjecturable	cosmopolitise
intransigeant	understrapper	commandership	conjecturally	cosmopolitism
intransigence	underwhelming	commemoration	conjugateness	costeffective
intrapersonal	undisciplined	commemorative	conjugational	cottonpicking
intravenously	unearthliness	commemoratory	conjunctional	counteraction
intricateness	unemotionally	commensurable	conjunctively	counteractive
intrinsically	unenlightened	commensurably	connaturality	counterattack
introgression	unequivocally	commercialise	connectedness	counterchange
introspection	unestablished	commercialism	consanguinity	countercharge
introspective	unexceptional	commercialist	conscientious	counterfeiter
introversible	unfamiliarity	commiseration	consciousness	counterstroke
intrusiveness	unfashionable	commiserative		counterweight
intuitiveness	unfashionably	communication	consciousness	counterweight

countinghouse	morphogenesis	somniloquence	spermatoblast	crystallinity
courteousness	morphogenetic	sophistically	spermatogenic	draftsmanship
courtsmartial	morphological	sophisticated	spermatophore	draggletailed
doctrinairism	mortification	sorrowfulness	spermatophyte	dramatisation
documentalist	mothercountry	soulsearching	spheroidicity	dramaturgical
documentation	mouldingboard	soundingboard	sphygmography	dreamlessness
dodecaphonist	mountainously	southeasterly	spindlelegged	dressimprover
domestication	mountebankery	southeastward	spindleshanks	dressingtable
domiciliation	mourningcloak	southwesterly	spinelessness	erroneousness
doublecrosser	mourningpaper	southwestward	spinninghouse	fractionalise
doubledealing	mouthwatering	sovietologist	spinningwheel	fractionation
doubleglazing	noiselessness	toastmistress	spiritualness	fractiousness
doublejointed	nomenclatural	tolerableness	splendiferous	fragmentarily
doubletongued	nonaggression	tonguelashing	splenetically	fragmentation
doubtlessness	nonappearance	tonguetwister	spontaneously	freeselection
followthrough	nonattendance	tonsillectomy	sportsmanlike	frequentation
foolhardiness	noncollegiate	toothsomeness	sportsmanship	frequentative
foraminiferal	noncompliance	topographical	sprightliness	frighteningly
foreknowledge	nonconducting	topologically	sprocketwheel	frightfulness
forementioned	nonconforming	topsyturvydom	equestrianism	frivolousness
foresightedly	nonconformism	tortoiseshell	equidistantly	frontogenesis
forgetfulness	nonconformist	toxicological	equilibration	fruitlessness
formalisation	nonconformity	toxoplasmosis	equiponderant	frustratingly
formidability	nondeductable	vocationalism	equiponderate	gracelessness
formulisation	nonfigurative	voicelessness	equipotential	graminivorous
fortification	nonforfeiting	volatilisable	equivocalness	grammatically
fortississimo	nonfulfilment	volcanologist	squandermania	granddaughter
fortunateness	nongovernment	volumenometer	squarebashing	grandfatherly
fortunehunter	nonproductive	voluntariness	squeamishness	grandiloquent
fortuneteller	nonresistance	voluntaristic	squeezability	grandmotherly
fossiliferous	nonreturnable	voraciousness	arbitrariness	graphological
fossilisation	nonsensically	vouchsafement	arbitrational	gratification
gonadotrophic	normalisation	wonderfulness	arboriculture	gravitational
gonadotrophin	northeasterly	wonderworking	archaeologist	greensickness
goniometrical	northeastward	woodengraving	archaeopteryx	grotesqueness
goodnaturedly	northwesterly	woolgathering	archbishopric	irrationalise
hocuspocussed	northwestward	worldlyminded	archdeaconate	irrationalism
hollowhearted	nostalgically	worrisomeness	archidiaconal	irrationalist
homeomorphism	notoriousness	worthlessness	archimandrite	irrationality
homoeomorphic	pococurantism	zoogeographer	architectonic	irreclaimable
homoeopathist	pointillistic	zoogeographic	architectural	irreclaimably
homogeneously	pointlessness	apathetically	argentiferous	irrecoverable
homoiothermal	polarographic	apheliotropic	argumentation	irrecoverably
homoiothermic	poliomyelitis	apocalyptical	argumentative	irrefrangible
homosexuality	polliniferous	appellatively	arithmetician	irreligionist
honorifically	polyadelphous	applicability	aromatisation	irreligiously
horizontality	polycarbonate	applicatively	arthritically	irreplaceable
horripilation	polychromatic	apportionment	artificiality	irrepressible
horsechestnut	polycotyledon	apprehensible	brachycephaly	irrepressibly
horsewhipping	polydactylous	appropriately	brachydactyly	irresponsible
horticultural	polyhistorian	appropriation	brachypterous	irresponsibly
housebreaking	polypropylene	appropriative	brainlessness	irretrievable
jollification	polysynthesis	approximately	brainstorming	irretrievably
loathsomeness	polysynthetic	approximation	breechloading	irreverential
longsuffering	ponderability	approximative	brilliantness	irritableness
moderatorship	ponderousness	epeirogenesis	broadmindedly	orangeblossom
modernisation	pontification	epigrammatise	broadspectrum	orchestration
Mohammedanism	porcellaneous	epigrammatist	brokenhearted	oreographical
mollification	postclassical	epiphenomenal	brotherliness	organogenesis
momentariness	postcommunion	epiphenomenon	brutalisation	organotherapy
momentousness	postoperative	openheartedly	crackerbarrel	ornamentation
Monarchianism	postulational	operativeness	craftsmanship	ornithologist
moneygrubbing	potentiometer	ophthalmology	craniological	orthocephalic
monochromatic	powerlessness	opinionatedly	credulousness	orthognathism
monocotyledon	roentgenogram	opisthobranch	criminalistic	orthognathous
monodactylous	roentgenology	opportuneness	criminologist	practicalness
monogrammatic	rollercoaster	opportunistic	crosscultural	pragmatically
monometallism	rontgenoscopy	oppositionist	crossgartered	prairieoyster
monometallist	sobermindness	opprobriously	crosshatching	prayermeeting
monomolecular	socialisation	spasmodically	crosspurposes	precautionary
mononucleosis	sociocultural	specification	crossquestion	precentorship
monophthongal	socioeconomic	spectacularly	cruiserweight	precipitantly
Monophysitism	softpedalling	spectrography	cryobiologist	precipitately
monosyllabism	solderingiron	spectrometric	cryptanalysis	precipitation
monosymmetric	solemnisation	spectroscopic	cryptanalytic	precipitative
Monotheletism	solicitorship	speculatively	cryptographer	precipitously
monotrematous	solidungulate	spelaeologist	cryptographic	preconception
monstrousness	somatological	speleological	cryptological	predatoriness
monumentalise	somnambulator	Spencerianism	crystalgazing	predestinator

predicability	proparoxytone	assassination	stratigraphic	outstandingly
predicamental	prophetically	assertiveness	stratocumulus	pulverisation
predicatively	proportionate	asserveration	stratospheric	punctiliously
predominantly	propositional	assiduousness	strawcoloured	puritanically
predomination	proprietorial	associateship	streetwalking	purposelessly
preengagement	proprioceptor	associativity	strenuousness	purposiveness
preengineered	prosopography	Assyriologist	streptococcal	pusillanimity
prefatorially	prospectively	asthenosphere	streptococcus	pusillanimous
preferability	prostaglandin	asthmatically	strikebreaker	quadragesimal
prefiguration	prosthodontia	astonishingly	structuralism	quadrennially
prefigurative	protectionism	astronautical	structuralist	quadricipital
prefigurement	protectionist	astrophysical	structureless	quadrilateral
prehistorical	protectorship	eschatologist	stylistically	quadrillionth
prejudicially	proteinaceous	eschscholtzia	auctioneering	quadripartite
preliminarily	Protestantism	essentialness	audaciousness	quadrumvirate
prematureness	protohistoric	establishment	Australianism	quadruplicate
premeditation	protonotarial	isochronously	authentically	quadruplicity
premeditative	protuberantly	isomerisation	authenticator	qualification
premillennial	provincialise	isometrically	authorisation	qualificatory
premonitorily	provincialism	isostatically	authoritarian	qualitatively
preoccupation	provincialist	osteomyelitis	authoritative	quarrelsomely
preordainment	provinciality	ostreiculture	autobiography	quartermaster
preordination	provisionally	pseudoarchaic	autocatalysis	quartziferous
preparatively	prudentialism	pseudomorphic	autocatalytic	querulousness
preparatorily	prudentialist	pseudoscience	autocephalous	questioningly
preponderance	prudentiality	psilanthropic	autochthonism	questionnaire
preponderancy	traceableness	psychasthenia	autochthonous	quicktempered
prepositional	tractableness	psychoanalyse	autoeroticism	quickwittedly
prepossessing	Tractarianism	psychoanalyst	automatically	quincentenary
prepossession	traditionally	psychodynamic	autonomically	quincuncially
prepreference	tranquilliser	psychogenesis	bumptiousness	quingentenary
PreRaphaelite	transatlantic	psychogenetic	bureaucratise	quinquagenary
prescientific	transcendence	psychokinesis	burglariously	Quinquagesima
presidentship	transcendency	psychokinetic	businesswoman	quinquevalent
prestigiously	transcription	psychological	butterfingers	quintillionth
presumptively	transcriptive	psychometrics	butterflyfish	quintuplicate
pretentiously	transformable	psychometrist	buttonthrough	rudimentarily
pretermission	transgression	psychophysics	curvilinearly	runningstitch
pretermitting	transgressive	psychosomatic	customariness	Russification
preternatural	transistorise	psychosurgery	dulcification	subcontractor
prevarication	transitionary	psychotherapy	Eucharistical	subeditorship
pricelessness	translational	psychrometric	fullfashioned	subirrigation
primigravidae	transliterate	atheistically	funambulation	sublieutenant
primitiveness	translocation	atlantosaurus	functionalism	submachinegun
primogenitary	translucently	atmospherical	functionalist	subordinately
primogenitive	translucidity	atomistically	fundamentally	subordination
primogeniture	transmigrator	atrociousness	gubernatorial	subordinative
primordiality	transmissible	attainability	guilelessness	subpostmaster
principalship	transmittable	attentiveness	guiltlessness	subreptitious
prismatically	transmutation	attributively	hundredweight	subsaturation
prizefighting	transmutative	ethnocentrism	judgeadvocate	subsequential
probationally	transnational	italicisation	judgmatically	subserviently
problematical	transparently	pteridologist	judiciousness	substantially
processionary	transpiration	stabilisation	jurisprudence	substantively
processionist	transpiratory	stainlessness	justification	substantivise
proconsulship	transportable	stalkinghorse	justificative	substitutable
procrastinate	transposition	staminiferous	justificatory	substructural
procuratorial	transshipment	standoffishly	juxtaposition	subternatural
professoriate	transshipping	statelessness	lucrativeness	subterraneous
professorship	transversally	statesmanlike	ludicrousness	subtilisation
profitability	traumatically	statesmanship	luxuriousness	subversionary
profitsharing	treacherously	stationmaster	Muhammadanism	suffocatingly
progenitorial	treasurership	statistically	multicellular	suffraganship
prognosticate	tremulousness	steadfastness	multicoloured	suffumigation
progressional	triangularity	steeplechaser	multinational	sulphureously
progressively	triangulation	steppingstone	multinucleate	summarisation
progressivism	tributariness	stercoraceous	multiplicable	sumptuousness
prohibitively	tricentennial	stereographic	multitudinous	superabundant
projectionist	trichromatism	stereoscopist	mummification	superaddition
prolegomenary	trigonometric	sterilisation	musicological	superannuable
prolegomenous	triliteralism	sternforemost	mutagenically	supercalender
proliferation	tritheistical	stickingplace	mutualisation	supercritical
proliferative	troglodytical	stigmatically	nucleoprotein	superdominant
proliferously	troublesomely	stirpiculture	nullification	supereminence
prolification	troublousness	stoichiometry	numerological	superfamilies
promiscuously	trustworthily	stoloniferous	numismatology	superfetation
pronounceable	wrongheadedly	stomatologist	nutritionally	superficially
pronouncement	ascertainable	strangulation	outgeneralled	superfluidity
pronunciation	ascertainment	strategically	outspokenness	superfluously

superhumanity	expressionist	tyrannosaurus	gratification	standoffishly
superlatively	expropriation	xylographical	gravitational	statelessness
supernational	expurgatorial	zygodactylous	healthfulness	statesmanlike
supernumerary	exquisiteness	————	heartbreaking	statesmanship
superordinate	extemporarily	anachronistic	heartlessness	stationmaster
superphysical	extensibility	anachronously	heartsickness	statistically
superposition	extensionally	anaerobically	imaginatively	swallowtailed
supersaturate	extensiveness	anagrammatise	inadvertently	swashbuckling
supersensible	extermination	anagrammatism	inanimateness	teachableness
superstitious	exterminatory	analogousness	inappreciable	thalassocracy
supersubtlety	exteroceptive	anaphrodisiac	inappreciably	thanklessness
supervenience	exterritorial	apathetically	inappropriate	thaumaturgist
supplantation	extracellular	availableness	inattentively	toastmistress
supplementary	extragalactic	beatification	italicisation	traceableness
suppositional	extrajudicial	beauteousness	leadpoisoning	tractableness
supranational	extraordinary	blackguardism	leatherjacket	Tractarianism
surreptitious	extraphysical	blameableness	loathsomeness	traditionally
surrogateship	extrapolation	blamelessness	meadowsaffron	tranquilliser
tuberculation	extratropical	blanketflower	nearsightedly	transatlantic
turkeygobbler	extravagantly	blasphemously	orangeblossom	transcendence
vulcanisation	extravasation	blastogenesis	peaceableness	transcendency
vulcanologist	extravascular	boardinghouse	phalansterian	transcription
vulgarisation	extrinsically	brachycephaly	phanerogamous	transcriptive
vulnerability	cyberneticist	brachydactyly	pharisaically	transformable
availableness	cylindrically	brachypterous	pharmaceutics	transgression
evangelically	cytochemistry	brainlessness	pharmaceutist	transgressive
everlastingly	dysfunctional	brainstorming	pharmacologic	transistorise
evocativeness	gymnastically	chalcoography	pharmacopoeia	transitionary
overabundance	gymnospermous	challengeable	plaintiveness	translational
overbearingly	gynaecocratic	challengingly	planimetrical	transliterate
overconfident	gynaecologist	changeability	platiniferous	translocation
overcredulous	gynandromorph	changefulness	platitudinise	translucently
overelaborate	hybridisation	characterless	platitudinous	translucidity
overemphasise	hydraulically	chateaubriand	platyhelminth	transmigrator
overindulgent	hydrocephalic	clairaudience	plausibleness	transmissible
overpopulated	hydrocephalus	clandestinely	practicalness	transmittable
overqualified	hydrochloride	clarification	pragmatically	transmutation
oversensitive	hydrocracking	coagulability	prairieoyster	transmutative
overstatement	hydrodynamics	coarsegrained	prayermeeting	transnational
oversubscribe	hydroelectric	crackerbarrel	quadragesimal	transparently
overvaluation	hydrogenation	craftsmanship	quadrennially	transpiration
ovoviviparous	hydromedusoid	craniological	quadricipital	transpiratory
owneroccupier	hydrometrical	deathlessness	quadrilateral	transportable
swallowtailed	hydrostatical	diageotropism	quadrillionth	transposition
swashbuckling	hydrosulphide	diagnostician	quadripartite	transshipment
Swedenborgian	hydrosulphite	diagrammatise	quadrumvirate	transshipping
swordsmanship	hydroxylamine	dialectically	quadruplicate	transversally
axiomatically	hymenopterous	diametrically	quadruplicity	traumatically
examinatorial	hyperboloidal	diaphragmatic	qualification	unaccompanied
exanthematous	hypercritical	diathermanous	qualificatory	unaccountable
exasperatedly	hypermetrical	draftsmanship	qualitatively	unaccountably
exceptionable	hypermetropia	draggletailed	quarrelsomely	unadulterated
exceptionably	hypermetropic	dramatisation	quartermaster	unambiguously
exceptionally	hyperphysical	dramaturgical	quartziferous	unanimousness
excessiveness	hypertrophied	elaborateness	reaffirmation	unanticipated
excitableness	hypnoanalysis	evangelically	realistically	unarticulated
exclusiveness	hypnotisation	examinational	rearcommodore	wearisomeness
excommunicate	hypochondriac	examinatorial	rearrangement	weatherbeaten
excrescential	hypoglycaemia	exanthematous	rhadamanthine	ambassadorial
excursiveness	hypothecation	exasperatedly	RhaetoRomanic	ambidexterity
excusableness	myrmecologist	featherheaded	rhapsodically	ambidexterous
exemplariness	mystification	featherstitch	scandalmonger	ambiguousness
exhibitionism	oystercatcher	featherweight	scarification	ambitiousness
exhibitionist	pyrheliometer	flagellantism	searchwarrant	arbitrariness
existentially	pyrimethamine	fractionalise	seaworthiness	arbitrational
expansibility	pyrotechnical	fractionation	shabbygenteel	arboriculture
expansiveness	syllabication	fractiousness	Shakespearean	bibliographer
expectoration	symbiotically	fragmentarily	Shakespearian	bibliographic
expeditionary	symbolisation	fragmentation	shamelessness	bibliolatrist
expeditiously	symmetrically	glaciological	shapelessness	bibliolatrous
expensiveness	symphonically	glamorisation	sharecropping	bibliological
explanatorily	symphoniously	gracelessness	sharpshooting	bibliophilism
explorational	synallagmatic	graminivorous	skateboarding	bibliophilist
explosiveness	synchronistic	grammatically	slangingmatch	cabinetmaking
exponentially	synchronously	granddaughter	spasmodically	cobelligerent
expostulation	syntactically	grandfatherly	stabilisation	cyberneticist
expostulatory	synthetically	grandiloquent	stainlessness	embarrassment
expressionism	typologically	grandmotherly	stalkinghorse	embellishment
	typographical	graphological	staminiferous	embranglement

embrittlement	deciduousness	lecherousness	uncertainness	pedagogically
embryogenesis	declaratively	lickerishness	uncircumcised	pedestrianise
embryological	decomposition	lucrativeness	uncleanliness	pedestrianism
fibrovascular	decompression	macaronically	uncomfortable	radioactivity
gubernatorial	decontaminate	machicolation	uncomfortably	radiolocation
habitableness	decontrolling	machinegunner	uncompetitive	radiotelegram
hybridisation	decortication	mackerelshark	uncomplaining	redescription
laboriousness	decrepitation	macrocephalic	uncomplicated	redevelopment
liberationist	dichlamydeous	macromolecule	unconceivable	reduplication
librarianship	dichotomously	mechanisation	unconcernedly	reduplicative
sabrerattling	dictatorially	microanalysis	unconditional	rudimentarily
sobermindness	doctrinairism	microcephalic	unconditioned	sadomasochism
subcontractor	documentalist	micrococcocci	unconformable	sadomasochist
subeditorship	documentation	microdetector	unconquerable	sedentariness
subirrigation	eccentrically	micronutrient	unconsciously	sedimentation
sublieutenant	encapsulation	microorganism	unconstrained	seditiousness
submachinegun	encephalogram	microphyllous	uncoordinated	seductiveness
subordinately	encompassment	microscopical	vacillatingly	sidesplitting
subordination	encouragement	microtonality	vicariousness	tiddledywinks
subordinative	encouragingly	necessitarian	viceadmiralty	underachiever
subpostmaster	encyclopaedia	necessitation	vicepresident	undercarriage
subreptitious	encyclopaedic	necessitously	victimisation	underclothing
subsaturation	encyclopedism	nectariferous	vocationalism	undereducated
subsequential	encyclopedist	nickeliferous	audaciousness	underemphasis
subserviently	eschatologist	nucleoprotein	deductibility	underemployed
substantially	eschscholtzia	occasionalism	dodecaphonist	underestimate
substantively	Eucharistical	occasionalist	endocrinology	underexposure
substantivise	exceptionable	occasionality	hydraulically	undergraduate
substitutable	exceptionably	occidentalise	hydrocephalic	underhandedly
substructural	exceptionally	Occidentalism	hydrocephalus	understanding
subternatural	excessiveness	Occidentalist	hydrochloride	understrapper
subterraneous	excitableness	oecologically	hydrocracking	underwhelming
subtilisation	exclusiveness	orchestration	hydrodynamics	undisciplined
subversionary	excommunicate	picturepalace	hydroelectric	acetification
tablespoonful	excrescential	picturesquely	hydrogenation	acetylcholine
tuberculation	excursiveness	pococurantism	hydromedusoid	breechloading
umbelliferous	excusableness	recalcitrance	hydrometrical	cheerlessness
unbelievingly	facetiousness	receptibility	hydrostatical	chemoreceptor
accelerometer	facultatively	receptiveness	hydrosulphide	clearheadedly
acceptability	hocuspocussed	recessiveness	hydrosulphite	clearinghouse
accessibility	incandescence	reciprocality	hydroxylamine	cleistogamous
accidentalism	incarceration	reciprocation	indefatigable	coeducational
accidentprone	incardination	reciprocative	indefatigably	coenaesthesis
acclimatation	inclusiveness	recombination	independently	credulousness
accommodating	incombustible	recommendable	indescribable	dreamlessness
accommodation	incommunicado	recomposition	indescribably	dressimprover
accommodative	incompetently	reconcilement	indeterminacy	dressingtable
accompaniment	inconceivable	reconsolidate	indeterminate	electioneerer
accoutrements	inconceivably	reconstructor	indeterminism	electrocution
accreditation	incondensable	recrimination	indeterminist	electrologist
acculturation	incongruously	recriminative	indifferently	electromagnet
acculturative	inconsequence	recriminatory	indiscernible	electrometric
alcoholically	inconsiderate	recrudescence	indiscernibly	electromotive
alcoholometer	inconsistence	recrystallise	indispensable	electrophorus
alcoholometry	inconsistency	rectangularly	indispensably	electroscopic
archaeologist	inconspicuous	rectification	indisposition	electrostatic
archaeopteryx	incontestable	rectilinearly	indissociable	electrovalent
archbishopric	incontestably	saccharimeter	indistinctive	elephantiasis
archdeaconate	incontinently	saccharimetry	individualise	energetically
archidiaconal	inconvenience	saccharometer	individualism	epeirogenesis
archimandrite	inconveniency	sacerdotalise	individualist	everlastingly
architectonic	inconvertible	sacerdotalism	individuality	exemplariness
architectural	inconvertibly	sacerdotalist	individuation	freeselection
ascertainable	inconvincible	sacramentally	indoctrinator	frequentation
ascertainment	incorporation	sacrificially	inductiveness	frequentative
auctioneering	incorporative	sacrosanctity	industrialise	greensickness
baccalaureate	incorporeally	secondariness	industrialism	haematologist
backformation	incorrectness	secretarybird	industrialist	heebiejeebies
backpedalling	incorruptible	secretaryship	industriously	identicalness
backscratcher	incorruptibly	sicklefeather	judgeadvocate	ideographical
backwardation	incorruptness	socialisation	judgmatically	ideologically
bacteriolysis	incredibility	sociocultural	judiciousness	ineducability
bacteriolytic	incredulously	socioeconomic	Kidderminster	ineffableness
bacteriophage	incrementally	tachistoscope	ludicrousness	ineffectively
cacographical	incriminatory	technicalness	mediatisation	ineffectually
cicatrisation	incurableness	technological	mediterranean	inefficacious
deceitfulness	incuriousness	uncircumcised	moderatorship	inefficiently
deceptiveness	incuriousness	uncleanliness	modernisation	ineligibility
decerebration	lackadaisical	unceremonious	paddlesteamer	inevitability

inexhaustible	premonitorily	unearthliness	argentiferous	unhealthiness
inexhaustibly	preoccupation	unemotionally	argumentation	abiologically
inexorability	preordainment	unenlightened	argumentative	acidification
inexpediently	preordination	unequivocally	daguerreotype	adiabatically
inexpensively	preparatively	unestablished	degranulation	animadversion
inexperienced	preparatorily	unexceptional	digestibility	animalisation
inexpressible	preponderance	wheelerdealer	ingeniousness	arithmetician
inexpressibly	preponderancy	affectionless	ingenuousness	axiomatically
laevorotation	prepositional	affenpinscher	ingurgitation	brilliantness
laevorotatory	prepossessing	affirmatively	jiggerypokery	chieftainship
liebfraumilch	prepossession	afforestation	legislatively	chinkerinchee
mnemotechnics	prepreference	affreightment	legislatorial	climactically
oceanographer	PreRaphaelite	anfractuosity	lightfingered	climatologist
oceanographic	prescientific	defeasibility	lightheadedly	climbingframe
oleomargarine	presidentship	defectiveness	lightmindedly	criminalistic
openheartedly	prestigiously	defencelessly	lightsomeness	criminologist
operativeness	presumptively	defensibility	lignification	deipnosophist
oreographical	pretentiously	deferentially	Maginotminded	enigmatically
overabundance	pretermission	defervescence	magisterially	epigrammatise
overbearingly	pretermitting	defibrination	magnanimously	epigrammatist
overconfident	preternatural	deforestation	magnetisation	epiphenomenal
overcredulous	prevarication	deformational	magnetomotive	epiphenomenon
overelaborate	pseudoarchaic	differentiate	magnetosphere	existentially
overemphasise	pseudomorphic	diffusiveness	magnification	faithlessness
overindulgent	pseudoscience	effectiveness	magnificently	flirtatiously
overpopulated	pteridologist	effervescence	magniloquence	frighteningly
overqualified	querulousness	effervescency	megacephalous	frightfulness
oversensitive	questioningly	efficaciously	megasporangia	frivolousness
overstatement	questionnaire	efflorescence	negligibility	guilelessness
oversubscribe	reembarkation	infallibilism	negotiability	guiltlessness
overvaluation	reexamination	infallibilist	niggardliness	hairsplitting
paediatrician	rheumatically	infallibility	nightmarishly	idiomatically
paedomorphism	roentgenogram	infeasibility	nightwatchman	idiosyncratic
phenomenalise	roentgenology	inferentially	organogenesis	imitativeness
phenomenalist	sheepshearing	infinitesimal	organotherapy	knickerbocker
phenomenology	sleeplessness	inflexibility	pigeonchested	laissezpasser
phenylalanine	smellingsalts	inflexionless	pigeonhearted	leishmaniasis
piezoelectric	specification	inflorescence	pigeonlivered	leisureliness
plenitudinous	spectacularly	influentially	pigheadedness	meistersinger
plenteousness	spectrography	informational	regardfulness	neighbourhood
plentifulness	spectrometric	informatively	regimentation	noiselessness
plethorically	spectroscopic	infundibulate	regretfulness	opinionatedly
pneumatically	speculatively	infuriatingly	regurgitation	opisthobranch
pneumatolysis	spelaeologist	lifepreserver	righteousness	painstakingly
pneumatolytic	speleological	nefariousness	righthandedly	painterliness
pneumatometer	Spencerianism	offensiveness	sagaciousness	philanthropic
pneumatophore	spermatoblast	offhandedness	sightlessness	philhellenism
pneumogastric	spermatogenic	officiousness	signalisation	philhellenist
pneumonectomy	spermatophore	referentially	significantly	philosophical
precautionary	spermatophyte	reflexibility	signification	philosophiser
precentorship	steadfastness	reforestation	significative	pointillistic
precipitantly	steeplechaser	reformability	ungrammatical	pointlessness
precipitately	steppingstone	reformational	vegetarianism	pricelessness
precipitation	stercoraceous	refractometer	zygodactylous	primigravidae
precipitative	stereographic	refrigeration	achromaticity	primitiveness
precipitously	stereoscopist	softpedalling	apheliotropic	primogenitary
preconception	sterilisation	suffocatingly	atheistically	primogenitive
predatoriness	sternforemost	suffraganship	ethnocentrism	primogeniture
predestinator	Swedenborgian	suffumigation	exhibitionism	primordiality
predicability	theanthropism	unfamiliarity	exhibitionist	principalship
predicamental	theatricalise	unfashionable	ichthyography	prismatically
predicatively	theatricalism	unfashionably	ichthyologist	prizefighting
predominantly	theatricality	unfeelingness	ichthyosaurus	psilanthropic
predomination	thenceforward	unflinchingly	inhospitality	quicktempered
preengagement	theologically	unforgettable	Mohammedanism	quickwittedly
preengineered	theoretically	unforgettably	Muhammadanism	quincentenary
prefatorially	thereinbefore	unforthcoming	ochlocratical	quincuncially
preferability	theriomorphic	unfortunately	ophthalmology	quingentenary
prefiguration	thermochemist	aggiornamento	schadenfreude	quinquagenary
prefigurative	thermodynamic	agglomeration	schematically	Quinquagesima
prefigurement	thermogenesis	agglomerative	schizocarpous	quinquevalent
prehistorical	thermonuclear	agglutination	schizogenesis	quintillionth
prejudicially	thermophilous	agglutinative	schizophrenia	quintuplicate
preliminarily	thermoplastic	aggravatingly	schizophrenic	reimbursement
prematureness	thermosetting	algebraically	scholarliness	reincarnation
premeditation	thermotropism	angiospermous	scholasticism	reinforcement
premeditative	treacherously	anglicisation	schoolteacher	reinstatement
premeditative	treasurership	AngloAmerican	spheroidicity	reintegration
premillennial	tremulousness	AngloCatholic	sphygmography	reinvigorator

scientologist	deliriousness	selenographer	syllabication	demythologise
scintillating	dulcification	selenographic	talkativeness	dimensionally
scintillation	enlightenment	selenological	telegrammatic	dimensionless
seismographer	falsification	selfabasement	telencephalon	domestication
seismographic	felicitations	selfaddressed	teleportation	domiciliation
seismological	feloniousness	selfadjusting	telerecording	gametogenesis
shiftlessness	filterability	selfappointed	televisionary	gymnastically
sniftingvalve	followthrough	selfapproving	tolerableness	gymnospermous
spindlelegged	fullfashioned	selfasserting	valuelessness	hemicellulose
spindleshanks	galactosaemia	selfassertion	villeggiatura	hemiparasitic
spinelessness	galvanisation	selfassertive	volatilisable	hemispherical
spinninghouse	halfheartedly	selfassurance	volcanologist	homeomorphism
spinningwheel	halfsovereign	selfassuredly	volumenometer	homoeomorphic
spiritualness	hallucination	selfawareness	voluntariness	homoeopathist
stickingplace	hallucinative	selfcentredly	voluntaristic	homogeneously
stigmatically	hallucinatory	selfcollected	vulcanisation	homoiothermal
stirpiculture	helminthiasis	selfcommunion	vulcanologist	homoiothermic
thigmotropism	helminthology	selfconceited	vulgarisation	homosexuality
thimblerigged	helterskelter	selfcondemned	vulnerability	hymenopterous
thimblerigger	hilariousness	selfconfessed	wellapPointed	immarcescible
triangularity	hollowhearted	selfconfident	xylographical	immaterialise
triangulation	illogicalness	selfconscious	admeasurement	immaterialism
tributariness	illustriously	selfconsuming	administrable	immaterialist
tricentennial	jollification	selfcontained	administrator	immateriality
trichromatism	kaleidoscopic	selfcontented	admirableness	immediateness
trigonometric	malacological	selfconvicted	admissibility	immiscibility
triliteralism	malacostracan	selfcriticism	admonishingly	immovableness
tritheistical	maladaptation	selfdeceiving	atmospherical	immunological
unicameralism	maladjustment	selfdeception	bamboozlement	immunotherapy
unicameralist	maladminister	selfdeceptive	bombastically	immutableness
unimpassioned	maladroitness	selfdefeating	bumptiousness	lamellibranch
unimpeachable	malariologist	selfdependent	campanologist	limitlessness
uninformative	maliciousness	selfdirecting	camphoraceous	mammaliferous
unintelligent	malleableness	selfdirection	combativeness	membranaceous
unintentional	Malthusianism	selfdiscovery	combinatorial	momentariness
uninterrupted	mellifluously	selfdispraise	commandership	momentousness
voicelessness	melodiousness	selfeducation	commemoration	mummification
whimsicalness	melodramatics	selfevidently	commemorative	nemathelminth
whithersoever	melodramatise	selfexecuting	commemoratory	nomenclatural
enjoyableness	melodramatist	selfexistence	commensurable	numerological
injudiciously	millefeuilles	selffertility	commensurably	numismatology
injuriousness	millennialism	selfforgetful	commercialise	reminiscently
objectionable	millionairess	selfgenerated	commercialism	remonstrantly
objectionably	mollification	selfgoverning	commercialist	remonstration
objectiveness	multicellular	selfimportant	commiseration	remonstrative
objectivistic	multicoloured	selfinduction	commiserative	remorselessly
rejuvenescent	multinational	selfindulgent	communication	removableness
allegorically	multinucleate	selfinflicted	communicative	semeiological
allelomorphic	multiplicable	selfinsurance	communicatory	semiautomatic
atlantosaurus	multitudinous	selfknowledge	communisation	semibarbarian
balkanisation	nullification	selfopinioned	communitarian	semibarbarism
balsamiferous	obliviousness	selfpityingly	commutability	semicivilised
BaltoSlavonic	palaeographer	selfpollinate	compagination	semiconductor
beleaguerment	palaeographic	selfpossessed	companionable	semiconscious
belleslettres	palaeontology	selfpropelled	companionably	semilogarithm
belligerently	palaeozoology	selfrecording	companionless	semiparasitic
bildungsroman	palatableness	selfregarding	companionship	semipermanent
calcification	palletisation	selfreproving	comparability	semipermeable
calculatingly	palynological	selfrepugnant	comparatively	semiporcelain
calligraphist	polarographic	selfrestraint	compartmental	somatological
callisthenics	poliomyelitis	selfrevealing	compassionate	somnambulator
Calvinistical	polliniferous	selfrighteous	compatibility	somniloquence
chlamydomonas	polyadelphous	selfsacrifice	compendiously	summarisation
chlamydospore	polycarbonate	selfsatisfied	competitively	sumptuousness
coldbloodedly	polychromatic	selfslaughter	complainingly	symbiotically
coldheartedly	polycotyledon	selfsterility	complaisantly	symbolisation
collaboration	polydactylous	selfsufficing	complementary	symmetrically
collaborative	polyhistorian	selfsupported	complexedness	symphonically
collaterality	polypropylene	selfsurrender	complicatedly	symphoniously
colleagueship	polysynthesis	selfsustained	complimentary	temerariously
collectedness	polysynthetic	selftormentor	compositeness	temperamental
collectorship	pulverisation	silvertongued	compositional	temperateness
collieshangie	religiousness	solderingiron	comprehension	tempestuously
colloquialism	rollercoaster	solemnisation	comprehensive	temporalities
colourfulness	salaciousness	solicitorship	compressional	temporariness
cylindrically	salmonellosis	solidungulate	computational	temporisation
deleteriously	scleroprotein	splendiferous	dematerialise	timeconsuming
deliciousness	selectiveness	splenetically	demonstration	unmeaningness
deliquescence	selenocentric	sulphureously	demonstrative	unmentionable

amniocentesis	constrainedly	monochromatic	tantalisation	glorification
annexationist	constructable	monocotyledon	tantalisingly	glossographer
beneficiation	constructible	monodactylous	tenaciousness	goodnaturedly
canaliculated	consumptively	monogrammatic	tendentiously	grotesqueness
candlelighter	containership	monometallism	tenderhearted	inoffensively
candlesnuffer	contamination	monometallist	tentativeness	inopportunely
cannibalistic	contaminative	monomolecular	tintinnabular	inorganically
centreforward	contemplation	mononucleosis	tintinnabulum	isochronously
centrifugally	contemplative	monophthongal	tonguelashing	isomerisation
centripetally	contentedness	Monophysitism	tonguetwister	isometrically
cinematically	contentiously	monosyllabism	tonsillectomy	isostatically
cinematograph	continentally	monosymmetric	unnaturalness	knowledgeable
cinquecentist	contortionist	Monotheletism	unnecessarily	knowledgeably
concatenation	contrabandist	monotrematous	vantageground	neoclassicism
concavoconvex	contrabassoon	monstrousness	venerableness	neoclassicist
conceitedness	contraception	monumentalise	venereologist	neoplasticism
concentration	contraceptive	nonaggression	ventriloquial	odontoglossum
concentrative	contractility	nonappearance	ventriloquise	odontological
concentricity	contractually	nonattendance	ventriloquism	odoriferously
conceptualise	contradiction	noncollegiate	ventriloquist	onomatopoetic
conceptualism	contradictory	noncompliance	venturesomely	ovoviviparous
conceptualist	contrafagotto	nonconducting	venturousness	phonautograph
concertmaster	contrapuntist	nonconforming	viniculturist	phosphoretted
concessionary	contrariously	nonconformism	windowshopper	photochemical
conchological	contravention	nonconformist	winterberries	photochromics
concomitantly	controversial	nonconformity	wonderfulness	photochromism
concretionary	convalescence	nondeductable	wonderworking	photoelectric
concupiscence	conventionary	nonfigurative	xanthochroism	photoelectron
concupiscible	conversazione	nonforfeiting	zinjanthropus	photoemission
condescension	conversazioni	nonfulfilment	abortifacient	photoemissive
conditionally	convertiplane	nongovernment	acotyledonous	photoperiodic
conduciveness	convexoconvex	nonproductive	agonistically	photopositive
conductorship	convocational	nonresistance	amorphousness	photoreceptor
condylomatous	convulsionary	nonreturnable	anomalistical	probationally
confabulation	dangerousness	nonsensically	anomalousness	problematical
confabulatory	denationalise	obnoxiousness	anonymousness	processionary
confectionary	dendritically	omnicompetent	apocalyptical	processionist
confectionery	denticulation	ornamentation	aromatisation	proconsulship
confederation	fantastically	owneroccupier	atomistically	procrastinate
confederative	funambulation	panegyrically	biodegradable	procuratorial
confessionary	functionalism	panicstricken	bioenergetics	professoriate
confidingness	functionalist	pantagruelian	biogeographer	professorship
configuration	fundamentally	pantagruelism	biotechnology	profitability
conflagration	generalisable	pantagruelist	bloodboltered	profitsharing
conflictingly	generalissimo	pantheistical	bloodcurdling	progenitorial
confraternity	gentlemanlike	pantisocratic	bloodlessness	prognosticate
confrontation	gonadotrophic	pendulousness	bloodrelation	progressional
conglomeratic	gonadotrophin	penetrability	Bloomsburyite	progressively
congratulator	goniometrical	penetratingly	bookingoffice	progressivism
congressional	gynaecocratic	penetratively	broadmindedly	prohibitively
congresswoman	gynaecologist	penitentially	broadspectrum	projectionist
congruousness	gynandromorph	Pennsylvanian	brokenhearted	prolegomenary
conjecturable	honorifically	pennyfarthing	brotherliness	prolegomenous
conjecturally	hundredweight	pennypinching	choreographer	proliferation
conjugateness	ignominiously	penuriousness	choreographic	proliferative
conjugational	innocuousness	ponderability	closedcircuit	proliferously
conjunctional	innoxiousness	ponderousness	clothesbasket	prolification
conjunctively	kinematically	pontification	cooperatively	promiscuously
connaturality	kinematograph	punctiliously	crosscultural	pronounceable
connectedness	lancecorporal	randomisation	crossgartered	pronouncement
consanguinity	lancesergeant	renegotiation	crosshatching	pronunciation
conscientious	landownership	rontgenoscopy	crosspurposes	proparoxytone
consciousness	languishingly	runningstitch	crossquestion	prophetically
consecutively	lineengraving	sanctimonious	deodorisation	proportionate
consenescence	linseywoolsey	sanitationist	deontological	propositional
consentaneity	longsuffering	sansculottism	egocentricity	proprietorial
consentaneous	manageability	sensationally	evocativeness	proprioceptor
consequential	manganiferous	senselessness	floricultural	prosopography
conservatoire	mangoldwurzel	sentientiously	floristically	prospectively
considerately	Manichaeanism	sensitisation	flourishingly	prostaglandin
consideration	manifestation	sensitiveness	foolhardiness	prosthodontia
consolidation	manifestative	sententiously	frontogenesis	protectionism
consolidative	manipulatable	sentimentally	geocentricism	protectionist
consolidatory	manneristical	singlehearted	geochronology	protectorship
conspicuously	mensurability	synallagmatic	geometrically	proteinaceous
constellation	mineralogical	synchronistic	geomorphology	Protestantism
constellatory	ministerially	synchronously	geostationary	protohistoric
consternation	Monarchianism	syntactically	geotropically	protonotarial
constrainable	moneygrubbing	synthetically	globetrotting	protuberantly

provincialise
provincialism
provincialist
provinciality
provisionally
reorientation
rhodochrosite
scolopendrium
scorbutically
scorification
scorpiongrass
shockabsorber
shootingbrake
shootingrange
shootingstick
shorttempered
shoulderblade
shoulderstrap
smokelessness
smoothingiron
snowblindness
spontaneously
sportsmanlike
sportsmanship
stoichiometry
stoloniferous
stomatologist
swordsmanship
thoroughbrace
thoroughgoing
thoroughpaced
thoughtlessly
thoughtreader
toothsomeness
troglodytical
troublesomely
troublousness
unobtrusively
violoncellist
wholesomeness
woodengraving
woolgathering
wrongheadedly
zoogeographer
zoogeographic
amphiprostyle
amplification
appellatively
applicability
applicatively
apportionment
apprehensible
appropriately
appropriation
appropriative
approximately
approximation
approximative
capaciousness
caprification
cephalothorax
copartnership
dependability
depersonalise
deprecatingly
emphysematous
expansibility
expansiveness
expectoration
expeditionary
expeditiously
expensiveness
explanatorily
explorational
explosiveness
exponentially
expostulation
expostulatory
expressionism

expressionist
expropriation
expurgatorial
haphazardness
heptasyllabic
hyperboloidal
hypercritical
hypermetrical
hypermetropia
hypermetropic
hyperphysical
hypertrophied
hypnoanalysis
hypnotisation
hypochondriac
hypoglycaemia
hypothecation
impalpability
impartibility
impassability
impassibility
impassiveness
impeccability
impecuniosity
impenetration
imperceptible
imperceptibly
impercipience
imperfectness
imperialistic
imperiousness
impermissible
impersonalise
impersonality
impersonation
impertinently
imperturbable
imperturbably
impetuousness
implacability
implicatively
impolitically
imponderables
importunately
impossibility
impracticable
impracticably
impractically
impressionism
impressionist
improbability
impropriation
improvability
improvidently
improvisation
improvisatory
impulsiveness
kapellmeister
lepidopterist
lepidopterous
leptocephalic
leptospirosis
naphthylamine
nephelometric
opportuneness
opportunistic
oppositionist
opprobriously
papaveraceous
paperhangings
papillomatous
peptonisation
rapaciousness
rapturousness
repetitionary
repetitiously
replenishment
reprehensible
reprehensibly

representable
reproachfully
reproachingly
republicanise
republicanism
republication
repulsiveness
separableness
separationist
septentrional
sophistically
sophisticated
superabundant
superaddition
superannuable
supercalender
supercritical
superdominant
supereminence
superfamilies
superfetation
superficially
superfluidity
superfluously
superhumanity
superlatively
supernational
supernumerary
superordinate
superphysical
superposition
supersaturate
supersensible
superstitious
supersubtlety
supervenience
supplantation
supplementary
suppositional
supranational
taperecording
topographical
topologically
topsyturvydom
typographical
typologically
unprecedented
unpredictable
unpretentious
unpromisingly
unputdownable
vapourishness
acquiescently
acquiescingly
exquisiteness
inquisitional
inquisitively
inquisitorial
requisiteness
sequentiality
sequestration
unqualifiedly
unquestioning
acrimoniously
acrobatically
acrylonitrile
aerodynamical
agreeableness
agriculturist
aircraftwoman
airworthiness
atrociousness
barbarisation
barbarousness
barefacedness
barrelchested
Berkeleianism
birefringence
bureaucratise

burglariously
carboniferous
carbonisation
carcinomatous
cardiographer
carnivorously
cartilaginous
cerebrospinal
ceremonialism
ceremonialist
ceremoniously
certification
certificatory
chrematistics
Christmastide
Christmastime
chromatically
chromatograph
chromatolytic
chromatophore
chromospheric
chronographic
chronological
chrysanthemum
circumambient
circumference
circumfluence
circumspectly
circumvallate
circumvention
cornification
corporativism
correlatively
correlativity
correspondent
corresponsive
corrigibility
corroboration
corroborative
corroboratory
corrosiveness
corruptionist
corticotropic
corticotropin
curvilinearly
derequisition
derestriction
dermatologist
egregiousness
erroneousness
ferociousness
ferrimagnetic
ferroconcrete
ferroelectric
ferromagnetic
fertilisation
foraminiferal
foreknowledge
forementioned
foresightedly
forgetfulness
formalisation
formidability
formulisation
fortification
fortissississimo
fortunateness
fortunehunter
fortuneteller
garnetiferous
garrulousness
germanisation
gerontocratic
gerontologist
harbourmaster
hardheartedly
harmonisation
hermaphrodite

hermeneutical
herpetologist
horizontality
horripilation
horsechestnut
horsewhipping
horticultural
irrationalise
irrationalism
irrationalist
irrationality
irreclaimable
irreclaimably
irrecoverable
irrecoverably
irrefrangible
irreligionist
irreligiously
irreplaceable
irrepressible
irrepressibly
irresponsible
irresponsibly
irretrievable
irretrievably
irreverential
irritableness
jerrybuilding
jurisprudence
laryngoscopic
martyrisation
martyrologist
mercenariness
mercerisation
merchandising
mercilessness
meritoriously
mirthlessness
morphogenesis
morphogenetic
morphological
mortification
myrmecologist
nervelessness
normalisation
northeasterly
northeastward
northwesterly
northwestward
parabolically
paradoxically
parallelogram
paramagnetism
paranormality
paraphernalia
parasitically
parasiticidal
parasynthesis
parasynthetic
parenthetical
parliamentary
parthenocarpy
participation
participative
participatory
particoloured
particularise
particularism
particularist
particularity
partridgewood
perambulation
perambulatory
percussionist
perdurability
peregrination
perfectionism
perfectionist
perfunctorily

perichondrial	verifiability	dispossession	misconception	authorisation
perichondrium	verisimilarly	dispraisingly	miserableness	authoritarian
periodisation	vermiculation	disproportion	misgovernment	authoritative
perishability	vernacularise	disrespectful	mismanagement	autobiography
perissodactyl	vernacularism	dissemblingly	mistrustfully	autocatalysis
permutability	vernacularity	dissemination	mistrustingly	autocatalytic
perpendicular	vernalisation	disseminative	misunderstand	autocephalous
perseveration	versicoloured	disseveration	misunderstood	autochthonism
perspectively	versification	dissimilarity	musicological	autochthonous
perspicacious	vertiginously	dissimilation	mystification	autoeroticism
perspicuously	voraciousness	dissimilitude	nostalgically	automatically
pervasiveness	worldlyminded	dissimulation	observational	autonomically
phraseologist	worrisomeness	dissolubility	obsessiveness	bathymetrical
phreatophytic	worthlessness	dissoluteness	obstinateness	battlecruiser
phrenetically	Zarathustrian	dissymetrical	obstructively	betweenwhiles
phrenological	absorbability	distastefully	oystercatcher	butterfingers
porce!laneous	abstractional	distinctively	passementerie	butterflyfish
puritanically	aesthetically	distinguished	passionflower	buttonthrough
purposelessly	answerability	distressfully	pestiferously	catechisation
purposiveness	assassination	distressingly	piscicultural	categorically
pyrheliometer	assertiveness	distributable	postclassical	cottonpicking
pyrimethamine	asserveration	distrustfully	postcommunion	cytochemistry
pyrotechnical	assiduousness	dysfunctional	postoperative	deterioration
sarcastically	associateship	essentialness	postulational	deteriorative
scrapmerchant	associativity	fasciculation	pusillanimity	determinately
scripturalism	Assyriologist	fascinatingly	pusillanimous	determination
scripturalist	Australianism	Fascistically	resentfulness	determinative
scrumptiously	basidiomycete	festschriften	resistibility	deterministic
SerboCroatian	businesswoman	fissiparously	resolvability	detrimentally
serendipitous	cosmopolitise	fossiliferous	resourcefully	entertainment
sergeantmajor	cosmopolitism	fossilisation	resplendently	entomological
serialisation	costeffective	gasteropodous	restoratively	entomophagous
sericulturist	customariness	gastrocnemius	restrictively	entomophilous
seriousminded	dastardliness	gastroenteric	resuscitation	entomostracan
serologically	descriptively	gastrological	resuscitative	establishment
sorrowfulness	desegregation	gastronomical	Russification	extemporarily
sprightliness	desirableness	gesticulation	sesquiplicate	extensibility
sprocketwheel	desperateness	gesticulative	tastelessness	extensionally
strangulation	destructively	gesticulatory	testification	extensiveness
strategically	destructivity	histrionicism	unselfishness	extermination
stratigraphic	desultoriness	insatiability	unsociability	exterminatory
stratocumulus	disadvantaged	inscriptional	unsubstantial	exteroceptive
stratospheric	disaffectedly	insectivorous	unsuitability	exterritorial
strawcoloured	disaffirmance	insensateness	unsymmetrical	extracellular
streetwalking	disappearance	insensibility	visionariness	extragalactic
strenuousness	disarticulate	insensitively	visualisation	extrajudicial
streptococcal	disciplinable	insensitivity	actinomorphic	extraordinary
streptococcus	discoloration	insidiousness	actinomycetes	extraphysical
strikebreaker	discommodious	insignificant	actinomycosis	extrapolation
structuralism	disconcerting	insinuatingly	actualisation	extratropical
structuralist	disconcertion	insociability	alternatively	extravagantly
structureless	disconformity	insolubleness	anthelminthic	extravasation
surreptitious	disconnection	inspectorship	anthropogenic	extravascular
surrogateship	discontinuity	inspirational	anthropometry	extrinsically
teratological	discontinuous	instantaneity	anthropopathy	heterogeneity
tercentennial	discreditable	instantaneous	anthropophagi	heterogeneous
tergiversator	discreditably	instinctively	anthropophagy	heterogenesis
terminability	discretionary	institutional	anthroposophy	heterogenetic
terminational	discriminator	instructional	Antichristian	heteromorphic
terminatively	disembodiment	instructively	anticlimactic	heteropterous
terpsichorean	disengagement	insubordinate	anticlockwise	heterosporous
terrestrially	disfigurement	insubstantial	anticoagulant	heterothallic
territorially	disgracefully	insufficience	antihistamine	heterotrophic
terrorisation	disharmonious	insufficiency	antilogarithm	intangibility
thrasonically	dishonourable	insupportable	antinomianism	integumentary
threateningly	dishonourably	insupportably	antipersonnel	intelligencer
threecornered	disintegrator	insusceptible	antiscorbutic	intelligently
threequarters	disinterested	justification	arthritically	intemperately
thremmatology	disinvestment	justificative	artificiality	intensiveness
thrillingness	disjunctively	justificatory	asthenosphere	intentionally
tortoiseshell	dismantlement	masculineness	asthmatically	intercalation
turkeygobbler	dismemberment	masterfulness	astonishingly	intercellular
tyrannosaurus	disobediently	mesencephalon	astronautical	intercolonial
unrelentingly	disparagement	mesmerisation	astrophysical	intercolumnar
unremittingly	disparagingly	misanthropist	attainability	intercropping
unrighteously	disparateness	miscegenation	attentiveness	intercultural
veraciousness	dispassionate	miscellaneous	attributively	intercurrence
verbalisation	displantation	mischievously	authentically	interdentally
verbigeration	disposability	miscomprehend	authenticator	interdigitate

interestingly	octocentenary	equipotential	revolutionism	disarticulate
intergalactic	ontogenically	equivocalness	revolutionist	dreamlessness
interjectural	ontologically	faultlessness	sovietologist	embarrassment
interlacement	orthocephalic	feudalisation	vivaciousness	encapsulation
interlocution	orthognathism	feuilletonism	vivisectional	establishment
interlocutory	orthognathous	feuilletonist	bewilderingly	expansibility
interlocutrix	osteomyelitis	fruitlessness	powerlessness	expansiveness
intermarriage	ostreiculture	frustratingly	sewingmachine	foraminiferal
intermediator	outgeneralled	glutinousness	unwarrantable	funambulation
intermittence	outspokenness	housebreaking	unwarrantably	galactosaemia
international	outstandingly	knuckleduster	unwholesomely	gonadotrophic
interoceptive	paterfamilias	laughableness	unwillingness	gonadotrophin
interosculate	paternalistic	laughingstock	dexterousness	gynaecocratic
interparietal	pathogenicity	mouldingboard	juxtaposition	gynaecologist
interpellator	pathognomonic	mountainously	lexicographer	gynandromorph
interpersonal	patriotically	mountebankery	lexicographic	hazardousness
interpolation	patronisingly	mourningcloak	luxuriousness	hilariousness
interpolative	petrification	mourningpaper	taxonomically	immarcescible
interposition	petrochemical	mouthwatering	toxicological	immaterialise
interpretable	petroliferous	neurastheniac	toxoplasmosis	immaterialism
interpretress	potentiometer	neurovascular	vexatiousness	immaterialist
interpunction	ratiocination	pluralisation	cryobiologist	immateriality
interrelation	ratiocinative	pluripresence	cryptanalysis	impalpability
interrogation	rationalistic	prudentialism	cryptanalytic	impartibility
interrogative	rattlebrained	prudentialist	cryptographer	impassability
interrogatory	retentiveness	prudentiality	cryptographic	impassibility
interruptible	retranslation	sculpturesque	cryptological	impassiveness
interspecific	retroactively	soulsearching	crystalgazing	incandescence
interspersion	retroactivity	soundingboard	crystallinity	incarceration
interstratify	retrogression	southeasterly	phycoerythrin	incardination
intertropical	retrogressive	southeastward	phyllophagous	infallibilism
intraarterial	retrospection	southwesterly	physiognomist	infallibilist
intracellular	retrospective	southwestward	physiognapher	infallibility
intramuscular	ritualisation	squandermania	physiographic	insatiability
intransigeant	tetrasyllable	squarebashing	physiological	intangibility
intransigence	titillatingly	squeamishness	physiotherapy	invariability
intrapersonal	untrustworthy	squeezability	phytoplankton	irrationalise
intravenously	viticulturist	tautologously	psychasthenia	irrationalism
intricateness	vitrification	thundershower	psychoanalyse	irrationalist
intrinsically	waterproofing	thunderstruck	psychoanalyst	irrationality
introgression	aluminiferous	thurification	psychodynamic	macaronically
introspection	aluminisation	trustworthily	psychogenesis	malacological
introspective	bouillabaisse	vouchsafement	psychogenetic	malacostracan
introversible	boundlessness	adventuresome	psychokinesis	maladaptation
intrusiveness	bounteousness	adventurously	psychokinetic	maladjustment
intuitiveness	bountifulness	adversatively	psychological	maladminister
lethargically	boustrophedon	advertisement	psychometrics	maladroitness
letterperfect	brutalisation	advisableness	psychometrist	malariologist
litigiousness	cauterisation	devastatingly	psychophysics	manageability
materfamilias	chuckleheaded	developmental	psychosomatic	megacephalous
materialistic	churchmanship	devolutionary	psychosurgery	megasporangia
mathematician	counteraction	devolutionist	psychotherapy	metagrobolise
matriculation	counteractive	divertisement	psychrometric	metalliferous
matrilineally	counterattack	eavesdropping	stylistically	metallisation
metagrobolise	counterchange	environmental	hazardousness	metallography
metalliferous	countercharge	invariability	—————————————	metallurgical
metallisation	counterfeiter	inventiveness	adiabatically	metamorphoses
metallography	counterstroke	inventorially	ambassadorial	metamorphosis
metallurgical	counterweight	investigation	assassination	metaphosphate
metamorphoses	countinghouse	investigative	atlantosaurus	metaphysician
metamorphosis	courteousness	investigatory	attainability	metastability
metaphosphate	courtsmartial	invidiousness	audaciousness	misanthropist
metaphysician	cruiserweight	invincibility	broadmindedly	Mohammedanism
metastability	dauntlessness	inviolability	broadspectrum	Monarchianism
meteorologist	deuteragonist	inviolateness	canaliculated	Muhammadanism
Methodistical	Deuteronomist	invisibleness	capaciousness	mutagenically
metonymically	doublecrosser	involuntarily	chlamydomonas	nefariousness
metrification	doubledealing	levelcrossing	chlamydospore	nemathelminth
mitochondrion	doubleglazing	navigableness	cicatrisation	nonaggression
mothercountry	doublejointed	revaccination	clearheadedly	nonappearance
mutagenically	doubletongued	revelationist	clearinghouse	nonattendance
mutualisation	doubtlessness	revendication	copartnership	occasionalism
nationalistic	ecumenicalism	reverberation	dematerialise	occasionalist
nitrification	educationally	reverberative	denationalise	occasionality
nitrobacteria	equestrianism	reverberatory	devastatingly	oceanographer
nitrocompound	equidistantly	reverentially	disadvantaged	oceanographic
notoriousness	equilibration	reversibility	disaffectedly	organogenesis
nutritionally	equiponderant	revolutionary	disaffirmance	organotherapy
obtrusiveness	equiponderate	revolutionise	disappearance	ornamentation

palaeographer	doubleglazing	electromotive	punctiliously	prudentialism
palaeographic	doublejointed	electrophorus	quicktempered	prudentialist
palaeontology	doubletongued	electroscopic	quickwittedly	prudentiality
palaeozoology	doubtlessness	electrostatic	saccharimeter	quadragesimal
palatableness	elaborateness	electrovalent	saccharimetry	quadrennially
papaveraceous	globetrotting	evocativeness	saccharometer	quadricipital
parabolically	harbourmaster	fasciculation	sanctimonious	quadrilateral
paradoxically	heebiejeebies	fascinatingly	sarcastically	quadrillionth
parallelogram	liebfraumilch	Fascistically	shockabsorber	quadripartite
paramagnetism	membranaceous	fractionalise	specification	quadrumvirate
paranormality	probationally	fractionation	spectacularly	quadruplicate
paraphernalia	problematical	fractiousness	spectrography	quadruplicity
parasitically	SerboCroatian	functionalise	spectrometric	randomisation
parasiticidal	shabbygenteel	functionalist	spectroscopic	rhadamanthine
parasynthesis	stabilisation	geocentricism	speculatively	rhodochrosite
parasynthetic	symbiotically	geochronology	stickingplace	solderingiron
pedagogically	symbolisation	glaciological	subcontractor	Swedenborgian
perambulation	tributariness	gracelessness	synchronistic	tendentiously
perambulatory	unobtrusively	inscriptional	synchronously	tenderhearted
phraseologist	verbalisation	isochronously	teachableness	tiddledywinks
polarographic	verbigeration	knickerbocker	tercentennial	traditionally
rapaciousness	aircraftwoman	knuckleduster	traceableness	unadulterated
recalcitrance	anachronistic	lancecorporal	tractableness	windowshopper
regardfulness	anachronously	lancesergeant	Tractarianism	wonderfulness
revaccination	apocalyptical	masculineness	tricentennial	wonderworking
sagaciousness	baccalaureate	mercenariness	trichromatism	woodengraving
salaciousness	blackguardism	mercerisation	unaccompanied	accelerometer
schadenfreude	brachycephaly	merchandising	unaccountable	acceptability
scrapmerchant	brachydactyly	mercilessness	unaccountably	accessibility
separableness	brachypterous	miscegenation	unicameralism	admeasurement
separationist	calcification	miscellaneous	unicameralist	adventuresome
somatological	calculatingly	mischievously	voicelessness	adventurously
squandermania	carcinomatous	miscomprehend	volcanologist	adversatively
squarebashing	chuckleheaded	misconception	vouchsafement	advertisement
steadfastness	circumambient	neoclassicism	vulcanisation	affectionless
strangulation	circumference	neoclassicist	vulcanologist	affenpinscher
strategically	circumfluence	noncollegiate	acidification	agreeableness
stratigraphic	circumspectly	noncompliance	bildungsroman	algebraically
stratocumulus	circumvallate	nonconducting	biodegradable	allegorically
stratospheric	circumvention	nonconforming	candlelighter	allelomorphic
strawcoloured	concatenation	nonconformism	candlesnuffer	alternatively
synallagmatic	concavoconvex	nonconformist	cardiographer	anaerobically
tenaciousness	conceitedness	nonconformity	coeducational	annexationist
teratological	concentration	peaceableness	coldbloodedly	apheliotropic
theanthropist	concentrative	percussionist	coldheartedly	appellatively
theatricalise	concentricity	phycoerythrin	condescension	argentiferous
theatricalism	conceptualise	piscicultural	conditionally	ascertainable
theatricality	conceptualism	porcellaneous	conduciveness	ascertainment
thrasonically	conceptualist	practicalness	conductorship	assertiveness
treacherously	concertmaster	precautionary	condylomatous	asserveration
treasurership	concessionary	precentorship	credulousness	atheistically
triangularity	conchological	precipitantly	dendritically	attentiveness
triangulation	concomitantly	precipitately	deodorisation	barefacedness
tyrannosaurus	concretionary	precipitation	feudalisation	beleaguerment
unearthliness	concupiscence	precipitative	fundamentally	beneficiation
unfamiliarity	concupiscible	precipitously	goodnaturedly	bioenergetics
unfashionable	crackerbarrel	preconception	hardheartedly	birefringence
unfashionably	descriptively	pricelessness	hundredweight	breechloading
unnaturalness	disciplinable	processionary	inadvertently	bureaucratise
unwarrantable	discoloration	processionist	ineducability	catechisation
unwarrantably	discommodious	proconsulship	Kidderminster	categorically
veraciousness	disconcerting	procrastinate	landownership	cerebrospinal
vexatiousness	disconcertion	procuratorial	leadpoisoning	ceremonialism
vicariousness	disconformity	psychasthenia	meadowsaffron	ceremonialist
vivaciousness	disconnection	psychoanalyse	nondeductable	ceremoniously
vocationalism	discontinuity	psychoanalyst	paddlesteamer	cheerlessness
volatilisable	discontinuous	psychodynamic	paediatrician	chieftainship
voraciousness	discreditable	psychogenesis	paedomorphism	chrematistics
Zarathustrian	discreditably	psychogenetic	pendulousness	cinematically
bamboozlement	discretionary	psychokinesis	perdurability	cinematograph
barbarisation	discriminator	psychokinetic	ponderability	cobelligerent
barbarousness	dulcification	psychological	ponderousness	coreligionist
bombastically	educationally	psychometrics	predatoriness	cyberneticist
carboniferous	egocentricity	psychometrist	predestinator	deceitfulness
carbonisation	electioneerer	psychophysics	predicability	deceptiveness
combativeness	electrocution	psychosomatic	predicamental	decerebration
combinatorial	electrologist	psychosurgery	predicatively	defeasibility
doublecrosser	electromagnet	psychotherapy	predominantly	defectiveness
doubledealing	electrometric	psychrometric	predomination	defencelessly

defensibility	immediateness	interspersion	receptiveness	threateningly
deferentially	impeccability	interstratify	recessiveness	threecornered
defervescence	impecuniosity	intertropical	redescription	threequarters
deleteriously	impenetration	inventiveness	redevelopment	thremmatology
dependability	imperceptible	inventorially	referentially	timeconsuming
depersonalise	imperceptibly	investigation	renegotiation	tolerableness
derequisition	impercipience	investigative	repetitionary	tuberculation
derestriction	imperfectness	investigatory	repetitiously	umbelliferous
desegregation	imperialistic	irreclaimable	resentfulness	unbelievingly
deterioration	imperiousness	irreclaimably	retentiveness	unceremonious
deteriorative	impermissible	irrecoverable	revelationist	uncertainness
determinately	impersonalise	irrecoverably	revendication	underachiever
determination	impersonality	irrefrangible	reverberation	undercarriage
determinative	impersonation	irreligionist	reverberative	underclothing
deterministic	impertinently	irreligiously	reverberatory	undereducated
developmental	imperturbable	irreplaceable	reverentially	underemphasis
digestibility	imperturbably	irrepressible	reversibility	underemployed
dimensionally	impetuousness	irrepressibly	RhaetoRomanic	underestimate
dimensionless	indefatigable	irresponsible	sacerdotalise	underexposure
disembodiment	indefatigably	irresponsibly	sacerdotalism	undergraduate
disengagement	independently	irretrievable	sacerdotalist	underhandedly
divertisement	indescribable	irretrievably	schematically	understanding
dodecaphonist	indescribably	irreverential	scientologist	understrapper
domestication	indeterminacy	kaleidoscopic	scleroprotein	underwhelming
eavesdropping	indeterminate	kapellmeister	sedentariness	unfeelingness
eccentrically	indeterminism	kinematically	selectiveness	unhealthiness
effectiveness	indeterminist	kinematograph	selenocentric	unmeaningness
effervescence	infeasibility	lamellibranch	selenographer	unmentionable
effervescency	inferentially	levelcrossing	selenographic	unnecessarily
egregiousness	ingeniousness	liberationist	selenological	unrelentingly
embellishment	ingenuousness	lifepreserver	semeiological	unremittingly
encephalogram	insectivorous	lineengraving	serendipitous	unselfishness
entertainment	insensateness	materfamilias	sheepshearing	vegetarianism
equestrianism	insensibility	materialistic	sidesplitting	venerableness
essentialness	insensitively	mesencephalon	sleeplessness	venereologist
exceptionable	insensitivity	meteorologist	sobermindness	viceadmiralty
exceptionably	integumentary	mineralogical	solemnisation	vicepresident
exceptionally	intelligencer	miserableness	spheroidicity	waterproofing
excessiveness	intelligently	moderatorship	splendiferous	wheelerdealer
expectoration	intemperately	modernisation	splenetically	confabulation
expeditionary	intensiveness	momentariness	squeamishness	confabulatory
expeditiously	intentionally	momentousness	squeezability	confectionary
expensiveness	intercalation	moneygrubbing	steeplechaser	confectionery
extemporarily	intercellular	necessitarian	streetwalking	confederation
extensibility	intercolonial	necessitation	strenuousness	confederative
extensionally	intercolumnar	necessitously	streptococcal	confessionary
extensiveness	intercropping	nomenclatural	streptococcus	confidingness
extermination	intercultural	numerological	subeditorship	configuration
exterminatory	intercurrence	objectionable	superabundant	conflagration
exteroceptive	interdentally	objectionably	superaddition	conflictingly
exterritorial	interdigitate	objectiveness	superannuable	confraternity
facetiousness	interestingly	objectivistic	supercalender	confrontation
foreknowledge	intergalactic	observational	supercritical	craftsmanship
forementioned	interjectural	obsessiveness	superdominant	differentiate
foresightedly	interlacement	offensiveness	supereminence	diffusiveness
freeselection	interlocution	osteomyelitis	superfamilies	disfigurement
gametogenesis	interlocutory	owneroccupier	superfetation	draftsmanship
generalisable	interlocutrix	panegyrically	superficially	dysfunctional
generalissimo	intermarriage	paperhangings	superfluidity	halfheartedly
greensickness	intermediator	parenthetical	superfluously	halfsovereign
gubernatorial	intermittence	paterfamilias	superhumanity	ineffableness
heterogeneity	international	paternalistic	superlatively	ineffectively
heterogeneous	interoceptive	pedestrianise	supernational	ineffectually
heterogenesis	interosculate	pedestrianism	supernumerary	inefficacious
heterogenetic	interparietal	penetrability	superordinate	inefficiently
heteromorphic	interpellator	penetratingly	superphysical	inoffensively
heteropterous	interpersonal	penetratively	superposition	nonfigurative
heterosporous	interpolation	peregrination	supersaturate	nonforfeiting
heterothallic	interpolative	phreatophytic	supersensible	nonfulfilment
heterotrophic	interposition	phrenetically	superstitious	perfectionism
homeomorphism	interpretable	phrenological	supersubtlety	perfectionist
hymenopterous	interpretress	pigeonchested	supervenience	perfunctorily
hyperboloidal	interpunction	pigeonhearted	taperecording	prefatorially
hypercritical	interrelation	pigeonlivered	telegrammatic	preferability
hypermetrical	interrogation	potentiometer	telencephalon	prefiguration
hypermetropia	interrogative	powerlessness	teleportation	prefigurative
hypermetropic	interrogatory	preengagement	telerecording	prefigurement
hyperphysical	interruptible	preengineered	televisionary	professoriate
hypertrophied	interspecific	receptibility	temerariously	professorship

profitability	burglariously	bathymetrical	arbitrational	lepidopterous
profitsharing	coagulability	cephalothorax	artificiality	lexicographer
reaffirmation	conglomeratic	dichlamydeous	assiduousness	lexicographic
selfabasement	congratulator	dichotomously	availableness	limitlessness
selfaddressed	congressional	disharmonious	basidiomycete	litigiousness
selfadjusting	congresswoman	dishonourable	bewilderingly	ludicrousness
selfappointed	congruousness	dishonourably	bouillabaisse	Maginotminded
selfapproving	dangerousness	emphysematous	brainlessness	magisterially
selfasserting	diageotropism	eschatologist	brainstorming	maliciousness
selfassertion	diagnostician	eschscholtzia	businesswoman	Manichaeanism
selfassertive	diagrammatise	Eucharistical	cabinetmaking	manifestation
selfassurance	disgracefully	haphazardness	Christmastide	manifestative
selfassuredly	draggletailed	lecherousness	Christmastime	manipulatable
selfawareness	enigmatically	lethargically	clairaudience	mediatisation
selfcentredly	epigrammatise	lightfingered	cleistogamous	mediterranean
selfcollected	epigrammatist	lightheadedly	cruiserweight	meritoriously
selfcommunion	flagellantism	lightmindedly	cylindrically	ministerially
selfconceited	forgetfulness	lightsomeness	deciduousness	musicological
selfcondemned	fragmentarily	Machiavellian	defibrination	nationalistic
selfconfessed	fragmentation	machicolation	deliciousness	navigableness
selfconfident	frighteningly	machinegunner	deliquescence	numismatology
selfconscious	frightfulness	mathematician	deliriousness	obliviousness
selfconsuming	imaginatively	mechanisation	desirableness	occidentalise
selfcontained	jiggerypokery	Methodistical	disintegrator	Occidentalism
selfcontented	judgeadvocate	mothercountry	disinterested	Occidentalist
selfconvicted	judgmatically	naphthylamine	disinvestment	officiousness
selfcriticism	languishingly	nephelometric	domiciliation	omnicompetent
selfdeceiving	laughableness	nightmarishly	efficaciously	ornithologist
selfdeception	laughingstock	nightwatchman	enlightenment	panicstricken
selfdeceptive	longsuffering	offhandedness	environmental	papillomatous
selfdefeating	manganiferous	orchestration	epeirogenesis	penitentially
selfdependent	mangoldwurzel	orthocephalic	equidistantly	perichondrial
selfdirecting	misgovernment	orthognathism	equilibration	perichondrium
selfdirection	neighbourhood	orthognathous	equiponderant	periodisation
selfdiscovery	niggardliness	pathogenicity	equiponderate	perishability
selfdispraise	nongovernment	pathognomonic	equipotential	perissodactyl
selfeducation	outgeneralled	pigheadedness	equivocalness	plaintiveness
selfevidently	pragmatically	prehistorical	excitableness	poliomyelitis
selfexecuting	progenitorial	prohibitively	exhibitionism	prairieoyster
selfexistence	prognosticate	pyrheliometer	exhibitionist	puritanically
selffertility	progressional	righteousness	felicitations	pusillanimity
selfforgetful	progressively	righthandedly	feuilletonism	pusillanimous
selfgenerated	progressivism	sightlessness	feuilletonist	pyrimethamine
selfgoverning	sergeantmajor	sophistically	fruitlessness	radioactivity
selfimportant	singlehearted	sophisticated	goniometrical	radiolocation
selfinduction	stigmatically	tachistoscope	habitableness	radiotelegram
selfindulgent	tergiversator	technicalness	hemicellulose	ratiocination
selfinflicted	thigmotropism	technological	hemiparasitic	ratiocinative
selfinsurance	tonguelashing	unwholesomely	hemispherical	rationalistic
selfknowledge	tonguetwister	accidentalism	horizontality	reciprocality
selfopinioned	trigonometric	accidentprone	immiscibility	reciprocation
selfpityingly	troglodytical	acrimoniously	indifferently	reciprocative
selfpollinate	vulgarisation	actinomorphic	indiscernible	regimentation
selfpossessed	zoogeographer	actinomycetes	indiscernibly	religiousness
selfpropelled	zoogeographic	actinomycosis	indispensable	reminiscently
selfrecording	amphiprostyle	administrable	indispensably	resistibility
selfregarding	anthelminthic	administrator	indisposition	rudimentarily
selfreproving	anthropogenic	admirableness	indissociable	sanitationist
selfrepugnant	anthropometry	admissibility	indistinctive	schizocarpous
selfrestraint	anthropopathy	advisableness	individualise	schizogenesis
selfrevealing	anthropophagi	affirmatively	individualism	schizophrenia
selfrighteous	anthropophagy	aggiornamento	individualist	schizophrenic
selfsacrifice	anthroposophy	agriculturist	individuality	scripturalism
selfsatisfied	archaeologist	ambidexterity	individuation	scripturalist
selfslaughter	archaeopteryx	ambidexterous	infinitesimal	sedimentation
selfsterility	archbishopric	ambiguousness	insidiousness	seditiousness
selfsufficing	archdeaconate	ambitiousness	insignificant	semiautomatic
selfsupported	archidiaconal	amniocentesis	insinuatingly	semibarbarian
selfsurrender	archimandrite	angiospermous	invidiousness	semibarbarism
selfsustained	architectonic	Antichristian	invincibility	semicivilised
selftormentor	architectural	anticlimactic	inviolability	semiconductor
shiftlessness	arthritically	anticlockwise	inviolateness	semiconscious
sniftingvalve	asthenosphere	anticoagulant	invisibleness	semilogarithm
suffocatingly	asthmatically	antihistamine	irritableness	semiparasitic
suffraganship	authentically	antilogarithm	judiciousness	semipermanent
suffumigation	authenticator	antinomianism	jurisprudence	semipermeable
anagrammatise	authorisation	antipersonnel	legislatively	semiporcelain
anagrammatism	authoritarian	antiscorbutic	legislatorial	serialisation
biogeographer	authoritative	arbitrariness	lepidopterist	sericulturist

seriousminded	chalcoography	spelaeologist	isomerisation	grandiloquent
sewingmachine	challengeable	speleological	isometrically	grandmotherly
socialisation	challengingly	stalkinghorse	mammaliferous	gymnastically
sociocultural	collaboration	stoloniferous	mesmerisation	gymnospermous
socioeconomic	collaborative	stylistically	mismanagement	hypnoanalysis
solicitorship	collaterality	sublieutenant	mnemotechnics	hypnotisation
solidungulate	colleagueship	swallowtailed	mummification	identicalness
sovietologist	collectedness	syllabication	myrmecologist	inanimateness
sprightliness	collectorship	tablespoonful	normalisation	lignification
stainlessness	collieshangie	thalassocracy	onomatopoetic	magnanimously
stoichiometry	colloquialism	triliteralism	permutability	magnetisation
strikebreaker	declaratively	uncleanliness	prematureness	magnetomotive
subirrigation	dialectically	unflinchingly	premeditation	magnetosphere
thrillingness	efflorescence	villeggiatura	premeditative	magnification
titillatingly	exclusiveness	violoncellist	premillennial	magnificently
toxicological	explanatorily	wellapPointed	premonitorily	magniloquence
uncircumcised	explorational	wholesomeness	primigravidae	manneristical
undisciplined	explosiveness	woolgathering	primitiveness	mountainously
unrighteously	faultlessness	worldlyminded	primogenitary	mountebankery
unwillingness	followthrough	aluminiferous	primogenitive	odontoglossum
vacillatingly	foolhardiness	aluminisation	primogeniture	odontological
verifiability	fullfashioned	animadversion	primordiality	openheartedly
verisimilarly	guilelessness	animalisation	promiscuously	opinionatedly
viniculturist	guiltlessness	anomalistical	reembarkation	orangeblossom
visionariness	hallucination	anomalousness	reimbursement	painstakingly
viticulturist	hallucinative	aromatisation	salmonellosis	painterliness
vivisectional	hallucinatory	atomistically	shamelessness	Pennsylvanian
conjecturable	healthfulness	blameableness	staminiferous	pennyfarthing
conjecturally	hollowhearted	blamelessness	stomatologist	pennypinching
conjugateness	implacability	chemoreceptor	submachinegun	phanerogamous
conjugational	implicatively	climactically	summarisation	phenomenalise
conjunctional	inclusiveness	climatologist	symmetrically	phenomenalism
conjunctively	ineligibility	climbingframe	terminability	phenomenalist
disjunctively	inflexibility	commandership	terminational	phenomenology
prejudicially	inflexionless	commemoration	terminatively	phenylalanine
projectionist	inflorescence	commemorative	thimblerigged	phonautograph
zinjanthropus	influentially	commemoratory	thimblerigger	planimetrical
backformation	italicisation	commensurable	tremulousness	plenitudinous
backpedalling	jollification	commensurably	unambiguously	plenteousness
backscratcher	malleableness	commercialise	unemotionally	plentifulness
backwardation	mellifluously	commercialism	unimpassioned	pointillistic
balkanisation	millefeuilles	commercialist	unimpeachable	pointlessness
Berkeleianism	millennialism	commiseration	vermiculation	principalship
bookingoffice	millionairess	commiserative	whimsicalness	pronounceable
brokenhearted	mollification	communication	agonistically	pronouncement
lackadaisical	mouldingboard	communicative	anonymousness	pronunciation
lickerishness	negligibility	communicatory	blanketflower	quincentenary
mackerelshark	nucleoprotein	communisation	boundlessness	quincuncially
nickeliferous	nullification	communitarian	bounteousness	quingentenary
Shakespearean	ochlocratical	commutability	bountifulness	quinquagenary
Shakespearian	palletisation	cosmopolitise	cannibalistic	Quinquagesima
sicklefeather	phalansterian	cosmopolitism	carnivorously	quinquevalent
smokelessness	philanthropic	criminalistic	changeability	quintillionth
talkativeness	philhellenism	criminologist	changefulness	quintuplicate
turkeygobbler	philhellenist	dermatologist	chinkerinchee	reincarnation
acclimatation	philosophical	diametrically	clandestinely	reinforcement
agglomeration	philosophiser	dismantlement	coenaesthesis	reinstatement
agglomerative	phyllophagous	dismemberment	connaturality	reintegration
agglutination	polliniferous	dramatisation	connectedness	reinvigorator
agglutinative	preliminarily	dramaturgical	cornification	roentgenogram
amplification	prolegomenary	ecumenicalism	counteraction	roentgenology
analogousness	prolegomenous	examinational	counteractive	runningstitch
anglicisation	proliferation	examinatorial	counterattack	scandalmonger
AngloAmerican	proliferative	exemplariness	counterchange	scintillating
AngloCatholic	proliferously	formalisation	countercharge	scintillation
applicability	prolification	formidability	counterfeiter	signalisation
applicatively	psilanthropic	formulisation	counterstroke	significantly
belleslettres	qualification	geometrically	counterweight	signification
belligerently	qualificatory	geomorphology	countinghouse	significative
bibliographer	qualitatively	germanisation	craniological	slangingmatch
bibliographic	realistically	glamorisation	dauntlessness	somnambulator
bibliolatrist	reflexibility	graminivorous	deontological	somniloquence
bibliolatrous	replenishment	grammatically	ethnocentrism	soundingboard
bibliological	rollercoaster	haematologist	evangelically	Spencerianism
bibliophilism	scolopendrium	harmonisation	exanthematous	spindlelegged
bibliophilist	sculpturesque	helminthiasis	frontogenesis	spindleshanks
brilliantness	smellingsalts	helminthology	garnetiferous	spinelessness
calligraphist	soulsearching	hermaphrodite	granddaughter	spinninghouse
callisthenics		hermeneutical	grandfatherly	spinningwheel

```
spontaneously  axiomatically  inconsistency  resourcefully  corporativism
standoffishly  bloodboltered  inconspicuous  revolutionary  cryptanalysis
thanklessness  bloodcurdling  incontestable  revolutionise  cryptanalytic
thenceforward  bloodlessness  incontestably  revolutionism  cryptographer
thundershower  bloodrelation  incontinently  revolutionist  cryptographic
thunderstruck  Bloomsburyite  inconvenience  sadomasochism  cryptological
tranquilliser  cacographical  inconveniency  sadomasochist  deipnosophist
transatlantic  chromatically  inconvertible  scholarliness  desperateness
transcendence  chromatograph  inconvertibly  scholasticism  diaphragmatic
transcendency  chromatolytic  inconvincible  schoolteacher  disparagement
transcription  chromatophore  incorporation  secondariness  disparagingly
transcriptive  chromospheric  incorporative  serologically  disparateness
transformable  chronographic  incorporeally  shootingbrake  dispassionate
transgression  chronological  incorrectness  shootingrange  displantation
transgressive  colourfulness  incorruptible  shootingstick  disposability
transistorise  cryobiologist  incorruptibly  smoothingiron  dispossession
transitionary  cytochemistry  incorruptness  sprocketwheel  dispraisingly
translational  decomposition  indoctrinator  subordinately  disproportion
transliterate  decompression  informational  subordination  elephantiasis
translocation  decontaminate  informatively  subordinative  epiphenomenal
translucently  decontrolling  inhospitality  taxonomically  epiphenomenon
translucidity  decortication  innocuousness  theologically  graphological
transmigrator  deforestation  innoxiousness  theoretically  herpetologist
transmissible  deformational  insociability  topographical  inappreciable
transmittable  demonstration  insolubleness  topologically  inappreciably
transmutation  demonstrative  involuntarily  toxoplasmosis  inappropriate
transmutative  devolutionary  laboriousness  typographical  inopportunely
transnational  devolutionist  melodiousness  typologically  inspectorship
transparently  disobediently  melodramatics  uncomfortable  inspirational
transpiration  encompassment  melodramatise  uncomfortably  morphogenesis
transpiratory  encouragement  melodramatist  uncompetitive  morphogenetic
transportable  encouragingly  metonymically  uncomplaining  morphological
transposition  endocrinology  mitochondrion  uncomplicated  neoplasticism
transshipment  enjoyableness  monochromatic  unconceivable  nonproductive
transshipping  entomological  monocotyledon  unconcernedly  perpendicular
transversally  entomophagous  monodactylous  unconditional  preparatively
unanimousness  entomophilous  monogrammatic  unconditioned  preparatorily
unanticipated  entomostracan  monometallism  unconformable  preponderance
unenlightened  erroneousness  monometallist  unconquerable  preponderancy
uninformative  excommunicate  monomolecular  unconsciously  prepositional
unintelligent  exponentially  mononucleosis  unconstrained  prepossessing
unintentional  expostulation  monophthongal  uncoordinated  prepossession
uninterrupted  expostulatory  Monophysitism  unforgettable  prepreference
vernacularise  feloniousness  monosyllabism  unforgettably  proparoxytone
vernacularism  ferociousness  monosymmetric  unforthcoming  prophetically
vernacularity  gerontocratic  Monotheletism  unfortunately  proportionate
vernalisation  gerontologist  monotrematous  unsociability  propositional
vulnerability  homoeomorphic  negotiability  vapourishness  proprietorial
wrongheadedly  homoeopathist  notoriousness  xylographical  proprioceptor
abiologically  homogeneously  obnoxiousness  zygodactylous  purposelessly
absorbability  homoiothermal  octocentenary  anaphrodisiac  purposiveness
accommodating  homoiothermic  oecologically  bumptiousness  resplendently
accommodation  homosexuality  oleomargarine  campanologist  rhapsodically
accommodative  honorifically  ontogenically  camphoraceous  shapelessness
accompaniment  hypochondriac  ontologically  compagination  steppingstone
accoutrements  hypoglycaemia  opportuneness  companionable  subpostmaster
acrobatically  hypothecation  opportunistic  companionably  sulphureously
admonishingly  ideographical  oppositionist  companionless  sumptuousness
aerodynamical  ideologically  oreographical  companionship  supplantation
afforestation  idiomatically  pococurantism  comparability  supplementary
alcoholically  idiosyncratic  preoccupation  comparatively  suppositional
alcoholometer  ignominiously  preordainment  compartmental  symphonically
alcoholometry  illogicalness  preordination  compassionate  symphoniously
apportionment  immovableness  pyrotechnical  compatibility  temperamental
arboriculture  impolitically  recombination  compendiously  temperateness
associateship  imponderables  recommendable  competitively  tempestuously
associativity  importunately  recomposition  complainingly  temporalities
astonishingly  impossibility  reconcilement  complaisantly  temporariness
atmospherical  incombustible  reconsolidate  complementary  temporisation
atrociousness  incommunicado  reconstructor  complexedness  terpsichorean
autobiography  incompetently  reforestation  complicatedly  cinquecentist
autocatalysis  inconceivable  reformability  complimentary  frequentation
autocatalytic  inconceivably  reformational  compositeness  frequentative
autocephalous  incondensable  remonstrantly  compositional  sesquiplicate
autochthonism  incongruously  remonstration  comprehension  unequivocally
autochthonous  inconsecutive  remonstrative  comprehensive  abortifacient
autoeroticism  inconsequence  remorselessly  compressional  accreditation
automatically  inconsiderate  removableness  computational  achromaticity
autonomically  inconsistence  resolvability  cooperatively  affreightment
```

aggravatingly	hydrochloride	overemphasise	supranational	dressingtable
amorphousness	hydrocracking	overindulgent	surreptitious	exasperatedly
anfractuosity	hydrodynamics	overpopulated	surrogateship	existentially
apprehensible	hydroelectric	overqualified	swordsmanship	falsification
appropriately	hydrogenation	oversensitive	terrestrially	fissiparously
appropriation	hydromedusoid	overstatement	territorially	fossiliferous
appropriative	hydrometrical	oversubscribe	terrorisation	fossilisation
approximately	hydrostatical	overvaluation	tetrasyllable	frustratingly
approximation	hydrosulphide	patriotically	thereinbefore	geostationary
approximative	hydrosulphite	patronisingly	theriomorphic	glossographer
astronautical	hydroxylamine	petrification	thermochemist	horsechestnut
astrophysical	impracticable	petrochemical	thermodynamic	horsewhipping
attributively	impracticably	petroliferous	thermogenesis	housebreaking
barrelchested	impractically	pharisaically	thermonuclear	isostatically
boardinghouse	impressionism	pharmaceutics	thermophilous	laissezpasser
caprification	impressionist	pharmaceutist	thermoplastic	leishmaniasis
characterless	improbability	pharmacologic	thermosetting	leisureliness
choreographer	impropriation	pharmacopoeia	thermotropism	linseywoolsey
choreographic	improvability	pluralisation	thoroughbrace	meistersinger
churchmanship	improvidently	pluripresence	thoroughgoing	mensurability
clarification	improvisation	PreRaphaelite	thoroughpaced	monstrousness
coarsegrained	improvisatory	pteridologist	thurification	noiselessness
correlatively	incredibility	quarrelsomely	unarticulated	nonsensically
correlativity	incredulously	quartermaster	ungrammatical	opisthobranch
correspondent	incrementally	quartziferous	unprecedented	outspokenness
corresponsive	incriminatory	querulousness	unpredictable	outstandingly
corrigibility	inorganically	rearcommodore	unpretentious	passementerie
corroboration	intraarterial	rearrangement	unpromisingly	passionflower
corroborative	intracellular	recrimination	untrustworthy	perseveration
corroboratory	intramuscular	recriminative	vitrification	perspectively
corrosiveness	intransigeant	recriminatory	wearisomeness	perspicacious
corruptionist	intransigence	recrudescence	worrisomeness	perspicuously
courteousness	intrapersonal	recrystallise	balsamiferous	phosphoretted
courtsmartial	intravenously	refractometer	blasphemously	physiognomist
decrepitation	intricateness	refrigeration	blastogenesis	physiographer
degranulation	intrinsically	regretfulness	boustrophedon	physiographic
deprecatingly	introgression	reorientation	closedcircuit	physiological
detrimentally	introspection	reprehensible	consanguinity	physiotherapy
disrespectful	introspective	reprehensibly	conscientious	prescientific
embranglement	introversible	representable	consciousness	presidentship
embrittlement	intrusiveness	reproachfully	consecutively	prestigiously
embryogenesis	jerrybuilding	reproachingly	consenescence	presumptively
embryological	librarianship	retranslation	consentaneity	prismatically
energetically	lucrativeness	retroactively	consentaneous	prosopography
everlastingly	macrocephalic	retroactivity	consequential	prospectively
excrescential	macromolecule	retrogression	conservatoire	prostaglandin
expressionism	matriculation	retrogressive	considerately	prosthodontia
expressionist	matrilineally	retrospection	consideration	questioningly
expropriation	metrification	retrospective	consolidation	questionnaire
extracellular	microanalysis	sabrerattling	consolidative	Russification
extragalactic	microcephalic	sacramentally	consolidatory	sansculottism
extrajudicial	micrococcocci	sacrificially	conspicuously	seismographer
extraordinary	microdetector	sacrosanctity	constellation	seismographic
extraphysical	micronutrient	scarification	constellatory	seismological
extrapolation	microorganism	scorbutically	consternation	sensationally
extratropical	microphyllous	scorification	constrainable	senselessness
extravagantly	microscopical	scorpiongrass	constrainedly	sensitisation
extravasation	microtonality	searchwarrant	constructable	sensitiveness
extravascular	mourningcloak	secretarybird	constructible	spasmodically
extrinsically	mourningpaper	secretaryship	consumptively	subsaturation
ferrimagnetic	nearsightedly	secretiveness	crosscultural	subsequential
ferroconcrete	neurastheniac	sharecropping	crossgartered	subserviently
ferroelectric	neurovascular	sharpshooting	crosshatching	substantially
ferromagnetic	nitrification	shorttempered	crosspurposes	substantively
fibrovascular	nitrobacteria	sorrowfulness	crossquestion	substantivise
flirtatiously	nitrocompound	spermatoblast	crystalgazing	substitutable
floricultural	nonresistance	spermatogenic	crystallinity	substructural
floristically	nonreturnable	spermatophore	dissemblingly	swashbuckling
garrulousness	nutritionally	spermatophyte	dissemination	toastmistress
glorification	obtrusiveness	spiritualness	disseminative	tonsillectomy
hairsplitting	odoriferously	sportsmanlike	dissemination	topsyturvydom
heartbreaking	operativeness	sportsmanship	dissimilarity	trustworthily
heartlessness	opprobriously	stercoraceous	dissimilation	unestablished
heartsickness	ostreiculture	stereographic	dissimilitude	versicoloured
horripilation	overabundance	stereoscopist	dissimulation	versification
hybridisation	overbearingly	sterilisation	dissolubility	abstractional
hydraulically	overconfident	sternforemost	dissoluteness	acetification
hydrocephalic	overcredulous	stirpiculture	dissymetrical	acetylcholine
hydrocephalus	overelaborate	subreptitious	dressimprover	acotyledonous

aesthetically	fortification	particularism	vantageground	reduplication
apathetically	fortississimo	particularist	ventriloquial	reduplicative
arithmetician	fortunateness	particularity	ventriloquise	regurgitation
auctioneering	fortunehunter	partridgewood	ventriloquism	rejuvenescent
Australianism	fortuneteller	peptonisation	ventriloquist	republicanise
bacteriolysis	gasteropodous	pestiferously	venturesomely	republicanism
bacteriolytic	gastrocnemius	photochemical	venturousness	republication
bacteriophage	gastroenteric	photochromics	vertiginously	repulsiveness
BaltoSlavonic	gastrological	photochromism	victimisation	requisiteness
battlecruiser	gastronomical	photoelectric	weatherbeaten	resuscitation
beatification	gentlemanlike	photoelectron	whithersoever	resuscitative
biotechnology	geotropically	photoemission	winterberries	rheumatically
brotherliness	gesticulation	photoemissive	worthlessness	ritualisation
brutalisation	gesticulative	photoperiodic	xanthochroism	scrumptiously
butterfingers	gesticulatory	photopositive	acculturation	seductiveness
butterflyfish	glutinousness	photoreceptor	acculturative	sequentiality
buttonthrough	gratification	phytoplankton	acquiescently	sequestration
cartilaginous	grotesqueness	picturepalace	acquiescingly	shoulderblade
cauterisation	helterskelter	picturesquely	actualisation	shoulderstrap
centreforward	heptasyllabic	platiniferous	argumentation	structuralism
centrifugally	histrionicism	platitudinise	argumentative	structuralist
centripetally	horticultural	platitudinous	beauteousness	structureless
certification	ichthyography	platyhelminth	daguerreotype	thaumaturgist
certificatory	ichthyologist	plethorically	deductibility	thoughtlessly
chateaubriand	ichthyosaurus	pontification	desultoriness	thoughtreader
clothesbasket	imitativeness	postclassical	documentalist	traumatically
containership	inattentively	postcommunion	documentation	troublesomely
contamination	instantaneity	postoperative	excursiveness	troublousness
contaminative	instantaneous	postulational	excusableness	unputdownable
contemplation	instinctively	pretentiously	expurgatorial	unqualifiedly
contemplative	institutional	pretermission	exquisiteness	unquestioning
contentedness	instructional	pretermitting	facultatively	unsubstantial
contentiously	instructively	preternatural	flourishingly	unsuitability
continentally	justification	protectionism	hocuspocussed	valuelessness
contortionist	justificative	protectionist	illustriously	visualisation
contrabandist	justificatory	protectorship	immunological	volumenometer
contrabassoon	juxtaposition	proteinaceous	immunotherapy	voluntariness
contraception	leatherjacket	Protestantism	immutableness	voluntaristic
contraceptive	leptocephalic	protohistoric	impulsiveness	Calvinistical
contractility	leptospirosis	protonotarial	incurableness	convalescence
contractually	letterperfect	protuberantly	incuriousness	conventionary
contradiction	loathsomeness	rapturousness	inductiveness	conversazione
contradictory	Malthusianism	rattlebrained	industrialise	conversazioni
contrafagotto	martyrisation	rectangularly	industrialism	convertiplane
contrapuntist	martyrologist	rectification	industrialist	convexoconvex
contrariously	masterfulness	rectilinearly	industriously	convocational
contravention	mirthlessness	restoratively	infundibulate	convulsionary
controversial	mistrustfully	restrictively	infuriatingly	curvilinearly
corticotropic	mistrustingly	rontgenoscopy	ingurgitation	frivolousness
corticotropin	mortification	sententiously	injudiciously	galvanisation
costeffective	mouthwatering	sentimentally	injuriousness	gravitational
cottonpicking	multicellular	septentrional	inquisitional	inevitability
customariness	multicoloured	skateboarding	inquisitively	laevorotation
dastardliness	multinational	softpedalling	inquisitorial	laevorotatory
deathlessness	multinucleate	southeasterly	insubordinate	nervelessness
denticulation	multiplicable	southeastward	insubstantial	ovoviviparous
destructively	multitudinous	southwesterly	insufficience	pervasiveness
destructivity	mystification	southwestward	insufficiency	prevarication
deuteragonist	nectariferous	statelessness	insupportable	provincialise
Deuteronomist	northeasterly	statesmanlike	insupportably	provincialism
dexterousness	northeastward	statesmanship	insusceptible	provincialist
diathermanous	northwesterly	stationmaster	intuitiveness	provinciality
dictatorially	northwestward	statistically	luxuriousness	provisionally
distastefully	nostalgically	subternatural	misunderstand	pulverisation
distinctively	obstinateness	subterraneous	misunderstood	silvertongued
distinguished	obstructively	subtilisation	monumentalise	subversionary
distressfully	ophthalmology	syntactically	mutualisation	airworthiness
distressingly	oystercatcher	synthetically	penuriousness	answerability
distributable	pantagruelian	tantalisation	plausibleness	betweenwhiles
distrustfully	pantagruelism	tantalisingly	pneumatically	knowledgeable
doctrinairism	pantagruelist	tastelessness	pneumatolysis	knowledgeably
faithlessness	pantheistical	tautologously	pneumatolytic	seaworthiness
fantastically	pantisocratic	tentativeness	pneumatometer	snowblindness
featherheaded	parthenocarpy	testification	pneumatophore	inexhaustible
featherstitch	participation	tintinnabular	pneumogastric	inexhaustibly
featherweight	participative	tintinnabulum	pneumonectomy	inexorability
fertilisation	participatory	toothsomeness	pseudoarchaic	inexpediently
festschriften	particoloured	tortoiseshell	pseudomorphic	inexpensively
filterability	particularise	tritheistical	pseudoscience	inexperienced

inexpressible	contaminative	operativeness	vulcanisation	hypochondriac
inexpressibly	convalescence	overabundance	vulcanologist	impeccability
reexamination	dastardliness	pantagruelian	vulgarisation	impecuniosity
unexceptional	declaratively	pantagruelism	wellapPointed	indoctrinator
acrylonitrile	defeasibility	pantagruelist	zinjanthropus	inductiveness
Assyriologist	degranulation	pervasiveness	acrobatically	innocuousness
chrysanthemum	dermatologist	phalansterian	adiabatically	insectivorous
demythologise	dictatorially	philanthropic	algebraically	insociability
encyclopaedia	disharmonious	phonautograph	archbishopric	irreclaimable
encyclopaedic	dismantlement	phreatophytic	autobiography	irreclaimably
encyclopedism	disparagement	pluralisation	cerebrospinal	irrecoverable
encyclopedist	disparagingly	polyadelphous	climbingframe	irrecoverably
laryngoscopic	disparateness	precautionary	coldbloodedly	judiciousness
palynological	dispassionate	predatoriness	cryobiologist	lexicographer
polyadelphous	distastefully	prefatorially	defibrination	lexicographic
polycarbonate	dramatisation	prematureness	disobediently	ludicrousness
polychromatic	dramaturgical	preparatively	establishment	malacological
polycotyledon	educationally	preparatorily	exhibitionism	malacostracan
polydactylous	embranglement	PreRaphaelite	exhibitionist	maliciousness
polyhistorian	eschatologist	prevarication	insubordinate	Manichaeanism
polypropylene	Eucharistical	probationally	insubstantial	megacephalous
polysynthesis	evocativeness	proparoxytone	overbearingly	mitochondrion
polysynthetic	explanatorily	psilanthropic	parabolically	monochromatic
prayermeeting	extracellular	rectangularly	reembarkation	monocotyledon
sphygmography	extragalactic	reexamination	reimbursement	musicological
unsymmetrical	extrajudicial	refractometer	republicanise	objectionable
piezoelectric	extraordinary	retranslation	republicanism	objectionably
prizefighting	extraphysical	rhadamanthine	republication	objectiveness
——————	extrapolation	ritualisation	scorbutically	objectivistic
actualisation	extratropical	sacramentally	semibarbarian	octocentenary
admeasurement	extravagantly	sarcastically	semibarbarism	officiousness
aggravatingly	extravasation	selfabasement	shabbygenteel	omnicompetent
anfractuosity	extravascular	selfaddressed	snowblindness	overconfident
animadversion	fantastically	selfadjusting	thimblerigged	overcredulous
animalisation	feudalisation	selfappointed	thimblerigger	panicstricken
anomalistical	formalisation	selfapproving	troublesomely	perichondrial
anomalousness	fundamentally	selfasserting	troublousness	perichondrium
apocalyptical	galvanisation	selfassertion	unambiguously	pococurantism
archaeologist	germanisation	selfassertive	unsubstantial	polycarbonate
archaeopteryx	gymnastically	selfassurance	affectionless	polychromatic
aromatisation	haematologist	selfassuredly	agriculturist	polycotyledon
baccalaureate	haphazardness	selfawareness	Antichristian	postclassical
balkanisation	heptasyllabic	semiautomatic	anticlimactic	postcommunion
balsamiferous	hermaphrodite	sensationally	anticlockwise	preoccupation
barbarisation	hydraulically	serialisation	anticoagulant	prescientific
barbarousness	imitativeness	signalisation	associateship	principalship
beleaguerment	implacability	socialisation	associativity	quincentenary
bombastically	impracticable	somnambulator	atrociousness	quincuncially
brutalisation	impracticably	spelaeologist	audaciousness	rapaciousness
bureaucratise	impractically	squeamishness	autocatalysis	rearcommodore
campanologist	infeasibility	stomatologist	autocatalytic	reincarnation
cephalothorax	instantaneity	submachinegun	autocephalous	revaccination
characterless	instantaneous	subsaturation	autochthonism	sagaciousness
climactically	intraarterial	summarisation	autochthonous	salaciousness
climatologist	intracellular	supranational	breechloading	sansculottism
coenaesthesis	intramuscular	syllabication	capaciousness	searchwarrant
collaboration	intransigeant	syntactically	catechisation	seductiveness
collaborative	intransigence	talkativeness	chalcoography	selectiveness
collaterality	intrapersonal	tantalisation	churchmanship	selfcentredly
combativeness	intravenously	tantalisingly	conscientious	selfcollected
commandership	juxtaposition	tentativeness	consciousness	selfcommunion
compagination	lackadaisical	tetrasyllable	cytochemistry	selfconceited
companionable	lethargically	thalassocracy	deductibility	selfcondemned
companionably	librarianship	threateningly	defectiveness	selfconfessed
companionless	lucrativeness	ungrammatical	deliciousness	selfconfident
companionship	magnanimously	unhealthiness	dodecaphonist	selfconscious
comparability	mammaliferous	unicameralism	domiciliation	selfconsuming
comparatively	manganiferous	unicameralist	effectiveness	selfcontained
compartmental	mechanisation	unmeaningness	efficaciously	selfcontented
compassionate	mediatisation	unqualifiedly	encyclopaedia	selfconvicted
compatibility	mismanagement	vantageground	encyclopaedic	selfcriticism
concatenation	mutualisation	verbalisation	encyclopedism	semicivilised
concavoconvex	nectariferous	vernacularise	encyclopedist	semiconductor
confabulation	neurastheniac	vernacularism	endocrinology	semiconscious
confabulatory	niggardliness	vernacularity	expectoration	sericulturist
connaturality	normalisation	vernalisation	felicitations	solicitorship
consanguinity	nostalgically	viceadmiralty	ferociousness	Spencerianism
containership	offhandedness	visualisation	galactosaemia	sprocketwheel
contamination	onomatopoetic	volcanologist	hemicellulose	stercoraceous

```
stoichiometry  selfdirecting  consentaneity  letterperfect  prudentiality
structuralism  selfdirection  consentaneous  lickerishness  pulverisation
structuralist  selfdiscovery  consequential  lineengraving  pyrheliometer
structureless  selfdispraise  conservatoire  linseywoolsey  reflexibility
tenaciousness  solidungulate  contemplation  mackerelshark  regretfulness
thenceforward  soundingboard  contemplative  magnetisation  replenishment
timeconsuming  spindlelegged  contentedness  magnetomotive  reprehensible
toxicological  spindleshanks  contentiously  magnetosphere  reprehensibly
treacherously  standoffishly  conventionary  malleableness  representable
unaccompanied  steadfastness  conversazione  manneristical  rollercoaster
unaccountable  subeditorship  conversazioni  masterfulness  sabrerattling
unaccountably  swordsmanship  convertiplane  mathematician  secretarybird
unexceptional  thundershower  convexoconvex  mercenariness  secretaryship
unnecessarily  thunderstruck  cooperatively  mercerisation  secretiveness
unsociability  worldlyminded  correlatively  mesmerisation  selfeducation
veraciousness  zygodactylous  correlativity  millefeuilles  selfevidently
viniculturist  accreditation  correspondent  millennialism  selfexecuting
viticulturist  affreightment  corresponsive  miscegenation  selfexistence
vivaciousness  agreeableness  costeffective  miscellaneous  senselessness
voraciousness  answerability  daguerreotype  mothercountry  sententiously
accidentalism  anthelminthic  dangerousness  myrmecologist  septentrional
accidentprone  apprehensible  decrepitation  nephelometric  sequentiality
aerodynamical  asthenosphere  deprecatingly  nervelessness  sequestration
ambidexterity  authentically  desperateness  nickeliferous  sergeantmajor
ambidexterous  authenticator  deuteragonist  noiselessness  Shakespearean
archdeaconate  autoeroticism  Deuteronomist  nondeductable  Shakespearian
assiduousness  bacteriolysis  dexterousness  nonresistance  shamelessness
basidiomycete  bacteriolytic  diageotropism  nonreturnable  shapelessness
bloodboltered  bacteriophage  dialectically  nonsensically  sharecropping
bloodcurdling  barrelchested  diametrically  nucleoprotein  silvertongued
bloodlessness  belleslettres  differentiate  orchestration  skateboarding
bloodrelation  Berkeleianism  dismemberment  ostreiculture  smokelessness
boardinghouse  betweenwhiles  disrespectful  outgeneralled  solderingiron
boundlessness  biodegradable  dissemblingly  overelaborate  sovietologist
broadmindedly  biogeographer  dissemination  overemphasise  speleological
broadspectrum  biotechnology  disseminative  oystercatcher  spinelessness
clandestinely  blameableness  disseveration  palaeographer  squeezability
deciduousness  blamelessness  ecumenicalism  palaeographic  statelessness
disadvantaged  brokenhearted  egocentricity  palaeontology  statesmanlike
equidistantly  butterfingers  excrescential  palaeozoology  statesmanship
expeditionary  butterflyfish  expressionism  palletisation  stereographic
expeditiously  cauterisation  expressionist  passementerie  stereoscopist
gonadotrophic  chateaubriand  filterability  peaceableness  streetwalking
gonadotrophin  choreographer  flagellantism  perfectionism  subreptitious
granddaughter  choreographic  forgetfulness  perfectionist  subsequential
grandfatherly  closedcircuit  garnetiferous  perpendicular  subserviently
grandiloquent  colleagueship  gasteropodous  perseveration  subternatural
grandmotherly  collectedness  geocentricism  phanerogamous  subterraneous
immediateness  collectorship  geometrically  pigheadedness  subversionary
injudiciously  commemoration  globetrotting  ponderability  surreptitious
insidiousness  commemorative  gracelessness  ponderousness  Swedenborgian
invidiousness  commemoratory  grotesqueness  porcellaneous  symmetrically
lepidopterist  commensurable  guilelessness  prayermeeting  tablespoonful
lepidopterous  commensurably  gynaecocratic  precentorship  tastelessness
maladaptation  commercialise  gynaecologist  predestinator  temperamental
maladjustment  commercialism  helterskelter  preferability  temperateness
maladminister  commercialist  hermeneutical  premeditation  tempestuously
maladroitness  compendiously  herpetologist  premeditative  tendentiously
melodiousness  competitively  homoeomorphic  pretentiously  tenderhearted
melodramatics  conceitedness  homoeopathist  pretermission  tercentennial
melodramatise  concentration  horsechestnut  pretermitting  terrestrially
melodramatist  concentrative  horsewhipping  preternatural  thereinbefore
monodactylous  concentricity  housebreaking  pricelessness  threecornered
mouldingboard  conceptualise  impressionism  prizefighting  threequarters
occidentalise  conceptualism  impressionist  processionary  traceableness
Occidentalism  conceptualist  incredibility  processionist  tricentennial
Occidentalist  concertmaster  incredulously  professoriate  turkeygobbler
paradoxically  concessionary  incrementally  professorship  uncleanliness
polydactylous  condescension  inflexibility  progenitorial  unfeelingness
pseudoarchaic  confectionary  inflexionless  projectionist  unprecedented
pseudomorphic  confectionery  inspectorship  prolegomenary  unpredictable
pseudoscience  confederation  isomerisation  prolegomenous  unpretentious
scandalmonger  confederative  isometrically  protectionism  unquestioning
schadenfreude  confessionary  jiggerypokery  protectionist  valuelessness
selfdeceiving  conjecturable  judgeadvocate  protectorship  villeggiatura
selfdeception  conjecturally  Kidderminster  proteinaceous  voicelessness
selfdeceptive  connectedness  lancecorporal  Protestantism  vulnerability
selfdefeating  consecutively  lancesergeant  prudentialism  wholesomeness
selfdependent  consenescence  lecherousness  prudentialist  winterberries
```

wonderfulness topographical psychogenetic collieshangie intrinsically
wonderworking typographical psychokinesis combinatorial intuitiveness
woodengraving unrighteously psychokinetic commiseration italicisation
zoogeographer woolgathering psychological commiserative jollification
zoogeographic wrongheadedly psychometrics conditionally justification
artificiality xylographical psychometrist confidingness justificative
backformation aesthetically psychophysics configuration justificatory
barefacedness alcoholically psychosomatic considerately kaleidoscopic
beneficiation alcoholometer psychosurgery consideration lignification
birefringence alcoholometry psychotherapy continentally Machiavellian
chieftainship anachronistic psychrometric cornification machicolation
disaffectedly anachronously saccharimeter corrigibility machinegunner
disaffirmance anaphrodisiac saccharimetry corticotropic magnification
fullfashioned antihistamine saccharometer corticotropin magnificently
indefatigable apathetically southeasterly craniological magniloquence
indefatigably arithmetician southeastward criminalistic matriculation
indifferently brachycephaly southwesterly criminologist matrilineally
ineffableness brachydactyly southwestward curvilinearly mellifluously
ineffectively brachypterous sulphureously deceitfulness mercilessness
ineffectually brotherliness swashbuckling denticulation metrification
inefficacious camphoraceous symphonically detrimentally millionairess
inefficiently clothesbasket symphoniously disciplinable mollification
inoffensively coldheartedly synchronistic disfigurement mortification
insufficience conchological synchronously dissimilarity multicellular
insufficiency deathlessness synthetically dissimilation multicoloured
irrefrangible diaphragmatic teachableness dissimilitude multinational
liebfraumilch diathermanous toothsomeness dissimulation multinucleate
manifestation elephantiasis trichromatism distinctively multiplicable
manifestative epiphenomenal tritheistical distinguished multitudinous
reaffirmation epiphenomenon vouchsafement dulcification mummification
reinforcement faithlessness weatherbeaten embrittlement mystification
selffertility featherheaded whithersoever examinational negligibility
selfforgetful featherstitch worthlessness examinatorial nitrification
uninformative featherweight xanthochroism exquisiteness nonfigurative
verifiability foolhardiness acclimatation extrinsically nullification
allegorically frighteningly acetification falsification nutritionally
ambiguousness frightfulness acidification fasciculation obstinateness
cacographical geochronology acquiescently fascinatingly odoriferously
categorically graphological acquiescingly Fascistically opinionatedly
changeability halfheartedly agonistically ferrimagnetic overindulgent
changefulness hardheartedly aluminiferous fertilisation ovoviviparous
desegregation ichthyography aluminisation fissiparously paediatrician
draggletailed ichthyologist amphiprostyle floricultural pantisocratic
egregiousness ichthyosaurus amplification floristically parliamentary
energetically inexhaustible anglicisation formidability participation
enlightenment inexhaustibly applicability fortification participative
evangelically isochronously applicatively fortississimo participatory
homogeneously laughableness archidiaconal fossiliferous particoloured
hypoglycaemia laughingstock archimandrite fossilisation particularise
ideographical leatherjacket architectonic gesticulation particularism
illogicalness leishmaniasis architectural gesticulative particularist
inorganically loathsomeness atheistically gesticulatory particularity
insignificant Malthusianism atomistically glaciological passionflower
integumentary merchandising attainability glorification patriotically
litigiousness mirthlessness attributively glutinousness pestiferously
manageability mischievously auctioneering graminivorous petrification
metagrobolise morphogenesis beatification gratification pharisaically
monogrammatic morphogenetic belligerently gravitational physiognomist
mutagenically morphological bibliographer heebiejeebies physiographer
navigableness mouthwatering bibliographic helminthiasis physiographic
nonaggression neighbourhood bibliolatrist helminthology physiological
ontogenically northeasterly bibliolatrous homoiothermal physiotherapy
orangeblossom northeastward bibliological homoiothermic piscicultural
oreographical northwesterly bibliophilism horripilation planimetrical
panegyrically northwestward bibliophilist horticultural platiniferous
pedagogically openheartedly bookingoffice hybridisation platitudinise
peregrination ophthalmology calcification imaginatively platitudinous
quingentenary pantheistical calligraphist implicatively plenitudinous
religiousness parthenocarpy callisthenics inanimateness pluripresence
renegotiation philhellenism Calvinistical incriminatory polliniferous
rontgenoscopy philhellenist cannibalistic ineligibility pontification
selfgenerated plethorically caprification inevitability precipitantly
selfgoverning polyhistorian carcinomatous inquisitional precipitately
slangingmatch prophetically cardiographer inquisitively precipitation
sphygmography psychasthenia carnivorously inquisitorial precipitative
sprightliness psychoanalyse cartilaginous inspirational precipitously
telegrammatic psychoanalyst certification instinctively predicability
thoughtlessly psychodynamic certificatory institutional predicamental
thoughtreader psychogenesis clarification intricateness predicatively

prefiguration	triliteralism	impalpability	automatically	sadomasochist
prefigurative	unanimousness	impolitically	axiomatically	schematically
prefigurement	unflinchingly	impulsiveness	Bloomsburyite	scrumptiously
prehistorical	unsuitability	infallibilism	ceremonialism	sedimentation
preliminarily	verbigeration	infallibilist	ceremonialist	seismographer
premillennial	vermiculation	infallibility	ceremoniously	seismographic
presidentship	versicoloured	insolubleness	chlamydomonas	seismological
primigravidae	versification	intelligencer	chlamydospore	solemnisation
primitiveness	vertiginously	intelligently	chrematistics	spasmodically
profitability	victimisation	involuntarily	chromatically	spermatoblast
profitsharing	vitrification	irreligionist	chromatograph	spermatogenic
prohibitively	wearisomeness	irreligiously	chromatolytic	spermatophore
proliferation	worrisomeness	kapellmeister	chromatophore	spermatophyte
proliferative	blackguardism	knowledgeable	chromospheric	stigmatically
proliferously	blanketflower	knowledgeably	cinematically	thaumaturgist
prolification	chinkerinchee	lamellibranch	cinematograph	thermochemist
promiscuously	chuckleheaded	levelcrossing	decomposition	thermodynamic
provincialise	crackerbarrel	metalliferous	decompression	thermogenesis
provincialism	foreknowledge	metallisation	disembodiment	thermonuclear
provincialist	knickerbocker	metallography	documentalist	thermophilous
provinciality	knuckleduster	metallurgical	documentation	thermoplastic
provisionally	quicktempered	neoclassicism	dreamlessness	thermosetting
pteridologist	quickwittedly	neoclassicist	encompassment	thermotropism
qualification	selfknowledge	neoplasticism	enigmatically	thigmotropism
qualificatory	shockabsorber	oecologically	entomological	thremmatology
qualitatively	stalkinghorse	ontologically	entomophagous	traumatically
realistically	stickingplace	paddlesteamer	entomophilous	uncomfortable
recrimination	strikebreaker	papillomatous	entomostracan	uncomfortably
recriminative	thanklessness	parallelogram	excommunicate	uncompetitive
recriminatory	abiologically	phyllophagous	extemporarily	uncomplaining
rectification	accelerometer	problematical	foraminiferal	uncomplicated
rectilinearly	acculturation	pusillanimity	forementioned	unfamiliarity
refrigeration	acculturative	pusillanimous	fragmentarily	unremittingly
reorientation	acrylonitrile	rattlebrained	fragmentation	unsymmetrical
requisiteness	allelomorphic	recalcitrance	funambulation	volumenometer
runningstitch	antilogarithm	repulsiveness	grammatically	actinomorphic
Russification	apheliotropic	resolvability	idiomatically	actinomycetes
sacrificially	appellatively	resplendently	ignominiously	actinomycosis
scarification	availableness	revelationist	incombustible	administrable
scorification	battlecruiser	revolutionary	incommunicado	administrator
selfimportant	bewilderingly	revolutionise	incompetently	admonishingly
selfinduction	bouillabaisse	revolutionism	intemperately	adventuresome
selfindulgent	brilliantness	revolutionist	judgmatically	adventurously
selfinflicted	burglariously	scholarliness	kinematically	affenpinscher
selfinsurance	canaliculated	scholasticism	kinematograph	antinomianism
semeiological	candlelighter	semilogarithm	metamorphoses	argentiferous
sensitisation	candlesnuffer	serologically	metamorphosis	astonishingly
sensitiveness	challengeable	shoulderblade	Mohammedanism	atlantosaurus
sentimentally	challengingly	shoulderstrap	monometallism	attentiveness
significantly	cobelligerent	sicklefeather	monometallist	autonomically
signification	complainingly	singlehearted	monomolecular	bioenergetics
significative	complaisantly	smellingsalts	monumentalise	brainlessness
somniloquence	complementary	supplantation	Muhammadanism	brainstorming
sophistically	complexedness	supplementary	oleomargarine	businesswoman
sophisticated	complicatedly	swallowtailed	ornamentation	cabinetmaking
specification	complimentary	synallagmatic	paramagnetism	chronographic
spiritualness	conflagration	theologically	perambulation	chronological
stabilisation	conflictingly	thrillingness	perambulatory	cylindrically
staminiferous	conglomeratic	tiddledywinks	pharmaceutics	decontaminate
stationmaster	coreligionist	titillatingly	pharmaceutist	decontrolling
statistically	desultoriness	topologically	pharmacologic	defencelessly
sterilisation	developmental	troglodytical	pharmacopoeia	defensibility
stylistically	devolutionary	typologically	pneumatically	deipnosophist
sublieutenant	devolutionist	umbelliferous	pneumatolysis	demonstration
subtilisation	dichlamydeous	unbelievingly	pneumatolytic	demonstrative
symbiotically	displantation	unenlightened	pneumatometer	dependability
tachistoscope	doublecrosser	unrelentingly	pneumatophore	diagnostician
tergiversator	doubledealing	unselfishness	pneumogastric	dimensionally
terminability	doubleglazing	unwillingness	pneumonectomy	dimensionless
terminational	doublejointed	vacillatingly	pragmatically	disengagement
terminatively	doubletongued	wheelerdealer	prismatically	disintegrator
territorially	embellishment	accommodating	pyrimethamine	disinterested
testification	equilibration	accommodation	recombination	disinvestment
theriomorphic	everlastingly	accommodative	recommendable	eccentrically
thurification	facultatively	accompaniment	recomposition	erroneousness
tintinnabular	feuilletonism	acrimoniously	regimentation	essentialness
tintinnabulum	feuilletonist	argumentation	rheumatically	expansibility
tonsillectomy	gentlemanlike	argumentative	rudimentarily	expansiveness
traditionally	ideologically	asthmatically	sadomasochism	expensiveness

exponentially reconstructor contortionist leptocephalic prepossessing
extensibility reminiscently convocational leptospirosis prepossession
extensionally remonstrantly corporativism macrocephalic primogenitary
extensiveness remonstration corroboration macromolecule primogeniture
feloniousness remonstrative corroborative mangoldwurzel primogeniture
gerontocratic resentfulness corroboratory meadowsaffron primordiality
gerontologist retentiveness corrosiveness meteorologist proconsulship
goodnaturedly revendication cosmopolitise Methodistical pronounceable
greensickness scientologist cosmopolitism microanalysis pronouncement
gynandromorph secondariness cottonpicking microcephalic proportionate
hymenopterous sedentariness customariness micrococcocci propositional
immunological selenocentric deodorisation microdetector prosopography
immunotherapy selenographer dichotomously micronutrient protohistoric
impenetration selenographic discoloration microorganism protonotarial
imponderables selenological discommodious microphyllous purposelessly
incandescence serendipitous disconcerting microscopical purposiveness
inconceivable sewingmachine disconcertion microtonality radioactivity
inconceivably spinninghouse disconformity miscomprehend radiolocation
incondensable spinningwheel disconnection misconception radiotelegram
incongruously splendiferous discontinuity misgovernment randomisation
inconsecutive splenetically discontinuous mnemotechnics ratiocination
inconsequence squandermania dishonourable nationalistic ratiocinative
inconsiderate stainlessness dishonourably neurovascular rationalistic
inconsistence sternforemost disposability nitrobacteria reproachfully
inconsistency strangulation dispossession nitrocompound reproachingly
inconspicuous strenuousness dissolubility noncollegiate restoratively
incontestable taxonomically dissoluteness noncompliance retroactively
incontestably technicalness efflorescence nonconducting retroactivity
incontinently technological elaborateness nonconforming retrogression
inconvenience telencephalon ethnocentrism nonconformism retrogressive
inconveniency theanthropism explorational nonconformist retrospection
inconvertible triangularity explosiveness nonconformity retrospective
inconvertibly triangulation expropriation nonforfeiting rhodochrosite
inconvincible tyrannosaurus ferroconcrete nongovernment sacrosanctity
infinitesimal unconceivable ferroelectric ochlocratical salmonellosis
infundibulate unconcernedly ferromagnetic opprobriously schoolteacher
ingeniousness unconditional fibrovascular orthocephalic scolopendrium
ingenuousness unconditioned followthrough orthognathism seaworthiness
insensateness unconformable frivolousness orthognathous selfopinioned
insensibility unconquerable geomorphology osteomyelitis SerboCroatian
insensitively unconsciously glamorisation paedomorphism seriousminded
insensitivity unconstrained goniometrical pathogenicity sociocultural
insinuatingly unmentionable gymnaspermous pathognomonic socioeconomic
intangibility voluntariness harbourmaster patronisingly sorrowfulness
intensiveness voluntaristic harmonisation peptonisation stoloniferous
intentionally achromaticity hollowhearted periodisation subcontractor
inventiveness aggiornamento homeomorphism petrochemical subpostmaster
inventorially agglomeration hydrocephalic petroliferous suffocatingly
invincibility agglomerative hydrocephalus phenomenalise suppositional
laryngoscopic airworthiness hydrochloride phenomenalism surrogateship
Maginotminded amniocentesis hydrocracking phenomenalist symbolisation
mesencephalon analogousness hydrodynamics phenomenology tautologously
metonymically angiospermous hydroelectric philosophical temporalities
misanthropist AngloAmerican hydrogenation philosophiser temporariness
misunderstand AngloCatholic hydromedusoid photochemical temporisation
misunderstood appropriately hydrometrical photochromics terrorisation
momentariness appropriation hydrostatical photochromism thoroughbrace
momentousness appropriative hydrosulphide photoelectric thoroughgoing
mononucleosis approximately hydrosulphite photoelectron thoroughpaced
mourningcloak approximation hydroxylamine photoemission tortoiseshell
mourningpaper approximative hypnoanalysis photoemissive trigonometric
nomenclatural astronautical hypnotisation photoperiodic uncoordinated
oceanographer astrophysical improbability photopositive unemotionally
oceanographic authorisation impropriation photoreceptor unpromisingly
offensiveness authoritarian improvability phycoerythrin unwholesomely
organogenesis authoritative improvidently phytoplankton violoncellist
organotherapy BaltoSlavonic improvisation piezoelectric visionariness
palynological bamboozlement improvisatory pigeonchested windowshopper
paranormality buttonthrough inexorability pigeonhearted acceptability
parenthetical carboniferous inflorescence pigeonlivered amorphousness
phrenetically carbonisation introgression poliomyelitis antipersonnel
phrenological chemoreceptor introspection postoperative backpedalling
plaintiveness colloquialism introspective preconception blasphemously
potentiometer compositeness introversible predominantly conspicuously
preengagement compositional inviolability predomination deceptiveness
preengineered concomitantly inviolateness premonitorily disappearance
prognosticate consolidation laevorotation preponderance encapsulation
reconcilement consolidative laevorotatory preponderancy encephalogram
reconsolidate consolidatory landownership prepositional equiponderant

equiponderate	quinquevalent	deterministic	incorporative	opportuneness
equipotential	tranquilliser	diagrammatise	incorporeally	opportunistic
exasperatedly	absorbability	disarticulate	incorrectness	owneroccupier
exceptionable	abstractional	discreditable	incorruptible	paperhangings
exceptionably	admirableness	discreditably	incorruptibly	partridgewood
exceptionally	adversatively	discretionary	incorruptness	paterfamilias
exemplariness	advertisement	discriminator	incurableness	paternalistic
hemiparasitic	affirmatively	disgracefully	incuriousness	penuriousness
inappreciable	afforestation	dispraisingly	inferentially	polarographic
inappreciably	aircraftwoman	disproportion	informational	powerlessness
inappropriate	alternatively	distressfully	informatively	prairieoyster
independently	anaerobically	distressingly	infuriatingly	preordainment
inexpediently	anagrammatise	distributable	ingurgitation	preordination
inexpensively	anagrammatism	distrustfully	injuriousness	prepreference
inexperienced	anthropogenic	divertisement	inscriptional	procrastinate
inexpressible	anthropometry	doctrinairism	instructional	progressional
inexpressibly	anthropopathy	effervescence	instructively	progressively
inopportunely	anthropophagi	effervescency	intercalation	progressivism
insupportable	anthropophagy	embarrassment	intercellular	proprietorial
insupportably	anthroposophy	entertainment	intercolonial	proprioceptor
irreplaceable	apportionment	environmental	intercolumnar	quadragesimal
irrepressible	arboriculture	epeirogenesis	intercropping	quadrennially
irrepressibly	arthritically	epigrammatise	intercultural	quadricipital
leadpoisoning	ascertainable	epigrammatist	intercurrence	quadrilateral
lifepreserver	ascertainment	excursiveness	interdentally	quadrillionth
manipulatable	assertiveness	expurgatorial	interdigitate	quadripartite
metaphosphate	asserveration	extermination	interestingly	quadrumvirate
metaphysician	Assyriologist	exterminatory	intergalactic	quadruplicate
monophthongal	Australianism	exteroceptive	interjectural	quadruplicity
Monophysitism	centreforward	exterritorial	interlacement	quarrelsomely
nonappearance	centrifugally	flourishingly	interlocution	rearrangement
outspokenness	centripetally	gastrocnemius	interlocutory	referentially
overpopulated	cheerlessness	gastroenteric	interlocutrix	reforestation
paraphernalia	clairaudience	gastrological	intermarriage	reformability
perspectively	clearheadedly	gastronomical	intermediator	reformational
perspicacious	clearinghouse	generalisable	intermittence	regardfulness
perspicuously	comprehension	generalissimo	international	regurgitation
phosphoretted	comprehensive	geotropically	interoceptive	remorselessly
polypropylene	compressional	gubernatorial	interosculate	restrictively
prospectively	concretionary	hazardousness	interparietal	reverberation
receptibility	confraternity	heterogeneity	interpellator	reverberative
receptiveness	confrontation	heterogeneous	interpersonal	reverberatory
reciprocality	congratulator	heterogenesis	interpolation	reverentially
reciprocation	congressional	heterogenetic	interpolative	reversibility
reciprocative	congresswoman	heteromorphic	interposition	sacerdotalise
reduplication	congruousness	heteropterous	interpretable	sacerdotalism
reduplicative	contrabandist	heterosporous	interpretress	sacerdotalist
scorpiongrass	contrabassoon	heterothallic	interpunction	scleroprotein
scrapmerchant	contraception	heterotrophic	interrelation	selfrecording
scripturalism	contraceptive	hilariousness	interrogation	selfregarding
scripturalist	contractility	histrionicism	interrogative	selfreproving
sculpturesque	contractually	honorifically	interrogatory	selfrepugnant
selfpityingly	contradiction	hundredweight	interruptible	selfrestraint
selfpollinate	contradictory	hyperboloidal	interspecific	selfrevealing
selfpossessed	contrafagotto	hypercritical	interspersion	selfrighteous
selfpropelled	contrapuntist	hypermetrical	interstratify	separableness
semiparasitic	contrariously	hypermetropia	intertropical	separationist
semipermanent	contravention	hypermetropic	invariability	sobermindness
semipermeable	controversial	hyperphysical	laboriousness	spheroidicity
semiporcelain	copartnership	hypertrophied	liberationist	squarebashing
sharpshooting	cyberneticist	immarcescible	luxuriousness	subirrigation
sheepshearing	decerebration	impartibility	macaronically	subordinately
sleeplessness	decortication	imperceptible	malariologist	subordination
softpedalling	deferentially	imperceptibly	materfamilias	subordinative
steeplechaser	defervescence	impercipience	materialistic	suffraganship
steppingstone	deforestation	imperfectness	membranaceous	superabundant
stirpiculture	deformational	imperialistic	mineralogical	superaddition
streptococcal	deliriousness	imperiousness	miserableness	superannuable
streptococcus	dendritically	impermissible	mistrustfully	supercalender
teleportation	depersonalise	impersonalise	mistrustingly	supercritical
toxoplasmosis	descriptively	impersonality	moderatorship	superdominant
unimpassioned	desirableness	impersonation	modernisation	supereminence
unimpeachable	destructively	impertinently	Monarchianism	superfamilies
vicepresident	destructivity	imperturbable	nefariousness	superfetation
deliquescence	deterioration	imperturbably	nonproductive	superficially
derequisition	deteriorative	importunately	notoriousness	superfluidity
overqualified	determinately	incarceration	numerological	superfluously
quinquagenary	determination	incardination	observational	superhumanity
Quinquagesima	determinative	incorporation	obstructively	superlatively

supernational	festschriften	resuscitation	courtsmartial	Monotheletism
supernumerary	foresightedly	resuscitative	craftsmanship	monotrematous
superordinate	freeselection	rhapsodically	cryptanalysis	monstrousness
superphysical	glossographer	selfsacrifice	cryptanalytic	mountainously
superposition	hairsplitting	selfsatisfied	cryptographer	mountebankery
supersaturate	halfsovereign	selfslaughter	cryptographic	naphthylamine
supersensible	hemispherical	selfsterility	cryptological	negotiability
superstitious	hocuspocussed	selfsufficing	crystalgazing	nemathelminth
supersubtlety	homosexuality	selfsupported	crystallinity	nightmarishly
supervenience	idiosyncratic	selfsurrender	dauntlessness	nightwatchman
taperecording	illustriously	selfsustained	deleteriously	nonattendance
telerecording	immiscibility	sidesplitting	dematerialise	odontoglossum
temerariously	impassability	soulsearching	demythologise	odontological
theoretically	impassibility	terpsichorean	denationalise	opisthobranch
tolerableness	impassiveness	thrasonically	deontological	ornithologist
tuberculation	impossibility	transatlantic	doubtlessness	outstandingly
unceremonious	indescribable	transcendence	draftsmanship	painterliness
uncertainness	indescribably	transcendency	electioneerer	palatableness
uncircumcised	indiscernible	transcription	electrocution	penetrability
underachiever	indiscernibly	transcriptive	electrologist	penetratingly
undercarriage	indispensable	transformable	electromagnet	penetratively
underclothing	indispensably	transgression	electrometric	penitentially
undereducated	indisposition	transgressive	electromotive	plenteousness
underemphasis	indissociable	transistorise	electrophorus	plentifulness
underemployed	indistinctive	transitionary	electroscopic	pointillistic
underestimate	industrialise	translational	electrostatic	pointlessness
underexposure	industrialism	transliterate	electrovalent	practicalness
undergraduate	industrialist	translocation	exanthematous	prestigiously
underhandedly	industriously	translucently	excitableness	prostaglandin
understanding	inhospitality	translucidity	existentially	prosthodontia
understrapper	insusceptible	transmigrator	facetiousness	punctiliously
underwhelming	investigation	transmissible	faultlessness	puritanically
unearthliness	investigative	transmittable	flirtatiously	pyrotechnical
unforgettable	investigatory	transmutation	fractionalise	quartermaster
unforgettably	invisibleness	transmutative	fractionation	quartziferous
unforthcoming	irresponsible	transnational	fractiousness	questioningly
unfortunately	irresponsibly	transparently	frontogenesis	questionnaire
unwarrantable	jurisprudence	transpiration	fruitlessness	quintillionth
unwarrantably	laissezpasser	transpiratory	frustratingly	quintuplicate
venerableness	legislatively	transportable	functionalism	reintegration
venereologist	legislatorial	transposition	functionalist	repetitionary
ventriloquial	longsuffering	transshipment	gametogenesis	repetitiously
ventriloquise	magisterially	transshipping	geostationary	RhaetoRomanic
ventriloquism	megasporangia	transversally	guiltlessness	righteousness
ventriloquist	metastability	treasurership	habitableness	righthandedly
vicariousness	ministerially	undisciplined	healthfulness	roentgenogram
waterproofing	monosyllabism	unfashionable	heartbreaking	roentgenology
accessibility	monosymmetric	unfashionably	heartlessness	sanctimonious
admissibility	nearsightedly	verisimilarly	heartsickness	sanitationist
advisableness	necessitarian	vivisectional	hypothecation	scintillating
ambassadorial	necessitation	whimsicalness	identicalness	scintillation
antiscorbutic	necessitously	abortifacient	immaterialise	seditiousness
assassination	numismatology	ambitiousness	immaterialism	selftormentor
atmospherical	obsessiveness	arbitrariness	immaterialist	shiftlessness
backscratcher	occasionalism	arbitrational	immateriality	shootingbrake
Christmastide	occasionalist	beauteousness	immutableness	shootingrange
Christmastime	occasionalist	blastogenesis	impetuousness	shootingstick
chrysanthemum	oppositionist	bounteousness	inattentively	shorttempered
cleistogamous	oversensitive	bountifulness	indeterminacy	sightlessness
coarsegrained	overstatement	boustrophedon	indeterminate	smoothingiron
crosscultural	oversubscribe	bumptiousness	indeterminism	sniftingvalve
crossgartered	painstakingly	cicatrisation	indeterminist	somatological
crosshatching	parasitically	constellation	insatiability	spectacularly
crosspurposes	parasiticidal	constellatory	irrationalise	spectrography
crossquestion	parasynthesis	consternation	irrationalism	spectrometric
cruiserweight	parasynthetic	constrainable	irrationalist	spectroscopic
derestriction	pedestrianise	constrainedly	irrationality	spontaneously
devastatingly	pedestrianism	constructable	irretrievable	sportsmanlike
digestibility	Pennsylvanian	constructible	irretrievably	sportsmanship
domestication	perishability	counteraction	irritableness	strategically
dressimprover	perissodactyl	counteractive	isostatically	stratigraphic
dressingtable	phraseologist	counterattack	lightfingered	stratocumulus
eavesdropping	plausibleness	counterchange	lightheadedly	stratospheric
equestrianism	polysynthesis	countercharge	lightmindedly	substantially
eschscholtzia	polysynthetic	counterfeiter	lightsomeness	substantively
excessiveness	recessiveness	counterstroke	limitlessness	substantivise
excusableness	redescription	counterweight	mediterranean	substitutable
expostulation	reinstatement	countinghouse	meistersinger	substructural
expostulatory	resistibility	courteousness	meritoriously	sumptuousness

teratological	mensurability	schizophrenic	grammatically	saccharometer
theatricalise	nonfulfilment	———————	habitableness	sadomasochism
theatricalism	obtrusiveness	abstractional	hemiparasitic	sadomasochist
theatricality	pendulousness	acrobatically	hypnoanalysis	sanitationist
toastmistress	percussionist	adiabatically	idiomatically	scandalmonger
tractableness	perdurability	admirableness	immovableness	schematically
Tractarianism	perfunctorily	advisableness	immutableness	scholarliness
trustworthily	permutability	agreeableness	incurableness	scholasticism
unanticipated	picturepalace	aircraftwoman	indefatigable	selfsacrifice
unarticulated	picturesquely	anagrammatise	indefatigably	selfsatisfied
unestablished	postulational	anagrammatism	ineffableness	semibarbarian
unintelligent	prejudicially	AngloAmerican	inexhaustible	semibarbarism
unintentional	presumptively	annexationist	inexhaustibly	semiparasitic
uninterrupted	procuratorial	asthmatically	inorganically	separableness
unnaturalness	pronunciation	Australianism	intraarterial	separationist
unobtrusively	protuberantly	autocatalysis	irritableness	sergeantmajor
unputdownable	querulousness	autocatalytic	isostatically	shockabsorber
vegetarianism	rapturousness	automatically	judgeadvocate	spectacularly
vexatiousness	recrudescence	availableness	judgmatically	spermatoblast
vocationalism	resourcefully	axiomatically	kinematically	spermatogenic
volatilisable	sesquiplicate	backwardation	kinematograph	spermatophore
Zarathustrian	speculatively	barefacedness	laughableness	spermatophyte
accoutrements	suffumigation	blameableness	liberationist	spontaneously
agglutination	tonguelashing	burglariously	Machiavellian	stigmatically
agglutinative	tonguetwister	chateaubriand	maladaptation	substantially
bildungsroman	tremulousness	chrematistics	malleableness	substantively
calculatingly	tributariness	chromatically	membranaceous	substantivise
cinquecentist	unadulterated	chromatograph	merchandising	suffraganship
circumambient	unequivocally	chromatolytic	microanalysis	superabundant
circumference	untrustworthy	chromatophore	mineralogical	superaddition
circumfluence	vapourishness	chrysanthemum	miserableness	superannuable
circumspectly	venturesomely	cinematically	moderatorship	supplantation
circumvallate	venturousness	cinematograph	monodactylous	teachableness
circumvention	equivocalness	clairaudience	mountainously	temerariously
coagulability	immovableness	colleagueship	navigableness	thaumaturgist
coeducational	inadvertently	complainingly	neoclassicism	tolerableness
colourfulness	individualise	complaisantly	neoclassicist	traceableness
communication	individualism	conflagration	neoplasticism	tractableness
communicative	individualist	confraternity	oleomargarine	Tractarianism
communicatory	individuality	congratulator	ophthalmology	transatlantic
communisation	individuation	contrabandist	outstandingly	traumatically
communitarian	irreverential	contrabassoon	overvaluation	uncleanliness
commutability	obliviousness	contraception	paediatrician	underachiever
computational	overvaluation	contraceptive	palatableness	unestablished
concupiscence	papaveraceous	contractility	paramagnetism	unimpassioned
concupiscible	redevelopment	contractually	parliamentary	vegetarianism
conduciveness	reinvigorator	contradiction	peaceableness	venerableness
conductorship	rejuvenescent	contradictory	pharmaceutics	woolgathering
conjugateness	removableness	contrafagotto	pharmaceutist	zygodactylous
conjugational	televisionary	contrapuntist	pharmacologic	absorbability
conjunctional	backwardation	contrariously	pharmacopoeia	attributively
conjunctively	strawcoloured	contravention	pigheadedness	bloodboltered
consumptively	annexationist	cryptanalysis	pneumatically	cannibalistic
convulsionary	innoxiousness	cryptanalytic	pneumatolysis	collaboration
corruptionist	obnoxiousness	crystalgazing	pneumatolytic	collaborative
credulousness	acetylcholine	crystallinity	pneumatometer	confabulation
diffusiveness	acotyledonous	desirableness	pneumatophore	confabulatory
disjunctively	anonymousness	diagrammatise	polycarbonate	corroboration
dysfunctional	bathymetrical	dichlamydeous	polydactylous	corroborative
encouragement	condylomatous	disgracefully	pragmatically	corroboratory
encouragingly	dissymetrical	displantation	prismatically	disembodiment
exclusiveness	embryogenesis	dispraisingly	procrastinate	funambulation
formulisation	embryological	dodecaphonist	prostaglandin	heartbreaking
fortunateness	emphysematous	efficaciously	psychasthenia	housebreaking
fortunehunter	enjoyableness	elephantiasis	puritanically	hyperboloidal
fortuneteller	jerrybuilding	enigmatically	quadragesimal	improbability
frequentation	martyrisation	enjoyableness	radioactivity	incombustible
frequentative	martyrologist	epigrammatise	rearrangement	jerrybuilding
garrulousness	moneygrubbing	epigrammatist	reembarkation	neighbourhood
hallucination	pennyfarthing	everlastingly	reincarnation	nitrobacteria
hallucination	pennypinching	excitableness	removableness	opprobriously
hallucinatory	phenylalanine	excusableness	reproachfully	overabundance
inclusiveness	platyhelminth	flirtatiously	reproachingly	perambulation
ineducability	recrystallise	foolhardiness	retroactively	perambulatory
influentially	topsyturvydom	fullfashioned	retroactivity	prohibitively
intrusiveness	horizontality	generalisable	revelationist	protuberantly
languishingly	schizocarpous	generalissimo	rheumatically	recombination
leisureliness	schizogenesis	geostationary	saccharimeter	reverberation
masculineness	schizophrenia	goodnaturedly	saccharimetry	reverberative

reverberatory	intercalation	unconcernedly	accidentalism	doubleglazing
selfabasement	intercellular	undercarriage	accidentprone	doublejointed
skateboarding	intercolonial	underclothing	acquiescently	doubletongued
swashbuckling	intercolumnar	undisciplined	acquiescingly	energetically
syllabication	intercropping	unprecedented	aesthetically	epiphenomenal
amniocentesis	intercultural	vermiculation	afforestation	epiphenomenon
anfractuosity	intercurrence	vernacularise	ambidexterity	erroneousness
anglicisation	intracellular	vernacularism	ambidexterous	evangelically
AngloCatholic	intricateness	vernacularity	antipersonnel	exasperatedly
antiscorbutic	invincibility	versicoloured	apathetically	existentially
applicability	italicisation	accreditation	archaeologist	exponentially
applicatively	lancecorporal	animadversion	archaeopteryx	featherheaded
backscratcher	leptocephalic	archidiaconal	archdeaconate	featherstitch
biotechnology	levelcrossing	bewilderingly	argumentation	featherweight
bloodcurdling	machicolation	closedcircuit	argumentative	ferroelectric
characterless	macrocephalic	confederation	autocephalous	forementioned
climactically	matriculation	confederative	backpedalling	fragmentarily
coeducational	mesencephalon	confidingness	battlecruiser	fragmentation
collectedness	microcephalic	considerately	beauteousness	freeselection
collectorship	micrococcocci	consideration	betweenwhiles	frequentation
conduciveness	Monarchianism	cylindrically	bioenergetics	frequentative
conductorship	multicellular	dependability	blanketflower	gentlemanlike
confectionary	multicoloured	eavesdropping	bounteousness	halfheartedly
confectionery	myrmecologist	formidability	brotherliness	hardheartedly
conjecturable	nitrocompound	granddaughter	businesswoman	heebiejeebies
conjecturally	nomenclatural	gynandromorph	cabinetmaking	hemicellulose
connectedness	ochlocratical	hazardousness	candlelighter	homogeneously
consecutively	orthocephalic	hybridisation	candlesnuffer	homosexuality
convocational	participation	hydrodynamics	centreforward	hundredweight
corticotropic	participative	imponderables	challengeable	hydroelectric
corticotropin	participatory	incandescence	challengingly	immaterialise
crosscultural	particoloured	incardination	changeability	immaterialism
defencelessly	particularise	incondensable	changefulness	immaterialist
denticulation	particularism	incredibility	chinkerinchee	immateriality
deprecatingly	particularist	incredulously	cinquecentist	impenetration
dialectically	particularity	infundibulate	clandestinely	inadvertently
eschscholtzia	perfectionism	interdentally	clothesbasket	inattentively
ethnocentrism	perfectionist	interdigitate	coarsegrained	independently
extracellular	petrochemical	kaleidoscopic	coenaesthesis	indeterminacy
fasciculation	photochemical	lackadaisical	coldheartedly	indeterminate
ferroconcrete	photochromics	Methodistical	collieshangie	indeterminism
festschriften	photochromism	microdetector	complementary	indeterminist
floricultural	piscicultural	misunderstand	complexedness	ineffectively
gesticulation	predicability	misunderstood	comprehension	ineffectually
gesticulative	predicamental	nondeductable	comprehensive	inexpediently
gesticulatory	predicatively	periodisation	compressional	inexpensively
gynaecocratic	preoccupation	polyadelphous	concretionary	inexperienced
gynaecologist	projectionist	prejudicially	congressional	inferentially
hallucination	protectionism	premeditation	congresswoman	influentially
hallucinative	protectionist	premeditative	constellation	inoffensively
hallucinatory	protectorship	preordainment	constellatory	interestingly
horsechestnut	ratiocination	preordination	consternation	irreverential
horticultural	ratiocinative	presidentship	counteraction	knickerbocker
hydrocephalic	recalcitrance	pteridologist	counteractive	knowledgeable
hydrocephalus	reconcilement	recrudescence	counterattack	knowledgeably
hydrochloride	redescription	regardfulness	counterchange	laissezpasser
hydrocracking	refractometer	revendication	countercharge	leatherjacket
hypercritical	resuscitation	sacerdotalise	counterfeiter	manageability
immarcescible	resuscitative	sacerdotalism	counterstroke	manifestation
immiscibility	revaccination	sacerdotalist	counterweight	manifestative
impeccability	rhodochrosite	secondariness	courteousness	mediterranean
imperceptible	SerboCroatian	selfaddressed	crackerbarrel	megacephalous
imperceptibly	sharecropping	selfadjusting	cruiserweight	meistersinger
impercipience	sociocultural	selfeducation	decerebration	monometallism
implacability	strawcoloured	serendipitous	deferentially	monometallist
implicatively	submachinegun	shoulderblade	deforestation	monumentalise
impracticable	suffocatingly	shoulderstrap	deleteriously	mountebankery
impracticably	supercalender	splendiferous	dematerialise	mutagenically
impractically	supercritical	squandermania	diathermanous	northeasterly
incarceration	syntactically	subordinately	discreditable	northeastward
inconceivable	telencephalon	subordination	discreditably	occidentalise
inconceivably	threecornered	subordinative	discretionary	Occidentalism
indescribable	transcendence	superdominant	disobediently	Occidentalist
indescribably	transcendency	unconditional	distressfully	octocentenary
indiscernible	transcription	unconditioned	distressingly	ontogenically
indiscernibly	transcriptive	unpredictable	documentalist	openheartedly
ineducability	tuberculation	unputdownable	documentation	orangeblossom
inspectorship	uncircumcised	viceadmiralty	doublecrosser	ornamentation
insusceptible	unconceivable	accelerometer	doubledealing	overbearingly

oversensitive	supplementary	proliferation	regurgitation	administrable
paddlesteamer	synthetically	proliferative	retrogression	administrator
painterliness	taperecording	proliferously	retrogressive	admonishingly
pantheistical	telerecording	prolification	roentgenogram	affreightment
papaveraceous	thenceforward	qualification	roentgenology	ambitiousness
parthenocarpy	theoretically	qualificatory	sewingmachine	antihistamine
penitentially	thundershower	rectification	strangulation	apheliotropic
perspectively	thunderstruck	Russification	surrogateship	arboriculture
philhellenism	tiddledywinks	sacrificially	transgression	archbishopric
philhellenist	tonguelashing	scarification	transgressive	arthritically
photoelectric	tonguetwister	scorification	triangularity	artificiality
photoelectron	tritheistical	significantly	triangulation	associateship
photoemission	unceremonious	signification	undergraduate	associativity
photoemissive	undereducated	significative	unforgettable	Assyriologist
phraseologist	underemphasis	specification	unforgettably	astonishingly
phrenetically	underemployed	steadfastness	vantageground	atrociousness
phycoerythrin	underestimate	sternforemost	verbigeration	audaciousness
piezoelectric	underexposure	superfamilies	vertiginously	autobiography
plenteousness	unexceptional	superfetation	villeggiatura	basidiomycete
prepreference	unimpeachable	superficially	amorphousness	beneficiation
problematical	unintelligent	superfluidity	Antichristian	boardinghouse
progressional	unintentional	superfluously	apprehensible	bountifulness
progressively	uninterrupted	testification	autochthonism	brilliantness
progressivism	unnecessarily	thurification	autochthonous	bumptiousness
prophetically	unrelentingly	transformable	blasphemously	canaliculated
prospectively	venereologist	uncomfortable	breechloading	capaciousness
pyrimethamine	vivisectional	uncomfortably	catechisation	centrifugally
pyrotechnical	volumenometer	unconformable	churchmanship	centripetally
quadrennially	weatherbeaten	unselfishness	clearheadedly	clearinghouse
quarrelsomely	wheelerdealer	versification	crosshatching	climbingframe
quartermaster	whithersoever	vitrification	cytochemistry	complicatedly
quincentenary	acetification	analogousness	demythologise	complimentary
quingentenary	acidification	beleaguerment	encephalogram	conceitedness
rattlebrained	amplification	belligerently	enlightenment	conflictingly
redevelopment	beatification	biodegradable	exanthematous	conscientious
referentially	calcification	blackguardism	healthfulness	consciousness
reforestation	caprification	calligraphist	hypochondriac	conspicuously
regimentation	certification	compagination	hypothecation	containership
reintegration	certificatory	configuration	lightheadedly	coreligionist
rejuvenescent	clarification	conjugateness	Manichaeanism	countinghouse
reorientation	cornification	conjugational	metaphosphate	cryobiologist
resplendently	costeffective	corrigibility	metaphysician	deliciousness
reverentially	disaffectedly	crossgartered	mitochondrion	deliriousness
righteousness	disaffirmance	disengagement	monochromatic	denationalise
rontgenoscopy	dulcification	disfigurement	monophthongal	dendritically
rudimentarily	falsification	expurgatorial	Monophysitism	descriptively
schadenfreude	fortification	extragalactic	Monotheletism	deterioration
sedimentation	glorification	hydrogenation	naphthylamine	deteriorative
selfcentredly	grandfatherly	incongruously	nemathelminth	discriminator
selfdeceiving	gratification	ineligibility	opisthobranch	distributable
selfdeception	imperfectness	ingurgitation	ornithologist	doctrinairism
selfdeceptive	indifferently	intangibility	paperhangings	domiciliation
selfdefeating	insufficience	intergalactic	paraphernalia	dressimprover
selfdependent	insufficiency	introgression	perichondrial	dressingtable
selffertility	jollification	laryngoscopic	perichondrium	egregiousness
selfgenerated	justification	miscegenation	perishability	electioneerer
selfrecording	justificative	moneygrubbing	phosphoretted	equidistantly
selfregarding	justificatory	negligibility	platyhelminth	equilibration
selfreproving	lightfingered	nonaggression	polychromatic	exhibitionism
selfrepugnant	lignification	nonfigurative	prosthodontia	exhibitionist
selfrestraint	magnification	orthognathism	protohistoric	expeditionary
selfrevealing	magnificently	orthognathous	reprehensible	expeditiously
semipermanent	materfamilias	pantagruelian	reprehensibly	facetiousness
semipermeable	mellifluously	pantagruelism	righthandedly	felicitations
sicklefeather	metrification	pantagruelist	searchwarrant	feloniousness
singlehearted	millefeuilles	pathogenicity	smoothingiron	ferociousness
socioeconomic	mollification	pathognomonic	sprightliness	flourishingly
softpedalling	mortification	preengagement	stoichiometry	foraminiferal
soulsearching	mummification	preengineered	superhumanity	foresightedly
southeasterly	mystification	prefiguration	thoughtlessly	fractionalise
southeastward	nitrification	prefigurative	thoughtreader	fractionation
spelaeologist	nullification	prefigurement	treacherously	fractiousness
Spencerianism	odoriferously	primigravidae	underhandedly	functionalism
splenetically	paterfamilias	primogenitary	unfashionable	functionalist
squarebashing	pennyfarthing	primogenitive	unfashionably	grandiloquent
strategically	pestiferously	primogeniture	unrighteously	hilariousness
strikebreaker	petrification	prolegomenary	wrongheadedly	histrionicism
sublieutenant	pontification	prolegomenous	Zarathustrian	honorifically
supereminence	prizefighting	refrigeration	abortifacient	identicalness

ignominiously	quadrilateral	maladjustment	interlacement	spinelessness
illogicalness	quadrillionth	sprocketwheel	interlocution	stabilisation
immediateness	quadripartite	acetylcholine	interlocutory	stainlessness
imperialistic	questioningly	acotyledonous	interlocutrix	statelessness
imperiousness	questionnaire	actualisation	inviolability	steeplechaser
impolitically	quintillionth	animalisation	inviolateness	sterilisation
incuriousness	rapaciousness	anomalistical	irreclaimable	subtilisation
individualise	reaffirmation	anomalousness	irreclaimably	superlatively
individualism	reinvigorator	anthelminthic	irreplaceable	symbolisation
individualist	religiousness	anticlimactic	kapellmeister	synallagmatic
individuality	reminiscently	anticlockwise	knuckleduster	tantalisation
individuation	repetitiously	apocalyptical	lamellibranch	tantalisingly
inefficacious	repetitiously	appellatively	legislatively	tastelessness
inefficiently	restrictively	baccalaureate	legislatorial	tautologously
infinitesimal	sagaciousness	barrelchested	limitlessness	thanklessness
infuriatingly	salaciousness	Berkeleianism	magniloquence	thimblerigged
ingeniousness	sanctimonious	blamelessness	mammaliferous	thimblerigger
injudiciously	scintillating	bloodlessness	mangoldwurzel	thrillingness
injuriousness	scintillation	bouillabaisse	masculineness	titillatingly
innoxiousness	scorpiongrass	boundlessness	matrilineally	tonsillectomy
insatiability	seditiousness	brainlessness	mercilessness	toxoplasmosis
inscriptional	selfdirecting	brutalisation	metalliferous	translational
insidiousness	selfdirection	calculatingly	metallisation	transliterate
insociability	selfdiscovery	cartilaginous	metallography	translocation
invariability	selfdispraise	cephalothorax	metallurgical	translucently
invidiousness	selfpityingly	cheerlessness	mirthlessness	translucidity
invisibleness	selfrighteous	chuckleheaded	miscellaneous	tremulousness
irrationalise	semicivilised	coagulability	mutualisation	troublesomely
irrationalism	sesquiplicate	cobelligerent	nephelometric	troublousness
irrationalist	shootingbrake	coldbloodedly	nervelessness	umbelliferous
irrationality	shootingrange	condylomatous	nickeliferous	unadulterated
irreligionist	shootingstick	consolidation	noiselessness	unfeelingness
irreligiously	slangingmatch	consolidative	noncollegiate	unhealthiness
judiciousness	smellingsalts	consolidatory	nonfulfilment	unqualifiedly
laboriousness	sniftingvalve	convalescence	normalisation	unwholesomely
languishingly	solicitorship	convulsionary	nostalgically	unwillingness
laughingstock	soundingboard	correlatively	overelaborate	vacillatingly
litigiousness	spinninghouse	correlativity	papillomatous	valuelessness
luxuriousness	spinningwheel	credulousness	parallelogram	verbalisation
malariologist	stalkinghorse	curvilinearly	pendulousness	vernalisation
maliciousness	steppingstone	dauntlessness	petroliferous	visualisation
materialistic	stickingplace	deathlessness	phenylalanine	voicelessness
melodiousness	stirpiculture	discoloration	pluralisation	worldlyminded
mischievously	stratigraphic	dissolubility	pointlessness	worthlessness
mouldingboard	subeditorship	dissoluteness	porcellaneous	acclimatation
mourningcloak	substitutable	doubtlessness	postclassical	accommodating
mourningpaper	technicalness	draggletailed	postulational	accommodation
nearsightedly	televisionary	dreamlessness	powerlessness	accommodative
nefariousness	tenaciousness	embellishment	premillennial	achromaticity
negotiability	terpsichorean	encyclopaedia	pricelessness	affirmatively
notoriousness	thereinbefore	encyclopaedic	pusillanimity	agglomeration
obliviousness	tortoiseshell	encyclopedism	pusillanimous	agglomerative
obnoxiousness	transistorise	encyclopedist	pyrheliometer	anonymousness
occasionalism	transitionary	establishment	querulousness	archimandrite
occasionalist	unambiguously	exemplariness	radiolocation	arithmetician
occasionality	unanticipated	faithlessness	rectilinearly	balsamiferous
officiousness	unarticulated	faultlessness	reduplication	bathymetrical
oppositionist	unbelievingly	fertilisation	reduplicative	broadmindedly
ostreiculture	unenlightened	feudalisation	republicanise	circumambient
parasitically	unequivocally	feuilletonism	republicanism	circumference
parasiticidal	unfamiliarity	feuilletonist	republication	circumfluence
partridgewood	unremittingly	flagellantism	ritualisation	circumspectly
penuriousness	unsociability	formalisation	schoolteacher	circumvallate
perspicacious	ventriloquial	formulisation	selfslaughter	circumvention
perspicuously	ventriloquise	fossiliferous	senselessness	commemoration
plausibleness	ventriloquism	fossilisation	serialisation	commemorative
plentifulness	ventriloquist	frivolousness	shamelessness	commemoratory
pointillistic	veraciousness	fruitlessness	shapelessness	concomitantly
polyhistorian	verifiability	garrulousness	shiftlessness	consumptively
practicalness	verisimilarly	gracelessness	sightlessness	contamination
prairieoyster	vexatiousness	guilelessness	signalisation	contaminative
prescientific	vicariousness	guiltlessness	sleeplessness	contemplation
prestigiously	vivaciousness	heartlessness	smokelessness	contemplative
principalness	vocationalism	hypoglycaemia	snowblindness	customariness
proprietorial	volatilisable	infallibilism	socialisation	deformational
proprioceptor	voraciousness	infallibilist	somniloquence	determinately
proteinaceous	whimsicalness	infallibility	speculatively	determination
punctiliously	extrajudicial	intelligencer	spindlelegged	determinative
quadricipital	interjectural	intelligently	spindleshanks	deterministic

detrimentally	thremmatology	embranglement	prudentialism	blastogenesis
discommodious	toastmistress	examinational	prudentialist	camphoraceous
dismemberment	transmigrator	examinatorial	prudentiality	cardiographer
dissemblingly	transmissible	explanatorily	psilanthropic	categorically
dissemination	transmittable	extrinsically	rationalistic	ceremonialism
disseminative	transmutation	fascinatingly	rectangularly	ceremonialist
dissimilarity	transmutative	foreknowledge	replenishment	ceremoniously
dissimilation	unanimousness	fortunateness	retranslation	chalcoography
dissimilitude	ungrammatical	fortunehunter	runningstitch	choreographer
dissimulation	unicameralism	fortuneteller	salmonellosis	choreographic
dissymetrical	unicameralist	galvanisation	selfinduction	chromospheric
excommunicate	unpromisingly	geocentricism	selfindulgent	chronographic
extermination	unsymmetrical	germanisation	selfinflicted	chronological
exterminatory	victimisation	glutinousness	selfinsurance	conchological
ferrimagnetic	alternatively	graminivorous	selfknowledge	confrontation
ferromagnetic	aluminiferous	gubernatorial	sententiously	conglomeratic
fundamentally	aluminisation	harmonisation	septentrional	controversial
goniometrical	asthenosphere	helminthiasis	sequentiality	craniological
grandmotherly	astronautical	helminthology	solemnisation	cryptographer
homeomorphism	attainability	hermeneutical	staminiferous	cryptographic
hydromedusoid	authentically	imaginatively	stoloniferous	cryptological
hydrometrical	authenticator	insignificant	subcontractor	deipnosophist
hypermetrical	balkanisation	instantaneity	supernational	deontological
hypermetropia	bildungsroman	instantaneous	supernumerary	developmental
hypermetropic	bookingoffice	instinctively	supranational	diageotropism
impermissible	brokenhearted	international	Swedenborgian	diagnostician
inanimateness	buttonthrough	intransigeant	tendentiously	disproportion
incommunicado	Calvinistical	intransigence	tercentennial	embryogenesis
incrementally	campanologist	intrinsically	terminability	embryological
incriminatory	carboniferous	lineengraving	terminational	entomological
informational	carbonisation	machinegunner	terminatively	entomophagous
informatively	carcinomatous	magnanimously	tintinnabular	entomophilous
intermarriage	combinatorial	manganiferous	tintinnabulum	entomostracan
intermediator	commandership	mechanisation	transnational	environmental
intermittence	commensurable	mercenariness	tricentennial	epeirogenesis
intramuscular	commensurably	micronutrient	trigonometric	equiponderant
leishmaniasis	communication	millennialism	tyrannosaurus	equiponderate
lightmindedly	communicative	misconception	unflinchingly	equipotential
macromolecule	communicatory	mismanagement	unmeaningness	equivocalness
maladminister	communisation	modernisation	violoncellist	exteroceptive
mathematician	communitarian	multinational	visionariness	extraordinary
miscomprehend	companionable	multinucleate	volcanologist	frontogenesis
Mohammedanism	companionably	nationalistic	vulcanisation	gametogenesis
Muhammadanism	companionless	nonconducting	vulcanologist	gastrocnemius
nightmarishly	companionship	nonconforming	woodengraving	gastroenteric
noncompliance	compendiously	nonconformism	zinjanthropus	gastrological
numismatology	concentration	nonconformist	abiologically	gastronomical
osteomyelitis	concentrative	nonconformity	acrimoniously	geotropically
overemphasise	concentricity	nonsensically	acrylonitrile	glaciological
paedomorphism	conjunctional	obstinateness	actinomorphic	glossographer
passementerie	conjunctively	offhandedness	actinomycetes	gonadotrophic
phenomenalise	consanguinity	outgeneralled	actinomycosis	gonadotrophin
phenomenalism	consenescence	overindulgent	alcoholically	graphological
phenomenalist	consentaneity	paternalistic	alcoholometer	halfsovereign
phenomenology	consentaneous	patronisingly	alcoholometry	heterogeneity
planimetrical	contentedness	peptonisation	allegorically	heterogeneous
poliomyelitis	contentiously	perfunctorily	allelomorphic	heterogenesis
predominantly	continentally	perpendicular	anaerobically	heterogenetic
predomination	conventionary	phalansterian	anthropogenic	heteromorphic
preliminarily	cottonpicking	philanthropic	anthropometry	heteropterous
presumptively	criminalistic	pigeonchested	anthropopathy	heterosporous
randomisation	criminologist	pigeonhearted	anthropophagi	heterothallic
recommendable	cyberneticist	pigeonlivered	anthropophagy	heterotrophic
recrimination	degranulation	platiniferous	anthroposophy	homoeomorphic
recriminative	disconcerting	polliniferous	anticoagulant	homoeopathist
recriminatory	disconcertion	precentorship	antilogarithm	homoiothermal
reexamination	disconformity	preconception	antinomianism	homoiothermic
reformability	disconnection	premonitorily	auctioneering	horizontality
reformational	discontinuity	preponderance	autonomically	hymenopterous
rhadamanthine	discontinuous	preponderancy	backformation	ideologically
sacramentally	dishonourable	pretentiously	bamboozlement	immunological
scrapmerchant	dishonourably	proconsulship	bibliographer	immunotherapy
selfimportant	disjunctively	progenitorial	bibliographic	inopportunely
sentimentally	dismantlement	pronunciation	bibliolatrist	insubordinate
sobermindness	distinctively	protonotarial	bibliolatrous	interoceptive
somnambulator	distinguished	provincialise	bibliological	interosculate
sphygmography	dysfunctional	provincialism	bibliophilism	irrecoverable
squeamishness	ecumenicalism	provincialist	bibliophilist	irrecoverably
suffumigation	egocentricity	provinciality	biogeographer	leadpoisoning

lepidopterist	reinforcement	xanthochroism	PreRaphaelite	declaratively
lepidopterous	renegotiation	zoogeographer	prosopography	defibrination
lexicographer	RhaetoRomanic	zoogeographic	recomposition	deodorisation
lexicographic	rhapsodically	accompaniment	scolopendrium	desegregation
macaronically	schizocarpous	affenpinscher	scrumptiously	desperateness
Maginotminded	schizogenesis	amphiprostyle	selfappointed	deuteragonist
malacological	schizophrenia	appropriately	selfapproving	Deuteronomist
malacostracan	schizophrenic	appropriation	selfopinioned	dexterousness
meritoriously	scleroprotein	appropriative	sidesplitting	diaphragmatic
metamorphoses	seismographer	astrophysical	subreptitious	differentiate
metamorphosis	seismographic	atmospherical	superphysical	disharmonious
microorganism	seismological	conceptualise	superposition	disparagement
millionairess	selenocentric	conceptualism	surreptitious	disparagingly
monocotyledon	selenographer	conceptualist	transparently	disparateness
monomolecular	selenographic	concupiscence	transpiration	efflorescence
morphogenesis	selenological	concupiscible	transpiratory	elaborateness
morphogenetic	selfcollected	corruptionist	transportable	electrocution
morphological	selfcommunion	cosmopolitise	transposition	electrologist
musicological	selfconceited	cosmopolitism	uncompetitive	electromagnet
nonproductive	selfcondemned	crosspurposes	uncomplaining	electrometric
nucleoprotein	selfconfessed	decomposition	uncomplicated	electromotive
numerological	selfconfident	decompression	waterproofing	electrophorus
oceanographer	selfconscious	decrepitation	wellapPointed	electroscopic
oceanographic	selfconsuming	disappearance	colloquialism	electrostatic
odontoglossum	selfcontained	disciplinable	consequential	electrovalent
odontological	selfcontented	encompassment	crossquestion	embarrassment
oecologically	selfconvicted	expropriation	subsequential	encouragement
omnicompetent	selfforgetful	extemporarily	threequarters	encouragingly
ontologically	selfgoverning	extraphysical	unconquerable	endocrinology
opinionatedly	selfpollinate	extrapolation	aggiornamento	Eucharistical
organogenesis	selfpossessed	fissiparously	airworthiness	explorational
organotherapy	selftormentor	hairsplitting	algebraically	exterritorial
outspokenness	semeiological	hemispherical	anachronistic	filterability
overconfident	semiconductor	hermaphrodite	anachronously	frustratingly
overpopulated	semiconscious	hocuspocussed	anaphrodisiac	gasteropodous
owneroccupier	semilogarithm	horripilation	answerability	geochronology
palaeographer	semiporcelain	hyperphysical	arbitrariness	geomorphology
palaeographic	serologically	impalpability	arbitrational	glamorisation
palaeontology	somatological	impropriation	authorisation	helterskelter
palaeozoology	spasmodically	incompetently	authoritarian	ideographical
palynological	speleological	incorporation	authoritative	inappreciable
parabolically	spheroidicity	incorporative	autoeroticism	inappreciably
paradoxically	standoffishly	incorporeally	bacteriolysis	inappropriate
paranormality	stationmaster	indispensable	bacteriolytic	incorrectness
passionflower	stercoraceous	indispensably	bacteriophage	incorruptible
patriotically	stereographic	indisposition	barbarisation	incorruptibly
pedagogically	stereoscopist	inhospitality	barbarousness	incorruptness
phrenological	stratocumulus	insupportable	birefringence	inexorability
phyllophagous	stratospheric	insupportably	bloodrelation	inexpressible
physiognomist	superordinate	intemperately	boustrophedon	inexpressibly
physiographer	swallowtailed	interparietal	butterfingers	inflorescence
physiographic	symbiotically	interpellator	butterflyfish	inspirational
physiological	symphonically	interpersonal	cacographical	interrelation
physiotherapy	symphoniously	interpolation	cauterisation	interrogation
plethorically	taxonomically	interpolative	cerebrospinal	interrogative
pneumogastric	technological	interposition	chemoreceptor	interrogatory
pneumonectomy	teleportation	interpretable	cicatrisation	interruptible
polarographic	teratological	interpretress	colourfulness	irrefrangible
polycotyledon	theologically	interpunction	commercialise	irrepressible
postcommunion	theriomorphic	intrapersonal	commercialism	irrepressibly
prognosticate	thermochemist	irresponsible	commercialist	irretrievable
pseudoarchaic	thermodynamic	irresponsibly	comparability	irretrievably
pseudomorphic	thermogenesis	jurisprudence	comparatively	isochronously
pseudoscience	thermonuclear	juxtaposition	compartmental	isomerisation
psychoanalyse	thermophilous	megasporangia	concertmaster	jiggerypokery
psychoanalyst	thermoplastic	microphyllous	conservatoire	Kidderminster
psychodynamic	thermosetting	multiplicable	constrainable	laevorotation
psychogenesis	thermotropism	nonappearance	constrainedly	laevorotatory
psychogenetic	thigmotropism	pennypinching	constructable	lecherousness
psychokinesis	thrasonically	photoperiodic	constructible	leisureliness
psychokinetic	timeconsuming	photopositive	contortionist	lethargically
psychological	topologically	phytoplankton	conversazione	letterperfect
psychometrics	toxicological	pluripresence	conversazioni	librarianship
psychometrist	troglodytical	postoperative	cooperatively	lickerishness
psychophysics	typologically	precipitantly	corporativism	liebfraumilch
psychosomatic	unaccompanied	precipitately	daguerreotype	lifepreserver
psychosurgery	unaccountable	precipitation	dangerousness	ludicrousness
psychotherapy	unaccountably	precipitative	dastardliness	mackerelshark
rearcommodore	uninformative	precipitously	convertiplane	maladroitness

manneristical	tenderhearted	extensibility	professoriate	agglutinative
martyrisation	terrorisation	extensionally	professorship	apportionment
martyrologist	theatricalise	extensiveness	promiscuously	architectonic
masterfulness	theatricalism	fantastically	propositional	architectural
melodramatics	theatricality	Fascistically	Protestantism	argentiferous
melodramatise	topographical	floristically	provisionally	aromatisation
melodramatist	trichromatism	fortississimo	purposelessly	ascertainable
mensurability	typographical	greensickness	purposiveness	ascertainment
mercerisation	uncoordinated	grotesqueness	realistically	assertiveness
mesmerisation	unobtrusively	gymnastically	recessiveness	atlantosaurus
metagrobolise	unwarrantable	gymnospermous	reconsolidate	attentiveness
meteorologist	unwarrantably	heartsickness	reconstructor	chieftainship
monogrammatic	vapourishness	heptasyllabic	recrystallise	Christmastide
monotrematous	venturesomely	hydrostatical	remonstrantly	Christmastime
monstrousness	venturousness	hydrosulphide	remonstration	cleistogamous
mothercountry	vicepresident	hydrosulphite	remonstrative	climatologist
nectariferous	vulgarisation	impassability	remorselessly	collaterality
niggardliness	vulnerability	impassibility	representable	combativeness
nonforfeiting	winterberries	impassiveness	repulsiveness	commutability
oreographical	wonderfulness	impersonalise	requisiteness	compatibility
overcredulous	wonderworking	impersonality	retrospection	competitively
oystercatcher	xylographical	impersonation	retrospective	computational
penetrability	accessibility	impossibility	reversibility	concatenation
penetratingly	admeasurement	impressionism	sacrosanctity	conditionally
penetratively	admissibility	impressionist	sarcastically	connaturality
perdurability	adversatively	impulsiveness	selfasserting	copartnership
peregrination	agonistically	inclusiveness	selfassertion	deceitfulness
phanerogamous	ambassadorial	inconsecutive	selfassertive	deceptiveness
photoreceptor	angiospermous	inconsequence	selfassurance	decontaminate
picturepalace	assassination	inconsiderate	selfassuredly	decontrolling
picturesquely	atheistically	inconsistence	sequestration	decortication
polypropylene	atomistically	inconsistency	Shakespearean	deductibility
ponderability	BaltoSlavonic	inconspicuous	Shakespearian	defectiveness
ponderousness	belleslettres	indissociable	sharpshooting	derestriction
prayermeeting	Bloomsburyite	infeasibility	sheepshearing	dermatologist
preferability	bombastically	inquisitional	sophistically	desultoriness
preparatively	brainstorming	inquisitively	sophisticated	devastatingly
preparatorily	broadspectrum	inquisitorial	sportsmanlike	diametrically
pretermission	callisthenics	insensateness	sportsmanship	dichotomously
pretermitting	commiseration	insensibility	statesmanlike	dictatorially
preternatural	commiserative	insensitively	statesmanship	digestibility
prevarication	compassionate	insensitivity	statistically	disarticulate
primordiality	compositeness	insubstantial	stylistically	disintegrator
procuratorial	compositional	intensiveness	subpostmaster	disinterested
proparoxytone	concessionary	interspecific	supersaturate	divertisement
proportionate	condescension	interspersion	supersensible	domestication
psychrometric	confessionary	interstratify	superstitious	dramatisation
pulverisation	correspondent	introspection	supersubtlety	dramaturgical
rapturousness	corresponsive	introspective	suppositional	eccentrically
reciprocality	corrosiveness	intrusiveness	swordsmanship	educationally
reciprocation	courtsmartial	lancesergeant	tablespoonful	effectiveness
reciprocative	craftsmanship	leptospirosis	tachistoscope	embrittlement
resourcefully	defeasibility	lightsomeness	tempestuously	entertainment
restoratively	defensibility	loathsomeness	terrestrially	equestrianism
rollercoaster	demonstration	microscopical	tetrasyllable	eschatologist
sabrerattling	demonstrative	necessitarian	thalassocracy	essentialness
seaworthiness	depersonalise	necessitation	toothsomeness	evocativeness
selfcriticism	diffusiveness	necessitously	transshipment	exceptionable
selfpropelled	dimensionally	neurastheniac	transshipping	exceptionably
silvertongued	dimensionless	nonresistance	unconsciously	exceptionally
solderingiron	dispassionate	obsessiveness	unconstrained	expectoration
spectrography	disposability	obtrusiveness	understanding	expostulation
spectrometric	dispossession	offensiveness	understrapper	expostulatory
spectroscopic	disrespectful	orchestration	unquestioning	extratropical
subirrigation	distastefully	panicstricken	unsubstantial	facultatively
subserviently	draftsmanship	pantisocratic	untrustworthy	forgetfulness
substructural	emphysematous	percussionist	vouchsafement	frighteningly
subternatural	encapsulation	perissodactyl	wearisomeness	frightfulness
subterraneous	excessiveness	pervasiveness	wholesomeness	galactosaemia
subversionary	exclusiveness	pharisaically	worrisomeness	garnetiferous
summarisation	excrescential	philosophical	acceptability	geometrically
synchronistic	excursiveness	philosophiser	accoutrements	gerontocratic
synchronously	expansibility	predestinator	acculturation	gerontologist
telegrammatic	expansiveness	prehistorical	acculturative	globetrotting
temperamental	expensiveness	prepositional	adventuresome	gravitational
temperateness	explosiveness	prepossessing	adventurously	haematologist
temporalities	expressionism	prepossession	advertisement	herpetologist
temporariness	expressionist	processionary	affectionless	hypertrophied
temporisation	exquisiteness	processionist	agglutination	hypnotisation

illustriously	regretfulness	mistrustingly	transversally	astronautical
imitativeness	reinstatement	mononucleosis	followthrough	attainability
impartibility	resentfulness	obstructively	hollowhearted	baccalaureate
impertinently	resistibility	overqualified	horsewhipping	bouillabaisse
imperturbable	retentiveness	oversubscribe	landownership	brilliantness
imperturbably	scientologist	phonautograph	meadowsaffron	cacographical
importunately	scripturalism	pococurantism	mouthwatering	calculatingly
incontestable	scripturalist	precautionary	nightwatchman	cannibalistic
incontestably	sculpturesque	pronounceable	northwesterly	cartilaginous
incontinently	secretarybird	pronouncement	northwestward	changeability
indistinctive	secretaryship	quadrumvirate	quickwittedly	chieftainship
indoctrinator	secretiveness	quadruplicate	selfawareness	circumambient
inductiveness	sedentariness	quadruplicity	sorrowfulness	coagulability
industrialise	seductiveness	quincuncially	southwesterly	coeducational
industrialism	selectiveness	quinquagenary	southwestward	coldheartedly
industrialist	selfsterility	Quinquagesima	trustworthily	combinatorial
industriously	sensationally	quinquevalent	underwhelming	commutability
inevitability	sensitisation	quintuplicate	windowshopper	comparability
insectivorous	sensitiveness	reimbursement	approximately	comparatively
institutional	shorttempered	revolutionary	approximation	computational
intentionally	sovietologist	revolutionise	approximative	conjugateness
intertropical	spiritualness	revolutionism	convexoconvex	conjugational
intuitiveness	stomatologist	revolutionist	hydroxylamine	constrainable
inventiveness	streetwalking	sansculottism	inflexibility	constrainedly
inventorially	streptococcal	scorbutically	inflexionless	convocational
investigation	streptococcus	selfsufficing	reflexibility	cooperatively
investigative	structuralism	selfsupported	selfexecuting	corporativism
investigatory	structuralist	selfsurrender	selfexistence	correlatively
isometrically	structureless	selfsustained	aerodynamical	correlativity
lucrativeness	subsaturation	semiautomatic	brachycephaly	criminalistic
magisterially	symmetrically	sericulturist	brachydactyly	crossgartered
magnetisation	talkativeness	seriousminded	brachypterous	crosshatching
magnetomotive	tentativeness	solidungulate	chlamydomonas	customariness
magnetosphere	territorially	strenuousness	chlamydospore	declaratively
mediatisation	theanthropism	sulphureously	ichthyography	decontaminate
metastability	threateningly	sumptuousness	ichthyologist	deformational
microtonality	topsyturvydom	thoroughbrace	ichthyosaurus	dependability
ministerially	traditionally	thoroughgoing	idiosyncratic	deprecatingly
misanthropist	tributariness	thoroughpaced	linseywoolsey	desperateness
mnemotechnics	triliteralism	tranquilliser	metonymically	deuteragonist
momentariness	uncertainness	treasurership	monosyllabism	devastatingly
momentousness	unearthliness	unnaturalness	monosymmetric	diaphragmatic
multitudinous	unemotionally	viniculturist	panegyrically	disadvantaged
nonattendance	unforthcoming	viticulturist	parasynthesis	disengagement
nonreturnable	unfortunately	aggravatingly	parasynthetic	disparagement
nutritionally	unmentionable	asseveration	Pennsylvanian	disparagingly
objectionable	unpretentious	carnivorously	polysynthesis	disparateness
objectionably	unsuitability	concavoconvex	polysynthetic	disposability
objectiveness	voluntariness	defervescence	shabbygenteel	elaborateness
objectivistic	voluntaristic	disadvantaged	turkeygobbler	embarrassment
onomatopoetic	agriculturist	disinvestment	haphazardness	encephalogram
operativeness	ambiguousness	disseveration	quartziferous	encompassment
opportuneness	assiduousness	effervescence	squeezability	encouragement
opportunistic	bureaucratise	effervescency	————————	encouragingly
overstatement	congruousness	extravagantly	absorbability	entertainment
painstakingly	deciduousness	extravasation	acceptability	examinational
palletisation	deliquescence	extravascular	acclimatation	examinatorial
parenthetical	derequisition	fibrovascular	accompaniment	exemplariness
pedestrianise	destructively	improvability	achromaticity	explanatorily
pedestrianism	destructivity	improvidently	adversatively	explorational
permutability	devolutionary	improvisation	affirmatively	expurgatorial
phreatophytic	devolutionist	improvisatory	aggravatingly	extragalactic
plaintiveness	distrustfully	inconvenience	algebraically	extravagantly
platitudinise	harbourmaster	inconveniency	alternatively	extravasation
platitudinous	hydraulically	inconvertible	ambassadorial	extravascular
plenitudinous	impecuniosity	inconvertibly	AngloCatholic	facultatively
potentiometer	impetuousness	inconvincible	answerability	fascinatingly
predatoriness	ingenuousness	intravenously	anticoagulant	ferrimagnetic
prefatorially	innocuousness	introversible	appellatively	ferromagnetic
prematureness	insinuatingly	misgovernment	applicability	fibrovascular
primitiveness	insolubleness	neurovascular	applicatively	filterability
probationally	instructional	nongovernment	arbitrariness	fissiparously
profitability	instructively	observational	arbitrational	formidability
profitsharing	integumentary	ovoviviparous	archdeaconate	fortunateness
qualitatively	involuntarily	perseverance	archimandrite	frustratingly
quicktempered	longsuffering	resolvability	ascertainable	granddaughter
radiotelegram	Malthusianism	selfevidently	ascertainment	grandfatherly
receptibility	manipulatable	supervenience	associateship	gravitational
receptiveness	mistrustfully	tergiversator	associativity	gubernatorial

halfheartedly	painstakingly	transnational	beneficiation	retroactively
haphazardness	paperhangings	transparently	brachycephaly	retroactivity
hardheartedly	paterfamilias	tributariness	bureaucratise	rollercoaster
ideographical	paternalistic	typographical	canaliculated	schizocarpous
imaginatively	penetrability	uncertainness	cinquecentist	selenocentric
immediateness	penetratingly	undercarriage	closedcircuit	selfdeceiving
impalpability	penetratively	underhandedly	commercialise	selfdeception
impassability	pennyfarthing	unimpeachable	commercialism	selfdeceptive
impeccability	perdurability	unsociability	commercialist	selfrecording
imperialistic	perishability	unsuitability	complicatedly	selfsacrifice
implacability	permutability	unwarrantable	condescension	socioeconomic
implicatively	pharisaically	unwarrantably	conflictingly	spectacularly
improbability	phenylalanine	vacillatingly	conjunctional	stirpiculture
improvability	ponderability	verifiability	conjunctively	stratocumulus
inanimateness	postclassical	visionariness	conspicuously	taperecording
ineducability	postulational	voluntariness	contraception	technicalness
inevitability	predicability	voluntaristic	contraceptive	telerecording
inexorability	predicamental	vouchsafement	contractility	terpsichorean
informational	predicatively	vulnerability	contractually	thermochemist
informatively	preengagement	xylographical	destructively	unanticipated
infuriatingly	preferability	admirableness	destructivity	unarticulated
insatiability	preordainment	advisableness	disconcerting	unconsciously
insensateness	preparatively	agreeableness	disconcertion	underachiever
insinuatingly	preparatorily	anaerobically	disgracefully	unflinchingly
insociability	procuratorial	availableness	disjunctively	violoncellist
inspirational	profitability	blameableness	distinctively	vivisectional
intercalation	pseudoarchaic	Bloomsburyite	doublecrosser	whimsicalness
intergalactic	psychoanalyse	contrabandist	dysfunctional	xanthochroism
interlacement	psychoanalyst	contrabassoon	efficaciously	zygodactylous
intermarriage	pusillanimity	decerebration	equivocalness	backpedalling
international	pusillanimous	desirableness	excrescential	brachydactyly
interparietal	qualitatively	dismemberment	exteroceptive	chlamydomonas
intricateness	quinquagenary	dissemblingly	gastrocnemius	chlamydospore
invariability	Quinquagesima	distributable	identicalness	commandership
inviolability	rationalistic	enjoyableness	illogicalness	compendiously
inviolateness	reformability	equilibration	ineffectively	contradiction
irreclaimable	reformational	excitableness	ineffectually	contradictory
irreclaimably	reinstatement	excusableness	inefficacious	dastardliness
irrefrangible	resolvability	habitableness	inefficiently	discreditable
irreplaceable	restoratively	immovableness	injudiciously	discreditably
lackadaisical	rhadamanthine	immutableness	instinctively	disobediently
legislatively	righthandedly	incurableness	instructional	doubledealing
legislatorial	sabrerattling	ineffableness	instructively	hundredweight
leishmaniasis	sacrosanctity	insolubleness	interoceptive	individualise
liebfraumilch	secondariness	invisibleness	microscopical	individualism
manageability	secretarybird	irritableness	misconception	individualist
Manichaeanism	secretaryship	laughableness	monodactylous	individuality
materfamilias	sedentariness	malleableness	mononucleosis	individuation
materialistic	selfabasement	miserableness	mothercountry	inexpediently
mathematician	selfawareness	mountebankery	obstructively	judgeadvocate
melodramatics	selfslaughter	navigableness	ostreiculture	knowledgeable
melodramatise	soulsearching	orangeblossom	owneroccupier	knowledgeably
melodramatist	southeasterly	oversubscribe	oystercatcher	mangoldwurzel
mensurability	southeastward	palatableness	perfunctorily	niggardliness
mercenariness	speculatively	peaceableness	perspectively	nonconducting
metastability	squeezability	plausibleness	perspicacious	nonproductive
mismanagement	steadfastness	rattlebrained	perspicuously	offhandedness
momentariness	suffocatingly	removableness	pharmaceutics	overindulgent
monogrammatic	supercalender	separableness	pharmaceutist	partridgewood
mouthwatering	superfamilies	shockabsorber	pharmacologic	perpendicular
Muhammadanism	superlatively	somnambulator	pharmacopoeia	pigheadedness
multinational	supernational	squarebashing	pigeonchested	preponderance
nationalistic	supersaturate	strikebreaker	polydactylous	preponderancy
negotiability	supranational	superabundant	practicalness	primordiality
neurovascular	surrogateship	Swedenborgian	preconception	psychodynamic
nightmarishly	synallagmatic	teachableness	promiscuously	rhapsodically
nightwatchman	telegrammatic	tolerableness	pronunciation	selfaddressed
nitrobacteria	temperamental	traceableness	prospectively	selfinduction
northeasterly	temperateness	tractableness	provincialise	selfindulgent
northeastward	temporalities	unestablished	provincialism	softpedalling
numismatology	temporariness	venerableness	provincialist	spasmodically
observational	terminability	winterberries	provinciality	superaddition
obstinateness	terminational	abstractional	pyrotechnical	thermodynamic
openheartedly	terminatively	acetylcholine	quadricipital	tiddledywinks
oreographical	thremmatology	arboriculture	radioactivity	troglodytical
overbearingly	titillatingly	artificiality	reproachfully	uncoordinated
overelaborate	topographical	barefacedness	reproachingly	undereducated
overqualified	toxoplasmosis	barrelchested	resourcefully	acotyledonous
overstatement	translational	battlecruiser	restrictively	agglomeration

agglomerative	hydromedusoid	multicellular	southwestward	selfsufficing
amniocentesis	hydrometrical	nemathelminth	spindlelegged	sicklefeather
apprehensible	hypermetrical	nervelessness	spindleshanks	sorrowfulness
architectonic	hypermetropia	noiselessness	spinelessness	standoffishly
architectural	hypermetropic	nonappearance	sprocketwheel	thenceforward
arithmetician	hypothecation	nonattendance	squandermania	wonderfulness
asserveration	immarcescible	nongovernment	stainlessness	abiologically
bathymetrical	imperceptible	northwesterly	statelessness	affreightment
belligerently	imperceptibly	northwestward	steeplechaser	antilogarithm
Berkeleianism	imperfectness	odoriferously	superfetation	bibliographer
bewilderingly	imponderables	orthocephalic	supersensible	bibliographic
blamelessness	inappreciable	outgeneralled	supervenience	bildungsroman
blasphemously	inappreciably	overcredulous	tastelessness	biogeographer
bloodlessness	incandescence	parallelogram	telencephalon	blastogenesis
bloodrelation	incarceration	paraphernalia	tergiversator	bookingoffice
boundlessness	incompetently	passementerie	thanklessness	cardiographer
brainlessness	inconceivable	pathogenicity	thimblerigged	choreographer
cheerlessness	inconceivably	perseveration	thimblerigger	choreographic
chemoreceptor	incondensable	pestiferously	threateningly	chronographic
chuckleheaded	inconsecutive	phenomenalise	transcendence	coarsegrained
clearheadedly	inconsequence	phenomenalism	transcendency	colleagueship
collaterality	incontestable	phenomenalist	transversally	conflagration
commiseration	incontestably	phenomenology	treacherously	consanguinity
commiserative	inconvenience	photoperiodic	triliteralism	coreligionist
concatenation	inconveniency	photoreceptor	troublesomely	cryptographer
confederation	inconvertible	picturepalace	unbelievingly	cryptographic
confederative	inconvertibly	picturesquely	uncompetitive	distinguished
conscientious	incorrectness	planimetrical	unconceivable	doubleglazing
consenescence	incrementally	platyhelminth	unconcernedly	embranglement
considerately	indifferently	pointlessness	unforgettable	embryogenesis
consideration	indiscernible	polyadelphous	unforgettably	epeirogenesis
continentally	indiscernibly	postoperative	unicameralism	foresightedly
convalescence	indispensable	powerlessness	unicameralist	frontogenesis
cyberneticist	indispensably	prairieoyster	unprecedented	gametogenesis
cytochemistry	inexpressible	prescientific	unpretentious	glossographer
dauntlessness	inexpressibly	presidentship	unsymmetrical	heterogeneity
deathlessness	inflorescence	pricelessness	unwholesomely	heterogeneous
defencelessly	insusceptible	primogenitary	valuelessness	heterogenesis
defervescence	intemperately	primogenitive	vantageground	heterogenetic
deliquescence	intercellular	primogeniture	venturesomely	ideologically
desegregation	interdentally	proliferation	verbigeration	irreligionist
detrimentally	interjectural	proliferative	vicepresident	irreligiously
differentiate	intermediator	proliferously	voicelessness	lethargically
disaffectedly	interpellator	proprietorial	worthlessness	lexicographer
disappearance	interpersonal	protuberantly	wrongheadedly	lexicographic
disintegrator	interrelation	purposelessly	abortifacient	lineengraving
disinterested	intracellular	quicktempered	aircraftwoman	morphogenesis
disinvestment	intrapersonal	quinquevalent	bountifulness	morphogenetic
disseveration	intravenously	radiotelegram	butterfingers	nearsightedly
dissymetrical	introversible	recommendable	butterflyfish	nostalgically
doubtlessness	irrepressible	recrudescence	centreforward	oceanographer
draggletailed	irrepressibly	refrigeration	centrifugally	oceanographic
dreamlessness	knuckleduster	remorselessly	changefulness	odontoglossum
effervescence	lancesergeant	reprehensible	circumference	oecologically
effervescency	leisureliness	reprehensibly	circumfluence	ontologically
efflorescence	leptocephalic	representable	colourfulness	organogenesis
emphysematous	lifepreserver	reverberation	contrafagotto	palaeographer
ethnocentrism	lightheadedly	reverberative	costeffective	palaeographic
exanthematous	limitlessness	reverberatory	deceitfulness	paramagnetism
extracellular	machinegunner	roentgenogram	disconformity	pedagogically
faithlessness	mackerelshark	roentgenology	forgetfulness	physiognomist
faultlessness	macrocephalic	sacramentally	frightfulness	physiographer
feuilletonism	magisterially	salmonellosis	healthfulness	physiographic
feuilletonist	mercilessness	scolopendrium	honorifically	pneumogastric
fortunehunter	mesencephalon	scrapmerchant	longsuffering	polarographic
fortuneteller	microcephalic	selfexecuting	masterfulness	prestigiously
frighteningly	microdetector	selfsterility	nonconforming	prostaglandin
fruitlessness	millefeuilles	senselessness	nonconformism	psychogenesis
fundamentally	ministerially	sentimentally	nonconformist	psychogenetic
gastroenteric	mirthlessness	shamelessness	nonconformity	quadragesimal
goniometrical	miscegenation	shapelessness	nonforfeiting	rectangularly
gracelessness	mischievously	shiftlessness	nonfulfilment	reintegration
guilelessness	misgovernment	shorttempered	plentifulness	reinvigorator
guiltlessness	misunderstand	shoulderblade	prepreference	runningstitch
heartlessness	misunderstood	shoulderstrap	regardfulness	schizogenesis
hermeneutical	mnemotechnics	sightlessness	regretfulness	seismographer
hydrocephalic	Mohammedanism	sleeplessness	resentfulness	seismographic
hydrocephalus	Monotheletism	smokelessness	selfdefeating	selenographer
hydrogenation	monotrematous	southwesterly	selfinflicted	selenographic

selfregarding	anticlimactic	determination	improvisation	metalliferous
selfrighteous	apportionment	determinative	improvisatory	metallisation
semilogarithm	approximately	deterministic	impulsiveness	Methodistical
serologically	approximation	diffusiveness	incardination	metrification
shabbygenteel	approximative	digestibility	inclusiveness	modernisation
stereographic	archidiaconal	dimensionally	inconsiderate	mollification
strategically	argentiferous	dimensionless	inconsistence	mortification
stratigraphic	aromatisation	disaffirmance	inconsistency	mountainously
suffraganship	assassination	disarticulate	incontinently	mummification
theologically	assertiveness	dispraisingly	inconvincible	mutualisation
thermogenesis	attentiveness	dissemination	incredibility	mystification
thoroughbrace	authorisation	disseminative	incriminatory	necessitarian
thoroughgoing	authoritarian	dissimilarity	indistinctive	necessitation
thoroughpaced	authoritative	dissimilation	inductiveness	necessitously
topologically	bacteriolysis	dissimilitude	ineligibility	nectariferous
turkeygobbler	bacteriolytic	divertisement	infallibilism	negligibility
typologically	bacteriophage	domestication	infallibilist	nickeliferous
unambiguously	balkanisation	dramatisation	infallibility	nitrification
unenlightened	balsamiferous	dulcification	infeasibility	nonresistance
villeggiatura	barbarisation	ecumenicalism	inflexibility	normalisation
woodengraving	beatification	educationally	inflexionless	nullification
zoogeographer	birefringence	effectiveness	infundibulate	nutritionally
zoogeographic	broadmindedly	embellishment	ingurgitation	objectionable
astrophysical	brutalisation	endocrinology	inhospitality	objectionably
atmospherical	calcification	essentialness	inquisitional	objectiveness
biotechnology	Calvinistical	establishment	inquisitively	objectivistic
brokenhearted	caprification	Eucharistical	inquisitorial	obsessiveness
comprehension	carboniferous	evocativeness	insectivorous	obtrusiveness
comprehensive	carbonisation	exceptionable	insensibility	offensiveness
eschscholtzia	catechisation	exceptionably	insensitively	operativeness
extraphysical	cauterisation	exceptionally	insensitivity	ovoviviparous
festschriften	certification	excessiveness	insignificant	palletisation
hemispherical	certificatory	exclusiveness	insufficience	pantheistical
hermaphrodite	cicatrisation	excursiveness	insufficiency	participation
hollowhearted	clarification	expansibility	intangibility	participative
horsechestnut	cobelligerent	expansiveness	intelligencer	participatory
horsewhipping	combativeness	expensiveness	intelligently	patronisingly
hydrochloride	communication	explosiveness	intensiveness	pennypinching
hyperphysical	communicative	exquisiteness	intentionally	peptonisation
microphyllous	communicatory	extensibility	interdigitate	peregrination
misanthropist	communisation	extensionally	intermittence	periodisation
Monarchianism	communitarian	extensiveness	intrusiveness	pervasiveness
parenthetical	compagination	extermination	intuitiveness	petrification
petrochemical	companionable	exterminatory	inventiveness	petroliferous
photochemical	companionably	exterritorial	investigation	plaintiveness
photochromics	companionless	falsification	investigative	platiniferous
photochromism	companionship	fertilisation	investigatory	pluralisation
pigeonhearted	compatibility	feudalisation	invincibility	polliniferous
PreRaphaelite	competitively	formalisation	irretrievable	pontification
rhodochrosite	complainingly	formulisation	irretrievably	potentiometer
sharpshooting	complaisantly	fortification	isomerisation	precipitantly
sheepshearing	compositeness	fossiliferous	italicisation	precipitately
singlehearted	compositional	fossilisation	jollification	precipitation
submachinegun	concomitantly	galvanisation	justification	precipitative
superphysical	concupiscence	garnetiferous	justificative	precipitously
tenderhearted	concupiscible	germanisation	justificatory	predominantly
theanthropism	conditionally	glamorisation	lamellibranch	predomination
transshipment	conduciveness	glorification	leadpoisoning	preengineered
transshipping	confidingness	graminivorous	librarianship	prejudicially
underwhelming	consolidation	gratification	lickerishness	preliminarily
unearthliness	consolidative	greensickness	lightfingered	premeditation
unforthcoming	consolidatory	hallucination	lightmindedly	premeditative
accessibility	contamination	hallucinative	lignification	premonitorily
accreditation	contaminative	hallucinatory	lucrativeness	preordination
acetification	cornification	harmonisation	magnanimously	prepositional
acidification	corrigibility	heartsickness	magnetisation	prevarication
actualisation	corrosiveness	horripilation	magnification	primitiveness
admissibility	curvilinearly	hybridisation	magnificently	prizefighting
advertisement	deceptiveness	hypnotisation	maladminister	probationally
affectionless	decortication	imitativeness	mammaliferous	progenitorial
affenpinscher	decrepitation	immiscibility	manganiferous	prohibitively
agglutination	deductibility	impartibility	manneristical	prolification
agglutinative	defeasibility	impassibility	martyrisation	propositional
aluminiferous	defectiveness	impassiveness	masculineness	protohistoric
aluminisation	defensibility	impercipience	matrilineally	provisionally
amplification	defibrination	impermissible	mechanisation	pulverisation
anglicisation	deodorisation	impertinently	mediatisation	purposiveness
animalisation	derequisition	impossibility	mercerisation	pyrheliometer
anomalistical	determinately	improvidently	mesmerisation	qualification

qualificatory	suppositional	embryological	unintelligent	acrylonitrile
quartziferous	syllabication	entomological	ventriloquial	aerodynamical
quickwittedly	symbolisation	evangelically	ventriloquise	aggiornamento
randomisation	talkativeness	ferroelectric	ventriloquism	argumentation
ratiocination	tantalisation	flagellantism	ventriloquist	argumentative
ratiocinative	tantalisingly	freeselection	viniculturist	auctioneering
recalcitrance	temporisation	gastrological	viticulturist	betweenwhiles
receptibility	tentativeness	generalisable	volatilisable	boardinghouse
receptiveness	terrorisation	generalissimo	actinomorphic	ceremonialism
recessiveness	testification	glaciological	actinomycetes	ceremonialist
recombination	theatricalise	grandiloquent	actinomycosis	ceremoniously
reconcilement	theatricalism	graphological	allelomorphic	challengeable
recrimination	theatricality	hairsplitting	anagrammatise	challengingly
recriminative	thrillingness	hemicellulose	anagrammatism	chrysanthemum
recriminatory	thurification	hydraulically	AngloAmerican	clearinghouse
rectification	toastmistress	hydroelectric	anthelminthic	climbingframe
rectilinearly	traditionally	immunological	antinomianism	confrontation
reduplication	tranquilliser	malacological	autonomically	containership
reduplicative	transliterate	manipulatable	Christmastide	copartnership
reexamination	transmigrator	mellifluously	Christmastime	countinghouse
reflexibility	transmissible	mineralogical	churchmanship	cryptanalysis
regurgitation	transmittable	miscellaneous	complementary	cryptanalytic
replenishment	transpiration	monomolecular	complimentary	deferentially
republicanise	transpiratory	monosyllabism	conglomeratic	disconnection
republicanism	tritheistical	morphological	courtsmartial	displantation
republication	umbelliferous	multiplicable	craftsmanship	doctrinairism
repulsiveness	unconditional	musicological	diagrammatise	documentalist
requisiteness	unconditioned	nomenclatural	dichlamydeous	documentation
resistibility	undisciplined	noncollegiate	discommodious	dressingtable
resuscitation	unemotionally	numerological	discriminator	elephantiasis
resuscitative	unfashionable	odontological	disharmonious	environmental
retentiveness	unfashionably	ophthalmology	draftsmanship	epiphenomenal
revaccination	unfeelingness	overvaluation	dressimprover	epiphenomenon
revendication	unmeaningness	palynological	epigrammatise	equiponderant
reversibility	unmentionable	parabolically	epigrammatist	equiponderate
ritualisation	unpredictable	Pennsylvanian	gentlemanlike	existentially
Russification	unpromisingly	philhellenism	heteromorphic	exponentially
sacrificially	unqualifiedly	philhellenist	homoeomorphic	foraminiferal
scarification	unselfishness	photoelectric	integumentary	forementioned
scorification	unwillingness	photoelectron	kapellmeister	fragmentarily
secretiveness	vapourishness	phrenological	Kidderminster	fragmentation
seductiveness	verbalisation	physiological	metonymically	frequentation
selectiveness	vernalisation	phytoplankton	monosymmetric	frequentative
selfcriticism	versification	piezoelectric	omnicompetent	gastronomical
selfevidently	vertiginously	pigeonlivered	parliamentary	homogeneously
selfexistence	victimisation	pointillistic	photoemission	horizontality
selfopinioned	visualisation	porcellaneous	photoemissive	hypnoanalysis
sensationally	vitrification	premillennial	postcommunion	idiosyncratic
sensitisation	vulcanisation	psychological	prayermeeting	ignominiously
sensitiveness	vulgarisation	punctiliously	pretermission	impecuniosity
serendipitous	doublejointed	quadrilateral	pretermitting	inattentively
serialisation	selfadjusting	quadrillionth	problematical	independently
signalisation	outspokenness	quarrelsomely	pseudomorphic	inexpensively
significantly	psychokinesis	quintillionth	psychometrics	inferentially
signification	psychokinetic	redevelopment	psychometrist	influentially
significative	agriculturist	sansculottism	quadrumvirate	inoffensively
smoothingiron	alcoholically	scandalmonger	rearcommodore	inorganically
snowblindness	alcoholometer	scintillating	sanctimonious	involuntarily
sobermindness	alcoholometry	scintillation	selfcommunion	landownership
socialisation	Australianism	seismological	sewingmachine	laughingstock
solderingiron	BaltoSlavonic	selenological	sportsmanlike	macaronically
solemnisation	belleslettres	selfcollected	sportsmanship	membranaceous
specification	bibliolatrist	selfpollinate	statesmanlike	merchandising
spheroidicity	bibliolatrous	semeiological	statesmanship	microanalysis
splendiferous	bibliological	sericulturist	supereminence	millennialism
squeamishness	breechloading	sidesplitting	supplementary	millionairess
stabilisation	candlelighter	somatological	swordsmanship	monumentalise
staminiferous	chronological	speleological	taxonomically	mouldingboard
sterilisation	conchological	superfluidity	theriomorphic	mourningcloak
stoichiometry	constellation	superfluously	unaccompanied	mourningpaper
stoloniferous	constellatory	technological	unceremonious	mutagenically
subirrigation	craniological	teratological	underemphasis	occidentalise
subordinately	cryptological	tonguelashing	underemployed	Occidentalism
subordination	crystalgazing	tonsillectomy	ungrammatical	Occidentalist
subordinative	crystallinity	toxicological	verisimilarly	octocentenary
subtilisation	deontological	uncomplaining	viceadmiralty	ontogenically
suffumigation	disciplinable	uncomplicated	accidentalism	opinionatedly
summarisation	domiciliation	underclothing	accidentprone	ornamentation
superficially		unfamiliarity	acrimoniously	orthognathism

orthognathous	unrelentingly	dichotomously	intercolonial	phanerogamous
outstandingly	volumenometer	dictatorially	intercolumnar	philosophical
overconfident	accommodating	discoloration	interlocution	philosophiser
oversensitive	accommodation	disembodiment	interlocutory	phosphoretted
palaeontology	accommodative	dishonourable	interlocutrix	photopositive
parasynthesis	ambiguousness	dishonourably	interpolation	phraseologist
parasynthetic	ambitiousness	egregiousness	interpolative	phreatophytic
parthenocarpy	amorphousness	electioneerer	interposition	plenteousness
passionflower	anachronistic	electrocution	interrogation	polypropylene
pathognomonic	anachronously	electrologist	interrogative	ponderousness
penitentially	analogousness	electromagnet	interrogatory	predatoriness
pneumonectomy	anaphrodisiac	electrometric	inventorially	prefatorially
polysynthesis	anomalousness	electromotive	invidiousness	prolegomenary
polysynthetic	anonymousness	electrophorus	irrationalise	prolegomenous
preternatural	anticlockwise	electroscopic	irrationalism	proparoxytone
pronounceable	antiscorbutic	electrostatic	irrationalist	proprioceptor
pronouncement	apheliotropic	electrovalent	irrationality	prosopography
proteinaceous	archaeologist	encyclopaedia	irresponsible	prosthodontia
puritanically	archaeopteryx	encyclopaedic	irresponsibly	protonotarial
quadrennially	assiduousness	encyclopedism	isochronously	psychrometric
quincentenary	Assyriologist	encyclopedist	judiciousness	pteridologist
quincuncially	asthenosphere	erroneousness	juxtaposition	querulousness
quingentenary	atlantosaurus	eschatologist	kaleidoscopic	questioningly
rearrangement	atrociousness	expectoration	laboriousness	questionnaire
referentially	audaciousness	extemporarily	laevorotation	radiolocation
regimentation	autobiography	extrapolation	laevorotatory	rapaciousness
rejuvenescent	autoeroticism	facetiousness	lancecorporal	rapturousness
reorientation	barbarousness	feloniousness	laryngoscopic	reciprocality
resplendently	basidiomycete	ferociousness	lecherousness	reciprocation
reverentially	beauteousness	ferroconcrete	lightsomeness	reciprocative
rontgenoscopy	bloodboltered	foreknowledge	litigiousness	recomposition
rudimentarily	bounteousness	fractionalise	loathsomeness	reconsolidate
schadenfreude	boustrophedon	fractionation	ludicrousness	religiousness
sedimentation	bumptiousness	fractiousness	luxuriousness	righteousness
selfcentredly	campanologist	frivolousness	machicolation	sacerdotalise
selfconceited	capaciousness	functionalism	macromolecule	sacerdotalism
selfcondemned	carcinomatous	functionalist	magnetomotive	sacerdotalist
selfconfessed	carnivorously	galactosaemia	magnetosphere	sagaciousness
selfconfident	cephalothorax	garrulousness	magniloquence	salaciousness
selfconscious	cerebrospinal	gasteropodous	maladroitness	scientologist
selfconsuming	chalcoography	geochronology	malariologist	scorpiongrass
selfcontained	cleistogamous	gerontocratic	maliciousness	seditiousness
selfcontented	climatologist	gerontologist	martyrologist	selfknowledge
selfconvicted	coldbloodedly	glutinousness	megasporangia	selfpropelled
selfgenerated	collaboration	grandmotherly	melodiousness	skateboarding
semiconductor	collaborative	gynaecocratic	metagrobolise	somniloquence
semiconscious	commemoration	gynaecologist	metallography	sovietologist
sergeantmajor	commemoratory	haematologist	metaphosphate	spectrography
shootingbrake	commemorative	hazardousness	meteorologist	spectrometric
shootingrange	concavoconvex	herpetologist	micrococcocci	spectroscopic
shootingstick	condylomatous	hilariousness	microtonality	spelaeologist
slangingmatch	congruousness	histrionicism	mitochondrion	sphygmography
smellingsalts	consciousness	hocuspocussed	momentousness	sternforemost
sniftingvalve	convexoconvex	homeomorphism	monstrousness	stomatologist
solidungulate	corroboration	hyperboloidal	multicoloured	strawcoloured
soundingboard	corroborative	hypochondriac	myrmecologist	strenuousness
spinninghouse	corroboratory	ichthyography	nefariousness	streptococcal
spinningwheel	corticotropic	ichthyologist	neighbourhood	streptococcus
spontaneously	corticotropin	ichthyosaurus	nephelometric	sumptuousness
stalkinghorse	cosmopolitise	imperiousness	nitrocompound	superdominant
stationmaster	cosmopolitism	impersonalise	notoriousness	superposition
steppingstone	courteousness	impersonality	obliviousness	synchronistic
stickingplace	credulousness	impersonation	obnoxiousness	synchronously
substantially	criminologist	impetuousness	occasionalism	tautologously
substantively	cryobiologist	inappropriate	occasionalist	tenaciousness
substantivise	dangerousness	incorporation	occasionality	territorially
subternatural	deciduousness	incorporative	officiousness	threecornered
superannuable	decomposition	incorporeally	onomatopoetic	toothsomeness
supplantation	deliciousness	incuriousness	opisthobranch	transformable
symphonically	deliriousness	indisposition	ornithologist	translocation
symphoniously	demythologise	indissociable	paedomorphism	transportable
thereinbefore	denationalise	ingeniousness	pantisocratic	transposition
thermonuclear	depersonalise	ingenuousness	papillomatous	tremulousness
thrasonically	dermatologist	injuriousness	particoloured	trichromatism
timeconsuming	desultoriness	innocuousness	pendulousness	trigonometric
tintinnabular	deterioration	innoxiousness	penuriousness	troublousness
tintinnabulum	deteriorative	insidiousness	perichondrial	trustworthily
uncleanliness	Deuteronomist	insupportable	perichondrium	tyrannosaurus
unintentional	dexterousness	insupportably	perissodactyl	unanimousness

uncomfortable	schizophrenic	hypertrophied	selffertility	extrinsically
uncomfortably	scleroprotein	illustriously	selfforgetful	flourishingly
unconformable	selfappointed	immaterialise	selfsurrender	fortississimo
unputdownable	selfapproving	immaterialism	selftormentor	fullfashioned
venereologist	selfdependent	immaterialist	semibarbarian	helterskelter
venturousness	selfimportant	immateriality	semibarbarism	heterosporous
veraciousness	selfreproving	impropriation	semiparasitic	impressionism
versicoloured	selfrepugnant	inadvertently	semipermanent	impressionist
vexatiousness	selfsupported	incongruously	semipermeable	interestingly
vicariousness	sesquiplicate	indescribable	semiporcelain	interosculate
vivaciousness	Shakespearean	indescribably	SerboCroatian	intransigeant
vocationalism	Shakespearian	indeterminacy	sharecropping	intransigence
volcanologist	tablespoonful	indeterminate	Spencerianism	intrinsically
voraciousness	thermophilous	indeterminism	stercoraceous	languishingly
vulcanologist	thermoplastic	indeterminist	subterraneous	malacostracan
wearisomeness	unexceptional	indoctrinator	sulphureously	Malthusianism
wholesomeness	wellapPointed	industrialise	supercritical	manifestation
worrisomeness	grotesqueness	industrialism	superordinate	manifestative
angiospermous	accelerometer	industrialist	symmetrically	meadowsaffron
anthropogenic	accoutrements	industriously	teleportation	mistrustfully
anthropometry	allegorically	inexperienced	temerariously	mistrustingly
anthropopathy	amphiprostyle	inopportunely	thundershower	neoclassicism
anthropophagi	Antichristian	insubordinate	thunderstruck	neoclassicist
anthropophagy	antipersonnel	intercropping	Tractarianism	neoplasticism
anthroposophy	appropriately	interpretable	transcription	nonsensically
autocephalous	appropriation	interpretress	transcriptive	paddlesteamer
bibliophilism	appropriative	intertropical	transgression	percussionist
bibliophilist	backformation	intraarterial	transgressive	phalansterian
brachypterous	backscratcher	introgression	treasurership	polyhistorian
broadspectrum	backwardation	irreverential	undergraduate	prepossessing
centripetally	biodegradable	isometrically	uninformative	prepossession
consumptively	bioenergetics	jurisprudence	uninterrupted	processionary
contemplation	brotherliness	knickerbocker	unnaturalness	processionist
contemplative	burglariously	leatherjacket	vegetarianism	proconsulship
contrapuntist	calligraphist	levelcrossing	waterproofing	procrastinate
correspondent	camphoraceous	mediterranean	weatherbeaten	professoriate
corresponsive	categorically	meistersinger	wheelerdealer	professorship
cottonpicking	chinkerinchee	meritoriously	whithersoever	profitsharing
descriptively	consternation	metamorphoses	acquiescently	prognosticate
developmental	contrariously	metamorphosis	acquiescingly	progressional
disproportion	counteraction	microorganism	administrable	progressively
disrespectful	counteractive	moneygrubbing	administrator	progressivism
dodecaphonist	counterattack	monochromatic	admonishingly	pseudoscience
entomophagous	counterchange	nonaggression	afforestation	psychasthenia
entomophilous	countercharge	ochlocratical	antihistamine	psychosomatic
geomorphology	counterfeiter	oleomargarine	archbishopric	psychosurgery
geotropically	counterstroke	opprobriously	astonishingly	reforestation
gymnospermous	counterweight	painterliness	businesswoman	reminiscently
heteropterous	crackerbarrel	panegyrically	candlesnuffer	retranslation
homoeopathist	cruiserweight	pantagruelian	chromospheric	sadomasochism
hymenopterous	cylindrically	pantagruelism	circumspectly	sadomasochist
inconspicuous	daguerreotype	pantagruelist	clandestinely	scholasticism
inscriptional	decompression	papaveraceous	clothesbasket	selfasserting
interspecific	decontrolling	paranormality	coenaesthesis	selfassertion
interspersion	deleteriously	pedestrianise	collieshangie	selfassertive
introspection	dematerialise	pedestrianism	commensurable	selfassurance
introspective	derestriction	phycoerythrin	commensurably	selfassuredly
lepidopterist	diametrically	plethorically	compassionate	selfdiscovery
lepidopterous	diathermanous	pluripresence	compressional	selfdispraise
leptospirosis	eavesdropping	pococurantism	concessionary	selfinsurance
letterperfect	eccentrically	polycarbonate	confessionary	selfpossessed
maladaptation	equestrianism	polychromatic	congressional	selfrestraint
megacephalous	exasperatedly	primigravidae	congresswoman	selfsustained
miscomprehend	expropriation	quartermaster	conversazione	seriousminded
noncompliance	extraordinary	reaffirmation	conversazioni	stereoscopist
nucleoprotein	extratropical	redescription	convulsionary	stratospheric
overemphasise	featherheaded	reembarkation	deforestation	subversionary
overpopulated	featherstitch	reimbursement	deipnosophist	televisionary
phyllophagous	featherweight	reincarnation	diagnostician	thalassocracy
presumptively	foolhardiness	reinforcement	dispassionate	thermosetting
principalship	geometrically	retrogression	dispossession	tortoiseshell
psychophysics	globetrotting	retrogressive	distressfully	transistorise
quadripartite	gynandromorph	RhaetoRomanic	distressingly	underestimate
quadruplicate	harbourmaster	saccharimeter	distrustfully	unimpassioned
quadruplicity	heartbreaking	saccharimetry	entomostracan	unnecessarily
quintuplicate	hemiparasitic	saccharometer	equidistantly	windowshopper
retrospection	housebreaking	scholarliness	everlastingly	acrobatically
retrospective	hydrocracking	selfdirecting	expressionism	adiabatically
schizophrenia	hypercritical	selfdirection	expressionist	aesthetically

agonistically	exhibitionism	prophetically	transitionary	metallurgical
airworthiness	exhibitionist	proportionate	traumatically	micronutrient
anfractuosity	expeditionary	protectionism	tricentennial	multinucleate
annexationist	expeditiously	protectionist	unadulterated	multitudinous
apathetically	fantastically	protectorship	unconstrained	nondeductable
arthritically	Fascistically	Protestantism	understanding	nonfigurative
asthmatically	felicitations	prudentialism	understrapper	nonreturnable
atheistically	flirtatiously	prudentialist	unhealthiness	opportuneness
atomistically	floristically	prudentiality	unquestioning	opportunistic
authentically	followthrough	psilanthropic	unremittingly	overabundance
authenticator	geocentricism	psychotherapy	unrighteously	particularise
autocatalysis	geostationary	pyrimethamine	unsubstantial	particularism
autocatalytic	gonadotrophic	realistically	untrustworthy	particularist
autochthonism	gonadotrophin	reconstructor	woolgathering	particularity
autochthonous	goodnaturedly	recrystallise	zinjanthropus	perambulation
automatically	grammatically	refractometer	acculturation	perambulatory
axiomatically	gymnastically	remonstrantly	acculturative	piscicultural
blanketflower	helminthiasis	remonstration	admeasurement	platitudinise
bombastically	helminthology	remonstrative	adventuresome	platitudinous
brainstorming	heterothallic	renegotiation	adventurously	plenitudinous
buttonthrough	heterotrophic	repetitionary	attributively	prefiguration
cabinetmaking	homoiothermal	repetitiously	beleaguerment	prefigurative
callisthenics	homoiothermic	revelationist	blackguardism	prefigurement
characterless	hydrostatical	revolutionary	bloodcurdling	prematureness
chrematistics	idiomatically	revolutionise	chateaubriand	preoccupation
chromatically	immunotherapy	revolutionism	clairaudience	scripturalism
chromatograph	impenetration	revolutionist	colloquialism	scripturalist
chromatolytic	impolitically	rheumatically	confabulation	sculpturesque
chromatophore	impracticable	sanitationist	confabulatory	selfeducation
cinematically	impracticably	sarcastically	configuration	sociocultural
cinematograph	impractically	schematically	connaturality	spiritualness
climactically	indefatigable	schoolteacher	consecutively	strangulation
collectedness	indefatigably	scorbutically	consequential	structuralism
collectorship	infinitesimal	scrumptiously	constructable	structuralist
compartmental	inspectorship	seaworthiness	constructible	structureless
conceitedness	instantaneity	selfpityingly	crosscultural	sublieutenant
concentration	instantaneous	selfsatisfied	crosspurposes	subsaturation
concentrative	insubstantial	semiautomatic	crossquestion	subsequential
concentricity	interstratify	sententiously	degranulation	substructural
conceptualise	isostatically	separationist	denticulation	superhumanity
conceptualism	judgmatically	septentrional	disfigurement	supernumerary
conceptualist	kinematically	sequentiality	dissimulation	supersubtlety
concertmaster	kinematograph	sequestration	dissolubility	swashbuckling
concretionary	liberationist	silvertongued	dissoluteness	threequarters
conductorship	Maginotminded	solicitorship	dramaturgical	topsyturvydom
confectionary	moderatorship	sophistically	encapsulation	translucently
confectionery	monocotyledon	sophisticated	excommunicate	translucidity
confraternity	monometallism	spermatoblast	expostulation	transmutation
congratulator	monometallist	spermatogenic	expostulatory	transmutative
conjecturable	monophthongal	spermatophore	extrajudicial	triangularity
conjecturally	neurastheniac	spermatophyte	fasciculation	triangulation
connectedness	oppositionist	splenetically	floricultural	tuberculation
consentaneity	orchestration	sprightliness	funambulation	unaccountable
consentaneous	organotherapy	statistically	gesticulation	unaccountably
contentedness	paediatrician	stigmatically	gesticulative	uncircumcised
contentiously	panicstricken	stylistically	gesticulatory	unconquerable
contortionist	parasitically	subcontractor	horticultural	unfortunately
conventionary	parasiticidal	subeditorship	hydrosulphide	unobtrusively
convertiplane	patriotically	subpostmaster	hydrosulphite	vermiculation
corruptionist	perfectionism	subreptitious	imperturbable	vernacularise
demonstration	perfectionist	substitutable	imperturbably	vernacularism
demonstrative	philanthropic	superstitious	importunately	vernacularity
dendritically	phonautograph	surreptitious	incombustible	Zarathustrian
devolutionary	phrenetically	symbiotically	incommunicado	animadversion
devolutionist	physiotherapy	syntactically	incorruptible	circumvallate
diageotropism	pneumatically	synthetically	incorruptibly	circumvention
dialectically	pneumatolysis	tachistoscope	incorruptness	conservatoire
discontinuity	pneumatolytic	tempestuously	incredulously	contravention
discontinuous	pneumatometer	tendentiously	inexhaustible	controversial
discretionary	pneumatophore	tercentennial	inexhaustibly	halfsovereign
dismantlement	polycotyledon	terrestrially	institutional	irrecoverable
distastefully	pragmatically	thaumaturgist	intercultural	irrecoverably
doubletongued	precautionary	theoretically	intercurrence	Machiavellian
egocentricity	precentorship	thermotropism	interpunction	selfgoverning
embrittlement	predestinator	thigmotropism	interruptible	selfrevealing
energetically	prehistorical	thoughtlessly	intramuscular	semicivilised
enigmatically	pretentiously	thoughtreader	jerrybuilding	subserviently
enlightenment	prismatically	tonguetwister	maladjustment	unequivocally
equipotential	projectionist	transatlantic	matriculation	linseywoolsey

searchwarrant	identicalness	applicability	supersubtlety	mortification
streetwalking	illogicalness	attainability	terminability	multinucleate
swallowtailed	inefficacious	bouillabaisse	thereinbefore	mummification
wonderworking	instantaneity	changeability	unsociability	mystification
ambidexterity	instantaneous	chateaubriand	unsuitability	nitrification
ambidexterous	insubstantial	clothesbasket	verifiability	nitrobacteria
complexedness	librarianship	coagulability	vulnerability	nondeductable
homosexuality	lightheadedly	commutability	weatherbeaten	nullification
paradoxically	manipulatable	comparability	acetification	owneroccupier
underexposure	meadowsaffron	compatibility	acidification	pantisocratic
apocalyptical	membranaceous	corrigibility	amplification	petrification
heptasyllabic	microanalysis	crackerbarrel	anticlockwise	photoreceptor
hydrodynamics	millionairess	deductibility	archdeaconate	pontification
hydroxylamine	miscellaneous	defeasibility	architectonic	prejudicially
hypoglycaemia	monometallism	defensibility	architectural	prevarication
jiggerypokery	monometallist	dependability	beatification	prolification
metaphysician	mountebankery	digestibility	calcification	pronounceable
Monophysitism	nomenclatural	disposability	caprification	pronouncement
naphthylamine	nonappearance	dissolubility	certification	proprioceptor
osteomyelitis	ochlocratical	expansibility	certificatory	pseudoscience
poliomyelitis	opinionatedly	extensibility	chemoreceptor	qualification
tetrasyllable	orthognathism	filterability	clarification	qualificatory
worldlyminded	orthognathous	formidability	communication	quincuncially
bamboozlement	oystercatcher	immiscibility	communicative	radiolocation
laissezpasser	papaveraceous	impalpability	communicatory	reciprocality
palaeozoology	perspicacious	impartibility	concavoconvex	reciprocation
————	phytoplankton	impassability	constructable	reciprocative
abortifacient	pneumogastric	impassibility	constructible	rectification
aerodynamical	pococurantism	impeccability	convexoconvex	reduplication
aggiornamento	porcellaneous	implacability	cornification	reduplicative
antilogarithm	practicalness	impossibility	counterchange	reinforcement
archidiaconal	PreRaphaelite	improbability	countercharge	reminiscently
autocatalysis	preternatural	improvability	decortication	republicanise
autocatalytic	primigravidae	incredibility	disaffectedly	republicanism
backpedalling	principalship	ineducability	disarticulate	republication
backscratcher	problematical	ineligibility	domestication	revendication
BaltoSlavonic	proteinaceous	inevitability	dulcification	Russification
bibliolatrist	Protestantism	inexorability	ecumenicalism	sacrificially
bibliolatrous	quadrilateral	infallibilism	electrocution	scarification
biodegradable	quadripartite	infallibilist	falsification	scorification
blackguardism	recrystallise	infallibility	fortification	selfconceited
brachydactyly	schizocarpous	infeasibility	gerontocratic	selfdiscovery
calligraphist	searchwarrant	inflexibility	glorification	selfeducation
camphoraceous	selfregarding	infundibulate	gratification	selfexecuting
Christmastide	semilogarithm	insatiability	greensickness	semiporcelain
Christmastime	semiparasitic	insensibility	gynaecocratic	significantly
churchmanship	sewingmachine	insociability	heartsickness	signification
circumvallate	skateboarding	intangibility	hocuspocussed	significative
clearheadedly	softpedalling	invariability	hypoglycaemia	specification
complicatedly	spiritualness	invincibility	hypothecation	steeplechaser
consentaneity	sportsmanlike	inviolability	idiosyncratic	stereoscopist
consentaneous	sportsmanship	knickerbocker	imperfectness	streptococcal
conservatoire	squarebashing	lamellibranch	inappreciable	streptococcus
contrabandist	statesmanlike	manageability	inappreciably	substructural
contrabassoon	statesmanship	mensurability	inconsecutive	superficially
contrafagotto	stercoraceous	metagrobolise	incorrectness	swashbuckling
conversazione	streetwalking	metastability	indissociable	syllabication
conversazioni	subternatural	negligibility	insufficience	testification
counteraction	subterraneous	negotiability	insufficiency	theatricalise
counteractive	suffraganship	opisthobranch	interjectural	theatricalism
counterattack	swordsmanship	overelaborate	interlacement	theatricality
courtsmartial	technicalness	penetrability	interlocution	thurification
craftsmanship	threequarters	perdurability	interlocutory	translocation
cryptanalysis	tintinnabular	perishability	interlocutrix	translucently
cryptanalytic	tintinnabulum	permutability	interosculate	translucidity
disappearance	tonguelashing	polycarbonate	irreplaceable	unforthcoming
doctrinairism	uncomplaining	ponderability	jollification	unimpeachable
draftsmanship	undergraduate	predicability	justification	unpredictable
equivocalness	understanding	preferability	justificative	versification
essentialness	ungrammatical	profitability	justificatory	vitrification
exasperatedly	unnaturalness	receptibility	lignification	accommodating
felicitations	unsubstantial	reflexibility	magnification	accommodation
flagellantism	whimsicalness	reformability	magnificently	accommodative
gentlemanlike	wrongheadedly	resistibility	metrification	acotyledonous
hemiparasitic	absorbability	resolvability	micrococcocci	ambassadorial
homoeopathist	acceptability	reversibility	mnemotechnics	anaphrodisiac
hydrocracking	accessibility	semibarbarian	mollification	backwardation
hydrostatical	admissibility	semibarbarism		clairaudience
hypnoanalysis	answerability	squeezability		consolidation

consolidative	disconnection	preponderance	schadenfreude	spinningwheel
consolidatory	disgracefully	preponderancy	selfconfessed	stalkinghorse
disembodiment	dismemberment	prepossessing	selfconfident	steppingstone
equiponderant	dispossession	prepossession	selfsufficing	stickingplace
equiponderate	disrespectful	prepreference	splendiferous	subirrigation
extrajudicial	distastefully	psychogenesis	staminiferous	suffumigation
extraordinary	doubledealing	psychogenetic	standoffishly	synallagmatic
foolhardiness	embryogenesis	psychometrics	stoloniferous	tautologously
hydromedusoid	enlightenment	psychometrist	umbelliferous	transmigrator
improvidently	epeirogenesis	quadragesimal	unqualifiedly	vantageground
inconsiderate	equipotential	rejuvenescent	vouchsafement	acetylcholine
independently	excrescential	resourcefully	anticoagulant	admonishingly
insubordinate	exteroceptive	retrogression	autobiography	affreightment
intermediator	ferroelectric	retrogressive	bioenergetics	airworthiness
knuckleduster	freeselection	retrospection	boardinghouse	archbishopric
merchandising	frontogenesis	retrospective	cartilaginous	astonishingly
Mohammedanism	gametogenesis	schizogenesis	chalcoography	autocephalous
Muhammadanism	gymnospermous	schoolteacher	challengeable	autochthonism
multitudinous	halfsovereign	selenocentric	challengingly	autochthonous
outstandingly	heartbreaking	selfasserting	clearinghouse	barrelchested
overcredulous	heebiejeebies	selfassertion	cleistogamous	bibliophilism
perissodactyl	hemispherical	selfassertive	climbingframe	bibliophilist
platitudinise	heterogeneity	selfdeceiving	cobelligerent	buttonthrough
platitudinous	heterogeneous	selfdeception	countinghouse	callisthenics
plenitudinous	heterogenesis	selfdeceptive	crystalgazing	chuckleheaded
prosthodontia	heterogenetic	selfdefeating	desegregation	collieshangie
resplendently	hollowhearted	selfdependent	deuteragonist	dodecaphonist
selfcondemned	homogeneously	selfdirecting	diaphragmatic	entomophagous
selfevidently	horsechestnut	selfdirection	disengagement	entomophilous
semiconductor	housebreaking	selfgenerated	disintegrator	featherheaded
spheroidicity	hydroelectric	selfgoverning	disparagement	flourishingly
superaddition	infinitesimal	selfrevealing	disparagingly	followthrough
superordinate	integumentary	shabbygenteel	dressingtable	foresightedly
unprecedented	interoceptive	Shakespearean	encouragement	fortunehunter
wheelerdealer	interpretable	Shakespearian	encouragingly	fullfashioned
accoutrements	interpretress	sheepshearing	extravagantly	geomorphology
angiospermous	interspecific	sicklefeather	ferrimagnetic	helminthiasis
AngloAmerican	interspersion	singlehearted	ferromagnetic	helminthology
animadversion	introgression	spontaneously	ichthyography	heterothallic
atmospherical	introspection	subsequential	intelligencer	homoiothermal
auctioneering	introspective	sulphureously	intelligently	homoiothermic
barefacedness	irrecoverable	supplementary	interdigitate	immunotherapy
beleaguerment	irrecoverably	tenderhearted	interrogation	languishingly
belleslettres	irretrievable	tercentennial	interrogative	megacephalous
blastogenesis	irretrievably	thermogenesis	interrogatory	monophthongal
brachycephaly	irreverential	thermosetting	investigation	nearsightedly
broadspectrum	kapellmeister	tonsillectomy	investigative	neurastheniac
brokenhearted	landownership	tortoiseshell	investigatory	organotherapy
centripetally	letterperfect	transgression	knowledgeable	overemphasise
characterless	Machiavellian	transgressive	knowledgeably	philanthropic
cinquecentist	Manichaeanism	treasurership	laughingstock	phyllophagous
circumference	misconception	tricentennial	machinegunner	physiotherapy
circumvention	monomolecular	unadulterated	metallography	pigeonchested
collectedness	morphogenesis	unconquerable	microorganism	profitsharing
commandership	morphogenetic	underwhelming	mismanagement	psilanthropic
complementary	nonaggression	unrighteously	mouldingboard	psychophysics
complexedness	noncollegiate	violoncellist	mourningcloak	psychotherapy
complimentary	nonforfeiting	winterberries	mourningpaper	pyrimethamine
comprehension	offhandedness	aluminiferous	oleomargarine	pyrotechnical
comprehensive	organogenesis	argentiferous	partridgewood	reproachfully
conceitedness	osteomyelitis	balsamiferous	phanerogamous	reproachingly
condescension	outspokenness	blanketflower	preengagement	schizophrenia
confraternity	parenthetical	carboniferous	prizefighting	schizophrenic
conglomeratic	parliamentary	counterfeiter	prosopography	seaworthiness
connectedness	petrochemical	fossiliferous	quinquagenary	selfrighteous
consequential	pharmaceutics	garnetiferous	Quinquagesima	terpsichorean
containership	pharmaceutist	insignificant	rearrangement	thermochemist
contentedness	photochemical	longsuffering	selfforgetful	thermophilous
contraception	photoelectric	mammaliferous	shootingbrake	thoroughbrace
contraceptive	photoelectron	manganiferous	shootingrange	thoroughgoing
contravention	piezoelectric	metalliferous	shootingstick	thoroughpaced
controversial	pigeonhearted	nectariferous	slangingmatch	underachiever
copartnership	pigheadedness	nickeliferous	smellingsalts	unenlightened
costeffective	pluripresence	overconfident	sniftingvalve	unflinchingly
crossquestion	pneumonectomy	passionflower	solidungulate	unhealthiness
daguerreotype	poliomyelitis	petroliferous	soundingboard	windowshopper
decompression	prayermeeting	platiniferous	spectrography	woolgathering
disconcerting	preconception	polliniferous	sphygmography	xanthochroism
disconcertion	premillennial	quartziferous	spinninghouse	zinjanthropus

abiologically	devolutionist	intransigeant	psychokinesis	verisimilarly
acrimoniously	dialectically	intransigence	psychokinetic	viceadmiralty
acrobatically	diametrically	intrinsically	punctiliously	villeggiatura
acrylonitrile	disciplinable	irreclaimable	puritanically	volatilisable
adiabatically	discontinuity	irreclaimably	quadricipital	leatherjacket
aesthetically	discontinuous	irreligionist	realistically	helterskelter
agonistically	discreditable	irreligiously	redescription	painstakingly
alcoholically	discreditably	isometrically	renegotiation	reembarkation
algebraically	discretionary	isostatically	repetitionary	admirableness
allegorically	discriminator	jerrybuilding	repetitiously	advisableness
anaerobically	disobediently	judgmatically	revelationist	agreeableness
annexationist	dispassionate	Kidderminster	revolutionary	archaeologist
anthelminthic	domiciliation	kinematically	revolutionise	Assyriologist
Antichristian	eccentrically	lackadaisical	revolutionism	availableness
antinomianism	efficaciously	leptospirosis	revolutionist	bamboozlement
apathetically	energetically	lethargically	rhapsodically	blameableness
appropriately	enigmatically	liberationist	rheumatically	bloodboltered
appropriation	entertainment	macaronically	saccharimeter	bloodrelation
appropriative	equestrianism	maladroitness	saccharimetry	brotherliness
arthritically	evangelically	Malthusianism	sanitationist	butterflyfish
artificiality	exhibitionism	meritoriously	sarcastically	campanologist
ascertainable	exhibitionist	metonymically	schematically	cannibalistic
ascertainment	expeditionary	millennialism	scorbutically	circumfluence
asthmatically	expeditiously	Monarchianism	scrumptiously	climatologist
atheistically	expressionism	multiplicable	selfsatisfied	confabulation
atomistically	expressionist	mutagenically	semicivilised	confabulatory
Australianism	expropriation	nonfulfilment	sententiously	constellation
authentically	extrinsically	nonsensically	separationist	constellatory
authenticator	fantastically	nostalgically	sequentiality	contemplation
automatically	Fascistically	oecologically	serologically	contemplative
autonomically	flirtatiously	ontogenically	sidesplitting	cosmopolitise
axiomatically	floristically	ontologically	sophistically	cosmopolitism
beneficiation	foraminiferal	oppositionist	sophisticated	criminalistic
Berkeleianism	fortississimo	opprobriously	spasmodically	criminologist
bombastically	generalisable	panegyrically	Spencerianism	crosscultural
burglariously	generalissimo	parabolically	splenetically	cryobiologist
butterfingers	geometrically	paradoxically	statistically	crystallinity
candlelighter	geostationary	parasitically	stigmatically	dastardliness
categorically	geotropically	parasiticidal	strategically	defencelessly
ceremonialism	grammatically	patriotically	stylistically	degranulation
ceremonialist	gymnastically	pedagogically	submachinegun	demythologise
ceremoniously	hairsplitting	pedestrianise	subreptitious	denticulation
chieftainship	honorifically	pedestrianism	subserviently	dermatologist
chinkerinchee	horsewhipping	percussionist	subversionary	desirableness
chrematistics	hydraulically	perfectionism	supercritical	dismantlement
chromatically	hypercritical	perfectionist	supereminence	dissemblingly
cinematically	ideologically	perpendicular	superstitious	dissimilarity
climactically	idiomatically	pharisaically	surreptitious	dissimilation
closedcircuit	ignominiously	photoemission	symbiotically	dissimilitude
colloquialism	illustriously	photoemissive	symmetrically	dissimulation
commercialise	immaterialise	phrenetically	symphonically	doubleglazing
commercialism	immaterialism	pigeonlivered	symphoniously	electrologist
commercialist	immaterialist	plethorically	syntactically	embranglement
compassionate	immateriality	pneumatically	synthetically	embrittlement
compendiously	impecuniosity	pragmatically	taxonomically	encapsulation
concessionary	impolitically	precautionary	televisionary	encephalogram
concretionary	impracticable	predestinator	temerariously	enjoyableness
confectionary	impracticably	preordainment	tendentiously	eschatologist
confectionery	impractically	prestigiously	theologically	excitableness
confessionary	impressionism	pretentiously	theoretically	excusableness
constrainable	impressionist	pretermission	thrasonically	expostulation
constrainedly	impropriation	pretermitting	topologically	expostulatory
contentiously	inconceivable	primordiality	Tractarianism	extracellular
contortionist	inconceivably	prismatically	transcription	extragalactic
contradiction	inconspicuous	processionary	transcriptive	extrapolation
contradictory	indefatigable	processionist	transitionary	fasciculation
contrariously	indefatigably	projectionist	transshipment	floricultural
conventionary	indescribable	pronunciation	transshipping	funambulation
convertiplane	indescribably	prophetically	traumatically	gerontologist
convulsionary	indoctrinator	proportionate	typologically	gesticulation
coreligionist	industrialise	protectionism	unanticipated	gesticulative
corruptionist	industrialism	protectionist	uncertainness	gesticulatory
cottonpicking	industrialist	provincialise	uncomplicated	gynaecologist
cylindrically	industriously	provincialism	unconceivable	habitableness
deleteriously	inefficiently	provincialist	unconsciously	haematologist
dematerialise	inexpediently	provinciality	uncoordinated	hemicellulose
dendritically	inexperienced	prudentialism	unfamiliarity	heptasyllabic
derestriction	injudiciously	prudentialist	unquestioning	herpetologist
devolutionary	inorganically	prudentiality	vegetarianism	horripilation

horticultural	quadrillionth	electrometric	compagination	matrilineally
hydrochloride	quadruplicate	electromotive	complainingly	microtonality
hydrosulphide	quadruplicity	emphysematous	concatenation	miscegenation
hydrosulphite	quintillionth	environmental	confidingness	mitochondrion
hydroxylamine	quintuplicate	epigrammatise	conscientious	mountainously
hyperboloidal	radiotelegram	epigrammatist	consternation	nonattendance
ichthyologist	rationalistic	exanthematous	contamination	occasionalism
immovableness	reconcilement	harbourmaster	contaminative	occasionalist
immutableness	reconsolidate	indeterminacy	continentally	occasionality
imperialistic	remorselessly	indeterminate	curvilinearly	opportuneness
incredulously	removableness	indeterminism	defibrination	opportunistic
incurableness	retranslation	indeterminist	denationalise	overabundance
ineffableness	salmonellosis	lightsomeness	depersonalise	paperhangings
insolubleness	scholarliness	loathsomeness	determinately	paramagnetism
intercalation	scientologist	Maginotminded	determination	passementerie
intercellular	scintillating	magnanimously	determinative	pathogenicity
intercolonial	scintillation	magnetomotive	deterministic	pennypinching
intercolumnar	selfcollected	materfamilias	detrimentally	peregrination
intercultural	selfinflicted	melodramatics	Deuteronomist	perichondrial
intergalactic	selfpollinate	melodramatise	differentiate	perichondrium
interpellator	separableness	melodramatist	disadvantaged	phenomenalise
interpolation	sesquiplicate	monogrammatic	dissemination	phenomenalism
interpolative	sociocultural	monosymmetric	disseminative	phenomenalist
interrelation	sovietologist	monotrematous	electioneerer	phenomenology
intracellular	spelaeologist	nephelometric	endocrinology	physiognomist
invisibleness	spindlelegged	nitrocompound	ethnocentrism	predominantly
irritableness	sprightliness	ophthalmology	excommunicate	predomination
laughableness	stomatologist	papillomatous	extermination	preengineered
leisureliness	strangulation	paranormality	exterminatory	preliminarily
machicolation	strawcoloured	paterfamilias	ferroconcrete	preordination
mackerelshark	supercalender	postcommunion	fractionalise	prescientific
macromolecule	teachableness	predicamental	fractionation	presidentship
malariologist	temporalities	prolegomenary	frighteningly	primogenitary
malleableness	tetrasyllable	prolegomenous	functionalism	primogenitive
martyrologist	thermoplastic	psychrometric	functionalist	primogeniture
materialistic	thoughtlessly	quartermaster	fundamentally	psychoanalyse
matriculation	tolerableness	quicktempered	gastrocnemius	psychoanalyst
meteorologist	traceableness	reaffirmation	gastroenteric	pusillanimity
miserableness	tractableness	rearcommodore	geochronology	pusillanimous
mononucleosis	tranquilliser	scandalmonger	hallucination	quadrennially
monosyllabism	transatlantic	selfcommunion	hallucinative	questioningly
Monotheletism	triangularity	selftormentor	hallucinatory	questionnaire
multicellular	triangulation	semipermanent	histrionicism	ratiocination
multicoloured	tuberculation	semipermeable	hydrodynamics	ratiocinative
myrmecologist	uncleanliness	seriousminded	hydrogenation	recombination
naphthylamine	unearthliness	shorttempered	hypochondriac	recommendable
nationalistic	unestablished	spectrometric	impersonalise	recrimination
navigableness	unintelligent	stationmaster	impersonality	recriminative
nemathelminth	venerableness	subpostmaster	impersonation	recriminatory
niggardliness	venereologist	superdominant	impertinently	rectilinearly
noncompliance	vermiculation	superfamilies	importunately	reexamination
odontoglossum	vernacularise	superhumanity	incardination	reincarnation
orangeblossom	vernacularism	supernumerary	incommunicado	reprehensible
ornithologist	vernacularity	telegrammatic	incondensable	reprehensibly
overqualified	versicoloured	temperamental	incontinently	representable
painterliness	volcanologist	toothsomeness	inconvenience	revaccination
palatableness	vulcanologist	trichromatism	inconveniency	rhadamanthine
parallelogram	anagrammatise	trigonometric	inconvincible	righthandedly
particoloured	anagrammatism	uncircumcised	incrementally	roentgenogram
particularise	anticlimactic	uninformative	incriminatory	roentgenology
particularism	approximately	wearisomeness	indispensable	sacramentally
particularist	approximation	wholesomeness	indispensably	sacrosanctity
particularity	approximative	worldlyminded	indistinctive	scolopendrium
paternalistic	backformation	worrisomeness	interdentally	scorpiongrass
peaceableness	basidiomycete	accompaniment	interpunction	selfopinioned
perambulation	blasphemously	affenpinscher	intravenously	sentimentally
perambulatory	cabinetmaking	agglutination	irrationalise	smoothingiron
phenylalanine	carcinomatous	agglutinative	irrationalism	snowblindness
philhellenism	circumambient	amniocentesis	irrationalist	sobermindness
philhellenist	compartmental	anachronistic	irrationality	solderingiron
phraseologist	concertmaster	anachronously	irrefrangible	subordinately
piscicultural	condylomatous	apprehensible	irresponsible	subordination
platyhelminth	cytochemistry	archimandrite	irresponsibly	subordinative
plausibleness	decontaminate	assassination	isochronously	superannuable
pointillistic	developmental	biotechnology	leishmaniasis	supersensible
polyadelphous	diagrammatise	birefringence	lightfingered	supervenience
prostaglandin	diathermanous	brilliantness	lightmindedly	synchronistic
pteridologist	dichotomously	broadmindedly	maladminister	synchronously
purposelessly	electromagnet	candlesnuffer	masculineness	threateningly

thrillingness	extratropical	selfrecording	microcephalic	crosspurposes
transcendence	gastrological	semeiological	omnicompetent	cryptographer
transcendency	gastronomical	semiautomatic	onomatopoetic	cryptographic
unaccountable	glaciological	sensationally	oreographical	customariness
unaccountably	globetrotting	SerboCroatian	orthocephalic	decerebration
underhandedly	grandiloquent	sharecropping	ovoviviparous	demonstration
unfeelingness	graphological	sharpshooting	participation	demonstrative
unfortunately	gynandromorph	silvertongued	participative	desultoriness
unmeaningness	heteromorphic	socioeconomic	participatory	deterioration
unpretentious	homoeomorphic	solicitorship	philosophical	deteriorative
unwarrantable	hypertrophied	somatological	philosophiser	diageotropism
unwarrantably	immunological	speleological	phreatophytic	dictatorially
unwillingness	inflexionless	spermatoblast	picturepalace	disaffirmance
vertiginously	inspectorship	spermatogenic	polypropylene	discoloration
vocationalism	intentionally	spermatophore	preoccupation	disfigurement
accelerometer	intercropping	spermatophyte	selfdispraise	disinterested
actinomorphic	intertropical	stoichiometry	selfpropelled	disseveration
affectionless	kinematograph	subeditorship	selfsupported	doublecrosser
alcoholometer	levelcrossing	Swedenborgian	serendipitous	dramaturgical
alcoholometry	linseywoolsey	tablespoonful	stratospheric	egocentricity
allelomorphic	malacological	tachistoscope	telencephalon	equilibration
amphiprostyle	microscopical	taperecording	topographical	exemplariness
anthropogenic	mineralogical	technological	typographical	expectoration
anthropometry	moderatorship	telerecording	unaccompanied	extemporarily
anthropopathy	monochromatic	teratological	underemphasis	festschriften
anthropophagi	morphological	thalassocracy	underemployed	fissiparously
anthropophagy	mothercountry	thenceforward	underexposure	geocentricism
anthroposophy	musicological	theriomorphic	undisciplined	glossographer
apportionment	nonconforming	toxicological	xylographical	gonadotrophic
bacteriolysis	nonconformism	traditionally	inconsequence	gonadotrophin
bacteriolytic	nonconformist	turkeygobbler	magniloquence	halfheartedly
bacteriophage	nonconformity	unceremonious	somniloquence	haphazardness
bibliological	numerological	underclothing	acculturation	hardheartedly
bookingoffice	nutritionally	unemotionally	acculturative	hermaphrodite
brainstorming	objectionable	unequivocally	admeasurement	heterotrophic
breechloading	objectionably	unfashionable	adventuresome	homeomorphism
centreforward	odontological	unfashionably	adventurously	impenetration
chlamydomonas	palaeozoology	unmentionable	agglomeration	imperturbable
chlamydospore	palynological	ventriloquial	agglomerative	imperturbably
chromatograph	parthenocarpy	ventriloquise	antiscorbutic	imponderables
chromatolytic	pathognomonic	ventriloquism	arbitrariness	incarceration
chromatophore	pharmacologic	ventriloquist	asserveration	inconvertible
chronological	pharmacopoeia	volumenometer	battlecruiser	inconvertibly
cinematograph	phonautograph	waterproofing	belligerently	incorporation
coldbloodedly	phrenological	wellapPointed	bewilderingly	incorporative
collectorship	physiological	wonderworking	bibliographer	incorporeally
companionable	pneumatolysis	apocalyptical	bibliographic	indifferently
companionably	pneumatolytic	archaeopteryx	biogeographer	indiscernible
companionless	pneumatometer	boustrophedon	bloodcurdling	indiscernibly
companionship	pneumatophore	cacographical	bureaucratise	insupportable
conchological	polychromatic	chromospheric	cardiographer	insupportably
conditionally	potentiometer	circumspectly	carnivorously	intemperately
conductorship	prairieoyster	dressimprover	choreographer	intercurrence
correspondent	precentorship	electrophorus	choreographic	intermarriage
corresponsive	prehistorical	encyclopaedia	chronographic	interparietal
craniological	probationally	encyclopaedic	coarsegrained	interpersonal
cryptological	professoriate	encyclopedism	coldheartedly	interstratify
decontrolling	professorship	encyclopedist	collaboration	intrapersonal
deipnosophist	protectorship	gasteropodous	collaborative	introversible
deontological	provisionally	heterosporous	collaterality	inventorially
dimensionally	pseudomorphic	hydrocephalic	commemoration	lancecorporal
dimensionless	psychological	hydrocephalus	commemorative	lancesergeant
discommodious	psychosomatic	ideographical	commemoratory	lexicographer
disconformity	pyrheliometer	imperceptible	commiseration	lexicographic
disharmonious	redevelopment	imperceptibly	commiserative	lineengraving
disproportion	refractometer	impercipience	concentration	magisterially
doublejointed	reinvigorator	inappropriate	concentrative	mediterranean
doubletongued	RhaetoRomanic	incorruptible	concentricity	megasporangia
eavesdropping	rollercoaster	incorruptibly	confederation	mercenariness
educationally	rontgenoscopy	incorruptness	confederative	metallurgical
embryological	saccharometer	insusceptible	configuration	ministerially
entomological	sadomasochism	interruptible	conflagration	misanthropist
epiphenomenal	sadomasochist	jiggerypokery	connaturality	miscomprehend
epiphenomenon	sanctimonious	laissezpasser	considerately	misgovernment
eschscholtzia	sansculottism	leptocephalic	consideration	misunderstand
exceptionable	seismological	macrocephalic	corroboration	misunderstood
exceptionably	selenological	mesencephalon	corroborative	momentariness
exceptionally	selfappointed	metamorphoses	corroboratory	nightmarishly
extensionally	selfimportant	metamorphosis	crossgartered	nonfigurative

nongovernment	structuralism	convalescence	lickerishness	southeasterly
nonreturnable	structuralist	counterstroke	lifepreserver	southeastward
nucleoprotein	structureless	dauntlessness	limitlessness	southwesterly
oceanographer	subcontractor	deathlessness	magnetisation	southwestward
oceanographic	subsaturation	decomposition	magnetosphere	spectroscopic
odoriferously	temporariness	defervescence	maladjustment	spindleshanks
openheartedly	tergiversator	deliquescence	manneristical	spinelessness
orchestration	terrestrially	deodorisation	martyrisation	squeamishness
outgeneralled	territorially	derequisition	mechanisation	stabilisation
overbearingly	theanthropism	disinvestment	mediatisation	stainlessness
paediatrician	thermotropism	dispraisingly	meistersinger	statelessness
paedomorphism	thigmotropism	distressfully	mercerisation	steadfastness
palaeographer	thimblerigged	distressingly	mercilessness	sterilisation
palaeographic	thimblerigger	divertisement	mesmerisation	subtilisation
panicstricken	thoughtreader	doubtlessness	metallisation	summarisation
paraphernalia	threecornered	dramatisation	metaphosphate	superposition
pennyfarthing	topsyturvydom	dreamlessness	metaphysician	symbolisation
perseveration	transformable	effervescence	Methodistical	tantalisation
pestiferously	transparently	effervescency	mirthlessness	tantalisingly
phosphoretted	transpiration	efflorescence	modernisation	tastelessness
photochromics	transpiratory	electroscopic	Monophysitism	temporisation
photochromism	transportable	electrostatic	mutualisation	terrorisation
photoperiodic	transversally	embarrassment	neoclassicism	thanklessness
physiographer	treacherously	embellishment	neoclassicist	thundershower
physiographic	tributariness	encompassment	nervelessness	thunderstruck
polarographic	triliteralism	establishment	neurovascular	timeconsuming
postoperative	trustworthily	Eucharistical	noiselessness	toastmistress
predatoriness	uncomfortable	extravasation	nonresistance	toxoplasmosis
prefatorially	uncomfortably	extravascular	normalisation	transmissible
prefiguration	unconcernedly	faithlessness	northeasterly	transposition
prefigurative	unconformable	faultlessness	northeastward	tritheistical
prefigurement	unconstrained	featherstitch	northwesterly	troublesomely
prematureness	undercarriage	fertilisation	northwestward	tyrannosaurus
proliferation	understrapper	feudalisation	oversensitive	unimpassioned
proliferative	unicameralism	fibrovascular	oversubscribe	unnecessarily
proliferously	unicameralist	formalisation	palletisation	unobtrusively
protuberantly	uninterrupted	formulisation	pantheistical	unpromisingly
pseudoarchaic	verbigeration	fossilisation	patronisingly	unselfishness
rattlebrained	visionariness	fruitlessness	peptonisation	unwholesomely
reconstructor	voluntariness	galactosaemia	periodisation	valuelessness
refrigeration	voluntaristic	galvanisation	photopositive	vapourishness
reintegration	woodengraving	germanisation	picturesquely	venturesomely
remonstrantly	zoogeographer	glamorisation	pluralisation	verbalisation
remonstration	zoogeographic	gracelessness	pointlessness	vernalisation
remonstrative	actualisation	guilelessness	postclassical	vicepresident
reverberation	advertisement	guiltlessness	powerlessness	victimisation
reverberative	aluminisation	harmonisation	pricelessness	visualisatioh
reverberatory	anglicisation	heartlessness	progressional	voicelessness
rhodochrosite	animalisation	hybridisation	progressively	vulcanisation
scleroprotein	anomalistical	hypnotisation	progressivism	vulgarisation
scrapmerchant	antipersonnel	ichthyosaurus	protohistoric	whithersoever
scripturalism	aromatisation	immarcescible	pulverisation	worthlessness
scripturalist	asthenosphere	impermissible	quarrelsomely	Zarathustrian
sculpturesque	atlantosaurus	improvisation	randomisation	abstractional
secondariness	authorisation	improvisatory	recomposition	accidentalism
secretarybird	balkanisation	incandescence	recrudescence	accidentprone
secretaryship	barbarisation	incombustible	reimbursement	acclimatation
sedentariness	bildungsroman	inconsistence	replenishment	accreditation
seismographer	blamelessness	inconsistency	ritualisation	achromaticity
seismographic	bloodlessness	incontestable	runningstitch	administrable
selenographer	boundlessness	incontestably	selfabasement	administrator
selenographic	brainlessness	indisposition	selfconscious	adversatively
selfaddressed	brutalisation	inexhaustible	selfconsuming	affirmatively
selfapproving	businesswoman	inexhaustibly	selfexistence	afforestation
selfawareness	Calvinistical	inexpensively	selfpossessed	aggravatingly
selfreproving	carbonisation	inexpressible	semiconscious	agriculturist
selfsacrifice	catechisation	inexpressibly	senselessness	aircraftwoman
selfsterility	cauterisation	inflorescence	sensitisation	alternatively
selfsurrender	cerebrospinal	inoffensively	serialisation	ambidexterity
septentrional	cheerlessness	interposition	shamelessness	ambidexterous
sequestration	cicatrisation	intramuscular	shapelessness	AngloCatholic
shoulderblade	communisation	irrepressible	shiftlessness	antihistamine
shoulderstrap	complaisantly	irrepressibly	shockabsorber	apheliotropic
soulsearching	compressional	isomerisation	sightlessness	appellatively
squandermania	concupiscence	italicisation	signalisation	applicatively
stereographic	concupiscible	juxtaposition	sleeplessness	arbitrational
sternforemost	congressional	kaleidoscopic	smokelessness	argumentation
stratigraphic	congresswoman	laryngoscopic	socialisation	argumentative
strikebreaker	consenescence	leadpoisoning	solemnisation	arithmetician

associateship	fascinatingly	necessitarian	sacerdotalist	changefulness
associativity	feuilletonism	necessitation	scholasticism	colleagueship
attributively	feuilletonist	necessitously	sedimentation	colourfulness
authoritarian	forementioned	neoplasticism	selfcentredly	commensurable
authoritative	fortunateness	nightwatchman	selfcontained	commensurably
autoeroticism	fortuneteller	numismatology	selfcontented	conceptualise
bathymetrical	fragmentarily	observational	selfcriticism	conceptualism
brachypterous	fragmentation	obstinateness	selffertility	conceptualist
calculatingly	frequentation	obstructively	selfrestraint	congratulator
cephalothorax	frequentative	occidentalise	selfsustained	congruousness
chrysanthemum	frustratingly	Occidentalism	sergeantmajor	conjecturable
clandestinely	goniometrical	Occidentalist	sericulturist	conjecturally
coeducationally	grandfatherly	octocentenary	speculatively	consanguinity
coenaesthesis	grandmotherly	ornamentation	sprocketwheel	consciousness
combinatorial	gravitational	overstatement	sublieutenant	conspicuously
communitarian	gubernatorial	paddlesteamer	substantially	contrapuntist
comparatively	heteropterous	palaeontology	substantively	courteousness
competitively	horizontality	parasynthesis	substantivise	credulousness
compositeness	hydrometrical	parasynthetic	suffocatingly	dangerousness
compositional	hymenopterous	penetratingly	superfetation	deceitfulness
computational	hypermetrical	penetratively	superlatively	deciduousness
concomitantly	hypermetropia	penitentially	supernational	deliciousness
conflictingly	hypermetropic	perfunctorily	supersaturate	deliriousness
confrontation	imaginatively	perspectively	supplantation	dexterousness
conjugateness	immediateness	phalansterian	suppositional	dishonourable
conjugational	implicatively	planimetrical	supranational	dishonourably
conjunctional	inadvertently	polydactylous	surrogateship	distinguished
conjunctively	inanimateness	polyhistorian	swallowtailed	distributable
consecutively	inattentively	polysynthesis	teleportation	egregiousness
consumptively	incompetently	polysynthetic	temperateness	erroneousness
contractility	ineffectively	postulational	terminational	facetiousness
contractually	ineffectually	precipitantly	terminatively	feloniousness
convocational	inferentially	precipitately	thremmatology	ferociousness
cooperatively	influentially	precipitation	titillatingly	forgetfulness
corporativism	informational	precipitative	transistorise	fractiousness
correlatively	informatively	precipitously	translational	frightfulness
correlativity	infuriatingly	predicatively	transliterate	frivolousness
corticotropic	ingurgitation	premeditation	transmittable	garrulousness
corticotropin	inhospitality	premeditative	transmutation	glutinousness
crosshatching	inopportunely	premonitorily	transmutative	goodnaturedly
cyberneticist	inquisitional	preparatively	transnational	granddaughter
declaratively	inquisitively	preparatorily	uncompetitive	grotesqueness
decrepitation	inquisitorial	prepositional	unconditional	hazardousness
deferentially	inscriptional	presumptively	unconditioned	healthfulness
deforestation	insensateness	procrastinate	underestimate	hermeneutical
deformational	insensitively	procuratorial	unexceptional	hilariousness
deprecatingly	insensitivity	progenitorial	unforgettable	homosexuality
descriptively	insinuatingly	prognosticate	unforgettably	imperiousness
desperateness	inspirational	prohibitively	unintentional	impetuousness
destructively	instinctively	propositional	unrelentingly	incongruously
destructivity	institutional	proprietorial	unremittingly	incuriousness
devastatingly	instructional	prospectively	unsymmetrical	individualise
diagnostician	instructively	protonotarial	vacillatingly	individualism
disjunctively	interestingly	psychasthenia	viniculturist	individualist
disparateness	intermittence	qualitatively	viticulturist	individuality
displantation	international	quickwittedly	vivisectional	individuation
dissoluteness	intraarterial	quincentenary	zygodactylous	ingeniousness
dissymetrical	intricateness	quingentenary	ambiguousness	ingenuousness
distinctively	inviolateness	radioactivity	ambitiousness	injuriousness
distrustfully	involuntarily	recalcitrance	amorphousness	innocuousness
documentalist	laevorotatory	referentially	analogousness	innoxiousness
documentation	laevorotatory	reforestation	anfractuosity	insidiousness
draggletailed	legislatively	reformational	anomalousness	invidiousness
dysfunctional	legislatorial	regimentation	anonymousness	judiciousness
elaborateness	lepidopterist	regurgitation	arboriculture	jurisprudence
elephantiasis	lepidopterous	reinstatement	assiduousness	laboriousness
entomostracan	malacostracan	reorientation	astronautical	lecherousness
equidistantly	maladaptation	requisiteness	atrociousness	liebfraumilch
everlastingly	manifestation	restoratively	audaciousness	litigiousness
examinational	manifestative	restrictively	baccalaureate	ludicrousness
examinatorial	mathematician	resuscitation	barbarousness	luxuriousness
existentially	microdetector	resuscitative	beauteousness	maliciousness
explanatorily	micronutrient	retroactively	Bloomsburyite	masterfulness
explorational	mistrustfully	retroactivity	bounteousness	mellifluously
exponentially	mistrustingly	reverentially	bountifulness	melodiousness
expurgatorial	monodactylous	rudimentarily	bumptiousness	millefeuilles
exquisiteness	monumentalise	sabrerattling	canaliculated	momentousness
exterritorial	mouthwatering	sacerdotalise	capaciousness	moneygrubbing
facultatively	multinational	sacerdotalism	centrifugally	monstrousness

nefariousness	diffusiveness	accidentalism	collaboration	displantation
neighbourhood	effectiveness	acclimatation	collaborative	dissemination
nonconducting	electrovalent	accommodating	collaterality	disseminative
nonproductive	evocativeness	accommodation	collieshangie	disseveration
notoriousness	excessiveness	accommodative	colloquialism	dissimilarity
obliviousness	exclusiveness	accreditation	commemoration	dissimilation
obnoxiousness	excursiveness	acculturation	commemorative	dissimulation
officiousness	expansiveness	acculturative	commemoratory	documentalist
ostreiculture	expensiveness	acetification	commercialise	documentation
overindulgent	explosiveness	acidification	commercialism	domestication
overpopulated	extensiveness	actualisation	commercialist	domiciliation
overvaluation	graminivorous	afforestation	commiseration	doubledealing
pantagruelian	imitativeness	agglomeration	commiserative	doubleglazing
pantagruelism	impassiveness	agglomerative	communication	draggletailed
pantagruelist	impulsiveness	agglutination	communicative	dramatisation
pendulousness	inclusiveness	agglutinative	communicatory	dulcification
penuriousness	inductiveness	aluminisation	communisation	ecumenicalism
perspicuously	insectivorous	amplification	communitarian	electromagnet
plenteousness	intensiveness	anagrammatise	compagination	electrovalent
plentifulness	intrusiveness	anagrammatism	complaisantly	emphysematous
ponderousness	intuitiveness	anglicisation	concatenation	encapsulation
proconsulship	inventiveness	animalisation	concentration	encyclopaedia
promiscuously	judgeadvocate	anticlimactic	concentrative	encyclopaedic
psychosurgery	lucrativeness	antihistamine	conceptualise	entomophagous
querulousness	mischievously	antinomianism	conceptualism	epigrammatise
rapaciousness	objectiveness	appropriately	conceptualist	epigrammatist
rapturousness	objectivistic	appropriation	concertmaster	equestrianism
rectangularly	obsessiveness	appropriative	concomitantly	equidistantly
regardfulness	obtrusiveness	approximately	condylomatous	equilibration
regretfulness	offensiveness	approximation	confabulation	exanthematous
religiousness	operativeness	approximative	confabulatory	expectoration
resentfulness	Pennsylvanian	argumentation	confederation	expostulation
righteousness	pervasiveness	argumentative	confederative	expostulatory
sagaciousness	plaintiveness	aromatisation	configuration	expropriation
salaciousness	primitiveness	artificiality	conflagration	extemporarily
seditiousness	purposiveness	assassination	confrontation	extermination
selfadjusting	quadrumvirate	asserveration	connaturality	exterminatory
selfassurance	quinquevalent	atlantosaurus	considerately	extragalactic
selfassuredly	receptiveness	Australianism	consideration	extrapolation
selfinduction	recessiveness	authorisation	consolidation	extravagantly
selfindulgent	repulsiveness	authoritarian	consolidative	extravasation
selfinsurance	retentiveness	authoritative	consolidatory	falsification
selfrepugnant	secretiveness	autocephalous	constellation	fasciculation
selfslaughter	seductiveness	backformation	constellatory	fertilisation
somnambulator	selectiveness	backwardation	consternation	feudalisation
sorrowfulness	selfconvicted	balkanisation	contamination	formalisation
spectacularly	sensitiveness	barbarisation	contaminative	formulisation
stirpiculture	talkativeness	beatification	contemplation	fortification
stratocumulus	tentativeness	beneficiation	contemplative	fossilisation
strenuousness	unbelievingly	Berkeleianism	cornification	fractionalise
substitutable	betweenwhiles	bibliographer	corroboration	fractionation
sumptuousness	counterweight	bibliographic	corroborative	fragmentarily
superabundant	cruiserweight	biogeographer	corroboratory	fragmentation
superfluidity	featherweight	bloodrelation	crackerbarrel	frequentation
superfluously	foreknowledge	bouillabaisse	cryptographer	frequentative
tempestuously	hundredweight	breechloading	cryptographic	funambulation
tenaciousness	mangoldwurzel	brokenhearted	crystalgazing	functionalism
thaumaturgist	selfknowledge	brutalisation	decerebration	functionalist
thermonuclear	tonguetwister	bureaucratise	decortication	galactosaemia
tremulousness	unputdownable	cabinetmaking	decrepitation	galvanisation
troublousness	untrustworthy	calcification	defibrination	germanisation
unambiguously	proparoxytone	caprification	deforestation	gesticulation
unanimousness	actinomyces	carbonisation	degranulation	gesticulative
unarticulated	actinomycosis	carcinomatous	dematerialise	gesticulatory
undereducated	astrophysical	cardiographer	demonstration	glamorisation
venturousness	dichlamydeous	catechisation	demonstrative	glorification
veraciousness	extraphysical	cauterisation	denationalise	glossographer
vexatiousness	hyperphysical	ceremonialism	denticulation	gratification
vicariousness	microphyllous	ceremonialist	deodorisation	hallucination
vivaciousness	monocotyledon	certification	depersonalise	hallucinative
voraciousness	phycoerythrin	certificatory	desegregation	hallucinatory
wonderfulness	polycotyledon	choreographer	deterioration	harbourmaster
assertiveness	psychodynamic	choreographic	deteriorative	harmonisation
attentiveness	selfpityingly	chronographic	determinately	heartbreaking
combativeness	superphysical	cicatrisation	determination	heterothallic
conduciveness	thermodynamic	clarification	determinative	hollowhearted
corrosiveness	tiddledywinks	cleistogamous	diagrammatise	homosexuality
deceptiveness	troglodytical	clothesbasket	diathermanous	horizontality
defectiveness	————	coarsegrained	discoloration	horripilation

housebreaking	mechanisation	physiographer	resuscitative	tenderhearted
hybridisation	mediatisation	physiographic	retranslation	terrorisation
hydrodynamics	mediterranean	picturepalace	revaccination	testification
hydrogenation	megacephalous	pigeonhearted	revendication	theatricalise
hydroxylamine	megasporangia	pluralisation	reverberation	theatricalism
hypnotisation	melodramatics	polarographic	reverberative	theatricality
hypoglycaemia	melodramatise	pontification	reverberatory	thermoplastic
hypothecation	melodramatist	postoperative	ritualisation	thurification
ichthyosaurus	mercerisation	precipitantly	rollercoaster	Tractarianism
immaterialise	mesmerisation	precipitately	rudimentarily	transatlantic
immaterialism	metallisation	precipitation	Russification	translocation
immaterialist	metrification	precipitative	sacerdotalise	transmutation
immateriality	microorganism	predominantly	sacerdotalism	transmutative
impenetration	microtonality	predomination	sacerdotalist	transpiration
impersonalise	millennialism	prefiguration	scarification	transpiratory
impersonality	miscegenation	prefigurative	schoolteacher	triangularity
impersonation	modernisation	preliminarily	scintillating	triangulation
imponderables	Mohammedanism	premeditation	scintillation	trichromatism
importunately	mollification	premeditative	scorification	triliteralism
impropriation	Monarchianism	preoccupation	scripturalism	tuberculation
improvisation	monosyllabism	preordination	scripturalist	tyrannosaurus
improvisatory	monotrematous	prevarication	sedimentation	unaccompanied
incarceration	monumentalise	primordiality	seismographer	unconstrained
incardination	mortification	profitsharing	seismographic	understrapper
incorporation	Muhammadanism	proliferation	selenographer	unfamiliarity
incorporative	mummification	proliferative	selenographic	unfortunately
incriminatory	mutualisation	prolification	selfcontained	unicameralism
individualise	mystification	pronunciation	selfdefeating	unicameralist
individualism	naphthylamine	prostaglandin	selfeducation	uninformative
individualist	necessitarian	protonotarial	selfrevealing	unnecessarily
individuality	necessitation	protuberantly	selfsustained	vegetarianism
individuation	nitrification	provincialise	semibarbarian	verbalisation
industrialise	nonfigurative	provincialism	semibarbarism	verbigeration
industrialism	normalisation	provincialist	semipermanent	vermiculation
industrialist	nullification	provinciality	sensitisation	vernacularise
ingurgitation	occasionalism	prudentialism	sequentiality	vernacularism
inhospitality	occasionalist	prudentialist	sequestration	vernacularity
intemperately	occasionality	prudentiality	SerboCroatian	vernalisation
intercalation	occidentalise	psychoanalyse	serialisation	versification
intergalactic	Occidentalism	psychoanalyst	Shakespearean	victimisation
interpolation	Occidentalist	pulverisation	Shakespearian	villeggiatura
interpolative	oceanographer	pyrimethamine	sheepshearing	visualisation
interrelation	oceanographic	qualification	sicklefeather	vitrification
interrogation	oleomargarine	qualificatory	signalisation	vocationalism
interrogative	orchestration	quartermaster	significantly	vulcanisation
interrogatory	ornamentation	quinquevalent	signification	vulgarisation
interstratify	outgeneralled	radiolocation	significative	woodengraving
investigation	overemphasise	randomisation	singlehearted	zoogeographer
investigative	overvaluation	ratiocination	specification	zoogeographic
investigatory	ovoviviparous	ratiocinative	Spencerianism	antiscorbutic
involuntarily	palaeographer	rattlebrained	stabilisation	circumambient
irrationalise	palaeographic	reaffirmation	stationmaster	impertubable
irrationalism	palletisation	reciprocality	stereographic	imperturbably
irrationalist	papillomatous	reciprocation	sterilisation	indescribable
irrationality	paranormality	reciprocative	strangulation	indescribably
isomerisation	participation	recombination	stratigraphic	moneygrubbing
italicisation	participative	recrimination	structuralism	mouldingboard
jollification	participatory	recriminatory	structuralist	shootingbrake
justification	particularise	rectification	subcontractor	shoulderblade
justificative	particularism	reduplication	subirrigation	soundingboard
justificatory	particularist	reduplicative	subordinately	spermatoblast
laevorotation	particularity	reembarkation	subordination	thoroughbrace
laevorotatory	pedestrianise	reexamination	subordinative	tintinnabular
laissezpasser	pedestrianism	reforestation	subpostmaster	tintinnabulum
leatherjacket	Pennsylvanian	refrigeration	subsaturation	turkeygobbler
lexicographer	peptonisation	regimentation	subtilisation	abiologically
lexicographic	perambulation	regurgitation	suffumigation	abortifacient
lignification	perambulatory	reincarnation	summarisation	acrobatically
lineengraving	peregrination	reintegration	superfetation	actinomycetes
machicolation	perissodactyl	remonstrantly	superhumanity	actinomycosis
magnetisation	perseveration	remonstration	supplantation	adiabatically
magnification	petrification	remonstrative	swallowtailed	aesthetically
maladaptation	phanerogamous	renegotiation	syllabication	agonistically
Malthusianism	phenomenalise	reorientation	symbolisation	alcoholically
Manichaeanism	phenomenalism	republicanise	tantalisation	algebraically
manifestation	phenomenalist	republicanism	teleportation	allegorically
manifestative	phenylalanine	republication	temporisation	anaerobically
martyrisation	phyllophagous	resuscitation		apathetically
matriculation				archidiaconal

arthritically	intrinsically	splenetically	barrelchested	imitativeness
asthmatically	introspection	statistically	belligerently	immediateness
atheistically	introspective	stercoraceous	bioenergetics	immovableness
atomistically	isometrically	stigmatically	blameableness	immunotherapy
authentically	isostatically	strategically	brachypterous	immutableness
authenticator	judgmatically	stylistically	callisthenics	impassiveness
automatically	kaleidoscopic	symbiotically	carboniferous	impertinently
autonomically	kinematically	symmetrically	challengeable	improvidently
axiomatically	laryngoscopic	symphonically	chemoreceptor	impulsiveness
bombastically	lethargically	syntactically	chuckleheaded	inadvertently
brachydactyly	macaronically	synthetically	circumspectly	inanimateness
broadspectrum	membranaceous	taxonomically	cobelligerent	inclusiveness
camphoraceous	metonymically	thalassocracy	colleagueship	incompetently
categorically	micrococcoci	theologically	combativeness	inconsiderate
chromatically	monomolecular	theoretically	compartmental	incontinently
cinematically	mourningcloak	thermonuclear	compositeness	incorporeally
climactically	multiplicable	thrasonically	conduciveness	incurableness
concupiscence	mutagenically	tonsillectomy	conjugateness	independently
concupiscible	neurovascular	topologically	corrosiveness	indifferently
consenescence	nightwatchman	traumatically	counterfeiter	inductiveness
contradiction	nonconducting	typologically	counterweight	ineffableness
contradictory	nonproductive	uncircumcised	cruiserweight	inefficiently
convalescence	nonsensically	uncomplicated	curvilinearly	inexpediently
costeffective	nostalgically	undereducated	deceptiveness	inexperienced
cottonpicking	oecologically	unequivocally	defectiveness	insensateness
counteraction	ontogenically	archimandrite	defencelessly	insolubleness
counteractive	ontologically	barefacedness	desirableness	intelligencer
crosshatching	oversubscribe	biodegradable	desperateness	intelligently
cylindrically	panegyrically	bloodcurdling	developmental	intensiveness
defervescence	papaveraceous	broadmindedly	diffusiveness	interlacement
deliquescence	parabolically	clearheadedly	disengagement	intraarterial
dendritically	paradoxically	coldbloodedly	disfigurement	intricateness
derestriction	parasitically	collectedness	disinterested	intrusiveness
dialectically	parasiticidal	complexedness	dismantlement	intuitiveness
diametrically	parthenocarpy	conceitedness	disobediently	inventiveness
disconnection	patriotically	connectedness	disparagement	inviolateness
disrespectful	pedagogically	contentedness	disparateness	invisibleness
eccentrically	pennypinching	dichlamydeous	dissoluteness	irreplaceable
effervescence	perpendicular	discommodious	divertisement	irritableness
effervescency	perspicacious	haphazardness	effectiveness	knowledgeable
efflorescence	pharisaically	hypochondriac	elaborateness	knowledgeably
electroscopic	photoelectric	jurisprudence	electioneerer	laughableness
energetically	photoelectron	lightheadedly	electrometric	lepidopterist
enigmatically	phrenetically	lightmindedly	embranglement	lepidopterous
evangelically	piezoelectric	mitochondrion	embrittlement	lifepreserver
extravascular	plethorically	nonattendance	encouragement	lightsomeness
extrinsically	pneumatically	offhandedness	encyclopedism	loathsomeness
fantastically	pneumonectomy	overabundance	encyclopedist	longsuffering
Fascistically	pragmatically	perichondrial	enjoyableness	lucrativeness
ferroconcrete	prismatically	perichondrium	environmental	macromolecule
ferroelectric	prophetically	pigheadedness	equiponderant	magnificently
fibrovascular	proteinaceous	recommendable	equiponderate	malleableness
floristically	pseudoarchaic	righthandedly	evocativeness	mammaliferous
freeselection	puritanically	scolopendrium	excessiveness	manganiferous
geometrically	realistically	snowblindness	excitableness	masculineness
geotropically	recrudescence	sobermindness	exclusiveness	matrilineally
grammatically	retrospection	transcendence	excursiveness	metalliferous
gymnastically	retrospective	transcendency	excusableness	microdetector
honorifically	rhapsodically	undergraduate	expansiveness	miscomprehend
hydraulically	rheumatically	underhandedly	expensiveness	miserableness
hydrocracking	sacrosanctity	wrongheadedly	explosiveness	mismanagement
hydroelectric	sadomasochism	acquiescently	exquisiteness	mononucleosis
ideologically	sadomasochist	admeasurement	extensiveness	monosymmetric
idiomatically	sarcastically	admirableness	featherheaded	Monotheletism
immarcescible	schematically	adventuresome	featherweight	mouthwatering
impolitically	scorbutically	advertisement	fortunateness	navigableness
impracticable	scrapmerchant	advisableness	fortuneteller	nectariferous
impracticably	selfconscious	agreeableness	fossiliferous	nephelometric
impractically	selfdirecting	aluminiferous	garnetiferous	neurastheniac
incandescence	selfdirection	ambidexterity	gastrocnemius	nickeliferous
inconspicuous	selfinduction	ambidexterous	grotesqueness	objectiveness
inconvincible	semiconscious	argentiferous	habitableness	obsessiveness
indistinctive	serologically	assertiveness	heebiejeebies	obstinateness
inefficacious	sewingmachine	associateship	helterskelter	obtrusiveness
inflorescence	sophistically	attentiveness	heteropterous	octocentenary
inorganically	sophisticated	auctioneering	homoiothermal	offensiveness
interpunction	soulsearching	availableness	homoiothermic	omnicompetent
interspecific	spasmodically	balsamiferous	hundredweight	operativeness
intramuscular	spectroscopic	bamboozlement	hymenopterous	opportuneness

organotherapy	semipermeable	intransigeant	replenishment	correlatively
overstatement	semiporcelain	intransigence	spindleshanks	correlativity
paddlesteamer	sensitiveness	irrefrangible	spinninghouse	corrigibility
palatableness	separableness	kinematograph	squeamishness	cosmopolitise
pantagruelian	spectrometric	lancesergeant	stalkinghorse	cosmopolitism
pantagruelism	spindlelegged	lightfingered	steeplechaser	criminalistic
pantagruelist	splendiferous	malacological	stratospheric	crystallinity
paramagnetism	staminiferous	metallurgical	telencephalon	customariness
partridgewood	sternforemost	mineralogical	thundershower	cyberneticist
peaceableness	stoloniferous	morphological	topographical	cytochemistry
pervasiveness	strikebreaker	musicological	typographical	dastardliness
petroliferous	structureless	noncollegiate	underemphasis	declaratively
phalansterian	sublieutenant	numerological	unimpeachable	decomposition
philhellenism	subserviently	odontological	unselfishness	decontaminate
philhellenist	supercalender	palynological	vapourishness	deductibility
phosphoretted	supernumerary	paperhangings	xylographical	defeasibility
photoreceptor	surrogateship	phonautograph	absorbability	defensibility
physiotherapy	talkativeness	phrenological	abstractional	deferentially
pigeonchested	teachableness	physiological	acceptability	deformational
plaintiveness	temperamental	psychological	accessibility	dependability
platiniferous	temperateness	scorpiongrass	accompaniment	deprecatingly
plausibleness	tentativeness	seismological	achromaticity	derequisition
polliniferous	thereinbefore	selenological	acquiescingly	descriptively
prayermeeting	thermochemist	selfrepugnant	admissibility	destructively
predicamental	thoughtlessly	selfslaughter	admonishingly	destructivity
preengagement	thoughtreader	semeiological	adversatively	desultoriness
preengineered	tolerableness	smoothingiron	affirmatively	deterministic
prefigurement	toothsomeness	solderingiron	aggravatingly	devastatingly
prematureness	traceableness	somatological	airworthiness	diagnostician
PreRaphaelite	tractableness	speleological	alternatively	dictatorially
primitiveness	transliterate	spermatogenic	anachronistic	digestibility
prolegomenary	translucently	technological	anaphrodisiac	disembodiment
prolegomenous	transparently	teratological	answerability	disjunctively
pronounceable	trigonometric	thoroughgoing	appellatively	disparagingly
pronouncement	umbelliferous	thrillingness	applicability	disposability
proprioceptor	unprecedented	toxicological	applicatively	dispraisingly
psychotherapy	venerableness	unfeelingness	arbitrariness	dissemblingly
psychrometric	vouchsafement	unmeaningness	arbitrational	dissimilitude
purposelessly	wearisomeness	unwillingness	arithmetician	dissolubility
purposiveness	weatherbeaten	AngloCatholic	associativity	distinctively
quartziferous	wheelerdealer	betweenwhiles	astonishingly	distinguished
quincentenary	wholesomeness	boardinghouse	attainability	distressingly
quingentenary	woolgathering	boustrophedon	attributively	doctrinairism
quinquagenary	worrisomeness	cacographical	autoeroticism	doublejointed
Quinquagesima	bookingoffice	cephalothorax	bewilderingly	dysfunctional
radiotelegram	climbingframe	chromospheric	bibliophilism	egocentricity
rearrangement	disgracefully	chrysanthemum	bibliophilist	elephantiasis
receptiveness	distastefully	clearinghouse	brotherliness	encouragingly
recessiveness	distressfully	coenaesthesis	calculatingly	entomophilous
reconcilement	distrustfully	counterchange	cannibalistic	everlastingly
rectilinearly	foraminiferal	countercharge	cartilaginous	examinational
reimbursement	meadowsaffron	countinghouse	challengingly	excommunicate
reinforcement	mistrustfully	electrophorus	changeability	exemplariness
reinstatement	reproachfully	embellishment	clairaudience	existentially
reminiscently	resourcefully	establishment	clandestinely	expansibility
remorselessly	anthropogenic	grandfatherly	coagulability	explorational
removableness	bibliological	grandmotherly	coeducational	exponentially
repulsiveness	birefringence	hydrocephalic	commutability	extensibility
requisiteness	candlelighter	hydrocephalus	comparability	extrajudicial
resplendently	centrifugally	ideographical	comparatively	extraordinary
retentiveness	chromatograph	leptocephalic	compatibility	facultatively
sculpturesque	chronological	lickerishness	competitively	fascinatingly
secretiveness	cinematograph	macrocephalic	complainingly	festschriften
seductiveness	conchological	mesencephalon	compositional	filterability
selectiveness	confidingness	metamorphoses	compressional	flourishingly
selfabasement	contrafagotto	metamorphosis	computational	foolhardiness
selfaddressed	craniological	microcephalic	concentricity	forementioned
selfawareness	cryptological	mnemotechnics	conflictingly	formidability
selfcollected	deontological	oreographical	congressional	frighteningly
selfconceited	dramaturgical	orthocephalic	conjugational	frustratingly
selfcondemned	embryological	parasynthesis	conjunctional	fullfashioned
selfconfessed	entomological	parasynthetic	conjunctively	geocentricism
selfcontented	gastrological	philosophical	consanguinity	gravitational
selfevidently	glaciological	philosophiser	consecutively	helminthiasis
selfforgetful	granddaughter	phreatophytic	consumptively	histrionicism
selfpossessed	graphological	polysynthesis	contractility	imaginatively
selfpropelled	immunological	polysynthetic	convocational	immiscibility
selfsurrender	indefatigable	prizefighting	cooperatively	impalpability
selftormentor	indefatigably	psychasthenia	corporativism	impartibility

impassability	materfamilias	propositional	temporalities	frightfulness
impassibility	materialistic	prospectively	temporariness	healthfulness
impeccability	mathematician	pseudoscience	terminability	heptasyllabic
impercipience	meistersinger	pusillanimity	terminational	hypnoanalysis
imperialistic	mensurability	pusillanimous	terminatively	identicalness
implacability	mercenariness	quadrennially	terrestrially	illogicalness
implicatively	merchandising	quadrillionth	territorially	intercellular
impossibility	metaphysician	quadrumvirate	thermophilous	interpellator
improbability	metastability	quadruplicate	thimblerigged	intracellular
improvability	millefeuilles	quadruplicity	thimblerigger	jerrybuilding
inappreciable	millionairess	qualitatively	threateningly	Machiavellian
inappreciably	ministerially	questioningly	titillatingly	masterfulness
inattentively	mistrustingly	quincuncially	tonguetwister	microanalysis
incommunicado	momentariness	quintillionth	translational	microphyllous
inconvenience	Monophysitism	quintuplicate	translucidity	monocotyledon
inconveniency	multinational	radioactivity	transnational	monometallism
incredibility	multitudinous	rationalistic	transposition	monometallist
indeterminacy	nationalistic	receptibility	tributariness	multicellular
indeterminate	negligibility	recomposition	unbelievingly	multinucleate
indeterminism	negotiability	reconsolidate	uncleanliness	nonfulfilment
indeterminist	neoclassicism	referentially	uncompetitive	osteomyelitis
indisposition	neoclassicist	reflexibility	uncomplaining	ostreiculture
indissociable	neoplasticism	reformability	unconditional	overindulgent
ineducability	niggardliness	reformational	unconditioned	overpopulated
ineffectively	nightmarishly	reproachingly	underachiever	passionflower
ineligibility	noncompliance	resistibility	underestimate	pharmacologic
inevitability	nonforfeiting	resolvability	unearthliness	plentifulness
inexorability	objectivistic	restoratively	unestablished	pneumatolysis
inexpensively	observational	restrictively	unexceptional	pneumatolytic
infallibilism	obstructively	retroactively	unflinchingly	poliomyelitis
infallibilist	opportunistic	retroactivity	unhealthiness	polycotyledon
infallibility	outstandingly	reverentially	unimpassioned	practicalness
infeasibility	overbearingly	reversibility	unintelligent	principalship
inferentially	overconfident	sacrificially	unintentional	proconsulship
inflexibility	overqualified	scholarliness	unobtrusively	recrystallise
influentially	oversensitive	scholasticism	unpromisingly	rectangularly
informational	paediatrician	seaworthiness	unqualifiedly	regardfulness
informatively	painstakingly	secondariness	unrelentingly	regretfulness
infuriatingly	painterliness	sedentariness	unremittingly	resentfulness
inoffensively	panicstricken	selfappointed	unsociability	salmonellosis
inquisitional	paterfamilias	selfconfident	unsuitability	selfindulgent
inquisitively	paternalistic	selfconvicted	vacillatingly	selfknowledge
insatiability	pathogenicity	selfcriticism	verifiability	semicivilised
inscriptional	patronisingly	selfdeceiving	vicepresident	softpedalling
insensibility	penetrability	selffertility	visionariness	somnambulator
insensitively	penetratingly	selfinflicted	vivisectional	sorrowfulness
insensitivity	penetratively	selfopinioned	voluntariness	spectacularly
insignificant	penitentially	selfpityingly	voluntaristic	spiritualness
insinuatingly	perdurability	selfpollinate	vulnerability	stirpiculture
insociability	perishability	selfsacrifice	wellapPointed	streetwalking
inspirational	permutability	selfsterility	worldlyminded	technicalness
instinctively	perspectively	selfsufficing	anticlockwise	tetrasyllable
institutional	photoperiodic	septentrional	greensickness	tranquilliser
instructional	photopositive	serendipitous	heartsickness	unarticulated
instructively	platitudinise	seriousminded	swashbuckling	underemployed
insubordinate	platitudinous	sesquiplicate	arboriculture	underwhelming
insufficience	plenitudinous	speculatively	autocatalysis	undisciplined
insufficiency	pointillistic	spheroidicity	autocatalytic	unnaturalness
intangibility	ponderability	sprightliness	backpedalling	verisimilarly
interdigitate	postulational	squeezability	bacteriolysis	violoncellist
interestingly	predatoriness	standoffishly	bacteriolytic	whimsicalness
intermediator	predicability	substantially	blanketflower	wonderfulness
international	predicatively	substantively	bountifulness	accelerometer
interparietal	prefatorially	substantivise	canaliculated	accoutrements
interposition	preferability	suffocatingly	changefulness	aerodynamical
invariability	prejudicially	superaddition	chromatolytic	aggiornamento
inventorially	preparatively	superdominant	circumvallate	alcoholometer
invincibility	prepositional	superfamilies	colourfulness	alcoholometry
inviolability	presumptively	superficially	congratulator	anthropometry
juxtaposition	primogenitary	superfluidity	cryptanalysis	chlamydomonas
kapellmeister	primogenitive	superlatively	cryptanalytic	diaphragmatic
languishingly	primogeniture	supernational	deceitfulness	disaffirmance
legislatively	procrastinate	superordinate	decontrolling	epiphenomenal
leishmaniasis	profitability	superposition	equivocalness	epiphenomenon
leisureliness	prognosticate	supervenience	eschscholtzia	gastronomical
Maginotminded	progressional	suppositional	essentialness	gynandromorph
magisterially	progressively	supranational	extracellular	irreclaimable
maladminister	progressivism	synchronistic	foreknowledge	irreclaimably
manageability	prohibitively	tantalisingly	forgetfulness	liebfraumilch

monochromatic	exceptionally	traditionally	expeditiously	palaeontology
monogrammatic	excrescential	tricentennial	explanatorily	palaeozoology
nemathelminth	extensionally	unceremonious	expressionism	parallelogram
pathognomonic	ferrimagnetic	uncertainness	expressionist	particoloured
petrochemical	ferromagnetic	unconcernedly	expurgatorial	percussionist
photochemical	flagellantism	uncoordinated	exterritorial	perfectionism
platyhelminth	frontogenesis	understanding	feuilletonism	perfectionist
pneumatometer	gametogenesis	unemotionally	feuilletonist	perfunctorily
polychromatic	gentlemanlike	unfashionable	fissiparously	perspicuously
potentiometer	heterogeneity	unfashionably	flirtatiously	pestiferously
psychosomatic	heterogeneous	unmentionable	gasteropodous	phenomenology
pyrheliometer	heterogenesis	unputdownable	geochronology	photochromics
refractometer	heterogenetic	unsubstantial	geomorphology	photochromism
RhaetoRomanic	indiscernible	acetylcholine	geostationary	phraseologist
saccharimeter	indiscernibly	acotyledonous	gerontologist	physiognomist
saccharimetry	indoctrinator	acrimoniously	gonadotrophic	polycarbonate
saccharometer	inflexionless	adventurously	gonadotrophin	polyhistorian
semiautomatic	instantaneity	ambassadorial	graminivorous	precautionary
sergeantmajor	instantaneous	anachronously	gubernatorial	precipitously
slangingmatch	insubstantial	anfractuosity	gynaecologist	premonitorily
squandermania	integumentary	annexationist	haematologist	preparatorily
stoichiometry	intentionally	antipersonnel	helminthology	prestigiously
stratocumulus	irreverential	archaeologist	hermaphrodite	pretentiously
synallagmatic	Kidderminster	archbishopric	herpetologist	processionary
telegrammatic	librarianship	archdeaconate	heterosporous	processionist
toxoplasmosis	miscellaneous	Assyriologist	heterotrophic	procuratorial
transformable	misgovernment	autochthonism	homogeneously	progenitorial
unconformable	morphogenesis	autochthonous	hydrochloride	projectionist
volumenometer	morphogenetic	biotechnology	hyperboloidal	proliferously
affectionless	mountebankery	blasphemously	ichthyologist	promiscuously
anthelminthic	nongovernment	burglariously	ignominiously	proportionate
apportionment	nonreturnable	campanologist	illustriously	proprietorial
ascertainable	nutritionally	carnivorously	impecuniosity	prosthodontia
ascertainment	objectionable	ceremoniously	impressionism	protectionism
blastogenesis	objectionably	climatologist	impressionist	protectionist
butterfingers	organogenesis	combinatorial	incongruously	pteridologist
chieftainship	outspokenness	compassionate	incredulously	punctiliously
chinkerinchee	paraphernalia	compendiously	industriously	quarrelsomely
churchmanship	parliamentary	concavoconvex	injudiciously	rearcommodore
cinquecentist	phytoplankton	concessionary	inquisitorial	repetitionary
circumvention	pococurantism	concretionary	insectivorous	repetitiously
companionable	porcellaneous	confectionary	intercolonial	revelationist
companionably	predestinator	confectionery	intravenously	revolutionary
companionless	premillennial	confessionary	irreligionist	revolutionise
companionship	preordainment	conspicuously	irreligiously	revolutionism
complementary	probationally	contentiously	isochronously	revolutionist
complimentary	Protestantism	contortionist	jiggerypokery	rhodochrosite
comprehension	provisionally	contrariously	judgeadvocate	roentgenogram
comprehensive	psychodynamic	conventionary	knickerbocker	roentgenology
condescension	psychogenesis	convexoconvex	leadpoisoning	sanitationist
conditionally	psychogenetic	convulsionary	legislatorial	scandalmonger
consentaneity	psychokinesis	coreligionist	liberationist	scientologist
consentaneous	psychokinetic	corruptionist	linseywoolsey	scleroprotein
consequential	pyrotechnical	criminologist	magnanimously	scrumptiously
constrainable	questionnaire	cryobiologist	magnetomotive	selfapproving
constrainedly	sanctimonious	daguerreotype	malariologist	selfdiscovery
contrabandist	schizogenesis	deleteriously	martyrologist	selfreproving
contrapuntist	selenocentric	demythologise	mellifluously	selfsupported
contravention	selfdependent	dermatologist	meritoriously	sententiously
correspondent	sensationally	deuteragonist	metagrobolise	separationist
corresponsive	shabbygenteel	Deuteronomist	meteorologist	sharpshooting
craftsmanship	silvertongued	devolutionary	misanthropist	shockabsorber
dimensionally	socioeconomic	devolutionist	mischievously	sovietologist
dimensionless	sportsmanlike	diageotropism	monophthongal	spelaeologist
disciplinable	sportsmanship	dichotomously	mountainously	spontaneously
discontinuity	statesmanlike	discretionary	multicoloured	stereoscopist
discontinuous	statesmanship	dispassionate	myrmecologist	stomatologist
discriminator	submachinegun	dodecaphonist	necessitously	strawcoloured
disharmonious	subsequential	doublecrosser	nucleoprotein	streptococcal
doubletongued	subterraneous	efficaciously	numismatology	streptococcus
draftsmanship	suffraganship	electrologist	odontoglossum	subversionary
educationally	superabundant	electromotive	odoriferously	sulphureously
embryogenesis	supereminence	encephalogram	onomatopoetic	superfluously
enlightenment	supplementary	endocrinology	ophthalmology	symphoniously
entertainment	swordsmanship	eschatologist	oppositionist	synchronously
epeirogenesis	tercentennial	examinatorial	opprobriously	tablespoonful
equipotential	thermodynamic	exhibitionism	orangeblossom	tautologously
exceptionable	thermogenesis	exhibitionist	ornithologist	televisionary
exceptionably	threecornered	expeditionary	overelaborate	temerariously

tempestuously	transcriptive	inspectorship	viceadmiralty	impermissible
tendentiously	transshipment	intercurrence	winterberries	impetuousness
terpsichorean	transshipping	intermarriage	wonderworking	incondensable
theanthropism	unanticipated	interspersion	xanthochroism	incuriousness
thermotropism	grandiloquent	irrecoverable	zinjanthropus	indispensable
thigmotropism	picturesquely	irrecoverably	affenpinscher	indispensably
thremmatology	ventriloquial	lamellibranch	ambiguousness	inexpressible
transistorise	ventriloquise	landownership	ambitiousness	inexpressibly
transitionary	ventriloquism	leptospirosis	amorphousness	infinitesimal
treacherously	ventriloquist	letterperfect	amphiprostyle	ingeniousness
troublesomely	actinomorphic	malacostracan	analogousness	ingenuousness
unambiguously	administrable	metallography	anomalousness	injuriousness
unconsciously	administrator	micronutrient	anonymousness	innocuousness
underexposure	allelomorphic	moderatorship	anthroposophy	innoxiousness
unforthcoming	angiospermous	neighbourhood	Antichristian	insidiousness
unquestioning	AngloAmerican	nonappearance	apprehensible	interpersonal
unrighteously	animadversion	nonconforming	assiduousness	intrapersonal
untrustworthy	antilogarithm	nonconformism	astrophysical	introgression
unwholesomely	apheliotropic	nonconformist	atrociousness	introversible
venereologist	atmospherical	nonconformity	audaciousness	invidiousness
venturesomely	autobiography	opisthobranch	barbarousness	irrepressible
versicoloured	baccalaureate	pantisocratic	beauteousness	irrepressibly
vertiginously	bathymetrical	philanthropic	blamelessness	irresponsible
volcanologist	beleaguerment	planimetrical	bloodlessness	irresponsibly
vulcanologist	bildungsroman	precentorship	boundlessness	judiciousness
waterproofing	blackguardism	prehistorical	bounteousness	laboriousness
whithersoever	Bloomsburyite	preponderance	brainlessness	lackadaisical
windowshopper	brainstorming	preponderancy	bumptiousness	laughingstock
accidentprone	buttonthrough	prepreference	capaciousness	lecherousness
anthropopathy	centreforward	professoriate	cheerlessness	levelcrossing
anthropophagi	chalcoography	professorship	chlamydospore	limitlessness
anthropophagy	characterless	prosopography	chrematistics	litigiousness
asthenosphere	chateaubriand	protectorship	Christmastide	ludicrousness
bacteriophage	circumference	pseudomorphic	Christmastime	luxuriousness
brachycephaly	closedcircuit	psilanthropic	congruousness	mackerelshark
calligraphist	collectorship	psychosurgery	consciousness	maliciousness
cerebrospinal	commandership	quadripartite	contrabassoon	melodiousness
chromatophore	commensurable	recalcitrance	courteousness	mercilessness
contraception	commensurably	reinvigorator	credulousness	mirthlessness
contraceptive	conductorship	schadenfreude	crossquestion	misunderstand
convertiplane	confraternity	schizocarpous	dangerousness	misunderstood
crosspurposes	conglomeratic	schizophrenia	dauntlessness	momentousness
deipnosophist	conjecturable	schizophrenic	deathlessness	monstrousness
eavesdropping	conjecturally	searchwarrant	deciduousness	nefariousness
exteroceptive	containership	selfasserting	decompression	nervelessness
extratropical	controversial	selfassertion	deliciousness	noiselessness
homeomorphism	copartnership	selfassertive	deliriousness	nonaggression
horsewhipping	corticotropic	selfassurance	dexterousness	notoriousness
hydrosulphide	corticotropin	selfassuredly	dispossession	obliviousness
hydrosulphite	courtsmartial	selfcentredly	doubtlessness	obnoxiousness
hypertrophied	disappearance	selfdispraise	dreamlessness	officiousness
intercropping	disconcerting	selfgenerated	egregiousness	pendulousness
interoceptive	disconcerting	selfgoverning	embarrassment	penuriousness
intertropical	disconformity	selfimportant	encompassment	photoemission
lancecorporal	dishonourable	selfinsurance	erroneousness	photoemissive
magnetosphere	dishonourably	selfrecording	extraphysical	plenteousness
metaphosphate	disintegrator	selfregarding	facetiousness	pluripresence
microscopical	dismemberment	selfrestraint	faithlessness	pneumogastric
misconception	disproportion	semilogarithm	faultlessness	pointlessness
mourningpaper	dissymetrical	shootingrange	feloniousness	ponderousness
nitrocompound	dressimprover	skateboarding	ferociousness	postclassical
paedomorphism	entomostracan	solicitorship	fortississimo	powerlessness
pharmacopoeia	followthrough	spectrography	fractiousness	prepossessing
pneumatophore	gerontocratic	sphygmography	frivolousness	prepossession
polyadelphous	goniometrical	subeditorship	fruitlessness	pretermission
preconception	goodnaturedly	Swedenborgian	garrulousness	pricelessness
quadricipital	gymnospermous	taperecording	generalisable	quadragesimal
quicktempered	gynaecocratic	telerecording	generalissimo	querulousness
redescription	halfsovereign	thaumaturgist	glutinousness	rapaciousness
redevelopment	hemispherical	thenceforward	gracelessness	rapturousness
selfdeception	heteromorphic	theriomorphic	guilelessness	rejuvenescent
selfdeceptive	homoeomorphic	threequarters	guiltlessness	religiousness
sharecropping	hydrometrical	transmigrator	hazardousness	reprehensible
shorttempered	hypermetrical	treasurership	heartlessness	reprehensibly
spermatophore	hypermetropia	unadulterated	hemiparasitic	retrogression
spermatophyte	hypermetropic	unconquerable	hilariousness	retrogressive
stickingplace	ichthyography	undercarriage	horsechestnut	righteousness
thoroughpaced	idiosyncratic	unsymmetrical	hyperphysical	rontgenoscopy
transcription	inappropriate	vantageground	imperiousness	sagaciousness

salaciousness	disaffectedly	presidentship	magniloquence	categorically
seditiousness	discreditable	pretermitting	mangoldwurzel	centrifugally
selfadjusting	discreditably	preternatural	mothercountry	centripetally
selfsatisfied	disinvestment	problematical	overcredulous	chalcoography
semiparasitic	distributable	protohistoric	owneroccupier	challengeable
senselessness	dressingtable	psychometrics	pharmaceutics	chromatically
shamelessness	electrostatic	psychometrist	pharmaceutist	chuckleheaded
shapelessness	ethnocentrism	quadrilateral	postcommunion	cinematically
shiftlessness	Eucharistical	quickwittedly	reconstructor	climactically
shootingstick	exasperatedly	representable	selfcommunion	commensurable
shoulderstrap	featherstitch	rhadamanthine	selfconsuming	commensurably
sightlessness	felicitations	runningstitch	selfexecuting	companionable
sleeplessness	floricultural	sabrerattling	semiconductor	companionably
smellingsalts	foresightedly	sacramentally	sericulturist	conditionally
smokelessness	fundamentally	sansculottism	solidungulate	conglomeratic
spinelessness	gastroenteric	selfexistence	somniloquence	congratulator
squarebashing	globetrotting	selfrighteous	superannuable	conjecturable
stainlessness	hairsplitting	sentimentally	supersaturate	conjecturally
statelessness	halfheartedly	sidesplitting	timeconsuming	constrainable
steppingstone	hardheartedly	sociocultural	uninterrupted	constructable
strenuousness	hermeneutical	southeasterly	viniculturist	continentally
sumptuousness	homoeopathist	southeastward	viticulturist	contractually
superphysical	horticultural	southwesterly	BaltoSlavonic	counterchange
supersensible	hydrostatical	southwestward	inconceivable	countercharge
tachistoscope	hypercritical	steadfastness	inconceivably	curvilinearly
tastelessness	imperceptible	subreptitious	irretrievable	cylindrically
tenaciousness	imperceptibly	substitutable	irretrievably	deferentially
tergiversator	imperfectness	substructural	pigeonlivered	dendritically
thanklessness	incombustible	subternatural	primigravidae	detrimentally
tonguelashing	inconsistence	supercritical	sniftingvalve	dialectically
tortoiseshell	inconsistency	superstitious	topsyturvydom	diametrically
transgression	incontestable	supersubtlety	unconceivable	diaphragmatic
transgressive	incontestably	surreptitious	aircraftwoman	dictatorially
transmissible	inconvertible	thermosetting	businesswoman	dimensionally
transversally	inconvertibly	thunderstruck	congresswoman	disadvantaged
tremulousness	incorrectness	toastmistress	spinningwheel	disaffirmance
troublousness	incorruptible	transmittable	sprocketwheel	disappearance
unanimousness	incorruptibly	transportable	tiddledywinks	disciplinable
valuelessness	incorruptness	tritheistical	basidiomycete	discreditable
venturousness	incrementally	troglodytical	butterflyfish	discreditably
veraciousness	inexhaustible	trustworthily	monodactylous	discriminator
vexatiousness	inexhaustibly	unaccountable	polydactylous	dishonourable
vicariousness	insupportable	unaccountably	polypropylene	dishonourably
vivaciousness	insupportably	uncomfortable	prairieoyster	disintegrator
voicelessness	insusceptible	uncomfortably	proparoxytone	distributable
volatilisable	intercultural	underclothing	psychophysics	dressingtable
voraciousness	interdentally	unenlightened	secretarybird	eccentrically
worthlessness	interjectural	unforgettable	secretaryship	educationally
acrylonitrile	intermittence	unforgettably	zygodactylous	electrostatic
affreightment	interpretable	ungrammatical	conversazione	elephantiasis
amniocentesis	interpretress	unpredictable	conversazioni	energetically
anomalistical	interruptible	unpretentious	————————————	enigmatically
apocalyptical	maladjustment	unwarrantable	abiologically	entomostracan
archaeopteryx	maladroitness	unwarrantably	acrobatically	evangelically
architectonic	manipulatable	Zarathustrian	adiabatically	exceptionable
architectural	manneristical	agriculturist	administrable	exceptionally
astronautical	Methodistical	anticoagulant	administrator	exceptionally
backscratcher	nearsightedly	battlecruiser	aesthetically	existentially
belleslettres	nitrobacteria	candlesnuffer	agonistically	exponentially
bibliolatrist	nomenclatural	circumfluence	alcoholically	extensionally
bibliolatrous	nondeductable	contractually	algebraically	extrinsically
bloodboltered	nonresistance	disarticulate	allegorically	fantastically
brilliantness	northeasterly	electrocution	anaerobically	Fascistically
Calvinistical	northeastward	fortunehunter	anthropopathy	featherheaded
centripetally	northwesterly	hemicellulose	apathetically	floristically
coldheartedly	northwestward	hocuspocussed	arthritically	fundamentally
complicatedly	ochlocratical	hydromedusoid	ascertainable	generalisable
conscientious	openheartedly	inconsecutive	asthmatically	geometrically
conservatoire	opinionatedly	inconsequence	atheistically	geotropically
constructable	orthognathism	ineffectually	atomistically	gerontocratic
constructible	orthognathous	infundibulate	authentically	grammatically
continentally	oystercatcher	inopportunely	authenticator	gymnastically
counterattack	pantheistical	intercolumnar	autobiography	gynaecocratic
counterstroke	parenthetical	interlocution	automatically	helminthiasis
crosscultural	passementerie	interlocutory	autonomically	heptasyllabic
crossgartered	pennyfarthing	interlocutrix	axiomatically	honorifically
detrimentally	phycoerythrin	interosculate	biodegradable	hydraulically
differentiate	piscicultural	knuckleduster	bombastically	hydrocephalic
disadvantaged	prescientific	machinegunner	canaliculated	hydrocephalus

ichthyography	nonsensically	sophistically	imponderables	skateboarding
ideologically	nostalgically	sophisticated	moneygrubbing	superabundant
idiomatically	nutritionally	spasmodically	monosyllabism	superfluidity
idiosyncratic	objectionable	spectacularly	secretarybird	taperecording
imperturbable	objectionably	spectrography	turkeygobbler	telerecording
imperturbably	oecologically	sphygmography	achromaticity	translucidity
impolitically	ontogenically	spindleshanks	affenpinscher	understanding
impracticable	ontologically	splenetically	anticlimactic	vicepresident
impracticably	opisthobranch	squandermania	arithmetician	accelerometer
impractically	orthocephalic	statistically	autoeroticism	accoutrements
inappreciable	overabundance	steeplechaser	backscratcher	actinomycetes
inappreciably	overpopulated	stigmatically	basidiomycete	aggiornamento
inconceivable	paddlesteamer	strategically	chinkerinchee	alcoholometer
inconceivably	panegyrically	strikebreaker	circumspectly	alcoholometry
incondensable	pantisocratic	stylistically	closedcircuit	amniocentesis
incontestable	parabolically	substantially	concentricity	anthropogenic
incontestably	paradoxically	substitutable	cyberneticist	anthropometry
incorporeally	paraphernalia	superannuable	diagnostician	archaeopteryx
incrementally	parasitically	superficially	egocentricity	baccalaureate
indefatigable	parthenocarpy	symbiotically	excommunicate	birefringence
indefatigably	patriotically	symmetrically	extragalactic	blastogenesis
indescribable	pedagogically	symphonically	extrajudicial	bloodboltered
indescribably	penitentially	synallagmatic	geocentricism	boustrophedon
indispensable	pharisaically	syntactically	histrionicism	broadmindedly
indispensably	phrenetically	synthetically	incommunicado	camphoraceous
indissociable	plethorically	taxonomically	insignificant	chromospheric
indoctrinator	pneumatically	telegrammatic	intergalactic	chrysanthemum
ineffectually	polychromatic	telencephalon	judgeadvocate	circumference
inferentially	pragmatically	tergiversator	knickerbocker	circumfluence
influentially	predestinator	terrestrially	leatherjacket	clairaudience
inorganically	prefatorially	territorially	macromolecule	clearheadedly
insupportable	prejudicially	tetrasyllable	mathematician	coenaesthesis
insupportably	preponderance	theologically	metaphysician	coldbloodedly
intentionally	preponderancy	theoretically	microdetector	coldheartedly
interdentally	prismatically	thermodynamic	neoclassicism	complicatedly
intermediator	probationally	thoroughpaced	neoclassicist	concupiscence
interpellator	pronounceable	thoughtreader	neoplasticism	consenescence
interpretable	prophetically	thrasonically	oystercatcher	consentaneity
intrinsically	prosopography	topologically	paediatrician	consentaneous
inventorially	provisionally	traditionally	panicstricken	constrainedly
irreclaimable	psychodynamic	transformable	pathogenicity	convalescence
irreclaimably	psychosomatic	transmigrator	perissodactyl	crossgartered
irrecoverable	puritanically	transmittable	prognosticate	defervescence
irrecoverably	quadrennially	transportable	quadruplicate	deliquescence
irreplaceable	questionnaire	transversally	quadruplicity	dichlamydeous
irretrievable	quincuncially	traumatically	quintuplicate	disaffectedly
irretrievably	realistically	typologically	reconstructor	effervescence
isometrically	recalcitrance	unaccountable	rejuvenescent	effervescency
isostatically	recommendable	unaccountably	rontgenoscopy	efflorescence
judgmatically	rectangularly	unadulterated	scholasticism	electioneerer
kinematically	rectilinearly	unanticipated	schoolteacher	embryogenesis
knowledgeable	referentially	unarticulated	selfcollected	encyclopaedia
knowledgeably	reinvigorator	uncomfortable	selfconvicted	encyclopaedic
lamellibranch	representable	uncomfortably	selfcriticism	epeirogenesis
leishmaniasis	reverentially	uncomplicated	selfinflicted	epiphenomenal
leptocephalic	RhaetoRomanic	unconceivable	selfsufficing	epiphenomenon
lethargically	rhapsodically	unconformable	semiconductor	exasperatedly
macaronically	rheumatically	unconquerable	sesquiplicate	ferrimagnetic
macrocephalic	sacramentally	uncoordinated	spheroidicity	ferromagnetic
magisterially	sacrificially	undereducated	streptococcal	foraminiferal
malacostracan	sarcastically	underemphasis	streptococcus	foreknowledge
manipulatable	schematically	unemotionally	subcontractor	foresightedly
matrilineally	scorbutically	unequivocally	tachistoscope	frontogenesis
mesencephalon	selfassurance	unfashionable	blackguardism	galactosaemia
metallography	selfdispraise	unfashionably	breechloading	gametogenesis
metonymically	selfgenerated	unforgettable	contrabandist	gastroenteric
microcephalic	selfinsurance	unforgettably	correspondent	goodnaturedly
ministerially	selfrestraint	unimpeachable	encyclopedism	grandfatherly
monochromatic	semiautomatic	unmentionable	encyclopedist	grandmotherly
monogrammatic	semipermeable	unpredictable	gasteropodous	halfheartedly
mourningpaper	sensationally	unputdownable	hermaphrodite	halfsovereign
multiplicable	sentimentally	unwarrantable	jerrybuilding	hardheartedly
mutagenically	sergeantmajor	unwarrantably	overconfident	heterogeneity
nonappearance	serologically	verisimilarly	rearcommodore	heterogeneous
nonattendance	shootingrange	viceadmiralty	reconsolidate	heterogenesis
noncompliance	slangingmatch	volatilisable	selfconfident	heterogenetic
nondeductable	smellingsalts	weatherbeaten	selfdependent	hypoglycaemia
nonresistance	sniftingvalve	wheelerdealer	selfrecording	impercipience
nonreturnable	somnambulator	heebiejeebies	selfregarding	incandescence

inconsequence	spermatogenic	anthropophagi	cryptological	oreographical
inconsistence	stercoraceous	anthropophagy	deontological	osteomyelitis
inconsistency	stoichiometry	asthenosphere	differentiate	palynological
inconvenience	stratospheric	bacteriophage	discommodious	pantheistical
inconveniency	submachinegun	brachycephaly	disharmonious	paperhangings
inflorescence	subterraneous	calligraphist	dissymetrical	parasiticidal
instantaneity	supereminence	candlelighter	draggletailed	parenthetical
instantaneous	supervenience	chromatophore	dramaturgical	perspicacious
insufficience	thermogenesis	crosshatching	embryological	petrochemical
insufficiency	threecornered	deipnosophist	entomological	philosophical
intercurrence	transcendence	granddaughter	Eucharistical	philosophiser
intermittence	transcendency	homeomorphism	extraphysical	photochemical
interparietal	unconcernedly	homoeopathist	extratropical	phrenological
intransigeant	underachiever	hydrosulphide	featherstitch	physiological
intransigence	underhandedly	hydrosulphite	featherweight	planimetrical
jurisprudence	unenlightened	hypertrophied	felicitations	platyhelminth
lancesergeant	unqualifiedly	mackerelshark	gastrological	poliomyelitis
lightfingered	volumenometer	magnetosphere	gastronomical	postclassical
lightheadedly	whithersoever	metaphosphate	glaciological	prehistorical
lightmindedly	wrongheadedly	miscomprehend	goniometrical	prescientific
magniloquence	bookingoffice	neighbourhood	graphological	primigravidae
membranaceous	butterflyfish	nightwatchman	hemiparasitic	problematical
miscellaneous	candlesnuffer	orthognathism	hemispherical	professoriate
monocotyledon	festschriften	orthognathous	hermeneutical	psychological
morphogenesis	letterperfect	paedomorphism	hundredweight	pyrotechnical
morphogenetic	meadowsaffron	pennyfarthing	hydrometrical	quadragesimal
multinucleate	overqualified	pennypinching	hydrostatical	quadricipital
nearsightedly	selfsacrifice	phycoerythrin	hyperboloidal	rattlebrained
nitrobacteria	selfsatisfied	pneumatophore	hypercritical	reprehensible
northeasterly	thereinbefore	polyadelphous	hypermetrical	reprehensibly
northwesterly	waterproofing	pseudoarchaic	hyperphysical	runningstitch
onomatopoetic	archaeologist	rhadamanthine	ideographical	sanctimonious
openheartedly	Assyriologist	sadomasochism	immarcescible	seismological
opinionatedly	butterfingers	sadomasochist	immunological	selenological
organogenesis	campanologist	scrapmerchant	imperceptible	selfconceited
papaveraceous	climatologist	selfslaughter	imperceptibly	selfconscious
parasynthesis	criminologist	sewingmachine	impermissible	selfcontained
parasynthetic	cryobiologist	soulsearching	inappropriate	selfsustained
passementerie	demythologise	spermatophore	incombustible	semeiological
pigeonlivered	dermatologist	spermatophyte	inconvertible	semicivilised
pluripresence	doubletongued	spinningwheel	inconvertibly	semiconscious
pneumatometer	electrologist	sprocketwheel	inconvincible	semilogarithm
polycotyledon	electromagnet	squarebashing	incorruptible	semiparasitic
polysynthesis	encephalogram	tonguelashing	incorruptibly	smoothingiron
polysynthetic	entomophagous	tortoiseshell	indiscernible	solderingiron
porcellaneous	eschatologist	trustworthily	indiscernibly	somatological
potentiometer	gerontologist	underclothing	inefficacious	speleological
preengineered	gynaecologist	abortifacient	inexhaustible	subreptitious
prepreference	haematologist	aerodynamical	inexhaustibly	supercritical
proteinaceous	herpetologist	AngloAmerican	inexpressible	superphysical
pseudoscience	ichthyologist	anomalistical	inexpressibly	supersensible
psychasthenia	malariologist	antilogarithm	infinitesimal	superstitious
psychogenesis	martyrologist	apocalyptical	insusceptible	surreptitious
psychogenetic	meteorologist	apprehensible	intermarriage	swallowtailed
psychokinesis	myrmecologist	astronautical	interruptible	technological
psychokinetic	ornithologist	astrophysical	interspecific	teratological
pyrheliometer	overindulgent	atmospherical	intertropical	tiddledywinks
quadrilateral	parallelogram	bathymetrical	introversible	topographical
quicktempered	phraseologist	battlecruiser	irrefrangible	toxicological
quickwittedly	phyllophagous	betweenwhiles	irrepressible	tranquilliser
recrudescence	psychosurgery	bibliological	irrepressibly	transmissible
refractometer	pteridologist	bouillabaisse	irresponsible	tritheistical
righthandedly	radiotelegram	cacographical	irresponsibly	troglodytical
saccharimeter	roentgenogram	Calvinistical	lackadaisical	typographical
saccharimetry	scientologist	cerebrospinal	liebfraumilch	unceremonious
saccharometer	selfindulgent	chateaubriand	malacological	uncircumcised
schadenfreude	silvertongued	chronological	manneristical	unconstrained
schizogenesis	sovietologist	circumambient	metallurgical	undercarriage
schizophrenia	spelaeologist	coarsegrained	Methodistical	undisciplined
schizophrenic	spindlelegged	conchological	micronutrient	ungrammatical
selfassuredly	stomatologist	concupiscible	microscopical	unpretentious
selfcentredly	Swedenborgian	conscientious	mineralogical	unsymmetrical
selfexistence	thaumaturgist	constructible	morphological	xylographical
selfknowledge	thimblerigged	conversazione	musicological	cabinetmaking
selfrighteous	thimblerigger	conversazioni	nemathelminth	cottonpicking
shorttempered	unintelligent	counterfeiter	noncollegiate	heartbreaking
somniloquence	venereologist	counterweight	numerological	housebreaking
southeasterly	volcanologist	craniological	ochlocratical	hydrocracking
southwesterly	vulcanologist	cruiserweight	odontological	jiggerypokery

mountebankery	horizontality	palaeozoology	unsuitability	transshipment
phytoplankton	immaterialise	pantagruelian	verifiability	troublesomely
streetwalking	immaterialism	pantagruelism	violoncellist	underestimate
wonderworking	immaterialist	pantagruelist	vocationalism	underwhelming
absorbability	immateriality	paranormality	vulnerability	unforthcoming
acceptability	immiscibility	paterfamilias	zygodactylous	unwholesomely
accessibility	impalpability	penetrability	accompaniment	venturesomely
accidentalism	impartibility	perdurability	admeasurement	vouchsafement
acetylcholine	impassability	perishability	advertisement	acotyledonous
admissibility	impassibility	permutability	affreightment	acquiescently
affectionless	impeccability	phenomenalise	angiospermous	acquiescingly
answerability	impersonalise	phenomenalism	antihistamine	admirableness
anticoagulant	impersonality	phenomenalist	apportionment	admonishingly
applicability	implacability	phenomenology	ascertainment	advisableness
artificiality	impossibility	picturepalace	bamboozlement	aggravatingly
attainability	improbability	polydactylous	beleaguerment	agreeableness
autocephalous	improvability	polypropylene	brainstorming	airworthiness
backpedalling	incredibility	ponderability	cleistogamous	ambiguousness
bibliophilism	individualise	predicability	Deuteronomist	ambitiousness
bibliophilist	individualism	preferability	disconformity	amorphousness
biotechnology	individualist	PreRaphaelite	disembodiment	analogousness
bloodcurdling	individuality	primordiality	disengagement	annexationist
ceremonialism	industrialise	profitability	disfigurement	anomalousness
ceremonialist	industrialism	provincialise	disinvestment	anonymousness
changeability	industrialist	provincialism	dismantlement	antinomianism
characterless	ineducability	provincialist	dismemberment	antipersonnel
circumvallate	ineligibility	provinciality	disparagement	arbitrariness
coagulability	inevitability	prudentialism	divertisement	archdeaconate
collaterality	inexorability	prudentialist	embarrassment	assertiveness
colloquialism	infallibilism	prudentiality	embranglement	assiduousness
commercialise	infallibilist	psychoanalyse	embrittlement	astonishingly
commercialism	infallibility	psychoanalyst	encompassment	atrociousness
commercialist	infeasibility	quinquevalent	encouragement	attentiveness
commutability	inflexibility	receptibility	enlightenment	audaciousness
companionless	inflexionless	reciprocality	entertainment	Australianism
comparability	infundibulate	recrystallise	establishment	autochthonism
compatibility	inhospitality	reflexibility	gastrocnemius	autochthonous
conceptualise	insatiability	reformability	gymnospermous	availableness
conceptualism	insensibility	resistibility	hydrodynamics	barbarousness
conceptualist	insociability	resolvability	hydroxylamine	barefacedness
connaturality	intangibility	reversibility	intercolumnar	beauteousness
contractility	interosculate	roentgenology	interlacement	belligerently
convertiplane	invariability	sabrerattling	maladjustment	Berkeleianism
corrigibility	invincibility	sacerdotalise	misgovernment	bewilderingly
decontrolling	inviolability	sacerdotalism	mismanagement	blameableness
deductibility	irrationalise	sacerdotalist	naphthylamine	blamelessness
defeasibility	irrationalism	scripturalism	nonconforming	bloodlessness
defensibility	irrationalist	scripturalist	nonconformism	boundlessness
dematerialise	irrationality	selffertility	nonconformist	bounteousness
denationalise	linseywoolsey	selfpropelled	nonconformity	bountifulness
dependability	Machiavellian	selfrevealing	nonfulfilment	brainlessness
depersonalise	manageability	selfsterility	nongovernment	brilliantness
digestibility	materfamilias	semiporcelain	overstatement	brotherliness
dimensionless	megacephalous	sequentiality	phanerogamous	bumptiousness
disarticulate	mensurability	shoulderblade	photochromics	calculatingly
disposability	metagrobolise	softpedalling	photochromism	callisthenics
dissolubility	metastability	solidungulate	physiognomist	capaciousness
documentalist	microphyllous	spermatoblast	preengagement	cartilaginous
doubledealing	microtonality	sportsmanlike	prefigurement	challengingly
ecumenicalism	millefeuilles	squeezability	preordainment	changefulness
electrovalent	millennialism	statesmanlike	pronouncement	cheerlessness
endocrinology	monodactylous	stickingplace	pusillanimity	clandestinely
entomophilous	monometallism	structuralism	pusillanimous	collectedness
expansibility	monometallist	structuralist	pyrimethamine	collieshangie
extensibility	monumentalise	structureless	quarrelsomely	colourfulness
filterability	mourningcloak	superfamilies	rearrangement	combativeness
formidability	negligibility	supersubtlety	reconcilement	compartmental
fortuneteller	negotiability	swashbuckling	redevelopment	compassionate
fractionalise	numismatology	terminability	reimbursement	complainingly
functionalism	occasionalism	theatricalise	reinforcement	complaisantly
functionalist	occasionalist	theatricalism	reinstatement	complexedness
gentlemanlike	occasionality	theatricality	replenishment	compositeness
geochronology	occidentalise	thermonuclear	selfabasement	concavoconvex
geomorphology	Occidentalism	thermophilous	selfcondemned	conceitedness
helminthology	Occidentalist	thremmatology	selfconsuming	concessionary
helterskelter	ophthalmology	triliteralism	selfconsuming	concomitantly
hemicellulose	outgeneralled	unicameralism	sternforemost	concretionary
heterothallic	overcredulous	unicameralist	thermochemist	conduciveness
homosexuality	palaeontology	unsociability	timeconsuming	confectionary

confectionery	expansiveness	infuriatingly	objectiveness	regardfulness
confessionary	expeditionary	ingeniousness	obliviousness	regretfulness
confidingness	expensiveness	ingenuousness	obnoxiousness	religiousness
conflictingly	explosiveness	injuriousness	obsessiveness	reminiscently
confraternity	expressionism	innocuousness	obstinateness	remonstrantly
congruousness	expressionist	innoxiousness	obtrusiveness	removableness
conjugateness	exquisiteness	inopportunely	octocentenary	repetitionary
connectedness	extensiveness	insensateness	offensiveness	reproachingly
consanguinity	extraordinary	insidiousness	offhandedness	republicanise
consciousness	extravagantly	insinuatingly	officiousness	republicanism
contentedness	facetiousness	insolubleness	operativeness	repulsiveness
contortionist	faithlessness	insubordinate	opportuneness	requisiteness
conventionary	fascinatingly	intelligencer	oppositionist	resentfulness
convexoconvex	faultlessness	intelligently	outspokenness	resplendently
convulsionary	feloniousness	intensiveness	outstandingly	retentiveness
coreligionist	ferociousness	intercolonial	overbearingly	revelationist
corrosiveness	feuilletonism	interestingly	painstakingly	revolutionary
corruptionist	feuilletonist	intricateness	painterliness	revolutionise
courteousness	flourishingly	intrusiveness	palatableness	revolutionism
credulousness	foolhardiness	intuitiveness	patronisingly	revolutionist
crystallinity	forgetfulness	inventiveness	peaceableness	righteousness
customariness	fortunateness	invidiousness	pedestrianise	sagaciousness
dangerousness	fortunehunter	inviolateness	pedestrianism	salaciousness
dastardliness	fractiousness	invisibleness	pendulousness	sanitationist
dauntlessness	frighteningly	irreligionist	penetratingly	scandalmonger
deathlessness	frightfulness	irritableness	penuriousness	scholarliness
deceitfulness	frivolousness	judiciousness	percussionist	seaworthiness
deceptiveness	fruitlessness	laboriousness	perfectionism	secondariness
deciduousness	frustratingly	languishingly	perfectionist	secretiveness
decontaminate	garrulousness	laughableness	pervasiveness	sedentariness
defectiveness	geostationary	leadpoisoning	phenylalanine	seditiousness
deliciousness	glutinousness	lecherousness	philhellenism	seductiveness
deliriousness	gracelessness	leisureliness	philhellenist	selectiveness
deprecatingly	greensickness	liberationist	pigheadedness	selfappointed
desirableness	grotesqueness	lickerishness	plaintiveness	selfawareness
desperateness	guilelessness	lightsomeness	platitudinise	selfcommunion
desultoriness	guiltlessness	limitlessness	platitudinous	selfcontented
deuteragonist	habitableness	litigiousness	plausibleness	selfevidently
devastatingly	haphazardness	loathsomeness	plenitudinous	selfgoverning
developmental	hazardousness	lucrativeness	plenteousness	selfpityingly
devolutionary	healthfulness	ludicrousness	plentifulness	selfpollinate
devolutionist	heartlessness	luxuriousness	pointlessness	selfrepugnant
dexterousness	heartsickness	machinegunner	polycarbonate	selfsurrender
diathermanous	hilariousness	Maginotminded	ponderousness	selftormentor
diffusiveness	identicalness	magnificently	postcommunion	semipermanent
discretionary	illogicalness	maladroitness	powerlessness	senselessness
disobediently	imitativeness	maliciousness	practicalness	sensitiveness
disparagingly	immediateness	malleableness	precautionary	separableness
disparateness	immovableness	Malthusianism	precipitantly	separationist
dispassionate	immutableness	Manichaeanism	predatoriness	seriousminded
dispraisingly	imperfectness	masculineness	predicamental	shamelessness
dissemblingly	imperiousness	masterfulness	predominantly	shapelessness
dissoluteness	impertinently	mediterranean	prematureness	shiftlessness
distressingly	impetuousness	megasporangia	premillennial	sightlessness
dodecaphonist	impressionism	meistersinger	pricelessness	sleeplessness
doublejointed	impressionist	melodiousness	primitiveness	smokelessness
doubtlessness	improvidently	mercenariness	processionary	snowblindness
dreamlessness	impulsiveness	mercilessness	processionist	sobermindness
effectiveness	inadvertently	microorganism	procrastinate	sorrowfulness
egregiousness	inanimateness	mirthlessness	projectionist	Spencerianism
elaborateness	inclusiveness	miserableness	prolegomenary	spinelessness
encouragingly	incompetently	mistrustingly	prolegomenous	spiritualness
enjoyableness	incontinently	mnemotechnics	proportionate	sprightliness
environmental	Mohammedanism	mothercountry	prostaglandin	squeamishness
equestrianism	incorrectness	momentariness	prosthodontia	stainlessness
equidistantly	incorruptness	momentousness	protectionism	statelessness
equivocalness	incurableness	Monarchianism	protectionist	steadfastness
erroneousness	incuriousness	monophthongal	protuberantly	strenuousness
essentialness	independently	monstrousness	purposiveness	sublieutenant
everlastingly	indeterminacy	mothercountry	querulousness	subserviently
evocativeness	indeterminate	Muhammadanism	questioningly	subversionary
excessiveness	indeterminism	multitudinous	quincentenary	suffocatingly
excitableness	indeterminist	navigableness	quingentenary	sumptuousness
exclusiveness	indifferently	nefariousness	quinquagenary	supercalender
excursiveness	inductiveness	nervelessness	rapaciousness	superdominant
excusableness	ineffableness	neurastheniac	rapturousness	superhumanity
exemplariness	inefficiently	niggardliness	receptiveness	superordinate
exhibitionism	inexpediently	noiselessness	recessiveness	tablespoonful
exhibitionist	inexperienced	notoriousness		

```
talkativeness BaltoSlavonic spectroscopic accidentprone particularist
tantalisingly bildungsroman spinninghouse acrylonitrile particularity
tastelessness blanketflower stalkinghorse agriculturist perfunctorily
teachableness boardinghouse supernational aluminiferous perichondrial
technicalness businesswoman suppositional ambassadorial perichondrium
televisionary buttonthrough supranational ambidexterity petroliferous
temperamental cephalothorax terminational ambidexterous phalansterian
temperateness chlamydomonas thoroughgoing archimandrite phonautograph
temporariness clearinghouse thundershower argentiferous physiotherapy
tenaciousness coeducational toxoplasmosis auctioneering pigeonhearted
tentativeness compositional translational authoritarian platiniferous
tercentennial compressional transnational balsamiferous polliniferous
thanklessness computational unconditional bibliolatrist polyhistorian
threateningly congressional unconditioned bibliolatrous preliminarily
thrillingness congresswoman underemployed brachypterous premonitorily
titillatingly conjugational unexceptional brokenhearted preparatorily
tolerableness conjunctional unimpassioned carboniferous procuratorial
toothsomeness conservatoire unintentional chromatograph profitsharing
traceableness contrafagotto vantageground cinematograph progenitorial
tractableness convocational vivisectional climbingframe proprietorial
Tractarianism corticotropic xanthochroism cobelligerent protonotarial
transatlantic corticotropin zinjanthropus combinatorial psychometrics
transitionary countinghouse actinomorphic communitarian psychometrist
translucently crosspurposes allelomorphic counterstroke psychotherapy
transparently deformational archbishopric crackerbarrel quadrumvirate
tremulousness dressimprover bibliographer dissimilarity quartziferous
tributariness dysfunctional bibliographic doctrinairism rudimentarily
tricentennial electrophorus biogeographer equiponderant scolopendrium
troublousness electroscopic cardiographer equiponderate scorpiongrass
unaccompanied examinational chemoreceptor ethnocentrism searchwarrant
unanimousness explorational chlamydospore examinatorial selfsupported
unbelievingly followthrough choreographer explanatorily semibarbarian
uncertainness forementioned choreographic expurgatorial semibarbarism
uncleanliness fullfashioned chronographic extemporarily sericulturist
uncomplaining gravitational cryptographer exterritorial Shakespearean
unearthliness gynandromorph cryptographic ferroconcrete Shakespearian
unfeelingness hypermetropia diageotropism fossiliferous sheepshearing
unflinchingly hypermetropic eavesdropping fragmentarily shockabsorber
unhealthiness informational glossographer garnetiferous shootingbrake
unmeaningness inquisitional gonadotrophic graminivorous singlehearted
unnaturalness inscriptional gonadotrophin gubernatorial splendiferous
unprecedented inspirational heteromorphic heteropterous staminiferous
unpromisingly institutional heterotrophic heterosporous stoloniferous
unquestioning instructional homoeomorphic hollowhearted supernumerary
unrelentingly international horsewhipping homoiothermal supersaturate
unremittingly interpersonal intercropping homoiothermic tenderhearted
unselfishness intrapersonal lexicographer hydrochloride terpsichorean
unwillingness kaleidoscopic lexicographic hymenopterous thalassocracy
vacillatingly lancecorporal misanthropist hypochondriac thoroughbrace
valuelessness laryngoscopic oceanographer immunotherapy thunderstruck
vapourishness leptospirosis oceanographic inconsiderate toastmistress
vegetarianism metamorphoses owneroccupier inquisitorial transistorise
venerableness metamorphosis palaeographer insectivorous transliterate
venturousness micrococcocci palaeographic interpretress triangularity
veraciousness mononucleosis photoreceptor intraarterial umbelliferous
vexatiousness mouldingboard physiographer involuntarily unfamiliarity
vicariousness multinational physiographic kinematograph unnecessarily
visionariness nitrocompound polarographic legislatorial untrustworthy
vivaciousness observational proprioceptor lepidopterist vernacularise
voicelessness passionflower pseudomorphic lepidopterous vernacularism
voluntariness pathognomonic schizocarpous lifepreserver vernacularity
voraciousness pharmacologic seismographer longsuffering viniculturist
wearisomeness pharmacopoeia seismographic mammaliferous viticulturist
wellapPointed philanthropic selenographer manganiferous winterberries
whimsicalness photoperiodic selenographic mangoldwurzel woolgathering
wholesomeness postulational sharecropping metalliferous Zarathustrian
wonderfulness prepositional stereographic millionairess adventuresome
worldlyminded progressional stereoscopist mitochondrion anachronistic
worrisomeness propositional stratigraphic mouthwatering anaphrodisiac
worthlessness protohistoric theanthropism necessitarian anfractuosity
abstractional psilanthropic theriomorphic nectariferous animadversion
actinomycosis quadrillionth thermotropism nickeliferous associateship
aircraftwoman quintillionth thigmotropism oleomargarine barrelchested
AngloCatholic reformational transshipping organotherapy cannibalistic
anthroposophy salmonellosis understrapper overelaborate chieftainship
apheliotropic selfopinioned uninterrupted oversubscribe churchmanship
arbitrational septentrional windowshopper ovoviviparous clothesbasket
archidiaconal socioeconomic zoogeographer particularise colleagueship
architectonic soundingboard zoogeographic particularism collectorship
```

commandership	selfaddressed	cauterisation	derestriction	hybridisation
companionship	selfconfessed	certification	desegregation	hydroelectric
comprehension	selfpossessed	certificatory	deterioration	hydrogenation
comprehensive	solicitorship	chrematistics	deteriorative	hypnotisation
concertmaster	sportsmanship	Christmastide	determinately	hypothecation
condescension	standoffishly	Christmastime	determination	impenetration
conductorship	statesmanship	cicatrisation	determinative	impersonation
containership	stationmaster	cinquecentist	diagrammatise	importunately
contrabassoon	subeditorship	circumvention	discoloration	impropriation
controversial	subpostmaster	clarification	disconcerting	improvisation
copartnership	suffraganship	collaboration	disconcertion	improvisatory
corresponsive	surrogateship	collaborative	disconnection	incarceration
craftsmanship	swordsmanship	commemoration	displantation	incardination
criminalistic	synchronistic	commemorative	disproportion	inconsecutive
cytochemistry	thermoplastic	commemoratory	disrespectful	incorporation
decompression	thoughtlessly	commiseration	dissemination	incorporative
defencelessly	tonguetwister	commiserative	disseminative	incriminatory
deterministic	transgression	communication	disseveration	indisposition
disinterested	transgressive	communicative	dissimilation	indistinctive
dispossession	treasurership	communicatory	dissimilitude	individuation
distinguished	underexposure	communisation	dissimulation	ingurgitation
doublecrosser	unestablished	compagination	documentation	insubstantial
draftsmanship	voluntaristic	complementary	domestication	integumentary
fortississimo	acclimatation	complimentary	domiciliation	intemperately
generalissimo	accommodating	concatenation	dramatisation	intercalation
harbourmaster	accommodation	concentration	dulcification	interdigitate
hocuspocussed	accommodative	concentrative	electrocution	interlocution
hydromedusoid	accreditation	condylomatous	electrometric	interlocutory
impecuniosity	acculturation	confabulation	electromotive	interlocutrix
imperialistic	acculturative	confabulatory	emphysematous	interoceptive
inspectorship	acetification	confederation	encapsulation	interpolation
interspersion	acidification	confederative	epigrammatise	interpolative
introgression	actualisation	configuration	epigrammatist	interposition
kapellmeister	afforestation	conflagration	equilibration	interpunction
Kidderminster	agglomeration	confrontation	equipotential	interrelation
knuckleduster	agglomerative	consequential	eschscholtzia	interrogation
laissezpasser	agglutination	considerately	exanthematous	interrogative
landownership	agglutinative	consideration	excrescential	interrogatory
levelcrossing	aluminisation	consolidation	expectoration	interstratify
librarianship	amphiprostyle	consolidative	expostulation	introspection
maladminister	amplification	consolidatory	expostulatory	introspective
materialistic	anagrammatise	constellation	expropriation	investigation
merchandising	anagrammatism	constellatory	extermination	investigative
moderatorship	anglicisation	consternation	exterminatory	investigatory
nationalistic	animalisation	contamination	exteroceptive	irreverential
nightmarishly	anthelminthic	contaminative	extrapolation	isomerisation
nonaggression	Antichthones	contemplation	extravasation	italicisation
objectivistic	appropriately	contemplative	falsification	jollification
odontoglossum	appropriation	contraception	fasciculation	justification
opportunistic	appropriative	contraceptive	ferroelectric	justificative
orangeblossom	approximately	contradiction	fertilisation	justificatory
overemphasise	approximation	contradictory	feudalisation	juxtaposition
paternalistic	approximative	contrapuntist	flagellantism	laevorotation
photoemission	arboriculture	contravention	formalisation	laevorotatory
photoemissive	argumentation	cornification	formulisation	laughingstock
pigeonchested	argumentative	corroboration	fortification	lignification
pointillistic	aromatisation	corroborative	fossilisation	machicolation
prairieoyster	assassination	corroboratory	fractionation	magnetisation
precentorship	asserveration	cosmopolitise	fragmentation	magnetomotive
prepossessing	authorisation	cosmopolitism	freeselection	magnification
prepossession	authoritative	costeffective	frequentation	maladaptation
presidentship	backformation	counteraction	frequentative	manifestation
pretermission	backwardation	counteractive	funambulation	manifestative
principalship	balkanisation	counterattack	galvanisation	martyrisation
proconsulship	barbarisation	courtsmartial	germanisation	matriculation
professorship	beatification	crossquestion	gesticulation	mediatisation
protectorship	belleslettres	daguerreotype	gesticulative	melodramatics
psychophysics	beneficiation	decerebration	gesticulatory	melodramatise
purposelessly	bioenergetics	decomposition	glamorisation	melodramatist
quartermaster	bloodrelation	decortication	globetrotting	mercerisation
Quinquagesima	brachydactyly	decrepitation	glorification	mesmerisation
rationalistic	broadspectrum	defibrination	gratification	metallisation
remorselessly	brutalisation	deforestation	hairsplitting	metrification
retrogression	bureaucratise	degranulation	hallucination	miscegenation
retrogressive	calcification	demonstration	hallucinative	misconception
rhodochrosite	caprification	demonstrative	hallucinatory	misunderstand
rollercoaster	carbonisation	denticulation	harmonisation	misunderstood
sculpturesque	carcinomatous	deodorisation	horripilation	modernisation
secretaryship	catechisation	derequisition	horsechestnut	

mollification	qualification	significative	dichotomously	tendentiously
Monophysitism	qualificatory	socialisation	discontinuity	tintinnabular
monosymmetric	radiolocation	solemnisation	discontinuous	tintinnabulum
Monotheletism	randomisation	specification	disgracefully	treacherously
monotrematous	ratiocination	spectrometric	distastefully	tyrannosaurus
mortification	ratiocinative	stabilisation	distressfully	unambiguously
mummification	reaffirmation	steppingstone	distrustfully	unconsciously
mutualisation	reciprocation	sterilisation	efficaciously	undergraduate
mystification	reciprocative	stirpiculture	expeditiously	unrighteously
necessitation	recombination	strangulation	extracellular	ventriloquial
nephelometric	recomposition	subirrigation	extravascular	ventriloquise
nitrification	recrimination	subordinately	fibrovascular	ventriloquism
nonconducting	recriminative	subordination	fissiparously	ventriloquist
nonfigurative	recriminatory	subordinative	flirtatiously	versicoloured
nonforfeiting	rectification	subsaturation	floricultural	vertiginously
nonproductive	redescription	subsequential	grandiloquent	adversatively
normalisation	reduplication	subtilisation	homogeneously	affirmatively
nucleoprotein	reduplicative	suffumigation	horticultural	alternatively
nullification	reembarkation	summarisation	ichthyosaurus	appellatively
omnicompetent	reexamination	superaddition	ignominiously	applicatively
orchestration	reforestation	superfetation	illustriously	associativity
ornamentation	refrigeration	superposition	incongruously	attributively
ostreiculture	regimentation	supplantation	inconspicuous	comparatively
oversensitive	regurgitation	supplementary	incredulously	competitively
overvaluation	reincarnation	syllabication	industriously	conjunctively
palletisation	reintegration	symbolisation	injudiciously	consecutively
papillomatous	remonstration	tantalisation	intercellular	consumptively
paramagnetism	remonstrative	teleportation	intercultural	cooperatively
parliamentary	renegotiation	temporalities	interjectural	corporativism
participation	reorientation	temporisation	intracellular	correlatively
participative	republication	terrorisation	intramuscular	correlativity
participatory	resuscitation	testification	intravenously	declaratively
peptonisation	resuscitative	thermosetting	irreligiously	descriptively
perambulation	retranslation	threequarters	isochronously	destructively
perambulatory	retrospection	thurification	magnanimously	destructivity
peregrination	retrospective	tonsillectomy	mellifluously	disjunctively
periodisation	revaccination	transcription	meritoriously	distinctively
perseveration	revendication	transcriptive	mischievously	facultatively
petrification	reverberation	translocation	mistrustfully	imaginatively
pharmaceutics	reverberative	transmutation	monomolecular	implicatively
pharmaceutist	reverberatory	transmutative	mountainously	inattentively
phosphoretted	ritualisation	transpiration	multicellular	ineffectively
photoelectric	Russification	transpiratory	multicoloured	inexpensively
photoelectron	sacrosanctity	transposition	necessitously	informatively
photopositive	sansculottism	triangulation	neurovascular	inoffensively
piezoelectric	scarification	trichromatism	nomenclatural	inquisitively
pluralisation	scintillating	trigonometric	odoriferously	insensitively
pneumogastric	scintillation	tuberculation	opprobriously	insensitivity
pneumonectomy	scleroprotein	uncompetitive	particoloured	instinctively
pococurantism	scorification	unfortunately	perpendicular	instructively
pontification	sedimentation	uninformative	perspicuously	legislatively
postoperative	selenocentric	unsubstantial	pestiferously	lineengraving
prayermeeting	selfadjusting	verbalisation	picturesquely	obstructively
precipitately	selfasserting	verbigeration	piscicultural	penetratively
precipitation	selfassertion	vermiculation	precipitously	perspectively
precipitative	selfassertive	vernalisation	prestigiously	predicatively
preconception	selfdeception	versification	pretentiously	preparatively
predomination	selfdeceptive	victimisation	preternatural	presumptively
prefiguration	selfdefeating	villeggiatura	proliferously	progressively
prefigurative	selfdirecting	visualisation	promiscuously	progressivism
premeditation	selfdirection	vitrification	punctiliously	prohibitively
premeditative	selfeducation	vulcanisation	repetitiously	prospectively
preoccupation	selfexecuting	vulgarisation	reproachfully	qualitatively
preordination	selfforgetful	acrimoniously	resourcefully	radioactivity
pretermitting	selfimportant	adventurously	scrumptiously	restoratively
prevarication	selfinduction	anachronously	sententiously	restrictively
primogenitary	sensitisation	antiscorbutic	sociocultural	retroactively
primogenitive	sequestration	architectural	spontaneously	retroactivity
primogeniture	SerboCroatian	atlantosaurus	stratocumulus	selfapproving
prizefighting	serendipitous	blasphemously	strawcoloured	selfdeceiving
proliferation	serialisation	burglariously	substructural	selfdiscovery
proliferative	shabbygenteel	carnivorously	subternatural	selfreproving
prolification	sharpshooting	ceremoniously	sulphureously	speculatively
pronunciation	shootingstick	compendiously	superfluously	substantively
proparoxytone	shoulderstrap	conspicuously	symphoniously	substantivise
Protestantism	sicklefeather	contentiously	synchronously	superlatively
psychrometric	sidesplitting	contrariously	tautologously	terminatively
pulverisation	signalisation	crosscultural	temerariously	unobtrusively
quadripartite	signification	deleteriously	tempestuously	woodengraving

anticlockwise	metaphosphate	constructable	shockabsorber	numerological
centreforward	misunderstand	constructible	substitutable	ochlocratical
northeastward	mouldingboard	disciplinable	superannuable	odontological
northwestward	multinucleate	discreditable	supersensible	oreographical
partridgewood	noncollegiate	discreditably	tetrasyllable	palynological
southeastward	northeastward	dishonourable	transformable	pantheistical
southwestward	northwestward	dishonourably	transmissible	parenthetical
thenceforward	octocentenary	distributable	transmittable	petrochemical
autocatalysis	organotherapy	dressingtable	transportable	philosophical
autocatalytic	overelaborate	exceptionable	unaccountable	photochemical
bacteriolysis	parliamentary	exceptionably	unaccountably	phrenological
bacteriolytic	phonautograph	generalisable	uncomfortable	physiological
Bloomsburyite	physiotherapy	heptasyllabic	uncomfortably	planimetrical
chromatolytic	picturepalace	immarcescible	unconceivable	postclassical
cryptanalysis	polycarbonate	imperceptible	unconformable	prehistorical
cryptanalytic	precautionary	imperceptibly	unconquerable	problematical
hypnoanalysis	primogenitary	impermissible	unfashionable	psychological
microanalysis	processionary	imperturbable	unfashionably	pyrotechnical
phreatophytic	procrastinate	imperturbably	unforgettable	seismological
pneumatolysis	professoriate	impracticable	unforgettably	selenological
pneumatolytic	prognosticate	impracticably	unimpeachable	semeiological
topsyturvydom	prolegomenary	inappreciable	unmentionable	somatological
crystalgazing	proportionate	inappreciably	unpredictable	speleological
doubleglazing	pseudoarchaic	incombustible	unputdownable	streptococcal
	psychotherapy	inconceivable	unwarrantable	streptococcus
anthropophagi	quadrumvirate	inconceivably	unwarrantably	supercritical
anthropophagy	quadruplicate	incondensable	volatilisable	superphysical
anticoagulant	quincentenary	incontestable	aerodynamical	technological
archdeaconate	quingentenary	incontestably	AngloAmerican	teratological
baccalaureate	quinquagenary	inconvertible	anomalistical	thoroughpaced
bacteriophage	quintuplicate	inconvertibly	apocalyptical	topographical
brachycephaly	reconsolidate	inconvincible	astronautical	toxicological
centreforward	repetitionary	incorruptible	astrophysical	tritheistical
chateaubriand	revolutionary	incorruptibly	atmospherical	troglodytical
chromatograph	scorpiongrass	indefatigable	bathymetrical	typographical
cinematograph	scrapmerchant	indefatigably	bibliological	ungrammatical
circumvallate	searchwarrant	indescribable	cacographical	unsymmetrical
climbingframe	selfimportant	indescribably	Calvinistical	xylographical
compassionate	selfpollinate	indiscernible	chronological	boustrophedon
complementary	selfrepugnant	indiscernibly	conchological	broadmindedly
complimentary	semiporcelain	indispensable	craniological	chuckleheaded
concessionary	sesquiplicate	indispensably	cryptological	clearheadedly
concretionary	shootingbrake	indissociable	deontological	coldbloodedly
confectionary	shoulderblade	inexhaustible	dissymetrical	coldheartedly
confessionary	solidungulate	inexhaustibly	dramaturgical	complicatedly
conventionary	soundingboard	inexpressible	embryological	constrainedly
convertiplane	southeastward	inexpressibly	entomological	disaffectedly
convulsionary	southwestward	insupportable	entomostracan	encyclopaedia
counterattack	spermatoblast	insupportably	Eucharistical	encyclopaedic
decontaminate	stickingplace	insusceptible	extraphysical	exasperatedly
devolutionary	sublieutenant	interpretable	extratropical	featherheaded
differentiate	subversionary	interruptible	gastrological	foreknowledge
disarticulate	superabundant	introversible	gastronomical	foresightedly
discretionary	superdominant	irreclaimable	glaciological	goodnaturedly
dispassionate	supernumerary	irreclaimably	goniometrical	halfheartedly
equiponderant	superordinate	irrecoverable	graphological	hardheartedly
equiponderate	supersaturate	irrecoverably	hemispherical	hyperboloidal
excommunicate	supplementary	irrefrangible	hermeneutical	lightheadedly
expeditionary	televisionary	irreplaceable	hydrometrical	lightmindedly
extraordinary	thalassocracy	irrepressible	hydrostatical	Maginotminded
geostationary	thenceforward	irrepressibly	hypercritical	monocotyledon
immunotherapy	thoroughbrace	irresponsible	hypermetrical	nearsightedly
inappropriate	transitionary	irresponsibly	hyperphysical	openheartedly
incommunicado	transliterate	irretrievable	ideographical	opinionatedly
inconsiderate	undercarriage	irretrievably	immunological	parasiticidal
indeterminacy	underestimate	knowledgeable	inexperienced	photoperiodic
indeterminate	undergraduate	knowledgeably	intelligencer	polycotyledon
infundibulate	administrable	manipulatable	intertropical	primigravidae
insignificant	apprehensible	multiplicable	lackadaisical	prostaglandin
insubordinate	ascertainable	nondeductable	malacological	quickwittedly
integumentary	biodegradable	nonreturnable	malacostracan	righthandedly
interdigitate	challengeable	objectionable	manneristical	selfassuredly
intermarriage	commensurable	objectionably	metallurgical	selfcentredly
interosculate	commensurably	pronounceable	Methodistical	selfknowledge
intransigeant	companionable	recommendable	micrococcocci	selfsurrender
judgeadvocate	companionably	reprehensible	microscopical	seriousminded
kinematograph	concupiscible	reprehensibly	mineralogical	supercalender
lancesergeant	conjecturable	representable	morphological	thoughtreader
mackerelshark	constrainable	semipermeable	musicological	topsyturvydom

unconcernedly	consciousness	feloniousness	judiciousness	polypropylene
underhandedly	consecutively	ferociousness	laboriousness	ponderousness
unqualifiedly	considerately	ferroconcrete	laughableness	powerlessness
worldlyminded	consumptively	foolhardiness	lecherousness	practicalness
wrongheadedly	contentedness	forgetfulness	legislatively	precipitately
abortifacient	cooperatively	fortunateness	leisureliness	predatoriness
accompaniment	correlatively	fractiousness	letterperfect	predicatively
admeasurement	correspondent	frightfulness	lickerishness	preengagement
admirableness	corrosiveness	frivolousness	lightsomeness	prefigurement
adversatively	courteousness	fruitlessness	limitlessness	prematureness
advertisement	credulousness	garrulousness	litigiousness	preordainment
advisableness	customariness	glutinousness	loathsomeness	preparatively
affectionless	dangerousness	gracelessness	lucrativeness	presumptively
affirmatively	dastardliness	grandiloquent	ludicrousness	pricelessness
affreightment	dauntlessness	greensickness	luxuriousness	primitiveness
agreeableness	deathlessness	grotesqueness	magnetosphere	progressively
airworthiness	deceitfulness	guilelessness	maladjustment	prohibitively
alternatively	deceptiveness	guiltlessness	maladroitness	pronouncement
ambiguousness	deciduousness	habitableness	maliciousness	prospectively
ambitiousness	declaratively	haphazardness	malleableness	psychosurgery
amorphousness	defectiveness	hazardousness	masculineness	purposiveness
analogousness	deliciousness	healthfulness	masterfulness	qualitatively
anomalousness	deliriousness	heartlessness	mediterranean	quarrelsomely
anonymousness	descriptively	heartsickness	melodiousness	querulousness
appellatively	desirableness	hilariousness	mercenariness	quinquevalent
applicatively	desperateness	identicalness	mercilessness	rapaciousness
apportionment	destructively	illogicalness	micronutrient	rapturousness
appropriately	desultoriness	imaginatively	millionairess	rearrangement
approximately	determinately	imitativeness	mirthlessness	receptiveness
arbitrariness	dexterousness	immediateness	miscomprehend	recessiveness
ascertainment	diffusiveness	immovableness	miserableness	reconcilement
assertiveness	dimensionless	immutableness	misgovernment	redevelopment
assiduousness	disembodiment	impassiveness	mismanagement	regardfulness
asthenosphere	disengagement	imperfectness	momentariness	regretfulness
atrociousness	disfigurement	imperiousness	momentousness	reimbursement
attentiveness	disinvestment	impetuousness	monstrousness	reinforcement
attributively	disjunctively	implicatively	mountebankery	reinstatement
audaciousness	dismantlement	importunately	navigableness	rejuvenescent
availableness	dismemberment	impulsiveness	nefariousness	religiousness
bamboozlement	disparagement	inanimateness	nervelessness	removableness
barbarousness	disparateness	inattentively	niggardliness	replenishment
barefacedness	dissoluteness	inclusiveness	noiselessness	repulsiveness
basidiomycete	distinctively	incorrectness	nonfulfilment	requisiteness
beauteousness	divertisement	incorruptness	nongovernment	resentfulness
beleaguerment	doubtlessness	incurableness	notoriousness	restoratively
blameableness	dreamlessness	incuriousness	nucleoprotein	restrictively
blamelessness	effectiveness	inductiveness	objectiveness	retentiveness
bloodlessness	egregiousness	ineffableness	obliviousness	retroactively
boundlessness	elaborateness	ineffectively	obnoxiousness	righteousness
bounteousness	electrovalent	inexpensively	obsessiveness	sagaciousness
bountifulness	embarrassment	inflexionless	obstinateness	salaciousness
brainlessness	embellishment	informatively	obstructively	scholarliness
brilliantness	embranglement	ingeniousness	obtrusiveness	scleroprotein
brotherliness	embrittlement	ingenuousness	offensiveness	seaworthiness
bumptiousness	encompassment	injuriousness	offhandedness	secondariness
butterfingers	encouragement	innocuousness	officiousness	secretiveness
capaciousness	enjoyableness	innoxiousness	omnicompetent	sedentariness
changefulness	enlightenment	inoffensively	operativeness	seditiousness
characterless	entertainment	inopportunely	opportuneness	seductiveness
cheerlessness	equivocalness	inquisitively	outspokenness	selectiveness
circumambient	erroneousness	insensateness	overconfident	selfabasement
clandestinely	essentialness	insensitively	overindulgent	selfawareness
cobelligerent	establishment	insidiousness	overstatement	selfconfident
collectedness	evocativeness	insolubleness	painterliness	selfdependent
colourfulness	excessiveness	instinctively	palatableness	selfdiscovery
combativeness	excitableness	instructively	peaceableness	selfindulgent
companionless	exclusiveness	intemperately	pendulousness	semipermanent
comparatively	excursiveness	intensiveness	penetratively	senselessness
competitively	excusableness	interlacement	penuriousness	sensitiveness
complexedness	exemplariness	interpretress	perspectively	separableness
compositeness	expansiveness	intricateness	pervasiveness	shabbygenteel
conceitedness	expensiveness	intrusiveness	pharmacopoeia	Shakespearean
conduciveness	explosiveness	intuitiveness	picturesquely	shamelessness
confectionery	exquisiteness	inventiveness	pigheadedness	shapelessness
confidingness	extensiveness	invidiousness	plaintiveness	shiftlessness
congruousness	facetiousness	inviolateness	plausibleness	sightlessness
conjugateness	facultatively	invisibleness	plenteousness	sleeplessness
conjunctively	faithlessness	irritableness	plentifulness	smokelessness
connectedness	faultlessness	jiggerypokery	pointlessness	snowblindness

sobermindness	candlesnuffer	chronographic	acrylonitrile	catechisation
sorrowfulness	disrespectful	churchmanship	actualisation	cauterisation
speculatively	interspecific	colleagueship	admissibility	ceremonialism
spinelessness	prescientific	collectorship	afforestation	ceremonialist
spinningwheel	selfforgetful	commandership	agglomeration	certification
spiritualness	tablespoonful	companionship	agglomerative	changeability
sprightliness	acquiescingly	conductorship	agglutination	chrematistics
sprocketwheel	admonishingly	containership	agglutinative	Christmastide
squeamishness	aggravatingly	copartnership	agriculturist	Christmastime
stainlessness	astonishingly	craftsmanship	aluminisation	cicatrisation
statelessness	bewilderingly	cryptographer	ambassadorial	cinquecentist
steadfastness	calculatingly	cryptographic	ambidexterity	circumvention
strenuousness	challengingly	distinguished	amplification	clarification
structureless	collieshangie	draftsmanship	anagrammatise	climatologist
subordinately	complainingly	glossographer	anagrammatism	coagulability
substantively	conflictingly	gonadotrophic	anaphrodisiac	collaboration
sumptuousness	counterweight	gonadotrophin	anfractuosity	collaborative
superlatively	cruiserweight	heteromorphic	anglicisation	collaterality
supersubtlety	deprecatingly	heterotrophic	animadversion	colloquialism
talkativeness	devastatingly	homoeomorphic	animalisation	combinatorial
tastelessness	disadvantaged	inspectorship	annexationist	commemoration
teachableness	disparagingly	landownership	answerability	commemorative
technicalness	dispraisingly	lexicographer	Antichristian	commercialise
temperateness	dissemblingly	lexicographic	anticlockwise	commercialism
temporariness	distressingly	librarianship	antihistamine	commercialist
tenaciousness	encouragingly	moderatorship	antinomianism	commiseration
tentativeness	everlastingly	nightmarishly	applicability	commiserative
terminatively	fascinatingly	oceanographer	appropriation	communication
terpsichorean	featherweight	oceanographic	appropriative	communicative
thanklessness	flourishingly	oystercatcher	approximation	communisation
thermonuclear	frighteningly	palaeographer	approximative	communitarian
threequarters	frustratingly	palaeographic	archaeologist	commutability
thrillingness	hundredweight	physiographer	archimandrite	compagination
toastmistress	infuriatingly	physiographic	argumentation	comparability
tolerableness	insinuatingly	polarographic	argumentative	compatibility
toothsomeness	interestingly	precentorship	arithmetician	comprehension
tortoiseshell	languishingly	presidentship	aromatisation	comprehensive
traceableness	megasporangia	principalship	artificiality	concatenation
tractableness	meistersinger	proconsulship	assassination	concentration
transshipment	mistrustingly	professorship	asseveration	concentrative
tremulousness	monophthongal	protectorship	associativity	concentricity
tributariness	outstandingly	pseudomorphic	Assyriologist	conceptualise
troublesomely	overbearingly	schoolteacher	attainability	conceptualism
troublousness	painstakingly	secretaryship	auctioneering	conceptualist
unanimousness	patronisingly	seismographer	Australianism	condescension
uncertainness	penetratingly	seismographic	authorisation	confabulation
uncleanliness	pharmacologic	selenographer	authoritarian	confederation
unearthliness	questioningly	selenographic	authoritative	confederative
unfeelingness	reproachingly	sicklefeather	autochthonism	configuration
unfortunately	scandalmonger	solicitorship	autoeroticism	conflagration
unhealthiness	selfpityingly	sportsmanship	backformation	confraternity
unintelligent	spindlelegged	standoffishly	backpedalling	confrontation
unmeaningness	submachinegun	statesmanship	backwardation	connaturality
unnaturalness	suffocatingly	stereographic	balkanisation	consanguinity
unobtrusively	tantalisingly	stratigraphic	barbarisation	consentaneity
unselfishness	thimblerigged	subeditorship	beatification	consequential
unwholesomely	thimblerigger	suffraganship	beneficiation	conservatoire
unwillingness	threateningly	surrogateship	Berkeleianism	consideration
valuelessness	titillatingly	swordsmanship	bibliolatrist	consolidation
vapourishness	unbelievingly	theriomorphic	bibliophilism	consolidative
venerableness	unflinchingly	treasurership	bibliophilist	constellation
venturesomely	unpromisingly	unestablished	bioenergetics	consternation
venturousness	unrelentingly	zoogeographer	blackguardism	contamination
veraciousness	unremittingly	zoogeographic	bloodcurdling	contaminative
vexatiousness	vacillatingly	absorbability	bloodrelation	contemplation
vicariousness	actinomorphic	acceptability	Bloomsburyite	contemplative
vicepresident	affenpinscher	accessibility	bookingoffice	contortionist
visionariness	allelomorphic	accidentalism	brainstorming	contrabandist
vivaciousness	anthelminthic	acclimatation	breechloading	contraception
voicelessness	associateship	accommodating	brutalisation	contraceptive
voluntariness	backscratcher	accommodation	bureaucratise	contractility
voraciousness	bibliographer	accommodative	butterflyfish	contradiction
vouchsafement	bibliographic	accreditation	cabinetmaking	contrapuntist
wearisomeness	biogeographer	acculturation	calcification	contravention
whimsicalness	cardiographer	acculturative	calligraphist	controversial
wholesomeness	chieftainship	acetification	callisthenics	coreligionist
wonderfulness	chinkerinchee	acetylcholine	campanologist	cornification
worrisomeness	choreographer	achromaticity	caprification	corporativism
worthlessness	choreographic	acidification	carbonisation	correlativity

```
corresponsive   domiciliation   gynaecologist   infallibilist   melodramatics
corrigibility   doubledealing   haematologist   infallibility   melodramatise
corroboration   doubleglazing   hairsplitting   infeasibility   melodramatist
corroborative   dramatisation   halfsovereign   inflexibility   mensurability
corruptionist   dulcification   hallucination   ingurgitation   mercerisation
cosmopolitise   eavesdropping   hallucinative   inhospitality   merchandising
cosmopolitism   ecumenicalism   harmonisation   inquisitorial   mesmerisation
costeffective   egocentricity   heartbreaking   insatiability   metagrobolise
cottonpicking   electrocution   heebiejeebies   insensibility   metallisation
counteraction   electrologist   hermaphrodite   insensitivity   metaphysician
counteractive   electromotive   herpetologist   insociability   metastability
courtsmartial   encapsulation   heterogeneity   instantaneity   meteorologist
criminologist   encyclopedism   histrionicism   insubstantial   metrification
crosshatching   encyclopedist   homeomorphism   intangibility   microorganism
crossquestion   epigrammatise   homoeopathist   intercalation   microtonality
cryobiologist   epigrammatist   homosexuality   intercolonial   millennialism
crystalgazing   equestrianism   horizontality   intercropping   misanthropist
crystallinity   equilibration   horripilation   interlocution   miscegenation
cyberneticist   equipotential   horsewhipping   interoceptive   misconception
decerebration   eschatologist   housebreaking   interpolation   mitochondrion
decomposition   ethnocentrism   hybridisation   interpolative   mnemotechnics
decompression   examinatorial   hydrochloride   interposition   modernisation
decontrolling   excrescential   hydrocracking   interpunction   Mohammedanism
decortication   exhibitionism   hydrodynamics   interrelation   mollification
decrepitation   exhibitionist   hydrogenation   interrogation   Monarchianism
deductibility   expansibility   hydrosulphide   interrogative   moneygrubbing
defeasibility   expectoration   hydrosulphite   interspersion   monometallism
defensibility   explanatorily   hydroxylamine   interstratify   monometallist
defibrination   expostulation   hypertrophied   intraarterial   Monophysitism
deforestation   expressionism   hypnotisation   introgression   monosyllabism
degranulation   expressionist   hypochondriac   introspection   Monotheletism
deipnosophist   expropriation   hypothecation   introspective   monumentalise
dematerialise   expurgatorial   ichthyologist   invariability   mortification
demonstration   extemporarily   immaterialise   investigation   mouthwatering
demonstrative   extensibility   immaterialism   investigative   Muhammadanism
demythologise   extermination   immaterialist   invincibility   mummification
denationalise   exteroceptive   immateriality   inviolability   mutualisation
denticulation   exterritorial   immiscibility   involuntarily   myrmecologist
deodorisation   extrajudicial   impalpability   irrationalise   mystification
dependability   extrapolation   impartibility   irrationalism   naphthylamine
depersonalise   extravasation   impassability   irrationalist   necessitarian
derequisition   falsification   impassibility   irrationality   necessitation
derestriction   fasciculation   impeccability   irreligionist   negligibility
dermatologist   fertilisation   impecuniosity   irreverential   negotiability
desegregation   feudalisation   impenetration   isomerisation   neoclassicism
destructivity   feuilletonism   impersonalise   italicisation   neoclassicist
deterioration   feuilletonist   impersonality   jerrybuilding   neoplasticism
deteriorative   filterability   impersonation   jollification   neurastheniac
determination   flagellantism   implacability   justification   nitrification
determinative   formalisation   impossibility   justificative   nonaggression
deuteragonist   formidability   impressionism   juxtaposition   nonconducting
Deuteronomist   formulisation   impressionist   laevorotation   nonconforming
devolutionist   fortification   improbability   leadpoisoning   nonconformism
diageotropism   fortississimo   impropriation   legislatorial   nonconformist
diagnostician   fossilisation   improvability   lepidopterist   nonconformity
diagrammatise   fractionalise   improvisation   levelcrossing   nonfigurative
digestibility   fractionation   incarceration   liberationist   nonforfeiting
discoloration   fragmentarily   incardination   lignification   nonproductive
disconcerting   fragmentation   inconsecutive   lineengraving   normalisation
disconnection   freeselection   incorporation   longsuffering   nullification
disconformity   frequentation   incorporative   Machiavellian   occasionalism
disconnection   frequentative   incredibility   machicolation   occasionalist
discontinuity   funambulation   indeterminism   magnetisation   occasionality
displantation   functionalism   indeterminist   magnetomotive   occidentalise
disposability   functionalist   indisposition   magnification   Occidentalism
dispossession   galvanisation   indistinctive   maladaptation   Occidentalist
disproportion   gastrocnemius   individualise   malariologist   oleomargarine
dissemination   generalissimo   individualism   Malthusianism   oppositionist
disseminative   gentlemanlike   individualist   manageability   orchestration
disseveration   geocentricism   individuality   Manichaeanism   ornamentation
dissimilarity   germanisation   individuation   manifestation   ornithologist
dissimilation   gerontologist   industrialise   manifestative   orthognathism
dissimulation   gesticulation   industrialism   martyrisation   overemphasise
dissolubility   gesticulative   industrialist   martyrologist   overqualified
doctrinairism   glamorisation   ineducability   materfamilias   oversensitive
documentalist   globetrotting   ineligibility   mathematician   oversubscribe
documentation   glorification   inevitability   matriculation   overvaluation
dodecaphonist   gratification   inexorability   mechanisation   owneroccupier
domestication   gubernatorial   infallibilism   mediatisation   paediatrician
```

paedomorphism	PreRaphaelite	resolvability	serialisation	transcriptive
palletisation	pretermission	resuscitation	sericulturist	transgression
pantagruelian	pretermitting	resuscitative	sewingmachine	transgressive
pantagruelism	prevarication	retranslation	Shakespearian	transistorise
pantagruelist	primogenitive	retroactivity	sharecropping	translocation
paramagnetism	primordiality	retrogression	sharpshooting	translucidity
paranormality	prizefighting	retrogressive	sheepshearing	transmutation
participation	processionist	retrospection	shootingstick	transmutative
participative	procuratorial	retrospective	sidesplitting	transpiration
particularise	profitability	revaccination	signalisation	transposition
particularism	profitsharing	revelationist	signification	transshipping
particularist	progenitorial	revendication	significative	triangularity
particularity	progressivism	reverberation	skateboarding	triangulation
paterfamilias	projectionist	reverberative	socialisation	tricentennial
pathogenicity	proliferation	reversibility	softpedalling	trichromatism
pedestrianise	proliferative	revolutionise	solemnisation	triliteralism
pedestrianism	prolification	revolutionism	soulsearching	trustworthily
penetrability	pronunciation	revolutionist	sovietologist	tuberculation
Pennsylvanian	proprietorial	rhadamanthine	specification	unaccompanied
pennyfarthing	protectionism	rhodochrosite	spelaeologist	uncompetitive
pennypinching	protectionist	ritualisation	Spencerianism	uncomplaining
peptonisation	Protestantism	rudimentarily	spheroidicity	underclothing
perambulation	protonotarial	Russification	sportsmanlike	understanding
percussionist	provincialise	sabrerattling	squarebashing	underwhelming
perdurability	provincialism	sacerdotalise	squeezability	unfamiliarity
peregrination	provincialist	sacerdotalism	stabilisation	unforthcoming
perfectionism	provinciality	sacerdotalist	statesmanlike	unicameralism
perfectionist	prudentialism	sacrosanctity	stereoscopist	unicameralist
perfunctorily	prudentialist	sadomasochism	sterilisation	uninformative
perichondrial	prudentiality	sadomasochist	stomatologist	unnecessarily
perichondrium	psychometrics	sanitationist	strangulation	unquestioning
periodisation	psychometrist	sansculottism	streetwalking	unsociability
perishability	psychophysics	scarification	structuralism	unsubstantial
permutability	pteridologist	scholasticism	structuralist	unsuitability
perseveration	pulverisation	scientologist	subirrigation	vegetarianism
petrification	pusillanimity	scintillating	subordination	venereologist
phalansterian	pyrimethamine	scintillation	subordinative	ventriloquial
pharmaceutics	quadripartite	scolopendrium	subsaturation	ventriloquise
pharmaceutist	quadruplicity	scorification	subsequential	ventriloquism
phenomenalise	qualification	scripturalism	substantivise	ventriloquist
phenomenalism	questionnaire	scripturalist	subtilisation	verbalisation
phenomenalist	Quinquagesima	secretarybird	suffumigation	verbigeration
phenylalanine	radioactivity	sedimentation	summarisation	verifiability
philhellenism	radiolocation	selfadjusting	superaddition	vermiculation
philhellenist	randomisation	selfapproving	superfamilies	vernacularise
photochromics	ratiocination	selfasserting	superfetation	vernacularism
photochromism	ratiocinative	selfassertion	superfluidity	vernacularity
photoemission	reaffirmation	selfassertive	superhumanity	vernalisation
photoemissive	receptibility	selfcommunion	superposition	versification
photopositive	reciprocality	selfconsuming	supplantation	victimisation
phraseologist	reciprocation	selfcriticism	swashbuckling	viniculturist
physiognomist	reciprocative	selfdeceiving	Swedenborgian	violoncellist
platitudinise	recombination	selfdeception	syllabication	visualisation
pluralisation	recomposition	selfdeceptive	symbolisation	viticulturist
pococurantism	recrimination	selfdefeating	tantalisation	vitrification
polyhistorian	recriminative	selfdirecting	taperecording	vocationalism
ponderability	recrystallise	selfdirection	teleportation	volcanologist
pontification	rectification	selfdispraise	telerecording	vulcanisation
postcommunion	redescription	selfeducation	temporalities	vulcanologist
postoperative	reduplication	selfexecuting	temporisation	vulgarisation
prayermeeting	reduplicative	selffertility	tercentennial	vulnerability
precipitation	reembarkation	selfgoverning	terminability	waterproofing
precipitative	reexamination	selfinduction	terrorisation	winterberries
preconception	reflexibility	selfrecording	testification	wonderworking
predicability	reforestation	selfregarding	thaumaturgist	woodengraving
predomination	reformability	selfreproving	theanthropism	woolgathering
preferability	refrigeration	selfrestraint	theatricalise	xanthochroism
prefiguration	regimentation	selfrevealing	theatricalism	Zarathustrian
prefigurative	regurgitation	selfsacrifice	theatricality	sergeantmajor
preliminarily	reincarnation	selfsatisfied	thermochemist	clothesbasket
premeditation	reintegration	selfsterility	thermosetting	knickerbocker
premeditative	remonstration	selfsufficing	thermotropism	leatherjacket
premillennial	remonstrative	semibarbarian	thigmotropism	panicstricken
premonitorily	renegotiation	semibarbarism	thoroughgoing	strikebreaker
preoccupation	reorientation	sensitisation	thurification	abiologically
preordination	republicanise	separationist	timeconsuming	acrobatically
preparatorily	republicanism	sequentiality	tonguelashing	adiabatically
prepossessing	republication	sequestration	Tractarianism	aesthetically
prepossession	resistibility	SerboCroatian	transcription	agonistically

alcoholically	interdentally	stigmatically	disappearance	septentrional
algebraically	intracellular	strategically	dysfunctional	shootingrange
allegorically	intramuscular	stratocumulus	effervescence	somniloquence
anaerobically	intrinsically	stylistically	effervescency	spermatogenic
AngloCatholic	inventorially	substantially	efflorescence	spindleshanks
apathetically	isometrically	superficially	electromagnet	squandermania
arthritically	isostatically	swallowtailed	epiphenomenal	supereminence
asthmatically	judgmatically	symbiotically	epiphenomenon	supernational
atheistically	kinematically	symmetrically	examinational	supervenience
atomistically	leptocephalic	symphonically	explorational	suppositional
authentically	lethargically	syntactically	forementioned	supranational
automatically	liebfraumilch	synthetically	fullfashioned	terminational
autonomically	macaronically	taxonomically	gravitational	tiddledywinks
axiomatically	macrocephalic	telencephalon	horsechestnut	transcendence
betweenwhiles	magisterially	terrestrially	impercipience	transcendency
bombastically	matrilineally	territorially	incandescence	translational
categorically	mesencephalon	theologically	inconsequence	transnational
centrifugally	metonymically	theoretically	inconsistence	unconditional
centripetally	microcephalic	thrasonically	inconsistency	unconditioned
chromatically	millefeuilles	tintinnabular	inconvenience	unconstrained
cinematically	ministerially	tintinnabulum	inconveniency	undisciplined
climactically	mistrustfully	topologically	inflorescence	unenlightened
conditionally	monomolecular	traditionally	informational	unexceptional
conjecturally	multicellular	transversally	inquisitional	unimpassioned
continentally	mutagenically	traumatically	inscriptional	unintentional
contractually	neurovascular	turkeygobbler	inspirational	vivisectional
cylindrically	nonsensically	typologically	institutional	accidentprone
deferentially	nostalgically	unemotionally	instructional	acotyledonous
dendritically	nutritionally	unequivocally	insufficience	adventuresome
detrimentally	oecologically	viceadmiralty	insufficiency	aluminiferous
dialectically	ontogenically	wheelerdealer	intercolumnar	ambidexterous
diametrically	ontologically	aircraftwoman	intercurrence	angiospermous
dictatorially	orthocephalic	bildungsroman	intermittence	argentiferous
dimensionally	outgeneralled	businesswoman	international	autocephalous
disgracefully	panegyrically	chrysanthemum	interpersonal	autochthonous
distastefully	parabolically	congresswoman	intransigence	balsamiferous
distressfully	paradoxically	galactosaemia	intrapersonal	bibliolatrous
distrustfully	paraphernalia	homoiothermal	jurisprudence	biotechnology
draggletailed	parasitically	homoiothermic	lamellibranch	brachypterous
eccentrically	patriotically	hypoglycaemia	machinegunner	camphoraceous
educationally	pedagogically	infinitesimal	magniloquence	carboniferous
energetically	penitentially	nightwatchman	multinational	carcinomatous
enigmatically	perpendicular	paddlesteamer	nemathelminth	cartilaginous
evangelically	pharisaically	psychodynamic	nonappearance	certificatory
exceptionally	phrenetically	quadragesimal	nonattendance	chlamydospore
existentially	plethorically	socioeconomic	noncompliance	chromatophore
exponentially	pneumatically	thermodynamic	nonresistance	cleistogamous
extensionally	pragmatically	abstractional	observational	commemoratory
extracellular	prefatorially	accoutrements	opisthobranch	communicatory
extravascular	prejudicially	aggiornamento	overabundance	condylomatous
extrinsically	prismatically	anthropogenic	paperhangings	confabulatory
fantastically	probationally	antipersonnel	pathognomonic	conscientious
Fascistically	prophetically	arbitrational	platyhelminth	consentaneous
fibrovascular	provisionally	archidiaconal	pluripresence	consolidatory
floristically	puritanically	architectonic	postulational	constellatory
fortuneteller	quadrennially	BaltoSlavonic	preponderance	contrabassoon
fundamentally	quincuncially	birefringence	preponderancy	contradictory
geometrically	realistically	cerebrospinal	prepositional	conversazione
geotropically	referentially	chlamydomonas	prepreference	conversazioni
grammatically	reproachfully	circumference	progressional	corroboratory
gymnastically	resourcefully	circumfluence	propositional	counterstroke
heterothallic	reverentially	clairaudience	pseudoscience	diathermanous
honorifically	rhapsodically	coarsegrained	psychasthenia	dichlamydeous
hydraulically	rheumatically	coeducational	quadrillionth	discommodious
hydrocephalic	sacramentally	compositional	quintillionth	discontinuous
hydrocephalus	sacrificially	compressional	rattlebrained	disharmonious
ideologically	sarcastically	computational	recalcitrance	emphysematous
idiomatically	schematically	concupiscence	recrudescence	endocrinology
impolitically	scorbutically	congressional	reformational	entomophagous
imponderables	selfpropelled	conjugational	RhaetoRomanic	entomophilous
impractically	sensationally	conjunctional	schizophrenia	exanthematous
incorporeally	sentimentally	consenescence	schizophrenic	expostulatory
incrementally	serologically	convalescence	selfassurance	exterminatory
ineffectually	smellingsalts	convocational	selfcondemned	felicitations
inferentially	sniftingvalve	counterchange	selfcontained	fossiliferous
influentially	sophistically	defervescence	selfexistence	garnetiferous
inorganically	spasmodically	deformational	selfinsurance	gasteropodous
intentionally	splenetically	deliquescence	selfopinioned	geochronology
intercellular	statistically	disaffirmance	selfsustained	geomorphology

gesticulatory	selfrighteous	lancecorporal	epeirogenesis	treacherously
graminivorous	semiconscious	lightfingered	expeditiously	unambiguously
gymnospermous	serendipitous	meadowsaffron	fissiparously	uncircumcised
hallucinatory	spermatophore	monosymmetric	flirtatiously	unconsciously
helminthology	splendiferous	multicoloured	frontogenesis	underemphasis
hemicellulose	staminiferous	nephelometric	gametogenesis	unrighteously
heterogeneous	steppingstone	nitrobacteria	helminthiasis	vertiginously
heteropterous	stercoraceous	nomenclatural	heterogenesis	accelerometer
heterosporous	sternforemost	northeasterly	hocuspocussed	acquiescently
hydromedusoid	stoloniferous	northwesterly	homogeneously	actinomycetes
hymenopterous	subreptitious	parallelogram	hypnoanalysis	administrator
improvisatory	subterraneous	parthenocarpy	ignominiously	alcoholometer
inconspicuous	superstitious	particoloured	illustriously	alcoholometry
incriminatory	surreptitious	passementerie	incongruously	anachronistic
inefficacious	tachistoscope	photoelectric	incredulously	anthropometry
insectivorous	thereinbefore	photoelectron	industriously	anthropopathy
instantaneous	thermophilous	phycoerythrin	injudiciously	anticlimactic
interlocutory	thremmatology	piezoelectric	intravenously	antilogarithm
interrogatory	tonsillectomy	pigeonlivered	irreligiously	antiscorbutic
investigatory	transpiratory	piscicultural	isochronously	authenticator
justificatory	umbelliferous	pneumogastric	laissezpasser	autocatalytic
laevorotatory	unceremonious	preengineered	leishmaniasis	bacteriolytic
laughingstock	unpretentious	preternatural	leptospirosis	barrelchested
lepidopterous	zygodactylous	protohistoric	linseywoolsey	belligerently
mammaliferous	anthroposophy	psychrometric	magnanimously	brokenhearted
manganiferous	apheliotropic	quadrilateral	mellifluously	canaliculated
megacephalous	autobiography	quicktempered	meritoriously	candlelighter
membranaceous	chalcoography	radiotelegram	metamorphoses	cannibalistic
metalliferous	corticotropic	rectangularly	metamorphosis	chemoreceptor
microphyllous	corticotropin	rectilinearly	microanalysis	chromatolytic
miscellaneous	electroscopic	roentgenogram	mischievously	circumspectly
misunderstood	hypermetropia	selenocentric	mononucleosis	compartmental
monodactylous	hypermetropic	shorttempered	morphogenesis	complaisantly
monotrematous	ichthyography	shoulderstrap	mountainously	concertmaster
mourningcloak	kaleidoscopic	smoothingiron	necessitously	concomitantly
multitudinous	laryngoscopic	sociocultural	odontoglossum	conglomeratic
nectariferous	metallography	solderingiron	odoriferously	congratulator
neighbourhood	mourningpaper	southeasterly	opprobriously	contrafagotto
nickeliferous	philanthropic	southwesterly	orangeblossom	counterfeiter
numismatology	prosopography	spectacularly	organogenesis	criminalistic
ophthalmology	psilanthropic	spectrometric	parasynthesis	cryptanalytic
orthognathous	spectrography	stalkinghorse	perspicuously	cytochemistry
overcredulous	spectroscopic	stratospheric	pestiferously	deterministic
ovoviviparous	sphygmography	strawcoloured	philosophiser	developmental
palaeontology	understrapper	substructural	pneumatolysis	diaphragmatic
palaeozoology	windowshopper	subternatural	polysynthesis	discriminator
papaveraceous	zinjanthropus	threecornered	precipitously	disintegrator
papillomatous	sculpturesque	trigonometric	prestigiously	disinterested
participatory	archaeopteryx	tyrannosaurus	pretentiously	disobediently
partridgewood	archbishopric	verisimilarly	proliferously	doublejointed
perambulatory	architectural	versicoloured	promiscuously	electrostatic
perspicacious	atlantosaurus	acrimoniously	psychogenesis	environmental
petroliferous	belleslettres	actinomycosis	psychokinesis	equidistantly
phanerogamous	bloodboltered	adventurously	punctiliously	extragalactic
phenomenology	broadspectrum	amniocentesis	purposelessly	extravagantly
phyllophagous	cephalothorax	anachronously	remorselessly	featherstitch
platiniferous	chromospheric	autocatalysis	repetitiously	ferrimagnetic
platitudinous	countercharge	bacteriolysis	salmonellosis	ferromagnetic
plenitudinous	crackerbarrel	battlecruiser	schizogenesis	festschriften
pneumatophore	crosscultural	blasphemously	scrumptiously	fortunehunter
pneumonectomy	crossgartered	blastogenesis	selfaddressed	gerontocratic
polliniferous	curvilinearly	bouillabaisse	selfconfessed	granddaughter
polyadelphous	electioneerer	burglariously	selfpossessed	gynaecocratic
polydactylous	electrometric	carnivorously	semicivilised	harbourmaster
porcellaneous	electrophorus	ceremoniously	sententiously	helterskelter
prolegomenous	encephalogram	coenaesthesis	spontaneously	hemiparasitic
proparoxytone	ferroelectric	compendiously	steeplechaser	heterogenetic
proteinaceous	floricultural	conspicuously	sulphureously	hollowhearted
pusillanimous	foraminiferal	contentiously	superfluously	idiosyncratic
qualificatory	gastroenteric	contrariously	symphoniously	imperialistic
quartziferous	grandfatherly	crosspurposes	synchronously	impertinently
rearcommodore	grandmotherly	cryptanalysis	tautologously	improvidently
recriminatory	gynandromorph	defencelessly	temerariously	inadvertently
reverberatory	horticultural	deleteriously	tempestuously	incompetently
roentgenology	hydroelectric	dichotomously	tendentiously	incontinently
rontgenoscopy	ichthyosaurus	doublecrosser	thermogenesis	independently
sanctimonious	intercultural	efficaciously	thoughtlessly	indifferently
schizocarpous	interjectural	elephantiasis	toxoplasmosis	indoctrinator
selfconscious	interlocutrix	embryogenesis	tranquilliser	inefficiently

inexpediently
intelligently
intergalactic
intermediator
interparietal
interpellator
kapellmeister
Kidderminster
knuckleduster
magnificently
maladminister
materialistic
microdetector
monochromatic
monogrammatic
morphogenetic
mothercountry
nationalistic
objectivistic
onomatopoetic
opportunistic
osteomyelitis
overpopulated
pantisocratic
parasynthetic
paternalistic
perissodactyl
phosphoretted
photoreceptor
phreatophytic
phytoplankton
pigeonchested
pigeonhearted
pneumatolytic
pneumatometer
pointillistic
poliomyelitis
polychromatic
polysynthetic
potentiometer
prairieoyster
precipitantly
predestinator
predicamental
predominantly
proprioceptor
prosthodontia
protuberantly
psychogenetic
psychokinetic
psychosomatic
pyrheliometer
quadricipital
quartermaster
rationalistic
reconstructor
refractometer
reinvigorator
reminiscently
remonstrantly
resplendently
rollercoaster
runningstitch
saccharimeter
saccharimetry
saccharometer
selfappointed
selfcollected
selfconceited
selfcontented
selfconvicted
selfevidented
selfgenerated
selfinflicted
selfslaughter
selfsupported
selftormentor
semiautomatic
semiconductor

semilogarithm
semiparasitic
significantly
singlehearted
slangingmatch
somnambulator
sophisticated
stationmaster
stoichiometry
subcontractor
subpostmaster
subserviently
synallagmatic
synchronistic
telegrammatic
temperamental
tenderhearted
tonguetwister
thermoplastic
transatlantic
translucently
transmigrator
transparently
unadulterated
unanticipated
unarticulated
uncomplicated
uncoordinated
undereducated
uninterrupted
unprecedented
untrustworthy
volumenometer
voluntaristic
weatherbeaten
wellapPointed
arboriculture
boardinghouse
buttonthrough
clearinghouse
closedcircuit
countinghouse
dissimilitude
doubletongued
followthrough
macromolecule
nitrocompound
ostreiculture
primogeniture
schadenfreude
silvertongued
spinninghouse
stirpiculture
thunderstruck
underexposure
vantageground
villeggiatura
concavoconvex
convexoconvex
dressimprover
lifepreserver
underachiever
whithersoever
blanketflower
passionflower
thundershower
amphiprostyle
brachydactyly
daguerreotype
psychoanalyse
spermatophyte
underemployed
eschscholtzia
mangoldwurzel
—————————
abstractional
aerodynamical

aircraftwoman
ambassadorial
anaphrodisiac
AngloAmerican
anomalistical
Antichristian
apocalyptical
arbitrational
archidiaconal
architectural
arithmetician
astronautical
astrophysical
atmospherical
authoritarian
bathymetrical
bibliological
bildungsroman
businesswoman
cacographical
Calvinistical
cephalothorax
cerebrospinal
chlamydomonas
chronological
coeducational
combinatorial
communitarian
compartmental
compositional
compressional
computational
conchological
congressional
congresswoman
conjugational
conjunctional
consequential
controversial
convocational
courtsmartial
craniological
crosscultural
cryptological
deformational
deontological
developmental
diagnostician
dissymetrical
dramaturgical
dysfunctional
embryological
encephalogram
entomological
entomostracan
environmental
epiphenomenal
equipotential
Eucharistical
examinational
examinatorial
excrescential
explorational
expurgatorial
exterritorial
extracellular
extrajudicial
extraphysical
extratropical
extravascular
fibrovascular
floricultural
foraminiferal
gastrological
gastronomical
glaciological
goniometrical
graphological
gravitational

gubernatorial
hemispherical
hermeneutical
homoiothermal
horticultural
hydrometrical
hydrostatical
hyperboloidal
hypercritical
hypermetrical
hyperphysical
hypochondriac
ideographical
immunological
infinitesimal
informational
inquisitional
inquisitorial
inscriptional
inspirational
institutional
instructional
insubstantial
intercellular
intercolonial
intercolumnar
intercultural
interjectural
international
interparietal
interpersonal
intertropical
intraarterial
intracellular
intramuscular
intrapersonal
irreverential
lackadaisical
lancecorporal
legislatorial
Machiavellian
malacological
malacostracan
manneristical
materfamilias
mathematician
mediterranean
metallurgical
metaphysician
Methodistical
microscopical
mineralogical
monomolecular
monophthongal
morphological
mourningcloak
multicellular
multinational
musicological
necessitarian
neurastheniac
neurovascular
nightwatchman
nomenclatural
numerological
observational
ochlocratical
odontological
oreographical
paediatrician
palynological
pantagruelian
pantheistical
parallelogram
parasiticidal
parenthetical
paterfamilias
Pennsylvanian
perichondrial

perpendicular
petrochemical
phalansterian
philosophical
photochemical
phrenological
physiological
piscicultural
planimetrical
polyhistorian
postclassical
postulational
predicamental
prehistorical
premillennial
prepositional
preternatural
primigravidae
problematical
procuratorial
progenitorial
progressional
propositional
proprietorial
protonotarial
psychological
pyrotechnical
quadragesimal
quadricipital
quadrilateral
radiotelegram
reformational
roentgenogram
seismological
selenological
semeiological
semibarbarian
septentrional
SerboCroatian
Shakespearean
Shakespearian
shoulderstrap
sociocultural
somatological
speleological
streptococcal
subsequential
substructural
subternatural
supercritical
supernational
superphysical
suppositional
supranational
Swedenborgian
technological
temperamental
teratological
tercentennial
terminational
terpsichorean
thermonuclear
tintinnabular
topographical
toxicological
translational
transnational
tricentennial
tritheistical
troglodytical
typographical
unconditional
unexceptional
ungrammatical
unintentional
unsubstantial
unsymmetrical
ventriloquial
vivisectional

xylographical	transcendence	Maginotminded	swallowtailed	prosopography
Zarathustrian	transcendency	maladminister	temporalities	semilogarithm
oversubscribe	Christmastide	mangoldwurzel	tenderhearted	spectrography
bioenergetics	dissimilitude	meistersinger	thimblerigged	sphygmography
birefringence	hydrochloride	metamorphoses	thimblerigger	untrustworthy
bookingoffice	hydrosulphide	millefeuilles	thoroughpaced	actinomorphic
callisthenics	incommunicado	mourningpaper	thoughtreader	actinomycosis
chrematistics	schadenfreude	multicoloured	threecornered	allelomorphic
circumference	shoulderblade	oceanographer	thundershower	amniocentesis
circumfluence	accelerometer	outgeneralled	tonguetwister	anachronistic
clairaudience	actinomycetes	overpopulated	tranquilliser	AngloCatholic
concupiscence	affenpinscher	overqualified	turkeygobbler	anthelminthic
consenescence	alcoholometer	owneroccupier	unaccompanied	anthropogenic
convalescence	antipersonnel	oystercatcher	unadulterated	anticlimactic
counterattack	backscratcher	paddlesteamer	unanticipated	antiscorbutic
defervescence	barrelchested	palaeographer	unarticulated	apheliotropic
deliquescence	battlecruiser	panicstricken	uncircumcised	archbishopric
disaffirmance	belleslettres	particoloured	uncomplicated	architectonic
disappearance	betweenwhiles	passionflower	unconditioned	associateship
effervescence	bibliographer	philosophiser	unconstrained	autocatalysis
effervescency	biogeographer	phosphoretted	uncoordinated	autocatalytic
efflorescence	blanketflower	physiographer	underachiever	bacteriolysis
featherstitch	bloodboltered	pigeonchested	undereducated	bacteriolytic
hydrodynamics	brokenhearted	pigeonhearted	underemployed	BaltoSlavonic
impercipience	canaliculated	pigeonlivered	understrapper	bibliographic
incandescence	candlelighter	pneumatometer	undisciplined	blastogenesis
inconsequence	candlesnuffer	potentiometer	unenlightened	cannibalistic
inconsistence	cardiographer	prairieoyster	unestablished	chieftainship
inconsistency	chinkerinchee	preengineered	unimpassioned	choreographic
inconvenience	choreographer	pyrheliometer	uninterrupted	chromatolytic
inconveniency	chuckleheaded	quartermaster	unprecedented	chromospheric
indeterminacy	clothesbasket	quicktempered	versicoloured	chronographic
inflorescence	coarsegrained	rattlebrained	volumenometer	churchmanship
insufficience	concavoconvex	refractometer	weatherbeaten	closedcircuit
insufficiency	concertmaster	rollercoaster	wellapPointed	coenaesthesis
intercurrence	convexoconvex	saccharimeter	wheelerdealer	colleagueship
intermittence	counterfeiter	saccharometer	whithersoever	collectorship
intransigence	crackerbarrel	scandalmonger	windowshopper	collieshangie
jurisprudence	crossgartered	schoolteacher	winterberries	commandership
lamellibranch	crosspurposes	seismographer	worldlyminded	companionship
laughingstock	cryptographer	selenographer	zoogeographer	conductorship
letterperfect	disadvantaged	selfaddressed	interstratify	conglomeratic
liebfraumilch	disinterested	selfappointed	anthropophagi	containership
magniloquence	distinguished	selfcollected	anthropophagy	copartnership
melodramatics	doublecrosser	selfconceited	bacteriophage	corticotropic
micrococcocci	doublejointed	selfcondemned	biotechnology	corticotropin
mnemotechnics	doubletongued	selfconfessed	buttonthrough	craftsmanship
nonappearance	draggletailed	selfcontained	counterchange	criminalistic
nonattendance	dressimprover	selfcontented	countercharge	cryptanalysis
noncompliance	electioneerer	selfconvicted	endocrinology	cryptanalytic
nonresistance	electromagnet	selfgenerated	followthrough	cryptographic
opisthobranch	featherheaded	selfinflicted	foreknowledge	deterministic
overabundance	festschriften	selfopinioned	geochronology	diaphragmatic
pharmaceutics	forementioned	selfpossessed	geomorphology	draftsmanship
photochromics	fortunehunter	selfpropelled	halfsovereign	electrometric
picturepalace	fortuneteller	selfsatisfied	helminthology	electroscopic
pluripresence	fullfashioned	selfslaughter	intermarriage	electrostatic
preponderance	glossographer	selfsupported	numismatology	elephantiasis
preponderancy	granddaughter	selfsurrender	ophthalmology	embryogenesis
prepreference	harbourmaster	selfsustained	palaeontology	encyclopaedia
pseudoscience	heebiejeebies	semicivilised	palaeozoology	encyclopaedic
psychometrics	helterskelter	seriousminded	paperhangings	epeirogenesis
psychophysics	hocuspocussed	shabbygenteel	phenomenology	eschscholtzia
recalcitrance	hollowhearted	shockabsorber	roentgenology	extragalactic
recrudescence	hypertrophied	shorttempered	selfknowledge	ferrimagnetic
runningstitch	imponderables	sicklefeather	shootingrange	ferroelectric
selfassurance	inexperienced	silvertongued	thrematology	ferromagnetic
selfexistence	intelligencer	singlehearted	undercarriage	frontogenesis
selfinsurance	kapellmeister	sophisticated	anthropopathy	galactosaemia
selfsacrifice	Kidderminster	spindlelegged	anthroposophy	gametogenesis
shootingstick	knickerbocker	spinningwheel	antilogarithm	gastroenteric
slangingmatch	knuckleduster	sprocketwheel	autobiography	gerontocratic
somniloquence	laissezpasser	stationmaster	chalcoography	gonadotrophic
stickingplace	leatherjacket	steeplechaser	counterweight	gonadotrophin
supereminence	lexicographer	strawcoloured	cruiserweight	gynaecocratic
supervenience	lifepreserver	strikebreaker	featherweight	helminthiasis
thalassocracy	lightfingered	subpostmaster	hundredweight	hemiparasitic
thoroughbrace	linseywoolsey	supercalender	ichthyography	heptasyllabic
thunderstruck	machinegunner	superfamilies	metallography	heterogenesis

heterogenetic	presidentship	adversatively	contentiously	geotropically
heteromorphic	principalship	aesthetically	continentally	goodnaturedly
heterothallic	proconsulship	affirmatively	contractually	grammatically
heterotrophic	professorship	aggravatingly	contrariously	grandfatherly
homoeomorphic	prostaglandin	agonistically	cooperatively	grandmotherly
homoiothermic	prosthodontia	alcoholically	correlatively	gymnastically
hydrocephalic	protectorship	algebraically	curvilinearly	halfheartedly
hydroelectric	protohistoric	allegorically	cylindrically	hardheartedly
hydromedusoid	pseudoarchaic	alternatively	declaratively	homogeneously
hypermetropia	pseudomorphic	amphiprostyle	defencelessly	honorifically
hypermetropic	psilanthropic	anachronously	deferentially	hydraulically
hypnoanalysis	psychasthenia	anaerobically	deleteriously	ideologically
hypoglycaemia	psychodynamic	apathetically	dendritically	idiomatically
idiosyncratic	psychogenesis	appellatively	deprecatingly	ignominiously
imperialistic	psychogenetic	applicatively	descriptively	illustriously
inspectorship	psychokinesis	apprehensible	destructively	imaginatively
intergalactic	psychokinetic	appropriately	determinately	immarcescible
interlocutrix	psychosomatic	approximately	detrimentally	imperceptible
interspecific	psychrometric	arthritically	devastatingly	imperceptibly
kaleidoscopic	rationalistic	ascertainable	dialectically	impermissible
landownership	RhaetoRomanic	asthmatically	diametrically	impertinently
laryngoscopic	salmonellosis	astonishingly	dichotomously	imperturbable
leishmaniasis	schizogenesis	atheistically	dictatorially	imperturbably
leptocephalic	schizophrenia	atomistically	dimensionally	implicatively
leptospirosis	schizophrenic	attributively	disaffectedly	impolitically
lexicographic	scleroprotein	authentically	disciplinable	importunately
librarianship	secretaryship	automatically	discreditable	impracticable
macrocephalic	seismographic	autonomically	discreditably	impracticably
materialistic	selenocentric	axiomatically	disgracefully	impractically
megasporangia	selenographic	belligerently	dishonourable	improvidently
metamorphosis	semiautomatic	bewilderingly	dishonourably	inadvertently
microanalysis	semiparasitic	biodegradable	disjunctively	inappreciable
microcephalic	semiporcelain	blasphemously	disobediently	inappreciably
moderatorship	socioeconomic	bombastically	disparagingly	inattentively
monochromatic	solicitorship	brachycephaly	dispraisingly	incombustible
monogrammatic	spectrometric	brachydactyly	dissemblingly	incompetently
mononucleosis	spectroscopic	broadmindedly	distastefully	inconceivable
monosymmetric	spermatogenic	burglariously	distinctively	inconceivably
morphogenesis	sportsmanship	calculatingly	distressfully	incondensable
morphogenetic	squandermania	carnivorously	distressingly	incongruously
nationalistic	statesmanship	categorically	distributable	incontestable
nephelometric	stereographic	centrifugally	distrustfully	incontestably
nitrobacteria	stratigraphic	centripetally	dressingtable	incontinently
nucleoprotein	stratospheric	ceremoniously	eccentrically	inconvertible
objectivistic	subeditorship	challengeable	educationally	inconvertibly
oceanographic	suffraganship	challengingly	efficaciously	inconvincible
onomatopoetic	surrogateship	chromatically	encouragingly	incorporeally
opportunistic	swordsmanship	cinematically	energetically	incorruptible
organogenesis	synallagmatic	circumspectly	enigmatically	incorruptibly
orthocephalic	synchronistic	clandestinely	equidistantly	incredulously
osteomyelitis	telegrammatic	clearheadedly	evangelically	incrementally
palaeographic	theriomorphic	climactically	everlastingly	indefatigable
pantisocratic	thermodynamic	coldbloodedly	exasperatedly	indefatigably
paraphernalia	thermogenesis	coldheartedly	exceptionable	independently
parasynthesis	thermoplastic	commensurable	exceptionably	indescribable
parasynthetic	toxoplasmosis	commensurably	exceptionally	indescribably
passementerie	transatlantic	companionable	existentially	indifferently
paternalistic	treasurership	companionably	expeditiously	indiscernible
pathognomonic	trigonometric	comparatively	explanatorily	indiscernibly
pharmacologic	underemphasis	compendiously	exponentially	indispensable
pharmacopoeia	voluntaristic	competitively	extemporarily	indispensably
philanthropic	zoogeographic	complainingly	extensionally	indissociable
photoelectric	counterstroke	complaisantly	extravagantly	industriously
photoperiodic	gentlemanlike	complicatedly	extrinsically	ineffectively
phreatophytic	shootingbrake	concomitantly	facultatively	ineffectually
phycoerythrin	spindleshanks	concupiscible	fantastically	inefficiently
physiographic	sportsmanlike	conditionally	fascinatingly	inexhaustible
piezoelectric	statesmanlike	conflictingly	Fascistically	inexhaustibly
pneumatolysis	tiddledywinks	conjecturable	fissiparously	inexpediently
pneumatolytic	abiologically	conjecturally	flirtatiously	inexpensively
pneumogastric	acquiescently	conjunctively	floristically	inexpressible
pointillistic	acquiescingly	consecutively	flourishingly	inexpressibly
polarographic	acrimoniously	considerately	foresightedly	inferentially
poliomyelitis	acrobatically	conspicuously	fragmentarily	influentially
polychromatic	acrylonitrile	constrainable	frighteningly	informatively
polysynthesis	adiabatically	constrainedly	frustratingly	infuriatingly
polysynthetic	administrable	constructable	fundamentally	injudiciously
precentorship	admonishingly	constructible	generalisable	inoffensively
prescientific	adventurously	consumptively	geometrically	inopportunely

inorganically	ontologically	retroactively	transversally	convertiplane
inquisitively	openheartedly	reverentially	traumatically	correspondent
insensitively	opinionatedly	rhapsodically	treacherously	cottonpicking
insinuatingly	opprobriously	rheumatically	troublesomely	crosshatching
instinctively	outstandingly	righthandedly	trustworthily	crystalgazing
instructively	overbearingly	rudimentarily	typologically	decontrolling
insupportable	painstakingly	sacramentally	unaccountable	disconcerting
insupportably	panegyrically	sacrificially	unaccountably	disembodiment
insusceptible	parabolically	sarcastically	unambiguously	disengagement
intelligently	paradoxically	schematically	unbelievingly	disfigurement
intemperately	parasitically	scorbutically	uncomfortable	disinvestment
intentionally	patriotically	scrumptiously	uncomfortably	dismantlement
interdentally	patronisingly	selfassuredly	unconceivable	dismemberment
interestingly	pedagogically	selfcentredly	unconcernedly	disparagement
interpretable	penetratingly	selfevidently	unconformable	divertisement
interruptible	penetratively	selfpityingly	unconquerable	doubledealing
intravenously	penitentially	semipermeable	unconsciously	doubleglazing
intrinsically	perfunctorily	sensationally	underhandedly	eavesdropping
introversible	perspectively	sententiously	unemotionally	electrovalent
inventorially	perspicuously	sentimentally	unequivocally	embarrassment
involuntarily	pestiferously	serologically	unfashionable	embellishment
irreclaimable	pharisaically	significantly	unfashionably	embranglement
irreclaimably	phrenetically	sophistically	unflinchingly	embrittlement
irrecoverable	picturesquely	southeasterly	unforgettable	encompassment
irrecoverably	plethorically	southwesterly	unforgettably	encouragement
irrefrangible	pneumatically	spasmodically	unfortunately	enlightenment
irreligiously	pragmatically	spectacularly	unimpeachable	entertainment
irreplaceable	precipitantly	speculatively	unmentionable	equiponderant
irrepressible	precipitately	splenetically	unnecessarily	establishment
irrepressibly	precipitously	spontaneously	unobtrusively	felicitations
irresponsible	predicatively	standoffishly	unpredictable	globetrotting
irresponsibly	predominantly	statistically	unpromisingly	grandiloquent
irretrievable	prefatorially	stigmatically	unputdownable	hairsplitting
irretrievably	prejudicially	strategically	unqualifiedly	heartbreaking
isochronously	preliminarily	stylistically	unrelentingly	horsewhipping
isometrically	premonitorily	subordinately	unremittingly	housebreaking
isostatically	preparatively	subserviently	unrighteously	hydrocracking
judgmatically	preparatorily	substantially	unwarrantable	hydroxylamine
kinematically	prestigiously	substantively	unwarrantably	insignificant
knowledgeable	presumptively	substitutable	unwholesomely	intercropping
knowledgeably	pretentiously	suffocatingly	vacillatingly	interlacement
languishingly	prismatically	sulphureously	venturesomely	intransigeant
legislatively	probationally	superannuable	verisimilarly	jerrybuilding
lethargically	progressively	superficially	vertiginously	lancesergeant
lightheadedly	prohibitively	superfluously	volatilisable	leadpoisoning
lightmindedly	proliferously	superlatively	wrongheadedly	levelcrossing
macaronically	promiscuously	supersensible	adventuresome	lineengraving
macromolecule	pronounceable	symbiotically	Christmastime	longsuffering
magisterially	prophetically	symmetrically	climbingframe	maladjustment
magnanimously	prospectively	symphonically	fortississimo	merchandising
magnificently	protuberantly	symphoniously	generalissimo	micronutrient
manipulatable	provisionally	synchronously	pneumonectomy	miscomprehend
matrilineally	punctiliously	syntactically	Quinquagesima	misgovernment
mellifluously	puritanically	synthetically	tonsillectomy	mismanagement
meritoriously	purposelessly	tantalisingly	abortifacient	misunderstand
metonymically	quadrennially	tautologously	accidentprone	moneygrubbing
ministerially	qualitatively	taxonomically	accommodating	mouthwatering
mischievously	quarrelsomely	temerariously	accompaniment	naphthylamine
mistrustfully	questioningly	tempestuously	acetylcholine	nitrocompound
mistrustingly	quickwittedly	tendentiously	admeasurement	nonconducting
mountainously	quincuncially	terminatively	advertisement	nonconforming
multiplicable	realistically	terrestrially	affreightment	nonforfeiting
mutagenically	recommendable	territorially	anticoagulant	nonfulfilment
nearsightedly	rectangularly	tetrasyllable	antihistamine	nongovernment
necessitously	rectilinearly	theologically	apportionment	oleomargarine
nightmarishly	referentially	theoretically	ascertainment	omnicompetent
nondeductable	reminiscently	thoughtlessly	auctioneering	overconfident
nonreturnable	remonstrantly	thrasonically	backpedalling	overindulgent
nonsensically	remorselessly	threateningly	bamboozlement	overstatement
northeasterly	repetitiously	titillatingly	beleaguerment	pennyfarthing
northwesterly	reprehensible	topologically	bloodcurdling	pennypinching
nostalgically	reprehensibly	tortoiseshell	brainstorming	phenylalanine
nutritionally	representable	traditionally	breechloading	polypropylene
objectionable	reproachfully	transformable	cabinetmaking	prayermeeting
objectionably	reproachingly	translucently	chateaubriand	preengagement
obstructively	resourcefully	transmissible	circumambient	prefigurement
odoriferously	resplendently	transmittable	cobelligerent	preordainment
oecologically	restoratively	transparently	conversazione	prepossessing
ontogenically	restrictively	transportable	conversazioni	pretermitting

prizefighting accommodation degranulation interpunction proliferation
profitsharing accreditation demonstration interrelation prolification
pronouncement acculturation denticulation interrogation pronunciation
proparoxytone acetification deodorisation interspersion proprioceptor
pyrimethamine acidification derequisition introgression pulverisation
quinquevalent actualisation derestriction introspection qualification
rearrangement administrator desegregation investigation radiolocation
reconcilement afforestation deterioration isomerisation randomisation
redevelopment agglomeration determination italicisation ratiocination
reimbursement agglutination discoloration jollification reaffirmation
reinforcement aluminisation disconcertion justification reciprocation
reinstatement amplification disconnection juxtaposition recombination
rejuvenescent anglicisation discriminator laevorotation recomposition
replenishment animadversion disintegrator lignification reconstructor
rhadamanthine animalisation displantation machicolation recrimination
sabrerattling appropriation dispossession magnetisation rectification
scintillating approximation disproportion magnification redescription
scrapmerchant argumentation dissemination maladaptation reduplication
searchwarrant aromatisation disseveration manifestation reembarkation
selfabasement assassination dissimilation martyrisation reexamination
selfadjusting asserveration dissimulation matriculation reforestation
selfapproving authenticator documentation meadowsaffron refrigeration
selfasserting authorisation domestication mechanisation regimentation
selfconfident backformation domiciliation mediatisation regurgitation
selfconsuming backwardation dramatisation mercerisation reincarnation
selfdeceiving balkanisation dulcification mesencephalon reintegration
selfdefeating barbarisation electrocution mesmerisation reinvigorator
selfdependent beatification encapsulation metallisation remonstration
selfdirecting beneficiation epiphenomenon metrification renegotiation
selfexecuting bloodrelation equilibration microdetector reorientation
selfgoverning boustrophedon expectoration miscegenation republication
selfimportant brutalisation expostulation misconception resuscitation
selfindulgent calcification expropriation misunderstood retranslation
selfrecording caprification extermination mitochondrion retrogression
selfregarding carbonisation extrapolation modernisation retrospection
selfreproving catechisation extravasation mollification revaccination
selfrepugnant cauterisation falsification monocotyledon revendication
selfrestraint certification fasciculation mortification reverberation
selfrevealing chemoreceptor fertilisation mummification ritualisation
selfsufficing cicatrisation feudalisation mutualisation Russification
semipermanent circumvention formalisation mystification scarification
sewingmachine clarification formulisation necessitation scintillation
sharecropping collaboration fortification neighbourhood scorification
sharpshooting commemoration fossilisation nitrification sedimentation
sheepshearing commiseration fractionation nonaggression selfassertion
sidesplitting communication fragmentation normalisation selfcommunion
skateboarding communisation freeselection nullification selfdeception
softpedalling compagination frequentation orangeblossom selfdirection
soulsearching comprehension funambulation orchestration selfeducation
squarebashing concatenation galvanisation ornamentation selfinduction
steppingstone concentration germanisation overvaluation selftormentor
streetwalking condescension gesticulation palletisation semiconductor
sublieutenant confabulation glamorisation participation sensitisation
superabundant confederation glorification partridgewood sequestration
superdominant configuration gratification peptonisation sergeantmajor
swashbuckling conflagration hallucination perambulation serialisation
taperecording confrontation harmonisation peregrination signalisation
telerecording congratulator horripilation periodisation signification
thermosetting consideration hybridisation perseveration smoothingiron
thoroughgoing consolidation hydrogenation petrification socialisation
timeconsuming constellation hypnotisation photoelectron solderingiron
tonguelashing consternation hypothecation photoemission solemnisation
transshipment contamination impenetration photoreceptor somnambulator
transshipping contemplation impersonation phytoplankton specification
uncomplaining contrabassoon impropriation pluralisation stabilisation
underclothing contraception improvisation polycotyledon sterilisation
understanding contradiction incarceration pontification strangulation
underwhelming contravention incardination postcommunion subcontractor
unforthcoming cornification incorporation precipitation subirrigation
unintelligent corroboration indisposition preconception subordination
unquestioning counteraction individuation predestinator subsaturation
vantageground crossquestion indoctrinator predomination subtilisation
vicepresident decerebration ingurgitation prefiguration suffumigation
vouchsafement decomposition intercalation premeditation summarisation
waterproofing decompression interlocution preoccupation superaddition
wonderworking decortication intermediator preordination superfetation
woodengraving decrepitation interpellator prepossession superposition
woolgathering defibrination interpolation pretermission supplantation
acclimatation deforestation interposition prevarication syllabication

symbolisation	incriminatory	Assyriologist	dastardliness	frivolousness
tantalisation	integumentary	atrociousness	dauntlessness	fruitlessness
telencephalon	interlocutory	attentiveness	deathlessness	functionalism
teleportation	interrogatory	audaciousness	deceitfulness	functionalist
temporisation	investigatory	Australianism	deceptiveness	garrulousness
tergiversator	jiggerypokery	autochthonism	deciduousness	geocentricism
terrorisation	justificatory	autoeroticism	defectiveness	gerontologist
testification	laevorotatory	availableness	deipnosophist	glutinousness
thurification	mackerelshark	barbarousness	deliciousness	gracelessness
topsyturvydom	magnetosphere	barefacedness	deliriousness	greensickness
transcription	mothercountry	beauteousness	dematerialise	grotesqueness
transgression	mouldingboard	Berkeleianism	demythologise	guilelessness
translocation	mountebankery	bibliolatrist	denationalise	guiltlessness
transmigrator	northeastward	bibliophilism	depersonalise	gynaecologist
transmutation	northwestward	bibliophilist	dermatologist	habitableness
transpiration	octocentenary	blackguardism	desirableness	haematologist
transposition	ostreiculture	blameableness	desperateness	haphazardness
triangulation	parliamentary	blamelessness	desultoriness	hazardousness
tuberculation	participatory	bloodlessness	deuteragonist	healthfulness
verbalisation	perambulatory	boardinghouse	Deuteronomist	heartlessness
verbigeration	pneumatophore	bouillabaisse	devolutionist	heartsickness
vermiculation	precautionary	boundlessness	dexterousness	hemicellulose
vernalisation	primogenitary	bounteousness	diageotropism	herpetologist
versification	primogeniture	bountifulness	diagrammatise	hilariousness
victimisation	processionary	brainlessness	diffusiveness	histrionicism
visualisation	prolegomenary	brilliantness	dimensionless	homeomorphism
vitrification	psychosurgery	brotherliness	disparateness	homoeopathist
vulcanisation	qualificatory	bumptiousness	dissoluteness	ichthyologist
vulgarisation	questionnaire	bureaucratise	doctrinairism	identicalness
chromatograph	quincentenary	butterflyfish	documentalist	illogicalness
cinematograph	quingentenary	calligraphist	dodecaphonist	imitativeness
daguerreotype	quinquagenary	campanologist	doubtlessness	immaterialise
gynandromorph	rearcommodore	capaciousness	dreamlessness	immaterialism
immunotherapy	recriminatory	ceremonialism	ecumenicalism	immaterialist
kinematograph	repetitionary	ceremonialist	effectiveness	immediateness
organotherapy	reverberatory	changefulness	egregiousness	immovableness
parthenocarpy	revolutionary	characterless	elaborateness	immutableness
phonautograph	saccharimetry	cheerlessness	electrologist	impassiveness
physiotherapy	secretarybird	cinquecentist	encyclopedism	imperfectness
psychotherapy	selfdiscovery	clearinghouse	encyclopedist	imperiousness
rontgenoscopy	soundingboard	climatologist	enjoyableness	impersonalise
tachistoscope	southeastward	collectedness	epigrammatise	impetuousness
alcoholometry	southwestward	colloquialism	epigrammatist	impressionism
anthropometry	spermatophore	colourfulness	equestrianism	impressionist
arboriculture	stirpiculture	combativeness	equivocalness	impulsiveness
asthenosphere	stoichiometry	commercialise	erroneousness	inanimateness
butterfingers	subversionary	commercialism	eschatologist	inclusiveness
centreforward	supernumerary	commercialist	essentialness	incorrectness
certificatory	supplementary	companionless	ethnocentrism	incorruptness
chlamydospore	televisionary	complexedness	evocativeness	incurableness
chromatophore	thenceforward	compositeness	excessiveness	incuriousness
commemoratory	thereinbefore	conceitedness	excitableness	indeterminism
communicatory	threequarters	conceptualise	exclusiveness	indeterminist
complementary	transitionary	conceptualism	excursiveness	individualise
complimentary	transpiratory	conceptualist	excusableness	individualism
concessionary	underexposure	conduciveness	exemplariness	individualist
concretionary	villeggiatura	confidingness	exhibitionism	inductiveness
confabulatory	accidentalism	congruousness	exhibitionist	industrialise
confectionary	admirableness	conjugateness	expansiveness	industrialism
confectionery	advisableness	connectedness	expensiveness	industrialist
confessionary	affectionless	consciousness	explosiveness	ineffableness
conservatoire	agreeableness	contentedness	expressionism	infallibilism
consolidatory	agriculturist	contortionist	expressionist	infallibilist
constellatory	airworthiness	contrabandist	exquisiteness	inflexionless
contradictory	ambiguousness	contrapuntist	extensiveness	ingeniousness
conventionary	ambitiousness	coreligionist	facetiousness	ingenuousness
convulsionary	amorphousness	corporativism	faithlessness	injuriousness
corroboratory	anagrammatise	corrosiveness	faultlessness	innocuousness
cytochemistry	anagrammatism	corruptionist	feloniousness	innoxiousness
devolutionary	analogousness	cosmopolitise	ferociousness	insensateness
discretionary	annexationist	cosmopolitism	feuilletonism	insidiousness
expeditionary	anomalousness	countinghouse	feuilletonist	insolubleness
expostulatory	anonymousness	courteousness	flagellantism	intensiveness
exterminatory	anticlockwise	credulousness	foolhardiness	interpretress
extraordinary	antinomianism	criminologist	forgetfulness	intricateness
geostationary	arbitrariness	cryobiologist	fortunateness	intrusiveness
gesticulatory	archaeologist	customariness	fractionalise	intuitiveness
hallucinatory	assertiveness	cyberneticist	fractiousness	inventiveness
improvisatory	assiduousness	dangerousness	frightfulness	invidiousness

inviolateness	offensiveness	republicanism	tentativeness	artificiality
invisibleness	offhandedness	repulsiveness	thanklessness	associativity
irrationalise	officiousness	requisiteness	thaumaturgist	attainability
irrationalism	operativeness	resentfulness	theanthropism	baccalaureate
irrationalist	opportuneness	retentiveness	theatricalise	basidiomycete
irreligionist	oppositionist	revelationist	theatricalism	Bloomsburyite
irritableness	ornithologist	revolutionise	thermochemist	changeability
judiciousness	orthognathism	revolutionism	thermotropism	circumvallate
laboriousness	outspokenness	revolutionist	thigmotropism	coagulability
laughableness	overemphasise	righteousness	thrillingness	collaterality
lecherousness	paedomorphism	sacerdotalise	toastmistress	commutability
leisureliness	painterliness	sacerdotalism	tolerableness	comparability
lepidopterist	palatableness	sacerdotalist	toothsomeness	compassionate
liberationist	pantagruelism	sadomasochism	traceableness	compatibility
lickerishness	pantagruelist	sadomasochist	tractableness	concentricity
lightsomeness	paramagnetism	sagaciousness	Tractarianism	confraternity
limitlessness	particularise	salaciousness	transistorise	connaturality
litigiousness	particularism	sanitationist	tremulousness	consanguinity
loathsomeness	particularist	sansculottism	tributariness	consentaneity
lucrativeness	peaceableness	scholarliness	trichromatism	contractility
ludicrousness	pedestrianise	scholasticism	triliteralism	contrafagotto
luxuriousness	pedestrianism	scientologist	troublousness	correlativity
maladroitness	pendulousness	scorpiongrass	unanimousness	corrigibility
malariologist	penuriousness	scripturalism	uncertainness	crystallinity
maliciousness	percussionist	scripturalist	uncleanliness	decontaminate
malleableness	perfectionism	seaworthiness	unearthliness	deductibility
Malthusianism	perfectionist	secondariness	unfeelingness	defeasibility
Manichaeanism	pervasiveness	secretiveness	unhealthiness	defensibility
martyrologist	pharmaceutist	sedentariness	unicameralism	dependability
masculineness	phenomenalise	seditiousness	unicameralist	destructivity
masterfulness	phenomenalism	seductiveness	unmeaningness	differentiate
melodiousness	phenomenalist	selectiveness	unnaturalness	digestibility
melodramatise	philhellenism	selfawareness	unselfishness	disarticulate
melodramatist	philhellenist	selfcriticism	unwillingness	disconformity
mercenariness	photochromism	selfdispraise	valuelessness	discontinuity
mercilessness	phraseologist	semibarbarism	vapourishness	dispassionate
metagrobolise	physiognomist	senselessness	vegetarianism	disposability
meteorologist	pigheadedness	sensitiveness	venerableness	dissimilarity
microorganism	plaintiveness	separableness	venereologist	dissolubility
millennialism	platitudinise	separationist	ventriloquise	egocentricity
millionairess	plausibleness	sericulturist	ventriloquism	equiponderate
mirthlessness	plenteousness	shamelessness	ventriloquist	excommunicate
misanthropist	plentifulness	shapelessness	venturousness	expansibility
miserableness	pococurantism	shiftlessness	veraciousness	extensibility
Mohammedanism	pointlessness	sightlessness	vernacularise	ferroconcrete
momentariness	ponderousness	sleeplessness	vernacularism	filterability
momentousness	powerlessness	smokelessness	vexatiousness	formidability
Monarchianism	practicalness	snowblindness	vicariousness	hermaphrodite
monometallism	predatoriness	sobermindness	viniculturist	heterogeneity
monometallist	prematureness	sorrowfulness	violoncellist	homosexuality
Monophysitism	pricelessness	sovietologist	visionariness	horizontality
monosyllabism	primitiveness	spelaeologist	viticulturist	hydrosulphite
Monotheletism	processionist	Spencerianism	vivaciousness	immateriality
monstrousness	progressivism	spermatoblast	vocationalism	immiscibility
monumentalise	projectionist	spinelessness	voicelessness	impalpability
Muhammadanism	protectionism	spinninghouse	volcanologist	impartibility
myrmecologist	protectionist	spiritualness	voluntariness	impassability
navigableness	Protestantism	sprightliness	voraciousness	impassibility
nefariousness	provincialise	squeamishness	vulcanologist	impeccability
neoclassicism	provincialism	stainlessness	wearisomeness	impecuniosity
neoclassicist	provincialist	stalkinghorse	whimsicalness	impersonality
neoplasticism	prudentialism	statelessness	wholesomeness	implacability
nervelessness	prudentialist	steadfastness	wonderfulness	impossibility
niggardliness	psychoanalyse	stereoscopist	worrisomeness	improbability
noiselessness	psychoanalyst	sternforemost	worthlessness	improvability
nonconformism	psychometrist	stomatologist	xanthochroism	inappropriate
nonconformist	pteridologist	strenuousness	absorbability	inconsiderate
notoriousness	purposiveness	structuralism	acceptability	incredibility
objectiveness	querulousness	structuralist	accessibility	indeterminate
obliviousness	rapaciousness	structureless	accoutrements	individuality
obnoxiousness	rapturousness	substantivise	achromaticity	ineducability
obsessiveness	receptiveness	sumptuousness	admissibility	ineligibility
obstinateness	recessiveness	talkativeness	aggiornamento	inevitability
obtrusiveness	recrystallise	tastelessness	ambidexterity	inexorability
occasionalism	regardfulness	teachableness	anfractuosity	infallibility
occasionalist	regretfulness	technicalness	answerability	infeasibility
occidentalise	religiousness	temperateness	applicability	inflexibility
Occidentalism	removableness	temporariness	archdeaconate	infundibulate
Occidentalist	republicanise	tenaciousness	archimandrite	inhospitality

insatiability	superhumanity	nickeliferous	electromotive	BaltoSlavonic
insensibility	superordinate	odontoglossum	exteroceptive	bibliographic
insensitivity	supersaturate	orthognathous	frequentative	cannibalistic
insociability	supersubtlety	overcredulous	gesticulative	choreographic
instantaneity	terminability	ovoviviparous	hallucinative	chromatolytic
insubordinate	theatricality	papaveraceous	inconsecutive	chromospheric
intangibility	transliterate	papillomatous	incorporative	chronographic
interdigitate	translucidity	perichondrium	indistinctive	conglomeratic
interosculate	triangularity	perspicacious	interoceptive	corticotropic
invariability	underestimate	petroliferous	interpolative	criminalistic
invincibility	undergraduate	phanerogamous	interrogative	cryptanalytic
inviolability	unfamiliarity	phyllophagous	introspective	cryptographic
irrationality	unsociability	platiniferous	investigative	deterministic
judgeadvocate	unsuitability	platitudinous	justificative	diaphragmatic
manageability	verifiability	plenitudinous	magnetomotive	electrometric
mensurability	vernacularity	polliniferous	manifestative	electroscopic
metaphosphate	viceadmiralty	polyadelphous	nonfigurative	electrostatic
metastability	vulnerability	polydactylous	nonproductive	encyclopaedic
microtonality	acotyledonous	porcellaneous	oversensitive	extragalactic
multinucleate	aluminiferous	prolegomenous	participative	ferrimagnetic
negligibility	ambidexterous	proteinaceous	photoemissive	ferroelectric
negotiability	angiospermous	pusillanimous	photopositive	ferromagnetic
nemathelminth	argentiferous	quartziferous	postoperative	gastroenteric
noncollegiate	atlantosaurus	sanctimonious	precipitative	gerontocratic
nonconformity	autocephalous	schizocarpous	prefigurative	gonadotrophic
occasionality	autochthonous	scolopendrium	premeditative	gynaecocratic
overelaborate	balsamiferous	sculpturesque	primogenitive	hemiparasitic
paranormality	bibliolatrous	selfconscious	proliferative	heptasyllabic
particularity	brachypterous	selfforgetful	ratiocinative	heterogenetic
pathogenicity	broadspectrum	selfrighteous	reciprocative	heteromorphic
penetrability	camphoraceous	semiconscious	recriminative	heterothallic
perdurability	carboniferous	serendipitous	reduplicative	heterotrophic
perishability	carcinomatous	splendiferous	remonstrative	homoeomorphic
permutability	cartilaginous	staminiferous	resuscitative	homoiothermic
platyhelminth	chrysanthemum	stercoraceous	retrogressive	hydrocephalic
polycarbonate	cleistogamous	stoloniferous	retrospective	hydroelectric
ponderability	condylomatous	stratocumulus	reverberative	hypermetropic
predicability	conscientious	streptococcus	selfassertive	hypochondriac
preferability	consentaneous	submachinegun	selfdeceptive	idiosyncratic
PreRaphaelite	diathermanous	subreptitious	significative	imperialistic
primordiality	dichlamydeous	subterraneous	sniftingvalve	intergalactic
procrastinate	discommodious	superstitious	subordinative	interspecific
professoriate	discontinuous	surreptitious	transcriptive	kaleidoscopic
profitability	disharmonious	tablespoonful	transgressive	laryngoscopic
prognosticate	disrespectful	thermophilous	transmutative	leptocephalic
proportionate	electrophorus	tintinnabulum	uncompetitive	lexicographic
provinciality	emphysematous	tyrannosaurus	uninformative	macrocephalic
prudentiality	entomophagous	umbelliferous	archaeopteryx	materialistic
pusillanimity	entomophilous	unceremonious	perissodactyl	microcephalic
quadrillionth	exanthematous	unpretentious	—————————	monochromatic
quadripartite	fossiliferous	zinjanthropus	encyclopaedia	monogrammatic
quadrumvirate	garnetiferous	zygodactylous	eschscholtzia	monosymmetric
quadruplicate	gasteropodous	accommodative	galactosaemia	morphogenetic
quadruplicity	gastrocnemius	acculturative	hypermetropia	nationalistic
quintillionth	graminivorous	agglomerative	hypoglycaemia	nephelometric
quintuplicate	gymnospermous	agglutinative	megasporangia	neurastheniac
radioactivity	heterogeneous	appropriative	nitrobacteria	objectivistic
receptibility	heteroporous	approximative	paraphernalia	oceanographic
reciprocality	heterosporous	argumentative	pharmacopoeia	onomatopoetic
reconsolidate	horsechestnut	authoritative	prosthodontia	opportunistic
reflexibility	hydrocephalus	collaborative	psychasthenia	orthocephalic
reformability	hymenopteran	commemorative	Quinquagesima	palaeographic
resistibility	ichthyosaurus	commiserative	schizophrenia	pantisocratic
resolvability	inconspicuous	communicative	squandermania	parasynthetic
retroactivity	inefficacious	comprehensive	villeggiatura	paternalistic
reversibility	insectivorous	concentrative	actinomorphic	pathognomonic
rhodochrosite	instantaneous	confederative	allelomorphic	pharmacologic
sacrosanctity	lepidopterous	consolidative	anachronistic	philanthropic
selffertility	mammaliferous	contaminative	anaphrodisiac	photoelectric
selfpollinate	manganiferous	contemplative	AngloCatholic	photoperiodic
selfsterility	megacephalous	contraceptive	anthelminthic	phreatophytic
sequentiality	membranaceous	corresponsive	anthropogenic	physiographic
sesquiplicate	metalliferous	corroborative	anticlimactic	piezoelectric
smellingsalts	microphyllous	costeffective	antiscorbutic	pneumatolytic
solidungulate	miscellaneous	counteractive	apheliotropic	pneumogastric
spermatophyte	monodactylous	demonstrative	archbishopric	pointillistic
spheroidicity	monotrematous	deteriorative	architectonic	polarographic
squeezability	multitudinous	determinative	autocatalytic	polychromatic
superfluidity	nectariferous	disseminative	bacteriolytic	polysynthetic

```
prescientific quicktempered asthenosphere dishonourable intransigence
protohistoric rattlebrained authoritative dispassionate introspective
pseudoarchaic secretarybird baccalaureate disseminative introversible
pseudomorphic selfaddressed bacteriophage dissimilitude investigative
psilanthropic selfappointed basidiomycete distributable irrationalise
psychodynamic selfcollected biodegradable dressingtable irreclaimable
psychogenetic selfconceited birefringence effervescence irrecoverable
psychokinetic selfcondemned Bloomsburyite efflorescence irrefrangible
psychosomatic selfconfessed boardinghouse electromotive irreplaceable
psychrometric selfcontained bookingoffice epigrammatise irrepressible
rationalistic selfcontented bouillabaisse equiponderate irresponsible
RhaetoRomanic selfconvicted bureaucratise exceptionable irretrievable
schizophrenic selfgenerated challengeable excommunicate judgeadvocate
seismographic selfinflicted chinkerinchee exteroceptive jurisprudence
selenocentric selfopinioned chlamydospore ferroconcrete justificative
selenographic selfpossessed Christmastide foreknowledge knowledgeable
semiautomatic selfpropelled Christmastime fractionalise macromolecule
semiparasitic selfsatisfied chromatophore frequentative magnetomotive
socioeconomic selfsupported circumference generalisable magnetosphere
spectrometric selfsustained circumfluence gentlemanlike magniloquence
spectroscopic semicivilised circumvallate gesticulative manifestative
spermatogenic seriousminded clairaudience hallucinative manipulatable
stereographic shorttempered clearinghouse hemicellulose melodramatise
stratigraphic silvertongued climbingframe hermaphrodite metagrobolise
stratospheric singlehearted collaborative hydrochloride metaphosphate
synallagmatic sophisticated collieshangie hydrosulphide monumentalise
synchronistic soundingboard commemorative hydrosulphite multinucleate
telegrammatic southeastward commensurable hydroxylamine multiplicable
theriomorphic southwestward commercialise immarcescible naphthylamine
thermodynamic spindlelegged commiserative immaterialise nonappearance
thermoplastic strawcoloured communicative imperceptible nonattendance
transatlantic swallowtailed companionable impercipience noncollegiate
trigonometric tenderhearted compassionate impermissible noncompliance
voluntaristic thenceforward comprehensive impersonalise nondeductable
zoogeographic thimblerigged concentrative imperturbable nonfigurative
barrelchested thoroughpaced conceptualise impracticable nonproductive
bloodboltered threecornered concupiscence inappreciable nonresistance
brokenhearted unaccompanied concupiscible inappropriate nonreturnable
canaliculated unadulterated confederative incandescence objectionable
centreforward unanticipated conjecturable incombustible occidentalise
chateaubriand unarticulated consenescence inconceivable oleomargarine
chuckleheaded uncircumcised conservatoire incondensable ostreiculture
coarsegrained uncomplicated consolidative inconsecutive overabundance
crossgartered unconditioned constrainable inconsequence overelaborate
disadvantaged unconstrained constructable inconsiderate overemphasise
disinterested uncoordinated constructible inconsistence oversensitive
distinguished undereducated contaminative incontestable oversubscribe
doublejointed underemployed contemplative inconvenience participative
doubletongued undisciplined contraceptive inconvertible particularise
draggletailed unenlightened convalescence inconvincible passementerie
featherheaded unestablished conversazione incorporative pedestrianise
forementioned unimpassioned convertiplane incorruptible phenomenalise
fullfashioned uninterrupted corresponsive indefatigable phenylalanine
hocuspocussed unprecedented corroborative indescribable photoemissive
hollowhearted vantageground cosmopolitise indeterminate photopositive
hydromedusoid versicoloured costeffective indiscernible picturepalace
hypertrophied wellapPointed counteractive indispensable platitudinise
inexperienced worldlyminded counterchange indissociable pluripresence
lightfingered accidentprone countercharge indistinctive pneumatophore
Maginotminded accommodative counterstroke individualise polycarbonate
miscomprehend acculturative countinghouse industrialise polypropylene
misunderstand acetylcholine daguerreotype inexhaustible postoperative
misunderstood acrylonitrile decontaminate inexpressible precipitative
mouldingboard administrable defervescence inflorescence prefigurative
multicoloured adventuresome deliquescence infundibulate premeditative
neighbourhood agglomerative dematerialise insubordinate preponderance
nitrocompound agglutinative demonstrative insufficience prepreference
northeastward amphiprostyle demythologise insupportable PreRaphaelite
northwestward anagrammatise denationalise insusceptible primigravidae
outgeneralled anticlockwise depersonalise intercurrence primogenitive
overpopulated antihistamine deteriorative interdigitate primogeniture
overqualified apprehensible determinative intermarriage procrastinate
particoloured appropriative diagrammatise intermittence professoriate
partridgewood approximative differentiate interoceptive prognosticate
phosphoretted arboriculture disaffirmance interosculate proliferative
pigeonchested archdeaconate disappearance interpolative pronounceable
pigeonhearted archimandrite disarticulate interpretable proparoxytone
pigeonlivered argumentative disciplinable interrogative proportionate
preengineered ascertainable discreditable interruptible provincialise
```

pseudoscience	transliterate	selfreproving	compressional	malacological
psychoanalyse	transmissible	selfrevealing	computational	mangoldwurzel
pyrimethamine	transmittable	selfsufficing	conchological	manneristical
quadripartite	transmutative	sharecropping	congressional	metallurgical
quadrumvirate	transportable	sharpshooting	conjugational	Methodistical
quadruplicate	unaccountable	sheepshearing	conjunctional	microscopical
questionnaire	uncomfortable	sidesplitting	consequential	mineralogical
quintuplicate	uncompetitive	skateboarding	controversial	monophthongal
ratiocinative	unconceivable	softpedalling	convocational	morphological
rearcommodore	unconformable	soulsearching	courtsmartial	multinational
recalcitrance	unconquerable	squarebashing	crackerbarrel	musicological
reciprocative	undercarriage	streetwalking	craniological	nomenclatural
recommendable	underestimate	swashbuckling	crosscultural	numerological
reconsolidate	underexposure	taperecording	cryptological	observational
recriminative	undergraduate	telerecording	deformational	ochlocratical
recrudescence	unfashionable	thermosetting	deontological	odontological
recrystallise	unforgettable	thoroughgoing	developmental	oreographical
reduplicative	unimpeachable	timeconsuming	disrespectful	palynological
remonstrative	uninformative	tonguelashing	dissymetrical	pantheistical
reprehensible	unmentionable	transshipping	dramaturgical	parasiticidal
representable	unpredictable	uncomplaining	dysfunctional	parenthetical
republicanise	unputdownable	underclothing	embryological	perichondrial
resuscitative	unwarrantable	understanding	entomological	perissodactyl
retrogressive	ventriloquise	underwhelming	environmental	petrochemical
retrospective	vernacularise	unforthcoming	epiphenomenal	philosophical
reverberative	volatilisable	unquestioning	equipotential	photochemical
revolutionise	accommodating	waterproofing	Eucharistical	phrenological
rhadamanthine	auctioneering	wonderworking	examinational	physiological
rhodochrosite	backpedalling	woodengraving	examinatorial	piscicultural
sacerdotalise	bloodcurdling	woolgathering	excrescential	planimetrical
schadenfreude	brainstorming	butterflyfish	explorational	postclassical
sculpturesque	breechloading	buttonthrough	expurgatorial	postulational
selfassertive	cabinetmaking	chromatograph	exterritorial	predicamental
selfassurance	cottonpicking	cinematograph	extrajudicial	prehistorical
selfdeceptive	crosshatching	featherstitch	extraphysical	premillennial
selfdispraise	crystalgazing	followthrough	extratropical	prepositional
selfexistence	decontrolling	gynandromorph	floricultural	preternatural
selfinsurance	disconcerting	kinematograph	foraminiferal	problematical
selfknowledge	doubledealing	lamellibranch	gastrological	procuratorial
selfpollinate	doubleglazing	liebfraumilch	gastronomical	progenitorial
selfsacrifice	eavesdropping	nemathelminth	glaciological	progressional
semipermeable	globetrotting	opisthobranch	goniometrical	propositional
sesquiplicate	hairsplitting	phonautograph	graphological	proprietorial
sewingmachine	heartbreaking	platyhelminth	gravitational	protonotarial
shootingbrake	horsewhipping	quadrillionth	gubernatorial	psychological
shootingrange	housebreaking	quintillionth	hemispherical	pyrotechnical
shoulderblade	hydrocracking	runningstitch	hermeneutical	quadragesimal
significative	intercropping	slangingmatch	homoiothermal	quadricipital
sniftingvalve	jerrybuilding	anthropophagi	horticultural	quadrilateral
solidungulate	leadpoisoning	conversazioni	hydrometrical	reformational
somniloquence	levelcrossing	micrococcocci	hydrostatical	seismological
spermatophore	lineengraving	counterattack	hyperboloidal	selenological
spermatophyte	longsuffering	laughingstock	hypercritical	selfforgetful
spinninghouse	merchandising	mackerelshark	hypermetrical	semeiological
sportsmanlike	moneygrubbing	mourningcloak	hyperphysical	septentrional
stalkinghorse	mouthwatering	shootingstick	ideographical	shabbygenteel
statesmanlike	nonconducting	thunderstruck	immunological	sociocultural
steppingstone	nonconforming	abstractional	infinitesimal	somatological
stickingplace	nonforfeiting	aerodynamical	informational	speleological
stirpiculture	pennyfarthing	ambassadorial	inquisitional	spinningwheel
subordinative	pennypinching	anomalistical	inquisitorial	sprocketwheel
substantivise	prayermeeting	antipersonnel	inscriptional	streptococcal
substitutable	prepossessing	apocalyptical	inspirational	subsequential
superannuable	pretermitting	arbitrational	institutional	substructural
supereminence	prizefighting	archidiaconal	instructional	subternatural
superordinate	profitsharing	architectural	insubstantial	supercritical
supersaturate	sabrerattling	astronautical	intercolonial	supernational
supersensible	scintillating	astrophysical	intercultural	superphysical
supervenience	selfadjusting	atmospherical	interjectural	suppositional
tachistoscope	selfapproving	bathymetrical	international	supranational
tetrasyllable	selfasserting	bibliological	interparietal	tablespoonful
theatricalise	selfconsuming	cacographical	interpersonal	technological
thereinbefore	selfdeceiving	Calvinistical	intertropical	temperamental
thoroughbrace	selfdefeating	cerebrospinal	intraarterial	teratological
transcendence	selfdirecting	chronological	intrapersonal	tercentennial
transcriptive	selfexecuting	coeducational	irreverential	terminational
transformable	selfgoverning	combinatorial	lackadaisical	topographical
transgressive	selfrecording	compartmental	lancecorporal	tortoiseshell
transistorise	selfregarding	compositional	legislatorial	toxicological

translational pedestrianism businesswoman expectoration mesmerisation
transnational perfectionism calcification expostulation metallisation
tricentennial perichondrium caprification expropriation metaphysician
tritheistical phenomenalism carbonisation extermination metrification
troglodytical philhellenism catechisation extrapolation miscegenation
typographical photochromism cauterisation extravasation misconception
unconditional pococurantism certification falsification mitochondrion
unexceptional progressivism cicatrisation fasciculation modernisation
ungrammatical protectionism circumvention fertilisation mollification
unintentional Protestantism clarification festschriften monocotyledon
unsubstantial provincialism collaboration feudalisation mortification
unsymmetrical prudentialism commemoration formalisation mummification
ventriloquial radiotelegram commiseration formulisation mutualisation
vivisectional republicanism communication fortification mystification
xylographical revolutionism communisation fossilisation necessitarian
accidentalism roentgenogram communitarian fractionation necessitation
anagrammatism sacerdotalism compagination fragmentation nightwatchman
antilogarithm sadomasochism comprehension freeselection nitrification
antinomianism sansculottism concatenation frequentation nonaggression
Australianism scholasticism concentration funambulation normalisation
autochthonism scolopendrium condescension galvanisation nucleoprotein
autoeroticism scripturalism confabulation germanisation nullification
Berkeleianism selfcriticism confederation gesticulation orchestration
bibliophilism semibarbarism configuration glamorisation ornamentation
blackguardism semilogarithm conflagration glorification overvaluation
broadspectrum Spencerianism confrontation gonadotrophin paediatrician
ceremonialism structuralism congresswoman gratification palletisation
chrysanthemum theanthropism consideration halfsovereign panicstricken
colloquialism theatricalism consolidation hallucination pantagruelian
commercialism thermotropism constellation harmonisation participation
conceptualism thigmotropism consternation horripilation Pennsylvanian
corporativism tintinnabulum contamination hybridisation peptonisation
cosmopolitism topsyturvydom contemplation hydrogenation perambulation
diageotropism Tractarianism contrabassoon hypnotisation peregrination
doctrinairism trichromatism contraception hypothecation periodisation
ecumenicalism triliteralism contradiction impenetration perseveration
encephalogram unicameralism contravention impersonation petrification
encyclopedism vegetarianism cornification impropriation phalansterian
equestrianism ventriloquism corroboration improvisation photoelectron
ethnocentrism vernacularism corticotropin incarceration photoemission
exhibitionism vocationalism counteraction incardination phycoerythrin
expressionism xanthochroism crossquestion incorporation phytoplankton
feuilletonism acclimatation decerebration indisposition pluralisation
flagellantism accommodation decomposition individuation polycotyledon
functionalism accreditation decompression ingurgitation polyhistorian
geocentricism acculturation decortication intercalation pontification
histrionicism acetification decrepitation interlocution postcommunion
homeomorphism acidification defibrination interpolation precipitation
immaterialism actualisation deforestation interposition preconception
impressionism afforestation degranulation interpunction predomination
indeterminism agglomeration demonstration interrelation prefiguration
individualism agglutination denticulation interrogation premeditation
industrialism aircraftwoman deodorisation interspersion preoccupation
infallibilism aluminisation derequisition introgression preordination
irrationalism amplification derestriction introspection prepossession
Malthusianism anglicisation desegregation investigation pretermission
Manichaeanism AngloAmerican deterioration isomerisation prevarication
microorganism animadversion determination italicisation proliferation
millennialism animalisation diagnostician jollification prolification
Mohammedanism Antichristian discoloration justification pronunciation
Monarchianism appropriation disconcertion juxtaposition prostaglandin
monometallism approximation disconnection laevorotation pulverisation
Monophysitism argumentation displantation lignification qualification
monosyllabism arithmetician dispossession Machiavellian radiolocation
Monotheletism aromatisation disproportion machicolation randomisation
Muhammadanism assassination dissemination magnetisation ratiocination
neoclassicism asseveration disseveration magnification reaffirmation
neoplasticism authorisation dissimilation malacostracan reciprocation
nonconformism authoritarian dissimulation maladaptation recombination
occasionalism backformation documentation manifestation recomposition
Occidentalism backwardation domestication martyrisation recrimination
odontoglossum balkanisation domiciliation mathematician rectification
orangeblossom barbarisation dramatisation matriculation redescription
orthognathism beatification dulcification meadowsaffron reduplication
paedomorphism beneficiation electrocution mechanisation reembarkation
pantagruelism bildungsroman encapsulation mediatisation reexamination
parallelogram bloodrelation entomostracan mediterranean reforestation
paramagnetism boustrophedon epiphenomenon mercerisation refrigeration
particularism brutalisation equilibration mesencephalon regimentation

regurgitation	versification	intelligencer	zoogeographer	connectedness
reincarnation	victimisation	intercellular	accoutrements	conscientious
reintegration	visualisation	intercolumnar	acotyledonous	consciousness
remonstration	vitrification	intermediator	actinomycetes	consentaneous
renegotiation	vulcanisation	interpellator	actinomycosis	contentedness
reorientation	vulgarisation	intracellular	admirableness	corrosiveness
republication	weatherbeaten	intramuscular	advisableness	courteousness
resuscitation	Zarathustrian	kapellmeister	affectionless	credulousness
retranslation	aggiornamento	Kidderminster	agreeableness	crosspurposes
retrogression	contrafagotto	knickerbocker	airworthiness	cryptanalysis
retrospection	fortississimo	knuckleduster	aluminiferous	customariness
revaccination	generalissimo	laissezpasser	ambidexterous	dangerousness
revendication	incommunicado	lexicographer	ambiguousness	dastardliness
reverberation	associateship	lifepreserver	ambitiousness	dauntlessness
ritualisation	chieftainship	machinegunner	amniocentesis	deathlessness
Russification	churchmanship	maladminister	amorphousness	deceitfulness
scarification	colleagueship	meistersinger	analogousness	deceptiveness
scintillation	collectorship	microdetector	angiospermous	deciduousness
scleroprotein	commandership	monomolecular	anomalousness	defectiveness
scorification	companionship	mourningpaper	anonymousness	deliciousness
sedimentation	conductorship	multicellular	arbitrariness	deliriousness
selfassertion	containership	neurovascular	argentiferous	desirableness
selfcommunion	copartnership	oceanographer	assertiveness	desperateness
selfdeception	craftsmanship	owneroccupier	assiduousness	desultoriness
selfdirection	draftsmanship	oystercatcher	atlantosaurus	dexterousness
selfeducation	inspectorship	paddlesteamer	atrociousness	diathermanous
selfinduction	landownership	palaeographer	attentiveness	dichlamydeous
semibarbarian	librarianship	passionflower	audaciousness	diffusiveness
semiporcelain	moderatorship	perpendicular	autocatalysis	dimensionless
sensitisation	precentorship	philosophiser	autocephalous	discommodious
sequestration	presidentship	photoreceptor	autochthonous	discontinuous
SerboCroatian	principalship	physiographer	availableness	disharmonious
serialisation	proconsulship	pneumatometer	bacteriolysis	disparateness
Shakespearean	professorship	potentiometer	balsamiferous	dissoluteness
Shakespearian	protectorship	prairieoyster	barbarousness	doubtlessness
signalisation	secretaryship	predestinator	barefacedness	dreamlessness
signification	shoulderstrap	proprioceptor	beauteousness	effectiveness
smoothingiron	solicitorship	pyrheliometer	belleslettres	egregiousness
socialisation	sportsmanship	quartermaster	betweenwhiles	elaborateness
solderingiron	statesmanship	reconstructor	bibliolatrous	electrophorus
solemnisation	subeditorship	refractometer	bioenergetics	elephantiasis
specification	suffraganship	reinvigorator	blameableness	embryogenesis
stabilisation	surrogateship	rollercoaster	blamelessness	emphysematous
sterilisation	swordsmanship	saccharimeter	blastogenesis	enjoyableness
strangulation	treasurership	saccharometer	bloodlessness	entomophagous
subirrigation	accelerometer	scandalmonger	boundlessness	entomophilous
submachinegun	administrator	schoolteacher	bounteousness	epeirogenesis
subordination	affenpinscher	seismographer	bountifulness	equivocalness
subsaturation	alcoholometer	selenographer	brachypterous	erroneousness
subtilisation	authenticator	selfslaughter	brainlessness	essentialness
suffumigation	backscratcher	selfsurrender	brilliantness	evocativeness
summarisation	battlecruiser	selftormentor	brotherliness	exanthematous
superaddition	bibliographer	semiconductor	bumptiousness	excessiveness
superfetation	biogeographer	sergeantmajor	butterfingers	excitableness
superposition	blanketflower	shockabsorber	callisthenics	exclusiveness
supplantation	candlelighter	sicklefeather	camphoraceous	excursiveness
Swedenborgian	candlesnuffer	somnambulator	capaciousness	excusableness
syllabication	cardiographer	stationmaster	carboniferous	exemplariness
symbolisation	chemoreceptor	steeplechaser	carcinomatous	expansiveness
tantalisation	choreographer	strikebreaker	cartilaginous	expensiveness
telencephalon	concertmaster	subcontractor	changefulness	explosiveness
teleportation	congratulator	subpostmaster	characterless	exquisiteness
temporisation	counterfeiter	supercalender	cheerlessness	extensiveness
terpsichorean	cryptographer	tergiversator	chlamydomonas	facetiousness
terrorisation	discriminator	thermonuclear	chrematistics	faithlessness
testification	disintegrator	thimblerigger	cleistogamous	faultlessness
thurification	doublecrosser	thoughtreader	coenaesthesis	felicitations
transcription	dressimprover	thundershower	collectedness	feloniousness
transgression	electioneerer	tintinnabular	colourfulness	ferociousness
translocation	extracellular	tonguetwister	combativeness	foolhardiness
transmutation	extravascular	tranquilliser	companionless	forgetfulness
transpiration	fibrovascular	transmigrator	complexedness	fortunateness
transposition	fortunehunter	turkeygobbler	compositeness	fossiliferous
triangulation	fortuneteller	underachiever	conceitedness	fractiousness
tuberculation	glossographer	understrapper	conduciveness	frightfulness
verbalisation	granddaughter	volumenometer	condylomatous	frivolousness
verbigeration	harbourmaster	wheelerdealer	confidingness	frontogenesis
vermiculation	helterskelter	whithersoever	congruousness	fruitlessness
vernalisation	indoctrinator	windowshopper	conjugateness	gametogenesis

garnetiferous	lepidopterous	pervasiveness	sleeplessness	wearisomeness
garrulousness	leptospirosis	petroliferous	smellingsalts	whimsicalness
gasteropodous	lickerishness	phanerogamous	smokelessness	wholesomeness
gastrocnemius	lightsomeness	pharmaceutics	snowblindness	winterberries
glutinousness	limitlessness	photochromics	sobermindness	wonderfulness
gracelessness	litigiousness	phyllophagous	sorrowfulness	worrisomeness
graminivorous	loathsomeness	pigheadedness	spindleshanks	worthlessness
greensickness	lucrativeness	plaintiveness	spinelessness	zinjanthropus
grotesqueness	ludicrousness	platiniferous	spiritualness	zygodactylous
guilelessness	luxuriousness	platitudinous	splendiferous	abortifacient
guiltlessness	maladroitness	plausibleness	sprightliness	accompaniment
gymnospermous	maliciousness	plenitudinous	squeamishness	admeasurement
habitableness	malleableness	plenteousness	stainlessness	advertisement
haphazardness	mammaliferous	plentifulness	staminiferous	affreightment
hazardousness	manganiferous	pneumatolysis	statelessness	agriculturist
healthfulness	masculineness	pointlessness	steadfastness	annexationist
heartlessness	masterfulness	poliomyelitis	stercoraceous	anticoagulant
heartsickness	materfamilias	polliniferous	stoloniferous	apportionment
heebiejeebies	megacephalous	polyadelphous	stratocumulus	archaeologist
helminthiasis	melodiousness	polydactylous	strenuousness	ascertainment
heterogeneous	melodramatics	polysynthesis	streptococcus	Assyriologist
heterogenesis	membranaceous	ponderousness	structureless	bamboozlement
heteropterous	mercenariness	porcellaneous	subreptitious	beleaguerment
heterosporous	mercilessness	powerlessness	subterraneous	bibliolatrist
hilariousness	metalliferous	practicalness	sumptuousness	bibliophilist
hydrocephalus	metamorphoses	predatoriness	superfamilies	calligraphist
hydrodynamics	metamorphosis	prematureness	superstitious	campanologist
hymenopterous	microanalysis	pricelessness	surreptitious	ceremonialist
hypnoanalysis	microphyllous	primitiveness	talkativeness	cinquecentist
ichthyosaurus	millefeuilles	prolegomenous	tastelessness	circumambient
identicalness	millionairess	proteinaceous	teachableness	climatologist
illogicalness	mirthlessness	psychogenesis	technicalness	closedcircuit
imitativeness	miscellaneous	psychokinesis	temperateness	clothesbasket
immediateness	miserableness	psychometrics	temporalities	cobelligerent
immovableness	mnemotechnics	psychophysics	temporariness	commercialist
immutableness	momentariness	purposiveness	tenaciousness	conceptualist
impassiveness	momentousness	pusillanimous	tentativeness	contortionist
imperfectness	monodactylous	quartziferous	thanklessness	contrabandist
imperiousness	mononucleosis	querulousness	thermogenesis	contrapuntist
impetuousness	monotrematous	rapaciousness	thermophilous	coreligionist
imponderables	monstrousness	rapturousness	threequarters	correspondent
impulsiveness	morphogenesis	receptiveness	thrillingness	corruptionist
inanimateness	multitudinous	recessiveness	tiddledywinks	counterweight
inclusiveness	navigableness	regardfulness	toastmistress	criminologist
inconspicuous	nectariferous	regretfulness	tolerableness	cruiserweight
incorrectness	nefariousness	religiousness	toothsomeness	cryobiologist
incorruptness	nervelessness	removableness	toxoplasmosis	cyberneticist
incurableness	nickeliferous	repulsiveness	traceableness	deipnosophist
incuriousness	niggardliness	requisiteness	tractableness	dermatologist
inductiveness	noiselessness	resentfulness	tremulousness	deuteragonist
ineffableness	notoriousness	retentiveness	tributariness	Deuteronomist
inefficacious	objectiveness	righteousness	troublousness	devolutionist
inflexionless	obliviousness	sagaciousness	tyrannosaurus	disembodiment
ingeniousness	obnoxiousness	salaciousness	umbelliferous	disengagement
ingenuousness	obsessiveness	salmonellosis	unanimousness	disfigurement
injuriousness	obstinateness	sanctimonious	unceremonious	disinvestment
innocuousness	obtrusiveness	schizocarpous	uncertainness	dismantlement
innoxiousness	offensiveness	schizogenesis	uncleanliness	dismemberment
insectivorous	offhandedness	scholarliness	underemphasis	disparagement
insensateness	officiousness	scorpiongrass	unearthliness	divertisement
insidiousness	operativeness	seaworthiness	unfeelingness	documentalist
insolubleness	opportuneness	secondariness	unhealthiness	dodecaphonist
instantaneous	organogenesis	secretiveness	unmeaningness	electrologist
intensiveness	orthognathous	sedentariness	unnaturalness	electromagnet
interpretress	osteomyelitis	seditiousness	unpretentious	electrovalent
intricateness	outspokenness	seductiveness	unselfishness	embarrassment
intrusiveness	overcredulous	selectiveness	unwillingness	embellishment
intuitiveness	ovoviviparous	selfawareness	valuelessness	embranglement
inventiveness	painterliness	selfconscious	vapourishness	embrittlement
invidiousness	palatableness	selfrighteous	venerableness	encompassment
inviolateness	papaveraceous	semiconscious	venturousness	encouragement
invisibleness	paperhangings	senselessness	veraciousness	encyclopedist
irritableness	papillomatous	sensitiveness	vexatiousness	enlightenment
judiciousness	parasynthesis	separableness	vicariousness	entertainment
laboriousness	paterfamilias	serendipitous	visionariness	epigrammatist
laughableness	peaceableness	shamelessness	vivaciousness	equiponderant
lecherousness	pendulousness	shapelessness	voicelessness	eschatologist
leishmaniasis	penuriousness	shiftlessness	voluntariness	establishment
leisureliness	perspicacious	sightlessness	voraciousness	exhibitionist

expressionist	reinstatement	anthropometry	conjecturally	energetically
featherweight	rejuvenescent	anthropopathy	conjunctively	enigmatically
feuilletonist	replenishment	anthropophagy	connaturality	equidistantly
functionalist	revelationist	anthroposophy	consanguinity	evangelically
gerontologist	revolutionist	apathetically	consecutively	everlastingly
grandiloquent	sacerdotalist	appellatively	consentaneity	exasperatedly
gynaecologist	sadomasochist	applicability	considerately	exceptionably
haematologist	sanitationist	applicatively	consolidatory	exceptionally
herpetologist	scientologist	appropriately	conspicuously	existentially
homoeopathist	scrapmerchant	approximately	constellatory	expansibility
horsechestnut	scripturalist	arthritically	constrainedly	expeditionary
hundredweight	searchwarrant	artificiality	consumptively	expeditiously
ichthyologist	selfabasement	associativity	contentiously	explanatorily
immaterialist	selfconfident	asthmatically	continentally	exponentially
impressionist	selfdependent	astonishingly	contractility	expostulatory
indeterminist	selfimportant	atheistically	contractually	extemporarily
individualist	selfindulgent	atomistically	contradictory	extensibility
industrialist	selfrepugnant	attainability	contrariously	extensionally
infallibilist	selfrestraint	attributively	conventionary	exterminatory
insignificant	semipermanent	authentically	convulsionary	extraordinary
interlacement	separationist	autobiography	cooperatively	extravagantly
intransigeant	sericulturist	automatically	correlatively	extrinsically
irrationalist	sovietologist	autonomically	correlativity	facultatively
irreligionist	spelaeologist	axiomatically	corrigibility	fantastically
lancesergeant	spermatoblast	belligerently	corroboratory	fascinatingly
leatherjacket	stereoscopist	bewilderingly	crystallinity	Fascistically
lepidopterist	sternforemost	biotechnology	curvilinearly	filterability
letterperfect	stomatologist	blasphemously	cylindrically	fissiparously
liberationist	structuralist	bombastically	cytochemistry	flirtatiously
maladjustment	sublieutenant	brachycephaly	declaratively	floristically
malariologist	superabundant	brachydactyly	deductibility	flourishingly
martyrologist	superdominant	broadmindedly	defeasibility	foresightedly
melodramatist	thaumaturgist	burglariously	defencelessly	formidability
meteorologist	thermochemist	calculatingly	defensibility	fragmentarily
micronutrient	transshipment	carnivorously	deferentially	frighteningly
misanthropist	unicameralist	categorically	deleteriously	frustratingly
misgovernment	unintelligent	centrifugally	dendritically	fundamentally
mismanagement	venereologist	centripetally	dependability	geochronology
monometallist	ventriloquist	ceremoniously	deprecatingly	geometrically
myrmecologist	vicepresident	certificatory	descriptively	geomorphology
neoclassicist	viniculturist	chalcoography	destructively	geostationary
nonconformist	violoncellist	challengingly	destructivity	geotropically
nonfulfilment	viticulturist	changeability	determinately	gesticulatory
nongovernment	volcanologist	chromatically	detrimentally	goodnaturedly
occasionalist	vouchsafement	cinematically	devastatingly	grammatically
Occidentalist	vulcanologist	circumspectly	devolutionary	grandfatherly
omnicompetent	archaeopteryx	clandestinely	dialectically	grandmotherly
oppositionist	cephalothorax	clearheadedly	diametrically	gymnastically
ornithologist	concavoconvex	climactically	dichotomously	halfheartedly
overconfident	convexoconvex	coagulability	dictatorially	hallucinatory
overindulgent	interlocutrix	coldbloodedly	digestibility	hardheartedly
overstatement	abiologically	coldheartedly	dimensionally	helminthology
pantagruelist	absorbability	collaterality	disaffectedly	heterogeneity
particularist	acceptability	commemoratory	disconformity	homogeneously
percussionist	accessibility	commensurably	discontinuity	homosexuality
perfectionist	achromaticity	communicatory	discreditably	honorifically
pharmaceutist	acquiescently	commutability	discretionary	horizontality
phenomenalist	acquiescingly	companionably	disgracefully	hydraulically
philhellenist	acrimoniously	comparability	dishonourably	ichthyography
phraseologist	acrobatically	comparatively	disjunctively	ideologically
physiognomist	adiabatically	compatibility	disobediently	idiomatically
preengagement	admissibility	compendiously	disparagingly	ignominiously
prefigurement	admonishingly	competitively	disposability	illustriously
preordainment	adventurously	complainingly	dispraisingly	imaginatively
processionist	adversatively	complaisantly	dissemblingly	immateriality
projectionist	aesthetically	complementary	dissimilarity	immiscibility
pronouncement	affirmatively	complicatedly	dissolubility	immunotherapy
protectionist	aggravatingly	complimentary	distastefully	impalpability
provincialist	agonistically	concentricity	distinctively	impartibility
prudentialist	alcoholically	concessionary	distressfully	impassability
psychoanalyst	alcoholometry	concomitantly	distressingly	impassibility
psychometrist	algebraically	concretionary	distrustfully	impeccability
pteridologist	allegorically	conditionally	eccentrically	impecuniosity
quinquevalent	alternatively	confabulatory	educationally	imperceptibly
rearrangement	ambidexterity	confectionary	effervescency	impersonality
reconcilement	anachronously	confectionery	efficaciously	impertinently
redevelopment	anaerobically	confessionary	egocentricity	imperturbably
reimbursement	anfractuosity	conflictingly	encouragingly	implacability
reinforcement	answerability	confraternity	endocrinology	implicatively

impolitically	interstratify	painstakingly	pusillanimity	spontaneously
importunately	intravenously	palaeontology	quadrennially	squeezability
impossibility	intrinsically	palaeozoology	quadruplicity	standoffishly
impracticably	invariability	panegyrically	qualificatory	statistically
impractically	inventorially	parabolically	qualitatively	stigmatically
improbability	investigatory	paradoxically	quarrelsomely	stoichiometry
improvability	invincibility	paranormality	questioningly	strategically
improvidently	inviolability	parasitically	quickwittedly	stylistically
improvisatory	involuntarily	parliamentary	quincentenary	subordinately
inadvertently	irrationality	parthenocarpy	quincuncially	subserviently
inappreciably	irreclaimably	participatory	quingentenary	substantially
inattentively	irrecoverably	particularity	quinquagenary	substantively
incompetently	irreligiously	pathogenicity	radioactivity	subversionary
inconceivably	irrepressibly	patriotically	realistically	suffocatingly
incongruously	irresponsibly	patronisingly	receptibility	sulphureously
inconsistency	irretrievably	pedagogically	reciprocality	superficially
incontestably	isochronously	penetrability	recriminatory	superfluidity
incontinently	isometrically	penetratingly	rectangularly	superfluously
inconveniency	isostatically	penetratively	rectilinearly	superhumanity
inconvertibly	jiggerypokery	penitentially	referentially	superlatively
incorporeally	judgmatically	perambulatory	reflexibility	supernumerary
incorruptibly	justificatory	perdurability	reformability	supersubtlety
incredibility	kinematically	perfunctorily	reminiscently	supplementary
incredulously	knowledgeably	perishability	remonstrantly	symbiotically
incrementally	laevorotatory	permutability	remorselessly	symmetrically
incriminatory	languishingly	perspectively	repetitionary	symphonically
indefatigably	legislatively	perspicuously	repetitiously	symphoniously
independently	lethargically	pestiferously	reprehensibly	synchronously
indescribably	lightheadedly	pharisaically	reproachfully	syntactically
indeterminacy	lightmindedly	phenomenology	reproachingly	synthetically
indifferently	linseywoolsey	phrenetically	resistibility	tantalisingly
indiscernibly	macaronically	physiotherapy	resolvability	tautologously
indispensably	magisterially	picturesquely	resourcefully	taxonomically
individuality	magnanimously	plethorically	resplendently	televisionary
industriously	magnificently	pneumatically	restoratively	temerariously
ineducability	manageability	pneumonectomy	restrictively	tempestuously
ineffectively	matrilineally	ponderability	retroactively	tendentiously
ineffectually	mellifluously	pragmatically	retroactivity	terminability
inefficiently	mensurability	precautionary	reverberatory	terminatively
ineligibility	meritoriously	precipitantly	reverentially	terrestrially
inevitability	metallography	precipitately	reversibility	territorially
inexhaustibly	metastability	precipitously	revolutionary	thalassocracy
inexorability	metonymically	predicability	rhapsodically	theatricality
inexpediently	microtonality	predicatively	rheumatically	theologically
inexpensively	ministerially	predominantly	righthandedly	theoretically
inexpressibly	mischievously	prefatorially	roentgenology	thoughtlessly
infallibility	mistrustfully	preferability	rontgenoscopy	thrasonically
infeasibility	mistrustingly	prejudicially	rudimentarily	threateningly
inferentially	mothercountry	preliminarily	saccharimetry	thremmatology
inflexibility	mountainously	premonitorily	sacramentally	titillatingly
influentially	mountebankery	preparatively	sacrificially	tonsillectomy
informatively	mutagenically	preparatorily	sacrosanctity	topologically
infuriatingly	nearsightedly	preponderancy	sarcastically	traditionally
inhospitality	necessitously	prestigiously	schematically	transcendency
injudiciously	negligibility	presumptively	scorbutically	transitionary
inoffensively	negotiability	pretentiously	scrumptiously	translucently
inopportunely	nightmarishly	primogenitary	selfassuredly	translucidity
inorganically	nonconformity	primordiality	selfcentredly	transparently
inquisitively	nonsensically	prismatically	selfdiscovery	transpiratory
insatiability	northeasterly	probationally	selfevidently	transversally
insensibility	northwesterly	processionary	selffertility	traumatically
insensitively	nostalgically	profitability	selfpityingly	treacherously
insensitivity	numismatology	progressively	selfsterility	triangularity
insinuatingly	nutritionally	prohibitively	sensationally	troublesomely
insociability	objectionably	prolegomenary	sententiously	trustworthily
instantaneity	obstructively	proliferously	sentimentally	typologically
instinctively	occasionality	promiscuously	sequentiality	unaccountably
instructively	octocentenary	prophetically	serologically	unambiguously
insufficiency	odoriferously	prosopography	significantly	unbelievingly
insupportably	oecologically	prospectively	sophistically	uncomfortably
intangibility	ontogenically	protuberantly	southeasterly	unconcernedly
integumentary	ontologically	provinciality	southwesterly	unconsciously
intelligently	openheartedly	provisionally	spasmodically	underhandedly
intemperately	ophthalmology	prudentiality	spectacularly	unemotionally
intentionally	opinionatedly	psychosurgery	spectrography	unequivocally
interdentally	opprobriously	psychotherapy	speculatively	unfamiliarity
interestingly	organotherapy	punctiliously	spheroidicity	unfashionably
interlocutory	outstandingly	puritanically	sphygmography	unflinchingly
interrogatory	overbearingly	purposelessly	splenetically	unforgettably

unfortunately	unrighteously	venturesomely	wrongheadedly
unnecessarily	unsociability	verifiability	
unobtrusively	unsuitability	verisimilarly	
unpromisingly	untrustworthy	vernacularity	
unqualifiedly	unwarrantably	vertiginously	
unrelentingly	unwholesomely	viceadmiralty	
unremittingly	vacillatingly	vulnerability	

14 letter words

abovementioned	archidiaconate	campanological	comprehensibly
absentmindedly	archiepiscopal	campylotropous	compulsiveness
absorptiveness	architectonics	cantankerously	concavoconcave
abstemiousness	arithmetically	capitalisation	conceivability
abstractedness	arrhythmically	capriciousness	concelebration
abstractionism	arrondissement	carcinogenesis	concentrically
abstractionist	articulateness	cardiovascular	concessionaire
acceleratingly	artificialness	cartographical	conclusiveness
acceptableness	associationism	castrametation	concretisation
accomplishable	astronomically	catachrestical	condescendence
accomplishment	astrophysicist	catechetically	conditionality
accountability	asymmetrically	categorisation	conductibility
accumulatively	asymptotically	censoriousness	confidentially
accustomedness	asynchronously	centralisation	conformability
achondroplasia	attainableness	centrifugation	conglomeration
achromatically	attractiveness	chancellorship	conglutination
acknowledgment	audiofrequency	changeableness	conglutinative
administration	Augustinianism	characteristic	congratulation
administrative	auspiciousness	charitableness	congratulative
administratrix	authentication	chemoreception	congratulatory
advantageously	autobiographer	chemoreceptive	congregational
adventitiously	autobiographic	chemosynthesis	conjunctivitis
aerobiological	autocratically	chickenhearted	conquistadores
aerobiotically	autoradiograph	chickenlivered	consanguineous
aerodynamicist	autosuggestion	chincherinchee	conscienceless
aesthesiometer	avariciousness	chivalrousness	conservational
aetiologically	backscattering	Christological	conservatively
affectionately	backscratching	chromatography	consociational
aforementioned	bacteriologist	chronometrical	conspiratorial
Africanisation	bacteriostasis	cinematography	constitutional
aggrandisement	bacteriostatic	circuitousness	constitutively
aggressiveness	barometrically	circumambiency	constructional
agrobiological	basidiomycetes	circumambulate	constructively
airconditioner	bastardisation	circumbendibus	constructivism
Albigensianism	bathingmachine	circumlittoral	constructivist
allegorisation	beautification	circumlocution	consubstantial
allelomorphism	behaviouristic	circumlocutory	consuetudinary
alphabetically	beneficialness	circumnavigate	contagiousness
alphanumerical	bibliographise	circumspection	contemptuously
altruistically	bibliomaniacal	circumstantial	conterminously
amateurishness	biodegradation	circumvolution	contiguousness
ambassadorship	bioelectricity	classconscious	continuousness
ambidextrously	bioengineering	classification	contractedness
anagrammatical	biographically	classificatory	contradictable
anthropography	bioluminescent	claustrophobia	contradictious
anthropologist	biosystematics	claustrophobic	contraindicate
anthropometric	bituminisation	clearsightedly	contraposition
anticipatively	blackmarketeer	climatological	contrapositive
anticonvulsant	blockaderunner	coessentiality	contrapuntally
antidepressant	bloodthirstily	colourfastness	controllership
antifederalist	boardingschool	colourlessness	controvertible
antiperspirant	boisterousness	combustibility	contumaciously
antiphlogistic	boroughEnglish	commensurately	contumeliously
antiquarianism	bougainvillaea	commensuration	conventionally
antiscriptural	bouleversement	commissaryship	conversational
antiseptically	bowdlerisation	commissionaire	convertibility
antithetically	brachycephalic	committeewoman	convexoconcave
aphoristically	breathlessness	commodiousness	convincingness
apologetically	breathtakingly	commonsensical	convulsiveness
apophthegmatic	bremsstrahlung	communications	coordinateness
apoplectically	Brobdingnagian	comparableness	copperbottomed
apothegmatical	bronchiectasis	compassionable	coquettishness
appendicectomy	bullheadedness	compatibleness	correspondence
apprehensively	butterfingered	compensational	correspondency
apprenticeship	butterflyscrew	complexionless	corruptibility
archaeological	calamitousness	compossibility	corticosteroid
archetypically	calcareousness	comprehensible	corticosterone

corticotrophic	diplomatically	electrodeposit	forthrightness
corticotrophin	disaffiliation	electrodynamic	fortuitousness
cosmographical	disaffirmation	electrostatics	fortunetelling
cosmopolitical	disappointment	electrotherapy	forwardlooking
cotemporaneous	disapprobation	electrothermal	fraternisation
councilchamber	disapprobative	electrothermic	friendlessness
councillorship	disapprobatory	electrovalency	fructification
counsellorship	disapprovingly	elementariness	fullyfashioned
counterbalance	disarrangement	embarrassingly	fundamentalism
counterculture	disassociation	emblematically	fundamentalist
countercurrent	disciplinarian	emulsification	fundamentality
countermeasure	discolouration	enantiomorphic	galactopoietic
counterplotted	discombobulate	encephalograph	gelatinisation
countrydancing	discomfortable	encyclopaedism	genealogically
courageousness	discommendable	encyclopaedist	generalisation
creditableness	disconcertment	endoradiosonde	generalpurpose
crinkumcrankum	disconformable	endosmotically	geocentrically
crossfertilise	disconnectedly	enharmonically	geographically
crosspollinate	disconsolately	enterprisingly	gerontological
crossreference	disconsolation	entertainingly	goodfellowship
cryptaesthesia	discontentedly	enthronisation	goodhumouredly
crystallisable	discontentment	entomostracous	goodtemperedly
cucurbitaceous	discontinuance	epexegetically	gramineousness
cumbersomeness	discountenance	epidemiologist	grandiloquence
cumulativeness	discouragement	epigrammatical	gratuitousness
curvilinearity	discouragingly	epistemologist	gregariousness
cyanocobalamin	discourteously	erythropoiesis	groundlessness
deceivableness	discriminating	eschatological	gynaecological
decimalisation	discrimination	esterification	gynandromorphy
decolonisation	discriminative	ethnologically	gyrostabiliser
decolorisation	discriminatory	etymologically	haematogenesis
deconsecration	discursiveness	eulogistically	hagiographical
decorativeness	disdainfulness	euphuistically	halfpennyworth
defenestration	disembarkation	eutrophication	hallucinogenic
definitiveness	disembowelment	Evangelicalism	handicraftsman
degenerateness	disenchantment	evangelisation	handkerchieves
dehumanisation	disenfranchise	exasperatingly	harmoniousness
delectableness	disenthralment	exceptionality	heartsearching
deliberateness	disequilibrium	exclaustration	hebetudinosity
deliberatively	disfurnishment	excommunicable	hereditariness
delightfulness	disgruntlement	excommunicator	hermaphroditic
delocalisation	disheartenment	excruciatingly	heroworshipper
demisemiquaver	disinclination	exhaustibility	heterochromous
demobilisation	disincorporate	exhaustiveness	heteromorphism
democratically	disinfestation	exhilaratingly	heteromorphous
demonetisation	disingenuously	existentialism	heterophyllous
demoralisation	disinheritance	existentialist	heterothallism
denazification	disintegration	experientially	hierarchically
denominational	disintegrative	experimentally	hieroglyphical
denumerability	disjointedness	expressionless	highhandedness
departmentally	disorderliness	expressiveness	highmindedness
dependableness	disorientation	extemporaneity	histochemistry
deplorableness	dispensability	extemporaneous	histopathology
depolarisation	dispiritedness	extensionality	historiography
dermatological	disputatiously	extinguishable	histrionically
despicableness	disquisitional	extinguishment	hobbledehoyish
despiritualise	disrespectable	extracorporeal	hocuspocussing
despitefulness	dissertational	extraneousness	holometabolism
destructionist	dissociability	extravehicular	holometabolous
determinedness	distemperature	factitiousness	homoeomorphism
detestableness	distensibility	faintheartedly	homogenisation
detoxification	distributional	fallaciousness	homotransplant
devitalisation	distributively	fantasticality	honourableness
dextrorotation	diverticulitis	farsightedness	horrorstricken
dextrorotatory	divertissement	fastidiousness	horticulturist
diachronically	dodecasyllable	favourableness	humidification
diagnostically	dolichocephaly	featherbrained	hydrocoralline
diagrammatical	dolomitisation	ferrimagnetism	hydrodynamical
dialectologist	doublebreasted	ferromagnesian	hydrographical
diamantiferous	ecclesiastical	ferromagnetism	hydromechanics
diamondiferous	ecclesiologist	fictitiousness	hygroscopicity
diaphanousness	econometrician	figurativeness	hyperbolically
dicotyledonous	educationalist	flagitiousness	hypercalcaemia
dieselectric	effervescently	flatfootedness	hypercatalexis
differentiable	effortlessness	floriculturist	hypercriticise
differentially	egalitarianism	foraminiferous	hypercriticism
diffractometer	eigenfrequency	forbiddingness	hyperglycaemia
diminutiveness	electioneering	foreordination	hyperirritable
dinoflagellate	electrobiology	formidableness	hypersensitive

hypersonically	indecorousness	intertwinement	microcircuitry
hypocoristical	indefiniteness	intolerability	microcomponent
hypocritically	indemonstrable	intractability	microeconomics
hypodermically	indestructible	intramolecular	microminiature
hypostatically	indestructibly	intransitively	microprocessor
hypothetically	indeterminable	intrinsicality	microsporangia
hypothyroidism	indifferentism	introductorily	microstructure
hysterectomise	indifferentist	intuitionalism	microtechnique
iatrochemistry	indiscerptible	intuitionalist	militarisation
ichthyological	indiscoverable	invariableness	millenarianism
ichthyophagous	indiscreetness	invincibleness	mineralisation
ichthyosaurian	indiscriminate	inviolableness	ministerialist
iconographical	indistinctness	irreconcilable	miraculousness
idealistically	indivisibility	irreconcilably	misapplication
identification	indoctrination	irreducibility	misappropriate
idiopathically	indubitability	irrefutability	miscalculation
illconditioned	ineffectuality	irremovability	misinformation
illegitimately	inevitableness	irreproachable	mistranslation
illimitability	inexorableness	irreproachably	monkeybusiness
illiterateness	inexpressively	irreproducible	monochromatism
illustrational	infectiousness	irresoluteness	monopolisation
illustratively	infelicitously	irrespectively	monosaccharide
imaginableness	inflammability	irrevocability	monotonousness
immaculateness	inflectionally	Johannisberger	morganatically
immethodically	inflectionless	judgematically	mountaineering
immobilisation	inflexibleness	jurisdictional	multifariously
immoderateness	infralapsarian	justifiability	multilaterally
imparisyllabic	infrangibility	knickerbockers	multinucleated
impassableness	infrastructure	knighterrantry	multiplication
impassibleness	ingloriousness	kremlinologist	multiplicative
imperativeness	ingratiatingly	lasciviousness	myrmecological
impermeability	inharmoniously	latitudinarian	myrmecophagous
imperviousness	inheritability	lefthandedness	myrmecophilous
implacableness	inimitableness	legalistically	mysteriousness
implausibility	inordinateness	legitimisation	mythologically
implementation	inscrutability	liberalisation	narrowmindedly
imponderabilia	insatiableness	libertarianism	naturalisation
impoverishment	insensibleness	libidinousness	necessarianism
impracticality	inseparability	licentiousness	neglectfulness
impregnability	insignificance	lightheartedly	neocolonialism
impressibility	insignificancy	linguistically	neuroanatomist
impressionable	instrumentally	liturgiologist	neurochemistry
impressiveness	insufficiently	longheadedness	neuropathology
improvableness	insuperability	longitudinally	neuroscientist
inadequateness	insuppressible	longwindedness	neutralisation
inadvisability	insurmountable	loquaciousness	newfangledness
inalienability	insurmountably	lovingkindness	nightblindness
inalterability	insurrectional	lugubriousness	nitrocellulose
inappositeness	intangibleness	lyophilisation	nitroglycerine
inappreciation	integrationist	macrocephalous	noctambulation
inappreciative	intellectually	macroeconomics	nomenclatorial
inapproachable	intelligential	magniloquently	nonbelligerent
inarticulately	intelligentsia	malappropriate	noncommunicant
inarticulation	intercessional	malcontentedly	nonconcurrence
inartistically	intercessorial	malodorousness	noncooperation
inauspiciously	intercommunion	manageableness	noninvolvement
incapacitation	intercommunity	marketgardener	nonperformance
incautiousness	interdependent	martyrological	nonrestrictive
incestuousness	interferential	marvellousness	nonsensicality
incommensurate	interferometer	massproduction	northeastwards
incommodiously	interferometry	mathematically	northnortheast
incommunicable	intergradation	matriarchalism	northnorthwest
incommunicably	interjectional	meddlesomeness	northwestwards
incompleteness	interlineation	meditativeness	noteworthiness
incompressible	interlocutress	megasporangium	numismatically
incompressibly	intermediately	megasporophyll	nutritiousness
inconclusively	intermediation	Mephistopheles	obsequiousness
inconsequently	intermigration	meretriciously	obstreperously
inconsiderable	intermittently	mesdemoiselles	obstructionism
inconsiderably	intermolecular	metallographer	obstructionist
inconsistently	internationale	metaphorically	oecumenicalism
incontrollable	interpellation	metaphysically	oleaginousness
inconveniently	interpenetrate	metapsychology	omnivorousness
incoordination	interplanetary	metempsychosis	oneirocritical
incorporeality	interpretation	meteorological	openhandedness
incredibleness	interpretative	methodological	openmindedness
indecipherable	interpretively	meticulousness	ophthalmoscope
indecisiveness	intersectional	microbiologist	ophthalmoscopy
indecomposable	intersexuality	microcephalous	opinionatively

oppressiveness photosensitise proletarianise reconstruction
optimistically photosensitive proletarianism reconstructive
organisational photosynthesis prolocutorship recoverability
organometallic photosynthetic propaedeutical rectangularity
ornithological phototelegraph propagandistic redintegration
orthochromatic phraseological propitiatorily redistribution
orthographical phthalocyanine propitiousness redistributive
ostentatiously physiognomical proportionable reflectiveness
osteoarthritis phytogeography proportionably refractoriness
outgeneralling phytopathology proportionally refrangibility
outlandishness pianoaccordian proprietorship regardlessness
outrageousness pigeonbreasted proprioceptive regeneratively
overabundantly pisciculturist proscriptively regressiveness
overcapitalise pistilliferous prosencephalic regularisation
overcommitment planetstricken prosencephalon rehabilitation
overcompensate pleasurability prosperousness reintroduction
overconfidence pleonastically protectiveness reinvigoration
overestimation pluviometrical prothonotarial rejuvenescence
overexcitement pneumatologist protozoologist relentlessness
overindulgence pneumoconiosis protrusiveness relinquishment
overpopulation poikilothermal providentially remarkableness
overpoweringly poikilothermic pseudaesthesia reminiscential
overproduction politicisation pseudepigrapha remonetisation
oversubscribed polymerisation pseudepigraphy remorsefulness
overwhelmingly polymorphously pseudomorphism reorganisation
oxyhaemoglobin polysaccharide pseudomorphous repetitiveness
pachydermatous polytheistical pseudonymously representation
palaeethnology popularisation psilanthropism representative
palaeobotanist portentousness psilanthropist reproductively
papilionaceous possessiveness psychoanalysis repudiationist
paradoxicality postmastership psychoanalytic resinification
parallelepiped postmillennial psychochemical resistlessness
parapsychology postpositional psychodynamics respectability
parasitologist postpositively psychoneurosis respectfulness
paratactically potentiometric psychoneurotic responsibility
pardonableness practicability psychophysical responsiveness
parenchymatous pragmaticality psychosomatics restorationism
parsimoniously praiseworthily psychosurgical restorationist
partridgeberry prearrangement pteridological restrictionist
passionateness precariousness publicspirited resurrectional
pasteurisation precociousness pugnaciousness retrogradation
pathogenically predesignation purposefulness revalorisation
pathologically predestinarian pyrheliometric revengefulness
patresfamilias predestination Pythagoreanism revivification
penetrableness predeterminate quadragenarian rheumatologist
perceptibility predictability quadrisyllabic rhinencephalic
perceptiveness predisposition quadrisyllable rhinencephalon
percutaneously prefabrication quantification ridiculousness
peremptoriness preferentially quantitatively rigidification
perfectibility premeditatedly quarterbinding roadworthiness
perfidiousness premillenarian quattrocentism robustiousness
periodontology preponderantly quattrocentist roentgenoscopy
peripateticism preposterously quinquagesimal rontgenography
perishableness presbyterially quinquennially Rosicrucianism
permissibility prescriptively quintessential roundaboutness
permissiveness presentability radicalisation Russianisation
perniciousness presentational radioautograph Sabbatarianism
personableness presentimental radiochemistry sacramentalism
persuasiveness presumptuously radiosensitive sacramentalist
pertinaciously presupposition radiostrontium sacramentarian
perturbational prettification radiotelegraph sacrilegiously
pestilentially preventability radiotelephone salubriousness
petrochemistry preventiveness radiotelephony sanctification
petrographical probabiliorism radiotherapist sanguification
petrologically probabiliorist rambunctiously sanguinariness
phantasmagoria proceleusmatic rampageousness saponification
phantasmagoric procrastinator reasonableness satisfactorily
pharmaceutical prodigiousness rebelliousness sauropterygian
pharmacologist productiveness recapitulation scandalisation
pharmacopoeial professionally recapitulative scandalousness
phenobarbitone professorially recapitulatory scatterbrained
phenylbutazone profitableness recolonisation schematisation
philanthropise progenitorship recommencement schismatically
philanthropist prognosticator recommendation scholastically
philologically progressionary recommendatory schoolchildren
phlegmatically progressionism reconciliation schoolmistress
phosphorescent progressionist reconciliatory scientifically
photochemistry prohibitionism reconnaissance scintillometer
photoperiodism prohibitionist reconstitution scrubbingbrush

scrupulousness	simplemindedly	substantivally	thyrotoxicosis
scurrilousness	simplification	substitutional	tintinnabulary
seasonableness	simultaneously	substitutively	tintinnabulate
secularisation	singlebreasted	subversiveness	tintinnabulous
segregationist	singlehandedly	successfulness	topsyturviness
selfabnegation	singlemindedly	successionally	traditionalism
selfabsorption	skimbleskamble	successiveness	traditionalist
selfaccusation	slanderousness	sufferableness	tragicomically
selfaccusatory	slatternliness	suggestibility	traitorousness
selfadjustment	slaughterhouse	suggestiveness	transcendental
selfadmiration	slaughterously	sulphanilamide	transcendently
selfassumption	snaggletoothed	superabundance	transformation
selfcomplacent	sociologically	superannuation	transformative
selfconfidence	sociopolitical	superciliously	transitionally
selfconsequent	solicitousness	superconductor	transitiveness
selfconsistent	solidification	superelevation	transitoriness
selfcontrolled	solitudinarian	supereminently	transliterator
selfcorrecting	solubilisation	supererogation	transmigration
selfdependence	somnambulation	supererogatory	transmigratory
selfdestroying	somnambulistic	superficiality	transplantable
selfdetermined	sophistication	superfoetation	transportation
selfdiscipline	soporiferously	superincumbent	transsexualism
selfeffacement	soteriological	superinduction	transvaluation
selfeffacingly	souldestroying	superintendent	transversality
selfemployment	southeastwards	supernaturally	tremendousness
selfenergising	southwestwards	superphosphate	tridimensional
selfexplaining	spatiotemporal	superscription	Trinitarianism
selfexpression	specialisation	supersensitive	trivialisation
selffertilised	spectrographic	supersonically	tropologically
selfflattering	spectroscopist	superstructure	troubleshooter
selffulfilling	speechlessness	superterranean	tumultuousness
selfgovernment	spermatogenous	supervisorship	twodimensional
selfimmolation	spermatogonium	supposititious	tyrannicalness
selfimportance	spermatophytic	supralapsarian	ubiquitousness
selfinductance	sphaerocrystal	supramaxillary	ultimogeniture
selfindulgence	sphygmographic	suprasegmental	ultramicrotome
selfinterested	spindleshanked	surefootedness	ultramontanism
selfpartiality	spinthariscope	susceptibility	ultramontanist
selfperception	spiritlessness	susceptiveness	ultrasonically
selfpossession	spiritualistic	suspensiveness	ultrastructure
selfpreserving	spirituousness	suspiciousness	umbrageousness
selfproclaimed	spirochaetosis	swordswallower	unaccommodated
selfpropelling	sprightfulness	sycophantishly	unaccomplished
selfpropulsion	springcleaning	symmetrisation	unacknowledged
selfprotection	squadronleader	symptomatology	unaffectedness
selfregulating	stadholdership	synchronically	unappreciative
selfrepression	stampcollector	systematically	unapproachable
selfrespectful	standardbearer	tachistoscopic	unattractively
selfrespecting	staphylococcus	tachygraphical	unbecomingness
selfrestrained	stationariness	tatterdemalion	uncircumcision
selfrevelation	statuesqueness	tautologically	uncommunicable
selfsatisfying	steganographer	teleologically	uncompromising
selfsufficient	stertorousness	telepathically	uncongeniality
selfsuggestion	stigmatisation	telephonically	unconscionable
selfsupporting	stochastically	telephotograph	uncontrollable
selfsustaining	stoicheiometry	telescopically	uncontrollably
selftormenting	stoichiometric	tergiversation	uncontroverted
semicentennial	stomatological	terminableness	unconventional
semiconducting	stoutheartedly	terminological	unconvincingly
semielliptical	stratification	territorialise	uncorroborated
semiofficially	strikebreaking	territorialism	underdeveloped
sensationalism	strongmindedly	territorialist	underemphasise
sensationalist	stultification	territoriality	undergraduette
sensualisation	stumblingblock	terrorstricken	undermentioned
sentimentalise	stupendousness	testimonialise	undernourished
sentimentalism	subalternation	tetradactylous	understandable
sentimentalist	subconsciously	tetragrammaton	understandably
sentimentality	subcontinental	thalassography	understatement
septuagenarian	subcontrariety	thanksoffering	undervaluation
seriocomically	subinfeudation	theocratically	undesirability
serviceability	subjectiveness	therianthropic	uneconomically
servomechanism	sublieutenancy	thermochemical	unemphatically
sesquipedalian	submersibility	thermodynamics	unenterprising
Shakespeareana	submicroscopic	thermoelectric	unenthusiastic
Shakespeariana	submissiveness	thimblerigging	unexpectedness
shamefacedness	substantialism	thoughtfulness	unfaithfulness
shortsightedly	substantialist	thoughtreading	unflatteringly
shovehalfpenny	substantiality	threadbareness	unfriendliness
silicification	substantiation	thriftlessness	ungraciousness

ungratefulness
unhesitatingly
unidimensional
unidirectional
uniformitarian
unintelligible
unintelligibly
universalistic
unmannerliness
unmentionables
unpalatability
unpleasantness
unpremeditated
unprofessional
unquestionable
unquestionably
unremunerative
unreservedness
unsatisfactory
unscrupulously
unsociableness
unsuccessfully
untruthfulness
uproariousness
utilitarianism
vaingloriously
valetudinarian
vasodilatation
vasodilatatory
vegetativeness
venereological
verisimilitude
verticillaster
vicechancellor
vicepresidency
victoriousness
villainousness
vindictiveness
vituperatively
viviparousness
vivisectionist
vociferousness
volatilisation
volcanological
volumetrically
voluminousness
voluptuousness
vulcanological
vulnerableness
watercolourist
watertightness
weakmindedness
weightlessness
weltanschauung
westernisation
whippersnapper
whortleberries
windowdressing
windowshopping
wonderstricken
worshipfulness
Zoroastrianism
————
backscattering
backscratching
bacteriologist
bacteriostasis
bacteriostatic
barometrically
basidiomycetes
bastardisation
bathingmachine
calamitousness
calcareousness
campanological
campylotropous
cantankerously
capitalisation
capriciousness

carcinogenesis
cardiovascular
cartographical
castrametation
catachrestical
catechetically
categorisation
factitiousness
faintheartedly
fallaciousness
fantasticality
farsightedness
fastidiousness
favourableness
galactopoietic
haematogenesis
hagiographical
halfpennyworth
hallucinogenic
handicraftsman
handkerchieves
harmoniousness
iatrochemistry
lasciviousness
latitudinarian
macrocephalous
macroeconomics
magniloquently
malappropriate
malcontentedly
malodorousness
manageableness
marketgardener
martyrological
marvellousness
massproduction
mathematically
matriarchalism
narrowmindedly
naturalisation
pachydermatous
palaeethnology
palaeobotanist
papilionaceous
paradoxicality
parallelepiped
parapsychology
parasitologist
paratactically
pardonableness
parenchymatous
parsimoniously
partridgeberry
passionateness
pasteurisation
pathogenically
pathologically
patresfamilias
radicalisation
radioautograph
radiochemistry
radiosensitive
radiostrontium
radiotelegraph
radiotelephone
radiotelephony
radiotherapist
rambunctiously
rampageousness
Sabbatarianism
sacramentalism
sacramentalist
sacramentarian
sacrilegiously
salubriousness
sanctification
sanguification
sanguinariness
saponification

satisfactorily
sauropterygian
tachistoscopic
tachygraphical
tatterdemalion
tautologically
vaingloriously
valetudinarian
vasodilatation
vasodilatatory
watercolourist
watertightness
abovementioned
absentmindedly
absorptiveness
abstemiousness
abstractedness
abstractionism
abstractionist
obsequiousness
obstreperously
obstructionism
obstructionist
ubiquitousness
acceleratingly
acceptableness
accomplishable
accomplishment
accountability
accumulatively
accustomedness
achondroplasia
achromatically
acknowledgment
ecclesiastical
ecclesiologist
econometrician
ichthyological
ichthyophagous
ichthyosaurian
iconographical
scandalisation
scandalousness
scatterbrained
schematisation
schismatically
scholastically
schoolchildren
schoolmistress
scientifically
scintillometer
scrubbingbrush
scrupulousness
scurrilousness
administration
administrative
administratrix
advantageously
adventitiously
educationalist
idealistically
identification
idiopathically
aerobiological
aerobiotically
aerodynamicist
aesthesiometer
aetiologically
beautification
behaviouristic
beneficialness
censoriousness
centralisation
centrifugation
deceivableness
decimalisation
decolonisation
decolorisation
deconsecration

decorativeness
defenestration
definitiveness
degenerateness
dehumanisation
delectableness
deliberateness
deliberatively
delightfulness
delocalisation
demisemiquaver
demobilisation
democratically
demonetisation
demoralisation
denazification
denominational
denumerability
departmentally
dependableness
deplorableness
depolarisation
dermatological
despicableness
despiritualise
despitefulness
destructionist
determinedness
detestableness
detoxification
devitalisation
dextrorotation
dextrorotatory
featherbrained
ferrimagnetism
ferromagnesian
ferromagnetism
gelatinisation
genealogically
generalisation
generalpurpose
geocentrically
geographically
gerontological
heartsearching
hebetudinosity
hereditariness
hermaphroditic
heroworshipper
heterochromous
heteromorphism
heteromorphous
heterophyllous
heterothallism
lefthandedness
legalistically
legitimisation
meddlesomeness
meditativeness
megasporangium
megasporophyll
Mephistopheles
meretriciously
mesdemoiselles
metallographer
metaphorically
metaphysically
metapsychology
metempsychosis
meteorological
methodological
meticulousness
necessarianism
neglectfulness
neocolonialism
neuroanatomist
neurochemistry
neuropathology
neuroscientist

neutralisation	revengefulness	terminableness	thermoelectric
newfangledness	revivification	terminological	thimblerigging
oecumenicalism	seasonableness	territorialise	thoughtfulness
penetrableness	secularisation	territorialism	thoughtreading
perceptibility	segregationist	territorialist	threadbareness
perceptiveness	selfabnegation	territoriality	thriftlessness
percutaneously	selfabsorption	terrorstricken	thyrotoxicosis
peremptoriness	selfaccusation	testimonialise	whippersnapper
perfectibility	selfaccusatory	tetradactylous	whortleberries
perfidiousness	selfadjustment	tetragrammaton	airconditioner
periodontology	selfadmiration	vegetativeness	bibliographise
peripateticism	selfassumption	venereological	bibliomaniacal
perishableness	selfcomplacent	verisimilitude	biodegradation
permissibility	selfconfidence	verticillaster	bioelectricity
permissiveness	selfconsequent	weakmindedness	bioengineering
perniciousness	selfconsistent	weightlessness	biographically
personableness	selfcontrolled	weltanschauung	bioluminescent
persuasiveness	selfcorrecting	westernisation	biosystematics
pertinaciously	selfdependence	affectionately	bituminisation
perturbational	selfdestroying	aforementioned	cinematography
pestilentially	selfdetermined	Africanisation	circuitousness
petrochemistry	selfdiscipline	effervescently	circumambiency
petrographical	selfeffacement	effortlessness	circumambulate
petrologically	selfeffacingly	aggrandisement	circumbendibus
reasonableness	selfemployment	aggressiveness	circumlittoral
rebelliousness	selfenergising	agrobiological	circumlocution
recapitulation	selfexplaining	egalitarianism	circumlocutory
recapitulative	selfexpression	chancellorship	circumnavigate
recapitulatory	selffertilised	changeableness	circumspection
recolonisation	selfflattering	characteristic	circumstantial
recommencement	selffulfilling	charitableness	circumvolution
recommendation	selfgovernment	chemoreception	diachronically
recommendatory	selfimmolation	chemoreceptive	diagnostically
reconciliation	selfimportance	chemosynthesis	diagrammatical
reconciliatory	selfinductance	chickenhearted	dialectologist
reconnaissance	selfindulgence	chickenlivered	diamantiferous
reconstitution	selfinterested	chincherinchee	diamondiferous
reconstruction	selfpartiality	chivalrousness	diaphanousness
reconstructive	selfperception	Christological	dicotyledonous
recoverability	selfpossession	chromatography	dieselelectric
rectangularity	selfpreserving	chronometrical	differentiable
redintegration	selfproclaimed	phantasmagoria	differentially
redistribution	selfpropelling	phantasmagoric	diffractometer
redistributive	selfpropulsion	pharmaceutical	diminutiveness
reflectiveness	selfprotection	pharmacologist	dinoflagellate
refractoriness	selfregulating	pharmacopoeial	diplomatically
refrangibility	selfrepression	phenobarbitone	disaffiliation
regardlessness	selfrespectful	phenylbutazone	disaffirmation
regeneratively	selfrespecting	philanthropise	disappointment
regressiveness	selfrestrained	philanthropist	disapprobation
regularisation	selfrevelation	philologically	disapprobative
rehabilitation	selfsatisfying	phlegmatically	disapprobatory
reintroduction	selfsufficient	phosphorescent	disapprovingly
reinvigoration	selfsuggestion	photochemistry	disarrangement
rejuvenescence	selfsupporting	photoperiodism	disassociation
relentlessness	selfsustaining	photosensitise	disciplinarian
relinquishment	selftormenting	photosensitive	discolouration
remarkableness	semicentennial	photosynthesis	discombobulate
reminiscential	semiconducting	photosynthetic	discomfortable
remonetisation	semielliptical	phototelegraph	discommendable
remorsefulness	semiofficially	phraseological	disconcertment
reorganisation	sensationalism	phthalocyanine	disconformable
repetitiveness	sensationalist	physiognomical	disconnectedly
representation	sensualisation	phytogeography	disconsolately
representative	sentimentalise	phytopathology	disconsolation
reproductively	sentimentalism	rheumatologist	discontentedly
repudiationist	sentimentalist	rhinencephalic	discontinuance
resinification	sentimentality	rhinencephalon	discountenance
resistlessness	septuagenarian	Shakespeareana	discouragement
respectability	seriocomically	Shakespeariana	discouragingly
respectfulness	serviceability	shamefacedness	discourteously
responsibility	servomechanism	shortsightedly	discriminating
responsiveness	sesquipedalian	shovehalfpenny	discrimination
restorationism	teleologically	thalassography	discriminative
restorationist	telepathically	thanksoffering	discriminatory
restrictionist	telephonically	theocratically	discursiveness
resurrectional	telephotograph	therianthropic	disdainfulness
retrogradation	telescopically	thermochemical	disembarkation
revalorisation	tergiversation	thermodynamics	disembarkation

disembowelment simplemindedly immobilisation indecisiveness
disenchantment simplification immoderateness indecomposable
disenfranchise simultaneously imparisyllabic indecorousness
disenthralment singlebreasted impassableness indefiniteness
disequilibrium singlehandedly impassibleness indemonstrable
disfurnishment singlemindedly imperativeness indestructible
disgruntlement tintinnabulary impermeability indestructibly
disheartenment tintinnabulate imperviousness indeterminable
disinclination tintinnabulous implacableness indifferentism
disincorporate vicechancellor implausibility indifferentist
disinfestation vicepresidency implementation indiscerptible
disingenuously victoriousness imponderabilia indiscoverable
disinheritance villainousness impoverishment indiscreetness
disintegration vindictiveness impracticality indiscriminate
disintegrative vituperatively impregnability indistinctness
disjointedness viviparousness impressibility indivisibility
disorderliness vivisectionist impressionable indoctrination
disorientation windowdressing impressiveness indubitability
dispensability windowshopping improvableness ineffectuality
dispiritedness skimbleskamble omnivorousness inevitableness
disputatiously Albigensianism umbrageousness inexorableness
disquisitional allegorisation anagrammatical inexpressively
disrespectable allelomorphism anthropography infectiousness
dissertational alphabetically anthropologist infelicitously
dissociability alphanumerical anthropometric inflammability
distemperature altruistically anticipatively inflectionally
distensibility blackmarketeer anticonvulsant inflectionless
distributional blockaderunner antidepressant inflexibleness
distributively bloodthirstily antifederalist infralapsarian
diverticulitis classconscious antiperspirant infrangibility
divertissement classification antiphlogistic infrastructure
eigenfrequency classificatory antiquarianism ingloriousness
fictitiousness claustrophobia antiscriptural ingratiatingly
figurativeness claustrophobic antiseptically inharmoniously
hierarchically clearsightedly antithetically inheritability
hieroglyphical climatological enantiomorphic inimitableness
highhandedness electioneering encephalograph inordinateness
highmindedness electrobiology encyclopaedism insatiableness
histochemistry electrodeposit encyclopaedist inscrutability
histopathology electrodynamic endoradiosonde insensibleness
historiography electrostatics endosmotically inseparability
histrionically electrotherapy enharmonically insignificance
liberalisation electrothermal enterprisingly insignificancy
libertarianism electrothermic entertainingly instrumentally
libidinousness electrovalency enthronisation insufficiently
licentiousness elementariness entomostracous insuperability
lightheartedly flagitiousness inadequateness insuppressible
linguistically flatfootedness inadvisability insurmountable
liturgiologist floriculturist inalienability insurmountably
microbiologist illconditioned inalterability insurrectional
microcephalous illegitimately inappositeness intangibleness
microcircuitry illimitability inappreciation integrationist
microcomponent illiterateness inappreciative intellectually
microeconomics illustrational inapproachable intelligential
microminiature illustratively inarticulately intelligentsia
microprocessor oleaginousness inarticulation intercessional
microsporangia planetstricken inartistically intercessorial
microstructure pleasurability inauspiciously intercommunion
microtechnique pleonastically incapacitation intercommunity
militarisation pluviometrical incautiousness interdependent
millenarianism slanderousness incestuousness interferential
mineralisation slatternliness incommensurate interferometer
ministerialist slaughterhouse incommodiously interferometry
miraculousness slaughterously incommunicable intergradation
misapplication ultimogeniture incommunicably interjectional
misappropriate ultramicrotome incompleteness interlineation
miscalculation ultramontanism incompressible interlocutress
misinformation ultramontanist incompressibly intermediately
mistranslation ultrasonically inconclusively intermediation
nightblindness ultrastructure inconsequently intermigration
nitrocellulose amateurishness inconsiderable intermittently
nitroglycerine ambassadorship inconsiderably intermolecular
pianoaccordian ambidextrously inconsistently internationale
pigeonbreasted embarrassingly incontrollable interpellation
pisciculturist emblematically inconveniently interpenetrate
pistilliferous emulsification incoordination interplanetary
ridiculousness imaginableness incorporeality interpretation
rigidification immaculateness incredibleness interpretative
silicification immethodically indecipherable interpretively

intersectional	unsuccessfully	contumeliously	northnortheast
intersexuality	untruthfulness	conventionally	northnorthwest
intertwinement	boardingschool	conversational	northwestwards
intolerability	boisterousness	convertibility	noteworthiness
intractability	boroughEnglish	convexoconcave	poikilothermal
intramolecular	bougainvillaea	convincingness	poikilothermic
intransitively	bouleversement	convulsiveness	politicisation
intrinsicality	bowdlerisation	coordinateness	polymerisation
introductorily	coessentiality	copperbottomed	polymorphously
intuitionalism	colourfastness	coquettishness	polysaccharide
intuitionalist	colourlessness	correspondence	polytheistical
invariableness	combustibility	correspondency	popularisation
invincibleness	commensurately	corruptibility	portentousness
inviolableness	commensuration	corticosteroid	possessiveness
knickerbockers	commissaryship	corticosterone	postmastership
knighterrantry	commissionaire	corticotrophic	postmillennial
oneirocritical	committeewoman	corticotrophin	postpositional
pneumatologist	commodiousness	cosmographical	postpositively
pneumoconiosis	commonsensical	cosmopolitical	potentiometric
snaggletoothed	communications	cotemporaneous	roadworthiness
unaccommodated	comparableness	councilchamber	robustiousness
unaccomplished	compassionable	councillorship	roentgenoscopy
unacknowledged	compatibleness	counsellorship	rontgenography
unaffectedness	compensational	counterbalance	Rosicrucianism
unappreciative	complexionless	counterculture	roundaboutness
unapproachable	compossibility	countercurrent	sociologically
unattractively	comprehensible	countermeasure	sociopolitical
unbecomingness	comprehensibly	counterplotted	solicitousness
uncircumcision	compulsiveness	countrydancing	solidification
uncommunicable	concavoconcave	courageousness	solitudinarian
uncompromising	conceivability	dodecasyllable	solubilisation
uncongeniality	concelebration	dolichocephaly	somnambulation
unconscionable	concentrically	dolomitisation	somnambulistic
uncontrollable	concessionaire	doublebreasted	sophistication
uncontrollably	conclusiveness	foraminiferous	soporiferously
uncontroverted	concretisation	forbiddingness	soteriological
unconventional	condescendence	foreordination	souldestroying
unconvincingly	conditionality	formidableness	southeastwards
uncorroborated	conductibility	forthrightness	southwestwards
underdeveloped	confidentially	fortuitousness	topsyturviness
underemphasise	conformability	fortunetelling	vociferousness
undergraduette	conglomeration	forwardlooking	volatilisation
undermentioned	conglutination	goodfellowship	volcanological
undernourished	conglutinative	goodhumouredly	volumetrically
understandable	congratulation	goodtemperedly	voluminousness
understandably	congratulative	hobbledehoyish	voluptuousness
understatement	congratulatory	hocuspocussing	wonderstricken
undervaluation	congregational	holometabolism	worshipfulness
undesirability	conjunctivitis	holometabolous	Zoroastrianism
uneconomically	conquistadores	homoeomorphism	aphoristically
unemphatically	consanguineous	homogenisation	apologetically
unenterprising	conscienceless	homotransplant	apophthegmatic
unenthusiastic	conservational	honourableness	apoplectically
unexpectedness	conservatively	horrorstricken	apothegmatical
unfaithfulness	consociational	horticulturist	appendicectomy
unflatteringly	conspiratorial	Johannisberger	apprehensively
unfriendliness	constitutional	longheadedness	apprenticeship
ungraciousness	constitutively	longitudinally	epexegetically
ungratefulness	constructional	longwindedness	epidemiologist
unhesitatingly	constructively	loquaciousness	epigrammatical
unidimensional	constructivism	lovingkindness	epistemologist
unidirectional	constructivist	monkeybusiness	openhandedness
uniformitarian	consubstantial	monochromatism	openmindedness
unintelligible	consuetudinary	monopolisation	ophthalmoscope
unintelligibly	contagiousness	monosaccharide	ophthalmoscopy
universalistic	contemptuously	monotonousness	opinionatively
unmannerliness	conterminously	morganatically	oppressiveness
unmentionables	contiguousness	mountaineering	optimistically
unpalatability	continuousness	noctambulation	spatiotemporal
unpleasantness	contractedness	nomenclatorial	specialisation
unpremeditated	contradictable	nonbelligerent	spectrographic
unprofessional	contradictious	noncommunicant	spectroscopist
unquestionable	contraindicate	nonconcurrence	speechlessness
unquestionably	contraposition	noncooperation	spermatogenous
unremunerative	contrapositive	noninvolvement	spermatogonium
unreservedness	contrapuntally	nonperformance	spermatophytic
unsatisfactory	controllership	nonrestrictive	sphaerocrystal
unscrupulously	controvertible	nonsensicality	sphygmographic
unsociableness	contumaciously	northeastwards	spindleshanked

spinthariscope	presentational	pseudaesthesia	outlandishness
spiritlessness	presentimental	pseudepigrapha	outrageousness
spiritualistic	presumptuously	pseudepigraphy	publicspirited
spirituousness	presupposition	pseudomorphism	pugnaciousness
spirochaetosis	prettification	pseudomorphous	purposefulness
sprightfulness	preventability	pseudonymously	quadragenarian
springcleaning	preventiveness	psilanthropism	quadrisyllabic
uproariousness	probabiliorism	psilanthropist	quadrisyllable
squadronleader	probabiliorist	psychoanalysis	quantification
archaeological	proceleusmatic	psychoanalytic	quantitatively
archetypically	procrastinator	psychochemical	quarterbinding
archidiaconate	prodigiousness	psychodynamics	quattrocentism
archiepiscopal	productiveness	psychoneurosis	quattrocentist
architectonics	professionally	psychoneurotic	quinquagesimal
arithmetically	professorially	psychophysical	quinquennially
arrhythmically	profitableness	psychosomatics	quintessential
arrondissement	progenitorship	psychosurgical	Russianisation
articulateness	prognosticator	attainableness	subalternation
artificialness	progressionary	attractiveness	subconsciously
brachycephalic	progressionism	ethnologically	subcontinental
breathlessness	progressionist	etymologically	subcontrariety
breathtakingly	prohibitionism	pteridological	subinfeudation
bremsstrahlung	prohibitionist	stadholdership	subjectiveness
Brobdingnagian	proletarianise	stampcollector	sublieutenancy
bronchiectasis	proletarianism	standardbearer	submersibility
creditableness	prolocutorship	staphylococcus	submicroscopic
crinkumcrankum	propaedeutical	stationariness	submissiveness
crossfertilise	propagandistic	statuesqueness	substantialism
crosspollinate	propitiatorily	steganographer	substantialist
crossreference	propitiousness	stertorousness	substantiality
cryptaesthesia	proportionable	stigmatisation	substantiation
crystallisable	proportionably	stochastically	substantivally
erythropoiesis	proportionally	stoicheiometry	substitutional
fraternisation	proprietorship	stoichiometric	substitutively
friendlessness	proprioceptive	stomatological	subversiveness
fructification	proscriptively	stoutheartedly	successfulness
gramineousness	prosencephalic	stratification	successionally
grandiloquence	prosencephalon	strikebreaking	successiveness
gratuitousness	prosperousness	strongmindedly	sufferableness
gregariousness	protectiveness	stultification	suggestibility
groundlessness	prothonotarial	stumblingblock	suggestiveness
irreconcilable	protozoologist	stupendousness	sulphanilamide
irreconcilably	protrusiveness	utilitarianism	superabundance
irreducibility	providentially	audiofrequency	superannuation
irrefutability	traditionalism	Augustinianism	superciliously
irremovability	traditionalist	auspiciousness	superconductor
irreproachable	tragicomically	authentication	superelevation
irreproachably	traitorousness	autobiographer	supereminently
irreproducible	transcendental	autobiographic	supererogation
irresoluteness	transcendently	autocratically	supererogatory
irrespectively	transformation	autoradiograph	superficiality
irrevocability	transformative	autosuggestion	superfoetation
kremlinologist	transitionally	bullheadedness	superincumbent
organisational	transitiveness	butterfingered	superinduction
organometallic	transitoriness	butterflyscrew	superintendent
ornithological	transliterator	cucurbitaceous	supernaturally
orthochromatic	transmigration	cumbersomeness	superphosphate
orthographical	transmigratory	cumulativeness	superscription
practicability	transplantable	curvilinearity	supersensitive
pragmaticality	transportation	eulogistically	supersonically
praiseworthily	transsexualism	euphuistically	superstructure
prearrangement	transvaluation	eutrophication	superterranean
precariousness	transversality	fullyfashioned	supervisorship
precociousness	tremendousness	fundamentalism	supposititious
predesignation	tridimensional	fundamentalist	supralapsarian
predestinarian	Trinitarianism	fundamentality	supramaxillary
predestination	trivialisation	humidification	suprasegmental
predeterminate	tropologically	judgematically	surefootedness
predictability	troubleshooter	jurisdictional	susceptibility
predisposition	associationism	justifiability	susceptiveness
prefabrication	astronomically	lugubriousness	suspensiveness
preferentially	astrophysicist	multifariously	suspiciousness
premeditatedly	asymmetrically	multilaterally	tumultuousness
premillenarian	asymptotically	multinucleated	vulcanological
preponderantly	asynchronously	multiplication	vulnerableness
preposterously	eschatological	multiplicative	avariciousness
presbyterially	esterification	numismatically	Evangelicalism
prescriptively	ostentatiously	nutritiousness	evangelisation
presentability	osteoarthritis	outgeneralling	overabundantly

overcapitalise anagrammatical slaughterously accumulatively
overcommitment avariciousness snaggletoothed accustomedness
overcompensate beautification spatiotemporal archaeological
overconfidence blackmarketeer stadholdership archetypically
overestimation boardingschool stampcollector archidiaconate
overexcitement brachycephalic standardbearer archiepiscopal
overindulgence chancellorship staphylococcus architectonics
overpopulation changeableness stationariness backscattering
overpoweringly characteristic statuesqueness backscratching
overproduction charitableness thalassography bacteriologist
oversubscribed classconscious thanksoffering bacteriostasis
overwhelmingly classification traditionalism bacteriostatic
swordswallower classificatory traditionalist cucurbitaceous
twodimensional claustrophobia tragicomically deceivableness
exasperatingly claustrophobic traitorousness decimalisation
exceptionality cyanocobalamin transcendental decolonisation
exclaustration diachronically transcendently decolorisation
excommunicable diagnostically transformation deconsecration
excommunicator diagrammatical transformative decorativeness
excruciatingly dialectologist transitionally dicotyledonous
exhaustibility diamantiferous transitiveness ecclesiastical
exhaustiveness diamondiferous transitoriness ecclesiologist
exhilaratingly diaphanousness transliterator encephalograph
existentialism egalitarianism transmigration encyclopaedism
existentialist enantiomorphic transmigratory encyclopaedist
experientially Evangelicalism transplantable eschatological
experimentally evangelisation transportation exceptionality
expressionless exasperatingly transsexualism exclaustration
expressiveness featherbrained transvaluation excommunicable
extemporaneity flagitiousness transversality excommunicator
extemporaneous flatfootedness unaccommodated excruciatingly
extensionality fraternisation unaccomplished factitiousness
extinguishable gramineousness unacknowledged fictitiousness
extinguishment grandiloquence unaffectedness hocuspocussing
extracorporeal gratuitousness unappreciative incapacitation
extraneousness heartsearching unapproachable incautiousness
extravehicular imaginableness unattractively incestuousness
oxyhaemoglobin inadequateness weakmindedness incommensurate
cyanocobalamin inadvisability Albigensianism incommodiously
gynaecological inalienability ambassadorship incommunicable
gynandromorphy inalterability ambidextrously incommunicably
gyrostabiliser inappositeness bibliographise incompleteness
hydrocoralline inappreciation bibliomaniacal incompressible
hydrodynamical inappreciative embarrassingly incompressibly
hydrographical inapproachable emblematically inconclusively
hydromechanics inarticulately hebetudinosity inconsequently
hygroscopicity inarticulation hobbledehoyish inconsiderable
hyperbolically inartistically liberalisation inconsiderably
hypercalcaemia inauspiciously libertarianism inconsistently
hypercatalexis phantasmagoria libidinousness incontrollable
hypercriticise phantasmagoric publicspirited inconveniently
hypercriticism pharmaceutical rebelliousness incoordination
hyperglycaemia pharmacologist robustiousness incorporeality
hyperirritable pharmacopoeial Sabbatarianism incredibleness
hypersensitive pianoaccordian subalternation licentiousness
hypersonically planetstricken subconsciously macrocephalous
hypocoristical practicability subcontinental macroeconomics
hypocritically pragmaticality subcontrariety microbiologist
hypodermically praiseworthily subinfeudation microcephalous
hypostatically quadragenarian subjectiveness microcircuitry
hypothetically quadrisyllabic sublieutenancy microcomponent
hypothyroidism quadrisyllable submersibility microeconomics
hysterectomise quantification submicroscopic microminiature
lyophilisation quantitatively submissiveness microprocessor
myrmecological quarterbinding substantialism microsporangia
myrmecophagous quattrocentism substantialist microstructure
myrmecophilous quattrocentist substantiality microtechnique
mysteriousness reasonableness substantiation necessarianism
mythologically roadworthiness substantivally noctambulation
pyrheliometric scandalisation substitutional oecumenicalism
Pythagoreanism scandalousness substitutively pachydermatous
sycophantishly scatterbrained subversiveness recapitulation
symmetrisation seasonableness umbrageousness recapitulative
symptomatology Shakespeareana unbecomingness recapitulatory
synchronically Shakespeariana acceleratingly recolonisation
systematically shamefacedness acceptableness recommencement
tyrannicalness slanderousness accomplishable recommendation
——————————————— slatternliness accomplishment recommendatory
amateurishness slaughterhouse accountability reconciliation

reconciliatory	underemphasise	presbyterially	lugubriousness
reconnaissance	undergraduette	prescriptively	magniloquently
reconstitution	undermentioned	presentability	megasporangium
reconstruction	undernourished	presentational	megasporophyll
reconstructive	understandable	presentimental	neglectfulness
recoverability	understandably	presumptuously	nightblindness
rectangularity	understatement	presupposition	organisational
sacramentalism	undervaluation	prettification	organometallic
sacramentalist	undesirability	preventability	pigeonbreasted
sacramentarian	breathlessness	preventiveness	pugnaciousness
sacrilegiously	breathtakingly	pseudaesthesia	regardlessness
secularisation	bremsstrahlung	pseudepigrapha	regeneratively
sociologically	chemoreception	pseudepigraphy	regressiveness
sociopolitical	chemoreceptive	pseudomorphism	regularisation
successfulness	chemosynthesis	pseudomorphous	rigidification
successionally	clearsightedly	pseudonymously	segregationist
successiveness	coessentiality	pteridological	suggestibility
sycophantishly	creditableness	rheumatologist	suggestiveness
tachistoscopic	dieselelectric	roentgenoscopy	ungraciousness
tachygraphical	electioneering	specialisation	ungratefulness
uncircumcision	electrobiology	spectrographic	vegetativeness
uncommunicable	electrodeposit	spectroscopist	achondroplasia
uncompromising	electrodynamic	speechlessness	achromatically
uncongeniality	electrostatics	spermatogenous	aphoristically
unconscionable	electrotherapy	spermatogonium	behaviouristic
uncontrollable	electrothermal	spermatophytic	dehumanisation
uncontrollably	electrothermic	steganographer	enharmonically
uncontroverted	electrovalency	stertorousness	ethnologically
unconventional	elementariness	theocratically	exhaustibility
unconvincingly	epexegetically	therianthropic	exhaustiveness
uncorroborated	gregariousness	thermochemical	exhilaratingly
vicechancellor	haematogenesis	thermodynamics	ichthyological
vicepresidency	hierarchically	thermoelectric	ichthyophagous
victoriousness	hieroglyphical	tremendousness	ichthyosaurian
vociferousness	idealistically	uneconomically	inharmoniously
audiofrequency	identification	unemphatically	inheritability
dodecasyllable	ineffectuality	unenterprising	Johannisberger
endoradiosonde	inevitableness	unenthusiastic	ophthalmoscope
endosmotically	inexorableness	unexpectedness	ophthalmoscopy
hydrocoralline	inexpressively	affectionately	rehabilitation
hydrodynamical	kremlinologist	defenestration	schematisation
hydrographical	oleaginousness	definitiveness	schismatically
hydromechanics	oneirocritical	differentiable	scholastically
indecipherable	openhandedness	differentially	schoolchildren
indecisiveness	openmindedness	diffractometer	schoolmistress
indecomposable	overabundantly	effervescently	sphaerocrystal
indecorousness	overcapitalise	effortlessness	sphygmographic
indefiniteness	overcommitment	infectiousness	unhesitatingly
indemonstrable	overcompensate	infelicitously	arithmetically
indestructible	overconfidence	inflammability	boisterousness
indestructibly	overestimation	inflectionally	chickenhearted
indeterminable	overexcitement	inflectionless	chickenlivered
indifferentism	overindulgence	inflexibleness	chincherinchee
indifferentist	overpopulation	infralapsarian	chivalrousness
indiscerptible	overpoweringly	infrangibility	climatological
indiscoverable	overproduction	infrastructure	crinkumcrankum
indiscreetness	oversubscribed	lefthandedness	epidemiologist
indiscriminate	overwhelmingly	reflectiveness	epigrammatical
indistinctness	phenobarbitone	refractoriness	epistemologist
indivisibility	phenylbutazone	refrangibility	existentialism
indoctrination	pleasurability	sufferableness	existentialist
indubitability	pleonastically	unfaithfulness	faintheartedly
judgematically	pneumatologist	unflatteringly	friendlessness
meddlesomeness	pneumoconiosis	unfriendliness	idiopathically
meditativeness	prearrangement	aggrandisement	inimitableness
radicalisation	precariousness	aggressiveness	knickerbockers
radioautograph	precociousness	Augustinianism	knighterrantry
radiochemistry	predesignation	degenerateness	opinionatively
radiosensitive	predestinarian	eigenfrequency	philanthropise
radiostrontium	predestination	figurativeness	philanthropist
radiotelegraph	predeterminate	hagiographical	philologically
radiotelephone	predictability	highhandedness	poikilothermal
radiotelephony	predisposition	highmindedness	poikilothermic
radiotherapist	prefabrication	hygroscopicity	psilanthropism
redintegration	preferentially	ingloriousness	psilanthropist
redistribution	premeditatedly	ingratiatingly	quinquagesimal
redistributive	premillenarian	legalistically	quinquennially
ridiculousness	preponderantly	legitimisation	quintessential
underdeveloped	preposterously	lightheartedly	reintroduction

reinvigoration	salubriousness	combustibility	congratulatory
rhinencephalic	selfabnegation	commensurately	congregational
rhinencephalon	selfabsorption	commensuration	conjunctivitis
scientifically	selfaccusation	commissaryship	conquistadores
scintillometer	selfaccusatory	commissionaire	consanguineous
skimbleskamble	selfadjustment	committeewoman	conscienceless
spindleshanked	selfadmiration	commodiousness	conservational
spinthariscope	selfassumption	commonsensical	conservatively
spiritlessness	selfcomplacent	communications	consociational
spiritualistic	selfconfidence	comparableness	conspiratorial
spirituousness	selfconsequent	compassionable	constitutional
spirochaetosis	selfconsistent	compatibleness	constitutively
stigmatisation	selfcontrolled	compensational	constructional
thimblerigging	selfcorrecting	complexionless	constructively
tridimensional	selfdependence	compossibility	constructivism
Trinitarianism	selfdestroying	comprehensible	constructivist
trivialisation	selfdetermined	comprehensibly	consubstantial
ubiquitousness	selfdiscipline	compulsiveness	consuetudinary
unidimensional	selfeffacement	cumbersomeness	contagiousness
unidirectional	selfeffacingly	cumulativeness	contemptuously
uniformitarian	selfemployment	demisemiquaver	conterminously
unintelligible	selfenergising	demobilisation	contiguousness
unintelligibly	selfexplaining	democratically	continuousness
universalistic	selfexpression	demonetisation	contractedness
utilitarianism	selffertilised	demoralisation	contradictable
vaingloriously	selfflattering	diminutiveness	contradictious
weightlessness	selffulfilling	homoeomorphism	contraindicate
whippersnapper	selfgovernment	homogenisation	contraposition
rejuvenescence	selfimmolation	homotransplant	contrapositive
acknowledgment	selfimportance	humidification	contrapuntally
allegorisation	selfinductance	immaculateness	controllership
allelomorphism	selfindulgence	immethodically	controvertible
bullheadedness	selfinterested	immobilisation	contumaciously
calamitousness	selfpartiality	immoderateness	contumeliously
calcareousness	selfperception	nomenclatorial	conventionally
colourfastness	selfpossession	numismatically	conversational
colourlessness	selfpreserving	rambunctiously	convertibility
delectableness	selfproclaimed	rampageousness	convexoconcave
deliberateness	selfpropelling	remarkableness	convincingness
deliberatively	selfpropulsion	reminiscential	convulsiveness
delightfulness	selfprotection	remonetisation	denazification
delocalisation	selfregulating	remorsefulness	denominational
dolichocephaly	selfrepression	semicentennial	denumerability
dolomitisation	selfrespectful	semiconducting	dinoflagellate
eulogistically	selfrespecting	semielliptical	fantasticality
fallaciousness	selfrestrained	semiofficially	fundamentalism
fullyfashioned	selfrevelation	simplemindedly	fundamentalist
galactopoietic	selfsatisfying	simplification	fundamentality
gelatinisation	selfsufficient	simultaneously	genealogically
halfpennyworth	selfsuggestion	somnambulation	generalisation
hallucinogenic	selfsupporting	somnambulistic	generalpurpose
holometabolism	selfsustaining	symmetrisation	gynaecological
holometabolous	selftormenting	symptomatology	gynandromorphy
illconditioned	silicification	tumultuousness	handicraftsman
illegitimately	solicitousness	unmanneriness	handkerchieves
illimitability	solidification	unmentionables	honourableness
illiterateness	solitudinarian	beneficialness	linguistically
illustrational	solubilisation	cantankerously	longheadedness
illustratively	sulphanilamide	censoriousness	longitudinally
malappropriate	teleologically	centralisation	longwindedness
malcontentedly	telepathically	centrifugation	manageableness
malodorousness	telephonically	cinematography	mineralisation
militarisation	telephotograph	concavoconcave	ministerialist
millenarianism	telescopically	conceivability	monkeybusiness
multifariously	valetudinarian	concelebration	monochromatism
multilaterally	villainousness	concentrically	monopolisation
multinucleated	volatilisation	concessionaire	monosaccharide
multiplication	volcanological	conclusiveness	monotonousness
multiplicative	volumetrically	concretisation	nonbelligerent
palaeethnology	voluminousness	condescendence	noncommunicant
palaeobotanist	voluptuousness	conditionality	nonconcurrence
phlegmatically	vulcanological	conductibility	noncooperation
politicisation	vulnerableness	confidentially	noninvolvement
polymerisation	weltanschauung	conformability	nonperformance
polymorphously	administration	conglomeration	nonrestrictive
polysaccharide	administrative	conglutination	nonsensicality
polytheistical	administratrix	conglutinative	omnivorousness
relentlessness	campanological	congratulation	ornithological
relinquishment	campylotropous	congratulative	penetrableness

rontgenography	proletarianise	impoverishment	circumstantial
sanctification	proletarianism	impracticality	circumvolution
sanguification	prolocutorship	impregnability	correspondence
sanguinariness	propaedeutical	impressibility	correspondency
sensationalism	propagandistic	impressionable	corruptibility
sensationalist	propitiatorily	impressiveness	corticosteroid
sensualisation	propitiousness	improvableness	corticosterone
sentimentalise	proportionable	Mephistopheles	corticotrophic
sentimentalism	proportionably	oppressiveness	corticotrophin
sentimentalist	proportionally	papilionaceous	curvilinearity
sentimentality	proprietorship	popularisation	dermatological
singlebreasted	proprioceptive	repetitiveness	farsightedness
singlehandedly	proscriptively	representation	ferrimagnetism
singlemindedly	prosencephalic	representative	ferromagnesian
synchronically	prosencephalon	reproductively	ferromagnetism
tintinnabulary	prosperousness	repudiationist	foraminiferous
tintinnabulate	protectiveness	saponification	forbiddingness
tintinnabulous	protozoologist	septuagenarian	foreordination
venereological	protrusiveness	sophistication	formidableness
vindictiveness	providentially	soporiferously	forthrightness
windowdressing	reorganisation	superabundance	fortuitousness
windowshopping	shortsightedly	superannuation	fortunetelling
wonderstricken	shovehalfpenny	superciliously	forwardlooking
abovementioned	stochastically	superconductor	gerontological
aforementioned	stoicheiometry	superelevation	gyrostabiliser
apologetically	stoichiometric	supereminently	harmoniousness
apophthegmatic	stomatological	supererogation	hereditariness
apoplectically	stoutheartedly	supererogatory	hermaphroditic
apothegmatical	swordswallower	superficiality	heroworshipper
biodegradation	thoughtfulness	superfoetation	horrorstricken
bioelectricity	thoughtreading	superincumbent	horticulturist
bioengineering	tropologically	superinduction	irreconcilable
biographically	troubleshooter	superintendent	irreconcilably
bioluminescent	twodimensional	supernaturally	irreducibility
biosystematics	whortleberries	superphosphate	irrefutability
blockaderunner	alphabetically	superscription	irremovability
bloodthirstily	alphanumerical	supersensitive	irreproachable
Brobdingnagian	appendicectomy	supersonically	irreproachably
bronchiectasis	apprehensively	superstructure	irreproducible
coordinateness	apprenticeship	superterranean	irresoluteness
crossfertilise	capitalisation	supervisorship	irrespectively
crosspollinate	capriciousness	supposititious	irrevocability
crossreference	copperbottomed	supralapsarian	jurisdictional
econometrician	departmentally	supramaxillary	marketgardener
floriculturist	dependableness	suprasegmental	martyrological
geocentrically	deplorableness	topsyturviness	marvellousness
geographically	depolarisation	unpalatability	meretriciously
goodfellowship	diplomatically	unpleasantness	miraculousness
goodhumouredly	euphuistically	unpremeditated	morganatically
goodtemperedly	experientially	unprofessional	myrmecological
groundlessness	experimentally	coquettishness	myrmecophagous
iconographical	expressionless	loquaciousness	myrmecophilous
inordinateness	expressiveness	unquestionable	narrowmindedly
lyophilisation	hyperbolically	unquestionably	northeastwards
neocolonialism	hypercalcaemia	aerobiological	northnortheast
phosphorescent	hypercatalexis	aerobiotically	northnorthwest
photochemistry	hypercriticise	aerodynamicist	northwestwards
photoperiodism	hypercriticism	agrobiological	paradoxicality
photosensitise	hyperglycaemia	airconditioner	parallelepiped
photosensitive	hyperirritable	arrhythmically	parapsychology
photosynthesis	hypersonically	arrondissement	parasitologist
photosynthetic	hypocoristical	barometrically	paratactically
phototelegraph	hypocritically	boroughEnglish	pardonableness
probabiliorism	hypodermically	carcinogenesis	parenchymatous
probabiliorist	hypostatically	cardiovascular	parsimoniously
proceleusmatic	hypothetically	cartographical	partridgeberry
procrastinator	hypothyroidism	chromatography	perceptibility
prodigiousness	imparisyllabic	chronometrical	perceptiveness
productiveness	impassableness	circuitousness	percutaneously
professionally	impassibleness	circumambiency	peremptoriness
professorially	imperativeness	circumambulate	perfectibility
profitableness	impermeability	circumbendibus	perfidiousness
progenitorship	imperviousness	circumlittoral	periodontology
prognosticator	implacableness	circumlocution	peripateticism
progressionary	implausibility	circumlocutory	perishableness
progressionism	implementation	circumnavigate	permissibility
progressionist	imponderabilia	circumspection	permissiveness
prohibitionism			perniciousness
prohibitionist			personableness

persuasiveness	discourteously	postpositively	heterochromous
pertinaciously	discriminating	resinification	heteromorphism
perturbational	discrimination	resistlessness	heteromorphous
phraseological	discriminative	respectability	heterophyllous
portentousness	discriminatory	respectfulness	heterothallism
purposefulness	discursiveness	responsibility	iatrochemistry
pyrheliometric	disdainfulness	responsiveness	intangibleness
scrubbingbrush	disembarkation	restorationism	integrationist
scrupulousness	disembowelment	restorationist	intellectually
seriocomically	disenchantment	restrictionist	intelligential
serviceability	disenfranchise	resurrectional	intelligentsia
servomechanism	disenthralment	Rosicrucianism	intercessional
sprightfulness	disequilibrium	Russianisation	intercessorial
springcleaning	disfurnishment	sesquipedalian	intercommunion
stratification	disgruntlement	susceptibility	intercommunity
strikebreaking	disheartenment	susceptiveness	interdependent
strongmindedly	disinclination	suspensiveness	interferential
surefootedness	disincorporate	suspiciousness	interferometer
tergiversation	disinfestation	systematically	interferometry
terminableness	disingenuously	testimonialise	intergradation
terminological	disinheritance	unsatisfactory	interjectional
territorialise	disintegration	unscrupulously	interlineation
territorialism	disintegrative	unsociableness	interlocutress
territorialist	disjointedness	unsuccessfully	intermediately
territoriality	disorderliness	vasodilatation	intermediation
terrorstricken	disorientation	vasodilatatory	intermigration
threadbareness	dispensability	westernisation	intermittently
thriftlessness	dispiritedness	aetiologically	intermolecular
tyrannicalness	disputatiously	altruistically	internationale
unremunerative	disquisitional	anthropography	interpellation
unreservedness	disrespectable	anthropologist	interpenetrate
uproariousness	dissertational	anthropometric	interplanetary
verisimilitude	dissociability	anticipatively	interpretation
verticillaster	distemperature	anticonvulsant	interpretative
worshipfulness	distensibility	antidepressant	interpretively
Zoroastrianism	distributional	antifederalist	intersectional
absentmindedly	distributively	antiperspirant	intersexuality
absorptiveness	fastidiousness	antiphlogistic	intertwinement
abstemiousness	histochemistry	antiquarianism	intolerability
abstractedness	histopathology	antiscriptural	intractability
abstractionism	historiography	antiseptically	intramolecular
abstractionist	histrionically	antithetically	intransitively
aesthesiometer	hysterectomise	articulateness	intrinsicality
associationism	insatiableness	artificialness	introductorily
auspiciousness	inscrutability	astronomically	intuitionalism
basidiomycetes	insensibleness	astrophysicist	intuitionalist
bastardisation	inseparability	attainableness	latitudinarian
castrametation	insignificance	attractiveness	liturgiologist
cosmographical	insignificancy	authentication	mathematically
cosmopolitical	instrumentally	autobiographer	matriarchalism
despicableness	insufficiently	autobiographic	metallographer
despiritualise	insuperability	autocratically	metaphorically
despitefulness	insuppressible	autoradiograph	metaphysically
destructionist	insurmountable	autosuggestion	metapsychology
disaffiliation	insurmountably	bathingmachine	metempsychosis
disaffirmation	insurrectional	bituminisation	meteorological
disappointment	justifiability	butterfingered	methodological
disapprobation	lasciviousness	butterflyscrew	meticulousness
disapprobative	massproduction	catachrestical	mythologically
disapprobatory	mesdemoiselles	catechetically	naturalisation
disapprovingly	misapplication	categorisation	nitrocellulose
disarrangement	misappropriate	cotemporaneous	nitroglycerine
disassociation	miscalculation	determinedness	noteworthiness
disciplinarian	misinformation	detestableness	nutritiousness
discolouration	mistranslation	detoxification	optimistically
discombobulate	mysteriousness	enterprisingly	orthochromatic
discomfortable	obsequiousness	entertainingly	orthographical
discommendable	obstreperously	enthronisation	ostentatiously
disconcertment	obstructionism	entomostracous	osteoarthritis
disconformable	obstructionist	esterification	outgeneralling
disconnectedly	passionateness	eutrophication	outlandishness
disconsolately	pasteurisation	extemporaneity	outrageousness
disconsolation	pestilentially	extemporaneous	pathogenically
discontentedly	pisciculturist	extensionality	pathologically
discontentment	pistilliferous	extinguishable	patresfamilias
discontinuance	possessiveness	extinguishment	petrochemistry
discountenance	postmastership	extracorporeal	petrographical
discouragement	postmillennial	extraneousness	petrologically
discouragingly	postpositional	extravehicular	phthalocyanine

potentiometric	physiognomical	prearrangement	electioneering
Pythagoreanism	phytogeography	recapitulation	electrobiology
retrogradation	phytopathology	recapitulatory	electrodeposit
satisfactorily	psychoanalysis	recapitulatory	electrodynamic
soteriological	psychoanalytic	regardlessness	electrostatics
tatterdemalion	psychochemical	rehabilitation	electrotherapy
tetradactylous	psychodynamics	remarkableness	electrothermal
tetragrammaton	psychoneurosis	revalorisation	electrothermic
ultimogeniture	psychoneurotic	sphaerocrystal	electrovalency
ultramicrotome	psychophysical	squadronleader	fructification
ultramontanism	psychosomatics	stratification	geocentrically
ultramontanist	psychosurgical	subalternation	illconditioned
ultrasonically	thyrotoxicosis	tyrannicalness	inscrutability
ultrastructure	————	unfaithfulness	knickerbockers
untruthfulness	advantageously	unmannerliness	lasciviousness
vituperatively	ambassadorship	unpalatability	malcontentedly
watercolourist	attainableness	unsatisfactory	miscalculation
watertightness	behaviouristic	volatilisation	neocolonialism
bougainvillaea	breathlessness	Brobdingnagian	noncommunicant
bouleversement	breathtakingly	combustibility	nonconcurrence
councilchamber	calamitousness	cumbersomeness	noncooperation
councillorship	catachrestical	doublebreasted	perceptibility
counsellorship	clearsightedly	forbiddingness	perceptiveness
counterbalance	denazification	hobbledehoyish	percutaneously
counterculture	departmentally	nonbelligerent	pisciculturist
countercurrent	disaffiliation	probabiliorism	practicability
countermeasure	disaffirmation	probabiliorist	precariousness
counterplotted	disappointment	rambunctiously	precociousness
countrydancing	disapprobation	Sabbatarianism	proceleusmatic
courageousness	disapprobative	airconditioner	procrastinator
doublebreasted	disapprobatory	blackmarketeer	psychoanalysis
educationalist	disapprovingly	blockaderunner	psychoanalytic
emulsification	disarrangement	brachycephalic	psychochemical
fructification	disassociation	carcinogenesis	psychodynamics
mountaineering	embarrassingly	chickenhearted	psychoneurosis
neuroanatomist	enharmonically	chickenlivered	psychoneurotic
neurochemistry	exhaustibility	circuitousness	psychophysical
neuropathology	exhaustiveness	circumambiency	psychosomatics
neuroscientist	foraminiferous	circumambulate	psychosurgical
neutralisation	galactopoietic	circumbendibus	sanctification
pluviometrical	gelatinisation	circumlittoral	specialisation
roundaboutness	gynaecological	circumlocution	spectrographic
sauropterygian	gynandromorphy	circumlocutory	spectroscopist
scurrilousness	idealistically	circumnavigate	stochastically
souldestroying	immaculateness	circumspection	subconsciously
southeastwards	imparisyllabic	circumstantial	subcontinental
southwestwards	impassableness	circumvolution	subcontrariety
squadronleader	impassibleness	concavoconcave	successfulness
stultification	incapacitation	conceivability	successionally
stumblingblock	incautiousness	concelebration	successiveness
stupendousness	inharmoniously	concentrically	susceptibility
tautologically	insatiableness	concessionaire	susceptiveness
advantageously	intangibleness	conclusiveness	synchronically
adventitiously	invariableness	concretisation	unaccommodated
devitalisation	Johannisberger	diachronically	unaccomplished
diverticulitis	legalistically	disciplinarian	unacknowledged
divertissement	malappropriate	discolouration	uneconomically
favourableness	manageableness	discombobulate	unscrupulously
invariableness	megasporangium	discomfortable	volcanological
invincibleness	megasporophyll	discommendable	vulcanological
inviolableness	metallographer	disconcertment	biodegradation
lovingkindness	metaphorically	disconformable	bowdlerisation
revalorisation	metaphysically	disconnectedly	cardiovascular
revengefulness	metapsychology	disconsolately	condescendence
revivification	miraculousness	disconsolation	conditionality
viviparousness	misapplication	discontentedly	conductibility
vivisectionist	misappropriate	discontentment	creditableness
bowdlerisation	oleaginousness	discontinuance	disdainfulness
newfangledness	organisational	discountenance	epidemiologist
dextrorotation	organometallic	discouragement	fundamentalism
dextrorotatory	palaeethnology	discouragingly	fundamentalist
asymmetrically	palaeobotanist	discourteously	fundamentality
asymptotically	paradoxicality	discriminating	goodfellowship
asynchronously	parallelepiped	discrimination	goodhumouredly
cryptaesthesia	parapsychology	discriminative	goodtemperedly
crystallisable	parasitologist	discriminatory	handicraftsman
erythropoiesis	paratactically	discursiveness	handkerchieves
etymologically	phraseological	educationalist	inadequateness
oxyhaemoglobin	pleasurability		inadvisability

meddlesomeness	heterophyllous	mineralisation	ineffectuality
mesdemoiselles	heterothallism	necessarianism	newfangledness
pardonableness	hyperbolically	nomenclatorial	perfectibility
predesignation	hypercalcaemia	noteworthiness	perfidiousness
predestinarian	hypercatalexis	obsequiousness	prefabrication
predestination	hypercriticise	ostentatiously	preferentially
predeterminate	hypercriticism	osteoarthritis	professionally
predictability	hyperglycaemia	parenchymatous	professorially
predisposition	hyperirritable	penetrableness	profitableness
prodigiousness	hypersensitive	peremptoriness	selfabnegation
productiveness	hypersonically	phlegmatically	selfabsorption
quadragenarian	illegitimately	pigeonbreasted	selfaccusation
quadrisyllabic	immethodically	potentiometric	selfaccusatory
quadrisyllable	imperativeness	rebelliousness	selfadjustment
roadworthiness	impermeability	regeneratively	selfadmiration
stadholdership	imperviousness	relentlessness	selfassumption
traditionalism	incestuousness	repetitiveness	selfcomplacent
traditionalist	indecipherable	revengefulness	selfconfidence
tridimensional	indecisiveness	schematisation	selfconsequent
twodimensional	indecomposable	scientifically	selfconsistent
unidimensional	indecorousness	soteriological	selfcontrolled
unidirectional	indefiniteness	speechlessness	selfcorrecting
vindictiveness	indemonstrable	superabundance	selfdependence
windowdressing	indestructible	superannuation	selfdestroying
windowshopping	indestructibly	superciliously	selfdetermined
wonderstricken	indeterminable	superconductor	selfdiscipline
absentmindedly	infectiousness	superelevation	selfeffacement
acceleratingly	infelicitously	supereminently	selfeffacingly
acceptableness	inheritability	supererogation	selfemployment
adventitiously	insensibleness	supererogatory	selfenergising
affectionately	inseparability	superficiality	selfexplaining
allegorisation	integrationist	superfoetation	selfexpression
allelomorphism	intellectually	superincumbent	selffertilised
appendicectomy	intelligential	superinduction	selfflattering
beneficialness	intelligentsia	superintendent	selffulfilling
bioelectricity	intercessional	supernaturally	selfgovernment
bioengineering	intercessorial	superphosphate	selfimmolation
catechetically	intercommunion	superscription	selfimportance
categorisation	intercommunity	supersensitive	selfinductance
cinematography	interdependent	supersonically	selfindulgence
cotemporaneous	interferential	superstructure	selfinterested
deceivableness	interferometer	superterranean	selfpartiality
defenestration	interferometry	supervisorship	selfperception
degenerateness	intergradation	surefootedness	selfpossession
delectableness	interjectional	teleologically	selfpreserving
dependableness	interlineation	telepathically	selfproclaimed
determinedness	interlocutress	telephonically	selfpropelling
detestableness	intermediately	telephotograph	selfpropulsion
disembarkation	intermediation	telescopically	selfprotection
disembowelment	intermigration	threadbareness	selfregulating
disenchantment	intermittently	unbecomingness	selfrepression
disenfranchise	intermolecular	underdeveloped	selfrespectful
disenthralment	internationale	underemphasise	selfrespecting
disequilibrium	interpellation	undergraduette	selfrestrained
diverticulitis	interpenetrate	undermentioned	selfrevelation
divertissement	interplanetary	undernourished	selfsatisfying
dodecasyllable	interpretation	understandable	selfsufficient
effervescently	interpretative	understandably	selfsuggestion
eigenfrequency	interpretively	understatement	selfsupporting
encephalograph	intersectional	undervaluation	selfsustaining
enterprisingly	intersexuality	undesirability	selftormenting
entertainingly	intertwinement	unhesitatingly	sufferableness
esterification	irreconcilable	unmentionables	unaffectedness
exceptionality	irreconcilably	unremunerative	uniformitarian
experientially	irreducibility	unreservedness	anagrammatical
experimentally	irrefutability	valetudinarian	biographically
extemporaneity	irremovability	vegetativeness	bougainvillaea
extemporaneous	irreproachable	venereological	conglomeration
extensionality	irreproachably	vicechancellor	conglutination
foreordination	irreproducible	vicepresidency	conglutinative
friendlessness	irresoluteness	watercolourist	congratulation
genealogically	irrespectively	watertightness	congratulative
generalisation	irrevocability	confidentially	congratulatory
generalpurpose	liberalisation	conformability	congregational
hebetudinosity	libertarianism	differentiable	diagnostically
hereditariness	licentiousness	differentially	diagrammatical
heterochromous	meretriciously	diffractometer	disgruntlement
heteromorphism	metempsychosis	disfurnishment	epigrammatical
heteromorphous	meteorological	halfpennyworth	flagitiousness

geographically	antifederalist	redintegration	neglectfulness
gregariousness	antiperspirant	redistribution	outlandishness
imaginableness	antiphlogistic	redistributive	philanthropise
judgematically	antiquarianism	relinquishment	philanthropist
knighterrantry	antiscriptural	reminiscential	philologically
linguistically	antiseptically	resinification	proletarianise
longheadedness	antithetically	resistlessness	proletarianism
longitudinally	articulateness	revivification	prolocutorship
longwindedness	artificialness	ridiculousness	psilanthropism
morganatically	audiofrequency	rigidification	psilanthropist
outgeneralling	basidiomycetes	Rosicrucianism	publicspirited
pragmaticality	capitalisation	satisfactorily	reflectiveness
progenitorship	Christological	schismatically	souldestroying
prognosticator	decimalisation	semicentennial	stultification
progressionary	definitiveness	semiconducting	sublieutenancy
progressionism	deliberateness	semielliptical	thalassography
progressionist	deliberatively	semiofficially	unflatteringly
sanguification	delightfulness	seriocomically	unpleasantness
sanguinariness	demisemiquaver	silicification	utilitarianism
singlebreasted	devitalisation	sociologically	villainousness
singlehandedly	diminutiveness	sociopolitical	asymmetrically
singlemindedly	disinclination	solicitousness	asymptotically
snaggletoothed	disincorporate	solidification	bremsstrahlung
steganographer	disinfestation	solitudinarian	chemoreception
stigmatisation	disingenuously	sprightfulness	chemoreceptive
suggestibility	disinheritance	springcleaning	chemosynthesis
suggestiveness	disintegration	stoicheiometry	climatological
tergiversation	disintegrative	stoichiometric	commensurately
tragicomically	dolichocephaly	strikebreaking	commensuration
weightlessness	exhilaratingly	subinfeudation	commissaryship
alphabetically	extinguishable	thriftlessness	commissionaire
alphanumerical	extinguishment	traitorousness	committeewoman
anthropography	hagiographical	ultimogeniture	commodiousness
anthropologist	humidification	uncircumcision	commonsensical
anthropometric	illimitability	verisimilitude	communications
archaeological	illiterateness	viviparousness	cosmographical
archetypically	indifferentism	vivisectionist	cosmopolitical
archidiaconate	indifferentist	vociferousness	dermatological
archiepiscopal	indiscerptible	conjunctivitis	diamantiferous
architectonics	indiscoverable	disjointedness	diamondiferous
arrhythmically	indiscreetness	subjectiveness	elementariness
authentication	indiscriminate	backscattering	etymologically
bathingmachine	indistinctness	backscratching	formidableness
disheartenment	indivisibility	marketgardener	gramineousness
enthronisation	insignificance	monkeybusiness	haematogenesis
eschatological	insignificancy	poikilothermal	harmoniousness
euphuistically	invincibleness	poikilothermic	hermaphroditic
highhandedness	inviolableness	Shakespeareana	inimitableness
highmindedness	jurisdictional	Shakespeariana	kremlinologist
lightheartedly	latitudinarian	weakmindedness	myrmecological
mathematically	legitimisation	apologetically	myrmecophagous
Mephistopheles	libidinousness	bibliographise	myrmecophilous
methodological	lovingkindness	bibliomaniacal	permissibility
mythologically	meditativeness	bioluminescent	permissiveness
nightblindness	meticulousness	bouleversement	premeditatedly
orthochromatic	militarisation	bullheadedness	premillenarian
orthographical	ministerialist	deplorableness	shamefacedness
oxyhaemoglobin	misinformation	dialectologist	skimbleskamble
pachydermatous	noninvolvement	diplomatically	stampcollector
pathogenically	numismatically	ecclesiastical	stomatological
pathologically	omnivorousness	ecclesiologist	stumblingblock
phthalocyanine	oneirocritical	egalitarianism	submersibility
prohibitionism	optimistically	emblematically	submicroscopic
prohibitionist	ornithological	emulsification	submissiveness
pyrheliometric	papilionaceous	exclaustration	symmetrisation
Pythagoreanism	periodontology	fallaciousness	terminableness
sophistication	peripateticism	fullyfashioned	terminological
tachistoscopic	perishableness	hallucinogenic	thimblerigging
tachygraphical	politicisation	implacableness	tremendousness
administration	praiseworthily	implausibility	unemphatically
administrative	radicalisation	implementation	acknowledgment
administratrix	radioautograph	inalienability	asynchronously
aetiologically	radiochemistry	inalterability	bronchiectasis
Africanisation	radiosensitive	inflammability	chancellorship
Albigensianism	radiostrontium	inflectionally	changeableness
ambidextrously	radiotelegraph	inflectionless	chincherinchee
anticipatively	radiotelephone	inflexibleness	councilchamber
anticonvulsant	radiotelephony	ingloriousness	councillorship
antidepressant	radiotherapist	millenarianism	counsellorship

counterbalance	aerobiotically	indoctrination	proportionable
counterculture	aerodynamicist	intolerability	proportionably
countercurrent	agrobiological	malodorousness	proportionally
countermeasure	aphoristically	monochromatism	proprietorship
counterplotted	arrondissement	monopolisation	proprioceptive
countrydancing	associationism	monosaccharide	purposefulness
crinkumcrankum	autobiographer	monotonousness	rampageousness
cyanocobalamin	autobiographic	pleonastically	respectability
econometrician	autocratically	recolonisation	respectfulness
enantiomorphic	autoradiograph	recommencement	responsibility
ethnologically	autosuggestion	recommendation	responsiveness
Evangelicalism	barometrically	recommendatory	simplemindedly
evangelisation	bloodthirstily	reconciliation	simplification
faintheartedly	boroughEnglish	reconciliatory	staphylococcus
grandiloquence	chromatography	reconnaissance	stupendousness
iconographical	chronometrical	reconstitution	sulphanilamide
identification	colourfastness	reconstruction	supposititious
magniloquently	colourlessness	reconstructive	suspensiveness
mountaineering	decolonisation	recoverability	suspiciousness
openhandedness	decolorisation	remonetisation	symptomatology
openmindedness	deconsecration	remorsefulness	tropologically
opinionatively	decorativeness	saponification	unappreciative
perniciousness	delocalisation	scholastically	unapproachable
phantasmagoria	demobilisation	schoolchildren	whippersnapper
phantasmagoric	democratically	schoolmistress	conquistadores
phenobarbitone	demonetisation	soporiferously	disquisitional
phenylbutazone	demoralisation	strongmindedly	sesquipedalian
pianoaccordian	denominational	sycophantishly	ubiquitousness
planetstricken	depolarisation	theocratically	achromatically
pugnaciousness	detoxification	uncommunicable	aforementioned
quantification	dicotyledonous	uncompromising	aggrandisement
quantitatively	dinoflagellate	uncongeniality	aggressiveness
quinquagesimal	disorderliness	unconscionable	altruistically
quinquennially	disorientation	uncontrollable	apprehensively
quintessential	dolomitisation	uncontrollably	apprenticeship
reintroduction	effortlessness	uncontroverted	astronomically
reinvigoration	endoradiosonde	unconventional	astrophysicist
rhinencephalic	endosmotically	unconvincingly	attractiveness
rhinencephalon	entomostracous	uncorroborated	avariciousness
roentgenoscopy	eulogistically	unsociableness	boardingschool
roundaboutness	excommunicable	uproariousness	capriciousness
scandalisation	excommunicator	vasodilatation	characteristic
scandalousness	favourableness	vasodilatatory	charitableness
scintillometer	gerontological	Zoroastrianism	coordinateness
slanderousness	gyrostabiliser	apophthegmatic	correspondence
somnambulation	heroworshipper	apoplectically	correspondency
somnambulistic	holometabolism	auspiciousness	corruptibility
spindleshanked	holometabolous	campanological	courageousness
spinthariscope	homoeomorphism	campylotropous	disrespectable
standardbearer	homogenisation	comparableness	eutrophication
thanksoffering	homotransplant	compassionable	excruciatingly
transcendental	honourableness	compatibleness	expressionless
transcendently	hypocoristical	compensational	expressiveness
transformation	hypocritically	complexionless	extracorporeal
transformative	hypodermically	compossibility	extraneousness
transitionally	hypostatically	comprehensible	extravehicular
transitiveness	hypothetically	comprehensibly	ferrimagnetism
transitoriness	hypothyroidism	compulsiveness	ferromagnesian
transliterator	idiopathically	copperbottomed	ferromagnetism
transmigration	immobilisation	cryptaesthesia	floriculturist
transmigratory	immoderateness	despicableness	heartsearching
transplantable	imponderabilia	despiritualise	hierarchically
transportation	impoverishment	despitefulness	hieroglyphical
transsexualism	incommensurate	diaphanousness	horrorstricken
transvaluation	incommodiously	dispensability	hydrocoralline
transversality	incommunicable	dispiritedness	hydrodynamical
Trinitarianism	incommunicably	disputatiously	hydrographical
unenterprising	incompleteness	inappositeness	hydromechanics
unenthusiastic	incompressible	inappreciation	hygroscopicity
unintelligible	incompressibly	inappreciative	iatrochemistry
unintelligibly	inconclusively	inapproachable	impracticality
vaingloriously	inconsequently	lyophilisation	impregnability
vulnerableness	inconsiderable	nonperformance	impressibility
absorptiveness	inconsiderably	preponderantly	impressionable
accomplishable	inconsistently	preposterously	impressiveness
accomplishment	incontrollable	propaedeutical	improvableness
accountability	inconveniently	propagandistic	inarticulately
achondroplasia	incoordination	propitiatorily	inarticulation
aerobiological	incorporeality	propitiousness	inartistically

incredibleness	spirochaetosis	presupposition	histopathology
infralapsarian	stertorousness	proscriptively	historiography
infrangibility	supralapsarian	prosencephalic	histrionically
infrastructure	supramaxillary	prosencephalon	horticulturist
ingratiatingly	suprasegmental	prosperousness	hysterectomise
inordinateness	swordswallower	reasonableness	ichthyological
intractability	territorialise	Russianisation	ichthyophagous
intramolecular	territorialism	seasonableness	ichthyosaurian
intransitively	territorialist	sensationalism	instrumentally
intrinsicality	territoriality	sensationalist	justifiability
introductorily	terrorstricken	sensualisation	lefthandedness
macrocephalous	tetradactylous	substantialism	martyrological
macroeconomics	tetragrammaton	substantialist	mistranslation
matriarchalism	therianthropic	substantiality	multifariously
microbiologist	thermochemical	substantiation	multilaterally
microcephalous	thermodynamics	substantivally	multinucleated
microcircuitry	thermoelectric	substitutional	multiplication
microcomponent	thyrotoxicosis	substitutively	multiplicative
microeconomics	ultramicrotome	topsyturviness	mysteriousness
microminiature	ultramontanism	worshipfulness	neutralisation
microprocessor	ultramontanist	abstemiousness	noctambulation
microsporangia	ultrasonically	abstractedness	northeastwards
microstructure	ultrastructure	abstractionism	northnortheast
microtechnique	umbrageousness	abstractionist	northnorthwest
narrowmindedly	unfriendliness	aesthesiometer	northwestwards
neuroanatomist	ungraciousness	amateurishness	obstreperously
neurochemistry	ungratefulness	apothegmatical	obstructionism
neuropathology	unpremeditated	arithmetically	obstructionist
neuroscientist	unprofessional	bacteriologist	ophthalmoscope
nitrocellulose	untruthfulness	bacteriostasis	ophthalmoscopy
nitroglycerine	whortleberries	bacteriostatic	partridgeberry
nonrestrictive	biosystematics	bastardisation	pasteurisation
nutritiousness	boisterousness	butterfingered	pertinaciously
oppressiveness	censoriousness	butterflyscrew	perturbational
outrageousness	classconscious	cantankerously	pestilentially
overabundantly	classification	cartographical	photochemistry
overcapitalise	classificatory	castrametation	photoperiodism
overcommitment	coessentiality	centralisation	photosensitise
overcompensate	consanguineous	centrifugation	photosensitive
overconfidence	conscienceless	contagiousness	photosynthesis
overestimation	conservational	contemptuously	photosynthetic
overexcitement	conservatively	conterminously	phototelegraph
overindulgence	consociational	contiguousness	phytogeography
overpopulation	conspiratorial	continuousness	phytopathology
overpoweringly	constitutional	contractedness	pistilliferous
overproduction	constitutively	contradictable	portentousness
oversubscribed	constructional	contradictious	postmastership
overwhelmingly	constructively	contraindicate	postmillennial
patresfamilias	constructivism	contraposition	postpositional
petrochemistry	constructivist	contrapositive	postpositively
petrographical	consubstantial	contrapuntally	prettification
petrologically	consuetudinary	controllership	protectiveness
pharmaceutical	crossfertilise	controvertible	prothonotarial
pharmacologist	crosspollinate	contumaciously	protozoologist
pharmacopoeial	crossreference	contumeliously	protrusiveness
pteridological	crystallisable	corticosteroid	quattrocentism
quarterbinding	dieselelectric	corticosterone	quattrocentist
refractoriness	dissertational	corticotrophic	rectangularity
refrangibility	dissociability	corticotrophin	restorationism
regressiveness	epistemologist	destructionist	restorationist
reorganisation	exasperatingly	dextrorotation	restrictionist
representation	existentialism	dextrorotatory	rontgenography
representative	existentialist	distemperature	scatterbrained
reproductively	farsightedness	distensibility	sentimentalise
retrogradation	massproduction	distributional	sentimentalism
sacramentalism	nonsensicality	distributively	sentimentalist
sacramentalist	parsimoniously	erythropoiesis	sentimentality
sacramentarian	passionateness	factitiousness	septuagenarian
sacrilegiously	personableness	fantasticality	slatternliness
sauropterygian	persuasiveness	fastidiousness	southeastwards
scurrilousness	phosphorescent	featherbrained	southwestwards
segregationist	physiognomical	fictitiousness	spatiotemporal
shortsightedly	possessiveness	flatfootedness	stationariness
spermatogenous	presbyterially	forthrightness	statuesqueness
spermatogonium	prescriptively	fortuitousness	systematically
spermatophytic	presentability	fortunetelling	tatterdemalion
spiritlessness	presentational	fraternisation	tautologically
spiritualistic	presentimental	gratuitousness	testimonialise
spirituousness	presumptuously	histochemistry	tintinnabulary

tintinnabulate	convexoconcave	intransitively	salubriousness
tintinnabulous	convincingness	loquaciousness	scrubbingbrush
unattractively	convulsiveness	miscalculation	skimbleskamble
verticillaster	curvilinearity	morganatically	solubilisation
victoriousness	inevitableness	newfangledness	stumblingblock
weltanschauung	marvellousness	noctambulation	thimblerigging
westernisation	pluviometrical	outlandishness	troubleshooter
accumulatively	preventability	outrageousness	affectionately
accustomedness	preventiveness	overabundantly	Africanisation
Augustinianism	providentially	oxyhaemoglobin	anticipatively
beautification	serviceability	philanthropise	anticonvulsant
bituminisation	servomechanism	philanthropist	articulateness
claustrophobia	shovehalfpenny	phthalocyanine	associationism
claustrophobic	subversiveness	precariousness	asynchronously
coquettishness	trivialisation	prefabrication	autocratically
cucurbitaceous	universalistic	probabiliorism	bronchiectasis
cumulativeness	forwardlooking	probabiliorist	catachrestical
dehumanisation	epexegetically	propaedeutical	catechetically
denumerability	inexorableness	propagandistic	chancellorship
figurativeness	inexpressively	psilanthropism	chincherinchee
groundlessness	unexpectedness	psilanthropist	conscienceless
hocuspocussing	encyclopaedism	pugnaciousness	councilchamber
illustrational	encyclopaedist	Pythagoreanism	councillorship
illustratively	polymerisation	rampageousness	delectableness
inauspiciously	polymorphously	rectangularity	delocalisation
indubitability	polysaccharide	refractoriness	democratically
insufficiently	polytheistical	refrangibility	dodecasyllable
insuperability	sphygmographic	Sabbatarianism	dolichocephaly
insuppressible ———————		sacramentalism	encyclopaedism
insurmountable	aggrandisement	sacramentalist	encyclopaedist
insurmountably	alphabetically	sacramentarian	galactopoietic
insurrectional	alphanumerical	selfabnegation	hypocoristical
intuitionalism	archaeological	selfabsorption	hypocritically
intuitionalist	attractiveness	selfaccusation	immaculateness
liturgiologist	bastardisation	selfaccusatory	indecipherable
loquaciousness	bougainvillaea	selfadjustment	indecisiveness
lugubriousness	calcareousness	selfadmiration	indecomposable
naturalisation	campanological	selfassumption	indecorousness
oecumenicalism	cantankerously	sensationalism	indoctrination
pneumatologist	characteristic	sensationalist	infectiousness
pneumoconiosis	chivalrousness	somnambulation	irreconcilable
popularisation	climatological	somnambulistic	irreconcilably
pseudaesthesia	comparableness	steganographer	meticulousness
pseudepigrapha	compassionable	stomatological	miraculousness
pseudepigraphy	compatibleness	supralapsarian	monochromatism
pseudomorphism	concavoconcave	supramaxillary	overcapitalise
pseudomorphous	consanguineous	suprasegmental	overcommitment
pseudonymously	contagiousness	tetradactylous	overcompensate
regularisation	courageousness	tetragrammaton	overconfidence
rejuvenescence	dermatological	thalassography	prescriptively
repudiationist	diamantiferous	threadbareness	proscriptively
resurrectional	disdainfulness	ultramicrotome	radicalisation
rheumatologist	educationalist	ultramontanism	ridiculousness
robustiousness	eschatological	ultramontanist	Rosicrucianism
salubriousness	exclaustration	ultrasonically	selfcomplacent
scrubbingbrush	extracorporeal	ultrastructure	selfconfidence
scrupulousness	extraneousness	umbrageousness	selfconsequent
secularisation	extravehicular	unflatteringly	selfconsistent
simultaneously	fallaciousness	ungraciousness	selfcontrolled
slaughterhouse	fantasticality	ungratefulness	selfcorrecting
slaughterously	forwardlooking	uproariousness	semicentennial
solubilisation	fundamentalism	villainousness	semiconducting
stoutheartedly	fundamentalist	volcanological	silicification
thoughtfulness	fundamentality	vulcanological	solicitousness
thoughtreading	genealogically	weltanschauung	speechlessness
troubleshooter	gregariousness	Zoroastrianism	stoicheiometry
tumultuousness	haematogenesis	aerobiological	stoichiometric
unquestionable	hermaphroditic	aerobiotically	theocratically
unquestionably	hierarchically	agrobiological	unaccommodated
unsuccessfully	implacableness	autobiographer	unaccomplished
vituperatively	implausibility	autobiographic	unbecomingness
volumetrically	impracticality	deliberateness	unsociableness
voluminousness	inflammability	deliberatively	unsuccessfully
voluptuousness	infralapsarian	demobilisation	vicechancellor
abovementioned	infrangibility	immobilisation	aerodynamicist
chivalrousness	infrastructure	indubitability	ambidextrously
conventionally	ingratiatingly	lugubriousness	antidepressant
conversational	intractability	presbyterially	basidiomycetes
convertibility	intramolecular	rehabilitation	bloodthirstily

boardingschool	dispensability	reflectiveness	integrationist
Brobdingnagian	disrespectable	regressiveness	manageableness
coordinateness	dissertational	representation	oleaginousness
grandiloquence	distemperature	representative	phlegmatically
hereditariness	distensibility	respectability	reorganisation
humidification	ecclesiastical	respectfulness	rontgenography
hypodermically	ecclesiologist	rhinencephalic	selfgovernment
immoderateness	elementariness	rhinencephalon	slaughterhouse
inordinateness	emblematically	segregationist	slaughterously
irreducibility	epexegetically	selfeffacement	snaggletoothed
libidinousness	epidemiologist	selfeffacingly	sphygmographic
malodorousness	expressionless	selfemployment	sprightfulness
paradoxicality	expressiveness	selfenergising	thoughtfulness
pseudaesthesia	fraternisation	selfexplaining	thoughtreading
pseudepigrapha	geocentrically	selfexpression	vaingloriously
pseudepigraphy	gynaecological	semielliptical	aesthesiometer
pseudomorphism	homoeomorphism	Shakespeareana	apophthegmatic
pseudomorphous	hysterectomise	Shakespeariana	apothegmatical
pseudonymously	implementation	shamefacedness	arithmetically
repudiationist	impregnability	shovehalfpenny	brachycephalic
rigidification	impressibility	sphaerocrystal	bullheadedness
roundaboutness	impressionable	stupendousness	diachronically
scandalisation	impressiveness	subjectiveness	diaphanousness
scandalousness	inadequateness	submersibility	erythropoiesis
selfdependence	incredibleness	subversiveness	featherbrained
selfdestroying	inflectionally	successfulness	forthrightness
selfdetermined	inflectionless	successionally	goodhumouredly
selfdiscipline	inflexibleness	successiveness	highhandedness
slanderousness	judgematically	sufferableness	ichthyological
solidification	marketgardener	suggestibility	ichthyophagous
souldestroying	marvellousness	suggestiveness	ichthyosaurian
spindleshanked	mathematically	susceptibility	knighterrantry
squadronleader	mesdemoiselles	susceptiveness	lefthandedness
standardbearer	millenarianism	suspensiveness	longheadedness
swordswallower	monkeybusiness	symmetrisation	lyophilisation
vasodilatation	myrmecological	systematically	northeastwards
vasodilatatory	myrmecophagous	tatterdemalion	northnortheast
abovementioned	myrmecophilous	tremendousness	northnorthwest
abstemiousness	mysteriousness	universalistic	northwestwards
aforementioned	neglectfulness	unpleasantness	openhandedness
aggressiveness	nonbelligerent	unpremeditated	ophthalmoscope
amateurishness	nonperformance	unquestionable	ophthalmoscopy
apprehensively	nonrestrictive	unquestionably	prothonotarial
apprenticeship	nonsensicality	vulnerableness	psychoanalysis
archetypically	oppressiveness	westernisation	psychoanalytic
authentication	outgeneralling	wonderstricken	psychochemical
bacteriologist	overestimation	antifederalist	psychodynamics
bacteriostasis	overexcitement	artificialness	psychoneurosis
bacteriostatic	palaeethnology	beneficialness	psychoneurotic
biodegradation	palaeobotanist	dinoflagellate	psychophysical
bouleversement	pasteurisation	disaffiliation	psychosomatics
butterfingered	patresfamilias	disaffirmation	psychosurgical
butterflyscrew	perceptibility	flatfootedness	southeastwards
commensurately	perceptiveness	goodfellowship	southwestwards
commensuration	perfectibility	indefiniteness	stadholdership
compensational	planetstricken	indifferentism	staphylococcus
conceivability	portentousness	indifferentist	stochastically
concelebration	possessiveness	ineffectuality	sulphanilamide
concentrically	predesignation	insufficiently	synchronically
concessionaire	predestinarian	irrefutability	weightlessness
condescendence	predestination	selffertilised	worshipfulness
conservational	predeterminate	selfflattering	archidiaconate
conservatively	preferentially	selffulfilling	archiepiscopal
contemptuously	premeditatedly	surefootedness	architectonics
conterminously	presentability	thriftlessness	attainableness
conventionally	presentational	unaffectedness	auspiciousness
conversational	presentimental	vociferousness	avariciousness
convertibility	preventability	Albigensianism	bathingmachine
convexoconcave	preventiveness	allegorisation	bibliographise
copperbottomed	proceleusmatic	categorisation	bibliomaniacal
coquettishness	professionally	changeableness	capriciousness
correspondence	professorially	delightfulness	carcinogenesis
correspondency	progenitorship	eulogistically	cardiovascular
cumbersomeness	proletarianise	Evangelicalism	charitableness
dialectologist	proletarianism	evangelisation	commissaryship
dieselelectric	prosencephalic	homogenisation	commissionaire
differentiable	prosencephalon	illegitimately	committeewoman
differentially	protectiveness	insignificance	conditionality
disheartenment	pyrheliometric	insignificancy	confidentially

contiguousness	selfinductance	kremlinologist	spermatogonium
continuousness	selfindulgence	legalistically	spermatophytic
convincingness	selfinterested	meddlesomeness	stigmatisation
corticosteroid	sentimentalise	metallographer	thermochemical
corticosterone	sentimentalism	papilionaceous	thermodynamics
corticotrophic	sentimentalist	parallelepiped	thermoelectric
corticotrophin	sentimentality	popularisation	ultimogeniture
creditableness	serviceability	rebelliousness	uncommunicable
curvilinearity	sophistication	recolonisation	uncompromising
deceivableness	spatiotemporal	regularisation	unremunerative
despicableness	specialisation	revalorisation	volumetrically
despiritualise	spiritlessness	scholastically	voluminousness
despitefulness	spiritualistic	secularisation	weakmindedness
disciplinarian	spirituousness	simplemindedly	absentmindedly
dispiritedness	stationariness	simplification	achondroplasia
egalitarianism	sublieutenancy	simultaneously	administration
factitiousness	submicroscopic	singlebreasted	administrative
farsightedness	submissiveness	singlehandedly	administratrix
fastidiousness	suspiciousness	singlemindedly	advantageously
ferrimagnetism	tachistoscopic	subalternation	adventitiously
fictitiousness	tergiversation	tumultuousness	appendicectomy
flagitiousness	terminableness	unpalatability	arrondissement
floriculturist	terminological	accomplishable	bioengineering
forbiddingness	territorialise	accomplishment	chronometrical
formidableness	territorialism	accumulatively	deconsecration
gramineousness	territorialist	asymmetrically	defenestration
handicraftsman	territoriality	barometrically	definitiveness
horticulturist	testimonialise	bituminisation	degenerateness
imaginableness	therianthropic	calamitousness	demonetisation
inalienability	tintinnabulary	chromatography	dependableness
inevitableness	tintinnabulate	cinematography	diagnostically
inimitableness	tintinnabulous	cotemporaneous	diminutiveness
intrinsicality	traditionalism	decimalisation	disenchantment
intuitionalism	traditionalist	dehumanisation	disenfranchise
intuitionalist	tragicomically	denominational	disenthralment
justifiability	tridimensional	denumerability	disinclination
lasciviousness	Trinitarianism	disembarkation	disincorporate
longitudinally	trivialisation	disembowelment	disinfestation
magniloquently	twodimensional	dolomitisation	disingenuously
matriarchalism	unfaithfulness	entomostracous	disinheritance
Mephistopheles	unfriendliness	excommunicable	disintegration
multifariously	unidimensional	excommunicator	disintegrative
multilaterally	unidirectional	extemporaneity	eigenfrequency
multinucleated	utilitarianism	extemporaneous	extensionality
multiplication	verticillaster	foraminiferous	extinguishable
multiplicative	vindictiveness	highmindedness	extinguishment
nutritiousness	blackmarketeer	holometabolism	friendlessness
opinionatively	blockaderunner	holometabolous	gerontological
overindulgence	chickenhearted	illimitability	groundlessness
parsimoniously	chickenlivered	incommensurate	gynandromorphy
passionateness	crinkumcrankum	incommodiously	imponderabilia
perfidiousness	handkerchieves	incommunicable	inconclusively
permissibility	knickerbockers	incommunicably	inconsequently
permissiveness	strikebreaking	incompleteness	inconsiderable
perniciousness	thanksoffering	incompressible	inconsiderably
pertinaciously	unacknowledged	incompressibly	inconsistently
pestilentially	acceleratingly	indemonstrable	incontrollable
physiognomical	allelomorphism	irremovability	inconveniently
pisciculturist	apoplectically	metempsychosis	insensibleness
pistilliferous	bioelectricity	oecumenicalism	intangibleness
pluviometrical	bowdlerisation	openmindedness	invincibleness
poikilothermal	complexionless	optimistically	Johannisberger
poikilothermic	conclusiveness	peremptoriness	licentiousness
predictability	conglomeration	pharmaceutical	lovingkindness
predisposition	conglutination	pharmacologist	misinformation
premillenarian	conglutinative	pharmacopoeial	nomenclatorial
prodigiousness	cumulativeness	pneumatologist	noninvolvement
profitableness	decolonisation	pneumoconiosis	organisational
prohibitionism	decolorisation	polymerisation	organometallic
prohibitionist	depolarisation	polymorphously	ostentatiously
propitiatorily	doublebreasted	postmastership	parenchymatous
propitiousness	exhilaratingly	postmillennial	pleonastically
providentially	hobbledehoyish	pragmaticality	potentiometric
pteridological	idealistically	recommencement	prognosticator
publicspirited	infelicitously	recommendation	reconciliation
Russianisation	intellectually	recommendatory	reconciliatory
sacrilegiously	intelligential	rheumatologist	reconnaissance
selfimmolation	intelligentsia	schematisation	reconstitution
selfimportance	intolerability	spermatogenous	reconstruction

reconstructive	horrorstricken	radiotelegraph	prosperousness
redintegration	hydrocoralline	radiotelephone	recapitulation
regeneratively	hydrodynamical	radiotelephony	recapitulative
relentlessness	hydrographical	radiotherapist	recapitulatory
relinquishment	hydromechanics	reasonableness	scrupulousness
reminiscential	hygroscopicity	reproductively	selfpartiality
remonetisation	iatrochemistry	responsibility	selfperception
resinification	iconographical	responsiveness	selfpossession
revengefulness	illconditioned	restorationism	selfpreserving
saponification	improvableness	restorationist	selfproclaimed
scientifically	incoordination	retrogradation	selfpropelling
springcleaning	inexorableness	sauropterygian	selfpropulsion
strongmindedly	ingloriousness	schoolchildren	selfprotection
subinfeudation	introductorily	schoolmistress	stampcollector
tyrannicalness	inviolableness	seasonableness	sycophantishly
uncongeniality	macrocephalous	semiofficially	telepathically
unconscionable	macroeconomics	seriocomically	telephonically
uncontrollable	malcontentedly	servomechanism	telephotograph
uncontrollably	meteorological	sociologically	unappreciative
uncontroverted	methodological	sociopolitical	unapproachable
unconventional	microbiologist	spirochaetosis	unemphatically
unconvincingly	microcephalous	subconsciously	unexpectedness
unmannerliness	microcircuitry	subcontinental	vicepresidency
unmentionables	microcomponent	subcontrariety	vituperatively
achromatically	microeconomics	supposititious	viviparousness
acknowledgment	microminiature	tautologically	voluptuousness
aetiologically	microprocessor	teleologically	whippersnapper
airconditioner	microsporangia	terrorstricken	antiquarianism
apologetically	microstructure	thyrotoxicosis	disequilibrium
astronomically	microtechnique	tropologically	obsequiousness
astrophysicist	mythologically	uneconomically	quinquagesimal
audiofrequency	narrowmindedly	uniformitarian	quinquennially
cartographical	neocolonialism	unprofessional	absorptiveness
censoriousness	neuroanatomist	victoriousness	abstractedness
chemoreception	neurochemistry	windowdressing	abstractionism
chemoreceptive	neuropathology	windowshopping	abstractionist
chemosynthesis	neuroscientist	acceptableness	anagrammatical
commodiousness	nitrocellulose	antiperspirant	anthropography
commonsensical	nitroglycerine	antiphlogistic	anthropologist
compossibility	noncommunicant	asymptotically	anthropometric
conformability	nonconcurrence	conspiratorial	aphoristically
consociational	noncooperation	disappointment	autoradiograph
cosmographical	orthochromatic	disapprobation	biographically
cosmopolitical	orthographical	disapprobative	castrametation
cyanocobalamin	osteoarthritis	disapprobatory	centralisation
deplorableness	pardonableness	disapprovingly	centrifugation
diamondiferous	pathogenically	encephalograph	clearsightedly
diplomatically	pathologically	exasperatingly	comprehensible
discolouration	periodontology	exceptionality	comprehensibly
discombobulate	personableness	halfpennyworth	concretisation
discomfortable	petrochemistry	idiopathically	congratulation
discommendable	petrographical	inappositeness	congratulative
disconcertment	petrologically	inappreciation	congratulatory
disconformable	phenobarbitone	inappreciative	congregational
disconnectedly	philologically	inapproachable	contractedness
disconsolately	photochemistry	incapacitation	contradictable
disconsolation	photoperiodism	inexpressively	contradictious
discontentedly	photosensitise	inseparability	contraindicate
discontentment	photosensitive	insuperability	contraposition
discontinuance	photosynthesis	insuppressible	contrapositive
discountenance	photosynthetic	irreproachable	contrapuntally
discouragement	phototelegraph	irreproachably	controllership
discouragingly	phytogeography	irreproducible	controvertible
discourteously	phytopathology	malappropriate	cucurbitaceous
disjointedness	pianoaccordian	massproduction	decorativeness
dissociability	pigeonbreasted	metaphorically	demoralisation
econometrician	precociousness	metaphysically	departmentally
ethnologically	preponderantly	metapsychology	destructionist
etymologically	preposterously	misapplication	determinedness
eutrophication	prolocutorship	misappropriate	dextrorotation
ferromagnesian	proportionable	monopolisation	dextrorotatory
ferromagnetism	proportionably	overpopulation	diagrammatical
foreordination	proportionally	overpoweringly	diffractometer
hagiographical	protozoologist	overproduction	disarrangement
harmoniousness	purposefulness	parapsychology	discriminating
hieroglyphical	radioautograph	peripateticism	discrimination
histochemistry	radiochemistry	phosphorescent	discriminative
histopathology	radiosensitive	postpositional	discriminatory
historiography	radiostrontium	postpositively	disgruntlement

disorderliness	liturgiologist	bremsstrahlung	verisimilitude
disorientation	mineralisation	Christological	vivisectionist
distributional	mistranslation	classconscious	antithetically
distributively	naturalisation	classification	beautification
diverticulitis	neutralisation	classificatory	boisterousness
divertissement	obstreperously	claustrophobia	breathlessness
effervescently	obstructionism	claustrophobic	breathtakingly
effortlessness	obstructionist	coessentiality	capitalisation
embarrassingly	oneirocritical	counsellorship	constitutional
endoradiosonde	partridgeberry	crossfertilise	constitutively
enharmonically	prearrangement	crosspollinate	constructional
enterprisingly	procrastinator	crossreference	constructively
entertainingly	progressionary	demisemiquaver	constructivism
enthronisation	progressionism	detestableness	constructivist
epigrammatical	progressionist	disassociation	counterbalance
esterification	proprietorship	emulsification	counterculture
experientially	proprioceptive	endosmotically	countercurrent
experimentally	protrusiveness	gyrostabiliser	countermeasure
figurativeness	quadragenarian	hocuspocussing	counterplotted
generalisation	quadrisyllabic	hypostatically	countrydancing
generalpurpose	quadrisyllable	illustrational	cryptaesthesia
geographically	regardlessness	illustratively	crystallisable
heterochromous	remarkableness	impassableness	devitalisation
heteromorphism	remorsefulness	impassibleness	dicotyledonous
heteromorphous	restrictionist	inauspiciously	electioneering
heterophyllous	resurrectional	incestuousness	electrobiology
heterothallism	scurrilousness	indestructible	electrodeposit
histrionically	selfregulating	indestructibly	electrodynamic
hyperbolically	selfrepression	indiscerptible	electrostatics
hypercalcaemia	selfrespectful	indiscoverable	electrotherapy
hypercatalexis	selfrespecting	indiscreetness	electrothermal
hypercriticise	selfrestrained	indiscriminate	electrothermic
hypercriticism	selfrevelation	indistinctness	electrovalency
hyperglycaemia	soporiferously	irresoluteness	enantiomorphic
hyperirritable	soteriological	irrespectively	epistemologist
hypersensitive	superabundance	jurisdictional	existentialism
hypersonically	superannuation	megasporangium	existentialist
imparisyllabic	superciliously	megasporophyll	faintheartedly
imperativeness	superconductor	ministerialist	fructification
impermeability	superelevation	monosaccharide	gelatinisation
imperviousness	supereminently	necessarianism	goodtemperedly
incorporeality	supererogation	numismatically	heartsearching
inharmoniously	supererogatory	oversubscribed	hebetudinosity
inheritability	superficiality	parasitologist	homotransplant
inscrutability	superfoetation	perishableness	hypothetically
instrumentally	superincumbent	phraseological	hypothyroidism
insurmountable	superinduction	pleasurability	identification
insurmountably	superintendent	polysaccharide	illiterateness
insurrectional	supernaturally	praiseworthily	immethodically
intercessional	superphosphate	redistribution	inalterability
intercessorial	superscription	redistributive	inarticulately
intercommunion	supersensitive	resistlessness	inarticulation
intercommunity	supersonically	robustiousness	inartistically
interdependent	superstructure	satisfactorily	indeterminable
interferential	superterranean	schismatically	insatiableness
interferometer	supervisorship	selfsatisfying	latitudinarian
interferometry	uncircumcision	selfsufficient	legitimisation
intergradation	uncorroborated	selfsuggestion	lightheartedly
interjectional	underdeveloped	selfsupporting	meditativeness
interlineation	underemphasise	selfsustaining	meretriciously
interlocutress	undergraduette	telescopically	militarisation
intermediately	undermentioned	transcendental	monotonousness
intermediation	undernourished	transcendently	mountaineering
intermigration	understandable	transformation	nightblindness
intermittently	understandably	transformative	ornithological
intermolecular	understatement	transitionally	paratactically
internationale	undervaluation	transitiveness	penetrableness
interpellation	unscrupulously	transitoriness	phantasmagoria
interpenetrate	venereological	transliterator	phantasmagoric
interplanetary	watercolourist	transmigration	politicisation
interpretation	watertightness	transmigratory	polytheistical
interpretative	accustomedness	transplantable	practicability
interpretively	ambassadorship	transportation	prettification
intersectional	antiscriptural	transsexualism	quantification
intersexuality	antiseptically	transvaluation	quantitatively
intertwinement	Augustinianism	transversality	quarterbinding
invariableness	autosuggestion	undesirability	quattrocentism
liberalisation	backscattering	unhesitatingly	quattrocentist
libertarianism	backscratching	unreservedness	quintessential

reintroduction	incautiousness	diffractometer	superabundance
repetitiveness	linguistically	disheartenment	superannuation
roentgenoscopy	percutaneously	dodecasyllable	telepathically
sanctification	persuasiveness	endoradiosonde	therianthropic
scatterbrained	perturbational	epigrammatical	trivialisation
scintillometer	presumptuously	exhilaratingly	unpalatability
selftormenting	presupposition	figurativeness	unpleasantness
shortsightedly	productiveness	generalisation	vegetativeness
slatternliness	rambunctiously	generalpurpose	viviparousness
solitudinarian	sanguification	geographically	alphabetically
spectrographic	sanguinariness	highhandedness	consubstantial
spectroscopist	sensualisation	idiopathically	cucurbitaceous
spinthariscope	septuagenarian	imperativeness	disembarkation
stertorousness	sesquipedalian	incapacitation	disembowelment
stoutheartedly	statuesqueness	inseparability	hyperbolically
stratification	ubiquitousness	lefthandedness	microbiologist
stultification	untruthfulness	liberalisation	nightblindness
substantialism	behaviouristic	matriarchalism	overabundantly
substantialist	impoverishment	meditativeness	phenobarbitone
substantiality	inadvisability	militarisation	prefabrication
substantiation	indivisibility	mineralisation	probabiliorism
substantivally	irrevocability	mistranslation	probabiliorist
substitutional	omnivorousness	monosaccharide	prohibitionism
substitutively	recoverability	mountaineering	prohibitionist
symptomatology	reinvigoration	naturalisation	scrubbingbrush
traitorousness	rejuvenescence	neuroanatomist	selfabnegation
unattractively	revivification	neutralisation	selfabsorption
unenterprising	heroworshipper	openhandedness	antiscriptural
unenthusiastic	longwindedness	ophthalmoscope	attractiveness
unintelligible	noteworthiness	ophthalmoscopy	auspiciousness
unintelligibly	overwhelmingly	osteoarthritis	avariciousness
unsatisfactory	roadworthiness	overcapitalise	backscattering
valetudinarian	detoxification	paratactically	backscratching
vegetativeness	arrhythmically	peripateticism	capriciousness
volatilisation	biosystematics	persuasiveness	characteristic
whortleberries	campylotropous	phantasmagoria	classconscious
accountability	fullyfashioned	phantasmagoric	conductibility
altruistically	martyrological	pharmaceutical	consociational
bioluminescent	pachydermatous	pharmacologist	corticosteroid
boroughEnglish	phenylbutazone	pharmacopoeial	corticosterone
circuitousness	tachygraphical	pianoaccordion	corticotrophic
circumambiency	topsyturviness	pleonastically	corticotrophin
circumambulate	denazification	pneumatologist	cyanocobalamin
circumbendibus	————————	polysaccharide	despicableness
circumlittoral	abstractedness	popularisation	dialectologist
circumlocution	abstractionism	postmastership	disenchantment
circumlocutory	abstractionist	pragmaticality	disinclination
circumnavigate	Africanisation	procrastinator	disincorporate
circumspection	anagrammatical	pseudaesthesia	dissociability
circumstantial	autoradiograph	quadragenarian	excruciatingly
circumvolution	biographically	radicalisation	extracorporeal
colourfastness	blockaderunner	radioautograph	fallaciousness
colourlessness	capitalisation	regularisation	floriculturist
combustibility	castrametation	reorganisation	gynaecological
communications	centralisation	rheumatologist	hallucinogenic
compulsiveness	chromatography	roundaboutness	handicraftsman
conductibility	cinematography	Russianisation	histochemistry
conjunctivitis	congratulation	scandalisation	horticulturist
conquistadores	congratulative	scandalousness	hydrocoralline
consubstantial	congratulatory	schematisation	hypercalcaemia
consuetudinary	contractedness	scholastically	hypercatalexis
contumaciously	contradictable	secularisation	hypercriticise
contumeliously	contradictious	selfpartiality	hypercriticism
convulsiveness	contraindicate	selfsatisfying	iatrochemistry
corruptibility	contraposition	sensualisation	implacableness
discursiveness	contrapositive	septuagenarian	impracticality
disfurnishment	contrapuntally	specialisation	inconclusively
disputatiously	cryptaesthesia	spermatogenous	indiscerptible
disquisitional	crystallisable	spermatogonium	indiscoverable
euphuistically	cumulativeness	spermatophytic	indiscreetness
excruciatingly	decimalisation	standardbearer	indiscriminate
exhaustibility	decorativeness	stigmatisation	inflectionally
exhaustiveness	dehumanisation	stochastically	inflectionless
favourableness	delocalisation	substantialism	intercessional
fortuitousness	demoralisation	substantialist	intercessorial
fortunetelling	depolarisation	substantiality	intercommunion
gratuitousness	devitalisation	substantiation	intercommunity
hallucinogenic	diagrammatical	substantivally	intractability
honourableness	diaphanousness	sulphanilamide	invincibleness

loquaciousness	providentially	macroeconomics	interferential
macrocephalous	pteridological	manageableness	interferometer
microcephalous	regardlessness	meddlesomeness	interferometry
microcircuitry	reproductively	microeconomics	justifiability
microcomponent	selfadjustment	northeastwards	misinformation
myrmecological	selfadmiration	obstreperously	multifariously
myrmecophagous	tetradactylous	oecumenicalism	satisfactorily
myrmecophilous	threadbareness	oxyhaemoglobin	selfeffacement
neglectfulness	underdeveloped	palaeethnology	selfeffacingly
neurochemistry	acceleratingly	phraseological	semiofficially
nitrocellulose	aesthesiometer	polymerisation	shamefacedness
nomenclatorial	Albigensianism	praiseworthily	subinfeudation
orthochromatic	ambidextrously	progressionary	superficiality
parenchymatous	antidepressant	progressionism	superfoetation
perfectibility	antifederalist	progressionist	transformation
perniciousness	antiperspirant	propaedeutical	transformative
petrochemistry	antiseptically	prosperousness	unprofessional
photochemistry	apoplectically	pseudepigrapha	apologetically
pisciculturist	apothegmatical	pseudepigraphy	biodegradation
precociousness	archaeological	quarterbinding	bioengineering
predictability	archiepiscopal	quintessential	boroughEnglish
productiveness	asymmetrically	recoverability	cartographical
prolocutorship	barometrically	regeneratively	contagiousness
protectiveness	bioelectricity	rejuvenescence	contiguousness
publicspirited	boisterousness	remonetisation	cosmographical
pugnaciousness	bowdlerisation	rontgenography	courageousness
radiochemistry	bullheadedness	scatterbrained	disingenuously
reconciliation	chancellorship	selfdependence	epexegetically
reconciliatory	changeableness	selfdestroying	extinguishable
reflectiveness	chickenhearted	selfdetermined	extinguishment
refractoriness	chickenlivered	selffertilised	farsightedness
respectability	coessentiality	selfperception	hagiographical
respectfulness	complexionless	selfregulating	hieroglyphical
selfaccusation	comprehensible	selfrepression	hydrographical
selfaccusatory	comprehensibly	selfrespectful	hyperglycaemia
seriocomically	concretisation	selfrespecting	iconographical
serviceability	congregational	selfrestrained	impregnability
spirochaetosis	consuetudinary	selfrevelation	intangibleness
stampcollector	counsellorship	semicentennial	intergradation
subjectiveness	counterbalance	simplemindedly	liturgiologist
submicroscopic	counterculture	singlebreasted	lovingkindness
superciliously	countercurrent	singlehandedly	nitroglycerine
superconductor	countermeasure	singlemindedly	orthographical
suspiciousness	counterplotted	slanderousness	outrageousness
telescopically	defenestration	slatternliness	pathogenically
tragicomically	degenerateness	souldestroying	petrographical
transcendental	deliberateness	southeastwards	phytogeography
transcendently	deliberatively	statuesqueness	prodigiousness
uncircumcision	demisemiquaver	strikebreaking	propagandistic
ungraciousness	demonetisation	sublieutenancy	Pythagoreanism
unsuccessfully	denumerability	superelevation	rampageousness
verticillaster	doublebreasted	supereminently	retrogradation
vindictiveness	epistemologist	supererogation	revengefulness
watercolourist	Evangelicalism	supererogatory	roentgenoscopy
achondroplasia	evangelisation	unaffectedness	segregationist
appendicectomy	exasperatingly	underemphasise	springcleaning
archidiaconate	existentialism	unenterprising	strongmindedly
arrondissement	existentialist	unexpectedness	tachygraphical
commodiousness	featherbrained	unfriendliness	tetragrammaton
confidentially	goodfellowship	unintelligible	umbrageousness
dependableness	goodtemperedly	unintelligibly	uncongeniality
disorderliness	halfpennyworth	unreservedness	undergraduette
fastidiousness	handkerchieves	venereological	antiphlogistic
forbiddingness	hobbledehoyish	vituperatively	antithetically
formidableness	holometabolism	vivisectionist	apprehensively
friendlessness	holometabolous	vociferousness	asynchronously
groundlessness	homogenisation	volumetrically	breathlessness
gynandromorphy	hypodermically	whippersnapper	breathtakingly
hydrodynamical	illiterateness	audiofrequency	bronchiectasis
imponderabilia	immoderateness	crossfertilise	catachrestical
incredibleness	impoverishment	disaffiliation	catechetically
interdependent	inalienability	disaffirmation	chincherinchee
introductorily	inalterability	disenfranchise	delightfulness
jurisdictional	indeterminable	disinfestation	disinheritance
methodological	ineffectuality	eigenfrequency	dolichocephaly
pachydermatous	insuperability	fullyfashioned	encephalograph
perfidiousness	intolerability	indifferentism	faintheartedly
periodontology	knickerbockers	indifferentist	hypothetically
premeditatedly	longheadedness	insufficiently	hypothyroidism

```
immethodically  emulsification  scurrilousness  sacrilegiously
lightheartedly  enantiomorphic  selfdiscipline  schoolchildren
metaphorically  esterification  sesquipedalian  schoolmistress
metaphysically  eulogistically  silicification  selfflattering
monochromatism  euphuistically  simplification  semielliptical
ornithological  experientially  solicitousness  skimbleskamble
overwhelmingly  experimentally  solidification  snaggletoothed
perishableness  foraminiferous  solubilisation  sociologically
phosphorescent  fortuitousness  soporiferously  spindleshanked
polytheistical  fructification  soteriological  stumblingblock
shovehalfpenny  gelatinisation  stratification  supralapsarian
slaughterhouse  grandiloquence  stultification  tautologically
slaughterously  gratuitousness  substitutional  teleologically
speechlessness  hereditariness  substitutively  thimblerigging
spinthariscope  highmindedness  superincumbent  transliterator
sprightfulness  histrionically  superinduction  tropologically
stoicheiometry  humidification  superintendent  troubleshooter
stoichiometric  hyperirritable  transitionally  vaingloriously
stoutheartedly  idealistically  transitiveness  whortleberries
sycophantishly  identification  transitoriness  abovementioned
telephonically  illegitimately  ubiquitousness  abstemiousness
telephotograph  illimitability  undesirability  achromatically
thoughtfulness  immobilisation  unhesitatingly  aforementioned
thoughtreading  imparisyllabic  unsatisfactory  arithmetically
unemphatically  inadvisability  unsociableness  bioluminescent
unenthusiastic  inarticulately  vasodilatation  blackmarketeer
vicechancellor  inarticulation  vasodilatatory  circumambiency
administration  inartistically  verisimilitude  circumambulate
administrative  indecipherable  villainousness  circumbendibus
administratrix  indecisiveness  volatilisation  circumlittoral
aerobiological  indefiniteness  voluminousness  circumlocution
aerobiotically  indivisibility  weakmindedness  circumlocutory
agrobiological  indubitability  worshipfulness  circumnavigate
altruistically  infelicitously  interjectional  circumspection
anticipatively  inheritability  remarkableness  circumstantial
aphoristically  inordinateness  aetiologically  circumvolution
artificialness  insatiableness  campylotropous  contemptuously
associationism  invariableness  chivalrousness  contumaciously
autobiographer  kremlinologist  compulsiveness  contumeliously
autobiographic  legalistically  concelebration  determinedness
basidiomycetes  legitimisation  convulsiveness  diplomatically
beautification  libidinousness  curvilinearity  discombobulate
behaviouristic  linguistically  dieselelectric  discomfortable
beneficialness  longwindedness  dinoflagellate  discommendable
bituminisation  lyophilisation  discolouration  distemperature
boardingschool  oleaginousness  encyclopaedism  econometrician
bougainvillaea  openmindedness  encyclopaedist  emblematically
Brobdingnagian  optimistically  ethnologically  endosmotically
calamitousness  organisational  etymologically  enharmonically
centrifugation  papilionaceous  genealogically  epidemiologist
circuitousness  parasitologist  infralapsarian  excommunicable
classification  partridgeberry  intellectually  excommunicator
classificatory  politicisation  intelligential  ferrimagnetism
conceivability  postmillennial  intelligentsia  ferromagnesian
conquistadores  practicability  interlineation  ferromagnetism
conscienceless  prettification  interlocutress  fundamentalism
conspiratorial  proprietorship  inviolableness  fundamentalist
constitutional  proprioceptive  magniloquently  fundamentality
constitutively  quadrisyllabic  marvellousness  hydromechanics
coordinateness  quadrisyllable  metallographer  impermeability
councilchamber  quantification  miscalculation  implementation
councillorship  quantitatively  multilaterally  incommensurate
definitiveness  recapitulation  mythologically  incommodiously
demobilisation  recapitulative  neocolonialism  incommunicable
denazification  recapitulatory  nonbelligerent  incommunicably
denominational  rehabilitation  parallelepiped  inflammability
detoxification  reinvigoration  pathologically  inharmoniously
discriminating  reminiscential  pestilentially  insurmountable
discrimination  repetitiveness  petrologically  insurmountably
discriminative  repudiationist  phenylbutazone  intermediately
discriminatory  resinification  philologically  intermediation
disdainfulness  restrictionist  phthalocyanine  intermigration
disjointedness  revivification  pistilliferous  intermittently
disorientation  rigidification  poikilothermal  intermolecular
disquisitional  sanctification  poikilothermic  intramolecular
distributional  sanguification  premillenarian  judgematically
distributively  sanguinariness  proceleusmatic  mathematically
dolomitisation  saponification  pyrheliometric  mesdemoiselles
electioneering  scintillometer  rebelliousness  microminiature
```

noctambulation	illconditioned	anticonvulsant	selfcorrecting
noncommunicant	imaginableness	bibliographise	selfgovernment
numismatically	infrangibility	bibliomaniacal	selfpossession
parsimoniously	insignificance	cardiovascular	selftormenting
phlegmatically	insignificancy	categorisation	semiconducting
presumptuously	internationale	chronometrical	spatiotemporal
recommencement	intransitively	conglomeration	stadholdership
recommendation	intrinsicality	controllership	stationariness
recommendatory	Johannisberger	controvertible	stertorousness
sacramentalism	malcontentedly	decolonisation	surefootedness
sacramentalist	millenarianism	decolorisation	symptomatology
sacramentalism	morganatically	dextrorotation	thermochemical
schismatically	multinucleated	dextrorotatory	thermodynamics
selfemployment	newfangledness	diagnostically	thermoelectric
selfimmolation	nonconcurrence	enthronisation	traitorousness
selfimportance	nonsensicality	entomostracous	ultimogeniture
sentimentalise	northnortheast	flatfootedness	unaccommodated
sentimentalism	northnorthwest	heroworshipper	unaccomplished
sentimentalist	outgeneralling	heterochromous	unbecomingness
sentimentality	outlandishness	heteromorphism	absorptiveness
servomechanism	overindulgence	heteromorphous	accomplishable
somnambulation	pardonableness	heterophyllous	accomplishment
somnambulistic	personableness	heterothallism	astrophysicist
sphygmographic	pertinaciously	homoeomorphism	corruptibility
supramaxillary	philanthropise	hypocoristical	cosmopolitical
systematically	philanthropist	inappositeness	cotemporaneous
testimonialise	pigeonbreasted	indecomposable	crosspollinate
transmigration	portentousness	indecorousness	disappointment
transmigratory	preponderantly	indemonstrable	disapprobation
tridimensional	presentability	irreconcilable	disapprobative
twodimensional	presentational	irreconcilably	disapprobatory
ultramicrotome	presentimental	irremovability	disapprovingly
ultramontanism	preventability	irresoluteness	disciplinarian
ultramontanist	preventiveness	irrevocability	enterprisingly
uncommunicable	progenitorship	malodorousness	eutrophication
undermentioned	prosencephalic	monopolisation	extemporaneity
unidimensional	prosencephalon	monotonousness	extemporaneous
unpremeditated	psilanthropism	noncooperation	hermaphroditic
accountability	psilanthropist	noteworthiness	histopathology
aggrandisement	rambunctiously	omnivorousness	hocuspocussing
airconditioner	reasonableness	oneirocritical	inauspiciously
alphanumerical	reconnaissance	opinionatively	incompleteness
apprenticeship	rectangularity	organometallic	incompressible
astronomically	refrangibility	overcommitment	incompressibly
attainableness	responsibility	overcompensate	incorporeality
authentication	responsiveness	overconfidence	insuppressible
bathingmachine	rhinencephalic	overpopulation	interpellation
campanological	rhinencephalon	overpoweringly	interpenetrate
cantankerously	seasonableness	palaeobotanist	interplanetary
carcinogenesis	selfenergising	paradoxicality	interpretation
commensurately	selfinductance	passionateness	interpretative
commensuration	selfindulgence	physiognomical	interpretively
commonsensical	selfinterested	pluviometrical	irrespectively
communications	steganographer	pneumoconiosis	malappropriate
compensational	stupendousness	polymorphously	megasporangium
concentrically	subconsciously	postpositional	megasporophyll
conjunctivitis	subcontinental	postpositively	metempsychosis
consanguineous	subcontrariety	prognosticator	microprocessor
continuousness	supernaturally	prothonotarial	misapplication
conventionally	suspensiveness	pseudomorphism	misappropriate
convincingness	terminableness	pseudomorphous	multiplication
diamantiferous	terminological	pseudonymously	multiplicative
diamondiferous	tintinnabulary	psychoanalysis	neuropathology
disconcertment	tintinnabulate	psychoanalytic	perceptibility
disconformable	tintinnabulous	psychochemical	perceptiveness
disconnectedly	tremendousness	psychodynamics	peremptoriness
disconsolately	tyrannicalness	psychoneurosis	photoperiodism
disconsolation	unacknowledged	psychoneurotic	phytopathology
discontentedly	undernourished	psychophysical	presupposition
discontentment	uneconomically	psychosomatics	sauropterygian
discontinuance	unmannerliness	psychosurgical	sociopolitical
dispensability	volcanological	recolonisation	superphosphate
distensibility	vulcanological	revalorisation	susceptibility
elementariness	weltanschauung	roadworthiness	susceptiveness
extraneousness	allegorisation	selfcomplacent	transplantable
fortunetelling	allelomorphism	selfconfidence	transportation
geocentrically	anthropography	selfconsequent	uncompromising
gramineousness	anthropologist	selfconsistent	inadequateness
harmoniousness	anthropometric	selfcontrolled	relinquishment

autocratically	mysteriousness	hypersonically	Zoroastrianism
bacteriologist	nonperformance	impassableness	absentmindedly
bacteriostasis	overproduction	impassibleness	acceptableness
bacteriostatic	penetrableness	impressibility	accustomedness
bastardisation	perturbational	impressionable	advantageously
butterfingered	prearrangement	impressiveness	adventitiously
butterflyscrew	precariousness	inconsequently	affectionately
calcareousness	preferentially	inconsiderable	apophthegmatic
censoriousness	prescriptively	inconsiderably	archetypically
chemoreception	proportionable	inconsistently	architectonics
chemoreceptive	proportionably	infrastructure	arrhythmically
colourfastness	proportionally	insensibleness	asymptotically
colourlessness	proscriptively	intersectional	Augustinianism
comparableness	quattrocentism	intersexuality	bloodthirstily
conformability	quattrocentist	Mephistopheles	charitableness
conservational	reintroduction	metapsychology	Christological
conservatively	restorationism	microsporangia	claustrophobia
constructional	restorationist	microstructure	claustrophobic
constructively	resurrectional	necessarianism	climatological
constructivism	Rosicrucianism	neuroscientist	committeewoman
constructivist	salubriousness	nonrestrictive	compatibleness
conterminously	selfpreserving	oppressiveness	conditionality
conversational	selfproclaimed	overestimation	coquettishness
convertibility	selfpropelling	parapsychology	creditableness
copperbottomed	selfpropulsion	patresfamilias	delectableness
countrydancing	selfprotection	permissibility	departmentally
crossreference	spectrographic	permissiveness	dermatological
cumbersomeness	spectroscopist	photosensitise	despitefulness
democratically	sphaerocrystal	photosensitive	detestableness
deplorableness	squadronleader	photosynthesis	disenthralment
despiritualise	submersibility	photosynthetic	disintegration
diachronically	subversiveness	possessiveness	disintegrative
differentiable	sufferableness	predesignation	disputatiously
differentially	synchronically	predestinarian	diverticulitis
disarrangement	tatterdemalion	predestination	divertissement
discursiveness	terrorstricken	predisposition	educationalist
disfurnishment	theocratically	preposterously	effortlessness
dispiritedness	unappreciative	professionally	egalitarianism
dissertational	unapproachable	professorially	entertainingly
electrobiology	unattractively	purposefulness	eschatological
electrodeposit	uncorroborated	radiosensitive	exceptionality
electrodynamic	unidirectional	radiostrontium	factitiousness
electrostatics	uniformitarian	reconstitution	fictitiousness
electrotherapy	universalistic	reconstruction	flagitiousness
electrothermal	uproariousness	reconstructive	galactopoietic
electrothermic	vicepresidency	regressiveness	gerontological
electrovalency	victoriousness	remorsefulness	gyrostabiliser
embarrassingly	vulnerableness	representation	haematogenesis
erythropoiesis	westernisation	representative	hypostatically
favourableness	wonderstricken	selfassumption	illustrational
foreordination	aggressiveness	Shakespeareana	illustratively
forthrightness	ambassadorship	Shakespeariana	incautiousness
forwardlooking	biosystematics	shortsightedly	incestuousness
fraternisation	bremsstrahlung	sophistication	incontrollable
gregariousness	chemosynthesis	submissiveness	indestructible
hierarchically	clearsightedly	successfulness	indestructibly
historiography	combustibility	successionally	indistinctness
homotransplant	commissaryship	successiveness	indoctrination
honourableness	commissionaire	suggestibility	inevitableness
horrorstricken	compassionable	suggestiveness	infectiousness
hypocritically	compossibility	superscription	ingratiatingly
hysterectomise	concessionaire	supersensitive	inimitableness
inappreciation	condescendence	supersonically	intertwinement
inappreciative	correspondence	superstructure	intuitionalism
inapproachable	correspondency	supposititious	intuitionalist
incoordination	deconsecration	suprasegmental	knighterrantry
inexorableness	disassociation	swordswallower	libertarianism
inexpressively	disrespectable	tachistoscopic	licentiousness
ingloriousness	ecclesiastical	thalassography	longitudinally
insurrectional	ecclesiologist	thanksoffering	marketgardener
integrationist	exhaustibility	transsexualism	microtechnique
irreproachable	exhaustiveness	ultrasonically	ministerialist
irreproachably	expressionless	ultrastructure	nutritiousness
irreproducible	expressiveness	unconscionable	ostentatiously
lugubriousness	extensionality	understandable	percutaneously
martyrological	fantasticality	understandably	phototelegraph
massproduction	heartsearching	understatement	planetstricken
meretriciously	hygroscopicity	unquestionable	potentiometric
meteorological	hypersensitive	unquestionably	predeterminate

profitableness	obsequiousness	democratically	satisfactorily
proletarianise	obstructionism	dependableness	schismatically
proletarianism	obstructionist	deplorableness	seasonableness
propitiatorily	oversubscribed	despicableness	segregationist
propitiousness	pasteurisation	detestableness	selfflattering
radiotelegraph	pleasurability	dinoflagellate	shamefacedness
radiotelephone	protrusiveness	diplomatically	shovehalfpenny
radiotelephony	quinquagesimal	disarrangement	simultaneously
radiotherapist	quinquennially	disembarkation	southeastwards
redintegration	ridiculousness	disputatiously	spinthariscope
redistribution	scrupulousness	egalitarianism	sufferableness
redistributive	selffulfilling	embarrassingly	supernaturally
relentlessness	selfsufficient	emblematically	supralapsarian
resistlessness	selfsuggestion	encephalograph	supramaxillary
robustiousness	selfsupporting	entertainingly	sycophantishly
Sabbatarianism	selfsustaining	favourableness	systematically
scientifically	solitudinarian	ferrimagnetism	terminableness
sensationalism	unremunerative	ferromagnesian	tetradactylous
sensationalist	unscrupulously	ferromagnetism	theocratically
simultaneously	valetudinarian	formidableness	transvaluation
spiritlessness	bouleversement	fullyfashioned	Trinitarianism
spiritualistic	concavoconcave	gyrostabiliser	unattractively
spirituousness	deceivableness	histopathology	undervaluation
stomatological	effervescently	homotransplant	unemphatically
subalternation	extravehicular	honourableness	unsociableness
superterranean	imperviousness	hypercalcaemia	utilitarianism
symmetrisation	improvableness	hypercatalexis	vicechancellor
territorialise	inconveniently	hypostatically	vulnerableness
territorialism	lasciviousness	imaginableness	circumbendibus
territorialist	noninvolvement	impassableness	copperbottomed
territoriality	supervisorship	implacableness	discombobulate
thriftlessness	tergiversation	improvableness	distributional
thyrotoxicosis	transvaluation	inevitableness	distributively
topsyturviness	transversality	inexorableness	doublebreasted
traditionalism	unconventional	infralapsarian	monkeybusiness
traditionalist	unconvincingly	inimitableness	noctambulation
Trinitarianism	undervaluation	insatiableness	oversubscribed
tumultuousness	acknowledgment	integrationist	palaeobotanist
uncontrollable	narrowmindedly	internationale	perturbational
uncontrollably	northwestwards	invariableness	phenylbutazone
uncontroverted	southwestwards	inviolableness	pigeonbreasted
unfaithfulness	windowdressing	judgematically	roundaboutness
unflatteringly	windowshopping	libertarianism	singlebreasted
ungratefulness	convexoconcave	longheadedness	somnambulation
unmentionables	inflexibleness	manageableness	somnambulistic
untruthfulness	overexcitement	mathematically	strikebreaking
utilitarianism	selfexplaining	millenarianism	superabundance
voluptuousness	selfexpression	morganatically	threadbareness
watertightness	aerodynamicist	multifariously	abstractedness
weightlessness	brachycephalic	multilaterally	abstractionism
accumulatively	dicotyledonous	necessarianism	abstractionist
amateurishness	ichthyological	neuropathology	apoplectically
antiquarianism	ichthyophagous	northeastwards	artificialness
articulateness	ichthyosaurian	numismatically	beneficialness
autosuggestion	monkeybusiness	ostentatiously	bioelectricity
conclusiveness	presbyterially	pardonableness	brachycephalic
conglutination	staphylococcus	penetrableness	condescendence
conglutinative	protozoologist	percutaneously	conjunctivitis
crinkumcrankum	————	perishableness	contractedness
destructionist	acceptableness	personableness	convincingness
diminutiveness	achromatically	pertinaciously	destructionist
discountenance	advantageously	phenobarbitone	diffractometer
discouragement	ambassadorship	phlegmatically	disconcertment
discouragingly	antiquarianism	phytopathology	heterochromous
discourteously	associationism	prearrangement	hierarchically
disequilibrium	attainableness	profitableness	hygroscopicity
disgruntlement	autocratically	proletarianise	inarticulately
exclaustration	backscattering	proletarianism	inarticulation
goodhumouredly	blackmarketeer	propagandistic	incapacitation
hebetudinosity	bullheadedness	psychoanalysis	ineffectuality
immaculateness	changeableness	psychoanalytic	infelicitously
implausibility	charitableness	quinquagesimal	irreducibility
inscrutability	circumambiency	reasonableness	irrevocability
instrumentally	circumambulate	reconnaissance	macroeconomics
irreducibility	comparableness	remarkableness	microeconomics
irrefutability	contumaciously	repudiationist	miscalculation
latitudinarian	creditableness	restorationism	monosaccharide
meticulousness	deceivableness	restorationist	neuroscientist
miraculousness	delectableness	Sabbatarianism	nonconcurrence

obstructionism	conscienceless	photosensitise	centrifugation
obstructionist	contumeliously	photosensitive	classification
oneirocritical	courageousness	phototelegraph	classificatory
overexcitement	crossfertilise	phytogeography	colourfastness
paratactically	crossreference	polytheistical	denazification
pharmaceutical	cryptaesthesia	predeterminate	detoxification
pharmacologist	deconsecration	preferentially	discomfortable
pharmacopoeial	despitefulness	proceleusmatic	disconformable
pianoaccordian	dieselelectric	proprietorship	emulsification
pneumoconiosis	differentiable	providentially	esterification
politicisation	differentially	pseudaesthesia	fructification
polysaccharide	disinfestation	purposefulness	humidification
practicability	disingenuously	quinquennially	identification
prosencephalic	disinheritance	radiosensitive	nonperformance
prosencephalon	disintegration	radiotelegraph	patresfamilias
psychochemical	disintegrative	radiotelephone	prettification
rambunctiously	disorderliness	radiotelephony	quantification
restrictionist	disorientation	rampageousness	resinification
rhinencephalic	econometrician	recommencement	revivification
rhinencephalon	effervescently	recommendation	rigidification
schoolchildren	epexegetically	recommendatory	sanctification
selfaccusation	experientially	redintegration	sanguification
selfaccusatory	extraneousness	remorsefulness	saponification
springcleaning	extravehicular	representation	selfeffacement
superscription	faintheartedly	representative	selfeffacingly
thermochemical	fortunetelling	resurrectional	selfsufficient
unaffectedness	fundamentalism	revengefulness	semiofficially
unconscionable	fundamentalist	roentgenoscopy	silicification
unexpectedness	fundamentality	sacramentalism	simplification
vivisectionist	gramineousness	sacramentalist	solidification
aggrandisement	heartsearching	sacramentarian	soporiferously
airconditioner	hydromechanics	sacrilegiously	stratification
antifederalist	hypersensitive	selfenergising	stultification
autoradiograph	hypothetically	selfpreserving	apothegmatical
bastardisation	hysterectomise	sentimentalise	autosuggestion
blockaderunner	impermeability	sentimentalism	bathingmachine
contradictable	implementation	sentimentalist	bibliographise
contradictious	imponderabilia	sentimentality	congregational
diamondiferous	inappreciation	serviceability	consanguineous
endoradiosonde	inappreciative	servomechanism	infrangibility
forbiddingness	incommensurate	skimbleskamble	marketgardener
foreordination	inconsequently	snaggletoothed	newfangledness
forwardlooking	inconveniently	southwestwards	physiognomical
hebetudinosity	indifferentism	spindleshanked	quadragenarian
hobbledehoyish	indifferentist	stoicheiometry	rectangularity
illconditioned	indiscerptible	stoutheartedly	refrangibility
incoordination	inexpressively	subalternation	reinvigoration
latitudinarian	insurrectional	subinfeudation	selfregulating
outlandishness	intellectually	supersensitive	selfsuggestion
overindulgence	intercessional	superterranean	septuagenarian
partridgeberry	intercessorial	suprasegmental	ultimogeniture
preponderantly	interdependent	tergiversation	apophthegmatic
propaedeutical	interferential	thermoelectric	arrhythmically
psychodynamics	interferometer	thimblerigging	astrophysicist
selfinductance	interferometry	transcendental	bloodthirstily
selfindulgence	interjectional	transcendently	boroughEnglish
solitudinarian	intermediately	transsexualism	comprehensible
stupendousness	intermediation	transversality	comprehensibly
tatterdemalion	interpellation	tridimensional	disenchantment
thermodynamics	interpenetrate	troubleshooter	disenthralment
tremendousness	intersectional	twodimensional	eutrophication
valetudinarian	intersexuality	umbrageousness	farsightedness
windowdressing	irrespectively	unappreciative	hermaphroditic
abovementioned	knighterrantry	uncongeniality	histochemistry
aforementioned	lightheartedly	unconventional	iatrochemistry
alphabetically	macrocephalous	underdeveloped	neurochemistry
antithetically	microcephalous	undermentioned	orthochromatic
apologetically	microtechnique	ungratefulness	parenchymatous
apprehensively	ministerialist	unidimensional	petrochemistry
architectonics	nitrocellulose	unidirectional	photochemistry
arithmetically	northwestwards	unmannerliness	radiochemistry
bouleversement	outgeneralling	unpremeditated	radiotherapist
calcareousness	outrageousness	unprofessional	singlehandedly
catechetically	overwhelmingly	unsuccessfully	spirochaetosis
chemoreception	pachydermatous	vicepresidency	superphosphate
chemoreceptive	parallelepiped	whortleberries	unfaithfulness
chincherinchee	pathogenically	beautification	untruthfulness
concelebration	pestilentially	butterfingered	abstemiousness
confidentially	photoperiodism	butterflyscrew	adventitiously

affectionately	jurisdictional	circumlocution	unintelligibly
appendicectomy	justifiability	circumlocutory	vasodilatation
archidiaconate	lasciviousness	colourlessness	vasodilatatory
arrondissement	licentiousness	controllership	volatilisation
Augustinianism	liturgiologist	councilchamber	weightlessness
auspiciousness	loquaciousness	councillorship	absentmindedly
avariciousness	lugubriousness	counsellorship	allelomorphism
bacteriologist	meretriciously	crystallisable	anagrammatical
bacteriostasis	microbiologist	decimalisation	bibliomaniacal
bacteriostatic	microcircuitry	delocalisation	castrametation
bioengineering	microminiature	demobilisation	chronometrical
bioluminescent	mountaineering	demoralisation	conformability
bronchiectasis	mysteriousness	devitalisation	conglomeration
capriciousness	nutritiousness	dicotyledonous	conterminously
censoriousness	obsequiousness	disciplinarian	crinkumcrankum
clearsightedly	perfidiousness	disinclination	demisemiquaver
commodiousness	perniciousness	effortlessness	departmentally
communications	potentiometric	Evangelicalism	diagrammatical
compatibleness	precariousness	evangelisation	discommendable
conditionality	precociousness	friendlessness	discriminating
consociational	predesignation	generalisation	discrimination
contagiousness	premeditatedly	generalpurpose	discriminative
contraindicate	prescriptively	goodfellowship	discriminatory
cucurbitaceous	probabiliorism	grandiloquence	epigrammatical
curvilinearity	probabiliorist	groundlessness	epistemologist
despiritualise	prodigiousness	hieroglyphical	experimentally
determinedness	progenitorship	hyperglycaemia	goodhumouredly
disaffiliation	prohibitionism	immaculateness	goodtemperedly
disaffirmation	prohibitionist	immobilisation	heteromorphism
disequilibrium	propitiatorily	incompleteness	heteromorphous
dispiritedness	propitiousness	inconclusively	homoeomorphism
dissociability	proscriptively	interplanetary	indecomposable
diverticulitis	pugnaciousness	irresoluteness	inflammability
divertissement	pyrheliometric	liberalisation	instrumentally
ecclesiastical	rebelliousness	lyophilisation	legitimisation
ecclesiologist	reconciliation	marvellousness	narrowmindedly
educationalist	reconciliatory	meticulousness	noncommunicant
epidemiologist	robustiousness	mineralisation	organometallic
exceptionality	salubriousness	miraculousness	overcommitment
excruciatingly	scientifically	misapplication	overcompensate
extensionality	scrubbingbrush	monopolisation	oxyhaemoglobin
factitiousness	sensationalism	multiplication	pluviometrical
fallaciousness	sensationalist	multiplicative	pseudomorphism
fastidiousness	shortsightedly	naturalisation	pseudomorphous
fictitiousness	stoichiometric	neutralisation	schoolmistress
flagitiousness	stumblingblock	nightblindness	selfadmiration
forthrightness	superciliously	nitroglycerine	selfcomplacent
gregariousness	superficiality	nomenclatorial	selfimmolation
hallucinogenic	supervisorship	nonbelligerent	simplemindedly
harmoniousness	supposititious	ophthalmoscope	singlemindedly
historiography	suspiciousness	ophthalmoscopy	strongmindedly
hypocritically	traditionalism	pistilliferous	supereminently
impassibleness	traditionalist	postmillennial	symptomatology
imperviousness	transliterator	premillenarian	unaccommodated
inauspiciously	transmigration	radicalisation	unaccomplished
incautiousness	transmigratory	regardlessness	unbecomingness
inconsiderable	tyrannicalness	rehabilitation	underemphasise
inconsiderably	ultramicrotome	relentlessness	uniformitarian
inconsistently	unconvincingly	resistlessness	verisimilitude
incredibleness	ungraciousness	ridiculousness	aerodynamicist
indistinctness	unmentionables	scandalisation	Africanisation
infectiousness	uproariousness	scandalousness	Albigensianism
inflexibleness	verticillaster	scintillometer	anticonvulsant
ingloriousness	victoriousness	scrupulousness	bituminisation
ingratiatingly	watertightness	scurrilousness	boardingschool
insensibleness	selfadjustment	selffulfilling	bougainvillaea
insignificance	cantankerously	semielliptical	Brobdingnagian
insignificancy	lovingkindness	sensualisation	chickenhearted
insufficiently	accomplishable	solubilisation	chickenlivered
intangibleness	accomplishment	specialisation	circumnavigate
intelligential	accumulatively	speechlessness	coessentiality
intelligentsia	acknowledgment	spiritlessness	coordinateness
interlineation	antiphlogistic	stadholdership	decolonisation
intermigration	articulateness	staphylococcus	dehumanisation
intermittently	breathlessness	superelevation	denominational
intuitionalism	capitalisation	thriftlessness	diaphanousness
intuitionalist	centralisation	transplantable	disconnectedly
invincibleness	chancellorship	trivialisation	discountenance
Johannisberger	circumlittoral	unintelligible	disdainfulness

disfurnishment asymptotically irreproducible tropologically
disgruntlement autobiographer magniloquently ultramontanism
disjointedness autobiographic martyrological ultramontanist
enthronisation basidiomycetes massproduction ultrasonically
existentialism behaviouristic megasporangium unacknowledged
existentialist campanological megasporophyll unapproachable
foraminiferous campylotropous mesdemoiselles uncorroborated
fraternisation carcinogenesis metallographer undernourished
gelatinisation Christological metaphorically uneconomically
halfpennyworth classconscious meteorological vaingloriously
highhandedness climatological methodological venereological
highmindedness concavoconcave microcomponent volcanological
homogenisation convexoconcave misinformation vulcanological
impregnability corticosteroid myrmecological watercolourist
inalienability corticosterone myrmecophagous anthropography
indefiniteness corticotrophic myrmecophilous anthropologist
indemonstrable corticotrophin mythologically anthropometric
inordinateness cosmopolitical neocolonialism anticipatively
irreconcilable cotemporaneous noninvolvement antidepressant
irreconcilably crosspollinate northnortheast antiseptically
kremlinologist cyanocobalamin northnorthwest archiepiscopal
lefthandedness dermatological ornithological biographically
libidinousness diachronically overproduction contemptuously
longwindedness disappointment papilionaceous contraposition
mistranslation disassociation parsimoniously contrapositive
monotonousness discolouration pathologically contrapuntally
neuroanatomist disembowelment periodontology correspondence
oecumenicalism disincorporate petrologically correspondency
oleaginousness dolichocephaly philologically disrespectable
openhandedness electioneering phosphorescent distemperature
openmindedness electrobiology phraseological geographically
opinionatively electrodeposit phthalocyanine heterophyllous
overconfidence electrodynamic poikilothermal indecipherable
passionateness electrostatics poikilothermic microsporangia
prothonotarial electrotherapy proprioceptive noncooperation
pseudonymously electrothermal protozoologist obstreperously
psychoneurosis electrothermic pteridological overcapitalise
psychoneurotic electrovalency Pythagoreanism overpopulation
recolonisation enantiomorphic quattrocentism predisposition
rejuvenescence encyclopaedism quattrocentist presumptuously
reorganisation encyclopaedist reintroduction presupposition
rontgenography endosmotically selfproclaimed pseudepigrapha
Russianisation enharmonically selfpropelling pseudepigraphy
sanguinariness erythropoiesis selfpropulsion psychophysical
selfabnegation eschatological selfprotection selfdependence
selfconfidence ethnologically seriocomically selfemployment
selfconsequent etymologically sociologically selfexplaining
selfconsistent extemporaneity sociopolitical selfexpression
selfcontrolled extemporaneous soteriological selfimportance
semicentennial extracorporeal spectrographic selfrepression
semiconducting flatfootedness spectroscopist selfsupporting
stationariness galactopoietic sphaerocrystal sesquipedalian
substantialism genealogically sphygmographic Shakespeareana
substantialist gerontological squadronleader Shakespeariana
substantiality gynaecological stampcollector unscrupulously
substantiation haematogenesis steganographer worshipfulness
substantivally histrionically stomatological acceleratingly
sulphanilamide hocuspocussing superconductor achondroplasia
superannuation hydrocoralline superfoetation allegorisation
superincumbent hyperbolically supersonically amateurishness
superinduction hypersonically surefootedness antiperspirant
superintendent ichthyological synchronically antiscriptural
therianthropic ichthyophagous tautologically asynchronously
tintinnabulary ichthyosaurian teleologically audiofrequency
tintinnabulate immethodically telephonically backscratching
tintinnabulous inapproachable telephotograph biodegradation
unfriendliness incommodiously telescopically boisterousness
unremunerative incorporeality terminological bowdlerisation
villainousness indiscoverable territorialise cartographical
voluminousness inharmoniously territorialism catachrestical
weakmindedness insurmountable territorialist categorisation
westernisation insurmountably territoriality chivalrousness
accustomedness intercommunion testimonialise claustrophobia
aerobiological intercommunity thanksoffering claustrophobic
aerobiotically interlocutress thyrotoxicosis conspiratorial
aetiologically intermolecular tragicomically cosmographical
agrobiological intramolecular transformation counterbalance
archaeological irreproachable transformative counterculture
astronomically irreproachably transportation countercurrent

countermeasure	prosperousness	expressiveness	windowshopping
counterplotted	quarterbinding	horrorstricken	wonderstricken
decolorisation	recoverability	idealistically	absorptiveness
degenerateness	redistribution	imparisyllabic	accountability
deliberateness	redistributive	implausibility	apprenticeship
deliberatively	regeneratively	impressibility	asymmetrically
denumerability	regularisation	impressionable	attractiveness
depolarisation	retrogradation	impressiveness	authentication
dextrorotation	revalorisation	inadvisability	barometrically
dextrorotatory	roadworthiness	inappositeness	biosystematics
disapprobation	scatterbrained	inartistically	breathtakingly
disapprobative	secularisation	indecisiveness	bremsstrahlung
disapprobatory	selfcorrecting	indivisibility	calamitousness
disapprovingly	selffertilised	intransitively	characteristic
discouragement	selfpartiality	intrinsicality	chromatography
discouragingly	selfperception	legalistically	cinematography
discourteously	selftormenting	linguistically	circuitousness
disenfranchise	slanderousness	meddlesomeness	combustibility
disheartenment	slatternliness	metempsychosis	committeewoman
eigenfrequency	standardbearer	nonsensicality	concentrically
enterprisingly	stertorousness	oppressiveness	concretisation
exasperatingly	submicroscopic	optimistically	conductibility
exhilaratingly	supererogation	organisational	conglutination
featherbrained	supererogatory	permissibility	conglutinative
gynandromorphy	symmetrisation	permissiveness	congratulation
hagiographical	tachygraphical	persuasiveness	congratulative
handicraftsman	tetragrammaton	phantasmagoria	congratulatory
handkerchieves	traitorousness	phantasmagoric	constitutional
heroworshipper	uncompromising	planetstricken	constitutively
hydrographical	uncontrollable	pleonastically	consuetudinary
hypercriticise	uncontrollably	possessiveness	conventionally
hypercriticism	uncontroverted	postmastership	convertibility
hyperirritable	undergraduette	postpositional	coquettishness
hypocoristical	undesirability	postpositively	corruptibility
hypodermically	unenterprising	procrastinator	cumulativeness
iconographical	unreservedness	professionally	decorativeness
illiterateness	vituperatively	professorially	definitiveness
illustrational	viviparousness	prognosticator	delightfulness
illustratively	vociferousness	progressionary	demonetisation
immoderateness	whippersnapper	progressionism	dialectologist
impoverishment	administration	progressionist	diamantiferous
inalterability	administrative	protrusiveness	diminutiveness
incompressible	administratrix	psychosomatics	discontentedly
incompressibly	aesthesiometer	psychosurgical	discontentment
incontrollable	aggressiveness	publicspirited	discontinuance
indecorousness	altruistically	quadrisyllabic	dissertational
indestructible	aphoristically	quadrisyllable	dolomitisation
indestructibly	circumspection	quintessential	elementariness
indeterminable	circumstantial	regressiveness	exhaustibility
indiscreetness	commensurately	reminiscential	exhaustiveness
indiscriminate	commensuration	responsibility	fantasticality
indoctrination	commissaryship	responsiveness	figurativeness
inseparability	commissionaire	scholastically	fortuitousness
insuperability	commonsensical	selfabsorption	geocentrically
insuppressible	compassionable	selfassumption	gratuitousness
intergradation	compensational	selfdestroying	hereditariness
interpretation	compossibility	selfdiscipline	heterothallism
interpretative	compulsiveness	selfpossession	holometabolism
interpretively	concessionaire	selfrespectful	holometabolous
intolerability	conclusiveness	selfrespecting	idiopathically
knickerbockers	conquistadores	selfrestrained	illegitimately
malappropriate	consubstantial	selfsustaining	illimitability
malodorousness	conversational	souldestroying	imperativeness
matriarchalism	convulsiveness	statuesqueness	impracticality
microprocessor	cumbersomeness	stochastically	indubitability
militarisation	defenestration	subconsciously	inflectionally
misappropriate	diagnostically	submersibility	inflectionless
monochromatism	disconsolately	submissiveness	infrastructure
noteworthiness	disconsolation	subversiveness	inheritability
omnivorousness	discursiveness	successfulness	inscrutability
orthographical	dispensability	successionally	intractability
osteoarthritis	disquisitional	successiveness	irrefutability
pasteurisation	distensibility	suspensiveness	malcontentedly
petrographical	dodecasyllable	terrorstricken	meditativeness
pleasurability	entomostracous	thalassography	Mephistopheles
polymerisation	eulogistically	universalistic	microstructure
polymorphously	euphuistically	unpleasantness	neglectfulness
popularisation	exclaustration	unsatisfactory	nonrestrictive
prefabrication	expressionless	weltanschauung	overestimation

palaeethnology	understandably	archidiaconate	lightheartedly
parasitologist	understatement	articulateness	marketgardener
perceptibility	unflatteringly	backscratching	neuroanatomist
perceptiveness	unhesitatingly	bibliomaniacal	nomenclatorial
peremptoriness	unpalatability	biodegradation	opinionatively
perfectibility	unquestionable	breathtakingly	organisational
peripateticism	unquestionably	cardiovascular	orthographical
philanthropise	vegetativeness	cartographical	passionateness
philanthropist	vindictiveness	circumnavigate	patresfamilias
pneumatologist	volumetrically	colourfastness	perturbational
portentousness	Zoroastrianism	commissaryship	petrographical
pragmaticality	alphanumerical	compensational	pleasurability
predestinarian	constructional	conceivability	practicability
predestination	constructively	conformability	predictability
predictability	constructivism	congregational	presentability
preposterously	constructivist	conservational	presentational
presbyterially	contiguousness	conservatively	preventability
presentability	continuousness	consociational	propitiatorily
presentational	excommunicable	conspiratorial	quantitatively
presentimental	excommunicator	conversational	recoverability
preventability	extinguishable	coordinateness	regeneratively
preventiveness	extinguishment	cosmographical	respectability
productiveness	floriculturist	degenerateness	retrogradation
proportionable	horticulturist	deliberateness	sanguinariness
proportionably	inadequateness	deliberatively	selfeffacement
proportionally	incestuousness	denominational	selfeffacingly
protectiveness	incommunicable	denumerability	serviceability
psilanthropism	incommunicably	discouragement	singlehandedly
psilanthropist	introductorily	discouragingly	spiritualistic
quantitatively	longitudinally	disenchantment	spirochaetosis
radiostrontium	multinucleated	disenfranchise	stationariness
recapitulation	overabundantly	dispensability	stoutheartedly
recapitulative	pisciculturist	dissertational	swordswallower
recapitulatory	prolocutorship	dissociability	symptomatology
reconstitution	radioautograph	ecclesiastical	tachygraphical
reconstruction	relinquishment	elementariness	tetragrammaton
reconstructive	reproductively	exasperatingly	threadbareness
reflectiveness	Rosicrucianism	excruciatingly	tintinnabulary
refractoriness	spiritualistic	exhilaratingly	tintinnabulate
remonetisation	spirituousness	faintheartedly	tintinnabulous
repetitiveness	sublieutenancy	hagiographical	transplantable
respectability	topsyturviness	handicraftsman	unapproachable
respectfulness	tumultuousness	heartsearching	undergraduette
rheumatologist	uncircumcision	hereditariness	understandable
sauropterygian	uncommunicable	holometabolism	understandably
schematisation	unenthusiastic	holometabolous	understatement
selfdetermined	voluptuousness	hydrographical	undesirability
selfinterested	cardiovascular	iconographical	unhesitatingly
selfsatisfying	circumvolution	illimitability	universalistic
slaughterhouse	conceivability	illiterateness	unpalatability
slaughterously	conservational	illustrational	unpleasantness
solicitousness	conservatively	illustratively	vasodilatation
sophistication	controvertible	immaculateness	vasodilatatory
spatiotemporal	irremovability	immoderateness	vituperatively
spermatogenous	selfgovernment	impermeability	acceptableness
spermatogonium	selfrevelation	impregnability	attainableness
spermatophytic	intertwinement	inadequateness	changeableness
sprightfulness	overpoweringly	inadvisability	charitableness
stigmatisation	praiseworthily	inalienability	comparableness
subcontinental	swordswallower	inalterability	compatibleness
subcontrariety	ambidextrously	inapproachable	concelebration
subjectiveness	complexionless	indubitability	counterbalance
substitutional	paradoxicality	inflammability	creditableness
substitutively	archetypically	ingratiatingly	cyanocobalamin
suggestibility	chemosynthesis	inheritability	deceivableness
suggestiveness	countrydancing	inordinateness	delectableness
superstructure	hydrodynamical	inscrutability	dependableness
susceptibility	hypothyroidism	inseparability	deplorableness
susceptiveness	metaphysically	insuperability	despicableness
tachistoscopic	metapsychology	intergradation	detestableness
telepathically	parapsychology	interplanetary	electrobiology
thoughtfulness	photosynthesis	intolerability	favourableness
thoughtreading	photosynthetic	intractability	featherbrained
transitionally	———————————	irrefutability	formidableness
transitiveness	acceleratingly	irremovability	gyrostabiliser
transitoriness	accountability	irreproachable	honourableness
ubiquitousness	accumulatively	irreproachably	imaginableness
ultrastructure	aerodynamicist	irrevocability	impassableness
understandable	anticipatively	justifiability	impassibleness

implacableness	polysaccharide	departmentally	weightlessness
improvableness	proprioceptive	dicotyledonous	crossreference
incredibleness	quattrocentism	discommendable	delightfulness
inevitableness	quattrocentist	disconcertment	despitefulness
inexorableness	reminiscential	disconnectedly	disdainfulness
inflexibleness	reproductively	discontentedly	insignificance
inimitableness	resurrectional	discontentment	insignificancy
insatiableness	Rosicrucianism	disrespectable	neglectfulness
insensibleness	satisfactorily	distemperature	overconfidence
intangibleness	selfdiscipline	effortlessness	purposefulness
invariableness	selfperception	eigenfrequency	remorsefulness
invincibleness	selfproclaimed	experimentally	respectfulness
inviolableness	servomechanism	friendlessness	revengefulness
knickerbockers	shamefacedness	groundlessness	scientifically
manageableness	sphaerocrystal	histochemistry	selfconfidence
pardonableness	subconsciously	hobbledehoyish	selffulfilling
penetrableness	superficiality	iatrochemistry	selfsufficient
perishableness	superincumbent	incompleteness	sprightfulness
personableness	tetradactylous	incompressible	successfulness
profitableness	tyrannicalness	incompressibly	thanksoffering
quarterbinding	ultramicrotome	indiscreetness	thoughtfulness
reasonableness	unappreciative	instrumentally	unfaithfulness
remarkableness	unattractively	insuppressible	ungratefulness
scatterbrained	unidirectional	interpretation	unsatisfactory
seasonableness	weltanschauung	interpretative	untruthfulness
sufferableness	ambassadorship	interpretively	worshipfulness
terminableness	bullheadedness	malcontentedly	advantageously
uncorroborated	countrydancing	neurochemistry	aetiologically
unsociableness	electrodeposit	noncooperation	autobiographer
vulnerableness	electrodynamic	obstreperously	autobiographic
whortleberries	highhandedness	organometallic	autosuggestion
appendicectomy	highmindedness	overpoweringly	boardingschool
architectonics	immethodically	peripateticism	Brobdingnagian
chemoreception	incommodiously	petrochemistry	carcinogenesis
chemoreceptive	inconsiderable	pharmaceutical	clearsightedly
communications	inconsiderably	photochemistry	dinoflagellate
concavoconcave	intermediately	pluviometrical	disintegration
constructional	intermediation	premillenarian	disintegrative
constructively	irreproducible	preponderantly	ethnologically
constructivism	lefthandedness	preposterously	etymologically
constructivist	longheadedness	presbyterially	ferrimagnetism
contumaciously	longitudinally	propaedeutical	ferromagnesian
convexoconcave	longwindedness	prosencephalic	ferromagnetism
councilchamber	massproduction	prosencephalon	forthrightness
counterculture	openhandedness	psychoneurosis	genealogically
countercurrent	openmindedness	psychoneurotic	haematogenesis
crinkumcrankum	overproduction	quadragenarian	intelligential
deconsecration	reintroduction	radiochemistry	intelligentsia
disassociation	semiconducting	radiotherapist	intermigration
diverticulitis	stadholdership	regardlessness	metallographer
dolichocephaly	standardbearer	rejuvenescence	mythologically
handkerchieves	superinduction	relentlessness	partridgeberry
hocuspocussing	unfriendliness	resistlessness	pathologically
hydromechanics	unpremeditated	rhinencephalic	petrologically
hysterectomise	weakmindedness	rhinencephalon	philologically
inappreciation	acknowledgment	sauropterygian	predesignation
inappreciative	antifederalist	selfabnegation	quinquagesimal
inauspiciously	apophthegmatic	selfdependence	redintegration
insufficiently	audiofrequency	selfdetermined	sacrilegiously
insurrectional	biosystematics	selfgovernment	selfsuggestion
intellectually	blockaderunner	selfinterested	shortsightedly
interjectional	boroughEnglish	selfrevelation	sociologically
interlocutress	brachycephalic	septuagenarian	spectrographic
intersectional	breathlessness	sesquipedalian	sphygmographic
introductorily	bronchiectasis	Shakespeareana	steganographer
irreconcilable	cantankerously	Shakespeariana	suprasegmental
irreconcilably	castrametation	slaughterhouse	tautologically
irrespectively	catachrestical	slaughterously	teleologically
jurisdictional	characteristic	soporiferously	transmigration
matriarchalism	chronometrical	spatiotemporal	transmigratory
meretriciously	circumbendibus	speechlessness	tropologically
metapsychology	colourlessness	spiritlessness	watertightness
microtechnique	committeewoman	superelevation	biographically
monosaccharide	commonsensical	superfoetation	chickenhearted
multinucleated	comprehensible	tatterdemalion	extravehicular
parapsychology	comprehensibly	thriftlessness	geographically
pertinaciously	condescendence	ultimogeniture	heterochromous
phthalocyanine	conglomeration	unflatteringly	heterophyllous
pianoaccordian	controvertible	unremunerative	heterothallism

hierarchically	depolarisation	lovingkindness	sanguification
idiopathically	detoxification	lyophilisation	saponification
indecipherable	devitalisation	meditativeness	scandalisation
palaeethnology	diamantiferous	mesdemoiselles	schematisation
philanthropise	diamondiferous	militarisation	schoolmistress
philanthropist	diminutiveness	mineralisation	secularisation
psilanthropism	disappointment	misapplication	selfadmiration
psilanthropist	disciplinarian	monopolisation	selfsatisfying
psychochemical	discontinuance	multiplication	semielliptical
psychophysical	discriminating	multiplicative	semiofficially
schoolchildren	discrimination	narrowmindedly	sensualisation
telepathically	discriminative	naturalisation	silicification
thermochemical	discriminatory	neuroscientist	simplemindedly
windowshopping	discursiveness	neutralisation	simplification
absentmindedly	disfurnishment	nightblindness	singlemindedly
absorptiveness	disinclination	nonbelligerent	solidification
accomplishable	disquisitional	nonsensicality	solitudinarian
accomplishment	distensibility	oecumenicalism	solubilisation
aesthesiometer	dolomitisation	oppressiveness	sophistication
Africanisation	emulsification	outlandishness	specialisation
aggrandisement	endoradiosonde	overcapitalise	stigmatisation
aggressiveness	enterprisingly	overestimation	stoicheiometry
airconditioner	entertainingly	overexcitement	stratification
allegorisation	enthronisation	paradoxicality	strongmindedly
amateurishness	esterification	pasteurisation	stultification
antiscriptural	eutrophication	perceptibility	subcontinental
apprenticeship	Evangelicalism	perceptiveness	subjectiveness
archiepiscopal	evangelisation	perfectibility	submersibility
artificialness	exhaustibility	permissibility	submissiveness
attractiveness	exhaustiveness	permissiveness	subversiveness
authentication	expressionless	persuasiveness	successionally
autoradiograph	expressiveness	pistilliferous	successiveness
bastardisation	extinguishable	politicisation	suggestibility
beautification	extinguishment	polymerisation	suggestiveness
beneficialness	fantasticality	polytheistical	sulphanilamide
bituminisation	figurativeness	popularisation	supereminently
bloodthirstily	foraminiferous	possessiveness	susceptibility
bowdlerisation	forbiddingness	postpositional	susceptiveness
butterfingered	foreordination	postpositively	suspensiveness
capitalisation	fraternisation	pragmaticality	symmetrisation
categorisation	fructification	predestinarian	transitionally
centralisation	gelatinisation	predestination	transitiveness
circumlittoral	generalisation	prefabrication	trivialisation
classification	hebetudinosity	presentimental	unbecomingness
classificatory	homogenisation	prettification	unconscionable
combustibility	humidification	preventiveness	uniformitarian
commissionaire	hypercriticise	productiveness	unquestionable
compassionable	hypercriticism	professionally	unquestionably
complexionless	hypocoristical	proportionable	valetudinarian
compossibility	identification	proportionably	vegetativeness
compulsiveness	illconditioned	proportionally	verisimilitude
concessionaire	illegitimately	protectiveness	vindictiveness
conclusiveness	immobilisation	protrusiveness	volatilisation
concretisation	imperativeness	pseudepigrapha	westernisation
conductibility	implausibility	pseudepigraphy	aerobiological
conglutination	impoverishment	quantification	agrobiological
conglutinative	impracticality	radicalisation	archaeological
conterminously	impressibility	recolonisation	butterflyscrew
contradictable	impressionable	reconnaissance	campanological
contradictious	impressiveness	reconstitution	chancellorship
conventionally	inappositeness	redistribution	chickenlivered
convertibility	incapacitation	redistributive	Christological
convincingness	incoordination	reflectiveness	climatological
convulsiveness	indecisiveness	refrangibility	controllership
coquettishness	indefiniteness	regressiveness	contumeliously
corruptibility	indiscriminate	regularisation	cosmopolitical
cumulativeness	indivisibility	rehabilitation	councillorship
decimalisation	indoctrination	relinquishment	counsellorship
decolonisation	infelicitously	remonetisation	crosspollinate
decolorisation	inflectionally	reorganisation	crystallisable
decorativeness	inflectionless	repetitiveness	dermatological
definitiveness	infrangibility	resinification	dieselelectric
dehumanisation	intertwinement	responsibility	disaffiliation
delocalisation	intransitively	responsiveness	disequilibrium
demisemiquaver	intrinsicality	revalorisation	encephalograph
demobilisation	irreducibility	revivification	eschatological
demonetisation	latitudinarian	rigidification	floriculturist
demoralisation	legitimisation	Russianisation	forwardlooking
denazification	liberalisation	sanctification	gerontological

goodfellowship	unaccommodated	sentimentalise	discomfortable
gynaecological	uncircumcision	sentimentalism	disconformable
horticulturist	uneconomically	sentimentalist	disconsolately
hyperbolically	abovementioned	sentimentality	disconsolation
hypercalcaemia	aforementioned	simultaneously	ecclesiologist
ichthyological	apprehensively	slatternliness	educationalist
intermolecular	Augustinianism	squadronleader	epidemiologist
interpellation	bioengineering	stumblingblock	epistemologist
intramolecular	bioluminescent	superannuation	exceptionality
martyrological	chemosynthesis	superconductor	extensionality
meteorological	classconscious	supersensitive	extraneousness
methodological	confidentially	supersonically	factitiousness
myrmecological	conscienceless	sycophantishly	fallaciousness
newfangledness	contraindicate	synchronically	fastidiousness
nitrocellulose	curvilinearity	telephonically	fictitiousness
noninvolvement	determinedness	testimonialise	flagitiousness
ornithological	diachronically	transcendental	fortuitousness
overwhelmingly	differentiable	transcendently	goodhumouredly
parallelepiped	differentially	tridimensional	gramineousness
phototelegraph	disarrangement	twodimensional	grandiloquence
phraseological	disingenuously	ultramontanism	gratuitousness
pisciculturist	disorientation	ultramontanist	gregariousness
postmillennial	electioneering	ultrasonically	gynandromorphy
probabiliorism	enharmonically	uncommunicable	harmoniousness
probabiliorist	excommunicable	uncongeniality	heteromorphism
pteridological	excommunicator	unconventional	heteromorphous
radiotelegraph	experientially	unconvincingly	historiography
radiotelephone	fundamentalism	undermentioned	homoeomorphism
radiotelephony	fundamentalist	unidimensional	hygroscopicity
reconciliation	fundamentality	vicechancellor	imperviousness
reconciliatory	halfpennyworth	abstemiousness	incautiousness
scintillometer	hallucinogenic	achondroplasia	incestuousness
selfemployment	histrionically	affectionately	incontrollable
selfexplaining	homotransplant	allelomorphism	indecorousness
shovehalfpenny	hydrodynamical	anthropography	infectiousness
sociopolitical	hypersensitive	anthropologist	ingloriousness
soteriological	hypersonically	anthropometric	intuitionalism
springcleaning	implementation	antiphlogistic	intuitionalist
stampcollector	incommensurate	asynchronously	kremlinologist
stomatological	incommunicable	auspiciousness	lasciviousness
superciliously	incommunicably	avariciousness	libidinousness
terminological	inconveniently	bacteriologist	licentiousness
thermoelectric	indistinctness	bacteriostasis	liturgiologist
transvaluation	inharmoniously	bacteriostatic	loquaciousness
undervaluation	interlineation	boisterousness	lugubriousness
unintelligible	interpenetrate	calamitousness	macroeconomics
unintelligibly	microminiature	calcareousness	malappropriate
venereological	mountaineering	capriciousness	malodorousness
verticillaster	neocolonialism	censoriousness	marvellousness
volcanological	overabundantly	chivalrousness	meddlesomeness
vulcanological	papilionaceous	chromatography	Mephistopheles
watercolourist	parsimoniously	cinematography	meticulousness
accustomedness	pathogenically	circuitousness	microbiologist
alphanumerical	percutaneously	circumlocution	microeconomics
anagrammatical	periodontology	circumlocutory	microprocessor
apothegmatical	pestilentially	circumvolution	microsporangia
arrhythmically	photosensitise	claustrophobia	miraculousness
astronomically	photosensitive	claustrophobic	misappropriate
basidiomycetes	photosynthesis	commodiousness	monochromatism
bathingmachine	photosynthetic	conditionality	monotonousness
circumambiency	physiognomical	contagiousness	mysteriousness
circumambulate	prearrangement	contiguousness	nonperformance
countermeasure	preferentially	continuousness	nutritiousness
diagrammatical	propagandistic	contraposition	obsequiousness
enantiomorphic	providentially	contrapositive	oleaginousness
epigrammatical	psychoanalysis	copperbottomed	omnivorousness
hypodermically	psychoanalytic	correspondence	outrageousness
indeterminable	quinquennially	correspondency	oxyhaemoglobin
intercommunion	radiosensitive	courageousness	palaeobotanist
intercommunity	recommencement	cumbersomeness	parasitologist
microcomponent	recommendation	dextrorotation	peremptoriness
ophthalmoscope	recommendatory	dextrorotatory	perfidiousness
ophthalmoscopy	representation	dialectologist	perniciousness
overcommitment	representative	diaphanousness	pharmacologist
phantasmagoria	roentgenoscopy	disapprobation	pharmacopoeial
phantasmagoric	sacramentalism	disapprobative	phytogeography
selftormenting	sacramentalist	disapprobatory	pneumatologist
seriocomically	sacramentarian	disapprovingly	pneumoconiosis
tragicomically	scrubbingbrush	discombobulate	portentousness

potentiometric	galactopoietic	nonrestrictive	pseudaesthesia
praiseworthily	generalpurpose	northnortheast	quintessential
precariousness	goodtemperedly	northnorthwest	selfconsequent
precociousness	ichthyophagous	oneirocritical	selfconsistent
predisposition	indecomposable	orthochromatic	selfpossession
presupposition	infralapsarian	outgeneralling	selfpreserving
prodigiousness	interdependent	pachydermatous	skimbleskamble
professorially	macrocephalous	phenobarbitone	southeastwards
propitiousness	microcephalous	phosphorescent	southwestwards
prosperousness	myrmecophagous	photoperiodism	spectroscopist
prothonotarial	myrmecophilous	pigeonbreasted	spindleshanked
protozoologist	overcompensate	predeterminate	supervisorship
pseudomorphism	polymorphously	proletarianise	troubleshooter
pseudomorphous	prescriptively	proletarianism	unenthusiastic
psychosomatics	proscriptively	Pythagoreanism	unprofessional
pugnaciousness	publicspirited	radiostrontium	unsuccessfully
pyrheliometric	selfcomplacent	reconstruction	vicepresidency
rampageousness	selfpropelling	reconstructive	whippersnapper
rebelliousness	selfpropulsion	Sabbatarianism	abstractedness
refractoriness	selfrespectful	selfcorrecting	abstractionism
reinvigoration	selfrespecting	selfenergising	abstractionist
rheumatologist	selfsupporting	selfexpression	achromatically
ridiculousness	supralapsarian	selfrepression	administration
robustiousness	telescopically	singlebreasted	administrative
rontgenography	unaccomplished	spinthariscope	administratrix
roundaboutness	underemphasise	strikebreaking	adventitiously
salubriousness	unenterprising	subalternation	aerobiotically
scandalousness	inconsequently	subcontrariety	alphabetically
scrupulousness	magniloquently	superscription	altruistically
scurrilousness	statuesqueness	superstructure	ambidextrously
selfabsorption	antidepressant	superterranean	antiseptically
selfimmolation	antiquarianism	tergiversation	antithetically
selfimportance	asymmetrically	territorialise	aphoristically
sensationalism	barometrically	territorialism	apologetically
sensationalist	bibliographise	territorialist	apoplectically
slanderousness	blackmarketeer	territoriality	arithmetically
solicitousness	bouleversement	thimblerigging	associationism
spermatogenous	bremsstrahlung	thoughtreading	asymptotically
spermatogonium	chincherinchee	topsyturviness	autocratically
spermatophytic	concentrically	transformation	backscattering
spirituousness	cotemporaneous	transformative	bioelectricity
staphylococcus	crossfertilise	transportation	campylotropous
stertorousness	disaffirmation	transversality	catechetically
stoichiometric	disembarkation	Trinitarianism	circumstantial
stupendousness	disenthralment	ultrastructure	coessentiality
submicroscopic	disincorporate	unmannerliness	conjunctivitis
supererogation	disinheritance	utilitarianism	conquistadores
supererogatory	disorderliness	vaingloriously	consubstantial
superphosphate	doublebreasted	volumetrically	contemptuously
suspiciousness	egalitarianism	windowdressing	contractedness
tachistoscopic	extemporaneity	Zoroastrianism	corticotrophic
thalassography	extemporaneous	Albigensianism	corticotrophin
traditionalism	extracorporeal	antiperspirant	cucurbitaceous
traditionalist	geocentrically	arrondissement	defenestration
traitorousness	hermaphroditic	corticosteroid	democratically
transitoriness	hydrocoralline	corticosterone	despiritualise
tremendousness	hyperirritable	cryptaesthesia	destructionist
tumultuousness	hypothyroidism	disinfestation	diagnostically
ubiquitousness	imponderabilia	divertissement	diffractometer
umbrageousness	incorporeality	effervescently	diplomatically
uncompromising	indifferentism	electrostatics	discountenance
uncontrollable	indifferentist	embarrassingly	discourteously
uncontrollably	indisceptible	fullyfashioned	disgruntlement
uncontroverted	infrastructure	heroworshipper	disheartenment
ungraciousness	interferential	ichthyosaurian	disjointedness
unmentionables	interferometer	inconsistently	dispiritedness
uproariousness	interferometry	indemonstrable	disputatiously
victoriousness	knighterrantry	inexpressively	econometrician
villainousness	libertarianism	intercessional	electrotherapy
viviparousness	megasporangium	intercessorial	electrothermal
vociferousness	megasporophyll	Johannisberger	electrothermic
voluminousness	metaphorically	metaphysically	emblematically
voluptuousness	microcircuitry	mistranslation	endosmotically
archetypically	microstructure	northeastwards	entomostracous
circumspection	millenarianism	northwestwards	epexegetically
counterplotted	ministerialist	oversubscribed	eulogistically
encyclopaedism	misinformation	progressionary	euphuistically
encyclopaedist	multifariously	progressionism	exclaustration
erythropoiesis	necessarianism	progressionist	existentialism

existentialist	systematically	imparisyllabic	impregnability
farsightedness	telephotograph	metempsychosis	impressibility
flatfootedness	terrorstricken	nitroglycerine	inadvisability
fortunetelling	theocratically	parenchymatous	inalienability
histopathology	therianthropic	pseudonymously	inalterability
horrorstricken	transliterator	psychodynamics	indivisibility
hypercatalexis	unaffectedness	quadrisyllabic	indubitability
hypocritically	unemphatically	quadrisyllable	inflammability
hypostatically	unexpectedness	thermodynamics	infrangibility
hypothetically	vivisectionist	————————————	inheritability
idealistically	wonderstricken	anagrammatical	inscrutability
inartistically	behaviouristic	apothegmatical	inseparability
ineffectuality	centrifugation	artificialness	insuperability
integrationist	commensurately	bathingmachine	intolerability
intermittently	commensuration	beneficialness	intractability
internationale	congratulation	bibliographise	irreducibility
judgematically	congratulative	bremsstrahlung	irrefutability
legalistically	congratulatory	circumstantial	irremovability
linguistically	consanguineous	communications	irrevocability
mathematically	constitutional	conquistadores	Johannisberger
morganatically	constitutively	consubstantial	justifiability
multilaterally	consuetudinary	cotemporaneous	perceptibility
neuropathology	contrapuntally	counterbalance	perfectibility
noteworthiness	discolouration	countrydancing	permissibility
numismatically	distributional	cucurbitaceous	phenobarbitone
obstructionism	distributively	cyanocobalamin	pleasurability
obstructionist	inarticulately	diagrammatical	practicability
optimistically	inarticulation	disenthralment	predictability
ostentatiously	inconclusively	electrovalency	presentability
osteoarthritis	indestructible	encyclopaedism	preventability
paratactically	indestructibly	encyclopaedist	recoverability
phlegmatically	insurmountable	epigrammatical	redistribution
phytopathology	insurmountably	extemporaneity	redistributive
planetstricken	irresoluteness	extemporaneous	refrangibility
pleonastically	miscalculation	heterothallism	respectability
poikilothermal	monkeybusiness	hydrocoralline	responsibility
poikilothermic	noctambulation	hydrodynamical	serviceability
postmastership	noncommunicant	hypercatalexis	standardbearer
premeditatedly	nonconcurrence	ichthyosaurian	submersibility
presumptuously	overindulgence	imponderabilia	suggestibility
procrastinator	overpopulation	megasporangium	susceptibility
progenitorship	phenylbutazone	outgeneralling	tintinnabulary
prognosticator	proceleusmatic	papilionaceous	tintinnabulate
prohibitionism	psychosurgical	phantasmagoria	tintinnabulous
prohibitionist	recapitulation	phantasmagoric	undesirability
prolocutorship	recapitulative	premeditatedly	unpalatability
proprietorship	recapitulatory	psychoanalysis	apprenticeship
radioautograph	rectangularity	psychoanalytic	archidiaconate
rambunctiously	selfaccusation	selfexplaining	authentication
repudiationist	selfaccusatory	selfsustaining	beautification
restorationism	selfadjustment	Shakespeareana	bronchiectasis
restorationist	selfassumption	Shakespeariana	circumlocution
restrictionist	selfinductance	subcontrariety	circumlocutory
roadworthiness	selfindulgence	tyrannicalness	classification
schismatically	selfregulating	unsatisfactory	classificatory
scholastically	somnambulation	accountability	conscienceless
segregationist	somnambulistic	circumambiency	contradictable
selfcontrolled	subinfeudation	circumambulate	contradictious
selfdestroying	substitutional	combustibility	denazification
selffertilised	substitutively	compossibility	detoxification
selfflattering	superabundance	conceivability	disconnectedly
selfpartiality	undernourished	conductibility	disrespectable
selfprotection	unscrupulously	conformability	effervescently
selfrestrained	anticonvulsant	convertibility	emulsification
selfsustaining	bougainvillaea	corruptibility	esterification
semicentennial	electrovalency	denumerability	eutrophication
snaggletoothed	indiscoverable	disapprobation	Evangelicalism
souldestroying	underdeveloped	disapprobative	fantasticality
stochastically	unreservedness	disapprobatory	fructification
sublieutenancy	disembowelment	discombobulate	humidification
substantialism	unacknowledged	dispensability	hypercalcaemia
substantialist	intersexuality	dissociability	hyperglycaemia
substantiality	supramaxillary	distensibility	identification
substantiation	thyrotoxicosis	exhaustibility	impracticality
substantivally	transsexualism	holometabolism	inapproachable
superintendent	astrophysicist	holometabolous	indestructible
supernaturally	dodecasyllable	illimitability	indestructibly
supposititious	hieroglyphical	impermeability	indistinctness
surefootedness	hyperglycaemia	implausibility	intrinsicality

irreproachable	dieselelectric	simultaneously	poikilothermal
irreproachably	dinoflagellate	singlebreasted	poikilothermic
metempsychosis	discountenance	spirochaetosis	polymorphously
microcircuitry	discourteously	springcleaning	polysaccharide
microprocessor	disembowelment	stadholdership	roadworthiness
misapplication	disheartenment	strikebreaking	servomechanism
multiplication	disjointedness	sublieutenancy	shortsightedly
multiplicative	dispiritedness	superintendent	spindleshanked
nitroglycerine	dolichocephaly	surefootedness	therianthropic
nonsensicality	doublebreasted	thermochemical	troubleshooter
oecumenicalism	electioneering	thermoelectric	underemphasise
oversubscribed	electrodeposit	thoughtreading	watertightness
paradoxicality	farsightedness	transliterator	weltanschauung
pragmaticality	flatfootedness	unaffectedness	abstractionism
prefabrication	fortunetelling	underdeveloped	abstractionist
prettification	goodtemperedly	unexpectedness	achromatically
quantification	haematogenesis	unreservedness	adventitiously
recommencement	highhandedness	weakmindedness	aerobiotically
resinification	highmindedness	whortleberries	aetiologically
revivification	inconsiderable	windowdressing	Albigensianism
rigidification	inconsiderably	diamantiferous	alphabetically
sanctification	incorporeality	diamondiferous	altruistically
sanguification	indecipherable	foraminiferous	antiquarianism
saponification	indifferentism	handicraftsman	antiseptically
selfeffacement	indifferentist	pistilliferous	antithetically
selfeffacingly	indiscoverable	shovehalfpenny	aphoristically
selfinductance	indiscreetness	thanksoffering	apologetically
semiofficially	intelligential	anthropography	apoplectically
silicification	intelligentsia	antiphlogistic	archetypically
simplification	interdependent	apophthegmatic	arithmetically
solidification	interferential	centrifugation	arrhythmically
sophistication	interlineation	chromatography	associationism
spectroscopist	intermolecular	cinematography	astronomically
staphylococcus	interpenetrate	disarrangement	asymmetrically
stratification	intramolecular	discouragement	asymptotically
stultification	lefthandedness	discouragingly	Augustinianism
unapproachable	longheadedness	historiography	autocratically
uncircumcision	longwindedness	nonbelligerent	barometrically
unconvincingly	mountaineering	oxyhaemoglobin	biographically
vicechancellor	multilaterally	phytogeography	bougainvillaea
acknowledgment	neuroscientist	prearrangement	catechetically
biodegradation	newfangledness	pseudepigrapha	chickenlivered
consuetudinary	openhandedness	pseudepigraphy	chincherinchee
contraindicate	openmindedness	rontgenography	coessentiality
dicotyledonous	overcompensate	scrubbingbrush	concentrically
intergradation	parallelepiped	selfabnegation	conjunctivitis
overabundantly	partridgeberry	selfenergising	consanguineous
propagandistic	percutaneously	spermatogenous	contumaciously
recommendation	phosphorescent	spermatogonium	contumeliously
recommendatory	phototelegraph	stumblingblock	cosmopolitical
retrogradation	pigeonbreasted	supererogation	crystallisable
sesquipedalian	postmastership	supererogatory	democratically
subinfeudation	postmillennial	thalassography	destructionist
superconductor	proprioceptive	clearsightedly	diachronically
transcendental	psychochemical	councilchamber	diagnostically
transcendently	Pythagoreanism	electrotherapy	diplomatically
undergraduette	quattrocentism	electrothermal	disaffiliation
abstractedness	quattrocentist	electrothermic	disassociation
accustomedness	quinquagesimal	forthrightness	disequilibrium
advantageously	quintessential	fullyfashioned	disinheritance
alphanumerical	radiotelegraph	handkerchieves	disputatiously
antidepressant	radiotelephone	heroworshipper	egalitarianism
appendicectomy	radiotelephony	histopathology	electrobiology
autosuggestion	reminiscential	hobbledehoyish	emblematically
bioengineering	selfconsequent	hydromechanics	endosmotically
bioluminescent	selfcorrecting	ichthyophagous	enharmonically
bullheadedness	selfexpression	macrocephalous	epexegetically
carcinogenesis	selfperception	matriarchalism	ethnologically
chemoreception	selfpossession	metapsychology	etymologically
chemoreceptive	selfpreserving	microcephalous	eulogistically
chickenhearted	selfpropelling	microtechnique	euphuistically
circumspection	selfprotection	monosaccharide	excommunicable
committeewoman	selfrepression	myrmecophagous	excommunicator
contractedness	selfrespectful	myrmecophilous	existentialism
controllership	selfrespecting	neuropathology	existentialist
countermeasure	selfsuggestion	noteworthiness	extravehicular
crossreference	selftormenting	osteoarthritis	genealogically
curvilinearity	semicentennial	parapsychology	geocentrically
determinedness	shamefacedness	phytopathology	geographically

gyrostabiliser publicspirited acceptableness recapitulatory
hierarchically quarterbinding anthropologist rectangularity
histrionically rambunctiously attainableness remarkableness
hyperbolically reconciliation bacteriologist rheumatologist
hyperirritable reconciliatory changeableness seasonableness
hypersonically repudiationist charitableness selfcomplacent
hypocritically restorationism circumvolution selfimmolation
hypodermically restorationist comparableness selfindulgence
hypostatically restrictionist compatibleness selfproclaimed
hypothetically Rosicrucianism congratulation selfregulating
idealistically Sabbatarianism congratulative selfrevelation
idiopathically sacrilegiously congratulatory slatternliness
immethodically schismatically counterplotted somnambulation
inappreciation scholastically creditableness somnambulistic
inappreciative schoolchildren crosspollinate spiritualistic
inartistically scientifically deceivableness squadronleader
inauspiciously segregationist delectableness stampcollector
incommodiously selfconfidence dependableness sufferableness
incommunicable selfconsistent deplorableness sulphanilamide
incommunicably selfdiscipline despicableness swordswallower
inconveniently selffertilised detestableness terminableness
indeterminable selffulfilling dialectologist unaccomplished
inharmoniously selfpartiality disconsolately unacknowledged
insignificance selfsufficient disconsolation uncontrollable
insignificancy seriocomically disgruntlement uncontrollably
insufficiently sociologically disorderliness unfriendliness
integrationist sociopolitical dodecasyllable universalistic
intermediately spinthariscope ecclesiologist unmannerliness
intermediation stochastically epidemiologist unscrupulously
internationale subconsciously epistemologist unsociableness
irreconcilable substantialism favourableness verisimilitude
irreconcilably substantialist formidableness verticillaster
judgematically substantiality honourableness vulnerableness
legalistically substantiation imaginableness aerodynamicist
libertarianism substantivally imparisyllabic anthropometric
linguistically superciliously impassableness biosystematics
longitudinally superficiality impassibleness cumbersomeness
mathematically superscription implacableness disaffirmation
meretriciously supersonically improvableness gynandromorphy
metaphorically suppositclause inarticulately histochemistry
metaphysically supramaxillary inarticulation iatrochemistry
microminiature synchronically incontrollable illegitimately
millenarianism systematically incredibleness indiscriminate
ministerialist tautologically inevitableness intercommunion
morganatically teleologically inexorableness intercommunity
multifariously telepathically inflexibleness meddlesomeness
mythologically telephonically inimitableness misinformation
necessarianism telescopically insatiableness monochromatism
neocolonialism territorialise insensibleness neurochemistry
nonrestrictive territorialism intangibleness overestimation
numismatically territorialist interpellation overwhelmingly
obstructionism territorialist invariableness pachydermatous
obstructionist testimonialise invincibleness parenchymatous
oneirocritical theocratically inviolableness patresfamilias
optimistically thimblerigging kremlinologist petrochemistry
ostentatiously thyrotoxicosis liturgiologist photochemistry
overcommitment tragicomically manageableness potentiometric
overconfidence Trinitarianism microbiologist predeterminate
paratactically tropologically miscalculation presentimental
parsimoniously ultrasonically mistranslation pseudonymously
pathogenically unappreciative multinucleated psychosomatics
pathologically uncommunicable nitrocellulose pyrheliometric
pertinaciously uncongeniality noctambulation radiochemistry
petrologically uneconomically overindulgence selfassumption
philologically unemphatically overpopulation spatiotemporal
phlegmatically unenthusiastic parasitologist stoichiometric
photoperiodism unintelligible pardonableness suprasegmental
pleonastically unintelligibly penetrableness tatterdemalion
probabiliorism unpremeditated perishableness tetragrammaton
probabiliorist utilitarianism personableness transformation
procrastinator vaingloriously pharmacologist transformative
prognosticator vicepresidency pneumatologist uncompromising
progressionary vivisectionist profitableness absentmindedly
progressionism volumetrically protozoologist affectionately
progressionist Zoroastrianism quadrisyllabic asynchronously
prohibitionism blackmarketeer quadrisyllable bibliomaniacal
prohibitionist breathtakingly reasonableness boroughEnglish
proletarianise disembarkation recapitulation Brobdingnagian
proletarianism skimbleskamble recapitulative butterfingered

circumbendibus	traditionalist	snaggletoothed	discolouration
commonsensical	transplantable	soteriological	discomfortable
comprehensible	ultimogeniture	stoicheiometry	disconcertment
comprehensibly	unbecomingness	stomatological	disconformable
condescendence	understandable	successionally	disintegration
conditionality	understandably	supervisorship	disintegrative
conglutination	unmentionables	telephotograph	distemperature
conglutinative	unpleasantness	terminological	econometrician
conterminously	valetudinarian	transitionally	elementariness
contrapuntally	whippersnapper	unaccommodated	entomostracous
convincingness	aerobiological	unconscionable	exclaustration
correspondence	aesthesiometer	uncorroborated	faintheartedly
correspondency	agrobiological	unquestionable	featherbrained
departmentally	ambassadorship	unquestionably	heartsearching
disappointment	archaeological	venereological	hereditariness
disciplinarian	autoradiograph	volcanological	heterochromous
discommendable	campanological	vulcanological	heteromorphism
discontentedly	chancellorship	watercolourist	heteromorphous
discontentment	Christological	windowshopping	homoeomorphism
discontinuance	climatological	achondroplasia	horrorstricken
discriminating	commissionaire	antiperspirant	intermigration
discrimination	compassionable	antiscriptural	knighterrantry
discriminative	complexionless	brachycephalic	lightheartedly
discriminatory	concavoconcave	cartographical	marketgardener
disenchantment	concessionaire	claustrophobia	metallographer
disenfranchise	conventionally	claustrophobic	microsporangia
disinclination	convexoconcave	cosmographical	nonconcurrence
educationalist	councillorship	disincorporate	noncooperation
entertainingly	counsellorship	extracorporeal	nonperformance
exceptionality	dermatological	hagiographical	obstreperously
experimentally	diffractometer	hieroglyphical	overpoweringly
extensionality	enantiomorphic	hydrographical	peremptoriness
ferrimagnetism	encephalograph	hygroscopicity	philanthropise
ferromagnesian	endoradiosonde	iconographical	philanthropist
ferromagnetism	erythropoiesis	indiscerptible	planetstricken
forbiddingness	eschatological	malappropriate	praiseworthily
foreordination	expressionless	Mephistopheles	preponderantly
hebetudinosity	forwardlooking	microcomponent	preposterously
incoordination	galactopoietic	misappropriate	presbyterially
indoctrination	gerontological	orthographical	professorially
instrumentally	goodfellowship	petrographical	pseudomorphism
insurmountable	gynaecological	pharmacopoeial	pseudomorphous
insurmountably	hallucinogenic	prosencephalic	psilanthropism
interplanetary	hermaphroditic	prosencephalon	psilanthropist
intertwinement	hypothyroidism	rhinencephalic	psychosurgical
intuitionalism	ichthyological	rhinencephalon	radiotherapist
intuitionalist	impressionable	semielliptical	redintegration
latitudinarian	indecomposable	spermatophytic	refractoriness
lovingkindness	inflectionally	tachygraphical	reinvigoration
macroeconomics	inflectionless	audiofrequency	sanguinariness
malcontentedly	interferometer	demisemiquaver	sauropterygian
microeconomics	interferometry	eigenfrequency	scatterbrained
narrowmindedly	knickerbockers	grandiloquence	selfabsorption
nightblindness	martyrological	administration	selfadmiration
noncommunicant	megasporophyll	administrative	selfcontrolled
palaeethnology	meteorological	administratrix	selfdestroying
pneumoconiosis	methodological	allelomorphism	selfdetermined
predesignation	myrmecological	ambidextrously	selfgovernment
predestinarian	ophthalmoscope	antifederalist	selfimportance
predestination	ophthalmoscopy	autobiographer	selfinterested
premillenarian	ornithological	autobiographic	selfrestrained
psychodynamics	orthochromatic	behaviouristic	slaughterhouse
quadragenarian	phraseological	bioelectricity	slaughterously
quinquennially	physiognomical	blockaderunner	soporiferously
selfdependence	pianoaccordian	bloodthirstily	souldestroying
sensationalism	professionally	campylotropous	spectrographic
sensationalist	progenitorship	cantankerously	sphaerocrystal
septuagenarian	prolocutorship	characteristic	sphygmographic
simplemindedly	proportionable	commensurately	stationariness
singlehandedly	proportionably	commensuration	steganographer
singlemindedly	proportionally	commissaryship	stoutheartedly
solitudinarian	proprietorship	concelebration	superterranean
strongmindedly	pteridological	conglomeration	terrorstricken
subalternation	radioautograph	controvertible	threadbareness
subcontinental	radiostrontium	corticotrophic	transitoriness
superabundance	roentgenoscopy	corticotrophin	transmigration
supereminently	scintillometer	crinkumcrankum	transmigratory
thermodynamics	selfemployment	deconsecration	ultramicrotome
traditionalism	selfsupporting	defenestration	undernourished

unenterprising	militarisation	congregational	northnorthwest
unflatteringly	mineralisation	conservational	northwestwards
unremunerative	monkeybusiness	conservatively	opinionatively
wonderstricken	monopolisation	consociational	organisational
accomplishable	naturalisation	conspiratorial	organometallic
accomplishment	neutralisation	constitutional	overcapitalise
Africanisation	outlandishness	constitutively	overexcitement
aggrandisement	pasteurisation	constructional	palaeobotanist
allegorisation	photosensitise	constructively	passionateness
amateurishness	photosensitive	constructivism	periodontology
apprehensively	politicisation	constructivist	peripateticism
archiepiscopal	polymerisation	conversational	perturbational
arrondissement	polytheistical	coordinateness	pestilentially
astrophysicist	popularisation	copperbottomed	phenylbutazone
bacteriostasis	predisposition	corticosteroid	photosynthesis
bacteriostatic	presupposition	corticosterone	photosynthetic
bastardisation	proceleusmatic	crossfertilise	pisciculturist
bituminisation	radicalisation	cryptaesthesia	pluviometrical
boardingschool	radiosensitive	degenerateness	postpositional
bouleversement	recolonisation	deliberateness	postpositively
bowdlerisation	reconnaissance	deliberatively	preferentially
breathlessness	regardlessness	denominational	prescriptively
capitalisation	regularisation	dextrorotation	presentational
cardiovascular	rejuvenescence	dextrorotatory	propitiatorily
catachrestical	relentlessness	differentiable	proscriptively
categorisation	relinquishment	differentially	prothonotarial
centralisation	remonetisation	disinfestation	providentially
classconscious	reorganisation	disorientation	pseudaesthesia
colourfastness	resistlessness	disquisitional	quantitatively
colourlessness	revalorisation	dissertational	reconstitution
concretisation	Russianisation	distributional	regeneratively
contraposition	scandalisation	distributively	rehabilitation
contrapositive	schematisation	electrostatics	representation
coquettishness	schoolmistress	exasperatingly	representative
decimalisation	secularisation	excruciatingly	reproductively
decolonisation	selfaccusation	exhilaratingly	resurrectional
decolorisation	selfaccusatory	experientially	sacramentalism
dehumanisation	selfadjustment	floriculturist	sacramentalist
delocalisation	selfsatisfying	fundamentalism	sacramentarian
demobilisation	sensualisation	fundamentalist	satisfactorily
demonetisation	solubilisation	fundamentality	selfflattering
demoralisation	specialisation	horticulturist	sentimentalise
depolarisation	speechlessness	hypercriticise	sentimentalism
devitalisation	spiritlessness	hypercriticism	sentimentalist
disfurnishment	stigmatisation	hysterectomise	sentimentality
divertissement	submicroscopic	illconditioned	southeastwards
dolomitisation	superphosphate	illiterateness	southwestwards
ecclesiastical	supersensitive	illustrational	substitutional
effortlessness	supralapsarian	illustratively	substitutively
embarrassingly	symmetrisation	immaculateness	superfoetation
enterprisingly	tachistoscopic	immoderateness	sycophantishly
enthronisation	tergiversation	implementation	symptomatology
evangelisation	thriftlessness	inadequateness	tetradactylous
extinguishable	transversality	inappositeness	transportation
extinguishment	tridimensional	incapacitation	ultramontanism
fraternisation	trivialisation	incompleteness	ultramontanist
friendlessness	twodimensional	inconsistently	unattractively
gelatinisation	unidimensional	indefiniteness	unconventional
generalisation	unprofessional	indemonstrable	undermentioned
groundlessness	unsuccessfully	infelicitously	understatement
homogenisation	volatilisation	ingratiatingly	unhesitatingly
homotransplant	weightlessness	inordinateness	unidirectional
hypersensitive	westernisation	insurrectional	uniformitarian
hypocoristical	abovementioned	intellectually	vasodilatation
immobilisation	acceleratingly	interjectional	vasodilatatory
impoverishment	accumulatively	intermittently	vituperatively
incommensurate	aforementioned	interpretation	abstemiousness
incompressible	airconditioner	interpretative	anticonvulsant
incompressibly	anticipatively	interpretively	auspiciousness
inconclusively	architectonics	intersectional	avariciousness
inexpressively	articulateness	intransitively	boisterousness
infralapsarian	backscattering	introductorily	calamitousness
insuppressible	backscratching	irresoluteness	calcareousness
intercessional	castrametation	irrespectively	capriciousness
intercessorial	chemosynthesis	jurisdictional	censoriousness
legitimisation	chronometrical	neuroanatomist	chivalrousness
liberalisation	circumlittoral	nomenclatorial	circuitousness
lyophilisation	compensational	northeastwards	commodiousness
mesdemoiselles	confidentially	northnortheast	contagiousness

contemptuously	reintroduction	reflectiveness	denazification
contiguousness	remorsefulness	regressiveness	depolarisation
continuousness	respectfulness	repetitiveness	despiritualise
counterculture	revengefulness	responsiveness	detoxification
countercurrent	ridiculousness	subjectiveness	devitalisation
courageousness	robustiousness	submissiveness	dextrorotation
delightfulness	roundaboutness	subversiveness	dextrorotatory
despiritualise	salubriousness	successiveness	disaffiliation
despitefulness	scandalousness	suggestiveness	disaffirmation
diaphanousness	scrupulousness	superelevation	disapprobation
disdainfulness	scurrilousness	susceptiveness	disapprobative
disingenuously	selfpropulsion	suspensiveness	disapprobatory
diverticulitis	semiconducting	topsyturviness	disassociation
extraneousness	slanderousness	transitiveness	disciplinarian
factitiousness	solicitousness	uncontroverted	discolouration
fallaciousness	spirituousness	vegetativeness	disconsolately
fastidiousness	sprightfulness	vindictiveness	disconsolation
fictitiousness	statuesqueness	basidiomycetes	discriminating
flagitiousness	stertorousness	butterflyscrew	discrimination
fortuitousness	stupendousness	electrodynamic	discriminative
generalpurpose	successfulness	halfpennyworth	discriminatory
goodhumouredly	superannuation	heterophyllous	disembarkation
gramineousness	superincumbent	phthalocyanine	disinclination
gratuitousness	superinduction	psychophysical	disinfestation
gregariousness	supernaturally	——————————	disintegration
harmoniousness	superstructure	administration	disintegrative
hocuspocussing	suspiciousness	administrative	disorientation
imperviousness	thoughtfulness	administratrix	distemperature
incautiousness	traitorousness	affectionately	dolomitisation
incestuousness	transsexualism	Africanisation	doublebreasted
inconsequently	transvaluation	Albigensianism	educationalist
indecorousness	tremendousness	allegorisation	egalitarianism
ineffectuality	tumultuousness	antifederalist	electrostatics
infectiousness	ubiquitousness	antiquarianism	emulsification
infrastructure	ultrastructure	Augustinianism	enthronisation
ingloriousness	umbrageousness	authentication	entomostracous
interlocutress	undervaluation	autobiographer	esterification
intersexuality	unfaithfulness	autobiographic	eutrophication
irreproducible	ungraciousness	bastardisation	Evangelicalism
lasciviousness	ungratefulness	beautification	evangelisation
libidinousness	untruthfulness	biodegradation	exceptionality
licentiousness	uproariousness	biosystematics	exclaustration
loquaciousness	victoriousness	bituminisation	existentialism
lugubriousness	villainousness	bowdlerisation	existentialist
magniloquently	viviparousness	Brobdingnagian	extensionality
malodorousness	vociferousness	capitalisation	fantasticality
marvellousness	voluminousness	castrametation	featherbrained
massproduction	voluptuousness	categorisation	foreordination
meticulousness	worshipfulness	centralisation	fraternisation
microstructure	absorptiveness	centrifugation	fructification
miraculousness	aggressiveness	chickenhearted	fundamentalism
monotonousness	attractiveness	classification	fundamentalist
mysteriousness	circumnavigate	classificatory	fundamentality
neglectfulness	compulsiveness	coessentiality	gelatinisation
nutritiousness	conclusiveness	commensurately	generalisation
obsequiousness	convulsiveness	commensuration	homogenisation
oleaginousness	cumulativeness	concelebration	humidification
omnivorousness	decorativeness	concretisation	hydromechanics
outrageousness	definitiveness	conditionality	hypercalcaemia
overproduction	diminutiveness	conglomeration	hyperglycaemia
perfidiousness	disapprovingly	conglutination	ichthyophagous
perniciousness	discursiveness	conglutinative	identification
pharmaceutical	exhaustiveness	congratulation	illegitimately
portentousness	expressiveness	congratulative	immobilisation
precariousness	figurativeness	congratulatory	implementation
precociousness	imperativeness	councilchamber	impracticality
presumptuously	impressiveness	countermeasure	inappreciation
prodigiousness	indecisiveness	crinkumcrankum	inappreciative
propaedeutical	meditativeness	curvilinearity	inarticulately
propitiousness	noninvolvement	decimalisation	inarticulation
prosperousness	oppressiveness	decolonisation	incapacitation
psychoneurosis	perceptiveness	decolorisation	incoordination
psychoneurotic	permissiveness	deconsecration	incorporeality
pugnaciousness	persuasiveness	defenestration	indoctrination
purposefulness	possessiveness	dehumanisation	ineffectuality
rampageousness	preventiveness	delocalisation	infralapsarian
rebelliousness	productiveness	demobilisation	intergradation
reconstruction	protectiveness	demonetisation	interlineation
reconstructive	protrusiveness	demoralisation	intermediately

intermediation	recapitulative	substantiation	bathingmachine
intermigration	recapitulatory	sulphanilamide	biographically
interpellation	recolonisation	superannuation	boardingschool
interpretation	recommendation	superelevation	cardiovascular
interpretative	recommendatory	supererogation	catechetically
intersexuality	reconciliation	supererogatory	circumspection
intrinsicality	reconciliatory	superficiality	classconscious
intuitionalism	rectangularity	superfoetation	concentrically
intuitionalist	redintegration	superterranean	cucurbitaceous
knighterrantry	regularisation	supralapsarian	democratically
latitudinarian	rehabilitation	symmetrisation	diachronically
legitimisation	reinvigoration	tatterdemalion	diagnostically
liberalisation	remonetisation	tergiversation	dieselelectric
libertarianism	reorganisation	territorialise	diplomatically
lyophilisation	representation	territorialism	disenfranchise
macrocephalous	representative	territorialist	emblematically
matriarchalism	resinification	territoriality	endosmotically
metallographer	retrogradation	testimonialise	enharmonically
microcephalous	revalorisation	thermodynamics	epexegetically
microminiature	revivification	thoughtreading	ethnologically
microsporangia	rigidification	traditionalism	etymologically
militarisation	Rosicrucianism	traditionalist	eulogistically
millenarianism	Russianisation	transformation	euphuistically
mineralisation	Sabbatarianism	transformative	excommunicable
ministerialist	sacramentalism	transmigration	excommunicator
misapplication	sacramentalist	transmigratory	extravehicular
miscalculation	sacramentarian	transportation	genealogically
misinformation	sanctification	transsexualism	geocentrically
mistranslation	sanguification	transvaluation	geographically
monochromatism	saponification	transversality	heartsearching
monopolisation	scandalisation	Trinitarianism	hierarchically
monosaccharide	scatterbrained	trivialisation	histrionically
multiplication	schematisation	ultramontanism	hyperbolically
multiplicaton	secularisation	ultramontanist	hypersonically
myrmecophagous	selfabnegation	unappreciative	hypocritically
naturalisation	selfaccusation	uncongeniality	hypodermically
necessarianism	selfaccusatory	underemphasise	hypostatically
neocolonialism	selfadmiration	undervaluation	hypothetically
neutralisation	selfcomplacent	unenthusiastic	idealistically
noctambulation	selfimmolation	uniformitarian	idiopathically
noncooperation	selfpartiality	unmentionables	immethodically
nonsensicality	selfproclaimed	unremunerative	inartistically
oecumenicalism	selfregulating	utilitarianism	incommunicable
organometallic	selfrestrained	valetudinarian	incommunicably
overabundantly	selfrevelation	vasodilatation	infrastructure
overcapitalise	sensationalism	vasodilatatory	insignificance
overestimation	sensationalist	verticillaster	insignificancy
overpopulation	sensualisation	volatilisation	intermolecular
pachydermatous	sentimentalise	weltanschauung	intramolecular
palaeobotanist	sentimentalism	westernisation	irreproducible
paradoxicality	sentimentalist	whippersnapper	judgematically
parenchymatous	sentimentality	Zoroastrianism	knickerbockers
pasteurisation	septuagenarian	disequilibrium	legalistically
phenylbutazone	servomechanism	imponderabilia	linguistically
phthalocyanine	sesquipedalian	partridgeberry	massproduction
pigeonbreasted	silicification	scrubbingbrush	mathematically
politicisation	simplification	stumblingblock	metaphorically
polymerisation	singlebreasted	achromatically	metaphysically
polysaccharide	skimbleskamble	aerobiotically	microstructure
popularisation	solidification	aetiologically	morganatically
pragmaticality	solitudinarian	alphabetically	mythologically
predesignation	solubilisation	altruistically	nonrestrictive
predestinarian	somnambulation	antiseptically	numismatically
predestination	sophistication	antithetically	optimistically
prefabrication	specialisation	aphoristically	overproduction
premillenarian	spectrographic	apologetically	papilionaceous
preponderantly	sphygmographic	apoplectically	paratactically
prettification	spindleshanked	appendicectomy	pathogenically
proletarianise	springcleaning	archetypically	pathologically
proletarianism	steganographer	archiepiscopal	petrologically
prothonotarial	stigmatisation	arithmetically	philologically
psychodynamics	stratification	arrhythmically	phlegmatically
psychosomatics	strikebreaking	astronomically	pleonastically
Pythagoreanism	stultification	asymmetrically	prognosticator
quadragenarian	subalternation	asymptotically	reconstruction
quantification	subinfeudation	autocratically	reconstructive
radicalisation	substantialism	backscratching	reintroduction
radiotherapist	substantialist	barometrically	rejuvenescence
recapitulation	substantiality	basidiomycetes	schismatically

scholastically	unreservedness	inconsequently	sufferableness
scientifically	vicepresidency	inconsistently	suggestiveness
selfcorrecting	weakmindedness	inconveniently	supereminently
selfprotection	absorptiveness	incredibleness	suprasegmental
selfrespectful	acceptableness	indecisiveness	susceptiveness
selfrespecting	aggrandisement	indefiniteness	suspensiveness
selfsufficient	aggressiveness	inevitableness	terminableness
semiconducting	anthropometric	inexorableness	thanksoffering
seriocomically	apprenticeship	inflexibleness	threadbareness
sociologically	arrondissement	inimitableness	transcendental
stochastically	articulateness	inordinateness	transcendently
submicroscopic	attainableness	insatiableness	transitiveness
superinduction	attractiveness	insensibleness	unacknowledged
supersonically	backscattering	insufficiently	uncontroverted
superstructure	bioengineering	intangibleness	understatement
synchronically	blackmarketeer	intermittently	unsociableness
systematically	bouleversement	interplanetary	vegetativeness
tachistoscopic	changeableness	intertwinement	vicechancellor
tautologically	charitableness	invariableness	vindictiveness
teleologically	comparableness	invincibleness	vulnerableness
telepathically	compatibleness	inviolableness	selfsatisfying
telephonically	compulsiveness	irresoluteness	unsuccessfully
telescopically	conclusiveness	Johannisberger	acknowledgment
theocratically	conscienceless	magniloquently	aerobiological
thermoelectric	convulsiveness	manageableness	agrobiological
thyrotoxicosis	coordinateness	meddlesomeness	archaeological
tragicomically	corticosteroid	meditativeness	autoradiograph
tropologically	corticosterone	mesdemoiselles	boroughEnglish
ultrasonically	creditableness	microprocessor	butterfingered
ultrastructure	cumbersomeness	mountaineering	campanological
uncommunicable	cumulativeness	multinucleated	Christological
uneconomically	deceivableness	nitroglycerine	climatological
unemphatically	decorativeness	nonbelligerent	convincingness
unsatisfactory	definitiveness	noninvolvement	dermatological
volumetrically	degenerateness	oppressiveness	encephalograph
absentmindedly	delectableness	overexcitement	eschatological
abstractedness	deliberateness	pardonableness	forbiddingness
accustomedness	dependableness	passionateness	gerontological
bullheadedness	deplorableness	penetrableness	gynaecological
circumbendibus	despicableness	perceptiveness	hallucinogenic
condescendence	detestableness	perishableness	ichthyological
conquistadores	diamantiferous	permissiveness	martyrological
contractedness	diamondiferous	personableness	meteorological
correspondence	diminutiveness	persuasiveness	methodological
correspondency	disarrangement	pistilliferous	myrmecological
determinedness	discouragement	poikilothermal	ornithological
discommendable	discursiveness	poikilothermic	overindulgence
disjointedness	disgruntlement	possessiveness	phantasmagoria
dispiritedness	divertissement	potentiometric	phantasmagoric
farsightedness	effervescently	prearrangement	phototelegraph
flatfootedness	electioneering	presentimental	phraseological
hermaphroditic	electrotherapy	preventiveness	psychosurgical
highhandedness	electrothermal	productiveness	pteridological
highmindedness	electrothermic	profitableness	radioautograph
lefthandedness	encyclopaedism	protectiveness	radiotelegraph
longheadedness	encyclopaedist	protrusiveness	selfindulgence
longwindedness	exhaustiveness	pyrheliometric	soteriological
lovingkindness	expressiveness	reasonableness	stomatological
marketgardener	favourableness	recommencement	telephotograph
narrowmindedly	ferrimagnetism	reflectiveness	terminological
newfangledness	ferromagnesian	regressiveness	thimblerigging
nightblindness	ferromagnetism	remarkableness	unbecomingness
openhandedness	figurativeness	repetitiveness	unintelligible
openmindedness	foraminiferous	responsiveness	unintelligibly
overconfidence	formidableness	seasonableness	venereological
selfconfidence	honourableness	selfeffacement	volcanological
selfdependence	illiterateness	selfflattering	vulcanological
shamefacedness	imaginableness	selfinterested	accomplishable
simplemindedly	immaculateness	spermatogenous	accomplishment
singlehandedly	immoderateness	squadronleader	amateurishness
singlemindedly	impassableness	stampcollector	brachycephalic
strongmindedly	impassibleness	standardbearer	bremsstrahlung
superabundance	imperativeness	statuesqueness	cartographical
surefootedness	implacableness	stoichiometric	chemosynthesis
unaccommodated	impressiveness	subcontinental	claustrophobia
unaffectedness	improvableness	subjectiveness	claustrophobic
understandable	inadequateness	submissiveness	coquettishness
understandably	inappositeness	subversiveness	cosmographical
unexpectedness	incompleteness	successiveness	cryptaesthesia

disfurnishment	differentially	organisational	undermentioned
extinguishable	disapprovingly	overpoweringly	undernourished
extinguishment	discouragingly	overwhelmingly	undesirability
hagiographical	disorderliness	patresfamilias	unenterprising
hieroglyphical	dispensability	perceptibility	unflatteringly
hydrographical	disquisitional	peremptoriness	unfriendliness
iconographical	dissertational	perfectibility	unhesitatingly
impoverishment	dissociability	peripateticism	unidimensional
inapproachable	distensibility	permissibility	unidirectional
irreproachable	distributional	perturbational	universalistic
irreproachably	distributively	pestilentially	unmannerliness
Mephistopheles	econometrician	petrochemistry	unpalatability
metempsychosis	elementariness	phenobarbitone	unprofessional
northnortheast	embarrassingly	photochemistry	verisimilitude
northnorthwest	enterprisingly	photosensitise	vituperatively
orthographical	entertainingly	photosensitive	wonderstricken
outlandishness	erythropoiesis	planetstricken	achondroplasia
petrographical	exasperatingly	pleasurability	anticonvulsant
photosynthesis	excruciatingly	pneumoconiosis	artificialness
photosynthetic	exhaustibility	postpositional	beneficialness
prosencephalic	exhilaratingly	postpositively	bougainvillaea
prosencephalon	experientially	practicability	counterbalance
pseudaesthesia	fullyfashioned	predeterminate	counterculture
relinquishment	galactopoietic	predictability	cyanocobalamin
rhinencephalic	handkerchieves	predisposition	delightfulness
rhinencephalon	hereditariness	preferentially	despitefulness
slaughterhouse	heroworshipper	presbyterially	dinoflagellate
spermatophytic	histochemistry	prescriptively	disdainfulness
tachygraphical	horrorstricken	presentability	disembowelment
unapproachable	hygroscopicity	presentational	disenthralment
abovementioned	hypercriticise	presupposition	diverticulitis
acceleratingly	hypercriticism	preventability	dodecasyllable
accountability	hypersensitive	professorially	electrovalency
accumulatively	hypothyroidism	propagandistic	fortunetelling
aerodynamicist	iatrochemistry	proscriptively	gyrostabiliser
aforementioned	illconditioned	providentially	heterophyllous
airconditioner	illimitability	quantitatively	heterothallism
anticipatively	illustrational	quinquennially	hydrocoralline
antiperspirant	illustratively	radiochemistry	hypercatalexis
antiphlogistic	impermeability	radiosensitive	imparisyllabic
apprehensively	implausibility	recoverability	incontrollable
astrophysicist	impregnability	refractoriness	irreconcilable
behaviouristic	impressibility	refrangibility	irreconcilably
bibliomaniacal	inadvisability	regeneratively	neglectfulness
bioelectricity	inalienability	reproductively	outgeneralling
breathtakingly	inalterability	respectability	oxyhaemoglobin
characteristic	inconclusively	responsibility	psychoanalysis
circumambiency	indiscriminate	resurrectional	psychoanalytic
circumnavigate	indivisibility	roadworthiness	purposefulness
combustibility	indubitability	sanguinariness	quadrisyllabic
compensational	inexpressively	selfeffacingly	quadrisyllable
compossibility	inflammability	selfenergising	remorsefulness
conceivability	infrangibility	selfexplaining	respectfulness
conductibility	ingratiatingly	selfsustaining	revengefulness
confidentially	inheritability	semiofficially	schoolchildren
conformability	inscrutability	serviceability	selffertilised
congregational	inseparability	slatternliness	selffulfilling
conservational	insuperability	somnambulistic	selfpropelling
conservatively	insurrectional	spiritualistic	selfpropulsion
consociational	intercessional	stationariness	sprightfulness
constitutional	interjectional	submersibility	successfulness
constitutively	interpretively	substitutional	supramaxillary
constructional	intersectional	substitutively	swordswallower
constructively	intolerability	suggestibility	thoughtfulness
constructivism	intractability	supersensitive	tyrannicalness
constructivist	intransitively	susceptibility	uncontrollable
consuetudinary	irreducibility	sycophantishly	uncontrollably
contraindicate	irrefutability	terrorstricken	underdeveloped
contraposition	irremovability	topsyturviness	unfaithfulness
contrapositive	irrespectively	transitoriness	ungratefulness
conversational	irrevocability	tridimensional	untruthfulness
convertibility	jurisdictional	twodimensional	worshipfulness
corruptibility	justifiability	ultimogeniture	aesthesiometer
crossfertilise	monkeybusiness	unaccomplished	apophthegmatic
crosspollinate	myrmecophilous	unattractively	diffractometer
deliberatively	neurochemistry	uncircumcision	disconformable
denominational	noncommunicant	uncompromising	hydrodynamical
denumerability	noteworthiness	unconventional	interferometer
differentiable	opinionatively	unconvincingly	interferometry

nonperformance	bacteriologist	prohibitionist	indecipherable
orthochromatic	campylotropous	propitiatorily	indemonstrable
physiognomical	cantankerously	protozoologist	indiscoverable
proceleusmatic	conspiratorial	pseudonymously	malappropriate
psychochemical	contemptuously	psilanthropism	misappropriate
scintillometer	conterminously	psilanthropist	multilaterally
selfdetermined	contumaciously	rambunctiously	nonconcurrence
stoicheiometry	contumeliously	repudiationist	osteoarthritis
superincumbent	corticotrophic	restorationism	oversubscribed
tetragrammaton	corticotrophin	restorationist	phytogeography
thermochemical	counterplotted	restrictionist	pianoaccordian
carcinogenesis	destructionist	rheumatologist	pluviometrical
chincherinchee	dialectologist	sacrilegiously	postmastership
circumstantial	dicotyledonous	satisfactorily	progenitorship
commissionaire	discourteously	segregationist	prolocutorship
compassionable	disincorporate	selfcontrolled	proprietorship
complexionless	disingenuously	selfdestroying	pseudepigrapha
concavoconcave	disputatiously	simultaneously	pseudepigraphy
concessionaire	ecclesiologist	slaughterously	psychoneurosis
consanguineous	electrobiology	snaggletoothed	psychoneurotic
consubstantial	epidemiologist	soporiferously	publicspirited
conventionally	epistemologist	souldestroying	rontgenography
convexoconcave	extracorporeal	spectroscopist	selfpreserving
cotemporaneous	forwardlooking	spermatogonium	selfsupporting
countrydancing	gynandromorphy	staphylococcus	Shakespeareana
discountenance	hebetudinosity	subconsciously	Shakespeariana
disheartenment	heterochromous	superciliously	stadholdership
electrodynamic	histopathology	symptomatology	subcontrariety
expressionless	hobbledehoyish	troubleshooter	supernaturally
extemporaneity	holometabolism	ultramicrotome	supervisorship
extemporaneous	holometabolous	unscrupulously	thalassography
haematogenesis	hysterectomise	vaingloriously	therianthropic
impressionable	inauspiciously	vivisectionist	transliterator
indeterminable	incommodiously	allelomorphism	uncorroborated
indifferentism	infelicitously	bibliographise	whortleberries
indifferentist	inharmoniously	chemoreception	abstemiousness
inflectionally	integrationist	chemoreceptive	antidepressant
inflectionless	intercessorial	dolichocephaly	auspiciousness
intelligential	internationale	electrodeposit	autosuggestion
intelligentsia	introductorily	heteromorphism	avariciousness
interdependent	kremlinologist	heteromorphous	bioluminescent
interferential	liturgiologist	homoeomorphism	bloodthirstily
longitudinally	macroeconomics	homotransplant	boisterousness
megasporangium	meretriciously	megasporophyll	breathlessness
microtechnique	metapsychology	parallelepiped	butterflyscrew
neuroscientist	microbiologist	proprioceptive	calamitousness
overcompensate	microcomponent	pseudomorphism	calcareousness
postmillennial	microeconomics	pseudomorphous	capriciousness
procrastinator	multifariously	radiotelephone	censoriousness
professionally	neuroanatomist	radiotelephony	chivalrousness
proportionable	neuropathology	selfabsorption	circuitousness
proportionably	nomenclatorial	selfassumption	colourlessness
proportionally	obstreperously	selfdiscipline	commodiousness
quarterbinding	obstructionism	selfperception	commonsensical
quattrocentism	obstructionist	shovelhalfpenny	comprehensible
quattrocentist	ostentatiously	spatiotemporal	comprehensibly
quintessential	palaeethnology	superphosphate	contagiousness
radiostrontium	parapsychology	superscription	contiguousness
reminiscential	parasitologist	windowshopping	continuousness
selfgovernment	parsimoniously	selfconsequent	courageousness
selftormenting	percutaneously	alphanumerical	crystallisable
semicentennial	periodontology	ambassadorship	diaphanousness
sublieutenancy	pertinaciously	anthropography	effortlessness
successionally	pharmacologist	chancellorship	endoradiosonde
superintendent	pharmacopoeial	chromatography	extraneousness
transitionally	philanthropise	chronometrical	factitiousness
unconscionable	philanthropist	cinematography	fallaciousness
unquestionable	photoperiodism	controllership	fastidiousness
unquestionably	phytopathology	councillorship	fictitiousness
abstractionism	pneumatologist	counsellorship	flagitiousness
abstractionist	polymorphously	countercurrent	fortuitousness
advantageously	preposterously	crossreference	friendlessness
adventitiously	presumptuously	enantiomorphic	gramineousness
ambidextrously	probabiliorism	generalpurpose	gratuitousness
anthropologist	probabiliorist	goodhumouredly	gregariousness
archidiaconate	progressionary	goodtemperedly	groundlessness
architectonics	progressionism	historiography	harmoniousness
associationism	progressionist	inconsiderable	hocuspocussing
asynchronously	prohibitionism	inconsiderably	imperviousness

incautiousness	voluptuousness	demisemiquaver	counterbalance
incestuousness	weightlessness	discombobulate	crystallisable
incompressible	windowdressing	discontinuance	cyanocobalamin
incompressibly	anagrammatical	eigenfrequency	demisemiquaver
indecomposable	antiscriptural	floriculturist	democratically
indecorousness	apothegmatical	grandiloquence	departmentally
infectiousness	bacteriostasis	horticulturist	diachronically
ingloriousness	bacteriostatic	ichthyosaurian	diagnostically
insuppressible	bronchiectasis	incommensurate	differentiable
lasciviousness	catachrestical	intellectually	differentially
libidinousness	circumlittoral	intercommunion	diplomatically
licentiousness	clearsightedly	intercommunity	discomfortable
loquaciousness	colourfastness	microcircuitry	discommendable
lugubriousness	communications	nitrocellulose	disconformable
malodorousness	contradictable	pisciculturist	discontinuance
marvellousness	contradictious	reconstitution	discountenance
meticulousness	contrapuntally	redistribution	disinheritance
miraculousness	controvertible	redistributive	disrespectable
monotonousness	copperbottomed	superconductor	dodecasyllable
mysteriousness	cosmopolitical	tintinnabulary	electrodynamic
nutritiousness	departmentally	tintinnabulate	emblematically
obsequiousness	diagrammatical	tintinnabulous	endosmotically
oleaginousness	disappointment	undergraduette	enharmonically
omnivorousness	discomfortable	watercolourist	epexegetically
ophthalmoscope	disconcertment	chickenlivered	ethnologically
ophthalmoscopy	disconnectedly	conjunctivitis	etymologically
outrageousness	discontentedly	substantivally	eulogistically
perfidiousness	discontentment	committeewoman	euphuistically
perniciousness	disenchantment	goodfellowship	excommunicable
phosphorescent	disinheritance	halfpennyworth	excommunicator
portentousness	disrespectable	northeastwards	experientially
precariousness	ecclesiastical	northwestwards	experimentally
precociousness	epigrammatical	southeastwards	extinguishable
prodigiousness	experimentally	southwestwards	genealogically
propitiousness	faintheartedly	commissaryship	geocentrically
prosperousness	forthrightness	sauropterygian	geographically
psychophysical	handicraftsman	selfemployment	hierarchically
pugnaciousness	hyperirritable	sphaerocrystal	historiography
quinquagesimal	hypocoristical	tetradactylous	histrionically
rampageousness	indestructible	————————————	hyperbolically
rebelliousness	indestructibly	accomplishable	hyperirritable
reconnaissance	indiscerptible	achondroplasia	hypersonically
regardlessness	indiscreetness	achromatically	hypocritically
relentlessness	indistinctness	aerobiotically	hypodermically
resistlessness	instrumentally	aetiologically	hypostatically
ridiculousness	insurmountable	alphabetically	hypothetically
robustiousness	insurmountably	altruistically	idealistically
roentgenoscopy	interlocutress	anthropography	idiopathically
salubriousness	interpenetrate	antiseptically	immethodically
scandalousness	lightheartedly	antithetically	imparisyllabic
scrupulousness	malcontentedly	aphoristically	impressionable
scurrilousness	oneirocritical	apologetically	inapproachable
selfconsistent	overcommitment	apophthegmatic	inartistically
selfexpression	pharmaceutical	apoplectically	incommunicable
selfpossession	polytheistical	archetypically	incommunicably
selfrepression	praiseworthily	arithmetically	inconsiderable
selfsuggestion	premeditatedly	arrhythmically	inconsiderably
slanderousness	propaedeutical	astronomically	incontrollable
solicitousness	roundaboutness	asymmetrically	indecipherable
speechlessness	schoolmistress	asymptotically	indecomposable
spinthariscope	selfadjustment	autocratically	indemonstrable
spiritlessness	selfimportance	bacteriostasis	indeterminable
spirituousness	selfinductance	bacteriostatic	indiscoverable
stertorousness	semielliptical	barometrically	inflectionally
stupendousness	shortsightedly	bibliomaniacal	insignificance
suspiciousness	sociopolitical	biographically	insignificancy
thriftlessness	spirochaetosis	brachycephalic	instrumentally
traitorousness	stoutheartedly	bronchiectasis	insurmountable
tremendousness	supposititious	catechetically	insurmountably
tumultuousness	transplantable	chromatography	intellectually
ubiquitousness	unpleasantness	cinematography	irreconcilable
umbrageousness	unpremeditated	commissionaire	irreconcilably
ungraciousness	watertightness	compassionable	irreproachable
uproariousness	audiofrequency	concentrically	irreproachably
victoriousness	blockaderunner	concessionaire	judgematically
villainousness	circumambulate	confidentially	legalistically
viviparousness	circumlocution	contradictable	linguistically
vociferousness	circumlocutory	contrapuntally	longitudinally
voluminousness	circumvolution	conventionally	mathematically

metaphorically	unapproachable	electrovalency	heteromorphous
metaphysically	uncommunicable	erythropoiesis	homoeomorphism
morganatically	unconscionable	extemporaneity	megasporophyll
multilaterally	uncontrollable	extemporaneous	praiseworthily
multinucleated	uncontrollably	faintheartedly	pseudomorphism
mythologically	uncorroborated	galactopoietic	pseudomorphous
nonperformance	understandable	goodhumouredly	radiotelephone
northeastwards	understandably	goodtemperedly	radiotelephony
northwestwards	uneconomically	grandiloquence	superphosphate
numismatically	unemphatically	haematogenesis	aerobiological
optimistically	unpremeditated	hallucinogenic	agrobiological
orthochromatic	unquestionable	handkerchieves	alphanumerical
paratactically	unquestionably	hypercalcaemia	anagrammatical
pathogenically	volumetrically	hypercatalexis	apothegmatical
pathologically	superincumbent	hyperglycaemia	archaeological
pestilentially	unmentionables	interferometer	campanological
petrologically	aerodynamicist	interferometry	cartographical
philologically	astrophysicist	lightheartedly	catachrestical
phlegmatically	bioelectricity	malcontentedly	Christological
phytogeography	bioluminescent	marketgardener	chronometrical
pleonastically	butterflyscrew	Mephistopheles	circumbendibus
preferentially	chincherinchee	narrowmindedly	classconscious
presbyterially	concavoconcave	nonconcurrence	climatological
proceleusmatic	contraindicate	northnortheast	commonsensical
procrastinator	convexoconcave	overconfidence	communications
professionally	countrydancing	overindulgence	comprehensible
professorially	econometrician	papilionaceous	comprehensibly
prognosticator	entomostracous	partridgeberry	conjunctivitis
proportionable	horrorstricken	pharmacopoeial	contradictious
proportionably	hygroscopicity	photosynthesis	controvertible
proportionally	hypercriticise	photosynthetic	cosmographical
prosencephalic	hypercriticism	premeditatedly	cosmopolitical
prosencephalon	noncommunicant	pseudaesthesia	dermatological
providentially	ophthalmoscope	rejuvenescence	diagrammatical
pseudepigrapha	ophthalmoscopy	scintillometer	diverticulitis
pseudepigraphy	peripateticism	selfconfidence	ecclesiastical
quadrisyllabic	phosphorescent	selfdependence	epigrammatical
quadrisyllable	planetstricken	selfindulgence	eschatological
quinquennially	roentgenoscopy	Shakespeareana	featherbrained
reconnaissance	selfcomplacent	shortsightedly	gerontological
rhinencephalic	spinthariscope	shovehalfpenny	gynaecological
rhinencephalon	stampcollector	simplemindedly	gyrostabiliser
rontgenography	staphylococcus	singlehandedly	hagiographical
schismatically	superconductor	singlemindedly	hermaphroditic
scholastically	terrorstricken	stoicheiometry	hieroglyphical
scientifically	wonderstricken	stoutheartedly	hydrodynamical
selfimportance	encyclopaedism	strongmindedly	hydrographical
selfinductance	encyclopaedist	undergraduette	hypocoristical
semiofficially	hypothyroidism	vicepresidency	ichthyological
seriocomically	interdependent	anthropologist	iconographical
sociologically	photoperiodism	bacteriologist	imponderabilia
southeastwards	pianoaccordian	Brobdingnagian	incompressible
southwestwards	quarterbinding	circumnavigate	incompressibly
squadronleader	schoolchildren	dialectologist	indestructible
standardbearer	superintendent	ecclesiologist	indestructibly
stochastically	thoughtreading	epidemiologist	indiscerptible
sublieutenancy	unacknowledged	epistemologist	insuppressible
substantivally	absentmindedly	ichthyophagous	irreproducible
successionally	aesthesiometer	kremlinologist	malappropriate
superabundance	audiofrequency	liturgiologist	martyrological
supernaturally	basidiomycetes	megasporangium	meteorological
supersonically	butterfingered	microbiologist	methodological
synchronically	carcinogenesis	myrmecophagous	microcircuitry
systematically	chemosynthesis	parasitologist	microtechnique
tautologically	chickenlivered	pharmacologist	misappropriate
teleologically	circumambiency	pneumatologist	myrmecological
telepathically	clearsightedly	protozoologist	oneirocritical
telephonically	condescendence	rheumatologist	ornithological
telescopically	consanguineous	sauropterygian	orthographical
tetragrammaton	correspondence	thimblerigging	osteoarthritis
thalassography	correspondency	allelomorphism	oversubscribed
theocratically	cotemporaneous	backscratching	parallelepiped
tragicomically	crossreference	bathingmachine	petrographical
transitionally	cryptaesthesia	bibliographise	pharmaceutical
transliterator	cucurbitaceous	boardingschool	phraseological
transplantable	diffractometer	disenfranchise	physiognomical
tropologically	disconnectedly	dolichocephaly	pluviometrical
ultrasonically	discontentedly	heartsearching	polytheistical
unaccommodated	eigenfrequency	heteromorphism	propaedeutical

psychochemical	impracticality	substantialism	archidiaconate
psychophysical	impregnability	substantialist	architectonics
psychosurgical	impressibility	substantiality	articulateness
pteridological	inadvisability	suggestibility	artificialness
publicspirited	inalienability	superficiality	associationism
quinquagesimal	inalterability	supramaxillary	attainableness
scatterbrained	incorporeality	susceptibility	attractiveness
selfdetermined	indivisibility	symptomatology	Augustinianism
selffertilised	indubitability	tatterdemalion	auspiciousness
selfproclaimed	ineffectuality	territorialise	avariciousness
selfrestrained	inflammability	territorialism	beneficialness
selfsufficient	inflectionless	territorialist	blockaderunner
semielliptical	infrangibility	territoriality	boisterousness
Shakespeariana	inheritability	testimonialise	breathlessness
sociopolitical	inscrutability	tetradactylous	breathtakingly
soteriological	inseparability	tintinnabulary	bullheadedness
stomatological	insuperability	tintinnabulate	calamitousness
subcontrariety	intersexuality	tintinnabulous	calcareousness
supposititious	intolerability	traditionalism	capriciousness
tachygraphical	intractability	traditionalist	censoriousness
terminological	intrinsicality	transsexualism	changeableness
thermochemical	intuitionalism	transversality	charitableness
unintelligible	intuitionalist	uncongeniality	chivalrousness
unintelligibly	irreducibility	undesirability	circuitousness
venereological	irrefutability	unpalatability	colourfastness
volcanological	irremovability	vicechancellor	colourlessness
vulcanological	irrevocability	accomplishment	commodiousness
forwardlooking	justifiability	acknowledgment	comparableness
knickerbockers	macrocephalous	aggrandisement	compatibleness
strikebreaking	matriarchalism	arrondissement	compulsiveness
accountability	mesdemoiselles	bouleversement	conclusiveness
antifederalist	metapsychology	councilchamber	consuetudinary
boroughEnglish	microcephalous	disappointment	contagiousness
bougainvillaea	ministerialist	disarrangement	contiguousness
bremsstrahlung	myrmecophilous	disconcertment	continuousness
circumambulate	neocolonialism	discontentment	contractedness
coessentiality	neuropathology	discouragement	convincingness
combustibility	nitrocellulose	disembowelment	convulsiveness
complexionless	nonsensicality	disenchantment	coordinateness
compossibility	oecumenicalism	disenthralment	coquettishness
conceivability	organometallic	disfurnishment	courageousness
conditionality	outgeneralling	disgruntlement	creditableness
conductibility	overcapitalise	disheartenment	crinkumcrankum
conformability	palaeethnology	divertissement	crosspollinate
conscienceless	paradoxicality	extinguishment	cumbersomeness
convertibility	parapsychology	heterochromous	cumulativeness
corruptibility	patresfamilias	hysterectomise	deceivableness
crossfertilise	perceptibility	impoverishment	decorativeness
denumerability	perfectibility	intertwinement	definitiveness
despiritualise	periodontology	macroeconomics	degenerateness
dinoflagellate	permissibility	microeconomics	delectableness
discombobulate	phytopathology	neuroanatomist	deliberateness
dispensability	pleasurability	noninvolvement	delightfulness
dissociability	practicability	overcommitment	dependableness
distensibility	pragmaticality	overexcitement	deplorableness
educationalist	predictability	prearrangement	despicableness
electrobiology	presentability	psychodynamics	despitefulness
Evangelicalism	preventability	recommencement	destructionist
exceptionality	recoverability	relinquishment	determinedness
exhaustibility	refrangibility	selfadjustment	detestableness
existentialism	respectability	selfeffacement	diaphanousness
existentialist	responsibility	selfemployment	dicotyledonous
expressionless	sacramentalism	selfgovernment	diminutiveness
extensionality	sacramentalist	skimbleskamble	disapprovingly
fantasticality	selfcontrolled	sulphanilamide	discouragingly
fortunetelling	selfdiscipline	thermodynamics	discursiveness
fundamentalism	selffulfilling	understatement	disdainfulness
fundamentalist	selfpartiality	absorptiveness	disjointedness
fundamentality	selfpropelling	abstemiousness	disorderliness
heterophyllous	sensationalism	abstractedness	dispiritedness
heterothallism	sensationalist	abstractionism	effervescently
histopathology	sentimentalise	abstractionist	effortlessness
holometabolism	sentimentalism	acceleratingly	egalitarianism
holometabolous	sentimentalist	acceptableness	elementariness
homotransplant	sentimentality	accustomedness	embarrassingly
hydrocoralline	serviceability	aggressiveness	enterprisingly
illimitability	sesquipedalian	Albigensianism	entertainingly
impermeability	stumblingblock	amateurishness	exasperatingly
implausibility	submersibility	antiquarianism	excruciatingly

exhaustiveness	libidinousness	rampageousness	Trinitarianism
exhilaratingly	licentiousness	reasonableness	tumultuousness
expressiveness	longheadedness	rebelliousness	tyrannicalness
extraneousness	longwindedness	reflectiveness	ubiquitousness
factitiousness	loquaciousness	refractoriness	ultramontanism
fallaciousness	lovingkindness	regardlessness	ultramontanist
farsightedness	lugubriousness	regressiveness	umbrageousness
fastidiousness	magniloquently	relentlessness	unaffectedness
favourableness	malodorousness	remarkableness	unbecomingness
fictitiousness	manageableness	remorsefulness	unconvincingly
figurativeness	marvellousness	repetitiveness	unexpectedness
flagitiousness	meddlesomeness	repudiationist	unfaithfulness
flatfootedness	meditativeness	resistlessness	unflatteringly
forbiddingness	meticulousness	respectfulness	unfriendliness
formidableness	microcomponent	responsiveness	ungraciousness
forthrightness	microsporangia	restorationism	ungratefulness
fortuitousness	millenarianism	restorationist	unhesitatingly
friendlessness	miraculousness	restrictionist	unmannerliness
gramineousness	monkeybusiness	revengefulness	unpleasantness
gratuitousness	monotonousness	ridiculousness	unreservedness
gregariousness	mysteriousness	roadworthiness	unsociableness
groundlessness	necessarianism	robustiousness	untruthfulness
harmoniousness	neglectfulness	Rosicrucianism	uproariousness
hereditariness	newfangledness	roundaboutness	utilitarianism
highhandedness	nightblindness	Sabbatarianism	vegetativeness
highmindedness	noteworthiness	salubriousness	victoriousness
honourableness	nutritiousness	sanguinariness	villainousness
hydromechanics	obsequiousness	scandalousness	vindictiveness
illiterateness	obstructionism	scrupulousness	viviparousness
imaginableness	obstructionist	scurrilousness	vivisectionist
immaculateness	oleaginousness	seasonableness	vociferousness
immoderateness	omnivorousness	segregationist	voluminousness
impassableness	openhandedness	selfeffacingly	voluptuousness
impassibleness	openmindedness	selfexplaining	vulnerableness
imperativeness	oppressiveness	selfsustaining	watertightness
imperviousness	outlandishness	semicentennial	weakmindedness
implacableness	outrageousness	servomechanism	weightlessness
impressiveness	overabundantly	shamefacedness	worshipfulness
improvableness	overpoweringly	slanderousness	Zoroastrianism
inadequateness	overwhelmingly	slatternliness	abovementioned
inappositeness	palaeobotanist	solicitousness	aforementioned
incautiousness	pardonableness	speechlessness	airconditioner
incestuousness	passionateness	spermatogenous	archiepiscopal
incompleteness	penetrableness	spermatogonium	circumlittoral
inconsequently	perceptiveness	spindleshanked	claustrophobia
inconsistently	peremptoriness	spiritlessness	claustrophobic
inconveniently	perfidiousness	spirituousness	committeewoman
incredibleness	perishableness	sprightfulness	compensational
indecisiveness	permissiveness	springcleaning	congregational
indecorousness	perniciousness	stationariness	conquistadores
indefiniteness	personableness	statuesqueness	conservational
indiscreetness	persuasiveness	stertorousness	consociational
indiscriminate	phthalocyanine	stupendousness	constitutional
indistinctness	portentousness	subcontinental	constructional
inevitableness	possessiveness	subjectiveness	conversational
inexorableness	postmillennial	submissiveness	copperbottomed
infectiousness	precariousness	subversiveness	denominational
inflexibleness	precociousness	successfulness	disquisitional
ingloriousness	predeterminate	successiveness	dissertational
ingratiatingly	preponderantly	sufferableness	distributional
inimitableness	presentimental	suggestiveness	electrodeposit
inordinateness	preventiveness	supereminently	endoradiosonde
insatiableness	prodigiousness	superterranean	fullyfashioned
insensibleness	productiveness	suprasegmental	halfpennyworth
insufficiently	profitableness	surefootedness	illconditioned
intangibleness	progressionary	susceptiveness	illustrational
integrationist	progressionism	suspensiveness	insurrectional
intercommunion	progressionist	suspiciousness	intercessional
intercommunity	prohibitionism	terminableness	interjectional
intermittently	prohibitionist	thoughtfulness	intersectional
internationale	proletarianise	threadbareness	jurisdictional
invariableness	proletarianism	thriftlessness	metempsychosis
invincibleness	propitiousness	topsyturviness	organisational
inviolableness	prosperousness	traitorousness	oxyhaemoglobin
irresoluteness	protectiveness	transcendental	perturbational
knighterrantry	protrusiveness	transcendently	phantasmagoria
lasciviousness	pugnaciousness	transitiveness	phantasmagoric
lefthandedness	purposefulness	transitoriness	pneumoconiosis
libertarianism	Pythagoreanism	tremendousness	postpositional

presentational	nomenclatorial	unaccomplished	disassociation
psychoneurosis	nonbelligerent	uncircumcision	discolouration
psychoneurotic	phototelegraph	uncompromising	disconsolately
resurrectional	pisciculturist	underemphasise	disconsolation
slaughterhouse	pistilliferous	undernourished	discriminating
spatiotemporal	poikilothermal	unenterprising	discrimination
spirochaetosis	poikilothermic	unenthusiastic	discriminative
submicroscopic	polysaccharide	universalistic	discriminatory
substitutional	predestinarian	verticillaster	disembarkation
swordswallower	premillenarian	windowdressing	disinclination
tachistoscopic	probabiliorism	administration	disinfestation
therianthropic	probabiliorist	administrative	disintegration
thyrotoxicosis	propitiatorily	administratrix	disintegrative
tridimensional	prothonotarial	affectionately	disorientation
troubleshooter	quadragenarian	Africanisation	distemperature
twodimensional	radioautograph	allegorisation	dolomitisation
unconventional	radiotelegraph	anthropometric	electrostatics
underdeveloped	rectangularity	appendicectomy	emulsification
undermentioned	sacramentarian	authentication	enthronisation
unidimensional	satisfactorily	autosuggestion	esterification
unidirectional	schoolmistress	bastardisation	eutrophication
unprofessional	scrubbingbrush	beautification	evangelisation
autobiographer	selfflattering	biodegradation	exclaustration
autobiographic	septuagenarian	biosystematics	ferrimagnetism
campylotropous	solitudinarian	bituminisation	ferromagnetism
corticotrophic	supralapsarian	blackmarketeer	foreordination
corticotrophin	telephotograph	bloodthirstily	fraternisation
enantiomorphic	thanksoffering	bowdlerisation	fructification
generalpurpose	uncontroverted	capitalisation	gelatinisation
heroworshipper	uniformitarian	castrametation	generalisation
metallographer	valetudinarian	categorisation	homogenisation
philanthropise	watercolourist	centralisation	humidification
philanthropist	whortleberries	centrifugation	hypersensitive
psilanthropism	ambassadorship	chemoreception	identification
psilanthropist	anticonvulsant	chemoreceptive	illegitimately
radiotherapist	antidepressant	circumlocution	immobilisation
spectrographic	antiphlogistic	circumlocutory	implementation
spectroscopist	apprenticeship	circumspection	inappreciation
sphygmographic	behaviouristic	circumstantial	inappreciative
steganographer	chancellorship	circumvolution	inarticulately
whippersnapper	characteristic	classification	inarticulation
windowshopping	commissaryship	classificatory	incapacitation
antiperspirant	controllership	commensurately	incoordination
autoradiograph	councillorship	commensuration	indifferentism
backscattering	counsellorship	concelebration	indifferentist
bioengineering	countermeasure	concretisation	indoctrination
chickenhearted	doublebreasted	conglomeration	infrastructure
conspiratorial	ferromagnesian	conglutination	intelligential
corticosteroid	goodfellowship	conglutinative	intelligentsia
corticosterone	handicraftsman	congratulation	interferential
countercurrent	hebetudinosity	congratulatory	intergradation
curvilinearity	histochemistry	congratulatory	interlineation
diamantiferous	hocuspocussing	consubstantial	intermediately
diamondiferous	iatrochemistry	contraposition	intermediation
disciplinarian	microprocessor	contrapositive	intermigration
disequilibrium	neurochemistry	counterculture	interpellation
disincorporate	overcompensate	counterplotted	interplanetary
electioneering	petrochemistry	decimalisation	interpretation
electrotherapy	photochemistry	decolonisation	interpretative
electrothermal	pigeonbreasted	decolorisation	legitimisation
electrothermic	postmastership	deconsecration	liberalisation
encephalograph	progenitorship	defenestration	lyophilisation
extracorporeal	prolocutorship	dehumanisation	massproduction
floriculturist	propagandistic	delocalisation	microminiature
foraminiferous	proprietorship	demobilisation	microstructure
gynandromorphy	radiochemistry	demonetisation	militarisation
horticulturist	selfenergising	demoralisation	mineralisation
ichthyosaurian	selfexpression	denazification	misapplication
incommensurate	selfinterested	depolarisation	miscalculation
infralapsarian	selfpossession	detoxification	misinformation
intercessorial	selfpropulsion	devitalisation	mistranslation
interlocutress	selfrepression	dextrorotation	monochromatism
interpenetrate	singlebreasted	dextrorotatory	monopolisation
introductorily	somnambulistic	dieselelectric	multiplication
Johannisberger	sphaerocrystal	disaffiliation	multiplicative
latitudinarian	spiritualistic	disaffirmation	naturalisation
monosaccharide	stadholdership	disapprobation	neuroscientist
mountaineering	supervisorship	disapprobative	neutralisation
nitroglycerine	sycophantishly	disapprobatory	noctambulation

noncooperation	selfrespecting	percutaneously	interplanetary
nonrestrictive	selfrevelation	pertinaciously	malappropriate
overestimation	selfsuggestion	polymorphously	misappropriate
overpopulation	selfsupporting	preposterously	noncommunicant
overproduction	selftormenting	presumptuously	northnortheast
pachydermatous	semiconducting	pseudonymously	overcompensate
parenchymatous	sensualisation	rambunctiously	phototelegraph
pasteurisation	silicification	sacrilegiously	predeterminate
phenobarbitone	simplification	selfconsequent	progressionary
photosensitise	snaggletoothed	simultaneously	radioautograph
photosensitive	solidification	slaughterously	radiotelegraph
politicisation	solubilisation	soporiferously	Shakespeareana
polymerisation	somnambulation	subconsciously	Shakespeariana
popularisation	sophistication	superciliously	superphosphate
potentiometric	specialisation	unscrupulously	supramaxillary
predesignation	stigmatisation	unsuccessfully	telephotograph
predestination	stoichiometric	vaingloriously	tintinnabulary
predisposition	stratification	weltanschauung	tintinnabulate
prefabrication	stultification	accumulatively	accomplishable
presupposition	subalternation	anticipatively	circumbendibus
prettification	subinfeudation	apprehensively	claustrophobia
proprioceptive	substantiation	conservatively	claustrophobic
psychosomatics	superannuation	constitutively	compassionable
pyrheliometric	superelevation	constructively	comprehensible
quantification	supererogation	constructivism	comprehensibly
quattrocentism	supererogatory	constructivist	contradictable
quattrocentist	superfoetation	deliberatively	controvertible
quintessential	superinduction	distributively	councilchamber
radicalisation	superscription	illustratively	crystallisable
radiosensitive	supersensitive	inconclusively	differentiable
radiostrontium	superstructure	inexpressively	discomfortable
recapitulation	symmetrisation	interpretively	discommendable
recapitulative	tergiversation	intransitively	disconformable
recapitulatory	thermoelectric	irrespectively	disrespectable
recolonisation	transformation	opinionatively	dodecasyllable
recommendation	transformative	postpositively	excommunicable
recommendatory	transmigration	prescriptively	extinguishable
reconciliation	transmigratory	proscriptively	hyperirritable
reconciliatory	transportation	quantitatively	imparisyllabic
reconstitution	transvaluation	regeneratively	impressionable
reconstruction	trivialisation	reproductively	inapproachable
reconstructive	ultimogeniture	selfpreserving	incommunicable
redintegration	ultramicrotome	substitutively	incommunicably
redistribution	ultrastructure	unattractively	incompressible
redistributive	unappreciative	vituperatively	incompressibly
regularisation	undervaluation	northnorthwest	inconsiderable
rehabilitation	unremunerative	hobbledehoyish	inconsiderably
reintroduction	unsatisfactory	psychoanalysis	incontrollable
reinvigoration	vasodilatation	psychoanalytic	indecipherable
reminiscential	vasodilatatory	selfdestroying	indecomposable
remonetisation	verisimilitude	selfsatisfying	indemonstrable
reorganisation	volatilisation	souldestroying	indestructible
representation	westernisation	spermatophytic	indestructibly
representative	advantageously	phenylbutazone	indeterminable
resinification	adventitiously	———————	indiscerptible
retrogradation	ambidextrously	anticonvulsant	indiscoverable
revalorisation	antiscriptural	antidepressant	insuppressible
revivification	asynchronously	antiperspirant	insurmountable
rigidification	cantankerously	archidiaconate	insurmountably
Russianisation	cardiovascular	autoradiograph	irreconcilable
sanctification	contemptuously	bougainvillaea	irreconcilably
sanguification	conterminously	circumambulate	irreproachable
saponification	contumaciously	circumnavigate	irreproachably
scandalisation	contumeliously	concavoconcave	irreproducible
schematisation	discourteously	consuetudinary	oversubscribed
secularisation	disingenuously	contraindicate	oxyhaemoglobin
selfabnegation	disputatiously	convexoconcave	proportionable
selfabsorption	extravehicular	crosspollinate	proportionably
selfaccusation	inauspiciously	dinoflagellate	quadrisyllabic
selfaccusatory	incommodiously	discombobulate	quadrisyllable
selfadmiration	infelicitously	disincorporate	skimbleskamble
selfassumption	inharmoniously	dolichocephaly	transplantable
selfconsistent	intermolecular	electrotherapy	unapproachable
selfcorrecting	intramolecular	encephalograph	uncommunicable
selfimmolation	meretriciously	homotransplant	unconscionable
selfperception	multifariously	incommensurate	uncontrollable
selfprotection	obstreperously	indiscriminate	uncontrollably
selfregulating	ostentatiously	internationale	understandable
selfrespectful	parsimoniously	interpenetrate	understandably

unintelligible	stoutheartedly	diminutiveness	inexorableness
unintelligibly	strongmindedly	disappointment	inexpressively
unquestionable	absorptiveness	disarrangement	infectiousness
unquestionably	abstemiousness	disconcertment	inflectionless
aerobiological	abstractedness	disconsolately	inflexibleness
agrobiological	acceptableness	discontentment	ingloriousness
alphanumerical	accomplishment	discouragement	inimitableness
anagrammatical	accumulatively	discursiveness	inordinateness
apothegmatical	accustomedness	disdainfulness	insatiableness
archaeological	acknowledgment	disembowelment	insensibleness
bibliomaniacal	affectionately	disenchantment	intangibleness
campanological	aggrandisement	disenthralment	interdependent
cartographical	aggressiveness	disfurnishment	interlocutress
catachrestical	amateurishness	disgruntlement	intermediately
Christological	anticipatively	disheartenment	interpretively
chronometrical	apprehensively	disjointedness	intertwinement
climatological	arrondissement	disorderliness	intransitively
commonsensical	articulateness	dispiritedness	invariableness
cosmographical	artificialness	distributively	invincibleness
cosmopolitical	attainableness	divertissement	inviolableness
dermatological	attractiveness	effortlessness	irresoluteness
diagrammatical	auspiciousness	elementariness	irrespectively
ecclesiastical	avariciousness	exhaustiveness	knickerbockers
epigrammatical	beneficialness	expressionless	lasciviousness
eschatological	bioluminescent	expressiveness	lefthandedness
gerontological	blackmarketeer	extinguishment	libidinousness
gynaecological	boisterousness	extracorporeal	licentiousness
hagiographical	bouleversement	extraneousness	longheadedness
hieroglyphical	breathlessness	factitiousness	longwindedness
hydrodynamical	bullheadedness	fallaciousness	loquaciousness
hydrographical	calamitousness	farsightedness	lovingkindness
hypocoristical	calcareousness	fastidiousness	lugubriousness
ichthyological	capriciousness	favourableness	malodorousness
iconographical	censoriousness	fictitiousness	manageableness
martyrological	changeableness	figurativeness	marvellousness
meteorological	charitableness	flagitiousness	meddlesomeness
methodological	chivalrousness	flatfootedness	meditativeness
myrmecological	circuitousness	forbiddingness	meticulousness
oneirocritical	colourfastness	formidableness	microcomponent
ornithological	colourlessness	forthrightness	miraculousness
orthographical	commensurately	fortuitousness	monkeybusiness
petrographical	commodiousness	friendlessness	monotonousness
pharmaceutical	comparableness	gramineousness	mysteriousness
phraseological	compatibleness	gratuitousness	neglectfulness
physiognomical	complexionless	gregariousness	newfangledness
pluviometrical	compulsiveness	groundlessness	nightblindness
polytheistical	conclusiveness	harmoniousness	nonbelligerent
propaedeutical	conscienceless	hereditariness	noninvolvement
psychochemical	conservatively	highhandedness	northnorthwest
psychophysical	constitutively	highmindedness	noteworthiness
psychosurgical	constructively	honourableness	nutritiousness
pteridological	contagiousness	illegitimately	obsequiousness
semielliptical	contiguousness	illiterateness	oleaginousness
sociopolitical	continuousness	illustratively	omnivorousness
soteriological	contractedness	imaginableness	openhandedness
staphylococcus	convincingness	immaculateness	openmindedness
stomatological	convulsiveness	immoderateness	opinionatively
tachygraphical	coordinateness	impassableness	oppressiveness
terminological	coquettishness	impassibleness	outlandishness
thermochemical	countercurrent	imperativeness	outrageousness
venereological	courageousness	imperviousness	overcommitment
volcanological	creditableness	implacableness	overexcitement
vulcanological	cumbersomeness	impoverishment	pardonableness
absentmindedly	cumulativeness	impressiveness	passionateness
clearsightedly	deceivableness	improvableness	penetrableness
disconnectedly	decorativeness	inadequateness	perceptiveness
discontentedly	definitiveness	inappositeness	peremptoriness
faintheartedly	degenerateness	inarticulately	perfidiousness
goodhumouredly	delectableness	incautiousness	perishableness
goodtemperedly	deliberateness	incestuousness	permissiveness
lightheartedly	deliberatively	incompleteness	perniciousness
malcontentedly	delightfulness	inconclusively	personableness
narrowmindedly	dependableness	incredibleness	persuasiveness
premeditatedly	deplorableness	indecisiveness	phosphorescent
shortsightedly	despicableness	indecorousness	portentousness
simplemindedly	despitefulness	indefiniteness	possessiveness
singlehandedly	determinedness	indiscreetness	postpositively
singlemindedly	detestableness	indistinctness	prearrangement
squadronleader	diaphanousness	inevitableness	precariousness

precociousness	suspiciousness	postmastership	constructivist
prescriptively	terminableness	progenitorship	consubstantial
preventiveness	thoughtfulness	prolocutorship	contraposition
prodigiousness	threadbareness	proprietorship	contrapositive
productiveness	thriftlessness	snaggletoothed	convertibility
profitableness	topsyturviness	spectrographic	corruptibility
propitiousness	traitorousness	sphygmographic	countrydancing
proscriptively	transitiveness	stadholdership	crossfertilise
prosperousness	transitoriness	steganographer	curvilinearity
protectiveness	tremendousness	supervisorship	decimalisation
protrusiveness	tumultuousness	sycophantishly	decolonisation
pugnaciousness	tyrannicalness	unaccomplished	decolorisation
purposefulness	ubiquitousness	undernourished	deconsecration
quantitatively	umbrageousness	abstractionism	defenestration
rampageousness	unaffectedness	abstractionist	dehumanisation
reasonableness	unattractively	accountability	delocalisation
rebelliousness	unbecomingness	administration	demobilisation
recommencement	understatement	administrative	demonetisation
reflectiveness	unexpectedness	aerodynamicist	demoralisation
refractoriness	unfaithfulness	Africanisation	denazification
regardlessness	unfriendliness	Albigensianism	denumerability
regeneratively	ungraciousness	allegorisation	depolarisation
regressiveness	ungratefulness	allelomorphism	despiritualise
relentlessness	unmannerliness	anthropologist	destructionist
relinquishment	unpleasantness	antifederalist	detoxification
remarkableness	unreservedness	antiquarianism	devitalisation
remorsefulness	unsociableness	architectonics	dextrorotation
repetitiveness	untruthfulness	associationism	dialectologist
reproductively	uproariousness	astrophysicist	disaffiliation
resistlessness	vegetativeness	Augustinianism	disaffirmation
respectfulness	victoriousness	authentication	disapprobation
responsiveness	villainousness	autosuggestion	disapprobative
revengefulness	vindictiveness	backscattering	disassociation
ridiculousness	vituperatively	backscratching	disciplinarian
roadworthiness	viviparousness	bacteriologist	discolouration
robustiousness	vociferousness	bastardisation	disconsolation
roundaboutness	voluminousness	bathingmachine	discriminating
salubriousness	voluptuousness	beautification	discrimination
sanguinariness	vulnerableness	bibliographise	discriminative
scandalousness	watertightness	biodegradation	disembarkation
schoolmistress	weakmindedness	bioelectricity	disenfranchise
scrupulousness	weightlessness	bioengineering	disequilibrium
scurrilousness	worshipfulness	biosystematics	disinclination
seasonableness	selfrespectful	bituminisation	disinfestation
selfadjustment	acceleratingly	bloodthirstily	disintegration
selfcomplacent	breathtakingly	boroughEnglish	disintegrative
selfconsequent	disapprovingly	bowdlerisation	disorientation
selfconsistent	discouragingly	Brobdingnagian	dispensability
selfeffacement	embarrassingly	capitalisation	dissociability
selfemployment	enterprisingly	castrametation	distensibility
selfgovernment	entertainingly	categorisation	dolomitisation
selfsufficient	exasperatingly	centralisation	ecclesiologist
shamefacedness	excruciatingly	centrifugation	econometrician
slanderousness	exhilaratingly	chemoreception	educationalist
slatternliness	ingratiatingly	chemoreceptive	egalitarianism
solicitousness	Johannisberger	circumlocution	electioneering
speechlessness	microsporangia	circumspection	electrostatics
spiritlessness	overpoweringly	circumstantial	emulsification
spirituousness	overwhelmingly	circumvolution	encyclopaedism
sprightfulness	selfeffacingly	classification	encyclopaedist
stationariness	unacknowledged	coessentiality	enthronisation
statuesqueness	unconvincingly	combustibility	epidemiologist
stertorousness	unflatteringly	commensuration	epistemologist
stupendousness	unhesitatingly	commissionaire	esterification
subcontrariety	ambassadorship	compossibility	eutrophication
subjectiveness	apprenticeship	conceivability	Evangelicalism
submissiveness	autobiographer	concelebration	evangelisation
substitutively	autobiographic	concessionaire	exceptionality
subversiveness	chancellorship	concretisation	exclaustration
successfulness	chincherinchee	conditionality	exhaustibility
successiveness	commissaryship	conductibility	existentialism
sufferableness	controllership	conformability	existentialist
suggestiveness	corticotrophic	conglomeration	extemporaneity
superincumbent	corticotrophin	conglutination	extensionality
superintendent	councillorship	conglutinative	fantasticality
superterranean	counsellorship	congratulation	ferrimagnetism
surefootedness	enantiomorphic	congratulative	ferromagnesian
susceptiveness	goodfellowship	conspiratorial	ferromagnetism
suspensiveness	metallographer	constructivism	floriculturist

foreordination	intuitionalism	postmillennial	Russianisation
fortunetelling	intuitionalist	practicability	Sabbatarianism
forwardlooking	irreducibility	pragmaticality	sacramentalism
fraternisation	irrefutability	praiseworthily	sacramentalist
fructification	irremovability	predesignation	sacramentarian
fundamentalism	irrevocability	predestinarian	sanctification
fundamentalist	justifiability	predestination	sanguification
fundamentality	kremlinologist	predictability	saponification
gelatinisation	latitudinarian	predisposition	satisfactorily
generalisation	legitimisation	prefabrication	sauropterygian
heartsearching	liberalisation	premillenarian	scandalisation
hebetudinosity	libertarianism	presentability	schematisation
heteromorphism	liturgiologist	presupposition	secularisation
heterothallism	lyophilisation	prettification	segregationist
hobbledehoyish	macroeconomics	preventability	selfabnegation
hocuspocussing	massproduction	probabiliorism	selfabsorption
holometabolism	matriarchalism	probabiliorist	selfaccusation
homoeomorphism	megasporangium	progressionism	selfadmiration
homogenisation	microbiologist	progressionist	selfassumption
horticulturist	microeconomics	prohibitionism	selfcorrecting
humidification	militarisation	prohibitionist	selfdestroying
hydrocoralline	millenarianism	proletarianise	selfdiscipline
hydromechanics	mineralisation	proletarianism	selfenergising
hygroscopicity	ministerialist	propitiatorily	selfexplaining
hypercriticise	misapplication	proprioceptive	selfexpression
hypercriticism	miscalculation	prothonotarial	selfflattering
hypersensitive	misinformation	protozoologist	selffulfilling
hypothyroidism	mistranslation	pseudomorphism	selfimmolation
hysterectomise	monochromatism	psilanthropism	selfpartiality
ichthyosaurian	monopolisation	psilanthropist	selfperception
identification	monosaccharide	psychodynamics	selfpossession
illimitability	mountaineering	psychosomatics	selfpreserving
immobilisation	multiplication	Pythagoreanism	selfpropelling
impermeability	multiplicative	quadragenarian	selfpropulsion
implausibility	naturalisation	quantification	selfprotection
implementation	necessarianism	quarterbinding	selfregulating
impracticality	neocolonialism	quattrocentism	selfrepression
impregnability	neuroanatomist	quattrocentist	selfrespecting
impressibility	neuroscientist	quintessential	selfrevelation
inadvisability	neutralisation	radicalisation	selfsatisfying
inalienability	nitroglycerine	radiosensitive	selfsuggestion
inalterability	noctambulation	radiostrontium	selfsupporting
inappreciation	nomenclatorial	radiotherapist	selfsustaining
inappreciative	noncooperation	recapitulation	selftormenting
inarticulation	nonrestrictive	recapitulative	semicentennial
incapacitation	nonsensicality	recolonisation	semiconducting
incoordination	obstructionism	recommendation	sensationalism
incorporeality	obstructionist	reconciliation	sensationalist
indifferentism	oecumenicalism	reconstitution	sensualisation
indifferentist	outgeneralling	reconstruction	sentimentalise
indivisibility	overcapitalise	reconstructive	sentimentalism
indoctrination	overestimation	recoverability	sentimentalist
indubitability	overpopulation	rectangularity	sentimentality
ineffectuality	overproduction	redintegration	septuagenarian
inflammability	palaeobotanist	redistribution	serviceability
infralapsarian	paradoxicality	redistributive	servomechanism
infrangibility	parasitologist	refrangibility	sesquipedalian
inheritability	pasteurisation	regularisation	silicification
inscrutability	patresfamilias	rehabilitation	simplification
inseparability	perceptibility	reintroduction	solidification
insuperability	perfectibility	reinvigoration	solitudinarian
integrationist	peripateticism	reminiscential	solubilisation
intelligential	permissibility	remonetisation	somnambulation
intercessorial	pharmacologist	reorganisation	sophistication
intercommunion	pharmacopoeial	representation	souldestroying
intercommunity	philanthropise	representative	specialisation
interferential	philanthropist	repudiationist	spectroscopist
intergradation	photoperiodism	resinification	spermatogonium
interlineation	photosensitise	respectability	springcleaning
intermediation	photosensitive	responsibility	stigmatisation
intermigration	phthalocyanine	restorationism	stratification
interpellation	pianoaccordian	restorationist	strikebreaking
interpretation	pisciculturist	restrictionist	stultification
interpretative	pleasurability	retrogradation	subalternation
intersexuality	pneumatologist	revalorisation	subinfeudation
intolerability	politicisation	revivification	submersibility
intractability	polymerisation	rheumatologist	substantialism
intrinsicality	polysaccharide	rigidification	substantialist
introductorily	popularisation	Rosicrucianism	substantiality

substantiation	astronomically	prosencephalic	grandiloquence
suggestibility	asymmetrically	prosencephalon	hallucinogenic
sulphanilamide	asymptotically	providentially	illconditioned
superannuation	autocratically	quinquennially	illustrational
superelevation	barometrically	rhinencephalic	insignificance
supererogation	biographically	rhinencephalon	insignificancy
superficiality	brachycephalic	schismatically	insurrectional
superfoetation	cardiovascular	scholastically	intercessional
superinduction	catechetically	scientifically	interjectional
superscription	concentrically	selfcontrolled	intersectional
supersensitive	confidentially	semiofficially	jurisdictional
supralapsarian	contrapuntally	seriocomically	marketgardener
susceptibility	conventionally	sociologically	nonconcurrence
symmetrisation	democratically	stochastically	nonperformance
tatterdemalion	departmentally	substantivally	organisational
tergiversation	diachronically	successionally	overconfidence
territorialise	diagnostically	supernaturally	overindulgence
territorialism	differentially	supersonically	perturbational
territorialist	diplomatically	synchronically	postpositional
territoriality	emblematically	systematically	presentational
testimonialise	endosmotically	tautologically	reconnaissance
thanksoffering	enharmonically	teleologically	rejuvenescence
thermodynamics	epexegetically	telepathically	resurrectional
thimblerigging	ethnologically	telephonically	scatterbrained
thoughtreading	etymologically	telescopically	selfconfidence
traditionalism	eulogistically	theocratically	selfdependence
traditionalist	euphuistically	tragicomically	selfdetermined
transformation	experientially	transitionally	selfimportance
transformative	experimentally	tropologically	selfinductance
transmigration	extravehicular	ultrasonically	selfindulgence
transportation	genealogically	uneconomically	selfrestrained
transsexualism	geocentrically	unemphatically	shovehalfpenny
transvaluation	geographically	unmentionables	sublieutenancy
transversality	hierarchically	unsuccessfully	substitutional
Trinitarianism	histrionically	vicechancellor	superabundance
trivialisation	hyperbolically	volumetrically	tridimensional
ultramontanism	hypersonically	committeewoman	twodimensional
ultramontanist	hypocritically	copperbottomed	unconventional
unappreciative	hypodermically	cyanocobalamin	undermentioned
uncircumcision	hypostatically	electrodynamic	unidimensional
uncompromising	hypothetically	electrothermal	unidirectional
uncongeniality	idealistically	electrothermic	unprofessional
underemphasise	idiopathically	handicraftsman	vicepresidency
undervaluation	immethodically	hypercalcaemia	appendicectomy
undesirability	imponderabilia	hyperglycaemia	boardingschool
unenterprising	inartistically	poikilothermal	campylotropous
uniformitarian	inflectionally	poikilothermic	circumlocutory
unpalatability	instrumentally	quinquagesimal	classconscious
unremunerative	intellectually	selfproclaimed	classificatory
utilitarianism	intermolecular	abovementioned	communications
valetudinarian	intramolecular	aforementioned	congratulatory
vasodilatation	judgematically	airconditioner	consanguineous
vivisectionist	legalistically	audiofrequency	contradictious
volatilisation	linguistically	blockaderunner	corticosteroid
watercolourist	longitudinally	circumambiency	corticosterone
westernisation	mathematically	compensational	cotemporaneous
whortleberries	Mephistopheles	condescendence	cucurbitaceous
windowdressing	mesdemoiselles	congregational	dextrorotatory
windowshopping	metaphorically	conservational	diamantiferous
Zoroastrianism	metaphysically	consociational	diamondiferous
crinkumcrankum	morganatically	constitutional	dicotyledonous
horrorstricken	multilaterally	constructional	disapprobatory
planetstricken	mythologically	conversational	discriminatory
spindleshanked	numismatically	correspondence	electrobiology
terrorstricken	optimistically	correspondency	entomostracous
wonderstricken	organometallic	counterbalance	extemporaneous
achromatically	paratactically	crossreference	foraminiferous
aerobiotically	pathogenically	denominational	generalpurpose
aetiologically	pathologically	discontinuance	heterochromous
alphabetically	pestilentially	discountenance	heteromorphous
altruistically	petrologically	disinheritance	heterophyllous
antiseptically	philologically	disquisitional	histopathology
antithetically	phlegmatically	dissertational	holometabolous
aphoristically	pleonastically	distributional	ichthyophagous
apologetically	preferentially	eigenfrequency	macrocephalous
apoplectically	presbyterially	electrovalency	metapsychology
archetypically	professionally	endoradiosonde	microcephalous
arithmetically	professorially	featherbrained	myrmecophagous
arrhythmically	proportionally	fullyfashioned	myrmecophilous

neuropathology	adventitiously	interferometry	Brobdingnagian
nitrocellulose	ambidextrously	intermittently	campanological
ophthalmoscope	asynchronously	knighterrantry	cardiovascular
ophthalmoscopy	bacteriostasis	magniloquently	cartographical
pachydermatous	bronchiectasis	microcircuitry	catachrestical
palaeethnology	cantankerously	multinucleated	Christological
papilionaceous	carcinogenesis	neurochemistry	chronometrical
parapsychology	chemosynthesis	orthochromatic	circumlittoral
parenchymatous	contemptuously	osteoarthritis	circumstantial
periodontology	conterminously	overabundantly	climatological
phenobarbitone	contumaciously	petrochemistry	committeewoman
phenylbutazone	contumeliously	photochemistry	commonsensical
phytopathology	cryptaesthesia	photosynthetic	compensational
pistilliferous	discourteously	pigeonbreasted	congregational
pseudomorphous	disingenuously	preponderantly	conservational
radiotelephone	disputatiously	presentimental	consociational
radiotelephony	electrodeposit	proceleusmatic	conspiratorial
recapitulatory	erythropoiesis	procrastinator	constitutional
recommendatory	gyrostabiliser	prognosticator	constructional
reconciliatory	haematogenesis	propagandistic	consubstantial
roentgenoscopy	inauspiciously	psychoanalytic	conversational
selfaccusatory	incommodiously	psychoneurotic	cosmographical
spermatogenous	infelicitously	publicspirited	cosmopolitical
spinthariscope	inharmoniously	radiochemistry	denominational
stumblingblock	intelligentsia	scintillometer	dermatological
supererogatory	meretriciously	selfinterested	diagrammatical
supposititious	metempsychosis	singlebreasted	disciplinarian
symptomatology	microprocessor	somnambulistic	disquisitional
tetradactylous	multifariously	spermatophytic	dissertational
tintinnabulous	obstreperously	sphaerocrystal	distributional
transmigratory	ostentatiously	spiritualistic	ecclesiastical
ultramicrotome	parsimoniously	stampcollector	econometrician
unsatisfactory	percutaneously	stoicheiometry	electrothermal
vasodilatatory	pertinaciously	subcontinental	epigrammatical
anthropography	photosynthesis	superconductor	eschatological
archiepiscopal	pneumoconiosis	supereminently	extracorporeal
chromatography	polymorphously	suprasegmental	extravehicular
cinematography	preposterously	tetragrammaton	ferromagnesian
gynandromorphy	presumptuously	transcendental	gerontological
heroworshipper	pseudaesthesia	transcendently	gynaecological
historiography	pseudonymously	transliterator	hagiographical
parallelepiped	psychoanalysis	troubleshooter	handicraftsman
phytogeography	psychoneurosis	unaccommodated	hieroglyphical
pseudepigrapha	rambunctiously	uncontroverted	hydrodynamical
pseudepigraphy	sacrilegiously	uncorroborated	hydrographical
rontgenography	selffertilised	undergraduette	hypocoristical
submicroscopic	simultaneously	unenthusiastic	ichthyological
tachistoscopic	slaughterously	universalistic	ichthyosaurian
thalassography	soporiferously	unpremeditated	iconographical
therianthropic	spirochaetosis	verticillaster	illustrational
underdeveloped	subconsciously	bremsstrahlung	infralapsarian
whippersnapper	superciliously	counterculture	insurrectional
microtechnique	thyrotoxicosis	countermeasure	intelligential
administratrix	unscrupulously	distemperature	intercessional
anthropometric	vaingloriously	infrastructure	intercessorial
antiscriptural	aesthesiometer	microminiature	interferential
butterfingered	antiphlogistic	microstructure	interjectional
butterflyscrew	apophthegmatic	scrubbingbrush	intermolecular
chickenlivered	bacteriostatic	slaughterhouse	intersectional
circumlittoral	basidiomycetes	superstructure	intramolecular
conquistadores	behaviouristic	ultimogeniture	jurisdictional
dieselelectric	characteristic	ultrastructure	latitudinarian
halfpennyworth	chickenhearted	verisimilitude	martyrological
northeastwards	conjunctivitis	weltanschauung	meteorological
northwestwards	counterplotted	demisemiquaver	methodological
partridgeberry	diffractometer	handkerchieves	myrmecological
phantasmagoria	diverticulitis	swordswallower	nomenclatorial
phantasmagoric	doublebreasted	hypercatalexis	oneirocritical
potentiometric	effervescently	megasporophyll	organisational
pyrheliometric	excommunicator	—————————	ornithological
schoolchildren	galactopoietic	aerobiological	orthographical
southeastwards	hermaphroditic	agrobiological	patresfamilias
southwestwards	histochemistry	alphanumerical	perturbational
spatiotemporal	iatrochemistry	anagrammatical	petrographical
standardbearer	inconsequently	antiscriptural	pharmaceutical
stoichiometric	inconsistently	apothegmatical	pharmacopoeial
thermoelectric	inconveniently	archaeological	phraseological
achondroplasia	insufficiently	archiepiscopal	physiognomical
advantageously	interferometer	bibliomaniacal	pianoaccordian

pluviometrical	reconnaissance	unaccommodated	intelligentsia
poikilothermal	rejuvenescence	unaccomplished	metempsychosis
polytheistical	selfconfidence	unacknowledged	microsporangia
postmillennial	selfdependence	uncontroverted	organometallic
postpositional	selfimportance	uncorroborated	orthochromatic
predestinarian	selfinductance	underdeveloped	osteoarthritis
premillenarian	selfindulgence	undermentioned	oxyhaemoglobin
presentational	stumblingblock	undernourished	phantasmagoria
presentimental	sublieutenancy	unmentionables	phantasmagoric
propaedeutical	superabundance	unpremeditated	photosynthesis
prothonotarial	thermodynamics	verticillaster	photosynthetic
psychochemical	vicepresidency	whippersnapper	pneumoconiosis
psychophysical	endoradiosonde	whortleberries	poikilothermic
psychosurgical	monosaccharide	wonderstricken	postmastership
pteridological	northeastwards	electrobiology	potentiometric
quadragenarian	northwestwards	histopathology	proceleusmatic
quinquagesimal	polysaccharide	metapsychology	progenitorship
quintessential	southeastwards	neuropathology	prolocutorship
reminiscential	southwestwards	palaeethnology	propagandistic
resurrectional	sulphanilamide	parapsychology	proprietorship
sacramentarian	verisimilitude	periodontology	prosencephalic
sauropterygian	abovementioned	phytopathology	pseudaesthesia
semicentennial	aesthesiometer	symptomatology	psychoanalysis
semielliptical	aforementioned	anthropography	psychoanalytic
septuagenarian	airconditioner	chromatography	psychoneurosis
sesquipedalian	autobiographer	cinematography	psychoneurotic
sociopolitical	basidiomycetes	gynandromorphy	pyrheliometric
solitudinarian	blackmarketeer	historiography	quadrisyllabic
soteriological	blockaderunner	phytogeography	rhinencephalic
spatiotemporal	bougainvillaea	pseudepigrapha	somnambulistic
sphaerocrystal	butterfingered	pseudepigraphy	spectrographic
stomatological	butterflyscrew	rontgenography	spermatophytic
subcontinental	chickenhearted	thalassography	sphygmographic
substitutional	chickenlivered	achondroplasia	spiritualistic
superterranean	chincherinchee	administratrix	spirochaetosis
supralapsarian	conquistadores	ambassadorship	stadholdership
suprasegmental	copperbottomed	anthropometric	stoichiometric
tachygraphical	councilchamber	antiphlogistic	submicroscopic
terminological	counterplotted	apophthegmatic	supervisorship
thermochemical	demisemiquaver	apprenticeship	tachistoscopic
transcendental	diffractometer	autobiographic	therianthropic
tridimensional	doublebreasted	bacteriostasis	thermoelectric
twodimensional	featherbrained	bacteriostatic	thyrotoxicosis
unconventional	fullyfashioned	behaviouristic	unenthusiastic
unidimensional	gyrostabiliser	brachycephalic	universalistic
unidirectional	handkerchieves	bronchiectasis	absentmindedly
uniformitarian	heroworshipper	carcinogenesis	acceleratingly
unprofessional	horrorstricken	chancellorship	accomplishable
valetudinarian	illconditioned	characteristic	accumulatively
venereological	interferometer	chemosynthesis	achromatically
volcanological	Johannisberger	claustrophobia	advantageously
vulcanological	marketgardener	claustrophobic	adventitiously
architectonics	Mephistopheles	commissaryship	aerobiotically
audiofrequency	mesdemoiselles	conjunctivitis	aetiologically
biosystematics	metallographer	controllership	affectionately
circumambiency	multinucleated	corticosteroid	alphabetically
condescendence	oversubscribed	corticotrophic	altruistically
correspondence	parallelepiped	corticotrophin	ambidextrously
correspondency	pigeonbreasted	councillorship	anticipatively
counterbalance	planetstricken	counsellorship	antiseptically
crossreference	publicspirited	cryptaesthesia	antithetically
discontinuance	scatterbrained	cyanocobalamin	aphoristically
discountenance	schoolchildren	dieselelectric	apologetically
disinheritance	scintillometer	diverticulitis	apoplectically
eigenfrequency	selfcontrolled	electrodeposit	apprehensively
electrostatics	selfdetermined	electrodynamic	archetypically
electrovalency	selffertilised	electrothermic	arithmetically
grandiloquence	selfinterested	enantiomorphic	arrhythmically
hydromechanics	selfproclaimed	erythropoiesis	astronomically
insignificance	selfrestrained	galactopoietic	asymmetrically
insignificancy	singlebreasted	goodfellowship	asymptotically
macroeconomics	snaggletoothed	haematogenesis	asynchronously
microeconomics	spindleshanked	hallucinogenic	autocratically
nonconcurrence	squadronleader	hermaphroditic	barometrically
nonperformance	standardbearer	hypercalcaemia	biographically
overconfidence	steganographer	hypercatalexis	bloodthirstily
overindulgence	swordswallower	hyperglycaemia	breathtakingly
psychodynamics	terrorstricken	imparisyllabic	cantankerously
psychosomatics	troubleshooter	imponderabilia	catechetically

clearsightedly	illustratively	percutaneously	uncontrollable
commensurately	immethodically	pertinaciously	uncontrollably
compassionable	impressionable	pestilentially	unconvincingly
comprehensible	inapproachable	petrologically	understandable
comprehensibly	inarticulately	philologically	understandably
concentrically	inartistically	phlegmatically	uneconomically
confidentially	inauspiciously	pleonastically	unemphatically
conservatively	incommodiously	polymorphously	unflatteringly
constitutively	incommunicable	postpositively	unhesitatingly
constructively	incommunicably	praiseworthily	unintelligible
contemptuously	incompressible	preferentially	unintelligibly
conterminously	incompressibly	premeditatedly	unquestionable
contradictable	inconclusively	preponderantly	unquestionably
contrapuntally	inconsequently	preposterously	unscrupulously
controvertible	inconsiderable	presbyterially	unsuccessfully
contumaciously	inconsiderably	prescriptively	vaingloriously
contumeliously	inconsistently	presumptuously	vituperatively
conventionally	incontrollable	professionally	volumetrically
crystallisable	inconveniently	professorially	appendicectomy
deliberatively	indecipherable	propitiatorily	ultramicrotome
democratically	indecomposable	proportionable	accomplishment
departmentally	indemonstrable	proportionably	acknowledgment
diachronically	indestructible	proportionally	aggrandisement
diagnostically	indestructibly	proscriptively	anticonvulsant
differentiable	indeterminable	providentially	antidepressant
differentially	indiscerptible	pseudonymously	antiperspirant
diplomatically	indiscoverable	quadrisyllable	arrondissement
disapprovingly	inexpressively	quantitatively	backscattering
discomfortable	infelicitously	quinquennially	backscratching
discommendable	inflectionally	rambunctiously	bathingmachine
disconformable	ingratiatingly	regeneratively	bioengineering
disconnectedly	inharmoniously	reproductively	bioluminescent
disconsolately	instrumentally	sacrilegiously	bouleversement
discontentedly	insufficiently	satisfactorily	bremsstrahlung
discouragingly	insuppressible	schismatically	communications
discourteously	insurmountable	scholastically	corticosterone
disingenuously	insurmountably	scientifically	countercurrent
disputatiously	intellectually	selfeffacingly	countrydancing
disrespectable	intermediately	semiofficially	disappointment
distributively	intermittently	seriocomically	disarrangement
dodecasyllable	internationale	shortsightedly	disconcertment
dolichocephaly	interpretively	simplemindedly	discontentment
effervescently	intransitively	simultaneously	discouragement
embarrassingly	introductorily	singlehandedly	discriminating
emblematically	irreconcilable	singlemindedly	disembowelment
endosmotically	irreconcilably	skimbleskamble	disenchantment
enharmonically	irreproachable	slaughterously	disenthralment
enterprisingly	irreproachably	sociologically	disfurnishment
entertainingly	irreproducible	soporiferously	disgruntlement
epexegetically	irrespectively	stochastically	disheartenment
ethnologically	judgematically	stoutheartedly	divertissement
etymologically	legalistically	strongmindedly	electioneering
eulogistically	lightheartedly	subconsciously	extinguishment
euphuistically	linguistically	substantivally	fortunetelling
exasperatingly	longitudinally	substitutively	forwardlooking
excommunicable	magniloquently	successionally	heartsearching
excruciatingly	malcontentedly	superciliously	hocuspocussing
exhilaratingly	mathematically	supereminently	homotransplant
experientially	megasporophyll	supernaturally	hydrocoralline
experimentally	meretriciously	supersonically	impoverishment
extinguishable	metaphorically	sycophantishly	interdependent
faintheartedly	metaphysically	synchronically	intertwinement
genealogically	morganatically	systematically	microcomponent
geocentrically	multifariously	tautologically	mountaineering
geographically	multilaterally	teleologically	nitroglycerine
goodhumouredly	mythologically	telepathically	nonbelligerent
goodtemperedly	narrowmindedly	telephonically	noncommunicant
hierarchically	numismatically	telescopically	noninvolvement
histrionically	obstreperously	theocratically	outgeneralling
hyperbolically	opinionatively	tragicomically	overcommitment
hyperirritable	optimistically	transcendently	overexcitement
hypersonically	ostentatiously	transitionally	phenobarbitone
hypocritically	overabundantly	transplantable	phenylbutazone
hypodermically	overpoweringly	tropologically	phosphorescent
hypostatically	overwhelmingly	ultrasonically	phthalocyanine
hypothetically	paratactically	unapproachable	prearrangement
idealistically	parsimoniously	unattractively	quarterbinding
idiopathically	pathogenically	uncommunicable	radiotelephone
illegitimately	pathologically	unconscionable	radiotelephony

recommencement
relinquishment
selfadjustment
selfcomplacent
selfconsequent
selfconsistent
selfcorrecting
selfdestroying
selfdiscipline
selfeffacement
selfemployment
selfenergising
selfexplaining
selfflattering
selffulfilling
selfgovernment
selfpreserving
selfpropelling
selfregulating
selfrespecting
selfsatisfying
selfsufficient
selfsupporting
selfsustaining
selftormenting
semiconducting
Shakespeareana
Shakespeariana
shovehalfpenny
souldestroying
springcleaning
strikebreaking
superincumbent
superintendent
thanksoffering
thimblerigging
thoughtreading
uncompromising
understatement
unenterprising
weltanschauung
windowdressing
windowshopping
administration
Africanisation
allegorisation
authentication
autosuggestion
bastardisation
beautification
biodegradation
bituminisation
boardingschool
bowdlerisation
capitalisation
castrametation
categorisation
centralisation
centrifugation
chemoreception
circumlocution
circumspection
circumvolution
classification
commensuration
concelebration
concretisation
conglomeration
conglutination
congratulation
contraposition
decimalisation
decolonisation
decolorisation
deconsecration
defenestration
dehumanisation
delocalisation
demobilisation

demonetisation
demoralisation
denazification
depolarisation
detoxification
devitalisation
dextrorotation
disaffiliation
disaffirmation
disapprobation
disassociation
discolouration
disconsolation
discrimination
disembarkation
disinclination
disinfestation
disintegration
disorientation
dolomitisation
emulsification
enthronisation
esterification
eutrophication
evangelisation
exclaustration
excommunicator
foreordination
fraternisation
fructification
gelatinisation
generalisation
homogenisation
humidification
identification
immobilisation
implementation
inappreciation
inarticulation
incapacitation
incoordination
indoctrination
intercommunion
intergradation
interlineation
intermediation
intermigration
interpellation
interpretation
legitimisation
liberalisation
lyophilisation
massproduction
microprocessor
militarisation
mineralisation
misapplication
miscalculation
misinformation
mistranslation
monopolisation
multiplication
naturalisation
neutralisation
noctambulation
noncooperation
overestimation
overpopulation
overproduction
pasteurisation
politicisation
polymerisation
popularisation
predesignation
predestination
predisposition
prefabrication
presupposition
prettification

procrastinator
prognosticator
prosencephalon
quantification
radicalisation
recapitulation
recolonisation
recommendation
reconciliation
reconstitution
reconstruction
redintegration
redistribution
regularisation
rehabilitation
reintroduction
reinvigoration
remonetisation
reorganisation
representation
resinification
retrogradation
revalorisation
revivification
rhinencephalon
rigidification
Russianisation
sanctification
sanguification
saponification
scandalisation
schematisation
secularisation
selfabnegation
selfabsorption
selfaccusation
selfadmiration
selfassumption
selfexpression
selfimmolation
selfperception
selfpossession
selfpropulsion
selfprotection
selfrepression
selfrevelation
selfsuggestion
sensualisation
silicification
simplification
solidification
solubilisation
somnambulation
sophistication
specialisation
stampcollector
stigmatisation
stratification
stultification
subalternation
subinfeudation
substantiation
superannuation
superconductor
superelevation
supererogation
superfoetation
superinduction
superscription
symmetrisation
tatterdemalion
tergiversation
tetragrammaton
transformation
transliterator
transmigration
transportation
transvaluation
trivialisation

uncircumcision
undervaluation
vasodilatation
vicechancellor
volatilisation
westernisation
autoradiograph
electrotherapy
encephalograph
ophthalmoscope
ophthalmoscopy
phototelegraph
radioautograph
radiotelegraph
roentgenoscopy
spinthariscope
telephotograph
circumlocutory
classificatory
commissionaire
concessionaire
congratulatory
consuetudinary
counterculture
countermeasure
dextrorotatory
disapprobatory
discriminatory
distemperature
histochemistry
iatrochemistry
infrastructure
interferometry
interplanetary
knickerbockers
knighterrantry
microcircuitry
microminiature
microstructure
neurochemistry
partridgeberry
petrochemistry
photochemistry
progressionary
radiochemistry
recapitulatory
recommendatory
reconciliatory
selfaccusatory
stoicheiometry
supererogatory
superstructure
supramaxillary
tintinnabulary
transmigratory
ultimogeniture
ultrastructure
unsatisfactory
vasodilatatory
absorptiveness
abstemiousness
abstractedness
abstractionism
abstractionist
acceptableness
accustomedness
aerodynamicist
aggressiveness
Albigensianism
allelomorphism
amateurishness
anthropologist
antifederalist
antiquarianism
articulateness
artificialness
associationism
astrophysicist
attainableness

attractiveness	existentialist	interlocutress	portentousness
Augustinianism	expressionless	intuitionalism	possessiveness
auspiciousness	expressiveness	intuitionalist	precariousness
avariciousness	extraneousness	invariableness	precociousness
bacteriologist	factitiousness	invincibleness	preventiveness
beneficialness	fallaciousness	inviolableness	probabiliorism
bibliographise	farsightedness	irresoluteness	probabiliorist
boisterousness	fastidiousness	kremlinologist	prodigiousness
boroughEnglish	favourableness	lasciviousness	productiveness
breathlessness	ferrimagnetism	lefthandedness	profitableness
bullheadedness	ferromagnetism	libertarianism	progressionism
calamitousness	fictitiousness	libidinousness	progressionist
calcareousness	figurativeness	licentiousness	prohibitionism
capriciousness	flagitiousness	liturgiologist	prohibitionist
censoriousness	flatfootedness	longheadedness	proletarianise
changeableness	floriculturist	longwindedness	proletarianism
charitableness	forbiddingness	loquaciousness	propitiousness
chivalrousness	formidableness	lovingkindness	prosperousness
circuitousness	forthrightness	lugubriousness	protectiveness
colourfastness	fortuitousness	malodorousness	protozoologist
colourlessness	friendlessness	manageableness	protrusiveness
commodiousness	fundamentalism	marvellousness	pseudomorphism
comparableness	fundamentalist	matriarchalism	psilanthropism
compatibleness	generalpurpose	meddlesomeness	psilanthropist
complexionless	gramineousness	meditativeness	pugnaciousness
compulsiveness	gratuitousness	meticulousness	purposefulness
conclusiveness	gregariousness	microbiologist	Pythagoreanism
conscienceless	groundlessness	millenarianism	quattrocentism
constructivism	harmoniousness	ministerialist	quattrocentist
constructivist	hereditariness	miraculousness	radiotherapist
contagiousness	heteromorphism	monkeybusiness	rampageousness
contiguousness	heterothallism	monochromatism	reasonableness
continuousness	highhandedness	monotonousness	rebelliousness
contractedness	highmindedness	mysteriousness	reflectiveness
convincingness	hobbledehoyish	necessarianism	refractoriness
convulsiveness	holometabolism	neglectfulness	regardlessness
coordinateness	homoeomorphism	neocolonialism	regressiveness
coquettishness	honourableness	neuroanatomist	relentlessness
courageousness	horticulturist	neuroscientist	remarkableness
creditableness	hypercriticise	newfangledness	remorsefulness
crossfertilise	hypercriticism	nightblindness	repetitiveness
cumbersomeness	hypothyroidism	nitrocellulose	repudiationist
cumulativeness	hysterectomise	northnortheast	resistlessness
deceivableness	illiterateness	northnorthwest	respectfulness
decorativeness	imaginableness	noteworthiness	responsiveness
definitiveness	immaculateness	nutritiousness	restorationism
degenerateness	immoderateness	obsequiousness	restorationist
delectableness	impassableness	obstructionism	restrictionist
deliberateness	impassibleness	obstructionist	revengefulness
delightfulness	imperativeness	oecumenicalism	rheumatologist
dependableness	imperviousness	oleaginousness	ridiculousness
deplorableness	implacableness	omnivorousness	roadworthiness
despicableness	impressiveness	openhandedness	robustiousness
despiritualise	improvableness	openmindedness	Rosicrucianism
despitefulness	inadequateness	oppressiveness	roundaboutness
destructionist	inappositeness	outlandishness	Sabbatarianism
determinedness	incautiousness	outrageousness	sacramentalism
detestableness	incestuousness	overcapitalise	sacramentalist
dialectologist	incompleteness	palaeobotanist	salubriousness
diaphanousness	incredibleness	parasitologist	sanguinariness
diminutiveness	indecisiveness	pardonableness	scandalousness
discursiveness	indecorousness	passionateness	schoolmistress
disdainfulness	indefiniteness	penetrableness	scrubbingbrush
disenfranchise	indifferentism	perceptiveness	scrupulousness
disjointedness	indifferentist	peremptoriness	scurrilousness
disorderliness	indiscreetness	perfidiousness	seasonableness
dispiritedness	indistinctness	peripateticism	segregationist
ecclesiologist	inevitableness	perishableness	sensationalism
educationalist	inexorableness	permissiveness	sensationalist
effortlessness	infectiousness	perniciousness	sentimentalise
egalitarianism	inflectionless	personableness	sentimentalism
elementariness	inflexibleness	persuasiveness	sentimentalist
encyclopaedism	ingloriousness	pharmacologist	servomechanism
encyclopaedist	inimitableness	philanthropise	shamefacedness
epidemiologist	inordinateness	philanthropist	slanderousness
epistemologist	insatiableness	photoperiodism	slatternliness
Evangelicalism	insensibleness	photosensitise	slaughterhouse
exhaustiveness	intangibleness	pisciculturist	solicitousness
existentialism	integrationist	pneumatologist	spectroscopist

speechlessness	circumnavigate	respectability	representative
spiritlessness	coessentiality	responsibility	supersensitive
spirituousness	combustibility	selfpartiality	transformative
sprightfulness	compossibility	sentimentality	unappreciative
stationariness	conceivability	serviceability	unremunerative
statuesqueness	conditionality	subcontrariety	————————
stertorousness	conductibility	submersibility	achondroplasia
stupendousness	conformability	substantiality	bougainvillaea
subjectiveness	contraindicate	suggestibility	claustrophobia
submissiveness	convertibility	superficiality	cryptaesthesia
substantialism	corruptibility	superphosphate	hypercalcaemia
substantialist	crosspollinate	susceptibility	hyperglycaemia
subversiveness	curvilinearity	territoriality	imponderabilia
successfulness	denumerability	tintinnabulate	intelligentsia
successiveness	dinoflagellate	transversality	microsporangia
sufferableness	discombobulate	uncongeniality	phantasmagoria
suggestiveness	disincorporate	undergraduette	pseudaesthesia
surefootedness	dispensability	undesirability	pseudepigrapha
susceptiveness	dissociability	unpalatability	Shakespeareana
suspensiveness	distensibility	campylotropous	Shakespeariana
suspiciousness	exceptionality	circumbendibus	anthropometric
terminableness	exhaustibility	classconscious	antiphlogistic
territorialise	extemporaneity	consanguineous	apophthegmatic
territorialism	extensionality	contradictious	autobiographic
territorialist	fantasticality	cotemporaneous	bacteriostatic
testimonialise	fundamentality	crinkumcrankum	behaviouristic
thoughtfulness	halfpennyworth	cucurbitaceous	brachycephalic
threadbareness	hebetudinosity	diamantiferous	characteristic
thriftlessness	hygroscopicity	diamondiferous	claustrophobic
topsyturviness	illimitability	dicotyledonous	corticotrophic
traditionalism	impermeability	disequilibrium	dieselelectric
traditionalist	implausibility	entomostracous	electrodynamic
traitorousness	impracticality	extemporaneous	electrothermic
transitiveness	impregnability	foraminiferous	enantiomorphic
transitoriness	impressibility	heterochromous	galactopoietic
transsexualism	inadvisability	heteromorphous	hallucinogenic
tremendousness	inalienability	heterophyllous	hermaphroditic
Trinitarianism	inalterability	holometabolous	imparisyllabic
tumultuousness	incommensurate	ichthyophagous	organometallic
tyrannicalness	incorporeality	macrocephalous	orthochromatic
ubiquitousness	indiscriminate	megasporangium	phantasmagoric
ultramontanism	indivisibility	microcephalous	photosynthetic
ultramontanist	indubitability	microtechnique	poikilothermic
umbrageousness	ineffectuality	myrmecophagous	potentiometric
unaffectedness	inflammability	myrmecophilous	proceleusmatic
unbecomingness	infrangibility	pachydermatous	propagandistic
underemphasise	inheritability	papilionaceous	prosencephalic
unexpectedness	inscrutability	parenchymatous	psychoanalytic
unfaithfulness	inseparability	pistilliferous	psychoneurotic
unfriendliness	insuperability	pseudomorphous	pyrheliometric
ungraciousness	intercommunity	radiostrontium	quadrisyllabic
ungratefulness	interpenetrate	selfrespectful	rhinencephalic
unmannerliness	intersexuality	spermatogenous	somnambulistic
unpleasantness	intolerability	spermatogonium	spectrographic
unreservedness	intractability	staphylococcus	spermatophytic
unsociableness	intrinsicality	supposititious	sphygmographic
untruthfulness	irreducibility	tetradactylous	spiritualistic
uproariousness	irrefutability	tintinnabulous	stoichiometric
utilitarianism	irremovability	administrative	submicroscopic
vegetativeness	irrevocability	chemoreceptive	tachistoscopic
victoriousness	justifiability	concavoconcave	therianthropic
villainousness	malappropriate	conglutinative	thermoelectric
vindictiveness	misappropriate	congratulative	unenthusiastic
viviparousness	nonsensicality	contrapositive	universalistic
vivisectionist	overcompensate	convexoconcave	abovementioned
vociferousness	paradoxicality	disapprobative	aforementioned
voluminousness	perceptibility	discriminative	butterfingered
voluptuousness	perfectibility	disintegrative	chickenhearted
vulnerableness	permissibility	hypersensitive	chickenlivered
watercolourist	pleasurability	inappreciative	copperbottomed
watertightness	practicability	interpretative	corticosteroid
weakmindedness	pragmaticality	multiplicative	counterplotted
weightlessness	predeterminate	nonrestrictive	doublebreasted
worshipfulness	predictability	photosensitive	featherbrained
Zoroastrianism	presentability	proprioceptive	fullyfashioned
accountability	preventability	radiosensitive	illconditioned
archidiaconate	recoverability	recapitulative	multinucleated
bioelectricity	rectangularity	reconstructive	oversubscribed
circumambulate	refrangibility	redistributive	parallelepiped

pigeonbreasted	hysterectomise	territorialise	bibliomaniacal
publicspirited	impressionable	testimonialise	boardingschool
scatterbrained	inappreciative	tintinnabulate	campanological
selfcontrolled	inapproachable	transformative	cartographical
selfdetermined	incommensurate	transplantable	catachrestical
selffertilised	incommunicable	ultimogeniture	Christological
selfinterested	incompressible	ultramicrotome	chronometrical
selfproclaimed	inconsiderable	ultrastructure	circumlittoral
selfrestrained	incontrollable	unappreciative	circumstantial
singlebreasted	indecipherable	unapproachable	climatological
snaggletoothed	indecomposable	uncommunicable	commonsensical
spindleshanked	indemonstrable	unconscionable	compensational
unaccommodated	indestructible	uncontrollable	congregational
unaccomplished	indeterminable	underemphasise	conservational
unacknowledged	indiscerptible	undergraduette	consociational
uncontroverted	indiscoverable	understandable	conspiratorial
uncorroborated	indiscriminate	unintelligible	constitutional
underdeveloped	infrastructure	unquestionable	constructional
undermentioned	insignificance	unremunerative	consubstantial
undernourished	insuppressible	verisimilitude	conversational
unpremeditated	insurmountable	backscattering	cosmographical
accomplishable	internationale	backscratching	cosmopolitical
administrative	interpenetrate	bioengineering	denominational
archidiaconate	interpretative	bremsstrahlung	dermatological
bathingmachine	irreconcilable	countrydancing	diagrammatical
bibliographise	irreproachable	discriminating	disquisitional
chemoreceptive	irreproducible	electioneering	dissertational
chincherinchee	malappropriate	fortunetelling	distributional
circumambulate	microminiature	forwardlooking	ecclesiastical
circumnavigate	microstructure	heartsearching	electrothermal
commissionaire	microtechnique	hocuspocussing	epigrammatical
compassionable	misappropriate	mountaineering	eschatological
comprehensible	monosaccharide	outgeneralling	extracorporeal
concavoconcave	multiplicative	quarterbinding	gerontological
concessionaire	nitrocellulose	selfcorrecting	gynaecological
condescendence	nitroglycerine	selfdestroying	hagiographical
conglutinative	nonconcurrence	selfenergising	hieroglyphical
congratulative	nonperformance	selfexplaining	hydrodynamical
contradictable	nonrestrictive	selfflattering	hydrographical
contraindicate	ophthalmoscope	selffulfilling	hypocoristical
contrapositive	overcapitalise	selfpreserving	ichthyological
controvertible	overcompensate	selfpropelling	iconographical
convexoconcave	overconfidence	selfregulating	illustrational
correspondence	overindulgence	selfrespecting	insurrectional
corticosterone	phenobarbitone	selfsatisfying	intelligential
counterbalance	phenylbutazone	selfsupporting	intercessional
counterculture	philanthropise	selfsustaining	intercessorial
countermeasure	photosensitise	selftormenting	interferential
crossfertilise	photosensitive	semiconducting	interjectional
crosspollinate	phthalocyanine	souldestroying	intersectional
crossreference	polysaccharide	springcleaning	jurisdictional
crystallisable	predeterminate	strikebreaking	martyrological
despiritualise	proletarianise	thanksoffering	megasporophyll
differentiable	proportionable	thimblerigging	meteorological
dinoflagellate	proprioceptive	thoughtreading	methodological
disapprobative	quadrisyllable	uncompromising	myrmecological
discombobulate	radiosensitive	unenterprising	nomenclatorial
discomfortable	radiotelephone	weltanschauung	oneirocritical
discommendable	recapitulative	windowdressing	organisational
disconformable	reconnaissance	windowshopping	ornithological
discontinuance	reconstructive	autoradiograph	orthographical
discountenance	redistributive	boroughEnglish	perturbational
discriminative	rejuvenescence	encephalograph	petrographical
disenfranchise	representative	halfpennyworth	pharmaceutical
disincorporate	selfconfidence	hobbledehoyish	pharmacopoeial
disinheritance	selfdependence	phototelegraph	phraseological
disintegrative	selfdiscipline	radioautograph	physiognomical
disrespectable	selfimportance	radiotelegraph	pluviometrical
distemperature	selfinductance	scrubbingbrush	poikilothermal
dodecasyllable	selfindulgence	telephotograph	polytheistical
endoradiosonde	sentimentalise	stumblingblock	postmillennial
excommunicable	skimbleskamble	aerobiological	postpositional
extinguishable	slaughterhouse	agrobiological	presentational
generalpurpose	spinthariscope	alphanumerical	presentimental
grandiloquence	sulphanilamide	anagrammatical	propaedeutical
hydrocoralline	superabundance	antiscriptural	prothonotarial
hypercriticise	superphosphate	apothegmatical	psychochemical
hyperirritable	supersensitive	archaeological	psychophysical
hypersensitive	superstructure	archiepiscopal	psychosurgical

```
pteridological  servomechanism  fraternisation  resinification
quinquagesimal  spermatogonium  fructification  retrogradation
quintessential  substantialism  gelatinisation  revalorisation
reminiscential  territorialism  generalisation  revivification
resurrectional  traditionalism  handicraftsman  rhinencephalon
selfrespectful  transsexualism  homogenisation  rigidification
semicentennial  Trinitarianism  horrorstricken  Russianisation
semielliptical  ultramontanism  humidification  sacramentarian
sociopolitical  utilitarianism  ichthyosaurian  sanctification
soteriological  Zoroastrianism  identification  sanguification
spatiotemporal  administration  immobilisation  saponification
sphaerocrystal  Africanisation  implementation  sauropterygian
stomatological  allegorisation  inappreciation  scandalisation
subcontinental  authentication  inarticulation  schematisation
substitutional  autosuggestion  incapacitation  schoolchildren
suprasegmental  bastardisation  incoordination  secularisation
tachygraphical  beautification  indoctrination  selfabnegation
terminological  biodegradation  infralapsarian  selfabsorption
thermochemical  bituminisation  intercommunion  selfaccusation
transcendental  bowdlerisation  intergradation  selfadmiration
tridimensional  Brobdingnagian  interlineation  selfassumption
twodimensional  capitalisation  intermediation  selfexpression
unconventional  castrametation  intermigration  selfimmolation
unidimensional  categorisation  interpellation  selfperception
unidirectional  centralisation  interpretation  selfpossession
unprofessional  centrifugation  latitudinarian  selfpropulsion
venereological  chemoreception  legitimisation  selfprotection
volcanological  circumlocution  liberalisation  selfrepression
vulcanological  circumspection  lyophilisation  selfrevelation
abstractionism  circumvolution  massproduction  selfsuggestion
Albigensianism  classification  militarisation  sensualisation
allelomorphism  commensuration  mineralisation  septuagenarian
antiquarianism  committeewoman  misapplication  sesquipedalian
associationism  concelebration  miscalculation  silicification
Augustinianism  concretisation  misinformation  simplification
constructivism  conglomeration  mistranslation  solidification
crinkumcrankum  conglutination  monopolisation  solitudinarian
disequilibrium  congratulation  multiplication  solubilisation
egalitarianism  contraposition  naturalisation  somnambulation
encyclopaedism  corticotrophin  neutralisation  sophistication
Evangelicalism  cyanocobalamin  noctambulation  specialisation
existentialism  decimalisation  noncooperation  stigmatisation
ferrimagnetism  decolonisation  overestimation  stratification
ferromagnetism  decolorisation  overpopulation  stultification
fundamentalism  deconsecration  overproduction  subalternation
heteromorphism  defenestration  oxyhaemoglobin  subinfeudation
heterothallism  dehumanisation  pasteurisation  substantiation
holometabolism  delocalisation  pianoaccordian  superannuation
homoeomorphism  demobilisation  planetstricken  superelevation
hypercriticism  demonetisation  politicisation  supererogation
hypothyroidism  demoralisation  polymerisation  superfoetation
indifferentism  denazification  popularisation  superinduction
intuitionalism  depolarisation  predesignation  superscription
libertarianism  detoxification  predestinarian  superterranean
matriarchalism  devitalisation  predestination  supralapsarian
megasporangium  dextrorotation  predisposition  symmetrisation
millenarianism  disaffiliation  prefabrication  tatterdemalion
monochromatism  disaffirmation  premillenarian  tergiversation
necessarianism  disapprobation  presupposition  terrorstricken
neocolonialism  disassociation  prettification  tetragrammaton
obstructionism  disciplinarian  prosencephalon  transformation
oecumenicalism  discolouration  quadragenarian  transmigration
peripateticism  disconsolation  quantification  transportation
photoperiodism  discrimination  radicalisation  transvaluation
probabiliorism  disembarkation  recapitulation  trivialisation
progressionism  disinclination  recolonisation  uncircumcision
prohibitionism  disinfestation  recommendation  undervaluation
proletarianism  disintegration  reconciliation  uniformitarian
pseudomorphism  disorientation  reconstitution  valetudinarian
psilanthropism  dolomitisation  reconstruction  vasodilatation
Pythagoreanism  econometrician  redintegration  volatilisation
quattrocentism  emulsification  redistribution  westernisation
radiostrontium  enthronisation  regularisation  wonderstricken
restorationism  esterification  rehabilitation  ambassadorship
Rosicrucianism  eutrophication  reintroduction  apprenticeship
Sabbatarianism  evangelisation  reinvigoration  chancellorship
sacramentalism  exclaustration  remonetisation  commissaryship
sensationalism  ferromagnesian  reorganisation  controllership
sentimentalism  foreordination  representation  councillorship
```

counsellorship	commodiousness	haematogenesis	myrmecophilous
goodfellowship	communications	handkerchieves	mysteriousness
postmastership	comparableness	harmoniousness	neglectfulness
progenitorship	compatibleness	hereditariness	newfangledness
prolocutorship	complexionless	heterochromous	nightblindness
proprietorship	compulsiveness	heteromorphous	northeastwards
stadholdership	conclusiveness	heterophyllous	northwestwards
supervisorship	conjunctivitis	highhandedness	noteworthiness
aesthesiometer	conquistadores	highmindedness	nutritiousness
airconditioner	consanguineous	holometabolous	obsequiousness
autobiographer	conscienceless	honourableness	oleaginousness
blackmarketeer	contagiousness	hydromechanics	omnivorousness
blockaderunner	contiguousness	hypercatalexis	openhandedness
cardiovascular	continuousness	ichthyophagous	openmindedness
councilchamber	contractedness	illiterateness	oppressiveness
demisemiquaver	contradictious	imaginableness	osteoarthritis
diffractometer	convincingness	immaculateness	outlandishness
excommunicator	convulsiveness	immoderateness	outrageousness
extravehicular	coordinateness	impassableness	pachydermatous
gyrostabiliser	coquettishness	impassibleness	papilionaceous
heroworshipper	cotemporaneous	imperativeness	pardonableness
interferometer	courageousness	imperviousness	parenchymatous
intermolecular	creditableness	implacableness	passionateness
intramolecular	cucurbitaceous	impressiveness	patresfamilias
Johannisberger	cumbersomeness	improvableness	penetrableness
marketgardener	cumulativeness	inadequateness	perceptiveness
metallographer	deceivableness	inappositeness	peremptoriness
microprocessor	decorativeness	incautiousness	perfidiousness
procrastinator	definitiveness	incestuousness	perishableness
prognosticator	degenerateness	incompleteness	permissiveness
scintillometer	delectableness	incredibleness	perniciousness
squadronleader	deliberateness	indecisiveness	personableness
stampcollector	delightfulness	indecorousness	persuasiveness
standardbearer	dependableness	indefiniteness	photosynthesis
steganographer	deplorableness	indiscreetness	pistilliferous
superconductor	despicableness	indistinctness	pneumoconiosis
swordswallower	despitefulness	inevitableness	portentousness
transliterator	determinedness	inexorableness	possessiveness
troubleshooter	detestableness	infectiousness	precariousness
verticillaster	diamantiferous	inflectionless	precociousness
vicechancellor	diamondiferous	inflexibleness	preventiveness
whippersnapper	diaphanousness	ingloriousness	prodigiousness
absorptiveness	dicotyledonous	inimitableness	productiveness
abstemiousness	diminutiveness	inordinateness	profitableness
abstractedness	discursiveness	insatiableness	propitiousness
acceptableness	disdainfulness	insensibleness	prosperousness
accustomedness	disjointedness	intangibleness	protectiveness
aggressiveness	disorderliness	interlocutress	protrusiveness
amateurishness	dispiritedness	invariableness	pseudomorphous
architectonics	diverticulitis	invincibleness	psychoanalysis
articulateness	effortlessness	inviolableness	psychodynamics
artificialness	electrostatics	irresoluteness	psychoneurosis
attainableness	elementariness	knickerbockers	psychosomatics
attractiveness	entomostracous	lasciviousness	pugnaciousness
auspiciousness	erythropoiesis	lefthandedness	purposefulness
avariciousness	exhaustiveness	libidinousness	rampageousness
bacteriostasis	expressionless	licentiousness	reasonableness
basidiomycetes	expressiveness	longheadedness	rebelliousness
beneficialness	extemporaneous	longwindedness	reflectiveness
biosystematics	extraneousness	loquaciousness	refractoriness
boisterousness	factitiousness	lovingkindness	regardlessness
breathlessness	fallaciousness	lugubriousness	regressiveness
bronchiectasis	farsightedness	macrocephalous	relentlessness
bullheadedness	fastidiousness	macroeconomics	remarkableness
calamitousness	favourableness	malodorousness	remorsefulness
calcareousness	fictitiousness	manageableness	repetitiveness
campylotropous	figurativeness	marvellousness	resistlessness
capriciousness	flagitiousness	meddlesomeness	respectfulness
carcinogenesis	flatfootedness	meditativeness	responsiveness
censoriousness	foraminiferous	Mephistopheles	revengefulness
changeableness	forbiddingness	mesdemoiselles	ridiculousness
charitableness	formidableness	metempsychosis	roadworthiness
chemosynthesis	forthrightness	meticulousness	robustiousness
chivalrousness	fortuitousness	microcephalous	roundaboutness
circuitousness	friendlessness	microeconomics	salubriousness
circumbendibus	gramineousness	miraculousness	sanguinariness
classconscious	gratuitousness	monkeybusiness	scandalousness
colourfastness	gregariousness	monotonousness	schoolmistress
colourlessness	groundlessness	myrmecophagous	scrupulousness

scurrilousness aerodynamicist restorationist conductibility
seasonableness aggrandisement restrictionist confidentially
shamefacedness anthropologist rheumatologist conformability
slanderousness anticonvulsant sacramentalist congratulatory
slatternliness antidepressant segregationist conservatively
solicitousness antifederalist selfadjustment constitutively
southeastwards antiperspirant selfcomplacent constructively
southwestwards arrondissement selfconsequent consuetudinary
speechlessness astrophysicist selfconsistent contemptuously
spermatogenous bacteriologist selfeffacement conterminously
spiritlessness bioluminescent selfemployment contrapuntally
spirituousness bouleversement selfgovernment contumaciously
spirochaetosis constructivist selfsufficient contumeliously
sprightfulness countercurrent sensationalist conventionally
staphylococcus destructionist sentimentalist convertibility
stationariness dialectologist spectroscopist correspondency
statuesqueness disappointment substantialist corruptibility
stertorousness disarrangement superincumbent curvilinearity
stupendousness disconcertment superintendent deliberatively
subjectiveness discontentment territorialist democratically
submissiveness discouragement traditionalist denumerability
subversiveness disembowelment ultramontanist departmentally
successfulness disenchantment understatement dextrorotatory
successiveness disenthralment vivisectionist diachronically
sufferableness disfurnishment watercolourist diagnostically
suggestiveness disgruntlement butterflyscrew differentially
supposititious disheartenment administratrix diplomatically
surefootedness divertissement absentmindedly disapprobatory
susceptibleness ecclesiologist acceleratingly disapprovingly
suspensiveness educationalist accountability disconnectedly
suspiciousness electrodeposit accumulatively disconsolately
terminableness encyclopaedist achromatically discontentedly
tetradactylous epidemiologist advantageously discouragingly
thermodynamics epistemologist adventitiously discourteously
thoughtfulness existentialist aerobiotically discriminatory
threadbareness extinguishment aetiologically disingenuously
thriftlessness floriculturist affectionately dispensability
thyrotoxicosis fundamentalist alphabetically disputatiously
tintinnabulous homotransplant altruistically dissociability
topsyturviness horticulturist ambidextrously distensibility
traitorousness impoverishment anthropography distributively
transitiveness indifferentist anticipatively dolichocephaly
transitoriness integrationist antiseptically effervescently
tremendousness interdependent antithetically eigenfrequency
tumultuousness intertwinement aphoristically electrobiology
tyrannicalness intuitionalist apologetically electrotherapy
ubiquitousness kremlinologist apoplectically electrovalency
umbrageousness liturgiologist appendicectomy embarrassingly
unaffectedness microbiologist apprehensively emblematically
unbecomingness microcomponent archetypically endosmotically
unexpectedness ministerialist arithmetically enharmonically
unfaithfulness neuroanatomist arrhythmically enterprisingly
unfriendliness neuroscientist astronomically entertainingly
ungraciousness nonbelligerent asymmetrically epexegetically
ungratefulness noncommunicant asymptotically ethnologically
unmannerliness noninvolvement asynchronously etymologically
unmentionables northnortheast audiofrequency eulogistically
unpleasantness northnorthwest autocratically euphuistically
unreservedness obstructionist barometrically exasperatingly
unsociableness overcommitment bioelectricity exceptionality
untruthfulness overexcitement biographically excruciatingly
uproariousness palaeobotanist bloodthirstily exhaustibility
vegetativeness parasitologist breathtakingly exhilaratingly
victoriousness pharmacologist cantankerously experientially
villainousness philanthropist catechetically experimentally
vindictiveness phosphorescent chromatography extemporaneity
viviparousness pisciculturist cinematography extensionality
vociferousness pneumatologist circumambiency faintheartedly
voluminousness prearrangement circumlocutory fantasticality
voluptuousness probabiliorist classificatory fundamentality
vulnerableness progressionist clearsightedly genealogically
watertightness prohibitionist coessentiality geocentrically
weakmindedness protozoologist combustibility geographically
weightlessness psilanthropist commensurately goodhumouredly
whortleberries quattrocentist compossibility goodtemperedly
worshipfulness radiotherapist comprehensibly gynandromorphy
abstractionist recommencement conceivability hebetudinosity
accomplishment relinquishment concentrically hierarchically
acknowledgment repudiationist conditionality histochemistry

histopathology	introductorily	praiseworthily	substantivally
historiography	irreconcilably	predictability	substitutively
histrionically	irreducibility	preferentially	successionally
hygroscopicity	irrefutability	premeditatedly	suggestibility
hyperbolically	irremovability	preponderantly	superciliously
hypersonically	irreproachably	preposterously	supereminently
hypocritically	irrespectively	presbyterially	supererogatory
hypodermically	irrevocability	prescriptively	superficiality
hypostatically	judgematically	presentability	supernaturally
hypothetically	justifiability	presumptuously	supersonically
iatrochemistry	knighterrantry	preventability	supramaxillary
idealistically	legalistically	professionally	susceptibility
idiopathically	lightheartedly	professorially	sycophantishly
illegitimately	linguistically	progressionary	symptomatology
illimitability	longitudinally	propitiatorily	synchronically
illustratively	magniloquently	proportionably	systematically
immethodically	malcontentedly	proportionally	tautologically
impermeability	mathematically	proscriptively	teleologically
implausibility	meretriciously	providentially	telepathically
impracticality	metaphorically	pseudepigraphy	telephonically
impregnability	metaphysically	pseudonymously	telescopically
impressibility	metapsychology	quantitatively	territoriality
inadvisability	microcircuitry	quinquennially	thalassography
inalienability	morganatically	radiochemistry	theocratically
inalterability	multifariously	radiotelephony	tintinnabulary
inarticulately	multilaterally	rambunctiously	tragicomically
inartistically	mythologically	recapitulatory	transcendently
inauspiciously	narrowmindedly	recommendatory	transitionally
incommodiously	neurochemistry	reconciliatory	transmigratory
incommunicably	neuropathology	recoverability	transversality
incompressibly	nonsensicality	rectangularity	tropologically
inconclusively	numismatically	refrangibility	ultrasonically
inconsequently	obstreperously	regeneratively	unattractively
inconsiderably	ophthalmoscopy	reproductively	uncongeniality
inconsistently	opinionatively	respectability	uncontrollably
inconveniently	optimistically	responsibility	unconvincingly
incorporeality	ostentatiously	roentgenoscopy	understandably
indestructibly	overabundantly	rontgenography	undesirability
indivisibility	overpoweringly	sacrilegiously	uneconomically
indubitability	overwhelmingly	satisfactorily	unemphatically
ineffectuality	palaeethnology	schismatically	unflatteringly
inexpressively	paradoxicality	scholastically	unhesitatingly
infelicitously	parapsychology	scientifically	unintelligibly
inflammability	paratactically	selfaccusatory	unpalatability
inflectionally	parsimoniously	selfeffacingly	unquestionably
infrangibility	partridgeberry	selfpartiality	unsatisfactory
ingratiatingly	pathogenically	semiofficially	unscrupulously
inharmoniously	pathologically	sentimentality	unsuccessfully
inheritability	perceptibility	seriocomically	vaingloriously
inscrutability	percutaneously	serviceability	vasodilatatory
inseparability	perfectibility	shortsightedly	vicepresidency
insignificancy	periodontology	shovehalfpenny	vituperatively
instrumentally	permissibility	simplemindedly	volumetrically
insufficiently	pertinaciously	simultaneously	
insuperability	pestilentially	singlehandedly	
insurmountably	petrochemistry	singlemindedly	
intellectually	petrologically	slaughterously	
intercommunity	philologically	sociologically	
interferometry	phlegmatically	soporiferously	
intermediately	photochemistry	stochastically	
intermittently	phytogeography	stoicheiometry	
interplanetary	phytopathology	stoutheartedly	
interpretively	pleasurability	strongmindedly	
intersexuality	pleonastically	subconsciously	
intolerability	polymorphously	subcontrariety	
intractability	postpositively	sublieutenancy	
intransitively	practicability	submersibility	
intrinsicality	pragmaticality	substantiality	

15 letter words

abiogenetically	acknowledgeable	agriculturalist	anaesthesiology
acanthocephalan	acknowledgement	airconditioning	anaesthetically
acclimatisation	acquisitiveness	alphabetisation	anisotropically
accommodatingly	adventurousness	ambidexterously	ankylostomiasis
accountableness	aerodynamically	Americanisation	annihilationism
achondroplastic	affranchisement	amphitheatrical	antepenultimate

anthropocentric	conceptualistic	discommendation	extracurricular
anthropogenesis	condescendingly	disconcertingly	extraillustrate
anthropological	confessionalism	discontinuously	extraordinarily
anthropomorphic	confessionalist	disenchantingly	familiarisation
anthropopathism	confidentiality	disentanglement	fantasticalness
anthropophagous	configurational	disgracefulness	fashionableness
anticlericalism	congratulations	dishearteningly	fissiparousness
antimonarchical	conjunctionally	disillusionment	flibbertigibbet
antisabbatarian	connoisseurship	disinflationary	foresightedness
antitrinitarian	conscientiously	disinterestedly	formularisation
antivivisection	consecutiveness	disorganisation	fourdimensional
apocalyptically	consentaneously	dispassionately	fragmentariness
approachability	consequentially	disproportional	frenchification
appropriateness	conservationist	disreputability	gastroenteritis
approximatively	considerateness	disrespectfully	gentlemanliness
arboriculturist	conspicuousness	dissatisfaction	geochronologist
archiepiscopate	constructionism	dissatisfactory	geomorphologist
architecturally	constructionist	distastefulness	gleichschaltung
argumentatively	consubstantiate	distinctiveness	governorgeneral
Aristotelianism	contemplatively	distinguishable	grandiloquently
arterialisation	contemporaneity	distinguishably	greatgrandchild
atherosclerosis	contemporaneous	distrustfulness	gynandromorphic
atherosclerotic	contemptibility	dithyrambically	halfheartedness
atmospherically	contentiousness	diversification	hardheartedness
atrabiliousness	contractability	dolichocephalic	heartbreakingly
authoritatively	contractibility	doublebarrelled	heliotropically
autographically	contradictorily	downheartedness	Hellenistically
autoradiography	contravallation	dramaturgically	hendecasyllabic
bacteriological	controversially	dyslogistically	hendecasyllable
bibliographical	conventionalise	ecclesiasticism	hermaphroditism
bioastronautics	conventionalism	ecclesiological	hermeneutically
biogeochemistry	conventionalist	echinodermatous	heterochromatic
biogeographical	conventionality	eclaircissement	heterodactyloos
bioluminescence	conversationist	efficaciousness	heterogeneously
blameworthiness	correspondingly	electrification	heterosexuality
bloodguiltiness	cosmopolitanism	electroanalysis	historiographer
brachistochrone	counterapproach	electrochemical	historiographic
brachycephalous	counterattacker	electrodynamics	hobbledehoyhood
brachydactylous	counterirritant	electrokinetics	homogeneousness
broadmindedness	countermovement	electromagnetic	hospitalisation
carnivorousness	counterplotting	electromyograph	humanitarianism
cerebrovascular	crossopterygian	electronegative	hydrodynamicist
ceremoniousness	cryptanalytical	electrophoresis	hydropathically
chloramphenicol	cryptocommunist	electrophoretic	hydrostatically
Christadelphian	crystallisation	electropositive	hypercatalectic
chromatographic	crystallography	emancipationist	hypercritically
chronogrammatic	Czechoslovakian	enantiomorphism	hyperthyroidism
chronologically	decalcification	enantiomorphous	ideographically
churrigueresque	decarbonisation	encephalography	illimitableness
cinematographer	decarburisation	enfranchisement	illustriousness
cinematographic	decolourisation	entrepreneurial	imaginativeness
circumferential	decontamination	episcopalianism	immortalisation
circumnavigator	defencelessness	epistemological	immunochemistry
circumscription	deleteriousness	epitheliomatous	impenetrability
circumspectness	demagnetisation	equalitarianism	imperishability
circumstantiate	demonstrability	equiprobability	impermeableness
circumvallation	demonstrational	etherealisation	imponderability
civilianisation	demonstratively	ethnocentricity	importunateness
coconsciousness	demystification	euphemistically	impracticalness
coinstantaneous	denitrification	Europeanisation	imprescriptible
coldbloodedness	departmentalise	everlastingness	impressionistic
coldheartedness	departmentalism	exchangeability	improvisatorial
collenchymatous	dermatoglyphics	excommunication	inaccessibility
commonplaceness	descriptiveness	excommunicative	inadmissibility
communalisation	desensitisation	excommunicatory	inapplicability
communicability	desexualisation	exemplification	inapprehensible
communicatively	dessertspoonful	exhibitionistic	inappropriately
compartmentally	destructibility	expeditiousness	inattentiveness
compassionately	destructiveness	experientialism	incalculability
compendiousness	determinateness	experientialist	incommensurable
competitiveness	detribalisation	experimentalise	incommensurably
complementarily	developmentally	experimentalism	incommunicative
complementarity	devitrification	experimentalist	incomparability
complicatedness	differentiation	experimentation	incompatibility
compositionally	disadvantageous	experimentative	incomprehension
comprehensively	disaffectedness	expressionistic	incongruousness
compressibility	disagreeability	extemporisation	inconsequential
computerisation	disappointingly	exteriorisation	inconsiderately
conceivableness	disarticulation	externalisation	inconsideration

inconspicuously	irreparableness	palaeoanthropic	prestigiousness
incorrigibility	irresistibility	palaeobotanical	pretentiousness
indefeasibility	irreversibility	palaeogeography	preternaturally
indefensibility	irrevocableness	palaeographical	problematically
indemnification	jurisprudential	palaeomagnetism	processionalist
indeterminately	kindheartedness	palaeontologist	procrastination
indetermination	lackadaisically	pantheistically	professionalise
indeterministic	levelheadedness	paradoxicalness	professionalism
indigestibility	lexicographical	parasympathetic	prognostication
indisciplinable	lightheadedness	parenthetically	prognosticative
indissolubility	lightmindedness	parliamentarian	progressiveness
indistinctively	logarithmically	parliamentarism	prohibitiveness
individualistic	logographically	parthenogenesis	properispomenon
indubitableness	longsightedness	parthenogenetic	proportionalist
ineffaceability	macroscopically	particularistic	proportionality
ineffectiveness	magnetoelectric	penetrativeness	proportionately
ineffectualness	malacopterygian	perfunctoriness	prosenchymatous
inefficaciously	maldistribution	peripatetically	protozoological
inexcusableness	malpractitioner	peristaltically	provocativeness
inexpensiveness	manicdepressive	perpendicularly	pseudepigraphic
inexplicability	manoeuvrability	personalisation	psychologically
infinitesimally	margaritiferous	personification	psychometrician
inflammableness	marketgardening	perspicaciously	psychopathology
infrangibleness	materialisation	perspicuousness	psychophysicist
infundibuliform	mechanistically	pessimistically	psychotherapist
injudiciousness	mellifluousness	pharisaicalness	pulchritudinous
innumerableness	Mephistophelean	pharmacological	punctiliousness
inoffensiveness	Mephistophelian	phenomenalistic	purposelessness
inopportuneness	meritoriousness	phenomenologist	pusillanimously
inquisitiveness	meroblastically	phenylketonuria	pyroelectricity
inquisitorially	metamathematics	philanthropical	pyrotechnically
inscrutableness	methamphetamine	philosophically	quadruplication
insensitiveness	microanalytical	phonautographic	quarrelsomeness
inseparableness	micromillimetre	phosphorescence	quarterfinalist
insignificantly	microphotograph	phosphorylation	quatercentenary
instantaneously	microsporangium	photochemically	quickwittedness
instructiveness	microsporophyll	photoconducting	quinquagenarian
instrumentalism	miniaturisation	photoconductive	quintuplication
instrumentalist	misapprehension	photoelectronic	radioautography
instrumentality	misapprehensive	photojournalism	radiogoniometer
instrumentation	mischievousness	photojournalist	radiotelegraphy
insubordination	misconstruction	photolithograph	rationalisation
insurrectionary	mistrustfulness	photomechanical	reafforestation
insurrectionist	monosymmetrical	photomicrograph	reapportionment
intellectualise	morphologically	photosensitiser	reconcilability
intellectualism	multitudinously	photosynthesise	reconsideration
intellectualist	nationalisation	phototelegraphy	reconsolidation
intellectuality	nearsightedness	phrenologically	reestablishment
intelligibility	necessitousness	physicochemical	regionalisation
intemperateness	necromantically	physiographical	remonstratively
intensification	neighbourliness	physiologically	remorselessness
interchangeable	neurophysiology	physiotherapist	repetitiousness
interchangeably	neuropsychiatry	phytogeographic	reproachfulness
interclavicular	noncommissioned	picturepostcard	reproducibility
intercollegiate	noncontributory	picturesqueness	resourcefulness
interconnection	nongovernmental	pithecanthropus	respectableness
interdependence	noninterference	platitudinarian	resurrectionism
interdependency	nonintervention	pleasurableness	resurrectionist
interdigitation	nonprofessional	plenipotentiary	retrogressively
interfascicular	nonprofitmaking	pleuropneumonia	retrospectively
interferometric	nonsensicalness	plumbaginaceous	rhombencephalon
interjectionary	northeastwardly	pneumatological	rhynchocephalia
internalisation	northwestwardly	polycrystalline	righthandedness
internationally	notwithstanding	polyunsaturated	rightmindedness
interpretership	numismatologist	postmillenarian	ritualistically
interprovincial	obstructiveness	povertystricken	roentgenography
interrogatively	oceanographical	practicableness	romanticisation
interscholastic	odoriferousness	precipitousness	rontgenotherapy
interstratified	omnidirectional	predeterminable	rudimentariness
interventionism	ontogenetically	prehistorically	sadomasochistic
interventionist	openheartedness	prepositionally	sanctimoniously
intolerableness	ophthalmologist	prepossessingly	saprophytically
intractableness	ophthalmoscopic	PreRaphaelitism	schistosomiasis
introsusception	opinionatedness	Presbyterianise	schoolmastering
intussusception	opprobriousness	Presbyterianism	selfabandonment
intussusceptive	ornithorhynchus	presentationism	selfaffirmation
involuntariness	orthopsychiatry	presentationist	selfapprobation
invulnerability	overconfidently	preservationist	selfcastigation
irrationalistic	overdevelopment	prestidigitator	selfcentredness

selfcomplacency	superconducting	underestimation	saprophytically
selfconfidently	superconductive	underprivileged	vasoconstrictor
selfconsciously	superficialness	underproduction	warmbloodedness
selfconsequence	superfluousness	understandingly	warmheartedness
selfconsistency	superheterodyne	unexceptionable	warrantableness
selfconstituted	superimposition	unexceptionably	abiogenetically
selfcontainment	superincumbence	unexceptionally	obstructiveness
selfdeprecating	superinducement	unintelligently	acanthocephalan
selfdeprecatory	superintendence	unintentionally	acclimatisation
selfdestruction	superintendency	unobjectionable	accommodatingly
selfdestructive	superlativeness	unparliamentary	accountableness
selfdetermining	supernaturalise	unprecedentedly	achondroplastic
selfdevelopment	supernaturalism	unprepossessing	acknowledgeable
selfdistrustful	supernaturalist	unpretentiously	acknowledgement
selfexamination	supersaturation	unquestioningly	acquisitiveness
selfexplanatory	superstitiously	unrealistically	ecclesiasticism
selffertilising	superstructural	unrighteousness	ecclesiological
selfforgetfully	supplementarily	unsophisticated	echinodermatous
selffulfillment	supplementation	unsportsmanlike	eclaircissement
selfgratulation	supportableness	unsubstantially	oceanographical
selfhumiliation	suppositionally	unsymmetrically	schistosomiasis
selfimprovement	surreptitiously	unwholesomeness	schoolmastering
selfindulgently	susceptibleness	vasoconstrictor	adventurousness
selfopinionated	sycophantically	ventriloquially	ideographically
selfpollination	syllabification	ventriloquistic	odoriferousness
selfpropagating	syllogistically	venturesomeness	aerodynamically
selfrealisation	symmetricalness	vertiginousness	cerebrovascular
selfregistering	sympathetically	vicechamberlain	ceremoniousness
selfreplicating	symptomatically	vicissitudinous	decalcification
selfreproachful	synchronisation	warmbloodedness	decarbonisation
selfreprovingly	systematisation	warmheartedness	decarburisation
selfrighteously	technologically	warrantableness	decolourisation
selfsacrificing	telegraphically	weatherboarding	decontamination
selfsufficiency	telephotography	wellconditioned	defencelessness
semiconsciously	temperamentally	wellintentioned	deleteriousness
semicylindrical	tempestuousness	wrongheadedness	demagnetisation
semidocumentary	tendentiousness	zoogeographical	demonstrability
semiindependent	therapeutically	———————————————	demonstrational
semitransparent	therianthropism	bacteriological	demonstratively
sententiousness	thermochemistry	carnivorousness	demystification
serviceableness	thoughtlessness	familiarisation	denitrification
sesquicentenary	thunderstricken	fantasticalness	departmentalise
shootinggallery	topographically	fashionableness	departmentalism
shrinkresistant	totalitarianism	gastroenteritis	dermatoglyphics
significatively	transcriptional	halfheartedness	descriptiveness
singleheartedly	transferability	hardheartedness	desensitisation
sleepingdraught	transfiguration	lackadaisically	desexualisation
socialistically	transfigurement	macroscopically	dessertspoonful
sociolinguistic	transgressively	magnetoelectric	destructibility
softheartedness	transilluminate	malacopterygian	destructiveness
sophisticatedly	transliteration	maldistribution	determinateness
speakingtrumpet	transmutability	malpractitioner	detribalisation
spectroscopical	transparentness	manicdepressive	developmentally
speculativeness	transplantation	manoeuvrability	devitrification
speechification	transpositional	margaritiferous	gentlemanliness
spermatogenesis	treacherousness	marketgardening	geochronologist
spermatogenetic	treasonableness	materialisation	geomorphologist
splendiferously	trigonometrical	nationalisation	heartbreakingly
spontaneousness	trinitrotoluene	palaeoanthropic	heliotropically
stadtholdership	trisyllabically	palaeobotanical	Hellenistically
stampcollecting	troublesomeness	palaeogeography	hendecasyllabic
standardisation	trueheartedness	palaeographical	hendecasyllable
standoffishness	trustworthiness	palaeomagnetism	hermaphroditism
stereochemistry	trypanosomiasis	palaeontologist	hermeneutically
stereoisomerism	typographically	pantheistically	heterochromatic
stoicheiometric	ultracentrifuge	paradoxicalness	heterodactyloos
straightforward	ultramicroscope	parasympathetic	heterogeneously
stratigraphical	unaccommodating	parenthetically	heterosexuality
stretcherbearer	unceremoniously	parliamentarian	levelheadedness
subordinateness	unchallengeable	parliamentarism	lexicographical
subpostmistress	unchangeability	parthenogenesis	mechanistically
substantialness	uncommunicative	parthenogenetic	mellifluousness
substantiveness	uncomplainingly	particularistic	Mephistophelean
substitutionary	uncomplimentary	radioautography	Mephistophelian
substratosphere	uncomprehending	radiogoniometer	meritoriousness
subterraneously	unconditionally	radiotelegraphy	meroblastically
suburbanisation	unconsciousness	rationalisation	metamathematics
sulphureousness	undemonstrative	sadomasochistic	methamphetamine
superabundantly	underemployment	sanctimoniously	nearsightedness

necessitousness	sesquicentenary	disappointingly	ambidexterously
necromantically	technologically	disarticulation	Americanisation
neighbourliness	telegraphically	discommendation	amphitheatrical
neurophysiology	telephotography	disconcertingly	emancipationist
neuropsychiatry	temperamentally	discontinuously	imaginativeness
penetrativeness	tempestuousness	disenchantingly	immortalisation
perfunctoriness	tendentiousness	disentanglement	immunochemistry
peripatetically	ventriloquially	disgracefulness	impenetrability
peristaltically	ventriloquistic	dishearteningly	imperishability
perpendicularly	venturesomeness	disillusionment	impermeableness
personalisation	vertiginousness	disinflationary	imponderability
personification	weatherboarding	disinterestedly	importunateness
perspicaciously	wellconditioned	disorganisation	impracticalness
perspicuousness	wellintentioned	dispassionately	imprescriptible
pessimistically	affranchisement	disproportional	impressionistic
reafforestation	efficaciousness	disreputability	improvisatorial
reapportionment	agriculturalist	disrespectfully	omnidirectional
reconcilability	chloramphenicol	dissatisfaction	anaesthesiology
reconsideration	Christadelphian	dissatisfactory	anaesthetically
reconsolidation	chromatographic	distastefulness	anisotropically
reestablishment	chronogrammatic	distinctiveness	ankylostomiasis
regionalisation	chronologically	distinguishable	annihilationism
remonstratively	churrigueresque	distinguishably	antepenultimate
remorselessness	pharisaicalness	distrustfulness	anthropocentric
repetitiousness	pharmacological	dithyrambically	anthropogenesis
reproachfulness	phenomenalistic	diversification	anthropological
reproducibility	phenomenologist	fissiparousness	anthropomorphic
resourcefulness	phenylketonuria	historiographer	anthropopathism
respectableness	philanthropical	historiographic	anthropophagous
resurrectionism	philosophically	kindheartedness	anticlericalism
resurrectionist	phonautographic	lightheadedness	antimonarchical
retrogressively	phosphorescence	lightmindedness	antisabbatarian
retrospectively	phosphorylation	microanalytical	antitrinitarian
selfabandonment	photochemically	micromillimetre	antivivisection
selfaffirmation	photoconducting	microphotograph	enantiomorphism
selfapprobation	photoconductive	microsporangium	enantiomorphous
selfcastigation	photoelectronic	microsporophyll	encephalography
selfcentredness	photojournalism	miniaturisation	enfranchisement
selfcomplacency	photojournalist	misapprehension	entrepreneurial
selfconfidently	photolithograph	misapprehensive	inaccessibility
selfconsciously	photomechanical	mischievousness	inadmissibility
selfconsequence	photomicrograph	misconstruction	inapplicability
selfconsistency	photosensitiser	mistrustfulness	inapprehensible
selfconstituted	photosynthesise	picturepostcard	inappropriately
selfcontainment	phototelegraphy	picturesqueness	inattentiveness
selfdeprecating	phrenologically	pithecanthropus	incalculability
selfdeprecatory	physicochemical	righthandedness	incommensurable
selfdestruction	physiographical	rightmindedness	incommensurably
selfdestructive	physiologically	ritualistically	incommunicative
selfdetermining	physiotherapist	significatively	incomparability
selfdevelopment	phytogeographic	singleheartedly	incompatibility
selfdistrustful	rhombencephalon	vicechamberlain	incomprehension
selfexamination	rhynchocephalia	vicissitudinous	incongruousness
selfexplanatory	shootinggallery	alphabetisation	inconsequential
selffertilising	shrinkresistant	blameworthiness	inconsiderately
selfforgetfully	therapeutically	bloodguiltiness	inconsideration
selffulfillment	therianthropism	electrification	inconspicuously
selfgratulation	thermochemistry	electroanalysis	incorrigibility
selfhumiliation	thoughtlessness	electrochemical	indefeasibility
selfimprovement	thunderstricken	electrodynamics	indefensibility
selfindulgently	airconditioning	electrokinetics	indemnification
selfopinionated	bibliographical	electromagnetic	indeterminately
selfpollination	bioastronautics	electromyograph	indetermination
selfpropagating	biogeochemistry	electronegative	indeterministic
selfrealisation	biogeographical	electrophoresis	indigestibility
selfregistering	bioluminescence	electrophoretic	indisciplinable
selfreplicating	cinematographer	electropositive	indissolubility
selfreproachful	cinematographic	flibbertigibbet	indistinctively
selfreprovingly	circumferential	gleichschaltung	individualistic
selfrighteously	circumnavigator	illimitableness	indubitableness
selfsacrificing	circumscription	illustriousness	ineffaceability
selfsufficiency	circumspectness	platitudinarian	ineffectiveness
semiconsciously	circumstantiate	pleasurableness	ineffectualness
semicylindrical	circumvallation	plenipotentiary	inefficaciously
semidocumentary	civilianisation	pleuropneumonia	inexcusableness
semiindependent	differentiation	plumbaginaceous	inexpensiveness
semitransparent	disadvantageous	sleepingdraught	inexplicability
sententiousness	disaffectedness	ultracentrifuge	infinitesimally
serviceableness	disagreeability	ultramicroscope	inflammableness

infrangibleness	unparliamentary	fourdimensional	irresistibility
infundibuliform	unprecedentedly	governorgeneral	irreversibility
injudiciousness	unprepossessing	hobbledehoyhood	irrevocableness
innumerableness	unpretentiously	homogeneousness	ornithorhynchus
inoffensiveness	unquestioningly	hospitalisation	orthopsychiatry
inopportuneness	unrealistically	logarithmically	practicableness
inquisitiveness	unrighteousness	logographically	precipitousness
inquisitorially	unsophisticated	longsightedness	predeterminable
inscrutableness	unsportsmanlike	monosymmetrical	prehistorically
insensitiveness	unsubstantially	morphologically	prepositionally
inseparableness	unsymmetrically	noncommissioned	prepossessingly
insignificantly	unwholesomeness	noncontributory	PreRaphaelitism
instantaneously	coconsciousness	nongovernmental	Presbyterianise
instructiveness	coinstantaneous	noninterference	Presbyterianism
instrumentalism	coldbloodedness	nonintervention	presentationism
instrumentalist	coldheartedness	nonprofessional	presentationist
instrumentality	collenchymatous	nonprofitmaking	preservationist
instrumentation	commonplaceness	nonsensicalness	prestidigitator
insubordination	communalisation	northeastwardly	prestigiousness
insurrectionary	communicability	northwestwardly	pretentiousness
insurrectionist	communicatively	notwithstanding	preternaturally
intellectualise	compartmentally	polycrystalline	problematically
intellectualism	compassionately	polyunsaturated	processionalist
intellectualist	compendiousness	postmillenarian	procrastination
intellectuality	competitiveness	povertystricken	professionalise
intelligibility	complementarily	roentgenography	professionalism
intemperateness	complementarity	romanticisation	prognostication
intensification	complicatedness	rontgenotherapy	prognosticative
interchangeable	compositionally	socialistically	progressiveness
interchangeably	comprehensively	sociolinguistic	prohibitiveness
interclavicular	compressibility	softheartedness	properispomenon
intercollegiate	computerisation	sophisticatedly	proportionalist
interconnection	conceivableness	topographically	proportionality
interdependence	conceptualistic	totalitarianism	proportionately
interdependency	condescendingly	zoogeographical	prosenchymatous
interdigitation	confessionalism	apocalyptically	protozoological
interfascicular	confessionalist	approachability	provocativeness
interferometric	confidentiality	appropriateness	transcriptional
interjectionary	configurational	approximatively	transferability
internalisation	congratulations	episcopalianism	transfiguration
internationally	conjunctionally	epistemological	transfigurement
interpretership	connoisseurship	epitheliomatous	transgressively
interprovincial	conscientiously	openheartedness	transilluminate
interrogatively	consecutiveness	ophthalmologist	transliteration
interscholastic	consentaneously	ophthalmoscopic	transmutability
interstratified	consequentially	opinionatedness	transparentness
interventionism	conservationist	opprobriousness	transplantation
interventionist	considerateness	speakingtrumpet	transpositional
intolerableness	conspicuousness	spectroscopical	treacherousness
intractableness	constructionism	speculativeness	treasonableness
introsusception	constructionist	speechification	trigonometrical
intussusception	consubstantiate	spermatogenesis	trinitrotoluene
intussusceptive	contemplatively	spermatogenetic	trisyllabically
involuntariness	contemporaneity	splendiferously	troublesomeness
invulnerability	contemporaneous	spontaneousness	trueheartedness
ontogenetically	contemptibility	equalitarianism	trustworthiness
pneumatological	contentiousness	equiprobability	trypanosomiasis
unaccommodating	contractability	arboriculturist	wrongheadedness
unceremoniously	contractibility	archiepiscopate	pseudepigraphic
unchallengeable	contradictorily	architecturally	psychologically
unchangeability	contravallation	argumentatively	psychometrician
uncommunicative	controversially	Aristotelianism	psychopathology
uncomplainingly	conventionalise	arterialisation	psychophysicist
uncomplimentary	conventionalism	brachistochrone	psychotherapist
uncomprehending	conventionalist	brachycephalous	atherosclerosis
unconditionally	conventionality	brachydactylous	atherosclerotic
unconsciousness	conversationist	broadmindedness	atmospherically
undemonstrative	correspondingly	crossopterygian	atrabiliousness
underemployment	cosmopolitanism	cryptanalytical	etherealisation
underestimation	counterapproach	cryptocommunist	ethnocentricity
underprivileged	counterattacker	crystallisation	stadtholdership
underproduction	counterirritant	crystallography	stampcollecting
understandingly	countermovement	dramaturgically	standardisation
unexceptionable	counterplotting	fragmentariness	standoffishness
unexceptionably	dolichocephalic	frenchification	stereochemistry
unexceptionally	doublebarrelled	grandiloquently	stereoisomerism
unintelligently	downheartedness	greatgrandchild	stoicheiometric
unintentionally	foresightedness	irrationalistic	straightforward
unobjectionable	formularisation	irreparableness	stratigraphical

stretcherbearer	dyslogistically	substratosphere	indubitableness
authoritatively	gynandromorphic	subterraneously	radioautography
autographically	hydrodynamicist	suburbanisation	radiogoniometer
autoradiography	hydropathically	acclimatisation	radiotelegraphy
euphemistically	hydrostatically	accommodatingly	rudimentariness
Europeanisation	hypercatalectic	accountableness	sadomasochistic
humanitarianism	hypercritically	archiepiscopate	undemonstrative
jurisprudential	hyperthyroidism	architecturally	underemployment
multitudinously	pyroelectricity	bacteriological	underestimation
numismatologist	pyrotechnically	coconsciousness	underprivileged
pulchritudinous	sycophantically	decalcification	underproduction
punctiliousness	syllabification	decarbonisation	understandingly
purposelessness	syllogistically	decarburisation	Americanisation
pusillanimously	symmetricalness	decolourisation	Czechoslovakian
quadruplication	sympathetically	decontamination	electrification
quarrelsomeness	symptomatically	ecclesiasticism	electroanalysis
quarterfinalist	synchronisation	ecclesiological	electrochemical
quatercentenary	systematisation	encephalography	electrodynamics
quickwittedness	typographically	exchangeability	electrokinetics
quinquagenarian	Czechoslovakian	excommunication	electromagnetic
quintuplication	———————————————	excommunicative	electromyograph
rudimentariness	acanthocephalan	excommunicatory	electronegative
subordinateness	anaesthesiology	incalculability	electrophoresis
subpostmistress	anaesthetically	incommensurable	electrophoretic
substantialness	blameworthiness	incommensurably	electropositive
substantiveness	brachistochrone	incommunicative	everlastingness
substitutionary	brachycephalous	incomparability	exemplification
substratosphere	brachydactylous	incompatibility	frenchification
subterraneously	dramaturgically	incomprehension	gleichschaltung
suburbanisation	emancipationist	incongruousness	greatgrandchild
sulphureousness	enantiomorphic	inconsequential	ideographically
superabundantly	enantiomorphous	inconsiderately	ineffaceability
superconducting	fragmentariness	inconsideration	ineffectiveness
superconductive	grandiloquently	inconspicuously	ineffectualness
superficialness	heartbreakingly	incorrigibility	inefficaciously
superfluousness	imaginativeness	lackadaisically	inexcusableness
superheterodyne	inaccessibility	macroscopically	inexpensiveness
superimposition	inadmissibility	mechanistically	inexplicability
superincumbence	inapplicability	microanalytical	oceanographical
superinducement	inapprehensible	micromillimetre	openheartedness
superintendence	inappropriately	microphotograph	overconfidently
superintendency	inattentiveness	microsporangium	overdevelopment
superlativeness	nearsightedness	microsporophyll	phenomenalistic
supernaturalise	pharisaicalness	necessitousness	phenomenologist
supernaturalism	pharmacological	necromantically	phenylketonuria
supernaturalist	platitudinarian	picturepostcard	pleasurableness
supersaturation	practicableness	picturesqueness	plenipotentiary
superstitiously	quadruplication	reconcilability	pleuropneumonia
superstructural	quarrelsomeness	reconsideration	pneumatological
supplementarily	quarterfinalist	reconsolidation	precipitousness
supplementation	quatercentenary	socialistically	predeterminable
supportableness	reafforestation	sociolinguistic	prehistorically
suppositionally	reapportionment	sycophantically	prepositionally
surreptitiously	stadtholdership	technologically	prepossessingly
susceptibleness	stampcollecting	unceremoniously	PreRaphaelitism
everlastingness	standardisation	unchallengeable	Presbyterianise
overconfidently	standoffishness	unchangeability	Presbyterianism
overdevelopment	transcriptional	uncommunicative	presentationism
exchangeability	transferability	uncomplainingly	presentationist
excommunication	transfiguration	uncomplimentary	preservationist
excommunicative	transfigurement	uncomprehending	prestidigitator
excommunicatory	transgressively	unconditionally	prestigiousness
exemplification	transilluminate	unconsciousness	pretentiousness
exhibitionistic	transliteration	vicechamberlain	preternaturally
expeditiousness	transmutability	vicissitudinous	pseudepigraphic
experientialism	transparentness	hydrodynamicist	reestablishment
experientialist	transplantation	hydropathically	roentgenography
experimentalise	transpositional	hydrostatically	sleepingdraught
experimentalism	unaccommodating	indefeasibility	speakingtrumpet
experimentalist	weatherboarding	indefensibility	spectroscopical
experimentation	ambidexterously	indemnification	speculativeness
experimentative	arboriculturist	indeterminately	speechification
expressionistic	bibliographical	indetermination	spermatogenesis
extemporisation	hobbledehoyhood	indeterministic	spermatogenetic
exteriorisation	subordinateness	indigestibility	stereochemistry
externalisation	subpostmistress	indisciplinable	stereoisomerism
extracurricular	substantialness	indissolubility	therapeutically
extraillustrate	substantiveness	indistinctively	therianthropism
extraordinarily	substitutionary	individualistic	thermochemistry

treacherousness	palaeogeography	immunochemistry	rontgenotherapy
treasonableness	palaeographical	numismatologist	sanctimoniously
unexceptionable	palaeomagnetism	remonstratively	sententiousness
unexceptionably	palaeontologist	remorselessness	singleheartedly
unexceptionally	polycrystalline	romanticisation	synchronisation
affranchisement	polyunsaturated	semiconsciously	tendentiousness
defencelessness	pulchritudinous	semicylindrical	ventriloquially
differentiation	selfabandonment	semidocumentary	ventriloquistic
efficaciousness	selfaffirmation	semiindependent	venturesomeness
enfranchisement	selfapprobation	semitransparent	apocalyptically
infinitesimally	selfcastigation	symmetricalness	bioastronautics
inflammableness	selfcentredness	sympathetically	biogeochemistry
infrangibleness	selfcomplacency	symptomatically	biogeographical
infundibuliform	selfconfidently	temperamentally	bioluminescence
softheartedness	selfconsciously	tempestuousness	bloodguiltiness
argumentatively	selfconsequence	annihilationism	broadmindedness
lightheadedness	selfconsistency	cinematographer	crossopterygian
lightmindedness	selfconstituted	cinematographic	geochronologist
logarithmically	selfcontainment	conceivableness	geomorphologist
logographically	selfdeprecating	conceptualistic	inoffensiveness
magnetoelectric	selfdeprecatory	condescendingly	inopportuneness
regionalisation	selfdestruction	confessionalism	odoriferousness
righthandedness	selfdestructive	confessionalist	phonautographic
rightmindedness	selfdetermining	confidentiality	phosphorescence
significatively	selfdevelopment	configurational	phosphorylation
achondroplastic	selfdistrustful	congratulations	photochemically
atherosclerosis	selfexamination	conjunctionally	photoconducting
atherosclerotic	selfexplanatory	connoisseurship	photoconductive
echinodermatous	selffertilising	conscientiously	photoelectronic
etherealisation	selfforgetfully	consecutiveness	photojournalism
ethnocentricity	selffulfillment	consentaneously	photojournalist
exhibitionistic	selfgratulation	consequentially	photolithograph
ophthalmologist	selfhumiliation	conservationist	photomechanical
ophthalmoscopic	selfimprovement	considerateness	photomicrograph
schistosomiasis	selfindulgently	conspicuousness	photosensitiser
schoolmastering	selfopinionated	constructionism	photosynthesise
abiogenetically	selfpollination	constructionist	phototelegraphy
anisotropically	selfpropagating	consubstantiate	problematically
Aristotelianism	selfrealisation	contemplatively	processionalist
coinstantaneous	selfregistering	contemporaneity	procrastination
episcopalianism	selfreplicating	contemporaneous	professionalise
epistemological	selfreproachful	contemptibility	professionalism
epitheliomatous	selfreprovingly	contentiousness	prognostication
flibbertigibbet	selfrighteously	contractability	prognosticative
neighbourliness	selfsacrificing	contractibility	progressiveness
opinionatedness	selfsufficiency	contradictorily	prohibitiveness
philanthropical	splendiferously	contravallation	properispomenon
philosophically	sulphureousness	controversially	proportionalist
quickwittedness	syllabification	conventionalise	proportionality
quinquagenarian	syllogistically	conventionalism	proportionately
quintuplication	telegraphically	conventionalist	prosenchymatous
trigonometrical	telephotography	conventionality	protozoological
trinitrotoluene	wellconditioned	conversationist	provocativeness
trisyllabically	wellintentioned	denitrification	rhombencephalon
unintelligently	atmospherically	fantasticalness	shootinggallery
unintentionally	commonplaceness	gentlemanliness	spontaneousness
injudiciousness	communalisation	gynandromorphic	stoicheiometric
acknowledgeable	communicability	hendecasyllabic	thoughtlessness
acknowledgement	communicatively	hendecasyllable	troublesomeness
ankylostomiasis	compartmentally	innumerableness	unobjectionable
chloramphenicol	compassionately	kindheartedness	wrongheadedness
coldbloodedness	compendiousness	longsightedness	zoogeographical
coldheartedness	competitiveness	manicdepressive	alphabetisation
collenchymatous	complementarily	manoeuvrability	amphitheatrical
deleteriousness	complementarity	miniaturisation	approachability
dolichocephalic	complicatedness	monosymmetrical	appropriateness
eclaircissement	compositionally	noncommissioned	approximatively
halfheartedness	comprehensively	noncontributory	departmentalise
heliotropically	compressibility	nongovernmental	departmentalism
Hellenistically	computerisation	noninterference	euphemistically
illimitableness	demagnetisation	nonintervention	expeditiousness
illustriousness	demonstrability	nonprofessional	experientialism
malacopterygian	demonstrational	nonprofitmaking	experientialist
maldistribution	demonstratively	nonsensicalness	experimentalise
malpractitioner	demystification	omnidirectional	experimentalism
mellifluousness	familiarisation	ornithorhynchus	experimentalist
multitudinously	homogeneousness	pantheistically	experimentation
palaeoanthropic	humanitarianism	penetrativeness	experimentative
palaeobotanical	immortalisation	punctiliousness	expressionistic

hypercatalectic	irresistibility	fissiparousness	intercollegiate
hypercritically	irreversibility	gastroenteritis	interconnection
hyperthyroidism	irrevocableness	historiographer	interdependence
impenetrability	jurisprudential	historiographic	interdependency
imperishability	margaritiferous	hospitalisation	interdigitation
impermeableness	marketgardening	inscrutableness	interfascicular
imponderability	meritoriousness	insensitiveness	interferometric
importunateness	meroblastically	inseparableness	interjectionary
impracticalness	morphologically	insignificantly	internalisation
imprescriptible	northeastwardly	instantaneously	internationally
impressionistic	northwestwardly	instructiveness	interpretership
improvisatorial	paradoxicalness	instrumentalism	interprovincial
Mephistophelean	parasympathetic	instrumentalist	interrogatively
Mephistophelian	parenthetically	instrumentality	interscholastic
opprobriousness	parliamentarian	instrumentation	interstratified
repetitiousness	parliamentarism	insubordination	interventionism
reproachfulness	parthenogenesis	insurrectionary	interventionist
reproducibility	parthenogenetic	insurrectionist	intolerableness
saprophytically	particularistic	misapprehension	intractableness
sophisticatedly	perfunctoriness	misapprehensive	introsusception
superabundantly	peripatetically	mischievousness	intussusception
superconducting	peristaltically	misconstruction	intussusceptive
superconductive	perpendicularly	mistrustfulness	materialisation
superficialness	personalisation	obstructiveness	metamathematics
superfluousness	personification	pessimistically	methamphetamine
superheterodyne	perspicaciously	postmillenarian	nationalisation
superimposition	perspicuousness	pusillanimously	notwithstanding
superincumbence	phrenologically	resourcefulness	ontogenetically
superinducement	purposelessness	respectableness	orthopsychiatry
superintendence	pyroelectricity	resurrectionism	pithecanthropus
superintendency	pyrotechnically	resurrectionist	rationalisation
superlativeness	serviceableness	sesquicentenary	retrogressively
supernaturalise	shrinkresistant	susceptibleness	retrospectively
supernaturalism	straightforward	systematisation	ritualistically
supernaturalist	stratigraphical	unsophisticated	totalitarianism
supersaturation	stretcherbearer	unsportsmanlike	ultracentrifuge
superstitiously	surreptitiously	unsubstantially	ultramicroscope
superstructural	unrealistically	unsymmetrically	churrigueresque
supplementarily	unrighteousness	vasoconstrictor	counterapproach
supplementation	vertiginousness	antepenultimate	counterattacker
supportableness	warmbloodedness	anthropocentric	counterirritant
suppositionally	warmheartedness	anthropogenesis	countermovement
topographically	warrantableness	anthropomorphic	counterplotting
typographically	cosmopolitanism	anthropopathism	doublebarrelled
unparliamentary	descriptiveness	anthropophagous	equalitarianism
unprecedentedly	desensitisation	anticlericalism	equiprobability
unprepossessing	desexualisation	antimonarchical	fourdimensional
unpretentiously	dessertspoonful	antisabbatarian	neurophysiology
acquisitiveness	destructibility	antitrinitarian	neuropsychiatry
inquisitiveness	destructiveness	antivivisection	plumbaginaceous
inquisitorially	disadvantageous	arterialisation	thunderstricken
unquestioningly	disaffectedness	authoritatively	trueheartedness
aerodynamically	disagreeability	autographically	trustworthiness
agriculturalist	disappointingly	autoradiography	adventurousness
airconditioning	disarticulation	determinateness	civilianisation
atrabiliousness	discommendation	detribalisation	developmentally
carnivorousness	disconcertingly	dithyrambically	devitrification
cerebrovascular	discontinuously	entrepreneurial	diversification
ceremoniousness	disenchantingly	extemporisation	governorgeneral
Christadelphian	disentanglement	exteriorisation	involuntariness
chromatographic	disgracefulness	externalisation	invulnerability
chronogrammatic	dishearteningly	extracurricular	levelheadedness
chronologically	disillusionment	extraillustrate	povertystricken
circumferential	disinflationary	extraordinarily	downheartedness
circumnavigator	disinterestedly	heterochromatic	unwholesomeness
circumscription	disorganisation	heterodactyloos	lexicographical
circumspectness	dispassionately	heterogeneously	cryptanalytical
circumstantiate	disproportional	heterosexuality	cryptocommunist
circumvallation	disreputability	intellectualise	crystallisation
correspondingly	disrespectfully	intellectualism	crystallography
dermatoglyphics	dissatisfaction	intellectualist	physicochemical
Europeanisation	dissatisfactory	intellectuality	physiographical
foresightedness	distastefulness	intelligibility	physiologically
formularisation	distinctiveness	intemperateness	physiotherapist
hardheartedness	distinguishable	intensification	phytogeographic
hermaphroditism	distinguishably	interchangeable	psychologically
hermeneutically	distrustfulness	interchangeably	psychometrician
irrationalistic	dyslogistically	interclavicular	psychopathology
irreparableness	fashionableness		psychophysicist

psychotherapist	electrophoresis	heterosexuality	unceremoniously
rhynchocephalia	electrophoretic	hypercatalectic	undemonstrative
trypanosomiasis	electropositive	hypercritically	underemployment
———————	geochronologist	hyperthyroidism	underestimation
atrabiliousness	inaccessibility	impenetrability	underprivileged
bioastronautics	inscrutableness	imperishability	underproduction
broadmindedness	mischievousness	impermeableness	understandingly
decalcification	misconstruction	indefeasibility	unrealistically
decarbonisation	noncommissioned	indefensibility	vicechamberlain
decarburisation	noncontributory	indemnification	confessionalism
demagnetisation	practicableness	indeterminately	confessionalist
departmentalise	precipitousness	indetermination	confidentiality
departmentalism	processionalist	indeterministic	configurational
disadvantageous	procrastination	insensitiveness	differentiation
disaffectedness	psychologically	inseparableness	halfheartedness
disagreeability	psychometrician	intellectualise	ineffaceability
disappointingly	psychopathology	intellectualism	ineffectiveness
disarticulation	psychophysicist	intellectualist	ineffectualness
eclaircissement	psychotherapist	intellectuality	inefficaciously
equalitarianism	pulchritudinous	intelligibility	inoffensiveness
greatgrandchild	punctiliousness	intemperateness	perfunctoriness
gynandromorphic	quickwittedness	intensification	professionalise
humanitarianism	sanctimoniously	interchangeable	professionalism
incalculability	spectroscopical	interchangeably	reafforestation
irrationalistic	speculativeness	interclavicular	selfabandonment
logarithmically	susceptibleness	intercollegiate	selfaffirmation
malacopterygian	synchronisation	interconnection	selfapprobation
metamathematics	unaccommodating	interdependence	selfcastigation
misapprehension	coldbloodedness	interdependency	selfcentredness
misapprehensive	coldheartedness	interdigitation	selfcomplacency
oceanographical	condescendingly	interfascicular	selfconfidently
palaeoanthropic	hardheartedness	interferometric	selfconsciously
palaeobotanical	hendecasyllabic	interjectionary	selfconsequence
palaeogeography	hendecasyllable	internalisation	selfconsistency
palaeographical	inadmissibility	internationally	selfconstituted
palaeomagnetism	kindheartedness	interpretership	selfcontainment
palaeontologist	maldistribution	interprovincial	selfdeprecating
paradoxicalness	predeterminable	interrogatively	selfdeprecatory
parasympathetic	quadruplication	interscholastic	selfdestruction
pleasurableness	stadtholdership	interstratified	selfdestructive
romanticisation	tendentiousness	interventionism	selfdetermining
speakingtrumpet	adventurousness	interventionist	selfdevelopment
straightforward	anaesthesiology	irreparableness	selfdistrustful
stratigraphical	anaesthetically	irresistibility	selfexamination
totalitarianism	antepenultimate	irreversibility	selfexplanatory
treacherousness	arterialisation	irrevocableness	selffertilising
treasonableness	atherosclerosis	levelheadedness	selfforgetfully
unparliamentary	atherosclerotic	materialisation	selffulfillment
doublebarrelled	cerebrovascular	necessitousness	selfgratulation
flibbertigibbet	ceremoniousness	parenthetically	selfhumiliation
hobbledehoyhood	cinematographer	penetrativeness	selfimprovement
problematically	cinematographic	phrenologically	selfindulgently
unobjectionable	defencelessness	povertystricken	selfopinionated
airconditioning	deleteriousness	repetitiousness	selfpollination
apocalyptically	desensitisation	sleepingdraught	selfpropagating
brachistochrone	desexualisation	speechification	selfrealisation
brachycephalous	determinateness	splendiferously	selfregistering
brachydactylous	developmentally	stretcherbearer	selfreplicating
circumferential	disenchantingly	superabundantly	selfreproachful
circumnavigator	disentanglement	superconducting	selfreprovingly
circumscription	diversification	superconductive	selfrighteously
circumspectness	encephalography	superficialness	selfsacrificing
circumstantiate	etherealisation	superfluousness	selfsufficiency
circumvallation	expeditiousness	superheterodyne	biogeochemistry
conceivableness	experientialism	superimposition	biogeographical
conceptualistic	experientialist	superincumbence	congratulations
Czechoslovakian	experimentalise	superinducement	disgracefulness
descriptiveness	experimentalism	superintendence	fragmentariness
discommendation	experimentalist	superintendency	imaginativeness
disconcertingly	experimentation	superlativeness	longsightedness
discontinuously	experimentative	supernaturalise	margaritiferous
electrification	extemporisation	supernaturalism	neighbourliness
electroanalysis	exteriorisation	supernaturalist	nongovernmental
electrochemical	externalisation	supersaturation	prognostication
electrodynamics	foresightedness	superstitiously	prognosticative
electrokinetics	governorgeneral	superstructural	progressiveness
electromagnetic	heterochromatic	telegraphically	singleheartedly
electromyograph	heterodactyloos	telephotography	trigonometrical
electronegative	heterogeneously	trueheartedness	zoogeographical

alphabetisation	radiogoniometer	phenomenologist	reconcilability
amphitheatrical	radiotelegraphy	phenylketonuria	reconsideration
anthropocentric	rationalisation	phonautographic	reconsolidation
anthropogenesis	regionalisation	plenipotentiary	remonstratively
anthropological	rudimentariness	quinquagenarian	remorselessness
anthropomorphic	schistosomiasis	quintuplication	resourcefulness
anthropopathism	semiconsciously	rhynchocephalia	sadomasochistic
anthropophagous	semicylindrical	roentgenography	schoolmastering
archiepiscopate	semidocumentary	significatively	shootinggallery
architecturally	semiindependent	spontaneousness	subordinateness
authoritatively	semitransparent	standardisation	sycophantically
dishearteningly	shrinkresistant	standoffishness	topographically
dithyrambically	socialistically	thunderstricken	typographically
euphemistically	sociolinguistic	transcriptional	uncommunicative
exchangeability	stoicheiometric	transferability	uncomplainingly
fashionableness	unrighteousness	transfiguration	uncomplimentary
lightheadedness	vicissitudinous	transfigurement	uncomprehending
lightmindedness	conjunctionally	transgressively	unconditionally
mechanistically	lackadaisically	transilluminate	unconsciousness
Mephistophelean	marketgardening	transliteration	unsophisticated
Mephistophelian	acclimatisation	transmutability	vasoconstrictor
methamphetamine	bibliographical	transparentness	compartmentally
orthopsychiatry	bioluminescence	transplantation	compassionately
pithecanthropus	collenchymatous	transpositional	compendiousness
prehistorically	dyslogistically	trinitrotoluene	competitiveness
prohibitiveness	ecclesiasticism	unintelligently	complementarily
righthandedness	ecclesiological	unintentionally	complementarity
rightmindedness	Hellenistically	wrongheadedness	complicatedness
sophisticatedly	inflammableness	abiogenetically	compositionally
technologically	mellifluousness	accommodatingly	comprehensively
unchallengeable	parliamentarian	accountableness	compressibility
unchangeability	parliamentarism	achondroplastic	computerisation
unwholesomeness	philanthropical	aerodynamically	cryptanalytical
agriculturalist	philosophically	arboriculturist	cryptocommunist
ambidexterously	syllabification	atmospherically	dispassionately
annihilationism	syllogistically	autographically	disproportional
anticlericalism	wellconditioned	autoradiography	hospitalisation
antimonarchical	wellintentioned	bloodguiltiness	inapplicability
antisabbatarian	blameworthiness	chloramphenicol	inapprehensible
antitrinitarian	commonplaceness	chromatographic	inappropriately
antivivisection	communalisation	chronogrammatic	inopportuneness
Christadelphian	communicability	chronologically	malpractitioner
civilianisation	communicatively	coconsciousness	morphologically
denitrification	cosmopolitanism	decolourisation	nonprofessional
devitrification	dermatoglyphics	decontamination	nonprofitmaking
disillusionment	dramaturgically	demonstrability	perpendicularly
disinflationary	exemplification	demonstrational	prepositionally
disinterestedly	formularisation	demonstratively	prepossessingly
dolichocephalic	geomorphologist	disorganisation	properispomenon
echinodermatous	hermaphroditism	Europeanisation	proportionalist
efficaciousness	hermeneutically	excommunication	proportionality
equiprobability	plumbaginaceous	excommunicative	proportionately
exhibitionistic	rhombencephalon	excommunicatory	purposelessness
familiarisation	stampcollecting	homogeneousness	reapportionment
gleichschaltung	symmetricalness	ideographically	respectableness
heliotropically	warmbloodedness	immortalisation	subpostmistress
illimitableness	warmheartedness	imponderability	sulphureousness
indigestibility	acanthocephalan	importunateness	supplementarily
indisciplinable	acknowledgeable	incommensurable	supplementation
indissolubility	acknowledgement	incommensurably	supportableness
indistinctively	carnivorousness	incommunicative	suppositionally
individualistic	coinstantaneous	incomparability	sympathetically
infinitesimally	connoisseurship	incompatibility	symptomatically
insignificantly	counterapproach	incomprehension	temperamentally
jurisprudential	counterattacker	incongruousness	tempestuousness
lexicographical	counterirritant	inconsequential	trypanosomiasis
manicdepressive	countermovement	inconsiderately	unsportsmanlike
meritoriousness	counterplotting	inconsideration	sesquicentenary
miniaturisation	downheartedness	inconspicuously	affranchisement
nationalisation	emancipationist	incorrigibility	Americanisation
noninterference	enantiomorphism	intolerableness	approachability
nonintervention	enantiomorphous	involuntariness	appropriateness
numismatologist	ethnocentricity	logographically	approximatively
omnidirectional	frenchification	manoeuvrability	churrigueresque
ornithorhynchus	grandiloquently	meroblastically	correspondingly
peripatetically	magnetoelectric	monosymmetrical	detribalisation
peristaltically	openheartedness	ontogenetically	disreputability
pusillanimously	opinionatedness	pyroelectricity	disrespectfully
radioautography	phenomenalistic	pyrotechnically	enfranchisement

entrepreneurial	personification	phytogeographic	extracurricular
everlastingness	perspicaciously	picturepostcard	extraillustrate
expressionistic	perspicuousness	picturesqueness	extraordinarily
extracurricular	pessimistically	platitudinarian	fantasticalness
extraillustrate	phosphorescence	postmillenarian	hermaphroditism
extraordinarily	phosphorylation	pretentiousness	impracticalness
fourdimensional	physicochemical	preternaturally	inflammableness
heartbreakingly	physiographical	protozoological	infrangibleness
hydrodynamicist	physiologically	quatercentenary	instantaneously
hydropathically	physiotherapist	rontgenotherapy	intractableness
hydrostatically	Presbyterianise	sententiousness	lackadaisically
impracticalness	Presbyterianism	softheartedness	margaritiferous
imprescriptible	presentationism	subterraneously	mechanistically
impressionistic	presentationist	systematisation	methamphetamine
improvisatorial	preservationist	ventriloquially	miniaturisation
infrangibleness	prestidigitator	ventriloquistic	philanthropical
intractableness	prestigiousness	venturesomeness	phonautographic
introsusception	prosenchymatous	vertiginousness	PreRaphaelitism
macroscopically	reestablishment	weatherboarding	ritualistically
microanalytical	substantialness	acquisitiveness	selfabandonment
micromillimetre	substantiveness	argumentatively	selfaffirmation
microphotograph	substitutionary	illustriousness	selfapprobation
microsporangium	substratosphere	immunochemistry	socialistically
microsporophyll	trisyllabically	indubitableness	syllabification
nearsightedness	trustworthiness	infundibuliform	sympathetically
necromantically	bacteriological	injudiciousness	therapeutically
neurophysiology	contemplatively	innumerableness	trypanosomiasis
neuropsychiatry	contemporaneity	inquisitiveness	ultracentrifuge
odoriferousness	contemporaneous	inquisitorially	ultramicroscope
opprobriousness	contemptibility	insubordination	unchallengeable
overconfidently	contentiousness	insurrectionary	unchangeability
overdevelopment	contractability	insurrectionist	unrealistically
pharisaicalness	contractibility	intussusception	warrantableness
pharmacological	contradictorily	intussusceptive	atrabiliousness
PreRaphaelitism	contravallation	invulnerability	cerebrovascular
quarrelsomeness	controversially	pleuropneumonia	coldbloodedness
quarterfinalist	destructibility	pneumatological	exhibitionistic
reproachfulness	destructiveness	pseudepigraphic	flibbertigibbet
reproducibility	distastefulness	resurrectionism	indubitableness
retrogressively	distinctiveness	resurrectionist	insubordination
retrospectively	distinguishable	ritualistically	meroblastically
saprophytically	distinguishably	suburbanisation	plumbaginaceous
spermatogenesis	distrustfulness	thoughtlessness	Presbyterianise
spermatogenetic	epitheliomatous	troublesomeness	Presbyterianism
stereochemistry	fantasticalness	unquestioningly	rhombencephalon
stereoisomerism	gastroenteritis	unsubstantially	troublesomeness
surreptitiously	gentlemanliness	conventionalise	unsubstantially
therapeutically	historiographer	conventionalism	warmbloodedness
therianthropism	historiographic	conventionalist	agriculturalist
thermochemistry	inattentiveness	conventionality	anticlericalism
ultracentrifuge	instantaneously	conversationist	conscientiously
ultramicroscope	instructiveness	provocativeness	dolichocephalic
unprecedentedly	instrumentalism	serviceableness	efficaciousness
unprepossessing	instrumentalist	notwithstanding	emancipationist
unpretentiously	instrumentality	inexcusableness	episcopalianism
warrantableness	instrumentation	inexpensiveness	frenchification
anisotropically	mistrustfulness	inexplicability	gleichschaltung
Aristotelianism	multitudinously	unexceptionable	inaccessibility
conscientiously	northeastwardly	unexceptionably	inexcusableness
consecutiveness	northwestwardly	unexceptionally	lexicographical
consentaneously	obstructiveness	ankylostomiasis	malacopterygian
consequentially	ophthalmologist	demystification	manicdepressive
conservationist	ophthalmoscopic	polycrystalline	overconfidently
considerateness	pantheistically	polyunsaturated	polycrystalline
conspicuousness	parthenogenesis	unsymmetrically	rhynchocephalia
constructionism	parthenogenetic	———————————————	selfcastigation
constructionist	particularistic	affranchisement	selfcentredness
consubstantiate	photochemically	alphabetisation	selfcomplacency
crossopterygian	photoconducting	apocalyptically	selfconfidently
crystallisation	photoconductive	compartmentally	selfconsciously
crystallography	photoelectronic	compassionately	selfconsequence
dessertspoonful	photojournalism	dermatoglyphics	selfconsistency
dissatisfaction	photojournalist	dispassionately	selfconstituted
dissatisfactory	photolithograph	dissatisfaction	selfcontainment
episcopalianism	photomechanical	dissatisfactory	semiconsciously
epistemological	photomicrograph	distastefulness	semicylindrical
fissiparousness	photosensitiser	dramaturgically	speechification
nonsensicalness	photosynthesise	enfranchisement	stoicheiometric
personalisation	phototelegraphy	exchangeability	treacherousness

unaccommodating	palaeobotanical	hardheartedness	vertiginousness
unexceptionable	palaeogeography	kindheartedness	wellintentioned
unexceptionably	palaeographical	mischievousness	unobjectionable
unexceptionally	palaeomagnetism	morphologically	quickwittedness
vasoconstrictor	palaeontologist	neighbourliness	speakingtrumpet
vicechamberlain	perpendicularly	northeastwardly	ankylostomiasis
wellconditioned	pithecanthropus	northwestwardly	civilianisation
aerodynamically	predeterminable	openheartedness	complementarily
ambidexterously	presentationism	ophthalmologist	complementarity
bloodguiltiness	presentationist	ophthalmoscopic	complicatedness
broadmindedness	preservationist	pantheistically	decalcification
disadvantageous	pretentiousness	parthenogenesis	decolourisation
expeditiousness	preternaturally	parthenogenetic	developmentally
fourdimensional	processionalist	psychologically	disillusionment
grandiloquently	professionalise	psychometrician	doublebarrelled
injudiciousness	professionalism	psychopathology	equalitarianism
omnidirectional	properispomenon	psychophysicist	everlastingness
overdevelopment	prosenchymatous	psychotherapist	familiarisation
paradoxicalness	pyroelectricity	pulchritudinous	gentlemanliness
pseudepigraphic	quatercentenary	selfhumiliation	hobbledehoyhood
selfdeprecating	respectableness	softheartedness	incalculability
selfdeprecatory	selfexamination	sulphureousness	intellectualise
selfdestruction	selfexplanatory	synchronisation	intellectualism
selfdestructive	sententiousness	trueheartedness	intellectualist
selfdetermining	stereochemistry	warmheartedness	intellectuality
selfdevelopment	stereoisomerism	weatherboarding	intelligibility
selfdistrustful	subterraneously	acclimatisation	intolerableness
semidocumentary	surreptitiously	acquisitiveness	involuntariness
standardisation	susceptibleness	Americanisation	invulnerability
standoffishness	symmetricalness	amphitheatrical	levelheadedness
thunderstricken	systematisation	archiepiscopate	problematically
bacteriological	temperamentally	architecturally	pusillanimously
biogeochemistry	tempestuousness	bibliographical	singleheartedly
biogeographical	tendentiousness	carnivorousness	supplementarily
blameworthiness	unprecedentedly	confidentiality	supplementation
collenchymatous	unprepossessing	configurational	totalitarianism
compendiousness	unpretentiously	considerateness	accommodatingly
competitiveness	unquestioningly	detribalisation	antimonarchical
conceivableness	zoogeographical	distinctiveness	argumentatively
conceptualistic	disaffectedness	distinguishable	ceremoniousness
condescendingly	indefeasibility	distinguishably	chromatographic
confessionalism	indefensibility	eclaircissement	cinematographer
confessionalist	ineffaceability	fashionableness	cinematographic
consecutiveness	ineffectiveness	fissiparousness	excommunication
consentaneously	ineffectualness	hospitalisation	excommunicative
consequentially	inefficaciously	imaginativeness	excommunicatory
conservationist	inoffensiveness	inquisitiveness	extemporisation
contemplatively	reafforestation	inquisitorially	fragmentariness
contemporaneity	selffertilising	maldistribution	illimitableness
contemporaneous	selfforgetfully	mellifluousness	inadmissibility
contemptibility	selffulfillment	Mephistophelean	incommensurable
contentiousness	abiogenetically	Mephistophelian	incommensurably
conventionalise	autographically	multitudinously	incommunicative
conventionalism	demagnetisation	notwithstanding	incomparability
conventionalist	disagreeability	odoriferousness	incompatibility
conventionality	homogeneousness	opinionatedness	incomprehension
conversationist	ideographically	parliamentarian	indemnification
correspondingly	indigestibility	parliamentarism	innumerableness
dessertspoonful	insignificantly	particularistic	intemperateness
differentiation	logographically	pessimistically	metamathematics
dishearteningly	ontogenetically	pharisaicalness	pharmacological
disreputability	rontgenotherapy	physicochemical	pneumatological
disrespectfully	selfgratulation	physiographical	postmillenarian
ecclesiasticism	telegraphically	physiologically	rudimentariness
ecclesiological	thoughtlessness	physiotherapist	sadomasochistic
entrepreneurial	topographically	platitudinarian	spermatogenesis
euphemistically	typographically	plenipotentiary	spermatogenetic
expressionistic	unrighteousness	precipitousness	thermochemistry
Hellenistically	wrongheadedness	prehistorically	uncommunicative
hendecasyllabic	annihilationism	prohibitiveness	uncomplainingly
hendecasyllable	brachistochrone	selfimprovement	uncomplimentary
hermeneutically	brachycephalous	selfindulgently	uncomprehending
imprescriptible	brachydactylous	semiindependent	undemonstrative
impressionistic	coldheartedness	serviceableness	unsymmetrically
magnetoelectric	Czechoslovakian	significatively	achondroplastic
manoeuvrability	downheartedness	sophisticatedly	adventurousness
marketgardening	epitheliomatous	straightforward	chronogrammatic
nonsensicalness	geochronologist	therianthropism	chronologically
palaeoanthropic	halfheartedness	trinitrotoluene	coconsciousness

decontamination	noncommissioned	telephotography	interferometric
defencelessness	noncontributory	unsophisticated	interjectionary
demonstrability	nongovernmental	quinquagenarian	internalisation
demonstrational	opprobriousness	anthropocentric	internationally
demonstratively	orthopsychiatry	anthropogenesis	interpretership
desensitisation	personalisation	anthropological	interprovincial
disenchantingly	personification	anthropomorphic	interrogatively
disentanglement	phenomenalistic	anthropopathism	interscholastic
disinflationary	phenomenologist	anthropophagous	interstratified
disinterestedly	philosophically	arboriculturist	interventionism
echinodermatous	photochemically	arterialisation	interventionist
gynandromorphic	photoconducting	atherosclerosis	logarithmically
humanitarianism	photoconductive	atherosclerotic	malpractitioner
immunochemistry	photoelectronic	autoradiography	materialisation
impenetrability	photojournalism	chloramphenicol	mistrustfulness
imponderability	photojournalist	churrigueresque	nonprofessional
incongruousness	photolithograph	comprehensively	nonprofitmaking
inconsequential	photomechanical	compressibility	obstructiveness
inconsiderately	photomicrograph	congratulations	pleuropneumonia
inconsideration	photosensitiser	contractability	povertystricken
inconspicuously	photosynthesise	contractibility	procrastination
infinitesimally	phototelegraphy	contradictorily	progressiveness
infundibuliform	phytogeographic	contravallation	quadruplication
insensitiveness	prepositionally	controversially	quarrelsomeness
intensification	prepossessingly	decarbonisation	remorselessness
noninterference	proportionalist	decarburisation	resurrectionism
nonintervention	proportionality	departmentalise	resurrectionist
oceanographical	proportionately	departmentalism	selfrealisation
parenthetically	protozoological	descriptiveness	selfregistering
phrenologically	provocativeness	destructibility	selfreplicating
prognostication	purposelessness	destructiveness	selfreproachful
prognosticative	radioautography	determinateness	selfreprovingly
reconcilability	radiogoniometer	disarticulation	selfrighteously
reconsideration	radiotelegraphy	disgracefulness	subordinateness
reconsolidation	rationalisation	disorganisation	suburbanisation
remonstratively	regionalisation	disproportional	superabundantly
romanticisation	reproachfulness	distrustfulness	superconducting
shrinkresistant	reproducibility	diversification	superconductive
splendiferously	retrogressively	etherealisation	superficialness
technologically	retrospectively	experientialism	superfluousness
unconditionally	saprophytically	experientialist	superheterodyne
unconsciousness	schoolmastering	experimentalise	superimposition
acknowledgeable	selfopinionated	experimentalism	superincumbence
acknowledgement	sociolinguistic	experimentalist	superinducement
airconditioning	subpostmistress	experimentation	superintendence
anisotropically	supportableness	experimentative	superintendency
approachability	suppositionally	exteriorisation	superlativeness
appropriateness	syllogistically	externalisation	supernaturalise
approximatively	trigonometrical	gastroenteritis	supernaturalism
authoritatively	unsportsmanlike	governorgeneral	supernaturalist
commonplaceness	unwholesomeness	heterochromatic	supersaturation
compositionally	antepenultimate	heterodactyloos	superstitiously
connoisseurship	conspicuousness	heterogeneously	superstructural
cosmopolitanism	disappointingly	heterosexuality	unceremoniously
discommendation	encephalography	hypercatalectic	underemployment
disconcertingly	equiprobability	hypercritically	underestimation
discontinuously	Europeanisation	hyperthyroidism	underprivileged
dyslogistically	exemplification	immortalisation	underproduction
ethnocentricity	inapplicability	imperishability	understandingly
geomorphologist	inapprehensible	impermeableness	unparliamentary
heliotropically	inappropriately	importunateness	ventriloquially
historiographer	inexpensiveness	incorrigibility	ventriloquistic
historiographic	inexplicability	inscrutableness	anaesthesiology
hydrodynamicist	inopportuneness	instructiveness	anaesthetically
hydropathically	inseparableness	instrumentalism	antisabbatarian
hydrostatically	irreparableness	instrumentalist	atmospherically
improvisatorial	misapprehension	instrumentality	bioastronautics
introsusception	misapprehensive	instrumentation	Christadelphian
macroscopically	peripatetically	insurrectionary	coinstantaneous
microanalytical	perspicaciously	insurrectionist	crossopterygian
micromillimetre	perspicuousness	interchangeable	demystification
microphotograph	phosphorescence	interchangeably	foresightedness
microsporangium	phosphorylation	interclavicular	illustriousness
microsporophyll	reapportionment	intercollegiate	indisciplinable
misconstruction	selfpollination	interconnection	indissolubility
nationalisation	selfpropagating	interdependence	indistinctively
necromantically	sleepingdraught	interdependency	intussusception
neurophysiology	stampcollecting	interdigitation	intussusceptive
neuropsychiatry	sycophantically	interfascicular	irresistibility

jurisprudential	roentgenography	pharmacological	reproducibility
longsightedness	sanctimoniously	plumbaginaceous	splendiferously
monosymmetrical	semitransparent	pneumatological	subordinateness
nearsightedness	shootinggallery	procrastination	unconditionally
necessitousness	spectroscopical	radioautography	abiogenetically
numismatologist	spontaneousness	reestablishment	ambidexterously
parasympathetic	stadtholdership	reproachfulness	antepenultimate
peristaltically	stratigraphical	sadomasochistic	archiepiscopate
pleasurableness	stretcherbearer	selfcastigation	argumentatively
schistosomiasis	substantialness	selfsacrificing	coldheartedness
selfsacrificing	substantiveness	spermatogenesis	complementarily
selfsufficiency	substitutionary	spermatogenetic	complementarity
transcriptional	substratosphere	spontaneousness	comprehensively
transferability	symptomatically	standardisation	compressibility
transfiguration	trustworthiness	substantialness	counterapproach
transfigurement	unintelligently	substantiveness	counterattacker
transgressively	unintentionally	superabundantly	counterirritant
transilluminate	accountableness	therianthropism	countermovement
transliteration	bioluminescence	alphabetisation	counterplotting
transmutability	circumferential	consubstantiate	deleteriousness
transparentness	circumnavigator	decarbonisation	doublebarrelled
transplantation	circumscription	decarburisation	downheartedness
transpositional	circumspectness	detribalisation	epistemological
treasonableness	circumstantiate	heartbreakingly	epitheliomatous
vicissitudinous	circumvallation	neighbourliness	etherealisation
acanthocephalan	communalisation	opprobriousness	Europeanisation
antitrinitarian	communicability	prohibitiveness	flibbertigibbet
Aristotelianism	communicatively	selfabandonment	fragmentariness
constructionism	computerisation	suburbanisation	gentlemanliness
constructionist	conjunctionally	syllabification	halfheartedness
counterapproach	consubstantiate	Americanisation	hardheartedness
counterattacker	formularisation	consecutiveness	hobbledehoyhood
counterirritant	perfunctoriness	decalcification	homogeneousness
countermovement	picturepostcard	defencelessness	impenetrability
counterplotting	picturesqueness	disenchantingly	inaccessibility
cryptanalytical	polyunsaturated	ethnocentricity	inattentiveness
cryptocommunist	resourcefulness	extracurricular	indefeasibility
crystallisation	sesquicentenary	hendecasyllabic	indefensibility
crystallography	speculativeness	hendecasyllable	indeterminately
deleteriousness	venturesomeness	hypercatalectic	indetermination
denitrification	antivivisection	hypercritically	indeterministic
devitrification	individualistic	impracticalness	indigestibility
electrification	irreversibility	incalculability	ineffectiveness
electroanalysis	irrevocableness	indisciplinable	ineffectualness
electrochemical	desexualisation	interchangeable	inexpensiveness
electrodynamics	dithyrambically	interchangeably	innumerableness
electrokinetics	phenylketonuria	interclavicular	inoffensiveness
electromagnetic	trisyllabically	intercollegiate	intolerableness
electromyograph	───────────────	interconnection	irreversibility
electronegative	antisabbatarian	intractableness	kindheartedness
electrophoresis	approachability	particularistic	northeastwardly
electrophoretic	autoradiography	photochemically	ontogenetically
electropositive	chloramphenicol	photoconducting	openheartedness
enantiomorphism	chromatographic	photoconductive	overdevelopment
enantiomorphous	cinematographer	physicochemical	pantheistically
epistemological	cinematographic	pithecanthropus	parthenogenesis
greatgrandchild	congratulations	provocativeness	parthenogenetic
heartbreakingly	contractability	reconcilability	photoelectronic
inattentiveness	contractibility	respectableness	problematically
indeterminately	contradictorily	serviceableness	progressiveness
indetermination	contravallation	stampcollecting	pseudepigraphic
indeterministic	cryptanalytical	stretcherbearer	pyrotechnically
irrationalistic	crystallisation	superconducting	quarrelsomeness
lightheadedness	crystallography	superconductive	quarterfinalist
lightmindedness	disgracefulness	transcriptional	rhombencephalon
meritoriousness	dishearteningly	ultracentrifuge	rontgenotherapy
ornithorhynchus	efficaciousness	unprecedentedly	rudimentariness
penetrativeness	everlastingness	achondroplastic	selfcentredness
practicableness	ineffaceability	confidentiality	selfdeprecating
prestidigitator	inseparableness	considerateness	selfdeprecatory
prestigiousness	irreparableness	gynandromorphic	selfdestruction
punctiliousness	malpractitioner	hydrodynamicist	selfdestructive
pyrotechnically	metamathematics	imponderability	selfdetermining
quarterfinalist	microanalytical	infundibuliform	selfdevelopment
quintuplication	ophthalmologist	interdependence	selffertilising
reestablishment	ophthalmoscopic	interdependency	selfrealisation
repetitiousness	parliamentarian	interdigitation	selfregistering
righthandedness	parliamentarism	lackadaisically	selfreplicating
rightmindedness	peripatetically	manicdepressive	selfreproachful

selfreprovingly	connoisseurship	intellectualism	conventionalism
singleheartedly	conscientiously	intellectualist	conventionalist
softheartedness	conspicuousness	intellectuality	conventionality
supplementarily	descriptiveness	intelligibility	demagnetisation
supplementation	emancipationist	meroblastically	disconcertingly
thunderstricken	enantiomorphism	phenylketonuria	discontinuously
trueheartedness	enantiomorphous	photolithograph	distinctiveness
unceremoniously	equalitarianism	pusillanimously	distinguishable
underemployment	exhibitionistic	pyroelectricity	distinguishably
underestimation	expeditiousness	ritualistically	enfranchisement
unexceptionable	experientialism	schoolmastering	exchangeability
unexceptionably	experientialist	socialistically	externalisation
unexceptionally	experimentalise	sociolinguistic	governorgeneral
unintelligently	experimentalism	speculativeness	Hellenistically
unintentionally	experimentalist	superlativeness	hermeneutically
unobjectionable	experimentation	transliteration	imaginativeness
warmheartedness	experimentative	trisyllabically	indemnification
weatherboarding	exteriorisation	troublesomeness	infrangibleness
disaffectedness	extraillustrate	unchallengeable	insignificantly
disinflationary	familiarisation	unparliamentary	instantaneously
interfascicular	foresightedness	unrealistically	internalisation
interferometric	fourdimensional	unwholesomeness	internationally
mellifluousness	grandiloquently	warmbloodedness	invulnerability
odoriferousness	humanitarianism	acclimatisation	mechanistically
selfaffirmation	illimitableness	accommodatingly	misconstruction
significatively	imperishability	bioluminescence	nationalisation
superficialness	inadmissibility	broadmindedness	noncontributory
superfluousness	individualistic	circumferential	nonsensicalness
transferability	indubitableness	circumnavigator	perfunctoriness
transfiguration	inefficaciously	circumscription	perpendicularly
transfigurement	infinitesimally	circumspectness	personalisation
bloodguiltiness	injudiciousness	circumstantiate	personification
configurational	irrationalistic	circumvallation	philanthropical
disorganisation	irresistibility	contemplatively	polyunsaturated
dyslogistically	logarithmically	contemporaneity	presentationism
greatgrandchild	longsightedness	contemporaneous	presentationist
incongruousness	materialisation	contemptibility	pretentiousness
phytogeographic	mischievousness	determinateness	prosenchymatous
radiogoniometer	nearsightedness	discommendation	rationalisation
retrogressively	omnidirectional	euphemistically	regionalisation
roentgenography	perspicaciously	excommunication	selfindulgently
straightforward	perspicuousness	excommunicative	semiindependent
syllogistically	postmillenarian	excommunicatory	sententiousness
transgressively	practicableness	impermeableness	supernaturalise
vertiginousness	prestidigitator	incommensurable	supernaturalism
acanthocephalan	prestigiousness	incommensurably	supernaturalist
dolichocephalic	punctiliousness	incommunicative	tendentiousness
encephalography	repetitiousness	inflammableness	trigonometrical
frenchification	sanctimoniously	lightmindedness	trypanosomiasis
gleichschaltung	selfdistrustful	methamphetamine	unchangeability
levelheadedness	selfrighteously	micromillimetre	warrantableness
lightheadedness	sesquicentenary	necromantically	wellintentioned
ornithorhynchus	shootinggallery	noncommissioned	ankylostomiasis
phosphorescence	sleepingdraught	numismatologist	anthropocentric
phosphorylation	speakingtrumpet	pessimistically	anthropogenesis
rhynchocephalia	stratigraphical	phenomenalistic	anthropological
righthandedness	substitutionary	phenomenologist	anthropomorphic
speechification	superimposition	photomechanical	anthropopathism
stadtholdership	superincumbence	photomicrograph	anthropophagous
stoicheiometric	superinducement	rightmindedness	antimonarchical
superheterodyne	superintendence	selfimprovement	Aristotelianism
sycophantically	superintendency	systematisation	atherosclerosis
telephotography	totalitarianism	transmutability	atherosclerotic
thoughtlessness	transilluminate	ultramicroscope	bibliographical
treacherousness	ventriloquially	uncommunicative	biogeochemistry
unrighteousness	ventriloquistic	unsymmetrically	biogeographical
unsophisticated	interjectionary	accountableness	ceremoniousness
vicechamberlain	photojournalism	affranchisement	chronogrammatic
wrongheadedness	photojournalist	airconditioning	chronologically
annihilationism	shrinkresistant	collenchymatous	controversially
antivivisection	anticlericalism	commonplaceness	crossopterygian
arboriculturist	apocalyptically	communicability	cryptocommunist
arterialisation	coldbloodedness	communicatively	Czechoslovakian
atrabiliousness	disillusionment	compendiousness	decolourisation
brachistochrone	exemplification	conjunctionally	developmentally
churrigueresque	formularisation	consentaneously	disproportional
civilianisation	inapplicability	contentiousness	echinodermatous
complicatedness	inexplicability	conventionalise	episcopalianism
conceivableness	intellectualise	conventionalise	extraordinarily

fashionableness	interprovincial	pulchritudinous	sophisticatedly
gastroenteritis	jurisprudential	quatercentenary	subpostmistress
heterochromatic	microphotograph	resourcefulness	supersaturation
heterodactyloos	misapprehension	resurrectionism	superstitiously
heterogeneously	misapprehensive	resurrectionist	superstructural
heterosexuality	neurophysiology	selfgratulation	suppositionally
immunochemistry	neuropsychiatry	selfpropagating	tempestuousness
inopportuneness	orthopsychiatry	semitransparent	unconsciousness
insubordination	plenipotentiary	spectroscopical	understandingly
irrevocableness	precipitousness	substratosphere	unquestioningly
lexicographical	PreRaphaelitism	subterraneously	unsubstantially
malacopterygian	saprophytically	supportableness	vicissitudinous
meritoriousness	selfapprobation	synchronisation	adventurousness
morphologically	selfopinionated	telegraphically	amphitheatrical
nonprofessional	surreptitiously	temperamentally	anaesthesiology
nonprofitmaking	susceptibleness	topographically	anaesthetically
oceanographical	therapeutically	typographically	anisotropically
opinionatedness	transparentness	unsportsmanlike	architecturally
overconfidently	transplantation	venturesomeness	bioastronautics
palaeoanthropic	transpositional	acquisitiveness	Christadelphian
palaeobotanical	uncomplainingly	coconsciousness	coinstantaneous
palaeogeography	uncomplimentary	compassionately	competitiveness
palaeographical	uncomprehending	compositionally	computerisation
palaeomagnetism	underprivileged	condescendingly	decontamination
palaeontologist	underproduction	confessionalism	demystification
paradoxicalness	unprepossessing	confessionalist	departmentalise
phrenologically	consequentially	correspondingly	departmentalism
physiographical	antitrinitarian	demonstrability	dermatoglyphics
physiologically	authoritatively	demonstrational	disarticulation
physiotherapist	autographically	demonstratively	disentanglement
pleuropneumonia	bacteriological	desensitisation	disinterestedly
prognostication	cerebrovascular	dispassionately	dissatisfaction
prognosticative	compartmentally	disrespectfully	dissatisfactory
psychologically	conservationist	distastefulness	dramaturgically
psychometrician	constructionism	diversification	heliotropically
psychopathology	constructionist	ecclesiasticism	hospitalisation
psychophysicist	conversationist	ecclesiological	hyperthyroidism
psychotherapist	denitrification	expressionistic	illustriousness
reafforestation	dessertspoonful	fantasticalness	immortalisation
reapportionment	devitrification	hydrostatically	importunateness
selfcomplacency	differentiation	imprescriptible	indistinctively
selfconfidently	disagreeability	impressionistic	magnetoelectric
selfconsciously	dithyrambically	inconsequential	marketgardening
selfconsequence	eclaircissement	inconsiderately	miniaturisation
selfconsistency	electrification	inconsideration	multitudinously
selfconstituted	electroanalysis	inconspicuously	noninterference
selfcontainment	electrochemical	indissolubility	nonintervention
selfforgetfully	electrodynamics	inquisitiveness	notwithstanding
selfpollination	electrokinetics	inquisitorially	parenthetically
semiconsciously	electromagnetic	insensitiveness	peristaltically
semidocumentary	electromyograph	intensification	phototelegraphy
standoffishness	electronegative	interscholastic	platitudinarian
stereochemistry	electrophoresis	interstratified	povertystricken
stereoisomerism	electrophoretic	introsusception	predeterminable
symptomatically	electropositive	intussusception	radiotelegraphy
technologically	equiprobability	intussusceptive	romanticisation
thermochemistry	geochronologist	macroscopically	schistosomiasis
treasonableness	geomorphologist	maldistribution	symmetricalness
unaccommodating	historiographer	Mephistophelean	sympathetically
undemonstrative	historiographic	Mephistophelian	trinitrotoluene
vasoconstrictor	ideographically	microsporangium	unpretentiously
wellconditioned	inapprehensible	microsporophyll	agriculturalist
zoogeographical	inappropriately	necessitousness	desexualisation
appropriateness	incorrigibility	pharisaicalness	destructibility
atmospherically	insurrectionary	philosophically	destructiveness
conceptualistic	insurrectionist	photosensitiser	distrustfulness
cosmopolitanism	interrogatively	photosynthesise	inexcusableness
disappointingly	logographically	prehistorically	inscrutableness
disreputability	margaritiferous	prepositionally	instructiveness
entrepreneurial	penetrativeness	prepossessingly	instrumentalism
extemporisation	picturepostcard	processionalist	instrumentalist
fissiparousness	picturesqueness	professionalise	instrumentality
hermaphroditism	polycrystalline	professionalism	instrumentation
hydropathically	preservationist	purposelessness	involuntariness
incomparability	preternaturally	reconsideration	manoeuvrability
incompatibility	properispomenon	reconsolidation	mistrustfulness
incomprehension	proportionalist	remonstratively	obstructiveness
intemperateness	proportionality	remorselessness	phonautographic
interpretership	proportionately	retrospectively	pleasurableness

quadruplication	northeastwardly	obstructiveness	phenomenologist
quinquagenarian	numismatologist	perfunctoriness	photomechanical
quintuplication	openheartedness	perspicaciously	photosensitiser
selffulfillment	palaeoanthropic	perspicuousness	phototelegraphy
selfhumiliation	penetrativeness	pharmacological	phytogeographic
selfsufficiency	peristaltically	practicableness	picturepostcard
sulphureousness	personalisation	prosenchymatous	picturesqueness
carnivorousness	pharisaicalness	pyrotechnically	predeterminable
disadvantageous	pithecanthropus	quatercentenary	purposelessness
improvisatorial	provocativeness	reproachfulness	pyroelectricity
interventionism	pusillanimously	resourcefulness	radiotelegraphy
interventionist	quinquagenarian	selfsacrificing	remorselessness
nongovernmental	rationalisation	semidocumentary	resurrectionism
acknowledgeable	regionalisation	sesquicentenary	resurrectionist
acknowledgement	righthandedness	stereochemistry	roentgenography
blameworthiness	selfabandonment	thermochemistry	serviceableness
northwestwardly	selfexamination	unconsciousness	stoicheiometric
quickwittedness	selfgratulation	unobjectionable	superheterodyne
trustworthiness	selfrealisation	airconditioning	therapeutically
approximatively	semitransparent	autoradiography	transferability
selfexamination	softheartedness	brachydactylous	treacherousness
selfexplanatory	speculativeness	compendiousness	troublesomeness
aerodynamically	substratosphere	contradictorily	ultracentrifuge
brachycephalous	suburbanisation	echinodermatous	unprecedentedly
brachydactylous	superlativeness	heterodactyloos	unpretentiously
monosymmetrical	supernaturalise	hobbledehoyhood	unsymmetrically
parasympathetic	supernaturalism	individualistic	unwholesomeness
Presbyterianise	supernaturalist	perpendicularly	venturesomeness
Presbyterianism	supersaturation	prestidigitator	wrongheadedness
semicylindrical	sycophantically	selfindulgently	circumferential
protozoological	systematisation	semiindependent	nonprofessional
———————————————	telegraphically	alphabetisation	nonprofitmaking
acclimatisation	temperamentally	anticlericalism	selfaffirmation
Americanisation	topographically	architecturally	selfsufficiency
arterialisation	transparentness	computerisation	standoffishness
autographically	trueheartedness	confidentiality	bibliographical
Christadelphian	typographically	conscientiously	biogeographical
civilianisation	vicechamberlain	considerateness	chronogrammatic
coinstantaneous	warmheartedness	defencelessness	churrigueresque
coldheartedness	antisabbatarian	demagnetisation	distinguishable
communalisation	doublebarrelled	differentiation	distinguishably
decontamination	palaeobotanical	disaffectedness	exchangeability
desexualisation	reestablishment	disagreeability	foresightedness
detribalisation	superabundantly	disinterestedly	heterogeneously
disadvantageous	affranchisement	ethnocentricity	infrangibleness
disentanglement	approachability	experientialism	lexicographical
disorganisation	arboriculturist	experientialist	longsightedness
dithyrambically	biogeochemistry	gastroenteritis	marketgardening
downheartedness	brachycephalous	hermeneutically	nearsightedness
encephalography	coconsciousness	impermeableness	oceanographical
etherealisation	collenchymatous	imponderability	palaeogeography
Europeanisation	complicatedness	inapprehensible	palaeographical
externalisation	condescendingly	incommensurable	physiographical
familiarisation	conjunctionally	incommensurably	plumbaginaceous
fissiparousness	conspicuousness	inconsequential	prestigiousness
formularisation	contractability	insurrectionary	selfregistering
halfheartedness	contractibility	insurrectionist	selfrighteously
hardheartedness	cryptocommunist	intellectualise	stratigraphical
hendecasyllabic	destructibility	intellectualism	unchangeability
hendecasyllable	destructiveness	intellectualist	zoogeographical
hospitalisation	disconcertingly	intellectuality	amphitheatrical
hydropathically	disgracefulness	intemperateness	anaesthesiology
hypercatalectic	distinctiveness	interdependence	anaesthetically
ideographically	eclaircissement	interdependency	atmospherically
imaginativeness	efficaciousness	interferometric	comprehensively
immortalisation	enfranchisement	interjectionary	disenchantingly
incomparability	heterochromatic	interventionism	hermaphroditism
incompatibility	immunochemistry	interventionist	hyperthyroidism
indefeasibility	imprescriptible	invulnerability	interchangeable
interfascicular	ineffaceability	levelheadedness	interchangeably
internalisation	ineffectiveness	lightheadedness	microphotograph
internationally	ineffectualness	manicdepressive	neurophysiology
kindheartedness	inefficaciously	mischievousness	notwithstanding
lackadaisically	injudiciousness	nongovernmental	parenthetically
logographically	instructiveness	noninterference	photochemically
materialisation	interscholastic	nonintervention	PreRaphaelitism
meroblastically	irrevocableness	northwestwardly	saprophytically
nationalisation	macroscopically	odoriferousness	singleheartedly
necromantically	malpractitioner	phenomenalistic	straightforward

stretcherbearer	superficialness	psychometrician	electromyograph
sympathetically	suppositionally	sanctimoniously	electronegative
acquisitiveness	syllabification	schoolmastering	electrophoresis
antitrinitarian	syllogistically	selfcomplacency	electrophoretic
approximatively	transfiguration	selfhumiliation	electropositive
authoritatively	transfigurement	superimposition	enantiomorphism
bacteriological	transliteration	supplementarily	enantiomorphous
bioluminescence	ultramicroscope	supplementation	equiprobability
broadmindedness	unconditionally	symptomatically	extemporisation
communicability	unparliamentary	unaccommodating	exteriorisation
communicatively	unrealistically	unceremoniously	geochronologist
competitiveness	unsophisticated	underemployment	governorgeneral
compositionally	vertiginousness	abiogenetically	inappropriately
decalcification	vicissitudinous	aerodynamically	indissolubility
demystification	phenylketonuria	antepenultimate	intercollegiate
denitrification	acknowledgeable	antimonarchical	interconnection
desensitisation	acknowledgement	argumentatively	interrogatively
determinateness	agriculturalist	ceremoniousness	irrationalistic
devitrification	annihilationism	circumnavigator	magnetoelectric
disarticulation	atrabiliousness	cryptanalytical	neighbourliness
dissatisfaction	chronologically	fashionableness	ornithorhynchus
dissatisfactory	crystallisation	fragmentariness	philosophically
diversification	crystallography	homogeneousness	phosphorescence
dyslogistically	disinflationary	inattentiveness	phosphorylation
ecclesiasticism	epitheliomatous	indefensibility	photoconducting
ecclesiological	extraillustrate	inexpensiveness	photoconductive
electrification	grandiloquently	inoffensiveness	photojournalism
euphemistically	interclavicular	involuntariness	photojournalist
exemplification	mellifluousness	microanalytical	physicochemical
frenchification	morphologically	ontogenetically	plenipotentiary
Hellenistically	ophthalmologist	opinionatedness	protozoological
historiographer	ophthalmoscopic	overconfidently	radiogoniometer
historiographic	photoelectronic	palaeontologist	reconsolidation
improvisatorial	phrenologically	parthenogenesis	rhynchocephalia
inapplicability	physiologically	parthenogenetic	schistosomiasis
inconsiderately	postmillenarian	preternaturally	selfpropagating
inconsideration	psychologically	rhombencephalon	spectroscopical
incorrigibility	punctiliousness	rontgenotherapy	stadtholdership
indemnification	quarrelsomeness	rudimentariness	stampcollecting
indisciplinable	selffulfillment	selfcentredness	superconducting
indistinctively	selfpollination	selfconfidently	superconductive
inexplicability	semicylindrical	selfconsciously	synchronisation
infundibuliform	superfluousness	selfconsequence	telephotography
inquisitiveness	technologically	selfconsistency	transpositional
inquisitorially	transilluminate	selfconstituted	trigonometrical
insensitiveness	transplantation	selfcontainment	trustworthiness
insignificantly	trisyllabically	semiconsciously	trypanosomiasis
intelligibility	unchallengeable	shootinggallery	unprepossessing
intensification	uncomplainingly	sleepingdraught	warmbloodedness
interdigitation	uncomplimentary	speakingtrumpet	anthropocentric
lightmindedness	unintelligently	spontaneousness	anthropogenesis
margaritiferous	ventriloquially	substantialness	anthropological
mechanistically	ventriloquistic	substantiveness	anthropomorphic
micromillimetre	chloramphenicol	superincumbence	anthropopathism
necessitousness	complementarise	superinducement	anthropophagous
pantheistically	complementarity	superintendence	archiepiscopate
personification	departmentalise	superintendency	commonplaceness
pessimistically	departmentalism	therianthropism	contemplatively
photolithograph	discommendation	treasonableness	contemporaneity
photomicrograph	epistemological	undemonstrative	contemporaneous
precipitousness	experimentalise	unintentionally	contemptibility
prepositionally	experimentalism	vasoconstrictor	correspondingly
prohibitiveness	experimentalist	wellconditioned	crossopterygian
properispomenon	experimentation	acanthocephalan	descriptiveness
pulchritudinous	experimentative	accommodatingly	developmentally
quickwittedness	fourdimensional	blameworthiness	disproportional
reconcilability	gentlemanliness	carnivorousness	disrespectfully
reconsideration	inflammableness	cerebrovascular	emancipationist
rightmindedness	instrumentalism	coldbloodedness	episcopalianism
ritualistically	instrumentalist	cosmopolitanism	geomorphologist
romanticisation	instrumentality	decarbonisation	inconspicuously
selfopinionated	instrumentation	dermatoglyphics	malacopterygian
significatively	monosymmetrical	disappointingly	methamphetamine
socialistically	noncommissioned	dolichocephalic	microsporangium
sociolinguistic	palaeomagnetism	electroanalysis	microsporophyll
speechification	parasympathetic	electrochemical	pleuropneumonia
splendiferously	parliamentarian	electrodynamics	pseudepigraphic
stereoisomerism	parliamentarism	electrokinetics	psychopathology
subordinateness	problematically	electromagnetic	psychophysicist

quadruplication	circumspectness	maldistribution	conservationist
quintuplication	circumstantiate	Mephistophelean	contravallation
retrospectively	compassionately	Mephistophelian	controversially
selfapprobation	compressibility	metamathematics	manoeuvrability
selfdeprecating	confessionalism	noncontributory	overdevelopment
selfdeprecatory	confessionalist	peripatetically	preservationist
selfexplanatory	connoisseurship	philanthropical	selfdevelopment
selfimprovement	consubstantiate	phonautographic	ambidexterously
selfreplicating	conversationist	physiotherapist	paradoxicalness
selfreproachful	Czechoslovakian	pneumatological	apocalyptically
selfreprovingly	dispassionately	prehistorically	hydrodynamicist
unexceptionable	distrustfulness	Presbyterianise	photosynthesise
unexceptionably	everlastingness	Presbyterianism	polycrystalline
unexceptionally	expressionistic	presentationism	povertystricken
achondroplastic	gleichschaltung	presentationist	────────────────
anisotropically	heterosexuality	pretentiousness	accountableness
appropriateness	imperishability	proportionalist	aerodynamically
bioastronautics	impressionistic	proportionality	annihilationism
counterapproach	inaccessibility	proportionately	antimonarchical
counterattacker	inadmissibility	psychotherapist	brachydactylous
counterirritant	indigestibility	remonstratively	circumnavigator
countermovement	inexcusableness	repetitiousness	circumvallation
counterplotting	irresistibility	respectableness	complicatedness
deleteriousness	misconstruction	selfdetermining	conceivableness
dishearteningly	mistrustfulness	sententiousness	consentaneously
entrepreneurial	neuropsychiatry	sophisticatedly	conservationist
extraordinarily	nonsensicalness	spermatogenesis	contravallation
flibbertigibbet	orthopsychiatry	spermatogenetic	conversationist
greatgrandchild	polyunsaturated	subpostmistress	counterapproach
gynandromorphic	prepossessingly	substitutionary	counterattacker
heartbreakingly	processionalist	superstitiously	cryptanalytical
heliotropically	procrastination	superstructural	disenchantingly
hypercritically	professionalise	supportableness	disinflationary
illustriousness	professionalism	surreptitiously	doublebarrelled
incomprehension	prognostication	susceptibleness	ecclesiasticism
incongruousness	prognosticative	tempestuousness	electroanalysis
indeterminately	progressiveness	tendentiousness	emancipationist
indetermination	sadomasochistic	thoughtlessness	episcopalianism
indeterministic	selfcastigation	totalitarianism	equalitarianism
innumerableness	selfdestruction	understandingly	fashionableness
inopportuneness	selfdestructive	unquestioningly	gentlemanliness
inseparableness	selfdistrustful	unrighteousness	greatgrandchild
insubordination	underestimation	unsportsmanlike	heterodactyloos
interpretership	accountableness	unsubstantially	humanitarianism
interprovincial	Aristotelianism	warrantableness	hydrostatically
intolerableness	chromatographic	wellintentioned	illimitableness
irreparableness	cinematographer	adventurousness	impermeableness
irreversibility	cinematographic	bloodguiltiness	indubitableness
jurisprudential	compartmentally	configurational	inefficaciously
meritoriousness	conceptualistic	consecutiveness	inexcusableness
misapprehension	congratulations	consequentially	inflammableness
misapprehensive	consentaneously	constructionism	innumerableness
omnidirectional	contentiousness	constructionist	inscrutableness
opprobriousness	conventionalise	decarburisation	inseparableness
pleasurableness	conventionalism	decolourisation	instantaneously
quarterfinalist	conventionalist	disillusionment	interchangeable
reafforestation	conventionality	disreputability	interchangeably
reapportionment	demonstrability	dramaturgically	interclavicular
retrogressively	demonstrational	excommunication	intolerableness
selffertilising	demonstratively	excommunicative	intractableness
selfforgetfully	dessertspoonful	excommunicatory	irreparableness
shrinkresistant	discontinuously	extracurricular	irrevocableness
standardisation	distastefulness	importunateness	levelheadedness
subterraneously	equalitarianism	incalculability	lightheadedness
sulphureousness	exhibitionistic	incommunicative	marketgardening
symmetricalness	expeditiousness	introsusception	microanalytical
thunderstricken	fantasticalness	intussusception	opinionatedness
transcriptional	humanitarianism	intussusception	palaeomagnetism
transgressively	hydrostatically	miniaturisation	perspicaciously
trinitrotoluene	illimitableness	multitudinously	pleasurableness
uncomprehending	impenetrability	particularistic	polyunsaturated
underprivileged	impracticalness	platitudinarian	practicableness
underproduction	indubitableness	radioautography	PreRaphaelitism
weatherboarding	infinitesimally	reproducibility	presentationism
ankylostomiasis	inscrutableness	transmutability	presentationist
atherosclerosis	instantaneously	uncommunicative	preservationist
atherosclerotic	interstratified	antivivisection	preternaturally
brachistochrone	intractableness	circumvallation	problematically
circumscription	logarithmically	conceivableness	psychopathology

respectableness	brachycephalous	wellintentioned	conventionality
schoolmastering	circumferential	decalcification	counterirritant
serviceableness	complementarily	demystification	deleteriousness
subterraneously	complementarity	denitrification	disappointingly
supportableness	comprehensively	devitrification	discontinuously
symptomatically	condescendingly	diversification	dispassionately
totalitarianism	consequentially	electrification	eclaircissement
transplantation	controversially	exemplification	efficaciousness
treasonableness	departmentalise	frenchification	epitheliomatous
trisyllabically	departmentalism	indemnification	exhibitionistic
uncomplainingly	disagreeability	insignificantly	expeditiousness
understandingly	discommendation	intensification	expressionistic
unparliamentary	disconcertingly	overconfidently	fantasticalness
unsubstantially	disgracefulness	personification	hypercritically
warrantableness	disrespectfully	quarterfinalist	illustriousness
wrongheadedness	distastefulness	selfconfidently	impracticalness
antisabbatarian	echinodermatous	selffulfillment	impressionistic
equiprobability	entrepreneurial	selfsufficiency	inconspicuously
infundibuliform	exchangeability	speechification	infrangibleness
weatherboarding	experimentalise	splendiferously	injudiciousness
acanthocephalan	experimentalism	standoffishness	lackadaisically
architecturally	experimentalist	syllabification	meritoriousness
atherosclerosis	experimentation	dermatoglyphics	noncommissioned
atherosclerotic	experimentative	incorrigibility	nonprofitmaking
circumscription	fourdimensional	intelligibility	nonsensicalness
communicability	heartbreakingly	interdigitation	opprobriousness
communicatively	heterogeneously	interrogatively	paradoxicalness
constructionism	heterosexuality	quinquagenarian	perpendicularly
constructionist	hobbledehoyhood	selfforgetfully	pharisaicalness
disaffectedness	homogeneousness	shootinggallery	plumbaginaceous
disarticulation	incomprehension	sleepingdraught	prestidigitator
dolichocephalic	ineffaceability	speakingtrumpet	prestigiousness
electrochemical	infinitesimally	transfiguration	pretentiousness
gleichschaltung	instrumentalism	transfigurement	processionalist
inapplicability	instrumentalist	affranchisement	professionalise
inexplicability	instrumentation	approachability	professionalism
insurrectionary	interpretership	biogeochemistry	proportionalist
insurrectionist	magnetoelectric	collenchymatous	proportionality
intellectualise	misapprehension	enfranchisement	proportionately
intellectualism	misapprehensive	foresightedness	pseudepigraphic
intellectualist	nonprofessional	geomorphologist	punctiliousness
intellectuality	omnidirectional	heterochromatic	repetitiousness
interjectionary	ontogenetically	immunochemistry	selfaffirmation
photomechanical	overdevelopment	imperishability	selfhumiliation
photomicrograph	palaeogeography	inapprehensible	selfregistering
physicochemical	parenthetically	interscholastic	semicylindrical
pyroelectricity	parliamentarian	logarithmically	sententiousness
reproducibility	parliamentarism	longsightedness	sophisticatedly
resurrectionary	peripatetically	metamathematics	stoicheiometric
resurrectionist	phenylketonuria	methamphetamine	superstitiously
rhombencephalon	photochemically	nearsightedness	surreptitiously
rhynchocephalia	photoelectronic	philanthropical	susceptibleness
romanticisation	prepossessingly	physiotherapist	symmetricalness
significatively	Presbyterianise	prosenchymatous	tendentiousness
superficialness	Presbyterianism	psychophysicist	transcriptional
superincumbence	psychometrician	psychotherapist	uncomplimentary
ultramicroscope	quatercentenary	pyrotechnically	unconsciousness
accommodatingly	reafforestation	reproachfulness	underprivileged
Christadelphian	resourcefulness	selfrighteously	unquestioningly
electrodynamics	retrogressively	stereochemistry	electrokinetics
extraordinarily	retrospectively	thermochemistry	arterialisation
inconsiderately	selfdetermining	airconditioning	commonplaceness
inconsideration	selfdevelopment	antivivisection	communalisation
insubordination	semiindependent	appropriateness	contemplatively
multitudinously	sesquicentenary	archiepiscopate	cosmopolitanism
platitudinarian	shrinkresistant	atrabiliousness	crystallisation
reconsideration	singleheartedly	autoradiography	crystallography
standardisation	spontaneousness	bloodguiltiness	Czechoslovakian
superinducement	stretcherbearer	ceremoniousness	defencelessness
unprecedentedly	sulphureousness	coconsciousness	desexualisation
wellconditioned	supplementarily	compassionately	detribalisation
abiogenetically	supplementation	compendiousness	encephalography
acknowledgeable	sympathetically	confessionalism	etherealisation
acknowledgement	transgressively	confessionalist	externalisation
amphitheatrical	unchallengeable	contentiousness	extraillustrate
anaesthesiology	unchangeability	contradictorily	hospitalisation
anaesthetically	uncomprehending	conventionalise	immortalisation
Aristotelianism	unrighteousness	conventionalism	incalculability
atmospherically		conventionalist	indissolubility

intercollegiate	incommunicative	pneumatological	kindheartedness
internalisation	indistinctively	prehistorically	lexicographical
materialisation	interconnection	protozoological	maldistribution
micromillimetre	interventionism	psychologically	manoeuvrability
nationalisation	interventionist	rontgenotherapy	miniaturisation
particularistic	irrationalistic	sadomasochistic	noncontributory
peristaltically	lightmindedness	sanctimoniously	nongovernmental
personalisation	necromantically	spermatogenesis	noninterference
phototelegraphy	palaeoanthropic	spermatogenetic	nonintervention
postmillenarian	phenomenalistic	technologically	oceanographical
purposelessness	phenomenologist	trinitrotoluene	odoriferousness
quadruplication	photoconducting	unceremoniously	openheartedness
quintuplication	photoconductive	underproduction	ornithorhynchus
radiotelegraphy	photosensitiser	ventriloquially	palaeographical
rationalisation	photosynthesise	ventriloquistic	phosphorescence
reconcilability	pithecanthropus	warmbloodedness	phosphorylation
reconsolidation	pleuropneumonia	apocalyptically	physiographical
reestablishment	pusillanimously	autographically	predeterminable
regionalisation	radiogoniometer	chloramphenicol	remonstratively
remorselessness	righthandedness	circumspectness	selfapprobation
selfexplanatory	rightmindedness	counterplotting	selfdeprecating
selfpollination	roentgenography	electrophoresis	selfdeprecatory
selfrealisation	selfabandonment	electrophoretic	selfimprovement
selfreplicating	selfopinionated	electropositive	selfreproachful
stadtholdership	semitransparent	ideographically	selfreprovingly
stampcollecting	sociolinguistic	inappropriately	selfsacrificing
thoughtlessness	subordinateness	indisciplinable	softheartedness
transilluminate	suburbanisation	interdependence	stratigraphical
unintelligently	superconducting	interdependency	superstructural
approximatively	superconductive	logographically	transferability
compartmentally	sycophantically	manicdepressive	transparentness
countermovement	synchronisation	parasympathetic	treacherousness
decontamination	ultracentrifuge	philosophically	trueheartedness
developmentally	uncommunicative	picturepostcard	trustworthiness
dithyrambically	unpretentiously	selfcomplacency	warmheartedness
electromagnetic	vertiginousness	selfpropagating	zoogeographical
electromyograph	achondroplastic	superimposition	compressibility
enantiomorphism	anisotropically	telegraphically	connoisseurship
enantiomorphous	anthropocentric	topographically	dessertspoonful
indeterminately	anthropogenesis	typographically	disillusionment
indetermination	anthropological	underemployment	dissatisfaction
indeterministic	anthropomorphic	inconsequential	dissatisfactory
monosymmetrical	anthropopathism	adventurousness	dyslogistically
ophthalmologist	anthropophagous	anticlericalism	euphemistically
ophthalmoscopic	bacteriological	bibliographical	Hellenistically
selfexamination	bioastronautics	biogeographical	hendecasyllabic
subpostmistress	chromatographic	blameworthiness	hendecasyllable
temperamentally	chronologically	carnivorousness	improvisatorial
trigonometrical	cinematographer	chronogrammatic	inaccessibility
unaccommodating	cinematographic	coldheartedness	inadmissibility
vicechamberlain	coldbloodedness	computerisation	indefeasibility
Americanisation	contemporaneity	configurational	indefensibility
antitrinitarian	contemporaneous	considerateness	inexpensiveness
bioluminescence	correspondingly	decarburisation	inoffensiveness
broadmindedness	cryptocommunist	decolourisation	interfascicular
civilianisation	disproportional	demonstrability	introsusception
coinstantaneous	ecclesiological	demonstrational	intussusception
confidentiality	epistemological	demonstratively	intussusceptive
conscientiously	grandiloquently	disinterestedly	irreversibility
decarbonisation	gynandromorphic	downheartedness	mechanistically
determinateness	heliotropically	dramaturgically	meroblastically
differentiation	historiographer	extemporisation	northeastwardly
disadvantageous	historiographic	exteriorisation	northwestwardly
disentanglement	interprovincial	extracurricular	notwithstanding
disorganisation	macroscopically	familiarisation	pantheistically
electronegative	Mephistophelean	fissiparousness	pessimistically
ethnocentricity	Mephistophelian	formularisation	picturesqueness
Europeanisation	microphotograph	governorgeneral	polycrystalline
excommunication	microsporangium	halfheartedness	povertystricken
excommunicative	microsporophyll	hardheartedness	progressiveness
excommunicatory	morphologically	hermaphroditism	properispomenon
experientialism	palaeobotanical	impenetrability	quarrelsomeness
experientialist	parthenogenesis	imponderability	ritualistically
gastroenteritis	parthenogenetic	imprescriptible	schistosomiasis
geochronologist	pharmacological	incomparability	selfconsciously
hydrodynamicist	phonautographic	intemperateness	selfconsequence
importunateness	phrenologically	interferometric	selfconsistency
incommensurable	physiologically	interstratified	selfconstituted
incommensurably	phytogeographic	invulnerability	semiconsciously

socialistically	prognostication	antisabbatarian	inexcusableness
spectroscopical	prognosticative	approachability	inflammableness
stereoisomerism	prohibitiveness	appropriateness	infrangibleness
syllogistically	provocativeness	approximatively	innumerableness
thunderstricken	pulchritudinous	argumentatively	inscrutableness
transpositional	quickwittedness	authoritatively	inseparableness
troublesomeness	radioautography	bibliographical	intolerableness
trypanosomiasis	reapportionment	biogeographical	intractableness
undemonstrative	rudimentariness	cerebrovascular	irreparableness
unprepossessing	selfcastigation	chronogrammatic	irrevocableness
unrealistically	selfcentredness	circumstantiate	pleasurableness
unsophisticated	selfcontainment	commonplaceness	practicableness
unsportsmanlike	selfdestruction	communicability	respectableness
unwholesomeness	selfdestructive	communicatively	serviceableness
vasoconstrictor	selfdistrustful	conceptualistic	supportableness
venturesomeness	selffertilising	configurational	susceptibleness
acclimatisation	selfgratulation	considerateness	treasonableness
acquisitiveness	speculativeness	consubstantiate	trisyllabically
agriculturalist	straightforward	contemplatively	vicechamberlain
alphabetisation	substantialness	contractability	warrantableness
ambidexterously	substantiveness	demonstrability	anthropocentric
ankylostomiasis	substratosphere	demonstrational	brachydactylous
argumentatively	superheterodyne	demonstratively	contradictorily
authoritatively	superintendence	determinateness	disrespectfully
brachistochrone	superintendency	disagreeability	fantasticalness
circumstantiate	superlativeness	disreputability	heterodactyloos
competitiveness	supernaturalise	electromagnetic	impracticalness
compositionally	supernaturalism	equiprobability	inconspicuously
conjunctionally	supernaturalist	exchangeability	indistinctively
consecutiveness	supersaturation	fragmentariness	inefficaciously
consubstantiate	suppositionally	heartbreakingly	interfascicular
contemptibility	systematisation	hydrodynamicist	introsusception
contractability	telephotography	hypercatalectic	intussusception
contractibility	therianthropism	impenetrability	intussusceptive
crossopterygian	transliteration	imperishability	neuropsychiatry
demagnetisation	transmutability	imponderability	nonsensicalness
descriptiveness	unconditionally	importunateness	omnidirectional
desensitisation	underestimation	improvisatorial	orthopsychiatry
destructibility	unexceptionable	inapplicability	paradoxicalness
destructiveness	unexceptionably	incalculability	perpendicularly
dishearteningly	unexceptionally	incomparability	perspicaciously
disreputability	unintentionally	individualistic	pharisaicalness
distinctiveness	unobjectionable	ineffaceability	photoelectronic
distrustfulness	unsymmetrically	inexplicability	retrospectively
everlastingness	vicissitudinous	intemperateness	sadomasochistic
flibbertigibbet	antepenultimate	interrogatively	selfconsciously
fragmentariness	arboriculturist	interstratified	semiconsciously
hydropathically	churrigueresque	involuntariness	sophisticatedly
hypercatalectic	conceptualistic	invulnerability	spectroscopical
imaginativeness	congratulations	irrationalistic	symmetricalness
inattentiveness	conspicuousness	lexicographical	acknowledgeable
incompatibility	distinguishable	manoeuvrability	acknowledgement
indigestibility	distinguishably	oceanographical	broadmindedness
ineffectiveness	hermeneutically	palaeographical	coldbloodedness
ineffectualness	incongruousness	parasympathetic	jurisprudential
inopportuneness	individualistic	particularistic	levelheadedness
inquisitiveness	jurisprudential	phenomenalistic	lightheadedness
inquisitorially	mellifluousness	physiographical	lightmindedness
insensitiveness	neighbourliness	reconcilability	photoconducting
instructiveness	perspicuousness	remonstratively	photoconductive
internationally	photojournalism	rudimentariness	righthandedness
involuntariness	photojournalist	selfcontainment	rightmindedness
irresistibility	selfindulgently	selfexplanatory	selfabandonment
malacopterygian	semidocumentary	selfpropagating	sleepingdraught
malpractitioner	substitutionary	significatively	stadtholdership
margaritiferous	superabundantly	singleheartedly	superconducting
misconstruction	superfluousness	stratigraphical	superconductive
mistrustfulness	tempestuousness	subordinateness	underproduction
necessitousness	therapeutically	transferability	warmbloodedness
numismatologist	cerebrovascular	transmutability	wrongheadedness
obstructiveness	mischievousness	unchangeability	acanthocephalan
palaeontologist	hyperthyroidism	zoogeographical	ambidexterously
penetrativeness	neurophysiology	accountableness	biogeochemistry
perfunctoriness	neuropsychiatry	conceivableness	bioluminescence
photolithograph	orthopsychiatry	dithyrambically	Christadelphian
plenipotentiary	saprophytically	fashionableness	churrigueresque
precipitousness	————————	illimitableness	circumspectness
prepositionally	accommodatingly	impermeableness	compartmentally
procrastination	amphitheatrical	indubitableness	connoisseurship

crossopterygian	shootinggallery	extemporisation	selfopinionated
defencelessness	sociolinguistic	exteriorisation	selfpollination
developmentally	spermatogenesis	externalisation	selfrealisation
dishearteningly	spermatogenetic	extraordinarily	selfreplicating
disinterestedly	technologically	familiarisation	selfsacrificing
dolichocephalic	autographically	flibbertigibbet	selfsufficiency
electronegative	chloramphenicol	formularisation	speculativeness
immunochemistry	electrochemical	frenchification	speechification
inapprehensible	electrophoresis	hospitalisation	standardisation
inconsiderately	electrophoretic	imaginativeness	standoffishness
inconsideration	gleichschaltung	immortalisation	subpostmistress
interdependence	hobbledehoyhood	imprescriptible	substantialness
interdependency	hydropathically	inaccessibility	substantiveness
malacopterygian	ideographically	inadmissibility	suburbanisation
metamathematics	incomprehension	inattentiveness	superficialness
methamphetamine	logographically	incommunicative	superlativeness
monosymmetrical	misapprehension	incompatibility	suppositionally
phosphorescence	misapprehensive	incorrigibility	syllabification
phototelegraphy	ornithorhynchus	indefeasibility	synchronisation
physiotherapist	philosophically	indefensibility	systematisation
plenipotentiary	photolithograph	indemnification	transpositional
pleuropneumonia	photomechanical	indeterminately	uncommunicative
postmillenarian	physicochemical	indetermination	uncomplainingly
PreRaphaelitism	telegraphically	indeterministic	unconditionally
psychotherapist	therianthropism	indigestibility	underestimation
purposelessness	topographically	ineffectiveness	unexceptionable
quinquagenarian	typographically	inexpensiveness	unexceptionably
radiotelegraphy	uncomprehending	inoffensiveness	unexceptionally
reconsideration	acclimatisation	inquisitiveness	unintelligently
remorselessness	acquisitiveness	insensitiveness	unintentionally
rhombencephalon	affranchisement	insignificantly	unobjectionable
rhynchocephalia	alphabetisation	instructiveness	wellconditioned
selfconsequence	Americanisation	insubordination	antepenultimate
selfdeprecating	anticlericalism	intelligibility	anthropological
selfdeprecatory	antitrinitarian	intensification	arboriculturist
selfforgetfully	arterialisation	interdigitation	Aristotelianism
splendiferously	civilianisation	internalisation	atherosclerosis
stereochemistry	communalisation	internationally	atherosclerotic
superheterodyne	competitiveness	irresistibility	bacteriological
superintendence	compositionally	irreversibility	bloodguiltiness
superintendency	compressibility	maldistribution	circumvallation
temperamentally	computerisation	malpractitioner	congratulations
thermochemistry	conjunctionally	margaritiferous	contravallation
thoughtlessness	consecutiveness	materialisation	counterplotting
transliteration	contemptibility	miniaturisation	cryptanalytical
transparentness	contractibility	multitudinously	dermatoglyphics
trigonometrical	cosmopolitanism	nationalisation	ecclesiological
unprecedentedly	crystallisation	noncontributory	episcopalianism
disgracefulness	decalcification	obstructiveness	epistemological
dissatisfaction	decarbonisation	overconfidently	indisciplinable
dissatisfactory	decarburisation	penetrativeness	intercollegiate
distastefulness	decolourisation	personalisation	magnetoelectric
distrustfulness	decontamination	personification	microanalytical
mistrustfulness	demagnetisation	platitudinarian	micromillimetre
noninterference	demystification	prepositionally	overdevelopment
reproachfulness	denitrification	procrastination	pharmacological
resourcefulness	descriptiveness	prognostication	pneumatological
straightforward	desensitisation	prognosticative	protozoological
anthropogenesis	desexualisation	progressiveness	selfcomplacency
chromatographic	destructibility	prohibitiveness	selfdevelopment
chronologically	destructiveness	provocativeness	selfhumiliation
cinematographer	detribalisation	pusillanimously	selfindulgently
cinematographic	devitrification	quadruplication	stampcollecting
disentanglement	disillusionment	quarterfinalist	underemployment
dramaturgically	disorganisation	quintuplication	aerodynamically
governorgeneral	distinctiveness	radiogoniometer	anthropomorphic
historiographer	distinguishable	rationalisation	cryptocommunist
historiographic	distinguishably	reapportionment	gynandromorphic
morphologically	diversification	reconsolidation	logarithmically
palaeomagnetism	electrification	reestablishment	photochemically
parthenogenesis	electrokinetics	regionalisation	predeterminable
parthenogenetic	enfranchisement	reproducibility	semidocumentary
phonautographic	etherealisation	romanticisation	uncomplimentary
phrenologically	Europeanisation	selfcastigation	unparliamentary
physiologically	everlastingness	selfconfidently	unsportsmanlike
phytogeographic	excommunication	selfconsistency	bioastronautics
prestidigitator	excommunicative	selfexamination	complementarily
pseudepigraphic	excommunicatory	selffertilising	complementarity
psychologically	exemplification	selffulfillment	comprehensively

condescendingly	expressionistic	Mephistophelian	coldheartedness
consentaneously	fissiparousness	properispomenon	complicatedness
consequentially	geochronologist	semiindependent	confidentiality
correspondingly	geomorphologist	transcriptional	conscientiously
departmentalise	hermaphroditism	grandiloquently	conservationist
departmentalism	homogeneousness	picturesqueness	constructionism
disappointingly	illustrationism	ventriloquially	constructionist
discommendation	impressionistic	ventriloquistic	conversationist
discontinuously	incongruousness	antimonarchical	counterattacker
disenchantingly	injudiciousness	atmospherically	differentiation
electroanalysis	inquisitorially	circumferential	disadvantageous
entrepreneurial	interferometric	circumscription	disaffectedness
experimentalise	interscholastic	contemporaneity	disinflationary
experimentalism	mellifluousness	contemporaneous	downheartedness
experimentalist	meritoriousness	controversially	dyslogistically
experimentation	mischievousness	counterirritant	emancipationist
experimentative	necessitousness	disconcertingly	ethnocentricity
fourdimensional	numismatologist	disproportional	euphemistically
gentlemanliness	odoriferousness	doublebarrelled	experientialism
greatgrandchild	ophthalmologist	echinodermatous	experientialist
heterogeneously	ophthalmoscopic	equalitarianism	foresightedness
instantaneously	opprobriousness	extracurricular	gastroenteritis
instrumentalism	palaeogeography	heterochromatic	halfheartedness
instrumentalist	palaeontologist	humanitarianism	hardheartedness
instrumentality	perfunctoriness	hyperthyroidism	Hellenistically
instrumentation	perspicuousness	inappropriately	hermeneutically
interchangeable	phenomenologist	manicdepressive	hydrostatically
interchangeably	picturepostcard	marketgardening	hypercritically
interconnection	precipitousness	microsporangium	insurrectionary
nongovernmental	prestigiousness	microsporophyll	insurrectionist
parliamentarian	pretentiousness	misconstruction	intellectualise
parliamentarism	processionalist	neighbourliness	intellectualism
plumbaginaceous	professionalise	philanthropical	intellectualist
pyrotechnically	professionalism	photojournalism	intellectuality
quatercentenary	proportionalist	photojournalist	interjectionary
sanctimoniously	proportionality	photomicrograph	interpretership
semicylindrical	proportionately	prehistorically	interventionism
sesquicentenary	punctiliousness	Presbyterianise	interventionist
subterraneously	quarrelsomeness	Presbyterianism	kindheartedness
superabundantly	radioautography	selfaffirmation	longsightedness
supplementarily	repetitiousness	selfcentredness	mechanistically
supplementation	roentgenography	selfdestruction	meroblastically
transplantation	schistosomiasis	selfdestructive	microphotograph
unceremoniously	selfapprobation	selfdetermining	nearsightedness
unchallengeable	selfimprovement	selfdistrustful	necromantically
understandingly	selfreproachful	stretcherbearer	nonprofitmaking
unsubstantially	selfreprovingly	totalitarianism	northeastwardly
wellintentioned	sententiousness	ultramicroscope	northwestwardly
adventurousness	spontaneousness	unsymmetrically	notwithstanding
ankylostomiasis	stereoisomerism	anaesthesiology	ontogenetically
atrabiliousness	stoicheiometric	antivivisection	openheartedness
autoradiography	substratosphere	archiepiscopate	opinionatedness
brachistochrone	sulphureousness	ecclesiasticism	palaeoanthropic
carnivorousness	superfluousness	eclaircissement	palaeobotanical
ceremoniousness	superimposition	incommensurable	pantheistically
coconsciousness	telephotography	incommensurably	parenthetically
compassionately	tempestuousness	infinitesimally	peripatetically
compendiousness	tendentiousness	lackadaisically	peristaltically
confessionalism	treacherousness	neurophysiology	pessimistically
confessionalist	troublesomeness	noncommissioned	phenylketonuria
conspicuousness	trypanosomiasis	nonprofessional	photosynthesise
contentiousness	unaccommodating	photosensitiser	pithecanthropus
conventionalise	unconsciousness	prepossessingly	polycrystalline
conventionalism	unquestioningly	reafforestation	polyunsaturated
conventionalist	unrighteousness	retrogressively	povertystricken
conventionality	unwholesomeness	schoolmastering	presentationism
countermovement	venturesomeness	selfregistering	presentationist
crystallography	vertiginousness	semitransparent	preservationist
Czechoslovakian	weatherboarding	shrinkresistant	preternaturally
deleteriousness	achondroplastic	transgressively	problematically
dispassionately	anisotropically	unprepossessing	psychometrician
efficaciousness	anthropopathism	abiogenetically	psychopathology
electropositive	anthropophagous	airconditioning	pyroelectricity
enantiomorphism	brachycephalous	anaesthetically	quickwittedness
enantiomorphous	counterapproach	annihilationism	resurrectionism
encephalography	dessertspoonful	apocalyptically	resurrectionist
epitheliomatous	heliotropically	architecturally	ritualistically
exhibitionistic	macroscopically	blameworthiness	rontgenotherapy
expeditiousness	Mephistophelean	coinstantaneous	saprophytically

selfconstituted	pharisaicalness	quadruplication	selfrighteously	
selfrighteously	photomechanical	quintuplication	semidocumentary	
socialistically	plumbaginaceous	selfdeprecating	semiindependent	
softheartedness	polycrystalline	selfdeprecatory	softheartedness	
speakingtrumpet	selfcomplacency	selfreplicating	spermatogenesis	
substitutionary	selfreproachful	selfsufficiency	spermatogenetic	
superstitiously	shootinggallery	speechification	stadtholdership	
surreptitiously	sophisticatedly	superinducement	stampcollecting	
sycophantically	substantialness	superstructural	subterraneously	
syllogistically	superficialness	syllabification	trueheartedness	
sympathetically	symmetricalness	uncommunicative	uncomplimentary	
symptomatically	unsportsmanlike	condescendingly	uncomprehending	
therapeutically	weatherboarding	correspondingly	unparliamentary	
thunderstricken	approachability	discommendation	unprepossessing	
trinitrotoluene	communicability	greatgrandchild	vicechamberlain	
trueheartedness	compressibility	hermaphroditism	warmbloodedness	
trustworthiness	contemptibility	marketgardening	warmheartedness	
ultracentrifuge	contractability	overconfidently	wrongheadedness	
undemonstrative	contractibility	pulchritudinous	margaritiferous	
unpretentiously	demonstrability	reconsolidation	selfsacrificing	
unrealistically	destructibility	selfconfidently	acknowledgeable	
unsophisticated	disagreeability	semicylindrical	acknowledgement	
vasoconstrictor	disreputability	superabundantly	autoradiography	
warmheartedness	equiprobability	unaccommodating	crystallography	
agriculturalist	exchangeability	understandingly	electromagnetic	
disarticulation	impenetrability	vicissitudinous	electronegative	
extraillustrate	imperishability	anthropocentric	encephalography	
inconsequential	imponderability	anthropogenesis	flibbertigibbet	
indissolubility	inaccessibility	antivivisection	interchangeable	
ineffectualness	inadmissibility	atherosclerosis	interchangeably	
infundibuliform	inapplicability	atherosclerotic	palaeogeography	
inopportuneness	incalculability	broadmindedness	phototelegraphy	
pulchritudinous	incomparability	chloramphenicol	radioautography	
selfgratulation	incompatibility	circumferential	radiotelegraphy	
superincumbence	incorrigibility	coldbloodedness	roentgenography	
superinducement	indefeasibility	coldheartedness	selfcastigation	
supernaturalise	indefensibility	complicatedness	selfindulgently	
supernaturalism	indigestibility	consentaneously	selfpropagating	
supernaturalist	indissolubility	disaffectedness	telephotography	
supersaturation	ineffaceability	downheartedness	unchallengeable	
superstructural	inexplicability	electrochemical	unintelligently	
transfiguration	intelligibility	entrepreneurial	anthropophagous	
transfigurement	invulnerability	foresightedness	blameworthiness	
transilluminate	irresistibility	gastroenteritis	brachycephalous	
vicissitudinous	irreversibility	governorgeneral	Mephistophelean	
circumnavigator	maldistribution	halfheartedness	Mephistophelian	
interclavicular	manoeuvrability	hardheartedness	neuropsychiatry	
interprovincial	noncontributory	heterogeneously	orthopsychiatry	
nonintervention	reconcilability	incomprehension	palaeoanthropic	
underprivileged	reproducibility	inconsequential	photosynthesise	
heterosexuality	selfapprobation	instantaneously	pithecanthropus	
collenchymatous	stretcherbearer	intercollegiate	psychopathology	
electrodynamics	transferability	interconnection	rontgenotherapy	
electromyograph	transmutability	interpretership	sadomasochistic	
hendecasyllabic	unchangeability	introsusception	trustworthiness	
hendecasyllable	anticlericalism	intussusception	abiogenetically	
phosphorylation	antimonarchical	intussusceptive	aerodynamically	
prosenchymatous	archiepiscopate	jurisprudential	airconditioning	
psychophysicist	brachistochrone	kindheartedness	anaesthesiology	
	circumspectness	levelheadedness	anaesthetically	
anthropopathism	commonplaceness	lightheadedness	anisotropically	
bioastronautics	decalcification	lightmindedness	annihilationism	
coinstantaneous	demystification	longsightedness	apocalyptically	
congratulations	denitrification	magnetoelectric	Aristotelianism	
contemporaneity	devitrification	manicdepressive	atmospherically	
contemporaneous	diversification	misapprehension	autographically	
disadvantageous	electrification	misapprehensive	chronologically	
dissatisfaction	excommunication	nearsightedness	circumnavigator	
dissatisfactory	excommunicative	noninterference	circumscription	
electroanalysis	excommunicatory	nonintervention	confidentiality	
fantasticalness	exemplification	openheartedness	conscientiously	
gleichschaltung	frenchification	opinionatedness	conservationist	
impracticalness	incommunicative	parthenogenesis	constructionism	
ineffectualness	indemnification	parthenogenetic	constructionist	
microsporangium	insignificantly	physicochemical	conversationist	
nonsensicalness	intensification	quickwittedness	differentiation	
notwithstanding	personification	righthandedness	disinflationary	
palaeobotanical	prognostication	rightmindedness	dithyrambically	
paradoxicalness	prognosticative	selfcentredness	dramaturgically	

dyslogistically	symptomatically	nonprofitmaking	dessertspoonful
emancipationist	technologically	prosenchymatous	disillusionment
episcopalianism	telegraphically	pusillanimously	ecclesiological
equalitarianism	therapeutically	quarrelsomeness	electromyograph
euphemistically	topographically	schistosomiasis	electrophoresis
experientialism	totalitarianism	selfaffirmation	electrophoretic
experientialist	trisyllabically	selfdetermining	epistemological
extracurricular	typographically	stereochemistry	gynandromorphic
heliotropically	unceremoniously	stereoisomerism	heterochromatic
Hellenistically	underprivileged	stoicheiometric	hobbledehoyhood
hermeneutically	unpretentiously	superincumbence	hyperthyroidism
humanitarianism	unrealistically	thermochemistry	internationally
hydropathically	unsophisticated	transilluminate	microphotograph
hydrostatically	unsymmetrically	troublesomeness	microsporophyll
hypercritically	heartbreakingly	trypanosomiasis	overdevelopment
ideographically	accountableness	underestimation	pharmacological
inappropriately	achondroplastic	unwholesomeness	phenylketonuria
indisciplinable	Christadelphian	venturesomeness	philanthropical
inefficaciously	circumvallation	circumstantiate	photolithograph
infinitesimally	conceivableness	compartmentally	photomicrograph
insurrectionary	conceptualistic	compassionately	pneumatological
insurrectionist	contravallation	confessionalism	prepositionally
interclavicular	disarticulation	confessionalist	properispomenon
interfascicular	disentanglement	consubstantiate	protozoological
interjectionary	fashionableness	conventionalise	radiogoniometer
interprovincial	gentlemanliness	conventionalism	reapportionment
interventionism	geochronologist	conventionalist	selfabandonment
interventionist	geomorphologist	conventionality	selfdevelopment
lackadaisically	hendecasyllabic	decontamination	selfopinionated
logarithmically	hendecasyllable	developmentally	spectroscopical
logographically	hypercatalectic	dishearteningly	straightforward
macroscopically	illimitableness	dispassionately	suppositionally
mechanistically	impermeableness	electrodynamics	trinitrotoluene
meroblastically	individualistic	electrokinetics	ultramicroscope
micromillimetre	indubitableness	everlastingness	unconditionally
morphologically	inexcusableness	exhibitionistic	underemployment
necromantically	inflammableness	expressionistic	unexceptionable
neurophysiology	infrangibleness	extraordinarily	unexceptionably
ontogenetically	infundibuliform	impressionistic	unexceptionally
pantheistically	innumerableness	inapprehensible	unintentionally
parenthetically	inscrutableness	indeterminately	unobjectionable
peripatetically	inseparableness	indetermination	acanthocephalan
peristaltically	interscholastic	indeterministic	bibliographical
perspicaciously	intolerableness	inopportuneness	biogeographical
pessimistically	intractableness	insubordination	counterapproach
philosophically	irrationalistic	interdependence	dolichocephalic
photochemically	irreparableness	interdependency	imprescriptible
photosensitiser	irrevocableness	multitudinously	lexicographical
phrenologically	neighbourliness	palaeomagnetism	oceanographical
physiologically	numismatologist	photojournalism	palaeographical
predeterminable	ophthalmologist	photojournalist	physiographical
prehistorically	palaeontologist	platitudinarian	rhombencephalon
Presbyterianise	phenomenalistic	plenipotentiary	rhynchocephalia
Presbyterianism	phenomenologist	postmillenarian	semitransparent
presentationism	phosphorylation	processionalist	stratigraphical
presentationist	pleasurableness	procrastination	zoogeographical
preservationist	practicableness	professionalise	selfconsequence
prestidigitator	PreRaphaelitism	professionalism	agriculturalist
problematically	respectableness	proportionalist	ambidexterously
psychologically	selffertilising	proportionality	chromatographic
pyrotechnically	selffulfillment	proportionately	churrigueresque
resurrectionism	selfgratulation	quarterfinalist	cinematographer
resurrectionist	serviceableness	quinquagenarian	cinematographic
ritualistically	supportableness	selfexamination	counterirritant
sanctimoniously	susceptibleness	selfexplanatory	crossopterygian
saprophytically	treasonableness	selfpollination	doublebarrelled
selfconsciously	warrantableness	superintendence	enantiomorphism
selfconstituted	ankylostomiasis	superintendency	enantiomorphous
selfcontainment	biogeochemistry	temperamentally	ethnocentricity
selfhumiliation	chronogrammatic	transparentness	fragmentariness
semiconsciously	collenchymatous	uncomplainingly	historiographer
shrinkresistant	cryptocommunist	unprecedentedly	historiographic
socialistically	echinodermatous	unquestioningly	inconsiderately
substitutionary	epitheliomatous	anthropological	inconsideration
superstitiously	hydrodynamicist	anthropomorphic	inquisitorially
surreptitiously	immunochemistry	bacteriological	involuntariness
sycophantically	interferometric	compositionally	malacopterygian
syllogistically	metamathematics	conjunctionally	particularistic
sympathetically	nongovernmental	counterplotting	perfunctoriness

phonautographic	rationalisation	retrospectively	superfluousness
physiotherapist	reestablishment	schoolmastering	tempestuousness
phytogeographic	regionalisation	selfforgetfully	tendentiousness
povertystricken	remorselessness	selfregistering	treacherousness
pseudepigraphic	retrogressively	sesquicentenary	unconsciousness
psychometrician	romanticisation	significatively	underproduction
psychotherapist	selfconsistency	subordinateness	unrighteousness
pyroelectricity	selfrealisation	supplementarily	ventriloquially
reconsideration	standardisation	supplementation	ventriloquistic
rudimentariness	standoffishness	transcriptional	vertiginousness
singleheartedly	subpostmistress	transplantation	acquisitiveness
sleepingdraught	substratosphere	transpositional	competitiveness
speakingtrumpet	suburbanisation	trigonometrical	consecutiveness
splendiferously	superimposition	unsubstantially	countermovement
superheterodyne	synchronisation	wellconditioned	Czechoslovakian
supernaturalise	systematisation	wellintentioned	descriptiveness
supernaturalism	thoughtlessness	adventurousness	destructiveness
supernaturalist	transgressively	architecturally	distinctiveness
supersaturation	accommodatingly	atrabiliousness	imaginativeness
therianthropism	amphitheatrical	carnivorousness	inattentiveness
thunderstricken	antepenultimate	ceremoniousness	ineffectiveness
transfiguration	antisabbatarian	coconsciousness	inexpensiveness
transfigurement	antitrinitarian	compendiousness	inoffensiveness
transliteration	appropriateness	connoisseurship	inquisitiveness
ultracentrifuge	approximatively	conspicuousness	insensitiveness
undemonstrative	arboriculturist	contentiousness	instructiveness
vasoconstrictor	argumentatively	deleteriousness	obstructiveness
acclimatisation	authoritatively	discontinuously	penetrativeness
affranchisement	bloodguiltiness	disgracefulness	progressiveness
alphabetisation	brachydactylous	distastefulness	prohibitiveness
Americanisation	communicatively	distrustfulness	provocativeness
arterialisation	complementarily	efficaciousness	selfimprovement
bioluminescence	complementarity	expeditiousness	selfreprovingly
cerebrovascular	configurational	fissiparousness	speculativeness
civilianisation	consequentially	grandiloquently	substantiveness
communalisation	considerateness	heterosexuality	superlativeness
comprehensively	contemplatively	homogeneousness	northeastwardly
computerisation	contradictorily	illustriousness	northwestwardly
controversially	cosmopolitanism	incommensurable	cryptanalytical
crystallisation	counterattacker	incommensurably	dermatoglyphics
decarbonisation	demonstrational	incongruousness	microanalytical
decarburisation	demonstratively	inconspicuously	ornithorhynchus
decolourisation	departmentalise	injudiciousness	———
defencelessness	departmentalism	intellectualise	acclimatisation
demagnetisation	determinateness	intellectualism	achondroplastic
desensitisation	disappointingly	intellectualist	agriculturalist
desexualisation	disconcertingly	intellectuality	alphabetisation
detribalisation	disenchantingly	mellifluousness	Americanisation
disinterestedly	disproportional	meritoriousness	anthropophagous
disorganisation	disrespectfully	mischievousness	anticlericalism
distinguishable	ecclesiasticism	misconstruction	antisabbatarian
distinguishably	experimentalise	mistrustfulness	antitrinitarian
eclaircissement	experimentalism	necessitousness	Aristotelianism
electropositive	experimentalist	odoriferousness	arterialisation
enfranchisement	experimentative	opprobriousness	brachycephalous
etherealisation	heterodactyloos	perpendicularly	chromatographic
Europeanisation	importunateness	perspicuousness	cinematographer
extemporisation	improvisatorial	photoconducting	cinematographic
exteriorisation	indistinctively	photoconductive	circumvallation
externalisation	instrumentalism	picturesqueness	civilianisation
extraillustrate	instrumentalist	pleuropneumonia	collenchymatous
familiarisation	instrumentality	polyunsaturated	communalisation
formularisation	instrumentation	precipitousness	compassionately
fourdimensional	intemperateness	prestigiousness	complementarily
hospitalisation	interdigitation	pretentiousness	complementarity
immortalisation	interrogatively	preternaturally	computerisation
internalisation	interstratified	punctiliousness	confessionalism
materialisation	malpractitioner	repetitiousness	confessionalist
miniaturisation	methamphetamine	reproachfulness	confidentiality
nationalisation	monosymmetrical	resourcefulness	contravallation
noncommissioned	omnidirectional	selfdestruction	conventionalise
nonprofessional	parasympathetic	selfdestructive	conventionalism
ophthalmoscopic	parliamentarian	selfdistrustful	conventionalist
personalisation	parliamentarism	sententiousness	conventionally
phosphorescence	photoelectronic	sociolinguistic	cosmopolitanism
picturepostcard	quatercentenary	spontaneousness	counterattacker
prepossessingly	reafforestation	sulphureousness	crystallisation
psychophysicist	remonstratively	superconducting	Czechoslovakian
purposelessness		superconductive	decalcification

decarbonisation	northeastwardly	antivivisection	coldbloodedness
decarburisation	northwestwardly	apocalyptically	coldheartedness
decolourisation	parliamentarian	atmospherically	complicatedness
decontamination	parliamentarism	autographically	disaffectedness
demagnetisation	personalisation	bioluminescence	downheartedness
demystification	personification	cerebrovascular	foresightedness
denitrification	phonautographic	chronologically	halfheartedness
departmentalise	phosphorylation	dissatisfaction	hardheartedness
departmentalism	photojournalism	dissatisfactory	interdependence
desensitisation	photojournalist	dithyrambically	interdependency
desexualisation	physiotherapist	dramaturgically	kindheartedness
detribalisation	phytogeographic	dyslogistically	levelheadedness
devitrification	platitudinarian	euphemistically	lightheadedness
differentiation	postmillenarian	extracurricular	lightmindedness
disarticulation	Presbyterianise	greatgrandchild	longsightedness
discommendation	Presbyterianism	heliotropically	nearsightedness
disorganisation	processionalist	Hellenistically	openheartedness
dispassionately	procrastination	hermeneutically	opinionatedness
diversification	professionalise	hydropathically	quickwittedness
echinodermatous	professionalism	hydrostatically	righthandedness
electrification	prognostication	hypercritically	rightmindedness
electrodynamics	prognosticative	ideographically	selfcentredness
electronegative	proportionalist	interclavicular	softheartedness
episcopalianism	proportionality	interconnection	superintendence
epitheliomatous	proportionately	interfascicular	superintendency
equalitarianism	prosenchymatous	lackadaisically	trueheartedness
etherealisation	pseudepigraphic	logarithmically	warmbloodedness
Europeanisation	psychotherapist	logographically	warmheartedness
excommunication	quadruplication	macroscopically	wrongheadedness
excommunicative	quarterfinalist	magnetoelectric	accountableness
excommunicatory	quinquagenarian	mechanistically	acknowledgeable
exemplification	quintuplication	meroblastically	acknowledgement
experientialism	rationalisation	misconstruction	acquisitiveness
experientialist	reafforestation	morphologically	affranchisement
experimentalise	reconsideration	necromantically	appropriateness
experimentalism	reconsolidation	ontogenetically	churrigueresque
experimentalist	regionalisation	ophthalmoscopic	commonplaceness
experimentation	romanticisation	pantheistically	competitiveness
experimentative	selfaffirmation	parenthetically	conceivableness
extemporisation	selfapprobation	peripatetically	consecutiveness
exteriorisation	selfcastigation	peristaltically	considerateness
externalisation	selfdeprecating	pessimistically	countermovement
extraordinarily	selfdeprecatory	philosophically	descriptiveness
familiarisation	selfexamination	phosphorescence	destructiveness
formularisation	selfexplanatory	photochemically	determinateness
frenchification	selfgratulation	photoconducting	disentanglement
heterosexuality	selfhumiliation	photoconductive	distinctiveness
historiographer	selfpollination	phrenologically	doublebarrelled
historiographic	selfpropagating	physiologically	eclaircissement
hospitalisation	selfrealisation	plumbaginaceous	electrokinetics
humanitarianism	selfreplicating	prehistorically	enfranchisement
immortalisation	semitransparent	problematically	fashionableness
inappropriately	sleepingdraught	psychologically	grandiloquently
incommunicative	speechification	pyrotechnically	hypercatalectic
inconsiderately	standardisation	ritualistically	illimitableness
inconsideration	suburbanisation	saprophytically	imaginativeness
indemnification	superabundantly	selfcomplacency	impermeableness
indeterminately	supernaturalise	selfdestruction	importunateness
indetermination	supernaturalism	selfdestructive	inattentiveness
insignificantly	supernaturalist	selfreproachful	indubitableness
instrumentalism	supplementarily	socialistically	ineffectiveness
instrumentalist	supplementation	stampcollecting	inexcusableness
instrumentality	syllabification	superconducting	inexpensiveness
instrumentation	synchronisation	superconductive	inflammableness
insubordination	systematisation	sycophantically	infrangibleness
intellectualise	totalitarianism	syllogistically	innumerableness
intellectualism	transfiguration	sympathetically	inoffensiveness
intellectualist	transliteration	symptomatically	inopportuneness
intellectuality	transplantation	technologically	inquisitiveness
intensification	unaccommodating	telegraphically	inscrutableness
interdigitation	uncommunicative	therapeutically	insensitiveness
internalisation	undemonstrative	topographically	inseparableness
interscholastic	underestimation	trisyllabically	instructiveness
materialisation	superincumbence	typographically	intemperateness
metamathematics	abiogenetically	underproduction	interchangeable
methamphetamine	aerodynamically	unrealistically	interchangeably
miniaturisation	anaesthetically	unsophisticated	interferometric
nationalisation	anisotropically	unsymmetrically	intolerableness
nonprofitmaking		broadmindedness	intractableness

```
irreparableness   rhynchocephalia   interrogatively   polycrystalline
irrevocableness   standoffishness   interstratified   reproachfulness
margaritiferous   stratigraphical   involuntariness   resourcefulness
marketgardening   zoogeographical   invulnerability   selffulfillment
Mephistophelean   accommodatingly   irrationalistic   shootinggallery
Mephistophelian   ankylostomiasis   irresistibility   substantialness
nongovernmental   antepenultimate   irreversibility   superficialness
obstructiveness   approachability   malpractitioner   symmetricalness
overconfidently   approximatively   manoeuvrability   trinitrotoluene
palaeomagnetism   argumentatively   neighbourliness   underprivileged
penetrativeness   authoritatively   neuropsychiatry   chronogrammatic
photosynthesise   biogeochemistry   noncommissioned   electrochemical
picturesqueness   blameworthiness   nonprofessional   heterochromatic
pleasurableness   bloodguiltiness   omnidirectional   infinitesimally
practicableness   communicability   orthopsychiatry   micromillimetre
progressiveness   communicatively   particularistic   physicochemical
prohibitiveness   comprehensively   perfunctoriness   pleuropneumonia
provocativeness   compressibility   phenomenalistic   properispomenon
quarrelsomeness   conceptualistic   povertystricken   radiogoniometer
quatercentenary   condescendingly   prepossessingly   anthropocentric
respectableness   configurational   PreRaphaelitism   anthropogenesis
rontgenotherapy   consequentially   psychometrician   chloramphenicol
schoolmastering   contemplatively   psychophysicist   circumferential
selfconfidently   contemptibility   pulchritudinous   coinstantaneous
selfimprovement   contractability   pyroelectricity   compositionally
selfindulgently   contractibility   reconcilability   conjunctionally
selfregistering   controversially   remonstratively   contemporaneity
serviceableness   correspondingly   reproducibility   contemporaneous
sesquicentenary   counterirritant   retrogressively   disillusionment
speculativeness   demonstrability   retrospectively   electromagnetic
stereoisomerism   demonstrational   rudimentariness   governorgeneral
stoicheiometric   demonstratively   sadomasochistic   incomprehension
stretcherbearer   destructibility   schistosomiasis   inconsequential
subordinateness   disagreeability   selfdetermining   indisciplinable
substantiveness   disappointingly   selffertilising   internationally
superinducement   disconcertingly   selfreprovingly   interprovincial
superlativeness   disenchantingly   selfsacrificing   jurisprudential
supportableness   dishearteningly   selfsufficiency   microsporangium
susceptibleness   disproportional   significatively   misapprehension
transfigurement   disreputability   sociolinguistic   misapprehensive
treasonableness   ecclesiasticism   stereochemistry   nonintervention
troublesomeness   electropositive   superimposition   notwithstanding
unchallengeable   equiprobability   thermochemistry   ornithorhynchus
unintelligently   ethnocentricity   thunderstricken   palaeobotanical
unwholesomeness   exchangeability   transcriptional   parthenogenesis
venturesomeness   exhibitionistic   transferability   parthenogenetic
warrantableness   expressionistic   transgressively   phenylketonuria
disrespectfully   flibbertigibbet   transilluminate   photomechanical
selfforgetfully   fourdimensional   transmutability   predeterminable
anthropological   fragmentariness   transpositional   prepositionally
bacteriological   gentlemanliness   trustworthiness   reapportionment
circumnavigator   heartbreakingly   trypanosomiasis   selfabandonment
disadvantageous   hermaphroditism   ultracentrifuge   selfcontainment
ecclesiological   hydrodynamicist   unchangeability   selfopinionated
electromyograph   hyperthyroidism   uncomplainingly   semidocumentary
epistemological   immunochemistry   understandingly   semiindependent
everlastingness   impenetrability   unquestioningly   spermatogenesis
intercollegiate   imperishability   unsubstantially   spermatogenetic
microphotograph   imponderability   vasoconstrictor   suppositionally
pharmacological   impressionistic   ventriloquially   uncomplimentary
photolithograph   inaccessibility   ventriloquistic   uncomprehending
photomicrograph   inadmissibility   vicissitudinous   unconditionally
pneumatological   inapplicability   wellconditioned   unexceptionable
protozoological   incalculability   wellintentioned   unexceptionably
acanthocephalan   incomparability   disgracefulness   unexceptionally
antimonarchical   incompatibility   distastefulness   unintentionally
bibliographical   incorrigibility   distrustfulness   unobjectionable
biogeographical   indefeasibility   electroanalysis   unparliamentary
brachistochrone   indefensibility   fantasticalness   unsportsmanlike
distinguishable   indeterministic   gleichschaltung   airconditioning
distinguishably   indigestibility   hendecasyllabic   ambidexterously
dolichocephalic   indissolubility   hendecasyllable   anaesthesiology
lexicographical   indistinctively   impracticalness   annihilationism
oceanographical   individualistic   ineffectualness   archiepiscopate
palaeographical   ineffaceability   mistrustfulness   conscientiously
parasympathetic   inexplicability   nonsensicalness   consentaneously
physiographical   infundibuliform   paradoxicalness   conservationist
reestablishment   inquisitorially   perpendicularly   constructionism
rhombencephalon   intelligibility   pharisaicalness   constructionist
```

contradictorily	palaeogeography	plenipotentiary	meroblastically
conversationist	photoelectronic	prestidigitator	morphologically
dessertspoonful	phototelegraphy	selfconsistency	necromantically
discontinuously	pithecanthropus	selfconstituted	neuropsychiatry
disinflationary	polyunsaturated	singleheartedly	ontogenetically
emancipationist	preternaturally	sophisticatedly	orthopsychiatry
geochronologist	radioautography	subpostmistress	palaeogeography
geomorphologist	radiotelegraphy	superstructural	pantheistically
heterogeneously	roentgenography	temperamentally	parenthetically
improvisatorial	semicylindrical	transparentness	peripatetically
inconspicuously	stadtholdership	unprecedentedly	peristaltically
inefficaciously	straightforward	arboriculturist	perpendicularly
instantaneously	telephotography	bioastronautics	pessimistically
insurrectionary	trigonometrical	cryptocommunist	philosophically
insurrectionist	vicechamberlain	entrepreneurial	photochemically
interjectionary	weatherboarding	maldistribution	phototelegraphy
interventionism	adventurousness	noncontributory	phrenologically
interventionist	atrabiliousness	selfconsequence	physiologically
multitudinously	carnivorousness	speakingtrumpet	polyunsaturated
neurophysiology	ceremoniousness	brachydactylous	predeterminable
numismatologist	coconsciousness	crossopterygian	prehistorically
ophthalmologist	compendiousness	heterodactyloos	prepositionally
palaeontologist	conspicuousness	hobbledehoyhood	prestidigitator
perspicaciously	contentiousness	malacopterygian	preternaturally
phenomenologist	defencelessness	underemployment	problematically
presentationism	deleteriousness	———————————————	psychologically
presentationist	efficaciousness	abiogenetically	pyrotechnically
preservationist	expeditiousness	acanthocephalan	radioautography
psychopathology	fissiparousness	acknowledgeable	radiotelegraphy
pusillanimously	homogeneousness	aerodynamically	rhombencephalon
resurrectionism	illustriousness	anaesthetically	rhynchocephalia
resurrectionist	inapprehensible	anisotropically	ritualistically
sanctimoniously	incongruousness	ankylostomiasis	roentgenography
selfconsciously	injudiciousness	apocalyptically	saprophytically
selfrighteously	manicdepressive	architecturally	schistosomiasis
semiconsciously	mellifluousness	atmospherically	selfopinionated
splendiferously	meritoriousness	autographically	socialistically
substitutionary	mischievousness	autoradiography	stretcherbearer
subterraneously	necessitousness	chronogrammatic	suppositionally
superheterodyne	odoriferousness	chronologically	sycophantically
superstitiously	opprobriousness	circumnavigator	syllogistically
surreptitiously	perspicuousness	compartmentally	sympathetically
therianthropism	precipitousness	compositionally	symptomatically
unceremoniously	prestigiousness	conjunctionally	technologically
unpretentiously	pretentiousness	consequentially	telegraphically
Christadelphian	punctiliousness	controversially	telephotography
circumscription	purposelessness	crystallography	temperamentally
dermatoglyphics	remorselessness	developmentally	therapeutically
enantiomorphism	repetitiousness	distinguishable	topographically
enantiomorphous	selfdistrustful	distinguishably	trisyllabically
introsusception	sententiousness	dithyrambically	trypanosomiasis
intussusception	shrinkresistant	dolichocephalic	typographically
intussusceptive	spontaneousness	dramaturgically	unchallengeable
microsporophyll	sulphureousness	dyslogistically	unconditionally
overdevelopment	superfluousness	encephalography	unexceptionable
philanthropical	tempestuousness	euphemistically	unexceptionably
selfdevelopment	tendentiousness	heliotropically	unexceptionally
spectroscopical	thoughtlessness	Hellenistically	unintentionally
substratosphere	treacherousness	hendecasyllabic	unobjectionable
amphitheatrical	ultramicroscope	hendecasyllable	unrealistically
anthropomorphic	unconsciousness	hermeneutically	unsophisticated
architecturally	unprepossessing	heterochromatic	unsubstantially
atherosclerosis	unrighteousness	hydropathically	unsymmetrically
atherosclerotic	vertiginousness	hydrostatically	ventriloquially
autoradiography	anthropopathism	hypercritically	flibbertigibbet
connoisseurship	circumspectness	ideographically	counterattacker
counterapproach	circumstantiate	incommensurable	ecclesiasticism
crystallography	compartmentally	incommensurably	ethnocentricity
electrophoresis	congratulations	indisciplinable	hydrodynamicist
electrophoretic	consubstantiate	infinitesimally	hypercatalectic
encephalography	counterplotting	inquisitorially	interprovincial
gastroenteritis	cryptanalytical	interchangeable	ornithorhynchus
gynandromorphic	developmentally	interchangeably	picturepostcard
incommensurable	disinterestedly	internationally	povertystricken
incommensurably	extraillustrate	lackadaisically	psychometrician
interpretership	imprescriptible	logarithmically	psychophysicist
monosymmetrical	microanalytical	logographically	pyroelectricity
noninterference	photosensitiser	macroscopically	selfsacrificing
palaeoanthropic	picturepostcard	mechanistically	thunderstricken

ultramicroscope	epistemological	instrumentality	condescendingly
vasoconstrictor	gastroenteritis	intellectualise	consecutiveness
hyperthyroidism	imprescriptible	intellectualism	conservationist
notwithstanding	inapprehensible	intellectualist	considerateness
semiindependent	intercollegiate	intellectuality	conspicuousness
superheterodyne	lexicographical	intelligibility	constructionism
uncomprehending	microanalytical	invulnerability	constructionist
weatherboarding	monosymmetrical	irresistibility	contentiousness
anthropogenesis	oceanographical	irreversibility	conversationist
bioluminescence	palaeobotanical	manoeuvrability	correspondingly
coinstantaneous	palaeographical	Mephistophelean	cosmopolitanism
contemporaneity	pharmacological	Mephistophelian	cryptocommunist
contemporaneous	philanthropical	neurophysiology	defencelessness
disadvantageous	photomechanical	photojournalism	deleteriousness
disinterestedly	photosensitiser	photojournalist	descriptiveness
electromagnetic	physicochemical	polycrystalline	dessertspoonful
electrophoresis	physiographical	processionalist	destructiveness
electrophoretic	plenipotentiary	professionalise	determinateness
governorgeneral	pneumatological	professionalism	disaffectedness
interdependence	protozoological	proportionalist	disappointingly
interdependency	semicylindrical	proportionality	disconcertingly
micromillimetre	spectroscopical	psychopathology	disenchantingly
noninterference	stratigraphical	quarterfinalist	disgracefulness
parasympathetic	trigonometrical	reconcilability	dishearteningly
parthenogenesis	zoogeographical	reproducibility	disinflationary
parthenogenetic	Czechoslovakian	shootinggallery	distastefulness
phosphorescence	nonprofitmaking	supernaturalise	distinctiveness
plumbaginaceous	agriculturalist	supernaturalism	distrustfulness
properispomenon	anaesthesiology	supernaturalist	downheartedness
radiogoniometer	anticlericalism	transferability	efficaciousness
selfcomplacency	approachability	transmutability	emancipationist
selfconsequence	brachycephalous	unchangeability	episcopalianism
selfconsistency	brachydactylous	unsportsmanlike	equalitarianism
selfsufficiency	communicability	vicechamberlain	everlastingness
singleheartedly	compressibility	acknowledgement	expeditiousness
sophisticatedly	confessionalism	affranchisement	fantasticalness
spermatogenesis	confessionalist	antepenultimate	fashionableness
spermatogenetic	confidentiality	countermovement	fissiparousness
superincumbence	contemptibility	disentanglement	foresightedness
superintendence	contractability	disillusionment	fragmentariness
superintendency	contractibility	eclaircissement	gentlemanliness
underprivileged	conventionalise	electrodynamics	grandiloquently
unprecedentedly	conventionalism	enfranchisement	halfheartedness
infundibuliform	conventionalist	methamphetamine	hardheartedness
interstratified	conventionality	overdevelopment	heartbreakingly
ultracentrifuge	demonstrability	reapportionment	homogeneousness
anthropophagous	departmentalise	reestablishment	humanitarianism
crossopterygian	departmentalism	selfabandonment	illimitableness
geochronologist	destructibility	selfcontainment	illustriousness
geomorphologist	disagreeability	selfdevelopment	imaginativeness
malacopterygian	disreputability	selffulfillment	impermeableness
microsporangium	doublebarrelled	selfimprovement	importunateness
numismatologist	equiprobability	speakingtrumpet	impracticalness
ophthalmologist	exchangeability	superinducement	inattentiveness
palaeontologist	experientialism	transfigurement	incongruousness
phenomenologist	experientialist	underemployment	indubitableness
anthropopathism	experimentalise	accommodatingly	ineffectiveness
Christadelphian	experimentalism	accountableness	ineffectualness
dermatoglyphics	experimentalist	acquisitiveness	inexcusableness
enantiomorphism	heterodactyloos	adventurousness	inexpensiveness
enantiomorphous	heterosexuality	airconditioning	inflammableness
greatgrandchild	impenetrability	annihilationism	infrangibleness
hobbledehoyhood	imperishability	appropriateness	injudiciousness
microsporophyll	imponderability	Aristotelianism	innumerableness
selfreproachful	inaccessibility	atrabiliousness	inoffensiveness
substratosphere	inadmissibility	blameworthiness	inopportuneness
amphitheatrical	inapplicability	bloodguiltiness	inquisitiveness
anthropological	incalculability	broadmindedness	inscrutableness
antimonarchical	incomparability	carnivorousness	insensitiveness
bacteriological	incompatibility	ceremoniousness	inseparableness
bibliographical	incorrigibility	circumspectness	insignificantly
biogeographical	indefeasibility	coconsciousness	instructiveness
chloramphenicol	indefensibility	coldbloodedness	insurrectionary
circumstantiate	indigestibility	coldheartedness	insurrectionist
congratulations	indissolubility	commonplaceness	intemperateness
consubstantiate	ineffaceability	compendiousness	interjectionary
cryptanalytical	inexplicability	competitiveness	interventionism
ecclesiological	instrumentalism	complicatedness	interventionist
electrochemical	instrumentalist	conceivableness	intolerableness

intractableness	superficialness	northeastwardly	disorganisation
involuntariness	superfluousness	northwestwardly	dispassionately
irreparableness	superlativeness	parliamentarian	dissatisfaction
irrevocableness	supportableness	parliamentarism	dissatisfactory
kindheartedness	susceptibleness	photolithograph	diversification
levelheadedness	symmetricalness	photomicrograph	echinodermatous
lightheadedness	tempestuousness	platitudinarian	electrification
lightmindedness	tendentiousness	postmillenarian	electrokinetics
longsightedness	thoughtlessness	quinquagenarian	electronegative
marketgardening	totalitarianism	rontgenotherapy	electropositive
mellifluousness	transilluminate	schoolmastering	epitheliomatous
meritoriousness	transparentness	selfregistering	etherealisation
mischievousness	treacherousness	semitransparent	Europeanisation
mistrustfulness	treasonableness	stereoisomerism	excommunication
nearsightedness	troublesomeness	subpostmistress	excommunicatory
necessitousness	trueheartedness	supplementarily	exemplification
neighbourliness	trustworthiness	achondroplastic	experimentation
nongovernmental	uncomplainingly	biogeochemistry	experimentative
nonsensicalness	unconsciousness	churrigueresque	extemporisation
obstructiveness	understandingly	conceptualistic	exteriorisation
odoriferousness	unintelligently	connoisseurship	externalisation
openheartedness	unquestioningly	exhibitionistic	familiarisation
opinionatedness	unrighteousness	expressionistic	formularisation
opprobriousness	unwholesomeness	immunochemistry	frenchification
overconfidently	venturesomeness	impressionistic	gleichschaltung
paradoxicalness	vertiginousness	incomprehension	hermaphroditism
penetrativeness	vicissitudinous	indeterministic	hospitalisation
perfunctoriness	warmbloodedness	individualistic	immortalisation
perspicuousness	warmheartedness	interpretership	inappropriately
pharisaicalness	warrantableness	interscholastic	incommunicative
picturesqueness	wrongheadedness	irrationalistic	inconsequential
pleasurableness	atherosclerosis	manicdepressive	inconsiderately
practicableness	atherosclerotic	misapprehension	inconsideration
precipitousness	configurational	misapprehensive	indemnification
prepossessingly	counterapproach	particularistic	indeterminately
Presbyterianise	demonstrational	phenomenalistic	indetermination
Presbyterianism	disproportional	photosynthesise	instrumentation
presentationism	fourdimensional	sadomasochistic	insubordination
presentationist	malpractitioner	selffertilising	intensification
preservationist	noncommissioned	sociolinguistic	interconnection
prestigiousness	nonprofessional	stadtholdership	interdigitation
pretentiousness	omnidirectional	stereochemistry	interferometric
progressiveness	ophthalmoscopic	thermochemistry	internalisation
prohibitiveness	palaeoanthropic	unprepossessing	introsusception
provocativeness	photoelectronic	ventriloquistic	intussusception
pulchritudinous	pithecanthropus	acclimatisation	intussusceptive
punctiliousness	pleuropneumonia	alphabetisation	jurisprudential
purposelessness	transcriptional	Americanisation	magnetoelectric
quarrelsomeness	transpositional	anthropocentric	maldistribution
quatercentenary	wellconditioned	antivivisection	materialisation
quickwittedness	wellintentioned	arterialisation	metamathematics
remorselessness	anthropomorphic	bioastronautics	miniaturisation
repetitiousness	archiepiscopate	circumferential	misconstruction
reproachfulness	chromatographic	circumscription	nationalisation
resourcefulness	cinematographer	circumvallation	noncontributory
respectableness	cinematographic	civilianisation	nonintervention
resurrectionism	gynandromorphic	collenchymatous	palaeomagnetism
resurrectionist	historiographer	communalisation	personalisation
righthandedness	historiographic	compassionately	personification
rightmindedness	phonautographic	computerisation	phosphorylation
rudimentariness	physiotherapist	contravallation	photoconducting
selfcentredness	phytogeographic	counterirritant	photoconductive
selfconfidently	pseudepigraphic	counterplotting	PreRaphaelitism
selfdetermining	psychotherapist	crystallisation	procrastination
selfindulgently	therianthropism	decalcification	prognostication
selfreprovingly	antisabbatarian	decarbonisation	prognosticative
sententiousness	antitrinitarian	decarburisation	proportionately
serviceableness	arboriculturist	decolourisation	prosenchymatous
sesquicentenary	brachistochrone	decontamination	quadruplication
softheartedness	complementarily	demagnetisation	quintuplication
speculativeness	complementarity	demystification	rationalisation
spontaneousness	contradictorily	denitrification	reafforestation
standoffishness	electromyograph	desensitisation	reconsideration
subordinateness	entrepreneurial	desexualisation	reconsolidation
substantialness	extraillustrate	detribalisation	regionalisation
substantiveness	extraordinarily	devitrification	romanticisation
substitutionary	improvisatorial	differentiation	selfaffirmation
sulphureousness	margaritiferous	disarticulation	selfapprobation
superabundantly	microphotograph	discommendation	

selfcastigation	interrogatively	semicylindrical	inappropriately
selfdeprecating	remonstratively	spectroscopical	inattentiveness
selfdeprecatory	retrogressively	stratigraphical	incongruousness
selfdestruction	retrospectively	trigonometrical	inconsiderately
selfdestructive	significatively	zoogeographical	indeterminately
selfdistrustful	transgressively	disinterestedly	indistinctively
selfexamination	straightforward	northeastwardly	indubitableness
selfexplanatory	electroanalysis	northwestwardly	ineffectiveness
selfgratulation	————————	singleheartedly	ineffectualness
selfhumiliation	antepenultimate	sophisticatedly	inexcusableness
selfpollination	archiepiscopate	unprecedentedly	inexpensiveness
selfpropagating	circumstantiate	accountableness	inflammableness
selfrealisation	consubstantiate	acknowledgement	infrangibleness
selfreplicating	counterapproach	acquisitiveness	injudiciousness
semidocumentary	counterirritant	adventurousness	innumerableness
shrinkresistant	disinflationary	affranchisement	inoffensiveness
speechification	electromyograph	appropriateness	inopportuneness
stampcollecting	extraillustrate	approximatively	inquisitiveness
standardisation	insurrectionary	argumentatively	inscrutableness
stoicheiometric	intercollegiate	atrabiliousness	insensitiveness
suburbanisation	interjectionary	authoritatively	inseparableness
superconducting	microphotograph	blameworthiness	instructiveness
superconductive	photolithograph	bloodguiltiness	intemperateness
superimposition	photomicrograph	broadmindedness	interrogatively
supersaturation	picturepostcard	carnivorousness	intolerableness
supplementation	plenipotentiary	ceremoniousness	intractableness
syllabification	quatercentenary	circumspectness	involuntariness
synchronisation	rontgenotherapy	coconsciousness	irreparableness
systematisation	semidocumentary	coldbloodedness	irrevocableness
transfiguration	sesquicentenary	coldheartedness	kindheartedness
transliteration	shrinkresistant	commonplaceness	levelheadedness
transplantation	straightforward	communicatively	lightheadedness
unaccommodating	substitutionary	compassionately	lightmindedness
uncommunicative	transilluminate	compendiousness	longsightedness
uncomplimentary	uncomplimentary	competitiveness	mellifluousness
undemonstrative	unparliamentary	complicatedness	Mephistophelean
underestimation	vicechamberlain	comprehensively	meritoriousness
underproduction	acknowledgeable	conceivableness	mischievousness
unparliamentary	distinguishable	consecutiveness	mistrustfulness
ambidexterously	distinguishably	considerateness	nearsightedness
cerebrovascular	flibbertigibbet	conspicuousness	necessitousness
conscientiously	hendecasyllabic	contemplatively	neighbourliness
consentaneously	hendecasyllable	contentiousness	nonsensicalness
discontinuously	imprescriptible	countermovement	obstructiveness
disrespectfully	inapprehensible	defencelessness	odoriferousness
extracurricular	incommensurable	deleteriousness	openheartedness
heterogeneously	incommensurably	demonstratively	opinionatedness
inconspicuously	indisciplinable	descriptiveness	opprobriousness
inefficaciously	interchangeable	destructiveness	overdevelopment
instantaneously	interchangeably	determinateness	paradoxicalness
interclavicular	predeterminable	disaffectedness	penetrativeness
interfascicular	unchallengeable	disentanglement	perfunctoriness
multitudinously	unexceptionable	disgracefulness	perspicuousness
perspicaciously	unexceptionably	disillusionment	pharisaicalness
phenylketonuria	unobjectionable	dispassionately	picturesqueness
pusillanimously	amphitheatrical	distastefulness	pleasurableness
sanctimoniously	anthropological	distinctiveness	practicableness
selfconsciously	antimonarchical	distrustfulness	precipitousness
selfconstituted	bacteriological	downheartedness	prestigiousness
selfforgetfully	bibliographical	eclaircissement	pretentiousness
selfrighteously	biogeographical	efficaciousness	progressiveness
semiconsciously	chloramphenicol	enfranchisement	prohibitiveness
sleepingdraught	cryptanalytical	everlastingness	proportionately
splendiferously	ecclesiological	expeditiousness	provocativeness
subterraneously	electrochemical	fantasticalness	punctiliousness
superstitiously	epistemological	fashionableness	purposelessness
superstructural	lexicographical	fissiparousness	quarrelsomeness
surreptitiously	microanalytical	foresightedness	quickwittedness
trinitrotoluene	monosymmetrical	fragmentariness	reapportionment
unceremoniously	oceanographical	gentlemanliness	reestablishment
unpretentiously	palaeobotanical	halfheartedness	remonstratively
approximatively	palaeographical	hardheartedness	remorselessness
argumentatively	pharmacological	homogeneousness	repetitiousness
authoritatively	philanthropical	illimitableness	reproachfulness
communicatively	photomechanical	illustriousness	resourcefulness
comprehensively	physicochemical	imaginativeness	respectableness
contemplatively	physiographical	impermeableness	retrogressively
demonstratively	pneumatological	importunateness	retrospectively
indistinctively	protozoological	impracticalness	righthandedness

rightmindedness	interpretership	dissatisfaction	intensification
rudimentariness	ornithorhynchus	diversification	interconnection
selfabandonment	phonautographic	ecclesiasticism	interdigitation
selfcentredness	phytogeographic	electrification	internalisation
selfcontainment	pseudepigraphic	electrodynamics	interprovincial
selfdevelopment	stadtholdership	electrokinetics	interstratified
selffulfillment	acclimatisation	electronegative	interventionism
selfimprovement	agriculturalist	electropositive	interventionist
semiindependent	airconditioning	emancipationist	introsusception
semitransparent	alphabetisation	enantiomorphism	intussusception
sententiousness	Americanisation	entrepreneurial	intussusceptive
serviceableness	annihilationism	episcopalianism	invulnerability
shootinggallery	anthropopathism	equalitarianism	irresistibility
significatively	anticlericalism	equiprobability	irreversibility
softheartedness	antisabbatarian	etherealisation	jurisprudential
speculativeness	antitrinitarian	ethnocentricity	malacopterygian
spontaneousness	antivivisection	Europeanisation	maldistribution
standoffishness	approachability	exchangeability	manicdepressive
subordinateness	arboriculturist	excommunication	manoeuvrability
subpostmistress	Aristotelianism	excommunicative	marketgardening
substantialness	arterialisation	exemplification	materialisation
substantiveness	bioastronautics	experientialism	Mephistophelian
substratosphere	Christadelphian	experientialist	metamathematics
sulphureousness	circumferential	experimentalism	methamphetamine
superficialness	circumscription	experimentalist	microsporangium
superfluousness	circumvallation	experimentation	miniaturisation
superinducement	civilianisation	experimentative	misapprehension
superlativeness	communalisation	extemporisation	misapprehensive
supportableness	communicability	exteriorisation	misconstruction
susceptibleness	complementarily	externalisation	nationalisation
symmetricalness	complementarity	extraordinarily	nonintervention
tempestuousness	compressibility	familiarisation	nonprofitmaking
tendentiousness	computerisation	formularisation	notwithstanding
thoughtlessness	confessionalism	frenchification	numismatologist
transfigurement	confessionalist	geochronologist	ophthalmologist
transgressively	confidentiality	geomorphologist	palaeomagnetism
transparentness	conservationist	greatgrandchild	palaeontologist
treacherousness	constructionism	hermaphroditism	parliamentarian
treasonableness	constructionist	heterosexuality	parliamentarism
trinitrotoluene	contemporaneity	hospitalisation	personalisation
troublesomeness	contemptibility	humanitarianism	personification
trueheartedness	contractability	hydrodynamicist	phenomenologist
trustworthiness	contractibility	hyperthyroidism	phosphorylation
unconsciousness	contradictorily	immortalisation	photoconducting
underemployment	contravallation	impenetrability	photoconductive
unrighteousness	conventionalise	imperishability	photojournalism
unwholesomeness	conventionalism	imponderability	photojournalist
venturesomeness	conventionalist	improvisatorial	photosynthesise
vertiginousness	conventionality	inaccessibility	physiotherapist
warmbloodedness	conversationist	inadmissibility	platitudinarian
warmheartedness	cosmopolitanism	inapplicability	polycrystalline
warrantableness	counterplotting	incalculability	postmillenarian
wrongheadedness	crossopterygian	incommunicative	PreRaphaelitism
dessertspoonful	cryptocommunist	incomparability	Presbyterianise
selfdistrustful	crystallisation	incompatibility	Presbyterianism
selfreproachful	Czechoslovakian	incomprehension	presentationism
accommodatingly	decalcification	inconsequential	presentationist
condescendingly	decarbonisation	inconsideration	preservationist
correspondingly	decarburisation	incorrigibility	processionalist
disappointingly	decolourisation	indefeasibility	procrastination
disconcertingly	decontamination	indefensibility	professionalise
disenchantingly	demagnetisation	indemnification	professionalism
dishearteningly	demonstrability	indetermination	prognostication
heartbreakingly	demystification	indigestibility	prognosticative
prepossessingly	denitrification	indissolubility	proportionalist
selfreprovingly	departmentalise	ineffaceability	proportionality
sleepingdraught	departmentalism	inexplicability	psychometrician
uncomplainingly	dermatoglyphics	instrumentalism	psychophysicist
underprivileged	desensitisation	instrumentalist	psychotherapist
understandingly	desexualisation	instrumentality	pyroelectricity
unquestioningly	destructibility	instrumentation	quadruplication
anthropomorphic	detribalisation	insubordination	quinquagenarian
chromatographic	devitrification	insurrectionist	quintuplication
cinematographer	differentiation	intellectualise	rationalisation
cinematographic	disagreeability	intellectualism	reafforestation
connoisseurship	disarticulation	intellectualist	reconcilability
gynandromorphic	discommendation	intellectuality	reconsideration
historiographer	disorganisation	intelligibility	reconsolidation
historiographic	disreputability		

```
regionalisation  dolichocephalic  phosphorescence  instantaneously
reproducibility  doublebarrelled  photoelectronic  multitudinously
resurrectionism  dramaturgically  pleuropneumonia  parthenogenesis
resurrectionist  dyslogistically  properispomenon  perspicaciously
romanticisation  euphemistically  selfcomplacency  photosensitiser
schoolmastering  extracurricular  selfconsequence  pusillanimously
selfaffirmation  heliotropically  selfconsistency  sanctimoniously
selfapprobation  Hellenistically  selfsufficiency  schistosomiasis
selfcastigation  hermeneutically  superincumbence  selfconsciously
selfdeprecating  hydropathically  superintendence  selfrighteously
selfdestruction  hydrostatically  superintendency  semiconsciously
selfdestructive  hypercritically  transcriptional  spermatogenesis
selfdetermining  ideographically  transpositional  splendiferously
selfexamination  infinitesimally  wellconditioned  subterraneously
selffertilising  inquisitorially  wellintentioned  superstitiously
selfgratulation  interclavicular  anaesthesiology  surreptitiously
selfhumiliation  interfascicular  anthropophagous  trypanosomiasis
selfpollination  internationally  brachistochrone  unceremoniously
selfpropagating  lackadaisically  brachycephalous  unpretentiously
selfrealisation  logarithmically  brachydactylous  achondroplastic
selfregistering  logographically  coinstantaneous  atherosclerotic
selfreplicating  macroscopically  collenchymatous  biogeochemistry
selfsacrificing  mechanistically  congratulations  chronogrammatic
speechification  meroblastically  contemporaneous  circumnavigator
stampcollecting  morphologically  disadvantageous  conceptualistic
standardisation  necromantically  dissatisfactory  electromagnetic
stereoisomerism  ontogenetically  echinodermatous  electrophoretic
suburbanisation  pantheistically  enantiomorphous  exhibitionistic
superconducting  parenthetically  epitheliomatous  expressionistic
superconductive  peripatetically  excommunicatory  gastroenteritis
superimposition  peristaltically  heterodactyloos  grandiloquently
supernaturalise  pessimistically  hobbledehoyhood  heterochromatic
supernaturalism  philosophically  infundibuliform  hypercatalectic
supernaturalist  photochemically  margaritiferous  immunochemistry
supersaturation  phrenologically  neurophysiology  impressionistic
supplementarily  physiologically  noncontributory  indeterministic
supplementation  prehistorically  plumbaginaceous  individualistic
syllabification  prepositionally  prosenchymatous  insignificantly
synchronisation  preternaturally  psychopathology  interscholastic
systematisation  problematically  pulchritudinous  irrationalistic
therianthropism  psychologically  selfdeprecatory  micromillimetre
totalitarianism  pyrotechnically  selfexplanatory  neuropsychiatry
transferability  rhombencephalon  ultramicroscope  nongovernmental
transfiguration  rhynchocephalia  vicissitudinous  orthopsychiatry
transliteration  ritualistically  autoradiography  overconfidently
transmutability  saprophytically  crystallography  parasympathetic
transplantation  selfforgetfully  encephalography  parthenogenetic
unaccommodating  socialistically  ophthalmoscopic  particularistic
unchangeability  suppositionally  palaeoanthropic  phenomenalistic
uncommunicative  sycophantically  palaeogeography  polyunsaturated
uncomprehending  syllogistically  phototelegraphy  prestidigitator
undemonstrative  sympathetically  pithecanthropus  radiogoniometer
underestimation  symptomatically  radioautography  sadomasochistic
underproduction  technologically  radiotelegraphy  selfconfidently
unprepossessing  telegraphically  roentgenography  selfconstituted
unsportsmanlike  temperamentally  speakingtrumpet  selfindulgently
weatherboarding  therapeutically  telephotography  selfopinionated
counterattacker  topographically  churrigueresque  sociolinguistic
povertystricken  trisyllabically  anthropocentric  spermatogenetic
thunderstricken  typographically  governorgeneral  stereochemistry
abiogenetically  unconditionally  interferometric  superabundantly
acanthocephalan  unexceptionally  magnetoelectric  thermochemistry
aerodynamically  unintentionally  perpendicularly  unintelligently
anaesthetically  unrealistically  phenylketonuria  unsophisticated
anisotropically  unsubstantially  stoichiometric   vasoconstrictor
apocalyptically  unsymmetrically  stretcherbearer  ventriloquistic
architecturally  ventriloquially  superstructural  gleichschaltung
atmospherically  bioluminescence  ambidexterously  ultracentrifuge
autographically  configurational  ankylostomiasis  microsporophyll
cerebrovascular  demonstrational  anthropogenesis  superheterodyne
chronologically  disproportional  atherosclerosis  ───────────────
compartmentally  fourdimensional  conscientiously  acanthocephalan
compositionally  interdependence  consentaneously  amphitheatrical
conjunctionally  interdependency  discontinuously  anthropological
consequentially  malpractitioner  electroanalysis  antimonarchical
controversially  noncommissioned  electrophoresis  antisabbatarian
developmentally  noninterference  heterogeneously  antitrinitarian
disrespectfully  nonprofessional  inconspicuously  bacteriological
dithyrambically  omnidirectional  inefficaciously  bibliographical
```

biogeographical	malpractitioner	spermatogenesis	inquisitorially
cerebrovascular	noncommissioned	spermatogenetic	insignificantly
Christadelphian	photosensitiser	stadtholdership	instantaneously
circumferential	polyunsaturated	stoicheiometric	interchangeable
configurational	povertystricken	trypanosomiasis	interchangeably
crossopterygian	radiogoniometer	ventriloquistic	internationally
cryptanalytical	selfconstituted	vicechamberlain	interrogatively
Czechoslovakian	selfopinionated	unsportsmanlike	lackadaisically
demonstrational	speakingtrumpet	abiogenetically	logarithmically
disproportional	stretcherbearer	accommodatingly	logographically
ecclesiological	thunderstricken	acknowledgeable	macroscopically
electrochemical	underprivileged	aerodynamically	mechanistically
entrepreneurial	unsophisticated	ambidexterously	meroblastically
epistemological	wellconditioned	anaesthetically	microsporophyll
extracurricular	wellintentioned	anisotropically	morphologically
fourdimensional	anaesthesiology	apocalyptically	multitudinously
governorgeneral	neurophysiology	approximatively	necromantically
improvisatorial	psychopathology	architecturally	northeastwardly
inconsequential	ultracentrifuge	argumentatively	northwestwardly
interclavicular	autoradiography	atmospherically	ontogenetically
interfascicular	crystallography	authoritatively	overconfidently
interprovincial	encephalography	autographically	pantheistically
jurisprudential	palaeogeography	chronologically	parenthetically
lexicographical	phototelegraphy	communicatively	peripatetically
malacopterygian	radioautography	compartmentally	peristaltically
Mephistophelean	radiotelegraphy	compassionately	perpendicularly
Mephistophelian	roentgenography	complementarily	perspicaciously
microanalytical	sleepingdraught	compositionally	pessimistically
monosymmetrical	telephotography	comprehensively	philosophically
nongovernmental	achondroplastic	condescendingly	photochemically
nonprofessional	ankylostomiasis	conjunctionally	phrenologically
oceanographical	anthropocentric	conscientiously	physiologically
omnidirectional	anthropogenesis	consentaneously	predeterminable
palaeobotanical	anthropomorphic	consequentially	prehistorically
palaeographical	atherosclerosis	contemplatively	prepositionally
parliamentarian	atherosclerotic	contradictorily	prepossessingly
pharmacological	chromatographic	controversially	preternaturally
philanthropical	chronogrammatic	correspondingly	problematically
photomechanical	cinematographic	demonstratively	proportionately
physicochemical	conceptualistic	developmentally	psychologically
physiographical	connoisseurship	disappointingly	pusillanimously
platitudinarian	dolichocephalic	disconcertingly	pyrotechnically
pneumatological	electroanalysis	discontinuously	remonstratively
postmillenarian	electromagnetic	disenchantingly	retrogressively
protozoological	electrophoresis	dishearteningly	retrospectively
psychometrician	electrophoretic	disinterestedly	ritualistically
quinquagenarian	exhibitionistic	dispassionately	sanctimoniously
semicylindrical	expressionistic	disrespectfully	saprophytically
spectroscopical	gastroenteritis	distinguishable	selfconfidently
stratigraphical	gynandromorphic	distinguishably	selfconsciously
superstructural	hendecasyllabic	dithyrambically	selfforgetfully
transcriptional	heterochromatic	dramaturgically	selfindulgently
transpositional	historiographic	dyslogistically	selfreprovingly
trigonometrical	hypercatalectic	euphemistically	selfrighteously
zoogeographical	impressionistic	extraordinarily	semiconsciously
bioastronautics	indeterministic	grandiloquently	significatively
bioluminescence	individualistic	greatgrandchild	singleheartedly
counterapproach	interferometric	heartbreakingly	socialistically
dermatoglyphics	interpretership	heliotropically	sophisticatedly
electrodynamics	interscholastic	Hellenistically	splendiferously
electrokinetics	irrationalistic	hendecasyllable	subterraneously
interdependence	magnetoelectric	hermeneutically	superabundantly
interdependency	ophthalmoscopic	heterogeneously	superstitiously
metamathematics	palaeoanthropic	hydropathically	supplementarily
noninterference	parasympathetic	hydrostatically	suppositionally
phosphorescence	parthenogenesis	hypercritically	surreptitiously
selfcomplacency	parthenogenetic	ideographically	sycophantically
selfconsequence	particularistic	imprescriptible	syllogistically
selfconsistency	phenomenalistic	inapprehensible	sympathetically
selfsufficiency	phenylketonuria	inappropriately	symptomatically
superincumbence	phonautographic	incommensurable	technologically
superintendence	photoelectronic	incommensurably	telegraphically
superintendency	phytogeographic	inconsiderately	temperamentally
cinematographer	pleuropneumonia	inconspicuously	therapeutically
counterattacker	pseudepigraphic	indeterminately	topographically
doublebarrelled	rhynchocephalia	indisciplinable	transgressively
flibbertigibbet	sadomasochistic	indistinctively	trisyllabically
historiographer	schistosomiasis	inefficaciously	typographically
interstratified	sociolinguistic	infinitesimally	unceremoniously

unchallengeable	crystallisation	speechification	constructionism
uncomplainingly	decalcification	standardisation	constructionist
unconditionally	decarbonisation	suburbanisation	contentiousness
understandingly	decarburisation	superimposition	conventionalise
unexceptionable	decolourisation	supersaturation	conventionalism
unexceptionally	decontamination	supplementation	conventionalist
unexceptionally	demagnetisation	syllabification	conversationist
unintelligently	demystification	synchronisation	cosmopolitanism
unintentionally	denitrification	systematisation	cryptocommunist
unobjectionable	desensitisation	transfiguration	defencelessness
unprecedentedly	desexualisation	transliteration	deleteriousness
unpretentiously	detribalisation	transplantation	departmentalise
unquestioningly	devitrification	underestimation	departmentalism
unrealistically	differentiation	underproduction	descriptiveness
unsubstantially	disarticulation	vasoconstrictor	destructiveness
unsymmetrically	discommendation	electromyograph	determinateness
ventriloquially	disorganisation	microphotograph	disaffectedness
acknowledgement	dissatisfaction	photolithograph	disgracefulness
affranchisement	diversification	photomicrograph	distastefulness
airconditioning	electrification	rontgenotherapy	distinctiveness
brachistochrone	etherealisation	ultramicroscope	distrustfulness
congratulations	Europeanisation	biogeochemistry	downheartedness
counterirritant	excommunication	disinflationary	ecclesiasticism
countermovement	exemplification	dissatisfactory	efficaciousness
counterplotting	experimentation	excommunicatory	emancipationist
disentanglement	extemporisation	immunochemistry	enantiomorphism
disillusionment	exteriorisation	infundibuliform	episcopalianism
eclaircissement	externalisation	insurrectionary	equalitarianism
enfranchisement	familiarisation	interjectionary	everlastingness
gleichschaltung	formularisation	micromillimetre	expeditiousness
marketgardening	frenchification	neuropsychiatry	experientialism
methamphetamine	heterodactyloos	noncontributory	experientialist
nonprofitmaking	hobbledehoyhood	orthopsychiatry	experimentalise
notwithstanding	hospitalisation	picturepostcard	experimentalism
overdevelopment	immortalisation	plenipotentiary	experimentalist
photoconducting	incomprehension	quatercentenary	fantasticalness
polycrystalline	inconsideration	selfdeprecatory	fashionableness
reapportionment	indemnification	selfexplanatory	fissiparousness
reestablishment	indetermination	semidocumentary	foresightedness
schoolmastering	instrumentation	sesquicentenary	fragmentariness
selfabandonment	insubordination	shootinggallery	gentlemanliness
selfcontainment	intensification	stereochemistry	geochronologist
selfdeprecating	interconnection	straightforward	geomorphologist
selfdetermining	interdigitation	substitutionary	halfheartedness
selfdevelopment	internalisation	substratosphere	hardheartedness
selffertilising	introsusception	thermochemistry	hermaphroditism
selffulfillment	intussusception	uncomplimentary	homogeneousness
selfimprovement	maldistribution	unparliamentary	humanitarianism
selfpropagating	materialisation	accountableness	hydrodynamicist
selfregistering	miniaturisation	acquisitiveness	hyperthyroidism
selfreplicating	misapprehension	adventurousness	illimitableness
selfsacrificing	misconstruction	agriculturalist	illustriousness
semiindependent	nationalisation	annihilationism	imaginativeness
semitransparent	nonintervention	anthropopathism	impermeableness
shrinkresistant	personalisation	anticlericalism	importunateness
stampcollecting	personification	appropriateness	impracticalness
superconducting	phosphorylation	arboriculturist	inattentiveness
superheterodyne	prestidigitator	Aristotelianism	incongruousness
superinducement	procrastination	atrabiliousness	indubitableness
transfigurement	prognostication	blameworthiness	ineffectiveness
trinitrotoluene	properispomenon	bloodguiltiness	ineffectualness
unaccommodating	quadruplication	broadmindedness	inexcusableness
uncomprehending	quintuplication	carnivorousness	inexpensiveness
underemployment	rationalisation	ceremoniousness	inflammableness
unprepossessing	reafforestation	circumspectness	infrangibleness
weatherboarding	reconsideration	coconsciousness	injudiciousness
acclimatisation	reconsolidation	coldbloodedness	innumerableness
alphabetisation	regionalisation	coldheartedness	inoffensiveness
Americanisation	rhombencephalon	commonplaceness	inopportuneness
antivivisection	romanticisation	compendiousness	inquisitiveness
arterialisation	selfaffirmation	competitiveness	inscrutableness
chloramphenicol	selfapprobation	complicatedness	insensitiveness
circumnavigator	selfcastigation	conceivableness	inseparableness
circumscription	selfdestruction	confessionalism	instructiveness
circumvallation	selfexamination	confessionalist	instrumentalism
civilianisation	selfgratulation	consecutiveness	instrumentalist
communalisation	selfhumiliation	conservationist	insurrectionist
computerisation	selfpollination	considerateness	intellectualise
contravallation	selfrealisation	conspicuousness	intellectualism

intellectualist	sententiousness	inexplicability	interscholastic
intemperateness	serviceableness	instrumentality	irrationalistic
interventionism	softheartedness	intellectuality	magnetoelectric
interventionist	speculativeness	intelligibility	ophthalmoscopic
intolerableness	spontaneousness	intercollegiate	palaeoanthropic
intractableness	standoffishness	invulnerability	parasympathetic
involuntariness	stereoisomerism	irresistibility	parthenogenetic
irreparableness	subordinateness	irreversibility	particularistic
irrevocableness	subpostmistress	manoeuvrability	phenomenalistic
kindheartedness	substantialness	proportionality	phonautographic
levelheadedness	substantiveness	pyroelectricity	photoelectronic
lightheadedness	sulphureousness	reconcilability	phytogeographic
lightmindedness	superficialness	reproducibility	pseudepigraphic
longsightedness	superfluousness	transferability	sadomasochistic
mellifluousness	superlativeness	transilluminate	sociolinguistic
meritoriousness	supernaturalise	transmutability	spermatogenetic
mischievousness	supernaturalism	unchangeability	stoicheiometric
mistrustfulness	supernaturalist	anthropophagous	ventriloquistic
nearsightedness	supportableness	brachycephalous	doublebarrelled
necessitousness	susceptibleness	brachydactylous	greatgrandchild
neighbourliness	symmetricalness	churrigueresque	hobbledehoyhood
nonsensicalness	tempestuousness	coinstantaneous	interstratified
numismatologist	tendentiousness	collenchymatous	noncommissioned
obstructiveness	therianthropism	contemporaneous	picturepostcard
odoriferousness	thoughtlessness	dessertspoonful	polyunsaturated
openheartedness	totalitarianism	disadvantageous	selfconstituted
ophthalmologist	transparentness	echinodermatous	selfopinionated
opinionatedness	treacherousness	enantiomorphous	straightforward
opprobriousness	treasonableness	epitheliomatous	underprivileged
palaeomagnetism	troublesomeness	margaritiferous	unsophisticated
palaeontologist	trueheartedness	microsporangium	wellconditioned
paradoxicalness	trustworthiness	ornithorhynchus	wellintentioned
parliamentarism	unconsciousness	pithecanthropus	acknowledgeable
penetrativeness	unrighteousness	plumbaginaceous	antepenultimate
perfunctoriness	unwholesomeness	prosenchymatous	archiepiscopate
perspicuousness	venturesomeness	pulchritudinous	bioluminescence
pharisaicalness	vertiginousness	selfdistrustful	brachistochrone
phenomenologist	warmbloodedness	selfreproachful	churrigueresque
photojournalism	warmheartedness	vicissitudinous	circumstantiate
photojournalist	warrantableness	electronegative	consubstantiate
photosynthesise	wrongheadedness	electropositive	conventionalise
physiotherapist	antepenultimate	excommunicative	departmentalise
picturesqueness	approachability	experimentalise	distinguishable
pleasurableness	archiepiscopate	incommunicative	electronegative
practicableness	circumstantiate	intussusceptive	electropositive
precipitousness	communicability	manicdepressive	excommunicative
PreRaphaelitism	complementarity	misapprehensive	experimentalise
Presbyterianise	compressibility	photoconductive	experimentalism
Presbyterianism	confidentiality	prognosticative	extraillustrate
presentationism	consubstantiate	selfdestructive	hendecasyllable
presentationist	contemporaneity	superconductive	imprescriptible
preservationist	contemptibility	uncommunicative	inapprehensible
prestigiousness	contractability	undemonstrative	incommensurable
pretentiousness	contractibility	———————————————	incommunicative
processionalist	conventionality	phenylketonuria	indisciplinable
professionalise	demonstrability	pleuropneumonia	intellectualise
professionalism	destructibility	rhynchocephalia	interchangeable
progressiveness	disagreeability	achondroplastic	intercollegiate
prohibitiveness	disreputability	anthropocentric	interdependence
proportionalist	equiprobability	anthropomorphic	intussusceptive
provocativeness	ethnocentricity	atherosclerotic	manicdepressive
psychophysicist	exchangeability	chromatographic	methamphetamine
psychotherapist	extraillustrate	chronogrammatic	micromillimetre
punctiliousness	heterosexuality	cinematographic	misapprehensive
purposelessness	impenetrability	conceptualistic	noninterference
quarrelsomeness	imperishability	dolichocephalic	phosphorescence
quarterfinalist	imponderability	electromagnetic	photoconductive
quickwittedness	inaccessibility	electrophoretic	photosynthesise
remorselessness	inadmissibility	exhibitionistic	polycrystalline
repetitiousness	inapplicability	expressionistic	predeterminable
reproachfulness	incalculability	gynandromorphic	Presbyterianise
resourcefulness	incomparability	hendecasyllabic	professionalise
respectableness	incompatibility	heterochromatic	prognosticative
resurrectionism	incorrigibility	historiographic	selfconsequence
resurrectionist	indefeasibility	hypercatalectic	selfdestructive
righthandedness	indefensibility	impressionistic	substratosphere
rightmindedness	indigestibility	indeterministic	superconductive
rudimentariness	indissolubility	individualistic	superheterodyne
selfcentredness	ineffaceability	interferometric	superincumbence

superintendence	selfreproachful	diversification	transplantation
supernaturalise	semicylindrical	electrification	underestimation
transilluminate	spectroscopical	etherealisation	underproduction
trinitrotoluene	stratigraphical	Europeanisation	vicechamberlain
ultracentrifuge	superstructural	excommunication	connoisseurship
ultramicroscope	transcriptional	exemplification	interpretership
unchallengeable	transpositional	experimentation	stadtholdership
uncommunicative	trigonometrical	extemporisation	cerebrovascular
undemonstrative	zoogeographical	exteriorisation	cinematographer
unexceptionable	annihilationism	externalisation	circumnavigator
unobjectionable	anthropopathism	familiarisation	counterattacker
unsportsmanlike	anticlericalism	formularisation	extracurricular
airconditioning	Aristotelianism	frenchification	historiographer
counterplotting	confessionalism	hospitalisation	interclavicular
gleichschaltung	constructionism	immortalisation	interfascicular
marketgardening	conventionalism	incomprehension	malpractitioner
nonprofitmaking	cosmopolitanism	inconsideration	photosensitiser
notwithstanding	departmentalism	indemnification	prestidigitator
photoconducting	ecclesiasticism	indetermination	radiogoniometer
schoolmastering	enantiomorphism	instrumentation	stretcherbearer
selfdeprecating	episcopalianism	insubordination	vasoconstrictor
selfdetermining	equalitarianism	intensification	accountableness
selffertilising	experientialism	interconnection	acquisitiveness
selfpropagating	experimentalism	interdigitation	adventurousness
selfregistering	hermaphroditism	internalisation	ankylostomiasis
selfreplicating	humanitarianism	introsusception	anthropogenesis
selfsacrificing	hyperthyroidism	intussusception	anthropophagous
stampcollecting	infundibuliform	malacopterygian	appropriateness
superconducting	instrumentalism	maldistribution	atherosclerosis
unaccommodating	intellectualism	materialisation	atrabiliousness
uncomprehending	interventionism	Mephistophelean	bioastronautics
unprepossessing	microsporangium	Mephistophelian	blameworthiness
weatherboarding	palaeomagnetism	miniaturisation	bloodguiltiness
counterapproach	parliamentarism	misapprehension	brachycephalous
electromyograph	photojournalism	misconstruction	brachydactylous
microphotograph	PreRaphaelitism	nationalisation	broadmindedness
photolithograph	Presbyterianism	nonintervention	carnivorousness
photomicrograph	presentationism	parliamentarian	ceremoniousness
amphitheatrical	professionalism	personalisation	circumspectness
anthropological	resurrectionism	personification	coconsciousness
antimonarchical	stereoisomerism	phosphorylation	coinstantaneous
bacteriological	supernaturalism	platitudinarian	coldbloodedness
bibliographical	therianthropism	postmillenarian	coldheartedness
biogeographical	totalitarianism	povertystricken	collenchymatous
chloramphenicol	acanthocephalan	procrastination	commonplaceness
circumferential	acclimatisation	prognostication	compendiousness
configurational	alphabetisation	properispomenon	competitiveness
cryptanalytical	Americanisation	psychometrician	complicatedness
demonstrational	antisabbatarian	quadruplication	conceivableness
dessertspoonful	antitrinitarian	quinquagenarian	congratulations
disproportional	antivivisection	quintuplication	consecutiveness
ecclesiological	arterialisation	rationalisation	considerateness
electrochemical	Christadelphian	reafforestation	conspicuousness
entrepreneurial	circumscription	reconsideration	contemporaneous
epistemological	circumvallation	reconsolidation	contentiousness
fourdimensional	civilianisation	regionalisation	defencelessness
governorgeneral	communisation	rhombencephalon	deleteriousness
improvisatorial	computerisation	romanticisation	dermatoglyphics
inconsequential	contravallation	selfaffirmation	descriptiveness
interprovincial	crossopterygian	selfapprobation	destructiveness
jurisprudential	crystallisation	selfcastigation	determinateness
lexicographical	Czechoslovakian	selfdestruction	disadvantageous
microanalytical	decalcification	selfexamination	disaffectedness
microsporophyll	decarbonisation	selfgratulation	disgracefulness
monosymmetrical	decarburisation	selfhumiliation	distastefulness
nongovernmental	decolourisation	selfpollination	distinctiveness
nonprofessional	decontamination	selfrealisation	distrustfulness
oceanographical	demagnetisation	speechification	downheartedness
omnidirectional	demystification	standardisation	echinodermatous
palaeobotanical	denitrification	suburbanisation	efficaciousness
palaeographical	desensitisation	superimposition	electroanalysis
pharmacological	desexualisation	supersaturation	electrodynamics
philanthropical	detribalisation	supplementation	electrokinetics
photomechanical	devitrification	syllabification	electrophoresis
physicochemical	differentiation	synchronisation	enantiomorphous
physiographical	disarticulation	systematisation	epitheliomatous
pneumatological	discommendation	thunderstricken	everlastingness
protozoological	disorganisation	transfiguration	expeditiousness
selfdistrustful	dissatisfaction	transliteration	fantasticalness

fashionableness	pulchritudinous	interventionist	disagreeability
fissiparousness	punctiliousness	numismatologist	disappointingly
foresightedness	purposelessness	ophthalmologist	disconcertingly
fragmentariness	quarrelsomeness	overdevelopment	discontinuously
gastroenteritis	quickwittedness	palaeontologist	disenchantingly
gentlemanliness	remorselessness	phenomenologist	dishearteningly
halfheartedness	repetitiousness	photojournalist	disinflationary
hardheartedness	reproachfulness	physiotherapist	disinterestedly
heterodactyloos	resourcefulness	presentationist	dispassionately
homogeneousness	respectableness	preservationist	disreputability
illimitableness	righthandedness	processionalist	disrespectfully
illustriousness	rightmindedness	proportionalist	dissatisfactory
imaginativeness	rudimentariness	psychophysicist	distinguishably
impermeableness	schistosomiasis	psychotherapist	dithyrambically
importunateness	selfcentredness	quarterfinalist	dramaturgically
impracticalness	sententiousness	reapportionment	dyslogistically
inattentiveness	serviceableness	reestablishment	encephalography
incongruousness	softheartedness	resurrectionist	equiprobability
indubitableness	speculativeness	selfabandonment	ethnocentricity
ineffectiveness	spermatogenesis	selfcontainment	euphemistically
ineffectualness	spontaneousness	selfdevelopment	exchangeability
inexcusableness	standoffishness	selffulfillment	excommunicatory
inexpensiveness	subordinateness	selfimprovement	extraordinarily
inflammableness	subpostmistress	semiindependent	grandiloquently
infrangibleness	substantialness	semitransparent	heartbreakingly
injudiciousness	substantiveness	shrinkresistant	heliotropically
innumerableness	sulphureousness	sleepingdraught	Hellenistically
inoffensiveness	superficialness	speakingtrumpet	hermeneutically
inopportuneness	superfluousness	superinducement	heterogeneously
inquisitiveness	superlativeness	supernaturalist	heterosexuality
inscrutableness	supportableness	transfiguration	hydropathically
insensitiveness	susceptibleness	underemployment	hydrostatically
inseparableness	symmetricalness	abiogenetically	hypercritically
instructiveness	tempestuousness	accommodatingly	ideographically
intemperateness	tendentiousness	aerodynamically	immunochemistry
intolerableness	thoughtlessness	ambidexterously	impenetrability
intractableness	transparentness	anaesthesiology	imperishability
involuntariness	treacherousness	anaesthetically	imponderability
irreparableness	treasonableness	anisotropically	inaccessibility
irrevocableness	troublesomeness	apocalyptically	inadmissibility
kindheartedness	trueheartedness	approachability	inapplicability
levelheadedness	trustworthiness	approximatively	inappropriately
lightheadedness	trypanosomiasis	architecturally	incalculability
lightmindedness	unconsciousness	argumentatively	incommensurably
longsightedness	unrighteousness	atmospherically	incomparability
margaritiferous	unwholesomeness	authoritatively	incompatibility
mellifluousness	venturesomeness	autographically	inconsiderately
meritoriousness	vertiginousness	autoradiography	inconspicuously
metamathematics	vicissitudinous	biogeochemistry	incorrigibility
mischievousness	warmbloodedness	chronologically	indefeasibility
mistrustfulness	warmheartedness	communicability	indefensibility
nearsightedness	warrantableness	communicatively	indeterminately
necessitousness	wrongheadedness	compartmentally	indigestibility
neighbourliness	acknowledgement	compassionately	indissolubility
nonsensicalness	affranchisement	complementarily	indistinctively
obstructiveness	agriculturalist	complementarity	ineffaceability
odoriferousness	arboriculturist	compositionally	inefficaciously
openheartedness	confessionalist	comprehensively	inexplicability
opinionatedness	conservationist	compressibility	infinitesimally
opprobriousness	constructionist	condescendingly	inquisitorially
ornithorhynchus	conventionalist	confidentiality	insignificantly
paradoxicalness	conversationist	conjunctionally	instantaneously
parthenogenesis	counterirritant	conscientiously	instrumentality
penetrativeness	countermovement	consentaneously	insurrectionary
perfunctoriness	cryptocommunist	consequentially	intellectuality
perspicuousness	disentanglement	contemplatively	intelligibility
pharisaicalness	disillusionment	contemporaneity	interchangeably
picturesqueness	eclaircissement	contemptibility	interdependency
pithecanthropus	emancipationist	contractability	interjectionary
pleasurableness	enfranchisement	contractibility	internationally
plumbaginaceous	experientialist	contradictorily	interrogatively
practicableness	experimentalist	controversially	invulnerability
precipitousness	flibbertigibbet	conventionality	irresistibility
prestigiousness	geochronologist	correspondingly	irreversibility
pretentiousness	geomorphologist	crystallography	lackadaisically
progressiveness	hydrodynamicist	demonstrability	logarithmically
prohibitiveness	instrumentalist	demonstratively	logographically
prosenchymatous	insurrectionist	destructibility	macroscopically
provocativeness	intellectualist	developmentally	manoeuvrability

mechanistically	proportionately	shootinggallery	uncomplainingly
meroblastically	psychologically	significatively	uncomplimentary
morphologically	psychopathology	singleheartedly	unconditionally
multitudinously	pusillanimously	socialistically	understandingly
necromantically	pyroelectricity	sophisticatedly	unexceptionably
neurophysiology	pyrotechnically	splendiferously	unexceptionally
neuropsychiatry	quatercentenary	stereochemistry	unintelligently
noncontributory	radioautography	substitutionary	unintentionally
northeastwardly	radiotelegraphy	subterraneously	unparliamentary
northwestwardly	reconcilability	superabundantly	unprecedentedly
ontogenetically	remonstratively	superintendency	unpretentiously
orthopsychiatry	reproducibility	superstitiously	unquestioningly
overconfidently	retrogressively	supplementarily	unrealistically
palaeogeography	retrospectively	suppositionally	unsubstantially
pantheistically	ritualistically	surreptitiously	unsymmetrically
parenthetically	roentgenography	sycophantically	ventriloquially
peripatetically	rontgenotherapy	syllogistically	
peristaltically	sanctimoniously	sympathetically	
perpendicularly	saprophytically	symptomatically	
perspicaciously	selfcomplacency	technologically	
pessimistically	selfconfidently	telegraphically	
philosophically	selfconsciously	telephotography	
photochemically	selfconsistency	temperamentally	
phototelegraphy	selfdeprecatory	therapeutically	
phrenologically	selfexplanatory	thermochemistry	
physiologically	selfforgetfully	topographically	
plenipotentiary	selfindulgently	transferability	
prehistorically	selfreprovingly	transgressively	
prepositionally	selfrighteously	transmutability	
prepossessingly	selfsufficiency	trisyllabically	
preternaturally	semiconsciously	typographically	
problematically	semidocumentary	unceremoniously	
proportionality	sesquicentenary	unchangeability	